CHAMBERS 21st CENTURY DICTIONARY

EDITOR-IN-CHIEF
MAIRI ROBINSON

SENIOR EDITOR
GEORGE DAVIDSON

CHAMBERS

CHAMBERS
An imprint of Chambers Harrap Publishers Ltd
7 Hopetoun Crescent, Edinburgh, EH7 4AY

First published by Chambers 1996
This updated edition first published 1999

A CIP catalogue record for this book is available from the British Library

We have made every effort to mark as such all words which we believe to be trademarks.
We should also like to make it clear that the presence of a word in the dictionary, whether marked or unmarked, in no way affects its legal status as a trademark.

ISBN 0 550 14210 X Standard
ISBN 0 550 14250 9 Thumb-indexed

Typeset in Great Britain by Cambridge University Press
Printed and bound in Great Britain by Clays Ltd, St Ives plc

CONTENTS

PREFACE

Chambers 21st Century Dictionary looks at the English language from a fresh perspective. The needs of the reader are always paramount, and this will be immediately apparent on comparing it with any other dictionary. Drawn from the unique Chambers database of language and reference materials, this new dictionary provides in one volume an exceptional range of information about English and how to use it.

In this dictionary, we have tried to make the information easy to find. Items are arranged as far as possible in separate articles. The user should therefore normally look for an item as a headword in its own right. This includes complex items such as **backfire**, **elder statesman**, **ghetto-blaster** and **the man in the street**.

Very few defined items are buried or 'nested' inside others, except for idioms (such as **on the make**) and phrasal verbs (such as **make up**), which are normally nested within the entry for the first principal word, in both these cases at **make**. Derivative words often appear as entries in their own right (eg **occasional**), but when they are straightforward they may be nested (eg **palindromic**), and where their meaning is obvious, they may also be left undefined (eg **bitterness**).

Guidance on pronunciation is given in the International Phonetic Alphabet, using a broad phonemic transcription of British English (ie a systematic representation of the pronunciation of British English speakers as a whole, not that of any individual speaker). An explanation of the symbols used is supplied at the foot of the dictionary pages in two separate sets on consecutive page openings. These cover first, the basic sounds of English, and second, common sounds in foreign words used in English.

One of the principal aims of this book is to help the readers to use English more confidently and effectively, and many of the special features of the dictionary have been designed with this in mind. For example, the fact that we give the past tense and present participle for base forms of all verbs means that readers should never have difficulty spelling these forms. In addition the Usage Panels give further information on aspects of English where there is frequent uncertainty, and provide practical unfussy help in dealing with such matters. They often give advice, too, on matters of style, eg by suggesting Plain English alternatives to over-pompous or stuffy word-choices.

The additional Information Panels and Tables are designed to draw together strands of information normally scattered throughout the alphabetical text: for example, French words and phrases used in English or the codewords used for letters of the alphabet in radio communication. These enable whole areas of information to be identified and explored together, a facility normally denied to the user of dictionaries.

A major challenge in the compilation of any English dictionary lies in the need to explain how words are used in conjunction with other words; after all, we speak and write phrases and sentences, and meanings emerge from the interaction of words rather than merely from the individual words themselves. Chambers dictionaries are justly famous for their excellence in exemplifying and explaining the idiomatic aspects of language. In this dictionary, we go still further in this process, and include phrasal verbs in this generous treatment, by explaining idioms and phrases in their typical surroundings (or *collocation*). This will be especially noticeable in highly functional and productive words such as *get* and *turn*, which often have little meaning in themselves and derive their meaning from the words that accompany them. No other dictionary for native speakers of English attempts this on such a scale.

We have made every effort to include as much information as possible that will be immediately useful to users from a wide range of ages, and we have paid particular attention to the vocabulary of modern life and culture. However any reference book, no matter what its size, can only provide a selection from a vast number of items available for consideration. There are thought to be over 500 000 words and wordgroups on record in English. The compiler's art lies in making a judicious selection, but it can be only a selection, and no two compilers will make the same choices. The publishers will therefore be pleased to receive suggestions for inclusion in future editions.

Thanks are due to many individuals and institutions for information and advice, and especially Compulexis Ltd, Charlton-on-Otmoor, Oxford, and the Centre for Speech Technology Research, University of Edinburgh, for their help in the preliminary stages of this book. We believe that the text presented here will find a permanent place as a standard source of information for family and general reference.

Mairi Robinson
June 1996

CONTRIBUTORS

Publishing Director
Robert Allen

Editor-in-Chief and Managing Editor
Mairi Robinson

Senior Editor
George Davidson

EDITORIAL TEAM

Text Editors
Serenella Flackett
Lesley Johnston
Judyth Lightbody
Fiona McPherson
Patricia Marshall
Martin Mellor
Susan Rennie

External Editors and Readers
Virginia Klein
M A Ruth Martin
Howard Sargeant
Catherine Schwarz
Agnes Young

Usage and Information Panels
Robert Allen
Howard Sargeant

Science Editor
Jo Hargreaves

Science Contributor
Bill Houston

New Words from Chambers Wordtrack
Martin Mellor

Administrative and Editorial Support
Anne Benson
Helen Bleck
Elaine McAdam
Louise McGinnity
Marian Shepherd
Shona Sutherland
Isabelle Vitale

COMPUTING

Computing Officer
Ilona Bellos-Morison

Computing Support
Dave Sparks
Alastair Sutherland

A BRIEF GUIDE TO THE DICTIONARY

We **spell out the past tense and present participle of all verbs** in full.

We give generous examples of the **idioms** in which a headword is used, introducing each with a •.

Phrasal verbs are given on their own in a tinted box after the main part of the entry, each preceded by ▪.

Some entries have additional **alternative headwords**. These are given in the same typeface as the headword, and are preceded by 'and'. For variant spellings, see note at **coomb** below.

Help with pronunciation is given for most multi-syllable words except as explained below at **cooking apple**.

Geographical labels are given where a meaning or form is restricted geographically.

Etymologies, introduced by ⓒ, give date of first use in English, followed by the source of the word or other interesting information about its origin.

Pronunciation help is not given for unambiguous monosyllables, obvious derivatives, or compounds whose parts are found elsewhere in the dictionary or are themselves unambiguous.

Usage examples are given, in a distinctive typeface, to illustrate the meanings. Each is preceded by □.

Appropriate contexts of use are given for some meanings. This is an example illustrating the context of an adjective. Compare note at **comb** below.

Straightforward derivatives are nested within their base entries either with or without a definition. Compare note at **faulty** opposite.

Parts of speech are marked with traditional labels, mostly in full, eg *noun*, *verb*, *adverb*. Some of the longer labels are given as abbreviations, eg *adj*, *conj*. In addition main parts of speech within an entry are picked out by being preceded by the symbol ▻.

We **spell out the plural of nouns** where there could be any problem.

Main entry **cross-references** are given for nested material which would be alphabetically more than five entries removed from the entry in which it is nested.

Variant spellings are given in a different typeface from the headword, and are preceded by 'or'. For alternative headwords, see note at **cookery book** above.

Appropriate contexts of use are given for some meanings. This is an example illustrating the context of a noun.

cook ▻ *verb* (*cooked*, *cooking*) **1** *tr & intr* to prepare (food) or be prepared by heating. **2** *colloq* to alter (accounts, etc) dishonestly. ▻ *noun* someone who cooks or prepares food. • **cook the books** to falsify accounts, records, etc. • **cook someone's goose** see under GOOSE. • **cook with gas** or **electricity** *colloq* to be successful. • **What's cooking?** *colloq* What's happening?; What's the plan? ⓒ Anglo-Saxon *coc*, from Latin *coquus*.

▪ **cook something up** **1** *colloq* to concoct or invent it. **2** *Black slang* to prepare (a drug, especially heroin) for use, by heating.

cookery book and **cookbook** ▻ *noun* a book of recipes.

cookie /'kʊkɪ/ ▻ *noun* (*cookies*) **1** *chiefly N Amer* a biscuit. **2** *Scottish* a bun. **3** *colloq* a person □ *a smart cookie.* • **That's the way the cookie crumbles** *N Amer colloq* That's the way it goes; That's how things usually turn out. ⓒ 18c: from Dutch *koekje*, diminutive of *koek* cake.

cooking apple and **cooker** ▻ *noun* an apple sour in taste, which is used for cooking rather than eating raw. Compare EATING APPLE.

cool ▻ *adj* **1** between cold and warm; fairly cold. **2** pleasantly fresh; free of heat □ *a cool breeze.* **3** calm; laid-back □ *He was very cool under pressure.* **4** lacking enthusiasm; unfriendly □ *a cool response.* **5** impudent; audacious; brazen. **6** said of a large sum: exact; at least □ *made a cool million.* **7** *colloq* admirable; excellent. **8** said of colours: suggestive of coolness, typically pale and containing blue. **9** sophisticated. ▻ *noun* **1** a cool part or period; coolness □ *the cool of the evening.* **2** *colloq* self-control; composure □ *keep your cool.* ▻ *verb* (*cooled*, *cooling*) *tr & intr* (*often* **cool down** or **off**) **1** to become cool. **2** to become less interested or enthusiastic □ *Martin had cooled towards Pat since her behaviour at the office party.* • **coolly** *adverb* in a cool manner. • **coolness** *noun.* • **Cool it!** *colloq* Calm down! • **cool one's heels** to be kept waiting. • **play it cool** to deal with a situation calmly but warily. ⓒ Anglo-Saxon *col.*

▪ **cool something down** or **off** to make it cool.

coolant /'kuːlənt/ ▻ *noun* **1** a liquid or gas used as a cooling agent, especially to absorb and remove heat from its source in a system such as a car radiator, nuclear reactor, etc. **2** a liquid or gas that is used to cool the edge of a cutting tool during machining.

cool box and **cool bag** ▻ *noun* an insulated container, used to keep food cool.

cooler ▻ *noun* **1** a container or device for cooling things. **2** *slang* prison. **3** a drink made from wine and fruit juice.

coolie ▻ *noun* (*coolies*) *offensive* **1** an unskilled native labourer in Eastern countries. **2** *S Afr* an Indian. ⓒ 17c: probably from Tamil *kuli* hired person.

cooling-off period ▻ *noun* an interval for reflection and negotiation before taking action.

cooling tower ▻ *noun* a tall, hollow structure in which water heated during industrial processes is cooled for re-use.

coolly and **coolness** see under COOL

coomb, **coombe**, **comb** or **combe** /kuːm/ ▻ *noun* **1** in *S England:* a short deep valley. **2** a deep hollow in a hillside. ⓒ Anglo-Saxon *cumb* valley.

faucet /'fɔːsɪt/ ▻ *noun* **1** a TAP[2] fitted to a barrel. **2** *N Amer* a TAP[2] on a washbasin, etc. ⓘ 15c in sense 1: from French *fausset* peg.

fault /fɔːlt/ ▻ *noun* **1** a weakness or failing in character. **2** a flaw or defect in an object or structure. **3** a misdeed or slight offence. **4** responsibility for something wrong □ *all my fault*. **5** *geol* a break or crack in the Earth's crust, resulting in the slippage of a rock mass. **6** *tennis, etc* an incorrectly placed or delivered serve. **7** *showjumping* a penalty for refusing or failing to clear a fence. ▻ *verb* (***faulted***, ***faulting***) **1** *intr* to commit a fault. **2** to blame someone. • **at fault 1** culpable; to blame. **2** said of dogs: unable to find the scent. • **find fault with something** or **someone** to criticize it or them, especially excessively or unfairly; to complain about it or them. • **to a fault** to too great an extent. ⓘ 14c in *noun* 2: from French *faute*.

faultless ▻ *adj* perfect; without fault or defect. • **faultlessly** *adverb*. • **faultlessness** *noun*.

fault plane ▻ *noun, geol* the surface along which two rock masses on either side of a fault rub against each other.

faulty /'fɔːltɪ/ ▻ *adj* (***faultier***, ***faultiest***) **1** having a fault or faults. **2** said particularly of a machine or instrument: not working correctly. • **faultily** *adverb*. • **faultiness** *noun*.

faun /fɔːn/ ▻ *noun, Roman mythol* a mythical creature with a man's head and body and a goat's horns, hind legs and tail. ⓘ 14c: from Latin *Faunus* a rural deity worshipped by shepherds and farmers.

fauna /'fɔːnə/ ▻ *noun* (***faunas*** or ***faunae*** /-niː/) **1** the wild animals of a particular region, country, or time period. **2** a book or list giving descriptions of such animals. Compare FLORA. • **faunal** *adj*. ⓘ 18c: Latin *Fauna* goddess of living creatures, sister of Faunus (see FAUN).

fauteuil /'foutɜːɪ/ ▻ *noun* **1** an armchair. **2** a theatre seat. ⓘ 18c: French, from Latin *faldistolium* FALDSTOOL.

Fauvism /'fouvɪzəm/ ▻ *noun, art* a painting style adopted by a group of Expressionists, including Matisse, who regarded a painting as essentially a two-dimensional decoration in colour for communicating emotion, and not necessarily imitating nature. • **Fauvist** *noun, adj*. ⓘ Early 20c: from French *fauve* wild beast.

faux ami / *French* fozami/ ▻ *noun* (***faux amis***) a word in a foreign language that looks similar to one in one's own language, but has a rather different meaning, eg *prétendre* is French meaning 'claim' or 'assert', not 'pretend'.

faux pas /fou pɑː/ ▻ *noun* (*plural* ***faux pas*** /fou pɑː/) an embarrassing blunder, especially a social blunder. ⓘ 17c: French, meaning 'false step'.

favela /fɑː'veɪlə/ ▻ *noun* (***favelas***) especially in Brazil: a shanty town. ⓘ 1960s: Portuguese.

favour or (*N Amer*) **favor** /'feɪvə(r)/ *noun* **1** a kind or helpful action performed out of goodwill. **2** the liking, approval or goodwill of someone. **3** unfair preference. **4** a knot of ribbons worn as a badge of support for a particular team, political party, etc. **5** *historical* something given or worn as a token of affection. **6** (**favours**) *euphemistic old use* a woman's consent to lovemaking or sexual liberties. ▻ *verb* (***favoured***, ***favouring***) **1** to regard someone or something with goodwill. **2** to treat someone or something with preference, or over-indulgently. **3** to prefer; to support. **4** said of circumstances: to give an advantage to someone or something. **5** *old use* to look like (eg one's mother or father). **6** *affected* to be wearing (a colour, etc). • **favourer** *noun*. • **in favour of something** or **someone 1** having a preference for it or them. **2** to their benefit. **3** in support or approval of them. • **in** or **out**

We give words as **cross-references** (in the special cross-reference typeface) within other definitions to alert readers to useful further information at the other entry.

Help with pronunciation is given for monosyllables where there might be any ambiguity or uncertainty. Compare note at **cooking apple**.

Subject labels are given where a meaning or form is used within a specific area of knowledge or sphere of reference.

We regard it as normal for verbs to be transitive (ie have an object), so **we only mark verbs when they are used intransitively**.

Appropriate contexts of use are given for some definitions. This is another example illustrating the context of an adjective.

Compounds are given as separate entries from their base words.

We **spell out the comparative and superlative of adjectives** where there could be a problem.

Many **derivatives** are given as separate entries from their base words (as here **faulty** is a derivative of **fault**). This is done when they are important words in their own right, eg with many meanings and perhaps with further derivatives based on them (as here **faultily** and **faultiness**). Compare **coolly** under **cool**.

We give **extra help with pronunciation** for parts of words other than their base forms where this is necessary, eg as here where their plural may be difficult, or sometimes for their different parts of speech; eg **record** is pronounced differently as a noun and as a verb.

We give **headwords in italics** if they normally appear in italics in print, eg especially foreign words which are not naturalized in English.

For **any foreign words which are not common in English** we normally give their pronunciation in their own language, and label the pronunciation as eg *French*. For more information on this see the Usage Panels in the dictionary on the Pronunciation of French, German, Latin and Spanish in English.

Foreign words which are common in English we give as ordinary headwords (ie no italics) and also with naturalized English pronunciations, eg using English vowel sounds rather than those of the original language.

When a particular form or variant of the headword (commonly its plural) is used in some but not all of its senses the **form is given in brackets** before the relevant definition. The principal exception is compound nouns which become hyphenated when they are used as adjectives. This is the norm, and also extremely common, so we do not give the form in brackets, but merely give an example of it in use. So eg ***a dead end***, but ***a dead-end job***.

Register labels pinpoint stylistic level or degree of formality.

ABBREVIATIONS USED IN THE DICTIONARY

In the interests of clarity, editorial abbreviations have been kept to a minimum. When they are used, this is either to save space, where this can be done without distracting the user (eg *adjective* is shortened to *adj*), or to give a special status to the information which would not be conveyed by ordinary prose (eg 11c used to represent 'eleventh century'). Most of the abbreviations are in the subject labels.

Afr	Africa, African
agric	agriculture
Amer	America, American
astrol	astrology
astron	astronomy
Austral	Australia, Australian
bacteriol	bacteriology
biochem	biochemistry
biol	biology
bot	botany
Brit	Britain, British
c	century (eg 15c)
c.	circa (ie approximately)
Can	Canada, Canadian
Caribb	Caribbean
chem	chemistry
cinematog	cinematography
C of E	Church of England
colloq	colloquial
conj	conjunction
crystallog	crystallography
derog	derogatory
E	East
EC	European Community
ecol	ecology
econ	economy
elec	electricity
Eng	English
eng	engineering
entomol	entomology
EU	European Union
gemmol	gemmology
geog	geography
geol	geology
geom	geometry
hortic	horticulture
image tech	image technology
intr	intransitive
IVR	International Vehicle Registration
math	mathematics
mech	mechanics
meteorol	meteorology
mythol	mythology
N	North
naut	nautical
NZ	New Zealand
ophthalmol	ophthalmology
ornithol	ornithology
palaeog	palaeography
palaeontol	palaeontology
pathol	pathology
pharmacol	pharmacology
philos	philosophy
photog	photography
physiol	physiology
prep	preposition
psychoanal	psychoanalysis
psychol	psychology
relig	religion
S	South
sociol	sociology
technol	technology
telecomm	telecommunications
teleg	telegraphy
theat	theatre
tr	transitive
trig	trigonometry
TV	television
US	United States
vet	veterinary
W	West
zool	zoology

In addition, the following symbols are used

- ▻ to mark a principal part-of -speech
- □ to mark a usage example
- ● to mark a nested derivative or idiom
- ■ to mark a phrasal verb
- Ⓘ to mark an etymology
- ☆ to mark a recommendation
- ✓ to mark a correct usage
- × to mark an incorrect usage
- ? to mark a disputed usage

A

A[1] or **a** /eɪ/ ▻ *noun* (*As, A's* or *a's*) **1** the first letter of the English alphabet. **2** (**A**) *music* **a** the sixth note on the scale of C major; **b** the musical key which has this note as its base. **3** (*usually* **A**) someone or something of first class, first in a sequence, or belonging to a class arbitrarily designated A. **4** *medicine* one of the four blood types in the ABO BLOOD GROUP SYSTEM. **5** the principal series of paper sizes, ranging from **A0** (841 x 1189mm) to **A10** (26 x 37mm). • **from A to B** from one place or point to another. • **from A to Z** from beginning to end.

A[2] ▻ *abbreviation* **1** absolute (temperature). **2** *cards* ace. **3** acre or acres. **4** *music* alto. **5** ammeter. **6** ampere or amperes. **7** angstrom. **8** area. **9** argon. **10** atomic weight. **11** *IVR* Austria.

a[1] (used before a consonant or consonant sound, eg *a boy, a one*) /ə/ or for emphasis /eɪ/ or (used before a vowel or vowel sound, eg *an egg, an hour*) **an** /an, ən/ ▻ *indefinite article* **1** used chiefly with a singular noun, usually where the thing referred to has not been mentioned before, or where it is not a specific example known to the speaker or listener. Compare THE. **2** used before a word describing quantity ◻ ***a dozen eggs.*** **3 a** any or every ◻ ***A fire is hot***; **b** used after *not* or *never*: any at all ◻ ***not a chance.*** **4** each or every; per ◻ ***once a day.*** **5** one of a specified type ◻ ***He thinks he's a real Romeo.*** ◷ Anglo-Saxon *an* one.

> ***a***
>
> Some people use **an** before words beginning with a weakly sounded *h*, eg *an hotel, an historic occasion.* This use of **an** is no more nor less correct than **a**; however, it is sometimes regarded as old-fashioned.

a[2] ▻ *abbreviation* **1** acceleration. **2** acre or acres. **3** adjective. **4** are or ares. **5** area. **6** *ante* (Latin), before.

a[3] see A[1]

a', aw or **a** /ɔː/ ▻ *adj* alternative *Scots* spellings of ALL.

a-[1] /ə/ ▻ *prefix, signifying* **1** to or towards ◻ ***ashore.*** **2** in the process or state of something ◻ ***abuzz*** ◻ ***a-roving.*** **3** on ◻ ***afire.*** **4** in ◻ ***asleep.*** ◷ Anglo-Saxon *an*, originally a preposition; sense 2 is still productive.

a-[2] /eɪ, a, ə/ or (before a vowel, and in scientific compounds before *h*) **an-** /an, ən/ ▻ *prefix, signifying* not; without; opposite to ◻ ***amoral*** ◻ ***ahistorical*** ◻ ***anaemia*** ◻ ***anhydrous.*** ◷ Greek.

Å ▻ *symbol* Ångström or angstrom.

A1 ▻ *adj* **1** first-rate or excellent. **2** said of a ship: in first-class condition. ◷ 19c: the symbol used for a first-class vessel in Lloyd's Register of Shipping.

AA ▻ *abbreviation* **1** Alcoholics Anonymous, an international association for alcoholics who are trying to give up alcohol completely. **2** anti-aircraft. **3** Automobile Association, a British organization which helps drivers with breakdowns or technical problems, gives road travel information, etc. See also RAC.

AAA ▻ *abbreviation* **1** *Brit* /ðə θriː 'eɪz/ Amateur Athletic Association. **2** *US* American Automobile Association. See also AA sense 3.

AAM ▻ *abbreviation* air-to-air missile.

A & R ▻ *abbreviation* artists and repertoire.

A & R man ▻ *noun* a person whose job is to check out new bands, singers, comedians, etc with a view to offering them a recording contract, the opportunity of playing live, etc. Being notorious for never being able to make their minds up, these people have earned the nickname of 'Um & Er men'.

aardvark /'ɑːdvɑːk/ ▻ *noun* a nocturnal African burrowing mammal with a thick set body, large snout and donkey-like ears. ◷ 19c: from Dutch *aarde* earth + *vark* pig.

Aaron's rod /'ɛərənz—/ ▻ *noun* a tall stiff flowering plant; a MULLEIN

AB[1] ▻ *noun, medicine* one of the four blood types in the ABO BLOOD GROUP SYSTEM.

AB[2] ▻ *abbreviation* **1** *Brit* able seaman. **2** *N Amer, especially US*: *Artium Baccalaureus* (Latin), Bachelor of Arts.

ab- /ab, əb/ ▻ *prefix, signifying* opposite to; from; away from ◻ ***abnormal.*** ◷ Latin.

abaca /'abəkə/ ▻ *noun* (***abacas***) **1** the fibre from a plant grown in the Philippine Islands. Also **Manila hemp**. **2** the plant itself.

aback /ə'bak/ ▻ *adverb* (*always* **taken aback**) surprised or shocked, especially by something unpleasant or unexpected. ◷ Anglo-Saxon *on bæc* backwards.

abacus /'abəkəs/ ▻ *noun* (***abaci*** /-saɪ/ or ***abacuses***) **1** an arithmetical calculating device, known to the Greeks, Romans and other ancient peoples, consisting of several rows of beads strung on horizontal wires or rods mounted in a frame. **2** *archit* the flat upper part of a column or capital. ◷ 17c in sense 1; 16c in sense 2: Latin, from Greek *abax* drawing-board.

abaft /ə'bɑːft/ *naut* ▻ *adverb* in or towards the stern of a ship. ▻ *prep* behind. ◷ Anglo-Saxon A-[1] + *beæftan* after.

abalone /abə'loʊnɪ/ ▻ *noun* (***abalones***) a marine gastropod mollusc which has a single flattened oval shell lined with bluish MOTHER-OF-PEARL, with a series of holes around the edge. ◷ 19c: from American Spanish *abulón*.

abandon /ə'bandən/ ▻ *verb* (***abandoned, abandoning***) **1** to give something up completely ◻ ***abandon hope.*** **2** to leave (a person, post of responsibility, etc), usually intending not to return. **3** to leave (a place of danger or difficulty, etc), intending either not to return at all or not until the danger or difficulty is past. **4** to give something up to another person's control. ▻ *noun* uncontrolled or uninhibited behaviour. • **abandonment** *noun*. • **abandon ship** said of the crew and passengers: to leave a ship at sea when it is in danger of sinking. ◷ 14c: from French *abandoner* to put under someone's control.

> ▪ **abandon oneself to something** to let oneself be overcome by (strong emotion, passion, etc).

abandoned /ə'bandənd/ ▻ *adj* **1** deserted. **2** having, or behaving as if one has, no sense of shame or morality. • **abandonedly** *adverb*.

abandonee /əbandə'niː/ ▻ *noun* (***abandonees***) *law* an insurer to whom a wreck has been abandoned.

abase /ə'beɪs/ ▻ *verb* (***abased, abasing***) to humiliate or degrade (someone else or oneself). • **abasement** *noun*. ◷ 15c: from French *abaissier*, from Latin *bassus* low.

abashed /ə'baʃt/ ▻ *adj* embarrassed or disconcerted, especially because of shyness. ◷ 14c as *abayste*: from French *esbahir* to astound.

abate /əˈbeɪt/ ⊳ *verb* (***abated***, ***abating***) *tr & intr* to become or make less strong or severe. • **abatement** *noun*. ◷ 13c: from French *abatre* to demolish.

abattoir /ˈabətwɑː(r)/ ⊳ *noun* a slaughterhouse. ◷ 19c: from French *abatre* to demolish.

abbacy /ˈabəsɪ/ ⊳ *noun* (***abbacies***) the office or authority of an abbot or abbess. ◷ 15c: from Latin *abbatia*.

abbess /ˈabəs/ ⊳ *noun* (***abbesses***) a woman in charge of a group of nuns living in an abbey. Compare ABBOT. ◷ 13c: from French *abbesse*.

abbey /ˈabɪ/ ⊳ *noun* (***abbeys***) **1** a group of nuns or monks living as a community under an abbot or abbess. **2** the buildings occupied by such a community. **3** a church associated with such a community. ◷ 13c: from French *abeie*.

abbot /ˈabət/ ⊳ *noun* the man in charge of a group of monks living in an abbey. Compare ABBESS. ◷ Anglo-Saxon *abbod*: from Latin *abbas*, from Aramaic *abba* father.

abbr. or **abbrev.** ⊳ *abbreviation* **1** abbreviated. **2** abbreviation.

abbreviate /əˈbriːvɪeɪt/ ⊳ *verb* (***abbreviated***, ***abbreviating***) to shorten, especially to represent (a long word) by a shortened form. ◷ 15c: from Latin *abbreviare*, *abbreviatum* to shorten.

abbreviation ⊳ *noun* **1** a shortening of a word written instead of a whole word, eg *approx.* for *approximately*. Compare ACRONYM, CONTRACTION, INITIALISM. **2** the act or process of abbreviating something, or the result of this.

Some Common Abbreviations

AD	*anno Domini*, in the year of our Lord
AH	*anno Hegirae*, in the year of the Hegira, the Muslim era
am	*ante meridiem*, before noon
BC	before Christ
c	*circa*, about
cf	*confer*, compare
do	*ditto*, the same thing
eg	*exempli gratia*, for example
et al	*et alibi*, and elsewhere
et alii, aliae *or* alia	*and other* (people or things)
et cetera	*et cetera*, and so on
et seq, seqq.	*et sequens*, *sequentes*, or *sequentia*, and that, or those, following
ff	following (pages, lines, etc)
fl	*floruit*, flourished
ibid	*ibidem*, in the same place of a book, chapter, etc already mentioned
ie	*id est*, that is, that is to say
l, ll	line, lines
loc cit	*loco citato*, in the passage or place just quoted
ms, mss	manuscript, manuscripts
NB, nb	*nota bene*, note well
nem con	*nemine contradicente*, without opposition
op cit	*opere citato*, in the work or book just quoted
p, pp	page, pages
pm	*post meridiem*, in the afternoon
PS	postscript, an addition to a letter, etc
pto	please turn over
qed	*quod erat demonstrandum*, which was to be demonstrated (ie proved)
qv, qqv	*quod vide*, see this item, these items
sc	*scilicet*, namely
sv	*sub verbo* or *sub voce*, under the word or heading specified
v	*versus*, against; *vide*, see
viz	*videlicet*, namely
vs	*versus*, against

ABC[1] ⊳ *noun* (***ABCs*** or ***ABC's***) **1** the alphabet. **2** the basic facts about a subject, especially when arranged alphabetically in a book. **3** an alphabetical guide.

ABC[2] ⊳ *abbreviation* **1** American Broadcasting Company. **2** Australian Broadcasting Corporation.

abdicate /ˈabdɪkeɪt/ ⊳ *verb* (***abdicated***, ***abdicating***) **1** *tr & intr* to give up one's right to (the throne). **2** to refuse or fail to carry out (one's responsibilities). • **abdication** *noun*. ◷ 16c: from Latin *ab-* away + *dicare*, *dicatum* to proclaim.

abdomen /ˈabdəmən, abˈdoʊmən/ ⊳ *noun, zool, anatomy* **1** in vertebrates: the lower part of the main body cavity, containing the digestive, excretory and reproductive organs. **2** in arthropods, eg insects: the rear part of the body, behind the head and the thorax. • **abdominal** /abˈdɒmɪnəl/ *adj*. ◷ 17c: Latin.

abduct /əbˈdʌkt/ ⊳ *verb* (***abducted***, ***abducting***) to take someone away illegally by force or deception. ◷ 19c: from Latin *abducere*, *abductum* to lead away.

abduction /əbˈdʌkʃən/ ⊳ *noun* the illegal taking away of someone by force or deception. ◷ 18c: from Latin *abductio* a leading away.

abductor /əbˈdʌktə(r)/ ⊳ *noun* **1** a person who abducts someone. **2** *anatomy* any muscle that acts to move a body part away from the mid line of the body.

abeam /əˈbiːm/ ⊳ *adverb* in a line at right angles to the length of a ship or aircraft. ◷ 19c: A-[1] + BEAM.

Aberdeen Angus /ˈabədiːn ˈaŋgəs/ ⊳ *noun* an early-maturing breed of hornless beef cattle with short black hair. ◷ 19c: developed from a mixture of breeds in *Aberdeen*shire and *Angus*, former counties in Scotland.

Aberdonian /abəˈdoʊnɪən/ ⊳ *noun* a citizen or inhabitant of, or person born in, Aberdeen, NE Scotland. Also *as adj*. ◷ 17c: from Latin *Aberdonia* Aberdeen.

aberrance /aˈbɛrəns/ and **aberrancy** /-sɪ/ ⊳ *noun* (***aberrances*** or ***aberrancies***) a departure from what is normal. ◷ 17c: see ABERRANT.

aberrant /aˈbɛrənt/ ⊳ *adj* differing or departing from what is normal or accepted as standard. • **aberrantly** *adverb*. ◷ 19c: from Latin *aberrare* to wander away.

aberration /abəˈreɪʃən/ ⊳ *noun* **1** a temporary, usually brief and often surprising change from what is normal or accepted as standard. **2** a usually temporary, brief and sudden drop in standards of behaviour, thought, etc. **3** *optics* the failure of a lens in an optical system to form a perfect image, usually due to the properties of the lens material.

abet /əˈbɛt/ ⊳ *verb* (***abetted***, ***abetting***) *especially law* to help or encourage someone to do something wrong, especially to commit an offence. See also AID AND ABET at AID. • **abetter** or (*especially law*) **abettor** *noun*. ◷ 14c, meaning 'to urge on': from French *abeter*.

abeyance /əˈbeɪəns/ ⊳ *noun* **1** said of laws, customs, etc: the condition of not being used or followed, usually only temporarily □ ***fall into abeyance***. **2** said of a position, eg a peerage: the state of not being filled or occupied, usually only temporarily. ◷ 16c: from French *abeance*, from *a* to + *baer* to gape.

ABH ⊳ *abbreviation* actual bodily harm.

abhor /əbˈhɔː(r)/ ⊳ *verb* (***abhorred***, ***abhorring***) to hate or dislike (usually something one considers morally wrong) very much. ◷ 15c: from Latin *ab-* from or away + *horrere* to shudder.

abhorrence /əbˈhɒrəns/ ⊳ *noun* **1** a feeling of hatred or disgust. **2** a person or thing that is abhorred.

abhorrent ⊳ *adj* (*especially* **abhorrent to someone**) hated or disliked by them. • **abhorrently** *adverb*.

abide /əˈbaɪd/ ⊳ *verb* (***abided*** or ***abode*** /əˈboʊd/, ***abiding***) **1** (*especially with negatives and in questions*) to put up with or tolerate someone or something □ *We cannot* *abide dishonesty.* **2** *intr, old use* to remain. **3** *intr, old use* to live (in a specified place). **4** *old use* to wait for something or someone. ◷ Anglo-Saxon *abidan*.

■ **abide by something** to follow, stay faithful to or obey (a decision, rule, etc).

abiding /ə'baɪdɪŋ/ ▷ *adj* permanent, lasting or continuing for a long time. • **abidingly** *adverb*.

ability /ə'bɪlɪtɪ/ ▷ *noun* (***abilities***) **1** the power, skill or knowledge to do something. **2** great skill or intelligence. ◷ 14c: from French *ableté*, remodelled in English on its ultimate origin, Latin *habilitas* suitability, though the spelled *h-* was dropped again by 1700.

-ability see under -ABLE

ab init. ▷ *abbreviation*: *ab initio* /ab ɪ'nɪʃɪoʊ/ (Latin), from the beginning.

abiogenesis /eɪbaɪoʊ'dʒɛnəsɪs/ ▷ *noun* the origination of living matter by non-living matter; spontaneous generation. Also called AUTOGENESIS. • **abiogenetic** /-dʒə'nɛtɪk/ *adj*. ◷ 1870: coined by T H Huxley, from A-[2] + BIO- + GENESIS..

abject /'abdʒɛkt/ ▷ *adj* **1** said of living conditions, etc: extremely sad, miserable or poor; wretched. **2** said of people or their actions: showing lack of courage or pride, etc; submissive □ ***an abject apology***. • **abjectly** *adverb*. • **abjectness** *noun*. ◷ 15c, meaning 'rejected': from Latin *abjicere*, *abjectum* to throw away.

abjure /əb'dʒʊə(r)/ ▷ *verb* (***abjured***, ***abjuring***) *formal* to promise solemnly, especially under oath, to stop believing or doing something. • **abjuration** /abdʒʊ'reɪʃən/ *noun*. ◷ 16c: from Latin *ab* away + *jurare* to swear.

abl. ▷ *abbreviation* ablative.

ablate /ə'bleɪt/ ▷ *verb* (***ablated***, ***ablating***) to remove or decrease something by the process of ablation.

ablation ▷ *noun* **1** *medicine* the removal of an organ, body tissue, tumour, etc, especially by surgical means. **2** any loss or removal of material caused by melting, evaporation, erosion, weathering, etc. **3** *aeronautics* the deliberate removal of material from a nose cone, spacecraft, etc in order to provide thermal protection against damage to the underlying structure caused by heat friction on re-entering the atmosphere. ◷ 16c: from Latin *ablatio* taking away.

ablative /'ablətɪv/ *grammar*, ▷ *noun* (abbreviation **abl.**) **1** in eg Latin: the form or CASE of a noun, pronoun or adjective which expresses the place, means, manner or instrument of an action. **2** a noun, etc in this case. ▷ *adj* belonging to or in this case. • **ablatival** /-'taɪvəl/ *adj*. ◷ 15c: from Latin *ablativus*, from *ablatus* carried off or removed.

ablaut /'ablaʊt/ ▷ *noun*, *linguistics* a variation in the vowel in the different inflections or tenses of a word, eg *song, sing, sang, sung*. ◷ 19c: German, from *ab* off + *Laut* sound.

ablaze /ə'bleɪz/ ▷ *adj* **1** burning, especially strongly. **2** brightly lit. **3** (*usually* **ablaze with something**) feeling (an emotion) with great passion. 14c: A-[1] sense 2 + BLAZE[1].

able /'eɪbəl/ ▷ *adj* (***abler*** /'eɪblə(r)/, ***ablest***) **1** having the necessary knowledge, power, time, opportunity, etc to do something. **2** clever or skilful. • **ability** see separate entry. • **ably** /'eɪblɪ/ *adverb*. ◷ 14c: from Latin *habilis* handy.

-able /əbəl/ ▷ *suffix, forming adjectives, signifying* **1** that may or must be □ ***eatable*** □ ***payable***. **2** that may be the subject of something □ ***objectionable***. **3** that is suitable for something □ ***fashionable***. See also -IBLE. • **-ability** *suffix, forming nouns*. • **-ably** *suffix, forming adverbs*. ◷ From Latin *-abilis*.

able-bodied ▷ *adj* fit and healthy.

able seaman ▷ *noun* (abbreviation **AB**) a sailor able to perform all duties, with more training and a higher rating than an ORDINARY SEAMAN.

ablution /ə'bluːʃən/ ▷ *noun* (*usually* **ablutions**) **1 a** the washing of the body, the hands or the ritual vessels as part of a religious ceremony; **b** *RC Church* (**ablution**) the wine and water used to rinse the chalice and the priest's hands, and drunk by the priest. **2** *colloq or facetious* the ordinary washing of oneself. **3** a place for washing oneself in a camp, on board ship, etc. ◷ 14c, in alchemy: from Latin *abluere* to wash away.

ably see under ABLE

-ably see under -ABLE

ABM ▷ *abbreviation* anti-ballistic missile, a type of rocket which can destroy an enemy's ballistic missile in the air.

abnegation /abnə'geɪʃən/ ▷ *noun, formal* **1** the act of giving up something one has or would like to have. **2** the act of renouncing a doctrine, etc. ◷ 16c: from Latin *abnegare* to deny.

abnormal /ab'nɔːməl/ ▷ *adj* not normal; different from what is expected or usual. • **abnormality** *noun* (***abnormalities***). • **abnormally** *adverb*. ◷ 19c: from French *anormal*, from Greek *anomalos*.

abnormal load ▷ *noun* in road transport: a larger or heavier load than is generally carried.

Abo or **abo** /'aboʊ/ ▷ *noun* (***Abos***) *offensive, slang* an Australian aborigine. ▷ *adj* aboriginal. ◷ 20c shortening.

aboard /ə'bɔːd/ ▷ *adverb, prep* **1** on, on to, in or into (a ship, train, aircraft, etc). **2** *naut* alongside. ◷ 16c as *aborde*.

ABO blood group system ▷ *noun, medicine* a system by which human blood is classified into four groups (A, B, AB and O) according to the antigens carried by the red blood cells.

abode[1] /ə'boʊd/ ▷ *noun, formal* the house or place where one lives; a dwelling. • **of no fixed abode** *Brit law* having no regular home or address. ◷ 17c in this sense; 13c as *abade*, meaning 'a wait or delay': from ABIDE.

abode[2] *past tense, past participle of* ABIDE

abolish /ə'bɒlɪʃ/ ▷ *verb* (***abolished***, ***abolishing***) to stop or put an end to (customs, laws, etc). ◷ 15c: from French *abolir*.

abolition /abə'lɪʃən/ ▷ *noun* **1** the act of abolishing something; the state of being abolished. **2** *historical* the abolishing of slavery.

abolitionist ▷ *noun* someone who seeks to abolish a custom or practice, especially capital punishment or (*formerly*) slavery. • **abolitionism** *noun*.

abomasum /aboʊ'meɪsəm/ ▷ *noun* (***abomasa*** /-sə/) *zool* the fourth or true stomach of a ruminant animal. ◷ 18c: Latin, from *ab* away from + *omasum* tripe or paunch.

A-bomb see under ATOM BOMB

abominable /ə'bɒmɪnəbəl/ ▷ *adj* **1** greatly disliked or found loathsome, usually because morally bad. **2** *colloq* very bad. • **abominably** *adverb*. ◷ 14c: from Latin *abominari*; see ABOMINATE.

abominable snowman ▷ *noun* a YETI. ◷ 1920s: a loose translation of Tibetan *metohkangmi*, literally 'snowfield man-bear'.

abominate /ə'bɒmɪneɪt/ ▷ *verb* (***abominated***, ***abominating***) to dislike or hate something greatly; to find it loathsome. ◷ 17c: from Latin *abominari* to turn away from something because it is believed to be ill-omened.

abomination /əbɒmɪ'neɪʃən/ ▷ *noun* **1** anything one hates, dislikes greatly or finds loathsome. **2** great dislike or hatred.

aboriginal /abə'rɪdʒɪnəl/ ▷ *adj* **1** said of inhabitants: earliest known; indigenous. **2** referring to the Aboriginals of Australia or one of their languages. ▻ *noun* (**Aboriginal**) a member of a people who were the original inhabitants of Australia. • **aboriginally** *adverb*. ◷ 17c: from ABORIGINE + -AL.

> ***Aboriginal, Aborigine***
>
> • When referring to Australian inhabitants, the preferred forms for the noun are **Aborigine** in the singular and **Aboriginals** in the plural; **Aboriginal** is preferred as an adjective.

aborigine /abə'rɪdʒɪnɪ/ ▻ *noun* (***aborigines***) **1** (*also* **Aborigine**) an Aboriginal. **2** a member of any people who were the first to live in a country or region, especially as compared to later arrivals. ◷ 16c: from Latin *aborigines* a race of pre-Roman inhabitants of Italy, from *ab origine* from the beginning.

abort /ə'bɔːt/ ▻ *verb* (***aborted, aborting***) **1** *intr* to expel (an embryo or fetus) spontaneously from the uterus before it is capable of surviving independently; to miscarry. **2** *intr* said of a baby: to be lost in this way. **3** to induce termination of pregnancy, by surgical procedures or the use of drugs, before the embryo or fetus is capable of surviving independently. **4** *tr & intr* to stop (a plan, space flight, etc), or to be stopped, earlier than expected and before reaching a successful conclusion, usually because of technical problems or danger. **5** *biol* to fail to grow or develop to maturity. **6** *computing* to stop the execution of (a program) before it has been completed, either because it is unsuitable or because it cannot continue owing to an error or system failure. ◷ 16c: from Latin *abortus* miscarried, from *aboriri* to miscarry.

abortifacient /əbɔːtɪ'feɪʃənt/ ▻ *adj, medicine* causing abortion. ▻ *noun* a drug or other agent that causes abortion.

abortion /ə'bɔːʃən/ ▻ *noun* **1** *medicine* the removal of an embryo or fetus from the uterus before it is sufficiently developed to survive independently, deliberately induced by the use of drugs or by surgical procedures. Also called **termination** or **induced abortion**. **2** *medicine* the spontaneous expulsion of an embryo or fetus from the uterus before it is sufficiently developed to survive independently. Also called MISCARRIAGE, **spontaneous abortion**. **3** the failure of a plan, project, etc. **4** anything which has failed to grow properly or enough. ◷ 16c: from Latin *abortio*; see ABORT.

abortionist /ə'bɔːʃənɪst/ ▻ *noun* **1** someone who carries out (especially illegal) abortions. **2** someone who supports or condones the practice of carrying out abortions.

abortion pill ▻ *noun* a drug taken orally that brings about abortion in the early stages of pregnancy.

abortive /ə'bɔːtɪv/ ▻ *adj* **1** unsuccessful. **2** checked in its development. **3** *biol* incompletely developed or imperfectly formed; primitive. • **abortively** *adverb*.

aboulia see ABULIA

abound /ə'baʊnd/ ▻ *verb* (***abounded, abounding***) *intr* to exist in large numbers. • **abounding** *adj* abundant. ◷ 14c: from Latin *abundare* to overflow.

> ■ **abound in** or **with something** to be rich in it or filled with it.

about /ə'baʊt/ ▻ *prep* **1** concerning or relating to someone or something; on the subject of them or it. **2** near to something. **3** around or centring on something. **4** here and there in or at points throughout something. **5** all around or surrounding someone or something. **6** occupied or busy with something ▫ *What are you about?* **7** on the person of someone ▫ *don't have the letter about me.* ▻ *adverb* **1** nearly or just over; approximately. **2** nearby; close ▫ *Is there anyone about?* **3** scattered here and there. **4** all around; in all directions. **5** in or to the opposite direction ▫ *turn about.* **6** on the move; in action ▫ *be up and about again after an illness.* • **about to do something** on the point of doing it. • **it's about time someone did something** they ought to have done it already. • **not about to do something** determined not to do it. • **that's about it** or **about all** *colloq* almost everything that needs to be said or done has been. ◷ Anglo-Saxon *onbutan*.

about turn and **about face** ▻ *noun* **1** a turn made so that one is facing in the opposite direction. **2** a complete change of direction. ▻ *verb* (**about-turn** or **about-face**) *intr* to turn round so as to be facing in the opposite direction.

above /ə'bʌv/ ▻ *prep* **1** higher than or over something. **2** more or greater than something in quantity or degree. **3** higher or superior to someone in rank, importance, ability, etc. **4** too good or great for a specified thing ▫ *above petty quarrels.* **5** too good, respected, etc to be affected by or subject to something. **6** too difficult to be understood by, or beyond the abilities of, someone. ▻ *adverb* **1** at, in or to a higher position, place, rank, etc. **2 a** in an earlier passage of written or printed text; **b** *in compounds* ▫ *above-mentioned.* **3** *literary* in heaven. ▻ *adj* appearing or mentioned in an earlier or preceding passage of written or printed text. ▻ *noun* (**the above**) something already mentioned. • **above all** most of all; more than anything else. • **above and beyond** more than is required by or in addition to a specified thing. • **above oneself** having an inflated opinion of one's importance; conceited or arrogant. ◷ Anglo-Saxon *abufan*.

above-board ▻ *adj* honest; open; not secret. ◷ 17c: from card-playing use, in which putting one's hand below the board would imply foul play.

above-the-line ▻ *adj* **1** *econ* relating to that part of the Government's expenditure and revenue allowed for in its original estimates and provided for by taxation. **2** *bookkeeping* relating to the expenditure and revenue detailed in a company's profit and loss account. Compare BELOW-THE-LINE.

Abp ▻ *abbreviation* Archbishop.

abr. ▻ *abbreviation* **1** abridged. **2** abridgement.

abracadabra /abrəkə'dabrə/ ▻ *exclamation* a word which supposedly has magic power, often used by people when doing magic tricks. ◷ 17c: first appearance is in a 2c Latin poem.

abrade /ə'breɪd/ ▻ *verb* (***abraded, abrading***) to scrape or wear something away, especially by rubbing. ◷ 17c: from Latin *abradere* to scrape away.

abranchiate /ə'braŋkɪeɪt/ ▻ *adj, zool* without gills. ◷ 19c: A-[2] + Greek *branchia* gills + -ATE 4.

abrasion /ə'breɪʒən/ ▻ *noun* **1** a damaged area of skin, rock, etc which has been worn away by scraping or rubbing. **2** the act of scraping or rubbing away. ◷ 17c.

abrasive /ə'breɪsɪv, -zɪv/ ▻ *adj* **1** said of a material: capable of wearing away the surface of skin, wood, etc by rubbing and scraping. **2** said of a material: used to smooth or polish another surface by rubbing. **3** relating to the process of abrasion. **4** said of people or their actions: likely to offend others by being harsh and rude. ▻ *noun* any hard material, such as sandpaper, pumice or emery, that is used to wear away the surface of other materials, usually in order to smooth or shape them. • **abrasively** *adverb*. • **abrasiveness** *noun*. ◷ 19c: see ABRADE.

abreaction /abrɪ'akʃən/ ▻ *noun, psychiatry* the release of emotional tension associated with a repressed memory, which may occur spontaneously or be deliberately induced by the use of psychotherapy, hypnosis, etc. ◷ 20c.

abreast /ə'brɛst/ ▻ *adverb* side by side and facing in the same direction. • **abreast of something** up to date concerning it; having the most recent information ▫ *keep abreast of events.* ◷ 15c.

abridge /əˈbrɪdʒ/ ▷ *verb* (***abridged, abridging***) to make (a book, etc) shorter. • **abridged** *adj*. • **abridgement** or **abridgment** *noun*. ⓒ 14c: from French *abregier*, from Latin *abbreviare* to abbreviate.

abroad /əˈbrɔːd/ ▷ *adverb* **1** in or to a foreign country or countries. **2** in circulation; at large. **3** over a wide area; in different directions. **4** *old use* out of or away from one's home. ⓒ 13c as *abrod*: A-[1] + BROAD.

abrogate /ˈabrəgeɪt/ ▷ *verb* (***abrogated, abrogating***) to cancel (a law, agreement, etc) formally or officially. • **abrogation** *noun*. ⓒ 16c: from Latin *abrogare*.

abrupt /əˈbrʌpt/ ▷ *adj* (*sometimes* ***abrupter, abruptest***) **1** sudden and unexpected; very quick. **2** said especially of speech, etc: rather sharp and rude. **3** steep. • **abruptly** *adverb*. • **abruptness** *noun*. ⓒ 16c: from Latin *abrumpere* to break off.

ABS ▷ *abbreviation, autos* anti-lock braking system.

abscess /ˈabses/ ▷ *noun* (***abscesses***) *pathol* a localized collection of pus in a cavity surrounded by inflamed tissue, usually caused by bacterial infection. ⓒ 17c: from Latin *abscessus* going away.

abscissa /abˈsɪsə/ ▷ *noun* (***abscissas*** or ***abscissae*** /-ˈsɪsiː/) *math* in coordinate geometry: the first of a pair of numbers *x* and *y*, known as the *x*-coordinate, which specifies the distance of a point from the vertical or *y*-axis. See also ORDINATE. ⓒ 17c: from Latin *abscissus* cut off.

abscond /əbˈskɒnd/ ▷ *verb* (***absconded, absconding***) *intr* to depart or leave quickly and usually secretly, especially because one has done something wrong and wants to avoid punishment or arrest. • **absconder** *noun*. ⓒ 16c: from Latin *abscondere* to hide.

abseil /ˈabseɪl, -saɪl/ ▷ *verb* (***abseiled, abseiling***) *intr, mountaineering* to go down a rock face, etc using a double rope wound round the body and fixed to a point higher up. ▷ *noun* an act of abseiling. • **abseiling** *noun*. ⓒ 20c: from German *abseilen*, from *ab* down + *Seil* rope.

absence /ˈabsəns/ ▷ *noun* **1** the state of being away, eg from work. **2** the time when a person is away, eg from work. **3** the state of not existing or of being lacking. • **absence of mind** a lack of attention or concentration. ⓒ 14c: from Latin *absentia*, from *abesse* to be away.

absent ▷ *adj* /ˈabsənt/ **1** not in its or one's expected place; not present. **2** not existing, especially where normally to be expected. **3** visibly not paying attention or concentrating. ▷ *verb* /abˈsent/ (***absented, absenting***) (*now always* **absent oneself**) to stay away from a meeting, gathering, etc. • **absently** *adverb* in a way which shows one is not paying attention or concentrating. ⓒ 14c.

absentee /absənˈtiː/ ▷ *noun* (***absentees***) someone who is not present at a particular or required time, or in a particular place. • **absenteeism** *noun* continual absence from work, school, etc.

absentia see IN ABSENTIA

absent-minded ▷ *adj* not noticing what one is doing or what is going on around one, especially because one is thinking about something else; preoccupied. • **absent-mindedly** *adverb*. • **absent-mindedness** *noun*.

absinthe or **absinth** /ˈabsɪnθ/ ▷ *noun* a strong green alcoholic drink flavoured with substances from certain plants, such as aniseed and wormwood. ⓒ 17c: French, from Latin *absinthium* wormwood.

absolute /ˈabsəluːt, -ljuːt/ ▷ *adj* **1** complete; total; perfect. **2** without limits; not controlled by anything or anyone else. **3** certain; undoubted. **4** not measured in comparison with other things; not relative ▫ *an absolute standard*. **5** pure; not mixed with anything else. **6** *grammar* **a** said of a clause or phrase: standing alone, ie not dependent on the rest of the sentence. Compare RELATIVE *adj* 5b. **b** said of an adjective or a transitive verb: standing alone, ie without a noun or an object respectively. ▷ *noun* **1** a rule, standard, etc which is thought to be true or right in all situations. **2** (**the absolute**) *philos* that which can exist without being related to anything else. • **absoluteness** *noun*. ⓒ 14c: from Latin *absolutus* loosened or separate, from *absolvere* (see ABSOLVE).

absolutely ▷ *adverb* **1** completely. **2** independently of anything else. **3** *colloq* in actual fact; really; very much. **4** *with negatives* at all ▫ ***absolutely nothing*** ▫ ***absolutely no use***. **5** yes; certainly.

absolute majority ▷ *noun* in an election: a number of votes for a candidate which is greater than the number of votes received by all the other candidates put together. Compare RELATIVE MAJORITY.

absolute pitch see PERFECT PITCH

absolute temperature ▷ *noun* temperature measured from ABSOLUTE ZERO on the KELVIN SCALE.

absolute zero ▷ *noun, physics* the lowest temperature theoretically possible, 0 K on the KELVIN SCALE, equivalent to -273.15°C or -459.67°F, at which atoms and molecules have minimal KINETIC ENERGY.

absolution /absəˈluːʃən, -ˈljuːʃən/ ▷ *noun* the formal forgiving of a person's sins, especially by a priest. ⓒ 12c: from Latin *absolutio* acquittal.

absolutism /ˈabsəluːtɪzəm, -ljuːtɪzəm/ ▷ *noun* the theory or practice of government by a person who has total power. • **absolutist** *noun, adj*. See also AUTOCRACY, DESPOTISM.

absolve /əbˈzɒlv, əbˈsɒlv/ ▷ *verb* (***absolved, absolving***) **1** (*usually* **absolve someone from** or **of something**) to release them or pronounce them free from a promise, duty, blame, etc. **2** said of a priest: to forgive someone formally for the sins they have committed. ⓒ 16c: from Latin *absolvere* to loosen.

absorb /əbˈsɔːb, əbˈzɔːb/ ▷ *verb* (***absorbed, absorbing***) **1** to take in or suck up (knowledge, etc). **2** *scientific* to take up or receive (matter or energy, eg water or radiation). **3** to receive or take something in as part of oneself or itself. **4** to engage all of (someone's attention or interest). **5** to reduce or lessen (the shock, force, impact, etc of something). **6** *physics* to take up (energy) without reflecting or emitting it. • **absorbability** *noun*. • **absorbable** *adj*. • **absorbed** *adj* engrossed; intently interested. • **absorbedly** *adverb*. • **absorbing** *adj* engrossing; fascinating. • **absorbingly** *adverb*. ⓒ 15c: from Latin *ab* away or from + *sorbere* to suck in.

absorbency ▷ *noun* (***absorbencies***) **1** the ability or capacity to absorb liquids, etc. **2** the degree to which something is able to absorb liquids, etc.

absorbent /əbˈsɔːbənt, -z-/ ▷ *adj* able to absorb liquids, etc. ▷ *noun, medicine, etc* something that absorbs liquids, etc.

absorbing and **absorbingly** see under ABSORB.

absorptance /əbˈsɔːptəns/ ▷ *noun, physics* a measure of the ability of a body to absorb radiation, measured as the ratio of energy absorbed by that body to the energy that is incident on it.

absorption ▷ *noun* **1** the act of taking in, sucking up or absorbing, or the process of being taken in, absorbed, etc. **2** the state of having all one's interest or attention occupied by something. ⓒ 16c: from Latin *absorptio*.

absorptive ▷ *adj* capable of absorbing. ⓒ 17c.

abstain /əbˈsteɪn/ ▷ *verb* (***abstained, abstaining***) *intr* (*usually* **abstain from something** or **from doing something**) **1** to choose not to take, have, do or undertake it. **2** to formally record one's intention not to vote in an election. • **abstainer** *noun*. See also ABSTENTION, ABSTINENCE. ⓒ 14c: from Latin *ab* away or from + *tenere* to hold.

abstemious /əbˈstiːmɪəs/ ▷ *adj* said of people, habits, etc: moderate or restrained in what one eats or drinks;

taking food, alcohol, etc in very limited amounts. • **abstemiously** *adverb*. • **abstemiousness** *noun*. ⓘ 17c: from Latin *abstemius*, from *abs* away or from + *temetum* strong drink.

abstention /əb'stɛnʃən/ ▻ *noun* **1** the act of choosing not to do something. **2 a** a refusal to vote; **b** someone who has abstained from voting; **c** an instance of abstaining from voting. ⓘ 16c: from Latin *abstinere* to abstain.

abstinence /'abstɪnəns/ ▻ *noun* the practice or state of choosing not to do or take something, especially to drink alcohol. • **abstinent** *adj*. • **abstinently** *adverb*. ⓘ 13c: from Latin *abstinere* to abstain.

abstract ▻ *adj* /'abstrakt/ **1** referring to something which exists only as an idea or quality. **2** concerned with ideas and theory rather than with things which really exist or could exist. **3** said of an art form, especially painting: that represents the subject by shapes and patterns, etc rather than in the shape or form it actually has. Compare CONCRETE *adj* 2 **4** *grammar* said of a noun: denoting a quality, condition or action rather than a physical thing. Compare CONCRETE *adj* 4. ▻ *noun* /'abstrakt/ **1** a brief statement of the main points (of a book, speech, etc). **2** an abstract idea, theory, etc. **3** an example of abstract painting, etc. ▻ *verb* /ab'strakt/ (***abstracted***, ***abstracting***) **1** to take out or remove something. **2** to summarize (a book, speech, etc). **3** to generalize about something from particular instances. • **abstractly** *adverb*. • **abstractness** *noun*. • **in the abstract** in theory rather than in reality. ⓘ 14c, meaning 'derived': from Latin *abs* away or from + *trahere* to draw.

abstracted /ab'straktɪd/ ▻ *adj* said of a person: thinking about something so much that they do not notice what is happening around them. • **abstractedly** *adverb*. • **abstractedness** *noun*.

abstract expressionism ▻ *noun, art* a development that began in 1940s America, in which the artist's abstract representations (see ABSTRACT *adj* 3) are animated by the expression of their feelings.

abstraction /ab'strakʃən/ ▻ *noun* **1** the act, or an example of, abstracting something. **2** something which exists as a general idea rather than as an actual example. **3** the state of thinking about something so much that one does not notice what is happening around one. **4** an example of abstract art.

abstruse /ab'struːs/ ▻ *adj* hard to understand. • **abstrusely** *adverb*. • **abstruseness** *noun*. ⓘ 16c: from Latin *abstrusus* pushed away.

absurd /əb'sɜːd, əb'zɜːd/ ▻ *adj* (***absurder***, ***absurdest***) **1** not at all suitable or appropriate. **2** ridiculous; silly. • **absurdity** *noun* (***absurdities***). • **absurdly** *adverb*. • **absurdness** *noun*. ⓘ 16c: from Latin *absurdus* out of tune.

ABTA /'abtə/ ▻ *abbreviation* Association of British Travel Agents.

abulia or **aboulia** /ə'buːlɪə, ə'bjuːlɪə/ ▻ *noun, psychiatry* a reduction in or absence of willpower, a common symptom of schizophrenia. ⓘ 19c: Latin, from Greek, usually meaning 'ill-advisedness', but used once to mean 'indecision'.

abundance /ə'bʌndəns/ ▻ *noun* **1** a large amount, sometimes more than is needed. **2** wealth. ⓘ 14c: French, from Latin *abundare* to overflow.

abundant /ə'bʌndənt/ ▻ *adj* existing in large amounts. • **abundant in something** having or providing a large amount or variety of something.

abundantly ▻ *adverb* **1** very; completely. **2** in large amounts.

abuse ▻ *verb* /ə'bjuːz/ (***abused***, ***abusing***) **1** to use (one's position, power, etc) wrongly. **2** to misuse something, especially to use (drugs) improperly. **3** to treat someone or something cruelly or wrongly. **4** to betray (a confidence). **5** to speak rudely or insultingly to or about someone. ▻ *noun* /ə'bjuːs/ **1** wrong use of one's position, power, etc. **2** (*also* **drug abuse**) the excessive use of alcohol, drugs or other harmful substances, especially as distinguished from the more severe form of dependence known as ADDICTION. **3** bad or cruel treatment of someone or something. **4** (*also* **child abuse**) the physical, mental or emotional maltreatment of a child by one of its parents or another adult. **5** an evil or corrupt practice. **6** rude or insulting words said to or about someone. ⓘ 15c: from Latin *abusus*, past participle of *abuti* to misuse.

abusive /ə'bjuːsɪv, -zɪv/ ▻ *adj* insulting or rude; using insulting or rude language. • **abusively** *adverb*. • **abusiveness** *noun*.

abut /ə'bʌt/ ▻ *verb* (***abutted***, ***abutting***) **1** *intr* (*usually* **abut against** or **on something**) said of countries, areas of land, buildings, etc: to join, touch or lean against another. **2** to lean on or touch something □ ***a wall abutting the house***. ⓘ 15c: from French *abouter* to touch with an end.

abutment ▻ *noun, archit, engineering* the support at the end of an arch, eg in a bridge or similar structure.

abuzz /ə'bʌz/ ▻ *adj* in a state of noisy activity or excitement. ⓘ 19c: A-[1] sense 2 + BUZZ.

abysmal /ə'bɪzməl/ ▻ *adj* **1** *colloq* extremely bad. **2** very deep; very great □ ***abysmal ignorance***. • **abysmally** *adverb*. ⓘ 19c: from French *abisme* abyss.

abyss /ə'bɪs/ ▻ *noun* (***abysses***) **1** a very large and deep chasm. **2** hell. **3** anything that seems to be bottomless or unfathomable. **4** a deep part of the ocean, generally more than 2 000m below the surface. ⓘ 14c as *abyssus*: from Latin *abyssus*, from Greek *abyssos* bottomless.

AC ▻ *abbreviation* **1** ALTERNATING CURRENT. Compare DC and AC/DC. **2** *ante Christum* (Latin), before Christ. **3** appellation contrôlée.

Ac ▻ *symbol, chem* actinium.

a/c ▻ *abbreviation, bookkeeping, etc* **1** account. **2** account current.

acacia /ə'keɪʃə/ ▻ *noun* (***acacias***) **1** any of various trees and shrubs found mainly in Australia, Africa and S America, most of which bear large spines and clusters of small yellow flowers. Also called WATTLE. **2** the false acacia or ROBINIA. ⓘ 16c in sense 1: from Greek *akakia*.

academe /'akədiːm/ ▻ *noun, formal* or *literary* **1** the world of scholars. **2** academic life. ⓘ 19c; 16c as *Academe*, meaning 'ACADEMY'.

academia /akə'diːmɪə/ ▻ *noun* the scholarly world or life. ⓘ 1950s.

academic /akə'dɛmɪk/ ▻ *adj* **1** to do with learning, study, education or teaching. **2** to do with a university, college or academy. **3** theoretical rather than practical. **4** of no practical importance, eg because impossible or unreal □ ***What we would do with a car is quite academic, since we can't afford one.*** **5** said of a person: fond of or having an aptitude for intellectual pursuits. **6** said of a person: too interested in intellectual pursuits at the expense of practicalities. ▻ *noun* a member of the teaching or research staff at a university or college. • **academically** *adverb*. • **academicism** /-mɪsɪzəm/ *noun*.

academicals ▻ *plural noun* academic robes.

academician /əkadə'mɪʃən/ ▻ *noun* a member of an ACADEMY (sense 2), especially the Royal Academy of Arts, the French *Académie Française* or the Russian Academy of Sciences.

academy /ə'kadəmɪ/ ▻ *noun* (***academies***) **1** a school or college that gives training in a particular subject or skill. **2** a society which encourages the study of science, literature, art or music. **3** in Scotland: a secondary school. ⓘ 16c in sense 2: from Greek *Akademeia* the garden outside Athens where the philosopher Plato taught, named after the hero *Akademos*.

Academy Award see OSCAR

Acadian /əˈkeɪdɪən/ ▻ *noun* **1** a native or inhabitant of the Atlantic provinces of Canada, especially a French-speaking one. **2** a native or inhabitant of Louisiana, especially one descended from the 18c emigrants from the Atlantic provinces of Canada. ◷ 18c: from French *Acadie* Acadia, from Micmac Indian *akade* abundance.

acanthus /əˈkanθəs/ ▻ *noun* (***acanthuses***) **1** any of various perennial plants with spiny leaves and bracts, including ornamental species cultivated for their white, pink or purple flowers and attractive foliage. **2** *archit* a conventionalized carving of an acanthus leaf used as a decoration, eg on columns or plaster mouldings. ◷ 17c: from Greek *akanthos*.

a cappella /akəˈpɛlə/ ▻ *adj, adverb* said of choral music: unaccompanied. ◷ 19c: Italian, literally 'in the church style'.

ACAS /ˈeɪkas/ ▻ *abbreviation* Advisory, Conciliation and Arbitration Service, a British organization which helps settle disagreements between employers and workers.

acatalectic /eɪkatəˈlɛktɪk, a-/ ▻ *adj* said of verse: having the full number of syllables. ◷ 16c: from Greek *akatalektos*; see A-[2] and CATALECTIC.

acc. ▻ *abbreviation* **1** (*also* **acct**) *bookkeeping* account. **2** (*also* **accus.**) *grammar* accusative.

accede /əkˈsiːd/ ▻ *verb* (***acceded***, ***acceding***) *intr* (*often* **accede to something**) **1** to take office, especially (as **accede to the throne**) to become king or queen. **2** to agree ▫ *accede to the proposal*. **3** to join with others in a formal agreement. ◷ 15c: from Latin *accedere* to go near.

accede to

☆ PLAIN ENGLISH alternatives in sense 2 are **agree to, grant, allow**.

accelerando /akseləˈrandoʊ, atʃɛl-/ ▻ *adverb, adj, music* increasingly faster. ◷ 19c: Italian.

accelerate /əkˈsɛləreɪt/ ▻ *verb* (***accelerated***, ***accelerating***) **1** *tr & intr* to increase the speed of something. **2** *intr* to be completed more quickly. **3** to make something happen sooner. ◷ 16c: from Latin *accelerare*.

acceleration /əksɛləˈreɪʃən/ ▻ *noun* **1** *physics* the rate of change of velocity with time, equal to FORCE (*noun* 9) divided by MASS[1] (*noun* 1). **2** any increase in the speed or rate at which a vehicle moves or a process occurs. **3** the ability of a motor vehicle, etc, to accelerate.

accelerator /əkˈsɛləreɪtə(r)/ ▻ *noun* **1** *engineering, autos* a pedal or lever designed to control the speed of an electric motor or engine by varying the amount of electric current or fuel supplied. **2** *physics* a piece of apparatus designed to increase the velocity of charged atomic particles, eg a cyclotron. **3** *chem* any substance that increases the rate at which a process occurs, eg a catalyst.

accent ▻ *noun* /ˈaksənt/ **1 a** the particular way words are pronounced by people who live in a particular place, belong to a particular social group, etc; **b** (**accents**) *poetic* way of speaking; speech. **2** emphasis or stress put on a particular syllable in speaking. **3** a mark put over a vowel to show how it is pronounced, eg ACUTE, GRAVE[3] or CIRCUMFLEX. Compare DIACRITIC. **4** a feature, mark or characteristic which makes something distinct or special. **5** *music* emphasis or stress placed on certain notes or chords. **6** *art* a highlight or other touch which emphasizes a particular effect. ▻ *verb* /əkˈsɛnt/ (***accented***, ***accenting***) **1** to pronounce something with an accent. **2** to mark an accent on (a written letter or syllable). **3** to emphasize or stress. • **accentless** *adj*. ◷ 14c: from Latin *accentus*.

accentuate /əkˈsɛntʃʊeɪt/ ▻ *verb* (***accentuated***, ***accentuating***) **1** to emphasize or make something more evident or prominent. **2** to mark something with an accent. • **accentuation** *noun*. ◷ 18c: from Latin *accentuare*.

accept /əkˈsɛpt/ ▻ *verb* (***accepted***, ***accepting***) **1** to agree or be willing to take or receive (something offered). **2** *tr & intr* to agree to (a suggestion, proposal, etc). **3** to agree to do (a job, etc) or take on (a responsibility, etc). **4** to believe something to be true or correct. **5** to be willing to listen to and follow (advice, etc). **6** to be willing to suffer or take (blame, etc). **7** to allow someone into a group, treat them as a colleague, etc. **8** to tolerate something calmly. **9** to promise to pay (a bill of exchange). ◷ 14c: from Latin *acceptare* to receive.

acceptable ▻ *adj* **1** worth accepting. **2** welcome or pleasing; suitable. **3** good enough, but usually only just; tolerable. • **acceptability** or **acceptableness** *noun*. • **acceptably** *adverb*.

acceptance ▻ *noun* **1** the act or state of accepting something. **2** favourable or positive reception of something. **3** a written or formal answer to an invitation, etc accepting it. **4 a** a formal agreement to pay a bill of exchange; **b** a bill which has been accepted in this way.

acceptor /əkˈsɛptə(r)/ ▻ *noun* **1** an organization or individual that accepts a bill of exchange. **2** *chem* any molecule or ion that accepts electrons from a DONOR. **3** *electronics* a small quantity of an impurity that is added to a SEMICONDUCTOR in order to increase its conductivity by attracting electrons, which leave 'holes' that behave like positive charges.

access /ˈaksɛs/ ▻ *noun* (***accesses***) **1** a means of approaching or entering a place. **2** the right, opportunity or ability to use, approach, meet with or enter something. **3** *computing* the right and opportunity to LOG ON to a computer system, and to read and edit files that are held within it, often requiring the entry of a password. **4** *computing* the possibility of transferring data to and from a memory device. **5** *formal or old use* a sudden and usually brief period of strong emotion. ▻ *verb* (***accesses***, ***accessed***, ***accessing***) to locate or retrieve (information stored in the memory of a computer). ◷ 14c: from Latin *accessus*, from *ad* to + *cedere* to go.

access

A word often confused with this one is **excess**.

accessary see ACCESSORY

access broadcasting and **access television** ▻ *noun* radio and TV programmes made independently by groups with a minority interest or viewpoint.

Access card ▻ *noun, trademark* a credit card issued by various banks.

accessible /əkˈsɛsɪbəl/ ▻ *adj* **1** able to be reached easily. **2** willing to talk to or have friendly discussions with other people. **3** easy to understand and enjoy or get some benefit from. • **accessibility** *noun*. • **accessibly** *adverb*.

accession /əkˈsɛʃən/ ▻ *noun* **1** the act or process of taking up a new office or responsibility, or of becoming a king or queen. **2** a person or thing added, eg a new book to a library. **3** the formal act of agreeing to, and coming under the rules of, an international agreement or treaty. ◷ 17c: French, from Latin *accedere* to accede.

accessory /əkˈsɛsərɪ/ ▻ *noun* (***accessories***) **1** something additional to, but less important than, something else. **2** an item of dress, such as a bag, hat, etc which goes with a dress, coat, etc. **3** (*sometimes* **accessary**) *law* someone who helps a criminal do something wrong. ▻ *adj* adding to something but only in a minor way. • **accessory before** or **after the fact** *law* someone who helps a criminal before or after the crime. ◷ 17c as *accessory*; 15c as *accessary*: from Latin *accessorius*.

access road ▻ *noun* a minor road built specially to give access to a house, motorway, etc.

access television see ACCESS BROADCASTING

access time ▷ *noun, computing* the time interval between the issue of a command requesting the retrieval of data from memory, and the stage at which data is finally obtained.

acciaccatura /ətʃakə'tʊərə/ ▷ *noun* (***acciaccaturas***) *music* a short GRACE NOTE, which does not take any time from the note on which it leans. Compare APPOGGIATURA. ◎ 19c: Italian, from *acciaccare* to crush.

accidence /'aksɪdəns/ ▷ *noun, technical* the part of grammar that deals with the inflections of words, eg to indicate the plural or past tense. ◎ 15c: from Latin *accidentia* chance.

accident /'aksɪdənt/ ▷ *noun* **1** an unexpected event which causes damage or harm. **2** something which happens without planning or intention; chance □ *managed it by accident.* ◎ 14c: from Latin *accidere* to happen.

accidental /aksɪ'dɛntəl/ ▷ *adj* **1** happening or done by accident; not planned. **2** incidental; not essential. ▷ *noun* **1** in written music: a sign, such as a sharp or flat, put in front of a note to show that it is to be played higher or lower than the key signature indicates. **2** something which is not a necessary feature of something. ● **accidentally** *adverb.*

accident-prone ▷ *adj* said of a person: frequently causing or involved in accidents, usually minor ones.

accidie /'aksɪdɪ/ ▷ *noun, especially formal, church* or *old use* sloth; torpor. ◎ 13c: French, from Greek *akedia*; used in the Middle Ages in Latin (as *acedia*) and English as a name for Sloth, one of the SEVEN DEADLY SINS.

acclaim /ə'kleɪm/ ▷ *verb* (***acclaimed, acclaiming***) **1** (*usually* **acclaim someone as something**) to declare them to be a specified thing, with noisy enthusiasm. **2** to receive or welcome someone or something with noisy enthusiasm. ▷ *noun* **1** acclamation. **2** CRITICAL ACCLAIM. ◎ 17c: from Latin *acclamare*, from *ad* to + *clamare* to shout.

acclamation /aklə'meɪʃən/ ▷ *noun* approval or agreement demonstrated by applause or shouting. ◎ 16c.

acclimatize or **acclimatise** /ə'klaɪmətaɪz/ ▷ *verb* (***acclimatized, acclimatizing***) *tr & intr* to make or become accustomed to a new place, situation, climate, etc. *US equivalent* **acclimate** /'akləmeɪt, ə'klaɪmət/ (***acclimated, acclimating***). ● **acclimatization** *noun.* ◎ 19c as *acclimatize*; 18c as *acclimate*: from French *acclimater*, from *climat* climate.

acclivity /ə'klɪvɪtɪ/ ▷ *noun* (***acclivities***) *formal* an upward slope. Compare DECLIVITY. ● **acclivitous** *adj.* ◎ 17c: from Latin *acclivitas*, from *clivus* sloping.

accolade /'akəleɪd/ ▷ *noun* **1** a sign or expression of great praise or approval. **2** a touch on the shoulder with a sword when giving a person a knighthood. ◎ 17c: French, from Italian *accollare* to embrace round the neck.

accommodate /ə'kɒmədeɪt/ ▷ *verb* (***accommodated, accommodating***) **1** to provide someone with a place in which to stay. **2** to be large enough for something; to be able to hold it. **3** to oblige someone; to do them a favour. **4** to adapt or adjust something in order to make it more acceptable to or appropriate for something else. ◎ 16c: from Latin *accommodare* to adapt.

accommodating /ə'kɒmədeɪtɪŋ/ ▷ *adj* helpful; willing to do what another person wants. ● **accommodatingly** *adverb.*

accommodation /əkɒmə'deɪʃən/ ▷ *noun* **1** (*also N Amer, especially US* **accommodations**) a room or rooms in a house or hotel in which to live. **2** willingness to accept other people's wishes, etc. **3** adaptation or adjustment. **4** (*also N Amer, especially US* **accommodations**) a reserved place on a bus, train, ship or aircraft. **5** *biol* in vertebrates: adjustment of the shape of the lens of the eye by CILIARY MUSCLES, in order to focus on distant and nearby objects.

accommodation

This is often misspelt as **accomodation**: there should be two *m*'s as well as two *c*'s.

accommodation address ▷ *noun* an address used on letters to a person who cannot give, or does not want to give, their permanent address.

accommodation ladder ▷ *noun* a small ladder on the outside of a large ship by means of which one can get to or from a smaller boat.

accompaniment ▷ *noun* **1** something that happens or exists at the same time as something else, or which comes with something else. **2** music played to accompany or support a singer or another instrument.

accompanist ▷ *noun* someone who plays a musical instrument to accompany or support a singer or another player.

accompany /ə'kʌmpənɪ/ ▷ *verb* (***accompanies, accompanied, accompanying***) **1** to come or go with someone. **2** to be done or found with something □ *The series is accompanied by an illustrated book.* **3** to play a musical instrument to support someone who is playing another instrument or singing. ◎ 15c: from French *accompagnier*, from *a* to + *compaignon* companion.

accomplice /ə'kʌmplɪs/ ▷ *noun* someone who helps another commit a crime. ◎ 15c as *complice*, from Latin *complex* joined; the *ac-* spelling begins in 16c, perhaps from a wrong division of *a complice*.

accomplish /ə'kʌmplɪʃ/ ▷ *verb* (***accomplishes, accomplished, accomplishing***) **1** to manage to do something. **2** to complete. ● **accomplishable** *adj.* ◎ 14c: from French *acomplir.*

accomplished /ə'kʌmplɪʃt/ ▷ *adj* **1** expert or skilled. **2** completed or finished.

accomplishment ▷ *noun* **1** a social or other skill developed through practice. **2** something special or remarkable which has been done; an achievement. **3** the finishing or completing of something.

accord /ə'kɔːd/ ▷ *verb* (***accorded, according***) *rather formal* to give someone (a welcome, etc) or grant them (permission, a request, etc). ▷ *noun* agreement or consent; harmony. ● **of one's own accord** willingly; without being told to or forced to. ● **with one accord** with everyone in agreement and acting at the same time. ◎ 12c: from French *acorder*, from Latin *cor* heart.

■ **accord with someone** or **something** to agree or be in harmony with them.

accordance ▷ *noun* agreement or harmony □ *in accordance with the law.* ◎ 14c.

of one's own accord, on one's own account

● **Of one's own accord** refers to willingness or initiative; **on one's own account** refers to benefit or advantage; but the two often overlap in meaning and are frequently confused or used imprecisely □ *I had been doing a little searching on my own account* □ *She had undertaken of her own accord not to tell anyone else.*

according /ə'kɔːdɪŋ/ ▷ *adverb* **1** (*usually* **according to someone**) as said or told by them □ *According to my doctor I am not contagious.* **2** (*usually* **according to something**) **a** in agreement with it □ *live according to one's principles*; **b** in proportion to it □ *Give to each according to his need.* **3** (*usually* **according as**) *formal* in proportion as; depending on whether □ *pay according as one is able.*

accordingly /ə'kɔːdɪŋlɪ/ ▷ *adverb* **1** in an appropriate way □ *act accordingly.* **2** therefore; for that reason.

accordion /ə'kɔːdɪən/ ▷ *noun* **a**) a portable musical instrument consisting of two box-like parts joined by a folding bellows-like middle section, which produces sound by forcing air over metal reeds, the melody being produced by means of buttons; **b**) (*also* **piano accordion**) a variety of this, which also has a piano-like keyboard on the right-hand box. • **accordionist** *noun*. ◷ 19c: from German *Akkordion*, from French *accorder* or Italian *accordare* to harmonize.

accordion pleats ▷ *plural noun* pleating with very narrow folds like the bellows section of an accordion.

accost /ə'kɒst/ ▷ *verb* (*accosted*, *accosting*) **1** to approach someone and speak to them, especially boldly or in a threatening way. **2** said of a prostitute: to offer to have sexual intercourse with someone in return for money. ◷ 16c: from French *acoster*, from Latin *ad* to + *costa* rib.

account /ə'kaʊnt/ ▷ *noun* **1** a description or report. **2** an explanation, especially of one's behaviour. **3 a** an arrangement by which a bank or building society allows a person to have banking or credit facilities; **b** a deposit of money in a bank or building society. **4** a statement of the money owed to a person or company for goods or services. **5** (*usually* **accounts**) a record of money received and spent. **6** an arrangement by which a shop allows a person to buy goods on credit and pay for them later. **7** *stock exchange* the period of time (usually a fortnight) by the end of which accounts must be settled. **8** a company or a specific area of business within a company which is dealt with by a PR firm or an advertising agency. **9** *now especially with negatives* importance or value ▫ *of little or no account*. ▷ *verb* (*accounted*, *accounting*) *formal* to consider someone or something to be as specified ▫ *accounted them all fools*. • **bring someone to account** to punish them for something wrong that has been done. • **by all accounts** according to general opinion. • **call someone to account** to demand an explanation from them for their action or behaviour. • **give a good** or **poor account of oneself** to give a good or bad performance; to make a good or bad impression. • **hold someone to account** to consider them responsible. • **leave something out of account** not to consider (a problem, factor, etc) when making a decision, calculation, etc. • **on account 1** said of goods: to be paid for at a later date. **2** said of a sum: as partial payment. • **on account of something** because of it. • **on no account** not for any reason. • **on one's own account 1** on one's own responsibility. **2** for one's own benefit. • **on someone's account** on their behalf; for their sake. • **put something to good account** to use a situation, ability, etc to one's advantage. • **take something into account** or **take account of something** to make allowances for or consider (a problem, opinion or other factor) when making a decision or assessment. • **turn something to good account** to use it to one's advantage. ◷ 14c as *acont* in senses 4, 5, 9 and in basic sense 'counting or reckoning': from French *aconter* to count.

■ **account for something 1** to give a reason or explanation for it. **2** to make or give a reckoning of (money spent, etc).

■ **account for something** or **someone** to succeed in destroying or disposing of it or them.

accountable ▷ *adj* **1** responsible; having to explain or defend one's actions or conduct. **2** explicable. • **accountability** or **accountableness** *noun*. • **accountably** *adverb*.

accountancy /ə'kaʊntənsɪ/ ▷ *noun* the profession or business of an accountant. ◷ 19c.

accountant /ə'kaʊntənt/ ▷ *noun* a person whose profession is to prepare, keep or audit the financial records of a business company, etc. ◷ 16c; 15c in old sense 'someone accountable'.

account-book ▷ *noun* a book for keeping accounts in (see ACCOUNT *noun* 5).

accounting ▷ *noun* the skill or practice of preparing or keeping the financial records of a company, etc.

accoutrements /ə'kuːtrəmənts/ ▷ *plural noun* **1** equipment. **2** a soldier's equipment apart from clothing and weapons. ◷ 16c: from French *accoustrer* to equip.

accredit /ə'krɛdɪt/ ▷ *verb* (*accredited*, *accrediting*) **1** to state officially that something is of a satisfactory standard. **2** *NZ* to accept (a student) for university on the basis of work done in school rather than a public examination. • **accreditation** *noun*. ◷ 17c: from French *accréditer*.

■ **accredit something to someone** or **accredit someone with something** to attribute (a saying, action, etc) to them.

■ **accredit someone to** or **at a place** to send (an ambassador or diplomat) to (a foreign country) with official authority.

accredited /ə'krɛdɪtɪd/ ▷ *adj* **1** officially recognized. **2** said of a belief, etc: generally accepted. **3** said of cattle or milk: officially stated to be of a satisfactory standard and free of disease.

accrete /ə'kriːt/ ▷ *verb* (*accreted*, *accreting*) **1** *tr & intr* to form or grow together. **2** *intr* to become attached. ◷ 18c: from Latin *accrescere*, *accretum*.

accretion /ə'kriːʃən/ ▷ *noun, formal or technical* **1** an extra layer of material which has formed on something else. **2** the process of separate things growing into one. **3** *geol* a gradual increase in land area resulting from offshore deposition of sediment carried by river currents, tides or wave action. **4** an increase in size of a particle, eg a hailstone, as a result of the formation of additional outer layers. • **accretive** *adj*. ◷ 17c: from Latin *accretio* growing together.

accrue /ə'kruː/ ▷ *verb* (*accrued*, *accruing*) **1** *intr* **a** to come in addition, as a product, result or development; **b** to be added as interest. **2** to collect ▫ *accrued a collection of antique vases*. • **accrual** *noun*. ◷ 15c: from French *acrue*, from Latin *accrescere* to grow together.

■ **accrue to someone** or **something 1** to accrue (sense 1) to them or it. **2** to fall to them or it naturally.

acct see under ACC.

acculturation /əkʌltʃə'reɪʃən/ *chiefly US* ▷ *noun* the process whereby one group of people becomes more like another group of people in behaviour, customs, etc, usually because of living near them for a long time. • **acculturate** *verb* (*acculturated*, *acculturating*) *tr & intr* to change or cause (a group of people) to change in this way. ◷ 19c: from Latin *ad* to + CULTURE.

accumulate /ə'kjuːmjʊleɪt/ ▷ *verb* (*accumulated*, *accumulating*) **1** to collect or gather something in an increasing quantity. **2** *intr* to grow greater in number or quantity. ◷ 16c: from Latin *accumulare*, from *cumulus* heap.

accumulation /əkjuːmjʊ'leɪʃən/ ▷ *noun* **1** the activity or process of accumulating. **2** a heap or mass.

accumulative /ə'kjuːmjʊlətɪv/ ▷ *adj* **1** becoming greater over a period of time. **2** tending to gather or buy, etc many things. • **accumulatively** *adverb*.

accumulator /ə'kjuːmjʊleɪtə(r)/ ▷ *noun* **1** *elec engineering* a storage battery that can be recharged by passing a current through it from an external direct current supply. **2** *horse-racing* (*also* **accumulator bet**) *Brit* a bet on four or more races, where the original money bet and any money won are bet on the next race, so that the better either wins a lot of money or loses it all. **3** *computing* a part of the memory of a computer that is used as a temporary store for the results of an arithmetical calculation or logic operation.

accuracy /'akjʊrəsɪ/ ▷ *noun* (*accuracies*) exactness; the state of being absolutely correct and making no mistakes, especially through careful effort.

accurate /ˈakjʊrət/ ▷ *adj* **1** absolutely correct; making no mistakes. **2** agreeing exactly with the truth or a standard. • **accurately** *adverb*. • **accurateness** *noun*. ⓒ 17c: from Latin *accuratus* performed with care.

accursed /əˈkɜːsɪd, əˈkɜːst/ ▷ *adj* **1** *colloq* disliked or hated. **2** having been cursed. • **accursedly** *adverb* damnably. ⓒ Anglo-Saxon *acursod*.

accusation /akjʊˈzeɪʃən/ ▷ *noun* **1** the act of accusing someone of having done something wrong. **2** *law* a statement charging a person with having committed a crime.

accus. see under ACC.

accusative /əˈkjuːzətɪv/ (abbreviation **acc.** or **accus.**) *grammar* ▷ *noun* **1** in certain languages, eg Latin, Greek and German: the form or CASE[2] (sense 7b) of a noun, pronoun or adjective when it is the object of an action or the point towards which something is moving. **2** a noun, etc in this case. ▷ *adj* belonging to or in this case. • **accusatival** /-ˈtaɪvəl/ *adj*. ⓒ 15c: from Latin *accusativus*.

accusatorial /əkjuːzəˈtɔːrɪəl/ ▷ *adj* said of a legal system, etc: in which the prosecutor is a different person from the judge. Compare INQUISITORIAL.

accusatory /əˈkjuːzətərɪ, akjuːˈzeɪtərɪ/ ▷ *adj* containing or consisting of accusation.

accuse /əˈkjuːz/ ▷ *verb* (***accused***, ***accusing***) (*usually* **accuse someone of something**) to charge them with (an offence). • **accuser** *noun*. • **accusing** *adj*. • **accusingly** *adverb*. • **the accused** the person or people accused of an offence. • **stand accused** *law* to appear in court charged with an offence. ⓒ 13c: from Latin *accusare*.

accustom /əˈkʌstəm/ ▷ *verb* (***accustomed***, ***accustoming***) (*usually* **accustom someone** or **oneself to something**) to make them or oneself familiar with it. ⓒ 15c: from French *acostumer*.

accustomed /əˈkʌstəmd/ ▷ *adj* usual; customary. • **accustomedness** *noun*. • **accustomed to someone** used to them. • **accustomed to something** familiar with or experienced in it.

AC/DC or **ac/dc** /eɪsiːˈdiːsiː/ ▷ *abbreviation*, *elec* alternating current/direct current. ▷ *adj*, *slang* sexually attracted to both men and women; bisexual.

ace /eɪs/ ▷ *noun* **1** *cards* the card in each of the four suits with a single symbol on it, having either the highest value or the value one. **2** *colloq* someone who is extremely good at something. **3** a fighter pilot who has shot down many enemy aircraft. **4** *tennis* a serve that is so fast and cleverly placed that the opposing player cannot hit the ball back. ▷ *adj*, *colloq* excellent. • **an ace up one's sleeve** a hidden or secret advantage, argument, etc that will help one to beat an opponent. • **hold all the aces** to be in a powerful or winning position. • **play one's ace** to put into action a plan for the final defeat of one's opponent. • **within an ace of something** or **of doing something** very close to it □ *came within an ace of winning*. ⓒ 13c as *as*: French, from Latin *as* a unit.

-acea /eɪsɪə/ ▷ *combining form*, *biol*, *forming plural nouns* in the classification of living organisms: used in the names of orders and classes □ *Crustacea*. ⓒ Latin neuter plural form of *-aceus* -ACEOUS.

-aceae /eɪsiiː/ ▷ *combining form*, *bot*, *forming plural nouns* in the classification of the plant kingdom: used in the names of plant families □ *Rosaceae*. ⓒ Latin feminine plural form of *-aceus* -ACEOUS.

-aceous /eɪʃəs/ ▷ *combining form*, *forming adjectives*, *denoting* relating or related to, or resembling, etc □ *rosaceous* □ *herbaceous*. ⓒ From Latin *-aceus*.

acerbic /əˈsɜːbɪk, aˈsɜːbɪk/ ▷ *adj* **1** bitter and sour in taste. **2** bitter and harsh in manner, speech, etc. ⓒ 19c.

acerbity /əˈsɜːbɪtɪ/ ▷ *noun* **1** applied to taste: sourness; bitterness. **2** applied to language or temper: harshness; sharpness. ⓒ 17c: from Latin *acerbus* sour.

acet- /asət, əˈsɛt/ or (before a consonant) **aceto-** /asɪtoʊ, əsiːtoʊ, asɪˈtɒ/ ▷ *combining form*, *signifying* derived from ACETIC ACID.

acetabulum /asəˈtabjʊləm/ ▷ *noun* (***acetabula*** /-lə/) **1** *anatomy* a cup-like socket in the pelvic girdle into which the ball-shaped head of the femur fits. **2** *zool* in insects: the cavity in the thorax into which a leg inserts. **3** in certain invertebrates, eg tapeworms: a sucker. ⓒ 17c; 14c in original sense 'a vinegar-cup': Latin, from *acetum* vinegar + *-abulum* a receptacle.

acetaldehyde /asɪˈtaldɪhaɪd/ ▷ *noun*, *chem* (formula CH_3CHO) a colourless volatile pungent liquid used as a solvent and reducing agent, and also in compounds such as PARALDEHYDE.

acetate /asəˈteɪt/ ▷ *noun* **1** a salt or ester of acetic acid. Also called **ethanoate**. **2** any of various synthetic fibres that are made from cellulose acetate. ⓒ 19c.

acetic /əˈsiːtɪk, əˈsɛtɪk/ ▷ *adj* consisting of or like vinegar. ⓒ 19c: from Latin *acetum* vinegar.

acetic acid ▷ *noun* a clear colourless viscous liquid with acidic properties and a characteristic pungent odour, present in vinegar, and formed by the fermentation of alcohol. Also called **ethanoic acid**.

aceto- see ACET-

acetone /ˈasətoʊn/ ▷ *noun*, *chem* (formula CH_3COCH_3) a colourless flammable volatile liquid with a characteristic pungent odour, widely used as a solvent for paints and varnishes, and as a raw material in the manufacture of plastics. Also called PROPANONE. ⓒ 19c.

acetyl /ˈasətaɪl, -tɪl, əˈsiːtɪl/ ▷ *noun*, *chem* the radical of acetic acid. ⓒ 19c: from ACETIC + -YL.

acetylene /əˈsɛtɪliːn, -lɪn/ ▷ *noun*, *chem* (formula C_2H_2) a colourless highly flammable gas with a sweet odour, used in lighting, oxyacetylene welding, and the manufacture of organic compounds. ⓒ 19c.

acetyl-salicylic acid ▷ *noun*, *chem* the chemical name for ASPIRIN.

ache /eɪk/ ▷ *verb* (***ached***, ***aching***) *intr* **1** to feel a dull continuous pain. **2** to be the source of a dull continuous pain. ▷ *noun* a dull continuous pain. • **aching** or **achy** *adj* (***achier***, ***achiest***). ⓒ Anglo-Saxon *acan* to ache, and *æce* an ache.

■ **ache for something** to want it very much.

achieve /əˈtʃiːv/ ▷ *verb* (***achieved***, ***achieving***) **1** to reach, realize or attain (a goal, ambition, etc), especially through hard work. **2** to earn or gain (a reputation, etc). **3** *intr* to be successful. • **achievable** *adj*. • **achiever** *noun*. ⓒ 14c: from French *achever*.

achievement ▷ *noun* **1** the gaining of something, usually after working hard for it. **2** something that has been done or gained by effort.

achievement age ▷ *noun* the level of an individual's educational achievement as determined by comparing his or her score in a test with the average score of other people of the same age.

achievement quotient ▷ *noun* (abbreviation **AQ**) ratio of ACHIEVEMENT AGE to chronological age.

Achilles' heel /əˈkɪliːz —/ ▷ *noun* a person's weak or vulnerable point. ⓒ 19c: named after Achilles, a hero in Homer's *Iliad*, who was invulnerable to weapons except in his heel, by which he had been held when being dipped in the river Styx as a baby, in an attempt by his mother to ensure his immortality.

Achilles' tendon ▷ *noun*, *anatomy* the tendon situated at the back of the ankle, that connects the muscles in the calf of the leg to the heelbone.

aching and **achy** see under ACHE

achondroplasia /eɪkɒndroʊˈpleɪʒə, ə-/ *medicine* ▷ *noun* an inherited form of DWARFISM, in which the arms and legs are abnormally short, but the head and body are of normal size. • **achondroplastic** *adj.* ◷ 19c: from Greek *achondros* without cartilage + *plassein* to form or mould.

achromat /'akroumat/ and **achromatic lens** ▻ *noun, image tech* a lens designed to minimize CHROMATIC ABERRATION. ◷ 20c.

achromatic /akrou'matɪk, eɪ-/ ▻ *adj* **1** without colour. **2** said of a lens: capable of transmitting light without separating it into its constituent colours. • **achromatically** *adverb.* • **achromaticity** /əkroumə'tɪsɪtɪ/ or **achromatism** /ə'kroumətɪzəm/ *noun.* ◷ 18c.

acid /'asɪd/ ▻ *noun* **1** *chem* any of a group of compounds that have a sour or sharp taste, turn blue litmus paper red, and react with bases to form salts. **2** any sour substance. **3** *slang* LSD. ▻ *adj* **1** sour to taste. **2** said of remarks, etc: expressing bitterness or anger. **3** said of soil, etc: having an acid reaction. **4** *chem* containing or having the properties of an acid. **5** *pop music* relating to ACID HOUSE. • **acidly** *adverb.* • **put the acid on someone** *Austral & NZ colloq* to pressurize them. ◷ 17c: from Latin *acidus* sour.

acid drop ▻ *noun* a sweet flavoured with tartaric acid.

acid-head ▻ *noun, drug-taking slang* someone who takes hallucinogenic drugs. ◷ 1960s: from ACID *noun* 3.

acid house or **Acid House** ▻ *noun* a type of electronically produced disco music with a repetitive hypnotic beat, often associated with the use of certain drugs (especially ECSTASY), and usually played at large all-night parties. Compare ACID ROCK. ◷ 1960s: ACID *noun* 3 + HOUSE 11.

acidic /ə'sɪdɪk/ ▻ *adj* like, or containing, acid.

acidify /ə'sɪdɪfaɪ/ ▻ *verb* (***acidifies, acidified, acidifying***) *tr & intr* to make or become acid. • **acidification** *noun.* ◷ 18c.

acidity /ə'sɪdɪtɪ/ ▻ *noun* (***acidities***) **1** the quality of being acid or sour. **2** *chem* the extent to which a given solution is acid, as indicated by its PH VALUE.

acidosis /asɪ'dousɪs/ ▻ *noun, pathol* a condition in which there is excessive acid in the blood, eg as in diabetes or in kidney disease. ◷ 20c.

acid rain ▻ *noun, ecol* rain or any other form of precipitation containing dissolved sulphur dioxide and nitrogen oxides that have been released into the atmosphere as a result of the burning of fossil fuels. ◷ 1850s.

acid rock ▻ *noun* a type of rock music featuring bizarre electronic and instrumental effects. ◷ 1960s: ACID *noun* 3 + ROCK[2] *noun* 2.

the acid test ▻ *noun* a decisive test to determine whether something is genuine or valid. ◷ 20c in this sense: originally (19c) a test using acid to determine whether a substance contained gold.

acidulate /ə'sɪdjʊleɪt/ ▻ *verb* (***acidulated, acidulating***) to make something slightly acid or sour. • **acidulated** *adj.* ◷ 18c.

acidulous /ə'sɪdjʊləs/ ▻ *adj* **1** slightly sour. **2** sharp or caustic in speech. ◷ 18c: from Latin *acidulus.*

acinus /'asɪnəs/ ▻ *noun* (***acini*** /-naɪ/) *bot* one of the small fruits that make up a composite fruit like the raspberry. ◷ 18c, meaning 'berry that grows in clusters': Latin, meaning 'berry'.

ack-ack /'akak/ *World War II slang* ▻ *adj* ANTI-AIRCRAFT. ▻ *noun* anti-aircraft fire. ◷ British World War I signallers' code for the letters *AA*, standing for *anti-aircraft.*

acknowledge /ək'nɒlɪdʒ/ ▻ *verb* (***acknowledged, acknowledging***) **1** to admit or accept the truth of (a fact or situation). **2** to accept something as valid or legal; to recognize it. **3** to report that one has received (what has been sent). **4** to express thanks for something. **5** to show that one has noticed or recognized someone, by greeting them, nodding one's head, etc. **6** to accept someone as something; to accept someone's claim to be something. • **acknowledged** *adj.* ◷ 16c: from earlier *acknow* to acknowledge + KNOWLEDGE.

acknowledgement or **acknowledgment** ▻ *noun* **1** the act of acknowledging someone or something. **2** something done, given or said to acknowledge something.

acme /'akmɪ/ ▻ *noun* the highest point of achievement, success, excellence, etc. ◷ 16c: from Greek *akme* point.

acne /'aknɪ/ ▻ *noun, pathol* a skin disorder, common in adolescence, caused by overactivity of the sebaceous glands, especially on the face, chest and back. ◷ 19c: perhaps from Greek *akme* point.

acolyte /'akəlaɪt/ ▻ *noun* **1** *Christianity* someone who assists a priest in certain religious ceremonies. **2** an assistant or attendant. ◷ 16c: from Latin *acolytus,* from Greek *akolouthos* follower.

aconite /'akənaɪt/ ▻ *noun* **1** any of various herbaceous plants, especially **monkshood** or WOLFSBANE, which has hooded bluish-purple flowers, and roots containing a toxic alkaloid compound formerly used to poison wolves. **2** the narcotic analgesic drug obtained from the roots of this plant, now generally regarded as too toxic for medicinal applications. ◷ 16c: from Latin *aconitum.*

acorn /'eɪkɔːn/ ▻ *noun* the nut-like fruit of the oak tree, which has a cup-shaped outer case (the **acorn-cup**). ◷ Anglo-Saxon *æcern.*

acoustic /ə'kuːstɪk/ and (especially in senses 1 and 3) **acoustical** ▻ *adj* **1** relating to, producing or operated by sound. **2** relating to acoustics. **3** relating to the sense of hearing. **4** said of a musical instrument, eg a guitar or piano: amplifying the sound by means of its body, not using an electrical amplifier. **5** said of building materials, etc: designed so as to reduce the disturbance caused by excessive noise. • **acoustically** *adverb.* ◷ 17c as *acoustique*: from Greek *akoustikos,* from *akouein* to hear.

acoustic coupler ▻ *noun* **1** *computing* a device that is used to transmit digital data along telephone lines to and from the MODEM of a computer terminal, without making direct connections to the telephone system. **2** any device that is used to convert electrical signals to sound signals, or vice versa.

acoustician /akʊ'stɪʃən/ ▻ *noun* **1** a scientist who specializes in ACOUSTICS. **2** a person whose job is to make or repair acoustic instruments.

acoustic phonetics ▻ *noun* the branch of phonetics that is specifically concerned with studying, measuring and analysing the frequency and amplitude of the vibrations and air movement that are produced when speech sounds are made. Compare ARTICULATORY PHONETICS, AUDITORY PHONETICS, PHONOLOGY.

acoustics /ə'kuːstɪks/ ▻ *plural noun* the characteristics of a room, concert hall, theatre, etc that determine the nature and quality of sounds such as music and speech heard within it. ▻ *singular noun* the scientific study of the production and properties of sound waves. ◷ 17c as *singular noun*: from ACOUSTIC.

acquaint /ə'kweɪnt/ ▻ *verb* (***acquainted, acquainting***) now only in phrases below. ◷ 13c: from French *acointer.*

- **acquaint someone with something** to make them aware of or familiar with it.
- **be acquainted with someone** to know them personally but only slightly.
- **become acquainted with someone** to get to know them personally.
- **be acquainted with something** to be familiar with it ▫ *Are you acquainted with her books?*

acquaintance ▻ *noun* **1** slight knowledge of something or someone. **2** someone whom one knows slightly. • **acquaintanceship** *noun*. • **make someone's acquaintance** to get to know them.

acquiesce /akwɪˈɛs/ ▷ *verb* (***acquiesced***, ***acquiescing***) *intr* (*usually* **acquiesce in** or **to something**) to accept it or agree to it without objection. • **acquiescence** *noun*. • **acquiescent** *adj*. • **acquiescently** *adverb*. Ⓒ 17c: from Latin *acquiescere*.

> ***acquiesce***
>
> **Acquiesce in** is the more usual construction and covers all uses. You will sometimes find **acquiesce to**, especially when there is a strong sense of submission □ *The political struggle of men and women refusing to acquiesce to the oppressive forces of capitalist society.* This is however sometimes considered to be incorrect.

acquire /əˈkwaɪə(r)/ ▷ *verb* (***acquired***, ***acquiring***) **1** to get, gain or develop something, especially through skill or effort. **2** to achieve or reach (a reputation). Ⓒ 15c: from Latin *acquirere*.

acquired immune deficiency syndrome and **acquired immunodeficiency syndrome** see AIDS

acquired immunity ▷ *noun* the level of resistance to infection in a person resulting from exposure to foreign substances or micro-organisms. Compare NATURAL IMMUNITY.

acquired taste ▷ *noun* **1** a liking for something that develops as one has more experience of it. **2** a thing liked in this way.

acquirement ▷ *noun* something learned or developed through hard work and not a natural gift.

acquisition /akwɪˈzɪʃən/ ▷ *noun* **1** something obtained or acquired, especially through hard work or effort. **2** a valuable addition to a group, a collection, etc. **3** the act of obtaining, developing or acquiring a skill, etc. Ⓒ 14c: from Latin *acquisitio*.

acquisitive /əˈkwɪzɪtɪv/ ▷ *adj* very eager to obtain and possess things. • **acquisitively** *adverb*. • **acquisitiveness** *noun*. Ⓒ 19c; 16c in an obsolete grammatical sense: from Latin *acquisitivus*.

acquit /əˈkwɪt/ ▷ *verb* (***acquitted***, ***acquitting***) (*often* **acquit someone of something**) said of a court or jury, etc: to declare a person accused of a crime to be innocent. • **acquit oneself** to behave or perform in a specified way □ *acquitted themselves with distinction.* Ⓒ 13c, meaning 'settle (a debt)': from French *aquiter*.

acquittal /əˈkwɪtəl/ ▷ *noun* **1** a declaration in a court of law that someone is not guilty of the crime, etc of which they have been accused. **2** performance of a duty.

acre /ˈeɪkə(r)/ ▷ *noun* **1** in the imperial system: a measure of land area equal to 4840 square yards (4047 sq m). **2** (*usually* **acres**) *colloq, loosely* a large area. • **acreage** /ˈeɪkərɪdʒ/ *noun* the number of acres in a piece of land. Ⓒ Anglo-Saxon *æcer* field.

acrid /ˈakrɪd/ ▷ *adj* **1** having a very bitter and pungent smell or taste. **2** said of speech, manner, etc: sharp or bitter. • **acridity** /aˈkrɪdɪtɪ/ *noun*. • **acridly** *adverb*. Ⓒ 18c; 16c as *acridity*: from Latin *acer* sharp or keen.

Acrilan /ˈakrɪlan/ ▷ *noun, trademark* an acrylic fibre.

acrimony /ˈakrɪmənɪ/ ▷ *noun* bitterness in feeling, temper or speech. • **acrimonious** /-ˈmoʊnɪəs/ *adj*. • **acrimoniously** *adverb*. Ⓒ 16c: from Latin *acrimonia*.

acro- /akroʊ, akrə, əˈkrɒ/ ▷ *combining form, signifying* **1** tip, point or extremity. **2** summit or height. Ⓒ From Greek *akron* tip, and *akros* highest.

acrobat /ˈakrəbat/ ▷ *noun* an entertainer, eg in a circus, who performs skilful balancing acts and other athletic tricks. • **acrobatic** *adj*. • **acrobatically** *adverb*. Ⓒ 19c: from French *acrobate*, from Greek *akrobatos* walking on tiptoe.

acrobatics /akrəˈbatɪks/ ▷ *singular noun* the art or skill of an acrobat. ▷ *plural noun* acrobatic movements.

acromegaly /akroʊˈmɛgəlɪ/ ▷ *noun, pathol* a disorder characterized by abnormal enlargement of the face, hands and feet, caused by overproduction of growth hormone. Ⓒ 19c: from Greek *akron* extremity + *megal-* big.

acronym /ˈakrənɪm/ ▷ *noun* a word made from the first letters or syllables of other words, and usually pronounced as a word in its own right, eg *NATO*. Compare ABBREVIATION, CONTRACTION, INITIALISM. • **acronymic** *adj*. Ⓒ 1940s: from Greek *akron* point or tip + *onyma* name.

acrophobia /akrəˈfoʊbɪə/ ▷ *noun, psychol* fear of heights or high places. • **acrophobic** *adj, noun*. Ⓒ 19c.

acropolis /əˈkrɒpəlɪs/ ▷ *noun* (***acropolises***) the upper fortified part or citadel of an ancient Greek city, now especially Athens. Ⓒ 19c in this sense: from Greek *akropolis*, from *akron* point or summit + *polis* city.

across /əˈkrɒs/ ▷ *prep* **1** to, at or on the other side of something. **2** from one side of something to the other. **3** so as to cross something □ *arms folded across the chest.* ▷ *adverb* **1** to, at or on the other side. **2** from one side to the other. **3** in a crossword: in the horizontal direction □ *6 across.* Compare DOWN *adverb* 10. • **across the board** *adverb* or **across-the-board** *adj* generally or general; applying in all cases □ *an across-the-board increase in pay.* Ⓒ 15c as *adverb* meaning 'crossed' or 'crosswise': A-^{1} + CROSS.

acrostic /əˈkrɒstɪk/ ▷ *noun* a poem or puzzle in which the first, last or middle letters in each line, or a combination of these, form a word or proverb. Ⓒ 16c: from Greek *akron* end + *stichos* line.

acrylic /əˈkrɪlɪk/ ▷ *noun* any of various synthetic products derived from acrylic acid, especially ACRYLIC FIBRE, ACRYLIC PAINT or ACRYLIC RESIN. ▷ *adj* relating to, containing or derived from acrylic acid. Ⓒ 19c as *acrylic acid*; otherwise 20c: from Latin *acer* sharp + *olere* to smell.

acrylic acid ▷ *noun, chem* a highly reactive colourless liquid with a pungent odour and acidic properties, used in the manufacture of acrylic resins, acrylic fibres, adhesives, artists' acrylic paint, etc.

acrylic fibre ▷ *noun* a synthetic fibre derived from acrylic acid, used for making knitwear and other clothing, etc. Often shortened to ACRYLIC.

acrylic paint ▷ *noun, art* a synthetic paint derived from acrylic acid, which is soluble in water but may also be applied in a thick impasto, and therefore can be used for a combination of watercolour and oil-painting techniques. Often shortened to ACRYLIC.

acrylic resin ▷ *noun* any of numerous synthetic resins used to make artificial fibres, lenses for optical instruments, protective coatings, waxes, paints and adhesives.

ACT ▷ *abbreviation* **1** ADVANCE CORPORATION TAX. **2** Australian Capital Territory.

act ▷ *noun* **1** a thing done; a deed. **2** the process of doing something □ *caught in the act.* **3** behaviour that is intended to make an impression on people and is not a sincere expression of feeling □ *Her shyness is just an act.* **4 a** a short piece of entertainment, usually one of a series in a variety show; **b** the person or people performing this. **5** a major division of a play, opera, etc. Compare SCENE. **6** (*often* **Act**) a formal decision reached, or a law passed, by a law-making body. **7** (**Acts**) *formal* the written proceedings of a society or committee. ▷ *verb* (***acted***, ***acting***) **1** *intr* to behave or function in a specified way □ *act tough* □ *acting strangely.* **2** *intr* to do something; to take action □ *need to act fast.* **3** *intr* to perform in a play or film. **4 a** to perform (a part) in a play or film; **b**) to perform (a play). **5** to play the part of someone or something □ *to act the fool.* **6** *intr* to show feelings one does not really have. ● **actable** *adj.* ● **actability** *noun.* ● **act of God** an event beyond human control, especially a natural disaster such as an earthquake. ● **act one's age** to behave appropriately for one's age. ● **get in on the act** *colloq* to start taking part in some profitable activity, plan, etc in order to share in the benefits. ● **get one's act together** *colloq* to become organized and ready for action, especially in relation to a specific undertaking. ⓒ 14c; late 15c as *verb*: from Latin *actum* thing done.

■ **act as someone** or **something** to perform the actions or functions of (a specified person or thing) □ *He acted as caretaker until an appointment was made.*

■ **act for someone** to stand in as substitute for them.

■ **act on** or **upon someone** or **something** to have an effect or influence on them or it.

■ **act on** or **upon something** to follow (advice, etc); to obey (instructions, etc).

■ **act something out** to express (one's feelings, fears, etc) in one's behaviour, usually unconsciously.

■ **act up** *colloq* **1** said of a machine, etc: to fail or function erratically. **2** to behave badly.

acting ▻ *noun* the profession or art of performing in a play or film. ▻ *adj* temporarily doing someone else's job or duties □ *the acting headmaster.*

actinide /'aktɪnaɪd/ ▻ *noun* any of a series of radioactive elements, from atomic number 89 upwards. ⓒ 19c.

actinium /ak'tɪnɪəm/ ▻ *noun, chem* (symbol **Ac**, atomic number 89) a silvery-white radioactive metal found in uranium ores, used as a source of ALPHA PARTICLES. ⓒ 19c: from Greek *aktis* ray (from its being radioactive).

action /'akʃən/ ▻ *noun* **1** the process of doing something □ *put ideas into action.* **2** something done. **3** activity, force or energy □ *a woman of action.* **4** a movement or gesture. **5** the working part of a machine, instrument, etc; a mechanism. **6** a battle; fighting □ *saw action in Korea.* **7** (**the action**) the events of a play, film, etc. **8** *colloq* (**the action**) exciting activity or events going on around one □ *get a piece of the action.* **9** a legal case. ● **out of action** not working. ⓒ 14c: from Latin *actio*, from *agere* to do or drive.

actionable ▻ *adj* giving reasonable grounds for legal action.

action committee and **action group** ▻ *noun* a committee or group who are chosen in order to take active measures to achieve some desired end.

action movie ▻ *noun* a cinema film with a fast-moving plot and many scenes containing elaborate stunts, special effects, minimal characterization and often, but not necessarily, much violence.

action-packed ▻ *adj, colloq* filled with exciting activity.

action painting ▻ *noun, art* an American version of TACHISM in which paint is dripped, spattered or smeared on to the canvas. ⓒ 1950s.

action potential ▻ *noun, physiol* the change in electrical potential across the membrane of a nerve cell when an impulse is being conducted. Compare RESTING POTENTIAL

action replay ▻ *noun* on television: the repeating of a piece of recorded action, eg the scoring of a goal in football, usually in slow motion or from another angle. *N Amer equivalent* INSTANT REPLAY.

action stations ▻ *plural noun* **1** positions taken by soldiers ready for battle. **2** *colloq* posts assumed or manned in readiness for any special combined task or action. ▻ *exclamation* **1** an instruction to take up these positions. **2** a general instruction to prepare for action.

activate /'aktɪveɪt/ ▻ *verb* (***activated, activating***) **1** to make something start working or go into operation. **2** to increase the energy of something. **3** to make (a material) radioactive. **4** to increase the speed of or to cause (a chemical reaction). **5** to increase the capacity of (carbon or charcoal) to ABSORB impurities, especially gases. **6** to increase the biological activity of (sewage) by treatment with air and bacteria. ● **activation** *noun.* ● **activator** *noun.* ⓒ 17c: ACTIVE + -ATE 1.

active /'aktɪv/ ▻ *adj* **1** said of a person, etc: moving, working and doing things; full of energy. **2** said of a machine, etc: operating; working. **3** having an effect □ *the active ingredients.* **4** said of a volcano: liable to erupt; not extinct. **5** *physics* radioactive. **6** *grammar* (abbreviation **act.**) **a** denoting or relating to a verbal construction in which the subject performs the action or has the state described by the verb, as in *the man fell, smoking kills you* and *God exists*. Compare PASSIVE; **b** denoting or relating to the verb in such a construction. ▻ *noun, grammar* **1** (*also* **active voice**) the form or forms that an active verb takes. **2** an active verb or construction. ● **actively** *adverb.* ⓒ 14c: from Latin *activus.*

active immunity ▻ *noun, medicine* immunity produced by stimulating the body to produce its own antibodies.

active list ▻ *noun* a list of full-pay officers engaged in or available for active service.

active service ▻ *noun* military service in the battle area.

activist /'aktɪvɪst/ ▻ *noun* someone who is very active, especially as a member of a political group. ● **activism** *noun.*

activity /ak'tɪvɪtɪ/ ▻ *noun* (***activities***) **1** the state of being active or busy. **2** (*often* **activities**) something that people do, especially for pleasure, interest, exercise, etc. **3** *physics* the rate at which the atoms of a radioactive substance disintegrate per unit of time. ⓒ 16c: from Latin *activitas.*

activity holiday ▻ *noun* a holiday which offers participation and usually training or coaching in a leisure activity, often a sport.

act of parliament see STATUTE

actor /'aktə(r); *affected* 'aktɔː(r)/ ▻ *noun* a man or woman who performs in plays or films, especially as their profession. ● **actorish** or **actorly** *adj* affectedly theatrical. ⓒ 16c; 14c, meaning 'agent': Latin, meaning 'doer'.

actress ▻ *noun* (***actresses***) a female actor. ● **actressy** *adj* said of a woman: affectedly theatrical.

ACTT ▻ *abbreviation, Brit* Association of Cinematograph, Television and Allied Technicians.

actual /'aktʃʊəl/ ▻ *adj* **1** existing as fact; real. **2** not imagined, estimated or guessed. **3** current; present. ⓒ 14c as *actuel*, meaning 'demonstrated by one's actions': from Latin *actualis.*

actual bodily harm ▻ *noun* (abbreviation **ABH**) *law* a criminal offence involving a less serious attack than GRIEVOUS BODILY HARM.

actuality /aktʃʊ'alɪtɪ/ ▻ *noun* (***actualities***) **1** fact; reality. **2** (*usually* **actualities**) an existing condition or fact.

actually ▻ *adverb* **1** really; in fact. **2** usually said in surprise or disagreement: as a matter of fact.

actuary /'aktʃʊərɪ/ ▻ *noun* (***actuaries***) someone who calculates insurance risks, and gives advice to insurance companies, etc on what premiums to set. ● **actuarial** /-'ɛərɪəl/ *adj.* ● **actuarially** *adverb.* ⓒ 19c in this sense; 16c in old sense 'clerk': from Latin *actuarius* clerk.

actuate /ˈaktʃʊeɪt/ ▷ *verb* (***actuated***, ***actuating***) to make (a mechanism, etc) go into action. • **actuation** *noun*. ⓒ 17c in this sense: from Latin *actuare*, from *actus* act.

■ **be actuated by something** to be made to act the way one does because of it.

acuity /əˈkjuːɪtɪ/ ▷ *noun* **1** sharpness or acuteness, eg of the mind or senses. **2** (*especially* **visual acuity**) sharpness of vision. ⓒ 16c: Latin, literally 'point', from *acus* needle.

acumen /ˈakjʊmən/ ▷ *noun* the ability to judge quickly and well; keen insight. ⓒ 16c: from Latin *acumen* point.

acupressure /ˈakjʊprɛʃə(r)/ ▷ *noun*, *alternative medicine* pressure instead of needles applied at specified points (**acupoints**). • **acupressurist** *noun*. See also AN MO, DO-IN, JIN SHIN DO, SHIATSU. ⓒ 1950s in this sense: from ACUPUNCTURE + PRESSURE 2.

acupuncture /ˈakjʊpʌŋktʃə(r)/ ▷ *noun*, *alternative medicine* a traditional Chinese method of healing in which symptoms are relieved by the insertion of thin needles at specified points (**acupoints**) beneath the skin, now widely recognized by orthodox medical practitioners. • **acupuncturist** *noun*. ⓒ 17c, meaning 'pricking with a needle': from Latin *acus* needle + PUNCTURE.

acute /əˈkjuːt/ ▷ *adj* (***acuter***, ***acutest***) **1** said of the senses: keen, good or sharp; penetrating. **2** said of mental powers, etc: quick and very good. **3** said of a disease or symptoms: arising suddenly and often severe, but of short duration □ *acute bronchitis* □ *acute pain*. Compare CHRONIC. **4** said of any bad condition or situation: extremely severe □ *acute drought*. **5** said of hospital accommodation: intended for patients with acute illnesses. **6** said of a sound: high, sharp and shrill. **7** *math* said of an angle: less than 90°. Compare REFLEX *adj* 5, OBTUSE 3. ▷ *noun* (*also* **acute accent**) a sign placed above a vowel in some languages, either to indicate a particular pronunciation of the vowel, as with *é* in French, or, as in Spanish, to indicate that the vowel is to be stressed. • **acutely** *adverb*. • **acuteness** *noun*. ⓒ 16c: from Latin *acuere* to sharpen.

-acy /əsɪ/ ▷ *combining form*, *forming nouns* (*plural* ***-acies***), *signifying* **1** a quality □ *accuracy*. **2** a state, condition, office, etc □ *supremacy* □ *piracy*. ⓒ From Latin *-acia*.

acyl group /ˈeɪsɪl —, ˈasɪl —/ ▷ *noun*, *chem* the radical RCO-, where R is ALIPHATIC. ⓒ 20c: from ACID + -YL.

AD ▷ *abbreviation* in dates: *Anno Domini* (Latin), in the year of our Lord, used together with a figure to indicate a specified number of years after that in which Christ was once thought to have been born. Compare BC, BCE. See also COMMON ERA.

AD

AD is used with dates to denote the current era. It should, strictly speaking, precede the year number, as *AD 2000*, but *2000 AD* is now common and acceptable. It is also legitimate to write eg *the 6th century AD*.

ad ▷ *noun*, *colloq* an ADVERTISEMENT.

adage /ˈadɪdʒ/ ▷ *noun* a proverb or maxim. ⓒ 16c: French.

adagio /əˈdɑːdʒɪoʊ/ *music* ▷ *adverb* slowly. ▷ *adj* slow. ▷ *noun* (***adagios***) a piece of music to be played in this way; a slow movement. ⓒ 18c: Italian, from *ad agio* at ease.

Adam /ˈadəm/ ▷ *noun* the first man, according to the Biblical account in the Book of Genesis. • **not know someone from Adam** to be unable to distinguish or recognize them at all. ⓒ 16c: Hebrew, meaning 'man'.

adamant /ˈadəmənt/ ▷ *adj* completely determined; not likely to change one's mind or opinion. • **adamantly** *adverb*. ⓒ Anglo-Saxon, meaning 'an extremely hard stone', from French *adamaunt*, from Latin *adamas* hard steel.

adamantine /adəˈmantaɪn/ *adj* extremely hard; immovable or impenetrable. ⓒ 14c: from Latin *adamantinus*; see ADAMANT.

Adam's apple ▷ *noun*, *anatomy* the projection of the THYROID cartilage, more prominent in men than in women, lying just beneath the skin at the front of the throat. ⓒ 18c.

adapt /əˈdapt/ ▷ *verb* (***adapted***, ***adapting***) **1** *tr & intr* to change something, oneself, etc so as to fit new circumstances, etc; to make something suitable for a new purpose. **2** to alter or modify something. • **adaptive** *adj*. ⓒ 17c: from Latin *ad* to + *aptare* to fit.

adaptable ▷ *adj* **1** said of a person: good at fitting into new circumstances, situations, etc. **2** said of a machine, device, etc: that can be adapted. • **adaptability** *noun*.

adaptation /adəpˈteɪʃən/ ▷ *noun* **1** a thing which is adapted. **2** the process of adapting. **3** *biol* a particular change in the structure, function or behaviour of a living organism that improves its chances of survival in its environment.

adaptive see under ADAPT

adaptor or **adapter** ▷ *noun* **1** a device designed to connect two parts of different sizes. **2** a device that enables a plug and socket with incompatible terminals to be connected, or that allows more than one electrical appliance to be powered from a single socket. **3** a person who adapts.

ADC ▷ *abbreviation* **1** aide-de-camp. **2** analogue-to-digital converter.

add ▷ *verb* (***added***, ***adding***) **1** (*also* **add something together**) to put together or combine (two or more things). **2** (*also* **add something up**) **a** to calculate the sum of two or more numbers or quantities in order to obtain their total value □ *When we added our money, it was more than we thought.* **b** *intr* (*also* **add up**) to carry out the process of addition. **3** to say or write something further □ *They added a remark about the bad weather.* • **added** *adj* additional; extra. ⓒ 14c: from Latin *addere*, from *ad* to + *dare* to put.

■ **add something in** to include it, especially as an extra.

■ **add something on** to attach it to something else. See also ADD-ON.

■ **add something to something else** to put them together, so that they are counted or regarded together □ *We'll add our money to yours.*

■ **add up** *colloq* to make sense; to be coherent. See also *verb* 2b above.

■ **add up to something** to be the equivalent of it or amount to it □ *It all adds up to a great success.*

added value ▷ *noun*, *econ* VALUE ADDED.

addendum /əˈdɛndəm/ ▷ *noun* (*plural* ***addenda*** /əˈdɛndə/) **1** an addition. **2** (*usually* **addenda**) an extra piece of text added to the end of a book. ⓒ 18c: Latin, from *addere* to add.

adder /ˈadə(r)/ ▷ *noun* the common European VIPER, a brown, olive or greyish snake with a dark zigzag line running down its back. It is the only poisonous snake found in the UK, but is seldom fatal to humans. ⓒ Anglo-Saxon *nædre*; around the 14c the old form *a nadder* became understood to be *an adder*.

addict /ˈadɪkt/ ▷ *noun* **1** someone who is physically or psychologically dependent on the habitual intake of a drug such as alcohol, nicotine, heroin, etc. **2** *colloq* someone who is extremely fond of a hobby, etc □ *a chess addict*. ⓒ 16c: see ADDICTED.

addicted /əˈdɪktɪd/ ▷ *adj* **1** (*especially* **addicted to something**) dependent on it (especially a drug). **2** unable to give it up, eg a habit. ◷ 16c, meaning 'devoted or attached to something': from obsolete verb *addict* to make oneself over or surrender (especially oneself), from Latin *addicere* to surrender.

addiction /ə'dɪkʃən/ ▻ *noun* **1** the state of being addicted. **2** a habit that has become impossible to break, especially one involving physical and psychological dependence on the intake of harmful substances such as alcohol or narcotic drugs.

addictive /ə'dɪktɪv/ ▻ *adj* relating to or tending to cause addiction; habit-forming □ ***addictive drugs***.

adding machine ▻ *noun* a device for performing basic arithmetical calculations.

addition /ə'dɪʃən/ ▻ *noun* **1** the act or operation of adding. **2** someone or something that is added. **3** *math* the combination of two or more numbers in such a way as to obtain their sum. • **in addition** as well; besides. • **in addition to something** as well as or besides it. ◷ 15c: from Latin *additio*, from *addere* to add.

addition reaction ▻ *noun, chem* a chemical reaction in which one molecule combines with another to form a third, more complex, molecule without the formation of a by-product such as water.

additional ▻ *adj* extra; more than usual. • **additionally** *adverb*.

additive /'adɪtɪv/ ▻ *noun* any chemical substance that is deliberately added to another substance, usually in small quantities, for a specific purpose, eg a food flavouring or colouring. ▻ *adj, math* relating to addition. ◷ 1940s as a *noun*; 17c as an *adj*: from Latin adjective *additivus*.

addle /'adəl/ ▻ *verb* (***addled***, ***addling***) **1** to confuse or muddle. **2** *intr* said of an egg: to go bad. • **addled** *adj*. ◷ Anglo-Saxon *adela* mud.

addle-brained, **addle-headed** and **addle-pated** ▻ *adj* said of a person: confused; crazy.

add-on ▻ *noun* **1** anything added to supplement something else. **2** *computing* any device that can be added to a basic computer system in order to increase its capabilities, eg extra memory or an extra program. **3** an extra charge added to the basic charge of something.

address ▻ *noun* /ə'drɛs; *chiefly US* 'adrɛs/ (***addresses***) **1** the number or name of the house or building, and the name of the street and town, where a person lives or works. **2** *rather formal* a speech or lecture. **3** *computing* a number giving the place in a computer memory where a particular piece of information is stored. ▻ *verb* /ə'drɛs/ (***addresses***, ***addressed***, ***addressing***) **1** to put the name and address on (an envelope, etc). **2** to make a speech, give a lecture, etc to (a group of people). **3** to speak to someone. **4** to give one's attention to (a problem, etc). ◷ 15c, meaning 'to direct (words) to someone'; 14c, meaning 'to arrange or prepare': from French *adresser*.

■ **address oneself to someone** to speak or write to them.

■ **address oneself to something** to deal with (a problem, matter, etc).

address book ▻ *noun* a notebook, usually with alphabetical thumb-index, in which names and addresses can be entered.

addressee /adrɛ'siː/ ▻ *noun* (***addressees***) the person to whom a letter, etc is addressed.

adduce /ə'dʒuːs/ ▻ *verb* (***adduced***, ***adducing***) to mention (a fact) as a supporting reason, piece of evidence, etc. • **adducible** *adj*. ◷ 17c: from Latin *ducere* to lead.

adenine /'adəniːn/ ▻ *noun, biochem* a base, derived from PURINE, which is one of the four bases found in NUCLEIC ACID. See also CYTOSINE, GUANINE, THYMINE.

adenoidal /adə'nɔɪdəl/ ▻ *adj, anatomy, etc* **1** relating to the adenoids. **2** said of a person: having swollen adenoids. **3** said of the voice: having the blocked nasal tone normally associated with swollen adenoids.

adenoids /'adənɔɪdz/ ▻ *plural noun, anatomy* a pair of lymph glands located in the upper part of the throat at the back of the nasal cavity, which may become infected and swollen and require surgical removal, especially in children. ◷ 19c: from Greek *adenoiedes*, from *aden* gland.

adenosine diphosphate see ADP

adenosine triphosphate see ATP

adept ▻ *adj* /'adɛpt, ə'dɛpt/ (***adepter***, ***adeptest***) (*often* **adept at something**) skilful at doing it; proficient. ▻ *noun* /'adɛpt/ an expert at something. • **adeptly** *adverb*. • **adeptness** *noun*. ◷ 17c: from Latin *adeptus* having attained something.

adequate /'adəkwət/ ▻ *adj* **1** enough; sufficient. **2** (*usually* **adequate to something**) competent to do a particular job, task, etc. **3** only just satisfactory. • **adequacy** /-kwəsɪ/ *noun*. • **adequately** *adverb*. • **adequateness** *noun*. ◷ 17c: from Latin *adaequatus* made equal.

à deux /a dø/ *adverb* for or consisting of two people □ *dinner à deux*. ◷ 19c: French.

adhere /əd'hɪə(r)/ ▻ *verb* (***adhered***, ***adhering***) *intr* (*often* **adhere to something**) **1** to stick or remain fixed to something. **2** to remain loyal to (a religion, etc). **3** to follow (a plan, rule, etc) exactly. ◷ 16c: from Latin *adhaerere*.

adherent /əd'hɪərənt/ ▻ *noun* a follower; a supporter. ▻ *adj* sticking or adhering. • **adherence** *noun*.

adhesion /əd'hiːʒən/ ▻ *noun* **1** the process of sticking or adhering. **2** the sticking together of two surfaces, especially by means of an adhesive. **3** *physics* the attraction between atoms or molecules of different substances, eg water and glass, that produces surface tension effects. See also COHESION. **4** *pathol* (*often* ***adhesions***) a mass or band of fibrous connective tissue that develops, especially after surgery or injury, between membranes or other structures which are normally separate. ◷ 17c: from Latin *adhaesio*.

adhesive /əd'hiːsɪv, -zɪv/ ▻ *adj* sticky; able to make things stick together. ▻ *noun* any substance that is used to bond two surfaces together. ◷ 18c: from ADHERE.

ad hoc /ad hɒk/ ▻ *adj* ▻ *adverb* for one particular purpose, situation, etc only □ ***employed on an ad hoc basis***. ◷ 17c: Latin, meaning 'for this purpose'.

ad hocery /ad 'hɒkərɪ/ ▻ *noun* (***ad hoceries***) *facetious* the use of ad hoc measures; improvisation or pragmatism. ◷ 20c.

ad hominem /ad 'hɒmɪnɛm/ *adj, adverb* **1** appealing to one's audience's prejudices rather than their reason. **2** attacking one's opponent's character rather than their argument. ◷ 16c: Latin, literally 'to the man'.

adieu /ə'djuː/ ▻ *noun* (***adieus*** or ***adieux*** /-z/) a goodbye. ▻ *exclamation* goodbye. ◷ 14c: French, from *à* to + *dieu* God.

Adi Granth see GRANTH

ad infinitum /ad ɪnfɪ'naɪtəm/ ▻ *adverb* for ever; without limit. ◷ 17c: Latin.

adipose /'adɪpoʊs, -z/ ▻ *adj, technical* relating to, containing or consisting of fat; fatty. ◷ 18c: from Latin *adiposus*, from *adeps* soft fat.

adipose tissue ▻ *noun, anatomy, medicine* body tissue that provides insulation and serves as an energy reserve, consisting of large spherical cells specialized for the storage of fat and oil.

adj. ▻ *abbreviation* adjective.

adjacent /ə'dʒeɪsənt/ ▻ *adj* (*often* **adjacent to something**) lying beside or next to it. • **adjacency** *noun*.

• **adjacently** *adverb*. ⓒ 15c: from Latin *adjacere* to lie by the side of.

adjacent, adjoining

There is sometimes confusion between **adjacent** and **adjoining**. **Adjacent** things can be close to or next to each other, but not necessarily touching □ *He dodged into an adjacent alley* □ *The noise from an adjacent bus station.* **Adjoining** things are next to and touching each other □ *The bathroom adjoining her hotel room* □ *A lease of land adjoining a road.*

adjective /ˈadʒəktɪv/ *grammar* ▻ *noun* (abbreviation **adj.**) a word that describes or modifies a noun or pronoun, as *dark* describes *hair* in *She has dark hair*, and *sad* describes *him* in *The story made him sad*. • **adjectival** /-ˈtaɪvəl/ *adj.* • **adjectivally** *adverb*. ⓒ 16c in this sense: from Latin *adjicere*, adjectum to attach or associate.

adjoin /əˈdʒɔɪn/ ▻ *verb* (**adjoined**, **adjoining**) to be next to and joined to something. • **adjoining** *adj.* ⓒ 14c: from French *ajoindre*, from Latin *ad* to + *jungere* to join.

adjourn /əˈdʒɜːn/ ▻ *verb* (**adjourned**, **adjourning**) **1** to put off (a meeting, etc) to another time. **2** to finish (a meeting, etc), intending to continue it at another time or place. **3** *intr* to move to another place, usually for refreshment or rest. **4** *intr* to finish a meeting and separate. • **adjournment** *noun*. ⓒ 14c: from French *ajorner*.

Adjt ▻ *abbreviation* Adjutant.

Adjt-Gen. ▻ *abbreviation* Adjutant-General.

adjudge /əˈdʒʌdʒ/ ▻ *verb* (**adjudged**, **adjudging**) to declare or judge officially. ⓒ 14c: from French *ajuger*, from Latin *adjudicare* to adjudicate.

adjudicate /əˈdʒuːdɪkeɪt/ ▻ *verb* (**adjudicated**, **adjudicating**) **1** *intr* to act as judge in a court, competition, etc. **2** to give a decision on (a disagreement between two parties, etc). • **adjudication** *noun*. • **adjudicator** *noun*. ⓒ 17c: from Latin *adjudicare*, from *judex* judge.

adjunct /ˈadʒʌŋkt/ ▻ *noun* **1** something attached or added to something else but not an essential part of it. **2** a person who is below someone else in rank. **3** *grammar* a word or clause that adds information about the subject, etc of a sentence. ⓒ 16c: from Latin *adjungere* to join to.

adjure /əˈdʒʊə(r)/ ▻ *verb* (**adjured**, **adjuring**) *formal* to request, beg or command someone formally or solemnly. • **adjuration** /adʒʊˈreɪʃən/ *noun*. ⓒ 14c, meaning 'to bind someone with an oath': from Latin *adjurare* to swear something with an oath.

adjust /əˈdʒʌst/ ▻ *verb* (**adjusted**, **adjusting**) **1** to change something or oneself, etc slightly so as to be more suitable for a situation, etc. **2** to change or alter something, especially only slightly, to make it more correct or accurate. **3** to calculate or assess (the amount of money payable in an insurance claim, etc). **4** *intr* (*often* **adjust to something**) to change so that one fits in with it or becomes suited to it. • **adjustable** *adj.* • **adjustably** *adverb*. • **adjuster** *noun*. • **adjustment** *noun*. ⓒ 17c: from French *ajuster*.

adjutant /ˈadʒʊtənt/ ▻ *noun* an army officer who does administrative work. • **adjutancy** *noun* (**adjutancies**). ⓒ 17c: from Latin *adjutare* to assist.

adjutant bird ▻ *noun* a large Indian stork or crane. ⓒ 18c as *adjutant*: so called because of its stiff stalking gait.

adjutant-general ▻ *noun* (**adjutants-general**) *military* the head of a department of the GENERAL STAFF which deals with administration and personnel.

ADL ▻ *abbreviation* Activity of Daily Living, one of a number of activities used to measure the extent of someone's incapacity, eg for insurance purposes.

ad-lib /adˈlɪb/ ▻ *verb* (**ad-libbed**, **ad-libbing**) *tr & intr* **1** to say something without preparation, especially as a departure from a prepared text or to fill time. **2** to improvise (music, etc). ▻ *adj* said of speeches, etc: made up as the speaker speaks; improvised. ▻ *adverb* (**ad lib**) **1** without preparation. **2** *colloq* without limit; freely. • **ad-libber** *noun*. • **ad-libbing** *noun*. ⓒ 19c as adverb; 20c otherwise: short for Latin *ad libitum* at pleasure.

Adm. ▻ *abbreviation* Admiral.

adman /ˈadman/ ▻ *noun*, *colloq* a person whose job is to produce or write advertisements.

admin /ˈadmɪn, adˈmɪn/ ▻ *noun*, *colloq* ADMINISTRATION 1.

administer /ədˈmɪnɪstə(r)/ ▻ *verb* (**administered**, **administering**) **1** to manage, govern or direct (one's affairs, an organization, etc). **2** to give out something formally □ *administer justice*. **3** to supervise a person taking (an oath). **4** to apply or provide (medicine). **5** to give □ *administer a rebuke*. **6** *intr* to act as an administrator. ⓒ 14c: from Latin *administrare*.

administrate ▻ *verb* (**administrated**, **administrating**) *tr & intr* to administer. ⓒ 17c.

administration /ədmɪnɪˈstreɪʃən/ ▻ *noun* **1** the directing, managing or governing of a company's affairs, etc. **2** a period of government by a particular party, etc. **3** *N Amer, especially US* a period of government by a particular president □ *the Nixon administration*. **4** the group of people who manage a company's affairs or run the business of government. ⓒ 14c: from Latin *administratio*.

administrative /ədˈmɪnɪstrətɪv/ ▻ *adj* relating to or concerned with administration. • **administratively** *adverb*.

administrator /ədˈmɪnɪstreɪtə(r)/ ▻ *noun* someone who manages, governs, directs, etc the affairs of an organization, estate, etc.

admirable /ˈadmɪrəbəl/ ▻ *adj* **1** worthy of being admired. **2** very good; excellent. • **admirably** *adverb*.

admiral /ˈadmɪrəl/ ▻ *noun* **1** a high-ranking officer in the navy (see table at RANK). **2** a name applied to several species of butterfly □ *red admiral*. ⓒ 15c in this sense; 13c, meaning 'Saracen ruler': from French *amiral*, from Arabic *amir-al-bahr* lord of the sea.

admiral of the fleet ▻ *noun* the highest-ranking admiral in the Royal Navy.

Admiralty /ˈadmɪrəltɪ/ ▻ *noun* (*usually* **the Admiralty**) *Brit, historical* the government department that managed the Royal Navy until the responsibility passed to the Ministry of Defence in 1964.

admire /ədˈmaɪə(r)/ ▻ *verb* (**admired**, **admiring**) to regard with respect or approval. • **admiration** /admɪˈreɪʃən/ *noun*. • **admiring** *adj.* • **admiringly** *adverb*. ⓒ 16c: from Latin *admirari*.

admirer ▻ *noun* **1** someone who admires a particular person or thing. **2** a man who is attracted to a particular woman.

admissible /ədˈmɪsɪbəl/ ▻ *adj* that can be allowed or accepted, especially as proof in a court of law □ *admissible evidence*. • **admissibility** *noun*. ⓒ 17c: from Latin *admissibilis*, from *admittere* to admit.

admission /ədˈmɪʃən/ ▻ *noun* **1** the act of allowing someone or something in or of being allowed in. **2** the cost of entry. **3 a** an act of admitting the truth of something; **b** something admitted or conceded. ⓒ 15c: from Latin *admissio*.

admit /ədˈmɪt/ ▻ *verb* (**admitted**, **admitting**) **1** *tr & intr* to agree to the truth of something, especially unwillingly. **2** (*also* **admit to something**) to agree that one is responsible for (a deed or action, especially an offence or wrongdoing). **3** to allow someone to enter. **4** (*also* **admit someone to something**) to allow them to take part in it; to accept them as a member or patient of it. **5** *formal* to have the capacity for something □ *a room admitting forty people*. ⓒ 15c: from Latin *admittere*.

■ **admit of something** *formal* to allow it as possible or valid.

admittance ▻ *noun* **1** the right to enter; permission to enter. **2** the act of entering; entry. **3** *physics* the reciprocal of IMPEDANCE, usually expressed in siemens, which gives a measure of how readily an alternating current flows through a circuit.

admittedly ▻ *adverb* as is known to be true; as one must admit.

admixture /əd'mɪkstʃə(r)/ ▻ *noun, chiefly technical* **1** anything that is added to the main ingredient of a mixture. **2** the mixture itself. **3** any material, other than cement, aggregate or water, that is added to wet concrete in order to improve its properties. ◷ 17c: from Latin *ad* to + *miscere* to mix.

admonish /əd'mɒnɪʃ/ ▻ *verb* (***admonishes, admonished, admonishing***) **1** to warn. **2** to scold or tell someone off firmly but mildly. **3** to advise or urge. • **admonishment** *noun*. ◷ 14c: from French *amonester*.

admonition /admə'nɪʃən/ ▻ *noun* a scolding or warning. ◷ 14c: from Latin *admonitio*, from *admonere* to admonish.

admonitory /ədm'ɒnɪtərɪ/ ▻ *adj* containing a scolding or warning. ◷ 16c.

ADN ▻ *abbreviation, IVR* People's Democratic Republic of Yemen (capital Aden).

ad nauseam /ad 'nɔːzɪam/ ▻ *adverb* **1** to the point of producing disgust; to a loathsome or objectionable extent. **2** excessively. ◷ 17c: Latin, meaning 'to the point of sickness'.

ado /ə'duː/ ▻ *noun* (*ados*) difficulty or trouble; fuss or bustle. • **without more** or **further ado** without any more delay; immediately; promptly. ◷ 14c in this sense; 13c as *at do* to do.

adobe /ə'doʊbɪ/ ▻ *noun* **1** a kind of building material made of clay and straw, and dried in the sun. **2** a sun-dried brick made from such material. **3** a building made from such bricks. ◷ 18c: Spanish, from Arabic *at tub* the brick.

adolescent /adə'lɛsənt/ ▻ *adj* **1** said of a young person: at the stage of development between childhood and adulthood, or between puberty and adulthood. **2** relating to or typical of this state. **3** *colloq* said of behaviour: of the kind often associated with adolescence; silly and immature. ▻ *noun* a young person between childhood and adulthood, or between puberty and adulthood. • **adolescence** *noun* this stage of development. ◷ 15c: from Latin *adolescere* to grow up; compare ADULT.

Adonis /ə'doʊnɪs, ə'dɒnɪs/ ▻ *noun* (***Adonises***) a handsome young man. ◷ 17c: in Greek mythology, a young man loved by the goddess Aphrodite.

adopt /ə'dɒpt/ ▻ *verb* (***adopted, adopting***) **1** *tr & intr* to take (a child of other parents) into one's own family, becoming its legal parent. **2** to take up (a habit, position, policy, etc). **3** to take (an idea, etc) over from someone else. **4** to choose formally (especially a candidate for an election). **5** said of a local authority: to take over responsibility for the upkeep of (a road) from private owners. • **adopted** *adj*. • **adoption** *noun*. ◷ 16c: from Latin *adoptare*, from *optare* to choose.

> ***adopted, adoptive***
>
> These words are sometimes confused: *adopted* children are adopted by their *adoptive* parents.

adoptive ▻ *adj* that adopts or is adopted.

adorable /ə'dɔːrəbəl/ ▻ *adj* **1** worthy of being adored. **2** *colloq* very charming and attractive. • **adorableness** *noun*. • **adorably** *adverb*. ◷ 18c in this sense; 17c, meaning 'worthy of worship'.

adore /ə'dɔː(r)/ ▻ *verb* (***adored, adoring***) **1** to love someone deeply. **2** *colloq* to like something very much. **3** to worship (a god). • **adoration** /adə'reɪʃən/ *noun*. • **adorer** *noun*. • **adoring** *adj*. • **adoringly** *adverb*. ◷ 14c in sense 3: from Latin *adorare*, from *ad* to + *orare* to pray.

adorn /ə'dɔːn/ ▻ *verb* (***adorned, adorning***) **1** to decorate. **2** to add beauty to something. • **adornment** *noun*. ◷ 14c: from Latin *adornare* to fit something out.

ADP ▻ *abbreviation* **1** *computing* automatic data processing, the use of computer systems to process information, especially business data, with little or no human assistance. **2** *biochem* adenosine diphosphate, an organic compound formed in living cells by the breakdown of ATP, during which process energy is released.

ad rem *adverb, adj* **1** to the point. **2** to the purpose. ◷ 17c: Latin. literally 'to the matter'.

adrenal /ə'driːnəl, 'adrənəl/ ▻ *adj, anatomy* **1** referring or relating to the kidneys. **2** situated on or near the kidneys. **3** referring or relating to the adrenal glands. ◷ 19c: from Latin *ad* to + RENAL.

adrenal cortex ▻ *noun, zool, anatomy* the outer part of the ADRENAL GLANDs, which secretes steroid hormones.

adrenal gland ▻ *noun, zool, anatomy* in mammals: either of a pair of flattened endocrine glands, situated one above each kidney, that secrete adrenaline and various steroid hormones, including sex hormones.

adrenalin or **adrenaline** /ə'drɛnəlɪn/ ▻ *noun, biol* **1** a hormone secreted by the adrenal glands in response to fear, excitement or anger, which causes an increase in heartbeat and blood pressure and diverts blood away from the intestines and towards the muscles. **2** this hormone produced synthetically, used to reduce blood loss during surgery, and to treat asthma. ◷ Early 20c: ADRENAL + -INE[2].

adrift /ə'drɪft/ ▻ *adj, adverb* **1** said of a boat: not tied up; floating about without being steered. **2** without help or guidance. **3** *colloq* off course. ◷ 17c: A-[1] + DRIFT.

adroit /ə'drɔɪt/ ▻ *adj* quick and clever in action or thought. • **adroitly** *adverb*. • **adroitness** *noun*. ◷ 17c: from French *à droit* according to the right, or rightly.

adsorb /əd'sɔːb, -z-/ ▻ *verb* (***adsorbed, adsorbing***) *technical* said of a solid, eg charcoal, or more rarely a liquid: to accumulate a thin layer of atoms or molecules of (a solid, liquid, or gas) on its surface. • **adsorbent** *adj*. • **adsorption** *noun*. ◷ 19c: from Latin *sorbere* to suck in.

adsorbent ▻ *noun* a substance on whose surface adsorption takes place.

aduki bean /ə'duːkɪ —/ or **adzuki bean** /adzuːkɪ —/ ▻ *noun* a type of KIDNEY BEAN grown especially in China and Japan. ◷ 18c as *adsuki*: from Japanese *azuki* red bean.

adulate /'adjʊleɪt/ ▻ *verb* (***adulated, adulating***) to praise or flatter someone far too much. • **adulation** *noun*. • **adulator** *noun*. • **adulatory** *adj*. ◷ 18c, from 15c *adulation*: from Latin *adulari* to fawn upon.

adult /'adʌlt, ə'dʌlt/ ▻ *adj* **1** fully grown; mature. **2** typical of, or suitable for, a fully grown person. **3** said especially of films: containing sexually explicit or indecent scenes, and therefore regarded as unsuitable for children. ▻ *noun* a fully grown person, animal, bird or plant. • **adulthood** *noun*. ◷ 16c: from Latin *adultus* grown-up, from *adolescere* to grow up; compare ADOLESCENT.

adulterant ▻ *noun* a substance with which something is adulterated.

adulterate /ə'dʌltəreɪt/ ▻ *verb* (***adulterated, adulterating***) to debase something or render it impure, by mixing it with something inferior or harmful. • **adulteration** *noun*. ◷ 16c: from Latin *adulterare*, adulteratum to defile.

adultery /ə'dʌltərɪ/ ▻ *noun* sexual relations willingly undertaken between a married person and a person who is not their spouse. • **adulterer** *noun*. • **adulteress** *noun*. • **adulterous** *adj*. • **adulterously** *adverb*. ⓘ 15c; 14c as *avowtery*: from Latin *adulterare*, *adulteratum* to defile.

adulthood see under ADULT

adumbrate /ˈadʌmbreɪt, əˈdʌm-/ ▷ *verb* (***adumbrated***, ***adumbrating***) *formal, literary, etc* **1** to indicate or describe in a general way. **2** to suggest or indicate (something likely to happen in the future); to foreshadow. **3** to throw a shadow over something. • **adumbration** *noun*. ⓘ 16c: from Latin *adumbrare*, adumbratum to shade in or sketch.

adv. ▷ *abbreviation, grammar* adverb.

advance /ədˈvɑːns/ ▷ *verb* (***advanced***, ***advancing***) **1** *tr & intr* to put, move or go forward, sometimes in a threatening way. **2** *intr* to make progress. **3** to help the progress of something; to improve or promote. **4** to propose or suggest (an idea, etc). **5** to put something at an earlier time or date than that previously planned. **6** *tr & intr* said of a value, price or rate: to increase. ▷ *noun* **1** progress; a move forward. **2** a payment made before it is due. **3** money lent to someone. **4** an increase, especially in price. **5** (*especially* **advances**) a friendly or sexual approach to a person. ▷ *adj* done, made or given beforehand. • **advance someone something** to lend them (a sum of money), especially on security, or pay them (money) before payment is due. • **in advance** ahead in time, place or development. ⓘ 16c; 13c as *avaunce*: from French *avancer*, from Latin *abante* in front.

advance corporation tax ▷ *noun* (abbreviation **ACT**) a UK tax deducted in advance from gross dividends and paid by the company to the Inland Revenue.

advanced ▷ *adj* **1** having progressed or developed well or far. **2** modern; new or revolutionary.

advanced gas-cooled reactor ▷ *noun* (abbreviation **AGR**) a type of NUCLEAR REACTOR that operates at high temperatures, using carbon dioxide gas as a coolant and graphite as a moderator.

Advanced level see A LEVEL

advanced passenger train ▷ *noun, Brit* (abbreviation **APT**) a lightweight electrically-powered train, designed to run at 250km/h (156mph) and to tilt on curves, which did not progress beyond the prototype stage.

Advanced Supplementary level see AS LEVEL

advance factory ▷ *noun* a factory built to encourage development, in the expectation that a company will take it over.

advancement ▷ *noun* **1** progress and development. **2** promotion in rank or improvement in status. **3** payment in advance.

advantage /ədˈvɑːntɪdʒ/ ▷ *noun* **1** a favourable circumstance; benefit or usefulness. **2** a circumstance that may help one to succeed, win, etc. **3** superiority over another. **4** *tennis* the point scored after DEUCE. ▷ *verb* (***advantaged***, ***advantaging***) to benefit someone or improve their position. • **have the advantage of someone** to know something that is not known to them; to be in a better position than them. • **take advantage of someone** or **something** **1** to make use of a situation, a person's good nature, etc in such a way as to benefit oneself. **2** *old use* to seduce someone. • **to advantage** in such a way as to emphasize the good qualities □ *shows off her figure to advantage*. • **to one's advantage** of benefit or importance to one. • **turn something to advantage** to use a circumstance, situation, etc in such a way as to get some benefit from it. ⓘ 14c: from French *avantage*, from *avant* before; see also ADVANCE.

advantaged ▷ *adj* having a good social or financial situation.

advantageous /advənˈteɪdʒəs/ ▷ *adj* giving help or benefit in some way. • **advantageously** *adverb*. • **advantageousness** *noun*.

advent /ˈadvɛnt/ ▷ *noun* **1** coming or arrival; first appearance. **2** (**Advent**) *Christianity* the period which includes the four Sundays before Christmas. **3** (**Advent**) *Christianity* the first or second coming of Christ. ⓘ 12c in sense 2: from Latin *adventus* arrival.

Adventist /ˈadvəntɪst/ ▷ *noun, Christianity* a member of a group which believes the second coming of Christ will happen very soon. ⓘ 19c.

adventitious /advənˈtɪʃəs/ ▷ *adj* **1** happening by chance; accidental. **2** *biol* denoting tissues or organs that grow in an unusual position, eg a root growing upwards from a stem. • **adventitiously** *adverb*. ⓘ 17c: from Latin *adventicius* coming from the outside.

adventure /ədˈvɛntʃə(r)/ ▷ *noun* **1** an exciting and often dangerous experience. **2** the excitement of risk or danger □ *a sense of adventure*. ⓘ 13c in old sense 'chance': from Latin *adventura* something about to happen.

adventure playground ▷ *noun* a playground with things for children to climb on and equipment for them to build with.

adventurer and **adventuress** ▷ *noun* **1** a man or woman, respectively, who is willing to use any means, dishonest, immoral or dangerous, to make money, obtain power, etc. **2** a man or woman who is eager for adventure.

adventurous ▷ *adj* **1** ready to act boldly and take risks; enjoying adventure; daring. **2** full of excitement, danger, daring activities, etc. • **adventurously** *adverb*. • **adventurousness** *noun*.

adverb /ˈadvɜːb/ *grammar* ▷ *noun* (abbreviation **adv.**) a word which describes or adds to the meaning of a verb, adjective or another adverb, such as *very* and *quietly* in *They were talking very quietly*. • **adverbial** /ədˈvɜːbɪəl/ *adj*. • **adverbially** *adverb*. ⓘ 16c: from Latin *adverbium* a word added after.

adversarial /advəˈsɛərɪəl/ ▷ *adj* **1** involving opposition □ *adversarial politics*. **2** hostile.

adversary /ˈadvəsərɪ/ ▷ *noun* (***adversaries***) **1** an opponent in a competition, etc. **2** an enemy. ⓘ 14c: from Latin *adversarius*.

adverse /ˈadvɜːs, ədˈvɜːs/ ▷ *adj* (*sometimes* ***adverser***, ***adversest***) **1** unfavourable to one's interests. **2** disapproving. **3** hurtful. **4** said of a wind: coming from in front of one and not from behind. • **adversely** *adverb*. ⓘ 14c: from Latin *adversus* hostile.

> ***adverse***
>
> A word sometimes confused with this one is **averse**.

adversity /ədˈvɜːsɪtɪ/ ▷ *noun* (***adversities***) **1** circumstances that cause trouble or sorrow. **2** an event or circumstance that causes trouble or sorrow; a misfortune.

advert¹ /ˈadvɜːt/ ▷ *noun, colloq* an ADVERTISEMENT. Also called AD. ⓘ 19c: abbreviation.

advert² /ədˈvɜːt/ ▷ *verb* (***adverted***, ***adverting***) now only in phrase below. ⓘ 15c: from French *avertir*, from Latin *advertere* to direct attention to something.

> ■ **advert to something** *formal* to refer to it or mention it in speaking or writing.

advertise or (*US sometimes*) **advertize** /ˈadvətaɪz, advəˈtaɪz/ ▷ *verb* (***advertised***, ***advertising***; *US sometimes* ***advertized***, ***advertizing***) **1** to draw attention to or describe (goods for sale, services offered, etc) in newspapers, on TV, etc, to encourage people to buy or use them. **2** (*usually* **advertise for something** or **someone**) to ask for or seek it or them by putting a notice in a newspaper, shop window, etc. **3** to make something known publicly or generally. • **advertiser** *noun*. • **advertising** *noun* the business or profession of producing advertisements for goods. ⓘ 16c: from French *avertir*, from Latin *advertere* to direct attention to.

advertisement /əd'vɜːtɪsmənt, -tɪz-/ ▻ *noun* **1** a public notice, announcement, picture, etc in a newspaper, on a wall in the street, etc, which advertises something. **2** a short television film advertising something. Often shortened to AD, ADVERT.

advertorial /advɜː'tɔːrɪəl/ ▻ *noun* an advertisement presented as if it is editorial material. Also *as adj*. ◷ 20c: from *advert*ise and edit*orial*.

advice /əd'vaɪs/ ▻ *noun* **1** suggestions or opinions given to someone about what they should do in a particular situation. **2** *business* an official note about a transaction, etc. ● **take advice 1** to ask someone for an opinion about what one should do. **2** to act on advice given. ◷ 13c as *avys*: from French *avis*.

> **advices**
>
> ☆ PLAIN ENGLISH alternatives for sense 2 (used in the plural) are **suggestions, opinion, comments**.

advice note ▻ *noun, commerce* a document sent by a supplier of goods to a buyer informing them that the goods ordered have been despatched.

advisable /əd'vaɪzəbəl/ ▻ *adj* **1** said of action to be taken, etc: to be recommended; wise. **2** sensible. ● **advisability** *noun*. ● **advisably** *adverb*.

advise /əd'vaɪz/ ▻ *verb* (***advised, advising***) **1** to give advice to someone. **2** to recommend something. **3** (*usually* **advise someone of something**) to inform them about it. **4** *tr & intr* to act as an adviser to someone. ◷ 13c, meaning 'watch': from French *aviser*.

> **advise**
>
> ☆ PLAIN ENGLISH alternatives in sense 3 are **inform, tell, let (someone) know**.

advised /əd'vaɪzd/ ▻ *adj, especially in compounds* considered; judged □ ***well-advised*** □ ***ill-advised***.

advisedly ▻ *adverb* after careful thought; on purpose.

adviser or **advisor** ▻ *noun* **1** someone who advises. **2** *Brit* a teacher appointed by an education authority to advise on the teaching and development of their subject. ● **advisorate** *noun* the body of advisers appointed by an education authority.

advisory /əd'vaɪzərɪ/ ▻ *adj* appointed in order to give advice.

advocaat /'advoʊkɑː, -kɑːt/ ▻ *noun* a liqueur made from raw eggs, sugar and brandy. ◷ 20c: from Dutch *advocaatenborrel* lawyers' drink (so called because it supposedly cleared the throat).

advocacy /'advəkəsɪ/ ▻ *noun* (***advocacies***) **1** recommendation or active support of an idea, etc. **2** the function or job of an advocate, eg in a particular trial. ◷ 15c.

advocate ▻ *noun* /'advəkət/ **1** especially in Scotland: a lawyer who speaks for the defence or prosecution in a trial. See also BARRISTER, SOLICITOR. **2** someone who supports or recommends an idea, proposal, etc. ▻ *verb* /'advəkeɪt/ (***advocated, advocating***) to recommend or support (an idea, proposal, etc), especially in public. ◷ 14c: from French *avocat*, from Latin *advocatus* legal adviser.

advt ▻ *abbreviation* advertisement.

adze or (*US*) **adz** /adz/ ▻ *noun* a tool with an arched blade set at right angles to its handle, used for cutting and shaping wood. ◷ Anglo-Saxon *adesa*.

adzuki bean see ADUKI BEAN

AEA ▻ *abbreviation, Brit* Atomic Energy Authority.

aegis /'iːdʒɪs/ ▻ *noun* (***aegises***) protection or patronage. ● **under the aegis of someone** or **some organization** under their supervision, support or patronage. ◷ 18c: from Greek *aigis* the shield of Zeus, in Greek mythology.

aegrotat /'aɪgroʊtat/ ▻ *noun* in some universities: a medical certificate, or a degree or CREDIT (*noun* 9) awarded, when illness has prevented someone from taking examinations, etc. ◷ 19c: Latin, literally 'he or she is ill'.

-aemia, (*US*) **-emia** /'iːmɪə/ or **-haemia**, (*US*) **-hemia** /'hiːmɪə/ ▻ *combining form, denoting* the presence of specified substances, especially to excess, in the blood □ ***leukaemia***.

aeolian harp /ɪ'oʊlɪən —/ ▻ *noun* a box-like musical instrument which has strings stretched across a hole, and which makes musical sounds when the wind passes through it. ◷ 18c: from Greek *Aiolus*, god of the winds.

aeon see EON

aerate /'ɛəreɪt/ ▻ *verb* (***aerated, aerating***) **1** to expose something to or mix it with air or oxygen, eg to OXYGENATE (the blood). **2** to charge (a liquid) with carbon dioxide or some other gas, eg when making fizzy drinks. See also CARBONATE *verb* 1. ● **aerated** *adj*. ● **aeration** *noun*. ◷ 18c: from Latin *aer* air.

aerial /'ɛərɪəl/ ▻ *noun* a wire, rod or other device, especially on a radio or television receiver, used to receive or transmit electromagnetic waves, especially radio waves. Also called ANTENNA. ▻ *adj* **1** relating to or found in the air. **2** like air. **3** ethereal. **4** relating to or using aircraft. ◷ 17c as *adj*; 20c as *noun*: from Latin *aerius*, from *aer* air.

aerie see EYRIE

aero- /ɛəroʊ/ ▻ *combining form, signifying* **1** air □ ***aerodynamics***. **2** aircraft □ ***aerodrome***. ◷ From Greek *aer* air.

aerobatics ▻ *plural noun* spectacular or dangerous manoeuvres, such as flying upside down or looping the loop, in an aircraft or glider. ▻ *singular noun* the art of performing such manoeuvres in the air. ● **aerobatic** *adj*. ◷ 1917: from AERO-, modelled on ACROBATICS.

aerobe /'ɛəroʊb/ ▻ *noun, biol* any organism that requires oxygen in order to obtain energy from the breakdown of carbohydrates or other foodstuffs by the process of respiration. Compare ANAEROBE. ◷ 19c: from French *aérobie*, from Greek *aer* air + *bios* life.

aerobic /ɛə'roʊbɪk/ ▻ *adj* **1** *biol* said of an organism: requiring oxygen in order to obtain energy from the breakdown of carbohydrates or other foodstuffs by the process of respiration. **2** relating to aerobics. **3** said of or relating to some forms of physical exercise, eg walking, jogging, swimming: producing an increase in the rate at which the body uses oxygen. **4** *biol* said of a form of respiration in living organisms: in which oxygen is required for the complete oxidation of foodstuffs, especially carbohydrates. ◷ 19c: from AEROBE.

aerobics ▻ *singular noun* a system of physical exercise consisting of rapidly repeated, energetic movements, which increases the supply of oxygen in the blood and strengthens the heart and lungs. ▻ *plural noun* energetic exercises. ◷ 1960s.

aerodrome /'ɛərədroʊm/ ▻ *noun, Brit* an area of land and its associated buildings, smaller than an airport, used for the take-off and landing of private and military aircraft. ◷ Early 20c.

aerodynamic ▻ *adj* **1** relating to AERODYNAMICS. **2** making effective use of aerodynamics so as to minimize air resistance and drag. ● **aerodynamically** *adverb*.

aerodynamics ▻ *singular noun* the scientific study of the movement of air or other gases relative to stationary or moving solid bodies immersed in them, eg the flow of air round bridges, buildings, aircraft, cars, etc. ▻ *plural noun* the qualities required for fast and efficient movement through the air. ◷ Early 19c.

aerofoil ▻ *noun* any body or part shaped so as to provide lift or thrust when it is moving through the air, eg the wings, tail fins and propeller blades of an aeroplane. ◷ Early 20c.

aerogramme or **aerogram** ▷ *noun* a thin piece of paper on which to write letters for sending by air, designed so that it can be folded and sealed without being put into an envelope. Also called **air letter**. ◷ 1960s.

aeronautics ▷ *singular noun* the scientific study of travel through the Earth's atmosphere. • **aeronautic** or **aeronautical** *adj*. ◷ 18c: from Latin *aeronautica*.

aeroplane ▷ *noun* a powered machine used for travelling in the air, that is heavier than air and supported in its flight by fixed wings. ◷ 19c: French.

> ***aeroplane, airplane***
>
> **Aeroplane** is the standard form in British English. **Airplane** is the normal form in American English, and it is sometimes found in British English also.

aerosol /ˈɛərəsɒl/ ▷ *noun* **1** a suspension of fine particles of a solid or liquid suspended in a gas. **2** a can containing a product, eg paint, polish or insecticide mixed with a PROPELLANT, that can be sprayed to produce such a suspension. ◷ 1920s: from AERO- + *solution*.

aerospace ▷ *noun* **1** the Earth's atmosphere and the space beyond it, considered as a zone available for the flight of aircraft and spacecraft. **2** *as adj* referring to the branches of technology or industry concerned with the design, development, manufacture and sale of aircraft and spacecraft □ ***the aerospace industry***. ◷ 1950s.

aesthete /ˈiːsθiːt/ or (*US*) **esthete** /ˈɛsθiːt/ ▷ *noun* someone who has or claims to have a special appreciation of art and beauty. ◷ 19c: from Greek *aisthetes* one who perceives.

aesthetic or (*US*) **esthetic** /ɪsˈθɛtɪk, ɛs-/ ▷ *adj* **1** able to appreciate beauty. **2** artistic; tasteful. **3** relating to aesthetics. • **aesthetically** *adverb*. ◷ 19c: from Greek *aisthetikos*, from *aisthanesthai* to perceive.

aesthetics ▷ *singular noun* **1** the branch of philosophy concerned with the study of the principles of beauty, especially in art. **2** the principles of good taste and the appreciation of beauty.

aestival or (*US*) **estival** /ˈiːstɪvəl, ˈɛstɪ-/ ▷ *adj* referring or relating to summer.

aestivate or (*US*) **estivate** /ˈiːstɪveɪt, ˈɛstɪ-/ ▷ *verb* (***aestivated***, ***aestivating***) said of certain animals: to survive the hot summer months in a dormant or torpid state. Compare HIBERNATE. ◷ 17c, meaning 'to spend the summer', from Latin *aestivare*, from *aestas* summer.

aestivation or (*US*) **estivation** ▷ *noun*, *biol* **1** in certain animals, eg tropical amphibians: a state of inactivity that enables them to survive prolonged periods of heat or drought. **2** the arrangement of the petals and sepals in a flower bud.

aet. ▷ *abbreviation*: *aetatis* (Latin), aged □ *aet. 34*. ◷ 19c; 17c as *aetat.*: literally 'of age'.

aether see under ETHER *noun* 3, 4

aetiology or (*US*) **etiology** /iːtɪˈɒlədʒɪ/ ▷ *noun* (***aetiologies*** or ***etiologies***) **1** the science or philosophy of causes. **2** the scientific study of the causes or origins of disease. **3** the cause of a specific disease. • **aetiological** *adj*. • **aetiologically** *adverb*. ◷ 17c in these senses; 16c, meaning 'cause': from Greek *aitia* cause.

AEU ▷ *abbreviation*, *Brit* Amalgamated Engineering Union.

AF ▷ *abbreviation* **1** Anglo-French. **2** audio frequency.

afar /əˈfɑː(r)/ ▷ *adverb* at a distance; far away. • **from afar** from a great distance. ◷ Anglo-Saxon, as *of feor* from far.

AFC ▷ *abbreviation* **1** Air Force Cross. **2** Association Football Club.

affable /ˈafəbəl/ ▷ *adj* pleasant and friendly in manner; easy to talk to. • **affability** *noun*. • **affably** *adverb*. ◷ 16c: from Latin *affabilis*, from *affari* to speak to.

affair /əˈfɛə(r)/ ▷ *noun* **1** a concern, matter or thing to be done. **2** an event or connected series of events. **3** a sexual relationship between two people, usually when at least one of them is married to someone else. **4** (**affairs**) matters of importance and public interest □ *current affairs*. **5** (**affairs**) private or public business matters □ *put my affairs in order*. ◷ 13c: from French *afaire*, from *faire* to do.

affect[1] ▷ *verb* /əˈfɛkt/ (***affected***, ***affecting***) **1** to have an effect on someone or something. **2** to cause someone to feel strong emotions, especially sadness or pity. **3** said of diseases: to attack or infect. ▷ *noun* /ˈafɛkt/ *psychol* **1** the emotion linked with a particular idea or mental image. **2** the predominant mood, feelings or emotions in a person's mental state. ◷ 17c: from Latin *afficere*.

> ***affect***
>
> A word often confused with this one is **effect**.

affect[2] /əˈfɛkt/ ▷ *verb* (***affected***, ***affecting***) **1** to pretend to feel or have (eg an illness or emotion). **2** to use, wear, etc something in a way that is intended to attract attention □ ***affect fast cars***. ◷ 15c, meaning 'to aim at': from Latin *affectare* to aim at, from *afficere*.

affectation /afɪkˈteɪʃən/ ▷ *noun* **1** unnatural behaviour or pretence which is intended to impress people. **2** the act of pretending.

affected ▷ *adj* **1** not genuine; false or pretended. **2** said of a manner of speaking or behaving: put on to impress people. • **affectedly** *adverb*.

affecting ▷ *adj* causing people to feel strong emotion, especially sadness, pity, sympathy, joy, etc.

affection /əˈfɛkʃən/ ▷ *noun* **1** a feeling of love or strong liking. **2** (**affections**) feelings. **3** a disease. ◷ 13c: from Latin *affectio*, from AFFECT[1].

affectionate ▷ *adj* showing love or fondness. • **affectionately** *adverb*. • **affectionateness** *noun*.

affective ▷ *adj*, *technical* **1** relating to, arising from, or influencing emotion. **2** *psychol* relating to an AFFECT[1]. • **affectively** *adverb*. • **affectivity** /afɛkˈtɪvɪtɪ/ *noun*. ◷ 17c.

afferent /ˈafərənt/ ▷ *adj* **1** *anatomy* said especially of a nerve or blood vessel: leading inwards or towards a central part. **2** *physiol* said of a nerve or neurone: carrying nerve impulses from the sense organs and other sensory receptors to the brain and spinal cord. Compare EFFERENT. ◷ 19c: from Latin *afferre*, from *ad* to + *ferre* to carry.

affiance /əˈfaɪəns/ ▷ *verb* (***affianced***, ***affiancing***) (*usually* **be affianced to someone**) *old use* to be or become engaged to be married to them. ◷ 17c in this construction; 14c meaning 'faith': from French *afiancer* to pledge in marriage.

affidavit /afəˈdeɪvɪt/ ▷ *noun*, *law* a written statement, sworn to be true by the person who makes it, for use as evidence in a court of law. ◷ 17c: Latin, meaning 'he or she has sworn on oath'.

affiliate ▷ *verb* /əˈfɪlɪeɪt/ (***affiliated***, ***affiliating***) *tr & intr* (*usually* **be affiliated with** or **to something**) to connect or associate a person or organization with a group or a larger organization. ▷ *noun* /əˈfɪlɪət/ a person or organization, etc that has an association with a group or larger body. • **affiliation** *noun*. ◷ 18c: from Latin *affiliatus* adopted.

affiliation order ▷ *noun*, *law* a court order instructing a man to pay money towards the support of his illegitimate child.

affinity /əˈfɪnɪtɪ/ ▷ *noun* (***affinities***) **1** a strong natural liking for or feeling of attraction or closeness towards someone or something. **2** (*usually* **affinity with someone**) relationship to them, especially by marriage. **3** similarity in appearance, structure, etc, especially one that suggests relatedness. **4** (*usually* **affinity for something**) chemical attraction between substances; readiness to combine chemically with another substance and remain in combination. ⓘ 14c: from Latin *affinitas*, from *affinis* neighbouring.

affinity card ▷ *noun* a credit card linked to a particular charity, to which the issuing bank pays a fee on issue and subsequent donations according to the credit level. ⓘ 1970s, originally US.

affirm /əˈfɜːm/ ▷ *verb* (**affirmed**, **affirming**) **1** to state something positively and firmly; to state something as a fact. **2** to uphold or confirm (an idea, belief, etc). **3** *intr* in a court of law: to promise solemnly to tell the truth, as opposed to SWEARing a religious oath. • **affirmation** *noun*. ⓘ 14c: from French *afermer*, from Latin *firmare* to make firm.

affirmative /əˈfɜːmətɪv/ ▷ *adj* expressing agreement; giving the answer 'yes'. Opposite of NEGATIVE. ▷ *noun* an affirmative word or phrase. • **affirmatively** *adverb*. ⓘ 17c.

affirmative action ▷ *noun, especially US* positive steps taken to ensure that minority groups are not discriminated against, especially as regards employment. See also POSITIVE DISCRIMINATION. ⓘ 1960s.

affix ▷ *verb* /əˈfɪks/ (**affixes**, **affixed**, **affixing**) to attach or fasten. ▷ *noun* /ˈafɪks/ (**affixes**) *grammar* a word-forming element of one or more syllables which can be added to a word to form another, related, word, eg *un-* in *unhappy* or *-ness* in *sadness*; a PREFIX, SUFFIX or INFIX. ⓘ 16c: from Latin *affigere*, *affixum* to fasten to.

afflict /əˈflɪkt/ ▷ *verb* (**afflicted**, **afflicting**) to cause someone physical or mental suffering. ⓘ 14c: from Latin *affligere*, *afflictum* to cast down.

> ***afflict***
>
> A word sometimes confused with this one is **inflict**.

affliction ▷ *noun* **1** distress or suffering. **2** a cause of this.

affluent /ˈafluənt/ ▷ *adj* having more than enough money; rich. • **affluence** *noun*. • **affluently** *adverb*. ⓘ 18c in this sense; 14c, meaning 'flowing': from Latin *affluere* to flow freely.

affluent society ▷ *noun* a society in which the ordinary person can afford many things once regarded as luxuries.

afford /əˈfɔːd/ ▷ *verb* (**afforded**, **affording**) **1** (used with *can, could, be able to*) **a** to have enough money, time, etc to spend on something; **b** to be able to do something, or allow it to happen, without risk. **2** to give; to provide □ *a room affording a view of the sea*. • **affordability** *noun*. • **affordable** *adj*. ⓘ Anglo-Saxon *geforthian* to further or promote.

afforest /əˈfɒrəst/ ▷ *verb* (**afforested**, **afforesting**) to carry out the process of afforestation on (a piece of land). ⓘ 16c: from Latin *afforestare*.

afforestation ▷ *noun* the process whereby a forest is established for the first time on bare or cultivated land, either by planting seeds, or by transplanting seedlings or young trees.

affray /əˈfreɪ/ ▷ *noun* (**affrays**) a fight in a public place; a breach of the peace by fighting. ⓘ 14c: from French *esfrei*.

affricate /ˈafrɪkət/ ▷ *noun, phonetics* a consonant sound that begins as a plosive and becomes a fricative, such as *ch* in *church*.

affront /əˈfrʌnt/ ▷ *noun* an insult, especially one delivered in public. ▷ *verb* (**affronted**, **affronting**) **1** to insult someone, especially in public. **2** to offend the pride of someone; to embarrass. ⓘ 14c: from French *afronter* to slap in the face.

AFG ▷ *abbreviation, IVR* Afghanistan.

Afghan /ˈafgan/ ▷ *adj* belonging or relating to Afghanistan, a republic in S Asia, its inhabitants or their language. ▷ *noun* **1** (*also* **Afghani**) a citizen or inhabitant of, or person born in, Afghanistan. **2** the official language of Afghanistan; PASHTO. **3** (*also* **Afghan hound**) a type of tall thin dog with long silky hair, originally used for hunting. ⓘ 18c: Pashto.

aficionado /əfɪʃɪəˈnɑːdoʊ/ ▷ *noun* (**aficionados**) someone who takes an enthusiastic interest in a particular sport or pastime. ⓘ 19c: Spanish.

afield /əˈfiːld/ ▷ *adverb* **1** to or at a distance. **2** away from home □ *far afield*. ⓘ Anglo-Saxon as *on felda*; see A-[1] + FIELD.

afire /əˈfaɪə(r)/ ▷ *adj, adverb* on fire; burning. ⓘ Anglo-Saxon as *afure*; see A-[1] + FIRE.

aflame /əˈfleɪm/ ▷ *adj* **1** in flames; burning. **2** very excited. ⓘ 16c: A-[1] + FLAME.

aflatoxin /afləˈtɒksɪn/ ▷ *noun, biol* a toxic substance, produced by a fungus, which contaminates stored corn, soya beans, peanuts, etc in warm humid regions, and causes cancer in some animals. ⓘ 1960s: from *Aspergillus flavus* (one of the fungi producing this) + TOXIN.

afloat /əˈfloʊt/ ▷ *adj, adverb* **1** floating. **2** at sea; aboard ship. **3** out of debt; financially secure. ⓘ Anglo-Saxon as *aflote*; see A-[1] + FLOAT.

AFM ▷ *abbreviation* audio frequency modulation.

afoot /əˈfʊt/ ▷ *adj, adverb* being prepared or already in progress or operation □ *There is trouble afoot.* ⓘ Anglo-Saxon as *a fote*; see A-[1] + FOOT.

afore /əˈfɔː(r)/ ▷ *adverb, prep, old use or dialect* before. ⓘ Anglo-Saxon as *on foran* in front.

afore- /əˈfɔː(r)/ ▷ *combining form, signifying* before; previously.

aforementioned ▷ *adj* already mentioned. • **the aforementioned** the person or group of people already mentioned.

aforesaid ▷ *adj* said or mentioned already.

aforethought ▷ *adj* premedicated. • **with malice aforethought** *law* said of a criminal act: done deliberately; planned beforehand.

a fortiori /eɪ fɔːtɪˈɔːraɪ/ *adverb* for a stronger reason. Also *as adj* □ *an afortiori argument.* ⓘ 17c: Latin, literally 'from the stronger thing'.

AFP ▷ *abbreviation* alpha-fetoprotein.

afraid /əˈfreɪd/ ▷ *adj* **1** (*often* **afraid of someone** or **something**) feeling fear; frightened of them or it. **2** (*usually* **afraid to do something**) reluctant to do it out of fear or concern for the consequences. **3** as a polite formula of regret: sorry □ *I'm afraid we're going to be late.* ⓘ 14c as *afrayed*, past participle of the obsolete verb *affray* to disturb or frighten.

afresh /əˈfrɛʃ/ ▷ *adverb* again, especially from the beginning; with a fresh start. ⓘ 16c: A-[1] + FRESH.

African /ˈafrɪkən/ ▷ *adj* belonging or relating to the continent of Africa, its inhabitants, or their languages. ▷ *noun* a citizen or inhabitant of, or person born in, Africa. ⓘ Anglo-Saxon as *noun* in plural: from Latin *Africanus*.

African-American or (*somewhat dated*) **Afro-American** ▷ *noun* an American whose ancestors were originally brought from Africa as slaves. ▷ *adj* belonging or relating to African-Americans, their music, culture, etc. Also called **Black American**.

African buffalo see BUFFALO

Africander /afrɪ'kandə(r)/ ▷ *noun* a S African breed of cattle. © 19c, originally also meaning 'Afrikaner': from Dutch *Afrikaander* an inhabitant of Africa.

African elephant see under ELEPHANT

Africanize or **Africanise** ▷ *verb* (***Africanized, Africanizing***) **1** to make something African. **2** to replace people of other races with Africans in (eg a company or the civil service). © 19c.

African violet ▷ *noun* any of various perennial tropical African plants, widely cultivated as house plants, with rounded hairy leaves and violet, bluish-purple, pink or white flowers.

Afrikaans /afrɪ'kɑːns/ ▷ *noun* one of the official languages of S Africa, developed from Dutch. © 20c: Dutch, meaning 'African'.

Afrikaner /afrɪ'kɑːnə(r)/ ▷ *noun* a white inhabitant of S Africa, especially one of Dutch descent, whose native language is Afrikaans. © 19c: Afrikaans.

Afro /'afroʊ/ ▷ *noun* (***Afros***) a hairstyle consisting of thick bushy curls standing out from the head.

Afro- /'əfroʊ/ ▷ *combining form, signifying* African. © From Latin *Afer* African.

Afro-American see AFRICAN-AMERICAN

Afro-Caribbean ▷ *noun* a person living in the Caribbean whose ancestors originally came from Africa. ▷ *adj* relating to Afro-Caribbeans, their music, culture, etc.

aft /ɑːft/ ▷ *adverb, adj, chiefly naut* at or towards the stern, rear or tail. © Anglo-Saxon *æftan* behind.

after /'ɑːftə(r)/ ▷ *prep* **1** coming later in time than something. **2** following someone or something in position; behind. **3** next to and following something in importance, order, arrangement, etc. **4** because of something; considering □ ***You can't expect to be promoted after that mistake.*** **5** in spite of something □ ***He's still no better after all that medicine.*** **6** about someone or something □ ***ask after her.*** **7** in pursuit of someone or something □ ***run after him.*** **8** said of a painting or other work of art: in the style or manner of (someone else). **9** by or with the same name as someone or something; with a name derived from that of (someone else) □ ***called her Mary after her aunt.*** **10** *N Amer, especially US* past (an hour) □ ***It's twenty after six.*** ▷ *adverb* **1** later in time. **2** behind in place. ▷ *conj* after the time when. ▷ *adj* **1** later; following □ ***in after years.*** **2** *naut* further towards the stern of a ship □ ***the after deck.*** See also AFT. • **after all** **1** in spite of all that has happened or has been said or done. **2** contrary to what is or was expected □ ***The shop was closed after all.*** • **after one's own heart** of exactly the kind one likes. • **after you** please go before me. © Anglo-Saxon *æfter*.

■ **be after someone** or **something** to be pursuing or chasing (a person or animal).

afterbirth ▷ *noun, zool, medicine* the placenta, blood and ruptured membranes expelled from the uterus after the birth of a mammal.

afterburner ▷ *noun* **1** *aeronautics* a device which injects fuel into the hot exhaust gases of a turbojet in order to obtain increased thrust. **2** an additional burner in an exhaust pipe, designed to burn off any remaining combustible gas. • **afterburning** *noun*.

aftercare ▷ *noun* care and support given to someone after a period of treatment, a surgical operation, a prison sentence, etc.

afterdamp ▷ *noun* a poisonous gas arising in coalmines after an explosion of FIREDAMP.

after-effect ▷ *noun* a circumstance or event, usually an unpleasant one, that follows as the result of something.

afterglow ▷ *noun* **1** a glow remaining in the sky after the Sun has set. **2** an impression or feeling, usually a pleasant one, that remains when the experience, etc that caused it is over.

after-image ▷ *noun* an image that persists for a time after one has stopped looking at an object.

afterlife ▷ *noun* the continued existence of one's spirit or soul after one's death.

aftermath /'ɑːftəmɑːθ/ ▷ *noun* circumstances that follow and are a result of something, especially a great and terrible event. © 16c, meaning 'second mowing': from Anglo-Saxon *mæth* mowing.

afternoon /ɑːftənuːn/ ▷ *noun* the period of the day between noon and the evening. © 14c.

afters ▷ *singular noun, Brit colloq* dessert; pudding.

aftersales service ▷ *noun* service offered by a retailer to a customer following the purchase of goods, eg advice on installation, repair, provision of spare parts, etc.

aftershave ▷ *noun* a perfumed lotion for a man to put on his face after shaving. Also called **aftershave lotion**.

aftershock ▷ *noun* a small earthquake that follows the main shock of a large earthquake, and originates at or near its epicentre.

aftertaste ▷ *noun* the taste that remains in the mouth or comes into it after one has eaten or drunk something.

after-tax ▷ *adj* said of profits: remaining after tax has been paid. Compare PRE-TAX.

afterthought ▷ *noun* an idea thought of after the main plan, etc has been formed; a later thought or modification.

afterwards and (*especially US*) **afterward** ▷ *adverb* later; following an earlier event.

AFV ▷ *abbreviation* armoured fighting vehicle.

AG ▷ *abbreviation* **1** Adjutant-General. **2** *Aktiengesellschaft* (German), plc. **3** (*also* **A-G**) Attorney-General.

Ag ▷ *symbol, chem* silver. © From Latin *argentum* silver.

Aga /'ɑːgə/ ▷ *noun* (***Agas***) *trademark* a type of large permanently lit cooking stove with multiple ovens, some models of which also heat water. © 1930s: acronym from Swedish *(Svenska) Aktienbolager Gasackumulator* (Swedish) Gas Accumulator Company, the original manufacturers.

again /ə'gɛn, ə'geɪn/ ▷ *adverb* **1** once more; another time. **2** back to (a previous condition or situation, etc) □ ***get well again.*** **3** in addition □ ***twice as much again.*** **4** however; on the other hand □ ***He might come, but then again he might not.*** **5** further; besides. • **again and again** very often; repeatedly. © Anglo-Saxon *ongean* back.

against /ə'gɛnst, ə'geɪnst/ ▷ *prep* **1** close to or leaning on something; in contact with it. **2** into collision with something or someone. **3** in opposition to something. **4** in contrast to something □ ***against a dark background.*** **5** with a bad or unfavourable effect on someone or something □ ***His youth is against him.*** **6** as a protection from someone or something. **7** *old use* in anticipation of or preparation for something. **8** in return for something □ ***the exchange rate against the franc.*** • **as against something** in comparison with it. • **have something against someone** or **something** to have a reason for disliking or disapproving of them or it. © 12c as *ageines*, meaning 'in front of'.

Aga Khan /'ɑːgə kɑːn/ ▷ *noun* the title of the head of the Ismaili Muslims. © 19c: Turkish, literally 'lord master'.

agapanthus /agə'panθəs/ ▷ *noun* (***agapanthuses***) a S African plant with strap-shaped leathery leaves and bell-shaped blue (or rarely white) flowers in large heads on long leafless stalks. © 19c: Latin, from Greek *agape* love + *anthos* flower.

agape¹ /ə'geɪp/ *adj* **1** said of the mouth: gaping; open wide. **2** said of a person: very surprised. © 17c.

agape² /ˈagəpeɪ/ *noun* Christian brotherly love, as distinct from erotic love. ◷ 17c: Greek, meaning 'love'.

agar /ˈeɪgə(r), -gɑː(r)/ and **agar-agar** ▷ *noun, medicine, cookery* a gelatinous substance extracted from certain red seaweeds, used as the main ingredient of solid culture media for growing bacteria, etc, and also used as a food stabilizer and thickening agent. ◷ 19c: Malay.

agaric /ˈagərɪk, əˈgarɪk/ ▷ *noun, bot* any of various fungi that produce an umbrella-shaped spore-bearing structure with a central vertical stem supporting a circular cap, eg FIELD MUSHROOM, DEATH CAP. ◷ 16c, meaning 'tree-fungus': from Latin *agaricum*.

Aga-saga ▷ *noun* (*Aga-sagas*) *facetious* any popular novel whose plot revolves around the anxieties of a middle-class housewife or family, especially one set in a rural English community.

agate /ˈagət/ ▷ *noun, mineralogy* a fine-grained variety of chalcedony consisting of concentrically arranged bands of two or more colours, used as a semiprecious stone in jewellery and ornaments. ◷ 16c: from French *agathes*.

agave /əˈgɑːvɪ, -geɪ-/ ▷ *noun* (*agaves*) *bot* any of various evergreen perennial plants, native to Central and S America, with fleshy sword-shaped, often spiny, leaves arranged in a rosette, and tall flower stalks with branched flower-heads. ◷ 19c: Greek female name.

age /eɪdʒ/ ▷ *noun* **1** the period of time during which a person, animal, plant or phenomenon has lived or existed. **2** a particular stage in life □ *old age*. **3** *psychol* one's developmental equivalent in years compared with the average for one's chronological age. **4** the fact or time of being old. **5** in the Earth's history: an interval of time during which specific life forms, physical conditions, geological events, etc were dominant □ *the Ice Age*. **6** (*usually* **ages**) *colloq* a very long time. ▷ *verb* (***aged*** /eɪdʒd/, ***ageing*** or ***aging***) **1** *intr* to show signs of growing old. **2** *intr* to grow old. **3** *intr* to mature. **4** to make someone seem older or look old. • **ageing** or **aging** *noun, adj*. • **act** or **be one's age** to behave sensibly. • **come of age** to become legally old enough to have an adult's rights and duties. • **of an age** of the same, or a similar, age. • **over age** too old. • **under age** too young to be legally allowed to do something, eg buy alcoholic drink. ◷ 13c: from French *aage*, from Latin *aetas*.

-age /ɪdʒ, ɑːʒ/ ▷ *suffix, forming nouns, signifying* **1** a collection, set or group □ *baggage*. **2** an action or process □ *breakage*. **3** the result of an action or event □ *wreckage*. **4** a condition □ *bondage*. **5** a home, house or place □ *orphanage* □ *anchorage*. **6** cost or charge □ *postage*. **7** rate □ *dosage*. ◷ French.

aged /eɪdʒd in sense 1, ˈeɪdʒɪd in senses 2 and 3/ ▷ *adj* **1** having a specified age. **2** very old. **3** (**the aged**) old people as a group (see THE sense 4b).

age group and **age bracket** ▷ *noun* the people between two particular ages, considered as a group.

ageing see under AGE

ageism or **agism** ▷ *noun* the practice of treating people differently, and usually unfairly, on the grounds of age only, especially because they are too old. • **ageist** or **agist** *noun, adj*. ◷ 1960s.

ageless ▷ *adj* never growing old or fading; never looking older. • **agelessness** *noun*.

age limit ▷ *noun* the age under or over which one may not do something.

agency /ˈeɪdʒənsɪ/ ▷ *noun* (**agencies**) **1** an office or business that provides a particular service, eg matching workers with employers in specific areas. **2** an active part played by someone or something in bringing something about; instrumentality. **3** *N Amer, especially US* a government department providing a particular service. **4** the business of an agent. ◷ 17c: from Latin *agere* to do.

agenda /əˈdʒendə/ ▷ *singular noun* (***agendas***) **1** a list of things to be done or discussed. **2** a written list of subjects to be dealt with at a meeting, etc. • **on the agenda** waiting or needing to be dealt with. ◷ 20c: Latin, meaning 'things needing to be done'.

agent /ˈeɪdʒənt/ ▷ *noun* **1 a** someone who represents an organization and acts on its behalf; **b** someone who deals with someone else's business matters, etc. **2** (*also* **secret agent**) a spy. **3** a substance that produces a particular effect. **4** someone who is the cause of something. **5** *grammar* the person who performs an action, eg the subject of an active verb or noun, etc preceded by *by* in a passive construction. ◷ 16c: from Latin *agens*, from *agere* to do.

agent-general ▷ *noun* (***agents-general***) a representative in the UK of an Australian state or a Canadian province. ◷ 19c.

agent noun ▷ *noun, non-technical* a noun that denotes a person or machine, etc that does a specified thing, eg *farmer* or *accelerator*.

Agent Orange ▷ *noun* a highly poisonous herbicide, used as a defoliant to remove the leaves from plants, including crops, during the Vietnam War. ◷ 1960s: named after the colour-coding stripe on the container.

agent provocateur / *French* aʒɑ̃pʀɔvɔkatœʀ/ ▷ *noun* (***agents provocateurs*** / *French* aʒɑ̃pʀɔvɔkatœʀ/) someone employed to lead others in illegal acts for which they will be punished. ◷ 19c: French.

age of consent ▷ *noun* the age at which consent to sexual intercourse is permitted by law.

age-old ▷ *adj* done, known, etc for a very long time and hallowed by its antiquity.

agglomerate ▷ *verb* /əˈglɒməreɪt/ (***agglomerated***, ***agglomerating***) *tr & intr* to make into or become an untidy mass. ▷ *noun* /-rət/ **1** an untidy mass or collection of things. **2** *geol* a type of volcanic rock consisting of a mass of coarse angular fragments of solidified lava embedded in a matrix of ashy material. ▷ *adj* /-rət/ formed into a mass. • **agglomeration** *noun*. ◷ 17c: from Latin *agglomerare*, *agglomeratum* to wind on to a ball.

agglutinate /əˈgluːtɪneɪt/ ▷ *verb* (***agglutinated***, ***agglutinating***) **1** to stick or glue together. **2** *biol* said of red blood cells, bacteria, etc: to clump together forming a visible PRECIPITATE, eg as a result of mixing blood cells from two incompatible blood groups. **3** *tr & intr, grammar* said of a language: to create (words) by joining together (simpler words or word elements, each of which corresponds to a particular element of meaning). • **agglutination** *noun*. • **agglutinative** *adj*. ◷ 16c: from Latin *agglutinare*, *agglutinatum* to glue together.

aggrandize or **aggrandise** /əˈgrandaɪz/ ▷ *verb* (***aggrandized***, ***aggrandizing***) **1** to increase the power, wealth, etc of (a person, country, etc). **2** to make someone or something seem greater than they really are. • **aggrandizement** /əˈgrandɪz-/ *noun*. ◷ 17c: from French *aggrandir*.

aggravate /ˈagrəveɪt/ ▷ *verb* (***aggravated***, ***aggravating***) **1** to make (a bad situation, an illness, etc) worse. **2** *colloq* to make someone angry; to annoy them. • **aggravating** *adj*. • **aggravatingly** *adverb*. • **aggravation** *noun*. ◷ 16c: from Latin *aggravare*, *aggravatum* to make heavier or worse.

> ***aggravate***
>
> Sense 2 is well established, especially in spoken English, although it is sometimes regarded as incorrect. It is also found in the form **aggravating**, meaning 'annoying'.

aggravated ▷ *adj, law* said of an offence: made more serious, eg by violence □ *aggravated burglary*.

aggregate ▷ *noun* /ˈagrəgət/ **1** a collection of separate units brought together; a total. **2** *civil engineering, building* any material, especially sand, gravel or crushed stone, that is mixed with cement to form concrete. **3** *geol* a mass of soil grains or rock particles, or a mixture of both. ▷ *adj* /ˈagrəgət/ formed of separate units combined together. ▷ *verb* /-geɪt/ (***aggregated***, ***aggregating***) **1** *tr & intr* to combine or be combined into a single unit or whole. **2** *colloq* to amount in total to something. **3** *formal* to add someone as a member to a society, group, etc. ● **aggregation** *noun*. ● **in the aggregate** taken all together. ● **on aggregate** in total. ⓘ 15c: from Latin *aggregare*, *aggregatum* to herd or bring together.

aggression /əˈgrɛʃən/ ▷ *noun* **1** the act of attacking another person or country without being provoked. **2** an instance of hostile behaviour towards someone. **3** the tendency to make unprovoked attacks. **4** hostile feelings or behaviour. ⓘ 17c: from Latin *aggredi*, *agressus* to attack.

aggressive ▷ *adj* **1** always ready to attack; hostile. **2** strong and determined; self-assertive. **3** said of an action: hostile. ● **aggressively** *adverb*. ● **aggressiveness** *noun*.

aggressor ▷ *noun* in a fight, war, etc: the person, group or country that attacks first, especially if the attack is unprovoked.

aggrieved /əˈgriːvd/ ▷ *adj* **1** angry, hurt or upset because one feels that one has been badly or unfairly treated. **2** *law* having suffered because of someone else's illegal behaviour. ⓘ 13c: from French *agrever* to press heavily upon.

aggro /ˈagroʊ/ ▷ *noun, Brit slang* **1** fighting; violent or threatening behaviour. **2** problems or difficulties. ⓘ 1960s: shortening of AGGRAVATION or AGGRESSION.

aghast /əˈgɑːst/ ▷ *adj* filled with fear or horror. ⓘ Anglo-Saxon *gæstan* to frighten.

agile /ˈadʒaɪl/ or (*US*) /ˈadʒəl/ ▷ *adj* (*sometimes* ***agiler***, ***agilest***) able to move, change direction, etc quickly and easily; nimble; active. ● **agilely** *adverb*. ● **agility** /əˈdʒɪlɪtɪ/ *noun*. ⓘ 16c: from Latin *agilis*, from *agere* to do.

agin /əˈgɪn/ ▷ *prep, dialect or colloq* against. ⓘ 19c: a variant of AGAIN in an obsolete meaning.

aging see under AGE

agism see under AGEISM

agitate /ˈadʒɪteɪt/ ▷ *verb* (***agitated***, ***agitating***) **1** to excite or trouble (a person, their feelings, nerves, etc). **2** *intr* to stir up public opinion for or against an issue. **3** to stir or shake (a liquid) vigorously, usually in order to mix it with another liquid or to dissolve a solid in it. ● **agitated** *adj*. ● **agitatedly** *adverb*. ⓘ 16c: from Latin *agitare*, *agitatum*.

agitation /adʒɪˈteɪʃən/ ▷ *noun* **1** public discussion for or against something. **2** a disturbed or nervous state of mind; anxiety.

agitato /adʒɪˈtɑːtoʊ/ *music* ▷ *adverb* in an agitated restless manner. ▷ *adj* agitated; restless and wild. ▷ *noun* a passage to be played in this way. ⓘ 19c: Italian.

agitator /ˈadʒɪteɪtə(r)/ ▷ *noun* **1** someone who tries continually to stir up public feeling, especially over serious political or social issues. **2** a tool or machine for stirring or shaking a liquid.

agitprop /ˈadʒɪtprɒp/ ▷ *noun* the spreading of political propaganda, especially by communists. ⓘ 1930s: from Russian *Agitpropbyuro* the department of the Central Committee of the Communist Party responsible for *agitatsiya* agitation + *propaganda* propaganda.

aglet /ˈaglət/ ▷ *noun* the metal tag on the end of a lace. ⓘ 15c: from French *aiguillette* little needle.

aglitter /əˈglɪtə(r)/ ▷ *adj* glittering; sparkling. ⓘ 19c.

aglow /əˈgloʊ/ ▷ *adj* shining with colour or warmth; glowing. ⓘ 19c.

AGM ▷ *abbreviation* ANNUAL GENERAL MEETING.

agnail *noun* a HANGNAIL.

agnate /ˈagneɪt/ ▷ *adj* in genealogy, etc: **1** related on one's father's side or through a male ancestor, sometimes exclusively with male links. **2** related in any way. ▷ *noun* a person related to another on their father's side or through a male ancestor. ⓘ 16c: from Latin *agnatus*, literally 'born in addition', from *ad* in addition + *gnasci* to be born.

agnostic /agˈnɒstɪk/ ▷ *noun* someone who believes that one can know only about material things and so believes that nothing can be known about the existence of God. ▷ *adj* relating to this view. ● **agnosticism** /-stɪsɪzəm/ *noun*. Compare ATHEISM, THEISM, DEISM. ⓘ 19c, coined by T H Huxley: from Greek *agnostos* not known or not knowable.

ago /əˈgoʊ/ ▷ *adverb* in the past; earlier. ⓘ 14c: originally (as *agon*) past participle of Anglo-Saxon *agan* to pass by.

> ***ago***
>
> **Ago** follows the noun it refers to; usually it is followed by **that** and not **since**:
>
> ✓ *It is months ago that I last saw her.*
>
> **?** *It is months ago since I last saw her.*
>
> ☆ RECOMMENDATION: use either **since** or **ago** alone:
>
> ✓ *It is months since I last saw her.*
>
> ✓ *I last saw her months ago.*

agog /əˈgɒg/ ▷ *adj* very interested and excited; eager to know more. ▷ *adverb* eagerly; expectantly. ⓘ 16c: perhaps from French *en gogues* in fun.

agonize or **agonise** /ˈagənaɪz/ ▷ *verb* (***agonized***, ***agonizing***) **1** *intr* (*especially* **agonize about** or **over something**) to worry intensely or suffer great anxiety about it. **2** to cause great anxiety or worry to someone. ● **agonized** *adj* suffering or showing great anxiety, worry or agony. ● **agonizing** *adj* causing great bodily or mental suffering. ⓘ 16c: from Greek *agonizesthai* to struggle.

agony /ˈagənɪ/ ▷ *noun* (***agonies***) severe bodily or mental pain. ⓘ 14c: from Greek *agonia* struggle.

agony aunt ▷ *noun, colloq* **1** a person (usually a woman, or a man with a female nom-de-plume) who answers letters sent in to an agony column, or who gives similar advice on radio or TV. **2** *also loosely* a woman who acts as an adviser to friends and acquaintances about their personal problems. See also AGONY UNCLE.

agony column ▷ *noun* part of a newspaper or magazine where advice is offered to readers who write in with their problems. See also PROBLEM PAGE.

agony uncle ▷ *noun, colloq* a man who does the same work, or takes the same role, as an AGONY AUNT.

agoraphobia /agərəˈfoʊbɪə/ *psychol* ▷ *noun* an irrational fear of open spaces or public places. ● **agoraphobe** *noun*. ● **agoraphobic** *adj, noun*. ⓘ 19c: from Greek *agora* market-place + -PHOBIA.

AGR ▷ *abbreviation* ADVANCED GAS-COOLED REACTOR.

agrarian /əˈgrɛərɪən/ ▷ *adj* **1** relating to land or its management. **2** relating to the uses of land, especially agriculture or the cultivation of plants. ⓘ 18c: from Latin *agrarius*, from *ager* field.

agree /əˈgriː/ ▷ *verb* (***agreed***, ***agreeing***) *usually intr* **1** (*often* **agree with someone** or **something** or **about something**) to be of the same opinion as them about it. **2** (*usually* **agree to something**) to say yes to (a suggestion, request or instruction). **3** (*usually* **agree on** or **upon something**) to reach a joint decision about it after discussion. **4** to reach agreement about something. **5** (*often* **agree with something**) *grammar* to have the same number, person, gender or case. ● **agree to differ** said of two or more people, groups, etc: to agree to accept each other's different opinions. ● **be agreed** to have reached the same conclusion. ⓘ 14c: from French *agreer*.

■ **agree with someone** usually said of food: to be suitable or good for them □ *Milk doesn't agree with me.*

■ **agree with something** to be consistent with it.

agreeable ▻ *adj* **1** said of things: pleasant. **2** said of people: friendly. **3** (*usually* **agreeable to something**) said of people: willing to accept (a suggestion, etc). • **agreeability** or **agreeableness** *noun*.

agreeably ▻ *adverb* **1** pleasantly. **2** (*especially* **agreeably to** or **with something**) corresponding to or in accordance with it.

agreement ▻ *noun* **1** a contract or promise. **2** a joint decision made after discussion. **3** the state of holding the same opinion. **4** *grammar* the state of having the same number, person, gender or case. Also called **concord**.

agribusiness /'agrɪbɪznɪs/ or **agrobusiness** ▻ *noun* all the operations of supplying the market with farm produce taken together, including growing, provision of farm machinery, distribution, etc. ⓒ 20c, originally US: from *agriculture* or *agro-* + BUSINESS.

agrichemical ▻ *adj* said of fruit and vegetables: treated with chemicals after being harvested.

agriculturalist /agrɪ'kʌltʃərəlɪst/ and **agriculturist** /-'kʌltʃərɪst/ ▻ *noun* **1** an expert on agriculture. **2** a farmer.

agriculture /'agrɪkʌltʃə(r)/ ▻ *noun* the cultivation of the land in order to grow crops or raise animal livestock as a source of food or other useful products, eg wool or cotton. • **agricultural** /-'kʌltʃərəl/ *adj*. ⓒ 17c: from Latin *ager* field + *cultura* cultivation.

agrimony /'agrɪmənɪ/ ▻ *noun* (***agrimonies***) an erect perennial plant which has pairs of small leaflets alternating with large ones, and small yellow flowers in long terminal spikes. ⓒ 15c: Latin, from Greek *argemone* a type of poppy.

agro- /agroʊ, ə'grɒ/ ▻ *combining form, signifying* agricultural □ *agrochemical.*

agronomy /ə'grɒnəmɪ/ ▻ *noun* the scientific study of the cultivation of field crops and soil management. • **agronomist** *noun*. ⓒ 19c.

aground /ə'graʊnd/ ▻ *adj, adverb* said of ships: stuck on the bottom of the sea or rocks, usually in shallow water. ⓒ 16c in this sense; 13c in obsolete sense 'on the ground'.

ague /'eɪgjuː/ ▻ *noun* **1** a fit of shivering. **2** malaria. **3** *old use* a burning fever. ⓒ 14c: from French *fièvre ague* acute fever.

AH ▻ *abbreviation* used in the Islamic dating system: *anno Hegirae* (Latin), in the year of the HEGIRA, ie counting from AD 622.

ah /ɑː/ ▻ *exclamation* expressing surprise, sympathy, admiration, pleasure, etc, according to the intonation of the speaker's voice. ⓒ 13c.

aha /ə'hɑː, ɑː'hɑː/ ▻ *exclamation* expressing pleasure, satisfaction, triumph or surprise, according to the intonation of the speaker's voice. ⓒ 14c.

ahead /ə'hɛd/ ▻ *adverb* **1** at or in the front; forwards. **2** earlier in time; before □ *arrived ahead of me.* **3** in the lead; further advanced □ *ahead on points.* • **ahead of someone** or **something** in advance of them or it. • **get ahead** to make progress, especially socially. ⓒ 16c: A-[1] + HEAD.

ahem /ə'hɛm, ə'həm/ ▻ *exclamation* a sound made in the back of the throat, used to gain people's attention or to express doubt or disapproval. ⓒ 18c.

ahimsa /ə'hɪmsə/ ▻ *noun* in Hinduism, Buddhism and especially Jainism: the principle of respect for all life and the practice of non-injury to living things. ⓒ 19c: Sanskrit.

-aholic or **-oholic** /ə'hɒlɪk/ *colloq* ▻ *combining form, forming adjectives and nouns, signifying* addicted to, or a person addicted to (a specified thing) □ *workaholic.* • **-aholism** or **-oholism** *noun*. ⓒ Modelled on ALCOHOLIC.

ahoy /ə'hɔɪ/ ▻ *exclamation, naut* a shout to greet or attract the attention of another ship. ⓒ 18c.

AI ▻ *abbreviation* **1** artificial insemination. **2** artificial intelligence.

AID ▻ *abbreviation* artificial insemination by donor (now called DI).

aid /eɪd/ ▻ *noun* **1** help. **2** help or support in the form of money, supplies or services given to people who need it. **3** (*often in compounds*) a person or thing that helps do something □ *a hearing-aid.* ▻ *verb* (***aided, aiding***) **1** to help or support someone. **2** to help something happen; to promote it. • **aid and abet** *law* to help and encourage someone to do something wrong, especially disobey the law. • **in aid of someone** or **something** in support of them or it. • **what's this in aid of?** *colloq* what is the reason for, or purpose of, this? ⓒ 15c: from French *aidier*.

aide /eɪd/ ▻ *noun* a confidential assistant or adviser, especially to the head of a government. ⓒ 18c: short form of AIDE-DE-CAMP.

aide-de-camp /eɪddə'kɑ̃/ or (*chiefly US*) **aid-de-camp** ▻ *noun* (***aides-de-camp, aids-de-camp*** /eɪddə'kɑ̃/) an officer in the armed forces who acts as assistant to a senior officer. ⓒ 17c: French.

aide-mémoire /eɪdmɛm'wɑː(r)/ ▻ *noun* (***aides-mémoire*** /eɪdmɛm'wɑː(r)/) something that helps one to remember something, especially a note listing the main points mentioned in a paper, speech, etc. ⓒ 19c: French, literally 'help-memory'.

AIDS or **Aids** /eɪdz/ ▻ *abbreviation*, acquired immune deficiency (or immunodeficiency) syndrome, a disease caused by infection with the human immunodeficiency virus (HIV), transmitted in blood, semen and vaginal fluids, and which destroys the immune system, leaving the body susceptible to potentially fatal infections. ⓒ 1980s.

AIDS-related complex ▻ *noun* (abbreviation **ARC**), *pathol* a condition that manifests prior to the onset of full-blown AIDS, characterized by fever, weight loss, thrush, shingles and a general feeling of malaise.

aiguille /eɪ'gwiːl/ ▻ *noun* a sharp, needle-like pinnacle of rock. ⓒ 19c: French, literally 'needle'.

AIH ▻ *abbreviation* artificial insemination by husband.

aikido /aɪ'kiːdoʊ/ ▻ *noun* a Japanese form of self-defence, based on a system of locks and holds and the movements of the attacker or opponent. ⓒ 1950s: Japanese, from *ai* to harmonize + *ki* breath or spirit + *do* way.

ail /eɪl/ ▻ *verb* (***ailed, ailing***) **1** *intr* to be ill and weak. **2** *old use* to cause pain or trouble to someone. • **ailing** *adj* ill; in poor health. ⓒ Anglo-Saxon *eglan* to trouble.

aileron /'eɪlərɒn/ ▻ *noun, aeronautics* one of a pair of hinged flaps situated at the rear edge of each wing of an aircraft, used to control roll about the craft's longitudinal axis. ⓒ 20c: French diminutive of *aile* wing.

ailment ▻ *noun* an illness, especially a minor one.

ailuro- /aɪ'lʊəroʊ, eɪ-/ or (before a vowel) **ailur-** ▻ *combining form, signifying* cat. ⓒ From Greek *ailouros* cat.

aim /eɪm/ ▻ *verb* (***aimed, aiming***) **1** *tr & intr* (*usually* **aim at** or **for someone** or **something**) to point or direct a weapon, attack, remark, etc at them or it. **2** *intr* to plan, intend or try. ▻ *noun* **1** what a person, etc intends to do; the achievement aimed at. **2** the ability to hit what is aimed at □ *good aim.* • **take aim** to point a weapon at a target so as to be ready to fire. ⓒ 14c: from French *esmer*, from Latin *aestimare* to estimate.

aimless ▻ *adj* without any purpose. • **aimlessly** *adverb*. • **aimlessness** *noun*.

ain't /eɪnt/ ▷ *contraction, colloq* **1** am not; is not; are not. **2** has not; have not.

aioli or **aïoli** /aɪˈoʊliː/ ▷ *noun cookery* a garlic-flavoured mayonnaise. ◷ 20c: French, from Provençal *ai* garlic + *oli* oil.

air /ɛə(r)/ ▷ *noun* **1** the invisible odourless tasteless mixture of gases that forms the atmosphere surrounding the Earth, essential for the survival of all living organisms that depend on oxygen for respiration. **2** the space above and around the Earth, where birds and aircraft fly. **3** moving air; a light breeze; a draught. **4** an appearance, look or manner □ *with a nonchalant air.* **5** (**airs**) behaviour intended to impress others, to show off, etc □ *put on airs* □ *airs and graces.* **6** a tune. **7** *in compounds* **a** relating to air or the air; **b** relating to aircraft. ▷ *verb* (*aired, airing*) **1** *tr & intr* **a** to hang (laundry) in a warm dry place to make it completely dry or to remove unpleasant smells; **b** said of laundry: to be hung in a warm dry place for this purpose. **2** *tr & intr* **a** to let fresh air into (a room, etc); **b** said of a room, etc: to become cooler or fresher in this way. **3** to warm (the sheets and blankets of a bed, especially one that has not been used recently). **4** to make (one's thoughts, opinions, etc) known publicly. **5** *old use* to make a show of or parade something. **6** *tr & intr, N Amer, especially US* to broadcast something, or be broadcast, on radio or television. ● **by air** in an aircraft. ● **a change of air** a beneficial change from one's usual routine. ● **clear the air** see under CLEAR. ● **in the air 1** said of proposals, etc: undecided; not definitely going ahead. **2** said of opinions, news, etc: being generally considered, thought or talked about. ● **into thin air** completely; mysteriously and leaving no trace. ● **off the air** no longer or not yet being broadcast on radio or television. ● **on the air** being broadcast on radio or television. ● **take the air** and **take to the air** see under TAKE. ● **up in the air 1** said of proposals, etc: undecided; not definitely going ahead. **2** said of a person: **a** excited; **b** angry. ◷ 13c: French, from Greek *aer.*

air ambulance ▷ *noun* a specially equipped aircraft that can attend accident scenes which are not easily accessible, or is used to take patients from remote places to hospital or to transfer them between hospitals quickly, etc.

air bag ▷ *noun* in a vehicle: a safety device consisting of a bag that inflates automatically in a collision to protect the occupants.

air base ▷ *noun* an operational centre for military aircraft.

air bed ▷ *noun* an inflated mattress.

air bladder ▷ *noun, biol* **1** a cavity or sac containing air. **2** a SWIM BLADDER.

airborne ▷ *adj* **1** said of aircraft, etc: flying in the air, having just taken off. **2** transported by air.

Airborne Warning and Control System ▷ *noun* (abbreviation **AWACS**) a radar system mounted on an aircraft, used to detect enemy planes and to control weapons or planes directed against them.

air brake ▷ *noun* in lorries, railway rolling stock, etc: a mechanism whereby the pressure of compressed air acting on a piston is used to stop or slow down a moving part.

air brick ▷ *noun* a brick with small holes, put into the side of a building to allow ventilation.

airbrush ▷ *noun* **1** a device for painting which uses compressed air to form a spray. **2** in computer graphics: a tool for achieving a similar effect. ▷ *verb* (***airbrushed, airbrushing***) **1** to paint something using an airbrush. **2** to retouch (a photograph). **3** to improve (the image of someone or something) by masking defects. ● **airbrushed** *adj.* ● **airbrushing** *noun.*

Airbus ▷ *noun, trademark* an aircraft which can carry a large number of passengers, especially on short flights.

air chief marshal ▷ *noun, Brit* an officer in the air force. See table at RANK.

air commodore ▷ *noun, Brit* an officer in the air force. See table at RANK.

air-compressor ▷ *noun, engineering* a machine that takes in air at atmospheric pressure, compresses it and delivers it at higher pressure.

air-conditioning ▷ *noun* **1** any system that is used to control the temperature, relative humidity or purity of air, and to circulate it in an enclosed space such as a room, building or motor vehicle. **2** the control of room temperature, etc using such a system. ● **air-conditioned** *adj.* ● **air-conditioner** *noun.*

air-cooled ▷ *adj* said of an engine: cooled by a current of air.

air cover ▷ *noun* **1** the use of aircraft to protect against enemy attack. **2** such protection. **3** the protecting aircraft.

aircraft ▷ *singular or plural noun* any structure, machine or vehicle that is designed for travelling through air supported by its own buoyancy or by the action of air on its surfaces, eg an aeroplane or helicopter.

aircraft carrier ▷ *noun* a large naval warship with a flat deck which aircraft can take off from and land on.

aircraftman and **aircraftwoman** ▷ *noun, Brit* a person of the lowest rank in the air force.

aircrew ▷ *noun* the people in an aircraft who are responsible for flying it and looking after the passengers. Often shortened to CREW. Compare GROUND CREW.

air cushion ▷ *noun* **1** a cushion that can be filled with air. **2** a pocket of down-driven air used for supporting a hovercraft, etc.

air-drop ▷ *noun* a delivery of military equipment, troops, supplies, etc by parachute. ▷ *verb* to deliver (supplies, etc) by parachute.

Airedale /ˈɛədeɪl/ and **Airedale terrier** ▷ *noun* (***Airedales*** or ***Airedale terriers***) a breed of large terrier.

airer /ˈɛərə(r)/ ▷ *noun* a frame on which clothes are dried.

airfield ▷ *noun* an open expanse that is used by aircraft for landing and take-off. Compare AIRSTRIP.

air force ▷ *noun* that part of a country's defence forces which uses aircraft for fighting.

airframe ▷ *noun* the body of an aircraft as opposed to its engines.

air freight ▷ *noun* **1** the transport of freight by air. **2** the cost of this. ▷ *verb* (**air-freight**) to transport (freight) by air.

air frost ▷ *noun, meteorol* a temperature of the air (not the ground) of below 0°.

airgun ▷ *noun* a gun that uses air under pressure to fire small pellets.

airhead ▷ *noun, slang* an idiot.

airhole ▷ *noun* **1** a hole for the passage of air, usually for ventilation. **2** a hole in ice where animals come up to breathe.

air hostess ▷ *noun, Brit* a female FLIGHT ATTENDANT. See also STEWARDESS.

airier, **airiest**, **airily** and **airiness** see under AIRY

airing ▷ *noun* **1** the act of airing (laundry, a room, the sheets, etc on a bed, etc) or fact of being aired. **2** the stating and discussing of opinions, etc publicly. **3** a short walk, etc taken in order to get some fresh air.

airing-cupboard ▷ *noun* a heated cupboard in which laundry is put to become completely dry and warm.

air lane ▷ *noun* in aviation: a route through the air regularly used by aircraft.

air layering ▷ *noun, hortic* the LAYERING of shoots, not by bending them down to root in the soil, but by enclosing them in compost, etc at their current place of growth.

airless ▷ *adj* **1** said of the weather: unpleasantly warm, with no wind. **2** said of a room: lacking fresh air; stuffy.

air letter see AEROGRAMME

airlift ▷ *noun* the transporting of large numbers of people or large amounts of goods in aircraft when other routes are blocked. ▷ *verb* to transport (people, goods, etc) in this way.

airline ▷ *noun* **1** a company or organization which provides a regular transport service for passengers or cargo by aircraft. **2** a tube which transports air under pressure, eg for divers.

airliner ▷ *noun* a large passenger aircraft.

airlock ▷ *noun* **1** a bubble of air or gas that obstructs or blocks the flow of liquid through a pipe. **2** an airtight chamber with two entrances, which enables a person to move between two areas on either side of it with different air pressures, eg between a space vehicle and outer space without air escaping, or between air and water, eg between a submarine and the sea without water entering.

airmail ▷ *noun* **1** the system of carrying mail by air. **2** mail carried by air. ▷ *verb* to send something by airmail.

airman and **airwoman** ▷ *noun* a pilot or member of the crew of an aeroplane, especially in an air force.

air marshal ▷ *noun, Brit* an officer in the air force. See table at RANK. Also *Austral, NZ*.

air miss ▷ *noun* in aviation: a situation in which two aircraft on different routes come dangerously close together.

air piracy ▷ *noun* the hijacking of an aircraft.

airplane ▷ *noun, N Amer* an aeroplane.

airplane

See Usage Note at **aeroplane**.

airplay ▷ *noun* the broadcasting of recorded music, especially pop music, on the radio.

air pocket ▷ *noun* an area of reduced pressure in the air, or a downward current, which can cause an aircraft to suddenly lose height.

air pollution ▷ *noun, ecol* the contamination of the air with noxious substances such as vehicle exhaust fumes, by-products from industrial processes, etc.

airport ▷ *noun* a place where civil aircraft arrive and depart, with facilities for passengers and cargo, etc.

air power ▷ *noun* military power in terms of aircraft.

air pump ▷ *noun* a device for pumping air out or in.

air raid ▷ *noun* an attack by enemy aircraft.

air-rifle ▷ *noun* a rifle that is fired by air under pressure.

air-sea rescue ▷ *noun* the use of both aircraft and boats to rescue people from the sea.

airship ▷ *noun* a power-driven steerable aircraft that consists of a streamlined envelope or hull containing helium gas, with an engine and a GONDOLA (sense 2) suspended from it, now used mainly for aerial photography and advertising. Also called DIRIGIBLE.

air shot ▷ *noun, golf, cricket* an attempted stroke that fails to connect with the ball.

airsick ▷ *adj* affected by nausea due to the motion of an aircraft. • **airsickness** *noun*.

airside ▷ *noun* in aviation: the area of an airport with direct access to the aircraft, entry to which is controlled. Also *as adj* and *adverb*.

airspace ▷ *noun* the part of the atmosphere directly above a country, considered as part of that country.

airspeed ▷ *noun* the speed of an aircraft, missile, etc in relation to the air through which it is moving.

airstrip ▷ *noun* a strip of ground where aircraft can land and take off but which has no facilities. Compare AIRFIELD.

air terminal ▷ *noun* an office or other place in a town from where passengers are taken, usually by bus, to an airport nearby.

airtight ▷ *adj* **1** said of a container, etc: which air cannot get into, out of, or through. **2** said of an opinion, argument, etc: having no weak points.

airtime ▷ *noun* on TV or radio: the length of time given to a particular item, programme or topic.

air-to-air ▷ *adj* said of a weapon: fired from one aircraft to another in flight.

air-traffic control ▷ *noun* a system or organization which manages the movement of aircraft and sends instructions to aircraft by radio communication. • **air-traffic controller** *noun*.

air vice-marshal ▷ *noun, Brit* an officer in the air force. See table at RANK. Also *Austral, NZ*.

airwaves ▷ *plural noun* **1** *informal* the RADIO WAVES used for radio and television broadcasting. **2** the particular frequencies used for such broadcasting.

airway ▷ *noun* **1** a passage for air, especially for ventilation. **2** in the body: the route by which oxygen reaches the lungs, from the nose or mouth via the windpipe. **3** a route regularly followed by aircraft. **4** (**airways**) used as part of an airline name. **5** *especially US* a radio channel.

airwoman see AIRMAN

airworthy ▷ *adj* said of aircraft: in a condition to fly safely. • **airworthiness** *noun*.

airy /ˈɛərɪ/ ▷ *adj* (***airier, airiest***) **1** with plenty of fresh cool air. **2** not thinking about or dealing with something as seriously as one should; flippant. **3** unconcerned; nonchalant. **4** lively; light-hearted. • **airily** *adverb*. • **airiness** *noun*.

airy-fairy ▷ *adj, colloq* showing or suggesting a lack of sense or good planning; not based on facts or on awareness of real situations. ◷ 19c: originally alluding to a phrase in Tennyson, 'airy, fairy Lilian' (*Lilian*, 1830).

aisle /aɪl/ ▷ *noun* **1** a passage between rows of seats, eg in an aircraft, theatre, or church. **2** the side part of the inside of a church. ◷ 14c as *ele*: from Latin *ala* wing; spelling influenced by ISLE.

aisle

There is sometimes a spelling confusion between **aisle** and **isle**.

aitch /eɪtʃ/ ▷ *noun* (***aitches***) the letter H or h. • **drop one's aitches** to fail to pronounce the sound of the letter *h* when it comes at the beginning of words. ◷ 16c as *ache*: from French *ache*.

aitchbone /ˈeɪtʃboʊn/ ▷ *noun* **1** the rump bone in cattle. **2** a cut of beef from this. ◷ 15c as *hach-boon*, the result of wrong division (compare ADDER) of earlier forms such as 13c *nage* (bone): from French *nache*, from Latin *natis* buttocks.

ajar /əˈdʒɑː(r)/ ▷ *adj, adverb* partly open. ◷ 18c; 16c as *on char*, from Anglo-Saxon *on* on + *cierr* turn.

AK ▷ *abbreviation, US state* Alaska. Also written **Alas.**

AKA or **aka** ▷ *abbreviation* also known as.

akimbo /əˈkɪmboʊ/ ▷ *adj, adverb* with hands on hips and elbows bent outward. ◷ 15c as *in kenebowe* in a sharp bend.

akin /ə'kɪn/ ⊳ *adj* **1** similar; being of the same kind. **2** related by blood. ⓒ 16c: from *a* (obsolete short form of *of*) + KIN.

AL ⊳ *abbreviation* **1** *US state* Alabama. Also written **Ala. 2** *IVR* Albania.

Al ⊳ *symbol, chem* aluminium.

-al /əl/ ⊳ *suffix* **1** *forming adjectives, signifying* related to someone specified □ ***parental*. 2** *forming nouns, signifying* the action of doing something specified □ ***arrival***. See also -IAL. ⓒ From Latin adjectival suffix *-alis*.

à la /ɑːlɑː/ ⊳ *prep* in the manner or style of someone or something specified: **a** in literature, art, etc: followed by the name of a writer, etc, or by a French adjective based on the name of a country □ ***à la Henry James*** □ ***à la Russe***; **b** in cookery: followed by the name of a person or (usually) by a French adjective based on the name of a region or town, etc □ ***à la Bordelaise***. ⓒ 16c: French.

alabaster /'aləbɑːstə(r), -ba-/ ⊳ *noun* a type of white stone used for ornaments, etc. ⊳ *adj* made of or like alabaster. ⓒ 14c: from Greek *alabastros* a perfume bottle made of alabaster.

à la carte /ɑː lɑː kɑːt/ ⊳ *adverb* ⊳ *adj* said of a meal in a restaurant: with each dish priced and ordered separately. Compare TABLE D'HÔTE. ⓒ 19c: French.

alacrity /ə'lakrɪtɪ/ ⊳ *noun* quick and cheerful enthusiasm. ⓒ 16c: from Latin *alacritas*.

à la mode /ɑː lɑː moʊd/ ⊳ *adj, adverb* in fashion; according to current fashion. ⓒ 17c: French, meaning 'in the fashion'.

alarm /ə'lɑːm/ ⊳ *noun* **1** sudden fear produced by awareness of danger. **2** a noise warning of danger. **3** a bell, etc which sounds to warn of danger or, eg on a clock, to wake a person from sleep. **4** an alarm clock. ⊳ *verb* (***alarmed***, ***alarming***) **1** to frighten. **2** to warn someone of danger. **3** to fit or switch on an alarm on (a house, car, etc). • **give**, **raise** or **sound the alarm** to give warning of danger by shouting, ringing a bell, etc. ⓒ 14c: from French *alarme*, from Italian *all'arme* to arms.

alarm clock ⊳ *noun* a clock that can be set to make a noise at a particular time, usually to wake someone up.

alarming ⊳ *adj* disturbing or frightening. • **alarmingly** *adverb*.

alarmist ⊳ *noun* someone who spreads unnecessary alarm. ⊳ *adj* causing unnecessary alarm. • **alarmism** *noun*.

Alas. see under AK

alas /ə'las, ə'lɑːs/ ⊳ *exclamation, old or literary* expressing grief or misfortune. ⓒ 13c: from French *ha* ah + *las* wretched, from Latin *lassus* weary.

alb ⊳ *noun* a long white garment reaching to the feet, worn by some Christian priests. ⓒ Anglo-Saxon: from Latin *albus* white.

Albanian /al'beɪnɪən/ ⊳ *adj* belonging or relating to Albania, a republic in the W part of the Balkan peninsula, its inhabitants, or their language. ⊳ *noun* **1** a citizen or inhabitant of, or person born in, Albania. **2** the official language of Albania.

albatross /'albətrɒs/ ⊳ *noun* (***albatrosses***) **1** a large seabird, found mainly in the southern oceans, with a powerful hooked beak, a stout body, long narrow wings, and white plumage with black (or sometimes brown) patches. **2** an oppressive and inescapable fact or influence from one's past. **3** *golf* a score of three under par. Compare BIRDIE 2, EAGLE 3, BOGEY². ⓒ 17c: from Portuguese *alcatraz* pelican; sense 2 is derived from Coleridge's *Ancient Mariner*.

albeit /ɔːl'biːɪt/ ⊳ *conj* even if; although. ⓒ 14c as *al be it* although it be.

albinism /'albɪnɪzəm/ ⊳ *noun, biol* in a living organism: the inherited lack of pigmentation, which in vertebrates is caused by a lack of the enzyme responsible for the production of the dark pigment MELANIN. ⓒ 19c, also as *albinoism*.

albino /al'biːnoʊ or (*US*) al'baɪnoʊ/ ⊳ *noun* (***albinos***) *biol* **1** in an animal or human: an abnormal lack of pigmentation in the hair, skin and eyes. **2** in a plant: a total or partial lack of CHLOROPHYLL or other pigments. ⓒ 18c: Portuguese, from Latin *albus* white.

album /'albəm/ ⊳ *noun* **1** a book with blank pages for holding photographs, stamps, autographs, etc. **2** a record, CD, etc which contains multiple tracks. ⓒ 17c: from Latin *album* blank tablet, from *albus* white.

albumen /'albjʊmən, al'bjuːmən/ ⊳ *noun, zool* in the eggs of birds and some reptiles: the nutritive material surrounding the yolk; the white of an egg. ⓒ 16c: Latin, from *albus* white.

albumin /al'bjuːmɪn, 'albjʊmɪn/ ⊳ *noun, biochem* any of various water-soluble globular proteins that coagulate when heated, found in egg white, milk, blood serum, etc. ⓒ 19c.

alchemy /'alkəmɪ/ ⊳ *noun* the forerunner of modern chemistry, which centred around attempts to convert ordinary metals into gold, and to discover a universal remedy for illness, known as the elixir of life. • **alchemist** *noun*. ⓒ 14c as *alkamy*: from Arabic *al* the + *kimiya*, from Greek *kemeia* transmutation.

alcheringa /altʃə'rɪŋgə/ ⊳ *noun* in Aboriginal folklore: DREAM TIME. ⓒ 19c: Aboriginal.

alcohol /'alkəhɒl/ ⊳ *noun* **1** *chem* any of numerous organic chemical compounds containing one or more hydroxyl groups, used as solvents for dyes, resins, varnishes, perfume oils, etc, and as fuels. **2** ETHANOL, especially when used as an intoxicant in alcoholic beverages. **3** any drink containing this liquid, such as wine or beer. ⓒ 19c in sense 1; 16c in obsolete sense 'a fine powder', especially 'a sublimate': medieval Latin, from Arabic *al* the + *kohl* kohl.

alcohol abuse ⊳ *noun* excessive drinking of alcohol, to the point where it becomes harmful.

alcoholic /alkə'hɒlɪk/ ⊳ *adj* **1** relating to, containing or having the properties of alcohol. **2** relating to alcoholism. ⊳ *noun* a person who suffers from alcoholism. • **alcoholically** *adverb*.

alcoholism /'alkəhɒlɪzəm/ ⊳ *noun, pathol* **1** a severe and potentially fatal condition caused by physical dependence on alcohol, habitual and extensive consumption of which impairs physical and mental health. **2** *loosely* heavy drinking habits.

alcove /'alkoʊv/ ⊳ *noun* a recess in the wall of a room or garden. ⓒ 17c: from Spanish *alcoba*, from Arabic *al* the + *qubbah* vault.

aldehyde /'aldəhaɪd/ ⊳ *noun* any of numerous organic chemical compounds formed by the oxidation of alcohols, including aromatic compounds which are used as flavourings and perfumes. ⓒ 19c: abbreviation of Latin *alcohol dehydrogenatum* alcohol with hydrogen removed.

al dente /al 'dente, -tɪ/ ⊳ *adj, cookery* said of pasta and vegetables: cooked so as to remain firm when bitten. ⓒ 20c: Italian, literally 'to the tooth'.

alder /'ɔːldə(r)/ ⊳ *noun* **1** any of various deciduous trees and shrubs with dark greyish-brown fissured bark, oval or rounded leaves with toothed margins, and male and female flowers in CATKINs on separate plants. **2** the timber of this tree, which is resistant to underwater rot and is used to make bridges and piles. Anglo-Saxon *alor*.

alderman /'ɔːldəmən/ ⊳ *noun* **1** in England and Wales until 1974: a member of a town, county or borough council elected by fellow councillors, below the rank of mayor. **2** in the US and Canada: a member of the governing body of a city. • **aldermanship** *noun*. ⓒ 13c in sense 1; Anglo-Saxon *ealdormann* a nobleman of the highest rank.

Alderney /ˈɔːldənɪ/ ▷ *noun* a small dairy cow of a breed which originated in Alderney; now also a cow from the other Channel Islands. 🕒 18c.

Aldis lamp /ˈɔːldɪs—/ ▷ *noun* a portable lamp for signalling in Morse code. 🕒 20c: named after its inventor A C W Aldis (died 1953).

aldrin /ˈɔːldrɪn/ ▷ *noun* a chlorinated hydrocarbon used as a contact insecticide. 🕒 20c: from the name of the German chemist K Alder (1902–58)

ale /eɪl/ ▷ *noun* **1** a light-coloured beer, higher in alcohol content than LAGER and with a fuller body, flavoured with hops. **2** beer. 🕒 Anglo-Saxon *ealu*.

aleatory /ˈeɪlɪətərɪ, alɪˈeɪ-/ and **aleatoric** /-əˈtɒrɪk/ ▷ *adj, technical* **1** depending on chance. **2** said of music: in which chance influences the choice of notes. 🕒 17c as *aleatory*; 20c as *aleatoric*: from Latin *aleator* dice-player.

alee /əˈliː/ ▷ *adverb, naut* on or towards the lee side. 🕒 14c.

alehouse ▷ *noun, old use* an inn or public house.

Alemannic /aləˈmanɪk/ ▷ *noun* the High German dialect of Switzerland, Alsace, etc. 🕒 18c: from Latin *Alemanni*, a people of SW Germany.

aleph /ˈalɪf, ˈɑː-/ ▷ *noun* the first letter of the Phoenician and Hebrew alphabets. 🕒 13c: Hebrew, literally 'ox', because the shape of the letter resembles an ox's head.

alert /əˈlɜːt/ ▷ *adj* (***alerter, alertest***) **1** thinking and acting quickly. **2** *especially* **alert to something**) watchful and aware of (a danger, etc). ▷ *noun* **1** a warning of danger. **2** the period of time covered by such a warning. ▷ *verb* (***alerted, alerting***) (*usually* **alert someone to something**) to warn them of (a danger); to make them aware of (a fact or circumstance). • **alertly** *adverb*. • **alertness** *noun*. • **on the alert** watchful. 🕒 17c: from French *alerte*, from Italian *all'erta* to the watchtower.

Aleut /ˈalɪuːt/ ▷ *noun* (***Aleut*** or ***Aleuts***) **1** a member of a people, related to the INUIT, who inhabit the Aleutian Islands and part of Alaska. **2** the language of this people. ▷ *adj* (*also* **Aleutian**) /əˈluːʃən/ belonging or relating to this people or their language. 🕒 18c: Russian, probably from a native word.

A level /eɪ —/ (*in full* **Advanced level**) ▷ *noun* **1** an examination in a single subject in England, Wales and N Ireland for which school and college students study until about the age of 18. **2** a pass in such an examination. Compare HIGHER. Also as *adj* □ ***A-level pass.***

alewife ▷ *noun* a fish related to the herring, common off the NE coast of America. 🕒 17c; perhaps referring to its corpulent shape.

alexanders /aləgˈzɑːndəz/ ▷ *noun* an umbelliferous plant whose stems were formerly eaten as celery is now. 🕒 Anglo-Saxon *alexandre*.

Alexander technique /alɪgˈzaːndə —/ ▷ *noun* a system of body awareness designed to improve posture and movement and avoid physical strain. 🕒 20c: named after its originator, the Australian-born physiotherapist F M Alexander (died 1955).

Alexandrian /aləgˈzɑːndrɪən/ ▷ *adj* referring to Alexandria in Egypt, especially as a Hellenistic centre of education, literature and culture, sometimes as being erudite and critical rather than original and creative.

alexandrine /aləgˈzɑːndraɪn, -driːn/ ▷ *noun, poetry* a verse of six iambic feet (in English) or twelve syllables (in French). ▷ *adj* said of verse: written in alexandrines. 🕒 16c: French, from the name *Alexandre*, Alexander the Great being the subject of an Old French romance written in this metre.

alexandrite /aləgˈzɑːndraɪt/ ▷ *noun* a dark green mineral, a kind of CHRYSOBERYL. 🕒 19c: named after Alexander I of Russia, as it was discovered on the day of his majority.

alexia /aˈlɛksɪə/ ▷ *noun, pathol* loss of the ability to read, caused by brain disease. Compare APHASIA, DYSLEXIA. 🕒 19c: from A-[2] + Greek *lexis* speech.

alfalfa /alˈfalfə/ ▷ *noun* **1** a perennial plant of the pulse family with purple flowers and spirally twisted pods, widely cultivated as a forage crop, especially in the USA. Also called LUCERNE. **2** the young leaves and shoots of this plant, eaten as a salad vegetable, etc. 🕒 19c: Spanish, from Arabic *al-fasfasah*.

alfresco /alˈfrɛskoʊ/ ▷ *adverb* in the open air. ▷ *adj* open-air. 🕒 18c: Italian *al fresco* in the fresh air.

algae /ˈalgiː, ˈaldʒiː/ ▷ *plural noun* (*singular* ***alga*** /ˈalgə/) a large and very diverse group of mainly aquatic organisms, ranging from single-celled members of the plant PLANKTON to large multicellular seaweeds. 🕒 16c as *alga*: Latin, meaning 'seaweed'.

algebra /ˈaldʒəbrə/ ▷ *noun* the branch of mathematics that uses letters and symbols to represent variable quantities and numbers, and to express generalizations about them. • **algebraic** /-ˈbreɪɪk/ *adj*. • **algebraically** *adverb*. • **algebraist** /-ˈbreɪɪst/ *noun*. 🕒 16c: Italian and Spanish, from Arabic *al-jebr*, from *al* the + *jebr* reunion of broken parts.

-algia /aldʒɪə/ ▷ *combining form, medicine, signifying* pain in the part of the body specified □ ***neuralgia.*** 🕒 From Greek *algos* pain.

alginate /ˈaldʒɪneɪt/ ▷ *noun* a salt of alginic acid, found in seaweeds, and used in food manufacturing as a thickening agent. 🕒 1930s.

alginic acid /alˈdʒɪnɪk —/ ▷ *noun* an acid obtained from certain seaweeds, used in plastics, medicine, as a food-thickening agent, etc. 🕒 19c: from ALGA.

ALGOL or **Algol** /ˈalgɒl/ ▷ *noun, computing* a high-level programming language, formerly widely used for scientific problem solving. 🕒 1950s: contraction of *algo*rithmic *l*anguage.

Algonquian /alˈgɒŋkwɪən/ or **Algonkian** /-kɪən/ ▷ *noun* **1** a family of Native American languages, including Natick, Shawnee, Ojibwa, Cheyenne, etc, spoken over a wide area. **2** a member of any Native American people that speaks one of these languages. ▷ *adj* relating to this family of languages or its speakers. 🕒 19c: from ALGONQUIN.

Algonquin /alˈgɒŋkwɪn/ or **Algonkin** /-kɪn/ ▷ *noun* **1** a major group of Native American peoples in the valley of the Ottawa and around the northern tributaries of the St Lawrence. **2** an individual belonging to this group. **3** their language. ▷ *adj* Algonquian. 🕒 17c, also as *Algoumequin*: French Canadian, perhaps from Micmac (a Native American language spoken in parts of Canada) *algoomaking* at the place of spearing fish.

algorithm /ˈalgərɪðəm/ ▷ *noun* **1** any procedure involving a series of steps that is used to find the solution to a specific problem, eg to solve a mathematical equation. **2** *computing* the sequence of operations, often represented visually by means of a flow chart, that are to be performed by and form the basis of a computer program. • **algorithmic** /-ˈrɪðmɪk/ *adj*. 🕒 1930s in sense 1: from earlier *algorism* arithmetic, from Latin *algorismus*, named after Al-Khwarizmi, a 9c Arab mathematician.

alias /ˈeɪlɪəs/ ▷ *noun* (***aliases***) a false or assumed name. ▷ *adverb* also known as □ ***John Smith, alias Mr X.*** See also AKA. 🕒 16c: Latin, meaning 'at another time' or 'otherwise'.

aliasing /ˈeɪlɪəsɪŋ/ ▷ *noun, image tech* image imperfections arising from insufficiently detailed input to a RASTER display and resulting eg in a diagonal line appearing stepped. 🕒 20c.

alibi /ˈalɪbaɪ/ ▷ *noun* (***alibis***) **1** a plea of being somewhere else when a crime was committed. **2** *colloq* an excuse.

▷ *verb* (***alibied, alibiing***) to provide an alibi for someone. ◷ 18c: Latin, meaning 'elsewhere'.

Alice band ▷ *noun* /a'lɪs —/ a wide hair-band of coloured ribbon or other material, worn flat round the head. ◷ 1950s: as Alice wore in the illustrations by Tenniel to Lewis Carroll's *Through the Looking Glass* (1872).

Alice-in-Wonderland ▷ *adj* as if happening in a dream or fantasy; unreal; irrational. ◷ 1920s: from Lewis Carroll's *Alice's Adventures in Wonderland* (1865).

alicyclic /alɪ'saɪklɪk/ ▷ *adj, chem* said of organic compounds: having the properties of aliphatic compounds but containing a ring of carbon atoms instead of an open chain. ◷ 19c: from *ali*phatic + CYCLIC.

alien /'eɪlɪən/ ▷ *noun* **1** a foreign-born resident of a country who has not adopted that country's nationality. **2** *especially science fiction* an inhabitant of another planet. **3** *bot* a plant introduced to an area by human agency rather than by nature. ▷ *adj* **1** foreign. **2** (*usually* **alien to someone** or **something**) not in keeping with them or it; unfamiliar. ◷ 14c: from Latin *alienus* foreign.

alienable ▷ *adj, law* said of property: able to be transferred to another owner. ◷ 17c.

alienate /'eɪlɪəneɪt/ ▷ *verb* (***alienated, alienating***) **1** to make someone become unfriendly or estranged. **2** to make someone feel unwelcome or isolated. **3** *law* to transfer ownership of (property) to another person. ● **alienation** *noun*. ◷ 16c; 15c as obsolete *adj*, meaning 'estranged': from Latin *alienatus*, from *alienus* foreign.

alight[1] /ə'laɪt/ ▷ *adj* **1** on fire. **2** lighted up; excited. ◷ 15c.

alight[2] /ə'laɪt/ ▷ *verb* (***alighted*** or ***alit*** /ə'lɪt/, ***alighting***) *intr* **1** (*often* **alight from something**) *rather formal or old use* to get down from or out of (a vehicle). **2** said of a bird, etc: to land, come to rest or perch. ◷ Anglo-Saxon *alihtan*.

■ **alight on something** **1** to alight (sense 2) on it. **2** to come upon it by chance. Compare LIGHT UPON.

align /ə'laɪn/ ▷ *verb* (***aligned, aligning***) **1** to put something in a straight line or bring it into line. **2** to bring (someone, a country, etc) into agreement with others, or with a political belief, cause, etc. **3** *intr* to come into alignment with someone or something. ● **alignment** *noun*. ◷ 17c: from French *à ligne* into line.

alike /ə'laɪk/ ▷ *adj* like one another; similar. ▷ *adverb* in a similar manner. ◷ Anglo-Saxon *gelic*.

aliment /'alɪmənt/ ▷ *noun* **1** *chiefly formal or old use* nourishment; food. **2** *Scots law* payment for the maintenance of a spouse or relative. ● **alimentation** *noun*. ◷ 15c: from Latin *alimentum* food, from *alere* to nourish.

alimentary /alɪ'mɛntərɪ/ ▷ *adj* **1** relating to digestion. **2** relating to food, diet or nutrition.

alimentary canal ▷ *noun, anatomy* in vertebrates: a tubular organ extending from the mouth to the anus, along which food passes, and in which it is digested. Also called **digestive tract**.

alimentation see under ALIMENT

alimony /'alɪmənɪ/ ▷ *noun, law* money for support paid by a man to his wife or by a woman to her husband, when they are legally separated or divorced. See also MAINTENANCE. ◷ 17c: from Latin *alimonia* nourishment.

aliphatic /alɪ'fatɪk/ ▷ *adj, chem* said of an organic compound: having carbon atoms arranged in chains rather than in rings. Compare AROMATIC 2. ◷ 19c: from Greek *aleiphar* oil.

aliphatic compound /alɪ'fatɪk —/ ▷ *noun* any of a major class of organic chemical compounds which have carbon atoms arranged in straight or branched chains, rather than in rings, eg ALKANES, ALKENE.

aliquot /'alɪkwɒt/ ▷ *noun* **1** (*also* **aliquot part**) *math* a number or quantity into which a given number or quantity can be exactly divided without any remainder □ ***3 is an aliquot part of 9.*** **2** *chem* a sample of a material or chemical substance that is analysed in order to determine its properties. ◷ 16c: Latin, meaning 'some' or 'several'.

alit *past tense, past participle of* ALIGHT[2]

alive /ə'laɪv/ ▷ *adj* **1** living; having life; in existence. **2** lively; active. **3** (*usually* **alive to something**) aware of it; responsive to it. **4** (*usually* **alive with something**) full of it; abounding in it. ● **alive and kicking** *colloq* living and active. ● **come alive** *colloq* to become more animated. ● **look alive** to get on with something; to hurry up. Also *as exclamation*. ◷ Anglo-Saxon *on life* in life.

alkali /'alkəlaɪ/ ▷ *noun* (***alkalis*** or ***alkalies***) *chem* a hydroxide of any of various metallic elements, eg sodium or potassium, that dissolves in water to produce an alkaline solution, and neutralizes acids to form salts. ◷ 14c as *alcaly*: from Arabic *al-qali* calcinated ashes.

alkaline /'alkəlaɪn/ ▷ *adj, chem* **1** relating to or having the properties of an alkali. **2** denoting a solution with a pH greater than 7, owing to the presence of an excess of hydroxide ions. ● **alkalinity** /-'lɪnɪtɪ/ *noun*. ◷ 17c.

alkaloid /'alkəlɔɪd/ ▷ *noun, biochem* any of numerous nitrogen-containing organic compounds with toxic or medicinal properties that occur naturally in certain plants, eg caffeine, nicotine. ◷ 19c.

alkane /'alkeɪn/ ▷ *noun, chem* the general name for a hydrocarbon of the methane series of general formula C_nH_{2n+2}.

alkene /'alkiːn/ ▷ *noun, chem* any of the unsaturated hydrocarbons of the ethylene series, of general formula C_nH_{2n}.

all /ɔːl/ ▷ *adj* **1** the whole amount, number or extent of something; every. **2** the greatest possible □ *run with all speed.* **3** any whatever □ *beyond all doubt.* ▷ *noun* **1** every one of the people or things concerned; the whole of something. **2** one's whole strength, resources, etc □ *give one's all.* ▷ *adverb* **1** entirely; quite. **2** *colloq* very □ *go all shy.* **3** used in giving the score in various games: on each side □ *30 all.* See also A'. ● **all along** the whole time. ● **all and sundry** everyone. ● **all but …** very nearly … □ *He all but drowned.* ● **all for something** extremely enthusiastic about it. ● **all found** said of accommodation charges: including all possible extra costs, such as meals, electricity and laundry. ● **all in 1** *colloq* exhausted. **2** with all expenses included. ● **all in all** considering everything. ● **all over** finished. ● **all over someone** *colloq* excessively demonstrative towards them. ● **all over something** everywhere in or on it □ *all over the world.* ● **all over the place** *colloq* in a disorganized muddle. ● **all right** see separate entry. ● **all systems go!** everything is in working order or ready to start. ● **all that …** or **as … as all that** *with negatives and in questions* particularly … □ *He's not as bad as all that.* ● **all the best!** *colloq* good luck! ● **all there** *usually with negatives, colloq* completely sane; mentally alert. ● **all the same** see under SAME. ● **all told 1** including everyone or everything. **2** taking everything into account. ● **all up with someone** or **something 1** at an end for them or it. **2** beyond all hope for them. ● **and all that** etcetera. ● **at all** *with negatives and in questions* **1** in the least. **2** in any way. ● **for all that** in spite of it. ● **in all** all together. ● **that's her**, *etc* **all over** *colloq* that's exactly what one would expect from her, etc. ● **when all is said and done** *colloq* all things considered; after all. ◷ Anglo-Saxon *eall*.

alla breve /'alə 'breɪvɪ, — -veɪ/ *music* ▷ *adverb, adj* played quickly with two beats to the bar instead of four. ▷ *noun* a piece of music to be played in this way. ◷ 19c: Italian, meaning 'to the time of the breve', there originally being one breve to the bar.

all-American ▷ *adj* typically American in quality, appearance, etc.

allantois /a'lantouɪs/ ▷ *noun* (***allantoides*** /-ɪdiːz/) a membranous sac-like appendage for effecting oxygenation in the embryos of mammals, birds and reptiles. • **allantoic** /alən'touɪk/ *adj.* ⓘ 19c: from Greek *allas, allantos* sausage.

allay /ə'leɪ/ ▻ *verb* (***allayed, allaying***) to make (pain, fear, suspicion, etc) less intense. ⓘ Anglo-Saxon *alecgan.*

the All Blacks ▻ *plural noun* the New Zealand international rugby team. ⓘ 20c: from their all-black rugby strip.

all clear ▻ *noun* a signal or statement that the threat of danger is over.

allegation /alə'geɪʃən/ ▻ *noun* an unsupported claim, statement or assertion, especially an unfavourable or depreciatory one. ⓘ 15c: from Latin *allegatio,* from *allegare* to allege.

allege /ə'lɛdʒ/ ▻ *verb* (***alleged, alleging***) to claim or declare something to be the case, usually without proof. • **alleged** *adj* presumed and claimed, but not proved, to be as stated. • **allegedly** /ə'lɛdʒɪdlɪ/ *adverb.* ⓘ 13c: from French *aleguer* to allege, mixed with *alegier* to justify or lighten.

allegiance /ə'li:dʒəns/ ▻ *noun* commitment and duty to obey and be loyal to a government, sovereign, etc. ⓘ 14c as *aliegiaunce:* from French *liege* liege.

allegorical /alə'gɒrɪkəl/ ▻ *adj* **1** being or containing an ALLEGORY. **2** characteristic of or like an allegory. • **allegorically** *adverb.*

allegorize or **allegorise** /'aləgəraɪz/ ▻ *verb* (***allegorized, allegorizing***) to put (a story, etc) in the form of an allegory. ⓘ 16c.

allegory /'aləgərɪ/ ▻ *noun* (***allegories***) **1** a story, play, poem, picture, etc in which the characters represent moral or spiritual ideas or messages. **2** symbolism of this sort. ⓘ 14c: from French *allegorie,* from Greek *allos* other + *agoreuein* to speak in public.

allegretto /alə'grɛtou/ *music* ▻ *adverb* in a fairly quick and lively manner (less brisk than ALLEGRO). ▻ *adj* fairly quick and lively. ▻ *noun* (***allegrettos***) a piece of music to be played in this way. ⓘ 18c: Italian.

allegro /ə'lɛgrou/ *music* ▻ *adverb* in a quick lively manner. ▻ *adj* quick and lively. ▻ *noun* (***allegros***) a piece of music to be played in this way. ⓘ 18c: Italian.

allele /ə'li:l/ ▻ *noun, genetics* any of the possible alternative forms of the same gene, of which every individual inherits two (one from each parent), different combinations of which produce different characteristics. Also called **allelomorph**. ⓘ 20c: from Greek *allelos* one another.

all-electric ▻ *adj* using only electricity for heating and lighting.

alleluia see HALLELUJAH

all-embracing ▻ *adj* including everything; missing nothing out.

allergen /'alədʒən/ ▻ *noun, medicine* any foreign substance, usually a protein, that induces an allergic reaction in the body of a person who is hypersensitive to it, eg pollen. ⓘ 20c: from ALLERGY, modelled on ANTIGEN.

allergic /ə'lɜ:dʒɪk/ ▻ *adj* **1** (**allergic to something**) having an allergy caused by abnormal sensitivity to it. **2** relating to or caused by an allergy ▫ *an allergic reaction.*

allergic reaction ▻ *noun, pathol* a hypersensitive reaction of the body to an ALLERGEN, consisting eg of hay fever or a rash, or in severe cases, extreme shock.

allergic rhinitis see under HAY FEVER

allergy /'alədʒɪ/ ▻ *noun* (***allergies***) **1** *pathol* a hypersensitive reaction of the body to certain foreign substances known as ALLERGENs, which may be caused by specific foods, inhalation of dust or pollen, contact with the hair of dogs, cats, etc, and certain drugs. **2** *colloq* a dislike. ⓘ 20c: from Greek *allos* other + *ergia* activity.

alleviate /ə'li:vɪeɪt/ ▻ *verb* (***alleviated, alleviating***) to make (pain, a problem, suffering, etc) less severe. • **alleviation** *noun.* ⓘ 16c: from Latin *alleviare* to lighten.

alleviate

☆ PLAIN ENGLISH alternatives are **ease, lessen, reduce**.

alley /'alɪ/ ▻ *noun* (***alleys***) **1** (*also* **alleyway**) a narrow passage behind or between buildings. **2** a long narrow channel used for bowling or skittles. **3** a path through a garden or park. ⓘ 14c in sense 3: from French *alee* passage, from *aler* to go.

All Fools' Day ▻ *noun* April Fool's Day.

All Hallows Eve see HALLOWE'EN

alliance /ə'laɪəns/ ▻ *noun* **1** the state of being allied. **2** an agreement or treaty by which people, countries, etc ally themselves with one another. ⓘ 14c: French; see ALLY.

allied /'alaɪd, ə'laɪd/ ▻ *adj* **1 a** joined by political agreement or treaty; **b** (**Allied**) belonging or referring to Britain and her allies in World Wars I and II ▫ *Allied troops.* **2** similar; related.

the Allies /— 'alaɪz/ ▻ *plural noun, historical* Britain and her wartime allies: **a** in World War I: Britain, France and Russia (the Triple Entente), plus Japan and Italy; **b** in World War II: Britain, France, USSR, USA, Poland, China and the Commonwealth countries.

allies *plural of* ALLY

alligator /'alɪgeɪtə(r)/ ▻ *noun* either of two species of a large reptile similar to a crocodile but with a broader head and blunter snout, and teeth that do not protrude over its jaws. ⓘ 16c as *aligarto:* from Spanish *el lagarto* the lizard.

all-important ▻ *adj* essential; crucial.

all-in wrestling ▻ *noun* a style of wrestling with few rules or restrictions.

alliterate /ə'lɪtəreɪt/ ▻ *verb* (***alliterated, alliterating***) *intr* to use or show alliteration. • **alliterative** /-rətɪv/ *adj.* • **alliteratively** *adverb.*

alliteration /əlɪtə'reɪʃən/ ▻ *noun* the repetition of the same sound at the beginning of each word or each stressed word in a phrase, as in *sing a song of sixpence.* Compare ASSONANCE. ⓘ 17c: from Latin *alliteratio,* from *ad* to + *littera* letter.

all-night ▻ *adj* **1** said of eg a shop: open all night. **2** said of eg an entertainment: lasting all night.

allo- /alou, alə, ə'lɒ/ *chiefly technical* ▻ *combining form, signifying* **1** other. **2** different. **3** one of a group which forms a unit. ⓘ From Greek *allos* other or different.

allocable /'aləkəbəl/ ▻ *adj* said of financial resources: able to be assigned or allocated.

allocate /'aləkeɪt/ ▻ *verb* (***allocated, allocating***) to give, set apart or assign something to someone or for some particular purpose. • **allocation** *noun.* ⓘ 17c: from Latin *ad* to + *locus* place.

all-or-nothing ▻ *adj* that must be accepted in its entirety or not at all.

allot /ə'lɒt/ ▻ *verb* (***allotted, allotting***) **1** to give (a share of or place in something) to each member of a group. **2** to assign something to a specific purpose. ⓘ 16c: from French *aloter.*

allotment ▻ *noun* **1** *Brit* one of the subdivisions of a larger piece of public ground rented to individuals to grow vegetables, etc. **2** the act of allotting. **3** an amount allotted.

allotrope /'aloutroup/ *chem* ▻ *noun* any of the two or more structural forms in which some elements can exist, often due to differences in crystal structure, eg graphite and diamond (allotropes of carbon). • **allotropic** /-'trɒpɪk/ *adj.* ⓘ 19c: from ALLOTROPY.

allotropy /ə'lɒtrəpɪ/ ▻ *noun, chem* the existence of an element in ALLOTROPES. ⓘ 19c: from Greek *allotropia* variation.

all-out ▻ *adj* **1** using all one's strength, powers, etc. **2** said eg of a strike: with everyone participating. Also *as adverb* (**all out**).

all-over ▻ *adj* covering the entire surface or body.

allow /əˈlaʊ/ ▻ *verb* (***allowed***, ***allowing***) **1** to permit (someone to do something, something to happen, etc). **2** to assign or allocate □ *allow £10 for food.* **3** to admit or agree to (a point, claim, etc). **4** to permit (oneself to do something). ⓒ 16c in these senses; 13c, meaning 'to accept or approve of': from French *alouer.*

■ **allow for something** to take it into consideration when judging or deciding something.

■ **allow of something** to permit it to happen or exist.

allowable ▻ *adj* able to be admitted or accepted. ● **allowably** *adverb.*

allowance ▻ *noun* **1** a fixed sum of money, amount of something, etc given regularly. **2** money given for expenses. **3** something allowed. ● **make allowances for someone** to judge them less severely, or expect less of them, because of particular circumstances applying to them. ● **make allowances for something** to take it into consideration in one's plans.

alloy ▻ *noun* /ˈalɔɪ/ (***alloys***) a material consisting of a mixture of two or more metals, or a metal and a non-metal, eg steel, bronze, brass. ▻ *verb* /əˈlɔɪ/ (***alloyed***, ***alloying***) **1** to mix (one metal with another). **2** to debase. **3** to temper or modify. ⓒ 16c: from French *alei*, from Latin *alligare* to bind.

all-powerful ▻ *adj* supremely powerful; omnipotent.

all-purpose ▻ *adj* useful for many different purposes.

all right or *sometimes* **alright** ▻ *adj* **1** unhurt; safe; feeling fine. **2** just about adequate, satisfactory, etc. **3** (**all-right**) *colloq* admirable; genuine; cool □ *an all-right kind of a guy.* ▻ *exclamation* **1** used simply as a greeting □ *All right? How's it going?* **2 a** used to signal agreement or approval □ *All right, you can go*; **b** (*sometimes* **awl right**) *slang* used to signal great approval □ *You got tickets to see Julian Cope? Awl right!* ▻ *adverb* **1** satisfactorily; properly. **2** *colloq* used to reinforce what has just been said □ *It's broken all right.* ● **a bit of all right** *colloq* someone or something much approved of, especially someone good-looking or sexy □ *Cor! He's a bit of all right!* ● **be all right with someone** *colloq* to be agreeable to them □ *I'll see you at eight, if that's all right with you.* ⓒ 19c.

all right, alright

A usage difficulty arises because **all right** is used at different levels of formality; in more casual use (eg in recorded conversation) it is often written as **alright**, influenced by words like **almighty** and **altogether**. The spelling is also influenced when **all** seems to be inappropriate in a particular context

? *Everything will be alright*

? *Have you settled in alright?*

☆ RECOMMENDATION: use **all right,** especially in writing for readers who are precise about the use of language.

all-risks ▻ *adj* said of insurance: covering every risk except for a few specifically excluded, such as war, depreciation, etc.

all-round ▻ *adj* **1** having many different skills, especially sporting ones □ *an all-round player.* **2** including everyone or everything □ *an all-round education.* ▻ *adverb* (**all round**) everywhere; in every respect □ *All round, the situation of the refugees looks desperate.*

all-rounder ▻ *noun* someone who has a lot of different skills.

All Saints' Day ▻ *noun* a Christian festival held on 1 November to commemorate all church saints collectively. See also HALLOWE'EN.

all-seater ▻ *adj* said of a sports stadium, especially a football ground: having no space for standing spectators □ *Pittodrie is now an all-seater stadium.* ⓒ 1990: its currency is due to the legislation which followed the Hillsborough disaster (1989).

all-singing all-dancing ▻ *adj, colloq or facetious* having many special features, especially ones that are gimmicky or not absolutely necessary, but which add to the product's desirability □ *an all-singing all-dancing video recorder.*

All Souls' Day ▻ *noun, RC Church* the day, 2 November, set aside for praying for souls in purgatory.

allspice /ˈɔːlspaɪs/ ▻ *noun* **1** an aromatic spice prepared from the dried unripe berries of a small tropical evergreen tree, used to flavour foods, especially meat. **2** the PIMENTO tree, cultivated mainly in Jamaica, that yields this spice. Also called JAMAICAN PEPPER. ⓒ 17c: from ALL + SPICE and so called because the flavour is supposed to combine that of cinnamon, nutmeg and cloves.

all-star ▻ *adj* said of a sports team or the cast of a show: consisting entirely of top players or performers.

all-terrain ▻ *adj* said of certain vehicles, bikes, etc: designed for travelling over rough country as well as normal road surfaces, etc.

all-time ▻ *adj, colloq* **1** said of a record, especially a sporting one: best to date; unsurpassed. **2** of great and permanent importance □ *one of the all-time greats of jazz.*

allude /əˈluːd, əˈljuːd/ ▻ *verb* (***alluded***, ***alluding***) *intr* (*usually* **allude to something**) to mention it indirectly or speak about it in passing. ⓒ 16c: from Latin *alludere* to play with.

allure /əˈlʊə(r), əˈljʊə(r)/ ▻ *noun* **1** attractiveness, appeal or charm. **2** the ability to exert appeal, charm, etc. ▻ *verb* (***allured***, ***alluring***) to attract, charm or fascinate. ⓒ 15c: from French *alurer*, from *lurer* to lure.

allurement ▻ *noun* **1** the act of alluring. **2** fascination or attraction. **3** someone or something that is thought to be fascinating, attractive, charming, appealing, etc.

alluring ▻ *adj* enticing; seductive; attractive. ● **alluringly** *adverb.*

allusion /əˈluːʒən, əˈljuː-/ ▻ *noun* **1** any indirect reference to something else. **2** *literary theory* **a** a reference, either explicit or veiled, to something else which an author uses deliberately, aware that only readers who are 'in the know' will understand it; **b** such devices thought of collectively □ *'The Waste Land' is full of erudite allusion.* ⓒ 16c: from Latin *allusio*, from *alludere* to play with.

allusive /əˈluːsɪv, əˈljuː-/ ▻ *adj* **1** referring indirectly to something. **2** having or abounding in allusions. ● **allusively** *adverb.*

alluvium /əˈluːvɪəm, əˈljuːvɪəm/ ▻ *noun* (***alluvia*** /-vɪə/) fine particles of silt, clay, mud and sand that are carried and deposited by rivers. ● **alluvial** *adj.* ⓒ 17c: from Latin *alluvius* washed against.

ally ▻ *noun* /ˈalaɪ/ (***allies***) **1** a country, state, sovereign, etc that has formally agreed to help and support another, especially in times of war. **2 a** someone who is willing to side with someone else over an issue □ *allies in the fight against local vandalism*; **b** a friend. ▻ *verb* /əˈlaɪ/ (***allies***, ***allied***, ***allying***) **1** said of a country, state, sovereign, etc: to join or become joined politically or militarily with another, especially with a formal agreement. **2** said of an individual or group: to join or become joined with someone else or another group through a shared view or stance on a particular matter. ● **allied** and **the Allies** see separate entries. ⓒ 13c: from French *alier*, from Latin *ligare* to bind.

almacantar see ALMUCANTAR

alma mater /ˈalmə ˈmɑːtə(r), — ˈmeɪtə(r)/ ▻ *noun* (***alma maters***) the school, college or university that someone used to attend. See also ALUMNUS. ⓒ 19c: Latin, literally 'bountiful mother'.

almanac /ˈɔːlmənak, ˈal-/ ▷ *noun* a book, published yearly, with a calendar, information about the phases of the Moon and stars, dates of religious festivals, public holidays, etc. ◎ 14c: from Latin *almanach*, from Arabic *al* the + *manakh* calendar.

almighty /ɔːlˈmaɪtɪ/ ▷ *adj* **1** having complete power ◻ *Almighty God.* **2** *colloq* very great ◻ *an almighty crash.* ▷ *adverb, colloq* extremely ◻ *hit her almighty hard.* ◎ Anglo-Saxon *ælmihtig*.

the Almighty ▷ *noun, Christianity* God.

almond /ˈɑːmənd/ ▷ *noun* **1** a kind of small tree related to the peach. **2** the nut-like seed from the fruit of this tree. **3** *as adj* **a** made from or containing almonds ◻ *almond paste*; **b** belonging or relating to this kind of tree ◻ *almond blossom.* ◎ 14c: from French *almande*.

almond-eyed ▷ *adj* with narrow oval eyes, often used euphemistically to refer to someone of oriental appearance.

almoner /ˈɑːmənə(r), ˈalmənə(r)/ ▷ *noun, historical* **1** *Brit old use* a medical social worker. **2** someone who distributed money, food, etc as charity. ◎ 14c: from French *aumoner*, from Latin *eleemosynator* an alms-giver.

almost /ˈɔːlmoust/ ▷ *adverb* nearly but not quite. ◎ Anglo-Saxon *ælmæst*.

alms /ɑːmz/ ▷ *plural noun, historical* charity donations of money, food, etc to the poor. ◎ Anglo-Saxon *ælmesse*, from Greek *eleemosyne* compassion.

alms-house ▷ *noun, Brit, historical* a place where the aged, poor, etc were supported by charity.

almucantar /almjʊˈkantə(r)/ or **almacantar** /-mə-/ ▷ *noun, astron* **1** a small circle of the celestial sphere parallel to the horizontal plane. **2** *old use* an instrument once used for measuring astronomical amplitude. ◎ 14c: from French *almicantarat* or *almucantarat*, from Arabic *almuqantarah* the sundials.

Alnico /ˈalnɪkou/ ▷ *noun, trademark* an alloy containing iron, nickel, aluminium, cobalt and copper, used to make permanent magnets. ◎ 1930s: from *al*uminium + *ni*ckel + *co*balt.

aloe /ˈalou/ ▷ *noun* (*aloes*) **1** any of various succulent African plants with tall trunk-like stems, long sword-shaped fleshy leaves with spiny edges, and bell-shaped or tubular yellow to red flowers. **2** (*usually* **aloes**) the dried juice of the leaves of this plant, formerly used as a purgative drug known as **bitter aloes**. ◎ 14c: from Latin *aloe*.

aloe vera /ˈalou ˈveɪrə/ ▷ *noun* **1** a species of ALOE plant, the leaves of which contain a juice that is said to have healing properties. **2** the juice of the leaves of this plant, used in skin lotions, ointments, shampoos, etc.

aloft /əˈlɒft/ ▷ *adverb* **1** in the air; overhead ◻ *held the trophy aloft.* **2** *naut* in a ship's rigging. ◎ 13c: from Norse *a lopti* in the sky.

aloha /əˈlouhə, -hɑː/ ▷ *exclamation* ▷ *noun* in Hawaii and the S Pacific: a greeting that is given when meeting or parting from someone. ◎ 18c: Hawaiian, from Maori *aroha* love, affection or pity.

alone /əˈloun/ ▷ *adj, adverb* **1** by oneself. **2** without anyone else ◻ *The idea was mine alone.* **3** apart from other people. **4** lonely. ● **go it alone** *colloq* to act on one's own and without help. ● **leave alone** or **leave well alone** see under LEAVE[1]. ● **let alone** see under LET[1]. ● **not alone** joined by others ◻ *You're not alone in thinking she's nuts.* ◎ 13c: from English *al one* wholly by oneself.

along /əˈlɒŋ/ ▷ *adverb* **1** in some direction ◻ *Her old banger just chugs along.* **2 a** in accompaniment ◻ *could sing along to any Nirvana track*; **b** in the company of someone else or with others ◻ *went along with Kurt to the gig.* **3** into a more advanced state ◻ *coming along nicely.* ▷ *prep* **1** by the side of something or near something. **2** down the length of or down part of the length of something ◻ *The shops are just along that street.* ● **all along** see under ALL. ● **along with something** or **someone 1** in addition to it or them ◻ *Along with the CD, you get a free poster.* **2** in conjunction with it or them. ● **be along** *colloq* to arrive, call, visit, etc ◻ *said he'd be along about six.* ● **go along with someone** or **something** and **go along for the ride** see under GO. ◎ Anglo-Saxon *andlang*.

alongside ▷ *prep* close to the side of something. ▷ *adverb* to or at the side. ◎ 18c.

aloof /əˈluːf/ ▷ *adj* unfriendly and distant. ▷ *adverb* away; apart; distant. ● **aloofly** *adverb.* ● **aloofness** *noun.* ◎ 16c: from A-[1] + nautical *loof* the after-part of a ship's bow.

alopecia /aləˈpiːʃə/ ▷ *noun, pathol* baldness, either of the hereditary type, such as the normal gradual loss of head hair in men, or of the type caused by disease or old age. ◎ 14c: from Greek *alopekia* fox-mange.

aloud /əˈlaud/ ▷ *adverb* **1** loud enough to be able to be heard; not silently ◻ *reading aloud.* **2** loudly. ◎ 14c.

ALP ▷ *abbreviation* Australian Labor Party.

alp /alp/ ▷ *noun* **1** a high mountain. **2** in Switzerland: pasture land on a mountainside. ◎ 16c: from Latin *Alpes* the name for the Alps, a mountain range in Switzerland, France and Italy.

alpaca /alˈpakə/ ▷ *noun* (*alpacas*) **1** a herbivorous hoofed S American mammal, closely related to the LLAMA, reared mainly for its long straight black, white or reddish-brown fleece. **2 a** the fine silky wool obtained from this animal; **b** cloth made from it. ◎ Early 19c: Spanish, from Aymara *alpaqa*, the local Peruvian name for the animal.

alpenstock /ˈalpənstɒk/ ▷ *noun* a long stout stick, usually with a metal point at the bottom end, that hikers, hill and mountain climbers, etc use to help them along. ◎ 19c: German, from *Alpen* the Alps + *Stock* a stick.

alpha /ˈalfə/ ▷ *noun* **1** the first letter of the Greek alphabet. See table at GREEK ALPHABET. **2** *Brit* **a** a mark given to an exam paper or other piece of work that denotes a first class grade; **b** (**alpha plus** or **alpha minus**) a mark above or below alpha respectively. **3** *astron* the brightest star in a constellation. **4** (**Alpha**) *communications* in the NATO alphabet: the word used to denote the letter 'A' (see table at NATO ALPHABET). **5** *as adj* **a** *chem* designating one of two or more isomeric forms of a compound; **b** *zool* referring to the most dominant member of a hierarchical group ◻ *That gorilla is the alpha female.* ● **alpha and omega** the beginning and the end. ◎ 14c: Greek, from Hebrew and Phoenician *aleph* an ox or a leader, the original hieroglyph being in the form of an ox's head.

alphabet /ˈalfəbet/ ▷ *noun* a set of letters, characters, symbols, etc, usually arranged in a fixed order that, by convention, are used to represent the spoken form of a language in writing and printing. ◎ 16c: from Latin *alphabetum*, from Greek *alpha* + *beta*, the first two letters of the Greek alphabet.

alphabetical /alfəˈbetɪkəl/ and **alphabetic** ▷ *adj* **1** in the order of the letters, characters, symbols, etc of an alphabet. **2** in the form of an alphabet. ● **alphabetically** *adverb.*

alphabetize or **alphabetise** ▷ *verb* (*alphabetized, alphabetizing*) to arrange or list in the correct alphabetical order. ◎ 19c: ALPHABET + -IZE.

alpha decay ▷ *noun, physics* a form of radioactive decay in which a radioactive nucleus spontaneously emits an ALPHA PARTICLE that is identical to a helium nucleus. See also BETA DECAY.

alpha-fetoprotein /alfəfiːtouˈproutiːn/ ▷ *noun, medicine* (abbreviation **AFP**) a type of protein that is formed in the liver of the developing human fetus and which can be detected in varying amounts in the mother's blood by a blood test, and in the amniotic fluid using AMNIOCENTESIS, a high level indicating the possibility of SPINA BIFIDA and a low one that the baby might have DOWN'S SYNDROME. ⓘ 1970s.

alphanumeric /alfənjʊ'mɛrɪk/ and **alphanumerical** ▷ *adj* **1** *computing* denoting characters, codes or data that consist of letters of the alphabet and numerals, and do not include punctuation marks or special characters. Compare GRAPHICS CHARACTER. **2** said of a machine: using letters of the alphabet and numerals. • **alphanumerically** *adverb*. ⓘ 1950s: from *alpha*bet + *numeric*al.

alpha particle ▷ *noun, physics* a positively charged particle with a low energy content, identical to the nucleus of a helium atom, produced by radioactive decay. See also BETA PARTICLE.

alpha ray ▷ *noun, physics* a stream of ALPHA PARTICLES.

alpha rhythm and **alpha wave** ▷ *noun, physiol* a slow-frequency wave of normal electrical activity produced by the relaxed human brain, which can be recorded by an ELECTROENCEPHALOGRAPH. Compare BETA RHYTHM, DELTA RHYTHM.

alpha test ▷ *noun, computing* an initial test of new software that is done by the manufacturer.

alphorn /'alphɔːn/ and **alpenhorn** /'alpənhɔːn/ ▷ *noun* a long straight or slightly curved horn, made of wood and bark with an upturned bell and used, especially in the Alps, for calling cattle home from the hillside but usually played as a musical instrument. ⓘ 19c: from German *Alpen* the Alps + HORN.

alpine /'alpaɪn/ ▷ *adj* **1** belonging or relating to alps or high mountains. **2** (**Alpine**) belonging or relating to the Alps. ▷ *noun* a plant that grows in high mountain areas. ⓘ 17c: from Latin *alpinus*.

Alpine skiing ▷ *noun* a name that encompasses the three racing events of DOWNHILL, SLALOM and GIANT SLALOM. Compare NORDIC sense 3.

already /ɔːl'rɛdɪ, ɒl-/ ▷ *adverb* **1** before the present time or the time in question □ ***We've already paid.*** **2** so soon or so early □ ***It was already lunchtime and he'd got nothing done.*** ⓘ 14c as *al redy* meaning 'completely ready'.

alright ▷ *adj* an alternative spelling of ALL RIGHT.

> ***alright***
>
> See Usage Note at **all right**.

Alsatian /al'seɪʃən/ ▷ *noun* **1** a GERMAN SHEPHERD DOG. **2** someone born or living in Alsace, a region in NE France. ▷ *adj* relating or belonging to Alsace. ⓘ 17c, although the name for the dog was not adopted until around 1920: from Latin *Alsatia* Alsace.

also /'ɔːlsoʊ/ ▷ *adverb* **1** in addition; as well as. **2** moreover; besides. ⓘ Anglo-Saxon *alswa* all so or wholly.

also-ran ▷ *noun* **1** a horse, dog, person, etc not finishing in one of the top three places in a race. **2** someone who is considered to be unimportant, undistinguished, unaccomplished, etc.

alstroemeria /alstrə'mɪərɪə/ ▷ *noun* (***alstroemerias***) a tuberous perennial plant originally from S America, highly valued for its brightly coloured flowers. ⓘ 18c: named after the Swedish naturalist, Claude Alströmer (1736–96).

alt /alt/ ▷ *noun, music* a high tone in a voice or instrument. • **in alt** in the octave above the treble stave beginning with G. ⓘ 16c: from Latin *altum* high.

alt. ▷ *abbreviation* **1** alternate. **2** altitude. **3** alto.

Altaic /al'teɪɪk/ ▷ *adj, linguistics* denoting a family of languages spoken from the Balkan Peninsula to the NE of Asia, which includes TURKIC, MONGOLIAN and TUNGUS. ▷ *noun* the languages that form this family. ⓘ 19c: from French *altaique* of the Altai mountains in Asia.

altar /'ɔːltə(r), 'ɒl-/ ▷ *noun* **1** a table, raised structure, etc where sacrifices are made to a god. **2** *Christianity* the table at the front of a church, consecrated for use during communion. ⓘ Anglo-Saxon, from Latin *altaria* a high place.

altar boy ▷ *noun, RC Church, C of E* a young man or boy who assists a priest during a service.

altarpiece ▷ *noun* a religious picture or carving, often in either two or three parts, that is placed above and behind an altar. See also DIPTYCH, TRIPTYCH. ⓘ 17c.

alter /'ɔːltə(r), 'ɒl-/ ▷ *verb* (***altered, altering***) *tr & intr* to change; to become, or make something or someone become, different. • **alterable** *adj*. ⓘ 14c: from French *alterer*, from Latin *alter* other.

alteration ▷ *noun* **1** a change that has been made to something. **2** the act of changing something; the state of being changed. **3** (**alterations**) **a** home improvements; **b** changes to clothing, curtains, etc, especially ones that will make them fit better. ⓘ 14c.

altercate /'ɔːltəkeɪt, 'ɒl-/ ▷ *verb* (***altercated, altercating***) *intr* to argue or dispute, especially angrily, heatedly, etc. • **altercation** *noun*. ⓘ 16c: from Latin *altercari*, *altercatus* to dispute with another, from *alter* other.

alter ego /'ɔːltər 'iːgoʊ, —'ɛgoʊ/ ▷ *noun* **1** someone's second or alternative character □ ***Her aggressive alter ego surfaces when she drinks too much.*** **2** a close and trusted friend. ⓘ 16c: Latin, literally 'another I'.

alternate /ɒl'tɜːnət as *adj* and *noun*, 'ɔːltəneɪt/ as *verb* ▷ *adj* **1** said of two feelings, states, conditions, etc: arranged or coming one after the other in turn □ ***alternate layers of pasta and sauce.*** **2** every other; one out of two. **3** *bot* said of leaves, petals, etc: appearing singly and regularly at either side of a stem. ▷ *verb* (***alternated, alternating***) *tr & intr* **1** said of two things: to succeed or make them succeed each other by turns □ ***Helen and Mike alternate their days off.*** **2** said of an electric current, etc: to reverse direction in a regular pattern. See ALTERNATING CURRENT. ▷ *noun* / *also* (*orig US*) 'ɔːltənət/ a substitute, especially a person who covers in someone's absence. • **alternately** *adverb*. ⓘ 16c: from Latin *alternare*, *alternatum* to do one thing after another.

> ■ **alternate between something and something else** to change from one thing to another by turns □ ***He alternates between fits of depression and periods of euphoria.***
>
> ■ **alternate from something to something else** to change from it to another □ ***Her mood swings alternate from one extreme to the other.***
>
> ■ **alternate** or **alternate something with someone** or **something** to swap or substitute with them or it, especially regularly or continually.

> ***alternate, alternative***
>
> These words are often confused with each other.

alternate angles ▷ *plural noun, geom* a pair of angles that lie on opposite sides and at opposite ends of a line (or TRANSVERSAL) that cuts two other lines.

alternating current ▷ *noun* (abbreviation **AC**) an electric current that reverses its direction of flow with a constant frequency, and is therefore continuously varying. Compare DIRECT CURRENT.

alternation ▷ *noun* a pattern or sequence of repeated change from one action, state, etc to another and back again.

alternation of generations ▷ *noun, biol* the occurrence within the life cycle of certain living organisms, eg ferns and mosses, of a sexually reproducing generation that alternates with an asexually reproducing generation. ◷ 19c.

alternative /ɒl'tɜːnətɪv/ ▷ *adj* **1** said of, strictly speaking, two, but often used of more than two, possibilities: secondary or different, especially in terms of being less favourable as a choice □ ***had to make alternative travel plans.*** **2** said of a lifestyle, culture, etc: outside the conventionally accepted ways of doing something and therefore thought of by adherents as preferable. ▷ *noun* **1** the possibility of having the option to choose, strictly speaking, between two things but often used of more than two or of an unknown number □ ***We had no alternative but to take the train.*** **2** something that represents another possible option □ ***Going by train is always an alternative.*** ● **alternatively** *adverb*. ◷ 16c: from Latin *alternare* to ALTERNATE.

alternative birth and **alternative birthing** ▷ *noun* any method of childbirth that tends to avoid any form of medical or technological intervention, eg underwater birthing or various kinds of 'natural' childbirth, etc.

alternative comedy ▷ *noun* comedy which relies heavily on black humour, surrealist concepts, etc and which does not resort to traditional joke-telling, such as that based on racial or gender stereotyping.

alternative energy ▷ *noun, ecol* energy derived from sources other than nuclear power or the burning of fossil fuels, eg WIND POWER, WAVE POWER, SOLAR ENERGY.

alternative medicine and **complementary medicine** ▷ *noun* the treatment of diseases and disorders using procedures other than those traditionally practised in orthodox medicine, eg ACUPUNCTURE, CHIROPRACTIC, HOMEOPATHY, OSTEOPATHY.

alternative technology see INTERMEDIATE TECHNOLOGY

Alternative Vote ▷ *noun, politics* a system of casting votes that affords voters the opportunity of placing candidates in order of preference. If none of the candidates has the required majority based on the first-choice votes, the candidate with the fewest votes is eliminated and their votes are re-examined so that the candidates who appear as second choices are now taken into account as first choices. Compare PROPORTIONAL REPRESENTATION. ◷ 1910.

alternator /'ɔːltəneɪtə(r)/ ▷ *noun, elec engineering* an electricity generator that produces ALTERNATING CURRENT by means of one or more coils rotating in a magnetic field.

althaea or (*US*) **althea** /al'θiːə/ ▷ *noun* (***althaeas***) a plant such as the hollyhock and marshmallow that has bright, usually pink, flowers. ◷ 17c: from Greek *althaia* marsh mallow.

althorn /'althɔːn/ ▷ *noun, music* a brass instrument of the SAXHORN family. ◷ 19c.

although /ɔːl'ðoʊ/ ▷ *conj* in spite of the fact that; apart from the fact that; though. ◷ 14c as *al thogh* all though.

altimeter /'altɪmiːtə(r), 'ɔːl-/ ▷ *noun, aeronautics* a device used in aircraft for measuring height above sea or ground level, by means of differences in atmospheric pressure or (**radio altimeter**) by means of the time taken for a radio wave from an aircraft to be reflected back. ◷ Early 20c: from Latin *altus* high + -METER 1.

altitude /'altɪtʃuːd, 'ɔːltɪ-/ ▷ *noun* **1** height, especially above sea level, of a mountain, aircraft, etc. **2** *astron* the angular distance between a celestial body and the horizon. See also AZIMUTH. **3** *geom* in a plane or solid figure: the distance from an angle or VERTEX to the side opposite the vertex (the BASE). ◷ 14c: from Latin *altitudo* height.

altitude sickness see MOUNTAIN SICKNESS

alto /'altoʊ, 'ɔːl-/ ▷ *noun* (***altos***) **1** the lowest female singing voice. Also called CONTRALTO. **2** the singing voice of a COUNTER-TENOR. **3** someone with either of these types of singing voice. **4** a part or piece of music written for a voice or instrument at this pitch. ▷ *adj* said of a musical instrument, etc: having a high pitch □ ***alto sax.*** ◷ 16c: Italian, from Latin *altus* high.

alto clef ▷ *noun, music* **1** a sign (𝄡) placed at the beginning of a piece of written music, which fixes the note middle C on the middle line of the stave which follows. **2** *loosely* the alto stave in a piece of music, pitched between the treble and bass clefs and used eg for viola music.

altocumulus /altoʊ'kjuːmjʊləs/ ▷ *noun* (***altocumuli*** /-laɪ/) *meteorol* white or grey clouds of the cumulus family that occur at altitudes of about 2 000m to 7 000m, and usually indicate fine weather. ◷ 19c: from Latin *altus* high + CUMULUS.

altogether /ɔːltə'gɛðə(r), 'ɔːltəgɛðə(r)/ ▷ *adverb* **1** completely. **2 a** on the whole □ ***It rained a bit but altogether it was a wonderful holiday***; **b** taking everything into consideration □ ***Altogether the holiday cost £500.*** ● **in the altogether** *colloq* naked. ◷ Anglo-Saxon *al togædere*, from *al* all + *togædere* to gather.

alto-relievo /'altoʊrə'liːvoʊ/ ▷ *noun* (***alto-relievos***) *art* another name for HIGH RELIEF. Compare BAS-RELIEF. ◷ 18c: from Italian *alto-rilievo*.

altostratus /altoʊ'strɑːtəs/ ▷ *noun* (***altostrati*** /-taɪ/) *meteorol* greyish sheetlike clouds of the stratus family that occur at altitudes of about 2 000m to 7 000m, and usually give a warning of warm rainy weather. ◷ 19c: from Latin *altus* high + STRATUS.

altricial /al'trɪʃəl/ *zool* ▷ *adj* said of the young of certain birds: hatching at a relatively immature stage, without feathers and blind, and so needing a great deal of parental care. ▷ *noun* a bird that produces such chicks. Compare PRECOCIAL, NIDICOLOUS. ◷ 19c: from Latin *alere* to nourish.

altruism /'altrʊɪzəm/ ▷ *noun* an unselfish concern for the welfare of others. ● **altruist** *noun* someone who shows such concern. ● **altruistic** *adj*. ● **altruistically** *adverb*. ◷ 19c: from French *altruisme*, from Italian *altrui* of or to others.

ALU ▷ *abbreviation, computing* ARITHMETIC LOGIC UNIT.

alula /'aljʊlə/ ▷ *noun* (***alulae*** /-liː/ or ***alulas***) *zool* a group of feathers, usually three to six in number, that grows from the first digit in some birds. Also called BASTARD WING. ◷ 18c: Latin diminutive of *ala* a wing.

alum /'aləm/ ▷ *noun* **1** *chem* aluminium potassium sulphate, a white crystalline compound used in dyeing and tanning, and as a medical astringent to stop bleeding. **2** any of various double-sulphate salts with a similar composition to this compound. ◷ 14c: from Latin *alumen*.

alumina /ə'luːmɪnə, ə'ljuː-/ ▷ *noun, chem* a white crystalline compound that is the main ingredient of BAUXITE and that also occurs in the form of the mineral CORUNDUM. ◷ 18c: from Latin *alumen* ALUM.

aluminium /aljʊ'mɪnɪəm, alʊ-/ or (*N Amer*) **aluminum** /ə'luːmɪnəm/ ▷ *noun, chem* (symbol **Al**, atomic number 13) a silvery-white light metallic element that forms strong alloys which are used in the construction of aircraft and other vehicles, door and window frames, household utensils, drink cans, etc. See also BAUXITE. ◷ 1812: from Latin *alumen* ALUM.

aluminize or **aluminise** /ə'luːmɪnaɪz/ ▷ *verb* (***aluminized***, ***aluminizing***) to coat (a mirror or other surface) with aluminium. ◷ 1930s.

aluminosilicate /aluːmɪnoʊ'sɪlɪkət/ ▷ *noun, chem* a chemical compound, consisting mainly of ALUMINA and SILICA, that is found in many rocks and minerals, and is also a constituent of glass and some ceramics. ◷ Early 20c.

aluminous /ə'luːmɪnəs/ ▷ *adj, chem* consisting of, containing or resembling ALUM, ALUMINA or ALUMINIUM. ◷ 16c.

alumna /əˈlʌmnə/ ▻ *noun* (***alumnae*** /-niː/) a female ALUMNUS. ⓒ 19c: Latin.

alumnus /əˈlʌmnəs/ ▻ *noun* (***alumni*** /-naɪ/) a former pupil or student of a school, college or university. See also ALMA MATER. ⓒ 17c: Latin, meaning 'a fosterchild', from *alere* to nourish.

alveolar /alvɪˈoʊlə(r)/ ▻ *adj* **1** *anatomy* referring or relating to the sockets in the upper jaw where the teeth are held in place □ ***Just behind the front teeth is the alveolar ridge.*** **2** *phonetics* said of a speech sound: produced by putting the tip of the tongue against this part of the mouth. ▻ *noun, phonetics* a consonant such as a 't' or a 'd' sound that can be produced in this way. ⓒ 18c: from Latin *alveolus* small cavity.

alveolus /alvɪˈoʊləs/ ▻ *noun* (***alveoli*** /-laɪ/) **1** *anatomy* (*also* **pulmonary alveolus**) in the lungs: any of the millions of tiny thin-walled air sacs in which oxygen from inhaled air is exchanged for carbon dioxide from the bloodstream. **2** *anatomy* (*also* **dental alveolus**) a tooth socket in the jaw bone. **3** *zool* any small depression in the surface of an organ. ⓒ 18c: Latin, meaning 'small cavity'.

always /ˈɔːlweɪz, -wɪz/ ▻ *adverb* **1** on every occasion. **2** continually; time and time again. **3** whatever happens; if necessary □ ***signed the letter 'Always yours'.*** See also AYE². ⓒ 13c as *alles weis*, genitive of *all way*, from Anglo-Saxon *ealne weg*.

alyssum /ˈalɪsəm, əˈlɪsəm/ ▻ *noun* any of various low-growing bushy plants with narrow leaves and white, yellow or purple cross-shaped flowers, widely cultivated as an ornamental plant. See also SWEET ALYSSUM. ⓒ 16c: from Greek *alysson*.

Alzheimer's disease /ˈaltshaɪməz —/ ▻ *noun, pathol* an incurable disease, usually occurring in middle age or later, in which degeneration of the brain cells results in gradual loss of memory, confusion, etc, eventually leading to total disintegration of the personality. ⓒ Early 20c: named after the German neurologist, Alois Alzheimer (1864-1915), who first identified it.

AM ▻ *abbreviation* AMPLITUDE MODULATION.

Am ▻ *symbol, chem* americium.

am /əm, am/ ▻ *verb* used with *I*: the 1st person singular of the present tense of BE.

a.m., am, **A.M.** or **AM** ▻ *abbreviation* ANTE MERIDIEM.

amadavat see AVADAVAT

amalgam /əˈmalgəm/ ▻ *noun* **1** a mixture or blend. **2** *chem* an alloy of mercury with one or more other metals, especially silver, which forms a soft paste on mixing but later hardens, used in dentistry to fill holes in drilled teeth. ⓒ 15c: from Latin *amalgama*.

amalgamate /əˈmalgəmeɪt/ ▻ *verb* (***amalgamated, amalgamating***) **1** *tr & intr* to join together or unite to form a single unit, organization, etc. **2** *intr* said of metals: to form an alloy with mercury. ⓒ 17c.

amalgamation ▻ *noun* the action or process of blending, merging or joining two or more things together.

amanita /aməˈnaɪtə/ ▻ *noun* (***amanitas***) *biol* any of various fungi some of which, eg FLY AGARIC, are poisonous. ⓒ 19c: from Greek *amanitai* a type of fungus.

amanuensis /əmanjʊˈɛnsɪs/ ▻ *noun* (***amanuenses*** /-siːz/) a literary assistant or secretary, especially one who writes from dictation or copies from manuscripts. ⓒ 17c: Latin, from *servus a manu* a handwriting servant.

amaranth /ˈamərانθ/ ▻ *noun* **1** any of various species of plant that produce spikes of small brightly coloured flowers, eg LOVE-LIES-BLEEDING. **2** a dark red dye obtained from the flowers of this plant, or manufactured artificially, used as a food colouring. **3** *poetic* a fabled flower that never fades, and is regarded as a symbol of immortality. ⓒ 17c: from Greek *amarantos* everlasting.

amaretto /aməˈrɛtoʊ/ ▻ *noun* an almond-flavoured liqueur from Italy. ⓒ 20c: Italian, from *amaro* bitter.

amaryllis /aməˈrɪlɪs/ ▻ *noun* **1** any of various plants, especially a S African species with strap-shaped leaves and large pink or white trumpet-shaped scented flowers. **2** *loosely* any of various tropical American plants, hybrids of which are popular house plants, that produce large trumpet-shaped red, pink or white flowers on a long stalk in winter before the leaves appear. ⓒ 18c: Latin; also a conventional name for a country girl or shepherdess in Greek and Latin literature.

amass /əˈmas/ ▻ *verb* (***amasses, amassed, amassing***) to gather or collect (money, possessions, knowledge, points, etc), especially in great quantity. ⓒ 15c: from French *amasser*, from *mass* MASS¹ *noun* 3.

amateur /ˈamətə(r), aməˈtɜː(r)/ ▻ *noun* **1** someone who takes part in a sport, pastime, etc as a hobby and without being paid for it. **2** someone who is not very skilled in an activity, etc. **3** *as adj* **a** unskilled or non-professional □ ***liked to play the amateur detective***; **b** for, relating to or done by those who are not professional □ ***amateur dramatics.*** • **amateurism** *noun*. ⓒ 18c: French, from Latin *amator* lover.

amateurish ▻ *adj* characteristic of an amateur; not particularly skilful; inexperienced. • **amateurishly** *adverb*. • **amateurishness** *noun*. ⓒ 19c.

amatory /ˈamətərɪ/ ▻ *adj* belonging or relating to, or showing, sexual love or desire. • **amatorial** /-ˈtɔːrɪəl/ *adj*. • **amatorially** *adverb*. ⓒ 16c: from Latin *amatorius* loving.

amaurosis /amɔːˈroʊsɪs/ ▻ *noun, pathol* an eye condition that affects the OPTIC NERVE and which results in partial or total blindness, often without any external signs of damage to the eye. ⓒ 17c: from Greek *amauroun* to grow dim or dark.

amaze /əˈmeɪz/ ▻ *verb* (***amazed, amazing***) to surprise someone greatly; to astonish them. • **amazed** *adj*. • **amazedly** /əˈmeɪzɪdlɪ/ *adverb*. • **amazement** *noun*. ⓒ Anglo-Saxon *amasian*.

amazing ▻ *adj* astonishing; wonderful. • **amazingly** *adverb*.

Amazon /ˈaməzən/ ▻ *noun* **1** a member of a legendary nation of women warriors, eg from Scythia or S America. **2** (*usually* **amazon**) any tall, well-built, strong woman, especially one who is good at sport. ⓒ 14c: Greek, in folk etymology believed to be from *a-* without + *mazos* breast, referring to the legend (which has no verifiable basis in fact) that the Scythian women warriors cut off their right breasts in order to use the bow better.

amazon /ˈaməzən/ ▻ *noun* any of several types of tropical American parrot. ⓒ 19c: named after the Amazon river in S America.

amazon ant ▻ *noun* any of several types of small European and American red ant, some of which practise the habit of capturing and enslaving young ants of other species.

Amazonian /aməˈzoʊnɪən/ ▻ *adj* **1** relating to or like an AMAZON. **2** relating to or in the region of the River Amazon, the world's largest river, which rises in the Andes, flows through Brazil and empties into the Atlantic □ ***the Amazonian rainforest.*** ⓒ 16c.

ambassador /amˈbasədə(r)/ ▻ *noun* **1** a diplomat of the highest rank permanently appointed by a government, head of state, sovereign, etc to act on their behalf or to be their official representative in some foreign country, state, etc. See also HIGH COMMISSIONER. **2** a representative, messenger or agent □ ***believed himself to be an ambassador of good taste.*** • **ambassadorial** /ambasəˈdɔːrɪəl/ *adj*. • **ambassadorship** *noun*. ⓒ 14c: from French *ambassateur*, from Latin *ambactus* servant.

ambassadress /amˈbasədrəs/ ▻ *noun* (***ambassadresses***) **1** a woman ambassador. **2** the wife of an ambassador.

amber /ˈambə(r)/ ▻ *noun, geol* **1** a transparent yellow or reddish fossilized resin that was exuded by coniferous trees, often carved and polished and used to make jewellery, ornaments, etc, and which sometimes contains insects, etc trapped within it. **2** the yellow or reddish-brown colour of this substance. Also *as adj*. **3** a traffic light that serves as a means of delaying the change-over in traffic flow, in the UK appearing on its own between green for 'go' and red for 'stop' but appearing simultaneously with red to mark the transition the other way between red and green. ⓒ 14c: from Latin *ambar*, from Arabic *anbar* ambergris.

amber gambler ▷ *noun, Brit colloq* a driver who, instead of reading an amber light as a cautionary sign, either speeds up in order to avoid having to wait until the next green light appears or sets off from stationary, usually at high speed, while the red light is still showing.

ambergris /ˈambəgriːs, -griː/ ▷ *noun* a pale-grey waxy substance with a strong smell, produced in the intestines of sperm whales, and widely used until recently in the perfume industry. ⓒ 15c: from French *ambre gris* grey amber.

amberjack ▷ *noun* any of several varieties of tropical and subtropical fish that live in the Atlantic. ⓒ 19c.

ambi- /ambɪ/ ▷ *prefix, denoting* both; on both sides. ⓒ Latin, from *ambo* both.

ambiance see AMBIENCE

ambidextrous /ambɪˈdɛkstrəs/ ▷ *adj* able to use both hands equally well. • **ambidextrously** *adverb*. ⓒ 17c: from Latin *ambidexter*, from *dexter* right-handed.

ambience or **ambiance** /ˈambɪəns, ˈɒmbɪɒns/ ▷ *noun* the surroundings or atmosphere of a place. ⓒ 19c: from Latin AMBIENT.

ambient /ˈambɪənt/ ▷ *adj* **1** said of air, temperature, etc: surrounding. **2** referring to restful and relaxing beatless music, usually played at low volume to create atmosphere. ⓒ 17c: from Latin *ambiens*, from *ambire* to go about, from AMBI- + *ire* to go.

ambiguity /ambɪˈgjuːɪtɪ/ ▷ *noun* (***ambiguities***) **1** uncertainty of meaning. **2** a word or statement that can be interpreted in more than one way. **3** *literary theory* **a** a word, statement, concept, theme, etc that can be interpreted in more than one way and which is employed deliberately because of this □ ***the ambiguity of the relationships in Nabokov***; **b** such devices thought of collectively □ ***Joyce's use of ambiguity can be seen as very Post-Modern.*** ⓒ 15c: from Latin *ambiguus*, from *ambi-* both ways + *agere* to drive + -ITY.

ambiguous /amˈbɪgjʊəs/ ▷ *adj* having more than one possible meaning; not clear. • **ambiguously** *adverb*. • **ambiguousness** *noun*. ⓒ 16c: from Latin *ambiguus*.

ambiguous, ambivalent

• Strictly, **ambiguous** refers to the meaning and significance of things, whereas **ambivalent** refers to the emotional feelings of people □ *Note the ambiguous sentences at the beginning of her new book* □ *Somali men tend to be very ambivalent in their attitudes towards these women.*

• However, **ambivalent** is often used where you might expect **ambiguous**: ? *The term is rather ambivalent in English, having both good senses and bad senses.*

ambisexual ▷ *adj* belonging or relating to, or affecting, both male and female.

ambisonics ▷ *singular noun* a system for reproducing high-fidelity sound using multiple channels.

ambit /ˈambɪt/ ▷ *noun* **1** range or extent. **2** circumference or boundary. ⓒ 14c: from Latin *ambitus* a going round.

ambition /amˈbɪʃən/ ▷ *noun* **1** a strong desire for success, fame or power. **2** a thing someone wants to do or achieve. ⓒ 14c: French, from Latin *ambitus*.

ambitious /amˈbɪʃəs/ ▷ *adj* **1** having a strong desire for success, etc. **2** enterprising or daring, but requiring hard work and skill □ ***an ambitious plan.*** **3** bold; presumptuous □ ***He was being far too ambitious thinking he could play that piece.*** • **ambitiously** *adverb*. • **ambitiousness** *noun*. ⓒ 14c.

ambivalence /amˈbɪvələns/ and **ambivalency** ▷ *noun, originally psychol* the concurrent adherence to two opposite or conflicting views, feelings, etc about someone or something. • **ambivalent** *adj*. • **ambivalently** *adverb*. ⓒ 1912: from German *Ambivalenz*, from AMBI-, modelled on 'equivalence'; see EQUIVALENT.

ambivalent

See Usage Note at **ambiguous**.

amble /ˈambəl/ ▷ *verb* (***ambled, ambling***) *intr* **1** to walk without hurrying; to stroll. **2** said of a horse, etc: to walk by lifting the two feet on the same side together and then lifting the two feet on the other side together and so move in a smooth, flowing way. ▷ *noun* **1** a leisurely walk. **2** a horse's ambling walk (see *verb* 2). ⓒ 14c: from French *ambler*, from Latin *ambulare* to walk.

amblyopia /amblɪˈoʊpɪə/ ▷ *noun, pathol* a form of vision impairment, especially one that is caused by damage to the retina or optic nerve by noxious substances. ⓒ 18c: from Greek *amblys* dull + *ops* the eye.

ambroid /ˈambrɔɪd/ and **amberoid** /ˈambərɔɪd/ ▷ *noun* amber that has been moulded or pressed and combined with other substances. ⓒ Late 19c.

ambrosia /amˈbroʊzɪə/ ▷ *noun* **1** *Greek mythol* **a** *most commonly* the food of the gods, believed to give them eternal youth and beauty; **b** *sometimes* the drink of the gods, also believed to have these properties. Compare NECTAR 2. **2** something with a delicious taste or smell. • **ambrosial** *adj*. • **ambrosially** *adverb*. • **ambrosian** *adj*. ⓒ 16c: Greek, from *ambrotos* immortal.

ambulance /ˈambjʊləns/ ▷ *noun* a specially equipped vehicle for carrying sick or injured people to hospital. ⓒ 1920s in this sense; 19c: from Latin *ambulare* to walk about.

ambulance chaser ▷ *noun, US slang* a lawyer who contrives to have a case-load that consists mainly of lucrative DAMAGES suits on behalf of accident victims, having approached them either at the scene of the accident or shortly afterwards. ⓒ 19c.

ambulant /ˈambjʊlənt/ ▷ *adj* **1** said especially of someone who is sick or injured: walking or able to walk. **2** said of a disease or injury: not requiring the patient to stay in bed. ⓒ 17c: from Latin *ambulans*.

ambulatory /ˈambjʊlətərɪ/ ▷ *adj* **1** belonging or relating to or designed for walking. **2** moving from place to place. **3** not permanent, especially in legal terms. ⓒ 17c: from Latin *ambulator* a walker, from *ambulare* to walk about.

ambuscade /ambəˈskeɪd/ ▷ *noun* an ambush. ▷ *verb* (***ambuscaded, ambuscading***) to ambush. ⓒ 16c: from French *embuscade*.

ambush /ˈambʊʃ/ ▷ *noun* (***ambushes***) **1** the act of lying in wait to attack someone by surprise. **2** an attack made in this way. **3** the person or people making such an attack. **4** the place of concealment from which the attack is made. ▷ *verb* (***ambushes, ambushed, ambushing***) to lie in wait for someone or attack them in this way. ⓒ 14c: from French *embuschier* to place men in the woods.

ameba an alternative *US* spelling of AMOEBA

ameer see EMIR

ameliorate /əˈmiːlɪəreɪt/ ▷ *verb* (***ameliorated, ameliorating***) *tr & intr* to make or become better. ⓒ 18c: from French *ameillorer*, from Latin *melior* better.

amelioration ▷ *noun* **1** making better; improvement. **2** *linguistics* a semantic change where a word's previous sense is superseded by one that is more positive. Compare DETERIORATION. ⓒ 18c.

amen /ɑːˈmɛn, eɪ-/ ▻ *exclamation* usually said at the end of a prayer, hymn, etc: so be it. • **say amen to something** *colloq* to be glad it is over, out of the way, etc. ⓒ Anglo-Saxon: Hebrew, literally 'certainly'.

amenable /əˈmiːnəbəl/ ▻ *adj* **1** (*especially* **amenable to something**) ready to accept (someone else's idea, proposal, advice, guidance, etc) □ *He was not amenable to her suggestion that they go on holiday together.* **2** legally responsible. • **amenability** *noun*. • **amenableness** *noun*. • **amenably** *adverb*. ⓒ 16c: Anglo-French, from *amener* (from *à mener*) to lead to.

amend /əˈmɛnd/ ▻ *verb* (***amended, amending***) to correct, improve or make minor changes to (especially a book, document, etc). Compare EMEND. • **amendable** *adj*. • **make amends for something** to make up for or compensate for (some injury, insult, etc). ⓒ 14c: from French *amender*, from Latin *emendare*.

amend, emend

A word often confused with this one is **emend**, which refers specifically to the correction of errors in written texts.

amendment ▻ *noun* **1** an addition or alteration, especially to a motion, official document, etc. **2** an act of correcting or improving something.

amenity /əˈmiːnɪtɪ, əˈmɛ-/ ▻ *noun* (***amenities***) **1** a valued public facility. **2** anything that makes life more comfortable and pleasant. **3** pleasantness of situation. ⓒ 15c: from Latin *amoenus* pleasant.

amenorrhoea or **amenorrhea** /eɪmɛnəˈrɪə, a-/ ▻ *noun, medicine* the absence or stopping of normal menstruation. ⓒ Early 19c: from A-[1] + MENORRHOEA.

Amerasian /amərˈeɪʒən/ ▻ *adj* relating or referring to someone of mixed American and Asian parentage. ▻ *noun* someone who is of mixed American and Asian parentage, especially someone whose father was a serviceman in Korea or Vietnam. ⓒ 1966: from *American* + *Asian*.

American /əˈmɛrɪkən/ ▻ *adj* **1** belonging or relating to the United States of America, a federal republic in N America, its inhabitants, or their languages. **2** belonging or relating to the American continent, its inhabitants, or their languages. ▻ *noun* a citizen or inhabitant of, or person born in, the United States of America, or the American continent. ⓒ 16c: named after the Italian navigator, Amerigo Vespucci (1454-1512).

Americana /əmɛrɪˈkɑːnə/ ▻ *noun* a collection of objects that are typically American. ⓒ 1840s: AMERICA + -ANA.

American cream soda see CREAM SODA

the American Dream ▻ *noun* the naive belief that the political, economic and social systems of America are all integrally designed to allow each individual an equal chance of being successful. ⓒ 1931.

American eagle ▻ *noun* another name for the BALD EAGLE, especially when used as the emblem of the USA.

American Express ▻ *noun, trademark* the name of an international organization that offers various financial services, such as the provision of credit cards, for its customers. Also called **Amex**. ⓒ 1950s.

American football ▻ *noun* **1** a team game with 11 players on both sides, similar to RUGBY but where forward passing is allowed and much emphasis is put on set-piece moves. **2** the oval ball used in this sport. ⓒ 19c.

American Indian and **Amerindian** /aməˈrɪndɪən/ ▻ *adj* relating or referring to any of the indigenous peoples of America, the languages they speak, their culture, etc. ▻ *noun* a member of any of the indigenous peoples of America. See also NATIVE AMERICAN. ⓒ 18c.

Americanism ▻ *noun* a word, phrase, custom, etc that is characteristic of Americans □ *Americanisms such as 'Have a nice day!'*

Americanize or **Americanise** ▻ *verb* (***Americanized, Americanizing***) to make or become more typical or characteristic of America, especially in terms of culture, customs, language, etc. • **Americanized** *adj*. ⓒ 18c.

American plan ▻ *noun, US* an all-inclusive deal in renting hotel accommodation where the cost of meals is included along with the cost of the room. Compare EUROPEAN PLAN, FULL BOARD ⓒ 1850s.

American Sign Language ▻ *noun* (abbreviation **ASL**) a sign system for communication developed for the deaf, where hand gestures are interpreted by their relative position to the upper part of the body. Also called AMESLAN. ⓒ 1960.

American tournament see ROUND ROBIN 2

americium /aməˈrɪsɪəm, -ʃɪəm/ ▻ *noun, chem* (symbol **Am**, atomic number 95) a silvery-white radioactive metallic element, used as a source of ALPHA PARTICLES, that occurs naturally in trace amounts and is produced artificially by bombarding plutonium with neutrons. ⓒ 1945: named after America (where it was discovered by G T Seaborg, R A James and L O Morgan) + -IUM 1.

Amerindian /ameˈrɪndɪən/ ▻ *adj* **1** relating or referring to any of the indigenous peoples of America. **2** denoting a family of over 1 000 languages used by the indigenous peoples of N, Central and S America which is divided into North American, Meso-American, and South American. ▻ *noun* **1** a member of any of the indigenous peoples of America. **2** the languages forming the Amerindian family. See also NATIVE AMERICAN.

Ameslan /ˈaməslan/ ▻ *noun* AMERICAN SIGN LANGUAGE. ⓒ 1972: from *Am*erican *S*ign *Lan*guage.

amethyst /ˈaməθɪst/ ▻ *noun* **1** a pale- to deep-purple transparent or translucent variety of the mineral QUARTZ used as a gemstone. **2** the purple or violet colour of this gemstone. ⓒ 13c: from Greek *amethystos* not drunken, referring to the notion that the stone was supposed to prevent drunkenness.

Amex ▻ *abbreviation* AMERICAN EXPRESS.

Amharic /amˈharɪk/ ▻ *noun* the official language of Ethiopia, related to Hebrew and Arabic. ▻ *adj* belonging or relating to, or in, this language. ⓒ 17c: named after Amhara, a province of Ethiopia.

amiable /ˈeɪmɪəbəl/ ▻ *adj* friendly, pleasant and good-tempered. • **amiability** *noun*. • **amiableness** *noun*. • **amiably** *adverb*. ⓒ 14c: from Latin *amicabilis* amicable, later confused with French *amable* lovable.

amiable, amicable

There is often confusion between **amiable** and **amicable**: **amiable** refers to people or their moods, personalities and expressions, whereas **amicable** refers to the relations between people.

amianthus /amɪˈanθəs/ or **amiantus** ▻ *noun* a variety of silky ASBESTOS. ⓒ 17c: from Latin *amiantus*, from Greek *amiantos* unsullied.

amicable /ˈamɪkəbəl/ ▻ *adj* **1** friendly. **2** done in a reasonably friendly manner □ *They managed an amicable parting.* • **amicability** *noun*. • **amicableness** *noun*. • **amicably** *adverb*. ⓒ 16c: from Latin *amicabilis*, from *amicus* a friend.

amicus curiae /əˈmaɪkʌs ˈkjʊərɪiː/ ▻ *noun* (***amici curiae*** /-kaɪ —/) *law* a person or group of people not directly involved in a case, but who may give advice about it. ⓒ 17c: Latin, meaning 'friend of the court'.

amid /əˈmɪd/ and **amidst** ▷ *prep* in the middle of something; among. ◷ Anglo-Saxon *onmiddan* in the centre.

amide /ˈamaɪd/ ▷ *noun, chem* **1** any member of a class of organic compounds that contain the $CONH_2$ group, formed when one or more of the hydrogen atoms of ammonia is replaced by an acyl group. **2** any member of a class of inorganic compounds that contain the NH_2^- ion, formed when one of the hydrogen atoms of ammonia is replaced by a metal. ◷ 19c: from *am*monia + -IDE.

amidships ▷ *adverb* in, into or near the middle of a ship. ◷ 17c.

amigo /əˈmiːgoʊ, a-/ ▷ *noun* (***amigos***) *chiefly US* especially in Spanish-speaking areas: a term used to address a friend or comrade. ◷ 19c: Spanish, meaning 'friend'.

amine /ˈamiːn, ˈamaɪn/ ▷ *noun, chem* any member of a class of organic compounds, produced by decomposing organic matter, in which one or more of the hydrogen atoms of ammonia has been replaced by an organic group. ◷ 19c: from *am*monia + -INE[2].

amino acid /əˈmiːnoʊ —/ ▷ *noun* any of a group of water-soluble organic compounds that contain an amino ($-NH_2$) group and a carboxyl ($-COOH$) group, and form the individual subunits of proteins.

amino group ▷ *noun, chem* the $-NH_2$ group in amino acids and other nitrogen-containing organic compounds.

amir see EMIR

Amish /ˈɑːmɪʃ, ˈa-/ ▷ *adj* belonging or relating to an ultra-conservative branch of the **Mennonite** church, formed around 1693, some American sects of which still insist on strict dress and behaviour codes for its members. ▷ *noun* a member of this church. ◷ 19c: named after the Swiss anabaptist leader Jacob Amman (c. 1645-c. 1730).

amiss /əˈmɪs/ ▷ *adj* wrong; out of order □ *knew something was amiss when she saw him crying.* ▷ *adverb* wrongly. • **take something amiss** to be upset or offended by it □ *took it amiss when she didn't phone.* ◷ 13c: from A-[1] sense 2 + MISS[1].

amitosis /amɪˈtoʊsɪs/ *biol* ▷ *noun* a simple form of cell division in which normal chromosome formation and separation do not occur. • **amitotic** /-ˈtɒtɪk/ *adj.* • **amitotically** *adverb.* Compare MITOSIS. ◷ 19c.

amity /ˈamɪtɪ/ ▷ *noun* friendship; friendliness. ◷ 15c: from French *amitie*, from Latin *amicus* a friend.

ammeter /ˈamiːtə(r)/ ▷ *noun, elec engineering* a device used for measuring electric current in a circuit, usually in amperes. ◷ 19c: from *am*pere + METER[1].

ammo /ˈamoʊ/ ▷ *noun, colloq* short form of AMMUNITION. ◷ Early 20c.

ammonia /əˈmoʊnɪə/ *chem* ▷ *noun* **1** (formula NH_3) a colourless pungent gas formed naturally by the bacterial decomposition of proteins, etc, and also manufactured industrially, used in liquefied form as a refrigerant, and in the form of its compounds in fertilizers and explosives. **2** an alkaline solution of ammonia in water, used as a bleach and household cleaning agent. Also called **ammonium hydroxide, liquid ammonia**. ◷ 18c: from Latin *sal ammoniacus* = SAL AMMONIAC.

ammonite /ˈamənaɪt/ ▷ *noun* **1** *zool* an extinct marine cephalopod mollusc with a flat, tightly coiled shell, widespread during the Mesozoic era. **2** *geol* the fossilized remains, especially the shell, of this animal. ◷ 18c: from Latin *Cornu Ammonis* horn of Ammon, apparently because of the fossil's tightly spiralled appearance.

ammonium /əˈmoʊnɪəm/ ▷ *noun, chem* a positively charged ion formed by the reaction of ammonia with acid, found in many salts, especially ammonium chloride (SAL AMMONIAC) and ammonium carbonate (SAL VOLATILE). ◷ Early 18c: from AMMONIA + -IUM 1.

ammonium hydroxide see AMMONIA sense 2

ammunition /amjʊˈnɪʃən/ ▷ *noun* **1** bullets, shells, bombs, etc made to be fired from a weapon. See also AMMO. **2** anything that can be used against someone in an argument, etc. ◷ 17c: from French *amunition*, from an apparent confusion of *la munition* a warning.

amnesia /amˈniːzɪə, -ˈniːʒə/ ▷ *noun, pathol* the loss or impairment of memory, caused by physical injury, disease, drugs or emotional trauma. • **amnesiac** *noun* someone suffering from amnesia. • **amnesic** /-ˈniːzɪk/ *adj.* ◷ 17c: from Greek *amnestia* forgetfulness.

amnesty /ˈamnəstɪ/ ▷ *noun* (***amnesties***) **1** a general pardon, especially for people convicted or accused of political crimes. **2** a period of time when people can admit to crimes, hand in weapons, etc in the knowledge that they will not be prosecuted. ◷ 16c: from Greek *amnestia* oblivion.

amnio /ˈamnɪoʊ/ ▷ *noun* (***amnios***) *colloq* short form of AMNIOCENTESIS.

amniocentesis /amnɪoʊsɛnˈtiːsɪs/ ▷ *noun* (***amniocenteses*** /-tiːsiːz/) *obstetrics* a procedure that involves the insertion of a hollow needle through the abdominal wall into the uterus of a pregnant woman, enabling a small quantity of AMNIOTIC FLUID to be drawn off in order to test for fetal abnormalities such as DOWN'S SYNDROME. ◷ 1950s: from AMNION + Greek *kentesis* puncture.

amnion /ˈamnɪən, -ɒn/ ▷ *noun* (***amnia*** /ˈamnɪə/) *anatomy* the innermost membrane that surrounds the embryo of mammals, birds and reptiles. ◷ 17c: from Greek *amnos* a little lamb.

amniotic fluid ▷ *noun, zool* in mammals, birds and reptiles: the clear fluid that surrounds and protects the embryo, found in the space between the embryo and the amnion.

amn't /ˈamənt/ ▷ *contraction, Scots, usually in questions* am not □ *I'm going too, amn't I?*

amoeba or (*N Amer*) **ameba** /əˈmiːbə/ ▷ *noun* (***amoebae*** /əˈmiːbiː/ or ***amoebas***) *zool* any of numerous microscopic PROTOZOAN animals, including some disease-causing parasites, that inhabit water or damp soil and have no fixed shape, but move by continually pushing out pseudopodia (see PSEUDOPODIUM) in different directions. • **amoebic** or **amebic** *adj.* ◷ 19c: from Greek *amoibe* change.

amok /əˈmɒk, əˈmʌk/ or **amuck** ▷ *adverb* • **run amok** or **amuck** to rush about violently and out of control. ◷ 19c: from Malay *amoq* frenzied.

among /əˈmʌŋ/ and **amongst** ▷ *prep* used of more than two things, people, etc: **1** in the middle of them □ *among friends.* **2** between them □ *divide it among them.* **3** in the group or number of them □ *among his best plays.* **4** with one another □ *decide among yourselves.* ◷ Anglo-Saxon *ongemang* mingling in.

> ***among***
>
> See Usage Note at **between**.

amontillado /əmɒntɪˈlɑːdoʊ, -ljɑː-/ ▷ *noun* (***amontillados***) a Spanish light medium-dry sherry. ◷ 19c: named after Montilla a town in S Spain.

amoral /eɪˈmɒrəl, a-/ ▷ *adj* having no moral standards or principles. Compare IMMORAL. • **amorality** *noun.* • **amorally** *adverb.* ◷ 19c: A-[2] + MORAL.

> ***amoral, immoral***
>
> • **Amoral** means 'having no morality', whereas **immoral** means 'violating a morality' □ *We live in a more impersonal, amoral, and uncertain modern world* □ *It is immoral to be rich when so many people are starving and homeless.*

amorist /ˈamərɪst/ ▷ *noun* **1** a lover. **2** someone who writes about love. ⓘ 16c: from Latin *amor* + -IST 2.

amoroso /aməˈroʊsoʊ/ ▷ *noun* (***amorosos***) a deep-coloured sweet sherry. ⓘ 1870s: Spanish and Italian, meaning 'a lover'.

amorous /ˈamərəs/ ▷ *adj* showing, feeling or relating to love, especially sexual love. • **amorously** *adverb*. ⓘ 14c: from Latin *amorosus*, from *amor* love.

amorphous /əˈmɔːfəs/ ▷ *adj* **1** without definite shape or structure. **2** *chem* said of rocks, chemicals, etc: without a crystalline structure. **3** without any clearly defined or thought-out purpose, identity, etc. ⓘ 18c: from Greek *amorphos* shapeless.

amortization or **amortisation** ▷ *noun* **1** the process of amortizing a debt. **2** the money used for this. ⓘ 17c.

amortize or **amortise** /əˈmɔːtaɪz/ ▷ *verb* (***amortized***, ***amortizing***) **1** to gradually pay off (a debt) by regular payments of money. **2** to gradually write off (the initial cost of an asset) over a period. ⓘ 14c: from French *amortir* to bring to death.

amount /əˈmaʊnt/ ▷ *noun* a quantity; a total or extent □ *a large amount of money* □ *didn't put in a great amount of effort*. ▷ *verb* (***amounted***, ***amounting***) (*always* **amount to something**) to be equal to it or add up to it in size, number, significance, etc □ *Their assets amounted to several millions* □ *If you don't study, you'll never amount to anything*. • **any amount of something** *colloq* a great deal of it. • **no amount of something** *colloq* not even the greatest imaginable quantity of it □ *No amount of evidence could have persuaded him otherwise*. ⓘ 14c: from French *amonter* to climb up.

amour /əˈmʊə(r), aˈmʊə(r)/ ▷ *noun*, *old use* a love affair, especially one that is kept secret. ⓘ 13c: French, meaning 'love'.

amour-propre /*French* amuʀpʀɔpʀ/ ▷ *noun* self-esteem. ⓘ 18c: French, literally 'love of self'.

amp ▷ *noun* **1** an AMPERE. **2** *colloq* an AMPLIFIER.

amperage /ˈampərɪdʒ/ ▷ *noun* the magnitude or strength of an electric current expressed in AMPERES.

ampere /ˈampɛə(r)/ ▷ *noun* (symbol **A**) the SI unit of electric current, equivalent to one COULOMB per second, defined as the current that would produce a force of $2 \times 10^{-7} Nm^{-1}$ between two parallel conductors of infinite length placed 1m apart in a vacuum. ⓘ 19c: named after the French physicist André Marie Ampère (1775–1836).

ampersand /ˈampəsand/ ▷ *noun* the symbol &, which means 'and'. ⓘ 1830s: from *and per se and* meaning '& when it appears by itself means *and*'.

amphetamine /amˈfɛtəmiːn, -mɪn/ ▷ *noun*, *medicine* any of various potentially addictive synthetic drugs, formerly used as appetite suppressants to treat obesity, now seldom prescribed but often used illegally to produce a sense of well-being and mental alertness. Also (*slang*) called SPEED. ⓘ 1930s: from the chemical name *a*lpha*m*ethyl*phe*ne*t*hyl*amine*.

amphi- /ˈamfɪ/ ▷ *combining form, denoting* both, or on both sides or ends. ⓘ Greek, meaning 'both' or 'on both sides'.

amphibian /amˈfɪbɪən/ ▷ *noun* **1** *zool* any of numerous cold-blooded vertebrates belonging to the class **amphibia**, eg frogs, toads and newts, the adults of which live partly or entirely on land but return to water to lay their eggs, which hatch to form fish-like larvae or tadpoles that breathe by means of gills. **2** a vehicle that can operate both on land and in water. ▷ *adj* referring or relating to these kinds of animals or vehicles. ⓘ 17c: from Greek *amphibia* creatures that live in both environments, from *amphi* both + *bios* life.

amphibious /amˈfɪbɪəs/ ▷ *adj* **1** *zool* said of a living organism: capable of living both on land and in water. **2** said of vehicles, equipment, etc: designed to be operated or used both on land, and on or in water, usually for military or rescue purposes. **3** said of a military operation: using troops that have been conveyed across the sea or other water before landing on enemy-held territory. **4** having, showing or combining different, usually discreditable, qualities. • **amphibiously** *adverb*. • **amphibiousness** *noun*. ⓘ 17c.

amphibole /ˈamfɪboʊl/ ▷ *noun* *mineralogy* any of various complex silicate minerals that are widely distributed in igneous and metamorphic rocks, eg HORNBLENDE. ⓘ 19c: from Greek *amphibolos* ambiguous, from *amphi-* + *ballein* to throw.

amphibolite ▷ *noun, mineralogy* rock that is composed mainly of AMPHIBOLE. ⓘ 1830s.

amphibology /amfɪˈbɒlədʒɪ/ and **amphiboly** /amˈfɪbəlɪ/ ▷ *noun* a piece of language whose grammatical construction makes the meaning ambiguous, as in *She could see the girl with her binoculars*. • **amphibolic** /-ˈbɒlɪk/ or **amphibological** /-bəˈlɒdʒɪkəl/ *adj*. ⓘ 14c: from Greek *amphibolia* ambiguity + -LOGY.

amphibrach /ˈamfɪbrak/ ▷ *noun* in verse: a metrical foot consisting of a long syllable with one short syllable either side of it, eg 'vacation'. • **amphibrachic** /-ˈbrakɪk/ *adj*. ⓘ 16c: from Greek *amphi* both sides + *brachys* short.

amphimacer /amˈfɪməsə(r)/ ▷ *noun* in verse: a metrical foot consisting of a short syllable with one long syllable either side of it, eg 'multitude'. ⓘ 16c: from Greek *amphi* both sides + *makros* long.

amphimixis /amfɪˈmɪksɪs/ ▷ *noun*, *biol* sexual reproduction where there is a fusing of the male and female GAMETE. ⓘ 19c: from AMPHI- + Greek *mixis* intercourse or mingling.

amphipod /ˈamfɪpɒd/ ▷ *noun*, *zool* any of numerous species belonging to an order of CRUSTACEANS with different pairs of legs adapted for swimming, walking or jumping, eg sandhoppers, freshwater shrimps. ⓘ 19c.

amphisbaena /amfɪsˈbiːnə/ ▷ *noun* (***amphisbaenae*** /-niː/ or ***amphisbaenas***) **1** any of several worm-like tropical American lizards that are camouflaged so that the tail resembles a head, making it very difficult to tell one end from the other. **2** *Greek & Roman mythol* a poisonous serpent which was believed to have a head at each end, enabling it to move in either direction. ⓘ 16c: from Greek *amphisbaina*, from *amphis* both ways + *bainein* to go.

amphistomous /amˈfɪstəməs/ ▷ *adj*, *zool* said of certain worms, leeches, etc: having a mouth-like opening or sucker at both ends of their body. ⓘ 19c: from Greek *amphis* both ways + *stoma* mouth.

amphitheatre /ˈamfɪθɪətə(r)/ ▷ *noun* **1** in ancient Greek and Roman architecture: an oval or round building without a roof, with tiers of seats for spectators built around a central open area which was used for staging drama and as a place of gladiatorial combat, etc. **2** *modern archit* a tiered gallery in a theatre, lecture hall, etc. ⓘ 16c: from Greek *amphitheatron*.

amphora /ˈamfərə/ ▷ *noun* (***amphoras*** or ***amphorae*** /ˈamfəriː/) *archaeol, etc* a large narrow-necked Greek or Roman jar with a handle on either side, used for storing liquids such as wine or oil. ⓘ 15c: Greek.

amphoric /amˈfɒrɪk/ ▷ *adj*, *medicine* sounding like the noise of someone blowing into a bottle □ *an amphoric cough*. ⓘ 19c: from AMPHORA.

amphoteric /amfoʊˈtɛrɪk/ ▷ *adj*, *chem* said of a compound: having the properties of both an acid and a base. ⓘ 19c: from Greek *amphoteros* both.

ampicillin or **Ampicillin** /ampɪˈsɪlən/ ▷ *noun*, *medicine*, *trademark* a type of semi-synthetic penicillin used as an antibiotic in the treatment of various infections. ⓘ 1960s: from *amino* + *penicillin*.

ample /ˈampəl/ ▷ *adj* (***ampler***, ***amplest***) **1** more than enough; plenty. **2** extensive; abundant. **3** *euphemistic* said of people or parts of the body: very large or fat □ *cradled the baby in her ample bosom*. • **amply** *adverb*. ◷ 15c: from Latin *amplus* abundant.

amplification /amplɪfɪˈkeɪʃən/ ▻ *noun* **1** the act, process or result of amplifying something. **2 a** material added to a report, story, etc to expand or explain it; **b** a story or account with details added. **3** *electronics* the magnification or the amount of magnification of a sound's loudness or the strength of an electrical current, signal, etc. **4** *genetics* the formation, either naturally or by artificial stimulation, of multiple copies of a particular gene or DNA sequence. Also called **gene amplification**. ◷ 16c.

amplifier /ˈamplɪfaɪə(r)/ ▻ *noun* **1** an electronic device that amplifies the strength of an electrical or radio signal without appreciably altering its characteristics, used in audio equipment, radio and television sets, etc. **2** *photog* a lens that enlarges the field of vision.

amplify /ˈamplɪfaɪ/ ▻ *verb* (***amplifies, amplified, amplifying***) **1** to increase the strength of (an electrical or radio signal) by transferring power from an external energy source. **2** *tr & intr* to add details or further explanation to an account, story, etc. ◷ 15c: from Latin *amplificare*, from *amplus* abundant.

amplitude /ˈamplɪtjuːd/ ▻ *noun* **1** spaciousness, wide range or extent. **2** abundance. **3** *physics* in any quantity that varies in periodic cycles, such as a wave or vibration: the maximum displacement from its mean position, eg the angle between the vertical and the peak position in the swing of a pendulum. **4** *astron* the difference between the maximum and minimum brightness of a VARIABLE STAR. ◷ 16c: from Latin *amplitudo*, from *amplus* abundant.

amplitude modulation ▻ *noun*, *telecomm* (abbreviation **AM**) in radio transmission: the process whereby the amplitude of the CARRIER WAVE is made to increase or decrease instantaneously in response to variations in the characteristics of the signal being transmitted. Compare FREQUENCY MODULATION. ◷ 1920s.

amply see under AMPLE

ampoule or (*US*) **ampule** /ˈampuːl/ ▻ *noun*, *medicine* a small sealed container, usually of glass or plastic, containing one sterile dose of a drug for injection. ◷ 17c: French, from Latin *ampulla* a small rounded flask.

ampulla /amˈpʊlə/ ▻ *noun* (***ampullae*** /amˈpʊliː/) **1** *anatomy* the dilated end of a duct or canal. **2** *zool* any small membranous vesicle. **3** *archaeol, etc* a small round glass bottle with two handles, used by ancient Romans for holding oil, perfume or wine. **4** a container for oil, water or wine used in religious ceremonies. ◷ 14c: Latin, meaning 'a small rounded flask' and thought to be a diminutive of AMPHORA.

amputate /ˈampjʊteɪt/ ▻ *verb* (***amputated, amputating***) *surgery* to remove (all or part of a limb), usually in cases of severe injury, or following death or decay of the tissue caused by gangrene or frostbite. • **amputation** *noun*. ◷ 17c: from Latin *amputare* to cut off.

amputee /ampjʊˈtiː/ ▻ *noun* (***amputees***) someone who has had a limb surgically removed. ◷ 20c.

amrita or **amreeta** /amˈriːtɑː/ ▻ *noun*, *Hinduism* an ambrosial drink of the gods believed to bestow immortality. ◷ Early 19c: from Sanskrit *a-* without + *mrta* death.

amt ▻ *abbreviation* amount.

amuck see AMOK

amulet /ˈamjʊlət/ ▻ *noun* a small object, charm or jewel worn to protect the wearer from witchcraft, evil, disease, etc. ◷ 15c: from Latin *amuletum*.

amuse /əˈmjuːz/ ▻ *verb* (***amused, amusing***) **1** to make someone laugh. **2** to keep someone entertained and interested. ◷ 15c: from French *amuser* to cause to muse.

amused ▻ *adj* **1** made to laugh. **2** entertained; happily occupied. • **amusedly** /əˈmjuːzɪdlɪ/ *adverb*.

amusement ▻ *noun* **1** the state of being amused. **2** something that amuses. **3** a machine for riding on or playing games of chance.

amusement arcade ▻ *noun*, *Brit* a place where people can play fruit machines, slot machines, pinball machines, video games, etc.

amusement park ▻ *noun*, *N Amer* a place of outdoor entertainment with side shows, stalls, shooting ranges and rides such as ghost trains, ferris wheels, etc. *Brit equivalent* FUNFAIR.

amusing ▻ *adj* mildly funny, diverting or entertaining. • **amusingly** *adverb*.

amygdala /əˈmɪgdələ/ ▻ *noun* (***amygdalae*** /-liː/) *anatomy* an almond-shaped body part, such as a lobe of the cerebellum or one of the palatal tonsils. ◷ 16c: Latin, literally 'almond'.

amygdalate /əˈmɪgdəleɪt/ and **amygdalaceous** /əmɪgdəˈleɪʃəs/ ▻ *adj, bot, etc* resembling, related to or producing almonds.

amygdale /əˈmɪgdeɪl/ and **amygdule** /əˈmɪgdjuːl/ ▻ *noun*, *geol* a cavity formed by escaping gas in a lava flow which then becomes filled with a mineral such as quartz. • **amygdaloid** /-dəlɔɪd/ *adj* said of rock, etc: having amygdales. ◷ 19c: from Latin *amygdala* an almond.

amylase /ˈamɪleɪs/ ▻ *noun* *biochem* any of various enzymes present in digestive juices, which play a part in the breakdown of starch and glycogen. ◷ 19c: from Greek *amylon* starch + -ASE.

Amytal /ˈamɪtal/ ▻ *noun*, *trademark* a white crystalline powder used as a sedative. Also called **sodium amytal**.

an /ən, an/ see A[1]

> ***an***
>
> See Usage Note at **a**[1].

an- see A-[2]

-an /ən, an/, **-ean** and **-ian** /ɪən/ ▻ *suffix* **1** *forming adjectives and nouns, signifying* belonging to, relating to or coming from a specified place □ *Roman remains*. **2** *forming adjectives and nouns, signifying* dating from or typical of the reign of a specified ruler □ *Georgian architecture*. **3** *forming adjectives and nouns, signifying* adhering to the beliefs or teachings of a specified leader □ *the Lutheran church*. **4** *biol, forming adjectives and nouns, denoting* belonging to a specified class or order □ *lobsters, crabs and shrimps are all crustaceans*. **5** *forming nouns, denoting* an expert in a specified subject □ *politician*.

ana /ˈɑːnə/ ▻ *singular noun* (***anas***) a collection of anecdotes, literary gossip, special possessions, etc, especially one that belongs or relates to an author. ▻ *plural noun* such anecdotes, possessions, etc. ◷ 18c: from -ANA.

-ana /ˈɑːnə, ˈeɪnə/ and **-iana** /ɪɑːnə/ ▻ *suffix, denoting* things belonging to or typical of a particular person or period □ *Shakespeariana* □ *Victoriana*. See also -IA. ◷ 17c: from Latin *-anum* belonging or referring to someone specified.

Anabaptist ▻ *noun*, *Christianity* a member of various groups of believers who adopted the more radical elements of the 16c Reformation and advocated the baptism of believing adults only, refusing to recognize infant baptism. • **Anabaptism** *noun*. Also called **Rebaptizer**. ◷ 16c: from Latin *anabaptismus*, from Greek *ana* over again + *baptein* to bathe.

anabas /ˈanəbas/ ▻ *noun* an E Indian fish that sometimes leaves the water and has even been known to climb trees in search of prey. ◷ 19c: from Greek *ana* up + *bainein* to go.

anabatic wind /anə'batɪk—/ ▷ *noun, meteorol* a local upward-moving wind, which most commonly develops in a valley, and reaches speeds of 10 to 15 metres per second. Compare KATABATIC WIND. ⓒ Early 20c: from Greek *ana* up + *bainein* to go.

anableps /'anəblɛps/ ▷ *noun* (*plural* ***anableps***) any of several varieties of bony fish with open air-bladders and projecting eyes that are divided in two, each part being specialized for seeing either in the water or out of it. Also called **four-eyed fish**. ⓒ 18c: from Greek *ana* up + *blepein* to look.

anabolic steroid /anə'bɒlɪk—/ ▷ *noun, biochem* any of various synthetic male sex hormones that promote tissue growth, prescribed to aid weight gain in the elderly and seriously ill, and sometimes used illegally in many sports to increase muscle bulk and strength. ⓒ 1960s: from ANABOLISM.

anabolism /ə'nabəlɪzəm/ ▷ *noun, biochem* in the cells of living organisms: the process whereby complex molecules such as proteins, fats and carbohydrates are manufactured from smaller molecules. • **anabolic** /anə'bɒlɪk/ *adj*. Compare CATABOLISM. ⓒ 19c: from Greek *ana* up + *bole* throw + -ISM 3.

anachronism /ə'nakrənɪzəm/ ▷ *noun* **1** the attribution of something to a historical period in which it did not exist. **2** a person, thing or attitude that is or appears to be out of date and old-fashioned. • **anachronistic** *adj*. • **anachronistically** *adverb*. ⓒ 17c: from Greek *ana* backwards + *chronos* time.

anacoluthia /anəkə'lu:θɪə, -'lju:θɪə/ ▷ *noun, rhetoric* a sentence where the second part does not fit grammatically with the first part. ⓒ 19c: from AN- + Greek *akolouthos* following.

anacoluthon /anəkə'lu:θən/ ▷ *noun* (***anacolutha*** /-ə/) *rhetoric* an instance of anacoluthia. ⓒ 18c: from AN- + Greek *akolouthos* following.

anaconda /anə'kɒndə/ ▷ *noun* the largest snake, a non-venomous constrictor of the BOA family, native to tropical S America, which has an olive green body covered with large round black spots. ⓒ 17c.

anaemia or **anemia** /ə'ni:mɪə/ ▷ *noun, pathol* an abnormal reduction in the amount of the oxygen-carrying pigment HAEMOGLOBIN in the red blood cells, characterized by pallid skin, fatigue and breathlessness, and caused by blood loss, iron deficiency, destruction of or impaired production of red blood cells, etc. ⓒ 19c: from AN- + Greek *haima* blood.

anaemic ▷ *adj* **1** suffering from anaemia. **2** pale or weak. **3** spiritless; lacking in energy. • **anaemically** *adverb*. ⓒ 19c.

anaerobe /'anəroub/ ▷ *noun, biol* any organism that does not require oxygen in order to obtain energy from the breakdown of carbohydrates or other foodstuffs by the process of respiration, or that cannot survive in the presence of oxygen. Compare AEROBE. ⓒ 19c: from French *anaerobie*.

anaerobic /anə'roubɪk/ ▷ *adj, biol* **1** denoting an organism, especially a bacterium, that does not require oxygen in order to obtain energy from the breakdown of carbohydrates or other foodstuffs by the process of respiration, or that cannot survive in the presence of oxygen. **2** *biochem* denoting a form of respiration in which oxygen is not required for the breakdown of foodstuffs, especially of carbohydrates. Compare AEROBIC. ⓒ 19c.

anaerobiosis /anɛəroubaɪ'ousɪs/ ▷ *noun* life in the absence of oxygen.

anaesthesia or (*US*) **anesthesia** /anɪs'θi:zɪə/ and **anaesthesis** or (*US*) **anesthesis** /anɪs'θi:sɪs/ ▷ *noun* **1** a reversible loss of sensation in all or part of the body, usually induced by drugs which may be inhaled or injected intravenously, but sometimes induced by acupuncture or hypnosis. **2** partial or complete loss of sensation, caused by disease or injury. ⓒ 18c: from AN- + Greek *aisthesis* feeling.

anaesthetic or (*US*) **anesthetic** /anəs'θɛtɪk/ ▷ *noun* any agent, especially a drug, capable of producing anaesthesia. See also GENERAL ANAESTHETIC, LOCAL ANAESTHETIC. ▷ *adj* denoting an agent or procedure (eg acupuncture) that is capable of producing anaesthesia in this way. • **anaesthetically** *adverb*. ⓒ 19c.

anaesthetist /ən'i:sθətɪst/ or (*US*) **anesthetist** /ə'nɛs-/ ▷ *noun* **1** *Brit* a medically qualified doctor who is trained to administer anaesthetics. *US equivalent* **anesthesiologist** /anɪsθi:zɪ'ɒlədʒɪst/. **2** *US* someone, often a nurse, who has been specifically trained in the administration of anaesthetics to patients. ⓒ 19c.

anaesthetize, **anaesthetise** /ə'ni:sθətaɪz/ or (*US*) **anesthetize** /ə'nɛs-/ ▷ *verb* (***anaesthetized***, ***anaesthetizing***) to give an anaesthetic to someone. • **anaesthetization** *noun*. ⓒ 19c.

anaglyph /'anəglɪf/ ▷ *noun* **1** an ornament, such as a cameo, in low relief. **2** *photog* a picture that is made up of two prints of the same thing taken from slightly different angles in complementary colours, usually red and green, so that, when it is looked at through glasses with a lens of each of these colours, a three-dimensional effect is produced. ⓒ 17c in sense 1; late 19c in sense 2: from Greek *anaglyphos* in low relief.

anaglypta /anə'glɪptə/ ▷ *noun* plain white wallpaper with a raised, usually geometric, pattern on it, which is often painted over. ⓒ 19c: Latin, meaning 'in low relief', originally a trademark.

anagnorisis /anag'nɔ:rɪsɪs/ ▷ *noun* (***anagnorises*** /-si:s/) a *dénouement*, especially in classical Greek tragedy but now used more loosely, extending even to popular genres like the detective novel, where the protagonist recognizes someone or makes some discovery that is vital to the resolution of the plot. ⓒ Early 18c: Greek, meaning 'recognition'.

anagram /'anəgram/ ▷ *noun* a word, phrase or sentence that is formed by changing the order of the letters of another word, phrase or sentence. Compare PALINDROME. ⓒ 16c: from Greek *ana* back + *gramma* a letter.

anal /'eɪnəl/ ▷ *adj* **1** relating to or in the region of the anus. **2** *psychoanal* **a** belonging to the period of a child's development that involves an increased focus on the anus and excretion and which, in FREUDIAN theory, is believed to follow the ORAL stage and to precede the PHALLIC and GENITAL stages; **b** showing a predilection towards being preoccupied with such things as getting one's own way, tidiness, cleanliness, money, etc which, in Freudian theory, is thought to have its roots in a fixation at the anal stage in childhood. **3** *informal* fastidious, over-fussy, pedantic. • **anally** *adverb* □ ***anally retentive***. ⓒ 19c: from ANUS + -AL 1.

analgesia /anəl'dʒi:zɪə, -sɪə/ ▷ *noun, physiol* a reduction in or loss of the ability to feel pain, without loss of consciousness or deadening of sensation, either deliberately induced by pain-killing drugs, eg aspirin, or a symptom of diseased or damaged nerves. ⓒ 18c: from AN- + Greek *algeein* to feel pain.

analgesic /anəl'dʒi:zɪk, -sɪk/ ▷ *noun* any drug or other agent that relieves pain, eg paracetamol, morphine. ▷ *adj* having the effect of relieving pain. ⓒ 18c.

analog an alternative *US* spelling of ANALOGUE.

analogical and **analogically** see under ANALOGY

analogize or **analogise** /ə'nalədgaɪz/ ▷ *verb* (***analogized***, ***analogizing***) to use analogy, especially in order to clarify a point or for rhetorical effect. ⓒ 17c: from ANALOGY + -IZE.

analogous /ə'naləgəs/ ▷ *adj* **1** similar or alike in some way. **2** *biol* denoting plant or animal structures that are similar in function, but have evolved completely independently of each other in different plant or animal groups, eg the wings of insects and birds. Compare HOMOLOGOUS. • **analogously** *adverb*. • **analogousness** *noun*. • **be analogous to something** to have similar characteristics to it or to function in the same way as it. ◷ 17c: from Latin *analogus*, from Greek *analogos* proportionate.

analogue or (*US*) **analog** /'anəlɒg/ ▷ *noun* **1** something regarded in terms of its similarity or parallelism to something else. **2** *biol* any organ or part of an animal or plant that is similar in function, though not in origin, to an organ or part in a different organism. **3** *chem* a chemical compound, especially a drug, that differs slightly in structure and properties from its parent compound, and is often used because it has fewer side-effects, is more potent, etc. ▷ *adj* said of a device or physical quantity: changing continuously rather than in a series of discrete steps, and therefore capable of being represented by an electric voltage □ ***analogue computer***. Compare DIGITAL. ◷ Early 19c: from Greek *analogos* proportionate.

analogue computer or **analog computer** ▷ *noun, computing* a computer in which data is stored and processed in the form of continually varying signals representing the changing size of a physical quantity, rather than in the form of individual numerical values. Compare DIGITAL COMPUTER.

analogue-to-digital converter ▷ *noun* (abbreviation **ADC**) an integrated circuit that allows a digital computer to accept and make use of data from an analogue device.

analogy /ə'nalədʒɪ/ ▷ *noun* (***analogies***) **1** a likeness or similarity in some ways. **2** a way of reasoning which makes it possible to explain one thing or event by comparing it with something else. **3** *linguistics* an imitation of a linguistic pattern already prominent elsewhere, eg when a child says *foots* instead of *feet* it is due to an analogy with the regular plural formation of adding *-s* to the singular form. • **analogical** *adj*. • **analogically** *adverb*. ◷ 16c: from Greek *analogia*, from *analogos* proportionate.

analysand /ə'nalɪzand/ ▷ *noun, psychoanal* someone who is being psychoanalyzed.

analyse or (*US*) **analyze** /'anəlaɪz/ ▷ *verb* (***analysed, analysing***) **1** to examine the structure or content of something in detail, eg to examine data in order to discover the general principles underlying a particular phenomenon. **2** to resolve or separate something into its component parts. **3** to detect and identify the different chemical compounds present in (a mixture), or to determine the relative proportions of the different components in (a mixture). **4** to psychoanalyse someone. ◷ 18c: from Greek *ana* up + *lyein* to loosen.

analysis /ə'nalɪsɪs/ ▷ *noun* (***analyses*** /-siːz/) **1** a detailed examination of the structure and content of something. **2** a statement of the results of such an examination. **3** short for PSYCHOANALYSIS. • **in the final** or **last analysis** after everything has been considered. ◷ 16c: from Greek *ana* up + *lyein* to loosen.

analysis of variance ▷ *noun, statistics* a widely-used procedure to separate the different factors which cause variance.

analyst /'anəlɪst/ ▷ *noun* **1** someone who is skilled in analysis, especially chemical, political or economic. **2** short form of **psychoanalyst** (see PSYCHOANALYSIS).

analytic /anə'lɪtɪk/ and **analytical** ▷ *adj* **1** concerning or involving analysis. **2** examining or able to examine things in detail to learn or make judgements about them. • **analytically** *adverb*.

analytical geometry see COORDINATE GEOMETRY

analytic language ▷ *noun, linguistics* a language such as Chinese or Samoan in which grammatical function is indicated by word order rather than by inflection.

analytic philosophy ▷ *noun* a movement of the first half of the 20c, particularly associated with Bertrand Russell and the early work of Ludwig Wittgenstein, in which the analysis of language is held to be the basis for the resolution of philosophical issues.

anamnesis /anam'niːsɪs/ ▷ *noun* (***anamneses*** /-siːz/) **1** the ability to remember past events; recollection. **2** someone's own account of their medical history. • **anamnestic** *adj*. ◷ Late 19c: from Greek *anamimneskein* to recall.

anamorphic lens /anə'mɔːfɪk —/ ▷ *noun* **1** a device incorporated into a film projector that converts standard 35mm film format into a widescreen image. **2** *cinematog* a camera lens that condenses a widescreen image so that it will fit on to a standard 35mm film. ◷ 1950s: from ANAMORPHOSIS.

anamorphosis /anə'mɔːfəsɪs, anəmɔː'foʊsɪs/ ▷ *noun* (***anamorphoses*** /-siːz/) in drawing and painting: an image executed in trick perspective so that it is distorted when seen from a normal viewpoint but appears in normal proportion when seen from a particular angle, or reflected in a curved mirror. ◷ 18c: Greek, meaning 'a transformation'.

anapaest /'anəpiːst/ ▷ *noun* in verse: a metrical foot that consists of two short or unstressed syllables followed by a long or stressed one. • **anapaestic** *adj*. ◷ 16c: from Greek *anapaistos*, literally 'reversed', because this kind of foot is the reverse of the DACTYL.

anaphase /'anəfeɪz/ ▷ *noun, genetics* the stage of MITOSIS during which the chromosomes move to opposite ends of the cell by means of a spindle composed of protein fibres that is formed in the cytoplasm. See also METAPHASE, PROPHASE, TELOPHASE. ◷ 19c: from Greek *ana* up or back + PHASE.

anaphora /ə'nafərə/ ▷ *noun* **1** *rhetoric* the repetition of a word or group of words at the start of a sequence of clauses, sentences, lines of poetry, etc. **2** *grammar* the use of another, usually smaller, unit of language to refer to something that has already been mentioned (the ANTECEDENT), eg in the sentence *Peter isn't here - he left an hour ago*, instead of repeating *Peter*, the pronoun *he* is used. • **anaphoric** /anə'fɒrɪk/ *adj* □ ***anaphoric reference***. ◷ 1930s in sense 2; 16c in sense 1: Greek, from *ana* back + *pherein* to bear.

anaphylaxis /anafɪ'laksɪs/ ▷ *noun, medicine* a sudden severe hypersensitive reaction to the injection of a particular foreign substance or antigen, eg certain drugs, into the body of a person who has already been exposed to that substance and is abnormally sensitive to it. • **anaphylactic** *adj*. ◷ Early 20c: from Greek *ana* back + *phylaxis* protection.

anarchist /'anəkɪst/ ▷ *noun* **1** someone who believes that governments and laws are unnecessary and should be abolished, and that society would function perfectly well if it were based on some unwritten agreement that each individual's talents were put to good co-operative use. **2** someone who tries to overthrow the government by violence. **3** someone who tries to cause disorder of any kind. • **anarchism** *noun*. • **anarchistic** *adj*. • **anarchistically** *adverb*. ◷ 17c: from ANARCHY.

anarchy /'anəkɪ/ ▷ *noun* **1 a** confusion and lack of order because of the failure or breakdown of law and government; **b** confusion and lack of order of any kind. **2** the absence of law and government without any implication of ensuing chaos, where the traditional hierarchical systems are replaced by an unwritten agreement that each individual's talents, rights, liberties, etc should be highly valued. **3** a spurning or disavowal of the importance of authority of any kind. • **anarchic** /an'ɑːkɪk/ *adj*. • **anarchically** *adverb*. ◷ 16c: from Greek *anarchia* lack of a ruler.

anastrophe see INVERSION sense 5

anathema /ə'naθəmə/ ▷ *noun* (***anathemas***) **1** someone or something that is detested or abhorred. **2** *Christianity* a person or doctrine that has been cursed or denounced. **3** a curse. ⓘ 16c: Latin, meaning 'an excommunicated person', from Greek, meaning 'an offering'.

anathematize or **anathematise** /ə'naθəmətaɪz/ ▷ *verb* (***anathematized***, ***anathematizing***) to curse or denounce. • **anathematization** *noun*. ⓘ 16c.

Anatolian /anə'toʊlɪən/ ▷ *noun* a group of extinct languages, including Hittite, spoken c.2 000BC in Anatolia, an area now in present-day Turkey and Syria. ▷ *adj* relating to this group of languages.

anatomist /ə'natəmɪst/ ▷ *noun* a scientist who specializes in anatomy.

anatomy /ə'natəmɪ/ ▷ *noun* (***anatomies***) **1** the scientific study of the structure of living organisms, including humans, especially as determined by dissection and microscopic examination. **2** the art of dissection. **3** the physical structure of an organism, especially the internal structure. **4** any close examination, analysis or study of something. **5** *non-technical* someone's body. • **anatomical** /anə'tɒmɪkəl/ *adj*. • **anatomically** *adverb*. ⓘ 14c: from Greek *ana* up + *temnein* to cut.

ANC ▷ *abbreviation* African National Congress.

-ance /əns/ ▷ *suffix, forming nouns, denoting* a state, quality, condition or action □ *abundance* □ *performance*. ⓘ From French *-ance*, from Latin *-antia*.

ancestor /'ansəstə(r)/ ▷ *noun* **1** someone, usually more distant than a grandparent, from whom a person is directly descended. **2** a plant or animal that another type of plant or animal has evolved from. **3** something thought of as a forerunner □ *the camera obscura, ancestor of the cinema*. ⓘ 13c: from Latin *antecessor*, from *ante* before + *cedere* to go.

ancestral /an'sɛstrəl/ ▷ *adj* belonging to or inherited from one's ancestors □ *the ancestral home*.

ancestry /'ansɪstrɪ/ ▷ *noun* (***ancestries***) lineage or family descent, especially when it can be traced back over many generations.

anchor /'aŋkə(r)/ ▷ *noun* **1** a heavy piece of metal attached by a cable to a ship and put overboard so that the barbs catch in the seabed or riverbed to restrict the ship's movement. **2** anything that acts as a weight to secure something else. **3** anything that gives security or stability. **4** *athletics* the last person to run in a relay race. **5** *TV, radio* the person in the studio who provides the links with outside broadcast reporters, between commercial breaks, etc. ▷ *verb* (***anchored***, ***anchoring***) **1** to fasten (a ship) using an anchor. **2** to fasten anything securely. **3** *intr* to drop an anchor and become moored by it; to be moored by an anchor. **4** *TV, radio* to sit in a studio and provide the links with outside broadcast reporters, between commercial breaks, etc. • **at anchor** said of a ship: secured by an anchor. • **cast anchor** to put an anchor overboard in order to restrict a ship's movement. • **ride at anchor** said of a ship: to have a restricted amount of movement because its anchor is in use. • **weigh anchor** to raise a ship's anchor in order to allow it to sail. ⓘ Anglo-Saxon *ancor*.

anchorage ▷ *noun* **1** a place where a ship may anchor. **2** a safe place in which to rest. **3** the act of anchoring. **4** the fee charged for the use of an anchoring place.

anchorite /aŋkə'rait/ ▷ *noun* someone who lives alone or separate from other people, usually for religious reasons. ⓘ 15c: from Greek *anachoretes*, from *anachorein* to withdraw.

anchorman see ANCHOR *noun* 4 and 5.

anchovy /'antʃəvɪ, an'tʃoʊvɪ/ ▷ *noun* (***anchovies***) any of numerous species of small fish related to the herring, with a pungent flavour, widely used as a garnish, and as a flavouring for fish pastes and other foods. ⓘ 16c: from Spanish *anchoa* and Portuguese *anchova* a small fish.

ancien régime / *French* ɑ̃sjɛ̃ reʒim/ ▷ *noun* (***anciens régimes*** /ɑ̃sjɛ̃ reʒim/) **1** the French political, social and royal systems that were in place before the Revolution of 1789. **2** any outmoded system. ⓘ 18c: French, meaning 'old rule'.

ancient /'eɪnʃənt/ ▷ *adj* **1** dating from very long ago. **2** very old. **3** dating from before the end of the Western Roman Empire in 476 AD. Compare MEDIEVAL, MODERN 1. ▷ *noun* **1** (*usually* **ancients**) people who lived in ancient times, especially the Greeks, Romans and Hebrews. **2** *archaic* a very old person, usually a male, who is venerated for his supposed wisdom. • **anciently** *adverb*. ⓘ 14c: from French *ancien* old.

ancient Briton see BRITON

Ancient Greek see GREEK

ancient history ▷ *noun* **1** the history of the countries surrounding the Mediterranean Sea, especially Greece, Asia Minor, Italy and Egypt, especially that prior to the end of the Western Roman Empire in AD 476. **2** *colloq* information, news, etc that has been well known for a long time.

ancient monument ▷ *noun* any edifice deemed to be of historical interest, and usually under the protection of the government.

ancillary /an'sɪlərɪ/ ▷ *adj* **1** helping or giving support to something else, eg medical services. **2** being used as an extra. ▷ *noun* someone or something used as support or back-up. ⓘ 17c: from Latin *ancillaris*, from *ancilla* maidservant.

-ancy /ənsɪ/ ▷ *suffix* forming nouns corresponding to adjectives in -ANT □ *expectancy* □ *vacancy*. ⓘ from Latin *-antia*.

AND ▷ *abbreviation, IVR* Andorra.

and /and, ənd, ən/ ▷ *conj* **1 a** used to show addition: □ *dogs and cats*; **b** used in sums of addition: □ *two and two make four*. **2 a** used to connect an action that follows as a result or reason of a previous one: □ *fall and bang one's head*; **b** used to connect an action that follows sequentially on from another: □ *boil the kettle and make the tea*. **3** used to show repetition or duration: □ *She cried and cried*. **4** used to show progression: □ *The crowd got bigger and bigger*. **5** used to show variety or contrast: □ *discussed the ins and outs of it*. **6** used after some verbs instead of *to*: □ *come and try* □ *go and get it*. ▷ *noun* an unspecified problem or matter □ *no ifs or ands about it*. ⓘ Anglo-Saxon.

and

Although it is sometimes regarded as poor style, it is not ungrammatical to begin a sentence with **and.** Indeed, many writers have done so with considerable effect. It is also common in conversation and in forms of English in which a looser grammatical structure is appropriate.

andalusite /andə'lu:saɪt/ ▷ *noun, geol* a variety of mineral aluminium silicate found in metamorphic rocks, which is an important indicator of the pressure and temperature of metamorphism in rocks. ⓘ 19c: from Andalusia in Spain where it was first found + -ITE 4.

andante /an'dantɪ, -teɪ/ *music* ▷ *adverb, adj* in a slow, steady manner. ▷ *noun* a piece of music to be played in this way. ⓘ 18c: Italian, from *andare* to go.

andiron /'andaɪən/ ▷ *noun* a decorated iron bar, usually one of a pair, for supporting logs and coal in a big fireplace. ⓘ 14c: from French *andier*.

and/or ▷ *conj* either or both of two possibilities stated □ *cakes and/or biscuits*.

andro- /androʊ, an'drɒ/ or (before a vowel) **andr-** ▷ *combining form, denoting* male. ⓘ From Greek *andro-* male.

androecium /an'dri:sɪəm/ ▷ *noun* (***androecia*** /-sɪə/) *bot* the male reproductive parts of a flower, consisting of the stamens. ⓘ 19c: from ANDRO- + Greek *oikion* house.

androgen /ˈandrədʒən/ ▷ *noun* **1** *physiol* any of a group of steroid hormones, produced mainly by the testes, that control the growth and functioning of the male sex organs and the appearance of male secondary sexual characteristics. **2** a synthetic form of any of these hormones. Compare OESTROGEN. ◷ 1930s.

androgynous /anˈdrɒdʒɪnəs/ ▷ *adj* **1** *biol* denoting an animal or plant that shows both male and female characteristics, especially one that possesses both male and female sex organs; hermaphrodite. **2** showing both male and female traits, eg a woman who resembles a man in outward appearance. ◷ 17c: from Greek *androgynos*, from *aner, andros* a man + *gyne* woman.

android /ˈandrɔɪd/ ▷ *noun* a robot that resembles a human being in form or features. ▷ *adj* relating to or resembling a human being. ◷ 18c.

andrology /anˈdrɒlədʒɪ/ ▷ *noun* the branch of medicine concerned with the diagnosis and treatment of diseases and disorders that affect the reproductive organs of the male body. ◷ 1980s: modelled on GYNAECOLOGY.

Andromeda galaxy /anˈdrɒmɪdə —/ and **Andromeda nebula** ▷ *noun, astron* a bright spiral galaxy in the constellation Andromeda, about 2.2m light years away from Earth, the largest of the nearby galaxies, the nearest to the Milky Way and the most distant object visible to the naked eye. ◷ 18c: named after Andromeda who, in Greek mythology, was the daughter of Cepheus and Cassiopeia.

-ane /eɪn/ ▷ *suffix, chem, forming nouns, denoting* a hydrocarbon derivative □ *propane*.

anecdotal /anəkˈdoutəl/ ▷ *adj* **1** consisting of or in the nature of anecdotes. **2** said of information, etc: based on chance accounts rather than first hand knowledge or experience. • **anecdotalist** *noun*. • **anecdotally** *adverb*. ◷ 19c.

anecdote /ˈanəkdout/ ▷ *noun* a short entertaining account of an incident. • **anecdotage** *noun*. • **anecdotist** *noun*. ◷ 17c: from Greek *anekdota* unpublished things.

anechoic /anəˈkouɪk/ ▷ *adj* **1** *physics* denoting a room, chamber, etc, in which there is little or no reflection of sound, and hence no echoes. **2** denoting wall tiles that absorb sound and so prevent reflection of sound waves by the wall. ◷ 1940s.

anemia an alternative *N Amer, especially US* spelling of ANAEMIA.

anemometer /anəˈmɒmɪtə(r)/ ▷ *noun* a device for measuring wind speed, used in meteorology, wind-tunnels, etc. Also called **wind gauge**. ◷ 18c: from Greek *anemos* wind + -METER 1.

anemone /əˈnɛmənɪ/ ▷ *noun* **1** *bot* any of several plants of the buttercup family, especially a cultivated species with red, purple, blue or white cup-shaped flowers on tall slender stems. **2** *zool* short form of SEA ANEMONE. ◷ 16c: Greek, meaning 'daughter of the wind'.

anencephaly /anənˈsɛfəlɪ, -ˈkɛfəlɪ/ ▷ *noun* the congenital absence of the brain or part of the brain. • **anencephalic** /-səˈfalɪk, -kə-/ *adj*. • **anencephalous** *adj*. ◷ 19c.

aneroid /ˈanərɔɪd/ ▷ *noun, meteorol* a type of barometer used to measure atmospheric pressure and to estimate altitude. Also called **aneroid barometer**. ◷ 19c: from A-[2] + Greek *neros* wet + -OID.

anesthesia an alternative *N Amer, especially US* spelling of ANAESTHESIA.

anesthesiologist *US* see ANAESTHETIST

anesthetic an alternative *N Amer, especially US* spelling of ANAESTHETIC

aneurysm or **aneurism** /ˈanjərɪzəm, ˈjʊə-/ ▷ *noun, pathol* a balloon-like swelling in the wall of an artery, caused by a congenital defect in the muscular wall, or by a disorder such as ARTERIOSCLEROSIS. • **aneurysmal** *adj*. ◷ 17c: from Greek *aneurysma*, from *ana* up + *eurynein* to widen.

anew /əˈnjuː/ ▷ *adverb* **1** once more, again. **2** in a different way. ◷ Anglo-Saxon *of niowe*.

angel /ˈeɪndʒəl/ ▷ *noun* **1 a** a messenger or attendant of God; **b** in the traditional medieval hierarchy of nine ranks of angels: a member of the ninth (lowest) rank of such beings. Compare SERAPH, CHERUB, THRONE, DOMINION, VIRTUE, POWER, PRINCIPALITY, ARCHANGEL. **2** a representation of this in the form of a human being with a halo and wings. **3** *colloq* a good, helpful, pure or beautiful person. **4** *colloq* someone who puts money into an enterprise, particularly a theatrical production. **5** *colloq* someone who works in the nursing profession. **6** *colloq* short for HELL'S ANGEL. ◷ Anglo-Saxon: from Greek *angelos* messenger.

angel cake and **angel food cake** ▷ *noun, US* a light sponge cake.

angel dust ▷ *noun, drug-taking slang* the street name of the hallucinogenic drug PCP, abuse of which can lead to serious psychological disturbances. ◷ 1960s.

angelfish ▷ *noun* **1** any of various unrelated fishes, so called because their pectoral fins resemble wings. **2** any of various S American freshwater fishes of this type, popular in tropical aquaria, which have a very deep body, flattened from side to side and covered with dark vertical stripes, and elongated pectoral fins. **3** any of various small brightly coloured marine fishes with a deep body and a sharp backward-pointing spine on the gill cover. **4** the monkfish.

angelic /anˈdʒɛlɪk/ ▷ *adj* said of someone's face, expression, temperament, behaviour, etc: like that of an angel, especially in being pure, innocent, beautiful, etc. • **angelically** *adverb*.

angelica /anˈdʒɛlɪkə/ ▷ *noun* **1** any of various tall perennial plants with leaves divided into oval leaflets, and clusters of white or greenish flowers. **2** pieces of the young stem and leaf stalks of this plant, crystallized in sugar and used as a food flavouring and cake decoration. ◷ 16c: from Latin *herba angelica* angelic herb.

angel shark see MONKFISH

angels on horseback ▷ *plural noun* oysters wrapped in slices of bacon, grilled until crisp and served on toast.

angelus /ˈandʒələs/ ▷ *noun, Christianity* **1** a Roman Catholic prayer said in the morning, at noon and at sunset, in honour of the Incarnation. **2** a bell rung to announce these prayers. ◷ 18c: from Latin *Angelus domini* the angel of the Lord, the opening words of the prayer.

anger /ˈaŋgə(r)/ ▷ *noun* a feeling of great displeasure or annoyance, usually brought on by some real or perceived injustice, injury, etc. ▷ *verb* (***angered***, ***angering***) to cause this kind of feeling in someone; to displease. ◷ 13c: from Norse *angr* trouble.

angina /anˈdʒaɪnə/ ▷ *noun, pathol* **1** severe pain behind the chest-bone, often spreading to the left shoulder and arm, usually induced by insufficient blood supply to the heart muscle during exertion, which is commonly caused by thickening of the artery walls. Also called **angina pectoris**. **2** inflammation of the throat. ◷ 18c in sense 1; 16c in sense 2: from Latin *angina* a throat disease, from *angere* to choke.

angio- /andʒiəʊ, andʒɪˈɒ/ or (*before a vowel*) **angi-** /ˈandʒi/ ▷ *combining form, denoting* some kind of vessel, eg one that carries blood or lymph or which contains seeds □ *angiogram* □ *angiosperm*. ◷ From Greek *angeion* a vessel.

angiogenesis ▷ *noun, physiol* the growth of new blood vessels, eg in the developing embryo, in a tumour, etc. ◷ 19c.

angiogram ▷ *noun, medicine* a type of x-ray photograph that is achieved by ANGIOGRAPHY. ◷ 1930s.

angiography /andʒɪ'ɒgrəfɪ/ ▷ *noun, medicine* the examination and recording of the condition of blood vessels by x-ray after they have had some agent such as iodine injected into them so that the vessels are more clearly defined. ◷ 1930s.

angioma ▷ *noun, pathol* a benign tumour composed of a mass of blood or lymphatic vessels. ◷ 19c.

angiosperm /'andʒɪoʊspɜːm/ ▷ *noun, bot* any member of a division of plants that characteristically produce flowers and bear ovules that develop into seeds which are enclosed within an ovary the wall of which develops into a fruit. Compare GYMNOSPERM. ◷ 19c: from ANGIO- + Greek *sperma* seed.

Angle /'aŋgəl/ ▷ *noun* a member of a N German tribe who settled in N and E England in the 5c, forming the kingdoms of Northumbria, Mercia and East Anglia, whose name was subsequently given to 'England' and 'English'. See also SAXON, ANGLO-SAXON. ◷ Anglo-Saxon *engle* the people of *Angulus*, a district of Holstein so called because of its hook shape.

angle^1 /'aŋgəl/ ▷ *noun* **1** *math* a measure of the rotation of a line about a point, usually measured in degrees, radians or revolutions. **2** the point where two lines or planes intersect. **3** the extent to which one line slopes away from another. **4** a corner. **5** a point of view; an aspect; a way of considering or being involved in something. ▷ *verb* (***angled, angling***) **1** *tr & intr* to move in or place at an angle. **2** to present a news story, information, etc from a particular point of view. ◷ 14c: from Latin *angulum* a corner.

angle^2 /'aŋgəl/ ▷ *verb* (***angled, angling***) to use a rod and line for catching fish. ◷ Anglo-Saxon *angul* hook.

■ **angle for something** to try to get it in a devious or indirect way □ *angled for an invitation to the party.*

angle bracket ▷ *noun* either of the symbols < or >, used in a variety of fields, eg mathematics, science, linguistics, editing, etc, where the left-pointing one is used to indicate the beginning of some statement or formula and the right-pointing one its end.

angle iron, angle and **angle bar** ▷ *noun* an L-shaped piece of iron or steel used in structural work.

angle of incidence ▷ *noun, physics* the angle between a ray, eg a light ray, that strikes a surface, eg glass, and a line drawn perpendicular to that surface at the point where the ray strikes the surface.

angle of reflection ▷ *noun, physics* the angle between a ray, eg a light ray, leaving a reflecting surface, eg glass, and a line drawn perpendicular to that surface at the point where the ray leaves the surface.

angle of refraction ▷ *noun, physics* the angle between a ray, eg a light ray, that is refracted at an interface between two different media, eg water and glass, and a line drawn perpendicular to that interface at the point where the ray is refracted.

anglepoise /'aŋgəlpɔɪz/ ▷ *noun* a reading lamp that can be put into a variety of different positions. Also called **anglepoise lamp**. ◷ 1940s.

angler ▷ *noun* **1** someone who fishes with a rod and line. **2** any of several different varieties of fish which either have spiny dorsal fins, often luminous, specially adapted to lure their prey, or which have long filaments around the area of the head and mouth, used to capture their prey. Also called **angler fish**.

Anglican /'aŋglɪkən/ ▷ *adj* relating to the Church of England or another Church in communion with it. ▷ *noun* a member of an Anglican Church. • **Anglicanism** *noun*. ◷ 13c: from Latin *Anglicanus*, from *Anglus* English.

Anglicism /'aŋglɪsɪzəm/ ▷ *noun* **1** an English word, phrase or idiom, especially one that slips into a sentence in another language. **2** a custom or characteristic that is peculiar to the English. ◷ 17c: from ANGLICIZE + -ISM 6.

anglicize or **anglicise** /'aŋglɪsaɪz/ ▷ *verb* (***anglicized, anglicizing***) to make something English in form or character. • **anglicization** *noun*. ◷ 18c: from Latin *Anglus* English.

angling ▷ *noun* the action or sport of catching fish with rod, line and hook, eg freshwater fishing, fly fishing, game fishing, coarse fishing and deep sea fishing. ◷ 15c.

Anglo /'aŋgloʊ/ ▷ *noun* (***Anglos***) **1** someone who is neither black nor of Latin-American descent, especially in the US. **2** an English-speaking Canadian. ◷ 1940s in sense 1; 1800 in sense 2.

Anglo- /'aŋgloʊ/ ▷ *combining form, denoting* **1** English □ *Anglophobic*. **2** British □ *Anglo-American*. ◷ 16c: from Latin *Anglus* English.

Anglo-Catholic ▷ *noun* a member of an Anglican Church which emphasizes the Church's Catholic traditions. Also *as adj*. • **Anglo-Catholicism** *noun*.

Anglocentric ▷ *adj* having a focus that is skewed in favour of things that are English or British, especially to the exclusion of other things. ◷ 19c.

Anglo-Indian ▷ *noun* **1** someone of British descent who has lived in India for a long time. **2** someone of mixed English and Indian descent. Also *as adj*.

Anglo-Irish ▷ *adj* **1 a** referring or relating to the community of people living in Ireland who are of English descent; **b** (**the Anglo-Irish**) such people as a group (see THE 4b). **2** referring or relating to anything that is of joint concern to the English or British and the Irish. ▷ *noun* the variety of English spoken in Ireland.

Anglo-Irish Agreement ▷ *noun* an agreement signed in 1985 between the British and the Irish governments, but bitterly opposed by Ulster Unionists, which stated that there would be regular consultation and exchange of information on all matters of political, legal and security importance and that there would never be any change in N Ireland's constitutional status without recourse to the people of the Republic.

Anglo-Norman ▷ *noun* **1** a blending of Norman French and English, used in England for around two centuries after the conquest, mainly to facilitate commercial transactions between the Normans and the natives. **2** someone of Norman descent who settled in England, Scotland or Wales after 1066. Also *as adj*. ◷ 18c.

anglophile or **Anglophile** /'aŋgloʊfaɪl/ ▷ *noun* someone who admires England and the English. • **anglophilia** /-'fɪlɪə/ *noun*. ◷ 1860s.

anglophobe or **Anglophobe** /'aŋgloʊfoʊb/ ▷ *noun* someone who hates or fears England and the English. • **anglophobia** *noun*. ◷ 18c.

anglophone or **Anglophone** /'aŋgloʊfoʊn/ **1** *noun* someone who speaks English, especially in a context where other languages are also spoken. ▷ *adj* belonging or relating to English-speaking people, countries, etc. ◷ 20c.

Anglo-Saxon /aŋgloʊ'saksən/ ▷ *noun* **1** a member of any of the Germanic tribes, the ANGLES, the JUTES and the SAXONS, who settled in England in the 5c and formed the HEPTARCHY of Essex, Wessex, Sussex, Kent, East Anglia, Mercia and Northumbria. **2** the English language before about 1150. Also called **Old English**. **3** English as thought of in terms of its plain, usually monosyllabic, words including most of the taboo ones. **4** any English-speaking White person, usually one of Germanic descent. ▷ *adj* **1 a** belonging or relating to the Germanic peoples who settled in England; **b** belonging or relating to the early form of the English language. **2** said of any English speech or writing: blunt and to the point; tending to avoid longer polysyllabic words. **3** belonging or relating to the shared cultural, legal, political, etc aspects of British and American life ▫ *traditional Anglo-Saxon values.* ◷ Anglo-Saxon, as plural noun *Angulseaxan*; 8c Latin *Angli Saxones*.

angora or **Angora** /aŋˈɡɔːrə/ ▻ *noun* the wool or cloth made from the soft silky wool of the Angora goat. ▻ *adj* **1** denoting a breed of domestic goat that originated in Turkey, but is now widely bred for its soft silky wool, known as mohair. **2** denoting a breed of rabbit, native to the island of Madeira, that produces fine white silky wool. **3** denoting a breed of domestic cat, not recognized in the UK, with a long smooth white coat, a long body, pointed head and full tail. ◷ Early 19c: an earlier form (used until 1930) of the name Ankara, capital of Turkey.

angostura bitters /aŋɡəsˈtjʊərə —/ ▻ *noun, trademark* a blend of GENTIAN and herbs, used as a flavouring in cocktails and other alcoholic drinks, and some fruit juices. ◷ 1870s: named after Angostura, now called Ciudad Bolivar, a town in Venezuela where it was first made.

angry /ˈaŋɡrɪ/ ▻ *adj* (***angrier***, ***angriest***) **1** feeling or showing annoyance, resentment, wrath, disapproval, etc. **2** irritable, cross, ill-tempered, etc ▫ *an angry expression.* **3** said of a wound, rash, etc: red and sore. **4** dark and stormy ▫ *an angry sky.* • **angrily** *adverb*. • **be angry about something** to feel or express annoyance over it. • **be angry at something** or **someone** to be irritated by or indignant about it or them. • **be angry with someone or something** to feel or express displeasure, disappointment, etc towards them or it. ◷ 14c: from ANGER.

angst /aːŋst/ ▻ *noun* **1** a feeling of apprehension, anxiety or foreboding. **2** in EXISTENTIALISM: a feeling of alarm that stems from the realization that the course one's life takes is one's own responsibility rather than being predetermined. **3** *in compounds* ▫ *angst-ridden.* ◷ 19c: German and Danish, meaning 'fear'.

angstrom or **ångstrom** /ˈaŋstrəm/ ▻ *noun* (symbol **Å**) a unit of length equal to 10^{-10}m, formerly used to measure wavelengths of electromagnetic radiation and the sizes of molecules and atoms, but in the SI system now replaced by the NANOMETRE. ◷ 19c: named after the Swedish physicist Anders J Ångström (1814-1874).

anguish /ˈaŋɡwɪʃ/ ▻ *noun* severe mental distress or torture. ▻ *verb* (***anguishes***, ***anguished***, ***anguishing***) *tr & intr* to suffer or cause to suffer severe mental distress or torture. ◷ 13c: from Latin *angustia* tightness.

angular /ˈaŋɡjʊlə(r)/ ▻ *adj* **1** said of someone or part of someone's body, etc: thin and bony. **2** said of actions, movement, etc: awkward or ungainly. **3** having sharp edges or corners. **4** measured by an angle ▫ *angular distance.* • **angularly** *adverb*. • **angularity** *noun*. ◷ 16c: from Latin *angularis*.

angular momentum ▻ *noun, physics* for a particle moving about an axis: the product of its angular velocity and its moment of inertia about the axis of rotation.

anhydride /anˈhaɪdraɪd/ ▻ *noun, chem* any chemical compound formed by the removal of water from another compound, especially an acid. ◷ 19c: AN- + HYDRIDE.

anhydrous /anˈhaɪdrəs/ ▻ *adj* denoting a chemical compound that contains no water, especially one that lacks water of crystallization ▫ *anhydrous copper sulphate.* ◷ Early 19c: AN- + HYDROUS.

aniconic /anaɪˈkɒnɪk/ ▻ *adj* said of imagery of gods, etc: not in recognizable animal or human form. • **aniconism** *noun*. • **aniconist** *noun*. ◷ 19c.

anil /ˈanɪl/ ▻ *noun* **1** a leguminous W Indian plant from which indigo is obtained. **2** the indigo dye itself. ◷ 18c: from Arabic *al* the + *nila* dark blue.

aniline /ˈanɪlɪn, ˈanɪliːn/ ▻ *noun* a colourless oily highly toxic liquid organic compound, used in the manufacture of rubber, plastics, drugs, dyes and photographic chemicals. ◷ 19c: from ANIL.

anima /ˈanɪmə/ ▻ *noun, psychol* **1** a Jungian term for the 'inner' personality as opposed to the personality presented in public. **2** a Jungian term for the feminine side of the male unconscious. Compare ANIMUS. ◷ 1920s: Latin, meaning 'spirit' or 'soul'.

animadvert /anɪmadˈvɜːt/ ▻ *verb* (***animadverted***, ***animadverting***) *tr & intr* (*often* **animadvert upon something**) to criticize or censure it. • **animadversion** *noun*. ◷ 16c: from Latin *animadvertere* to turn the mind to something.

animal /ˈanɪməl/ ▻ *noun* **1 a** *zool* any member of the kingdom of organisms that are capable of voluntary movement, have specialized sense organs that allow rapid response to stimuli, and lack chlorophyll and cell walls; **b** any of these excluding human beings. **2** someone who behaves in a rough uncivilized way. **3** *colloq* (*usually* **an altogether different animal**) a person or thing ▫ *This new multimedia PC is a completely different animal.* ▻ *adj* **1** belonging or relating to, from or like, an animal ▫ *free of animal fat.* **2** relating to physical desires; brutal; sensual ▫ *She found it hard to control her animal passions.* ◷ 14c: Latin, from *anima* breath.

animalcule /anɪˈmalkjuːl/ ▻ *noun* (***animalcules*** or ***animalcula*** /-lə/) *formerly* any microscopic animal, ie one that cannot be seen by the naked eye. ◷ 17c: from Latin *animalculum*, diminutive of *animal* animal.

animal experimentation ▻ *noun* any type of experiment performed on living animals, especially in order to test the effects of chemical compounds such as new drugs, cosmetics, food additives and pesticides.

animal husbandry ▻ *noun* the branch of agriculture concerned with the breeding, care and feeding of domestic animals.

animalism ▻ *noun* **1** a display of or obsession with anything that is physical as opposed to the spiritual or intellectual. **2** the belief that humans are no better than other animals. • **animalist** *noun*. ◷ 19c.

animality /anɪˈmalɪtɪ/ ▻ *noun* **1** someone's animal nature or behaviour. **2** the state of being an animal, especially a lower animal.

animalize or **animalise** ▻ *verb* (***animalized***, ***animalizing***) to make someone brutal or sensual. ◷ 19c.

animal kingdom ▻ *noun* **1** *biol* in the classification of living organisms: the rank which includes all ANIMALS (sense 1a). **2** all of the animals thought of collectively.

animal magnetism ▻ *noun, often facetious* the capacity to appear attractive, especially in a sexual way.

animal rights ▻ *noun* the rights of animals to exist without being exploited by humans.

animate ▻ *verb* /ˈanɪmeɪt/ **1** to give life to someone or something. **2** to make something lively. **3** to record (drawings) on film in such a way as to make the images seem to move. ▻ *adj* /ˈanɪmət/ alive. ◷ 16c: from Latin *animare* to breathe.

animated ▻ *adj* **1** lively; spirited ▫ *an animated discussion.* **2** living. **3** moving as if alive ▫ *animated cartoons.* • **animatedly** *adverb*.

animated cartoon see CARTOON 2

animation /anɪˈmeɪʃən/ ▻ *noun* **1** liveliness; vivacity. **2 a** the techniques used to record still drawings on film in such a way as to make the images seem to move; **b** any sequence of these images.

animator /ˈanɪmeɪtə(r)/ ▻ *noun* someone who makes the original drawings that will be put together to produce an animated film or cartoon.

animatronics /anɪməˈtrɒnɪks/ ▻ *singular noun, cinematog* in film-making: the art of animating a life-like figure of a person, animal, etc, by means of computer technology.

animism /ˈanɪmɪzəm/ ▻ *noun* the belief that plants and natural phenomena such as rivers, mountains, etc have souls. • **animist** *noun*. • **animistic** *adj*. ◷ 19c: from Latin *anima* soul.

animosity /anɪˈmɒsɪtɪ/ ▻ *noun* (***animosities***) a strong dislike or hatred. • **animosity between two people** or **groups** a mutual loathing that exists between them □ *The animosity between the two brothers was long-standing.* ◷ 17c; 15c in the obsolete sense 'spiritedness' or 'bravery': from Latin *animositas*, from *animosus* spirited or hot-tempered.

animus /ˈanɪməs/ ▻ *noun* **1** a feeling of strong dislike or hatred. **2** *psychol* a Jungian term for the masculine side of the female unconscious. Compare ANIMA. ◷ Early 19c in sense 1; 1920s in sense 2: Latin, meaning 'spirit', 'soul'.

anion /ˈanaɪən/ ▻ *noun, chem* any negatively charged ION, which moves towards the ANODE during ELECTROLYSIS. Compare CATION. • **anionic** /anaɪˈɒnɪk/ *adj*. ◷ 19c: Greek, meaning 'going up'.

anise /ˈanɪs/ ▻ *noun* an annual plant with small umbelliferous flowers and small greyish-brown aromatic fruits containing liquorice-flavoured seeds. ◷ 14c: from Greek *anison*.

aniseed /ˈanisiːd/ ▻ *noun* the liquorice-flavoured seeds of the anise plant, used as a food flavouring in cakes and other baked products, sweets, liqueurs and other beverages. ◷ 14c.

aniseed ball ▻ *noun* a small round hard sweet that tastes of aniseed. ◷ 1920s.

Anjou Blanc / *French* ɑ̃ʒu blɑ̃/ ▻ *noun* a dry white wine produced in the western Loire region of France and made from blends of such grape varieties as Chenin Blanc, Chardonnay and Sauvignon.

ankh /aŋk/ ▻ *noun* the ancient Egyptian symbol of life in the form of a T-shaped cross with a loop above the horizontal bar. ◷ 19c: Egyptian, meaning 'life'.

ankle /ˈaŋkəl/ ▻ *noun* **1** the joint that connects the leg and the foot. **2** the part of the leg just above the foot. **3** *in compounds* □ *ankle-boots* □ *ankle-length*. ◷ Anglo-Saxon *ancleow*.

ankle-biter and **ankle-nipper** ▻ *noun, slang* a child.

anklet /ˈaŋklət/ ▻ *noun* a chain or ring worn around the ankle. ◷ Early 19c.

ankylosaur /ˈaŋkɪləsɔː(r)/ ▻ *noun* a small plant-eating dinosaur, known from the Cretaceous period, that had a small head, a flattened body covered with rectangular bony plates, and short legs. ◷ Early 20c: from Greek *ankylos* crooked + *sauros* lizard.

ankylosis /aŋkɪˈloʊsɪs/ ▻ *noun* a disorder characterized by immobility or stiffening of a joint, the bones of which often become fixed in an abnormal position, as a result of injury, disease, surgery, etc. ◷ 18c: from Greek *ankylos* crooked + -OSIS 2.

anlage /ˈanlɑːgə/ (***anlagen*** /-gən/ or ***anlages***) *noun, biol* a group of cells that can be identified as a future body part. Also called **primordium**. ◷ Late 19c: from German *anlagen* to establish.

an mo or **anmo** /an ˈmo/ ▻ *noun, Chinese medicine* a remedial system in which massage of specific areas of the body affects corresponding internal organs. ◷ Chinese, from *an* pressing + *mo* stroking.

annals /ˈanəlz/ ▻ *plural noun* **1 a** yearly historical records of events; **b** recorded history in general. **2** (**annal**) a single entry in a historical record or an entry relating to one particular year. **3** regular reports of the work of an organization. • **annalist** *noun*. • **annalistic** *adj*. ◷ 16c: from Latin *libri annales* yearly books.

annates /ˈaneɪts/ ▻ *plural noun, RC Church* a special payment made by newly-appointed bishops, etc to the pope. ◷ 16c: from Latin *annata*, from *annus* year.

annatto or **anatto** /əˈnatoʊ/ ▻ *noun* **1** an American tree that produces pulpy seeds from which a yellowish-red dye is obtained. **2** the dye itself, used to colour fabric, butter, cheese, etc. Also called ROUCOU. ◷ 17c.

anneal /əˈniːl/ ▻ *verb* (***annealed***, ***annealing***) **1** *engineering* to heat (a material such as metal or glass) and then slowly cool it in order to make it softer, less brittle and easier to work. **2** to toughen (the will, the determination, etc). • **annealing** *noun*. ◷ Anglo-Saxon *onælan* to burn.

annelid /ˈanəlɪd/ ▻ *noun, zool* any member of a phylum of invertebrate animals that characteristically have long soft cylindrical bodies composed of many similar ring-shaped segments, eg the earthworm or the leech. ◷ 19c: from Latin *annellus* little ring.

annex ▻ *verb* /əˈnɛks/ (***annexed***, ***annexing***) **1** to take possession of land or territory, especially by conquest or occupation. **2** to add or attach something to something larger. **3** *colloq* to take without permission. ▻ *noun* /ˈanɛks/ an alternative *US* spelling of ANNEXE. ◷ 14c: from Latin *adnectere*, *adnexum* to tie or bind.

annexation /anəkˈseɪʃən/ ▻ *noun* **1** annexing. **2** something annexed. • **annexational** *adj*. • **annexationism** *noun*. ◷ 17c.

annexe or (*US*) **annex** /ˈanɛks/ ▻ *noun* **1** an additional room, building, area, etc that provides supplementary space. **2** anything that has been added to something else, especially an extra clause, appendix, etc in a document. ◷ 19c in sense 1, which takes its spelling directly from French and which subsequently influenced the other sense; 17c in sense 2: French, meaning 'something joined'.

annihilate /əˈnaɪəleɪt/ ▻ *verb* (***annihilated***, ***annihilating***) **1** to destroy something completely. **2** to defeat, crush or humiliate someone, especially in an argument, debate, sporting contest, etc. **3** *physics* said of a particle: to be destroyed as a result of a collision with its corresponding ANTIPARTICLE. • **annihilation** *noun*. ◷ 16c: from Latin *annihilare*, from *nihil* nothing.

anniversary /anɪˈvɜːsərɪ/ ▻ *noun* (***anniversaries***) **1** a date on which some event took place in a previous year. **2** the celebration of this event on the same date each year. **3** *as adj* □ *an anniversary present*. ◷ 13c: from Latin *anniversarius*, from *annus* year + *vertere* to turn.

Wedding Anniversaries

In many Western countries, different wedding anniversaries have become associated with gifts of different materials. There is some variation between countries.

1st	Cotton	14th	Ivory
2nd	Paper	15th	Crystal
3rd	Leather	20th	China
4th	Fruit, Flowers	25th	Silver
5th	Wood	30th	Pearl
6th	Sugar	35th	Coral
7th	Copper, Wool	40th	Ruby
8th	Bronze, Pottery	45th	Sapphire
9th	Pottery, Willow	50th	Gold
10th	Tin	55th	Emerald
11th	Steel	60th	Diamond
12th	Silk, Linen	70th	Platinum
13th	Lace		

Anno Domini or **anno Domini** /ˈanoʊ ˈdɒmɪnaɪ, — -niː/ ▻ *adverb* AD. ▻ *noun, colloq* old age. ◷ 16c: Latin, meaning 'in the year of our Lord'.

annotate /ˈanoʊteɪt/ ▻ *verb* (***annotated***, ***annotating***) to add notes and explanations to (a book, article, etc). • **annotator** *noun*. ◷ 18c: from Latin *annotare* to put a note to something.

annotated ▷ *adj* augmented with explanatory or critical notes about the text, the author, etc.

annotation ▷ *noun* **1** the making of notes. **2** an explanatory note or comment. ◷ 15c.

announce /əˈnaʊns/ ▷ *verb* (***announced, announcing***) **1** to make something known publicly □ *announced the birth in the paper.* **2** to make (an arrival, especially of a guest or some form of transport) known. **3** to declare in advance □ *The sign announced next week's sale.* **4** to be a sign of something □ *dark clouds announcing a storm.* **5** *intr, US* to declare oneself to be running as a candidate, especially for the presidency or a governorship □ *She announced for governor.* ◷ 15c: from Latin *annuntiare* to report.

announcement ▷ *noun* **1** a public or official statement, notice or advertisement. **2** the act of announcing. ◷ 18c.

announcer ▷ *noun* someone who introduces programmes or reads the news on radio or TV. ◷ 1920s.

annoy /əˈnɔɪ/ ▷ *verb* (***annoyed, annoying***) **1** to anger or distress. **2** to harass or pester. • **annoyed** *adj.* • **annoying** *adj.* • **annoyingly** *adverb.* ◷ 13c: from Latin *inodiare* to cause aversion.

annoyance ▷ *noun* **1** something that annoys. **2** the act of annoying. **3** the state of being annoyed. ◷ 14c.

annual /ˈanjʊəl/ ▷ *adj* **1** done or happening once a year or every year □ *her annual holiday.* **2** lasting for a year. ▷ *noun* **1** *bot* a plant that germinates, flowers, produces seed, and dies within a period of one year, eg marigold. See also BIENNIAL, PERENNIAL. **2** a book published every year or every alternate year, especially one for children which is based on a comic or TV series. • **annually** *adverb.* ◷ 14c: from Latin *annualis*, from *annus* year.

annual general meeting ▷ *noun* (abbreviation **AGM**) a meeting of a public company, society, etc held once a year when financial and other reports are presented, and official elections are held, etc.

annualize or **annualise** ▷ *verb* (***annualized, annualizing***) to calculate (rates of interest, inflation, etc) for a year based on the figures for only part of it. ◷ 1950s.

annual percentage rate ▷ *noun* APR.

annual ring ▷ *noun, bot* any of the concentric rings, each formed during one growing season, that are visible in a cross-section of the stem of a woody plant, eg certain trees, and which are often used to estimate the age of the plant. See also DENDROCHRONOLOGY. ◷ 19c.

annuity /əˈnjuːɪtɪ/ ▷ *noun* (***annuities***) **1** a yearly grant or allowance. **2** money that has been invested to provide a fixed amount of interest every year. ◷ 15c: from Latin *annuitas*, from *annus* year.

annuity share ▷ *noun, finance* a share in a SPLIT CAPITAL TRUST that is highly geared towards income.

annul /əˈnʌl/ ▷ *verb* (***annulled, annulling***) to declare publicly that a marriage, legal contract, etc is no longer valid. • **annulment** see separate entry. ◷ 15c: from Latin *annullare*, from *nullus* none.

annular /ˈanjʊlə(r)/ ▷ *adj* referring or relating to a ring or rings; ring-shaped. • **annularity** *noun.* ◷ 16c: from Latin *annularis*; see ANNULUS.

annular eclipse ▷ *noun, astron* an eclipse in which a thin ring of light can be seen around the edge of the obscuring body, eg a solar eclipse during which a ring of sunlight remains visible around the Moon's shadow. Compare PARTIAL ECLIPSE, TOTAL ECLIPSE.

annulate /ˈanjʊlət/ ▷ *adj* formed from or marked with rings. ◷ 19c: see ANNULUS.

annulet /ˈanjʊlət/ ▷ *noun* **1** a small ring. **2** *archit* a decorative ring on a column. ◷ 16c: see ANNULUS.

annulment ▷ *noun* **1** the act of annulling. **2** the formal ending of a marriage, legal contract, etc. ◷ 15c.

annulus /ˈanjʊləs/ ▷ *noun* (***annuli*** /-laɪ/) **1** *geom* the figure formed by two concentric circles on a plane surface, ie a disc with a central hole. **2** *biol* any ring-shaped structure, eg the ring of cells that surrounds the spore-bearing structure in ferns, and by constriction causes the structure to rupture and release its spores. ◷ 16c, meaning 'a ring or ring-shaped object': medieval Latin, from classical Latin *anulus* ring.

annunciate /əˈnʌnsɪeɪt/ ▷ *verb* (***annunciated, annunciating***) to declare publicly or officially. ◷ 16c: from Latin *annuntiare* to report.

the Annunciation /ənʌnsɪˈeɪʃən/ ▷ *noun, Christianity* **1** the announcement by the Angel Gabriel to Mary that she would be the mother of Christ (Luke 1.26-38). **2** the festival, held on 25 March, celebrating this. Also called LADY DAY. ◷ 15c: from Latin *annuntiare* to report.

annus horribilis /ˈanʊs hɒˈriːbɪlɪs/ ▷ *noun* (***anni horribiles*** /ˈaniː hɒˈriːbɪleɪz/) a year of great sorrow or misfortune. ◷ The phrase was brought into prominence through its use by Queen Elizabeth II in November 1992: Latin, meaning 'terrifying year'.

annus mirabilis /ˈanʊs mɪˈrabɪlɪs/ ▷ *noun* (***anni mirabiles*** /ˈaniː mɪˈrabɪleɪz/) a year that is auspicious or remarkable in some way. ◷ 17c: Latin, meaning 'wonderful year'.

anobiid /aˈnoʊbɪɪd/ ▷ *noun* any of several varieties of coleopterous beetle, including the DEATHWATCH BEETLE and WOODWORM, whose heads are covered by a prominent hood.

anode /ˈanoʊd/ ▷ *noun* **1** in an electrolytic cell: the positive electrode, towards which negatively charged ions, usually in solution, are attracted. **2** the negative terminal of a battery. Compare CATHODE. • **anodal** *adj.* • **anodic** *adj.* ◷ 19c: from Greek *anodos* way up, from *ana* up + *hodos* way.

anodize or **anodise** /ˈanədaɪz/ ▷ *verb* (***anodized, anodizing***) to coat (an object made of metal, especially aluminium) with a thin protective oxide film by making that object the ANODE in a cell to which an electric current is applied. ◷ 1930s.

anodyne /ˈanoʊdaɪn/ ▷ *noun* **1** a medicine or drug that relieves or alleviates pain. **2** anything that has a palliative effect, especially to hurt feelings, mental distress, etc. ▷ *adj* able to relieve physical pain or mental distress. ◷ 16c: from Greek *an-* without + *odyne* pain.

anoint /əˈnɔɪnt/ ▷ *verb* (***anointed, anointing***) to put oil or ointment on (someone's head, feet, etc), usually as part of a religious ceremony, eg baptism. • **anointed** (*often* **the anointed**) *adj.* • **anointer** *noun.* • **anointment** *noun.* ◷ 14c: from Latin *inungere* from *ungere* to smear with oil.

anointing of the sick ▷ *noun, RC Church* the act of anointing a person who is very ill or dying, with consecrated oil.

anomalous /əˈnɒmələs/ ▷ *adj* different from the usual; irregular; peculiar. • **anomalously** *adverb.* ◷ 17c: from Greek *an-* not + *homalos* even.

anomaly /əˈnɒməlɪ/ ▷ *noun* (***anomalies***) **1** something that is unusual or different from what is expected. **2** divergence from what is usual or expected. • **anomalistic** *adj.* • **anomalistically** *adverb.* ◷ 16c.

anomie or **anomy** /ˈanəmɪ/ ▷ *noun* (***anomies***) *sociol* **1** a lack of regard for the generally accepted social or moral standards either in an individual or in a social group. **2** the state or condition of having no regard for the generally accepted social or moral standards. ◷ First coined by the French sociologist Emile Durkheim (1858–1917) in *Suicide* (1897), and first attested in English in the 1930s: from Greek *anomia* lawlessness.

anon[1] /əˈnɒn/ *abbreviation* anonymous.

anon[2] /əˈnɒn/ *adverb, old use* some time soon. ◷ Anglo-Saxon *on an* into one.

anonymous /əˈnɒnɪməs/ ▷ *adj* **1** having no name. **2** said of a piece of writing, an action, etc: from or by someone whose name is not known or not given □ *anonymous testing for the virus.* **3** without character; nondescript. • **anonymity** /anəˈnɪmɪtɪ/ *noun*. • **anonymously** *adverb*. • **anonymousness** *noun*. ⓒ 17c: from Greek *an-*, without + *onoma* name.

anopheles /əˈnɒfəliːz/ ▷ *noun* any of various kinds of mosquito many of which are germ-carrying, including the mosquito that transmits malaria. ⓒ 19c: Greek, meaning 'useless'.

anorak /ˈanərak/ ▷ *noun* **1** a hooded waterproof jacket. **2** *slang* **a** someone who is obsessively involved in something that is generally regarded as boring, unfashionable and not worthy of such commitment; **b** *as adj* □ *an anorak attitude.* • **anoraky** *adj* □ *the anoraky image of the internet.* ⓒ 1920s: originally an Inuit word for a hooded jacket made from skin and decorated with embroidery and beads.

anorexia /anəˈrɛksɪə/ ▷ *noun* **1** loss of appetite. **2** the common name for ANOREXIA NERVOSA. ⓒ 16c: Latin, from Greek, meaning 'lack of desire'.

anorexia nervosa /— nɜːˈvoʊsə/ ▷ *noun* a psychological disorder, mainly affecting adolescent girls and young women, characterized by a significant decrease in body weight, deliberately induced by refusal to eat because of an obsessive desire to lose weight. See also BULIMIA NERVOSA. ⓒ 19c.

anorexic /anɒˈrɛksɪk/ ▷ *noun* someone who suffers from anorexia or anorexia nervosa. ▷ *adj* **1** relating to or suffering from anorexia or anorexia nervosa. **2** relating to loss of appetite for food.

anosmia /aˈnɒzmɪə/ ▷ *noun, pathol* loss of the sense of smell. • **anosmatic** /-ˈmatɪk/ *adj*. • **anosmic** *adj*. ⓒ Early 19c: from Greek *an-* not + *osme* smell.

another /əˈnʌðə(r)/ ▷ *adj* ▷ *pronoun* **1** one more □ *Do you want another?* **2** one of a different kind □ *I've tried that wine, now let me try another.* **3** someone or something that is like or is thought to be like someone or something else □ *Ritchey Manic - another Kurt Cobain?* • **in another world** *euphemistic* daydreaming; not paying full attention. • **on another planet** *colloq* out of touch with reality; in a very drunk or drugged state. • **one another** see separate entry. ⓒ 14c: originally *an other*.

A N Other /eɪ ɛn ˈʌðə(r)/ ▷ *noun* used to denote a person whose name is so far unknown, eg in a list of participants, etc.

anoxia /aˈnɒksɪə/ ▷ *noun, pathol* **1** a complete lack of oxygen in the tissues. **2** *sometimes* oxygen deficiency. • **anoxic** *adj*. ⓒ 1930s: AN- + *oxygen* + -IA[1].

ansaphone see under ANSWERING MACHINE

ansate /ˈanseɪt/ ▷ *adj* fitted with a handle or handles or with something that will serve as a handle. ⓒ 19c: from Latin *ansa* handle.

anserine /ˈansəraɪn, -riːn/ ▷ *adj* **1** *technical* referring to or like a goose. **2** stupid □ *gave an anserine reply.* ⓒ 19c: from Latin *anser* goose.

answer /ˈɑːnsə(r)/ ▷ *noun* **1** something said or done in response to a question, request, letter, particular situation, etc □ *His answer to his sacking was to hit the bottle.* **2** (**the answer**) **a** the solution □ *Winning the lottery would be the answer to all our problems*; **b** the solution to a mathematical problem. ▷ *verb* (***answered***, ***answering***) **1** *tr & intr* to make a spoken or written reply to something or someone □ *answered the letter* □ *answered quietly.* **2** to react or respond to something (especially a doorbell, the telephone, someone calling one's name, etc). **3 a** to solve (especially a maths problem); **b** to write in response to (an exam question); **c** to offer a reply as the correct solution to (any question or problem). **4** *intr* to retaliate □ *The UN answered with their own heavy artillery fire.* **5** to put up a defence to or offer an explanation for something □ *answered the charges of alleged corruption.* **6 a** to suit □ *A better hammer would answer her purpose*; **b** to fulfil □ *A bigger house would answer the needs of this growing family.* • **answer in the negative** or **positive** to say 'No' or 'Yes'. • **answer the description of something** to match or be the same as it. . ⓒ Anglo-Saxon *andswaru*.

■ **answer back** to reply rudely, especially to someone supposedly in authority.

■ **answer for something a** to be punished for it; **b** to be liable for (one's own actions, etc); **c** to speak up on behalf of someone else.

■ **answer to (a name)** to respond to it; to be called ... □ *The cat answers to Poppy.*

■ **answer to someone** to have to account to them.

■ **answer with something** to give (a signal) in response to something, rather than giving a conventional reply □ *answered with a huge smile.*

answerable ▷ *adj* (*usually* **answerable to someone for something**) accountable to them for it. • **answerability** *noun*. ⓒ 16c.

answering machine, **answerphone** and **ansaphone** /ˈɑːnsəfoun/ ▷ *noun* a tape-recording device attached to a telephone, which automatically answers incoming calls by playing a pre-recorded message to the caller and recording the caller's message for subsequent playback. ⓒ 1960s.

answering service ▷ *noun* an organization which takes messages and answers telephone calls for its customers. ⓒ 1940s.

ant ▷ *noun* any of numerous social insects belonging to the same order as bees and wasps, characterized by the possession of elbowed antennae and a narrow waist, often equipped with a protective sting, and usually lacking wings. • **have ants in one's pants** *colloq* **1** to be extremely restless or fidgety. **2** to be impatiently eager to get on with something. ⓒ Anglo-Saxon *æmette*.

-ant /ənt/ ▷ *combining form* **1** *forming adjectives, signifying* **a** being in a specified state; **b** performing a specified action or function. **2** *forming nouns, signifying* someone or something that performs a specified action □ *assistant* □ *anticonvulsant.* ⓒ Latin present participle ending of first conjugation verbs; compare -ENT.

antacid /anˈtasɪd/ *medicine* ▷ *noun*, an alkaline substance that neutralizes excess acidity in the digestive juices of the stomach, and is used to relieve pain and discomfort caused by indigestion, peptic ulcer, etc. ▷ *adj* said of a substance, especially a medicine: able to neutralize excess acid in the stomach. ⓒ 18c: from ANTI- + ACID.

antagonism /anˈtagənɪzəm/ ▷ *noun* **1** openly expressed dislike or opposition. **2** *physiol* the opposing action between one muscle or group of muscles and another. **3** *biochem* inhibition of or interference with the growth or action of one organism or substance by another. ⓒ 19c: from ANTAGONIZE.

antagonist /anˈtagənɪst/ ▷ *noun* **1** an opponent or enemy. **2** *physiol* a muscle whose contraction opposes the action of another muscle. **3** *pharmacol* a drug, hormone or other chemical substance which has the opposite effect to that of another drug, hormone or chemical substance in the body, and so inhibits it. ⓒ 1830s.

antagonistic ▷ *adj* hostile; actively opposing. • **antagonistically** *adverb*.

antagonize or **antagonise** /anˈtagənaɪz/ ▷ *verb* (***antagonized***, ***antagonizing***) **1** to make someone feel anger or hostility. **2** to irrritate. **3** to counteract the action of (a muscle). ⓒ 17c: from Greek *antagonizesthai* to oppose or rival.

Antarctic /ant'ɑːktɪk/ ▻ *noun* (**the Antarctic**) the area round the South Pole. ▻ *adj* relating to this area. ⓒ 14c: from Greek *antarktikos* opposite the Arctic or North.

antbird ▻ *noun, zool* a forest-dwelling bird, native to the New World tropics, so called because it follows ant armies, feeding on the insects, spiders, lizards, etc that they disturb. ⓒ 19c.

ante /'antɪ/ ▻ *noun* (***antes***) **1** a stake put up by a player, usually in poker, but also in other card games, before receiving any cards. **2** an advance payment. ▻ *verb* (***anted, anteing***) to put up as a stake. • **raise** or **up the ante 1** to increase the stakes in a card game, especially poker. **2** to elevate the importance of something. ⓒ 19c: from Latin *ante* before.

■ **ante up** *colloq, especially US* to pay.

ante- /'antɪ/ ▻ *prefix* before in place or time □ ***anteroom*** □ ***antenatal***. ⓒ Latin, meaning 'before'.

anteater ▻ *noun* any of various Central and S American mammals, related to armadillos and sloths, with a long cylindrical snout and an untidily bushy tail.

antecedent /antɪ'siːdənt/ ▻ *noun* **1** an event or circumstance which precedes another. **2** *grammar* a word or phrase that some other word, usually a RELATIVE pronoun, relates to, eg *in the man who came to dinner, who* is a relative pronoun and its antecedent is *the man*. See also ANAPHORA. **3** *logic* the hypothetical or conditional proposition that a premiss depends on. **4** (*usually* **antecedents**) **a** someone's past history; **b** someone's ancestry. ▻ *adj* going before in time. • **antecedence** *noun*. ⓒ 14c: from Latin *antecedens, -entis* going before.

antechamber ▻ *noun* an ANTEROOM

antedate /antɪ'deɪt/ ▻ *verb* **1** to belong to an earlier period than (some other date). **2** to put a date (on a document, letter, etc) that is earlier than the actual date. ⓒ 16c.

antediluvian /antɪdɪ'luːvɪən, -daɪ-/ ▻ *adj* **1** belonging to the time before THE FLOOD. **2** *facetious* very old or old-fashioned. ⓒ 17c: from ANTE- + Latin *dilivium* flood.

antefix ▻ *noun* (***antefixes*** or ***antefixa***) *usually* **antifixes** or **antifixa** an ornamental tile, etc used, especially in ancient buildings, to cover up the place at the eaves and cornices where the ordinary roof tiles end. ⓒ 19c: from ANTE- + Latin *figare* to fix.

antelope /'antəloʊp/ ▻ *noun* (***antelope*** or ***antelopes***) any of various species of hoofed mammal with a smooth brown or grey coat and usually with paired horns, found mainly in Africa, eg gazelle, springbok, gnu. ⓒ 15c: from Greek *antholops*.

antemeridian /antɪmə'rɪdɪən/ ▻ *adj* referring or relating to the morning. Compare POSTMERIDIAN. ⓒ 17c: from ANTE MERIDIEM.

ante meridiem /antɪ mə'rɪdɪəm/ ▻ *adj* (abbreviation **a.m.**, **am**, **A.M.** or **AM**) indicating the time from midnight to midday. Compare POST MERIDIEM. ⓒ 16c: Latin, meaning 'before noon'.

antenatal ▻ *adj* **1** formed or occurring before birth. **2** relating to the health and care of women during pregnancy. ▻ *noun, colloq* a medical check-up or examination for pregnant women, usually arranged regularly throughout pregnancy. ⓒ 19c: from ANTE- + Latin *natalis* pertaining to birth.

antenna /an'tɛnə/ ▻ *noun* **1** (***antennae*** /-niː/) in certain invertebrate animals, especially insects and crustaceans: one of a pair of long slender jointed structures on the head which act as feelers but are also concerned with the sense of smell. **2** (***antennas***) an AERIAL. ⓒ 15c in sense 1; early 20c in sense 2: Latin, meaning 'yard of a mast'.

antepenultimate ▻ *adj* third from last. ▻ *noun* anything that is in third last position. ⓒ 18c.

ante-post ▻ *adj* said of betting or betting odds: offered before the day of the race, etc. ⓒ Early 20c.

anterior /an'tɪərɪə(r)/ ▻ *adj* **1** earlier in time. **2 a** at or nearer the front; **b** *zool* at or near the head; **c** *bot* growing away from the main stem. Compare POSTERIOR. ⓒ 17c: Latin, meaning 'fore', from *ante* before.

anteroom ▻ *noun* a small room which opens into another, more important, room. ⓒ 18c.

anteversion /antɪ'vɜːʃən/ ▻ *noun* the abnormal tilting forward of some body part, especially the womb. ⓒ 1830s: from ANTE- + Latin *vertere* to turn.

anthelion /an'θiːlɪən/ ▻ *noun, astron* a luminous white spot that occasionally appears in the sky directly opposite the Sun. ⓒ 17c: from Greek *anti* opposite + *helios* sun.

anthelminthic /anθɛl'mɪnθɪk/ ▻ *adj* having the effect of destroying or expelling intestinal worms. ▻ *noun* a drug that has this effect. ⓒ 17c: from Greek *anti* against + *helmins, helminthos* a worm.

anthem /'anθəm/ ▻ *noun* **1** a song of praise or celebration, especially a NATIONAL ANTHEM. **2** a piece of music for a church choir, usually set to a Biblical text, sung at church services. ⓒ Anglo-Saxon *antefn*, from Latin *antiphona* a hymn or psalm.

anther /'anθə(r)/ ▻ *noun* in flowering plants: the two-lobed structure at the tip of the stamen which contains the pollen sacs within which the pollen grains are produced. ⓒ 16c: from Greek *anthos* flower.

antheridium /anθə'rɪdɪəm/ ▻ *noun, bot* in ferns, mosses, liverworts, algae, etc: the organ in which the male GAMETEs develop. ⓒ 19c: a diminutive of ANTHER.

antherozoid /anθəroʊ'zoɪd/ ▻ *noun, bot* in ferns, mosses, liverworts, algae, etc: the MOTILE male gamete, which usually develops in an ANTHERIDIUM. ⓒ 19c: from ANTHER + Greek *zoion* animal.

anthesis /an'θiːsɪs/ ▻ *noun, bot* **1** the opening of a flower-bud. **2** the period of time during which a flower is in full bloom. ⓒ 19c: from Greek *anthesis* flowering.

ant hill ▻ *noun* a heap of earth, leaves, twigs, etc that ants pile up over their nest.

antho- /anθoʊ, an'θɒ/ ▻ *combining form, denoting* a flower. ⓒ From Greek *anthos* a flower.

anthocyanin /anθoʊ'saɪənɪn/ ▻ *noun, bot* any of a group of pigments that are found in certain cells in plants, and are responsible for many of the red, purple and blue colours of flowers, fruits and leaves. ⓒ 19c.

anthologize or **anthologise** ▻ *verb* (***anthologized, anthologizing***) **1** to include in an anthology. **2** *intr* to compile an anthology. • **anthologist** *noun*. ⓒ Late 19c.

anthology /an'θɒlədʒɪ/ ▻ *noun* (***anthologies***) **1** a collection of poems, usually by different authors but with some kind of thematic link. **2** a collection of other creative writing □ ***an anthology of punk songs***. ⓒ 17c.

anthophore /'anθoʊfɔː(r)/ ▻ *noun, bot* the elongated stalk which in some flowers raises the RECEPTACLE (sense 2) above the CALYX.

anthracite /'anθrəsaɪt/ ▻ *noun* a hard shiny black coal that burns with a short blue flame, generating much heat but little or no smoke, and widely used for domestic heating. ⓒ Early 19c: from Greek *anthrax* coal.

anthracosis /anθrə'koʊsɪs/ ▻ *noun* a disease of the lungs, mainly affecting coal miners, caused by inhalation of coal dust. Also (*colloq*) called **coal miner's lung**. Compare SILICOSIS, ASBESTOSIS.

anthrax /'anθraks/ ▻ *noun, pathol* **1** an acute infectious disease, mainly affecting sheep and cattle, which can be transmitted to humans by contact with infected meat, hides, excrement, etc, and is often fatal if left untreated. **2** an ulcer or sore caused by this disease. ⓒ 14c: from Greek *anthrax* coal or a carbuncle.

anthropo- /anθroʊpoʊ, anθrə'pɒ/ ▻ *combining form, denoting* belonging to or like human beings. ⓒ From Greek *anthropos* man.

anthropocentric ▷ *adj* having or regarding mankind as the central element of existence. • **anthropocentrically** *adverb*. • **anthropocentrism** or **anthropocentricism** *noun*. ◷ 19c.

anthropoid /ˈanθrəpɔɪd/ ▷ *adj* **1** belonging, referring or relating to, or like, a human being in form. **2** belonging, referring or relating to, or like, an ape. ▷ *noun* **1** (also **anthropoid ape**) any of the apes that shows a relatively close resemblance to a human, eg a chimpanzee or gorilla. **2** any PRIMATE. • **anthropoidal** *adj*. ◷ 19c.

anthropology /anθrəˈpɒlədʒɪ/ ▷ *noun* the multidisciplinary study and analysis of the origins and characteristics of human beings and their societies, customs and beliefs. • **anthropological** *adj*. • **anthropologically** *adverb*. • **anthropologist** *noun*. ◷ 16c.

anthropometry /anθrəˈpɒmɪtrɪ/ ▷ *noun* the study of the sizes of human bodies or their parts, especially the comparison of sizes at different ages, in different races, etc. • **anthropometric** *adj*. ◷ 19c.

anthropomorphism /anθrəpəˈmɔːfizəm/ ▷ *noun* the ascribing of a human form or human characteristics or attributes such as behaviour, feelings, beliefs, etc to animals, gods, inanimate objects, etc. • **anthropomorphic** *adj*. • **anthropomorphically** *adverb*. • **anthropomorphous** *adj*. ◷ 18c.

anthropomorphize or **anthropomorphise** ▷ *verb* (***anthropomorphized***, ***anthropomorphizing***) *tr & intr* to ascribe a human form or human behaviour, characteristics, etc to (an animal, god or inanimate object). ◷ 19c.

anthropophagy /anθrəˈpɒfədʒɪ/ ▷ *noun* CANNIBALISM.

anthroposophy /anθrəˈpɒsəfɪ/ ▷ *noun* **1** human wisdom. **2** the movement whose main belief is that, through meditation and awareness, people can heighten their own spirituality and commune with a shared universal spirituality. • **anthroposophist** *noun*. ◷ Early 19c in sense 1; early 20c in sense 2, originated by the Austrian social philosopher, Rudolph Steiner (1861–1925), who believed this could be achieved through education with an emphasis on art, myth, drama, etc and that this would be especially useful for children with learning difficulties.

anthurium /anˈθuːrɪəm/ ▷ *noun* a plant that is highly valued as a house plant because of its flamboyantly stripey leaves and its unusual spike of flowers at the end of a long slender stalk which are surrounded by a large white or red conical bract. ◷ 19c: from Greek *anthos* flower + *oura* a tail.

anti /ˈantɪ/ ▷ *adj*, *informal* opposed to (a particular policy, party, ideology, etc). ▷ *noun* (***antis***) someone who is opposed to something, especially a particular policy, party, ideology, etc. Compare PRO[1]. ◷ 18c: from Greek *anti* against.

anti- /antɪ, antaɪ/ *prefix, signifying* **1** opposed to □ ***anti-vivisectionist march***. **2** designed for retaliation against or for the immobilization or destruction of □ ***anti-aircraft fire***. **3** opposite to □ ***anticlockwise*** □ ***anticlimax***. **4** said mainly of drugs, remedies, etc: having the effect of counteracting, inhibiting, resisting, neutralizing or reversing □ ***antidepressant*** □ ***antibiotic*** □ ***antitoxin***. **5** said of a device, product, etc: preventing; having a counteracting effect □ ***antifreeze*** □ ***anti-lock braking system***. **6** different from what might be expected, especially in being less worthy, satisfying, etc; unconventional □ ***antihero***. **7** set up as a rival or alternative □ ***Antichrist*** □ ***antipope***. Compare PRO- [1]. ◷ Greek, meaning 'against'.

anti-aircraft ▷ *adj* said of a gun or missile: designed for use against enemy aircraft. ◷ 1910.

antibiosis /antɪbaɪˈoʊsɪs/ ▷ *noun* a relationship between two organisms that is not beneficial to one or both of them. Compare SYMBIOSIS 1. ◷ 19c.

antibiotic /antɪbaɪˈɒtɪk/ ▷ *noun* a substance, produced or derived from a micro-organism, that can selectively destroy or inhibit other bacteria or fungi without damaging the host, eg penicillin, widely used in the treatment of bacterial infections. ▷ *adj* having the property of or relating to antibiotics. ◷ 1940s in this sense; 19c, meaning 'injurious to life'.

antibody /ˈantɪbɒdɪ/ ▷ *noun* (***antibodies***) a protein that is produced by certain white blood cells in response to the presence in the body of an ANTIGEN, and forms an important part of the body's immune response. ◷ Early 20c.

antic /ˈantɪk/ ▷ *noun* (*often* **antics**) a playful caper or trick. ◷ 16c: from Italian *antico* ancient, an obsolete name for the grotesque faces of carved figures from ancient Rome, which were rediscovered in 16c.

Some words with *anti-* prefixed: see ANTI- for numbered senses specified below

anti-abortion *adj* sense 1.
anti-abortionist *adj, noun* sense 1.
anti-ageing *adj* sense 4.
anti-allergenic *adj* sense 4.
anti-American *adj, noun* sense 1.
anti-apartheid *adj* sense 1.
anti-art *adj, noun* senses 1 and 6.
anti-attrition *adj* sense 2.
antibacterial *adj* sense 4.
antiballistic *adj* sense 2.
antibigotry *noun* sense 1.
antibilious *adj* sense 4.
anti-Black *adj* sense 1.
anti-British *adj* sense 1.
anti-bugging *adj* sense 2.
antibureaucratic *adj* sense 2.
anti-Calvinism *noun* sense 1.
anti-Calvinist *adj, noun* sense 1.
anticapitalist *adj, noun* senses 1 and 2.
anti-Catholic *adj, noun* sense 1.
anticensorship *noun* sense 1.
anti-Christian *adj, noun* sense 1.
antichurch *adj* sense 1.
anticlassical *adj* sense 1.
anti-clotting *adj* sense 4.
anticolonial *adj, noun* sense 1.
anti-Communism *noun* sense 1.
anti-Communist *adj, noun* sense 1.
anticonformist *adj, noun* sense 1.
anticonstitutional *adj* sense 2.
anticorrosive *adj, noun* sense 5.
anticrime *adj* sense 5.
anticruelty *adj* sense 1.
antidemocratic *adj* sense 1 and 2.
anti-devolutionist *noun, adj* sense 1.
antidiscrimination *noun* sense 1.
antidisestablishmentarianism *noun* sense 1.
antidiuretic *adj, noun* sense 4.
antidrug *adj* sense 1.
antidumping *noun, as adj* senses 1 and 5.
antiemetic *adj, noun* sense 4.
anti-English *adj* sense 1.
anti-establishment *adj, noun* sense 1.
anti-European *adj* sense 1.
anti-expansionism *noun* sense 1.
anti-expansionist *adj, noun* sense 1.
antifascism *noun* sense 1.
antifascist *adj, noun* sense 1.
antifebrile *adj, noun* sense 4.
antifederalism *noun* sense 1.
antifederalist *adj, noun* sense 1.
antifeminism *noun* sense 1.
antifeminist *adj, noun* sense 1.

anticathode /antɪ'kaθoud/ ▻ *noun* a metal plate opposite the CATHODE, especially one in an X-RAY tube which is the target for the rays emitted by the cathode and which itself emits the X-rays. ◷ Early 20c.

Antichrist /'antɪkraɪst/ ▻ *noun* **1** an enemy of Christ. **2** *Christianity* the great enemy of Christ, expected by the early Church to appear and reign over the world before Christ's SECOND COMING. **3** (*usually* **antichrist**) *colloq* someone who holds opinions or who acts in ways that are contrary to those that are generally accepted □ ***Frank's dismissal of Wordsworth made him into some kind of antichrist.*** ◷ 14c: from ANTI- 7 + CHRIST.

anticipate /an'tɪsɪpeɪt/ ▻ *verb* (***anticipated, anticipating***) **1** to see what will be needed or wanted in the future and do what is necessary in advance. **2** to predict something and then act as though it is bound to happen. **3** to expect something. **4** to look forward to something. **5** to know beforehand □ ***could anticipate his every move.*** **6** *tr & intr* to mention or think something before the proper time. **7** to do or use something before the proper time. **8** to foil or preclude □ ***anticipated the attack.*** • **anticipator** *noun*. • **anticipatory** *adj*. • **anticipatorily** *adverb*. ◷ 16c: from Latin *anticipare, anticipatum*, from *ante* before + *capere* to take.

> ***anticipate***
>
> The use of **anticipate** in sense 3, meaning 'expect' or 'foresee', is often regarded as incorrect, but it is an established meaning that carries stronger connotations of forestalling or preventing than 'expect' does. However:
>
> ☆ PLAIN ENGLISH alternative in sense 3 is often **expect**.

anticipation ▻ *noun* **1** a feeling of excited expectation □ ***waited with anticipation for the birth.*** **2** knowledge gained in advance; a foretaste. **3** *music* the introduction of part of a chord before the whole chord is actually played. **4** doing or making use of something before the proper time. • **in anticipation** with the belief, knowledge, hope, etc. ◷ 16c.

anticlerical ▻ *adj* opposed to public and political power being held by members of the clergy. • **anticlericalism** *noun*. ◷ 19c.

anticlimax /antɪ'klaɪmaks/ ▻ *noun* a dull or disappointing end or dénouement to a series of events, a film, novel, visit, etc which had earlier promised to be more interesting, exciting, satisfying, etc. • **anticlimactic** /-'maktɪk/ *adj*. ◷ 18c.

anticline /'antɪklaɪn/ ▻ *noun, geol* a geological fold in the form of an arch, formed as a result of compressional forces acting in a horizontal plane on rock strata. • **anticlinal** *adj*. Compare SYNCLINE. ◷ 1860s: from ANTI- 3 + Greek *klinein* to lean.

anticlockwise ▻ *adverb, adj* in the opposite direction to the direction that the hands of a clock move. ◷ 19c.

anticoagulant ▻ *noun, medicine* a drug or other substance that prevents or slows the clotting of blood, used to prevent the formation of blood clots, or to break up existing clots, eg in the treatment of thrombosis. ▻ *adj* having or relating to this kind of effect. ◷ Early 20c.

anticonvulsant *medicine* ▻ *noun* a drug that is used to prevent or reduce convulsions, especially in epilepsy. ▻ *adj* having or relating to this kind of effect. ◷ Early 20c.

antics see under ANTIC

anticyclone *meteorol* ▻ *noun* an area of relatively high atmospheric pressure from which light winds spiral outward in the opposite direction to that of the Earth's rotation, generally associated with calm settled weather. Also called **high**. Compare CYCLONE 1. • **anticyclonic** *adj*. ◷ 19c: ANTI- (sense 3) + CYCLONE.

antidepressant ▻ *noun, medicine* any drug that prevents or relieves the symptoms of depression. ▻ *adj* having or relating to this effect. ◷ 1960s.

antidote /'antɪdout/ ▻ *noun* **1** any agent, eg a drug, that counteracts or prevents the action of a poison. **2** anything that acts as a means of preventing, relieving or counteracting something else. ◷ 15c: from Greek *antidoton* a remedy, from *anti* against + *didonai* to give.

antifreeze ▻ *noun* **1** any substance that is added to water or some other liquid in order to lower its freezing point. **2** a mixture of ethylene glycol and water, widely used to protect cooling systems that rely on circulating water, eg the radiators of motor vehicles. ◷ Early 20c.

antigen /'antɪdʒən/ ▻ *noun, biol* any foreign substance (usually a protein), eg a bacterium or virus, that stimulates the body's immune system to produce antibodies. ◷ Early 20c: from *anti*body + -GEN.

Some words with *anti-* prefixed: see ANTI- for numbered senses specified below

antifog *adj* sense 5.
anti-Freudian *adj, noun* sense 1.
antifriction *adj* sense 5.
antifungal *adj* sense 4.
antigay *adj* sense 1 + GAY *noun*.
antiglare *adj* sense 5.
antigod *noun* sense 7.
antigovernment *adj* sense 1.
antigovernmental *adj* sense 2.
antigravity *noun* sense 5.
anti-hunting *adj* sense 1.
antihypertensive *adj, noun* sense 4.
anti-imperialism *noun* sense 1.
anti-imperialist *adj, noun* sense 1.
anti-inflammatory *adj, noun* sense 1
anti-inflationary *adj* sense 2.
anti-Irish *adj* sense 1.
anti-isolationism *noun* sense 1.
anti-isolationist *adj, noun* senses 1 and 2.
antimagnetic *adj* sense 5.
antimalarial *adj* sense 4.
anti-Masonic *adj* sense 1.
antimetabolite *noun* sense 3.
antimilitant *adj, noun* sense 1.
antimissile *adj* sense 2.
antimonarchical *adj* sense 1.
antinational *adj* sense 1.
antinationalist *adj, noun* sense 1.
antinoise *adj* sense 5.
antipapal *adj* sense 1.
antipatriotic *adj* sense 3.
antiperistaltic *adj* sense 4.
antipersonnel *adj* sense 2.
antipollutant *noun, adj* sense 5.
antipollution *adj, noun* sense 1.
antipornographic *adj* senses 1 and 2.
antiprotectionist *adj, noun* senses 1 and 2.
antipruritic *adj, noun* sense 4.
antipsychotic *adj, noun* sense 4.
anti-recessionary *adj* sense 2.
anti-resonance *adj* sense 5.
anti-rust *adj* sense 5.
antisatellite *adj* sense 2.
antiself *noun* sense 7.
antislavery *noun* sense 1.
antismoking *adj* sense 1.
antiterrorism *noun* sense 2.
antiterrorist *adj, noun* sense 2.
antitheft *adj* sense 2.
antitheistic *adj* sense 1.
antitype *noun* sense 3.
anti-union *adj* sense 1.
antiwar *adj* sense 1.
antiwrinkle *adj* senses 4 and 5.
anti-Zionism *noun* sense 1.
anti-Zionist *adj, noun* sense 1.

antihero ▷ *noun* (***antiheroes***) a principal character in a novel, play, film, etc who either lacks the conventional qualities of a hero or whose circumstances do not allow for any kind of heroic action. • **antiheroic** *adj.* ◷ 19c in this sense; 18c in more general sense 'someone who is the opposite of a hero'.

antiheroine ▷ *noun* a female antihero. ◷ 1960s.

antihistamine ▷ *noun, medicine* any of a group of drugs that counteract the effects of histamines produced in allergic reactions such as hay fever, and which are also used to prevent travel sickness, etc. ◷ 1930s.

anti-icer ▷ *noun* a piece of equipment fitted to an aircraft to prevent ice forming. ◷ 1930s.

antiknock ▷ *noun* any substance that is added to petrol in order to reduce KNOCK (noun 5), especially in the engines of motor vehicles. ◷ 1920s.

anti-lock or **anti-locking** ▷ *adj* said of a braking system: fitted with a special sensor that prevents the wheels of a vehicle locking when the brakes are applied vigorously. See also ABS.

antilogarithm ▷ *noun, math* the number whose logarithm to a specified base is a given number. Often shortened to **antilog**. See also LOGARITHM. • **antilogarithmic** *adj.* ◷ 18c.

antimacassar /antɪmə'kasə(r)/ ▷ *noun* a covering for the back of a chair to stop it getting dirty. ◷ 19c: ANTI- 5 + *macassar* the proprietary name for an oil once used on hair.

antimatter ▷ *noun* a substance that is composed entirely of ANTIPARTICLES. ◷ 1950s.

antimere /'antɪmɪə(r)/ ▷ *noun, zool* any of the equivalent segments into which a radially symmetrical animal may be divided. • **antimeric** /-'merɪk/ *adj.* ◷ 19c: ANTI- 3 + Greek *meros* a part.

antimonide /an'tɪmənaɪd/ ▷ *noun, chem* a compound of antimony with another element, such as hydrogen or a metal, or with an organic radical. ◷ 19c.

antimony /'antɪmənɪ/ ▷ *noun, chem* (symbol **Sb**, atomic number 51) a brittle bluish-white metallic element used to increase the hardness of lead alloys, and also used in storage batteries, semiconductors, flameproofing, paints, ceramics and enamels. ◷ 15c: from Latin *antimonium*.

antinephritic *medicine* ▷ *adj* having the effect of reducing or counteracting disease, inflammation, etc in the kidneys. ▷ *noun* a drug or remedy that has this effect. ◷ 17c: from ANTI- 4 + Greek *nephros* kidney.

antineutrino ▷ *noun* the ANTIPARTICLE to the NEUTRINO. ◷ 1930s.

antineutron ▷ *noun* the ANTIPARTICLE to the NEUTRON. ◷ 1940s.

antinode ▷ *noun, physics* a point halfway between the nodes in a STANDING WAVE, that indicates a position of maximum displacement or intensity. ◷ 19c.

antinomian /antɪ'noʊmɪən/ ▷ *adj* denoting the view that Christians do not have to observe moral law. ▷ *noun* someone who holds this view. ◷ 17c: from *Antinomi*, the Latin name of a 16c German sect that believed this, from Greek *nomos* law.

antinomy /an'tɪnəmɪ/ ▷ *noun* (***antinomies***) **1** a contradiction between two laws or beliefs that are reasonable in themselves. **2** a conflict of authority. ◷ 16c: from Greek *nomos* law.

antinovel ▷ *noun* a piece of prose in which the traditional, conventional or generally accepted elements such as plot, characterization, etc have deliberately been abandoned. ◷ 1950s.

antinuclear ▷ *adj* **1 a** opposed to the use of nuclear weapons; **b** opposed to the building of nuclear power stations and to the use of nuclear power as a fuel. **2** designed for retaliation against, or for the immobilization or destruction of, nuclear weapons. ◷ 1950s.

antioxidant /antɪ'ɒksɪdənt/ *chem* ▷ *noun* a substance, especially an additive in foods, plastics, etc, that slows down the oxidation of other substances. ▷ *adj* having this effect. ◷ 1930s.

antiparticle ▷ *noun, physics* a subatomic particle which has the opposite electrical charge, magnetic moment and spin from other subatomic particles of the same mass, eg the POSITRON is the antiparticle of the ELECTRON. ◷ 1930s.

antipasto /antɪ'pastoʊ/ ▷ *noun* (***antipasti*** /antɪ'pastiː/) any of a variety of cold food such as marinated vegetables and fish, pork sausage, mushroom salad, etc served either as a cocktail snack or at the beginning of a meal to sharpen the appetite. ◷ 1930s: Italian, meaning 'before food'.

antipathetic ▷ *adj* (*usually* **antipathetic to something**) arousing or having a strong aversion to it. • **antipathetical** *adj.* • **antipathetically** *adverb*. ◷ 17c: from *antipathy*, modelled on the Greek *adj* from *antipathetikos*.

antipathy /an'tɪpəθɪ/ ▷ *noun* (***antipathies***) **1** a feeling of strong dislike or hostility. **2** the object that such a feeling is directed towards. ◷ 17c: from Greek *antipatheia*, from *pathos* feeling.

anti-personnel ▷ *adj* said of weapons and bombs: designed to attack and kill people rather than destroy buildings, other weapons, etc. ◷ 1930s.

antiperspirant /antɪ'pɜːspərənt/ ▷ *noun* a preparation in aerosol, roll-on or stick form applied to the skin, especially under the armpits, in order to reduce perspiration and so minimize smells and clothing stains. ▷ *adj* counteracting perspiration □ *antiperspirant spray*. ◷ 1940s: ANTI- 4 + PERSPIRE + -ANT 2.

antiphon /'antɪfɒn/ ▷ *noun* a hymn or psalm sung alternately by two groups of singers. • **antiphonal** /an'tɪfənəl/ *adj.* • **antiphonally** *adverb*. • **antiphony** /an'tɪfənɪ/ *noun* the antiphonal rendition of a musical piece. ◷ 16c: from Greek *antiphonos* sounding in response.

antipodes /an'tɪpədiːz/ ▷ *plural noun* (*usually* **the Antipodes**) two points on the Earth's surface that are diametrically opposite each other, especially Australia and New Zealand as being opposite Europe. • **antipodal** *adj.* • **antipodean** /-'dɪən/ *adj, noun*. ◷ 14c: from Greek *antipous*, *-podos*.

antipope ▷ *noun* a pope elected in opposition to one already canonically chosen. ◷ 13c.

antipyretic /antɪpaɪə'retɪk/ ▷ *adj* denoting any drug that reduces or prevents fever, eg aspirin, paracetamol. ▷ *noun* any drug that has this effect. ◷ 17c.

antiquarian /antɪ'kweərɪən/ ▷ *adj* referring or relating to, or dealing in, antiques and or rare books. ▷ *noun* an antiquary. ◷ 17c.

antiquary /'antɪkwərɪ/ ▷ *noun* (***antiquaries***) someone who collects, studies or deals in antiques or antiquities. ◷ 16c: from Latin *antiquarius*, from *antiquus* ancient.

antiquated /'antɪkweɪtɪd/ ▷ *adj* old and out of date; old-fashioned. ◷ 17c: from Latin *antiquare* to make old.

antique /an'tiːk/ ▷ *noun* **1** a piece of furniture, china, etc which is old and often valuable, and is sought after by collectors. **2** (**the Antique**) ancient Classical art, especially sculpture from Greek and Roman times, which has been a source of motifs and a model for style for artists since the Renaissance. ▷ *adj* **1** old and often valuable. **2** *colloq* old-fashioned. ◷ 16c: from Latin *antiquus* ancient.

antiquity /an'tɪkwɪtɪ/ ▷ *noun* (*plural* in sense 3 only ***antiquities***) **1** ancient times, especially before the end of the Roman Empire in AD 476. **2** great age. **3** (**antiquities**) works of art or buildings surviving from ancient times. ◷ 14c: from Latin *antiquitas*, from *antiquus* ancient.

antiracism ▷ *noun* opposition to prejudice or persecution on grounds of race, often accompanied by the active promotion of policies that encourage equality and tolerance in groups of different racial origins. • **antiracist** *adj, noun*.

anti-roll bar ▷ *noun* a rigid bar built into the suspension of a motor vehicle to prevent it from overturning in the event of a collision or other accident. ◷ 1960s.

antirrhinum /antɪˈraɪnəm/ ▷ *noun* any of various bushy perennial plants with large brightly coloured two-lipped flowers, including many ornamental varieties. Also called SNAPDRAGON. ◷ 16c: from Greek *antirrhinon*, from *rhis, rhinos* nose.

antiscorbutic ▷ *adj* said of a drug, remedy, etc: having the effect of preventing or curing scurvy. ▷ *noun* a drug or remedy that has this effect. ◷ 17c.

anti-semite ▷ *noun* someone who is hostile to or prejudiced against Jews. • **antisemitic** *adj*. • **antisemitism** *noun*. ◷ 19c.

antisepsis ▷ *noun* the destruction or containment of germs. ◷ 19c.

antiseptic ▷ *adj* **1** denoting any substance that kills or inhibits the growth of bacteria and other micro-organisms, but is not toxic to the skin, and so can be used to clean wounds, etc. **2** denoting any substance that has this effect, eg alcohol or iodine. **3** *informal* indifferent; boring; lacking in passion, enthusiasm, etc □ ***gave an antiseptic account of his trip.*** ▷ *noun* a drug or other substance that has this effect. ◷ 18c.

antiserum /ˈantɪsɪərəm/ ▷ *noun* (***antisera*** /-sɪərə/) a blood serum containing antibodies that are specific for, and neutralize the effects of, a particular antigen, used in vaccines. ◷ 19c: a contraction of *antitoxin serum*.

antisexism ▷ *noun* ANTISEXIST ideology.

antisexist ▷ *adj* **1** opposed to language, behaviour, rules, etc that might discriminate against someone solely on grounds of their gender. **2** designed to prevent sexism □ ***introduced antisexist measures.*** ▷ *noun* a devotee of ANTISEXISM. ◷ 1980s.

antisocial ▷ *adj* **1** reluctant to mix socially with other people. **2** said of behaviour: harmful or annoying to the community in general. • **antisocially** *adverb*. ◷ 18c.

antistatic ▷ *adj* denoting any substance that prevents the accumulation of static electric charges on the surface of vinyl records, clothing, etc, as a result of friction during operation or wear. ◷ 1930s.

antistrophe /anˈtɪstrəfɪ/ ▷ *noun* in ancient Greek drama: **1** the return movement by the CHORUS (sense 7), which follows the STROPHE. **2** the choral song delivered during this movement. ◷ 17c.

antitank ▷ *adj* said of weapons: designed to destroy or immobilize military tanks. ◷ 1915.

antithesis /anˈtɪθəsɪs/ ▷ *noun* (***antitheses*** /-siːz/) **1** a direct opposite of something. **2** the placing together of contrasting ideas, words or themes in any oral or written argument, especially to produce an effect. • **antithetic** /antɪˈθɛtɪk/ or **antithetical** *adj*. • **antithetically** *adverb*. ◷ 16c: Greek, meaning 'opposition', from *antithenai* to set something against something else.

antitoxin /antɪˈtɒksɪn/ ▷ *noun, medicine* a type of antibody, produced by the body or deliberately introduced into it by vaccination, which neutralizes a toxin that has been released by invading bacteria, viruses, etc. ◷ 19c.

antitrades ▷ *plural noun* winds that blow above and in the opposite direction to TRADE WINDS. ◷ 19c.

anti-trust /antɪˈtrʌst/ ▷ *adj, N Amer, especially US* said of a law, policy, etc: having the effect of protecting small companies and trade from domination by monopolies. ◷ 19c.

antivenin /antɪˈvɛnɪn/ or **antivenene** /-vəˈniːn/ ▷ *noun* an antidote to a venom, especially that of a snake. ◷ 19c.

anti-vivisection ▷ *noun* opposition to scientific experiments on living animals. • **antivivisectionist** *adj, noun*. ◷ 19c.

antler /ˈantlə(r)/ ▷ *noun* either of a pair of solid bony outgrowths, which may or may not be branched, on the head of an animal belonging to the deer family. • **antlered** *adj*. ◷ 14c: from French *antoillier* the branch of a stag's horn.

antler moth ▷ *noun* a European nocturnal moth with wing markings that resemble antlers, the larvae of which can cause massive destruction to pastures and grassland. ◷ 17c.

antonomasia /antənəˈmeɪzɪə/ ▷ *noun* **1** the use of a title or epithet to address or refer to someone or something rather than using the proper name name, eg *the Iron Lady* to refer to Margaret Thatcher or *Auld Reekie* to refer to Edinburgh. **2** the use of someone's name to convey some quality that is associated with that name, eg *Gazza* in *Philip is the Gazza of the primary school football team*. ◷ 16c: Greek, from *onomazein* to name.

antonym /ˈantənɪm/ ▷ *noun* a word that in certain contexts is the opposite in meaning to another word, eg *straight* has many antonyms, eg *curved, unconventional, gay, indirect*. • **antonymous** *adj*. ◷ 19c: from ANTI- + Greek *onoma* name; compare SYNONYM.

antrorse /anˈtrɔːs/ ▷ *adj, biol* turning or pointing forward or upwards. ◷ 19c: from Latin *antrorsus* bent up or forward.

antrum /ˈantrəm/ ▷ *noun* (***antra*** /ˈantrə/) *anatomy* **1** a cavity or sinus, especially in a bone. **2** the part of the stomach next to the opening that leads into the duodenum. ◷ 14c: from Greek *antron* cave.

ANU ▷ *abbreviation* Australian National University.

anuresis /anjʊəˈriːsɪs/ ▷ *noun, pathol* the retention of urine in the bladder. ◷ 19c: from AN- + Greek *ouresis* urination.

anuria /anˈjʊərɪə/ ▷ *noun, pathol* failure or inability of the kidneys to produce urine. ◷ 19c: from AN- + -URIA.

anus /ˈeɪnəs/ ▷ *noun* the opening at the end of the alimentary canal, through which the faeces are expelled from the body. See ANAL. ◷ 17c: Latin, meaning 'ring'.

anvil /ˈanvɪl/ ▷ *noun* **1** a heavy iron block on which metal objects can be hammered into shape. **2** *non-technical* the INCUS. ◷ Anglo-Saxon *anfilte*.

anxiety /aŋˈzaɪɪtɪ/ ▷ *noun* (***anxieties***) **1** a strong feeling of fear or distress which occurs as a normal response to a dangerous or stressful situation, symptoms of which may include trembling, sweating, rapid pulse rate, dry mouth, nausea, etc. **2** *informal* a worry □ ***My one anxiety is that the flight might be late.*** **3** *psychiatry* a form of neurosis characterized by excessive and lasting fear, often for no apparent reason. ◷ 16c in sense 1: from Latin *anxietas*; see also ANXIOUS.

anxious /ˈaŋʃəs, ˈaŋk-/ ▷ *adj* **1 a** worried, nervous or fearful; **b** (**anxious about something**) worried, nervous, or fearful about what will or may happen □ ***anxious about her job security***; **c** (**anxious for someone** or **something**) concerned about them or it □ ***anxious for his safety.*** **2** causing worry, fear or uncertainty □ ***an anxious moment.*** **3** very eager □ ***anxious to do well.*** • **anxiously** *adverb*. • **anxiousness** *noun*. ◷ 17c: from Latin *anxius* troubled in the mind, from *angere* to press tightly.

any /ˈɛnɪ/ ▷ *adj* **1** one, no matter which □ ***can't find any answer.*** **2** some, no matter which □ ***have you any apples?*** **3** *with negatives and in questions* even a very small amount of something □ ***won't tolerate any nonsense.*** **4**

indefinitely large □ ***have any number of dresses.*** **5** every, no matter which □ ***Any child could tell you.*** ▷ *pronoun* any one or any amount. ▷ *adverb, with negatives and in questions* in any way whatever □ ***It isn't any better.*** ◷ Anglo-Saxon *ænig.*

anybody /ˈɛnɪbədɪ, -bɒdɪ/ ▷ *pronoun* **1** any person, no matter which □ ***There wasn't anybody home.*** **2** an important person □ ***Everybody who is anybody will be invited.*** **3** some ordinary person □ ***She's not just anybody, you know.*** ◷ 15c: formerly written as two words.

anyhow ▷ *adverb* **1** in spite of what has been said, done, etc; anyway. **2** carelessly; in an untidy state. ● **any old how** randomly; in a dishevelled state. □ ***pulled her clothes on any old how.***

anyone ▷ *pronoun* ANYBODY.

anyplace ▷ *adverb, N Amer, especially US* ANYWHERE. □ ***Is there anyplace to get a coffee nearby?***

anything ▷ *pronoun* a thing of any kind; a thing, no matter which. ▷ *adverb* in any way; to any extent □ ***She isn't anything like her sister.*** ● **anything but ...** not at all ... □ ***was anything but straightforward.*** ● **like anything** *colloq* with great speed or enthusiasm. ● **anything from ...** in a possible range from (a specified number) □ ***could cost anything from fifty to five hundred pounds.***

anyway ▷ *conj* used as a sentence connector or when resuming an interrupted piece of dialogue: and so □ ***Anyway, you'll never guess what he did next.*** ▷ *adverb* **1** nevertheless; in spite of what has been said, done, etc □ ***I don't care what you think, I'm going anyway.*** **2** in any way or manner □ ***Try and get it done anyway you can.***

anywhere ▷ *adverb* in, at or to any place. ▷ *pronoun* any place.

Anzac /ˈanzak/ ▷ *noun* **1** (*sometimes* **ANZAC**) the Australia and New Zealand Army Corps, a unit made up of troops from both countries which fought during World War I in the Middle East and on the Western Front. **2** a soldier serving in this unit. ◷ 1915: acronym.

AOB or **a.o.b.** and **AOCB** or **a.o.c.b.** ▷ *abbreviation* any other business or any other competent business, the last item on the agenda for a meeting, when any matter not already dealt with may be raised.

AOC ▷ *abbreviation* APPELLATION D'ORIGINE CONTRÔLÉE

A1 or **A-1** /eɪˈwʌn/ ▷ *adj, colloq* first-class; being of the highest quality.

aorist /ˈɛərɪst, ˈeɪərɪst/ ▷ *noun, grammar* a tense of a verb in some inflected languages, especially Greek, that expresses action in simple past time with no implications of completion, duration or repetition □ ***The aorist in Greek is similar to the past in English.*** Also *as adj.* ● **aoristic** *adj.* ● **aoristically** *adverb.* ◷ 16c: from Greek *aoristos* indefinite, from A-^{2} + *horistos* limited.

aorta /eɪˈɔːtə/ ▷ *noun* (**aortas**) *anatomy* in mammals: the main artery in the body, which carries oxygenated blood from the heart to the smaller arteries that in turn supply the rest of the body. ● **aortic** *adj.* ◷ 16c: from Greek *aorte* something that is hung.

AP ▷ *abbreviation* Associated Press.

apace /əˈpeɪs/ ▷ *adverb, literary* quickly. ◷ 14c: from A-^{1} + PACE^1.

Apache /əˈpatʃɪ/ ▷ *noun* (***Apaches***) **1** a Native N American people who formerly lived nomadically in New Mexico and Arizona. **2** a member of this people. **3** the language of this people. ◷ 18c: from Zuni (the language of another N American native people) *apachu* enemy, the name the Zuni gave to the Navaho people.

apanage see APPANAGE

apart /əˈpɑːt/ ▷ *adverb* **1** in or into pieces □ ***come apart.*** **2** separated by a certain distance or time □ ***The villages are about 6 miles apart.*** **3** to or on one side □ ***set apart for special occasions.*** **4** disregarded, not considered, taken account of, etc □ ***joking apart.*** **5** distinguished by some unique quality □ ***a breed apart.*** ● **apart from someone** or **something** not including them or it; except for them or it; leaving them or it out of consideration □ ***Everyone enjoyed the party apart from Andy.*** ◷ 14c: from French *à part* to one side.

apartheid /aˈpɑːtheɪt, -haɪt/ ▷ *noun* **1** an official state policy, especially that operating in South Africa until 1992, of keeping different races segregated in such areas as housing, education, sport, etc, together with the privileging of one race, in the case of South Africa the White minority, over any others. **2** any segregationist policy □ ***Traditionally working men's clubs operate gender apartheid.*** ◷ 1940s: Afrikaans, from *apart* apart + *-heid* hood.

apartment /əˈpɑːtmənt/ ▷ *noun* **1** (abbreviation **apt**) a single room in a house or flat. **2** (**apartments**) a set of rooms used for accommodation, usually in a large building. **3** *N Amer* a self-contained set of rooms for living in, usually all on one floor, in a large building that is divided into a number of similar units. *Brit equivalent* FLAT^2. ◷ 17c: from French *appartement,* from Latin *appartire* to apportion.

apatetic /apəˈtɛtɪk/ ▷ *adj, zool* said of the coloration or markings of an animal, etc: closely resembling those of another creature or species, or closely resembling its surroundings. Compare SEMATIC. ◷ 19c: from Greek *apatetikos* deceitful.

apathetic /apəˈθɛtɪk/ ▷ *adj* feeling or showing little or no emotion; indifferent; uncaring. ● **apathetically** *adverb.* ◷ 18c: from APATHY by analogy with PATHETIC.

apathy /ˈapəθɪ/ ▷ *noun* **1** lack of interest or enthusiasm. **2** lack of emotion. ◷ 17c: from A-^{2} + Greek *pathos* feeling.

apatite /ˈapətaɪt/ ▷ *noun, geol* a common phosphate mineral, widely distributed in small amounts in many igneous and metamorphic rocks. ◷ Early 19c: from Greek *apate* deceit, from its confusing similarity to other minerals.

apatosaurus ▷ *noun* a huge semi-aquatic dinosaur of the Jurassic period that had massive limbs, a small head, a long neck and a whip-like tail, and is thought to have been herbivorous. Formerly called **brontosaurus.** ◷ From Greek *apate* deceit + *sauros* lizard.

ape /eɪp/ ▷ *noun* **1** any of several species of primate that differ from most monkeys, and resemble humans, in that they have a highly developed brain, lack a tail and are capable of walking upright. **2** *non-technical* any monkey or primate. **3** a mimic. **4** an ugly, stupid or clumsy person. ▷ *verb* (***aped, aping***) to imitate (someone's behaviour, speech, habits, etc). ● **apery** *noun.* ● **go ape** *N Amer slang* to go completely crazy. See also APISH. ◷ Anglo-Saxon as *apa.*

apeman ▷ *noun* any of various extinct primates thought to have been intermediate in development between humans and the higher apes.

aperient /əˈpɪərɪənt/ ▷ *adj* having a mild laxative effect. ▷ *noun* a drug or other remedy that has this effect. ◷ 17c: from Latin *aperire* to open.

aperitif /əpɛrɪˈtiːf/ ▷ *noun* an alcoholic drink taken before a meal to stimulate the appetite. ◷ 19c: from French *apéritif,* from Latin *aperire* to open.

aperture /ˈapətʃə(r)/ ▷ *noun* **1** a small hole or opening. **2** the opening through which light enters an optical instrument such as a camera or telescope. **3** the effective diameter of the lens in such an instrument. ◷ 17c: from Latin *apertura,* from *aperire* to open.

APEX /ˈeɪpɛks/ ▷ *abbreviation* **1** Advance Purchase Excursion, a reduced fare that is available on some air and train tickets when they are booked a certain period in advance. **2** *Brit* Association of Professional, Executive, Clerical and Computer Staff.

apex /ˈeɪpɛks/ ▻ *noun* (*apexes* or *apices* /ˈeɪpɪsiːz/) **1** the highest point or tip. **2** *geom* the highest point of a plane or solid figure relative to some line or plane. **3** a climax or pinnacle. See also APICAL. ⌚ 17c: Latin, meaning 'peak'.

aphaeresis or **apheresis** /əˈfɪərəsɪs/ ▻ *noun, phonetics* the omission of a sound or syllable (or sometimes more than one) at the beginning of a word, eg *telephone* becomes *phone*, where the missing element is sometimes suggested by an apostrophe as in *'gator* for *alligator*. Compare APHESIS, APOCOPE. ⌚ 17c: from Greek *aphairein* to remove.

aphagia /əˈfeɪdʒɪə/ ▻ *noun, pathol* **1** inability or unwillingness to eat. **2** inability to swallow or difficulty in swallowing. ⌚ 19c: from A-^{2} + Greek *phagein* to eat.

aphasia /əˈfeɪzɪə/ ▻ *noun, psychol* loss or impairment of the ability to speak or write, or to understand the meaning of spoken or written language, which in right-handed people is caused by damage to the left side of the brain. ⌚ 19c: from A-^{2} + Greek *phanai* to speak.

aphelion /aˈfiːlɪən, apˈhiːlɪən/ ▻ *noun* (***aphelia*** /aˈfiːlɪə/) the point in a planet's orbit when it is farthest from the Sun. See also PERIHELION, APOGEE. ⌚ 17c: from Greek *apo* from + *helios* Sun.

aphesis /ˈafəsɪs/ ▻ *noun, phonetics* the gradual weakening and disappearance of an unstressed vowel at the beginning of a word, eg *alone* becomes *lone*. • **aphetic** /əˈfɛtɪk/ *adj* ▫ *an aphetic vowel.* • **aphetically** *adverb*. Compare APHAERESIS, APOCOPE. ⌚ 19c: from Greek *aphienai* to set free.

aphid /ˈeɪfɪd/ or **aphis** ▻ *noun* (***aphids*** or ***aphides*** /-diːz/) any of numerous small bugs, including serious plant pests, which have a soft pear-shaped body, a small head and slender beak-like mouthparts that are used to pierce plant tissues and suck the sap, eg greenfly, blackfly. ⌚ 18c.

aphonia /eɪˈfoʊnɪə/ ▻ *noun* inability to speak, which may be caused by hysteria, laryngitis or some other disorder of the larynx, or by brain damage. ⌚ 18c: from A-^{2} + Greek *phone* voice.

aphorism /ˈafərɪzəm/ ▻ *noun* a short and often clever or humorous saying expressing some well-known truth, eg *A little knowledge is a dangerous thing*. • **aphorist** *noun*. • **aphoristic** *adj*. ⌚ 16c: from Greek *aphorizein* to define.

aphotic /eɪˈfoʊtɪk/ ▻ *adj* **1** *bot* said of a plant: able to grow in the absence of sunlight. **2** said of an oceanic zone: below c.1500m (4900ft), ie below the depth that photosynthesis can take place. ⌚ Early 20c: from A-^{2} + Greek *phos, photos* light.

aphrodisiac /afrəˈdɪzɪak/ ▻ *noun* a food, drink or drug that is said to stimulate sexual desire, eg oysters, ginseng. ▻ *adj* sexually exciting or arousing. • **aphrodisiacal** *adj*. ⌚ 19c: from Greek *aphrodisiakos*, from *Aphrodite* the goddess of love.

aphtha /ˈafθə/ ▻ *noun* (***aphthae*** /ˈafθiː, ˈafθaɪ/) **1** *technical* THRUSH^2. **2** (**aphthae**) the small white ulcers that appear on mucus membranes in conditions such as thrush. ⌚ 17c: Greek, meaning 'spot' or 'speck'.

aphyllous /əˈfɪləs/ ▻ *adj, bot* said of some plants: naturally leafless. • **aphylly** *noun*. ⌚ 19c: from A-^{2} + Greek *phyllon* leaf.

apian /ˈeɪpɪən/ ▻ *adj* referring or relating to bees.

apiarist /ˈeɪpɪərɪst/ ▻ *noun* a bee-keeper.

apiary /ˈeɪpɪərɪ/ ▻ *noun* (*apiaries*) a place where honey bees are kept, usually for the purpose of breeding and honey production, but sometimes to aid the pollination of seed and fruit crops. • **apiarian** /-ˈɛərɪən/ *adj*. ⌚ 17c: from Latin *apiarium*, from *apis* bee.

apical /ˈapɪkəl, ˈeɪ-/ ▻ *adj* **1** belonging to, at or forming an apex. **2** *phonetics* said of a sound: articulated with the tip of the tongue, eg /t/ and /d/. ⌚ 19c: from APEX.

apiculture /ˈeɪpɪkʌltʃə(r)/ ▻ *noun* the rearing and breeding of honey bees, especially on a commercial scale, to obtain honey, beeswax or royal jelly. • **apicultural** *adj*. • **apiculturist** *noun*. ⌚ 19c: from Latin *apis* bee + *cultura* tending.

apiece /əˈpiːs/ ▻ *adverb* to, for, by or from each one ▫ *They all chipped in £5 apiece.* ⌚ 15c: originally two words.

apish /ˈeɪpɪʃ/ ▻ *adj* **1** like an ape. **2** imitative, especially in a way that is fawning, unimaginative or lacking in originality. **3** affected; silly. ⌚ 16c.

aplasia /əˈpleɪzɪə/ *pathol* the congenital absence or malformation of an organ or other body part. • **aplastic** *adj*. ⌚ 19c: from A-^{2} + Greek *plassein* to form.

aplastic anaemia ▻ *noun, pathol* a condition characterized by the inability of the bone marrow to generate blood cells properly.

aplenty /əˈplɛntɪ/ ▻ *adverb* in great numbers or abundance. ⌚ 19c: A-^{1} + PLENTY.

aplomb /əˈplɒm/ ▻ *noun* calm self-assurance and poise. ⌚ 19c: from French *à plomb* straight up and down, according to the plumb line.

apnoea or (*US*) **apnea** /apˈnɪə/ ▻ *noun, pathol* a temporary cessation of breathing, which occurs in some adults during sleep, and in some newborn babies. ⌚ 18c: from Greek *apnoia* breathlessness.

apocalypse /əˈpɒkəlɪps/ ▻ *noun* **1** (**Apocalypse**) the last book of the New Testament, also called the REVELATION of St John, which describes the end of the world. **2** any revelation of the future, especially future destruction or violence. ⌚ 12c: from Greek *apocalypsis* uncovering, from *apokalyptein* to disclose.

apocalyptic /əpɒkəˈlɪptɪk/ ▻ *adj* **1** belonging to or like an apocalypse. **2** said of an event: signalling or foretelling an upheaval, disaster, etc. • **apocalyptically** *adverb*.

apocarpous /apoʊˈkɑːpəs/ ▻ *adj, bot* said of the ovaries of certain flower families: having separate CARPELS. Compare SYNCARPOUS. ⌚ 19c: from Greek *apo* away + *karpos* fruit + -OUS.

apochromatic /apəkroʊˈmatɪk/ ▻ *adj* said of a lens: relatively free from chromatic and spherical aberration. • **apochromat** /-ˈkroʊmat/ *noun* a lens that is apochromatic. • **aprochromatism** *noun*. ⌚ 19c: from Greek *apo* away + CHROMATIC 1.

apocope /əˈpɒkəpɪ/ ▻ *noun, phonetics* the loss of pronunciation of the final sound or sounds of a word, either because they are weakly stressed, eg the gradual disappearance of the inflected endings in English, or for reasons of economy in colloquial speech, eg *television* becomes *telly*, or to shorten longish forenames, eg *Patricia* becomes *Pat*. ⌚ 16c: from Greek *apokoptein* to cut off.

apocrine /ˈapəkraɪn/ ▻ *adj* **1** denoting any of various sweat glands located in hairy regions of the body. **2** denoting any secretion that contains part of the cytoplasm of the secretory cell. ⌚ 1920s: from Greek *apo* away + *crine*, from *krinein* to separate.

Apocrypha /əˈpɒkrɪfə/ ▻ *plural noun* those books of the Bible included in the ancient Greek and Latin versions of the Old Testament but not in the Hebrew version, and which are excluded from modern Protestant Bibles but included in Roman Catholic and Orthodox Bibles. Compare PSEUDEPIGRAPHA. ⌚ 14c: from Greek *apocryphos* hidden.

apocryphal /əˈpɒkrɪfəl/ ▻ *adj* **1** being of doubtful authenticity. **2** said of a story, etc: unlikely to be true; mythical. **3** (**Apocryphal**) belonging, relating or referring to the Apocrypha. • **apocryphally** *adverb*.

apodal /ˈapədəl/ and **apodous** /ˈapədəs/ ▻ *adj, zool* **1** said of snakes, eels, etc: lacking feet; lacking limbs, especially hind ones ▫ *The slow-worm is one example of* *an apodal lizard.* **2** said of fish: lacking the ventral fin. ⓘ Early 18c: from A-^{2} + Greek *pous, podos* foot.

apodictic /apəˈdɪktɪk/ or **apodeictic** /-ˈdaɪktɪk/ ▷ *adj* **1** proved to be true by demonstration. **2** *philos* said of a proposition: in Kantian terms, necessarily true. • **apodictically** *adverb.* ⓘ 17c: from Greek *apodeiktikos* clearly demonstrating.

apodosis /əˈpɒdəsɪs/ ▷ *noun* (***apodoses*** /əˈpɒdəsiːz/) *grammar, logic* the consequent clause in a conditional sentence or propositon, eg in *If Winter comes, can Spring be far behind?* the part following the comma is the 'apodosis'. Compare PROTASIS. ⓘ 17c: Greek, from *apodidonai* to give back.

apogamy /əˈpɒgəmɪ/ ▷ *noun, bot* the absence of sexual reproduction as found in some species of fern where new plants can develop without the fusion of gametes. • **apogamous** *adj.* • **apogamously** *adverb.* ⓘ 19c: from Greek *apo* away + -GAMY.

apogee /ˈapoʊdʒiː/ ▷ *noun* **1** *astron* the point in the orbit of the Moon or an artifical satellite around the Earth when it is at its greatest distance from the Earth. Compare PERIGEE, APHELION. **2** *physics* the greatest height reached by a missile whose velocity is not high enough for it to escape from a gravitational field. **3** any culminating point or pinnacle. ⓘ 16c: from Greek *apo* away + *gaia* Earth.

apolitical /eɪpəˈlɪtɪkəl/ ▷ *adj* not interested or active in politics. • **apolitically** *adverb.*

Apollo /əˈpɒloʊ/ ▷ *noun* (***Apollos***) any of a series of US manned spacecraft designed for exploration around, and sometimes landing on, the Moon.

apollo /əˈpɒləʊ/ ▷ *noun* (***apollos***) a stunningly handsome young man. ⓘ Named after Apollo, one of the twelve Olympian Greek gods, famed for his beauty and associated with light, music, poetry, archery, medicine, the care of flocks and herds and also with prophecy.

apologetic /əpɒləˈdʒɛtɪk/ ▷ *adj* showing or expressing regret for a mistake or offence. • **apologetical** *adj.* • **apologetically** *adverb.*

apologia /apəˈloʊdʒɪə/ ▷ *noun* (***apologias***) a formal statement in defence of a belief, cause, someone's behaviour, etc.

apologist /əˈpɒlədʒɪst/ ▷ *noun* someone who formally defends a belief or cause.

apologize or **apologise** /əˈpɒlədʒaɪz/ ▷ *verb* (***apologized, apologizing***) *intr* **1** to acknowledge a mistake or offence and express regret for it. **2** to offer a formal written statement in defence of a belief, cause, someone's behaviour, etc. ⓘ 16c: from APOLOGY.

apology /əˈpɒlədʒɪ/ ▷ *noun* (***apologies***) **1** an expression of regret for a mistake or offence. **2** a formal defence of a belief or cause. • **apology for something** a poor example of it □ *You're a ridiculous apology for a man!* ⓘ 16c: from Greek *apologia*, from *apologeisthai* to speak in defence, from *apo* away + *logos* speech.

aponeurosis /apoʊnjʊəˈroʊsɪs/ ▷ *noun, anatomy* a thin flat tendinous sheet of tissue important in the attachment of muscles to bones, other muscles, etc and in forming sheaths around muscles. • **aponeurotic** *adj.* ⓘ 17c: from Greek *apo* away + *neuron* tendon.

apophthegm or **apothegm** /ˈapəθɛm/ ▷ *noun* a short saying expressing some general truth, usually one that is snappier than an APHORISM. • **apophthegmatic** *adj.* ⓘ 16c: from Greek *apophthegma*, from *apo* forth + *phthengesthai* to speak.

apophyge /əˈpɒfɪdʒɪ/ ▷ *noun, archit* the outward curve of a COLUMN where it rises from its BASE or merges into its CAPITAL^2. ⓘ 16c: Greek, meaning 'escape'.

apophysis /əˈpɒfɪsɪs/ ▷ *noun* (***apophyses*** /-siːz/) **1** *biol* any naturally occurring knobbly outgrowth such as on bones, especially vertebrae, pine cone scales, moss stalks, etc. **2** *geol* a branch of rock that forms an offshoot from the main mass of igneous rock. ⓘ 17c: Greek, meaning 'offshoot'.

apoplectic /apoʊˈplɛktɪk/ ▷ *adj* **1** characteristic of, suffering from, causing or relating to apoplexy. **2** *colloq* red-faced and seething with anger. ▷ *noun* someone who has apoplexy. • **apoplectically** *adverb.* ⓘ 17c: from APOPLEXY.

apoplexy /ˈapəplɛksɪ/ ▷ *noun* the former name for a STROKE (sense 9) caused by a cerebral haemorrhage. ⓘ 14c: from Greek *apoplexia* being struck down, from *apoplessein* to disable by a stroke.

aport /əˈpɔːt/ ▷ *adj, adverb, naut* on or towards the port side. ⓘ 17c: A-^{1} + PORT^2.

aposematic /apəsiːˈmatɪk/ ▷ *noun* said of the colouring or markings of certain animals, especially poisonous ones: startling or garish and so serving as a warning and deterrent to predators. ⓘ 19c: from Greek *apo* away + SEMATIC.

apostasy /əˈpɒstəsɪ/ ▷ *noun* (***apostasies***) the relinquishment or rejection of one's religion or principles or of one's affiliation to a specified political party, etc. ⓘ 14c: from Greek *apo* away + *stasis* standing.

apostate /əˈpɒsteɪt, -stət/ ▷ *noun* someone who rejects a religion, belief, political affiliation, etc that they previously held. ▷ *adj* relating to or involved in this kind of rejection. ⓘ 14c: from APOSTASY.

apostatize or **apostatise** /aˈpɒstətaɪz/ ▷ *verb* (***apostatized, apostatizing***) *intr* to abandon one's religion, beliefs, principles, etc. ⓘ 16c: from APOSTASY.

a posteriori /eɪ pɒstɛrɪˈɔːraɪ/ ▷ *adj, adverb* said of an argument or reasoning: working from effect to cause or from particular cases to general principles; based on observation or experience. Compare A PRIORI. ⓘ 17c: Latin, meaning 'from the latter'.

apostle /əˈpɒsəl/ ▷ *noun* **1** *Christianity* (*often* **Apostle**) someone sent out to preach about Christ in the early church, especially one of the twelve original DISCIPLES. **2** any enthusiastic champion or supporter of a cause, belief, etc. ⓘ Anglo-Saxon *apostol*: from Greek *apostolos*, from *apo* away + *stellein* to send.

Apostles' Creed ▷ *noun, Christianity* a succinct summary, dating back to 3c, of the main principles and ideology behind the Christian faith, widely used in Roman Catholic and Protestant churches and recognized by Orthodox Churches, which stresses both the threefold nature of God (as Father, Son and Holy Spirit) and the work of Christ as God's representative on Earth.

apostolic /apəˈstɒlɪk/ ▷ *adj* **1** relating to the apostles in the early Christian Church, or to their teaching. **2** relating to the Pope, thought of as the successor to the Apostle Peter □ *the Apostolic See.* • **apostolical** *adj.* • **apostolically** *adverb.*

apostolic succession ▷ *noun, Christianity* the theory in the Christian Church (notably the Roman Catholic Church) that certain spiritual powers believed to have been conferred on the first Apostles by Christ have been handed down from one generation of bishops to the next in an unbroken chain of transmission.

apostrophe^1 /əˈpɒstrəfɪ/ ▷ *noun* a punctuation mark (') that in English is used to show that there has been an omission of a letter or letters, eg in a contraction such as *I'm* for *I am*, or as a signal for the possessive such as *Ann's book.* ⓘ 16c: French, from Greek *apostrephein* to turn away, and originally pronounced with only three syllables as /ˈapəstrəf/, but later influenced by the pronunciation of following entry.

apostrophe^2 /əˈpɒstrəfɪ/ ▷ *noun* (***apostrophized, apostrophizing***) *rhetoric* a passage in a speech, poem, etc which digresses to pointedly address a person (especially dead or absent) or thing. • **apostrophic** /apəˈstrɒfɪk/ *adj.* ⓘ 16c: Latin, from Greek, meaning 'a turning away'.

apostrophe

- An **apostrophe** can be used to indicate possession, with or without an extra *s* □ *the child's dog* □ *the children's clothes* □ *James's ball* □ *Robert Burns's letters* □ *the boys' mothers.*
- Should you write an extra *s* or not?

☆ WRITE WHAT YOU SAY. If an extra *s* sounds too clumsy to say, leave it out in writing □ *Moses' laws* □ *Xerxes' army* □ *the Mercedes' engine.*

- An apostrophe can also be used to indicate that letters or numbers have been dropped to produce a shortened form □ *I'd say so* □ *she'll get you back* □ *we can't comment* □ *sounds of the '60s.*
- Apostrophes are no longer used with former clipped forms such as *bus, plane* and *phone.* These are now treated as full forms in their own right.
- Note that *and* abbreviated to *'n'* has two apostrophes.
- An apostrophe can also be used to clarify some plurals, especially plurals of short words □ *do's and don'ts* □ *several unpleasant set-to's* □ *Dot your i's and cross your t's* □ *three lbw's in three balls.*
- Note that in dates both *'s* and *s* are permissible:

✓ *Were you around in the 60's?*
✓ *It's been law since the 1930s.*

apostrophize or **apostrophise** /əˈpɒstrəfaɪz/ ▷ *verb* ▷ *rhetoric* to address someone or something in an APOSTROPHE².

apothecary /əˈpɒθəkərɪ/ ▷ *noun* (***apothecaries***) *old use* a chemist licensed to dispense drugs. ⓒ 14c: from Greek *apotheke* storehouse.

apothegm see APOPHTHEGM

apothem /ˈapəθɛm/ ▷ *noun, math* the perpendicular from the centre of a regular polygon to any of its sides. ⓒ 19c: from Greek *apo* away + *tithenai* to place.

apotheosis /əpɒθɪˈoʊsɪs/ ▷ *noun* (***apotheoses*** /-siːz/) **1 a** the action of raising someone to the rank of a god; **b** the state of being raised to the rank of a god. **2 a** glorification or idealization of someone or something; **b** an ideal embodiment. ⓒ 16c: Greek, from *apo* completely + *theoun* to deify, from *theos* god.

appal or (*N Amer*) **appall** /əˈpɔːl/ ▷ *verb* (***appals*** or ***appalls, appalled, appalling***) to shock, dismay or horrify. ⓒ 14c: from French *appallir* to grow pale.

appalling ▷ *adj* **1** causing feelings of shock or horror. **2** *colloq* extremely bad □ *His cooking is appalling.* • **appallingly** *adverb.*

appanage or **apanage** /ˈapənɪdʒ/ ▷ *noun* **1 a** the provision made for the maintenance of younger children, especially the younger sons of a king; **b** land or property that is set aside for this. **2** a benefit that traditionally goes along with certain jobs, eg a company car or a tied house. ⓒ 17c: from French *apaner* to give the means of subsistence to, related to Latin *panis* bread.

apparatchik /apəˈratʃɪk/ ▷ *noun* (***apparatchiks*** or ***appartchiki*** /-tʃɪkiː/) **1** a member of a communist bureaucracy or party machine. **2** a bureaucratic official in a corporation, organization, political party, etc. ⓒ 1940s: Russian, from *apparat* apparatus or machine.

apparatus /apəˈreɪtəs, apəˈrɑːtəs/ ▷ *noun* (***apparatuses*** or ***apparatus***) **1** the equipment needed for a specified purpose, especially in a science laboratory, gym, military campaign, etc. **2** an organization or system made up of many different parts. **3** a machine with a specified purpose □ *breathing apparatus.* ⓒ 16c: Latin, from *apparare* to prepare for something.

apparel /əˈparəl/ ▷ *noun, old use, formal* clothing. ⓒ 14c: from French *apareiller* to make fit.

apparent /əˈparənt, əˈpɛərənt/ ▷ *adj* **1** easy to see or understand; obvious. **2** seeming to be real but perhaps not actually so. **3** *physics* said of the results of an experiment, etc: obtained by observation alone and usually without taking certain variables into account. • **apparently** *adverb.* See also HEIR APPARENT. ⓒ 14c: from Latin *apparere* to come into sight.

apparent horizon see HORIZON

apparent time and **apparent solar time** ▷ *noun* the true time as shown by the shadow of a sundial at a particular place and moment, as opposed to the mean time shown on a watch or clock, etc.

apparition /apəˈrɪʃən/ ▷ *noun* **1** a sudden unexpected appearance, especially of a ghost. **2** a ghost. **3** the action of suddenly appearing or of becoming visible. ⓒ 16c: from Latin *apparitio* an appearance, from *apparere* to appear.

appeal /əˈpiːl/ ▷ *noun* **1 a** an urgent or formal request for help, money, medical aid, food, etc; **b** a request made in a pleading or heartfelt way. **2** *law* **a** an application or petition to a higher authority or law court to carry out a review of a decision taken by a lower one; **b** a review and its outcome as carried out by such an authority or court; **c** a case that is under such review; **d** *as adj* □ *the appeal court.* **3** the quality of being attractive, interesting, pleasing, etc. **4** *cricket* a request made to the umpire from the fielding side to declare that a batsman is out. ▷ *verb* (***appealed, appealing***) *intr* **1** to make an urgent or formal request □ *appealed for calm.* **2** *law* to request a higher authority or law court to review a decision given by a lower one. **3** *cricket* **a** to ask the umpire to call a batsman out; **b** to ask the umpire whether a batsman is out or not. **4** to be attractive, interesting, pleasing, etc □ *Some brands of cat food appeal more than others.* • **appealing** *adj* attractive. • **appealingly** *adverb.* ⓒ 14c: from Latin *appellare* to address.

■ **appeal to someone** or **something a** to call on or address them or it; **b** to implore or beg them or it.

appear /əˈpɪə(r)/ ▷ *verb* (***appeared, appearing***) *intr* **1** to become visible or come into sight. **2** to develop □ *Flaws in his design soon appeared.* **3** to seem. **4** to present oneself formally or in public, eg on stage. **5** to be present in a law court as either accused or counsel. **6** to be published. ⓒ 14c: from Latin *apparere* to come forth.

appearance /əˈpɪərəns/ ▷ *noun* **1** an act or instance of appearing □ *his appearance on TV.* **2** the outward or superficial look of someone or something □ *He never bothered much with his appearance.* **3** illusion; pretence □ *the appearance of being a reasonable person.* **4** (**appearances**) the outward show or signs by which someone or something is judged or assessed □ *appearances can be deceptive.* • **keep up appearances** to put on an outward public show that things are normal, stable, etc when they are not. • **put in** or **make an appearance** to attend a meeting, party, etc only briefly, especially out of politeness, duty, etc. • **to all appearances** so far as it can be seen. ⓒ 14c.

appease /əˈpiːz/ ▷ *verb* (***appeased, appeasing***) **1** to calm, quieten, pacify, etc, especially by making some kind of concession. **2** to satisfy or allay (a thirst, appetite, doubt, etc). • **appeaser** *noun.* • **appeasing** *adj.* • **appeasingly** *adverb.* ⓒ 14c: from French *apesier* to bring to peace.

appeasement ▷ *noun* **1** the act, state or process of appeasing or of being appeased. **2** a policy of achieving peace by making concessions.

appellant /əˈpɛlənt/ ▷ *noun* **a** someone who makes an appeal to a higher court to review the decision of a lower one; **b** someone who makes any appeal. ▷ *adj* belonging, relating or referring to an appeal or appellant. ⓒ 14c: from Latin *appellare* to address.

appellate /əˈpɛlɪt/ ▷ *adj, law* **1** concerned with appeals. **2** said of a court, tribunal, etc: having the authority to review and, if necessary, overturn the earlier decision of another court. ◷ 18c: from Latin *appellare* to address.

appellation /apə'leɪʃən/ ▷ *noun, formal* **1** a name or title. **2** the act of giving a name or title to someone or something. ◷ 15c: from Latin *appellare* to address.

appellation contrôlée / *French* apɛlasjɔ̃ kɔ̃tʀole/ and ***appellation d'origine controlée*** / *French* — dɔʀiʒin —/ ▷ *noun* (abbreviation **AC** or **AOC**) **1** the system which within France designates and controls the names especially of wine, but also of cognac, armagnac, calvados and some foods, guaranteeing the authenticity of the producing region and the methods of production, and which outside France protects the generic names from misappropriation. **2** the highest designation of French wine awarded under this system. Compare VDQS, VIN DE PAYS.

appellative /ə'pɛlətɪv/ ▷ *noun* **1** a designated name or title. **2** *grammar* a technical name for COMMON NOUN. ◷ 16c: from Latin *appellare* to address.

append /ə'pɛnd/ ▷ *verb* (***appended, appending***) to add or attach something to a document, especially as a supplement, footnote, etc. ◷ 17c: from Latin *appendere* to hang.

appendage /ə'pɛndɪdʒ/ ▷ *noun* **1** anything added or attached to a larger or more important part. **2** *zool* a part or organ, eg a leg, antenna, etc, that extends from the main body of animals such as insects, crustaceans, etc. **3** *bot* an offshoot, eg a branch, leaf, etc, that sprouts from the stem of a plant. ◷ 17c.

appendectomy /apɛn'dɛktəmɪ/ or **appendicectomy** /əpɛndɪ'sɛktəmɪ/ ▷ *noun* (***appendectomies*** or ***appendicectomies***) *surgery* an operation for the surgical removal of the appendix, the commonest surgical emergency. ◷ 19c: from APPENDIX + -ECTOMY.

appendicitis /əpɛndɪ'saɪtɪs/ ▷ *noun, pathol* inflammation of the appendix, causing abdominal pain and vomiting, and usually treated by surgical removal of the organ.

appendix /ə'pɛndɪks/ ▷ *noun* (***appendixes*** or ***appendices*** /ə'pɛndɪsiːz/) **1** a section containing extra information, notes, etc at the end of a book or document. **2** *anatomy* a short tube-like sac attached to the lower end of the caecum at the junction of the small and large intestines. **3** anything that is supplementary to something else. ◷ 16c: Latin, from *appendere* to hang.

apperceive /apə'siːv/ ▷ *verb* (***apperceived, apperceiving***) **1** to be consciously aware of understanding something. **2** *psychol* to be consciously aware of assimilating (some new information or understanding) to the mass of knowledge or understanding that is already held. ◷ 14c: from French *aperceveir*, from Latin *percipere* to seize.

apperception /apə'sɛpʃən/ ▷ *noun* **1** the mind's awareness of itself as a conscious agent. **2** the act of apperceiving. ◷ 18c.

appertain /apə'teɪn/ ▷ *verb, intr* (*usually* **appertain to something**) to belong or relate to it. ◷ 14c: from Latin *pertinere* to belong.

appetent /'apətənt/ ▷ *adj* showing an eager natural craving. • **appetence** or **appetency** *noun*. ◷ 15c: from Latin *petere* to seek.

appetite /'apətaɪt/ ▷ *noun* **a** a natural physical desire, especially for food; **b** the extent to which someone enjoys their food; the capacity someone has for eating □ *always has a very poor appetite.* • **have an appetite for something** to favour or enjoy it. ◷ 14c: from Latin *appetitus*, from *petere* to seek after.

appetizer or **appetiser** /'apətaɪzə(r)/ ▷ *noun* a small amount of food or drink taken before a meal to stimulate the appetite.

appetizing or **appetising** ▷ *adj* **1** stimulating the appetite, especially by looking or smelling delicious; tasty. **2** enticing; tempting □ *The book had the appetizing title 'American Psycho'.* • **appetizingly** *adverb*. ◷ 17c: from French *appetissant*.

applaud /ə'plɔːd/ ▷ *verb* (***applauded, applauding***) **1** *intr* to show approval by clapping. **2** to express approval of something □ *He applauded her brave attempt.* ◷ 16c: from Latin *applaudere*, from *plaudere* to clap.

applause /ə'plɔːz/ ▷ *noun* **1** approval or appreciation shown by clapping. **2** critical or public approval or appreciation in general □ *published her first novel to great applause.* ◷ 16c: from Latin *applausus*, from *plaudere* to clap.

apple /'apəl/ ▷ *noun* **1** any of numerous varieties of a small deciduous tree with pink or white flowers and edible fruit. **2** the firm round edible fruit of this tree, which has a green, red or yellow skin and white flesh, and is eaten fresh or cooked, or used to make fruit juice, cider, etc. **3** *in compounds* □ *apple-blossom* □ *apple-corer.* **4** *as adj* □ *apple-green.* • **Adam's apple** see separate entry. • **apples and pears** *Cockney rhyming slang* stairs. • **in apple-pie order** neat and tidy. • **the apple of one's eye** someone's favourite person □ *That baby is just the apple of her eye.* • **the Big Apple** see separate entry. • **upset the apple cart** to disrupt carefully made plans. ◷ Anglo-Saxon *æppel*.

apple jack ▷ *noun* the US name for CIDER.

apple-pie bed ▷ *noun* a bed that, as a joke, has been made up with the sheets doubled up so that the person cannot get into it.

apple sauce ▷ *noun* a sauce made from stewed apples, traditionally served with roast pork.

apple strudel /— 'struːdəl/ ▷ *noun* a cake originating in Austria, made from very thin wafers of pastry wrapped around a filling of apples and raisins flavoured with cinnamon.

Appleton layer /'apəltən —/ ▷ *noun, physics* the F-LAYER. ◷ 1930s: named after the British physicist, Edward V Appleton (1892–1965).

appliance /ə'plaɪəns/ ▷ *noun* **1** any electrical device, usually a tool or machine, that is used to perform a specific task, especially in the home, eg a washing machine, iron or toaster. **2** the act of putting something into use, practice, operation, etc □ *the appliance of science.* **3** *old use* a fire engine. ◷ 17c: from APPLY.

applicable /ə'plɪkəbəl, 'aplɪkəbəl/ ▷ *adj* **1** relevant; to the point. **2** suitable; appropriate. **3** able to be applied. ◷ 17c: from Latin *applicare* to apply.

applicant /'aplɪkənt/ ▷ *noun* someone who has applied for a job, a university place, a grant, etc. ◷ 15c: from Latin *applicare* to apply.

application /aplɪ'keɪʃən/ ▷ *noun* **1** a formal written or verbal request, proposal or submission, eg for a job. **2 a** the act of putting something on (something else); **b** something put on (something else) □ *stopped the squeak with an application of oil.* **3** the act of using something for a particular purpose □ *the application of statistics to interpret the data.* **4** *computing* a specific task or function that a computer system or program is designed to perform, eg payroll processing, stock control. **5** *computing, colloq* an applications package. **6** dedication; persistent effort □ *Her application to the job is astounding.* **7** relevance; usefulness □ *religion and its application to today's world.* ◷ 15c: from Latin *applicare* to apply.

applications package ▷ *noun, computing* a set of integrated programs designed for a particular purpose, usually to perform a specific task, eg word-processing, database or spreadsheet.

applications program ▷ *noun, computing* a computer program written to perform a specific task, eg word-processing.

applicator /'aplɪkeɪtə(r)/ ▷ *noun* **1** a device, eg on a tube of cream, etc, designed for putting something on to or into something else. **2** *as adj* □ ***applicator tampons.*** ⓒ 17c: from Latin *applicare* to apply.

applied /ə'plaɪd/ ▷ *adj* said of a skill, theory, etc: put to practical use □ ***applied linguistics.*** Compare PURE 5.

appliqué /ə'pliːkeɪ/ ▷ *noun* **1** a decorative technique whereby pieces of differently textured and coloured fabrics are cut into various shapes and stitched onto each other. **2** work produced using this technique. ▷ *verb* (***appliquéd, appliquéing***) to use this technique to create (a decorative article). ⓒ 19c: French, meaning 'applied'.

apply /ə'plaɪ/ ▷ *verb* (***applies, applied, applying***) **1** *intr* to make a formal request, proposal or submission, eg for a job. **2** to put something on to something else. **3** to put or spread something on a surface □ ***applied three coats of paint.*** **4** *intr* to be relevant or suitable □ ***thinks the rules don't apply to her.*** **5** to put (a skill, rule, theory, etc) to practical use □ ***Try to understand the principles before applying the theory.*** ⓒ 14c: from Latin *applicare* to attach.

■ **apply oneself to something** to give one's full attention or energy to (a task, etc).

appoggiatura /əpɒdʒɪə'tʊərə/ ▷ *noun* (***-turas*** or ***-ture*** /-tʊəreɪ/) *music* an ornamental note that is not essential to the melody but which leans on the following note, taking half its time from it. Compare ACCIACCATURA. ⓒ 18c: from Italian *appoggiare* to lean upon.

appoint /ə'pɔɪnt/ ▷ *verb* (***appointed, appointing***) **1** *tr & intr* to give someone a job or position. **2** to fix or agree on (a date, time or place) □ ***They appointed Thursday at noon as the deadline.*** **3** to equip or furnish □ ***The rooms were beautifully appointed in Art Deco style.*** ● **appointee** *noun.* ⓒ 14c: from French *apointer*, from *point* point.

appointed ▷ *adj* **1** said of an arranged time, place, etc: fixed upon; settled in advance □ ***met her at the appointed hour.*** **2** *in compounds* furnished; equipped □ ***a well-appointed kitchen.***

appointment /ə'pɔɪntmənt/ ▷ *noun* **1** an arrangement to meet someone. **2 a** the act of giving someone a job or position; **b** the job or position someone is given; **c** the person who is given a job or position. **3** (**appointments**) *formal* equipment and furnishings. ● **by appointment** at a time arranged in advance □ ***saw his clients only by appointment.*** ● **by appointment to someone** a designation appended to the name of a supplier of goods or services, etc to show that it has been chosen and approved by someone, especially by some royal figure □ ***was delighted to have 'by appointment to HRH Princess Margaret' after the firm's name.***

apportion /ə'pɔːʃən/ ▷ *verb* to share out fairly or equally. ● **apportionable** *adj.* ● **apportionment** *noun.* ⓒ 16c: from French *portioner* to share.

apposite /'apəzɪt, -zaɪt/ ▷ *adj* suitable; well chosen; appropriate. ● **appositely** *adverb.* ● **appositeness** *noun.* ⓒ 17c: from Latin *appositus*, from *ponere* to place or put.

apposition /apə'zɪʃən/ ▷ *noun* **1** *grammar* a construction in which a series of nouns or noun phrases have the same grammatical status and refer to the same person or thing and give further information about them or it, eg *Poppy, the cat* or *the archdruid himself, Julian Cope*. **2** *bot* growth in the thickness of cell walls created by new material being put down in layers. ⓒ 15c: from Latin *appositio, appositionis*, from *apponere* to put something next to something else.

appraisal /ə'preɪzəl/ ▷ *noun* **1** evaluation; estimation of quality. **2** any method of doing this.

appraise /ə'preɪz/ ▷ *verb* (***appraised, appraising***) **1** to decide the value or quality of (someone's skills, ability, etc). **2** to put a price on (a house, property, etc), especially officially. ● **appraisable** *adj.* ● **appraisement** *noun.* ● **appraiser** *noun.* ⓒ 16c: from French *aprisier*, from *prisier* to prize.

appraise, apprise

● **Appraise** means 'to evaluate', **apprise** means 'to inform':

✓ *There was a magnificent belvedere for appraising the surroundings*

✓ *The judge had not been apprised properly of her wishes.*

● Sometimes, **appraise** is used where you might expect **apprise**:

✗ *I had my hand up for about ten minutes, and I thought our friend on your right had appraised you of that.* See also Usage Note at **apprise**.

appreciable /ə'priːʃəbəl/ ▷ *adj* noticeable; significant; able to be measured or noticed □ ***The new motorway makes an appreciable difference to the travelling time.*** ● **appreciably** *adverb.* ⓒ Early 19c: from APPRECIATE.

appreciate /ə'priːʃɪeɪt, -sɪ-/ ▷ *verb* (***appreciated, appreciating***) **1** to be grateful or thankful for something. **2** to be aware of the value, quality, etc of something. **3** to understand or be aware of something. **4** *usually intr* to increase in value. ● **appreciative** *adj.* ● **appreciatively** *adverb.* ⓒ 17c: from Latin *appretiare*, from *pretium* price.

appreciation ▷ *noun* **1** gratitude or thanks. **2** sensitive understanding and enjoyment of the value or quality of something □ ***an appreciation of good music.*** **3** the state of knowing or being aware of something. **4** an increase in value. ● **show (one's) appreciation 1** to give an indication of one's gratitude, eg by way of a gift, etc □ ***Here are some flowers to show my appreciation.*** **2** to give an indication of one's enjoyment of something, eg by clapping, cheering, etc. ⓒ 15c.

apprehend /aprɪ'hɛnd/ ▷ *verb* (***apprehended, apprehending***) **1** to arrest. **2** to understand. ⓒ 14c: from Latin *apprehendere* to lay hold of.

apprehension /aprɪ'hɛnʃən/ ▷ *noun* **1** uneasy concern about the imminent future; fear or anxiety. **2** the act of capturing and arresting someone or something □ ***Her apprehension was hindered by his lies.*** **3** understanding. ⓒ 14c.

apprehensive /aprɪ'hɛnsɪv/ ▷ *adj* anxious or worried; uneasily concerned about the imminent future. ● **apprehensively** *adverb.* ● **apprehensiveness** *noun.*

apprentice /ə'prɛntɪs/ ▷ *noun* **1 a** someone, usually a young person, who works for an agreed period of time, often for very low pay, in order to learn a craft or trade; **b** *as adj* □ ***an apprentice hairdresser.*** **2** anyone who is relatively unskilled at something or just beginning to learn something. ▷ *verb* (***apprenticed, apprenticing***) to take someone on as an apprentice. ⓒ 14c: from French *apprentis*, from Latin *apprehendere* to lay hold of.

apprenticeship ▷ *noun* **1** the status of an apprentice. **2** the statutory time of training for a trade, etc, now varying according to the trade but formerly seven years. ● **to serve one's apprenticeship** to be employed as an apprentice with the view to getting a qualification in a specified trade or craft after a set number of years. ⓒ 16c.

apprise /ə'praɪz/ ▷ *verb* (***apprised, apprising***) (*usually* **apprize someone of something**) to give them information about it. ⓒ 17c: from French *appris*, from *apprendre* to learn.

apprise

See Usage Note at **appraise**.

☆ PLAIN ENGLISH alternatives are **tell (someone something), inform someone or something)**.

appro /'aproʊ/ ▷ *noun* ● **on appro** *colloq* on approval. See under APPROVAL.

approach /əˈproʊtʃ/ ▷ *verb* (***approaches***, ***approached***, ***approaching***) **1** *tr & intr* to come near or nearer in space, time, quality, character, state, etc □ ***It's approaching one o'clock*** □ ***Few can approach her beautiful singing voice.*** **2** to begin to deal with, think about, etc (a problem, subject, etc) □ ***They approached the project from an entirely new angle.*** **3** to contact someone, especially when wanting to suggest, propose, sell, etc something, especially something illegal or underhand □ ***was approached by a drug dealer.*** ▷ *noun* **1** the act of coming near. **2** a way to, or means of reaching, a place. **3** a request for help, support, etc; a suggestion or proposal. **4** a way of considering or dealing with a problem, etc □ ***a new approach.*** **5** the course that an aircraft follows as it comes in to land. **6** *golf* the shot that is played onto the putting green. • **make approaches to someone** to suggest something underhand to them or to try to influence them to do something underhand. ⊙ 14c: from Latin *appropiare* to draw near.

approachable ▷ *adj* **1** friendly and ready to listen and help. **2** capable of being reached. **3** accessible; comparatively easy to understand □ ***gave a very approachable account of Freud.*** • **approachability** *noun*. ⊙ 16c.

approbation /aproʊˈbeɪʃən/ ▷ *noun* approval; consent. • **approbatory** /əˈproʊbətərɪ, aprəˈbeɪtərɪ/ *adj*. ⊙ 14c: from Latin *approbatio*, from *approbare* to approve.

appropriate ▷ *adj* /əˈproʊprɪət/ suitable or proper. ▷ *verb* /-eɪt/ (***appropriated***, ***appropriating***) **1** to take something as one's own, especially without permission. **2** to put (money) aside for a particular purpose. • **appropriately** *adverb*. • **appropriateness** *noun*. • **appropriation** *noun*. • **appropriator** *noun*. ⊙ 16c: from Latin *appropriare*, from *proprius* one's own.

approval ▷ *noun* **1** a favourable opinion; esteem. **2** official permission. • **on approval** said of goods for sale: able to be returned if not satisfactory. ⊙ 17c.

approve /əˈpruːv/ ▷ *verb* (***approved***, ***approving***) **1** to agree to or permit. **2** *intr* (**approve of someone** or **something**) to be pleased with or think well of them or it. • **approving** *adj*. • **approvingly** *adverb*. ⊙ 14c: from Latin *approbare* to approve of.

approx. ▷ *abbreviation* approximate, approximately.

approximate ▷ *adj* /əˈprɒksɪmət/ almost exact or accurate. ▷ *verb* /-meɪt/ (***approximated***, ***approximating***) *tr & intr* to come close to something in value, quality, accuracy, etc. • **approximately** *adverb*. ⊙ 17c: from Latin *approximare*, from *proximus* nearest.

approximation /əprɒksɪˈmeɪʃən/ ▷ *noun* **1** a figure, answer, etc which is almost exact. **2** the process of estimating a figure, etc. ⊙ 17c.

appurtenance /əˈpɜːtənəns/ ▷ *noun* (*usually* **appurtenances**) an accessory to, or minor detail of, something larger, especially in reference to property-owning rights. ⊙ 14c: from French *apertenance*, from Latin *appertinere* to belong.

APR ▷ *abbreviation* annual percentage rate, an annual rate of interest calculated from figures relating to periods shorter or longer than a year and supplied in order to allow potential customers to compare the rates offered by competing financial institutions.

Apr or **Apr.** ▷ *abbreviation* April.

apraxia /eɪˈpraksɪə, ə-/ ▷ *noun*, *pathol* an inability to make deliberate movements with accuracy, usually as a result of brain disease. ⊙ 19c: Greek, meaning 'inaction'.

après-ski /apreˈskiː/ ▷ *noun* **1** the relaxation and entertainment that is enjoyed after a day's skiing. **2** *as adj* □ ***an après-ski party.*** ⊙ 1950s: French, meaning 'after-ski'.

apricot /ˈeɪprɪkɒt/ ▷ *noun* **1** a small deciduous tree with oval toothed leaves and white or pale pink flowers. **2** the small edible fruit of this plant, which has yellow flesh and a soft furry yellowish-orange skin, eaten fresh, or used to make jams, preserves, etc. **3** the colour of this fruit. Also *as adj*. ⊙ 16c: from Portuguese *albricoque*, from Latin *praecox* early-ripening.

April /ˈeɪprɪl/ ▷ *noun* **1** the fourth month of the year which has 30 days and which follows March and comes before May. **2** *as adj* □ ***April showers.*** ⊙ 12c.

April fool ▷ *noun* **1** someone who has had a practical joke played on them on 1 April. **2** a practical joke played on this date. ⊙ 17c.

April Fool's Day and **All Fool's Day** ▷ *noun* 1 April, the day when traditionally throughout Europe people play practical jokes on one another. ⊙ 19c.

a priori /eɪ praɪˈɔːraɪ, — priː-/ ▷ *adj*, *adverb* **1** said of an argument or reasoning: working from cause to effect or from general principles to particular cases. **2** verified by one's own previous knowledge or by someone or something else. Compare A POSTERIORI. ⊙ 18c: Latin, meaning 'from what is before'.

apron /ˈeɪprən/ ▷ *noun* **1 a** a piece of cloth, plastic, etc tied around the waist and worn over the front of clothes to protect them; **b** any similar cloth worn as part of the distinctive or ceremonial dress of certain groups, eg by members of the clergy, Freemasons, etc. **2** a hard-surface area at an airport where aircraft are loaded. **3** *theat* the part of the stage that can still be seen when the curtain is closed, which in Elizabethan times jutted right out into the audience. **4** *golf* the area of fairway around the green. **5** a SKIRT (sense 4). • **tied to someone's apron strings** usually said of a boy or man: completely dominated by and dependent on them, especially a mother or wife. ⊙ 15c: from 14c *napron*, from French *naperon*, a diminutive of *nappe* a tablecloth.

apropos /aprəˈpoʊ, ˈaprəpoʊ/ ▷ *adj* said of remarks: suitable or to the point. ▷ *adverb* by the way; appropriately. • **apropos of something** with reference to it. ⊙ 17c: French, meaning 'to the purpose'.

apse /aps/ ▷ *noun* (***apses*** /ˈapsɪz/) a semicircular recess, especially when arched and domed and at the east end of a church. ⊙ 19c: from Greek *apsis* arch, from *haptein* to fasten.

apsis /ˈapsɪs/ ▷ *noun* (***apsides*** /ˈapsɪdiːz, apˈsaɪdiːz/) either of two points in the orbit of a planet, satellite, etc, that lie furthest from or closest to the body about which it is orbiting. See also APHELION, PERIHELION. ⊙ 17c: Greek, meaning 'arch'.

APT ▷ *abbreviation* advanced passenger train.

apt /apt/ ▷ *adj* **1** suitable. **2** clever or quick to learn. • **aptly** *adverb*. • **aptness** *noun*. • **apt at something** ready and quick to learn or understand it □ ***She is apt at foreign languages.*** • **apt to do something** inclined or likely to do it □ ***Harry is apt to have illusions.*** ⊙ 14c: from Latin *aptus* fit.

apt. or **apt** ▷ *abbreviation* apartment.

apterous /ˈaptərəs/ ▷ *adj*, *zool* without wings. ⊙ 18c: from Greek *apteros* wingless.

apteryx /ˈaptərɪks/ ▷ *noun* (***apteryxes***) any flightless bird belonging to the KIWI family, found in New Zealand. ⊙ Early 19c: from Greek *a* without + *pteryx* wing.

aptitude /ˈaptɪtʃuːd/ ▷ *noun* **1** (*usually* **aptitude for something**) a natural skill or talent □ ***showed a real aptitude for playing the piano.*** **2** intelligence; speed in learning or understanding □ ***Her aptitude in maths is astounding.*** **3** suitability. **4** *as adj* □ ***aptitude test.*** ⊙ 17c: from Latin *aptitudo*, from *aptus* fit.

AQ ▷ *abbreviation* achievement quotient.

aq. or **Aq.** ▷ *abbreviation* **1** *aqua* (Latin), water. **2** aqueous.

aqua- /akwə/ and **aqui-** /akwɪ/ ▷ *combining form*, denoting water □ ***aqualung.***

aquaculture and **aquiculture** ▷ *noun*, *agric* the practice of using the sea, lakes and rivers for cultivating aquatic animals eg fish, shellfish and plants eg seaweed, especially for consumption as food. ⊙ 19c.

aqua fortis ▷ *noun, old use* the early scientific name for NITRIC ACID. ◷ 17c: Latin, meaning 'strong water'.

aqualung ▷ *noun* a device that enables a diver to breathe under water, consisting of a mouth tube connected to one or more cylinders of compressed air strapped to the diver's back.

aquamarine /akwəmə'riːn/ ▷ *noun* **1** *geol* a transparent bluish-green gemstone that is a variety of the mineral beryl. **2** the colour of this gemstone. ◷ 16c: Latin, meaning 'sea water'.

aquaplane ▷ *noun* a board similar to a water ski but shorter and wider so that the rider puts both feet on it while being towed along at high speed by a motor boat. ▷ *verb, intr* **1** to ride on an aquaplane. **2** said of a vehicle: to slide along out of control on a thin film of water, the tyres having lost contact with the road surface. ● **aquaplaning** *noun* the sport of riding aquaplanes. ◷ Early 20c.

aqua regia /'akwə 'riːdʒə/ ▷ *noun* a highly corrosive mixture of one part concentrated nitric acid to three parts concentrated hydrochloric acid, which dissolves all metals except silver. ◷ 17c: Latin, meaning 'royal water', so called because it dissolves gold and platinum which are thought of as the 'noble' metals.

aquarelle /akwə'rɛl/ ▷ *noun* **1** a method of painting using very transparent watercolours. **2** a painting, often of flowers or a landscape, that is produced using this method. ◷ 19c: from Italian *aquarella* a watercolour.

aquarium /ə'kwɛərɪəm/ ▷ *noun* (***aquariums*** or ***aquaria*** /-rɪə/) **1** a glass tank that fish, other water animals and water plants are kept in so that they can be observed or displayed. **2** a building in a zoo, etc with several of these tanks. ◷ 19c: from Latin *aquarius* of water.

Aquarius /ə'kwɛərɪəs/ ▷ *noun* **1** *astron* a large but dim southern constellation of the zodiac, lying between Pisces and Capricornus. **2** *astrol* **a** the eleventh sign of the zodiac; **b** a person born between 21 January and 19 February, under this sign. ● **Aquarian** *adj*. See table at ZODIAC. ◷ 14c: Latin, meaning 'water-carrier'.

aquatic /ə'kwatɪk/ ▷ *adj* **1** denoting any organism that lives or grows in, on or near water. **2** said of sports: taking place in water. ▷ *noun* **1** an aquatic animal or plant. **2** (**aquatics**) water sports. ◷ 17c in sense 1; 15c, meaning 'watery' or 'rainy': from Latin *aquaticus* watery.

aquatint /'akwətɪnt/ ▷ *noun* **1** a method of INTAGLIO etching that gives a transparent granular effect similar to that of watercolour. **2** a picture produced using this method of etching. ▷ *verb, tr & intr* to etch using this technique. ◷ 18c: from Italian *aqua tinta*, from Latin *aqua tincta* dyed water.

aquavit /'akwəvɪt, -viːt/ ▷ *noun* a Scandanavian spirit made from potatoes and other starch-rich plants such as grains and flavoured with caraway seeds, traditionally drunk like schnapps without being diluted. ◷ 19c: the Scandanavian form of AQUA VITAE.

aqua vitae /'akwə 'viːtaɪ, — 'vaɪtiː/ ▷ *noun* a strong alcoholic drink, especially brandy. ◷ 15c: Latin, meaning 'water of life'.

aqueduct /'akwɪdʌkt/ ▷ *noun* a channel or canal that carries water, especially one that is in the form of a tall bridge across a valley, river, etc. ◷ 16c: from Latin *aqua* water + *ducere* to lead.

aqueous /'eɪkwɪəs, 'a-/ ▷ *adj* **1** relating to water. **2** denoting a solution that contains water, or in which water is the solvent. ◷ 17c: from Latin *aqua* water.

aqueous humour ▷ *noun, anatomy* the clear liquid between the lens and the cornea of the eye. Compare VITREOUS HUMOUR.

aqueous solution ▷ *noun, chem* any solution in which the solvent is water.

aquiculture /akwɪ'kʌltʃʊə(r)/ ▷ *noun* **1** a variant of AQUACULTURE. **2** another name for HYDROPONICS.

aquifer /'akwɪfə(r)/ ▷ *noun, geol* any body of water-bearing rock that is highly porous and permeable to water and can be tapped directly by sinking wells or pumping the water into a reservoir. ◷ Early 20c: from AQUA- + Latin *ferre* to carry.

aquilegia /akwɪ'liːdʒə/ ▷ *noun* (***aquilegias***) a columbine. ◷ 16c: from Latin *aquilegus*.

aquiline /'akwɪlaɪn/ ▷ *adj* **1** relating to or referring to, or like, an eagle. **2** said of someone's nose: curved like an eagle's beak. Also called ROMAN NOSE. ◷ 17c: from Latin *aquila* eagle.

aquiver /ə'kwɪvə(r)/ ▷ *adverb* in a trembling or excited state ▫ ***Frank went all aquiver whenever he saw Pat.*** ◷ 1880s.

AR ▷ *abbreviation, US state* Arkansas.

Ar ▷ *symbol, chem* ARGON

-ar[1] ▷ *combining form, forming adjectives, denoting* belonging to or having the quality of something ▫ ***polar*** ▫ ***muscular.***

-ar[2] ▷ *combining form, forming nouns, signifying* someone who carries out the action of the attached verb ▫ ***liar.***

Arab /'arəb/ ▷ *noun* **1** a member of a Semitic people living in the Middle East and N Africa. **2** a breed of horse that is famous for its intelligence, grace and speed. ◷ 17c: from Greek *Araps*.

Arab, Arabian, Arabic

- **Arab** generally refers to people and to political entities, as in **the Arabs, an Arab, Arab countries, leaders, nations, neighbours, oil imports, pride**.
- **Arabian** has geographical and cultural reference, as in **Arabian desert, onyx, peninsula**, and also occurs as part of **Saudi Arabian**.
- **Arabic** refers as a noun and adjective principally to language.

arabesque /arə'bɛsk/ ▷ *noun* **1** *ballet* a position in which the dancer stands with one leg stretched out backwards and the body bent forwards from the hips. **2** a complex flowing design of leaves, flowers, etc woven together. **3** a short ornate piece of music. ◷ 17c: from Italian *arabesco* in the Arabian style.

Arabian /ə'reɪbɪən/ ▷ *adj* belonging, relating or referring to Arabia or the Arabs. ▷ *noun* an ARAB (sense 1).

Arabic /'arəbɪk/ ▷ *noun* the Semitic language of the Arabs. ▷ *adj* belonging, relating or referring to Arabs, their language or culture.

arabica /ə'rabɪkə/ ▷ *noun* a variety of coffee that is grown in S America, especially Brazil. ◷ 1920s.

Arabic numeral ▷ *noun* any of the symbols 0, 1, 2, 3, 4, 5, 6, 7, 8 and 9, which are based on Arabic characters. Compare ROMAN NUMERALS.

Arabist ▷ *noun* someone who is an expert in, or student of, Arabic culture, history, language, etc.

arable /'arəbəl/ ▷ *adj, agric* **1** said of land: suitable or used for ploughing and growing crops. **2** denoting a crop that has to be sown on ploughed land, eg cereals, potatoes, root crops. ◷ 16c: from Latin *arare* to plough.

arachnid /ə'raknɪd/ ▷ *noun* any invertebrate animal belonging to the class which includes spiders, scorpions, mites, ticks, and harvestmen. ◷ 19c: from Greek *arachne* spider.

arachnoid /ə'raknɔɪd/ ▷ *adj* **1** relating to or resembling an ARACHNID. **2** resembling a spider's web or cobweb. **3** *bot* covered in, or made up of, long thin delicate fibres. ▷ *noun, anatomy* (**arachnoid membrane**) the middle of the three membranes that cover the brain and spinal cord, so called because it resembles a cobweb in texture. See also MENINGES. ◷ 18c.

arachnology /arak'nɒlədʒɪ/ ▷ *noun* the study of ARACHNIDS. • **arachnological** /əraknə'lɒdʒɪkəl/ *adj*. • **arachnologist** *noun*. ◷ 19c.

arachnophobia /əraknə'foʊbɪə/ ▷ *noun* a morbid and usually irrational fear of spiders. • **arachnophobe** *noun* someone who suffers from this kind of fear. ◷ 20c: from Greek *arachne* spider + -PHOBIA.

aragonite /ə'ragənaɪt, 'arə-/ ▷ *noun*, *geol* a mineral form of calcium carbonate that occurs in some alpine metamorphic rocks, sedimentary rocks and the shells of certain molluscs. ◷ Early 19c: from Aragon, a province in Spain where it was first found.

arak see under ARRACK

aralia /ə'reɪlɪə/ ▷ *noun* a plant of the ivy family that is often cultivated as a decorative house plant. ◷ 18c.

Aramaic /arə'meɪɪk/ ▷ *noun* any of a group of ancient northern Semitic languages that are still spoken in parts of the Middle East today. ▷ *adj* referring, relating or belonging to, or written in, one of these languages. ◷ 1830s: from Greek *Aramaios* of Aram, an ancient name for Syria.

Aran /'arən/ ▷ *adj* **1** belonging, relating or referring to the Aran Islands, three islands that lie off the W coast of Ireland. **2** *knitting* a type of knitwear originating from these islands and characterized by its use of undyed wool and complex cabled patterns. ▷ *noun* a jumper or cardigan of this type. ◷ Early 20c.

Arapaho /ə'rapəhoʊ/ ▷ *noun* (*Arapaho* or *Arapahos*) **1** a member of a Native American Plains tribe who now live mainly in Oklahoma and Wyoming. **2** the Algonquian language that these people speak. ◷ Early 19c: from Crow *allapaho* many tattoo marks.

arbiter /'ɑːbɪtə(r)/ ▷ *noun* **1** someone who has the authority or influence to settle arguments or disputes between other people. **2** someone who has great influence in matters of style, taste, etc. • **arbitress** /'ɑːbɪtrəs/ *noun, somewhat rare* a female arbitrator. ◷ 16c.

arbitrary /'ɑːbɪtrərɪ/ ▷ *adj* **1** capricious; whimsical. **2** discretionary; based on subjective factors or random choice and not on objective principles. **3** said of a government or of someone in a position of power: dictatorial, authoritarian or high-handed. • **arbitrarily** *adverb*. • **arbitrariness** *noun*. ◷ 16c: from Latin *arbitrarius* uncertain.

arbitrate /'ɑːbɪtreɪt/ ▷ *verb* (*arbitrated*, *arbitrating*) **1** *intr* to help the parties involved in a dispute or disagreement find grounds for agreement. **2** to submit to or settle by arbitration. • **arbitrator** *noun*. ◷ 16c: from Latin *arbitrari* to give a judgement.

arbitration /ɑːbɪ'treɪʃən/ ▷ *noun* the settling of a dispute, especially an industrial one, between two or more groups by some neutral person who is acceptable to all concerned. See ACAS. ◷ 14c.

arbor /'ɑːbə(r)/ ▷ *noun* **1** a tree-like structure. **2** the axle or spindle on which a revolving cutting tool, eg a reamer, is mounted. **3** the axle of a wheel in a clock or watch. ◷ 17c: Latin, meaning 'tree'.

arboreal /ɑː'bɔːrɪəl/ ▷ *adj* **1** relating to or resembling a tree. **2** denoting an animal that lives mainly in trees. ◷ 17c: from Latin *arbor* tree.

arboreous /ɑː'bɔːrɪəs/ ▷ *adj* **1** densely wooded. **2** relating to trees. **3** tree-shaped; tree-like. ◷ 17c: from Latin *arbor* tree.

arborescent /ɑːbə'rɛsənt/ ▷ *adj* resembling a tree in shape, size or other characteristic, eg by having a woody main stem. • **arborescence** *noun*. ◷ 17c: from Latin *arbor* tree.

arboretum /ɑːbə'riːtəm/ ▷ *noun* (*arboreta* /-tə/) *bot* a botanical garden where trees and shrubs are grown and displayed for scientific, educational and recreational purposes. ◷ 19c: Latin, meaning 'a place where trees are grown'.

arboriculture /'ɑːbɔːrɪkʌltʃə(r)/ ▷ *noun* the cultivation of trees and shrubs, especially for ornamental or scientific purposes, rather than for profit. • **arboricultural** *adj*. • **arboriculturist** *noun*. ◷ 19c: from Latin *arbor* tree + *cultura* tending.

arbour /'ɑːbə(r)/ ▷ *noun* a shady area in a garden formed by trees or climbing plants, usually with a seat. ◷ 14c: from Latin *herba* grass, influenced by Latin *arbor* tree.

Arbroath smokie /ɑː'broʊθ 'smoʊkɪ/ ▷ *noun* (— ***smokies***) *Scottish* an unsplit smoked haddock. ◷ 19c: named after Arbroath, a fishing town on the E coast of Scotland.

ARC ▷ *abbreviation* **1** Aeronautical Research Council. **2** the Agriculture Research Council, superseded first by the Agriculture and Food Research Council, and then by the Biotechnology and Biological Sciences Research Council. **3** AIDS-RELATED COMPLEX. ◷ 1980s.

arc ▷ *noun* **1** a continuous section of a circle or other curve. **2** the graduated scale of an instrument or device that is used to measure angles. **3** a continuous electric discharge, giving out heat and light, that is maintained across the space between two electrodes, used in welding, etc. Also called ELECTRIC ARC. **4** something that is curved or that appears curved in shape, eg a rainbow. **5** *astron* a part of the path that a planet, satellite, etc appears to make. ▷ *verb* (*arced*, *arcing*) **1** to form an arc. **2** to move in an apparent arc. ◷ 16c: from Latin *arcus* bow.

arcade /ɑː'keɪd/ ▷ *noun* **1** a covered walk or passage, usually lined with shops. **2** a row of arches supporting a roof, wall, etc. **3** an AMUSEMENT ARCADE. ◷ 17c: French, from Italian *arcata* an arch.

arcade game ▷ *noun* any of a variety of electronic or mechanical games, such as video games, one-armed bandits or pinball machines that are played in an amusement arcade. ◷ 1970s.

Arcadian /ɑː'keɪdɪən/ ▷ *adj* characterized by simple rural pleasures. ▷ *noun* someone who enjoys such pleasures. ◷ 16c: from Greek *Arcadia*, a hilly area in the Peloponnesus thought to be ideal in its rural tranquillity.

arcane /ɑː'keɪn/ ▷ *adj* mysterious, secret or obscure; understood only by a few; difficult to understand. • **arcanely** *adverb*. • **arcaneness** *noun*. ◷ 16c: from Latin *arcanus*, from *arcere* to shut up.

arch[1] /ɑːtʃ/ ▷ *noun* (*arches*) **1** a curved structure forming an opening, and consisting of wedge-shaped stones or other pieces supporting each other by mutual pressure, used to sustain an overlying weight such as a roof or bridge, or for ornament. **2** anything shaped like an arch, especially a monument. **3** the bony structure of the foot between the heel and the toes, normally having an upward curve. **4** one of the four possible configurations of human FINGERPRINTS. ▷ *verb* (*arches*, *arched*, *arching*) **1** to form an arch. **2** to span something like an arch. ◷ 14c: from Latin *arcus* bow.

arch[2] /ɑːtʃ/ ▷ *adj* **1** (*usually in compounds*) chief, principal □ *their arch enemy, the Penguin.* **2** most experienced □ *that arch crime writer, Jim Thompson.* **3** cunning, knowing □ *gave an arch look.* **4** self-consciously playful or coy. • **archly** see separate entry. • **archness** *noun*. ◷ 17c: from ARCH- as in such combinations as 'arch-villain'.

arch- /ɑːtʃ/ or **archi-** /ɑːkɪ/ ▷ *combining form* **1** chief; most important; highest-ranking □ *archduke.* **2** most esteemed, feared, extreme, etc of its kind □ *arch-conservative* □ *arch-criminal.* ◷ Anglo-Saxon *arce*, from Greek *archos* chief, from *archein* to rule.

Archaean or (*US*) **Archean** /ɑː'kɪən/ ▷ *adj*, *geol* denoting the earlier of the two geological eons into which the Precambrian period is divided, extending from the time of formation of the Earth to about 2 500 million years ago. ⓘ 19c: from Greek *archaios* ancient.

archaebacterium /ɑːkɪbak'tɪərɪəm/ ▷ *noun* (***archaebacteria*** /-rɪə/) *biol* any of various different kinds of micro-organisms which resemble ordinary bacteria in size and in the primitive nature of their structure but which evolved separately, probably about 3-4 billion years ago, so that the organization of their molecules is unique. • **archaebacterial** *adj.* ⓘ 1970s.

archaeo- or (*US*) **archeo-** /ɑːkɪoʊ, ɑːkɪ'ɒ/ ▷ *combining form, indicating* ancient; primitive □ *archaeology*. ⓘ From Greek *archaios*, from *archein* to begin.

archaeology or (*US*) **archeology** /ɑːkɪ'ɒlədʒɪ/ ▷ *noun* the excavation and subsequent study of the physical remains of earlier civilizations, especially buildings and artefacts, which now benefits from advances in scientific techniques such as CARBON DATING. • **archaeological** or **archeological** /ɑːkɪə'lɒdʒɪkəl/ *adj.* • **archaeologically** or **archeologically** *adverb.* • **archaeologist** or **archeologist**. ⓘ 17c.

archaeometry /ɑːkɪ'ɒmɪtrɪ/ ▷ *noun* the use of technical and scientific methods in archaeology, especially to help in the dating of objects. • **archaeometric** *adj.* • **archaeometrist** *noun.* ⓘ 1950s.

archaeopteryx /ɑːkɪ'ɒptərɪks/ ▷ *noun* the oldest fossil bird, known from the Jurassic period in Europe, which had feathers, but differed from modern birds in having a long bony tail supported by vertebrae, and sharp teeth on both jaws. ⓘ 19c: ARCHAEO- + Greek *pteryx* wing.

archaic /ɑː'keɪɪk/ ▷ *adj* **1** ancient; relating or referring to, or from, a much earlier period. **2** out of date; old-fashioned. **3** said of a word, phrase, etc: no longer in general use, but sometimes used for special effect. • **archaically** *adverb.* ⓘ 19c: from Greek *archaikos*, from *archaios* ancient.

archaism /'ɑːkeɪɪzəm/ ▷ *noun* **1** an archaic word, expression or style. **2** the deliberate use of archaic words, expressions or style. ⓘ 17c: from Greek *archaizein* to copy the language of the ancient writers.

archaize or **archaise** /'ɑːkeɪaɪz/ ▷ *verb* (***archaized***, ***archaizing***) to make something archaic in appearance or style. ⓘ 19c.

archangel /'ɑːkeɪndʒəl, ɑːk'eɪndʒəl/ ▷ *noun* **a** an angel of the highest rank; **b** in the traditional medieval hierarchy of nine ranks of angels: an angel of the eighth (second-lowest) rank. Compare SERAPH, CHERUB, THRONE, DOMINION, VIRTUE, POWER, PRINCIPALITY, ANGEL. ⓘ 11c.

archbishop ▷ *noun* a chief BISHOP who is in charge of all the other bishops, clergy and churches in a particular area. ⓘ Anglo-Saxon *arcebiscop*.

archbishopric ▷ *noun* **1** the office of an archbishop. **2** the area that is governed by an archbishop. Also called SEE², DIOCESE.

archdeacon ▷ *noun, C of E* a member of the clergy who ranks just below a bishop. See ARCHIDIACONAL. • **archdeaconry** *noun* **1** the office or duties of an archdeacon. **2** the house in which an archdeacon lives. ⓘ Anglo-Saxon *arcediacon*.

archdiocese ▷ *noun, C of E* the area under the control of an archbishop.

archduchess ▷ *noun* **1** *historical* a princess in the Austrian royal family. **2** the wife of an archduke.

archduchy ▷ *noun* the area ruled by an archduke.

archduke ▷ *noun* the title of some princes, especially formerly the son of the Emperor of Austria.

arched /ɑːtʃt/ ▷ *adj* **1** having an arch or arches. **2** shaped like an arch.

archegonium /ɑːkə'goʊnɪəm/ ▷ *noun* (***-ia*** /-ɪə/) in ferns, mosses, liverworts, etc, and in many gymnosperms: the often flask-shaped structure in which the female gamete develops. ⓘ 19c: from ARCH- + Greek *gonos* seed.

archenemy /ɑːtʃ'ɛnəmɪ/ ▷ *noun* **1** a chief enemy. **2** the Devil.

archeology an alternative *US* spelling of ARCHAEOLOGY.

archer /'ɑːtʃə(r)/ ▷ *noun* **1** someone who uses a bow and arrow. **2** (**the Archer**) the constellation and sign of the zodiac SAGITTARIUS. ⓘ 13c: from French *archier*, from Latin *arcus* bow.

archer fish ▷ *noun* a freshwater fish found in S and SE Asia and Australia that spits jets of water at insects, knocking them into the water and then eating them. ⓘ 19c.

archery /'ɑːtʃərɪ/ ▷ *noun* the art or sport of shooting with a bow and arrow. ⓘ 15c.

archetype /'ɑːkɪtaɪp/ ▷ *noun* **1** an original model; a prototype. **2** a perfect example. • **archetypal** /ɑːkɪ'taɪpəl/ *adj.* • **archetypally** *adverb.* ⓘ 16c: from Greek *arche* beginning + *typos* model.

archfiend ▷ *noun* the Devil.

archi- see ARCH-

archidiaconal /ɑːkɪdaɪ'akənəl/ ▷ *adj* referring or relating to an archdeacon or archdeaconry.

archiepiscopal ▷ *adj* relating or referring to an archbishop or an archbishopric. ⓘ 17c: from Greek *archiepiskopos* archbishop.

archil see ORCHIL

archimandrite /ɑːkɪ'mandraɪt/ ▷ *noun, Christianity* a priest in the Greek Orthodox Church who is in charge of a group of monks. ⓘ 16c: from ARCHI- + Greek *mandra* monastery.

Archimedes' principle /ɑːkɪ'miːdiːz —/ ▷ *noun, physics* the law which states that, when a body is wholly or partly immersed in a liquid, the weight of the fluid displaced by the body is equal to the weight of the body. ⓘ Named after the Greek philosopher, mathematician and scientist, Archimedes (c.287–212 BC).

Archimedes screw ▷ *noun* a device for raising water against gravity, especially for irrigation, consisting of a spiral screw that rotates inside an inclined close-fitting cylinder.

archipelago /ɑːkɪ'pɛləgoʊ/ ▷ *noun* (***archipelagos***) *geog* a group or chain of islands separated from each other by narrow bodies of water. ⓘ 16c: from Italian *arcipelago*, from ARCHI- + Greek *pelagos* sea.

architect /'ɑːkɪtɛkt/ ▷ *noun* **1** someone who is professionally qualified to design buildings and other large structures and supervise their construction. **2** someone who is responsible for creating or initiating something □ *the architect of the European Community*. ⓘ 16c: from Greek *archi tekton* master-builder.

architectonic /'ɑːkɪtɛktɒnɪk/ ▷ *adj* **1** belonging, relating or referring to architecture. **2** relating to the science of systematizing knowledge. • **architectonics** *singular noun* **1** the science of architecture. **2** the science of systematizing knowledge. ⓘ 17c: from Greek *architektonikos* relating to architecture.

architecture /'ɑːkɪtɛktʃə(r)/ ▷ *noun* **1** the art, science and profession of designing buildings, ships and other large structures and supervising their construction. **2 a** a specified historical, regional, etc style of building design, especially when it is thought of as fine art □ *Victorian architecture*; **b** the buildings built in any particular style. **3** the way in which anything is physically constructed or designed. **4** *computing* the general specification and configuration of the internal design of computer or local area network. • **architectural** *adj.* • **architecturally** *adverb.* ⓘ 16c: from Latin *architectura*.

architrave /ˈɑːkɪtreɪv/ ⊳ *noun* **1** *archit* a beam that forms the bottom part of an ENTABLATURE and which rests across the top of a row of columns. **2** a moulded frame around a door or window. ◷ 16c: French, from Latin *trabes* beam.

archive /ˈɑːkaɪv/ ⊳ *noun* **1** (*usually* **archives**) **a** a collection of old public documents, records, etc; **b** a place where such documents are kept. **2** *computing* a place for keeping data or files which are seldom used or needed. ⊳ *verb* (***archived***, ***archiving***) **1** to store (documents, data, etc) in an archive. **2** *computing* to move and store (files or data that are not often used or needed) out of a computer's internal memory. • **archival** *adj.* ◷ 17c: French, from Greek *archeion* public office or records, from *arkhe* government.

archive material ⊳ *noun* TV and radio recordings that are stored in case they are needed for showing in the future □ ***archive material from the war.***

archivist /ˈɑːkɪvɪst/ ⊳ *noun* someone who collects, keeps, catalogues, records, etc archives.

archivolt /ˈɑːkɪvoʊlt/ ⊳ *noun, archit* the underside curve of an arch or the decorative moulding around it. ◷ 18c: from Latin *arcus* arch + *volta* vault.

archly ⊳ *adverb* cleverly; slyly; in a self-consciously playful manner. ◷ 17c: from ARCH[2].

arch stone see VOUSSOIR

archway ⊳ *noun* a passage or entrance under an arch or arches.

arc light ⊳ *noun* a type of electric lighting source in which the current flows through ionized gas between two electrodes to produce a very bright white illuminated arc and which is used when intense light is needed, eg at the scene of a disaster.

arco /ˈɑːkoʊ/ *music* ⊳ *noun* the bow of a stringed instrument. ⊳ *adverb* (*also* **coll arco**) a direction to the player of a stringed instrument to resume using the bow after a PIZZICATO passage. ◷ 18c: Italian, meaning 'bow'.

Arctic /ˈɑːktɪk/ ⊳ *noun* (**the Arctic**) the area round the North Pole. ⊳ *adj* **1** belonging or relating to this area. **2** (**arctic**) *colloq* extremely cold □ ***arctic conditions.*** ◷ 14c as *adj* 1: from Greek *arktikos*, from *arktos* the constellation of the Bear.

Arctic Circle ⊳ *noun* **1** the imaginary circular line parallel to the equator at a latitude of 66° 32′N, which forms a boundary around the area of the north pole. **2** the area of the Earth that lies within this line. ◷ 16c.

Arctic fox ⊳ *noun* either of two species of fox, widespread on Arctic land masses, one of which is white in winter and brown in summer, the other being pale blue-grey in winter and darker blue-grey in summer. ◷ 18c.

Arctic tern ⊳ *noun* a small tern that breeds in areas around the Arctic before migrating south to the Antarctic, which travels further than any other migratory bird. ◷ 19c.

arctoid /ˈɑːktɔɪd/ ⊳ *adj* relating to or resembling a bear. ◷ 19c: from Greek *arktos* bear.

arctophile /ˈɑːktoʊfaɪl/ ⊳ *noun* someone who collects or is very fond of teddy bears. ◷ 20c: from Greek *arktos* bear + -PHILE.

Arcturus /ɑːkˈtjʊərəs/ ⊳ *noun, astron* the brightest star in the constellation Boötes, and the fourth brightest star in the sky. Also called ALPHA BOÖTIS. ◷ 14c: from Greek *Arktouros*, from *arktos* bear + *ouros* guard.

arc welding ⊳ *noun, engineering* a form of welding in which two pieces of metal are joined by raising the temperature of, and so melting, the material at the joint by means of a continuous electric arc. ◷ 19c.

ardent /ˈɑːdənt/ ⊳ *adj* **1** enthusiastic; eager. **2** burning; passionate. • **ardently** *adverb*. ◷ 14c: from Latin *ardere* to burn.

ardour /ˈɑːdə(r)/ ⊳ *noun* a great enthusiasm or passion. ◷ 14c: from Latin *ardor*, from *ardere* to burn.

arduous /ˈɑːdjʊəs/ ⊳ *adj* **1** difficult; needing a lot of work, effort or energy. **2** steep. • **arduously** *adverb*. • **arduousness** *noun*. ◷ 16c: from Latin *arduus* steep.

are[1] /ɑː(r)/ ⊳ *verb* used with *you*, *we* and *they*: the 2nd person singular and 1st, 2nd and 3rd person plural of the present tense of BE □ ***You are here*** □ ***We are alive*** □ ***Here they are.***

are[2] /ɑː(r)/ ⊳ *noun* a unit of land measure equal to $100m^2$. ◷ Early 19c: from French *are*, from Latin *area* open space.

are[3] /ɑː(r)/ ⊳ *noun colloq* someone who has passed through the stage of being a WANNABE and made it □ ***a room full of wannabes and one or two ares.*** Also *as adj* □ ***After his CD was issued he saw himself as an are songwriter rather than a wannabe one.*** ◷ 1990s.

area /ˈɛərɪə/ ⊳ *noun* (***areas***) **1** a measure of the size of any surface, measured in square units, eg m^2. **2** a region or part. **3** any space set aside for a particular purpose. **4** the range of a subject, activity or topic. **5** an open space in front of a building's basement. ◷ 16c: Latin, meaning 'open space'.

area code ⊳ *noun, N Amer* a three-digit number used before the local phone number when making long-distance calls.

areca /ˈarɪkə/ ⊳ *noun* (***arecas***) a tall palm tree found in SE Asia which produces the BETEL NUT. ◷ 16c: from Malayalam *adekka* which denotes the way the nuts grow in clusters.

arena /əˈriːnə/ ⊳ *noun* (***arenas***) **1** an area surrounded by seats, for public shows, sports contests, etc. **2** a place of great activity, especially conflict □ ***the political arena.*** **3** the open area in the middle of an amphitheatre. ◷ 17c: Latin, meaning 'sanded area for combats', 'sand'.

arenaceous /arəˈneɪʃəs/ ⊳ *adj* **1** *geol* said of rocks or deposits: resembling sand or composed mainly of sand; granular. Compare ARGILLACEOUS, RUDACEOUS. **2** *bot* said of plants: thriving in sandy soil. ◷ 17c: from Latin *arena* sand + -ACEOUS.

arena stage see THEATRE-IN-THE-ROUND

aren't /ɑːnt/ ⊳ *contraction* **1** are not □ ***They aren't coming.*** **2** *in questions* am not □ ***Aren't I lucky?*** Compare AIN'T, AMN'T. ◷ 18c.

areola /əˈrɪələ/ ⊳ *noun* (***areolae*** /-liː/ or ***areolas***) *anatomy* **1** the ring of brownish or pink pigmented tissue surrounding a nipple. **2** the part of the iris that surrounds the pupil of the eye. ◷ 17c: from Latin, a diminutive of *area* open space.

arête /əˈrɛt/ ⊳ *noun, mountaineering* a sharp ridge or rocky ledge on the side of a mountain. ◷ 19c: French, from Latin *arista* ear of corn or fish bone.

argali /ˈɑːgəlɪ/ ⊳ *noun* (*plural* ***argali***) a wild sheep found in the arid mountainous regions of central Asia, the males of which have huge curly horns. ◷ 18c: the Mongolian word for this kind of sheep.

argentiferous /ɑːdʒənˈtɪfərəs/ ⊳ *adj* containing silver. ◷ Early 19c: from Latin *argentum* silver + -FEROUS.

Argentinian /ɑːdʒənˈtɪnɪən/ and **Argentine** /ˈɑːdʒəntiːn, -taɪn/ ⊳ *adj* belonging, relating or referring to Argentina, a republic in SE South America, or its inhabitants. ⊳ *noun* a citizen or inhabitant of, or person born in, Argentina.

argil /ˈɑːdʒɪl/ ⊳ *noun* white clay, especially the kind used in pottery. ◷ 16c: from Latin *argilla* white clay.

argillaceous /ɑːdʒɪˈleɪʃəs/ ⊳ *adj, geol* said of rocks or deposits: resembling clay or composed mainly of clay; finely grained. Compare ARENACEOUS 1, RUDACEOUS. ◷ 18c: from Latin *argilla* white clay + -ACEOUS.

arginine /ˈɑːdʒɪniːn, -naɪn/ ⊳ *noun, biochem* one of the essential amino acids found in plant and animal proteins. ◷ 19c.

argol /'ɑːgɒl/ ▻ *noun* the harmless crystalline potassium deposit that is left on the sides of wine vats during fermentation. Also called **tartrate**. ◷ 14c.

argon /'ɑːgɒn/ ▻ *noun, chem* (symbol **Ar**, atomic number 18) a colourless odourless inert gas, one of the noble gases, used to provide inert atmospheres in light bulbs, discharge tubes, and in arc welding. ◷ 19c: from A-[2] + Greek *ergon* work.

argot /'ɑːgoʊ/ ▻ *noun* slang that is only used and understood by a particular group of people. ◷ 19c: French, of obscure origin and once confined only to the slang spoken by thieves.

arguable /'ɑːgjʊəbəl/ ▻ *adj* **1** capable of being argued or disputed. **2** said of a proposition, statement, etc: capable of being maintained. • **arguably** *adverb*.

argue /'ɑːgjuː/ ▻ *verb* (***argued, arguing***) **1** *tr & intr* to put forward one's case, especially in a clear and well-ordered manner ▫ *argued the point very eloquently*. **2** *intr* to quarrel or disagree. **3** to show or be evidence for something ▫ *It argues a degree of enthusiasm on their part*. • **arguer** *noun*. ◷ 14c: from Latin *arguere* to prove.

■ **argue about** or **over something** to disagree over it ▫ *argued over money*.

■ **argue with someone** to quarrel with them verbally, especially heatedly or angrily.

argument /'ɑːgjʊmənt/ ▻ *noun* **1** a quarrel or unfriendly discussion. **2** a reason for or against an idea, etc. **3** the use of reason in making decisions. **4** a summary of the theme or subject of a book, etc. • **for argument's sake** or **for the sake of argument** said in order to dismiss less important details so that the main issue or issues can be dealt with ▫ *For the sake of argument, let's say I got the time of the meeting wrong*. ◷ 14c: from Latin *argumentum*, from *arguere* to prove.

argumentation /ɑːgjʊmən'teɪʃən/ ▻ *noun* sensible and methodical reasoning.

argumentative /ɑːgjʊ'mɛntətɪv/ ▻ *adj* fond of arguing; always ready to quarrel. • **argumentatively** *adverb*.

argy-bargy /'ɑːdʒɪ 'bɑːdʒɪ/ ▻ *noun* **1** a dispute, especially when it remains relatively good-natured. **2** a bickering argument or disagreement. ▻ *verb* (***argy-bargies, argy-bargied, argy-bargying***) *intr* to dispute or disagree. ◷ 19c.

argyle /ɑː'gaɪl/ ▻ *adj* said of socks, jumpers, etc: having a diamond pattern in two or more colours. ▻ *noun* **1** a diamond pattern on knitwear, etc. **2** /'ɑːgaɪl/ a garment with this pattern, especially socks or a jumper ▫ *Frank got a pair of argyles for his birthday*. ◷ 18c: a variant of *Argyll*, because the pattern was based on the tartan of Campbell of Argyll.

aria /'ɑːrɪə/ ▻ *noun* (***arias***) *music* a long accompanied song for one voice, especially in an opera or oratorio. ◷ 18c: Italian, meaning 'air'.

Arian[1] or **Arien** /'ɛərɪən/ ▻ *noun* someone who is born under the sign of ARIES. ▻ *adj* born under or characteristic of the sign of ARIES. ◷ Early 20c.

Arian[2] /'ɛərɪən/ ▻ *noun* someone who believes in the doctrine of **Arianism**, ultimately pronounced heretical in the 4c, according to which Christ is not divine but only the first and highest of all created beings. ▻ *adj* relating to or following Arius, the originator of the doctrine, or Arianism.

arid /'arɪd/ ▻ *adj* **1** denoting a region or climate characterized by very low rainfall, often supporting only desert vegetation. **2** lacking interest; dull. • **aridity** /ə'rɪdɪtɪ/ *noun*. • **aridly** *adverb*. ◷ 17c: from Latin *aridus*, from *arere* to be dry.

ariel /'ɛərɪəl/ ▻ *noun* a type of gazelle found in W Asia and Africa. ◷ 19c: from Arabic *aryl* stag.

Aries /'ɛəriːz, 'ɛəriiːz/ ▻ *noun* **1** *astron* the Ram, a small zodiacal constellation situated between Pisces and Taurus. **2** *astrol* **a** the first sign of the zodiac; **b** a person born between 21 March and 20 April, under this sign. Also called ARIAN. See table at ZODIAC. ◷ 14c: from Latin *aries* ram.

arietta /arɪ'ɛtə/ ▻ *noun, music* a light short air, usually with no second part. ◷ 18c: Italian diminutive of *aria*.

aright /ə'raɪt/ ▻ *adverb, old use* correctly. ◷ Anglo-Saxon *ariht*.

arioso /ɑːrɪ'oʊzoʊ, a-/ *music* ▻ *adverb* in a melodious manner. ▻ *adj* melodious. ▻ *noun* (***ariosos*** or ***ariosi*** /-ziː/) a piece of music to be played in this way. ◷ 18c: Italian, meaning 'airy'.

arise /ə'raɪz/ ▻ *verb* (***arose*** /ə'roʊz/, ***arisen*** /ə'rɪzən/, ***arising***) *intr* **1** to come into being. **2** to get up or stand up. **3** to come to notice. **4** to move or grow in an upwards direction. ◷ Anglo-Saxon *arisan*.

■ **arise from** or **out of something** to result from or be caused by it.

arista /ə'rɪstə/ ▻ *noun* (***aristae*** /-stiː/) a bristly part found on the ears of some cereals and grasses. ◷ 17c: Latin.

aristo /'arɪstoʊ, ə'rɪstoʊ/ ▻ *noun* (***aristos***) *colloq, often derog* short form of ARISTOCRAT.

aristocracy /arɪ'stɒkrəsɪ/ ▻ *noun* (***aristocracies***) **1** the highest social class, usually owning land and having titles; the nobility. **2 a** this class as a ruling body; **b** government by this class; **c** a country or state that is governed by this class. **3** people considered to be the best representatives of something ▫ *The French have long been considered the aristocracy of art cinema*. ◷ 16c: from Greek *aristos* best + -CRACY.

aristocrat /'arɪstəkrat, ə'rɪ-/ ▻ *noun* **1** a member of the aristocracy. **2** someone or something that is well-respected or considered amongst the best in its class.

aristocratic ▻ *adj* **1** belonging, relating or referring to the aristocracy. **2** proud and noble-looking. **3** stylish. • **aristocratically** *adverb*.

Aristotelian /arɪstə'tiːlɪən/ ▻ *adj* relating to Aristotle or his ideas. ▻ *noun* a student or follower of Aristotle. ◷ 17c: named after the Greek philosopher, Aristotle (384–322 BC).

arithmetic ▻ *noun* /ə'rɪθmətɪk/ **1** the branch of mathematics that uses numbers to solve theoretical or practical problems, mainly by the processes of addition, subtraction, multiplication and division. **2** any calculation that involves the use of numbers. **3** skill, knowledge or understanding in this field. ▻ *adj* /arɪθ'mɛtɪk/ (*also* **arithmetical**) relating to arithmetic. • **arithmetically** *adverb*. • **arithmetician** /ərɪθmə'tɪʃən/ *noun*. ◷ 13c: from Greek *arithmeein* to reckon, from *arithmos* number.

arithmetic logic unit ▻ *noun* (abbreviation **ALU**) *computing* in the CENTRAL PROCESSING UNIT of a computer: the circuit or set of circuits that performs a set of arithmetic operations and a set of logical operations of a computer.

arithmetic mean see under MEAN[3]

arithmetic progression ▻ *noun* a sequence of numbers such that each number differs from the preceding and following ones by a constant amount, eg 4, 10, 16, 22 …

Ariz. ▻ *abbreviation US state* Arizona.

Ark. ▻ *abbreviation US state* Arkansas.

ark ▻ *noun* **1** *Bible* the vessel built by Noah in which his family and animals survived the Flood. **2** (**Ark**) *Judaism* a chest or cupboard in a synagogue in which the law scrolls are kept. ◷ Anglo-Saxon *arc*, from Latin *arca* chest.

arkose /ɑː'koʊs/ ▻ *noun* a type of sandstone that is rich in FELDSPAR. ◷ 19c: French.

arm[1] ▻ *noun* **1 a** in humans: either of the two upper limbs of the body, from the shoulders to the hands; **b** a limb of an octopus, squid, starfish, etc. **2** anything shaped like or similar to this □ *the arm of the record player.* **3** the sleeve of a garment. **4** the part of a chair, etc that supports a person's arm. **5** a section or division of a larger group, eg of the army, etc. **6** power and influence □ *the long arm of the law.* • **armless** *adj.* • **armlike** *adj.* • **arm in arm** with arms linked together. • **at arm's length** at a distance, especially to avoid becoming too friendly. • **with open arms** wholeheartedly; in a very friendly way. ⓒ Anglo-Saxon *earm.*

arm[2] ▻ *noun* (*usually* **arms**) **1** a weapon □ *nuclear arms* □ *firearm.* **2** fighting; soldiering. **3** a heraldic design that, along with others, makes up the symbol of a family, school, country, etc. ▻ *verb* (***armed***, ***arming***) **1** to equip (with weapons). **2** to prepare (a bomb) for use. • **bear arms** to serve as a soldier. • **lay down one's arms** to stop fighting. • **take up arms** to begin fighting. • **under arms** armed and ready to fight. • **up in arms** openly angry and protesting. ⓒ 14c: from Latin *arma.*

■ **arm someone against something** to protect them from it or from its effects. See also ARMED.

■ **arm someone with something** to supply them with it as protection against or preparation for something. □ *He armed her with some inside knowledge.*

armada /ɑːˈmɑːdə, ɑːˈmeɪdə/ ▻ *noun* **1** a fleet of ships. **2** (**the Armada**) *historical* the fleet of Spanish ships sent to attack England in 1588. ⓒ 16c: Spanish, from Latin *armata* armed forces.

armadillo /ɑːməˈdɪloʊ/ ▻ *noun* (***armadillos***) a small nocturnal burrowing American mammal, the head and body of which are covered with horny plates. ⓒ 16c: Spanish, from *armado* armed man.

Armageddon /ɑːməˈgɛdən/ ▻ *noun* **1** a large-scale and bloody battle, especially the final battle between good and evil before the Day of Judgement, as described in the New Testament (Revelation 16.16). **2** any war, battle or conflict. ⓒ Early 19c: from Hebrew *har megiddon* a place in northern Palestine and site of many Old Testament battles.

Armagnac /ˈɑːmənjak/ ▻ *noun* a high-quality dry French brandy. ⓒ 19c: named after a district in the Gers department of France which was formerly known by this name.

Armalite /ˈɑːməlaɪt/ ▻ *noun, trademark* a small-bore high-velocity assault rifle. ⓒ 1950s: from ARM[2] + LITE.

armament /ˈɑːməmənt/ ▻ *noun* **1** (**armaments**) weapons or military equipment. **2** preparation for war. ⓒ 17c: from Latin *armamenta,* from *armare* to arm.

armature /ˈɑːmətʃə(r)/ ▻ *noun* **1** *engineering* the moving part of an electromagnetic device in which a voltage is induced by a magnetic field, eg the rotating wire-wound coil of an electric motor or generator. **2** a piece of soft iron placed across the two poles of a permanent magnet that is not in use, in order to preserve its magnetic properties. Also called KEEPER (sense *6*). **3** a wire or wooden framework that forms the support for a sculpture as it is being modelled. ⓒ 16c: from Latin *armatura* armour.

armband ▻ *noun* **1** a strip of cloth worn round the arm, usually to indicate an official position, such as being captain of a team, or as a sign of mourning. **2** an inflatable plastic band worn round the arm by someone who is learning to swim.

armchair ▻ *noun* **1** a comfortable chair with arms at each side. **2** *as adj* taking no active part; taking an interest in the theory of something rather than its practice □ *an armchair detective.* ⓒ 17c.

armed /ɑːmd/ ▻ *adj* **1** supplied with arms. **2** said of a weapon or bomb: ready for use. • **armed to the teeth** very heavily armed indeed. • **armed with something** equipped with a means of attack or defence.

armed forces and **armed services** ▻ *noun* the military forces of a country, such as the army, air force and navy, thought of collectively.

Armenian /ɑːˈmiːnɪən/ ▻ *adj* belonging or relating to Armenia, a republic in S Transcaucasia, the area extending from the CAUCASIAN regions to the Turkish and Iranian frontiers, its inhabitants, or their language. ▻ *noun* **1** a citizen or inhabitant of, or person born in, Armenia. **2** the official language of Armenia.

armful ▻ *noun* (***armfuls***) an amount that can be held in someone's arms.

armhole ▻ *noun* the opening at the shoulder of a garment where the arm goes through.

armiger /ˈɑːmɪdʒə(r)/ ▻ *noun* **1** someone who is entitled to bear heraldic arms. **2** *old use* an esquire who would carry the shield, etc of a medieval knight. ⓒ 16c: from Latin *armiger* an armour-bearer.

armistice /ˈɑːmɪstɪs/ ▻ *noun* an agreement between warring factions to suspend all fighting so that they can discuss peace terms; a truce. ⓒ 17c: from Latin *armistitium,* from *arma* arms + *sistere* to stop.

Armistice Day ▻ *noun* the anniversary of the day (11 Nov 1918) when fighting in World War I ended and which, since the end of World War II, has been combined with REMEMBRANCE DAY.

armlet /ˈɑːmlɪt/ ▻ *noun* a band or bracelet worn round the arm.

armorial /ɑːˈmɔːrɪəl/ ▻ *adj* relating to heraldry or coats of arms. ▻ *noun* a book that catalogues coats of arms. ⓒ 16c: from Latin *arma* arms.

armour or (*US*) **armor** /ˈɑːmə(r)/ ▻ *noun* **1** *historical* a metal or chainmail, etc suit or covering worn by men or horses to protect them against injury in battle. **2** metal covering to protect ships, tanks, etc against damage from weapons. **3** armoured fighting vehicles as a group. **4** a protective covering on some animals and plants. **5** heraldic designs and symbols. **6** *in compounds* □ *armour-clad.* • **armoured** *adj.* ⓒ 13c: from French *armure,* from Latin *armatura* armour.

armoured car ▻ *noun* **1** a light-armoured fighting vehicle, usually with four-wheel drive and armed with a machine gun or small-calibre cannon on a rotating turret, first developed just before 1914 and mainly used on the battlefield for reconnaissance and rear area protection. **2** a security vehicle protected by armour plating and usually used for the transportation of valuables, cash, etc.

armoured fighting vehicle ▻ *noun* (abbreviation **AFV**) any military vehicle running either on tracks or on wheels, such as a tank, armoured car, armoured personnel carrier, armoured reconnaissance vehicle, etc that is protected and strengthened by metal armour.

armourer ▻ *noun* **1** someone whose job is to make or repair suits of armour, weapons, etc. **2** someone in charge of a regiment's arms.

armour-plate ▻ *noun* strong metal or steel for protecting ships, tanks, etc. • **armour-plated** *adj.* • **armour-plating** *noun.*

armoury /ˈɑːmərɪ/ ▻ *noun* (***armouries***) **1** a place where arms are kept. **2** a collection of arms and weapons. **3** *US* a place where arms are manufactured. **4** the bank of knowledge, skills, etc that someone can call on when necessary □ *had many cunning wiles in her armoury.*

armpit ▻ *noun* the hollow under the arm at the shoulder.

arms race ▻ *noun* an ongoing contest between two or more countries to achieve superiority in effectiveness and quantity of weapons.

arm wrestling ▻ *noun* a contest between two people seated opposite each other at a table with their hands locked together and their elbows on the table, who then try to use their strength to push their opponent's arm down onto the table while still keeping their own elbow in contact with the table.

army /'ɑːmɪ/ ▻ *noun* (***armies***) **1** a large number of people armed and organized for fighting on land. **2** the military profession. **3** a large number □ ***an army of Rangers supporters.*** **4** a group of people organized for a particular cause □ ***Salvation Army.*** ◷ 14c: from French *armee*, from Latin *armare* to arm.

army ant ▻ *noun* any of various predatory ants found mainly in tropical America which live in temporary nests and move around in huge swarms in search of food.

arnica /'ɑːnɪkə/ ▻ *noun* **1** a composite plant with yellow flowers, found in N temperate and arctic zones and valued for its medicinal properties. **2** a tincture made from the dried heads of the flowers of this plant, used in the treatment of bruises and sprains, but unsuitable for treating open wounds. ◷ 18c.

A-road ▻ *noun* in the UK: a main or principal road that can either be a dual or a single carriageway. Compare B-ROAD.

aroma /ə'roʊmə/ ▻ *noun* (***aromas***) **1** a distinctive, usually pleasant, smell that a substance has or gives off. **2** a subtle quality or charm. ◷ 13c: Greek, meaning 'spice'.

aromatherapy ▻ *noun* a form of therapy involving the use of essential plant oils, generally in combination with massage, to treat physical ailments, anxiety, depression, etc. • **aromatherapist** *noun*.

aromatic /arə'matɪk/ ▻ *adj* **1** having a strong, but sweet or pleasant smell. **2** *chem* said of an organic compound: having carbon atoms arranged in one or more rings rather than in chains. See also ALIPHATIC. ▻ *noun* anything, such as a herb, plant, drug, etc, that gives off a strong fragrant smell. • **aromatically** *adverb*.

aromatic compound ▻ *noun, chem* any of a major class of organic chemical compounds, usually with a strong odour, that contain one or more BENZENE RINGs or that resemble BENZENE in their chemical properties, eg benzene, naphthalene.

aromatize or **aromatise** ▻ *verb* (***aromatized, aromatizing***) to introduce a flavour or smell to (a product). ◷ 1990s.

-arooney or **-erooney** /ə'ruːnɪ/ ▻ *suffix, colloq* a facetious diminutive ending □ ***Here's a quidarooney.***

arose *past tense of* ARISE

around /ə'raʊnd/ ▻ *adverb* **1** on every side; in every direction □ ***tended to throw his money around.*** **2** here and there; in different directions; in or to different places; with or to different people, etc □ ***could see for miles around*** □ ***It's best to shop around.*** **3** approximately □ ***This cinema seats around 100.*** **4** somewhere in the vicinity □ ***waited around.*** ▻ *prep* **1** on all sides of something. **2** in all directions from (a specified point) □ ***The land around here is very fertile.*** **3** over; in all directions □ ***Toys were scattered around the floor.*** **4** so as to surround or encircle; so as to make a circuit of something. **5** reached by making a turn or partial turn about □ ***The shop is around the corner.*** **6** somewhere in or near □ ***The village must be around here.*** **7** approximately in or at; about. • **all around** everywhere to be seen □ ***The signs of spring are all around.*** • **be around 1** to be in existence. **2** to be prominent in a particular field □ ***But will 'REM' still be around in ten years' time?*** • **be up and around** to be fit enough to get up out of bed, especially after an illness, etc. • **fool around** see under FOOL. • **get around** *colloq* **1** said of a rumour, gossip, etc: to become known. **2** to become experienced by doing a variety of different things or going to a variety of different places. **3** to move or travel □ ***gets around by bus.*** **4** to overcome □ ***Having more staff would get around the problem.*** • **get around to something** or **to doing something** to tackle it or do it, especially eventually or reluctantly. • **have been around 1** *colloq* to have had a great deal of experience of life. **2** *euphemistic* to have had numerous sexual liaisons.

arouse /ə'raʊz/ ▻ *verb* (***aroused, arousing***) **1** to cause or produce (an emotion, reaction, sexual desire or response, etc). **2** to cause to become awake or active. • **arousal** *noun*. ◷ 16c: A³ 2 + ROUSE.

ARP ▻ *abbreviation* air-raid precautions.

arpeggio /ɑː'pɛdʒɪoʊ/ ▻ *noun* (***arpeggios***) a chord whose notes are played one at a time in rapid succession rather than simultaneously. Also called BROKEN CHORD. ◷ 18c: from Italian *arpeggiare* to play the harp.

arquebus /'ɑːkwɪbəs/ and **harquebus** /hɑː-/ ▻ *noun, historical* an early type of portable gun. ◷ 15c: from Dutch *hakebusse*, from *hake* hook + *busse* gun.

arr ▻ *abbreviation* **1** *music* arranged by. **2** arrival; arrives.

arrack or **arak** /'arək/ ▻ *noun* an alcoholic drink made in Eastern and Middle Eastern countries from grain or rice and sugar and sometimes coconut juice. ◷ 16c: from Arabic *araq* sweat.

arraign /ə'reɪn/ ▻ *verb* (***arraigned, arraigning***) **1** to bring someone (usually someone who is already in custody) to a court of law to answer a criminal charge or charges. **2** to find fault with someone; to accuse them. • **arraigner** *noun*. • **arraignment** *noun*. ◷ 14c: from French *aresnier*, from Latin *adrationare* to talk reasonably to.

arrange /ə'reɪndʒ/ ▻ *verb* (***arranged, arranging***) **1** to put into the proper or desired order □ ***arranged the flowers.*** **2** to settle the plans for something □ ***arranged their holiday.*** **3** to make a mutual agreement. **4** to make (a piece of music) suitable for particular voices or instruments. **5** to adapt (a play, novel, etc), especially for broadcast on TV or radio. ◷ 14c: from French *arangier*, from *rangier* to put in a row.

■ **arrange for something** to agree it □ ***arranged for a delivery.***

■ **arrange with someone (to do something)** to come to an agreement with or settle with them (to do it) □ ***arrange with him to take time off.***

arranged ▻ *adj* **1** in order, settled. **2** said of a marriage: settled by people other than the bride and groom, usually through the mutual agreement of both sets of parents, rather than by the partners freely choosing each other.

arrangement ▻ *noun* **1** a plan or preparation for some future event. **2** the act of putting things into a proper order or pattern. **3** the order, pattern, etc which results from things being arranged. **4** an agreement. **5** a piece of music which has been made suitable for particular voices or instruments. **6** a play, novel, etc that has been specially adapted for broadcast on TV or radio.

arrant /'arənt/ ▻ *adj* out-and-out; notorious □ ***an arrant liar.*** ◷ 14c: a variant of ERRANT, meaning 'wandering' which, through common collocations such as *arrant thief* and *arrant coward*, came to mean 'notorious'.

arras /'arəs/ ▻ *noun* a colourful woven tapestry, often depicting figures and animals in outdoor scenes, especially hunting ones, used as a wall hanging or for concealing an alcove or door. ◷ 14c: named after the town of Arras in N France which was famous for manufacturing this type of fabric.

array /ə'reɪ/ ▻ *noun* **1** a large and impressive number, display or collection. **2** a well-ordered arrangement, especially a military one □ ***troops in battle array.*** **3** *math* an arrangement of numbers or other items of data in rows and columns, eg a matrix. **4** *computing* an arrangement of individual elements of data in such a way that any element can be located and retrieved. **5** *poetic* fine clothes. ▻ *verb* (***arrayed, arraying***) **1** to put in order; to display. **2** to dress (someone or oneself) in fine clothes. ◷ 13c: from French *areer* to arrange.

arrears /əˈrɪəz/ ▻ *plural noun* an amount or quantity which still needs to be done or paid back. • **in arrears 1** late in paying money that is owed, in doing the required work, or in meeting some obligation. **2** in a state of having the agreed, usually monthly, repayments overdue. ⓒ 17c: from French *arere*, from Latin *ad* to + *retro* back, behind.

arrest /əˈrɛst/ ▻ *verb* (***arrested, arresting***) **1** to take someone into custody, especially by legal authority. **2 a** to stop or slow down the progress of (growth, development, etc); **b** to stop or slow down the progress of (a disease, etc). **3** to catch or attract (someone's attention). **4** *intr, pathol* to suffer a CARDIAC ARREST. **5** under Scots and maritime law: to seize (assets, property, freight, etc) by legal warrant. ▻ *noun* **1** the act of taking, or state of being taken, into custody, especially by the police. **2** a stopping. **3** a halting or slowing down in the progress, development or growth of something; the act of doing this. • **arrestable** *adj* □ *an arrestable offence.* • **arrester** *noun.* • **under arrest** taken into police custody pending a decision on whether or not there is sufficient grounds to make formal charges. ⓒ 14c: from French *arester*, from Latin *ad* to + *restare* to stand still.

arresting ▻ *adj* **1** strikingly individual or attractive. **2** performing an act of taking someone into custody □ *Iain was the arresting officer.*

arrhythmia /əˈrɪðmɪə, eɪ-/ ▻ *noun, physiol* any change from the normal rhythm of the heartbeat. • **arrhythmic** *adj.* • **arrhythmically** *adverb.*

arris /ˈarɪs/ ▻ *noun* (***arrises***) *archit* a sharp edge on stone, metal or wood where two surfaces meet. ⓒ 17c: from French *arête* a sharp ridge.

arris rail ▻ *noun, archit* a wooden or metal rail of triangular section.

arris tile ▻ *noun, archit* an angular roofing tile used where hips and ridges intersect.

arrival /əˈraɪvəl/ ▻ *noun* **1 a** the act of coming to a destination; **b** *as adj* □ *the arrival lounge.* **2** someone or something that has arrived. **3** *colloq* the attainment of recognition, success, etc □ *'Reservoir Dogs' marked Tarantino's arrival as a bankable director.*

arrive /əˈraɪv/ ▻ *verb* (***arrived, arriving***) *intr* **1** to reach a place during a journey or come to a destination at the end of a journey. **2** *colloq* to be successful or to attain recognition □ *thought he had really arrived when he bought his first Armani suit.* **3** said of a baby: to be born. **4** said of a thing: to be brought, delivered, etc □ *The letter arrived by second post.* **5** to come about, happen or occur at last □ *The day arrived when a decision had to be made.* • **arrive on the scene** to become known or popular □ *Punk arrived on the scene in '77.* ⓒ 13c: from French *ariver*, from Latin *ad* to + *ripa* shore.

■ **arrive at something** to come to (a conclusion, decision, etc).

arrogant /ˈarəgənt/ ▻ *adj* said of someone or their behaviour: aggressively and offensively self-assertive; having or showing too high an opinion of one's own abilities or importance; impudently over-presumptive. • **arrogance** /ˈarəgəns/ *noun.* • **arrogantly** *adverb.* ⓒ 14c: from Latin *arrogare* to claim as one's own, from *rogare* to ask.

arrogate /ˈarəgeɪt/ ▻ *verb* (***arrogated, arrogating***) **1** to claim a responsibility, power, etc without having any legal right to do so. **2** to attribute, ascribe to someone else, or demand on behalf of someone else without any right or justification. • **arrogation** /arəˈgeɪʃən/ *noun.* ⓒ 16c: from Latin *arrogare* to claim as own's own, from *ad* to + *rogare* to ask.

arrow /ˈaroʊ/ ▻ *noun* **1** a thin straight stick with a sharp point at one end and feathers at the other, which is fired from a bow either at a scoring target as in archery, or at prey or an enemy. **2** any arrow-shaped thing that acts as a symbol or sign, especially one showing the way to go or the position of something. ⓒ Anglo-Saxon *arwe.*

arrowhead ▻ *noun* the pointed tip of an arrow.

arrowroot ▻ *noun* **1** a tropical perennial plant cultivated in tropical regions for its swollen underground tubers, which produce a highly digestible form of starch. **2** the fine-grained starch obtained from the tubers of this plant, used as a food thickener. **3** any similar starch obtained from the tubers or roots of other plants. ⓒ 17c: named after its former use by S American Indians to treat wounds made by poisoned arrows.

arrowwood ▻ *noun* a N American tree with particularly straight stems which are very suitable for making arrows.

arse /ɑːs/ or (*N Amer*) **ass** /as/ (*slang* in all senses except perhaps *noun* 1) ▻ *noun* (***arses*** or ***asses***) **1** the buttocks. **2** someone who is held in great contempt. **3** a woman, especially when she is considered in terms of her sexual availability, willingness or competence □ *Check out that tasty piece of arse!* **4** sexual intercourse or gratification. **5** *in compounds* □ *He's a bit of a wild-arse.* ▻ *verb* (***arsed, arsing***) (*also* **arse about** or **around**) to behave in a stupid, irritating way. • **arsed** *adj, in compounds* having buttocks of a specified kind □ *fat-arsed* □ *big-arsed.* • **be arsed** *usually with negatives and in questions* to take the trouble; to feel up to or motivated to doing something □ *I can't be arsed going out.* • **get one's arse in gear** to become motivated to start doing something □ *so hungover I couldn't get my arse in gear all day.* • **my arse!** an exclamation expressing utter disbelief □ *You're saying it only cost 20 quid? My arse!* ⓒ Anglo-Saxon *ears.* Many of the compounds of this word are of American origin and have been adopted with the American spelling ASS and are, therefore, given under that spelling rather than here.

arse bandit ▻ *noun, slang* **1** a homosexual. **2** someone who engages in anal sex.

arsehole or (*N Amer*) **asshole** ▻ *noun, slang* **1** the anus. **2** a fool; someone whose behaviour, opinion, etc is not highly regarded. **3** a place or thing that is loathed and despised. • **arseholed** *adj* extremely drunk.

arse-licker or (*N Amer*) **ass-licker** and **arse-kisser** or (*N Amer*) **ass-kisser** *slang* ▻ *noun* someone who behaves in an overly sycophantic way. Also called BROWN-NOSE. • **arse-licking** or **arse-kissing** *noun* the act of flattering someone and currying favour with them in order to win some personal advantage.

arsenal /ˈɑːsənəl/ ▻ *noun* **1** a store for weapons, explosives, etc. **2** a factory or workshop where weapons are made, repaired or serviced. **3** the weapons, etc available to a country or group. **4** a supply of something that can be called upon when necessary and used to one's advantage, usually destructively. ⓒ 16c: from Arabic *dar* house + *sina`ah* of handicrafts.

arsenic /ˈɑːsənɪk/ ▻ *noun* **1** (symbol **As**, atomic number 33) a metalloid chemical element that occurs in three different forms, the commonest and most stable of which is a highly toxic grey shiny solid. **2** a powerful poison, an oxide of arsenic, used in insecticides, rodent poisons, etc, and formerly used in medical drugs to treat syphilis. • **arsenical** /ɑːˈsɛnɪkəl/ *adj, noun.* • **arsenious** /ɑːˈsiːnɪəs/ *adj.* ⓒ 14c: from Greek *arsenikon* yellow orpiment, which is an ore of arsenic.

arsenide /ˈɑːsənaɪd/ ▻ *noun, chem* a compound of arsenic with another element, such as hydrogen or a metal, or with an organic radical. ⓒ 19c.

arsenite /ˈɑːsənaɪt/ ▻ *noun, chem* a salt of arsenious acid. ⓒ Early 19c.

arsine /ˈɑːsiːn, ˈɑːsaɪn/ ▻ *noun, chem* **1** a poisonous colourless gas used by the military. **2** a compound that has the same structure as ammonia or an amine, but with arsenic instead of nitrogen. ⓒ 19c.

arson /ˈɑːsən/ ▻ *noun* the crime under English law of deliberately setting fire to a building, etc and which in Scots law is termed **fire-raising**. • **arsonist** *noun* someone who commits this type of crime, especially habitually. ⓒ 17c: from Latin *arsio*, from *ardere* to burn.

art[1] /ɑːt/ ▷ *noun* **1 a** the creation of works of beauty, especially visual ones; **b** such creations thought of collectively. **2** human skill and work as opposed to nature. **3** a skill, especially one gained through practice □ *the lost art of conversation.* **4** *colloq* cunning schemes. ● **art for art's sake** the concept that any form of creativity should be valued for its own merits alone, rather than measured against some fixed set of criteria that is laid down by the art establishment. See also ARTS, FINE ART. ⓒ 13c: from Latin *ars.*

art[2] /ɑːt/ ▷ *verb, archaic* used with *thou*: the 2nd person singular of the present tense of BE. ⓒ Anglo-Saxon *eart*, part of the irregular declension of *beon* to be.

art cinema ▷ *noun* the production of cinema films in which profit and attracting big audiences are secondary considerations, and where the emphasis is on achieving an artistically and aesthetically pleasing look, sometimes to such an extent that plot, action, characterization, etc become of little or no importance.

art deco or **Art Deco** /— 'dekoʊ/ ▷ *noun* a style of interior design, originally of the 1920s and 1930s, characterized by highly angular geometric shapes and strong colours, whose influence spilled over into such fields as architecture, jewellery design, etc and later to mass-produced furniture, carpets, etc. ⓒ 1960s: a shortening of French *art décoratif* decorative art, from the name of the Paris exhibition *L'Exposition Internationale des Arts Décoratifs et Industriels Modernes* which was held in 1925.

artefact or **artifact** /'ɑːtəfakt/ ▷ *noun* **1** a handcrafted object, eg a tool, a cave painting, etc, especially one that is historically or archaeologically interesting. **2** anything that has been manipulated or self-consciously constructed for a specific purpose, especially if it is subsequently shown to be so □ *The statistical data was nothing but an election-rigging artefact.* **3** something mass-produced and usually cheap □ *those nasty touristy artefacts.* ⓒ 19c: from Latin *arte factum*, from *ars* skill + *facere* to make.

artemisia /ɑːtɪ'mɪzɪə/ ▷ *noun, bot* any of various aromatic herbs and shrubs with silvery hair-covered leaves and small yellow flowers, including several species with medicinal properties. ⓒ 14c: named after *Artemis*, the Greek goddess of the moon and hunting.

arterial /ɑː'tɪərɪəl/ ▷ *adj* **1** affecting, relating to or like an artery or arteries. **2** said of a road, etc: connecting large towns or cities; main, especially with lots of minor branches. ⓒ 19c.

arteriole /ɑː'tɪərɪoʊl/ ▷ *noun, anatomy* a small artery.

arteriosclerosis /ɑːtɪərɪoʊsklə'roʊsɪs, -sklɪə-/ ▷ *noun* (***arterioscleroses*** /-siːz/) *pathol* a disease of the arteries, often associated with ageing or high blood pressure, characterized by thickening of the artery walls, loss of elasticity, and eventual obstruction of blood flow. See also ATHEROSCLEROSIS. ⓒ 19c: from ARTERY + SCLEROSIS.

artery /'ɑːtərɪ/ ▷ *noun* (***arteries***) **1** *anatomy* a blood vessel that carries oxygenated blood from the heart to the body tissues, the only exception being the pulmonary artery, which conveys deoxygenated blood from the heart to the lungs. Compare VEIN. **2** a main road, railway or shipping lane. ⓒ 14c: from Greek *arteria* windpipe.

artesian basin /ɑː'tiːzɪən, -ʒən —/ ▷ *noun, geol* a shallow basin-shaped AQUIFER surrounded above and below by rocks that are impermeable to water, so that groundwater confined under pressure in the aquifer will rise to the surface without the need for pumping if a well is drilled into it.

artesian well ▷ *noun, geol* a deep well that is drilled into an AQUIFER in an ARTESIAN BASIN, so that the water trapped there under pressure is forced to flow upward in the well, often used as a source of drinking water. ⓒ 19c: named after *Arteis* (now called *Artois*), an old province in France where it was common to draw water by this method.

art film see ART MOVIE

art form ▷ *noun* **1** a form of music or literature that conforms to certain established traditions, eg the sonnet must have 14 lines, must be in iambic pentameter and must have a specific rhyme scheme. **2** any genre of art or any activity that can be seen as an expression of artistic creativity.

artful ▷ *adj* **1** cunning, especially in being able to achieve what one wants, often by illicit or underhand means. **2** skilful. ● **artfully** *adverb.* ● **artfulness** *noun.* ⓒ 17c.

art house ▷ *noun* a cinema that shows ART MOVIES rather than mainstream or Hollywood movies. ⓒ 1950s.

arthritic /ɑː'θrɪtɪk/ ▷ *noun* someone who is suffering from arthritis. ▷ *adj* relating to or typical of arthritis.

arthritis /ɑː'θraɪtɪs/ ▷ *noun, pathol* inflammation of one or more joints, associated with swelling, pain, redness, local heat, and often restricted movement of the affected part. See also OSTEOARTHRITIS, RHEUMATOID ARTHRITIS. ⓒ 16c: from Greek *arthron* joint + -ITIS 1.

arthropod /'ɑːθrəpɒd/ ▷ *noun, zool* any invertebrate animal of the **Arthropoda** (/ɑː'θrɒpədə/, the largest phylum in the animal kingdom, that includes insects, crustaceans, ARACHNIDs, and MYRIAPODs). ⓒ 19c: from Greek *arthron* joint + -POD.

artic /ɑː'tɪk, 'ɑːtɪk/ ▷ *abbreviation, colloq* articulated lorry.

artichoke /'ɑːtɪtʃoʊk/ ▷ *noun* **1** a GLOBE ARTICHOKE. **2** a JERUSALEM ARTICHOKE. ⓒ 16c: from Arabic *al-kharshuf.*

article /'ɑːtɪkəl/ ▷ *noun* **1** a thing or object, especially one that has been mentioned previously. **2** a short written composition in a newspaper, magazine, etc. **3** a clause or paragraph in a document, legal agreement, etc. **4** *grammar* the definite article 'the' or the indefinite article 'a' or 'an'. **5** *colloq, usually derog* a person □ *You lazy article!* ▷ *verb* (***articled, articling***) to bind (a trainee or apprentice, especially in the legal profession) for a set number of years, at the end of which the trainee or apprentice is qualified. ● **article of something** a single item belonging to that class of objects □ *an article of clothing* □ *articles of furniture.* ● **genuine article** *colloq* something that is not counterfeit. ⓒ 13c: from Latin *articulus* little joint.

articled ▷ *adj* said of a trainee lawyer, accountant, etc: bound by a legal contract while working in an office to learn the job.

articular /ɑː'tɪkjʊlə(r)/ ▷ *adj* relating to or associated with a joint of the body. ⓒ 15c: from Latin *articularis*, from *articulus* little joint.

articulate ▷ *verb* (***articulated, articulating***) /ɑː'tɪkjʊleɪt/ **1** *tr & intr* to pronounce (words) or speak clearly and distinctly. **2** to express (thoughts, feelings, ideas, etc) clearly. **3** *intr, physiol* to be attached by way of a joint □ *The carpals articulate with the metacarpals.* ▷ *adj* /ɑː'tɪkjʊlət/ **1 a** skilled at expressing one's thoughts clearly; **b** said of a speech or a piece of writing: clearly presented, well-argued and to the point. **2** said of speech sounds: pronounced clearly and distinctly so that each sound can be heard. **3** having joints. ● **articulately** *adverb.* ● **articulateness** *noun.* ⓒ 16c: from Latin *articulare*, *articulatum* to divide into distinct parts.

articulated /ɑː'tɪkjʊleɪtɪd/ ▷ *adj* having joints.

articulated lorry ▷ *noun* (*sometimes* shortened to ARTIC) a large lorry that has a pivot between the cab and the main part, making it easier to manoeuvre, especially round corners, into loading bays, etc. ⓒ 1920s.

articulation /ɑːtɪkjʊ'leɪʃən/ ▷ *noun* **1** the act of speaking or expressing an idea in words. **2** *phonetics* **a** the process involved in uttering separate speech sounds; **b** the act of uttering separate speech sounds. **3** the state of being jointed together. **4** a joint.

articulator /ɑːˈtɪkjʊleɪtə(r)/ ▻ *noun* **1 a** someone who speaks, especially by voicing the unspoken worries, thoughts, etc of others; **b** someone who speaks in a specified way. **2** *phonetics* one of the vocal parts that is used in the delivery of a speech sound, eg a movable one such as the tongue or either of the lips, or a fixed one such as the teeth, alveolar ridge, palate, etc.

articulatory phonetics ▻ *singular noun* the branch of phonetics that is specifically concerned with how speech sounds are physically made, especially by observing, studying and measuring the movement of the various vocal organs, often by using x-rays, photography and electromyography. Compare ACOUSTIC PHONETICS, AUDITORY PHONETICS, PHONOLOGY.

artifact see ARTEFACT

artifice /ˈɑːtɪfɪs/ ▻ *noun* **1 a** a clever trick; a crafty plan or ploy; **b** clever trickery; cunning. **2 a** a piece of crafty fraudulence; **b** crafty fraudulence. ⓒ 16c: from Latin *artificium*, from *ars*, *artis* art + *facere* to make.

artificer /ɑːˈtɪfɪsə(r)/ ▻ *noun* **1** a skilled craftsman. **2** a wily or inventive creator or craftsman. **3** a mechanic in the army or navy.

artificial /ɑːtɪˈfɪʃəl/ ▻ *adj* **1** made by human effort; not occurring naturally. **2** imitating something natural, especially in order to become a cheaper substitute for the natural product. **3** said of someone, their behaviour, etc: not genuine or sincere; premeditated, rehearsed. • **artificiality** *noun*. • **artificially** *adverb*. ⓒ 14c: from Latin *artificialis*.

artificial insemination (abbreviation **AI**) ▻ *noun, medicine* the introduction of semen into the vagina of a woman or female animal by artificial means in order to facilitate conception. See also AID, AIH.

artificial intelligence ▻ *noun* (abbreviation **AI**) the development and use of computer systems that can perform some of the functions normally associated with human intelligence, such as learning, problem-solving, decision-making, and pattern recognition.

artificial language ▻ *noun* **1** a language, eg ESPERANTO, that is specially invented to make international communication easier, especially one that is intended to be used in the fields of business and education. See also AUXILIARY LANGUAGE, NATURAL LANGUAGE. **2** an invented language used in computer programming. See also COMPUTER LANGUAGE.

artificial radioactivity ▻ *noun, physics* a form of radioactivity that results from the absorption of ionizing radiation, eg alpha particles or neutrons, by a stable substance that is not normally radioactive.

artificial respiration ▻ *noun* respiration that is stimulated and maintained manually, eg by the 'kiss of life', or mechanically, eg using a respirator, by forcing air in and out of the lungs when normal spontaneous breathing has stopped. See MOUTH-TO-MOUTH.

artificial satellite ▻ *noun, astron* a man-made spacecraft that is placed in orbit round the Earth or round a celestial object such as a planet, eg to relay communications signals or to obtain information for weather forecasting, navigation, military purposes, etc.

artillery /ɑːˈtɪlərɪ/ ▻ *noun* (***artilleries***) **1** large guns for use on land. **2** the part of an army equipped with such guns. ⓒ 14c: from French *artillier* to arm.

artisan /ɑːtɪˈzan, ˈɑːtɪzan/ ▻ *noun* someone who does skilled work with their hands. ⓒ 16c: French, from Latin *artitus* skilled.

artist /ˈɑːtɪst/ ▻ *noun* **1** someone who produces works of art, especially paintings. **2** someone who is skilled at some particular thing. **3** an artiste. **4** *in compounds, slang* someone who takes part in a specified activity such as drinking, fraudulent deals, etc habitually or to excess □ *con artist*. ⓒ 16c.

artist, artiste

In sense 3, **artist** is now common in the meaning for which **artiste** was formerly more common, but is now often regarded as somewhat old-fashioned or affected.

artiste /ɑːˈtiːst/ ▻ *noun* **1** a professional performer, especially a singer or dancer, in a theatre, circus, etc. **2** someone whose job is thought to involve a degree of creativity, eg in hairdressing, cooking, etc. ⓒ 19c: French.

artistic ▻ *adj* **1** relating to or characteristic of art or artists. **2** liking, or skilled in, painting, music, etc. **3** made or done with skill and good taste. • **artistically** *adverb*.

artistry ▻ *noun* artistic skill and imagination.

artless ▻ *adj* **1** simple and natural in manner. **2** honest, not deceitful. • **artlessly** *adverb*. • **artlessness** *noun*.

art movie and **art film** ▻ *noun* a cinema film made in the ART CINEMA style.

art nouveau /ɑː nuːˈvoʊ/ ▻ *noun* a style of art, architecture and interior design that flourished towards the end of the 19c, characterized by the use of flowing curved lines that resemble plant stems interlaced with highly stylized flowers and leaves. ⓒ 1899: French, meaning 'new art'.

the arts ▻ *noun* **1** literature, music, theatre, dance, cinema, painting, sculpture, etc thought of collectively. **2** the branch of knowledge that covers the study of subjects such as literature, philosophy, languages, etc that are generally considered to be non-scientific and non-vocational.

arts and crafts ▻ *noun* the application of artistic design to things that have a practical purpose, especially as advocated by the Arts and Crafts movement of the late 19c, which sought to counteract the loss of the traditional craftsman.

arts centre ▻ *noun* a building or buildings used for exhibitions, dramatic productions, music, poetry readings, etc.

art therapy ▻ *noun, psychol* art used as a means of communication, or as a creative activity, in order to gain insight into psychological and emotional disorders, and to aid recovery.

artwork ▻ *noun* any original material in the form of illustrations, drawings, design, etc, produced by an artist, illustrator or designer for reproduction in a book, magazine or other printed medium.

arty ▻ *adj* (***artier***, ***artiest***) *colloq* affectedly or ostentatiously artistic. • **arty-farty** or **artsy-fartsy** *adj, colloq* pretentiously or snobbishly artistic □ *those arty-farty French movies*.

arty-crafty ▻ *adj* quaintly artistic, especially when produced by a non-professional craftsman or artist.

arum /ˈɛərəm/ ▻ *noun* any of various perennial plants with a characteristic flower-head consisting of numerous tiny flowers around the base of a club-shaped SPADIX which is enclosed by a leaf-like SPATHE, eg cuckoo pint. ⓒ 16c: from Greek *aron*.

arum lily ▻ *noun* a perennial S African plant of the arum family, with large leaves shaped like arrow-heads and a yellow cylindrical SPADIX surrounded by a white, yellow or pink petal-like SPATHE, often used in floristry.

arundinaceous /ərʌndɪˈneɪʃəs/ ▻ *adj* resembling a reed. ⓒ 17c: from Latin *harundo*, *harundinis* reed + -ACEOUS.

arvo /ˈɑːvoʊ/ ▻ *noun* (***arvos***) *Austral colloq* afternoon. ⓒ 1930s abbreviation.

-ary ▷ *suffix* **1** *forming adjectives, denoting* connected with or pertaining to something □ ***customary***. **2** *forming nouns, denoting* someone who is connected with or engaged in something □ ***adversary*** □ ***secretary***. **3** *forming nouns, denoting* something connected with or employed in something; a place for something □ ***dictionary*** □ ***apiary***. ◷ From Latin *-arius*.

Aryan /ˈɛərɪən/ ▷ *noun* **1** *historical* in Nazi ideology: a European not of Jewish descent, especially someone of the northern European type with blonde hair and blue eyes, believed to be racially superior to members of any other race. **2** a member of the peoples speaking any of the Indo-European languages, now especially the Indo-Iranian languages. ▷ *adj* belonging, relating or referring to Aryans or the Aryan languages. ◷ 19c: from Sanskrit *arya* noble.

aryl /ˈarɪl/ ▷ *adj, chem* in an organic chemical compound: referring or relating to the group produced by removal of a hydrogen atom from an aromatic hydrocarbon. ◷ Early 20c: from *a*romatic + -YL.

arytenoid or **arytaenoid** /arɪˈtiːnɔɪd/ *anatomy* ▷ *adj, denoting* the cartilages in the larynx that are involved in controlling the vibrations of the vocal cords. ▷ *noun* one of these cartilages. ◷ 17c: from Greek *arytainoeides* shaped like a ladle or pitcher.

As ▷ *symbol, chem* arsenic.

as[1] /əz, az/ ▷ *conj* **1** when; while; during □ ***met him as I was coming out of the shop***. **2** because; since □ ***didn't go as it was raining***. **3** in the manner that □ ***fussing as only a mother can***. **4** that which; what □ ***Do as you're told***. **5** to the extent that □ ***Try as he might, he still couldn't reach***. **6** for instance □ ***large books, as this one for example***. **7** in the same way that □ ***married late in life, as his father had done***. **8** used to refer to something previously said, done, etc: like; just like □ ***As Frank says, the job won't be easy***. ▷ *prep* in the role of something □ ***speaking as her friend***. ▷ *adverb* equally □ ***It was really hot yesterday, but I don't think today is as hot***. ● **as … as …** used in similes and for comparison: denoting that the things compared are the same or share the expected quality or characteristic □ ***as sly as a fox*** □ ***as sly as his brother*** □ ***not as sly as he used to be***. ● **as for** or **to something** or **someone** with regard to it or them; concerning it or them □ ***And as for Harry, he's just mad***. ● **as from** or **as of** starting on or at (a particular time) □ ***As from Monday, we'll be open till ten***. ● **as if!** *colloq* short form of *as if I would* etc: an exclamation that questions or negates what has just been said. ● **as if** or **as though** as he, she, etc would if □ ***behaved as if nothing had happened***. ● **as it is** the way things are at the moment □ ***I think you've drunk enough as it is***. ● **as it were** in a way; to some extent. ● **as much** the same; what amounts to that □ ***I thought as much***. ● **as well** also. ● **as yet** until now. ● **so as to** in order to. ◷ Anglo-Saxon *eallswa* just as.

as[2] /as/ ▷ *noun* (*asses*) an ancient Roman copper coin. ◷ 17c: Latin.

ASA ▷ *abbreviation* **1** *Brit* Advertising Standards Authority. **2** *Brit* Amateur Swimming Association. **3** American Standards Association, used eg in labelling photographic film speeds.

asafoetida /asəˈfɛtɪdə, -ˈfiː-/ ▷ *noun* a gum resin with an unpleasant smell of onions formerly used medicinally, now widely used as an ingredient in Indian cooking. ◷ 14c: from Latin *asa* gum (from Persian *aza* mastic) + Latin *foetida* fetid.

asana /ˈɑːsənə/ ▷ *noun* any of the various positions in YOGA.

ASAP or **asap** ▷ *abbreviation* as soon as possible.

asbestos /azˈbɛstɒs, as-/ ▷ *noun, geol* any of a group of fibrous silicate minerals that are highly resistant to heat and chemically inert, formerly used in fireproof curtains, protective clothing, felt, plaster, roofing materials, etc, but now known to cause asbestosis and lung cancer. ◷ 14c: Greek, meaning 'inextinguishable'.

asbestosis ▷ *noun* a chronic inflammatory disease of the lungs, caused by inhalation of asbestos dust over a long period. Compare ANTHRACOSIS, SILICOSIS. ◷ 1920s: from ASBESTOS + -OSIS 2.

ascarid /ˈaskərɪd/ ▷ *noun* a parasitic nematode worm, such as the roundworm, that infests the gut of humans and pigs, causing diarrhoea, vomiting and attendant weight loss. ◷ 14c: from Greek *ascaris* an intestinal worm.

ascend /əˈsɛnd/ ▷ *verb* (***ascended, ascending***) *tr & intr* **1** to climb, go or rise up □ ***The Moon ascended the night sky***. **2** *intr* to slope upwards □ ***The path ascended steeply***. **3** *intr* to rise to a higher point, level, degree, etc □ ***ascended to the position of chairman***. ● **ascend the throne** to become king or queen. ◷ 14c: from Latin *ascendere* to climb up.

ascendancy, **ascendency**, **ascendance** or **ascendence** ▷ *noun* controlling or dominating power.

ascendant or **ascendent** ▷ *adj* **1** having more influence or power. **2** *astrol* rising over the eastern horizon. ▷ *noun* **1** supremacy; increasing influence or power. **2** *astrol* the sign of the zodiac rising over the eastern horizon at the time of an event, especially birth. ● **in the ascendant** showing an increase in power, domination, authority, wealth, etc.

ascender ▷ *noun* **1** someone or something that goes or climbs up. **2** *printing* **a** any upper case letter; **b** any lower case letter which has an upper stem, etc, eg 'b', 'd', 'i', etc; **c** the part of a lower-case letter above the main body of the letters.

ascending ▷ *adj* **1** rising; moving upwards. **2** from the lowest to the highest, the least to the greatest, or the worst to the best □ ***in ascending order***.

ascension /əˈsɛnʃən/ ▷ *noun* **1** an act of climbing or moving upwards. **2** (**Ascension**) *Christianity* Christ's believed passing into heaven on the fortieth day after the RESURRECTION (see RESURRECTION 3a), as told in Acts 1. ● **Ascension Day** the fortieth day after Easter Sunday, when Christ's Ascension is celebrated. Also called **Holy Thursday**. ◷ 14c: from Latin *ascensio*, from *ascendere* to ascend.

ascent /əˈsɛnt/ ▷ *noun* **1** the act of climbing, ascending or rising □ ***a meteoric ascent to fame***. **2** an upward slope.

ascertain /asəˈteɪn/ ▷ *verb* (***ascertained, ascertaining***) to find out; to discover (the truth, etc). ● **ascertainable** *adj*. ● **ascertainment** *noun*. ◷ 15c: from French *acertener* to make certain.

> ***ascertain***
>
> ☆ PLAIN ENGLISH alternatives are **find out, discover, establish**.

ascesis /əˈsiːsɪs/ ▷ *noun* the custom, observance or practice of self-discipline. ◷ 19c: from Greek *askesis*, from *askeein* to practise, train.

ascetic /əˈsɛtɪk/ ▷ *noun* someone who shuns or abstains from all physical comfort and pleasure, especially someone who does so in solitude and for religious reasons. ▷ *adj* characterized by the shunning of or abstinence from physical pleasure and comfort; self-denying. ● **ascetically** *adverb*. ● **asceticism** *noun*. ◷ 17c: from Greek *asketikos*, from *askeein* to practise, train.

asceticism /əˈsɛtɪsɪzəm/ ▷ *noun* the philosophy or practice of self-denial of physical pleasures or comforts.

asci *plural of* ASCUS

ASCII /ˈaskiː/ ▷ *noun, computing* in digital computing systems: the most common way of representing text characters by binary code, widely used for storage of text and for transmission of data between computers. ◷

1960s: an acronym of *A*merican *S*tandard *C*ode for *I*nformation *I*nterchange.

ascomycete /askoumaɪ'siːt/ ▷ *noun, biol* any member of a large subdivision of fungi characterized by the formation of ASCI, eg truffles, morels, most yeasts and many parasitic fungi. • **ascomycetous** *adj.* 19c: from Greek *askos* a bag or bladder + *mykes* a mushroom.

ascorbic acid /ə'skɔːbɪk —/ ▷ *noun* VITAMIN C. 1930s: from A-^{2} + *scorbutic*.

ascospore /'askəspɔː(r)/ ▷ *noun* a spore, usually one of eight, produced in the ASCUS of an ASCOMYCETE.

ascribe /ə'skraɪb/ ▷ *verb* to attribute; assign ▫ ***ascribed their success to hard work.*** • **ascribable** *adj.* 15c: from Latin *ascribere* to enrol, from *ad-* to + *scribere* to write.

ascus /'askəs/ ▷ *noun* (***asci*** /'asəɪ, 'askaɪ/) *bot* in ascomycete fungi: a small elongated sac-like reproductive structure that contains (usually eight) ASCOSPORES. 1830s: from Greek *askos* a bag or bladder.

asdic or **Asdic** /'azdɪk/ ▷ *noun* the name for the ultrasonic system of submarine detection used by warships of the Royal Navy until 1963, which, since then, has been known as SONAR. 1930s: an acronym of *A*nti-*S*ubmarine *D*etection *I*nvestigation *C*ommittee, the body set up in 1917 to develop the system.

ASE ▷ *abbreviation* Association for Science Education.

-ase /eɪz/ ▷ *suffix, chem, forming nouns, indicating* an enzyme ▫ ***amylase.***

ASEAN or **Asean** /'asɪan/ ▷ *noun* an acronym for Association of South East Asian Nations.

aseismic /eɪ'saɪzmɪk/ ▷ *adj* **1** said of a particular geographical area: not liable to earthquakes. **2** said of buildings, bridges, roads, etc: designed and constructed so as to withstand damage by earthquakes. 19c: A-^{2} + SEISMIC.

asepalous /eɪ'sɛpələs/ ▷ *adj, bot* said of a plant or flower: without sepals.

asepsis /eɪ'sepsɪs/ ▷ *noun* (***asepses*** /-siːz/) **1** the condition of being free from germs or other infection-causing micro-organisms. **2** the methods involved in achieving this kind of condition. • **aseptic** *adj, noun.* 19c: A-^{2} + SEPSIS.

asexual /eɪ'sekʃuəl/ ▷ *adj* **1** denoting reproduction that does not involve sexual processes, and in which genetically identical offspring are produced from a single parent, eg budding of yeasts or vegetative propagation in plants. **2** without functional sexual organs. **3** lacking in sexuality. • **asexuality** *noun.* • **asexually** *adverb.* 19c.

asexual reproduction ▷ *noun, biol* a form of reproduction in which new individuals are produced from a single parent without the involvement of gametes and fertilization, and all the offspring are genetically identical to the parent and to each other. Compare SEXUAL REPRODUCTION.

ASH /aʃ/ ▷ *abbreviation* Action on Smoking and Health, a British organization that campaigns against tobacco smoking.

ash^{1} /aʃ/ ▷ *noun* (***ashes*** /'aʃɪz/) **1 a** the dusty residue that remains after something has been burnt; **b** *in compounds* ▫ ***ashtray.*** **2** the powdery dust that is put out by an erupting volcano. **3** a silvery grey colour. **4** (**ashes**) **a** the remains of a body after cremation; **b** charred remains. • **ashy** *adj.* Anglo-Saxon *asce*.

ash^{2} /aʃ/ ▷ *noun* (***ashes*** /'aʃɪz/) **1** any of various species of deciduous tree or shrub with compound leaves, small clusters of greenish flowers and winged fruits. **2** the strong pale timber obtained from this tree, used to make tool handles, furniture, hockey sticks, etc. Anglo-Saxon *æsc*.

ash^{3} /aʃ/ ▷ *noun* **1** the digraph *æ*, originally a runic symbol and used in Anglo-Saxon to represent a fronted *a*. **2** in the International Phonetic Alphabet: the symbol that traditionally, although not in this dictionary, is used to represent the vowel in English words like *pat*. Anglo-Saxon *æsc*.

ashamed /ə'ʃeɪmd/ ▷ *adj* **1** troubled by feelings of guilt, embarrassment, humiliation, etc. **2** (*usually* **ashamed of someone** or **something**) embarrassed or humiliated by them or it ▫ ***ashamed of his humble roots.*** **3** (*usually* **ashamed that** …) feeling guilty, embarrassed, etc because … ▫ ***ashamed that he hadn't been kinder to her.*** **4** hesitant or reluctant (to do something) because of embarrassment, guilt, fear of disapproval, etc ▫ ***He was not ashamed to say he had taken drugs.*** • **ashamedly** /ə'ʃeɪmɪdlɪ/ *adverb.* Anglo-Saxon *ascamian* to feel shame.

ashcan ▷ *noun, N Amer, especially US* a dustbin.

ashen ▷ *adj* said of a face: grey or very pale, usually from shock, illness, etc.

the Ashes /'aʃɪz/ ▷ *plural noun, cricket* a trophy that contains the charred remains of a stump that was burnt on the 1883 England tour of Australia, awarded to the team that wins any of the regular series of cricket matches played between England and Australia, the award or otherwise being referred to as 'winning, losing or retaining the Ashes'. 19c: so called because of a mock obituary notice to mark the death of English cricket that appeared after England's spectacular drubbing by Australia; the notice ran 'In Affectionate Remembrance of English Cricket Which died at the Oval on 29th August, 1882. Deeply lamented by a large circle of friends and acquaintances. R.I.P. N.B.-The body will be cremated and the ashes taken to Australia.'.

ashet /'aʃət/ ▷ *noun, Scots & Northern dialect* a large oval plate or dish, usually used for serving meat. 16c: from French *assiette* a plate.

ashlar or **ashler** /'aʃlə(r)/ ▷ *noun* **1** a large square-cut stone that is used for building or facing walls. **2** masonry made of ashlars. 14c: from French *aiseler*, from Latin *axilla* small plank.

ashore /ə'ʃɔː(r)/ ▷ *adverb* **1** to, towards or onto the shore or land. **2** on land as opposed to at sea.

ashram /'aʃrəm/ ▷ *noun* a place of retreat, especially in India, for a holy-man or for a religious community, where members lead lives of austere self-discipline. Early 20c: from Sanskrit *asrama* a hermitage, from *a* near or towards + *srama* earnest endeavour.

ashtray ▷ *noun* a dish or other container where smokers can put the ash, butts, etc from cigarettes, pipes, joints, etc.

Ash Wednesday ▷ *noun, Christianity* the first day of LENT, so called because of the practice (especially in the Roman Catholic Church) of sprinkling ashes on the heads of penitents.

Asian /'eɪʃən, 'eɪʒən/ ▷ *adj* belonging or relating to the continent of Asia, its inhabitants or its languages. ▷ *noun* **1** an inhabitant of, or person born in, Asia. **2** someone of Asian descent. 16c: from Greek *Asianos*.

Asian elephant see under ELEPHANT

Asiatic /eɪʃɪ'atɪk, eɪzɪ'atɪk/ ▷ *adj* belonging or relating to Asia or Asians. ▷ *noun, offensive* an Asian. 17c: from Greek *Asiatikos*.

Asiatic

Asiatic is often considered offensive when applied to people.

aside /ə'saɪd/ ▷ *adverb* **1** on, to, towards or over to one side. **2** away from everyone else ▫ ***took him aside to give him the bad news.*** **3** in a direction away from oneself ▫ ***tossed the magazine aside in disgust.*** **4** out of mind, consideration, etc, especially temporarily ▫ ***tried to put***

his worries aside. ▷ *noun* **1** words said by a character in a play which the audience can hear, but which the other characters cannot. **2** a remark that is not related to the main subject of a conversation. • **aside from something** apart from or not including it □ *Aside from the weather, we had a wonderful time.* • **put something aside** to keep it for some special time or purpose □ *put money aside for their holidays.* • **set something aside** *law* to declare (a verdict, sentence, etc) invalid; to quash it.

A-side /'eɪ—/ ▷ *noun* on a record, usually a single: **a** the side which holds the track that is being more actively promoted; **b** the track concerned. Compare B-SIDE.

asinine /'asɪnaɪn/ ▷ *adj* **1** relating to or resembling an ass. **2** stupid; idiotic; stubborn. • **asininity** /asɪ'nɪnɪtɪ/ *noun.* • **asininely** *adverb.* ⓘ 17c: from Latin *asininus*, from *asinus* ass.

ask /ɑːsk/ ▷ *verb* (***asked***, ***asking***) **1** *tr & intr* to question someone about something □ *asked her qualifications.* **2** to call for an answer to (a question) □ *asked what qualifications she had.* **3** to inquire about □ *ask the way.* **4** to invite □ *asked him to the dance.* **5** to expect □ *don't ask a lot of him.* • **for the asking** on request. ⓘ Anglo-Saxon *ascian.*

■ **ask after someone** to show concern about their health.

■ **ask for someone** or **something** to make a request for them or it □ *asked for directions.*

■ **ask for something** *informal* to behave in such a way as to deserve it □ *That's just asking for trouble.*

■ **ask someone out** to invite them on a date.

■ **ask someone over** to invite them round, especially to one's own house.

askance /ə'skans, ə'skɑːns/ ▷ *adverb* sideways. • **look askance at someone** or **something** to consider them or it with suspicion or disapproval. ⓘ 16c.

askew /ə'skjuː/ ▷ *adverb, adj* squint; not properly straight or level; awry. ⓘ 16c.

asking price ▷ *noun* the proposed selling price of something, set by the seller. ⓘ 18c.

ASL ▷ *abbreviation* American Sign Language.

asleep /ə'sliːp/ ▷ *adj* **1** in a sleeping state. **2** *colloq* not paying attention. **3** said of limbs, hands, feet, etc: numb. ▷ *adverb* into a sleeping state □ *fall asleep.* • **sound asleep** in a very deep sleep. ⓘ Anglo-Saxon *on slæpe.*

ASLEF /'azlɛf/ ▷ *abbreviation* Associated Society of Locomotive Engineers and Firemen.

AS level or (*in full*) **Advanced Supplementary level** ▷ *noun* **1** an examination designed to provide supplementary A-LEVEL study for A-level students, covering a smaller syllabus than the corresponding A level examination. **2** a pass in such an examination.

ASM ▷ *abbreviation* air-to-surface missile.

asocial /eɪ'soʊʃəl/ ▷ *adj* **1** not social; antisocial; not gregarious. **2** hostile to, or against the interests of, society.

asp ▷ *noun* **1** any of various small venomous S European snakes, often with dark slanting markings on the back of the body, and an upturned snout. **2** the Egyptian cobra, a venomous African snake, said to have caused the death of the Egyptian queen, Cleopatra. ⓘ 14c: from Greek *aspis.*

asparagine /ə'sparədʒɪn, -dʒiːn/ ▷ *noun, biochem* an amino acid, derived from aspartic acid, that is a requirement of the human diet and an important nitrogen reserve in many plants. ⓘ 19c: so called because it was first discovered in ASPARAGUS.

asparagus /ə'sparəgəs/ ▷ *noun* **1** any of several species of plant with cylindrical green shoots or 'spears' that function as leaves, the true leaves being reduced to scales. **2** the harvested shoots of this plant, which can be cooked and eaten as a vegetable. ⓘ 15c: from Greek *asparagos.*

aspartame /ə'spɑːteɪm/ ▷ *noun* an artificial sweetener, 200 times sweeter than sugar but without the bitter aftertaste of saccharin, widely used in the food industry and by diabetics and dieters. ⓘ 1970s: from ASPARTIC ACID.

aspartic acid /ə'spɑːtɪk/ ▷ *noun, biochem* an amino acid formed by the hydrolysis of asparagine. ⓘ 19c.

aspect /'aspɛkt/ ▷ *noun* **1** a particular or distinct part or element of a problem, subject, etc □ *probed every aspect of the murder case.* **2** a particular way of considering a matter □ *It's a very serious matter from all aspects.* **3 a** the appearance something has to the eye □ *a lush green aspect*; **b** a look or appearance, especially of a face □ *a worried aspect.* **4** the direction something faces □ *a garden with a southern aspect.* **5 a** *astron, astrol* the position of a planet in relation to the Sun as viewed from the Earth; **b** *astrol* any of the different influences that these positions are believed to have on the star signs □ *Aries is under the benign aspect of Venus just now.* **6** *grammar* a verbal form in certain languages, eg Russian and other Slavonic languages, that expresses features such as simple action, repetition, beginning, duration, continuity, completedness, habituality, etc. • **aspectual** /a'spɛktʃʊəl/ *adj.* ⓘ 14c: from Latin *aspectus*, from *ad* to + *specere* to look.

aspect ratio ▷ *noun* **1** *cinematog* the comparative ratio of width to height of an image on a TV or cinema screen. **2** *aeronautics* the ratio of the wingspan to the mean chord of an aerofoil.

aspen /'aspən/ ▷ *noun* a deciduous tree of the poplar family, widespread in Europe, with smooth greyish-brown bark and round or oval greyish-green leaves that tremble in the slightest breeze. ⓘ Anglo-Saxon *æspe.*

asperity /a'spɛrɪtɪ/ ▷ *noun* (***asperities***) roughness, bitterness or harshness, especially of temper. ⓘ 17c: from Latin *asper* rough.

aspersion /as'pɜːʃən/ ▷ *noun* • **cast aspersions on someone** or **something** to make a damaging or spiteful remark. ⓘ 16c: from Latin *aspergere, aspersum* from *spergere* to sprinkle.

asphalt /'asfalt/ ▷ *noun* **a** a brown or black semi-solid bituminous material that occurs in natural deposits and is also prepared synthetically by distillation from petroleum; **b** this material used in the construction industry for roofing, or mixed with rock chips or gravel to make paving and road-surfacing materials. ▷ *verb* (***asphalted***, ***asphalting***) to cover with asphalt. • **asphaltic** *adj.* ⓘ 14c: from Greek *asphaltos.*

asphodel /'asfədɛl/ ▷ *noun* any of various perennial plants of the lily family, native to S Europe, with long narrow leaves and yellow or white star-shaped flowers, including many species that grow in damp habitats, eg bog asphodel. ⓘ 16c: from Greek *asphodelos*; related to DAFFODIL.

asphyxia /as'fɪksɪə/ ▷ *noun* suffocation caused by any factor that interferes with respiration and prevents oxygen from reaching the body tissues, such as choking, drowning or inhaling poisonous gases. ⓘ 18c: Greek, originally meaning 'absence of pulse' from *sphyxis* pulse.

asphyxiate /as'fɪksɪeɪt/ ▷ *verb* (***asphyxiated***, ***asphyxiating***) *tr & intr* **1** to stop or cause to stop breathing. **2** to suffocate. • **asphyxiation** *noun.* ⓘ 19c.

aspic /'aspɪk/ ▷ *noun* a savoury jelly made from meat or fish stock and sometimes flavoured with port, Madeira or sherry, and used as a glaze or to make a mould for terrines, fish, eggs, etc. ⓘ 18c.

aspidistra /aspɪ'dɪstrə/ ▷ *noun* (***aspidistras***) an evergreen perennial plant with long-lasting broad leathery leaves, and dull-purple bell-shaped flowers produced at ground level, widely grown as a house plant. ⓘ 19c: from Greek *aspis* shield.

aspirant /'aspɪrənt, ə'spaɪərənt/ ▷ *noun* someone who works hard to achieve something, especially a position of great status. ▷ *adj* trying to achieve a higher position.

aspirate ▷ *noun* /ˈaspɪrət/ *phonetics* **a** the sound represented in English and several other languages by the letter *h*; **b** a voiceless plosive sound such as /p/, /t/ or /k/ that has an audible breathiness after the stop has been released. ▷ *verb* (***aspirated***, ***aspirating***) /ˈaspɪreɪt/ **1** *phonetics* **a** to pronounce a word with an *h* sound as opposed to 'dropping' it, eg to give the word *hedgehog* its full phonetic value, rather than saying *'edge'og*, as in some varieties of English; **b** to give a voiceless plosive an audible breathiness after the stop has been released. **2** to withdraw (liquid, gas or solid debris) from a cavity by suction. ◷ 17c: from Latin *aspirare*, from *spirare* to breathe.

aspiration /aspɪˈreɪʃən/ ▷ *noun* **1 a** eager desire; ambition; **b** a hope or an ambition. **2** the removal of fluid from a cavity in the body such as a cyst or an inflamed joint, or from the mouth during dental treatment, by suction using an aspirator.

aspirator /ˈaspɪreɪtə(r)/ ▷ *noun* **1** a device used to withdraw liquid, gas or solid debris from a cavity of the body, eg during dental treatment. **2** a device that is used to draw air or other gases through bottles or other vessels.

aspire /aˈspaɪə(r)/ ▷ *verb* (***aspired***, ***aspiring***) (*usually* **aspire to** or **after something**) to have a strong desire to achieve or reach (an objective or ambition) □ *aspired to greatness.* ◷ 15c: from Latin *aspirare*, from *spirare* to breathe.

aspirin /ˈasprɪn, ˈaspɪrɪn/ ▷ *noun* **1** an analgesic drug that is widely used to relieve mild to moderate pain and to reduce inflammation and fever, and is sometimes also used in daily doses to prevent coronary thrombosis and stroke in susceptible individuals. **2** a tablet of this drug. ◷ 19c: originally a trademark, from German *Acetylirte Spirsäure* acetylated spiraeic acid.

aspiring /əˈspaɪərɪŋ/ ▷ *adj* ambitious; hopeful of becoming something specified □ *an aspiring novelist.*

ass¹ /as/ ▷ *noun* (*asses*) **1** any of various species of hoofed mammal resembling, but smaller than, a horse, with longer ears, a grey or brownish coat, a short erect mane, and a characteristic bray. **2** *colloq* a stupid person. ◷ Anglo-Saxon *assa*.

ass² /as/ ▷ *noun, N Amer, especially US slang* **1** ARSE. **2** the anus. **3** a sexual partner or a possible sexual conquest □ *a sexy piece of ass.* **4** the self or the person, especially when used for emphasis or to express anger, contempt, etc □ *Get your ass out here!* **5** *in compounds, denoting* a person of a specified kind □ *smart-ass.* • **-assed** *in compounds* **1** having buttocks of a specified kind □ *fat-assed.* **2** having a specified kind of temperament or character □ *wild-assed.* • **drag, haul** or **tear ass** to move very fast. • **get one's ass in a sling** to be in deep trouble. • **kick ass 1** to have or assume power □ *The LA cops don't kick ass like they used to.* **2** said of forms of entertainment: to be vigorous and powerful □ *They're a live band that always kicks ass.* • **my ass** an expression of disbelief or contempt. • **out on one's ass** sacked; rejected. • **put one's ass on the line** to risk something or to take the responsibility for something. • **up to one's ass in something** totally overwhelmed by it □ *up to my ass in paperwork.* • **work one's ass off** to put a lot of effort into something. • **up your ass** an exclamation of contemptuous dismissal or rejection.

assail /əˈseɪl/ ▷ *verb* (***assailed***, ***assailing***) **1** to make a strong physical attack. **2** to attack with a barrage of hostile words; to criticize. **3** to agitate, especially mentally. **4** to face up to something with the intention of mastering it. • **assailable** *adj.* • **assailer** *noun.* ◷ 13c: from Latin *ad* to + *salire* to leap.

assailant ▷ *noun* someone who attacks something or someone, either verbally or physically.

Assam /aˈsam/ ▷ *noun* a type of Indian tea that is made from small broken leaves with golden tips, which give a strongish full-bodied taste. ◷ 19c: named after the state of Assam in N India.

Assamese /asəˈmiːz/ ▷ *noun* a language spoken in the eastern parts of N and Central India. ▷ *adj* relating to, or spoken or written in, Assamese. ◷ 1820s: from Assam a state in N India.

assassin /əˈsasɪn/ ▷ *noun* someone who kills someone else, especially for political or religious reasons. ◷ 16c: from Arabic *hashshashin* hashish-eaters, originally applied to Muslim fanatics who would give themselves Dutch courage in this way before setting off on murder missions during the Crusades.

assassinate /əˈsasɪneɪt/ ▷ *verb* (***assassinated***, ***assassinating***) **1** to murder, especially for political or religious reasons. **2** to destroy (someone's reputation) by slander, malicious rumour, etc. • **assassination** *noun.*

assassin bug ▷ *noun* a small bug that feeds mainly on the body fluids of small arthropods, although several species suck the blood of vertebrates and are carriers of disease.

assault /əˈsɔːlt/ ▷ *noun* **1** a violent physical or verbal attack. **2** *law* any act that causes someone to feel physically threatened, which is considered reckless or intentional, and which need not necessarily involve any physical contact, eg pointing a gun at someone. Compare ASSAULT AND BATTERY. **4** *euphemistic* rape or attempted rape. ▷ *verb* (***assaulted***, ***assaulting***) to make an assault on someone or something. ◷ 13c: from French *asaut*, from Latin *saltus* leap.

assault and battery ▷ *noun, law* the act of threatening to physically attack someone which is then followed by an actual physical attack, even when any damage sustained is minimal.

assault course ▷ *noun* an obstacle course with walls, pools, nets, etc, used especially for training soldiers who might come across similar obstructions in the field.

assay /əˈseɪ, ˈaseɪ/ ▷ *noun, metallurgy* the analysis and assessment of the composition and purity of a metal in an ore or mineral, or of a chemical compound in a mixture of compounds. ▷ *verb* (***assayed***, ***assaying***) to perform such an analysis on, or to determine the commercial value of (an ore or mineral) on the basis of such an analysis. ◷ 14c: from French *assaier* to attempt.

assegai or **assagai** /ˈasəgaɪ/ ▷ *noun* (***assegais***) a thin light iron-tipped wooden spear used in southern Africa. ◷ 17c: from Arabic *az-zagayah* the spear.

assemblage ▷ *noun* /əˈsɛmblɪdʒ/ **1** a collection of people or things. **2 a** a gathering together; **b** the act of gathering together; **c** the state of being gathered together. **3** / *also* asɑ̃blaʒ/ the technique (popular in the 1950s at the time of the revival of DADAism) of assembling and fixing together various materials, eg paper, wood, metal, sacks, rubbish or even crushed motor cars, or objects that occur naturally such as grasses, stones, shells, etc to create a work of art that functions as a three-dimensional whole. See also COLLAGE, FOUND OBJECT.

assemble /əˈsɛmbəl/ ▷ *verb* (***assembled***, ***assembling***) **1** *tr & intr* to gather or collect together. **2** to put together (the parts of something, such as a machine, a piece of furniture, etc). ◷ 13c: from French *assembler*, from Latin *simul* together.

assembler ▷ *noun, computing* a computer program designed to convert a program written in assembly language into one written in machine code.

assembly /əˈsɛmblɪ/ ▷ *noun* (***assemblies***) **1** a group of people gathered together, especially for a meeting. **2 a** the act of assembling; **b** the state of being assembled. **3** the procedure of putting together the parts of something, such as a machine, a piece of furniture, etc.

assembly language ▷ *noun* a low-level programming language that uses mnemonic codes to represent machine code programs.

assembly line ▷ *noun* a continuous series of machines and workers that an article, product, etc passes along in the stages of its manufacture.

assent /ə'sɛnt/ ▻ *noun* consent or approval, especially official. See also ROYAL ASSENT. ▻ *verb* (***assented, assenting***) (*often* **assent to something**) to agree to it. ⓒ 13c: from Latin *assentari*, from *ad-* to + *sentire* to feel or think.

assert /ə'sɜːt/ ▻ *verb* (***asserted, asserting***) **1** to state firmly. **2** to insist on or defend (one's rights, opinions, etc). • **assert oneself** to state one's wishes, defend one's opinions, etc confidently and vigorously. ⓒ 17c: from Latin *asserere*, from *ad-* to + *serere* to join.

assertion /ə'sɜːʃən/ ▻ *noun* **1** a positive or strong statement or claim. **2** the act of making such a claim or statement.

assertive ▻ *adj* said of someone or their attitude: inclined to expressing wishes and opinions in a firm and confident manner; pushy. • **assertively** *adj*. • **assertiveness** *noun*. ⓒ 16c: from ASSERT.

assertiveness training ▻ *noun* a system whereby more positive behaviour patterns are learned, mainly by adopting a more self-confident non-aggressive approach to dealing with difficult people or situations. ⓒ 1970s.

assess /ə'sɛs/ ▻ *verb* (***assesses, assessed, assessing***) **1** to judge the quality or importance of something. **2** to estimate the cost, value, etc of something. **3** to fix the amount of (a fine or tax). ⓒ 15c: from Latin *assidere* to sit by.

assessment ▻ *noun* **1** the act of judging the quality of something, especially pupils' or students' work. **2** evaluation; estimation. **3** a valuation or estimate. **4** an amount to be paid.

assessor ▻ *noun* **1** someone who assesses the importance or quality of something, eg the performance of pupils, students, workers, etc. **2** someone who evaluates the extent of damage and the cost of repair, eg in an insurance claim. **3** someone who assesses the value of property, etc for taxation. **4** someone who advises a judge, etc on technical matters.

asset /'asɛt/ ▻ *noun* anything that is considered valuable or useful, such as a skill, quality, person, etc □ ***He is a real asset to the company.***

assets ▻ *plural noun, accounting* **1** the total value of the property and possessions of a person or company, especially when thought of in terms of whether or not it is enough to cover any debts. Compare LIABILITIES. **2** *law* the total property that belonged to someone who has died and which is then at the disposal of an executor for the payment of any outstanding debts, legacies, etc. **3** any property, possessions, shares, money, etc held by someone or by a company, etc. ⓒ 16c: from French *asetz* enough.

asset-stripping ▻ *noun* the practice of buying an unsuccessful company at a low price and selling off its assets separately for a profit and with no regard for the future welfare of the company or its employees.

asset-stripper ▻ *noun* a person or company that performs or attempts to perform ASSET-STRIPPING.

asseverate /ə'sɛvəreɪt/ ▻ *verb* (***asseverated, asseverating***) to state solemnly. ⓒ 18c: from Latin *asseverare* to assert solemnly.

asshole see ARSEHOLE

assiduity /asɪ'djuːɪtɪ/ ▻ *noun* (***assiduities***) constant care and attention that is shown towards someone, or to what one is doing. ⓒ 17c.

assiduous /ə'sɪdjʊəs/ ▻ *adj* **1** hard-working. **2** done carefully and exactly. • **assiduously** *adverb*. • **assiduousness** *noun*. ⓒ 17c: from Latin *assiduus* sitting down to, and hence, persistent.

assign /ə'saɪn/ ▻ *verb* (***assigned, assigning***) **1** to give (a task, etc) to someone. **2** to appoint someone to a position or task. **3** to fix (a time, place, etc) for a purpose. **4** to attribute or ascribe. **5** *law, formerly* to hand over (a title, property, interest, etc) to someone else by contract. • **assignable** *adj*. ⓒ 13c: from Latin *assignare*, from *signare* to mark out.

assignation /asɪg'neɪʃən/ ▻ *noun* **1** a secret appointment to meet, especially between lovers. **2** *Scots law* an ASSIGNMENT (sense 3).

assignee /asɪ'niː/ ▻ *noun, law* someone to whom property, interest, etc is given by contract.

assignment /ə'saɪnmənt/ ▻ *noun* **1 a** a task or duty that has been selected for someone to do; **b** an exercise that is set for students, etc. **2** the act of assigning. **3** *law* a transfer of property, interest, etc to someone else.

assignor /asɪ'nɔː(r)/ ▻ *noun, law* someone who gives property, interest, etc by contract.

assimilate ▻ *verb* /ə'sɪmɪleɪt/ (***assimilated, assimilating***) **1** to become familiar with and understand (facts, information, etc) completely. **2** *tr & intr* to become part of, or make (people) part of, a larger group, especially when they are of a different race, culture, etc. **3** *biol* said of a plant or animal: to manufacture complex organic compounds. **4** *tr & intr, phonetics* said of a sound, usually a consonant: to change due to the influence of an immediately adjacent sound, eg *d* assimilates to *g* in *broadcast*. **5** to cause something to become similar to something else. ▻ *noun* /-lət/ *biol* any of the complex organic compounds initially produced by green plants and certain bacteria that manufacture complex molecules from simple molecules obtained from the environment. ⓒ 17c: from Latin *ad* to + *similis* like.

assimilation /əsɪmɪ'leɪʃən/ ▻ *noun* **1** *biol* in green plants and certain bacteria: the manufacture of complex organic compounds from simple molecules obtained from the environment. **2** *physiol* in animals: the manufacture of complex organic compounds, such as proteins and fats, from simple molecules derived from digested food material. **3** *phonetics* **a** the process whereby a sound is ASSIMILATED (sense 4). **b** an instance of this happening. Compare ELISION.

assist /ə'sɪst/ ▻ *verb* (***assisted, assisting***) *tr & intr* to help. ⓒ 16c: from Latin *assistere*, from *ad* beside + *sistere* to take a stand.

> ***assist***
>
> ☆ PLAIN ENGLISH alternatives are **help, aid**.

assistance ▻ *noun* **1** help. **2** an act of helping.

assistant ▻ *noun* **1** a person whose job is to help someone of higher rank, position, etc. **2** a person whose job is to serve customers in a shop □ ***sales assistant***.

assizes /ə'saɪzɪz/ ▻ *plural noun, formerly* in England and Wales: court sittings which used to be held at regular intervals in each county and which were presided over by itinerant judges, but whose criminal jurisdiction was transferred to the Crown Court under the Courts Act of 1971. ⓒ 14c: from Latin *assidere* to sit beside.

assoc. ▻ *abbreviation* **1** associated. **2** association.

associate ▻ *verb* (***associated, associating***) /ə'soʊʃɪeɪt, -sɪ-/ **1** to connect in the mind □ ***associate lambs with spring.*** **2** *intr* to mix socially □ ***don't associate with him.*** **3** to involve (oneself) in a group because of shared views or aims. **4** *intr* to join with people for a common purpose. ▻ *noun* /-ət/ **1** a business partner or colleague. **2** a companion or friend. **3** someone who is admitted to a society, institution, etc without full membership. ▻ *adj* /-ət/ **1** joined with another, especially in a business □ ***an associate director.*** **2** not having full membership of a society, institution, etc. **3** attendant; accompanying □ ***suffering from a cold and all its associate miseries.*** ⓒ 14c: from Latin *associare*, from *ad* to + *socius* united.

associated ▻ *adj* (*usually* **Associated**) used in the name of a company to show that it has been formed from several smaller companies.

Associated Press ▷ *noun* (abbreviation **AP**) the world's largest newsgathering co-operative, based in New York.

association ▷ *noun* **1** an organization or club. **2** a friendship or partnership. **3** a connection in the mind. **4** the act of associating.

Association Football see under FOOTBALL

associative ▷ *adj, math* said of an arithmetical process: resulting in the same answer, no matter which way the elements are grouped together.

assonance /'asənəns/ ▷ *noun, prosody* a correspondence or resemblance in the sounds of words or syllables, either between their vowels, eg in *meet* and *bean*, or between their consonants, eg in *keep* and *cape*. Compare ALLITERATION, RHYME. ⓒ 18c: from Latin *assonare* to sound.

assorted /ə'sɔːtɪd/ ▷ *adj* **1** mixed; consisting of or containing various different kinds □ *assorted chocolates*. **2** arranged in sorts; classified. ⓒ 18c: from French *assorter*, from Latin *sors, sortis* kind, a voter's lot.

assortment ▷ *noun* a mixed collection.

assuage /ə'sweɪdʒ/ ▷ *verb* (***assuaged, assuaging***) to make (a pain, sorrow, hunger, etc) less severe. ⓒ 14c: from Latin *suavis* mild, sweet.

assume /ə'sjuːm, ə'suːm/ ▷ *verb* (***assumed, assuming***) **1** to accept something without proof; to take for granted. **2** to take on (a responsibility, duty, etc). **3** to take on or adopt (an appearance, quality, etc) □ *an issue assuming immense importance*. **4** to pretend to have or feel. ● **assumable** *adj*. ● **assumably** *adverb*. ⓒ 15c: from Latin *assumere*, from *sumere* to take.

assumed ▷ *adj* **1** false; not genuine □ *an assumed name*. **2** accepted as true before proof is available. ● **assumedly** /-mɪdlɪ/ *adverb*.

assuming ▷ *adj* said of someone or their attitude: arrogant; presumptuous. ▷ *conj* if it is taken as a fact □ *Assuming that the meal won't cost too much, we should have enough money left*. ● **assumingly** *adverb*.

Assumption ▷ *noun, Christianity* **1** the taking up to heaven of the Virgin Mary. **2** the feast held on 15 August when Roman Catholics celebrate this.

assumption /ə'sʌmʃən, ə'sʌmpʃən/ ▷ *noun* **1** something that is accepted as true without proof. **2** the act of accepting something as true without proof. **3** the act of assuming in other senses. ● **assumptive** *adj*. ⓒ 13c: from Latin *assumptio*, from *assumere* to take to oneself.

assurance ▷ *noun* **1** a promise, guarantee or statement that something is true. **2** confidence and poise. **3** *Brit* insurance, especially life insurance.

assurance, insurance

There is often confusion between **assurance** and **insurance**: with **assurance**, you have a guarantee of payment of a fixed sum at an agreed time, whereas with **insurance**, a variable sum is payable only if certain circumstances occur, eg fire or theft.

assure /ə'ʃʊə(r), ə'ʃɔː(r)/ ▷ *verb* (***assured, assuring***) **1** to state positively and confidently; to guarantee. **2** to make (an event, etc) certain □ *Her hard work assured her success*. **3** *Brit* to insure something (especially one's life). ● **assurable** *adj*. ● **assurer** *noun*. ⓒ 14c: from French *aseurer*, from Latin *securus* safe.

assured ▷ *adj* **1** said of someone or their attitude, behaviour, etc: confident and poised. **2** certain to happen. ● **assuredly** /-rɪdlɪ/ *adverb*.

assurgent /ə'sɜːdʒənt/ ▷ *adj* **1** *bot* said of stems, leaves, etc: curving or growing upwards. **2** aggressively ambitious. ● **assurgency** *noun*.

Assyrian /ə'sɪrɪən/ *historical* ▷ *noun* **1** an inhabitant of Assyria, an empire that, from 1530-612 BC, extended from the E Mediterranean to Iran, and from the Persian Gulf to the mountains of E Turkey. **2** the now extinct Semitic language of Assyria. ▷ *adj* belonging, relating or referring to Assyria, its people, language or culture. ⓒ 16c: from Greek *Assyrios*.

Assyriology ▷ *noun* the study of Assyrian archaeology, culture, language, history, etc. ● **Assyriologist** *noun*.

AST ▷ *abbreviation* Atlantic Standard Time.

astatic /ə'statɪk, eɪ-/ ▷ *adj* **1** lacking the tendency to remain in a fixed position; unstable. **2** *physics* without any tendency to change position. **3** *physics* without directional characteristics. ⓒ 19c.

astatine /'astətiːn, -tɪn/ ▷ *noun, chem* (symbol **At**, atomic number 85) a radioactive chemical element, the heaviest of the halogens, that occurs naturally in trace amounts and is produced artificially by bombarding bismuth with alpha particles. ⓒ 1940s: from Greek *astatos* unstable.

aster /'astə(r)/ ▷ *noun* **1** any of numerous mainly perennial plants with daisy-like flower-heads consisting of a central yellow disc of true flowers surrounded by blue, purple, pink or white rays, eg Michaelmas daisy. **2** *biol* in a cell dividing by mitosis: the star-shaped structure that radiates out from each of the two centrosomes. ⓒ 18c: from Greek *aster* star.

asterisk /'astərɪsk/ ▷ *noun* a star-shaped symbol (*) used **a** in printing and writing: to mark a cross-reference to a footnote, an omission, etc; **b** *linguistics* to indicate that the form of the word that follows it is unattested; **c** *grammar* to indicate that what follows is in some way unacceptable. ▷ *verb* (***asterisked, asterisking***) to mark with an asterisk. ⓒ 17c: from Greek *asteriskos* small star.

astern /ə'stɜːn/ ▷ *adverb, adj* **1** in or towards the stern. **2** backwards. **3** behind. ⓒ 17c.

asteroid /'astərɔɪd/ ▷ *noun* any of thousands of small rocky objects, 1km to 1000km in diameter, that orbit around the Sun, mainly between the orbits of Mars and Jupiter. Also called **minor planet**. ▷ *adj* star-shaped. ⓒ Early 19c: from Greek *asteroeides* star-like.

asthenia /as'θiːnɪə/ ▷ *noun, pathol* a condition characterized by an abnormal lack of energy or strength; weakness. ⓒ Early 19c: from Greek *astheneia* weakness.

asthenic /as'θenɪk/ ▷ *adj* **1** characterized by or relating to ASTHENIA. **2** said of a physical type: distinguished by having a relatively small trunk and long slim limbs and sometimes associated with exhibiting schizoid personality traits. Compare ATHLETIC 3, PYKNIC, LEPTOSOME. ▷ *noun* someone of this physical type. ⓒ 18c.

asthenosphere /as'θenəsfɪə(r)/ ▷ *noun, geol* the upper layer of the MANTLE (sense 3) that lies immediately beneath the Earth's crust. ⓒ Early 20c.

asthma /'asmə, 'asθmə or (*US*) 'azmə/ ▷ *noun* a respiratory disorder in which breathlessness and wheezing occur, caused by excessive contraction of muscles in the walls of the air passages, most commonly associated with allergic reactions, but sometimes precipitated by infections, physical exertion, stress, etc. ⓒ 14c: Greek, meaning 'laboured breathing', from *azein* to breathe hard.

asthmatic /as'matɪk/ ▷ *adj* relating to or suffering from asthma. ▷ *noun* someone who suffers from asthma. ● **asthmatically** *adverb*.

astigmatic /astɪg'matɪk/ ▷ *adj* relating to, affected by or correcting astigmatism □ *astigmatic lenses*. ▷ *noun* someone who has astigmatism.

astigmatism /ə'stɪgmətɪzəm/ ▷ *noun* a defect in a lens, especially abnormal curvature of the lens or cornea of the eye, which causes distortion of the image of an object, and is corrected by wearing spectacles or contact lenses that produce exactly the opposite degree of distortion. ⓒ 19c: from A-[2] + Greek *stigma* point.

astir /ə'stɜː(r)/ ▻ *adj, adverb* **1** awake and out of bed. **2** in a state of motion or excitement. Ⓒ Early 19c.

astonish /ə'stɒnɪʃ/ ▻ *verb* (***astonishes, astonished, astonishing***) to surprise greatly. • **astonished** *adj.* Ⓒ 16c: related to French *estoner*, from Latin *tonare* to thunder.

astonishing ▻ *adj* wonderful or surprising; extraordinary. • **astonishingly** *adverb.*

astonishment ▻ *noun* wonder; complete surprise.

astound /ə'staʊnd/ ▻ *verb* (***astounded, astounding***) to amaze or shock. • **astounded** *adj.* • **astounding** *adj.* • **astoundingly** *adverb.* Ⓒ 17c as *verb*; 14c as *past participle*, meaning 'stunned'.

astr. and **astron.** ▻ *abbreviation* **1** astronomy. **2** astronomical. **3** astronomer.

astragal /'astrəgəl/ ▻ *noun, archit* **1** a small circular moulding, often round a column. **2** *Scottish* a glazing bar. Ⓒ 17c: from Greek *astragalos* 'moulding' or 'ankle-bone'.

astrakhan /astrə'kan, -kɑːn/ ▻ *noun* **1** a kind of fur made from the dark tightly-curled wool and skin of very young or stillborn lambs, which is used to line and trim coats, make hats, etc. **2** a cloth made to resemble this fur. Ⓒ 18c: named after Astrakhan, a city on the Volga in SE Russia, where the use of this fur originated.

astral /'astrəl/ ▻ *adj* belonging or relating to, consisting of, or like, the stars; starry. Ⓒ 17c: from Latin *astralis*, from *astrum* star.

astray /ə'streɪ/ ▻ *adj, adverb* out of the right or expected way. • **go astray 1** to become lost. **2** to start behaving in a way that is considered unacceptable ▫ *started taking drugs and then went completely astray.* • **lead someone astray** see under LEAD[1]. Ⓒ 14c: A-[1] + STRAY.

astride /ə'straɪd/ ▻ *adverb* **1** with a leg on each side. **2** with legs apart. ▻ *prep* **1** with a leg on each side of something. **2** stretching across. Ⓒ 17c: A-[1] + STRIDE.

astringent /ə'strɪndʒənt/ ▻ *adj* **1** severe and harsh. **2** said of a substance: causing cells to shrink. ▻ *noun* a substance that causes cells to shrink, used in medical preparations to stop bleeding from minor cuts, and in throat lozenges, cosmetic lotions to harden and protect the skin, antiperspirants, etc. • **astringency** *noun.* • **astringently** *adverb.* Ⓒ 16c: from Latin *astringere* to draw tight.

astro- /astroʊ, ə'strɒ/ ▻ *combining form, denoting* stars or space. Ⓒ From Greek *astron* star.

astrodome ▻ *noun* **1** a transparent covering over the fuselage of an aircraft that allows astronomical observations to be made. **2** *US* a sports centre or arena that has a transparent domed roof. Ⓒ 1940s.

astrol. ▻ *abbreviation* astrology.

astrolabe /'astroʊleɪb/ ▻ *noun, astron, formerly* a navigational instrument used to observe the positions of the Sun and bright stars, and to estimate the local time by determining the altitude of the Sun or specific stars above the horizon. Ⓒ 14c: from ASTRO- + Greek *lambanein* to take.

astrology /ə'strɒlədʒɪ/ ▻ *noun* the study of the movements of the stars and planets and the interpretation of these movements in terms of how they are thought to exert influences on people's lives, character traits, etc. • **astrologer** *noun.* • **astrological** *adj.* • **astrologically** *adverb.* Ⓒ 14c: ASTRO- + -LOGY.

astrometry /ə'strɒmətrɪ/ ▻ *noun, astron* the branch of astronomy concerned with the precise measurement of the positions of stars, planets and other celestial bodies on the celestial sphere. Ⓒ 19c: ASTRO- + -METRY 1.

astronaut /'astrənɔːt/ ▻ *noun* someone who is trained to travel in a space vehicle. See also COSMONAUT. Ⓒ 1920s: from ASTRO-, modelled on AERONAUT.

astronautics /astrə'nɔːtɪks/ ▻ *singular noun* the science of travel in space. • **astronautical** or **astronautic** *adj.* • **astronautically** *adverb.*

Astronomer Royal ▻ *noun* **1** *formerly* the title of the Director of the Royal Greenwich Observatory. **2** since 1972, an honorary title awarded to a distinguished British astronomer.

astronomical /astrə'nɒmɪkəl/ and **astronomic** ▻ *adj* **1** said of numbers, amounts, prices, etc: large; extreme. **2** relating to astronomy. • **astronomically** *adverb.*

astronomical unit ▻ *noun* (abbreviation **AU**) *astron* the mean distance between the Earth and the Sun, about 149.6 million km (93 million ml), which is used to measure distances within the solar system.

astronomical year see SOLAR YEAR

astronomy /ə'strɒnəmɪ/ ▻ *noun* the scientific study of celestial bodies, including the planets, stars and galaxies, as well as interstellar and intergalactic space, and the universe as a whole. Ⓒ 13c: ASTRO- + -NOMY.

astrophysics ▻ *singular noun* the application of physical laws and theories to astronomical objects and phenomena, especially stars and galaxies, with the aim of deriving theoretical models to explain their behaviour. • **astrophysical** *adj.* • **astrophysicist** *noun.* Ⓒ 19c.

Astroturf ▻ *noun, trademark* a type of artificial grass surface for sports grounds. Ⓒ 1960s: from *astro*dome + TURF.

astute /ə'stjuːt/ ▻ *adj* said of someone or their ideas, attitude, etc: having or showing the ability to judge and act intelligently and decisively; mentally perceptive; shrewd. • **astutely** *adverb.* • **astuteness** *noun.* Ⓒ 17c: from Latin *astutus* crafty.

asunder /ə'sʌndə(r)/ ▻ *adverb* **1** apart or into pieces ▫ *ripped my heart asunder.* **2** *archaic* in or into a separate place or position. Ⓒ Anglo-Saxon *onsundran.*

asylum /ə'saɪləm/ ▻ *noun* (***asylums***) **1** a place of safety or protection. **2** *historical* a mental hospital. • **give** or **grant asylum to someone** said of a country, state, etc: to offer them the opportunity to stay, especially when return to their own country might put them in jeopardy. See also POLITICAL ASYLUM. Ⓒ 15c: from Greek *asylon* sanctuary, from A- not + *sylon* right of seizure.

asymmetric /eɪsɪ'metrɪk, a-/ and **asymmetrical** ▻ *adj* lacking symmetry. • **asymmetrically** *adverb.*

asymmetry /eɪ'sɪmətrɪ, a-/ ▻ *noun* a lack of symmetry. Ⓒ 17c.

asymptote /'asɪmtoʊt, 'asɪmp-/ ▻ *noun* **1** *geom* a line, usually a straight one, which is continually approached by a curve that never actually meets the line. **2** something that seems as though it might be conclusive or might concur with something else, but never quite does so. • **asymptotic** /asɪm'tɒtɪk/ *adj.* • **asymptotical** *adj.* • **asymptotically** *adverb.* Ⓒ 17c: from Greek *asymptotos* not falling together.

asynchronism /eɪ'sɪŋkrənɪzəm, a-/ ▻ *noun* the absence of a correspondence in time. • **asynchronous** *adj.* • **asynchronously** *adverb.* • **asynchrony** *noun.* Ⓒ 19c.

asyndeton /a'sɪndətən, -tɒn/ ▻ *noun, grammar* **1** the omission of a conjunction in a construction. **2** a construction where no conjunctions are used. • **asyndetic** /asɪn'detɪk/ *adj.* • **asyndetically** *adverb.* Ⓒ 16c: from Greek *asyndetos* not bound together.

asynergy /ə'sɪnədʒɪ/ and **asynergia** /asɪ'nɜːdʒɪə/ ▻ *noun, pathol* lack of co-ordination between muscles or other body parts which usually work together. Ⓒ 19c.

asystole /eɪ'sɪstəlɪ, a'sɪstəlɪ/ ▻ *noun, pathol* absence or cessation of heartbeat. • **asystolic** /asɪs'tɒlɪk/ *adj.* Ⓒ 19c.

At ▻ *symbol, chem* astatine.

at /ət, at/ ▻ *prep* **1** used to indicate position or place: in, within, on, near, etc ▫ *worked at a local factory.* **2** towards, in the direction of something ▫ *working at* *getting fit.* **3** used to indicate a position in time: **a** around; on the stroke of □ ***The train arrives at six***; **b** having reached the age of □ ***At 17 you can start to drive.*** **4** with, by, beside, next to, etc □ ***annoyed at her.*** **5** engaged in; occupied with □ ***children at play.*** **6** for; in exchange for □ ***sold it at a profit.*** **7** in a state of □ ***at liberty.*** • **at it** or **at it again a** doing something (again); **b** *euphemistic* having sexual intercourse; **c** *colloq* committing crimes. ⓘ Anglo-Saxon *æt.*

atabrin an alternative *US* spelling of ATEBRIN

ataman /ˈatəman/ ▻ *noun* (***atamans***) an elected Cossack leader of a village or military division. ⓘ 19c: from Russian, from Polish *hetman* head man.

ataractic /atəˈraktɪk/ and **ataraxic** /atəˈraksɪk/ ▻ *adj* **1** calm. **2** *medicine* **a** said of a drug or other form of treatment: inducing calmness.

ataraxia /ˈatəraksɪə/ and **ataraxy** /atəˈraksɪ/ ▻ *noun* calmness. ⓘ 17c: Greek.

atavism /ˈatəvɪzəm/ ▻ *noun* **1** a resemblance to ancestors rather than immediate parents. **2** reversion to an earlier, especially more primitive, type. ⓘ 19c: from Latin *atavus* great-great-great-grandfather.

atavistic ▻ *adj* **1** relating to or resembling ancestors. **2** relating to or involving reversion to an earlier type.

ataxia /əˈtaksɪə/ and **ataxy** /əˈtaksɪ/ ▻ *noun, pathol* inability of the brain to co-ordinate voluntary movements of the limbs, resulting in jerky movements and a staggering gait, and caused by a disorder of the sensory nerves or by disease of the cerebellum. ⓘ 17c: Greek, meaning 'disorder'.

ATC ▻ *abbreviation* Air Training Corps.

ate *past tense of* EAT

-ate[1] /eɪt, ət/ ▻ *suffix* **1** *forming verbs, denoting* cause to be or have □ ***hyphenate.*** **2** *forming nouns, denoting* a salt □ ***carbonate.*** Compare -IDE, -ITE. **3** *forming adjectives, denoting* having, showing features of, like or related to □ ***passionate.*** ⓘ From the Latin participial ending *-atus.*

-ate[2] ▻ *suffix, forming nouns, denoting* rank, profession, or group □ ***doctorate*** □ ***magistrate*** □ ***electorate.*** ⓘ From the Latin collective noun ending *-atus.*

atebrin or (*US*) **atabrin** /ˈatəbrɪn/ ▻ *noun, trademark* the proprietary names for the artificial anti-malarial drug **mepacrine**. ⓘ 1932.

atelectasis /atəˈlɛktəsɪs/ ▻ *noun* lack of full dilation, especially of the lung or lungs, eg of a newborn baby, or of an adult suffering from a tumour, etc. • **atelectatic** /atɪlɛkˈtatɪk/ *adj.* ⓘ 19c: from Greek *ateles* imperfect + *ektasis* extension.

atelier /əˈtɛlɪeɪ; *French* atəlje/ ▻ *noun* **1** a workshop or artist's studio. **2** *formerly* a short form of *atelier libre,* meaning 'free studio' which, in the 19c, was a place where artists could, on the payment of a small fee, meet up with other artists to paint, discuss ideas, etc and which often provided models, although no formal teaching was done. ⓘ 19c: French.

a tempo /ɑː ˈtɛmpoʊ/ ▻ *adverb, adj, music* a direction to play: **a** in the stated timing; **b** in the previous timing. ⓘ 18c: Italian, meaning 'in time'.

Atharva-veda see VEDA

atheism /ˈeɪθiːɪzəm/ ▻ *noun* the belief that there is no god. • **atheist** *noun.* • **atheistic** or **atheistical** *adj.* • **atheistically** *adverb.* Compare AGNOSTICISM, THEISM, DEISM. ⓘ 16c: from Greek *atheos* godless.

athematic /aθɪˈmatɪk, eɪ-/ ▻ *adj, music* not composed of tunes. • **athematically** *adverb.* ⓘ 1930s; 1890s in obsolete sense used in prescriptive grammar.

Athenian /əˈθiːnɪən/ ▻ *adj* belonging or relating to Athens, the capital city of Greece, or its inhabitants. ▻ *noun* a citizen or inhabitant of, or person born in, Athens.

atheroma /aθəˈroʊmə/ ▻ *noun* (***atheromas*** or ***atheromata*** /-tə/) *pathol* in atherosclerosis: a fatty deposit that develops on the inner surface of an artery wall. ⓘ 19c; 18c in obsolete sense meaning 'a cyst filled with a porridge-like substance': from Greek *athere* gruel + -OMA.

atherosclerosis /aθəroʊskləˈroʊsɪs/ ▻ *noun* (***atheroscleroses*** /-siːz/) *pathol* a form of ARTERIOSCLEROSIS in which cholesterol and other fatty substances are deposited on the inner walls of arteries, making them narrow and eventually obstructing the flow of blood. • **atherosclerotic** /-ˈrɒtɪk/ *adj.* ⓘ Early 20c: from Greek *athere* gruel + SCLEROSIS.

athlete /ˈaθliːt/ ▻ *noun* **1** someone who trains for and competes in field and track events such as running events, the high jump, long jump, pole vault, etc. **2** someone who is good at sports. **3** someone who has strength, stamina, expertise, etc in a specified field □ ***a sexual athlete.*** ⓘ 16c: from Greek *athlos* contest.

-athlete see -ATHLON

athlete's foot ▻ *noun, informal* a fungal infection of the foot, caused by a type of ringworm, and usually characterized by itching lesions on the skin between the toes. *Technical equivalent* TINEA PEDIS.

athletic /aθˈlɛtɪk/ ▻ *adj* **1** said of someone or their build: physically fit and strong. **2** relating to athletics. **3** said of a physical type: distinguished by having well-developed muscles and a body that is in proportion. Compare ASTHENIC 2, PYKNIC, LEPTOSOME. • **athletical** *adj.* • **athletically** *adverb.* • **athleticism** /-sɪzəm/ *noun.*

athletics ▻ *singular noun* competitive track and field sports such as running, jumping, throwing and walking events.

-athlon /aθlɒn/ ▻ *combining form, denoting* a sporting event in which individual competitors take part in a specified number of different disciplines □ ***decathlon.*** • **-athlete** /ˈaɪliːt/ *noun* such a competitor □ ***pentathlete.*** ⓘ Greek, meaning 'contest'.

-athon /əθɒn/ or (after a vowel) **-thon** /θɒn/ ▻ *combining form, denoting* something that takes a long time to complete, especially an event that involves raising money for charity □ ***telethon.*** ⓘ 1930s: modelled on MARATHON.

athwart /əˈθwɔːt/ ▻ *adverb* transversely. ▻ *prep* across, from side to side of. ⓘ 17c: A-[1] + THWART.

-atic /atɪk/ ▻ *suffix, forming adjectives, denoting* belonging, relating or tending to do or be something specific □ ***Asiatic*** □ ***systematic*** □ ***lunatic.***

-ation /eɪʃən/ ▻ *suffix, forming nouns, denoting* an action, process, condition, result, etc □ ***expectation*** □ ***mechanization*** □ ***representation.*** See also -ION.

atishoo /əˈtɪʃuː/ ▻ *exclamation, indicating* the sound of a sneeze. ▻ *noun* (***atishoos***) a sneeze. ▻ *verb* (***atishooed, atishooing***) *intr* to make the sound of a sneeze. ⓘ 19c.

-ative /ətɪv/ ▻ *suffix, forming adjectives, denoting* having a specified attribute or tendency □ ***authoritative*** □ ***talkative.***

Atlantic /ətˈlantɪk, at-/ ▻ *noun* (**the Atlantic**) the Atlantic Ocean, an ocean bounded by Europe and Africa to the East, and by N and S America to the West. ▻ *adj* belonging, relating or referring to the area of the Atlantic Ocean □ ***Atlantic fishing.*** ⓘ 17c: from Greek *Atlantikos,* from *Atlas,* so named because the ocean lies beyond this range of mountains in N Africa.

Atlantic Standard Time ▻ *noun* (abbreviation **AST**) the most easterly of the TIME ZONES of the US and Canada, 4 hours behind GREENWICH MEAN TIME.

atlas /ˈatləs/ ▻ *noun* (***atlases*** /-səz/) **1** a book of maps and geographical charts. **2** a book of any other kind of charts. **3** *anatomy* in vertebrates: the topmost vertebra of the spine, which joins the skull to the spine and pivots on the axis vertebra, enabling nodding movements of the head to be made. ⓘ 16c: in Greek mythology Atlas was a Titan who was condemned to support the sky on his shoulders, hence the application of his name to the vertebra, and in early collections of maps a representation of him often appeared as the frontispiece.

ATM ▷ *abbreviation* automated or automatic teller machine. See CASH MACHINE.

atman /'ɑːtmən/ ▷ *noun, Hinduism* the human soul or essential self, which, in the teachings of the UPANISHADS, is seen as being one with the Absolute, and is identified with Brahman. ◷ 18c: Sanskrit, meaning 'self' or 'soul'.

atmolysis /at'mɒlɪsɪs/ ▷ *noun* (***atmolyses*** /-siːz/) a method of separating or partially separating mixed gases or vapours that relies on the fact that they will pass through a porous substance at different rates. ◷ 19c: from Greek *atmos* vapour + LYSIS.

atmometer /at'mɒmɪtə(r)/ ▷ *noun, physics* an instrument for measuring the amount or rate of evaporation of water from a moist surface into the atmosphere. ◷ Early 19c: from Greek *atmos* + -METER 1.

atmosphere /'atməsfɪə(r)/ ▷ *noun* **1** the layer of gas surrounding a planet, especially the Earth, and held to it by gravity. **2** the air in a particular place ▫ ***the humid atmosphere of the greenhouse.*** **3** the mood of a book, film, painting, piece of music, etc or the general impression that it gives ▫ ***the sultry atmosphere of film noir.*** **4** the general or prevailing climate or mood ▫ ***an atmosphere of jubilation.*** **5** a unit of ATMOSPHERIC PRESSURE, equal to normal air pressure at sea level. ◷ 17c: from Greek *atmos* vapour + *sphaira* ball.

atmospheric /atməs'ferɪk/ ▷ *adj* **1** relating to, or occurring within, the Earth's atmosphere ▫ ***atmospheric pollution.*** **2** said of a place, work of art, literature, etc: evocative of a particular mood or feeling. • **atmospherical** *adj.* • **atmospherically** *adverb.*

atmospheric pressure ▷ *noun, physics* the pressure exerted by the atmosphere at any point on the Earth's surface, due to the weight of the air above it.

atmospherics ▷ *plural noun* radio-frequency electromagnetic radiation, produced by natural electrical disturbances in the Earth's atmosphere, eg lightning discharges, that interferes with radio communications. Also called ATMOSPHERIC INTERFERENCE.

atoll /'atɒl, ə'tɒl/ ▷ *noun* a continuous or broken circle of coral reef that surrounds a lagoon, and is itself surrounded by open sea. ◷ 17c: from *atollon*, a native name applied to the Maldive Islands, which are typical examples of this kind of formation.

atom /'atəm/ ▷ *noun* **1** the smallest unit of a chemical element that can display the properties of that element, and which is capable of combining with other atoms to form molecules. **2** *formerly* the smallest particle of matter capable of existing. **3** *non-technical* a very small amount or quantity; a tiny piece. ◷ 15c: from Greek *atomos* something that cannot be divided, from *temnein* to cut.

atom bomb and **atomic bomb** ▷ *noun* a powerful explosive device that derives its force from the sudden release of enormous amounts of nuclear energy during nuclear fission. Also called NUCLEAR BOMB.

atomic /ə'tɒmɪk/ ▷ *adj* **1** relating to atoms. **2** obtained by atomic phenomena, especially nuclear fission ▫ ***atomic weapons.*** • **atomically** *adverb.*

atomic clock ▷ *noun, physics* a precise clock that measures time by using the regular oscillations of individual atoms or molecules to regulate its movement.

atomic energy see NUCLEAR ENERGY

atomicity /atə'mɪsɪtɪ/ ▷ *noun, chem* **1** the number of atoms in a molecule of a chemical element. **2** the state or fact of existing in the form of atoms.

atomic mass unit ▷ *noun, chem* an arbitrary unit, used to denote the masses of individual atoms or molecules, which is equal to one twelfth of the mass of an atom of the carbon-12 isotope of carbon. Also called **dalton**.

atomic number ▷ *noun, chem* (symbol **Z**) the number of protons in the nucleus of an atom of a particular element.

atomic pile ▷ *noun, formerly* a NUCLEAR REACTOR.

atomic theory ▷ *noun, chem* the hypothesis that all atoms of the same element are alike and that a compound can be formed by the union of atoms of different elements in some simple ratio.

atomic weight ▷ *noun, formerly* alternative name for RELATIVE ATOMIC MASS.

atomism /'atəmɪzəm/ ▷ *noun* a philosophical tradition that dates back to c.500 BC which maintains that everything that exists is made up of minute indivisible particles, and that all phenomena must be explained in terms of such 'fundamental particles' and their interactions in space.

atomize or **atomise** ▷ *verb* (***atomized, atomizing***) **1** to reduce to atoms or small particles. **2** to reduce (a liquid) to a spray or mist of fine droplets by passage through a nozzle or jet under pressure. **3** to destroy by means of atomic weapons. ◷ 19c; 17c, meaning 'to believe in ATOMISM'.

atomizer or **atomiser** /'atəmaɪzə(r)/ ▷ *noun* a container that releases liquid, containing eg perfume, medicine, etc, as a fine spray.

atom smasher ▷ *noun, non-technical* an ACCELERATOR (sense 2).

atonal /eɪ'toʊnəl, a-/ ▷ *adj, music* lacking tonality; not written in a particular key. • **atonalism** *noun.* • **atonality** *noun.* • **atonally** *adverb.* ◷ 1920s.

atone /ə'toʊn/ ▷ *verb* (***atoned, atoning***) (*also* **atone for something**) to make amends for (a wrongdoing, crime, sin, etc). ◷ 17c: back-formation from ATONEMENT.

atonement ▷ *noun* **1** an act of making amends for, making up for, or paying for a wrongdoing, crime, sin, etc. **2** (**Atonement**) *Christianity* the reconciliation of God and man through the sufferings and death of Christ. ◷ 16c: from earlier *at onement*, meaning 'in harmony'.

atony /'atənɪ/ ▷ *noun* **1** *pathol* lack of normal muscle tone. **2** *phonetics* lack of stress or accent. ◷ 17c: from Greek *atonia* slackness.

atop /ə'tɒp/ ▷ *adverb* on top; at the top. ▷ *prep* on top of, or at the top of, something. ◷ 17c.

-ator /eɪtə(r)/ ▷ *suffix, forming nouns, denoting* someone or something that performs a specified action ▫ ***commentator.***

ATP ▷ *abbreviation, biochem* adenosine triphosphate, an organic compound that is the main form in which energy is stored in the cells of living organisms. Compare ADP 2.

atrium /'eɪtrɪəm, 'ɑː-/ ▷ *noun* (***atria*** /'eɪtrɪə, 'ɑːtrɪə/ or ***atriums***) **1** a central court or entrance hall in an ancient Roman house. **2** a court in a public space, such as a shopping mall, office block, hotel, etc, that has galleries around it, often several storeys high and usually with a glass-domed roof that allows in plenty of natural light. **3** *anatomy* either of the two upper chambers of the heart that receive blood from the veins. Also called AURICLE. **4** *anatomy* any of various other chambers or cavities in the body. • **atrial** *adj.* ◷ 16c: Latin in sense 1.

atrocious /ə'troʊʃəs/ ▷ *adj* **1** *colloq* very bad. **2** extremely cruel or wicked. • **atrociously** *adverb.* • **atrociousness** *noun.* ◷ 17c: from Latin *atrox* cruel, from *ater* black.

atrocity /ə'trɒsɪtɪ/ ▷ *noun* (***atrocities***) **1** wicked or cruel behaviour. **2** an act of wickedness or cruelty. ◷ 16c: from Latin *atrox* cruel, from *ater* black.

atrophy /'atrəfɪ/ ▷ *verb* (***atrophies, atrophied, atrophying***) *tr & intr* **1** to make or become weak and thin through lack of use or nourishment. **2** to diminish or die away; to cause to diminish or die away □ *Love and respect had atrophied with the passing years.* ▷ *noun* the process of atrophying. ⓒ 17c: from Greek *atrophia* lack of nourishment, from *trephein* to feed.

atropine /'atrəpɪn, -piːn/ or **atropin** /-pɪn/ ▷ *noun, medicine* a poisonous alkaloid drug, obtained from DEADLY NIGHTSHADE, which is used as a premedication before general anaesthesia, as a treatment for peptic ulcers, and for dilating the pupil during eye examinations. Also called **belladonna**. ⓒ 1830s: from *Atropos* the name of the Fate who, in Greek mythology, cut the thread of life.

Att. ▷ *abbreviation* Attorney.

attach /ə'tatʃ/ ▷ *verb* (***attaches, attached, attaching***) **1** to fasten or join. **2** to associate (oneself) with or join □ *attached herself to the local Greenpeace.* **3** to attribute or assign □ *attach great importance to detail.* **4** *law* to arrest someone or seize (property) with legal authority. ⓒ 14c: from French *atachier* to fasten.

■ **be attached to someone** or **something** to be fond of them or it □ *Nelly is very attached to her cat.*

■ **attach to something** to be connected with or form part of it.

attaché /ə'taʃeɪ/ ▷ *noun* (***attachés*** /-ʃeɪz/) **1** a junior official in an embassy. **2** someone who is connected to a diplomatic department, etc because they have some specialized knowledge. ⓒ 19c: French, meaning 'attached'.

attaché-case ▷ *noun* a small rigid leather case for holding documents, etc.

attached ▷ *adj* **1** joined; connected. **2** said of someone: in a relationship, especially a sexual one. • **attached at the hip** *colloq* inseparable.

attachment ▷ *noun* **1 a** an act or means of fastening; **b** the state of being fastened. **2** liking or affection □ *His attachment for the car was obsessive.* **3** an extra part that can be fitted to a machine, often used for changing its function slightly □ *a diffuser attachment for the hairdryer.* **4** a legal seizure of a person or property. **5** a temporary period of working with a different group.

attack /ə'tak/ ▷ *verb* (***attacked, attacking***) **1** to make a sudden violent attempt to hurt, damage or capture. **2** to criticize strongly in speech or writing. **3** *intr* to make an attack. **4** to begin to do something with enthusiasm or determination. **5** to begin to damage □ *Plaque attacks the teeth.* **6** *intr* to take the initiative in a game, contest, etc to attempt to score a goal, points, etc. ▷ *noun* **1** an act or the action of attacking. **2** a sudden spell of illness □ *an attack of 'flu.* **3** (**the attack**) the players, eg the strikers, forwards, etc in a team sport whose job is to score goals, points, etc. Compare THE DEFENCE at DEFENCE 7, THE MIDFIELD at MIDFIELD 2. • **attackable** *adj.* • **attacker** *noun* someone who makes a physical, verbal, sporting, etc attack. • **to be on the attack** *sport* to take up an offensive position. ⓒ 17c: from Italian *attaccare.*

attacking ▷ *adj* **1** said of a team: ready and willing to seize goal- or point-scoring opportunities. **2** said of a match, sport, etc: enterprising and creating plenty of goal- or point-scoring chances.

attain /ə'teɪn/ ▷ *verb* (***attained, attaining***) **1** to complete successfully; to accomplish; to achieve. **2** to reach (in space or time) □ *attained the summit* □ *attained the grand age of one hundred.* ⓒ 14c: from Latin *tangere* to touch.

attain

☆ PLAIN ENGLISH alternatives are **reach, achieve**.

attainable ▷ *adj* capable of being achieved. • **attainability** *noun.* • **attainableness** *noun.*

attainder /ə'teɪndə(r)/ ▷ *noun, formerly law* the loss of someone's civil rights following their conviction for felony or for an act of treason. ⓒ 15c: from French *atteindre* to attain.

attainment ▷ *noun* **1** achievement, especially after some effort. **2** the act of achieving something. **3** something that is achieved.

attar /'atə(r), 'atɑː(r)/ and **attar of roses** ▷ *noun* a fragrant essential oil that is distilled from rose petals, especially those of the damask rose. ⓒ 18c: from Persian *atir* perfumed.

attempt /ə'tɛmt, ə'tɛmpt/ ▷ *verb* (***attempted, attempting***) **1** to try. **2** to try to climb (a mountain, etc). **3** to try to master, tackle, answer, etc (a problem, etc). ▷ *noun* an effort; an endeavour. • **make an attempt at something** to try to do it. • **make an attempt on someone's life** to try to kill them. • **make an attempt on something 1** to try to climb (a mountain, etc). **2** to try to master or tackle (a mountainous difficulty). ⓒ 14c: from Latin *attemptare* to strive after.

attend /ə'tɛnd/ ▷ *verb* (***attended, attending***) **1** *tr & intr* to be present at something. **2** to go regularly to (eg school, church, etc). **3** to go along with; to accompany □ *higher prices attended by a lowering in demand.* **4** to wait upon; to serve □ *had to attend the princess's every need.* • **attender** *noun.* ⓒ 13c: from Latin *attendere*, from *ad-* to + *tendere* to stretch.

■ **attend on** or **upon someone** to wait upon or serve them.

■ **attend on** or **upon something** to follow as a result of it.

■ **attend to someone** or **something** to take care of them or it or to take action over them or it.

attendance ▷ *noun* **1** the act of attending. **2** the number of people attending. **3** regularity of attending.

attendance allowance ▷ *noun, Brit* money that is allocated by the government to severely disabled people who are in need of care so that they can pay for a nurse, etc to help them.

attendant ▷ *noun* **1** someone whose job is to help, guide or give some other service, especially to the public □ *museum attendant.* **2** someone who serves or waits upon someone else □ *the queen and her attendants.* **3** something that accompanies something else. ▷ *adj* **1** being in or giving attendance. **2** accompanying □ *attendant responsibilities.*

attention /ə'tɛnʃən/ ▷ *noun* **1** the act of concentrating or directing the mind. **2** notice; awareness □ *The problem has recently come to my attention.* **3** special care and consideration □ *attention to detail.* **4** *in compounds* □ *attention-seeking behaviour.* **5** (**attentions**) *old use* an act of politeness or courtship. **6** *military* **a** a position in which one stands rigidly erect with heels together and hands by one's sides; **b** (**Attention!**) a command to take up this position. • **pay attention to something 1** to listen to or concentrate on it closely. **2** to take care or heed of it □ *paid little attention to his appearance.* ⓒ 14c: from Latin *attentio, attentionis* from *attendere* to attend.

attentive ▷ *adj* **1** said of someone or their attitude: characterized by showing close concentration; alert and watchful. **2** considerate; polite and courteous. • **attentively** *adverb.* • **attentiveness** *noun.*

attenuate /ə'tɛnjʊeɪt/ ▷ *verb* (***attenuated, attenuating***) **1** *tr & intr* to make or become thin and weak. **2** to reduce the strength or value of something. **3** *physics* said of sound, radiation, electric current, etc: to decrease in intensity as a result of absorption or scattering on passing through a medium. **4** *medicine* during the production of certain vaccines: to treat bacteria or viruses in such a way as to diminish greatly their capacity to cause disease, while retaining their ability to evoke an immune response. ⓒ 16c: from Latin *attenuare* to make thin, from *tenuis* thin.

attenuated ▷ *adj* **1** thin. **2** thinned; diluted. **3** tapering.

attenuation ▷ *noun* **1** the process of making something slender. **2** reduction in strength, virulence, etc. **3** *physics* a reduction in amplitude or intensity of sound, electromagnetic radiation, etc, caused by absorption, scattering or friction as it passes through a medium.

attest /əˈtɛst/ ▷ *verb* (***attested, attesting***) **1** to affirm or be proof of the truth or validity of something. **2** to be evidence of something. ◷ 16c: from Latin *attestari*, from *ad* to + *testari* to bear witness.

■ **attest to something** to certify that it is so; to witness or bear witness to it, especially by giving a sworn written or verbal statement.

attestation /atɛˈsteɪʃən/ ▷ *noun* **1** an act of attesting. **2** the administration of an oath.

attested ▷ *adj* **1** said of a fact, statement, etc: supported by evidence or proof. **2** said of a written form of a word or phrase: substantiated by its occurrence at a specified date □ ***The word 'filofax' is attested as early as the 1920s.*** **3** *Brit* said of cattle: officially certified as being free from disease, especially tuberculosis.

Att. Gen. ▷ *abbreviation* Attorney General.

Attic /ˈatɪk/ ▷ *adj* **1** relating to ancient Athens or Attica, or the form of Greek spoken there. **2** said of a literary style: elegant but simple. ▷ *noun* the form of Greek spoken in ancient Athens. ◷ 16c: from Greek *Attikos* of Attica.

attic /ˈatɪk/ ▷ *noun* a space or room at the top of a house under the roof. ◷ 17c: from ATTIC because, in classical Greek architecture, the decoration of the topmost part of a building was particularly important, and this came to be thought of as typifying Attic style.

attire /əˈtaɪə(r)/ ▷ *noun* clothes, especially formal or elegant ones. ▷ *verb* (***attired, attiring***) *tr & intr, chiefly literary or formal* to dress or adorn or be dressed or adorned □ ***helped to attire the bride*** □ ***She was attired all in black.*** ◷ 13c: from French *atirier* to put in order.

attitude /ˈatɪtjuːd/ ▷ *noun* **1** a way of thinking or behaving. **2** a hostile or resentful manner. **3** (*sometimes* **Attitude**) *colloq* said of someone, music, style, etc: self-assured presence, especially in being unconventional or outrageous □ ***wears her clothes with real Attitude.*** **4** a position of the body. **5** a pose, especially adopted for dramatic effect □ ***strike an attitude.*** **6** the angle made by the axes of an aircraft or space vehicle in relation to some plane, especially the relative airflow or the Earth's surface. ◷ 17c: French, from Latin *aptitudo* suitability.

attitudinize or **attitudinise** ▷ *verb* (***attitudinized, attitudinizing***) to adopt an opinion or position for effect. • **attitudinizer** *noun*.

attorney /əˈtɜːnɪ/ ▷ *noun* (***attorneys***) **1** someone able to act for another in legal or business matters. **2** *N Amer* a lawyer. • **power of attorney** see separate entry. ◷ 14c: from French *atourner* to turn over to.

Attorney General ▷ *noun* (***Attorneys General*** or ***Attorney Generals***) **1** in the UK (apart from Scotland where the equivalent post is held by the **Lord Advocate**): the principal law officer and chief legal counsel to the Crown, who also holds a ministerial position (although not a cabinet one) and a seat in the House of Commons. **2** in other countries, eg US, Australia, New Zealand, etc: the chief law officer or chief government law officer. **3** (**attorney general**) in some US states: another term for a PUBLIC PROSECUTOR.

attract /əˈtrakt/ ▷ *verb* (***attracted, attracting***) **1** to cause (attention, notice, a crowd, interest, etc) to be directed towards oneself, itself, etc □ ***Her new film attracted much criticism.*** **2** to draw or pull (towards itself), especially by exerting some force or power; to be drawn or pulled (towards something that exerts some force or power) □ ***This type of screen attracts a lot of dust.*** **3** to arouse liking or admiration in someone; to be attractive to them. ◷ 15c: from Latin *trahere* to draw.

attraction ▷ *noun* **1** the act or power of attracting. **2** someone or something that attracts. **3** *physics* a force that tends to pull two objects closer together, such as that between opposite electric charges or opposite magnetic poles. Opposite of REPULSION at REPULSE.

attractive ▷ *adj* **1** appealing; enticing □ ***an attractive salary.*** **2** good-looking. **3** capable of attracting attention, etc. • **attractively** *adverb*. • **attractiveness** *noun*.

attribute ▷ *verb* /əˈtrɪbjuːt/ (***attributed*** /-bjʊtɪd/, ***attributing*** /-bjʊtɪŋ/) (*always* **attribute something to someone** or **something**) to think of it as being written, made, said, or caused by them or it; to ascribe it to them or it □ ***attributed the accident to human error.*** ▷ *noun* /ˈatrɪbjuːt/ a quality, characteristic, feature, etc, usually one that has positive or favourable connotations □ ***One of her great attributes is her sharp wit.*** • **attributable** /əˈtrɪbjʊtəbəl/ *adj* • **attribution** /atrɪˈbjuːʃən/ *noun*. • **attributor** /əˈtrɪbjʊtə(r)/ *noun*. ◷ 15c: from Latin *attribuere*, from *tribuere* to bestow.

attributive /əˈtrɪbjʊtɪv/ ▷ *adj, grammar* said of an adjective or noun in a noun phrase: placed before the noun it modifies, eg the adjective 'young' in *young girl* and the noun 'buffet' in *buffet car*, as opposed to a PREDICATIVE use after the noun. • **attributively** *adverb*. • **attributiveness** *noun*.

attrition /əˈtrɪʃən/ ▷ *noun* **1** a rubbing together; friction. **2** *military* a relentless wearing down of an enemy's strength, morale, etc, especially by continual attacks □ ***war of attrition.*** **3** *geol* the process whereby rock fragments become worn, smooth and smaller in size while being transported by water, wind or gravity. ◷ 14c: from Latin *attritio*, from *atterere* to rub.

attune /əˈtjuːn/ ▷ *verb* (***attuned, attuning***) **1** (*often* **attune to** or **become attuned to something**) to adjust to or prepare for (a situation, etc). **2** to put (a musical instrument, an orchestra, etc) into tune. • **attunement** *noun*. ◷ 16c: from TUNE.

at. wt. or **At. wt.** ▷ *abbreviation* atomic weight.

atypical /eɪˈtɪpɪkəl/ ▷ *adj* not typical, representative, usual, etc. • **atypically** *adverb*.

AU or **a.u.** ▷ *abbreviation* **1** angstrom unit. **2** astronomical unit.

Au ▷ *symbol, chem* gold. ◷ From Latin *aurum*.

aubergine /ˈoʊbəʒiːn/ ▷ *noun* **1** a bushy perennial plant with large leaves and funnel-shaped violet flowers, widely cultivated for its edible fruit. **2** the large cylindrical or egg-shaped edible fruit of this plant, with a smooth skin that is usually deep purple in colour, eaten as a vegetable, especially in moussaka and ratatouille. *N Amer & Austral equivalent* EGG-PLANT. **3** a deep purple colour. ▷ *adj* deep purple in colour. ◷ 18c.

aubrietia /ɔːˈbriːʃə/ ▷ *noun* (***aubrietias***) any of numerous varieties of dwarf perennial plant with greyish leaves and purple, lilac, blue or pink cross-shaped flowers, widely cultivated as an ornamental plant in rock gardens. ◷ 19c: named after the French painter of flowers and animals, Claude Aubriet (1668–1743).

auburn /ˈɔːbən/ ▷ *adj* especially said of hair: reddish-brown. ◷ 15c: from Latin *alburnus* whitish, from *albus* white.

au courant / *French* okurã/ ▷ *adj* aware of the present situation, developments, etc; well read in current affairs. ◷ 18c: French, meaning 'in the stream or current'.

auction /ˈɔːkʃən, ˈɒk-/ ▷ *noun* a public sale in which each item is sold to the person who offers the most money. ▷ *verb* (***auctioned, auctioning***) to sell something in an auction. See also ROUP. Compare DUTCH AUCTION. • **auctionary** *adj*. ◷ 17c: from Latin *auctio*, *auctionis* an increase.

■ **auction something off** to sell it to the highest bidder.

auction bridge ▷ *noun, cards* a form of bridge where the players bid for the right to name the trump suit and each odd trick counts towards the score. Compare CONTRACT BRIDGE.

auctioneer ▷ *noun* a person whose job is to conduct an auction by cataloguing and announcing the LOTs (sense 6) and presiding over the bids.

audacious /ɔːˈdeɪʃəs/ ▷ *adj* **1** bold and daring. **2** disrespectful; impudent. • **audaciously** *adverb*. • **audaciousness** *noun*. Ⓢ 16c: from Latin *audax* bold.

audacity /ɔːˈdasɪtɪ/ ▷ *noun* **1** boldness. **2** flagrant rejection of convention or disregard for what is generally held to be 'proper'. Ⓢ 15c: from Latin *audacitas* boldness.

audible /ˈɔːdɪbəl/ ▷ *adj* loud enough to be heard. • **audibility** *noun*. • **audibly** *adverb*. Ⓢ 16c: from Latin *audire* to hear.

audience /ˈɔːdɪəns/ ▷ *noun* **1 a** a group of people watching a performance, eg of a play, concert, film, etc; **b** a group of people listening to a speech, lecture, etc. **2** the people reached by a film, TV or radio broadcast, book, magazine, etc. **3** a formal interview with an important person. Ⓢ 14c: from Latin *audientia*, from *audire* to hear.

audio /ˈɔːdɪoʊ/ ▷ *noun* reproduction of recorded or broadcast sound. ▷ *adj* **1** relating to hearing or sound. **2** relating to the recording and broadcasting of sound. **3** relating to, or operating at, audio frequencies. Ⓢ Early 20c: from Latin *audire* to hear.

audio- /ˈɔːdɪoʊ/ ▷ *combining form, denoting* **1** sound, especially broadcast sound. **2** hearing. **3** audio frequencies.

audio frequency ▷ *noun* any frequency that can be detected by the human ear, in the range 20 to 20 000Hz for normal hearing.

audiogram ▷ *noun, medicine* a record of a person's hearing ability, in the form of a graph, as measured by an audiometer.

audiometer /ɔːdɪˈɒmɪtə(r)/ ▷ *noun* **1** *medicine* a device that measures a person's hearing ability at different sound frequencies, used in the diagnosis of deafness. **2** an instrument that is used to measure the intensity of sounds. • **audiometric** /ɔːdɪoʊˈmɛtrɪk/ *adj*. • **audiometrically** *adverb*. • **audiometrist** /-ˈɒmətrɪst/ *noun*. • **audiometry** /-ˈɒmətrɪ/ *noun*. Ⓢ 1870s.

audio-typist ▷ *noun* a person whose job is to listen to a recording that has been made on a dictation machine and transfer the data into the form of typed letters, etc. • **audio-typing** *noun*.

audiovisual ▷ *adj* **1** concerned simultaneously with seeing and hearing. **2** said of a device or teaching method: using both sound and vision, especially in the form of film strips, video recordings, television programmes or computer programs, as a teaching or training aid. • **audiovisually** *adverb*.

audiovisual aid ▷ *noun* (abbreviation **AVA**) any aid to teaching, lecturing, etc that uses sound or pictures, eg slides, acetates for overhead projectors, cassettes in language laboratories, videos in film studies, etc.

audit /ˈɔːdɪt/ ▷ *noun* an official inspection of an organization's accounts by an accountant. ▷ *verb* (***audited, auditing***) to examine (accounts) officially. Ⓢ 15c: from Latin *audire* to hear.

audition /ɔːˈdɪʃən/ ▷ *noun* a test of the suitability of an actor, singer, musician, etc for a particular part or role, which involves them giving a short performance. ▷ *verb* (***auditioned, auditioning***) *tr & intr* to test or be tested by means of an audition. Ⓢ 19c; 16c, meaning 'the action or power of hearing': from Latin *auditio*, from *audire* to hear.

auditor ▷ *noun* a person who is professionally qualified to audit accounts.

auditorium /ɔːdɪˈtɔːrɪəm/ ▷ *noun* (***auditoriums*** or ***auditoria*** /-rɪə/) the part of a theatre, hall, etc where the audience sits. Ⓢ 18c: Latin, meaning 'a lecture-room'.

auditory /ˈɔːdɪtərɪ, -trɪ/ ▷ *adj* belonging, relating or referring to hearing or the organs involved in hearing. Ⓢ 16c: from Latin *audire* to hear.

auditory phonetics ▷ *noun* the branch of phonetics that is specifically concerned with a hearer's perception of sounds, especially speech sounds. Compare ACOUSTIC PHONETICS, ARTICULATORY PHONETICS, PHONOLOGY.

AUEW ▷ *abbreviation* Amalgamated Union of Engineering Workers.

au fait /oʊ ˈfeɪ/ ▷ *adj* (*usually* **au fait with something**) well informed about or familiar with it. Ⓢ 18c: French, meaning 'to the point'.

Aug. ▷ *abbreviation* August.

auger /ˈɔːgə(r)/ ▷ *noun* **1** a hand-tool with a corkscrew-like point for boring holes in wood. **2** a similar but larger implement for boring holes in the ground. Ⓢ Anglo-Saxon *nafogar*; in 15c this became *a nauger*, which was subsequently mistaken as *an auger*.

aught /ɔːt/ ▷ *pronoun, with negatives and questions and in conditional clauses: archaic or literary* anything. Ⓢ Anglo-Saxon *awiht* any person.

augment /ɔːgˈmɛnt/ ▷ *verb* (***augmented, augmenting***) *tr & intr* to make or become greater in size, number, strength, amount, etc. • **augmentable** *adj*. • **augmentation** /-mənˈteɪ-/ *noun*. • **augmentative** /-ˈmɛntətɪv/ *adj*. • **augmentor** *noun*. Ⓢ 15c: from Latin *augere* to increase.

augmented ▷ *adj* **1** having become or been made greater in size, etc. **2** *music* said of an interval: increased by a semitone. Compare DIMINISHED 2.

au gratin /oʊ ˈgratɛ̃/ and **gratin** ▷ *adj, cookery* said of a dish: covered with breadcrumbs, or grated cheese, or a combination of both, cooked in the oven and/or browned under the grill, so that a crisp, golden topping is formed. Ⓢ Early 19c: French, meaning 'with the burnt scrapings'.

augur /ˈɔːgə(r), ˈɔːgjə(r)/ ▷ *verb* (***augured, auguring***) *intr* (*usually* **augur well** or **ill**) to be a good or bad sign for the future. Ⓢ 15c: Latin, meaning 'a soothsayer'.

augury /ˈɔːgjʊrɪ/ ▷ *noun* (***auguries***) **1** a sign or omen. **2** the practice of predicting the future.

August /ˈɔːgəst/ ▷ *noun* the eighth month of the year, which follows July and comes before September, and which contains 31 days. Ⓢ Anglo-Saxon: from Latin, named after Augustus Caesar, the first Roman emperor.

august /ɔːˈgʌst/ ▷ *adj* noble; imposing. • **augustly** *adverb*. • **augustness** *noun*. Ⓢ 17c: from Latin *augustus* grand.

Augustan /ɔːˈgʌstən/ ▷ *adj* **1 a** belonging, relating or referring to, or characteristic of, the reign of the Roman emperor Augustus Caesar; **b** said of Latin literature of this period, especially that written by Horace, Virgil and Ovid. **2** said of other literatures, such as those that flourished in 17c France and 18c England: imitative of the style of these Roman writers. See also NEOCLASSICISM. ▷ *noun* a writer of one of the Augustan Ages. Ⓢ 18c: from Latin *Augustanus* relating to Augustus Caesar.

Augustinian /ɔːgəˈstɪnɪən/ ▷ *adj* relating or referring to Saint Augustine, his teachings or any religious order founded in his name. ▷ *noun* a monk of one of these orders or a follower of Saint Augustine's doctrines. • **Augustinianism** *noun*. Ⓢ 17c: named after Saint Augustine (AD 354–430) whose beliefs and writings profoundly influenced the Christian Church.

Augustinian friars, Augustinian hermits, Austin friars and **Austin hermits** ▷ *noun* the Order of the Hermit Friars of St Augustine, a religious order which established missions and monasteries throughout the world and many famous hospitals.

auk /ɔːk/ ▻ *noun* any of various species of small diving seabirds with a heavy body, black and white plumage, and short wings, found in cool northern seas. ◷ 16c: from Norse *alka*.

au lait /oʊ'leɪ/ ▻ *adj* served or prepared with milk □ *café au lait*. ◷ French, meaning 'with milk'.

auld /ɔːld/ ▻ *adj*, *Scots* old. ◷ Anglo-Saxon *ald*.

auld lang syne /ɔːld laŋ saɪn/ ▻ *noun*, *Scots* days of long ago, especially those remembered nostalgically. ◷ 17c: Scots, literally 'old long since'.

Auld Reekie /ɔːld riːkɪ/ ▻ *noun*, *Scottish* a nickname for Edinburgh. ◷ Early 19c: Scots, meaning 'Old Smokie', from the 19c perception of how polluted the air in the city was.

au naturel /oʊ natjʊə'rɛl/ ▻ *adverb*, *adj* **1 a** said of food: uncooked or cooked in a simple way, usually without seasoning, eg steamed vegetables; **b** said of a method of cooking: without butter, sauce, seasoning, etc. **2** naked. ◷ Early 19c: French, meaning 'naturally'.

aunt /ɑːnt/ ▻ *noun* **1** the sister of one's father or mother. **2** the wife of one's uncle. **3** a close female friend of a child's parents. ◷ 13c: from Latin *amita* father's sister.

Auntie ▻ *noun*, *informal* the BBC.

auntie or **aunty** ▻ *noun* **(*aunties*)** *colloq* an aunt.

Aunt Sally /— salɪ/ ▻ *noun* **(*Aunt Sallies*)** **1** a game in which sticks or balls are thrown at a dummy in the form of an old woman with a pipe, with the object of knocking the pipe out of the dummy's mouth. **2** any target of abuse. ◷ 19c.

au pair /oʊ 'pɛə(r)/ ▻ *noun* **(*au pairs*)** a young person from abroad, usually female, who, in order to learn the language, lives with a family and helps with housework, looking after children, etc in return for board and lodging. ◷ 19c: French, meaning 'on equality', the term originally having been applied to the arrangement made between a family and a young person.

aura /'ɔːrə/ ▻ *noun* **(*auras* or *aurae* /-riː/)** **1** a distinctive character or quality around a person or in a place. **2** a fine substance coming out of something, especially that supposedly coming from and surrounding the body, which many mystics claim is visible as a faint light. **3** *pathol* an unusual sensation that precedes the onset of an attack, especially such a sensation occurring before a migraine attack or an epileptic seizure. ● **aural** *adj*. ◷ 14c: Greek, meaning 'breeze'.

aural /'ɔːrəl/ ▻ *adj* relating to the sense of hearing or to the ears. ● **aurally** *adverb*. ◷ 1840s: from Latin *auris* ear.

> ***aural***
>
> A word often confused with this one is **oral**.

Aura-Soma /'ɔːrə-soʊmə/ ▻ *noun*, *alternative medicine* a form of therapy using coloured oils, herbs and energies created by crystals. ◷ 1980s: from AURA (sense 2) + Greek *soma* body.

aureate /'ɔːrɪət, -eɪt/ ▻ *adj* **1 a** made of or covered in gold; gilded; **b** golden in colour. **2** said of a speech, someone's speaking or writing style, etc: elaborately ornamental. ● **aureately** *adverb*. ● **aureateness** *noun*. ◷ 15c: from Latin *aureus* golden, from *aurum* gold.

aureole /'ɔːrɪoʊl/ and **aureola** /ɔː'rɪələ/ ▻ *noun* **1** a bright disc of light that surrounds the head or, less usually, the whole body of a holy figure, eg a saint, Christ, the Virgin Mary, etc, in Christian painting and iconography. **2** a less common name for a HALO. **3** *astron* a hazy bluish-white halo surrounding the Sun or Moon. **4** *astron* a corona. **5** *geol* a ring-shaped area of metamorphosed rock surrounding an igneous intrusion. ◷ 13c: from Latin *aureolus* golden.

au revoir /oʊ rəv'wɑː(r)/ ▻ *exclamation* goodbye. ▻ *noun* **(*au revoirs* /-z/)** a farewell. ◷ 17c: French, meaning 'until the next seeing'.

auricle /'ɔːrɪkəl, 'ɒ-/ ▻ *noun*, *anatomy* **1** the outer part of the ear. **2** the ear-shaped tip of the ATRIUM of the heart. **3** any ear-shaped appendage. ◷ 17c: from Latin *auricula* little ear.

auricular /ɔː'rɪkjʊlə(r), ɒ-/ ▻ *adj* **1** belonging or relating to the ear or sense of hearing. **2** known by hearing or report. **3** shaped like an ear. **4** relating to an auricle.

auricular therapy ▻ *noun*, *alternative medicine* acupuncture treatment using points on the ear that are related to specific parts of the body.

auriferous /ɔː'rɪfərəs/ ▻ *adj* said of a substance, mineral deposit, etc: containing or yielding gold. ◷ 18c: from Latin *aurum* gold.

aurochs /'ɔːrɒks, 'ɑʊərɒks/ ▻ *noun* (*plural* ***aurochs***) an extinct wild ox, considered to be the ancestor of domestic cattle, and depicted in numerous Stone Age cave paintings. Also called URUS. ◷ 18c: from German *urohso*, from *uro* bison + *ohso* ox.

aurora /ə'rɔːrə/ ▻ *noun* **(*auroras* /-rəz/ or *aurorae* /-riː/)** **1** *astron* the appearance of diffuse bands of coloured lights in the night sky, most often observed from the Arctic and Antarctic regions, caused by a burst of charged particles from the Sun which collide with oxygen and nitrogen atoms in the upper atmosphere to produce electrical discharges. See also AURORA AUSTRALIS, AURORA BOREALIS. **2** *poetic* the dawn. ◷ 15c: Latin, meaning 'dawn'.

aurora australis /— ɒ'streɪlɪs, — ɔː'strɑːlɪs/ ▻ *noun* **(*auroras* or *aurorae* /-riː —/)** the name given to the aurora visible in the southern hemisphere. Also called **the southern lights**. ◷ 18c: Latin, meaning 'southern aurora'.

aurora borealis /— bɔːrɪ'eɪlɪs, — bɔːrɪ'ɑːlɪs/ ▻ *noun* **(*auroras* or *aurorae* /-riː —/)** the name given to the aurora visible in the northern hemisphere. Also called **the northern lights**. ◷ 17c: Latin, meaning 'northern aurora'.

aurous /'ɔːrəs/ ▻ *adj*, *chem* said of compounds: containing gold, especially in the monovalent state. ◷ 19c: from Latin *aurum* gold.

AUS ▻ *abbreviation*, *IVR* Australia.

auscultate /'ɔːskəlteɪt, 'ɒ-/ ▻ *verb* **(*auscultated*, *auscultating*)** to examine someone by auscultation. ● **auscultative** *adj*. ● **auscultator** *noun*. ● **auscultatory** *adj*.

auscultation ▻ *noun*, *medicine* the practice of listening, especially with a stethoscope, to the sounds produced by the movement of blood or air within the heart, lungs, etc, in order to ascertain their physical state and diagnose any abnormalities. ◷ 19c; 17c, meaning 'the act of listening': from Latin *auscultare* to listen.

auspice /'ɔːspɪs, 'ɒ-/ ▻ *noun* (*usually* **auspices**) protection; patronage. ● **under the auspices of someone** or **something** with their or its help, support or guidance. ◷ 17c: from Latin *auspicium* the action of foretelling the future by watching birds.

auspicious /ɔː'spɪʃəs/ promising future success; favourable. ● **auspiciously** *adverb*. ● **auspiciousness** *noun*.

Aussie /'ɒzɪ, 'ɒsɪ/ ▻ *noun*, *adj*, *colloq* Australian.

austere /ɒ'stɪə(r), ɔː-/ ▻ *adj* **1** severely simple and plain. **2** serious; severe; stern. **3** severe in self-discipline. ● **austerely** *adverb*. ◷ 14c: from Greek *austeros* making the tongue dry and rough.

austerity /ɒ'stɛrɪtɪ, ɔː-/ ▻ *noun* **(*austerities*)** **1** the state of being austere; strictness or harshness. **2** severe simplicity of dress, lifestyle, etc. **3** a period of economic depression.

Austin see under AUGUSTINIAN

austral /'ɔːstrəl/ ▻ *adj* southern. ◷ 14c: from Latin *Auster* the south wind.

Australasian /ɒstrəˈleɪʒən, -ʃən, ɔː-/ ▷ *adj* belonging or relating to Australia, New Zealand and the nearby Pacific islands, their inhabitants, or their language. ▷ *noun* a citizen or inhabitant of, or person born in, Australia, New Zealand or the nearby Pacific islands. ◷ 18c.

Australia Day ▷ *noun* a public holiday in Australia, held on 26 January or the first Monday after that, to celebrate the landing of the British in 1788.

Australian /ɒˈstreɪlɪən, ɔː-/ ▷ *adj* belonging or relating to Australia, a continent and country in the southern hemisphere, or its inhabitants. ▷ *noun* a citizen or inhabitant of, or person born in, Australia. ◷ 18c: from AUSTRAL.

Australian Rules and **Australian Rules Football** ▷ *singular noun* a team game with 18 players on each side, that combines features of both ASSOCIATION FOOTBALL and RUGBY and which is played on an oval pitch with a large rugby-like ball which may be carried, kicked or punched, the object being to score by kicking the ball between either of two pairs of goalposts which have no crossbars. Also called **national code**.

australopithecine /ɒstrəloʊˈpɪθəsaɪn, ɔː-/ ▷ *noun* any of several kinds of extinct anthropoid apes whose fossil remains were first discovered in southern Africa in the 1920s, some of which are believed to be over 4.5 million years old. ▷ *adj* belonging, relating or referring to this kind of ape. ◷ 1920s: from Latin *australis* southern + Greek *pithekos* ape.

Austrian /ˈɒstrɪən, ˈɔː-/ ▷ *adj* belonging or relating to Austria, a republic in central Europe, or its inhabitants. ▷ *noun* a citizen or inhabitant of, or person born in, Austria. ◷ 18c: from German *Österreich* Eastern Kingdom.

Austrian blind ▷ *noun* a type of decorative window covering that consists of material in a series of gathered vertical panels that may be drawn up to form a frill at the top of the window.

Austro-¹ /ɒstroʊ, ɔː-/ ▷ *combining form, denoting* southern □ *Austro-Asiatic*. ◷ 19c: from Latin *australis* southern.

Austro-² /ɒstroʊ, ɔː-/ ▷ *combining form, denoting* belonging, relating or referring to Austria □ *the Austro-Hungarian Empire*. ◷ 19c.

Austro-Asiatic ▷ *noun* a family of languages which consists of over 100 different languages that are spoken in parts of Vietnam, Thailand, Laos, Malaysia, Burma (Myanmar), India, etc. ▷ *adj* belonging, relating or referring to the languages of this family.

Austronesian /ɒstroʊˈniːʒən, -ˈniːzɪən/ ▷ *noun* a language family which includes around 700 languages divided into two main groups — approximately 400 languages spoken in Madagascar, Malaysia, Indonesia, the Philippines, Taiwan, and W New Guinea, and a smaller eastern group spoken in Melanesia, Micronesia, and Polynesia. ▷ *adj* belonging, relating or referring to the languages of this group.

AUT ▷ *abbreviation* Association of University Teachers.

autacoid /ˈɔːtəkɔɪd/ ▷ *noun, physiol* any naturally occurring internal secretion such as adrenaline, thyroxine, insulin, etc that either stimulates or inhibits reactions in the body. ◷ Early 20c: from AUTO- + Greek *akos* remedy.

autarchy /ˈɔːtɑːkɪ/ ▷ *noun* (***autarchies***) government of a country by a ruler who has absolute power. ● **autarchic** /ɔːˈtɑːkɪk/ or **autarchical** *adj*. ● **autarchist** *noun*. ◷ 17c: from Greek *autarchos* an absolute ruler.

autarky /ˈɔːtɑːkɪ/ ▷ *noun* (***autarkies***) **1** a system or policy of economic self-sufficiency in a country, state, etc where tariffs and other trade barriers are erected so that international trade is hindered or prevented altogether. **2** a country, state, etc that operates this kind of economic system or policy. ● **autarkic** /ɔːˈtɑːkɪk/ or **autarkical** *adj*. ● **autarkist** *noun*. ◷ 1930s; 17c, meaning 'self-sufficiency', from Greek *autarkeia* self-sufficiency.

auteur /oʊˈtɜː(r)/ ▷ *noun* a film director, especially one whose work is regarded as having some distinctively personal quality about it. ● **auteurism** *noun*. ● **auteurist** *noun, adj*.

authentic /ɔːˈθɛntɪk/ ▷ *adj* **1** genuine. **2** reliable; trustworthy; true to the original. **3** *music* said of a Gregorian MODE (sense 4a): consisting of notes within the octave above the FINAL. Compare PLAGAL. ● **authentically** *adverb*. ● **authenticity** /ɔːɪənˈtɪsɪtɪ/ *noun*. ◷ 14c: from Greek *authentikos* original.

authenticate /ɔːˈθɛntɪkeɪt/ ▷ *verb* (***authenticated, authenticating***) to prove something to be true or genuine. ● **authentication** *noun*. ● **authenticator** *noun*.

author /ˈɔːθə(r)/ ▷ *noun* **1 a** the writer of a book, article, play, etc; **b** someone who writes professionally. **2** the creator or originator of an idea, event, etc □ *the author of the peace plan*. ▷ *verb* (***authored, authoring***) to be the author of (a book, article, play, etc). ● **authorial** /ɔːˈθɔːrɪəl/ *adj*. ◷ 14c: from Latin *auctor*.

> ***authoress***
>
> Like some other words in -ess, this is now commonly regarded as affected and condescending.

authoress /ˈɔːθərɛs/ ▷ *noun, old use* a woman writer.

authoritarian /ɔːθɒrɪˈtɛərɪən/ ▷ *adj* in favour of, insisting on, characterized by, etc strict authority. ▷ *noun* an authoritarian person. ● **authoritarianism** *noun*.

authoritative /ɔːˈθɒrɪtətɪv/ ▷ *adj* **1** accepted as a reliable source of knowledge. **2** having authority; official. ● **authoritatively** *adverb*. ● **authoritativeness** *noun*.

> ***authoritarian, authoritative***
>
> These words are often confused with each other.

authority /ɔːˈθɒrɪtɪ, ə-/ ▷ *noun* (***authorities***) **1 a** the power or right to control or judge others, or to have the final say in something; **b** this kind of power when it is delegated to someone else. **2** a position which has such a power or right. **3** (*sometimes* **authorities**) the person or people who have power, especially political or administrative □ *reported them to the authorities*. **4** the ability to influence others, usually as a result of knowledge or expertise. **5** well-informed confidence □ *Betty delivered her lecture with authority*. **6** an expert □ *an authority on birds*. **7** a passage in a book used to support a statement. ● **have it on authority** to know about something from a reliable source. ◷ 14c: from French *autorite*, from Latin *auctoritas*, from *auctor* author.

authorize /ˈɔːθəraɪz/ or **authorise** ▷ *verb* (***authorized, authorizing***) **1** to give someone the power or right to do something. **2** to give permission for something. ● **authorization** *noun*. ● **authorizer** *noun*. ◷ 14c: from French *autoriser*, from Latin *auctorizare*, from *auctor* author.

Authorized Version ▷ *noun* the English translation of the Bible that was first published in 1611 under the direction of King James VI and I. Often shortened to **Auth. Ver.** Also called **King James Bible, King James Version**.

authorship ▷ *noun* **1** the origin or originator of a particular piece of writing. **2** the profession of writing.

Auth. Ver. ▷ *abbreviation* Authorized Version.

autism /ˈɔːtɪzəm/ ▷ *noun, psychol* a mental disorder that develops in early childhood and is characterized by learning difficulties, inability to relate to other people and the outside world, and repetitive body movements. ● **autistic** *adj*. ● **autistically** *adverb*. ◷ Early 20c: from AUTO- + -ISM 5.

auto /ˈɔːtoʊ/ ▻ *noun* (*autos*) **1** *N Amer* a motor car. **2** *in compounds* □ *autocross*. ⓒ 19c: a shortened form of AUTOMOBILE.

auto- /ɔːtoʊ, ɔːˈtɒ/ or (before a vowel) **aut-** ▻ *combining form* **1** self; same; by or of the same person or thing □ *autobiography*. **2** self-acting □ *automatic*. **3** self-induced. ⓒ From Greek *autos* self.

autobahn /ˈɔːtoʊbɑːn; *German* ˈaʊtobaːn/ ▻ *noun* a motorway in Austria, Switzerland or Germany. ⓒ 1930s: German *Auto* car + *Bahn* road.

autobiographical ▻ *adj* **1** relating to or in the nature of autobiography. **2** said of a film, book, etc: containing elements that might be interpreted as having come from the life of the director, author, etc. • **autobiographically** *adverb*.

autobiography ▻ *noun* (*autobiographies*) **1** someone's own account of their life. **2** the literary genre of accounts of people's lives as recorded by themselves. • **autobiographer** *noun*. ⓒ 18c: AUTO- 1 + BIOGRAPHY.

autocatalysis ▻ *noun* (*autocatalyses*) *chem* a catalytic reaction that is catalysed by one of the products of that reaction. ⓒ 19c.

autocephalous /ɔːtoʊˈsɛfələs, -kɛfələs/ ▻ *adj*, *Christianity* **1** said of certain branches of the Eastern church: having its own head or chief. **2** said of a bishop: having no higher authority to answer to. ⓒ 19c.

autochanger ▻ *noun* **1** a mechanism fitted to a record player which allows a small stack of records to be put on the spindle and which then lets them fall onto the turntable one at a time. **2** a record player that has this type of mechanism.

autochthon /ɔːˈtɒkθɒn/ ▻ *noun* (*autochthons* or *autochthones* /-ɪniːz/) **1** a member of the group of the earliest known inhabitants of a country or region; an aborigine. **2** a plant or animal native to a specific country or region. • **autochthonic** /ɔːtɒkˈɪɒnɪk/ *adj*. ⓒ 17c: from Greek *autochthones* not settlers, indigenous inhabitants.

autoclave /ˈɔːtoʊkleɪv/ ▻ *noun* a strong steel container that can be made airtight and filled with pressurized steam in order to sterilize equipment, eg surgical instruments. ⓒ 19c: from AUTO- 1 + Latin *clavis* key or *clavus* nail.

autocracy /ɔːˈtɒkrəsɪ/ ▻ *noun* (*autocracies*) **1** absolute government by one person; dictatorship. **2** the rule of such a person. **3** a country, state, society, etc that is governed by one person. See also MONOCRACY. ⓒ 17c: from AUTO- 1 + Greek *kratos* power.

autocrat /ˈɔːtəkrat/ ▻ *noun* **1** a ruler with absolute power. **2** an authoritarian person. • **autocratic** *adj*. • **autocratically** *adverb*. ⓒ 19c: from Greek *autokrates* absolute.

autocross /ˈɔːtoʊkrɒs/ ▻ *noun* a motor-racing sport for cars of varying classes that takes place against the clock over a rough grass track of between 500 and 800yd (c.455–730m). Compare MOTOCROSS, RALLYCROSS.

Autocue ▻ *noun*, *trademark*, *TV* a screen hidden from the camera which slowly displays a script line by line, so that the newscaster or speaker can read the script but appears to be speaking without a prompt. ⓒ 1950s.

auto-da-fé /ɔːtoʊdəˈfeɪ/ ▻ *noun* (*autos-da-fé*) **1** *historical* the ceremonial passing of sentence on heretics by the Spanish Inquisition. **2** the public burning of a heretic who had been sentenced by the Inquisition. ⓒ 18c: Portuguese, meaning 'act of the faith'.

autodestruct ▻ *verb*, *intr* to blow itself up. ⓒ 1970s.

autodidact /ɔːtoʊˈdaɪdakt/ ▻ *noun* someone who has taught himself or herself to do something. • **autodidactic** /-ˈdaktɪk/ *adj*. ⓒ 16c: from AUTO- 1 + Greek *didaskein* to teach.

autodyne /ˈɔːtoʊdaɪn/ ▻ *adj*, *radio* said of an electronic circuit: configured so that the same elements and valves are used both as oscillator and detector. ⓒ Early 20c: from AUTO- 1 + Greek *dynamis* power.

autoeroticism or **autoerotism** ▻ *noun*, *psychol* sexual arousal of oneself; masturbation. • **autoerotic** *adj*. • **autoerotically** *adverb*. ⓒ 19c.

autogamy /ɔːˈtɒgəmɪ/ ▻ *noun*, *bot* in flowering plants: self-fertilization. • **autogamic** /ɔːtoʊˈgamɪk/ or **autogamous** *adj*. ⓒ 19c.

autogenics /ɔːtoʊˈdʒɛnɪks/ ▻ *singular noun*, *medicine* a system of relaxation, also used in the treatment of psychosomatic disorders, that is designed to facilitate voluntary control of bodily tension. ⓒ 1960s: from Greek *autogenes* self-produced.

autogenesis see under ABIOGENESIS

autogenous /ɔːˈtɒdʒənəs/ ▻ *adj* **1** self-generated; independent. **2** said of a vaccine, graft, etc: derived from bacteria or tissue obtained from the patient's own body. **3** denoting a type of welding or soldering that is done by melting the metals together and, if a filler metal is used, it is of the same metal □ *autogenous soldering*. • **autogenously** *adverb*. ⓒ 19c: from Greek *autogenes* self-produced.

autogiro or **autogyro** ▻ *noun* a type of aircraft that differs from a helicopter in that its rotor blades are not mechanically powered, but produce lift because they are turned by the air (rather like the sails of a windmill) when the aircraft is moving forwards. ⓒ 1920s: from Greek *auto-* + Spanish *giro*, from Latin *gyrus* circle, originally a trademark and invented by the Spanish engineer, Don Juan de la Cierva (1895-1936).

autograph ▻ *noun* **1** someone's signature, especially a famous person's, that is kept as a souvenir. **2** a literary or musical manuscript in the author's or composer's own handwriting. ▻ *verb* (*autographed*, *autographing*) to sign (a photograph, book, poster, etc). • **autographic** /-ˈgrafɪk/ *adj*. • **autographically** *adverb*. ⓒ 17c: from Greek *autographos* written with one's own hand.

autograph book and **autograph album** ▻ *noun* a book or album that contains a collection of signatures, especially those of famous people.

autography /ɔːˈtɒgrəfɪ/ ▻ *noun* **1 a** the act of writing something in one's own handwriting; **b** something that has been handwritten. **2** the copying of a piece of writing or a drawing, etc by replicating it exactly.

autoharp ▻ *noun* a stringed musical instrument similar to a ZITHER, plucked either with the fingers or with a plectrum, which has a set of dampers that allow chords to be played, and which is commonly used in country-and-western music. ⓒ 19c.

autoimmunity ▻ *noun*, *physiol* the production by the body of antibodies that attack constituents of its own tissues, treating them as foreign material. • **autoimmune** *adj*.

autolysis /ɔːˈtɒlɪsɪs/ ▻ *noun*, *biol* the breakdown of cells or tissues by enzymes produced within them, which occurs either as a symptom of certain diseases and disorders, or after the death of those cells or tissues. ⓒ Early 20c.

automat /ˈɔːtəmat, ɔːtəˈmat/ ▻ *noun*, *N Amer* **1** a fast-food outlet where hot and cold food may be bought from automatic vending machines. **2** an automatic vending machine.

automate /ˈɔːtəmeɪt/ ▻ *verb* (*automated*, *automating*) to apply automation to (a technical process) □ *This plant was automated back in the 70s*. ⓒ 1950s: a back-formation from AUTOMATION.

automated /ˈɔːtəmeɪtɪd/ ▻ *adj* said of a factory, production process, etc: mechanized and automatic, and often under the control of a computer.

automated telling machine and **automatic telling machine** see ATM

automatic /ɔːtə'matɪk/ ▻ *adj* **1** said of a machine or device: capable of operating on its own by means of a self-regulating mechanism, and requiring little human control once it has been activated. **2** said of an action: done without thinking; unconscious; spontaneous. **3** happening as a necessary and inevitable result □ ***The gravity of the offence meant an automatic driving ban.*** **4** said of a firearm: able to reload itself and so capable of firing continuously. Compare SEMI-AUTOMATIC. **5** said of a motor vehicle: having automatic transmission. ▻ *noun* **1** an automatic firearm. **2** a vehicle with automatic transmission. **3** a washing machine that operates automatically. Compare TWIN TUB, WASHER-DRYER. • **automatically** *adverb*. ◷ 18c: from Greek *automatos* acting independently.

automatic pilot and **autopilot** ▻ *noun* an electronic control device that automatically steers a vehicle, especially an aircraft, space vehicle or ship. Also called **autopilot**. • **on automatic pilot** displaying automatic or involuntary actions or behaviour resulting from fatigue, boredom or abstraction.

automatic transmission ▻ *noun* in a motor vehicle: a system that allows the gears to be selected and engaged automatically in response to variations in speed, gradient, etc, as opposed to a manually controlled gearbox.

automatic writing ▻ *noun* a piece of spontaneous writing that apparently flows from someone involuntarily, which in pre-Freudian times was thought to be someone from the spirit world trying to get in touch, but which is now believed to be outpourings from the unconscious.

automation /ɔːtə'meɪʃən/ ▻ *noun* the use of automatic machinery in manufacturing and data-processing, so that entire procedures can be automatically controlled with minimal or no human intervention.

automatism /ɔː'tɒmətɪzəm/ ▻ *noun* **1** the quality or state of being automatic or of acting mechanically. **2** action that happens unconsciously, eg sleepwalking, automatic writing, etc. **3** a technique used by some artists, writers, etc in which normal conscious thought is suspended in the belief that a purer creative impulse will ensue. • **automatist** *noun*. ◷ 19c: from AUTOMATON.

automaton /ɔː'tɒmətən/ ▻ *noun* (***automatons*** or ***automata*** /-tə/) **1** a machine or robot that has been programmed to perform specific actions in a manner imitative of a human or animal, especially such a device used as a toy, amusement or decoration. **2** someone who acts like a machine, according to routine and without thinking. ◷ 17c: from Greek *automatos* acting independently.

automobile /'ɔːtəməbiːl/ ▻ *noun, N Amer* a motor car. ◷ 19c: French, from Latin *mobilis* mobile.

automobilia /ɔːtəmə'bɪlɪə, -'biːlɪə/ ▻ *plural noun* items connected with cars or motoring that are considered collectable or interesting. ◷ 20c: from AUTO, modelled on MEMORABILIA.

automotive /ɔːtə'moutɪv/ ▻ *adj* **1** relating to motor vehicles. **2** self-propelling. ◷ 19c: from AUTO- 1 + Latin *movere* to move.

autonomic /ɔːtə'nɒmɪk/ ▻ *adj* **1** self-governing. **2** relating, referring or belonging to the autonomic nervous system. • **autonomically** *adverb*.

autonomic nervous system ▻ *noun* (abbreviation **ANS**) *physiol* that part of the nervous system which supplies the glands, heart muscle and smooth muscle, and which consists of the SYMPATHETIC NERVOUS SYSTEM and PARASYMPATHETIC NERVOUS SYSTEM.

autonomous /ɔː'tɒnəməs/ ▻ *adj* **1** said of a country, state, etc: self-governing. **2** independent of others. **3** in Kantian philosophy, said of the will: guided by its own principles. • **autonomously** *adverb*.

autonomy /ɔː'tɒnəmɪ/ ▻ *noun* (***autonomies***) **1** the power or right of self-government, administering one's own affairs, etc. **2** freedom from the intervention of others □ ***A single currency is seen to threaten our financial autonomy.*** **3** personal freedom or independence. **4** in Kantian philosophy: the doctrine that stresses the freedom of the will. ◷ 17c: from AUTO- 1 + Greek *nomos* law.

autopilot see AUTOMATIC PILOT

autopista /'ɑutoupiːsta/ ▻ *noun* in Spain: a motorway. ◷ 1950s: Spanish, meaning 'car track'.

autoplasty /'ɔːtouplastɪ/ ▻ *noun, surgery* the use of the patient's own tissue or organ in grafting or transplantation. • **autoplastic** *adj*. ◷ 19c.

autopsy /'ɔːtɒpsɪ, ɔː'tɒpsɪ/ ▻ *noun* (***autopsies***) **1** a POSTMORTEM. **2** any dissection and analysis. ◷ 17c: from Greek *autopsia* seeing with one's own eyes.

autoradiography ▻ *noun, physics, biol* a photographic technique for showing the positions of radioactively labelled molecules within the cells or tissues of a specimen. • **autoradiographic** *adj*.

auto-reverse ▻ *noun* a feature on a cassette recorder, etc, that causes automatic playing of the reverse side of a tape after completion of the first side.

autorickshaw ▻ *noun* in India: a light three-wheeled vehicle powered by a motorcycle engine.

autoroute /'ɔːtouruːt/ ▻ *noun* in France and other French-speaking countries: a motorway. ◷ 1960s: French, meaning 'car road'.

autosome /'ɔːtousoum/ ▻ *noun, genetics* a chromosome other than a sex chromosome. • **autosomal** *adj*. ◷ Early 20c.

autostrada /'ɔːtoustrɑːdə/ ▻ *noun* (***autostradas***) in Italy: a motorway. ◷ 1920s: Italian, meaning 'car road'.

auto-suggestion /ɔːtousə'dʒɛstʃən/ ▻ *noun, psychol* a form of psychotherapy that involves repeating ideas to oneself in order to change attitudes or habits, eg to reduce anxiety. • **autosuggestive** *adj*.

autotimer ▻ *noun* a facility on a cooker that allows the oven to come on and go off at preset times.

autotomy /ɔː'tɒtəmɪ/ ▻ *noun* a reflex reaction in certain animals in which part of the body drops off, especially in order to allow them to escape when being attacked, eg some lizards shed their tails in this way.

autotrophism /ɔːtə'troufɪzəm/ ▻ *noun, biol* the ability to manufacture complex organic compounds from simple inorganic molecules obtained from the environment, as occurs in green plants and certain bacteria. • **autotrophic** *adj*. Compare HETEROTROPHY. ◷ 1930s: from Greek *trophe* food.

autotype ▻ *noun* **1** a technique of photographic reproduction in monochrome that uses a carbon pigment to give a print that is less susceptible to fading of the image. **2** a print made using this technique. **3** a facsimile; an exact reproduction of a manuscript, etc. ◷ 19c: modelled on PROTOTYPE.

autumn /'ɔːtəm/ ▻ *noun* **1** the season of the year, between summer and winter, when leaves change colour and fall and harvests ripen. **2** a period of maturity before decay. • **autumnal** /ɔː'tʌmnəl/ *adj*. • **autumnally** *adverb*. *N Amer equivalent* FALL. ◷ 14c: from Latin *autumnus*.

autumnal equinox see under EQUINOX

autumn crocus ▻ *noun* a plant that produces corms and has lance-shaped glossy leaves, so called because its lilac goblet-shaped flowers appear during the autumn. Also called **meadow saffron**.

autunite /'ɔːtənaɪt/ ▻ *noun, mineralogy* a common yellow or green fluorescent mineral that occurs in uranium deposits. ◷ 19c: named after the town of Autun in France, one of the places that supplies the mineral.

auxesis /ɔːk'siːsɪs/ ▻ *noun, biol* growth in plant or animal tissue that results from an increase in cell size as opposed to an increase in cell number. ◷ 19c; 16c, meaning 'gradual increase of intensity of meaning': Greek, from *auxein* to grow.

auxiliary /ɔːɡ'zɪlɪərɪ/ ▷ *adj* **1** helping or supporting □ *auxiliary nurse.* **2** additional or extra. ▷ *noun* (***auxiliaries***) **1** a helper □ *nursing auxiliary.* **2** (**auxiliaries**) foreign troops that help and support another nation that is engaged in a war. **3** *grammar* an AUXILIARY VERB. ◷ 17c: from Latin *auxiliarius*, from *auxilium* help.

auxiliary language ▷ *noun* **1** a NATURAL LANGUAGE that people of different speech communities adopt to aid communication, eg English and French are often used in this way in many parts of Africa, particularly in the spheres of trade and education. **2** an ARTIFICIAL LANGUAGE such as ESPERANTO.

auxiliary verb ▷ *noun, grammar* a verb, such as *be, do, have, can, shall, may* or *must,* used with other verbs (**lexical verbs**, such as *come, eat, sing* or *use*), to indicate TENSE, MOOD, VOICE, ASPECT, etc, as in *I must go, you will go, they are going, they have been sent, I do not know.* See also MODAL.

auxin /'ɔːksɪn/ ▷ *noun, bot* any of numerous plant hormones that promote growth of plant tissues by an increase in the size of existing cells, rather than an increase in cell number, and are used commercially as rooting powders and weedkillers. ◷ 1930s: from Greek *auxein* to increase.

AV ▷ *abbreviation* **1** (*also* **av**) audiovisual. **2** Authorized Version (of the Bible).

av. ▷ *abbreviation* **1** average. **2** avoirdupois.

AVA ▷ *abbreviation* audiovisual aid(s).

ava[1] or **ava'** /ə'vɑː/ ▷ *adverb, Scots* at all □ *disnae mak sense ava.* ◷ 18c: Scots, an elided form of *of all.*

ava[2] an alternative spelling of KAVA

avadavat /avədə'vat/ or **amadavat** /amə-/ ▷ *noun* a small Indian songbird related to the weaverbirds. ◷ 17c: from *Ahmadabad,* the name of a town in Gujarat.

avail /ə'veɪl/ ▷ *verb* (***availed, availing***) *tr & intr* to help or be of use. ▷ *noun* use; advantage. ◷ 14c: from French *valoir* to be worth, from Latin *valere* to be strong.

> ■ **avail oneself of something** to make use of it or take advantage of it.

> ***avail oneself of something***
>
> ☆ PLAIN ENGLISH alternatives are **use it, make use of it**.

available ▷ *adj* **1** able or ready to be obtained or used. **2** *colloq* not romantically or sexually involved with anyone. • **availability** *noun.* • **availably** *adverb.*

avalanche /'avəlɑːntʃ, -lɑːnʃ/ ▷ *noun* **1** the rapid movement of a large mass of snow or ice down a mountain slope under the force of gravity. **2** a sudden appearance or onslaught of a large number of people or things or a large amount of something □ *His book met with an avalanche of criticism.* ▷ *verb* (***avalanched, avalanching***) *intr* to come down like an avalanche. ◷ 18c: French.

avant-garde /avɑ̃'ɡɑːd/ ▷ *noun* the writers, painters, musicians, etc whose ideas and techniques are considered the most modern or advanced of their time, regarded collectively. ▷ *adj* said of a work of art, a piece of literature, a film, idea, movement, etc: characterized by daring modernity; innovative. • **avant-gardism** *noun.* • **avant-gardist** or **avant-gardiste** *noun.* ◷ 15c: French, meaning 'vanguard'.

avarice /'avərɪs/ ▷ *noun* excessive desire for money, possessions, etc; greed. • **avaricious** /avə'rɪʃəs/ *adj.* • **avariciously** *adverb.* • **avariciousness** *noun.* ◷ 14c: from Latin *avaritia,* from *avere* to crave.

avatar /'avətɑː(r)/ ▷ *noun* **1** *Hinduism* the appearance of a god, especially Vishnu, in human or animal form. **2** the visual manifestation of something abstract. ◷ 18c: from Sanskrit *ava* down + *tarati* he passes over.

Ave[1] and **Av.** ▷ *abbreviation* used in addresses: Avenue.

Ave[2] /'ɑːvɪ/ and **Ave Maria** /— mə'riːə/ ▷ *noun* (***Aves*** or ***Ave-Marias***) a prayer to the Virgin Mary. See also HAIL MARY. ◷ 13c: Latin, meaning 'Hail Mary', the opening words of the angel's greeting to Mary in Luke 1.28.

avenge /ə'vɛndʒ/ ▷ *verb* (***avenged, avenging***) to carry out some form of retribution for (some previous wrongdoing). • **avenger** *noun.* ◷ 14c: from French *avengier,* from Latin *vindicare* to claim as one's own.

avenue /'avənjuː/ ▷ *noun* (***avenues***) **1 a** a broad road or street, often with trees along the sides; **b** (**Avenue**) a street title in an address. **2** a tree-lined approach to a house. **3** a means, way or approach. ◷ 17c: French, from Latin *venire* to come.

aver /ə'vɜː(r)/ ▷ *verb* (***averred, averring***) **1** to state firmly and positively. **2** *law* to prove something to be true. ◷ 14c: from French *averer,* from Latin *verus* true.

average /'avərɪdʒ/ ▷ *noun* **1** the usual or typical amount, extent, quality, number, etc. **2** *statistics* any number that is representative of a group of numbers or other data, especially the arithmetic mean, which is equal to the sum of a set of *n* numbers, divided by *n*. Same as MEAN[3] (sense 2a). Compare MEDIAN 3, MODE 5. **3** *cricket* **a** the mean number of runs that a batsman scores in a single innings. Also called **batting average**. **b** the mean number of runs per wicket conceded by a bowler in a tour, season, etc. Also called **bowling average**. ▷ *adj* **1** usual or ordinary □ *an average sort of a day.* **2** estimated by taking an average □ *of average height.* **3** mediocre □ *gave a pretty average performance.* ▷ *verb* (***averaged, averaging***) **1** to obtain the numerical average of (several numbers). **2** to amount to on average □ *Her speed averaged 90mph on the motorway.* • **on average** usually; normally; typically. ◷ 15c: from Arabic *awariya* damaged goods.

> ■ **average out** to result in an average or balance □ *It averaged out at 3 each.*

averse /ə'vɜːs/ ▷ *adj* (*always* **averse to something**) reluctant about or opposed to it. • **aversely** *adverb.* • **averseness** *noun.* ◷ 16c: from Latin *aversus,* from *ab* away from + *vertere* to turn.

> ***averse***
>
> A word sometimes confused with this one is **adverse**.

aversion /ə'vɜːʃən/ ▷ *noun* **1** a strong dislike. **2** something or someone that is the object of strong dislike □ *Anchovies are my real aversion.*

aversion therapy ▷ *noun, psychiatry* a form of behaviour therapy that aims to eliminate an undesirable habit or a compulsive form of behaviour by repeatedly linking it with an unpleasant stimulus, eg by linking the taste of alcohol with feelings of nausea.

avert /ə'vɜːt/ ▷ *verb* (***averted, averting***) **1** to turn away □ *avert one's eyes.* **2** to prevent (especially danger) □ *Quick reactions averted the accident.* ◷ 15c: from Latin *avertere,* from *ab* away from + *vertere* to turn.

Avesta /ə'vɛstɑː/ ▷ *noun* the holy scriptures of ZOROASTRIANISM. ◷ Early 19c.

Avestan /ə'vɛstən/ and **Avestic** /ə'vɛstɪk/ ▷ *noun* a language that belongs to the Iranian group of the Indo-Iranian branch of the Indo-European family of languages and which has texts dating back to 6c BC. ◷ Early 19c.

avgolemono /avɡə'lɛmənoʊ/ ▷ *noun* a type of Greek soup made from chicken stock, lemon juice and egg yolks. ◷ 1960s: from Modern Greek *augo* egg + *lemono* lemon.

avian /'eɪvɪən/ ▻ *adj* belonging, relating or referring to birds. ⓘ 19c: from Latin *avis* bird.

aviary /'eɪvɪərɪ/ ▻ *noun* (***aviaries***) a large enclosed area where birds are kept. • **aviarist** *noun*. ⓘ 16c: from Latin *aviarium*, from *avis* bird.

aviation /eɪvɪ'eɪʃən/ ▻ *noun* **1** the science or practice of mechanical flight through the air, especially by powered aircraft. **2** the production, design and operation of aircraft. **3** the aircraft industry. ⓘ 19c: from Latin *avis* bird.

aviator /'eɪvɪeɪtə(r)/ ▻ *noun, old use* an aircraft pilot.

aviculture /'eɪvɪkʌltʃə(r), 'avɪ-/ ▻ *noun* the care and rearing of birds. • **aviculturist** *noun*. ⓘ 19c: from Latin *avis* bird + *cultura* tending.

avid /'avɪd/ ▻ *adj* very enthusiastic □ *an avid film-goer*. • **avidly** *adverb*. • **avidity** /ə'vɪdɪtɪ/ *noun*. • **avid for something** eagerly wanting it. ⓘ 18c: from Latin *avidus*, from *avere* to crave.

avidin /'avɪdɪn/ ▻ *noun* a protein found in egg-white, which combines with BIOTIN in such a way that it prevents the biotin from being absorbed. ⓘ 1940s: from AVID + biot*in*.

avifauna /'eɪvɪfɔːnə, 'avɪ-/ ▻ *noun* the bird-life of a specific area. • **avifaunal** *adj*. ⓘ 19c: from Latin *avis* bird + FAUNA.

avionics /eɪvɪ'ɒnɪks/ **1** *singular noun, aeronautics* the scientific study of the development and use of electronic and electrical devices for aircraft and spacecraft. **2** *plural noun, aeronautics* the electrical and electronic equipment that is on board an aircraft or spacecraft or that is used in connection with controlling its flight. ⓘ 1940s: from AVIATION, modelled on ELECTRONICS.

AVM ▻ *abbreviation* **1** automatic vending machine. **2** *Brit* Air Vice-Marshal.

avocado /avə'kɑːdoʊ/ ▻ *noun* (***avocados***) **1** a tropical evergreen tree of the laurel family, with large oval leaves, small yellowish flowers and a pear-shaped fruit. **2** the edible pear-shaped fruit of this tree, which has a rough thick greenish-brown skin and creamy flesh which is eaten fresh. Also called **avocado pear** or **alligator pear**. **3** the greyish-green colour of the flesh of this fruit. Also *as adj*. ⓘ 17c: from Nahuatl *ahuacatl* testicle, so called because of the resemblance of the fruit's stone to a testicle in the scrotum.

avocation /avə'keɪʃən/ ▻ *noun, old use* **1** a diversion or distraction from one's main occupation; a hobby. **2** *colloq* someone's usual occupation. ⓘ 17c: from Latin *avocatio*, from *vocare* to call.

avocet /'avəsɛt/ ▻ *noun* any of various large wading birds with black and white plumage, long legs and a long slender upward curving bill. ⓘ 18c: from French *avocette*.

Avogadro's constant and **Avogadro's number** /avə'gɑːdroʊz —/ ▻ *noun, chem* the number of atoms, molecules or ions that are present in a MOLE[4] of any substance, having a value of 6.02×10^{23}. ⓘ 19c: named after the Italian scientist, Amedeo Avogadro (1776–1856), professor of physics at Turin.

Avogadro's law and **Avogadro's rule** ▻ *noun, chem* the law which states that, under the same conditions of temperature and pressure, equal volumes of all gases contain the same number of molecules. ⓘ 19c: see AVOGADRO'S CONSTANT.

avoid /ə'vɔɪd/ ▻ *verb* (***avoided, avoiding***) **1** to keep away from (a place, person, action, etc). **2** to stop, prevent, manage not to do, or escape something. • **avoidable** *adj*. • **avoidably** *adverb*. • **avoider** *noun*. • **avoid someone** or **something like the plague** to keep away from them or it completely. ⓘ 14c: from French *avoidier* to empty out.

avoidance ▻ *noun* the act of avoiding or shunning someone or something.

avoid, evade

• **Avoid** is neutral in meaning; **evade** implies an element of personal effort often involving cunning or deceit. Typically you evade more seriously unwelcome things such as arrest, detection, identification, taxes and (quite often) the truth □ *The drop in revenue was largely due to efforts to evade the poll tax* □ *For once they managed to evade the searchlights and dodge the guard-dogs*. You can avoid them too, but more usually you avoid things that are more routinely unwelcome and more easily dealt with □ *What can I do to avoid catching head lice?* □ *It is best to avoid continuous hard braking*.

• Note that **tax avoidance** is legal, and **tax evasion** is illegal. In 1979, the UK Institute of Economic Affairs invented the word **avoision** so as not to have to choose always between avoidance and evasion, but the term has not caught on.

avoirdupois /avwɑːdjʊ'pwɑː, avədə'pɔɪz/ ▻ *noun* (abbreviation **av.**) a system of units of mass based on a pound (0.45kg) consisting of 16 ounces, formerly widely used in English-speaking countries, but now increasingly replaced by SI units. ▻ *adj* referring or relating to this system of units. ⓘ 14c: from French *aveir de peis* goods of weight.

avow /ə'vaʊ/ ▻ *verb* (***avowed, avowing***) to state openly; to declare or admit. • **avowable** *adj*. • **avowed** /ə'vaʊd/ *adj*. • **avowedly** /ə'vaʊɪdlɪ/ *adverb*. • **avower** *noun*. ⓘ 13c: from Latin *advocare* to appeal to.

avowal ▻ *noun* **1** a declaration, acknowledgement or confession. **2** an act of avowing; the action of avowing.

avuncular /ə'vʌŋkjʊlə(r)/ ▻ *adj* relating to or like an uncle, especially in being kind and caring. ⓘ 19c: from Latin *avunculus* maternal uncle, from *avus* grandfather.

aw[1] /ɔː/ ▻ *exclamation, colloq* **1** used to express disappointment, commiseration, sympathy, etc □ *Aw! What a shame!* **2** used to express girly delight □ *Aw! Look at that reeeally cute kitten!*

aw[2] see A'

awa or **awa'** /ə'wɔː/ an alternative *Scots* spelling of AWAY

AWACS /'eɪwaks/ ▻ *abbreviation* airborne warning and control system.

await /ə'weɪt/ ▻ *verb* (***awaited, awaiting***) **1** *formal* to wait for something. **2** to be in store for someone. ⓘ 14c; 13c, meaning 'to keep a watch for': from French *awaitier* to lie in wait for.

awake /ə'weɪk/ ▻ *verb* (***awoke*** /ə'woʊk/, ***awoken*** /ə'woʊkən/, ***awaking***) *tr & intr* **1** to stop sleeping or cause to stop sleeping. **2** to become active or cause to become active. ▻ *adj* **1** not sleeping. **2** alert or aware. • **keep someone** or **something awake** to prevent them or it from sleeping. ⓘ Anglo-Saxon *awacian*.

■ **awake to something** to become conscious or aware of it □ *suddenly awoke to the fact that he was no longer young*.

awake, awaken

See Usage Note at **wake**.

awaken /ə'weɪkən/ ▻ *verb* (***awakened, awakening***) *tr & intr* **1** to wake up. **2** to arouse (feelings, etc). **3** to stir or evoke □ *The photo awakened happy memories*. ⓘ Anglo-Saxon *awacian*.

award /ə'wɔːd/ ▻ *verb* (***awarded, awarding***) (*always* **award something to someone** or **award someone something**) **1** to present or grant them it, especially in recognition of some achievement □ *Cannes awarded Tarantino the Palme d'Or*. **2** *law* to decide and declare (a right or claim to something) □ *The judge awarded custody to the father*. ▻ *noun* **1** a payment, prize, etc, especially one given in recognition of an achievement, etc. **2** a legal judgement granting something. ◷ 14c: from French *awarder*, from *esguarder* to observe.

aware /əˈwɛə(r)/ ▷ *adj* **1** (*often* **aware of something** or **someone**) acquainted with or mindful of it or them. **2** (**aware that ...**) conscious that .... **3** well informed □ *ecologically aware.* ◷ Anglo-Saxon *gewær*.

awareness ▷ *noun* the fact or state of being aware, or conscious, especially of matters that are particularly relevant or topical □ *AIDS awareness.*

awash /əˈwɒʃ/ ▷ *adj, adverb* **1** *colloq* covered or flooded with water. **2** *naut* level or on a level with the surface of the water. • **awash with something** over-abundantly supplied with it; covered by a large amount of it □ *The streets are awash with top grade cocaine.* ◷ 19c.

away /əˈweɪ/ ▷ *adverb* **1** from one place, position, person or time towards another; off. **2** in or to the usual or proper place □ *put the books away.* **3** into the distance; into extinction □ *fade away.* **4** apart; remote □ *stay away from the bustle of the city.* **5** continuously; repeatedly; relentlessly □ *talk away.* **6** aside; in another direction □ *looked away.* **7** promptly; without hesitation; now □ *Any questions? Ask away!* **8** said of a sporting event: on the opponent's ground. **9** used with verbs such as *while, fritter, sleep*: wastefully; idly □ *whiled away his days smoking and drinking* □ *frittered away her money on expensive clothes.* ▷ *adj* **1** not present; not at home. **2** distant □ *not far away.* **3** said of a sporting event: played on the opponent's ground □ *away game.* ▷ *noun* a match played or won by a team playing on their opponent's ground. • **away with the fairies** distracted; mad; doolally. • **Away you go!** an expression of disbelief □ *Away you go! You never ate all that ice-cream yourself!* • **do away with someone** or **something** **1** *euphemistic* to kill them □ *hired a contract killer to do away with her husband.* **2** to stop or to get rid of it □ *Let's do away with the small talk and get down to business.* • **right** or **straight away** immediately □ *got promoted straight away.* ◷ Anglo-Saxon *aweg, onweg*.

awe /ɔː/ ▷ *noun* admiration, fear and wonder. ▷ *verb* (***awed, awing***) to fill with awe. • **in awe of someone** or **something** filled with admiration for them or it, but often slightly intimidated too. ◷ 13c: from Norse *agi* fear.

aweigh /əˈweɪ/ ▷ *adverb, naut* said of an anchor: in the process of being raised from the bottom of the sea. ◷ 17c.

awe-inspiring ▷ *adj* **1** causing or deserving awe. **2** *colloq* wonderful.

awesome ▷ *adj* **1** causing awe; dreaded. **2** *colloq* completely and utterly wonderful.

awestruck ▷ *adj* filled with awe.

awful ▷ *adj* **1** *colloq* very bad. **2** *colloq* very great □ *an awful shame.* **3** terrible or shocking. ▷ *adverb, non-standard* very □ *I'm awful busy.* • **awfully** /ˈɔːfəlɪ, ˈɔːflɪ/ *adverb* **1** very badly. **2** very □ *been awfully ill.* • **awfulness** *noun.*

awhile /əˈwaɪl/ ▷ *adverb* for a short time. ◷ Anglo-Saxon *æne hwil* a while.

awkward /ˈɔːkwəd/ ▷ *adj* **1** clumsy and ungraceful. **2** embarrassed or embarrassing □ *an awkward moment.* **3** difficult and dangerous □ *Careful, it's an awkward turning.* **4** difficult or inconvenient to deal with □ *an awkward customer.* • **awkwardly** *adverb.* • **awkwardness** *noun.* • **the** or **that awkward age** early adolescence. ◷ 14c, meaning 'turned the wrong way': from Norse *ofugr* turned the wrong way + -WARD.

awl /ɔːl/ ▷ *noun* a pointed tool used for boring small holes, especially in leather □ *a cobbler's awl.* See also BRADAWL. ◷ Anglo-Saxon *æl*.

awl right see ALL RIGHT 3

awn /ɔːn/ ▷ *noun* **1** *bot* in some grasses, eg barley: a small stiff bristle projecting from the lemma or glumes. **2** a similar structure projecting from a leaf tip or fruit. • **awned** *adj.* • **awnless** *adj.* ◷ 14c: from Norse *ogn*.

awning /ˈɔːnɪŋ/ ▷ *noun* a soft, often striped, plastic or canvas covering over the entrance or window of a shop, hotel, caravan, etc, that can be extended to give shelter from the sun or rain. ◷ 17c: originally only applied to this type of structure on the deck of a boat.

awoke, awoken see under AWAKE

AWOL or **A.W.O.L.** /ˈeɪwɒl/ ▷ *abbreviation* absent without leave, temporarily absent from one's place of duty, especially in the armed forces, without official permission.

AWRE ▷ *abbreviation* Atomic Weapons Research Establishment.

awry /əˈraɪ/ ▷ *adj, adverb* **1** twisted to one side. **2** wrong; amiss. ◷ 14c.

axe or (*US*) **ax** /aks/ ▷ *noun* (***axes*** /ˈaksɪz/) a hand-tool with a long handle and a heavy metal blade, used for cutting down trees, chopping wood, etc. **2** *slang* **a** a guitar; **b** *formerly* a saxophone. **3** *in compounds* □ *pick-axe.* ▷ *verb* (***axed, axing***) **1 a** to get rid of, dismiss or put a stop to something □ *30 jobs were axed*; **b** to reduce (costs, services, etc). **2** to chop with an axe. • **have an axe to grind** to have a personal, often selfish, reason for being involved in something. ◷ Anglo-Saxon *æcs*.

axe-breaker ▷ *noun, Austral* any of several native hardwood trees.

axel /ˈaksəl/, **single axel** and **Axel-Paulsen jump** ▷ *noun, ice-skating* a jump in figure skating in which the skater starts from the forward outside edge of one skate, makes a turn and a half in the air, and comes down on the backward outside edge of the other skate. A similar jump but with two and a half turns in the air is called a **double axel** and one with three and a half turns is a **triple axel**. ◷ 1930s: named after the Norwegian skater, Axel Paulsen (1855–1938).

axeman ▷ *noun* (***axemen***) **1** someone who wields an axe. **2** someone who cuts budgets, etc.

axes *plural of* AXE, AXIS

axial /ˈaksɪəl/ ▷ *adj* relating to, forming or placed along an axis. • **axiality** *noun.* • **axially** *adverb.* ◷ 19c.

axial skeleton ▷ *noun* the bones of the skull and the vertebral column, around which the rest of the skeleton is symmetrically arranged.

axil /ˈaksɪl/ ▷ *noun, bot* the angle between the upper surface of a leaf or stem and the stem or branch from which it grows. • **axillar** or **axillary** *adj.* ◷ 18c: from Latin *axilla* armpit.

axiology /aksɪˈɒlədʒɪ/ ▷ *noun, philos* the theory of moral and aesthetic values. • **axiological** /aksɪəˈlɒdʒɪkəl/ *adj.* • **axiologically** *adverb.* • **axiologist** /aksɪˈɒlədʒɪst/ *noun.* ◷ Early 20c: from Greek *axios* worthy.

axiom /ˈaksɪəm/ ▷ *noun* **1** a proposition, fact, principle, etc which, because it is long-established, is generally accepted as true. **2** a maxim. **3** a self-evident statement. ◷ 15c: from Greek *axios* worthy.

axiomatic /aksɪəˈmatɪk/ and **axiomatical** ▷ *adj* **1** obvious; self-evident. **2** containing or based on axioms. • **axiomatically** *adverb.*

axis /ˈaksɪs/ ▷ *noun* (***axes*** /ˈaksiːz/) **1** an imaginary straight line around which an object, eg a planet, rotates. **2** an imaginary straight line around which an object is symmetrical. **3** *geom* one of the lines of reference used to specify the position of points on a graph, eg the horizontal *x*-axis and vertical *y*-axis in Cartesian COORDINATES. **4** *anatomy* in vertebrates: the second cervical vertebra of the spine, which articulates with the ATLAS vertebra and enables the head to be moved from side to side. • **axial** *adj.* • **axially** *adverb.* • **axile** *adj* coinciding with an axis. ◷ 16c: from Latin *axis* axletree, the Earth's axis.

axle /ˈaksəl/ ▷ *noun* a fixed or rotating rod designed to carry a wheel or one or more pairs of wheels which may be attached to it, driven by it, or rotate freely on it. ● **axled** *adj.* ⓒ 16c: from Norse *oxul.*

Axminster /ˈaksmɪnstə(r)/ ▷ *noun, trademark* a type of patterned carpet with a short close pile. ⓒ Early 19c: named after the town in Devon.

axolotl /aksəˈlɒtəl, ˈaksəlɒtəl/ ▷ *noun* a rare salamander, found in certain Mexican lakes, that is unusual in that it generally lays eggs while still in its aquatic larval stage, and only rarely leaves the water and develops into an adult. Also called **mole salamander**. ⓒ 18c: from Nahuatl *atl* water + *xolotl* servant.

axon /ˈaksɒn/ ▷ *noun, anatomy* the long extension of a neurone which carries nerve impulses outward away from the CELL BODY. ⓒ 19c: Greek, meaning 'axis'.

ayah /ˈaɪə/ ▷ *noun, formerly* in India and other parts of the British Empire: a governess, lady's maid or children's nurse, especially one who is of Asian origin. ⓒ 18c: from Hindi *aya*, from Portuguese *aia*, Latin *avia* grandmother.

ayatollah or **Ayatollah** /aɪəˈtɒlə/ ▷ *noun* **1** in the hierarchy of Shi'ite religious leaders in Iran: someone who can demonstrate a highly advanced knowledge of the Islamic religion and laws. See also IMAM, MAHDI. **2** any dictatorial or influential person. ⓒ 1950s: from Arabic *ayatullah* miraculous sign of God.

aye¹ or **ay** /aɪ/ ▷ *adverb, chiefly dialect* yes. ▷ *noun* **1** a vote in favour of something, especially in the House of Commons. **2** someone who votes in favour of something. Opposite of NAY. See also YEA. ⓒ 16c.

aye² or **ay** /aɪ/ ▷ *adverb, Scots and N Eng dialect* always; still; continually □ *Och, he's aye skiving aff.* ⓒ 13c: from Norse *ei* ever.

aye-aye /ˈaɪaɪ/ ▷ *noun* a nocturnal tree-living primitive primate, native to Madagascar, which has a shaggy coat, a long bushy tail, large ears and extremely long slender fingers. ⓒ 18c: from Malagasy *aiay.*

Ayrshire /ˈɛəʃə(r)/ ▷ *noun, Brit* **1** a breed of dairy cow. **2** a type of bacon. ⓒ 19c: named after the county in SW Scotland.

ayurveda /ˈɑːjʊveɪdə/ ▷ *noun, Hinduism* an ancient system of Hindu medicine, still widely practised in India, involving numerous forms of treatment, eg herbal remedies, fasting, bathing, special diets, enemas, massage, prayers and yoga. ● **ayurvedic** /-ˈveɪdɪk/ *adj.* ⓒ Early 20c: Sanskrit, from *ayur* life + *veda* knowledge.

AZ ▷ *abbreviation US state* Arizona.

az- see AZO-

azalea /əˈzeɪljə/ ▷ *noun* (***azaleas***) **1** any of various deciduous shrubs closely related to the evergreen rhododendron, especially hybrid varieties with large clusters of funnel-shaped pink, orange, red, yellow, white or purple flowers. **2** the flower of this plant. ⓒ 18c: from Greek *azaleos* dry, because it is supposed to prefer drier soil conditions.

azan /ɑːˈzɑːn/ ▷ *noun* any of the five calls to Muslim public prayer that are chanted daily by the MUEZZIN from the minaret of a mosque. ⓒ 19c: from Arabic *adhan* invitation.

azathioprine /azəˈθaɪəpriːn/ ▷ *noun, surgery* a synthetic drug that is used to suppress the body's natural immune system following the transplant of an organ and in the treatment of rheumatoid arthritis. ⓒ 1960s.

azeotrope /əˈzɪətroʊp/ ▷ *noun, chem* a mixture of liquids which boils at a constant temperature and whose constituents do not change on distillation. ● **azeotropic** /eɪzɪəˈtrɒpɪk/ *adj.* ⓒ Early 20c: from A-² + Greek *zeein* to boil + Greek *tropos* a turn.

Azerbaijani /azəbaɪˈdʒɑːnɪ/ ▷ *adj* belonging or relating to Azerbaijan, a republic in the Caucasus Mountains in East Central Asia, its inhabitants, or their language. ▷ *noun* **1** a citizen or inhabitant of, or person born in, Azerbaijan. **2** the language spoken in Azerbaijan, which belongs to the TURKIC branch of the ALTAIC family.

azide /ˈeɪzaɪd/ ▷ *noun, chem* any member of a large class of compounds that are synthesized from **hydrazoic acid** (formula HN_3). ⓒ Early 20c.

azidothymidine /eɪzɪdoʊˈθaɪmɪdiːn/ ▷ *noun* AZT.

azimuth /ˈazɪməθ/ ▷ *noun* in astronomy and surveying: the bearing of an object, eg a planet or star, measured in degrees as the angle around the observer's horizon clockwise from north, which is the zero point. See also ALTITUDE. ● **azimuthal** /azɪˈmʌθəl/ *adj.* ⓒ 14c: from Arabic *al* the + *sumut* directions.

azine /ˈeɪziːn, -zɪn/ ▷ *noun, chem* an organic chemical compound consisting of a six-membered ring composed of carbon and nitrogen atoms, eg pyridine. ⓒ 19c: from AZO + -INE².

azo- /eɪzoʊ/ or (*before a vowel*) **az-** ▷ *combining form, denoting* a compound that contains nitrogen □ *azobenzine.*

azobenzine ▷ *noun* a yellow or orange crystalline substance used in making dyes.

azo-compound ▷ *noun, chem* a compound that has two nitrogen atoms attached to another atom, usually a carbon one.

azo-dye ▷ *noun* a dye that contains an azo-compound.

azoic /əˈzoʊɪk, eɪ-/ ▷ *adj* **1** showing no trace of life. **2** *geol* said of a period or age: showing no traces of organic remains. ⓒ 19c: from A-² + Greek *zoion* animal.

azonal /eɪˈzoʊnəl, a-/ ▷ *adj* not confined to, or arranged in, zones or regions. ⓒ 19c.

AZT ▷ *abbreviation* azidothymidine, a drug that is used in the treatment of AIDS. ⓒ 1970s.

Aztec /ˈaztɛk/ ▷ *noun* **1** a group of Mexican Indian peoples whose great empire was overthrown by the Spanish in the 16c. **2** an individual belonging to this group of peoples. **3** their language. Also called **Nahuatl**. ▷ *adj* belonging or referring to this group or their language. ● **Aztecan** *adj.* ⓒ 18c: from Nahuatl *Aztecatl*, from *Aztlan* the name of the region they inhabited.

azure /ˈaʒə(r), ˈeɪʒʊə(r)/ ▷ *adj* **1** deep sky-blue in colour. **2** *heraldry* blue. ▷ *noun* **1** a deep sky-blue colour. **2** *poetic* the sky. ⓒ 14c: from Persian *lajward* lapis lazuli.

azygous /ˈazɪgəs/ ▷ *adj, biol* said of body parts, organs, etc: occurring or developing singly; without a counterpart. ● **azygously** *adverb.* ⓒ 17c: from A-² + Greek *zygon* yoke.

B

B ▷ *symbol, physics* bel.

B¹ or **b** /biː/ ▷ *noun* (***Bs, B's*** or ***b's***) **1** the second letter of the English alphabet. **2** (*usually* **B**) the second highest grade or quality, or a mark indicating this. **3** (**B**) *music* **a** the seventh note on the scale of C major; **b** the musical key which has this note as its base.

B² ▷ *abbreviation* **1** Bachelor. **2** *music* bass. **3** *IVR* Belgium. **4** on pencils: black.

B³ ▷ *symbol* **1** *chess* bishop. **2** *chem* boron.

b. ▷ *abbreviation* **1** born. **2** *cricket* bowled.

BA ▷ *abbreviation* **1** Bachelor of Arts. **2** British Academy. **3** British Airways.

Ba ▷ *symbol, chem* barium.

BAA ▷ *abbreviation* British Airports Authority.

baa /bɑː/ ▷ *noun* the cry of a sheep or lamb. ▷ *verb* (***baas, baaed, baaing***) *intr* to make this cry; to bleat. ⊙ 16c: imitating the sound.

baba /ˈbɑːbɑː/ and **rum baba** ▷ *noun* a type of small sponge cake soaked in a rum-flavoured syrup. ⊙ 19c: French, from Polish, meaning 'old woman'; the cake was introduced to France by the court of the exiled Polish King Stanislaus I.

babble /ˈbabəl/ ▷ *verb* (***babbled, babbling***) **1** *tr & intr* to talk or say something quickly, especially in a way that is hard to understand. **2** *intr, colloq* to talk foolishly. **3** *intr, formal, literary* said of a stream, etc: to make a low murmuring sound. **4** to give away (a secret) carelessly. • **babbling** *adj* **1** said eg of gently flowing water: making a murmuring sound. **2** said of a person: making incomprehensible sounds. ⊙ 13c: probably imitating the sound.

babe /beɪb/ ▷ *noun* **1** *N Amer colloq* (often used as a term of affection) a girl or young woman. **2** *literary & old use* a baby. **3** someone who is stunningly sexy and beautiful, especially a woman. ⊙ 14c in sense 2: probably imitating the sound made by a baby.

babel /ˈbeɪbəl/ ▷ *noun* **1** a confused sound of voices. **2** a scene of noise and confusion. ⊙ 17c: from Hebrew *Babel*, the place where, according to the biblical account, God caused people to speak different languages.

Babinski reflex and **Babinski effect** /bəˈbɪnskɪ/ ▷ *noun, physiol* a reflex curling upwards of the big toe when the outer side of the foot is stroked, normal in children up to two years of age. ⊙ 20c: named after the French neurologist Joseph Babinski (1857–1932).

baboon /bəˈbuːn/ ▷ *noun* **1** any of various large ground-dwelling mainly African monkeys, which have a long dog-like muzzle, large teeth and a long tail. **2** *derog* a clumsy or stupid person. ⊙ 14c: from French *babuin*.

babushka /bəˈbuːʃkə/ ▷ *noun* (***babushkas***) an old Russian woman. ⊙ 20c: Russian, meaning 'grandmother', diminutive of *baba* old woman.

baby /ˈbeɪbɪ/ ▷ *noun* (***babies***) **1** a newborn or very young child or animal. **2** an unborn child. **3** the youngest member of a group. **4** *derog* a childish person. **5** *colloq* a person's own particular project, responsibility, etc. **6** *colloq, especially N Amer* a term of affection for a girl or woman. ▷ *verb* (***babies, babied, babying***) to treat someone as a baby. • **babyhood** *noun*. • **babyish** *adj, derog* childish; immature. • **babyishly** *adverb*. • **be left holding the baby** *colloq* to be left with the responsibility for something. • **throw the baby out with the bathwater** *colloq* to give up or throw away the important part of something when getting rid of an unwanted part. ⊙ 14c: probably imitating the sound a baby makes.

baby blues see POSTNATAL DEPRESSION

baby boomer ▷ *noun* a person born during a boom in the birth rate, especially that which followed World War II.

baby bouncer (*Brit*) and **baby jumper** (*N Amer*) ▷ *noun* a harness or seat suspended, eg from a door frame, on elastic straps, etc in which a young baby can amuse itself. ⊙ 19c: originally US.

Baby Buggy ▷ *noun, trademark* a collapsible pushchair for a baby or toddler.

baby doll ▷ *noun* **1** a doll in the form of a baby. **2** a woman with an innocent childlike appearance and personality.

baby doll pyjamas ▷ *plural noun* women's pyjamas with a loose top and very short bottoms with elasticated legs.

Babygro /ˈbeɪbɪgroʊ/ ▷ *noun* (***Babygros***) *trademark* an all-in-one stretch-fabric suit for a baby.

baby-sit ▷ *verb, tr & intr* to look after a child, usually in its own home, while the parents are out. • **baby-sitter** *noun* a person who looks after a child while the parents are out. • **baby-sitting** *noun*. ⊙ 20c: the verb is a back-formation from BABY-SITTER.

baby snatcher ▷ *noun* **1** *colloq* a CRADLE-SNATCHER. **2** a person who steals a baby, especially from its pram.

baby talk ▷ *noun* a way, naturally adopted by most parents, in which adults talk to very young children, mimicking their immature speech forms.

baby tooth see MILK TOOTH

baby-walker ▷ *noun* a frame with a seat and wheels in which babies can sit and move about before they have learnt to walk unaided.

BAC ▷ *abbreviation* British Aircraft Corporation.

Bacardi /bəˈkɑːdɪ/ ▷ *noun; trademark* a type of rum, originally produced in the West Indies.

baccalaureate /bakəˈlɔːrɪət/ ▷ *noun* **1** *formal* a BACHELOR's degree. **2** a diploma of a lower status than a degree. ⊙ 17c: from French *baccalauréat*, from Latin *baccalaureus* bachelor.

baccarat /ˈbakərɑː/ ▷ *noun* a card game in which players bet money against the banker. ⊙ 19c: French.

bacchanal /bakəˈnal/ ▷ *noun* **1** *literary* a noisy and drunken party. **2** a follower of Bacchus, the god of wine and pleasure in ancient Greece and Rome. ⊙ 16c: from Latin *bacchanalis*.

bacchanalia /bakəˈneɪlɪə/ ▷ *plural noun* drunken celebrations; orgies. • **bacchanalian** *adj* characteristic of a bacchanal; riotous. ⊙ 17c: Latin, meaning 'feasts in honour of Bacchus'.

baccy /ˈbakɪ/ ▷ *noun* (***baccies***) *colloq* tobacco. ⊙ 18c.

bachelor /ˈbatʃələ(r)/ ▷ *noun* **1** an unmarried man. **2** (**Bachelor**) a person who has taken a first university degree □ *Bachelor of Arts/Science*. See also MASTER (*noun* 7). • **bachelorhood** *noun*. ⊙ 13c: from French *bacheler* a young man aspiring to knighthood.

Bach flower healing /bɑːk — — / ▷ *noun, alternative medicine* a form of therapy in which the healing properties of flowers are used to treat disease by relieving mental and emotional symptoms which are thought to be its cause. ◷ 20c: named after the British physician, Edward Bach (1880–1936).

bacillus /bəˈsɪləs/ ▷ *noun* (***bacilli*** / -laɪ/) *biol* any of a large group of rod-shaped GRAM-POSITIVE bacteria that are widely distributed in soil and air, including many species that cause food spoilage and serious diseases such as tuberculosis and tetanus. ◷ 19c: Latin, meaning 'little stick'.

> ***bacillus***
>
> See Usage Note at **bacterium**.

back ▷ *noun* **1 a** the rear part of the human body from the neck to the base of the spine; **b** the spinal column itself. **2** the upper part of an animal's body. **3** the part of an object that is opposite to or furthest from the front □ *The back of the house faces north.* **4** the side of an object that is not normally seen or used. **5** the upright part of a chair. **6** *sport* a player whose usual position is behind the forwards (see FORWARD *noun*), and who in most sports is a defender, but who (eg in rugby) may also attack. ▷ *adj* **1** located or situated behind or at the back □ *through the back door.* **2** concerning, belonging to or from an earlier date □ *back pay.* **3** away from or behind something, especially something more important □ *back roads.* ▷ *adverb* **1** to or towards the rear; away from the front. **2** in or into an original position or condition □ *when I get back from holiday.* **3** in return or in response □ *hit back.* **4** in or into the past □ *look back to happier days.* ▷ *verb* (***backed***, ***backing***) **1** to help or support someone or something, usually with money. **2** *tr & intr* (*usually* **back away, out** or **out of something**, or **back up**) to move or cause something to move backwards, away from or out of something. **3** to bet on the success of (a horse, etc). **4** (*sometimes* **back someone** or **something up**) to provide a back or support for them. **5** to accompany (a singer) with music. **6** to lie at the back of something. **7** *intr, naut* said of the wind: to change direction anticlockwise. Compare VEER. **8** to countersign or endorse (eg a cheque). • **the back of beyond** a very remote isolated place. • **back to front 1** with the back where the front should be. **2** in the wrong order. • **get off someone's back** *colloq* to stop annoying or troubling them. • **have one's back to the wall** *colloq* to be in a very difficult or desperate situation. • **put one's back into something** *colloq* to carry out (a task) with all one's energy. • **put someone's back up** *colloq* to make them annoyed or resentful. • **see the back of someone** or **something** *colloq* to be rid of or finished with (an unpleasant or tiresome person or thing). ◷ Anglo-Saxon *bæc*.

■ **back down** to concede an argument or claim, especially under pressure or opposition.

■ **back off 1** to move backwards or retreat. **2** to back down.

■ **back on to something** said of a building, etc: to have its back next to or facing it.

■ **back out of something** to withdraw from (a promise or agreement, etc).

■ **back someone up** to support or assist them.

■ **back something up** to copy (computer data) on to a disk or tape. See also BACKUP.

■ **back up on something** *Austral* to repeat (an action) immediately.

backache ▷ *noun* a pain in the back.

backbeat see BREAKBEAT

backbench ▷ *noun* a seat in the House of Commons for members who do not hold an official position either in the government or in the opposition. Also *as adj* □ ***backbench spokesperson.*** • **backbencher** *noun*. Compare CROSS BENCH, FRONT BENCH.

backbite *colloq* ▷ *verb, intr* to speak unkindly about someone who is absent. • **backbiting** *noun* unkind remarks about someone who is absent. ◷ 12c.

backboard ▷ *noun* **1** a board laid under a mattress to support the back while sleeping. **2** *basketball* a rigid vertical panel placed above and behind the basket to deflect the ball.

backbone ▷ *noun* **1** the spine. **2** in both physical and abstract senses: the main support of something □ *the backbone of a company.* **3** firmness and strength of character. ◷ 13c.

backbreaker ▷ *noun* **1** a very hard or tiring task or job, etc. **2** *wrestling* a hold in which one's opponent is pressed down on their back over one's knee or shoulder.

backbreaking ▷ *adj* said of a task, etc: extremely hard or tiring.

back burner ▷ *noun* the rear burner on a stove, used especially for keeping a pot simmering when it doesn't need immediate attention. • **keep** or **place** or **put something on the back burner** to set it aside, postpone work on it, or keep it in reserve for later consideration or action.

backchat ▷ *noun, Brit* impertinent or rude replies, especially to a superior. ◷ Early 20c, originally military slang.

backcloth and **backdrop** ▷ *noun* the painted cloth at the back of a stage, forming part of the scenery.

backcomb ▷ *verb* to comb (the hair) towards the roots to make it look thicker.

backcourt ▷ *noun* **1** *tennis* the part of the court behind the service line. **2** in other games: the part of the court nearest the baseline.

back-cross ▷ *noun, genetics* a cross between a hybrid and a parent.

backdate ▷ *verb* **1** to put a date on (a document, etc) that is earlier than the actual date. **2** to make something effective from a date in the past □ *The pay-rise was backdated to January.*

backdoor ▷ *adj* applied to an activity done secretly and often dishonestly □ *a backdoor deal.* ▷ *noun* (*usually* **the back door**) a clandestine or illicit means of achieving an objective □ *got into power by the back door.* ◷ 16c.

backdrop see BACKCLOTH

backer ▷ *noun* a person who gives financial BACKING (sense 1) to a project, etc.

backfill ▷ *verb* to refill (eg foundations or an excavation) with earth or other material. ▷ *noun* the material used for backfilling.

backfire ▷ *verb, intr* **1** said of an engine or vehicle: to make a loud bang as the result of an explosion of accumulated unburnt or partially burned gases in the exhaust or inlet system. **2** said of a plan, etc: to go wrong and have a bad effect on the person who originated it. ◷ Early 20c in these senses.

back-formation ▷ *noun, grammar* **1** the making of a new word as if it were the root or simpler form of an existing word. **2** a word made in this way, eg *laze* from *lazy*. ◷ Late 19c.

backgammon ▷ *noun* a board game for two people, with pieces moved according to the throws of a dice. ◷ 17c: from BACK + *gamen* game; the same game was called *tables* until the 17c.

background ▷ *noun* **1** the space behind the main figures of a picture. **2** the events or circumstances that precede and help to explain an event, etc. **3** a person's social origins or education, etc. **4** a less noticeable or less public position □ *prefers to stay in the background.* ⓒ 17c.

background heating ▻ *noun* heating which provides a low level of warmth but which requires supplementing for complete comfort.

background music ▻ *noun* music which is intended to provide an accompaniment to something, eg a dinner party, in an inobtrusive way so as not to impede conversation.

background processing ▻ *noun, computing* processing carried out non-interactively, when work placed in a **background queue** is attended to as resources become available.

background radiation ▻ *noun, physics, astron* naturally occurring radiation detectable anywhere on Earth, resulting from COSMIC RAYS from outer space, and from natural radioactive substances on Earth, eg certain rocks.

backhand ▻ *noun* **1** *tennis, squash, etc* a stroke made with the back of the hand turned towards the ball. Compare FOREHAND. **2** handwriting with the letters sloping backwards.

backhanded *adj* **1** *tennis* said of a stroke: made with or as a backhand. **2** said of a compliment: ambiguous or doubtful in effect.

backhander *noun* **1** *tennis* a backhand stroke of a ball. **2** *colloq* a bribe. ⓒ 17c.

backing ▻ *noun* **1** support, especially financial support. **2** material, etc that supports the back of something. **3** music accompanying a singer. Also *as adj* □ *backing group.*

backing store ▻ *noun, computing* a large-capacity computer data store supplementary to a computer's main memory.

backlash ▻ *noun* **1** a sudden violent reaction to an action or situation, etc. **2** a jarring or recoil between parts of a machine that do not fit together properly. ⓒ 1920s; 19c in sense 2.

backless ▻ *adj* lacking or not requiring a back □ *backless swimsuit.*

backlist ▻ *noun* a publisher's list of previously issued titles that are still in print.

backlog ▻ *noun* a pile or amount of uncompleted work. ⓒ 1950s; 17c, meaning 'the log at the back of the fire'.

backmarker ▻ *noun* in a race: a competitor at the back of the field.

back number ▻ *noun* **1** a copy or issue of a newspaper or magazine that is earlier than the current one. **2** *colloq* a person or thing that is out of date or no longer useful.

backpack ▻ *noun, N Amer, especially US* a rucksack. ▻ *verb, intr* to go hiking with a pack on one's back. • **backpacker** *noun.* • **backpacking** *noun.* ⓒ Early 20c.

back passage ▻ *noun, colloq* the RECTUM.

back-pedal ▻ *verb, intr* **1** to turn the pedals on a bicycle backwards. **2** to withdraw rapidly or suddenly from one's previous opinion or course of action.

back projection ▻ *noun* **1** the technique of projecting an image from film, transparency or video on to a translucent screen, to be viewed from the opposite side. **2** *cinematog* this technique used to project a static or moving scene on to a screen which forms a background to action taking place in front of the screen, both then being filmed together to create a single image.

back room ▻ *noun* **1** a place where secret work or activity takes place. **2** *as adj* (*usually* **backroom**) applied to important work done secretly behind the scenes, or to someone who does such work □ *backroom boys.*

back scratcher ▻ *noun* a long-handled implement with which to scratch one's back.

back scratching ▻ *noun, colloq* doing favours for people in return for other favours, to the advantage of both parties.

back seat ▻ *noun* an inferior or unimportant position □ *take a back seat.*

back-seat driver ▻ *noun, derog* a person, especially a passenger in a car, who gives unwanted advice.

back shift ▻ *noun* **1** a group of workers whose working period comes between the day shift and the night shift. **2** this period.

backside ▻ *noun, colloq* the buttocks. ⓒ 16c in this sense; 15c in the general sense 'back' or 'rear'.

back slang ▻ *noun* a type of language in which words are spelt backwards and pronounced according to the new spelling, as in *neetrith* (thirteen) and *yob* (boy). ⓒ 19c.

backslapping ▻ *adj* vigorously and demonstratively cheery.

backslide ▻ *verb, intr* to relapse into former bad behaviour, habits, etc. • **backslider** *noun.* • **backsliding** *noun.* ⓒ 16c.

backspace ▻ *verb, intr* to move the carriage of a typewriter, or a computer cursor, back one or more spaces. ▻ *noun* (*sometimes* **backspacer** or **backspace key**) the key on a typewriter or computer keyboard used for backspacing. • **backspacing** *noun.*

backspin ▻ *noun, sport* the spinning of a ball in the opposite direction to the way it is travelling, which reduces the speed of the ball when it hits a surface. See also SIDESPIN at SIDE, TOPSPIN.

backstage ▻ *adverb* behind a theatre stage. ▻ *adj* not seen by the public.

backstitch *needlecraft* ▻ *noun* a stitch in which the needle enters in the middle of, and comes out in front of, the previous stitch. ▻ *verb, tr & intr* to sew (a seam, etc) using this stitch.

backstop ▻ *noun* **1** a wall or screen which acts as a barrier in various sports. **2** *baseball* **a** the CATCHER; **b** the position of catcher. **3** someone or something that provides extra support or protection.

backstreet ▻ *noun* **1** a street away from a town's main streets. **2** *as adj* secret or illicit; going on or carried out in, or as if in, a backstreet □ *a backstreet abortion.*

backstroke ▻ *noun* a swimming stroke performed on the back, with the arms raised alternately in a backward circular motion, and the legs kicked in a paddling action. ⓒ 17c, meaning 'a return stroke or blow'.

backswing ▻ *noun, sport* the first stage in the swing of a club or racket, etc, when it is swung back and away from the ball.

backtrack ▻ *verb intr* **1** to return the way one came. **2** to reverse one's previous opinion or course of action. ⓒ 20c: originally US.

back translation ▻ *noun* the re-translation of a translated text into the original language, used to test the quality of the original translation.

backup ▻ *noun* **1** support; assistance. **2** *computing* **a** a procedure for backing up data for security purposes; **b** a copy made by this procedure. See also BACK SOMETHING UP at BACK. **3** *sport, especially US* a reserve player.

backward /ˈbakwəd/ ▻ *adj* **1** directed behind or towards the back. **2** less advanced than normal in mental, physical or intellectual development. **3** reluctant or shy. ▻ *adverb* backwards. • **backwardness** *noun.* ⓒ 13c: originally a variant of *abackward.*

backwards or *sometimes* **backward** ▻ *adverb* **1** towards the back or rear. **2** with one's back facing the direction of movement □ *walk backwards out of the room.* **3** in reverse order □ *counting backwards.* **4** in or into a worse state □ *felt her career going backwards.*

• **backwards and forwards** first in one direction, and then in the opposite direction. • **bend** or **fall** or **lean over backwards** *colloq* to try extremely hard to please or accommodate someone. • **know something backwards** *colloq* to know it thoroughly. ◷ 16c: from BACKWARD.

backwash ▷ *noun* **1** waves washed backwards by the movement of a ship or oars, etc through the water. **2** a repercussion.

backwater ▷ *noun* **1** a pool of stagnant water connected to a river. **2** *derog* an isolated place, not affected by what is happening elsewhere.

backwoods ▷ *plural noun* **1** remote uncleared forest. **2** a remote region. ◷ 18c.

backwoodsman ▷ *noun* **1** a person who lives in the backwoods. **2** a coarse person.

backyard ▷ *noun* **1** *Brit* a yard at the back of a house. **2** *N Amer* a garden at the rear of a house.

baclava see BAKLAVA

bacon /ˈbeɪkən/ ▷ *noun* meat from the back and sides of a pig, usually salted or smoked. • **bring home the bacon** *colloq* **1** to provide material support; to earn the money. **2** to accomplish a task successfully. • **save someone's bacon** *colloq* to rescue them from a difficult situation. ◷ 14c: French.

bacteraemia or **bacteremia** /baktəˈriːmɪə/ ▷ *noun, medicine* the presence of bacteria in the blood. ◷ 19c.

bacteria /bakˈtɪərɪə/ ▷ *plural noun* (*rare singular* ***bacterium*** /-rɪəm/ *biol* an extremely diverse group of microscopic and usually single-celled organisms that occur in soil, water and air, including many parasitic species that cause numerous infectious diseases. See also PROKARYOTE. • **bacterial** *adj*. ◷ 19c: from Greek *bakterion* little stick.

bacterium, bacillus

Although both are commonly used to refer to microscopic organisms that cause disease, **bacillus** is, strictly speaking, correctly used only when referring to members of a particular group of **bacteria**, many of which are harmless.

bacteriology /baktɪərɪˈɒlədʒɪ/ ▷ *noun* the scientific study of bacteria and their effects. • **bacteriological** *adj*. • **bacteriologist** *noun* a scientist who specializes in bacteriology. ◷ 19c.

bacteriophage /bakˈtɪərɪoʊfeɪdʒ/ ▷ *noun* any of numerous viruses that infect bacteria, widely used in genetic research. Often shortened to PHAGE. ◷ 1920s: from Greek *phagein* to eat.

Bactrian camel /ˈbaktrɪən —/ ▷ *noun* a camel with two humps, native to central Asia, widely used as a means of transport, and also reared for its meat. Compare DROMEDARY. ◷ 17c: from Bactria, an ancient country in NW Asia.

bad ▷ *adj* (***worse***, ***worst***; *slang* ***badder***, ***baddest***) **1** not good. **2** wicked; immoral. **3** naughty. **4** (**bad at something**) not skilled or clever (at some activity). **5** (**bad for someone**) harmful to them. **6** unpleasant; unwelcome. **7** rotten; decayed. **8** serious; severe ◻ ***a bad cold.*** **9** unhealthy; injured; painful ◻ ***a bad leg.*** **10** sorry, upset or ashamed ◻ ***feel bad about what happened.*** **11** not valid; worthless ◻ ***a bad cheque.*** **12** *slang* very good. ▷ *adverb, N Amer colloq* badly; greatly; hard ◻ ***needs the money bad.*** ▷ *noun* **1** evil; badness ◻ ***take the good with the bad.*** **2** unpleasant events. • **badly** and **badness** see separate entries. • **go bad** said especially of food: to spoil; to become rotten or rancid. • **go to the bad** said of a person: to become morally bad. • **in a bad way** **1** very ill. **2** in serious trouble. • **not bad** *colloq* quite good. • **not half bad** *colloq* very good. • **take the bad with the good** to accept unpleasant facts or events along with pleasant ones. • **too bad** *colloq* unfortunate (often used to dismiss a problem or unsatisfactory situation that cannot, or will not, be put right). ◻ ***She's still not happy with it, but that's just too bad.*** ◷ 13c.

badass /ˈbadas/ *N Amer slang* ▷ *adj* (*also* **badassed**) **1** touchy; difficult. **2** tough; intimidating. ▷ *noun* a difficult person. ◷ 1960s: BAD + ASS[2]

bad blood and **bad feeling** ▷ *noun* angry or bitter feelings.

bad debt ▷ *noun* a debt which will never be paid.

baddy ▷ *noun* (***baddies***) *colloq* a criminal or villain, especially one in a film or book, etc.

bade *past tense of* BID[2]

bad faith ▷ *noun* dishonesty; treachery.

bad feeling see BAD BLOOD

badge /badʒ/ ▷ *noun* **1** a small emblem or mark worn to show rank, membership of a society, etc. **2** any distinguishing feature or mark. ◷ 14c as *bage*: originally a knight's emblem.

badger[1] /ˈbadʒə(r)/ ▷ *noun* a small stocky burrowing mammal with a short tail and short powerful legs, especially a European species with white fur on its head and two broad black stripes running from behind its ears to the tip of its muzzle. ◷ 16c: probably from BADGE, because of the white mark on its forehead.

badger[2] ▷ *verb* (***badgered***, ***badgering***) to pester or worry someone ◻ ***keeps badgering me to contribute.*** ◷ 18c: from BADGER[1], the sense based on the analogy of badger baiting.

bad hair day ▷ *noun, colloq* a feeling of slight depression when you would rather stay at home than face the world, particularly because you cannot find the right clothes to wear. ◷ 1990s: Californian teenage slang.

badinage /ˈbadɪnɑːʒ/ ▷ *noun* playful bantering talk. ◷ 17c: French, from *badiner* to jest.

bad language ▷ *noun* coarse words and swearing.

badly ▷ *adverb* (***worse***, ***worst***) **1** poorly; inefficiently ◻ ***a badly recorded tape.*** **2** unfavourably ◻ ***came off badly in the review.*** **3** extremely; severely ◻ ***badly in arrears with the rent.*** • **badly off** poor; hard up.

badminton /ˈbadmɪntən/ ▷ *noun* a game for two or four players played with rackets and a SHUTTLECOCK which is hit across a high net. ◷ 19c: named after Badminton House in SW England, where it was first played.

badmouth ▷ *verb, colloq, especially N Amer* to criticize or malign someone or something. ◷ 1940s.

badness ▷ *noun* **1** being bad. **2** poor or evil quality.

bad news ▷ *noun* **1 a** any unwelcome, upsetting or irritating event; **b** a report of any such event. **2** *slang* a troublesome or irritating person.

bad-tempered ▷ *adj* easily annoyed or made angry. • **bad-temperedly** *adverb*.

bad trip ▷ *noun, colloq* an episode of terrifying hallucinations and physical discomfort resulting from taking a drug, especially LSD.

BAe ▷ *abbreviation* British Aerospace.

Baedeker /ˈbeɪdɪkə(r), ˈbeɪdɛkə(r)/ ▷ *noun* a guidebook. ◷ 19c: originally the name for any of the famous series published by Karl Baedeker (1801–59).

BAF ▷ *abbreviation* British Athletics Federation.

baffle /ˈbafəl/ ▷ *verb* (***baffled***, ***baffling***) **1** to confuse or puzzle. **2** to hinder or frustrate (plans, etc). ▷ *noun* (*also* **baffle-board** or **baffle-plate** or **baffler**) a device for controlling the flow of gas, liquid or sound through an opening. • **bafflement** *noun*. • **baffling** *adj*. • **bafflingly** *adverb*. ◷ 16c: perhaps related to French *befe* mockery.

BAFTA /'baftə/ ▻ *noun* British Academy of Film and Television Arts.

bag¹ ▻ *noun* **1** a container made of a soft material with an opening at the top, for carrying things. **2** a BAGFUL. **3** an amount of fish or game caught. **4** (**bags**, *especially* **bags of something**) *colloq* a large amount of something. **5** *offensive colloq* a woman, especially an unpleasant or ugly one. **6** (**bags**) loose wide-legged trousers. **7** *slang* a quantity of drugs, especially heroin, in a paper or other container. ● **bag and baggage** completely ◻ *clear out bag and baggage.* ● **in the bag** *colloq* as good as secured or done. ⓒ 13c.

bag² ▻ *verb* (***bagged***, ***bagging***) **1** *tr & intr* (*also* **bag something up**) to put something into a bag. **2** to kill (game) ◻ *bagged six pheasants.* **3** *colloq* to obtain or reserve (a seat, etc). **4** *tr & intr* said especially of clothes: to hang loosely or bulge. ● **bags I** or **bags** or **bagsy** *children's slang* I want to do or have, etc (the thing specified); I lay claim to it ◻ *Bags I sit in the front.* ⓒ 15c: in the nautical sense (of a sail) 'to swell out or bulge': from BAG¹.

bagatelle /bagə'tɛl/ ▻ *noun* **1** a game played on a board with holes into which balls are rolled. **2** an unimportant thing ◻ *a mere bagatelle.* **3** a short piece of light music. ⓒ 17c: French, from Italian *bagatella* a trick or trifle.

bagel or **beigel** /'beɪgəl/ ▻ *noun* a hard ring-shaped bread roll. ⓒ 1930s: from Yiddish *beygel*.

bagful ▻ *noun* (***bagfuls***) the amount a bag can hold.

baggage /'bagɪdʒ/ ▻ *noun* (*plural* in sense 2 only ***baggages***) **1** a traveller's luggage. **2** *usually humorous, colloq* an annoying or unpleasant woman. **3** the portable equipment of an army. ⓒ 15c: from French *bagage* LUGGAGE.

baggage car ▻ *noun, N Amer* a railway luggage van.

baggage reclaim ▻ *noun* **1** the process whereby travellers, especially those travelling long-distance, collect their baggage on arrival at their destination. **2** the area in an airport terminal, etc where travellers collect their baggage on arrival.

baggy ▻ *adj* (***baggier***, ***baggiest***) hanging loose or bulging. ● **baggily** *adverb*. ● **bagginess** *noun*.

bag lady ▻ *noun* a homeless woman who carries her belongings around with her in carrier bags.

bag of bones ▻ *noun, colloq* an extremely thin person or animal.

bagpipes ▻ *plural noun* a musical instrument consisting of a bag into which air is blown through a fingered reed pipe (the CHANTER) by means of which the melody is also created. It sometimes also has other drone pipes which produce single sustained low notes. ● **bagpiper** (often shortend to PIPER) *noun*.

BAgr or **BAgric** ▻ *abbreviation* Bachelor of Agriculture.

baguette /ba'gɛt/ ▻ *noun* **1** a long narrow French loaf. **2** a precious stone cut in a long rectangle. **3** *archit* a small moulding like an ASTRAGAL, with a semicircular cross-section. ⓒ 18c in sense 3: French.

bah /bɑː/ ▻ *exclamation* expressing displeasure, scorn or disgust.

Bahai or **Baha'i** /bə'hɑːiː/ ▻ *noun* (*plural* in sense 2 only ***Bahais*** or ***Baha'is***) *relig* **1** Bahaism. **2** a believer or follower of Bahaism. ● **Bahaism** or **Baha'ism** *noun* a religion, originally from Persia, which follows the teaching of *Baha Ullah* (1817–92) and emphasizes the oneness of God, the harmony of all people, world unity and peace, universal education, etc. ● **Bahaist** or **Baha'ist** *adj, noun*. ⓒ 19c: from Persian *baha* splendour.

bail¹ ▻ *noun* **1** the temporary release of a person awaiting trial, secured by the payment of money and/or the imposition of special conditions. **2** money required as security for a person's temporary release while awaiting trial. ▻ *verb* (***bailed***, ***bailing***) (*usually* **bail someone out**) **1** to provide bail for them. **2** *colloq* to help them out of difficulties, especially by lending them money. ● **forfeit bail** or *informal* **jump bail** to fail to return for trial after being released on bail. ● **on bail** said of a person: released once bail money has been given to the court. ● **put up** or **stand** or **go bail** to provide bail for a prisoner. ⓒ 14c: French, meaning 'custody'.

bail² or **bale** ▻ *verb* (***bailed***, ***baling***; ***baled***, ***bailing***) (*usually* **bail out** or **bale out**) **1** *tr & intr* to remove (water) from a boat with a bucket or scoop. **2** *intr* to escape from an aeroplane by jumping out. ⓒ 17c: from French *baille* bucket.

bail³ ▻ *noun* (*usually* **bails**) *cricket* one of the cross-pieces laid on top of the STUMPS.

bail⁴ ▻ *noun* on a typewriter or printer, etc: a hinged bar that holds the paper against the PLATEN.

bailey /'beɪlɪ/ ▻ *noun* (***baileys***) **1** the outer wall of a castle. **2** a courtyard within the wall. ⓒ 13c: from French *baille* enclosure.

Bailey bridge /'beɪlɪ —/ ▻ *noun* a temporary bridge that can be assembled rapidly from prefabricated pieces of welded steel. ⓒ 1940s: designed by Sir Donald Bailey (1901–85).

bailiff /'beɪlɪf/ ▻ *noun* **1** an officer of a lawcourt, especially one with the power to seize the property of a person who has not paid money owed to the court. **2** a person who looks after property for its owner. ⓒ 13c, meaning 'administrator of a district': from French *baillier* to control or hand over.

bailiwick /'beɪlɪwɪk/ ▻ *noun, now often slightly facetious* one's area of jurisdiction. ⓒ 15c, originally meaning 'a bailiff's area of jurisdiction'.

Baily's beads /'beɪlɪz —/ ▻ *plural noun, astron* a broken ring of bright spots of sunlight, seen around the edges of the Moon immediately before and after a total eclipse of the Sun, and caused by sunlight shining between mountains and valleys on the extreme rim of the Moon. ⓒ 19c: described in detail in 1836 by the astronomer Francis Baily.

bain-marie / *French* bɛ̃ma'riː/ ▻ *noun* (***bain-maries***) *cookery* a pan filled with hot water in which a container of food can be cooked gently or kept warm. ⓒ 19c: French, literally 'bath of Mary', from medieval Latin *balneum Mariae*, 'Maria' being the name of an alleged alchemist.

Bairam /'baɪrɑːm, baɪ'rɑːm/ ▻ *noun* the name of two Muslim festivals, the **Lesser Bairam** lasting for three days at the end of Ramadan, and the **Greater Bairam** lasting for four days at the end of the Islamic year. ⓒ 16c: from Turkish *bayram* festival.

bairn /beərn/ ▻ *noun, dialect* a child. ⓒ Anglo-Saxon *beran*, from *bearn* to bear.

bait ▻ *noun* **1** food put on a hook or in a trap to attract fish or animals. **2** anything intended to attract or tempt. **3** (*also* **bate**) *slang* a rage. ▻ *verb* (***baited***, ***baiting***) **1** to put food on or in (a hook or trap). **2** to harass or tease (a person or animal) wilfully. **3** to set dogs on (another animal, eg a badger). ● **baiting** *noun, especially in compounds* ◻ *bear-baiting.* ⓒ 13c: from Norse *beita* to make something bite.

baited

There is often a spelling confusion between **baited** and **bated**.

baize /beɪz/ ▻ *noun* a woollen cloth, usually green and used as a covering on snooker and card tables, etc. ⓒ 16c: from French *baies*, from Latin *badius* chestnut-coloured.

Bajan /'beɪdʒən/ ▻ *adj, Caribb colloq* Barbadian.

bake ▻ *verb* (***baked***, ***baking***) **1** *tr & intr* to cook (cakes, bread, vegetables, etc) using dry heat in an oven. **2** *tr & intr* to dry or harden by heat from the sun or a fire. **3** *intr, colloq* to be extremely hot. ⓒ Anglo-Saxon *bacan*.

baked beans ▷ *plural noun* haricot beans baked in tomato sauce and usually tinned.

bakehouse ▷ *noun, old use* a bakery.

Bakelite /ˈbeɪkəlaɪt/ ▷ *noun, trademark* a type of hard plastic formerly used to make dishes, buttons, etc. ⓒ 1909: named after L H Baekeland (1863–1944), its Belgian-born US inventor.

baker ▷ *noun* a person who bakes and sells bread and cakes, etc, especially as their profession.

baker's dozen ▷ *noun* thirteen. ⓒ 16c: the term derives from the practice common among bakers in medieval times of supplying an extra loaf or roll with every batch of twelve, so as to avoid being penalized for supplying underweight goods.

bakery ▷ *noun* (***bakeries***) a place where bread, cakes, etc are made or sold.

baking ▷ *adj* (*also* **baking hot**) extremely hot, especially from the sun. ▷ *noun* **1** the process by which bread and cakes, etc are baked. **2** the quantity baked at one time.

baking powder and **baking soda** see under BICARBONATE OF SODA

baklava or **baclava** /ˈbakləvə/ ▷ *noun* a rich cake of Middle-Eastern origin made of layers of FILO pastry, with a filling of honey, nuts and spices. ⓒ 17c as *bocklava*: Turkish.

baksheesh /ˈbakʃiːʃ/ ▷ *noun* in some Eastern countries: money given as a tip or present. ⓒ 18c: from Persian *bakshish*.

balaclava /baləˈklɑːvə/ and **balaclava helmet** ▷ *noun* a warm knitted hat that covers the head and neck, with an opening for the face. ⓒ 19c: from *Balaklava* in the Crimea, in southern Ukraine.

balalaika /baləˈlaɪkə/ ▷ *noun* (***balalaikas***) a Russian stringed musical instrument with a triangular body, a neck like a guitar, and normally three strings. ⓒ 18c: Russian.

balance /ˈbaləns/ ▷ *noun* **1** a state of physical stability in which the weight of a body is evenly distributed. **2** an instrument for weighing, usually with two dishes hanging from a bar supported in the middle. **3** the amount by which the two sides of a financial account (money spent and money received) differ. **4** an amount left over. **5** a state of mental or emotional stability. **6** a state existing when two opposite forces are equal. **7** something that is needed to create such equality. **8** a device which regulates the speed of a clock or watch. *verb* (***balanced***, ***balancing***) **1** *tr & intr* to be in, or put something into, a state of physical balance. **2** (*often* **balance something against something else**) to compare two or more things in one's mind; to compare their respective advantages and disadvantages. **3** to find the difference between money put into an account and money taken out of it, and to make them equal □ ***balance the books***. **4** *intr* (*also* **balance out**) to be or become equal in amount. • **in the balance** not yet decided. • **on balance** having taken all the advantages and disadvantages into consideration. ⓒ 14c as *noun* 2: from Latin *bilanx* having two scales.

balanced ▷ *adj* **1** in a state of balance. **2** fair; considering all sides of an argument, etc. **3** said of a person: calm and sensible.

balance of payments ▷ *noun, econ* the difference in value between the amount of money coming into a country and the amount going out of it, over a period of time.

balance of power ▷ *noun* the equal distribution of political or military power, with no one nation or group having supremacy. • **hold the balance of power** to be in a position where either of two equal and opposed groups or individuals can be made more powerful than the other through one's support.

balance of trade ▷ *noun, econ* the difference in value of a country's imports and exports.

balance sheet ▷ *noun* a summary and balance of financial accounts.

balance wheel ▷ *noun* a wheel in a watch, etc which regulates the beat or rate.

balcony /ˈbalkənɪ/ ▷ *noun* (***balconies***) **1** a platform surrounded by a wall or railing, projecting from the wall of a building. **2** an upper tier in a theatre or cinema. ⓒ 17c: from Italian *balcone*.

bald /bɛːld/ ▷ *adj* **1** said of a person: having little or no hair on their head. **2** said of birds or animals: **a** not having any feather or fur; **b** having white markings on the face. **3** bare or plain □ ***the bald truth***. • **balding** *adj* becoming bald. • **baldly** in a plain and often hurtful way □ ***told them baldly they were not wanted***. • **baldness** *noun* the partial or total loss of hair from parts of the body where it normally grows, especially the head. *Technical equivalent* ALOPECIA. • **bald as a coot** completely bald. ⓒ 15c: from the bird's area of bare white skin on the forehead. ⓒ 14c: perhaps from *balled* rounded.

baldacchino /bɛːldəˈkiːnoʊ/ or **baldachin** or **baldaquin** /-kɪn/ ▷ *noun* (***baldacchinos***) **1** a canopy, especially one supported at each corner by a pole and carried over a sacred object in a religious procession, or placed over a throne, altar or pulpit. **2** *archit* especially over the high altar in a Baroque church: a fixed structure with a canopy supported at each corner by a column. ⓒ 16c as *baldakin*, meaning 'a rich brocade': from Italian *baldacchino*, from *Baldacco* Baghdad, where the silk used for such canopies originally came from.

bald eagle ▷ *noun* a large N American eagle, the national emblem of the USA, so called because its head and neck are covered with distinctive white feathers, whereas the rest of its plumage is black.

balderdash /ˈbɛːldədaʃ/ ▷ *noun, dated* nonsense. ⓒ 16c.

bald-faced ▷ *adj* said of a lie: arrant; out-and-out.

bald-headed ▷ *adj* having a bald head. ▷ *adverb, slang* without restraint; without regard for the consequences.

balding, **baldly** and **baldness** see under BALD

baldric or **baldrick** /ˈbɛːldrɪk/ ▷ *noun, historical* a broad leather belt or silk sash, worn around the waist or over the right shoulder to support a sword or bugle, etc. ⓒ 13c: from French *baudrei*.

bale¹ ▷ *noun* a large tied bundle of a commodity such as hay or cloth. ▷ *verb* (***baled***, ***baling***) to make (hay, etc) into bales. ⓒ 14c: French.

bale² see BAIL²

baleen /bəˈliːn, baˈliːn/ ▷ *noun* whalebone. ⓒ 14c: from Latin *balaena* whale.

baleen whale ▷ *noun* any of various whales which have strips of whalebone in their mouths to enable them to strain KRILL from the water.

baleful ▷ *adj* **1** evil; harmful. **2** threatening; gloomy. • **balefully** *adverb* with menace; threateningly. • **balefulness** *noun*. ⓒ Anglo-Saxon *bealufull*, from *bealu* evil.

baler ▷ *noun* a machine for making bales of hay, etc.

balk or **baulk** /bɛːk, bɛːlk/ ▷ *verb* (***balked***, ***balking***) **1** *intr* (*usually* **balk at something**) to hesitate, or refuse to go on, because of some obstacle. **2** to check or block. ▷ *noun, snooker, etc* the part of the table behind a line (called the **balk line**) near one end, from within which the start and restarts are made. ⓒ 14c, meaning 'to plough in ridges', from Anglo-Saxon *balca* ridge.

Balkan /ˈbɔːlkən/ ▷ *adj* belonging or relating to the peninsula in SE Europe (called the **Balkans**) which is surrounded by the Adriatic, Aegean and Black seas, or to its peoples or its countries. ⓒ 19c.

Balkanize or **Balkanise** (*also without capital*) /'bɔːlkənaɪz/ ▷ *verb* (***Balkanized***, ***Balkanizing***) to break up (a country or area) into mutually hostile areas. • **Balkanization** (*also without capital*) *noun*. ⓒ 1920s: coined because this process took place in the Balkans in the 18c and early 20c; the use has been given new life by the hostilities of the 1990s in Yugoslavia.

ball¹ /bɔːl/ ▷ *noun* **1** a round or roundish object used in some sports. **2** anything round or nearly round in shape □ *a ball of wool*. Also *in compounds* □ *a snowball*. **3** the act of throwing a ball, or the way a ball is thrown. **4** a rounded fleshy part of the body □ *the ball of the foot*. **5** (*usually* **balls**) *coarse slang* a testicle (see also separate entry BALLS). ▷ *verb* (***balled***, ***balling***) *tr & intr* to form or gather into a ball. • **have the ball at one's feet** to have the opportunity to do something. • **on the ball** *colloq* well-informed; alert. • **play ball** *colloq* to co-operate. • **start** or **set** or **keep the ball rolling** to begin or continue an activity, conversation, etc. ⓒ 13c: from Norse *böllr*.

ball² /bɔːl/ ▷ *noun* **1** a formal social meeting for dancing. **2** *colloq* an enjoyable time □ *We had a ball*. ⓒ 17c: from French *bal*.

ballad /'baləd/ ▷ *noun* **1** a slow, usually romantic song. **2** a poem or song with short verses, which tells a popular story. ⓒ 15c: from Provençal *balada* dance.

ballade /ba'lɑːd/ ▷ *noun* **1** a poem consisting of verses grouped in threes, with a repeated refrain and an ENVOY 2. **2** *music* a short lyrical piece for piano. ⓒ 14c: an earlier form of BALLAD.

ball-and-socket joint ▷ *noun* a joint, especially one in the body (eg the shoulder joint) in which the ball-shaped end of one part fits into the cup-shaped end of the other part, allowing rotation on various axes.

ballast /'baləst/ ▷ *noun* **1** heavy material used to keep a ship steady when it is carrying little or no cargo, or to weigh down and stabilize a hot-air balloon. **2** broken rocks or stones used as a base for roads and railway lines. **3** anything used to give a steadying influence, or lend weight or stability. ⓒ 16c: probably from Swedish *bar* bare + *last* load.

ball-bearing ▷ *noun* **1** an arrangement of small steel balls between the moving parts of some machines, to help reduce friction. **2** one of these balls.

ball-boy and **ball-girl** ▷ *noun, tennis* a boy or girl who collects balls that go out of play, supplies balls to the server, etc.

ballcock ▷ *noun* a floating ball that rises and falls with the water level in a tank or cistern and, by means of a hinged rod to which it is attached, operates a valve controlling the inflow of water. ⓒ 18c.

ballerina /balə'riːnə/ ▷ *noun* (***ballerinas***) a female ballet-dancer, especially one who takes leading roles. ⓒ 18c: Italian, from *ballare* to dance.

ballet /'baleɪ, ba'leɪ/ ▷ *noun* **1** a classical style of dancing and mime, using set steps and body movements. **2** the art of activity of dancing in this style □ *I'm learning ballet*. **3** a single performance or work in this style. **4** a troupe of dancers giving such performances □ *touring with the Scottish Ballet*. • **balletic** /ba'letɪk/ *adj*. • **balletically** *adverb*. ⓒ 17c: French, diminutive of *bal* dance.

ballet-dancer ▷ *noun* a dancer of BALLET.

ball game ▷ *noun* **1 a** a game played with a ball; **b** *N Amer* a baseball game. **2** *colloq* a situation or state of affairs □ *a whole new ball game*.

ballier and **balliest** see under BALLY

ballistic /bə'lɪstɪk/ ▷ *adj* **1** referring or relating to projectiles □ *ballistic weapons*. **2 a** referring to BALLISTICS; **b** operating according to the observable rules of BALLISTICS, or under the force of gravity. • **go ballistic** *slang* **1** to go sky-high; to rocket upward at speed □ *Prices in our area have gone ballistic*. **2** said of a person: to fly into a rage; to blow up. ⓒ 18c: from Latin *ballista* a military machine for throwing large rocks at buildings, etc.

ballistic missile ▷ *noun* a type of missile which is initially guided but drops on its target under the force of gravity.

ballistics ▷ *singular noun* **1** the scientific study of the movement, behaviour and effects of projectiles, such as bullets, rockets and guided missiles. **2** the study of the effects and processes of firing in relation to a firearm. **3** a department, group of people, etc expert in ballistics □ *Send the rifle to ballistics for examination*. ⓒ 18c, from BALLISTIC.

balloon /bə'luːn/ ▷ *noun* **1** a small, usually brightly-coloured, rubber pouch with a neck, that can be inflated with air or gas and used as a toy or decoration, etc. **2** a large bag made of light material and filled with a light gas or hot air, designed to float in the air carrying people, or weather-recording instruments, etc in a basket underneath. **3** a balloon-shaped outline containing the words or thoughts of a character in a cartoon. ▷ *verb* (***ballooned***, ***ballooning***) **1** *intr* to swell out like a balloon. **2** *intr* to increase dramatically □ *Food prices ballooned this spring*. **3** *intr* to travel by balloon. **4** *Brit* to kick or propel by some other means (a ball, etc) high into the air. **5** to inflate. • **ballooning** *noun*. • **balloonist** *noun* a person who travels in a balloon, especially for recreation. • **when the balloon goes up** when the trouble, fuss or excitement starts ⓒ 1920s phrase; in World War I observation balloons were launched soon before an attack was to begin. ⓒ 16c in the sense 'large ball' or 'football': from Italian *ballone*.

ballot /'balət/ ▷ *noun* **1 a** a method or system of voting, usually in secret, by putting a marked paper into a box or other container; **b** an act or occasion of voting by this system. **2** the total number of votes recorded in an election □ *The ballot supported the management*. **3** a BALLOT PAPER or small ball, etc used in voting. ▷ *verb* (***balloted***, ***balloting***) **1** to take the vote or ballot of (a group of people). **2** *intr* (*especially* **ballot for something**) to vote by ballot (in favour of it). ⓒ 16c: from Italian *ballotta* little ball.

ballot box ▷ *noun* **1** the box into which voters put marked ballot papers. **2** the system of voting in secret by ballot, especially as a sign of political freedom □ *Power lies in the ballot box*.

ballot paper ▷ *noun* a piece of paper used for voting in a ballot. Often shortened to **ballot**.

ballot-rigging ▷ *noun* dishonest manipulation of a ballot, to produce false results.

ball park ▷ *noun, originally US* **1** a baseball field. **2** a sphere of activity. ▷ *adj* (*usually* **ballpark**) approximate □ *ballpark figures*. • **in the right ballpark** approximately correct or relevant.

ballpeen hammer or **ballpein hammer** /bɔːlpiːn —/ ▷ *noun* a type of hammer used especially for beating metal, which has a rounded head (or PEEN) opposite its hammering head.

ballpoint and **ballpoint pen** ▷ *noun* a pen which has a tiny ball as the writing point, around which the ink flows as it is moved across the paper.

ballroom ▷ *noun* a large room with a spacious dance floor, in which balls (see BALL²) are held.

ballroom dancing ▷ *noun* a formal kind of social dancing, in which couples dance to music with a strict rhythm.

balls *coarse slang* ▷ *singular noun* **1** *N Amer, especially US* courage or bravery □ *It took balls to stand up and admit it*. **2** rubbish; nonsense. Also *as exclamation*. **3** a balls-up. ⓒ 19c in sense 2; 20c in other senses: from BALL¹ *noun* 5.

■ **balls something up** (***ballsed***, ***ballsing***) *Brit* to make a complete mess of it; to bungle it.

balls-up ▻ *noun, Brit, coarse slang* a mess; something confused or bungled □ *made a total balls-up of the accounts.*

ballsy /bɔːlzɪ/ ▻ *adj* (***ballsier, ballsiest***) *slang, especially US* gutsy, tough and courageous. Ⓒ 1940s: from BALLS.

bally /'balɪ/ ▻ *adj* (***ballier, balliest***) *dated Brit colloq* a mild form of BLOODY, but almost meaningless. Ⓒ 19c.

ballyhoo /balɪ'huː/ ▻ *noun* (***ballyhoos***) *colloq* **1** a noisy confused situation. **2** noisy or sensational publicity or advertising. ▻ *verb* (***ballyhooed, ballyhooing***) to make a ballyhoo about something or someone; to create loud publicity or sensationalism over it or them. Ⓒ Early 20c.

balm /bɑːm/ ▻ *noun* **1** an oil obtained from certain types of trees, having a pleasant smell and used in healing or reducing pain. **2** a fragrant and healing ointment. **3 a** an aromatic plant, especially one of the mint family; **b** (*also* **lemon balm**) a LABIATE herbaceous plant with an aroma similar to that of lemon. **4** something comforting to either the body or the spirit. Ⓒ 14c: from French *basme.*

balmoral /bal'mɒrəl/ ▻ *noun* a round flat bonnet with a pompom on the top, worn by certain Scottish regiments. Compare GLENGARRY. Ⓒ 19c: named after Balmoral, the royal residence in Aberdeenshire.

balmy[1] /'bɑːmɪ/ ▻ *adj* (***balmier, balmiest***) said of the air: warm and soft. • **balmily** *adverb.* • **balminess** *noun.* Ⓒ 18c in this sense; 16c in obsolete sense 'fragrant': from BALM.

balmy[2] /'bɑːmɪ/ ▻ *adj* (***balmier, balmiest***) an altered spelling of BARMY, which is now the more common form.

baloney or **boloney** /bə'loʊnɪ/ ▻ *noun, slang* nonsense. Also *as exclamation.* Ⓒ 1920s: perhaps from the *Bologna* sausage.

balsa /'bɛːlsə, 'bɒlsə/ ▻ *noun* (***balsas***) **1** a tropical American tree. **2** (*also* **balsa-wood**) the very lightweight wood of this tree. Ⓒ 18c in obsolete sense 'raft' or 'light fishing-boat': from Spanish, meaning 'raft'.

balsam /'bɔːlsəm/ ▻ *noun* **1** a pleasant-smelling thick sticky substance obtained from some trees and plants, used to make medicines and perfumes. **2** a tree or plant from which this substance is obtained. **3** an aromatic, sticky or oily ointment, or similar healing and soothing preparation made from this substance. • **balsamic** /bɔːl'samɪk/ *adj* **1** like, or made with, balsam. **2** aromatic. **3** said of a preparation: soothing; healing. Ⓒ Anglo-Saxon: from Greek *balsamon.*

balti /'bɔːltɪ/ ▻ *noun* **1** in Indian cookery: a style of curry, originating in Britain, in which the food is cooked in and eaten out of the same wok-like dish. **2** the pan in which this is cooked. Often *as adj* □ *balti bar.* Ⓒ 1990s: Hindi, meaning 'bucket' or 'scoop', from the shape of the dish in which it is cooked.

Baltic /'bɔːltɪk/ ▻ *adj* **1** belonging or relating to the sea which separates Scandinavia from Germany and Russia. **2 a** belonging or relating to Estonia, Latvia or Lithuania, three independent (and formerly Soviet) states adjoining the Baltic Sea; **b** belonging or relating to the inhabitants or languages of these states. **3** belonging or relating to an Indo-European language group which includes Latvian and Lithuanian. Ⓒ 16c: from Latin *Balticus.*

baluster /'baləstə(r)/ ▻ *noun* any one of a series of posts or pillars supporting a rail. Ⓒ 17c: from French *balustre.*

balustrade /balə'streɪd/ ▻ *noun* a row of posts or pillars, joined by a rail, on the edge of a balcony, staircase, bridge, etc. Ⓒ 17c: French, from *balustre* BALUSTER.

bamboo /bam'buː/ ▻ *noun* (*plural* in sense 1 only ***bamboos***) **1** a tall grass that rarely flowers found mainly in tropical regions, with jointed hollow woody stems and deciduous leaves. **2** the stems of this grass, used in furniture-making, basketry, building, etc and as a garden cane. Ⓒ 16c: probably from Malay *bambu.*

bamboozle /bam'buːzəl/ ▻ *verb* (***bamboozled, bamboozling***) *colloq* **1** to trick or cheat someone. **2** to confuse someone. • **bamboozlement** *noun.* Ⓒ 18c.

ban ▻ *noun* an official order stating that something is not allowed □ *a ban on advertising.* ▻ *verb* (***banned, banning***) **1** to forbid something. **2** to forbid someone from going somewhere or doing something, especially officially or formally □ *banned him from the club* □ *ban you from driving.* Ⓒ Anglo-Saxon *bannan* in the original *verb* sense 'to summon'; 13c as *noun* in obsolete sense 'a summons or proclamation'.

banal /bə'nɑːl/ ▻ *adj* boring or trivial; not saying, doing or providing, etc anything interesting or original □ *a banal speech.* • **banality** /bə'nalɪtɪ/ *noun* (***banalities***) **1** something which is boring, trivial, uninteresting or unoriginal. **2** the state of being boring, trivial, etc. • **banally** *adverb.* Ⓒ 18c: French, originally applied to a lord's mill, bakehouse, etc which local people were required to use, from which developed the sense 'common to all', and later 'commonplace'.

banana /bə'nɑːnə/ ▻ *noun* (***bananas***) **1** a large perennial SE Asian plant, superficially resembling a tree, that is cultivated throughout the tropics as a staple food crop. **2** the long curved fruit of this plant, which is often sold as an unblemished yellow fruit, but which is not fully ripe until it is flecked with brown spots. • **be** or **go bananas** *slang* to be or become crazy. Ⓒ 16c: from the native name in Guinea.

banana republic ▻ *noun, derog* a poor country whose economy is dependent on foreign capital. Ⓒ 1930s.

banana skin ▻ *noun* **1** the outer covering of a banana. **2** *colloq* something which happens unexpectedly, or something which is said without sufficient thought, and which causes embarrassment or difficulty.

banana split ▻ *noun* a dish consisting of banana cut from end to end and filled with ice cream, decorated with cream, fruit, nuts, etc.

bancassurance /baŋkə'ʃʊərəns/ ▻ *noun* the selling of insurance policies by banks and building societies, through wholly-owned subsidiary companies of these, rather than by insurance companies. Ⓒ 20c: from BANK[1] + ASSURANCE.

band[1] ▻ *noun* **1** a flat narrow strip of cloth, metal, paper, etc used to hold things together or as a decoration. **2** a stripe of colour or strip of material differing from its background or surroundings. **3** a belt for driving machinery. **4** a group or range of radio frequencies between two limits. Also *in compounds* □ *waveband.* **5** a range of values between two limits. ▻ *verb* (***banded, banding***) to fasten or mark something with a band. Ⓒ 12c: from French *bande.*

band[2] ▻ *noun* **1** a group of people with a common purpose or interest. **2** a group of musicians who play music other than classical music □ *a rock band.* ▻ *verb* (***banded, banding***) (*usually* **band together** or **band someone together**) to act as a group, or to organize (people) to act as a group or to work for a common purpose. Ⓒ 15c: from French *bande.*

bandage /'bandɪdʒ/ ▻ *noun* a strip of cloth for winding round a wound or a broken limb. ▻ *verb* (***bandaged, bandaging***) to wrap (especially a wound or a broken limb) in a bandage. Ⓒ 16c: French.

Band-aid ▻ *noun, trademark, especially N Amer* a type of sticking-plaster with attached dressing, for covering minor wounds. *Brit equivalent* ELASTOPLAST and PLASTER. ▻ *adj* (*usually without capital*) said of policies, etc: makeshift or temporary.

bandana or **bandanna** /ban'danə/ ▻ *noun* (***bandanas*** or ***bandannas***) a large brightly-coloured cotton or silk square, folded and worn around the neck or head. Ⓒ 18c: from Hindi *bandhnu* or badnu a type of dyeing.

B and B or **B & B** or **b & b** ▻ *noun* (*plural* ***B and B's, B & B's*** or ***b & b's***) a BED AND BREAKFAST.

bandbox ▻ *noun* a light round box for holding hats.

bandeau /ˈbandoʊ, banˈdoʊ/ ▻ *noun* (***bandeaux*** /-doʊz/) a narrow band of soft material worn around the head. ◷ 18c: French.

banded ▻ *adj* marked with a stripe or stripes of a different colour.

banderilla /bandəˈriːljə/ ▻ *noun* (***banderillas***) a dart with a streamer, stuck by bullfighters into the bull's neck. • **banderillero** /-rɪlˈjɛəroʊ/ ▻ *noun* (***banderilleros***) a bullfighter who uses banderillas. ◷ 18c: Spanish.

banderole /ˈbandəroʊl/ ▻ *noun* **1** a long narrow flag, usually with a forked end. **2** a flat ribbon-like band carved into a stone wall, etc with writing on it. ◷ 16c: French.

bandicoot /ˈbandɪkuːt/ ▻ *noun* a nocturnal MARSUPIAL, found in Australia, Tasmania and Papua New Guinea, with elongated hindlegs and a long flexible snout. ▻ *verb* (***bandicooted***, ***bandicooting***) *Austral* to remove (potatoes) from the ground without disturbing the tops of the plants. ◷ 18c: from Telugu (an Indian language) *pandikokku* pig-rat.

bandier and **bandiest** see under BANDY[2]

banding ▻ *noun, Brit education* the division of children in the final year of primary school into three groups according to ability, in order to obtain an even spread in the mixed-ability classes usual in comprehensive schools.

bandit /ˈbandɪt/ ▻ *noun* (***bandits*** or ***banditti*** /-ˈdɪtiː/) an armed robber, especially a member of a gang that attacks travellers or isolated homes and villages. ◷ 16c: from Italian *bandito* outlaw.

bandmaster ▻ *noun* the conductor of a musical band, especially a brass band.

bandog /ˈbandɒg/ ▻ *noun* **1** a dog bred for exceptional ferocity, usually a cross between an American pit bull terrier and a mastiff, rottweiler or Rhodesian ridgeback. **2** an aggressive dog kept chained or tied up. ◷ 15c as *band-dogge* in sense 2: from BAND[1] in the old sense 'chain' or 'strap'.

bandoleer or **bandolier** /bandəˈlɪə(r)/ ▻ *noun* a leather shoulder belt, especially one for carrying bullets. ◷ 16c: from French *bandouillere*.

band-saw ▻ *noun* a saw consisting of a blade with teeth attached to a metal band which moves very fast around two wheels.

bandsman ▻ *noun* a member of a musical band, especially a brass band.

bandstand ▻ *noun* a platform with a roof, often in a park, where bands play music.

bandwagon ▻ *noun* • **jump** or **climb on the bandwagon** to join, or show interest in, an activity or movement that is fashionable or likely to succeed and in which one previously had no interest, especially to do so for the sake of personal gain or to improve one's public image. ◷ 19c: the BANDWAGON was originally the wagon or lorry at the head of a parade, on which the band played.

bandwidth ▻ *noun, telecomm* **1** the width or spread of the range of frequencies used for the transmission of radio or TV signals. **2** the space in the frequency-domain occupied by signals of a specified nature, eg TV, radar, telephone-quality speech, etc.

bandy[1] /ˈbandɪ/ ▻ *verb* (***bandies***, ***bandied***, ***bandying***) (*usually* **bandy something about** or **around**) **1** to pass (a story, information, etc) from one person to another. **2** to mention (someone's name) in rumour. • **bandy words with someone** to exchange angry words with them ▫ *Don't bandy words with me!* ◷ 16c.

bandy[2] /ˈbandɪ/ ▻ *adj* (***bandier***, ***bandiest***) said of a person's or animal's legs: curved or bending wide apart at the knees. Also *in compounds* ▫ *bandy-legged.* ◷ 17c.

bane /beɪn/ ▻ *noun* the cause of trouble or evil ▫ *the bane of my life.* ◷ Anglo-Saxon *bana* murderer.

baneful ▻ *adj* evil; causing harm.

bang[1] /baŋ/ ▻ *noun* **1** a sudden loud explosive noise. **2** a heavy blow. **3** *coarse slang* an act of sexual intercourse. **4** *slang* an injection of an illegal drug. ▻ *verb* (***banged***, ***banging***) *tr & intr* **1** to make, or cause something to make, a loud noise by hitting, dropping or closing it violently, etc ▫ *went out and banged the door behind her.* **2** to hit something sharply, especially by accident ▫ *banged her elbow on the table.* **3** to make, or cause something to make, the sound of an explosion. **4** *coarse slang* to have sexual intercourse with someone. ▻ *adverb, colloq* **1** exactly ▫ *bang on time.* **2** suddenly. • **bang goes something** *colloq* that is the end of it ▫ *Bang go my chances of promotion.* • **bang one's head against a brick wall** to waste one's time trying to achieve something that has little or no chance of success. • **bang on** *colloq* exactly on target; exactly as required. • **go with** or **go off with a bang** to be a great success. ◷ 16c: from Norse *banga* to hammer.

■ **bang away** *colloq* to make a continuous noise by hitting something ▫ *banging away on an old typewriter.*

■ **bang on** *colloq* to speak at great length about something, especially repetitively and boringly ▫ *forever banging on about what he did in the war.*

■ **bang someone up** *slang* to imprison them; to shut them up in a cell.

bang[2] /baŋ/ (*usually* **bangs**) *N Amer, especially US* ▻ *noun* hair cut in a straight line across the forehead. *Brit equivalent* FRINGE. ▻ *verb* (***banged***, ***banging***) to cut the hair in this way. ◷ 19c: probably from *bangtail* a short tail.

banger ▻ *noun* **1** *colloq* a sausage. **2** *colloq* an old car, usually one that is noisy and in poor condition. **3** a loud firework.

Bangla see under BENGALI

bangle /ˈbaŋgəl/ ▻ *noun* a piece of jewellery in the form of a solid band, worn round the arm or leg. ◷ 18c: from Hindi *bangri* glass ring.

banian see BANYAN

banish /ˈbanɪʃ/ ▻ *verb* (***banished***, ***banishing***) **1** to send someone away from a place, usually from the country they were born in. **2** to put (thoughts, etc) out of one's mind. • **banishment** *noun* the act or an instance of banishing someone. ◷ 14c: from French *bannir*.

banister or **bannister** /ˈbanɪstə(r)/ ▻ *noun* (*usually* **banisters**) a row of posts and the hand-rail they support, running up the side of a staircase. ◷ 17c: from BALUSTER.

banjax /ˈbandʒaks, banˈdʒaks/ ▻ *verb* (***banjaxes***, ***banjaxed***, ***banjaxing***) to ruin, stymie or destroy. ◷ 1930s: Anglo-Irish.

banjo /ˈbandʒoʊ, banˈdʒoʊ/ ▻ *noun* (***banjos*** or ***banjoes***) a stringed musical instrument with a long neck and a round body, played like a guitar. • **banjoist** *noun.* ◷ 18c: probably of African origin.

bank[1] ▻ *noun* **1** a financial organization which keeps money in accounts for its clients, lends money, exchanges currency, etc. **2** a box in which money can be saved, especially by children. See also PIGGY BANK. **3** a place where something is stored or collected for later use. Also *in compounds* ▫ *blood bank* ▫ *databank.* **4** in some games: a stock of money controlled by one of the players (the BANKER). ▻ *verb* (***banked***, ***banking***) **1** to put (money) into a bank. **2** *intr* to have a bank account ▫ *They bank with Lloyds.* • **break the bank** in gambling: to win from eg a casino the sum of money fixed as the limit it is willing to lose in any one day. ◷ 15c, meaning 'a moneylender's shop': from French *banque*.

■ **bank on something** to rely on it or expect it.

bank[2] ⊳ *noun* **1** the side or slope of a hill. **2** the ground at the edge of a river or lake, etc. Also *in compounds*. **3** a long raised pile of earth or snow, etc. **4** (*also* **sandbank**) a raised area of sand under the sea. **5** a mass of cloud, mist or fog. ⊳ *verb* (***banked***, ***banking***) **1** to enclose something with a bank, or form a bank to it. **2** *tr & intr* said of an aircraft: to change direction, with one wing higher than the other. **3** (*also* **bank up**) to cover (a fire) with a large amount of coal to keep it burning slowly for a long time. ◷ 13c.

■ **bank up** to form a bank or banks.

■ **bank something up** to form it into a bank or banks.

bank[3] ⊳ *noun* a collection of similar things arranged in rows ▫ *a bank of switches*. ◷ 16c: from French *banc* bench.

bankable ⊳ *adj* (used especially in the film industry) likely to ensure profitability. • **bankability** *noun*.

bank account ⊳ *noun* an arrangement by which a person or company keeps money in a bank and takes it out when needed.

bank book ⊳ *noun* a book that records the amounts of money put into and taken out of a bank account.

bank card and **banker's card** ⊳ *noun* a CHEQUE CARD or DEBIT CARD.

bank charge ⊳ *noun* a sum charged periodically, eg monthly, by a bank to a customer's account as the price for handling transactions (not usually applied now as long as the account stays in credit to a specified level).

bank draft ⊳ *noun* a written order sent from one bank to another bank for paying money to a customer.

banker[1] ⊳ *noun* **1** a person who owns or manages a bank. **2** in some games: a person in charge of the bank (see BANK[1] *noun* 4).

banker[2] ⊳ *noun*, *Austral*, *NZ* a river that has risen up to, or is overflowing, its banks. • **run a banker** said of a river: to be overflowing or reaching up to its banks.

banker's draft ⊳ *noun* a bill of exchange obtained from a bank by one of its customers, enabling the purchase of goods, etc by the presentation of the draft to the seller, the bank debiting the customer's account with that amount.

banker's order see STANDING ORDER 1

bank holiday ⊳ *noun* in the UK: any one of several days in the year on which banks are closed, usually observed as a public holiday.

banking ⊳ *noun* the business done by a bank or banker.

banknote ⊳ *noun* a special piece of paper, issued by a bank, which serves as money, being payable to the bearer on demand. Also called BILL (see BILL[1] *noun* 3).

bankroll ⊳ *noun* money resources; funds. ⊳ *verb*, *colloq*, *chiefly N Amer* to finance; to provide the capital for something.

bankrupt /'baŋkrʌpt/ ⊳ *noun* **1** someone who is legally recognized, by a court adjudication order, as not being able to pay their debts. **2** someone whose character is completely lacking in a specified respect, or drained of a specified quality, etc ▫ *a moral bankrupt*. ⊳ *adj* **1** not having money to pay one's debts; insolvent. **2** exhausted of or lacking (some quality, etc) ▫ *bankrupt of ideas*. ⊳ *verb* (***bankrupted***, *past participle* ***bankrupt***, ***bankrupting***) to make someone bankrupt. • **bankruptcy** /-rʌpsɪ/ *noun* (***bankruptcies***) a state of being bankrupt. ◷ 16c: from French *banqueroute*, altered under the influence of Latin *banca rupta* bank broken.

banksia /'baŋksɪə/ ⊳ *noun* (***banksias***) an Australian shrub or small tree with small sharply-toothed leathery leaves and cream, orange, red or purplish flowers on spectacular spherical or cylindrical flower-heads. ◷ 19c: named after the British botanist Sir Joseph Banks (1744–1820).

bank switching ⊳ *noun*, *computing* a method of accessing more memory than can normally be addressed at one time, by switching between one bank of memory and another.

banner /'banə(r)/ ⊳ *noun* **1** a large piece of cloth or cardboard, with a design or slogan, etc, carried or displayed at public meetings and parades. **2 a** *loosely* a military flag; **b** *strictly* a square flag bearing the coat of arms or other insignia of a lord, king or emperor, etc and used as a battle standard. **3** a BANNER HEADLINE. **4** a slogan, theme or catchword, etc used to identify or proclaim one's principles or beliefs. ◷ 13c in sense 2: from French *baniere*.

banner headline ⊳ *noun* a newspaper headline written in large letters across the width of the page.

bannister see BANISTER

bannock /'banək/ ⊳ *noun*, *dialect* a small flat round cake, usually made from oatmeal. ◷ Anglo-Saxon *bannuc*.

banns /banz/ ⊳ *plural noun* a public announcement in church of two people's intention to marry ▫ *The banns have already been published*. • **forbid the banns** to make formal objection to a projected marriage. ◷ 14c: from Anglo-Saxon *bannan* to summon.

banquet /'baŋkwɪt/ ⊳ *noun* **1** a sumptuous formal dinner. **2** *loosely* an elaborate meal. ⊳ *verb* (***banqueted***, ***banqueting***) **1** *intr* to eat or take part in a banquet. **2** to entertain (guests, etc) with a banquet. ◷ 15c: French, from *banc* a seat.

banqueting-house ⊳ *noun* a building, often sumptuously decorated, used for formal dinners and similar entertainment, receptions, ceremonial occasions, etc.

banquette /baŋ'kɛt, bɒŋ'kɛt/ ⊳ *noun* **1** a built-in wall-sofa used instead of individual seats, eg in a restaurant. **2** *archit* a raised walkway inside a parapet or on the bottom of a trench. ◷ 17c in sense 2: French, from Italian *banchetta* little seat.

banshee /'banʃiː, ban'ʃiː/ ⊳ *noun* (***banshees***) *especially Irish & Scottish folklore* a female spirit whose sad wailing outside a house warn that a member of the family will die in the near future. ◷ 18c: from Irish Gaelic *bean sídhe* woman of the fairies.

bantam /'bantəm/ ⊳ *noun* **1** a small breed of farm chicken. **2** a small but forceful person. ◷ 18c: probably from *Bantam* in Java, from where such chickens may have been first imported.

bantamweight ⊳ *noun* **1** a class for boxers, wrestlers and weightlifters of not more than a specified weight (53.5 kg in professional boxing, slightly more in the other sports). **2** a boxer, etc of this weight. ◷ 19c.

banter /'bantə(r)/ ⊳ *noun* light-hearted friendly talk. ⊳ *verb* (***bantered***, ***bantering***) *tr & intr* to tease someone or joke ▫ *The men bantered noisily at the back* ▫ *Don't banter your brother so*. • **bantering** *noun*, *adj*. ◷ 17c.

Bantu /'bantuː, ban'tuː/ ⊳ *noun* (*plural* ***Bantu***) **1** a group of languages spoken in southern and central Africa. **2** *plural* the group of peoples who speak these languages ▫ *Bantu are predominant here*. **3** *offensive* a Black speaker of one of these languages. ⊳ *adj* belonging or relating to the Bantu languages or Bantu-speaking people ▫ *numerous Bantu dialects*. ◷ 19c: a Bantu word, meaning 'people'.

Bantustan /bantu'stɑːn/ ⊳ *noun*, *often offensive* (official term later HOMELAND) any of the partially self-governing regions of South Africa populated and administered by Blacks before the end of apartheid in 1994. ◷ 1940s: from BANTU + *-stan*, modelled on Hindustan.

banyan or **banian** /'banjan/ ⊳ *noun* an Indian fruit tree with branches from which shoots grow down into the ground and take root. ⓒ 17c: from Portuguese *banian*, from Gujarati *vaniyo* man of the trading caste or merchant.

banzai /'banzaɪ/ ▷ *noun* (***banzais***) ▷ *exclamation* **1** a Japanese battle-cry and salute to the emperor. **2** a Japanese exclamation of joy used on happy occasions. ⓒ 19c: Japanese, literally '10,000 years', ie (may you live) forever.

baobab /'beɪoʊbab/ ▷ *noun* a large deciduous African tree with a massive soft trunk which serves as a water store, and a relatively small crown. ⓒ 17c.

BAOR ▷ *abbreviation* British Army of the Rhine.

bap ▷ *noun, Scots & N Eng dialect* a large flat elliptical breakfast roll. ⓒ 16c.

baptise see BAPTIZE

baptism /'baptɪzəm/ ▷ *noun* **1** the religious ceremony of baptizing a person by immersion in, or sprinkling with, water. **2** an experience regarded as initiating someone into a society or group, etc. See also BAPTISM OF FIRE. • **baptismal** /bap'tɪzməl/ *adj.*

baptism of fire ▷ *noun* (***baptisms of fire***) **1** a soldier's first experience of battle. **2** a difficult or frightening first experience of something.

baptist ▷ *noun* **1** a person who baptizes or baptized, especially John the Baptist. **2** (**Baptist**) a member of a Christian group which believes that only people who are able to profess their religious beliefs should be baptized into the church, and that this should be by complete immersion in water.

baptistery or **baptistry** /'baptɪstrɪ/ ▷ *noun* (***baptisteries*** or ***baptistries***) **1** the part of a church where baptisms are carried out, whether a separate building or part of the church. **2** a tank of water for baptisms in a Baptist church.

baptize or **baptise** /bap'taɪz/ ▷ *verb* (***baptized, baptizing***) **1** to dip or immerse someone in, or sprinkle them with, water as a sign of them having become a member of the Christian Church (in the case of babies, this is usually accompanied by name-giving). **2** to give a name to someone ☐ *He was baptized Harold.* Compare CHRISTEN (sense 1). ⓒ 13c: from Greek *baptizein* to immerse.

bar¹ ▷ *noun* **1** a block of some solid substance ☐ *bar of soap.* **2** a rod or long piece of a strong rigid material used as a fastening, weapon, obstruction, etc. **3** anything that prevents, restricts or hinders, such as a non-physical barrier ☐ *colour bar* ☐ *a bar on alcohol.* **4** a line or band of colour or light, etc, especially a stripe on a heraldic shield. **5** a room or counter in a restaurant or hotel, etc, or a separate establishment, where alcoholic drinks are sold and drunk. **6** *in compounds* a small café where drinks and snacks are served ☐ *coffee bar* ☐ *snack bar.* **7** *in compounds* a counter where some specified service is available ☐ *a heel bar.* **8** **a** (*also* **bar-line**) a vertical line marked on music, dividing it into sections of equal value; **b** one of these sections. **9** the rail in a law court where the accused person stands. **10** (**the Bar**) the profession of barristers and advocates. **11** a raised area of sand, mud or stones, etc at the mouth of a river or harbour. **12** an addition to a medal, usually to show that it has been won more than once ☐ *DSO and bar.* **13** in salary statements: a level beyond which one cannot rise unless certain conditions, eg concerning the amount of advanced work one does, are met. ▷ *verb* (***barred, barring***) **1** to fasten something with a bar. **2** (*often* **bar someone from something**) to forbid, prohibit, prevent them from entering (eg a place or event), doing something, etc ☐ *The landlord barred him for a month.* **3** to hinder, obstruct or prevent someone's progress ☐ *tried to bar his way.* **4** to mark something with a stripe or bar. ▷ *prep* except; except for ☐ *CID have now interviewed every suspect, bar one.* See also BARRING. • **be called to the Bar** in the UK: to be admitted as a barrister or advocate. • **behind bars** in prison. ⓒ 12c: from French *barre*.

bar² ▷ *noun, physics, meteorol, etc* in the metric system: a unit of pressure, especially atmospheric pressure, 10^{15} newtons per square metre. See also MILLIBAR. ⓒ Early 20c: from Greek *baros* weight.

Barbadian /bɑː'beɪdɪən/ ▷ *adj* belonging or relating to Barbados, an independent island state in the E Caribbean, or its inhabitants. ▷ *noun* a citizen or inhabitant of, or person born in, Barbados. ⓒ 18c.

barb ▷ *noun* **1** a point on a hook facing in the opposite direction to the main point, which makes it difficult to pull the hook out. **2** a humorous but hurtful remark. **3** one of the threadlike structures forming a feather's web. ▷ *verb* (***barbed, barbing***) to fit or provide something with barbs or a barb. See also BARBED. ⓒ 14c in obsolete sense 'beard' and then applied to a comparable projection or appendage: from Latin *barba* beard.

barbarian /bɑː'bɛərɪən/ ▷ *noun* **1** someone who is cruel and wild in behaviour. **2** an uncivilized and uncultured person. ▷ *adj* cruel and wild; uncivilized ☐ *under attack from barbarian tribes.* ⓒ 14c: from Greek *barbaros* foreign.

barbaric /bɑː'barɪk/ ▷ *adj* **1** cruel and brutal; excessively harsh or vicious. **2** coarse and rude; uncivilized. • **barbarically** *adverb.* ⓒ 15c.

barbarism /'bɑːbərɪzəm/ ▷ *noun* **1** the state of being uncivilized, coarse, uncivilized, etc. **2** a cruel, coarse or ignorant act. **3** a piece of spoken language which is considered coarse or ungrammatical. ⓒ 15c.

barbarity /bɑː'barɪtɪ/ ▷ *noun* (***barbarities***) barbarism (in senses 1 and 2). ⓒ 16c.

barbarous /'bɑːbərəs/ ▷ *adj* **1** uncultured and uncivilized. **2** extremely cruel or brutal. **3** coarse or rude. • **barbarously** *adverb.* ⓒ 15c: from Latin *barbarus*, from Greek *barbaros* foreign, or literally 'stammering', referring to the unfamiliar sound of foreign languages.

Barbary ape /'bɑːbərɪ — / ▷ *noun* a type of MACAQUE, native to mountainous regions of N Africa, and also found in Gibraltar. ⓒ 19c: from *Barbary* the old name for the regions along the N coast of Africa, the country of the *Berbers*.

barbecue /'bɑːbɪkjuː/ ▷ *noun* (***barbecues***) **1** a frame on which food is grilled over an open fire, especially a charcoal fire. **2** a portable grill for cooking food in this way. **3** food cooked in this way. **4** a party held out of doors at which food is cooked on a barbecue. ▷ *verb* (***barbecued, barbecueing***) to cook (food) on a barbecue, often coating it with a highly-seasoned sauce (a **barbecue sauce**). ⓒ 18c: from S American Arawak *barbacòa* a framework of sticks.

barbed ▷ *adj* **1** having a barb or barbs. **2** said of a remark: spiteful or vindictive.

barbed wire ▷ *noun* wire with short sharp points twisted on at intervals, used for making fences, etc.

barbel /'bɑːbəl/ ▷ *noun* **1** a large freshwater fish of the carp family, widespread in European rivers, which has a slender body and four long sensory feelers or **barbels** around its mouth. **2** (*also* **barbule**) a fleshy whisker-like outgrowth covered with taste buds, found around the mouth or nostril of some fishes, especially catfish and barbels. ⓒ 15c: from Latin *barba* beard.

barbell ▷ *noun* a bar with heavy metal weights at each end, used for weightlifting exercises.

barber /'bɑːbə(r)/ ▷ *noun* someone who cuts and styles men's hair and shaves their beards. ⓒ 14c: from French *barbeor*, from Latin *barba* beard.

barberry /'bɑːbərɪ/ ▷ *noun* (***barberries***) a bushy plant or shrub with thorns, yellow flowers and red berries. ⓒ 15c: from Latin *berberis*.

barbershop ▷ *noun* **1** a type of singing in which usually four men sing in close harmony without musical accompaniment. **2** the premises in which a barber works.

barbet /ˈbɑːbət/ ▷ *noun* a plump brightly-coloured tropical bird that has a beardlike growth of feathers at the base of its large bill. ◷ 19c: from Latin *barba* beard.

barbican /ˈbɑːbɪkən/ ▷ *noun* a tower over the outer gate of a castle or town, for the purpose of defending the gate. ◷ 13c: from French *barbacane*.

barbie ▷ *noun, Austral colloq* a barbecue. ◷ 1970s.

barbiturate /bɑːbɪˈtjʊərət/ ▷ *noun, medicine* a salt or ester of **barbituric acid**, used as a source of sedative and hypnotic drugs, eg sleeping pills and anaesthetics, but now increasingly being replaced by safer and less addictive drugs. ◷ 1920s.

Barbour /ˈbɑːbə(r)/ *trademark* and **Barbour jacket** ▷ *noun* a strong waterproof jacket, especially one made of green waxed cotton.

barbule /ˈbɑːbjuːl/ ▷ *noun, zool* **1** any of numerous parallel hairlike filaments on the barbs of a feather. **2** a BARBEL (sense 2). ◷ 19c.

barcarole or **barcarolle** /ˈbɑːkəroul, -ˈrɒl/ ▷ *noun* a gondolier's song, or a piece of music with a similar rhythm. ◷ 18c: from Italian *barcarola* boat-song.

BArch ▷ *abbreviation* Bachelor of Architecture.

bar chart and **bar graph** ▷ *noun* a graph which shows values or amounts by means of vertical bars. Compare PIE CHART.

bar code ▷ *noun* a series of numbers and black parallel lines of varying thickness, commonly used on product labels such as food packaging and book jackets, that represents information about the product for sales checkouts, stock control, etc. See also EPOS. • **bar-coded** *adj*. ◷ 1970s.

bard /bɑːd/ ▷ *noun* **1** *literary* a poet. **2** a poet who has won a prize at the Eisteddfod in Wales. • **bardic** *adj*. ◷ 15c: Scottish and Irish Gaelic, meaning 'poet'.

bare /bɛə(r)/ ▷ *adj* (*barer*, *barest*) **1** not covered by clothes; naked. **2** without the usual or natural covering □ *bare trees*. **3** empty □ *The cupboard was bare*. **4** simple; plain □ *the bare facts*. **5** basic; essential □ *the bare necessities*. ▷ *verb* (*bared*, *baring*) to uncover □ *He bared his chest*. • **barely** see separate entry. • **bareness** *noun*. • **bare one's heart** or **soul** to make known one's private thoughts and feelings. • **with one's bare hands** without using weapons or tools □ *pulled down the wall with his bare hands*. ◷ Anglo-Saxon *bær*.

bareback ▷ *adverb, adj* on a horse without a saddle □ *often rode bareback* □ *bareback riders*.

bare bones ▷ *plural noun* the essential facts □ *the bare bones of the case*.

barefaced ▷ *adj* **1** having no shame or regret; impudent □ *a barefaced lie*. **2** beardless; with the face uncovered. • **barefacedly** /-ˈfeɪsɪdlɪ/ *adverb* without shame; openly.

barefoot or **barefooted** ▷ *adj, adverb* not wearing shoes or socks.

bareheaded ▷ *adj, adverb* not wearing a hat, scarf or other head-covering.

bareknuckle ▷ *adj* **1** without boxing gloves on □ *bareknuckle fighter*. **2** fiercely aggressive □ *The meeting turned into a bareknuckle encounter*.

barelegged ▷ *adj, adverb* with the legs uncovered.

barely ▷ *adverb* **1** scarcely or only just □ *barely enough food*. **2** plainly or simply □ *barely furnished*.

bareness see under BARE

barf ▷ *verb* (*barfed*, *barfing*) *intr, slang, originally US* to vomit. ◷ 1950s.

bargain /ˈbɑːgɪn/ ▷ *noun* **1** an agreement made between people buying and selling things, offering and accepting services, etc □ *strike a bargain*. **2** something offered for sale, or bought, at a low price. ▷ *verb* (*bargained*, *bargaining*) *intr* (*often* **bargain with someone**) to discuss the terms for buying or selling, etc. • **bargainer** *noun, especially in compounds* a person, especially someone of a specified kind, who bargains □ *a hard bargainer*. • **drive a hard bargain** to enter into an agreement only after bargaining hard for the best terms. • **into the bargain** in addition; besides □ *lost his job, and his home into the bargain*. ◷ 14c: from French *bargaine*.

■ **bargain something away** to lose it by bargaining badly.

■ **bargain for something** to be prepared for it □ *We hadn't bargained for a flood*.

■ **bargain on something** *especially with negatives* to rely on it or expect it to happen □ *wasn't bargaining on my mum arriving so early*.

barge /bɑːdʒ/ ▷ *noun* **1** a long flat-bottomed boat used on rivers and canals. **2** a large boat, often decorated, used in ceremonies, celebrations, etc. ▷ *verb* (*barged*, *barging*) *intr* (*especially* **barge about** or **around**) to move in a clumsy ungraceful way. ◷ 14c: French, from Latin *barga*.

■ **barge in** to interrupt a conversation, especially rudely or abruptly.

■ **barge into someone** or **something** to hit or knock them or it clumsily or roughly □ *She barged right into him*.

■ **barge past** or **through** to make one's way rudely or roughly □ *barged past, ignoring the queue*.

bargeboard ▷ *noun, archit* a board, often a decorated one, along the edge of a gable. ◷ 19c.

bargee /bɑːˈdʒiː/ ▷ *noun* (*bargees*) a person in charge of a barge. Also called **bargeman**.

bargepole ▷ *noun* (*bargepoles*) a long pole used to move or guide a barge. • **not touch something** or **someone with a bargepole** *colloq* to refuse to have anything to do with it or them □ *That job sounds terrible — I wouldn't touch it with a bargepole*.

bar graph see BAR CHART

barite /ˈbɛəraɪt/ ▷ *noun, geol* BARYTES.

baritone /ˈbarɪtoun/ ▷ *noun, music* **1** the second lowest male singing voice, between bass and tenor. **2** a singer with such a voice. **3** in written music: a part for such a voice. **4** an instrument with a range between bass and tenor in the saxophone, horn, oboe, etc families. ▷ *adj* referring to the pitch and compass of a baritone □ *He plays baritone sax*. ◷ 17c: from Italian *baritono*, from Greek *barytonos* deep-sounding.

barium /ˈbɛərɪəm/ ▷ *noun* (symbol **Ba**, atomic number 56) *chem* a soft silvery-white metallic element, soluble compounds of which burn with a green flame and are used in fireworks and flares, and as paint pigments. ◷ 19c: from Greek *barys* heavy.

barium meal ▷ *noun, medicine* a preparation of barium sulphate and water, drunk by a patient prior to X-ray of their digestive system, because it cannot be penetrated by X-rays and so forms an opaque shadow showing the outline of the stomach and intestines.

bark[1] ▷ *noun* the short sharp cry of a dog or fox, etc. ▷ *verb* (*barked*, *barking*) *intr* to make this sound. • **bark up the wrong tree** *colloq* to have the wrong idea, follow a mistaken course of action or investigation, etc ◷ 19c, originally US: from raccoon-hunting, in which dogs are used to locate raccoons up in the trees ◷ Anglo-Saxon *beorcan*.

■ **bark out something** to speak it loudly and sharply.

bark[2] ▷ *noun, bot* the tough protective outer layer consisting mainly of dead cells, that covers the stems and roots of woody plants, eg trees. ▷ *verb* (*barked*, *barking*)

1 to scrape or rub off the skin from (one's leg, etc) □ ***barked her shin when she fell.*** **2** to strip or remove the bark from (a tree, etc). ⓘ 14c: from Norse *börkr.*

bark³ see BARQUE

barker ▷ *noun* **1** a person who stands outside a circus or show, etc who shouts to attract customers. **2** a person or animal that barks (see BARK¹).

barley /'bɑːlɪ/ ▷ *noun* (***barleys***) **1** a cereal of the grass family which bears a dense head of grains with long slender AWNS (sense1), and is an important crop in north temperate regions because it is relatively tolerant of low temperatures and poor soil. **2** (*also* **barleycorn**) the grain of this plant, used as feed for animal livestock and, when partially germinated, also used in the brewing of beer and the production of whisky. ⓘ Anglo-Saxon *bærlic* referring to barley.

barley sugar ▷ *noun* a kind of hard orange-coloured sweet, made by melting and cooling sugar, or formerly by boiling sugar in a liquid in which barley has been boiled.

barley water ▷ *noun* a drink made from water in which barley has been boiled, usually with orange or lemon juice added.

bar-line see BAR¹ *noun* 8

barm ▷ *noun* the froth formed on fermenting liquor. ⓘ Anglo-Saxon *beorma*; see also BARMY.

barmaid and **barman** ▷ *noun* a woman or man who serves drinks in a bar or public house. Also called **barperson**. *N Amer equivalent* BARTENDER.

bar mitzvah /bɑː 'mɪtsvə/ ▷ *noun* **1** a Jewish ceremony in which a boy (usually aged 13) formally accepts full religious responsibilities. **2** a boy for whom this ceremony is conducted. **3** the festivities held in recognition of this event. ⓘ 19c: Hebrew, literally 'son of the law'.

barmy ▷ *adj* (***barmier, barmiest)*** *colloq* crazy; mentally unsound. ⓘ 16c in original sense 'bubbling or fermenting' or 'full of BARM'.

barn ▷ *noun* **1** a building in which grain or hay, etc is stored, or for housing cattle, etc. **2** a large bare building. ● **Were you born in a barn?** *colloq* said as a complaint to someone who comes into a house or room, etc leaving the door wide open, ie Do you like, or are you accustomed to, cold draughty places? ⓘ Anglo-Saxon *beren*, from *bere* barley + *ærn* house.

barnacle /'bɑːnəkl/ ▷ *noun* a marine CRUSTACEAN with a shell consisting of several plates, which cements itself firmly by means of its head to rocks, hulls of boats, and other underwater objects. ⓘ 16c.

barnacle goose ▷ *noun* a wild black-and-white goose of N Europe. Often shortened to **barnacle**. ⓘ 13c: as *bernekke*: the bird was believed to hatch from the goose-necked barnacle, a type of limpet found attached to floating timbers, and from which feathery clouds were seen protruding into the water.

barn dance ▷ *noun* **1** a kind of party at which there is music and country dancing, originally held in a barn. **2** a particular kind of country dance, especially a SQUARE DANCE.

barney /'bɑːnɪ/ ▷ *noun* (***barneys***) *colloq* a rough noisy quarrel. ⓘ 19c.

barn owl ▷ *noun* an owl, found in forests and open country worldwide, which has a pale heart-shaped face and feathered legs.

barnstorm ▷ *verb, intr* **1** to tour a country, stopping briefly in each town to give theatrical performances. **2** *N Amer* to travel about the country making political speeches just before an election. ● **barnstormer** *noun.* ⓘ 19c: the theatrical performances were often formerly given in barns.

barnyard ▷ *noun* the area around or adjoining a barn.

barograph /'barougrɑːf/ ▷ *noun, meteorol* a type of BAROMETER that produces a continuous printed chart which records fluctuations in atmospheric pressure over a period of time. ⓘ 19c: from Greek *baros* weight + -GRAPH1.

barometer /bə'rɒmɪtə(r)/ ▷ *noun* **1** *meteorol* an instrument which measures atmospheric pressure, especially in order to predict changes in the weather or to estimate height above sea level. See also ANEROID. **2** anything that indicates a change □ ***a barometer of public opinion.*** ● **barometric** /barou'metrɪk/ *adj.* ● **barometrically** *adverb.* ⓘ 17c: from Greek *baros* weight + -METER.

baron /'barən/ ▷ *noun* **1** a man holding the lowest rank of the British nobility. **2** a powerful businessman in a specified industry □ ***oil baron.*** ⓘ 13c: from Latin *baro, baronis* man.

baroness /'barənes, -'nes/ ▷ *noun* (***baronesses***) **1** a baron's wife. **2** a woman holding the title of baron in her own right.

baronet /'barənət/ ▷ *noun* (abbreviation **Bart**) in the UK: **a** a hereditary title ranking below that of baron, not part of the PEERAGE; **b** a man holding such a title. ● **baronetcy** *noun* (***baronetcies***) the rank or title of a baronet. ⓘ 17c: diminutive of BARON.

baronial /bə'rounɪəl/ ▷ *adj* **1** relating to or suitable for a baron or barons. **2** grand; stately □ ***a baronial hall.*** **3** *archit* referring to a turreted building style especially favoured formerly by the Scottish land-holding class.

barony /'barənɪ/ ▷ *noun* (***baronies***) **1** the rank of baron. **2** land belonging to a baron. **3** *Scottish* a large freehold estate or manor, even though not carrying with it a baron's title or rank. **4** *Irish* a division of a county.

baroque /bə'rɒk/ ▷ *noun* **1** (*also* **Baroque**) a bold complex decorative style of architecture, art, decoration and music, popular in Europe from the late 16c to the early 18c. **2** (*usually* **the Baroque**) this period in European cultural history. ▷ *adj* (*also* **Baroque**) **1** built, designed or written, etc in such a style. **2** said of ornamentation, etc: flamboyant or extravagant. ⓘ 18c: French, from Portuguese *barroco* an irregularly shaped pearl.

barperson see under BARMAID

barque or **bark** /bɑːk/ ▷ *noun* **1** a small sailing ship with three masts. **2** *literary* any boat or small ship. ⓘ 15c: French, from Latin *barca* small boat.

barrack¹ /'barək/ ▷ *noun* (*usually* **barracks**) a building or group of buildings for housing soldiers □ ***sent the men back to barracks.*** ▷ *verb* (***barracked, barracking***) **1** to house (soldiers) in barracks. **2** *intr* to lodge in barracks. ⓘ 17c: from French *baraque* hut.

barrack² /'barək/ ▷ *verb* (***barracked, barracking***) *tr & intr, chiefly Brit* to shout and laugh rudely or hostilely at (a speaker, sports team, etc). See also HECKLE, JEER. ● **barracking** *noun.* ⓘ 19c.

■ **barrack for someone** *Austral & NZ* to support, or shout encouragement to them.

barrack-room ▷ *adj* said of humour, etc: somewhat coarse; not suitable for polite company.

barrack-room lawyer ▷ *noun* a person who, although unqualified, insists on giving advice. ⓘ 1940s: originally, any argumentative soldier who queried military procedure.

barracuda /barə'kjuːdə, -'kuːdə/ ▷ *noun* (***barracuda*** or ***barracudas***) a large tropical sea fish which feeds on other fish and sometimes attacks people. ⓘ 17c: Spanish.

barrage /'barɑːʒ/ ▷ *noun* **1** *military* a long burst of gunfire which keeps an enemy back while soldiers move forward. **2** a large number of things, especially questions or criticisms, etc, coming in quickly and sharply one after the other. **3** a man-made barrier across a river. ⓘ 19c: French, from *barrer* to block.

barrage balloon ▷ *noun* a large balloon attached to the ground by a cable and often with a net hanging from it, used to prevent attack by low-flying aircraft. ◎ 1920s.

barre /bɑːr/ ▷ *noun, ballet* a rail fixed to a wall at waist level, which dancers use to balance themselves while exercising. ◎ 20c: French, literally 'bar'.

barred ▷ *adj* **1** having, marked or fitted with bars □ *a barred window.* **2** closed off; blocked □ *found our way barred.*

barrel[1] /'barəl/ ▷ *noun* **1** a large round container with a flat top and bottom and curving out in the middle, usually made of planks of wood held together with metal bands. **2** a BARRELFUL. **3** a measure of capacity, especially of industrial oil. **4** the long hollow tube-shaped part of a gun or pen, etc. • **have someone over a barrel** to be in a position to get whatever one wants from them; to have them in one's power □ *They've got me over a barrel, - if I don't co-operate I'll lose my job* ◎ 19c: US expression probably alluding to the helpless position of someone laid over a barrel to clear their lungs after being rescued from drowning. • **scrape the bottom of the barrel** see under SCRAPE. ◎ 14c: from French *baril*.

barrel[2] /'barəl/ ▷ *verb* (***barrelled***, ***barrelling***; *US* ***barreled***, ***barreling***) **1** to put something in barrels. **2** *intr, colloq* (*usually* **barrel along** or **past**, *etc*) to move at great speed □ *huge lorries barrelling past us.* ◎ 15c.

barrel-chested ▷ *adj* said of a person: having a large rounded chest or rib cage.

barrelful ▷ *noun* (***barrelfuls***) the amount a barrel can hold.

barrel organ ▷ *noun* a large mechanical instrument which plays music when a handle is turned.

barrel roll ▷ *noun, aerobatics* a complete revolution on the longitudinal axis.

barrel vault ▷ *noun, archit* a vault with a simple semi-cylindrical roof. • **barrel-vaulted** *adj.*

barren /'barən/ ▷ *adj* **1** said of a woman: not able to bear children. **2** said of land or soil, etc: not able to produce crops or fruit, etc. **3** not producing results □ *All my efforts proved barren.* **4** dull; unresponsive. • **barrenness** *noun.* • **barren of something** lacking in or devoid of (a specified quality, etc). ◎ 13c: from French *brahaigne*.

barricade /'barɪkeɪd/ ▷ *noun* a barrier, especially an improvised one made of anything which can be piled up quickly, eg to block a street. ▷ *verb* (***barricaded***, ***barricading***) to block or defend something with a barricade. ◎ 17c: French, from *barrique* barrel, because barricades were often made from barrels.

■ **barricade someone** or **oneself in** to shut them or oneself off behind a barrier.

barrier /'barɪə(r)/ ▷ *noun* **1** a fence, gate or bar, etc put up to defend, block, protect, separate, etc. **2** any thing or circumstance, etc that separates people, items, etc. Often *in compounds* □ *a language barrier.* ◎ 14c: from French *barriere*.

barrier cream ▷ *noun* cream used to protect the skin, especially the skin on the hands, from damage or infection.

barrier method ▷ *noun* any method of contraception that uses an artificial barrier to trap the sperm, either at the point of ejaculation (eg a CONDOM) or in the vagina (eg a CAP (see *noun* 9) or SPERMICIDE).

barrier nursing ▷ *noun* the nursing of infectious patients in isolation from other patients to avoid infecting other patients with an illness unrelated to their original one.

barrier reef ▷ *noun* a long narrow actively-growing coral reef that lies parallel to the coast of a continent or encircles a volcanic island, but is separated from the land by a wide and deep lagoon.

barring /'bɑːrɪŋ/ ▷ *prep* except for; leaving a specified thing out of consideration □ *We shall be there by two o'clock, barring accidents.*

barrister /'barɪstə(r)/ ▷ *noun* in England and Wales: a lawyer qualified to act for someone in the higher law courts. ◎ 15c: either from Latin *barra* bar, or from BAR[1], originally referring to the partition inside the Inns of Court which separated the benchers from the junior counsel and the public, etc.

bar-room ▷ *noun* in a hotel or clubhouse, etc: a room in which there is a bar where alcoholic drinks are served.

barrow[1] /'baroʊ/ ▷ *noun* **1** a small one-wheeled cart used to carry tools, earth, etc. **2** a larger cart, with two or four wheels, from which goods are often sold in the street. ◎ 14c as *barewe*: from Anglo-Saxon *bearwe* a bier.

barrow[2] /'baroʊ/ ▷ *noun, archaeol* a large pile of earth over an ancient grave. ◎ Anglo-Saxon *beorg*, originally meaning 'hill'.

barrow boy ▷ *noun* a boy or man who sells goods from a barrow.

Bart ▷ *abbreviation* (*also* **Bart.**) Baronet.

bartender ▷ *noun, N Amer* someone who serves drinks in a bar; a barperson.

barter /'bɑːtə(r)/ ▷ *verb* (***bartered***, ***bartering***) *tr & intr* to trade or exchange (goods or services) without using money. ▷ *noun* trade by exchanging goods rather than by selling them for money. • **barterer** *noun.* ◎ 15c: from French *barater* to trick or cheat.

baryon /'barɪɒn/ ▷ *noun, physics* a heavy subatomic particle involved in strong interactions with other subatomic particles and composed of three QUARKS bound together by GLUON. See also HADRON, HYPERON, NUCLEON. ◎ 1950s: from Greek *barys* heavy + -ON.

barytes /bə'raɪtiːz/ ▷ *noun, geol* the mineral form of barium sulphate, the chief ore of barium. Also called **barite**. ◎ 18c: from Greek *barys* heavy.

BAS ▷ *abbreviation* **1** Bachelor of Agricultural Science. **2** British Antarctic Survey.

basal /'beɪsəl/ ▷ *adj* **1** at, referring to or forming a base. **2** at the lowest level.

basalt /'basəlt/ ▷ *noun, geol* a fine-grained dark volcanic rock, formed by the solidification of thin layers of molten lava that spread out following a volcanic eruption. • **basaltic** /bə'sɔːltɪk/ *adj.* ◎ 17c: from Greek *basanites*.

bascule /'baskjuːl/ ▷ *noun* **1** an apparatus one end of which rises as the other sinks. **2** (*also* **bascule bridge**) a bridge whose roadway section rises when a counterpoise section descends into a pit. ◎ 17c: French, meaning 'a see-saw'.

base[1] ▷ *noun* **1** the lowest part or bottom; the part which supports something or on which something stands. **2** the origin, root or foundation of something. **3** the headquarters or centre of activity or operations. **4** a starting point. **5** the main part of a mixture □ *Rice is the base of this dish.* **6** *chem* any of a group of chemical compounds that can neutralize an acid to form a salt and water. **7** *baseball* any one of four fixed points on the pitch which players run between. **8** *math* in a numerical system: the number of different symbols used, eg in the BINARY number system the base is two, because only the symbols 0 and 1 are used. **9** *math* in logarithms: the number that, when raised to a certain power (see POWER *noun* 12), has a logarithm equal in value to that power. **10** *geom* the line or surface, usually horizontal, on which a geometric figure rests. ▷ *verb* (***based***, ***basing***) to make or form a base for something or someone. • **get to** or **make first base** see under FIRST. • **off base** *US colloq* wrong; mistaken. ◎ 14c: French, from Latin *basis* pedestal.

■ **base someone** or **something in** or **at somewhere** to post or place them, or give it a headquarters or centre of operations, in or at a specified place.

■ **base something on something** to use it as the basis for something; to found or establish (an argument, etc) on it.

■ **base out** *US* said of prices, etc: to BOTTOM OUT.

base² /beɪs/ ▻ *adj* **1** lacking morals; wicked. **2** not pure. **3** low in value. • **basely** *adverb*. • **baseness** *noun* immorality; wickedness. ◎ 14c as *bas*: from Latin *bassus* low or short.

baseball ▻ *noun* **1** a game played by two teams of nine people using a truncheon-shaped bat and a ball, in which the person batting attempts to run as far as possible round a diamond-shaped pitch formed by four BASEs, aiming to get back to the HOME PLATE to score a run. **2** the ball used in this game. ◎ 19c.

baseless ▻ *adj* having no cause or foundation □ *baseless fears.*

baseline ▻ *noun* **1** one of the two lines which mark the ends of a tennis court. **2** an amount or value taken as a basis for comparison.

basement /'beɪsmənt/ ▻ *noun* the lowest floor of a building, usually below ground level.

base metal ▻ *noun* any metal that readily corrodes, tarnishes or oxidizes on exposure to air, moisture or heat, eg zinc, copper, lead. Opposite of NOBLE METAL.

baseness see under BASE²

base rate ▻ *noun, finance* the rate used by a bank as the base or starting point in fixing its INTEREST RATES to customers.

bases *plural of* BASE¹, BASE², BASIS

BASF ▻ *abbreviation*: *Badische Anilin und Soda-Fabrik* (German), Baden Aniline and Soda Manufactory, a chemical company.

bash ▻ *verb* (***bashed, bashing***) *colloq* **1** to strike or smash something bluntly; to beat or batter. **2** to attack something or someone harshly or maliciously with words □ *likes to bash the unions.* ▻ *noun* (***bashes***) **1** a heavy blow or knock. **2** a mark made by a heavy blow □ *Did he notice the bash on the car door?* **3** *slang* a noisy party. • **have a bash** or **have a bash at something** *colloq* to have a try; to make an attempt at it □ *had a bash at making a soufflé.* ◎ 17c.

■ **bash something down** or **in** to damage or break (eg a door) by striking it very hard.

■ **bash into something** or **someone** to collide violently with it or them.

■ **bash someone** or **something up** to attack them or it physically and violently.

basher ▻ *noun, especially in compounds* someone or something that bashes a specified thing □ *union-basher.* See also BIBLE-BASHER

bashful ▻ *adj* lacking confidence; shy; self-conscious. • **bashfully** *adverb*. • **bashfulness** *noun*. ◎ 16c: from obsolete *bash* to disconcert, abash or lose confidence.

bashing ▻ *noun, colloq* **1** *sometimes in compounds* an instance of severe physical or verbal assault □ *The gang gave Carter a bashing* □ *got such an ear-bashing when I got home.* **2** *especially in compounds* the practice or activity of making strong and often unjustified physical or verbal attacks on a person or group of people one dislikes or is opposed to □ *gay-bashing.* **3** any of various other activities associated with the verb BASH (sense 1) □ *Bible-bashing.*

basho /'baʃoʊ/ ▻ *noun* (*plural* ***basho***) *sumo* a tournament. ◎ 20c: Japanese, literally 'place'.

BASIC or **Basic** /'beɪsɪk/ ▻ *noun* a high-level computer programming language that is relatively simple to learn and has been widely adopted as a standard language by microcomputer manufacturers. ◎ 1960s: acronym from *Beginner's All-purpose Symbolic Instruction Code.*

basic /'beɪsɪk/ ▻ *adj* **1** referring to or forming the base or basis of something. **2** belonging to, or at, a very simple or low level □ *Her grasp of French is basic* □ *basic arithmetic.* **3** without additions □ *basic salary.* **4** *chem* referring or relating to, or forming, a base or bases. **5** *chem* having a pH value greater than 7.0. ▻ *noun* (*usually* **the basics**) the essential parts or facts; the simplest principles. • **basically** *adverb*. ◎ 19c: from BASE¹.

basic process and **basic-oxygen process** ▻ *noun, engineering* the most widely used method of steel production, in which oxygen is blown at high pressure through molten pig iron.

basidium /bə'sɪdɪəm/ ▻ *noun* (*plural* ***basidia*** /-dɪə/) *biol* in fungi: a terminal club-shaped reproductive structure which contains spores. ◎ 19c: from Latin *basis* BASE¹.

basil /'bazɪl/ ▻ *noun* a bushy aromatic annual plant with purplish-green oval leaves and white or purplish flowers, widely cultivated as a culinary herb. ◎ 15c: from Greek *basilikon*, meaning 'royal', suggesting that it may have been used in a royal potion or lotion.

basilar /'bazɪlə(r), 'basɪ-/ ▻ *adj, especially anatomy* relating to, situated at or growing from the base. ◎ 16c: from Latin *basilaris*, irregularly formed from BASIS.

basilica /bə'zɪlɪkə, -'sɪl-/ ▻ *noun* (***basilicas***) **1** an ancient Roman public hall, with a rounded wall at one end and a row of stone pillars along each side, used as a lawcourt, for public assemblies or for commerce. **2** a church shaped like this. ◎ 16c: from Greek *basilike* hall, from *basilikos* royal.

basilisk /'bazɪlɪsk, 'basɪ-/ ▻ *noun* **1** *mythol* a snake which can kill people by breathing on them or looking at them. **2** a type of lizard found in S America. ◎ 14c: from Greek *basiliskos* little king.

basin /'beɪsən/ ▻ *noun* **1** a wide open dish, especially one for holding water. **2** a bowl or sink in a bathroom, etc for washing oneself in. **3** a BASINFUL. **4** a valley or area of land drained by a river, or by the streams running into a river. **5** the deep part of a harbour; a dock. **6** *geol* a large depression into which sediments deposit. **7** *geol* a gently folded structure in which beds dip inwards from the margin to the centre. ◎ 13c: from French *bacin*, from Latin *bacinum* water vessel.

basinful ▻ *noun* (***basinfuls***) the amount a basin can hold. • **have a basinful of something** *colloq* to have more than enough of it □ *I've had a basinful of his whining.*

basis /'beɪsɪs/ ▻ *noun* (*plural* ***bases*** /-siːz/) **1** a principle on which an idea or theory, etc is based. **2** a foundation or starting point □ *a basis for discussion.* **3** the main part of a mixture □ *using tomato as the basis for the sauce.* ◎ 16c in its original meaning 'the lowest part'.

bask /bɑːsk/ ▻ *verb* (***basked, basking***) *intr* **1** to lie in comfort, especially in warmth or sunshine □ *spent all day basking on the beach.* **2** to enjoy and take great pleasure □ *basking in her approval.* ◎ 14c: from Norse *bathask* to bathe.

basket /'bɑːskɪt/ ▻ *noun* **1 a** a container made of plaited or interwoven twigs, rushes, canes or similar flexible material, often with a handle across the top; **b** any similar container. **2** a BASKETFUL. **3** *basketball* **a** either of the nets into which the ball is thrown to score a goal; **b** a goal scored. **4** a collection of similar or related ideas or things, eg the **basket of currencies** (*econ*) the group of European currencies in fixed proportions that is used as a standard against which to assess and control the value of any participating currency, or merely to assess the value of a non-participating currency. ◎ 13c.

basketball ▻ *noun* **1** a game in which two teams of five players score by throwing a ball into a net (called a

basket) fixed horizontally in a raised position at each end of the court and move the ball around by passing and/or dribbling (see DRIBBLE). **2** the ball used in this game. ⓘ 19c.

basket case ▷ *noun, slang* **1** a nervous wreck; someone unable to cope. **2** someone or something completely incapacitated, worn out or useless. ⓘ Early 20c: originally US, applied to a person with both arms and legs amputated; in sense 1 the term refers to the practice of teaching mental patients basketwork as therapy.

basket chair ▷ *noun* a chair made from strips of wood or cane woven together.

basketful ▷ *noun* (***basketfuls***) the amount a basket can hold.

basketry ▷ *noun* (***basketries***) the art or business of making baskets and similar articles of BASKETWORK.

basketweave ▷ *noun* a form of weaving using two or more yarns in the warp and weft to produce an effect similar to BASKETWORK.

basketwork ▷ *singular noun* **1** articles made of strips of wood, cane, twigs or similar flexible material, woven together. **2** the art of making such articles.

basking shark ▷ *noun* a large but harmless shark, the second-largest living fish, which lives in oceanic surface waters and feeds entirely on plankton.

basmati /baz'matɪ/ and **basmati rice** ▷ *noun* a type of long-grain rice that is naturally aromatic, eaten especially with Indian food.

Basque /bɑːsk/ ▷ *noun* **1** a member of a people living in the western Pyrenees, in Spain and France. **2** the language spoken by these people, that is unrelated to any other European language. ▷ *adj* belonging or relating to the Basque people or their language □ ***Basque nationalism.*** ⓘ 19c: French, from Latin *Vasco*.

basque /bɑːsk/ ▷ *noun* **1** a tight-fitting bodice for women, often with a continuation below the waist to the hips, worn either as an undergarment or as a lightweight top. Compare BODY *noun* 13, BUSTIER. **2** a continuation of a bodice extending below the waist. **3** a similar area on a skirt, to which pleats or gathers are often attached. **4** a short-skirted jacket. ⓘ 19c, originally in sense 2, applying to a man's waistcoat: from BASQUE.

bas-relief /bɑːrɪ'liːf/ ▷ *noun, art* **1** sculpture in which the relief figures are only slightly raised from the stone or wood from which they are carved, none of them being fully undercut. **2** this technique in sculpture. See RELIEF 8. ⓘ 17c: French, literally 'low relief', from Italian *basso rilievo*.

bass¹ /beɪs/ ▷ *noun* (***basses***) *music* **1** the lowest male singing voice. **2** a singer with such a voice. **3** a musical part written for such a voice or for an instrument of the lowest range. **4** *colloq* a bass instrument, especially a bass guitar or a double-bass □ ***Introducing, on bass, Alan King.*** **5 a** low frequency sound as output from an amplifier, etc □ ***The bass is too heavy on this track***; **b** a knob or dial that adjusts this sound □ ***fiddled with the bass on the stereo.*** ▷ *adj* said of a musical instrument, voice or sound: low in pitch and range. ⓘ 15c as *bas* (see etymology of BASE²): the Italian form *basso* later influenced the spelling in musical contexts.

bass² /bas/ ▷ *noun* (***bass*** or ***basses***) **1** a marine fish, found in European coastal waters, which has a greenish-grey body with silvery sides, spiny fins, and is an important commercial and sport fish. **2** any of various freshwater and marine fishes, especially N American species, which have spiny fins similar to those of the common bass. ⓘ 16c as *bace*: from Anglo-Saxon *bærs* perch.

bass clef /beɪs —/ ▷ *noun, music* **1** a sign (𝄢) placed at the beginning of a piece of written music, which fixes the note F below middle C on the fourth line of the stave which follows. Also called **F-clef**. **2** *loosely* the bass stave in a piece of music.

bass drum /beɪs —/ ▷ *noun* a large drum that produces a very low sound.

basset /'basɪt/ and **basset hound** ▷ *noun* a breed of dog with a long body, smooth hair, short legs and long drooping ears. ⓘ 17c: French, from an old diminutive of *bas* low or short.

basset horn /'basɪt — / ▷ *noun* a musical instrument of the clarinet family, with a lower range of pitch than that of a standard clarinet. ⓘ 19c: a partial translation of French *cor de bassette* and Italian *corno di bassetto*; see etymology of BASSET.

bass guitar and (*especially colloq*) **bass** /beɪs/ ▷ *noun* a guitar, usually an electric one, similar in pitch and range to the double-bass, frequently used in popular music bands to provide the bass sound and rhythm (see BASS¹).

bassinet /'basɪnɛt/ ▷ *noun* **1** a baby's basket-like bed or pram, usually covered at one end with a hood. **2** a bed for the care of a baby in hospital, often made of plastic material, with necessary equipment provided. ⓘ 19c: French diminutive of *bassin* basin.

bassist /'beɪsɪst/ ▷ *noun* a person who plays a bass guitar or double-bass.

bassoon /bə'suːn/ ▷ *noun* a large woodwind instrument which produces a very low sound, formed of a long jointed wooden pipe doubled back on itself, fitted with metal keys and a curved crook with a double reed. • **bassoonist** *noun*. ⓘ 18c: from Italian *bassone*, from *basso* low.

bast ▷ *noun* **1** *bot* the conductive material in a plant; PHLOEM. **2** threads of the soft inner bark of some trees, woven together and used to make ropes, mats, etc. ⓘ Anglo-Saxon *bæst*.

bastard /'bɑːstəd, 'bastəd/ ▷ *noun* **1** *often offensive* a child born of parents not married to each other. **2** *coarse slang* **a** a term of abuse or sympathy for a man □ ***What a rotten bastard!*** □ ***poor bastard!***; **b** a man generally; a chap □ ***lucky bastard.*** **3** *coarse slang* something annoying or difficult □ ***This wallpaper is a bastard to hang.*** ▷ *adj* **1** said of a person: born to parents not married to each other; ILLEGITIMATE □ ***bastard son.*** **2** not genuine, standard, original or pure □ ***bastard copy.*** • **bastardy** *noun* (***bastardies***) the state of being a bastard. ⓘ 13c: French; the term may have meant 'someone conceived on a pack-saddle' (French *bast*), since these were used as makeshift beds.

bastardize or **bastardise** ▷ *verb* (***bastardized, bastardizing***) to make something less genuine or pure. • **bastardization** *noun*. • **bastardized** *adj*.

baste¹ /beɪst/ ▷ *verb* (***basted, basting***) to pour hot fat, butter or juices over something (especially roasting meat), during cooking. ⓘ 15c.

baste² /beɪst/ ▷ *verb* (***basted, basting***) to sew (eg a seam) with temporary loose stitches. Also TACK. ⓘ 15c: from French *bastir*, from German *besten* to sew.

baste³ /beɪst/ ▷ *verb* (***basted, basting***) to beat someone or something soundly; to thrash them. • **basting** *noun* □ ***That boy deserves a basting.*** ⓘ 16c.

bastinado /bastɪ'neɪdoʊ/ ▷ *noun* (***bastinadoes***) beating of the soles of the feet with a stick as a form of torture or punishment. ▷ *verb* (***bastinadoed, bastinadoing***) to beat someone on the soles of the feet with a stick. ⓘ 16c: from Spanish *bastonada*, from *bastón* a stick.

bastion /'bastɪən/ ▷ *noun* **1** a kind of tower which sticks out at an angle from a castle wall. **2** a person, place or thing regarded as a defender of a principle, etc □ ***He is a bastion of religious freedom.*** ⓘ 16c: French, from Italian *bastione*, from *bastire* to build.

BASW ▷ *abbreviation* British Association of Social Workers.

BAT ▷ *abbreviation* British-American Tobacco Company.

bat¹ ▷ *noun* **1** a shaped piece of wood, with a flat or curved surface, for hitting the ball in cricket, baseball, table-tennis, etc. Compare RACKET. **2** *chiefly cricket* a batsman or batswoman. **3** a flat round short-handled signalling device used by a BATSMAN (sense 2) to guide aircraft on the ground. **4** a quick and usually gentle or inoffensive blow with a flat hand or other flat-sided object, etc. ▷ *verb* (***batted, batting***) **1** *intr, cricket, baseball, etc* to take a turn at hitting a ball with a bat; to have an innings □ *get a chance to bat before lunch.* **2** to hit something with, or as if with, a bat. ● **off one's own bat** unaided. ⓒ Anglo-Saxon *batt* club or stick.

bat² ▷ *noun* any of numerous species of small nocturnal mammals which have a fur-covered body and membranous wings, and in most cases hunt for food in darkness by relying mainly on ECHOLOCATION. ● **have bats in the belfry** *colloq* to be crazy or slightly mad. See also BATS, BATTY. ● **like a bat out of hell** *colloq* very fast. ⓒ 16c; 14c as *bakke*.

bat³ ▷ *verb* (***batted, batting***) to open and close (one's eyelids) very quickly, usually to attract sympathy or admiration □ *batted her eyelashes coyly at him.* ● **not bat an eye** or **eyelid** *colloq, originally US* to show no surprise or emotion □ *He didn't bat an eye when he heard the news.* ⓒ 17c as a variant of *bate* (used of a hawk) to flutter or flap (when on the leash).

batch¹ ▷ *noun* **1** a number of things or people dealt with at the same time □ *a batch of loaves* □ *saw another batch of applicants today.* **2** in banking: **a** a number of credit items and the corresponding debit items listed to ensure that the totals of each agree; **b** (**the batch**) the process of listing and agreeing the items in such a batch □ *This cheque hasn't been through the batch yet.* ▷ *verb* (***batched, batching***) **1** to arrange or treat something in batches. **2** *computing* to deal with (data) by batch processing. ⓒ 15c as *bache*, meaning 'a baking' or 'a quantity of bread baked in one baking', from Anglo-Saxon *bacan* to bake.

batch² ▷ *verb* (***batched, batching***) *intr, Austral & NZ colloq* said of a man: to cook and clean, etc for himself. ⓒ 19c: from *bach* short for BACHELOR.

batch file ▷ *noun, computing* a text file containing a series of commands which are executed in order when the name of the file is called.

batch processing ▷ *noun, computing* the processing of several batches of similar data by a single computer at the same time.

bate see under BAIT

bated ▷ *adj* diminished; restrained. Now usually only used in the phrase ● **with bated breath** hushed and tense with excitement, fear or anxiety □ *watched with bated breath as the lion-tamer entered the cage.* ⓒ 14c: from *bate* to lessen, moderate or beat down, from ABATE.

> ***bated***
>
> There is often a spelling confusion between **bated** and **baited**.

bath /bɑːθ/ ▷ *noun* (***baths*** /bɑːðz, bɑːθs/) **1** a large open container for water, in which to wash the whole body while sitting in it. **2** an act of washing the body in a bath. **3** the water filling a bath □ *run a bath.* **4** (**the baths**) a public swimming pool. **5** *in compounds* a liquid with or in which something is washed, heated or steeped, etc, as a medicinal or cleansing treatment, etc or as part of a technical process such as developing photographs □ *acid bath* □ *baby bath.* **6** *especially in compounds* a container in which something is washed, heated, or steeped, etc, of appropriate size and shape for the specific purpose □ *an eye bath.* ▷ *verb* (***bathed, bathing***) **1** to wash someone or something in a bath □ *Have you bathed the children?* **2** *intr* (*also* **have a bath**, or **take a bath**) to wash oneself in a bath □ *She baths every evening.* See also BATHE². ⓒ Anglo-Saxon *bæth*.

Bath bun ▷ *noun* a small sweet spicy cake containing dried fruit. ⓒ 19c: named after Bath in SW England where they were originally made.

Bath chair or **bath chair** ▷ *noun, especially formerly* a large wheeled and usually hooded chair in which an invalid can be pushed. ⓒ 19c: named after Bath in SW England where they were used at the spa.

bathcube ▷ *noun* a small block of bath salts.

bathe /beɪð/ ▷ *verb* (***bathed, bathing***) **1** *intr* to swim in the sea, etc for pleasure. **2** *intr, chiefly N Amer* to wash oneself in a bath; to take a bath. **3** to wash or treat (part of the body, etc) with water, or with a liquid, etc to clean it or to lessen pain □ *Bathe the wound every hour.* **4** (*often* **bathe something** or **someone in** or **with something**) to cover and surround it or them (eg in light); to suffuse □ *Sunlight bathed the room.* ▷ *noun* (***bathes***) an act of swimming in the sea, etc; a swim or dip. ⓒ Anglo-Saxon *bathian* to wash.

> ***bathe, bath***
>
> In British English, **bathe** refers to swimming, or to therapeutic washing, eg of wounds or sore feet; **bath** is the verb for washing yourself or someone in a bath. In the past tense, the same form **bathed** is used (with different pronunciations when spoken), which contributes to the uncertainty. In American English, **bathe** has both meanings.

bather /ˈbeɪðə(r)/ ▷ *noun* **1** a person who bathes or is bathing. **2** (**bathers**) *Austral & NZ* a swimming costume □ *Hang your bathers up to dry.*

bathetic /bəˈθɛtɪk/ ▷ *adj* said of speech or writing: characterized by BATHOS.

bathing cap ▷ *noun* a tight rubber cap worn on the head to keep the hair dry and out of the way when swimming.

bathing costume ▷ *noun* a swimming costume or swimsuit.

batholith /ˈbaθoulɪθ/ ▷ *noun, geol* a large igneous rock mass, typically granite, that has intruded while molten into the surrounding rock. Also called **batholite** /-laɪt/. ⓒ Early 20c: from Greek *bathos* depth + -LITH.

Bath Oliver ▷ *noun* a type of plain biscuit, usually eaten with cheese. ⓒ 19c: named after Dr William Oliver of Bath who devised the recipe in the 18c.

bathos /ˈbeɪθɒs/ ▷ *noun* in speech or writing: a sudden descent from very important, serious or beautiful ideas to very ordinary or trivial ones. ⓒ 18c in this sense: Greek, meaning 'depth'.

> ***bathos***
>
> A word sometimes confused with this one is **pathos**.

bathrobe ▷ *noun* a loose towelling coat used especially before and after taking a bath.

bathroom ▷ *noun* **1** a room containing a bath and now usually other washing facilities, a lavatory, etc. **2** *especially N Amer* a room with a lavatory.

bath salts ▷ *plural noun* a sweet-smelling substance in the form of large soluble grains, which perfumes and softens the water in a bath.

bathtub ▷ *noun* **1** *especially N Amer* a BATH (*noun* 1). **2** an unfixed moveable bath without taps.

bathy- /baθɪ/ ▷ *combining form, signifying* deep. ⓒ From Greek *bathys* deep.

bathymetry /baˈθɪmətrɪ/ ▷ *noun, geol* the measurement of the depths of sea-bottom features in large bodies of water, especially by ECHO-SOUNDING. ⓒ 19c.

bathyscaphe or **bathyscape** /ˈbaθɪskeɪf/ ▷ *noun* an electrically-powered crewed vessel with a spherical observation cabin on its underside, used for exploring the ocean depths. ⓘ 1940s: from Greek *skaphos* ship.

bathysphere ▷ *noun* a deep-sea observation chamber, consisting of a watertight steel sphere that is lowered and raised from a surface vessel, eg a ship, by means of cables, now largely superseded by the bathyscaphe. ⓘ 1930s.

batik /bəˈtiːk/ ▷ *noun* **1** a technique of printing coloured patterns on cloth, in which those parts not to be coloured or dyed are covered with wax. **2** cloth coloured by this method. ⓘ 19c: Malay, literally 'painted'.

batman ▷ *noun* an officer's personal servant in the armed forces. ⓘ 18c: from French *bât* pack-saddle.

baton /ˈbatən, -tɒn; *US* bəˈtɑːn/ ▷ *noun* **1** a light thin stick used by the conductor of an orchestra or choir, etc to direct them. **2** a short heavy stick carried by a policeman as a weapon. Also called TRUNCHEON. *N Amer equivalent* NIGHT STICK. **3** a short stick passed from one runner to another in a relay race. **4** a stick carried, tossed and twirled, etc by a person at the head of a marching band. • **under the baton of someone** said of a choir or orchestra, etc: conducted by them. ⓘ 16c, meaning 'a stick used as a weapon': from French *bâton* stick.

baton, batten

There is sometimes a spelling confusion between **baton** and **batten**.

baton charge ▷ *noun* an operation in which police officers, with batons drawn for use, make a swift forward movement against a hostile crowd.

baton round ▷ *noun, formal* a plastic or rubber bullet, as used in riot control.

bats ▷ *adj, colloq* crazy; BATTY[1]. ⓘ 1930s: from the phrase HAVE BATS IN THE BELFRY; see under BAT[2].

batsman ▷ *noun* **1** *chiefly cricket* (*also* **batswoman**) a man or woman who bats or is batting. Also called BAT. Compare BATTER[3]. **2** someone whose job is to assist aircraft to taxi into position, by signalling with a pair of lightweight bats.

battalion /bəˈtalɪən/ ▷ *noun* an army unit made up of several smaller companies (see COMPANY *noun* 6), and forming part of a larger BRIGADE. ⓘ 16c: Italian *battaglione* a squadron of soldiers.

batten /ˈbatən/ ▷ *noun* **1** a long flat piece of wood used for keeping other pieces in place. **2** a strip of wood used to fasten the covers over the hatches in a ship's deck, etc. ▷ *verb* (***battened, battening***) to fasten, strengthen or shut (eg a door) with battens. ▷ **batten down the hatches 1** *colloq* to prepare for a danger or crisis. **2** *naut* to fasten covers over the hatches in a ship's deck using battens, so as to secure them before a storm, etc. ⓘ 17c: a variant of BATON.

Battenburg /ˈbatənbɜːg/ and **Battenburg cake** ▷ *noun* an oblong marzipan-covered cake made typically of yellow and pink sponge which forms a chequered pattern when sliced. ⓘ 20c: presumed to be named after Battenberg, a town in Germany.

batter[1] /ˈbatə(r)/ ▷ *verb* (***battered, battering***) **1** *tr & intr* to strike or hit something or someone hard and often, or continuously. **2** to damage or wear something through continual use. • **battered** *adj* **1** said of a person: suffering repeated violence from someone else, especially from a partner or parent □ ***battered baby***. **2** said of an object: damaged or worn, through continual use □ ***a battered old raincoat***. • **battering** *noun* a beating. ⓘ 14c: from French *battre* to beat.

■ **batter something down** or **in** to break it down or destroy it by battering.

batter[2] /ˈbatə(r)/ ▷ *noun* a mixture of eggs, flour and either milk or water, beaten together and used in cooking, eg to coat fish or to make pancakes. • **battered** *adj* said of fish or other food: coated in batter and deep-fried. ⓘ 15c: probably from BATTER[1].

batter[3] /ˈbatə(r)/ ▷ *noun, especially baseball* a person who bats or is batting. See also BATSMAN.

battered baby syndrome and **battered child syndrome** ▷ *noun* a collection of symptoms, such as bruises, burns and fractures, found in a baby or young child, and caused by violence on the part of a parent or other adult suffering from social and psychological disturbance.

battering-ram ▷ *noun* a large wooden beam with a metal head, formerly used in war for breaking down walls or gates.

battery /ˈbatərɪ/ ▷ *noun* (***batteries***) **1** a device that converts chemical energy into electrical energy in the form of direct current, eg a car battery, or a DRY BATTERY used as a portable energy source in a torch, etc. See also DRY CELL, ELECTROLYTIC CELL. **2** a number of similar things kept, used, arranged or encountered, etc, especially if the effect is rather threatening or daunting □ ***On the table lay a whole battery of surgical instruments.*** **3 a** a long line of small tiered cages in which hens are kept, arranged so that the eggs they lay run down into wire containers outside the cages; **b** a similar arrangement of compartments for the intensive rearing of any other animal. **4** *law* intentional physical attack on a person, including touching the clothes or body in a threatening manner, not necessarily involving damage. See also ASSAULT AND BATTERY. **5 a** a group of heavy guns with their equipment; **b** the place where they are mounted. **6** a unit of artillery or its personnel. ⓘ 16c: from French *batterie*, from *battre* to strike or beat.

batting ▷ *noun* **1** in ball games such as cricket: using, managing, playing or hitting with a bat. **2** cotton fibre prepared in sheets and used for quilts, etc originally made by beating raw cotton by hand to remove impurities. ⓘ 17c: from BAT[1] in general sense of hitting with or using a bat.

batting average see under AVERAGE

battle /ˈbatəl/ ▷ *noun* **1** a fight between opposing armies, naval or air forces, etc or people. **2** a competition between opposing groups or people □ ***a battle of wits***. **3** a long or difficult struggle □ ***a battle for equality***. ▷ *verb* (***battled, battling***) *intr* **1** to fight. **2** to struggle; to campaign vigorously or defiantly. • **do battle** *especially literary* to fight. ⓘ 13c: ultimately from Latin *battuere* to beat.

battle-axe ▷ *noun* **1** *colloq* a fierce and domineering older woman. **2** *historical* a type of broad-bladed axe used in warfare in the Middle Ages. ⓘ 14c in sense 2: 19c US slang in sense 1.

battle-axe block ▷ *noun, Austral, NZ* a plot of land without a street frontage, with access to and from the street via a drive or lane.

battle-blouse and **battle-dress blouse** see BLOUSE *noun* 2

battle-cruiser ▷ *noun* a large warship, the same size as a battleship but faster and with fewer guns.

battle-cry ▷ *noun* **1** a shout given by soldiers charging into battle. **2** a slogan used to strengthen or arouse support for a cause or campaign, etc.

battledress ▷ *noun* a soldier's ordinary uniform.

battle fatigue and **combat fatigue** ▷ *noun, psychol, medicine* POST-TRAUMATIC STRESS DISORDER caused by the experience of military combat.

battlefield and **battleground** ▷ *noun* **1** the place at which a battle is or was fought. **2** a site, subject or area of intense disagreement □ ***a political battlefield***.

battlement /ˈbatəlmənt/ ▷ *noun* a low wall around the top of a castle, etc with gaps for shooting through. ⓘ 14c: from French *bataillement*, from *batailler* to provide something with ramparts.

battler ▻ *noun* **1 a)** someone who battles; **b** *now especially* a person who fights tirelessly and resolutely against difficult circumstances, etc. **2** *Austral, NZ* someone who scrapes a living by any means available.

battle royal ▻ *noun* (***battles royal***) **1 a** a big noisy argument or free-for-all; **b** a general brawl or meleé. **2** a fight involving more than two combatants, specifically one in which the last man or fighting cock left standing is the victor. ◷ 17c, originally in sense 2.

battleship ▻ *noun* the largest type of warship.

batty ▻ *adj* (***battier, battiest***) **1** *colloq* crazy; eccentric. **2** batlike; referring to a BAT². ◷ 16c in sense 2.

bauble /'bɔːbəl/ ▻ *noun* **1** a small cheap ornament or piece of jewellery; a trinket. **2** a round coloured decoration, made from fibre glass and hung on Christmas trees. ◷ 14c as *babel*: French, meaning 'a child's toy'.

baud /bɔːd/ and **baud rate** ▻ *noun* **1** *computing* in a computer system: the number of bits or other signalling elements that can be transmitted between computers per second. **2** *telecomm* in telegraphy: the number of pulses and spaces that can be transmitted per second. ◷ 1930s: named after French inventor J M E Baudot (1845–1903).

baulk see BALK

bauxite /'bɔːksaɪt/ ▻ *noun, geol* a white, yellow, red or brown clay-like substance, which is the main ore of aluminium and is formed by weathering of igneous rocks in tropical regions. ◷ 19c: French, named after Les Baux in S France, where it was first found.

bawdy /'bɔːdɪ/ ▻ *adj* (***bawdier, bawdiest***) said of language or writing, etc: containing coarsely humorous references to sex; lewd. • **bawdily** *adverb*. • **bawdiness** *noun*. ◷ 16c, meaning 'appropriate for or relating to a *bawd*' (the now archaic word for a woman who keeps a brothel): from French *baude* merry or dissolute.

bawl /bɔːl/ ▻ *verb* (***bawled, bawling***) (*also* **bawl out**) *tr & intr* to cry or shout loudly ◻ *a child bawling for its mother* ◻ *She bawled out the price rudely.* ◷ 15c: probably from Latin *baulare* to bark.

■ **bawl someone out** *colloq* to scold them angrily ◻ *Dad bawled me out before I could explain.*

bay¹ ▻ *noun* (***bays***) a body of water that forms a wide-mouthed indentation in the coastline, larger than a COVE. Compare GULF 1. ◷ 14c: from French *baie*.

bay² ▻ *noun* (***bays***) **1** an enclosed or partly enclosed area within a building, vessel, etc for storage or some other purpose. **2** *in compounds* a compartment for storing or carrying, eg in an aircraft ◻ *bomb bay*. **3 a** a PARKING BAY; **b** a LOADING BAY. **4** a small area of a room set back into a wall. See also BAY WINDOW. **5** *Brit* a section of side track in a railway station, especially one where a branch line terminates. ◷ 14c, meaning 'an opening in a wall' or 'space between two columns': from French *baer* to gape.

bay³ ▻ *adj* said of a horse: reddish-brown in colour, usually with black mane and tail. ▻ *noun* (***bays***) a bay-coloured horse. ◷ 14c: from Latin *badius* chestnut-coloured.

bay⁴ ▻ *noun* (***bays***) **1** any of various evergreen trees of the LAUREL family with shiny dark-green leaves, especially a species whose dried leaves are often used as a flavouring agent (**bayleaf**) during the cooking of soups and stews. Also called **bay tree, sweet bay**. **2** any of various other trees and shrubs, such as magnolias. **3** (*usually* **bays**) a wreath of bay leaves, traditionally worn on the head by champions in some competitions, etc. ◷ 15c in obsolete sense 'berry' (especially that of the bay tree): from Latin *baca*.

bay⁵ ▻ *verb* (***bayed, baying***) **1** *intr* said especially of large dogs: to make a deep howling bark or cry, especially when hunting. **2** *intr* said of a crowd, etc: to howl or shout loudly and with a deep menacing tone. **3** said especially of large dogs: to bay or howl at something ◻ *bay the moon*. **4** to utter something by baying ◻ *baying their welcome*. **5** to bring (a hunted animal) to bay. ▻ *noun* (***bays***) the baying sound of a dog, etc. • **at bay** said of a hunted animal: not able to escape, but forced to face its attacker or attackers. • **bring something** or **someone to bay** to trap it or them; to get (one's prey or opponent) into a position that leaves them no way out. • **keep something** or **someone at bay 1** to fight it or them off; to keep it or them from overwhelming (usually oneself) ◻ *keeping poverty at bay* ◻ *some soup to keep the cold at bay*. **2** to keep it or them at a distance ◻ *The boxer kept his opponent at bay.* ◷ 14c: from French *abai* barking; originally an imitation of the sound.

bayberry see WAX MYRTLE

bayonet /'beɪənɪt/ ▻ *noun* **1** a steel knife that fixes to the muzzle of a soldier's rifle. **2** (*also* **bayonet fitting**) a type of fitting for a light bulb or camera lens, etc in which prongs on its side fit into slots to hold it in place. ▻ *verb* (***bayoneted, bayoneting***) to stab someone or something with a bayonet. ◷ 17c: named after Bayonne in SW France, where they were first made.

bayou /'baɪuː/ ▻ *noun* (***bayous***) in the US: a marshy offshoot of a lake or river. ◷ 18c: Louisiana French, from Choctaw (a Native American language) *bayuk* little river.

bay window ▻ *noun* a three-sided or rounded window that juts out from the wall of a building. • **bay-windowed** *adj*.

bazaar /bə'zɑː(r)/ ▻ *noun* **1** a sale of goods, etc usually in order to raise money for a particular organization or purpose. **2** a shop selling miscellaneous goods. **3** in Eastern countries: a market place or exchange. ◷ 16c in sense 3: from Persian *bazar* market.

bazooka /bə'zuːkə/ ▻ *noun* (***bazookas***) a portable anti-tank gun which fires small rockets. ◷ 1940s: from the name of a toy wind-instrument (1930s) similar to the KAZOO.

bazouki see BOUZOUKI

BB ▻ *abbreviation* **1** Boys' Brigade. **2** on pencils: soft black.

BBB ▻ *abbreviation* on pencils: softest black.

BBBC ▻ *abbreviation* British Boxing Board of Control.

BBC ▻ *abbreviation* British Broadcasting Corporation.

BBFC ▻ *abbreviation* **1** British Board of Film Censors. **2** British Board of Film Classification.

BBSRC ▻ *abbreviation* Biotechnology and Biological Sciences Research Council.

BC ▻ *abbreviation* **1** in dates: before Christ, used together with a figure to indicate a specified number of years before that in which Christ was once thought to have been born. Compare AD, BCE. See also COMMON ERA. **2** *Canadian province* British Columbia.

BC

BC follows the year number ◻ *753 BC*. Compare Usage Note at **AD**.

BCC ▻ *abbreviation* British Council of Churches.

BCD ▻ *abbreviation, computing* binary-coded decimal.

BCE ▻ *abbreviation* in dates: before the Common Era, sometimes used instead of BC, as a culturally neutral notation. Compare AD.

BCG or **bcg** ▻ *abbreviation* bacillus Calmette-Guérin, a vaccine given to a person to prevent tuberculosis.

BCL ▻ *abbreviation* Bachelor of Common Law.

BCom or **BComm** ▻ *abbreviation* Bachelor of Commerce.

BD ▻ *abbreviation* **1** Bachelor of Divinity. **2** *IVR* Bangladesh.

BDA ▻ *abbreviation* British Dental Association.

BDI ▻ *abbreviation*: *Bundesverband des Deutschen Industrie* (German), Federation of German Industry.

BDS ▻ *abbreviation* **1** Bachelor of Dental Surgery. **2** *IVR* Barbados.

BE ▻ *abbreviation* **1** Bachelor of Education. **2** Bachelor of Engineering. **3** bill of exchange.

Be ▻ *symbol, chem* beryllium.

be /biː/ ▻ *verb* (***been***, ***being***; *present tense* ***am***, ***are***, ***is***; *past tense* ***was***, ***were***) *intr* **1** to exist or live □ ***I think, therefore I am.*** **2** to occur or take place □ ***Lunch is in an hour.*** **3** to occupy a position in space □ ***She is at home.*** **4** *in past tense* to go □ ***He's never been to Italy.*** **5** to remain or continue without change □ ***Let it be.*** **6** (as a COPULA) used to link a subject and what is said about it □ ***She is a doctor*** □ ***He is ill.*** **7** used with the INFINITIVE form of a verb to express a possibility, command, intention, outcome, etc □ ***if it were to rain*** □ ***We are to come tomorrow*** □ ***It was not to be.*** ▻ *auxiliary verb* **1** used with a past PARTICIPLE to form a PASSIVE construction □ ***The film was shown last night.*** **2** used with a present PARTICIPLE to form the PROGRESSIVE tenses □ ***He was running.*** • **be someone** to suit them □ ***That hat really isn't her.*** • **be that as it may** although that may be true. • **the be-all and end-all** the only important issue or overriding aim. ⓔ From Anglo-Saxon *beon* to live or exist, and Anglo-Saxon *weran* to be.

be- /bɪ/ ▻ *prefix, signifying* **1** all over or all around; thoroughly or completely □ ***beset*** □ ***befuddle*** □ ***bedeck.*** **2** considering something or someone as, or causing it or them to be or feel, a specified thing □ ***befriend*** □ ***belittle*** □ ***benumb.*** **3** having, covered with or affected by, a specified thing □ ***bejewelled*** □ ***beribboned*** □ ***bedevilled.*** **4** affecting someone or something by a particular action □ ***bereave*** □ ***betroth*** □ ***bewail.*** ⓔ 16c, originally meaning 'about': from Anglo-Saxon *bi-* by.

BEAB ▻ *abbreviation* British Electrical Approvals Board.

beach /biːtʃ/ ▻ *noun* (***beaches***) the sandy or stony shore of a sea or lake. ▻ *verb* (***beached***, ***beaching***) to push, pull or drive (especially a boat) on to a beach. ⓔ 16c, first as a dialect word, meaning SHINGLE[1].

beach-ball ▻ *noun* a large colourful and usually inflatable ball for playing games with at the beach, in the swimming pool, etc.

beachcomber /ˈbiːtʃkoumə(r)/ ▻ *noun* someone who searches beaches for things of interest or value washed up by the tide. • **beachcombing** *noun*. ⓔ 19c: originally meaning 'a long rolling wave', later someone who loafs about on the coast at a Pacific seaport.

beachhead ▻ *noun, military* an area of shore captured from the enemy, on which an army can land men and equipment. ⓔ 1940s: modelled (illogically) on BRIDGEHEAD.

beacon /ˈbiːkən/ ▻ *noun* **1** a warning or guiding device for aircraft or ships, eg a lighthouse or (*in full* **radio beacon**) a radio transmitter that broadcasts signals. **2** a fire on a hill, mountain or high ground, lit as a signal. **3** *Brit* chiefly in place names: a hill, etc on which a beacon could be lit. **4** something that warns of danger. **5** a BELISHA BEACON. ⓔ Anglo-Saxon *beacen* in obsolete sense 'a sign'; 14c in sense 2.

bead /biːd/ ▻ *noun* **1** a small and usually round ball made of glass or stone, etc strung with others, eg in a necklace. **2** (**beads**) a string of beads worn as jewellery, or one used when praying (a ROSARY). **3** a small drop of liquid □ ***beads of sweat.*** **4** BEADING. **5** the front sight of a gun. ▻ *verb* (***beaded***, ***beading***) to decorate something with beads or beading. • **beaded** *adj*. • **draw a bead on something** *colloq* to aim a gun at it. • **tell one's beads** to pray using a rosary. ⓔ Anglo-Saxon *bed* in obsolete sense 'a prayer', from *biddan* to pray.

beading ▻ *noun* **1** thin strips of patterned wood used to decorate the edges of furniture or walls, etc. **2** a small convex moulding formed on wood or other material. Also called BEAD.

beadle /ˈbiːdəl/ ▻ *noun Brit* **1** a person who leads formal processions in church or in some old universities and institutions. **2** in Scotland: a church officer who attends the minister. **3** *formerly* in England: a minor parish official who had the power to punish minor offences. ⓔ 16c: from Anglo-Saxon *bydel*, from *beodan* to proclaim.

beady ▻ *adj* (***beadier***, ***beadiest***) **1** *usually derog* said of a person's eyes: small, round and bright. **2** covered with beads or bubbles.

beady-eyed ▻ *adj* **1** said of a person or animal: with eyes that are small, round and bright. **2** said of a person: observant; sharp-eyed.

beagle /ˈbiːgəl/ ▻ *noun* a breed of small hunting-dog with a short coat. ▻ *verb* (***beagled***, ***beagling***) *intr* to hunt with beagles. • **beagler** *noun*. • **beagling** *noun*. ⓔ 15c: possibly from French *béguele*, from *baer* to gape + *goule* throat or mouth.

beak /biːk/ ▻ *noun* **1** the horny projecting jaws of a bird. Also called BILL. **2** any pointed projection that resembles this, eg the projecting jaws of certain fishes and other animals. **3** *slang* a nose, especially a big pointed one. **4** *Brit, dated slang* a headmaster, judge or magistrate. **5** *naut hist* an iron point projecting from the bow of an ancient galley, for ramming and piercing the enemy's vessel. • **beaked** *adj*. • **beaky** *adj*. ⓔ 13c: from French *bec*.

beaker /ˈbiːkə(r)/ ▻ *noun* **1** a large drinking-glass, or a large cup (often a plastic one) without a handle. **2** a deep glass container, usually one with a lip for pouring, used by chemists in laboratory work. **3** a BEAKERFUL. ⓔ 14c: from Norse *bikarr*.

beakerful ▻ *noun* (***beakerfuls***) the amount a beaker can hold.

be-all and end-all see under BE

beam /biːm/ ▻ *noun* **1** a long straight thick piece of wood, used eg as a main structural component in a building. **2** a ray or shaft of light □ ***the beam of a torch.*** **3** a broad radiant smile. **4** the widest part of a ship or boat. **5** one of the transverse timbers extending across the hull of a ship. **6** a raised narrow horizontal wooden bar on which gymnasts perform balancing exercises. **7** *physics* a directed flow of electromagnetic radiation (eg radio or X-rays) or of particles (eg atoms or electrons). **8** the part of a set of scales from which the weighing-pans hang. **9** *weaving* either of the two wooden or metal cylinders in a loom. **10** the main shaft of a deer's antler, or of a plough, anchor, etc. ▻ *verb* (***beamed***, ***beaming***) **1** *intr* to smile broadly with pleasure. **2** *intr* (*often* **beam down** or **out**) to shine. **3** to send out or transmit (eg rays of light, radio waves, etc). • **beaming** *adj, noun*. • **beam me up, Scotty** *humorous* get me out of this (dangerous, awkward, embarrassing, etc) situation, quickly! ⓔ 20c: a phrase used in the TV science-fiction series *Star Trek*, as an instruction to the chief engineer of the 'starship' to activate a 'beam' which can instantly transfer the speaker from a planet's surface or another spaceship, etc back to the ship. • **broad in the beam** see under BROAD. • **off beam** *colloq* wrong; misguided. • **on the beam** *colloq* on the right track. • **on one's beam ends** *Brit colloq* having only a very small amount of money or resources left; dangerously close to ruin or destitution ⓔ 19c, from nautical use: in severe gale conditions a sailing ship would be laid right over on her side, where the transverse timbers (ie the BEAMS) end. • **on the port** or **starboard beam** *naut* on the left or right side of a ship. ⓔ Anglo-Saxon, meaning 'tree'.

bean /biːn/ ▻ *noun* **1** a general name applied to the edible kidney-shaped seeds of plants belonging to the pea family, especially those of the runner bean. **2** any plant belonging to the pea family that bears such seeds, eg **broad bean**, **haricot bean**. **3** (*usually* **beans**) *cookery* a seed or young pod of such a plant, used as food. **4** any other seed that superficially resembles those of the pea family, eg coffee bean. **5** *colloq, with negatives* a small coin; a tiny amount of money □ ***I haven't got a bean*** □ ***Have you any cash left? Not a bean.*** **6** *US slang* a head or brain. **7** (**beans**) *US slang, especially with negatives* anything at all □ ***Don't ask him, he doesn't know beans.*** ▷ *verb* (***beaned, beaning***) *US slang* to hit someone on the head with something. ● **full of beans** *colloq* full of energy; very lively and cheerful. ● **know how many beans make five** *colloq* to be fully alert and clued-up; to know what's what. ● **old bean** see separate entry. ● **spill the beans** see under SPILL[1]. ◷ Anglo-Saxon.

bean bag ▷ *noun* **1** a small cloth bag filled with dried beans or something similar, used like a ball in children's games, etc. **2** a very large cushion filled with polystyrene chips or balls, etc, kept on the floor as seating.

beanfeast ▷ *noun, Brit colloq* **1** a party or celebration. **2** an annual dinner given by employers to their workers. ◷ 19c in sense 2: beans were perhaps considered the staple dish for such occasions.

beano /'biːnoʊ/ ▷ *noun* (***beanos***) *Brit colloq* a beanfeast or jollification. ◷ 19c: printers' abbreviation of BEANFEAST.

beanpole ▷ *noun* **1** a tall supporting pole for a bean plant to climb up as it grows. **2** *colloq* a tall thin person.

beansprout and **beanshoot** ▷ *noun* a young shoot of a bean plant, usually the mung bean plant, eaten as a vegetable especially in Chinese food.

beanstalk ▷ *noun* the stem of a bean plant.

bear[1] /bɛə(r)/ ▷ *verb* (*past tense* ***bore***, *past participle* ***borne*** or (in sense 7b) ***born***, *present participle* ***bearing***) **1** to support or sustain (a weight or load). **2** to take or accept □ ***bear the blame.*** **3** to put up with or tolerate something or someone. **4 a** to allow; to be fit or suitable for something □ ***It doesn't bear thinking about***; **b** to stand up to or be capable of withstanding something □ ***will not bear close scrutiny.*** **5** to bring or take something with one; to carry □ ***bearing gifts.*** **6** to produce □ ***bear fruit.*** **7 a** to give birth to (a child or offspring) □ ***She bore three children***; **b** in the passive using past participle *born* □ ***He was born in 1990***; **c** in the past tense using past participle *borne* □ ***Has she borne children?***; **d** in the passive using past participle *borne*, followed by *by* and the mother's name □ ***a child borne by Mary***; **e** with a direct and an indirect object to give birth to (the child of a man) □ ***She bore him a son.*** **8** to carry something in one's thought or memory □ ***bearing grudges.*** **9** to have □ ***bears no resemblance to his father.*** **10** to show or be marked by something □ ***Her cheeks bore the traces of tears.*** **11** *intr* to turn slightly in a given direction □ ***bear left.*** **12** to behave □ ***bear oneself well.*** ● **bear fruit** to be productive; to bring results. ● **bring something to bear** to apply or exert (especially pressure or influence), or bring something into operation. ◷ Anglo-Saxon *beran* to carry or support.

■ **bear down on** or **upon someone** or **something** to move threateningly towards them or it □ ***saw a lorry bearing down on them.***

■ **bear on something** to affect, concern or relate to it □ ***How does the new evidence bear on this case?***

■ **bear someone** or **something out** to support or confirm them or it □ ***The evidence bears out my original suspicions*** □ ***My colleagues will bear me out on this.***

■ **bear up** to remain strong or brave, etc under strain or difficult circumstances □ ***How is Jo bearing up after the accident?***

■ **bear with someone** to be patient with them □ ***Bear with me while I check this.***

bear[2] /bɛə(r)/ ▷ *noun* (***bears*** or ***bear***) **1 a** any of various large carnivorous animals with a heavily built body covered with thick fur, short powerful limbs, small eyes and ears, strong claws and a short tail. Also *in compounds* □ ***brown bear*** □ ***polar bear***; **2** a rough ill-mannered person. **3** a teddy bear. **4** *stock exchange* someone who sells shares, hoping to buy them back later at a much lower price. Compare LAME DUCK 4, BULL[1] *noun* 4. ▷ *verb* (***beared, bearing***) *stock exchange* **1** to act as a bear (sense 4 above). **2** to lower the price of (a stock) or to depress (a market) by selling speculatively. ● **bearish** *adj* **1** said of a person: like a bear in behaviour and manners; bad-tempered and rough. **2** *stock exchange* causing or linked with a fall in prices. ● **like a bear with a sore head** *colloq* said of a person: exceptionally touchy and bad-tempered. ● **the Great Bear** and **the Little Bear** see separate entries. ◷ Anglo-Saxon *bera*.

bearable ▷ *adj* able to be suffered or tolerated. ● **bearably** *adverb*.

bear-baiting ▷ *noun, historical* in 16c Britain: a popular sport (made illegal in 1835) in which a bear, chained to a stake or put into a pit, was attacked by dogs and bets were placed on the performance of individual dogs.

beard[1] /bɪəd/ ▷ *noun* **1** the hair that grows on a man's chin and neck. **2** a beard-like growth on the lower jaw of some animals, especially goats. **3** a hair-like growth on an ear of corn, grass, etc. See also AWN. ● **bearded** *adj*. ● **beardless** *adj*. ◷ Anglo-Saxon.

beard[2] /bɪəd/ ▷ *verb* (***bearded, bearding***) (*often* **beard someone in their den** or **beard the lion in his den**) to face, defy or oppose someone openly, boldly or resolutely □ ***I bearded the boss and insisted on an explanation.*** ◷ 16c; 15c in obsolete sense (said of a man) 'to get a beard'.

bearer /'bɛərə(r)/ ▷ *noun* **1** a person or thing that bears, carries or brings something. Also *in compounds* □ ***flag-bearer.*** **2** a person who helps carry equipment on an expedition. **3** a person who holds a banknote, cheque or other money order which can be exchanged for money. **4** a PALL-BEARER. **5** *Indian subcontinent, historical* a personal, household or hotel servant. **6** *as adj, finance* said of a bill or bond, etc: payable to the person who is in possession of it.

bear hug ▷ *noun, colloq* **1** a rough tight hug to the upper body. **2** *wrestling* a hold in which a wrestler wraps his arms tightly around his opponent's arms and upper body.

bearing /'bɛərɪŋ/ ▷ *noun* **1** the way a person stands, walks, behaves, etc □ ***a proud bearing.*** **2** (*usually* **bearing on something**) relevance to it □ ***That has no bearing on the situation.*** **3 a** the horizontal direction of a fixed point, or the path of a moving object, measured from a reference point on the Earth's surface, and normally expressed as an angle measured in degrees clockwise from the north; **b** (*usually* **bearings**) position or a calculation of position □ ***a ship's bearings*** □ ***compass bearing.*** **4** (**bearings**) *colloq* a sense or awareness of one's own position or surroundings □ ***lose one's bearings.*** **5** any part of a machine or device that supports another part, and allows free movement between the two parts, eg a BALL-BEARING. ◷ 13c: from BEAR[1].

bearing rein ▷ *noun* a fixed rein between the bit and the saddle, by which a horse's head is held up and its neck is made to arch.

bearish see under BEAR[2]

Béarnaise sauce /beɪə'neɪz/ or **Béarnaise** (*also without capital*) ▷ *noun, cookery* a rich sauce made from egg yolks, butter, shallots, tarragon, chervil and wine vinegar. ◷ 19c: French, named after *Bearn*, a region in SW France.

bearskin ▷ *noun* **1** the skin of a bear, used eg as a rug or cloak. **2** a tall fur cap worn as part of some military uniforms. See also BUSBY.

beast /biːst/ ▷ *noun* **1** any large wild animal, especially a four-footed one □ ***the beast of Exmoor.*** Compare BEAST OF BURDEN. **2** *colloq* a cruel brutal person. **3** *colloq* a difficult or unpleasant person or thing □ ***The catch on this bracelet is a beast to undo.*** ● **bring out the beast in someone** to cause them to behave brutishly; to expose the worst side of their nature. ◷ 13c as *beste*: French, from Latin *bestia*.

beastie ▷ *noun, Scots* or *humorous* a small animal, especially an insect or spider, etc. ⓘ 18c: Scots diminutive of BEAST.

beastly ▷ *adj* (*beastlier, beastliest*) **1** *colloq* unpleasant; horrid; disagreeable. **2** like a beast in actions or behaviour; fierce or brutal. See also BESTIAL. ▷ *adverb, colloq* extremely and unpleasantly □ *It was beastly hot.* • **beastliness** *noun*.

beast of burden ▷ *noun* an animal such as a donkey or bullock, used to carry or pull loads.

beat /biːt/ ▷ *verb* (*past tense* **beat**, *past participle* **beaten** or (*now rare*) **beat**, *present participle* **beating**) **1** to hit (a person, animal, etc) violently and repeatedly, especially to harm or punish them. **2** to strike something repeatedly, eg to remove dust or make a sound. **3** *intr* (*usually* **beat against** or **at** or **on something**) to knock or strike repeatedly □ *rain beating against the window.* **4** to defeat; to do something better, sooner or quicker than someone else □ *always beats me at chess.* **5** to be too difficult to be solved or understood by someone □ *The last puzzle had me beaten.* See also *it beats me* below. **6** (*sometimes* **beat something up**) to mix or stir thoroughly □ *Beat two eggs in a bowl.* **7** (*also* **beat something out**) **a** to make or shape it by repeatedly striking the raw material □ *beating out horseshoes on the forge*; **b** to flatten or reduce the thickness of it by beating. **8** *intr* to move in a regular pattern of strokes, etc □ *heard my heart beating.* **9** *tr & intr* to move rhythmically up and down □ *tent-flaps beating in the wind.* **10** (*usually* **beat time** or **beat out time**) to mark or show (musical time or rhythm) with the hand or a baton, etc. **11** (*especially* **beat someone** or **something back** or **down off**) to push, drive or force them or it away. **12** (*also* **beat up something**) *tr & intr* to strike (bushes or trees, etc) to force birds or animals into the open for shooting. ▷ *noun* **1** a regular recurrent stroke, or its sound □ *the beat of my heart.* **2 a** in music and poetry, etc: the basic pulse, unit of rhythm or accent □ *two beats to the bar* **b** the conductor's stroke of the hand or baton indicating such a pulse □ *Watch the beat* **c** in popular music: rhythm; a strong rhythmic pulse. **3** a regular or usual course or journey □ *a policeman on his beat.* **4 a** in the 1950s and 60s: a member or follower of the BEAT GENERATION; **b** a beatnik ▷ *adj, colloq, especially US* worn out; exhausted. • **beatable** *adj*. • **beater** *noun* a person or thing that beats in any sense, eg a person who rouses or beats up game for shooting, an electric or hand-operated device for beating, etc. Also *in compounds* □ *egg-beater.* • **beat about the bush** to talk tediously about a subject without coming to the main point. • **beat a hasty retreat** or **beat a retreat** to go away in a hurry, especially in order to escape or avoid an unpleasant or difficult situation. Compare *beat the retreat* below. • **beat it** *slang* to go away immediately and quickly. • **beat one's brains** or **beat one's brains out** *colloq* to puzzle long and hard over something. • **beat one's breast** to show unrestrained, wild or exaggerated signs of grief. • **beat someone's brains out** *colloq* to kill or seriously injure them by hitting them about the head. • **beat someone to it** to manage to do something before they can □ *I went back to tidy up, but someone had beaten me to it.* • **beat the bounds** *Brit* to perform a traditional ceremony of tracing out the parish boundaries by walking around them, formally striking the boundary stones, etc with willow twigs. See also COMMON-RIDING. • **beat the clock** to do or finish something within the time allowed. • **beat the pants** or **socks off someone** *colloq* to defeat them thoroughly. • **beat the rap** *slang, originally US* to escape without punishment. • **beat the retreat** to perform the military ceremony (**beating the retreat**) consisting of marching and military music, usually performed at dusk, originally marking the recall (by drum beat) of troops to their quarters. • **Can you beat it?** or **Can you beat that?** *colloq* as an expression of astonishment: Would you believe it, or that, to be possible, true, etc? • **dead beat** *colloq* very tired; exhausted. • **it beats me** *colloq* it is beyond my comprehension; I cannot understand it or work it out. • **off the beaten track** away from main roads and towns; isolated. • **you can't beat something** *colloq* there is no substitute for it, or nothing better than it. ⓘ Anglo-Saxon *beatan*.

■ **beat down 1** said of the sun: to give out great heat. **2** said of rain: to fall heavily.

■ **beat someone down** to force them to reduce the price of something by bargaining.

■ **beat something down** to strike it heavily until it collapses □ *beat the door down.*

■ **beat someone off** to check or put a stop to them, or succeed in overcoming them □ *Police beat off the protesters.*

■ **beat someone up** or (*US*) **beat up on someone** to punch, kick or hit them severely and repeatedly.

beat box ▷ *noun, colloq* a ghetto-blaster.

beaten ▷ *adj* **1** defeated or outmanoeuvred. **2** *colloq, especially Austral & NZ* exhausted or worn out. **3** made smooth or hard by beating or treading □ *beaten path.* **4** shaped and made thin by beating □ *beaten gold.*

beater see under BEAT

beat generation or **Beat Generation** ▷ *noun, originally US* a 1950s set of young people, specifically writers, who dissociated themselves from the aims, conventions and standards of contemporary society.

beatific /bɪəˈtɪfɪk/ ▷ *adj* **1** expressing or revealing supreme peaceful happiness □ *a beatific smile.* **2** making someone blessed or supremely happy. • **beatifically** *adverb*. ⓘ 17c: from Latin *beatificus*, from *beatus* blessed + *facere* to make.

beatify /bɪˈatɪfaɪ/ ▷ *verb* (**beatified, beatifying**) **1** *RC Church* to declare the blessed status of someone who has died, conferring the title 'Blessed' upon them, usually as the first step towards full canonization. **2** to make someone blessed, or eternally or supremely happy. • **beatification** *noun*. ⓘ 16c.

beating ▷ *noun* **1** (*often* **take a beating**) a physical assault or punishment. **2** a thorough defeat; a thrashing. • **take some beating** or **take a lot of beating** *colloq* to be of a very high standard, and therefore difficult to improve upon or defeat.

beatitude /bɪˈatɪtjuːd/ ▷ *noun* **1** (**the Beatitudes**) *Bible* the group of statements made by Christ during the Sermon on the Mount (in Matthew 5.3–11) about the kinds of people who receive God's blessing. **2** a state of blessedness or of extreme happiness and peace. **3** (**Your** or **His Beatitude**) *Orthodox Church* a title of respect given to a patriarch of the church. ⓘ 15c: from Latin *beatitudo*, from *beatus* blessed.

beat music ▷ *noun* popular music with a pronounced rhythm or beat, originally and especially that which evolved in Britain in the 1960s.

beatnik /ˈbiːtnɪk/ ▷ *noun* **1** a young person with scruffy or unconventional clothes, long hair, unusual lifestyle, etc. **2** in the 1950s and 60s: a member or follower of the BEAT GENERATION, who rejected the accepted social and political ideas, etc of the time. ⓘ 1950s: BEAT (*adj*) + -NIK.

beat-up ▷ *adj, colloq* old and worn; in very dilapidated or overused condition.

beau /boʊ/ ▷ *noun* (**beaux** or **beaus** /boʊz/) **1** *US or dated Brit* a boyfriend or male lover. **2** *old use* a DANDY (sense 1). ⓘ 17c in sense 2: French, meaning 'beautiful'.

Beaufort scale /ˈboʊfət —/ ▷ *noun, meteorol* a system for estimating wind speeds without using instruments. ⓘ 19c: devised by Sir Francis Beaufort (1774–1857).

beau monde / *French* bomɔ̃d/ ▷ *noun* (***beaux mondes*** or ***beau mondes*** /bomɔ̃d/) the world of fashion and high society. ⓘ 18c: French, literally 'beautiful world'.

beaut /bjuːt/ ▻ *adj, exclamation, colloq, chiefly Austral & NZ* excellent; fine. ▻ *noun* **1** *chiefly Austral, NZ & US* someone or something exceptionally beautiful, pleasing or remarkable; a BEAUTY (*noun* 3). **2** *Austral, NZ* someone or something remarkably bad or unpleasant. ⌚ 19c: short form of BEAUTIFUL.

beauteous /ˈbjuːtɪəs/ ▻ *adj, poetic* beautiful. • **beauteously** *adverb*. • **beauteousness** *noun*. ⌚ 15c.

beautician /bjuːˈtɪʃən/ ▻ *noun* a person who gives beauty treatment such as hair and skin treatments, make-up application, etc to women, especially in a beauty parlour. ⌚ 1920s.

beautiful /ˈbjuːtɪfəl/ ▻ *adj* **1** having an appearance or qualities which please the senses or give rise to admiration in the mind □ *a beautiful view* □ *a beautiful poem.* **2** *colloq* very enjoyable; excellent. • **beautifully** *adverb* **1** in a manner that pleases the senses □ *The stories are beautifully written.* **2** *colloq* very well □ *She behaved beautifully.*

beautify ▻ *verb* (***beautifies, beautified, beautifying***) to make something or someone beautiful, often by decorating it or them; to adorn or grace □ *a new window beautifying the church.* • **beautification** *noun*. • **beautifier** *noun*. ⌚ 16c.

beauty /ˈbjuːtɪ/ ▻ *noun* (***beauties***) **1** a quality pleasing to the senses, especially to the eye or ear, or giving aesthetic pleasure generally. **2** *colloq* an excellent example of something □ *a beauty of a black eye.* **3** a benefit or particular strength or quality □ *The beauty of the plan is its flexibility.* **4** a beautiful person, usually a woman or girl □ *She's a famous beauty.* ▻ *exclamation* (*also* **you beauty!**) *Austral & NZ colloq* enthusiastically expressing approval; great! ⌚ 13c: from French *biauté*, ultimately from Latin *bellus*.

beauty contest ▻ *noun* a competition in which young women are judged according to the beauty of their faces and bodies.

beauty parlour and **beauty salon** ▻ *noun* a place where women may go for beauty treatments such as hairdressing, facials, make-up, manicure, massage, etc. *US equivalent* **beauty shop**.

beauty queen ▻ *noun* the winner of a beauty contest.

beauty sleep ▻ *noun* sleep, particularly sleep taken before midnight, which is traditionally thought to be the most refreshing and beneficial to health.

beauty spot ▻ *noun* **1** a place of great natural beauty. **2** a small dark natural or artificial mark on the face, meant to enhance beauty.

beaux arts / *French* bozaʀ/ ▻ *plural noun* **1** the fine arts; FINE ART (see senses 1 and 3). **2** (**Beaux-Arts**) *archit* a decorative classical style of the late 19c, particularly popular in France.

beaver¹ /ˈbiːvə(r)/ ▻ *noun* **1** either of two species of a large semi-aquatic squirrel-like rodent with soft dark-brown fur, large incisor teeth, webbed hind feet and a broad flat scaly tail. See also LODGE *noun* 5. **2** its valuable fur. **3** a hat made of beaver fur. **4** (**Beaver** or **Beaver Scout**) a boy belonging to the most junior branch of the SCOUT movement. **5** *coarse slang, originally US* a woman's pubic region, especially the genitals. ⌚ Anglo-Saxon *beofor*.

beaver² /ˈbiːvə(r)/ ▻ *verb* (***beavered, beavering***) *intr* (*especially* **beaver away at something**) *colloq, chiefly Brit* to work very hard and persistently at something. ⌚ 1940s: from BEAVER¹, referring to the way beavers work away felling trees, damming streams and building their lodges.

bebop /ˈbiːbɒp/ ▻ *noun* (*often shortened to* **bop**) a variety of jazz music which added new harmonies, melodic patterns and highly syncopated rhythms to accepted jazz style. • **bebopper** *noun*. ⌚ 1940s: in imitation of two quavers in the typical bebop rhythm.

becalmed /bɪˈkɑːmd/ ▻ *adj* said of a sailing ship: motionless and unable to move because of lack of wind. ⌚ 16c.

became *past tense of* BECOME

because /bɪˈkɒz, -kəz/ ▻ *conj* for the reason that □ *I left the room because Dad called me.* • **because of something** or **someone** by reason of, or on account of, it or them □ *The whole class was punished because of you.* ⌚ 14c: shortened from the phrase '*by cause of*'.

> ***because***
>
> See Usage Note at **due**.

béchamel /beɪʃəmɛl/ and **béchamel sauce** ▻ *noun, cookery* a white sauce flavoured with onion and herbs and sometimes enriched with cream. ⌚ 18c: named after a French courtier, the Marquis de Béchamel (died 1703), who attended Louis XIV.

beck¹ ▻ *noun* now only used in the phrase • **at someone's beck and call** having to be always ready or at hand to carry out their orders or wishes. ⌚ 14c, meaning 'a signal with the finger or head', from Anglo-Saxon *biecnan* to beckon.

beck² ▻ *noun, N Eng dialect* a stream or brook. ⌚ 12c: from Norse *bekkr*.

beckon /ˈbɛkən/ ▻ *verb* (***beckoned, beckoning***) *tr & intr* to summon someone towards oneself, especially by making a sign or repeated gesture with the hand □ *Ann beckoned me over.* ⌚ Anglo-Saxon *biecnan*, from *beacen* a sign.

become /bɪˈkʌm/ ▻ *verb* (*past tense* ***became****, past participle* ***become****, present participle* ***becoming***) **1** *intr* to come or grow to be something; to develop into something □ *I became lazy* □ *He might become king.* **2** *formal* said especially of clothing: to suit, look good on or befit someone □ *That hat becomes you.* ⌚ Anglo-Saxon *becuman* in obsolete sense 'to come, approach or happen'.

> ■ **become of someone** or **something** to happen to them or it.

becoming ▻ *adj* **1** attractive □ *a most becoming outfit.* **2** said of behaviour, etc: suitable or proper. • **becomingly** *adverb*.

becquerel /ˈbɛkərɛl, -rəl/ ▻ *noun, physics* (symbol **Bq**) in the SI system: the unit of radioactivity, equivalent to one DISINTEGRATION of a radioactive source per second. See also CURIE. ⌚ 1970s: named after the French physicist A H Becquerel (1852–1908).

bed ▻ *noun* **1** a piece of furniture for sleeping on, generally a wooden and/or metal frame with a mattress and coverings, etc on it. **2** a place in which anything (eg an animal) sleeps or rests. **3** *colloq* sleep or rest □ *ready for bed.* **4** the bottom of a river, lake or sea. **5** an area of ground in a garden, for growing plants. Often *in compounds* □ *rose-bed.* **6** a flat surface or base, especially one made of slate, brick or tile, on which something can be supported or laid down. **7** a layer or STRATUM, eg of oysters, sedimentary rock, etc. **8** *colloq* sexual intercourse; marital relations □ *All he ever thinks about is bed.* **9** a place available for occupancy in a residential home, nursing home or hospital. ▻ *verb* (***bedded, bedding***) **1** *tr & intr* (*usually* **bed down** or **bed someone down**) to go to bed, or put someone in bed or in a place to sleep □ *bedded down on the sofa.* **2** (*usually* **bed something out**) to plant it in the soil, in a garden, etc. **3** to place or fix something firmly □ *Its base was bedded in concrete.* **4** *colloq* to have sexual intercourse with someone. **5** *tr & intr* to arrange something in or to form, layers. • **bed of roses** see separate entry. • **get out of bed on the wrong side** *colloq* to start the day in a bad mood. • **go to bed** *journalism, printing* said of a newspaper or magazine, etc: to go to press. • **go to bed with someone** *colloq* to have sexual intercourse with them. • **in bed with someone or something** *colloq* in close involvement or collusion with (a person, organization, company, etc). • **make one's bed and have to lie in it** to have to accept the disadvantages or problems that result from one's own actions or past decisions. • **make the bed** to make the bedclothes tidy after the bed has been slept in. • **put something to bed** *journalism, printing* to send (a newspaper or magazine, etc) to press. • **take to one's bed** to go to bed and remain there, because of illness, grief, etc. ⓘ Anglo-Saxon *bedd*.

BEd ▷ *abbreviation* Bachelor of Education.

bed and board ▷ *noun* lodgings and food.

bed and breakfast ▷ *noun* (***bed and breakfasts***) (abbreviation **B and B**, **B & B** or **b & b**) **1** at a guest-house, hotel, etc: overnight accommodation with breakfast included in the price. *US equivalent* ROOM AND BOARD. **2** a guest-house, etc that provides bed and breakfast accommodation. **3** *as adj, stock exchange* applied to the practice of selling shares late on one day and buying them back early on the next day in order to establish a loss for tax purposes while retaining the shares.

bedazzle /bɪ'dazəl/ ▷ *verb* **1** to dazzle or impress someone greatly. **2** to confuse or daze someone, due to the effect of bright light, or high glamour, impressiveness, excitement, etc. • **bedazzled** *adj*. • **bedazzlement** *noun*. ⓘ 16c.

bedbath ▷ *noun* a complete wash of the body of a person who is unable get out of bed. Also called **blanket bath**.

bedbug ▷ *noun* the common name for any of various species of household pest that infest bedding and feed on human blood.

bedclothes ▷ *plural noun* the sheets, blankets, etc used to cover a bed.

bedcover see BEDSPREAD

beddable ▷ *adj, colloq* sexually attractive.

bedding ▷ *noun* **1** bedclothes, and sometimes also mattress and pillows, etc. **2** straw or hay, etc for animals to sleep on. **3** a base layer or foundation on which something is bedded. **4** *geol* stratification.

bedding plant ▷ *noun* a young plant that is sufficiently well-grown for planting out in a garden.

beddy-byes ▷ *noun* used in speaking to young children: bed. Compare BYE-BYES.

bedeck /bɪ'dɛk/ ▷ *verb* to cover something or someone with decorations; to adorn. ⓘ 16c: from DECK².

bedevil /bɪ'dɛvəl/ ▷ *verb* (***bedevilled, bedevilling; US bedeviled, bedeviling***) **1** to cause continual difficulties or trouble to someone or something ▫ *The project was bedevilled by problems.* **2** to throw something or someone into utter confusion. • **bedevilment** *noun*. ⓘ 19c; 18c meaning 'to treat in a devilishly malignant way'.

bedfellow ▷ *noun* **1** a partner or associate ▫ *They make strange bedfellows.* **2** a person with whom one shares a bed. ⓘ 15c in sense 2.

bed-jacket ▷ *noun* a short light jacket worn over one's nightclothes when sitting up in bed.

bedlam /'bɛdləm/ ▷ *noun, colloq* a very noisy confused place or situation; a madhouse. ⓘ 16c as *Bedlam*, the popular name for St Mary of Bethlehem, a former lunatic asylum in London; 17c in current sense.

bed linen ▷ *noun* the sheets and pillowcases used on a bed.

Bedlington /'bɛdlɪŋtən/ and **Bedlington terrier** ▷ *noun* a UK breed of dog with a tapering muzzle, a curly, usually pale, coat and no obvious forehead in side view. ⓘ 19c: from Bedlington in NE England, where it was first bred.

bed of roses ▷ *noun* an easy or comfortable place or situation ▫ *Her life is no bed of roses these days.*

Bedouin /'bɛdʊɪn/ ▷ *noun* (***Bedouin*** or ***Bedouins***) a member of a nomadic tent-dwelling Arab tribe that lives in the deserts of the Middle East. Also **Beduin**. ⓘ 15c: from French *beduin*, from Arabic *badawi* desert-dweller.

bedpan ▷ *noun* a wide shallow pan used as a toilet by people who are unable to get out of bed.

bedpost ▷ *noun* the corner support of a bedstead. • **between you, me and the bedpost** *colloq* in strict confidence; just between ourselves.

bedraggled /bɪ'dragəld/ ▷ *adj* said of a person or animal: very wet and untidy. ⓘ 18c.

bed-rest ▷ *noun* **1** a period of confinement to bed, usually on medical orders. **2** a support for the back of a person sitting up in bed.

bedridden /'bɛdrɪdən/ ▷ *adj* not able to get out of bed, especially because of old age or sickness. ⓘ Anglo-Saxon, originally *bedrid* (later altered in imitation of RIDDEN, past participle of RIDE), from BED + *reda* rider.

bedrock ▷ *noun* **1** the solid rock forming the lowest layer under soil and rock fragments. **2** the basic principle or idea, etc on which something rests. Also *as adj* ▫ *unshakeable bedrock standards.* **3** *as adj* bottom or lowest.

bedroll ▷ *noun* bedding rolled up so as to be carried easily by a camper, etc.

bedroom ▷ *noun* **1** a room for sleeping in. **2** *as adj* **a** for, appropriate for or in, a bedroom ▫ *bedroom furniture*; **b** especially of a comedy or farce: involving or concerning a bedroom, or specifically activity between people in a bedroom, in nightclothes, etc.

Beds. ▷ *abbreviation, English county* Bedfordshire.

bedside ▷ *noun* the place or position next to a bed, especially that of a sick person.

bedside manner ▷ *noun* a doctor's way of talking to, reassuring, etc and generally dealing with, a patient in bed.

bedsitting-room (*formal*) and **bedsit** or **bedsitter** (*informal*) ▷ *noun, Brit* a single room used as a combined bedroom and sitting-room usually with basic cooking facilities, especially as cheap accommodation for a lodger or tenant.

bedsore ▷ *noun* an ulcer on a person's skin, caused by lying in bed for long periods. Also called PRESSURE SORE.

bedspread and **bedcover** ▷ *noun* a top cover for a bed.

bedstead /'bɛdstɛd/ ▷ *noun* the frame of a bed.

bedstraw ▷ *noun* a small plant with a fragile stem, narrow leaves arranged in whorls and tiny white, yellow or greenish flowers in open clusters.

bedtime ▷ *noun* the time for going to bed.

Beduin see BEDOUIN

bed-wetting ▷ *noun* accidental urination in bed at night.

bee¹ ▷ *noun* (***bees***) **1** any of numerous four-winged insects, the female of which almost always bears a sting, and some species of which live in colonies and are often kept for their honey, eg the BUMBLE BEE and HONEY BEE. **2** (*usually* **busy bee**) a busy industrious person. • **a bee in one's bonnet** an idea, especially a rather strange one, which has become an obsession. • **the bee's knees** *Brit colloq* a person or thing considered to be extremely special or good, etc. ⓘ Anglo-Saxon *beo*.

bee² ▷ *noun* (***bees***) *N Amer, especially US* a meeting of friends or neighbours to work on a particular task together (eg a **quilting bee**) or in competition (eg a **spelling-bee**). ⓘ 18c: possibly from a dialect word *been* meaning 'help from neighbours', from Anglo-Saxon *ben* a prayer or boon; or from BEE[1], alluding to the co-operative industrious behaviour of the bee.

the Beeb ▷ *noun, Brit colloq* the British Broadcasting Corporation. ⓒ 1960s: colloquial shortening of the abbreviation BBC.

beech ▷ *noun* (*beeches*) **1** (*also* **beech tree**) a deciduous tree or shrub with smooth grey bark, pale-green glossy leaves, and triangular edible fruits known collectively as **beech mast**. **2** (*also* **beechwood**) the hard straight-grained wood of this tree, widely used for furniture making. **3** a similar tree of a related genus, belonging to the southern hemisphere. • **beechy** *adj*. ⓒ Anglo-Saxon *bece*.

beef ▷ *noun* (*plural* in sense 3 ***beefs***, in sense 4 ***beeves***) **1** the flesh of a bull, cow or ox, used as food. **2** *colloq* muscle; vigorous muscular force or strength **3** *slang* a complaint or argument. **4 a** a steer or cow, especially one fattened for butchering; **b** its butchered carcass. ▷ *verb, intr, slang* (*often* **beef away** or **on about something**) to complain or grumble, especially vigorously or at length. ⓒ 13c: from French *boef* ox.

■ **beef something** up *colloq* **1** to make it stronger or heavier. **2** to make it more interesting or exciting.

beefalo /'biːfəloʊ/ ▷ *noun* (***beefalos*** or ***beefaloes***) a cross between a domestic cow and a N American buffalo, bred for its high-protein, low-fat meat. ⓒ 1970s: from BEEF + BUFFALO.

beefburger ▷ *noun* a piece of finely chopped beef, often with added ingredients, made into a flat round shape and grilled or fried. See also BURGER.

beefcake ▷ *plural noun, slang, often derog* very muscular men, especially when displayed in photographs, etc for their supposed physical attractiveness to women. Compare CHEESECAKE 2.

beef cattle ▷ *noun, agric* cows that are reared for their meat. Compare DAIRY CATTLE.

beefeater or **Beefeater** ▷ *noun, Brit* a Yeoman of the Guard, or a Yeoman Warder at the Tower of London, both of whom wear the same Tudor-style ceremonial uniform. ⓒ 17c: the name was apparently applied popularly in reference to the guards' strong healthy appearance.

beefsteak ▷ *noun* a thick slice of beef for grilling or frying.

beef tea ▷ *noun* a drink made from beef stock or the juice of chopped beef, often given (especially formerly) to sick or convalescent people to help stimulate the appetite.

beef tomato ▷ *noun* a particularly large fleshy variety of tomato.

beefy ▷ *adj* (***beefier***, ***beefiest***) **1** made of or like beef. **2** *colloq* said eg of a person: fleshy or muscular. • **beefily** *adverb*. • **beefiness** *noun*.

beehive ▷ *noun* **1** a box or hut in which bees are kept, and where they store their honey. **2** something dome-shaped like a traditional beehive, especially a high domed women's hairstyle very popular in the 1960s. **3** a place where a lot of people are working hard.

beekeeper ▷ *noun* a person who keeps bees for their honey, as a hobby, etc. • **beekeeping** *noun*.

beeline ▷ *noun* a straight line between two places. • **make a beeline for something** or **someone** to go directly or purposefully to it or them. ⓒ 19c: a bee is thought to take the most direct route back to its hive instinctively.

been *past participle of* BE

beep ▷ *noun* a short high-pitched sound, like that made by a car horn or by some electronic machines. ▷ *verb* (***beeped***, ***beeping***) *tr & intr* to produce a beep on or with something □ ***Do stop beeping the horn.*** • **beeper** *noun* a device that makes a beep, eg to attract someone's attention. ⓒ 1920s: imitating the sound.

beer /bɪə(r)/ ▷ *noun* **1** an alcoholic drink brewed by the slow fermentation of malted cereal grains, usually barley, flavoured with hops, eg ALE, LAGER and STOUT. **2** a glass, can or bottle of this drink. **3** *in compounds* any other fermented drink, often non-alcoholic □ ***ginger beer.*** • **beer and skittles** *Brit* fun; pleasure □ ***It hasn't been all beer and skittles while you were away.*** ⓒ Anglo-Saxon *beor*.

beer belly and **beer gut** ▷ *noun, colloq* a fat stomach or paunch resulting from drinking beer in quantity on a regular basis.

beer garden ▷ *noun* a garden, usually attached to a pub, where beer and other refreshments can be drunk.

beer-mat ▷ *noun* a small tablemat, usually made of cardboard, for standing a glass of beer, etc on.

beer-up ▷ *noun, Austral slang* a drinking-bout; a rowdy drunken party.

beery ▷ *adj* (***beerier***, ***beeriest***) **1** made of or like beer. **2** *colloq* affected by drinking beer. • **beerily** *adverb*.

beeswax ▷ *noun* **1** a solid yellowish substance produced by bees for making the cells in which they live. **2** this substance in a refined form, used especially as a wood-polish, in candles and other products. • **mind your own beeswax** or **none of your beeswax** *colloq, usually children's or facetious* it is no concern of yours; mind your own business.

beet ▷ *noun* **1** any of several types of plant with large round or carrot-shaped roots which are cooked and used as food, or for making sugar (called **beet sugar**). **2** (*also* **red beet**) *US* beetroot. ⓒ Anglo-Saxon *bete*.

beetle[1] /'biːtəl/ *noun* **1** any of numerous species of insect with thickened forewings that are not used for flight but modified to form rigid horny cases which cover and protect the delicate membranous hindwings. **2** (*usually* **Beetle**) *colloq* a particular type of small Volkswagen car with a rounded roof and bonnet, resembling a beetle in shape. **3** a game using dice, in which a drawing of a beetle is gradually assembled from its various parts. ▷ *verb* (***beetled***, ***beetling***) *intr* (*usually* **beetle about**, **around** or **away**) *Brit* to move quickly or as if in a hurry to get away; to scurry. ⓒ Anglo-Saxon *bitela*, from *biten* to bite; early 20c as *verb*.

beetle[2] /'biːtəl/ *noun* (*beetles*) a long-handled tool with a heavy head, for crushing, beating, driving in wedges, etc. ⓒ Anglo-Saxon *bietel*, from *beatan* to beat.

beetle[3] /'biːtəl/ *verb* (***beetled***, ***beetling***) *intr* to project or jut out; to overhang. • **beetling** *adj* □ ***beetling cliffs.*** ⓒ 17c: apparently first used as a verb by Shakespeare; derived from BEETLE-BROWED.

beetle-browed ▷ *adj* having bushy, overhanging or shaggy eyebrows. ⓒ 14c as *bitel-browed*: perhaps related to BEETLE[1].

beetroot ▷ *noun* a type of plant with a round dark-red root which is cooked and used as a vegetable. *US equivalent* BEET. ▷ *adj, Brit colloq* said of someone's complexion: deep or rosy red, especially as a result of embarrassment or exertion. ⓒ 16c.

beeves *plural of* BEEF *noun* 4

BEF ▷ *abbreviation* British Expeditionary Force.

befall /bɪ'fɔːl/ ▷ *verb* (***befell***, ***befallen***, ***befalling***) *old or literary* **1** *intr* to happen □ ***Stand firm, whatever befalls.*** **2** to happen to someone or something □ ***I alone knew what had befallen him.*** ⓒ Anglo-Saxon *befeallan* in the sense 'to fall' or 'to fall as by right or by fate'.

befit /bɪ'fɪt/ ▷ *verb* (***befitted***, ***befitting***) *formal* to be suitable or right for something or someone □ ***Such behaviour does not befit a man of his rank.*** • **befitting** *adj*. • **befittingly** *adverb*. ⓒ 15c: BE- 1 + FIT[1].

before /bɪ'fɔː(r)/ ▻ *prep* **1** earlier than something □ ***before noon.*** **2** ahead of or in front of someone or something. **3** in the presence of, or for the attention of, someone □ ***The question before us is a complex one.*** **4** rather than or in preference to someone or something □ ***Never put money before friendship.*** **5** *formal or literary* in the face of something □ ***draw back before the blast.*** ▻ *conj* **1** earlier than the time when something occurs □ ***Tidy up before Mum gets back.*** **2** rather than or in preference to doing something □ ***I'd die before I'd surrender.*** ▻ *adverb* **1** previously; in the past. **2** *now rare or formal* in front; ahead □ ***saints who have gone before.*** ◷ Anglo-Saxon *beforan.*

beforehand ▻ *adverb* **1** in advance; before a particular time or event. **2** in preparation or anticipation □ ***got the food ready beforehand.*** Compare BEHINDHAND. ◷ 13c: originally *before hand* or *before the hand.*

befoul /bɪ'faʊl/ ▻ *verb* to make something or someone foul or dirty; to soil. ◷ 14c.

befriend /bɪ'frɛnd/ ▻ *verb* **1** to become the friend of, or start a friendship with, someone □ ***was a lonely child until he befriended her.*** **2** to be friendly and helpful towards (a stranger, etc), eg as a conscious policy or service. ◷ 16c.

befuddle /bɪ'fʌdəl/ ▻ *verb* (used especially in the *passive*) to confuse someone, eg with the effects of alcohol □ ***I was befuddled by the wine and the noise.*** • **befuddled** *adj.* • **befuddlement** *noun.* ◷ 19c.

beg ▻ *verb* (***begged, begging***) *tr & intr* **1** to ask for (money or food, etc) □ ***forced to beg for scraps.*** **2** to ask earnestly or humbly □ ***Give me one chance, I beg you*** □ ***I beg your pardon*** □ ***begging for mercy.*** **3** said especially of an animal: to sit up on the hindquarters, or stand up on the back legs, with paws raised (like a dog asking for food or reward). • **beg the question 1** in an argument: to assume the truth of something which is in fact a part of what is still to be proved. **2** *colloq* to avoid giving an answer on a tricky matter; to dodge an awkward subject. • **beg to differ** to disagree. • **go begging** *colloq* to be unused or unwanted □ ***I'll have that sandwich if it's going begging.*** ◷ 13c: probably from Anglo-Saxon *bedecian.*

■ **beg off** to ask to be excused from, or to apologize for being unable to be present at, something one had previously agreed to attend, do, take part in, etc.

began see under BEGIN

beget /bɪ'gɛt/ ▻ *verb* (*past tense* ***begot*** or, especially in the Authorized Version of the Bible, ***begat***, *past participle* ***begotten***, *present participle* ***begetting***) **1** *rather formal* to cause; to give rise to something □ ***Envy begets strife.*** **2** especially in the Authorized Version of the Bible: to be the father of someone □ ***Abraham begat Isaac.*** ◷ Anglo-Saxon *begietan* in the sense 'to acquire' or 'get'.

beggar /'bɛgə(r)/ ▻ *noun* **1** a person who lives by begging. **2** *colloq, chiefly Brit* an affectionate or gently reproachful term for a person □ ***lucky beggar*** □ ***cheeky beggar.*** • **beggar description** or **belief** to be impossible to describe or believe □ ***That story beggars belief.*** • **beggars can't be choosers** if you are in need, you must accept whatever you are given or whatever becomes available, even if it is not what you would have chosen ideally.

beggarly ▻ *adj* extremely small or poor; paltry. • **beggarliness** *noun.*

beggar-my-neighbour ▻ *noun* **1** *cards* a game that goes on until one player has gained all the others' cards. **2** *as adj* profit-making at the expense of others □ ***beggar-my-neighbour policies.***

beggary ▻ *noun* extreme poverty; the state of being a beggar. ◷ 14c.

begging bowl ▻ *noun* a bowl used by beggars to collect donations of food or money in.

begging letter ▻ *noun* a letter asking for money, sent to an individual or an organization believed to be rich.

begin /bɪ'gɪn/ ▻ *verb* (*past tense* ***began***, *past participle* ***begun***, *present participle* ***beginning***) **1** *tr & intr* to start. **2** *tr & intr* to bring or come into being □ ***Our story begins in the summer of 1970*** □ ***when we began our family.*** **3** *intr* to start speaking. **4** *intr* to be the first, or to take the first step □ ***Nick, will you begin?*** **5** *intr, colloq* to have the ability or possibility to do something □ ***I can't even begin to understand.*** • **to begin with** at first; firstly. ◷ Anglo-Saxon.

■ **begin with someone** or **something** to deal with them or it first.

beginner ▻ *noun* **1** someone who is just starting to learn, or is still learning, how to do something. **2** a person who begins. • **beginner's luck** success achieved by someone inexperienced, eg in sport or a game of skill.

beginning ▻ *noun* **1** the point or occasion at which something begins. **2** an opening or first part of something.

begone /bɪ'gɒn/ ▻ *exclamation, poetic* or *old use* go away; be off with you! ◷ 14c.

begonia /bə'goʊnɪə/ ▻ *noun* (***begonias***) a kind of tropical plant with brightly coloured waxy flowers and unevenly shaped leaves. ◷ 18c: Latin, named after Michel Bégon (1638–1710), a French patron of botany.

begot and **begotten** see under BEGET

begrudge ▻ *verb* **1** to do, give or allow something unwillingly or with regret. **2** (*usually* **begrudge someone something**) to envy or resent them for it □ ***Don't begrudge him his success.*** • **begrudgingly** *adverb.* ◷ 14c.

beguile /bɪ'gaɪl/ ▻ *verb* (***beguiled, beguiling***) **1** to charm or captivate □ ***Her voice beguiled me.*** **2** (*sometimes* **beguile someone into** or **out of something**) to cheat, trick or deceive them into or out of it. **3** (*usually* **beguile away something**) to spend (time, etc) pleasantly □ ***beguile away the hours.*** • **beguilement** *noun.* • **beguiling** *adj* deceptively charming or amusing. • **beguilingly** *adverb.* ◷ 13c: from obsolete verb *guile* to deceive.

beguine /bɪ'giːn/ ▻ *noun* **1** a dance of French W Indian origin, in bolero rhythm. **2** a piece of music for this dance. ◷ 1930s: from French *béguin* flirtation.

begum /'beɪgəm, 'biː-/ ▻ *noun* **1** *Indian subcontinent* a Muslim woman of high rank. **2** (**Begum**) a title of respect given to a married Muslim woman. ◷ 18c: Urdu.

begun see under BEGIN

behalf /bɪ'hɑːf/ ▻ *noun* now usually only used in the phrases • **on** or (*N Amer*) **in behalf of someone** or **on** or (*N Amer*) **in someone's behalf 1** for, in or referring to their interests, or on their account □ ***acting purely on his own behalf.*** **2** speaking or acting, etc as a representative of someone or something. ◷ 14c as *behalve*: from Anglo-Saxon *be* by + *healfe* side.

on behalf of, on the part of

There is often confusion between **on behalf of** and **on the part of**: **on behalf of** means 'acting as a representative of', wheareas **on the part of** simply means 'by' or 'of'.

behave /bɪ'heɪv/ ▻ *verb* (***behaved, behaving***) **1** *intr* to act in a specified way □ ***behaving strangely*** □ ***behaved like an idiot.*** **2** *tr & intr* (*especially* **behave oneself**) to act or conduct oneself in a suitable, polite or orderly way □ ***Mind you behave yourself at the party*** □ ***If you don't behave, I'll take you home.*** ◷ 15c.

behaviour or (*US*) **behavior** /bɪ'heɪvɪə(r)/ ▻ *noun* **1** way of behaving; manners □ ***good behaviour.*** **2** *psychol* a response to a stimulus. • **be on one's best behaviour** to behave as well as one possibly can. • **behavioural** *adj.* • **behaviourally** *adv.* ◷ 15c.

behaviourism or (*US*) **behaviorism** ▷ *noun, psychol* the psychological theory that aims to interpret behaviour as being governed by CONDITIONING as opposed to internal processes (eg thoughts) and that by changing behaviour patterns, it is possible to treat psychological disorders. • **behaviourist** *noun*.

behaviour therapy ▷ *noun, psychol* a form of PSYCHOTHERAPY which aims to modify undesirable behaviour patterns, and is often used in the treatment of neuroses, eg phobias, which are assumed to be learned forms of behaviour.

behead /bɪˈhɛd/ ▷ *verb* to cut off the head of someone, usually as a form of capital punishment. • **beheading** *noun*. ⓔ Anglo-Saxon *beheafdian*, from *be-* off or away + *heafod* head.

beheld *past tense, past participle of* BEHOLD

behemoth /bɪˈhiːmɒɪ/ ▷ *noun* **1** *loosely* something huge or monstrous. **2** in the Authorized Version of the Bible: a huge beast, perhaps the hippopotamus (described in Job 40, from verse 15). ⓔ 14c: from Hebrew *b'hemoth*, plural of *b'hemah* beast.

behest /bɪˈhɛst/ ▷ *noun, formal or old use* a command or request. • **at the behest of someone** or **at someone's behest** at their request; when they asked or commanded. ⓔ 12c: from Anglo-Saxon *behæs* a vow or promise.

behind /bɪˈhaɪnd/ ▷ *prep* **1** at or towards the back or the far side of something or someone □ ***hiding behind the hedge.*** **2** later or slower than something; after in time □ ***behind schedule.*** **3** supporting □ ***We're all behind you.*** **4** in the past with respect to someone or something □ ***Those problems are all behind me now.*** **5** not as far advanced as someone or something □ ***Technologically, they are behind the Japanese.*** **6** being the cause or precursor of something □ ***reasons behind the decision.*** ▷ *adverb* **1** in or to the back or far side of something or someone. **2** remaining; in a place, etc that is or was being left or departed from □ ***Wait behind after class*** □ ***I left something behind.*** **3** following □ ***drove off, with the dog running behind.*** **4** in or into arrears □ ***fell behind with the rent.*** ▷ *adj* **1** not up to date; late □ ***behind with the payments.*** **2** not having progressed enough □ ***I got behind with my work.*** ▷ *noun* **1** *colloq* the part of the body a person sits on; the buttocks. **2** in Australian Rules football: a kick that scores one point, usually one in which the ball passes between a goal post and a BEHIND POST. • **behind someone's back** without their knowledge or permission. • **behind time** late. • **behind the times** out of date; old-fashioned. • **put something behind one** to try to forget (something unpleasant). ⓔ Anglo-Saxon *behindan*.

behindhand ▷ *adj* (following a verb) *rather formal or dated* **1** not up to date with regard to it; in arrears; behind □ ***has fallen behindhand with the payments*** □ ***I'm behindhand in my correspondence.*** **2** late; occurring later or progressing more slowly than expected □ ***The project is seriously behindhand.*** Compare BEFOREHAND.

behind post ▷ *noun* in Australian Rules football: one of two smaller posts positioned to either side of the main goalposts at each end of the pitch. See also BEHIND *noun* 2.

behold /bɪˈhoʊld/ *literary or old use* ▷ *verb* (***beheld, beholding***) to see; to look at something or someone □ ***Shall I behold his face?*** ▷ *exclamation* see!; look! See also LO. • **beholder** *noun, literary* an observer or onlooker □ ***the eye of the beholder.*** ⓔ Anglo-Saxon *behealdan* to hold or observe.

beholden ▷ *adj* now usually used in the phrase • **beholden to someone** *formal* owing them a debt or favour; grateful to them. ⓔ 14c: originally *past participle* of BEHOLD.

behove /bɪˈhoʊv/ or (*chiefly US*) **behoove** /bɪhuːv/ ▷ *verb* (***behove, behoving; behooved, behooving***) now only used impersonally as **it behoves someone** *old use or formal* to be necessary or fitting on their part □ ***It behoves me to tell you the truth.*** ⓔ Anglo-Saxon *behofian* to stand in need of.

beige /beɪʒ/ ▷ *noun* a very pale pinkish-brown or yellowish-brown colour. ▷ *adj* having, referring to, made in, etc this colour. ⓔ 19c: French.

beigel see BAGEL

being /ˈbiːɪŋ/ ▷ *noun* **1** existence; life □ ***come into being.*** **2** a living person or thing □ ***beings from another world.*** **3** essence; essential self or nature, especially that of a person □ ***She was like part of my very being.*** ⓔ 14c: the *verbal noun* and *present participle* of BE.

bejewelled ▷ *adj* wearing or decorated with jewels.

bel ▷ *noun, physics* (symbol **B**) a unit used to represent the ratio of two different power levels, eg of sound, equal to 10 decibels. ⓔ 1920s: named after the Scots-born US inventor Alexander Graham Bell (1847–1922).

belabour or (*US*) **belabor** /bɪˈleɪbə(r)/ ▷ *verb* (***belaboured, belabouring; belabored, belaboring***) *rather old use* **1** to argue about or discuss something at excessive length □ ***The professor belaboured the point for half an hour.*** **2** to attack or batter thoroughly, either physically or with words. ⓔ 16c.

belated /bɪˈleɪtɪd/ ▷ *adj* happening or coming late, or too late □ ***belated birthday greetings.*** • **belatedly** *adverb*. • **belatedness** *noun*. ⓔ 17c: from obsolete *belate* to make something late.

belay /bɪˈleɪ/ ▷ *verb* (***belayed, belaying***) **1** *mountaineering* to make (a climber) safe by tying their rope to a rock or a wooden or metal **belaying pin**. **2** *naut* to make (a rope) secure by winding it round a hook or peg, etc. ▷ *exclamation, naut* enough!; stop! ▷ *noun* (***belays***) **1** an act or method of belaying. **2** *mountaineering* a piece of rock used for belaying. ⓔ Anglo-Saxon verb *belecgan*, from BE- 1 + *lecgan* to lay.

bel canto /— ˈkantoʊ/ *music* ▷ *noun* a style of operatic singing that concentrates on beauty of tone and phrasing, agility, fluidity and effortless transition to, and sustaining of, the highest notes in the range. ▷ *adverb* in this style. ⓔ 19c: Italian, literally 'beautiful singing'.

belch /bɛltʃ/ ▷ *verb* (***belches, belched, belching***) **1** *intr* to give out air noisily from the stomach through the mouth; to burp. **2** (*also* **belch something out**) said of a chimney or volcano, etc: to send out (eg smoke) forcefully or in quantity. ▷ *noun* an act of belching. ⓔ Anglo-Saxon *bealcan*.

beleaguer /bɪˈliːgə(r)/ ▷ *verb* (***beleaguered, beleaguering***) **1** to cause someone bother or worry; to beset □ ***beleaguered her parents with constant demands.*** **2** to surround (eg a city) with an army and lay siege to it. • **beleaguered** *adj*. ⓔ 16c: from Dutch *belegeren* to besiege.

belfry /ˈbɛlfrɪ/ ▷ *noun* (***belfries***) **1** the upper part of a tower or steeple, where the bells are hung. **2** a tower for bells, usually attached to a church. • **have bats in the belfry** see under BAT². ⓔ 15c: from French *berfroi*, originally a movable wooden tower for use in warfare, later a watchtower.

Belgian /ˈbɛldʒən/ ▷ *adj* belonging or relating to Belgium, a kingdom of NW Europe, or its inhabitants. ▷ *noun* a citizen or inhabitant of, or person born in, Belgium. ⓔ 17c: from Latin *Belgae* a Celtic tribe which inhabited Belgium in Roman times.

belie /bɪˈlaɪ/ ▷ *verb* (***belied, belying***) **1** to show something to be untrue or false □ ***The new figures belied previous impressive reports.*** **2** to give a false idea or impression of something □ ***Her cheerful face belied the seriousness of the situation.*** **3** to fail to fulfil or justify (a hope, etc). ⓔ Anglo-Saxon *beleogan* to deceive by lying.

belief /bɪˈliːf/ ▷ *noun* **1** a principle or idea, etc accepted as true, especially without proof □ ***belief in the afterlife.*** **2** trust or confidence □ ***has no belief in people.*** **3** a person's religious faith. **4** a firm opinion. • **beyond belief** impossible to believe; incredible. ⓘ 12c as *bileafe*: from Anglo-Saxon *geleafa*.

believe /bɪ'liːv/ ▻ *verb* (***believed, believing***) **1** to accept what is said by someone as true □ *Why don't you believe me?* **2** (*sometimes* **believe something of someone**) to accept something said or proposed, eg about someone, as true □ *cannot believe his story* □ *cannot believe that of John.* **3** to think, assume or suppose □ *I believe she comes from Turkey.* • **believable** *adj.* • **believably** *adverb.* • **believer** *noun* a person who believes, especially someone who believes in God. • **believe it or not** or **can** or **would you believe it**? it seems incredible (but in fact it is true). • **not be able to believe one's ears** or **eyes** *colloq* to find it hard to believe what one is hearing or seeing. ⓘ Anglo-Saxon *belyfan*.

■ **believe in someone** to have trust or confidence in them.

■ **believe in something** or **someone 1** to be convinced of the existence of it or them □ *Do you believe in ghosts?* **2** to have religious faith, or other forms of conviction, about God or a Supreme being, etc.

■ **believe in something** to consider it right or good □ *I believe in being honest.*

Belisha beacon /bə'liːʃə — / ▻ *noun* in the UK: a tall black-and-white striped post beside a road, with a flashing orange light on top, marking a pedestrian crossing point. ⓘ 1934: named after L Hore-Belisha, the Minister of Transport who introduced these.

belittle /bɪ'lɪtəl/ ▻ *verb* (***belittled, belittling***) to treat something or someone as unimportant, or of little or no significance; to speak or write disparagingly about it or them. • **belittlement** *noun.* • **belittling** *adj.* • **belittlingly** *adverb.* ⓘ 18c.

bell[1] ▻ *noun* **1** a deep hollow object, usually one made of metal, rounded at one end and wide and open at the other, which makes a ringing sound when struck by the small hammer or CLAPPER fixed inside it. **2** any other device which makes a ringing or buzzing sound, eg an electric doorbell. **3** the sound made by such an object or device. **4** *Brit colloq* a telephone call □ *Give me a bell soon.* **5** *naut* the ringing of a bell on board ship to tell the number of half-hours that have passed in a four-hour watch □ *See me at six bells.* **6** anything shaped like a bell. ▻ *verb* (***belled, belling***) to attach or fit a bell to something. • **bell the cat** to do something daring and dangerous. ⓘ 18c: from the old fable in which some mice plan to hang a bell around the cat's neck to warn them of her approach, if a mouse could be found brave enough to take on the task.. • **ring a bell** see under RING[2]. ⓘ Anglo-Saxon *belle*.

bell[2] ▻ *verb* (***belled, belling***) *intr* said of a stag at rutting-time: to bellow with a loud roaring cry. ▻ *noun* this cry made by a rutting stag (see RUT[2]). ⓘ Anglo-Saxon *bellan* to roar.

belladonna /bɛlə'dɒnə/ (*plural* in sense 2 only ***belladonnas***) ▻ *noun* **1** DEADLY NIGHTSHADE. **2** any of various toxic alkaloid compounds, used medicinally, obtained from the deadly nightshade plant, eg ATROPINE. ⓘ 16c: from Italian *bella donna* beautiful lady; so called because ladies once used the drug cosmetically to enlarge the pupils of their eyes, and so enhance their beauty.

bellbird ▻ *noun* any of several Australian, New Zealand, Central and South American birds with a bell-like call.

bell-bottoms ▻ *plural noun* trousers which are much wider at the bottom of the leg than at the knee. Fashionable varieties of these since the 1960s are usually called FLARES. • **bell-bottomed** *adj* said of trousers: having bell-bottoms. ⓘ Late 19c.

bellboy and (*chiefly N Amer*) **bellhop** ▻ *noun* a man or boy who works in a hotel, carrying guests' bags and delivering messages, etc, who may be summoned by ringing a bell provided. *Brit equivalent* PORTER. See also DOORMAN. ⓘ 19c; BELLHOP dates from early 20c and was short for *bell-hopper*.

bell buoy ▻ *noun, naut* a buoy carrying a bell which is rung by the movement of the waves.

belle /bɛl/ ▻ *noun, dated* a beautiful woman. • **the belle of the ball** the most beautiful woman or girl at a dance or similar occasion. ⓘ 17c: French, feminine of *beau* beautiful or fine.

belles-lettres /bɛl'lɛtrə/ ▻ *plural noun* works of literature, especially poetry and essays, valued for their elegant style rather than their content. • **belletrist** /-'lɛtrɪst/ *noun.* ⓘ 18c: French, literally 'beautiful letters'.

bell-flower ▻ *noun* any member of a family of plants with bell-shaped flowers, especially the CAMPANULA.

bellhop see BELLBOY

bellicose /'bɛlɪkoʊs/ ▻ *adj* likely to, or seeking to, cause an argument or war; aggressive; warlike. • **bellicosity** /-'kɒsɪtɪ/ *noun.* ⓘ 15c: from Latin *bellicosus*, from *bellum* war.

belligerent /bə'lɪdʒərənt/ ▻ *adj* **1** aggressive and unfriendly; ready to argue. **2** fighting a war; engaged in conflict. ▻ *noun* a person, faction or country fighting a war. • **belligerence** and **belligerency** *noun.* • **belligerently** *adverb.* ⓘ 16c: from Latin *belligerare* to wage war.

bell jar ▻ *noun* a bell-shaped glass cover put over apparatus, experiments, etc in a laboratory, to stop gases escaping, etc, or used to protect a delicate decorative object from dust and damage. Also called **bell glass**.

bellow /'bɛloʊ/ ▻ *verb* (***bellowed, bellowing***) **1** *intr* to make a loud deep cry like that of a bull. **2** *tr & intr* (*often* **bellow out**) to shout something out loudly, especially in anger or pain. ▻ *noun* **1** the loud roar of a bull. **2** a deep loud sound or cry. ⓘ 14c: from Anglo-Saxon *bylgan*.

bellows /'bɛloʊz/ ▻ *singular or plural noun* **1** (*also* **a pair of bellows**) a device consisting of or containing a bag-like or box-like part with folds in it, which is squeezed to create a current of air, used eg to fan a fire. **2** on some cameras: a sleeve with bellows-like folds connecting the body of the camera to the lens, used when focusing on small close objects. • **bellows to mend** *especially sport* in a horse, etc: shortness of breath. ⓘ 13c as *belies* (plural of *bely* belly or bag): from Anglo-Saxon *belg* or *baelig* bag.

bell pull ▻ *noun* a handle or cord which operates a bell.

bell push ▻ *noun* a button which, when pressed, operates an electric bell.

bellringer ▻ *noun* a person who rings a bell at a church, or who plays music on the HANDBELL. • **bellringing** *noun* the art or practice of ringing bells; campanology.

bells and whistles ▻ *plural noun, colloq* additional features which are largely decorative rather than functional.

Bell's palsy ▻ *noun, pathol, medicine* a sudden paralysis of the muscles of one side of the face, caused by damage to the facial nerve, which results in distortion of the features and sometimes affects hearing and the sense of taste. ⓘ 19c: named after the Scottish surgeon Sir Charles Bell (1774–1842).

bell tent ▻ *noun* a bell-shaped tent with a central supporting pole.

bell tower ▻ *noun* a tower built to contain one or more bells. See also CAMPANILE.

bellwether ▻ *noun* **1** the leading sheep in a flock, that generally has a bell fastened around its neck. **2** *especially contemptuous* a ringleader; someone whose lead is followed blindly by others. ⓘ 15c.

belly /'bɛlɪ/ ▻ *noun* (***bellies***) **1** the part of the human body below the chest, containing the organs used for digesting food. **2** the stomach. **3** the lower or under part of an animal's body, which contains the stomach and other organs. **4** the deep interior of something, especially an interior space. **5** a swelling exterior part of something, eg the underside of a plane, the upper, convex side of a violin across which the strings are stretched, etc. **6** a part or surface of something which bulges out like a belly and is seen in terms of a container, eg the hollow side of a swelling sail, the wide body of a narrow-necked bottle, etc. ▻ *verb* (***bellies, bellied, bellying***) *tr & intr* (*usually* **belly out** or **belly something out**) to bulge out, or make something bulge or swell out. ⓘ Anglo-Saxon *belg* or *baelig* bag.

bellyache ▻ *noun, colloq* a pain in the belly; stomach ache. ▻ *verb, intr, slang* to complain noisily or repeatedly; to moan. • **bellyacher** *noun*. ⓘ Late 19c.

belly button ▻ *noun, colloq* the navel. Also called **tummy button**.

belly dance ▻ *noun* an erotic eastern dance performed by women, in which the belly and hips are moved around in a circling motion, often very fast. ▻ *verb* (**belly-dance**) *intr* to perform a belly dance. • **belly-dancer** *noun*. ⓘ Late 19c.

belly flop ▻ *noun* a dive into water in which the body hits the surface flat, instead of at an angle. ▻ *verb* (**belly-flop**) *intr* to perform a belly flop. ⓘ Late 19c.

bellyful ▻ *noun* (***bellyfuls***) **1** enough to eat. **2** *slang* (*usually* **a bellyful of something** or **someone**) more than enough, or more than one can bear (of it, them, or their behaviour, etc).

belly landing ▻ *noun* the landing of an aeroplane without using its wheels, usually because of a fault.

belly laugh ▻ *noun* a deep unrestrained laugh.

belong /bɪˈlɒŋ/ ▻ *verb* (***belonged, belonging***) *intr* **1 a** to have a proper place, or have the right qualities to fit (especially with or in something or someone); to go along or together with it or them ▫ ***Knives do not belong in this drawer*** ▫ ***My child belongs with me*** ▫ ***These two socks belong together***; **b** to be properly classified (in a class, section, under a heading, etc). **2** to be entirely acceptable on a social or personal level; to be at home, or to fit in ▫ ***It's a nice firm, but somehow I just don't belong.*** • **belonging** *noun* (*especially in* **a sense of belonging**) fitting in or acceptability within a group. ⓘ 14c intensive of *longen* to belong or to be suitable.

■ **belong to someone** or **something** to be their or its property or right.

■ **belong to something** to be a member of (a group, club, etc) or a native of (a place).

belongings ▻ *plural noun* personal possessions.

Belorussian or **Byelorussian** /bjɛləˈrʌʃən/ ▻ *adj* **1** belonging or relating to Belorussia (now officially the Republic of Belarus, a member state of the CIS), its inhabitants or their language. **2** *historical* White Russian; belonging or referring to Belorussia, a region to the west of Moscow. ▻ *noun* **1** a citizen or inhabitant of Belorussia. **2** the official language of Belorussia. ⓘ 1940s: from Russian *Belorussiya* White Russia, from *beliy* white.

beloved /bɪˈlʌvd, bɪˈlʌvɪd/ ▻ *adj, often in compounds* much loved; very dear ▫ ***my beloved wife*** ▫ ***well-beloved*** ▫ ***best-beloved.*** ▻ *noun, chiefly literary* or *old use* a person who is much loved. ⓘ 14c: from an obsolete verb *belove* to love.

below /bɪˈloʊ/ ▻ *prep* **1** lower in position, rank, amount, degree, number or status, etc than a specified thing ▫ ***40 degrees below zero.*** **2** not worthy of someone beneath them. **3** under the surface of something ▫ ***below water*** ▫ ***below deck.*** ▻ *adverb* **1** at, to or in a lower place, point or level. **2** further on in a book, etc ▫ ***See p 23 below.*** **3** *literary or archaic* on earth (as regarded from heaven), or in hell (as regarded from earth). • **below the belt** *colloq* unfair; not following the accepted rules of behaviour. ⓘ originally from boxing: a blow below the level of the belt is against the Queensberry Rules. ⓘ 14c as *biloogħe*, from *bi-* by + *looghe* low.

below-the-line ▻ *adj* **1** *econ* relating to that part of the Government's expenditure and revenue not allowed for in its original estimates. **2** *bookkeeping* relating to the expenditure and revenue listed separately from the normal financial details in a company's profit and loss account. Compare ABOVE-THE-LINE.

bel paese /bɛl pɑːˈeɪzɪ/ ▻ *noun* a mild creamy-textured Italian cheese. ⓘ 1930s: Italian, literally 'beautiful country'.

belt ▻ *noun* **1 a** a long narrow piece of leather or cloth worn around the waist to keep clothing in place, or for decoration, etc; **b** in certain sports, eg boxing and judo: a band worn around the waist signifying that the wearer has achieved a specific standard (eg BLACK BELT). **2** a SEAT-BELT. See also LAP BELT. **3** an area or zone, usually a relatively long and narrow one ▫ ***a belt of rain.*** **4** a band of rubber, etc moving the wheels, or round the wheels, of a machine. Often *in compounds* ▫ ***fan belt*** ▫ ***conveyor belt.*** **5** *slang* a hard blow. ▻ *verb* (***belted, belting***) **1** to put a belt around someone or something. **2** to beat someone or something with a belt. **3** *tr & intr* (*often* **belt into someone**) *colloq* to hit someone repeatedly. **4** *intr* (*especially* **belt along**) *colloq* to move very fast, especially in a specified direction ▫ ***belting along on his bike*** ▫ ***belted back home.*** **5** (*also* **belt something on**) to fasten it with, or on with, a belt. • **belted** *adj* **1** having or wearing a belt. **2** said especially of an animal: marked with a band of different colour. • **under one's belt** *colloq* said of an achievement, qualification, valuable experience, etc: firmly secured and in one's possession. ⓘ Anglo-Saxon: from Latin *balteus*.

■ **belt something** out *colloq* to sing or say it very loudly.

■ **belt up** *colloq* **1** to stop talking; to be quiet. **2** to fasten one's seat-belt.

belt-and-braces ▻ *adj* designed to protect against some possible event in two different ways, so as to make doubly sure or to double the chances of success ▫ ***a belt-and-braces policy.***

belter ▻ *noun, colloq* **1** something or someone that stands out from the others as strikingly admirable, enjoyable, thrilling, etc ▫ ***That goal was a belter*** ▫ ***She's a little belter.*** **2** a stirring song, suitable for belting out.

beltman ▻ *noun, Austral* the member of a life-saving team responsible for bringing the LIFELINE, attached to his belt, when he swims out to help someone in trouble.

beltway ▻ *noun, US* a road that goes around the outskirts of a town or an inner city area. *Brit equivalent* RINGROAD.

beluga /bəˈluːgə/ ▻ *noun* (***belugas***) **1** a kind of large sturgeon. **2** caviar from this type of sturgeon. **3** a white whale. ⓘ 16c: Russian, from *beliy* white.

belvedere /ˈbɛlvədɪə(r)/ ▻ *noun, archit* **1** a turret, lantern or room built on the top of a house, with open or glazed sides to provide a view or to let in light and air. **2** a SUMMERHOUSE on high ground. ⓘ 16c: Italian, from *bel* beautiful + *vedere* to see.

BEM ▻ *abbreviation* British Empire Medal.

bemoan ▻ *verb* to express great sadness or regret about something ▫ ***bemoaning the loss of his freedom.*** ⓘ Anglo-Saxon.

bemuse ▻ *verb* to puzzle or confuse someone. • **bemused** *adj* **1** bewildered; confused. **2** preoccupied; faraway in thought. • **bemusement** *noun*. ⓘ 18c.

ben[1] ▻ *noun, Scottish* especially in place names: a mountain or mountain peak ▫ ***Ben Nevis.*** ⓘ 18c: from Gaelic *beann*.

ben² ▷ *noun, Scots* the inner or better room or rooms of a house, which used to be reached through the **but** or kitchen. ▷ *prep, adverb* in, into or toward the inner or better room or rooms of (a house). ⓒ 14c as an adverb *binne*: from Anglo-Saxon *binnan* within.

bench /bɛntʃ/ ▷ *noun* **1** a long wooden or stone seat for seating several people. **2** a work-table for a carpenter, scientist, etc. **3** (**the bench** or **the Bench**) **a** the place where the judge or magistrate sits in court; **b** judges and magistrates as a group or profession. See also QUEEN'S BENCH. **4** *sport* especially in football and baseball: a seat for officials and reserve players, etc at a match. **5** *Brit* a seat in the House of Commons □ *took his seat in the back benches.* See also BACKBENCH, FRONT BENCH. • **on the bench 1** said of a person: holding the office of, or officiating as, a judge or bishop. **2** said of a football player: listed as a substitute. • **raise someone to the bench** to make them a judge or a bishop. ▷ *verb* (***benched***, ***benching***) **1** to provide or furnish something with benches. **2** to place something on a bench or benches, especially to exhibit (eg a dog) on a viewing platform at a show. **3** *sport, especially N Amer* to take (a player) out of a game, because of injury, infringement of the rules, etc. ⓒ Anglo-Saxon *benc*.

bencher ▷ *noun* **1** *Brit* a senior member of an INN OF COURT. **2** a person who sits on a bench in some official capacity. ⓒ 15c.

benchmark ▷ *noun* **1** anything taken or used as a standard or point of reference. **2** *surveying* a permanent mark cut on a post, building, etc giving the height above sea level of the land at that exact spot, used when measuring land and making maps. **3** *computing* a standard program used to compare the performance of different makes of computer. ⓒ 19c: originally in sense 2, in which *bench* referred to the temporary bracket used to support the surveyor's levelling-staff.

bend ▷ *verb* (***bent***, ***bending***) **1** *tr & intr* to make or become angled or curved. **2** *intr* to move or stretch in a curve. **3** *intr* (*usually* **bend down** or **over**) to move the top part of the body forward and down towards the ground. **4** *tr & intr* to submit or force someone or something to submit □ *bent them to his will.* **5** (*usually* **bend something** or **someone towards something**) to aim or direct (one's attention, etc) towards it. See also BENT. ▷ *noun* **1** a curve or bent part. **2** the act of curving or bending □ *Give that wire a bend.* See also THE BENDS. • **bendable** *adj*. • **bend over backwards** *Brit* to take great trouble or put oneself out (to be helpful, etc). • **bend the rules** to interpret the rules in one's favour, without actually breaking them. • **round the bend** *colloq* mad; crazy. ⓒ Anglo-Saxon.

bended ▷ *adj* now usually only used in the phrase • **on bended knee** kneeling down on one knee, or both knees. ⓒ 14c: an archaic *past participle* of BEND.

bender ▷ *noun* **1** *slang* a drunken spree; a spell of uncontrolled drinking. **2** a person or machine that bends.

the bends ▷ *singular or plural noun, non-technical* DECOMPRESSION SICKNESS. ⓒ Late 19c.

bendy ▷ *adj* (***bendier***, ***bendiest***) **1** having many bends or curves. **2** able to bend easily; flexible.

beneath /bɪ'niːθ/ ▷ *prep* **1** under; below; in a lower position, so as to be covered or hidden by something or someone. **2** not worthy of someone or something □ *He thinks the job is beneath him.* ▷ *adverb, rather formal or archaic* below; underneath □ *A new church was built, but the old vaults lay beneath.* ⓒ Anglo-Saxon *beneothan*.

Benedictine /bɛnɪ'dɪktɪn, -taɪn/ ▷ *noun* **1** a member of the Christian religious order (the **Order of St Benedict**) that follows the teachings of St Benedict of Nursia (480–543). **2** /-tiːn/ a brandy-based greenish-yellow liqueur first made by Benedictine monks in France in the 16c. Also *as adj*. ⓒ 15c.

benediction /bɛnɪ'dɪkʃən/ ▷ *noun, Christianity* **1** a prayer giving blessing, especially at the end of a religious service. **2** *RC Church* a short service in which the congregation is blessed. **3** *formal* blessedness. • **benedictory** *adj*. ⓒ 15c: from Latin *benedicere* to bless.

benefaction ▷ *noun* **1** a gift or donation from a benefactor. **2** an act of doing good; help or charity given. ⓒ 17c.

benefactor /'bɛnɪfaktə(r)/ ▷ *noun* a person who gives help, especially financial help, to an institution, cause or person. Also (if a female benefactor) **benefactress**. • **benefactory** *adj* **1** serving as a gift or donation. **2** belonging or referring to a benefactor. ⓒ 15c: from Latin *bene* good + *facere* to do.

benefice /'bɛnɪfɪs/ ▷ *noun* a position as a priest or minister, or other church office, and the income from land or buildings, etc which goes with it. • **beneficed** *adj* holding a benefice. ⓒ 14c: from Latin *beneficium* a favour, service or benefit.

beneficence /bɪ'nɛfɪsəns/ ▷ *noun, formal* **1** generosity. **2** a BENEFACTION. • **beneficent** *adj* actively kind and generous. • **beneficently** *adverb*. ⓒ 16c: from Latin *beneficentia*.

beneficial /bɛnɪ'fɪʃəl/ ▷ *adj* **1** having good results or benefits; advantageous. **2** *law* having the use of, and entitlement to the profits from, property. • **beneficially** *adverb*. ⓒ 15c: from Latin *beneficialis* generous.

beneficiary /bɛnɪ'fɪʃərɪ/ ▷ *noun* (***beneficiaries***) **1** a person who benefits from something. **2** *law* **a** a person who is entitled to estate or interest held for them by trustees; **b** a person who receives property or money, etc in a will, or benefits under an insurance policy, etc. Also *as adj*. ⓒ 17c.

benefit /'bɛnɪfɪt/ ▷ *noun* **1** something good gained or received. **2** advantage or sake □ *for your benefit.* **3** (*often* **benefits**) a payment made by a government or company insurance scheme, usually to someone who is ill or out of work □ *social security benefit.* **4** a concert, match, performance at a theatre, etc from which the profits are given to a particular cause, person or group of people in need. ▷ *verb* (***benefited***, ***benefiting***; *US also* ***benefitted***, ***benefitting***) **1** *intr* (*especially* **benefit from** or **by something**) to gain an advantage or receive something good from it or as a result of it. **2** to do good to someone. • **give someone the benefit of the doubt** in a case where some doubt remains: to assume that they are telling the truth, or are innocent, because there is not enough evidence to be certain that they are not. ⓒ 14c: from French *benfet*, from Latin *benefactum* good deed.

benefit of clergy ▷ *noun* **1** permission or sanction granted by the church. **2** *legal hist* exemption from the processes of the secular lawcourts granted to members of the clergy.

benefit society ▷ *noun* a FRIENDLY SOCIETY.

Benelux /'bɛnɪlʌks/ ▷ *noun* **1** an economic union between Belgium, the Netherlands and Luxembourg. **2** these three countries viewed or considered together. ⓒ 1947, originally formed as a customs union; a blend of the names.

benevolence /bə'nɛvələns/ ▷ *noun* **1** the desire to do good; kindness; generosity. **2** an act of kindness or generosity. ⓒ 14c: from Latin *bene* good + *volens* wishing.

benevolent ▷ *adj* **1** showing or involving kindness and generosity. **2** said of an organization, society, fund or enterprise: set up and run for the benefit of others rather than for profit; charitable. • **benevolently** *adverb*. ⓒ 15c.

BEng ▷ *abbreviation* Bachelor of Engineering.

Bengali /bɛŋ'gɔːlɪ, bɛn-/ ▷ *adj* belonging or relating to Bangladesh, a republic in S Asia, and the state of W Bengal in India, their inhabitants, or their language. ▷ *noun* **1** a citizen or inhabitant of, or person born in, Bangladesh or W Bengal. **2** (*also* **Bangla**) the official language of Bangladesh and the chief language of W Bengal. ◷ 19c: from Hindi *Bangali*.

benighted ▻ *adj, literary* said of eg a people, a land or a race: lacking intelligence or a sense of morality. ◷ 16c, from the obsolete verb *benight* to overcome with darkness.

benign /bɪ'naɪn/ ▻ *adj* **1** kind; gentle. **2** *medicine* **a** said of a disorder: not having harmful effects; of a mild form; **b** said specifically of a cancerous tumour: of a type that does not invade and destroy the surrounding tissue or spread to more distant parts. Compare MALIGNANT. **3** favourable; promising. • **benignly** *adverb*. ◷ 14c: from Latin *benignus*.

benignant /bə'nɪgnənt/ ▻ *adj* **1** *medicine* said of a disease or growth, etc: not fatal; a later and less common word for BENIGN. **2** kind. **3** favourable. • **benignancy** *noun* (***benignancies***). • **benignantly** *adverb*.

benignity /bə'nɪgnɪtɪ/ ▻ *noun* (***benignities***) **1** kindness; benevolence. **2** an act of kindness. ◷ 14c.

benny /'bɛnɪ/ ▻ *noun* (***bennies***) *slang* an amphetamine tablet. ◷ 1940s: an abbreviation of BENZEDRINE.

bent ▻ *adj* **1** not straight; curved or having a bend. **2** *Brit slang* **a** dishonest; corrupt ▫ *bent officers in the force*; **b** obtained dishonestly; stolen ▫ *bent goods*. **3** *Brit, derog slang* homosexual. **4** (*usually* **bent on** or **upon something**) having all one's attention or energy directed on it, or on doing it; intent or determined ▫ *bent on revenge*. ▻ *noun* **1** a natural inclination, liking or aptitude ▫ *shows a real bent for music*. **2** *bot* BENT GRASS. ▻ *verb, past tense, past participle of* BEND. • **bent as a nine bob note** *Brit slang* **1** said of a person: thoroughly dishonest. **2** said of property: obviously stolen or illicit. **3** said of a person: homosexual. ◷ 14c.

bent grass ▻ *noun, bot* any of various hardy perennial grasses used for pasture, lawns or hay. Also shortened to **bent**. ◷ 15c.

benthos /'bɛnθɒs/ ▻ *noun, biol* the living organisms that are found at the bottom of a sea or lake. • **benthic** *adj*. Compare PELAGIC. ◷ 19c: Greek, literally 'depth'.

bentonite /'bɛntənaɪt/ ▻ *noun, geol* a white, pale-green or pale-blue soft porous rock, capable of absorbing large quantities of water, and used in papermaking and as a bleaching and decolourizing agent. ◷ 19c: named after Fort Benton in Montana, USA where it was found.

bentwood ▻ *noun* wood artificially curved for making furniture, etc.

benumb /bɪ'nʌm/ ▻ *verb* **1** to make someone or something numb. **2** to stupefy (especially the senses or the mind). ◷ 15c.

Benzedrine /'bɛnzɪdriːn/ ▻ *noun, trademark* an AMPHETAMINE drug. See also BENNY. ◷ 1930s.

benzene /'bɛnziːn/ ▻ *noun, chem* (formula C_6H_6) an inflammable colourless liquid HYDROCARBON, mainly obtained from petroleum, that has an aromatic odour and is widely used as a solvent and in the manufacture of plastics, dyes, drugs and other organic chemicals. ◷ 19c: from BENZOIC ACID.

benzene ring ▻ *noun, chem* a ring consisting of six linked carbon atoms, as in a molecule of benzene.

benzine or **benzin** /'bɛnziːn/ ▻ *noun* a volatile mixture of HYDROCARBONs distilled from petroleum, used as a motor fuel and solvent, etc. ◷ 19c: originally the name given to BENZENE, with which it is still sometimes confused.

benzocaine /'bɛnzoʊkeɪn/ ▻ *noun, medicine* a white crystalline powder used as a local anaesthetic, especially to relieve painful skin conditions, and also administered by mouth to treat gastric ulcers. ◷ 1920s: from *benz*ic acid + *cocaine*.

benzodiazepine /bɛnzoʊdaɪ'azəpiːn, -'eɪzəpiːn/ ▻ *noun, medicine* any of various potentially addictive minor tranquillizer and hypnotic drugs, eg DIAZEPAM, now generally only used for short-term treatment of severe anxiety or insomnia. ◷ 1960s: from *benzo*ic acid + *diazepam* + -INE².

benzoic acid /bɛn'zoʊɪk — / ▻ *noun, chem* (formula C_6H_5COOH) a colourless or white crystalline compound, usually obtained from benzoin or cranberries, used as a fruit preservative, in cosmetics and anti-fungal medicines etc, and in the manufacture of organic compounds. ◷ 18c: from BENZOIN in which it is found.

benzoin /'bɛnzoʊɪn, -zɔɪn/ ▻ *noun* **1** the aromatic resinous sap of a tree native to Java and Sumatra, used in perfumery, incense, etc and as an expectorant, respiratory inhalant and antiseptic. **2** *chem* a highly toxic white crystalline compound used in the manufacture of organic compounds. ◷ 16c as *benjoin*: ultimately from Arabic *luban jawa* incense of Java.

benzoquinone see QUINONE

bequeath /bɪ'kwiːð, -'kwiːθ/ ▻ *verb* (***bequeathed***, ***bequeathing***) **1** to leave (personal property) in a will. **2** to pass on or give to posterity. ◷ Anglo-Saxon *becwethan* in obsolete sense 'to say or utter'.

bequest /bɪ'kwɛst/ ▻ *noun* **1** an act of leaving personal property in a will. **2** anything left or bequeathed in someone's will. ◷ 14c: from Anglo-Saxon *becwethan* (see BEQUEATH).

berate /bɪ'reɪt/ ▻ *verb* (***berated***, ***berating***) to scold someone severely. ◷ 16c: from BE- 1 + old verb *rate* to scold.

Berber /'bɜːbə(r)/ ▻ *noun* **1** any of several native Muslim tribes of N Africa. **2** an individual belonging to any of these tribes. **3** any of a group of Afro-Asiatic languages spoken by these people, eg TUAREG. ▻ *adj* belonging or relating to this group or their language. ◷ 18c: from Arabic *barbar*; the aboriginal N African tribes were given this name following the 7c Arab conquest.

bereave /bɪ'riːv/ ▻ *verb* (***bereaved***, ***bereaving***) **1** to widow, orphan or deprive someone of a close relative or friend by death. **2** to deprive or rob someone of something they value generally. • **bereaved** *adj* said of a person: **1** having recently suffered the death of a close relative or friend. Compare BEREFT. **2** (**the bereaved**) bereaved people as a group (see THE 4). • **bereavement** *noun* the death of a close relative or friend. ◷ Anglo-Saxon *bereafian* to rob or plunder.

bereft /bɪ'rɛft/ ▻ *adj* (*usually* **bereft of something**) deprived of it; having had something precious taken away (especially, in a formal context, some immaterial possession) ▫ *bereft of all hope* ▫ *I feel quite bereft without my radio*. Compare BEREAVED. ◷ 16c *past participle* of BEREAVE.

beret /'bɛreɪ, 'bɛrɪ; *N Amer* bə'reɪ/ ▻ *noun* a round flat cap made of wool or other soft material. ◷ 19c: from French *béret* cap.

berg¹ ▻ /bɜːg/ *noun, S Afr* a mountain. ◷ 19c: Afrikaans, from Dutch.

berg² ▻ /bɜːg/ *noun* short form of ICEBERG. ◷ 19c.

bergamot¹ /'bɜːgəmɒt/ ▻ *noun* **1** a small citrus tree that produces acidic pear-shaped fruits. **2** (*also* **bergamot oil**) the oil extracted from the rind of the fruit of this tree, widely used in perfumery. ◷ 17c: named after Bergamo in N Italy.

bergamot² /'bɜːgəmɒt/ ▻ *noun* a type of fine pear. ◷ 17c: ultimately from Turkish *begarmudu*, from *beg* prince + *armud* pear.

bergschrund /'bɛəkʃrʊnt/ ▻ *noun, geog* a deep crevasse, or a series of fissures, formed at or near the head of a mountain glacier, between the moving and stationary ice. ◷ 19c: German, literally 'mountain cleft'.

beribboned ▷ *adj* decorated with ribbons. ◷ 19c.

beriberi /ˈbɛrɪbɛrɪ/ ▷ *noun, pathol, medicine* a deficiency disease, most widespread in the tropics, caused by lack of THIAMINE, which results in inflammation of the nerves, paralysis of the limbs, OEDEMA and heart failure. ◷ 18c: from Sinhalese *beri* weakness.

berk or **burk** /bɜːk/ ▷ *noun, Brit slang* a fool or twit. ◷ 1930s: from Cockney rhyming slang *Berkeley Hunt*, for CUNT.

berkelium /bɜːˈkiːlɪəm, ˈbɜːklɪəm/ ▷ *noun, chem* (symbol **Bk**, atomic number 97) a radioactive metallic element manufactured artificially by bombarding americium-241 with ALPHA PARTICLES. ◷ 1950s: named after Berkeley in California, where it was first made.

Berks. /bɑːks/ ▷ *abbreviation, English county* Berkshire.

berley or **burley** /ˈbɜːlɪ/ ▷ *noun, Austral* **1** *colloq* humbug; rubbish. **2** *fishing* groundbait. ◷ 19c in sense 2.

berm /bɜːm/ ▷ *noun* a narrow ledge or path beside an embankment, road or canal, etc. ◷ 18c: from French *berme*.

Bermudan /bɜːˈmjuːdən/ ▷ *adj* belonging or relating to Bermuda, an island in the W Atlantic Ocean, or its inhabitants. ▷ *noun* a citizen or inhabitant of, or person born in, Bermuda. Also **Bermudian**.

Bermuda shorts or **Bermudas** ▷ *plural noun* knee-length shorts, usually made of brightly-patterned cotton fabric. ◷ 1950s.

Bermuda Triangle ▷ *noun* an area of the Atlantic between Florida, Bermuda and Puerto Rico, where there is an unusually high number of unexplained disappearances of ships and aircraft.

berry /ˈbɛrɪ/ ▷ *noun* (*berries*) **1** *bot* an INDEHISCENT fleshy fruit that contains anything from several to many seeds which are not surrounded by a stony protective layer, eg grape, cucumber, tomato, citrus fruits. **2** *loosely* any of the various small fleshy edible fruits that are not true berries, eg strawberry and raspberry. **3** *zool* a dark structure resembling a knob on the bill of a swan. **4** the egg of a crayfish or lobster. ◷ Anglo-Saxon *berie*.

berserk /bəˈzɜːk, bəˈsɜːk/ ▷ *adj* (*especially* **go berserk**) **1** violently angry; wild and destructive. **2** *colloq & facetious* furious; crazy. ▷ *noun* (*also* **berserker**) *historical* a Norse warrior who rushed into battle in a wild frenzied rage. ◷ 19c, originally as a *noun*: from Norse *berserkr*, probably from *bern* a bear + *serkr* coat.

berth /bɜːθ/ ▷ *noun* **1** a sleeping-place in a ship or train, etc. **2** a place in a port where a ship or boat can be tied up. **3** enough room for a ship to be able to turn round in. **4** *Brit colloq* a job or situation, especially a comfortable one. ▷ *verb* (*berthed*, *berthing*) **1** to tie up (a ship) in its berth. **2** *intr* said of a ship: to arrive at its berth; to moor. **3** to provide a sleeping-place for someone. ● **give someone** or **something a wide berth** to stay well away from them or it. ◷ 17c: a nautical term, possibly connected with BEAR[1].

berth

There is sometimes a spelling confusion between **berth** and **birth.**

beryl /ˈbɛrɪl/ ▷ *noun, geol* a hard mineral (beryllium aluminium silicate) that occurs in the form of green, blue, yellow or white crystals, used as a source of BERYLLIUM and as a gemstone, the most valuable varieties being AQUAMARINE and EMERALD. ◷ 14c: ultimately from Greek *beryllos*.

beryllium /bəˈrɪlɪəm/ ▷ *noun, chem* (symbol **Be**, atomic number 4) a silvery-grey metal, obtained from the mineral BERYL, used to make windows in X-ray tubes, and also used together with copper to make strong alloys. ◷ 19c.

beseech /bɪˈsiːtʃ/ ▷ *verb* (*besought* /bɪsɔːt/ or *beseeched, beseeching*) *formal or literary* to ask someone earnestly; to beg □ *Have mercy, we beseech you, O Lord.* ● **beseeching** *adj, noun.* ● **beseechingly** *adverb.* ◷ 12c: from BE- 1 + obsolete *sechen* to seek.

beset /bɪˈsɛt/ ▷ *verb* (*beset, besetting*) *now chiefly literary or formal* (*usually* **beset by** or **with something**) **1** to worry or harass someone, or to hamper or complicate something (with problems, temptations, obstacles, etc). **2** to surround, attack or beseige (a person or people) on every side. ◷ Anglo-Saxon *besettan* to surround or set about.

beside /bɪˈsaɪd/ ▷ *prep* **1** next to, by the side of or near something or someone. **2** not relevant to something □ *That is beside the point.* **3** as compared with something or someone □ *All beauty pales beside hers.* ● **beside oneself** in a state of uncontrollable anger, excitement or other emotion □ *By the time he arrived, I was beside myself.* □ *beside herself with worry.* ◷ 13c: from Anglo-Saxon *be* by + *sidan* side.

beside, besides

There is often confusion between **beside** and **besides**: **beside** means 'next to, at the side of', whereas **besides** means 'in addition to, other than'.

besides ▷ *prep* in addition to, as well as or apart from something or someone. ▷ *adverb* **1** also; as well □ *We saw three more besides.* **2** (often as a sentence connector) moreover; in any case □ *I don't want to go; besides, I'm not dressed.* ◷ 13c: from, and originally with the same meaning as, BESIDE.

besiege /bɪˈsiːdʒ/ ▷ *verb* **1** to surround (a town or stronghold) with an army in order to force it to surrender. **2** to gather round something or someone in a crowd; to surround □ *beseiged by excited fans.* **3** to annoy someone constantly or thoroughly; to plague or bother □ *She besieged me with questions.* **4** to inundate or overwhelm someone □ *besieged with offers of help.* ◷ 13c.

besmear /bɪˈsmɪə(r)/ ▷ *verb* **1** to smear or daub someone or something with something greasy, sticky or dirty, etc □ *face besmeared with oil.* **2** to besmirch or sully (someone's reputation, etc). ◷ Anglo-Saxon.

besmirch /bɪˈsmɜːtʃ/ ▷ *verb, formal* **1** to spoil or stain (the reputation, character, name, etc of someone). **2** to make something dirty. ◷ 16c.

besom /ˈbɪzəm, ˈbiːzəm/ ▷ *noun* **1** a large brush made from sticks tied to a long wooden handle. **2** *Scots & N Eng, derog* or *jocular* a woman □ *cheeky besom.* ◷ Anglo-Saxon *besma*; sense 2 may be unrelated.

besotted /bɪˈsɒtɪd/ ▷ *adj* **1** (*especially* **besotted by** or **with someone** or **something**) foolishly infatuated. **2** confused, especially through having drunk too much alcohol. ● **besottedly** *adverb.* ◷ 16c: from old verb *besot* to make foolish or sottish.

besought *past tense, past participle of* BESEECH

bespangle ▷ *verb* to decorate something with objects which shine or sparkle. ◷ 17c.

bespatter ▷ *verb* to cover something or someone with spots, splashes or large drops (especially of a dirty liquid). ◷ 17c.

bespeak ▷ *verb, formal* **1** to claim, engage or order something in advance. See also BESPOKE. **2** to show or be evidence of something. **3** to indicate something in advance; to foretell □ *This worrying news bespoke trouble ahead.* ◷ 16c.

bespectacled ▷ *adj* wearing spectacles or with marks around the eyes resembling spectacles.

bespoke /bɪˈspoʊk/ ▷ *adj, now rather formal* **1** said of clothes: made to fit a particular person, or made according to a particular person's requirements. See also MADE TO

MEASURE at MADE. Compare OFF-THE-PEG, READY-MADE, READY-TO-WEAR. **2** said of a tailor: making clothes to order, to fit individual customers and their requirements. ⓒ 18c in this use; see BESPEAK.

Bessemer process /ˈbɛsɪmə(r) — / ▻ *noun, technical* a process in which pig iron is converted into steel by blowing air through the molten iron. ⓒ 19c: named after the inventor, English engineer Sir Henry Bessemer (1813–98).

best ▻ *adj* (superlative of GOOD) **1** most excellent, suitable or desirable. **2** most successful, clever, able or skilled, etc. **3** the greatest or most ▫ *took the best part of an hour.* ▻ *adverb* (superlative of WELL[1]) **1** most successfully or skilfully, etc ▫ *Who did best in the test?* **2** more than, or better than, all others ▫ *I like her best* ▫ *Which hat looks best?* ▻ *noun* **1** (**the best**) the most excellent or suitable person or thing; the most desirable quality or result, etc ▫ *the best of the bunch.* **2** the greatest effort; one's utmost ▫ *Do your best.* **3** a person's finest clothes ▫ *Sunday best.* **4** (**the best**) victory or success ▫ *get the best of an argument.* **5** (*usually* **the best of something**) a winning majority from (a given number, etc) ▫ *the best of three.* ▻ *verb* (***bested, besting***) *colloq* to beat or defeat someone. • **all the best!** *colloq* said in parting, closing a telephone conversation, etc: best wishes; good luck; wishing you success, happiness, etc. • **as best one can** as well as one can. • **at best** considered in the most favourable way; in the best of circumstances. • **at the best of times** even in the most favourable circumstances. • **the best bet** or **your**, **our**, *etc* **best bet** *colloq* the (or your, our, etc) most appropriate course of action. • **best wishes** often written in greetings cards, etc: wishing you happiness, health, prosperity, success, etc. • **for the best** likely or intended to have the best results possible, especially in the long term or over all. • **had best do something** would find it wisest to do it ▫ *You had best find out straight away.* • **make the best of something** to do, etc as well as possible in unfavourable circumstances ▫ *It isn't what I wanted, but I'll just have to make the best of it.* • **put one's best foot forward** to make the best attempt possible. • **to the best of one's knowledge** or **belief** or **ability** as far as one knows, or believes, or is able. • **with the best of them** as successfully or as well as anyone. ⓒ Anglo-Saxon *betst*; 19c as *verb*.

best-before date ▻ *noun* a date stamped or printed on the packaging of a perishable product, especially food, to indicate the day or month by which it should be used or consumed. Compare SELL-BY DATE. ⓒ 1980s: from the usual wording 'Best before (a given date)'.

best boy ▻ *noun, cinema & TV, originally N Amer* the charge-hand electrician in a production crew, chief assistant to the GAFFER. ⓒ 1930s.

bestial /ˈbɛstɪəl/ ▻ *adj* **1** *derog* cruel; savage; brutish. **2** rude; unrefined; uncivilized. **3** sexually depraved. **4** like or referring to an animal in character, behaviour, etc. • **bestially** *adverb.* ⓒ 14c: from Latin *bestia* animal.

bestiality /bɛstɪˈalɪtɪ/ *noun* (***bestialities***) **1** disgusting or cruel behaviour. **2** sexual intercourse between a human and an animal.

bestiary /ˈbɛstɪərɪ/ ▻ *noun* (***bestiaries***) a kind of book popular in Europe in the Middle Ages, containing pictures and descriptions of animals, often used for moral instruction. ⓒ 19c: from Latin *bestiarium* a menagerie.

bestir /bɪˈstɜː(r)/ ▻ *verb, rather formal* or *archaic* now usually only used as • **bestir oneself** to make an effort to become active; to get oneself moving or busy. ⓒ 14c.

best man ▻ *noun* a bridegroom's chief attendant at a wedding, who has certain traditional responsibilities in the arrangements and ceremony, etc. See also GROOMSMAN. ⓒ 18c.

bestow /bɪˈstoʊ/ ▻ *verb* (***bestowed, bestowing***) (*usually* **bestow something on** or **upon someone**) *formal* to give or present (a title, award, quality, etc) to someone. • **bestowal** *noun.* ⓒ 14c: from Anglo-Saxon *stowen* to place.

bestraddle ▻ *verb* to stand or sit with one leg on either side of something; to straddle across something. ⓒ Early 19c.

bestrewn ▻ *adj, especially formal* or *literary* said of a surface, eg the ground, a floor, or table-top: littered or covered loosely, usually with things which have been thrown casually or scattered randomly ▫ *a beach bestrewn with shells.* ⓒ 19c: from Anglo-Saxon *bestreowian* to strew.

bestride /bɪˈstraɪd/ ▻ *verb* (***bestrode, bestridden, bestriding***) *formal or literary* **1** to sit or stand across something (eg a horse) with one leg on each side. **2** to stand over or across something in an imposing, protective or defensive manner. ⓒ Anglo-Saxon *bestridan*, from *stridan* to straddle.

bestseller ▻ *noun* **1** a book or other item which sells in large numbers. **2** the author of a bestselling book. • **bestselling** *adj* said of a book or other item: that sells in large numbers. ⓒ Early 19c.

bet ▻ *verb* (***bet*** or ***betted, betting***) **1** *tr & intr* to risk (a sum of money or other asset) on predicting the outcome or result of a future event, especially a race or other sporting event, in such a way that the better wins money if the outcome is as predicted, and loses the STAKE[2] if it is not ▫ *bet £5 on the favourite.* **2** (*usually* **bet someone something**) to make a bet (of a specified amount with someone in particular), so that if one's prediction is correct one wins (that amount from them), and if not, one loses (that amount to them) ▫ *She bet me £1 that you'd be late.* **3** *colloq* to feel sure or confident ▫ *I bet they'll be late.* ▻ *noun* **1** an act of betting. **2** a sum of money, or other asset, betted. **3** *colloq* an opinion or guess ▫ *My bet is that he's bluffing.* **4** *colloq* a choice of action or way ahead ▫ *Our best bet is to postpone the trip.* • **better** or *sometimes* **bettor** *noun* a person who bets. • **bet one's bottom dollar** to bet all one has. • **you bet** *slang, especially US* certainly; definitely; of course. ⓒ 16c.

beta /ˈbiːtə/ ▻ *noun* (***betas***) **1** the second letter of the Greek alphabet. See table at GREEK ALPHABET. **2** a mark indicating the second highest grade or quality. **3** the second in a series, or the second of two categories or types. ⓒ 14c: Greek.

beta-blocker ▻ *noun, medicine* a drug that slows the heartbeat, used to treat high blood pressure, angina, and abnormal heart rhythms. ⓒ 1970s.

betacarotene ▻ *noun, biochem* a form of the pigment CAROTENE, found in yellow and orange fruits and vegetables, that is converted to vitamin A in the body.

beta decay ▻ *noun, physics* a form of RADIOACTIVE DECAY in which a neutron in an atomic nucleus spontaneously breaks up into a PROTON (which remains within the nucleus) and an ELECTRON (which is emitted).

betake ▻ *verb, very formal or literary,* (*usually* **betake oneself**) to go; to take oneself to a specified place ▫ *betook himself to Rome.* ⓒ 13c, meaning 'to commit' or 'to hand over'.

beta particle ▻ *noun, physics* an ELECTRON or POSITRON produced when a neutron inside an unstable radioactive nucleus turns into a proton, or a proton turns into a neutron. ⓒ Early 20c.

beta ray ▻ *noun, physics* a stream of beta particles.

beta rhythm and **beta wave** ▻ *noun, physiol* a wave representing the normal electrical activity of the brain when a person is awake with their eyes open. Compare ALPHA RHYTHM, DELTA RHYTHM.

beta test *computing* ▻ *noun* a second round of tests run on new software before it is marketed, designed to recreate normal working conditions. • **beta testing** *noun.* ⓒ 1980s.

betatron ▻ *noun, physics* a type of PARTICLE ACCELERATOR, used in medicine and industry, which continuously increases the magnetic FLUX within the orbit of a charged particle. ⓒ 1940s.

betel /ˈbiːtəl/ ▷ *noun* **1** a palm, native to Asia, the fruit of which (the **betel nut**) is mixed with lime and chewed as a mild stimulant. **2** a preparation consisting of dried betel nut mixed with lime and wrapped in the leaf of a different plant (the **betel pepper**), chewed in the East as a mild stimulant. ◎ 16c: Portuguese, from Malayalam *vettila*.

bête noire /bɛt nwɑː(r)/ ▷ *noun* (***bêtes noires***) a person or thing that especially bothers, annoys or frightens someone. ◎ 19c: French, literally 'black beast'.

betide /bɪˈtaɪd/ ▷ *verb* (now limited to this form, as infinitive and 3rd person subjunctive) *literary or archaic* **1** *intr* to happen; to come to pass □ *whate'er may betide.* **2** to happen to someone; to befall them □ *Woe betide you.* ◎ 13c: from Anglo-Saxon *tidan* to befall.

betoken ▷ *verb* (***betokened, betokening***) *formal* to be evidence, or a sign or omen of something; to signify. ◎ 15c: from Anglo-Saxon *tacnian* to signify.

betook *past tense of* BETAKE

betray /bɪˈtreɪ/ ▷ *verb* (***betrayed, betraying***) **1** to hand over or expose (a friend or one's country, etc) to an enemy. **2** to give away or disclose (a secret, etc). **3** to break (a promise or confidence, etc) or to be unfaithful to someone □ *betray a trust* □ *could never betray his wife.* **4** to be evidence of something, especially something intended to be hidden □ *Her face betrayed her unhappiness.* • **betrayal** *noun.* • **betrayer** *noun.* ◎ 13c: ultimately from Latin *tradere* to hand over.

betrothal /bɪˈtroʊðəl/ ▷ *noun, formal* engagement to be married. ◎ 19c.

betrothed /bɪˈtroʊðd/ *formal or sometimes facetious,* ▷ *adj* said of a person: engaged to marry someone. ▷ *noun* a person to whom someone is betrothed. ◎ 16c: from the archaic verb *betroth* to plight one's TROTH.

better¹ /ˈbɛtə(r)/ ▷ *adj* (comparative of GOOD) **1** more excellent, suitable or desirable, etc. **2** (*usually* **better at something**) more successful, skilful, etc in doing it. **3** (comparative of WELL¹) (*especially* **be** or **feel** or **get better**) partly or fully improved in health or recovered from illness. **4** greater □ *the better part of a day.* ▷ *adverb* (comparative of WELL¹) **1** more excellently, successfully or fully, etc □ *You can see better from here.* **2** in or to a greater degree □ *knows the area better than I do.* ▷ *noun* **1** (*especially* **betters**) a person superior in quality or status, etc □ *Respect your elders and betters.* **2** (**the better**) the thing or person that is the more excellent or suitable, etc of two comparable things or people □ *This is the better of my two attempts.* ▷ *verb* (***bettered, bettering***) **1** to beat or improve on something □ *can't better his original score.* **2** to make something more suitable, desirable or excellent, etc □ *set out to better the conditions for the workers.* • **all the better for something** very much better as a result of it. • **better off** more affluent or fortunate; wealthier or in happier circumstances. • **better oneself** to improve one's position or social standing. • **for better or for worse** no matter what happens. • **get the better of someone** to gain the advantage over them; to outwit them. • **go one better than someone** to beat them by improving on what they have done, achieved or offered, etc. • **had better do something** ought to do it, especially in order to avoid some undesirable outcome. • **so much the better** that is, or would be, preferable. ◎ Anglo-Saxon *betera*; 14c as *verb* 2.

better² or **bettor** see under BET

better half ▷ *noun, jocular or patronizing* one's own, or someone else's, partner or spouse.

betterment ▷ *noun* **1** making better; improvement or advancement, especially in standard of life or status, etc □ *for the betterment of mankind.* **2** an improvement in the value of property.

betting ▷ *noun* gambling by predicting the outcome of some future event, especially a race or other sporting event. • **What's the betting...?** *colloq* I'd be willing to bet or guess (that a specified thing happens or has happened); it's very likely.

betting-shop ▷ *noun, Brit* a licensed establishment where the public can place bets; a bookmaker's.

between /bɪˈtwiːn/ ▷ *prep* **1** in, to, through or across the space dividing (two people, places, times, etc). **2** to and from □ *a regular bus service between Leeds and Bradford.* **3** in combination; acting together □ *They bought the house between them.* **4** shared out among □ *Divide the money between them.* **5** involving a choice between alternatives □ *choose between right and wrong.* **6** including; involving □ *a fight between rivals.* ▷ *adverb* (*also* **in between**) in or into the middle of (two points in space or time, etc) □ *time for a quick lunch between appointments.* • **between you and me** or **between ourselves** in confidence; privately; without informing anyone else. ◎ Anglo-Saxon *betweonum*, from *be* by + *twegen* two.

> ***between, among***
>
> • It is acceptable to use **between** with reference to more than two people or things □ *Viewers tend to switch between channels.* However, **among** is sometimes more appropriate when there is a distinct notion of sharing or distributing □ *Hand these out among all of you.* **Between** is more usual when individual people or things are named □ *Duties are divided between John, Margaret and Catherine.*

betweentimes ▷ *adverb* (*also* **in betweentimes**) during the intervals between other events.

betwixt /bɪˈtwɪkst/ ▷ *prep* ▷ *adverb, old use* between. • **betwixt and between** ▷ *adj* undecided; in a middle position. ◎ Anglo-Saxon *betweox*.

BeV ▷ *abbreviation, US, nuclear physics* billion electron-volts (where BILLION equals one thousand million). *Brit equivalent* GEV.

bevatron /ˈbɛvətrɒn/ ▷ *noun, nuclear physics* a type of PROTON ACCELERATOR that produces particles with an energy content of the order of billions of electron-volts. ◎ 1940s: from BEV + -TRON.

bevel /ˈbɛvəl/ ▷ *noun* **1** a sloping edge to a surface, meeting another surface at an angle between the horizontal and the vertical. **2** a tool which makes such a sloping edge on a piece of wood, stone or glass. ▷ *verb* (***bevelled, bevelling***; *US* ***beveled, beveling***) **1** to give a bevel or slant to (eg a piece of wood). **2** *intr* to slope at an angle. • **bevelled** *adj.* ◎ 16c; first used in heraldry referring to an angled line, and apparently from an older form of the French *beveau* a bevel (sense 2): ultimately from French *baer* to gape.

bevel gear ▷ *noun, engineering* a system of toothed wheels (**bevel wheels**) connecting shafts whose axes are at an angle to one another but in the same plane.

beverage /ˈbɛvərɪdʒ/ ▷ *noun, formal* a prepared drink, especially a hot drink (eg tea or coffee) or an alcoholic drink (eg beer). ◎ 14c: from French *bevrage*, from *beivre* to drink.

bevvy or **bevy** /ˈbɛvɪ/ *colloq* ▷ *noun* (***bevvies*** or ***bevies***) **1** alcoholic drink, or an individual alcoholic drink. **2** a drinking session. • **bevvied** said of a person: drunk; intoxicated. ◎ 19c: a colloquial shortening of BEVERAGE.

bevy /ˈbɛvɪ/ ▷ *noun* (***bevies***) **1** a group, especially and originally a group of women or girls. **2** a flock of larks, quails or swans. ◎ 15c.

bewail ▷ *verb, chiefly literary* to express great sorrow about something, or to lament over it □ *bewailing her tragic loss.* ◎ 14c.

beware /bɪˈwɛə(r)/ ▷ *verb* (not inflected in modern use, but used as an imperative or infinitive) **1** *intr* **a** (*usually* **beware of something**) to be careful of it; to be on one's guard □ *Beware of the dog;* **b** *rather formal or literary* (*usually* **beware that** or **lest something**) (with the subjunctive) to take care that one does, or does not, do something □ *should beware lest he fall.* **2** *old use or literary* to be on one's guard against something or someone □ *Beware the cruel hand of fate.* ◎ 13c: from BE (imperative) + *ware* cautious or wary.

Bewick's swan /ˈbjuːɪks — / ▷ *noun* the smallest of the European swans, with a short neck, small bill, a concave forehead and a characteristic musical goose-like honking call. ◎ 19c: named after the English illustrator Thomas Bewick (1753–1828).

bewilder /bɪˈwɪldə(r)/ ▷ *verb* (***bewildered, bewildering***) to confuse, disorientate or puzzle thoroughly, often by numerous things happening or moving at the same time or in rapid succession. • **bewildered** *adj.* • **bewildering** *adj.* • **bewilderingly** *adverb.* • **bewilderment** *noun.* ◎ 17c: from obsolete verb *wilder* to lose one's way.

bewitch /bɪˈwɪtʃ/ ▷ *verb* (***bewitches, bewitched, bewitching***) **1** to charm, fascinate or enchant □ *bewitched me with her smile.* **2** to cast a spell on, or use witchcraft on, someone or something. • **bewitching** *adj* alluring; charming. • **bewitchingly** *adverb.* ◎ 13c in sense 2: from *wicchen* to enchant, from Anglo-Saxon *wiccian* to use witchcraft.

beyond /bɪˈjɒnd/ ▷ *prep* **1** on the far side of something □ *beyond the hills.* **2** farther on than something in time or place. **3** out of the range, reach, power, understanding, possibility, etc of someone or something □ *It's quite beyond my comprehension.* **4** greater or better than something in amount, size, or level □ *beyond all our expectations.* **5** other than, or apart from, something □ *unable to help beyond giving money.* ▷ *adverb* farther away; to or on the far side of something. ▷ *noun* (**the beyond**) the unknown, especially life after death. • **beyond a joke** more than one can reasonably tolerate. • **beyond one** *colloq* **1** outside one's comprehension □ *It's beyond me how she did it.* **2** more than one is able to do □ *I'm afraid the task is beyond me.* ◎ Anglo-Saxon *begeondan.*

bezel /ˈbɛzəl/ ▷ *noun* **1** the sloped surface of a cutting tool. **2** a grooved rim which holds a watch-glass, precious gem, cover or dial of a panel instrument, etc in its setting. **3** a small indicator light on a dashboard or instrument panel. **4** an oblique side or face of a cut gem. ◎ 17c: from an unknown French word which preceded the modern French *biseau* a bevel or chamfer.

bezique /bɪˈziːk/ ▷ *noun* a card game for two, three or four players, using two packs of cards from which all cards of a value below seven have been removed. ◎ 19c: from French *bésigue.*

bf ▷ *abbreviation* **1** *Brit colloq* bloody fool. **2** *printing* bold face. **3** (*also* **b/f**) in accounts, etc: brought forward.

BFI ▷ *abbreviation* British Film Institute.

B-film see under B-MOVIE

BFPO ▷ *abbreviation* written on mail sent to British forces abroad, along with the number or name of the military unit: British Forces Post Office.

BG ▷ *abbreviation, IVR* Bulgaria.

BH ▷ *abbreviation, IVR* Belize, formerly called British Honduras.

Bh ▷ *symbol, chem* bohrium.

bhaji or **bhagee** /ˈbɑːdʒiː/ ▷ *noun* (***bhajis*** or ***bhagees***) *cookery* an Indian appetizer consisting of vegetables in a batter of flour and spices, formed into a ball and deep-fried. ◎ 20c: Hindi.

bhakti /ˈbʌktɪ/ ▷ *noun, Hinduism* loving devotion and surrender to God, recommended as the most effective path to salvation in most popular Hindu texts. ◎ 19c: Sanskrit, literally 'portion'.

bhang /baŋ/ ▷ *noun* the leaves and shoots of the CANNABIS plant, used as a narcotic and intoxicant. ◎ 16c: from Hindi *bhag.*

bhangra /ˈbaŋgrə/ ▷ *noun* a style of pop music created from a mix of traditional Punjabi and Western pop which originated among the British Asian community in the late 1970s. ◎ 1980s: Punjabi, the name of a traditional harvest dance.

bhindi /ˈbɪndɪ/ ▷ *noun* in Indian cookery: OKRA. ◎ 20c: Hindi.

bhp ▷ *abbreviation* brake horsepower.

Bhs or *formerly* **BHS** ▷ *abbreviation* British Home Stores, a British department store.

Bi ▷ *symbol, chem* bismuth.

bi[1] /baɪ/ *colloq* ▷ *adj* bisexual. ▷ *noun* (***bi's***) a bisexual person. ◎ 1960s; short form.

bi[2] /bɪː/ ▷ *noun, Chinese medicine* a blockage in the circulation of QI. ◎ Chinese, meaning 'paralysis'.

bi- /baɪ/ or (before a vowel) **bin-** /baɪn/ ▷ *prefix, signifying* **1** having, involving, using or consisting of two things or elements, etc □ *bifocal* □ *binaural.* **2** happening twice in every one (of something), or once in every two (of something) □ *bi-monthly.* **3** on or from both sides □ *bilateral.* **4** *chem* **a** applied to a salt or compound: containing twice the amount of the acid, etc shown in the prefixed word (eg BICARBONATE of soda indicates the presence of twice the quantity of carbonic acid present in CARBONATE of soda); **b** applied to a compound: containing two identical hydrocarbon groups □ *biphenyl. Technical equivalent* DI-. ◎ 14c: from Latin *bis* twice.

biannual ▷ *adj* occurring or produced, etc twice a year. • **biannually** *adverb.*

> ***biannual***
>
> A word often confused with this one is **biennial**.

bias /baɪəs/ ▷ *noun* (***biases***) **1** an inclination to favour or disfavour one side against another in a dispute, competition, etc; a prejudice. **2** a tendency or principal quality in a person's character □ *has a bias towards analytical work.* **3** *bowls, etc* **a** a weight on or in an object (eg a bowl) which makes it move in a particular direction; **b** a course in which such an object (especially a bowl) turns in a particular direction. **4** *dressmaking, etc* a line cut across the grain of a fabric. **5** *statistics* an unevenness or lack of balance in a result. **6** *electronics* the voltage applied to certain components to cause them to function only for a current of a given polarity, or only for currents greater than a given current. ▷ *verb* (***biased, biasing****; also* ***biassed, biassing***) **1** to influence or prejudice, especially unfairly or without objective grounds **2** to give a bias to something. • **biased** or **biassed** *adj* (*especially* **be biased against** or **towards someone** or **something**) predisposed to favour one side, group, person, etc rather than another. • **on the bias** diagonally; on the cross (of a fabric). ◎ 16c: from French *biais* slant.

bias binding ▷ *noun, dressmaking, etc* a long narrow folded strip of cloth cut on the bias, sewn on or into the hems or corners of garments, etc to make them strong.

biathlon /baɪˈaθlɒn/ ▷ *noun* an outdoor sporting event in which competitors cross a 20km (12.43ml) course on skis, stopping at intervals to shoot at targets with rifles. ◎ 1950s: from BI- 1, modelled on PENTATHLON.

biaxial /baɪˈaksɪəl/ ▷ *adj* said especially of a crystal: having two axes (see AXIS 2). ◎ 19c.

bib ▷ *noun* **1** a piece of cloth or plastic fastened under a baby's or child's chin to protect its clothes while eating or drinking. **2** the top part of an apron or overalls, covering the chest area. **3** a vest bearing their number worn by an athlete in a race or other competition. **4** a fish related to the cod and haddock, with a large BARBEL under its chin. • **best bib and tucker** *colloq* best clothes. • **stick** or **poke** or **put one's bib in** *Austral slang* to interfere; to butt in. ◎ 16c.

bibl. ▻ *abbreviation* **1** biblical. **2** bibliographical. **3** bibliography.

Bible /'baɪbəl/ ▻ *noun* **1 a** (**the Bible**) the sacred writings of the Christian Church, consisting of the Old and New Testaments; **b** (*sometimes* **bible**) a copy of these writings. Also *as adj* □ *Bible class.* **2 a** (**the Bible**) the Jewish Scriptures; the Old Testament or Hebrew Bible; **b** (*sometimes* **bible**) a copy of these. **3** (*usually* **bible**) an authoritative and comprehensive book on a particular subject, regarded as definitive. ◷ 14c: ultimately from Greek *biblos* a scroll or papyrus.

Bible-basher and **Bible-thumper** ▻ *noun, slang* a vigorous, aggressive or dogmatic Christian preacher.

Bible-bashing ▻ *noun, derog colloq* enthusiastic evangelical Christian preaching, especially in which the preacher thumps or brandishes a Bible.

Bible belt ▻ *noun, rather dated* those areas of the southern USA where the population is predominantly Christian fundamentalist. ◷ 1920s.

biblical or **Biblical** /'bɪblɪkəl/ ▻ *adj* **1** from, relating to or in accordance with the Bible. **2** resembling the Bible (specifically the Authorized Version of the Christian Bible) in style of language, imagery, etc.

biblio- /bɪblɪoʊ, bɪblɪ'ɒ/ ▻ *combining form, denoting* book or books. ◷ From Greek *biblion* book.

bibliography /bɪblɪ'ɒgrəfɪ/ ▻ *noun* (***bibliographies***) **1** a list of books by one author or on one subject. **2** a list of the books used as sources during the writing of a book or other written work, usually printed at the end of it. **3 a** the study, description or knowledge of books, in terms of their subjects, authors, editions, history, format, etc; **b** a book or other work on this subject. • **bibliographer** *noun.* • **bibliographic** or **bibliographical** *adj.* ◷ 17c; 19c in the current senses.

bibliomania ▻ *noun* a passionate enthusiasm for collecting or possessing books. • **bibliomaniac** *noun.* Also *as adj.* ◷ 18c.

bibliophile /'bɪblɪoʊfaɪl/ ▻ *noun* an admirer or collector of books. ◷ 19c.

bibulous /'bɪbjʊləs/ ▻ *adj, humorous* liking alcohol too much, or drinking too much of it. ◷ 17c: from Latin *bibulus* drinking freely, from *bibere* to drink.

bicameral /baɪ'kamərəl/ ▻ *adj* said of a legislative body: made up of two parts or chambers, such as the House of Commons and the House of Lords in the British parliament. • **bicameralism** *noun.* ◷ 19c: from Latin *camera* a chamber.

bicarbonate /baɪ'kɑːbənət/ ▻ *noun, chem* a common name for HYDROGEN CARBONATE. ◷ 19c.

bicarbonate of soda ▻ *noun, colloq* (often shortened to **bicarb** /'baɪkɑːb/) sodium bicarbonate, a white powder used in baking to make cakes, etc rise (as **baking soda** and **baking powder**), as an indigestion remedy, and for other purposes, eg in some fire extinguishers. Also called **soda.**

bicentenary /baɪsɛn'tiːnərɪ, -'tɛnərɪ/ ▻ *noun* (***bicentenaries***) *especially Brit* **1** a two-hundredth anniversary of an event. **2** a celebration held in honour of such an anniversary. ▻ *adj* marking, belonging to, referring to or in honour of a bicentenary. ◷ 19c.

bicentennial ▻ *noun & adj, chiefly N Amer, especially US* bicentenary. ◷ 19c.

biceps /'baɪsɛps/ ▻ *noun* (*plural* ***biceps***) *anatomy* any muscle that has two points of origin, especially the muscle at the front of the upper arm, which is used to flex the forearm. ◷ 17c: Latin, meaning 'two-headed', from BI- 1 + *caput* head.

bicker /'bɪkə(r)/ ▻ *verb* (***bickered, bickering***) *intr, colloq* to argue or quarrel in a petty way, especially about or over something trivial. • **bickering** *noun* tedious petty quarrelling. ◷ 14c as *biker*, meaning 'to fight or skirmish'.

Books of the Bible

Old Testament

Books of the Law (known as the Pentateuch)

Genesis	Numbers
Exodus	Deuteronomy
Leviticus	

Historical Books

Joshua	2 Kings
Judges	1 Chronicles
Ruth	2 Chronicles
1 Samuel	Ezra
2 Samuel	Nehemiah
1 Kings	Esther

Books of Poetry and Wisdom

Job	Ecclesiastes
Psalms	Song of Solomon
Proverbs	

Books of the Prophets

Isaiah	Jonah
Jeremiah	Micah
Lamentations	Nahum
Ezekiel	Habakkuk
Daniel	Zephaniah
Hosea	Haggai
Joel	Zechariah
Amos	Malachi
Obadiah	

New Testament

The Gospels and Acts

Matthew	John
Mark	Acts of the Apostles
Luke	

The Epistles or Letters

Romans	Titus
1 Corinthians	Philemon
2 Corinthians	Hebrews
Galatians	James
Ephesians	1 Peter
Philippians	2 Peter
Colossians	1 John
1 Thessalonians	2 John
2 Thessalonians	3 John
1 Timothy	Jude
2 Timothy	

Book of Revelation, or Apocalypse of St John

Apocrypha

1 Esdras	Prayer of Azariah
2 Esdras	Song of the Three Young Men
Tobit	
Judith	History of Susanna
Additions to Esther	Bel and the Dragon
Wisdom of Solomon	Prayer of Manasseh
Ecclesiasticus	1 Maccabees
Baruch	2 Maccabees
Epistle of Jeremiah	

The Roman Catholic Church includes Tobit, Judith, all of Esther, Maccabees 1 and 2, Wisdom of Solomon, Ecclesiasticus and Baruch in its canon.

bicolour or (*US*) **bicolor** and **bicoloured** or (*US*) **bicolored** ▻ *adj* composed of two colours; two-coloured. ◷ 19c.

biconcave ▷ *adj, physics* said of a structure, especially a lens: concave on both sides. ◷ 19c.

biconvex ▷ *adj, physics* said of a structure, especially a lens: convex on both sides. ◷ 19c.

bicultural ▷ *adj* belonging to, containing, having, combining or referring to two distinct cultures. • **biculturalism** *noun*. ◷ 1950s.

bicuspid /baɪˈkʌspɪd/ ▷ *adj* said especially of a tooth: having two cusps or points. ▷ *noun, N Amer* a PREMOLAR tooth. ◷ 19c.

bicycle /ˈbaɪsɪkəl/ ▷ *noun* a vehicle consisting of a metal frame with two wheels one behind the other, and a saddle between and above them, which is driven by turning pedals with the feet and steered by handlebars attached to the front wheel. Often shortened to BIKE, *sometimes* CYCLE. ▷ *verb* (***bicycled, bicycling***) *intr, rather formal* to ride a bicycle. Usually shortened to CYCLE, *sometimes* BIKE. • **bicyclist** /ˈbaɪsɪklɪst/ *noun, now rather formal* a cyclist. ◷ 19c: French, from BI- 1 + Greek *kyklos* a wheel or circle.

bicycle chain ▷ *noun* a metal chain that connects the pedals to the back wheel of a bicycle, and makes it move when the pedals are turned.

bicycle clip ▷ *noun* one of a pair of metal clips worn around the bottoms of a cyclist's trouser-legs, keeping the trousers close to the legs so that they do not catch in the bicycle chain.

bicycle pump ▷ *noun* a long thin pump for inflating bicycle tyres by hand.

bid[1] ▷ *verb* (***bid, bidding***) **1** *tr & intr* to offer (an amount of money) when trying to buy something, especially at an auction. **2** *tr & intr, cards* to state in advance (the number of tricks one will try to win). **3** *intr* (*especially* **bid for something**) to state a price one will charge for work to be done. ▷ *noun* **1** an offer of an amount of money in payment for something, especially at an auction. **2** *cards* a statement of how many tricks one proposes to win. **3** *colloq* especially in journalistic usage: an attempt to obtain or achieve something □ *a bid for freedom.* • **bidder** *noun*. • **bidding** see separate entry. • **bid fair** *formal* to seem likely. ◷ Anglo-Saxon *beodan* meaning 'to command' or 'summon'.

■ **bid in** said of the owner of an item for sale at an auction, or of their agent: to make a bid that is greater than the highest offer (and so retain the item). See also BUY IN.

■ **bid something up** to raise its market price by some artificial means, eg by bids that are not genuine.

bid[2] ▷ *verb* (*past tense* ***bade*** /bad, beɪd/, *past participle* ***bidden***, *present participle* ***bidding***) *formal, archaic or literary* **1** to express (a wish or greeting, etc) □ *We bid you welcome.* **2** (with an imperative) to command someone (to do a specified thing) □ *The king bade him kneel.* **3** (*often* **bid someone to something** or **to do something**) to invite them to it, or to do it □ *was bidden to the ceremony* □ *bid her to start.* ◷ Anglo-Saxon *biddan*, meaning 'to beg' or 'to pray'.

biddable ▷ *adj* **1** compliant; obedient; docile. **2** *cards* said of a hand or a suit: fit or suitable for bidding on.

bidding ▷ *noun* **1** a command, request or invitation. **2** the offers at an auction □ *start the bidding at £50.* **3** *cards* the act of making bids. • **be at someone's bidding** to be ready and available to carry out their orders or commands. • **do someone's bidding** to obey their orders or commands.

biddy /ˈbɪdɪ/ ▷ *noun* (***biddies***) *slang, chiefly derog* (*especially* **old biddy**) a woman, especially an old, doddery, fussy or cantankerous one. ◷ 18c, meaning 'an Irish maid-servant': presumably from the woman's name *Biddy*, short for *Bridget*.

bide /baɪd/ ▷ *verb* (*past tense* ***bided*** or ***bode***, *past participle* ***bided***, *present participle* ***biding***) *intr, Scots* or *old use* **1** to wait or stay. **2** to dwell or reside; to stay, especially temporarily. **3** to endure or tolerate. • **bide one's time** to wait patiently for a good opportunity or for the right moment. ◷ Anglo-Saxon *bidan*.

bidet /ˈbiːdeɪ/ ▷ *noun* a small low basin with taps, on which a person sits to wash their genital and anal areas. ◷ 17c, originally meaning 'a small horse': French, meaning 'a bidet' or (now old-fashioned) 'a pony'.

bi-directional ▷ *adj* **1** operating in two directions. **2** *computing, printing* said of a machine: that prints the lines of a text alternately left to right and right to left.

biennial /baɪˈɛnɪəl/ ▷ *adj* **1** said of an event: occurring once in every two years. **2** said especially of a plant: lasting two years. ▷ *noun* **1** *bot* a plant which takes two years to complete its life cycle, germinating and accumulating food reserves in the first year, and flowering, producing seed and dying during the second year, eg carrot. See also ANNUAL, PERENNIAL. **2** an event which takes place, or is celebrated, every two years. • **biennially** *adverb*. ◷ 17c: from Latin *biennium* two years, from *annus* year.

biennial

A word often confused with this one is **biannual**.

bier /bɪə(r)/ ▷ *noun* a movable stand on which a coffin rests or is transported. ◷ Anglo-Saxon *bær*.

biff *slang, especially Brit* ▷ *verb* (***biffed, biffing***) to hit someone or something very hard, usually with the fist. ▷ *noun* a hard sharp blow, usually with the fist; a punch. ◷ Late 19c: imitating the sound.

bifid /ˈbɪfɪd, ˈbaɪfɪd/ ▷ *adj, biol* divided into two parts by a deep split; forked. ◷ 17c: from Latin *bifidus*, from *findere, findus* to split.

bifocal /baɪˈfoʊkəl/ ▷ *adj* said of a lens: **1** having two different focal lengths. **2** said of spectacle or contact lenses: having two separate sections with different focal lengths, one for near vision, eg reading, and one for viewing distant objects. ◷ 19c.

bifocals ▷ *plural noun* a pair of glasses with BIFOCAL lenses, which allow the wearer to look at distant objects through the upper part of the lens, and to read or look at close objects through the lower part.

BIFU /ˈbɪfuː/ ▷ *abbreviation* Banking, Insurance and Finance Union.

bifurcate /ˈbaɪfəkeɪt/ ▷ *verb* (***bifurcated, bifurcating***) *intr, formal* said of roads, etc: to divide into two parts or branches; to fork. ▷ *adj* (*also* **bifurcated**) forked or branched into two parts. • **bifurcation** *noun*. ◷ 17c: from Latin *bifurcatus*, from *furca* fork.

big ▷ *adj* (***bigger, biggest***) **1** large or largest in size, amount, weight, number, power, etc. **2** significant or important to someone □ *You've got a big day tomorrow.* **3** important, powerful or successful, especially in a special area or line of business, etc □ *the big four banks* □ *He's big in the city.* **4** elder □ *my big sister.* **5** adult; grown-up □ *not big enough to go on your own.* **6** *often ironic* generous or magnanimous □ *That was big of him.* **7** boastful; extravagant; ambitious □ *big ideas.* **8** (*usually* **big on something**) *colloq, especially US* fond of or enthusiastic about it □ *She's very big on lace.* **9** *old use* in an advanced stage of pregnancy □ *big with child.* ▷ *adverb, colloq* **1** in a boastful, extravagant or ambitious way □ *likes to act big with his mates.* **2** greatly or impressively □ *Your idea went over big with the boss.* • **bigness** *noun*. • **big deal!** *ironic slang* an expression indicating that one is indifferent to, or not at all impressed by, what has just been said or done □ *So his father's the chairman, - big deal!* • **in a big way** *colloq* very much; strongly and enthusiastically. • **make it big** *colloq* to become successful and famous. • **too big for one's boots** *colloq* having an exaggerated view of one's importance; conceited. ◷ 14c.

bigamy /ˈbɪɡəmɪ/ ▷ *noun* (***bigamies***) the crime of being married to two wives or husbands at the same time. • **bigamist** *noun* a person who has committed bigamy. • **bigamous** *adj*. • **bigamously** *adverb*. ⓒ 13c: ultimately from Latin *bi-* twice + Greek *gamos* marriage.

the Big Apple ▷ *noun, US colloq* New York City. ⓒ 1920s: the term first came into use among US jazz musicians, and in the 1930s there was a Harlem nightclub and a jitterbug dance of this name; it may relate to the old jive term *apple* meaning 'the planet' or 'universe', and so 'any large place'.

Big Bang ▷ *noun* **1** a hypothetical model of the origin of the universe, now generally accepted, which postulates that all matter and energy were once concentrated into an unimaginably dense state, which underwent a gigantic explosion between 13 and 20 billion years ago. **2** *Brit colloq* the introduction, on 27 October 1986, of a momentous package of changes to the rules controlling the British Stock Exchange (including the abolition of the distinction between JOBBERS and BROKERS). ⓒ 1950s in sense 1.

Big Brother ▷ *noun* an all-powerful government or organization, etc, or its leader, keeping complete control over, and a continual watch on, its citizens. ⓒ 1950s: the name of the remote and tyrannical leader of Eurasia in George Orwell's novel *Nineteen Eighty-Four* (published 1949).

big business ▷ *noun* **1** powerful commercial and industrial organizations, especially considered as a group. **2** an activity that is commercially attractive or ambitious, or that is run with a view to making financial profit.

the Big C ▷ *noun, colloq* the disease cancer.

big cat ▷ *noun* a large member of the cat family, eg a lion or tiger.

big dipper ▷ *noun* **1** *now chiefly Brit* a rollercoaster. **2** (**the Big Dipper**) *especially N Amer* THE PLOUGH.

big end ▷ *noun, Brit* in an internal combustion engine: the larger end of the main CONNECTING-ROD.

Bigfoot ▷ *noun* in the mountaineering folklore of N America: a large hairy primate reputed to inhabit wilderness areas, equivalent to the YETI. ⓒ 1960s.

big game ▷ *noun* large animals, such as lions, tigers and elephants, etc hunted for sport.

big girl's blouse ▷ *noun, slang* someone who behaves in a sissy way.

biggish ▷ *adj* fairly big.

the big guns ▷ *plural noun, colloq* the most important or powerful people in an organization, etc.

biggy or **biggie** ▷ *noun* (***biggies***) *colloq* a large or important thing or person, especially as seen in comparison with others of a similar kind. ⓒ 1930s.

bighead ▷ *noun, colloq, derog* a conceited or arrogant person. • **bigheaded** *adj*. • **bigheadedness** *noun*. ⓒ 19c, first used figuratively in the US to mean 'conceit' or 'self-importance'.

big-hearted ▷ *adj* generous, kind and thoughtful. ⓒ 19c.

bighorn ▷ *noun* (***bighorns*** or ***bighorn***) either of two species of wild sheep (the N American and Siberian) that inhabit mountains, especially cliffs. ⓒ 18c: in both species the male has large curling horns.

bight /baɪt/ ▷ *noun* **1** a stretch of gently curving coastline. **2** a loose curve or loop in a length of rope. Anglo-Saxon *byht*, meaning 'a bend, corner or angle'.

bigmouth ▷ *noun, derog colloq* a boastful, or tactless, talkative person.

big name ▷ *noun, colloq* a celebrity; someone famous.

bigness see under BIG

big noise and (*chiefly Brit*) **big shot** ▷ *noun, originally & especially US colloq* an important, powerful or influential person.

big-note ▷ *verb noun, Austral colloq* (*usually* **big-note oneself** or **come the big-note**) to boast about oneself, or try to make oneself seem important □ *I know all about you, so don't come the big-note with me* □ *big-noting himself*. ⓒ 1940s.

bigot /ˈbɪɡət/ ▷ *noun* someone who is persistently prejudiced, especially about religion or politics, and refuses to tolerate the opinions of others. • **bigoted** *adj*. • **bigotry** *noun* (***bigotries***). ⓒ 16c, first meaning 'a superstitious hypocrite': French.

the Big Smoke ▷ *noun, slang* **1** *Brit* London **2** (*also* **the Smoke**) *especially Austral* any large city. ⓒ 19c.

big-ticket ▷ *adj, US colloq* expensive. ⓒ 1940s.

big time ▷ *noun, colloq* success in an activity or profession, especially in show business □ *hit the big time*.

big top ▷ *noun* a large round tent in which a circus gives its performances.

bigwig ▷ *noun, colloq* an important or powerful person. ⓒ 18c.

bijou /ˈbiːʒuː/ ▷ *noun* (***bijoux*** or ***bijous***) a small delicate jewel or trinket. ▷ *adj* small and elegant. • **bijouterie** *noun* jewellery or trinkets collectively. ⓒ 17c: French, from Breton *bizou* a ring.

bike /baɪk/ ▷ *noun, colloq* **1** a bicycle. **2** a motorcycle. ▷ *verb* (***biked, biking***) *intr* to ride a bicycle or motorcycle. • **biker** *noun* **1** someone who rides a motorcycle, especially a member of a motorcycle gang or group. *Austral & NZ colloq equivalent* BIKIE. **2** *rare* someone who rides a bicycle. Usually called CYCLIST. • **biking** *noun* the sport or pastime of cycling or riding a motorcycle. • **get off one's bike** *Austral slang, usually with negatives* to lose control of oneself, one's temper or emotions; to go crazy □ *Don't get off your bike, mate!* • **get on one's bike** *Brit colloq* to start making an effort; to get to work or take some determined action. • **on your bike** *Brit slang* **1** an expression of dismissal; clear off! push off! **2** an expression of disbelief; get away! ⓒ 19c: colloquial short form of BICYCLE.

bikeway ▷ *noun, chiefly N Amer* a lane or road, etc specially designed or set aside for the use of pedal cycles. *Brit equivalent* **cycleway**, **cycle path**.

bikini /bɪˈkiːnɪ/ ▷ *noun* (***bikinis***) **1** a small two-piece swimming costume for women. **2** (*usually* **bikinis**) a pair of scantily-cut briefs, especially ones for women. ⓒ 1940s: named after Bikini, an atoll in the Marshall Islands in the Pacific where atom-bomb experiments were first held in 1946; the bikini's effect was supposed to be similarly 'explosive'.

bilabial /baɪˈleɪbɪəl/ *phonetics* ▷ *adj* said of a consonant: made with both lips touching or almost touching each other, as with the letters *b* and *w*. Compare LABIAL. ▷ *noun* a bilabial consonant. ⓒ 19c.

bilateral /baɪˈlatərəl/ ▷ *adj* **1** said of a treaty, agreement, conference, talks, etc: involving the participation of, affecting, or signed or agreed by, two countries, parties or groups, etc. **2** having, belonging or referring to, or on, two sides. • **bilateralism** *noun* **1** equality, especially in the value of trade between two countries. **2** two-sidedness. • **bilaterally** *adverb*. ⓒ 18c in sense 2.

bilberry /ˈbɪlbərɪ/ ▷ *noun* **1** a small deciduous shrub, native to heaths and moorland of Europe and N Asia, which has bright green oval leaves and pink globular flowers. **2** the edible fruit of this plant, which is a round black berry with a bluish-white bloom. ⓒ 16c.

Bildungsroman / ˈbɪldʊŋsroʊmɑːn/ ▷ *noun* a novel concerning the early emotional or spiritual education, experience and development of its hero or heroine. ⓒ 20c: German, literally 'education novel'.

bile /baɪl/ ▷ *noun* **1** *biol* a thick yellowish-green alkaline liquid produced by the liver, stored by the gall bladder and secreted into the duodenum, where it plays a major role in the digestion of fats. **2** *literary* anger, irritability or bad temper. See also BILIOUS. ⓒ 17c: from Latin *bilis*; in early physiology, an excess of yellow bile in the body was thought to produce irritability.

bilge /bɪldʒ/ ▷ *noun* **1 a** the broadest part of a ship's bottom; **b** (*usually* **bilges**) the lowermost parts on the inside of a ship's hull, below the floorboards. **2** (*also* **bilge-water**) the dirty water that collects in a ship's bilge. **3** *rather dated colloq* rubbish; nonsense; drivel. ⓒ 16c: probably a variant of BULGE.

bilharzia /bɪl'hɑːzɪə/ ▷ *noun* (*plural* in sense 2 only ***bilharzias***) **1** *pathol* another name for the parasitic disease SCHISTOSOMIASIS. **2** *zool* another name for a SCHISTOSOME, a parasitic worm or fluke. ⓒ 19c: Latin, named after Theodor Bilharz (1825–62), the German parasitologist who discovered the schistosomes.

biliary /'bɪlɪərɪ/ ▷ *adj* concerned with, relating or belonging to bile, the bile ducts or the gall bladder.

bilingual /baɪ'lɪŋgwəl/ ▷ *adj* **1** written or spoken in two languages ◻ ***bilingual dictionary***. **2** said of a person: speaking two languages very well, especially with equal fluency. ▷ *noun* (*usually* **bilinguist**) a person who speaks two languages. • **bilingualism** *noun*. • **bilingually** *adverb* using or involving two languages. ⓒ 19c: from BI- 1 + Latin *lingua* tongue.

bilious /'bɪlɪəs/ ▷ *adj* **1 a** affected by or sick with a disorder relating to the secretion, especially excessive secretion, of BILE; **b** *loosely* nauseated; sick. **2** *derog* said of a colour: unpleasant and sickly; nauseous. **3** peevish; bad-tempered. **4** belonging or relating to BILE. • **biliously** *adverb*. • **biliousness** *noun*. ⓒ 16c: from Latin *biliosus*.

bilirubin /bɪlɪ'ruːbɪn/ ▷ *noun, biochem* a yellowish-orange pigment found in bile and formed from BILIVERDIN, excess of which in the blood causes JAUNDICE. ⓒ 19c: from Latin *bilis* bile + *ruber* red.

biliverdin /bɪlɪ'vɜːdɪn/ ▷ *noun, biochem* a green pigment found in bile, formed as the result of the breakdown of HAEM during the disintegration of old red blood cells. ⓒ 19c: from Latin *bilis* + *verd* as in VERDURE.

bilk ▷ *verb* (***bilked, bilking***) **1** to avoid paying someone money one owes them. **2** (*especially* **bilk someone out of something**) to cheat or trick them; to make them lose something, usually money, by dishonest means. **3** to elude; to escape from someone or something. • **bilker** *noun*. ⓒ 17c, originally a term in cribbage: perhaps a form of BALK.

the Bill and **the Old Bill** ▷ *singular or plural noun, Brit slang* the police force, or a member or members of the police force. ⓒ 1960s; the nickname probably arose because many policemen between the World Wars wore large walrus moustaches like that of 'Old Bill', a popular cartoon character of the time created by the British cartoonist B Bairnsfather (1888–1959).

bill¹ ▷ *noun* **1 a** a printed or written statement of the amount of money owed for goods or services received; an invoice; **b** such a statement for food and drink received in a restaurant or hotel. *US equivalent* CHECK; **c** the amount of money owed. **2** a written plan or draft for a proposed law. **3** *N Amer, especially US* a banknote. *Brit equivalent* NOTE. **4** an advertising poster. **5** a list of items, events or performers, etc; a programme of entertainment. ▷ *verb* (***billed, billing***) **1** to send or give a bill to someone, requesting payment for goods, etc; to charge ◻ ***Did they bill you for the wine?*** **2** to advertise or announce (a person or event) in a poster, etc ◻ ***was billed as Britain's best new comedy act***. • **fit** or **fill the bill** *colloq* to be suitable, or what is required. ⓒ 14c: from Latin *bulla* a seal or a document bearing a seal.

bill² ▷ *noun* **1** the beak of a bird. **2** any structure which resembles this in appearance or function. **3** a long thin piece of land that extends into the sea, eg Portland Bill. ▷ *verb* (***billed, billing***) (*especially* **bill and coo**) *colloq* **1** said of lovers: to kiss and whisper together affectionately. **2** said of birds such as doves: to touch and rub bills together. • **billed** *usually in compounds* having a specified kind of bill ◻ ***hard-billed*** ◻ ***duck-billed***. • **billing** *noun*. ⓒ Anglo-Saxon *bile*.

bill³ ▷ *noun* **1** *historical* a long-handled weapon with a concave or hook-shaped blade, or one with a hook-like spike. **2** a BILLHOOK. ⓒ Anglo-Saxon *bil*, originally meaning 'sword' or 'broadsword'.

billabong /'bɪləbɒŋ/ ▷ *noun, Austral* **1** a pool of water left when most of a river or stream has become dry. **2** a branch of a river which comes to an end without flowing into a sea, lake, or another river. ⓒ 19c: from Australian Aboriginal *billa* river + *bung* dead.

billboard ▷ *noun, especially N Amer* a large board, eg by a roadside or railway platform, on which advertising posters are displayed. *Brit equivalent* HOARDING.

billet¹ /'bɪlɪt/ ▷ *noun* **1** a house, often a private home, where soldiers are given food and lodging temporarily. **2** a formal order to a householder to provide lodgings for a soldier. **3** *colloq* an allocated sleeping- or resting-place. **4** *colloq, chiefly Brit* a job or occupation. ▷ *verb* (***billeted, billeting***) to give or assign lodging to, or to accommodate (soldiers, etc). ⓒ 15c, originally meaning 'a brief letter or note assigning quarters' (as sense 2): from French *billette* a letter or note.

billet² /'bɪlɪt/ ▷ *noun* **1** a small log or thick chunk of wood, eg for firewood. **2** a small bar of metal. **3** *archit* a Romanesque type of ornamental moulding formed of bands of regularly-spaced cylindrical or square blocks. ⓒ 15c: from French *billette*, from *bille* a log or small tree-trunk.

billet-doux /bɪlɪ'duː, bɪleɪ'duː/ ▷ *noun* (***billets-doux*** /-'duː, -'duːz/) *old use, literary or humorous* a love-letter. ⓒ 17c: French, from *billet* letter + *doux* sweet.

billfold ▷ *noun, N Amer* a soft case, pocketbook or wallet for holding banknotes, and often credit cards and documents, etc. ⓒ 19c, originally as *billfolder*.

billhook ▷ *noun* a wooden-handled cutting tool used for pruning, lopping off stems, etc, having a long curved blade with a sharp inner edge, and often a hooked tip. Also called **bill**.

billiard /'bɪlɪəd/ ▷ *noun, as adj* for, belonging or referring to the game of BILLIARDS ◻ ***billiard ball***.

billiards /'bɪlɪədz/ ▷ *singular noun* an indoor game played with a CUE² and coloured balls on a cloth-covered table with high cushioned edges (a **billiard table**), which has pockets at the sides and corners into which the balls can be struck to score points. Compare SNOOKER, POOL. ⓒ 16c: from French *billard*, from *bille* a narrow stick.

billing ▷ *noun* **1** the importance of a performer in a play or concert, especially as shown by the position of the name on the poster advertising the performance ◻ ***top billing***. **2** the making or sending out of bills or invoices. **3** in advertising or insurance, etc: the total amount of money or business received from customers or clients. **4** *N Amer* advertising or promotion. ⓒ 19c: from BILL¹.

Billings method ▷ *noun* a RHYTHM METHOD of family planning that involves examination of the cervical mucus for changes which indicate the time of ovulation. ⓒ 20c: named after the Australian physicians Drs Evelyn and John Billings who devised the method in the 1960s.

billion /'bɪlɪən/ ▷ *noun* (***billions*** or after a number ***billion***) **1** a thousand million (ie unit and nine zeros). **2** *formerly* in the UK and France, etc: a million million (ie unit and twelve zeros). **3** (*usually* **a billion** or **billions of something**) *colloq* a great number; lots ◻ ***I've got billions of things to do***. ⓒ 17c: French, modelled on MILLION.

billionaire /bɪljə'nɛə(r)/ and **billionairess** ▷ *noun* (***billionaires*** and ***billionairesses***) a person who owns money and property worth over a billion pounds, dollars, or a billion of their country's unit of currency. ⓘ 19c: modelled on MILLIONAIRE.

billionth ▷ *noun* a thousand millionth. ▷ *adj* **1** thousand millionth. **2** *colloq* umpteenth.

bill of exchange ▷ *noun* (***bills of exchange***) *finance* especially in international trade: a document promising payment of a specified sum of money, through a mutually convenient third party, to a certain person on a certain date or when payment is asked for.

bill of fare ▷ *noun* (***bills of fare***) a list of dishes or articles of food, etc available; a menu.

bill of lading ▷ *noun* (***bills of lading***; abbreviation **B/L**, *etc*) an official receipt signed by the shipowner or their master or agent, specifying the goods to be shipped, and stating the terms and conditions under which they will be transported.

bill of rights or **Bill of Rights** ▷ *noun* (***bills of rights***) a written declaration of the rights and privileges of the citizens of a country, or of the individual, eg the first ten amendments to the US Constitution (1791) and the British Declaration of Rights (1689).

bill of sale ▷ *noun* (***bills of sale***) *Eng law* a formal legal paper stating that something has been sold by one person to another.

billow /ˈbɪloʊ/ ▷ *verb* (***billowed***, ***billowing***) *intr* **1** said eg of smoke: to move in large waves or clouds. **2** (*usually* **billow out**) to swell or bulge, like a sail in the wind □ *Her cloak billowed out behind her.* ▷ *noun* **1** a rolling upward-moving mass of smoke or mist, etc. **2** *literary* a large wave. • **billowing** or **billowy** *adj*. ⓘ 16c as *noun* 2: from Norse *bylgja*.

billposter and **billsticker** ▷ *noun* a person who puts up advertising posters on walls or hoardings, etc. • **billposting** and **billsticking** *noun*. ⓘ 18c (as *billsticker*); 19c (as *billposter*); from BILL[1].

billy[1] and **billycan** ▷ *noun* (***billies***; ***billycans***) *Brit & especially Austral* a metal container with a lid and wire handle, used for carrying and boiling water in, cooking in, or eating and drinking from, especially when camping. • **boil the billy** *Austral colloq* to make a pot (or cup, etc) of tea; to take a break for food and drink. ⓘ 19c: probably from Scottish and Northern English dialect *billypot*, and *billy* a comrade or mate.

billy goat ▷ *noun* a male goat. Often shortened to **billy**. Compare NANNY GOAT. ⓘ 19c: from the name Billy.

billy-o or **billy-oh** /ˈbɪlɪoʊ/ ▷ *noun* now only usually in the phrase • **like billy-o** *dated Brit slang* very much; energetically, forcefully or rapidly. ⓘ 19c.

bilobate /baɪˈloʊbeɪt/ and **bilobed** /baɪˈloʊbd/ ▷ *adj* having or made up of two lobes. ⓘ 18c.

BIM ▷ *abbreviation* British Institute of Management.

bimanual ▷ *adj* using or performed with two hands. • **bimanually** *adverb*. ⓘ 19c.

bimbo /ˈbɪmboʊ/ ▷ *noun* (***bimbos***) *derog slang* a young woman who is physically attractive, but empty-headed. ⓘ Early 20c, US slang for a person of either sex, in a contemptuous or general sense: Italian, meaning 'baby' or 'small child'.

bimetallic /baɪməˈtalɪk/ ▷ *adj* **1** made of or using two metals. **2** said of a monetary system, etc: referring to, using or based on BIMETALLISM. ⓘ 19c.

bimetallic strip ▷ *noun*, *technical* in thermostats, etc: a strip consisting of two lengths of different metals welded or riveted together, which expand to different extents on heating and thus assume a curved shape and complete an electrical circuit when a certain temperature is reached.

bimetallism /baɪˈmɛtəlɪzəm/ ▷ *noun*, *econ* a monetary system in which two metals (usually gold and silver) are used in fixed relative values. ⓘ 19c.

bimonthly ▷ *adj* **1** occurring or produced, etc once every two months. **2** occurring or produced, etc twice a month. ▷ *adverb* **1** every two months. **2** twice a month. ⓘ 19c.

bin ▷ *noun* **1** a container for depositing or storing rubbish. **2** a container for storing some kinds of food. Often *in compounds* □ ***bread bin***. **3** a large industrial container for storing goods in large quantities. **4** a stand or case with sections in it, for storing bottles of wine. ▷ *verb* (***binned***, ***binning***) **1** to put (eg rubbish) into a bin. **2** to store (eg wine) in a bin. ⓘ Anglo-Saxon.

bin- see BI-

binary /ˈbaɪnərɪ/ ▷ *adj* **1** consisting of or containing two parts or elements. **2** *computing, math* denoting a system that consists of two components, especially a number system which uses the digits 0 and 1. See also BINARY SYSTEM. ▷ *noun* (***binaries***) **1** a thing made up of two parts. **2** *astron* a BINARY STAR. ⓘ 16c: from Latin *binarius*, from *bini* two by two.

binary code ▷ *noun*, *computing* a code of numbers that involves only two digits, 0 and 1. See also BINARY SYSTEM.

binary-coded decimal (abbreviation **BCD**) ▷ *noun*, *computing, etc* a numbering system in which each digit of a decimal number is written separately as a binary number.

binary star ▷ *noun*, *astron* (*also* **binary**) a system of two stars that share and orbit around the same centre of mass, and are held together by gravitational attraction. Also called **double star**.

binary system ▷ *noun*, *math & especially computing* a number system to the base 2 that uses only the binary digits 0 and 1, and that forms the basis of the internal coding of information in electronics and computers, especially where 1 and 0 represent on and off states of switches. Also called **binary notation**.

binary weapon ▷ *noun* a type of chemical weapon, usually an artillery shell packed with two chemicals which are individually harmless but which combine on detonation to form a deadly toxic agent.

binaural /baɪˈnɔːrəl, bɪ-/ ▷ *adj* **1** having, using or relating to two ears. **2** said of sound reproduction: using two separate sound channels. ⓘ 19c: BI- 1 + AURAL.

bin-bag ▷ *noun*, *Brit colloq* **1** a large strong plastic bag for rubbish, especially one for disposing of household refuse. **2** a BIN-LINER.

bind /baɪnd/ ▷ *verb* (***bound***, ***binding***) **1** to tie or fasten tightly. **2** (*often* **bind something up**) to tie or pass strips of cloth or bandage, etc around it. **3** to control or prevent someone or something from moving; to restrain them or it. See also BOUND[1]. **4** to make someone promise to do something. **5** to require or oblige someone to do something □ *He is legally bound to reply.* **6** to fasten together and put a cover on (the separate pages of a book). **7** to put a strip of cloth on the edge of something to strengthen it. **8** to cause (dry ingredients) to stick together. **9** *intr* to stick together; to become bound. **10** *intr* (*especially* **bind on about something**) *slang* to complain about it. ▷ *noun*, *colloq* **1** a difficult, tedious or annoying situation. **2** a restriction; something that limits or hampers one. ⓘ Anglo-Saxon *bindan*.

■ **bind someone over** *Brit law* to make them legally obliged to do a particular thing, especially to 'keep the peace' and not cause a disturbance. See also BOUND[1].

binder ▷ *noun* **1** a hard book-like cover in which loose pieces of paper can be kept in order. **2** a person or business that binds books. Also called **bookbinder**. **3** a cementing agent that causes loose particles of a mixture to adhere. **4 a** an attachment to a reaping machine, used for tying cut grain into bundles; **b** a reaping machine provided with such an attachment. • **bindery** *noun* (***binderies***) a place where books are bound.

binding ▷ *noun* **1** the part of a book cover on to which the pages are stuck. **2** cloth or tape, etc used to bind something. ▷ *adj* formally or legally obliging or constraining someone to do something □ *a binding contract.*

bindweed /ˈbaɪndwiːd/ ▷ *noun* **1** any of numerous perennial plants with funnel-shaped flowers consisting of five fused petals, including many climbing species which twine around the stems of other plants. *See also* CONVOLVULUS. **2** (*especially* **common bindweed**) a perennial European plant and persistent weed, which has long slender twining stems, arrowhead-shaped leaves, and funnel-shaped white or pink flowers.

binge /bɪndʒ/ ▷ *noun, colloq* a bout of over-indulgence, usually in eating and drinking. ▷ *verb* (***binged, bingeing*** or ***binging***) *intr* to indulge in a binge. ◎ 19c; apparently from a dialect verb meaning 'to soak'.

bingle /ˈbɪŋgəl/ ▷ *noun Austral slang* a car-crash; a smash. ◎ 1950s; in World War II slang 'a skirmish'.

bingo /ˈbɪŋgoʊ/ ▷ *noun* (***bingos***) a game of chance, especially one for cash prizes, in which each player has a card with a set of numbers on it, and may cover a number if it is called out at random by the **bingo-caller**, the winner being the first player with a card on which all or a certain sequence of the numbers have been called. Formerly called HOUSEY-HOUSEY and LOTTO. ▷ *exclamation* **1** the word shouted by the winner of a game of bingo. **2** indicating sudden or eventual success, discovery or pleasure. ◎ 1920s: perhaps simply an imitation of the sound of a bell rung when someone has won the game.

bin-liner ▷ *noun* a disposable plastic bag used as a lining inside a rubbish bin.

binman ▷ *noun, Brit* a refuse-collector. *N Amer equivalent* GARBAGE-MAN, GARBAGE COLLECTOR.

binnacle /ˈbɪnəkəl/ ▷ *noun, naut* a case for a ship's compass. ◎ 17c; its earlier form *bittacle* derived from Latin *habitaculum* a habitation or dwelling-place.

binocular /bɪˈnɒkjʊlə(r), baɪ-/ ▷ *adj* **1** relating to the use of both eyes simultaneously. **2** said of an optical instrument: that requires the use of both eyes simultaneously, producing a stereoscopic effect. ◎ 18c: from Latin *bini* two by two + *oculus* eye.

binoculars ▷ *plural noun* an optical instrument designed for viewing distant objects, consisting of two small telescopes arranged side by side so that the observer is able to use both eyes at once. ◎ 19c: short for *binocular glasses*.

binocular vision ▷ *noun* the ability of animals with forward-facing eyes to focus both eyes on an object at the same time, so that a single three-dimensional image is perceived.

binomial /baɪˈnoʊmɪəl/ ▷ *noun* **1** *math* an algebraic expression that contains two VARIABLES, eg 6x–3y. **2** *biol* in the taxonomic system (known as **binomial nomenclature**) introduced by Linnaeus: a two-part name for an animal or plant, made up of two Latin words, first the genus name (with an initial capital letter) and then the species name, eg *Homo sapiens*. ▷ *adj* **1** *math* containing two variables. **2** consisting of two names or terms. ◎ 16c: from BI- 1 + -NOMIAL.

binomial distribution ▷ *noun, statistics* the FREQUENCY DISTRIBUTION of the total number of outcomes of a particular kind in a predetermined number of independent trials, the probability of the outcome being constant at each trial.

binomial theorem ▷ *noun, math* a formula for finding any power of a BINOMIAL without lengthy multiplication, eg $(a + b)^2 = (a^2 + 2ab + b^2)$.

bint ▷ *noun, offensive slang* a girl or woman. ◎ 19c: Arabic, meaning 'daughter'.

binturong /ˈbɪntjʊrɒŋ/ ▷ *noun* a SE Asian carnivorous mammal of the civet family, with thick black fur and a prehensile tail. ◎ 19c: Malay.

bio- /baɪoʊ, baɪˈɒ/ ▷ *combining form, signifying* **1** relating to or involving, etc life or living things □ *biology* □ *biogenesis*. **2** relating to or like a life □ *biography*. **3** biological □ *biocontrol* □ *biorhythms*. ◎ From Greek *bios* life.

bioassay ▷ *noun, biol* the assessment of its effect concentration of a chemical substance by testing its effect on a living organism, eg its effect on plant or bacterial growth. ◎ Early 20c.

bioavailability ▷ *noun, biol* the extent to which, and rate at which, a drug administered eg by mouth is taken up by the body and reaches the tissues and organs it is intended to act upon. ◎ 1970s.

biochemistry ▷ *noun* the scientific study of the chemical compounds and chemical reactions that occur within the cells of living organisms. • **biochemical** *adj*. • **biochemist** *noun*. ◎ Late 19c.

biocontrol ▷ *noun* biological control.

biodegradable ▷ *adj* said of a substance or waste product, etc: capable of being broken down by bacteria, fungi or other living organisms, so that its constituents are released and can be recycled. • **biodegradeability** *noun*. • **biodegradation** *noun*. ◎ 1960s.

biodiversity ▷ *noun, biol* a measure of the number of different species of living organism that are present within a given area, also including the number of representatives of each species, and the variety of habitats within the area.

bioelectrotherapy ▷ *noun, alternative medicine* a form of therapy in which a low-energy electric current is applied to the skin.

bioenergetics ▷ *singular noun* **1** *biol* the scientific study of the use of energy by living organisms, including its conversion from one form to another. **2** REICHIAN THERAPY. ◎ Early 20c.

bioengineering and **biological engineering** ▷ *noun* **1** *medicine* the application of engineering methods and technology to biology and medicine, especially with regard to the design and manufacture of artificial limbs, hip joints, heart pacemakers, etc, to replace damaged, diseased or missing body parts. Also called **biomedical engineering**. **2** *biol* the application of engineering methods and technology to the biosynthesis of plant and animal products. See also BIOTECHNOLOGY. • **bioengineer** *noun*. ◎ 1960s.

biofeedback ▷ *noun, psychol* the technique whereby a person learns to control certain body functions (eg heart rate or blood pressure) by having them monitored and displayed by means of electronic instruments, so that the person becomes aware of them and can learn to control the underlying process. ◎ 1970s.

bioflavonoid ▷ *noun, biochem* vitamin P, a vitamin that regulates the permeability of the capillary walls, and is found naturally in citrus fruit, blackcurrants and rose-hips. Also called CITRIN or FLAVONOID. ◎ 1950s.

biofuel ▷ *noun* any fuel produced from organic matter, whether directly or (in the case of certain household, industrial and agricultural wastes, etc) indirectly through burning or fermentation processes. See also BIOGAS, BIOMASS 2.

biogas ▷ *noun* domestic or commercial gas (especially methane and carbon dioxide) produced by bacterial fermentation of naturally occurring materials such as animal manure and other organic waste; a type of BIOFUEL. ◎ 1970s.

biogenesis ▷ *noun, biol* the theory that living matter always arises from other, pre-existing, living matter. Compare SPONTANEOUS GENERATION. • **biogenetic** *adj*. ◎ 19c.

biogeography ▷ *noun, biol* the scientific study of the distributions of plants and animals. ◎ 19c.

biography /baɪˈɒgrəfɪ/ ▷ *noun* (***biographies***) **1** an account of a person's life, usually written by someone else and published or intended for publication. **2**

biographies as a specific art or branch of literature. • **biographer** *noun*. • **biographical** or **biographic** *adj*. • **biographically** *adverb*. 🕒 17c.

biol. ▷ *abbreviation* biology.

biological /baɪəˈlɒdʒɪkəl/ ▷ *adj* **1** relating to biology. **2** physiological. **3** said of a detergent: containing and using enzymes which are said to remove dirt of organic origin, eg blood, grass and egg stains. • **biologically** *adverb*.

biological clock ▷ *noun* a supposed natural mechanism inside the body which controls the rhythm of the body's functions. Also called **body clock**. 🕒 1950s.

biological control ▷ *noun, biol* the control of plant or animal pests: **a** by the introduction of natural predators or parasites, etc that are only harmful to the pest; **b** by interfering with the reproductive behaviour of the pest. Often shortened to **biocontrol**. 🕒 1920s.

biological engineering see BIOENGINEERING

biological rhythm see under BIORHYTHM

biological warfare ▷ *noun* the use of toxins and micro-organisms as weapons of war, to kill or incapacitate the enemy. 🕒 1940s.

biology /baɪˈɒlədʒɪ/ ▷ *noun* the scientific study of living organisms. • **biologist** *noun*. 🕒 19c.

bioluminescence ▷ *noun, biol* the emission of light by living organisms, such as certain insects, deep-sea fishes, etc.

biomagnetics ▷ *singular noun, alternative medicine* a type of therapy in which small magnets are placed on acupuncture points.

biomass ▷ *noun, biol, ecol* **1** the total mass of living organisms in an ecosystem, population or designated area at a given time. **2** vegetation or other plant material that can be converted into useful fuel, considered as a potential source of energy. 🕒 1930s.

biome /ˈbaɪoʊm/ ▷ *noun, biol* a major ecological community of living organisms, usually defined by the plant habitat with which they are associated, eg grassland, rainforest. 🕒 Early 20c: BIO- 1 + -OME.

biomechanics ▷ *singular noun* the mechanics of movement in living things. • **biomechanical** *adj*. 🕒 1930s.

biomedical engineering see under BIOENGINEERING

biometry /baɪˈɒmətrɪ/ and **biometrics** /-ˈmɛtrɪks/ ▷ *singular noun* the branch of biology concerned with the applications of statistical methods of analysis to biological systems. • **biometric** *adj*. 🕒 19c.

biomorphic art ▷ *noun* a type of abstract art which makes used of forms reminiscent of, but not necessarily drawn from, the shapes of living things. 🕒 19c: from Greek *bios* life + *morphe* form.

bionic /baɪˈɒnɪk/ ▷ *adj* **1** using, or belonging or relating to, BIONICS. **2** *colloq, science fiction* having extraordinary superhuman powers of speed or strength, etc. 🕒 1960s; sense 2 developed especially from the 1970s onward, due to the popularity of an American TV fiction series *The Six Million Dollar Man*, which featured a 'bionic man' whose body had been substantially rebuilt of bionic machinery (see BIONICS 2).

bionics ▷ *singular noun* **1** the study of how living organisms function, and the application of the principles observed to develop computers and other machines which work in similar ways. **2** the replacement of damaged parts of the body, such as limbs and heart valves, by electronic devices. 🕒 1960s: from BIO- 1, modelled on ELECTRONICS.

bionomics /baɪoʊˈnɒmɪks/ *singular noun* the study of the relationships between living organisms and their environment. *General equivalent* ECOLOGY. • **bionomic** *adj*. 🕒 19c (originally as *adj*): from BIO- 1, modelled on ECONOMIC.

biophysics ▷ *singular noun* the application of the ideas and methods of physics to the study of biological processes. • **biophysical** *adj*. • **biophysicist** *noun*. 🕒 19c.

biopic /ˈbaɪoʊpɪk/ ▷ *noun* a film telling the life-story of a famous person, frequently in an uncritically admiring or superficial way. 🕒 1950s: short for *bio*graphical *pic*ture.

biopsy /ˈbaɪɒpsɪ/ ▷ *noun* (***biopsies***) *pathol* **1** the removal and examination of a small piece of living tissue from an organ or part of the body in order to determine the nature of any suspected disease. **2** *loosely* the specimen of living tissue collected for a biopsy. 🕒 19c: from BIO- 1 + Greek *opsis* sight or appearance.

biorhythm ▷ *noun, biol* **1** a periodic change in the behaviour or physiology of many animals and plants (eg hibernation and migration), mediated by hormones which are in turn influenced by changes in day-length. **2** a CIRCADIAN rhythm associated eg with sleep, and independent of day-length. **3** any of three cyclical patterns which have been suggested as influencing physical, intellectual and emotional aspects of human behaviour. 🕒 1960s.

bioscope ▷ *noun, S Afr* a cinema. 🕒 19c.

-biosis /baɪˈoʊsɪs/ ▷ *combining form, forming nouns* (***-bioses*** /-siːz/) *signifying* a specified way of living □ *symbiosis*. 🕒 From Greek *biosis* way of life.

biosphere ▷ *noun* that part of the earth's surface and its atmosphere in which living organisms are known to exist. Also called **ecosphere**. 🕒 19c.

biosynthesis ▷ *noun* the manufacture by living organisms of complex organic compounds such as proteins and fats, etc from simpler molecules. • **biosynthetic** *adj*. 🕒 1930s.

biota /baɪˈoʊtə/ ▷ *noun, collective, ecol* the living organisms present in a particular area. 🕒 Early 20c: from Greek *biote* life.

biotechnology ▷ *noun, biol* the use of living organisms (eg bacteria), or the enzymes produced by them, in the industrial manufacture of useful products, or the development of useful processes, eg in energy production, processing of waste, manufacture of drugs and hormones, etc. 🕒 1940s.

biotic /baɪˈɒtɪk/ ▷ *adj* belonging or relating to life or living organisms. 🕒 19c; 17c in an obsolete sense referring only to common (ie secular) life.

-biotic ▷ *combining form* forming adjectives corresponding to nouns in -BIOSIS □ *symbiotic*.

biotin /ˈbaɪoʊtɪn/ ▷ *noun, biochem* a member of the vitamin B complex, produced by the bacteria that inhabit the gut of animals, and also found in yeast, liver, egg yolk, cereals and milk. Also called VITAMIN H. 🕒 1930s: from Greek *biotos* means of living.

bipartisan /baɪˈpɑːtɪzan/ ▷ *adj* belonging to, involving, supported by or consisting of two groups or political parties. • **bipartisanship** *noun*. 🕒 Early 20c.

bipartite /baɪˈpɑːtaɪt/ ▷ *adj* **1** consisting of or divided into two parts. **2** said of an agreement, etc: involving, affecting or agreed by two parties. 🕒 16c: from Latin *bipartitus*, from *bi*-BI- 1 + *partire* to divide.

biped /ˈbaɪpɛd/ ▷ *noun* an animal with two feet, eg man. ▷ *adj* (*also* **bipedal**) /baɪˈpiːdəl/ said of an animal: having two feet; walking on two feet. 🕒 17c: from BI- 1 + Latin *pes, pedis* foot.

biplane /ˈbaɪpleɪn/ ▷ *noun* an early type of aeroplane with two sets of wings, one above the other. 🕒 19c.

BIPM ▷ *abbreviation*: *Bureau International des Poids et Mesures* (French), International Bureau of Weights and Measures.

bipolar ▷ *adj* **1** having two poles or extremes. **2** belonging or relating to, or occurring at, both the North and the South Pole. **3** *electronics* said of a transistor: using both positive and negative charge carriers. • **bipolarity** *noun*. ⓘ 19c.

birch /bɜːtʃ/ ▷ *noun* (***birches***) **1** a slender deciduous tree or shrub of N temperate and Arctic regions, with smooth silvery-white bark that often peels off in long papery strips. **2** (*also* **birchwood**) the strong fine-textured wood of this tree, valued for furniture-making, and used to make plywood, charcoal, etc. **3** (**the birch**) **a** a birch rod, or a bundle of birch branches, formerly used to inflict physical punishment; **b** the punishment of being beaten or whipped with the birch. ▷ *adj* made of birch wood. ▷ *verb* (***birched***, ***birching***) to flog someone with a birch; to whip them. ⓘ Anglo-Saxon *berc* or *beorc*.

bird /bɜːd/ ▷ *noun* **1** any member of a class of warm-blooded vertebrate animals characterized by the possession of feathers, front limbs modified to form wings, and projecting jaws modified to form a horny beak. **2** *Brit slang, often considered offensive* a girl or woman. **3** *Brit slang* prison or a prison sentence □ ***just out of bird***. See also *do bird* below. **4** (**the bird**) *US slang* an obscene gesture of contempt, dismissal or defiance, etc, using a raised middle finger. See also *give someone the bird* 2 below. **5** *colloq, old use* a person, especially a strange or unusual one □ ***He's a funny old bird***. • **birder** *noun* a BIRDWATCHER. • **birding** *noun* BIRDWATCHING. • **birds of a feather** *Brit colloq* people who are like each other, who share the same ideas, habits or lifestyle, etc ⓘ 16c, in the proverb 'Birds of a feather (ie of the same species) flock together'. • **do bird** *Brit slang* to serve a prison sentence □ ***They did bird together at the Scrubs*** ⓘ 20c: short for BIRD-LIME, rhyming slang for TIME *noun* 11. • **get the bird** *slang* **1** said of a performer or entertainer, etc: to be hissed or jeered at, or booed, by an audience. **2** to be dismissed or sacked. • **give someone the bird** *slang* **1** *chiefly Brit* to criticize them severely or publicly. **2** *US* to make an obscene gesture of dismissal, etc (see *noun* 4 above) at them. • **go like a bird** *colloq* said of a machine, especially a car: to run very fast and smoothly. • **kill two birds with one stone** see under KILL. • **strictly for the birds** or **for the birds** *especially US colloq* worthless or unimportant; acceptable only to people who are stupid or weak, etc (in the speaker's eyes). ⓘ Anglo-Saxon *bridd* young bird.

birdbath ▷ *noun* a basin, usually one on a pedestal, set up outside for birds to bathe in.

bird-brained ▷ *adj, colloq* said of a person: silly or flighty; daft.

birdcage ▷ *noun* a cage, usually made of wire or wicker, for keeping a bird in.

birdcall ▷ *noun* **1** a bird's song. **2** an instrument for imitating the sound of birdsong.

bird-dog ▷ *noun, especially US* a dog trained to find or retrieve birds, etc shot by hunters. *British equivalent* GUNDOG.

bird-fancier ▷ *noun* a person who breeds cagebirds, either to keep or for sale. Compare BIRDWATCHER.

birdie ▷ *noun* (***birdies***) **1** *colloq* used by or to a child: a little bird. **2** *golf* a score of one stroke under PAR for a particular hole on a course. Compare ALBATROSS 3, BOGEY 2, EAGLE 3. ▷ *verb* (***birdied***, ***birdying***) *tr & intr, golf* to complete (a hole) with a birdie score. • **watch the birdie** *colloq* a humorous instruction to look at the camera when one's photograph is about to be taken.

birding see under BIRDWATCHER

bird-lime ▷ *noun* a sticky substance put on the branches of trees to catch small birds. Also called **lime**.

bird of paradise ▷ *noun* (***birds of paradise***) **1** any of various stout-billed brilliantly coloured birds, native to New Guinea and Australia, the male of which has elaborate tail plumes that form a fan over its back during its elaborate courtship displays. **2** the bird of paradise flower. ⓘ 17c.

bird of paradise flower ▷ *noun* an evergreen perennial tropical plant, widely cultivated for its conspicuous flower-heads which are composed of orange sepals and blue petals that emerge from a sheathing bract and resemble a bird of paradise in flight. ⓘ 19c.

bird of passage ▷ *noun* (***birds of passage***) **1** a bird that flies to different parts of the world as the seasons change; a migratory bird. **2** a person who constantly moves around and never settles in one place. ⓘ 18c.

bird of prey ▷ *noun* (***birds of prey***) any of several types of bird that kill other birds and small mammals for food, eg the owl, hawk and eagle. ⓘ 14c.

the birds and the bees ▷ *noun, colloq, euphemistic* sexual activity and reproduction. See also FACT OF LIFE 2.

birdseed ▷ *noun* **1** seed used for feeding cagebirds, etc, eg a mixture of small seeds such as hemp. **2** *slang* CHICKENFEED 2.

bird's-eye view ▷ *noun* **1** a wide general overall view from above. **2** a general impression. ⓘ 18c.

birdsfoot trefoil ▷ *noun* a small perennial plant, native to Europe, Asia and Africa, with leaves composed of five oval leaflets and flat-topped clusters of yellow flowers on stalks, often tinged with red. Also called **eggs-and-bacon**.

birdshot ▷ *noun* small pellets suitable for shooting birds.

bird's nest fern ▷ *noun* a perennial fern, native to Old World tropical forests, with bright-green undivided leaves that form a nest-like rosette in which HUMUS accumulates, into which the roots of the plants then grow to obtain nutrients and water.

bird's nest soup ▷ *noun* a spicy Chinese soup, made from the outer layers of the nest of the swallow, which is covered in a gelatinous substance secreted by the bird to construct the nest.

bird strike ▷ *noun* a collision between a bird or birds and the engine of an aeroplane.

bird table ▷ *noun* a table or raised platform for placing food on for wild birds to eat, out of reach of cats, etc.

birdwatcher ▷ *noun* a person who studies birds by observing them closely, especially as a hobby. Also called (*especially US* or *colloq*) **birder**. • **bird-watching** *noun* the scientific observation of birds in their natural habitat. Also called (*especially US* or *colloq*) **birding**.

biretta /bɪ'rɛtə/ ▷ *noun* (***birettas***) a stiff square cap with three flat upright projections on top, worn by Roman Catholic clergy, most commonly black (worn by priests), but also purple (worn by bishops) or red (worn by cardinals). ⓘ 16c: from Italian *berretta*, from Latin *birretum* cap.

biriani or **biryani** /bɪri'ɑːnɪ/ ▷ *noun* (***birianis*** or ***biryanis***) *cookery* a type of spicy Indian dish consisting mainly of rice, with meat or fish and vegetables, etc. ⓘ 20c: Urdu.

Biro /'baɪroʊ/ ▷ *noun* (***Biros***) *Brit trademark* a type of BALLPOINT pen. ⓘ 1940s: named after a Hungarian journalist, Laszlo Biró (1899–1985), its inventor.

birth /bɜːθ/ ▷ *noun* **1** the act or process of bearing children. Also called CHILDBIRTH. **2** the act or process of being born. See also NATIVITY. **3** family history or origin; ancestry; descent □ ***of humble birth***. **4** beginning; origins □ ***the birth of socialism***. Sometimes called GENESIS. • **give birth** said of a mother: to bear or produce (a baby). • **give birth to something** to produce or be the cause or origin of it. ⓘ 13c: from Norse *byrthr*.

birth

There is often a spelling confusion between **birth** and **berth**.

birth certificate ▷ *noun* an official document that records a person's birth, stating the date and place, the parents, etc.

birth control ▷ *noun* the prevention of pregnancy, especially by means of CONTRACEPTION. Also called **family planning**.

birthday ▷ *noun* **1** the anniversary of the day on which a person was born. **2** (*also* **birth day**) the day on which a person was born. ◷ 14c.

birthday honours ▷ *plural noun* in the UK: titles or medals awarded to people, public notice of which is given on the official birthday of the sovereign.

birthday suit ▷ *noun* used especially in the phrase • **in one's birthday suit** *humorous, colloq* completely naked. ◷ 18c, originally meaning a special suit of clothes for wearing on the sovereign's birthday.

birthing pool ▷ *noun* a portable pool in which a woman can sit partially immersed in water during labour and childbirth.

birthmark ▷ *noun* a blemish or mark that is present on the skin at birth and may be temporary (eg a STRAWBERRY MARK) or permanent (eg a PORT-WINE STAIN). *Technical equivalent* NAEVUS.

birthplace ▷ *noun* **1** the place where a person was born. **2** the place where something important or wellknown began □ *the birthplace of medicine.*

birth rate ▷ *noun* the ratio of the number of live births occurring over a period of a year in a given area per thousand inhabitants, or per thousand women of childbearing age.

birthright ▷ *noun* the rights a person may claim by being born into a particular family or social class, etc.

birth sign ▷ *noun, astrol* the SIGN OF THE ZODIAC under which a person was born.

birthstone ▷ *noun* a gemstone associated with the month in which a person was born, or with their BIRTH SIGN.

biryani see BIRIANI

biscuit /ˈbɪskɪt/ ▷ *noun* **1** *especially Brit* **a** a small thin sweet crisp cake, in any of numerous varieties or flavours, etc. *N Amer equivalent* COOKIE; **b** a small thin crisp plain or savoury cake □ *cheese and biscuits*. *N Amer equivalent* CRACKER. **2** *N Amer* an unsweetened scone, eaten eg with meat or gravy. **3** objects made from baked clay that have not been glazed. Also called **biscuitware** and BISQUE. **4** a pale golden brown or pale tan colour. Also called BISQUE. ▷ *adj* pale golden brown or pale tan in colour. • **biscuity** *adj* like a biscuit in flavour, texture or colour. • **take the biscuit** *Brit, ironic colloq* to surpass everything else that has happened; to be worse than anything □ *His last comment really took the biscuit* ◷ A 20c variant of *take the cake*.. ◷ 14c: ultimately from Latin *bis* twice + *coquere* to cook.

bisect /baɪˈsɛkt/ *math, etc,* ▷ *verb* (***bisected, bisecting***) to divide something into two equal parts. • **bisection** *noun*. • **bisector** *noun* a line that divides an angle, etc into two equal parts. ◷ 17c: from Latin *secare* to cut.

bisexual ▷ *adj* **1** sexually attracted to both males and females. Often *colloq* shortened to BI. **2** having the sexual organs of both male and female. Also HERMAPHRODITE. ▷ *noun* a bisexual person or organism, etc. Compare HETEROSEXUAL, HOMOSEXUAL, UNISEXUAL. • **bisexuality** *noun*. ◷ 19c.

bishop /ˈbɪʃəp/ ▷ *noun* **1** (*often* **Bishop**) *Christianity* a senior priest or minister in the Roman Catholic, Anglican and Orthodox Churches, in charge of a group of churches in an area, or of a DIOCESE. See also ARCHBISHOP, SUFFRAGAN. **2** *chess* (symbol **B**) a piece shaped like a bishop's mitre at the top, which may only be moved diagonally across the board. ◷ Anglo-Saxon *bisceop*: ultimately from Greek *episkopos* overseer.

bishopric /ˈbɪʃəprɪk/ ▷ *noun, Christianity* **1** the post or position of bishop. **2** the area under the charge of a bishop; a diocese. Also called SEE^{2}. ◷ Anglo-Saxon *bisceoprice*.

bismuth /ˈbɪzməθ, ˈbɪs-/ ▷ *noun, chem* (symbol **Bi**, atomic number 83) a hard silvery-white metallic element with a pinkish tinge, used to make lead alloys for use in fire-detection devices, electrical fuses, etc, the insoluble compounds of which are used to treat stomach upsets, skin disorders, etc. ◷ 17c: German.

bison /ˈbaɪsən/ ▷ *noun* (*plural* ***bison***) either of two species of large hoofed mammal with a dark-brown coat, broad humped shoulders, short upward-curving horns and long shaggy hair on its head, neck, shoulders and forelegs. ◷ 14c: Latin, probably of Germanic origin.

bisque^{1} /bɪsk, biːsk/ ▷ *noun, cookery* a thick rich soup, usually made from shellfish, cream and wine. ◷ 17c: French.

bisque^{2} /bɪsk/ ▷ *noun* a type of baked clay or china, which has not been glazed. ▷ *adj* pale golden-brown or pale tan in colour, like unglazed pottery. Also (in both *noun* and *adj* senses) BISCUIT. ◷ 17c as *noun*; 20c as *adj*: shortened and altered from BISCUIT.

bistable /ˈbaɪsteɪbəl/ ▷ *adj, telecomm, etc* said of a valve or transistor circuit: having two stable states. ▷ *noun, electronics, computing* a FLIP-FLOP 2. ◷ 1940s.

bistort /ˈbɪstɔːt/ ▷ *noun* any of various plants found mainly in northern temperate regions, with lance-shaped or oblong leaves and small white, pink or red flowers with terminal spikes. ◷ 16c: from Latin *bis* twice + *tortus* twisted, referring to its twisted root.

bistro /ˈbiːstroʊ/ ▷ *noun* (***bistros***) a small bar or informal restaurant. ◷ 1920s: French.

bisulphate ▷ *noun, chem* HYDROGENSULPHATE.

bit^{1} ▷ *noun* **1** a small piece, part or amount of something. **2** *Brit, old use, in compounds* a coin, especially a small coin □ *threepenny bit.* **3** *N Amer* (*only* **two-bits, four bits** or **six bits**) $12\frac{1}{2}$ cents (ie a quarter, a half, and three-quarters of a dollar, respectively). See also TWO-BIT. • **a bit** *colloq* **1** a short time or distance □ *Wait a bit.* **2** a little; slightly; rather □ *feel a bit of a fool.* **3** a lot □ *takes a bit of doing.* • **a bit much** or **thick** or **rich** *colloq* behaviour that is unacceptable, unreasonable or unfair. • **a bit of all right** *colloq* someone or something very much approved of. • **a bit of rough** see under ROUGH. • **a bit off** *Brit colloq* bad manners, taste or behaviour. • **a bit on the side** see separate entry. • **bit by bit** gradually; piecemeal. • **do one's bit** *colloq* to do one's fair share. • **not a bit** or **not a bit of it** not at all; not to any extent. ◷ Anglo-Saxon *bita* in obsolete sense 'a portion of something bitten off at one time'; see BITE.

bit^{2} ▷ *noun* **1** a small metal bar which a horse holds in its mouth as part of the bridle with which it is controlled. **2** (*also* **drill bit**) a tool with a cutting edge, which can be fitted into a drill and turned at high speed. See also BRACE AND BIT. **3** the part of a key which connects with the lever in a lock. • **champ at the bit** see under CHAMP^{1}. • **take** or **get the bit between one's teeth** to act decisively and with determination; to occupy or interest oneself keenly in something. ◷ 14c: from Anglo-Saxon *bite* an act of biting.

bit^{3} ▷ *noun, computing* a binary digit with a value of either 0 or 1, representing the smallest piece of information that can be dealt with by a computer. ◷ 1940s: a contraction of *binary digit.*

bit^{4} *past tense of* BITE

bitch ▷ *noun* (***bitches***) **1** a female of the dog family. **2** *offensive or derog slang* a bad-tempered, unpleasant or spiteful woman. **3** *slang* a difficult or unpleasant thing □ *Life's a bitch.* ▷ *verb* (***bitched, bitching***) **1** *intr* (*especially* **bitch about someone**) to complain or talk bitchily. **2**

(*often* **bitch something up**) to mess it up or spoil it. ⓒ Anglo-Saxon *bicce*.

bitchy ▷ *adj* (**bitchier**, **bitchiest**) *colloq* spiteful; petulantly bad-tempered or malicious. • **bitchily** *adverb*. • **bitchiness** *noun*. ⓒ 1930s.

bite /baɪt/ ▷ *verb* (**bit**, **bitten**, **biting**) **1** *tr & intr* (*sometimes* **bite something away** or **off** or **out**) to grasp, seize or tear with the teeth. **2** *tr & intr* said of snakes and insects: to puncture a victim's skin (with the fangs, mouthparts, etc) and suck blood. **3** *tr & intr* to smart or sting, or to make something do so. **4** *colloq* to annoy or worry □ *What's biting him?* **5** said of acid, etc: to eat into something chemically; to have a corrosive effect. **6** *intr* to start to have an effect, usually an adverse one □ *The spending cuts are beginning to bite.* **7** *intr, angling* said of fish: to be caught on the hook on a fishing line, by taking the bait into the mouth. **8** *intr* said of a wheel or screw, etc: to grip firmly. ▷ *noun* **1** an act or an instance of biting. **2** a wound or sting caused by biting. **3** a piece of something removed or taken, etc by biting; a mouthful □ *took a bite out of my apple.* **4** *colloq* a small amount of food □ *a bite to eat.* **5** strength, sharpness or bitterness of taste. **6** sharpness or incisiveness of words. **7** *angling* said of a fish: an act or an instance of biting or nibbling at the bait. • **biter** *noun*. • **biting** *noun*. • **bite off more than one can chew** to agree or attempt to do more than one can manage; to over-estimate what one is capable of. • **bite one's tongue** to restrain oneself from saying something one wants very much to say. • **bite someone's head off** *colloq* to reply to them with unexpected or unnecessary fierceness or anger. • **bite the bullet** to accept or face up to something unpleasant but unavoidable as bravely as possible. • **bite the dust** *colloq* **1** said of a plan or project, etc: to fail or come to nothing; to be unsuccessful. **2** said of a person: to fall down dead; to be killed. • **bite the hand that feeds you** to harm or show ingratitude towards a person who is being kind or helpful to you. • **put the bite on someone** *slang* to extort or borrow money from them. ⓒ Anglo-Saxon *bitan*.

▪ **bite something back** *colloq* to restrain oneself from saying it, as if by biting one's lips.

▪ **bite something in** in etching, etc: to eat out the lines of (a design, etc) with acid.

bitesize ▷ *adj* referring to a morsel of food which is small enough to be put into the mouth and eaten in one.

biting ▷ *adj* **1** bitterly and painfully cold. **2** said of a remark: sharp and hurtful; sarcastic. • **bitingly** *adverb*.

bit-mapping ▷ *noun, computing* a method of organizing the display on a computer screen so that each PIXEL is assigned to one or more bits (see BIT[3]) of memory, depending on the shading or number of colours required. • **bit map** *noun*. • **bit-mapped** *adj*. ⓒ 1970s.

bitonal /baɪ'toʊnəl/ ▷ *adj, music* said of a composition, etc: using two keys simultaneously. • **bitonality** *noun*. ⓒ 1920s.

bit on the side ▷ *noun* **1** an extramarital relationship. **2** someone with whom a person is having such a relationship.

bit-part ▷ *noun* a small acting part in a play or film.

bit player ▷ *noun* an actor who plays bit parts.

bits and pieces and **bits and bobs** ▷ *plural noun, Brit colloq* small objects or possessions; odds and ends.

bitten /'bɪtən/ *past participle of* BITE

bitter /'bɪtə(r)/ ▷ *adj* (**bitterer**, **bitterest**) **1** having a sharp, acid and often unpleasant taste. Compare SALT, SOUR, SWEET, SMOOTH. **2** feeling or causing sadness or pain □ *bitter memories.* **3** difficult to accept □ *a bitter disappointment.* **4** showing an intense persistent feeling of dislike, hatred or opposition □ *bitter resentment.* **5** said of words, etc: sharp; acrimonious. **6** said of the weather, etc: extremely and painfully cold. ▷ *noun, Brit* a type of beer with a slightly bitter taste, strongly flavoured with hops. Compare MILD *noun*. • **bitterly** *adverb* **1** in a bitter manner, especially with fierce resentment. **2** extremely; painfully □ *bitterly cold.* • **bitterness** *noun*. • **a bitter pill to swallow** something difficult or unpleasant to accept, such as an unwelcome fact. ⓒ Anglo-Saxon *biter*, from *bitan* to bite.

the bitter end ▷ *noun* **1** (*especially* **to the bitter end**) the very end of a task, etc, however unpleasant and in spite of difficulties; the absolute limit of one's strength, endurance or resources, etc □ *The play was dreadful, but we saw it through to the bitter end.* **2** *naut* the end of the cable or chain fastened to the BITTS on a ship. ⓒ 19c: probably referring to the nautical term *bitter* a turn of the anchoring cable around the bitts; once a rope has been paid out to the *bitter end*, there is no more rope available.

bitter lemon ▷ *noun* a lemon-flavoured carbonated soft drink.

bittern /'bɪtən/ ▷ *noun* a long-legged European bird that lives on or near water and makes a very loud deep sound. ⓒ 14c: from French *butor*.

bitter orange see under ORANGE

bitters ▷ *plural noun* a liquid made from bitter herbs or roots, used to help digestion or to flavour certain alcoholic drinks.

bittersweet ▷ *adj* pleasant and unpleasant, or bitter and sweet, at the same time □ *a bittersweet love story.* ▷ *noun* a plant, the stems of which taste first bitter and then sweet when chewed. Also called WOODY NIGHTSHADE. ⓒ 14c.

bitts ▷ *noun, naut* a pair of posts or BOLLARDS for fastening the anchoring cables, etc around on the deck of a ship. ⓒ 16c: perhaps from Norse *biti* a crossbeam.

bitty ▷ *adj* (**bittier**, **bittiest**) *colloq* consisting of small unrelated bits or parts, especially when put together awkwardly or untidily; scrappy; disjointed. • **bittiness** *noun*. ⓒ 19c.

bitumen /'bɪtjʊmɪn/ ▷ *noun* **1** any of various black solid or tarry flammable substances composed of an impure mixture of hydrocarbons, either occurring naturally or obtained by the distillation of petroleum, and which is used for surfacing roads and pavements, etc. **2** (**the bitumen**) *Austral colloq* a road with a tarred surface. • **bituminize** or **bituminise** /bɪ'tjuː-/ *verb* (**bituminized**, **bituminizing**) to mix with or make into bitumen. • **bituminous** *adj* containing or impregnated with bitumen. ⓒ 15c: the Latin word for PITCH[2] or ASPHALT.

bituminous coal ▷ *noun, geol* a dark brown or black coal containing more than 80% carbon, which burns with a smoky yellowish flame and is widely used for domestic and industrial purposes.

bivalent /baɪ'veɪlənt, 'bɪvələnt/ ▷ *adj, chem* DIVALENT. • **bivalency** *noun*. ⓒ 19c.

bivalve /'baɪvalv/ *zool* ▷ *adj* said of a mollusc: having a shell composed of two valves hinged together by a ligament. ▷ *noun* any of numerous mainly marine species of mollusc with a shell composed of two valves hinged together by a tough horny ligament, eg clam, cockle, mussel and scallop. Also called LAMELLIBRANCH. ⓒ 17c.

bivariate /baɪ'veərɪaɪt/ ▷ *adj, math* involving two variables. ⓒ 1920s.

bivouac /'bɪvʊak/ ▷ *noun* **1** a temporary camp or camping place without tents, especially one used by soldiers and mountaineers. **2** the making of such a camp, or camping out in one. ▷ *verb* (**bivouacked**, **bivouacking**) *intr* **1** to camp out temporarily at night without a tent. **2** to make such a camp. ⓒ 18c, originally meaning a NIGHT WATCH by a whole army: French, probably from Swiss German *Beiwacht* an additional guard at night.

bi-weekly ▷ *adj* **1** FORTNIGHTLY. **2** occurring or appearing twice a week. Sometimes SEMI-WEEKLY. Also *adverb.* ▻ *noun* a periodical issued twice a week, or once every two weeks.

bi-yearly ▻ *adj* **1** happening, issued or produced, etc twice a year. Also BIANNUAL. **2** happening, issued or produced, etc every two years. Also BIENNIAL. Also *adverb.*

bizarre /bɪˈzɑː(r)/ ▻ *adj* weirdly odd or strange. • **bizarrely** *adverb.* • **bizarreness** *noun.* ⓒ 17c: French, from Spanish *bizarro* gallant or brave, possibly from Basque *bizarra* a beard.

Bk ▻ *symbol, chem* berkelium.

bk ▻ *abbreviation* **1** bank. **2** book.

BL ▻ *abbreviation* **1** Bachelor of Law. **2** *formerly* British Leyland. **3** British Library.

B/L or **b/l** or **b.l.** ▻ *abbreviation* bill of lading.

blab ▻ *verb* (***blabbed***, ***blabbing***) **1** *tr & intr* (*usually* **blab something out**) to tell or divulge (a secret, etc). **2** *intr* to chatter foolishly or indiscreetly. • **blabbing** *noun, adj.* ⓒ 16c: from 14c noun *blabbe* a chatterer, later meaning 'idle talk'.

■ **blab on about something** *colloq* to talk incessantly about it.

blabber ▻ *verb* (***blabbered***, ***blabbering***) *intr* to talk nonsense, especially without stopping or without being understood; to babble. ▻ *noun* a blabbermouth. ⓒ 14c.

blabbermouth ▻ *noun, slang, originally US* a person who talks foolishly and indiscreetly; someone who blabs. ⓒ 1930s.

black ▻ *adj* (***blacker***, ***blackest***) **1** having the darkest colour, the same colour as coal; reflecting no light. **2** without any light; totally dark. **3** (*now usually* **Black**) used of people: dark-skinned, especially of African, West Indian or Australian Aboriginal origin. **4** (*usually* **Black**) belonging or relating to Black people. **5** said of coffee or tea: without added milk. **6** angry; threatening □ *black looks.* **7** dirty; soiled □ *came in from the garden with his hands black.* **8** sad, gloomy or depressed; dismal □ *a black mood.* **9** promising trouble; likely to be bad in some way □ *The future looks black.* **10** wicked or sinister; grim or macabre □ *black-hearted* □ *black comedy.* **11** said of goods, etc: not allowed by a trade union to be handled, especially during a strike. **12** said of income, etc: not reported in tax returns; illicit. ▻ *noun* **1** the colour of coal, etc, the darkest colour, or absence of colour. **2** anything which is black in colour, eg a black chess piece. **3** (*usually* **Black**) a dark-skinned person, especially one of African, West Indian or Australian Aboriginal origin. **4** black clothes worn when in mourning. **5** a black pigment or dye. **6** (*usually* **be in the black**) the credit side of an account; the state of not being in debt, eg to a bank Compare RED *noun* 6. ▻ *verb* (***blacked***, ***blacking***) **1** (*also* **blacken**) to make something black □ *The men blacked their faces with soot.* **2** to clean (shoes, etc) with black polish. **3** said of a trade union: to forbid work to be done on or with (certain goods). • **blackly** *adverb* in an angry or threatening way. • **blackness** *noun.* • **black in the face** purple in the face, due to exertion, anger, strangulation, etc. • **in black and white 1** in writing or in print. **2** having or using no colours, only black and white. • **in someone's black books** in trouble or disgrace, or out of favour with them ⓒ From the 16c; a *black book* was one in which the names of people deserving punishment were recorded. • **in the black** in credit; solvent; out of debt ⓒ From the bookkeeping practice of writing in black ink on the credit side of a ledger. ⓒ Anglo-Saxon *blæc.*

■ **black out** said of a person: to lose consciousness.

■ **black something out 1** to deprive it of light; to extinguish or cover (lights), or all lights in (a place). **2** to prevent (information) from being broadcast or published; to suppress (news, etc).

Black Africa ▻ *noun* the part of Africa south of the Sahara desert, where the population is mainly black.

Black American ▻ *noun* an AFRICAN-AMERICAN.

blackamoor /ˈblakəmʊə(r)/ ▻ *noun, old use, usually derog* a dark-skinned or black person.

black and blue ▻ *adj, colloq* said of a person or of a person's skin: covered in bruises.

black and white ▻ *adj* **1** used of photographs or TV images: having no colours except black, white, and shades of grey. **2** either good or bad, right or wrong, etc, with no compromise.

the black art see BLACK MAGIC

blackball ▻ *verb* **1** to vote against (a candidate for membership of something), originally by putting a black ball in the ballot box. **2** to refuse to see or speak to someone. • **blackballing** *noun.* ⓒ 18c.

black bean ▻ *noun* **1** in Asiatic cookery: a SOYA BEAN, as used in sauces, etc after fermenting, salting and seasoning. **2** any black bean of the same genus as the haricot or kidney bean. **3** an Australian tree with attractive wood.

black bear ▻ *noun* a bear belonging to either of two species, the American and the Asiatic black bear, usually black but sometimes brown in colour, the Asiatic sometimes having white markings.

black belt ▻ *noun, judo, karate, etc* 1 a belt indicating that the wearer has reached the highest possible level of skill. **2** a person who is entitled to wear a black belt.

blackberry ▻ *noun* **1** a thorny shrub which produces dark purple-coloured berries. **2** a berry from this shrub. Also called (*especially Scottish*) BRAMBLE.

blackbird ▻ *noun* **1** a small European bird, the male of which is black with a yellow beak. **2** any of various similar N American birds.

blackboard ▻ *noun* a black or dark-coloured board for writing on with chalk, used especially in schools.

black body ▻ *noun, physics* a hypothetical body that absorbs all the radiation that falls on it, reflecting none.

black books see IN SOMEONE'S BLACK BOOKS at BLACK

black box ▻ *noun* a FLIGHT RECORDER in an aircraft.

blackcap ▻ *noun* a small songbird, the male of which has a black-topped head.

blackcock ▻ *noun* the male of the BLACK GROUSE.

black comedy ▻ *noun* a kind of comedy (in narrative or dramatic form) which derives its often bitter humour from exposing and confronting the grotesque and absurd accidents and misfortunes of life.

the Black Country ▻ *noun* the industrialized West Midlands region of England, centred on Staffordshire, Warwickshire and Worcestershire. ⓒ 19c: from the smoke and grime produced by the heavy industries.

blackcurrant ▻ *noun* **1** a garden shrub grown for its small round black fruit. **2** the fruit of this shrub.

the Black Death ▻ *noun, historical* a virulent pneumonic and BUBONIC PLAGUE which spread across Europe from Asia in the 14c, killing approximately 25 million people. ⓒ 18c.

black economy ▻ *noun* unofficial business or trade, etc involving payment in cash or in kind, and not declared for tax purposes. Compare BLACK MARKET.

blacken ▻ *verb* (***blackened***, ***blackening***) **1** *tr & intr* to make or become black or very dark in colour. See also BLACK *verb* 1. **2** (*especially* **blacken someone's name**) to say something bad about them, or to attack their reputation, usually unfairly or untruthfully; to slander or libel them. ⓒ 14c.

black eye ▻ *noun* an eye with darkened bruised swollen skin around it, usually caused by a blow.

black-eye bean or **black-eyed bean** and (*US*) **black-eyed pea** ▻ *noun* **1** a plant with many varieties, widely cultivated for its seed pods containing beans which are usually creamy white with a black 'eye'. **2** the seed of this plant. Also called **cowpea.**

black-eyed Susan ▷ *noun* **1** a N American plant that has flowers with dark centres and yellow or orange rays. **2** a tropical African climbing plant that has yellow flowers with purple centres.

blackfly ▷ *noun* a small biting fly found near running water, including some species the females of which are bloodsuckers and serious pests of cattle.

Black Forest gateau ▷ *noun, cookery* a rich chocolate cake filled and topped with black cherries and cream. ⓒ 20c: named after the Black Forest, a forested mountain region in SW Germany.

black grouse ▷ *noun* a large northern European grouse, the male of which is black with a lyre-shaped tail and is called a **blackcock**, while the female is called a **grey hen**.

blackguard /'blagɑːd/ *dated or facetious* ▷ *noun* a rogue or villain; a contemptible scoundrel. • **blackguardly** *adj.* ⓒ 16c in obsolete sense 'the lowest form of servant'.

blackhead ▷ *noun* a small black spot on the skin caused by sweat blocking one of the skin's tiny pores or hair follicles. *Technical equivalent* COMEDO.

black hole ▷ *noun, astron* a region in space, believed to be formed when a large star has collapsed in on itself at the end of its life, with such a strong gravitational pull that not even light waves can escape from it. ⓒ 1960s.

black ice ▷ *noun* a type of ice that is thin and transparent, which forms on road surfaces, where the blackness of the road makes it barely visible and therefore highly dangerous.

blacking ▷ *noun, rather dated* black polish, especially for shining shoes or fireplaces, etc.

blackjack ▷ *noun* **1** *cards* **a** PONTOON[2] or a similar game; **b** a combination of an ace and a face-card in the game of blackjack. **2** *N Amer* a length of hard flexible leather, especially one used for hitting people; a cosh. **3** *antiq, etc* a large jug or tankard for holding drink, made of tarred leather. ▷ *verb, N Amer* (***blackjacked***, ***blackjacking***) **1** to hit someone with a blackjack (sense 2). **2** to pressurize or threaten someone into doing something. ⓒ 16c in sense 3.

black lead /— lɛd/ ▷ *noun* GRAPHITE.

blackleg *chiefly Brit* ▷ *noun, derog* a person who refuses to take part in a strike, or who works in a striker's place during a strike. Also called STRIKE-BREAKER and (*slang*) SCAB. ▷ *verb* (***blacklegged***, ***blacklegging***) *intr* to refuse to take part in a strike; to work as a blackleg. ⓒ 19c; 18c meaning 'a swindler'.

blacklist ▷ *noun* a list of people convicted or suspected of something, or not approved of, to be boycotted or excluded, etc. ▷ *verb* to put someone on such a list. ⓒ 17c as *noun*.

blackly see under BLACK

black magic and **the black art** ▷ *noun* magic which supposedly invokes the power of the devil to perform evil.

blackmail ▷ *verb* **1** to extort money, etc illegally from someone by threatening to reveal harmful information about them. **2** to try to influence someone by using unfair pressure or threats. ▷ *noun* an act of blackmailing someone. • **blackmailer** *noun.* ⓒ 16c in historical sense 'a payment made to robbers for protection': from BLACK *adj* 6 + obsolete *mail* payment of money.

Black Maria[1] / — mə'raɪə/ ▷ *noun, colloq* a police van for transporting prisoners. ⓒ 19c (originally US): thought perhaps to refer to Maria Lee, the landlady of a Boston lodging-house, because when the police needed help to constrain someone, they are said to have called upon the services of Maria, a very large strong black woman.

Black Maria[2] see HEARTS

black mark ▷ *noun* a sign or demonstration, etc of disapproval or criticism towards someone, or of a failure on their part. ⓒ 19c, literally a black cross or similar mark made against someone's name as an indication of failure, etc.

black market ▷ *noun* the illegal buying and selling, at high prices, of goods which are scarce, strictly regulated or in great demand. • **black-marketeer** *noun.* ⓒ 1930s; see BLACK *adj* 12.

black mass ▷ *noun* a blasphemous ceremony parodying the Christian mass, in which Satan is worshipped rather than God.

blackness see under BLACK

blackout ▷ *noun* **1** an enforced period during which all the lights in an area are turned out, eg during World War II as a precaution during an air raid at night. **2** an electrical power-failure or power-cut, putting out all the artificial light, etc in an area. **3** a sudden loss of memory or of consciousness. **4 a** a suppression or stoppage of news, information, communications, etc; **b** a stoppage in the transmission of radio or TV programmes. **5** *theat* the extinguishing of all the stage lighting to give sudden darkness on stage. See also BLACK OUT at BLACK.

black pepper ▷ *noun* pepper produced by grinding the dried fruits of the pepper plant without removing their dark outer covering.

Black Power or **black power** ▷ *noun* a movement seeking to increase the political, economic and social power and influence of Black people; originally and still mainly associated with US radical and activist politics. ⓒ 1950s.

black pudding ▷ *noun* a dark sausage made from pig's blood and fat, cereal, etc. Also called **blood pudding**.

Black Rod ▷ *noun* in the UK: the chief usher to the House of Lords and to the Chapter of the Garter, whose staff of office is an ebony rod surmounted by a golden lion, and who by tradition is sent to summon the members of the Commons to the Lords at the opening of Parliament. ⓒ 16c: the full title is 'Gentleman Usher of the Black Rod'.

black sheep ▷ *noun* a member of a family or group who is disapproved of in some way (eg for failing to succeed, conform or achieve, etc) and is seen as a source of shame or embarrassment, etc to the rest. ⓒ 18c.

Blackshirt ▷ *noun* **1** a member of the Italian Fascist Party before and during World War II. **2** *loosely* a Fascist. ⓒ 1920s: a translation of the Italian *camicia nera* black shirt (a distinctive part of the Fascist Party uniform).

blacksmith ▷ *noun* a person who makes and repairs by hand things made of iron, such as horseshoes. ⓒ 15c: a SMITH who works with BLACK metal (ie iron), as opposed to one who works with white metal (ie tin).

black spot ▷ *noun* **1** *chiefly Brit* a dangerous stretch of road where accidents often occur. **2** *chiefly Brit* an area where an adverse social condition is prevalent □ *an unemployment black spot.* **3** a fungal disease affecting plants, causing dark spots eg on the leaves of roses.

black stump ▷ *noun, Austral, NZ* a mythical distance marker on the edge of civilization. • **beyond the black stump** in the far distant outback.

black swan ▷ *noun* a swan native to Australia and Tasmania, with dark plumage.

blackthorn ▷ *noun* a thorny deciduous European shrub or small tree, with conspicuous black twigs on which small white flowers appear in early spring before the leaves have emerged, and which produces rounded bluish-black fruits known as SLOES.

black tie ▷ *noun* a black BOW TIE, especially one worn with a dinner jacket as part of a man's formal evening dress. ▻ *adj* (*usually* **black-tie**) said of a celebration or function: formal, at which guests are expected to wear evening dress.

blacktop ▻ *noun, N Amer* **1** bituminous material used for surfacing roads, etc. **2** a road or other surface covered with blacktop. Compare MACADAM, TARMAC, TARMACADAM. ◷ 1930s.

black velvet ▻ *noun* a drink consisting of champagne and stout in equal parts.

blackwater fever ▻ *noun* a type of malaria in which the urine becomes dark-coloured, due to the rapid destruction of red blood cells

black widow ▻ *noun* any of various species of venomous spider, especially a N American species, the female of which has a black shiny body and an almost spherical abdomen with a red hourglass-shaped marking. ◷ Early 20c: so called because the black-bodied female commonly eats the male after mating.

bladder /'bladə(r)/ ▻ *noun* **1** *anatomy* in all mammals, and some fish, amphibians and reptiles: a hollow sac-shaped organ with a thin muscular wall, in which urine produced by the kidneys is stored before it is discharged from the body. **2** any of various similar hollow organs in which liquid or gas is stored, eg the gall bladder of animals, or the swim bladder of bony fish. **3** a hollow bag made eg of leather, which can be stretched by filling it with air or liquid. **4** in certain plants: a hollow sac-like structure, especially one of the air-filled sacs at the tips of the fronds of BLADDER WRACK. ◷ Anglo-Saxon *blædre* blister or pimple.

bladder wrack ▻ *noun* a tough brown seaweed, so called because its fronds bear paired air-filled bladders that provide buoyancy in the water.

blade /bleɪd/ ▻ *noun* **1** the cutting part of a knife or sword, etc. **2** the flat, usually long and narrow, part of a leaf, petal or sepal. **3** the wide flat part of an oar, bat or propeller, or of certain tools and devices. **4** a broad flat bone, eg the SHOULDER BLADE (SCAPULA). **5** the runner of an ice-skate, that slides on the surface of the ice. **6** *Brit slang* a knife or switchblade. **7** the free flat part of the tongue just behind the tip. ◷ Anglo-Saxon *blæd*.

blag ▻ *verb* (***blagged, blagging***) *slang* **1** to rob or steal something. **2** to scrounge something; to get it for nothing □ *blagged his way into the club.* ▻ *noun* a theft or robbery; a scrounge. ● **blagger** *noun*. ◷ 1930s.

■ **blag on about something** or **blag about something** *colloq* to talk boastfully about it, often exaggerating the truth.

blah /blɑː/ *slang*, ▻ *noun* bunkum; pretentious nonsense. Also **blah-blah**. ▻ *verb* (***blahed, blahing***) *intr* to talk stupidly or insipidly. ● **blah blah blah** an expression used instead of repeating words which have already been said, often because they are not worth repeating anyway.

blain /bleɪn/ ▻ *noun* a boil or blister. ◷ Anglo-Saxon *blegen*.

blame /bleɪm/ ▻ *verb* (***blamed, blaming***) **1** (*especially* **blame someone for something** or **blame something on someone**) to consider them as responsible for (something bad, wrong or undesirable) □ *blames himself for the accident.* **2** to find fault with someone. ▻ *noun* (*especially* **the blame**) responsibility for something bad, wrong or undesirable □ *I refuse to take the blame.* ● **blamable** or **blameable** *adj*. ● **be to blame for something** to be responsible for (something bad, wrong or undesirable). ◷ 13c: from French *blasmer*, from Latin *blasphemare* to blaspheme.

blameless ▻ *adj* free from blame; innocent. ● **blamelessly** *adverb*. ● **blamelessness** *noun*.

blameworthy ▻ *adj* deserving blame.

blanch /blɑːntʃ/ ▻ *verb* (***blanches, blanched, blanching***) **1** to make something white by removing the colour. **2** *usually intr* to become pale or white (or occasionally to make someone or something turn pale or white), especially out of fear. **3** *cookery* to prepare (vegetables or meat) for cooking or freezing by boiling in water for a few seconds. **4** *cookery* to remove the skins from (almonds, etc) by soaking in boiling water. ◷ 15c: from French *blanchir*, from *blanc* white.

blancmange /blə'mɒndʒ, -'mɑ̃ʒ/ ▻ *noun* a cold sweet jelly-like pudding made with milk. ◷ 14c: from French *blanc* white + *manger* food.

bland ▻ *adj* (***blander, blandest***) *derog* **1** said of food: having a very mild taste; tasteless. **2** insipid; lacking interest. **3** said of a person or their actions: mild or gentle; showing no strong emotion. ● **blandly** *adverb*. ● **blandness** *noun*. ◷ 17c: from Latin *blandus* soft or smooth.

blandish /'blandɪʃ/ ▻ *verb* (***blandishes, blandished, blandishing***) to persuade by gentle flattery; to coax or cajole. ◷ 14c: from French *blandir*, from Latin *blandiri*, from *blandus* (see BLAND).

blandishments ▻ *plural noun* flattery intended to persuade. ◷ 16c.

blank /blaŋk/ ▻ *adj* (***blanker, blankest***) **1** said of paper: not written or printed on. **2** said of magnetic tape, etc: with no sound or pictures yet recorded on it. **3** with spaces left for details, information, a signature, etc □ *a blank form.* **4** not filled in; empty □ *Leave that space blank.* **5** showing no expression or interest □ *a blank look.* **6** having no thoughts or ideas □ *My mind went blank.* **7** without a break or relieving feature □ *a blank wall.* **8** sheer; absolute □ *blank refusal.* ▻ *noun* **1** an empty space; a void. **2** an empty space left (on forms, etc) to be filled in with particular information. **3** a printed form with blank spaces left for filling in. **4** a state of having no thoughts or ideas □ *My mind went a complete blank.* **5** a dash written in place of a word or letter. **6** a BLANK CARTRIDGE. **7** a roughly-shaped piece eg of metal, to be processed into a finished article. ▻ *verb* (***blanked, blanking***) **1** (*usually* **blank something off** or **out**) to hide it or form a screen in front of it. **2** *tr & intr* to produce blanks (sense 7) in a manufacturing process. ● **blankly** *adverb*. ● **blankness** *noun*. ● **draw a blank** *colloq* to get no results; to fail. ◷ 14c in the original sense of 'white' or 'colourless': from French *blanc* white.

blank cartridge ▻ *noun* a cartridge containing an explosive but no bullet.

blank cheque ▻ *noun* **1** a cheque which has been signed but on which the amount to be paid has been left blank. **2** complete freedom or authority.

blanket /'blaŋkɪt/ ▻ *noun* **1** a thick covering of wool or other material, used to cover beds or for wrapping a person in for warmth. **2** a thick layer or mass which covers or obscures something □ *a blanket of fog.* ▻ *adj* (used before the noun it describes) general; applying to or covering all cases, people, etc □ *blanket coverage* □ *a blanket rule.* ▻ *verb* (***blanketed, blanketing***) **1** to cover something with, or as if with, a blanket. **2** (*often* **blanket something out**) to keep it quiet, suppress it, or cover it up. **3** to cover or apply something in a general, comprehensive or indiscriminate way. ● **on the blanket** applied to IRA prisoners in jail: wearing blankets instead of prison clothes, as a protest against their having criminal rather than political status. ● **born on the wrong side of the blanket** illegitimately; out of wedlock. ◷ 14c, originally meaning 'rough, undyed or white woollen fabric'; from French *blankete*, from *blanc* white.

blanket bath see BEDBATH

blanket stitch ▻ *noun* a type of stitch used to strengthen and bind the edge of a piece of thick fabric, especially a blanket.

blanketweed ▻ *noun* a rapidly-spreading green threadlike alga that forms over the surface of ponds.

blankly and **blankness** see under BLANK

blank verse ▷ *noun, prosody* poetry which does not rhyme, especially that written in iambic pentameter.

blanquette / *French* blɑ̃kɛt/ ▷ *noun, cookery* a dish made with white meat such as chicken or veal, cooked in a white sauce. ⓘ 19c: French; related to BLANKET.

blare /blɛə(r)/ ▷ *verb* (***blared, blaring***) (*often* **blare out**) **1** *intr* to make a sound like a trumpet. **2** *tr & intr* to sound or say loudly and harshly. ▷ *noun* a loud harsh sound. ⓘ 15c, originally meaning 'to roar or howl (like a crying child), or bellow (like a calf)'.

blarney /'blɑːnɪ/ ▷ *noun* flattering words used to persuade, deceive or cajole. ▷ *verb* (***blarneyed, blarneying***) to persuade using flattery; to cajole or charm. ⓘ 19c: named after Blarney Castle, near Cork in Ireland: tradition has it that anyone who kisses the Blarney stone (an inscribed stone high up in one of its walls and very difficult to reach) receives the gift of charmingly persuasive talk.

blasé /'blɑːzeɪ, blɑː'zeɪ/ ▷ *adj* lacking enthusiasm or interest, or unconcerned, especially as a result of over-familiarity. ⓘ 19c: French, past participle of *blaser* to cloy.

blaspheme /blas'fiːm/ ▷ *verb* (***blasphemed, blaspheming***) **1** *tr & intr* to speak disrespectfully or rudely about God, a divine being or sacred matters. **2** *intr* to swear or curse using the name of God or referring to sacred things. • **blasphemer** *noun*. ⓘ 14c; see BLASPHEMY.

blasphemous /'blasfəməs/ ▷ *adj* applied to speech, writing, thoughts or ideas, etc: involving, containing or using blasphemy, involving the profane use of divine names used profanely. • **blasphemously** *adverb*.

blasphemous libel ▷ *noun, law* the offence (for which prosecution is rare) of insulting, ridiculing or denying the truth of the Christian religion, the Bible, the goodness or existence of God, etc in some scandalous or offensive manner. Also called BLASPHEMY.

blasphemy /'blasfəmɪ/ ▷ *noun* (***blasphemies***) **1 a** speaking about God or sacred matters in a disrespectful or rude way; **b** an action, word or sign that intentionally insults God, or something held sacred, in such a way. **2** *law* blasphemous libel. ⓘ 13c as *blasfemie*: from Latin *blasphemos* evil-speaking.

blast /blɑːst/ ▷ *noun* **1** an explosion, or the strong shock-waves spreading out from it. **2** a strong sudden stream or gust (of air or wind, etc). **3** a sudden loud sound of a trumpet or car horn, etc. **4** a sudden and violent outburst of anger or criticism. **5** *colloq, chiefly & originally US* a highly enjoyable or exciting event, occasion or activity, especially a party. ▷ *verb* (***blasted, blasting***) **1** to blow up (a tunnel or rock, etc) with explosives. **2** *tr & intr* (*especially* **blast out**) to make or cause to make a loud or harsh sound □ *Rock music blasted from the room.* **3** to destroy or damage something severely and beyond repair □ *blast one's hopes.* **4** to criticize severely, or to rage or curse at something or someone. **5** to wither or cause something to shrivel up. ▷ *exclamation* (*also* **blast it!**) *colloq* expressing annoyance or exasperation, etc. • **blaster** *noun* **1** a person or thing that blasts. **2** *golf* a sand-wedge. • **at full blast** at full power or speed, etc; with maximum effort or energy. ⓘ Anglo-Saxon *blæst*.

■ **blast off** said of a spacecraft: to take off from its launching pad.

blasted ▷ *adj, colloq* **1** (often used as an intensifier) annoying; damned; stupid; infuriating. **2** *slang* thoroughly drunk or high on drugs. **3** blighted. ▷ *adverb, colloq* (used as an intensifier) extremely □ *Do you have to go so blasted fast?*

blast furnace ▷ *noun* a tall furnace that is used to extract iron from iron ores such as haematite and magnetite.

blasting ▷ *noun* **1** blowing up with explosives. **2** swearing; cursing □ *What's all this damning and blasting about?*

blasto- /blastoʊ/ *biol* ▷ *combining form, denoting* a sprout, bud or germ □ *blastosphere.* ⓘ From Greek *blastos* bud.

blast-off ▷ *noun* **1** the moment at which a spacecraft or rocket-propelled missile is launched. **2** the launching of a spacecraft or rocket-propelled missile. See BLAST OFF at BLAST.

blastula /'blastjʊlə/ ▷ *noun* (***blastulas*** or ***blastulae*** /-liː/) *biol* a hollow sphere of cells, one cell thick, formed during the division process early in the development of a multicellular embryo. Also called **blastosphere**. ⓘ 19c: Latin; see BLASTO-.

blatant /'bleɪtənt/ ▷ *adj* **1** very obvious and without shame □ *a blatant lie.* **2** very noticeable and obtrusive. • **blatantly** *adverb*. ⓘ 16c: probably invented by Edmund Spenser (c.1552–99), perhaps influenced by Latin *blatire* to babble or chatter.

blather see under BLETHER

blaxploitation ▷ *noun* the commercial exploitation of Black characters or subjects, especially on film, TV, etc. ⓘ 1980s.

blaze[1] /bleɪz/ ▷ *noun* **1** a bright strong fire or flame. **2** a brilliant display □ *The garden was a blaze of colour.* **3** a sudden and sharp bursting out of feeling or emotion. **4** an intense burst or spate □ *a blaze of publicity* (see also BLAZE[3]). ▷ *verb* (***blazed, blazing***) *intr* **1** to burn or shine brightly. **2** *colloq* to show great emotion, especially to be furious □ *Keep out of her way—she's still blazing.* **3** (*often* **blaze away**) *intr* **a** said of a person: to fire a gun rapidly and without stopping; **b** said of a gun: to fire rapidly and without stopping. **4** (*usually* **blaze away at something**) *intr, colloq* to work very hard or vigorously. ⓘ Anglo-Saxon *blæse* torch.

■ **blaze up 1** to suddenly burn much more brightly. **2** to become very angry.

blaze[2] /bleɪz/ ▷ *noun* **1** a white mark or band on an animal's face. **2** a mark made on the bark of a tree, especially to show a route or path. ▷ *verb* (***blazed, blazing***) to mark (a tree or path, etc) with blazes. • **blaze a trail 1** to be the first to do, study or discover something, etc. **2** *literally* to make marks on trees, etc along one's route or trail, so that others may follow behind. ⓘ 17c: perhaps related to Dutch *bles* and Norse *blesi* a white blaze on a horse's head.

blaze[3] /bleɪz/ ▷ *verb* (***blazed, blazing***) (*especially* **blaze something abroad**) to make (news or information) widely known; to proclaim or publicize it openly or loudly. ⓘ 14c in the obsolete sense 'to blow (eg a horn)', from Dutch *blasen*.

blazer ▷ *noun* a light jacket, often in the colours of a school or club and sometimes worn as part of a uniform. • **blazered** *adj* wearing a blazer. ⓘ 19c; 17c in general sense of 'something or someone that blazes' (BLAZE[1]).

blazes ▷ *plural noun, slang* • **like blazes** with great speed, energy or enthusiasm. • **what the blazes!** an exclamation of surprise or bewilderment. Also used in various questions such as • **who** or **why** or **how the blazes ...?** □ *Why the blazes didn't you tell me?*

blazing ▷ *adj* **1** burning brightly. **2** *colloq* extremely angry; furious □ *a blazing row.*

blazon /'bleɪzən, 'blazən/ ▷ *verb* (***blazoned, blazoning***) **1** (*often* **blazon something abroad** or **forth** or **out**) to make it public. **2** *heraldry* to describe (a coat of arms) in technical terms. **3** (*usually* **blazon something with** or **on something**) *heraldry* to paint (names, designs, etc) on (a coat of arms). ▷ *noun, heraldry* a shield or coat of arms. • **blazonry** *noun* **1** a coat-of arms, or heraldic arms collectively. **2** the art of drawing, designing or deciphering coats of arms. ⓘ 14c: from French *blason* shield.

bleach /bliːtʃ/ ▷ *verb* (***bleaches, bleached, bleaching***) *tr & intr* to whiten or remove colour from (a substance) by exposure to sunlight or certain chemicals. ▷ *noun* **1** a liquid chemical used to bleach clothes, etc. **2** the process of bleaching. • **bleacher** *noun* any liquid chemical eg hydrogen peroxide, used to whiten or remove colour from cloth, paper, hair, etc. • **bleaching** *noun, adj.* ◐ Anglo-Saxon *blæcan*.

bleachers ▷ *plural noun, US* at a sports ground, etc: cheap open-air seats for spectators, usually tiered benches. ◐ 19c.

bleaching powder ▷ *noun* a white powder used in bleaching, a compound of calcium, chlorine and oxygen.

bleak /bliːk/ ▷ *adj* (*bleaker, bleakest*) **1** exposed and desolate. **2** cold and unwelcoming. **3** offering little or no hope. • **bleakly** *adverb*. • **bleakness** *noun*. ◐ 16c: from Anglo-Saxon *blac* pale.

bleary /'blɪərɪ/ ▷ *adj* (*blearier, bleariest*) **1** said of a person's eyes: red and dim, usually from tiredness or through crying. **2** blurred, indistinct and unclear. • **blearily** *adverb*. • **bleariness** *noun*. ◐ 14c.

bleary-eyed ▷ *adj* said of a person: with bleary, watery or tired-looking eyes.

bleat /bliːt/ ▷ *verb* (*bleated, bleating*) **1** *intr* to cry like a sheep, goat or calf. **2** (*usually* **bleat something out**) *tr & intr* to speak or say it foolishly and in a weak high voice. **3** *intr* (*sometimes* **bleat on about something**) *colloq* to complain whiningly about it. • **bleating** *noun, adj.* ◐ Anglo-Saxon *blætan*.

bleed /bliːd/ ▷ *verb* (*bled, bleeding*) **1** *intr* to lose or let out blood. **2** to remove or take blood from someone, etc. **3** *intr* said of plants, etc: to lose juice or sap. **4** to empty liquid or air from (a radiator, hydraulic brakes, etc). **5** *colloq* to obtain money from someone, usually illegally. **6** *intr* said of dye or paint: to come out of the material when wet; to run. **7** (*also* **bleed off**) *tr & intr, printing* said of an illustration or other printed matter: to extend or be extended beyond the trimmed size of a page. • **one's heart bleeds for someone** *usually ironic* one feels great pity for them, or one is very sad on their account. • **bleed like a pig** or **a stuck pig** to bleed copiously. ◐ Anglo-Saxon *bledan*.

bleeder ▷ *noun* **1** *non-technical* a sufferer from HAEMOPHILIA. **2** *Brit slang, dated* a fellow.

bleeding ▷ *adj, adverb, coarse Brit slang* (used as an intensifier) expressing anger or disgust; bloody ▫ *a bleeding fool* ▫ *He's bleeding lying*.

bleeding heart ▷ *noun* **1** *informal, usually derog* a person who is very soft-hearted and charitable; a do-gooder. **2** a name given to various plants, eg a Chinese perennial with pink-and-white heart-shaped pendulous flowers.

bleep /bliːp/ ▷ *noun* **1** a short high-pitched burst of sound, usually made by an electronic machine. **2** a BLEEPER. ▷ *verb* (*bleeped, bleeping*) **1** *intr* said of an electronic machine, etc: to give out a short high-pitched sound. **2** to call someone using a bleeper. **3** (*often* **bleep something out**) in a radio or TV broadcast: to replace (a word or words, usually something rude, offensive, or legally unable to be broadcast) with a bleep or similar sound. ◐ 1950s: probably imitating the sound.

bleeper ▷ *noun* a portable radio receiver that emits a single short bleeping sound when it picks up a signal, used especially to call a doctor or police officer carrying such a device. Also called PAGER. *N Amer equivalent* BEEPER.

blemish /'blɛmɪʃ/ ▷ *noun* (*blemishes*) a stain, mark or fault. ▷ *verb* (*blemishes, blemished, blemishing*) to stain or spoil the beauty of something. ◐ 14c, meaning 'to damage or deface': from French *blesmir* or *blamir* to wound or to make pale.

blench /blɛntʃ/ ▷ *verb* (*blenches, blenched, blenching*) *intr* to start back or move away, especially in fear. ◐ Anglo-Saxon *blencan*.

blend /blɛnd/ ▷ *verb* (*blended, blending*) **1** to mix (different sorts or varieties) into one. **2** *intr* (*often* **blend in**, *also* **blend with something**) to form a mixture or harmonious combination; to go well together. **3** to mix together, especially intimately or harmoniously. **4** *intr* said especially of colours: to shade gradually into another. ▷ *noun* **1** a mixture or combination. **2** *grammar, linguistics* a word formed by combining the sense and sound of two separate words, eg BRUNCH (for *breakfast* and *lunch*). Also called **portmanteau word**. ◐ 14c.

blende /blɛnd/ ▷ *noun* **1** any naturally occurring metal sulphide, eg zinc blende. **2** sphalerite, a mineral consisting mainly of zinc sulphide. ◐ 17c: from German *blenden* to deceive (because of its deceptive resemblance to GALENA.

blender ▷ *noun* **1** a machine for mixing food or especially for making it into a liquid or purée. See also FOOD PROCESSOR. **2** a person or thing that blends.

blenny /'blɛnɪ/ ▷ *noun* (*blennies*) the common name for any of various small fishes which have a long tapering slimy body, no scales, long pelvic fins, and jaws with many small teeth. ◐ 18c: from Greek *blennos* mucus or slime.

blepharitis /blɛfə'raɪtɪs/ ▷ *noun, pathol, medicine* inflammation of the eyelid or eyelids, with redness, irritation and often scaliness of the skin. ◐ 19c: from Greek *blepharon* eyelid.

blepharoplasty /'blɛfəroʊplastɪ/ ▷ *noun, surgery* plastic surgery to remove drooping or wrinkled skin from the eyelids. ◐ 19c: from Greek *blepharon* eyelid.

blepharospasm /'blɛfəroʊspazəm/ ▷ *noun, pathol, medicine* involuntary contraction of the muscles controlling the eyelid over a continued time, causing the eyelid to close. ◐ 19c.

blesbok /'blɛsbɒk/ ▷ *noun* a type of S African antelope with a large white blaze on its forehead, very similar to the BONTEBOK but with a brown rump. ◐ 19c: Afrikaans, from Dutch *bles* blaze + *bok* goat.

bless ▷ *verb* (*past tense* **blessed**, *past participle* **blessed** or **blest**, *present participle* **blessing**) **1** to ask for divine favour or protection for someone or something. **2 a** to make or pronounce someone or something holy; to consecrate; **b** to make the sign of the cross over someone or something or to cross (oneself). **3** to praise; to give honour or glory to (a deity). **4** to thank or be thankful for something ▫ *I bless the day I met him*. • **bless me** or **bless my soul** an expression of surprise, pleasure or dismay, etc. • **bless you!** or *sometimes* **God bless you! 1** said to a person who has just sneezed (originally as a superstitious call for God to protect them from illness). **2** an expression of affection, well-wishing or thanks, etc towards a person. ◐ Anglo-Saxon *bletsian* or *bledsian*, probably from *blod* blood (from the use of sacrificial blood in ancient blessing ceremonies).

■ **be blessed with something** to have the benefit or advantage of (some natural quality or attribute, eg good health).

blessed /'blɛsɪd, blɛst/ ▷ *adj* **1** (*also* **blest**) holy. **2** /'blɛsɪd/ *RC Church* said of a dead person, and used before their name as a title: pronounced holy by the Pope, usually as the first stage towards becoming a saint. **3** *euphemistic, colloq* (pronounced /'blɛsɪd/ when preceding its noun) damned; confounded ▫ *This blessed zip's stuck* ▫ *I'm blessed if I know what's wrong*. **4** very fortunate or happy. • **blessedly** /'blɛsɪdlɪ/ *adverb*. • **blessedness** /'blɛsɪdnəs/ *noun*.

blessed sacrament or **Blessed Sacrament** /'blɛsɪd —/ ▷ *noun, Christianity* the consecrated bread and wine (the **elements**), or specifically the bread or wafer (the **Host**), of the Eucharist or Communion service.

blessing ▷ *noun* **1** a wish or prayer for happiness or success. **2** *relig* **a** an act which invites the goodness of God to rest upon someone, often expressed by the placing of hands upon their head; **b** a short prayer said before or after a meal or church service, etc. **3** a cause of happiness, or sometimes of relief or comfort; a benefit or advantage. **4** approval or good wishes □ *They married without his blessing.* • **a blessing in disguise** something that has proved to be fortunate after seeming unfortunate. ◷ 18c: a phrase first used by James Hervey (1714–58) in his poem *Reflections on a Flower-Garden.* • **count one's blessings** to be grateful for what one has, rather than unhappy about what one does not have.

blether /ˈblɛðər/ or **blather** /ˈblaðə(r)/ ▻ *verb* (***blethered, blethering***) *intr* (*chiefly Scottish*) **1** to talk foolishly and long-windedly. **2** to chat or gossip idly. ▻ *noun* **1** long-winded nonsense. **2** a chat or gossip. • **blethering** *noun, adj.* ◷ 16c: from Norse *blathra.*

blew see under BLOW[1]

blight /blaɪt/ ▻ *noun* **1** a fungal disease of plants that usually attacks an entire crop, or (*in compounds*) one specific crop throughout a particular region □ *potato blight.* **2** a fungus that causes blight. **3** something or someone that has a damaging, distressing, or destructive effect on something, or that spoils it (*especially* **cast a blight on something**). **4** *often in compounds* **a** an ugly, decayed or neglected state or condition □ *urban blight*; **b** a district (usually an urban district) in such a condition. ▻ *verb* (***blighted, blighting***) **1** to affect with blight. **2** to harm or destroy. **3** to disappoint or frustrate □ *All our hopes were blighted.* • **blighted** *adj.* ◷ 17c.

blighter ▻ *noun, colloq, old use* **1** (often used as a term of mild abuse) a scoundrel or contemptible person, usually a man. **2** a fellow, especially a man one feels some sympathy for or envy of □ *poor old blighter* □ *lucky blighter.* ◷ 19c: originally and literally 'something that BLIGHTS'.

blimey /ˈblaɪmɪ/ ▻ *exclamation, Brit slang* expressing surprise or amazement. ◷ 19c: from *gorblimey*, a corruption of the phrase *God blind me.*

Blimp or **blimp** ▻ *noun* a very conservative old-fashioned reactionary person. • **blimpish** *adj.* ◷ 1930s: from the fat pompous cartoon character Colonel Blimp, used in anti-German and anti-government cartoons during World War II.

blimp ▻ *noun* **1** a type of large balloon or airship, used for publicity, observation or defence. **2** a soundproof cover for a film camera. ◷ Early 20c: originally (in World War I) an observation balloon.

blind /blaɪnd/ ▻ *adj* (***blinder, blindest***) **1** not able to see. **2** (**the blind**) blind people as a group; people suffering from BLINDNESS (see THE 4). **3** (*always* **blind to something**) unable or unwilling to understand or appreciate something unwelcome or undesirable □ *blind to his faults.* **4** unthinking; without reason or purpose □ *blind hatred.* **5** hidden from sight □ *blind entrance.* **6** not allowing sight of what is beyond □ *blind summit.* **7** said of flying, landing, navigating or bombing, etc: relying completely on instruments inside the craft, eg when conditions such as darkness or poor visibility do not allow direct visual contact. **8 a** having no openings or windows, etc □ *blind wall*; **b** blocked or walled up □ *blind arch.* **9** closed at one end □ *blind alley.* **10** said of a pastry case: cooked without a filling. **11** without preparation or previous knowledge □ *blind testing.* **12** said of a plant: failing to produce flowers. ▻ *adverb* **1** blindly; without being able to see. **2** without having seen, tested or gained proper knowledge of the item concerned □ *I can't believe that you bought the car blind.* ▻ *noun* **1** a screen to stop light coming through a window, eg one which rolls up (a ROLLER BLIND) or folds up (a VENETIAN BLIND) when not in use. *N American equivalent* WINDOW SHADE. **2** a person, action or thing which hides the truth or deceives. **3** anything which prevents sight or blocks out light. ▻ *verb* (***blinded, blinding***) **1** to make someone blind. **2** to make someone unreasonable or foolish, etc. • **blindly**, **blindness** see separate entries. • **blind as a bat** completely blind. • **blind drunk** *colloq* completely and helplessly drunk. • **not a blind bit of ...** *colloq* not the slightest bit of ...; not any ... □ *took not a blind bit of notice.* • **swear blind** *colloq* to state with certainty or declare emphatically □ *swore blind that he had already paid.* • **the blind leading the blind** someone inexperienced or incompetent helping another person to do something or telling them about it. • **turn a blind eye to something** to pretend not to notice it. ◷ 11c.

■ **blind someone to something** to make them unable to see it, or incapable of appreciating it □ *Jealousy blinded him to all reason.*

■ **blind someone with something** to confuse or dazzle them with it □ *tried to blind me with science.*

blind alley ▻ *noun* **1** a narrow road with an opening at one end only. **2** a situation, course of action or job, etc which is leading or will lead nowhere.

blind date ▻ *noun* **1** a date with a person of the opposite sex whom one has not met before, often arranged by a third person. **2** the person met on such a date.

blinder ▻ *noun* **1** *colloq* a heavy drinking session, especially over many hours or several days. **2** *colloq* a spectacular performance in a sporting activity or event □ *Trevor played a blinder today.* **3** (**blinders**) *N Amer* a horse's blinkers. **4** a person or thing that blinds.

blindfold ▻ *noun* a piece of cloth (often a handkerchief or scarf) used to cover the eyes to prevent a person from seeing. ▻ *adj, adverb* with one's eyes covered with a piece of cloth to prevent one seeing. ▻ *verb* to cover the eyes of someone to prevent them from seeing. ◷ 16c: from earlier *blindfellen* to strike someone blind, and its past participle *blindfelled* which became associated and combined with the word FOLD[1] (from the idea of folding a piece of cloth with which to cover the eyes).

blind gut ▻ *noun, anatomy* the CAECUM.

blinding ▻ *noun* **1** the act of making someone blind, especially violently. **2** the process of filling the cracks of a newly made road with grit. ▻ *adj* **1** said of a light, etc: intensely strong and bright, causing temporary lack of vision. **2** *colloq* said of a headache: severe or incapacitating. **3** clear and intense. • **blindingly** *adverb.*

blindly ▻ *adverb* **1** in a blind manner. **2** without seeing or thinking ahead □ *ran blindly on.*

blindman's-buff ▻ *noun* a children's game in which one child wears a blindfold and tries to catch the other children. ◷ 16c: traditionally the blindfolded child would give three slaps or *buffs* (short for *buffets*) to anyone they caught.

blindness ▻ *noun* **1** serious or total loss of vision in one or both eyes, caused by disease, injury or the normal ageing process. **2** lack of perception; thoughtlessness; recklessness.

blind side ▻ *noun* **1** the side on which a person cannot see and is blind to approaching danger, etc. **2** a person's weak point or BLIND SPOT 3. **3** *rugby* the part of the field between the scrum, etc and the touch-line nearer it. ▻ *verb* (**blind-side**) *especially N Amer* to take advantage of a person's blind side; to catch someone unawares, by, or as if by, approaching them from their blind side.

blind spot ▻ *noun* **1** on the retina of the eye: a small area from which no visual images can be transmitted, and where nerve fibres from the light-sensitive rods and cones lead into the optic nerve. **2** an area of poor reception within the normal range of radio transmission, caused by tall buildings or other obstructions. **3** a place where sight or vision is obscured because something is in the way or there is no means of viewing it from the position occupied. **4** any subject which a person either cannot understand, or refuses even to try to understand.

blind trust ▻ *noun* **1** uncritical and unquestioning confidence. **2** *especially N Amer, finance* a TRUST (*noun* 6) which manages the private capital and financial affairs of an influential public figure (especially a politician) without giving them any knowledge of specific investments, etc, so as to prevent any possible conflict of interest.

blindworm see SLOWWORM

blink ▻ *verb* (***blinked***, ***blinking***) **1** *intr* to shut and open the eyes again quickly, especially involuntarily. **2** to shut and open (an eyelid or an eye) very quickly. **3** (*usually* **blink something away** or **from** or **out of something**) to remove (tears, dust, a speck or smut, etc) from (the eye or eyes) by blinking □ ***Hastily she blinked away her tears.*** **4** *intr* said of a light: to flash on and off; to shine unsteadily. ▻ *noun* **1** an act of blinking. **2** a gleam or quick glimmer of light, such as a brief moment of sunshine. • **in the blink of an eye** quickly; suddenly. • **on the blink** *colloq* broken or not working properly. ⓘ 14c: a variant of BLENCH.

▪ **blink at something** **1** to refuse to recognize or accept (something unwelcome). **2** to show surprise or shock at the sight of it.

blinker ▻ *noun* **1** (*usually* **blinkers**) one of two small flat pieces of leather attached to a horse's bridle to prevent it from seeing sideways. *N Amer equivalent* BLINDERS. **2** *especially US* a light that blinks or flashes, usually as a signal, eg an indicator on a car used to show that the driver intends to turn, overtake or pull over. Also called WINKER. ▻ *verb* (***blinkered***, ***blinkering***) **1** to put blinkers on (a horse). **2** to limit or obscure the vision or awareness of (a person, etc).

blinkered ▻ *adj* **1** said of a horse: wearing blinkers. **2** *derog* said of a person: narrow in outlook; unwilling to consider the opinions of others.

blinking ▻ *adj, adverb, slang* used to express mild annoyance, frustration or disapproval, or as a general intensifier □ ***broke the blinking thing.*** ⓘ Early 20c in these senses: euphemism for BLOODY.

blip ▻ *noun* **1** a sudden sharp sound produced by a machine such as a monitor or radar screen. **2** a spot of bright light on a radar screen, showing the position of an object, or a sudden sharp peak in a line on a screen or monitor, showing a pulse or position, etc. **3 a** a short interruption, pause or irregularity in the expected pattern or course of something; **b** an unforeseen phenomenon, especially an economic one, that is claimed or expected to be temporary. ▻ *verb* (***blipped***, ***blipping***) **1** *intr* to make a blip. **2** *colloq* to hit or tap sharply □ ***blipped him on the head with his stick.*** ⓘ 1950s: imitating the sound.

bliss ▻ *noun* **1** very great happiness. **2** the special happiness of heaven. ⓘ Anglo-Saxon, from BLITHE.

blissful ▻ *adj* completely happy; utterly joyful. • **blissfully** *adverb*. • **blissfulness** *noun*. ⓘ 13c.

blister /ˈblɪstə(r)/ ▻ *noun* **1** a small swelling on or just beneath the surface of the skin, containing watery fluid and occasionally blood or pus, usually caused by friction or a burn. **2** a bubble in a thin surface coating of paint or varnish, etc or on the surface of previously molten metal or plastic that has solidified. ▻ *verb* (***blistered***, ***blistering***) **1** to make a blister or blisters occur on something □ ***The heat has blistered the windowsill.*** **2** *intr* said of hands or feet, etc: to come up in blisters. **3** to criticize or attack someone with sharp scathing language. • **blistered** *adj*. • **blistery** *adj*. ⓘ 14c: most probably from French *blestre*.

blistering ▻ *adj* **1** said of weather or conditions, etc: very hot; burning. **2** said of criticism, etc: viciously angry and aggressive. **3** said of pace or action, etc: intense; very hard or fast. • **blisteringly** *adverb*.

blister pack and **blister card** see under BUBBLE PACK

blithe /blaɪð/ ▻ *adj* (***blither***, ***blithest***) **1** happy; without worries or cares. **2** *derog* done without serious thought; casual. • **blithely** *adverb*. • **blitheness** *noun*. ⓘ Anglo-Saxon.

blithering /ˈblɪðərɪŋ/ ▻ *adj, derog colloq* stupid; jabbering; half-witted. ⓘ 19c: from *blither*, a form of BLETHER.

blithesome ▻ *adj, literary or old use* happy; cheerful and without any worries; blithe. ⓘ 18c.

BLitt ▻ *abbreviation*: *Baccalaureus Litterarum*, (Latin) Bachelor of Letters.

blitz /blɪts/ ▻ *noun* (***blitzes***) **1** a sudden strong attack, or period of such attacks, especially from the air. **2** (**the Blitz**) the German air raids on Britain in 1940. **3** (*especially* **have a blitz on something**) *colloq* a period of hard work, etc to get something (especially a cleaning or tidying job) finished or done quickly and thoroughly. **4** *Amer football* a charge against a quarterback by the defensive line-backers. ▻ *verb* (***blitzed***, ***blitzing***) **1** to attack, damage or destroy something as if by an air raid. **2** *colloq* to work hard at something for a short period; to have a blitz on it. • **blitzed** *adj, slang* thoroughly drunk or very high on drugs. ⓘ 1930s: from BLITZKRIEG.

blitzkrieg /ˈblɪtskriːg/ ▻ *noun* a blitz; a sudden and intensive attack to win a quick victory in war. ⓘ 1930s: German, literally 'lightning war'.

blizzard /ˈblɪzəd/ ▻ *noun* a severe snowstorm characterized by low temperatures and strong winds that blow large drifts of dry powdery snow upward from the ground, resulting in much reduced visibility. ⓘ 19c: probably imitating the sound of one.

bloat /bloʊt/ ▻ *verb* (***bloated***, ***bloating***) **1** (*sometimes* **bloat up**) *tr & intr* to swell or make something swell or puff out with air, pride, food, etc, especially unpleasantly or uncomfortably. **2** to prepare (fish, especially herring) by salting and half-drying in smoke. • **bloated** *adj*. • **bloatedness** *noun*. ⓘ 17c: perhaps from 13c *adj bloat* soft.

bloater ▻ *noun* a herring that has been salted in brine and partially smoked. ⓘ 19c.

blob ▻ *noun* **1** a small soft round mass of something. **2** a small drop of liquid. ⓘ 15c: an imitation of the sound of dripping.

bloc ▻ *noun* a group of countries or people, etc that have a common interest, purpose or policy. ⓘ Early 20c: French, meaning 'block' or 'group'.

block ▻ *noun* **1** a mass of solid wood, stone, ice or other hard material, usually with flat sides. **2 a** a piece of wood or stone, etc used for chopping and cutting on; **b** (**the block**) *historical* a piece of wood used for beheading, across which the condemned person laid their neck. **3** a wooden or plastic cube, used as a child's toy. **4** *slang* a person's head □ ***knock his block off.*** **5** a large building containing offices, flats, etc. *N Amer equivalent* APARTMENT HOUSE or APARTMENT BUILDING. **6 a** a group of buildings with roads on all four sides □ ***Let's take a walk around the block***; **b** the distance from one end of such a group of buildings to the other □ ***lives about a block away.*** **7** *Austral, NZ* an extensive area of land for settlement or farming, etc. **8** a compact mass, group or set. **9** a group of seats, tickets, votes, data, shares, etc thought of as a single unit. **10** something which causes or acts as a stopping of movement or progress, etc; an obstruction. Also *in compounds* □ ***road block.*** **11** *often in compounds* a psychological barrier preventing progress in thought or development, etc □ ***writer's block*** □ ***a mental block.*** **12** *sport, especially Amer football* obstruction of an opposing player. **13** *athletics, often in plural* a starting-block □ ***fast off the block.*** **14** (*also* **nerve block**) *medicine* the obstruction of nerve impulses to a particular area of the body by means of an injection of local anaesthetic. **15** a piece of wood or metal which has been cut to be used in printing. **16** *engineering* a pulley or set of pulleys mounted in a case, often with rope or chain passing over it, used as part of a lifting tackle. See also BLOCK AND TACKLE. ▻ *verb* (***blocked***, *blocking*) **1** to obstruct or impede; to put an obstacle in the way of someone or something. **2** to print (a design, title, etc) on (the cover of a book, piece of material, etc). **3** *cricket* to stop (a ball) with one's bat held upright and touching on the ground. **4** *tr & intr, sport* to obstruct the play or action of (an opposing player). **5** *medicine* to interrupt or obstruct (a normal physiological function), such as a nerve impulse, eg with an anaesthetic. **6** *theat* to practise the moves in (a scene, etc). • **blocked** *adj*. See also BLOCKED STYLE. • **blocker** see separate entry. • **do one's block** *slang, chiefly Austral & NZ* to become very angry or excited; to lose one's temper. ◷ 14c: from French *bloc*.

■ **block someone** or **something in 1** to prevent them or it from moving or from getting out; to confine them. **2** to draw or sketch them or it roughly, often simply to show their position in a layout.

■ **block something off** to restrict or limit the use of (an area or place, etc) □ *The police have blocked off several streets.*

■ **block something out 1** to shut out (eg light, or an idea, etc). **2** to draw or sketch it roughly. **3** *theat* to practise the moves in (a scene, etc).

■ **block something up 1** to block it completely. **2** to fill (a window or doorway, etc) with bricks, etc.

blockade /blɒ'keɪd/ ▷ *noun* the closing off of a port or region, etc by surrounding it with troops, ships and/or air-power, in order to prevent people or goods, etc from passing in and out, or to obtain a particular political aim or force a surrender. ▷ *verb* (***blockaded, blockading***) to impose a blockade on (a port or country, etc). ◷ 17c: BLOCK + *-ade* as in other military vocabulary of French origin, eg *enfilade*.

blockage /'blɒkɪdʒ/ ▷ *noun* **1 a** anything that causes a pipe or roadway, etc to be blocked. **2** the state of being blocked or the act of blocking.

block and tackle ▷ *noun, mech, engineering* **a** a device used for lifting heavy objects, consisting of a case or housing (the BLOCK) containing a pulley or system of pulleys and a rope or chain passed over it (the TACKLE); **b** a series of such ropes and blocks.

blockboard ▷ *noun, building* plywood board made from thin strips of soft wood bonded together and enclosed by two outer layers of veneer.

blockbuster ▷ *noun, colloq* **1** a highly popular and successful film, book or TV drama, etc. **2** an extremely powerful bomb that could destroy a whole block of buildings. ◷ 1940s in sense 2.

block capital and **block letter** ▷ *noun* a plain capital letter written in imitation of printed type.

blocked style ▷ *noun, typing, etc* the display style in which all text begins at the left margin, without centring, indenting or underscoring.

blocker ▷ *noun* **1** a person or thing that blocks in any sense. **2** *medicine, often in compounds* a substance, used as a drug, that prevents the production or operation of some other substance in the body. **3** *sport* a player who BLOCKS (*verb* 4).

blockhead ▷ *noun, derog colloq* a stupid person. ◷ 16c.

blockhouse ▷ *noun* **1** a small shelter made from reinforced concrete, used as a protected observation post for watching rocket launches, military operations, explosions, etc. **2** *historical* a small temporary fort. ◷ 16c.

block release ▷ *noun, Brit* release from employment for a period of weeks, or longer, in order to attend a course of study at college, etc.

block vote ▷ *noun* a vote by a single delegate, eg at a trade-union conference, that is counted as the number of people that delegate represents.

bloke /blouk/ *Brit colloq* ▷ *noun* a man or chap. • **blokedom** *noun*. • **blokeish** *adj* typical of, suited to or like, one of the blokes, ie an ordinary chap; matey or hearty in manner. • **blokey** *adj*. ◷ 19c: suggested derivations include Dutch *blok* a fool, and Shelta *loke* a man.

blond and (the feminine form) **blonde** /blɒnd/ ▷ *adj* **1** said of a person or people: having light-coloured hair, between pale yellowish-gold and very light chestnut, and usually fair or pale skin and blue or grey eyes. **2** said of a person's hair: light-coloured, between pale yellowish-gold and very light chestnut. ▷ *noun* a person with this colour of hair. Compare BRUNETTE. ◷ 15c: from Latin *blondus* yellow.

blond

Note the distinction between **blond** and **blonde**.

blood /blʌd/ ▷ *noun* **1** a fluid tissue that circulates in the arteries veins, and capillaries of the body as a result of muscular contractions of the heart. **2** relationship through belonging to the same family or race, etc; descent □ *of royal blood.* **3** near family □ *He's my own flesh and blood.* **4** bloodshed or murder; violence □ *When the ceasefire ends we shall see more blood.* **5** temper; passion □ *Watch out, his blood is up!* See also HUMOUR noun 6. **6** human nature, especially a person's innate or sensual nature. **7 a** life or vitality; lifeblood; **b** (*especially* **new blood** and **young blood**) a group of people seen as adding new strength, youth, young ideas, etc to an existing group. **8** *Brit, old use* a man, especially a rowdy or spirited young aristocrat, who is interested in fashion, etc and thinks a lot about his appearance. ▷ *verb* (***blooded, blooding***). **1** *hunting* to give (a young hound) its first taste of a freshly killed animal. **2** to give someone the first experience of (war or battle, etc). • **after** or **out for someone's blood** to be extremely angry with them and to want revenge, or to fight or hurt them. • **blood is thicker than water** one's obligations and loyalty towards one's own family are more important than those towards other people. • **in cold blood** deliberately or cruelly; showing no concern or passion. • **in one's** or **someone's blood** in one's or their character. • **make one's blood boil** to make one extremely angry. • **make someone's blood run cold** to frighten or horrify them. • **sweat blood** or *often* **sweat blood over something** to work very hard; to put strenuous effort into it. ◷ Anglo-Saxon *blod*.

blood-and-thunder ▷ *adj* said of a film or story, etc: including much violent action and excitement.

blood bank ▷ *noun* in a hospital or blood transfusion centre: a department where blood collected from donors is stored, categorized according to blood group, and tested for the presence of certain diseases prior to transfusion into patients. ◷ 1930s.

bloodbath ▷ *noun* a massacre; a savage murder of a number of people, involving much bloodshed.

blood brother ▷ *noun* **1** a man or boy who has promised to treat another as his brother, usually in a ceremony in which some of their blood has been mixed. **2** a true brother, by birth.

blood cell ▷ *noun* any of the cells that are present in the blood, ie an ERYTHROCYTE or a LEUCOCYTE. *Technical equivalent* HAEMOCYTE.

blood count ▷ *noun, medicine* a numerical calculation to determine the number of red or white blood cells in a known volume of blood.

bloodcurdling ▷ *adj* causing a strong chilling fear or horror, as if one's blood were congealing. • **bloodcurdlingly** *adverb*.

blood donation ▷ *noun* the procedure in which blood is collected from a BLOOD DONOR, to be stored until it is required for transfusion into a patient.

blood donor ▷ *noun* a person who donates blood under medical supervision for storage in a blood bank until it is required for transfusion into a patient with a compatible blood group.

blood doping and **blood packing** ▻ *noun* the illegal practice of temporarily increasing the oxygen-carrying capacity of an athlete's blood, by reinjecting them with their own red blood cells previously drawn off.

blooded /ˈblʌdɪd/ ▻ *adj* **1** *usually in compounds* (with hyphen) said of a person or animal: having blood or temperament of a specified kind □ ***hot-blooded*** □ ***red-blooded.*** **2** said of an animal, especially a horse: having pure blood or breeding; pedigreed.

blood group and **blood type** ▻ *noun, medicine* any one of the various types into which human blood is classified, eg A, B, AB or O (in the ABO BLOOD GROUP SYSTEM), rhesus positive or rhesus negative (see RHESUS FACTOR).

blood heat ▻ *noun* the normal temperature of human blood (37°C or 98.4°F).

bloodhound ▻ *noun* **1** a large breed of dog, known for its keen sense of smell, which has a powerful body with loose-fitting skin, a short tan or black and tan coat, long pendulous ears and a long deep muzzle. **2** *colloq* a detective, or anyone who follows a trail intently. ⓒ 14c.

bloodily and **bloodiness** see under BLOODY

bloodless ▻ *adj* **1** without violence or anybody being killed. **2** pale and lifeless; weak and sickly. **3** dull and tedious; without emotion or spirit. • **bloodlessly** *adverb.* • **bloodlessness** *noun.*

bloodletting ▻ *noun* **1** killing; bloodshed. **2** the removal of blood by opening a vein, formerly used to treat numerous diseases and disorders. (see also PHLEBOTOMY).

bloodline ▻ *noun* all the individuals in a family of animals, etc over a number of generations, especially when seen in terms of some inherited characteristic, pedigree, etc; strain, line or stock.

bloodlust ▻ *noun* an appetite or desire for bloodshed.

blood money ▻ *noun* money gained at the cost of someone's life: **a** money paid for committing murder; **b** money earned by supplying information that will cause someone to be convicted on a charge punishable by death, especially if the charge is false; **c** money paid in compensation to the relatives of a murdered person. ⓒ 16c.

blood orange ▻ *noun* a type of orange with flesh which is red or flecked with red.

blood packing see BLOOD DOPING

blood poisoning ▻ *noun* a serious condition caused by the presence of either bacterial toxins or large numbers of bacteria in the bloodstream. *Technical equivalent* SEPTICAEMIA and *especially* TOXAEMIA.

blood pressure ▻ *noun* the pressure of the blood within the blood vessels, especially the pressure within the arteries.

blood pudding see BLACK PUDDING

blood-red ▻ *adj* having the strong red colour of blood.

blood relation and **blood relative** ▻ *noun* a person related to one by birth, rather than by marriage.

bloodshed ▻ *noun* the shedding of blood or killing of people; slaughter.

bloodshot ▻ *adj* said of the eyes: having small streaks of red across the white of the eye due to inflamed blood vessels in the conjunctiva; red and irritated or swollen. ⓒ 15c.

blood sports ▻ *plural noun* sports that involve the killing of animals, eg fox-hunting.

bloodstain ▻ *noun* a stain caused by blood. • **bloodstained** *adj* **1** stained with blood. **2** marked or characterized by, or involving, bloodshed or murder □ ***a bloodstained history.***

bloodstock ▻ *noun, collective* horses that have been bred especially for racing; pedigree horses.

bloodstone ▻ *noun, geol* a type of CHALCEDONY, a fine-grained dark green variety of the mineral quartz, with red flecks.

bloodstream ▻ *noun* the flow of blood through the arteries, veins and capillaries of an animal's body.

bloodsucker ▻ *noun* **1** an animal that sucks blood, eg the leech. **2** *colloq* a person who extorts money from another, or who persistently sponges off them. • **bloodsucking** *adj.*

blood sugar ▻ *noun* the concentration of glucose in the bloodstream, which is kept within narrow limits by the action of certain hormones, especially INSULIN.

blood test ▻ *noun* a test in which a small amount of blood is analysed in order to determine its blood group, to detect the presence of alcohol or drugs, etc, to determine whether a particular disease is present, or to resolve paternity disputes.

bloodthirsty ▻ *adj* **1** eager for or fond of killing or violence. **2** said of a film, etc: including much violence and killing. • **bloodthirstily** *adverb.* • **bloodthirstiness** *noun.* ⓒ 16c.

blood transfusion ▻ *noun, medicine* the introduction of a volume of blood directly into a person's bloodstream in order to replace blood that has been lost as a result of injury, severe burns, surgery, etc, or blood that is of defective quality as a result of disease. See also TRANSFUSION.

blood type see BLOOD GROUP

blood typing ▻ *noun* **1** the identification of the BLOOD GROUP to which a blood-sample belongs. **2** the classification of blood according to blood groups.

blood vessel ▻ *noun* in the body of an animal: any tubular structure through which blood flows, ie an artery, vein or capillary.

bloody /ˈblʌdɪ/ ▻ *adj* (***bloodier***, ***bloodiest***) **1** stained or covered with blood □ ***a bloody nose.*** **2** involving or including much killing □ ***met in bloody combat.*** **3** *rather coarse slang* used as an intensifier expressing annoyance, etc but sometimes almost meaningless □ ***a bloody fool*** □ ***missed the bloody bus again.*** Also *as infix* □ ***im-bloody-possible.*** **4** murderous or cruel. ▻ *adverb, rather coarse slang* used as an intensifier; **a** expressing annoyance, etc but sometimes almost meaningless □ ***I wish you'd bloody listen***; **b** extremely □ ***We're bloody angry about it.*** ▻ *verb* (***bloodies***, ***bloodied***, ***bloodying***) to stain or cover something with blood. • **bloodily** *adverb.* • **bloodiness** *noun.* ⓒ Anglo-Saxon as *blodig.*

bloody Mary ▻ *noun* a drink made with vodka, tomato juice and seasoning.

bloody-minded ▻ *adj, derog* said of a person: deliberately unco-operative and inclined to cause difficulties for others. • **bloody-mindedness** *noun.*

bloom[1] /bluːm/ *noun* **1 a** a flower, especially one on a plant valued for its flowers; **b** such flowers or blossoms collectively. **2** the state of being in flower □ ***tulips in bloom.*** **3** a state of perfection or great beauty □ ***in the full bloom of youth.*** **4** a glow or flush on the skin. **5** a powdery or waxy coating on the surface of certain fruits (eg grapes) or leaves. **6** *biol* a rapid seasonal increase in the rate of growth of certain algae in lakes and ponds, etc, often as a result of pollution of the water by nitrate fertilizers applied to the surrounding land. ▻ *verb* (***bloomed***, ***blooming***) *intr* **1** said of a plant: to be in or come into flower. **2** to be in or achieve a state of great beauty or perfection. **3** said of a person, eg a child or an expectant mother: to be healthy; to be growing well; to flourish. • **bloomer** *noun.* ⓒ 13c: from Norse *blom.*

bloom² /bluːm/ *noun, engineering* a semi-finished mass or bar of iron or steel, larger and thicker than a BILLET. ⓒ Anglo-Saxon *bloma* a lump of metal.

bloomer¹ *noun, Brit colloq* an idiotic and embarrassing mistake. *US equivalent* BLOOPER. ⓒ 19c: a slang contraction of *blooming error* (see BLOOMING *adj 3*).

bloomer² *noun, Brit* a longish crusty loaf of white bread, with rounded ends and several diagonal slashes across the top. ⓒ 1930s.

bloomer³ see under BLOOM¹

bloomers ▷ *plural noun* **1** *colloq, facetious or old use* women's underpants or knickers, especially large or baggy ones. **2** (*also* **bloomer trousers**) *historical* loose trousers for women, gathered at the knee or ankle, to be worn (eg for cycling) with a close-fitting jacket and a skirt falling to just below the knee. ⓒ 19c in sense 2: named after Amelia Bloomer (1818–94), an American social reformer who thought women should adopt this style of dress.

blooming ▷ *adj* **1** said of a plant: flowering. **2** said of someone or something: healthy and flourishing. **3** *slang* used as an intensifier **a** expressing annoyance, etc; a euphemism for BLOODY *adj* 3 □ ***I've lost my blooming pen now***; **b** complete and utter □ ***a blooming idiot***. Also *as infix* □ ***fan-blooming-tastic***. **4** *literary* bright; beautiful. ▷ *adverb, slang* used as an intensifier **a** expressing annoyance, etc; a euphemism for BLOODY *adv*; **b** very or completely □ ***He went blooming crazy***.

bloop ▷ *noun* a howling sound on a soundtrack or made by a radio. ▷ *verb* (***blooped***, ***blooping***) *intr* said of a radio, etc: to make such a sound. ⓒ 1920s as *verb*: imitating the sound.

blooper ▷ *noun* **1** *slang, chiefly US* a stupid and embarrassing mistake; a bloomer. **2** a radio, etc that bloops.

blossom /ˈblɒsəm/ ▷ *noun* **1** a flower or mass of flowers, especially on a fruit tree. **2** the state of being in flower □ ***The trees are in blossom***. ▷ *verb* (***blossomed***, ***blossoming***) *intr* **1** said of a plant, especially a fruit tree or bush: to produce blossom or flowers. **2** (*sometimes* **blossom out**) to grow well or develop successfully; to thrive □ ***She has blossomed into a fine dancer***. • **blossoming** *adj*. • **blossomy** *adj*. ⓒ Anglo-Saxon *blostm*.

blot /blɒt/ ▷ *noun* **1** a spot or stain, especially of ink. **2** a spot or blemish which spoils the beauty of something. **3** a stain on a person's good reputation or character. **4** *Austral slang* the buttocks or anus. ▷ *verb* (***blotted***, ***blotting***) **1** to make a spot or stain on something, especially with ink. **2 a** to dry something with blotting-paper; **b** (*sometimes* **blot something up**) to soak up (excess liquid) by pressing eg a cloth, towel or tissue against it. • **blot one's copybook** to spoil one's good reputation, etc, especially by some foolish or unfortunate mistake. ⓒ 14c.

■ **blot something out 1** to hide it from sight □ ***A cloud blotted out the sun***. **2** to refuse to think about or remember (a painful memory). **3** to destroy or obliterate it.

blotch /blɒtʃ/ ▷ *noun* (***blotches***) a large irregular-shaped coloured patch or mark on the skin, etc. ▷ *verb* (***blotched***, ***blotching***) to cover or mark with blotches. • **blotchiness** *noun*. • **blotchy** *adj* (***blotchier***, ***blotchiest***) covered in blotches; discoloured in patches. ⓒ 17c: perhaps from BLOT.

blotter ▷ *noun* **1** a large sheet or pad of blotting paper with a hard backing. **2** *US* a record-book or log, especially a police charge-sheet.

blotting paper ▷ *noun* soft thick unsized paper for pressing against a document newly-written in ink, to dry it and to absorb any excess ink.

blotto /ˈblɒtoʊ/ ▷ *adj, rather dated Brit slang* helplessly drunk. ⓒ Early 20c, alluding to blotting up quantities of alcohol, and/or blotting out most of one's senses with it.

blouse /blaʊz/ ▷ *noun* **1** a woman's garment very similar to a shirt. **2** (*also* **battle-blouse** and **battle-dress blouse**) *especially formerly* a loose jacket belted or gathered in at the waist, forming part of a soldier's or airman's uniform. ▷ *verb* (***bloused***, ***blousing***) **1** to arrange (a garment or drapery, etc) in loose folds. **2** *intr* said of a garment, etc: to hang or puff out in loose folds. ⓒ 19c: French.

blouson /ˈbluːzɒn/ ▷ *noun* a loose jacket or top gathered in tightly at the waist. ⓒ Early 20c: French.

blow¹ /bloʊ/ ▷ *verb* (*past tense* ***blew***, *past participle* ***blown*** or (only in sense 12) ***blowed***, *present participle* ***blowing***) **1** *intr* said of a current of air or wind, etc: to be moving, especially rapidly. **2** (*often* **blow along** or **down**, *etc*) *tr & intr* to move or be moved by a current of air or wind, etc. **3** to send (a current of air) from the mouth. **4** to form or shape (eg bubbles, glass) by blowing air from the mouth. **5** (*often* **blow something off** or **out** or **in** or **up**, *etc*) to shatter or destroy something by an explosion. **6** to produce a sound from (an instrument, etc) by blowing into it. **7** to clear something by blowing through it □ ***blow one's nose***. **8** *colloq* **a** to make (an electric fuse) melt and so interrupt the circuit; **b** (*also* **blow out**) *intr* said of an electric fuse: to melt, causing an interruption in the flow of current. **9** to break into (a safe, etc) using explosives. **10** slang to spoil or bungle (an opportunity, etc) □ ***He had his chance, and he blew it***. **11** *slang* to spend a large amount of money, especially quickly or recklessly. **12** *slang* often used in mild curses, expressions of annoyance, astonishment, etc: to damn, curse or blast □ ***Blow the expense, let's get a taxi*** □ ***Well I'll be blowed, it's my old friend Pat!*** **13** (*often* **blow the gaff** or **blow one's** or **someone's cover**) *slang* to disclose or give away (something secret or confidential). **14** *tr & intr, chiefly US slang* to leave (a place) quickly and suddenly. **15** *intr* to breathe heavily □ ***puffing and blowing after the jog***. **16** said of a whale: to exhale a spout of air and water through a hole in the top of its head □ ***There she blows!*** **17** said of an insect, especially a fly: to deposit eggs on or in something. ▷ *noun* **1** an act or example of blowing. **2** a spell of exposure to fresh air □ ***Let's go for a blow on the cliffs***. ▷ *exclamation* (*also* **blow it**!) expressing annoyance; damn! • **blow hot and cold on something** or **someone** *colloq* to keep changing one's mind about (an idea, plan, person, etc), sometimes favouring or showing enthusiasm towards it or them, and sometimes opposing or showing no enthusiasm. ⓒ 16c: from Aesop's fable of the centaur who believed that, because a man could both warm his hands and cool his food by blowing on them, he must be able to blow hot and cold air from the same mouth. • **blow one's** or **someone's cover** *slang* to reveal one's or someone's true identity. • **blow one's** or **someone's mind** *slang* to become or make someone become intoxicated or ecstatic under the influence of a drug or of some exhilarating experience. • **blow one's own trumpet** *colloq* to praise oneself and one's own abilities and achievements. • **blow something sky-high** to destroy it completely. • **blow one's stack** or **top** *colloq* to explode in anger; to lose one's temper. • **blow the gaff** *Brit slang* to give away a secret; to inform or blab. • **blow the whistle on someone** *colloq* to inform on them, usually as they are engaged in something illegal or fraudulent. • **blow the whistle on something** *colloq* to bring (something deceitful or illegal, etc) to an abrupt end by exposing it. • **I'll be blowed** or **blow me!** or **blow me down!** *Brit slang* expressions of surprise, etc (see *verb* 12 above). ⓒ Anglo-Saxon *blawan*.

■ **blow someone away** *N Amer slang* **1** to murder them with a gun. 2 to surprise and excite them □ ***The percussion in the second movement just blew me away***.

■ **blow something away** or **off 1** to remove it by blowing. **2** to disprove (eg a hypothesis, theory, etc).

■ **blow in** *colloq* to turn up casually or unexpectedly. See also BLOW-IN.

■ **blow out a** said of a tyre: to burst; to puncture suddenly and forcibly when in use; **b** said of an electric fuse: to melt or blow (see *verb* 8b above); **c** (*usually* **blow itself out**) said of a storm, etc: to let up, or become weaker or extinguished. See also BLOW-OUT.

■ **blow something out 1** to put out (a flame, etc) by blowing. **2** to send (a window, etc) forcibly outwards as the result of an explosion.

■ **blow over** said of an incident, quarrel, threat, storm, etc: to pass by, especially without having any harmful or lasting effect; to die down or come to an end.

■ **blow through** *Austral colloq* to leave, especially quickly or abruptly. Also **shoot through**.

■ **blow up 1** *colloq* said of a person: to explode in anger. **2** to fill up or swell up with air or gas. **3** to explode □ *The truck hit the bridge and blew up.* See also *verb* 5 above.

■ **blow someone up** *colloq* **1** to lose one's temper with them. **2** to bring about their death by way of an explosion.

■ **blow something up 1** to inflate (eg a balloon). **2** to produce a larger version of (a photograph, etc). **3** *colloq* to make it seem more serious or important than it really is. **4** to destroy it by way of an explosion.

blow[2] /bloʊ/ ▷ *noun* **1** a forceful stroke or knock with the hand or with a weapon. **2** a sudden shock or misfortune. ● **at a blow** by a single action; suddenly. ● **come to blows** to start or end up fighting. ⓘ 15c, first as Northern English and Scots *blaw*.

blow-by-blow ▷ *adj, only before the noun* said of a description or account, etc: giving all the details precisely and in order.

blow-dry ▷ *verb* to dry (hair) in a particular style using a hand-held hairdrier. ▷ *noun* **1** an act or process of blow-drying. **2** a hairstyle created by blow-drying. ● **blow-drier** *noun* a hand-held hairdrier used for blow-drying. ⓘ 1970s.

blower ▷ *noun* **1** a device or machine that blows out a current of air. **2** (**the blower**) *Brit colloq* the telephone.

blowfly ▷ *noun* any of various species of fly whose eggs are laid in rotting flesh or excrement on which the hatched larvae subsequently feed, eg bluebottle.

blowhard ▷ *noun, colloq, chiefly US* a boastful or loudmouthed person.

blowhole ▷ *noun* **1** a hole in an area of surface ice, where marine mammals, eg seals, can go to breathe. **2** a hole or modified nostril on top of a whale's head, through which it BLOWS (*verb* 16). **3** *geol* a natural vent from the roof of a sea cave up to the ground surface, through which air and water are forced by breaking waves.

blow-in ▷ *noun, Austral derog, colloq* a person who has just recently turned up; a newcomer. See BLOW IN at BLOW.

blow job ▷ *noun, coarse slang* an act of oral stimulation of the male genitals. Also called FELLATIO.

blowlamp and (*especially N Amer*) **blowtorch** ▷ *noun* a small portable burner, usually fuelled with liquid gas, that produces an intense hot flame, used for paint-stripping, melting soft metal, etc.

blown see under BLOW[1]

blow-out ▷ *noun* **1** *colloq* a tyre-burst. **2** *oil industry* a violent escape of gas and oil from a well or on a rig, etc. **3** *colloq* a large meal at which one overindulges. **4** *elec engineering* **a** an incident in which a circuit is broken by a fuse blowing; **b** a blown (ie melted or burnt out) fuse. See BLOW SOMETHING OUT at BLOW.

blowpipe ▷ *noun* **1** in glass-blowing: a long narrow iron tube on which a mass of molten glass is gathered before air is forced down the tube to form a bubble of air within the glass, which can then be shaped as it cools. **2** a small often curved tube that carries a stream of air into a flame in order to concentrate and direct it, eg for brazing and soldering. **3** a blowtorch.

blow-up ▷ *noun* **1** *colloq* an enlargement of a photograph. **2** *colloq* a sudden explosion of temper. **3** an explosion. See also BLOW UP at BLOW[1].

blowy /ˈbloʊɪ/ ▷ *adj* (***blowier***, ***blowiest***) blustery; windy.

blowzy or **blowsy** /ˈblaʊzɪ/ ▷ *adj* (***blowzier***, ***blowziest***) *derog, colloq* said of a woman: **1** fat and red-faced or flushed. **2** dirty and dishevelled; slovenly. ⓘ 18c: from old dialect *blowze* a beggar woman or wench.

BLT ▷ *abbreviation* bacon, lettuce and tomato. ▷ *noun, colloq, originally US* a sandwich with this filling.

blub ▷ *verb* (***blubbed***, ***blubbing***) *intr, colloq* to weep or sob. ⓘ 19c: short for BLUBBER *verb*.

blubber /ˈblʌbə(r)/ ▷ *noun* **1** the fat of sea animals such as the whale. **2** *colloq* excessive body fat; flab. **3** *colloq* a bout of weeping or blubbering. ▷ *verb* (***blubbered***, ***blubbering***) *derog colloq* **1** *intr* to weep, especially noisily or unrestrainedly. **2** to say or try to say (words, etc) while weeping. **3** to make (the face, eyes, etc) swollen, red, unattractive, etc with weeping. ● **blubbering** *noun*. ● **blubbery** *adj*. ⓘ 17c in noun sense 1;14c as *blober*, meaning 'foam or bubbles on the surface of the sea' and 'to bubble up': imitating the sound.

bludge /blʌdʒ/ *Austral & NZ slang* ▷ *verb* (***bludged***, ***bludging***) **1** (*often* **bludge on someone**) *tr & intr* to scrounge; to impose on or sponge off someone. **2** *intr* to loaf about; to avoid work or other responsibilities. ▷ *noun* an easy job that requires no effort; a spell of loafing about. ⓘ Early 20c: back-formation from BLUDGER.

bludgeon /ˈblʌdʒən/ ▷ *noun* **1** a stick or club with a heavy end. **2** someone or something (eg a method, tactic or line of defence) that is effective but heavy-handed or crude. ▷ *verb* (***bludgeoned***, ***bludgeoning***) **1** to hit someone or something with or as if with a bludgeon. **2** (*usually* **bludgeon someone into something**) to force or bully them into doing it. ⓘ 18c.

bludger ▷ *noun, Austral & NZ slang* a scrounger or loafer; a person who bludges (sometimes used affectionately, in the same way as BASTARD). ⓘ 19c in the obsolete sense 'someone living off a prostitute's earnings': originally from BLUDGEON.

blue /bluː/ ▷ *adj* (***bluer***, ***bluest***) **1** with the colour of a clear cloudless sky; having any of the shades of this colour, which falls between green and violet on the SPECTRUM. **2** sad or depressed. See also BLUES. **3** said of a film or joke etc: pornographic or indecent. **4** politically conservative. **5** with a skin which is pale blue or purple because of the cold or from bruising, etc. ▷ *noun* **1** the colour of a clear cloudless sky; any blue shade or hue. **2** blue paint or dye. **3** blue material or clothes. **4** a person who has been chosen to represent a college or university at sport, especially at Oxford or Cambridge. **5** *Brit colloq* a supporter of the Conservative Party. **6** *Austral & NZ slang* an argument or fight. **7** *Austral & NZ colloq* a mistake; a bloomer. **8** (**Blue**) *Austral & NZ colloq* a nickname commonly given to a person with red hair, especially a man. **9** (*also* **washing-blue**) a blue liquid or powder (such as INDIGO) used in laundering whites. ▷ *verb* (***blues***, ***blued***, ***bluing*** or ***blueing***) **1** to make something blue. **2** to treat (laundry, linen, etc) with blue. ● **blueness** *noun*. ● **bluer** *adj*. ● **bluish** *adj*. ● **do something till one is blue in the face** to do it repeatedly but without any effect. ● **out of the blue** without warning; unexpectedly. ⓘ 13c as *blew*: from French *bleu*.

blue baby ▷ *noun* a newborn baby suffering from congenital heart disease that results in some or all of the deoxygenated blood being pumped around the body, instead of passing through the lungs, giving the skin and lips a bluish tinge. See CYANOSIS.

bluebell ▻ *noun* **1** a bulbous spring-flowering perennial plant with narrow shiny leaves and erect stems with one-sided clusters of bell-shaped flowers that are usually blue (also called WILD HYACINTH). **2** *Scottish, N Eng* the HAREBELL.

blueberry ▻ *noun* **1** any of various species of deciduous shrub, native to N America, with white or pinkish bell-shaped flowers and edible berries. Also called HUCKLEBERRY. **2** the bluish-black edible berry produced by this plant, which has a waxy bloom and contains numerous seeds.

bluebird ▻ *noun* **1** any of various birds of the thrush family, native to N and Central America, and so called because the male has bright blue plumage on its back. **2** any of various other birds with blue plumage.

blue-black ▻ *adj, noun* black with a tinge of blue; very dark blue.

blue blood ▻ *noun* royal or aristocratic ancestry. • **blue-blooded** *adj.* ◷ 19c: a translation of the Spanish *sangre azul*, probably referring originally to the 'blue blood' visible in the veins of the fair-skinned pure-blooded aristocratic old families of Castile (as distinct from those with darker skin, of Moorish blood or of mixed race, etc).

bluebottle ▻ *noun* **1** a large fly which has a characteristic noisy buzzing flight, and is so called because its abdomen has a metallic blue sheen. **2** *Austral & NZ* the PORTUGUESE MAN-OF-WAR. **3** the blue cornflower.

blue cheese ▻ *noun* cheese with veins of blue mould running through it, eg STILTON, and GORGONZOLA.

blue-chip *stock exchange, originally US* ▻ *adj* **1 a** said of industrial stocks and shares: considered reliable, secure and strong, having a good dividend yield and capital value, though less secure than GILT-EDGED ones; **b** said of a company, etc: considered secure, dependably profitable or reliable, and therefore prestigious; having blue-chip shares. **2** *loosely* prestigious and valuable. ▻ *noun* a blue-chip stock. ◷ 1920s: from the (high-value) *blue chip* in poker.

blue-collar ▻ *adj* said of workers: doing manual or unskilled work. Compare WHITE-COLLAR.

Blue Ensign see under ENSIGN

blue-eyed boy ▻ *noun, chiefly Brit & derog colloq* a boy or man who is a favourite; the one out of a group who is especially liked, encouraged, supported, etc.

blue flag ▻ *noun* a flag awarded to, and flown at, a beach which meets European Community standards of cleanliness and water purity.

blue funk ▻ *noun, slang* a state of great terror or cowardice.

bluegrass ▻ *noun* **1** a simple style of country music originating in Kentucky and popular in southern states of America, played on unamplified stringed instruments, especially banjo, fiddle and guitar. **2** any of several bluish-green grasses of Europe and N America, especially Kentucky. ◷ 18c in sense 2: the name was applied to the music in the 1950s, after a group called the *Blue Grass Boys*, from Kentucky (known as the Bluegrass state).

blue-green alga ▻ *noun, biol* the common name for any of a group of single-celled photosynthetic PROKARYOTIC organisms, often blue in colour owing to the presence of the pigment PHYCOCYANIN.

blue gum ▻ *noun* any of several species of Australian EUCALYPTUS with bluish leaves and strong wood.

blue jay ▻ *noun* a common N American jay with mainly blue plumage.

blue moon ▻ *noun, colloq* a very long but indefinite amount of time. • **once in a blue moon** very seldom; hardly ever. ◷ 19c: on rare occasions the Moon appears to be blue because of dust particles in the atmosphere.

blue movie and **blue film** see BLUE *adj* 3

blue murder ▻ *noun, colloq* used in phrases describing a terrible din or commotion. • **scream blue murder** to scream very loudly in pain, alarm, protest, anger, etc. Also **shout** or **cry**, *etc* **blue murder**. ◷ 19c: possibly connected with the archaic French oath *morbleu*, literally 'blue death'.

blueness see under BLUE

blue note ▻ *noun, music, especially jazz* a flattened note (usually a flattened third or seventh), characteristic of the BLUES.

blue-pencil ▻ *verb* to correct, edit or cut parts out of (a piece of writing); to censor. ◷ 1880s: during the 19c it had become the custom (originally among military censors) to use a blue pencil for correcting, emending and deleting, etc.

Blue Peter or **blue peter** ▻ *noun* a blue flag with a white square, flown on a ship which is about to set sail. ◷ 19c.

blueprint ▻ *noun* **1 a** a pattern, model or prototype; **b** a detailed original plan of work to be done to develop an idea, project or scheme, etc. **2** *technical* a photographic print of plans, engineering or architectural designs, etc consisting of white lines on a blue background, produced on **blueprint paper** sensitized with ferric salts. ▻ *verb* to make a blueprint of (a plan or project, etc). ◷ 19c in sense 2.

blue ribbon or **blue riband** ▻ *noun* **1** a first prize awarded in a competition, or some other very high distinction. **2** *Brit* the blue silk ribbon of the Order of the Garter.

blue rinse ▻ *noun, hairdressing* a bluish colouring for white or grey hair. ▻ *adj* (*also* **blue-rinse** or **blue-rinsed**) used, often disparagingly, of a supposedly typical middle-class, well-groomed, well-off lady.

blues ▻ *singular or plural noun* (*usually* **the blues**) **1** a feeling of sadness or depression. **2** slow melancholy jazz music of Black American origin, a typical piece consisting of three four-bar phrases and making use of BLUE NOTES. • **bluesy** *adj* like the blues. ◷ 18c, short for 'the blue devils'; early 20c in sense 2.

blue-sky and **blue-skies** ▻ *adj, originally US* **1** said of research, etc: having no immediate practical application; hypothetical. **2** said of stocks and securities, etc: financially unsound or fraudulent. ◷ Early 20c: the term came to be applied to anything unrealistic or fanciful, as an extension in sense from earlier simple attributive uses.

bluestocking ▻ *noun, often derog* a highly educated woman who is interested in serious academic subjects. ◷ 18c: the term originated when a group of London ladies (c.1750) held philosophical and literary meetings, in contrast to card-playing evening-parties, and came to be nicknamed the 'Blue Stocking Society' because at least one gentleman would attend dressed informally in blue worsted stockings (as opposed to formal black silk).

blue tit ▻ *noun* a small bird belonging to the tit family, which has a bright blue crown, wings and tail, and yellow underparts, and often hangs upside down while feeding.

blue whale ▻ *noun* a rare BALEEN WHALE of the RORQUAL family, the largest living animal (up to 30m long), which has a bluish body with pale spots, and feeds on krill.

bluey /'bluːɪ/ ▻ *adj* (*especially in compounds*) tending towards blue in colour □ *bluey-green eyes.* ▻ *noun* (*blueys*) *colloq* **1** *Austral* a bundle or swag, often wrapped in a blue blanket or cloth. **2** *Austral* a blanket. **3** an aerogramme.

bluff[1] ▻ *verb* (*bluffed, bluffing*) *tr & intr* to deceive or try to deceive someone by pretending to be stronger, cleverer or more determined, etc than one really is. ▻ *noun* an act of bluffing. • **bluff it out** *colloq* to keep up a deception, in order to avoid a difficult or embarrassing outcome. • **call**

someone's bluff to challenge or expose their bluff, by making them prove the genuineness of their claim, threat or promise, etc. ⓒ 19c: originally used in poker, meaning to conceal (by confident behaviour) the fact that one has poor cards: from Dutch *bluffen* to brag or boast.

■ **bluff someone into** or **out of something** to fool or trick them into it, or into giving it up or giving it away, by bluffing.

bluff² ▷ *adj* (**bluffer**, **bluffest**) **1** said of a person, character, manner, etc: rough, cheerful and honest; outspoken and hearty. **2** usually said of a cliff or of the bow of a ship: broad, steep and upright. ▷ *noun* a steep cliff or high bank of ground. • **bluffly** *adverb*. • **bluffness** *noun*. ⓒ 17c in sense 2: perhaps from obsolete Dutch *blaf* broad or flat.

bluish see under BLUE

blunder /ˈblʌndə(r)/ ▷ *noun* a foolish or thoughtless, and usually serious, mistake. ▷ *verb* (**blundered**, **blundering**) **1** *intr* to make a blunder. **2** (*especially* **blunder about** or **around** or **in** or **into** or **through**, *etc*) *intr* to act or move about awkwardly and clumsily. **3** to mismanage or bungle. • **blunderer** *noun*. • **blundering** *adj*. • **blunderingly** *adverb*. ⓒ 14c as *verb* meaning 'to move blindly or foolishly' and *noun* meaning 'confusion or bewilderment': possibly from Norse *blunda* to shut one's eyes.

blunderbuss /ˈblʌndəbʌs/ ▷ *noun* (**blunderbusses**) *historical* a type of musket with a wide barrel and a flared muzzle, for discharging a quantity of shot at close range. ⓒ 17c: altered (by influence of BLUNDER) from Dutch *donderbus*, from *donder* thunder + *bus* gun.

blunt /blʌnt/ ▷ *adj* (**blunter, bluntest**) **1** said of a pencil, knife or blade, etc: having no point or sharp edge. **2** dull; imperceptive. **3** said of a person, character or manner, etc: honest and direct in a rough way. ▷ *verb* (**blunted, blunting**) to make blunt or less sharp. • **bluntly** *adverb*. • **bluntness** *noun*. ⓒ 13c.

blur /blɜː(r)/ ▷ *noun* **1** a thing not clearly seen or heard, or happening too fast or too distantly, etc to be clearly seen, comprehended or recognized. **2** a smear or smudge. ▷ *verb* (**blurred**, **blurring**) **1** *tr & intr* to make or become less clear or distinct. **2** to rub over and smudge something. **3** to make (one's memory or judgement, etc) less clear. • **blurred** or **blurry** *adj* (**blurrier**, **blurriest**) smudged; indistinct. ⓒ 16c: perhaps a variant of BLEAR.

blurb /blɜːb/ ▷ *noun* **1** a brief description of a book, usually printed on the jacket in order to promote it. **2** *loosely* any brief descriptive printed passage to advertise, praise, list the credits, etc of someone or something. ⓒ Early 20c: invented by Gelett Burgess (1866–1951), an American author.

blurt /blɜːt/ ▷ *verb* (**blurted**, **blurting**) (*usually* **blurt something out**) to say it suddenly or without thinking of the effect or result. ⓒ 16c: probably imitating this action.

blush /blʌʃ/ ▷ *verb* (**blushed, blushing**) *intr* **1** to become red or pink in the face because of shame, embarrassment, excitement, joy, etc. **2** to feel ashamed or embarrassed. **3** *tr & intr, especially literary* to make or grow red or rosy. ▷ *noun* (**blushes**) **1** a red or pink glow on the skin of the face, caused by shame, embarrassment, excitement, joy, etc. **2** *especially literary* a pink rosy glow. • **blushing** *adj*. • **blushingly** *adverb*. ⓒ 14c, from Anglo-Saxon *blyscan* to shine or redden.

blusher ▷ *noun* a cosmetic cream or powder, usually in a pinkish shade, used to give colour to the cheeks.

bluster /ˈblʌstə(r)/ ▷ *verb* (**blustered, blustering**) **1** *intr* to speak in a boasting, angry or threatening way, often to hide fear. **2** *intr* said of the wind or waves, etc: to blow or move roughly. **3** to say something in a boasting, angry or threatening way. ▷ *noun* **1** speech that is ostentatiously boasting, angry or threatening. **2** the roaring noise of the wind or sea on a rough day. • **blusterer** *noun*. • **blustering** *adj*. • **blusteringly** *adverb*. • **blustery** *adj* said of the weather: rough and windy. ⓒ 16c: probably from German dialect *blustern* to blow violently.

blvd ▷ *abbreviation* boulevard.

BM ▷ *abbreviation* **1** Bachelor of Medicine. **2** British Museum.

BMA ▷ *abbreviation* British Medical Association.

BMEWS /bɪˈmjuːz/ ▷ *abbreviation* ballistic missile early warning system, or station.

BMJ ▷ *abbreviation* British Medical Journal.

BMI ▷ *abbreviation* body mass index.

B-movie ▷ *noun* a film, usually cheaply-produced and of mediocre or poor quality, made to support the main film in a cinema programme. Also (*chiefly Brit*) called **B-film**.

BMus ▷ *abbreviation* Bachelor of Music.

BMW ▷ *abbreviation*: Bayerische Motoren Werke (German), Bavarian motor works.

BMX ▷ *noun* **1** the sport of bicycle riding and racing over a rough track with obstacles. **2** (*also* **BMX bike**) a bicycle designed for BMX racing and also used for stunt-riding, with small wheels, high handle-bars and a sturdy frame. ⓒ 1970s (originally US): abbreviation of BICYCLE MOTOCROSS.

bn ▷ *abbreviation* **1** battalion. **2** billion.

BNFL ▷ *abbreviation* British Nuclear Fuels Limited.

BNSC ▷ *abbreviation* British National Space Centre.

b.o. ▷ *abbreviation* **1** (*also* **BO**) body odour. **2** box office. **3** branch office. **4** buyer's option.

BOA ▷ *abbreviation* British Olympic Association.

boa /ˈboʊə/ ▷ *noun* (**boas**) **1** a **boa constrictor**, or any similar snake of the mainly S American type that kill by winding themselves round their prey and crushing it. **2** *popularly* any large constricting snake. **3** a woman's long thin scarf, usually made of feathers or fur, worn wrapped around the neck. ⓒ 14c: Latin, meaning 'a kind of snake'.

boar /bɔː(r)/ ▷ *noun* (**boars** or **boar**) **1** a wild ancestor of the domestic pig, native to Europe, Africa and Asia, which has thick dark hair, and the male of which has tusks. **2** a mature uncastrated male pig. **3** the flesh of a boar (as meat). ⓒ Anglo-Saxon *bar*.

boar

There is sometimes a spelling confusion between **boar** and **boor**.

board /bɔːd/ ▷ *noun* **1** a long flat strip of wood. **2** *often in compounds* a piece of material resembling this, made from fibres compressed together □ *chipboard*. **3** *often in compounds* **a** a flat piece of wood or other hard solid material, used for a specified purpose or of a specified kind □ *notice board* □ *ironing board* □ *blackboard*; **b** a slab, table or other flat surface prepared for playing a game on □ *chessboard* □ *dart-board*. **4** thick stiff card used eg for binding books. **5** a person's meals, provided in return for money □ *bed and board*. **6** **a** an official group of people controlling or managing an organization, etc, or examining or interviewing candidates □ *a board of examiners*; **b** (*also* **board of directors**) a group of individual directors appointed by a company, who are collectively responsible for its management. **7** *US* the stock exchange, especially the New York Stock Exchange. **8** (**the boards**) a theatre stage □ *tread the boards*. **9** *naut* the side of a ship. ▷ *verb* (**boarded, boarding**) **1** to enter or get on to (a ship, aeroplane, bus, etc). **2** (*usually* **board something up**) to cover (a gap or entrance) with boards. **3** *intr* **a** to receive accommodation and meals in someone else's house, in return for payment □ *I boarded with Mrs Green*; **b** to receive accommodation and meals at school; to attend school as a BOARDER 2. **4** to provide someone with accommodation and meals in return for payment. **5** (*also* **board someone out**) to arrange for them to receive accommodation and meals away from home. • **above board** openly (see also separate entry ABOVE-BOARD). • **across the board** see under ACROSS. • **go by the board** *colloq* to be given up or ignored. ◎ From nautical usage (see *noun* 9 above): something that has fallen or been thrown, etc 'by the board' (ie overboard) and has disappeared for good. • **on board** on or into a ship or aeroplane, etc. • **sweep the board 1** to win everything or take all the prizes. **2** *cards, betting* to take (ie win) all the cards or money from the board (see *noun* 3 above). • **take something on board** to understand or accept (new ideas or responsibilities, etc). ◎ Anglo-Saxon *bord*.

boarder ▷ *noun* **1** a person who receives accommodation and meals in someone else's house, in return for payment. **2** a pupil who lives at school during term time.

board game ▷ *noun* a game (such as chess or draughts) played with pieces or counters that are moved on a specially designed board.

boarding ▷ *noun* **1** a structure or collection of wooden boards laid side by side. **2** the act of boarding a ship or aeroplane, etc.

boarding house ▷ *noun* a house in which people live and take meals as paying guests.

boarding pass and **boarding card** ▷ *noun* an official card issued by an airline, etc, which allows a person to board an aeroplane, etc.

boarding school ▷ *noun* a school at which all or most of the pupils live during term time. Compare DAY SCHOOL.

Board of Trade ▷ *noun* **1** *Brit* a ministry within the Department of Trade and Industry. **2** (**board of trade**) *US* a local chamber of commerce.

boardroom ▷ *noun* **1** a room in which the directors of a company meet. **2** the highest level of management of a company.

boardwalk ▷ *noun, N Amer, especially US* a footpath made of boards, especially on the seafront.

boast /boust/ ▷ *verb* (***boasted, boasting***) **1** *intr* (*often* **boast about** or **of something**) to talk with excessive pride about one's own abilities or achievements, etc. **2** to own or have (something it is right to be proud of) □ ***The hotel boasts magnificent views across the valley.*** ▷ *noun* **1** an act of boasting; a brag. **2** a thing one is proud of. • **boaster** *noun*. • **boasting** *noun, adj*. ◎ 14c as *bost*, probably originally meaning 'to speak in a loud voice'.

boastful ▷ *adj, usually derog* **1** given to boasting about oneself. **2** showing or characterized by boasting. • **boastfully** *adverb*. • **boastfulness** *noun*.

boat /bout/ ▷ *noun* **1** a small vessel for travelling over water. *Often in compounds* □ ***sailing boat*** □ ***rowing boat.*** **2** *colloq, loosely* a larger vessel; a ship. **3** *in compounds* a boat-shaped dish for serving sauce, etc □ ***gravy boat*** □ ***sauceboat.*** ▷ *verb* (***boated, boating***) **1** *intr* to sail or travel in a boat, especially for pleasure. **2** to put something into or convey something in a boat. • **in the same boat** said of people: finding themselves in the same difficult circumstances. • **miss the boat** to lose an opportunity. • **push the boat out** *colloq* to celebrate or entertain in a lavish or extravagant way. • **rock the boat** to disturb the balance or calmness of a situation. ◎ Anglo-Saxon *bat*.

boater ▷ *noun* **1** a straw hat with a flat top and a brim. **2** a person who boats. ◎ 17; 19c in sense 1, so called because it was a type of hat suitable for wearing when boating.

boathook ▷ *noun* a metal hook fixed to the end of a pole, used by someone on a boat for pushing off, pulling or pushing on something, etc.

boathouse ▷ *noun* a building in which boats are stored, especially by a lake or river.

boatie ▷ *noun* **1** *Austral & NZ colloq* a person who enjoys boating as a regular pastime or passion. **2** *Brit university slang* a rowing enthusiast.

boating ▷ *noun* the sailing or rowing, etc of boats for pleasure.

boatload ▷ *noun* **1** the number of people and/or the amount of cargo, etc that a boat can carry. **2** *colloq* a large but inexact quantity □ ***boatloads of jumble.***

boatman ▷ *noun* a man who is in charge of, or hires out, etc a small passenger-carrying boat or boats.

boat people ▷ *plural noun* refugees who have fled their country by boat.

boat race ▷ *noun* **1** a race between rowing boats. **2** (**the Boat Race**) *Brit* the boat race between Oxford and Cambridge university eights (see EIGHT *noun* 7) held every year on the River Thames.

boatswain or **bosun** /'bousən/ ▷ *noun* a warrant officer in the navy, or the foreman of a crew, who is in charge of a ship's lifeboats, rigging, sails, etc and its maintenance. ◎ 15c: from Anglo-Saxon *batswegen* boatman.

boat train ▷ *noun* a train which takes passengers to or from a ship.

bob¹ ▷ *verb* (***bobbed, bobbing***) **1** *intr* (*sometimes* **bob along** or **past**, *etc*) to move up and down quickly □ ***a stick bobbing along on the water.*** **2** to move (the head) up and down, usually as a greeting. **3** *intr* (*usually* **bob for something**) to try to catch (especially an apple floating on water or suspended on a string) with one's teeth, as a game. **4** *intr* to make a quick curtsy. ▷ *noun* **1** a quick up-and-down bouncing movement. **2** a quick curtsy. ◎ 14c.

■ **bob up** to appear or reappear suddenly.

bob² ▷ *noun* **1** a short hairstyle for women and children, with the hair cut square across the face and evenly all round the head. **2** a hanging weight on a clock's pendulum or plumbline, etc. **3** a bobsleigh. See also BITS AND BOBS at BITS AND PIECES. ▷ *verb* (***bobbed, bobbing***) **1** to cut (hair) in a bob. **2** to dock (a tail). **3** *intr* to ride on a bobsleigh. ◎ 20c in sense 1 (*noun* and *verb*); 14c as *bobbe* in the original (now dialect) sense 'a spray, bunch or cluster' (eg of flowers); later used to mean 'a rounded lump or knob', and hence BOBTAIL.

bob³ ▷ *noun* (*plural* ***bob***) *Brit colloq* **1** *old use* a shilling. **2** *loosely* (*usually* **a few bob** or **a bob or two**) a sum of money, especially a large amount □ ***I bet that cost a few bob!*** ◎ 18c.

bob⁴ ▷ *noun* • **bob's your uncle** *Brit colloq* an expression used to show that something should follow simply as a matter of course □ ***Just flick the switch and bob's your uncle!*** ◎ 19c phrase: from *Bob*, a pet-form of the name *Robert*.

bobbin ▷ *noun* a small cylindrical object on which thread or yarn, etc is wound, used in sewing and weaving machines. ◎ 16c: from French *bobine*.

bobble¹ ▷ *noun* **1** a small ball, often fluffy or made of tufted wool, used to decorate clothes or furnishings, etc, especially on the top of a knitted **bobble-hat**. **2** a little ball formed on the surface of a fabric during use, through rubbing, etc. • **bobbly** *adj*. ◎ 20c: diminutive of BOB².

bobble² ▷ *verb* (***bobbled, bobbling***) **1** *tr & intr* to bob rapidly or continuously. **2** *originally US, especially Amer football* to fumble; to bungle. ▷ *noun* **1** a bobbing motion, especially one that is rapid or repeated. **2** *chiefly US, especially Amer football* a fumble; a bungle or error. ◎ 19c: frequentative of BOB¹.

bobby ▷ *noun* (***bobbies***) *Brit colloq* a policeman. ◎ 19c: from the name *Bob*, after Sir Robert Peel (1788–1850) who founded the Metropolitan Police in 1828.

bobby-dazzler ▷ *noun, Brit colloq or dialect* anything overwhelmingly excellent, striking or showy, especially a strikingly attractive woman.

bobby-pin ▷ *noun, chiefly N Amer* a small flat wire clip for holding the hair in place. *British equivalent* HAIRGRIP.

bobby socks ▻ *plural noun, originally US* ankle socks, especially as worn by girls in their early teens, first popular in the 1940s and 50s.

bobcat ▻ *noun* a solitary nocturnal member of the cat family, native to mountains and deserts of N America, which has a brown coat with dark spots, white underparts and tufted ears.

bobsleigh and (*especially US*) **bobsled** ▻ *noun* **1** a sleigh with metal runners, used on snow and ice, made up of two short sledges coupled together. **2** *sport* a modified toboggan for two or more people, with a continuous seat, steel body, steering mechanism and brakes, for racing on ice-covered track. Compare LUGE. ▻ *verb, intr* to ride or race on a bobsleigh. • **bobsleighing** or **bobsledding** *noun* racing or riding on a bobsleigh. ⓘ 19c.

bobstays ▻ *plural noun, naut* ropes used to hold the BOWSPRIT down to the STEM, and counteract the strain of the foremast-stays.

bobtail ▻ *noun* **1** a short or cropped tail. **2** an animal having such a tail. See also RAGTAG AND BOBTAIL. • **bobtailed** *adj*. ⓘ 17c: see BOB[2].

Boche /bɒʃ/ *derog slang* ▻ *plural noun* (**the Boche**) the Germans, especially German soldiers. ▻ *singular noun* a German, especially a German soldier. ⓘ Early 20c: from French *boche* rascal, applied to Germans in World War I.

bod ▻ *noun, colloq* **1** a person or chap. **2** a body ▫ ***He's got a fantastic bod!*** ⓘ 18c in Scottish use probably short for Gaelic *bodach* an old man, later associated with *body*.

bode¹ ▻ /boʊd/ *verb* (***boded, boding***) to be a sign of something; to portend. • **bode ill** or **well** to be a bad or good sign for the future. ⓘ Anglo-Saxon as *bodian* in the obsolete sense 'to announce'.

bode² /boʊd/ see under BIDE

bodega /bɒ'diːgə, boʊ'deɪgə/ ▻ *noun* (***bodegas***) especially in Spain and other Spanish-speaking countries: **1** a wine-shop. **2** a warehouse for storing and maturing wine. ⓘ 19c: Spanish, from Latin *apotheca* storehouse.

bodge /bɒdʒ/ ▻ *verb* (***bodged, bodging***) *tr & intr, colloq* to make a mess of something; to do it badly or carelessly. ▻ *noun, colloq* a piece of poor or clumsy workmanship. ⓘ 16c: a variant of BOTCH.

Bodhisattva /bɒdɪ'satvə, -wə/ ▻ *noun, Buddhism* a person who has reached the state of enlightenment but postpones entry into NIRVANA in order to help others. ⓘ 19c: Sanskrit, from *bodhi* enlightenment + *sattva* being.

bodhran /boʊ'rɑːn/ ▻ *noun* a shallow one-sided drum often played in Scottish and Irish folk-music. ⓘ Irish Gaelic.

bodice /'bɒdɪs/ ▻ *noun* **1** the close-fitting upper part of a woman's dress, from shoulder to waist. **2** a woman's close-fitting waistcoat, worn over a blouse. **3** *formerly* a similar tight-fitting stiffened undergarment for women. ⓘ 16c: from *bodies*, plural of BODY.

bodice-ripper ▻ *noun, colloq, usually derog* a romantic novel or film, often an historical one, involving sex and violence.

bodied ▻ *adj, in compounds* having a body of the type specified ▫ ***able-bodied*** ▫ ***wide-bodied.***

bodily /'bɒdɪlɪ/ ▻ *adj* belonging or relating to, or performed by, the body. ▻ *adverb* **1** as a whole; taking the whole body ▫ ***carried me bodily to the car.*** **2** in person.

bodily function ▻ *noun* any of the processes or activities performed by or connected with the body, such as breathing, hearing and digesting.

bodkin /'bɒdkɪn/ ▻ *noun* a large blunt needle. ⓘ 14c as *bodekin* a small dagger or stiletto.

body /'bɒdɪ/ ▻ *noun* (***bodies***) **1** the whole physical structure of a person or animal. **2** the physical structure of a person or animal excluding the head and limbs. **3** a corpse. **4** the main or central part of anything, such as the main part of a vehicle which carries the load or passengers. **5** a person's physical needs and desires as opposed to spiritual concerns. **6** a substantial section or group ▫ ***a body of opinion.*** **7** a group of people regarded as a single unit. **8** a quantity or mass ▫ ***a body of water.*** **9** a distinct mass or object; a piece of matter ▫ ***a heavenly body*** ▫ ***a foreign body.*** **10** applied to wine, music, etc: a full or strong quality or tone; fullness. **11** thickness; substantial quality. **12** the opacity of a paint or pigment. **13** a legless tight-fitting one-piece garment for women, fastening at the crotch. Also (*especially formerly*) called **bodysuit**. **14** *colloq* a person. ▻ *verb* (***bodies, bodied, bodying***) (*often* **body something out**) to give it body or form. • **keep body and soul together** *often facetious* to remain alive, especially not to die of hunger. • **over my dead body** see under DEAD. • **in a body** said of a number of people: all together; acting all together. ⓘ Anglo-Saxon as *bodig*.

body bag ▻ *noun* a bag made of heavy material, closed with a zip, in which a dead body, especially the body of a war casualty or accident victim, is transported.

body blow ▻ *noun* **1** *boxing* a blow to the body, ie the torso. **2** a serious setback or misfortune.

body-building ▻ *noun* physical exercise designed to develop the muscles and strengthen the body. • **bodybuilder** *noun*.

body clock see under BIOLOGICAL CLOCK

bodyguard ▻ *noun* a person or group of people whose job is to accompany and give physical protection to an important person, etc.

body language ▻ *noun, psychol* the communication of information by means of conscious or unconscious gestures, attitudes, facial expressions, etc, rather than by words.

bodyline ▻ *noun, cricket* the policy of bowling the ball straight at the batsman so that it will strike the body. See also LEG THEORY.

body mass index ▻ *noun* (abbreviation **BMI**) an index of obesity calculated by dividing the person's weight in kilograms by the square of their height in metres.

body piercing ▻ *noun* the practice of piercing parts of the body other than the earlobes, eg nipples, navel, in order to insert metal studs or rings for decoration.

body politic ▻ *noun* (*usually* **the body politic**) all the people of a nation in their political capacity. ⓘ 16c.

body popping ▻ *noun* a form of dancing using robot-like movements, which became popular among young people in the 1980s. • **body popper** *noun*.

body shop ▻ *noun* a vehicle-body repair or construction shop.

body snatcher ▻ *noun, historical* a person who steals dead bodies from their graves, usually to sell them for dissection.

body stocking ▻ *noun* a tight-fitting one-piece garment worn next to the skin, covering all of the body and often the arms and legs.

bodysuit see BODY *noun* 13

body warmer ▻ *noun* a padded sleeveless jacket or JERKIN.

bodywork ▻ *noun* **1** the metal outer shell of a motor vehicle. **2** *alternative medicine* a term covering therapeutic techniques such as yoga, massage and t'ai chi ch'uan that release tensions and balance energies in the body and integrate mind, body and spirit. • **bodyworker** *noun* a therapist using bodywork techniques.

Boer /bɔː(r), bʊə(r)/ ▻ *noun* a descendant of the early Dutch settlers in S Africa. ▻ *adj* belonging or relating to the Boers. ⓘ 19c: Dutch, literally 'farmer'.

boeuf bourguignon / *French* bœf —/ ▻ *noun, cookery* a beef and vegetable casserole cooked in red wine.

boffin /ˈbɒfɪn/ ▻ *noun, Brit colloq* a scientist engaged in research, especially for the armed forces or the government. ⓔ 1940s.

bog ▻ *noun* **1** *ecol* a flat or domed area of wet spongy poorly-drained ground, composed of acid peat and slowly decaying plant material, and dominated by sphagnum moss, sedges, rushes, etc. **2** *coarse Brit, slang* a toilet. ▻ *verb* (***bogged***, ***bogging***) only in the phrases below. • **bogginess** *noun*. • **boggy** *adj* (***boggier***, ***boggiest***). ⓔ 14c: from Irish and Scottish Gaelic *bogach*, from *bog* soft.

■ **bog someone** or **something down** to prevent them or it from progressing by an overload of work, complications, etc.

■ **bog off** *coarse Brit slang* to go away or get lost.

bog asphodel ▻ *noun, bot* a perennial plant, native to boggy regions of NW Europe, which has yellow flowers that turn deep orange after fertilization, and woolly stamens.

bogey[1] or **bogy** /ˈboʊgɪ/ ▻ *noun* (***bogeys*** or ***bogies***) **1** an evil or mischievous spirit. **2** something especially feared or dreaded; a bugbear. **3** *slang* a piece of nasal mucus. ⓔ 19c: probably from *bogle*, a dialect word meaning 'a spectre or goblin'.

bogey[2] /ˈboʊgɪ/ ▻ *noun* (***bogeys***) *golf* **1** a score of one over PAR on a specific hole. **2** *formerly* the number of strokes that a competent golfer might expect to take for a given hole or course. • *verb* (***bogeyed***, ***bogeying***) to complete (a specified hole) in one over par. Compare BIRDIE 2, EAGLE 2, 3. ⓔ 19c: in 1890 a Major Wellman is said to have remarked that the hypothetical golfer able to play to this standard must be a regular *'Bogey Man'* (referring to a popular song of the time); thereafter this imaginary player came to be called *Colonel Bogey* and golfers would aim to 'beat the Colonel' or 'beat the Bogey'; see BOGEYMAN.

bogey[3] see BOGIE

bogeyman or **bogyman** ▻ *noun* a cruel or frightening person or creature, existing or imaginary, used to threaten or frighten children. ⓔ 19c: from BOGEY[1].

boggle /ˈbɒgəl/ ▻ *verb* (***boggled***, ***boggling***) *intr, colloq* **1** to be amazed or unable to understand or imagine □ *the mind boggles.* **2** (*usually* **boggle at something**) to hesitate or equivocate over it, out of surprise or fright, etc. ⓔ 16c: from *bogle* see; BOGEY[1].

boggy see under BOG

bogie or **bogey** /ˈboʊgɪ/ ▻ *noun* (***bogies*** or ***bogeys***), *mainly Brit* **1** a frame with four or six wheels used as part of a pivoting undercarriage, supporting part of a long vehicle such as a railway carriage. **2** (sometimes called **bogie truck**) a small low open truck or trolley, used to move coal, ores, concrete, etc. ⓔ 19c.

bogies see under BOGEY[1]

bog-standard ▻ *adj* mediocre; ordinary.

bogus /ˈboʊgəs/ ▻ *adj* false; not genuine. ⓔ 19c US cant: first used as a noun meaning 'apparatus for making counterfeit money'.

bogy see under BOGEY[1]

bohemian /boʊˈhiːmɪən, bə-/ ▻ *noun* **1** someone, especially a writer or an artist, who lives in a way which ignores standard customs and rules of social behaviour. **2** (**Bohemian**) a person from Bohemia, formerly a kingdom, later a part of the Czech Republic. ▻ *adj* **1** ignoring standard customs and rules of social behaviour. **2** (**Bohemian**) from or belonging or relating to Bohemia. • **bohemianism** (*also* **Bohemianism**) *noun*. ⓔ 19c; 16c in sense 2: from French *bohémien* a Bohemian or gypsy (from the belief that the gypsies came from Bohemia).

bohrium /ˈbɔːrɪəm/ ▻ *noun, chem* (symbol **Bh**, atomic number 107) a name proposed for the radioactive element UNNILSEPTIUM.

boil[1] /bɔɪl/ ▻ *verb* (***boiled***, ***boiling***) **1** *intr* said of a liquid: to change rapidly to a vapour on reaching a temperature known as the BOILING POINT, often with the formation of copious bubbles of vapour within the liquid. **2** *intr* said of a container, eg a kettle: to have contents that are boiling. **3 a** to make (a liquid) reach its boiling point rapidly; **b** to boil the contents of (a container). **4** *tr & intr* said of food: to cook or be cooked by heating in boiling liquid. **5** (*sometimes* **boil something up**) to bring (a liquid or its container) to a heat at which the liquid boils. **6** *tr & intr* said of food: to cook something or be cooked by boiling. **7** (*usually* **be boiling**) *colloq* **a** to be very hot □ *It's boiling in the car*; **b** to be extremely angry. **8** to treat something with boiling water, especially to clean it. **9** *intr* said of the sea, etc: to move and bubble violently as if boiling. ▻ *noun* (*usually* **a boil** or **the boil**) the act or point of boiling □ *Give it a boil for five minutes* □ *Reduce the heat as soon as the liquid reaches the boil.* • **come to the boil 1** to reach boiling point. **2** *colloq* said of a plan, affair or business deal, etc: to reach a critical point or state. • **go off the boil 1** to stop boiling; to fall below boiling point. **2** *colloq* to cease to be active, interested or involved, etc. ⓔ 13c: from French *boillir*, from Latin *bullire* to bubble.

■ **boil away** or **down** said of a liquid: to be lost or reduced by boiling.

■ **boil something away** or **down** to reduce (a liquid) by boiling.

■ **boil down to something** *colloq* to mean; to have it as the most important part or factor □ *It all boils down to a question of cost.*

■ **boil over 1** said of a liquid: to boil and flow over the edge of its container. **2** *colloq* to speak out angrily.

■ **boil up 1** said of a liquid: to reach boiling point (see also *verb* 3 above). **2** *colloq* to rise or develop to a dangerous level.

boil[2] /bɔɪl/ ▻ *noun* a reddened and often painful swelling in the skin, containing pus, and usually caused by bacterial infection of a hair follicle. ⓔ Anglo-Saxon *byl*.

boiled sweet ▻ *noun, mainly Brit* a hard sweet made from boiled sugar, often with added colouring and generally flavoured with fruit, mint, etc.

boiler ▻ *noun* **1** any closed vessel that is used to convert water into steam, especially by burning coal, oil or some other fuel, in order to drive a steam turbine, steamship, steam locomotive, etc. **2** an apparatus for heating a building's hot water supply. **3** a metal vessel or tub, etc for boiling and washing clothes in.

boilermaker ▻ *noun* an industrial metalworker.

boilersuit ▻ *noun* a one-piece suit worn over normal clothes to protect them while doing manual or heavy work. Also called OVERALLS. *US equivalent* COVERALLS.

boiling point ▻ *noun* **1** the temperature at which a particular substance changes from a liquid to a vapour, and which varies according to the air pressure. **2** a point of great anger or high excitement, etc at which emotions can no longer be controlled.

boisterous /ˈbɔɪstərəs/ ▻ *adj* **1** said of people, behaviour, etc: very lively, noisy and cheerful. **2** said of the sea, etc: rough and stormy; wild; turbulent. • **boisterously** *adverb*. • **boisterousness** *noun*. ⓔ 15c variant of 14c *boistous* meaning 'rough' or 'coarse'.

bolas /ˈboʊlɑːs/ ▻ *singular or plural noun* (***bolas*** or ***bolases***) a S American hunting missile made of two or more balls or stones strung together on a cord, used by swinging them around and then hurling them so as to entangle the animal's legs. ⓔ 19c: American Spanish, plural of 'ball'.

bold /boʊld/ ▻ *adj* (***bolder***, ***boldest***) **1** daring or brave; confident and courageous. **2** (**the bold**) bold people as a group (see THE 4b). **3** not showing respect; impudent. **4** striking and clearly marked; noticeable. **5** *printing* printed in boldface. • **boldly** *adverb.* • **boldness** *noun.* • **be so bold as to do something** to take the liberty of doing it; to dare to do it. • **bold as brass** completely shameless; extremely cheeky or forward. ⓒ Anglo-Saxon *beald.*

boldface ▻ *noun, printing* a typeface used for emphasis (eg in headings), in which the letters have blacker heavier strokes than in normal type, as in the word **boldface.** • *adj* (*also* **boldfaced**) said of type: printed in boldface.

bole /boʊl/ ▻ *noun* the trunk of a tree. ⓒ 14c: from Norse *bolr.*

bolero ▻ *noun* (*boleros*) **1** /bəˈlɛəroʊ/ **a** a traditional Spanish dance, generally danced by a couple; **b** the music for this dance, usually in triple time. **2** /*usually* ˈbɒləroʊ/ a short open jacket reaching not quite to the waist. ⓒ 18c: Spanish.

bolivar /ˈbɒlɪvɑː(r), bəˈliːvɑː(r)/ ▻ *noun* (*bolivars* or *bolivares* /-rɛs/) (symbol **SB**) the standard monetary unit of Venezuela. ⓒ 19c: after Simón Bolívar (1783–1830), national hero.

boliviano /bɒliːvɪˈɑːnoʊ/ ▻ *noun* (*bolivianos*) (symbol **b**) the standard monetary unit of Bolivia; the Bolivian dollar. ⓒ 19c: Spanish.

boll /boʊl/ ▻ *noun* a rounded capsule containing seeds, especially of a cotton or flax plant. ⓒ 14c, in obsolete sense 'a bubble', from *bolla* a bowl.

bollard /ˈbɒlɑːd, -ləd/ ▻ *noun* **1** *Brit* a small post used to mark a traffic island or to keep traffic away from a certain area. **2** a short but strong post on a ship or quay, etc around which ropes are fastened. ⓒ 19c in sense 2: probably from BOLE.

bollocking ▻ *noun, coarse slang* a severe telling-off or reprimand; a rollicking.

bollocks or **ballocks** /ˈbɒləks/ *coarse slang* ▻ *plural noun* the testicles. ▻ *singular noun* rubbish; nonsense □ ***Don't talk such bollocks.*** ▻ *exclamation* rubbish! nonsense!; a dismissive expression of disbelief. ⓒ 20c as *singular noun*; Anglo-Saxon as *beallucas plural noun* in sense 1.

boll weevil ▻ *noun* a small weevil, found in Mexico and the southern USA, the larvae of which infest and destroy young cotton bolls.

Bollywood ▻ *noun* the Indian commercial film industry, centred in Bombay. ⓒ 1980s: from *Bombay,* modelled on *Hollywood.*

Bolognese /bɒləˈneɪz/ ▻ *adj* **1** belonging or relating to the city of Bologna in N Italy or its inhabitants. **2** *cookery* said especially of pasta: served with a tomato and meat sauce, usually also containing mushrooms, garlic, etc. ▻ *noun* **1** a citizen or inhabitant of, or person born in, Bologna. **2** a Bolognese sauce.

boloney see BALONEY

Bolshevik /ˈbɒlʃəvɪk/ ▻ *noun* (*Bolsheviks* or *sometimes Bolsheviki* /-ˈʃəˈviːkɪ/) **1** *historical* a member of the radical faction of the Russian socialist party, which became the Communist Party in 1918 (compare MENSHEVIK). **2** a Russian communist. **3** (*often* **bolshevik**) *derog colloq* any radical socialist or revolutionary. ▻ *adj* **1** belonging or relating to the Bolsheviks. **2** communist. ⓒ Early 20c: Russian, from *bolshe* greater, either because they were in the majority at the 1903 party congress or because they favoured more extreme measures.

Bolshevist /ˈbɒlʃəvɪst/ ▻ *noun* a Bolshevik; an adherent of Bolshevism. ▻ *adj* belonging or relating to Bolshevism. • **Bolshevism** *noun* the political principles and philosophy of the Bolsheviks.

bolshie or **bolshy** /ˈbɒlʃɪ/ *Brit derog colloq* ▻ *adj* (*bolshier, bolshiest*) **1** bad-tempered and unco-operative; difficult or rebellious. **2** left-wing. ▻ *noun* (*bolshies*) a Bolshevik.

bolster /ˈboʊlstə(r)/ ▻ *verb* (*bolstered, bolstering*) (*often* **bolster something up**) to support it, make it stronger or hold it up □ ***Winning the competition really bolstered his confidence.*** ▻ *noun* **1** a long narrow, sometimes cylindrical, pillow. **2** any pad or support. **3** *building* a form of cold chisel, used in cutting stone slabs, etc. ⓒ Anglo-Saxon.

bolt¹ /boʊlt/ ▻ *noun* **1** a bar or rod that slides into a hole or socket to fasten a door or gate, etc. **2** a small thick round bar of metal, with a screw thread, used with a NUT to fasten things together. **3** a sudden movement or dash away, especially to escape from someone or something □ ***make a bolt for it.*** **4** a flash of lightning. **5** a short arrow fired from a crossbow. **6** a roll of cloth. ▻ *verb* (*bolted, bolting*) **1** to fasten (a door or window, etc) with a bolt. **2** to fasten together with bolts. **3** to eat (a meal, etc) very quickly. **4** *intr* to run or dash away suddenly and quickly. **5** *intr* said of a horse: to run away out of control. **6** *intr* said of a plant: to flower and produce seeds too early, usually in response to low temperatures. **7** *bot* said of a biennial: to behave like an annual. • **a bolt from the blue** a sudden, completely unexpected and usually unpleasant, event. ⓒ 19c: ie comparable to a thunderbolt coming out of a clear blue sky. • **bolt upright** absolutely straight and stiff. • **have shot one's bolt** to have made a last attempt to do something but to have failed. ⓒ 17c: like an archer who has only one bolt or arrow and is defenceless and unable to do more once he has fired it. ⓒ Anglo-Saxon.

bolt² or **boult** /boʊlt/ ▻ *verb* (*bolted, bolting; boulted, boulting*) **1** to pass (flour, etc) through a sieve. **2** to examine, sift or investigate. ⓒ 13c: from French *bulter.*

bolthole ▻ *noun, Brit colloq* **1** a refuge from danger; a secluded private place to hide away in. **2** a secret escape route or other means of escape. ⓒ 19c: from BOLT¹ *verb* 4.

bolus /ˈboʊləs/ ▻ *noun* (*boluses*) *technical, especially medicine* **1** a soft rounded mass, especially of chewed food. **2 a** a large pill; **b** a drug dose that is injected rapidly into a blood vessel. ⓒ 17c: Latin, from Greek *bolos* a lump.

bomb /bɒm/ ▻ *noun* **1** a hollow case or other device containing a substance capable of causing an explosion, fire or smoke, etc. See also LETTER BOMB, TIME BOMB. **2** (**the bomb**) the atomic bomb, or nuclear weapons collectively. **3** (**a bomb**) *Brit colloq* a lot of money. See also *go down like a bomb, go like a bomb, make a bomb* below. **4** *N Amer colloq* a failure, flop or fiasco □ ***The film was a bomb.*** **5** *Austral & NZ colloq* an old worn-out car. **6** *Amer football* a long pass. **7** *computing* a piece of programming, inserted into software, that can be activated to sabotage the system. **8** (*also* **volcanic bomb**) *geol* a rounded mass of lava thrown out by a volcano and hardened into volcanic rock. ▻ *verb* (*bombed, bombing*) **1** to attack or damage, etc with a bomb or bombs. **2** (*especially* **bomb along** or **off,** *etc*) *intr, colloq* to move or drive quickly □ ***bombing along the road.*** **3** *intr, N Amer colloq* to fail or flop badly. • **bomber** see separate entry. • **bombing** *noun.* • **go down like a bomb** or **go down a bomb** *colloq, chiefly Brit* to be a great success; to be received enthusiastically. • **go like a bomb** *colloq, chiefly Brit* **1** to move very quickly. **2** to go or sell, etc extremely well; to be very successful. • **make a bomb** *Brit colloq* to make or earn a great deal of money. ⓒ 17c: probably ultimately from Greek *bombos* a humming sound.

bombard /bɒmˈbɑːd/ ▻ *verb* (*bombarded, bombarding*) **1** to attack (a place, target, etc) with large, heavy guns or bombs. **2** to direct questions or abuse at someone very quickly and without stopping. **3** to batter or pelt something or someone heavily and persistently. **4** *physics* to subject (a target, especially an atom) to a stream of high-energy particles. • **bombardment** *noun.* ⓒ 16c, meaning 'to fire or attack with a *bombard*' (an early type of cannon for throwing stones).

bombardier /bɒmbəˈdɪə(r)/ ▻ *noun* **1** *Brit* a non-commissioned officer in the Royal Artillery. **2** the member of a bomber aircraft's crew who aims and releases the bombs. ⓒ 16c, meaning 'artillery-man': French.

bombast /ˈbɒmbast/ ▻ *noun* pretentious, boastful or insincere words having little real force or meaning. • **bombastic** /bɒmˈbastɪk/ *adj* said of language, etc: sounding impressive but insincere or meaningless. • **bombastically** *adverb*. ⓒ 16c, originally meaning 'cotton padding or wadding': ultimately from Greek *bombyx* silk.

Bombay duck ▻ *noun* a slender-bodied fish with large jaws and barb-like teeth, which is found in the tropical Indian Ocean and is an important food fish, often eaten dried with curry.

bomb calorimeter ▻ *noun, chem* an apparatus used to determine the amount of heat energy (often expressed as calories) released during the complete combustion of a fuel or food, etc.

bomb disposal ▻ *noun* the act, process or technique of removing unexploded bombs and detonating them or making them safe, as carried out by specially trained bomb squads.

bombe /bɒm; *French* bɔ̃b/ ▻ *noun, cookery* a dessert, usually ice cream, frozen in a round or melon-shaped mould. ⓒ 19c: French, meaning 'bomb'.

bombed ▻ *adj* (*also* **bombed out**) *slang* very drunk or high on drugs; stoned. ⓒ 1960s.

bomber /ˈbɒmə(r)/ ▻ *noun* **1** an aeroplane designed for carrying and dropping bombs. **2** a person who bombs something or who plants bombs. **3** *slang* a large strong cannabis joint. **4** *slang* an amphetamine capsule.

bomber jacket ▻ *noun* **1** a short jacket, usually with a zipped front and gathered in at the waist. **2** a thick leather jacket of this style as worn by British and American bomber pilots in World War II.

bombing run see RUN (*noun* 17)

bombora /bɒmˈbɔːrə/ ▻ *noun* (***bomboras***) *Austral, NZ* **1** a submerged reef. **2** a dangerous current or rough sea over such a reef. ⓒ 1930s: Aboriginal.

bomb scare and **bomb threat** ▻ *noun* **a** an incident in which a warning is received that a bomb or bombs have been planted in a certain location; **b** a state of alert or activity resulting from such a warning.

bombshell ▻ *noun* **1** a piece of surprising and usually disappointing or devastating news. **2** *colloq* a stunningly attractive woman. **3** *especially formerly* an artillery bomb.

bombsight ▻ *noun* a device for aiming and releasing bombs from an aeroplane.

bombsite ▻ *noun* **1** an area where buildings, etc have been destroyed by a bomb or an air-raid. **2** *colloq* an area of devastation; a chaotically untidy place.

bomb squad and **bomb disposal squad** ▻ *noun* a group of soldiers or police officers specially trained in BOMB DISPOSAL.

bona fide /ˈbounə ˈfaɪdɪ/ ▻ *adj* genuine or sincere; done or carried out in good faith ▫ ***a bona fide offer.*** ▻ *adverb* genuinely or sincerely; in good faith. ⓒ 16c as *adverb*: Latin.

bonanza /bəˈnanzə/ ▻ *noun* (***bonanzas***) **1** an unexpected and sudden source of good luck or wealth. **2** a large amount, especially of gold from a mine. **3** *N Amer* a rich mine or vein of precious ore such as gold or silver. ⓒ 19c: Spanish, literally 'calm sea'.

bonbon /ˈbɒnbɒn/ ▻ *noun* a sweet, especially a fancy chocolate- or sugar-coated piece of confectionery. ⓒ 18c: French, literally 'good-good', originally used by children.

bonce /bɒns/ ▻ *noun, Brit slang* the head. ⓒ 19c, at first meaning 'a large marble'.

bond ▻ *noun* **1** something used for tying, binding or holding. **2** (*usually* **bonds**) something which restrains or imprisons someone. **3** something that unites or joins people together ▫ ***a bond of friendship.*** **4** a binding agreement or promise. **5** *finance* a DEBENTURE. **6** *law* a written agreement to pay money or carry out the terms of a contract. **7** *chem* the strong force of attraction that holds together two atoms in a molecule or a crystalline salt; a chemical bond. **8** *building* the overlapping arrangement of one course of stones or bricks with another. ▻ *verb* (***bonded, bonding***) **1** to join, secure or tie together. **2** *intr* to hold or stick together securely. **3** *intr* said especially of a mother and newborn baby: to form a strong emotional attachment. **4** to put (goods) into a BONDED WAREHOUSE. • **bonding** *noun*. • **in** or **out of bond** said of goods: held in or out of a BONDED WAREHOUSE. ⓒ 13c: from Norse *band*.

bondage /ˈbɒndɪdʒ/ ▻ *noun* **1** slavery. **2** the state of being confined or imprisoned, etc; captivity. **3** a sadomasochistic sexual practice in which one partner is physically restrained with eg ropes, handcuffs or chains. ▻ *adj* said of clothes and accessories, specifically ones made of black leather: having chains, metal studs, buckles or similar aggressive-looking features, eg as worn by PUNKS (*noun* sense 2). ⓒ 14c: from Latin *bondagium*.

bonded warehouse ▻ *noun* a building in which goods are kept until customs or other duty on them is paid.

bond energy ▻ *noun, chem* the energy released or absorbed during the formation of a chemical bond.

bondholder ▻ *noun* a person who holds a bond or bonds issued by a public company, government or private person.

bond paper ▻ *noun* a type of very good quality writing paper. ⓒ 19c: so called because it was the kind used for bonds and similar documents.

bone /boun/ ▻ *noun* **1** the hard dense tissue that forms the skeleton of vertebrates, providing structural support for the body and serving as an attachment for muscles. **2** any of the components of the skeleton, made of this material. **3** (**bones**) the skeleton. **4** (*chiefly* **one's bones**) the body as the place where feelings or instincts come from ▫ ***I feel in my bones something is wrong.*** **5** a substance similar to human bone, such as ivory and whalebone, etc. **6** (**bones**) the basic or essential part. ▻ *verb* (***boned, boning***) **1** to take bone out of (meat, etc). **2** to make (a piece of clothing, eg a corset or bodice) stiff by adding strips of bone or some other hard substance. • **boned** *adj* **1** having bones. **2** said of meat, etc: having the bones removed. • **boneless** *adj* lacking bones; having the bones removed. • **have a bone to pick with someone** to have something to disagree or argue about with them. • **make no bones about something** **1** to admit or allow it without any fuss, bother or hesitation. **2** to be quite willing to say or do it openly. • **near** or **close to the bone** *colloq* said of speech, etc: **1** referring too closely to a subject which it would have been kind or tactful to avoid; upsettingly pointed or critical. **2** rather indecent or risqué. • **to the bone** **1** thoroughly and completely ▫ ***I was chilled to the bone.*** **2** to the minimum ▫ ***cut my living expenses to the bone.*** • **work one's fingers to the bone** to work very hard, until one is worn out. ⓒ Anglo-Saxon *ban*.

■ **bone up on something** *colloq* to learn or collect information about (a subject).

bone china ▻ *noun* a type of fine china or PORCELAIN made from clay mixed with ash from bones burnt in air, known as **bone ash**.

bone-dry ▻ *adj* completely dry; as dry as a bone.

bonehead ▻ *noun, slang* a stupid person; a blockhead. • **bone-headed** *adj*.

bone-idle ▻ *adj, colloq* utterly lazy.

bone marrow see MARROW 1

bone meal ▻ *noun* dried and ground bones, used as a plant fertilizer and as a supplement to animal feed.

bone of contention ▻ *noun* a point or subject over which there is argument or disagreement.

boner ▻ *noun, slang* **1** a blunder or howler. **2** *coarse* an erection of the penis.

boneshaker ▷ *noun, colloq* an old uncomfortable and unsteady vehicle, especially an early type of bicycle.

bonfire /ˈbɒnfaɪə(r)/ ▷ *noun* a large outdoor fire, for burning garden refuse, etc, or burned as a signal or as part of a celebration, eg on **Bonfire night** (see GUY FAWKES DAY). ⓒ 15c as *bonefire*, from BONE + FIRE: bones were formerly used as fuel.

bong /bɒŋ/ ▷ *noun* a long deep sound such as is made by a large bell. ▷ *verb* (***bonged, bonging***) *intr* to make such a sound. ⓒ 19c: imitating the sound.

bongo /ˈbɒŋgoʊ/ ▷ *noun* (***bongos*** or ***bongoes***) each of a pair of small, usually connected, drums held between the knees and played with the hands. Also called **bongo drum**. ⓒ 1920s: from American Spanish *bongó*; bongos originated in Cuba.

bonhomie /ˈbɒnɒmiː/ ▷ *noun* easy good nature; cheerful friendliness. ⓒ 19c: French, from *bon* good + *homme* man.

boniness see under BONY

bonk /bɒŋk/ ▷ *verb* (***bonked, bonking***) *tr & intr* **1** to bang or hit something. **2** *coarse slang* **a** to have sexual intercourse with someone ◻ *He's been bonking her for months*; **b** *intr* to have sexual intercourse. ▷ *noun* **1** the act of banging; a blow or thump. **2** *coarse slang* an act of sexual intercourse. ⓒ 1970s in sense 2; 1930s: imitating the sound.

bonkers /ˈbɒŋkəz/ ▷ *adj, chiefly Brit slang* mad or crazy. ⓒ 1940s, at first meaning 'slightly drunk'.

bon mot /bɔ̃ˈmoʊ/ ▷ *noun* (***bons mots*** /bɔ̃ˈmoʊ/) a short clever remark; a witticism. ⓒ 18c: French, literally 'good word'.

bonnet /ˈbɒnɪt/ ▷ *noun* **1** a type of hat fastened under the chin with ribbon, formerly worn by women but now worn especially by babies. **2** *Brit* the hinged cover over a motor vehicle's engine. *N Amer equivalent* HOOD. **3** *Scottish* a brimless cap made of soft fabric, worn by men or boys. **4** *naut* an additional part laced on to the foot of a JIB[1], etc to gather more wind. **5** a wire cowl over a chimney-top. ⓒ 14c as *bonet*: French.

bonny /ˈbɒnɪ/ ▷ *adj* (***bonnier, bonniest***) **1** *chiefly Scottish & N Eng* attractive; pretty. **2** looking very healthy and attractive, especially attractively plump. • **bonnily** *adverb*. ⓒ 15c: presumed to be from or related to French *bon* good.

bonsai /ˈbɒnsaɪ/ ▷ *noun* (*plural* ***bonsai***) **1** the ancient Japanese art of cultivating artificially miniaturized trees in small containers, by pruning the roots and shoots regularly and using wires to bend the branches to the desired shape. **2** a miniature tree cultivated in this way, eg pine, Japanese maple, cherry. ⓒ 1920s: Japanese, from *bon* tray or bowl + *sai* cultivation.

bontebok /ˈbɒntəbɒk/ ▷ *noun* a S African antelope, very similar to the BLESBOK, its coat having several shades of brown with white blaze, legs, rump and belly. ⓒ 18c: Afrikaans, from Dutch *bont* particoloured + *bok* goat.

bonus /ˈboʊnəs/ ▷ *noun* (***bonuses***) **1** an extra sum of money given on top of what is due as wages, interest or dividend, etc. **2** an unexpected extra benefit gained or given with something else. **3** *insurance* an additional sum of money payable to the holder of a policy when it matures. ⓒ 18c: Latin, meaning 'good'.

bonus issue ▷ *noun, finance* an issue of additional shares (**bonus shares**) to a company's shareholders in proportion to their existing shareholding, representing the conversion of reserves into capital.

bon vivant /*French* bɔ̃vivɑ̃/ ▷ *noun* (***bons*** or ***bon vivants*** /*French* bɔ̃vivɑ̃/) a person who enjoys good food and wine, or the good things of life generally. Also **bon viveur** (***bons*** or ***bon viveurs***) /bɔ̃viːvɜː/. ⓒ 17c: French, literally 'a good-living (person)'; *bon viveur* is a 19c English invention.

bon voyage /*French* bɔ̃vwajaʒ/ ▷ *exclamation* said to a person about to travel: expressing good wishes for a safe and pleasant journey. ⓒ 15c: French, literally 'good journey'.

bony /ˈboʊnɪ/ ▷ *adj* (***bonier, boniest***) **1** consisting of, made of or like bone. **2** full of bones. **3** said of a person or animal: thin, so that the bones are very noticeable. • **boniness** *noun*.

boo ▷ *exclamation, noun* (***boos***) a sound expressing disapproval, or made when trying to frighten or surprise someone. ▷ *verb* (***booed, booing***) *tr & intr* to shout 'boo' to express disapproval ◻ *The audience booed him off the stage*. • **he**, *etc* **can't, couldn't** or **wouldn't say boo to a goose** he, *etc* is very shy or easily frightened. ⓒ 19c.

boob[1] ▷ *noun, colloq* **1** (*also* **booboo**) a stupid or foolish mistake; a blunder. **2** *especially N Amer* a stupid or foolish person; a booby. ▷ *verb* (***boobed, boobing***) *intr, colloq* to make a stupid or foolish mistake. ⓒ Early 20c: short for BOOBY.

boob[2] ▷ *noun, slang* a woman's breast. ⓒ 1940s (originally US): short for *booby*, from the obsolete English word *bubby*.

boob tube ▷ *noun, slang* **1** a woman's tight-fitting garment made of stretch fabric covering the torso from midriff to armpit. **2** *N Amer* a TV set.

booby /ˈbuːbɪ/ ▷ *noun* (***boobies***) **1** any of various large tropical seabirds of the gannet family which have white plumage with dark markings, long powerful wings, a large head and a colourful conical bill. **2** *old use, colloq* a stupid or foolish person. ⓒ 17c in sense 2: probably from Spanish *bobo* a dolt.

booby prize ▷ *noun* a prize (usually a joke prize) for the lowest score, or for the person coming last, etc in a competition.

booby trap ▷ *noun* **1** a bomb or mine which is disguised so that it is set off by the victim. **2 a** something placed as a trap, eg a bucket of water, some books or a bag of flour, put on top of a door so as to fall on the person who opens the door; **b** a practical joke in which the victim is surprised by such a booby trap. ▷ *verb* (**booby-trap**) to put a booby trap in or on (a place). ⓒ 19c: from BOOBY.

boodle /ˈbuːdəl/ ▷ *noun, dated slang* money, especially money gained dishonestly or as a bribe, or counterfeit. ⓒ 19c: from Dutch *boedel* possessions.

boogie /ˈbuːgɪ/ *colloq* ▷ *verb* (***boogied, boogieing*** or ***boogying***) *intr* to dance to pop, rock or jazz music. ▷ *noun* **1** a dance, or dancing, to pop, rock or jazz music. **2** BOOGIE-WOOGIE or rock music with a repetitive rhythmic bass like boogie-woogie. ⓒ 1940s as *noun*.

boogie-woogie /ˈbuːgɪˈwuːgɪ/ ▷ *noun, music, originally US* a style of jazz piano music with a constantly repeated, strongly rhythmic bass, and melodic variations above. ⓒ Early 20c: a reduplication of old US slang *boogie* a Negro performer.

boo-hoo /buːˈhuː/ ▷ *exclamation, noun* (***boo-hoos***) the sound of noisy weeping. ▷ *verb* (***boo-hooed, boo-hooing***) *intr* to weep noisily. ⓒ 16c (19c as *verb*): imitating the sound.

book /bʊk/ ▷ *noun* **1** a number of printed pages bound together along one edge and protected by covers. **2** a piece of written work intended for publication, eg a novel, reference work, instruction manual, etc. **3** a number of sheets of blank paper bound together. Often *in compounds* ◻ *exercise book* ◻ *autograph book*. **4** (*usually* **the books**) a record or formal accounts of the business done by a company, society, etc. **5** a record of bets made with different people ◻ *kept a book on whether it would snow*. **6** (**the book**) *colloq* the current telephone directory. **7** (*usually* **Book**) a major division of a long literary work ◻ *Book IX of Paradise Lost*. **8** a number of stamps, matches or cheques, etc bound together. **9** (**the book**) an authoritative definitive source of information, instruction or accepted wisdom, etc on a given subject ◻ ***tried every trick in the book to get the car started.*** **10** (*usually* **the Book**) the Bible. **11** the words of an opera or musical. ▷ *verb* (***booked, booking***) **1** *tr & intr* to reserve (a ticket, seat, etc), or engage (a person's services) in advance ◻ ***Have you booked, sir?*** **2** said of a police officer, traffic warden, etc: to record the details of (a person who is being charged with an offence). **3** *football* said of a referee: to enter (a player's name) in a notebook as a record of an offence or serious violation of the rules. **4** to enter (a person's name, etc) in a book or list. ● **be in someone's good** or **bad books** to be in or out of favour with them. ● **be booked up** to have no more places or tickets available. ● **bring someone to book** to punish them or make them account for their behaviour. ● **by the book** strictly according to the rules ◻ ***I played it by the book and didn't take any chances.*** ● **in my book** in my opinion ◻ ***That amounts to cheating, in my book.*** ● **on the books** officially listed as a member, customer, etc. ● **suit someone's book** to be what they want or like. ● **take a leaf out of someone's book** to benefit from their example. ● **throw the book at someone** see under THROW. ⓘ Anglo-Saxon *boc*.

■ **book in** *especially Brit* **1** to sign one's name on the list of guests at a hotel. **2** to report one's arrival at a hotel or conference reception desk, airport CHECK-IN, etc. *N Amer equivalent* CHECK IN.

■ **book someone in** to reserve a place or room for them in a hotel, etc. *N Amer equivalent* CHECK IN, CHECK SOMEONE IN.

■ **book something up** to fix and reserve in advance the tickets and other arrangements for (a holiday, show, meal, etc).

bookable ▷ *adj* **1** said of seats for a performance, etc: able to be booked or reserved in advance. **2** said of an offence: liable to cause the offender to be charged.

bookbinder ▷ *noun* a person or business that binds books (see BIND *verb* 6). ● **bookbinding** *noun* the art or business of binding books.

bookcase ▷ *noun* a piece of furniture with shelves for books.

book club ▷ *noun* a club which sells books to its members at reduced prices and generally by mail order.

booked-up and **booked-out** ▷ *adj* said of a performance, restaurant, holiday, etc: full up or fully booked; unable to accept further reservations, bookings or appointments.

book end ▷ *noun* each of a pair of supports used to keep a row of books standing upright.

bookie ▷ *noun, mainly Brit colloq* a bookmaker.

booking ▷ *noun* **1** a reservation of a theatre seat, hotel room, seat on a plane or train, etc. **2** especially in sport: the recording of an offence with details of the offender. **3** an engagement for the services of a person or company, especially for a theatrical or musical performance, etc.

booking office ▷ *noun* an office where reservations are made or tickets sold, at a railway station, theatre, concert hall, etc.

bookish ▷ *adj, often derog* **1** extremely fond of reading and books. **2** learned and serious; having knowledge or opinions based on books rather than practical experience. ● **bookishness** *noun*.

bookkeeper ▷ *noun* a person who keeps a record of the financial transactions of a business or organization, etc. ● **bookkeeping** *noun* the practice or skill of keeping financial accounts (see ACCOUNT *noun* 5) in a regular and systematic manner. ⓘ 16c.

booklet ▷ *noun* a small book or pamphlet with a paper cover.

bookmaker ▷ *noun, mainly Brit* (often shortened to **bookie**). **1** a person whose job is to take bets on horse-races, etc and pay out winnings. **2** *colloq* a shop or premises used by a bookmaker for taking bets, etc. Also called **turf accountant**. ● **bookmaking** *noun*. ⓘ 19c; 16c, in the sense 'someone who makes books'.

bookmark and *sometimes* **bookmarker** ▷ *noun* a strip of leather, card, etc put in a book to mark a particular page, especially the reader's current place in the book.

bookmobile /bʊkməˈbiːl/ ▷ *noun, N Amer* a mobile library.

book of hours ▷ *noun* an often illustrated book containing the services and prayers used in the CANONICAL HOURS.

bookplate ▷ *noun* a piece of decorated paper stuck into the front of a book and bearing the owner's name, etc.

book price and **book value** ▷ *noun* the officially-recorded value of a commodity, which is not necessarily the market value.

bookseller ▷ *noun* a person who sells books as their profession.

bookshelf ▷ *noun* a shelf for standing books on.

bookshop and *US* **bookstore** ▷ *noun* a shop where books are sold.

bookstall ▷ *noun* a small shop in a station, etc where books, newspapers, magazines, etc are sold. Also called BOOKSTAND.

bookstand ▷ *noun* **1** a bookstall. **2** a stand or support for holding a book while reading.

book token ▷ *noun* a voucher worth a specified amount of money which can be used to buy books, usually placed in a card and given as a gift.

book value see BOOK PRICE

bookworm ▷ *noun* **1** *colloq* a person who is extremely fond of reading. **2** a type of small insect which feeds on the paper and glue used in books.

Boolean algebra /ˈbuːlɪən —/ ▷ *noun* a form of algebra, used to work out the logic for computer programs, that uses algebraic symbols and set theory to represent logic operations.

boom¹ ▷ *noun* a deep resounding sound, like that made by a large drum or gun. ▷ *verb* (***boomed, booming***) *intr* to make a deep resounding sound. ⓘ 15c as *verb*: probably imitating the sound.

■ **boom something out** to say it in a loud booming voice.

boom² ▷ *noun* **1** a sudden increase or growth in business, prosperity, activity, etc. **2** a period of such rapid growth or activity, etc. ▷ *verb* (***boomed, booming***) *intr* **1** said especially of a business: to become rapidly and suddenly prosperous, active or busy. **2** said of a commodity, etc: to increase sharply in value. ⓘ 19c, originally US: perhaps from BOOM¹.

boom³ ▷ *noun* **1** *naut* a pole to which the bottom of a ship's sail is attached, keeping the sail stretched tight. **2** a heavy pole or chain, or a barrier of floating logs, etc across the entrance to a harbour or across a river. **3** *cinema, TV, etc* a long pole with a microphone, camera or light attached to one end, allowing it to be held above the heads of people being filmed. ⓘ 17c: Dutch, meaning 'beam' or 'pole'.

boomerang /ˈbuːməraŋ/ ▷ *noun* **1** a piece of flat curved wood used by Australian Aborigines for hunting, often so balanced that, when thrown to a distance, it returns towards the person who threw it. **2** a malicious act or statement which harms the perpetrator rather than the intended victim. ▷ *verb* (***boomeranged, boomeranging***) *intr* said of an act or statement, etc: to go wrong and harm the perpetrator rather than the intended victim; to recoil or rebound. ⓘ 19c: from Dharuk (Australian Aboriginal language) *bumariny*.

boom town ▷ *noun* a town which has expanded rapidly and prospered, eg because of the arrival of a valuable new industry.

boon¹ ▷ *noun* **1** an advantage, benefit or blessing; something to be thankful for. **2** *old use* a gift or favour. ⓔ 12c: from Norse *bon* a prayer.

boon² ▷ *adj* close, convivial, intimate or favourite □ *a boon companion.* ⓔ 14c: from French *bon* good.

boondocks /'buːndɒks/ ▷ *plural noun* (*usually* **the boondocks**, often shortened to **the boonies**) *N Amer colloq* **1** wild or remote country. **2** a dull provincial or rural place. Compare THE STICKS. ⓔ 19s, first used by US soldiers returned from the Philippines: from Tagàlog *bundok* mountain.

boor /bʊə(r), bɔː(r)/ ▷ *noun, derog* a coarse person with bad manners. ⓔ 15c, meaning 'peasant': from Dutch *boer* farmer or peasant.

> ***boor***
>
> There is sometimes a spelling confusion between **boor** and **boar**.

boorish ▷ *adj* said of a person, or a person's manner: coarse, rough or rude. • **boorishly** *adverb.* • **boorishness** *noun.* ⓔ 16c.

boost ▷ *verb* (**boosted**, **boosting**) **1** to improve or encourage something or someone □ ***boost the spirits.*** **2** to make something greater or increase it; to raise □ ***boost profits*** □ ***boosted the power input.*** **3** to promote something by advertising. **4** *aerospace* to push (a spacecraft) into orbit by means of a BOOSTER (sense 3). ▷ *noun* **1** a piece of help or encouragement, etc. **2** a push upwards. **3** a rise or increase □ ***a boost in sales.*** ⓔ 19c, originally US.

booster ▷ *noun* **1** a person or thing that boosts. **2** (*also* **booster shot**) a dose of vaccine that is given in order to renew or increase the immune response to a previous dose of the same vaccine. **3** *aerospace* an engine in a rocket that provides additional thrust at some stage of the vehicle's flight. **4** (*also* **booster rocket**) a rocket that is used to launch a space vehicle, before another engine takes over. **5** *electronics* a radio-frequency amplifier that is used to amplify a weak TV or radio signal, and to rebroadcast such a signal so that it can be received by the general public. **6** any device to increase the effect of another mechanism. **7** *US* a keen supporter or promoter. **8** *US slang* a shoplifter.

boot¹ ▷ *noun* **1** an outer covering, made of leather or rubber, etc, for the foot and lower part of the leg. **2** *Brit* a compartment for luggage in a car, usually at the back. *N Amer equivalent* TRUNK. **3** *colloq* a hard kick. **4** (**the boot**) *colloq* dismissal from a job; the sack. **5** *historical* an instrument of torture used on the leg and foot. ▷ *verb* (**booted**, **booting**) **1** to kick. **2** (*usually* **boot someone** or **something out**) to throw them or it out, or remove them or it by force; **3** (*often* **boot something up**) *computing* to start or restart (a computer) by loading the programs which control its basic functions; to BOOTSTRAP it. **4** to put boots on someone. • **bootable** *adj, computing* able to be booted (*verb* 3). • **boots and all** *Austral, NZ* without reservation; all-out. • **put the boot in** *colloq* **1** to kick viciously. **2** to deliver further humiliation, hurt, torment, etc. • **the boot is on the other foot** or **leg** *colloq* the situation is now the reverse of what it was before, especially as regards advantage or responsibility, etc. ⓔ 14c: from French *bote.*

> ■ **boot someone out** to dismiss them from their job or home, etc.

boot² • **to boot** as well; in addition. ⓔ Anglo-Saxon *bot* an advantage or help.

bootee /buː'tiː,'buːtiː/ ▷ *noun* (**bootees**) **1** a soft knitted boot for a baby. **2** a short boot, such as a woman's ankle-length boot.

booth /buːð, buːθ/ ▷ *noun* (**booths**) **1** a small temporary roofed structure or tent, especially a covered stall at a fair or market. **2** a small partly-enclosed compartment, eg one in a restaurant containing a table and seating, or one intended for a specific purpose. Often *in compounds* □ ***polling booth*** □ ***telephone booth.*** ⓔ 13c, meaning 'a temporary dwelling': from Norse *buth.*

boot-jack ▷ *noun* a device which grips the heel of a boot, allowing the foot to be easily withdrawn.

bootlace ▷ *noun* a piece of cord, string or ribbon, etc used to tie up a boot.

bootlace tie ▷ *noun* a very thin stringlike necktie.

bootleg ▷ *verb* (**bootlegged**, **bootlegging**) **1** to make, sell or transport (alcoholic drink) illegally, especially in a time of prohibition. **2** to make or deal in (illicit goods such as unofficial recordings of copyright music). ▷ *noun* **1** illegally produced, sold or transported goods, especially alcoholic drink or recorded material. **2** the leg of a high boot. • **bootlegger** *noun.* • **bootlegging** *noun.* ⓔ 19c; 17c as *noun* 2: a *bootlegger* would conceal bottles of illegal liquor in his bootlegs.

bootless ▷ *adj, literary* useless; vain; unprofitable. ⓔ Anglo-Saxon, meaning 'without compensation'.

bootlicker ▷ *noun, colloq* a person who tries to gain the favour of someone in authority by flattery, excessive obedience, etc; a crawler or toady. • **bootlicking** *noun.* ⓔ 19c.

boots ▷ *noun, old use* a male employee at a hotel who carries guests' luggage, cleans their shoes, runs messages, etc. ⓔ 18c, from earlier *boot-catcher* someone who pulled off guests' boots.

boot sale see CAR BOOT SALE

bootstrap *computing* ▷ *noun* a short program used to boot up a computer by transferring the disk-operating system's program from storage on disk into a computer's working memory. ▷ *verb* to boot up (a computer) by activating the bootstrap program. • **pull oneself up by one's bootstraps** to get on by one's own efforts.

booty ▷ *noun* (**booties**) valuable goods taken in wartime or by force; plunder. ⓔ 15c *botye*: from Norse *byti*, from *byta* to divide.

booze *slang* ▷ *noun* **1** alcoholic drink. **2** a drinking session (also called BOOZE-UP). ▷ *verb* (**boozed**, **boozing**) *intr* to drink a lot of alcohol, or too much of it. • **on the booze** indulging in a bout of hard drinking. ⓔ 14c as *verb*: from Dutch *busen* to drink to excess.

boozer ▷ *noun, slang* **1** *Brit, Austral & NZ* a public house or bar. **2** a person who drinks a lot of alcohol.

booze-up ▷ *noun, Brit, Austral & NZ slang* a drinking-bout or an occasion when a lot of alcohol is drunk.

boozy ▷ *adj* (**boozier**, **booziest**) *slang* **1** said of an occasion, etc: including or entailing a lot of boozing; drunken. **2** said of a person: inclined to drink a lot of alcohol. • **boozily** *adverb.*

bop¹ *colloq* ▷ *verb* (**bopped**, **bopping**) *intr* to dance to popular music. ▷ *noun* **1** a dance to popular music. **2** BEBOP. • **bopper** *noun.* ⓔ 1940s, shortened from BEBOP.

bop² ▷ *colloq, often humorous verb* (**bopped**, **bopping**) to hit □ ***bopped him on the head with a saucepan.*** ▷ *noun* a blow or knock. ⓔ 1930s: imitating the sound.

boracic see BORIC

boracic acid see BORIC ACID

borage /'bɒrɪdʒ, 'bʌrɪdʒ/ ▷ *noun* an annual European plant with oval hairy leaves and small bright-blue star-shaped flowers, now widely cultivated as a herb for use in salads and medicinally. ⓔ 13c: from French *bourache.*

borak or **borack** /'bɔːrak/ ▷ *noun, Austral & NZ slang* nonsense or banter. • **poke borak at someone** to make fun of them, ridicule or jeer at them. ⓔ 19c: Australian Aboriginal.

borate /ˈbɔːreɪt/ ▷ *noun* a salt or ester of BORIC ACID.

borax /ˈbɔːraks/ ▷ *noun* (**boraxes**) a colourless crystalline salt or white greasy powder, found in saline lake deposits, used in the manufacture of enamels, ceramics and heat-resistant glass, and as a cleaning agent, mild antiseptic, astringent and source of BORIC ACID. Also called **sodium borate**. ◷ 14c as *boras*: from Latin *borax*, ultimately from Persian *burah*.

borborygmus /bɔːbəˈrɪgməs/ ▷ *noun* (*plural* **borborygmi** /-maɪ/) *medicine* the sound made by gas and fluid moving through the intestines; rumbling in the stomach. ◷ 18c: Latin, from Greek *borboryzein* to rumble.

Bordeaux /bɔːˈdoʊ/ ▷ *noun* wine, especially claret, made in the Bordeaux region of SW France. ◷ 15c.

bordello /bɔːˈdɛloʊ/ ▷ *noun* (**bordellos**) a brothel. ◷ 16c: Italian, from French *bordel* cabin or hut.

border /ˈbɔːdə(r)/ ▷ *noun* **1** a band or margin along the edge of something. **2** the boundary of a country or political region, etc. **3** the land on either side of a country's border. See also BORDERS. **4** (**the Border**) *Brit* the boundary between England and Scotland. **5** a narrow strip of ground planted with flowers, surrounding an area of grass. **6** any decorated or ornamental edge or trimming. ▷ *adj* belonging or referring to the border, or on the border. ▷ *verb* (**bordered**, **bordering**) **1** to be a border to, adjacent to, or on the border of something □ *An industrial estate borders the town.* **2** to provide something with a border. • **bordered** *adj*. ◷ 14c as *bordure*: French, from the same root as BOARD.

■ **border on something 1** to be nearly the same as a specified quality or condition, or verge on it □ *actions bordering on stupidity.* **2** (*also* **border upon** or **with something**) to come near or be adjacent to it.

Border collie ▷ *noun* a breed of very intelligent medium-sized, usually black and white, collie dog. ◷ 1940s.

borderer ▷ *noun* a person who lives on or comes from the border area of a country.

borderland ▷ *noun* **1** land at or near a country's border. **2** the undefined margin or condition between two states, eg between sleeping and waking.

borderline ▷ *noun* **1** the border between one thing, country, etc and another. **2** a line dividing two opposing or extreme conditions □ *the borderline between passing and failing.* ▷ *adj* on the border between one thing, state, etc and another; marginal □ *a borderline result.*

Borders ▷ *plural noun* **1** (**the Borders**) the area of land lying either side of the border between Scotland and England. **2** (**the Borders**) the area of Scotland bordering on England, especially between the Border and Lothian. **3** (*also* **Borders Council**) a local administrative area of southern Scotland, comprising Tweeddale, Ettrick and Lauderdale, Berwickshire and Roxburgh.

Border terrier ▷ *noun* a breed of small rough-haired terrier, usually black and tan, originally bred in the Borders for fox-hunting. ◷ Late 19c.

bore[1] /bɔː(r)/ ▷ *verb* (**bored**, **boring**) **1** (*often* **bore a hole in something**) to make a hole in it by drilling. **2** to produce (a borehole, tunnel or mine, etc) by drilling. **3** *intr* said of a racehorse or an athlete: to push against other competitors so as to gain advantage in a race. ▷ *noun* **1** the hollow barrel of a gun, or the cavity inside any such tube. **2 a** *in compounds* the diameter of the hollow barrel of a gun, especially to show which size bullets the gun requires □ *12-bore shotgun*; **b** the diameter of the cavity inside any such tube or pipe. Also called **calibre**, **gauge**. **3** a BOREHOLE. **4** *Austral* an artesian well. ◷ Anglo-Saxon *borian*.

bore[2] /bɔː(r)/ ▷ *verb* (**bored**, **boring**) to make someone feel tired and uninterested, by being dull, tedious, uninteresting, unimaginative, etc. ▷ *noun* **1** a dull, uninteresting or tedious person or thing. **2** *colloq* something that causes a certain amount of irritation or annoyance; a nuisance. • **bored** *adj* tired and uninterested from being unoccupied or under-occupied. • **boredom** *noun* the state of being bored. • **boring** *adj* tedious and uninteresting. • **boringly** *adverb*. ◷ 18c.

bore[3] /bɔː(r)/ ▷ *noun* a solitary high wave of water resembling a wall, that moves rapidly upstream, gradually losing height, caused by constriction of the spring tide as it enters a narrow shallow estuary. ◷ 17c: from Norse *bara* a wave or swell.

bore[4] see under BEAR[1]

borehole ▷ *noun* a deep narrow hole made by boring, especially one made in the ground to find oil or water, etc.

borer ▷ *noun* **1** a machine or tool for boring holes. **2** any of various animals, especially insects such as WOODWORM, that bore into wood, etc.

boric /ˈbɔːrɪk/ and **boracic** /bɒˈrasɪk/ ▷ *adj* relating to or containing BORON.

boric acid and **boracic acid** ▷ *noun, chem* (formula H_3BO_3) a water-soluble white or colourless crystalline solid obtained from BORAX, used in pharmaceutical products, glazes, enamels, glass, detergents, adhesives, explosives, and as a food preservative.

boring[1] ▷ *noun* **1** the act of making a hole in anything. **2** a hole made by boring (also called BORE and BOREHOLE). **3** (**borings**) the chips produced by boring. ◷ 19c: from BORE[2].

boring[2] see under BORE[2]

born /bɔːn/ ▷ *adj* **1** brought into being by birth □ *five children born on the same day.* **2** having a specified quality or ability as a natural attribute □ *a born leader.* **3** (**born to something**) destined to do it □ *born to lead men.* **4** *in compounds* having a specified status by birth □ *Scots-born* □ *freeborn.* ▷ *verb, past participle of* BEAR[1]. • **in all one's born days** *colloq* in all one's lifetime or experience. • **not born yesterday** alert; shrewd; not naive or foolish.

born, borne

These words are often confused with each other.

born-again ▷ *adj* **1** filled with a new spiritual life; converted or re-converted, especially to a fundamentalist or evangelical Christian faith. **2** *colloq* showing a new and passionate enthusiasm for some particular cause, activity or lifestyle, etc □ *a born-again vegetarian.* ◷ 1960s from the biblical passage (John 3) in which Jesus states that noone can see the kingdom of God unless they are *born again*.

borne ▷ *verb* see under BEAR[1]. ▷ *adj, in compounds* carried by a specified thing □ *airborne* □ *food-borne infection.*

boron /ˈbɔːrɒn/ ▷ *noun, chem* (symbol **B**) a non-metallic element consisting of a dark brown powder or black crystals, found only in compounds, eg BORAX and BORIC ACID, and used in semiconductors and as a component of control rods and shields in nuclear reactors . ◷ 19c: from *borax* + *carbon*.

borough /ˈbʌrə/ ▷ *noun* **1** (*also* **parliamentary borough**) in England: a town or urban area represented by at least one member of Parliament. **2** *historical* in England: a town with its own municipal council and special rights and privileges granted by royal charter. See also BURGH. **3** a division of a large town, especially of London or New York, for local-government purposes. **4** in some US states: a municipal corporation. ◷ Anglo-Saxon *burg* a city or fortified town.

borrow /ˈbɒroʊ/ ▷ *verb* (**borrowed**, **borrowing**) **1** to take something temporarily, usually with permission and with the intention of returning it. **2** *intr* to get money in this way, from a bank, etc. **3** to take, adopt or copy (words or ideas, etc) from another language or person, etc □ *images borrowed from traditional Russian folklore.* **4** *intr, golf* to make allowance for slope or wind, especially by putting the ball uphill of the hole. • **borrower** *noun.* • **borrowing** *noun* something borrowed, especially a word taken from one language into another. • **borrow trouble** *US colloq* to take a particular course of action that brings oneself extra problems that would otherwise have been avoided. *British equivalent* ASK FOR TROUBLE. • **live on borrowed time** see under LIVE[1]. ⓒ Anglo-Saxon *borgian*, from *borg* a pledge or security.

borscht /bɔːʃt/, **bortsch** /bɔːtʃ/ or **borsh** /bɔːʃ/ ▻ *noun* a Russian and Polish beetroot soup, often served with sour cream. ⓒ 19c: Russian.

borstal /ˈbɔːstəl/ ▻ *noun, Brit, formerly* an institution which was both a prison and a school, to which young criminals were sent, replaced in 1983 by DETENTION CENTRES and YOUTH CUSTODY CENTRES. ⓒ Early 20c: named after Borstal in Kent, where the first of these was established.

borzoi /ˈbɔːzɔɪ/ ▻ *noun* (*borzois*) a large breed of dog with a tall slender body, a long thin muzzle, a long tail and a long soft coat, formerly used by Russian aristocrats to hunt wolves. ⓒ 19c: Russian, literally 'swift'.

Bosch process /bɒʃ —/ ▻ *noun* an industrial process whereby hydrogen is obtained by reducing steam using carbon monoxide.

bosh ▻ *noun, exclamation, colloq* nonsense; foolish talk. ⓒ 19c: from Turkish *boş* worthless or empty.

Bosnian ▻ *adj* belonging or relating to Bosnia, a republic in SE Europe, or its inhabitants. ▻ *noun* a citizen or inhabitant of, or person born in, Bosnia. ⓒ 18c.

bosom /ˈbʊzəm/ ▻ *noun* **1** a person's chest or breast, now especially that of a woman. **2** (*sometimes* **bosoms**) *colloq* a woman's breasts. **3** a loving or protective centre □ *return to the bosom of one's family.* **4** *chiefly literary* the seat of emotions and feelings; the heart. **5** the part of a dress, etc covering the breasts and chest. • **bosomy** *adj* said of a woman: having large breasts. ⓒ Anglo-Saxon *bosm*.

bosom friend and **bosom buddy** ▻ *noun* a close or intimate friend.

boson /ˈboʊzɒn, -sɒn/ ▻ *noun, physics* a category of subatomic particle, the spin of which can only take values that are whole numbers or zero. ⓒ 1940s: named after S N Bose, an Indian physicist (1894–1974).

boss[1] ▻ *noun* (*bosses*) *colloq* **1** a person who employs others, or who is in charge of others; a leader, master or manager. **2** *especially US* the person who pulls the wires in political intrigues. ▻ *verb* (*bosses, bossed, bossing*) *colloq* **1** (*especially* **boss someone about** or **around**) to give them orders in a domineering way **2** to manage or control someone. ▻ *adj* **1** *US slang* excellent; great. **2** said of a person: chief. ⓒ 17c, originally US: from Dutch *baas* master.

boss[2] ▻ *noun* (*bosses*) **1** a round raised knob or stud on a shield, etc, usually for decoration. **2** *archit* a round raised decorative knob found where the ribs meet in a vaulted ceiling. **3** *mech* a thickened part of a shaft, to allow the attachment of other parts, or for strengthening. ▻ *verb* (*bosses, bossed, bossing*) to ornament something with bosses. • **bossed** *adj* embossed, or ornamented with bosses. ⓒ 14c: from French *boce*.

bossa nova /ˈbɒsə ˈnoʊvə/ ▻ *noun* (*bossa novas*) **1** a dance like the SAMBA, originally from Brazil. **2** music for this dance. ⓒ 1960s: Portuguese, from *bossa* trend + *nova* new.

boss-eyed ▻ *adj, Brit colloq* **1** having only one good eye. **2** cross-eyed. **3** crooked; squint. ⓒ 19c: from the dialect and slang word *boss* a mistake or bungle.

bossy ▻ *adj* (*bossier, bossiest*) *colloq* inclined (especially over-inclined) to give orders like a BOSS[1]; disagreeably domineering. • **bossily** *adverb.* • **bossiness** *noun.*

bossy-boots ▻ *noun* (*plural* **bossy-boots**) *colloq* a bossy domineering person.

bosun see BOATSWAIN

bot[1] or **bott** ▻ *noun* **1** the maggot of a BOTFLY, which lives as a parasite under the skin of the horse, sheep and other animals. **2** the diseased condition in horses and sheep, etc caused by this. ⓒ 15c.

bot[2] *Austral colloq* ▻ *noun* a cadger; a person who habitually sponges off others. ▻ *verb* (*botted, botting*) *tr & intr* to cadge. • **on the bot** cadging; on the scrounge. ⓒ 1930s from BOT[1], the parasite.

bot. ▻ *abbreviation* **1** botanical. **2** botany. **3** bottle.

botanic /bəˈtanɪk/ and **botanical** ▻ *adj* relating to BOTANY or plants. • **botanically** *adverb.* ⓒ 17c: ultimately from Greek *botanikos*, from *botane* a plant or herb.

botanic garden and **botanical garden** ▻ *noun* a garden in which an extremely diverse collection of plants, unlikely to be encountered together naturally, is developed and maintained for educational, scientific and conservation purposes.

botanist /ˈbɒtənɪst/ ▻ *noun* a person who specializes in, or has a detailed knowledge of, BOTANY.

botany /ˈbɒtənɪ/ ▻ *noun* (*botanies*) **1** the branch of biology concerned with the scientific study of plants, including their structure, function, ecology, evolution and classification. **2** the properties displayed by a specific plant group or plant community. ⓒ 17c: a back-formation from BOTANIC.

botch *colloq* ▻ *verb* (**botches, botched, botching**) (*especially* **botch something up**) **1** to do something badly and unskilfully; to make a mess or bad job of something. **2** to repair something carelessly or badly. ▻ *noun* (*botches*) (also **botch-up**) a badly or carelessly done piece of work, repair, etc. • **botched** *adj.* • **botcher** *noun.* • **botchy** *adj.* ⓒ 16c in current *verb* senses;14c as *bocchen*, meaning 'to patch'.

botfly or **bot fly** ▻ *noun* any of various two-winged insects, the larvae of which are parasitic on mammals, especially horses and sheep. See BOT[1].

both /boʊθ/ ▻ *adj, pronoun* (*sometimes* **both of something**) the two; the one and the other □ *She burnt both hands on the stove* □ *I'd like you both to help.* ▻ *adverb* as well. • **both something and something** not only one specified thing but also another specified thing □ *He is both rude and ignorant.* ⓒ 12c: from Norse *bathir*.

bother /ˈbɒðə(r)/ ▻ *verb* (*bothered, bothering*) **1** to annoy, worry or trouble someone. **2** *tr & intr* (*usually* **bother about something**; *sometimes* **bother one's head about something**) to worry about it □ *I'm bothered about the cost.* **3** *intr* (*especially* **bother about** or **with something**) to take the time or trouble to do it or consider it, etc □ *Don't bother to see me out* □ *We never bother with convention here* □ *I don't want to bother about cooking today.* ▻ *noun* **1** a minor trouble or worry. **2** a person or thing that causes bother. ▻ *exclamation, mainly Brit* expressing slight annoyance or impatience. • **I, they,** *etc* **cannot be bothered** I, they, etc consider something to be too much trouble. • **I, they,** *etc* **cannot be bothered with something** or **someone** I, they, etc find it or them very annoying or tiresome. ⓒ 18c: perhaps from Irish *bodhair* to annoy.

botheration *chiefly Brit colloq* ▻ *exclamation* expressing slight annoyance; bother! ▻ *noun* a minor trouble or worry. ⓒ 18c as *noun*.

bothersome ▻ *adj* causing bother or annoyance. ⓒ 19c.

bothy /ˈbɒθɪ/ ▻ *noun* (*bothies*) *chiefly Scottish* **1** a simple rough cottage or hut used as temporary accommodation or shelter. **2** a basically furnished dwelling for farm workers, etc. ⓒ 18c: probably altered from Gaelic *bothan* a hut.

bo tree /boʊ —/ ▷ *noun* a variety of Indian fig tree that Buddhists regard as sacred because Buddha's enlightenment is said to have happened below one of these trees. Also called pipal, etc. ⓘ 19c: from Sanskrit *bodhi* enlightenment or supreme knowledge.

bottle /ˈbɒtəl/ ▷ *noun* **1** a hollow glass or plastic container with a narrow neck, for holding liquids. **2** a BOTTLEFUL. **3** a baby's feeding bottle or the liquid in it. **4** *Brit slang* courage, nerve or confidence ◻ *He said he'd jump, but then he lost his bottle.* **5** (*usually* **the bottle**) *slang* drinking of alcohol, especially to excess (*especially* **hit** or **take to the bottle**). ▷ *verb* (**bottled**, **bottling**) to put something into, enclose or store it in bottles. ⓘ 14c: ultimately Latin *buttis* a cask.

■ **bottle something off** to draw (wine or spirits) from the cask and put into bottles.

■ **bottle out** *Brit slang* to lose one's courage and decide not to do something.

■ **bottle something up** to hold back or suppress (one's feelings about something).

bottle bank ▷ *noun* a large purpose-built container, usually in the street or a public place, into which people can put empty glass bottles and jars, etc to be collected and RECYCLEd. ⓘ 1970s.

bottlebrush ▷ *noun* **1** a brush for cleaning bottles, with bristles standing out on all sides of a central axis. **2** a name for various plants of a similar appearance, especially an Australian shrub with red or yellow flowers that grow in dense brush-like spikes.

bottle-feed ▷ *verb* to feed (a baby) with milk from a bottle rather than the breast. ● **bottle-feeding** *noun* the practice of feeding a baby from a bottle.

bottleful ▷ *noun* (**bottlefuls**) the amount a bottle can hold.

bottle gas and **bottled gas** ▷ *noun* liquefied butane or propane gas in containers, for use in cooking, heating, lighting, etc.

bottle glass ▷ *noun* a coarse green glass used for the manufacture of bottles, made using a mixture of sand, limestone and alkali.

bottle gourd see CALABASH

bottle green ▷ *noun* a dark-green colour. ▷ *adj* (**bottle-green**) dark green, like the colour of BOTTLE GLASS.

bottleneck ▷ *noun* **1** a place or thing which impedes or is liable to impede the movement of traffic, especially a narrow or partly-blocked part of a road. **2** a traffic hold-up, especially one caused by such a place or thing. **3** something which causes congestion and is an obstacle to progress.

bottlenose whale ▷ *noun* any of several toothed whales with a narrow projecting beak and a bulbous forehead.

bottle-opener ▷ *noun* any one of various kinds of device for opening bottles.

bottle party ▷ *noun* a party to which the guests each bring a bottle of wine or some other alcohol, etc.

bottler ▷ *noun* **1** a person or machine that bottles. **2** *Austral colloq* an excellent person or thing ◻ *a bottler of a game.*

bottom /ˈbɒtəm/ ▷ *noun* **1** the lowest position or part. **2** the point farthest away from the front, top, most important or most successful part ◻ *the bottom of the garden* ◻ *bottom of the class.* **3** the part of the body on which a person sits; the buttocks. **4** the base on which something stands or rests; the foundation. **5** (**the bottom**) the basic cause or origin ◻ *Let's to get to the bottom of the problem.* **6** the ground (or BED *noun* 4) underneath a sea, river or lake. **7** the part of a ship which is under the water. **8** the seat of a chair. **9** solidity of character; importance or influence. **10** especially applied to a horse: staying power; stamina. **11** the fundamental character or ingredient. ▷ *adj* lowest or last ◻ *the bottom rung of the ladder* ◻ *in bottom place.* ▷ *verb* (**bottomed**, **bottoming**) **1** to put a bottom on (a seat or container, etc). **2** *usually intr* said especially of a ship: to reach or touch the bottom. ● **at bottom** in reality; fundamentally. ● **be at the bottom of something** to be the basic cause of it. ● **from the bottom of one's heart** very sincerely. ● **get to the bottom of something** to discover the real cause of (a mystery or difficulty, etc). ● **the bottom has fallen out of the market** there has been a sudden fall in the market demand (for some commodity or product, etc). ● **touch** or **hit bottom** to reach the lowest point, eg in morale or personal circumstances. ⓘ Anglo-Saxon *botm*.

■ **bottom something on** or **upon something** to base or ground it on something.

■ **bottom out** said of prices, etc: to reach and settle at the lowest level, especially before beginning to rise again. *US equivalent* BASE OUT.

bottom drawer ▷ *noun, Brit* the clothes, linen and other household articles that a young woman is given and collects ready for use in her own home when she gets married. *US equivalent* HOPE CHEST. ⓘ 19c: because such items were commonly stored in the bottom of a chest of drawers, it became customary for a woman to say they were 'for her bottom drawer'.

bottomless ▷ *adj* extremely deep or plentiful.

bottom line ▷ *noun* **1** *colloq* the essential or most important factor or truth in a situation ◻ *The bottom line is no funds are available.* **2** the last line of a financial statement, showing profit or loss.

bottommost ▷ *adj* nearest the bottom.

botulism /ˈbɒtjʊlɪzəm/ ▷ *noun, pathol* a severe form of food poisoning, caused by swallowing a bacterial toxin that is most commonly found in canned raw meat, and is destroyed by cooking. ⓘ 19c: from Latin *botulus* sausage (from the shape of the bacteria).

bouclé /ˈbuːkleɪ/ ▷ *noun* (**bouclés**) **1** a type of wool with curled or looped threads, made with one thread looser than the others. **2** a material made from this. ▷ *adj* made of or referring to bouclé wool or material. ⓘ 19c: French, literally 'buckled' or 'curly'.

boudoir /ˈbuːdwɑː(r)/ ▷ *noun, rather old use* a woman's private sitting-room or bedroom. ⓘ 18c: French, literally 'a place for sulking in', from *bouder* to sulk or pout.

bouffant /ˈbuːfɒnt; *French* bufɑ̃/ ▷ *adj* said of a hairstyle, or a skirt, sleeve, dress, etc: very full and puffed out. ⓘ 1950s in hair sense; 19c in a dressmaking context: French, from *bouffer* to puff out.

bougainvillaea or **bougainvillea** /buːgənˈvɪlɪə/ ▷ *noun* (**bougainvillaeas**) any of various climbing S American shrubs with oval leaves and conspicuous flower-heads consisting of three small tubular flowers surrounded by large brightly coloured leaf-like bracts. ⓘ 19c: named after Louis Antoine de Bougainville (1729–1811), the first Frenchman to sail round the world.

bough /baʊ/ ▷ *noun* a branch of a tree. ⓘ Anglo-Saxon *bog*, also meaning 'the shoulder or limb of an animal', from *bugan* to bend.

bought *past tense, past participle of* BUY

bougie /ˈbuːʒiː/ ▷ *noun, medicine* an instrument which can be inserted into body passages, eg to deliver medication. ⓘ 18c: French, meaning 'a wax candle', from Bougie (modern Bujiya) in Algeria.

bouillabaisse /buːjəˈbɛs/ ▷ *noun, cookery* a thick spicy fish soup from Provence. ⓘ 19c: French.

bouillon /ˈbuːjɔ̃/ ▷ *noun* a thin clear soup or stock made by boiling meat and vegetables in water, often used as a basis for thicker soups. ⓘ 17c: French, from *bouillir* to boil.

boulder /ˈbouldə(r)/ ▻ *noun* a large piece of rock that has been rounded and worn smooth by weathering and abrasion during transport. See also ERRATIC. ◷ 17c, shortened from 14c *bulderston*.

boulder clay ▻ *noun, geol* a glacial deposit consisting of boulders of different sizes embedded in hard clay.

boules /buːl/ ▻ *singular noun* a form of BOWLS popular in France, played on rough ground, in which the players try to hit a small metal ball (the JACK) with larger balls rolled along the ground. Also called PÉTANQUE. ◷ Early 20c: plural of French *boule* BOWL[2].

boulevard /ˈbuːlvɑːd, -vɑː(r)/ ▻ *noun* a broad street in a town or city, especially one lined with trees. ◷ 18c: French, from German *Bollwerk* bulwark: the term was originally applied to a road built on a town's demolished fortifications.

boult see BOLT[2]

bounce /bauns/ ▻ *verb* (***bounced, bouncing***) **1** *intr* said of a ball, etc: to spring or jump back from a solid surface. **2** to make (a ball, etc) spring or jump back from a solid surface. **3** *intr* (*often* **bounce about** or **up**) to move or spring suddenly □ *Sparky bounced about the room excitedly.* **4** (*often* **bounce in** or **out**) to rush noisily, angrily or with a lot of energy, etc, in the specified direction □ *bounced out in a temper.* **5** *tr & intr, colloq* said of a cheque: to return or be returned without being paid, because of lack of funds in a bank account. **6** *colloq, especially US* to turn out, eject or dismiss someone (from a place or job, etc). ▻ *noun* **1** the ability to spring back or bounce well; springiness. **2** *colloq* energy and liveliness. **3** a jump or leap. **4** the act of springing back from a solid surface. ◷ 16c in sense 2, etc; 13c as *bunsen* in obsolete sense 'to beat or thump' : from Dutch *bonzen*.

■ **bounce back** to rapidly or easily recover one's health or good fortune after a difficult or adverse period.

bouncer ▻ *noun* **1** *colloq, originally US* a person employed by a club or restaurant, etc to stop unwanted guests such as drunks from entering, and to throw out people who cause trouble. **2** *cricket* a ball bowled so as to bounce and rise sharply off the ground. **3** someone or something that bounces.

bouncing ▻ *adj* **1** said especially of a baby: strong, healthy, and lively. **2** (*usually* **bouncing with something**) full of (eg energy).

bouncy ▻ *adj* (***bouncier, bounciest***) **1** able to bounce well, or tending to bounce. **2** said of a person: noticeably lively and energetic. • **bouncily** *adverb*. • **bounciness** *noun*.

bouncy castle ▻ *noun* a large structure which is inflated with air to form a large cushion with sides which a number of people, usually children, can climb onto without shoes and jump around on. ◷ 1970s.

bound[1] /baund/ ▻ *adj* **1** tied with or as if with a rope or other binding. **2** *in compounds* restricted to or by the specified thing □ *housebound* □ *snowbound.* **3** obliged. **4** said of a book: fastened with a permanent cover. ▻ *verb, past participle of* BIND. • **bound to do something** certain or obliged to do it □ *It is bound to happen* □ *We are bound to comply* □ *I feel bound to help.* • **bound up with something** closely linked with it. See also BIND. ◷ 14c, meaning 'confined by bonds', 'in prison'.

bound[2] /baund/ ▻ *adj* **1 a** (*usually* **bound for somewhere** or **something**) on the way to or going towards it; **b** *following an adverb* □ *homeward bound.* **2** *in compounds* going in a specified direction □ *southbound* □ *homebound flight.* ◷ 13c, meaning 'read' or 'prepared': from Norse *buinn*, past participle of *bua* to get ready.

bound[3] /baund/ ▻ *noun* **1** (*usually* **bounds**) a limit or boundary, eg of that which is reasonable or permitted □ *His arrogance knows no bounds.* **2** (*usually* **bounds**) a limitation or restriction. **3** (**bounds**) land generally within certain understood limits; the district. ▻ *verb* (***bounded, bounding***) **1** to form a boundary to or of something; to surround □ *The river bounds the estate to the east.* **2** to set limits or bounds to something; to restrict. • **out of bounds** usually said of a place: not to be visited or entered, etc; outside the permitted area or limits. ◷ 13c as *bunne* or *bodne*, specifically for a landmark showing the limit of an estate, etc: ultimately from Latin *bodina*.

bound[4] /baund/ ▻ *noun* **1** a jump or leap upwards. **2** a bounce (eg of a ball) back from a solid surface. ▻ *verb* (***bounded, bounding***) *intr* **1** (*often* **bound across, in, out, over** or **up**, *etc*) to spring or leap in the specified direction; to move energetically. **2** to move or run with leaps □ *The dog bounded across the field.* **3** said of a ball: to bounce back from a solid surface. ◷ 16c: from French *bondir* to spring.

boundary /ˈbaundərɪ/ ▻ *noun* (***boundaries***) **1** a line or border marking the farthest limit of an area, etc. **2** a final or outer limit, often an immaterial limit, to anything □ *the boundary of good taste.* **3** the marked limits of a cricket field. **4** *cricket* **a** a stroke that hits the ball across the boundary line, scoring four or six runs; **b** the score for such a stroke. ◷ 17c: from BOUND[3].

bounden /ˈbaundən/ ▻ *adj, formal or old use* which must be done; obligatory □ *It is my bounden duty.* ◷ 14c; old past participle of BIND.

bounder ▻ *noun, dated colloq* a badly-behaved person; a cad. ◷ 19c in this sense, from BOUND[4] *verb*.

boundless ▻ *adj* having no limit; extensive or vast. • **boundlessly** *adverb*. • **boundlessness** *noun*.

bounteous /ˈbauntɪəs/ ▻ *adj, literary* **1** generous; beneficent. **2** said of things: freely given; plentiful. • **bounteously** *adverb*. • **bounteousness** *noun*. ◷ 14c, from BOUNTY.

bountiful ▻ *adj, now chiefly literary* **1** said of a person, etc: bounteous; generous. **2** ample; plentiful. • **bountifully** *adverb*. ◷ 16c, from BOUNTY.

bounty /ˈbauntɪ/ ▻ *noun* (***bounties***) **1 a** a reward or premium given, especially by a government, as encouragement eg to kill or capture dangerous animals, criminals, etc; **b** *formerly* a payment or reward offered as an inducement to enter the army or other service. **2** *chiefly literary* the giving of things generously; generosity. **3** a generous gift. ◷ 13c as *bounte*, meaning 'goodness': from French *bonte*, from Latin *bonus* good.

bounty hunter ▻ *noun* a person who hunts down wanted criminals, animals or anything for which a reward has been offered.

bouquet /buˈkeɪ, bu-/ ▻ *noun* **1** a bunch of flowers arranged in an artistic way, given eg as a gift to a woman on a special occasion, or carried by a bride, etc. **2** the delicate smell of wine, etc. ◷ 18c: French, diminutive of *bois* a wood.

bouquet garni /ˈbuːkeɪ ˈgɑːniː/ ▻ *noun* (***bouquets garnis*** /ˈbuːkeɪ ˈgɑːniː/) *cookery* a small packet or bunch of mixed herbs used eg in stews to add flavour during cooking, but removed before serving. ◷ 19c: French, literally 'garnished bouquet'.

bourbon /ˈbɜːbən/ ▻ *noun* a type of whisky made from maize and rye, popular in the US. ◷ 19c: named after Bourbon county, Kentucky, where it was first made.

Bourbon /ˈbuəbɒn/and **Bourbon biscuit** ▻ *noun* (*also* **bourbon**) a type of biscuit consisting of two long rectangular chocolate-flavoured biscuits with a chocolate cream filling. ◷ 1930s in this sense, named after the Bourbon royal line of France and Spain.

bourdon /ˈbuədən/ ▻ *noun, music* **1** a bass stop in an organ or harmonium. **2** the DRONE bass of a bagpipe. ◷ 14c in obsolete sense 'a low accompanying voice': French, meaning 'a humming tone'; compare BURDEN[2].

Bourdon gauge /ˈbʊədɒn —/ ▻ *noun, engineering* an instrument for measuring the pressure of gases, which is indicated by a pointer on a circular scale, often attached to cylinders of compressed oxygen or other gases. ⓒ 20c: named after E.Bourdon (1808–84), French engineer.

bourgeois /ˈbʊəʒwɑː, ˈbɔːʒwɑː/ ▻ *noun* (*plural* ***bourgeois***) *usually derog* **1** a member of the middle class, especially someone regarded as politically conservative and socially self-interested. **2** a person with capitalist, materialistic or conventional values. ▻ *adj* **1** characteristic of the bourgeoisie; conventional or humdrum; conservative; materialistic. **2** belonging to the middle class or bourgeoisie. **3** in Marxist use: capitalist, exploitative of the working classes. ⓒ 16c: French, meaning 'a citizen' or 'townsman' (as distinct from a peasant or a member of the gentry), from *bourg* town.

the bourgeoisie /bʊəʒwɑːˈziː, bɔːʒ-/ ▻ *noun, derog* **1** the MIDDLE CLASSes, especially regarded as politically conservative and socially self-interested, etc. **2** in Marxist use: the capitalist classes. ⓒ 18c: French, from BOURGEOIS.

bourguignon / *French* buʀɡinjɔ̃/ ▻ *adj, cookery* applied to meat dishes, chiefly BOEUF BOURGUIGNON: stewed with onion, mushrooms and red wine (properly Burgundy wine). ⓒ Early 20c: French, meaning 'Burgundian' or 'in Burgundy style'.

bourn¹ /bɔːn, bʊən/ *noun, chiefly Southern Eng* a small stream. ⓒ 14c: a variant of BURN².

bourn² or **bourne** /bɔːn, bʊən/ *noun old use or literary* **1** a limit or bound. **2** a goal or destination. ⓒ 16c: French *bourne*, earlier *bodne* a boundary.

bourse /bʊəs, bɔːs/ ▻ *noun* **1** (*usually* **Bourse**) a European stock exchange, especially that in Paris. **2** an exchange where merchants meet for business. ⓒ 16c: French, literally 'purse'.

bout /baʊt/ ▻ *noun* **1** a period or turn of some activity; a spell or stint ◻ ***a drinking bout.*** **2** an attack or period of illness. **3** a boxing or wrestling match. ⓒ 16c: from obsolete *bought* a bend or turn.

boutique /buːˈtiːk/ ▻ *noun* **1** **a** a small shop, especially one selling fashionable clothes and accessories; **b** especially in the 1960s: a small, expensive, exclusive dress shop for women. **2** a small specialist business or agency operating within a larger business sphere, especially advertising, accountancy or investment services. **3** *as adj* applied to a business, agency, etc: small, specialist or exclusive ◻ ***boutique trading.*** ⓒ 18c: French, meaning 'a small shop'.

boutonnière see under BUTTONHOLE 2

bouzouki or **bazouki** /bəˈzuːkɪ/ ▻ *noun* (***bouzoukis***) a Greek musical instrument with a long neck and metal strings, related to the mandolin. ⓒ 1950s: modern Greek.

bovine /ˈboʊvaɪn/ ▻ *adj* **1** belonging or relating to, or characteristic of, cattle. **2** *derog* said of people: dull or stupid. • **bovinely** *adverb*. ⓒ 19c: from Latin *bovinus*, from *bos, bovis* an ox.

bovine somatotrophin ▻ *noun* (abbreviation **BST**) a hormone that increases milk production in cattle.

bovine spongiform encephalopathy / — spʌndʒɪfɔːm ɛŋkefəˈlɒpəθɪ/ ▻ *noun* (abbreviation **BSE**) a notifiable brain disease of cattle, characterized by spongy degeneration of the brain, nervousness, a clumsy gait and eventual collapse and death, and which is thought to be related to CREUTZFELDT-JAKOB DISEASE. Also (*colloq*) called **mad cow disease**.

Bovril /ˈbɒvrəl/ ▻ *noun, trademark* a concentrated beef extract used diluted as a drink or stock, and added to meat dishes, etc for flavour. ⓒ Invented in 1889: from Latin *bos, bovis* an ox or cow.

bovver boy /ˈbɒvə(r) —/ ▻ *noun, Brit slang* a violent young male troublemaker, specifically a member of a gang of hooligans commonly engaging in street fights using heavy, hobnailed **bovver boots** to kick their opponents. ⓒ 1970s: from the Cockney pronunciation of BOTHER.

bow¹ /baʊ/ ▻ *verb* (***bowed, bowing***) **1** (*also* **bow down**) to bend (the head or the upper part of the body) forwards and downwards ◻ ***bow one's head.*** **2** (*also sometimes* **bow down before someone** or **something**) *intr* to bend the head or the upper part of the body forwards and downwards, usually as a sign of greeting, respect, shame, etc or to acknowledge applause. **3** to express (eg thanks or acceptance) with a bow. **4** (*usually* **bow to something**) to accept or submit to it, especially unwillingly. ▻ *noun* an act of bowing. • **bow and scrape** *derog* to behave with excessive politeness or deference. • **take a bow** to acknowledge applause or recognition. ⓒ Anglo-Saxon *bugan* to bend.

■ **bow something** or **someone down** to crush it or them down.

■ **bow down to someone** to agree to obey them, or to submit to them.

■ **bow someone** in or **out**, *etc* to usher them in or out, etc with a formal or respectful bow.

■ **bow out** to stop taking part; to retire or withdraw.

bow² /boʊ/ ▻ *noun* **1** **a** a knot made with a double loop, to fasten the two ends of a lace, ribbon, or string, etc; **b** a lace, ribbon or string, etc tied in such a knot; **c** a looped knot of ribbons, etc used to decorate anything. **2** a weapon made of a piece of flexible curved wood or other material, bent by a string stretched between its two ends, for shooting arrows. **3** a long, thin piece of wood with horsehair stretched along its length, for playing the violin or cello, etc. **4** a single stroke or movement (up or down) of the bow while playing the violin or cello, etc. Also *in compounds* ◻ ***up-bow*** ◻ ***down-bow.*** **5** anything which is curved or bent in shape, eg a rainbow. ▻ *verb* (***bowed, bowing***) **1** *tr & intr* to bend or make something bend into a curved shape. **2** **a** to use a bow on (a violin or cello, etc); **b** *intr* in playing a stringed instrument: to use the bow; **c** to play (a passage, etc) with a specified kind of bowing; **d** to make (written music) with up-bows and down-bows. • **bowing** *noun* **1** the technique of using the bow when playing a stringed instrument. **2** a manner or style of using the bow. ⓒ Anglo-Saxon *boga* an arch or bow (senses 2 and 5).

bow³ /baʊ/ *naut* ▻ *noun* **1** (*often* **bows**) the front part of a ship or boat. **2** *rowing* the rower nearest the bow. • **on the bow** within 45° of the point right ahead. ⓒ 17c: from German dialect *boog* or Dutch *boeg* a ship's bow, or a shoulder.

bowdlerize or **bowdlerise** /ˈbaʊdləraɪz/ ▻ *verb* (***bowdlerized, bowdlerizing***) to remove passages or words from (a book or play, etc), especially on moral and social rather than aesthetic grounds; to expurgate, especially in an unnecessary or distorting way. • **bowdlerism** *noun*. • **bowdlerization** *noun*. • **bowdlerized** *adj*. ⓒ 19c: named after Dr T Bowdler (1754–1825), who published an expurgated Shakespeare in ten volumes in 1818.

bowel /ˈbaʊəl/ ▻ *noun* **1** an intestine, especially the large intestine in humans. **2** (*usually* **bowels**) the depths or innermost part of something, especially when deep or mysterious ◻ ***the bowels of the earth.*** ⓒ 14c: from French *buel*, from Latin *botellus* sausage.

bowel movement ▻ *noun* **1** an instance or act of defecation. **2** faeces; excrement.

bower /baʊə(r)/ ▻ *noun* **1** a place in a garden, etc which is enclosed and shaded from the sun by plants and trees. **2** *literary* a lady's private room or boudoir. ⓒ Anglo-Saxon *bur* a chamber.

bowerbird ▻ *noun* any of various species of bird native to Australia and New Guinea, so called because the males construct bowers out of twigs, usually decorated with flowers, berries, leaves, shells, etc, to attract the females.

bowie knife /ˈbouɪ —/ ▷ *noun* a strong single-edged curved sheath-knife with a blade about twelve inches long. ⓒ 19c: named after the US adventurer Colonel James Bowie (1790–1836) who popularized and perhaps invented it.

bowl¹ /boul/ ▷ *noun* **1** a round deep dish for mixing or serving food, or for holding liquids or flowers, etc. **2** a BOWLFUL. **3** the round hollow part of an object, eg of a spoon, pipe, lavatory, etc. **4** *especially US* a large bowl-shaped place or structure, such as a stadium or amphitheatre. ⓒ Anglo-Saxon *bolla*.

bowl² /boul/ ▷ *noun* **1 a** a heavy wooden ball for rolling, especially one for use in the game of BOWLS, made with a BIAS so as to run in a curve; **b** a similar metal ball used in BOULES. **2** an act, instance or turn of bowling, or of rolling the ball in bowls or tenpin bowling, etc. ▷ *verb* (***bowled, bowling***)**1** to roll (a ball or hoop, etc) smoothly along the ground. **2** *intr* to play bowls, or tenpin bowling, etc. **3** *tr & intr, cricket* to throw (the ball) towards the person batting at the wicket. **4** (*often* **bowl someone out**) *cricket* to put (the batsman) out by hitting the wicket with the ball. **5** (*sometimes* **bowl along** or **on**, *etc*) *intr* to roll or trundle along the ground. ⓒ 15c as *boule*: French, from Latin *bulla* a ball.

■ **bowl along** to move smoothly and quickly □ *bowling along in my little car.*

■ **bowl someone over 1** *colloq* to surprise, delight or impress them thoroughly. **2** to knock them over.

bow legs /bou —/ ▷ *plural noun* legs which curve out at the knees. • **bow-legged** *adj* said of a person: having bow legs. Also called BANDY-LEGGED.

bowler¹ /ˈboulə(r)/ *noun* **1** a person who bowls the ball in cricket, etc. **2** a person who plays bowls or goes bowling.

bowler² /ˈboulə(r)/ *noun* (*also* **bowler hat**) a hard, usually black, felt hat, with a rounded crown and a narrow curved brim. *US equivalent* DERBY. ⓒ 19c: named after Bowler, a 19c English hatter who designed it.

bowlful ▷ *noun* (***bowlfuls***) the amount a BOWL¹ can hold.

bowline /ˈboulɪn/ ▷ *noun, naut* **1** a rope used to keep a sail taut against the wind. **2** (*also* **bowline knot**) a knot which makes a loop that will not slip at the end of a piece of rope. ⓒ 14c: from German dialect *boline*, corresponding to BOW³ + LINE¹.

bowling ▷ *noun* **1** the game of BOWLS. **2** a game (eg especially TENPIN BOWLING) played indoors, in which a ball is rolled along an alley at a group of skittles, the object being to knock over as many as possible. **3** *cricket* the act, practice or a turn or spell of throwing the ball towards the person batting at the wicket.

bowling alley ▷ *noun* **1** a long narrow channel made of wooden boards, used in BOWLING. **2** a building containing several of these.

bowling average see under AVERAGE

bowling green ▷ *noun* an area of smooth grass set aside for the game of BOWLS.

bowls /boulz/ ▷ *singular noun* **1** a game played on smooth grass with bowls (see BOWL²), the object being to roll these as close as possible to a smaller ball called the JACK. **2** sometimes applied to the game of skittles, or to tenpin bowling.

bowman /ˈboumən/ ▷ *noun, chiefly old use* an archer. ⓒ 13c: from BOW² *noun* 2.

bowser /ˈbauzə(r)/ ▷ *noun* **1** a light tanker used for refuelling aircraft on an airfield. **2** *now chiefly Austral & NZ* a petrol pump. ⓒ originally a tradename.

bowshot /ˈbouʃɒt/ ▷ *noun* the distance to which an arrow can be shot from a bow.

bowsprit /ˈbousprɪt/ ▷ *noun, naut* a strong spar projecting from the front of a ship, often with ropes from the sails fastened to it. ⓒ 14c as *bouspret*: from German dialect *boch* bow (of a ship) + *spret* pole.

bowstring /ˈboustrɪŋ/ ▷ *noun* **1** *archery* the string on a bow, which is drawn back and then released to project the arrow. **2** *civil engineering* a horizontal tie on a bridge or girder.

bow tie /bou —/ ▷ *noun* a necktie which is tied in a double loop to form a horizontal bow at the collar, often worn in formal dress.

bow wave /bau —/ ▷ *noun* the wave created by the bow of a moving ship.

bow window /bou —/ ▷ *noun* a window which projects towards the centre, forming a curved shape. See also BAY WINDOW.

bow-wow /ˈbauwau/ ▷ *noun* **1** a child's word for a dog. **2** a dog's bark; a woof. ▷ *exclamation* an imitation of a dog's bark. ⓒ 16c as *exclamation*.

box¹ ▷ *noun* (***boxes***) **1** a container made from wood, cardboard or plastic, etc, usually square or rectangular and with a lid. **2** a boxful. **3 a** *in compounds* a small enclosed area, shelter or kiosk, etc for a specified purpose □ *telephone box* □ *sentry box* □ *witness box*; **b** in a theatre, etc: a separate compartment for a group of people, containing several seats; **c** (*often* **horse-box**) an enclosed area for a horse in a stable or vehicle. **4** an area in a field, pitch, road, printed page, etc marked out by straight lines. **5** (**the box**) *Brit colloq* **a**) the television; **b**) *football* the penalty box. **6** an individually allocated pigeonhole or similar container at a newspaper office or other agency, in which mail is collected to be sent on to, or collected by, the person it is intended for □ *Reply to box number 318.* See also PO BOX. **7** *often in compounds* a case or housing for protecting machinery, etc □ *gearbox*. **8** *cricket, etc* a lightweight padded shield to protect the genitals. **9** a gift of money given to tradesmen and *(formerly)* servants □ *a Christmas box.* **10** a small country house or lodge, used as a base for some sports, eg a SHOOTING-BOX. **11** a raised seat for the driver on a carriage. ▷ *verb* (***boxes, boxed, boxing***) **1** (*also* **box something up**) to put it into a box or boxes **2** (*especially* **box someone** or **something in** or **up**) to stop them or it from moving about; to confine or enclose them or it. **3** (*also* **box something up**) *Austral, NZ* **a** to mix up (different flocks of sheep) accidentally; **b** *colloq* to make a mess or muddle of it. **4** (*also* **box something up**) to fit or provide it with a box or boxes. • **boxed** *adj* contained in or provided with a box. • **boxlike** *adj*. • **box the compass** *naut* to name all the 32 points of the compass in their correct order. ⓒ Anglo-Saxon: from Latin *buxis*, from Greek *pyxis*.

box² ▷ *verb* (***boxes, boxed, boxing***) **1** *tr & intr* to fight with the hands formed into fists and protected by thick leather gloves, especially as a sport. **2** *colloq* to hit (especially someone's ears) with the fist, or sometimes the hand. ▷ *noun* (***boxes***) *colloq* (*usually* **a box on the ears**) a punch with the fist, or sometimes a cuff or slap, especially on the ears. • **box clever** *colloq* to act in a clever or cunning way; to be smart. ⓒ 16c as *verb*; 14c, meaning 'a blow'.

box³ ▷ *noun* (***boxes***) **1** (*also* **boxtree**) an evergreen shrub or small tree with small leathery paired leaves, glossy green above and paler underneath, and tiny green flowers lacking petals, widely used in formal gardens as a hedging plant, and for topiary. **2** (*also* **boxwood**) the hard durable fine-grained yellow wood of this tree, used eg for fine carving and inlay work. ⓒ Anglo-Saxon: from Latin *buxus*, from Greek *pyxos*.

boxcar and **box-wagon** ▷ *noun, N Amer* a closed railway goods-wagon.

boxer ▷ *noun* **1** a person who boxes, especially as a sport. **2** a large breed of dog with a muscular body, rounded compact head, soft pendulous ears and a short broad muzzle with pronounced jowls and a prominent lower jaw. Ⓒ Early 20c.

boxercise ▻ *noun* a workout involving a mixture of AEROBICS and movements simulating boxing blows. Ⓒ 1990s.

boxer shorts ▻ *plural noun* (sometimes shortened to **boxers**) loose shorts worn by men as underpants, with an elasticated waistband and a front opening. Ⓒ 1940s: from the loose shorts worn by a BOXER[1].

boxful ▻ *noun* (***boxfuls***) the amount a BOX[1] can hold.

box girder ▻ *noun, engineering* a hollow girder made of steel, timber or concrete, and having thin walls, often used in bridge construction.

boxing ▻ *noun* the sport or practice of fighting with the fists, especially wearing BOXING GLOVES.

Boxing Day ▻ *noun* **1** 26 December, the day after Christmas Day. **2** in the UK and the Commonwealth: the first weekday after Christmas, observed as a public holiday. Ⓒ 19c: so called because of the tradition of giving boxes (see BOX[1] *noun* 9) to the poor and to apprentices, etc on that day.

boxing glove ▻ *noun* each of a pair of thick padded leather gloves required to be worn by boxers since the introduction of the QUEENSBERRY RULES.

box junction ▻ *noun, Brit* an area at the intersection of a road junction, marked with a grid of yellow lines painted on the ground, which vehicles may enter only if the exit is clear.

box kite ▻ *noun* a kite in the form of a box with open ends.

box number ▻ *noun* a box, or the number of a box (BOX[1] *noun* 6) at a newspaper office or post office, etc to which mail, such as replies to advertisements, may be sent.

box office ▻ *noun* **1** an office at which theatre, cinema or concert tickets, etc are sold. **2 a** theatrical entertainment seen in terms of its commercial value, ie its takings ◻ ***The new show is wonderful box office***; **b** theatrical entertainment seen in terms of its popular appeal, ie its ability to attract an audience. Also (**box-office**) *as adj.*

box pleat ▻ *noun* on a skirt or dress: a large double pleat formed by folding the material in two pleats facing in opposite directions.

boxroom ▻ *noun, chiefly Brit* a small room, usually without a window, used to store bags and boxes, etc or as an extra bedroom.

boxy ▻ *adj* (***boxier, boxiest***) **1** shaped like a box. **2** said of clothes, etc: having a squarish or chunky appearance. • **boxiness** *noun.*

boy /bɔɪ/ ▻ *noun* (***boys***) **1** a male child. **2** a son ◻ ***Our youngest boy is still at school.*** **3** a young man, especially one regarded as still immature. **4** (**the boys**) *colloq* a group of male friends with whom a man regularly socializes ◻ ***Joe goes out with the boys once a week.*** **5** *colloq, usually in compounds* a man or youth with a specified function or skill, etc ◻ ***backroom boy*** ◻ ***post boy.*** **6** *S Afr, offensive* a black male servant. ▻ *exclamation* (*also* **oh boy!**) expressing excitement, surprise or pleasure. • **boys will be boys** said especially when referring to childish or foolish behaviour in men rather than in boys: boys cannot help behaving like boys, it is in their nature (so one must expect and put up with it). Ⓒ 14c as *boi.*

boycott /ˈbɔɪkɒt/ ▻ *verb* (***boycotted, boycotting***) **1** to refuse to have any business or social dealings with (a company or a country, etc), or to attend or take part in (negotiations, or a meeting, etc), usually as a form of disapproval or coercion. **2** to refuse to handle or buy (goods), as a way of showing disapproval or of exerting pressure, etc. ▻ *noun* an act or instance of boycotting. Ⓒ 19c: named after Captain C C Boycott (1832–97), an English land agent in Ireland, who was treated in this way by his neighbours in 1880, because of his harsh treatment of tenants.

boyfriend ▻ *noun* a regular male friend and companion, especially as a partner in a romantic or sexual relationship.

boyhood ▻ *noun* **1** the period of a man's life in which he is a boy. **2** the condition or state of being a boy.

boyish ▻ *adj* like a boy in appearance or behaviour ◻ ***boyish good looks.*** • **boyishly** *adverb.* • **boyishness** *noun.*

Boyle's law ▻ *noun, physics* a law which states that the volume of a given mass of gas at a constant temperature is inversely proportional to its pressure. Ⓒ 19c: named after Robert Boyle (1627–91), Anglo-Irish chemist.

boyo /ˈbɔɪoʊ/ ▻ *noun, colloq, chiefly Welsh & Irish* especially as a cheery or affectionate form of address: boy or young man. Ⓒ 19c.

Boys' Brigade ▻ *noun* (abbreviation **BB**) in the UK: an organization for boys which encourages discipline and self-respect, etc.

Boy Scout see SCOUT[1]

bozo /ˈboʊzoʊ/ ▻ *noun* (***bozos***) *slang, especially US* **1** a dim-witted fellow; a dope or wally. **2** a man or fellow generally. Ⓒ 1920s, originally in sense 2.

BP ▻ *abbreviation* **1** British Petroleum. **2** British Pharmacopoeia.

bp ▻ *abbreviation* **1** (*also* **b/p, B/P**) bills payable. **2** (*also* **Bp**) bishop. **3** (*also* **BP**) blood pressure. **4** boiling point.

BPharm. ▻ *abbreviation* Bachelor of Pharmacy.

BPhil ▻ *abbreviation*: *Baccalaureus Philosophiae* (Latin), Bachelor of Philosophy.

bpi ▻ *abbreviation, computing* **1** bits per inch. **2** bytes per inch.

BPM or **bpm** ▻ *abbreviation* said of dance music: beats per minute.

bps ▻ *abbreviation, computing* bits per second.

Bq ▻ *symbol* becquerel.

BR ▻ *abbreviation* **1** *IVR* Brazil. **2** *historical* British Rail.

Br[1] ▻ *abbreviation* **1** Britain. **2** British. **3** Brother.

Br[2] ▻ *symbol, chem* bromine.

br ▻ *abbreviation* **1** bank rate. **2** bedroom. **3** (*also* **b/r, B/R**) bills receivable.

br. ▻ *abbreviation* **1** branch. **2** bridge. **3** bronze. **4** brother. **5** brown.

bra /brɑː/ ▻ *noun* (***bras***) an undergarment worn by a woman to support and cover the breasts. • **braless** *adj* said of a woman: not wearing a bra. Ⓒ 1930s; short for BRASSIÈRE, and now the more commonly used word.

brace /breɪs/ ▻ *noun* (***braces***) **1** a device, usually made from metal, which supports, strengthens or holds two things together. Often *in compounds* ◻ ***wall brace*** ◻ ***orthopaedic brace.*** **2** (**braces**) *Brit* straps worn over the shoulders, for holding trousers up. *US equivalent* SUSPENDERS. **3** a wire device worn on the teeth (usually a child's teeth) to straighten them. **4** *building, etc* a tool used by carpenters and metalworkers to hold a BIT[2] and enable it to be rotated (see also BRACE AND BIT). **5** *printing* either of two symbols ({ or }) used to connect lines, figures, staves of music, parts of text, etc, indicating that they are to be taken together (compare BRACKET *noun* 1, PARENTHESIS). **6** (*in plural also* ***brace***) a pair or couple, especially of game birds. **7** *naut* a rope attached to a ship's YARD, used for adjusting the sails. See also MAINBRACE. ▻ *verb* (***braced, bracing***) **1** to make something tight or stronger, usually by supporting it in some way. **2** (*usually* **brace oneself**) to prepare and steady oneself for a blow or shock, etc ◻ ***Here comes the bump, so brace yourself!*** **3** to tone up, stimulate or invigorate someone □ *braced by the crisp November day*. See also BRACING. ● **bracer** *noun*. ⓒ 14c, meaning 'a pair of arms': from Latin *brachium* arm.

brace and bit ▷ *noun* a hand tool for drilling holes, consisting of a BRACE with the drilling BIT² in place.

bracelet /'breɪslɪt/ ▷ *noun* **1** a band or chain worn as a piece of jewellery round the arm or wrist. **2** (**bracelets**) *slang* handcuffs. ⓒ 15c: French from Latin *brachium* arm.

brachial /'breɪkɪəl, 'bra-/ ▷ *adj, technical* **1** belonging or relating to the arm. **2** like an arm in function, structure, etc. ⓒ 16c.

brachiate /'breɪkɪeɪt/ ▷ *adj* **1** *bot* having opposite widely spreading branches. **2** *zool* having arms. ⓒ 19c.

brachiopod /'breɪkɪəpɒd, 'bra-/ ▷ *noun* (***brachiopods*** or ***brachiopoda*** /-'ɒpədə/) *zool* any member of a phylum of marine invertebrate animals (**Brachiopoda**) with an asymmetrical chalky shell consisting of two unequal valves, and a short fleshy stalk projecting from the rear of the shell, used for anchorage to rock surfaces, etc. Also called **lampshell**. ⓒ 19c: from Greek *brachion* arm + *pous, podos* foot.

brachiosaurus /breɪkɪə'sɔːrəs, bra-/ ▷ *noun* (***brachiosauruses***) *palaeontol* the heaviest of the dinosaurs, that lived in the late Jurassic period and had a massive body, a small head and longer forelegs than hindlegs. ⓒ Early 20c: from Greek *brachion* arm + *sauros* lizard.

brachycephalic see CEPHALIC INDEX

bracing ▷ *adj* said of the wind, air, climate, etc: stimulatingly cold and fresh. ⓒ 18c: from BRACE *verb* 3.

bracken /'brakən/ ▷ *noun* the commonest species of fern in the UK, which has tall fronds, spreads rapidly by means of its underground rhizomes and is poisonous to livestock. ⓒ 14c.

bracket /'brakɪt/ ▷ *noun* **1** *non-technical* either member of several pairs of symbols, **< >**, **{ }**, **( )**, **[ ]**, used to group together or enclose words, figures, etc. *Technical equivalent* ANGLE BRACKET, BRACE *noun* 5, PARENTHESIS, SQUARE BRACKET. **2** *usually in compounds* a group or category falling within a certain range □ *income bracket* □ *out of my price bracket*. **3** an L-shaped piece of metal or strong plastic, used for attaching shelves, etc to walls. **4** a small shelf fastened to a wall. **5** *archit* a small projecting support, usually of stonework, eg in the form of a scroll. ▷ *verb* (***bracketed***, ***bracketing***) to enclose or group together (words, etc) in brackets. ⓒ 16c in *noun* sense 5: from French *braguette*, ultimately from Latin *bracae* breeches.

■ **bracket someone** or **something together** to put them or it into the same group or category.

bracket-creep ▷ *noun, finance* a phenomenon caused by INFLATION in which a rise in salary makes a taxpayer less well off, because it pushes them into a higher tax bracket.

brackish /'brakɪʃ/ ▷ *adj* said of water: slightly salty; somewhat salt rather than fresh. ● **brackishness** *noun*. ⓒ 16c: from Dutch *brak* salty.

bract ▷ *noun, bot* a modified leaf, usually smaller than a true leaf and green in colour, in whose AXIL an INFLORESCENCE develops. ● **bracteal** *adj*. ⓒ 18c: from Latin *bractea* a thin plate of metal or gold leaf.

brad ▷ *noun* a thin flattish nail, tapering in width, with the head either flush with the sides or slightly projecting on one side. ⓒ 13c: from Norse *broddr* a spike.

bradawl /'bradɔːl/ ▷ *noun* a small chisel-edged handtool for making holes in wood or leather, etc. ⓒ 19c: BRAD + AWL.

bradycardia /bradɪ'kɑːdɪə/ ▷ *noun, pathol* a condition in which the heartbeat is slower than normal (less than 50 to 60 beats per minute). ⓒ 19c: Latin, from Greek *bradys* slow + *kardia* heart.

brae /breɪ/ ▷ *noun* (**braes**) *Scottish* **1** a slope on a hill. **2** a sloping bank beside a river, loch or seashore, etc. **3** (**braes**) an upland or mountainous area. ⓒ 14c as *bra*: Norse, meaning 'eyelash'.

brackets

1. round brackets or parentheses

● These separate a comment off from the rest of the sentence □ *Applications (six copies) should be lodged with the Vice-Chancellor by 1 October* □ *The novels of Neil Gunn (1891–1973) have enjoyed a recent revival of critical interest.*

ALTERNATIVE STYLES: a pair of commas; *(more informal)* a pair of long dashes. Punctuation that belongs to the bracketed comment goes inside the brackets; punctuation belonging to the sentence as a whole goes outside the brackets:

✓ *This has caused a lot of pain (mental and physical).*

✗ *This has caused a lot of pain (mental and physical.)*

✓ *(This has caused a lot of pain, mental and physical.)* Avoid inserting a bracketed full sentence into another sentence:

✗ *The new regulations (six copies are enclosed for Board members) have been issued to all departments.*

✓ *The new regulations have been issued to all departments. (Six copies are enclosed for Board members.).*

✓ *The new regulations (six copies of which are enclosed for Board members) have been issued to all departments.* Where a bracketed full sentence does occur within another sentence, note that there is no capital letter and no full stop, but that there may be a question mark or exclamation mark □ *Jean Jones (have you seen her in action?) is the new club champion.*

● They are an economical way of indicating alternatives or options □ *Any candidate(s) must be formally proposed and seconded by two Club members.*

● They enclose numbers or letters that mark off items in a list □ *This project needs to be (1) carefully researched and (2) adequately funded.*

2. square brackets

● These enclose letters, words or phrases inserted as comments, corrections or explanations into a piece of quoted text, for example by an editor □ *He [St Stephen] was the earliest Christian martyr* □ *[St Stephen] was the earliest Christian martyr.*

brag /brag/ ▷ *verb* (***bragged***, ***bragging***) *intr, derog* to talk boastfully or too proudly about oneself, or what one has done, etc ▷ *noun* **1** a boastful statement or boastful talk. **2** a card game similar to poker. ● **braggingly** *adverb*. ⓒ 14c.

braggart /'bragət/ ▷ *noun* someone who brags a lot. ▷ *adj* boastful. ⓒ 16c: from French *bragard* vain or bragging.

Brahma /'brɑːmə/ ▷ *noun, Hinduism* **1** the creator God, the first god of the Hindu TRIMURTI of deities. Compare SHIVA, VISHNU. **2** (*also* **Brahman**) in Hindu thought: the eternal impersonal Absolute principle, the guiding principle beneath all reality. ⓒ 18c: Sanskrit.

Brahman or (*especially formerly*) **Brahmin** /'brɑːmən/ ▷ *noun* **1** a Hindu who belongs to the highest of the four major CASTES, traditionally the priestly order. **2** BRAHMA 2. **3** (*also* **brahmin bull** or **cow** or **ox**) the humped Indian ox or ZEBU, or a zebu cross. ● **Brahmanic** /-'manɪk/ or **Brahmanical** *adj*. ● **Brahmanism** *noun* **1** the religion and practices of the Brahmans. **2** the worship of Brahma, one of the early religions of India, from which the great religious themes and traditions of Hinduism evolved. ⓒ 15c: from Sanskrit *brahmana*, from *brahma* prayer or worship.

braid /breɪd/ ▷ *noun* **1** a band or tape, often made from threads of gold and silver twisted together, used as a decoration on uniforms, etc. **2** *now chiefly N Amer* a ropelike length of interwoven hair, consisting usually of three separate lengths which have been twisted together. *Brit equivalent* PLAIT. ▷ *verb* (***braided, braiding***) **1** to twist (several lengths of thread or hair, etc) together, placing one over the other in a regular sequence. **2** to decorate something with braid. • **braided** *adj.* • **braiding** *noun* braid decoration; work in braid. ◷ Anglo-Saxon *bregdan* to weave, or to move quickly, flash or change colour.

Braille or **braille** /breɪl/ ▷ *noun* a system of printing for the blind, in which printed characters are represented by raised dots which can be read by touch, each character formed by a different combination taken from a basic six-dot matrix. Also *as adj.* ▷ *verb* (***Brailled, Brailling***) to transcribe or print something in Braille. • **brailler** *noun* (*also* **braille-writer**) a machine for writing in Braille. ◷ 19c: named after Louis Braille (1809–52), who invented the system.

brain /breɪn/ ▷ *noun* **1** the highly developed mass of nervous tissue that co-ordinates and controls the activities of the central nervous system of animals. **2** (*especially* **brains**) *colloq* cleverness; intelligence □ *It takes brains to do that job.* **3** (*especially* **brains** or **the brains**) *colloq* a very clever person. **4** (*usually* **brains**) *colloq* a person who thinks up and controls a plan, etc □ *He was the brains behind the idea.* ▷ *verb* (***brained, braining***) *colloq* **1** to hit someone hard on the head. **2** to dash out or smash someone's brains. • **brained** *adj, especially in compounds* having a brain or brains of a specified type □ *hare-brained* □ *scatterbrained.* • **brainless** *adj.* • **brainlessly** *adverb.* • **have something on the brain** *colloq* to be unable to stop thinking about it; to be obsessed by it. • **pick someone's brains** see under PICK. ◷ Anglo-Saxon *brægen.*

brainchild ▷ *noun* a person's particular and original theory, idea or plan.

brain damage ▷ *noun* as a general and loose term: temporary or especially permanent injury or disease of the brain. • **brain-damaged** *adj.*

brain-dead ▷ *adj* denoting a person in whom brain death has occurred or has been diagnosed.

brain death ▷ *noun* the functional death of the centres in the brainstem that control breathing and other vital reflexes, so that the affected person is incapable of surviving without the aid of a ventilator. Also called **clinical death**.

brain drain ▷ *noun, colloq* the steady or continuing loss of scientists, academics, professionals, etc to another country, usually because the prospects and rewards are better.

brainier, **brainiest**, **brainily** and **braininess** see under BRAINY

brainless and **brainlessly** see under BRAIN

Braille alphabet

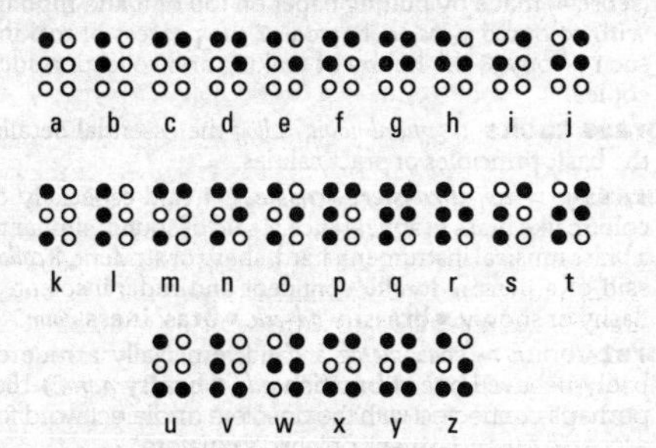

brainstem ▷ *noun, anatomy* the part of the brain that is connected to the top of the spinal cord, and consists of the MIDBRAIN, MEDULLA OBLONGATA and PONS.

brainstorm ▷ *noun* **1** *colloq* a sudden loss of the ability to think clearly and act properly or sensibly; a mental ABERRATION. **2** *N Amer colloq* a BRAINWAVE 1. ◷ 19c, meaning 'a sudden violent disturbance of the mind'.

brainstorming ▷ *noun, originally US* the practice of trying to solve problems or develop new ideas and strategies, etc by intensive group discussion in which suggestions and thoughts are put forward spontaneously.

brainteaser ▷ *noun* a difficult exercise or puzzle.

brainwash ▷ *verb* to force someone to change their beliefs or ideas, etc by applying continual and prolonged mental pressure. • **brainwashing** *noun* the process of subjecting someone to such mental pressure or systematic indoctrination, so as to change their beliefs, etc. ◷ 1950s, originally US: the *verb* is a back-formation from the *noun.*

brainwave ▷ *noun* **1** *colloq* a sudden, bright or clever idea; an inspiration. **2** a wave representing the pattern of electrical activity in the brain, recorded by electrodes placed on the scalp.

brainy ▷ *adj* (***brainier, brainiest***) *colloq* clever; intelligent. • **brainily** *adverb.* • **braininess** *noun.*

braise /breɪz/ ▷ *verb* (***braised, braising***) to cook (meat, vegetables, etc) slowly with a small amount of liquid in a closed dish, usually after browning in a little fat. • **braised** *adj* said of food, especially meat: cooked by braising. ◷ 18c: from French *braiser,* from *braise* live coals.

brake[1] /breɪk/ ▷ *noun* **1** a device used to slow down or stop a moving vehicle or machine, or to prevent the movement of a parked vehicle, eg by applying friction to the surface of a rotating part such as a wheel, brake drum or disc. **2** anything which makes something stop, prevents or slows down progress, etc □ *a brake on public spending.* **3** a SHOOTING BRAKE. **4** a toothed instrument for crushing flax or hemp. **5** (*also* **brake harrow**) a type of harrow for breaking up large lumps of hard earth. ▷ *verb* (***braked, braking***) **1** *intr* to apply or use a brake. **2** to use a brake to make (a vehicle) slow down or stop. **3** to crush (flax or hemp) by beating. ◷ 18c: related to BREAK.

brake[2] /breɪk/ ▷ *noun* an area of wild rough ground covered with low bushes, brushwood, etc; a thicket. ◷ 15c, originally referring to broken branches, stumps, etc: probably from a German dialect word, but also related to BREAK.

brake drum ▷ *noun, engineering* a revolving cylinder, attached to a rotating piece of machinery, eg the wheel of a car, against which the BRAKE SHOES press when the brake is applied.

brake fluid ▷ *noun, autos* in a hydraulic brake system: the fluid that transmits pressure from the brake pedal to the brake pistons.

brake horsepower ▷ *noun, engineering* (abbreviation **bhp**) the power developed by an engine as measured either by the force that must be applied to a friction brake in order to stop it, or by a dynamometer applied to the flywheel.

brake light ▷ *noun* any of the red lights at the back of a vehicle which light up when the driver applies the brakes.

brake parachute ▷ *noun* a parachute attached to the tail of some high performance aircraft, used as a brake when landing.

brake shoe ▷ *noun, engineering* either of two semicircular metal structures within a rotating BRAKE DRUM, which press against the inner wall of the drum when the brake is applied.

brakesman and (*US*) **brakeman** ▷ *noun* **1** a man who is responsible for operating the brake of a railway train. **2** *mining* a man who operates the winch or hoist.

braless see under BRA

bramble /'brambəl/ ▻ *noun* **1** (*also* **bramble-bush**) a blackberry bush. **2** any other wild prickly shrub. **3** *especially Scottish* a blackberry. ● **brambly** *adj.* ⓒ Anglo-Saxon *bremel*.

brambling ▻ *noun* a small bird of the finch family with an orange breast and shoulder patch, a white rump and a black tail. ⓒ 16c: from German *brämling*, equivalent to BROOM 2 + -LING1.

Bramley /bramlɪ/ ▻ *noun* (***Bramleys***) a popular variety of large cooking apple. Also called **Bramley seedling**. ⓒ 19c: named after M Bramley, a Nottinghamshire butcher, who is said to have been the first person to have grown this apple.

bran ▻ *noun* the outer covering of cereal grain, removed during the preparation of white flour, and often added to foods because it is an important source of vitamin B and dietary fibre. ⓒ 14c: French.

branch /brɑːntʃ/ ▻ *noun* (***branches***) **1** an offshoot arising from the trunk of a tree or the main stem of a shrub. **2** a main division of a railway line, river, road or mountain range. **3** a local office of a large company or organization. **4** a subdivision or section in a family, subject, group of languages, etc □ *works in a branch of geography called biogeography.* ▻ *verb* (***branched, branching***) *intr* (*especially* **branch off**) **1** to divide from the main part □ *a road branching off to the left.* **2** (*sometimes* **branch out** or **branch out from something**) to send out branches, or spread out from it as a branch or branches. ● **branched** *adj.* ● **branching** *adj, noun.* ● **branchless** *adj.* ● **branchy** *adj* (***branchier, branchiest***). ⓒ 14c: from French *branche*, from Latin *branca* an animal's paw.

■ **branch out** (*often* **branch out into something**) to develop different interests or projects, etc; to expand or diversify.

brand ▻ *noun* **1** a distinctive maker's name or trademark, symbol or design, etc used to identify a product or group of products. **2** a variety or type □ *a special brand of humour.* **3** an identifying mark on cattle, etc, usually burned on with a hot iron. **4** (*also* **branding-iron**) a metal instrument with a long handle and shaped end which can be heated and then used to burn identifying marks on cattle, etc. **5** a sign or mark of disgrace or shame. **6** a piece of burning or smouldering wood. **7** any of various fungoid diseases or blights affecting grain crops, eg mildew, rust and smut. **8** *literary* a torch. **9** *literary* a sword. ▻ *verb* (***branded, branding***) **1** to mark (cattle, etc) with a hot iron. **2** to give someone a bad name or reputation. **3** (*especially* **brand something upon someone's memory**) to impress (an incident or fact, etc) permanently on to their memory. **4** to give a brand (sense 1) to, or fix a brand or trademark, etc upon (a product or group of products). ⓒ Anglo-Saxon as *noun* 6.

brandish /'brandɪʃ/ ▻ *verb* (***brandishes, brandished, brandishing***) to flourish or wave (a weapon, etc) as a threat or display. ▻ *noun* a flourish or wave (of a weapon, etc). ⓒ 14c: from French *brandir*.

brand leader ▻ *noun* the brand of a particular product that has the largest share of the market; the best-selling brand.

brand name ▻ *noun* a tradename identifying a particular manufacturer's products; a make.

brand-new ▻ *adj* completely new. ⓒ 16c, from BRAND (ie like bright new metal just taken out of the fire).

brandy /'brandɪ/ ▻ *noun* (***brandies***) **1** a strong alcoholic drink distilled from grape wine. See also COGNAC. **2** a glass of this drink. **3** *in compounds* a strong alcoholic drink made from another type of wine or fermented fruit juice, or by steeping fruit in brandy □ *cherry brandy.* ● **brandied** *adj.* ⓒ 17c, originally as *brandwine:* from Dutch *brandewijn*, from *branden* to burn or distil + *wijn* wine.

brandy butter ▻ *noun* butter mixed with sugar and brandy, eaten especially with Christmas pudding or mince pies.

brandy glass ▻ *noun* a short-stemmed glass with a globe-shaped bowl, for drinking brandy from.

brandy snap ▻ *noun* a thin crisp biscuit flavoured with ginger (and originally with brandy), usually rolled up when still hot to form a hollow tube, and served filled with cream.

brant goose see BRENT GOOSE

bran tub ▻ *noun, Brit* a LUCKY DIP consisting of a tub filled with bran, paper or wood shavings, etc with prizes hidden in it.

brash /braʃ/ ▻ *adj* (***brasher, brashest***) **1** very loud, flashy or showy. **2** rude; impudent, overbearingly forward. **3** *US* reckless; impetuous. ● **brashly** *adverb.* ● **brashness** *noun.* ⓒ 19c.

brass /brɑːs/ ▻ *noun* (*plural* ***brasses*** or when treated as plural in collective senses 3 and 6 ***brass***) **1** an alloy of copper and zinc, which is strong and ductile, resistant to corrosion, and suitable for casting, used to make electrical fittings, screws, buttons, buckles, etc. **2** an ornament, tool or other object made of brass, or such objects collectively □ *polish the brass once a month.* See also BRAZIER2. **3** (*singular or plural noun*) **a** wind instruments made of brass, such as the trumpet and horn; **b** the people who play brass instruments in an orchestra. **4** a piece of flat brass with a figure, design or name, etc on it, usually found in a church, in memory of someone who has died. **5** (*also* **horse brass**) a small flat brass ornament with a design on it, for a horse's harness. **6** (*usually* **top brass** or **the brass**) *colloq* people in authority or of high military rank collectively. See also BRASS HAT. **7** (*especially* **the brass** or **the brass neck**) *colloq* over-confidence or effrontery; nerve □ *had the brass neck to send me the bill.* **8** *colloq, especially N Eng* money; cash. ▻ *adj* made of brass. ● **brassy** see separate entry. ● **brassed off** *Brit slang* fed up; annoyed. ⓒ Anglo-Saxon *bræs*.

■ **brass someone off** *Brit slang* to make them annoyed or fed up □ *He brasses me off.*

brass band ▻ *noun* a band consisting mainly of brass instruments.

brasserie /'brasəriː/ ▻ *noun* **1** a bar serving food. **2** a small and usually inexpensive restaurant, especially one serving French food, and originally beer. ⓒ 19c: French, meaning 'brewery', from *brasser* to brew.

brass-faced ▻ *adj, colloq* shameless; brazen; blatant.

brass hat ▻ *noun, Brit colloq* a high-ranking military officer or other top official. Compare BRASS *noun* 6. ⓒ 19c: so called because of the gold trimming on the hats of senior staff officers.

brassica /'brasɪkə/ ▻ *noun* (***brassicas***) any member of a genus of plants that includes several commercially important crop vegetables, eg cabbage, cauliflower, broccoli, brussels sprout, turnip, swede. ⓒ 19c: Latin, meaning 'cabbage'.

brassière /'brazɪə(r), -sɪə(r)/ ▻ *noun* the full name for BRA. ⓒ Early 20c: French, formerly meaning 'a bodice' (now 'a child's sleeved vest'), from *braciere* an arm protector, from *bras* arms.

brass neck see BRASS *noun* 7

brass rubbing ▻ *noun* **1** a copy of the design on a BRASS (sense 4) made by putting paper on top of it and rubbing with coloured wax or charcoal. **2** the process of making such a copy. **3** the hobby of making and collecting such copies.

brass tacks ▻ *plural noun, colloq* the essential details; the basic principles or practicalities.

brassy ▻ *adj* (***brassier, brassiest***) **1** said especially of colour: like brass in appearance. **2** said of sound: similar to a brass musical instrument; hard, sharp or strident. **3** *colloq* said of a person: loudly confident and rude; insolent. **4** flashy or showy. ● **brassily** *adverb.* ● **brassiness** *noun.*

brat /brat/ ▻ *noun, derog* a child, especially a rude or badly-behaved one. ● **brattish** *adj.* ● **bratty** *adj.* ⓒ 16c: perhaps connected with the obsolete or dialect word for a 'coarse outer garment' or 'child's pinafore'.

brat pack ▻ *noun, colloq, usually derog* a group of successful and popular young, especially teenage, male stars working in cinema or a similar creative field, with a reputation for rowdy high-spirited or insolent behaviour. • **bratpacker** *noun*. ⓒ 1980s.

bratwurst /'bratvʊəst/ ▻ *noun* a type of German pork sausage. ⓒ Late 19c: German.

bravado /brə'vɑːdoʊ/ ▻ *noun* (***bravados*** or ***bravadoes***) a display of confidence or daring, often a boastful and insincere one. ⓒ 16c: from Spanish *bravada*.

brave[1] /breɪv/ *adj* (***braver, bravest***) **1** said of a person, or their character, actions, etc: having or showing courage in facing danger or pain, etc; daring or fearless. **2** *chiefly literary or old use* fine or excellent, especially in appearance. **3** (**the brave**) brave people as a group (see THE 4b). ▻ *noun* (***braves***) *formerly* a warrior, especially one from a Native American tribe. ▻ *verb* (***braved, braving***) (*especially* **brave something out**) to meet or face up to (danger, pain, etc) boldly or resolutely; to defy □ *brave the storm*. • **bravely** *adverb* with bravery; boldly. • **bravery** *noun* a brave quality; being brave or courageous. ⓒ 15c: French, perhaps ultimately from Latin *barbarus* barbarous.

bravo /'brɑːvoʊ/ *exclamation* (*also* /brɑː'voʊ/ (*also* **brava** /-və/ when addressed to a woman, and **bravi** /-viː/ to a number of people) shouted to express one's appreciation at the end of a performance, etc: well done! excellent! ▻ *noun* (***bravos***) **1** a cry of 'bravo'. **2** (**Bravo**) *communications* in the NATO alphabet: the word used to represent the letter 'B' (see table at NATO ALPHABET). ⓒ 18c: Italian.

bravura /brə'vjʊərə/ ▻ *noun* (***bravuras***) **1** a display of great spirit, dash or daring. **2** *music* especially in vocal music: **a** virtuosity, spirit or brilliance in performance; **b** a piece or style requiring considerable technical ability. Also *as adj*. ⓒ 18c: Italian.

braw /brɔː/ ▻ *adj, chiefly Scots* fine or splendid. ⓒ 16c: Scots variant of BRAVE *adj* 2.

brawl /brɔːl/ ▻ *noun* a noisy quarrel or fight, especially in public; a punch-up. ▻ *verb* (***brawled, brawling***) *intr* to quarrel or fight noisily. • **brawler** *noun*. • **brawling** *noun*. ⓒ 14c as *verb*: perhaps from Dutch *brallen* to brag.

brawn /brɔːn/ ▻ *noun* **1** muscle; muscular or physical strength. **2** jellied meat made from pig's head and ox-feet, cut up, boiled and pickled. ⓒ 14c: from French *braon* meat, a thick fleshy part suitable for roasting.

brawny ▻ *adj* (***brawnier, brawniest***) muscular; strong. • **brawniness** *noun*. ⓒ 16c.

bray ▻ *verb* (***brayed, braying***) **1** *intr* said of an ass or donkey: to make its characteristic loud harsh cry. **2** *intr* said of a person: to make a loud harsh sound, often a harsh raucous laugh. **3** to say in a loud harsh voice. ▻ *noun* **1** the loud harsh braying sound made by an ass or donkey. **2** any loud harsh grating cry or sound; a noisy uproar. ⓒ 14c: from French *braire*.

Braz. ▻ *abbreviation* **1** Brazil. **2** Brazilian.

braze[1] ▻ *verb* (***brazed, brazing***) *engineering* to join (two pieces of metal) by melting an alloy with a lower melting point than either of the metals to be joined, and applying it to the joint. ⓒ 16c, meaning 'to expose to fire': from French *braise* live coals.

braze[2] ▻ *verb* (***brazed, brazing***) **1** to cover, make or decorate something with brass. **2** to make something hard like brass. ⓒ Anglo-Saxon *brasian*.

brazen /'breɪzən/ ▻ *adj* **1** (*also* **brazen-faced**) bold; impudent; shameless. **2** made of brass or like brass, especially in its colour or its loud harsh sound. • **brazenly** *adverb*. • **brazenness** *noun*. ▻ *verb* (***brazened, brazening***) only in phrase below. ⓒ Anglo-Saxon *bræsen* made of brass, from *bræs* brass.

■ **brazen something out** to face (an embarrassing or difficult situation) boldly and without showing shame or awkwardness.

brazier[1] /'breɪzɪə(r)/ ▻ *noun* a metal frame or container for holding burning coal or charcoal, used especially by people who have to work outside in cold weather. ⓒ 17c: from French *brasier*, from *braise* live coals.

brazier[2] /'breɪzɪə(r)/ ▻ *noun* a person who works in brass, eg casting objects in brass. ⓒ 15c: from BRAZE.

Brazil or **brazil** /brə'zɪl/ ▻ *noun* **1** (*also* **Brazil nut**) an edible type of long white oily nut with a hard three-sided shell, obtained from a tropical American tree. **2** (*sometimes* **Brazil wood**) a type of red wood from any of several tropical trees. ⓒ 14c in sense 2: the country of Brazil in S America was so named from the similarity of the red wood found there to that found in the East and known as *brasil*.

Brazilian ▻ *adj* belonging or relating to Brazil, a republic in east and central S America, or its inhabitants. ▻ *noun* a citizen or inhabitant of, or person born in, Brazil. ⓒ 17c.

brazing see BRAZE[1], BRAZE[2]

BRCS ▻ *abbreviation* British Red Cross Society (see RED CROSS).

BRE ▻ *abbreviation* **1** in the UK: Building Research Establishment. **2** *chiefly US* Bachelor of Religious Education.

breach /briːtʃ/ ▻ *noun* (***breaches***) **1** an act of breaking, especially breaking of a law or promise, etc, or a failure to fulfil or carry out a duty, promise, etc. **2** a serious disagreement; a break in relations, communications, etc. **3** a gap, break or hole. ▻ *verb* (***breached, breaching***) **1** to break (a promise, etc) or fail to carry out (a duty or commitment, etc). **2** to make an opening or hole in something. • **in breach of something** not following or agreeing with (a law or regulation, etc). • **step into the breach** see under STEP. ⓒ Anglo-Saxon *bryce*.

breach of confidence ▻ *noun* an act or instance of divulging information that was received in confidence; the giving away of a secret.

breach of contract ▻ *noun* failure to fulfil or keep to the terms of a contract.

breach of promise ▻ *noun* the breaking of a promise, especially a promise to marry someone.

breach of the peace ▻ *noun, law* **1** in England and Wales: a riot or disturbance which violates the public peace, involving harm to people or property, or fear of assault. **2** in Scotland: a disturbance of the public peace which might reasonably lead to the public being alarmed, and is classed as a crime.

bread /brɛd/ ▻ *noun* **1** one of the oldest and most important staple foods known to man, usually prepared from wheat or rye flour mixed with water or milk, kneaded into a dough with a leavening agent, eg yeast, and baked. **2** (*often* **daily bread**) food and the other things one needs to live; sustenance. **3** *slang* money. ▻ *verb* (***breaded, breading***) to cover (a piece of food) with breadcrumbs before cooking. • **breaded** *adj* □ *breaded haddock*. • **know which side one's bread is buttered** *colloq* to know how to act for one's own best advantage. • **like** or **want one's bread buttered on both sides** *colloq* to like or want to live in great comfort or luxury. • **take the bread out of someone's mouth** *colloq* to deprive them of their very means of living. ⓒ Anglo-Saxon.

bread and butter ▻ *noun* **1** bread that has been sliced and spread with butter. **2** a means of earning a living; subsistence. ▻ *adj* (**bread-and-butter**) **1** connected with making a living, or providing a means of living. **2** ordinary or routine. **3** said of a letter, etc: sent to someone to thank them for their hospitality, for a meal or stay, etc. **4** materialistic or practical.

bread basket ▻ *noun* **1** a basket for holding bread. **2** an area which produces large amounts of grain for export □ *the bread basket of Europe*. **3** *dated slang* the stomach.

breadboard ▻ *noun* **1** a wooden board on which bread, etc is cut. **2** a board for making a model of an electric circuit.

breadcrumb ▻ *noun* **1** (*usually* **breadcrumbs**) **a** bread crumbled into small pieces, used in cooking; **b** a commercially-produced version of this, usually coloured orange, used for dressing fish, etc. **2** a crumb of bread.

breadfruit ▷ *noun* (***breadfruit*** or ***breadfruits***) **1** a tall tropical SE Asian tree, cultivated throughout the Pacific islands and parts of S America. **2** the large oval edible starchy fruit of this tree, which when ripe can be roasted and baked whole and eaten. ⓒ 17c: so called because it has a texture similar to that of bread.

bread knife ▷ *noun* a large knife with a serrated edge, for slicing bread.

breadline ▷ *noun, originally US* a queue of poor or down-and-out people waiting for handouts of bread or other food, from charity or government sources. • **on the breadline** said of a person or people: having hardly enough food and money to live on; living at SUBSISTENCE level.

bread sauce ▷ *noun* a thick milk-based sauce made with breadcrumbs and seasoning, eaten especially with turkey or chicken.

breadstick ▷ *noun* a long thin stick of bread dough baked until crisp. Also called GRISSINO.

breadth /brɛdθ/ ▷ *noun* **1** the measurement from one side of something to the other; width or broadness. Compare LENGTH. **2** an area, section or extent (eg of cloth) taken as the full or standard width. **3** openness and willingness to understand and respect other people's opinions and beliefs, etc. **4** extent, size □ *impressed by the breath of his knowledge.* ⓒ 16c, from earlier *brede*, from Anglo-Saxon *brædu*.

breadthways and **breadthwise** ▷ *adverb* as seen or measured from one side to the other (rather than from one end to the other).

breadwinner ▷ *noun* the person who earns money to support a family.

break /breɪk/ ▷ *verb* (*past tense* ***broke***, *past participle* ***broken***, *present participle* ***breaking***) **1** *tr & intr* to divide or become divided into two or more parts as a result of stress or a blow □ *He broke my ruler in half.* **2 a** *intr* said of a machine or tool, etc: to become damaged, so as to stop working and be in need of repair; **b** to damage (a machine or tool, etc) in such a way. **3** to fracture a bone in (a limb, etc). **4** to burst or cut (the skin, etc). **5** to do something not allowed by (a law, agreement, promise, etc); to violate something □ *broke the rules.* **6** to exceed or improve upon (a sporting record, etc). **7** *intr* to stop work, etc for a short period of time □ *Let's break for tea.* **8** to interrupt (a journey, one's concentration, etc). **9** *intr* said of a boy's voice: to become lower in tone on reaching puberty. **10** to defeat or destroy something □ *break a strike.* **11** to force open with explosives □ *break a safe.* **12** *intr* said of a storm: to begin violently. **13** *tr & intr* said of news, etc: to make or become known □ *He was away when the story broke* □ *had to break the bad news to her.* **14** *intr* (*also* **break up**) to disperse or scatter □ *The crowd broke up.* **15** to reduce the force of (a fall or a blow, etc). **16** *intr* said of waves, etc: to collapse into foam. **17** to lose or disrupt the order or form of somethig □ *break ranks.* **18** *intr* said of the weather: to change suddenly, especially after a fine spell. **19** *tr & intr* to cut or burst through □ *break the silence* □ *sun breaking through the clouds.* **20** *intr* to come into being □ *day breaking over the hills.* **21** *tr & intr* to make or become weaker. **22** to make someone bankrupt; to destroy them financially. **23** to decipher (a code, etc). **24** to disprove (an alibi, etc). **25** to interrupt the flow of electricity in (a circuit). **26** *intr, snooker* to take the first shot at the beginning of a game. **27** *intr, tennis* (*also* **break service** and **break someone's service**) to win (an opponent's service game). **28** *intr, boxing* to come out of a clinch. **29** *intr, cricket* said of a ball: to change direction on hitting the ground. **30** (*usually* **break someone of something**) to make them give up (a bad habit, etc). ▷ *noun* **1** an act or result of breaking. **2 a** a pause, interval or interruption in some ongoing activity or situation □ *Let's take a break*; **b** (*also* **breaktime**) a short interval in work or lessons, etc □ *Come and see me at break. US equivalent* RECESS. **3** a change or shift from the usual or overall trend □ *a break in the weather.* **4** a sudden rush, especially to escape □ *make a break for it.* **5** *colloq* a chance or opportunity to show one's ability, etc, often a sudden or unexpected one □ *After that first break, his career took off* □ *Give me a break.* **6** *colloq* a piece of luck. Also *in compounds* □ *a bad break* □ *lucky break.* **7** *snooker, billiards, etc* a series of successful shots played one after the other. **8** *snooker, billiards, etc* the opening shot of a game. **9** *tennis* (*also* **break of service** or **service break**) an instance of breaking service (see *verb* 27 above). **10** *cricket* the change of direction made by a ball on striking the ground. **11** an interruption in the electricity flowing through a circuit. **12** *music* in jazz, etc: a short improvised solo passage. • **break camp** to pack up the equipment after camping. • **break cover** said eg of a fox: to make a dash from its hiding place; to come out of hiding. • **break into song, laughter**, *etc* to begin singing or laughing, etc, especially unexpectedly. • **break loose** or **free 1** to escape from control. **2** to become detached. • **break it down!** *Austral & NZ colloq* stop it!; cut it out! *British equivalent* GIVE OVER. • **break new** or **fresh ground** to do something in an original way. • **break someone's heart** to devastate them emotionally, usually by failing or betraying them in love. • **break something open** to open (a box, door, etc) by force. • **break step** said of soldiers, etc: to march out of step deliberately. • **break the back of something** to complete the heaviest or most difficult part of a job, etc. • **break the ice** *colloq* to overcome the first awkwardness or shyness, etc, especially on a first meeting or in a new situation. • **break wind** to release gas from the bowels through the anus; to fart. ⓒ Anglo-Saxon *brecan*.

■ **break away** *intr* **1** to escape from control, especially suddenly or forcibly. **2** to put an end to one's connection with a group or custom, etc, especially suddenly. See also BREAKAWAY.

■ **break away from** or **out from something** to make a sudden forward movement or burst of speed away or out from it.

■ **break down 1** said of a machine, etc: to stop working properly; to fail. **2** to collapse, disintegrate or decompose. **3** said of a person: to give way to one's emotions; to burst into tears. **4** said of human relationships: to be unsuccessful and so come to an end □ *The marriage has broken down irretrievably.* **5** said of a person: to suffer a nervous breakdown. See also BREAKDOWN.

■ **break something down 1** to use force to crush, demolish or knock it down. **2** to divide into separate parts and analyse it □ *We need to break down these figures.* See also BREAKDOWN.

■ **break even 1** to make neither a profit nor a loss in a transaction. **2** to reach the point at which income or revenue is exactly equal to spending or cost.

■ **break in 1** to enter a building by force, especially to steal things inside □ *Thieves broke in last night.* See also BREAK-IN. **2** (*also* **break in on something**) to interrupt (a conversation, etc).

■ **break someone in** to train or familiarize them in a new job or role.

■ **break something in 1** to use or wear (new shoes or boots, etc) so that they lose their stiffness, etc. **2** to train (a horse) to carry a saddle and a rider. See also BROKEN-IN.

■ **break off 1** to become detached by breaking □ *The top broke off.* **2** to come to an end abruptly. **3** to stop talking.

■ **break something off 1** to detach it by breaking. **2** to end (eg a relationship) abruptly.

■ **break out 1** to escape from a prison, etc using force. **2** to begin suddenly and usually violently □ *then war broke out.* **3** (*especially* **break out in something**) to become suddenly covered in (spots or a rash, etc). See also BREAKOUT.

■ **break through 1** to force a way through. **2** to make a new discovery or be successful, especially after a difficult or unsuccessful period. See also BREAKTHROUGH.

■ **break up 1** to break into pieces. **2** to come to an end; to finish □ *The meeting broke up early.* **3** said of people: to end a relationship or marriage □ *His parents have broken up.* **4** said of a school or a pupil: to end term and begin the holidays. See also BREAK-UP.

■ **break someone up** *N Amer colloq* to make them laugh convulsively □ *You break me up when you do that.*

■ **break something up 1** to divide it into pieces. **2** to make it finish or come to an end. See also BREAK-UP.

■ **break with someone** to stop associating with them.

breakable ▷ *adj* able to be broken. ▷ *noun* (*usually* **breakables**) a breakable object.

breakage ▷ *noun* **1** the act of breaking. **2** a broken object; damage caused by breaking. See also BREAK AWAY under BREAK.

breakaway ▷ *noun* an act of breaking away or escaping. ▷ *adj, always before its noun* that has broken away; separate □ *a breakaway republic.*

breakbeat and **backbeat** ▷ *noun* a short sample of rhythm (eg of drum beats) that is looped to create a new rhythm, often taken from old soul or jazz records and used in HOUSE MUSIC, HIP-HOP and DRUM-AND-BASS music.

breakdance and **breakdancing** ▷ *noun* an energetic style of dancing to rock or disco music, involving acrobatic jumps and twists, originally developed by young Black Americans. ● **breakdancer** *noun*.

breakdown ▷ *noun* **1 a** a failure in a machine or device; **b** *as adj* said especially of a road vehicle used in connection with a breakdown □ *a breakdown van.* **2** a failure or collapse of a process □ *a breakdown in communications.* **3** a process or act of dividing something into separate parts for analysis. **4** (*also* **nervous breakdown**) a failure or collapse in a person's mental health. **5** disintegration or decomposition. See BREAK DOWN, BREAK SOMETHING DOWN at BREAK.

breaker ▷ *noun* **1** a large wave which breaks on rocks or on the beach. **2** *slang* a person who broadcasts on Citizens' Band radio. **3** a person or thing that breaks something □ *The ship has gone to the breaker's yard.*

breakfast /ˈbrɛkfəst/ ▷ *noun* the first meal of the day, normally taken soon after getting up in the morning. ▷ *verb* (***breakfasted***, ***breakfasting***) *intr* to have breakfast. ⓒ 15c: from *break fast*, ie to begin eating again after a time of fasting.

breakfast TV ▷ *noun* TV programmes broadcast early in the morning, especially news and conversation, etc presented in an informal style.

break-in ▷ *noun* an illegal entry by force into a building, especially to steal property inside. See BREAK IN at BREAK.

breaking and entering ▷ *noun, formerly* the act or practice of breaking into a building to steal property inside. Now called BURGLARY. See also HOUSEBREAKING.

breaking point ▷ *noun* the point at which something, especially a person or relationship, can no longer stand up to a stress or strain, and breaks down.

breakneck ▷ *adj* said of speed: extremely fast, and usually dangerously fast.

break of day ▷ *noun, chiefly literary* dawn; daybreak.

breakout ▷ *noun* an act or instance of breaking out, especially an escape by force □ *a mass breakout from the city jail.* See BREAK OUT at BREAK.

break point ▷ *noun, tennis* **1** a point giving a player the opportunity to break the opposing player's service. See BREAK *verb* 27. **2** *computing* a point at which a computer program will stop running to allow checking, etc.

breakthrough ▷ *noun* **1** a decisive advance or discovery, especially in scientific research, opening the way to further developments. **2** an act of breaking through something. **3** *psychol* a sudden advance in a patient's treatment, usually after a long period without progress. See BREAK THROUGH at BREAK.

breakthrough bleeding ▷ *noun, medicine* the intermittent discharge of small amounts of blood through the vagina, especially during the first few months of use of hormone treatment, eg the contraceptive pill.

breaktime see BREAK *noun* 2b

break-up ▷ *noun* **1** the ending of a relationship or situation. **2** the dispersal, scattering or dividing up of something. See BREAK UP, BREAK SOMETHING UP at BREAK.

breakwater ▷ *noun* a strong wall or barrier built out from a beach to break the force of the waves. See also GROYNE and MOLE[5].

bream /briːm/ ▷ *noun* (*plural* ***bream***) **1** any of various freshwater fish of the carp family which have a deep body covered with silvery scales, and mouthparts which can be pushed out to form a tube for feeding. **2** (*usually* **sea bream**) an unrelated deep-bodied marine fish, several species of which are important food fish. ⓒ 14c: from French *bresme*.

breast /brɛst/ ▷ *noun* **1** *anatomy* in women: each of the two mammary glands, which form soft protuberances on the chest, each consisting of a group of milk-secreting glands embedded in fatty tissue. **2** the front part of the body between the neck and the belly □ *The robin has a red breast* □ *clutched it to his breast.* **3** the part of a garment covering the breast. **4** a swelling or curving slope □ *breast of the hill* □ *chimney breast.* **5** *now chiefly literary* the source or seat of emotions. ▷ *verb* (***breasted***, ***breasting***) **1** to face, confront or fight against something □ *breast the wind* □ *breasting his troubles bravely.* **2** *athletics* to touch (the tape) at the end of a race with the chest. **3** to come to the top of (a hill, etc). ● **make a clean breast of something** see under CLEAN. ⓒ Anglo-Saxon *breost*.

breastbone ▷ *noun, non-technical* the STERNUM.

breasted ▷ *adj, in compounds* having a breast or breasts of the specified type □ *pigeon-breasted* □ *double-breasted.*

breastfeed ▷ *verb, tr & intr* to feed (a baby) with milk from the breast. Also (*chiefly old use*) SUCKLE. ● **breastfed** *adj* said of a baby: fed with milk from the breast. ● **breastfeeding** *noun*.

breastplate ▷ *noun* a piece of armour which protects the chest.

breast pocket ▷ *noun* a pocket on the breast of a jacket or shirt, often used for keeping a handkerchief or pens, etc.

breaststroke ▷ *noun* a style of swimming breast-downwards in the water, in which the arms are pushed out in front and then pulled outward and backward together, while the legs are drawn up and then pushed out and back in a similar way.

breastwork ▷ *noun, fortification* a temporary wall built of earth for defensive purposes, reaching to about chest-height.

breath /brɛθ/ ▷ *noun* **1** *physiol* the air drawn into, and then expelled from, the lungs. **2** exhaled air as odour, vapour or heat □ *felt his breath on my face* □ *bad breath*. **3** a single inhalation of air □ *a deep breath*. **4** a faint breeze. **5** a slight hint, suggestion or rumour □ *not a breath of scandal*. **6** a slight trace of perfume, etc. **7** life; the power or ability to breathe □ *not while I have breath in my body*. • **a breath of fresh air** *colloq* **1** a walk in the open air. **2** a refreshing and invigorating change, new arrival, etc. • **catch one's breath** to stop breathing for a moment, from fear, amazement or pain, etc. • **draw breath 1** to breathe; to be alive. **2** *colloq, especially with negatives* to stop talking. • **get one's breath back 1** to begin breathing normally again after strenuous exercise. **2** to recover from a shock or surprise. • **hold one's breath 1** to stop oneself from breathing or from breathing out, especially when one is anxious, tense or trying to avoid being heard. **2** *colloq* to wait anxiously or expectantly; to expect some imminent change, result, outcome, etc □ *They are notoriously slow, so don't hold your breath!* • **in the same breath** *colloq* usually said of something spoken, at the very next moment; virtually at the same time. • **out of** or **short of breath** breathless, especially after strenuous exercise. • **take one's** or **someone's breath away** *colloq* to astound or amaze one or them (see also BREATHTAKING). • **under one's breath** in a whisper. • **waste one's breath** to speak without any effect or without being heeded. ⓒ Anglo-Saxon *bræth*.

breathable /ˈbriːðəbəl/ ▻ *adj* **1** said of a fabric, etc: able to BREATHE (sense 4). **2** said of air, etc: fit for breathing.

breathalyse or (*mainly US*) **breathalyze** /ˈbrɛθəlaɪz/ ▻ *verb* (***breathalysed, breathalysing; breathalyzed, breathalyzing***) to test (a driver) with a Breathalyser.

Breathalyser or (*mainly US*) **Breathalyzer** ▻ *noun, trademark* a device used to test the amount of alcohol on a driver's breath, consisting of a plastic bag containing alcohol-sensitive crystals which change colour when a certain concentration of alcohol vapour is blown through them. ⓒ 1960s: from *breath* + *analyser*.

breathe /briːð/ ▻ *verb* (***breathed, breathing***) **1** *tr & intr* to respire by alternately drawing air into and expelling it from the lungs. **2** *tr & intr* to say, speak or sound quietly; to whisper. **3** *intr* to take breath; to rest or pause □ *haven't had a moment to breathe*. **4** *intr* said of fabric or leather, etc: to allow air and moisture, etc to pass through. **5** *intr* said of wine: to develop flavour when exposed to the air. **6** to live; to continue to draw breath. **7** *intr* to blow softly □ *warm air breathing over my face*. **8** to show or express □ *She breathed confidence*. **9** to allow (eg a horse) to rest; to give breathing-space to something. • **breathe again** or **easily** or **easy** or **freely** *colloq* to relax or feel relieved after a period of anxiety, tension or fear. • **breathe down someone's neck** *colloq* to watch or supervise them so closely that they feel uncomfortable. • **breathe fire** *colloq* to speak very angrily; to be furious. • **breathe one's last** *euphemistic* to die. ⓒ 13c as *brethen*, from BREATH.

breather /ˈbriːðə(r)/ ▻ *noun* **1** *colloq* a short rest or break from work or exercise. **2** someone or something that breathes.

breathier, breathiest, breathily and **breathiness** see under BREATHY

breathing /ˈbriːðɪŋ/ ▻ *noun* **1** in terrestrial animals: the process whereby air is alternately drawn into the lungs and then expelled from them, as a result of which oxygen is taken into the body and carbon dioxide is released from it. **2** *phonetics* **a** (*also* **rough breathing**) a sign (ʽ) used in ancient Greek to indicate that the initial vowel is pronounced with an h- sound; **b** (*also* **smooth breathing**) a sign (ʼ) used in ancient Greek to indicate the absence of such an ASPIRATE.

breathing-space ▻ *noun* a short time allowed for rest; a brief respite. ⓒ 17c.

breathless /ˈbrɛθləs/ ▻ *adj* **1** having difficulty in breathing normally, because of illness or from hurrying, etc. **2** very eager or excited. **3** with no wind or fresh air □ *a breathless summer day*. **4** *literary* lifeless; dead □ *her breathless body*. • **breathlessly** *adverb*. • **breathlessness** *noun*.

breathtaking ▻ *adj* very surprising, exciting or impressive □ *a breathtaking view*. • **breathtakingly** *adverb*. ⓒ 19c.

breath test ▻ *noun, chiefly Brit* a test given to drivers to check the amount of alcohol in their blood, especially one using a BREATHALYSER.

breathy /ˈbrɛθɪ/ ▻ *adj* (***breathier, breathiest***) **1** said of a speaking voice: accompanied by a sound of unvocalized breathing. **2** said of a singing voice or instrumentalist: without proper breath control, causing an impure sound. • **breathily** *adverb*. • **breathiness** *noun*.

breccia /ˈbrɛtʃɪə/ ▻ *noun* (***breccias***) *geol* coarse sedimentary rock, composed of a mixture of angular rock cemented together by finer-grained material, and usually formed by processes such as landslides and geological faulting. ⓒ 18c: Italian, meaning 'rubble' or 'gravel'.

bred *past tense, past participle of* BREED

breech /briːtʃ/ ▻ *noun* (***breeches***) **1** the back part of a gun barrel, where it is loaded. **2** *old use* the lower back part of the body; the buttocks. See also BREECHES. ⓒ Anglo-Saxon *brec*, plural of *broc*, originally meaning 'a garment covering the loins and thighs' and also in sense 2.

breech birth and **breech delivery** ▻ *noun* the birth of a baby buttocks or feet first instead of in the normal head-first position.

breeches or (*chiefly N Amer*) **britches** /ˈbrɪtʃɪz/ ▻ *plural noun* **1** short trousers fastened usually just below the knee □ *riding breeches*. **2** *humorous, colloq* trousers. ⓒ 13c: plural of BREECH.

breeches buoy /ˈbriːtʃɪz — / ▻ *noun* a device, used especially for rescuing people from ships, consisting of a lifebuoy fitted with a strong canvas sling like a pair of breeches, in which a person is supported when being hauled along a rope to safety.

breeching /ˈbrɪtʃɪŋ/ ▻ *noun* in a horse's harness: a strap attached to the saddle, and passing around the horse's rump.

breech loader ▻ *noun* a firearm in which the charge is loaded at the breech. Compare MUZZLE-LOADER. • **breech-loading** *adj*.

breed ▻ *verb* (***bred, breeding***) **1** *intr* said of animals and plants: to reproduce sexually. **2** to make (animals or plants) reproduce sexually, sometimes in order to transmit certain selected characteristics from parents to offspring. **3** to make or produce (usually something bad) □ *Dirt breeds disease*. **4** to train, bring up or educate (children, etc). **5** *physics* to produce more fissile fuel that is consumed in a nuclear reaction. See also BREEDER REACTOR. ▻ *noun* **1** an artificially maintained subdivision within an animal species, especially farm livestock or pet animals, produced by domestication and selective breeding, eg Friesian cattle. **2** a race or lineage. **3** a kind or type □ *a new breed of salesman*. • **breeder** *noun* **1** someone or something that breeds, especially a person who breeds animals or plants for a living. **2** short for BREEDER REACTOR. ⓒ Anglo-Saxon *bredan* to produce, hatch or cherish offspring.

breeder reactor ▻ *noun* a type of nuclear reactor which produces more FISSILE material than it consumes as fuel, used mainly to produce plutonium-239 for the nuclear weapons industry. Compare FAST-BREEDER REACTOR. ⓒ 1940s.

breeding ▻ *noun* **1** *biol* controlling the manner in which plants or animals reproduce in such a way that certain characteristics are selected for and passed on to the next generation. **2** the result of a good education and training, social skills, manners, etc; upbringing. **3** the act of producing offspring; reproduction.

breeding ground ▻ *noun* **1** a place or situation, etc which encourages the development or creation of something usually regarded as bad □ *a breeding ground for crime.* **2** a place where animals or birds, etc produce their young.

breeze¹ /briːz/ ▻ *noun* **1** a gentle wind. **2** *colloq, especially N Amer* any job or situation which is effortless; a pleasantly simple task. ▻ *verb* (***breezed, breezing***) *intr, colloq* (*usually* **breeze into** or **out of somewhere** or **breeze along** or **in** or **out**, *etc*) to move briskly, in a cheery and confident manner □ *breezed into the room.* Ⓒ 16c, meaning 'a north-east wind': probably from Spanish *brisa*.

■ **breeze through something** *colloq* to do it easily and quickly.

breeze² /briːz/ ▻ *noun* ashes from coal, coke or charcoal, used in building materials such as BREEZEBLOCK. Ⓒ 18c: from French *braise* live coals.

breezeblock ▻ *noun* a type of brick made from BREEZE² and cement, used for building houses, etc. *US equivalent* CINDERBLOCK.

breezy ▻ *adj* (***breezier, breeziest***) **1** rather windy. **2** said of a person: lively, confident and casual □ *You're bright and breezy today.* • **breezily** *adverb.* • **breeziness** *noun.*

bren gun or **Bren gun** ▻ *noun* a light quick-firing machine-gun used during the World War II. Often shortened to **bren** or **Bren**. Ⓒ 1930s: from *Br*no in Czechoslovakia, where it was originally made + *En*field in England, where it was later made.

brent goose or (*especially N Amer*) **brant goose** ▻ *noun* the smallest and darkest of the black geese, which has a white marking on each side of the neck, and includes varieties with dark and pale bellies. Compare BARNACLE GOOSE with which it is often confused. Ⓒ 16c: perhaps from the obsolete term *branded* meaning 'brindled'.

brethren see under BROTHER

Breton /ˈbrɛtən, -tɒn/ ▻ *adj* **1** belonging or relating to Brittany, a region of NW France, its inhabitants, or their language. ▻ *noun* **1** a citizen or inhabitant of, or person born in, Brittany. **2** the Celtic language spoken in Brittany. Ⓒ 14c.

breve /briːv/ ▻ *noun* **1** a mark (˘) sometimes put over a vowel to show that it is short or unstressed. **2** *music* a note twice as long as a SEMIBREVE (now only rarely used). **3** *RC Church* a BRIEF (*noun* 4). Ⓒ 14c, meaning 'a royal mandate': from Latin *brevis* short.

breviary /ˈbriːvɪərɪ/ ▻ *noun* (***breviaries***) *RC Church* a book containing the hymns, prayers and psalms which form the daily service. See also DIVINE OFFICE. Ⓒ 17c; 16c meaning 'a brief statement': from Latin *breviarum* a summary.

brevity /ˈbrɛvɪtɪ/ ▻ *noun* (***brevities***) **1** using few words; conciseness □ *He admires brevity in speech.* **2** shortness of time □ *the brevity of this life.* Ⓒ 16c: probably from Anglo-French *brevete*, influenced by Latin *brevitas*, from *brevis* short.

brew ▻ *verb* (***brewed, brewing***) **1** to make (eg beer) by mixing, boiling and fermenting. **2** (*also* **brew up**) *tr & intr* to make (tea, coffee, etc) by mixing the leaves, grains, etc with boiling water. **3** *intr* to be in the process of brewing □ *Let the tea brew for a while.* **4** (*also* **brew up**) *intr* to get stronger and threaten □ *There's a storm brewing.* **5** (*especially* **brew up**) to plan or prepare something □ *brew up trouble.* ▻ *noun* **1** a drink produced by brewing, especially tea or beer. **2** an amount, especially an amount of beer, produced by brewing □ *last year's brew.* **3** the quality of what is brewed □ *a good strong brew.* **4** a concoction or mixture □ *a heady brew of passion and intrigue.* • **brewer** *noun* a person or company that brews and sells beer. • **brewing** *noun* **1** the act or process of making alcoholic drink, especially beer, from malt. **2** the quantity of beer, etc brewed at once. Ⓒ Anglo-Saxon *breowan*.

brewer's yeast ▻ *noun* a type of yeast used in the brewing of beer, and as a source of vitamins of the vitamin B complex for use in dietary supplements.

brewery ▻ *noun* (***breweries***) a place where beer and ale are brewed.

briar¹ or **brier** /braɪə(r)/ ▻ *noun* any of various prickly shrubs, especially a wild rose bush. Ⓒ Anglo-Saxon *brer*.

briar² or **brier** /braɪə(r)/ ▻ *noun* **1** a shrub or small tree, native to S Europe, the woody root of which is used to make tobacco pipes. **2** a tobacco pipe made from the root of this plant. Ⓒ 19c, originally *bruyer*: from French *bruyère* heath.

bribe /braɪb/ ▻ *noun* **1** a gift, usually of money, offered to someone to persuade them to do something illegal or improper. **2** something offered to someone in order to persuade them to behave in a certain way. ▻ *verb* (***bribed, bribing***) **1** *usually tr* to offer or promise a bribe, etc to someone. **2** to gain influence over or co-operation from someone, by offering a bribe. • **bribable** *adj.* • **briber** *noun.* • **bribery** *noun* **1** the act or practice of offering or taking bribes. **2** *law* the crime of deliberately using improper influence on public officials so as to win some advantage, eg the award of a contract. Ⓒ 14c, meaning 'something stolen' or 'plunder': apparently from a French word meaning 'a lump of bread given to a beggar'.

bric-à-brac /ˈbrɪkəbrak/ ▻ *noun* small objects of little financial value kept as decorations or ornaments; knick-knacks. Ⓒ 19c: French, from *à bric et à brac* at random.

brick /brɪk/ ▻ *noun* **1** a rectangular block of baked clay used for building. **2** the material used for making bricks. **3** a child's plastic or wooden building block, usually part of a set containing chiefly square or rectangular shapes. **4** something in the shape of a brick □ *a brick of ice cream.* **5** (**a brick**) *Brit colloq* a trusted, helpful, supportive person. ▻ *adj* **1** made of brick or of bricks □ *a brick wall.* **2** (*also* **brick-red**) having the dull brownish-red colour of ordinary bricks. ▻ *verb* (***bricked, bricking***) (*usually* **brick something in** or **over** or **up**) to close, cover, fill in or wall up (eg a window) with bricks. • **a brick short of a load** *colloq* not quite all there (see ALL THERE at ALL); rather dim-witted or slow. • **bang one's head against a brick wall** see under HEAD. • **make bricks without straw** to do a job without having the proper or necessary materials for it. Ⓒ 15c: from French *brique*, from Dutch *bricke*.

brickbat ▻ *noun* **1** an insult or criticism. **2** a piece of brick or anything hard thrown at someone. Ⓒ 16c in sense 2.

brickfield see under BRICKYARD

brickfielder ▻ *noun, Austral colloq* a hot dry dusty wind.

bricklayer ▻ *noun* in the building trade: a person who lays and builds with bricks. Often (*colloq*) shortened to **brickie**. • **bricklaying** *noun* the skill or practice of laying bricks in building.

brick-red see BRICK *adj* 2

brickwork ▻ *noun* **1** the part of a building, etc that is constructed of brick, eg the walls. **2** bricklaying.

brickworks ▻ *singular noun* a factory producing bricks.

brickyard ▻ *noun* a place where bricks are made. Also *formerly* (*chiefly Brit & Austral*) called **brickfield.**

bridal /ˈbraɪdəl/ ▻ *adj* belonging or relating to a bride or a wedding □ *bridal gown* □ *bridal suite.* Ⓒ Anglo-Saxon *brydeala*, originally a *noun* meaning 'wedding feast'; from *bryd* bride + *ealu* ale.

bride /braɪd/ ▻ *noun* a woman who has just been married, or is about to be married. Ⓒ Anglo-Saxon *bryd*.

bridegroom ▻ *noun* a man who has just been married, or is about to be married. Ⓒ Anglo-Saxon *brydguma*, from *bryd* bride + *guma* man.

bride-price ▻ *noun* especially in tribal societies: a price paid, usually in kind, to a bride's family by the bridegroom.

bridesmaid ▻ *noun* a girl or unmarried woman who attends the bride at a wedding. See also MAID OF HONOUR, MATRON OF HONOUR, PAGE[2], FLOWER GIRL

bridge[1] /brɪdʒ/ ▻ *noun* **1** a structure that spans a river, road, railway, valley, ravine or other obstacle, providing a continuous route across it for pedestrians, motor vehicles or trains. See also CANTILEVER BRIDGE, SUSPENSION BRIDGE. **2** anything that joins or connects two separate things or parts of something, or that connects across a gap. **3** on a ship: the narrow raised platform from which the captain and officers direct its course. **4** the hard bony upper part of the nose. **5** in a pair of spectacles: the part of the frame that rests on the bridge of the nose, connecting the two lenses. **6** on a violin, or guitar, etc: a thin, movable, upright piece of wood, etc which supports the strings and keeps them stretched tight. **7** *dentistry* a fixed replacement for one or more missing teeth, consisting of a partial denture that is permanently secured to one or more adjacent natural teeth. Also called **bridgework**. **8** *elec engineering* a type of electrical circuit for measuring RESISTANCE, etc. **9** *billiards, snooker, etc* a raised support with a long handle, on which the end of the CUE[2] can be rested, eg when playing an awkward shot. ▻ *verb* (***bridged, bridging***) **1** to form or build a bridge over (eg a river or railway). **2** to make a connection across something, or close the two sides of (a gap, etc) □ *managed to bridge our differences.* **3** *elec engineering* to make an electrical connection. ● **bridgeable** *adj.* ● **cross a bridge when one comes to it** to deal with a problem when it arises and not before. ⓒ Anglo-Saxon *brycg.*

bridge[2] /brɪdʒ/ ▻ *noun, cards* a game which developed from WHIST, for four people playing in pairs, in which the partner of the player who declares trumps (the **declarer**) lays down their cards face upwards, for the declarer to play them. See also AUCTION BRIDGE, CONTRACT BRIDGE. ⓒ 19c, when it was known also as *bridge whist* or *biritch.*

bridge-builder ▻ *noun* **1** a person who builds bridges. **2** a person who tries to settle a dispute or rift between two other people or parties. ● **bridge-building** *noun.*

bridgehead ▻ *noun* **1** *military* **a** an advanced position established inside enemy territory, from which an attack can be made; **b** a fortified position held at the end of a bridge which is nearest to the enemy. **2** a significant step forward or a position of advantage gained, from which major progress can be made. ⓒ Early 19c.

bridge roll ▻ *noun* a long thin soft bread roll. ⓒ 1920s.

bridgework see BRIDGE[1] *noun* 7

bridging loan ▻ *noun* a loan of money made, usually by a bank, to cover the period between having to pay for one thing, eg a new house, and receiving the funds to do so, eg the money from selling another house.

bridle /ˈbraɪdəl/ ▻ *noun* **1** the leather straps put on a horse's head which help the rider to control the horse. **2** anything used to control or restrain someone or something. ▻ *verb* (***bridled, bridling***) **1** to put a bridle on (a horse). **2** to bring something under control □ *bridle one's anger.* **3** (*especially* **bridle at something** or *sometimes* **bridle up**) *intr* to show anger or resentment, especially by moving the head upwards proudly or indignantly, like a horse being pulled up by the bridle □ *He bridled visibly at the price.* ⓒ Anglo-Saxon *bridel.*

bridle path and **bridle way** ▻ *noun* a path for riding or leading horses along.

Brie /briː/ ▻ *noun* a soft creamy French cheese with a whitish rind. ⓒ 19c: the name of the area in NE France where it is made.

brief /briːf/ ▻ *adj* (***briefer, briefest***) **1** lasting only a short time □ *a brief meeting.* **2** short or small □ *a brief pair of shorts.* **3** said of writing or speech: using few words; concise □ *a brief note.* ▻ *noun* **1** *law* **a** a summary of the facts and legal points of a case, prepared for the barrister who will be dealing with the case in court; **b** a case taken by a barrister; **c** *colloq* a barrister. **2** instructions given for a job or task. **3** (**briefs**) a woman's or man's close-fitting underpants without legs. **4** (*also* **breve** and **papal brief**) *RC Church* a letter from the Pope, less formal in nature than a papal BULL[3], written on a matter of discipline. ▻ *verb* (***briefed, briefing***) **1** to prepare someone by giving them instructions in advance. **2** *law* **a** to inform (a barrister) about a case by BRIEF (*noun* 1a); **b** to retain (a barrister) as counsel. ● **briefless** *adj* said of a barrister: holding no brief; without a client. ● **briefly** *adverb* **1** using few words □ *Let me explain it briefly.* **2** for a short time □ *visited her briefly at home.* ● **briefness** *noun* being brief, especially using few words; brevity. ● **hold a brief for someone** or **something** **1** *law* said of a barrister: to be retained as counsel for them or it. **2** to advocate something; to argue for them or it. ● **hold a brief** or **no brief for someone** or **something** to support or not to support (ie argue in favour of) them or it. ● **in brief** in few words; briefly. ⓒ 14c as *bref*: French, from Latin *brevis* short.

briefcase ▻ *noun* a light, usually flat, case for carrying papers, etc.

briefing ▻ *noun* **1** a meeting at which instructions and information are given, or any instance of making or giving a brief (see BRIEF *noun* 1a, 2). **2** the instructions or information given at such a meeting.

brier see BRIAR[1], BRIAR[2]

brig /brɪg/ ▻ *noun* **1** a type of sailing ship with two masts and square sails. **2** *originally US navy, slang* **a** a place of detention on board ship; **b** a prison. ⓒ 18c: shortened from BRIGANTINE.

Brig. ▻ *abbreviation* Brigadier.

brigade /brɪˈgeɪd/ ▻ *noun* **1** one of the subdivisions in the army, consisting eg of a group of regiments, usually commanded by a BRIGADIER. **2** *especially in compounds* a group of people, usually in uniform, organized for a specified purpose □ *the fire brigade.* ⓒ 17c: ultimately from Latin *briga* conflict or strife.

brigadier /brɪgəˈdɪə(r)/ ▻ *noun* **1** **a** an officer commanding a brigade; **b** in the British Army and Royal Marines: a staff officer. See table at RANK. **2** *US colloq* a brigadier general.

brigadier general ▻ *noun* in the US army: an officer ranking above a colonel. See table at RANK.

brigand /ˈbrɪgənd/ ▻ *noun* a member of a band of robbers, especially one operating in a remote mountain area. Also called BANDIT. ● **brigandage** or **brigandry** *noun.* ⓒ 15c: French, from Italian *brigante* a member of an armed band.

brigantine /ˈbrɪgəntiːn/ ▻ *noun* a type of sailing ship with two masts, that has its sails SQUARE-RIGGED on its foremast, and FORE-AND-AFT on its mainmast. Compare BRIG, SCHOONER. ⓒ 16c: from Italian *brigantino* a pirate ship.

Brig. Gen. ▻ *abbreviation* Brigadier General.

bright /braɪt/ ▻ *adj* (***brighter, brightest***) **1** giving out or shining with much light. **2** said of a colour: strong, light and clear. **3** lively; cheerful. **4** *colloq* clever and quick to learn □ *He's a bright boy, especially at maths.* **5** full of hope or promise □ *a bright future.* ▻ *adverb, literary* brightly □ *a fire burning bright.* ● **brightly** *adverb.* ● **brightness** *noun.* ● **as bright as a button** *colloq* said especially of a child: very intelligent and alert. ● **bright and early** very early in the morning; in good time. ● **look on the bright side** to be hopeful and consider the best features of something. ⓒ Anglo-Saxon *beorht* or byrht.

brighten ▻ *verb* (***brightened, brightening***) *tr & intr* (*often* **brighten up**) **1** to become, or make something or someone, bright or brighter. **2** to make or become happier or more cheerful □ *She brightened up at the news.*

the bright lights ▻ *plural noun* a big city seen as a place of entertainment and excitement.

bright spark ▻ *noun, often derog* a clever, or lively and eager, young person.

brill[1] /brɪl/ ▻ *noun* (***brills*** or ***brill***) a large flatfish, found mainly in shallow European coastal waters, which has a freckled sandy brown body and is valued as a food fish. ◷ 15c.

brill[2] ▻ *adj, dated Brit slang* excellent. ◷ 1980s: short for BRILLIANT 5.

brilliance and **brilliancy** ▻ *noun* **1** intense or sparkling brightness; radiance. **2** outstanding intelligence or technical skill □ *a display of musical brilliance.*

brilliant /ˈbrɪlɪənt/ ▻ *adj* **1** very bright and sparkling. **2** said of a colour: bright and vivid. **3** said of a person: showing outstanding intelligence or talent. **4** making a great display or show. **5** *colloq* excellent; exceptionally good. **6** (*usually* **brilliant-cut**) *technical* said of a gem, especially a diamond: cut so as to have a lot of facets, so that it sparkles brightly. ▻ *noun* a diamond or other gem. • **brilliantly** *adverb*. ◷ 17c: from French *brillant*, from *briller* to shine.

brilliantine /ˈbrɪljəntiːn/ ▻ *noun, old use* a perfumed oil used by men to make the hair shiny. • **brilliantined** *adj*. ◷ 19c: from French *brillantine*, from *brillant* shining.

brim ▻ *noun* **1** the top edge or lip of a cup, glass, bowl, etc □ *full to the very brim.* **2** the projecting edge of a hat. ▻ *verb* (***brimmed, brimming***) *intr* to be, or become, full to the brim □ *eyes brimming with tears.* • **brimless** *adj* said especially of a hat: not having a brim. ◷ 13c.

■ **brim over** *intr* to become full and begin to overflow.

■ **brim over with something** said of a person: to be unable to contain or control (eg happiness, or other emotion) □ *She was brimming over with excitement.*

brimful or **brimfull** ▻ *adj, following its noun* **1** (*sometimes* **brimful of** or **with something**) full to the brim □ *a bucket brimfull of money.* **2** said of eyes: brimming over with tears.

brimstone ▻ *noun, old use* sulphur. ◷ Anglo-Saxon *brynstan*, literally 'burning stone'.

brimstone butterfly ▻ *noun* a wide-winged butterfly, found in hedgerows, woodland margins and gardens, and so called because the male has brilliant yellow wings.

brindled /ˈbrɪndəld/ ▻ *adj* said of animals: brown or grey, and marked with streaks or patches of a darker colour. ◷ 15c as *brinded*, from earlier *brended*, from *brend* burnt.

brine /braɪn/ ▻ *noun* **1** very salty water, used for preserving food. **2** *literary* the sea □ *fell into the foaming brine.* See also BRINY. • **brinish** *adj*. ◷ Anglo-Saxon *bryne*.

bring /brɪŋ/ ▻ *verb* (***brought*** /brɔːt/, ***bringing***) **1** to carry or take something or someone to a stated or implied place or person □ *Bring the cup here.* **2** to make someone or something be in, or reach, a certain state □ *It brought him to his senses* □ *bring two new rules into effect.* **3** to make something or result in it □ *War brings misery.* **4** (*especially* **bring oneself to do something**) *usually with negatives* to persuade, make or force oneself to do (something unpleasant) □ *I can't bring myself to tell her.* **5** (*especially* **bring in something**) to be sold for (a stated price); to produce (a stated amount) as income. **6** to make (a charge or action, etc) against someone. **7** to give (evidence) to a court, etc. • **bringer** *noun*. • **bring home something** (*often* **bring something home to someone**) to prove or show it clearly. • **bring the house down** said of an actor or performer, etc: to receive ecstatic applause; to be brilliantly successful. • **bring something to bear** to make (pressure or influence) felt; to apply it. • **bring something to mind** to make it be remembered or thought about □ *That story brought to mind my student days.* • **bring up the rear** to come last or behind all the others. • **bring someone up short** to make them stop suddenly □ *The doorbell brought me up short.* ◷ Anglo-Saxon *bringan*.

■ **bring something about** to make it happen; to cause it.

■ **bring something** or **someone along 1** usually said of a person: to bring or convey (a thing or person) with them. **2** to help something develop □ *His visit brought the decorating along greatly.*

■ **bring something back** to make (a thought or memory) return.

■ **bring someone down 1** to make them sad or disappointed, etc. **2** to demean them.

■ **bring something down** to make it fall or collapse.

■ **bring something forth** *formal or old use* to give birth to or produce (an offspring, etc).

■ **bring something forward 1** to move (an arrangement, etc) to an earlier date or time. **2** to draw attention to it □ *I hesitate to bring the matter forward.* **3** *bookkeeping* to transfer (a partial sum) to the head of the next column.

■ **bring something in 1** to introduce it or make it effective, etc. **2** to produce (income or profit).

■ **bring something off** *colloq* to succeed in doing (something difficult) □ *It's really tricky, so I hope I can bring it off OK.*

■ **bring something on 1** to help it to develop or progress □ *The rain will bring on my seedlings.* **2** to make it happen or appear □ *This weather brings on my arthritis.*

■ **bring something out 1** (*often* **bring something out in someone**) to emphasize or clarify it □ *brings out the worst in me.* **2** to publish or release it □ *brought out a new novel.*

■ **bring someone out in something** to cause them to be affected with (spots or a rash, etc) □ *Cats bring me out in spots.*

■ **bring someone over** or **round** or **around** to convince them that one's own opinions, etc are right; to convert them to one's own side.

■ **bring someone round** to cause them to recover consciousness.

■ **bring someone to** to make (someone who is asleep or unconscious) wake up.

■ **bring something to** *naut* to bring (a ship) to a standstill.

■ **bring someone up** to care for and educate them when young.

■ **bring something up 1** to introduce (a subject) for discussion. **2** to vomit or regurgitate (something eaten).

bring and buy sale ▻ *noun, chiefly Brit* a charity sale to which people bring items to be sold, and at which they buy other items.

brinjal /ˈbrɪndʒɑːl/ ▻ *noun* especially in Indian cookery: the aubergine. ◷ 17c: an Anglo-Indian adaptation of Portuguese *berinjela*.

brink ▻ *noun* **1** the edge or border of a steep dangerous place or of a river. **2** the point immediately before something dangerous, unknown or exciting, etc starts or occurs □ *the brink of a new era* □ *the brink of disaster.* • **on the brink of something** at the very point or moment when it might start or occur, etc; extremely near it □ *on* *the brink of extinction.* ◑ 13c: probably Danish, meaning 'steepness' or 'slope'.

brinkmanship and **brinksmanship** ▷ *noun* especially in politics and international affairs: the art or practice of going to the very edge of a dangerous situation (eg war) before moving back or withdrawing. ◑ 1950s.

briny /'braɪnɪ/ ▷ *adj* (***brinier***, ***briniest***) said of water: very salty. ▷ *noun* (**the briny**) *colloq* the sea. ◑ 17c: from BRINE.

brioche /briː'ɒʃ/ ▷ *noun* a type of light soft cake-like bread or roll, made with a yeast dough, eggs and butter. ◑ 19c: French.

briquette or **briquet** /brɪ'kɛt/ ▷ *noun* a brick-shaped block made of compressed coal-dust or charcoal, etc, used for fuel. ◑ 19c: French, meaning 'little brick'.

brisk ▷ *adj* **1** lively, active or quick ▫ ***a brisk walk*** ▫ ***a brisk response.*** **2** said of the weather: pleasantly cold and fresh. • **briskly** *adverb*. • **briskness** *noun*. ◑ 16c: perhaps related to Welsh *brysg* brisk of foot.

brisket /'brɪskɪt/ ▷ *noun* **1** *cookery, etc* meat from next to the ribs of a bull or cow. **2** the breast or chest of a four-legged animal, especially of a bull or cow. ◑ 14c as *brusket*.

brisling /'brɪslɪŋ/ ▷ *noun* a small marine fish of the herring family, fished in Norwegian fjords, and usually processed and canned in oil. ◑ 19c: Norwegian.

bristle /'brɪsəl/ ▷ *noun* **1** a short stiff hair on an animal or plant. **2** something similar to this but man-made, used eg for brushes. ▷ *verb* (***bristled***, ***bristling***) **1** *tr & intr* said of an animal's or a person's hair: to stand upright and stiff. **2** (*usually* **bristle with something**) *intr* to show obvious anger or rage, etc ▫ ***bristling with resentment.*** **3** (*usually* **bristle with something**) *intr* to be covered or closely-packed with (upright objects) ▫ ***a room bristling with people.*** • **bristled** *adj*. • **bristling** *adj* said of a beard or eyebrows, etc: thick and rough. ◑ 14c as *brustel*, from Anglo-Saxon *byrst*.

bristly ▷ *adj* (***bristlier***, ***bristliest***) **1** having bristles; rough or prickly. **2** likely to be or tending to become quickly angry ▫ ***He's a bristly character.*** • **bristliness** *noun*.

bristols /'brɪstəlz/ ▷ *plural noun* (*especially* **pair of bristols**) *Brit slang* female breasts. ◑ 1960s: from Cockney rhyming slang *Bristol city* for TITTY.

Brit ▷ *noun, colloq* a British person ▫ ***the Brits abroad.***

Brit. ▷ *abbreviation* **1** Britain. **2** British.

Britain, British, British Isles, Great Britain, United Kingdom

Great Britain consists of England, Scotland and Wales; **United Kingdom** is a political term denoting 'the United Kingdom of Great Britain and Northern Ireland', and excludes the Isle of Man and the Channel Islands; **British Isles** is a geographical term which embraces the United Kingdom, the island of Ireland (ie including the Republic of Ireland), the Isle of Man, and the Channel Islands; **Britain** is a term with no official status, and is generally used to refer either to Great Britain or to the United Kingdom. **British** means 'relating to Britain', in either of the senses above.

Britannia /brɪ'tanjə/ ▷ *noun* **1** a female warrior wearing a helmet and carrying a shield and a trident, usually portrayed in a seated pose as an image or personification of Britain. **2** *historical* in the Roman empire: the province occupying the south of what is now Great Britain. **3** short for BRITANNIA METAL (*especially as adj*). ◑ Latin in sense 2.

Britannia metal ▷ *noun* a silvery-white alloy, consisting mainly of tin and antimony, used to make bearings and tableware.

Britannic /brɪ'tanɪk/ ▷ *adj, formal*, used in some official titles: belonging or relating to Britain ▫ ***His Britannic Majesty.*** ◑ 17c: from Latin *britannicus*, from BRITANNIA.

britches see BREECHES

Briticism /'brɪtɪsɪzəm/ and **Britishism** ▷ *noun* a word, phrase or custom, etc that is characteristic of the British or of the English spoken in Britain. Compare AMERICANISM, GALLICISM. ◑ 19c.

British /'brɪtɪʃ/ ▷ *adj* **1** belonging or relating to GREAT BRITAIN or its inhabitants. **2** belonging or relating to the British Empire or to the Commonwealth. **3** belonging or relating to the variety of English used in Britain. **4** (**the British**) the people of Great Britain as a group (see THE 4). ▷ *noun* **1** British English. **2** *historical* the language of the ancient Britons. • **Britisher** *US* a British person. • **Britishness** *noun*. ◑ Anglo-Saxon *Bryttisc*, from *Bryt* a Briton or Welshman.

the British Isles ▷ *noun* the group of islands consisting of Great Britain and Ireland, and all the other smaller islands around them, eg the Hebrides, Channel Islands and Isle of Man.

British Summer Time ▷ *noun* (abbreviation **BST**) the system of time (one hour ahead of GREENWICH MEAN TIME) used in Britain during the summer to give extra daylight in the evenings.

British thermal unit ▷ *noun, physics* (abbreviation **BTU**) in the imperial system: a unit of heat energy, equal to the amount of heat required to raise the temperature of one pound of water by one degree Fahrenheit, equivalent to 1054.5 joules or 252 calories.

Briton /'brɪtən/ ▷ *noun* **1** a British person. **2** (*also* **ancient Briton**) *historical* one of the Celtic people living in Southern Britain before the Roman conquest. ◑ 13c as *Breton*: French, from Latin *Britto, Brittonis*.

Britpop ▷ *noun* a melody-driven guitar music, with an emphasis on good song-writing, and often drawing inspiration from the music scene of the 1960s in Britain. ◑ 1990s.

brittle /'brɪtəl/ ▷ *adj* (***brittler, brittlest***) **1** said of a substance: hard but easily broken or likely to break. **2** sharp or hard in quality ▫ ***a brittle laugh.*** **3** said of a condition or state, etc: difficult to keep stable or controlled; fragile, easily damaged or disrupted ▫ ***a brittle relationship*** ▫ ***a brittle diabetic.*** ▷ *noun* (***brittles***) a type of hard crunchy toffee made from caramelized sugar and nuts. • **brittlely** or **brittly** *adverb*. • **brittleness** *noun*. ◑ 14c as *britul*, from Anglo-Saxon *breotan* to break in pieces.

brittle bone disease and **brittle bones** ▷ *noun, medicine* a hereditary disease, associated with an abnormality of the structural protein collagen, and characterized by abnormal fragility of the bones of the skeleton, resulting in fractures and physical deformities.

brittlestar ▷ *noun* a starfish-like ECHINODERM with five long slender fragile mobile arms radiating from a disc-like body.

BRN ▷ *abbreviation, IVR* Bahrain.

Bro. ▷ *abbreviation* (*plural* ***Bros***) Brother.

bro' see SOUL BROTHER

broach /broutʃ/ ▷ *verb* (***broaches***, ***broached***, ***broaching***) **1** to raise (a subject, especially one likely to cause arguments or problems) for discussion. **2** to open (a bottle, cask or barrel, etc) to remove liquid. **3** to open (a bottle or other container) and start using its contents ▫ ***broach a new jar of olives.*** ▷ *noun* (***broaches***) **1** a long tapering pointed tool for making and rounding out holes. **2** a roasting-spit. ◑ 13c as *broche*: ultimately from Latin *brochus* projecting.

broach

There is sometimes a spelling confusion between **broach** and **brooch**.

broad /brɔːd/ ▻ *adj* (***broader, broadest***) **1** large in extent from one side to the other □ *The sink is two foot broad.* Opposite of DEEP. **2** wide and open; spacious. **3** general, not detailed □ *a broad inquiry.* **4** clear; full □ *in broad daylight.* **5** strong; obvious □ *a broad hint.* **6** main; concentrating on the main elements rather than on detail □ *the broad facts of the case.* **7** tolerant or liberal □ *take a broad view.* **8** said of an accent or speech: strongly marked by local dialect or features □ *broad Scots.* **9** usually said of a joke or anecdote, etc: rather rude and vulgar. **10** *econ* said of money: belonging to one of the less LIQUID (*adj* 5) categories, eg money deposited in an account, etc so that it cannot be realized into cash without several months' notice. See M^2. ▻ *noun* **1** *N Amer, offensive slang* a woman. **2** (**the Broads**) a series of low-lying shallow lakes connected by rivers in E Anglia. **3** the broad part of something. • **broadly** *adverb* widely; generally □ *broadly speaking* □ *I broadly agree.* • **broadness** *noun.* • **broad in the beam** *colloq* said of a person: wide across the hips or buttocks. ⓒ Originally and literally used of a ship which is 'wide in proportion to its length' (see BEAM *noun* 4). • **have broad shoulders** said of a person: to be able to accept a great deal of responsibility. • **it's as broad as it is long** said of a situation or problem, etc: it makes no difference which way you look at it, approach it or deal with it, etc; the result will be the same either way. ⓒ Anglo-Saxon *brad.*

B-road ▻ *noun* in the UK: a secondary road. Compare A-ROAD.

broadband ▻ *adj* **1** *telecomm* across, involving or designed to operate across a wide range of frequencies. **2** *computing* capable of accommodating data from a variety of input sources, such as voice, telephone, TV, etc.

broad-based ▻ *adj* including a wide range of opinions, people, political groups, etc □ *a broad-based sample.*

broad bean ▻ *noun* **1** an annual plant of the bean family, cultivated worldwide for its large edible seeds, which grow in pods. **2** one of the large flattened pale green edible seeds of this plant, eaten as a vegetable, and sometimes used to feed livestock. ⓒ 18c.

broadcast ▻ *verb* (***broadcast, broadcasting***) **1** *tr & intr* to transmit (a radio or TV programme, speech, etc) for reception by the public. **2** *intr* to take part in a radio or TV broadcast. **3** to make something widely known. **4** to sow (seeds) by scattering them in all directions, especially by hand, as opposed to sowing in drills. ▻ *noun* **1** a radio or TV programme. **2** the transmission of a radio or TV programme for reception by the public. **3** the act or practice of broadcasting seed. ▻ *adj* **1** communicated or sent out by radio or TV □ *on broadcast news.* **2** widely known or scattered. ▻ *adverb* in all directions; widely. • **broadcaster** *noun* a person who takes part in broadcasts, especially on a regular or professional basis. • **broadcasting** *noun.* ⓒ 18c as *adjective* 2, relating to seed 'scattered over an entire area': BROAD *adj* + CAST *verb.*

Broad Church ▻ *noun* **1** a party within the Church of England that favours a broad and liberal interpretation of dogmatic definitions, doctrine, taking of creeds, etc. **2** (*usually* **broad church**) a political or other group or party, etc that is similarly liberal-minded and all-inclusive.

broadcloth ▻ *noun* a thick good-quality cloth made from wool, cotton or silk. ⓒ 15c.

broaden /ˈbrɔːdən/ ▻ *verb* (***broadened, broadening***) (*also* **broaden out**) *tr & intr* to become or make something broad or broader.

broad gauge ▻ *noun* a railway track that is wider than the standard size of STANDARD GAUGE. See GAUGE *noun.* Also (**broad-gauge**) *as adj.*

broadloom ▻ *adj* said especially of a carpet: woven on a wide loom to give broad widths.

broadly see under BROAD

broad-minded ▻ *adj* tolerant and accepting of other people's opinions, preferences, habits, etc; liberal. • **broad-mindedly** *adverb.* • **broad-mindedness** *noun.*

broadsheet ▻ *noun* **1** a newspaper printed on large sheets of paper, usually approximately 40 x 60cm (c.16 x 24in). Compare TABLOID. **2** a large sheet of paper, usually printed on one side only, for advertisements, etc.

broadside ▻ *noun* **1** a strongly critical verbal attack. **2** *navy* **a** all of the guns on one side of a warship; **b** the firing of all of these guns simultaneously. • **broadside on** sideways on. ⓒ 16c, literally 'the broad side' (of a ship).

broadsword ▻ *noun, old use* a heavy sword with a broad blade, chiefly used for cutting with a two-handed swinging action.

brocade /brəˈkeɪd/ ▻ *noun* a heavy silk fabric with a raised design on it, often one using gold or silver threads. • **brocaded** *adj.* ⓒ 16c as *brocardo* or *brocado*: from Italian *broccato*, from *brocco* a twisted thread or spike.

Broca's area /ˈbrɒkəz —/ ▻ *noun, anatomy* the region of the brain responsible for speech, located in the left frontal lobe in most right-handed people. ⓒ Late 19c: named after Paul Broca (1824–80), a French surgeon.

broccoli /ˈbrɒkəlɪ/ ▻ *noun* (*plural* in sense 1 only ***broccolis***) **1** a type of cultivated cabbage grown for its green leafy stalks and branched heads of flower buds. Also called **sprouting broccoli**. **2** the immature buds of this plant, eaten as a vegetable. ⓒ 17c: plural of Italian *broccolo* 'little shoot', from *brocco* a shoot.

broch /brɒk, brɒx/ ▻ *noun, archaeol* (*rare* except in Scotland) a circular tower built of dry stone, dating from the late Iron Age, with galleries in the thickness of the wall and an open central area. ⓒ 17c: from Norse *borg.*

brochette /brəˈʃɛt/ ▻ *noun, cookery* a small metal or wooden skewer for holding food together or steady while it is being cooked. ⓒ 15c: French, diminutive of *broche* a brooch or needle.

brochure /ˈbroʊʃʊə(r), ˈbroʊʃə(r)/ ▻ *noun* a booklet or pamphlet, especially one giving information or publicity about holidays, products, etc. ⓒ 18c: French, from *brocher* to stitch.

broderie anglaise /ˈbroʊdərɪ ɑ̃ˈgleɪz, ˈbrɒdrɪ ɑ̃ˈglɛz/ ▻ *noun* **1** a method of embroidery used for decorating cotton and linen, by forming openwork patterns of tiny holes and stitches. **2** fine embroidery-work of this kind. ⓒ 19c: French, literally 'English embroidery'.

brogue¹ /broʊg/ ▻ *noun,* (*usually* **brogues**) a type of strong heavy-soled leather outdoor shoe, typically patterned with decorative punched holes. ⓒ 16c: from Gaelic *bròg* shoe.

brogue² /broʊg/ ▻ *noun* a strong but gentle accent, especially the type of English spoken by an Irish person. ⓒ 18c.

broil /brɔɪl/ ▻ *verb* (***broiled, broiling***) **1** *chiefly N Amer* to grill (food). **2** *intr* to be extremely hot. • **broiler** *noun* **1** a small chicken suitable for broiling. **2** *especially N Amer* a grill. **3** *colloq* a very hot day. ⓒ 14c: from French *bruiller* to burn.

broke /broʊk/ ▻ *adj, colloq* **1** having no money; bankrupt. **2** short of money; hard-up. ▻ *verb, past tense, old past participle of* BREAK. • **go for broke** *slang* to risk everything one has left in a last attempt to win or succeed. ⓒ 17c.

broken ▻ *adj* **1** smashed; fractured. **2** disturbed or interrupted □ *broken sleep.* **3** not working properly. **4** said of a promise, agreement or law, etc: not kept; violated or infringed. **5** said of a marriage or family, etc: split apart by divorce. **6** said of language, especially speech: not perfect or fluent; halting. **7** usually said of a person: brought down, weakened and tired out, or with their life shattered, eg as a result of illness or misfortune □ *a broken man.* **8** BROKEN-IN 1. **9** with an uneven rough surface □ *broken ground.* **10** *music* played or written in ARPEGGIO form. ▻ *verb, past participle of* BREAK. • **brokenly** *adverb.* • **brokenness** *noun.* ⓒ 14c.

broken chord ▻ *noun, music* an ARPEGGIO.

broken-down ▻ *adj* **1** said of a machine, etc: not in working order. **2** said of an animal or person: not in good condition, spirits or health.

broken-hearted ▻ *adj* deeply hurt emotionally, or overwhelmed with sadness or grief, especially because of a disappointment or loss in love. • **broken-heartedly** *adverb*.

broken home ▻ *noun* a home that has been disrupted by the separation or divorce of parents.

broken-in ▻ *adj* **1** (*also* **broken**) said of an animal, especially a horse: made tame through training; trained for the saddle and/or bridle. **2** said of shoes, etc: made comfortable by being worn. See also BREAK IN SOMETHING at BREAK

brokenly and **brokenness** see under BROKEN

broken reed ▻ *noun* a weak person who cannot be relied on.

broken wind see HEAVES

broker ▻ *noun* **1** a person employed to buy and sell stocks and shares; a stockbroker. See also BROKER-DEALER. **2** *in compounds* a person who acts as an agent for other people in buying and selling goods or property □ *insurance broker* □ *commodity broker*. **3** a negotiator or middleman. **4** a person who buys and sells secondhand goods; a pawnbroker. ◷ 14c as *brocor*, originally meaning 'someone who broaches (eg a cask)': from Anglo-French *brocour*.

brokerage /'broukərɪdʒ/ ▻ *noun* **1** the profit taken by, or fee charged by, a broker for transacting business for other people; commission. **2** the business or office of a broker. ◷ 15c in sense 2.

broker-dealer ▻ *noun* in the UK stock exchange since the BIG BANG: a firm or a person officially combining the jobs of STOCKBROKER and STOCKJOBBER, but only able to act as one or the other in any single deal.

broking /'broukɪŋ/ ▻ *noun* the trade or business of a broker.

brolga ▻ *noun* (*brolgas*) a large grey Australian crane. Also called **native companion**.

brolly /'brɒlɪ/ ▻ *noun* (*brollies*) *chiefly Brit colloq* an UMBRELLA (sense 1). ◷ 19c.

bromeliad /brə'miːlɪad/ ▻ *noun, bot* any of numerous plants, most of which are EPIPHYTEs found in the canopy of tropical rainforests that typically have large strap-shaped fleshy leaves forming a rosette around a central cup in which water accumulates. The pineapple is a bromeliad. ◷ 19c: named after Olaus Bromel (1639–1705), the Swedish botanist.

bromide /'broumaɪd/ ▻ *noun* **1** *chem* any chemical compound that is a salt of HYDROBROMIC ACID, including various compounds used medicinally as sedatives, and silver bromide, which is used to coat photographic film. **2** *rather formal or old use* a much-used and now meaningless statement or phrase; a platitude. ◷ 19c: *bromine* + *-ide*.

bromide paper ▻ *noun* a type of paper with a surface that has been coated with silver bromide to make it sensitive to light, used for printing photographs.

bromine /'broumiːn, -maɪn/ ▻ *noun* (symbol **Br**) a non-metallic element consisting of a dark-red highly-corrosive liquid with a pungent smell, compounds of which are used in photographic film, water purification, anti-knock petrol additives, and in the manufacture of plastics and organic chemicals. ◷ 19c: from Greek *bromos* stink + -INE².

bronchi *plural of* BRONCHUS

bronchial /'brɒnkɪəl/ ▻ *adj, anatomy* relating to either of the two main airways to the lungs, known as the BRONCHI. • **bronchially** *adverb*.

bronchial tube ▻ *noun, anatomy* either of the two BRONCHI, or one of their smaller branches.

bronchiole /'brɒŋkɪoul/ ▻ *noun, anatomy* any of the minute branches of the BRONCHI. ◷ 19c.

bronchitic /brɒŋ'kɪtɪk/ *pathol* ▻ *adj* relating to or suffering from bronchitis. ▻ *noun* a person suffering from bronchitis.

bronchitis /brɒŋ'kaɪtɪs/ ▻ *noun, pathol* inflammation of the mucous membrane of the BRONCHI, characterized by coughing, contraction and narrowing of the bronchi, and fever, and usually caused by bacterial or viral infection, cigarette smoking or air pollution. ◷ 19c: from BRONCHUS + -ITIS.

bronchodilator /brɒŋkoudaɪ'leɪtə(r)/ ▻ *noun, medicine* any drug or other agent that relaxes the smooth muscle of the bronchi, causing the air passages in the lungs to widen, used to treat asthma and chronic bronchitis. ◷ Early 20c.

bronchoscope ▻ *noun, medicine* a device used to examine the interior of the lungs in order to diagnose a disease or disorder, or to remove tissue for a biopsy. ◷ 19c.

bronchus /'brɒŋkəs/ ▻ *noun* (*plural* ***bronchi*** /-kaɪ/) either of the two main airways to the lungs that branch off the lower end of the TRACHEA. ◷ 18c: from Greek *bronchos* windpipe.

bronco /'brɒŋkou/ ▻ *noun* (***broncos***) a wild or half-tamed horse from the western US. ◷ 19c: American Spanish, from Spanish *adj* meaning 'rough'.

brontosaurus /brɒntə'sɔːrəs/ and **brontosaur** ▻ *noun* (*plural* ***brontosauri*** /-raɪ/ and ***brontosaurs***) the former names for APATOSAURUS. ◷ 19c: from Greek *bronte* thunder + *sauros* lizard.

Bronx cheer /brɒŋks —/ ▻ *noun, US* a rude sound made with the tongue and lips, to show disapproval or contempt. *Brit equivalent* RASPBERRY. ◷ 1920s: named after the Bronx, a borough of New York City.

bronze /brɒnz/ ▻ *noun* **1** an alloy of copper and tin that is harder than pure copper, resistant to corrosion, and suitable for casting. **2** the dark orangey-brown colour of bronze. **3** a BRONZE MEDAL. **4** a work of art made of bronze. ▻ *adj* **1** made of bronze. **2** having the colour of bronze. ▻ *verb* (***bronzed***, ***bronzing***) **1** to give a bronze colour, surface or appearance to something. **2** *intr* to become the colour of bronze, or tanned. • **bronzed** *adj* having a bronze colour; suntanned. • **bronzy** *adj* (***bronzier***, ***bronziest***). ◷ 18c: French, from Italian *bronzo*.

Bronze Age ▻ *noun* (*usually* **the Bronze Age**) the period in the history of humankind, between about 3000 and 1000BC, when tools, weapons, etc were made out of bronze.

bronze medal ▻ *noun* in athletics and other competitive sports events, etc: a medal given to the competitor who comes third.

bronzing ▻ *noun* the process of giving or acquiring a bronze-like colour or surface.

brooch /broutʃ/ ▻ *noun* (***brooches***) a decoration or piece of jewellery with a hinged pin at the back for fastening it to clothes. ◷ 13c as *broche*: French; see BROACH *noun*.

> ***brooch***
>
> There is sometimes a spelling confusion between **brooch** and **broach**.

brood /bruːd/ ▻ *noun* **1** a number of young animals, especially birds, that are produced or hatched at the same time. **2** *colloq, usually humorous* all the children in a family. **3** a kind, breed or race of something. **4** *as adj*: **a** said of an animal: kept for breeding □ *brood mare*; **b** used for or relating to the brooding of offspring □ *brood-pouch*. ▻ *verb* (***brooded***, ***brooding***) *intr* **1** said of a bird: to sit on eggs in order to hatch them. **2** (*often* **brood about, on** or **over something**) to think anxiously or resentfully about it for a period of time. • **brooder** *noun*. ◷ Anglo-Saxon *brod*.

> ■ **brood over someone** or **somewhere** to hang over them or it as a threat □ ***The prospect of redundancy now broods over the town.***

brooding ▻ *adj* **1** said of a person: thinking anxiously or resentfully about something. **2** said of something threatening, oppressive, gloomy, etc: hanging closely over or around □ ***brooding stormclouds*** □ ***a brooding silence.*** • **broodingly** *adverb*.

broody ▻ *adj* (***broodier, broodiest***) **1** said of a bird: ready and wanting to brood. **2** said of a person: deep in anxious or resentful thought; moody. **3** *colloq* said of a woman: eager to have a baby. • **broodily** *adverb*. • **broodiness** *noun*. ◷ 16c.

brook[1] /brʊk/ *noun* a small stream. ◷ Anglo-Saxon *broc*.

brook[2] /brʊk/ *verb* (***brooked, brooking***) *formal, usually with negatives* to tolerate, endure or accept □ ***I shall brook no criticism.*** ◷ 16c in this sense; Anglo-Saxon *brucan*, meaning 'to enjoy'.

broom /bruːm/ ▻ *noun* **1 a** a long-handled sweeping brush, formerly made from the stems of the broom plant, but now usually made from straw or synthetic material; **b** a BESOM. **2** any of various deciduous shrubby plants of the pea family with white, purple or yellow flowers. **3** (**common broom**) a deciduous shrubby plant of the pea family, native to Europe, which has straight green ridged stems, small leaves and loose clusters of bright yellow flowers followed by black pods. ◷ Anglo-Saxon *brom*.

broomrape ▻ *noun* an annual or perennial plant that lacks chlorophyll, produces dense spikes of brownish flowers, has leaves reduced to scales and is parasitic on broom, ivy and members of the daisy family.

broomstick ▻ *noun* the long handle of a BROOM (sense 1).

Bros ▻ *abbreviation* / *sometimes* brɒs/ (used especially in the name of a company) Brothers.

broth /brɒθ/ ▻ *noun* **1** *cookery* **a** a thin clear soup made by boiling meat, fish or vegetables, etc in water (compare SCOTCH BROTH); **b** stock. **2** *scientific* broth (sense 1a) used as a medium for the culture of bacteria. ◷ Anglo-Saxon, from *breowan* to brew.

brothel /ˈbrɒθəl/ ▻ *noun* a house where men can go to have sexual intercourse with prostitutes for money (currently illegal in the UK and most of the US). ◷ 14c, meaning 'a worthless person' and later 'a prostitute', from Anglo-Saxon *brothen* ruined or worthless.

brother /ˈbrʌðə(r)/ ▻ *noun* (***brothers*** or (*archaic or formal except in sense 3*) ***brethren***) **1** a boy or man with the same natural parents as another person or people. Compare BROTHER-IN-LAW, HALF-BROTHER, STEPBROTHER. **2** a man belonging to the same group, society, church, trade union, etc as another or others. **3** (*plural* ***brethren***)a man who is a member of a religious group, especially a monk. **4** (*often* **brother-man**) a fellow-creature □ ***We are all brothers under the sun.*** **5** *especially US dialect or Black slang, also Brit facetious* as a form of address to a man: friend; mate. See also SOUL BROTHER. ◷ Anglo-Saxon *brothor*, plural *brether*.

brotherhood ▻ *noun* **1** an association of men formed for a particular purpose, especially a religious purpose. **2** friendliness, or a sense of companionship or unity, etc felt towards people one has something in common with. **3** the state of being a brother. See also FRATERNITY.

brother-in-law ▻ *noun* (***brothers-in-law***) **1** the brother of one's husband or wife. **2** the husband of one's sister. **3** the husband of the sister of one's own wife or husband.

brotherly ▻ *adj* like a brother; kind, affectionate. Compare FRATERNAL. • **brotherliness** *noun*.

brougham /ˈbruːəm/ ▻ *noun* **1** a type of light, closed carriage pulled by four horses, with a raised open seat for the driver. **2** an early type of motor car with the driver's seat uncovered. ◷ 19c: named after Lord Brougham (1778–1868).

brought *past tense, past participle of* BRING

brouhaha /ˈbruːhɑːhɑː/ ▻ *noun* (***brouhahas***) noisy, excited and confused activity; a commotion or uproar. ◷ 19c: French.

brow /braʊ/ ▻ *noun* **1** (*usually* **brows**) short form of EYEBROW. **2** the forehead □ ***a furrowed brow.*** **3** *literary* a person's appearance or expression □ ***a troubled brow.*** **4** the top of a hill, road or pass, etc; the summit. **5** the edge of a cliff, etc. ◷ Anglo-Saxon *bru*.

browbeat ▻ *verb* to frighten or intimidate someone by speaking angrily or sternly, or by looking fierce; to bully. • **browbeaten** *adj*. ◷ 16c.

brown /braʊn/ ▻ *adj* (***browner, brownest***) **1** having the colour of dark soil or wood, or any of various shades of this colour tending towards red or yellow. **2** said of bread, etc: made from wholemeal flour and therefore darker in colour than white bread. **3** having a dark skin or complexion. **4** having a skin tanned from being in the sun. ▻ *noun* **1** any of various dark earthy colours, like those of bark, tanned skin or coffee, etc. **2** brown paint, dye, pigment, material or clothes. ▻ *verb* (***browned, browning***) *tr & intr* to make or become brown by cooking, tanning in the sun, etc □ ***Brown the meat in a little oil.*** • **brownish** *adj* somewhat brown in colour. • **brownness** *noun*. • **browny** *adj* brownish. ◷ Anglo-Saxon *brun*.

brown alga ▻ *noun, biol* any member of a class of mainly marine algae, eg kelp, characterized by the presence of the brown pigment fucoxanthin which masks the green pigment chlorophyll.

brown bear ▻ *noun* a bear, native to the N hemisphere, which has a thick brown coat and a pronounced hump on its shoulders.

brown dwarf ▻ *noun, astron* a star with very low mass (less than 8% of that of the Sun) such that thermonuclear reactions cannot occur, its dim appearance being the result of contraction due to gravitational force and constant release of energy.

browned off ▻ *adj, colloq* **1** (*often* **browned off with something**) bored or fed up with it. **2** (*especially* **browned off with someone**) annoyed or fed up with them. **3** depressed or discouraged.

brown fat ▻ *noun* in humans and many other mammals: yellowish-brown adipose tissue composed of spherical fat cells containing small droplets of fat which are a major source of heat energy. ◷ 1950s.

brown goods ▻ *plural noun* electrical equipment of a type used for leisure, eg radio, TV, audio equipment, home computers, etc, as distinct from domestic appliances. Compare WHITE GOODS. ◷ 1970s: traditionally such goods were wooden-cased, ie brown in colour.

Brownian movement and **Brownian motion** /ˈbraʊnɪən—/ ▻ *noun, physics* the ceaseless random movement of small particles suspended in a liquid or gas, caused by the continual bombardment of the particles by molecules of the liquid or gas.

brownie ▻ *noun* (***brownies***) **1** *folklore* a friendly goblin or fairy, traditionally said to help with domestic chores. **2** *especially US* a small square piece of chewy chocolate cake containing nuts. ◷ 16c, originally meaning a 'little brown man'.

Brownie Guide and **Brownie** ▻ *noun* a young girl (between 7 and 11 years old) belonging to the junior section of the Guides (see GUIDE *noun* 4) Association in Britain, or of the Girl Scouts in the US. Compare CUB *noun* 2. • **Brownie Guider** *noun* a woman in charge of a group of Brownie Guides. ◷ Early 20c: so called because until

1990 the Brownies wore a brown uniform, now replaced by a yellow one.

brownie point or **Brownie point** ▻ *noun, colloq, usually ironic or facetious* an imaginary mark of approval awarded for doing something good or helpful, etc. ⌚ 1960s.

browning ▻ *noun, cookery, chiefly Brit* a substance used to turn gravy a rich brown colour.

brownish and **brownness** see under BROWN.

brown-nose *coarse, slang, especially US* ▻ *verb* (***brown-nosed, brown-nosing***) *tr & intr* to try to gain favour with someone or gain their approval in a very contemptible and obsequious way. ▻ *noun* an ARSE-LICKER. ⌚ 1930s.

brown owl ▻ *noun* **1** the tawny owl. **2** (**Brown Owl**) a BROWNIE GUIDER.

brown paper ▻ *noun* thick strong brown-coloured paper, used especially for wrapping up parcels sent through the post.

brown rat ▻ *noun* a common rat found worldwide. Also called **Norway rat**.

brown rice ▻ *noun* unpolished rice from which only the fibrous husk has been removed, leaving the yellowish-brown bran layer intact.

brown sauce ▻ *noun, chiefly Brit* a dark-brown savoury sauce made with fruit, spices and vinegar, etc, especially a commercially bottled variety.

Brownshirt ▻ *noun* **1** *historical* in Nazi Germany: a member of the Nazi political militia. Also called STORMTROOPER. **2** a member of any fascist organization. Compare BLACKSHIRT, REDSHIRT. ⌚ 1930s.

brownstone *US* ▻ *noun* **1** a dark reddish-brown sandstone, originally regarded as particularly popular among wealthy people for building their homes with. **2** a house or building made using brownstone.

brown study ▻ *noun, now rather dated* or *literary* (*usually* **be in a brown study**) **1** deep thought; preoccupation. **2** a state of absent-mindedness. ⌚ 16c: apparently from an obsolete sense of BROWN as 'gloomy'.

brown sugar ▻ *noun* sugar that is unrefined or only partially refined. See also DEMERARA, MUSCOVADO.

browse /braʊz/ ▻ *verb* (***browsed, browsing***) *tr & intr* **1** to look through a book, etc, or look around a shop, etc in a casual, relaxed or haphazard way. **2** said of certain animals, eg deer: to feed by continually nibbling on young buds, shoots, leaves and stems of trees and shrubs, as opposed to grazing. **3** *computing* to examine information stored in (a database, etc). ▻ *noun* **1** an act of browsing. **2** young shoots, twigs, leaves, etc used as food for cattle or other animals. • **browser** *noun* **1** someone or something that browses. **2** *computing* software that acts as an interface between the user and data on the Internet or an internal network. ⌚ 16c in *verb* and *noun* sense 2: from French *broust* a new shoot.

BRS ▻ *abbreviation* British Road Services.

BRU ▻ *abbreviation, IVR* Brunei.

brucellosis /bruːsəˈloʊsɪs/ ▻ *noun, vet medicine* an infectious disease, mainly affecting cattle, in which it causes reduced milk yields, infertility and abortion of calves, and which is sometimes transmitted to humans, as UNDULANT FEVER, by contact or by consumption of unpasteurized milk. ⌚ 1930s: Latin, from *Brucella* the bacteria causing the disease (named after Sir David Bruce (1855–1931), an Australian-born bacteriologist).

bruise /bruːz/ ▻ *noun* **1** an area of skin discoloration and swelling caused by the leakage of blood from damaged blood vessels following injury. *Technical equivalent* CONTUSION. **2** a similar injury to a fruit or plant, shown as a soft discoloured area. ▻ *verb* (***bruised, bruising***) **1** to mark and discolour (the surface of the skin or of a fruit, etc) in this way. **2** *intr* to develop bruises □ *I bruise easily.* **3** *tr & intr* to hurt or be hurt emotionally or mentally. **4** *cookery, etc* to crush or pound (eg berries, leaves, or other foods), generally to release the juices or flavour. • **bruised** *adj.* ⌚ Anglo-Saxon *brysan* to crush, merged with French *bruisier* to break.

bruiser ▻ *noun, colloq* a big strong person, especially one who likes fighting or who looks aggressive.

bruising ▻ *noun* dark-coloured marks which show on bruised skin. ▻ *adj* said eg of experience: hurting in an emotional or mental way.

bruit /bruːt/ *formal or old use* ▻ *verb* (***bruited, bruiting***) (*usually* **bruit something about** or **abroad** or **around**) to spread or report (news or rumours, etc). ▻ *noun* something widely rumoured. ⌚ 15c as *noun*: French, literally 'noise'.

brûlé or (in the feminine form) **brûlée** /bruˈleɪ/ ▻ *adj, cookery* with a coating of caramelized brown sugar on top. ⌚ 20c: French, literally 'burnt'.

brummagem /ˈbrʌmədʒəm/ ▻ *noun* something, especially imitation jewellery, that is showy, cheap and tawdry. ▻ *adj* showy; sham; tawdry; worthless. ⌚ 17c: from *Brummagem*, a local form of the name Birmingham, a town formerly known for its manufacture of counterfeit coins and low-quality goods.

Brummie or **Brummy** *Brit, colloq* ▻ *adj* belonging or relating to Birmingham, a city in central England, or its inhabitants. ▻ *noun* (***Brummies***) a citizen or inhabitant of, or person born in, Birmingham. ⌚ 1940s: from *Brummagem* (often shortened to *Brum*), the informal local name for Birmingham.

brunch /brʌntʃ/ ▻ *noun* (***brunches***) *colloq* a meal that combines breakfast and lunch, eaten around midday or late in the morning. ⌚ Late 19c: from *br*eakfast + l*unch*.

brunette or (*US*) **brunet** /bruˈnɛt/ ▻ *noun* a woman or girl with brown or dark hair. ▻ *adj* said of hair colour: brown, usually dark brown. Compare BLONDE. ⌚ 18c: French, from *brun* brown.

brunt ▻ *noun* (*especially* **bear the brunt of something**) the main force or shock of (a blow or attack, etc); the most damaging, burdensome or painful part of something. ⌚ 14c, meaning 'a sharp blow'.

bruschetta /bruˈskɛtə/ ▻ *noun* (***bruschettas*** or ***bruschette*** /-teɪ/) toasted white bread such as ciabatta coated in olive oil and topped with grilled tomatoes, olives, basil or other variations. ⌚ 1990s: Italian.

brush ▻ *noun* (***brushes***) **1** a tool with lengths of stiff nylon, wire, hair, bristles or something similar set into it, used for tidying the hair, cleaning, painting, etc. **2** an act of brushing □ *Give your hair a brush.* **3** a light grazing contact. **4** a short encounter, especially a fight or disagreement; a skirmish □ ***a brush with the law.*** **5** a fox's bushy brush-like tail. **6** *elec* a metal or carbon conductor that maintains sliding contact between the stationary and moving parts of an electric motor or generator. **7** BRUSHWOOD. ▻ *verb* (***brushed, brushing***) **1** to sweep, groom or clean, etc with a brush; to pass a brush over (eg the floor) or through (eg the hair). **2** (*often* **brush something** or **someone down**) to rub it or them with a brush, etc or with a sweeping movement, so as to remove dirt or dust, etc. **4** (*also* **brush against something** or **someone**) *tr & intr* to touch it or them lightly in passing. • **brusher** *noun*. • **brushed** *adj* **1** said of a fabric: treated by a brushing process so that it feels soft and warm. **2** smoothed, rubbed, straightened, etc with a brush. • **brushing** *noun*. ⌚ 14c: from French *brosse* brushwood.

- **brush something** or **someone aside** to dismiss or pay no attention to it or them.
- **brush something away** to remove it with a brush or a brushing movement.
- **brush something** or **someone off** to ignore or refuse to listen to it or them. See also BRUSH-OFF.

■ **brush something on** to apply it with a brush or a brushing movement.

■ **brush up** to make oneself clean or tidy one's appearance, etc. See also BRUSH-UP.

■ **brush something up** or **brush up on something** to improve or refresh one's knowledge of (a language or subject, etc).

brush fire ▷ *noun* a fire of dead and dry bushes and trees, which usually spreads quickly.

brush-off ▷ *noun* (*usually* **the brush-off**) *colloq* an act of ignoring, rebuffing or dismissing someone or something in an abrupt or offhand manner. • **give someone the brush-off** *colloq* especially in a romance or friendship: to rebuff or reject them; to finish with them in an offhand or blunt way.

brush-up ▷ *noun* an act of brushing up on something (eg a subject) □ *My French needs a brush-up before the holiday.* See BRUSH SOMETHING UP at BRUSH.

brushwood ▷ *noun* **1** dead, broken or lopped-off branches and twigs, etc from trees and bushes. **2** small trees and bushes on rough land. **3** rough land covered by such trees and bushes. Also called BRUSH.

brushwork ▷ *noun* **1** a particular technique or manner a painter uses to apply the paint to a canvas, etc. **2** work done with a brush.

brusque /brʌsk, brʊsk/ ▷ *adj* (***brusquer, brusquest***) said of a person or their manner, etc: blunt and often impolite; curt. • **brusquely** *adverb*. • **brusqueness** *noun*. ⓒ 17c: from Italian *brusco* sour or rough.

Brussels lace ▷ *noun* a fine type of PILLOW LACE or NEEDLEPOINT, especially with raised sprigs on a fine net ground. ⓒ 18c: originally made in Brussels, the capital of Belgium.

Brussels sprout or **brussels sprout** ▷ *noun* (*usually as plural* **Brussels sprouts** or (*colloq*) **sprouts**) **1** a type of cabbage, widely cultivated for its swollen edible buds, which develop in the leaf axils along the main stem. **2** these buds cooked and eaten as a vegetable. ⓒ 18c: first grown near Brussels, the capital of Belgium.

brut /bruːt/ ▷ *adj* said of wines, especially champagne: very dry. ⓒ 19c: French, literally 'rough' or 'raw'.

brutal /ˈbruːtəl/ ▷ *adj* **1** savagely cruel or violent. **2** ruthlessly harsh or unfeeling. **3** like, or belonging or relating to, a brute. • **brutalism** *noun* applied to art, architecture and literature, etc: deliberate crudeness or harshness of style. • **brutality** /brʊˈtalɪtɪ/ *noun* (***brutalities***) **1** a brutal act. **2** brutal behaviour or treatment. • **brutally** *adverb*. ⓒ 15c in sense 3: from Latin *brutalis*.

brutalize or **brutalise** ▷ *verb* (***brutalized, brutalizing***) **1** to make someone brutal. **2** to treat someone brutally. • **brutalization** *noun*. See also BRUTALISM at BRUTAL.

brute /bruːt/ ▷ *noun* **1** a cruel, brutal or violent person. **2** an animal other than humans, especially one of the larger mammals; a beast. ▷ *adj* **1** irrational or stupid; instinctive, not involving rational thought. **2** coarse, crudely sensual or animal-like. **3** in its natural or raw state; unrefined or unworked □ *brute nature.* ⓒ 15c: from Latin *brutus* heavy or irrational.

brute fact ▷ *noun* a fact presented on its own, without explanation.

brute force and **brute strength** ▷ *noun* sheer physical strength, with no thought or skill.

brutish ▷ *adj* like, or belonging or relating to, a brute; cruel or coarse. • **brutishly** *adverb*. • **brutishness** *noun*.

bryony /ˈbraɪənɪ/ ▷ *noun* (***bryonies***) **1** (*also* **black bryony**) a perennial climbing plant, related to the yam, which has heart-shaped or three-lobed glossy green leaves, and tiny yellowish-green flowers followed by bright-red highly poisonous berries. **2** (*also* **white bryony**) a perennial climbing plant, related to the pumpkin, which has lobed leaves and greenish-white flowers followed by bright-red highly poisonous berries. ⓒ 14c: from Latin *bryonia*.

bryophyte /ˈbraɪoʊfaɪt/ ▷ *noun* any member of the division (**Bryophyta** /-ˈɒfɪtə/) of the plant kingdom that includes mosses, liverworts and hornworts. ⓒ 19c: from Greek *bryon* a moss or liverwort + *phyton* plant.

BS ▷ *abbreviation* **1** Bachelor of Surgery. **2** *IVR* Bahamas. **3** British Standard or Standards, marked on manufactured goods that conform to an acceptable standard. See also BSI. **4** building society.

bs ▷ *abbreviation* **1** balance sheet. **2** bill of sale.

BSc ▷ *abbreviation* Bachelor of Science.

BSE ▷ *abbreviation* bovine spongiform encephalopathy.

BSI ▷ *abbreviation* British Standards Institution, an organization which controls the quality and safety standards, etc for a wide range of manufactured goods.

B-side ▷ *noun* on a record, usually a single: **a** the side which holds the less important, or less promoted, track; **b** the track concerned. Compare A-SIDE.

BSM ▷ *abbreviation* British School of Motoring.

BST ▷ *abbreviation* **1** bovine somatotrophin. **2** British Summer Time.

BT ▷ *abbreviation* British Telecom.

Bt ▷ *abbreviation* Baronet.

BTA ▷ *abbreviation* British Tourist Authority, an official body which promotes tourism and the tourist industry within the UK, and tourism to the UK from abroad.

BTEC ▷ *abbreviation* Business and Technician Education Council, a body which provides vocational training and qualifications in the UK.

BTU ▷ *abbreviation* British thermal unit.

bubble /ˈbʌbəl/ ▷ *noun* **1** a thin film of liquid forming a hollow sphere filled with air or gas, especially one which floats in liquid. **2** a ball of air or gas which has formed in a solid or liquid. **3** a dome made of clear plastic or glass. **4** an unrealistic or over-ambitious plan or scheme. **5** a sound of or like bubbling liquid. **6** *computing* see under BUBBLE MEMORY. ▷ *verb* (***bubbled, bubbling***) *intr* **1** to form or give off bubbles, or to rise in bubbles. **2** (*often* **bubble away**) to make the sound of bubbling liquid □ *water bubbling away in the pan.* ⓒ 14c as *bobel*.

■ **bubble over 1** to boil over. **2** (*especially as* **bubble over with something**) to be full of or bursting with (happiness, excitement, enthusiasm, good ideas, etc).

bubble and squeak ▷ *noun, cookery, chiefly Brit* left-over cooked cabbage and potatoes mixed together and then fried.

bubble bath ▷ *noun* a scented soapy liquid which is added to running bath water to make it bubble.

bubble chamber ▷ *noun, physics* a device that enables the movements of charged subatomic particles to be observed and photographed as trails of gas bubbles within a container of superheated liquid. See also CLOUD CHAMBER.

bubble gum ▷ *noun* a type of chewing gum which can be blown into bubbles.

bubble-jet ▷ *noun* a type of INKJET PRINTER which heats the ink in a fine tube to form a bubble, which then bursts and projects the ink on to the paper.

bubble memory ▷ *noun* a form of computer memory, relatively insensitive to shock and vibration, in which microscopic artificially-produced irregularities known as **magnetic bubbles** float in a thin film of magnetic material. ⓒ 1970s.

bubble pack ▷ *noun* a clear plastic bubble, usually stuck on to a cardboard backing, in which an article for sale is packed and displayed. Also called **blister pack**, **blister card**.

bubbly ▷ *adj* (***bubblier***, ***bubbliest***) **1** having bubbles, or being like bubbles □ *very bubbly lemonade.* **2** said of a person or their character: very lively and cheerful and full of high spirits. ▷ *noun* (***bubblies***) *colloq* champagne.

bubo /'bjuːboʊ/ ▷ *noun* (***buboes***) *pathol* a swollen tender lymph node, especially in the armpit or groin, commonly developing as a symptom of bubonic plague, syphilis or gonorrhoea. • **bubonic** *adj* **1** said of a disease, etc: characterized by the appearance of buboes. **2** relating to buboes. ◷ 14c: Latin, from Greek *boubon* the groin.

bubonic plague ▷ *noun, pathol* the commonest form of plague, caused by a bacterium which is transmitted to humans via fleas carried by rats, characterized by fever and the development of buboes, and known in the Middle Ages as the Black Death. ◷ 19c.

buccal /'bʌkəl/ ▷ *adj, anatomy* relating to the mouth or the inside of the cheek. ◷ 18c: from Latin *bucca* cheek.

buccaneer /bʌkə'nɪə(r)/ ▷ *noun* **1** ▷ *historical & literary* a pirate, especially an adventurer who attacked and plundered Spanish ships in the Caribbean during the 17c. **2** *derog* an opportunistic or unscrupulous businessman or politician, etc. ◷ 17c: from French *boucanier*, which originally meant 'someone who prepares smoked dried meat using a wooden gridiron' (as the French settlers in the Caribbean did); from *boucan*, the French word for both the gridiron and the dried meat.

buccaneering ▷ *adj* said of a person: living or acting as a buccaneer. ▷ *noun* piracy; unscrupulous adventuring.

buck[1] ▷ *noun* (***bucks*** or in senses 1 and 2 only ***buck***) **1** a male animal, especially a male deer, goat, antelope, rabbit, hare or kangaroo. Compare DOE. **2** *especially in compounds* an antelope □ *water buck.* **3** an act of bucking □ *The horse gave a huge buck.* **4** *old use* a lively fashionably-dressed young man. ▷ *verb* (***bucked***, ***bucking***) **1** *intr* said of a horse, etc: to make a series of rapid jumps into the air, with the back arched and legs held stiff, especially in an attempt to throw off a rider. **2** said of a horse, etc: to throw (a rider) from its back in this way. **3** *colloq* to oppose or resist (an idea or trend, etc). • **bucker** *noun*. ◷ Anglo-Saxon *buc* or bucca.

■ **buck up** *colloq* **1** to become more cheerful. **2** to hurry up.

■ **buck someone up** *colloq* to make them more cheerful.

■ **buck something up** *colloq* to improve or liven up (one's ways or ideas, etc).

buck[2] *noun*, ▷ *colloq* **1** *N Amer, Austral, NZ, etc* a dollar. **2** *S Afr* a rand. • **make a fast** or **quick buck** to make money quickly or easily, and often dishonestly. ◷ 19c: perhaps from BUCKSKIN, because deerskins were used as a unit of exchange by Native Americans and frontiersmen in the 19c US.

buck[3] *noun* **1** *cards* **a** in the game of poker: a token object placed before the person who is to deal the next hand and start the next jackpot, having won the previous one; **b** a counter or marker. **2** *colloq* responsibility, especially that of dealing with a problem. • **pass the buck** *colloq* to shift the responsibility for something on to someone else. • **the buck stops here** *colloq* this is where the final responsibility rests. ◷ 19c, from *buckhorn knife*, an item which used to be used as a *buck* in poker.

bucked ▷ *adj, Brit colloq* pleased and encouraged □ *I'm so bucked by your news.*

bucket /'bʌkɪt/ ▷ *noun* **1** a round open-topped container for holding or carrying liquids and solids such as sand, etc. **2** a BUCKETFUL □ *need about two buckets of water.* See also *rain, weep, etc buckets* below. **3** *colloq* a rubbish-bin or wastepaper basket. **4** *Austral colloq* an icecream tub. **5** *computing* a subdivision of a data file, used to locate data. **6** the scoop of a dredging machine. ▷ *verb* (***bucketed***, ***bucketing***) *colloq* **1** (*also* **bucket down**) *intr* said of rain: to pour down heavily. **2** (*especially* **bucket along** or **down**) *now usually intr* to drive or ride very hard or bumpily □ *bucketing down the hill.* **3** to put, lift or carry something in a bucket. • **kick the bucket** see under KICK. • **rain, weep,** *etc* **buckets** to rain or weep, etc long, hard and continuously. ◷ 13c: related to Anglo-French *buket* a pail, and Anglo-Saxon *buc* a pitcher.

bucketful ▷ *noun* (***bucketfuls***) the amount a bucket can hold.

bucket seat ▷ *noun* a small seat with a round back, for one person, eg in a car.

bucket shop ▷ *noun* **1** *especially Brit, rather derog colloq* a travel agent that sells cheap airline tickets, normally at the expense of the usual standards of reliability and insurance, etc. **2** *chiefly US* **a** an office where a person may deal in shares, gamble on the money market, etc; **b** a firm of stockbrokers with questionable or dishonest methods of dealing. ◷ 19c; originally US, meaning 'a shop or bar selling alcoholic drink from open buckets', the drink therefore being of questionable origin.

buckhorn and **buck's horn** ▷ *noun* horn from a buck, used for making handles for knives, etc.

buckle /'bʌkəl/ ▷ *noun* **1** a flat piece of metal or plastic, etc usually attached to one end of a strap or belt, with a pin in the middle which goes through a hole in the other end of the strap or belt to fasten it. **2** a curled, warped or bent condition. ▷ *verb* (***buckled***, ***buckling***) *tr & intr* **1** to fasten or be fastened with a buckle. **2** said eg of metal: to bend or become bent out of shape, especially as a result of great heat or force. • **buckled** *adj*. ◷ 14c: from Latin *buccula* 'the cheek-strap of a helmet', literally 'little cheek'.

■ **buckle down to something** *colloq* to begin working seriously on it.

■ **buckle to** or **buckle down** *colloq* to get down to some serious work.

■ **buckle under** to collapse or give in under strain.

buckler ▷ *noun* **1** *historical* a small round shield, usually with a raised centre. **2** *literary* someone or something that protects or shields. ◷ 13c: from French *bocler*, from *bocle* a BOSS[2].

Buckley's /'bʌklɪz/ and **Buckley's chance** ▷ *noun, Austral & NZ colloq* no chance at all □ *He's got Buckley's of catching that train.* ◷ 19c: perhaps named after William Buckley, a convict who escaped in 1803 and lived 32 years among the Aborigines before giving himself up.

buckminsterfullerene /bʌkmɪnstə'fʊləriːn/ ▷ *noun, chem* (formula C_{60}) an almost spherical molecule, thought to be an ingredient of soots, in which each carbon atom is bonded to three others, so that the surface of the molecule consists of 12 pentagons and 20 hexagons. Also called BUCKYBALL. ◷ 1990s: named after Richard Buckminster Fuller (1895–1983), US engineer, who designed geodesic domes of similar structure.

buck naked ▷ *adj, US colloq* stark naked. ◷ 20c.

buck passing ▷ *noun, derog colloq* the practice or habit of passing the responsibility for something on to another person. See PASS THE BUCK at BUCK[3].

buckram /'bʌkrəm/ ▷ *noun* cotton or linen stiffened with SIZE[2], used to line clothes or cover books, etc. ◷ 13c as *bukeram*, meaning 'a fine cotton or linen fabric': perhaps ultimately named after Bukhara, a town in central Asia once noted for its textiles.

Bucks. ▷ *abbreviation, English county* Buckinghamshire.

Buck's fizz or **buck's fizz** ▷ *noun* a drink consisting of champagne, or sparkling white wine, and orange juice. ◷ 1930s: named after Buck's Club, in London.

buckshee /bʌk'ʃiː/ ▷ *adj* ▷ *adverb, slang* free of charge; gratis. ◷ Early 20c, originally military slang: from BAKSHEESH.

buckshot ▷ *noun* a large type of lead shot used in hunting.

buckskin ▷ *noun* **1** the skin of a deer. **2** a soft strong greyish-yellow leather made from deerskin, or now often from sheepskin. **3** a strong smooth twilled woollen fabric. **4** (**buckskins**) breeches or a suit made of buckskin.

bucks party ▷ *noun, Austral, NZ* a STAG PARTY.

buckthorn ▷ *noun* **1** any of various northern temperate shrubs or small trees, especially a thorny deciduous shrub with bright-green oval toothed leaves and small yellowish-green sweetly-scented flowers followed by black berries. **2** the wood of this tree, formerly used to make charcoal. ◷ 16c.

bucktooth ▷ *noun* a large front tooth which sticks out. • **bucktoothed** *adj* said of a person: having large projecting front teeth. ◷ 18c: BUCK[1] *noun* 1 + TOOTH.

buckwheat ▷ *noun* **1** an erect fast-growing annual plant, native to Central Asia, with leathery spear-shaped leaves and terminal clusters of tiny pink or white flowers. **2** the greyish-brown triangular seeds of this plant, which are highly nutritious and can be cooked whole, or ground into flour and used to make bread, pancakes, porridge, etc. ◷ 16c: from Dutch *boekweit* beech wheat, because the nuts are similar in shape to beechnuts.

buckyball /'bʌkɪbɔːl/ ▷ *noun, chem* common name for BUCKMINSTERFULLERENE.

bucolic /bjʊ'kɒlɪk/ ▷ *adj* concerned with the countryside or people living there; pastoral; rustic. ▷ *noun, literary* a poem about the countryside or pastoral life. • **bucolically** *adverb*. ◷ 16c: from Greek *boukolos* herdsman.

bud[1] ▷ *noun* **1** in a plant: an immature knob-like shoot, often enclosed by protective scales, that will eventually develop into a leaf or flower. **2** a flower or leaf that is not yet fully open. Also *in compounds* □ ***rosebud***. **3** *biol* in yeasts and simple animals, eg hydra: a small outgrowth from the body of the parent that becomes detached and develops into a new individual capable of independent existence. **4** in an embryo: an outgrowth from which a limb develops. ▷ *verb* (***budded, budding***) **1** *intr* said of a plant, etc: to put out or develop buds. **2** *biol* said of a yeast or a simple animal, eg hydra: to reproduce asexually by the production of buds (*noun* 3). • **in bud** said of a plant: producing buds. • **nip something in the bud** to put a stop to it, or destroy it, at a very early stage. ◷ 14c.

bud[2] see under BUDDY

Buddhism /'bʊdɪzəm/ ▷ *noun* a world religion that originated in ancient India, founded by the Buddha, Siddhartha Gautama, in the 6c BC, and based on his teachings regarding spiritual purity and freedom from human concerns and desires. See also MAHAYANA, THERAVADA. • **Buddhist** *noun* a person who believes in and practises Buddhism. ▷ *adj* relating or belonging to Buddhism. ◷ 19c: from Sanskrit *buddha* wise or enlightened, from *budh* to awaken, notice or understand.

budding ▷ *noun* **1** *bot* the formation of buds on a plant shoot. **2** *bot* the artificial propagation of a plant by grafting of a bud. **3** *zool* a method of asexual reproduction involving the production of one or more outgrowths or buds that develop into new individuals. ▷ *adj* **budding** said of a person: developing; beginning to show talent in a specified area □ ***a budding pianist***.

buddleia /'bʌdlɪə/ ▷ *noun* (***buddleias***) any of various deciduous shrubs or small trees, native to China, with spear-shaped leaves and long pointed purple, lilac, orange-yellow or white fragrant flower-heads, widely cultivated in gardens because it attracts many butterflies. ◷ 18c: named after the English botanist Adam Buddle (died 1715).

buddy /'bʌdɪ/ ▷ *noun* (***buddies***) **1** *colloq, especially N Amer* (sometimes shortened to **bud**, especially when used as a term of address in these senses) **a** a friend or companion; **b** a term of address used to a man, often expressing a degree of annoyance or aggression, etc □ ***Watch it, buddy!*** **2** a volunteer who helps care for a person suffering from AIDS. ▷ *verb* (***buddied, buddying***) **1** (*usually* **buddy up**) *intr, chiefly US colloq* to become friendly □ ***The kids normally buddy up very quickly***. **2** to help care for someone suffering from AIDS. ◷ 19c: perhaps from the dialect word *butty* a companion, or a childish alteration of BROTHER.

buddy movie ▷ *noun, colloq* a film, usually with two central characters, that explores male or female camaraderie.

budge /bʌdʒ/ ▷ *verb* (***budged, budging***) *tr & intr* **1** to move, or to make something or someone move. **2** to change one's mind or opinions, or make someone change their mind or opinions □ ***Nothing will budge him on the matter***. ◷ 16c: from French *bouger*.

budgerigar /'bʌdʒərɪgɑː(r)/ ▷ *noun* **1** a small Australian parrot which has a yellow head with a blue patch on each cheek, bright-green underparts, a greyish-green back with black and yellow barred markings, and a long tapering blue tail. **2** any of numerous varieties of this bird produced by selective breeding, which are popular cagebirds. Often shortened to **budgie**. ◷ 19c: from Australian Aboriginal *gijirrigaa*.

budget /'bʌdʒɪt/ ▷ *noun* **1** a plan, especially one covering a particular period of time, specifying how money coming in, eg to a household or a business project, will be spent and allocated. **2** (**the Budget**) *Brit* a periodic assessment of and programme for national revenue and expenditure, proposed by the government and presented to parliament by the Chancellor of the Exchequer. **3** the amount of money set aside for a particular purpose □ ***used up my clothes budget for the year***. **4** *as adj* low in cost; economical □ ***budget holidays***. ▷ *verb* (***budgeted, budgeting***) **1** *intr* to calculate how much money one is earning and spending, so that one does not spend more than one has; to draw up a budget. **2** (*usually* **budget for something**) *intr* to plan, arrange or allow for (a specific expense) in a budget. **3** to provide (an amount of money, or sometimes time, etc) in a budget □ ***We budgeted £600 for the holiday***. • **budgetary** *adj* relating to or connected with a budget or financial planning. • **budgeting** *noun*. ◷ 15c in obsolete sense 'wallet' or 'bag': from French *bougette*, diminutive of *bouge* a pouch.

budget account ▷ *noun* **1** a bank account into which payments are made regularly by agreement so that regular bills can be paid. **2** an account with a shop into which regular, eg monthly, payments are made to cover purchases and sustain a credit level.

budgie /bʌdʒɪ/ ▷ *noun* (***budgies***) *colloq* a budgerigar.

buff[1] ▷ *noun, colloq, usually in compounds* a person who is enthusiastic about and knows a lot about a specified subject □ ***an opera buff*** □ ***a sports buff***. ◷ Early 20c, originally US; keen attenders at fires came to be nicknamed buffs because of the buff overcoats (see BUFF[2] *adj* 2) formerly worn by New York volunteer firemen.

buff[2] ▷ *noun* **1** a dull-yellowish colour. **2** a soft undyed leather. **3** (*sometimes* **buffer**) **a** a cloth or pad of buff (*noun* 2) or other material, used for polishing; **b** a revolving disk used for polishing metals, made of layers of cloth loaded with abrasive powder. ▷ *adj* **1** dull yellow in colour □ ***a buff envelope***. **2** made of buff (*noun* 2) □ ***a military buff coat***. ▷ *verb* (***buffed, buffing***) **1** (*also* **buff something up**) to polish it with a buff or a piece of soft material. **2** to make (leather) soft like buff. • **buffer** *noun* a person or thing that buffs or polishes. • **in the buff** *Brit colloq* naked. ◷ 16c, meaning 'a buffalo'; later meaning 'buffalo-hide' (or military wear made of this): from French *buffle* buffalo.

buffalo /'bʌfəloʊ/ ▷ *noun* (***buffalo*** or ***buffaloes***) **1** (*also* **African buffalo**) a member of the cattle family, native to

S and E Africa, which has a heavy black or brown body, thick horns curving upwards at their tips, and large drooping ears. **2** (*also* **Indian buffalo**) a member of the cattle family, native to SE Asia, the wild form of which has a black coat, although domesticated forms may also be grey, pink or white and are noted for their docility. **3** sometimes used generally to refer to the American BISON. ◷ 16c: Italian, or from Portuguese *bufalo*.

buffer[1] ▷ *noun* **1** an apparatus designed to take the shock when an object such as a railway carriage or a ship hits something, especially a device using springs, on a railway carriage, etc, or a cushion of rope on a ship. **2** a person or thing which protects from harm or shock, etc, or makes its impact less damaging or severe. **3** *computing* a temporary storage area for data that is being transmitted from the central processing unit to an output device such as a printer. **4** *chem* a chemical solution that maintains its pH at a constant level when an acid or alkali is added to it or when the solution is diluted. It is used to prepare solutions of a specific pH, eg for dyeing, food technology, medical treatment and brewing. ▷ *verb* (***buffered, buffering***) **1** *chem* to add a buffer to something. **2** to protect someone or something from shock. ● **buffered** *adj* **1** equipped with a buffer or buffers. **2** protected or cushioned. **3** *chem* with a buffer added. ◷ 19c: from obsolete verb *buff* to strike or make a dull-sounding impact.

buffer[2] ▷ *noun, Brit colloq* a rather foolish or dull person, especially a man.

buffer[3] see under BUFF[2]

buffer state and **buffer zone** ▷ *noun* a neutral country or zone situated between two others which are or may become hostile towards each other, making the outbreak of war less likely.

buffer stock ▷ *noun, finance* stock held in reserve to minimize the effect of price fluctuations, etc.

buffet[1] /ˈbufeɪ; *US* bəˈfeɪ/ ▷ *noun* **1 a** a meal set out on tables from which people help themselves; **b** a party or social occasion at which such a meal is provided. **2** a place, room or counter, etc where light meals and drinks may be bought and eaten. See also BUFFET CAR. **3** a sideboard or cupboard for holding china or glasses, etc. ◷ 18c in sense 3: French.

buffet[2] /ˈbʌfɪt/ ▷ *noun* **1** a blow with the hand or fist. **2** a stroke or blow, especially a heavy or repeated one □ *A sudden buffet of wind* □ *reeling from the buffets that fate had dealt her.* ▷ *verb* (***buffeted, buffeting***) **1** to strike or knock someone or something with the hand or fist. **2** to knock someone or something about; to batter them or it repeatedly □ *a ship buffeted by the waves.* ● **buffeting** *noun* **1** repeated knocks or blows. **2** irregular oscillation of any part of an aircraft, caused and maintained by an eddying wake from some other part. ◷ 13c: from French *buffe* a blow.

buffet car ▷ *noun* a carriage in a train, in which light meals, snacks and drinks can be bought.

buffoon /bəˈfuːn/ ▷ *noun, usually rather derog* **1** a person who sets out to amuse people with jokes and foolish or comic behaviour, etc; a clown. **2** someone who does stupid or foolish things; a fool. ● **buffoonery** *noun* comic or foolish behaviour. ◷ 16c: from Italian *buffone*.

bug[1] ▷ *noun* **1** the common name for any of thousands of insects with a flattened oval body and mouthparts modified to form a beak for piercing and sucking, eg aphids. **2** an insect living in dirty houses, etc and thought of as dirty. **3** *N Amer* a popular name for any kind of insect. **4** *colloq* a popular name for a bacterium or virus that causes infection or illness □ *a nasty stomach bug.* **5** *colloq* a small hidden microphone. **6** *colloq* a small fault in a machine or computer program which stops it from working properly. **7** *colloq* an obsession or craze □ *She caught the skiing bug.* ▷ *verb* (***bugged, bugging***) **1** *colloq* to hide a microphone in (a room, telephone, etc) so as to be able to listen in to any conversations carried on there. **2** *slang* to annoy or worry someone. **3** *US colloq* said of the eyes: to bulge or pop out (like the eyes of certain insects). ◷ 17c: perhaps connected with Anglo-Saxon *budda* a beetle.

bug[2] ▷ *verb* (***bugged, bugging***) (*usually* **bug out** or **off**) *intr, chiefly US, colloq* to leave or retreat quickly, especially in a panic. ◷ 1950s.

bugaboo /ˈbʌgəbuː/ ▷ *noun* (***bugaboos***) *chiefly US, colloq* an imaginary thing which causes fear or anxiety. Also called BUGBEAR, BOGEY. ◷ 18c.

bugbear ▷ *noun* **1** an object of fear, dislike or annoyance, especially when that fear, etc is irrational or needless. **2** *folklore* a hobgoblin or other imaginary creature in the form of a bear, invented to frighten young children. ◷ 16c in sense 2, from obsolete *bugge* a bogy, perhaps from Welsh *bwg* hobgoblin.

bug-eyed ▷ *adj* said of a person: with eyes bulging out from their face, eg from astonishment or exertion.

bugger /ˈbʌgə(r)/ *coarse slang* ▷ *noun* **1** a person who practises anal sex. **2** a person or thing considered to be difficult or awkward □ *He really is a bugger to work for.* **3** a person one feels affection or pity for □ *poor old bugger.* ▷ *verb* (***buggered, buggering***) **1** to practise anal sex with someone. **2** to tire or exhaust someone. **3** (*also* **bugger something up**) to spoil or ruin it □ *She completely buggered up our weekend.* ▷ *exclamation* (*also* **bugger it!**) expressing annoyance or frustration. ● **buggered** *adj* **1** exhausted; tired out. **2** ruined; broken □ *The TV's buggered.* **3** shocked; amazed □ *Well I'm buggered!* ● **bugger all** nothing at all. ● **not give a bugger** not to care at all. ◷ 16c in sense 3: from French *bougre*, from Latin *Bulgarus* a heretic (literally 'a Bulgarian'); a large number of heretical beliefs, including deviant sexual practices were thought in the Middle Ages to have come from the Balkans.

■ **bugger about** or **around** to waste time; to do things flippantly or without due attention.

■ **bugger someone about** to mislead them or cause them problems.

■ **bugger off** to go away; to clear off.

buggery ▷ *noun* anal sex. See also SODOMY.

buggy /ˈbʌgɪ/ ▷ *noun* (***buggies***) **1** a light open carriage pulled by one horse. **2** a light folding pushchair for a small child. **3** (*also* **baby buggy**) *N Amer, especially US* a pram. **4** *often in compounds* a small motorized vehicle, used for a specified purpose □ *beach buggy* □ *golf buggy.* ◷ 18c.

bugle[1] /ˈbjuːgəl/ ▷ *noun* a brass or copper instrument similar to a small trumpet but normally without any valves, used mainly for sounding military calls or fanfares, etc. ▷ *verb* (***bugled, bugling***) **1** *intr* to sound a bugle. **2** to sound (a call or signal, etc) or play (a fanfare, etc) on a bugle. ● **bugler** *noun.* ◷ 14c, at first meaning 'buffalo' and later short for *bugle horn*, which was a hunting horn made from the horn of a buffalo or wild ox: French, ultimately from Latin *bos* ox.

bugle[2] /ˈbjuːgəl/ ▷ *noun, bot* a creeping perennial plant of the mint family, native to northern temperate regions, which produces short spikes of blue or purple flowers. ◷ 13c: from Latin *bugula*.

bugloss /ˈbjuːglɒs/ ▷ *noun* (***buglosses***) *bot* any of several plants of the borage family, especially the **viper's bugloss**, which has strap-shaped leaves arranged in a basal rosette, and tall spikes of funnel-shaped flowers that are pink in bud and turn bright blue as they open. ◷ 16c: ultimately from Greek *bous* ox + *glossa* tongue.

build /bɪld/ ▷ *verb* (***built, building***) **1** to make or construct something from parts. **2** (*also* **build up**) *intr* to increase gradually in size, strength, amount, intensity, etc; to develop □ *Outside the excitement was building.* See also *build something up* below. **3** to make in a specified way or for a specified purpose □ *built to last* □ *a garden built for convenience.* **4** to control the building of something; to have something built □ *The government built two new housing schemes.* ▻ *noun* physical form, especially that of the human body; style of construction □ *He had a slim build.* ⓘ Anglo-Saxon *byldan.*

■ **build something in** or **on to something** to make it in such a way that it forms a permanent part of or addition to some larger thing □ *built a garage on to the side of the house.* See also BUILT-IN.

■ **build on something 1** to add it on by building. **2** to use (a previous success, etc) as a basis from which to develop. **3** to base (hopes, etc) or achieve (success, etc) on something □ *success built on hard work.*

■ **build someone** or **something up** to speak with great enthusiasm about them or it.

■ **build something up** to build it in stages or gradually. See also separate entries BUILD-UP, BUILT-UP.

builder ▻ *noun* **1** a person who builds, or organizes and supervises the building of, houses, etc. **2** anything which helps to develop or build something.

builders' merchant ▻ *noun* a trader who supplies building materials.

building ▻ *noun* **1** the business, process, art or occupation of constructing houses, etc. **2** a structure with walls and a roof, such as a house.

building block ▻ *noun* **1** a hollow or solid block, larger than a brick, made of concrete or other material. **2** a child's toy, usually a cube made of wood. **3** any of the separate parts out of which something is built.

building society ▻ *noun, Brit* a finance company that lends money to its members for buying or improving houses, and in which customers can invest money in accounts to earn interest. Many building societies now provide cheque accounts and other general banking services. ⓘ 19c.

build-up ▻ *noun* **1** a gradual increase. **2** a gradual approach to a conclusion or climax. **3** publicity or praise of something or someone given in advance of its or their appearance.

built *past tense, past participle of* BUILD

built-in ▻ *adj* **1** built to form part of the main structure or design of something, and not as a separate or free-standing object □ *The bedroom has built-in wardrobes.* **2** included as, forming or designed as a necessary or integral part of something □ *The deal comes with built-in insurance cover.* **3** inherent; present naturally, by genetic inheritance, etc.

built-up ▻ *adj* **1** said of land, etc: covered with buildings, especially houses. **2** increased in height by additions to the underside □ *built-up shoes.* **3** made up of separate parts.

bulb /bʌlb/ ▻ *noun* **1** in certain plants, eg tulip and onion: a swollen underground organ that functions as a food store and consists of a modified shoot, with overlapping layers of fleshy leaf bases or scales, and roots growing from its lower surface. **2** a flower grown from a bulb, eg a daffodil and hyacinth. **3** a light-bulb. **4** anything which is shaped like a pear or a bulb (sense 1). ⓘ 16c in obsolete sense 'onion': from Greek *bolbos* onion.

bulbous /'bʌlbəs/ ▻ *adj* **1** like a bulb in shape; fat, bulging or swollen. **2** having or growing from a bulb. • **bulbously** *adverb.* ⓘ 16c.

bulge /bʌldʒ/ ▻ *noun* **1** a swelling, especially where one would expect to see something flat. **2** a sudden and usually temporary increase, eg in population. ▻ *verb* (***bulged, bulging***) *intr* (*often* **bulge out** or **bulge with something**) to swell outwards □ *a sack bulging with presents.* • **bulging** *adj.* • **bulgy** *adj* (***bulgier, bulgiest***). ⓘ 13c, meaning 'bag' or 'pouch': from Latin *bulga* knapsack.

bulghur or **bulgur** /'bʌlgər/ ▻ *noun* wheat that has been boiled, dried, lightly milled and cracked. ⓘ 1930s: Turkish.

bulimia /bʊ'lɪmɪə/ ▻ *noun, medicine, psychol* **1** compulsive overeating, caused either by psychological factors or by damage to the hypothalamus of the brain. **2** BULIMIA NERVOSA. ⓘ 14c as *bulimy*, in sense 2: from Greek *boulimia*, from *bous* ox + *limos* hunger.

bulimia nervosa /— nɜː'voʊsə/ ▻ *noun, medicine, psychol* a psychological disorder, most common in female adolescents and young women, in which episodes of excessive eating are followed by self-induced vomiting or laxative abuse in an attempt to avoid any weight gain. ⓘ 19c: from BULIMIA + Latin *nervosus* nervous.

bulimic /'bʊ'lɪmɪk/ ▻ *adj* suffering from or relating to BULIMIA NERVOSA. ▻ *noun* a person suffering from bulimia nervosa.

bulk ▻ *noun* **1** size, especially when large and awkward. **2** the greater or main part of something □ *The bulk of the task is routine.* **3** a large body, shape, structure or person. **4** a large quantity □ *buy in bulk.* **5** roughage; dietary fibre. ▻ *verb* (*often* **bulk out** or *sometimes* **bulk up**) *tr & intr* to swell, fill out or increase in bulk, or to make something do so □ *Add some beans to bulk the casserole out a bit.* • **bulk large** to be or seem important □ *an issue which bulks large in his mind.* ⓘ 15c: from Norse *bulki* a heap or cargo.

bulk buying ▻ *noun* purchase of a commodity in a large quantity, usually at a reduced price, and by a single buyer on behalf of a number or group of consumers.

bulk carrier ▻ *noun* a ship which carries dry goods, such as grain, in bulk and unpackaged.

bulkhead ▻ *noun* a wall in a ship or aircraft, etc which separates one section from another, so that if one section is damaged, the rest is not affected. ⓘ 15c: from *bulk* a stall or framework + HEAD.

bulky ▻ *adj* (***bulkier, bulkiest***) large in size, filling a lot of space and awkward to carry or move. • **bulkily** *adverb.* • **bulkiness** *noun.*

bull[1] /bʊl/ ▻ *noun* **1** the uncastrated male of animals in the cattle family. **2** the male of the elephant, whale and some other large animals. **3** (**a** or **the Bull**) *astron, astrol* TAURUS. **4** *stock exchange* someone who buys shares hoping to sell them at a higher price at a later date. Compare BEAR[2] *noun* 4, LAME DUCK 4. **5** *colloq* a BULL'S-EYE (sense 1). **6** (*especially* **a bull of a man**) a well-built, powerful or aggressive man. ▻ *adj* **1** male □ *a bull walrus.* **2** *stock exchange* said of a market: favourable to the bulls (sense 4); rising. **3** massive; coarse; strong. • **take the bull by the horns** to deal boldly and positively with a challenge or difficulty. ⓘ 13c.

bull[2] /bʊl/ ▻ *noun* **1** *slang* nonsense; meaningless, pretentious talk. **2** an illogical nonsensical statement, eg 'If you don't receive this card, you must write and tell me'. **3** tedious and sometimes unnecessary routine tasks. ⓘ 17c in sense 2, originally 'a ludicrous joke'.

bull[3] /bʊl/ ▻ *noun* an official letter or written instruction from the Pope, with the papal seal attached. ⓘ 14c; 13c meaning only the seal itself: from Latin *bulla* a lead seal.

bull bar see under ROO-BAR

bulldog ▻ *noun* a breed of dog with a heavy body, a short brown or brown and white coat, a large square head with a flat upturned muzzle, short bowed legs and a short tail. ⓘ 16c.

bulldog ant ▻ *noun* a black or red Australian ant with a vicious sting. Sometimes shortened to **bull ant**.

bulldog clip ▻ *noun* a clip with a spring, used to hold papers together or on to a board.

bulldoze ▻ *verb* **1** to use a bulldozer to move, flatten or demolish something. **2** (*especially* **bulldoze someone into something**) to force them to do something they do not want to do; to intimidate or bully them. **3** to force or push something through against all opposition □ *bulldozed his scheme through the Council.* ⓘ 19c, originally US colloquial noun meaning 'a severe DOSE (*noun* 3) (of flogging)'.

bulldozer ▷ *noun* a large, powerful, heavy tractor with a vertical blade at the front, for pushing heavy objects, clearing the ground or making it level.

bull dust ▷ *noun, Austral, NZ* **1** *colloq* fine dust as found on outback roads. **2** *slang* nonsense; bullshit.

bullet /'bʊlɪt/ ▷ *noun* a small metal cylinder with a pointed or rounded end, for firing from a small gun or rifle. See also CARTRIDGE. ⓘ 16c: from French *boulette* little ball.

bulletin /'bʊlɪtɪn/ ▷ *noun* **1** a short official statement of news issued as soon as the news is known. **2** a short printed newspaper or leaflet, especially one produced regularly by a group or organization. ⓘ 17c in obsolete sense 'a short note or memo': from Italian *bullettino*, a diminutive ultimately from *bulla* BULL[3].

bulletin board ▷ *noun* **1** *N Amer* a noticeboard. **2** *computing* an electronic data system containing messages and programs accessible to a number of users.

bullet-proof ▷ *adj* said of a material, etc: strong enough to prevent bullets passing through.

bullet train ▷ *noun* a high-speed passenger train, especially in Japan.

bullfight ▷ *noun* a public show, especially in Spain and Portugal, etc in which people on horseback and on foot bait, and usually ultimately kill, a bull. • **bullfighter** *noun* a person who takes part in a bullfight. See also BANDERILLERO, MATADOR, TOREADOR. • **bullfighting** *noun.*

bullfinch ▷ *noun* a small bird of the finch family, native to Europe and Asia, the male of which has a short black bill, a conspicuous red breast, a bluish-grey back, white rump and black tail. ⓘ 13c.

bullfrog ▷ *noun* **1** any of various large frogs with a loud call. **2** the largest N American frog, up to 20cm long, which seldom leaves water.

bullhead ▷ *noun* a small bottom-dwelling freshwater fish, native to N Europe, which has a stout body and a broad flattened head.

bull-headed ▷ *adj, usually derog* impetuous and obstinate. • **bull-headedly** *adverb.* • **bull-headedness** *noun.*

bullhorn ▷ *noun, N Amer* a LOUDHAILER.

bull in a china shop ▷ *noun* someone who acts in a rough, careless or tactless way and is likely to cause damage, especially in a delicate situation.

bullion /'bʊlɪən/ ▷ *noun* **1** gold or silver that has not been coined, especially in large bars, or in mass. **2** *finance* in banks and building societies, etc: bulk amounts of money generally, sometimes both coin and paper money. ⓘ 14c as an Anglo-French word for MINT[2], which perhaps developed from French *bouillon* boiling.

bullish ▷ *adj* **1** *stock exchange* tending to cause, or hoping for, rising prices. **2** very confident about the future; strongly optimistic. **3** like a bull, especially in temper; bull-headed or aggressive. • **bullishly** *adverb.* • **bullishness** *noun.*

bull-mastiff ▷ *noun* a breed of dog, developed by crossing bulldogs and mastiffs, which has a thickset body, a short brown coat, soft ears and a powerful muzzle.

bull-necked ▷ *adj* said of a person: having a short thick strong neck.

bullock /'bʊlək/ ▷ *noun* **1** a young male ox. **2** a castrated bull. Also called STEER[2].

bull pen ▷ *noun* **1** *baseball* **a** a part of the field where the pitchers warm up during the game; **b** the pitchers as a group. **2** a PEN[2] for a bull.

bull point ▷ *noun, colloq* a key point, one that is significant, advantageous or important.

bullring ▷ *noun* an arena where bullfights take place.

bull's-eye ▷ *noun* **1** the small circular centre of a target used in shooting or darts, etc. **2** *darts, etc* a shot which hits this. **3** *colloq* anything which hits its target or achieves its aim, etc. **4** a large 'hard' round peppermint sweet. **5** a thick round disc of glass forming a window, especially on a ship. **6** a thick round boss in a sheet of glass. **7 a** a round lens in a lantern; **b**) a lantern with such a lens.

bullshit *coarse slang* ▷ *noun* **1** nonsense. **2** deceptive, insincere or pretentious talk. ▷ *verb* **1** to talk bullshit to someone, especially in order to deceive them. **2** *intr* to talk bullshit. • **bullshitter** *noun.* ⓘ 1940s.

bull terrier ▷ *noun* a breed of dog with a heavy body, short, smooth (usually white) coat, broad head with small eyes, pointed erect ears and a long tail, originally developed by crossing bulldogs and terriers.

bully[1] /'bʊlɪ/ ▷ *noun* (***bullies***) a person who hurts, frightens or torments weaker or smaller people. ▷ *verb* (***bullied, bullying***) **1** to act like a bully towards someone; to threaten or persecute them. **2** (*usually* **bully someone into something**) to force them to do something they do not want to do. ▷ *adj, exclamation, dated colloq* excellent; very good. • **bullying** *noun.* • **bully for you!** *colloq, now usually ironic* good for you! well done! ⓘ 16c, originally meaning 'sweetheart', but by the 18c 'ruffian' or BULLY BOY: from Dutch *boele* lover.

bully[2] /'bʊlɪ/ and **bully beef** ▷ *noun* especially in the armed services: corned beef; tinned or pickled beef. ⓘ 18c: from French *bouilli* boiled beef.

bully[3] /'bʊlɪ/ ▷ *verb* (***bullies, bullied, bullying***) *intr* (*usually* **bully off**) *hockey, formerly* to begin or re-start a game by performing a **bully** or **bully-off**, a move involving hitting one's stick three times against an opponent's before going for the ball. Now called PASS-BACK. ⓘ 19c.

bully boy ▷ *noun* (***bully boys***) *colloq* a rough aggressive person hired to bully and threaten people. Also (**bully-boy**) *as adj.* ⓘ 17c.

bulrush /'bʊlrʌʃ/ ▷ *noun* **1** a tall waterside plant with long narrow greyish leaves and one or two thick spikes of tightly packed dark-brown flowers. **2** *Bible* a papyrus plant. ⓘ 15c.

bulwark /'bʊlwək/ ▷ *noun* **1** a wall built as a defence, often one made of earth; a rampart. **2** a BREAKWATER or sea-wall. **3** someone or something that defends a cause or way of life, etc. **4** (*especially* **bulwarks**) *naut* the side of a ship projecting above the deck. ▷ *verb* (***bulwarked, bulwarking***) to defend or fortify something. ⓘ 15c: from Dutch *bolwerc*, from German *bol* plank + *werc* work.

bum[1] ▷ *noun, Brit colloq* **1** the buttocks. **2** *coarse* the anus. ⓘ 14c as *bom.*

bum[2] *colloq, especially N Amer & Austral* ▷ *noun* **1** someone who lives by begging; a tramp. **2** someone who is lazy and shows no sense of responsibility; a loafer. ▷ *adj* worthless; dud or useless. ▷ *verb* (***bummed, bumming***) **1** to get something by begging, borrowing or cadging □ *bum a lift.* **2** (*usually* **bum around** or **about**) *intr* to travel around, or spend one's time, doing nothing in particular. • **give someone the bum's rush** *slang* **1** to throw them out by force. **2** to dismiss them abruptly, roughly or rudely, from a job, etc. ⓘ 19c: probably short for BUMMER 2.

bum bag ▷ *noun, colloq* a small bag on a belt, worn round the waist, to keep money and valuables, etc in. ⓘ 1950s in skiing use.

bumble /'bʌmbəl/ ▷ *verb* (***bumbled, bumbling***) *intr* **1** (*often* **bumble about**) to move or do something in an awkward or clumsy way. **2** to speak in a confused or confusing way. • **bumbler** *noun*. • **bumbling** *adj* inept; blundering. ◷ 16c.

bumble-bee ▷ *noun* a large hairy black and yellow bee that forms smaller colonies than the honey bee and produces only small amounts of honey, but pollinates many flowers that are important food for livestock, eg clover. Also called **humble-bee**. ◷ 16c: from the old verb *bumble* to boom or buzz.

bumf or **bumph** ▷ *noun*, *Brit colloq*, *disparaging* miscellaneous useless leaflets, official papers and documents, etc. ◷ 19c: short for *bum-fodder*, ie lavatory paper; see BUM[1], FODDER.

bummer ▷ *noun* **1** *slang* a difficult or unpleasant thing □ *She failed again? What a bummer!* **2** a lazy or idle person. ◷ 19c in sense 2: perhaps from German *Bummler* loafer.

bump ▷ *verb* (***bumped, bumping***) **1** *tr & intr* (*especially* **bump into** or **against something** or **someone**) to knock or hit them or it, especially heavily or with a jolt. **2** to hurt or damage (eg one's head) by hitting or knocking it. **3** (*usually* **bump together**) *intr* said of two moving objects: to collide. **4** (*also* **bump along**) *intr* to move or travel with jerky or bumpy movements. **5** in air travel: to turn away (a passenger who holds a valid reservation for a seat on a flight) because the airline has allowed too many seats to be booked. **6** *cricket* **a** *intr* said of a cricket ball: to bounce up high on striking the pitch; **b** said of a bowler: to bowl (a ball) so as to do this. ▷ *noun* **1** a knock, jolt or collision. **2** a dull sound caused by a knock or collision, etc. **3** a lump or swelling on the body, especially one caused by a blow. **4** a lump on a road surface. **5** (**the bumps**) an old custom in which the friends and family of a person, usually a child, celebrating his or her birthday, lift them up by their arms and legs, and give them series of thumps against the ground (usually the same number as their new age, plus one for luck). • **with a bump** *colloq* with a harsh unpleasant suddenness □ *After the honeymoon, it was back to work with a bump.* ◷ 17c: imitating the sound.

- **bump into someone** *colloq* to meet them by chance.
- **bump someone off** *slang* to kill them.
- **bump something up** *colloq* to increase or raise (eg production or prices).

bumper ▷ *noun* **1** *Brit* a bar on the front or back of a motor vehicle which lessens the shock or damage if it hits anything. **2** a pad fitted around the inside of a cot to prevent a baby from bumping itself against the bars. **3** *US* a railway BUFFER. **4** something or someone that bumps, eg in cricket a delivery that bumps. **5** an exceptionally good or large example or measure. ▷ *adj* exceptionally good or large □ *a bumper edition.* • **bumper-to-bumper** said of traffic: in or consisting of solid queues, one car behind the other.

bumper car ▷ *noun* a car used in DODGEMS.

bumpkin /ˈbʌmkɪn, ˈbʌmp–/ ▷ *noun*, *colloq*, *usually derog* an awkward, simple or stupid person, especially a simple fellow who lives in the country. Also called **country bumpkin**. ◷ 16c: perhaps from Dutch *bommekijn* little barrel.

bump-start ▷ *verb* to start (a car) by pushing it and engaging the gears while it is moving. ▷ *noun* (**bump start**) an act or instance of bump-starting a car. See also JUMP-START.

bumptious /ˈbʌmpʃəs, ˈbʌmʃəs/ ▷ *adj* offensively or irritatingly conceited or self-important. • **bumptiously** *adverb*. • **bumptiousness** *noun*. ◷ 19c: probably a humorous combination of BUMP + FRACTIOUS.

bumpy ▷ *adj* (***bumpier, bumpiest***) **1** having a lot of bumps. **2** affected by bumps; rough □ *a bumpy ride.* • **bumpily** *adverb*. • **bumpiness** *noun*.

bum steer ▷ *noun*, *slang* something misleading, false or worthless; a dud.

bun ▷ *noun* **1** *especially Brit* **a** a small, round, usually sweetened, roll, often containing currants, etc; **b** a small round cake of various types, eg an individual sponge cake. **2** a mass of hair fastened in a round shape on the back of the head. **3** (**buns**) *US colloq* the buttocks or bottom. • **have a bun in the oven** *Brit humorous colloq* to be pregnant. ◷ 14c.

bunch /bʌntʃ/ ▷ *noun* (***bunches***) **1** a number of things fastened or growing together □ *gave me a bunch of roses.* **2** (*usually* **bunches**) long hair divided into two sections and tied separately at each side or the back of the head. **3** *colloq* a group or collection. **4** *colloq* a group of people; gang □ *The drama students are a strange bunch.* ▷ *verb* (***bunches, bunched, bunching***) *tr & intr* (*sometimes* **bunch up**) to group together in, or to form, a bunch or bunches. • **bunching** *noun* **1** gathering together in bunches. **2** a situation in which traffic on a motorway travels in groups with little, especially too little, distance between vehicles. ◷ 14c.

bunch of fives ▷ *noun*, *Brit slang* a clenched fist; a blow with a fist.

bunchy ▷ *adj* (***bunchier, bunchiest***) **1** resembling, growing in, or in the form of, a bunch or bunches. **2** bulging. • **bunchiness** *noun*.

bunco or **bunko** /ˈbʌŋkoʊ/ ▷ *noun* (***buncos*** or ***bunkos***) *US* a confidence trick in which the victim is swindled or taken somewhere and robbed. ◷ 19c: from Spanish *banca* a kind of card-game.

buncombe see BUNKUM

Bundestag /ˈbʊndəztɑːɡ/ ▷ *noun* the lower house of the German parliament. ◷ 1940s in this sense: German, from *Bund* confederation + *tagen* to confer.

bundle /ˈbʌndəl/ ▷ *noun* **1** a number of things loosely fastened or tied together. **2** a loose parcel, especially one contained in a cloth. **3** (*also* **vascular bundle**) *bot* one of many strands of conducting vessels or fibres, etc that serve to conduct water and nutrients and to provide mechanical support in the stems and leaves of higher plants. **4** *slang* a large amount of money □ *made a bundle on the deal.* ▷ *verb* (***bundled, bundling***) **1** (*often* **bundle something up**) to make it into a bundle or bundles. **2** (*often* **bundle something with something**) *marketing* to sell (a product) along with (another related product) as a single package. • **be a bundle of nerves** to be extremely nervous and jumpy. • **go a bundle on someone** or **something** *slang* to be enthusiastic about, or like, them or it very much. ◷ 14c.

- **bundle someone** or **something away**, **off** or **out**, *etc* to put them or it somewhere quickly and unceremoniously, roughly or untidily; to hustle □ *bundled him into a taxi.*
- **bundle someone up** *colloq* to wrap them up warmly □ *bundled her up in a blanket.*

bundle of fun and **bundle of laughs** ▷ *noun*, *colloq*, *usually ironic* an exuberant and entertaining person or situation □ *He's a right bundle of fun* □ *I'm getting a tooth out, which should be a bundle of laughs.*

bun fight ▷ *noun*, *Brit colloq* **1** a noisy tea party. **2** a noisy occasion or function.

bung[1] /bʌŋ/ ▷ *noun* a small round piece of wood, rubber or cork, etc used to close a hole eg in the bottom of a barrel or small boat, or in the top of a jar or other container. Sometimes called STOPPER or PLUG. ▷ *verb* (***bunged, bunging***) **1** (*especially* **bung something up**) **a** to block (a hole) with a bung; **b** *colloq, especially in passive* to block, plug or clog something □ *The sink is bunged up with dirt* □ *My nose is bunged up.* **2** *slang* to throw or put something somewhere in a careless way □ *Just bung my coat in there.* ◷ 15c: from Dutch *bonge* stopper.

bung[2] *Austral colloq* ⊳ *adj* **1** dead. **2** bankrupt. **3** ruined or useless. • **go bung 1** to die. **2** to fail or go bust. **3** to break down or go phut. ◷ 19c: from Aboriginal *bong* dead.

bung[3] /bʌŋ/ *criminal slang* ⊳ *noun* a bribe. ⊳ *verb* (***bunged, bunging***) to bribe someone. ◷ 1950s.

bungalow /'bʌŋgəloʊ/ ⊳ *noun* a single-storey house. ◷ 17c: from Gujarati *bangalo*, from Hindi *bangla* 'in the style of Bengal.

bungee jumping /'bʌndʒiː —/ ⊳ *noun* the sport or recreation in which a person jumps from a height with strong rubber ropes or cables attached to their ankles to ensure that they bounce up before they reach the ground. ◷ 1980s: from slang *bungie* or *bungy* india-rubber.

bunghole ⊳ *noun* a hole by which a barrel, etc is emptied or filled and into which a BUNG[1] is fitted.

bungle /'bʌŋgəl/ ⊳ *verb* (***bungled, bungling***) *tr & intr* to do something carelessly or badly; to spoil or mismanage (a job or procedure). ⊳ *noun* carelessly or badly done work; a mistake or foul-up. • **bungled** *adj*. • **bungler** *noun*. • **bungling** *noun, adj*. ◷ 16c.

bunion /'bʌnjən/ ⊳ *noun* a painful swelling on the first joint of the big toe. ◷ 18c: perhaps from French *buigne* a bump on the head.

bunk[1] ⊳ *noun* **1** a narrow bed attached to the wall in a cabin in a ship, caravan, etc. **2** a BUNK BED. **3** *colloq* a place to sleep □ *need a bunk for the night*. ⊳ *verb* (***bunked, bunking***) *intr, colloq* **1** (*especially* **bunk down**) to lie down and go to sleep, especially in some improvised place. **2** to occupy a bunk. ◷ 18c: probably from BUNKER.

bunk[2] *Brit slang* ⊳ *noun* (*usually* **do a bunk**) the act of running away; leaving the place where one ought to be, usually furtively □ *He did a bunk from gym*. ⊳ *verb* (***bunked, bunking***) only in phrase below. ◷ 19c.

■ **bunk off** to stay away from school or work, etc when one ought to be there.

bunk[3] see under BUNKUM

bunk bed ⊳ *noun* each of a pair of single beds fixed one on top of the other. Often shortened to BUNK.

bunker ⊳ *noun* **1** an obstacle on a golf course consisting of a hollow area containing sand. **2** (*also* **coal bunker**) a large container or cupboard for storing coal. **3** a compartment for storing fuel on board ship. **4** an underground bombproof shelter. ⊳ *verb* (***bunkered, bunkering***) **1** *golf* to play (the ball) into a bunker. **2** *tr & intr* to fill the bunker of (a ship) with fuel. ◷ 18c in sense 2; 16c Scots as *bonker*, meaning 'box', 'chest', or 'seat'.

bunkhouse ⊳ *noun* a building containing sleeping accommodation for workers, especially ranch workers.

bunko see BUNCO

bunkum or (*chiefly US*) **buncombe** /'bʌŋkəm/ ⊳ *noun, colloq* nonsense; foolish talk; claptrap. Often shortened to **bunk**. See also DEBUNK. ◷ 19c: named after Buncombe, a county in N Carolina, whose congressman is said to have excused a rambling speech in Congress on the grounds that he was only speaking for Buncombe.

bunk-up ⊳ *noun, colloq* a push or lifting action from below, to help someone climb up on to something. ◷ Early 20c: an alteration from the original dialect sense of BUNT to push or BUTT.

bunny ⊳ *noun* (***bunnies***) **1** (*also* **bunny rabbit**) a pet name or child's word for a RABBIT (*noun* 1). **2** *Austral colloq* a fool or dupe. ◷ 17c: from Scottish Gaelic *bun* bottom, or the tail of a rabbit, etc.

bunny girl ⊳ *noun* a club hostess or waitress who wears a scanty provocative costume which includes stylized rabbit's ears and tail. ◷ 1960s.

Bunsen burner /'bʌnsən—/ ⊳ *noun* a gas burner, used mainly in chemistry laboratories, with an adjustable inlet hole which allows the gas-air mixture to be controlled so as to produce a very hot flame with no smoke. ◷ 19c: named after its inventor R W Bunsen (1811–99), a German chemist.

bunt ⊳ *verb* (***bunted, bunting***) *tr & intr, baseball* to push or block (the ball) with the bat, rather than swinging at it. ⊳ *noun* **1** an act or instance of this. **2** a bunted ball. ◷ 19c: from a dialect word altered from BUTT[1] (see BUNK-UP).

bunting[1] ⊳ *noun* **1** a row of small cloth or paper flags on a string, hung usually as an outdoor decoration; streamers or other similar decorations hung on string. **2** thin loosely-woven cotton used to make flags, especially for ships. ◷ 18c.

bunting[2] ⊳ *noun* any of various small finch-like birds with a short stout bill and a sturdy body, usually with streaked brown plumage. ◷ 13c.

bunyip /'bʌnjɪp/ ⊳ *noun, Austral folklore* a frightening monster that lives in water-holes, lakes, swamps, etc. ◷ 19c: Aboriginal.

buoy /bɔɪ; *N Amer* 'buːɪ/ ⊳ *noun* (***buoys***) a brightly-coloured floating object fastened to the bottom of the sea by an anchor, to warn ships of rocks, etc or to mark channels, etc. See also LIFEBUOY, BREECHES BUOY. ⊳ *verb* (***buoyed, buoying***) **1** to mark (eg an obstruction or a channel) with a buoy or buoys. **2** (*usually* **buoy something up**) to keep it afloat. **3** (*usually* **buoy someone up**) to raise or lift their spirits; to encourage, cheer or excite them. **4** (*often* **buoy something up**) to sustain, support or boost it □ *profits were buoyed by the new economic confidence*. **5** *intr* to rise or float to the surface. ◷ 15c as *boye* a float.

buoyant /'bɔɪənt; *N Amer* buːjənt/ ⊳ *adj* **1** said of an object: able to float in or on the surface of a liquid. **2** said of a liquid or gas: able to keep an object afloat. **3** said of a person: cheerful; bouncy; resilient. **4** said of sales, profits, etc: tending to rise; increasing. **5** said of a business, etc: having increasing trade, rising profits, etc. • **buoyancy** *noun* (***buoyancies***) **1** the quality or capacity of being buoyant (in any of the senses). **2** the upward force exerted on an object that is immersed in or floating on the surface of a fluid (a liquid or gas), and is equal to the weight of fluid displaced. • **buoyantly** *adverb*. ◷ 16c.

BUPA /'buːpə/ ⊳ *abbreviation* British United Provident Association, , a private medical insurance scheme.

BUR ⊳ *abbreviation, IVR* Burma, now called Myanmar.

bur or **burr** /bɜː(r)/ ⊳ *noun* **1** any seed or fruit with numerous hooks or prickles which are caught in the fur or feathers of passing mammals and birds, and so dispersed over considerable distances. **2** any plant that produces such seeds or fruits. ◷ 14c.

Burberry /'bɜːbərɪ/ ⊳ *noun* (***Burberries***) *trademark* a type of good-quality raincoat made of strong waterproof fabric. ◷ Early 20c: named after Burberrys Ltd, the manufacturers.

burble /'bɜːbəl/ ⊳ *verb* (***burbled, burbling***) **1** (*often* **burble on** or **away**) *intr* to speak at length but with little meaning or purpose. **2** *intr* said of a stream, etc: to make a bubbling murmuring sound. **3** to say something in a way that is hard to understand, especially very quickly or incoherently. ⊳ *noun* **1** a bubbling murmuring sound. **2** a long incoherent or rambling stream of speech. ◷ 14c in sense 2: probably imitating the sound.

burbot /'bɜːbət/ ⊳ *noun* (***burbot*** or ***burbots***) a large fish, the only freshwater species in the cod family, and an important food fish in the former Soviet Union. ◷ 14c: from French *bourbotte*.

burden[1] /'bɜːdən/ ⊳ *noun* **1** something to be carried; a load. **2** a duty or obligation, etc which is difficult, time-consuming, costly, exacting or hard to endure. **3** the carrying of a load or loads □ *a beast of burden*. **4** *naut* (*also* **burthen** /'bɜːðən/) the amount of cargo a ship can carry; its capacity. ⊳ *verb* (***burdened, burdening***) **1** (*usually* **burden someone with something**) to weigh them down with a burden, difficulty, problem, etc; to trouble or impose upon them. **2** (*sometimes* **burden something** or **someone down**) to put a load on to it or them. ⓒ Anglo-Saxon as *byrthen*, from *beran* to bear.

burden² /ˈbɜːdən/ ▷ *noun* **1** the main theme, especially of a book or speech, etc. **2** a line repeated at the end of each verse of a song; a refrain. ⓒ 16c, originally meaning 'a bass accompaniment': from French *bourdon* a droning sound.

burden of proof ▷ *noun* **1** *law* the duty of a LITIGANT or PROSECUTOR to prove a fact in the law court. **2** *loosely* the responsibility for proving something.

burdensome ▷ *adj* difficult to carry, support or tolerate; onerous. ⓒ 16c.

burdock /ˈbɜːdɒk/ ▷ *noun* any of various perennial plants, native to Europe and Asia, with heart-shaped lower leaves and oval heads of tiny purple flowers, followed by spiny fruits or burrs. ⓒ 16c: BUR + DOCK³.

bureau /ˈbjʊəroʊ, bjʊˈroʊ/ ▷ *noun* (***bureaux*** or ***bureaus*** /-roʊz/) **1** *Brit* a desk for writing at, with drawers and usually a front flap which opens downwards to provide the writing surface. **2** *N Amer, especially US* a chest of drawers. **3** an office or department for business, especially for collecting and supplying information. **4** *N Amer* a government or newspaper department. ⓒ 17c: French, from *burel* a type of dark red cloth which was used for covering desks.

bureaucracy /bjʊˈrɒkrəsɪ/ ▷ *noun* (***bureaucracies***) **1** a system of government by officials who are responsible to their department heads and are not elected. **2** these officials as a group, especially when regarded as oppressive. **3** any system of administration in which matters are complicated by complex procedures and trivial rules. **4** a country governed by officials. ⓒ 19c: BUREAU + -CRACY.

bureaucrat /ˈbjʊəroʊkrat/ ▷ *noun* **1** a government official. **2** an official who follows rules rigidly, so creating delays and difficulties; someone who practises or believes in bureaucracy. • **bureaucratic** /-ˈkratɪk/ *adj.* • **bureaucratically** *adverb*.

bureaucratize or **bureaucratise** /bjʊˈrɒkrətaɪz/ ▷ *verb* (***bureaucratized, bureaucratizing***) **1** to form something into a bureaucracy; to make something bureaucratic. **2** to govern (a country or organization, etc) as a bureaucracy. • **bureaucratization** *noun*. ⓒ 19c.

bureau de change /— də ʃɑ̃ʒ/ ▷ *noun* (***bureaux de change***) a place where one can change money from one currency to another.

burette /bjʊˈrɛt/ ▷ *noun, chem* a long vertical glass tube marked with a scale and having a tap at the bottom, used to deliver controlled volumes of liquid, eg during chemical TITRATIONS. ⓒ 15c, meaning 'small cruet' or 'jug': French.

burgeon /ˈbɜːdʒən/ *literary* ▷ *verb* (***burgeoned, burgeoning***) (*sometimes* **burgeon forth**) *intr* **1** to grow or develop quickly; to flourish. **2** said of a plant: to bud or sprout. • **burgeoning** *adj*. ⓒ 14c: from French *burjon* bud or shoot.

burger /ˈbɜːɡə(r)/ ▷ *noun* **1** a hamburger. **2** *especially in compounds* a hamburger covered or flavoured with something □ ***cheeseburger***. **3** *especially in compounds* an item of food shaped like a hamburger but made of something different □ ***nutburger***. ⓒ 1930s: shortening of HAMBURGER.

burgess /ˈbɜːdʒɪs/ ▷ *noun* **1** *Brit, mainly formal or old use* **a** in England: an inhabitant or citizen of a BOROUGH, especially a person who has the right to elect people to government; **b** *formerly* in Scotland: an inhabitant or citizen of a BURGH. **2** *Brit, historical* an MP for a BOROUGH (senses 1 and 2) or a university. **3** *Brit, historical* a borough magistrate or town councillor. ⓒ 13c as *burgeis*: French, from Latin *burgus* borough.

burgh /ˈbʌrə/ ▷ *noun* in Scotland until 1975: an incorporated town or borough, with a certain amount of self-government under a town council. See also ROYAL BURGH. ⓒ 14c: Scots form of BOROUGH.

burgher /ˈbɜːɡə(r)/ ▷ *noun, rather old or facetious* a citizen of a town, especially a town on the Continent, or of a borough □ ***This outraged the respectable burghers of Cheltenham.*** ⓒ 16c: from German *burger*, from *burg* borough.

burglar /ˈbɜːɡlə(r)/ ▷ *noun, law* a person who commits the crime of BURGLARY. ⓒ 16c: from Anglo-French *burgler*, from Anglo-Latin *burglator*.

burglar alarm ▷ *noun* an alarm fitted to a building, which is activated by an intruder.

burglarize ▷ *verb* (***burglarized, burglarizing***) *tr & intr, US* to burgle. ⓒ 19c.

burglary ▷ *noun* (***burglaries***) *law* the crime of entering a building or other permanent structure illegally in order to steal, or to commit grievous bodily harm or rape. Compare ROBBERY. ⓒ 16c; see BURGLAR.

burgle /ˈbɜːɡəl/ ▷ *verb* (***burgled, burgling***) **1** to enter (a building, etc) illegally and steal from it; to steal from someone or something. **2** *intr* to commit burglary. *US equivalent* BURGLARIZE. ⓒ 19c: a back-formation from BURGLAR.

burgomaster /ˈbɜːɡoʊmɑːstə(r)/ ▷ *noun* a mayor of a town in Germany, Belgium, the Netherlands or Austria. ⓒ 16c: from Dutch *burgemeester*, from *burg* borough + *meester* master.

burgundy /ˈbɜːɡəndɪ/ ▷ *noun* (***burgundies***) **1** a French wine made in the Burgundy region, especially a red wine. **2** any similar red wine. **3** a deep or purplish red colour, the colour of red wine. ⓒ 17c.

burial /ˈbɛrɪəl/ ▷ *noun* **1** the burying of a dead body in a grave. Also *in compounds* and *as adj* □ ***burial-ground*** □ ***burial clothes***. **2** *archaeol* a grave and the remains found in it. ⓒ Anglo-Saxon *byrgels* tomb.

burin /ˈbjʊərɪn/ ▷ *noun* a tempered steel tool for engraving copper or wood, etc. ⓒ 17c: French.

burk see BERK

burl /bɜːl/ ▷ *noun* **1** a small knot or lump in wool or thread. **2** a KNOT (*noun* 7) in wood. ▷ *verb* (***burled, burling***) to remove the burls from (a fabric). ⓒ 15c: from French *bourle* a tuft of wool.

burlap /ˈbɜːlap/ ▷ *noun, especially N Amer* **1** a coarse canvas made from jute or hemp, used for sacks or wrappings. **2** a lighter material, made eg of flax, used for wall-coverings, etc. Also called HESSIAN. ⓒ 17c.

burlesque /bɜːˈlɛsk/ ▷ *noun* **1** a piece of literature, acting or some other presentation which exaggerates, demeans or mocks a serious subject or art form. See also TRAVESTY. **2** *N Amer, especially US* a type of theatrical entertainment involving humorous sketches, songs and usually strip-tease. ▷ *adj* belonging to or like a burlesque. ▷ *verb* (***burlesqued, burlesquing***) to make fun of something using burlesque; to make a burlesque of it. ⓒ 17c: French, from Italian *burlesco*, from *burla* jest.

burley see BERLEY

burly /ˈbɜːlɪ/ ▷ *adj* (***burlier, burliest***) said of a person: strong and heavy in build; big and sturdy. • **burliness** *noun*. ⓒ 13c as *borli* in obsolete sense 'stately' or 'imposing'.

Burmese /bɜːˈmiːz, ˈbɜːmiːz/ ▷ *adj* belonging or relating to Burma, a republic in SE Asia since 1989 called Myanmar, its inhabitants or their language. ▷ *noun* **1** a citizen or inhabitant of, or person born in, Burma. See also MYANMAN. **2** the official language of Burma. **3** a Burmese cat. ⓒ 19c.

Burmese cat ▷ *noun* a breed of short-haired domestic cat similar to the SIAMESE, but typically dark-brown with golden eyes.

burn¹ /bɜːn/ ▷ *verb* (***burned*** or ***burnt, burning***) **1** *tr & intr* to be on fire or set something on fire. **2** *tr & intr* to damage or injure, or be damaged or injured, by fire or heat. **3** to use something as fuel. **4** *tr & intr* to char or scorch, or become charred or scorched. **5** to make (a hole, etc) by or as if by fire or heat, etc □ *Acid can burn holes in material.* **6** *intr* to be or feel hot. **7** *tr & intr* to feel or make something feel a hot or stinging pain □ *Vodka burns my throat.* **8** (*usually* **be burning to do something**) *intr, colloq* to want to do it very much □ *is burning to get his revenge.* **9** (*especially* **be burning with something**) *intr* to feel strong emotion □ *was burning with shame.* **10** to use (coal, oil, etc) as fuel. **11** *tr & intr* (*now usually* **burn to death** or **burn alive**) to kill or die by fire. ▷ *noun* **1** an injury or mark caused by fire, heat, acid, friction, etc. **2** pain felt in a muscle, experienced as a result of the build-up of LACTIC ACID during demanding exercise. **3** an act of firing the engines of a space rocket so as to produce thrust. **4** (*also* **burn-up**) a very fast ride eg on a motorcycle or speedboat □ *went for a burn on the bike.* • **burn one's boats** or **bridges** *colloq* to do something which makes it impossible for one to return to one's former situation or way of life, etc; to destroy all chance of escape or retreat. • **burn the candle at both ends** to exhaust oneself by trying to do too much, usually by starting work very early in the morning and staying up late at night. • **burn one's fingers** or **get one's fingers burnt** *colloq* to suffer, often financially, as a result of getting involved in or interfering with something foolish, dangerous, risky, etc. • **burn a hole in one's pocket** said of money that one is very eager to spend: to be extremely difficult or tempting not to spend. See also MONEY TO BURN under MONEY. • **burn the midnight oil** to work late into the night. ⓒ Anglo-Saxon *biernan* to be on fire, and *bærnan* to cause to burn.

■ **burn down** said of a large structure such as a building: to be destroyed by fire or burnt to the ground.

■ **burn something down** to destroy (a building, etc) by fire.

■ **burn out 1** to burn up completely and be reduced to nothing. **2** said of a rocket engine: to stop working when the fuel is used up.

■ **burn someone** or **oneself out** to exhaust them or oneself by too much work or exercise.

■ **burn something out** to make it stop working from overuse or overheating.

■ **burn up 1** to be destroyed by fire, heat or acid, etc. **2** *N Amer slang* to become very angry. **3** said of a fire, etc: to increase in activity; to blaze or flare up. See also BURN-UP.

■ **burn someone up** *N Amer slang* to make them very angry □ *Her letter really burned me up.*

■ **burn something up 1** to destroy it by fire, heat or acid, etc. **2** said of an engine: to use up fuel in large quantities.

burn² /bɜːn/ ▷ *noun, chiefly Scottish* a small stream. ⓒ Anglo-Saxon *burna* brook.

burner ▷ *noun* **1** the part of a gas lamp or stove, etc which produces the flame. **2** a piece of equipment, etc for burning something. • **put something on the back burner** see under BACK BURNER.

burning ▷ *adj* **1** on fire. **2** feeling extremely hot. **3** very strong or intense □ *a burning desire.* **4** very important or urgent □ *the burning question.*

burning ghat see GHAT (sense 3)

burnish /ˈbɜːnɪʃ/ ▷ *verb* (***burnishes, burnished, burnishing***) to make (metal) bright and shiny by polishing. ▷ *noun* polish; lustre. • **burnished** *adj.* • **burnishing** *noun.* ⓒ 14c: from French *brunir* to burnish, literally 'to make brown'.

burnous /bɜːˈnuːs/ ▷ *noun* (***burnouses*** or ***burnous***) a long cloak with a hood, worn by Arabs. ⓒ 17c: from Arabic *burnus.*

burn-out ▷ *noun, especially US* **1** physical or emotional exhaustion caused by overwork or stress. **2** the point at which a rocket engine stops working when the fuel is used up.

burnt *a past tense and past participle of* BURN¹

burnt ochre ▷ *noun* a natural dark reddish-brown pigment made by heating OCHRE.

burnt offering ▷ *noun* **1** something offered and burned on an altar as a sacrifice, especially (in traditional Jewish ritual) a young sheep, goat, bullock or pigeon. **2** *facetious* a burnt or overcooked dish served up at a meal.

burnt sienna ▷ *noun* a natural dark reddish-brown pigment made by heating raw SIENNA.

burnt umber ▷ *noun* a natural rich brown pigment made by heating UMBER.

burn-up ▷ *noun* **1** *nuclear* a measure of the consumption of fuel in a nuclear reactor. **2** a BURN¹ (*noun* 4).

burp /bɜːp/ *colloq* ▷ *verb* (***burped, burping***) **1** *intr* to let air escape noisily from one's stomach through one's mouth. Also called BELCH. **2** to rub or pat (a baby) on the back to help get rid of air in its stomach. ▷ *noun* a belch. ⓒ 1930s: imitating the sound.

burr¹ /bɜː(r)/ ▷ *noun* **1** in some accents of English, such as that found in Northumberland: a rough 'r' sound pronounced at the back of the throat. **2** a continual humming sound made eg by a machine. **3** a rough edge on metal or paper. **4** a small rotary drill used by a dentist or surgeon. ▷ *verb* (***burred, burring***) **1** *intr* to make a burring sound. **2** to pronounce something with a burr. ⓒ 17c in sense 3; associated with BUR, but perhaps also an imitation of the sound.

burr² see BUR

burrito /bəˈriːtoʊ/ ▷ *noun* (***burritos***) *cookery* a Mexican dish consisting of a TORTILLA folded around a filling of meat, cheese, refried beans, etc. ⓒ 1940s: American Spanish, literally 'little donkey', from Spanish *burro* donkey.

burrow /ˈbʌroʊ/ ▷ *noun* **1** a hole in the ground, especially one dug by a rabbit or other small animal for shelter or defence. **2** *colloq* a cosy little refuge or bolt-hole. ▷ *verb* (***burrowed, burrowing***) **1** (*especially* **burrow in** or **into** or **through** or **under something**) *tr & intr* to make a hole or tunnel in or under it. **2** *intr* said of an animal: to make burrows or live in a burrow. **3** (*especially* **burrow away, down, in** or **into something**) *tr & intr* said of a person: to keep (oneself, or something belonging to oneself, etc) cosy, protected or hidden away, as if in a burrow; to hide, bury or sink. **4** (*usually* **burrow into something**) to search or investigate deeply into it. ⓒ 13c as *borow.*

bursa /ˈbɜːsə/ ▷ *noun* (***bursae*** /-siː/ or ***bursas***) *anatomy* a sac or pouch of liquid occurring at a point of friction between two structures, especially between a tendon and a bone. ⓒ 19c: from Latin, meaning 'a bag or pouch'.

bursar /ˈbɜːsə(r)/ ▷ *noun* **1** a treasurer in a school, college or university. **2** in Scotland and New Zealand: a student or pupil who has a bursary. • **bursarship** *noun.* ⓒ 13c: from Latin *bursarius,* from *bursa* a bag or purse.

bursary /ˈbɜːsərɪ/ ▷ *noun* (***bursaries***) **1** especially in Scotland and New Zealand: an award or grant of money made to a student; a scholarship. **2** the bursar's room in a school, college, etc.

bursitis /bɜːˈsaɪtɪs/ ▷ *noun, pathol, medicine* inflammation of a BURSA. ⓒ 19c.

burst /bɜːst/ ▷ *verb* (***burst, bursting***) **1** *tr & intr* to break or fly open or into pieces, usually suddenly and violently. **2** (*especially* **burst in, into** or **out of somewhere** or

something) *intr* to make one's way suddenly or violently into or out of it, etc □ *burst into the room.* **3** (*usually* **burst on to something**) *intr* to appear suddenly in (a specified circle or area) and be immediately important or noteworthy □ *burst on to the political scene.* **4** (*usually* **be bursting**) *intr* **a** (*also* **be bursting at the seams**) to be completely full; **b** to break open; to overflow, etc □ *My suitcase is bursting*; **c** (*usually* **be bursting with something**) to be overflowing with or unable to contain (one's excitement, vitality, anger or other emotion). **5** *technical* to tear apart the perforated sheets of (CONTINUOUS STATIONERY). ▻ *noun* **1** an instance of bursting or breaking open. Often *in compounds* □ *a tyre-burst.* **2** the place where something has burst or broken open, or the hole or break, etc made by it bursting. **3** a sudden, brief or violent period of some activity, eg speed, gunfire, applause, laughter. • **burst into flames** to begin burning suddenly and violently. • **burst into song** to begin singing, especially suddenly or unexpectedly. • **burst into tears** to begin weeping suddenly or unexpectedly. • **burst open** usually said of a door: to open suddenly and violently. • **burst out laughing** to begin laughing suddenly or unexpectedly. ◷ Anglo-Saxon *berstan.*

bursting ▻ *adj, colloq* **1** very eager to do something. **2** (*usually* **bursting with something**) brimful, as full as one can be, or too full, of (eg pride or joy). **3** urgently needing to urinate.

burthen see BURDEN[1] *noun* 4

burton /ˈbɜːtən/ *Brit slang* ▻ *noun* now only in the phrase **gone for a burton 1** lost for good, missing or no longer in existence. **2** dead, killed or drowned. **3** broken or destroyed. ◷ 1940s phrase; in World War II airforce slang, an airman who was missing, presumed dead, was said euphemistically to have 'gone for a Burton', probably referring to a type of beer made in Burton-upon-Trent, Staffordshire, and meaning that the airman had gone for a drink, ie 'into the drink' (the sea).

bury /ˈbɛrɪ/ ▻ *verb* (***buries, buried, burying***) **1** to place (a dead body) in a grave, the sea, etc. **2** to hide something in the ground. **3** to put something out of sight; to cover □ *bury one's face in one's hands.* **4** to put something out of one's mind or memory; to blot out □ *Let's bury our differences.* **5** to lose (a close relative) by death □ *She has already buried three husbands.* • **bury the hatchet** to stop quarrelling and become friends again . ◷ 18c: in Native American tradition, when the chiefs met to smoke the PEACE PIPE, hatchets and similar weapons would be buried ceremonially to show that hostilities were at an end. • **bury one's head in the sand** to refuse to think about or accept some unpleasant or unwelcome fact . ◷ 19c: from the old belief that the ostrich reacted to danger by burying its head in the sand, apparently thinking that if it could not see it could not be seen. ◷ Anglo-Saxon *byrgan.*

■ **bury oneself in something** to occupy oneself completely with it.

bus ▻ *noun* (***buses*** or (*chiefly US*) ***busses***) **1** a road vehicle, usually a large one, which carries passengers to and from established stopping points along a fixed route for payment. Originally called **omnibus**. See also DOUBLE-DECKER, MINIBUS. **2** *colloq* a car or aeroplane, especially one which is old and shaky. **3** *computing* a set of electrical conductors that form a channel or path along which data (in the form of digital signals) or power may be transmitted to and from all the main components of a computer. ▻ *verb* (***buses*** or ***busses***, ***bused*** or ***bussed***, ***busing*** or ***bussing***) **1** (*also* **bus it**) *intr* to go by bus. **2** *especially US* to transport (children) by bus to a school in a different area, as a way of promoting racial integration. **3** *N Amer* in a restaurant, etc: to clear away (dirty dishes) from tables, replace items, etc and help the waiting staff. See also BUS-BOY. • **miss the bus** to lose an opportunity. ◷ 19c: short for OMNIBUS.

bus-boy and **bus-girl** ▻ *noun, N Amer* a person who BUSes (*verb* 3); an assistant waiter or waitress.

busby /ˈbʌzbɪ/ ▻ *noun* (***busbies***) **1** a tall fur hat with a bag hanging on its right side, worn as part of some military uniforms, especially that of the HUSSAR. **2** *colloq* a BEARSKIN 2. ◷ 18c in the obsolete sense 'a large bushy wig'.

bus conductor ▻ *noun, especially formerly* a person whose job is to collect the fares from passengers on a bus, and to give out tickets.

bush[1] /bʊʃ/ ▻ *noun* (***bushes***) **1** a low woody perennial plant, especially one having many separate branches originating at or near ground level. See also SHRUB[1]. **2** (*usually* **the bush**) wild uncultivated land covered with shrubs or small trees, and ranging from open countryside to forest, especially in semi-arid regions of Africa, Australia or New Zealand. **3** something like a bush, especially in thickness, shape or density □ *a bush of hair.* • **beat about the bush** see under BEAT. • **go bush** *Austral & NZ colloq* **1** to go off into the bush. **2** to leave town or one's usual haunts; to disappear. **3** to abandon civilized life, or start living rough. ◷ 13c: from Norse *buskr*; some uses are from Dutch *bosch.*

bush[2] /bʊʃ/ ▻ *noun* (***bushes***) a sheet of thin metal lining a cylinder in which an axle revolves. ▻ *verb* (***bushed, bushing***) to provide (eg a bearing) with a bush. ◷ 16c: from Dutch *bussche* box.

bush-baby ▻ *noun* an agile nocturnal primate of sub-Saharan Africa with thick fur, large eyes and ears, a long tail and long hind legs. ◷ Early 20c.

bushed ▻ *adj, following its noun, colloq* **1** extremely tired. **2** *Austral, NZ* lost in the bush, or as if in the bush; bewildered.

bushel /ˈbʊʃəl/ ▻ *noun* **1** in the imperial system: a unit for measuring dry or liquid goods (especially grains, potatoes or fruit) by volume, equal to 8 gallons or 36.4 litres in the UK (35.2 litres in the USA). **2** a container with this capacity. **3** *colloq, especially US* a large amount or number. • **hide one's light under a bushel** to keep one's talents or good qualities hidden from other people. ◷ 14c: from French *boissiel.*

bushfire ▻ *noun, especially Austral & NZ* a fire in forest or scrub.

bushily and **bushiness** see under BUSHY

bushman ▻ *noun* **1** *Austral, NZ* someone who lives or travels in the bush. **2** (**Bushman**) a member of an almost extinct, small-statured, aboriginal race of nomadic huntsmen in S Africa. **3** (**Bushman**) any of the languages spoken by the Bushmen. ◷ 18c in sense 2: from Afrikaans *boschjesman.*

bushranger ▻ *noun* **1** *Austral, historical* an outlaw or escaped convict living in the bush. **2** *N Amer* a backwoodsman; someone who lives far from civilization.

bush shirt and **bush jacket** ▻ *noun* a light cotton jacket with four pockets and a belt.

bush telegraph ▻ *noun, chiefly Brit, humorous* the rapid spreading of information, rumours, etc, usually by word of mouth.

bushveld /ˈbʊʃfɛlt/ ▻ *noun, S Afr* VELD made up largely of woodland.

bushwalk *Austral, NZ* ▻ *verb, intr* to walk or hike through the bush as a leisure activity. ▻ *noun* a walk through the bush. • **bushwalker** *noun.* • **bushwalking** *noun.*

bushwhack ▻ *verb* **1** *originally & especially N Amer* to ambush someone usually in rough country. **2** *intr, N Amer, Austral, etc* to travel through woods or bush, especially by clearing a way through it. **3** *intr, N Amer* to fight in guerrilla warfare in bush country. **4** *intr, Austral, NZ* to work in the bush, especially as an unskilled labourer felling trees, etc.

• **bushwhacking** *noun*. ⓒ 19c: back-formation from BUSHWHACKER.

bushwhacker ▻ *noun* **1** *N Amer* a guerrilla fighter. **2** *N Amer, Austral, etc* someone who lives or travels in bush country. **3** *Austral colloq* a country bumpkin or backwoodsman. ⓒ 19c, literally 'someone who chops down (or WHACKS) the bush'.

bushy ▻ *adj* (***bushier***, ***bushiest***) **1** covered with bush or bushes. **2** said of hair, etc: thick and spreading. • **bushily** *adverb*. • **bushiness** *noun*. ⓒ 14c: from BUSH[1].

busier, **busies**, **busiest** and **busily** see under BUSY

business /'bɪznɪs, -nəs/ ▻ *noun* **1** the buying and selling of goods and services. Also called COMMERCE, TRADE. **2** a shop, firm or commercial company, etc. **3** a regular occupation, trade or profession. **4** the things that are one's proper or rightful concern ▫ ***mind your own business***. **5** serious work or activity ▫ ***get down to business***. **6** an affair or matter ▫ ***a nasty business***. **7** *colloq* a difficult or complicated problem; a bother or nuisance. **8** (**the business**) *slang* exactly what is required; the perfect thing or person, etc for the job. **9** commercial practice or policy ▫ ***Prompt invoicing is good business***. **10** economic or commercial dealings, activity, custom or contact ▫ ***I have some business with his company***. **11** the quantity or level of commercial activity ▫ ***Business is very poor this quarter***. **12** (*also* **stage business**) *theat* action on stage, as distinguished from dialogue. • **go out of business** to be unable to continue functioning as a business; to fold or go bankrupt. • **make it one's business to do something** to take a personal interest in or responsibility for doing it, or for seeing that it is done. • **on business** said of a person: in the process of doing business or something official. • **send someone about their business** to dismiss them or send them away abruptly. ⓒ Anglo-Saxon as *bisignes* meaning 'busyness', from *bisig* busy.

business card ▻ *noun* a card carried by a businessman or businesswoman, showing their name and designation, and the name, address and telephone number, etc of their company.

business class ▻ *noun* on an aeroplane, etc: CLUB CLASS.

business end ▻ *noun, colloq* (*especially* **the business end of something**) the part (of a tool or weapon, etc) which does the actual work that the item is intended for ▫ ***waving the business end of his knife at me***.

businesslike ▻ *adj* practical and efficient; methodical.

businessman and **businesswoman** ▻ *noun* a man or woman working in trade or commerce, especially at quite a senior level.

business park ▻ *noun* an area, usually on the edge of a town, especially designed to accommodate business offices and light industry.

business plan ▻ *noun* a plan laying out the objectives of a proposed business venture, its financial strategy, the products or service to be produced or supplied, and the estimated market, turnover, profits, return for investors, etc.

business studies ▻ *plural noun* the study of economic, financial and managerial matters, especially as part of a school, college or university course.

busk ▻ *verb* (***busked***, ***busking***) *intr, chiefly Brit* to sing, play music, etc in the street for money. • **busker** *noun* someone who performs in the street for money. • **busking** *noun*. ⓒ 19c.

bus lane ▻ *noun* a traffic lane chiefly for the use of buses, either for all or a specified part of the day.

busman's holiday ▻ *noun* leisure time spent doing what one normally does at work.

bus shelter ▻ *noun* an open-sided structure at a bus stop, that gives people waiting for a bus some protection against the weather.

bus stop ▻ *noun* **1** a stopping place for a bus, where passengers may board or alight from a bus. **2** a post or sign marking such a place.

bust[1] ▻ *noun* **1** the upper, front part of a woman's body; breasts or bosom. **2** a sculpture of a person's head, shoulders and upper chest. ⓒ 17c in sense 2: from French *buste*, from Italian *busto*.

bust[2] *colloq* ▻ *verb* (**bust** or **busted**, **busting**) **1** *tr & intr* to break or burst. **2** said of the police: to arrest someone ▫ ***He was busted for possession of marijuana***. **3** to raid or search someone or somewhere (especially in a search for illegal drugs) ▫ ***The club was busted last night***. **4** *N Amer, usually military* to demote. ▻ *noun, slang* **1** a police raid. **2** a drinking bout; a spree. ▻ *adj, colloq* **1** broken or burst. **2** having no money left; bankrupt or ruined. • **go bust** *colloq* to go bankrupt. ⓒ 19c: colloquial form of BURST.

bustard /'bʌstəd/ ▻ *noun* any one of various species of large ground-dwelling bird with speckled grey or brown plumage and long powerful legs, several species of which have been hunted almost to extinction. ⓒ 15c: from French *bistarde*, from Latin *avis tarda* slow bird (although it is not slow).

buster ▻ *noun, N Amer slang* a form of address (often used aggressively) for a man or boy. ▫ ***Hey, buster, get your hands off her!***

bustier[1] /'bʌstɪeɪ, 'bʊ-/ ▻ *noun, fashion* a short tight-fitting strapless bodice for women, worn as a bra and top combined. ⓒ 1980s: French, meaning 'bodice'.

bustier[2] and **bustiest** see under BUSTY

bustle[1] /'bʌsəl/ ▻ *verb* (***bustled***, ***bustling***) **1** (*usually* **bustle about**) *intr* to busy oneself in a brisk, energetic and/or noisy manner. **2** to make someone hurry or work hard, etc ▫ ***bustled her out of the room***. ▻ *noun* hurried, noisy and excited activity ▫ ***far away from the hustle and bustle***. • **bustler** *noun* a person who bustles or works with ostentatious haste. • **bustling** *adj* lively and busy. ⓒ 16c: probably from *buskle*, an obsolete verb meaning 'to prepare in a busy or energetic way'.

■ **bustle with something** said of a place: to be busy with or full of (eg excitement or people).

bustle[2] /'bʌsəl/ ▻ *noun, historical* a frame or pad for holding a skirt out from the back of the waist. ⓒ 18c.

bust-up ▻ *noun, colloq* **1** a quarrel; the ending of a relationship or partnership. **2** an explosion or collapse.

busty ▻ *adj* (***bustier***, ***bustiest***) *colloq* said of a woman: having large breasts.

busy /'bɪzɪ/ ▻ *adj* (***busier***, ***busiest***) **1** fully occupied; having much work to do. **2** full of activity ▫ ***a busy day*** ▫ ***a busy street***. **3** *N Amer, especially US* said of a telephone line, etc: in use. *Brit equivalent* ENGAGED. **4** constantly working or occupied. **5** said of a person: fussy and tending to interfere in the affairs of others. **6** said of a picture or design, etc: unrestful to the eye because too full of detail. ▻ *verb* (***busies***, ***busied***, ***busying***) chiefly in phrase below. • **busily** *adverb*. • **busyness** *noun*. ⓒ Anglo-Saxon *bisig*.

■ **busy someone** or **oneself with something** to occupy them or oneself with a task, etc; to make them or oneself busy.

busybody ▻ *noun* someone who is always interfering in other people's affairs. ⓒ 16c.

busy Lizzie ▻ *noun* any of various species of IMPATIENS, usually with pink, red or white flowers, widely grown as a house plant. ⓒ 1950s: so called because it is fast-growing.

but[1] ▻ *conj* **1** contrary to expectation ▫ ***She fell down but didn't hurt herself***. **2** in contrast ▫ ***You've been to Spain but I haven't***. **3** other than ▫ ***You can't do anything but wait***. **4** used to emphasize the word that follows it ▫ ***Nobody, but nobody, must go in there***. ▻ *prep* except ▫ ***They are all here but him***. ▻ *adverb* only ▫ ***I can but try***. ▻ *noun* an objection or doubt ▫ ***no buts about it*** ▫ ***too***

many ifs and buts. • **but for** were it not for; without □ ***I couldn't have managed but for your help.*** • **but that** *rather formal or old use* were it not that; except that □ ***There seemed no explanation but that he had done it.*** Ⓒ Anglo-Saxon *butan*, meaning 'outside of' or 'without', from *be* by + *utan* out.

> ***but***
>
> Although it is sometimes regarded as poor style, it is not ungrammatical to begin a sentence with **but**. Indeed, many writers have done so with considerable effect. It is also common in conversation and in forms of English in which a looser grammatical structure is appropriate.

but[2] see under BEN[2]

but and ben ▷ *noun* a two-roomed or very small house. See BEN[2].

butane /ˈbjʊteɪn/ ▷ *noun* (formula C_4H_{10}) a colourless highly flammable gas belonging to the alkane series of hydrocarbon compounds, and used in the manufacture of synthetic rubber, and in liquid form as a fuel supply for portable stoves, etc. Ⓒ 19c: from *butyric acid* (which gives rancid butter its smell), from Latin *butyrum* butter.

butch /bʊtʃ/ ▷ *adj* (***butcher, butchest***) *slang* said of a person: tough and strong-looking; aggressively masculine in manner or looks, etc. Ⓒ 1940s: from a boy's nickname in the US.

butcher /ˈbʊtʃə(r)/ ▷ *noun* **1** a person or shop that sells meat. **2** someone whose job is slaughtering animals and preparing the carcasses for use as food. **3** a person who kills people needlessly and savagely, or takes pleasure in killing. ▷ *verb* (***butchered, butchering***) **1** to kill and prepare (an animal) for sale as food. **2** to kill (especially a large number of people or animals) cruelly or indiscriminately. **3** *colloq* to ruin or make a botch of something □ ***The publisher butchered the preface I sent in.*** Ⓒ 13c as *bocher* or *boucher*, from French *bochier* or *bouchier* a person who kills and sells he-goats, from *boc* a he-goat.

butcher bird ▷ *noun* **1** any of six species of a bird, native to Australia and New Guinea, that has a large powerful hooked beak and impales its prey on thorns. **2** the name sometimes given to SHRIKEs that impale their prey on thorns.

butcher's broom ▷ *noun, bot* a stiff leathery dark-green European shrub which has true leaves reduced to scales, white flowers and red berries in the centre of flattened leaf-like branches.

butchery ▷ *noun* (***butcheries***) **1** the preparing of meat for sale as food; the trade of a butcher. **2** senseless, cruel or wholesale killing. **3** a slaughterhouse.

butler /ˈbʌtlə(r)/ ▷ *noun* the chief male servant in a house, specifically in charge of the wine cellar and dining table, etc, but usually also in charge of all the other servants and the general running of the household. Ⓒ 13c as *buteler*: from French *bouteillier*, from *botele* bottle.

butlery ▷ *noun* (***butleries***) the pantry in which the glassware, dinner service and silverware, etc is kept. Also called **butler's pantry**.

butt[1] ▷ *verb* (***butted, butting***) *tr & intr* **1** to push or hit hard or roughly with the head, in the way a ram or goat might. See also HEAD-BUTT. **2** (*especially* **butt against** or **on something**) to join or be joined end to end with it. ▷ *noun* **1** a blow with the head or horns. **2** the place where two edges join. Ⓒ 13c: from French *boter* to push or strike.

> ■ **butt in** *colloq* to interrupt or interfere.
>
> ■ **butt into something** to interrupt (eg a conversation, or someone's private affairs).

butt[2] ▷ *noun* **1** the unused end of a finished cigar or cigarette, etc. **2** the thick, heavy or bottom end of a tool or weapon □ ***a rifle butt.*** **3** *now chiefly N Amer colloq* the buttocks. Ⓒ 15c as *bott* or *but* in senses 2 and 3; related to BUTTOCK.

butt[3] ▷ *noun* **1** a person who is often a target of jokes, ridicule or criticism, etc. **2** a mound of earth behind a target on a shooting range, acting as a backstop. **3** a low mound behind which grouse-shooters, etc conceal themselves. Ⓒ 15c in sense 2: from French *but* a target.

butt[4] ▷ *noun* a large barrel for beer or rainwater, etc. Ⓒ 14c: from French *botte*, from Latin *buttis* cask.

butte /bjuːt/ ▷ *noun, geol* an isolated flat-topped residual hill with steep sides, formed by erosion of a MESA when a remnant of hard rock protects the softer rock underneath. Ⓒ Early 19c: French.

butter /ˈbʌtə(r)/ ▷ *noun* **1** a solid yellowish edible food, made from the fats in milk by churning, and used for spreading on bread, and in cooking. **2** *in compounds* any of various substances that resemble this food in appearance or texture □ ***peanut butter*** □ ***coconut butter.*** ▷ *verb* (***buttered, buttering***) to put butter on or in something. • **buttered** *adj.* • **buttery** *adj.* • **butter wouldn't melt in his** or **her**, *etc* **mouth** he or she, etc is utterly innocent, honest or well-behaved (used to imply that the speaker believes or knows that they are not) □ ***She always looks as if butter wouldn't melt in her mouth.*** Ⓒ Anglo-Saxon *butere*: from Latin *butyrum*, from Greek *boutyron*, probably meaning 'ox-cheese'.

> ■ **butter someone up** *colloq* to flatter them, usually in order to gain a favour.

butter bean ▷ *noun* **1** any of several varieties of lima bean which have large edible seeds. **2** the large pale flat edible seed of this plant.

butter cream ▷ *noun, cookery* butter and icing sugar beaten together, usually with flavouring and sometimes colouring, used to fill and top cakes. Also called **butter icing**.

buttercup ▷ *noun* any of various perennial plants, often found on damp soils, which have erect branched stems, lobed leaves and cup-shaped flowers, usually with five glossy yellow petals. Ⓒ 18c.

butter dish ▷ *noun* a dish in which butter is served at the table.

butterfingers ▷ *singular noun, colloq* a person who often drops things, or who does not manage to catch things. • **butter-fingered** *adj.* Ⓒ 19c: 17c *as adj.*

butterfly ▷ *noun* **1** the common name for any of thousands of species of insect which have four broad, often brightly coloured wings covered with tiny overlapping scales, and a long proboscis for sucking nectar from flowers. **2** a person who is not very serious, but is only interested in enjoying themselves □ ***a social butterfly.*** **3** (**butterflies**) *colloq* a nervous or fluttering feeling in the stomach □ ***always get dreadful butterflies before I go on stage.*** **4** BUTTERFLY STROKE. Ⓒ Anglo-Saxon *buter-fleoge*, from BUTTER + FLY[1].

butterfly kiss ▷ *noun* a caress given by fluttering the eyelashes against someone's skin.

butterfly nut and **butterfly screw** ▷ *noun* a screw or nut with two flat projections which allow it to be turned with the fingers. Also called WING NUT.

butterfly stroke ▷ *noun* a swimming stroke in which both arms are brought out of the water and over the head at the same time. Often shortened to BUTTERFLY.

butter icing see under BUTTER CREAM

butter knife ▷ *noun* a blunt knife for taking a portion of butter from a butter dish.

buttermilk ▷ *noun* the slightly sharp-tasting liquid left after all the butter has been removed from milk after churning.

butter muslin ▷ *noun* a thin loosely-woven cloth, originally used for wrapping butter.

butterpat ▷ *noun* **1** a small lump of butter. **2** a wooden implement used for shaping butter.

butterscotch ▷ *noun* **1** a kind of hard toffee made from butter and sugar. **2** a flavouring made from butterscotch or similar to it.

butterwort /ˈbʌtəwɜːt/ ▷ *noun, bot* a small carnivorous perennial plant with white, lilac or violet flowers and a rosette of oval leaves with a greasy coating on which insects become trapped and are then digested by enzymes secreted by the plant. ◷ 16c.

buttery[1] ▷ *noun* (***butteries***) **1** *Brit* a room, especially in a college or university, where food is kept and supplied to students. **2** a storeroom for bottles of liquor. ◷ 14c in sense 2: from French *boterie* a place for storing butts (see BUTT[4]).

buttery[2] see under BUTTER

buttock /ˈbʌtək/ ▷ *noun* (*usually* **buttocks**) each of the fleshy parts of the body between the base of the back and the top of the legs, on which a person sits. ◷ 14c: probably from BUTT[2].

button /ˈbʌtən/ ▷ *noun* **1** a small round piece of metal or plastic, etc sewn on to a piece of clothing, which fastens it by being passed through a buttonhole. **2** (*sometimes* **push button**) a small round disc pressed to operate a door or bell, etc □ *Press the button to call the lift.* **3** a small round object worn as decoration or a badge. **4** any small round object more or less like a button. **5** *computing* a small part on a mouse or joystick that is pressed to make it function. **6** *computing* a small shape on a VDU screen that a user clicks on to select an option. **7** anything of small value □ *not worth a button.* ▷ *verb* (***buttoned, buttoning***) **1** (*usually* **button something up**) to fasten or close it using a button or buttons. **2** *intr* to be capable of being fastened with buttons or a button □ *This dress buttons at the back.* • **buttoned up** *slang* **1** successfully arranged; safely in one's possession. **2** (*especially* **buttoned up about something**) said of a person: unwilling to talk about it; uncommunicative. • **on the button** *colloq* exactly right or correct; spot on. ◷ 14c as *botoun*: from French *bouton* any small projection, from *bouter* to push.

■ **button up** *slang* to stop talking; to shut up.

■ **button something up** *slang* to bring it to a successful conclusion.

button cell and **button cell battery** ▷ *noun* a small flat circular battery used to power a watch, etc.

buttonhole ▷ *noun* **1** a small slit or hole through which a button is passed to fasten a garment. **2** a flower or flowers worn in a buttonhole or pinned to a lapel. *US equivalent* **boutonnière** /buːtəˈnɪər/. ▷ *verb* **1** to stop someone, especially someone who is reluctant to engage in conversation, and force conversation on them. **2** to make buttonholes in something.

button mushroom ▷ *noun* the head of an unexpanded mushroom.

buttress /ˈbʌtrəs/ ▷ *noun* (***buttresses***) **1** *archit, civil engineering* a projecting support made of brick or masonry, etc built on to the outside of a wall. See also FLYING BUTTRESS. **2** any support or prop. ▷ *verb* (***buttresses, buttressed, buttressing***) **1** to support (a wall, etc) with buttresses. **2** to support or encourage (an argument, etc). ◷ 14c as *butres*: from French *bouter* to push.

butty ▷ *noun* (***butties***) *Brit, especially N Eng, colloq* a sandwich; a piece of bread and butter, as a snack. ◷ 19c: from BUTTER.

buxom /ˈbʌksəm/ ▷ *adj* said of a woman: **1** attractively plump, lively and healthy-looking. **2** having large or plumply rounded breasts; busty. • **buxomness** *noun.* ◷ 16c in sense 1; 12c as *buhsum*, in obsolete sense 'pliant' or 'obedient'.

buy /baɪ/ ▷ *verb* (***buys, bought, buying***) **1** *tr & intr* to obtain something by paying a sum of money for it. Opposite of SELL. **2** to be a means of obtaining something □ *There are some things money can't buy.* **3** to obtain something by giving up or sacrificing something else □ *success bought at the expense of happiness.* **4** *colloq* to believe or accept as true □ *I don't buy his story.* **5** (*sometimes* **buy someone off**) to bribe them □ *He can't be bought, he's thoroughly honest.* ▷ *noun* (*usually in* **a good buy** *or* **a bad buy**) a thing bought. • **buy time** *colloq* to gain more time before a decision or action, etc is taken. • **have bought it** *slang* to have been killed. ◷ Anglo-Saxon *bycgan.*

■ **buy something in 1** to buy a stock or supply of it. **2** at an auction: to buy it back for the owner when the RESERVE PRICE is not reached.

■ **buy into something** to buy shares or an interest in (a company, etc).

■ **buy someone off** to get rid of (a threatening person, etc) by paying them money.

■ **buy oneself out** to pay to be released from the armed forces.

■ **buy someone out** to pay to take over possession of something from them, especially to buy all the shares that they hold in a company. See also BUY-OUT.

■ **buy something up** to buy the whole stock of it.

buy-back ▷ *noun, commerce* an act or instance (either optional or obligatory) of the seller buying back all or part of what was previously sold, eg shares in a company.

buyer ▷ *noun* **1** a person who buys; a customer. **2** a person employed by a large shop or firm to buy goods on its behalf.

buyer's market ▷ *noun* a situation in which there are more goods for sale than people wanting to buy them, with the result that prices stay low. Compare SELLER'S MARKET.

buy-out ▷ *noun, commerce* the purchase of all the shares in a company in order to get control of it. See BUY SOMEONE OUT at BUY.

buzz ▷ *verb* (***buzzes, buzzed, buzzing***) **1** *intr* to make a continuous, humming or rapidly vibrating sound, like that made by the wings of an insect such as the bee. **2** *intr* to be filled with activity or excitement □ *a room buzzing with activity.* **3** *colloq* to call someone using a BUZZER. **4** *colloq* to call someone on the telephone. **5** *colloq* said of an aircraft: to fly very low over or very close to (another aircraft or a building, etc). ▷ *noun* (***buzzes***) **1** a humming or rapidly vibrating sound, such as that made by a bee. **2** *colloq* a telephone call □ *Give me a buzz from the station.* **3** *colloq* a very pleasant, excited, or exhilarated feeling; a kick or thrill □ *said that joy-riding gives him a real buzz.* **4** a low murmuring sound such as that made by many people talking. **5** *colloq* a rumour or whispered report. ◷ 14c: imitating the sound.

■ **buzz about** or **around** to move quickly or excitedly.

■ **buzz off** *colloq* to go away.

buzzard /ˈbʌzəd/ ▷ *noun* **1** any of several large hawks that resemble eagles in their effortless gliding flight, rising on warm air currents for long periods. **2** *N Amer* a vulture. ◷ 13c: from French *busard*, ultimately from Latin *buteo, buteonis* hawk.

buzzer ▷ *noun* an electrical device which makes a buzzing sound, used as a signal or for summoning someone, eg in a doctor's surgery or an office, etc.

buzz word ▷ *noun, colloq* a fashionable new word or expression, usually in a particular subject, social group, or profession, showing (or meant to show) that the person who uses it is very up-to-date or has specialized knowledge. ◷ 1960s.

BVM ▻ *abbreviation*: *Beata Virgo Maria* (Latin), Blessed Virgin Mary.

b/w or **B/W** ▻ *abbreviation* black and white.

bwana /'bwɑːnə/ ▻ *noun* (**bwanas**) *E Afr* often used as a form of address or respect: master; sir. ⓒ 19c: Swahili, ultimately from Arabic *abuna* our father.

by /baɪ/ ▻ *prep* **1** next to, beside or near □ ***standing by the door.*** **2** past □ ***I'll drive by the house.*** **3** through, along or across □ ***enter by the window.*** **4** (especially after a passive verb) used to indicate the person or thing that does, causes or produces, etc something □ ***He was bitten by a dog*** □ ***destroyed by fire.*** **5** used to show method or means □ ***travel by air*** □ ***sent by registered post.*** **6** not later than □ ***Be home by 10pm.*** **7** during □ ***escape by night.*** **8** used to show extent or amount □ ***bigger by six feet*** □ ***The price fell by £2*** □ ***worse by far.*** **9** used in stating rates of payment, etc □ ***paid by the hour.*** **10** according to □ ***It's 8.15 by my watch*** □ ***By my calculation, we're overdrawn.*** **11** used to show the part of someone or something held, taken or used, etc □ ***grabbed her by the throat*** □ ***pulling me by the hand.*** **12** used to show the number which must perform a mathematical operation on another □ ***divide six by two*** □ ***multiply three by four.*** **13** used in giving measurements and compass directions, etc □ ***a room measuring six feet by ten*** □ ***north-north-east by north.*** **14** used to show a specific quantity or unit, etc that follows another to bring about an increase or progression □ ***step by step*** □ ***little by little*** □ ***two by two.*** **15** with regard to someone or something □ ***do his duty by them.*** **16** in oaths, etc: in the name of, or strictly 'with the witness of' or 'in the presence of' (a specified deity, thing or person) □ ***I swear by all that's holy*** □ ***By God, you're right!*** **17** fathered or SIRED by □ ***two children by her first husband.*** ▻ *adverb* **1** near □ ***live close by.*** **2** past □ ***drive by without stopping.*** **3** aside; away; in reserve □ ***put money by.*** **4** *chiefly N Amer* to or at one's or someone's home, etc □ ***Come by for a drink later*** □ ***said he'd stop by after work.*** ▻ *noun* (**byes**) same as BYE[1]. • **by and by** *rather literary or old use* after a short time; at some time in the not-too-distant future. • **by and large** generally; all things considered. ⓒ 17c: originally a nautical expression, used in reference to a ship sailing both *by* (ie into the wind) and *large* (ie with the wind). • **by itself** see ITSELF. • **by oneself** **1** alone □ ***Sit by yourself over there.*** **2** without anyone else's help □ ***can't do it by myself.*** • **by the by** or **by the bye** or **by the way** *colloq* while I think of it; incidentally. ⓒ Anglo-Saxon *be* or *bi*.

by- or **bye-** ▻ *prefix, signifying* **1** minor, supplementary or less important □ ***by-law*** □ ***by-election.*** **2** indirect; running past, beside or apart from something □ ***byroad*** □ ***bypass.*** **3** incidental; occurring by way of something else □ ***by-product.*** **4** near □ ***bystander.***

bye[1] /baɪ ▻ *noun* **1** *sport, etc* a pass into the next round of a competition, given to a competitor or team that has not been given an opponent in the current round. **2** *cricket* a run scored from a ball which the batsman has not hit or touched. See also LEG-BYE, STEAL A BYE at STEAL. **3** *golf* the holes remaining after the match is decided, played as a subsidiary game. • **by the bye** see BY THE BY at BY. ⓒ 18c in sense 2, and first used to mean a minor or side event in sports such as cockfighting; an altered form of BY.

bye[2] /baɪ/ or **bye-bye** ▻ *exclamation, colloq* goodbye.

bye-byes ▻ *singular noun* used to children: sleep; bed (*especially* **go bye-byes** or **go to bye-byes**). Also called BEDDY-BYES. ⓒ 16c as a soothing sound in lullaby songs.

by-election ▻ *noun* an election held during the sitting of parliament, in order to fill a seat which has become empty because the member has died or resigned. Compare GENERAL ELECTION.

Byelorussian see BELORUSSIAN

by Gad see GAD[2]

bygone /'baɪgɒn/ ▻ *adj* former □ ***in bygone days.*** ▻ *noun* (**bygones**) **1** events, troubles or arguments which occurred in the past. **2** household articles or ornaments, etc from former times, which are not of the quality, age or significance to be valued as antiques. • **let bygones be bygones** to agree to forget past disagreements and differences. ⓒ 15c.

by-law or **bye-law** ▻ *noun* **1** *Brit* a law or rule made by a local authority or other body, rather than by the national government. **2** a rule imposed by a company or society, etc on its members. ⓒ 13c: probably from the obsolete word *byrlaw* local custom, from Norse *byjar-log* town law.

byline ▻ *noun* **1** *journalism* a line under the title of a newspaper or magazine article which gives the name of the author. **2** *football* the touchline.

byname ▻ *noun* another name, or an additional name, by which a person is known. Also called NICKNAME or (*literary*) SOBRIQUET. ⓒ 14c.

BYO ▻ *abbreviation* bring your own, usually meaning 'bring your own alcohol'.

BYOB ▻ *abbreviation, colloq* bring your own bottle (ie of drink, usually an alcoholic drink).

bypass ▻ *noun* **1** a major road which carries traffic on a route that avoids a city centre, town or congested area. **2** *medicine* the redirection of blood flow so as to avoid a blocked or diseased blood vessel, especially a coronary artery, usually by grafting a blood vessel taken from another part of the body. **3** a channel or pipe, etc which carries gas or electricity, etc when the main channel is blocked or congested. **4** an electrical circuit that carries current around one or more circuit components instead of through them. ▻ *verb* **1** to avoid (a congested or blocked place) by taking a route which goes round or beyond it. **2** to leave out or avoid (a step in a process), or ignore and not discuss something with (a person) □ ***managed to bypass the usual selection procedure.*** **3** to provide something with a bypass. **4** to direct (eg fluid, traffic or electricity) along a bypass.

bypath ▻ *noun* **1** an out-of-the-way, little-used or indirect path. **2** a BYROAD (sense 2). ⓒ 14c.

by-play ▻ *noun* especially in a play: less important action that happens at the same time as the main action.

by-product ▻ *noun* **1** a secondary and often commercially important product that is formed at the same time as the main product during a chemical reaction or manufacturing process. **2** an unexpected or extra result; a side effect. Compare END PRODUCT.

byre /baɪə(r)/ ▻ *noun, mainly Scots* a cowshed. ⓒ Anglo-Saxon, meaning 'stall' or 'shed'.

byroad and **byway** ▻ *noun* **1** a minor, secondary or secluded road. Also called SIDE-ROAD. **2** (*especially* **byway**) a line of thought or activity, etc not often taken by other people; an obscure area of interest. Sometimes called BYPATH. ⓒ 17c.

bystander ▻ *noun* a person who happens to be standing by, who sees but does not take part in what is happening; an onlooker. ⓒ 17c.

byte /baɪt/ ▻ *noun, computing* **1** a group of adjacent binary digits (see BIT[3]) that are handled as a single unit, especially a group of eight bits representing one alphanumerical character or two decimal digits. **2** the amount of storage space occupied by such a group. ⓒ 1960s: possibly from *binary digit eight*, or from BIT[3].

byword ▻ *noun* **1** a person or thing that is well known as an example of something □ ***a byword for luxury.*** **2** a common saying or proverb. ⓒ Anglo-Saxon in sense 2.

Byzantine /bɪ'zantaɪn, 'bɪzəntiːn, baɪ-/ ▻ *adj* **1** *historical* relating to Byzantium (later Constantinople and now the city of Istanbul, in Turkey) or the eastern part of the Roman Empire from AD 395 to 1453. **2** belonging or relating to the style of architecture and painting, etc developed in the Byzantine Empire, with domes, arches, stylized mosaics and icons, etc. **3** belonging or relating to the **Byzantine Church**, ie the Eastern or Orthodox Church. **4** secret, difficult to understand, and extremely intricate and complex; tortuous. **5** said eg of attitudes or policies: rigidly hierarchic; inflexible. ▷ *noun, historical* an inhabitant of Byzantium. ⓒ 18c: from Latin *byzantinus*.

C

C[1] or **c** /siː/ ⊳ *noun* (*Cs, C's* or *c's*) **1** the third letter of the English alphabet. **2** (*usually* **C**) the third highest grade or quality, or a mark indicating this. **3** (**C**) *music* the note on which the Western system of music is based. **4** a musical key with the note C as its base.

C[2] ⊳ *abbreviation* **1** Celsius. **2** centigrade. **3** century □ *C19*. **4** *IVR* Cuba.

C[3] ⊳ *symbol* **1** (*also* **c**) *centum* (Latin), the Roman numeral for 100. **2** *chem* carbon.

c[1] ⊳ *abbreviation* **1** centi-. **2** cubic.

c[2] ⊳ *symbol, physics* the speed of light.

c. ⊳ *abbreviation* **1** *cricket* caught. **2** cent. **3** century. **4** chapter. **5** (*also* **ca**) *circa* (Latin), approximately.

© ⊳ *symbol* copyright.

¢ ⊳ *symbol* cent.

CA ⊳ *abbreviation* **1** *US state* California. Also written **Cal**. **2** Chartered Accountant. Also *as noun* (*plural CAs*).

Ca ⊳ *symbol, chem* calcium.

ca ⊳ *abbreviation: circa* (Latin), approximately.

CAA ⊳ *abbreviation* Civil Aviation Authority.

CAB ⊳ *abbreviation* **1** Citizen's Advice Bureau. Also *as noun* (*plural* ***CABs*** or ***CABx***). **2** *US* Civil Aeronautics Board.

cab ⊳ *noun* **1** a taxi. **2** the driver's compartment in a lorry, railway engine, etc. **3** *historical* a horse-drawn carriage for hire. ◷ 19c: shortened from CABRIOLET.

cabal /kə'bal/ ⊳ *noun* **1** a small group formed within a larger body, for secret, especially political, discussion, planning, etc. **2** a political plot or conspiracy. ⊳ *verb* (***caballed, caballing***) to form a cabal; to plot. ◷ 17c: from French *cabale*, from CABBALA.

cabaret /'kabəreɪ/ ⊳ *noun* **1** entertainment with songs, dancing, etc at a restaurant or nightclub. **2** a restaurant or nightclub providing this. ◷ 20c in this sense; 17c in obsolete sense 'wooden dwelling': French, meaning 'tavern'.

cabbage /'kabɪdʒ/ ⊳ *noun* **1** any of several varieties of a leafy biennial plant, grown for its compact head of green, white or red edible leaves. **2** the leaves of this plant, which can be cooked, eaten raw in salads or pickled. **3** *derog* a dull inactive person. **4** *offensive* a person so severely brain-damaged or mentally subnormal as to be completely dependent on other people for survival. ◷ 14c: from French *caboche* head.

cabbage-white butterfly ⊳ *noun* a large butterfly, so called because it has white wings with black markings and its caterpillars are pests of plants belonging to the cabbage family.

cabbala, **cabala**, **kabala** or **kabbala** /kə'bɑːlə, 'kabələ/ ⊳ *noun* (***cabbalas***, *etc.*) **1** a secret traditional lore of Jewish rabbis, who can interpret hidden meanings in the Old Testament. **2** any mysterious or esoteric doctrine. ● **cabbalism** *noun*. ● **cabbalist** *noun*. ● **cabbalistic** or **cabbalistical** *adj*. ◷ 17c: Latin, from Hebrew *qabbalah* tradition, from *qabal* to receive.

cabby or **cabbie** ⊳ *noun* (***cabbies***) *colloq* a taxi-driver.

caber /'keɪbə(r)/ ⊳ *noun, Scottish athletics* a heavy wooden pole of c.3–4m in length, that must be carried upright and then tipped end over end, during a contest called **tossing the caber**. ◷ 16c: from Scottish Gaelic *cabar* pole.

Cabernet Sauvignon /'kabəneɪ 'souviːnjɒn/ ⊳ *noun* **1** a red grape variety originally from Bordeaux, now grown throughout the world. **2** the wine produced from this grape. ◷ 20c: French.

cabin /'kabɪn/ ⊳ *noun* **1** a small house, especially one made of wood. **2** a small room on a ship for living, sleeping or working in. **3 a** the passenger section of a plane; **b** the section at the front of a plane for pilot and crew. **4** the driving compartment of a large commercial vehicle. ⊳ *verb* (***cabined, cabining***) to shut up in a confined space. ◷ 14c: from French *cabane*, from Latin *capanna*.

cabin boy ⊳ *noun, historical* a boy who serves officers and passengers on board ship.

cabin crew ⊳ *noun* the members of an aircraft crew who attend to the passengers.

cabin cruiser see CRUISER 2

cabinet /'kabɪnət/ ⊳ *noun* **1** a piece of furniture with shelves and doors, for storing or displaying items. **2** the casing round a television set, music centre, etc. **3** (*often* **the Cabinet**) *Brit* an executive, policy-making body made up of senior ministers in charge of the various departments of government, who meet regularly for discussion with the prime minister. ◷ 16c: diminutive of CABIN.

cabinet-maker ⊳ *noun* a skilled craftsman who makes and repairs fine furniture. ● **cabinet-making** *noun*.

cabinet minister ⊳ *noun, politics* in the UK: a senior government minister who is a member of the CABINET (sense 3).

cabinet picture ⊳ *noun* a small easel painting, carefully executed in minute detail, which is intended for close viewing and suitable for display in a small private room.

cabin fever ⊳ *noun, Can* a state of severe depression or irritability brought on by spending long periods of time in isolated places or cramped conditions.

cable /'keɪbəl/ ⊳ *noun* **1** a strong wire cord or rope used for supporting loads, lifting, hauling, towing, etc. **2** two or more electrical wires bound together but separated from each other by insulating material, and covered by a protective outer sheath, used to carry electricity, telephone messages, television signals, etc. **3** *naut* a measure of length or depth, about 600 ft (200 m). **4** (*also* **cablegram**) a telegram sent by cable. **5** (*also* **cable stitch**) a pattern in knitting that looks like twisted cable. **6** short for CABLE TELEVISION. ⊳ *verb* (***cabled, cabling***) **1** to tie up or provide with a cable or cables. **2** *tr & intr* to send a cable, or send (a message) to someone by cable. **3** to provide with cable television. ◷ 13c: ultimately from Latin *capulum* halter.

cable car ⊳ *noun* a small carriage suspended from a continuous moving cable, for carrying passengers up or down a steep mountain, across a valley, etc.

cable television, **cable TV** and **cablevision** ⊳ *noun* a television broadcasting system in which television signals are relayed directly to individual subscribers by means of underground or overhead cables, instead of being broadcast by radio waves.

cabochon /'kabəʃɒn/ ⊳ *noun* a precious stone that is

polished but uncut. • **en cabochon** said of a precious stone: rounded on top but flat on the back, without facets. ⓘ 16c: from French *caboche*, from Latin *caput* head.

caboodle /kəˈbuːdəl/ ▷ *noun, colloq* (*especially* **the whole caboodle**) the whole lot; everything. ⓘ 19c: probably a corruption of KIT[1] + BOODLE.

caboose /kəˈbuːs/ ▷ *noun* **1** *N Amer* a guard's van on a railway train. **2** *naut* a ship's galley or kitchen. **3** *US* a CALABOOSE. ⓘ 18c: from Dutch *cabuse* ship's galley.

cabriole /ˈkabrɪoʊl/ ▷ *noun* a furniture leg ornamentally curved to resemble an animal's leg. ⓘ 19c in this sense; 18c in obsolete sense 'small armchair': French, meaning 'goat-like leap'.

cabriolet /kabrɪoʊˈleɪ/ ▷ *noun* **1** *historical* a light two-wheeled carriage drawn by one horse. **2** a car with a folding roof. ⓘ 18c: French, meaning 'little leap', from CABRIOLE.

cacao /kəˈkeɪoʊ, kəˈkɑːoʊ/ ▷ *noun* (***cacaos***) **1** a small evergreen tree, native to S and Central America, but widely cultivated in other tropical regions for its seeds. **2** the edible seed of this tree, used in the manufacture of drinks, chocolate and cocoa butter. ⓘ 16c: Spanish, from Aztec *cacauatl* cacao tree.

cachalot see SPERM WHALE

cache /kaʃ/ ▷ *noun* **1** a hiding-place, eg for weapons. **2** a collection of hidden things. ▷ *verb* (***cached, caching***) to put or collect in a cache. ⓘ 19c: French, from *cacher* to hide.

cache memory ▷ *noun, computing* an extremely fast part of the main store of computer memory, often used to execute instructions.

cachet /ˈkaʃeɪ, kaˈʃeɪ/ ▷ *noun* **1** something which brings one respect or admiration; a distinction. **2** a distinguishing mark. **3** an official seal. **4** a special commemorative postmark. **5** *old use, medicine* a small edible container for a pill, etc. ⓘ 17c: French, from *cacher* to hide.

cachexia /kaˈkɛksɪə, kə-/ ▷ *noun, pathol* a condition characterized by physical weakness, abnormally low body weight and general ill health, usually associated with a chronic disease such as cancer or tuberculosis. ⓘ 16c: Latin, from Greek *kachexia*, from *kakos* bad + *hexis* condition.

cack-handed /kakˈhandɪd/ ▷ *adj, colloq* **1** clumsy; awkward. **2** left-handed. • **cack-handedness** *noun*. ⓘ 19c: from dialect *cack* excrement.

cackle /ˈkakəl/ ▷ *noun* **1** the sound made by a hen or a goose. **2** *derog* a raucous laugh like this. **3** shrill, silly chatter. ▷ *verb* (***cackled, cackling***) *intr* **1** to laugh raucously. **2** to chatter noisily. **3** to utter as a cackle. • **cut the cackle** *colloq* to stop chatting aimlessly and come to the point. ⓘ 13c: imitating the sound.

CACM ▷ *abbreviation* Central American Common Market.

caco- /kakoʊ, kaˈkɒ/ ▷ *combining form, denoting* bad; unpleasant. ⓘ From Greek *kakos*.

cacography /kəˈkɒgrəfɪ/ ▷ *noun* bad handwriting or spelling. • **cacographer** *noun*. • **cacographic** /kakoʊˈgrafɪk/ *adj*. ⓘ 16c.

cacophony /kəˈkɒfənɪ/ ▷ *noun* (***cacophonies***) often said of music: a disagreeable combination of loud noises. • **cacophonous** *adj*. ⓘ 17c.

cactus /ˈkaktəs/ ▷ *noun* (***cacti*** /-taɪ/ or ***cactuses***) any of numerous mostly spiny plants, found mainly in the arid deserts of N and Central America, which usually store water in swollen, often barrel-like stems. ⓘ 18c in this sense; 17c referring to another plant: Latin, from Greek *kaktos* a prickly plant in Sicily.

cactus dahlia ▷ *noun* a variety of double-flowered dahlia with grill-like petals.

CAD ▷ *abbreviation* **1** computer-aided design. **2** compact audio disc.

cad ▷ *noun, Brit colloq* a man who behaves discourteously or dishonourably, especially towards a woman. • **caddish** *adj*. ⓘ 19c in this sense: probably short for CADET and CADDIE 2.

cadaver /kəˈdɑːvə(r)/ ▷ *noun, medicine* a human corpse, especially one used for dissection. ⓘ 16c: Latin.

cadaverous /kəˈdavərəs/ ▷ *adj* corpse-like in appearance; pale and gaunt. • **cadaverousness** *noun*.

caddie or **caddy** /ˈkadɪ/ ▷ *noun* (***caddies***) **1** someone whose job is to carry the golf clubs around the course for a golf-player. **2** in 18c urban Scotland: a messenger; an errand-boy. ▷ *verb* (***caddies, caddied, caddying***) *intr* (*also* **caddie for someone**) to act as a caddie. ⓘ 18c in sense 2; 17c in obsolete sense 'cadet': from French *cadet* cadet.

caddis and **caddis worm** ▷ *noun* the larva of the caddis fly, found in ponds and streams, which builds a protective cylindrical case around itself consisting of sand grains, fragments of shell, small pieces of twig and leaf fragments. ⓘ 17c.

caddis fly ▷ *noun* a small or medium-sized moth-like insect with brown or black wings covered with fine hairs. ⓘ 17c.

caddish see under CAD

caddy¹ /ˈkadɪ/ ▷ *noun* (***caddies***) **1** a small container for loose tea. **2** *US* any storage container. ⓘ 18c: from Malay *kati* a unit of weight equal to a small packet of tea.

caddy² see CADDIE

cadence /ˈkeɪdəns/ ▷ *noun* **1** a fall of pitch in the voice. **2** the rising and falling of the voice in speaking. **3** rhythm or beat. **4** *music* a succession of notes that closes a musical passage. ⓘ 14c: French, from Latin *cadere* to fall.

cadential /kəˈdɛnʃəl/ ▷ *adj* **1** pertaining to cadence. **2** pertaining to a cadenza.

cadenza /kəˈdɛnzə/ ▷ *noun* (***cadenzas***) *music* an elaborate virtuoso passage given by a solo performer towards the end of a movement. ⓘ 19c: Italian, from Latin *cadere* to fall.

cadet /kəˈdɛt/ ▷ *noun* **1** a student undergoing preliminary training for the armed forces or police. **2** a school pupil training in a cadet corps. **3** *formerly* a gentleman who entered the army without a commission, with a view to finding a career for himself. **4** a younger son. **5** in New Zealand: a person learning sheep-farming. ⓘ 17c: French, ultimately from Latin *caput* head.

cadet branch ▷ *noun* the part of a family descended from a younger son.

cadet corps ▷ *noun* an organized group, especially of school pupils, undergoing military training, although not necessarily as preparation for entry into the armed forces.

cadge /kadʒ/ ▷ *verb* (***cadged, cadging***) *tr & intr, derog* (*also* **cadge something from** or **off someone**) to get something (especially money or food) by scrounging or begging. • **cadger** *noun*. ⓘ 19c in this sense; 14c in obsolete sense 'to fasten'.

cadi, **kadi** or **qadi** /ˈkɑːdɪ, ˈkeɪdɪ/ ▷ *noun* (***cadis, etc***) in Muslim countries: a judge or magistrate. ⓘ 16c: from Arabic *qadi*.

cadmium /ˈkadmɪəm/ ▷ *noun, chem* (symbol **Cd**, atomic number 48) a soft bluish-white metallic element used in alloys, corrosion-resistant plating, control rods in nuclear reactors and nickel-cadmium batteries. ⓘ 19c: from Latin *cadmia*, from Greek *kadmeia* calamine.

cadmium yellow ▷ *noun* a vivid orange or yellow pigment consisting of cadmium sulphide.

cadre /ˈkadə(r), ˈkeɪdə(r), -drə/ ▷ *noun* **1** *military* a permanent core unit which can be expanded when required, eg by conscription. **2** an inner group of activists in a revolutionary party, especially a Communist one. **3** a member of a such a group. ◷ 19c: French, meaning 'framework', from Italian *quadro*, from Latin *quadrum* square.

CAE ▷ *abbreviation* **1** *Austral* College of Advanced Education. **2** *computing* computer-aided engineering, the use of computers to replace the manual control of machine tools by automatic control, in order to increase accuracy and efficiency.

caecilian /siːˈsɪlɪən/ ▷ *noun* a tropical amphibian with a worm-like body and no legs, which burrows into forest floors or river beds. ◷ 19c: from Latin *caecilia* a kind of lizard, from *caecus* blind.

caecum or (*especially US*) **cecum** /ˈsiːkəm/ ▷ *noun* (***caeca*** /-kə/) *anatomy* a blind-ended pouch, to the lower end of which the appendix is attached, at the junction of the small and large intestines. ● **caecal** *adj.* ◷ 18c: Latin, short for *intestinum caecum* blind-ended intestine.

Caenozoic see CENOZOIC

caesarean section or (*US*) **cesarean** /sɪˈzɛərɪən —/ ▷ *noun* a surgical operation in which a baby is delivered through an incision in the lower abdomen, usually performed when normal delivery through the vagina would place the mother or baby at risk. ◷ 17c: apparently named after Julius Caesar, who was said to have been the first child to be delivered by this method.

Caesar salad ▷ *noun* a salad made of lettuce dressed with olive oil, raw or semi-cooked egg, garlic and seasoning, topped with croutons. ◷ Early 20c: named after Caesar Cardini, the owner of a Mexican restaurant, who invented it.

caesium or (*US*) **cesium** /ˈsiːzɪəm/ ▷ *noun, chem* (symbol **Cs**, atomic number 55) a soft silvery-white metallic element formed by the fission of uranium, and used in photoelectric cells and certain optical instruments. ◷ 19c: Latin, from *caesius* bluish-grey.

caesura or **cesura** /sɪˈzjʊərə/ ▷ *noun* (***caesuras*** or ***caesurae***/-riː/) a pause near the middle of a line of verse. ◷ 16c: Latin, from *caedere, caesum* to cut.

café or **cafe** /ˈkafeɪ, ˈkafɪ, kaˈfeɪ/ ▷ *noun* (***cafés*** or ***cafes***) a restaurant (usually a small one) that serves light meals or snacks. ◷ 19c: French, meaning 'coffee'.

café au lait /kafeɪ oʊ ˈleɪ/ ▷ *noun* **1** coffee made with hot milk or with milk added. **2** the pale-brown colour of such coffee. ◷ 18c: French.

café noir /ˈkafeɪ ˈnwɑː(r)/ ▷ *noun* black coffee. ◷ 19c: French.

café society ▷ *noun* a set or group of people who patronize fashionable cafés, restaurants, etc.

cafeteria /kafəˈtɪərɪə/ ▷ *noun* (***cafeterias***) a self-service restaurant. ◷ 19c: American Spanish, meaning 'coffee shop'.

cafetière /kafəˈtjɛə(r)/ ▷ *noun* a coffee-pot with a plunger for separating the grounds from the liquid by pushing them to the bottom. ◷ 19c: French.

caffeine /ˈkafiːn/ ▷ *noun* a bitter-tasting alkaloid, found in coffee beans, tea leaves and cola nuts, a stimulant of the central nervous system. ● **caffeinated** *adj.* See also DECAFFEINATE. ◷ 19c: from French *caféine*, from *café* coffee.

CAFOD ▷ *abbreviation* Catholic Fund for Overseas Development.

caftan or **kaftan** /ˈkaftan/ ▷ *noun* **1** originally in Middle Eastern countries: a long loose-fitting robe, often tied at the waist, worn by men. **2** a similar garment worn by women in Western cultures. ◷ 16c: from Turkish *qaftan*.

cage /keɪdʒ/ ▷ *noun* **1** an enclosure, sometimes portable and usually with bars, in which captive birds and animals are kept. **2** in a mine: a lift which transports mineworkers up and down a shaft. **3** *often in compounds* any structure resembling a cage □ *the ribcage.* ▷ *verb* (***caged***, ***caging***) (*also* **cage someone in**) to put them in a cage; to imprison or confine them. ● **caged** *adj.* ● **rattle someone's cage** to provoke their anger. ◷ 13c: French, from Latin *cavea* hollow place, from *cavus* hollow.

cagebird ▷ *noun* a bird, such as a canary, suitable for keeping in a cage.

cagey or **cagy** /ˈkeɪdʒɪ/ ▷ *adj* (***cagier***, ***cagiest***) *colloq* secretive and cautious; not forthcoming. ● **cagily** *adverb.* ● **caginess** *noun.* ◷ 20c.

cagoule or **kagoule** /kəˈguːl/ ▷ *noun* (***cagoules*** or ***kagoules***) a lightweight waterproof hooded anorak, pulled on over the head and often reaching down to the knees. ◷ 1950s: French, meaning 'cowl'.

cahoots /kəˈhuːts/ ▷ *plural noun* ● **in cahoots with someone** *usually derog, colloq* working in close partnership with them, especially in the planning of something unlawful. ◷ 19c.

caiman see CAYMAN

Cain ● **raise Cain** see under RAISE.

Cainozoic see CENOZOIC

caique /kɑːˈiːk/ ▷ *noun* **1** a light narrow boat propelled by one or more oars, used in Turkish waters, particularly on the Bosporus. **2** any small rowing boat, skiff or lateen-rigged sailing vessel of the E Mediterranean, used mainly for island trade. ◷ 17c: French, from Turkish *kaik*.

cairn[1] /kɛən/ ▷ *noun* a heap of stones piled up to mark something, especially a grave or pathway. ◷ 16c: from Scottish Gaelic *carn*.

cairn[2] /kɛən/ and **cairn terrier** ▷ *noun* a small breed of dogs with short legs, a thick shaggy brown coat and erect ears, developed in Scotland and formerly used for flushing foxes out of their burrows. ◷ 20c: from Scottish Gaelic *carn* cairn; said to be because the dogs used to hunt amongst cairns.

cairngorm /kɛənˈgɔːm/ ▷ *noun, geol* a yellow or smoky-brown variety of the mineral quartz, often used as a gemstone. ◷ 18c: from Gaelic *carn gorm* blue cairn, so called because it is found in the Cairngorm mountains.

caisson /ˈkeɪsən, kəˈsuːn/ ▷ *noun* **1** a watertight rectangular or cylindrical chamber used to protect construction workers during the building of underwater foundations, bridges, piers, etc. **2** a tumbrel or ammunition wagon. **3** the pontoon or floating gate used to close a dry dock. **4** a kind of float which is used to raise sunken vessels out of the water for inspection. ◷ 18c: French, meaning 'large box', from *caisse* chest.

caisson disease see DECOMPRESSION SICKNESS

cajole /kəˈdʒoʊl/ ▷ *verb* (***cajoled***, ***cajoling***) (*usually* **cajole someone into something**) to persuade them using flattery, promises, etc; to coax. ● **cajolement** *noun.* ● **cajoler** *noun.* ● **cajolery** *noun.* ◷ 17c: from French *cajoler* to coax.

Cajun /ˈkeɪdʒən/ ▷ *noun* a member of a group of people living in Louisiana, descendants of 18c French colonists deported from Canada by the British authorities. ▷ *adj* of or relating to the Cajuns and their culture, especially their music and food. ◷ 19c: from *Acadian*, from Acadia, a French colony in eastern Canada.

cake /keɪk/ ▷ *noun* **1** a solid food made by baking a mixture of flour, fat, eggs, sugar, etc. **2** an individually baked portion of this food. **3** a portion of some other food pressed into a particular shape □ *fish cake.* **4** a solid block of a particular substance, eg soap, chocolate, etc. ▷ *verb* (***caked***, ***caking***) **1** *intr* to dry as a thick hard crust. **2** to cover in a thick crust □ *skin caked with blood.* ● **have one's cake and eat it** *colloq* to enjoy the advantages of two alternative courses of action, usually as an unattainable ideal since it is impossible to do both at the same time. ● **a piece of cake** *colloq* a very easy task. ● **sell** or **go like hot cakes** said especially of a new product: to be bought enthusiastically in large numbers. ◎ 13c: from Norse *kaka*.

cakehole ▷ *noun, slang* the mouth.

cakewalk ▷ *noun* **1** a prancing march with intricate improvised steps originally performed by Black Americans as part of a competition. **2** a dance developed from this. **3** *colloq* something accomplished with extreme ease. ▷ *verb, intr* **1** to perform a cakewalk. **2** to accomplish something with extreme ease. ◎ 19c: so called because the dance was originally performed for the prize of a cake.

Cal see CA

cal. ▷ *abbreviation* calorie.

calabash /'kaləbaʃ/ ▷ *noun* **1** (*also* **calabash tree**) an evergreen tree, native to tropical S America, which has clusters of lance-shaped leaves, bell-shaped flowers that are borne directly on the trunk and branches, and flask-shaped woody fruits. Also called BOTTLE GOURD. **2** a trailing or climbing vine, native to warm regions of the Old World, which has white flowers and woody bottle-shaped fruits. **3** the dried hollowed-out shell of one of these fruits used as a bowl or water container. ◎ 17c: from French *calebasse*.

calaboose /'kaləbu:s, kalə'bu:s/ ▷ *noun, N Amer slang* a small local prison. Also called CABOOSE. ◎ 19c: Louisiana French, from Spanish *calabozo* dungeon.

calabrese /kalə'breɪzeɪ, 'kaləbri:s/ ▷ *noun* a type of green sprouting broccoli. ◎ 20c: Italian, meaning 'Calabrian', relating to a region in SW Italy.

calamari /kalə'mɑ:rɪ/ ▷ *plural noun* in Mediterranean cookery: squid. ◎ Italian, plural of *calamaro* squid.

calamine /'kaləmaɪn/ ▷ *noun* **1** a fine pink powder containing zinc oxide and small amounts of ferric oxide, used in the form of a lotion or ointment to soothe insect bites and stings, and to treat sunburn, eczema and other skin complaints. **2** *N Amer* zinc ore consisting mainly of zinc oxide. ◎ 17c: French, from Latin *calamina*.

calamitous /kə'lamɪtəs/ ▷ *adj* disastrous, tragic or dreadful. • **calamitously** *adverb*.

calamity /kə'lamɪtɪ/ ▷ *noun* (***calamities***) **1** a catastrophe, disaster or serious misfortune causing great loss or damage. **2** a state of great misery or disaster. ◎ 15c: from French *calamité*, from Latin *calamitas* harm.

calc- see CALCI-

calcareous /kal'kɛərɪəs/ ▷ *adj* relating to, containing or resembling calcium carbonate; chalky. ◎ 17c: from Latin *calcarius*, from *calx, calcis* lime.

calceolaria /kalsɪoʊ'lɛərɪə/ ▷ *noun* (***calceolarias***) any of various annual and perennial plants and shrubs, native to Central and S America, with wrinkled leaves and characteristic two-lipped yellow, orange or red spotted flowers, the lower lip being inflated and pouch-like. ◎ 19c: from Latin *calceolus*, diminutive of *calceus* shoe.

calces *plural of* CALX

calci- /kalsɪ/ or (before a vowel) **calc-** /kals/ ▷ *combining form, denoting* calcium or lime. ◎ From Latin *calx* lime.

calcicole /'kalsɪkoʊl/ ▷ *noun bot* a plant that requires soil with a high lime or chalk content. ◎ 19c: from CALCI- + Latin *colere* to dwell.

calciferol /kal'sɪfərɒl/ ▷ *noun* VITAMIN D_2 (see VITAMIN D).

calciferous /kal'sɪfərəs/ ▷ *adj* **1** *chem* containing lime. **2** *biol* containing or producing calcium or calcium salts. ◎ 18c.

calcifuge /'kalsɪfju:dʒ/ ▷ *noun, bot* a plant that grows best in acid soil with a low lime or chalk content. ◎ 19c.

calcify /'kalsɪfaɪ/ ▷ *verb* (***calcified, calcifying***) *tr & intr* **1** to harden as a result of the deposit of calcium salts. **2** to change or be changed into lime. • **calcification** *noun*. ◎ 19c.

calcite /'kalsaɪt/ ▷ *noun, geol* a white or colourless mineral, composed of crystalline calcium carbonate, that is the main constituent of limestone and marble rocks. ◎ 19c.

calcium /'kalsɪəm/ ▷ *noun, chem* (abbreviation **Ca**, atomic number 20) a soft, silvery-white metallic element which occurs mainly in the form of calcium carbonate minerals such as chalk, limestone and marble, and which is an important constituent of bones, teeth, milk and plant cell walls. ◎ 19c: from CALX.

calcium carbide ▷ *noun, chem* (formula $\mathbf{CaC_2}$) a solid grey compound, formerly used to produce acetylene in acetylene lamps.

calcium carbonate ▷ *noun, chem* (formula $\mathbf{CaCO_3}$) a white powder or colourless crystals, occurring naturally as limestone, marble, chalk, etc, and also found in the bones and shells of animals, which is used in the manufacture of glass, cement, bleaching powder, etc.

calcium chloride ▷ *noun, chem* (formula $\mathbf{CaCl_2}$) a white crystalline compound that absorbs moisture from the atmosphere and is used to dry gases, and as a de-icing agent.

calcium hydroxide ▷ *noun, chem* (formula $\mathbf{Ca(OH)_2}$) a white crystalline powder that dissolves sparingly in water to form an alkaline solution, and which is used in the manufacture of mortar, cement, bleaching powder, whitewash and water softeners, and as a neutralizer for acid soil. See also SLAKED LIME.

calcium oxide ▷ *noun, chem* (formula **CaO**) a white chemical compound used in producing other calcium compounds, such as SLAKED LIME, and in agriculture as an alkali to reduce acidity in soil. Also called **lime**, **quicklime**, **unslaked lime**, **calx**.

calcium phosphate ▷ *noun, chem* (formula $\mathbf{Ca_3(PO_4)_2}$) a white crystalline salt which occurs in the mineral APATITE and which is essential for the formation of bones and teeth in animals, and for the healthy growth of plants.

calcium sulphate ▷ *noun, chem* (formula $\mathbf{CaSO_4}$) a white crystalline solid, occurring naturally as GYPSUM, which causes permanent hardness of water, and is used to make plaster of Paris, paint, paper, ceramics and blackboard chalk.

calculable /'kalkjʊləbəl/ ▷ *adj* **1** capable of being calculated. **2** predictable. • **calculability** *noun*. • **calculably** *adverb*.

calculate /'kalkjʊleɪt/ ▷ *verb* (***calculated, calculating***) **1** to work out, find out or estimate, especially by mathematical means. **2** (*often* **calculate on something**) *intr* to make plans that depend on or take into consideration some probability or possibility. **3** to intend or aim □ *The emergency measures were calculated to avoid mass redundancy.* ◎ 16c: from Latin *calculare* to calculate, from *calculus* a stone.

calculated ▷ *adj* intentional; deliberate.

calculated risk ▷ *noun* a possibility of failure that has been taken into consideration before some action is taken.

calculating ▷ *adj, derog* deliberately shrewd and selfish, especially in terms of how one can use other people and situations to benefit oneself. • **calculatingly** *adverb*.

calculation ▷ *noun* **1** the act or process of calculating. **2** something estimated or calculated. **3** *derog* the cold and deliberate use of people or situations to benefit oneself.

calculator ▷ *noun* **1** a small usually hand-held electronic device that is used to perform numerical calculations, especially addition, subtraction, multiplication, and division. **2** a person or thing that calculates.

calculus /'kalkjʊləs/ ▷ *noun* (***calculuses*** or ***calculi*** /-laɪ, -li:/) **1** the branch of mathematics concerned with the differentiation and integration of functions. See

DIFFERENTIAL CALCULUS, INTEGRAL CALCULUS. **2** *medicine* a hard stone-like mass consisting of calcium salts and other compounds, eg cholesterol, that forms within hollow body structures such as the kidney, urinary bladder, gall bladder or bile ducts. Also called CONCRETION. ◷ 17c: Latin, meaning 'pebble', diminutive of *calx* stone.

caldera /kal'dɛərə/ ▷ *noun* (***calderas***) *geol* a large crater formed when the remains of a volcano subside down into a magma chamber that has been emptied during a violent eruption. ◷ 19c: Spanish, meaning 'cauldron'.

Caledonian /kalɪ'dounɪən/ *especially formerly* ▷ *adj* belonging or relating to Scotland or its inhabitants. ▷ *noun, facetious* a citizen or inhabitant of, or person born in, Scotland. ◷ 17c: from Latin *Caledonia* Scotland.

calendar /'kaləndə(r)/ ▷ *noun* **1** any system by which the beginning, length and divisions of the year are fixed. **2** a booklet, chart or an adjustable device, that shows such an arrangement. **3** a timetable or list of important dates, events, appointments, etc. ▷ *verb* (***calendared, calendaring***) **1** to place or record in a calendar. **2** to analyse or index (documents). ◷ 13c: from Latin *calendrium* account book.

calendarize or **calendarise** /'kaləndəraɪz/ ▷ *verb, accounting* to divide (eg a budget) into equal units of time, usually months, within a year. ◷ 20c.

calendar month see MONTH

calender /'kaləndə(r)/ ▷ *noun* a machine consisting of a vertical arrangement of heated rollers through which paper or cloth is passed in order to give it a smooth shiny finish. ▷ *verb* (***calendered, calendering***) to give a smooth finish to (paper or cloth) by passing it through such a machine. ◷ 16c: from French *calandre*, from Greek *kylindros* cylinder, roller.

calends or **kalends** /'kaləndz, 'kalɛndz/ ▷ *plural noun* in the ancient Roman calendar: the first day of each month. ◷ 14c: from Latin *kalendae*.

calf[1] /kɑːf/ ▷ *noun* (***calves*** /kɑːvz/) **1** the young of any bovine animal, especially domestic cattle. **2** the young of certain other mammals, such as the elephant and whale. **3** a large mass of ice that has broken off a glacier or an iceberg. **4** CALFSKIN. ● **in calf** usually said of a cow: pregnant with a calf. ◷ Anglo-Saxon *cælf*.

calf[2] /kɑːf/ ▷ *noun* (***calves*** /kɑːvz/) the thick fleshy part of the back of the leg, below the knee. ◷ 14c: from Norse *kálfi*.

calf love see PUPPY LOVE

calfskin ▷ *noun* leather made from the skin of a calf.

calibrate /'kalɪbreɪt/ ▷ *verb* (***calibrated, calibrating***) **1** to mark a scale on (a measuring instrument) so that it can be used to take readings in suitable units. **2** to determine (a correct value) by comparison with an accurate standard. **3** to measure (the diameter of a gun barrel or tube). ◷ 19c: CALIBRE + -ATE[1] sense1.

calibrated airspeed ▷ *noun, aeronautics* an airspeed value obtained from an airspeed indicator and corrected for instrument error but not for altitude.

calibration /kalɪ'breɪʃən/ ▷ *noun* **1** the act of checking a measuring instrument against fixed standards and then marking a scale on it. **2** one of the individual marks on the scale of a measuring instrument. **3** any measurement that is made against a fixed standard.

calibre /'kalɪbə(r)/ ▷ *noun* **1** the internal diameter of a gun barrel or tube. **2** the outer diameter of a bullet, shell or other projectile. **3** quality; standard; ability. ◷ 16c: from French *calibre*, probably from Arabic *qalib* mould.

calico /'kalɪkou/ ▷ *noun* (***calicoes***) **1** a kind of cotton cloth, usually plain white or in its natural unbleached state. **2** *chiefly US* coarse cotton cloth, with a pattern printed usually on one side. ◷ 16c: named after Calicut, the town in India from where the cloth was first brought.

Calif. ▷ *abbreviation, US state* California.

Californian bees see GINGER BEER PLANT

californium /kalɪ'fɔːnɪəm/ ▷ *noun, chem* (abbreviation **Cf**, atomic number 98) a synthetic radioactive metallic element of the ACTINIDE series, produced by bombarding an isotope of CURIUM with alpha particles. ◷ 1950: named after California, where the element was first made.

calipash /'kalɪpaʃ/ ▷ *noun* (***calipashes***) the part of a turtle which is closest to the upper shell, composed of a greenish, gelatinous substance. ◷ 17c.

calipee /'kalɪpiː/ ▷ *noun* (***calipees***) the part of a turtle which is closest to the lower shell, composed of a yellowish gelatinous substance. ◷ 17c: originally meaning 'the lower shell'.

caliper the *US* spelling of CALLIPER.

caliph, **calif**, **kalif** or **khalif** /'keɪlɪf, 'ka-/ ▷ *noun* the chief Muslim civil and religious leader. ◷ 14c: from Arabic *khalifah* successor (of Muhammad).

caliphate ▷ *noun* the office, rank or government of, or area ruled by, a caliph.

call /kɔːl/ ▷ *verb* (***called, calling***) **1** *tr & intr* (*also* **call out**) to shout or speak loudly in order to attract attention or in announcing something. **2** to ask someone to come, especially with a shout. **3** to ask for a professional visit from someone □ ***call the doctor.*** **4** to summon or invite someone. **5** *tr & intr* to telephone. **6** to waken □ ***Tim was called at 6.30am.*** **7** *intr* to make a visit □ ***call at the grocer's.*** **8** *intr* to stop at a place during a journey □ ***Does the train call at York?*** **9** to give a name to someone or something □ ***They called their son Kurt.*** **10** to regard or consider something as something specified □ ***I call that strange.*** **11** to say or imply that someone is something specified, usually unpleasant □ ***Are you calling me a liar?*** **12** to summon or assemble people for (a meeting). **13** to announce or declare something □ ***call an election.*** **14** (*often* **call for something**) *tr & intr* to make a demand or appeal for it □ ***call a strike.*** **15** *tr & intr* in a card game: to make a bid or choose (a suit for trumps). **16** *intr* to predict which way a coin will land when tossed □ ***Heads or tails? You call!*** **17** said of an umpire, etc: to judge (a ball) to be in or out of play. **18** *intr* said of a bird, etc: to make its typical or characteristic sound. ▷ *noun* **1** a shout or cry. **2** the cry of a bird or animal. **3** an invitation; a summons. **4** a demand, request or appeal. **5** (*usually* **call on something**) a claim or demand for it □ ***too many calls on my time.*** **6** a brief visit. **7** an act of contacting someone by telephone; a telephone conversation. **8** a need or reason □ ***not much call for Latin teachers.*** **9** an act of waking someone, usually by arrangement. **10** a signal blown on a bugle, etc. **11** a feeling that one has been chosen to do a particular job; a vocation. **12** a player's turn to bid or choose trumps in a card game. **13** the decision of a referee, etc on whether a ball is in or out of play. **14** an instrument that imitates a bird's call. ● **caller** *noun* a person or thing that calls. ● **call collect** *N Amer, especially US* to have the telephone call one is making charged to the receiver of the call; to reverse the charges. ● **call something into question** to suggest reasons for doubting it. ● **call it a day** to decide to stop doing something, eg finish work, etc. ● **call someone** or **something to mind 1** to remember them. **2** to remind one of something. ● **call the shots** to be in command. ● **have first call on something** to have the right to (someone's help, attention, etc) before anyone else. ● **on call** said eg of a doctor: available if needed, eg to deal with an emergency. ● **within call** close enough to hear if called. ◷ Anglo-Saxon *ceallian*.

■ **call back** to visit or telephone again.

■ **call someone back 1** to contact them again or in return by telephone. **2** to summon them to return.

■ **call something down on someone** to try to inflict it on them as if from heaven.

■ **call for something** or **someone 1** to require them. **2** to collect or fetch them.

■ **call something forth** to elicit or evoke it.

■ **call someone in** to invite or request their help.

■ **call something in** to request the return of (eg library books, a batch of faulty products, etc).

■ **call in on** or **in at someone** to visit them, usually briefly.

■ **call something off 1** to cancel a meeting, arrangement, etc. **2** to order (an animal) to stop attacking someone. **3** to give orders for something to be stopped □ *We'll call off the search at midnight.*

■ **call on** or **upon someone 1** to visit them. **2** to appeal to them. **3** to request or invite them □ *The chairperson called on the secretary to read the minutes.*

■ **call on something** to gather or summon up (one's strength, etc).

■ **call people out 1** to instruct (workers) to strike. **2** to summon (eg the fire brigade, the gas board, etc) to help with an emergency, etc.

■ **call round** to make an informal visit.

■ **call someone up 1** to conscript them into the armed forces. See also CALL-UP. **2** *colloq* to telephone them.

■ **call something up 1** to cause (memories, images, etc) to come into the mind. **2** to retrieve (data) from a computer □ *She called up the file in order to print it out.*

Callanetics /kalə'nɛtɪks/ ▷ *singular noun, trademark* a method of exercise involving frequent repetition of small muscular movements, designed to improve muscle tone. ◷ 1980s: named after its US inventor, Callan Pinckney.

call box ▷ *noun* a public telephone box.

call girl ▷ *noun* a prostitute with whom appointments are made by telephone.

calligrapher /kə'lɪgrəfə(r)/ or **calligraphist** ▷ *noun* someone skilled in calligraphy.

calligraphy /kə'lɪgrəfɪ/ ▷ *noun* **1** handwriting as an art. **2** beautiful decorative handwriting. ● **calligraphic** /kalɪ'grafɪk/ *adj.* ◷ 17c: from Greek *kallos* beauty + *graphein* to write.

calling ▷ *noun* **1** a trade or profession. **2** an urge to follow a particular profession, especially the ministry or one involving the care of other people.

calling card ▷ *noun* **1** *N Amer* a VISITING-CARD. **2** an unmistakable and usually disagreeable sign, especially one deliberately left, that a particular person has been present.

calliope /kə'laɪəpɪ/ *noun* (*calliopes*) *N Amer* a keyboard musical instrument similar to an organ, with a set of whistles operated by steam or compressed air. ◷ 19c: Greek, meaning 'beautiful voice'.

calliper /'kalɪpə(r)/ ▷ *noun* **1** a measuring device, consisting of two hinged prongs attached to a scale, which is used to measure the linear distance between the prongs, eg in order to determine the diameters of pipes. **2** a splint for supporting an injured or paralysed leg by keeping it rigid and taking most of the weight of the body. ◷ 16c: variant of CALIBRE.

callisthenics /kalɪs'θɛnɪks/ ▷ *plural noun* a system of physical exercises to increase the strength and grace of the body. ● **callisthenic** *adj.* ◷ 19c: from Greek *kallos* beauty + *sthenos* strength.

callosity /kə'lɒsɪtɪ/ ▷ *noun* (*callosities*) **1** a callus. **2** hard-heartedness. ◷ 16c: from Latin *callositas*, from *callosus* callous.

callous /'kaləs/ *adj* unconcerned for the feelings of others; coldly and deliberately cruel. ● **callously** *adverb* unfeelingly; cruelly. ● **callousness** *noun* deliberate cruelty; brutality. ◷ 15c: from Latin *callosus* thick-skinned.

callow /'kaloʊ/ ▷ *adj, derog* young and inexperienced. ◷ Anglo-Saxon *calu* bald.

call sign and **call signal** ▷ *noun, communications* a word, letter or number that identifies a ship, plane, etc when communicating by radio, etc.

call-up ▷ *noun* an official order to join the armed forces as a conscript. See also CALL SOMEONE UP at CALL.

callus /'kaləs/ ▷ *noun* (*calluses*) **1** a thickened hardened pad of skin which develops on parts of the body that are subjected to constant friction or pressure, such as the palms of the hands and soles of the feet. **2** a mass of tissue, consisting of large thin-walled cells, that forms around a wound on the surface of a plant. **3** a mass of blood and connective tissue that forms around the exposed ends of a fractured bone as an important part of the healing process. ◷ 16c: Latin meaning, 'hardened skin or tissue'.

call waiting ▷ *noun, telecomm* a system whereby one is able to accept an incoming telephone call routed by another number, while holding a call on one's own number.

calm /kɑːm/ ▷ *adj* **1** relaxed and in control; not anxious, upset, angry, etc. **2** said of the weather, etc: still, quiet or peaceful; not rough or stormy. ▷ *noun* **1** peace, quiet and tranquillity. **2** stillness of weather. **3** a lack of sufficient wind for sailing. ▷ *verb* (*calmed*, *calming*) *tr & intr* **1** (*usually* **calm down**) to become calmer. **2** (*usually* **calm someone** or **something down**) to make them calmer. ● **calmly** *adverb*. ● **calmness** *noun*. ◷ 14c: from French *calme*, from Greek *kauma*, (a rest during) the heat of noon.

Calor gas /'kalə —/ ▷ *noun, trademark* a mixture of liquefied butane and propane gases, stored under pressure in metal cylinders, and used as a fuel supply for portable stoves, etc. ◷ 1930s: Latin, meaning 'heat' + GAS 3.

calorie /'kalərɪ/ ▷ *noun* (*calories*) **1** a metric unit denoting the amount of heat required to raise the temperature of one gram of water by 1°C (1K) at one atmospheric pressure, now replaced by the SI unit JOULE. Also called SMALL CALORIE. **2** (**Calorie**) *old use* a KILOCALORIE. ◷ 19c: French, from Latin *calor* heat.

calorific /kalə'rɪfɪk/ ▷ *adj* **1** referring or relating to, or generating, heat. **2** referring or relating to calories. ◷ 17c: from French *calorifique*, from Latin *calorificus* heat-making.

calorific value ▷ *noun, physics* the amount of heat produced during the complete combustion of the unit mass of a fuel or food.

calorimeter /kalə'rɪmɪtə(r)/ ▷ *noun, chem* an instrument for measuring the thermal properties of a substance, especially its calorific value. ◷ 18c: from Latin *calor* heat + -METER 1.

calque /kalk/ ▷ *noun* a compound word or phrase, adopted into a language, whose parts are a literal translation of the corresponding parts of the phrase in the language it has been borrowed from, eg in English, *superman* is a calque of German *Übermensch*. Also called **loan translation**. ◷ 20c: French, meaning 'copy', from *calquer* to trace a design.

calumet /'kaljʊmɛt/ ▷ *noun* a tobacco-pipe, smoked as a token of peace by Native Americans. Also called **peace pipe**, **pipe of peace**. ◷ 18c: French dialect, meaning 'pipe stem', from Latin *calamus* reed.

calumniate /kə'lʌmnɪeɪt/ ▷ *verb* (*calumniated*, *calumniating*) to accuse someone falsely; to slander. ● **calumniator** *noun*.

calumny /'kaləmnɪ/ ▷ *noun* (*calumnies*) **1** an untrue and malicious spoken statement about a person. **2** the act of uttering such a statement. ● **calumnious** /kə'lʌmnɪəs/ *adj*. ⓒ 16c: from Latin *calumnia* false accusation.

Calvados /'kalvədɒs, kalvə'dɒs/ ▷ *noun* a type of brandy made from cider or apple-pulp. ⓒ 20c: named after the department in N France where it is traditionally made.

calve /kaːv/ ▷ *verb* (*calved*, *calving*) *intr* **1** to give birth to (a calf). **2** said of a glacier or iceberg: to release (masses of ice) on breaking up.

calves *plural of* CALF[1], CALF[2]

Calvinism /'kalvɪnɪzəm/ ▷ *noun* the teachings of John Calvin, laying emphasis on mankind's inability to repent and believe in Christ without God's help, and on predestination. ● **Calvinist** *noun*. ● **Calvinistic** or **Calvinistical** *adj*.

calx /kalks/ ▷ *noun* (*calces* /'kalsiːz/ or *calxes* /'kalksɪz/) **1** the powdery metal oxide that remains after an ore has been roasted in air. **2** lime, or CALCIUM OXIDE. ⓒ 15c: Latin, meaning 'lime'.

Calypso /kə'lɪpsoʊ/ ▷ *noun, astron* the fourteenth moon of Saturn, measuring 30km in diameter. ⓒ 1980.

calypso /kə'lɪpsoʊ/ ▷ *noun* (*calypsos*) a type of popular song originating in the West Indies, usually dealing with current happenings in an amusing way, and often improvised by the singer. ⓒ 20c.

calyx /'keɪlɪks, 'ka-/ ▷ *noun* (*calyces* /-lɪsiːz/ , *calyxes* /-lɪksiːz/) *bot* the outermost WHORL (*noun* 1) of a flower, consisting of the SEPALs. It encloses the petals, STAMENs and CARPELs, and protects the developing flower bud. ⓒ 17c: Latin, from Greek *kalyx* covering or husk.

calzone /kalt'souneɪ/ ▷ *noun* (*calzones*) a folded round of pizza dough stuffed with a savoury filling. ⓒ 1940s: Italian, meaning 'trouser leg'.

CAM /kam/ ▷ *abbreviation*, *computing* computer-aided manufacture, the use of computers to control any part of a manufacturing process.

cam ▷ *noun, engineering* an irregular projection on a wheel or rotating shaft, shaped so as to transmit regular movement to another part in contact with it. ⓒ 18c: from Dutch *kam* comb.

camaraderie /kamə'rɑːdəriː/ ▷ *noun* a feeling of friendship and cheerful support for one another within a group or team of people. ⓒ 19c: French, from *camarade* comrade.

camber /'kambə(r)/ ▷ *noun* **1** a slight convexity on the upper surface of a road, ship's deck, wing section of an aeroplane, etc, designed to promote drainage of water. **2** the curve in the wings of an aeroplane. **3** a curved piece of timber. **4** a sideways inclination of the wheels at the front of a road vehicle. ▷ *verb* (*cambered*, *cambering*) *tr & intr* to form (a slight convexity) on the upper surface of a structure or to give (a slight convexity) to such a surface. ⓒ 17c: from French *cambre*, from Latin *camarus* curved inwards.

cambium /'kambɪəm/ ▷ *noun* (*cambia* or *cambiums*) *bot* in the roots and stems of woody plants: a layer of actively dividing cells between the XYLEM and the PHLOEM, which produces an increase in lateral growth or girth. ⓒ 17c: Latin, meaning 'exchange'.

Cambodian /kam'boudɪən/ ▷ *adj* belonging or relating to Cambodia, a republic in SE Asia, or its inhabitants. ▷ *noun* a citizen or inhabitant of, or person born in, Cambodia.

Cambrian /'kambrɪən/ ▷ *adj* **1** *geol* relating to the earliest geological period of the Palaeozoic era. See table at GEOLOGICAL TIME SCALE. **2** *geol* relating to rocks formed during this period. **3** relating to Wales and the Welsh. ▷ *noun* **1** *geol* the Cambrian period. **2** a Welsh person. ⓒ 17c: from Latin *Cambria*, from Welsh *Cymru* Wales.

cambric /'kambrɪk, 'keɪm-/ ▷ *noun* a fine white cotton or linen fabric. ⓒ 16c: from Flemish *Kameryk* Cambrai, the town in N France where the cloth was first made.

Cambs. ▷ *abbreviation* Cambridgeshire.

camcorder /'kamkɔːdə(r)/ ▷ *noun* a portable video camera that is used to record images and sound as electronic signals on a small cassette of video tape, which can then be played back through a standard television receiver using a videocassette recorder incorporated within the camera. ⓒ 1980s: a shortening of CAMERA + RECORDER.

came *past tense of* COME

camel /'kaməl/ ▷ *noun* **1** a large HERBIVOROUS mammal with a long neck and legs, coarse hair, a tufted tail and one or two humps on its back, which contain fat and act as a food reserve. **2** the pale brown colour of this animal. ⓒ Anglo-Saxon, from Latin *camellus*, Greek *kamelos*, of Semitic origin.

cameleer /kamə'lɪə(r)/ ▷ *noun* someone who drives or rides a camel.

camelhair ▷ *noun* **1** a soft, usually pale-brown cloth made from camels' hair. **2** hair from a squirrel's tail used to make paintbrushes.

camellia /kə'miːlɪə, kə'mɛlɪə/ ▷ *noun* (*camellias*) **1** an evergreen shrub, native to SE Asia, widely cultivated for its conspicuous white, pink or crimson flowers and glossy dark green leaves. **2** the flower of this plant. Also called **japonica**. ⓒ 18c: named after the plant collector Josef Kamel (1661–1706).

Camembert /'kaməmbɛə(r)/ ▷ *noun* a kind of soft white French cheese with a rich flavour and strong smell. ⓒ 19c: named after the village in N France where it was originally made.

cameo /'kamɪoʊ/ ▷ *noun* (*cameos*) **1** a smooth rounded gemstone with a raised design of a head in profile carved on it, especially one where the design is a different colour from the gemstone. Compare INTAGLIO (sense 1). **2** a piece of jewellery containing such a gemstone. **3** the design itself. **4** (*also* **cameo role**) a small part in a play or film performed by a well-known actor. **5** a short descriptive piece of writing. ⓒ 14c: from Italian *cammeo*.

camera[1] /'kamərə/ ▷ *noun* (*cameras*) **1** an optical device that focuses light from an object through a lens on to light-sensitive film, in order to record the image as a photograph. **2** a device in a television broadcasting system that converts visual images into electrical signals for transmission. ● **on camera** in front of the camera; being filmed. ⓒ 19c in sense 1; 18c in obsolete sense 'vaulted chamber': Latin, meaning 'vaulted chamber'.

camera[2] see IN CAMERA

camera lucida /— 'luːsɪdə, — 'ljuːsɪdə/ ▷ *noun* (*camera lucidas*) *optics* a mechanical aid used in conjunction with a microscope or other optical instrument, whereby the image of an object is projected through a prism onto paper, so enabling the observer to trace an accurate outline of the object. ⓒ 18c: Latin, meaning 'light chamber'.

cameraman ▷ *noun* in TV or film-making: someone who operates a camera.

camera obscura /— əb'skjʊərə/ ▷ *noun* (*camera obscuras*) a darkened box or room with a small hole in one wall or the roof, through which light from outside can enter, pass through a lens, and form an inverted image of the scene outside, which is projected on to the opposite wall or the floor, etc of the chamber. ⓒ 18c: Latin, meaning 'dark chamber'.

camera-shy ▷ *adj* having a dislike of being photographed.

camiknickers /'kamɪnɪkəz/ ▷ *plural noun* **1** loose-legged knickers for women, usually made from a silky material. **2** a woman's undergarment consisting of a camisole and knickers combined.

camisole /'kamɪsoul/ ▷ *noun* a woman's loose undergarment, with narrow shoulder straps for the top half of the body. ⓒ 19c: French, from Spanish *camisola*, diminutive of *camisa* shirt.

camomile or **chamomile** /ˈkaməmaɪl/ ▷ *noun* (*plural* in sense 1 only ***camomiles***) **1** a strongly scented perennial plant, native to Europe and SW Asia, which has finely divided leaves, and daisy-like flower-heads consisting of outer white ray florets and inner yellow disc florets. **2** the dried crushed flowers or leaves of this plant, used for their soothing medicinal properties, especially in the form of a herbal tea, or added to some types of shampoo. ⓒ 14c: French, from Latin *chamomilla*, from Greek *chamaimelon* earth apple (from the smell of the flowers).

camouflage /ˈkaməflɑːʒ, -flɑːdʒ/ ▷ *noun* **1** any device or means of disguising or concealing a person or animal, or of deceiving an adversary, especially by adopting the colour, texture, etc, of natural surroundings or backgrounds. **2** the use of such methods to conceal or disguise the presence of military troops (including soldiers' uniforms), equipment, vehicles or buildings, by imitating the colours of nature. **3** objects such as tree branches, undergrowth, etc, used to disguise military equipment, etc. **4** the colour pattern or other physical features that enable an animal to blend with its natural environment and so avoid detection by predators. ▷ *verb* (***camouflaged, camouflaging***) to disguise or conceal with some kind of camouflage. ⓒ 20c: French, from *camoufler* to disguise.

camp[1] ▷ *noun* **1** a piece of ground on which tents have been erected. **2** a collection of buildings, huts, tents, etc used as temporary accommodation or for short stays for a particular purpose. **3** a permanent site where troops are housed or trained. **4** *archaeol* an ancient fortified site. **5** a party or side in a dispute, etc; a group having a particular set of opinions, beliefs, etc. ▷ *verb* (***camped, camping***) *intr* to stay in a tent or tents, cooking meals in the open air, etc. ● **camping** *noun* living in a tent or makeshift accommodation, especially for recreation. ● **break camp** to take down tents, etc when leaving a campsite. ● **pitch camp** see under PITCH[1]. ⓒ 16c: French, from Latin *campus* field.

■ **camp out 1** to live and sleep in the open, with or without a tent. **2** to stay in temporary accommodation with a minimum of furniture, equipment, etc.

camp[2] *colloq, sometimes derog* ▷ *adj* **1** said of a man or his behaviour: using mannerisms that are typically associated with women, especially in a deliberate, exaggerated or theatrical way. **2** said of a man: homosexual. **3** theatrical and exaggerated, especially amusingly so. ▷ *noun* camp behaviour or style. ▷ *verb* (***camped, camping***) *intr* to behave in a camp way. ● **camp it up** to behave in an exaggerated theatrical way; to overact. ⓒ 20c.

■ **camp something up** to make it camp □ *He camped his performance up to make the character more lively.*

campaign /kamˈpeɪn/ ▷ *noun* **1** an organized series of actions intended to gain support for or build up opposition to a particular practice, group, etc. **2** the operations of an army while fighting in a particular area or to achieve a particular goal or objective. ▷ *verb* (***campaigned, campaigning***) *intr* (*usually* **campaign for** or **against something**) to organize or take part in a campaign. ● **campaigner** *noun*. ⓒ 17c in sense 2: from French *campagne* open countryside, ultimately from Latin *campus* field.

campanile /kampəˈniːlɪ/ ▷ *noun* especially in Italy: a free-standing bell tower, ie not attached to a church, etc. ⓒ 17c: Italian, from *campana* bell.

campanology /kampəˈnɒlədʒɪ/ ▷ *noun* **1** the art of bell-ringing and CHANGE-RINGING. **2** the study of bells. ● **campanologist** *noun*. ⓒ 19c: from Latin *campana* bell + -LOGY 1.

campanula /kamˈpanjʊlə/ ▷ *noun* (***campanulas***) any of numerous north temperate plants with bell-shaped flowers, usually blue but sometimes white or pink, borne either singly or in long flower-heads. Also called **bell-flower**. ⓒ 17c: Latin, diminutive of *campana* bell.

camp bed ▷ *noun* a light portable folding bed consisting of a metal or wooden frame with canvas stretched across it.

camper ▷ *noun* **1** someone who camps. **2** a motor vehicle equipped for sleeping in, with cooking and washing facilities, etc.

camp-follower ▷ *noun* **1** *derog* someone who supports a particular group, party, etc only because it is fashionable. **2** someone who travels about with an army or other moving group in order to earn money eg as a prostitute or by doing odd jobs for them.

camphor /ˈkamfə(r)/ ▷ *noun* a white or colourless crystalline compound with a strong aromatic odour, used as a plasticizer in the manufacture of celluloid, as a medicinal liniment and inhalant, and as an insect repellent. ● **camphoric** /kamˈfɒrɪk/ *adj*. ⓒ 14c: from Latin *camphora*, from Arabic *kafur*, from Malay *kapur* chalk.

camphorate /ˈkamfəreɪt/ ▷ *verb* (***camphorated, camphorating***) to treat or impregnate with camphor. ● **camphorated** *adj*.

camping see under CAMP[1]

campion /ˈkampɪən/ ▷ *noun* any of various annual or perennial north temperate plants, especially the red campion and white campion, which have bright pink and white flowers, respectively, and a tubular calyx. ⓒ 16c.

campsite ▷ *noun* a piece of land on which people are allowed to camp.

campus /ˈkampəs/ ▷ *noun* (***campuses***) **1** the grounds of a college or university. **2** a university or the university as an institution. **3** the academic world. ● **on campus** within university premises or grounds. ⓒ 18c: Latin, meaning 'field'.

campylobacter /ˈkampɪlɒbaktə(r)/ ▷ *noun, biol* a spiral-shaped bacterium that occurs in the reproductive and digestive tracts of humans and animals, causing diarrhoea and GASTRITIS in humans, and genital diseases in cattle and sheep. ⓒ 20c: from Greek *kampylos* bent + *bacterion* a little rod (from its shape).

CAMRA /ˈkamrə/ ▷ *abbreviation* Campaign for Real Ale.

camshaft ▷ *noun, engineering* a shaft to which one or more CAMs are attached.

can[1] ▷ *verb* (*past tense* ***could***) **1** to be able to □ *Can you lift that?* **2** to know how to □ *He can play the guitar.* **3** to feel able to; to feel it right to □ *How can you believe that?* **4** used to express surprise □ *Can it really be that late?* **5** used to express a possibility □ *The weather can change so quickly in the mountains.* **6** to have permission to □ *Can I take an apple?* **7** used when asking for help, etc □ *Can you give me the time?* See also CANNOT, CAN'T, COULD, COULDN'T. ⓒ Anglo-Saxon *cunnan* to know.

can, may

● Essentially, **can** denotes capability or capacity, and **may** denotes permission or opportunity. Because these two sets of meaning constantly overlap, the two words have become highly interchangeable, with **can** more versatile than **may** □ *Hospital trusts attract more staff and can determine their own pay rates* □ *You can do it when you come home from work.* In both these examples, **may** is also possible.
● Both **can** and **may** are used to denote what is probable or habitual □ *A quiet river on a summer's day may be a raging torrent in February* □ *Things can go dreadfully wrong at this stage.* When capability or capacity is predominant, **can** is used □ *I can't cope with life at the moment* □ *Can you see the point I am trying to make?*

can² ▻ *noun* **1** a sealed container, usually of tin plate or aluminium, used to preserve food and protect it from bacterial contamination, or to retain the carbon dioxide in fizzy drinks. **2** a large container made of metal or another material, for holding liquids, eg oil or paint. **3** the amount a can will hold. **4** (**the can**) *slang* prison. **5** *N Amer, slang* (*usually* **the can**) a lavatory. ▻ *verb* (***canned***, ***canning***) to seal (food or drink) in metal containers in order to preserve it. ● **carry the can** *colloq* to take the blame. ● **in the can** *colloq* completed; finished. ◷ Anglo-Saxon *canne*.

Can. ▻ *abbreviation* **1** Canada. **2** Canadian.

Canada Day ▻ *noun* in Canada: a public holiday on 1 July, commemorating the anniversary of the union of the provinces in 1867 which created the Dominion of Canada.

Canada goose ▻ *noun* a goose native to N America, and introduced to Europe and New Zealand, with a black head and neck and a white chin.

Canadian /kəˈneɪdɪən/ ▻ *adj* belonging or relating to Canada, an independent country in N America, or its inhabitants. ▻ *noun* a citizen or inhabitant of, or person born in, Canada.

canakin see CANNIKIN

canal /kəˈnal/ ▻ *noun* **1** an artificial channel or waterway, usually constructed to allow shipping to pass between two adjacent bodies of water, but sometimes built to improve irrigation or drainage of a particular area of land. **2** *anatomy* any tubular channel or passage that conveys air, fluids or semi-solid material from one part of the body to another, eg the ALIMENTARY CANAL. **3** *astron* any of the indistinct channel-like markings apparent on the surface of Mars when viewed through a telescope. ◷ 17c in sense 1; 15c in obsolete sense 'pipe, tube': from Latin *canalis* water pipe.

canal boat ▻ *noun* a barge.

canaliculus /kanəˈlɪkjʊləs/ ▻ *noun* (***canaliculi*** /-laɪ/) *anatomy* a small tube or furrow which connects the lacunae (see LACUNA 2) in some bones. ● **canalicular** *adj*. ● **canaliculate** or **canaliculated** *adj*. ◷ 19c in this sense; 16c in obsolete sense 'a channel': Latin diminutive of *canalis* pipe or groove.

canalize or **canalise** /ˈkanəlaɪz/ ▻ *verb* (***canalized***, ***canalizing***) **1** to make or convert into an artificial channel or system of channels, especially to deepen, widen or straighten (a river) in order to allow the passage of shipping or prevent flooding. **2** to guide or direct into a useful, practical or profitable course. ● **canalization** *noun*.

canapé /ˈkanəpeɪ, ˈkanəpɪ/ ▻ *noun* (***canapés***) a type of food often served at parties, etc consisting of a small piece of bread or toast spread or topped with something savoury. ◷ 19c: French, meaning 'sofa' or 'canapé'.

canard /ˈkanɑːd/ ▻ *noun* **1** a false report or piece of news; a rumour, hoax, etc. **2 a** a second wing fitted near the nose of an aircraft, to provide horizontal stability; **b** an aircraft with such a wing. ◷ 19c: French, meaning 'duck'.

canary /kəˈnɛərɪ/ ▻ *noun* (***canaries***) **1** a small finch, native to the Canary Islands, the Azores and Madeira, which has been bred to produce varieties with bright yellow plumage, and is very popular as a caged bird. **2** (*also* **canary yellow**) bright yellow. ▻ *adj* canary coloured. ◷ 16c: named after the Canary Islands.

canasta /kəˈnastə/ ▻ *noun* (*plural* in sense 2 only ***canastas***) **1** a card game similar to rummy played with two packs of cards, in which the aim is to collect sets of cards of the same value. **2** a MELD² of seven or more cards in this card game. ◷ 20c: Spanish, meaning 'basket'.

cancan /ˈkankan/ ▻ *noun* a lively dance originating in Parisian theatres, which is usually performed by dancing girls, who execute high kicks, raising their skirts to reveal their petticoats. ◷ 19c: French.

cancel /ˈkansəl/ ▻ *verb* (***cancelled***, ***cancelling***) **1** to stop (something already arranged) from taking place, by an official announcement, etc; to call off. **2** to stop (something in progress) from continuing. **3** *intr* to withdraw from an engagement, etc. **4** to tell a supplier that one no longer wants something. **5** to put an end to (an existing arrangement, rule, law, etc). **6** to delete or cross out something. **7** to put an official stamp on (eg a cheque or postage stamp) so that it cannot be re-used. **8** *math* to eliminate (common numbers or terms), especially to strike out (equal quantities) from opposite sides of an equation, or (common factors) from the NUMERATOR and DENOMINATOR of a fraction. **9** (*usually* **cancel something out**) to remove the effect of it, by having an exactly opposite effect; to counterbalance. **10** *computing* to stop (a process) before or shortly after it has started. ▻ *noun*, *printing* **1** the suppression of a printed leaf or sheet. **2 a** the leaf or sheet so cancelled; **b** more usually, the new one substituted. ◷ 14c: from French *canceller*, from Latin *cancellare* to cross out.

cancellate /ˈkansəleɪt/ or **cancellated** ▻ *adj* **1** marked with criss-crossed line. **2** *anatomy* having a lattice-like or porous structure.

cancellation /kansəˈleɪʃən/ ▻ *noun* **1** an act of cancelling. **2** something which has been cancelled, especially a theatre ticket which can then be transferred to another person.

Cancer /ˈkansə(r)/ ▻ *noun* **1** *astron* a faint constellation lying on the zodiac between Gemini and Leo. **2** *astrol* **a** the fourth sign of the zodiac; **b** a person born between 22 June and 22 July, under this sign. See table at ZODIAC. ◷ 14c: Latin, meaning 'crab'.

cancer /ˈkansə(r)/ ▻ *noun* **1** *pathol* any form of malignant tumour that develops when the cells of a tissue or organ multiply in an uncontrolled manner. **2** *pathol* a diseased area produced when a malignant tumour invades and destroys the surrounding tissues, and which if left untreated is generally fatal. **3** an evil within an organization, community, etc that is gradually destroying it. See also ONCOGENE. ● **cancerous** *adj*. ◷ 17c: Latin, meaning 'crab' or 'cancerous growth'.

candela /kanˈdɛlə, -ˈdiːlə/ ▻ *noun* (***candelas***) (symbol **cd**) the SI unit of luminous intensity, equal to the luminous intensity in a given direction of a source that emits monochromatic radiation of frequency 540 × 10^{-12}Hz and has a radiant intensity in that direction of 1/683 watts per steradian. ◷ 20c: Latin, meaning 'candle'.

candelabrum /kandəˈlɑːbrəm/ or (sometimes used wrongly as singular) **candelabra** ▻ *noun* (***candelabrums***, ***candelabra*** or ***candelabras***) a decorative candle-holder with branches for several candles, or a light fitting for overhead lights, designed in the same way. ◷ 19c: Latin, meaning 'candlestick', from *candela* candle.

candid /ˈkandɪd/ ▻ *adj* **1** honest and open about what one thinks; outspoken. **2** fair and impartial. **3** *colloq* said of a photograph: unposed for: taken without the subject's knowledge so as to catch them unawares in an informal situation. ● **candidly** *adverb*. ● **candidness** *noun*. ◷ 17c: from Latin *candidus* shining white, from *candere* to be white or to glisten.

candidate /ˈkandɪdət/ ▻ *noun* **1** someone who is competing with others for a job, prize, parliamentary seat, etc. **2** someone taking an examination. **3** a person or thing considered suitable for a particular purpose or likely to suffer a particular fate □ ***Jackie is a definite candidate for promotion.*** ● **candidacy** /ˈkandɪdəsɪ/ or **candidature** /ˈkandɪdətʃə(r)/ *noun* (***candidacies***). ◷ 17c: from Latin *candidatus* clothed in white, because Roman candidates always wore white.

candied /ˈkandɪd/ ▻ *adj* preserved or encrusted with sugar; crystallized.

candle /'kandəl/ ▻ *noun* a piece of wax or (especially formerly) tallow, usually cylindrical and formed around a wick, which is burnt to provide light. ▻ *verb* (***candled***, ***candling***) to test (eggs, etc) by examining against a bright light. ● **burn the candle at both ends** to exhaust oneself with work or activity from early morning till late in the night; to try to do too many things. ● **not fit** or **able to hold a candle to something** or **someone** to be noticeably inferior to them. ● **not worth the candle** said of a task, etc: not worth the trouble and effort it would take. ⓒ Anglo-Saxon *candel*.

candlelight ▻ *noun* **1** the light given by a candle or candles. **2** dusk.

candlelit ▻ *adj* lit by candles.

Candlemas /'kandəlməs/ ▻ *noun* in the Christian church: a festival held on 2 February celebrating the purification of the Virgin Mary after childbirth, at which candles are carried in procession. ⓒ Anglo-Saxon.

candlestick ▻ *noun* a holder, usually portable, for a candle.

candlewick ▻ *noun* a cotton fabric with a tufted surface formed by cut loops of thread, used for bedcovers, etc.

candour /'kandə(r)/ ▻ *noun* the quality of being candid; frankness and honesty. ⓒ 17c in this sense; 14c in obsolete sense 'brilliant whiteness': from Latin *candor* purity, sincerity.

C and W ▻ *abbreviation* country and western.

candy /'kandɪ/ ▻ *noun* (***candies***) *N Amer* **1** a sweet. **2** sweets or confectionery. **3** *drug-taking slang* any hard drug, usually cocaine or heroin. ▻ *verb* (***candies***, ***candied***, ***candying***) **1** to reduce (sugar) to a crystalline form by boiling and evaporating slowly. **2** to preserve (fruit, peel, etc) by boiling in sugar or syrup. **3** to coat or encrust with sugar or candied sugar. ⓒ 18c: from French *sucre candi* candied sugar, from Persian *qandi* sugar.

candyfloss ▻ *noun* a fluffy mass of spun sugar usually coloured and served on a stick.

candy stripe ▻ *noun* a textile fabric patterned with narrow stripes, usually pink or red, on a white background. ● **candy-striped** *adj*.

candytuft /'kandɪtʌft/ ▻ *noun* an annual or perennial evergreen plant, native to Europe and Asia, which has narrow leaves and flattened heads of small white or mauve flowers. ⓒ 17c: named after Candia, the town in Crete from which the plant was brought + TUFT.

cane /keɪn/ ▻ *noun* **1** the long jointed hollow or pithy stem of certain plants, especially various small palms (eg rattan) and larger grasses (eg bamboo and sugar cane). **2** SUGAR CANE. **3** the woody stem of a raspberry, blackberry or loganberry plant. **4** thin stems or strips cut from stems, eg of rattan, for weaving into baskets, etc. **5** a walking-stick. **6** a long slim stick for beating people as a punishment, or for supporting plants. ▻ *verb* (***caned***, ***caning***) **1** to beat someone with a cane as a punishment. **2** to construct or mend with cane. **3** *colloq* to beat or defeat. ● **caning** *noun* **1** a beating with a cane. **2** *colloq* a severe defeat or humiliation. ⓒ 14c: French, from Latin *canna*, from Greek *kanna* reed.

cane-sugar ▻ *noun* SUCROSE, especially that obtained from sugar-cane.

canful ▻ *noun* (***canfuls***) the amount a can will hold.

canikin see CANNIKIN

canine /'keɪnaɪn, 'kanaɪn/ ▻ *adj* **1** relating to or resembling a dog. **2** relating to the dog family in general, including wolves and foxes as well as the domestic dog. **3** relating to a canine tooth. ▻ *noun* **1** any animal belonging to the dog family, especially a domestic dog. **2** a CANINE TOOTH. ⓒ 17c: from Latin *caninus*, from *canis* dog.

canine distemper see DISTEMPER[1]

canine tooth ▻ *noun* in most mammals: any of the long sharp pointed teeth, two in each jaw, located between the incisors and premolars, and used for catching and killing prey and tearing flesh. Also called **eye tooth**. Compare INCISOR, MOLAR.

Canis Major /'keɪnɪs —/ ▻ *noun, astron* a small but very bright constellation in the southern hemisphere, lying partly in the Milky Way, and containing SIRIUS. ⓒ Latin, meaning 'greater dog'.

Canis Minor /'keɪnɪs —/ ▻ *noun, astron* a small constellation in the northern hemisphere, lying partly in the Milky Way. ⓒ Latin, meaning 'lesser dog'.

canister /'kanɪstə(r)/ ▻ *noun* **1** a metal or plastic container for storing tea or other dry foods. **2** *military* a metal cylinder filled with gas or metal shot, which explodes when thrown or fired. ⓒ 17c: from Latin *canistrum*, from Greek *kanastron* basket, from *kanna* reed.

canker /'kaŋkə(r)/ ▻ *noun* **1** a fungal, bacterial or viral disease of trees and woody shrubs, eg fruit trees, in which hardened tissue forms over sunken or cracked dead areas on the bark or near a wound. **2** ulceration of the lips, mouth or tongue. **3** an ulcerous disease of animals that causes several conditions, eg inflammation and decay of the hooves of horses, inflammation of the ears of cats and dogs. **4** an evil, destructive influence, etc. ● **cankerous** *adj*. ⓒ Anglo-Saxon *cancer*, from Latin *cancer* cancerous ulcer.

cannabis /'kanəbɪs/ ▻ *noun* **1** a narcotic drug, prepared from the leaves and flowers of the hemp plant, that produces euphoria or hallucinations when smoked or swallowed, and the use of which is prohibited in many countries. Also called **marijuana**, **hashish**, **pot**, **spliff**, **bhang**. **2** a common name for the hemp plant from which this drug is obtained. ⓒ 18c: Latin, from Greek *kannabis* hemp.

cannabis resin ▻ *noun* a resin obtained from the dried leaves and flowers of the cannabis plant, and used to make hashish.

canned ▻ *adj* **1** contained or preserved in cans. **2** *slang* drunk. **3** *colloq* previously recorded □ *canned laughter*.

cannelloni /kanə'loʊnɪ/ ▻ *plural noun* a kind of pasta in the form of large tubes, served with a filling of meat, cheese, etc. ⓒ 20c: Italian, from *cannello* tube.

cannery ▻ *noun* (***canneries***) a factory where goods are canned.

cannibal /'kanɪbəl/ ▻ *noun* **1** someone who eats human flesh. **2** an animal that eats others of its own kind. ⓒ 16c: from Spanish *Caníbales*, from *Caribes* the Caribs of the W Indies, who were once believed to be cannibals.

cannibalism ▻ *noun* the practice of eating human flesh. Also called **anthropophagy**. ● **cannibalistic** *adj*.

cannibalize or **cannibalise** ▻ *verb* (***cannibalized***, ***cannibalizing***) *colloq* to take parts from (a machine, vehicle, etc) for use in repairing another.

cannier, **canniest**, **cannily** and **canniness** see under CANNY

cannikin, **canakin** or **canikin** /'kanɪkɪn/ ▻ *noun* a small can, often used as a drinking vessel. ⓒ 16c: from Dutch *kanneken*.

cannon /'kanən/ ▻ *noun* (***cannons*** or in senses 1 and 2 only ***cannon***) **1** *historical* a large gun mounted on wheels. **2** a rapid-firing gun fitted to an aircraft or ship. **3** in billiards, pool and snooker: a shot in which the cue ball strikes one object ball and then strikes another. ▻ *verb* (***cannoned***, ***cannoning***) *intr* in billiards, pool and snooker: to play a cannon shot. ⓒ 16c: from French *canon*, from Italian *cannone*, from *canna* tube.

■ **cannon into something** to hit or collide with it while moving at speed.

■ **cannon off something** to hit it with force and bounce off it.

cannonade /kanən'eɪd/ ▻ *noun* a continuous bombardment by heavy guns. ▻ *verb* (***cannonaded, cannonading***) *tr & intr* to attack with or as if with a cannon. ⓘ 17c: from French *canonnade*, from Italian *cannonata* cannon shot.

cannonball ▻ *noun, historical* a ball, usually of iron, for shooting from a cannon.

cannon fodder ▻ *noun, colloq* soldiers regarded merely as material to be sacrificed in war.

cannot /'kanət, 'kanɒt, ka'nɒt/ ▻ *verb* can not. See also CAN'T. ● **cannot but** see under CAN'T.

cannula /'kanjʊlə/ ▻ *noun* (***cannulas*** or ***cannulae*** /-liː, -laɪ/) *surgery* a thin hollow tube used to introduce fluid to, or remove it from, body cavities. ⓘ 17c: Latin diminutive of *canna* reed.

canny /'kanɪ/ ▻ *adj* (***cannier, canniest***) **1** wise, clever and alert, especially in business matters; shrewd. **2** careful; cautious. **3** *Scots & N Eng dialect* nice; good. **4** *Scots* lucky. ● **cannily** *adverb*. ● **canniness** *noun*. ⓘ 17c: from CAN[1], in the sense 'to know how to'.

canoe /kə'nuː/ ▻ *noun* (***canoes***) a light narrow boat propelled manually by one or more single- or double-bladed paddles. ▻ *verb* (***canoed, canoeing***) *intr* to travel by canoe. ● **canoeing** *noun*. ● **canoeist** *noun*. ● **paddle one's own canoe** *colloq* **1** to manage without other people's help. **2** to look after one's own affairs; to mind one's own business. ⓘ 16c: from Spanish *canoa*.

canon /'kanən/ ▻ *noun* **1** a basic law, rule or principle. **2 a** a member of the clergy attached to a cathedral; **b** *C of E* a member of the clergy who has special rights with regard to the election of bishops. **3** an officially accepted collection of writing, eg on religion, or work considered to be by a particular writer. **4** in the Christian church: a list of saints. **5** a section of the Roman Catholic mass. **6** a piece of music, similar to a round, in which a particular sequence is repeated with a regular overlapping pattern, by different voices or instruments. ⓘ Anglo-Saxon: from Greek *kanon* rod or rule.

canonical /kə'nɒnɪkəl/ ▻ *adj* **1** according to, of the nature of or included in a canon. **2** regular. **3** orthodox or accepted. **4** ecclesiastical.

canonical hours ▻ *plural noun* **1** *now especially RC Church* **a** the hours appointed for prayer and devotion; **b** the services prescribed for these times, which are MATINS, LAUDS, TERCE, SEXT, NONE[2], VESPERS and COMPLINE. **2** in England: the hours when a marriage ceremony is able to be lawfully conducted in a parish church.

canonize or **canonise** /'kanənaɪz/ ▻ *verb* (***canonized, canonizing***) **1** to officially declare someone to be a saint. **2** to treat someone as a saint. **3** to approve something by the authority of the church. ● **canonization** *noun*.

canon law ▻ *noun* the law of the Christian church.

canoodle /kə'nuːdəl/ ▻ *verb* (***canoodled, canoodling***) *intr, colloq* to hug and kiss; to cuddle.

can-opener ▻ *noun* a small device for opening cans.

canopy /'kanəpɪ/ ▻ *noun* (***canopies***) **1** an ornamental covering hung over a bed, throne, etc. **2** a covering hung or held up over something or someone, usually for shelter. **3** a wide overhead covering. **4** *archit* a roof-like structure over an altar, recess, etc. **5** a transparent cover over the cockpit of an aeroplane. **6** *bot* the topmost layer of a wood or forest, consisting of the uppermost leaves and branches of trees. **7** the fabric part of a parachute, that opens like an umbrella. ● **canopied** *adj*. ⓘ 14c: from Greek *konopeion* a couch with a mosquito net.

canst /kanst/ ▻ *verb, archaic* the 2nd person singular of CAN[1], used with the pronoun THOU[1].

cant[1] /kant/ ▻ *noun* **1** *derog* insincere talk, especially with a false display of moral or religious principles. **2** the special slang or jargon of a particular group of people, eg thieves, lawyers, etc. ▻ *verb* (***canted, canting***) *intr* to talk using cant. ● **canting** *adj*. ● **cantingly** *adverb*. ⓘ 17c in sense 2; 16c in obsolete sense 'musical sound': from Latin *cantare* to chant.

cant[2] /kant/ ▻ *noun* **1** a slope. **2** a jerk or toss that makes something tilt. **3** a sloping or tilting position or plane. ▻ *verb* (***canted, canting***) *tr & intr* to tilt, slope or tip up. ⓘ 14c.

can't /kɑːnt/ ▻ *contraction* cannot. ● **one can't** or **cannot but** ... one has to ... or is obliged to ... □ *You can't but admire her perseverance.*

Cantab. ▻ *abbreviation* especially used in abbreviations of academic degrees: *Cantabrigiensis* (Latin), belonging to Cambridge □ *BA Cantab.*

cantabile /kan'tɑːbɪleɪ/ *music* ▻ *adverb* in a flowing and melodious manner. ▻ *adj* flowing and melodious. ▻ *noun* a piece of music to be played this way. ⓘ 18c: Italian, meaning 'suitable for singing'.

cantaloup or **cantaloupe** /'kantəluːp/ ▻ *noun* (***cantaloups*** or ***cantaloupes***) a type of large melon with a thick ridged skin and orange-coloured flesh. ⓘ 18c: French, from Italian Cantaluppi, the place where it was first cultivated in Europe.

cantankerous /kan'taŋkərəs/ ▻ *adj* bad-tempered; irritable. ● **cantankerously** *adverb*. ● **cantankerousness** *noun*. ⓘ 18c.

cantata /kan'tɑːtə/ ▻ *noun* (***cantatas***) a musical work, especially on a religious theme, which is sung, with parts for chorus and soloists. ⓘ 18c: Italian, meaning 'a thing to be sung', from *cantare* to sing.

canteen /kan'tiːn/ ▻ *noun* **1** a restaurant, especially a cafeteria, attached to a factory, office, etc for the use of employees. **2** a small shop selling food and drink in an army camp, etc. **3 a** a case containing cutlery; **b** the full set of cutlery contained in the case. **4** a flask for water, etc carried by soldiers or campers. ⓘ 18c: from French *cantine*, from Italian *cantina* cellar or cave.

canter /'kantə(r)/ ▻ *noun* a horse-riding pace between trotting and galloping. ▻ *verb* (***cantered, cantering***) *tr & intr* to move or cause to move at this pace. ⓘ 18c: shortened from *Canterbury gallop* the pace used by the pilgrims riding to Canterbury in the Middle Ages.

cantharides see SPANISH FLY

canticle /'kantɪkəl/ ▻ *noun* a non-metrical hymn or chant with a text taken from the Bible. ⓘ 13c: from Latin *canticulum*, diminutive of *canticum* song.

cantilever /'kantɪliːvə(r)/ ▻ *noun* **1** a beam or other support that projects from a wall to support a balcony, staircase, etc. **2** *engineering* a beam that is securely fixed at one end and hangs freely at the other, although it may be supported at some point along its length. ⓘ 17c: perhaps from CANT[2] + LEVER.

cantilever bridge ▻ *noun* a fixed bridge consisting of two outer spans that project towards one another and support a suspended central span, eg the Forth Bridge in Scotland.

canto /'kantoʊ/ ▻ *noun* (***cantos***) a section of a long poem. ⓘ 16c: Italian, meaning 'song', from Latin *canere* to sing.

canton /'kantɒn, kan'tɒn/ ▻ *noun* a division of a country, especially one of the separately governed regions of Switzerland. ▻ *verb* (***cantoned, cantoning***) **1** to divide into cantons. **2** /kən'tuːn/ *military* to provide (soldiers) with quarters. ⓘ 16c: French, from Italian *cantone*, from *canto* corner.

Cantonese /kantə'niːz/ ▻ *adj* belonging to or relating to Canton, an area in S China, its inhabitants, or their dialect of Chinese. ▻ *noun* (*plural* ***Cantonese***) **1** a citizen or inhabitant of, or person born in, Canton. **2** the dialect of Chinese spoken in Canton.

cantonment /kan'tɒnmənt, kən'tuːn-/ ▻ *noun, military* **1** *historical* a permanent military station in India. **2** the temporary quarters of an army on manoeuvres. **3** the winter quarters of an army.

cantor /'kantɔː(r)/ ▻ *noun* **1** *Judaism* in a synagogue service: a man who chants the liturgy and leads the congregation in prayer. **2** *Christianity* in a church service: someone who leads the choir. ⓘ 16c: Latin, meaning 'singer', from *canere* to sing.

canvas /'kanvəs/ ▻ *noun* (***canvases***) **1** a thick heavy coarse cloth, made from hemp or flax, used to make sails, tents, etc and for painting pictures on. **2 a** a painting done on a piece of canvas; **b** a piece of canvas prepared for painting. **3** the sails of a ship. **4** (**the canvas**) the floor of a boxing or wrestling ring, made from canvas. **5** *rowing* either of the covered end-sections of a rowing boat. ● **under canvas 1** in tents. **2** *naut* with sails spread. ⓘ 14c: from French *canevas*, from Latin *cannabis* hemp.

canvas, canvass

These words are often confused with each other.

canvass /'kanvəs/ ▻ *verb* (***canvassed, canvassing***) **1** *tr & intr* to ask for votes or support from someone. **2** to find out the opinions of, (voters, etc). **3** to discuss or examine (a question) in detail. ▻ *noun* (***canvasses***) a solicitation of information, votes, opinions, etc. ● **canvasser** *noun*. ⓘ 16c: from CANVAS in an obsolete sense 'to toss in a canvas sheet, eg as a punishment', thus 'to criticize severely'.

canyon /'kanjən/ ▻ *noun* a deep gorge or ravine with steep sides, usually cut into the bedrock of arid or semi-arid regions by the action of a stream or river. ⓘ 19c: from Spanish *cañón*, from *caña* tube or hollow, from Latin *canna* reed or pipe.

CAP ▻ *abbreviation* Common Agricultural Policy.

cap ▻ *noun* **1** any of various types of hat, eg with a flat or rounded crown and a peak. **2** a small hat often worn as an indication of occupation, rank, etc. **3** a lid, cover or top, eg for a bottle or pen. **4** (*also* **percussion cap**) a little metal or paper case containing a small amount of gunpowder that explodes when struck, used eg to make a noise in toy guns. **5** a protective or cosmetic covering fitted over a damaged or decayed tooth. **6** *also in compounds* a covering or top layer □ *icecap*. **7** the top or top part. **8 a** someone chosen for a team representing a country, etc; **b** the fact of being chosen for such a team. **9** (**the cap** or **Dutch cap**) a contraceptive device used by a woman, consisting of a rubber cover that fits over the CERVIX (sense 1) and prevents the male sperm entering. Also called **diaphragm**. ▻ *verb* (***capped, capping***) **1** to put a cap on or cover the top or end of something, with a cap. **2** to be or form the top of. **3** to choose someone for a national team. **4** to do better than, improve on or outdo someone or something □ *cap someone's achievement*. **5** to set an upper limit to (a tax), or to the tax-gathering powers of (a local authority). See also RATE-CAP. ● **cap in hand** humbly. ● **if the cap fits, wear it** *colloq* you can take the general criticism, etc personally if you think it applies to you. ● **set one's cap at someone** *colloq* said of a woman: to make obvious efforts to attract a particular man. ● **to cap it all** *colloq* as a final blow; to make matters worse. ⓘ Anglo-Saxon *cæppe*: from Latin *cappa* hooded cloak.

cap. ▻ *abbreviation* **1** capacity. **2** capital. **3** capital letter.

capability /keɪpə'bɪlɪtɪ/ ▻ *noun* (***capabilities***) **1** ability or efficiency. **2** a power or ability, often one that has not yet been made full use of □ *The USA has a strong nuclear capability*.

capable /'keɪpəbəl/ ▻ *adj* **1** clever; able; efficient. **2** (**capable of something**) **a** having the ability to do it; **b** having the disposition or temperament to do it □ *She was capable of plagiarism*. ● **capableness** *noun*. ● **capably** *adverb*. ⓘ 16c: French, from Latin *capabilis*, from *capere* to take.

capacious /kə'peɪʃəs/ ▻ *adj, formal* having plenty of room for holding things; roomy. ● **capaciously** *adverb*. ● **capaciousness** *noun*. ⓘ 17c: from Latin *capere* to take.

capacitance /kə'pasɪtəns/ ▻ *noun, elec* (SI unit FARAD) the ability of the conductors in a capacitor to store electric charge.

capacitor /kə'pasɪtə(r)/ ▻ *noun, elec* a device consisting of two conducting surfaces separated by a dielectric material, eg waxed paper, that can store energy in the form of electric charge.

capacity /kə'pasɪtɪ/ ▻ *noun* (***capacities***) **1 a** the amount that something can hold **b** *as adj* □ *a capacity crowd*. **2** the amount that a factory, etc can produce. **3** (**capacity for something**) the ability or power to achieve it □ *capacity for change*. **4** function; role. **5** mental ability or talent □ *Jim's capacity for maths was not enough to pass the exam*. **6** legal competence. ⓘ 15c: from French *capacité*, from Latin *capax* roomy.

caparison /kə'parɪsən/ ▻ *noun* **1** *historical* a decorative covering, harness, etc for a horse. **2** *formal* a fine set of clothes. ▻ *verb* (***caparisoned, caparisoning***) **1** to put a caparison on (especially a horse). **2** *formal, facetious* to dress up. ⓘ 16c: from French *caparasson*, from Spanish *caparazón* saddle cloth.

cape[1] /keɪp/ ▻ *noun* **1** a short cloak. **2** an extra layer of cloth attached to the shoulders of a coat, etc. ⓘ 16c: French, from Latin *cappa* hooded cloak.

cape[2] /keɪp/ ▻ *noun* a part of the coast that projects into the sea. ⓘ 14c: from French *cap*, ultimately from Latin *caput* head.

the Cape ▻ *noun* **1** the Cape of Good Hope, the most southerly part of Africa. **2** Cape Province in South Africa.

Cape Coloured ▻ *noun* in South Africa: relating to the COLOURED population of Cape Province.

caper[1] /'keɪpə(r)/ ▻ *verb* (***capered, capering***) *intr* to jump or dance about playfully. ▻ *noun* **1** a playful jump. **2** *old use* a playful trick or joke. **3** *derog* a scheme, activity, etc, especially something dishonest or illegal. ⓘ 16c: probably abbreviated from CAPRIOLE.

caper[2] /'keɪpə(r)/ ▻ *noun* **1** a small deciduous spiny shrub, native to S Europe, which has oval slightly fleshy leaves and conspicuous white or lilac flowers with a large number of long purple stamens. **2** a young flower bud of this plant, pickled in vinegar and used as a condiment. ⓘ 14c as *capers* (mistaken as a plural): from Latin *capparis*, from Greek *kapparis*.

capercaillie or **capercailzie** /kapə'keɪlɪ/ ▻ *noun* (***capercaillies*** or ***capercailzies***) either of two species of large game bird native to Europe and N Asia, the male of which is dark grey with a blue-green sheen on its neck and breast, and the female of which has speckled brown plumage. ⓘ 16c: from Scottish Gaelic *capull coille* horse of the wood.

capillarity /kapɪ'larɪtɪ/ ▻ *noun* the phenomenon, caused by surface tension effects, whereby a liquid such as water rises up a narrow tube placed in the liquid. Also called **capillary action**. ⓘ 19c: from French *capillarité*, from Latin *capillaris*, from *capillus* hair.

capillary /kə'pɪlərɪ; *US* 'kapɪlərɪ/ ▻ *noun* (***capillaries***) **1** a tube, usually made of glass, which has a very small diameter. **2** in vertebrates: the narrowest type of blood vessel, many of which form a network connecting the arteries with the veins. ▻ *adj* **1** said of a tube: having a very small diameter. **2** relating to capillarity. **3** hair-like. ⓘ 17c: from Latin *capillaris*, from *capillus* hair.

capita see PER CAPITA

capital[1] /'kapɪtəl/ ▻ *noun* **1** the chief city of a country, usually where the government is based. **2** a capital letter (see *adj* 2 below). **3** the total amount of money or wealth possessed by a person or business, etc, especially when used to produce more wealth. ▻ *adj* **1** principal; chief. **2**

said of a letter of the alphabet: in its large form, as used eg at the beginnings of names and sentences. Also called **upper-case**. **3** said of a crime: punishable by death. **4** *Brit old use, colloq* excellent. ● **make capital out of something** to use a situation or circumstance to one's advantage. ● **with a capital A**, *etc* in a very real or genuine sense □ *poverty with a capital P*. ⓒ 13c meaning 'relating to the head': French, from Latin *capitalis*, from *caput* head.

capital letter

A **capital letter** should be used for:

- the first letter of the first word in a sentence.
- the first letter of proper nouns, such as names of people and places, and words derived from them □ *Anne* □ *Bernard Smith* □ *the Australian cricket team* □ *the Irish Republic* □ *Shakespearian tragedy*.
- the first letter of all important words in titles, eg of people, plays, films and organizations □ *the Prince of Wales* □ *Admiral of the Fleet Lord Brown* □ *Cat on a Hot Tin Roof* □ *Raiders of the Lost Ark* □ *the Department of Social Services*.

Note that when an unimportant word is the first word in the title of a book, play or film, it must have a capital □ *The Mill on the Floss* □ *A Man for All Seasons* □ *In the Heat of the Night*.

- the first letter of brand names □ *a Milky Way* □ *a red Jaguar* □ *a new Hoover*.

capital² /ˈkapɪtəl/ ▻ *noun, archit* the slab of stone, etc, usually ornamentally carved, that forms the top section of a column or pillar. ⓒ 13c: from Latin *capitellum*, diminutive of *caput* head.

capital assets ▻ *plural noun* the things that a person or company owns which could be sold to raise capital.

capital expenditure ▻ *noun* the money that a company, etc uses to buy equipment, buildings, etc.

capital gains ▻ *plural noun* profits obtained from selling assets.

capital gains tax ▻ *noun, commerce* (abbreviation **CGT**) in the UK: a tax on the profit or gain obtained by selling or exchanging certain kinds of assets, eg machinery, land, shares, works of art, etc.

capital-intensive ▻ *adj* said of an industry, enterprise, etc: requiring a large amount of capital to keep it going. Compare LABOUR-INTENSIVE.

capitalism ▻ *noun* an economic system based on private, rather than state, ownership of businesses, factories, transport services, etc, with free competition and profit-making.

capitalist ▻ *noun* **1** someone who believes in capitalism. **2** *derog* a wealthy person, especially one who is obviously making a great deal of personal profit from business, etc. ▻ *adj* **1** believing in capitalism. **2** relating to capitalism. ● **capitalistic** *adj*.

capitalize or **capitalise** /ˈkapɪtəlaɪz/ ▻ *verb* (***capitalized, capitalizing***) **1** to write with a capital letter or in capital letters. **2** to sell (property, etc) in order to raise money. **3** to supply (a business, etc) with needed capital. ● **capitalization** *noun*.

■ **capitalize on something** to exploit (an asset, achievement, etc) to one's advantage.

capitally ▻ *adverb, Brit old use, colloq* in an excellent way.

capital punishment ▻ *noun* punishment of a crime by death.

capital sum ▻ *noun* a sum of money paid all at once, eg to someone insured.

capital transfer tax ▻ *noun* in the UK: a tax on the transference of wealth, payable on gifts of money or property over a certain value, which replaced DEATH DUTY in 1975, and was itself replaced in 1986 by INHERITANCE TAX.

capitation /kapɪˈteɪʃən/ ▻ *noun* a tax of so much paid per person. ⓒ 17c: from Latin *capitatio*, from *caput* head.

capitulate /kəˈpɪtʃʊleɪt/ ▻ *verb* (***capitulated, capitulating***) *intr* **1** to surrender formally, usually on agreed conditions. **2** to give in to argument or persuasion. ● **capitulation** *noun*. 16c, meaning 'to draw up (a document) under headings': from Latin *capitulare* to set out under headings.

capon /ˈkeɪpən, -pɒn/ ▻ *noun* a male chicken that has been castrated, usually by hormonal rather than surgical methods, in order to increase the tenderness of its flesh and fatten it for eating. ⓒ Anglo-Saxon *capun*: from Latin *capo, caponis*.

cappuccino /kapʊˈtʃiːnoʊ/ ▻ *noun* (***cappuccinos***) coffee with frothy hot milk and usually dusted with chocolate powder on top. ⓒ 1940s: Italian, meaning CAPUCHIN, because the colour of the coffee was thought to resemble the colour of these monks' habits.

capriccio /kaˈpriːtʃɪoʊ/ ▻ *noun* (***capricci*** /-ˈpriːtʃiː/ or ***capriccios***) **1** *music* (*also* **caprice**) a piece of music played in a free and lively style. **2** *art* a picture or print depicting a scene or incident that is largely a product of the artist's imagination, although it does contain some real features. ⓒ 17c: Italian, meaning 'sudden start or motion', perhaps shortened from *caporiccio* head with bristling hair.

capriccioso /kapriːtʃɪˈoʊsoʊ/ ▻ *adverb, music* in a free and lively manner.

caprice /kəˈpriːs/ ▻ *noun* **1** a sudden change of mind for no good or obvious reason. **2** a sudden strange wish or desire. **3** the tendency to have caprices. **4** a CAPPRICIO (sense1). ⓒ 17c: French, from Italian *capriccio* a sudden start.

capricious /kəˈprɪʃəs/ ▻ *adj* subject to sudden changes in behaviour, mood or opinion, often for no good reason. ● **capriciously** *adverb*. ● **capriciousness** *noun*.

Capricorn /ˈkaprɪkɔːn/ ▻ *noun* **1** (*also* **Capricornus**) *astron* a large but dim zodiacal constellation lying between Sagittarius and Aquarius. **2** *astrol* **a** the tenth sign of the zodiac; **b** a person born between 22 December and 19 January, under this sign. See table at ZODIAC. See also TROPIC. ⓒ 14c: from Latin *Capricornus*, from *caper* goat + *cornu* horn.

caprine /ˈkapraɪn/ ▻ *adj* belonging or relating to, or characteristic of, a goat. ⓒ 17c: from Latin *caprinus*, from *caper* goat.

caps. ▻ *abbreviation* capital letters.

capsicum /ˈkapsɪkəm/ ▻ *noun* **1** any of various tropical shrubs belonging to the potato family. **2** the red, green or yellow fruit of this plant, which has a hollow seedy interior, and is eaten raw in salads or cooked as a vegetable. See also PEPPER *noun* 2. ⓒ 18c: probably from Latin *capsa* box or case.

capsize /kapˈsaɪz/ ▻ *verb* (***capsized, capsizing***) **1** *intr* usually said of a boat: to tip over completely; to overturn. **2** to cause (a boat) to capsize. ● **capsizable** *adj*. ⓒ 18c.

capstan /ˈkapstən/ ▻ *noun* **1** a cylinder-shaped apparatus that is turned to wind a heavy rope or cable, eg that of a ship's anchor. **2** in a tape recorder: either of the shafts or spindles round which the tape winds. ⓒ 14c: from Provençal *cabestan*, from Latin *capistrum*, from *capere* to take hold of.

capsule /ˈkapsjuːl/ ▻ *noun* **1** a hard or soft soluble case, usually made of gelatine, containing a single dose of a powdered drug to be taken orally. **2** (*also* **space capsule**) a small spacecraft or a compartment within a spacecraft that houses the instruments and crew for the duration of a space flight. **3** *anatomy* a membranous sheath, sac or other structure that surrounds an organ or tissue, eg the capsule that surrounds the lens of the eye or the moving parts of a joint. **4** *bot* in some flowering plants, eg poppy: a dry dehiscent fruit, formed by the fusion of two or more carpels, that splits open to release its many seeds. **5** *biol* the gelatinous envelope of protein or polysaccharide that surrounds and protects certain bacteria. • **capsular** *adj.* ◷ 17c: French, from Latin *capsula*, diminutive of *capsa* box.

capsulize or **capsulise** /ˈkapsjuːlaɪz/ ▷ *verb* (***capsulized***, ***capsulizing***) to present (information) in a concise form.

Capt. ▷ *abbreviation* Captain.

captain /ˈkaptɪn/ ▷ *noun* **1** a leader or chief. **2** the commander of a ship. **3** the commander of a company of troops. **4** a naval officer below a commodore and above a commander in rank. **5** an army officer of the rank below major and above lieutenant. See table at RANK. **6** the chief pilot of a civil aircraft. **7** the leader of a team or side, or chief member of a club. ▷ *verb* (***captained***, ***captaining***) to be captain of something. • **captaincy** *noun* (***captaincies***). • **captainship** *noun.* ◷ 14c: from French *capitain*, from Latin *capitaneus* chief.

caption /ˈkapʃən/ ▷ *noun* **1** the words that accompany a photograph, cartoon, etc to explain it. **2** a heading given to a chapter, article, etc. **3** wording appearing on a television or cinema screen as part of a film or broadcast. ▷ *verb* (***captioned***, ***captioning***) to provide a caption or captions for something. ◷ 18c in sense 2; 14c in sense 'seizure, capture': from Latin *captio* act of seizing, from *capere* to take.

captious /ˈkapʃəs/ ▷ *adj* inclined to criticize and find fault. • **captiously** *adverb.* • **captiousness** *noun.* ◷ 14c: from Latin *captiosus* arguing falsely, from *captio* seizing.

captivate /ˈkaptɪveɪt/ ▷ *verb* (***captivated***, ***captivating***) to delight, charm or fascinate □ *He captivated me with his smile.* • **captivating** *adj.* • **captivatingly** *adverb.* • **captivation** *noun.* ◷ 16c: from Latin *captivare* to take captive.

captive /ˈkaptɪv/ ▷ *noun* a person or animal that has been caught or taken prisoner. ▷ *adj* **1** kept prisoner. **2** held so as to be unable to get away. **3** forced into a certain state or role □ *captive market.* • **captivity** /kapˈtɪvɪtɪ/ *noun* (***captivities***) the condition or period of being captive or imprisoned. ◷ 14c: from Latin *captivus* prisoner, from *captus* taken.

captor /ˈkaptə(r)/ ▷ *noun* someone who takes a person or animal captive. ◷ 17c: Latin.

capture /ˈkaptʃə(r)/ ▷ *verb* (***captured***, ***capturing***) **1** to catch; to take prisoner; to gain control of someone or something. **2** in a game, eg chess: to gain possession or control of (a piece, etc). **3** to succeed in recording (a subtle quality, etc) □ *The camera captured her smile.* ▷ *noun* **1** the capturing of someone or something. **2** the person or thing captured. **3** *physics* the process whereby a neutron is absorbed by a nucleus, and the excess energy produced is released as gamma radiation. • **capturer** *noun.* ◷ 16c: French, from Latin *captura*, from *capere* to take .

Capuchin /ˈkapjʊtʃɪn/ **1** *noun* a Franciscan order of monks, which stresses austerity and poverty. **2** a friar belonging to such an order. ▷ *adj* relating to this order. ◷ 16c: French, from Italian *cappuccio* hood.

capuchin /ˈkapjʊtʃɪn/ ▷ *noun* an acrobatic intelligent New World monkey with a PREHENSILE tail, formerly a popular pet for street musicians. ◷ 18c: French, from Italian *cappuccio* hood (because its thick hair resembles a monk's cowl).

capybara /kapɪˈbɑːrə/ ▷ *noun* (***capybaras***) the largest living rodent, native to Central and S America, which has a deep square snout, partially webbed toes and no tail. ◷ 18c: Portuguese, from Tupí.

car ▷ *noun* **1** a self-propelled four-wheeled road vehicle designed to carry passengers and powered by an internal combustion engine. Also called **motor car, automobile**. **2** *N Amer, often in compounds* a railway carriage or van □ *dining car.* **3** a passenger compartment in eg a balloon, airship, lift or cable railway. ◷ 14c: from French *carre*, from Latin *carra*, *carrum* two-wheeled cart.

carafe /kəˈraf/ ▷ *noun* a wide-necked bottle or flask for wine, etc, for use on the table. ◷ 18c: French, from Spanish *garrafa*, probably from Arabic *gharrafah* drinking vessel.

carambola /karəmˈboʊlə/ ▷ *noun* **1** a SE Asian tree. **2** the fruit of this tree, known as the **star fruit**. ◷ 16c: Portuguese, from Marathi (an Indian language) *karambal*.

caramel /ˈkarəməl, -mɛl/ ▷ *noun* **1** a brown substance with a characteristic flavour produced by heating sugar solution until it darkens, used as a food colouring and flavouring. **2** a toffee-like sweet made from sugar, animal fat and milk or cream. **3** a pale yellowish brown colour. ▷ *adj* **1** caramel-coloured. **2** made from caramel. ◷ 18c: French, from Spanish *caramelo*.

caramelize or **caramelise** /karəməlaɪz/ ▷ *verb* (***caramelized***, ***caramelizing***) **1** to change (sugar) into caramel. **2** *intr* to turn into caramel. • **caramelization** *noun.*

carapace /ˈkarəpeɪs/ ▷ *noun* **1** *zool* the hard thick shell, resembling a shield, that covers the upper part of the body of some tortoises, turtles and CRUSTACEANS. **2** a layer of heat-resistant tiles covering a spacecraft. ◷ 19c: French, from Spanish *carapacho*.

carat /ˈkarət/ ▷ *noun* **1** a unit of mass, equal to 0.2g, used to measure the mass of gemstones, especially diamonds. **2** a unit used to express the purity of gold in an alloy with another metal (usually copper), equal to the number of parts of gold in 24 parts of the alloy. ◷ 16c: French, from Arabic *qirat* 4-grain weight, from Greek *keration* carob bean, 3.3-grain weight.

caravan /ˈkarəvan/ ▷ *noun* **1** a large vehicle fitted for living in, designed for towing by a motor vehicle. **2** a large covered van, formerly pulled by horses, used as a travelling home by gypsies, etc. **3** *historical* a group of travellers, merchants, etc, usually with camels, crossing the desert as a large company for safety. ▷ *verb* (***caravanned***, ***caravanning***) *intr* to go travelling with or stay in a caravan. • **caravanning** *noun* holidaying in or travelling with a caravan. ◷ 16c: from Persian *karwan*.

caravanette /karəvəˈnɛt/ ▷ *noun* a motor vehicle with a compartment equipped for living in while touring. ◷ 1960s.

caravanserai or (*US*) **caravansery** /karəˈvansəraɪ/ ▷ *noun* (***caravanserais*** or ***caravanseries***) in some Eastern countries: an inn with a central courtyard for receiving caravans crossing the desert, etc. ◷ 16c: from Persian *karwansarai* caravan inn.

caravan site ▷ *noun* a place where caravans may be parked, permanently or temporarily, usually with washing facilities, toilets, a shop, etc.

caravel /ˈkarəvɛl/ or **carvel** /ˈkɑːvəl/ ▷ *noun* a light sailing vessel, usually with three masts, used for trade in the Mediterranean in the 14c–17c. ◷ 16c: from Portuguese *caravela*, diminutive of *caravo* ship, ultimately from Greek *karabos* crab.

caraway /ˈkarəweɪ/ ▷ *noun* **1** an annual plant, native to Europe and Asia, which has finely divided leaves and clusters of small white flowers with deeply notched petals. **2** caraway seed. ◷ 14c: from Arabic *karawiya*, from Greek *karon*.

caraway seed ▷ *noun* the dried ripe fruit of the caraway plant which contains an aromatic oil and is widely used as a spice for flavouring bread, cakes, cheese, etc.

carb. ▷ *abbreviation, colloq* a CARBURETTOR.

carbide /ˈkɑːbaɪd/ ▷ *noun, chem* any chemical compound consisting of carbon and another element (except for hydrogen), usually a metallic one.

carbine /ˈkɑːbaɪn/ ▷ *noun* a short light rifle. ◷ 17c: from French *carabine*, from *carabin* lightly-armed cavalryman.

carbohydrate /kɑːbə'haɪdreɪt/ ▷ *noun* any of a group of organic compounds, present in the cells of all living organisms, which consist of carbon, hydrogen and oxygen and are formed in green plants during photosynthesis. ◷ 19c: CARBON + HYDRATE.

carbolic acid see PHENOL

carbolic soap ▷ *noun* soap containing carbolic acid.

carbon /'kɑːbən/ ▷ *noun* **1** (symbol **C**, atomic number 6) a non-metallic element that occurs in various pure AMORPHOUS (sense 2) forms, such as coal, coke and charcoal, and as two crystalline ALLOTROPEs, namely DIAMOND and GRAPHITE. **2** a sheet of carbon paper. **3** a carbon copy. ◷ 18c: from French *carbone*, from Latin *carbo* charcoal.

carbonaceous /kɑːbə'neɪʃəs/ ▷ *adj* containing large amounts of, or resembling, carbon.

carbonate /kɑːbə'neɪt/ ▷ *noun chem* any salt of carbonic acid containing the CO_3^{2-} ion. ▷ *verb* (***carbonated, carbonating***) **1** to combine or treat (eg a liquid) with carbon dioxide, to make it fizzy. **2** *tr & intr* to turn into a carbonate. ▷ *adj* relating to such a compound. • **carbonated** *adj* said of a drink: made fizzy by being filled with carbon dioxide. • **carbonation** *noun*.

carbon black ▷ *noun, chem* a form of finely divided carbon, produced by partial combustion of natural gas or petroleum oil, which is used in pigments and printer's ink.

carbon copy ▷ *noun* **1** an exact duplicate copy of writing, typed matter, etc made using carbon paper. **2** *colloq* a person or thing that looks exactly like someone or something else.

carbon cycle ▷ *noun, chem* a series of reactions in which carbon, either as the free element or in the form of one of its compounds, is exchanged between living organisms and their non-living environment.

carbon dating ▷ *noun, archaeol* a scientific method of estimating the age of archaeological specimens, based on measurements of the radioactive ISOTOPE carbon-14, which is present in all living organisms, but on their death gradually decays and is not replaced.

carbon dioxide ▷ *noun, chem* (formula $\mathbf{CO_2}$) a colourless odourless tasteless gas, present in the atmosphere and formed during respiration. It is chemically unreactive and does not burn or support the combustion of other materials, and is used in fire-extinguishers.

carbon fibre ▷ *noun* a high-strength material prepared by heating textile fibres in the absence of air, used in fibre-reinforced plastics to make components of aeroplanes and rockets, and sports equipment, eg racquets and skis.

carbonic /kɑː'bɒnɪk/ ▷ *adj* said of a compound: containing carbon, especially carbon with a valency of four.

carbonic acid ▷ *noun* a weak acid formed by dissolving carbon dioxide in water.

carboniferous /kɑːbə'nɪfərəs/ ▷ *adj* **1** producing carbon or coal. **2** (**Carboniferous**) *geol* relating to the fifth geological period of the Palaeozoic era, characterized by extensive swampy forests which subsequently formed coal deposits. See table at GEOLOGICAL TIME SCALE. **3** *geol* relating to rocks formed during this period. ▷ *noun, geol* the Carboniferous period. ◷ 18c.

carbonization or **carbonisation** /kɑːbənaɪ'zeɪʃən/ ▷ *noun* the action or process of carbonizing.

carbonize or **carbonise** /'kɑːbənaɪz/ ▷ *verb* (***carbonized, carbonizing***) **1** *tr & intr* to convert or reduce (a substance containing carbon) into carbon, either by heating or by natural methods such as fossilization. **2** to coat (a substance) with a layer of carbon.

carbon monoxide ▷ *noun, chem* (formula **CO**) a poisonous colourless odourless gas formed by the incomplete combustion of carbon, eg in car-exhaust gases.

carbonnade /kɑːbə'nɑːd, -neɪd/ ▷ *noun* a beef stew made with beer. ◷ 19c: French.

carbon paper ▷ *noun* paper coated on one side with an ink-like substance containing carbon, which is placed between two or more sheets of paper so that a copy of what is produced on the top sheet is made on the lower sheets.

carbon steel ▷ *noun, engineering* steel containing carbon, with different properties according to the quantity of carbon used.

carbon tetrachloride see also TETRACHLOROMETHANE

carbonyl group /'kɑːbənɪl —/ ▷ *noun, chem* in certain organic chemical compounds, eg aldehydes and ketones: the C═O group, consisting of a carbon atom joined to an oxygen atom by a double bond.

car boot sale and **boot sale** ▷ *noun* a sale, usually in the open air, where people sell second-hand goods from their car boots or from stalls.

carborundum /kɑːbə'rʌndəm/ ▷ *noun, trademark, chem* an extremely hard black crystalline substance, consisting of silicon carbide, that is used as an abrasive and semiconductor. ◷ 19c: see CARBON and CORUNDUM.

carboxyl group /kɑː'bɒksɪl —/ ▷ *noun, chem* in certain organic chemical compounds: the -COOH group, characteristic of carboxylic acids.

carboxylic acid /kɑːbɒk'sɪlɪk —/ ▷ *noun, chem* an organic acid containing a carboxyl group bonded to hydrogen or a hydrocarbon, eg methanoic acid.

carboy /'kɑːbɔɪ/ ▷ *noun* (***carboys***) a large glass or plastic bottle, usually protected by a basketwork casing, used for storing or transporting corrosive liquids. ◷ 18c: from Persian *qaraba* glass flagon.

carbuncle /'kɑːbʌŋkəl/ ▷ *noun* **1** a cluster of boils on the skin, usually caused by bacterial infection, and characterized by the presence of several drainage ducts. **2** a rounded red gemstone, especially a garnet in uncut form. ◷ 13c: from Latin *carbunculus*, diminutive of *carbo* coal.

carburettor /kɑːbə'rɛtə(r)/ ▷ *noun* the part of an internal combustion engine in which the liquid fuel and air are mixed in the correct proportions and vaporized before being sucked into the cylinders. ◷ 19c: from obsolete *carburet* carbide.

carcass or **carcase** /'kɑːkəs/ ▷ *noun* (***carcasses*** or ***carcases***) **1** the dead body of an animal. **2** *colloq* the body of a living person. **3** the rotting remains of something, eg a ship. ◷ 14c: from French *carcasse*.

carcinogen /kɑː'sɪnədʒən, 'kɑː-/ ▷ *noun, pathol* any substance capable of causing cancer in a living tissue that is exposed to it, eg ionizing radiation, many chemical compounds, some viruses. • **carcinogenic** /kɑːsɪnə'dʒənɪk/ *adj*. ◷ 19c: from Greek *karkinos* cancer + -GEN1.

carcinogenesis /kɑːsɪnə'dʒɛnɪsɪs/ ▷ *noun, pathol* the production of cancerous cells in living tissue.

carcinoma /kɑːsɪ'noʊmə/ ▷ *noun* (***carcinomas***) *pathol* any cancer that occurs in the skin or in the tissue that lines the internal organs of the body, and which may then spread to other parts of the body via the bloodstream. ◷ 18c: Latin, from Greek *karkinos* cancer.

card[1] ▷ *noun* **1** a kind of thick, stiff paper or thin cardboard. **2** (*also* **playing card**) a rectangular piece of card bearing a design, usually one of a set, used eg for playing games, fortune-telling, etc. **3** a small rectangular piece of card or plastic, showing eg one's identity, job, membership of an organization, etc. **4** a small rectangular piece of stiff plastic issued by a bank, etc to a customer, used eg instead of cash or a cheque when making payments, as a guarantee for a cheque, for operating a cash machine, etc. See also CREDIT CARD, DEBIT CARD. **5** *computing* a piece of card on which information is stored in the form of punched holes or magnetic codes. **6** a piece of card, usually folded double and bearing a design and message, sent to someone on a special occasion □ *Christmas card.* **7** a postcard. **8** *old use, colloq* an amusing person. **9** *horse-racing* a RACECARD. **10** (**cards**) games played with playing cards. **11** (**cards**) an employee's personal documents held by their employer. ▻ *verb* (***carded, carding***) **1** to enter in card index. **2** *sport, especially football* (**be carded**) to be shown a YELLOW CARD or RED CARD by the referee, resulting in either a booking or dismissal from the field. ● **the cards are stacked against someone** or **something** *colloq* circumstances do not favour them. ● **get one's cards** *colloq* to be dismissed from one's job. ● **have a card up one's sleeve** in an argument or contest: to have something prepared, which can be used to one's advantage, but which has not yet been revealed to one's opponents. ● **hold all the cards** *colloq* to have the stronger or strongest position of opposing parties; to have all the advantages. ● **lay** or **put one's cards on the table** *colloq* to announce one's intentions, reveal one's thoughts, etc openly. ● **on the cards** *colloq* likely to happen. ● **play one's best, strongest** or **trump card** *colloq* to make use of one's strongest advantage. ● **play one's cards close to one's chest** to be secretive about one's intentions. ● **play one's cards right** *colloq* to make good use of one's opportunities and advantages. ⓘ 15c: from French *carte*, from Latin *charta*, from Greek *chartes* papyrus leaf.

card² ▻ *noun* a comb-like device with sharp teeth for removing knots and tangles from sheep's wool, etc before spinning, or for pulling across the surface of cloth to make it fluffy. ▻ *verb* (***carded, carding***) to treat (wool, fabric) with a card. ● **carding** *noun.* ⓘ 15c: from French *carde* teasel head, from Latin *carduus* thistle.

cardamom or **cardamum** /ˈkɑːdəməm/ or **cardamon** /ˈkɑːdəmən/ ▻ *noun* **1** a tropical perennial shrub, native to India and Sri Lanka, which has large hairy leaves and clusters of small white flowers with blue and yellow markings on the petals. **2** the dried aromatic seeds of this plant, which are used as a spice, especially in curry powder or paste. ⓘ 15c: from Greek *kardamomum*, from *kardamon* cress + *amomon* a spice.

cardboard ▻ *noun* a stiff material manufactured from pulped waste paper, used for making boxes, card, etc. ▻ *adj, derog* not realistic or life-like. ● **cardboardy** *adj.* ⓘ 19c.

cardboard city ▻ *noun, informal* an area in large cities where homeless people live or sleep, often using cardboard boxes, etc, as shelter.

card-carrying ▻ *adj* **1** officially registered as a member of a political party, etc and openly supporting it. **2** *colloq* strongly supporting.

cardiac /ˈkɑːdɪak/ ▻ *adj* **1** relating to or affecting the heart. **2** relating to the upper part of the stomach, in the region of the junction between the stomach and the oesophagus. ▻ *noun* someone suffering from heart disease. ⓘ 17c: from Greek *kardia* heart.

cardiac arrest ▻ *noun, pathol* the stopping of the heartbeat and therefore the pumping action of the heart, which may cause brain damage and death unless emergency treatment is given.

cardiac massage ▻ *noun* rhythmic stimulation of the heart, either by exerting manual pressure on the chest or by massaging the heart directly, in order to restart or maintain blood circulation after heart failure.

cardiac muscle ▻ *noun, anatomy* specialized muscle, found only in the walls of the heart, which consists of long fibres with unique physiological properties that enable them to expand and contract indefinitely.

cardigan /ˈkɑːdɪgən/ ▻ *noun* a long-sleeved knitted jacket that fastens down the front. ⓘ 19c: named after the 7th Earl of Cardigan (1797–1868).

cardinal /ˈkɑːdɪnəl/ ▻ *noun* **1** *RC Church* one of a group of leading clergy, who elect and advise the pope. **2** a CARDINAL NUMBER. See also ORDINAL 3. **3** either of two species of N American songbird, so called because the plumage of the male is bright red. **4** (*also* **cardinal red**) a bright red colour. ▻ *adj* highly important; principal. ⓘ 12c: from Latin *cardinalis* relating to a hinge, from *cardo* hinge.

cardinalate /ˈkɑːdɪnəleɪt/ and **cardinalship** ▻ *noun* **1** the rank or office of a cardinal. **2** the cardinals as a collective body.

cardinal number ▻ *noun* one of a series of numbers expressing quantity (eg 1, 2, 3, ...). Compare ORDINAL NUMBER.

cardinal point ▻ *noun* any of the four main points of the compass: north, south, east and west.

cardinal virtue ▻ *noun* any of the most important virtues, usually listed as justice, prudence, temperance, fortitude, faith, hope and charity.

cardinal vowels ▻ *noun, phonetics* a set of reference points for identifying the vowel sounds of a language based on the movements of the tongue and jaws, and separated by roughly regular acoustic intervals from each other. ⓘ 20c: devised by the British phonetician Daniel Jones (1881–1967).

carding see under CARD²

cardio- /ˈkɑːdɪoʊ/ or (before a vowel) **cardi-** ▻ *combining form, denoting* heart. ⓘ From Greek *kardia* heart.

cardiogram ▻ *noun* short for ELECTROCARDIOGRAM.

cardiograph ▻ *noun* short for ELECTROCARDIOGRAPH.

cardiographer /kɑːdɪˈɒgrəfə(r)/ ▻ *noun* someone who operates an ELECTROCARDIOGRAPH.

cardiography /kɑːdɪˈɒgrəfɪ/ ▻ *noun* the branch of medicine concerned with the recording of the movements of the heart.

cardiology /kɑːdɪˈɒlədʒɪ/ ▻ *noun* the branch of medicine concerned with the study of the structure, function and diseases of the heart. ● **cardiologist** *noun.* ⓘ 19c.

cardiopulmonary ▻ *adj, anatomy* relating to the heart and lungs.

cardiopulmonary resuscitation ▻ *noun* (abbreviation **CPR**) an emergency life-saving technique, involving heart massage alternating with the kiss of life. ⓘ 20c.

cardiovascular /kɑːdɪoʊˈvaskjʊlə(r)/ ▻ *adj, anatomy* relating to the heart and blood vessels. ⓘ 19c.

cardiovascular system see CIRCULATORY SYSTEM

cardphone ▻ *noun* a payphone operated with a phonecard. ⓘ 20c.

card-sharp or **card-sharper** ▻ *noun, derog* someone who makes a business out of cheating at card games played for money.

card table ▻ *noun* a small folding table, usually covered with green cloth, for playing card games on.

card vote ▻ *noun, Brit* a vote by representatives of bodies, with each representative's vote counting in proportion to the number of members that they represent.

care /kɛə(r)/ ▻ *noun* **1** attention and thoroughness. **2** caution; gentleness; regard for safety. **3** the activity of looking after someone or something, or the state of being looked after. **4** worry or anxiety. **5** a cause for worry; a responsibility. ▻ *verb* (***cared, caring***) *intr* **1** to mind or be upset by something, or the possibility of something. **2** (*usually* **care about** or **for someone** or **something**) to concern oneself about them or be interested in them. **3** to wish or be willing □ *Would you care to come?* ● **as if I**, *etc* **care** or **cared** *colloq* it doesn't matter to me, etc. ● **care of** (abbreviation **c/o**) written on letters, etc addressed to a person at someone else's address. ● **for all I**, *etc* **care** *colloq* without upsetting me, etc in the least. ● **have a care!** *old use* be more careful, considerate, etc. ● **I**, *etc* **couldn't care less** *colloq* it doesn't matter to me, etc in the least. ● **in care** being looked after by a local authority, etc, or in a hospital, etc, instead of at home. ● **take care** to be cautious, watchful or thorough. ● **take care of someone** or **something** **1** to look after them. **2** to attend to or organize them. ⓒ Anglo-Saxon *caru* anxiety or sorrow.

■ **care for someone** or **something** **1** to look after them. **2** to be fond of or love them. **3** to like or approve of them □ *I don't care for mushrooms.* **4** to have a wish or desire for them □ *Would you care for a drink?*

careen /kə'riːn/ ▻ *verb* (***careened, careening***) **1** to turn (a boat) over on its side for cleaning, etc. **2** *intr* said of a ship: to lean over to one side; to heel over. **3** *intr, N Amer, especially US* said of a vehicle, etc: to swerve or lurch violently from side to side. ⓒ 17c: ultimately from Latin *carina* keel.

career /kə'rɪə(r)/ ▻ *noun* **1** one's professional life; one's progress in one's job. **2** a job, occupation or profession. **3** one's progress through life generally. **4** a swift or headlong course. ▻ *verb* (***careered, careering***) *intr* to rush in an uncontrolled or headlong way. ⓒ 16c: from French *carrière* racecourse, from Latin *carriara* carriage road, from *carrus* wagon.

careerism ▻ *noun* concern with the advancement of one's career.

careerist ▻ *noun, sometimes derog* someone who is chiefly interested in the advancement or promotion of their career.

careers adviser and **careers officer** ▻ *noun* in schools, etc: someone whose job is to help young people choose a suitable career.

carefree ▻ *adj* having few worries; cheerful.

careful ▻ *adj* **1** giving or showing care and attention; thorough. **2** gentle; watchful or mindful; cautious. **3** taking care to avoid harm or damage. **4** (*usually* **careful of something**) protective of it. ● **carefully** *adverb*. ● **carefulness** *noun*.

careless ▻ *adj* **1** not careful or thorough enough; inattentive. **2** lacking or showing a lack of a sense of responsibility. **3** effortless □ *careless charm*. ● **carelessly** *adverb*. ● **carelessness** *noun*.

carer ▻ *noun* the person who has the responsibility for looking after an ill, disabled or otherwise dependent person.

caress /kə'rɛs/ ▻ *verb* (***caresses, caressed, caressing***) to touch or stroke gently and lovingly. ▻ *noun* (***caresses***) a gentle loving touch; a gentle embrace. ⓒ 17c: from French *caresse*, from Italian *carezza*, from Latin *carus* dear.

caret /'karət/ ▻ *noun* a mark (^) made on written or printed material to show where a missing word, letter, etc should be inserted. ⓒ 18c: Latin, meaning 'there is missing', from *carere* to be in need of.

caretaker ▻ *noun* **1** a person whose job is to look after a house or a public building, eg a school, especially at times when the building would otherwise be unoccupied. **2** *as adj* temporary; stopgap □ *caretaker president*.

caretaker speech see MOTHERESE

careworn ▻ *adj* worn out with or marked by worry and anxiety.

carfuffle, **kefuffle** or **kerfuffle** /kə'fʌfəl/ ▻ *noun, colloq* a commotion; agitation. ⓒ From Gaelic *car-* + Scots *fuffle* to disorder.

cargo /'kɑːgoʊ/ ▻ *noun* (***cargoes***) **1** the goods carried by a ship, aircraft or other vehicle. **2** any load. ⓒ 17c: Spanish, meaning 'burden'.

Carib ▻ *noun* (***Caribs*** or ***Carib***) **1** a group of Native American peoples of the Southern West Indies or Central and S America. **2** an individual belonging to this group of peoples. **3** their language. ▻ *adj* belonging or relating to this group or their langauge.

Caribbean /karɪ'bɪən, kə'rɪbɪən/ ▻ *adj* belonging or relating to **the Caribbean**, the part of the Atlantic and its islands between the West Indies and Central and S America, or its inhabitants. ▻ *noun* a citizen or inhabitant of, or person born in, the Caribbean.

caribou /'karɪbuː, karɪ'buː/ ▻ *noun* (***caribous*** /-buːz/ or ***caribou***) a large deer belonging to the same species as the reindeer, but which lives in vast herds in N America and Siberia. ⓒ 17c: Canadian French, from a Native American language.

caricature /'karɪkətʃʊə(r), karɪkə'tʃʊə(r)/ ▻ *noun* **1** a representation, especially a drawing, of someone with their most noticeable and distinctive features exaggerated for comic effect. **2** a ridiculously poor attempt at something. ▻ *verb* (***caricatured, caricaturing***) to make or give a caricature of someone. ● **caricaturist** *noun*. ⓒ 18c: French, from Italian *caricatura*, from *caricare* to distort.

CARICOM /'karɪkɒm/ ▻ *abbreviation* Caribbean Community.

caries /'kɛəriːz/ ▻ *noun* (*plural* ***caries***) the progressive decomposition and decay of a tooth or bone, accompanied by softening and discoloration. ⓒ 17c: Latin, meaning 'decay'.

carillon /kə'rɪljən, 'karɪljən/ ▻ *noun* **1** a set of bells hung usually in a tower and played mechanically or by means of a keyboard. **2** a tune played on such bells. **3** an organ stop that imitates a peal of bells. ⓒ 18c: French, from Latin *quaternion* probably meaning 'a set of four bells'.

caring /'kɛərɪŋ/ ▻ *adj* **1** showing concern for others; sympathetic and helpful. **2** professionally concerned with social, medical, etc welfare.

caring profession ▻ *noun* a job that involves looking after people's social or medical welfare.

carjacking ▻ *noun* the practice of hijacking a car with its driver and passengers. ⓒ 20c: from CAR + HIJACK.

Carmelite /'kɑːməlaɪt/ ▻ *noun* **1** a member of a Roman Catholic monastic order founded in the 12c. **2** a member of a contemplative order of nuns founded in the 15c. ▻ *adj* relating or belonging to these orders. ⓒ 15c: French, from Latin *Carmelita* inhabitant of Mount Carmel, where the order was founded.

carmine /'kɑːmaɪn, -mɪn/ ▻ *noun* **1** a deep red colour; crimson. **2** a red colouring substance obtained from the COCHINEAL insect. ▻ *adj* carmine-coloured. ⓒ 18c: from French *carmin*, from Latin *carminus*, from Arabic *qirmiz* KERMES.

carnage /'kɑːnɪdʒ/ ▻ *noun* great slaughter. ⓒ 16c: French, from Latin *carnaticum* payment in meat.

carnal /'kɑːnəl/ ▻ *adj* **1** belonging to the body or the flesh, as opposed to the spirit or intellect. **2** sexual. ● **carnality** *noun*. ● **carnally** *adverb*. ⓒ 15c: from Latin *caro, carnis* flesh.

carnassial tooth /kɑː'nasɪəl —/ ▻ *noun, anatomy* in carnivorous animals: a molar or premolar tooth that is adapted for tearing flesh. ⓒ 19c: from French *carnassier* flesh-eating, from Latin *caro, carnis* flesh.

carnation /kɑː'neɪʃən/ ▻ *noun* **1** a perennial plant, native to the Mediterranean region, with tufted leaves and strongly scented pink, white, red, yellow, orange or multicoloured flowers with spreading slightly frilled petals. **2** the flower of this plant. **3** a deep pink colour.

▷ *adj* carnation-coloured. ◷ 16c: from Latin *carnatio* flesh colour, from *caro* flesh.

carnauba /kɑːnɑːˈuːbə, -ˈnaʊbə/ ▷ *noun* (***carnaubas***) **1** (*also* **wax palm**) a Brazilian palm tree. **2** (*also* **carnauba wax**) the yellowish wax secreted from the young leaves of the tree, used in the manufacture of polishes, candles, etc. ◷ 19c: Brazilian Portuguese, from Tupí *karanaiwa*.

carnelian see CORNELIAN

carnival /ˈkɑːnɪvəl/ ▷ *noun* **1** a period of public festivity with eg street processions, colourful costumes, singing and dancing. **2** a circus or fair. **3** the period just before Lent, marked by revelry and feasting. ◷ 16c: from Italian *carnevale*, from Latin *carnelevarium*, probably from *caro* flesh + *levare* to remove, the original carnival being Shrove Tuesday, the day before the start of the Lent fast.

carnivore /ˈkɑːnɪvɔː(r)/ ▷ *noun* **1** an animal that feeds mainly on the flesh of other animals. **2** any of a group of mammals whose teeth are specialized for biting and tearing flesh, eg dogs, cats, seals, etc, including some omnivores and herbivores, eg panda. ◷ 19c: French, from Latin *carnivorus* flesh-eating.

carnivorous /kɑːˈnɪvərəs/ ▷ *adj* **1** denoting an animal, especially a mammal, that feeds mainly on the flesh of other vertebrate animals. **2** denoting a plant which traps animals, usually insects and small invertebrates, and secretes enzymes which digest the prey.

carob /ˈkarəb, ˈkarɒb/ ▷ *noun* **1** an evergreen tree, native to the Mediterranean region, which produces large reddish-brown seedpods rich in sugars and gums. Also called **locust tree**. **2** the edible seedpod of this tree, ground and used as a substitute for chocolate and as a food stabilizer, or as a feed for animal livestock. ◷ 16c: from French *carobe*, from Arabic *kharrub*.

carol /ˈkarəl/ ▷ *noun* a religious song, especially one sung at Christmas in honour of Christ's birth. ▷ *verb* (***carolled, carolling***) **1** *intr* to sing carols. **2** to sing joyfully. ◷ 16c in *noun* sense; 13c in obsolete sense 'a ring-dance': from French *carole*.

Carolingian /karəˈlɪndʒɪən/ ▷ *adj* relating or belonging to the dynasty founded by Charlemagne in W Europe, which ruled from 751 until 987. ▷ *noun* a member of such a dynasty.

carom /ˈkarəm/ ▷ *noun* a form of billiards popular in Europe, played on a table without pockets with the object of making CANNONS (see *noun* 3). ◷ 18c: short for *carambole* a cannon in billiards, from Spanish *carambola* the red ball in billiards.

carotene or **carotin** /ˈkarətiːn, -tɪn/ ▷ *noun, biochem* any of a number of reddish-yellow pigments, widely distributed in plants, that are converted to vitamin A in the body. ◷ 19c as *carotin*: German, from Latin *carota* carrot.

carotenoid or **carotinoid** /kəˈrɒtɪnɔɪd/ ▷ *noun, biochem* any of a group of plant pigments that absorb light during PHOTOSYNTHESIS.

carotid /kəˈrɒtɪd/ ▷ *noun* (*also* **carotid artery**) either of the two major arteries that supply blood to the head and neck. ▷ *adj* relating to either of these arteries. ◷ 17c: from Greek *karotides*, from *karos* stupor, because pressure on these arteries causes unconsciousness.

carousal /kəˈraʊzəl/ ▷ *noun* a drinking bout or party; a noisy revel.

carouse /kəˈraʊz/ ▷ *verb* (***caroused, carousing***) *intr* to take part in a noisy drinking party. ▷ *noun* CAROUSAL. ◷ 16c: from German *gar aus* all out, ie completely emptying the glass.

carousel /karəˈsɛl/ ▷ *noun* **1** a revolving belt in an airport, etc onto which luggage is unloaded so that passengers can collect it as it passes by. **2** a revolving case for holding photographic transparencies, for use in a projector. **3** *N Amer* a merry-go-round. ◷ 17c: from French *carrousel*, from Italian *carusello* a joust on horseback.

carp[1] /kɑːp/ ▷ *noun* (***carps*** or ***carp***) **1** a deep-bodied freshwater fish, found mainly in warm shallow waters of slow-flowing rivers and large lakes, which has two pairs of sensory barbels under its mouth. **2** any of various freshwater fishes found worldwide and characterized by soft fins and a sucker-like mouth. ◷ 15c: from French *carpe*, from Latin *carpa*.

carp[2] /kɑːp/ ▷ *verb* (***carped, carping***) *intr* (*often* **carp at someone** or **something**) to complain, find fault or criticize, especially unnecessarily. • **carper** *noun*. • **carping** *adj, noun*. • **carpingly** *adverb*. ◷ 16c in this sense; 13c in obsolete sense 'to speak': from Norse *karpa* to boast or dispute.

carpal *anatomy* ▷ *adj* relating to the CARPUS. ▷ *noun* in terrestrial vertebrates: any of the bones that form the carpus. ◷ 18c: from Latin *carpalis*, from Greek *karpos* wrist.

car park ▷ *noun* a building or piece of land where motor vehicles can be parked.

carpel /ˈkɑːpəl/ ▷ *noun, bot* the female reproductive part of a flowering plant, consisting of a STIGMA (sense 3), STYLE (sense 7) and OVARY (sense 2). • **carpellary** *adj*. ◷ 19c: from Greek *karpos* fruit.

carpenter /ˈkɑːpəntə(r)/ ▷ *noun* someone skilled in working with wood, eg in building houses, etc or in making and repairing fine furniture. ▷ *verb* (***carpentered, carpentering***) **1** *intr* to do the work of a carpenter. **2** to make by carpentry. ◷ 14c: from French *carpentier*, from Latin *carpentarius* person who builds wagons, from *carpentum* two-wheeled chariot.

carpentry /ˈkɑːpəntrɪ/ ▷ *noun* **1** the art or skill of a carpenter. **2** the body of work produced by a carpenter. ◷ 14c: from French *carpenterie*, from Latin *carpentaria* carriage-maker's workshop.

carper see under CARP[2]

carpet /ˈkɑːpɪt/ ▷ *noun* **1** a covering for floors and stairs, made of heavy, usually woven and tufted, fabric. **2** something that covers a surface like a carpet does □ *a carpet of rose petals*. **3** *prison slang* a prison sentence of three months. ▷ *verb* (***carpeted, carpeting***) **1** to cover something with or as if with a carpet. **2** *colloq* to reprimand or scold. • **on the carpet** *colloq* scolded or reprimanded verbally, by someone in authority. ◷ 14c: from French *carpite*, from Italian *carpita* woollen bed-covering, from Latin *carpere* to pluck or card wool.

carpet-bag ▷ *noun* an old-fashioned travelling-bag made of carpeting.

carpetbagger ▷ *noun, derog* a politician seeking election in a place where he or she is a stranger, with no local connections.

carpet bombing ▷ *noun* systematic bombing of a whole area.

carpeting ▷ *noun* **1** fabric used to make carpets. **2** carpets generally.

carpet shark see WOBBEGONG

carpet slippers ▷ *plural noun* slippers, especially men's, with the upper part made of carpeting or a fabric resembling it.

carpet-sweeper ▷ *noun* a long-handled device fitted with a revolving brush, that picks up dust, etc from carpets as it is pushed along.

car phone ▷ *noun* a portable telephone, operating by CELLULAR RADIO, for use in a car.

carping and **carpingly** see under CARP[2]

carport ▷ *noun* a roofed shelter for a car, usually attached to the side of a house.

carpus /ˈkɑːpəs/ ▷ *noun* (***carpi*** /-paɪ, -piː/) *anatomy* in terrestrial vertebrates: the set of small bones (eight in humans) that forms the wrist or corresponding part of the forelimb. ◷ 17c: Latin, from Greek *karpos*.

carrageen or **carragheen** /ˈkarəgiːn/ ▷ *noun* a type of purplish-red, edible seaweed found in the N Atlantic and used for making soup and a kind of blancmange, and also as an emulsifying and gelling agent. Also called **Irish moss**.

carrel or **carrell** /ˈkarəl/ ▷ *noun* a small individual compartment or desk in a library, for private study. ⓘ 20c in this sense: from obsolete *carole* enclosure for study in a cloister.

carriage /ˈkarɪdʒ/ ▷ *noun* **1** a four-wheeled horse-drawn passenger vehicle. **2** a railway coach for carrying passengers. **3** the process or cost of transporting goods. **4** a moving section of a machine, eg a typewriter, that carries some part into the required position. **5** a wheeled support for a gun. **6** the way one holds oneself when standing or walking. ⓘ 14c: from French *cariage*, from *carier* to carry.

carriage clock ▷ *noun* a small ornamental clock with a handle on top, originally used by travellers.

carriageway ▷ *noun* the part of a road used by vehicles, or a part used by vehicles travelling in one particular direction.

carrier ▷ *noun* **1** a person or thing that carries. **2** a person or firm that transports goods. **3** an individual who is infected by a disease-causing micro-organism, and who may remain without symptoms but is still capable of transmitting that organism to other individuals. **4** *genetics* an individual who carries a gene for a particular disorder without displaying signs or symptoms of that disorder, and who may pass on the gene to his or her offspring. **5** a vector. **6** *radio* a carrier wave. **7** *physics* a charge carrier, such as an electron. **8** a non-radioactive material mixed with, and chemically identical to, a radioactive compound. **9** a carrier bag.

carrier bag ▷ *noun* a plastic or paper bag with handles, supplied to shop customers for carrying purchased goods.

carrier pigeon ▷ *noun* any pigeon with homing instincts, especially one used for carrying messages.

carrier wave ▷ *noun, physics* in radio transmission: a continuously transmitted radio wave whose amplitude or frequency is made to increase or decrease instantaneously, in response to variations in the characteristics of the signal being transmitted.

carrion /ˈkarɪən/ ▷ *noun* **1** dead and rotting animal flesh. **2** anything vile. ⓘ 13c: from French *charogne*, ultimately from Latin *caro* flesh.

carrion crow ▷ *noun* a crow native to Europe and Asia, which usually has black plumage, and inhabits forest, grassland and cultivated land.

carrot /ˈkarət/ ▷ *noun* **1** a biennial plant with divided leaves, small white, pink, or yellow flowers borne in dense flat-topped clusters, and an edible orange root. **2** the large fleshy orange root of this plant, eaten raw in salads or cooked as a vegetable. **3** *colloq* something offered as an incentive □ ***The promise of an extra week's holiday was the carrot she needed to finish the job.*** • **carroty** *adj* said of hair: having a strong reddish colour. ⓘ 16c: from French *carrotte*, from Latin *carota*, from Greek *karaton*.

carry /ˈkarɪ/ ▷ *verb* (***carries, carried, carrying***) **1** to hold something in one's hands, have it in a pocket, bag etc, or support its weight on one's body, while moving from one place to another. **2** to bring, take or convey something. **3** to have on one's person □ ***He always carried some means of identification on him.*** **4** to be the means of spreading (a disease, etc) □ ***Mosquitos carry malaria.*** **5** to support □ ***The walls carry the roof.*** **6** to be pregnant with (a baby or babies). **7** to hold (oneself or a part of one's body) in a specified way □ ***She really carries herself well.*** **8** to bear (responsibilities, etc). **9** to bear the burden or expense of something. **10** to do the work of (someone who is not doing enough) in addition to one's own. **11** to print or broadcast □ ***The story surrounding the arms scandal was first carried by the tabloids.*** **12** to stock or sell. **13** to have, involve, etc □ ***He committed a crime carrying the death penalty.*** **14** *intr* said of a sound or the source of a sound: to be able to be heard a distance away. **15** to pass or agree to by majority vote. **16** to win the support of (voters, an audience, etc). **17** to bear the effects of something □ ***He carries his age well.*** **18** to take to a certain point □ ***carry politeness too far.*** **19** *math* to transfer (a figure) in a calculation from one column to the next. **20** *intr* said of a golf ball, etc: to travel (a certain distance). **21** *military* to capture (a town, etc). ▷ *noun* (***carries***) **1** an act of carrying. **2** *golf* the distance that the ball travels from when it is first struck to when it first touches the ground. **3** *N Amer* the land across which a vessel has to be transported between one navigable stretch and another. **4** the range of a gun. • **be** or **get carried away** *colloq* to become over-excited or over-enthusiastic. ⓘ 14c: from French *carier*, from Latin *carricare* to cart, from *carrus* car.

■ **carry something forward** to transfer (a number, amount, etc) to the next column, page or financial period.

■ **carry something off 1** to manage (an awkward situation, etc) well. **2** to win (a prize, etc). **3** to take something away by force. **4** to cause someone's death □ ***She was carried off by cancer.***

■ **carry on 1** to continue; to keep going. **2** *colloq* to make a noisy or unnecessary fuss. See also CARRY-ON.

■ **carry something on** to conduct or engage in (business, etc).

■ **carry on with someone** to have a love affair with them.

■ **carry something out** to accomplish it successfully.

■ **carry something over 1** to continue it on the following page, etc; to carry forward. **2** to postpone it.

■ **carry someone through** to help them to survive a difficult period, etc.

■ **carry something through** to complete or accomplish it.

carrycot ▷ *noun* a light box-like cot with handles, for carrying a baby.

carrying ▷ *adj* said of a voice: easily heard at a distance.

carry-on ▷ *noun* **1** an excitement or fuss. **2** a romance or love-affair.

carry-out ▷ *noun, Scottish colloq* **1** cooked food bought at a restaurant, etc for eating elsewhere. **2** a shop or restaurant supplying such food. **3** alcohol bought in a shop, pub, etc for drinking elsewhere.

car-sick ▷ *adj* feeling sick as a result of travelling in a car or other motor vehicle. • **car-sickness** *noun*.

cart ▷ *noun* **1** a two- or four-wheeled, horse-drawn vehicle for carrying goods or passengers. **2** a light vehicle pushed or pulled by hand. ▷ *verb* (***carted, carting***) **1** to carry in a cart. **2** (*often* **cart something around** or **off**, *etc*) *colloq* to carry or convey it. • **in the cart** *colloq* in difficulties. • **put the cart before the horse** to reverse the normal or logical order of doing something. ⓘ 13c: from Norse *kartr*.

carte see QUART[2]

carte blanche /kɑːtˈblɑ̃ʃ/ ▷ *noun* complete freedom of action or discretion □ ***She was given carte blanche by her boss to revolutionize the company.*** ⓘ 18c: French, meaning 'blank paper'.

cartel /kɑːˈtɛl/ ▷ *noun* a group of firms that agree, especially illegally, on similar fixed prices for their products, so as to reduce competition and keep profits high. ⓘ 20c in this sense; 16c in obsolete sense 'letter of defiance': French, from Italian *cartello*, diminutive of *carta* paper, letter.

carthorse ▻ *noun* a large strong horse bred for pulling heavy loads on farms, etc, and formerly used to pull carts and carriages.

Carthusian /kɑːˈθjuːzɪən, -ˈθuːzɪən/ ▻ *noun* **1** a Roman Catholic monastic order founded in 1084 whose members practise strict abstinence and live as solitaries. **2** a member of this order. ▻ *adj* relating or belonging to this order. ⌚ 14c: from Latin *Cartusianus* belonging to Chatrousse in France, where their first monastery was founded.

cartilage /ˈkɑːtɪlɪdʒ/ ▻ *noun* a tough flexible semi-opaque material that forms the skeleton of cartilaginous fish, while in other vertebrates, including humans, it forms the skeleton of the embryo, but is converted into bone before adulthood, persisting in the adults in structures such as the larynx and trachea. ● **cartilaginous** /kɑːtɪˈladʒɪnəs/ *adj.* ⌚ 16c: French, from Latin *cartilago, cartilaginis* gristle.

cartography /kɑːˈtɒgrəfɪ/ ▻ *noun* the art or technique of making or drawing maps. ● **cartographer** *noun.* ● **cartographic** /kɑːtoʊˈgrafɪk/ *adj.* ⌚ 19c: from French *carte* CHART + -GRAPHY 2.

carton /ˈkɑːtən/ ▻ *noun* **1** a plastic or cardboard container in which food or drink of various types is packaged for sale. **2** a cardboard box. ⌚ 19c: French, meaning 'pasteboard', from Italian *cartone* strong paper.

cartoon /kɑːˈtuːn/ ▻ *noun* **1** a humorous drawing in a newspaper, etc, often ridiculing someone or something. **2** (*also* **animated cartoon**) a film made by photographing a series of drawings, each showing the subjects in a slightly altered position, giving the impression of movement when the film is run at normal speed. **3** (*also* **strip cartoon**) a strip of drawings in a newspaper, etc showing a sequence of often humorous events. **4** a preparatory drawing of a subject done by an artist before attempting a large painting of it. ● **cartoonist** *noun* an artist who draws cartoons for newspapers, etc. ⌚ 17c: from Italian *cartone* strong paper, or a drawing on it.

cartouche /kɑːˈtuːʃ/ ▻ *noun, historical* **1** a paper case containing the explosive charge for a gun, etc; a cartridge. **2** *archit* a scroll-like ornament or decorative border with rolled ends. **3** in Egyptian hieroglyphics: an oval figure enclosing a royal or divine name. ⌚ 17c: French, from Italian *cartoccio* a cornet of paper, from Latin *charta* paper.

cartridge /ˈkɑːtrɪdʒ/ ▻ *noun* **1** a metal case containing the propellant charge for a gun. **2** the part of the pick-up arm of a record-player that contains the stylus. **3** a small plastic tube containing ink for loading into a fountain pen. **4** a plastic container holding a continuous loop of magnetic tape which can be easily inserted into and removed from a tape deck, video recorder, etc. **5** a plastic container holding photographic film, which can be inserted into and removed from a camera without exposing the film to light. ⌚ 16c: variant of CARTOUCHE.

cartridge belt ▻ *noun* a wide belt with a row of loops or pockets for gun cartridges.

cartridge paper ▻ *noun* a type of thick rough-surfaced paper for drawing or printing on, or for making cartridges.

cartwheel ▻ *noun* **1** the wheel of a cart. **2** an acrobatic movement in which one throws one's body sideways with the turning action of a wheel, supporting one's body weight on each hand and foot in turn. ▻ *verb, intr* to perform a cartwheel.

carve /kɑːv/ ▻ *verb* (*carved, carving*) **1** to cut (wood, stone, etc) into a shape. **2** to make something from wood or stone by cutting into it. **3** to produce (a design, inscription, etc) in wood or stone. **4** *tr & intr* to cut (meat) into slices; to cut (a slice) of meat. **5** (*sometimes* **carve something out**) to establish or create (an opportunity, etc) for oneself through personal effort ▫ *carve out a career.* ⌚ Anglo-Saxon *ceorfan.*

■ **carve something up 1** to cut it up into pieces. **2** *colloq* to divide (territory, spoils, etc), especially in a crude or wholesale manner. See also CARVE-UP.

■ **carve someone up** *slang* to attack and cut them with a knife.

carvel see CARAVEL

carvel-built ▻ *adj* said of the hull of a boat: built with planks laid flush (see FLUSH[2]). Compare CLINKER-BUILT.

carver ▻ *noun* **1** someone who carves. **2** a carving-knife.

carvery ▻ *noun* (*carveries*) a restaurant where meat is carved from a joint for customers on request.

carve-up ▻ *noun* a wholesale division, often dishonest, of territory or spoils. See also CARVE SOMETHING UP at CARVE.

carving ▻ *noun* a figure or pattern, etc produced by carving wood, stone, etc.

carving-fork ▻ *noun* a large fork with two long prongs, for holding meat steady during carving.

carving-knife ▻ *noun* a long sharp knife for carving meat.

car wash ▻ *noun* a drive-through facility at a petrol station, etc fitted with automatic equipment for washing cars.

caryatid /karɪˈatɪd, ˈkarɪətɪd/ ▻ *noun* (*caryatids* or *caryatides* /karɪˈatɪdiːz/) *archit* a carved female figure used as a support for a roof, etc, instead of a column or pillar. ⌚ 16c: from Greek *Karyatides* priestesses of the goddess Artemis at Caryae in S Greece.

Casanova /kasəˈnoʊvə/ ▻ *noun* (*Casanovas*) *derog* a man with a reputation for having many love affairs. ⌚ 20c: named after Giacomo Casanova (1725–98), an Italian adventurer noted for his sexual conquests with women.

cascade /kaˈskeɪd/ ▻ *noun* **1** a waterfall or series of waterfalls. **2** something resembling a waterfall in appearance or manner of falling. **3** a large number of things arriving or to be dealt with suddenly ▫ *The teen idols received a cascade of fan letters.* **4** a sequence of successive chemical, etc processes. **5** a sequence of stages in an electrical device, connected in such a way that each operates the next in the series. ▻ *verb* (*cascaded, cascading*) *intr* to fall like a waterfall. ⌚ 17c: French, from Italian *cascata* fall, from *cascare* to fall.

case[1] /keɪs/ ▻ *noun* **1** often *in compounds* a box, container or cover, used for storage, transportation, etc ▫ *suitcase.* **2** an outer covering, especially a protective one ▫ *watch case.* **3** *printing* a tray with compartments containing individual types, divided up in terms of their style and size. See UPPER CASE, LOWER CASE. **4** *bookbinding* the hard covers containing the text of a hardback book. ▻ *verb* (*cased, casing*) to put something in a case. ● **case a joint** *slang* to have a good look at a premises with the intention of robbing them. ⌚ 13c: from French *casse*, from Latin *capsa*, from *capere* to hold or take.

case[2] /keɪs/ ▻ *noun* **1** a particular occasion, situation or set of circumstances. **2** an example, instance or occurrence. **3** someone receiving some sort of treatment or care. **4** a matter requiring investigation. **5** a matter to be decided in a law court. **6** (*sometimes* **case for** or **against something**) the argument for or against something, presented as a set of arguments, statements, etc, with the relevant facts fully stated. **7** *grammar* **a** the relationship of a noun, pronoun or adjective to other words in a sentence; **b** one of the forms or categories indicating the relationship ▫ *nominative case.* **8** an odd character. ● **as the case may be** according to how things turn out. ● **be the case** to be true. ● **a case in point** a good example, relevant to the present discussion. ● **in any case** whatever happens; no matter what happens. ● **in case** so as to be prepared or safe (if a certain thing should happen). ● **in case of something** if a certain occurrence happens. • **in that case** if that happens, since that has happened, etc. ◷ 13c: from French *cas*, from Latin *casus* fall, chance, from *cadere* to fall.

casebook ▷ *noun* a written record of cases dealt with by a doctor, lawyer, etc.

case-harden ▷ *verb* **1** *metallurgy* to harden the surface layer of (steel) by diffusing carbon into it at a high temperature, so that the outer surface is tough and resistant to wear, while the inner core remains resistant to fracture. **2** *geol* said of a mineral: to form a coating on the surface of porous rock as a result of the evaporation of a solution containing that mineral. **3** to make someone insensitive or callous.

case history ▷ *noun* a record of relevant details from someone's past kept by a doctor, social worker, etc.

casein /ˈkeɪsiːn, –siːɪn/ ▷ *noun* a milk protein that is the main constituent of cheese. ◷ 19c: from Latin *caseus* cheese.

case law ▷ *noun* law based on decisions made about similar cases in the past, as distinct from STATUTE LAW.

case load ▷ *noun* the number of cases a doctor, lawyer, etc has to deal with at any particular time.

casement and **casement window** ▷ *noun* a window with vertical hinges that opens outwards like a door. ◷ 16c in this sense: from CASE[1] + -MENT.

casework ▷ *noun* social work concerned with the close study of the background and environment of individuals and families.

cash ▷ *noun* **1** coins or paper money, as distinct from cheques, credit cards, etc. **2** *colloq* money in any form. ▷ *verb* (***cashes, cashed, cashing***) to obtain or give cash in return for (a cheque, traveller's cheque, postal order, etc). • **cash down** *colloq* with payment immediately on purchase. • **cash on delivery** (abbreviation **c.o.d.**) with payment for goods immediately on delivery. ◷ 16c: from French *casse* box, from Latin *capsa* coffer.

▪ **cash something in** to exchange (tokens, vouchers, etc) for money.

▪ **cash in on something** *colloq* to make money, or profit in some other way, by exploiting a situation, etc.

▪ **cash up** *Brit colloq* said of a shopkeeper, etc: to count up the money taken, usually at the end of a day.

cash-and-carry ▷ *noun* (***cash-and-carries***) a large, often wholesale, shop where accredited customers pay for goods in cash and take them away immediately. ▷ *adj* said of a business, etc: using this system.

cash book ▷ *noun* a written record of all money paid out and received by a business, etc.

cash box ▷ *noun* a box, usually metal and with a lock, for keeping petty cash in.

cash card ▷ *noun* a card such as a credit card or debit card, issued by a bank or building society, allowing the holder to withdraw money from a cash machine.

cash crop ▷ *noun* a crop that is grown for sale rather than for consumption by the farmer's household or animal livestock.

cash desk ▷ *noun* a desk in a shop, etc at which one pays for goods.

cashew /kəˈʃuː, ˈkaʃuː/ ▷ *noun* **1** a small evergreen tree, native to tropical regions of Central and S America, which has oval leaves, and red flowers borne in terminal clusters. **2** (*also* **cashew nut**) the curved edible seed of this tree, which is rich in oil and protein. ◷ 17c: from Portuguese *cajú*, from Tupí *akaiu*.

cash flow ▷ *noun* the amount of money coming into and going out of a business, etc.

cashier[1] /kaˈʃɪə(r)/ ▷ *noun* in a business firm, bank, etc: any person who receives, pays out and generally deals with the cash. ◷ 16c: from French *caissier* treasurer, from *caisse* cash box.

cashier[2] /kaˈʃɪə(r)/ ▷ *verb* (***cashiered, cashiering***) to dismiss (an officer) from the armed forces in disgrace. ◷ 16c: from Dutch *kasseren*, from French *casser* to break or discharge, from Latin *quassare* to shatter.

cashless ▷ *adj* said of a transaction, etc: paid by credit card, debit card or other electronic transfer of money, rather than by cash or cheque.

cash machine and **cash dispenser** ▷ *noun* an electronic machine, usually fitted into the outside wall of a bank, from which one can obtain cash using one's personal cash card. Also called **ATM, hole-in-the-wall.**

cashmere /ˈkaʃmɪə(r), kaʃˈmɪə(r)/ ▷ *noun* **1** a type of very fine soft wool from a long-haired Asian goat. **2** a fabric made from this. ◷ 19c: named after Kashmir in N India, where shawls were woven from this wool.

cash point ▷ *noun* **1** the place in a shop, etc where money is taken for goods purchased. **2** a CASH MACHINE.

cash register ▷ *noun* a machine in a shop, etc that calculates and records the amount of each sale and from which change and a receipt are usually given.

casing /ˈkeɪsɪŋ/ ▷ *noun* **1** a protective covering, eg of plastic for electric cables. **2** a timber frame for a door or window.

casino /kəˈsiːnoʊ/ ▷ *noun* (***casinos***) a public building or room for gambling. ◷ 18c: Italian diminutive of *casa* house.

cask /kɑːsk/ ▷ *noun* **1** a barrel for holding liquids, especially alcoholic liquids. **2** the amount contained by a cask. ▷ *verb* (***casked, casking***) to put in a cask. ◷ 15c: from French *casque*, from Spanish *casco* an earthen pot.

casket /ˈkɑːskɪt/ ▷ *noun* **1** a small case for holding jewels, etc. **2** *N Amer* a coffin. ◷ 15c: perhaps from French *cassette*, diminutive of *cassa* box.

cassava /kəˈsɑːvə/ ▷ *noun* (***cassavas***) **1** a perennial shrubby plant native to Brazil, but cultivated throughout the tropics for its fleshy tuberous edible roots. Also called **manioc. 2** a starchy substance obtained from the root of this plant, and used to make cassava flour, bread, tapioca, laundry starch, etc. ◷ 16c: from Spanish *cazabe*, from Taino (a West Indies Native American language) *caçabi*.

casserole /ˈkasəroʊl/ ▷ *noun* **1** an ovenproof dish with a lid, in which meat, vegetables, etc can be cooked and served. **2** the food cooked and served in this kind of dish ▫ ***vegetable casserole***. ▷ *verb* (***casseroled, casseroling***) to cook in a casserole. ◷ 18c: French, from Provençal *casa*, from Latin *cattia* ladle, from Greek *kyathion*, diminutive of *kyathos* cup.

cassette /kəˈsɛt/ ▷ *noun* **1** a small, usually plastic, case, containing a long narrow ribbon of magnetic tape wound around two reels, that can be inserted into a suitable audio or video tape recorder for recording or playback. **2** a small lightproof plastic cartridge containing photographic film for loading into a camera. ◷ 18c: French, diminutive of *casse* box, from Italian *cassetta*.

cassette recorder and **cassette player** ▷ *noun* a machine that records or plays material on audio cassette.

cassette single ▷ *noun* a release by an artist or band in cassette format, usually with one lead track and up to two extra ones, with both sides of the cassette usually being identical.

Cassini /kəˈsiːnɪ/ ▷ *noun, space flight* a space probe scheduled by NASA and the European Space Agency for launch in 1997, and to go into orbit around Saturn in 2004.

Cassini's division /kəˈsiːnɪz —/ ▷ *noun, astron* a dark ring, consisting of a gap about 2 600km wide, concentric with the ring of Saturn and dividing it into two parts. ◷ 17c: named after the Italian-French astronomer Giovanni Domenico Cassini (1625–1712).

cassis /ka'siːs/ ▻ *noun* a syrupy blackcurrant drink or flavouring. ⓒ 19c: French.

cassiterite /kə'sɪtəraɪt/ ▻ *noun, geol* a hard black mineral, consisting mainly of tin oxide, that is the chief ore of tin. ⓒ 19c: from Greek *kassiteros* tin.

cassock /'kasək/ ▻ *noun* a long black or red garment worn in church by clergymen and male members of a church choir. ⓒ 17c in this sense; 16c in obsolete sense 'long loose coat': from French *casaque* type of coat.

cassowary /'kasəwərɪ, –wɛərɪ/ ▻ *noun* (***cassowaries***) a large flightless bird, native to New Guinea and N Australia, which has a bony crest on its head, bright blue or red naked skin on its neck and head, long bristle-like black feathers on its body, and dagger-like claws. ⓒ 17c: from Malay *kasuari*.

cast /kɑːst/ ▻ *verb* (*past tense, past participle* ***cast****, present participle* ***casting***) **1** to throw. **2** to direct (one's eyes, a glance, etc) on or over something. **3** to throw off or shed something □ *She cast her clothes in a heap.* **4** to project; to cause to appear □ *cast a shadow.* **5** *tr & intr* to throw (a fishing-line) out into the water. **6** to let down (an anchor). **7** to release someone or something from a secured state □ *They were cast adrift.* **8** said of animals: to get rid of or shed (a skin, horns, etc). **9** (*usually* **cast something off, aside** or **out**) to throw it off or away; to get rid of it. **10** to give (an actor) a part in a play or film; to distribute the parts in a film, play, etc. **11** to shape (molten metal, plastic, etc) by pouring it into a mould and allowing it to set. **12** to give or record (one's vote). **13** to work out (a horoscope). **14** to present (work, facts, etc) in a certain way. ▻ *noun* **1** a throw; an act of throwing (eg dice, a fishing-line). **2** an object shaped by pouring metal, plastic, etc, into a mould and allowing it to set. **3** (*also* **plaster cast**) a rigid casing, usually of gauze impregnated with plaster of Paris, moulded round a broken limb or other body part while the plaster is still wet, and then allowed to set in order to hold the broken bone in place while it heals. **4** the set of actors or performers in a play, opera, etc. **5** *formal* type, form, shape or appearance. **6** a slight tinge; a faint colour. **7** the slight turning inwards of an eye; a squint. **8** (*also* **casting**) a coiled heap of earth or sand thrown up by a burrowing worm, etc. ● **cast doubt on something** to express doubt about it. ● **cast of mind** a way of thinking. ● **cast one's mind back** to think about something in the past. ⓒ 13c: from Norse *kasta* to throw.

■ **cast about** or **around for something** **1** to look about for it. **2** to try to think of it □ *cast about for ideas.*

■ **be cast away** to be abandoned on a remote piece of land after shipwreck, etc. See also CASTAWAY.

■ **be cast down** to be depressed or discouraged.

■ **cast off** **1** to untie a boat ready to sail away. **2** to finish off and remove knitting from the needles. **3** *printing* to estimate how much space will be taken up by a piece of manuscript or typewritten copy. See also CAST-OFF.

■ **cast on** to form (stitches or knitting) by looping and securing wool, etc over the needles.

■ **cast up** to find the total of a column of figures, etc

■ **cast something up** **1** to mention (a person's past faults, etc) to them, as a reproach. **2** to throw (a body, etc) up on to a beach.

■ **cast up** to find the total of (a column of figures, etc).

cast, caste

These words are sometimes confused with each other.

castanets /kastə'nɛts/ ▻ *plural noun* a musical instrument used especially by Spanish dancers to accompany their movements, consisting of two hollow pieces of wood or plastic attached to each other by string, which are held in the palm and struck together rhythmically, using the middle finger. ⓒ 17c: from Spanish *castañeta*, from *castaña* chestnut, the wood used to make them.

castaway ▻ *noun* someone who has been shipwrecked. See also CAST SOMEONE AWAY at CAST. ▻ *adj* **1** cast adrift; shipwrecked. **2** rejected; worthless.

caste /kɑːst/ ▻ *noun* **1 a** any of the four hereditary social classes into which Hindu society is divided and which although not officially recognized by the state, are still entrenched in many areas of Indian society; **b** this system of social class division. **2** any system of social division based on inherited rank or wealth. ● **lose caste** to drop to a lower social class. ⓒ 17c in sense 1; 16c in obsolete general sense 'breed of men': from Portuguese *casta* breed or race, from Latin *castus* pure.

castellated /'kastəleɪtɪd/ ▻ *adj* said of a building: having turrets and battlements like those of a castle. ● **castellation** *noun* **1** building castles. **2** providing a house with battlements. **3** a castellated structure; a battlement. ⓒ 17c: from Latin *castellare, castellatum* to fortify.

caster[1] /'kɑːstə(r)/ ▻ *noun* **1** someone or something that casts. **2** (*also* **castor**) a closed container with holes in its lid, through which to sprinkle the contents, eg sugar or flour, over food.

caster[2] see CASTOR[1]

caster sugar ▻ *noun* finely crushed white sugar used in baking, etc.

castigate /'kastɪgeɪt/ ▻ *verb* (***castigated, castigating***) to criticize or punish severely. ● **castigation** *noun*. ⓒ 17c: from Latin *castigare, castigatum* to chastise.

casting ▻ *noun* **1** *engineering* the process of forming a solid object with a fixed shape by pouring molten material, eg metal, alloy, glass or plastic, into a mould and allowing it to cool and solidify. **2** an object formed in this way. **3** the process of choosing actors to take part in a production. **4** a CAST *noun* 8.

casting vote ▻ *noun* the deciding vote, used by a chairperson when the votes taken at a meeting, etc are equally divided.

cast iron ▻ *noun* any of a group of hard heavy alloys of iron, containing more carbon than steels, and cast into a specific shape when molten, used to make machine and engine parts, stoves, pipes, etc. ▻ *adj* (**cast-iron**) **1** made of cast iron. **2** very strong. **3** said of a rule or decision: firm; not to be altered. **4** said of an argument, etc: with no flaws, loopholes, etc.

castle /'kɑːsəl/ ▻ *noun* **1** a large, fortified, especially medieval, building with battlements and towers. **2** any fortified building. **3** a large mansion, especially the residence of a nobleman. **4** *chess* a piece that can be moved any number of empty squares forwards or backwards, but not diagonally. Also called **rook**. ▻ *verb* (***castled, castling***) *intr, chess* to make a move allowed once to each player in a game, in which the king is moved two squares along its rank towards either castle, and the castle is placed on the square the king has passed over. ⓒ 11c: from Latin *castellum* fort or fortress.

castles in the air and **castles in Spain** ▻ *plural noun* grand but impossible schemes; daydreams.

cast-off ▻ *noun* (***cast-offs***) **1** something, especially a garment, discarded or no longer wanted. **2** *printing* an estimate of the amount of space that will be taken up by a piece of manuscript or typewritten copy. See also CAST OFF at CAST. ▻ *adj* no longer needed; discarded.

castor[1] or **caster** /'kɑːstə(r)/ ▻ *noun* a small swivelling wheel fitted to the legs or underside of a piece of furniture so that it can be moved easily.

castor[2] see CASTER[1]

castor oil ▻ *noun* a yellow or brown non-drying oil obtained from the seeds of a tropical African plant, used as a lubricant and in soap manufacture, and formerly used medicinally as a laxative.

castrate /ka'streɪt/ ▻ *verb* (***castrated***, ***castrating***) **1** to remove the testicles of a male person or animal. **2** to deprive of vigour or strength. ● **castrated** *adj.* ● **castration** *noun.* ◷ 17c: from Latin *castrare, castratum.*

castrato /ka'strɑːtoʊ/ ▻ *noun* (***castrati*** /-tiː/ or ***castratos***) in 17c and 18c opera: a male singer castrated before puberty in order to preserve his soprano or contralto voice. ◷ 18c: Italian, from *castrare* to castrate.

casual /'kaʒʊəl, 'kazjʊəl/ ▻ *adj* **1** happening by chance. **2** careless; showing no particular interest or concern. **3** without serious intention or commitment ▫ *casual sex.* **4** said of clothes: informal. **5** said of work, etc: occasional; not permanent or regular. ▻ *noun* **1** an occasional worker. **2** (*usually* **casuals**) clothes suitable for informal wear. **3** (*usually* **casuals**) *Brit colloq* a young male, often one dressed in informal yet expensive clothes, and associated with violent behaviour especially at football grounds. ● **casually** *adverb.* ● **casualness** *noun.* ◷ 14c: from French *casuel*, from Latin *casualis* accidental, from *casus* event, from *cadere* to fall.

casualty /'kaʒʊəltɪ/ ▻ *noun* (***casualties***) **1** someone killed or hurt in an accident or war. **2** the casualty department of a hospital. **3** something that is lost, destroyed, sacrificed, etc as a result of some event.

casualty department and **casualty ward** ▻ *noun* the part of a hospital where people involved in accidents, etc are treated.

casuist /'kazjʊɪst, 'kaʒʊɪst/ ▻ *noun* someone who uses cleverly misleading arguments, especially to make things that are really morally wrong seem acceptable. ● **casuistic** /kazjʊ'ɪstɪk/ *adj.* ● **casuistry** *noun.* ◷ 17c: from French *casuiste*, from Latin *casus* case.

casus belli /'keɪsəs 'belaɪ, 'kɑːzʊs 'beliː/ ▻ *noun* (*plural* ***casus belli***) a circumstance or situation that causes a war. ◷ 19c: Latin, meaning 'occasion of war'.

CAT ▻ *abbreviation* **1** College of Advanced Technology. **2** computer-assisted training or computer-aided training. **3** a CAT SCANNER.

cat¹ ▻ *noun* **1** any of a wide range of carnivorous mammals, including large cats such as the lion, tiger, jaguar, leopard and cheetah, as well as the domestic cat. **2** the domestic cat, which has many different breeds. See also FELINE. **3** *derog, colloq* someone, especially a woman, with a spiteful tongue. **4** *slang* a person. **5** a CAT-O'-NINE-TAILS. ● **the cat's whiskers** or **pyjamas** *colloq* the best or greatest thing ▫ *Darren thinks he's the cat's whiskers.* ● **fight like cat and dog** *colloq* to quarrel ferociously. ● **let the cat out of the bag** *colloq* to give away a secret unintentionally. ● **like a cat on a hot tin roof** or **on hot bricks** *colloq* very nervous or uneasy. ● **like something the cat brought** or **dragged in** *colloq* messy, dirty, untidy or bedraggled in appearance. ● **no room to swing a cat** having very little space; cramped. ● **not have a cat in hell's chance** *colloq* to have absolutely no chance. ● **play cat and mouse with someone** to tease them cruelly by not letting them know exactly what one intends to do with them. ● **put** or **set the cat among the pigeons** to do something, often suddenly, that is generally upsetting or disturbing. ● **rain cats and dogs** *colloq* to rain very heavily, usually for a long time. ● **see which way the cat jumps** *colloq* to wait to see how a situation develops before taking action. ◷ Anglo-Saxon *catte*, from Latin *cattus.*

cat² ▻ *noun, colloq* short for CATALYTIC CONVERTER.

catabolism /kə'tabəlɪzəm/ ▻ *noun, biochem* the metabolic process whereby complex organic compounds in living organisms are broken down into simple molecules. ◷ 19c: from Greek *katabole* throwing down, from *kata* down + *ballein* to throw.

catachumen ▻ *noun* someone who is being taught about the main beliefs of Christianity.

cataclysm /'katəklɪzəm/ ▻ *noun* **1** an event, especially a political or social one, causing tremendous change or upheaval. **2** a terrible flood or other disaster. ● **cataclysmic** *adj.* ◷ 17c: from Greek *kataklysmos* flood, from *kata* down + *klyzein* to wash.

catacomb /'katəkuːm, 'katəkoʊm/ ▻ *noun* (*usually* **catacombs**) **1** an underground burial place, especially one consisting of a system of tunnels with recesses dug out for the tombs. **2** a system of winding underground tunnels. ◷ Anglo-Saxon *catacumbe*, from Latin *catacumbas.*

catafalque /'katəfalk/ ▻ *noun* a temporary platform on which a dead king or other important person lies in state, before or during the funeral. ◷ 17c: French, from Italian *catafalco.*

Catalan /'katəlan/ ▻ *adj* belonging or relating to Catalonia, an autonomous region of NE Spain, its inhabitants, or their language. ▻ *noun* **1** a citizen or inhabitant of, or person born in, Catalonia. **2** the official language of Catalonia.

catalectic /katə'lɛktɪk/ ▻ *adj* said of verse: lacking one syllable in the last foot. Compare ACATALECTIC. ◷ 16c: from Greek *katalektikos* incomplete.

catalepsy /'katəlɛpsɪ/ ▻ *noun* (***catalepsies***) **1** a trance-like state characterized by the abnormal maintenance of rigid body postures, and an apparent loss of sensation, most commonly associated with catatonia. **2** cataplexy in animals. ● **cataleptic** /katə'lɛptɪk/ *adj, noun.* ◷ 14c: from Latin *catalepsia*, from Greek *katalepsis* seizing, from *kata* down + *lambanein* to seize.

catalogue /'katəlɒg/ ▻ *noun* **1** a list of items arranged in a systematic order, especially alphabetically. **2** a brochure, booklet, etc containing a list of goods for sale. **3** a list or index of all the books in a library. **4** a series of things mentioned one by one as though in a list ▫ *the catalogue of his faults.* ▻ *verb* (***catalogued***, ***cataloguing***) **1** to make a catalogue of (a library, books, etc). **2** to enter (an item) in a catalogue. **3** to list or mention one by one ▫ *He catalogued her virtues.* ● **cataloguer** *noun.* ◷ 15c: French, from Latin *catalogus*, from Greek *katalegein* to reckon in a list, from *kata* down + *legein* to choose.

catalyse or *(US)* **catalyze** /'katəlaɪz/ ▻ *verb* (***catalysed***, ***catalysing***) *chem* said of a CATALYST: to alter the rate of (a chemical reaction), usually by increasing it, without itself undergoing any permanent chemical change.

catalysis /kə'taləsɪs/ ▻ *noun* (***catalyses*** /-siːz/) *chem* the process effected by a catalyst. ● **catalytic** /katə'lɪtɪk/ *adj.* ◷ 19c in this sense; 17c in obsolete sense 'dissolution': from Greek *katalysis* breaking up, from *katalyein* to dissolve, from *kata* down + *lyein* to loosen.

catalyst /'katəlɪst/ ▻ *noun* **1** *chem* any substance that CATALYSES a chemical reaction. **2** something or someone that speeds up the pace of something, or causes change.

catalytic converter ▻ *noun* a device fitted to the exhaust system of a motor vehicle that is designed to reduce toxic emissions from the engine and thereby reduce environmental pollution.

catalytic cracking ▻ *noun* in the petrochemical industry: the process by which long-chain hydrocarbons produced during petroleum refining are broken down into lighter, more useful short-chain products, using a catalyst.

catamaran /'katəməran, katəmə'ran/ ▻ *noun* **1** a sailing-boat with two hulls lying parallel to each other, joined across the top by the deck. **2** a raft made of logs or boats lashed together. ◷ 17c: from Tamil *kattumaram* tied wood.

cataplexis /katə'plɛksɪs/ ▻ *noun, zool* a physical state resembling death, adopted by some animals to discourage predators. ⌚ 19c: from Greek *kataplexis* astonishment.

cataplexy /ˈkatəplɛksɪ/ ▷ *noun, pathol* a sudden attack of muscular weakness, caused by strong emotion, eg laughter or anger, which affects the whole body and causes collapse without loss of consciousness. • **cataplectic** *adj.* ⌚ 19c: from Greek *kataplexis* astonishment, from *kata* down + *plessein* to strike.

catapult /ˈkatəpʌlt/ ▷ *noun* **1** a Y-shaped stick with an elastic or rubber band fitted between its prongs, used especially by children for firing stones, etc. **2** *historical* a weapon of war designed to fire boulders. **3** an apparatus on an aircraft-carrier for launching aircraft. ▷ *verb* (***catapulted, catapulting***) **1** to fire or send flying with, or as if with, a catapult. **2** *intr* to be sent flying as if from a catapult. ⌚ 16c: from Greek *katapeltes*, from *kata* against + *pallein* to throw.

cataract /ˈkatərakt/ ▷ *noun* **1** *pathol* an opaque area within the lens of the eye that produces blurring of vision, caused by ageing, injury, diabetes, exposure to ionizing radiation, or various hereditary disorders. **2** a succession of steep waterfalls within a river. **3** an immense rush of water, eg from a large waterfall that consists of a single vertical drop. ⌚ 16c in sense 1; 15c in obsolete sense 'flood-gates': from Greek *kataractes* waterfall, from *kata* down + *arassein* to dash.

catarrh /kəˈtɑː(r)/ ▷ *noun* inflammation of the mucuous membranes lining the nose and throat, causing an excessive discharge of thick mucus. • **catarrhal** *adj.* ⌚ 16c: from French *catarrhe*, from Latin *catarrhus*, from Greek *katarrheein* to flow down.

catastrophe /kəˈtastrəfɪ/ ▷ *noun* (***catastrophes***) **1** a terrible blow or calamity. **2** a great disaster, causing destruction, loss of life, etc. **3** a disastrous ending or conclusion of a play. **4** a violent event in the geological history of the Earth. **5** in catastrophe theory: a discontinuous change. • **catastrophic** /katəˈstrɒfɪk/ *adj.* • **catastrophically** *adverb.* ⌚ 16c: Greek, from *katastrephein* to overturn.

catastrophe theory ▷ *noun, math* a theory which states that continuous changes in the input of a system cause discontinuous changes in the output. ⌚ 20c.

catatonia /katəˈtoʊnɪə/ ▷ *noun* (***catatonias***) *pathol* an abnormal mental state characterized either by stupor, mutism and immobility, or by excessive excitement and violent or unco-ordinated activity. • **catatonic** /katəˈtɒnɪk/ *adj, noun.* ⌚ 19c: from Greek *kata* down + *tonos* tension.

cat burglar ▷ *noun* a burglar who breaks into buildings by climbing walls, water pipes, etc.

catcall ▷ *noun* a long shrill whistle expressing disagreement or disapproval. ▷ *verb, tr & intr* to whistle at someone in this way.

catch ▷ *verb* (*past tense, past participle* ***caught*** /kɔːt/, *present participle* ***catching***) **1** to stop (a moving object) and hold it. **2** to manage to get hold of or trap, especially after a hunt or chase. **3** to be in time to get, reach, see, etc something □ *catch the last post.* **4** to overtake or draw level with someone or something. **5** to discover someone or something in time to prevent or to encourage the development of something □ *The disease can be cured if caught early.* **6** to surprise someone doing something wrong or embarrassing □ *I caught them in a passionate clinch in the kitchen.* **7** to trick or trap. **8** to become infected with (a disease, etc). **9** *tr & intr* to become or cause to become accidentally attached or held □ *My dress caught on a nail.* **10** to hit □ *I caught him square on the chin.* **11** to manage to hear, see or understand something □ *I didn't quite catch your third point.* **12** to attract (attention, etc) □ *catch her eye.* **13** *intr* to start burning □ *The fire caught within seconds and spread to the library.* **14** to succeed in recording (a subtle quality, etc) □ *The artist caught her expression perfectly.* **15** *cricket* to put (a batsman) out by gathering the ball he has struck before it touches the ground. ▷ *noun* (***catches***) **1** an act of catching. **2** a small device for keeping a lid, door, etc closed. **3** something caught. **4** the total amount of eg fish caught. **5** a hidden problem or disadvantage; a snag; some unsuspected trick in a question, etc. **6** someone or something that it would be advantageous to get hold of, eg a certain person as a husband or wife. **7** a slight breaking sound in one's voice, caused by emotion. **8** a children's game of throwing and catching a ball. **9** *music* a humorous round sung by two or three people. • **catchable** *adj.* • **be caught short** see under SHORT. • **be** or **get caught up in something** to be or get involved in it, especially unintentionally. • **catch fire** to start burning. • **catch hold of something** to grasp or grab it. • **catch it** *colloq* to be scolded, punished, etc. • **catch sight of** or **catch a glimpse of someone** or **something** to see them only for a brief moment. ⌚ 13c: from French *cachier*, from Latin *captiare* to try to catch, from *capere* to seize.

■ **catch at something** to try to catch or hold it; to hold on to it briefly.

■ **catch on** *colloq* **1** to become popular. **2** (*sometimes* **catch on to something**) to understand it.

■ **catch someone out 1** to trick them into making a mistake. **2** to discover them or take them unawares in embarrassing circumstances.

■ **catch up 1** (*often* **catch up with someone**) to draw level with someone ahead. **2** (*sometimes* **catch up on something**) to bring oneself up to date with one's work, the latest news, etc. **3** to immerse or occupy □ *She was completely caught up in her studies.*

■ **catch something up** to pick it up or grab it hastily.

catch-22 ▷ *noun* a situation in which one is permanently frustrated and from which one cannot escape, since all possible courses of action either have undesirable consequences or lead inevitably to further frustration of one's aims. ⌚ 20c: named after the novel by Joseph Heller (born 1923).

catch-all ▷ *adj* said of a phrase in an agreement, etc: covering all possibilities.

catch crop ▷ *noun, agric* a fast-growing secondary crop that is either planted between the rows of a main crop, or grown in the time interval between two main crops. Compare INTERCROPPING.

catcher ▷ *noun* **1** someone who catches. **2** *baseball* the fielder who stands behind the batter.

catchiness see under CATCHY

catching ▷ *adj* **1** infectious. **2** captivating.

catchment ▷ *noun* **1** the area of land that is drained by a particular river system or lake. **2** the population within the catchment area of a school, hospital, etc.

catchment area ▷ *noun* **1** the area served by a particular school, hospital, etc, encompassing those people who are expected to make use of the facilities within it. **2** (*also* **drainage basin**) the area of land whose rainfall feeds a particular river, lake or reservoir.

catchpenny ▷ *noun, derog* something which is poor in quality but designed to appeal to the eye and sell quickly. Also *as adj* □ *a catchpenny watch.*

catch phrase ▷ *noun* a well-known and frequently used phrase or slogan, especially one associated with a particular celebrity.

catchup see KETCHUP 2

catchword ▷ *noun* **1** a much-repeated well-known word or phrase. **2** either of the words printed in the top corners of each page of a dictionary or encyclopedia, indicating the first and last entry to be found on that page. **3** the first word of a page, printed at the bottom of the previous page.

catchy ▷ *adj* (***catchier, catchiest***) **1** said of a song, etc: tuneful and easily remembered. **2** misleading; deceptive □ *a catchy exam question.* **3** spasmodic; intermittent □ *catchy rain.* ● **catchiness** *noun.*

catechetical /katə'kɛtɪkəl/ and **catechetic** ▷ *adj* relating to instruction using catechism, especially in Christianity. ● **catechetically** *adverb.*

catechism /'katəkɪzəm/ ▷ *noun* **1** a series of questions and answers about the Christian religion, or a book containing this, used for instruction. **2** any long series of difficult questions, eg in an interview. ● **catechismal** *adj.* ● **catechist** *noun.* ⓘ 16c: from Latin *catechismus*; see CATECHIZE.

catechize or **catechise** /'katəkaɪz/ ▷ *verb* (***catechized, catechizing***) **1** to instruct someone in the ways of the Christian faith, especially by means of a catechism. **2** to teach using a question-and-answer method. **3** to question someone very thoroughly. ● **catechizer** *noun.* ⓘ 15c: from Greek *katechizein*, from *katechein* to instruct orally.

categorial /katə'gɔːrɪəl/ ▷ *adj* relating or belonging to a category.

categorical /katə'gɒrɪkəl/ and **categoric** ▷ *adj* **1** said of a statement, refusal, denial, etc: absolute or definite; making no exceptions and giving no room for doubt or argument. **2** relating or belonging to a category. ● **categorically** *adverb.* ⓘ 16c: see CATEGORY.

categorization or **categorisation** ▷ *noun* classification.

categorize or **categorise** /'katəgəraɪz/ ▷ *verb* (***categorized, categorizing***) to put something into a category or categories; to classify something.

category /'katəgərɪ/ ▷ *noun* (***categories***) **1** a group of things, people or concepts classed together because of some quality or qualities they have in common. **2** in Aristotelian philosophy: any of the ten most basic modes of existence, including place, time, quantity, etc. **3** in Kantian philosophy: any of the conceptions of the understanding used to interpret the world. ⓘ 16c: from Latin *categoria*, from Greek *kategoria* accusation, affirmation, from *kategorein* to accuse or assert.

catenary /kə'tiːnərɪ; *US* 'katənərɪ/ ▷ *noun* (***catenaries***) **1** *math* the curve formed by a flexible chain or cable supported at both ends and hanging freely, acted on by no force other than gravity. **2** *engineering* a similar structure, consisting of an overhead cable, that is used to deliver electric current to an electric railway locomotive or tram. ⓘ 18c: from Latin *catena* chain.

cater /'keɪtə(r)/ ▷ *verb* (***catered, catering***) only in phrases below. ⓘ 17c as *verb*; 15c in obsolete sense 'a buyer of provisions': from French *acater* to buy.

■ **cater for someone** or **something 1** to supply food, accommodation or entertainment for them. **2** to make provision for them; to take them into account.

■ **cater to something** to indulge or pander to (unworthy desires, etc).

caterer /'keɪtərə(r)/ ▷ *noun* a person whose professional occupation is to provide food, etc for social occasions.

catering ▷ *noun* **1** the provision of food, etc. **2** the activity or job of a caterer.

caterpillar /'katəpɪlə(r)/ ▷ *noun* **1** the larva of a butterfly, moth or sawfly, which has a segmented worm-like body, often hairy or conspicuously patterned, several pairs of legs and strong jaws. **2** (*usually* **Caterpillar**) *trademark* **a** a continuous band or track made up of metal plates driven by cogs, used instead of wheels on heavy vehicles for travelling over rough surfaces; **b** a vehicle fitted with such tracks. ⓘ 15c: probably from French *chatepelose* hairy cat.

caterwaul /'katəwɔːl/ ▷ *verb* (***caterwauled, caterwauling***) *intr* **1** said of a cat: to make a loud high wailing noise. **2** to wail or shriek in this way. ▷ *noun* a loud high wail. ● **caterwauling** *noun.* ⓘ 14c: imitating the sound.

catfish ▷ *noun* any of several hundred mainly freshwater species of fish, all of which have long whisker-like sensory barbels around the mouth, and including several popular aquarium fish.

catflap ▷ *noun* a small door or flap, easily pushed open from either side, set into a door to allow a cat exit and entry.

catgut ▷ *noun* a strong cord made from the dried intestines of sheep and other animals (and formerly from those of cats), used in surgery for making stitches and ligatures, and also used for stringing violins, etc and (now rarely) tennis rackets.

Cath. ▷ *abbreviation* Catholic.

catharsis /kə'θɑːsɪs/ ▷ *noun* (***catharses*** /siːz/) **1** *psychoanal* the emotional relief that results either from allowing repressed thoughts and feelings to surface, as in psychoanalysis, or from an intensely dramatic experience. **2** the cleansing of the emotions through the elicitation of acute fear and pity in spectators of drama, especially tragedy. **3** *medicine* the process of clearing out or purging the bowels. ⓘ 19c: Latin, from Greek *kathairein* to purify.

cathartic /kə'θɑːtɪk/ ▷ *adj* (*also* **cathartical**) **1** resulting in catharsis. **2** cleansing; purgative. ▷ *noun, medicine* a purgative drug or medicine. ● **cathartically** *adverb.*

cathedral /kə'θiːdrəl/ ▷ *noun* the principal church of a DIOCESE, in which the bishop has his throne. ⓘ 13c: from Greek *kathedra* seat.

Catherine wheel /'kaθrɪn —/ ▷ *noun* a firework shaped like a wheel, which is fixed to a post, etc and rotates when set off. ⓘ 18c: named after St Catherine of Alexandria, who apparently escaped being martyred on a spiked wheel, only to be beheaded.

catheter /'kaθɪtə(r)/ ▷ *noun, medicine* a hollow slender flexible tube that can be introduced into a narrow opening or body cavity, usually in order to drain a liquid, especially urine, but sometimes used to introduce a liquid during diagnosis or treatment. ⓘ 17c: Latin, from Greek *katheter*, from *kathienai* to send down.

cathexis /kə'θɛksɪs/ ▷ *noun* (***cathexes*** /-siːz/) *psychol* a charge of mental energy directed towards a particular idea or object. ⓘ 20c: from Greek *kathexis* holding.

cathode /'kaθoʊd/ ▷ *noun* **1** in an electrolytic cell: the negative electrode, towards which positively charged ions, usually in solution, are attracted. **2** the positive terminal of a battery. Compare ANODE. ⓘ 19c: from Greek *kathodos* descent, from *kata* down + *hodos* way.

cathode-ray oscilloscope see under OSCILLOSCOPE

cathode rays ▷ *plural noun* a stream of electrons emitted from the surface of a cathode in a vacuum tube.

cathode-ray tube ▷ *noun* (abbreviation **CRT**) an evacuated glass tube in which streams of electrons, known as cathode rays, are produced, used to display images in television sets, the visual display units of computers, etc.

catholic /'kaθəlɪk/ ▷ *adj* **1** (**Catholic**) relating or belonging to the Roman Catholic Church. **2** (**Catholic**) relating to the whole Christian Church, especially before the East-West split of 1054, or to the Western Church before the split caused by the Reformation. **3** said especially of a person's interests and tastes: broad; wide-ranging. ▷ *noun* (**Catholic**) a member of the Roman Catholic Church. ⓘ 14c: from Greek *katholikos* universal.

Catholicism /kə'θɒlɪsɪzəm/ ▷ *noun* **1** the faith, dogma, etc of any Catholic Church. **2** short for ROMAN CATHOLICISM.

catholicity /kaθə'lɪsɪtɪ/ ▷ *noun* (*plural* in senses 1 and 2 only ***catholicities***) **1** universality. **2** liberality or breadth of view. **3** Catholicism.

cation /'kataɪən/ ▻ *noun, chem* any positively charged ion, which moves towards the CATHODE during ELECTROLYSIS. Compare ANION. ◷ 19c: from Greek *katienai* to go down.

catkin ▻ *noun, bot* in certain tree species, eg birch, hazel: a flowering shoot that bears many small unisexual flowers, adapted for wind pollination. ◷ 16c: from Dutch *kateken* kitten.

catmint and **catnip** ▻ *noun, bot* a square-stemmed perennial plant native to Europe and Asia, with oval toothed leaves and spikes of white two-lipped flowers spotted with purple. ◷ 13c: so called because the strong scent of the flowers is attractive to cats.

catnap ▻ *noun* a short sleep. ▻ *verb, intr* to doze; to sleep briefly, especially without lying down.

cat-o'-nine-tails ▻ *noun* (*plural* ***cat-o'-nine-tails***) *historical* a whip with nine knotted rope lashes, used as an instrument of punishment in the navy. Often shortened to **cat**.

CAT scanner ▻ *abbreviation, medicine* computer-assisted tomography or computed axial tomography scanner, a machine that produces X-ray images of cross-sectional 'slices' through the brain or other soft body tissues. Now usually called CT SCANNER.

cat's cradle ▻ *noun* a game with a long piece of string, which is looped over the fingers in a series of changing patterns, sometimes passed from person to person.

cat's eye ▻ *noun* **1** (**Catseye**) *trademark* a small glass reflecting device, one of a series set into the surface along the centre and sides of a road to guide drivers in the dark. **2** a type of precious stone which resembles the eye of a cat when light is reflected onto it.

cat's paw ▻ *noun* **1** a person used by someone else to perform an unpleasant job. **2 a** a slight breeze which ripples the surface of the sea; **b** the area rippled by such a breeze.

catsuit ▻ *noun* a close-fitting one-piece garment, combining trousers and top, usually worn by women.

catsup see KETCHUP 2

cattery /'katərɪ/ ▻ *noun* a place where cats are bred or looked after in their owner's absence.

cattle /'katəl/ ▻ *plural noun* **1** any of various large heavily built grass-eating mammals, including wild species, which are all horned, and domestic varieties. **2** any domesticated forms of this animal, farmed for their milk, meat and hides. ◷ 13c: from French *chatel*, from Latin *capitalis* wealth.

cattle cake ▻ *noun* a concentrated processed food for cattle, made from the compressed seeds of soya bean, groundnut and various other plants.

cattle grid ▻ *noun* a grid of parallel metal bars that covers a trench or depression in a road where it passes through a fence, designed to allow pedestrians and wheeled vehicles to pass unhindered, while preventing the passage of animal livestock.

cattleya /'katlɪə/ ▻ *noun* (***cattleyas***) a highly popular cultivated orchid, native to SE Asia and S America, which has swollen green bulb-like stems for storing water, and spikes of large yellow, pink or violet flowers. ◷ 19c: named after the English botanist William Cattley.

catty /'katɪ/ ▻ *adj* (***cattier***, ***cattiest***) **1** *informal* malicious; spiteful. **2** like a cat. • **cattily** or **cattishly** *adverb*. • **cattiness** or **cattishness** *noun*.

catwalk ▻ *noun* **1** a narrow walkway, usually at a high level, eg alongside a bridge. **2** the narrow raised stage along which models walk at a fashion show.

Caucasian /kɔː'keɪʒən/ ▻ *adj* **1** relating to the Caucasus, a mountain range between the Black Sea and the Caspian Sea, representing the boundary between Europe and Asia. **2** belonging to one of the light- or white-skinned races of mankind, inhabiting Europe, N Africa and W and Central Asia, although loosely thought of as white-skinned only. **3** denoting a family of 38 languages spoken in the area of the Caucasus mountains, which do not belong to the Indo-European, Semitic or Ural-Altaic groups. ▻ *noun* **1** an inhabitant or native of the Caucasus. **2 a** a member of the Caucasian race; **b** *loosely* a white-skinned person. **3** the languages forming the Caucasian family.

Caucasoid /'kɔːkəsɔɪd/ ▻ *adj* belonging to the Caucasian race.

caucus /'kɔːkəs/ ▻ *noun* (***caucuses***) **1** *sometimes derog* a small dominant group of people taking independent decisions within a larger organization. **2** *N Amer, especially US* a group of members of a political party, or a meeting of such a group for some purpose. ◷ 18c.

caudal /'kɔːdəl/ ▻ *adj, anatomy* **1** relating to, resembling, or in the position of a tail. **2** relating to the tail end of the body. ◷ 17c: from Latin *caudalis*, from *cauda* tail.

caudate /'kɔːdeɪt/ or **caudated** ▻ *adj, zool* having a tail or a tail-like appendage. ◷ 17c: from Latin *caudatus*, from *cauda* tail.

caught *past tense, past participle of* CATCH

caul /kɔːl/ ▻ *noun* **1** *anatomy* a membrane that sometimes surrounds an infant's head at birth, and consists of part of the AMNION. **2** *historical* a net or covering for the head. ◷ 14c: from French *cale* little cap.

cauldron or **caldron** /'kɔːldrən/ ▻ *noun* a very large metal pot, often with handles, for boiling or heating liquids. ◷ 13c: from French *cauderon*, from Latin *caldarium* hot bath.

cauliflower /'kɒlɪflaʊə(r)/ ▻ *noun* **1** a biennial plant that is a type of cultivated cabbage, widely cultivated for its edible flower-head. **2** the edible immature flower-head of this plant, consisting of a mass of creamy-white flower buds, which can be cooked and eaten as a vegetable. ◷ 16c as *colieflorie*: from Latin *cauliflora*, with spelling influenced by FLOWER.

cauliflower ear ▻ *noun* an ear permanently swollen and misshapen by injury, especially from repeated blows.

caulk /kɔːk/ ▻ *verb* (***caulked***, ***caulking***) **1** to fill up (the seams or joints of a boat) with OAKUM. **2** to make (a boat) watertight by this means. ◷ 15c: from French *cauquer* to press with force, from Latin *calcare* to trample.

causal ▻ *adj* **1** relating to or being a cause. **2** relating to cause and effect. • **causally** *adverb*. ◷ 16c: from Latin *causa* cause.

causality /kɔː'zalɪtɪ/ ▻ *noun* (***causalities***) **1** the relationship between cause and effect. **2** the principle that everything has a cause. **3** the process at work in the causing of something.

causation /kɔː'zeɪʃən/ ▻ *noun* **1** the relationship of cause and effect; causality. **2** the process of causing. • **causational** *adj*. ◷ 17c: from Latin *causatio*, from *causare*.

causative /'kɔːzətɪv/ ▻ *adj* **1** making something happen; producing an effect. **2** *grammar* expressing the action of causing. ▻ *noun* a causative verb. • **causatively** *adverb*. ◷ 15c: from Latin *causativus*.

cause /kɔːz/ ▻ *noun* **1** something which produces an effect; the person or thing through which something happens. **2** a reason or justification ▫ *There is no cause for concern.* **3** an ideal, principle, aim, etc, that people support and work for ▫ *She dedicated her life to the feminist cause.* **4** a matter that is to be settled by a lawsuit; the lawsuit itself. ▻ *verb* (***caused***, ***causing***) to produce as an effect; to bring about something. • **make common cause with someone** to co-operate with them, so as to achieve a common aim. ◷ 13c: from Latin *causa*.

'cause /kɒz, kəz/ ▻ *contraction, colloq* because.

cause célèbre /kouz sə'lɛb, kɔːz sɛ'lɛbrə; *French* koz selɛbʀ/ ▻ *noun* (***causes célèbres*** /kouz sə'lɛb, kɔːz sɛ'lɛbrə; *French* koz selðbʀ/) a legal case, or some other matter, that attracts much attention and causes controversy. ◷ 18c: French, meaning 'famous case'.

causeway /'kɔːzweɪ/ ▻ *noun* **1** a raised roadway crossing low-lying marshy ground or shallow water. **2** a stone-paved pathway. ◷ 15c: from French *caucie*, from Latin (*via*) *calciata* limestone-paved (way).

caustic /'kɔːstɪk, 'kɒ-/ ▻ *adj* **1** *chem* said of a chemical substance, eg sodium hydroxide: strongly alkaline and corrosive to living tissue. **2** said of remarks, etc: sarcastic; cutting; bitter. ▻ *noun* **1** CAUSTIC SODA. **2** *optics* the curve produced when parallel rays of light are reflected in a large concave mirror, or refracted by a convex lens. • **caustically** *adverb*. • **causticity** /kɔː'stɪsɪtɪ, kɒ'stɪsɪtɪ/ *noun*. ◷ 14c: from Latin *causticus*, from Greek *kaustikos* capable of burning.

caustic lime see SLAKED LIME

caustic soda see SODIUM HYDROXIDE

cauterize or **cauterise** /'kɔːtəraɪz/ ▻ *verb* (***cauterized***, ***cauterizing***) to destroy (living tissue) by the direct application of a heated instrument, an electric current, a laser beam, or a caustic chemical. • **cauterization** *noun*. ◷ 14c: from Latin *cauterizare*, from Greek *kauter* branding-iron.

caution /'kɔːʃən/ **1** care in avoiding danger; prudent wariness. **2** a warning. **3** a reprimand or scolding for an offence, accompanied by a warning not to repeat it. **4** *law* a warning from the police to someone suspected of an offence, that anything he or she says may be used as evidence. **5** *old use*, *colloq* an amusing person or thing. ▻ *verb* (***cautioned***, ***cautioning***) **1** *tr & intr* to warn or admonish someone. **2** to give someone a legal caution. ◷ 17c: French, from Latin *cautio*, from *cavere*, *cautum* to take heed.

cautionary /'kɔːʃənərɪ/ ▻ *adj* acting as or giving a warning □ *cautionary remarks*.

cautious /'kɔːʃəs/ ▻ *adj* having or showing caution; careful; wary. • **cautiously** *adverb*. • **cautiousness** *noun*.

cavalcade /kavəl'keɪd/ ▻ *noun* **1** a ceremonial procession of cars, horseback riders, etc. **2** any procession or parade. ◷ 17c in this sense; 16c in obsolete sense 'a ride on horseback': French, from Italian *cavalcata*, from Latin *caballicare* to ride on horseback, from *caballus* horse.

cavalier /kavə'lɪə(r)/ ▻ *noun* **1** *old use* a horseman or knight. **2** *old use* a courtly gentleman. **3** *facetious* a man acting as escort to a lady. **4** (**Cavalier**) *historical* a supporter of Charles I during the 17c English Civil War. ▻ *adj*, *derog* said of a person's behaviour, attitude, etc: thoughtless, offhand, casual or disrespectful. • **cavalierly** *adverb*. ◷ 16c: French, from Italian *cavaliere*, from Latin *caballarius* horseman.

cavalry /'kavəlrɪ/ ▻ *noun* (***cavalries***) **1** *usually historical* the part of an army consisting of soldiers on horseback. **2** the part of an army consisting of soldiers in armoured vehicles. Compare INFANTRY. ◷ 16c: from French *cavallerie*, from Italian *cavalleria*, from Latin *caballarius* horseman.

cavalryman ▻ *noun* a member of the cavalry.

cave[1] /keɪv/ ▻ *noun* **1** a large natural hollow chamber either underground, usually with an opening to the surface, or in the side of a mountain, hillside or cliff. **2** a small group of politicians who secede from their party over some issue. ▻ *verb* (***caved***, ***caving***) **1** to hollow something out. **2** *intr* to inhabit a cave, usually temporarily. ◷ 13c: French, from Latin *cava*, from *cavus* hollow.

■ **cave in 1** said of walls, a roof, etc: to collapse inwards. **2** *colloq* said of a person: to give way to persuasion. See also CAVE-IN.

cave[2] /'keɪvɪ/ ▻ *exclamation*, *school slang*, *dated* beware. • **keep cave** to keep watch; to be a lookout. ◷ 19c: Latin, imperative of *cavere* to beware.

cave art ▻ *noun* the art of the PALAEOLITHIC period, created c.30 000 years ago, including paintings preserved on the walls of limestone caves which depict hunting scenes and realistic drawings of animals, and small stone carvings.

caveat /'kavɪat, 'keɪ-/ ▻ *noun* **1** a warning. **2** *law* an official request that a court should not take some particular action without warning the person who is making the request. ◷ 16c: Latin, meaning 'let him or her beware', from *cavere* to beware.

caveat emptor /'kavɪat 'ɛmptɔː(r), 'keɪ- —/ ▻ *noun* the precept that a buyer should examine any goods they wish to purchase before doing so, as once they are sold the responsibility for the quality of the goods rests with them and no longer with the seller. ◷ 16c: Latin, meaning 'let the buyer beware'.

cave-in ▻ *noun* (***cave-ins***) **1** a collapse. **2** a submission or surrender. See also CAVE IN at CAVE[1].

caveman ▻ *noun* **1** (*also* **cave-dweller**) a person of prehistoric times, who lived in caves, etc. **2** *derog* a man who behaves in a crude, brutish way.

caver ▻ *noun* someone whose pastime is exploring caves.

cavern /'kavən/ ▻ *noun* a large cave or an underground chamber. ▻ *verb* (***caverned***, ***caverning***) **1** to enclose something in a cavern. **2** to hollow something out. ◷ 14c: from French *caverne*, from Latin *caverna* cave, from *cavus* hollow.

cavernous /'kavənəs/ ▻ *adj* **1** said of a hole or space: deep and vast. **2** said of rocks: full of caverns. • **cavernously** *adverb*.

cavetto /ka'vɛtou/ ▻ *noun* (***cavetti*** /-tiː/) *archit* a hollowed moulding with a curvature of a quarter of a circle, used chiefly in cornices, eg on ancient Egyptian buildings. ◷ 17c: Italian diminutive of *cavo*, from Latin *cavus* hollow.

caviar or **caviare** /'kavɪɑː(r), kavɪ'ɑː(r)/ ▻ *noun* the salted hard roe of the sturgeon, used as food and considered a delicacy. ◷ 16c: perhaps from Turkish *havyar*.

cavil /'kavɪl/ ▻ *verb* (***cavilled***, ***cavilling***) *intr* (*usually* **cavil at** or **about something**) to make trivial objections to something. ▻ *noun* a trivial objection. • **caviller** *noun*. ◷ 16c: from French, from Latin *cavillari* to scoff, from *cavilla* a jeering.

caving /'keɪvɪŋ/ ▻ *noun* the sport of exploring caves.

cavitation /kavɪ'teɪʃən/ ▻ *noun*, *physics* **1** the formation of cavities in a structure. **2** the formation of gas bubbles in a liquid. **3** the formation of a partial vacuum in a liquid moving at high speed.

cavity /'kavɪtɪ/ ▻ *noun* (***cavities***) **1** a hollow or hole. **2** a hole in a tooth, caused by decay. ◷ 16c: from French *cavité*, from Latin *cavitas* hollowness, from *cavus* hollow.

cavity wall ▻ *noun* a double wall with an airspace in between.

cavort /kə'vɔːt/ ▻ *verb* (***cavorted***, ***cavorting***) *intr* to jump or caper about. ◷ 19c.

cavy /'keɪvɪ/ ▻ *noun* (***cavies***) any of various rodents native to S America, including guinea pigs. ◷ 18c: from *Cabiai* the native name in French Guiana.

caw /kɔː/ ▻ *noun* the loud harsh cry of a crow or rook. ▻ *verb* (***cawed***, ***cawing***) *intr* to make such a cry. ◷ 16c: imitating the sound.

cay see KEY[2]

cayenne /keɪ'ɛn/ and **cayenne pepper** ▻ *noun* a hot spice made from the seeds of various types of

CAPSICUM. ◎ 18c as *cayan*, from Tupí, popularly associated with Cayenne in French Guiana.

cayman or **caiman** /'keɪmən/ ▷ *noun* (***caymans***) a reptile closely related to the alligator, native to tropical regions of Central and S America, which often has bony plates embedded in the skin of its belly. ◎ 16c: from Spanish *caimán*, from Carib.

CB ▷ *abbreviation* **1** Citizens' Band (Radio). **2** Companion of the Order of the Bath.

CBC ▷ *abbreviation* Canadian Broadcasting Corporation.

CBE ▷ *abbreviation* Commander of the Order of the British Empire.

CBI ▷ *abbreviation* **1** Confederation of British Industry, an association of UK employers that researches and reports to the government on the needs, problems and plans of business organization. **2** in the US: Central Bureau of Investigation.

CBS ▷ *abbreviation* Columbia Broadcasting System, a US broadcasting network.

CBSO ▷ *abbreviation* City of Birmingham Symphony Orchestra.

CC ▷ *abbreviation* **1** County Council. **2** Cricket Club.

cc ▷ *abbreviation* **1** carbon copy. **2** cubic centimetre.

CCC ▷ *abbreviation* County Cricket Club.

CCD ▷ *abbreviation, computing, electronics* charge-coupled device.

CCTV ▷ *abbreviation* closed-circuit television.

CD ▷ *abbreviation* **1** civil defence, or Civil Defence (Corps), a voluntary organization of civilians, active especially in World War II, trained to cope with the effects of enemy attack. **2** compact disc. **3** *Corps Diplomatique* (French), Diplomatic Corps, the body of diplomats in the service of any country.

Cd ▷ *symbol, chem* cadmium.

cd ▷ *abbreviation* candela.

CD-i or **CDI** ▷ *abbreviation* compact disc interactive, a type of CD-ROM that responds intelligently to instructions given by the user, and is used in conjunction with a computerized reader. Also written **ICD**.

CDN ▷ *abbreviation, IVR* Canada.

Cdr ▷ *abbreviation* Commander.

CD-ROM /siːdiː'rɒm/ ▷ *abbreviation, computing* compact disc read-only memory, a facility allowing examination, but not alteration, of a text on compact disc.

CDT ▷ *abbreviation, education* craft, design and technology.

CE or **C.E.** ▷ *abbreviation* **1** Church of England. **2** civil or chemical engineer. **3** Common Era. **4** *Communauté européene* (French), the mark required as the manufacturer's declaration of conformity with EU toy safety regulations on all toys since January 1990.

Ce ▷ *symbol, chem* cerium.

cease /siːs/ ▷ *verb* (***ceased, ceasing***) *tr & intr* to bring or come to an end. ● **without cease** *now only formal* continuously. ◎ 14c: from French *cesser*.

ceasefire ▷ *noun* (***ceasefires***) **1** a break in the fighting during a war, agreed to by all sides. **2** the order to stop firing.

ceaseless ▷ *adj* continuous; going on without a pause or break. ● **ceaselessly** *adverb*.

cebadilla see SABADILLA

cecal and **cecum** see CAECUM

cedar /'siːdə(r)/ ▷ *noun* **1** any of various tall coniferous trees belonging to the pine family, with a flat crown, widely spreading branches, needle-like leaves and reddish-brown bark. **2** (*also* **cedarwood**) the hard yellow sweet-smelling wood of this tree, used as building timber and for making furniture. ▷ *adj* made of cedar. ◎ 11c: from French *cedre*, from Greek *kedros*.

cede /siːd/ ▷ *verb* (***ceded, ceding***) **1** to hand over or give up something formally. **2** *intr* to yield or give way □ ***cede to a higher authority***. ◎ 17c: from Latin *cedere* to yield.

cedilla /sə'dɪlə/ ▷ *noun* (***cedillas***) **1** in French and Portuguese: a DIACRITIC put under *c* in some words, eg *façade*, to show that it is to be pronounced like *s*, not like *k*. **2** the same mark used under other letters in other languages to indicate various sounds. ◎ 16c: Spanish, meaning 'little c'.

Ceefax /'siːfaks/ ▷ *noun, trademark* a TELETEXT information service broadcast by the BBC. ◎ 1970s: from SEE + FACTS.

CEGB ▷ *abbreviation* Central Electricity Generating Board.

ceilidh /'keɪlɪ/ ▷ *noun* **1** in Scotland and Ireland: an informal social gathering, with songs, story-telling, music and dancing. **2** *Scottish* a public or private dance with Scottish traditional dancing only. ◎ 19c: Scottish Gaelic, meaning 'a visit'.

ceiling /'siːlɪŋ/ ▷ *noun* **1** the inner roof of a room, etc. **2** an upper limit. **3** the maximum height at which a specific aircraft is allowed to fly. **4** *meteorol* the height above the ground of the base of the cloud-layer. ◎ 16c in sense 1; 15c in obsolete sense 'panelling'.

celandine /'sɛləndaɪn/ ▷ *noun* a low-growing perennial plant, native to Europe and W Asia, which has heart-shaped dark-green leaves, and flowers with glossy golden-yellow petals that gradually fade to white. ◎ 13c: from Latin *chelidonia*, from Greek *chelidon* swallow, as the flowering of the plant was supposed to coincide with the arrival of the swallows in spring.

celeb /sə'lɛb/ ▷ *abbreviation, colloq* CELEBRITY 1.

celebrant /'sɛlɪbrənt/ ▷ *noun* someone who performs a religious ceremony.

celebrate /'sɛləbreɪt/ ▷ *verb* (***celebrated, celebrating***) **1** to mark (an occasion, especially a birthday or anniversary) with festivities. **2** *intr* to do something enjoyable to mark a happy occasion, anniversary, etc. **3** to give public praise or recognition to someone or something, eg in the form of a poem. **4** to conduct (a religious ceremony, eg a marriage or mass). ● **celebration** *noun*. ● **celebrator** *noun*. ● **celebratory** *adj*. ◎ 15c: from Latin *celebrare, celebratum* to honour, from *celeber* renowned.

celebrated ▷ *adj* famous; renowned.

celebrity /sə'lɛbrɪtɪ/ ▷ *noun* (***celebrities***) **1** a famous person. Often shortened to **celeb**. **2** fame or renown. ◎ 17c: from Latin *celebritas* fame.

celeriac /sə'lɛrɪak/ ▷ *noun* **1** a variety of celery, widely cultivated for the swollen edible base of its stem. **2** the swollen base of the stem of this plant, which is eaten raw in salads or cooked as a vegetable. ◎ 18c: from CELERY.

celerity /sə'lɛrɪtɪ/ ▷ *noun, formal* quickness; rapidity of motion or thought. ◎ 15c: from Latin *celeritas*, from *celer* swift.

celery /'sɛlərɪ/ ▷ *noun* (***celeries***) **1** a biennial plant, native to Europe, W Asia and Africa, which has shiny segmented leaves and tiny greenish-white flowers borne in flat-topped clusters. **2** the edible deeply grooved swollen leaf stalks of this plant, which can be eaten raw or cooked as a vegetable. ◎ 17c: from French *céleri*, from Italian dialect *sellaro*, from Greek *selinon* parsley.

celesta /sə'lɛstə/ ▷ *noun* (***celestas***) a keyboard instrument, resembling a small upright piano, from which soft bell-like sounds are produced by hammers striking steel plates suspended over wooden resonators. ◎ 19c: Latinization of French *céleste* heavenly.

celestial /sə'lɛstɪəl/ ▻ *adj* **1** belonging or relating to the sky □ *celestial bodies.* **2** belonging to heaven; heavenly; divine □ *celestial voices.* ● **celestially** *adverb.* ⓘ 14c: from Latin *celestialis*, from *caelum* the heavens.

celestial equator ▻ *noun, astron* the GREAT CIRCLE in which the plane of the Earth's equator meets the celestial sphere and divides it into northern and southern hemispheres.

celestial mechanics ▻ *noun* the branch of astronomy concerned with the movement of celestial bodies in gravitational fields.

celestial sphere ▻ *noun, astron* an infinitely large imaginary sphere on which the stars and other celestial bodies appear to lie when viewed by an observer at the centre of the sphere, represented by the Earth.

celiac see COELIAC

celibate /'sɛlɪbət/ ▻ *adj* **1** unmarried, especially in obedience to a religious vow. **2** having no sexual relations with anyone. ▻ *noun* someone who is unmarried, especially because of a religious vow. ● **celibacy** *noun.* ⓘ 17c: from Latin *caelebs* unmarried.

cell /sɛl/ ▻ *noun* **1** a small room occupied by an inmate in a prison or monastery. **2** *biol* the basic structural unit of all living organisms, consisting of a mass of protein material which is composed of the CYTOPLASM and usually a NUCLEUS (sense 2). **3** *elec* a device consisting of two ELECTRODES immersed in an ELECTROLYTE, for converting electrical energy into chemical energy. **4** a voltaic cell, which produces a current as a result of the conversion of chemical energy to electrical energy at the surface of two ELECTRODES immersed in an ELECTROLYTE. **5** one of the compartments in a honeycomb or in a similarly divided structure. **6** *radio* **a** a radio transmitter serving one of the geographical areas into which a country is divided for coverage by cellular radio; **b** one of these geographical areas. **7** *computing* a unit or area of storage, eg the smallest unit capable of storing a single bit. **8** a small unit of people (especially spies or terrorists) conducting their own operation within a larger organization. **9** *historical* a tiny one-roomed dwelling used by a hermit. ⓘ 12c: from Latin *cella* room or small apartment.

cellar /'sɛlə(r)/ ▻ *noun* **1** a room, usually underground, for storage, eg of wine. **2** a stock of wines. ▻ *verb* (***cellared, cellaring***) to store in a cellar. ⓘ 13c: from French *celer*, from Latin *cellarium* foodstore.

cellarage ▻ *noun* **1** the volume of cellar space in a building. **2** the charge made for storing goods in a cellar.

cell body ▻ *noun, anatomy* the enlarged part of a NEURONE, which contains the NUCLEUS (sense 2) and CYTOPLASM, and from which the AXON extends.

cell membrane see MEMBRANE 2

Cellnet ▻ *noun* in the UK: a system of mobile telecommunications using cellular radio.

cello /'tʃɛloʊ/ ▻ *noun* (***cellos***) a large stringed musical instrument of the violin family, which is played sitting, with the neck of the instrument resting against the player's shoulder. ● **cellist** /'tʃɛlɪst/ *noun* someone who plays the cello. ⓘ 19c: short for VIOLONCELLO.

Cellophane /'sɛləfeɪn/ ▻ *noun, trademark* a thin transparent sheeting manufactured from regenerated CELLULOSE, used mainly as a wrapping material for food and other products. ⓘ 20c: from CELLULOSE + Greek *phainein* to shine or appear.

cellphone ▻ *noun, radio* a portable telephone for use in a cellular radio system.

cellular /'sɛljʊlə(r)/ ▻ *adj* **1** composed of cells or divided into cell-like compartments. **2** containing many cavities or holes; porous. **3** knitted with an open pattern. **4** relating to cellular radio. ⓘ 18c: from Latin *cellularis*, from *cellula*, diminutive of *cella* room.

cellular radio ▻ *noun* a system of radio communication used especially for car phones, based on a network of small geographical areas called cells, each of which is served by a transmitter.

cellular therapy see LIVE-CELL THERAPY

cellule /'sɛljuːl/ ▻ *noun biol* a small cell. ⓘ 19c in this sense; 17c in obsolete sense 'a small compartment': from Latin *cellula*, diminutive of *cella* room.

cellulite /'sɛljʊlaɪt/ ▻ *noun* deposits of fat cells said to be resistant to changes in diet or exercise regime, and which give the skin a dimpled, pitted appearance. ⓘ 1960s: French.

celluloid /'sɛljʊlɔɪd/ ▻ *noun, trademark* **1** a transparent highly flammable plastic material made from CELLULOSE NITRATE and CAMPHOR, formerly widely used in photographic film, but now largely superseded by CELLULOSE ACETATE. **2** cinema film.

cellulose /'sɛljʊloʊs, -loʊz/ ▻ *noun* a complex carbohydrate that is the main constituent of plant cell walls, and is used in the manufacture of paper, rope, textiles, (eg cotton and linen) and plastics (eg Cellophane). ⓘ 18c: from CELLULE + -OSE.

cellulose acetate ▻ *noun, chem* a tough flexible non-flammable THERMOPLASTIC resin, prepared by treating cellulose with ACETIC ACID, and used to make photographic film, magnetic tape, lacquers, varnishes and acetate fibres, eg rayon.

cellulose nitrate ▻ *noun, chem* a highly flammable pulpy solid, prepared by treating cellulose with concentrated NITRIC ACID, and used as an explosive and propellant. It was formerly used in photographic film, plastics and lacquers.

cell wall ▻ *noun, bot* in plant cells: the relatively rigid outer wall that surrounds the membrane of the cell and consists mainly of CELLULOSE.

Celsius /'sɛlsɪəs/ ▻ *adj* (abbreviation **C**) relating to the Celsius scale.

Celsius

In stating temperatures, **Celsius** is now preferred, as a more specific term, to **centigrade**.

Celsius scale ▻ *noun* a scale of temperature, formerly known as the centigrade scale, in which the freezing point of water is 0°C and its boiling point is 100°C, with the temperature range between these fixed points being divided into 100 degrees. ⓘ 18c: named after Anders Celsius (1701–44), a Swedish astronomer and the inventor of the centigrade thermometer.

Celt /kɛlt, sɛlt/ or **Kelt** /kɛlt/ ▻ *noun* **1** a member of one of the ancient peoples that inhabited most parts of Europe in pre-Roman and Roman times, or of the peoples descended from them, eg in Scotland, Wales and Ireland. **2** someone who speaks a Celtic language. ⓘ 17c: from Latin *Celtae*.

Celtic or **Keltic** ▻ *adj* relating to the Celts or their languages. ▻ *noun* a branch of the Indo-European family of languages, including Gaelic, Welsh, Cornish and Breton.

cement /sə'mɛnt/ ▻ *noun* **1** a fine powder, composed of a mixture of clay and limestone, that hardens when mixed with water, and is used to make mortar and concrete. **2** any of various substances used as adhesives for bonding to a hard material. **3** *dentistry* any of various substances used to fill cavities in teeth. **4** another word for CEMENTUM. **5** *geol* any material, especially precipitated mineral salts, that binds loose particles of sediment together to form solid rock. ▻ *verb* (***cemented, cementing***) **1** to stick together with cement. **2** to apply cement. **3** to bind or make firm (eg a friendship). ⓘ 13c: from French *ciment*, from Latin *caementum* quarried stone.

cement, concrete

Note that **cement** is not the same as **concrete**, but is the bonding ingredient of it.

cementation /sɛmən'teɪʃən/ ▻ *noun* **1** the act of cementing. **2** the process of impregnating the surface of one substance with another by surrounding it with powder and applying heat, used in case-hardening and the conversion of glass into porcelain. **3** the process of injecting fluid cement mixture into a hole or cavity for strengthening purposes.

cementum ▻ *noun* the thin layer of hard bony tissue that anchors the roots of the teeth to the jaws. Also called **cement**.

cemetery /'sɛmətrɪ, 'sɛmətərɪ/ ▻ *noun* (***cemeteries***) a burial ground for the dead, especially one that is not attached to a church. ◷ 14c: from Latin *cemeterium*, from Greek *koimeterion* burial place, from *koiman* to put to sleep.

-cene /siːn/ *combining form, geol, denoting* any epoch in the Cenozoic era. [From Greek *kainos* new]

cenotaph /'sɛnətɑːf/ ▻ *noun* a tomb-like monument in honour of a person or persons buried elsewhere, especially soldiers killed in war. ◷ 17c: from French *cenotaphe*, from Greek *kenos* empty + *taphos* tomb.

Cenozoic or **Caenozoic** /siːnoʊ'zoʊɪk/ or **Cainozoic** /kaɪnoʊ'zoʊɪk/ ▻ *adj, geol, denoting* the most recent era of the Phanerozoic eon. ▻ *noun* (**the Cenozoic**) the Cenozoic era. See table at GEOLOGICAL TIME SCALE. ◷ 19c: from Greek *kainos* new + *zoe* life.

censer /'sɛnsə(r)/ ▻ *noun* a container in which incense is burnt, used eg in some churches. Also called **thurible**. ◷ 13c: from French *censier*, from Latin *incensarium*, from *incensum* incense.

censor /'sɛnsə(r)/ ▻ *noun* **1** an official who examines books, films, newspaper articles, etc, with the power to cut out any parts thought politically sensitive or offensive, and to forbid publication or showing altogether. **2** *historical* in ancient Rome: either of the two magistrates who kept account of the property of Roman citizens and watched over their morals. **3** someone who controls the actions and behaviour of others on moral grounds. **4** *psychol* an unconscious mechanism in the mind which inhibits the emergence of that which is painful to the conscious from the subconscious. ▻ *verb* (***censored, censoring***) **1** to alter or cut out parts of something, or forbid its publication, showing or delivery. **2** to act as a censor. • **censorial** /sɛn'sɔːrɪəl/ *adj*. ◷ 16c: Latin, from *censere* to estimate or assess.

censorious /sɛn'sɔːrɪəs/ ▻ *adj* inclined to find fault; severely critical. • **censoriously** *adverb*. • **censoriousness** *noun*. ◷ 16c: from Latin *censorius* relating to a censor.

censorship ▻ *noun* **1** the practice of censoring. **2** the job of a censor.

censure /'sɛnʃə(r)/ ▻ *noun* severe criticism or disapproval. ▻ *verb* (***censured, censuring***) to criticize severely or express strong disapproval of someone or something. • **censurable** *adj*. ◷ 17c in this sense; 14c in obsolete sense 'a spiritual punishment': French, from Latin *censura*, from *censere* to estimate or assess.

census /'sɛnsəs/ ▻ *noun* (***censuses***) **1** an official count of a population, carried out at periodic intervals, which covers information such as sex, age, job, etc. **2** any official count, eg of vehicles using a particular road, customers using a particular shop, etc. ◷ 17c: Latin, from *censere* to estimate or assess.

cent /sɛnt/ ▻ *noun* a currency unit of several countries, worth one hundredth of the standard unit, eg of the US dollar and the euro. ◷ 16c: from Latin *centum* a hundred.

cent. /sɛnt/ ▻ *abbreviation* **1** centigrade. **2** central. **3** century.

centaur /'sɛntɔː(r)/ ▻ *noun, Greek mythol* a creature with a man's head, arms and trunk, joined to the four-legged body of a horse. ◷ 14c: from Latin *centaurus*, from Greek *kentauros*.

Centaurus /sɛn'tɔːrəs/ ▻ *noun, astron* a large constellation in the S hemisphere.

centavo /sɛn'tɑːvoʊ/ ▻ *noun* (***centavos***) a currency unit of several countries, worth one hundredth of the standard unit, eg of the Columbian peso.

centenarian /sɛntə'nɛərɪən/ ▻ *noun* someone who is 100 years old or more. ▻ *adj* **1** 100 years old or more. **2** relating to a centenarian. ◷ 19c.

centenary /sɛn'tiːnərɪ/ ▻ *noun* (***centenaries***) the one-hundredth anniversary of some event, or the celebration of it. ▻ *adj* **1** occurring every 100 years. **2** relating to a period of 100 years. ◷ 17c: from Latin *centenarius* composed of one hundred.

centennial /sɛn'tɛnɪəl, sən-/ ▻ *noun, N Amer* a centenary. ▻ *adj* **1** relating to a period of 100 years. **2** occurring every 100 years. **3** lasting 100 years. ◷ 18c: from Latin *centum* 100 + *annus* year, modelled on BIENNIAL.

center the *N Amer* spelling of CENTRE.

centi- /sɛntɪ/ or (before a vowel) **cent-** /sɛnt/ ▻ *prefix, denoting* **1** one hundredth □ *centigram*. **2** one hundred □ *centipede*. ◷ From Latin *centum* hundred.

centigrade /'sɛntɪgreɪd/ ▻ *adj* ▻ *noun* (abbreviation **C**) the former name for the CELSIUS scale of temperature. ◷ 19c.

centigrade

See Usage Note at **Celsius**.

centigram or **centigramme** /'sɛntɪgram/ ▻ *noun* the one-hundredth part of a gram. ◷ 19c.

centilitre or (*US*) **centiliter** /'sɛntɪliːtə(r)/ ▻ *noun* the one-hundredth part of a litre. ◷ 19c.

centime /'sɒntiːm; *French* sɑ̃tim/ ▻ *noun* a currency unit of several countries, worth one hundredth of the standard unit, eg of the French franc. ◷ 19c: French, from *centiesme*, from Latin *centesimus* one-hundredth.

centimetre /'sɛntɪmiːtə(r)/ ▻ *noun* in the metric system: a basic unit of length equal to 0.01m (one hundredth of a metre). ◷ 19c.

centipede /'sɛntɪpiːd/ ▻ *noun* any of numerous species of terrestrial arthropod which have a long rather flat segmented body and usually either 15 or 23 pairs of legs, one pair for each body segment. ◷ 17c: from Latin *centipeda*, from CENTI- + *pes* foot.

central /'sɛntrəl/ ▻ *adj* **1** at or forming the centre of something. **2** near the centre of a city, etc; easy to reach. **3** principal or most important. • **centrality** *noun*. • **centrally** *adverb*. ◷ 17c: from Latin *centralis*, from *centrum* centre.

Central American ▻ *adj* belonging or relating to Central America, a geographical region that encompasses the independent states south of Mexico and north of S America (including Guatemala, El Salvador, Belize and Nicaragua), and their inhabitants. ▻ *noun* a citizen or inhabitant of, or person born in, Central America.

central bank ▻ *noun* a national bank acting as banker to the government, issuing currency, controlling the amount of credit in the country and having control over interest rates.

Central Criminal Court ▻ *noun* the official title of the OLD BAILEY.

central government ▻ *noun* the government that has power over a whole country, as distinct from local government.

central heating ▻ *noun* a system for heating a whole building, by means of pipes, radiators, etc connected to a central source of heat.

centralism /'sɛntrəlɪzəm/ ▻ *noun* the policy of bringing the administration of a country under central control, with a decrease in local administrative power. ● **centralist** *noun, adj.*

centrality see under CENTRAL

centralize or **centralise** ▻ *verb* (***centralized, centralizing***) *tr & intr* to bring under central control. ● **centralization** *noun.*

central locking ▻ *noun* in a motor vehicle: a system whereby all the doors (including the boot or trunk) are locked or unlocked automatically when the driver's door is locked.

centrally see under CENTRAL

centrally-heated ▻ *adj* provided with or warmed by central heating.

central nervous system ▻ *noun* in vertebrates: the part of the nervous system that is responsible for the co-ordination and control of the various body functions; it consists of the brain and spinal cord.

central processing unit ▻ *noun, computing* (abbreviation **CPU**) the part of a digital computer that controls and co-ordinates the operation of all the other parts, and that performs arithmetical and logical operations on data loaded into it. Also called **central processor**. See also MICROPROCESSOR.

central reservation ▻ *noun, Brit* a narrow strip of grass, concrete, etc dividing the two sides of a dual carriageway, especially a motorway.

centre or (*N Amer*) **center** /'sɛntə(r)/ ▻ *noun* **1** a part at the middle of something □ *chocolates with soft centres.* **2** a point inside a circle or sphere that is an equal distance from all points on the circumference or surface, or a point on a line at an equal distance from either end. **3** a point or axis round which a body revolves or rotates. **4** a central area. **5** *chiefly in compounds* a place where a specified activity is concentrated or specified facilities, information, etc are available □ *a sports centre.* **6** something that acts as a focus □ *the centre of attraction.* **7** a point or place from which activities are controlled □ *the centre of operations.* **8** a position that is at neither extreme, especially in politics. **9** in some field sports, eg football: **a** a position in the middle of the field; **b** a player in this position. ▻ *adj* at the centre; central. ▻ *verb* (***centred, centring***) **1** to place in or at the centre; to position centrally or symmetrically. **2** to adjust or focus (eg one's thoughts). **3** *tr & intr* (*often* **centre on** or **upon something**) to concentrate on it. ⓒ 14c: French, from Latin *centrum*, from Greek *kentron* sharp point, from *kentein* to prick.

> ***centre around***
>
> ● Although illogical, (**be**) **centred around** is a common alternative for (**be**) **centred on**, especially in spoken English □ *Talks were centred around the purchase of transport aircraft and weaponry.*
> ☆ PLAIN ENGLISH alternatives are **about, devoted to, concentrated on**.

centre-back ▻ *noun, football* **a** the position in the centre of defence; **b** a player in this position.

centreboard ▻ *noun* in a sailing boat or dinghy: a movable plate which can be let down through the keel to prevent sideways drift.

centrefold and **centre spread** ▻ *noun* **1 a** the sheet that forms the two central facing pages of a magazine, etc; **b** the illustration occupying it. **2 a** a photograph of a naked or nearly naked person on such pages; **b** the subject of the photograph.

centre-forward ▻ *noun, sport* in some field games: **a** the position in the centre of the front line; **b** a player in this position, usually a striker.

centre-half ▻ *noun, sport* in some field games: **a** the position in the centre of the half-back line; **b** the player in this position.

centre of gravity ▻ *noun, physics* a theoretical fixed point in a body about which its weight may be considered to be uniformly distributed.

centre of mass and **centre of inertia** ▻ *noun, physics* a theoretical fixed point in a body about which its whole mass may be considered to be concentrated.

centrepiece ▻ *noun* **1** a central or most important item. **2** an ornament or decoration for the centre of a table.

centre spread see CENTREFOLD

centri- /sɛntrɪ, sɛn'trɪ/ or **centro-** /sɛntroʊ/ or (before a vowel) **centr-** ▻ *combining form, denoting* a centre or middle. ⓒ From Latin *centrum*, from Greek *kentron* centre.

-centric /sɛntrɪk/ ▻ *combining form, denoting* a stated centre, focus, basis, etc □ *egocentric.*

centrifugal /sɛntrɪ'fjuːgəl, sɛn'trɪfjʊgəl/ ▻ *adj, physics* acting or moving away from the centre of a circle along which an object is moving, or away from the axis of rotation. Compare CENTRIPETAL. ⓒ 18c: from CENTRI- + Latin *fugere* to flee.

centrifugal force ▻ *noun* an apparent but non-existent force that seems to exert an outward pull on an object that is moving in a circular path. Compare CENTRIPETAL FORCE.

centrifuge /'sɛntrɪfjuːdʒ/ ▻ *noun* a device containing a rotating device that is used to separate solid or liquid particles of different densities, by spinning them at high speed in a tube in a horizontal circle, with the heaviest particles becoming sedimented in the form of a pellet at the end of the tube. ▻ *verb* (***centrifuged, centrifuging***) to subject something to centrifugal action. ⓒ 19c: from CENTRI- + Latin *fugere* to flee.

centriole /'sɛntrɪoʊl/ ▻ *noun, biol* in animal cells: a tiny cylindrical structure that plays an important role in cell division. ⓒ 19c: from German *Centriol*, from Latin *centriolum*, diminutive of *centrum* centre.

centripetal /sɛn'trɪpɪtəl, sɛntrɪ'piːtəl/ ▻ *adj, physics* acting or moving towards the centre of a circle along which an object is moving, or towards the axis of rotation. Compare CENTRIFUGAL. ⓒ 18c: from CENTRI- + Latin *petere* to seek.

centripetal force ▻ *noun* the force that is required to keep an object moving in a circular path. Compare CENTRIFUGAL FORCE.

centrist /'sɛntrɪst/ ▻ *adj* having moderate, non-extreme political opinions. ▻ *noun* someone holding such opinions. ● **centrism** *noun.* ⓒ 19c.

centromere /'sɛntroʊmɪə(r)/ ▻ *noun, genetics* the part of a chromosome that attaches it to the SPINDLE (sense 4) during cell division. ⓒ 20c: from CENTRO- + Greek *meros* part.

centurion /sɛn'tʃʊərɪən/ ▻ *noun, historical* in the army of ancient Rome: an officer in charge of a CENTURY (*noun* 5). ⓒ 14c: from Latin *centurio*, from *centum* 100.

century /'sɛntʃərɪ/ ▻ *noun* (***centuries***) **1** any 100-year period counted forwards or backwards from an important event, especially the birth of Christ. **2** a period of 100 years. **3** *cricket* a score of 100 runs made by a batsman in a single innings. **4** a score of 100. **5** *historical* in the army of ancient Rome: a company of (originally) 100 foot soldiers. ⓘ 16c: from Latin *centuria* a division of 100 things, from *centum* 100.

CEO ▷ *abbreviation* Chief Executive Officer.

cephalic /sɪ'falɪk, kɛ-/ ▷ *adj* relating to the head or the head region. ⓘ 16c: from French *céphalique*, from Greek *kephale* head..

-cephalic and **-cephalous** ▷ *combining form, forming adjectives, signifying* head or skull; headed □ *dolichocephalic.*

cephalic index ▷ *noun, anthropol* a skull's breadth as a percentage of its length, with skulls of different relative breadths termed **brachycephalic** /brakɪ-/ for a short broad head, **mesocephalic** /mɛsoʊ-, miːsoʊ-/ for a medium-sized head and **dolichocephalic** /dɒlɪkoʊ-/ for a long narrow head.

cephalo- /sɛfəloʊ, sɛfə'lɒ, kɛ-/ or (before a vowel) **cephal-** ▷ *combining form, denoting* head or skull □ *cephalopod.* ⓘ From Greek *kephale.*

cephalopod /'sɛfələpɒd, 'kɛ-/ ▷ *noun* any invertebrate animal belonging to a class of marine predatory molluscs with a highly developed brain and sense organs, eg squid, octopus, cuttlefish, nautilus. ⓘ 19c.

Cepheid variable /'siːfɪɪd —/ ▷ *noun, astron* any of a group of variable stars that pulsate on a very regular basis, every 1 to 100 days, used to measure distances in our own and nearby galaxies.

Cepheus /'siːfɪəs/ ▷ *noun, astron* a northern constellation, lying partly in the Milky Way, that includes the star Delta Cephei, the prototype of Cepheid variables. ⓘ 20c: named after a mythical king of Ethiopia.

ceramic /sə'ramɪk/ ▷ *noun* **1** any of a number of hard brittle materials, eg enamels, porcelain and brick, produced by moulding or shaping and then baking or firing clays at high temperatures. **2** an object made from such a material. ▷ *adj* relating to or made of such a material. ⓘ 19c: from Greek *keramikos*, from *keramos* potter's clay.

ceramics ▷ *singular noun* the art and technique of making pottery.

cere /sɪə(r)/ ▷ *noun* the bare wax-like patch at the base of the upper part of a bird's beak, containing the nostrils. ⓘ 15c: from French *cire*, from Latin *cera* wax.

cereal /'sɪərɪəl/ ▷ *noun* **1** a member of the grass family that is cultivated as a food crop for its nutritious edible seeds, ie grains, eg barley, wheat, rice, etc. **2** the grain produced. **3** a breakfast food prepared from this grain. ▷ *adj* relating to edible grains. ⓘ 19c: from Latin *Cerealis* relating to Ceres, goddess of agriculture.

cerebellum /sɛrə'bɛləm/ ▷ *noun* (***cerebella*** /-lə/) *anatomy* in vertebrates: the main part of the hindbrain, concerned primarily with the co-ordination of movement. ● **cerebellar** *adj.* ⓘ 16c: Latin diminutive of *cerebrum* brain.

cerebral /'sɛrəbrəl, sə'riːbrəl/ ▷ *adj* **1** relating to or in the region of the brain. **2** *often facetious* intellectual; using the brain rather than appealing to the emotions □ *a cerebral argument.* ⓘ 19c: from CEREBRUM.

cerebral cortex ▷ *noun, anatomy* in most vertebrates: the outer layer of the cerebral hemispheres of the brain, responsible for consciousness (including perception, memory and learning) and the initiation of voluntary movement.

cerebral haemorrhage ▷ *noun, pathol* bleeding from a ruptured blood vessel, usually an artery, within the brain, most often caused by HYPERTENSION or degenerative disease of the blood vessel concerned, which may result in stroke, coma or death.

cerebral hemisphere ▷ *noun, anatomy* in higher vertebrates: either of the two halves of the cerebrum, which in humans form the major part of the brain, with each hemisphere controlling the opposite side of the body.

cerebral palsy ▷ *noun, pathol* a failure of the brain to develop normally in young children due to brain damage before or around the time of birth, resulting in weakness, lack of co-ordination of the limbs, and often spastic paralysis.

cerebrate /'sɛrəbreɪt/ ▷ *verb* (***cerebrated, cerebrating***) *intr, facetious* to think; to use one's brain. ● **cerebration** *noun.*

cerebrospinal /sɛrəbroʊ'spaɪnəl/ ▷ *adj* relating to the brain and spinal cord together □ *cerebrospinal fluid.*

cerebrum /'sɛrəbrəm, sə'riːbrəm/ ▷ *noun* (***cerebrums*** or ***cerebra*** /-brə/) *anatomy* in higher vertebrates: the front part of the brain, consisting of two cerebral hemispheres linked by the CORPUS CALLOSUM, which initiates and co-ordinates all voluntary activity. ⓘ 17c: Latin.

ceremonial /sɛrə'moʊnɪəl/ ▷ *adj* relating to, used for or involving a ceremony. ▷ *noun* **1** a system of rituals. **2** *Christianity* **a** the stipulated order of ceremonies and rites; **b** a book containing this. ● **ceremonially** *adverb.* ⓘ 14c: from Latin *caerimonia* rite.

ceremonious /sɛrə'moʊnɪəs/ ▷ *adj* excessively formal. ● **ceremoniously** *adverb.* ⓘ 16c: from Latin *caerimoniosus* full of ceremony.

ceremony /'sɛrəmənɪ/ ▷ *noun* (***ceremonies***) **1** a ritual performed to mark a particular, especially public or religious, occasion. **2** formal politeness. **3** ceremonial rituals collectively. ● **stand on ceremony** to insist on behaving formally. ● **without ceremony** in a hasty informal way. ⓘ 14c: from Latin *caerimonia* sacredness or rite.

cerise /sə'riːz, sə'riːs/ ▷ *noun* a bright cherry-red colour. ▷ *adj* cerise-coloured. ⓘ 19c: French, meaning 'cherry'.

cerium /'sɪərɪəm/ ▷ *noun, chem* (abbreviation **Ce**, atomic number 58) a soft silvery-grey metallic element belonging to the LANTHANIDE series, used in catalytic converters, alloys for cigarette-lighter flints, etc. ⓘ 19c: named after the asteroid Ceres.

cermet /'sɜːmɛt/ ▷ *noun, engineering* **1** a hard strong composite material, resistant to corrosion and wear, made from a ceramic and a metal, and used to make cutting tools and brake linings. **2** a type of electronic resistor made of such material. ⓘ 20c: from CERAMIC + METAL.

CERN /sɜːn/ ▷ *abbreviation*: *Conseil Européen pour la Recherche Nucléaire* (French), European Organization for Nuclear Research, now known as the European Laboratory for Particle Physics.

ceroc /sə'rɒk/ ▷ *noun* a contemporary style of jive dancing to rock-and-roll music. ⓘ 20c: from French *Le Roc* dancing, on which it is based.

cert /sɜːt/ ▷ *noun, colloq* (*usually* **dead cert**) a certainty, especially a horse that is bound to win a race.

cert. ▷ *abbreviation* **1** certificate. **2** certified.

certain /'sɜːtən/ ▷ *adj* **1** proved or known beyond doubt □ *It is certain that the defendant knew Mr Wilson.* **2** (*sometimes* **certain about** or **of something**) having no doubt about it; absolutely sure. **3** used with reference to the future: definitely going to happen, etc; able to rely on or be relied on. **4** particular and, though known, not named or specified □ *a certain friend of yours.* **5** used before a person's name to indicate either their obscurity or one's own unfamiliarity with them □ *a certain Mrs Smith.* **6** said of a quality: undeniably present without being clearly definable □ *The beard gave his face a certain authority.* **7** some, though not much □ *That's true to a certain extent.* ▷ *pronoun* some □ *Certain of the team are not pulling their weight.* ● **for certain** definitely; without doubt. ● **make certain of something** to take action so as to ensure it or be sure about it. ⓘ 13c: French, from Latin *certus* sure.

certainly ▻ *adverb* **1** without any doubt. **2** definitely. **3** in giving permission: of course.

certainty ▻ *noun* (***certainties***) **1** something that cannot be doubted or is bound to happen. **2** freedom from doubt; the state of being sure. **3** the state of being bound to happen.

certifiable /ˈsɜːtɪfaɪəbəl/ ▻ *adj* **1** capable of or suitable for being certified. **2** *colloq* said of a person: mad; crazy.

certificate /səˈtɪfɪkət/ ▻ *noun* an official document that formally acknowledges or witnesses a fact, an achievement or qualification, or one's condition □ *marriage certificate.* ▻ *verb* /səˈtɪfɪkeɪt/ (***certificated, certificating***) to provide with a certificate. See also CERTIFY. ⓒ 15c: from Latin *certificare, certificatum* to certify.

certificated ▻ *adj* qualified by a particular course of training.

certificate of deposit ▻ *noun* a certificate representing a fixed-term interest-bearing deposit in large denominations, which may be bought and sold. ⓒ 1961: first introduced by a bank in New York.

certification /sɜːtɪfɪˈkeɪʃən/ ▻ *noun* **1** certifying or being certified. **2** a document that certifies something.

certified ▻ *adj* **1** possessing a certificate. **2** endorsed or guaranteed. **3** said of a person: insane.

certify /ˈsɜːtɪfaɪ/ ▻ *verb* (***certifies, certified, certifying***) **1** *tr & intr* to declare or confirm officially. **2** to declare someone legally insane. **3** to declare to have reached a required standard, passed certain tests, etc. See also CERTIFICATE. ● **certifier** *noun*. ⓒ 14c: from Latin *certificare*, from *certus* certain + *facere* to make.

certitude /ˈsɜːtɪtʃuːd/ ▻ *noun* a feeling of certainty. ⓒ 15c: from Latin *certitudo*, from *certus* certain.

cerumen /sɪˈruːmən/ ▻ *noun* EARWAX. ● **ceruminous** *adj*.

cervical /ˈsɜːvɪkəl, səˈvaɪkəl/ ▻ *adj* relating to or in the region of the cervix.

cervical smear ▻ *noun, medicine* the collection of a sample of cells from the cervix of the uterus for staining and examination under a microscope, in order to detect any abnormal changes indicative of cancer. Also called **smear test**.

cervine /ˈsɜːvaɪn/ ▻ *adj* relating to or resembling a deer. ⓒ 19c: from Latin *cervinus*, from *cervus* a deer.

cervix /ˈsɜːvɪks/ ▻ *noun* (***cervixes*** or ***cervices*** /sɜːˈvaɪsiːz/) **1** *anatomy* the neck of the uterus, consisting of a narrow passage leading to the inner end of the vagina. **2** *anatomy* the neck. ⓒ 18c: Latin, meaning 'neck'.

cesarian the *US* spelling of CAESARIAN

cesium the *US* spelling of CAESIUM

cessation /sɛˈseɪʃən/ ▻ *noun* a stopping or ceasing; a pause. ⓒ 14c: from Latin *cessatio*, from *cessare* to cease.

cession /ˈsɛʃən/ ▻ *noun* the giving up or yielding of territories, rights, etc to someone else. ⓒ 15c: from Latin *cessio*, from *cedere* to yield.

cesspit /ˈsɛspɪt/ ▻ *noun* **1** a pit for the collection and storage of sewage. **2** a foul and squalid place. ⓒ 19c.

cesspool ▻ *noun* **1** a tank, well, etc for the collection and storage of sewage and waste water. **2** a rotten and putrid place. ⓒ 17c.

cesura see CAESURA

cetacean /sɪˈteɪʃən/ ▻ *noun* in the animal kingdom: any animal belonging to the order which includes dolphins, porpoises and whales. ▻ *adj* relating or belonging to this group. ⓒ 19c: Latin, from Greek *ketos* whale.

cetane /ˈsiːteɪn/ ▻ *noun* a colourless liquid hydrocarbon found in petroleum, used as a solvent and in the determination of the cetane number of diesel fuel. Also called **hexadecane**. ⓒ 19c: from Latin *cetus* whale.

cetane number ▻ *noun* a measure of the ignition quality of diesel fuel when it is burnt in a standard diesel engine.

Cetus /ˈsiːtəs/ ▻ *noun, astron* the fourth largest constellation, which lies above the celestial equator, but is inconspicuous because it has few bright stars. ⓒ Latin, meaning 'whale'.

cevadilla see SABADILLA

Ceylonese /sɪlɒˈniːz/ *noun, adj* SRI LANKAN.

Cf ▻ *symbol, chem* californium.

cf ▻ *abbreviation*: *confer* (Latin), compare.

CFC ▻ *abbreviation* chlorofluorocarbon.

cg ▻ *abbreviation* centigram.

CGI or **CGLI** ▻ *abbreviation* City and Guilds (of London) Institute.

cgs unit ▻ *abbreviation, physics* centimetre-gram-second unit, a system of measurement based on the use of the centimetre, gram and second as the fundamental units of length, mass and time, respectively, for most purposes now superseded by SI units.

CH ▻ *abbreviation* **1** Companion of Honour, a British title awarded to people who have given particular service to the nation. **2** *IVR*: *Confederatio Helvetica* (Latin), Switzerland.

ch ▻ *abbreviation* **1** chapter. **2** CHAIN (*noun* 6). **3** *chess* check. **4** church.

Chablis /ˈʃabliː/ ▻ *noun* a dry white wine made in the Burgundy region of NE France. ⓒ 17c: named after the small French town near to where it is made.

cha-cha /ˈtʃɑːtʃɑː/ and **cha-cha-cha** ▻ *noun* (***cha-chas***) **1** a Latin American dance. **2** a piece of music for it. ▻ *verb* (***cha-chaed, cha-chaing***) *intr* to perform this dance. ⓒ 1950s: American Spanish.

chaconne /ʃaˈkɒn, ʃə-/ ▻ *noun* **1** an old slow Spanish dance. **2** a piece of music for it, written in the form of variations on a ground bass or a stereotyped harmonic progression in triple time with slow stately tempo. See also PASSACAGLIA. ⓒ 17c: French, from Spanish *chacona*, from Basque *chucun* pretty.

Chadian /ˈtʃadɪən/ ▻ *adj* belonging or relating to Chad, a republic in N central Africa, or its inhabitants. ▻ *noun* a citizen or inhabitant of, or person born in, Chad.

Chadic /ˈtʃadɪk/ ▻ *noun* a group of more than 100 languages, assigned to the Afro-Asiatic family of languages, which are spoken by c.25 million people in parts of Ghana and the Central African Republic. ▻ *adj* relating to this group of languages.

chador, **chadar** or **chuddar** /ˈtʃʌdə(r)/ ▻ *noun* a thick veil worn by Muslim women that covers the head and body. ⓒ 17c: Persian.

chafe /tʃeɪf/ ▻ *verb* (***chafed, chafing***) **1** *tr & intr* to make or become sore or worn by rubbing. **2** to make warm by rubbing. **3** *intr* (*also* **chafe at** or **under something**) to become angry or impatient □ *chafe at the rules.* ▻ *noun* an irritation caused by rubbing. ⓒ 14c: from French *chaufer* to heat, ultimately from Latin *calere* to be warm + *facere* to make.

chafer /ˈtʃeɪfə(r)/ ▻ *noun, also in compounds* any of various species of large nocturnal beetle, found mainly in the tropics, and including several pests □ *cock-chafer.* ⓒ Anglo-Saxon *ceafor*.

chaff¹ /tʃɑːf, tʃaf/ ▻ *noun* **1** the husks that form the outer covering of cereal grain, and are separated from the seeds during threshing. **2** chopped hay or straw used as animal feed or bedding. **3** worthless material. **4** thin strips of metallic foil fired into or dropped through the atmosphere in order to deflect radar signals and so prevent detection. ⓘ Anglo-Saxon *ceaf*.

chaff² /tʃɑːf, tʃaf/ ▷ *noun* light-hearted joking or teasing. ▷ *verb* (***chaffed, chaffing***) to tease or make fun of someone in a good-natured way. ⓘ 19c: probably from CHAFF¹.

chaffinch /ˈtʃafɪntʃ/ ▷ *noun* either of two birds of the finch family, especially a species with a blue crown, brown body, stout bill, conspicuous white wing bars and a greenish rump. ⓘ Anglo-Saxon *ceaffinc*.

chagrin /ˈʃagrɪn/ ▷ *noun* acute annoyance or disappointment. ▷ *verb* (***chagrined, chagrining***) to annoy or embarrass someone. ⓘ 18c in this sense; 17c in obsolete sense 'shagreen': French.

chain /tʃeɪn/ ▷ *noun* **1** a series of interconnecting links or rings, especially of metal, used for fastening, binding, holding, supporting, transmitting motion or, eg in jewellery, for ornament. **2** a series or progression □ *a chain of events*. **3** a number of shops, hotels, etc under common ownership or management. **4** (**chains**) something that restricts or frustrates. **5** *chem* a number of atoms of the same type that are joined in a line to form a molecule. **6** an old measure of length equal to 22 yards (c.20m). ▷ *verb* (***chained, chaining***) (*often* **chain someone** or **something up** or **down**) to fasten, bind or restrict with, or as if with, chains. ● **in chains** said of eg a prisoner or slave: bound by chains. ⓘ 13c: from French *chaeine*, from Latin *catena*.

chain gang ▷ *noun* a group of prisoners chained together for working outside the prison, to prevent escape.

chain letter ▷ *noun* a letter copied to a large number of people, especially with a request for and promise of something, eg money, with each recipient being asked to copy the letter to a stated number of acquaintances.

chainmail see MAIL²

chain of office ▷ *noun* a heavy ornamental chain worn round the neck as a symbol of office, eg by a mayor.

chain reaction ▷ *noun* **1** *physics* a nuclear reaction that is self-sustaining, eg nuclear fission, in which the splitting of atomic nuclei is accompanied by the release of neutrons, which themselves cause the splitting of more nuclei. **2** *chem* a chemical reaction that is self-sustaining because a change in one molecule causes many other molecules to undergo change, eg during combustion. **3** a series of events, each causing the next.

chainsaw ▷ *noun* a portable power-driven saw with cutting teeth linked together in a continuous chain, used mainly for cutting timber.

chain-smoke ▷ *verb, tr & intr* to smoke (cigarettes, etc) continuously, especially lighting each one from its predecessor. ● **chain-smoker** *noun*.

chain stitch ▷ *noun, needlecraft* an ornamental embroidery stitch which resembles the links of a chain.

chain store ▷ *noun* one of a series of shops, especially department stores, owned by the same company and selling the same range of goods.

chair /tʃɛə(r)/ ▷ *noun* **1** a seat for one person, with a back-support and usually four legs. **2** the office of chairman or chairwoman at a meeting, etc, or the person holding this office. **3** a professorship. **4** (**the chair**) *colloq N Amer, especially US* the electric chair as a means of capital punishment. ▷ *verb* (***chaired, chairing***) **1** to control or conduct (a meeting) as chairman or chairwoman. **2** *Brit* to lift up and carry (a victor, etc) in triumph. **3** to place someone in a seat of authority. ● **in the chair** acting as chairperson. ● **take the chair** to be chairperson. ⓘ 13: from French *chaiere*, from Latin *cathedra*, from Greek *kathedra* seat.

chairlift ▷ *noun* a series of seats suspended from a moving cable, for carrying skiers, etc up a mountain.

chairman, chairwoman and **chairperson** ▷ *noun* **1** someone who conducts or controls a meeting or debate. **2** someone who presides over a committee, board of directors, etc.

chaise /ʃeɪz/ ▷ *noun, historical* a light open two-wheeled horse-drawn carriage, for one or more persons. ⓘ 18c: French, meaning 'chair'.

chaise longue /ʃeɪzˈlɒŋ/ ▷ *noun* (***chaises longues*** /ʃeɪzˈlɒŋ, -lɒŋz/) a long seat with a back and one arm-rest, on which one can recline at full length. ⓘ 19c: French, meaning 'long chair'.

chakra /ˈtʃakrə/ ▷ *noun* (***chakras***) in yoga and alternative medicine: one of a number of centres of spiritual and physical energy in the body.

chalaza /kəˈleɪzə/ ▷ *noun* (***chalazas*** or ***chalazae*** /-ziː/) **1** *zool* in a bird's egg: one of a pair of twisted strands of albumen that hold the yolk sac in position. **2** *bot* in a plant ovule: the region at the base of the nucellus. ⓘ 18c: Latin, from Greek *chalaza* hailstone or lump.

chalcedony /kalˈsɛdənɪ, ˈkalsədounɪ/ ▷ *noun* (***chalcedonies***) *geol* a fine-grained variety of the mineral quartz, which occurs in various forms, including several semiprecious gemstones, eg agate, jasper, onyx. ● **chalcedonic** /-ˈdɒnɪk/ *adj*. ⓘ 14c: from Latin *chalcedonius*, from Greek *chalkedon* a kind of precious stone.

Chalcolithic /kalkouˈlɪθɪk/ ▷ *adj, geol* belonging or relating to the period of transition between the Neolithic and Bronze Ages when copper was already in use. See table at GEOLOGICAL TIME SCALE. ⓘ 20c: from Greek *chalkos* copper + *lithos* stone.

chalcopyrite /kalkouˈpaɪraɪt/ ▷ *noun, geol* a golden-yellow mineral, found in veins associated with igneous rocks, which is the main ore of copper. Also called COPPER PYRITES. ⓘ 19c: from Greek *chalkos* copper + PYRITE.

chalet /ˈʃaleɪ/ ▷ *noun* **1** a style of house typical of snowy Alpine regions, built of wood, with window-shutters and a heavy sloping wide-eaved roof. **2** a small cabin for holiday accommodation, especially one of a number at a holiday camp, etc. **3** a wooden villa. ⓘ 19c: Swiss French.

chalice /ˈtʃalɪs/ ▷ *noun* **1** *poetic* a wine cup; a goblet. **2** in the Christian church: the cup used for serving the wine at Communion or Mass. ⓘ Anglo-Saxon: French, from Latin *calix, calicis* cup.

chalk /tʃɔːk/ ▷ *noun* **1** a soft fine-grained porous rock, composed of calcium carbonate, often pure white or very light in colour, and formed from the shell fragments of minute marine organisms, used in paints, putty, cement, fertilizers, etc. **2** a material similar to this, usually calcium sulphate, or a stick of it, often coloured, used for writing and drawing, especially on a blackboard. ▷ *verb* (***chalked, chalking***) to write or mark in chalk. ● **chalk-like** *adj*. ● **by a long chalk** *colloq* by a considerable amount. ● **as different** or **as like as chalk and cheese** *colloq* completely different. ● **not by a long chalk** *colloq* not at all. ⓘ Anglo-Saxon *cealc*, from Latin *calx, calcis* limestone.

■ **chalk something up** to add an item to one's list of successes or experiences.

■ **chalk something up to someone** to add it to the account of money owed by or to them.

chalkboard ▷ *noun, N Amer* a blackboard.

chalky ▷ *adj* (***chalkier, chalkiest***) **1** like or consisting of chalk. **2** said eg of a face: very pale. ● **chalkiness** *noun*.

challenge /ˈtʃaləndʒ/ ▷ *verb* (***challenged, challenging***) **1** to call on someone to settle a matter by any sort of contest □ *challenge him to a duel*. **2** to cast doubt on something or call it in question □ *I shall challenge her right to borrow my key*. **3** to test, especially in a stimulating way □ *a task that challenges you*. **4** said of a guard or sentry: to order someone to stop and show official proof of identity, etc. **5** *law* to object to the inclusion of someone on a jury. ▷ *noun* **1** an invitation to a contest. **2** the questioning or doubting of something. **3** a problem or task that stimulates effort and interest. **4** an order from a guard or sentry to stop and prove identity. **5** *law* an objection to the inclusion of someone on a jury. ● **challenger** *noun*. ● **challenging** *adj*. ● **challengingly** *adverb*. ⓘ 13c: from French *chalenge*, from Latin *calumnia* trickery.

challenged ▷ *adj, usually in compounds* a supposedly neutral term, denoting some kind of handicap, impairment or disability □ *physically challenged* □ *vertically challenged*.

chalumeau /ʃaljʊˈmoʊ/ ▷ *noun* (***chalumeaux*** /-moʊ/) **1** an early reed-pipe which evolved into the clarinet at the beginning of the 18c. **2** the lowest register of the clarinet. ⓘ 18c: French, from Latin *calamellus*, diminutive of *calamus* reed.

Chamaeleon /kəˈmiːlɪən/ ▷ *noun, astron* a small faint constellation in the S hemisphere.

chamber /ˈtʃeɪmbə(r)/ ▷ *noun* **1** *old use* a room, especially a bedroom. **2** a hall for the meeting of an assembly, especially a legislative or judicial body. **3** one of the houses of which a parliament consists. **4** (**chambers**) a suite of rooms used by eg a judge or lawyer. **5** an enclosed space or hollow; a cavity. **6** the compartment in a gun into which the bullet or cartridge is loaded. **7** a room or compartment with a particular function □ *a decompression chamber*. ⓘ 13c: from French *chambre*, from Latin *camera* room.

chambered tomb ▷ *noun, archaeol* a megalithic monumental tomb from the Neolithic period, consisting of massive stone uprights with corbelled blocks as roofs, used for collective burial, originally in the E Mediterranean and later around the coasts of W Europe.

chamberlain /ˈtʃeɪmbəlɪn/ ▷ *noun* **1** someone who manages a royal or noble household. See also LORD CHAMBERLAIN. **2** the treasurer of a corporation, etc. ⓘ 13c: from French *chambrelenc*; see CHAMBER, -LING 1.

chambermaid ▷ *noun* a woman who cleans bedrooms in a hotel, etc.

chamber music ▷ *noun* music composed for a small group of players, suitable for performing in a room rather than a concert hall, with only one player to a part.

chamber of commerce ▷ *noun* an association of business people formed to promote local trade.

chamber orchestra ▷ *noun* a small orchestra that plays classical music.

chamberpot ▷ *noun* a receptacle for urine, etc for use in a bedroom.

chambray /ˈʃambreɪ/ ▷ *noun* a fine cotton or linen fabric, with interwoven white and coloured threads. ⓘ 19c: see CAMBRIC.

chambré /ˈʃɒmbreɪ; *French* ʃɑ̃bʀe/ ▷ *adj* said of wine: at room temperature. ⓘ 20c: French, meaning 'put into a room'.

chameleon /kəˈmiːlɪən/ ▷ *noun* **1** a slow-moving lizard, found mainly in Africa, whose granular skin changes colour rapidly in response to changes in its environment, acting as camouflage and as a means of communication with rivals. **2** someone who readily adapts to any new environment. **3** *derog* a changeable unreliable person. ● **chameleonic** or **chameleon-like** *adj*. ⓘ 14c: from Greek *chamaileon*, from *chamai* on the ground + *leon* lion.

chamfer /ˈtʃamfə(r)/ ▷ *verb* (***chamfered, chamfering***) to give a smooth rounded shape to (an edge or corner). ▷ *noun* a rounded or bevelled edge. ⓘ 16c: from French *chanfrein*, from *chant* edge + *fraindre* to break.

chamois ▷ *noun* (*plural* ***chamois***) **1** *singular and plural* /ˈʃamwɑː/ an agile hoofed mammal, native to S Europe, Asia Minor and the Caucasus region, which has short vertical horns with backward-pointing tips, and a long reddish-brown, brown or black coat. **2** /ˈʃamɪ/ soft suede leather, formerly made from the skin of this animal, but now usually made from the hides of sheep, lambs or goats. **3** /ˈʃamɪ/ (*plural* /-mɪz/) a piece of this used as a polishing cloth for glass, etc. Also written **shammy** (*plural* **shammies** /-mɪz/) and **shammy leather** or **chamois leather**. **4** a light fawn colour. ▷ *adj* chamois-coloured. ▷ *verb* /ˈʃamwɑː, ˈʃamɪ/ (***chamoised, chamoising***) **1** to prepare (leather) like chamois. **2** to polish something with a chamois. ⓘ 16c: French.

chamomile see CAMOMILE

champ¹ /tʃamp/ ▷ *verb* (***champed, champing***) *tr & intr* to munch noisily. ▷ *noun* the sound of munching. ● **champ at the bit** to be impatient to act. ⓘ 16c: imitative.

champ² /tʃamp/ ▷ *noun, colloq* a champion.

champagne /ʃamˈpeɪn/ ▷ *noun* **1** *strictly* a sparkling white wine made in the Champagne district of France, which is traditionally drunk at celebrations. **2** *loosely* any sparkling white wine. **3** a pale pinkish-yellow colour. **4** *as adj* **a** denoting an extravagant way of life □ *champagne lifestyle*; **b** relating to champagne □ *champagne bottle*. ▷ *adj* champagne-coloured. ⓘ 17c: named after Champagne, the French district where the wine was originally made.

champers /ˈʃampəz/ ▷ *singular noun, colloq* champagne.

champerty /ˈtʃampətɪ/ ▷ *noun* (***champerties***) *law* an illegal bargain between a party to litigation and an uninvolved third party, whereby the third party provides financial assistance in return for a share in the proceeds.

champion /ˈtʃampɪən/ ▷ *noun* **1** in games, competitions, etc: a competitor that has defeated all others. **2** the supporter or defender of a person or cause. ▷ *verb* (***championed, championing***) to strongly support or defend (a person or cause). ▷ *adj, N Eng dialect* excellent. ▷ *adverb, N Eng dialect* excellently. ⓘ 13c: French, from Latin *campio*, from *campus* battlefield or place for exercise.

championship ▷ *noun* **1** a contest held to find the champion. **2** the title or position of champion. **3** the strong defence or support of a cause or person.

champlevé /ˈʃampləveɪ; *French* ʃɑ̃ləve/ ▷ *noun* a technique of enamelling on metal, whereby the surface of the metal is first engraved with the pattern or image, and the engraved channels are then filled with vitreous pastes or powders of different colours, and then the metal is fired. ⓘ 19c: French, meaning 'raised field'.

chance /tʃɑːns/ ▷ *noun* **1** the way that things happen unplanned and unforeseen. **2** fate or luck; fortune. **3** an unforeseen and unexpected occurrence. **4** a possibility or probability. **5** a possible or probable success. **6** an opportunity □ *your big chance*. **7** risk; a gamble □ *take a chance*. ▷ *verb* (***chanced, chancing***) **1** to risk something. **2** *intr* to do or happen by chance □ *I chanced to meet her*. ● **chanceful** *adj*. ● **be in with a chance** to have some hope of success. ● **chance it** or **chance one's luck** or **chance one's arm** to take a risk, although the likelihood of success is slim. ● **chance would be a fine thing!** *colloq* some hope! ● **the chances are ...** it is likely that ... □ *I'll buy a ticket but the chances are I'll be busy that night*. ● **an eye to the main chance** a tendency to act from motives of personal advantage rather than consideration for others. ● **no chance** or **not a chance** no likelihood of success. ● **on the off chance** in hope rather than expectation. ● **an outside chance** a very faint possibility. ● **stand a good chance** to have a reasonable expectation of success. ● **take a chance on something** to act in the hope of it being the case. ● **take one's chance** or **chances** to risk an undertaking; to accept whatever happens. ⓘ 13c: from French *cheance*, from Latin *cadentia* falling.

■ **chance on** or **upon someone** or **something** to meet or find them by accident.

chance in a million ▻ *noun* **1** the faintest possibilty. **2** (*also* **chance of a lifetime**) an opportunity not to be missed.

chancel /ˈtʃɑːnsəl/ ▻ *noun* the eastern part of a church containing the altar, usually separated from the nave by a screen or steps. ◷ 14c: French, from Latin *cancellus*, from *cancelli* lattice, grating.

chancellery or **chancellory** ▻ *noun* (***chancelleries*** or ***chancellories***) **1** the rank of chancellor. **2** a chancellor's department or staff. **3** (*also* **chancery**) **a** the offices or residence of a chancellor; **b** the office of an embassy or consulate.

chancellor /ˈtʃɑːnsələ(r)/ ▻ *noun* **1** the head of the government in certain European countries. **2** a state or legal official of various kinds. See also LORD CHANCELLOR. **3** in the UK: the honorary head of a university. **4** in the US: the president of a university or college. • **chancellorship** *noun*. ◷ 11c: from French *chanceler*, from Latin *cancellarius* court usher.

Chancellor of the Exchequer ▻ *noun* in the British government: the chief minister of finance.

chance of a lifetime see CHANCE IN A MILLION 2

chancer ▻ *noun, colloq, derog* someone inclined to take any opportunity to profit, whether honestly or dishonestly.

chancery ▻ *noun* (***chanceries***) **1** (*also* **Chancery**) a division of the High Court of Justice. **2** a record office containing public archives. **3** a CHANCELLERY. • **in chancery 1** said of a legal case: being heard in a court of chancery. **2** in the charge of a Lord Chancellor. **3** in an awkward or difficult situation. ◷ 14c: a shortened form of CHANCELLERY.

chancre /ˈʃaŋkə(r)/ ▻ *noun* (***chancres***) *pathol* a small hard growth that develops in the primary stages of syphilis and certain other diseases. • **chancrous** *adj*. ◷ 17c: French, from Latin *cancer* crab or cancer.

chancy /ˈtʃɑːnsɪ/ ▻ *adj* (***chancier***, ***chanciest***) risky; uncertain. • **chanciness** *noun*.

chandelier /ʃandəˈlɪə(r)/ ▻ *noun* an ornamental light-fitting hanging from the ceiling, with branching holders for candles or light-bulbs. ◷ 17c: French, meaning 'candle-holder'; see CHANDLER.

chandler /ˈtʃɑːndlə(r)/ ▻ *noun* **1** a dealer in ship's supplies and equipment. **2** a dealer in certain other goods □ *corn chandler*. **3** *old use* a grocer. **4** *old use* a dealer in candles, oil, etc. • **chandlery** *noun* (***chandleries***) **1** a place where candles are kept. **2** goods sold by a chandler. ◷ 14c: from French *chandelier* dealer in candles, from Latin *candellarius*, from *candela* candle.

change /tʃeɪndʒ/ ▻ *verb* (***changed***, ***changing***) **1** *tr & intr* to make or become different. **2** to give, leave or substitute one thing for another. **3** to exchange (usually one's position) with another person, etc. **4** *tr & intr* (*often* **change into** or **out of something**) to remove (clothes, sheets, a baby's nappy, etc) and replace them with clean or different ones. **5** *tr & intr* (*sometimes* **change into something**) to make into or become something different. **6** to obtain or supply another kind of money □ *change pounds into francs*. **7** *tr & intr* to go from one vehicle, usually a train or bus, to another to continue a journey. **8** *tr & intr* to put a vehicle engine into (another gear). ▻ *noun* **1** the process of changing or an instance of it. **2** the replacement of one thing with another; the leaving of one thing for another. **3** a variation, especially a welcome one, from one's regular habit, etc □ *Let's eat out for a change*. **4** the leaving of (one vehicle) for another during a journey. **5** a fresh set (of clothes) for changing into. **6** (*also* **small** or **loose change**) coins as distinct from notes. **7** coins or notes given in exchange for ones of higher value. **8** money left over or returned from the amount given in payment. **9** (*usually* **changes**) any of the various orders in which a set of church bells can be rung. **10** (**the change**) *colloq* see CHANGE OF LIFE. • **change hands** to pass into different ownership. • **change one's mind** or **tune** to adopt a different intention or opinion. • **get no change out of someone** *colloq* to get no help from them. • **ring the changes** to do something which is often repeated in varying ways. • **changeful** *adj*. • **changer** *noun*. ◷ 13c: French, from Latin *cambire* to barter or exchange.

■ **change down** to change to a lower gear, when driving a motor vehicle.

■ **change over 1** to change from one preference or situation to another. **2** to exchange (jobs, roles, etc). **3** *sport* in a relay race: to hand over to a team-mate by exchanging a baton, making contact, etc. See also CHANGE-OVER.

■ **change up** to change to a higher gear, when driving a motor vehicle.

changeable ▻ *adj* **1** inclined or liable to change often; fickle. **2** able to be changed. • **changeably** *adverb*. • **changeability** or **changeableness** *noun*.

changeless ▻ *adj* never-changing. • **changelessly** *adverb*. • **changelessness** *noun*.

changeling ▻ *noun, folklore* a child substituted by the fairies for an unbaptized human baby. ◷ 16c.

change of heart ▻ *noun* a change of attitude often resulting in the reversal of a decision.

change of life ▻ *noun* the menopause. Also called **the change**.

change-over ▻ *noun* (***change-overs***) **1** a change from one preference, position, situation, etc to another. **2** *sport* in a relay race: the instance of handing over to or being freed by a team-mate, by exchanging a baton, making contact, etc. See also CHANGE OVER at CHANGE.

change-ringing ▻ *noun* a British form of bell-ringing, in which a set of differently tuned bells is rung in various permutations so that no sequence is sounded more than once. ◷ 17c: early sequences were devised by Cambridge printer Fabian Stedman.

changing-room ▻ *noun* **1** a room in a sports centre, etc where one can change one's clothes. **2** see FITTING-ROOM.

channel /ˈtʃanəl/ ▻ *noun* **1** any natural or artificially constructed water course, eg the bed of a stream or an irrigation channel. **2** the part of a river, waterway, etc, that is deep enough for navigation by ships. **3** a wide stretch of water, especially between an island and a continent, eg the English Channel. **4** *electronics* **a** the frequency band that is assigned for sending or receiving a clear radio or television signal; **b** a path along which electrical signals flow. **5** a groove, furrow or any long narrow cut, especially one along which something moves. **6** *computing* the path along which electrical signals representing data flow. **7** (*often* **channels**) a means by which information, etc is communicated, obtained or received. **8** a course, project, etc into which some resource may be directed □ *a channel for one's energies*. **9** (**the Channel**) the English Channel, the stretch of sea between England and France. ▻ *verb* (***channelled***, ***channelling***) **1** to make a channel or channels in something. **2** to convey (a liquid, information, etc) through a channel. **3** to direct (a resource, eg talent, energy, money) into a course, project, etc. ◷ 13c: from French *chanel*, from Latin *canalis* canal.

channel surfing ▻ *noun* browsing through the channels of cable or satellite TV. Compare SURF *verb* 3.

channel swimming ▻ *noun* the act of swimming across the English Channel from shore to shore.

Channel Tunnel ▻ *noun* a rail tunnel beneath the English Channel, which opened in 1994, linking Cheriton near Folkstone in England, with Sangatte near Calais in France. Also called **Chunnel**, **Eurotunnel**.

chanson de geste /*French* 'ʃɑ̃sɔ̃ də ʒɛst/ ▷ *noun* (***chansons de geste*** / *French* 'ʃɑ̃sɔ̃ də ʒɛst/) a type of Old French epic poem popular in the 12c–14c, which celebrated the exploits of noblemen and feudal lords. ◷ 19c: French, meaning 'song of deeds'.

chant /tʃɑːnt/ ▷ *verb* (***chanted***, ***chanting***) *tr & intr* **1** to recite in a singing voice. **2** to keep repeating, especially loudly and rhythmically. ▷ *noun* **1** a type of singing used in religious services for passages in prose, with a simple melody and several words sung on one note. **2** a phrase or slogan constantly repeated, especially loudly and rhythmically. **3** a simple song or melody. ● **chanting** *noun, adj.* ◷ 14c: from French *chanter*, from Latin *cantare*, from *canere* to sing.

chanter ▷ *noun* **1** on a set of bagpipes: the pipe on which the melody is played. **2** this pipe adapted for separate use as a practice instrument. **3** someone who chants.

chanterelle /tʃantə'rel, ʃantə'rɛl/ ▷ *noun* the bright yellow funnel-shaped fruiting body of a fungus, native to Europe and N America, which has soft apricot-scented edible flesh, and is highly prized as a delicacy. ◷ 18c: from French *chanterelle*, from Latin *cantharellus*, diminutive of *cantharus* tankard.

chantry /'tʃɑːntrɪ/ ▷ *noun* (***chantries***) **1** an endowment provided for the chanting of masses. **2** a chapel or part of a church so endowed. ◷ 14c: from French *chanterie*, from *chanter* sing.

chanty see SHANTY[2]

Chanukkah and **Hanukkah** /'hɑːnəkə; *Hebrew* xanu'ka/ ▷ *noun* an eight-day Jewish festival held annually in December commemorating the rededication of the temple at Jerusalem in 165 BC. Also called **Festival of Dedication, Festival of Lights**. ◷ 19c: Hebrew *hanukkah* consecration.

chaos /'keɪɒs/ ▷ *noun* **1** the formless shape of matter that is alleged to have existed before the Universe was given order. **2** complete confusion or disorder. **3** *physics* a state of disorder and irregularity that is an intermediate stage between highly ordered motion and entirely random motion. ● **chaotic** /keɪ'ɒtɪk/ *adj.* ● **chaotically** *adverb*. ◷ 16c in sense 1; 15c in obsolete sense 'a chasm': Greek.

chaos theory ▷ *noun* the theory that all phenomena thought of as being entirely random actually have some kind of underlying order.

chap[1] ▷ *noun, colloq* (*also* **chappie**) a man or boy; a fellow. ◷ 18c in this sense; 16c in sense 'a customer': shortened from CHAPMAN.

chap[2] ▷ *verb* (***chapped***, ***chapping***) *tr & intr* **1** said of the skin: to make or become cracked, roughened and red as a result of rubbing or exposure to cold. **2** *Scots, N Eng* to knock. ▷ *noun* **1** a cracked roughened red patch on the skin, formed in this way. **2** *Scots, N Eng* an act of knocking. ◷ 14c.

chap[3] ▷ *noun* **1** a jaw. **2** a cheek. ◷ 16c.

chap. ▷ *abbreviation* chapter.

chaparajos or **chaparejos** see under CHAPS

chaparral /ʃapə'ral, -'rɑːl, tʃapə'rɑːl, -'ral/ ▷ *noun* in the southwestern USA: a dense growth of low evergreen thorny shrubs and trees, often forming tangled thickets. ◷ 19c: Spanish, from *chapparro* evergreen oak.

chapati or **chapatti** /tʃə'pɑːtɪ/ ▷ *noun* (***chapati***, ***chapatis*** or ***chapaties***) in Indian cooking: a thin flat portion of unleavened bread. ◷ 19c: Hindi.

chapel /'tʃapəl/ ▷ *noun* **1** a recess within a church or cathedral, with its own altar. **2** a place of worship attached to a house, school, etc. **3** in England and Wales: **a** a place of Nonconformist worship; **b** the services held there. **4** in Scotland and N Ireland: **a** the place of worship for Roman Catholics or Episcopalians; **b** the services held there. **5** an association of workers in a newspaper office, or a printing- or publishing-house, usually belonging to a trade union. ◷ 13c: from French *chapele*, from Latin *cappella*, diminutive of *cappa* cloak, ie the cloak of St Martin, which was kept in a shrine, to which the word became attached.

chaperone or **chaperon** /'ʃapəroun/ ▷ *noun* (***chaperones*** or ***chaperons***) **1** *formerly* an older woman accompanying a younger unmarried one on social occasions, for respectability's sake. **2** an older person accompanying and supervising a young person or group of young people. ▷ *verb* (***chaperoned***, ***chaperoning***) to act as chaperone to someone. ◷ 18c in sense 1; 14c in historical sense 'hood': French, from *chape* hood.

chaplain /'tʃaplɪn/ ▷ *noun* a member of the clergy attached to a school, hospital or other institution, sometimes having a chapel, or to the armed forces. ● **chaplaincy** *noun* (***chaplaincies***) the position or office of chaplain. ◷ 12c: from French *chapelain*, from Latin *cappellanus* custodian of St Martin's cloak; see CHAPEL.

chaplet /'tʃaplət/ ▷ *noun* **1** a wreath of flowers or a band of gold, etc worn on the head. **2** *RC Church* **a** a string of beads, making up one-third of the rosary; **b** the prayers recited using this. **3** any string of beads. ◷ 14c: from French *chapel* wreath or hat.

chapman ▷ *noun, historical* a travelling dealer; a pedlar. ◷ Anglo-Saxon *ceapman*, from *ceap* trading.

chapped ▷ *adj* said of the skin and lips: dry and cracked.

chappie see CHAP[1]

chaps, chaparajos and **chaparejos** /ʃapə'reɪous/ ▷ *plural noun* a cowboy's protective leather riding leggings, worn over the trousers. ◷ 19c: from Spanish *chaparejos*.

chapter /'tʃaptə(r)/ ▷ *noun* **1** one of the numbered or titled sections into which a book is divided. **2** a period associated with certain happenings □ *University was an exciting chapter in my life.* **3** a sequence or series □ *a chapter of accidents.* **4** *N Amer* **a** a branch of a society; **b** a meeting of such a branch. **5 a** the body of canons of a cathedral, or of the members of a religious order; **b** a meeting of such people. **6** a division of the Acts of Parliament of a session. ▷ *verb* (***chaptered***, ***chaptering***) to divide into chapters. ● **chapter and verse** an exact reference, description of circumstances, etc quoted in justification of a statement, etc. ◷ 13c: from French *chapitre*, from Latin *capitulum*, diminutive of *caput* head.

chapter house ▷ *noun* the building used for the meetings of a cathedral, church, etc chapter.

char[1] /tʃɑː(r)/ ▷ *verb* (***charred***, ***charring***) **1** *tr & intr* to blacken or be blackened by burning; to scorch. **2** said of wood: to turn into charcoal by partial burning. ◷ 17c: shortened from CHARCOAL.

char[2] /tʃɑː(r)/ ▷ *verb* (***charred***, ***charring***) *intr* to do paid cleaning work in someone's house, an office, etc. ▷ *noun, colloq* a charwoman. ◷ Anglo-Saxon *cierran*.

char[3] /tʃɑː(r)/ ▷ *noun, slang* tea. ◷ 20c: from Chinese *cha*.

char[4] or **charr** /tʃɑː(r)/ *noun* (***char***, ***charr***, ***chars*** or ***charrs***) a fish related to and resembling the salmon, native to cool northern lakes and rivers, with minute scales, white spotted sides, and bright red flanks and belly.

charabanc /'ʃarəbaŋ/ ▷ *noun, dated* a single-decker coach for tours, sightseeing, etc. ◷ 19c: from French *char à bancs* carriage with seats.

character /'karəktə(r)/ ▷ *noun* **1** the combination of qualities that makes up a person's nature or personality. **2** the combination of qualities that typifies anything. **3** type or kind. **4** strong admirable qualities such as determination, courage, honesty, etc. **5** interesting qualities that make for individuality □ *a house with character.* **6** someone in a story or play. **7** an odd or amusing person. **8** *colloq* a person. **9** reputation □ *blacken someone's character.* **10** a letter, number or other written or printed symbol. **11** *computing* a symbol, which can be displayed on a screen or printed, represented by a finite length bit pattern, (see BIT 3), unique to it. ● **in** or **out of character** typical or untypical of a person's nature. Ⓒ 14c: Latin, from Greek *charakter* engraving tool, hence a distinctive mark impressed on something.

character actor ▻ *noun* an actor who specializes in playing eccentric characters.

character assassination ▻ *noun* the usually deliberate destruction of a person's good name, reputation, etc, by slander, rumour, etc.

character code ▻ *noun, computing* the particular binary code used to represent a character in a computer, eg ASCII.

characteristic ▻ *noun* **1** a distinctive quality or feature. **2** *math* the integral part of a logarithm. ▻ *adj* indicative of a distinctive quality or feature; typical □ *a characteristic feature.* ● **characteristically** *adverb*.

characterization or **characterisation** ▻ *noun* **1** an act of characterizing. **2** the process by which a writer builds up the characters in a story or play so that their individual personalities emerge. **3** the art of an actor in giving a convincing performance as a particular character.

characterize or **characterise** /'karəktəraɪz/ ▻ *verb* (***characterized, characterizing***) **1** to describe or give the chief qualities of someone or something. **2** to be a typical and distinctive feature of someone or something.

characterless ▻ *adj, derog* dull; uninteresting; lacking individuality.

character part ▻ *noun* a colourful part in a play or film, usually of an odd or eccentric person.

character sketch ▻ *noun* a quick description of someone, mentioning his or her chief qualities.

charade /ʃə'rɑːd, ʃə'reɪd/ ▻ *noun* **1** *derog* a ridiculous pretence; a farce. **2** a mime in charades. **3** (**charades**) a party game in which players mime each syllable of a word, or each word of a book title, etc in successive scenes, while the watching players try to guess the complete word or title. Ⓒ 18c: French, from Provençal *charrado* entertainment.

charcoal /'tʃɑːkoul/ ▻ *noun* **1** a black porous form of carbon produced by heating organic material, especially wood, in the absence of air, and which is used for adsorbing gases and clarifying liquids, as a fuel, and as an artist's material. **2** a stick of this used for making black line drawings. **3** a drawing done in charcoal. **4** (*also* **charcoal grey**) a dark grey colour. ▻ *adj* charcoal-coloured. Ⓒ 14c.

Chardonnay ▻ *noun* /'ʃɑːdəneɪ/ **1** a white grape variety, originally from the Burgundy region of France, now grown also in California, Australia, New Zealand, etc. **2** a dry white wine made from this grape. Ⓒ 20c: French.

charge /tʃɑːdʒ/ ▻ *verb* (***charged, charging***) **1** to ask for an amount as the price of something. **2** to ask someone to pay an amount for something. **3** to accuse someone officially of a crime. **4** *intr* to rush at someone or something in attack. **5** to rush. **6** *formal* to officially order someone to do something □ *She was charged to appear in court.* **7** to load (a gun, furnace, etc) with explosive, fuel, etc. **8** *formal & old use* to fill up □ *charge your glasses.* **9** *intr* said of a battery, capacitor, etc: to take up or store electricity. **10** to cause (a battery, capacitor, etc) to take up or store electricity. **11** to load or saturate □ *The liquid is made fizzy by charging it with carbon dioxide.* **12** to fill □ *The moment was charged with emotion.* ▻ *noun* **1** an amount charged; a price, fee, or cost. **2** control, care or responsibility □ *in charge of repairs.* **3** supervision or guardianship □ *The police arrived and took charge.* **4** something or someone, eg a child, that is in one's care. **5** something of which one is accused □ *a charge of murder.* **6** a rushing attack. **7** (*also* **electrical charge**) a deficiency or excess of electrons on a particular object, giving rise to a positive or negative charge, respectively. **8** the total amount of electricity stored by an insulated object such as an accumulator or capacitor. **9** a quantity of material appropriate for filling something. **10** an amount of explosive, fuel, etc, for loading into a gun, furnace, etc. **11** an order. **12** a task, duty or burden. **13** a debt or financial liability. ● **press** or **prefer charges** to charge someone officially with a crime, etc. Ⓒ 13c: French, from Latin *carricare* to load a vehicle.

■ **charge someone with something** to accuse them of (a crime, etc).

■ **be charged with something** to be given the task or responsibility of doing it.

■ **charge something to someone** to record it as a debt against them □ *Charge the breakages to me.*

chargeable ▻ *adj* **1** said of costs, etc: that may or should be charged to someone. **2** permitted or liable to be charged □ *A fee is chargeable for missed appointments.* **3** incurring tax or duty □ *chargeable assets.* **4** said of an offence: serious enough to justify a legal charge by the police.

charge card ▻ *noun* a small card issued by a store, which entitles the holder to buy goods on credit.

charge-coupled device ▻ *noun* **1** *computing* a unit of memory in which information is stored using electrically charged particles that circulate continuously through cells printed on a semiconductor. **2** *electronics* a semiconductor device that converts an optical image into an electronic signal, widely used in television cameras, home video cameras and camcorders, and for photography in astronomical research.

charged ▻ *adj* filled with excitement or other strong emotion □ *the charged atmosphere in the room.*

chargé d'affaires /ʃɑːʒeɪda'fɛə/ ▻ *noun* (***chargés d'affaires*** /ʃɑːʒeɪda'fɛə/) a deputy to, or substitute for, an ambassador. Ⓒ 18c: French, meaning 'person in charge of affairs'.

charge hand ▻ *noun* the deputy to a foreman in a factory, etc.

charge nurse ▻ *noun* a nurse in charge of a hospital ward, especially if a male; the equivalent of a SISTER.

charger ▻ *noun, historical* a strong horse used by a knight in battle, etc.

charily and **chariness** see under CHARY

chariot /'tʃarɪət/ ▻ *noun, historical* a two-wheeled vehicle pulled by horses, used in ancient times for warfare or racing. ● **charioteer** *noun* a chariot-driver. Ⓒ 14c: diminutive of French *char* carriage.

charisma /kə'rɪzmə/ ▻ *noun* (***charismata*** /–mətə/) **1** a strong ability to attract people, and inspire loyalty and admiration. **2** *relig* a divinely bestowed talent or power. ● **charismatic** /karɪz'matɪk/ *adj*. Ⓒ 17c: from Greek *charis* grace.

charismatic movement ▻ *noun, Christianity* a movement that emphasizes the power of the Holy Spirit at work within individuals, manifesting itself as an ability to heal, a talent for prophecy, etc.

charitable ▻ *adj* **1** having a kind and understanding attitude to others. **2** generous in assisting people in need. **3** relating to, belonging to, or in the nature of a charity □ *charitable institutions.* ● **charitableness** *noun*. ● **charitably** *adverb*. Ⓒ 14c: French, from *charite* charity.

charity /'tʃarɪtɪ/ ▻ *noun* (***charities***) **1** assistance given to those in need. **2** an organization established to provide such assistance. **3** a kind and understanding attitude towards, or judgement of, other people. **4** *Authorized*

Version compassionate love for others. ◷ 13c: from French *charite*, from Latin *caritas* love.

charlady see CHARWOMAN

charlatan /'ʃɑːlətən/ ▷ *noun, derog* someone posing as an expert in some profession, especially medicine. ● **charlatanism** *noun*. ◷ 17c: from French, from Italian *ciarlare* to chatter.

Charles's law ▷ *noun, physics* a law which states that, if the pressure remains constant, the volume of a given mass of gas is directly proportional to its absolute temperature. ◷ 18c: named after the French physicist Jacques Charles (1746–1823).

Charleston /'tʃɑːlstən/ ▷ *noun* a vigorous dance popular in the 1920s, its characteristic step being a pivot on one leg with a side-kick of the other from the knee. ◷ Early 20c: named after the town in South Carolina, USA, where the dance originated.

charlie /'tʃɑːlɪ/ ▷ *noun* **1** (*plural* **charlies**) *Brit colloq* a fool □ *a right charlie.* **2** (**Charlie**) *communications* in the NATO alphabet: the word used to denote the letter 'C' (see table at NATO ALPHABET). ◷ 20c.

charlock /'tʃɑːlək, -lɒk/ ▷ *noun* a rough hairy annual plant, related to mustard, with toothed and lobed leaves and yellow cross-shaped flowers. ◷ Anglo-Saxon *cerlic*.

charm /tʃɑːm/ ▷ *noun* **1** the power of delighting, attracting or fascinating. **2** (**charms**) delightful qualities possessed by a person, place, thing, etc. **3** an object believed to have magical powers. **4** a magical saying or spell. **5** a small ornament, especially of silver, worn on a bracelet. ▷ *verb* (**charmed, charming**) **1** to delight, attract or fascinate someone. **2** (*usually* **charm someone into** or **out of something**) to influence or persuade them by charm. ● **charmless** *adj*. ● **charmlessly** *adverb*. ● **work like a charm** to produce the desired result as if by magic. ◷ 13c: French *charme*, from Latin *carmen* song or spell.

charmed ▷ *adj* seemingly protected by magic.

charmer ▷ *noun* **1** *colloq* someone with an attractive winning manner. **2** *in compounds* a person who can control specified animals as if by magic □ *a snake-charmer.*

charming ▷ *adj* delightful; pleasing; attractive; enchanting. ● **charmingly** *adverb*.

charmless see under CHARM

charnel house /'tʃɑːnəl —/ ▷ *noun, historical* a building where dead bodies or bones are stored. ◷ 14c: French *charnel* burial place.

chart /tʃɑːt/ ▷ *noun* **1** a map, especially one designed as an aid to navigation by sea or air, or one on which weather developments are shown. **2** a sheet of information presented as a table, graph or diagram. **3** (**the charts**) *colloq* a weekly list of top-selling recordings, usually of pop music. ▷ *verb* (**charted, charting**) **1** to make a chart of something, eg part of the sea. **2** to plot (the course or progress of something). **3** *intr, colloq* to appear in the recording charts. ◷ 16c: from French *charte*, from Latin *charta* leaf of paper.

charter /'tʃɑːtə(r)/ ▷ *noun* **1** a formal deed guaranteeing the rights and privileges of subjects, issued by a sovereign or government. **2** a document in which the constitution and principles of an organization are presented. **3** a document creating a borough or burgh. **4** the hire of aircraft or ships for private use, or a contract for this. ▷ *verb* (**chartered, chartering**) **1** to hire (an aircraft, etc) for private use. **2** to grant a charter to someone. ◷ 13c: from French *chartre*, from Latin *charta* paper.

chartered ▷ *adj* **1** qualified according to the rules of a professional body that has a royal charter □ *chartered accountant.* **2** having been granted a CHARTER (*noun* 4) □ *a chartered plane.*

charterer ▷ *noun* **1** the holder of a charter; a freeholder. **2** someone who charters transport.

charter flight ▷ *noun* a flight in a chartered aircraft.

Chartism /'tʃɑːtɪzəm/ ▷ *noun, Brit historical* a political movement for the extension of political power to the working classes. ● **Chartist** *noun, adj*.

chartreuse /ʃɑː'trɜːz; *French* ʃaʀtʀøz/ ▷ *noun* a green or yellow liqueur made from aromatic herbs and brandy. ◷ 19c: named after the monastery of Chartreuse near Grenoble in France where it is produced.

charwoman /'tʃɑːwʊmən/ and **charlady** /'tʃɑːleɪdɪ/ ▷ *noun* a woman employed to clean a house, office, etc. ◷ 19c: from CHAR².

chary /'tʃɛərɪ/ ▷ *adj* (**charier, chariest**) (*usually* **chary of something**) **1** cautious or wary □ *chary of lending money.* **2** sparing; rather mean □ *chary of praise.* ● **charily** *adverb*. ● **chariness** *noun*. ◷ Anglo-Saxon *cearig* sorrowful or anxious.

Charybdis see under SCYLLA

chase¹ /tʃeɪs/ ▷ *verb* (**chased, chasing**) **1** (*often* **chase after someone**) to follow or go after them in an attempt to catch them. **2** (*often* **chase someone away** or **off**, *etc*) to drive or force them away, off, etc. **3** *intr* to rush; to hurry. **4** *colloq* to try to obtain or achieve something, especially with difficulty □ *too many applicants chasing too few jobs.* **5** *colloq* to pursue a particular matter urgently with someone □ *chase the post office about the missing parcel.* **6** *colloq* to pursue (a desired sexual partner) in an obvious way. ▷ *noun* **1** a pursuit. **2** (**the chase**) the hunting of animals, eg foxes. **3** *Brit* a large area of open land, originally where wild animals were kept for hunting. ● **give chase** to rush off in pursuit. ● **chase the dragon** *drug-taking slang* to inhale heroin. ◷ 13c: from French *chasser*, from Latin *captare* to try to catch.

■ **chase someone up** to speak to them in order to get something done.

■ **chase something up** to inquire about a matter or seek out information.

chase² /tʃeɪs/ ▷ *verb* (**chased, chasing**) to decorate (metal) with engraved or embossed work. ● **chasing** *noun*. ◷ 14c: short for ENCHASE.

chase³ ▷ *noun, printing* a metal frame that holds assembled type, or the FORME, in position for printing. ◷ 17c: from French *chas*, from a variant of Latin *capsa* case.

chaser /'tʃeɪsə(r)/ ▷ *noun* **1** *colloq* a drink taken after one of a different kind, eg beer after spirits. **2** a person, animal, etc that chases. **3** a horse for steeplechasing.

chasm /'kazəm/ ▷ *noun* **1** a deep crack or opening in the ground or in the floor of a cave. **2** a very wide difference in opinion, feeling, etc. ◷ 17c: from Greek *chasma*.

chassé /'ʃaseɪ/ ▷ *noun* (**chassés**) a gliding step used in ballroom dancing, etc. ▷ *verb* (**chasséd, chasséing**) *intr* to perform this step. ◷ 19c: French *chassé*.

chasseur /ʃa'sɜː(r)/ ▷ *adj, cookery* applied to a sauce or food cooked in a sauce containing mushrooms, shallots, white wine etc. ◷ 19c: French, meaning 'hunter'.

Chassid or **Chasid** /'ʃasɪd/ ▷ *noun* HASID.

chassis /'ʃasɪ/ ▷ *noun* (*plural* **chassis** /'ʃasɪz/) **1** the structural framework of a motor vehicle, to which the body and movable working parts eg wheels are attached. **2** *electronics* the rigid structural framework of an electronic device, such as a radio or television set, on which the circuit components, etc, are mounted. **3** an aeroplane's landing-gear. ◷ 20c: French, meaning 'frame'.

chaste /tʃeɪst/ ▷ *adj* **1** sexually virtuous or pure; refraining from sexual relations either outside marriage or altogether. **2** said of behaviour, etc: modest; decent. **3** said of clothes, jewellery, style, etc: simple; plain; unadorned. ● **chastely** *adverb*. ● **chasteness** *noun*. See CHASTITY. ◷ 13c: French, from Latin *castus*.

chasten /'tʃeɪsən/ ▷ *verb* (**chastened, chastening**) **1** to free someone from faults by punishing them. **2** to moderate or restrain something. ◷ 16c: from French *chastier* to punish.

chastise /tʃa'staɪz/ ▻ *verb* (***chastised, chastising***) **1** to punish someone severely, especially by beating. **2** to scold someone. ● **chastisement** *noun*. ⓒ 14c, from obsolete *chastien* to chasten.

chastity /'tʃastɪtɪ/ ▻ *noun* **1** the state of being CHASTE. **2** simplicity or plainness of style. ⓒ 13c: from French *chastete*, from Latin *castus* pure.

chastity belt ▻ *noun* a lockable garment covering the genitals in such a way as to prevent sexual intercourse, into which eg crusaders were said to lock their wives to ensure chastity in their absence.

chasuble /'tʃazjʊbəl, 'tʃas-/ ▻ *noun, Christianity* a long sleeveless garment, usually elaborately embroidered, worn by a priest when celebrating Mass or Communion. ⓒ 13c: French, from Latin *casubla* hooded cloak.

chat[1] ▻ *verb* (***chatted, chatting***) *intr* to talk or converse in a friendly informal way. ▻ *noun* informal familiar talk; a friendly conversation. ⓒ 16c: shortened from CHATTER.

■ **chat someone up** *informal* to speak to them flirtatiously, or with an ulterior motive.

chat[2] ▻ *noun* any of various songbirds belonging to several different families, and noted for their harsh chattering calls. ⓒ 17c: imitating the sound.

château /'ʃatoʊ/ ▻ *noun* (***châteaux*** /-toʊz; *French* -to/) **1** a French castle or country seat. **2** used in names of wines, especially from the Bordeaux area: a vineyard estate around a castle or house. ⓒ 18c: French, from Latin *castellum* castle.

Chateaubriand /ʃatoʊ'briːɑ̃/ ▻ *noun* a thick steak cut from grilled fillet of steak.

châtelaine /'ʃatəleɪn/ ▻ *noun, historical* **1** the mistress of a large house. **2** a chain or set of chains to which keys are attached, worn hanging from a woman's belt. ⓒ 19c: French, from CHÂTEAU.

chat show ▻ *noun* a TV or radio programme in which well-known people are interviewed informally.

chattel /'tʃatəl/ ▻ *noun* any kind of MOVEABLE property. ● **goods and chattels** all personal moveable possessions. ⓒ 13c: French *chatel*, from Latin *capitale* wealth.

chatter /'tʃatə(r)/ ▻ *verb* (***chattered, chattering***) *intr* **1** to talk rapidly and unceasingly, usually about trivial matters. **2** said of the teeth: to keep clicking together as a result of cold or fear. **3** said eg of monkeys or birds: to make rapid continuous high-pitched noises. ▻ *noun* **1** a sound similar to this. **2** idle talk or gossip. ● **chatterer** *noun*. ⓒ 13c: imitating the sound.

chatterbox ▻ *noun, derog* someone who is inclined to chatter.

chattering classes ▻ *noun, informal, derog* the usually well-educated section of society who engage in discussion of social, economic, political etc issues.

chatty /'tʃatɪ/ ▻ *adj* (***chattier, chattiest***) *colloq* **1** given to amiable chatting. **2** said of writing: friendly and informal in style. ● **chattily** *adverb*. ● **chattiness** *noun*.

chauffeur /'ʃoʊfə(r), ʃoʊ'fɜː(r)/ ▻ *noun* someone employed to drive a car for someone else. ▻ *verb* (***chauffeured, chauffeuring***) *tr & intr* to act as a driver for someone. ⓒ 20c: French, meaning 'stoker'.

chauffeuse /ʃoʊ'fɜːz/ ▻ *noun* a female chauffeur.

chauvinism /'ʃoʊvənɪzəm/ ▻ *noun, derog* an unreasonable belief, especially if aggressively expressed, in the superiority of one's own nation, sex, etc. ● **chauvinist** *noun, adj*. ● **chauvinistic** *adj*. ● **chauvinistically** *adverb*. ⓒ 19c: named after Nicolas Chauvin, a fanatically patriotic soldier under Napoleon.

ChB ▻ *abbreviation*: *Chirurgiae Baccalaureus* (Latin), Bachelor of Surgery.

cheap /tʃiːp/ ▻ *adj* **1** low in price; inexpensive. **2** being or charging less then the usual; good value for money. **3** low in price but of poor quality. **4** having little worth; valueless □ *War makes human life seem cheap.* **5** vulgar or nasty. ▻ *adverb, colloq* cheaply □ *Good houses don't come cheap.* ● **cheaply** *adverb*. ● **cheapness** *noun*. ● **cheap and nasty** offensively inferior and of low value. ● **dirt cheap** ridiculously cheap. ● **on the cheap** *derog* cheaply; with minimal expense. ⓒ Anglo-Saxon *ceap* trade, price or bargain.

cheapen ▻ *verb* (***cheapened, cheapening***) **1** to cause to appear cheap or not very respectable. **2** *tr & intr* to make or become cheaper.

cheapjack ▻ *noun, derog* a seller of cheap poor-quality goods. ▻ *adj* of poor quality.

cheapskate ▻ *noun, colloq derog* a mean, miserly person.

cheat /tʃiːt/ ▻ *verb* (***cheated, cheating***) **1** to trick, deceive or swindle. **2** (*usually* **cheat someone of** or **out of something**) to deprive them of it by deceit or trickery. **3** *intr* to act dishonestly so as to gain an advantage □ *cheat at cards.* **4** to escape (something unpleasant) by luck or skill □ *cheat death.* ▻ *noun* **1** someone who cheats. **2** a dishonest trick. ● **cheater** *noun*. ⓒ 14c: shortened from ESCHEAT.

■ **cheat on someone** *colloq* to be unfaithful to (one's spouse, lover etc), especially sexually.

check ▻ *verb* (***checked, checking***) **1** *tr & intr* to establish that something is correct or satisfactory, especially by investigation or enquiry; to verify □ *Will you check that I locked the front door?* **2** to hold back, prevent or restrain □ *He was about to complain, but checked himself.* **3** *colloq* to reproach or rebuke someone. **4** *N Amer* to mark something correct, etc with a tick. **5** *N Amer* to hand over or deposit something for safekeeping. **6** *chess* to put (the opposing king) into check. ▻ *noun* **1** an inspection or investigation made to find out about something or to ensure that something is as it should be. **2** a standard or test by means of which to check something. **3** a stoppage in, or control on, progress or development. **4** a pattern of squares □ *cotton with a purple check.* **5** *N Amer, especially US* a tick marked against something. **6** *N Amer, especially US* a cheque. **7** *N Amer* a restaurant bill. **8** *N Amer* a ticket or token for claiming something left in safekeeping. **9** *chess* the position of the king when directly threatened by an opposing piece. ● **checkable** *adj*. ● **checker** *noun*. ⓒ 14c: from French *eschec*, meaning 'check' in chess, from Persian *shah* king.

■ **check in** to report one's arrival at an air terminal or a hotel.

■ **check someone** or **something in 1** to register or report the arrival of someone, especially guests at a hotel or passengers at an air terminal. **2** to hand in (luggage for weighing and loading) at an air terminal. See also CHECK-IN.

■ **check something off** to mark (an item on a list) as dealt with.

■ **check out 1** to register one's departure, especially from a hotel on paying the bill. **2** *chiefly N Amer* said of information etc: to be satisfactory or consistent.

■ **check out someone** or **something** *especially N Amer colloq* to look at them or it □ *Check out the idiot in the corner.*

■ **check someone** or **something out** to investigate them or it thoroughly.

■ **check up on someone** or **something** to enquire into or examine them or it (eg evidence). See also CHECK-UP.

■ **check with something** said of information etc: to be consistent; to agree with (other information).

checked ▻ *adj* having a squared pattern □ *purple-checked cotton.*

checker¹ ▻ *noun* **1** someone who checks. **2** *N Amer* someone who operates a checkout at a supermarket.

checker² see CHEQUER

check-in ▻ *noun* at an air terminal: the desk at which passengers' tickets are checked and luggage weighed and accepted for loading. See also CHECK IN, CHECK SOMEONE OR SOMETHING IN at CHECK.

checklist ▻ *noun* a list of things to be done or systematically checked.

checkmate ▻ *noun* **1** *chess* a winning position, putting one's opponent's king under inescapable attack. **2** frustration or defeat. ▻ *verb* **1** *chess* to put the (opposing king) into checkmate. **2** to foil or outwit someone. ⓘ 14c: from Persian *shah mata* the king is dead.

checkout ▻ *noun* the pay desk in a supermarket.

checkpoint ▻ *noun* a place, eg at a frontier, where vehicles are stopped and travel documents officially checked.

check-up ▻ *noun* a thorough examination, especially a medical one. See also CHECK UP at CHECK.

cheek /tʃiːk/ ▻ *noun* **1** either side of the face below the eye; the fleshy wall of the mouth. **2** impudent speech or behaviour. **3** *colloq* either of the buttocks. ● **cheek by jowl** very close together. ● **turn the other cheek** to refuse to retaliate. ⓘ Anglo-Saxon *ceace* or *cece*.

cheekbone ▻ *noun* either of a pair of bones that lie beneath the prominent part of the cheeks.

cheeky ▻ *adj* (*cheekier*, *cheekiest*) impudent or disrespectful in speech or manner. ● **cheekily** *adverb*. ● **cheekiness** *noun*.

cheep /tʃiːp/ ▻ *verb* (*cheeped*, *cheeping*) *intr* said especially of young birds: to make high-pitched noises; to chirp. ▻ *noun* a sound of this sort. ⓘ 16c: imitating the sound.

cheer /tʃɪə(r)/ ▻ *noun* **1** a shout of approval or encouragement. **2** *old use* disposition; frame of mind □ *be of good cheer*. **3** *old use* merriment. **4** *old use* food and drink □ *Christmas cheer*. ▻ *verb* (*cheered*, *cheering*) *tr & intr* to show approval or encouragement of someone or something by shouting. ● **three cheers!** an exclamation encouraging people to give three shouts in celebration of something or in honour of someone □ *Three cheers for Nicholas!* ⓘ 13c: from French *chere* face.

■ **cheer someone on** to encourage them by shouting.

■ **cheer up** to become more cheerful.

■ **cheer someone up** to make them more cheerful.

cheerful ▻ *adj* **1** happy; optimistic. **2** in a good mood. **3** bright and cheering. **4** willing; glad; ungrudging. ● **cheerfully** *adverb*. ● **cheerfulness** *noun*.

cheerily and **cheeriness** see under CHEERY

cheering ▻ *adj* bringing comfort; making one feel glad or happier.

cheerio /tʃɪərɪ'oʊ/ ▻ *exclamation, Brit colloq* **1** goodbye. **2** cheers (sense 1). ▻ *noun* (*cheerios*) an act or instance of saying goodbye. ⓘ 20c: from CHEER.

cheerleader ▻ *noun* especially in the US: someone who leads organized cheering, applause, etc, especially at sports events.

cheerless ▻ *adj* dismal, depressing, dreary or dull. ● **cheerlessly** *adverb*. ● **cheerlessness** *noun*.

cheers ▻ *exclamation, Brit colloq* **1** used as a toast before drinking. **2** thank you. **3** goodbye. ⓘ 20c: from CHEER.

cheery ▻ *adj* (*cheerier*, *cheeriest*) cheerful; lively; jovial. ● **cheerily** *adverb*. ● **cheeriness** *noun*.

cheese¹ /tʃiːz/ *noun* **1** a solid or soft creamy food that is prepared from the curds of milk. **2** a wheel-shaped solid mass of this substance. **3** a flavoured food with the consistency of soft cheese, eg *lemon cheese*. ● **cheesed off** *Brit slang, dated* fed up or annoyed. ● **hard cheese!** *Brit slang* bad luck! ⓘ Anglo-Saxon *cyse*, from Latin *caseus*.

cheese² *noun* (*also* **the big cheese**) *slang* an important person. ⓘ 19c: perhaps from Urdu *chiz* thing.

cheese board ▻ *noun* **1** a board on which cheese is served. **2** the selection of cheeses served.

cheeseburger ▻ *noun* a hamburger served with a slice of cheese, usually in a bread roll.

cheesecake ▻ *noun* **1** a sweet cake with a pastry base, filled with cream cheese, sugar, eggs etc. **2** *slang, often derog* photographs of partially clothed women, especially when used to add sex appeal in advertising. Compare BEEFCAKE.

cheesecloth ▻ *noun* **1** a type of thin cloth used for pressing cheese. **2** a loosely woven cloth used for shirts, etc.

cheeseparing ▻ *adj, derog* mean with money; miserly. ▻ *noun* miserliness.

cheese plant see MONSTERA

cheese straw ▻ *noun* a long twig-shaped cheese-flavoured biscuit.

cheesy ▻ *adj* (*cheesier*, *cheesiest*) **1** like cheese eg in smell, flavour, etc. **2** *colloq* cheap, inferior. **3** said of a smile: wide, but probably insincere □ *a cheesy grin*.

cheetah /'tʃiːtə/ ▻ *noun* a large member of the cat family and the fastest land mammal, found in Africa and SW Asia, which has a tawny or grey coat with black spots, a small head, and very long legs. ⓘ 18c: from Hindi *cita*, from Sanskrit *cirta* speckled.

chef /ʃɛf/ ▻ *noun* a cook in a restaurant etc, especially the principal one, and usually a man. ⓘ 19c: French, meaning 'chief'.

chef d'œuvre /ʃeɪ'dɜːvrə/ ▻ *noun* (*chefs d'œuvre* /ʃeɪ'dɜːvrə/) an artist's or writer's masterpiece. ⓘ 17c: French, meaning 'chief (piece of) work'.

cheiromancy see CHIROMANCY

chelate /'kiːleɪt/ ▻ *noun, chem* any organic chemical compound, eg haemoglobin, in which a central metal ion is attached to one or more rings of atoms. ⓘ 20c: from Greek *chele* claw.

chemical /'kɛmɪkəl/ ▻ *adj* **1** relating to or used in the science of chemistry. **2** relating to a substance or substances that take part in or are formed by reactions in which atoms or molecules undergo changes. **3** relating to the properties of chemicals. ▻ *noun* a substance that has a specific molecular composition, and takes part in or is formed by reactions in which atoms or molecules undergo changes. ● **chemically** *adverb*. ⓘ 16c: from the earlier *chemic* relating to alchemy or chemistry.

chemical element ▻ *noun* a substance which cannot be broken down into simpler substances by chemical means, and which is composed of similar atoms that all have the same ATOMIC NUMBER.

chemical engineering ▻ *noun* the branch of engineering concerned with the design, manufacture, operation and maintenance of machinery and other equipment used for chemical processing on an industrial scale.

chemical equation ▻ *noun* a way of expressing a CHEMICAL REACTION symbolically.

chemical formula ▻ *noun* the representation of the chemical composition of a compound by means of symbols that represent atoms of an element.

chemical reaction ▻ *noun* the process whereby one or more substances react to form one or more different PRODUCT.

chemical symbol ▻ *noun* a single capital letter, or a combination of a capital letter and a small one, used to represent an atom of a particular chemical element in a chemical formula, eg the chemical symbol for copper is Cu.

Chemical Elements

Symbol	Element	Symbol derived from	Atomic no.
Ac	actinium	Greek *aktis* = ray	89
Ag	silver	Latin *argentum*	47
Al	aluminium	Latin *alumen* = alum	13
Am	americium	America	95
Ar	argon	Greek *argos* = inactive	18
As	arsenic	Latin *arsenicum*	33
At	astatine	Greek *astatos* = unstable	85
Au	gold	Latin *aurum*	79
B	boron	Persian *burah*	5
Ba	barium	Greek *barys* = heavy	56
Be	beryllium	Greek *beryllion* = beryl	4
Bi	bismuth	German (origin unknown)	83
Bk	berkelium	Berkeley, California	97
Br	bromine	Greek *bromos* = stench	35
C	carbon	Latin *carbo* = charcoal	6
Ca	calcium	Latin *calx* = lime	20
Cd	cadmium	Greek *kadmeia* = calamine	48
Ce	cerium	asteroid Ceres	58
Cf	californium	California	98
Cl	chlorine	Greek *chloros* = green	17
Cm	curium	Marie and Pierre Curie	96
Co	cobalt	German *Kobold* = goblin	27
Cr	chromium	Greek *chroma* = colour	24
Cs	caesium	Latin *caesium* = bluish-grey	55
Cu	copper	Cyprus	29
Dy	dysprosium	Greek *dysprositos*	66
Er	erbium	Ytterby, a Swedish town	68
Es	einsteinium	Einstein	99
Eu	europium	Europe	63
F	fluorine	Latin *fluor* = flow	9
Fe	iron	Latin *ferrum*	26
Fm	fermium	Fermi	100
Fr	francium	France	87
Ga	gallium	Latin *gallus* = cock	31
Gd	gadolinium	Gadolin, a Finnish chemist	64
Ge	germanium	Latin *Germania* = Germany	32
H	hydrogen	Greek *hydro* = water	1
He	helium	Greek *helios* = sun	2
Hf	hafnium	*Hafnia* = Copenhagen	72
Hg	mercury	Latin *hydrargyrum* = mercury	80
Ho	holmium	*Holmia* = Stockholm	67
I	iodine	Greek *ioeides* = violet	53
In	indium	its indigo spectrum	49
Ir	iridium	Latin *iris* = a rainbow	77
K	potassium	Latin *kalium*	19
Kr	krypton	Greek *kryptos* = hidden	36
La	lanthanum	Greek *lanthanein* = conceal	57
Li	lithium	Greek *lithos* = stone	3
Lu	lutetium	*Lutetia*, ancient name of Paris	71
Lw	lawrencium	Lawrence, US physicist	103
Md	mendelevium	Mendeleyev, Russian chemist	101
Mg	magnesium	Magnesia, district in Thessaly	12
Mn	manganese	Magnesia (as above)	25
Mo	molybdenum	Greek *molybdos* = lead	42
N	nitrogen	Greek *nitron* = saltpetre	7
Na	sodium	Latin *natrium*	11
Nb	niobium	Niobe (Greek myth)	41
Nd	neodymium	Greek *neos* = new + *didymos* = twin	60
Ne	neon	Greek *neos* = new	10
Ni	nickel	German, abbreviation of *Küpfernickel* = copper devil	28
No	nobelium	Nobel	102
Np	neptunium	planet Neptune	93
O	oxygen	Greek *oxys* = acid	8
Os	osmium	Greek *osme* = odour	76
P	phosphorus	Greek *phosphoros* = light-bearing	15
Pa	protactinium	Greek *protos* = first + *actinium*	91
Pb	lead	Latin *plumbum*	82
Pd	palladium	asteroid Pallas	46
Pm	promethium	Prometheus, stealer of fire from heaven (Greek myth)	61
Po	polonium	Poland	84
Pr	praseodymium	Greek *prasios* = green + *didymos* = twin	59
Pt	platinum	Spanish *plata* = silver	78
Pu	plutonium	planet Pluto	94
Ra	radium	Latin *radius* = ray	88
Rb	rubidium	Latin *rubidus* = red	37
Re	rhenium	Latin *Rhenus* = river Rhine	75
Rh	rhodium	Greek *rhodon* = rose	45
Rn	radon	radium emanation	86
Ru	ruthenium	*Ruthenia* = Russia	44
S	sulphur	Latin *sulfur*	16
Sb	antimony	Latin *stibium*	51
Sc	scandium	Scandinavia	21
Se	selenium	Greek *selene* = moon	34
Si	silicon	Latin *silex* = flint	14
Sm	samarium	Samarski, a Russian savant	62
Sn	tin	Latin *stannum*	50
Sr	strontium	Strontian, a Scottish village	38
Ta	tantalum	Tantalus (Greek myth)	73
Tb	terbium	Ytterby, a Swedish town	65
Tc	technetium	Greek *technetos* = artificial	43
Te	tellurium	Latin *tellus* = earth	52
Th	thorium	Norse god Thor	90
Ti	titanium	Latin *Titanes* = sons of the earth	22
Tl	thallium	Greek *thallos* = green shoot	81
Tm	thulium	Greek and Latin *Thule* = Northland	69
U	uranium	planet Uranus	92
Une	unnilennium	Greek *ennea* = nine	109
Unh	unnilhexium	Greek *hex* = six	106
Uno	unniloctium	Greek *octo* = eight	108
Unp	unnilpentium	Greek *pente* = five	105
Unq	unnilquadium	Latin *quattuor* = four	104
Uns	unnilseptium	Latin *septem* = seven	107
V	vanadium	Norse goddess Vanadis (Freya)	23
W	tungsten	wolfram	74
Xe	xenon	Greek *xenos* = stranger	54
Y	yttrium	Ytterby, a Swedish town	39
Yb	ytterbium	Ytterby, a Swedish town	70
Zn	zinc	German *zink*	30
Zr	zirconium	Persian *zargun* = gold-coloured	40

chemical toilet ▷ *noun* a toilet in which human waste is treated with chemicals, used where running water is not available, eg in a caravan.

chemical warfare ▷ *noun* warfare involving the use of toxic chemical substances, eg MUSTARD GAS and TEAR GAS, to kill, injure or temporarily incapacitate humans, or to damage or destroy animals, plants or non-living materials.

chemin de fer /ʃəˈmɛ̃ də fɛə(r)/ ▷ *noun* a variation of the card game baccarat. ⓘ 19c: French, meaning 'railway'.

chemise /ʃəˈmiːz/ ▻ *noun* a woman's shirt or loose-fitting dress. ⊙ 13c: French, from Latin *camisa* shirt.

chemist /ˈkɛmɪst/ ▻ *noun* **1** a scientist who specializes in chemistry. **2** someone qualified to dispense medicines; a pharmacist. **3** a shop dealing in medicines, toiletries, cosmetics, etc. ⊙ 16c: earlier *chymist* from Latin *alchimista* alchemist.

chemistry /ˈkɛmɪstrɪ/ ▻ *noun* (***chemistries***) **1** the scientific study of the composition, properties, and reactions of chemical elements and their compounds. **2** *colloq* emotional and psychological interaction experienced in a relationship. ⊙ 17c.

chemo- /ˈkɛmoʊ, ˈkiːmoʊ/ ▻ *combining form, signifying* **1** chemicals. **2** chemical reactions.

chemoreceptor ▻ *noun, biol* any sense organ that responds to stimulation by chemical substances.

chemotaxis ▻ *noun, biol* the movement of a whole organism in response to chemical stimulus. ⊙ 19c.

chemotherapy ▻ *noun, medicine* the treatment of a disease or disorder by means of drugs or other chemical compounds that are designed to destroy invading micro-organisms or specific areas of tissue, especially the treatment of cancer with cytotoxic drugs, as opposed to RADIOTHERAPY. ● **chemotherapeutic** *adj.*

chenille /ʃəˈniːl/ ▻ *noun* a soft shiny velvety fabric. ⊙ 18c: French, meaning 'caterpillar'.

cheong-sam /tʃɒŋˈsam/ ▻ *noun* a tightfitting high-necked dress with a slit skirt, worn by Chinese women. ⊙ 20c: Cantonese Chinese, meaning 'long jacket'.

cheque /tʃɛk/ ▻ *noun* a printed form on which to fill in instructions to one's bank to pay a specified sum of money from one's account to another account. ⊙ 18c: from CHECK.

cheque account ▻ *noun* a bank or building society account from which cheques can be drawn.

chequebook ▻ *noun* a book of cheques ready for use, printed with the account-holder's name and that of the bank issuing it.

chequebook journalism ▻ *noun, derog* the practice of paying enormous prices for exclusive rights to sensational material for newspaper stories.

cheque card ▻ *noun* a card issued to customers by a bank, guaranteeing payment of their cheques up to a stated amount.

chequer or (*US*) **checker** /ˈtʃɛkə(r)/ ▻ *noun* **1** a pattern of squares alternating in colour as on a chessboard. **2** one of the pieces used in the game of Chinese chequers. **3** *N Amer* one of the round pieces used in the game of draughts. See CHEQUERS. ▻ *verb* (***chequered, chequering***) to mark in squares of different colours. ⊙ 13c: from French *escheker* chessboard, from *eschec*, meaning 'check' in chess; see CHECK.

chequered ▻ *adj* **1** patterned with squares or patches of alternating colour. **2** said of a person's life, career, etc: eventful, with alternations of good and bad fortune.

chequered flag ▻ *noun* a black-and-white checked flag waved in front of the winner and subsequent finishers in a motor race.

chequers or (*US*) **checkers** ▻ *singular noun* the game of draughts.

cherish /ˈtʃɛrɪʃ/ ▻ *verb* (***cherishes, cherished, cherishing***) **1** to care for lovingly. **2** to take great care to keep (a tradition, etc) alive. **3** to cling fondly to (a hope, belief or memory). ⊙ 14c: from French *cherir*, from *cher* dear.

chernozem /ˈtʃɜːnəzɛm/ ▻ *noun, geol* a dark, highly fertile soil, rich in humus and soluble calcium salts, found in cool regions with low humidity, especially semi-arid grasslands. ⊙ 19c: Russian, from *chernyl* black + *zemlya* earth.

cheroot /ʃəˈruːt/ ▻ *noun* a cigar that is cut square at both ends. ⊙ 17c: from French *cheroute*, from Tamil *curuttu* roll.

cherry /ˈtʃɛrɪ/ ▻ *noun* (***cherries***) **1** a small round red, purplish or yellow fruit containing a small smooth stone surrounded by pulpy flesh, which may be sweet or sour, and can be eaten raw, or used in jams, pies, liqueurs, etc. **2** any of various small deciduous trees which bear this fruit. **3** the fine-grained reddish wood of this tree, which is highly prized for cabinetwork, panelling, and fine furniture. **4 a** a bright red colour; **b** *as adj* □ ***She bought some cherry lipstick.*** **5** *slang, especially US* **a** a virginity; **b** a virgin; **c** someone who has not had experience of something; a novice. ● **two bites** or **another bite at the cherry** *colloq* an unexpected further opportunity. ⊙ Anglo-Saxon *ciris* (mistaken for a plural), from Greek *kerasion*.

cherry brandy ▻ *noun* a liqueur made with brandy in which cherries have been steeped.

cherry picker ▻ *noun* a type of crane with a hydraulic arm ending with a platform, used to carry out inspections and work at high levels.

cherry-picking ▻ *noun, colloq* the business practice of rejecting insurance applications from those considered to be bad risks.

chert /tʃɜːt/ ▻ *noun, geol* flint. ⊙ 17c.

cherub /ˈtʃɛrəb/ ▻ *noun* **1** (*plural also* **cherubim** /ˈtʃɛrəbɪm/) **a** an angel, represented in painting and sculpture as a winged child; **b** in the traditional medieval hierarchy of nine ranks of angels: an angel of the second-highest rank. Compare SERAPH, THRONE, DOMINION, VIRTUE, POWER, PRINCIPALITY, ARCHANGEL, ANGEL. **2** a sweet, innocent and beautiful child. ● **cherubic** /tʃəˈruːbɪk/ *adj.* ● **cherubically** *adverb.* ⊙ Anglo-Saxon, from Hebrew *k'rubh*, plural *k'rubhim*.

chervil /ˈtʃɜːvɪl/ ▻ *noun* an annual plant, native to Europe and Asia, with small white flowers borne in flat-topped clusters, and smooth oblong fruits. It is widely cultivated for its aromatic leaves, which are used as a garnish and for flavouring salads, etc. ⊙ Anglo-Saxon *cherfelle*, from Greek *chairephyllon*.

Ches. ▻ *abbreviation, English county* Cheshire.

chess /tʃɛs/ ▻ *noun* a game of skill played on a chequered board by two people, each with 16 playing-pieces, the object of which is to trap the opponent's king. ⊙ 13c: from French *esches*, plural of *eschec* meaning 'check' in chess, from Persian *shah* king.

chessboard ▻ *noun* the board on which chess or draughts is played, divided into 64 squares alternately white and another colour (usually black).

chessman ▻ *noun* one of the 32 figures used as playing-pieces in chess.

chest ▻ *noun* **1** the front part of the body between the neck and the waist; the non-technical name for the thorax. **2** a large strong box used for storage or transport. **3** a small cabinet, eg for medicines. ● **get something off one's chest** *colloq* to relieve one's anxiety about a problem, wrongdoing, etc by talking about it openly. ⊙ Anglo-Saxon *cist, cest* box, from Latin *cista*.

chesterfield /ˈtʃɛstəfiːld/ ▻ *noun* **1** a heavily padded leather-covered sofa with arms and back of the same height. **2** a kind of long overcoat. ⊙ 19c: named after a 19c Earl of Chesterfield.

chestnut /ˈtʃɛsnʌt/ ▻ *noun* **1** (*also* **sweet chestnut**) a deciduous tree, native to S Europe and W Asia and widely cultivated elsewhere, which has simple toothed glossy leaves, erect catkins with yellow male flowers above and green female flowers below, and prickly globular fruits containing large edible nuts. **2** the large reddish-brown edible nut produced by this tree, which can be roasted and eaten. **3** (*also* **horse chestnut**) a large spreading deciduous tree, native to the Balkans and widely cultivated elsewhere, which has pyramidal spikes of white-petalled flowers with yellow and pink spots, and brown shiny inedible seeds, popularly known as CONKERS. **4** the hard timber of either of these trees. **5** a reddish-brown colour, especially of hair. **6** a reddish-brown horse. **7** an often-repeated joke or anecdote. ● **pull someone's chestnuts out of the fire** *colloq* to rescue them from difficulties. ⓒ 16c: from the earlier *chesten nut*, from Latin *castanea* chestnut tree.

chest of drawers ▻ *noun* a piece of furniture fitted with drawers, especially for holding clothes.

chesty ▻ *adj* (***chestier***, ***chestiest***) *colloq* **1** *Brit* liable to, suffering from or caused by illness affecting the lungs ▫ *a chesty cough*. **2** *colloq* said of a woman: having large breasts. ● **chestily** *adverb*. ● **chestiness** *noun*.

cheval glass /ʃə'val —/ ▻ *noun* a full-length mirror mounted on a stand with swivelling hinges that allow it to be positioned at any angle. ⓒ 19c: French *cheval* support (literally 'horse') + GLASS.

chevalier /ʃɛvə'lɪə(r), ʃə'valjeɪ/ ▻ *noun* **1** in France: a member of a modern order such as the Legion of Honour, or of one of the historical knighthood orders. **2** *old use* **a** a knight; **b** a chivalrous man. ⓒ 14c: French, from Latin *caballarius* horseman.

chevron /'ʃɛvrən/ ▻ *noun* **1** a V-shaped mark or symbol, especially one worn on a uniform sleeve to indicate non-commissioned rank. **2** on a road sign: a horizontal row of black and white V-shapes indicating a sharp bend ahead. ⓒ 14c: French, literally 'rafter'.

chevrotain /'ʃɛvroʊteɪn, -tən/ ▻ *noun* a ruminant mammal with a small stocky body and short slender legs, which is native to the tropical forests of Africa, India, Sri Lanka and SE Asia. Also called **mouse deer**. ⓒ 18c: French diminutive of *chevrot*, from *chèvre* she-goat.

chew /tʃuː/ ▻ *verb* (***chewed***, ***chewing***) **1** *tr & intr* to use the teeth to break up (food) inside the mouth before swallowing. **2** *tr & intr* (*sometimes* **chew at** or **on something**) to keep biting or nibbling it. ▻ *noun* **1** an act of chewing. **2** something for chewing, eg a sweet. ● **chew the rag** or **chew the fat** *slang* to argue a point, especially at length. ⓒ Anglo-Saxon *ceowan*.

■ **chew something up** to crush, damage or destroy it by chewing or as if by chewing ▫ *The machine chewed the cassette up*.

■ **chew on something** or **chew something over** *colloq* to consider it or discuss it at length.

chewing-gum ▻ *noun* a sticky sweet-flavoured substance for chewing without swallowing.

chewy ▻ *adj* (***chewier***, ***chewiest***) *colloq* requiring a lot of chewing. ● **chewiness** *noun*.

chez /ʃeɪ/ ▻ *prep* at the home of someone. ⓒ 18c: French.

chi and **ch'i** see QI

Chianti /kɪ'antɪ/ ▻ *noun* a dry, usually red, Italian wine. ⓒ 19c: named after the region in Italy where the wine was first produced.

chiaroscuro /kɪɑːroʊ'skʊəroʊ, –'skjʊəroʊ/ ▻ *noun* (***chiaroscuros***) **1** *art* the management of light and shade in a picture. **2** a monochrome painting. ⓒ 17c: Italian, meaning 'light-dark'.

chiasma /kaɪ'azmə/ ▻ *noun* (***chiasmas*** /-məz/ or ***chiasmata*** /-mətə/) **1** *genetics* during MEIOSIS: any region where homologous chromosomes remain in contact after they have begun to separate from each other, and where mutual exchange of genetic material occurs as a result of CROSSING OVER. **2** *anatomy* the point where the optic nerves cross each other in the brain. ⓒ 19c: Greek, meaning 'a cross-shaped mark'.

chic /ʃiːk/ ▻ *adj* said of clothes, people, etc: appealingly elegant or fashionable. ▻ *noun* stylishness; elegance. ● **chicly** *adverb*. ⓒ 19c: French.

chicane /ʃɪ'keɪn/ ▻ *noun* **1** *motor sport* on a motor-racing circuit: a series of sharp bends. **2** trickery; chicanery. ▻ *verb* (***chicaned***, ***chicaning***) **1** (*sometimes* **chicane someone into** or **out of something**) *old use* to cheat them. **2** *intr* to use trickery or chicanery. ⓒ 17c: French, meaning 'quibble'.

chicanery /ʃɪ'keɪnərɪ/ ▻ *noun* (***chicaneries***) **1** clever talk intended to mislead. **2** a dishonest argument. **3** trickery; deception.

chick /tʃɪk/ ▻ *noun* **1** the young of a bird, especially a domestic fowl such as a chicken, that has just hatched or is about to hatch. **2** *dated slang* a young woman. ⓒ 14c: shortened from CHICKEN.

chicken /'tʃɪkən/ ▻ *noun* **1** the domestic fowl, bred virtually worldwide for its meat and eggs. **2** the flesh of this animal used as food. **3** *derog slang* a cowardly person. **4** *slang* a youthful person. **5** *colloq* any of various games which involves daring someone to perform a dangerous activity. ▻ *adj, derog colloq* cowardly. ● **count one's chickens before they are hatched** to plan or act on the basis of some expectation which has not yet been fulfilled. ⓒ Anglo Saxon *cicen*.

■ **chicken out of something** to avoid or withdraw from (an activity or commitment) from lack of nerve or confidence.

chicken-and-egg situation ▻ *noun* a situation where one cannot tell which of two happenings is the cause and which is the effect.

chickenfeed ▻ *noun* **1** food for poultry. **2** something small and insignificant, especially a paltry sum of money.

chicken-hearted and **chicken-livered** ▻ *adj, derog, colloq* cowardly.

chickenpox ▻ *noun* an infectious viral disease which mainly affects children, characterized by a fever and an itchy rash of dark red spots.

chicken run ▻ *noun* a small strip of ground usually enclosed with wire netting, for keeping chickens.

chicken wire ▻ *noun* wire netting.

chickpea ▻ *noun* **1** a leafy branching annual plant with white or bluish flowers, cultivated for its wrinkled yellow pea-like edible seeds. **2** the edible seed of this plant, usually eaten boiled or roasted. ⓒ 16c: from earlier *chich pea*, from French *chiche*.

chickweed ▻ *noun* a low-growing sprawling annual plant, native to Europe, which has oval pointed leaves and tiny white flowers with deeply lobed petals. ⓒ 14c.

chicory /'tʃɪkərɪ/ ▻ *noun* (***chicories***) **1** a perennial plant, native to Europe, W Asia and N Africa, which has stalked lower leaves which may be toothed or lobed, stalkless upper leaves, bright blue flower-heads and a long stout tap root. **2** the dried root of this plant, which is often ground, roasted and blended with coffee. **3** the leaves of this plant, eaten raw as a salad vegetable. ⓒ 14c: from Greek *kichoreion*.

chide /tʃaɪd/ ▻ *verb* (*past tense* ***chided*** or ***chid***, *past participle* ***chidden*** or ***chided***, *present participle* ***chiding***) *chiefly literary* to scold or rebuke. ● **chiding** *noun* a scolding or a rebuke. ⓒ Anglo-Saxon *cidan*.

chief /tʃiːf/ ▻ *noun* **1** the head of a tribe, clan, etc. **2** a leader. **3** the person in charge of any group, organization, department, etc. ▻ *adj* **1** used in titles, etc: first in rank; leading ▫ *chief inspector*. **2** main; most important; principal. ● **in chief** mainly; especially; most of all. ⓒ 13c: from French *chef*, from Latin *caput* head.

chief constable ▻ *noun* in the UK: the officer commanding the police force of a county or region.

chief executive ▻ *noun* the top director of a business, organization, etc.

chiefly ▻ *adverb* **1** mainly. **2** especially; above all.

chief of staff ▻ *noun* (***chiefs of staff***) *military* **1** (**Chief of Staff**) the senior officer of each of the armed forces. **2** a senior staff officer.

chief petty officer ▻ *noun* a senior non-commissioned officer in the Royal Navy and the navies of some other countries.

chieftain /ˈtʃiːftən/ ▻ *noun* **1** the head of a tribe or clan. **2** a leader or commander. • **chieftaincy** or **chieftainship** *noun*. ⓘ 14c: from French *chevetaine*, from Latin *capitaneus* captain.

chiffchaff ▻ *noun* an insect-eating bird which belongs to a group of Old World warblers, and inhabits forest margins with thick undergrowth. ⓘ 18c: imitating the sound.

chiffon /ˈʃɪfɒn/ ▻ *noun* **1** a very fine transparent silk or nylon fabric. **2** *cookery* a light frothy mixture, made with beaten whites of eggs and used to make soufflés, cakes, etc. ⓘ 18c: French, from *chiffre* rag.

chiffonier or **chiffonnier** /ʃɪfəˈnɪə(r)/ ▻ *noun* **1** a tall elegant chest of drawers. **2** a low wide cabinet with an open or grille front. ⓘ 19c: French, meaning 'a container for scraps of fabric'.

chigger /ˈtʃɪgə(r)/, **chigoe** /ˈtʃɪgoʊ/ (*chigoes*) and **jigger** /ˈdʒɪgə(r)/ ▻ *noun* **1** the bright red larval stage of a mite, often found in damp fields in autumn, which is a parasite of vertebrates and feeds by sucking the blood of small mammals and humans, causing a rash and severe itching. Also called **harvestmite**. **2** a tropical flea, the pregnant female of which buries herself under the skin of the host, especially under the toenails in humans, causing great discomfort. Also called **sand flea**. ⓘ 17c: from Carib *chigo*.

chignon /ˈʃiːnjɔ̃, -jɒn/ ▻ *noun* a soft bun or coil of hair worn at the back of the neck. ⓘ 18c: French, meaning 'nape of the neck'.

chihuahua /tʃɪˈwɑːwə, -ˈwɑːwɑː/ ▻ *noun* (***chihuahuas***) the smallest domestic breed of dog, which has a tiny body and a disproportionately large head with a bulbous forehead, large widely spaced eyes and large ears. ⓘ 19c: named after the place in Mexico that it originally came from.

chi kung see QI GONG

chilblain /ˈtʃɪlbleɪn/ ▻ *noun* a painful red itchy swelling of the skin, especially on the fingers, toes or ears, caused by abnormal constriction of the blood vessels of the skin on exposure to cold. ⓘ 16c: from CHILL + BLAIN.

child /tʃaɪld/ ▻ *noun* (***children*** /ˈtʃɪldrən/) **1** a boy or girl between birth and physical maturity. **2** one's son or daughter. **3** someone lacking experience or understanding in something □ *an absolute child in financial matters.* **4** *derog* an innocent or naive person. **5** someone seen as a typical product of a particular historical period, movement, etc □ *He was a child of his time.* • **childish** *adj* **1** *derog* silly; immature. **2** relating to children or childhood; like a child. • **childishly** *adverb*. • **childishness** *noun*. • **childless** *adj*. • **childlessness** *noun*.• **childlike** *adj*. • **with child** *old use* pregnant. ⓘ Anglo-Saxon *cild*.

child abuse ▻ *noun* any form of physical, mental or emotional maltreatment of a child, eg neglect or sexual abuse, by either of its parents or another adult.

childbearing ▻ *noun* the act of giving birth to a child. ▻ *adj* suitable for or relating to the bearing of children □ *childbearing hips.*

child benefit ▻ *noun* a regular state allowance to parents for the upbringing of children below a certain age.

childbirth ▻ *noun* the process at the end of pregnancy whereby a mother gives birth to a child.

childhood ▻ *noun* the state or time of being a child.

child-lock ▻ *noun* **1** a device designed to prevent a child opening something such as a car door or a drawer. **2** a feature on equipment, eg a video recorder, which prevents settings being altered by a child playing with it.

childminder ▻ *noun* an officially registered person who looks after children, especially those with working parents, in return for payment.

childproof and **child-resistant** ▻ *adj* designed so as not to be able to be opened, operated, damaged, etc by a child □ *childproof lock.*

child's play ▻ *noun, colloq* a basic or simple task.

Child Support Agency ▻ *noun* (abbreviation **CSA**) a UK government body established in 1993 to administer the provisions of the Child Support Act by contacting and enforcing absent parents to pay child maintenance costs.

child welfare ▻ *noun* care of children's health and living conditions, as a branch of social work.

Chilean /ˈtʃɪlɪən/ ▻ *adj* belonging or relating to Chile, a republic in SW South America, or its inhabitants. ▻ *noun* a citizen or inhabitant of, or person born in, Chile.

Chile pine ▻ *noun* the MONKEY PUZZLE TREE

chili see CHILLI

chill ▻ *noun* **1** a feeling of coldness. **2** a cold that causes shivering, chattering teeth, pale skin, and a sensation of coldness, often preceding a fever, and commonly caused by exposure to a cold damp environment. **3** a feeling, especially sudden, of depression or fear. **4** a coldness of manner; hostility. ▻ *verb* (***chilled***, ***chilling***) **1** *tr & intr* to make or become cold. **2** to cause to feel cold. **3** to scare, depress or discourage. **4** to increase the hardness and density of (a molten metal) by pouring it into a (usually water-cooled) iron mould. • **take the chill off something** to warm it slightly. ⓘ Anglo-Saxon *ciele* cold.

■ **chill out** *slang* to relax or calm oneself, especially after a period of hard work or exercise.

chilled ▻ *adj* **1** made cold. **2** hardened by chilling. **3** preserved by chilling.

chill factor ▻ *noun* a means of assessing the extent to which weather conditions, especially wind speed, increase the cooling effect of low temperatures □ *wind-chill factor.*

chilli or **chili** /ˈtʃɪlɪ/ ▻ *noun* (***chillis*** or ***chillies***) **1** the fruit or 'pod' of one of the varieties of capsicum, which has a hot spicy flavour and is used in sauces, pickles, etc, or is dried and ground to a powder known as cayenne pepper and used as a spice. **2** CHILLI CON CARNE. ⓘ 17c: Aztec.

chilli con carne /ˈtʃɪlɪ kɒn ˈkɑːnɪ/ ▻ *noun* a spicy Mexican dish of minced meat and beans, flavoured with chilli. Also called CHILLI.

chilling ▻ *adj* frightening. • **chillingly** *adverb*.

chilly ▻ *adj* (***chillier***, ***chilliest***) **1** rather cold. **2** *colloq* unfriendly; hostile. • **chilliness** *noun*.

chime ▻ *noun* **1** an individual bell or a set of tuned bells. **2** the sound made by them. **3** (*usually* **chimes**) a percussion instrument consisting of hanging metal tubes that are struck with a hammer. ▻ *verb* (***chimed***, ***chiming***) **1** *intr* said of bells: to ring. **2** *tr & intr* said of a clock: to indicate (the time) by chiming. **3** *intr* to agree or harmonize □ *That chimes with what others say.* ⓘ 13c: formerly *chymbe belle*, probably from Anglo-Saxon *cimbal* cymbal.

■ **chime in** **1** to interrupt or join in a conversation, especially to repeat or agree with something. **2** to agree with someone or to fit in with them.

chimera or **chimaera** /kaɪˈmɪərə, kɪ-/ ▻ *noun* (***chimeras*** or ***chimaeras***) **1** a wild or impossible idea. **2** (**Chimera**) *Greek mythol* a fire-breathing monster, with the head of a lion, the body of a goat and the tail of a serpent. **3** a beast made up from various different animals, especially in art. **4** *biol* an organism made up of two or more genetically distinct tissues. ● **chimeric** or **chimerical** *adj* **1** relating to, or of the nature of, a chimera. **2** wild or fanciful. ● **chimerically** *adverb*. ◷ 14c: from Greek *chimaira* she-goat.

chimney /ˈtʃɪmnɪ/ ▷ *noun* (*chimneys*) **1** **a** a vertical structure made of brick, stone or steel, that carries smoke, steam, fumes or heated air away from a fireplace, stove, furnace or engine; **b** the top part of this, rising from a roof. **2** a vent in a volcano. **3** a glass funnel protecting the flame of a lamp. **4** *mountaineering* a steep narrow cleft in a rock face, just large enough for a mountaineer to enter and climb. ◷ 14c: from French *cheminee*, from Latin *camera caminata* room with a fireplace.

chimney breast ▷ *noun* a projecting part of a wall built round the base of a chimney.

chimneypot ▷ *noun* a short hollow rounded fitting, usually made of pottery, that sits in the opening at the top of a chimney.

chimney stack ▷ *noun* **1** a stone or brick structure rising from a roof, usually carrying several chimneys. **2** a very tall factory chimney.

chimney-sweep ▷ *noun* someone who cleans soot out of chimneys, especially for a living.

chimp ▷ *noun, colloq* a CHIMPANZEE.

chimpanzee /tʃɪmpanˈziː, -ənˈziː/ ▷ *noun* (*chimpanzees*) the most intelligent of the great apes, found in tropical rainforests of Africa, which has long coarse black hair on all parts of its body except its face, ears, hands, and feet. ◷ 18c: from W African.

chin ▷ *noun* the front protruding part of the lower jaw. ● **keep one's chin up** *colloq* to stay cheerful in spite of misfortune or difficulty. ● **take it on the chin** *colloq* to accept a difficulty or misfortune bravely. ◷ Anglo-Saxon *cinn*.

china /ˈtʃaɪnə/ ▷ *singular noun* **1** articles made from a fine translucent earthenware, originally from China. **2** articles made from similar materials. ▷ *adj* made of china. ◷ 17c: from Persian *chini* Chinese.

china clay see KAOLIN

Chinaman ▷ *noun* **1** *derog, old use* a Chinese man. **2** (*usually* **chinaman**) *cricket* a ball bowled by a left-handed bowler to a right-handed batsman, which spins from the off to the leg side.

China tea ▷ *noun* a kind of smoke-cured tea grown in China.

Chinatown ▷ *noun* in any city outside China: a district where most of the inhabitants are Chinese.

chinchilla /tʃɪnˈtʃɪlə/ ▷ *noun* (*chinchillas*) **1** a small mammal with a thick soft grey coat, a bushy tail and large round ears, native to the Andes of S America, and farmed worldwide for its fur. **2** the thick soft grey fur of this animal. **3** a breed of cat or a breed of rabbit with grey fur. ◷ 17c: Spanish diminutive of *chinche* bug.

chine[1] *noun* **1** the backbone. **2** a cut, especially of pork, which consists of part of the backbone and adjoining parts. **3** a steep-sided ridge. ▷ *verb* (*chined*, *chining*) to cut (the carcass of an animal) along the backbone. ◷ 14c: from French *eschine* backbone.

chine[2] *noun* a deep ravine, especially in S England. ◷ Anglo-Saxon *cinu* crevice.

Chinese /tʃaɪˈniːz/ ▷ *adj* belonging or relating to China, a state in central and E Asia, its inhabitants, or their language. ▷ *noun* **1** a citizen or inhabitant of, or person born in, China. **2** any of the closely related languages of the main ethnic group of China.

Chinese block see WOODBLOCK

Chinese cabbage and **Chinese leaves** ▷ *singular noun* a green vegetable, related to the cabbage, which is used raw in salads.

Chinese chequers ▷ *singular noun* a game in which players move pegs or marbles on a star-shaped board.

Chinese gooseberry see KIWI FRUIT

Chinese lantern ▷ *noun* **1** a collapsible paper lantern that is folded like a concertina. **2** an Asian plant with bright orange papery calyxes (see CALYX) resembling lanterns.

Chinese puzzle ▷ *noun* **1** a very difficult wooden puzzle, especially one that consists of a series of boxes which fit one inside the next. **2** any highly complicated puzzle or problem.

Chink, **Chinkie** or **Chinky** *offensive slang* ▷ *noun* (*Chinkies*) a Chinese person. ▷ *adj* Chinese.

chink[1] ▷ *noun* **1** a small slit or crack. **2** a narrow beam of light shining through such a crack. ● **chink in someone's armour** a significant weakness. ◷ 16c: related to CHINE[2].

chink[2] ▷ *noun* a faint short ringing noise; a clink □ *a chink of glasses*. ▷ *verb* (*chinked*, *chinking*) *tr & intr* to make or cause to make this noise. ◷ 16c: imitating the sound.

chinky or **chinkie** ▷ *noun* (*chinkies*) *slang* **1** a meal of Chinese food, especially a takeaway. **2** a Chinese restaurant. ◷ 20c: in these senses not intentionally offensive; compare CHINK.

chinless ▷ *adj, derog* **1** having a small weak, backwards-sloping chin. **2** having a weak indecisive character. See CHINLESS WONDER.

chinless wonder ▷ *noun, Brit colloq* a person, especially from the upper classes, who lacks strength of character.

chinoiserie /ʃɪnˈwɑːzəriː/ ▷ *noun* a European style of design and decoration which imitates or uses Chinese motifs and methods. ◷ 19c: French, from *chinois* Chinese.

chinos /ˈtʃiːnoʊz/ ▷ *plural noun* trousers made from the material **chino**, a strong khaki-like twilled cotton.

chinstrap ▷ *noun* a helmet strap which fastens under the chin.

chintz /tʃɪnts/ ▷ *noun* (*chintzes*) a cotton fabric printed generally in bright colours on a light background, especially used for soft furnishings. ◷ 17c: Gujarati *chints*, plural of *chint*.

chintzy ▷ *adj* (*chintzier*, *chintziest*) *derog* sentimentally or quaintly showy.

chinwag ▷ *noun, colloq* a chat.

chip ▷ *verb* (*chipped*, *chipping*) **1** (*sometimes* **chip at something**) to knock or strike small pieces off (a hard object or material). **2** *intr* to be broken off in small pieces; to have small pieces broken off. **3** to shape by chipping. **4** to cut (potatoes) into strips for frying. **5** *tr & intr, golf, football* to strike the ball so that it goes high up in the air over a short distance. ▷ *noun* **1** a small piece chipped off. **2** a place from which a piece has been chipped off □ *a big chip in the lid*. **3** *Brit* (*usually* **chips**) strips of deep-fried potato. See also FRENCH FRIES. **4** *N Amer* (*also* **potato chip**) a potato crisp. **5** in gambling: a plastic counter used as a money token. **6** *computing* a SILICON CHIP. **7** a small piece of stone. **8** short for CHIP SHOT. ● **chipped** *adj* **1** shaped or damaged by chips. **2** shaped into chips □ *chipped potatoes*. ● **a chip off the old block** *colloq* someone who strongly resembles one of their parents in personality, behaviour or appearance. ● **have a chip on one's shoulder** *colloq* to feel resentful about something, especially unreasonably. ● **have had one's chips** *colloq* **1** to have failed or been beaten. **2** to have been killed. ● **when the chips are down** *colloq* at the moment of crisis; when it comes to the point. ◷ Anglo-Saxon *cipp* log, ploughshare or beam.

■ **chip in** *colloq* **1** to interrupt. **2** *tr & intr* to contribute (eg money, time) □ *We all chipped in for the car.*

chipboard ▻ *noun* thin solid board made from compressed wood chips.

chipmunk /ˈtʃɪpmʌŋk/ ▻ *noun* any of several small ground squirrels, found in N America and N Asia, which have reddish-brown fur and a less bushy tail than that of tree squirrels. ⓒ 19c: from earlier *chitmunk*, from Ojibwa, a native N American language.

chipolata /tʃɪpəˈlɑːtə/ ▻ *noun* (***chipolatas***) a small sausage. ⓒ 19c: French, from Italian *cipolla* onion.

Chippendale /ˈtʃɪpəndeɪl/ ▻ *adj, furniture* denoting furniture made by, or imitating the style of, Thomas Chippendale (died 1779), with graceful elegant lines and detailed carving.

chipper ▻ *adj, N Amer colloq* said of a person: cheerful and lively. ⓒ 19c.

chippy ▻ *noun* (***chippies***) *Brit colloq* **1** a chip shop. **2** a carpenter or joiner.

chip shop ▻ *noun* a shop selling take-away meals of chips and other fried foods, especially fish.

chip shot ▻ *noun, golf, football* a short high shot or kick.

chiro- or **cheiro-** /kaɪərou, kaɪəˈrɒ/ ▻ *combining form, signifying* hand. ⓒ From Greek *cheir* hand.

chirography or **cheirography** ▻ *noun* handwriting or penmanship. ● **chirographer** *noun*. ● **chirographic** or **chirographical** *adj*. See also CALLIGRAPHY. ⓒ 17c.

chiromancy or **cheiromancy** ▻ *noun* PALMISTRY. ⓒ 16c.

chiropodist /kɪˈrɒpədɪst, ʃɪ-/ ▻ *noun* someone who treats minor disorders of the feet, eg corns. ● **chiropody** *noun* the diagnosis, treatment and prevention of foot disorders. ⓒ 19c: from CHIRO- + Greek *pous, podos* foot; the original practitioners treated hands as well as feet.

chiropractic ▻ *noun* a method of treating pain by manual adjustment of the spinal column, etc, so as to release pressure on the nerves. ● **chiropractor** *noun* someone who practises this. ⓒ 19c: from CHIRO- + Greek *praktikas* practical.

chirp /tʃɜːp/ ▻ *verb* (***chirped, chirping***) **1** *intr* said of birds, grasshoppers, etc: to produce a short high-pitched sound. **2** *tr & intr* to chatter or say something merrily. ▻ *noun* a chirping sound. ⓒ 15c: imitating the sound.

chirpy ▻ *adj* (***chirpier, chirpiest***) *colloq* lively and merry. ● **chirpily** *adverb*. ● **chirpiness** *noun*.

chirrup /ˈtʃɪrəp/ ▻ *verb* (***chirruped, chirruping***) *intr* said of some birds and insects: to chirp, especially in little bursts. ▻ *noun* a burst of chirping. ● **chirrupy** *adj*. ⓒ 16c: lengthened form of CHIRP and associated with CHEER UP.

chisel /ˈtʃɪzəl/ ▻ *noun* a hand tool which has a strong metal blade with a cutting edge at the tip, used for cutting and shaping wood or stone. ▻ *verb* (***chiselled, chiselling***) **1** to cut or shape (wood or stone) with a chisel. **2** *slang* to cheat. ⓒ 14c: from French *cisel*, from Latin *caesus* cut.

chit¹ ▻ *noun* **1** a short note or voucher recording money owed or paid. **2** a receipt or similar document. Also called **chitty** (***chitties***). ⓒ 18c: from Hindi *citthi*.

chit² ▻ *noun, derog* **a** a cheeky young girl; **b** a mere child. ⓒ 17c: related to KITTEN.

chitchat /ˈtʃɪttʃat/ ▻ *noun, colloq* **1** chatter. **2** gossip. ▻ *verb, intr* to gossip idly. ⓒ 18c: reduplicated form of CHAT.

chitin /ˈkaɪtɪn/ ▻ *noun, zool, biol* a complex carbohydrate substance that serves to strengthen the tough outer covering or cuticle of insects and crustaceans, and the cell walls of many fungi. ● **chitinous** *adj*. ⓒ 19c: French *chitine*, from Greek *chiton* tunic.

chitterlings /ˈtʃɪtəlɪŋz/ or **chitlings** /ˈtʃɪtlɪŋz/ ▻ *singular or plural noun* the intestines of a pig or another edible animal prepared as food. ⓒ 13c.

chivalrous /ˈʃɪvəlrəs/ ▻ *adj* **1 a** brave or gallant; **b** courteous or noble. **2** relating to medieval chivalry. ● **chivalrously** *adverb*. ● **chivalrousness** *noun*.

chivalry /ˈʃɪvəlrɪ/ ▻ *noun* **1** courtesy and protectiveness especially as shown towards women or the weak. **2** *historical* a code of moral and religious behaviour followed by medieval knights; the medieval system of knighthood. **3** *historical* a collective body of knights, noblemen etc. ⓒ 13c: from French *chevalerie*, from *chevalier* knight.

chive /tʃaɪv/ ▻ *noun* a plant of the onion family with purple flowers and long thin hollow leaves used as a flavouring or garnish. ⓒ 14c: from French *cive*, from Latin *caepa* onion.

chivvy or **chivy** /ˈtʃɪvɪ/ ▻ *verb* (***chivvies, chivvied, chivvying***) to harass or pester someone, especially to hurry or to get some task done. ⓒ 19c: a form of *chevy*, perhaps from the ballad *Chevy Chase*.

chlamydia /kləˈmɪdɪə/ *noun* (***chlamydiae*** /-dɪiː/ or ***chlamydias***) *medicine* **1** a virus-like bacterium that is parasitic in humans and animals, causing diseases such as TRACHOMA, PSITTACOSIS and urinogenital infections. **2** an infection caused by chlamydia, especially one transmitted sexually. It is now the most widespread form of SEXUALLY TRANSMITTED DISEASE in the US and is becoming increasingly common in the UK. ● **chlamydial** *adj*. ⓒ 1940s: Latin, from Greek *chlamys* a cloak.

chlor- see CHLORO-

chloral /ˈklɔːrəl/ ▻ *noun, medicine* an oily colourless toxic liquid with a pungent odour, produced by the chlorination of acetaldehyde, and used in the manufacture of DDT and the sedative and hypnotic drug **chloral hydrate**. Also called TRICHLOROETHANAL. ⓒ 19c: see CHLORINE and ALCOHOL.

chlorate /ˈklɔːreɪt/ ▻ *noun, chem* any salt of chloric acid, including several compounds that are used in defoliant weedkillers. ⓒ 19c.

chloric /ˈklɔːrɪk/ ▻ *adj, chem* relating to, containing or obtained from chlorine. ⓒ 19c.

chloride /ˈklɔːraɪd/ ▻ *noun* **1** *chem* ***a*** a compound of chlorine with another element or RADICAL (*noun* 3); **b** a salt of hydrochloric acid. **2** chloride of lime, a bleaching agent. ⓒ 19c.

chlorinate /ˈklɔːrɪneɪt, ˈklɒ-/ ▻ *verb* (***chlorinated, chlorinating***) to treat (eg water) with, or cause (a substance) to combine with, chlorine. ● **chlorinated** *adj*. ⓒ 19c.

chlorination /klɔːrɪˈneɪʃən, klɒ-/ ▻ *noun* **1** *chem* the formation of a **chlorinated compound**, an organic compound containing chlorine, as a result of a chemical reaction between chlorine and an organic compound. **2** the bleaching or disinfecting of a substance by treating it with chlorine.

chlorine /ˈklɔːriːn/ ▻ *noun, chem* (symbol **Cl**, atomic number 17) a greenish-yellow poisonous gas with a pungent smell, obtained from deposits of SODIUM CHLORIDE or potassium chloride, and from sea water, widely used as a disinfectant and bleach, and in the chemical industry. ⓒ 19c: CHLOR- + -INE²; named by Sir Humphrey Davy, because of its colour.

chloro- /klɔːrou, klɒ-/ or (before vowels) **chlor-** ▻ *combining form, signifying* **1** green. **2** chlorine. ⓒ Greek *chloros* green.

chlorofluorocarbon ▻ *noun, chem* (abbreviation **CFC**) a chemical compound composed of chlorine, fluorine and carbon, formerly widely used as an aerosol propellant and refrigerant, but now banned by many countries as a result of concern about the damaging effects of such compounds on the ozone layer. ⓒ 1940s.

chloroform /ˈklɔːrəfɔːm, ˈklɒ-/ ▻ *noun, chem* a colourless volatile sweet-smelling liquid, formerly used as an anaesthetic, and still used as a solvent and in the manufacture of organic chemicals. Also called **trichloromethane**. ▻ *verb* (***chloroformed, chloroforming***) to administer chloroform to someone. ⓒ 19c: see CHLORO- and FORMIC.

chlorophyll /'klɔːrəfɪl, 'klɒ-/ ▻ *noun, bot* the green pigment, found in the chloroplasts of all green plants, that absorbs light energy from the Sun during PHOTOSYNTHESIS. ⓒ 19c: from CHLORO- + Greek *phyllon* leaf.

chloroplast /'klɔːrəplast, 'klɒr-, -plɑːst/ ▻ *noun, bot* in the cytoplasm of photosynthetic cells of all green plants: any of many specialized membrane-bound structures containing the green pigment chlorophyll. ⓒ 19c: from CHLORO- + Greek *plastos* moulded.

choc /tʃɒk/ ▻ *noun, colloq* chocolate or a chocolate.

chocaholic or **chocoholic** /tʃɒkə'hɒlɪk/ ▻ *noun* someone who is addicted to chocolate. ⓒ Late 20c: from CHOCOLATE, modelled on ALCOHOLIC.

chock ▻ *noun* a heavy block or wedge used to prevent movement of a wheel, etc. ▻ *verb* (***chocked, chocking***) to wedge or immobilize something with chocks.

chock-a-block /tʃɒkə'blɒk/ and **chock-full** ▻ *adj* tightly jammed; crammed full □ *a room chock-a-block with people.* ⓒ 19c: originally a nautical term, referring to a tackle with two blocks close together.

chocolate /'tʃɒklət, 'tʃɒkələt/ ▻ *noun* **1** a food product, made from CACAO beans, that may be eaten on its own or used as a coating or flavouring. **2** an individual sweet made from or coated with this substance. **3** a drink made by dissolving a powder prepared from this substance in hot water or milk. Also called **hot chocolate**. **4** a dark-brown colour. ▻ *adj* **1** made from or coated with chocolate. **2** dark brown. ⓒ 17c: from Aztec *chocolatl*.

chocolate-box ▻ *adj, derog* over-pretty or sentimental, like the designs on boxes of chocolates.

chocolaty or **chocolatey** ▻ *adj* **1** made with or as if with chocolate. **2** tasting of or like chocolate. **3** coloured like chocolate.

choice /tʃɔɪs/ ▻ *noun* **1** the act or process of choosing. **2** the right, power, or opportunity to choose. **3** something or someone chosen. **4** a variety of things available for choosing between □ *a wide choice.* ▻ *adj* select; worthy of being chosen □ *choice cuts of meat.* ● **choiceness** *noun.* ● **from choice 1** willingly. **2** if given a choice. ● **of one's choice** selected according to one's own preference. ● **take one's choice** to choose whatever one wants. ⓒ 13c: from French *chois*.

choir /kwaɪə(r)/ ▻ *noun* **1** an organized group of trained singers, especially one that performs in church. **2** the area occupied by a choir, especially in a cathedral or large church; the chancel. **3** a group of instruments from the same family playing together. ⓒ 13c as *quer*, from French *cuer*, from Latin *chorus*.

choirboy and **choirgirl** ▻ *noun* a young boy or girl who sings in a church choir.

choirmaster and **choirmistress** ▻ *noun* the trainer of a choir.

choir stalls ▻ *plural noun* fixed wooden seats for the choir in the chancel of a church.

choke ▻ *verb* (***choked, choking***) **1** *tr & intr* to prevent or be prevented from breathing by an obstruction in the throat, fumes, emotion, etc. **2** to stop or interfere with breathing in this way. **3** *tr & intr* to make or become speechless from emotion □ *choking with rage.* **4** to fill up, block or restrict something. **5** to restrict the growth or development of □ *plants choked by weeds.* **6** *intr* to lose one's nerve when facing an important challenge. ▻ *noun* **1** the sound or act of choking. **2** *engineering* a valve in the carburettor of a petrol engine that reduces the air supply and so gives a richer fuel/air mixture while the engine is still cold. **3** (*also* **choke coil**) *electronics* a coil of wire that is included in a radio circuit in order to present a high impedance to the passage of audio-frequency or radio-frequency currents. ⓒ Anglo-Saxon *aceocian* to suffocate.

■ **choke something back** to suppress something indicative of feelings, especially tears, laughter or anger.

■ **choke someone off** to prevent them from continuing to speak.

■ **choke something off** to put a stop to it; to prevent it.

■ **choke something up** to fill or block it up completely.

choker ▻ *noun* **1** a close-fitting necklace or broad band of velvet, etc worn round the neck. **2** a person or thing that chokes.

cholecalciferol /kɒlɪkal'sɪfərɒl/ ▻ *noun* VITAMIN D_3 (see VITAMIN D).

choler /'kɒlə(r)/ ▻ *noun, dated* anger or irritability. See also HUMOUR noun 6. ● **choleric** *adj* irritable or bad-tempered. ⓒ 16c: from Greek *chole* bile.

cholera /'kɒlərə/ ▻ *noun, pathol* an acute and potentially fatal bacterial infection of the small intestine, characterized by severe vomiting and diarrhoea, and caused by ingestion of contaminated food or water. ● **choleraic** /kɒlə'reɪɪk/ *adj.* ⓒ 16c: from Greek *chole* bile.

cholesterol /kə'lɛstərɒl/ ▻ *noun, biochem* in animal cells: a STEROL which is an important constituent of all cell membranes and a precursor of many steroid hormones, and which is often associated with ATHEROSCLEROSIS when present at high levels in the blood. ⓒ 19c: from Greek *chole* bile + STEROL.

choline /'koʊlɪn, 'koʊliːn/ ▻ *noun, biochem* an organic compound that is a component of the neurotransmitter acetylcholine, and is also involved in the transport of fats in the body. ⓒ 19c: from Greek *chole* bile.

chomp ▻ *verb* (***chomped, chomping***) *tr & intr* to munch noisily. ▻ *noun* an act or sound of chomping. ⓒ 17c: variant of CHAMP[1].

Chomskyan or **Chomskian** /'tʃɒmskɪən/ ▻ *adj* referring or relating to the US linguist and political activist Noam Chomsky (born 1928), to his linguistic theories such as GENERATIVE GRAMMAR and those developed since then, or to his political theories.

choose /tʃuːz/ ▻ *verb* (***chose, chosen, choosing***) **1** *tr & intr* to take or select (one or more things or persons) from a larger number, according to one's own preference or judgement. **2** to decide; to think fit. **3** *intr* to be inclined; to like □ *I will leave when I choose.* ● **nothing** or **not much to choose between (people** or **things)** little difference in quality, value, etc between them. ● **pick and choose** to select with great care. ⓒ Anglo-Saxon *ceosan*.

choosy ▻ *adj* (***choosier, choosiest***) *colloq* difficult to please; fussy.

chop[1] ▻ *verb* (***chopped, chopping***) **1** to cut with a vigorous downward or sideways slicing action, with an axe, knife, etc. **2** to hit (a ball) with a sharp downwards stroke. **3** *colloq* to reduce or completely withdraw (funding, etc). ▻ *noun* **1** a slice of pork, lamb or mutton containing a bone, especially a rib. **2** a chopping action or stroke. **3** a sharp downward stroke given to a ball. **4** in boxing, karate etc: a short sharp blow. ● **for the chop** *colloq* about to be dismissed. ● **get the chop** *colloq* **1** to be dismissed from a job. **2** to be stopped or closed down □ *Our project got the chop.* ⓒ 14c: variant of CHAP[2].

■ **chop something off** to remove it by chopping.

chop[2] ▻ *verb* (***chopped, chopping***) ● **chop and change** to keep changing one's mind, plans, etc. ● **chop logic** to use over-subtle or complicated and confusing arguments.

See also CHOP-LOGIC. ◎ Anglo-Saxon *ceapian* to bargain or trade.

chop chop ▷ *exclamation* quickly! hurry up! ◎ 19c: Pidgin English, from Chinese.

chophouse ▷ *noun, colloq* a restaurant specializing in steak and chops.

chop-logic ▷ *noun* **1** over-subtle or complicated and confusing arguments. **2** someone who argues in this way. See also CHOP LOGIC at CHOP[2].

chopper ▷ *noun* **1** *colloq* a helicopter. **2** *colloq* a motorcycle with high handlebars. **3** a short-handled axe. **4** (**choppers**) *colloq* the teeth.

chopping-board ▷ *noun* a board on which vegetables, etc are chopped.

choppy ▷ *adj* (***choppier, choppiest***) said of the sea, weather etc: rather rough. ● **choppily** *adverb*. ● **choppiness** *noun*.

chops ▷ *plural noun* the jaws or mouth, especially of an animal. ● **lick one's chops** *colloq* to look forward to some pleasure with relish; to eagerly await. ◎ 16c: from *chap* the lower half of the cheek.

chopsticks ▷ *plural noun* a pair of slender sticks made from wood, plastic or ivory, which are held in one hand and used for eating with, chiefly in Oriental countries. ◎ 17c: from Pidgin English *chop* quick + STICK[1].

chop suey /tʃɒp'suːɪ/ ▷ *noun* a Chinese-style dish of chopped meat and vegetables fried in a sauce, usually served with rice. ◎ 19c: from Cantonese Chinese *jaahp seui* mixed bits.

choral /'kɔːrəl/ ▷ *adj* relating to, or to be sung by, a choir or chorus. Compare VOCAL, INSTRUMENTAL. ● **chorally** *adverb*. ◎ 17c: from Latin *choralis*, from *chorus* choir.

chorale or **choral** /kɒ'rɑːl/ ▷ *noun* **1** a hymn tune with a slow dignified rhythm and strong harmonization. **2** *N Amer, especially US* a choir or choral society. ◎ 19c: German *Choral*, short for *Choralgesang* choral singing.

choral society ▷ *noun* a group that meets regularly to practise and perform choral music.

chord[1] /kɔːd/ ▷ *noun, music* a combination of musical notes played together. ◎ 16c: earlier as *cord*, shortened from ACCORD.

chord[2] /kɔːd/ ▷ *noun* **1** *poetic* a string of a musical instrument. **2** *anatomy* another spelling of CORD. **3** *math* a straight line joining two points on a curve or curved surface. ● **strike a chord** to prompt a feeling of recognition or familiarity. ● **touch the right chord** to get the desired emotional or sympathetic response from someone. ◎ 16c: from Greek *chorde* string or gut.

Chordata /kɔː'deɪtə/ ▷ *noun, zool* in the animal kingdom: the PHYLUM which includes all animals that possess a NOTOCHORD at some stage of their development. ◎ 19c: from Greek *chorde* a string or intestine.

chordate /'kɔːdeɪt/ ▷ *noun, zool* any animal which belongs to the type that possesses a NOTOCHORD at some stage in their development. ◎ 19c: from Greek *chorde* a string or intestine..

chore /tʃɔː(r)/ ▷ *noun* **1** a domestic task. **2** a boring or unenjoyable task. ◎ 18c: see CHAR[2].

chorea /kɔː'rɪə, kə-/ ▷ *noun, pathol* either of two disorders of the nervous system that cause rapid involuntary movements of the limbs and sometimes of the face. See HUNTINGDON'S CHOREA, SYDENHAM'S CHOREA. ◎ 19c: Greek *choreia* dance.

choreograph /'kɒrɪəgrɑːf/ ▷ *verb* (***choreographed, choreographing***) to plan the choreography for (a dance, ballet, etc).

choreography /kɒrɪ'ɒgrəfɪ/ ▷ *noun* **1** the arrangement of the sequence and pattern of movements in dancing. **2** the steps of a dance or ballet. **3** the art of dancing. ● **choreographer** *noun*. ● **choreographic** /kɒrɪə'grafɪk/ *adj*. ◎ 18c: from Greek *choreia* dance + -GRAPHY 2.

chorion /'kɔːrɪɒn/ ▷ *noun* the outer membrane which surrounds a fetus. ◎ 16c: Greek, meaning 'outer membrane of the fetus'.

chorionic gonadotrophin /kɔːrɪ'ɒnɪk —/ ▷ *noun, physiol* in mammals: a hormone produced during pregnancy and whose presence in the urine forms the basis of many types of pregnancy test. Also called **human chorionic gonadotrophin**.

chorionic villus sampling ▷ *noun* a method of diagnosing abnormalities in a fetus by removing a tiny sample of placental tissue for analysis.

chorister /'kɒrɪstə(r)/ ▷ *noun* a singer in a choir, especially a church or cathedral choir. ◎ 14c as *queristre*: from French *quer* choir, influenced by Latin *chorista* singer in a choir.

choroid /'kɔːrɔɪd/ *anatomy* ▷ *adj* resembling or relating to the chorion. ▷ *noun* (*also* **choroid coat**) in the eye of terrestrial vertebrates: the layer of pigmented cells, rich in blood vessels, which lies between the retina and the sclerotic. ◎ 18c: from Greek *chorion* membrane.

chortle /'tʃɔːtəl/ ▷ *verb* (***chortled, chortling***) *intr* to laugh joyfully. ▷ *noun* a joyful laugh. ◎ 19c: invented by Lewis Carroll in *Through the Looking-glass*, combining CHUCKLE + SNORT.

chorus /'kɔːrəs/ ▷ *noun* (***choruses***) **1** a set of lines in a song, sung as a refrain after each verse. **2** a large choir. **3** a piece of music for such a choir. **4 a** the group of singers and dancers supporting the soloists in an opera or musical show; **b** *as adj* ◻ ***a chorus girl***. **5** something uttered by a number of people at the same time ◻ ***a chorus of 'No's'***. **6** *theat* an actor who delivers an introductory or concluding passage to a play. **7** *Greek theat* a group of actors, always on stage, who comment on developments in the plot. ▷ *verb* (***choruses, chorused, chorusing***) to say, sing or utter simultaneously. ● **in chorus** all together; in unison. ◎ 16c: Latin, meaning 'band of dancers, singers, etc'.

chose and **chosen** *past tense and past participle of* CHOOSE

chosen few ▷ *plural noun* a select or privileged group of people.

chough /tʃʌf/ ▷ *noun* a red-legged black bird of the crow family. ◎ 14c as *choghe*.

choux pastry /ʃuː —/ ▷ *noun* a very light pastry made with eggs. ◎ 19c: from French *pâte choux* cabbage paste.

chow[1] /tʃaʊ/ and **chow-chow** ▷ *noun* a breed of dog originally from China, with thick fur, a curled tail and a blue tongue. ◎ 19c: probably from Pidgin English.

chow[2] /tʃaʊ/ ▷ *noun, slang* food. ◎ 19c: from Pidgin English.

chowder /'tʃaʊdə(r)/ ▷ *noun, chiefly N Amer* a thick soup or stew made from clams or fish with vegetables. ◎ 18c: from French *chaudière* pot.

chow mein /tʃaʊ'meɪn/ ▷ *noun* a Chinese-style dish of chopped meat and vegetables, served with fried noodles. ◎ Early 20c: Chinese, meaning 'fried noodles'.

chrism or **chrisom** /'krɪzəm/ ▷ *noun, relig* **1** holy oil used for anointing in the Roman Catholic and Greek Orthodox Churches. **2** confirmation. ● **chrismal** *adj*. ◎ 13c: from Greek *chrisma* anointing.

Christ /kraɪst/ ▷ *noun* **1** the Messiah whose coming is prophesied in the Old Testament. **2** Jesus of Nazareth, or Jesus Christ, believed by Christians to be the Messiah. **3** a figure or picture of Jesus. ▷ *exclamation, offensive to many* a curse expressing surprise, anger, etc. ◎ Anglo-Saxon *Crist*: from Greek *christos* anointed.

Christadelphian /krɪstə'delfɪən/ ▷ *noun, Christianity* a member of a Christian sect which believes in conditional immortality. ◎ 19c: from Greek *Christos* Christ + *adelphos* brother.

christen /'krɪsən/ ▷ *verb* (***christened***, ***christening***) **1** to give a person, especially a baby, a name as part of the religious ceremony of receiving them into the Christian Church. Compare BAPTIZE. **2** to give a name or nickname to someone. **3** *humorous, colloq* to use something for the first time □ *Shall we christen the new wine glasses?* ● **christening** *noun* the ceremony of baptism. ◎ Anglo-Saxon *cristnian*, from *cristen* Christian.

Christendom /'krɪsəndəm/ ▷ *noun* **1** all Christians. **2** the parts of the world in which Christianity is the recognized religion. ◎ Anglo-Saxon, from *cristen* Christian + -DOM.

Christian /'krɪstʃən, 'krɪstɪən/ ▷ *noun* **1** someone who believes in, and follows the teachings and example of, Jesus Christ. **2** *colloq* someone of Christian qualities. ▷ *adj* **1** relating to Jesus Christ, the Christian religion or Christians. **2** *colloq* showing virtues associated with Christians, such as kindness, patience, tolerance and generosity. ◎ 16c: from Latin *Christianus*.

Christian era ▷ *noun* the period of time from the birth of Jesus Christ to the present.

Christianity /krɪstɪ'anɪtɪ/ ▷ *noun* **1** the religious faith based on the teachings of Jesus Christ. **2** the spirit, beliefs, principles and practices of this faith. **3** CHRISTENDOM.

christian name ▷ *noun* **1** *loosely* anyone's first or given name; a forename. Compare FIRST NAME, FORENAME. **2** the personal name given to a Christian at baptism.

christian name

Although this term has largely lost its Christian associations, a culturally neutral term such as **first name, forename** or **given name** is usually preferable.

Christian Science ▷ *noun* a religious movement, founded by Mary Baker Eddy in 1879, which emphasizes the power of spiritual healing rather than conventional medicine. ● **Christian Scientist** *noun* a follower of this religious movement.

Christmas /'krɪsməs/ ▷ *noun* **1** the annual Christian festival held on 25 December, which commemorates the birth of Christ. Also called **Christmas Day**. **2** the period of, mostly non-religious, celebration surrounding this date. ● **Christmassy** *adj* relating to or suitable for Christmas. ◎ Anglo-Saxon *Cristesmæsse* Christ's Mass.

Christmas box ▷ *noun* a small gift of money given at Christmas to the postmen or tradesmen who regularly serve the giver.

Christmas cactus ▷ *noun* a hybrid cactus which flowers in winter and has spineless arching green stems and magenta flowers.

Christmas cake ▷ *noun* a large rich iced fruitcake eaten especially at Christmas.

Christmas card ▷ *noun* a greeting-card sent at Christmas.

Christmas Eve ▷ *noun* 24 December, or the evening of this day.

Christmas pudding ▷ *noun* a rich steamed pudding containing dried fruit, spices etc, eaten especially at Christmas.

Christmas rose ▷ *noun* a type of evergreen HELLEBORE (sense 1) with white or pink flowers that bloom in the winter.

Christmas stocking ▷ *noun* a long sock or an ornamental equivalent, traditionally hung up by children on Christmas Eve to be filled with presents.

Christmas tree ▷ *noun* an evergreen tree, sometimes artificial, on which decorations, lights and presents are hung at Christmas.

Christology /krɪ'stɒlədʒɪ/ ▷ *noun, Christianity* the branch of theology concerned with the significance of Jesus Christ for the Christian faith. ◎ 17c.

chromakey /'kroʊməkiː/ ▷ *noun, TV* a special effect in which an area of strong colour (usually a blue background) can be removed from an image and replaced by a picture or background from another source. ◎ 1970s.

chromatic /kroʊ'matɪk/ ▷ *adj* **1** relating to colours; coloured. **2** *music* relating to, or using notes from, the CHROMATIC SCALE. See also DIATONIC. ● **chromatically** *adverb*. ● **chromaticism** /kroʊ'matɪsɪzəm/ *noun, music*. **3** using notes, intervals and chords foreign to the prevailing mode or key. ● **chromaticity** /-mə'tɪsɪtɪ/ *noun*. ◎ 17c: from Greek *chromatikos*, from *chroma* colour.

chromatic scale ▷ *noun, music* a scale which proceeds by SEMITONES.

chromatid /'kroʊmətɪd/ ▷ *noun, genetics* one of the two thread-like structures formed by the longitudinal division of a chromosome.

chromatin /'kroʊmətɪn/ ▷ *noun, biol* in a cell nucleus: the loose network of thread-like material, composed of DNA, RNA and proteins, which becomes organized into visible chromosomes at the time of cell division. ◎ 19c: from Greek *chroma* colour.

chromato- see CHROMO-

chromatography /kroʊmə'tɒgrəfɪ/ ▷ *noun, chem* a technique for separating the components of a mixture of liquids or gases, whereby a mobile PHASE (sense 5) containing a mixture of substances that are to be analysed is allowed to pass through a stationary phase composed of a liquid or solid. ◎ 1930s: from Greek *chroma* colour + -GRAPHY 2.

chromatophore /kroʊ'matəfɔː(r)/ ▷ *noun, zool* a pigment-bearing cell or structure within a cell, which in many animals contains pigment granules that can be dispersed or contracted, so enabling the animal to change colour. ◎ 19c: Greek *chroma* colour + -PHORE.

chrome /kroʊm/ ▷ *noun, non-technical* chromium, especially when used as a silvery plating for other metals. ▷ *verb* (***chromed***, ***chroming***) **1** in dyeing: to treat with a chromium solution. **2** to plate with chrome. ◎ 19c: French, from Greek *chroma* colour.

chrome yellow ▷ *noun* a yellow pigment of lead chromate.

chrominance /'kroʊmɪnəns/ ▷ *noun* **1** the difference in colour quality between any colour and a reference colour (usually a specified white) of equal brightness and specified colour quality. **2** in TV and video signals: the component that defines the colour as distinct from its brightness or LUMINANCE. ◎ 1950s: from *chromo-* + lum*inance*.

chromite /'kroʊmaɪt/ ▷ *noun, geol* a mineral, composed of chromium and iron oxides, that occurs as compact masses of black crystals with a metallic lustre and is the main source of chromium.

chromium /'kroʊmɪəm/ ▷ *noun, chem* (symbol **Cr**, atomic number 24) a hard silvery metallic element that is resistant to corrosion, which is used in electroplating and in alloys with iron and nickel to make stainless steel. ◎ 19c: a Latinized form of CHROME.

chromo- /kroʊmoʊ/ or **chromato-** /kroʊmətoʊ, kroʊ'matoʊ/ ▷ *combining form, signifying* **1** colour. **2** chromium. ◎ From Greek *chroma* colour.

chromophore /'kroʊməfɔː(r)/ ▷ *noun, chem* that part of a molecule of a chemical compound that gives rise to the colour of the compound. ● **chromophoric** /-'fɒrɪk/ *adj*.

chromosome /'kroʊməsoʊm/ ▷ *noun* in the nucleus of a cell: any of a number of microscopic thread-like structures that become visible as small rod-shaped bodies at the time of cell division, and which contain, in the form of DNA, all the genetic information needed for the development of the cell and the whole organism. ● **chromosomal** *adj*. Ⓒ 19c: see -SOME[2]

chromosome map ▻ *noun, genetics* a diagram showing the LOCI (see LOCUS sense 4) of genes along an individual chromosome.

chromosphere /ˈkroʊməsfɪə(r)/ or **chromatosphere** /kroʊˈmatə-/ ▻ *noun, astron* a layer of gas, mainly hydrogen, about 10 000km deep, that lies above the Sun's PHOTOSPHERE, and which can be seen as a thin crescent of pinkish-red light during a total eclipse of the Sun. Ⓒ 19c.

Chron. ▻ *abbreviation, Bible* Chronicles.

chron- /krɒn, kroʊn, krən/ or **chrono-** /krɒnə, kroʊnoʊ/ ▻ *combining form, signifying* time. Ⓒ Greek *chronos*.

chronic /ˈkrɒnɪk/ ▻ *adj* **1** said of a disease or symptoms: long-lasting, usually of gradual onset and often difficult to treat ◻ *chronic pain*. Compare ACUTE. **2** *Brit colloq* very bad; severe; grave ◻ *The film was chronic*. **3** habitual ◻ *a chronic dieter*. ● **chronically** *adverb*. ● **chronicity** *noun*. Ⓒ 16c: from Greek *chronikos* relating to time.

chronic fatigue syndrome see MYALGIC ENCEPHALOMYELITIS

chronicle /ˈkrɒnɪkəl/ ▻ *noun* (*often* **chronicles**) a record of historical events year by year in the order in which they occurred. ▻ *verb* (***chronicled***, ***chronicling***) to record (an event) in a chronicle. ● **chronicler** *noun*. Ⓒ 14c: diminutive of French *chronique*, from Greek *chronika* annals.

chronicle play ▻ *noun* a play based on recorded history, rather than myth or legend.

chrono- see CHRON-

chronological /krɒnəˈlɒdʒɪkəl/ ▻ *adj* **1** according to the order of occurrence. **2** relating to chronology. ● **chronologically** *adverb*.

chronology /krəˈnɒlədʒɪ/ ▻ *noun* (***chronologies***) **1** the study or science of determining the correct order of historical events. **2** the arrangement of events in order of occurrence. **3** a table or list showing events in order of occurrence. ● **chronologist** *noun*.

chronometer /krəˈnɒmɪtə(r)/ ▻ *noun* a type of watch or clock, used especially at sea, which is designed to keep accurate time in all conditions. ● **chronometric** /-ˈmɛtrɪk/ or **chronometrical** *adj*. ● **chronometrically** *adverb*.

chrysalis /ˈkrɪsəlɪs/ or **chrysalid** ▻ *noun* (***chrysalises*** or ***chrysalides*** /-ˈsalɪdiːz/) **1** the pupa of insects that undergo METAMORPHOSIS, eg butterflies, moths. **2** the protective case that surrounds the pupa. Ⓒ 17c: from Greek *chrysallis*, from *chrysos* gold.

chrysanthemum /krɪˈsanθəməm/ ▻ *noun* a garden plant of the daisy family, with large golden bushy flowers. Also (*colloq*) shortened to **chrysanth**. Ⓒ 16c: from Greek *chrysos* gold + *anthemon* flower.

chrysoberyl /krɪsəˈbɛrɪl/ ▻ *noun, geol* a green, yellow or brown mineral, some varieties of which are used as gemstones. Ⓒ 17c: from Greek *chrysos* gold + *beryllos* beryl.

chrysolite /ˈkrɪsəlaɪt/ ▻ *noun, geol* a light yellowish-green gemstone that is a variety of the mineral OLIVINE. Ⓒ 14c: from Greek *chrysos* gold + *lithos* stone.

chrysoprase /ˈkrɪsoʊpreɪz/ ▻ *noun, geol* a translucent bright green gemstone that is a variety of CHALCEDONY. Ⓒ 13c: from Greek *chrysos* gold + *prason* leek.

chub ▻ *noun* a small fat river-fish of the carp family. Ⓒ 15c.

chubby ▻ *adj* (***chubbier***, ***chubbiest***) plump, especially in a childishly attractive way. ● **chubbily** *adverb*. ● **chubbiness** *noun*. Ⓒ 18c.

chuck[1] ▻ *verb* (***chucked***, ***chucking***) **1** *colloq* to throw or fling. **2** to give (a child, etc) an affectionate tap under the chin. **3** *slang* to abandon or reject, especially a lover. ▻ *noun* **1** *colloq* a toss, fling or throw. **2** (**the chuck**) *slang* dismissal; rejection ◻ *gave her boyfriend the chuck*. **3** an affectionate tap under the chin. Ⓒ 16c.

■ **chuck something in** *colloq* to give it up or abandon it.

■ **chuck something out** *colloq* to get rid of it; to reject it.

■ **chuck someone out** *colloq* to order them to leave.

■ **chuck up** *colloq* to be sick; to vomit.

chuck[2] and **chuck steak** ▻ *noun* beef cut from the area between the neck and shoulder. Ⓒ 17c: variant of CHOCK.

chuck[3] ▻ *noun* a device for holding a piece of work in a lathe, or for holding the blade or bit in a drill. Ⓒ 17c: variant of CHOCK.

chuckle /ˈtʃʌkəl/ ▻ *verb* (***chuckled***, ***chuckling***) *intr* to laugh quietly, especially in a half-suppressed private way. ▻ *noun* an amused little laugh. Ⓒ 17c: probably from *chuck* to cluck like a hen.

chuddar see CHADOR

chuff ▻ *verb* (***chuffed***, ***chuffing***) *intr* said of a steam train: to progress with regular puffing noises. Ⓒ Early 20c: imitating the sound.

chuffed /tʃʌft/ ▻ *adj, Brit colloq* very pleased. Ⓒ 19c: from dialect *chuff* plump or swollen with pride.

chug ▻ *verb* (***chugged***, ***chugging***) *intr* said of a motor boat, motor car, etc: to progress while making a quiet thudding noise. ▻ *noun* a short dull thudding noise, typical of an engine. Ⓒ 19c: imitating the sound.

chukka boot ▻ *noun* a leather ankle boot worn when playing polo.

chukker /ˈtʃʌkə(r)/ or **chukka** ▻ *noun* any of the six periods of play in polo each of which normally lasts for seven and a half minutes. Ⓒ 19c: from Hindi *cakkar* round.

chum ▻ *noun, colloq* a close friend. ▻ *verb* (***chummed***, ***chumming***) **1** *intr* (*usually* **chum up with someone**) to make friends with them. **2** to accompany someone ◻ *She chummed me to the clinic*. ● **chummy** *adj* (***chummier***, ***chummiest***) *colloq* friendly. Ⓒ 19c: in this sense; perhaps from *chamber fellow* a fellow student, etc sharing one's room.

chump ▻ *noun* **1** *colloq* an idiot; a fool. **2** the thick end of anything, especially of a loin cut of lamb or mutton ◻ *a chump chop*. **3** a short thick heavy block of wood. **4** *Brit colloq* the head. ● **off one's chump** *Brit colloq* crazy; extremely foolish. Ⓒ 18c: perhaps a combination of CHUNK + LUMP.

chunder /ˈtʃʌndə(r)/ *slang, chiefly Austral* ▻ *verb* (***chundered***, ***chundering***) *intr* to vomit; to be sick. ▻ *noun* vomit. Ⓒ 1920s.

chunk ▻ *noun* **1** a thick, especially irregularly shaped, piece. **2** *colloq* a large or considerable amount. Ⓒ 17c: variant of CHUCK[3].

chunky ▻ *adj* (***chunkier***, ***chunkiest***) **1** thick-set; stockily or strongly built. **2** said of clothes, fabrics, etc: thick; bulky. **3** solid and strong. **4** containing chunks ◻ *chunky marmalade*.

Chunnel /ˈtʃʌnəl/ ▻ *noun, colloq* another name for the CHANNEL TUNNEL.

church /tʃɜːtʃ/ ▻ *noun* **1** a building for public Christian worship. **2** the religious services held in a church. **3** (**the Church**) the clergy as a profession ◻ *enter the Church*. **4** (*often* **the Church**) the clergy considered as a political group ◻ *quarrels between Church and State*. **5** (*usually* **Church**) any of many branches of Christians with their own doctrines, style of worship, etc ◻ *the Methodist*

Church. **6 a** the whole Christian establishment; **b** *as adj* ◻ ***studying church history***. Ⓒ Anglo-Saxon *cirice*: from Greek *kyriakon* (*doma*) the house of the Lord, from *kyrios* lord.

churchgoer ▻ *noun* someone who regularly attends church services.

churchman and **churchwoman** ▻ *noun* a member of the clergy or of a church.

Church of England ▻ *noun* the official state church in England, which is based on episcopal authority and has the sovereign as its head.

church officer ▻ *noun* in some churches: someone acting as church caretaker, with certain other duties.

Church of Scotland ▻ *noun* the national church in Scotland.

churchwarden ▻ *noun* **1** in the Church of England: either of two lay members of a congregation elected to look after the church's property, money, etc. **2** an old-fashioned long clay pipe.

churchyard ▻ *noun* the burial ground round a church.

churl /tʃɜːl/ ▻ *noun* an ill-bred surly person. ● **churlish** *adj* ill-mannered or rude. ● **churlishly** *adverb*. ● **churlishness** *noun*. Ⓒ Anglo-Saxon *ceorl* peasant.

churn /tʃɜːn/ ▻ *noun* **1** a machine in which milk is vigorously shaken to make butter. **2** a large milk can. ▻ *verb* (***churned***, ***churning***) **1 a** to make (butter) in a churn; **b** to turn (milk) into butter in a churn. **2** (*often* **churn something up**) to shake or agitate it violently. **3** *intr* said of a person's stomach: to be turning over in anticipation or excitement. Ⓒ Anglo-Saxon *ciern*.

■ **churn something out** to keep producing things of tedious similarity in large quantities.

chute¹ /ʃuːt/ *noun* **1** a sloping channel down which to send water, rubbish, etc. **2** a slide in a children's playground or swimming-pool. **3** a waterfall or rapid. Ⓒ 19c: French, from Latin *cadere* to fall.

chute² /ʃuːt/ *noun colloq* short for PARACHUTE.

chutney /ˈtʃʌtnɪ/ ▻ *noun* (***chutneys***) a type of pickle, originally from India, made with fruit, vinegar, spices, sugar, etc. Ⓒ 19c: from Hindi *chatni*.

chutzpah /ˈxʊtspə/ ▻ *noun, chiefly N Amer colloq* self-assurance bordering on impudence; audacity; effrontery. Ⓒ 19c: Yiddish.

chyle /kaɪl/ ▻ *noun, physiol* a milky fluid, consisting of LYMPH containing fats that have been absorbed from the small intestine during digestion. Ⓒ 17c: from Greek *chylos* juice.

chyme /kaɪm/ ▻ *noun, physiol* the partially digested food that passes into the duodenum and small intestine from the stomach. Ⓒ 17c: from Greek *chymos* juice.

CI ▻ *abbreviation* **1** Channel Islands. **2** *IVR*: *Côte d'Ivoire*, Ivory Coast.

Ci ▻ *symbol, physics* curie.

CIA ▻ *abbreviation* Central Intelligence Agency, the official US intelligence analysis organization responsible for external security. Compare FBI.

ciabatta /tʃəˈbɑːtə/ ▻ *noun* (***ciabattas*** or ***ciabatte*** /-teɪ/) **1** Italian bread with a sponge-like texture, made with olive oil. **2** a loaf of this bread. Ⓒ 20c: Italian, meaning 'slipper'.

ciao /tʃaʊ/ ▻ *exclamation* (***ciaos***) an informal Italian greeting used on meeting and parting, which has now become fashionable in English. Ⓒ 20c: Italian, a dialect alteration of *schiavo* I am your slave.

CIB ▻ *abbreviation* Chartered Institute of Bankers.

cicada /sɪˈkɑːdə, sɪˈkeɪdə/ and **cicala** /sɪˈkɑːlə/ ▻ *noun* (***cicadas*** or ***cicadae*** /–diː/; ***cicalas*** or ***cicale*** /-leɪ/) a large predominantly tree-dwelling HEMIPTEROUS insect of mainly tropical regions, the male of which is noted for its high-pitched warbling whistle, produced by vibrating tambourine-like membranes on either side of the body. Ⓒ 19c: Latin.

cicatrice /ˈsikətrɪs/ and **cicatrix** /ˈsɪkətrɪks/ ▻ *noun* (***cicatrices*** /-trɪsiːz, -ˈtraɪsiːz/ or ***cicatrixes***) **1** *medicine* the scar tissue that lies over a healed wound. **2** *bot* a scar on a plant, especially one marking the former point of attachment of a leaf, branch, etc. ● **cicatricial** /sɪkəˈtrɪʃəl/ *adj*. Ⓒ 15c: Latin *cicatrix*.

cicatrize /ˈsɪkətraɪz/ ▻ *verb* (***cicatrized***, ***cicatrizing***) *pathol* said of a wound: **1** to heal by generating a scar. **2** *intr* to become healed by the formation of a scar. ● **cicatrization** *noun*.

CICB ▻ *abbreviation, Brit* Criminal Injuries Compensation Board.

cicely /ˈsɪsəlɪ/ ▻ *noun* (***cicelies***) any of various umbelliferous plants related to CHERVIL, especially SWEET CICELY. Ⓒ 16c: from Greek *seselis*, with spelling influenced by the name *Cicely*.

CID ▻ *abbreviation* Criminal Investigation Department, the detective branch of the British police force.

-cide /saɪd/ or **-icide** ▻ *combining form, forming nouns, denoting* a person, substance or thing that kills ◻ ***pesticide***. Ⓒ From Latin *-cida* agent and *-cidium* act of killing, from *caedere* to cut down; modelled on words such as PATRICIDE in which the compound originates in Latin.

cider or **cyder** /ˈsaɪdə(r)/ ▻ *noun* an alcoholic drink made from apples. Ⓒ 14c: French, from Hebrew *shekhar* intoxicating liquor.

cigar /sɪˈgɑː(r)/ ▻ *noun* a long slender roll of tobacco leaves for smoking. Ⓒ 18c: from Spanish *cigarro*.

cigarette /sɪgəˈrɛt/ ▻ *noun* a tube of finely cut tobacco rolled in thin paper, for smoking. Ⓒ 19c: French diminutive of *cigare* cigar.

cigarette end and **cigarette butt** ▻ *noun* the unsmoked stub of a cigarette.

cigarette-holder ▻ *noun* a long slim mouthpiece into which a cigarette can be fitted for smoking.

cigarette-lighter ▻ *noun* a petrol- or gas-fuelled device with a flint, used for lighting cigarettes.

cigarillo /sɪgəˈrɪloʊ/ ▻ *noun* (***cigarillos***) a small cigar. Ⓒ 19c: Spanish diminutive of *cigarro* cigar.

cigar-shaped ▻ *adj* having an elongated oval shape with pointed ends.

ciggy /ˈsɪgɪ/ or **cig** /sɪg/ ▻ *noun* (***ciggies***) *colloq* short for CIGARETTE.

CII ▻ *abbreviation* Chartered Insurance Institute.

ciliary muscle /ˈsɪlɪərɪ —/ ▻ *noun, anatomy* a muscle that controls the curvature of the lens of the eye, by contracting to make it thin for viewing distant objects, or relaxing to make it thicker for viewing nearby objects. Ⓒ 18c: from Latin *cilium* eyelash.

ciliate /ˈsɪlɪeɪt/ ▻ *noun, zool* any of numerous microscopic single-celled organisms that typically possess CILIA and which are found free-living in all kinds of aquatic and terrestrial habitats, and as parasites. Ⓒ 18c: from Latin *cilium* eyelash.

cilium /ˈsɪlɪəm/ ▻ *noun* (***cilia*** /ˈsɪlɪə/) *biol* any of the short hair-like appendages that project from the surface of certain cells, and whose rhythmic movement aids cell locomotion, or causes movement of the water surrounding some single-celled aquatic organisms. Ⓒ 18c: Latin, meaning 'eyelash'.

cimbalom /ˈsɪmbələm/ ▻ *noun* a form of dulcimer used in Hungary and other E European countries. Ⓒ 19c: Hungarian, from Italian *cembala* cymbal.

C-in-C ▻ *abbreviation* Commander-in-Chief.

cinch /sɪntʃ/ ▻ *noun* (*cinches*) *colloq* **1** an easily accomplished task. **2** a certainty. ▻ *verb* (*cinches, cinched, cinching*) *colloq* to make certain of something. ⓘ 19c: from Spanish *cincha* saddle girth.

cinchona /sɪŋ'kounə/ ▻ *noun* (*cinchonas*) **1** any tree of the type yielding bark from which quinine and related by-products are obtained. **2** the dried bark of these trees. ⓘ 18c: named in honour of the Countess of Chinchon in Spain, who brought a supply of the bark to Spain from Peru.

cincture /'sɪŋktʃə(r)/ ▻ *noun, chiefly literary* a belt or girdle. ⓘ 16c: from Latin *cinctura*, from *cingere, cinctum* to gird.

cinder /'sɪndə(r)/ ▻ *noun* **1** a piece of burnt coal or wood. **2** (**cinders**) **a** ashes; **b** (*geol*) residue of lava. • **cindery** *adj*. ⓘ Anglo-Saxon *sinder* slag.

Cinderella /sɪndə'relə/ ▻ *noun* (*Cinderellas*) **1** someone who achieves recognition or fame after being unknown. **2** someone or something whose charms or merits go unnoticed. ⓘ 19c: named after the heroine of the fairy-tale *Cinderella*.

cine- /'sɪnɪ/ ▻ *adj, combining form, signifying* moving pictures □ *a cinecamera*. ⓘ Shortened from CINEMA.

cineaste or **cineast** /'sɪnɪast/ ▻ *noun* someone who is interested in, or who makes, cinema films. ⓘ Early 20c: French.

cinema /'sɪnəmə/ ▻ *noun* (*cinemas*)**1** a theatre in which motion pictures are shown. **2** cinemas in general. **3** (*usually* **the cinema**) **a** motion pictures or films generally; **b** the art or business of making films. • **cinematic** /-'matɪk/ *adj*. • **cinematically** *adverb*. ⓘ 19c, as *kinema*: shortened from CINEMATOGRAPH.

cinema film see FILM *noun* 2

cinema-goer ▻ *noun* someone who regularly attends the cinema.

cinematograph /sɪnə'matəgrɑːf/ ▻ *noun* an apparatus for taking and projecting a series of still photographs, each representing an instant of time, in rapid succession so as to present a single moving scene. ⓘ 19c: from Greek *kinema* motion + -GRAPH 1.

cinematography /sɪnəmə'tɒgrəfɪ/ ▻ *noun* the art of making motion pictures. • **cinematographer** *noun*. • **cinematographic** /-matə'grafɪk/ *adj*. ⓘ 19c: from Greek *kinema* motion + -GRAPHY 2.

cinéma vérité /sɪnəmə 'verɪteɪ/ ▻ *noun, cinema* a style of film production characterized by documentary treatment, giving the appearance of real life even for fictional drama. ⓘ 20c: French, literally 'truth cinema'.

Cinerama /sɪnə'rɑːmə/ ▻ *noun trademark* a method of film projection onto a wide curved screen using three projectors to give a three-dimensional effect. ⓘ 20c: from CINEMA, modelled on PANORAMA.

cineraria /sɪnə'reərɪə/ ▻ *noun* (*cinerarias*) *bot* **1** a dwarf shrub native to Africa and Madagascar, which has rounded lobed leaves, the undersurfaces densely covered with white hairs, and numerous red, deep blue, violet, or variegated daisy-like flowerheads. **2** a popular garden plant derived from a related species, native to the Canary Islands. ⓘ 16c: from Latin *cinerarius* relating to ashes.

cinerarium /sɪnə'reərɪəm/ ▻ *noun* (*cineraria* /-rɪə/) a place for keeping the ashes of the dead.

cinerary /'sɪnərərɪ/ ▻ *adj* **a** relating to ashes; **b** for holding ashes □ *a cinerary urn*. ⓘ 18c: from Latin *cinerarius* relating to ashes.

cinnabar /'sɪnəbɑː(r)/ ▻ *noun* **1** *geol* a bright red mineral form of mercury sulphide, the principal source of mercury and also used as a pigment. **2** a bright orange-red colour. **3** a large moth with red and black wings. ⓘ 15c: from Greek *kinnabari*.

cinnamon /'sɪnəmən/ ▻ *noun* **1 a** a spice obtained from the cured dried bark of a SE Asian tree; **b** any of various small evergreen trees which yield this bark. **2** a brownish-orange colour. Also *as adj*. ⓘ 15c: from Greek *kinnamon*.

cinquecento /tʃɪŋkwɪ'tʃentou/ ▻ *noun* Italian art and literature of the 16c Renaissance. ⓘ 18c: Italian, meaning '500', shortened from *milcinquecento* fifteen hundred, referring to the century 1500–99.

cinquefoil /'sɪŋkfɔɪl/ ▻ *noun* **1** a plant of the rose family with five-petalled flowers, typically yellow, white or purple, and leaves divided into five sections. **2** *heraldry* a five-petalled flower. **3** *archit* a design composed of five petal-like arcs, found at the top of an arch, in a circular window, etc. ⓘ 14c: from French *cincfoille*, from Latin *quinquefolium* five-leaved plant.

CIOB ▻ *abbreviation* Chartered Institute of Building.

CIPA ▻ *abbreviation* Chartered Institute of Patent Agents.

CIPFA ▻ *abbreviation* Chartered Institute of Public Finance and Accountancy.

cipher or **cypher** /'saɪfə(r)/ ▻ *noun* **1** a secret code. **2** something written in code. **3** the key to a code. **4** an interlaced set of initials; a monogram. **5** *math, old use* the symbol 0, used to fill blanks in writing numbers, but of no value itself. **6** a person or thing of little importance. **7** any Arabic numeral. ▻ *verb* (*ciphered, ciphering*) to write (a message, etc) in code. ⓘ 14c: from Latin *ciphra*, from Arabic *sifr* empty or zero.

circa /'sɜːkə/ ▻ *prep* (abbreviation **c.**) used especially with dates: about; approximately □ *circa 1250*. ⓘ 19c: Latin, meaning 'about' or 'around'.

circadian /sɜː'keɪdɪən/ ▻ *adj, biol* relating to a biological rhythm that is more or less synchronized to a 24-hour cycle, eg the pattern of sleeping and waking in adult humans. ⓘ 20c: from Latin *circa* around + *dies* day.

Circinus /'sɜːsɪnəs/ ▻ *noun, astron* the Compasses, a small obscure constellation in the southern hemisphere, lying in the Milky Way.

circle /'sɜːkəl/ ▻ *noun* **1** a perfectly round two-dimensional figure that is bordered by the CIRCUMFERENCE, every point of which is an equal distance from a fixed point within the figure called the CENTRE. **2** anything in the form of a circle. **3** a circular route, eg the orbit of a planet, etc. **4** in a theatre, auditorium etc: a gallery of seats above the main stalls □ *the dress circle*. **5** a series or chain of events, steps or developments, ending at the point where it began. See also VICIOUS CIRCLE. **6** a group of people associated in some way □ *his circle of acquaintances*. ▻ *verb* (*circled, circling*) **1** *tr & intr* **a** to move in a circle; **b** to move in a circle round something. **2** to draw a circle round something. • **circler** *noun*. • **come full circle 1** to complete a full cycle. **2** to reach or arrive back at the starting-point. • **go round in circles** to be trapped in an endless and frustrating cycle of repetitive discussion or activity. • **run round in circles** to rush around frantically, making little progress. ⓘ Anglo-Saxon *circul*, from Latin *circulus*.

circlet /'sɜːklət/ ▻ *noun* **1** a simple band or hoop of gold, silver, etc worn on the head. **2** a small circle. ⓘ 15c: from French *cerclet*, diminutive of *cercle* circle.

circotherm oven /'sɜːkəθɜːm —/ ▻ *noun* an oven with a fan to circulate internal hot air, designed to achieve uniformity of heating and to economize in heating and cooking time. Also called **fan oven**. ⓘ 20c.

circuit /'sɜːkɪt/ ▻ *noun* **1** a complete course, journey or route round something. **2** a race track, running-track, etc. **3** (*sometimes* **electric circuit**) a path consisting of various electrical devices joined together by wires, to allow an electric current to flow continuously through it. **4** the places or venues visited in turn and regularly by entertainers, etc. **5** a round of places made by a travelling judge. **6** a group of cinemas, theatres, etc under common control, with shows moving on from one to the next. **7** *sport* the round of tournaments in which competitors take part. ▻ *verb* (***circuited***, ***circuiting***) to go round. ⓒ 14c: French, from Latin *circuitus* round trip or revolution

circuit-breaker ▻ *noun* in an electric circuit: a device that automatically interrupts the circuit if the current exceeds a certain value.

circuitous /sə'kjuːɪtəs/ ▻ *adj* indirect; roundabout. • **circuitously** *adverb*. • **circuitousness** *noun*.

circuitry /'sɜːkɪtrɪ/ ▻ *noun* (***circuitries***) *elec* **1** a plan or system of circuits used in a particular electronic or electrical device. **2** the equipment or components making up such a system.

circuit training ▻ *noun* athletic training in the form of a repeated series of exercises.

circular /'sɜːkjʊlə(r)/ ▻ *adj* **1** having the form of a circle. **2** moving or going round in a circle, leading back to the starting-point. **3** said of reasoning, etc: illogical, since the truth of the premises cannot be proved without reference to the conclusion. **4** said of a letter, etc: addressed and copied to a number of people. ▻ *noun* a circular letter or notice. • **circularity** /-'larɪtɪ/ *noun* a circular form, position or quality. • **circularly** *adverb*. ⓒ 14c: from Latin *circularis*.

circularize or **circularise** /'sɜːkjʊləraɪz/ ▻ *verb* (***circularized***, ***circularizing***) **1** to send circulars to (people). **2** to make something circular.

circular saw ▻ *noun* a power-driven saw which has a rotating disc-shaped blade with a serrated edge.

circulate /'sɜːkjʊleɪt/ ▻ *verb* (***circulated***, ***circulating***) **1** *tr & intr* to move or cause to move round freely, especially in a fixed route □ *traffic circulating through the town.* **2** *tr & intr* to spread; to pass round □ *circulate the report.* **3** *intr* to move around talking to different people, eg at a party. • **circulatory** *adj*. ⓒ 17c: from Latin *circulare, circulatum* to encircle.

circulation /sɜːkjʊ'leɪʃən/ ▻ *noun* **1** the act or process of circulating. **2** *anatomy* in most animals: the system of blood vessels that supplies oxygenated blood pumped by the heart to all parts of the body, and that transports deoxygenated blood to the lungs. **3 a** the distribution of a newspaper or magazine; **b** the number of copies of it that are sold. • **in** or **out of circulation** **1** said of money: being, or not being, used by the public. **2** taking part, or not taking part, in one's usual social activities.

circulatory system ▻ *noun, anatomy, zool* the network of blood vessels which, along with the heart, transport materials such as blood, lymph, etc around the body. Also called **cardiovascular system**.

circum- /sɜːkəm/ ▻ *combining form, signifying* round about. ⓒ Latin, meaning 'about'.

circumcise /'sɜːkəmsaɪz/ ▻ *verb* (***circumcised***, ***circumcising***) **1** to cut away all or part of the foreskin of the penis of (a male), as a religious rite or medical necessity. **2** to cut away the clitoris and sometimes the labia of (a woman). ⓒ 13c: from Latin *circumcidere*.

circumcision /sɜːkəm'sɪʒən/ ▻ *noun* **1** in males: the surgical removal of all or part of the foreskin of the penis, usually performed during early childhood. **2** in females: the surgical removal of the clitoris and sometimes the labia. See also CLITORIDECTOMY. **3** (**Circumcision**) *Christianity* a festival celebrated on 1 January in honour of the circumcision of Christ, eight days after his birth.

circumference /sə'kʌmfərəns/ ▻ *noun* **1** *geom* the length of the boundary of a circle or other closed curve, or the length of a path around a sphere at its widest point. **2** the boundary of an area of any shape. **3** the distance represented by any of these. • **circumferential** /səkʌmfə'rɛnʃəl/ *adj*. ⓒ 14c: from French, from Latin *circum* about + *ferre* to carry.

circumflex /'sɜːkəmflɛks/ ▻ *noun* (***circumflexes***) (*also* **circumflex accent**) in some languages, eg French: a mark placed over a vowel, eg *ô*, *û*, as an indication of pronunciation, length or the omission of a letter formerly pronounced. ▻ *adj, anatomy* said of arteries, muscles, etc: bent or curved. ▻ *verb* (***circumflexes***, ***circumflexed***, ***circumflexing***) to bend round. ⓒ 16c: from Latin *circumflexus* bent.

circumfuse /sɜːkəm'fjuːz/ ▻ *verb* (***circumfused***, ***circumfusing***) **1** to pour (a liquid) around something. **2** to envelop something with a substance or as with a substance. • **circumfusion** *noun*. ⓒ 16c: from Latin *fundere, fusum* to pour.

circumlocution /sɜːkəmlə'kjuːʃən, -loʊ'kjuːʃən/ ▻ *noun* an unnecessarily long or indirect way of saying something. • **circumlocutory** *adj*. ⓒ 16c.

circumnavigate /sɜːkəm'navɪgeɪt/ ▻ *verb* (***circumnavigated***, ***circumnavigating***) to sail or fly round, especially the world. • **circumnavigation** *noun*. • **circumnavigator** *noun*. ⓒ 17c.

circumscribe /sɜːkəm'skraɪb/ ▻ *verb* (***circumscribed***, ***circumscribing***) **1** to put a boundary round or to draw a line round something. **2** to limit or restrict something. **3** *geom* to draw one geometrical figure round (another geometrical figure) so that they touch one another but do not intersect. Compare INSCRIBE. • **circumscription** *noun*. ⓒ 15c: from Latin *circumscribere, circumscriptum*.

circumspect /'sɜːkəmspɛkt/ ▻ *adj* cautious; prudent; wary. • **circumspection** *noun*. • **circumspectly** *adverb*. ⓒ 15c: from Latin *circumspicere, circumspectum*.

circumstance /'sɜːkəmstəns, -stɑːns/ ▻ *noun* **1** (*usually* **circumstances**) a fact, occurrence or condition, especially when relating to an act or event □ *died in mysterious circumstances.* **2** (**circumstances**) one's financial situation. **3** events that one cannot control; fate □ *a victim of circumstance.* **4** ceremony □ *pomp and circumstance.* • **in** or **under no circumstances** never, not for any reason at all. • **in** or **under the circumstances** the situation being what it is or was. • **reduced circumstances** poverty. ⓒ 13c: from Latin *circumstantia*.

circumstantial /sɜːkəm'stanʃəl/ ▻ *adj* **1** relating to or dependent on circumstance. **2** said of an account of an event: full of detailed description, etc. • **circumstantiality** *noun*. • **circumstantially** *adverb*.

circumstantial evidence ▻ *noun, law* evidence from which a conclusion or verdict is inferred but not proven.

circumstantiate /sɜːkəm'stanʃɪeɪt/ ▻ *verb* (***circumstantiated***, ***circumstantiating***) to support or prove by citing circumstances. • **circumstantiation** *noun*.

circumvent /sɜːkəm'vɛnt/ ▻ *verb* (***circumvented***, ***circumventing***) **1** to find a way of getting round or evading (a rule, law, etc). **2** to outwit or frustrate someone. **3** to surround so as to intercept or capture. • **circumvention** *noun*. ⓒ 16c: from Latin *circumvenire, circumventum* to surround, beset, deceive.

circus /'sɜːkəs/ ▻ *noun* (***circuses***) **1 a** a travelling company of performers including acrobats, clowns and often trained animals, etc; **b** a performance by such a company, traditionally in a circular tent. **2** *colloq* a scene of noisy confusion. **3** a travelling group of professional sportspeople, etc who put on displays □ *flying circus.* **4** (**Circus**) often in place names: **a** an open space, especially one roughly circular, at the junction of a number of streets □ *Oxford Circus*; **b** a circular terrace of houses. **5** in ancient Rome: an oval or circular open-air stadium for chariot-racing and other competitive sports. • **circussy** *adj*. ⓒ 16c: Latin, meaning 'circle', 'ring' or 'stadium'.

cirque /sɜːk/ ▻ *noun, geog* a deep semicircular hollow with steep side and back walls, located high on a mountain slope and formed as a result of glacial erosion. See COOMB (*noun* 2), CORRIE, CWM (*noun* 2). ⓒ 19c: French, from Latin *circus* ring.

cirrhosis /sə'roʊsɪs/ ▻ *noun, pathol* a progressive disease of the liver, especially alcohol related, which results in a wasting away of normal tissue, and an overgrowth of abnormal lumpy tissue. ⓘ 19c: from Greek *kirrhos* tawny, the colour of diseased liver + -OSIS.

cirriped /ˈsɪrɪpɛd/ or **cirripede** /-piːd/ ▷ *noun, zool* any of the class of sea creatures that includes barnacles. ⓘ 19c: from Latin *cirrus* curl + -PED.

cirrocumulus /sɪroʊˈkjuːmjʊləs/ ▷ *noun* (*cirrocumuli* /-laɪ/) *meteorol* a type of high cloud which consists of small masses of white clouds that form a rippled pattern. See also MACKEREL SKY. ⓘ 19c: from CIRRUS + CUMULUS.

cirrostratus /sɪroʊˈstrɑːtəs/ ▷ *noun* (*cirrostrati* /-taɪ/) *meteorol* a type of high cloud which forms a thin whitish layer with a fibrous appearance and is associated with the approach of a warm front of a depression. ⓘ 19c: from CIRRUS + STRATUS.

cirrus /ˈsɪrəs/ ▷ *noun* (*cirri* /-raɪ/) **1** *meteorol* a common type of high cloud composed of ice crystals, with a wispy fibrous or feathery appearance and which indicates fair weather. **2** *zool* a curved filament, found in barnacles. **3** *bot* a TENDRIL. ⓘ 19c: Latin, meaning 'curl'.

CIS ▷ *abbreviation* **1** Chartered Institute of Secretaries. **2** Commonwealth of Independent States, an organization, formed in 1991, consisting of the former republics of the Soviet Union, excluding the Baltic States.

cissy see SISSY

cist /sɪst/ ▷ *noun, archaeol* a chest-shaped tomb, lined and covered with slabs of stone. ⓘ 19c: Welsh, from Latin *cista* chest.

Cistercian /sɪsˈtɜːʃən/ ▷ *noun* a member of the religious order of Cistercians formed in 1098, who follow a strict rule with an emphasis on solitude, poverty and simplicity. ▷ *adj* belonging or relating to the Cistercians. ⓘ 17c: from Latin place name Cistercium, now Cîteaux, the site of the original abbey near Dijon.

cistern /ˈsɪstən/ ▷ *noun* **1** a tank storing water, usually in the roof-space of a house, or connected to a flushing toilet. **2** *archaeol* a natural underground reservoir. ⓘ 13c: from Latin *cisterna* reservoir.

cistron /ˈsɪstrən/ ▷ *noun, genetics* that part of a chain of DNA that is functionally equivalent to a gene. ⓘ 20c: from *cis-trans test* a test defining the unit of genetic function.

CIT ▷ *abbreviation* Chartered Institute of Transport.

citadel /ˈsɪtədəl, -dɛl/ ▷ *noun* **1** a fortress built close to or within a city, for its protection and as a place of refuge. **2** any stronghold or place of refuge. **3** a building in which the Salvation Army holds its meetings. ⓘ 16c: from Italian *cittadella*, diminutive of *città* city.

citation /saɪˈteɪʃən, sɪ-/ ▷ *noun* **1** the quoting or citing of something as example or proof. **2** a passage quoted from a book, etc. **3** *law* **a** a summons to appear in court; **b** the document containing the summons. **4** **a** a special official commendation or award for merit, bravery, etc; **b** a list of the reasons for such an award.

citation analysis ▷ *noun* the quantitative analysis of the use of bibliographical citations in academic publications.

cite /saɪt/ ▷ *verb* (*cited, citing*) **1** to quote (a book, its author or a passage from it) as an example or proof. **2** to mention as an example or illustration. **3** *law* **a** to summon someone to appear in court; **b** to name someone as being involved in a case. **4** to mention someone in an official report by way of commendation □ *cited for bravery*. • **citable** *adj*. ⓘ 15c: from French *citer* to summon.

CITES ▷ *abbreviation* Convention on International Trade in Endangered Species (of Wild Fauna and Flora).

citizen /ˈsɪtɪzən/ ▷ *noun* **1** an inhabitant of a city or town. **2** a native of a country or state, or a naturalized member of it. ⓘ 14c as *citesein*: from French *citeain*, from *cité* city.

citizenry ▷ *noun* (*citizenries*) the citizens of a town, country, etc.

citizen's arrest ▷ *noun* in some countries: an arrest made without a warrant by a member of the public.

Citizens' Band and **Citizens' Band Radio** ▷ *noun* (abbreviation **CB**) in the USA and many European countries: a band of radio frequencies, around 27 MHz, on which members of the public are permitted to send messages to each other.

citizenship ▷ *noun* **1** the status or position of a citizen. **2** the rights and duties of a citizen. **3** a person's conduct in relation to such duties.

citrate /ˈsɪtreɪt/ ▷ *noun, chem* a salt or ester of citric acid.

citric /ˈsɪtrɪk/ ▷ *adj* **1** derived from citric acid. **2** relating to or derived from citrus fruits. ⓘ 19c: see CITRUS.

citric acid ▷ *noun, chem* an organic acid present in the juice of citrus fruit, which is used as a food flavouring and ANTIOXIDANT.

citrin /ˈsɪtrɪn/ ▷ *noun* VITAMIN P. ⓘ 20c: from CITRUS.

citron /ˈsɪtrən/ ▷ *noun* **1** a fruit like a large lemon, with a thick sweet-smelling yellow rind. **2** the candied rind of this fruit, used for flavouring or decorating cakes, etc. **3** the small thorny evergreen Asian tree bearing the fruit. ⓘ 16c: French, from Latin *citrus* the citron tree.

citrus /ˈsɪtrəs/ ▷ *noun* (*citruses*) any of a group of edible fruits with a tough outer peel enclosing juicy flesh rich in vitamin C, citric acid and water. Also called **citrus fruit**. ⓘ 19c: Latin, meaning 'the citron tree'.

cittern /ˈsɪtɜːn/ or **cithern** /ˈsɪθɜːn/ or **cither** /ˈsɪθə(r)/ ▷ *noun* a plucked stringed instrument which resembles the lute and was popular in the 16c and 17c. ⓘ 16c: perhaps from *cither* + *gitterne* other obsolete name for a stringed instrument.

city /ˈsɪtɪ/ ▷ *noun* (*cities*) **1** any large town. **2** in the UK: a town with a royal charter and usually a cathedral. **3** the body of inhabitants of a city. **4** (**the City**) the business centre of a city, especially London. ⓘ 13c: from French *cité*, from Latin *civitas* state.

city desk ▷ *noun* in a newspaper office: the desk or department of the city editor.

city editor ▷ *noun* in a newspaper office: the financial editor.

city fathers ▷ *plural noun* **a** the magistrates of a city; **b** the members of a city's council.

city hall ▷ *noun* (*often* **City Hall**) **a** the local government of a city; **b** the building in which it is housed.

cityscape ▷ *noun* a view or picture of a city.

city slicker ▷ *noun* an over-sophisticated and worldly city-dweller.

city-state ▷ *noun, historical* a sovereign state consisting of a city and its dependencies.

civet /ˈsɪvɪt/ ▷ *noun* **1** (*also* **civet cat**) a small spotted and striped carnivorous mammal found in Asia and Africa. **2** a strong-smelling fluid secreted by glands near the reproductive organs of this animal, used in perfumes to make their scent last. See also MUSK. **3** the fur of the animal. ⓘ 16c: French *civette*, from Arabic *zabad* perfume.

civic /ˈsɪvɪk/ ▷ *adj* relating to a city, citizen or citizenship. • **civically** *adverb*. ⓘ 17c: from Latin *civicus* belonging to citizens, from *civis* citizen.

civic centre ▷ *noun* a place, sometimes a specially designed complex, where the administrative offices and chief public buildings of a city are grouped.

civics ▷ *singular noun* the study of local government and of the rights and duties of citizenship.

civil /ˈsɪvɪl/ ▷ *adj* **1** relating to the community □ *civil affairs*. **2** relating to or occurring between citizens □ *civil* *disturbances.* **3 a** relating to ordinary citizens; **b** not military, legal or religious. **4** *law* relating to cases about individual rights, etc, not criminal cases. **5** polite. ● **civilly** *adverb*. ⓒ 14c: from Latin *civilis* relating to citizens, from *civis* citizen.

civil defence ▻ *noun* **1** the organization and training of ordinary citizens to assist the armed forces in wartime, especially during enemy attack. **2** the body of people involved in this.

civil disobedience ▻ *noun* the refusal to obey regulations, pay taxes, etc as a form of non-violent protest, usually against the government.

civil engineering ▻ *noun* the branch of engineering concerned with the design, construction, and maintenance of roads, bridges, railways, tunnels, docks, etc as carried out by a **civil engineer** (see ENGINEER *noun* 2).

civilian /sɪˈvɪlɪən/ ▻ *noun* anyone who is not a member of the armed forces or the police force. ⓒ 14c: French *civilien* relating to civil law, from Latin *civilis* citizen.

civility /sɪˈvɪlɪtɪ/ ▻ *noun* (*civilities*) **1** politeness. **2 a** an act of politeness; **b** a polite remark or gesture. ⓒ 16c: French *civilité*, from Latin *civilitas* courtesy.

civilization or **civilisation** ▻ *noun* **1** a stage of development in human society that is socially, politically, culturally and technologically advanced. **2** the parts of the world that have reached such a stage. **3** the state of having achieved or the process of achieving such a stage. **4** *usually historical* a people and their society and culture □ *the Minoan civilization.* **5** built-up areas as opposed to wild, uncultivated or sparsely populated parts. **6** intellectual or spiritual enlightenment, as opposed to brutishness or coarseness.

civilize or **civilise** /ˈsɪvɪlaɪz/ ▻ *verb* (*civilized, civilizing*) **1** to lead out of a state of barbarity to a more advanced stage of social development. **2** to educate and enlighten morally, intellectually and spiritually. ⓒ 16c: French *civiliser*, from Latin *civilis* citizen.

civilized or **civilised** ▻ *adj* **1** socially, politically and technologically advanced. **2** agreeably refined, sophisticated or comfortable. **3** *facetious* trained to behave and speak politely.

civil law ▻ *noun* the part of a country's law that deals with the rights, etc of its citizens, rather than crimes.

civil liberty ▻ *noun* (*often* **civil liberties**) personal freedom of thought, word, action, etc and the right to exercise it.

civil list ▻ *noun* in the UK: the annual Parliamentary allowance to the sovereign and certain members of the Royal family for household expenses.

civil marriage ▻ *noun, law* a marriage performed by a civil magistrate or official, rather than by a clergyman.

civil rights ▻ *plural noun* the personal rights of any citizen of a country to freedom and equality, regardless of race, religion, sex or sexuality.

civil servant ▻ *noun* someone employed in the civil service.

civil service ▻ *noun* the body of officials employed by a government to administer the affairs of a country, excluding the military, naval, legislative and judicial areas.

civil war ▻ *noun* a war between citizens of the same state.

civvy /ˈsɪvɪ/ ▻ *noun* (*civvies*) *colloq* **1** a civilian. **2** (**civvies**) ordinary civilian clothes as opposed to a military uniform.

civvy street ▻ *noun, colloq* ordinary civilian life after service in the armed forces.

CJD ▻ *abbreviation* Creutzfeldt-Jakob disease.

CL ▻ *abbreviation, IVR* Sri Lanka.

Cl ▻ *symbol, chem* chlorine.

cl ▻ *abbreviation* centilitre.

clack ▻ *noun* a sharp noise made by one hard object striking another. ▻ *verb* (*clacked, clacking*) **1** *tr & intr* to make or cause something to make this kind of noise. **2** *intr* to talk noisily. ⓒ 13c: imitating the sound.

clad ▻ *adj, literary* **1** clothed. **2** covered. Also *in compounds* □ *velvet-clad* □ *stone-clad.* ▻ *verb* (*clad, cladding*) to cover one material with another, eg brick or stonework with a different material, especially to form a protective layer. ⓒ 14c: past tense and past participle of CLOTHE.

cladding ▻ *noun, engineering* **1** a thin covering applied to the external surface of a building in order to improve its appearance or to give it extra protection. **2** a thin layer of an expensive metal that is used to coat a cheaper metal. **3** in nuclear reactors: a thin layer of metal that covers the fuel elements and protects them from corrosion and also prevents the release of fission products into the coolant. **4** the process whereby one material is covered with another, and the two are then bonded together under conditions of high temperature and pressure.

cladistics /kləˈdɪstɪks/ ▻ *singular noun, biol* a system of animal and plant classification in which organisms are grouped together on the basis of similarities due to recent origin from a common ancestor. ⓒ 20c: from Greek *klados* branch.

claim ▻ *verb* (*claimed, claiming*) **1** to state something firmly, insisting on its truth □ *She claimed that she was innocent.* **2** to declare oneself (to be, to have done, etc). **3** to assert that one has something □ *He claimed no knowledge of the crime.* **4** *tr & intr* to demand or assert as a right □ *He claimed his prize.* **5** to take or use up something □ *The hurricane claimed 300 lives.* **6 a** to need; **b** to deserve; **c** to have a right to something □ *The baby claimed its mother's attention.* **7** to declare that one is the owner of something □ *I claimed my umbrella from the lost property office.* **8** to identify oneself as having responsibility or being responsible for something. **9** *intr* to make a claim or put in a claim for something, in acccordance with an insurance policy □ *He claimed for a new windscreen.* ▻ *noun* **1** a statement of something as a truth. **2** a demand, especially for something to which one has, or believes one has, a right □ *lay claim to the throne.* **3** a right to or reason for something □ *a claim to fame.* **4** something one has claimed, eg a piece of land or a sum of money. **5** a demand for compensation in the form of money, in accordance with an insurance policy etc. ● **claimable** *adj*. ● **claimant** *noun*. ● **jump a claim** to claim land containing gold, oil, etc which already belongs to someone else. ● **lay claim to something** to assert a right to it. ⓒ 13c: from Latin *clamare* to cry out.

clairvoyance /kleəˈvɔɪəns/ or **clairvoyancy** /-sɪ/ ▻ *noun* the alleged ability to see into the future, or know things that cannot be discovered through the normal range of senses. ⓒ 19c: French, literally 'clear-seeing', from *clair* clear + *voir* to see.

clairvoyant ▻ *adj* involving or claiming the power of clairvoyance. ▻ *noun* someone who claims to have the power of clairvoyance.

clam ▻ *noun* **1 a** any of various BIVALVE shellfish; **b** its edible flesh. **2** *colloq* an uncommunicative person. ▻ *verb* (*clammed, clamming*) *intr, chiefly US* to gather clams. ⓒ 16c: a shortening of *clamshell* a shell which clamps (see CLAMP[1]).

■ **clam up** *colloq* **1** to stop talking suddenly. **2** to refuse to speak or answer questions, etc.

clamant /ˈklamənt, ˈkleɪ-/ ▻ *adj* **1** noisy. **2** calling out aloud or earnestly. ⓒ 17c: from Latin *clamare* to cry out.

clamber /ˈklambə(r)/ ▻ *verb* (*clambered, clambering*) *intr* to climb using one's hands as well as one's feet. ▻ *noun* an act of clambering. ⓒ 15c: related to CLIMB.

clammy /'klamɪ/ ▻ *adj* (***clammier, clammiest***) **1** moist or damp, especially unpleasantly so. **2** said of the weather: humid. ● **clammily** *adverb*. ● **clamminess** *noun*. Ⓒ Anglo-Saxon *clæman* to smear.

clamour /'klamə(r)/ ▻ *noun* **1** a noise of shouting or loud talking. **2 a** a continuous outcry; **b** loud protesting or loud demands. **3** any persistent loud noise. ▻ *verb* (***clamoured, clamouring***) *intr* to make a loud continuous outcry. ● **clamorous** *adj*. ● **clamorously** *adverb*. ● **clamorousness** *noun*. Ⓒ 14c: French, from Latin *clamare* to cry out.

■ **clamour for something** to demand it noisily.

clamp¹ ▻ *noun* **1** a tool with adjustable jaws for gripping things firmly or pressing parts together. **2** a reinforcing or fastening device, used in woodwork, etc. **3** (*usually* **wheel clamp**) a heavy metal device fitted to the wheels of an illegally parked car, to prevent it being moved. ▻ *verb* (***clamped, clamping***) **1** to fasten together or hold with a clamp. **2** to fit a clamp to a wheel of (a parked car) to stop it being moved. **3** to hold, grip, shut or press tightly. Ⓒ 14c: from Dutch *klampe*.

■ **clamp down on something** or **someone** to put a stop to or to control it or them strictly.

clamp² ▻ *noun* a harvested root crop, silage, etc, piled into a mound out of doors, and covered with earth and straw as protection against cold. Ⓒ 16c: from Dutch *klamp* heap.

clampdown ▻ *noun* **a** a suppressive measure; **b** repression of activity □ *a clampdown on drugs*.

clan ▻ *noun* **1** in Scotland or among people of Scots origin: a group of families, generally with the same surname, and (especially formerly) led by a chief. **2** *humorous* one's family or relations. **3** a group of people who have similar interests, concerns, etc. **4** a division of a tribe. Ⓒ 14c: from Scottish Gaelic *clann* family, from Latin *planta* sprout.

clandestine /klan'dɛstɪn, 'klandɛstaɪn/ ▻ *adj* **1 a** concealed; **b** kept secret. **2** furtive; sly; surreptitious. ● **clandestinely** *adverb*. Ⓒ 16c: from Latin *clandestinus*, from *clam* secretly.

clang ▻ *verb* (***clanged, clanging***) *tr & intr* to ring or make something ring loudly and deeply. ▻ *noun* this ringing sound. Ⓒ 16c: from Latin *clangere* to resound.

clanger /'klaŋə(r)/ ▻ *noun, colloq* a tactless, embarrassing and all-too-obvious blunder. ● **drop a clanger** *colloq* to make such a blunder. Ⓒ 20c.

clangour /'klaŋgə(r)/ ▻ *noun, poetic* a loud resounding noise. Ⓒ 16c: from Latin *clangor*.

clank ▻ *noun* a sharp metallic sound like pieces of metal striking together. ▻ *verb* (***clanked, clanking***) *tr & intr* to make or cause something to make such a sound. Ⓒ 17c: imitating the sound.

clannish ▻ *adj, derog* said of a group of people: closely united, with little interest or trust in people not belonging to the group. ● **clannishly** *adverb*. ● **clannishness** *noun*.

clansman and **clanswoman** ▻ *noun* a member of a clan.

clap ▻ *verb* (***clapped, clapping***) **1** *tr & intr* to strike the palms of (one's hands) together with a loud noise, in order to mark (a rhythm), gain attention, etc. **2** *tr & intr* to applaud someone or something by clapping. **3** to strike someone softly with the palm of the hand, usually as a friendly gesture. **4** to place forcefully □ *clapped the book on the table*. **5** *colloq* to put someone suddenly or forcibly (into prison, chains, etc). **6** *Scottish* to pat □ *She clapped the friendly dog.* ▻ *noun* **1** an act of clapping. **2** the sudden loud explosion of noise made by thunder. ● **clap eyes on someone** or **something** *colloq* to see or catch sight of them. Ⓒ Anglo-Saxon *clæppan*.

the clap ▻ *noun, coarse slang* a venereal disease, especially gonorrhoea. Ⓒ 16c: perhaps from French *clapoir* venereal sore, from *clapier* brothel.

clapped out ▻ *adj, colloq* **1** said of a machine, etc: old, worn out and no longer working properly. **2** said of a person: exhausted.

clapper ▻ *noun* **1** the dangling piece of metal inside a bell that strikes against the sides to make it ring. **2** a device that produces a loud clattering noise, for scaring birds from crops, etc. ● **like the clappers** *colloq* very quickly; at top speed.

clapperboard ▻ *noun* a pair of hinged boards clapped together in front of the camera before and after shooting a piece of film, to help synchronize sound and vision.

claptrap ▻ *noun* **a** meaningless, insincere or pompous talk; **b** nonsense. Ⓒ 18c.

claque /klak/ ▻ *noun* **1** a group of people paid to applaud a speaker at a meeting or performer in a theatre, etc. **2** a circle of flatterers or admirers. Ⓒ 19c: French, meaning 'a clap', from *claquer* to clap.

claret /'klarət/ ▻ *noun* **1** a French red wine, especially from the Bordeaux area in SW France. **2** the deep reddish-purple colour of this wine. Ⓒ 14c: from French *clairet* clear wine, from Latin *clarus* clear.

clarify /'klarɪfaɪ/ ▻ *verb* (***clarifies, clarified, clarifying***) *tr & intr* **1** to make or become clearer or easier to understand. **2** said of butter, fat, etc: to make or become clear by heating. ● **clarification** *noun* the process of making clear. ● **clarifier** *noun*. Ⓒ 19c in this sense: from Latin *clarus* clear.

clarinet /klarɪ'nɛt/ ▻ *noun, music* a woodwind instrument with a cylindrical tube and a single REED (sense 2). ● **clarinettist** *noun* someone who plays the clarinet. Ⓒ 18c: French *clarinette*, diminutive of *clarin* clarion.

clarion /'klarɪən/ ▻ *noun, chiefly poetic, historical* an old kind of trumpet with a shrill sound, used to call men to arms, etc □ *a clarion call*. Ⓒ 14c: French, from Latin *clarus* clear.

clarity /'klarɪtɪ/ ▻ *noun* **1** the quality of being clear and pure. **2** the quality of being easy to see, hear or understand. **3** clearness and accuracy of thought, reasoning and expression. Ⓒ 17c: from Latin *claritas* clearness.

clarsach /'klɑːsəx/ ▻ *noun* in Scotland and Ireland: a small harp strung with wire. Ⓒ 15c: Scottish Gaelic.

clash ▻ *noun* **1** a loud noise, like that of metal objects striking each other. **2** a serious disagreement; a quarrel or argument. **3** a fight, battle or match. **4** the coinciding of two or more events, both or all of which one ought to or would like to attend. ▻ *verb* (***clashes, clashed, clashing***) **1** *tr & intr* said of metal objects, etc: to strike against each other noisily. **2** *intr* to fight; to have a battle. **3** *intr* said of commitments, etc: to coincide, usually not fortuitously. **4** *intr* said of colours, styles, etc: to be unpleasing or unharmonious together. Ⓒ 16c: imitating the sound.

■ **clash with someone** to disagree with them violently.

clasp /klɑːsp/ ▻ *noun* **1** a fastening on jewellery, a bag, etc made of two parts that link together. **2** a firm grip, or act of gripping. **3** *military* a bar on the ribbon of a medal. ▻ *verb* (***clasped, clasping***) **1** to hold or take hold of someone or something firmly. **2** to fasten or secure something with a clasp. Ⓒ 14c.

clasp knife ▻ *noun* a folding pocket knife, originally one held open by a catch.

class /klɑːs/ ▻ *noun* (***classes***) **1** a lesson or lecture. **2** a number of pupils taught together. **3** *especially US* the body of students that begin or finish university or school in the same year □ *class of '94*. **4** a category, kind or type, members of which share common characteristics. **5** a grade or standard. **6** any of the social groupings into which people fall according to their job, wealth, etc. **7** the system by which society is divided into such groups. **8** *colloq* **a** stylishness in dress, behaviour, etc; **b** good quality.

9 *biol* in taxonomy: any of the groups, eg *Mammalia* (the mammals), into which a PHYLUM in the animal kingdom or a DIVISION (sense 7) in the plant kingdom is divided, and which is in turn subdivided into one or more ORDERS (sense 11). ▻ *verb* (***classes, classed, classing***) **a** to regard someone or something as belonging to a certain class; **b** to put into a category. ● **in a class of its own** outstanding; with no equal. ◷ 17c: from Latin *classis* rank, class, division.

class-conscious ▻ *adj, derog* aware of one's own and other people's social class. ● **class-consciousness** *noun*.

classic /'klasɪk/ ▻ *adj* **1** made of or belonging to the highest quality; established as the best. **2** entirely typical. **3** simple, neat and elegant, especially in a traditional style. ▻ *noun* **1** an established work of literature. **2** an outstanding example of its type. **3** something, eg an item of clothing, which will always last, irrespective of fashions and fads □ *the little black dress, a classic of the 50s*. **4** (**Classic**) a celebrated annual sporting event, especially a horse race. See also THE CLASSICS. ● **classically** *adverb* **1** in a classic or classical way. **2** so as to be classical. ◷ 17c: from Latin *classicus* relating to classes, especially the best.

classical ▻ *adj* **1** said of literature, art, etc: **a** from ancient Greece and Rome; **b** in the style of ancient Greece and Rome. **2** said of architecture or the other arts: showing the influence of ancient Greece and Rome □ *a classical façade*. **3** said of music and arts related to it: having an established, traditional and somewhat formal style and form. **4** said of procedures, etc: following the well-known traditional pattern □ *the classical method of making pancakes*. **5** said of a shape, design, etc: simple; pure; without complicated decoration. **6** said of a language: being the older literary form. **7** said of an education: concentrating on Latin, Greek and the humanities.

classical music ▻ *noun* **a** *loosely* music which is relatively formal or 'serious', performed most often by orchestras in concert halls, opera houses and churches; **b** *strictly* the music of the 18c and early 19c, in which there were certain accepted conventions of form and structure used as a framework for the expression of ideas.

classical revival ▻ *noun* a form of Western art characterized by a return to the classical orders in architecture, an interest in themes from classical literature and an emphasis on the human form (with proportions based on Roman sculpture), as a central motif. See also NEOCLASSICAL.

classicism /'klasɪsɪzəm/ ▻ *noun* **1** in art and literature: a simple elegant style based on the Roman and Greek priciples of beauty, good taste, restraint and clarity. **2** a Latin or Greek idiom or form.

classicist ▻ *noun* someone who has studied classics, especially as a university subject.

the Classics ▻ *plural noun, Brit horse-racing* the five chief annual races of the flat season, comprising the Two Thousand Guineas, the One Thousand Guineas, the Derby, the Oaks and the St Leger.

classics ▻ *singular noun* (*often* **the Classics**) **a** the study of Latin and Greek; **b** the study of the literature and history of ancient Greece and Rome.

classification /klasɪfɪ'keɪʃən/ ▻ *noun* **1** the arrangement and division of things and people into classes. **2** a group or class into which a person or thing is put.

classified ▻ *adj* **1** arranged in groups or classes. **2** said of information: kept secret or restricted by the government. **3** said of a road: classed as a motorway or major route.

classified advertisement or **classified ad** ▻ *noun* a small advertisement in a newspaper or magazine, offering something for sale, advertising a job, etc.

classify /'klasɪfaɪ/ ▻ *verb* (***classifies, classified, classifying***) **1** to put into a particular group or category. **2** said of information: to declare it secret and not for publication. ● **classifiable** *adj*. ◷ 18c: from Latin *classis* class, division.

classless ▻ *adj* **1** said of a community, society etc: not divided into social classes. **2** not belonging to any particular social class. ● **classlessness** *noun*.

classmate ▻ *noun* a fellow pupil or student in one's class at school or college.

classroom ▻ *noun* a room in a school or college where classes are taught.

class war ▻ *noun* hostility between the various classes of society, especially between the working and the upper classes.

classy ▻ *adj* (***classier, classiest***) *colloq* **a** stylish or fashionable; **b** superior.

clastic /'klastɪk/ ▻ *adj, geol* said of sedimentary rock: composed of fragments, or **clasts**, of older rocks. Also called **fragmental**.

clatter /'klatə(r)/ ▻ *noun* a loud noise made by hard objects striking each other, or falling onto a hard surface. ▻ *verb* (***clattered, clattering***) *tr & intr* to make or cause to make this noise. ◷ Anglo-Saxon *clatrunge* clattering.

clause /klɔːz/ ▻ *noun* **1** *grammar* **a** a group of words that includes a subject and its related finite verb, and which may or may not constitute a sentence (eg *if time permits* and *we will come tomorrow*). See MAIN CLAUSE, SUBORDINATE CLAUSE; **b** a group of words with a similar grammatical function, but which has no expressed subject (eg *while running for the bus*), no finite verb (eg *time permitting*), or neither a subject nor a verb (eg *if possible*). **2** *law* a paragraph or section in a contract, will or act of parliament. ● **clausal** *adj*. ◷ 13c: from Latin *claudere, clausum* to close.

Clause 4 or **Clause IV** ▻ *noun* a clause which appeared in the Labour Party constitution committing the party to widespread public ownership of industry, such as coal, steel, rail, etc, and which was changed by the Labour Party in 1995 removing this commitment.

claustrophobia /klɔːstrə'foubɪə, klɒ-/ ▻ *noun* **1** an irrational fear of being in confined spaces, eg lifts, tunnels. **2** an uncomfortable feeling of being shut in or confined. ● **claustrophobic** *adj*. ◷ 19c: from Latin *claustrum* bolt or barrier + -PHOBIA.

clavichord /'klavɪkɔːd/ ▻ *noun* an early keyboard instrument with a soft tone. ◷ 15c: from Latin *clavis* key + *chorda* string.

clavicle /'klavɪkəl/ ▻ *noun, anatomy* in vertebrates: either of two short slender bones linking the shoulder-blades with the top of the breastbone. ◷ 17c: from Latin *clavicula*, diminutive of *clavis* key.

claw ▻ *noun* **1** a hard curved pointed nail on the end of each digit of the foot in birds, most reptiles and many mammals. **2** the foot of an animal or bird with a number of such nails. **3** any structure resembling a claw, eg the pincer of a crab or lobster or a sharp curved structure at the tip of the leg of certain insects. **4** something with the shape or action of a claw, eg part of a mechanical device. ▻ *verb* (***clawed, clawing***) *tr & intr* (*often* **claw at something**) to tear or scratch it with claws, nails or fingers. ◷ Anglo-Saxon *clawu*.

> ■ **claw something back** **1** said of a government: to recover money given away in benefits and allowances by imposing a new tax. **2** to regain something with difficulty (eg commercial advantage etc) □ *She clawed her way back to solvency*.

clawback ▻ *noun* **1** recovery of expenditure by taxation. **2** the process of clawing back extended to other situations.

clawed frog and **clawed toad** ▷ *noun* an African or S American aquatic frog, so called because it has claws on three hind toes.

claw hammer ▷ *noun* a hammer with one side of its head divided into two claws, for pulling out nails.

clay ▷ *noun* **1** *geol* a poorly draining soil consisting mainly of aluminium SILICATEs, which is pliable when wet and is used to make pottery, bricks, ceramics, etc. **2** earth or soil generally. **3** a prepared hard surface of a tennis court. **4** *poetic* the substance of which the human body is formed. ● **have feet of clay** said of a person of great merit: to have a weakness which was previously undiscovered. ● **clayey** *adj.* ⓒ Anglo-Saxon *clæg.*

clay court ▷ *noun* a tennis court with a hard surface made from clay or a similar substance.

claymation /kleɪˈmeɪʃən/ ▷ *noun, cinema* animation using clay or Plasticine figures.

clay mineral ▷ *noun, geol* any of various SILICATEs of aluminium that are the chief constituents of clay, and form fine flaky crystals which can absorb water, giving clay its characteristic plasticity when wet.

claymore ▷ *noun, historical* a two-edged broadsword used by Scottish highlanders. ⓒ 18c: from Scottish Gaelic *claidheamh mór* large sword.

clay pigeon ▷ *noun* a clay disc that is thrown up mechanically as a target in the sport of **clay pigeon shooting**.

clay pipe ▷ *noun* a tobacco pipe made of baked clay.

clean /kliːn/ ▷ *adj* (**cleaner**, **cleanest**) **1** free from dirt or contamination. **2** not containing anything harmful to health; pure. **3** pleasantly fresh □ *a clean taste.* **4** recently washed. **5** hygienic in habits □ *a clean animal.* **6** unused; unmarked □ *a clean sheet of paper.* **7** neat and even □ *a clean cut.* **8** simple and elegant □ *a ship with good clean lines.* **9** clear of legal offences □ *a clean driving licence.* **10** morally pure; innocent. **11** said of humour, etc: not offensive or obscene. **12** fair □ *a clean fight.* **13** *slang* not carrying drugs or offensive weapons. **14** *slang* **a** cured of drug addiction; **b** said of athletes, etc: free from drugs or banned substances when tested. **15** said of a wound: showing no signs of infection. **16** said of nuclear installations, etc: not producing a harmful level of radioactivity. **17** said of an aeroplane's landing gear: in a retracted position. **18** *relig* said of certain animals: allowed for people to eat. **19** said of musical sounds: pure and accurate. **20** absolute; complete □ *make a clean break.* ▷ *adverb* **1** *colloq* completely □ *I clean forgot.* **2** straight or directly; encountering no obstruction □ *sailed clean through the window.* ▷ *verb* (**cleaned**, **cleaning**) **1** *tr & intr* to make or become free from dirt. **2** *tr & intr* to dry-clean or be dry-cleaned. **3** *intr* to dust, polish floors and furniture, etc in a house or office, especially as a job. **4** to prepare (vegetables, etc) for cooking or eating by cutting away the inedible parts. ▷ *noun* **1** an act of cleaning. **2** *weightlifting* a lift of the weight as far as the shoulders, with the legs and arms bent. ● **cleanness** *noun.* ● **come clean** *colloq* to admit or tell the truth about something that one has previously concealed or lied about. ● **have clean hands** *colloq* to have no connection with the crime, etc in question. ● **make a clean breast of something** to confess or admit to having done it, especially through feelings of guilt. ● **show a clean pair of heels** to run away, especially quickly. ● **wipe the slate clean** see under SLATE[1]. ⓒ Anglo-Saxon *clæne.*

■ **clean someone out** *slang* to deprive or cheat them of money.

■ **clean something out** to clean (a room or cupboard, etc) thoroughly.

■ **clean up 1** to clean a place thoroughly. **2** *slang* to make a large profit □ *He cleaned up at the racetrack.*

■ **clean someone** or **something up** to make them or it clean; to get rid of a mess.

■ **clean up after someone** to clean up a mess, etc left by them.

clean bill of health ▷ *noun* a declaration that a person is healthy, or that a machine or organization is working satisfactorily.

clean-cut ▷ *adj* **1** pleasingly regular in outline or shape □ *clean-cut features.* **2** neat; respectable.

cleaner ▷ *noun* **1** someone employed to clean inside buildings, offices, etc. **2** a machine or substance used for cleaning. **3** (*usually* **cleaners**) a shop where clothes, etc can be taken for cleaning. ● **take someone to the cleaners** *colloq* to extort all or most of their money.

cleaning lady and **cleaning woman** ▷ *noun* a woman whose job is to clean inside a house, factory, office, etc.

clean-limbed ▷ *adj* having a tall slim shapely body.

clean-living ▷ *adj* leading a decent healthy existence.

cleanly *adverb* /ˈkliːnlɪ/ **1** in a clean way. **2** tidily; efficiently; easily. ▷ *adj* /ˈklɛnlɪ/ *dated* hygienic in one's personal habits. ● **cleanliness** /ˈklɛnlɪnəs/ *noun.*

clean-out ▷ *noun* **1** a thorough cleaning. **2** *colloq* a swindle.

clean room ▷ *noun* **1** an area in a factory where rigorous standards of cleanliness are maintained, especially during the manufacture of computer components and other sensitive equipment. **2** a special facility for handling material, especially that destined for use in space exploration, in a sterile and dust-free environment.

cleanse /klɛnz/ ▷ *verb* (**cleansed**, **cleansing**) **1** to clean or get rid of dirt from someone or something. **2 a** to purify someone or something; **b** to remove sin or guilt from someone. ⓒ Anglo-Saxon *clænsian.*

cleanser ▷ *noun* a substance that cleans, eg a cream or liquid for cleaning the face.

clean-shaven ▷ *adj* said of men: without facial hair.

clean sheet ▷ *noun* **1** a record (sense 6) with no blemishes □ *She had a clean sheet as a manager.* **2** *sport* a situation in which the goalkeeper or the team as a whole do not concede any goals □ *Main kept a clean sheet on Saturday.*

cleansing department ▷ *noun* the local-government department responsible for cleaning the streets and collecting rubbish.

clean slate ▷ *noun* a fresh start, especially after an error.

clean sweep ▷ *noun* **1** a complete or overwhelming success. **2** a complete change or clear-out.

clean-up ▷ *noun* a thorough cleaning.

clear ▷ *adj* **1** transparent; easy to see through. **2** said of weather, etc: not misty or cloudy. **3** said of the skin: healthy; unblemished by spots, etc. **4 a** easy to see, hear or understand; **b** lucid. **5** bright; sharp; well-defined □ *a clear photograph.* **6** said of vision: not obstructed. **7** said of musical sounds: pure and accurate. **8** certain; convinced; having no doubts or confusion □ *Are you clear about that point?* **9** definite; free of doubt, ambiguity or confusion. **10** capable of, or resulting from, accurate observation, logical thinking, etc. **11** evident; obvious. **12** free from obstruction □ *a clear path.* **13** well away from something; out of range of or contact with it □ *well clear of the rocks.* **14** free of it; no longer affected by it. **15** remaining after all charges, taxes, expenses, etc have been paid. **16** said of the conscience, etc: free from guilt, etc. **17** entire; without interruption □ *need a clear week to finish.* **18** free of appointments, etc. ▷ *adverb* **1** in a clear manner. **2** completely □ *get clear away.* **3** *N Amer* all the way □ *see clear to the hills.* **4** well away from something; out of the way of it □ *steer clear of trouble.* ▷ *verb* (**cleared**, **clearing**) **1** *tr & intr* to make or become clear, free of obstruction, etc. **2** to remove or move out of the way. **3** to prove or declare to be innocent or free from suspicion. **4** to get over or past something without touching □ *clear the fence.* **5** to make as profit over expenses. **6** to pass inspection by (customs). **7** to give or get official permission for (a plan, etc). **8** to approve someone for a special assignment, access to secret information, etc. **9** *tr & intr* said of a cheque: to pass from one bank to another through a clearing-house. **10** to decode. **11** to pay a debt. **12** *tr & intr* to give or receive clearance □ *The aeroplane was cleared for take-off.* ● **clearness** *noun.* ● **clear as mud** see under MUD. ● **clear the air** *colloq* to get rid of bad feeling, suspicion or tension, especially by frank discussion. ● **clear the decks** see under DECK[1]. ● **in the clear** no longer under suspicion, in difficulties, or in danger. ◷ 13c: from French *cler*, from Latin *clarus* clear.

■ **clear something away** to remove it.

■ **clear off** *colloq* to go away.

■ **clear something off** to finish paying debts, etc.

■ **clear out** *colloq* to go away.

■ **clear something out** to rid it of rubbish, etc.

■ **clear up 1** said of the weather: to brighten after rain, a storm, etc. **2** to get better □ *Her acne cleared up quickly.*

■ **clear something up 1** to tidy up a mess, room, etc. **2** to solve a mystery, etc.

clearance ▷ *noun* **1** the act of clearing. **2** the distance between one object and another passing beside or under it. **3** permission, or a certificate granting this □ *The plane was given clearance to land.* **4** (*in full* **security clearance**) official acknowledgement that one can be trusted not to pass secrets to an enemy.

clear-cut ▷ *adj* clear; sharp.

clear-headed ▷ *adj* capable of, or showing, clear logical thought. ● **clear-headedly** *adverb.*

clearing ▷ *noun* **1** an area in a forest, etc that has been cleared of trees, etc. *US equivalent* OPENING. **2** *Brit* the stage during the annual national process of application for places in higher education after the exam results are known, when a central agency attempts to match remaining places with appropriate candidates.

clearing bank ▷ *noun* a bank using the services of a central clearing-house.

clearing-house ▷ *noun* **1** an establishment that deals with transactions between its member banks. **2** a central agency that collects, organizes and distributes information.

clearly ▷ *adverb* **1** in a clear manner □ *speak clearly.* **2** obviously □ *Clearly, he's wrong.*

clear-out ▷ *noun* a clearing out of something, eg rubbish, possessions, etc.

clear-sighted ▷ *adj* capable of, or showing, accurate observation and good judgement. ● **clear-sightedly** *adverb.* ● **clear-sightedness** *noun.*

clearstory see CLERESTORY

clearway ▷ *noun* a stretch of road on which cars may not stop except in an emergency.

cleat ▷ *noun* **1** a wedge. **2** a piece of wood attached to a structure to give it extra support. **3** a device attached to parts of a ship for fastening ropes. ▷ *verb* (**cleated**, **cleating**) **1** to strengthen something with a cleat. **2** to fasten something to or by a cleat. ◷ 14c as *clete*: probably from CLOT.

cleavage /ˈkliːvɪdʒ/ ▷ *noun* **1** a series of cell divisions of an ovum immediately after it has been fertilized. **2** *biochem* the breakdown of a complex molecule into simpler molecules by the splitting of chemical bonds within its structure. **3** *geol* **a** the splitting of rocks into thin parallel sheets; **b** the splitting of a crystal in one or more specific directions to give smooth surfaces. **4** *colloq* the hollow between a woman's breasts, especially as revealed by a top with a low neck. ◷ 20c in sense 4; 19c in technical senses: from CLEAVE[1].

cleave[1] /kliːv/ ▷ *verb* (*past tense* **clove**, **cleft** or **cleaved**, *past participle* **cloven**, **cleft** or **cleaved**, *present participle* **cleaving**) *tr & intr, formal or literary* **1** to split or divide. **2** to cut or slice □ *cleave a way through the undergrowth.* See also CLOVEN. ● **cleavable** *adj.* ● **cleavableness** *noun.* ◷ Anglo-Saxon *cleofan*.

cleave[2] /kliːv/ ▷ *verb* (**cleaved**, **cleaving**) *intr* to cling or stick. ◷ Anglo-Saxon *cleofian*.

cleaver /ˈkliːvə(r)/ ▷ *noun* a knife with a large square blade, used especially by butchers for chopping meat. ◷ 16c: from CLEAVE[1].

cleavers ▷ *singular or plural noun* a Eurasian plant with a bristly stem and fruits that cling to clothes. Also called **goosegrass.** ◷ Anglo-Saxon *clife*.

clef /klɛf/ ▷ *noun, music* a symbol placed on a STAVE to indicate the pitch of the notes written on it. ◷ 16c: French, meaning 'key', from Latin *clavis*.

cleft[1] ▷ *noun* a split, fissure, wide crack or deep indentation. ◷ 13c: from CLEAVE[1].

cleft[2] ▷ *adj* split; divided. ● **in a cleft stick** in a difficult or awkward situation. ▷ *verb* see CLEAVE[1]. ◷ 14c: from CLEAVE[1].

cleft palate ▷ *noun, pathol* a fissure in the midline of the palate caused by the failure of the two sides of the mouth to meet and fuse together in the developing fetus. See also HARELIP.

cleg see HORSEFLY

clematis /ˈklɛmətɪs, kləˈmeɪtɪs/ ▷ *noun* (**clematises**) a garden climbing plant of the buttercup family, with purple, yellow or white flowers. ◷ 16c: from Greek *klematis* a name for several climbing plants.

clemency /ˈklɛmənsɪ/ ▷ *noun* **1** the quality of being clement. **2** mercy.

clement /ˈklɛmənt/ ▷ *adj* **1** said of the weather: mild; not harsh or severe. ● **clemently** *adverb* **1** mildly. **2** mercifully; in a merciful way. ◷ 15c: from Latin *clemens* mild, calm or merciful.

clementine /ˈklɛməntiːn, -taɪn/ ▷ *noun* a citrus fruit which is either a type of small tangerine, or a hybrid of an orange and a tangerine. ◷ 20c: French.

clench /klɛntʃ/ ▷ *verb* (**clenches**, **clenched**, **clenching**) **1** to close one's teeth or one's fists tightly, especially in anger. **2** to hold or grip firmly. ▷ *noun* (**clenches**) **1** the action of clenching. **2** a very tight grasp. ◷ Anglo-Saxon *beclencan* to hold fast.

clerestory or **clearstory** /ˈklɪəstɔːrɪ/ ▷ *noun* (**clerestories** or **clearstories**) *archit* **a** in a church: an upper row of windows in the nave wall, above the roof of the aisle; **b** a similar feature in another type of building. ◷ 15c: from CLEAR + STOREY.

clergy /ˈklɜːdʒɪ/ ▷ *singular or plural noun* (**clergies**) the ordained ministers of the Christian church, or the priests of any religion. ◷ 13c: French, from Latin *clericus* priest or clergyman.

clergyman and **clergywoman** ▷ *noun* a member of the clergy.

cleric /ˈklɛrɪk/ ▷ *noun* a clergyman. ◷ 17c: from Latin *clericus* priest, clergyman.

clerical /ˈklɛrɪkəl/ ▷ *adj* **1** relating to clerks, office workers or office work. **2** relating to the clergy.

clerical collar ▷ *noun* the stiff white collar, which fastens at the back, worn by clergymen. Also (*colloq*) called **dog-collar.**

clericalism ▷ *noun* the power or influence of the church.

clerihew /ˈklɛrɪhjuː/ ▷ *noun* a humorous poem about a famous person, consisting of two short couplets. ◎ 20c: named after E Clerihew Bentley (1875–1956), the English journalist and novelist who invented it.

clerk /klɑːk; *US* klɜːrk/ ▷ *noun* **1** in an office or bank: someone who deals with letters, accounts, records, files, etc. **2** in a law court: someone who keeps records or accounts. **3** a public official in charge of the records and business affairs of the town council. **4** an unordained or lay minister of the church. **5** *N Amer* a shop assistant or hotel receptionist. **6** *old use* a scholar or clergyman. ● **clerkish** *adj.* ● **clerkship** *noun.* ◎ Anglo-Saxon *clerc*, from Latin *clericus* priest or clergyman.

clerkess ▷ *noun* a female clerk.

clerk of works ▷ *noun* the person in charge of the construction and care of a building.

clever /ˈklɛvə(r)/ ▷ *adj* (*cleverer*, *cleverest*) **1** good or quick at learning and understanding. **2** skilful, dexterous, nimble or adroit. **3** well thought out; ingenious. ● **cleverly** *adverb.* ● **cleverness** *noun.* ◎ 16c as *cliver*, related to Anglo-Saxon *clifer* claw.

clever dick and **clever clogs** ▷ *noun, derog slang* someone who is over-sure of their cleverness.

clew /kluː/ ▷ *noun* **1** *naut* the corner of a ship's sail. **2** *old use* a ball of thread. ▷ *verb* (*clewed*, *clewing*) to coil up into a ball. ◎ Anglo-Saxon *cliewen* ball of thread.

■ **clew up** or **down** *naut* to haul a sail up or to let it down.

cliché /ˈkliːʃeɪ/ ▷ *noun* (*clichés*) *derog* **1** a once striking and effective phrase or combination of words which has become stale and hackneyed through overuse. **2 a** an overused idea or image; **b** a stereotype. ● **clichéd** or **cliché'd** *adj.* ◎ 19c: French, meaning 'a stereotype plate or stencil'.

click ▷ *noun* **1** a short sharp sound like that made by two parts of a mechanism locking into place. **2** *mech* a catch in a piece of machinery. **3** *phonetics* a click-like speech sound produced by a sucking action with the tongue which is characteristic of some African languages. **4 a** a situation in which two people who are attracted to each other hit it off; **b** the person with whom one hits it off in such a situation. ▷ *verb* (*clicked*, *clicking*) **1** *tr & intr* to make or cause to make a click. **2** *intr, colloq* to meet with approval. **3** *intr, colloq* to become clear or understood □ *The meaning clicked after a while.* **4** *computing* to press and release one of the buttons on a MOUSE in order to send an instruction to the computer to which it is attached. **5** *intr* said of two or more people: to instantly get along very well. ◎ 17c: imitating the sound.

■ **click with someone** *colloq* to become friendly with them.

click beetle *noun* a beetle which, if placed on its back, is able to right itself with a clicking sound. Also called **spring beetle**. See also WIREWORM.

clickety-click ▷ *noun* a persistent clicking noise.

client /ˈklaɪənt/ ▷ *noun* **1** someone using the services of a professional institution eg a bank, a law firm, an estate agent, etc. **2** a customer. **3** someone looked after by a social worker, etc. ◎ 17c: from Latin *cliens* dependant.

clientele /kliːɒnˈtɛl, kliːɑ̃-/ ▷ *noun* **1** the clients of a professional person, customers of a shopkeeper, etc. **2** people habitually attending a theatre, pub, club, etc. ◎ 16c: from Latin *clientela*, from *cliens* dependent.

cliff ▷ *noun* a high steep rock face, especially on the coast or the side of a mountain. ◎ Anglo-Saxon *clif*.

cliff-face ▷ *noun* the sheer or steep front of a cliff.

cliffhanger ▷ *noun* **1** a story that keeps one in suspense up to the end. **2** the ending of an episode of a serial story which leaves the audience in suspense. **3** an exciting situation, especially a contest, of which the conclusion is in doubt until the very last minute. ● **cliffhanging** *adj.*

climacteric /klaɪˈmaktərɪk, klaɪmakˈtɛrɪk/ ▷ *noun* **1** *biol* in living organisms: a period of changes, especially those associated with the menopause in women, and with a reduction in sexual desire in men. **2** *bot* in plants: an increase in respiration rate associated with the ripening of fruit. **3** a critical period. ▷ *adj* relating to such a period. ● **climacterical** *adj.* ◎ 16c: from Greek *klimakter* critical period.

climactic see under CLIMAX

climactic, climatic

These words are sometimes confused with each other.

climate /ˈklaɪmət/ ▷ *noun* **1** the average weather conditions of a particular region of the world over a long period of time, with regard to temperature, rainfall, air pressure, etc. **2** a part of the world considered from the point of view of its weather conditions □ *move to a warmer climate.* **3** a current trend in general feeling, opinion, policies, etc. ● **climatic** *adj.* ● **climatically** *adverb.* ◎ 14c: from Greek *klima* slope or inclination.

climatology /klaɪməˈtɒlədʒɪ/ ▷ *noun* the scientific study of climate. ● **climatological** *adj.* ● **climatologist** *noun.*

climax /ˈklaɪmaks/ ▷ *noun* (*climaxes*) **1** the high point or culmination of a series of events or of an experience. **2** a sexual orgasm. **3 a** *rhetoric* the arrangement of a series of sentences, etc, in order of increasing strength; **b** *loosely* the final term of the arrangement. ▷ *verb* (*climaxes*, *climaxed*, *climaxing*) *tr & intr* **1** to come or bring to a climax. **2** *intr* to experience sexual orgasm. ● **climactic** or **climactical** *adj.* ● **climactically** *adverb.* ◎ 16c: Latin, from Greek *klimax* ladder or climax.

climax community ▷ *noun, ecol* in the development of a community of plants and animals in a particular area: the final stage when the community remains relatively stable under the prevailing environmental conditions, eg oak woodland in the UK.

climb /klaɪm/ ▷ *verb* (*climbed*, *climbing*) **1** (*often* **climb up**) to mount or ascend (a hill, ladder, etc), often using hands and feet. **2** *tr & intr* to rise or go up □ *The aeroplane climbed steadily.* **3** *intr* to increase. **4** *intr* to slope upwards □ *The path started to climb suddenly.* **5** said of plants: to grow upwards using tendrils, etc. ▷ *noun* **1** an act of climbing. **2** a slope to be climbed. ● **climbable** *adj.* ◎ Anglo-Saxon *climban*.

■ **climb down 1** to descend. **2** to concede one's position on some issue, etc, especially publicly or humiliatingly.

■ **climb in** or **out** to reach somewhere with difficulty, especially using hands and feet.

climb-down ▷ *noun* a dramatic change of mind or concession, often humiliating.

climber ▷ *noun* **1** a climbing plant. **2** a mountaineer. **3** *derog* someone who is too obviously trying to rise through the social ranks. See also SOCIAL CLIMBER.

climbing ▷ *noun* the sport of climbing rock faces.

climbing-frame ▷ *noun* a strong framework of metal or wooden bars for children to climb around on.

climbing iron ▷ *noun* a metal frame with a horizontal spike, worn strapped to the feet as an aid in climbing trees, telegraph poles etc.

climbing perch ▷ *noun* an Asiatic freshwater fish with a special respiratory organ above the gills for breathing air. ◎ 19c: so called because it was believed to have the power to climb trees.

climbing plant ▻ *noun, bot* a plant which reaches toward the light by clinging to neighbouring plants, walls, or other supports. See also VINE.

clime /klaɪm/ ▻ *noun, chiefly poetic or humorous* a region of the world ▫ *foreign climes*. Ⓒ 16c: from Greek *klima* region or latitude.

clinch /klɪntʃ/ ▻ *verb* (***clinches, clinched, clinching***) **1** to settle something finally and decisively, eg an argument, deal, etc. **2** *intr, boxing, wrestling* said of contestants: to hold each other in a firm grip. **3** *intr, colloq* to embrace. **4** to bend over and hammer down the projecting point of a nail, etc, so as to secure it. ▻ *noun* (***clinches***) **1** an act of clinching. **2** *boxing, wrestling* an act of clinging to each other to prevent further blows, create a breathing space, etc. **3** *colloq* an embrace between lovers. Ⓒ 16c: variant of CLENCH.

clincher ▻ *noun* **1** a point, argument or circumstance that finally settles or decides a matter. **2** someone or something that clinches.

cline /klaɪn/ ▻ *noun, biol* a gradual change in the form of an animal or plant species across different parts of its geographical or environmental range. Ⓒ 20c: from Greek *klinein* to lean.

cling /klɪŋ/ ▻ *verb* (***clung, clinging***) *intr* **1** to hold firmly or tightly; to stick. **2** to be emotionally over-dependent. **3** to refuse to drop or let go. **4** said of clothes: to stick closely to the body ▫ *This skirt clings horrendously*. ▻ *noun* a CLINGSTONE. ● **clinger** *noun*. Ⓒ Anglo-Saxon *clingan*.

clingfilm ▻ *noun* a thin clear plastic material that adheres to itself, used for wrapping food, covering containers, etc.

clingstone ▻ *noun* **1** a fruit in which the flesh is firmly attached to the stone. **2** *as adj* signifying such a fruit ▫ *clingstone peach*. Compare FREESTONE.

clingy ▻ *adj* (***clingier, clingiest***) liable or tending to cling. ● **clinginess** *noun*.

clinic /ˈklɪnɪk/ ▻ *noun* **1** a private hospital or nursing home that specializes in the treatment and care of patients with particular diseases or disorders. **2** a department of a hospital or a health centre which specializes in one particular area, eg a family planning clinic. **3** a session during which patients are given medical treatment or advice in such a specialized area ▫ *an asthma clinic here every Monday*. **4** the instruction in examination and treatment of patients that is given to medical students, usually at the patient's bedside in a hospital ward. **5** a session in which an expert is available for consultation. Ⓒ 19c: from Greek *klinikos* relating to a sickbed.

clinical ▻ *adj* **1** relating to, or like, a clinic or hospital. **2** said of medical studies: based on, or relating to, direct observation and treatment of the patient, as distinct from theoretical or experimental work. **3** said of manner, behaviour, etc: cold; impersonal; unemotional or detached. **4** said of surroundings, etc: severely plain and simple, with no personal touches. ● **clinically** *adverb*.

clinical death see BRAIN DEATH.

clinical linguistics ▻ *noun* the application of linguistics to the analysis and treatment of disorders of spoken, written or signed language.

clinical psychology ▻ *noun* the practical application of psychological research findings to the diagnosis, treatment and prevention of a wide range of mental disorders.

clinical thermometer ▻ *noun* a thermometer consisting of a calibrated glass tube with a narrow bulb at one end containing mercury, used for measuring body temperature.

clinician /klɪˈnɪʃən/ ▻ *noun* a doctor who works directly with patients, in a clinic, etc, as opposed to conducting experimental or theoretical work.

clink[1] ▻ *noun* a short sharp ringing sound. ▻ *verb* (***clinked, clinking***) *tr & intr* to make or cause to make such a sound. Ⓒ 14c: perhaps from Dutch *klinken* to ring.

clink[2] ▻ *noun, slang* prison. Ⓒ 16c: originally the name of a prison in Southwark.

clinker[1] ▻ *noun* **1** a mass of fused ash or slag left unburnt in a furnace. **2** the cindery crust on a lava flow. **3** a very hard kind of brick. Ⓒ 17c: from Dutch *klinker* hard brick, from *klinken* to ring.

clinker[2] ▻ *noun, slang* **1** *Brit* something or someone that is popular or outstanding. **2** *chiefly US* **a** a mistake or failure; **b** something of poor quality.

clinker-built ▻ *adj* said of the hull of a boat: built with planks, each of which overlaps the one below it on the outside. Compare CARVEL-BUILT. Ⓒ 18c: from *clink*, a form of CLINCH *noun* 4.

clinkstone see PHONOLITE

clinometer /klaɪˈnɒmɪtə(r), klɪˈnɒmɪtə(r)/ ▻ *noun, surveying* any of various hand-held instruments used to measure the verticle angles of a slope. Ⓒ 18c: from Greek *klinein* to slope + -METER 1.

clint ▻ *noun, geol, chiefly Scottish* **1** one of a series of limestone blocks or ridges divided by fissures. **2** any exposed outcrop of hard flinty rock that forms a projection or ledge. **3** *curling* the first stone thrown. Ⓒ 14c: from Danish and Swedish *klint*.

clip[1] ▻ *verb* (***clipped, clipping***) **1** to cut (hair, wool, etc). **2** to trim or cut off the hair, wool or fur of (an animal). **3** to punch out a piece from (a ticket) to show that it has been used. **4** to cut (an article, etc) from a newspaper, etc. **5** *colloq* to hit or strike someone or something sharply. **6** to cut (a small amount) from something. **7** to excerpt a section from (a film, etc). ▻ *noun* **1** an act of clipping. **2** a short sequence extracted from a film. **3** *colloq* a sharp blow ▫ *a clip round the ear*. **4** *colloq* speed; rapid speed ▫ *going at a fair clip*. **5** *Austral, NZ* the total amount of wool shorn from sheep, at one time, place, etc. ● **clip someone's wings** to restrain their ambition, power or scope for activity. Ⓒ 12c: from Norse *klippa* to cut.

clip[2] ▻ *noun* **1** *often in compounds* any of various devices, usually small ones, for holding things together or in position ▫ *paper clip*. **2** (*also* **cartridge clip**) a container for bullets attached to a gun, that feeds bullets directly into it. **3** a piece of jewellery in the form of a clip which can be attached to clothing. ▻ *verb* (***clipped, clipping***) to fasten something with a clip. Ⓒ Anglo-Saxon *clyppan* to embrace or clasp.

clipboard ▻ *noun* a firm board with a clip at the top for holding paper, forms, etc which can be used as a portable writing surface.

clip-clop see CLOP

clip joint ▻ *noun, slang* a bar, restaurant or nightclub charging excessively high prices.

clip-on ▻ *adj* said eg of earrings: fastening with a clip.

clipped ▻ *adj* **1** said of the form of a word: shortened, eg *deli* from *delicatessen*. **2** said of speaking style: **a** tending to shorten vowels, omit syllables, etc; **b** curt and distinct.

clipper ▻ *noun* **1** *historical* a fast sailing ship with large sails. **2** someone or something which clips. Ⓒ 14c: from CLIP[1].

clippers ▻ *plural noun, often in compounds* a clipping device ▫ *nail clippers*.

clipping ▻ *noun* **1** a piece clipped off ▫ *hair clippings*. **2** a cutting from a newspaper, etc.

clique /kliːk/ ▻ *noun* (***cliques***) *derog* a group of friends, professional colleagues, etc who stick together and are hostile towards outsiders. ● **cliquey** /ˈkliːkɪ/ (***cliquier, cliquiest***) and **cliquish** /ˈkliːkɪʃ/ *adj* characteristic of a clique; socially exclusive. ● **cliquiness** or **cliquishness** *noun*. Ⓒ 18c: French from *cliquer* to click.

clitoridectomy /klɪtərɪ'dɛktəmɪ/ ▷ *noun* (*clitoridectomies*) the surgical removal of the clitoris. See also CIRCUMCISION 2.

clitoris /'klɪtərɪs, 'klaɪ-/ ▷ *noun* (*clitorises*) *anatomy* in female mammals: a small highly sensitive organ located in front of the opening of the vagina, which like the penis in males, becomes erect when sexually stimulated. ● **clitoral** *adj*. ⓘ 17c: from Greek *kleitoris*.

Cllr ▷ *abbreviation* Councillor.

cloaca /kloʊ'eɪkə, -'ɑːkə/ ▷ *noun* (*cloacae* /-'eɪsiː, -'ɑːkaɪ/) **1** *zool* in most vertebrates apart from mammals: the terminal region of the gut, into which the alimentary canal and the urinary and reproductive systems all open and discharge their contents. **2** a sewer. ● **cloacal** *adj*. ⓘ 18c: Latin meaning 'sewer', from *cluere* to purge.

cloak ▷ *noun* **1** a loose outdoor garment, usually sleeveless, fastened at the neck so as to hang from the shoulders. **2** a covering □ *a cloak of mist.* **3** a concealment or disguise □ *use one's job as a cloak for spying activities.* ▷ *verb* (*cloaked*, *cloaking*) to cover up or conceal something. ⓘ 13c: French *cloke*, from Latin *clocca* bell or bell-shaped cape.

cloak-and-dagger ▷ *noun, as adj* said of stories, situations, etc: full of adventure, mystery, plots, spying, etc □ *It was a typical cloak-and-dagger yarn.*

cloakroom ▷ *noun* especially in a public building: **a** a room where coats, hats, etc may be left; **b** a room containing a WC; **c** a room offering both these facilities.

clobber[1] ▷ /'klɒbə(r)/ *verb* (*clobbered*, *clobbering*) *colloq* **1** to beat or hit someone very hard. **2** to defeat someone completely. **3** to criticize someone severely. ⓘ 20c.

clobber[2] ▷ *noun, slang* **1** clothing. **2** personal belongings, equipment, etc.

cloche /klɒʃ/ ▷ *noun* **1** a transparent glass or, now usually, plastic covering, bell-shaped or tunnel shaped, for protecting young plants from frost, etc. **2** a woman's close-fitting dome-shaped hat. ⓘ 19c: French, meaning 'bell' and 'bell jar', from Latin *clocca* bell.

clock[1] ▷ *noun* **1** a device for measuring and indicating time, usually by means of a digital display or pointers on a dial. **2** *computing* an electronic device that synchronizes processes within a computer system, by issuing signals at a constant rate. **3** a device that synchronizes the timing in switching circuits, transmission systems, etc. **4** (*the clock*) *colloq* **a** a MILEOMETER; **b** a SPEEDOMETER. **5** (in full **time clock**) a device for recording the arrival and departure times of employees. **6** the downy seedhead of a dandelion. **7** *slang* the face. ▷ *verb* (*clocked*, *clocking*) **1** to measure or record (time) using such a device. **2** to record with a stopwatch the time taken by (a racer, etc) to complete a distance, etc. **3** *colloq* to travel at (a speed as shown on a speedometer). **4** *slang* to hit someone. **5** *colloq* to achieve (an officially attested time) in a race □ *He clocked 9.89 seconds in the final.* **6** *colloq* to turn back the mileometer of (a car), to display a lower figure than the actual mileage. **7** *slang* to observe or notice someone. ● **against the clock** with a time deadline. ● **beat the clock** to finish before the set time limit or deadline. ● **put back the clock** or **turn back the clock** to seek to return to the conditions of an earlier period. ● **round the clock** throughout the day and night. ● **watch the clock** to pay close attention to the time of day, especially in order not to exceed minimum working hours. ⓘ 14c as *clokke*: from Dutch *clocke* bell or clock.

■ **clock in** or **on** to record one's time of arrival at a place of work.

■ **clock out** or **off** to record one's time of departure from a place of work.

■ **clock up something** to reach (a speed), cover (a distance), or achieve (a score), etc.

clock[2] ▷ *noun* a decoration on the side of a sock, etc. ⓘ 16c.

clock tower ▷ *noun* a four-walled tower with a clock face on each wall.

clock-watcher ▷ *noun* an employee who pays close attention to the time, in expectation of the end of the working day, especially so as not to exceed minimum working hours.

clockwise ▷ *adj, adverb* moving, etc in the same direction as that in which the hands of a clock move.

clockwork ▷ *noun* a mechanism like that of some clocks, working by means of gears and a spring that must be wound periodically. ▷ *adj* operated by clockwork □ *a clockwork mouse.* ● **like clockwork** smoothly and with regularity; without difficulties.

clod ▷ *noun* **1** a lump of earth, clay, etc. **2** *colloq* a stupid person. ⓘ 15c as *clodde*, from Anglo-Saxon *clod-*, found in compounds, a variant of CLOT.

cloddish ▷ *adj* **1** like a clod or clods. **2** stupid. ● **cloddishly** *adverb*. ● **cloddishness** *noun*.

clodhopper ▷ *noun, colloq* **1** a clumsy person. **2** a large heavy boot or shoe. ● **clodhopping** *adj*. ⓘ 19c.

clog ▷ *noun* **1** a shoe carved entirely from wood, or having a thick wooden sole. **2** *Scots* a heavy block of wood. ▷ *verb* (*clogged*, *clogging*) *tr & intr* to obstruct or become obstructed so that movement is difficult or impossible. ● **clogged** *adj* choked up; blocked. ● **pop one's clogs** *slang* to die. ⓘ 14c.

■ **clog up** to block or choke up.

clog-dance ▷ *noun* a dance performed by people wearing clogs, with the noise made by the clogs keeping time to the music.

cloisonné /'klwazɒneɪ/ ▷ *noun* a form of decoration with the pattern being formed in wire and filled in using coloured enamel. ▷ *adj* decorated in this way. ⓘ 19c: French, meaning 'compartmented'.

cloister /'klɔɪstə(r)/ ▷ *noun* **1** a covered walkway built around a garden or quadrangle, which has an open colonnade on one side and a solid outer wall on the other. **2 a** a place of religious retreat, eg a monastery or convent; **b** the quiet secluded life of such a place. ▷ *verb* (*cloistered*, *cloistering*) to keep someone away from the problems of normal life in the world. ● **cloistered** *adj* secluded. ● **cloistral** *adj* **1** relating to or like a cloister. **2** living in a cloister. ⓘ 13c: from French *cloistre*, from Latin *claustrum* a bolt or bar.

clone ▷ *noun* **1** *biol* any of a group of genetically identical cells or organisms derived from a single parent cell or organism by asexual reproduction. **2** *biol* any of a large number of identical copies of a gene produced by genetic engineering. **3** *computing* an imitation of an existing computer or software product, usually cheaper, and produced by a different manufacturer. **4** *colloq* a person or thing that looks like a replica of someone or something else. ▷ *verb* (*cloned*, *cloning*) **1** to produce a set of identical cells or organisms from (a single parent cell or organism). **2** to produce many identical copies of (a gene) by genetic engineering. **3** to produce replicas of, or to copy something □ *cloned ideas.* ● **clonal** *adj*. ⓘ 20c: from Greek *klon* twig.

clonk ▷ *noun* a noise of a heavy, especially metal, object striking something. ▷ *verb* (*clonked*, *clonking*) **1** *intr* to make or cause to make this noise. **2** to hit. ⓘ 20c: imitating the sound.

clop ▷ *noun* **a** the hollow sound of a horse's hooves on hard ground; **b** any sound similar to this. ▷ *verb* (*clopped*, *clopping*) *intr* said of a horse: to walk along making this noise. Also called **clip-clop**, **clop-clop**. ⓘ 20c: imitating the sound.

close[1] /kloʊs/ ▷ *adj* **1** near in space or time; at a short distance. **2 a** near in relationship □ *a close relation*; **b**

intimate. **3** touching or almost touching. **4** tight; dense or compact; with little space between □ *a close fit.* **5** near to the surface □ *a close haircut.* **6** thorough; searching □ *a close reading.* **7** said of a contest, etc: with little difference between entrants, etc. **8** (*often* **close to something**) about to happen, on the point of doing it, etc □ *close to tears.* **9** similar to the original, or to something else □ *a close resemblance.* **10** uncomfortably warm; stuffy. **11** secretive. **12** mean □ *close with money.* **13** heavily guarded □ *under close arrest.* **14** *old use* shut; closed; confined. **15** said of an organization, etc: restricted in membership. ▷ *adverb* **1** *often in compounds* in a close manner; closely □ *close-fitting* □ *follow close behind.* **2** at close range. ● **closely** *adverb* **a** in a close way; **b** with close attention □ *shall watch them closely.* ● **closeness** *noun.* ● **at close quarters 1** at close range; near to someone or something. **2** said of fighting: hand-to-hand, one individual fighting another. ● **close at** or **to hand** near by; easily available. ● **close on** or **to** nearly; almost □ *close on a thousand.* ● **close to one's chest** without revealing one's intentions; secretive. ● **close to home** uncomfortably close to the truth, or to a sensitive matter. ⓒ 14c: from French *clos* closed, from Latin *claudere, clausum* to close.

close² /klouz/ ▷ *verb* (**closed, closing**) **1** *tr & intr* to shut. **2** (*sometimes* **close something off**) to block (a road, etc) so as to prevent use. **3** *tr & intr* said of shops, etc: to stop or cause to stop being open to the public for a period of time. **4** *tr & intr* said of a factory, business, etc: to stop or cause to stop operating permanently. **5** *tr & intr* to conclude; to come or bring to an end; to stop (discussion, etc of something) □ *He closed with a joke.* **6** *tr & intr* to join up or come together; to cause edges, etc, of something to come together. **7** to settle or agree on something □ *close a deal.* **8** *intr, econ* said of currency, shares, etc: to be worth (a certain amount) at the end of a period of trading □ *The pound closed three cents up on the dollar.* ▷ *noun* an end or conclusion. ● **close one's eyes to something** to pretend not to notice it. ● **close ranks 1** said of soldiers drawn up in line: to stand closer together so as to present a solid front to the enemy. **2** to unite in the face of a common threat or danger. ⓒ 13c: from French *clos,* from Latin *claudere* to close.

■ **close down 1** said of a business: to close permanently. **2** said of a television or radio station, etc: to stop broadcasting at the end of the day.

■ **close something down** to close it permanently.

■ **close in** said of days: to become shorter, while nights get longer.

■ **close in on someone** to approach and surround them.

■ **close on someone** to catch them up.

■ **close up** to move closer together.

■ **close something up** to bring it closer together □ *close up the gaps.*

■ **close with someone 1** to strike a bargain with them; to agree to (an offer, etc). **2** *old use* to begin fighting them.

close³ /klous/ ▷ *noun* **1** in Scotland, especially Glasgow: a narrow indoor passage leading from the street to the stair of a tenement building. **2** (**Close**) used as the name of a residential street, often a cul-de-sac □ *Brookside Close.* **3** the land and buildings surrounding and belonging to a cathedral. ⓒ 13c as *clos:* from Latin *clausum* enclosure.

close call see CLOSE SHAVE

close company ▷ *noun* a firm controlled by five or fewer people.

close corporation ▷ *noun* a firm which fills its own vacancies without outside interference.

closed ▷ *adj* **1** shut; blocked. **2** said of a community or society: exclusive, with membership restricted to a chosen few. ● **behind closed doors** said of court cases, football matches, etc: held privately, with the public being excluded.

closed book ▷ *noun* a person or subject that one cannot understand; a mystery.

closed circuit ▷ *noun* **1** a complete electrical circuit through which current flows when a voltage is applied. **2** a closed-circuit television system.

closed-circuit television ▷ *noun* a TV system serving a limited number of receivers, eg within a building, the signal being transmitted by cables or telephone links.

closed-end ▷ *adj, finance* said of an investment trust: offering shares up to a limited number.

closed-loop ▷ *adj* denoting a computer system in which performance is controlled by comparing an amount of output with an expected standard in order to identify and reduce deviations.

close-down ▷ *noun* **1** the permanent closing of a business. **2** *Brit TV* the closing of broadcasting on a particular channel at the end of the day.

closed set ▷ *noun, math* a set which includes the limits that define that set. Compare OPEN SET.

closed shop ▷ *noun* an establishment, eg a factory, which requires its employees to be members of a trade union. Compare OPEN SHOP.

closed syllable ▷ *noun, phonetics* a syllable ending in a consonant. Compare OPEN SYLLABLE.

close encounter ▷ *noun* **1** a direct confrontation with an extraterrestrial being. **2** any personal confrontation.

close-fisted and **close-handed** ▷ *adj, colloq* mean; miserly.

close harmony ▷ *noun, music* harmony in which the notes of chords lie close together.

close-hauled ▷ *adj, naut* with sails set for sailing as near to the wind as possible.

close-knit ▷ *adj* said of a group, community, etc: closely bound together.

close-lipped and **close-mouthed** ▷ *adj* reticent; saying little.

closely and **closeness** see CLOSE¹

close-range ▷ *adj* **1** in, at or within a short distance. **2** said eg of a gun: fired from very close by.

close-run ▷ *adj* said of a competition, election, etc: fiercely contested; having close results.

close season ▷ *noun* the time of year when it is illegal to kill certain birds, animals or fish for sport.

close shave and **close call** ▷ *noun* a narrow or lucky escape.

closet /ˈklɒzɪt/ ▷ *noun* **1** *chiefly N Amer* a cupboard. **2** *old use* a small private room. **3** *old use* a WATER CLOSET. **4** *as adj* secret; not openly declared □ *She was a closet gambler.* ▷ *verb* (**closeted, closeting**) to shut up or away in private, eg for confidential discussion. ● **be in the closet** *colloq* to keep something secret, especially one's homosexuality. ● **come out of the closet** *colloq* to admit something openly, especially one's homosexuality. ⓒ 14c: French diminutive of *clos* (see CLOSE¹).

close thing ▷ *noun* **1** a lucky escape. **2** something only just managed or achieved.

closet queen ▷ *noun, slang* a secret homosexual.

close-up ▷ *noun* **1** a photograph, television shot, etc taken at close range. **2** a detailed look or examination.

closing date ▷ *noun* the last possible date on which something can be done, sent in, etc.

closing-time ▷ *noun* the time when pubs must stop serving drinks and close.

clostridium /klɒ'strɪdɪəm/ ▷ *noun* (***clostridia*** /-dɪə/) *biol* a rod-shaped bacterium that occurs in soil and in the digestive tract of humans and animals, and which can cause botulism and tetanus. ◷ 19c: from Greek *kloster* spindle.

closure /'kloʊʒə(r)/ ▷ *noun* **1** the act of closing something, eg a business or a transport route. **2** a device for closing or sealing something. **3** a parliamentary procedure for cutting short a debate and taking an immediate vote. ▷ *verb* (***closured, closuring***) to use this procedure for ending a debate, etc. ◷ 16c: French, from Latin *clausura*, from *claudere, clausum* to close.

clot ▷ *noun* **1** a soft semi-solid mass, especially one formed during the coagulation of blood. **2** *Brit colloq* a fool. ▷ *verb* (***clotted, clotting***) *tr & intr* to form into clots. ◷ Anglo-Saxon *clott* lump or mass.

cloth /klɒθ/ ▷ *noun* **1** woven, knitted or felted material. **2** *often in compounds* a piece of fabric for a special use □ *tablecloth*. **3** (**the cloth**) the clergy. ◷ Anglo-Saxon *clath*.

cloth cap ▷ *noun* a flat cap, especially one made of tweed, with a stiff brim.

clothe /kloʊð/ ▷ *verb* (*past tense, past participle* ***clothed*** or ***clad***, *present participle* ***clothing***) **1** to cover or provide someone with clothes. **2** to dress someone. **3** to cover, conceal or disguise someone or something □ *hills clothed in mist*. See also CLAD. ◷ Anglo-Saxon *clathian*.

cloth-ears ▷ *noun, colloq* someone who does not hear what is being said to them, usually because of inattention. ● **cloth-eared** *adj*.

clothes /kloʊðz, kloʊz/ ▷ *plural noun* **1** articles of dress for covering the body, for warmth, decoration, etc. **2** BEDCLOTHES. ◷ Anglo-Saxon *clathas*, plural of *clath* cloth.

clothes horse ▷ *noun* **1** a hinged frame on which to dry or air clothes indoors. **2** *colloq, derisive* an extremely fashionable person who seems to be constantly wearing new clothes.

clothesline ▷ *noun* a rope, usually suspended outdoors, on which washed clothes, etc are hung to dry.

clothes moth ▷ *noun* any of the small drab moths whose larvae feed on dried organic matter, including woollen materials and fur.

clothes peg ▷ *noun* a small clip made from wood or plastic used for securing clothes to a clothesline.

clothes pole ▷ *noun* a fixed vertical pole to which a clothesline is tied.

clothes press ▷ *noun* a cupboard, usually with drawers, for keeping clothes in.

clothes prop ▷ *noun* a long pole usually made from wood, which is used to lift a clothesline to a higher position, in order to allow it to catch the full strength of the wind.

clothing /'kloʊðɪŋ/ ▷ *noun* **1** clothes collectively. **2** something forming a covering □ *a clothing of snow*. ◷ 13c: from CLOTHE.

cloth of gold ▷ *noun* a silk or woollen fabric interwoven with gold thread.

clotted cream ▷ *noun* thick cream made by slowly heating milk and taking the cream from the top. Also called **Devonshire cream**.

clotting factor ▷ *noun* any of a group of proteins in the blood essential in the process of blood clotting.

cloud /klaʊd/ ▷ *noun* **1** *meteorol* a visible floating mass of small water droplets or ice crystals suspended in the atmosphere above the Earth's surface. **2** a visible mass of particles of dust or smoke in the atmosphere. **3** a dark or dull spot. **4** a circumstance that causes anxiety. **5** a state of gloom, depression or suspicion. ▷ *verb* (***clouded, clouding***) **1** *tr & intr* (*usually* **cloud over** or **cloud something over**) to make or become misty or cloudy. **2** *intr* (*often* **cloud over**) said of the face: to develop a troubled expression □ *His face clouded at the terrible news*. **3** to make dull or confused. **4** to spoil or mar. ● **cloudless** *adj* said especially of the sky: having no clouds; clear and bright. ● **cloudlessly** *adverb*. ● **on cloud nine** *colloq* extremely happy. ● **under a cloud** in trouble or disgrace □ *He left the firm under a cloud*. ● **up in the clouds** *colloq* out of touch with reality. ● **with one's head in the clouds** *colloq* preoccupied with one's own thoughts. ◷ Anglo-Saxon *clud* hill or mass of rock.

■ **cloud over** to become overcast with clouds.

cloud base ▷ *noun, meteorol* the height above sea level of the lowest part of a cloud.

cloudburst ▷ *noun* a sudden heavy downpour of rain over a small area.

cloud chamber ▷ *noun, physics* a device for detecting SUBATOMIC PARTICLES moving through a gas. See also BUBBLE CHAMBER.

cloud-cuckoo-land ▷ *noun* the imaginary dwelling-place of over-optimistic people who refuse to see the problems of the real world.

cloudless see under CLOUD

cloudy ▷ *adj* (***cloudier, cloudiest***) **1** full of clouds; overcast. **2** said eg of a liquid: not clear; muddy. **3** confused; muddled. ● **cloudily** *adverb*. ● **cloudiness** *noun*.

clout /klaʊt/ ▷ *noun* **1** *colloq* a blow or cuff. **2** *colloq* influence or power. **3** *dialect* a piece of clothing. ▷ *verb* (***clouted, clouting***) *colloq* to hit or cuff. ◷ Anglo-Saxon *clut* piece of cloth.

clove^{1} /kloʊv/ ▷ *noun* **1** an evergreen tree belonging to the myrtle family, native to Indonesia, widely cultivated elsewhere. **2** (*usually* **cloves**) the strong-smelling dried flower-bud of this tree, used as a spice. ◷ 14c: from French *clou* nail, from the shape of the bud.

clove^{2} ▷ *noun* one of the sections into which a compound bulb, especially of garlic, naturally splits. ◷ Anglo-Saxon *clufu* bulb.

clove^{3} *past tense of* CLEAVE^{1}

clove gillyflower see GILLYFLOWER

cloven ▷ *adj, old use, poetic* split; divided. ▷ *verb* see under CLEAVE^{1}. ◷ 13c.

cloven hoof and **cloven foot** ▷ *noun* **a** the partially divided hoof of various mammals, including cattle, deer, sheep, goats and pigs; **b** in folklore, etc: the partly divided foot of the Devil. ● **cloven-hooved** and **cloven-footed** *adj*.

clover /'kloʊvə(r)/ ▷ *noun* a small herbaceous plant that grows wild in temperate regions and which has leaves divided into three leaflets and small dense red or white flowers. ● **in clover** *colloq* in great comfort and luxury. ◷ Anglo-Saxon *clæfre*.

cloverleaf ▷ *noun* a traffic arrangement in which one road passes over the top of another, and the roads connecting the two are in the shape of a four-leaved clover.

clown /klaʊn/ ▷ *noun* **1** in a circus or pantomime, etc: a comic performer, usually wearing ridiculous clothes and make-up. **2** someone who behaves comically. **3** *derog* a fool. ▷ *verb* (***clowned, clowning***) *intr* to play the clown. ● **clownery** *noun*. ● **clownish** *adj*. ● **clownishly** *adverb*. ● **clownishness** *noun*. ◷ 16c.

■ **clown about** or **around** to behave ridiculously.

cloy /klɔɪ/ ▷ *verb* (***cloyed, cloying***) **1** *intr* to become distasteful through excess, especially of sweetness. **2** to satiate to the point of disgust. ● **cloying** *adj*. ◷ 16c in this sense: variant of earlier *acloy*, originally meaning 'to nail', from Latin *clavus* nail.

cloze testing /kloʊz —/ ▷ *noun* a procedure used to establish a student's level of comprehension of a text, by removing words from it and having the student supply the missing words or give appropriate substitutes for them. ⓘ 20c: formed from CLOSURE.

club ▷ *noun* **1** a stick, usually thicker at one end, used as a weapon. **2** in various sports, especially golf: a stick with a specially shaped head, used to hit the ball. **3** an INDIAN CLUB. **4** a society or association. **5** the place where such a group meets. **6** a building with dining, reading and sleeping facilities for its members. **7** a NIGHTCLUB. **8** (**clubs**) one of the four suits of playing-cards, with black cloverleaf-shaped symbols. **9** one of the playing-cards of this suit. ▷ *verb* (***clubbed, clubbing***) to beat or strike (a person, animal, etc) with a club. • **clubber** *noun*. • **clubbing** *noun*. • **go clubbing** to go to and spend an evening at a nightclub □ *They go clubbing every weekend*. • **in the club** or **pudding club** *colloq* pregnant. • **join the club!** me too! ⓘ 13c: from Norse *klubba* cudgel.

■ **club together 1** to contribute money jointly for a special purpose. **2** to join together for a common end or purpose.

clubbable ▷ *adj* friendly; able to mix well socially.

clubbing ▷ *noun, pathol* a thickening of the tips of the fingers and toes. • **clubbed** *adj* said of the fingers and toes: thickened at the tips.

club class ▷ *noun* in an aeroplane: the standard of accommodation between first class and economy class. ▷ *adj* relating to this standard of travel. Also called **business class**.

club foot ▷ *noun, non-technical* a congenital deformity in which the foot is twisted down and turned inwards. Also (*technical*) called **talipes**.

clubhouse ▷ *noun* a building where a club meets, especially the premises of a sports club.

clubman and **clubwoman** ▷ *noun* someone who is a member of a lot of clubs.

clubmoss ▷ *noun, bot* a spore-bearing vascular plant related to ferns and horsetails, found mainly in moist tropical or subtropical regions.

clubroot ▷ *noun, bot* a fungal disease of plants of the cabbage family, characterized by gall-like swellings of the roots and discoloration of the leaves.

club sandwich ▷ *noun* a sandwich made up of three slices of bread containing two fillings.

club soda ▷ *noun, chiefly US* soda water.

cluck ▷ *noun* **1** the sound made by a hen. **2** any similar sound. ▷ *verb* (***clucked, clucking***) *intr* **1** said of a hen: to make such a sound. **2** to express disapproval by making a similar sound with the tongue. ⓘ 17c: imitating the sound.

clue /kluː/ ▷ *noun* **1** a fact or circumstance which helps towards the solution of a crime or a mystery. **2** in a crossword puzzle: a word or words representing, in a more or less disguised form, a problem to be solved. ▷ *verb* (***clued, cluing***) to direct or indicate by giving a clue. • **not have a clue** *colloq* to be completely ignorant about something. ⓘ 17c: variant of CLEW, from its use in finding the way out of a maze.

■ **clue someone in** or **up** *colloq* to inform them.

clued-up ▷ *adj, colloq* shrewd; knowledgeable.

clueless ▷ *adj, derog* stupid, incompetent or ignorant.

clump ▷ *noun* **1** a group or cluster of something, eg trees, plants or people standing close together. **2** a dull heavy sound, eg of treading feet. **3** a shapeless mass □ *a clump of weeds*. ▷ *verb* (***clumped, clumping***) **1** *intr* to walk with a heavy tread. **2** *tr & intr* to form into clumps. ⓘ 16c: related to Dutch *klompe* lump or mass.

clumpy ▷ *adj* (***clumpier, clumpiest***) **1** large and heavy □ *clumpy shoes*. **2** like a clump. • **clumpiness** *noun*.

clumsy /ˈklʌmzɪ/ ▷ *adj* (***clumsier, clumsiest***) **1** unskilful with the hands or awkward and ungainly in movement. **2** badly or awkwardly made. • **clumsily** *adverb*. • **clumsiness** *noun*. ⓘ 16c as *clumse*, meaning 'numb with cold': perhaps originally from Norse.

clung *past tense, past participle of* CLING

clunk ▷ *noun* the sound of a heavy object, especially a metal one, striking something. ▷ *verb* (***clunked, clunking***) *tr & intr* to make or cause to make such a sound. ⓘ 19c: imitating the sound.

clunky ▷ *adj* (***clunkier, clunkiest***) **1** making a clunking noise. **2** *colloq* **a** awkward, clumsy; **b** said of a piece of text: badly written. ⓘ 1960s.

cluster /ˈklʌstə(r)/ ▷ *noun* **1** a small group or gathering. **2** a number of flowers growing together on one stem. ▷ *verb* (***clustered, clustering***) *tr & intr* to form into a cluster or clusters. • **clustered** *adj*. • **clustery** *adj*. ⓘ Anglo-Saxon *clyster* bunch.

cluster bomb ▷ *noun* a bomb which opens on impact to throw out a number of smaller bombs.

clutch¹ ▷ *verb* (***clutches, clutched, clutching***) **1** to grasp something tightly. **2** *intr* (*usually* **clutch at something**) to try to grasp it. **3** *US* in a motor vehicle: to press the clutch pedal. ▷ *noun* (***clutches***) **1** (*usually* **clutches**) control or power. **2** any device for connecting and disconnecting two rotating shafts, especially the device in a motor vehicle that transmits or prevents the transmission of the driving force from engine to gearbox. **3** in a motor vehicle: the pedal operating this device. **4** a grasp. • **clutch** or **grasp at straws** to try anything, however unlikely, in one's desperation. ⓘ Anglo-Saxon *clyccan*.

clutch² ▷ *noun* (***clutches***) **1** a number of eggs laid in a single nest or at the same time. **2** a brood of newly hatched birds, especially chickens. **3** *colloq* a group or number. ▷ *verb* (***clutches, clutched, clutching***) to hatch. ⓘ 18c: from Norse *klekja* to hatch.

clutch bag ▷ *noun* a small handbag without handles, held in the hand or under the arm.

clutter /ˈklʌtə(r)/ ▷ *noun* an untidy accumulation of objects, or the confused overcrowded state caused by it. ▷ *verb* (***cluttered, cluttering***) (*often* **clutter something up**) to overcrowd it or make it untidy with accumulated objects. • **cluttered** *adj*. ⓘ 16c variant of earlier *clotter* from CLOT.

CM ▷ *abbreviation*: *Chirurgiae Magister* (Latin), Master of Surgery.

Cm ▷ *symbol, chem* curium.

cm ▷ *abbreviation* centimetre.

CMG ▷ *abbreviation, Brit* Companion of the Order of St Michael and St George.

CNAA ▷ *abbreviation* Council for National Academic Awards.

CND ▷ *abbreviation, Brit* Campaign for Nuclear Disarmament.

CNN ▷ *abbreviation, US* Cable News Network.

CNR ▷ *abbreviation* Canadian National Railway.

CO ▷ *abbreviation* **1** *IVR* Colombia. **2** *US state* Colorado. **3** Commanding Officer.

Co *symbol, chem* cobalt.

co- /koʊ/ ▷ *prefix, indicating* with; together; jointly □ *co-starring* □ *co-operate*. ⓘ Shortened from CON-.

c/o ▷ *abbreviation* care of.

coach ▷ *noun* (***coaches***) **1** a railway carriage. **2** a bus designed for long-distance travel. **3** *historical* a closed horse-drawn carriage. **4** a trainer or instructor, especially in sport. **5** a private tutor, especially one who prepares pupils for examinations. ▷ *verb* (***coaches, coached, coaching***) **1** *tr & intr* **a** to train in a sport, etc; **b** to teach privately. **2** *intr* to go or travel by coach. ● **coaching** *noun* **1** instruction or tuition. **2** *historical* travel by coach. ● **drive a coach and horses through something** *colloq* to point out obvious flaws in an argument, laws, etc and thereby refute it. ⓘ 16c: French *coche*, from Hungarian *kocsi*, named after Kocs in Hungary.

coachbuilder ▷ *noun* a person or organization whose business is to build the bodies of motor vehicles.

coachman ▷ *noun, historical* the driver of a horse-drawn coach.

coach party ▷ *noun* a group of people travelling by coach.

coach tour ▷ *noun* a holiday or outing on which people travel from place to place by coach.

coachwork ▷ *noun* the painted outer bodywork of a motor or rail vehicle.

coagulant ▷ *noun* a substance which causes or facilitates coagulation.

coagulate /koʊ'agjʊleɪt/ ▷ *verb* (***coagulated***, ***coagulating***) *tr & intr* **1** to cause (a liquid) to clot, curdle, or form a soft semi-solid mass. **2** said of a liquid: to become clotted or curdled, or to form a soft semi-solid mass. ▷ *noun* the soft semi-solid mass produced by this process. ● **coagulation** *noun* **1** the action or process of coagulating. **2** the forming or uniting into a mass. ● **coagulant** *noun* a substance capable of causing coagulation. ● **coagulator** *noun* something which coagulates. ● **coagulum** *noun* (***coagula*** /-ə/) a mass of coagulated matter. ⓘ 17c: from Latin *coagulare*, *coagulatum*.

coal /koʊl/ ▷ *noun* **1** a hard brittle CARBONACEOUS rock, usually black or brown in colour, formed by the compaction of partially decomposed plant material and used as a fuel. **2** a piece of this. ▷ *verb* (***coaled***, ***coaling***) *tr & intr* to take in or provide with coal. ● **coals to Newcastle** something brought to a place where it is already plentiful. ● **haul someone over the coals** *colloq* to scold them severely. ● **heap coals of fire on someone's head** to make them feel guilty by repaying evil with good. ⓘ Anglo-Saxon *col*.

coal bunker see BUNKER

coalesce /koʊə'lɛs/ ▷ *verb* (***coalesced***, ***coalescing***) *intr* to come together so as to form a single mass. ● **coalescence** *noun*. ● **coalescent** *adj*. ⓘ 17c: from Latin *co-* together + *alescere* to grow.

coalface ▷ *noun* **1** in a coal mine: the exposed surface from which coal is being cut. **2** the area where the essential practical work is carried on in any particular field of activity.

coalfield ▷ *noun* an area where there is coal underground.

coalfish see COLEY

coal-fired ▷ *adj* fuelled by coal.

coal gas ▷ *noun* a flammable gas, consisting mainly of hydrogen and methane, which is obtained by the DESTRUCTIVE DISTILLATION of coal and was formerly used as a fuel.

coalition /koʊə'lɪʃən/ ▷ *noun, politics* a combination or temporary alliance, especially between political parties. ● **coalitional** *adj*. ● **coalitionist** *noun*. ⓘ 18c: Latin *coalitio*, from *coalescere* to coalesce.

coalition government ▷ *noun, politics* government by, or a government made up of, representatives of two or more political parties forming a temporary alliance.

coal mine ▷ *noun* an underground deposit of coal prepared for excavation.

coal scuttle ▷ *noun* a fireside container for coal, usually in a domestic household.

coal tar ▷ *noun* a thick black liquid obtained as a by-product during the manufacture of coke and which was formerly a major source of organic compounds for the manufacture of drugs, dyes, etc.

coal tit ▷ *noun* a small bird belonging to the tit family, native to Europe, Asia and Africa, with a large head with a glossy black crown and white cheeks, and a characteristic white patch on the nape of its neck.

coaming /'koʊmɪŋ/ ▷ *noun, naut* the raised edging round the hatches on a ship, to keep out water.

coarse ▷ *adj* **1** rough or open in texture. **2** rough or crude; not refined. **3** said of behaviour, speech, etc: rude or offensive. ● **coarsely** *adverb*. ● **coarseness** *noun*. ⓘ 15c.

coarse fish ▷ *noun* a freshwater fish, other than trout and salmon. ● **coarse fishing** *noun* the sport of catching this type of fish.

coarsen ▷ *verb* (***coarsened***, ***coarsening***) *tr & intr* to make or become coarse.

coast ▷ *noun* **1** the zone of land that borders the sea. **2** the seaside. ▷ *verb* (***coasted***, ***coasting***) *intr* **1** to travel downhill, eg on a bicycle or in a motor vehicle, relying on gravity or momentum rather than power. **2** to progress smoothly and satisfactorily without much effort. ● **coastal** *adj*. ● **the coast is clear** *colloq* there is no danger of being spotted or caught. ⓘ 14c: from French *coste*, from Latin *costa* rib or side.

coaster ▷ *noun* **1** a vessel that sails along the coast taking goods to coastal ports. **2** a small mat or tray placed under a glass, bottle, decanter, etc to protect the table surface.

coastguard ▷ *noun* **1** an official organization stationed on the coast which rescues people at sea, prevents smuggling, etc. **2** a member of this organization.

coastline ▷ *noun* the shape of the coast, especially as seen on a map, or from the sea or air.

coat ▷ *noun* **1** an outer garment with long sleeves, typically reaching to the knees. **2** any similar garment, eg a jacket. **3** the hair, fur or wool of an animal. **4** a covering or application of something eg paint, dust, sugar, etc. ▷ *verb* (***coated***, ***coating***) to cover with a layer of something. ● **coating** *noun* **1** a covering or outer layer. **2** material for making a coat. ⓘ 13c: from French *cote*.

coat-hanger ▷ *noun* a shaped piece of wood, plastic or metal with a hook, on which to hang clothes.

coati /koʊ'ɑːtiː/ ▷ *noun* (***coatis***) a raccoon-like mammal, which has reddish-brown fur, a long narrow muzzle with an overhanging tip, and a long banded tail, and which lives in N and S America. ⓘ 17c: from Tupí *cuatim* literally 'belt nose'.

coating see under COAT

coat of arms ▷ *noun* (***coats of arms***) a heraldic design consisting of a shield bearing the special insignia of a particular person, family, organization or town.

coat of mail ▷ *noun* (***coats of mail***) *historical* a piece of protective armour made from interlinked metal rings.

coat-tails ▷ *plural noun* the two long pieces of material which hang down at the back of a man's tailcoat. ● **on someone's coat-tails** enjoying undeserved success as a result of someone else's achievement.

coauthor ▷ *noun* a joint author. ▷ *verb* to write a book, etc with one or more others.

coax /koʊks/ ▷ *verb* (***coaxes***, ***coaxed***, ***coaxing***) **1** (*often* **coax someone into** or **out of something**) to persuade them, using flattery, promises, kind words, etc. **2** to get something by coaxing. **3** to manipulate something patiently □ *I coaxed the key into the lock.* ● **coaxer** *noun*. ● **coaxingly** *adverb*. ⓘ 16c: from earlier *cokes* fool.

coaxial /koʊ'aksɪəl/ ▷ *adj* **1** having or mounted on a common axis. **2** *elec* said of a cable: consisting of a conductor in the form of a metal tube surrounding and insulated from a second conductor. ◷ 20c: from CO- + AXIS.

cob[1] ▷ *noun* **1** a short-legged sturdy horse used for riding. **2** a male swan. See also CYGNET, PEN[4]. **3** a hazelnut or hazel tree. **4** a CORNCOB. **5** *Brit* a loaf with a rounded top. ◷ 16c.

cob[2] ▷ *noun, Brit* a mixture of clay and straw, used as a building material. ◷ 17c.

cobalt /'koubɔːlt, 'koubɒlt/ ▷ *noun* **1** *chem* (symbol **Co**, atomic number 27) a hard silvery-white metallic element commonly used in ALLOYS to produce cutting tools and magnets. **2** a mixture of cobalt OXIDE and ALUMINA used as a bright blue pigment in paints, ceramics, etc. Also called **cobalt blue**. **3** the colour of this compound. ● **cobaltic** *adj.* ◷ 17c: from German *Kobold* goblin of the mines, the name given to the material by frustrated miners looking for silver.

cobalt-60 ▷ *noun, chem* a radioactive ISOTOPE of cobalt used in the treatment of cancer.

cobalt bomb ▷ *noun, chem* a theoretical hydrogen bomb encased in cobalt which, upon detonation, would release cobalt-60 dust into the atmosphere.

cobber /'kɒbə(r)/ ▷ *noun, Austral & NZ colloq* used as a form of address: a pal or mate. ◷ 19c.

cobble[1] ▷ *noun* a rounded stone used especially formerly to surface streets. Also called **cobblestone**. ▷ *verb* (***cobbled, cobbling***) to pave with cobblestones. ● **cobbled** *adj.* ◷ 16c.

cobble[2] ▷ *verb* (***cobbled, cobbling***) **1** to mend (shoes). **2** (*often* **cobble something together** or **up**) to assemble or put it together roughly or hastily. ◷ 15c: back-formation from COBBLER.

cobbler ▷ *noun* someone who makes or mends shoes. ◷ 13c.

cobblers ▷ *plural noun, Brit slang* **1** nonsense. **2** testicles. ◷ 20c: rhyming slang from *cobblers' awls*, ie *balls*.

cobblestone see under COBBLE[1]

cobelligerent ▷ *noun* a nation fighting a war on the side of another nation, although not necessarily an ally of it. ▷ *adj* co-operating in warfare alongside another country.

COBOL /'koubɒl/ ▷ *abbreviation* Common Business-Oriented Language, an English-based computer programming language used in commerce.

cobra /'koubrə, 'kɒ-/ ▷ *noun* (***cobras***) any of various species of venomous snake found in Africa and Asia which, when threatened, rear up and spread the skin behind the head to form a flattened hood. ◷ 19c: shortened from Portuguese *cobra de capello* snake with hood, from Latin *colubra* snake + *cappellus* hood.

cobweb ▷ *noun* **1** a web of fine sticky threads spun by a spider. **2** a single thread from this. **3** anything flimsy or easily broken. **4** (*usually* **cobwebs**) obscurity or mustiness. ● **cobwebby** *adj.* ◷ 14c as *coppeweb*: from Anglo-Saxon *atorcoppe* spider + WEB.

coca /'koukə/ ▷ *noun* **1** either of two S American shrubs whose leaves contain cocaine. **2** the leaves of the shrub chewed as a stimulant. ◷ 17c: Spanish, from Quechua *kuka*.

Coca-Cola /koukə'koulə/ ▷ *noun, trademark* a carbonated soft drink. Often shortened to **Coke**.

cocaine /kou'keɪn/ ▷ *noun, medicine* an addictive narcotic drug, obtained from the leaves of the coca plant, which is sometimes used medicinally as a local anaesthetic but more commonly used as an illegal stimulant. See also COKE[2].

coccus /'kɒkəs/ ▷ *noun* (***cocci*** /'kɒksaɪ/) *biol* a spherical bacterium. ◷ 19c: Latin, from Greek *kokkos* berry.

coccyx /'kɒksɪks/ ▷ *noun* (***coccyges*** /kɒk'saɪdʒiːz/) *anatomy* in humans and certain apes: a small triangular tail-like bone at the base of the spine. ◷ 17c: Latin, from Greek *kokkyx* cuckoo, from its triangular beak.

cochineal /'kɒtʃiniːl, kɒtʃɪ'niːl/ ▷ *noun* **1** a bright red pigment widely used as a food colouring, eg in alcoholic drinks. **2** an insect found in Mexico and the West Indies, the dried body of which yields this dye. ◷ 16c: from Spanish *cochinilla*, from Latin *coccineus* scarlet.

cochlea /'kɒklɪə/ ▷ *noun* (***cochleae*** /-iː/) *anatomy* in the inner ear of vertebrates: a hollow spirally coiled structure which converts the vibrations of sound waves into nerve impulses, which are then interpreted by the brain as sound. ● **cochlear** *adj.* ◷ 17c: Latin, meaning 'snail or snail shell' from Greek *kochlias* snail with a spiral shell.

cock[1] ▷ *noun* **1** a male bird, especially an adult male chicken. **2** a STOPCOCK. **3** the hammer of a gun which, when raised and let go by the trigger, produces the discharge. **4** *coarse slang* the penis. **5** *coarse slang* nonsense. **6** *slang* a pal, usually used as a form of address. ▷ *verb* (***cocked, cocking***) **1** *tr & intr* to lift; to stick up. **2** to turn in a particular direction □ ***cock an ear towards the door.*** **3** to draw back the hammer of a gun. **4** to set (one's hat) at an angle. ● **go off at half cock** to begin too soon, without being fully prepared. ◷ Anglo-Saxon *cocc*.

■ **cock something up** to make a mess of it; to do it badly □ ***He really cocked up his exams.*** See also COCK-UP.

cock[2] ▷ *noun* a small heap of hay, etc. ▷ *verb* to pile into such heaps. ◷ 15c: perhaps related to Norse *kökkr* lump.

cockade /kɒ'keɪd/ ▷ *noun, historical* a feather or a rosette of ribbon worn on the hat as a badge. ◷ 18c: a corruption of *cockard*, from French *coquarde*, from *coq*; see COCK[1].

cock-a-doodle-doo ▷ *noun* an imitation of the sound of a cock crowing.

cock-a-hoop ▷ *adj, colloq* **1** jubilant; exultant. **2** boastful.

cock-a-leekie ▷ *noun, Scottish* soup made from chicken and leeks. ◷ 18c: COCK[1] + LEEK.

cockamamie ▷ *noun, slang, chiefly US* ridiculous or incredible □ ***What a cockamamie thing to do!***

cock-and-bull story ▷ *noun, colloq* an unlikely story, especially one used as an excuse or explanation.

cockatiel or **cockateel** /kɒkə'tiːl/ ▷ *noun* a small crested Australian parrot of the cockatoo family.

cockatoo /kɒkə'tuː/ ▷ *noun* (***cockatoos***) any of 16 species of the parrot family usually found in woodland areas in Australasia, which are generally light-coloured with a brightly coloured erectile crest on their heads. ◷ 17c: from Malay *kakatua*.

cockatrice /'kɒkətrɪs, -traɪs/ ▷ *noun* **1** *mythol* a monster with the head, wings and legs of a cock and the body and tail of a serpent. See also BASILISK 1. **2** *Authorized Version* a poisonous snake. ◷ 14c: from French *cocatris*, from Latin *calcatrix* tracker, used for the Greek ICHNEUMON.

cockchafer ▷ *noun* a large grey-brown beetle. Also called **May beetle** and **May bug**. ◷ 18c: COCK[1] + CHAFER.

cock-crow ▷ *noun* dawn; early morning.

cocked hat ▷ *noun, historical* a three-cornered hat with upturned brim. ● **knock someone** or **something into a cocked hat** *colloq* to surpass them or it spectacularly or defeat them or it utterly.

cocker and **cocker spaniel** ▷ *noun, Brit* a small long-haired breed of spaniel with silky ears. ◷ 19c: from WOODCOCK, which the dogs were bred to hunt.

cockerel ▷ *noun* a young cock. ◷ 15c: diminutive of COCK[1].

cock-eyed ▷ *adj, colloq* **1** suffering from a squint. **2** crooked; lopsided. **3** senseless; crazy; impractical □ *cock-*

eyed schemes to make money. **4** drunk. ◷ 19c: from COCK[1].

cockfight ▻ *noun* a fight between cocks wearing sharp metal spurs. ● **cockfighting** *noun*.

cockily and **cockiness** see under COCKY

cocking piece see SPROCKET

cockle[1] /'kɒkəl/ ▻ *noun* any of about 200 species of edible BIVALVE shellfish with a rounded and ribbed shell. ● **warm the cockles of the heart** *colloq* to delight and gladden someone. ◷ 14c: French *coquille* shell.

cockle[2] /'kɒkəl/ ▻ *noun* a cornfield weed, especially the CORNCOCKLE.

cockleshell ▻ *noun* **1** the shell of the cockle. **2** any tiny insubstantial boat.

cockney /'kɒknɪ/ ▻ *noun* (***cockneys***) **1** (*often* **Cockney**) **a** *loosely* a native of London, especially of the East End; **b** *strictly* someone born within the sound of Bow Bell. **2** the dialect used by Cockneys. ▻ *adj* relating to Cockneys or their dialect. ◷ 17c in sense 1: from earlier *cokeney* a cock's egg ie a misshapen egg, later used as a contemptuous name for a town-dweller.

cock of the walk ▻ *noun* someone who is, or thinks themself, the most important one in a group.

cockpit ▻ *noun* **1** in an aircraft: the compartment for the pilot and crew. **2** in a racing-car: the driver's seat. **3** *naut* the part of a small yacht, etc which contains the wheel and tiller. **4** *historical* a pit into which cocks were put to fight each other. **5** any scene of prolonged conflict, especially in war. ◷ 16c.

cockroach ▻ *noun* (***cockroaches***) a large insect with a flattened body, long slender antennae and biting mouthparts, which feeds mainly nocturnally on decaying animal and vegetable matter. ◷ 17c: from Spanish *cucaracha*.

cockscomb and **coxcomb** /'kɒkskoʊm/ ▻ *noun* **1** the fleshy red crest on a cock's head. **2** a flower whose petals resemble this crest. **3** (**coxcomb**) *old use, derog* a foolishly vain or conceited fellow. ◷ 15c: sense 3 from the traditional JESTERS' comb-like cap.

cocksure ▻ *adj* foolishly over-confident. ● **cocksureness** *noun*. ◷ 17c.

cocktail ▻ *noun* **1** a mixed drink of spirits and other liquors. **2** a mixed dish especially of seafood and mayonnaise. **3** a mixture of different things □ *a cocktail of drink and drugs*. ◷ 19c.

cocktail dress ▻ *noun* a dress suitable for wear on semi-formal occasions.

cocktail stick ▻ *noun* a short thin pointed stick on which small items of food are served at parties, etc.

cock-up ▻ *noun* (***cock-ups***) *slang* a mess or muddle resulting from incompetence. See also COCK[1].

cocky ▻ *adj* (***cockier***, ***cockiest***) *derog* cheekily self-confident. ● **cockily** *adverb*. ● **cockiness** *noun*. ◷ 18c: from COCK[1].

coco see COCONUT

cocoa /'koʊkoʊ/ ▻ *noun* (***cocoas***) **1** the seed of the CACAO tree. **2** a powder prepared from the seeds of this tree after they have been fermented, dried and roasted. **3** a drink prepared by mixing this powder with hot milk or water. **4** a lightish brown colour. ◷ 18c: variant of CACAO.

cocoa bean ▻ *noun* one of the seeds from the CACAO tree after it has been fermented, removed from the pod and roasted.

cocoa butter ▻ *noun* a pale yellow fat obtained from cocoa beans, which is used in the manufacture of chocolate, cosmetics, etc.

coconut ▻ *noun* **1** (*also* **coconut palm, coco**) a tropical palm tree cultivated for its edible fruit. **2** the large single-seeded fruit of this tree, with a thick fibrous outer husk and a hard woody inner shell enclosing a layer of white edible flesh and a central cavity. ◷ 18c: from Portuguese *coco* grimace or ugly face, from the face-like markings on a coconut.

coconut shy ▻ *noun* at a fairground: a stall where people throw balls at coconuts to try to knock them off stands and thereby win a prize.

cocoon /kə'kuːn/ ▻ *noun* **1** the protective silky covering that many animals, eg spiders and earthworms, spin around their eggs. **2** a similar covering that a larva spins around itself before it develops into a pupa. ▻ *verb* (***cocooned***, ***cocooning***) **1** to wrap someone or something up as if in a cocoon. **2** to protect someone from the problems of everyday life. ◷ 17c: French *cocon*, from Provençal *coucoun* eggshell.

cocooning ▻ *noun* the practice of choosing to spend one's spare time with a partner or one's family, rather than taking part in more social activities.

cocotte /kɒ'kɒt/ ▻ *noun* a small lidded pot for oven and table use, usually intended for an individual portion. ◷ 20c: French, from *cocasse* a kind of pot.

co-counselling ▻ *noun* a form of self-help therapy in which two or more people take turns at being client and counsellor.

cod[1] ▻ *noun* (*plural* ***cod***) a large soft-finned fish, found mainly in the N Atlantic Ocean, which is popular in western countries as a food fish. Also called **codfish**. ◷ 14c.

cod[2] ▻ *noun, slang* **1** a hoax. **2** a parody. ▻ *verb* (***codded***, ***codding***) **1** to hoax someone. **2** to parody. ◷ 20c as *noun*, 19c as *verb*.

c.o.d. ▻ *abbreviation* cash on delivery.

coda /'koʊdə/ ▻ *noun* (***codas***) **1** *music* a passage added at the end of a movement or piece, to bring it to a satisfying conclusion. **2** a similar passage in a book, story, dance, etc. ◷ 18c: Italian, meaning 'tail', from Latin *cauda*.

coddle /'kɒdəl/ ▻ *verb* (***coddled***, ***coddling***) **1** to cook something (especially eggs) gently in hot, rather than boiling, water. **2** to pamper, mollycoddle or over-protect someone or something. ◷ 16c.

code ▻ *noun* **1** a system of words, letters or symbols, used in place of those really intended, for secrecy's or brevity's sake. **2** a set of signals for sending messages, etc. **3** a message in code. **4** *computing* a set of symbols that represent numbers, letters, etc in binary form so that information can be stored or exchanged between different computer systems, eg the ASCII code. **5** *computing* the set of written instructions or statements that make up a computer program. **6** a group of numbers and letters used as means of identification. **7** a set of principles of behaviour. **8** a systematically organized set of laws. **9** *telecomm* the number dialled before a personal telephone number when making a non-local call, in order to connect with the required area. ▻ *verb* (***coded***, ***coding***) **1** to put something into a code. **2** *computing* to generate a set of written instructions or statements that make up a computer program. ◷ 14c: French, from Latin *codex* book.

codeine /'koʊdiːn/ ▻ *noun, medicine* a morphine derivative that relieves mild to moderate pain, has a sedative effect and suppresses the coughing reflex. ◷ 19c: from Greek *kodeia* poppy head.

co-dependency ▻ *noun* the condition of seeking to fulfil one's own emotional needs by caring for or controlling a dependant. ● **co-dependant** *noun*.

code switching ▻ *noun, linguistics* a common feature of the speech of bilinguals, where a speaker changes from one language to another during a conversation with another bilingual from the same language background.

code word ▻ *noun* a word or phrase of special and secret significance, agreed on by its users for a purpose.

codex /ˈkoʊdɛks/ ▻ *noun* (***codices*** /koʊdɪsiːz/) an ancient manuscript volume, bound in book form. ⓒ 19c: Latin, meaning 'set of tablets' or 'book'.

codfish see under COD[1]

codger /ˈkɒdʒə(r)/ ▻ *noun, colloq* a man, especially an old and strange one. ⓒ 18c: perhaps a variant of CADGE.

codicil /ˈkoʊdɪsɪl, ˈkɒdɪsɪl/ ▻ *noun, law* a supplement to a will, which makes extra provisions or revokes some part of the original draft. ⓒ 15c: from Latin *codicillus*, diminutive of *codex* book.

codicology /koʊdɪˈkɒlədʒɪ/ ▻ *noun* the study of manuscripts and their physical make-up, excluding the writing. Compare PALAEOGRAPHY.

codify /ˈkoʊdɪfaɪ/ ▻ *verb* (***codifies, codified, codifying***) to arrange something into a systematic code, eg laws, etc. • **codification** *noun*. • **codifier** *noun*.

codling[1] /ˈkɒdlɪŋ/ ▻ *noun* a kind of cooking-apple, which has an elongated shape. ⓒ 15c as *querdling*.

codling[2] ▻ *noun* a young cod.

cod-liver oil ▻ *noun* a medicinal oil obtained from the livers of cod, rich in vitamins A and D.

codon /ˈkoʊdɒn/ ▻ *noun, genetics* in a molecule of DNA or messenger RNA: a set of three bases that is specific for one particular amino acid.

codpiece ▻ *noun, historical* a pouch attached to the front of a man's breeches, covering his genitals. ⓒ 15c: from an earlier sense of *cod* scrotum.

codswallop /ˈkɒdzwɒləp/ ▻ *noun, Brit slang* nonsense. ⓒ 20c.

co-ed /koʊˈɛd/ ▻ *abbreviation, colloq* coeducation or coeducational. ▻ *noun, N Amer, especially US* a female student in a co-educational school or college.

coeducation ▻ *noun* the teaching of pupils of both sexes in the same school or college. • **coeducational** *adj*. • **coeducationally** *adverb*.

coefficient /koʊɪˈfɪʃənt/ ▻ *noun* **1** *algebra* a number or other constant factor placed before a variable to signify that the variable is to be multiplied by that factor. **2** *physics* a number or parameter that is a measure of a specified property of a particular substance under certain conditions, eg the coefficient of viscosity.

coelacanth /ˈsiːləkanθ/ ▻ *noun* a primitive bony fish believed extinct until a live specimen was found in 1938. ⓒ 19c: from Greek *koilos* hollow + *akantha* spine.

coelenterate /sɪˈlɛntəreɪt, siː-/ ▻ *noun, zool* any member of the PHYLUM of invertebrate animals which have a single body cavity and usually show radial symmetry, eg jellyfish, sea anemones and corals. ⓒ 19c: from Greek *koilos* hollow + *enteron* intestine.

coeliac or (*especially US*) **celiac** /ˈsiːlɪak/ ▻ *adj* **1** relating to the abdomen. **2** relating to coeliac disease. ▻ *noun* someone suffering from coeliac disease. ⓒ 17c: from Greek *koilia* belly.

coeliac disease ▻ *noun, pathol* a condition in which the lining of the small intestine is abnormally sensitive to GLUTEN, leading to improper digestion and absorption of food.

coelom or (*especially US*) **celom** /ˈsiːloʊm/ ▻ *noun, zool* in multicellular animals: the main body cavity which typically forms the cavity around the gut in ANNELIDS, ECHINODERMS and VERTEBRATES. ⓒ 19c: from Greek *koiloma* cavity.

coenobite /ˈsiːnəbaɪt/ ▻ *noun* a member of a monastic community. • **coenobitic** /-ˈbɪtɪk/ *adj*. ⓒ 17c: from Greek *koinos* common + *bios* life.

co-enzyme ▻ *noun* an organic molecule whose presence is essential for the biochemical reactions of enzymes to take place, but which remains unaffected by the reactions. ⓒ 20c.

coerce /koʊˈɜːs/ ▻ *verb* (***coerced, coercing***) (*often* **coerce someone into something**) to force or compel them to do it, using threats, etc. • **coercible** *adj*. • **coercion** /koʊˈɜːʃən/ *noun*. • **coercive** *adj*. • **coercively** *adverb*. ⓒ 17c: from Latin *coercere* to restrain.

coeval /koʊˈiːvəl/ ▻ *adj, formal* belonging to the same age or period of time. ▻ *noun* someone or something from the same age or period of time. ⓒ 17c: from CO- + Latin *aevum* age.

co-exist ▻ *verb, intr* **1** to exist together, or simultaneously. **2** to live peacefully side by side in spite of differences, etc. • **co-existence** *noun*. • **co-existent** *noun*. ⓒ 17c.

co-extend ▻ *verb, tr & intr* to extend equally. • **co-extension** *noun*. • **co-extensive** *adj*. ⓒ 17c.

C of E ▻ *abbreviation* Church of England.

coffee /ˈkɒfɪ/ ▻ *noun* (***coffees***) **1** an evergreen tree or shrub which has oval leaves, white fragrant flowers and red fleshy fruits. **2** the seeds of this plant, called beans, roasted whole or ground to a powder. **3** a popular drink, usually containing CAFFEINE, which is prepared from the roasted and ground beans of the coffee plant. **4** the brown colour of the drink when mixed with milk. ⓒ 17c: from Turkish *kahveh*, from Arabic *qahwah* coffee or wine.

coffee bar ▻ *noun* a place where coffee and snacks are sold over a counter.

coffee bean ▻ *noun* the seed of the coffee plant, especially roasted in readiness for grinding to make coffee.

coffee break ▻ *noun* a pause during working hours, for a cup of coffee.

coffee house ▻ *noun, historical* an establishment serving coffee, used by fashionable people especially in the 18c.

coffee mill ▻ *noun* a machine for grinding coffee beans.

coffee shop ▻ *noun* a shop where coffee is sold and drunk, along with light snacks or meals.

coffee table ▻ *noun* a small low table.

coffee-table book ▻ *noun, often derog* a large expensive highly illustrated book, intended for browsing through rather than reading.

coffer /ˈkɒfə(r)/ ▻ *noun* **1** a large chest for holding valuables. **2** (**coffers**) a treasury or supply of funds. **3** *archit* a hollow or sunken section in the elaborate panelling or plasterwork of a ceiling. ⓒ 13c: from French *cofre*, from Greek *kophinos* basket.

cofferdam ▻ *noun* a watertight chamber allowing construction workers to carry out building work underwater. Compare CAISSON.

coffin /ˈkɒfɪn/ ▻ *noun* a box into which a corpse is put for cremation or burial. ▻ *verb* (***coffined, coffining***) to place in a coffin. *Amer equivalent* CASKET. ⓒ 16c: French *cofin*, from Greek *kophinos* basket.

cog ▻ *noun* **1** one of a series of teeth on the edge of a wheel or bar which engage with another series of teeth to bring about motion. **2** a small gear wheel. **3** someone unimportant in, though necessary to, a process or organization. ⓒ 13c as *cogge*, perhaps from Scandinavian origin.

cogent /ˈkoʊdʒənt/ ▻ *adj* said of arguments, reasons, etc: strong; persuasive; convincing. • **cogency** *noun* convincing or persuasive force. • **cogently** *adverb*. ⓒ 17c: French, from Latin *cogere* to drive together.

cogitate /ˈkɒdʒɪteɪt/ ▻ *verb* (***cogitated, cogitating***) *intr* to think deeply; to ponder. • **cogitation** *noun*. • **cogitative** *adj*. • **cogitator** *noun*. ⓒ 17c: from Latin *cogitare, cogitatum* to think.

cognac /ˈkɒnjak/ ▻ *noun* a high-quality French brandy. ⓒ 18c: named after the area in SW France.

cognate /ˈkɒɡneɪt/ ▷ *adj* **1** descended from or related to a common ancestor. **2** said of words or languages: derived from the same original form. **3** related; akin. ▷ *noun* something that is related to something else. • **cognately** *adverb*. • **cognateness** *noun*. • **cognation** *noun*. ◎ 17c: Latin *cognatus*, from *co-* with + *gnasci* to be born.

cognition /kɒɡˈnɪʃən/ ▷ *noun, psychol* the mental processes, such as perception, reasoning, problem-solving, etc, which enable humans to experience and process knowledge and information. ◎ 15c: Latin *cognitio* study or knowledge.

cognitive /ˈkɒɡnɪtɪv/ ▷ *adj* **1** relating to congition. **2** capable of cognition. • **cognitively** *adverb* in terms of cognition.

cognitive psychology ▷ *noun* a branch of psychology which studies the higher mental processes such as memory, reasoning, language, etc.

cognitive science ▷ *noun* the study of the mind.

cognitive therapy ▷ *noun, psychol* a form of psychotherapy in which the therapist helps the patient to change false or distorted perceptions of themselves and the world, in an attempt to alleviate disorders such as depression, addictive behaviour, etc.

cognizance or **cognisance** /ˈkɒɡnɪzəns, ˈkɒn-/ ▷ *noun* **1** knowledge; understanding; perception; awareness. **2** the range or scope of one's awareness or knowledge. **3** *law* the right of a court to deal with a particular matter. **4** *heraldry* a distinctive mark or sign. • **take cognizance of something** to take it into consideration. ◎ 14c: from French *conoisance*, from Latin *cognoscere* to know.

cognizant or **cognisant** ▷ *adj* aware of something or having knowledge of it.

cognomen /kɒɡˈnoʊmən/ ▷ *noun* (***cognomens*** or ***cognomina*** /-ˈnoʊmɪnə/) **1** *Roman history* a Roman's third name, often in origin an epithet or nickname, which became their family name. **2** a nickname or surname. ◎ 19c: from Latin *co-* with + *(g)nomen* name.

cognoscenti /kɒnjoʊˈʃɛntiː, kɒɡnəˈʃɛntiː/ ▷ *plural noun* knowledgeable or refined people; connoisseurs. ◎ 18c: Italian, from Latin *cognoscere* to know.

cogwheel ▷ *noun* a toothed wheel.

cohabit /koʊˈhabɪt/ ▷ *verb* (***cohabited***, ***cohabiting***) *intr* to live together as husband and wife, usually without being married. Sometimes shortened to **cohab**. • **cohabitation** *noun*. • **cohabiter** or **cohabitee** *noun* (***cohabitees***). ◎ 16c: from Latin *cohabitare* to live together.

cohere /koʊˈhɪə(r)/ ▷ *verb* (***cohered***, ***cohering***) *intr* **1** to stick together. **2** to be consistent; to have a clear logical connection or development. ◎ 16c: from Latin *cohaerere* to be connected.

coherence theory ▷ *noun, philos* **1** a theory of truth which maintains that a proposition is true if it fits into a network of propositions. **2** a theory of justification which maintains that a necessary condition for justifying a belief is that it should fit with the believer's other beliefs.

coherent /koʊˈhɪərənt/ ▷ *adj* **1** said of a description or argument: logically and clearly developed; consistent. **2** speaking intelligibly. **3** sticking together; cohering. **4** *physics* said of two or more radiating waves: denoting waves of electromagnetic radiation, eg light waves, that have the same frequency, and either the same PHASE (*noun* 4) or a constant phase difference, eg the light waves produced by a laser. • **coherence** *noun* **1** a sticking together. **2** consistency. • **coherently** *adverb*. ◎ 16c: French, from Latin *cohaerere* to be connected.

cohesion /koʊˈhiːʒən/ ▷ *noun* **1** the process or state of sticking together. **2** the tendency to unite or stick together. **3** *physics* the attraction between atoms or molecules of the same substance, which produces SURFACE TENSION. See also ADHESION. ◎ 17c: French, from Latin *cohaerere* to stick together.

cohesive /koʊˈhiːsɪv, -zɪv/ ▷ *adj* **1** having the power of cohering. **2** tending to unite into a mass. **3** *physics* denoting the forces of attraction that exist between atoms or molecules of the same substance.

cohort /ˈkoʊhɔːt/ ▷ *noun* **1** *historical* in the ancient Roman army: one of the ten divisions of a legion. **2** a band of warriors. **3** a group of people sharing a common quality or belief. **4** *colloq* a follower, supporter or companion. ◎ 15c: from Latin *cohors* enclosure or company of soldiers.

COHSE /ˈkoʊziː/ ▷ *abbreviation* Confederation of Health Service Employees.

coif[1] /kɔɪf/ ▷ *noun* a close-fitting cap worn especially by women in medieval times, or by nuns under a veil. ◎ 14c: French *coiffe*, from Latin *cofea* helmet.

coif[2] /kwɑːf/ ▷ *noun* a hairstyle. ▷ *verb* (***coiffed***, ***coiffing***) to dress (hair); to dress someone's hair. ◎ 19c in this sense; probably from COIFFURE.

coiffeur /kwɑːˈfɜː(r)/ and **coiffeuse** /kwɑːˈfɜːz/ ▷ *noun* (***coiffeurs*** /-fɜː(r), -fɜːz/ or ***coiffeuses*** /-fɜːz, -fɜːzɪz/) a male or female hairdresser respectively. ◎ 19c: French.

coiffure /kwɑːˈfʊə(r)/ ▷ *noun* a hairstyle. ▷ *verb* (***coiffured***, ***coiffuring***) to dress (hair); to dress someone's hair. ◎ 17c: French.

coil[1] ▷ *verb* (***coiled***, ***coiling***) *tr & intr* (*sometimes* **coil up**) to wind round and round in loops to form rings or a spiral. ▷ *noun* **1** something looped into rings or a spiral □ ***a coil of rope***. **2** a single loop in such an arrangement. **3** *elec* a conducting wire wound into a spiral, used to provide a magnetic field, to react mechanically by moving in response to a change in the existing magnetic field, or to introduce inductance into an electrical circuit. **4** *non-technical* an INTRAUTERINE DEVICE. ◎ 17c: from French *cueillir* to gather together.

coil[2] ▷ *noun, old use* trouble and tumult. • **this mortal coil** the troubles of life and the world. ◎ 16c.

coin ▷ *noun* **1** a small metal disc stamped for use as currency. **2** coins generally. ▷ *verb* (***coined***, ***coining***) **1 a** to manufacture (coins) from metal; **b** to make (metal) into coins. **2** to invent (a new word or phrase). • **be coining it in** *colloq* to be making a lot of money. • **the other side of the coin** the opposite way of looking at the issue under consideration. • **pay someone back in their own coin** to respond to their discourteous or unfair treatment with similar behaviour. • **to coin a phrase** *ironic* used to introduce an over-used expression. ◎ 14c: French meaning 'wedge' or 'die'.

coinage ▷ *noun* (*plural* in senses 4 only and 5 ***coinages***) **1** the process of coining. **2** coins. **3** the invention of something new. **4** a newly invented word or phrase. **5** the official currency of a country.

coin box ▷ *noun* a telephone or other machine operated by the insertion of coins.

coincide /koʊɪnˈsaɪd/ ▷ *verb* (***coincided***, ***coinciding***) *intr* **1** to happen at the same time. **2** to be the same; to agree. **3** to occupy the same position. ◎ 18c: from Latin *co-* together + *incidere* to happen.

coincidence /koʊˈɪnsɪdəns/ ▷ *noun* **1** the striking occurrence of events together or in sequence, without any causal connection. **2** the fact of being the same.

coincident ▷ *adj* **1** coinciding in space or time. **2** in agreement.

coincidental /koʊɪnsɪˈdɛntəl/ ▷ *adj* happening by coincidence. • **coincidentally** *adverb*.

coin-operated ▷ *adj* said of a machine: operating on the insertion of a coin. Often shortened to **coin-op**.

coir /kɔɪə(r)/ ▷ *noun* fibre from coconut shells, used for making ropes, matting, etc. ◎ 16c: from Malayalam (a language of S India) *kayaru* cord.

coition /koʊ'ɪʃən/ and **coitus** /'koʊɪtəs, kɔɪ-/ ▻ *noun* sexual intercourse. ● **coital** /'koʊɪtəl, kɔɪ-/ *adj.* ◎ 17c: from Latin *coire* to unite.

coitus interruptus /koʊɪtəs ɪntə'rʌptəs, kɔɪ- —/ ▻ *noun* an unreliable method of contraception where sexual intercourse is intentionally stopped before the ejaculation of semen into the vagina.

coitus reservatus ▻ *noun* /koʊɪtəs rɛzə'vɑːtəs, kɔɪ- —/ sexual intercourse in which ejaculation is deliberately avoided, so as to prolong coition.

Coke short for COCA-COLA

coke[1] /koʊk/ ▻ *noun* a brittle greyish-black porous solid consisting of the residue of carbon and ash after DESTRUCTIVE DISTILLATION, most commonly used as a smokeless fuel for domestic heating. ▻ *verb* (***coked, coking***) *tr & intr* to convert (coal) into this material. ◎ 17c: perhaps from N Eng dialect *colk* core.

coke[2] /koʊk/ ▻ *noun, colloq* cocaine when used as an illegal stimulant.

col /kɒl/ *noun* **1** *geol* in a mountain range: a pass between two adjacent peaks, or the lowest point in a ridge, often used for lines of communication, eg roads. **2** *meteorol* in a weather chart: a zone of low pressure and light winds between two ANTICYCLONES. ◎ 19c: French, meaning 'neck'.

Col. ▻ *abbreviation* **1** Colonel. **2** *US state* Colorado. **3** *Bible* Colossians.

col. ▻ *abbreviation* **1** colour. **2** column.

col- see CON-

cola or **kola** /'koʊlə/ ▻ *noun* (***colas*** or ***kolas***) **1** an evergreen tree, native to Africa but cultivated in other tropical regions for its seeds called COLA NUTS. **2** a soft drink flavoured with the extract obtained from the seeds of this tree. ◎ 18c: from W African *kolo* nut.

colander /'kʌləndə(r), 'kɒ- ▻ *noun* a perforated bowl made from metal or plastic used to drain the water from cooked vegetables, etc. ◎ 15c: from Latin *colare* to strain.

cola nut ▻ *noun* a seed of the cola tree, which contains caffeine and is used in soft drink flavourings and the manufacture of certain medicines.

cold /koʊld/ ▻ *adj* **1** low in temperature; not hot or warm. **2** lower in temperature than is normal, comfortable or pleasant. **3** said of food: cooked, but not eaten hot ▫ *cold meat*. **4** unfriendly. **5** comfortless; depressing. **6** *colloq* unenthusiastic ▫ *The suggestion left me cold*. **7** without warmth or emotion ▫ *a cold calculating person*. **8** sexually unresponsive. **9** said of colours: producing a feeling of coldness rather than warmth. **10** *colloq* unconscious, usually after a blow, fall, etc ▫ *out cold*. **11** dead. **12** said of someone trying to guess or find something: far from the answer or the hidden object. **13** said of a trail or scent: not fresh; too old to follow. ▻ *adverb* without preparation or rehearsal. ▻ *noun* **1** lack of heat or warmth; cold weather. **2** (*also Scottish* **the cold**) a highly contagious viral infection, which causes inflammation of the mucous membranes of the respiratory organs and whose symptoms include a sore throat, coughing and sneezing, and a congested nose. Also called **the common cold**. ● **coldly** *adverb* in an unfriendly manner. ● **coldness** *noun*. ● **catch cold** to become ill with a cold. ● **get cold feet** *colloq* **1** to lose courage. **2** to become reluctant to carry something out. ● **give someone the cold shoulder** *colloq* to respond aloofly to them; to rebuff or snub them. ● **in cold blood** deliberately and unemotionally. ● **make someone's blood run cold** to terrify or horrify them. ● **out in the cold** *colloq* ignored, disregarded and neglected by others. ● **pour** or **throw cold water on something** *colloq* to be discouraging or unenthusiastic about a plan, idea, etc. ◎ Anglo-Saxon *ceald*.

cold-blooded ▻ *adj* **1** said of all animals except mammals and birds eg fish, reptiles: having a body temperature that varies with the temperature of the surrounding environment. *Technical equivalent* **poikilothermic**. **2 a** lacking emotion; **b** callous or cruel. ● **cold-bloodedly** *adverb*. ● **cold-bloodedness** *noun*.

cold boot ▻ *noun, computing* a REBOOT activated by completely switching off and restarting a computer from the power source. Compare WARM BOOT.

cold calling and **cold canvassing** ▻ *noun* a marketing technique in which a sales representative contacts potential customers without advance warning.

cold chisel ▻ *noun* a strengthened chisel for cutting cold metal, stone, etc.

cold comfort ▻ *noun* no comfort at all.

cold cream ▻ *noun* a face cream for cleaning the skin and keeping it soft.

cold cuts ▻ *plural noun* slices of cold cooked meats.

cold frame ▻ *noun* a glass-covered frame which protects young plants growing outdoors from the cold weather.

cold front ▻ *noun, meteorol* the leading edge of an advancing mass of cold air moving under a retreating mass of warm air.

cold-hearted ▻ *adj* unkind. ● **cold-heartedly** *adverb*. ● **cold-heartedness** *noun*.

cold-shoulder ▻ *verb* to give someone the cold shoulder.

cold snap *noun* a sudden cold spell.

cold sore ▻ *noun* a patch of small blister-like spots on or near the lips, caused by the herpes simplex virus (see under HERPES).

cold storage ▻ *noun* **1** the storage of food, etc under refrigeration, in order to preserve it. **2** the state of being put aside or saved till another time; abeyance.

cold sweat ▻ *noun* a chill caused by a feeling of fear or nervousness.

cold turkey ▻ *noun, drug-taking slang* **1** a way of curing drug addiction by suddenly and completely stopping the use of drugs. **2** the unpleasant withdrawal symptoms suffered by a drug addict using this method.

cold war ▻ *noun* a state of hostility and antagonism between nations, without actual warfare, especially **the Cold War** that existed between the former Soviet Union and the West between 1945 and the late 1980s.

cole /koʊl/ ▻ *noun* any of various vegetables belonging to the cabbage family. ◎ Anglo-Saxon *cawl*, from Latin *caulis* cabbage.

colectomy /koʊ'lɛktəmɪ/ ▻ *noun* (***colectomies***) *medicine* the surgical removal of the colon. ◎ 19c: COLON + -ECTOMY.

coleopteran /kɒlɪ'ɒptərən/ ▻ *noun, zool* a member of the class of insects with forewings which have been modified so that they form a hard and horny protective case, eg beetles. ● **coleopterist** *noun* someone who studies and collects such insects. ● **coleopterous** *adj.* ◎ 19c: from Greek *koleos* sheath + *pteron* wing.

coleslaw /'koʊlslɔː/ ▻ *noun* a salad made with finely-cut raw cabbage, onion and carrots, etc, bound together, usually with mayonnaise. ◎ 19c: from Dutch *koolsla* cabbage salad.

coleus /'koʊlɪəs/ ▻ *noun* (***coleuses***) a perennial plant, native to Java, which is widely grown as a house plant for its ornamental and variegated leaves. ◎ 19c: from Greek *koleos* sheath.

coley /'koʊlɪ/ ▻ *noun* (***coleys***) a large edible fish belonging to the cod family with white or grey flesh, found in the inshore waters of the N Atlantic. Also called **coalfish, saithe**.

colic /'kɒlɪk/ ▻ *noun, pathol* severe spasmodic abdominal pain, usually caused in adults by constipation or partial or complete obstruction of the intestine. ● **colicky** *adj.* ⓒ 15c: from French *colique*, from Greek *kolen* (see COLON²).

coliseum or **colosseum** /kɒlə'sɪəm/ ▻ *noun* (***coliseums***) *historical* a large stadium or amphitheatre for sports and other entertainment. ⓒ 18c: from Latin *Colosseum* the largest amphitheatre in Rome.

colitis /koʊ'laɪtɪs, kɒ-/ ▻ *noun* inflammation of the COLON². ⓒ 19c: COLON² + -ITIS.

collaborate /kə'labəreɪt/ ▻ *verb* (***collaborated, collaborating***) *intr* **1** to work together with another or others on something. **2** *derog* to co-operate or collude with an enemy, especially one occupying one's own country. ● **collaboration** *noun.* ● **collaborationism** *noun* a policy of collaboration with an enemy. ● **collaborationist** *noun.* ● **collaborative** *adj.* ● **collaboratively** *adverb.* ● **collaborator** *noun.* ⓒ 19c: from Latin *com-* together + *laborare* to work.

collage /kɒ'lɑːʒ, 'kɒlɑːʒ/ ▻ *noun* **1** a design or picture made up of pieces of paper, cloth, photographs, etc glued onto a background surface. **2** the art of producing such works. ● **collagist** *noun.* ⓒ 20c: French, meaning 'pasting' or 'gluing'.

collagen /'kɒlədʒən/ ▻ *noun, biol* a tough fibrous protein of CONNECTIVE TISSUE found in skin, bones, teeth, cartilage, ligaments, etc. ⓒ 19c: from Greek *kolla* glue + -GEN 2.

collapse /kə'laps/ ▻ *verb* (***collapsed, collapsing***) **1** *intr* said of buildings, etc: to fall, give way or cave in. **2** *intr* said of people: **a** to fall or drop in a state of unconsciousness; to faint; **b** to drop in a state of exhaustion or helplessness. **3** *intr* to break down emotionally □ *She collapsed in a flood of tears.* **4** *intr* to fail suddenly and completely □ *Several firms collapsed.* **5** *tr & intr* to fold up compactly for storage or space-saving □ *You can collapse the table into a small box.* **6** *tr & intr* said of the lungs or blood vessels, etc: to become or cause to become flattened. **7** *intr, stock exchange* to suffer a sudden steep drop in value □ *The company's shares collapsed by the end of trading.* ▻ *noun* **1** a process or act of collapsing. **2** a breakdown. ● **collapsible** or **collapsable** *adj.* ● **collapsibility** or **collapsability** *noun.* ⓒ 18c: from Latin *collabi collapsus* to slide or fall.

collar /'kɒlə(r)/ ▻ *noun* **1 a** a band or flap of any of various shapes, folded over or standing up round the neck of a garment; **b** the neck of a garment generally. **2** something worn round the neck. **3** a band of leather, etc worn round the neck by an animal, especially a dog. **4** a padded leather device, fitted round a horse's neck, to ease the strain of pulling a vehicle. **5** a distinctively coloured ring of fur or feathers round the neck of certain mammals and birds. **6** a cut of meat, especially bacon, from the neck of an animal. **7** a ring-shaped fitting for joining two pipes, etc together. **8** any collar-like part. ▻ *verb* (***collared, collaring***) **1** to seize something by the collar. **2** *colloq* to catch or capture someone or something. **3** *colloq* to grab something for oneself. ● **collared** *adj.* ● **collarless** *noun.* ● **to have one's collar felt** *slang* to be arrested. ● **hot under the collar** *colloq* angry or flustered. ⓒ 13c: from French *colier*, from Latin *collum* neck.

collarbone ▻ *noun, non-technical* the CLAVICLE.

collate /kə'leɪt/ ▻ *verb* (***collated, collating***) **1** to study and compare (texts, evidence, etc). **2** to check and arrange (sheets of paper, pages of a book, etc) in order, ready for fastening together. **3** *bookbinding* to check the order of the SIGNATURES (sense 3) before binding. ● **collator** *noun* a person or device which collates. ⓒ 17c: from Latin *collatus*, past participle of *conferre* to put together or compare.

collateral /kə'latərəl, kɒ'latərəl/ ▻ *adj* **1** descended from a common ancestor, but through a different branch of the family. **2** additional; secondary in importance; subsidiary. **3** running parallel. ▻ *noun* **1** a collateral relative. **2** assets offered to a creditor as security for a loan. Also called **collateral security**. ● **collaterally** *adverb.* ⓒ 14c: from Latin *collateralis*, from *com-* with + *latus* side.

collateral damage ▻ *noun, military* incidental civilian casualties or damage to property, neither being the intended target.

collation /kə'leɪʃən, kɒ-/ ▻ *noun* **1** the act of collating. **2** *bookbinding* the description of a manuscript or book in terms of its pages, quires, etc. **3** *RC Church* a modest meal, permitted on fast days. **4** any light meal.

colleague /'kɒliːg/ ▻ *noun* a fellow-worker, especially in a profession. ⓒ 16c: from French *collègue*, from Latin *collega* partner or colleague.

collect¹ /kə'lɛkt/ ▻ *verb* (***collected, collecting***) **1** *tr & intr* to bring or be brought together; to gather. **2** to build up a collection of things of a particular type because of a interest in or enthusiasm for them □ *collect stamps.* **3** to call for someone or something; to fetch; to pick up □ *I'll collect you in the evening.* **4** *tr & intr* to get something from people, eg money owed or voluntary contributions, etc □ *offered to collect for Oxfam.* **5** to calm or control oneself; to get one's thoughts, etc under control. ▻ *adj, N Amer, especially US* said of a telephone call: paid for by the person receiving it. ▻ *adverb, N Amer, especially US* reversing the charges. ⓒ 16c: from Latin *collectus*, past participle of *colligere* to gather.

collect² /'kɒlɛkt/ ▻ *noun, Christianity* a short form of prayer used in the Anglican and Roman Catholic Churches. ⓒ 13c: from Latin *collecta*, shortened from *oratorio ad collectum* the title of a prayer, from *colligere* to gather.

collectable ▻ *adj* **1** capable of being collected. **2** desirable □ *a highly collectable item.* ▻ *noun* (*often* **collectables**) one of a set of items which are of interest to a collector.

collected ▻ *adj* **1** said of a writer's works: all published together in a single volume or a uniform set of volumes. **2** cool; calm; self-possessed. ● **collectedly** *adverb.* ● **collectedness** *noun.*

collection ▻ *noun* **1** the act of collecting. **2** an accumulated assortment of things of a particular type □ *a stamp collection.* **3** an amount of money collected. **4** the removal of mail from a postbox at scheduled times.

collective ▻ *adj* said of, belonging to or involving all the members of a group □ *a collective effort.* ▻ *noun* **a** an organized group or unit who run some kind of business, etc; **b** the individual members of such a group. ● **collectively** *adverb* together; as a whole.

collective bargaining ▻ *noun* talks between a trade union and a company's management to settle questions of pay and to negotiate working conditions.

collective farm ▻ *noun, agric* especially in the former Soviet bloc: a large state-controlled farm run on co-operative principles and formed by the merging of several smaller farms, previously owned by individuals. Compare KOLKHOZ.

collective noun ▻ *noun* a singular noun which refers to a group of people, animals, things, etc, such as *cast, flock, gang.*

collective nouns

● Collective nouns, or group nouns, are nouns like *committee, government, orchestra,* and *team,* which are singular in form but denote a number or group of individuals.

● Because of the special meaning they have, they can be treated as either singular or plural, depending on whether the group is being thought of as a unit or as a number of individuals.

● There are further notes at the entries for some of these words. See also the notes at **majority**, **none**.

collective security ▻ *noun, politics* the maintenance of security and territorial integrity by the collective actions of nation states.

collective unconscious ▻ *noun, psychoanal* that part of the unconscious mind which represents the accumulated experiences common to all mankind.

collectivize or **collectivise** ▻ *verb* (***collectivized, collectivizing***) to group (farms, factories, etc) into larger units and bring them under state control and ownership. • **collectivism** *noun* **1** the economic theory that industry should be carried on with a collective capital. **2** a system embodying this. • **collectivization** *noun.*

collector ▻ *noun, often in compounds, denoting* someone who collects, as a job or hobby □ *debt-collector* □ *stamp-collector.*

collector's item and **collector's piece** ▻ *noun* an object of great interest or value, which would interest a collector.

colleen /ˈkɒliːn, kɒˈliːn/ ▻ *noun, Irish* a girl. ⓒ 19c: from Irish Gaelic *cailín* girl.

college /ˈkɒlɪdʒ/ ▻ *noun* **1** an institution, either self-contained or part of a university, which provides higher education, further education or professional training. **2** one of a number of self-governing establishments that make up certain universities. **3** the staff and students of a college. **4** the buildings which make up a college. **5** (*often* **College**) a name used by some larger secondary schools. **6** a body of people with particular duties and rights. **7** an official body of members of a profession, concerned with maintaining standards, etc. ⓒ 14c: from Latin *collegium* group of associates or fellowship.

College of Arms ▻ *noun, Brit* a collegiate institute incorporated in 1483 that deals with the granting and designing of arms, tracing genealogies, etc. See also LYON KING OF ARMS.

College of Cardinals ▻ *noun, RC Church* the whole body of cardinals who elect and subsequently advise the Pope.

college of education ▻ *noun, Brit* a college specializing in the initial and in-service training of teachers.

collegiate /kəˈliːdʒɪət/ ▻ *adj* **1** said of, relating to or belonging to a college. **2** having the form of a college. **3** said of a university: consisting of individual colleges. ⓒ 16c: from Latin *collegiatus*, from *collegium* fellowship.

collegiate church ▻ *noun* **1** *C of E, RC Church* a church with a chapter of canons attached to it. **2** in Scotland: a church served by two or more clergymen of equal rank.

Colles' fracture /ˈkɒlɪs —/ ▻ *noun* a fracture of the radius near the wrist with backward displacement of the hand. ⓒ 19c: named after Abraham Colles (1773-1843), Irish surgeon.

collide /kəˈlaɪd/ ▻ *verb* (***collided, colliding***) *intr* **1** to crash together or crash into someone or something. **2** said of people: to disagree or clash. ⓒ 17c: Latin *collidere*, from *com-* with + *laedere* to strike.

collie /ˈkɒlɪ/ (***collies***) ▻ *noun* any of several medium-sized highly intelligent long-haired breeds of dog, usually black and white or brown and white, originally used for herding sheep. ⓒ 17c: perhaps from Scots *colle* coal, the breed having once been black.

collier /ˈkɒlɪə(r)/ ▻ *noun* **1** a coal-miner. **2 a** a ship that transports coal; **b** a crew member of such a ship. ⓒ 16c as *coliere*: from Anglo-Saxon *col* coal.

colliery /ˈkɒljərɪ/ ▻ *noun* (***collieries***) a coalmine with its surrounding buildings.

collimate /ˈkɒlɪmeɪt/ ▻ *verb* (***collimated, collimating***) **1** to make parallel. **2** to adjust the line of sight of a telescope, etc. • **collimation** *noun.* ⓒ 17c: from Latin *collimare*, a mistaken reading of *collineare* to bring into a straight line.

collimator ▻ *noun, physics* **1** any device for obtaining a beam of parallel rays of light, used to test the focal length of lenses, etc. **2** any device, eg a diaphragm made of radiation-absorbing material, used to limit the size and angle of spread of a beam of radiation or radioactive particles. **3** a small fixed telescope that is attached to a larger optical instrument, eg an astronomical telescope, to assist in preliminary alignment, eg to fix the larger telescope's line of sight on a particular celestial body. ⓒ 19c.

collinear /kɒˈlɪnɪə(r), koʊ-/ ▻ *adj, math* lying on the same straight line. • **collinearity** *noun.*

collision /kəˈlɪʒən/ ▻ *noun* **1** a violent meeting of objects; a crash. **2** a disagreement or conflict. ⓒ 15c: Latin, from *collidere* to strike together.

collision course ▻ *noun* a direction or course of action taken which, if followed, will result in collision with something or someone.

collocate /ˈkɒləkeɪt, ˈkɒloʊkeɪt/ ▻ *verb* (***collocated, collocating***) **1** to arrange or group together in some kind of order. **2** *grammar* said of a word: to occur frequently alongside another word, often as part of the construction that relates it to its context □ *'Different' collocates with 'from' and 'to', and sometimes with 'than'.* ⓒ 16c: from Latin *collocare* to place together.

collocation ▻ *noun* **1** grouping together in a certain order. **2** *grammar* the habitual co-occurrence of certain words; grammatical interdependence.

colloid /ˈkɒlɔɪd/ ▻ *noun, chem* an intermediate state between a SUSPENSION (sense 5) and a true SOLUTION (sense 3), in which fine particles of one substance are spread evenly throughout another. • **colloidal** *adj.* ⓒ 19c: from Greek *kolla* glue.

colloquial /kəˈloʊkwɪəl/ ▻ *adj* said of language or vocabulary: **a** informal; **b** used in familiar conversation rather than in formal speech or writing. • **colloquially** *adverb.* ⓒ 18c: from Latin *colloquium* conversation.

colloquialism ▻ *noun* a word or expression used in informal conversation.

colloquium /kəˈloʊkwɪəm/ ▻ *noun* (***colloquia*** /-ə/ or ***colloquiums***) an academic conference; a seminar. ⓒ 19c: Latin, meaning 'conversation'.

colloquy /ˈkɒləkwɪ/ ▻ *noun* (***colloquies***) a conversation; talk. ⓒ 16c: from Latin *colloquium* conversation, from *com-* with + *loquium* speaking.

collude /kəˈluːd, kəˈljuːd/ ▻ *verb* (***colluded, colluding***) *intr* to plot secretly with someone, especially with a view to committing fraud. ⓒ 16c: from Latin *colludere* to play with, to act collusively.

collusion /kəˈluːʒən, -ˈljuːʒən/ ▻ *noun* secret and illegal co-operation for the purpose of fraud or other criminal activity, etc. • **collusive** /kəˈluːsɪv, -ˈljuːsɪv/ *adj.* • **collusively** *adverb.* ⓒ 14c: French, from Latin *colludere, collusum* to play with, to act collusively.

collywobbles /ˈkɒlɪwɒbəlz/ ▻ *plural noun* (*usually* **the collywobbles**) *colloq* **1** pain or discomfort in the abdomen. **2** nervousness; apprehensiveness. ⓒ 19c: probably from COLIC + WOBBLE.

Colo. ▻ *abbreviation, US state* Colorado.

cologne see EAU DE COLOGNE

Colombian /kəˈlɒmbɪən/ ▻ *adj* belonging or relating to Colombia, a republic in the NW of S America, or its inhabitants. ▻ *noun* a citizen or inhabitant of, or person born in, Colombia.

colon[1] /ˈkoʊlɒn, -ən/ ▻ *noun* a punctuation mark (:), properly used to introduce a list, an example or an explanation. ⓒ 16c: Greek, meaning 'clause' or 'limb'.

> ***colon***
>
> A **colon**
>
> ● introduces a part of a sentence that explains or expands on what comes before □ *I have something to tell you: John is coming back tomorrow* □ *This is an excellent play: believable characters, gripping action and a totally unexpected ending.* Alternative style: an introductory word such as 'namely', preceded by a comma □; *There is one thing I would really like, namely a much larger house.*
>
> ● It introduces a list (no dash is needed):
>
> ✓ *To make the model, you will need the following things: a sheet of thin cardboard, string, glue, scissors.*
>
> ● It introduces a contrast □ *You may be sorry: I am delighted* □ *To err is human: to forgive, divine.*
>
> ALTERNATIVE STYLES: a semicolon □ *You may be sorry; I am delighted*; a comma and a conjunction □ *You may be sorry, but I am delighted.*
>
> ● It introduces direct speech □ *John suddenly shouted: 'Look out! He's coming back!'*
>
> ALTERNATIVE STYLE *(more common)* a comma □ *John suddenly shouted, 'Look out! He's coming back!'*

colon[2] /'koulɒn, -ən/ ▷ *noun, anatomy* in vertebrates: the large intestine lying between the CAECUM and RECTUM. ● **colonic** *adj.* 16c: Latin, from Greek *kolon* large intestine.

colonel /'kɜːnəl/ ▷ *noun* a senior army officer, in charge of a regiment. See table at RANK. ● **colonelcy** /'kɜːnəlsɪ/ *noun* (***colonelcies***) the rank or office of colonel. 16c: from Italian *colonello* leader of a regiment.

colonel-in-chief ▷ *noun* (***colonels-in-chief***) in the British Army: an honorary rank and title often held by a member of the Royal Family.

colonial /kə'lounɪəl/ ▷ *adj* **1** relating to, belonging to or living in a colony or colonies. **2** possessing colonies. ▷ *noun* an inhabitant of a colony. ● **colonially** *adverb.* 18c: see COLONY.

colonialism ▷ *noun, often derog* the policy of acquiring colonies, especially as a source of profit. Compare IMPERIALISM. ● **colonialist** *noun, adj.*

colonic see under COLON[2]

colonization or **colonisation** /kɒlənaɪ'zeɪʃən/ ▷ *noun* **1** the act of colonizing or the process of being colonized. **2** setting up a colony or colonies.

colonize or **colonise** /'kɒlənaɪz/ ▷ *verb* (***colonized, colonizing***) **1** *tr & intr* to establish a colony in (an area or country). **2** to settle (people) in a colony. **3** said of plants and animals: to spread into (a new habitat). **4** *US politics* **a** to put (political supporters) in an area where their votes could decide a closely fought election; **b** to fill (an area) with these voters. ● **colonist** *noun* **1** someone who settles in a colony. **2** a voter put in a certain area for election purposes. ● **colonizer** *noun.*

colonnade /kɒlə'neɪd/ ▷ *noun* **1** *archit* a row of columns placed at regular intervals. **2** a similar row of trees. ● **colonnaded** *noun.* 18c: French, from Latin *columna* column.

colony /'kɒlənɪ/ ▷ *noun* (***colonies***) **1 a** a settlement abroad established and controlled by the founding country; **b** the settlers living there; **c** the territory they occupy. **2** a group of the same nationality or occupation forming a distinctive community within a city, etc □ *writers' colony.* **3** *zool* **a** a group of animals or plants of the same species living together in close proximity, sometimes with physical connections between individual members, eg sponges, corals; **b** a large number of animals living together in a highly organized social group, eg bees, ants, termites. **4** *bacteriol* an isolated group of bacteria or fungi growing on a solid medium, usually from the same single cell. 16c: from Latin *colonia*, from *colonus* farmer or tiller, from *colere* to cultivate or inhabit.

colophon /'kɒləfɒn, -ən/ ▷ *noun* **1** an inscription at the end of a printed book or manuscript giving the name of the writer, printer, etc and place and date of production. **2** a publisher's ornamental mark or device. 17c: Latin, from Greek *kolophon* summit or finishing touch.

Colorado beetle /kɒlə'rɑːdou —/ ▷ *noun* a small beetle that has a yellow back with black stripes on its wing cases, which is a serious pest of potato crops.

colorant or **colourant** /'kʌlərənt/ ▷ *noun* a substance used for colouring. 19c: French, from Latin *colorare* to colour.

coloration or **colouration** /kʌlə'reɪʃən/ ▷ *noun* arrangement or combination of colours, especially in the markings of animals or plants. 17c: from Latin *colorare* to colour.

coloratura /kɒlərə'tuərə, -'tjuərə/ ▷ *noun, music* **1** an elaborate and intricate passage or singing style. **2** (*also* **coloratura soprano**) a soprano specializing in such singing. 18c: Italian, meaning 'colouring'.

colorimeter /kʌlə'rɪmɪtə(r), kɒlə-/ ▷ *noun, chem* a device for measuring the colour intensity of a solution, by comparing it with those of standard solutions which contain known concentrations of the constituent. ● **colorimetric** *adj.* ● **colorimetry** *noun.*

colossal /kə'lɒsəl/ ▷ *adj* **1** huge; vast. **2** *colloq* splendid; marvellous □ *a colossal view.* ● **colossally** *adverb* hugely. 18c: from COLOSSUS.

colosseum see COLISEUM

colossus /kə'lɒsəs/ ▷ *noun* (***colossi*** /-saɪ/ or ***colossuses***) **1** a gigantic statue. **2** an overwhelmingly powerful person or organization. 14c: Latin, from Greek *kolossos* gigantic statue.

colostomy /kə'lɒstəmɪ/ ▷ *noun* (***colostomies***) *surgery* an operation in which part of the colon is brought to the surface of the body through an incision in the abdomen, forming an artificial anus through which the colon can be emptied. 19c: from COLON[2] + -STOMY.

colostomy bag ▷ *noun* a device worn over the opening created by a colostomy, into which waste is passed.

colostrum /kə'lɒstrəm/ ▷ *noun, zool* in mammals: the yellowish milky fluid secreted by the mammary glands immediately before and after giving birth, which is followed by the secretion of the true milk. 16c: Latin.

colour or (*US*) **color** /'kʌlə(r)/ ▷ *noun* **1 a** the visual sensation produced when light of different wavelengths is absorbed by the cones of the retina and relayed, in the form of nerve impulses, to the brain; **b** the particular visual sensation produced in this way, depending upon the wavelength. **2** any of these variations or colours, often with the addition of black and white. **3** *photog, art* the use of some or all colours, as distinct from black and white only □ *in full colour.* **4** a colouring substance, especially paint. **5 a** the shade of a person's skin, as related to race; **b** the darker skin shades. **6** pinkness of the face or cheeks, usually indicating healthiness. **7** lively or convincing detail □ *add local colour to the story.* **8** richness of quality in music, or its mood and quality generally. See also COLOURS. ▷ *verb* (***coloured, colouring***) **1 a** to put colour on to something; **b** to paint or dye. **2** (*often* **colour something in**) to fill in (an outlined area or a black and white picture) with colour. **3** to influence □ *Personal feelings can colour one's judgement.* **4** *intr* to blush. ● **lend colour to something** to give it credence; to make it more believable. ● **nail one's colours to the mast** see under COLOURS. ● **off colour** *colloq* unwell. 13c: French, from Latin *color*.

colour bar ▷ *noun* social discrimination against people of different races.

colour-blind ▷ *adj* being unable to distinguish between certain colours, most commonly red and green, due to a congenital defect in the cone cells of the retina. ● **colour-blindness** *noun*.

colour code ▻ *noun* the systematic use of colour as a means of identification or classification, as in electrical wiring. ▻ *verb* (**colour-code**) to mark something with different colours for identification. ● **colour-coded** *adj*.

coloured ▻ *adj* **1** *also in compounds* having colour, or a specified colour □ *coloured paper*. **2 a** belonging to a dark-skinned race; **b** non-white. **3** (**Coloured**) *S Afr* being of mixed white and non-white descent. **4** distorted □ *Her judgement was coloured because of past experiences*. ▻ *noun* **1** someone of a dark-skinned race. **2** (**Coloured**) *S Afr* a person of mixed white and non-white descent.

colour-fast ▻ *adj* said of fabrics: dyed with colours that will not run or fade when washed.

colour filter ▻ *noun, photog* a transparent material which transmits light for only a selected portion of the visible SPECTRUM, partially or completely absorbing the remainder.

colourful ▻ *adj* **1** full of especially bright colour. **2** lively; vivid; full of interest or character. **3** said of a person's language: full of swear words. ● **colourfully** *adverb*.

colouring ▻ *noun* **1** a substance used to give colour, eg to food. **2** the applying of colour. **3** arrangement or combination of colour. **4** facial complexion, or this in combination with eye and hair colour.

colourist ▻ *noun* someone skilled in the use of colour, especially an artist.

colourize, **colourise** or (*US*) **colorize** ▻ *verb* (***colourized***, ***colourizing***) *cinema* to add colour to (a film made in black and white), with the aid of a computer. ● **colourization** *noun*.

colourless ▻ *adj* **1** without or lacking colour. **2** uninteresting; dull; lifeless □ *a colourless existence*. **3** pale. ● **colourlessly** *adverb*.

colours ▻ *plural noun* **1** the flag of a nation, regiment or ship. **2** the coloured uniform or other distinguishing badge awarded to team-members in certain games. **3** a badge of ribbons in colours representing a particular party, etc, worn to show support for it. **4** the coloured dress of a jockey and horse, identifying the horse's owner. ● **in one's true colours** as one really is. ● **nail one's colours to the mast** to announce openly one's irrevocable support for something or someone. ● **with flying colours** with great success.

colour scheme ▻ *noun* a choice or combination of colours in house decoration, etc.

colour sergeant ▻ *noun* a sergeant who carries the company's colours.

colour supplement ▻ *noun* an illustrated magazine accompanying a newspaper.

colour television ▻ *noun* a TV system in which separate signals corresponding to the three primary colours of light (red, blue and green) are used to form a full-colour image on the screen of a specially designed television receiver.

colour therapy ▻ *noun* a form of therapy which involves the selection and use of appropriate colours that are said to promote healing and well-being.

colourway ▻ *noun* a combination of colours in patterned material, etc.

Colt /koʊlt/ ▻ *noun, trademark* a type of small pistol. ◷ 19c: named after its inventor Samuel Colt (1814–62).

colt /koʊlt/ ▻ *noun* **1** a male horse or pony less than four years old. **2** a thoroughbred horse or pony less than five years old. **3** *sport* an inexperienced young team-player or a member of a junior team. ◷ Anglo-Saxon, meaning 'young ass'.

coltish ▻ *adj* youthfully awkward in movement or behaviour. ● **coltishly** *adverb*.

coltsfoot ▻ *noun* (***coltsfoot*** or ***coltsfoots***) a perennial wild plant with bright yellow flowers and large soft heart-shaped leaves. ◷ 16c: so called because of the shape of its leaves.

colugo /kɒ'luːgoʊ/ ▻ *noun* (***colugos***) a nocturnal mammal, native to SE Asia, with a large membrane between its fore and hind limbs extending to the tail, which it uses to glide through the air. Also called **flying lemur**. ◷ 18c: probably from a Malaysian word.

Columba /kə'lʌmbə/ ▻ *noun, astron* a small constellation in the southern hemisphere, lying near Canis Major. Also called **the Dove**.

columbine /'kɒləmbaɪn/ ▻ *noun* a perennial wild flower related to the buttercup. ◷ 13c: from French *colombine*, from Latin *columba* dove or pigeon; so called because its petals look like a group of pigeons.

columbium /kə'lʌmbɪəm/ ▻ *noun, chem* former name for NIOBIUM.

column /'kɒləm/ ▻ *noun* **1** *archit* a vertical pillar, usually cylindrical, with a base and a CAPITAL[2]. **2** something similarly shaped; a long and more or less cylindrical mass. **3** a vertical row of numbers. **4** a vertical strip of print on a newspaper page, etc. **5** a regular section in a newspaper concerned with a particular topic, or by a regular writer. **6** a troop of soldiers or vehicles standing or moving a few abreast. ● **columnar** *adj*. ● **columned** *adj*. ◷ 15c: from Latin *columna* pillar.

column inch ▻ *noun* the measure used in newspapers, etc, especially for advertisement spacing, being an area one column wide by one inch deep.

columnist /'kɒləmɪst, 'kɒləmnɪst/ ▻ *noun* someone who writes a regular section of a newspaper.

com- see CON-

coma[1] /'koʊmə/ ▻ *noun* (***comas***) a prolonged state of deep unconsciousness from which a person cannot be awakened, caused by head injury, brain damage, stroke, etc. ◷ 17c: from Greek *koma* deep sleep.

coma[2] /'koʊmə/ ▻ *noun* (***comae*** /-miː/) **1** *bot* a tuft of hairs attached to the TESTA of some seeds. **2** *bot* the arrangement of leaves at the top of a tree. **3** *astron* the envelope of gas and dust which forms around the NUCLEUS of a comet. **4** *optics* a defect in an optical system or the manifestation of it in which the image of a point appears as a blurred pear shape. ◷ 17c: Latin, from Greek *kome* hair of the head.

Coma Berenices /koʊmə berə'naɪsiːz/ ▻ *noun, astron* a small faint constellation of the northern hemisphere, noted for the large number of galaxies it contains.

comatose /koʊmətoʊs, -toʊz/ ▻ *adj* **1** in a coma. **2** *facetious* **a** very drowsy; **b** asleep. ◷ 18c: from Greek *koma* deep sleep.

comb /koʊm/ ▻ *noun* **1 a** a rigid toothed device for tidying and arranging the hair; **b** a similar device worn in the hair to keep it in place. **2** a toothed implement or part of a machine for disentangling, straightening and cleaning strands of wool or cotton. **3** an act of combing. **4** a honeycomb. **5** the fleshy serrated crest on the head of the male chicken or other cock bird. ▻ *verb* (***combed***, ***combing***) **1** to arrange, smooth or clean something with a comb. **2** to search (a place) thoroughly. ◷ Anglo-Saxon *camb*, *comb*.

■ **comb something out 1** to remove it from the hair by combing. **2** to search for and remove it.

combat /'kɒmbat, 'kʌm-/ ▻ *noun* fighting; a struggle or contest. ▻ *verb* (***combated***, ***combating***) to fight against someone or something; to oppose something. ◷ 16c: French, from *combattre* to fight, from Latin *com-* with + *battere* to fight.

combatant /ˈkɒmbətənt, ˈkʌm-/ ▻ *adj* involved in or ready for a fight. ▻ *noun* someone involved in or ready for a fight.

combat fatigue see BATTLE FATIGUE

combative ▻ *adj* inclined to fight or argue. ● **combativeness** *noun.*

combination /kɒmbɪˈneɪʃən/ ▻ *noun* **1** the process of combining or the state of being combined. **2 a** two or more things, people, etc combined; **b** the resulting mixture or union. **3** a sequence of numbers or letters for opening a combination lock. **4** *Brit* a motorcycle with sidecar. **5** *math* a SUBSET selected from a given set of numbers or objects, regardless of the order of selection. **6** *chem* **a** a union of chemical substances which forms a new compound; **b** the new compound formed. **7** (**combinations**) an old-fashioned one-piece undergarment combining long-sleeved vest and long underpants.

combination lock ▻ *noun* a lock which will only open when the numbered dial on it is turned to show a specific sequence of numbers.

combine /kəmˈbaɪn/ ▻ *verb* (***combined, combining***) *tr & intr* **1** to join together; to unite. **2 a** to possess (two contrasting qualities, etc) at the same time; **b** to manage or achieve (two different things) at the same time. **3** *chem* to coalesce or make things coalesce so as to form a new compound. ▻ *noun* /ˈkɒmbaɪn/ **1** a group of people or businesses associated for a common purpose. **2** *colloq* a combine harvester. ● **combinative** *adj.* ● **combinatory** *adj.* ⓒ 15c: from Latin *combinare*, from *com-* with + *bini* two together.

combine harvester ▻ *noun, agric* a machine used to harvest cereals and other arable crops, so called because it is equipped both to reap and thresh the crop.

combining form ▻ *noun, grammar* a word-forming element that occurs in combinations or compounds, eg *-lysis* in *electrolysis*.

combo /ˈkɒmboʊ/ ▻ *noun* (**combos**) *colloq* **a** a small jazz dance band; **b** *facetious* any band or group of musicians. ⓒ 20c: from COMBINATION.

combustible /kəmˈbʌstɪbəl/ ▻ *adj* **1 a** liable to catch fire and burn readily; **b** capable of being burnt as fuel. **2** easily angered; excitable. ▻ *noun* a combustible object or material. ● **combustibility** or **combustibleness** *noun.* ⓒ 16c: from Latin *combustibilis*, from *comburere*, *combustum* to burn up.

combustion /kəmˈbʌstjən, kɒm-/ ▻ *noun* **1** the process of catching fire and burning. **2** *chem* a chemical reaction in which a gas, liquid or solid is rapidly OXIDIZEd, producing heat and light. ⓒ 15c: French, from Latin *comburere, combustum* to burn up.

come /kʌm/ ▻ *verb* (*past tense* ***came***, *past participle* ***come***, *present participle* ***coming***) *intr* in most senses **1** to move in the direction of speaker or hearer. **2** to reach a place; to arrive. **3** (*usually* **come to** or **into something**) to reach (a certain stage or state) □ *come to power.* **4** to travel or traverse (a distance, etc). **5** (*often* **come to do** or **be something**) to happen □ *How did you come to hurt yourself?* **6** to enter one's consciousness or perception □ *come into view.* **7** to occupy a specific place in order, etc □ *In 'ceiling', 'e' comes before 'i'.* **8** to be available; to exist or be found □ *Those purple jeans come in several sizes.* **9** to become □ *come undone.* **10** to descend or result from something □ *This is what comes of being indulgent.* **11** to act the part of (a specified character); to pretend to be something □ *Don't come the innocent.* **12** *intr, colloq* to have a sexual orgasm. **13** on the arrival of (a particular point in time) □ *Come next Tuesday I'll be free.* ▻ *exclamation* used to reassure or admonish □ *Oh, come now, don't exaggerate.* ▻ *noun, slang* (*sometimes* **cum**) ejaculated semen. ● **Come again?** *colloq* Could you repeat that? ● **come and go** to reappear from time to time. ● **come apart** to fall to pieces. ● **come into one's own** to have the opportunity to display one's talents. ● **come it** *slang* to put on an act □ *Don't come it over me.* ● **Come off it!** *colloq* stop talking nonsense! ● **Come on! 1** Hurry up! **2** Don't talk rubbish! □ *The government is popular amongst the working class? Oh, come on!* **3** Cheer up! □ *Come on! Smile.* **4** Don't exaggerate. ● **come one's way** to become available. ● **come to grief** to be unsuccessful; to fail. ● **come to harm** to suffer or be hurt. ● **come to nothing** to fail. ● **come to something** to succeed. ● **come to** (**a decision**, *etc*) to decide, usually after some consideration. ● **come to oneself 1** to regain consciousness. **2** to calm down; to regain one's self-control. ● **have it coming to one** *colloq* to deserve whatever unpleasant fate befalls one. ● **not know whether one is coming or going** to be in a dazed or bewildered state. ● **when it comes to …** when it is a question or case of … □ *When it comes to hard work, he's your man.* ⓒ Anglo-Saxon *cuman.*

■ **come about 1** to happen. **2** *naut* to change direction.

■ **come across 1** to make a certain impression □ *Her speech came across well.* **2** *slang* said of a woman: to show willingness to sexual advances.

■ **come across something** or **someone** to meet or discover them accidentally □ *I came across my old toy soldier in the attic.*

■ **come across with something** *slang* to provide what is required or anticipated □ *He eventually came across with the money.*

■ **come along 1** to progress; to improve □ *His recovery was coming along nicely.* **2** to arrive. **3** often used as an exhortation to hurry up.

■ **come at something** or **someone 1** to attack them. **2** to approach them.

■ **come away** to become detached □ *The poster came away from the wall.*

■ **come back 1** to be recalled to mind □ *It's all coming back to me now.* **2** to become fashionable again □ *After an absence of over a decade, flares really came back.* **3** to return to something, usually after a period of time □ *I would like to come back here someday.* **4** said of a sportsperson: to return to competition after an enforced absence, eg an injury, etc.

■ **come back at someone** to answer them rudely.

■ **come between someone** or **something and someone** or **something else** to create a barrier or division between them.

■ **come by** to pass by or call in □ *Come by around seven and I'll give you that CD.*

■ **come by something** to obtain it, especially accidentally □ *How did you come by that cut?*

■ **come down 1** to lose one's social position □ *come down in the world.* **2** said of an heirloom, etc: to be inherited. **3** to leave university. **4** to decide. **5** to emerge from the state induced by a hallucinogenic or addictive drug. **6** to descend.

■ **come down on** or **upon someone** or **something** to deal with them severely; to be very disapproving □ *come down heavily on bullying.*

■ **come down to something** to be equivalent to it, in simple terms □ *It comes down to this: we stay or we leave.*

■ **come down with something** to develop (an illness).

■ **come for someone** or **something 1** to attack them. **2** to call to collect them or it □ *I'll come for you at seven.*

■ **come forward** to offer oneself □ *Several witnesses came forward.*

■ **come from** to be or have previously been a native or citizen of (a place) □ *She comes from Stoke.*

■ **come in 1** to arrive; to be received. **2** to have a particular role, function or use □ *This is where you come in* □ *would come in useful.* **3** said of the tide: to rise. **4** to become fashionable.

■ **come in for something** to deserve or incur it □ *came in for some criticism.*

■ **come into something** to inherit (money, etc.)

■ **come off 1** to become detached. **2** to succeed □ *The robbery came off exactly as planned.* **3** *informal* to take place □ *The robbery came off at exactly midnight.*

■ **come on 1** to start. **2** to prosper or make progress □ *She is coming on now that she has changed schools.* **3** to appear or make an entrance on stage. **4** *informal* to begin □ *He could feel the flu coming on.*

■ **come on to someone** *informal* to flirt with them or make sexual advances towards them.

■ **come out 1** said of the Sun or stars: to appear. **2** to become known; to become public □ *It came out that the government were involved in another scandal.* **3** to be removed □ *The mark should come out when the shirt is washed.* **4** to be released or made available □ *Their new album comes out on Monday.* **5** to go on strike □ *come out in sympathy.* **6** to declare one's opinion openly □ *come out in favour of the plan.* **7** to work out □ *can't get the sum to come out.* **8** to emerge in a specified position or state □ *come out well from the affair.* **9** said of a photograph: to be developed □ *come out nice and clear.* **10** *colloq* to declare openly that one is a homosexual. Compare OUT (*verb* 2). **11** *old use* said of a girl: to be launched in society.

■ **come out in something** to develop (a rash, etc) □ *come out in spots.*

■ **come out with something** to make (a remark, etc) □ *What will she come out with next?*

■ **come over 1** to change one's opinion or side □ *come over to our side.* **2** to make a specified impression □ *comes over well on television.* **3** *colloq* to feel or become □ *come over a bit faint.*

■ **come over someone** to affect them □ *What came over them?*

■ **come round 1** to regain consciousness. **2** to regain one's temper; to calm down. **3** to change one's opinion. **4** to recur in order or routine.

■ **come through 1** to survive. **2** to emerge successfully.

■ **come through for someone 1** to be there when they need you, especially in a time of crisis. **2** to complete what they have asked you do.

■ **come through something 1** to survive it. **2** to emerge from it successfully.

■ **come to** to regain consciousness.

■ **come to something** to reach or total (a sum of money).

■ **come under something** or **someone 1** to belong to (a category). **2** to be the responsibility of □ *Swimming-pools come under the local authority.*

■ **come up 1** to occur; to happen □ *I'll contact you if anything comes up.* **2** to be considered or discussed □ *The question didn't come up.* **3** to rise socially □ *come up in the world.*

■ **come up against someone** or **something** to be faced with them as an opponent, challenge, etc.

■ **come up to something** to extend to or reach (a level, standard, etc).

■ **come up to someone** to approach them.

■ **come up with something** to offer it; to put it forward □ *come up with an idea.*

■ **come upon something** or **someone** to discover it or them by chance.

comeback ▷ *noun* **1** a return to former success, or to the stage, etc after a period of retirement or obscurity □ *stage a comeback.* **2** a retort □ *Her comeback was biting.* **3** an opportunity for redress or retaliation.

comedian /kəˈmiːdɪən/ and **comedienne** /kəmiːdɪˈɛn/ ▷ *noun* **1** a male or female entertainer who tells jokes, performs comic sketches, etc. **2** an actor in comedy. **3** *facetious* a funny person. ◷ 17c: from COMEDY.

comedo /ˈkɒmɪdoʊ/ ▷ *noun* (***comedones*** /kɒmɪˈdoʊniːz/ or ***comedos***) *technical* a mass of fatty material forming a plug blocking one of the sebaceous ducts in the skin. *Non-technical equivalent* **blackhead**. ◷ 19c: Latin, meaning 'glutton'.

comedown ▷ *noun* **1** a decline in social status. **2** an anticlimax.

comedy /ˈkɒmədɪ/ ▷ *noun* (***comedies***) **1** a light amusing play or film. **2** in earlier literature: a play with a fortunate outcome. **3** such plays as a group or genre. Compare TRAGEDY. **4** funny incidents or situations. ◷ 14c: from Greek *komoidia*, from *komos* comic chorus + *aoidos* singer.

come-hither ▷ *adj, colloq* flirtatious; seductive □ *a come-hither look.*

comeliness ▷ *noun* a comely or attractive quality.

comely /ˈkʌmlɪ/ ▷ *adj* (***comelier, comeliest***) *dated* said of a person: attractive in a wholesome way. ◷ Anglo-Saxon *cymlic* beautiful.

come-on ▷ *noun, colloq* sexual encouragement □ *give someone the come-on.*

comer /ˈkʌmə(r)/ ▷ *noun, in compounds, denoting* someone who comes at the specified time □ *latecomers* □ *a newcomer.*

comestible /kəˈmɛstɪbəl/ ▷ *noun* (*usually* **comestibles**) *affected* something to eat. ◷ 19c: in this sense; French, from Latin *comedere* to eat up.

comet /ˈkɒmɪt/ ▷ *noun, astron* in the solar system: a small body consisting of a COMA (noun 4), a NUCLEUS and a TAIL, which is composed mainly of frozen gas, dust and rock and follows an elliptical orbit around the Sun. ◷ 13c: from Greek *kometes* long-haired, from *kome* hair.

come-uppance ▷ *noun, colloq* justified punishment or retribution □ *She got her come-uppance when no one voted for her.*

comfit /ˈkʌmfɪt/ ▷ *noun* a type of sweet, containing a sugar-coated nut, liquorice, etc. ◷ 15c: from French *confit*, from Latin *conficere* to prepare or make ready.

comfort /ˈkʌmfət/ ▷ *noun* **1** a state of contentedness or wellbeing. **2** relief from suffering, or consolation in grief. **3** a person or thing that provides such relief or consolation. **4** (*usually* **comforts**) something that makes for ease and physical wellbeing. ▷ *verb* (***comforted, comforting***) to relieve from suffering; to console or soothe. ◷ 13c: from French *conforter*, from Latin *confortare*.

comfortable ▷ *adj* **1** in a state of wellbeing, especially physical. **2** at ease. **3** providing comfort. **4** *colloq* financially secure. **5** said of a hospital patient, etc: in a stable condition. **6** quite large □ *win by a comfortable* *margin.* ⓘ 18c: from French *confortable*, from *conforter* to comfort.

comfortably ▷ *adverb* **1** so as to be comfortable. **2** in a comfortable way. ● **comfortably off** *colloq* financially secure; able to live in comfort.

comforter ▷ *noun* **1** someone who comforts. **2** *old use* a warm scarf. **3** *old use* a baby's dummy. **4** *N Amer, especially US* a quilt.

comfrey /'kʌmfrɪ/ ▷ *noun* (***comfreys***) a bristly, robust, perennial plant belonging to the borage family, with tubular white, pink or purple flowers, traditionally used medicinally. ⓘ 13c: from Latin *conferva* healing water plant.

comfy /'kʌmfɪ/ ▷ *adj* (***comfier***, ***comfiest***) *colloq* comfortable.

comic /'kɒmɪk/ ▷ *adj* **1** characterized by or relating to comedy; intended to amuse. **2** funny. ▷ *noun* **1** a comedian. **2** a paper or magazine, especially one aimed at children or teenagers, which includes strip cartoons, illustrated stories, etc. Also called **comic book**. ⓘ 16c: from Greek *komikos*, from *komos* comic chorus.

comical, comic

● Both words have the meaning 'causing laughter', and they are largely interchangeable □ *Her long body would have looked comical as she ran back and forth.* Only **comic** still has a direct association with comedy □ *He had a solo spot with a comic song.*

comical ▷ *adj* funny; amusing; humorous; ludicrous. ● **comicality** *noun*. ● **comically** *adverb*.

comic opera ▷ *noun* lighthearted opera with spoken dialogue as well as singing.

comic strip ▷ *noun* in a newspaper, magazine, etc: a brief story or episode told through a short series of cartoon drawings.

coming ▷ *noun* an arrival or approach. ▷ *adj* **1** *colloq* likely to succeed □ *the coming man.* **2** approaching □ *in the coming months.* ▷ *exclamation* used as a promise of arrival □ *Coming! I'll just put this away first.* ● **have it coming to one** to deserve what is about to happen to one. ● **up and coming 1** promising; progressing well. **2** approaching □ *the up and coming share issue.*

comings and goings ▷ *plural noun, colloq* bustle; activity; movement.

comity /'kɒmɪtɪ/ ▷ *noun* (***comities***) civility; politeness; courtesy. ⓘ 16c: from Latin *comitas*, from *comis* friendly.

comity of nations ▷ *noun* mutual respect and recognition between nations for one another's laws and customs.

comma /'kɒmə/ ▷ *noun* (***commas***) a punctuation mark (,) indicating a slight pause or break made for the sake of clarity, to separate items in a list, etc. ⓘ 16c: Latin, from Greek *comma* short clause.

command /kə'mɑːnd/ ▷ *verb* (***commanded***, ***commanding***) **1** to order formally. **2** to have authority over or be in control of someone or something. **3** to have at one's disposal. **4** to deserve or be entitled to something. **5** to look down over something □ *The window commands a view of the bay.* ▷ *noun* **1** an order. **2** control; charge. **3** knowledge of and ability to use something □ *a good command of the English language.* **4** a military unit or a district under one's command. **5** *military* a specialized section of an army, air force, etc □ *Bomber Command.* **6** *military* a group of high-ranking army officers, etc □ *the British High Command.* **7** an instruction to a computer to initiate a specific operation. **8** *Brit* a royal invitation. ⓘ 13c: from French *commander*, from Latin *com-* intensive + *mandare* to give in charge.

commandant /'kɒməndant, kɒmən'dant/ ▷ *noun* a commanding officer, especially of a prisoner-of-war camp or a military training establishment. ⓘ 17c: French, present participle of *commander* to command.

comma

A **comma**

● indicates a pause or slight break within a sentence □ *I'd give anything not to go, but I'm afraid I must* □ *Whatever you have to say, make it brief* □ *He had grown to like his little room, which, like his jacket pockets, was filled with possessions he had gathered over the years.*

Many commas of this kind are nowadays optional:

✓ *They're down at the pub, celebrating their win on the Lottery.*

✓ *They're down at the pub celebrating their win on the Lottery.*

However, always use a comma to separate the main clause from a dependent clause that comes before it □ *When he arrived home, the children ran to meet him.*

● It separates clauses between which there is a balance or contrast □ *You may be sorry, but I am delighted.*

ALTERNATIVE STYLES: a semicolon and no conjunction □ *You may be sorry; I am delighted;* a colon and no conjunction □ *You may be sorry: I am delighted.*

● It clarifies the structure or meaning of a sentence □ *She felt sick, and tired of looking at modern art* □ *For this week, only coats will be half-price.*

Note especially how the comma is used to distinguish between a 'defining relative clause' and a 'non-defining relative clause' □ *The students, who attend classes every day, are making good progress* (ie all the students) □ *The students who attend classes every day are making good progress* (ie only those who attend classes every day).

● It separates introductory words and inserted comments □ *I don't much like the idea. However, you can go if you want to* □ *I put it to you, ladies and gentlemen, that the government has earned your support.*

● It is used after 'yes' and 'no', and before 'please' □ *Yes, you're quite right* □ *No, I don't agree at all.* □ *Put the books down over there, please.*

● It is used before the name of a person being spoken to, and before other forms of address □ *Are you coming too, Jack?* □ *Will you answer the door, dear?*

● It separates groups of adjectives, phrases, nouns and adverbs, with an optional comma before the 'and' or 'or' □ *a cold, wet, windy day.* □ *I came for a holiday, I liked what I saw, I stayed — it's as simple as that* □ *I like football, tennis(,) and golf We need to deal with this quickly, quietly(,) and effectively* □ *Which do you do best — sing, dance(,) or paint?*

● It separates direct speech from the rest of the sentence □ *'I wouldn't stay now,' she said, 'even if you begged me'* □ *Peter at once said, 'I want to come too.'*

ALTERNATIVE STYLE: a colon, when the quoted speech comes last □ *Peter at once said: 'I want to come too.'*

● Although it is not incorrect, nowadays it is not usually used in letter-writing, either in the address or after 'Dear Sir' etc.

● It is used optionally in five-figure numbers and above, before every three figures counting from the left □ *35,000* □ *2,335,560.*

ALTERNATIVE STYLES: no comma and no space □ *35000*; a thin space and no comma □ *35 000.*

command economy ▷ *noun* a centrally controlled economy in which the state takes all economic decisions.

Also called **planned economy**. Compare MARKET ECONOMY, MIXED ECONOMY.

commandeer /kɒmən'dɪə(r)/ ▷ *verb* (***commandeered, commandeering***) **1** to seize (property) for military use in wartime, official use in an emergency, etc. **2** to seize without justification. ◷ 19c: from Afrikaans *kommandeer*, from French *commander* to command.

commander ▷ *noun* **1** someone who commands. **2** in the British navy: an officer just below captain in rank. See table at RANK. **3** a high-ranking police officer. **4** a senior member in some orders of knighthood. Also called **knight commander**.

commander in chief ▷ *noun* (***commanders in chief***) the officer in supreme command of a nation's forces.

commanding ▷ *adj* **1** powerful; leading; controlling. **2** in charge. **3** inspiring respect or awe. **4** favourable; giving good views all round □ *a house with a commanding position.*

commandment ▷ *noun* **1 a** a divine command; **b** (**Commandment**) *Authorized Version* one of the 10 rules given to Moses by God as the basis of a good life. **2** *literary* a command.

command module ▷ *noun, space flight* the section of a spacecraft from which operations are directed, and which serves as living quarters for the crew.

commando ▷ *noun* (***commandos***) **1** a unit of soldiers specially trained to carry out dangerous and difficult attacks or raids. **2** a member of such a unit. ◷ 18c: Portuguese, from *commandar* to command.

command paper ▷ *noun* a government document, originally one presented to parliament by command of the monarch. Compare GREEN PAPER, WHITE PAPER.

command performance ▷ *noun* a special performance of a play, etc at the request, and in the presence, of the monarch or head of state.

command post ▷ *noun* a temporary military headquarters.

commedia dell'arte /kɒ'meɪdɪə dɛl'ɑːteɪ/ ▷ *noun* Italian Renaissance comedy with stock characters and plots which are full of intrigue. ◷ 16c: Italian, meaning 'comedy of the arts'.

commemorate /kə'mɛməreɪt/ ▷ *verb* (***commemorated, commemorating***) **1** to honour the memory of (a person or event) with a ceremony, etc. **2** to be a memorial to someone or something. ● **commemoration** *noun*. ● **commemorative** *adj*. ◷ 16c: from Latin *commemorare, commemoratum* to keep in mind.

commence /kə'mɛns/ ▷ *verb* (***commenced, commencing***) *tr & intr* to begin. ◷ 14c: from French *commencier*, from Latin *com-* intensive + *initiare* to begin.

commencement ▷ *noun* **1** a beginning. **2** *N Amer* **a** a graduation ceremony for the conferment of degrees and diplomas; **b** the day on which this ceremony takes place.

commend /kə'mɛnd/ ▷ *verb* (***commended, commending***) to praise someone. ● **commendable** *adj* praiseworthy. ● **commendably** *adverb*. ● **commendatory** *adj* containing praise □ *commendatory letter.* ◷ 14c: from Latin *commendare*, from *com-* intensive + *mandare* to entrust.

■ **commend someone** or **something to someone** **1** to entrust it to them. **2** to recommend or make it acceptable to them □ *if the idea commends itself to you.*

commendation /kɒmən'deɪʃən/ ▷ *noun* **1** praise; approval. **2** a public award or honour.

commensal /kə'mɛnsəl/ *biol* ▷ *adj* said of two organisms of different species: living in close association with each other, with one gaining from the relationship, while the other remains unaffected by it. ▷ *noun* the organism in a commensal relationship which benefits from it. Compare HOST[1] (*noun* 5). ● **commensalism** such a partnership or association. Compare PARASITISM, SYMBIOSIS (sense 1). ◷ 19c in this sense; French, from Latin *commensalis*, from *com-* together + *mensa* table.

commensurable /kə'mɛnʃərəbəl, kə'mɛnsjʊrəbəl/ ▷ *adj* **1** *math* having a common factor. **2** denoting quantities whose ratio is a RATIONAL NUMBER. **3** denoting two or more quantities that can be measured in the same units. ◷ 16c: from Latin *commensurabilis*, from *com-* with + *mensurare* to measure.

commensurate ▷ *adj* **1** in equal proportion to something; appropriate to it. **2** equal in extent, quantity, etc to something. ● **commensurately** *adverb*. ◷ 17c: from Latin *commensuratus*.

comment /'kɒmɛnt/ ▷ *noun* **1** a remark or observation, especially a critical one. **2** talk, discussion or gossip. **3** an explanatory or analytical note on a passage of text. ▷ *verb* (***commented, commenting***) *tr & intr* (*often* **comment on something**) to make observations, remarks, etc. ● **no comment** usually said in response to a question from a journalist, etc: I have nothing to say. ◷ 15c: French.

commentary /'kɒməntərɪ/ ▷ *noun* (***commentaries***) **1** an ongoing description of an event, eg a football match, as it happens, that is broadcast on TV or radio. **2** an explanation accompanying a film, etc. **3** a set of notes explaining or interpreting points in a text, etc. ◷ 16c: from Latin *commentarium* notebook.

commentate ▷ *verb* (***commentated, commentating***) *intr* to give a RUNNING COMMENTARY. ◷ 20c: from COMMENTATOR.

commentator ▷ *noun* **1** a broadcaster who gives a commentary on an event, etc. **2** the writer of a textual commentary. ◷ 17c: Latin, meaning 'inventor' or 'author'.

commerce /'kɒmɜːs/ ▷ *noun* **1 a** the buying and selling of commodities and services; **b** trade, including banking, insurance, etc. **2** *old use* social dealings or communication. ◷ 16c: French, from Latin *commercium* trade.

commercial /kə'mɜːʃəl/ ▷ *adj* **1** relating to, engaged in or used for commerce. **2** profitable; having profit as the main goal. **3** paid for by advertising. ▷ *noun* a radio or TV advertisement. ● **commerciality** *noun*. ● **commercially** *adverb*. ◷ 17c: from Latin *commercium* trade.

commercial break ▷ *noun* on some TV and radio stations: a periodic interruption of programmes to allow the advertising of various products.

Commercial Court ▷ *noun* in England and Wales: a court within the Queen's Bench Division which hears major commercial cases, usually in private.

commercialism ▷ *noun* **1** commercial attitudes and aims. **2** undue emphasis on profit-making.

commercialize or **commercialise** ▷ *verb* (***commercialized, commercializing***) **1** *derisive* to exploit for profit, especially by sacrificing quality. **2** to make commercial. ● **commercialization** *noun*.

commercial traveller ▷ *noun* someone who travels around the country representing a company and selling their goods to other companies.

commercial vehicle ▷ *noun* a vehicle which carries goods or fare-paying passengers.

commie ▷ *noun, adj, colloq derog* short form of COMMUNIST.

comminute /'kɒmɪnjuːt/ ▷ *verb* (***comminuted, comminuting***) *technical* **1** to crush (a solid) into tiny pieces. **2** to divide (eg property) into small portions. ● **comminution** *noun*. ◷ 17c: from Latin *comminuere, comminutum* to lessen.

commis /'kɒmiː/ and **commis chef** ▷ *noun* (*plural* ***commis*** /'kɒmiːz/ or ***commis chefs***) an assistant or trainee waiter or chef. ◷ 20c: French, meaning 'deputy'.

commiserate /kə'mɪzəreɪt/ ▷ *verb* (***commiserated, commiserating***) *tr & intr* (*often* **commiserate with**

someone) to express one's sympathy for them. ● **commiseration** *noun*. ⓒ 17c: from Latin *commiserari*, *commiseratus* from *com-* with + *miserari* to lament.

commissar /kɒmɪ'sɑː(r)/ ▷ *noun* in the former Soviet Union: **1** the head of a government department. **2** a Communist Party official responsible for the political education of military units. ⓒ 20c: from Russian *komissar*, from Latin *commissarius* officer in charge.

commissarial /kɒmɪ'sɛərɪəl, –'sɑːrɪəl/ ▷ *adj* relating to or associated with a commissary. ⓒ 18c.

commissariat /kɒmɪ'sɛərɪət, -'sɑːrɪət/ ▷ *noun* **1** in the army: a department responsible for food supplies. **2** in the former Soviet Union: a government department. ⓒ 18c: from French (sense 1) and Russian (sense 2), from Latin *commissarius* officer in charge.

commissary /'kɒmɪsərɪ/ ▷ *noun* (**commissaries**) **1** in the army: an officer responsible for supplies and provisions. **2** *US* a store supplying provisions and equipment to a military force. **3** *originally US* a canteen serving a film studio, etc. **4** a deputy, especially one representing a bishop. ⓒ 14c: from Latin *commissarius* officer in charge.

commission /kə'mɪʃən/ ▷ *noun* **1 a** a formal or official request to someone to perform a task or duty; **b** the authority to perform such a task or duty; **c** the task or duty performed. **2 a** a military rank above the level of officer; **b** the document conferring this rank. **3** an order for a piece of work, especially a work of art. **4** a board or committee entrusted with a particular task □ *the equal rights commission.* **5** a fee or percentage given to an agent for arranging a sale, etc. **6** the act of committing (eg a crime). ▷ *verb* (**commissioned**, **commissioning**) **1** to give a commission or authority to someone. **2** to grant a military rank above a certain level to someone. **3** to request someone to do something. **4** to place an order for something, eg a work of art, etc. **5** to prepare (a ship) for active service. ● **in** or **out of commission** in or not in use or working condition. ⓒ 14c: French, from Latin *commissio*, from *committere* to commit.

commissionaire /kəmɪʃə'nɛə(r)/ ▷ *noun, chiefly Brit* a uniformed attendant at the door of a cinema, theatre, office or hotel. ⓒ 19c: French.

commissioned officer ▷ *noun* a military officer who holds a commission.

commissioner ▷ *noun* **1** a representative of the government in a district, department, etc. **2** a member of a commission. ● **commissionership** *noun*.

commit /kə'mɪt/ ▷ *verb* (**committed**, **committing**) **1** to carry out or perpetrate (a crime, offence, error, etc). **2** to have someone put in prison or a mental institution. **3** to promise or engage, especially oneself, for some undertaking, etc. **4** to dedicate oneself to a cause, etc from a sense of conviction □ *She committed herself to Christ.* **5** to entrust or give. **6** to send someone for trial in a higher court. ● **commit oneself** to make a definite irrevocable decision. ● **commit something to memory** to memorize it. ⓒ 14c: from Latin *committere* to put together or to join.

commitment ▷ *noun* **1 a** the act of committing someone or oneself; **b** the state of being committed. **2** dedication or devotion; strong conviction. **3** a usually irrevocable undertaking or responsibility. **4** *law* an official order for the imprisonment of someone. Also called **mittimus**.

committal ▷ *noun* **1** the action of committing someone to a prison or mental institution. **2** at a burial: the act of putting the coffin into the grave.

committee /kə'mɪtiː/ ▷ *noun* (**committees**) **1** a group of people selected by and from a larger body, eg a club, to undertake certain duties on its behalf. **2** a body specially appointed to undertake an investigation, enquiry, etc. ⓒ 17c.

committee stage ▷ *noun, politics* the stage between the second and third readings of a parliamentary bill, when it is examined in detail by members sitting in committee.

commode /kə'moʊd/ ▷ *noun* **1** a chair with a hinged seat, designed to conceal a chamber pot. **2** an ornate chest of drawers. ⓒ 18c: French, from Latin *commodus* convenient.

commodious ▷ *adj* comfortably spacious. ● **commodiously** *adverb*. ● **commodiousness** *noun*. ⓒ 15c: from Latin *commodus* convenient.

commodity /kə'mɒdɪtɪ/ ▷ *noun* (**commodities**) **1** something that is bought and sold, especially a manufactured product or raw material. **2** something, eg a quality, from the point of view of its value or importance in society □ *Courtesy is a scarce commodity.* ⓒ 15c: from French *commodité*, from Latin *commoditas* convenience.

commodity market and **commodity exchange** ▷ *noun, econ* a market where buyers and sellers of raw materials eg wool, sugar, coffee, wheat, metals, etc trade.

commodore /'kɒmədɔː(r)/ ▷ *noun* **1** in the navy: an officer just below a rear admiral in rank. See table at RANK. **2** the president of a yacht club. **3** the senior captain in charge of a fleet of merchant ships. ⓒ 17c: perhaps from Dutch, from French *commandeur* commander.

common /'kɒmən/ ▷ *adj* **1** often met with; frequent; familiar □ *a common mistake.* **2** shared by two or more people, things, etc □ *characteristics common to both animals.* **3** publicly owned. **4** said of a standard one has a right to expect □ *common decency.* **5** widespread □ *common knowledge.* **6** *derog* lacking taste or refinement; vulgar. **7 a** said of the ordinary type □ *the common cold*; **b** especially of plants and animals: general or ordinary □ *common toad* □ *common bindweed.* **8** not of high rank or class □ *the common people.* **9** *math* shared by two or more numbers □ *highest common factor.* ▷ *noun* **1** a piece of land that is publicly owned or available for public use. **2** *law* a right to something, or to do something, on someone else's land. **3** *slang* common sense. See also COMMONS. ● **commonly** *adverb*. ● **commonness** *noun*. ● **the common touch** an ability, in someone distinguished by accomplishment or rank, to relate sociably to ordinary people. ● **in common 1** said of two people with regard to their interests, etc: shared. **2** in joint use or ownership □ *a garden owned in common by the residents.* ● **make common cause** to co-operate to achieve a common aim. ⓒ 13c: as *commun*, from French *comun*, from Latin *communis*.

common denominator ▷ *noun* **1** *math* a whole number that is a multiple of each of the DENOMINATORS of two or more VULGAR FRACTIONS, eg 15 is a common denominator of $^1/_3$ and $^3/_5$. See also LOWEST COMMON DENOMINATOR. **2** something that enables comparison, agreement, etc between people or things.

commoner ▷ *noun* **1** someone who is not a member of the nobility. **2** at some English colleges: a student who is not on a scholarship.

Common Era ▷ *noun* (abbreviation **CE**) a culturally neutral term for the present era, reckoned since the birth of Christ, sometimes used instead of ANNO DOMINI. See also BCE.

common fraction see VULGAR FRACTION

common gender ▷ *noun, grammar* the GENDER of such nouns as *doctor*, *scientist*, *baby*, which have only one form that can refer to either sex. See also NEUTER.

common ground ▷ *noun* an area of mutual agreement or shared interest, often used as a starting-point for discussion.

common law ▷ *noun, law* the body of law based on custom and decisions by judges, in contrast to STATUTE law.

common-law ▷ *noun, as adj* denoting the relationship of two people who have lived together as husband and wife for a certain number of years but who have not been through a civil or religious ceremony □ *common-law marriage.*

the Common Market see under EUROPEAN ECONOMIC COMMUNITY

common noun ▷ *noun, grammar* a noun that is not a proper name and which can refer to any member of a class of things, eg *car, table, girl* as opposed to *Paris, John.* Compare PROPER NOUN.

common-or-garden ▷ *adj* ordinary; everyday.

commonplace ▷ *adj* **1** ordinary; everyday. **2** *derog* unoriginal; lacking individuality; trite. ▷ *noun* **1** *derog* a trite comment; a cliché. **2** an everyday occurrence. ⓒ 16c: a translation of the Latin phrase *locus communis* an argument widely used.

common-riding ▷ *noun* in the Scottish Borders: a ceremonial progress by riders on horseback around the boundaries of common land, traditionally intended to deter encroachment by neighbouring landowners and to guard against invasion by the English. See also BEAT THE BOUNDS at BEAT.

common room ▷ *noun* in a college, school, etc: a sitting-room for general use by students or one used by staff.

commons ▷ *plural noun* **1** *historical* (**the commons**) the ordinary people. **2** *old use, facetious* shared food rations. ▷ *singular noun* (**the Commons**) the House of Commons. ● **on short commons** having reduced rations.

common seal ▷ *noun* a true seal native to the N Pacific and N Atlantic oceans, usually grey with dark blotches.

common sense ▷ *noun* practical wisdom and understanding. ● **common-sense** and **common-sensical** ▷ *adj* having or noted for common sense.

common time ▷ *noun, music* a rhythm with four beats to the bar.

the Commonwealth ▷ *noun* (*in full* **the Commonwealth of Nations**) a voluntary association of countries or states which were all formerly ruled by Great Britain.

commonwealth ▷ *noun* **1** a country or state. **2** an association of states that have joined together for their common good. **3** a state in which the people hold power; a republic. **4** a title used by certain US states. ⓒ 16c.

Commonwealth Day ▷ *noun* a public holiday celebrated in many parts of the Commonwealth on the second Monday in March.

Commonwealth of Independent States see CIS

commotion /kəˈmoʊʃən/ ▷ *noun* **1** a disturbance; an upheaval. **2** noisy confusion; uproar. ⓒ 15c: from Latin *commovere* to move.

communal /ˈkɒmjʊnəl, kəˈmjuːnəl/ ▷ *adj* **1** relating or belonging to a community. **2** shared; owned in common. **3** relating to a commune or communes. ● **communally** *adverb.* ⓒ 19c: French, from Latin *communalis,* from *communis* common.

commune[1] /ˈkɒmjuːn/ ▷ *noun* **1** a number of unrelated families and individuals living together as a mutually supportive community, with shared accommodation, supplies, responsibilities, etc. **2** in some European countries: the smallest administrative unit locally governed. ⓒ 18c: French, from Latin *communis* common.

commune[2] /kəˈmjuːn/ ▷ *verb* (**communed, communing**) *intr* **1** to communicate intimately or confidentially. **2** to get close to or relate spiritually to (eg nature). ⓒ 16c in this sense; from French *comuner* to share, from *comun* common.

communicable /kəˈmjuːnɪkəbəl/ ▷ *adj* capable of being communicated. ⓒ 16c: French, from Latin *communicabilis,* from *communicare* to share or impart.

communicable disease ▷ *noun, pathol* an infectious or contagious disease that can be transmitted from one organism to another by direct physical contact, infected airborne droplets, etc.

communicant /kəˈmjuːnɪkənt/ ▷ *noun* **1** *Christianity* someone who receives communion. **2** someone who communicates or informs. ⓒ 16c: from Latin *communicare* to partake or impart.

communicate /kəˈmjuːnɪkeɪt/ ▷ *verb* (**communicated, communicating**) **1** *tr & intr* **a** to impart (information, ideas, etc); to make something known or understood; **b** to get in touch. **2** to pass on or transmit (a disease, feeling, etc). **3** *intr* to understand someone; to have a comfortable social relationship. **4** *intr* said of rooms, etc: to be connected □ *a communicating door.* **5** *intr, Christianity* to receive communion. ⓒ 16c: from Latin *communicare, communicatum* to share.

communication ▷ *noun* **1** **a** the process or act of communicating; **b** the exchanging or imparting of ideas and information, etc. **2** a piece of information, a letter or a message. **3** social contact. **4** (**communications**) the various electronic processes by which information is conveyed from one person or place to another, especially by means of wires, cables or radio waves. **5** (**communications**) means or routes used for moving troops or supplies. **6** (**communications**) the science and activity of transmitting information, etc.

communication cord ▷ *noun, Brit* in a railway carriage: a chain or cord which can be pulled in an emergency to stop the train.

communications satellite ▷ *noun, astron* an artificial satellite which orbits the Earth relaying radio, TV and telephone signals.

communication theory ▷ *noun* the application of information theory to human communication in general, where communication is seen as involving an information source which encodes a message to be transmitted through a channel to a receiver, where it is decoded and has an effect.

communicative /kəˈmjuːnɪkətɪv/ ▷ *adj* **1** sociable; talkative. **2** relating to communication □ *communicative skills.* ● **communicatively** *adverb.*

communion /kəˈmjuːnɪən/ ▷ *noun* **1** the sharing of thoughts, beliefs or feelings. **2** a group of people sharing the same religious beliefs. **3** (*also* **Holy Communion**) *Christianity* **a** a church service at which bread and wine are taken as symbols of Christ's body and blood; **b** the consecrated bread and wine. See also EUCHARIST. ⓒ 14c: from Latin *communio* mutual participation.

communiqué /kəˈmjuːnɪkeɪ/ ▷ *noun* (**communiqués**) an official bulletin, communication or announcement. ⓒ 19c: French, meaning 'something communicated', from *communiquer* to communicate.

communism /ˈkɒmjʊnɪzəm/ ▷ *noun* **1** a political ideology advocating a classless society, the abolition of private ownership and all sources of wealth and production being collectively owned and controlled by the people. **2** (**Communism**) a political movement founded on the principles of communism set out by Karl Marx. **3** the political and social system established on these principles in the former Soviet Union and other countries. ⓒ 19c: from French *communisme,* from *commun* common.

communist ▷ *noun* **1** a supporter of or believer in communism. **2** (*often* **Communist**) a member of a communist party. Often shortened to **commie.** ▷ *adj* **1** relating to communism. **2** believing in or favouring communism. Often shortened to **commie**.

communistic *adj* **1** believing in or favouring communism. **2** involving or favouring communal living and ownership.

communitarian /kəmjuːnɪ'tɛərɪən/ ▷ *noun* **1** a member of a community. **2** an advocate of community life.

community /kə'mjuːnɪtɪ/ ▷ *noun* (***communities***) **1 a** the group of people living in a particular place; **b** the place in which they live. **2** a group of people bonded together by a common religion, nationality or occupation □ *the Asian community.* **3** a religious or spiritual fellowship of people living together. **4** the quality or fact of being shared or common □ *community of interests.* **5** a group of states with common interests. **6** the public; society in general. **7** *biol* a naturally occurring group of different plant or animal species that occupy the same habitat and interact with each other. ⓘ 14c: from Latin *communitas* fellowship, from *communis* common.

community centre ▷ *noun* a place where members of a community may meet for social, sporting or educational activities.

community charge ▷ *noun, formerly* in Britain: a tax levied on individuals to pay for local services, known informally as the **poll tax**. See also RATES, COUNCIL TAX.

community council ▷ *noun* a group of lay people elected to look after local interests. ⓘ 20c.

community home ▷ *noun* in Britain: **1** an institution in which children are placed by local authorities when they are unable to live with their parents. **2** a similar institution for young offenders.

community policing ▷ *noun* a type of law enforcement whereby a police officer is assigned exclusively to a particular area in order to become familiar with it and with the residents.

community school and **community college** ▷ *noun, originally US* a school or college which is geared towards providing education for the whole community, irrespective of age.

community service ▷ *noun* unpaid work of benefit to the local community, sometimes prescribed for offenders as an alternative to a prison sentence.

community singing ▷ *noun* organized singing at a large gathering, with everyone taking part.

community work ▷ *noun* a form of social work that serves the needs of members of the local community.

commutate /'kɒmjʊteɪt/ ▷ *verb* (***commutated, commutating***) *electronics* to change an alternating current into a direct one and vice versa. ● **commutator** *noun* a device for changing electrical currents.

commutation ▷ *noun* **1** the act of being commuted or exchanged. **2** the act of changing an electrical current.

commutative /kə'mjuːtətɪv, 'kɒmjʊteɪtɪv/ ▷ *adj, math* said of an arithmetical process: performed on two quantities, the order of which does not affect the result, eg addition and multiplication, but not subtraction and division.

commute /kə'mjuːt/ ▷ *verb* (***commuted, commuting***) **1** *intr* to travel regularly between two places which are a significant distance apart, especially between home and work in a city, etc. **2** to alter (a criminal sentence) to one less severe. **3** to substitute; to convert. **4** to exchange (one type of payment) for another, eg a single payment for one made in instalments. ● **commutable** *adj.* ● **commutation** *noun.* ● **commuter** *noun* someone who regularly travels a significant distance between home and work. ⓘ 17c: from Latin *commutare* to alter or exchange.

compact[1] ▷ *adj* /'kɒmpakt/ **1** firm and dense in form or texture. **2** small, but with all essentials neatly contained. **3** neatly concise, packed tightly together. ▷ *verb* /kəm'pakt/ (***compacted, compacting***) to compress. ▷ *noun* /'kɒmpakt/ a small case for women's face powder, usually including a mirror. ● **compaction** *noun.* ● **compactly** *adverb.* ● **compactness** *noun.* ⓘ 14c: from Latin *compactus*, from *compingere* to put together closely.

compact[2] /'kɒmpakt/ ▷ *noun* a contract or agreement. ⓘ 16c: from Latin *compactum*, from *compacisci* to covenant together.

compact disc ▷ *noun* (abbreviation **CD**) a small aluminium disc used to record audio and/or visual information in the form of digital data, which can be played back on a specially designed machine. See also CD-ROM.

compact disc interactive see CD-I

compact disc read-only memory see CD-ROM

companion[1] /kəm'panjən/ ▷ *noun* **1** a friend, comrade or frequent associate. **2** someone who accompanies someone on a journey. **3** *historical* a woman employed by another woman to live or travel with her and to keep her company. **4** especially as a title: a book of advice; a handbook or guide. **5** one of a pair of matching objects. **6** (**Companion**) an honourable title denoting a low-ranking member of any of various orders of knighthood. ● **companionship** *noun.* ⓘ 13c: from French *compagnon*, from Latin *companio*, literally 'food-sharer', from *com-* together + *panis* bread.

companion[2] /kəm'panjən/ ▷ *noun, naut* a hatch admitting light to a cabin or lower deck. ⓘ 18c: from Dutch *kompanje* quarterdeck, from Italian *compagna* storeroom for provisions.

companionable ▷ *adj* friendly; sociable; comfortable as a companion. ● **companionably** *adverb.*

companion set ▷ *noun* a set of tools, consisting of a brush, poker, shovel and tongs, which are kept on a stand by the fireplace and used to tend a coal fire.

companionway ▷ *noun* on a ship: a staircase from a deck to a cabin, or between decks.

company /'kʌmpənɪ/ ▷ *noun* (***companies***) **1** the presence of another person or other people; companionship. **2** the presence of guests or visitors, or the people involved □ *expecting company.* **3** one's friends, companions or associates □ *get into bad company.* **4** a business organization. **5** a troop of actors or entertainers. **6** a military unit of about 120 men. **7** a ship's crew. **8** a gathering of people, at a social function, etc. ● **be good** or **bad company** to be an entertaining, or dreary, companion. ● **be in good company** to be not the only one in the same situation □ *You failed your exam? Well, you're in good company!* ● **in company with ...** together with ...; along with ... □ *in company with other reasons.* ● **keep someone company** to act as their companion. ● **part company with someone 1** to separate from them. **2** to disagree with them. ⓘ 13c: from French *compaignie*; see COMPANION.

company secretary ▷ *noun* a senior member of a business organization, concerned with financial and legal matters.

comparable /'kɒmpərəbəl, kəm'parəbəl/ ▷ *adj* **1** being of the same or equivalent kind. **2** able to be compared; similar enough to allow comparison. ● **comparability** *noun.* ● **comparably** *adverb.*

comparative /kəm'paratɪv/ ▷ *adj* **1** judged by comparison; as compared with others. **2** relating to, or using the method of, comparison. **3** as observed by comparing one another; relative □ *their comparative strengths.* **4** *grammar* said of adjectives and adverbs: in the form denoting a greater degree of the quality in question but not the greatest, formed either by using the suffix *-er* or the word *more*, eg *larger* or *more usual.* Compare POSITIVE, SUPERLATIVE. ▷ *noun, grammar* **1** a comparative adjective or adverb. **2** the comparative form of a word. ● **comparatively** *adverb.* ⓘ 15c: from Latin *comparativus*, from *comparare* to match.

comparative history ▷ *noun* a form of historical inquiry that studies the development of different societies within the same period of history, or similar phenomena across different periods, rather than concentrating on the development of one particular nation.

comparative linguistics ▷ *noun* **1** the study of the similarities and differences between languages and dialects. **2** the comparison of features found in their various forms in the historical development of a single language.

comparative literature ▷ *noun* the study of the literatures of different languages and nations and the relationships and similarities which may exist between them.

compare /kəm'pɛə(r)/ ▷ *verb* (***compared, comparing***) **1** to examine (items, etc) to see what differences or similarities they have. **2** *intr* (*often* **compare with something** or **someone**) to be comparable with it or them □ *He can't compare with his predecessor in ability.* **3** *intr* to relate (well, badly, etc) when examined □ *The two books compare well.* **4** *grammar* to state the positive, comparative and superlative forms often adjective or adverb. ● **beyond** or **without compare** *formal* without equal; incomparable. ● **compare notes** to exchange ideas and opinions. ⊙ 15c: from Latin *comparare* to match.

■ **compare someone** or **something to someone** or **something else** to liken them to each other □ *compare her to an angel.*

comparison /kəm'parɪsən, -zən/ ▷ *noun* **1** the process of, an act of or a reasonable basis for, comparing □ *There can be no comparison between them.* **2** *grammar* the POSITIVE (sense 14), COMPARATIVE (*adj* 4) and SUPERLATIVE (*adj* 1) forms of adjectives and adverbs. Also called **degrees of comparison**. ⊙ 14c: from French *comparaison*, from Latin *comparare* to match.

compartment /kəm'pɑːtmənt, kɒm-/ ▷ *noun* **1** a separated-off or enclosed section. **2** any of several enclosed sections into which some railway carriages are divided. ● **compartmental** /-'mɛntəl/ *adj*. ⊙ 16c: from French *compartiment*, from Latin *compartiri* to divide.

compartmentalize or **compartmentalise** /kɒmpɑːt'mɛntəlaɪz/ ▷ *verb* (***compartmentalized, compartmentalizing***) to divide, distribute or force into categories. ● **compartmentalization** *noun*.

compass /'kʌmpəs/ ▷ *noun* (***compasses***) **1** any device for finding direction, especially one consisting of a magnetized needle that swings freely on a pivot and points to magnetic north, from which true north can be calculated. See also GYROCOMPASS. **2** (*usually* **compasses**) a device consisting of two hinged legs, for drawing circles, measuring distances on maps, etc. Also called **pair of compasses**. **3** range or scope □ *within the compass of philosophy.* **4** *music* said of a voice or instrument: the range between the highest and lowest possible notes. ▷ *verb* (***compasses, compassed, compassing***) **1** to pass or go round. **2** to surround or enclose. **3** to accomplish or obtain. **4** to comprehend. ⊙ 13c: from French *compas*, from *compasser* to measure.

compassion /kəm'paʃən/ ▷ *noun* a feeling of sorrow and pity for someone in trouble. ● **compassionate** *adj* **1** inclined to pity or mercy. **2** merciful. ● **compassionately** *adverb*. ⊙ 14c: French, from Latin *compassio*, from *com*- with + *pati, passus* to suffer.

compassionate leave ▷ *noun* special absence from work granted in cases of bereavement.

compassion fatigue ▷ *noun* progressive disinclination to show compassion because of continued or excessive exposure to deserving cases.

compatible /kəm'patɪbəl/ ▷ *adj* (*often* **compatible with something** or **someone**) **1** able to associate or coexist agreeably. **2** consistent or congruous □ *His actions were not compatible with his beliefs.* **3** *computing* said of a program or device: capable of being used with a particular computer system, especially one produced by another manufacturer. **4** *engineering* said of a device or piece of machinery: capable of being used in conjunction with another, especially a newer version, without the need for special modification. ● **compatibility** *noun*. ● **compatibly** *adverb*. ⊙ 16c: French, from Latin *compatibilis*, from *compati* to suffer with.

compatriot /kəm'peɪtrɪət, -'patrɪət/ ▷ *noun* someone from one's own country; a fellow-citizen. ⊙ 17c: from Latin *compatriota*, from *com*- with + *patria* one's country.

compeer /kəm'pɪə(r)/ ▷ *noun* an equal; a companion or comrade. ⊙ 13c: from French *comper*, from Latin *com*- with + *per* equal or peer.

compel /kəm'pɛl/ ▷ *verb* (***compelled, compelling***) **1** to force; to drive. **2** to arouse; to elicit or evoke □ *Their plight compels sympathy.* ⊙ 14c: from Latin *compellere*, from *com*- together + *pellere* to force.

compelling ▷ *adj* **1** powerful; forcing one to agree, etc. **2** irresistibly fascinating. ● **compellingly** *adverb*.

compendious /kəm'pɛndɪəs/ ▷ *adj* concise but comprehensive. ● **compendiously** *adverb*. ● **compendiousness** *noun*. ⊙ 14c: from Latin *compendiosus*, from *compendium* summary.

compendium /kəm'pɛndɪəm/ ▷ *noun* (***compendiums*** or ***compendia*** /-dɪə/) **1** a concise summary; an abridgement. **2** a collection of boardgames, puzzles, etc in a single container. ⊙ 16c: Latin, meaning 'that which is weighed together', from *com*- together + *pendere* to weigh.

compensate /'kɒmpənseɪt/ ▷ *verb* (***compensated, compensating***) **1** to make amends to someone for loss, injury or wrong, especially by a suitable payment. **2** *intr* (*often* **compensate for something**) to make up for (a disadvantage, loss, imbalance, etc). ● **compensatory** *adj*. ⊙ 17c: from Latin *compensare, compensatum* to counterbalance.

compensation /kɒmpən'seɪʃən/ ▷ *noun* **1** the process of compensating. **2** something that compensates. **3** a sum of money awarded to make up for loss, injury, etc.

compere or **compère** /'kɒmpɛə(r)/ ▷ *noun* someone who hosts a radio or television show, introduces performers, etc. ▷ *verb* (***compered, compering***) *tr & intr* to act as compere for (a show). ⊙ 1930s: French, meaning 'godfather'.

compete /kəm'piːt/ ▷ *verb* (***competed, competing***) *intr* **1** to take part in a contest. **2** to strive or struggle □ *compete with other firms.* **3** said of a product, firm, etc: to give good value, be reasonably cheap, etc when compared to market rivals. ⊙ 17c: from Latin *competere* to coincide, ask for or seek.

competence /'kɒmpətəns/ and **competency** ▷ *noun* **1** capability; efficiency. **2** legal authority or capability. **3** *old use* sufficient income to live comfortably.

competent ▷ *adj* **1** efficient. **2** having sufficient skill or training to do something. **3** legally capable. ● **competently** *adverb*. ⊙ 14c: from Latin *competere* to meet, be sufficient.

competition /kɒmpə'tɪʃən/ ▷ *noun* **1** an event in which people compete. **2** the process or fact of competing. **3** rivals, eg in business or their products. **4** *biol* in a community of plants or animals: the simultaneous demand for the same limited resource, eg light or water, by two or more organisms or species, which leads to a struggle for continued survival. ⊙ 16c: from Latin *competitio* meeting together.

competitive /kəm'pɛtɪtɪv/ ▷ *adj* **1** involving rivalry. **2** characterized by competition; aggressive; ambitious. **3** said of a price or product: reasonably cheap; comparing well with those of market rivals. ● **competitively** *adverb*.

• **competitiveness** *noun*. ◷ 19c: from Latin *competere* to meet together.

competitor /kəm'pɛtɪtə(r)/ ▷ *noun* **a** a person, team, firm or product that competes; **b** a rival. ◷ 16c: Latin, from *competere* to meet together.

compilation /kɒmpɪ'leɪʃən, kɒmpaɪ'leɪʃən/ ▷ *noun* **1** the process of compiling. **2** a book, recording, etc that has been compiled.

compile /kəm'paɪl/ ▷ *verb* (***compiled, compiling***) **1 a** to collect and organize (information, etc) from different sources; **b** to produce (a list, reference book, etc) from information collected. **2** *computing* to create (a set of instructions written in machine code) from a source program written in a high-level programming language, using a compiler. ◷ 14c: from Latin *compilare* to plunder.

compiler ▷ *noun* **1** someone who compiles information, etc. **2** *computing* a program that converts a source program written in a high-level programming language into a set of instructions written in machine code that can be acted on by computer.

complacent /kəm'pleɪsənt/ ▷ *adj* **1** self-satisfied; smug. **2** too easily satisfied; disinclined to worry. • **complacence** or **complacency** *noun*. • **complacently** *adverb*. ◷ 15c as *complacence*, 18c as *complacent*: from Latin *complacere* to be pleasing.

complain /kəm'pleɪn/ ▷ *verb* (***complained, complaining***) *intr* to express dissatisfaction or displeasure. • **complainer** *noun*. • **complaining** *adj*. • **complainingly** *adverb*. ◷ 14c: from French *complaindre*, from Latin *complangere* to bewail.

■ **complain of something** to say that one is suffering from (a pain, disease, etc).

complainant ▷ *noun, law* a plaintiff.

complaint ▷ *noun* **1** the act of complaining. **2** an expression of dissatisfaction. **3** a grievance. **4** a disorder, illness, etc.

complaisant /kəm'pleɪzənt/ ▷ *adj* eager to please; obliging; amenable. • **complaisance** *noun*. • **complaisantly** *adverb*. ◷ 17c: French, from Latin *complacere* to be very pleasing to.

complement ▷ *noun* /'kɒmplɪmənt/ **1** something that completes or perfects; something that provides a needed balance or contrast. **2** (*often* **full complement**) the number or quantity required to make something complete, eg the crew of a ship. **3** *grammar* a word or phrase added to a verb to complete the PREDICATE of a sentence, eg *dark* in *It grew dark*. **4** *math* in set theory: all the members of a universal set that do not belong to a specified set S. **5** *geom* the amount by which an angle or arc falls short of a right angle or QUADRANT 4. **6** *biol* in blood serum: a group of proteins that combine with antibodies and thereby enhance the destruction of foreign particles following an immune response. ▷ *verb* /'kɒmplɪmɛnt/ (***complemented, complementing***) to be a complement to something. ◷ 14c: from Latin *complementum*, from *complere* to fill up.

complement, complementary

There is often a spelling confusion between **complement** and **compliment**, and between **complementary** and **complimentary**.

complementary ▷ *adj* **1** serving as a complement to something. **2** said of two or more things: complementing each other. **3** *physics* denoting either of a pair of coloured lights that, when mixed together in the correct intensities, produce the sensation of white light. • **complementarily** *adverb*.

complementary angle ▷ *noun* one of a pair of angles whose sum is 90 degrees. Compare CONJUGATE ANGLE, SUPPLEMENTARY ANGLE.

complementary medicine see ALTERNATIVE MEDICINE

complete /kəm'pliːt/ ▷ *adj* **1** whole; finished; with nothing missing. **2** thorough; utter; absolute; total ▫ ***a complete triumph***. **3** perfect. ▷ *verb* (***completed, completing***) **1 a** to finish; **b** to make complete or perfect. **2** to fill in (a form). • **completely** *adverb*. • **completeness** *noun*. • **completion** *noun*. • **complete with …** having the additional feature of … ▫ ***The car came complete with tinted windows.*** ◷ 14c: from Latin *complere, completum* to fill up.

complex /'kɒmplɛks/ ▷ *adj* **1** composed of many interrelated parts. **2** complicated; involved; tangled. ▷ *noun* (***complexes***) **1** something made of interrelating parts, eg a multi-purpose building ▫ ***a leisure complex***. **2** *psychoanal* a set of repressed thoughts and emotions that strongly influence an individual's behaviour and attitudes. **3** *colloq* an obsession or phobia. ◷ 17c: from Latin *complexus*, from *complectere* to encompass, to embrace.

complexion /kəm'plɛkʃən/ ▷ *noun* **1** the colour or appearance of the skin, especially of the face. **2** character or appearance ▫ ***That puts a different complexion on the matter.*** ◷ 16c: French, from Latin *complexio* combination.

complexity ▷ *noun* (***complexities***) **1** the quality of being complex. **2** a complication; an intricacy.

complex number ▷ *noun, math* the sum of a real and an imaginary number.

complex sentence ▷ *noun, grammar* a sentence which contains more than one clause.

compliance /kəm'plaɪəns/ ▷ *noun* **1** yielding. **2** agreement; assent. **3** submission. ◷ 17c: see COMPLY.

compliant /kəm'plaɪənt/ ▷ *adj* inclined to comply with or yield to the wishes of others; obedient; submissive. • **compliantly** *adverb*.

complicate /'kɒmplɪkeɪt/ ▷ *verb* (***complicated, complicating***) to add difficulties or intricacies to something; to make complex or involved. ◷ 17c: from Latin *complicare, complicatum* to fold together.

complicated ▷ *adj* **1** difficult to understand or deal with. **2** intricate; complex. **3** said of a fracture in a bone: accompanied by damage to surrounding tissue.

complication ▷ *noun* **1** the process of becoming complicated. **2** a circumstance that causes difficulties. **3** *pathol* a second and possibly worse disease or disorder that arises during the course of, and often as a result of, an existing one.

complicity /kəm'plɪsətɪ/ ▷ *noun* the state of being an accomplice in a crime or wrongdoing. ◷ 17c: from Latin *complex* closely connected.

compliment ▷ *noun* /'kɒmplɪmənt/ **1** an expression of praise, admiration or approval. **2** a gesture implying approval ▫ ***paid her the compliment of dancing with her.*** **3** (**compliments**) formal regards accompanying a gift, etc. ▷ *verb* /'kɒmplɪmɛnt/ (***complimented, complimenting***) (*often* **compliment someone on something**) **1** to congratulate them for it. **2** to praise them; to pay them a compliment. • **compliments of the season** *formal* a greeting appropriate to a certain time of the year, especially Christmas.

compliment, complimentary

There is often a spelling confusion between **compliment** and **complement**, and between **complimentary** and **complementary**.

complimentary ▷ *adj* **1** paying a compliment; admiring or approving. **2** given free.

compline or **complin** /'kɒmplɪn/ ▷ *noun now* especially *RC Church* the seventh of the CANONICAL HOURS, completing the set hours for prayer. ◷ 13c: from French *complie*, from Latin *completa hora* complete hour.

comply /kəm'plaɪ/ ▷ *verb* (***complies***, ***complied***, ***complying***) *intr* (*usually* **comply with something**) to act in obedience to an order, command, request, etc; to agree. ◷ 17c: from Italian *complire*, from Lating *complere* to fill up.

component /kəm'pounənt/ ▷ *noun* any of the parts or elements that make up a machine, engine, instrument, etc. ▷ *adj* functioning as one of the parts of something; constituent. • **componential** /kɒmpou'nɛnʃəl/ *adj*. ◷ 17c: from Latin *componere* to assemble into a whole.

componential analysis /kɒmpə'nɛnʃəl —/ ▷ *noun*, *semantics* the analysis of vocabulary into a series of basic identifying features or 'components' of meaning, eg *woman* could be analysed using the components 'female', 'adult' and 'human'.

comport /'kɒmpɔːt/ ▷ *verb* (***comported***, ***comporting***) (*always* **comport oneself**) to behave in a specified way. • **comportment** *noun* behaviour. ◷ 16c: from Latin *comportare* to carry together.

■ **comport with something** to suit or be appropriate to it.

compose /kəm'pouz/ ▷ *verb* (***composed***, ***composing***) **1** *tr & intr* to create (music). **2** to write (a poem, letter, article, etc). **3** to make up or constitute something. **4** to arrange as a balanced, artistic whole **5** to calm (oneself); to bring (thoughts, etc) under control. **6** to settle (differences between people in dispute). **7** *printing* to arrange (type) or set (a page, etc) in type ready for printing. ◷ 16c: from French *composer*, from Latin *componere* to put together.

composed /-zɪdlɪ/ ▷ *adj* said of a person: calm; controlled. • **composedly** /-zɪdlɪ/ *adverb*.

composer ▷ *noun* someone who composes, especially music.

composite /'kɒmpəzɪt, kɒm'pɒzɪt/ ▷ *adj* **1** made up of different parts, materials or styles. **2** *bot* belonging or relating to the *Compositae* (see noun 1 below) family. ▷ *noun* **1** *bot* a member of the largest family of flowering plants *Compositae* with a flower head consisting of a crowd of tiny florets often surrounded by a circle of bracts, eg daisy. **2** *chem* a combination of two or more materials which has superior properties to any of its individual components. **3** *archit* (*often* **Composite**) the most decorative of the five main orders (see ORDER *noun* 19) of architecture. Compare CORINTHIAN 2, DORIC, IONIC, TUSCAN. ▷ *verb* (***composited***, ***compositing***) to pool and combine proposals from local branches eg of a political party, etc, so as to produce a satisfactory list for discussion at a national level. ◷ 16c: from Latin *compositus*, from *componere* to put together.

composite cinematography ▷ *noun*, *cinema* motion picture photography involving the combination and blending of images from two or more different sources, eg live actors and miniature or painted settings.

composition /kɒmpə'zɪʃən/ ▷ *noun* **1** something composed, especially a musical or literary work. **2** the process of composing. **3** *art* arrangement, especially with regard to balance and visual effect □ *photographic composition*. **4** *old use* a school essay. **5** the constitution of something. **6** a synthetic material of any of various kinds. **7** *printing* the arrangement of pages of type ready for printing.

compositor /kɒm'pɒzɪtə(r)/ ▷ *noun*, *printing* someone who sets or arranges pages of type ready for printing.

compos mentis /'kɒmpɒs 'mɛntɪs/ ▷ *adj*, *law* sound in mind; perfectly rational. ◷ 17c: Latin.

compost /'kɒmpɒst/ ▷ *noun* a mixture of decomposed organic substances such as rotting vegetable matter, etc, which is used to enrich soil and nourish plants. Also *as adj* □ *compost heap*. ▷ *verb* (***composted***, ***composting***) **1** to treat with compost. **2** to convert (decaying organic matter) into compost. ◷ 14c: from Latin *composita*, from *componere* to put together.

composure /kəm'pouʒə(r)/ ▷ *noun* mental and emotional calmness; self-control. ◷ 17c: from COMPOSE.

compound[1] /'kɒmpaund/ ▷ *noun* **1** (*in full* **chemical compound**) *chem* a substance composed of two or more elements combined in fixed proportions and held together by chemical bonds. **2** something composed of two or more ingredients or parts. **3** a word made up of two or more words, eg *tablecloth*. Compare DERIVATIVE (*noun* 2). ▷ *adj* **1** composed of a number of parts or ingredients. **2** *grammar* said of a sentence: made up of two or more main clauses. ▷ *verb* /kəm'paund/ (***compounded***, ***compounding***) **1 a** to make (especially something bad) much worse; **b** to complicate or add to (a difficulty, error, etc). **2 a** to mix or combine (ingredients); **b** to make up (a mixture, etc) by doing this. **3** *law* to agree to overlook (an offence, etc) in return for payment. **4** *tr & intr* (*often* **compound with someone**) **a** to come to an agreement with them, especially a financial one; **b** to settle (a debt, etc) for less than the amount which is owed. ◷ 14c: from French *compondre*, from Latin *componere* to put together.

compound[2] /'kɒmpaund/ ▷ *noun* **1** in China, India, etc: an area enclosed by a wall or fence, containing a house or factory. **2 a** an enclosed area in a prison, used for a particular purpose; **b** a similar area in a concentration camp, prisoner-of-war camp, etc. **3** in S Africa: accommodation in which Black labourers are housed. ◷ 17c: probably from Malay *kampong* village.

compound eye ▷ *noun* in insects: an eye made up of many separate units.

compound fracture ▷ *noun*, *medicine* a type of bone fracture in which the overlying skin is pierced by the broken bone. Also called **open fracture**. Compare SIMPLE FRACTURE.

compound interest ▷ *noun* interest calculated on the original sum of money borrowed and on any interest already accumulated. Compare SIMPLE INTEREST.

compound time ▷ *noun*, *music* a TIME (*noun* 18) that has three, or a multiple of three, beats to a bar.

comprehend /kɒmprɪ'hɛnd/ ▷ *verb* (***comprehended***, ***comprehending***) **1 a** to understand; to grasp with the mind; **b** to envisage. **2** to include. ◷ 14c: from Latin *comprehendere* to grasp or seize.

comprehensible ▷ *adj* capable of being understood. • **comprehensibility** *noun*. • **comprehensibly** *adverb*. ◷ 16c: from Latin *comprehensibilis*.

comprehension ▷ *noun* **1 a** the process or power of understanding; **b** the scope or range of someone's knowledge or understanding. **2** a school exercise for testing students' understanding of a passage of text. ◷ 16c: from Latin *comprehensio*.

comprehensive ▷ *adj* **1** covering or including a large area or scope. **2** said of a school or education: providing teaching for pupils of all abilities aged between 11 and 18. ▷ *noun* a comprehensive school. • **comprehensiveness** *noun*. ◷ 17c: from Latin *comprehensivus*.

comprehensive school *noun* a school for pupils of all abilities aged between 11 and 18.

compress ▷ *verb* /kəm'prɛs/ (***compresses***, ***compressed***, ***compressing***) **1** to press, squeeze or squash together. **2** to reduce in bulk; to condense. **3** *computing* to pack (data) into the minimum possible space in computer memory. ▷ *noun* /'kɒmprɛs/ (***compresses***) a cloth or pad soaked in water and pressed against a part of the body to reduce swelling, stop bleeding, etc. • **compressible** /-'prɛsɪbəl/ *adj*. • **compressibility** *noun*. • **compressive** *adj*. ◷ 14c: from Latin *comprimere*, *compressum* to squeeze together.

compressed air ▷ *noun* air at more than atmospheric pressure.

compression /kəm'prɛʃən/ ▷ *noun* **1** the process of compressing or the state of being compressed. **2** the reduction in the volume of a substance, especially a gas, as a result of an increase in pressure. **3** the stroke that compresses the gases in an internal-combustion engine.

compressor ▷ *noun, engineering* a device that compresses a gas, especially air, by raising its pressure and decreasing its volume.

comprise /kəm'praɪz/ ▷ *verb* (***comprised***, ***comprising***) **1** to contain, include or consist of something specified. **2** to go together to make up something. ◷ 15c: from French *compris*, from Latin *comprehendere* to comprehend.

comprise

- When you say that A comprises Bs, you mean that Bs are the parts or elements of A:

✓ *The village school comprises one old building dating back to 1868 and two modern buildings.*

- Because it means the same as **consist of**, it is sometimes confused with this and followed by 'of', but this use is ungrammatical:

✗ *The instructions comprised of two sheets of A5 paper.*

compromise /'kɒmprəmaɪz/ ▷ *noun* **1** a settlement of differences agreed upon after concessions have been made on each side. **2** anything of an intermediate type which comes halfway between two opposing stages. ▷ *verb* (***compromised***, ***compromising***) **1** *intr* to make concessions; to reach a compromise. **2** to endanger or expose to scandal, by acting indiscreetly. **3 a** to settle (a dispute) by making concessions; **b** to relax (principles, etc). ◷ 15c: from French *compromis*, from Latin *compromittere* to promise reciprocally.

comptroller see CONTROLLER

compulsion /kɒm'pʌlʃən/ ▷ *noun* **1** the act of compelling or condition of being compelled. **2** an irresistible urge to perform a certain action, especially an irrational one. **3** *psychol* an action or ritual that is repeated many times, usually against the will, and which usually represents a form of OBSESSION (sense 2). ◷ 15c: French, from Latin *compulsio*, from *compellere* to compel.

compulsive ▷ *adj* **1** having the power to compel. **2** said of an action: resulting from a compulsion. **3** said of a person: acting on a compulsion. **4** said of a book, film, etc: holding the attention; fascinating. ● **compulsively** *adverb*. ◷ 17c: from Latin *compulsivus*.

compulsive, compulsory

These words are sometimes confused with each other.

compulsory /kəm'pʌlsərɪ/ ▷ *adj* **1** required by the rules, law, etc; obligatory. **2** involving compulsion. ● **compulsorily** *adverb*. ● **compulsoriness** *noun*. ◷ 16c: from Latin *compulsorius*.

compulsory purchase ▷ *noun* the purchase of property or land required for some public project, etc by a local authority, irrespective of the wishes of the owner.

compunction /kəm'pʌŋkʃən/ ▷ *noun* a feeling of guilt, remorse or regret. ● **compunctious** *adj*. ◷ 14c: from Latin *compungere* to prick sharply or sting.

computation /kɒmpjʊ'teɪʃən/ ▷ *noun* **1** the process or act of calculating or computing. **2** a result calculated or computed.

computational ▷ *adj* **1** involving calculation or computing. **2** denoting an error caused by arithmetical rounding of figures.

computational linguistics ▷ *noun* the application of the techniques and concepts used in computer science to the analysis of language, with special reference to artificial intelligence and information retrieval.

compute /kəm'pjuːt/ ▷ *verb* (***computed***, ***computing***) *tr & intr* **1** to calculate, estimate or reckon, especially with the aid of a computer. **2** to carry out (a computer operation). ● **computable** *adj*. ● **computing** see separate entry. ◷ 17c: from Latin *computare* to reckon.

computer ▷ *noun* an electronic device which processes data at great speed according to a PROGRAM (see under PROGRAMME) stored within the device. See also ANALOGUE (*adj*), DIGITAL (sense 2).

computer-aided design ▷ *noun* (abbreviation **CAD**) the use of a computer system to create and edit design drawings, by employing many of the techniques of COMPUTER GRAPHICS.

computerate /kəm'pjuːtərεɪt/ ▷ *adj* computer literate. ◷ 1980s: modelled on *literate*.

computer crime ▷ *noun* crime such as embezzlement which is committed through the manipulation of company finances, etc using a computer.

computer dating ▷ *noun* the introduction of possible romantic partners by an agency, by entering data supplied by clients into a computer which then matches them up according to common interests, etc.

computer game ▷ *noun, computing* a game on cassette, cartridge, disk or CD which is played on a home computer, with the player manipulating moving images on the screen by pressing certain keys, or using a control pad or joystick.

computer-generated ▷ *adj* said of an image, etc: produced by using a computer program.

computer generation ▷ *noun* the production of images, etc using a computer program.

computer generations ▷ *plural noun* five broad groups used to denote the different eras of technological development of digital computers, from **first-generation** (1945–55) denoting the early type of calculating and computing machines using THERMIONIC VALVES, to **fifth-generation** denoting the kind of computer expected to incorporate aspects of ARTIFICIAL INTELLIGENCE, and which will probably be capable of PARALLEL PROCESSING.

computer graphics ▷ *noun* the use of computers to display and manipulate information in graphical or pictorial form, either on a visual-display unit (VDU) or via a printer or plotter.

computerize or **computerise** ▷ *verb* (***computerized***, ***computerizing***) **a** to transfer (a procedure, operation, system, etc) to control by computer; **b** to organize (information, data, etc) by computer; **c** to install (computers) for this purpose. ● **computerization** *noun*.

computer language ▷ *noun* a defined set of numbers, symbols or words used to write a computer program. See HIGH-LEVEL LANGUAGE, LOW-LEVEL LANGUAGE.

computer-literate ▷ *adj* able to use computers, programs, etc.

computer literacy ▷ *noun* the ability to use computers. ● **computer literate** *adj*.

computer memory ▷ *noun* the part of a computer system that stores programs and data, either temporarily or permanently, and which is connected to the central processing unit of the computer. See RAM, ROM.

computer science ▷ *noun* the study of the design, development, operations and applications of computers. ● **computer scientist** *noun*.

computer virus see VIRUS 5

computing ▷ *noun* the act or process of using a computer.

comrade /'kɒmreɪd, -rəd/ ▷ *noun* **1 a** a friend or companion; **b** an associate, fellow worker, etc. **2** a fellow communist or socialist. ● **comradely** *adj*. ● **comradeship** *noun*. ◷ 16c: from French *camarade*, from

Spanish *camarada* the soldiers sharing a billet, from Latin *camera* room.

comrade-in-arms ▷ *noun* (*comrades-in-arms*) a fellow soldier or campaigner.

COMSAT or **comsat** /ˈkɒmsat/ ▷ *abbreviation*, *US* Communications Satellite.

con¹ *colloq* ▷ *noun* a CONFIDENCE TRICK. ▷ *verb* (*conned, conning*) to swindle or trick someone, especially after winning their trust.

con² ▷ *verb* (*conned, conning*) *old use* to read over and learn by heart. ⓒ 15c: from CAN¹ 2.

con³ or (*especially US*) **conn** ▷ *verb* (*conned, conning*) *naut* to direct the steering of (a ship). ⓒ 17c: from earlier *cond*, from French *conduire*, from Latin *conducere* to conduct.

con⁴ ▷ *noun* an argument against something. See also PROS AND CONS. ⓒ 16c: shortened from Latin *contra* against.

con⁵ ▷ *noun*, *prison slang* a prisoner or inmate. ⓒ 19c: shortened from CONVICT.

con-, **col-**, **com-** or **cor-** ▷ *prefix* found usually in words derived from Latin: with or together, sometimes used with emphatic or intensifying effect. ⓒ From Latin *com-*, form of *cum* together with.

conc ▷ *abbreviation*. **1** concentrated. **2** concentration.

concatenate /kəŋˈkatəneɪt, kən-/ ▷ *verb* (*concatenated, concatenating*) to link up, especially into a connected series. ● **concatenation** *noun* a series of items linked together in a chain-like way. ⓒ 16c: from Latin *concatenare*, *concatenatum*, from *con-* together + *catenare* to chain.

concave /ˈkɒnkeɪv/ ▷ *adj* said of a surface or shape: inward-curving, like the inside of a bowl. Compare CONVEX. ▷ *verb* (*concaved, concaving*) to make or become convex. ⓒ 14c: French, from Latin *concavus* vaulted, from *cavus* hollow.

concavity /kəŋˈkavɪtɪ/ ▷ *noun* (*concavities*) **1** the quality of being concave. **2** a hollow.

conceal /kənˈsiːl/ ▷ *verb* (*concealed, concealing*) **1** to hide; to place out of sight. **2** to keep secret. ● **concealer** *noun*. ● **concealment** *noun*. ⓒ 14c: from Latin *concelare*, from *con-* intensive + *celare* to hide.

concede /kənˈsiːd/ ▷ *verb* (*conceded, conceding*) **1** to admit to be true or correct. **2** to give or grant. **3** to yield or give up. **4** *intr* to admit defeat in (a contest, etc) before, or without continuing to, the end. ● **conceder** *noun*. ● **concede defeat** to admit to being beaten. ⓒ 17c: from Latin *concedere* to yield.

conceit /kənˈsiːt/ ▷ *noun* **1 a** an inflated opinion of oneself; **b** vanity. **2** *old use* a witty, fanciful or ingenious thought or idea. ⓒ 16c: from CONCEIVE, by analogy with *deceive*, *deceit*.

conceited ▷ *adj* **a** having too good an opinion of oneself; **b** vain. ● **conceitedly** *adverb*. ● **conceitedness** *noun*.

conceivable ▷ *adj* imaginable; possible ◻ *try every conceivable method*. ● **conceivability** *noun*. ● **conceivably** *adverb*.

conceive /kənˈsiːv/ ▷ *verb* (*conceived, conceiving*) **1** *tr & intr* to become pregnant. **2** to form from the union of an ovum and a sperm. **3** *tr & intr* (*often* **conceive of something**) to think of or imagine (an idea, etc). ⓒ 13c: from French *concever*, from Latin *concipere*.

concentrate /ˈkɒnsəntreɪt/ ▷ *verb* (*concentrated, concentrating*) **1** *intr* (*often* **concentrate on something** or **someone**) to give full attention and energy to them or it. **2** to focus ◻ *concentrate our efforts*. **3** *tr & intr* to bring or come together in one place. **4** *chem* to increase the strength of (a dissolved substance in a solution), either by adding more of it or by evaporating the solvent in which it is dissolved. **5** *chem* to make (a chemical substance) denser or purer. ▷ *noun* a concentrated liquid or substance. ● **concentrated** *adj* **1** attentive; focused. **2** contracted. **3** condensed; compressed. ⓒ 17c: from Latin *con-* together + *centrum* centre.

concentration /kɒnsənˈtreɪʃən/ ▷ *noun* **1** intensive mental effort. **2** the act of concentrating or the state of being concentrated. **3** the number of molecules or ions of a substance present in unit volume or weight of a solution or mixture. **4** a concentrate.

concentration camp ▷ *noun* a prison camp used to detain civilians who are not tolerated by the authorities, especially in Nazi Germany.

concentre ▷ *verb*, *tr & intr* to meet or cause to meet in a common centre. ⓒ 17c: from French *concentrer*, from Latin *concentrare*, from *centrum* centre.

concentric ▷ *adj*, *geom* said of circles, spheres, etc: having a common centre. ● **concentrically** *adverb*. ● **concentricity** *noun*. ⓒ 14c: from Latin *concentricus*.

concept /ˈkɒnsɛpt/ ▷ *noun* a notion; an abstract or general idea. ⓒ 17c: from Latin *conceptum*, from *concipere* to conceive.

conception ▷ *noun* **1** an idea or notion. **2** the origin or start of something, especially something intricate. **3** the act or an instance of conceiving. **4** *biol* the fertilization of an ovum by a sperm, the start of pregnancy. ⓒ 13c: French, from Latin *conceptio*, from *concipere* to conceive.

conceptual ▷ *adj* relating to or existing as concepts or conceptions. ● **conceptually** *adverb*.

conceptualism ▷ *noun*, *philos* any theory of universals, ie general terms and abstract objects, such as qualities, relations and numbers, that maintains that these are formed and constructed in the mind, and therefore exist only in the mind.

conceptualize or **conceptualise** ▷ *verb* (*conceptualized, conceptualizing*) to form a concept or idea of something. ● **conceptualization** *noun*.

concern /kənˈsɜːn/ ▷ *verb* (*concerned, concerning*) **1** to have to do with someone or something; to be about someone or something ◻ *It concerns your son*. **2** (*often* **be concerned about something** or **someone**) to worry, bother or interest. **3** to affect; to involve ◻ ***a perfectionist where food is concerned***. ▷ *noun* **1 a** worry or a cause of worry; **b** interest or a subject of interest. **2** someone's business or responsibility ◻ *That's my concern*. **3** an organization; a company or business. ● **concernment** *noun*. ⓒ 16c: from Latin *concernere* to distinguish or relate to.

concerned ▷ *adj* worried. ● **concernedly** /-nɪdlɪ/ *adverb*. ● **concernedness** *noun*. ● **concerned with something** or **someone** having to do with it or them; involving it or them.

concerning ▷ *prep* regarding; relating to; about.

concert ▷ *noun* /ˈkɒnsət/ **1** a musical performance given before an audience by singers or players. **2** agreement; harmony. ▷ *verb* /kənˈsɜːt/ (*concerted, concerting*) to endeavour or plan by arrangement. ● **in concert 1** jointly; in co-operation. **2** said of singers, musicians, etc: in a live performance. ⓒ 16c: French, from Italian *concerto*, from *concertare* to organize.

concerted /kənˈsɜːtɪd/ ▷ *adj* **1** planned and carried out jointly. **2** *music* arranged in parts.

concertina /kɒnsəˈtiːnə/ ▷ *noun* (*concertinas*) a musical instrument like a small accordion. ▷ *verb* (*concertinaed, concertinaing*) *tr & intr* to fold or collapse like a concertina. ⓒ 19c: from CONCERT + *-ina*.

concertino /kɒntʃəˈtiːnoʊ/ ▷ *noun* (*concertinos*) *music* **1** a short CONCERTO. **2** the group of solo musicians in a CONCERTO GROSSO. ⓒ 19c: Italian, meaning 'little concert'.

concert master ▷ *noun*, *US* a LEADER of an orchestra.

concerto /kən'tʃɛətoʊ, kɒn'tʃɜːtoʊ/ ▻ *noun* (*concertos* or *concerti* /-tiː/) *music* a composition for an orchestra and one or more solo performers. ⓘ 18c: Italian, meaning 'concert'.

concerto grosso ▻ *noun* (*concerti grossi* /-tiː -siː/) *music* **1** an orchestral work performed by solo musicians as well as the main body of the orchestra. **2** the main body of instruments in an orchestral work of this kind. See also RIPIENO. ⓘ 18c: Italian, meaning 'large concert'.

concert pitch ▻ *noun, music* the standard pitch to which instruments are tuned for concert performances.

concession /kən'sɛʃən/ ▻ *noun* **1** the act of conceding. **2** something conceded or allowed. **3** the right, granted under government licence, to extract minerals, etc in an area. **4** the right to conduct a business from within a larger concern. **5** a reduction in ticket prices, fares, etc for categories such as students, the elderly, the unwaged, etc. ● **concessionary** *adj* involving or obtained by a concession, especially a reduction in price □ *concessionary fares for students.* ● **concessive** *adj.* ⓘ 17c: from Latin *concessio* yielding, from *concedere* to concede.

concessionaire /kən'sɛʃənɛə(r)/ or (*US*) **concessioner** ▻ *noun* the holder of a mining or trading concession.

conch /kɒŋk, kɒntʃ/ ▻ *noun* (*conchs* /kɒŋks/ or *conches* /kɒntʃɪz/) **1** any of a family of large marine snails, native to warm shallow tropical waters, which have large colourful shells with a long narrow opening and an outer lip which is generally expanded to form a broad plate. **2** the large brightly coloured shell of this animal, used as a trumpet or valued as a collector's item. ⓘ 16c: from Latin *concha*, from Greek *konche* cockle or mussel.

conchology ▻ *noun* the study of the shells of molluscs. ● **conchologist** *noun.*

concierge /'kɒnsiːɛəʒ/ ▻ *noun* a warden or caretaker of a block of flats, especially one who lives on the premises.

conciliate /kən'sɪlɪeɪt/ ▻ *verb* (*conciliated, conciliating*) **1** to win over someone; to overcome the hostility of someone. **2** to reconcile (people in dispute, etc). ● **conciliation** *noun.* ● **conciliator** *noun.* ● **conciliatory** *adj* intended to placate or win over someone. ● **conciliatorily** *adverb.* ⓘ 16c: from Latin *conciliare, conciliatum* to unite in friendship, from *concilium* council.

concise /kən'saɪs/ ▻ *adj* brief but comprehensive. ● **concisely** *adverb.* ● **conciseness** or **concision** *noun.* ⓘ 16c: from Latin *concisus* cut short.

conclave /'kɒŋkleɪv, 'kɒn-/ ▻ *noun* **1** a private or secret meeting. **2** *RC Church* **a** the body of cardinals gathered to elect a new pope; **b** their meeting-place. ⓘ 14c: Latin, meaning 'a room that can be locked', from *con-* together + *clavis* key.

conclude /kəŋ'kluːd, kən-/ ▻ *verb* (*concluded, concluding*) **1** *tr & intr* to come or bring to an end. **2** to reach an opinion based on reasoning. **3** to settle or arrange □ *conclude a treaty with a neighbouring state.* ⓘ 15c: from Latin *concludere*, from *claudere* to close.

conclusion /kəŋ'kluːʒən, kən-/ ▻ *noun* **1** an end. **2** a reasoned judgement; an opinion based on reasoning □ *draw a conclusion.* **3** *logic* a statement validly deduced from a previous PREMISE. **4** settling of terms, an agreement, etc. **5** a result or outcome (of a discussion, event, etc). ● **in conclusion** finally; lastly. ● **jump to conclusions** to presume something without adequate evidence. ⓘ 14c: French, from Latin *conclusio*, from *concludere* to end.

conclusive /kəŋ'kluːsɪv, kən-/ ▻ *adj* said of evidence, proof, etc: decisive, convincing; leaving no room for doubt. ● **conclusively** *adverb.* ● **conclusiveness** *noun.* ⓘ 17c: from Latin *conclusivus*, from *concludere* to conclude.

concoct /kəŋ'kɒkt, kən-/ ▻ *verb* (*concocted, concocting*) **1** to make something, especially ingeniously from a variety of ingredients. **2** to invent (a story, excuse, etc). ● **concocter** or **concoctor** *noun.* ● **concoction** *noun.* ⓘ 17c in this sense: from Latin *concoctus* cooked together, from *coquere* to cook.

concomitant /kəŋ'kɒmɪtənt, kən-/ ▻ *adj* accompanying because of or as a result of something else. ▻ *noun* a concomitant thing, person, etc. ● **concomitantly** *adverb.* ⓘ 17c: from Latin *concomitari* to accompany.

concord /'kɒŋkɔːd, 'kɒn-/ ▻ *noun* **1** agreement; peace or harmony. **2** *grammar* AGREEMENT (sense 4). **3** *music* a combination of sounds which are harmonious to the ear. Opposite of DISCORD. **4** a treaty; a pact. ● **concordant** *adj.* ⓘ 13c: from French *concorde*, from Latin *concordia*, from *con* with + *cor* heart.

concordance ▻ *noun* **1** a state of harmony. **2** a book containing an alphabetical index of principal words used in a major work, usually supplying citations and their meaning. ⓘ 14c: from Latin *concordantia*, from Latin *concordare* to agree.

concordat /kɒn'kɔːdat/ ▻ *noun* an agreement between church and state, especially the Roman Catholic church and a secular government. ⓘ 17c: French, from Latin *concordare* to agree.

concourse /'kɒŋkɔːs/ ▻ *noun* **1** in a railway station, airport, etc: a large open area where people can gather. **2** a throng; a gathering. ⓘ 14c: from French *concours*.

concrete /'kɒŋkriːt/ ▻ *noun* a building material consisting of a mixture of cement, sand, gravel and water, which forms a hard rock-like mass when dry. ▻ *adj* **1** relating to such a material. **2** relating to items which can be felt, touched, seen, etc □ *concrete objects.* Compare ABSTRACT *adj* 3. **3** definite or positive, as opposed to vague or general □ *concrete evidence.* **4** *grammar* said of a noun: denoting a physical thing, eg *house*, rather than a quality, condition or action. Compare ABSTRACT *adj* 4. ▻ *verb* (*concreted, concreting*) **1** to cover with or embed in concrete. **2** *tr & intr* to solidify. ● **concretely** *adverb.* ● **concreteness** *noun.* ⓘ 16c: from Latin *concretus*, from *con-* together + *crescere* to grow.

concrete

See Usage Note at **cement**.

concrete art ▻ *noun* a term applied to various styles of non-figurative art in which the picture is constructed from geometrical forms and simple planes. ⓘ 1930.

concrete music see MUSIQUE CONCRÈTE

concrete poetry ▻ *noun* poetry which conveys meaning through the physical arrangement of the words on the page as well as through the words themselves.

concretion /kəŋ'kriːʃən, kən-/ ▻ *noun* **1** *pathol* a hard stony mass which forms in body tissues or natural cavities. See also CALCULUS 2. **2** *geol* a hard rounded nodule of mineral matter formed within the pores of a sedimentary or igneous rock as a result of precipitation of dissolved mineral salts. ⓘ 17c: from Latin *concretio*.

concubinage /kɒŋ'kjuːbɪnɪdʒ/ ▻ *noun* **1** the state of a man and a woman living together but not married to each other. **2** the status of a concubine.

concubine /'kɒŋkjʊbaɪn, 'kɒn-/ ▻ *noun* **1** *historical* a woman who lives with a man and has sexual intercourse with him, without being married to him. **2** in polygamous societies: a secondary wife. ⓘ 13c: from Latin *concubina*, from *con-* together + *cumbare* to lie.

concupiscence /kəŋ'kjuːpɪsəns, kən-/ ▻ *noun* strong desire, especially sexual. ● **concupiscent** *adj.* ⓘ 14c: from Latin *concupiscere* to long for.

concupiscent /kəŋ'kjuːpɪsənt, kən-/ ▻ *adj* lustful.

concur /kəŋ'kɜː(r), kən-/ ▻ *verb* (*concurred, concurring*) *intr* **1** to agree. **2** to happen at the same time; to coincide. ⓘ 16c: from Latin *con-* together + *currere* to run.

concurrence /kəŋˈkʌrəns, kən-/ ▷ *noun* **1** agreement; consent. **2** the coinciding of events, etc.

concurrent ▷ *adj* **1** happening or taking place simultaneously. **2** said of lines: meeting or intersecting; having a common point. **3** in agreement. ● **concurrently** *adverb*. ◷ 15c.

concuss /kəŋˈkʌs, kən-/ ▷ *verb* (***concusses, concussed, concussing***) **1** to cause concussion in someone. **2** to shake severely. ◷ 16c: from Latin *concutere, concussum* to shake together.

concussion ▷ *noun* **1** a violent shaking or jarring of the brain, caused by injury to the head eg as a result of a severe blow or fall, and usually resulting in temporary loss of consciousness. **2** a violent shock caused by the sudden contact of two bodies.

condemn /kənˈdɛm/ ▷ *verb* (***condemned, condemning***) **1** to declare something to be wrong or evil. **2** to pronounce someone guilty; to convict someone. **3** (*usually* **condemn someone to something**) **a** to sentence them to (a punishment, especially death); **b** to force into (a disagreeable fate). **4** to show the guilt of someone; to give away or betray someone □ *His obvious nervousness condemned him.* **5** to declare (a building) unfit to be used or lived in. ● **condemnation** *noun*. ● **condemnatory** *adverb*. ◷ 13c: from French *condemner*, from Latin *condemnare*, from *con-* together + *damnare* to convict.

condensation /kɒndənˈseɪʃən/ ▷ *noun* **1** *chem* the process whereby a gas or vapour turns into a liquid as a result of cooling. **2** *meteorol* the production of water droplets in the atmosphere. **3** *optics* the process of focusing a beam of light.

condensation reaction ▷ *noun, chem* a reaction in which two or more small molecules combine to form a larger one, with the elimination of a simpler byproduct, usually a molecule of water.

condense /kənˈdɛns/ ▷ *verb* (***condensed, condensing***) **1** to decrease the volume, size or density of (a substance). **2** said of a substance: to be reduced in volume, size or density. **3** to concentrate something. **4** *tr & intr* to undergo or cause to undergo condensation. **5** to express something more briefly; to summarize. ◷ 15c: from Latin *condensare* to compress, from *condensus* very dense.

condensed milk ▷ *noun* milk that has been concentrated and thickened by evaporation and to which sugar has been added as a preservative.

condenser ▷ *noun* **1** *elec* a CAPACITOR. **2** *chem* an apparatus for changing a vapour into a liquid by cooling it and allowing it to condense. **3** *optics* in a microscope, film projector, etc: a lens or series of lenses that is used to concentrate a light source.

condescend /kɒndɪˈsɛnd/ ▷ *verb* (***condescended, condescending***) *intr* **1** to act in a gracious manner towards those one regards as inferior. **2** to be gracious enough to do something, especially as though it were a favour. ● **condescending** *adj* **1** gracious. **2** offensively patronizing. ● **condescendingly** *adverb*. ● **condescension** *noun*. ◷ 15c: from Latin *condescendere*, from *descendere* to descend.

condign /kənˈdaɪn/ ▷ *adj* usually said of punishment: well-deserved; fitting. ● **condignly** *adverb*. ◷ 15c: from Latin *condignus*, from *dignus* worthy.

condiment /ˈkɒndɪmənt/ ▷ *noun* any seasoning or sauce, eg salt, pepper, mustard, etc, added to food at the table, to give extra flavour. ◷ 15c: from Latin *condimentum*, from *condire* to pickle.

condition /kənˈdɪʃən/ ▷ *noun* **1** a particular state of existence. **2** a state of health, fitness or suitability for use □ *out of condition.* **3** an ailment or disorder □ *a heart condition.* **4** (**conditions**) circumstances □ *poor working conditions.* **5** a requirement or qualification. **6** a term of contract. **7** *law* in a legal document, eg will, contract, etc: a clause which requires something to happen before the document can be enacted. **8** *math* a statement which must be true for a further statement to be true. ▷ *verb* (***conditioned, conditioning***) **1** to accustom or train someone or something to behave or react in a particular way; to influence them or it. **2** to prepare or train (a person or animal) for a certain activity or for certain conditions of living. **3** to subject (a person or animal) to a particular stimulus in order to secure, by training, a certain behavioural response that was not initially associated with that stimulus. **4** to affect or control; to determine. **5** to improve (the physical state of hair, skin, fabrics, etc) by applying a particular substance. ● **conditioner** *noun, often in compounds* a substance or apparatus which improves the condition of something, especially hair □ *hair conditioner* □ *fabric conditioner.* ● **on condition that …** only if … □ *I will go on condition that you come too.* ● **on no condition** absolutely not. ◷ 14c: from Latin *conditio*, from *condicere* to agree upon.

conditional ▷ *adj* **1** dependent on a particular condition, etc. **2** *grammar* expressing a condition on which something else is dependent, as in the first clause in 'If it rains, I'll stay at home'. Compare INDICATIVE, IMPERATIVE, SUBJUNCTIVE. ● **conditionality** *noun*. ● **conditionally** *adverb*.

conditioning ▷ *noun* **1** the process of making or becoming conditioned. **2** *psychol* a reflex response to a stimulus which depends upon the former experience of the individual, and can be modified, eg by rewarding or punishing a particular response so that it comes to occur more or less frequently.

condole /kənˈdoʊl/ ▷ *verb* (***condoled, condoling***) (*always* **condole with someone**) to express sympathy to them. ● **condolence** *noun* (*usually* **condolences**) an expression of sympathy □ *offer my condolences.* ◷ 17c in this sense: from Latin *con-* with + *dolere* to grieve.

condom /ˈkɒndɒm, -dəm/ ▷ *noun* a thin rubber sheath worn on the penis during sexual intercourse, to prevent conception and the spread of sexually transmitted diseases. See also FEMALE CONDOM. ◷ 18c.

condominium /kɒndəˈmɪnɪəm/ ▷ *noun* **1** *N Amer* **a** a building, eg office block, apartment block, etc in which each apartment is individually owned and any common areas, eg passageways, etc are commonly owned; **b** an individual apartment in such a block. Often shortened to **condo** (*plural* ***condos***). **2** a country which is controlled by two or more other countries. **3** joint sovereignty. ◷ 18c: from Latin *con-* with + *dominium* lordship.

condone /kənˈdoʊn/ ▷ *verb* (***condoned, condoning***) **1** to pardon or overlook (an offence or wrong). **2** *loosely* to tolerate. ● **condonable** *adj*. ◷ 19c: from Latin *condonare* to present or overlook, from *con-* intensive + *donare* to give.

condor /ˈkɒndɔː(r)/ ▷ *noun* either of two species of large American vulture, with a wingspan of up to 3m. ◷ 17c: Spanish, from Quechua *kuntur*.

conduce /kənˈdʒuːs/ ▷ *verb* (***conduced, conducing***) *intr* (*always* **conduce to something**) to help or contribute (to a result, especially a desirable one). ◷ 16c: from Latin *conducere*, from *con-* together + *ducere* to lead.

conducive ▷ *adj* (*often* **conducive to something**) likely to achieve a desirable result; encouraging □ *Good working conditions are conducive to a happy workforce.*

conduct ▷ *verb* /kənˈdʌkt/ (***conducted, conducting***) **1** to lead or guide. **2** to manage; to control □ *conduct the firm's business.* **3** *tr & intr* to direct the performance of an orchestra or choir by movements of the hands or by using a baton. **4** to transmit (heat or electricity) by CONDUCTION. **5** to direct, channel or convey □ *Hot air is conducted through the pipes.* **6** to behave (oneself) in a specified way □ *One should always conduct oneself with dignity.* ▷ *noun* /ˈkɒndʌkt/ **1** behaviour. **2** the managing or organizing of something. ◷ 15c: from Latin *conductus* guide.

conductance ▷ *noun* **a** the ability of a material to conduct heat or electricity; **b** in a direct current circuit: the reciprocal of RESISTANCE. See also CONDUCTIVITY.

conduction ▷ *noun* **1** the transmission of heat through a material from a region of higher temperature to one of lower temperature, without any movement of the material itself. **2** the flow of electricity through a material under the influence of an electric field, without any movement of the material itself. **3** the passage of a nerve impulse along a nerve fibre.

conductive education ▷ *noun* a system of teaching children (and sometimes adults) suffering from motor disorders (eg cerebral palsy) to achieve their maximum potential. The aim is to guide them to attain specific goals in their own way by providing a concentrated course of exercise and intellectual stimulation.

conductivity ▷ *noun* **1 a** a measure of the ability of a material to conduct electricity; **b** the reciprocal of RESISTIVITY. Also called **electrical conductivity**. **2** the ability of a material to conduct heat. Also called THERMAL CONDUCTIVITY.

conductor ▷ *noun* **1** the person who conducts a choir or orchestra. **2** (*in full* **thermal conductor**) a material that allows heat to flow through it by the process of conduction. **3** (*in full* **electrical conductor**) a material that allows electricity to flow through it by the process of conduction. **4** someone who collects fares from passengers on a bus, etc. **5** a leader or guide. **6** *N Amer* the official in charge of a train.

conductress ▷ *noun* a woman who collects fares from passengers on a bus, etc.

conduit /ˈkɒndjʊɪt, -dɪt/ ▷ *noun* **1** a channel, pipe, tube or duct through which a fluid, a liquid or a gas, may pass. Ⓒ 14c: French, from Latin *conductus* channel.

cone ▷ *noun* **1** *geom* a solid, three-dimensional figure with a flat base in the shape of a circle or ellipse, and a curved upper surface that tapers to a fixed point. **2** something similar to this in shape, eg a hollow pointed wafer for holding ice cream. **3** *anatomy* in the retina: a type of light-sensitive receptor cell specialized for the detection of colour, and which functions best in bright light. Compare ROD *noun* 6. **4** *bot* the reproductive structure of GYMNOSPERMS, consisting of a central axis bearing many overlapping SPOROPHYLLS. *Technical equivalent* **strobilus**. **5** a plastic cone-shaped bollard which is placed on the road temporarily, to divert traffic, cordon off an area, etc. Also called **traffic cone**. ▷ *verb* (***coned, coning***) to shape like a cone. Ⓒ 16c: from Greek *konos* pine cone or geometrical cone.

■ **cone something** or **somewhere off** to close off (an area or part of a road) with a line of traffic cones.

confab *colloq* ▷ *noun* a conversation. ▷ *verb* (***confabbed, confabbing***) *intr* to chat. Ⓒ 17c: from CONFABULATE.

confabulate /kənˈfabjʊleɪt/ ▷ *verb* (***confabulated, confabulating***) *intr, formal* **1** to talk, discuss or confer. **2** *psychiatry* to imagine experiences, usually to compensate for loss of memory. ● **confabulation** *noun*. Ⓒ 17c: from Latin *confabulari, confabulatus* to talk together.

confection ▷ *noun* **1** any sweet food, eg a cake, sweet, biscuit or pudding. **2** *dated, facetious* a fancy or elaborate garment. Ⓒ 14c: French, from Latin *confectio* preparation, from *conficere* to put together.

confectioner ▷ *noun* someone who makes or sells sweets or cakes.

confectioner's sugar ▷ *noun, US* ICING SUGAR.

confectionery ▷ *noun* (***confectioneries***) **1** sweets, biscuits and cakes. **2** the work or art of a confectioner.

confederacy ▷ *noun* (***confederacies***) **1** a league or alliance of states. **2** (**the Confederacy**) *US historical* the union of 11 southern states that seceded from the USA in 1860–1, so causing the American Civil War. **3** a conspiracy; an association formed for illegal purposes. Ⓒ 14c: from Latin *confoederatio* league.

confederate ▷ *noun* /kənˈfɛdərət/ **1** a member of a confederacy. **2** a friend or an ally; an accomplice or a fellow conspirator. **3** (**Confederate**) *US history* a supporter of the Confederacy. ▷ *adj* /-rət/ **1** allied; united. **2** (**Confederate**) *US history* belonging to the Confederacy. ▷ *verb* /-reɪt/ (***confederated, confederating***) *tr & intr* to unite into or become part of a confederacy. Ⓒ 14c: from Latin *confoederatus*, from *confoederare* to unite in a league.

confederation ▷ *noun* **1** the uniting of states into a league. **2** the league so formed.

confer /kənˈfɜː(r)/ ▷ *verb* (***conferred, conferring***) **1** *intr* to consult or discuss together. **2** (*usually* **confer something on someone**) to grant them (an honour or distinction). ● **conferment** *noun* the bestowal of an honour. Ⓒ 16c: from Latin *conferre* to bring together.

conference /ˈkɒnfərəns/ ▷ *noun* **1** a formally organized gathering for the discussion of matters of common interest or concern. **2** consultation; the formal exchanging of views □ *in conference with the Prime Minister*. **3** an assembly of representatives of an association, church denomination, etc. **4** an act of conferring. Ⓒ 16c: from Latin *conferentia*, from *conferre* to bring together.

conference call ▷ *noun* a telephone call or computer link-up in which it is possible for several people to participate simultaneously.

conferencing ▷ *noun* the practice of holding a business conference in which the participants are linked by telephone, video equipment and/or computer.

confess /kənˈfɛs/ ▷ *verb* (***confesses, confessed, confessing***) **1** *tr & intr* **a** to own up to (a fault, wrongdoing, etc); **b** to admit (a disagreeable fact, etc) reluctantly. **2** *tr & intr, Christianity* to declare (one's sins) to a priest or directly to God, in order to gain absolution. **3** said of a priest: to hear the confession of someone. ● **confessed** *adj* admitted. ● **confessedly** /-sɪdlɪ/ *adverb*. Ⓒ 14c: from French *confesser*.

confession ▷ *noun* **1** the admission of a sin, fault, crime, distasteful or shocking fact, etc. **2** *Christianity* the formal act of confessing one's sins to a priest. **3** a declaration of one's religious faith or principles □ *a confession of faith*. **4** a religious body with its own creed or set of beliefs.

confessional ▷ *noun* in a church: the small enclosed stall in a church where a priest sits when hearing confessions. ▷ *adj* relating to a confession.

confessor ▷ *noun* **1** *Christianity* a priest who hears confessions and gives spiritual advice. **2** *historical* someone whose holy life serves as a demonstration of his or her religious faith, but who does not suffer martyrdom. **3** someone who makes a confession. Ⓒ 13c: Latin, meaning 'martyr' or 'witness'.

confetti /kənˈfɛtɪ, kɒn-/ ▷ *noun* at a wedding: tiny pieces of coloured paper traditionally thrown over the bride and groom by the wedding guests. Ⓒ 19: Italian, plural of *confetto* sweetmeat.

confidant or **confidante** /kɒnfɪˈdant, ˈkɒnfɪdant/ ▷ *noun* a close friend (male or remale, respectively) with whom one discusses personal matters, especially concerning love affairs. Ⓒ 18c: an alternative of CONFIDENT, probably an attempt to render the pronunciation of the French *confident*(e), ultimately from Latin *confidere* to trust.

confide /kənˈfaɪd/ ▷ *verb* (***confided, confiding***) **1** to tell (a secret, etc) to someone. **2** to entrust someone (to someone's care). Ⓒ 15c: from Latin *confidere* to trust.

■ **confide in someone** **1** to speak freely and confidentially with them about personal matters. **2** to trust them.

confidence /ˈkɒnfɪdəns/ ▻ *noun* **1** trust or belief in a person or thing. **2** faith in one's own ability; self-assurance. **3** a secret, etc confided to someone. **4** a relationship of mutual trust. ● **in confidence** in secret; confidentially. ◐ 15c: from Latin *confidentia*.

confidence interval ▻ *noun, math* in statistical analyses: an interval that can with reasonable confidence (usually 95%) be expected to contain the true value of an unknown parameter.

confidence trick ▻ *noun* a form of swindle, usually involving money, in which the swindler first wins the trust of the victim. Often shortened to CON[1].

confident ▻ *adj* **1** (*sometimes* **confident of something**) certain; sure ▫ *confident of success.* **2** self-assured.

confidential /kɒnfɪˈdɛnʃəl/ ▻ *adj* **1** secret; not to be divulged. **2** trusted with private matters. **3** indicating privacy or secrecy ▫ *a confidential whisper.* ● **confidentiality** *noun.* ● **confidentially** *adverb.* ◐ 18c: from Latin *confidentia* confidence.

confiding ▻ *adj* trusting; unsuspicious. ● **confidingly** *adverb.*

configuration /kənfɪgjʊˈreɪʃən, kənfɪgəˈreɪʃən/ ▻ *noun* **1** the positioning or distribution of the parts of something, relative to each other. **2** an outline or external shape. **3 a** *chem* the spatial arrangement of atoms in a molecule; **b** *physics* the arrangement of electrons in orbitals around the nucleus of an atom. ◐ 17c: from Latin *configuratio*, from *configurare* to form or fashion.

confine /kənˈfaɪn/ ▻ *verb* (**confined**, **confining**) **1** to restrict or limit. **2** to prevent the spread of (eg a fire). **3** to keep prisoner. **4** said eg of ill health: to restrict someone's movement ▫ *Flu confined Yvonne to her bed for the whole week.* ● **be confined** said of a pregnant woman: to be about to give birth.

confined ▻ *adj* narrow; restricted.

confinement ▻ *noun* **1** the state of being shut up or kept in an enclosed space. **2** *old use* the period surrounding childbirth.

confirm /kənˈfɜːm/ ▻ *verb* (**confirmed**, **confirming**) **1** to provide support for the truth or validity of something ▫ *refused to confirm or deny the rumour.* **2** to finalize or make definite (a booking, arrangement etc). **3** said of an opinion, etc: to strengthen it or become more convinced in it. **4** to give formal approval to something; to establish officially ▫ *His appointment was confirmed at the interview.* **5** *Christianity* to accept someone formally into full membership of the Church. ● **confirmative** *adj.* ● **confirmatory** *adj* **1** giving additional strength to, eg an argument, etc. **2** confirming. ◐ 13c: from Latin *confirmare*, from *firmare* to strengthen, from *firmus* firm.

confirmation ▻ *noun* **1** the act of confirming. **2** proof or support. **3** finalization. **4** *Christianity* the religious ceremony in which someone is admitted to full membership of the church.

confirmed ▻ *adj* so firmly settled into a state, habit, etc as to be unlikely to change ▫ *confirmed bachelor.*

confiscate /ˈkɒnfɪskeɪt/ ▻ *verb* (**confiscated**, **confiscating**) to take away something from someone, usually as a penalty. ▻ *adj* forfeited. ● **confiscation** *noun.* ● **confiscator** *noun.* ● **confiscatory** *adj.* ◐ 16c: from Latin *confiscare* to transfer to the state treasury, from *fiscus* treasury.

conflagration /kɒnfləˈgreɪʃən/ ▻ *noun* a large destructive blaze. ◐ 17c: from Latin *conflagrare* to burn up.

conflate /kənˈfleɪt/ ▻ *verb* (**conflated**, **conflating**) to blend or combine (two things, especially two different versions of a text, story, etc) into a single whole. ● **conflation** *noun.* ◐ 17c: from Latin *conflare* to fuse, from *con-* together + *flare* to blow.

conflict ▻ *noun* /ˈkɒnflɪkt/ **1** disagreement; fierce argument; a quarrel. **2** a clash between different aims, interests, ideas, etc. **3** a struggle, fight or battle, usually on a lesser scale than a WAR. **4** *psychol* in an individual: a clash between two incompatible desires or needs, sometimes leading to emotional turmoil. ▻ *verb* /kənˈflɪkt/ (**conflicted**, **conflicting**) *intr* **1** to be incompatible or in opposition ▫ *The demands of a career often conflict with those of family life.* **2** to fight. ● **conflicting** *adj.* ● **confliction** *noun.* ◐ 15c: from Latin *confligere*, *conflictum* to dash together or clash.

conflict theory ▻ *noun, sociol* the theory that conflict and social division are inevitable in all social structures because the mechanisms by which society integrates and exercises control over its members are never wholly successful.

confluence /ˈkɒnfluəns/ and **conflux** /ˈkɒnflʌks/ ▻ *noun* (**confluxes**) **1 a** the meeting and flowing together of two or more rivers, streams, glaciers, etc. **b** the point where two rivers flow into one another. **2** a flowing together. **3** an act of meeting together. ● **confluent** *adj* **1** flowing together. **2** running into one. **3** uniting. ◐ 15c: from Latin *confluentia* flowing together.

conform /kənˈfɔːm/ ▻ *verb* (**conformed**, **conforming**) *intr* (*often* **conform to something**) to behave, dress, etc in obedience to some standard considered normal by the majority. ● **conformer** or **conformist** *noun.* ● **conformity** *noun.* ◐ 14c: from Latin *conformare* to shape.

■ **conform to something a** to obey (rules, etc); **b** to meet or comply with (standards, etc).

■ **conform to** or **with something** to be in agreement with it; to match or correspond to it.

conformable ▻ *adj* **1** corresponding or matching. **2** compliant; agreeable. **3** *geol* said of rock strata: lying in a parallel sequence, without interruption, as originally laid down.

conformation /kɒnfɔːˈmeɪʃən/ ▻ *noun* a shape, structure or arrangement of something.

confound /kənˈfaʊnd/ ▻ *verb* (**confounded**, **confounding**) **1** to puzzle; to baffle. **2** to defeat or thwart (enemies or their schemes). **3** to mix up or confuse (one thing with another). ● **Confound it!** used as an exclamation of annoyance: Damn it! ◐ 14c: from Latin *confundere* to pour together, throw into disorder or overthrow.

confounded ▻ *adj* **1** confused. **2** *colloq* used to indicate annoyance: damned ▫ *That boy's a confounded nuisance!* ● **confoundedly** *adverb* **1** *colloq* hatefully; shamefully. **2** cursedly.

confraternity ▻ *noun* a brotherhood, especially a religious or charitable one. ◐ 15c: from Latin *confraternitas*, from *confrater*, from *frater* brother.

confrère /ˈkɔ̃frɛə(r)/ ▻ *noun* a fellow member of one's profession, etc; a colleague. ◐ 18c in this sense; French, from Latin *con-* together with + *frater* brother.

confront /kənˈfrʌnt/ ▻ *verb* (**confronted**, **confronting**) **1** to face someone, especially defiantly or accusingly. **2** to prepare to deal firmly with something. **3** said of an unpleasant prospect: to present itself to someone. ● **confrontation** *noun* **1** an act of confronting. **2** a hostile meeting or exchange of words. ◐ 16c: from Latin *confrontari*, from *frons* forehead or brow.

■ **confront someone with something** to bring them face to face with it, especially when it is damning or revealing ▫ *decided to confront him with his error.*

Confucianism /kənˈfjuːʃənɪzəm, kɒn-/ ▻ *noun* the oldest school of Chinese thought, with emphasis on morality, consideration for others, obedience and good education. ● **Confucian** *adj, noun.* ● **Confucianist** *noun.* ◐ 19c: named after the Chinese philosopher Confucius (551–479BC), upon whose teaching the school of thought is based.

confuse /kənˈfjuːz/ ▻ *verb* (**confused**, **confusing**) **1** to put into a muddle or mess. **2** to mix up or fail to distinguish (things, ideas, people, etc) □ *confuse 'ascetic' with 'aesthetic'.* **3** to puzzle, bewilder or muddle. **4** to complicate. **5** to embarrass. ● **confused** *adj.* ● **confusedly** /-ɪdlɪ/ *adverb.* ● **confusing** *adj.* ● **confusingly** *adverb.* ⓒ 18c: from Latin *confundere, confusum* to mix.

confusion /kən'fjuːʒən/ ▻ *noun* **1** the act of confusing or state of being confused. **2** disorder; muddle. **3** mental bewilderment. ⓒ 14c: from Latin *confusio,* from *confundere* to mix.

confutation /kɒnfjʊ'teɪʃən/ ▻ *noun* **1** the action of confuting. **2** something that confutes a person, theory, etc.

confute /kən'fjuːt/ ▻ *verb* (***confuted, confuting***) to prove (a person, theory, etc) wrong or false. ⓒ 16c: from Latin *confutare* to refute.

conga /'kɒŋgə/ ▻ *noun* (***congas***) **1** an originally Cuban dance of three steps followed by a kick, performed by people moving in single file. **2** a tall narrow drum beaten with the fingers. ▻ *verb* (***congaed, congaing***) *intr* to dance the conga. ⓒ 1930sc: Spanish, the feminine of *congo* of the Congo river.

congé /kɔ̃ʒeɪ, 'kɒn-/ ▻ *noun* **1** permission to depart. **2** abrupt dismissal. ⓒ 16c: French.

congeal /kən'dʒiːl/ ▻ *verb* (***congealed, congealing***) *tr & intr* said of a liquid, especially blood: to thicken, coagulate or solidify, especially through cooling. ● **congealable** *adj.* ● **congealment** or **congelation** *noun.* ⓒ 15c: from Latin *congelare* to freeze completely.

congener /'kɒndʒiːnə(r)/ ▻ *noun* **1** a plant or animal of the same GENUS as another plant or animal. **2** in an alcoholic drink: a by-product which helps to determine its flavour, colour and strength. ⓒ 18c: Latin, from *con-* same + *genus* kind.

congenial /kən'dʒiːnɪəl/ ▻ *adj* **1** said of people: compatible; having similar interests. **2** pleasant or agreeable. ● **congeniality** *noun.* ● **congenially** *adverb.* ⓒ 17c: from Latin *con-* same + *genius* spirit.

congenital /kən'dʒenɪtəl/ ▻ *adj* **1** said of a disease, defect or deformity: present at or before birth, and either inherited, or caused by injury, infection or the presence of certain drugs or chemicals in the mother's body during pregnancy. **2** complete, as if from birth □ *a congenital idiot.* ● **congenitally** *adverb.* ⓒ 18c: from Latin *congenitus,* from *con-* with + *gignere* to give birth to.

conger /'kɒŋgə(r)/ ▻ *noun* a large marine eel, which can grow to lengths of 2.75m. ⓒ 14c: from Latin *conger.*

congeries /kɒn'dʒerɪiːz, kɒn'dʒɪəriːz/ ▻ *singular or plural noun* a miscellaneous accumulation; a confused heap. ⓒ 14c: Latin, from *congerere* to heap up.

congest /kən'dʒest/ ▻ *verb* (***congested, congesting***) *tr & intr* **1** to excessively crowd or become excessively crowded. **2** said of an organ: to accumulate or make something accumulate with blood, often causing inflammation. **3** said of the nose or other air passages: to block up with mucus. ● **congested** *adj.* ● **congestion** *noun.* ● **congestive** *adj.* ⓒ 19c: from Latin *congerere, congestum* to heap up.

conglomerate /kəŋ'glɒmərət, kən-/ ▻ *noun* **1** a miscellaneous collection or mass. **2** *geol* a sedimentary rock consisting of small rounded pebbles embedded in a fine matrix of sand or silt. **3** a business group composed of a large number of firms with diverse and often unrelated interests. ▻ *adj* composed of miscellaneous things. ▻ *verb* /-reɪt/ (***conglomerated, conglomerating***) *intr* to accumulate into a mass. ● **conglomeration** *noun.* ⓒ 17c: from Latin *conglomerare, conglomeratum* to roll together, from *glomerare* to form into a ball.

congrats ▻ *plural noun, colloq* often as an exclamation: a short form of CONGRATULATIONS.

congratulate /kəŋ'gratʃʊleɪt, kən-/ ▻ *verb* (***congratulated, congratulating***) (*usually* **congratulate someone on something**) **1** to express pleasure to someone at their success, good fortune, happiness, etc. **2** to consider (oneself) lucky or clever to have managed something □ *congratulated herself on her narrow escape.* ● **congratulation** *noun* **1** the action or an expression of congratulating. **2** (**congratulations**) often as an exclamation: an expression used to congratulate someone. ● **congratulative** or **congratulatory** *adj.* ⓒ 16c: from Latin *congratulari, congratulatus,* from *gratulari* to express one's joy.

congregate /'kɒŋgrəgeɪt/ ▻ *verb* (***congregated, congregating***) *tr & intr* to gather together into a crowd. ⓒ 15c: from Latin *congregare, congregatum,* from *gregare* to collect into a herd, from *grex* herd.

congregation ▻ *noun* **1** a gathering or assembly of people, especially for worship in church. **2** the people regularly attending a particular church. **3** an academic assembly. **4** *RC Church* an administrative board.

congregational ▻ *adj* **1** relating to or administered by a congregation or separate congregations. **2** (**Congregational**) pertaining to Congregationalism.

Congregationalism ▻ *noun, Christianity* a form of church government in which each individual congregation is responsible for the management of its own affairs. ● **Congregationalist** *noun.*

congress /'kɒŋgres/ ▻ *noun* (***congresses***) **1** a large, especially international, assembly of delegates, gathered for discussion. **2** in some countries: a name used for the law-making body. **3** (**Congress**) in the US: the federal legislature, consisting of two elected chambers called the Senate and the House of Representatives. ● **congressional** *adj.* ⓒ 16c: from Latin *congredi, congressus* to go together.

congressman and **congresswoman** ▻ *noun* someone who is a member of a congress.

congruent /'kɒŋgrʊənt/ ▻ *adj* **1** *geom* said of two or more figures: identical in size and shape. **2** *math* belonging or relating to two integers that have the same remainder when divided by a third integer. **3** (*often* **congruent with something**) suitable or appropriate to it. ● **congruence** or **congruency** *noun* **1** suitability or appropriateness. **2** agreement. **3** *math* the quality or relationship of being congruent. ● **congruently** *adverb.* ⓒ 15c: from Latin *congruere* to meet together.

congruous /'kɒŋgrʊəs/ ▻ *adj* (*often* **congruous with something**) **1** corresponding. **2** fitting; suitable. ● **congruity** *noun.* ● **congruously** *adverb.* ⓒ 16c: from Latin *congruus,* from *congruere* to meet together.

conic /'kɒnɪk/ and **conical** ▻ *adj, geom* **a** relating to a cone; **b** resembling a cone. ▻ *noun* (**conic**) CONIC SECTION. ⓒ 17c: from Greek *konikos,* from *konos* cone.

conic section ▻ *noun, geom* the curved figure produced when a plane (see PLANE² *noun* 1) intersects a cone. Depending on the angle of the cut, it may be a CIRCLE, ELLIPSE, HYPERBOLA or PARABOLA.

conifer /'kɒnɪfə(r), 'koʊ-/ ▻ *noun* any of various, mostly evergreen, trees and shrubs with narrow needle-like leaves, which produce their pollen and seeds in cones, eg pine, spruce, cedar, yew, etc. ● **coniferous** /kɒ'nɪfərəs/ *adj* being a conifer; cone-bearing. ⓒ 19c: Latin, from *conus* cone + *ferre* to carry.

conj. ▻ *abbreviation, grammar* conjunction.

conjecture /kən'dʒektʃə(r)/ ▻ *noun* **1** an opinion based on incomplete evidence. **2** the process of forming such an opinion. ▻ *verb* (***conjectured, conjecturing***) *intr* to make a conjecture. ● **conjectural** *adj.* ● **conjecturally** *adverb.* ⓒ 16c: from Latin *conjectura* conclusion, from *conjicere* to throw together.

conjoin /kən'dʒɔɪn/ ▻ *verb, tr & intr* to join together, combine or unite. ● **conjoined** *adj.* ⓒ 14c: from French *conjoindre.*

conjoint ▻ *adj* joint; associated; united. ● **conjointly** *adverb.*

conjugal /'kɒndʒʊgəl/ ▻ *adj* relating to marriage, or to the relationship between husband and wife. ● **conjugality** *noun.* ● **conjugally** *adverb.* ⌚ 16c: from Latin *conjugalis*, from *conjunx* spouse, from *con-* together + *jugum* yoke.

conjugal family ▻ *noun* the family of one's husband or wife.

conjugate ▻ *verb* /'kɒndʒʊgeɪt/ (***conjugated, conjugating***) **1** *grammar* **a** to give the inflected parts of (a verb), indicating number, person, tense, MOOD and VOICE; **b** *intr* said of a verb: to undergo inflection □ *The verb 'to be' does not conjugate like more regular verbs in English.* **2** *intr, biol* to reproduce by conjugation. ▻ *adj* /-gət/ **1** joined, connected or coupled. **2** *chem* said of an acid and base: related to each other in such a way that the acid is converted into the BASE[1] (*noun 6*) by losing a PROTON, and the base is converted into the acid by gaining a proton. **3** said of words: having a common origin. ▻ *noun* /-gət/ a conjugate word or thing. ⌚ 15c: from Latin *conjugare, conjugatum* to yoke together.

conjugate angle ▻ *noun* one of a pair of angles whose sum is 360 degrees. Compare COMPLEMENTARY ANGLE, SUPPLEMENTARY ANGLE.

conjugation /kɒndʒʊ'geɪʃən/ ▻ *noun* **1** *grammar* **a** the inflection of a verb to indicate number, person, tense, VOICE and MOOD; **b** a particular class of verbs having the same set of inflections. See also DECLENSION. **2** a uniting, joining or fusing. **3** *biol* a method of sexual reproduction which involves the fusion of GAMETES.

conjunction /kən'dʒʌŋkʃən/ ▻ *noun* **1** *grammar* a word used to link sentences, clauses or other words, eg *and, but, if, or, because*, etc. **2** a joining together; combination. **3** the coinciding of two or more events. **4** *astron, astrol* the alignment of two or more heavenly bodies, as seen from Earth. ● **in conjunction with something** together with it. ⌚ 14c: from Latin *conjunctio*, from *conjungere* to join with.

conjunctiva /kɒndʒʌŋk'taɪvə/ ▻ *noun* (***conjunctivas*** or ***conjunctivae*** /-viː/) *anatomy* in the eye of vertebrates: the thin mucous membrane that lines the eyelids and covers the exposed surface of the cornea at the front of the eyeball. ● **conjunctival** *adj.* ⌚ 16c: from Latin *membrana conjunctiva* conjunctive membrane.

conjunctive ▻ *adj* **1** connecting; linking. **2** *grammar* relating to conjunctions. ▻ *noun, grammar* a word or phrase used as a conjunction. ● **conjunctively** *adverb.* ⌚ 15c: from Latin *conjunctivus*, from *conjungere* to join together.

conjunctivitis /kən'dʒʌnktɪvaɪtɪs/ ▻ *noun* inflammation of the conjunctiva. Also called **pink eye**.

conjuncture /kən'dʒʌnktʃə(r)/ ▻ *noun* a combination of circumstances, especially one leading to a crisis. ⌚ 17c: from Latin *conjungere* to join together.

conjure /'kʌndʒə(r)/ ▻ *verb* (***conjured, conjuring***) **1** *intr* to perform magic tricks, especially ones which deceive the eye or seem to defy nature. **2** to summon (a spirit, demon, etc) to appear. **3** /kɒn'dʒʊə(r)/ *old use* to beg someone earnestly to do something. ● **conjurer** or **conjuror** *noun* someone who performs magic tricks, etc, especially for the entertainment of others. ● **conjuring** *noun.* ● **a name to conjure with** a name of great importance or significance. ⌚ 13c: from Latin *conjurare* to swear together.

■ **conjure something up 1** to produce it as though from nothing. **2** to call up, evoke or stir (images, memories, etc).

conk[1] ▻ *noun, slang* **1** the nose. **2** the head. **3** a blow, especially on the head or nose. ▻ *verb* (***conked, conking***) to hit someone on the nose or head. ⌚ 19c: probably a variant of CONCH.

conk[2] ▻ *verb, intr, slang* (*usually* **conk out**) **1** said of a machine, etc: to break down. **2** said of a person: to collapse with fatigue, etc. ⌚ 20c.

conker ▻ *noun, colloq* the brown shiny seed of the HORSE CHESTNUT tree. ⌚ 19c: probably dialectal, meaning 'snail shell', from CONQUER.

conkers ▻ *singular noun, Brit* a children's game played with conkers threaded onto strings, the aim of which is to shatter one's opponent's conker by hitting it with one's own.

con man ▻ *noun, colloq* a swindler who uses a CONFIDENCE TRICK.

Conn. ▻ *abbreviation, US state* Connecticut.

connect /kə'nɛkt/ ▻ *verb* (***connected, connecting***) (*usually* **connect to** or **with someone** or **something**) **1** *tr & intr* to join; to link. **2** to associate or involve □ *is connected with advertising.* **3** *tr & intr* to associate or relate mentally □ *We connected immediately.* **4** to join by telephone. **5** to relate by marriage or birth. **6** *intr* said of aeroplanes, trains, buses, etc: to be timed so as to allow transfer from one to another. **7** *intr, humorous* said of the fist, etc: to strike. **8** *intr, colloq* to make sense. **9** *intr, US colloq* to meet someone in order to get illegal drugs from them. ● **connectable** or **connectible** *adj.* ● **connector** or **connecter** *noun.* ● **well connected** with important or aristocratic relatives. ⌚ 17c: from Latin *con-* together + *nectere* to fasten.

■ **connect up** to set up a computer connection with the Internet, eg linking a home or office computer via a modem to a company offering Internet access

■ **connect something up** to link it with something else.

connecting rod ▻ *noun* **1** a rod or bar attached to two parts of a machine, so that motion in one part causes motion in another. **2** in an internal-combustion engine: the metal rod connecting the piston to the crankshaft.

connection or **connexion** /kə'nɛkʃən/ ▻ *noun* **1** the act of connecting or state of being connected. **2** something that connects; a link. **3** a relationship through marriage or birth. **4** an especially influential person whom one meets through one's job, etc; a contact. **5 a** a train, bus, etc timed so as to allow transfer to it from another passenger service; **b** the transfer from one vehicle to another. **6** *US colloq* a supplier of illegal drugs. ● **in connection with something** to do with it; concerning it. ● **in this connection** with reference to the matter being considered.

connective ▻ *adj* serving to connect. ▻ *noun* **1** something which connects. **2** *grammar* a word which links phrases, clauses, other words, etc. **3** *zool* a bundle of nerve fibres which unite two nerve centres.

connective tissue ▻ *noun, anatomy* any of several widely differing tissues, usually containing COLLAGEN, that provide the animal body and its internal organs with structural support, eg bone, cartilage, tendons, ligaments.

connector see under CONNECT

conning tower ▻ *noun* **1** the raised part of a submarine containing the periscope, which is additionally used as an entrance or exit. **2** the armoured WHEELHOUSE of a warship. ⌚ 19c: from CON[3].

connive /kə'naɪv/ ▻ *verb* (***connived, conniving***) *intr* (*often* **connive with someone**) to conspire or plot. ● **connivance** *noun.* ● **conniver** *noun.* ⌚ 17c: from Latin *connivere* to blink or shut the eyes.

■ **connive at something** to pretend not to notice a wrongdoing.

connoisseur /kɒnə'sɜː(r), 'kɒnəsɜː(r)/ ▻ *noun* someone who is knowledgeable about and a good judge of a particular subject, eg the arts, wine, food, etc. ⌚ 18c: French, from Latin *cognoscere* to become thoroughly acquainted with.

connote /kə'noʊt/ ▷ *verb* (***connoted, connoting***) *formal* **1** said of a word: to suggest, in addition to its literal meaning □ ***'Portly' somehow connotes pomposity.*** **2** to include as a condition; to imply. Compare DENOTE. ● **connotation** /kɒnə'teɪʃən/ **1** the act of connoting. **2** an idea, association or implication additional to the main idea or object expressed. ● **connotative** /kɒnə'teɪtɪv/ *adj.* Ⓒ 17c: from Latin *connotare* to mark in addition.

connubial /kə'njuːbɪəl/ ▷ *adj* pertaining to marriage or to relations between a husband and wife. ● **connubially** *adverb.* Ⓒ 17c: from Latin *connubialis*, from *connubium* marriage.

conquer /'kɒŋkə(r)/ ▷ *verb* (***conquered, conquering***) **1** to gain possession or dominion over (territory) by force. **2** to defeat or overcome. **3** to overcome or put an end to (a failing, difficulty, evil, etc) □ ***He eventually conquered his fear of flying.*** **4** to succeed in climbing, reaching, traversing, etc. **5** to become successful or a celebrity in something □ ***They were the latest British group to conquer America.*** **6** *intr* to win; to succeed. ● **conquerable** *adj.* ● **conquering** *adj.* ● **conqueror** *noun.* Ⓒ 13c: from French *conquerre*, from Latin *conquirere* to go in search of.

conquest /'kɒŋkwɛst/ ▷ *noun* **1** the act of conquering. **2** a conquered territory. **3** something won by effort or force. **4 a** someone whose affection or admiration has been won; **b** the winning of the admiration of such a person. Ⓒ 13c: from French *conqueste*, from Latin *conquista*, from *conquirere* to go in search of.

conquistador /kəŋ'kwɪstədɔː(r), kɒŋ'kiːstadɔː(r), kɒn-/ ▷ *noun* (***conquistadores*** /-'dɔːreɪz/ or ***conquistadors***) an adventurer or conqueror, especially one of the 16th-century Spanish conquerors of Peru and Mexico. Ⓒ 19c: Spanish, meaning 'conqueror', from *conquistar* to conquer.

consanguinity /kɒnsaŋ'gwɪnɪtɪ/ ▷ *noun* **1** relationship by blood; descent from a common ancestor. **2** a close relationship or connection. ● **consanguine** /-gwɪn/ or **consanguineous** /-'gwɪnɪəs/ *adj.* Ⓒ 14c: from Latin *consanguinitas* blood relationship, from *sanguis* blood.

conscience /'kɒnʃəns/ ▷ *noun* the moral sense of right and wrong that determines someone's thoughts and behaviour. ● **in all conscience** by any normal standard of fairness. ● **on one's conscience** making one feel guilty. Ⓒ 13c: French, from Latin *conscientia* knowledge within oneself, from *con* together + *scire* to know.

conscience money ▷ *noun* money paid to make amends for some kind of wrongdoing, so that one feels less guilty.

conscience-stricken ▷ *adj* feeling guilty over something one has done.

conscientious /kɒnʃɪ'ɛnʃəs, kɒnsɪ'ɛnʃəs/ ▷ *adj* **1** careful; thorough; painstaking. **2** guided by conscience. ● **conscientiously** *adverb.* ● **conscientiousness** *noun.* Ⓒ 17c: from Latin *conscientiosus.*

conscientious objector ▷ *noun* someone who refuses to serve in the armed forces on moral grounds.

conscious /'kɒnʃəs/ ▷ *adj* **1** awake, alert and aware of one's thoughts and one's surroundings. **2** aware; knowing □ ***She was conscious that someone was watching her.*** **3** deliberate □ ***I made a conscious effort to be polite.*** **4** *often in compounds* concerned, especially too concerned, with □ ***image-conscious.*** ▷ *noun* the part of the human mind which is responsible for such awareness, and is concerned with perceiving and reacting to external objects and events. ● **consciously** *adverb.* ● **consciousness** *noun* **1** the state of being conscious. **2** awareness. **3** *psychol* the physical and mental state of being awake and fully aware of one's environment, thoughts and feelings. Ⓒ 17c: from Latin *conscius* knowing something with others, from *scire* to know.

conscript ▷ *verb* /kən'skrɪpt/ (***conscripted, conscripting***) to enlist for compulsory military service. ▷ *noun* /'kɒnskrɪpt/ someone who has been conscripted. ● **conscription** *noun.* Ⓒ 18c: from Latin *conscribere, conscriptum* to enlist.

consecrate /'kɒnsəkreɪt/ ▷ *verb* (***consecrated, consecrating***) **1** to set something apart for a holy use; to make sacred; to dedicate something to God. **2** *Christianity* to sanctify (bread and wine) for the EUCHARIST. **3** to devote something to a special use. ● **consecration** *noun.* Ⓒ 15c: from Latin *consecrare, consecratum* to make sacred, from *sacer* sacred.

consecutive /kən'sɛkjʊtɪv, kɒn-/ ▷ *adj* **1** following one after the other; in sequence. **2** *grammar* expressing result or consequence. ● **consecution** *noun.* ● **consecutively** *adverb.* ● **consecutiveness** *noun.* Ⓒ 17c: from French *consécutif*, from Latin *consecutus*, from *consequi* to follow.

consensus /kən'sɛnsəs/ ▷ *noun* (***consensuses***) general feeling or agreement; the majority view. ● **consensual** /-'sɛnsjʊəl/ *adj* **1** *law* said of a contract, etc: based on consent. **2** *physiol* said of a part of the body: reacting to the stimulation of another part. Ⓒ 19c: Latin, meaning 'agreement', from *consentire* to agree.

consent /kən'sɛnt/ ▷ *verb* (***consented, consenting***) **1** *intr* (*often* **consent to something**) to give one's permission for it; to agree to it. **2** to agree to do something. ▷ *noun* agreement; assent; permission □ ***give one's consent.*** ● **age of consent** see separate entry. ● **by common consent** as is generally agreed. Ⓒ 13c: from Latin *consentire* to agree.

consenting adult ▷ *noun* someone over the age of 18 who consents to something, especially (*Brit*) a homosexual relationship.

consequence /'kɒnsəkwɛns/ ▷ *noun* **1** something that follows from, or is caused by, an action or set of circumstances. **2** a conclusion reached from reasoning. **3** importance or significance □ ***of no consequence.*** ● **in consequence (of)** as a result (of). ● **take the consequences** to accept the (often unpleasant) results from one's decision or action. Ⓒ 14c: French, from Latin *consequentia*, from *consequi* to follow.

consequent /'kɒnsəkwɛnt/ ▷ *adj* **1** following as a result. **2** following as an inference. **3** said of a stream: flowing in the same direction as the slope on which it was originally formed. Compare OBSEQUENT, SUBSEQUENT.

consequential /kɒnsə'kwɛnʃəl/ ▷ *adj* **1** significant or important. **2** said of a person: self-important; pompous. **3** following as a result. ● **consequentiality** *noun.* ● **consequentially** *adverb.* Ⓒ 17c: from Latin *consequentia*, from *consequi* to follow.

consequentialism ▷ *noun, ethics* a theory which states that the morality of an action is judged according to how good or bad its consequences are. ● **consequentialist** *noun.* Ⓒ 20c.

consequently ▷ *adverb* as a result; therefore.

conservable see under CONSERVE

conservancy /kən'sɜːvənsɪ/ ▷ *noun* (***conservancies***) **1** in the UK: a court or commission having authority to preserve a port, river or area of countryside, etc. **2** an area under special environmental protection. **3** the act of CONSERVATION, especially the official care of a river, forest, etc. Ⓒ 18c: from Latin *conservare* to CONSERVE.

conservation /kɒnsə'veɪʃən/ ▷ *noun* **1** the act of conserving; the state of being conserved. **2** the protection and preservation of the environment, its wildlife and its natural resources. **3** the preservation of historical artefacts, eg books, paintings, monuments, for future generations. ● **conservational** *adj.* ● **conservationist** *noun* **1** someone who is trained or qualified to manage the environment and natural resources. **2** someone who actively encourages or supports conservation, especially of the environment or natural resources. Ⓒ 14c: from Latin *conservatio*, from *conservare* to save.

conservation area ▻ *noun* an area, especially in a village, town or city, designated as being of special architectural or historic interest, and therefore protected from any alterations that may threaten its character.

conservation law ▻ *noun, physics* a law which states that in the interaction between particles, certain quantities, eg mass, energy, charge, etc, remain unchanged by the process.

conservation of energy ▻ *noun, physics* the law which states that the total energy of an isolated system remains constant, ie it can be converted into another form but it cannot be destroyed or created.

conservation of mass ▻ *noun, physics* the principle which states that the total mass of an isolated system remains constant, ie it cannot be destroyed or created.

conservatism ▻ *noun* **1** the inclination to preserve the existing state of affairs and to avoid especially sudden or radical change. **2** (**Conservatism**) the policies and principles of a Conservative Party.

conservative /kən'sɜːvətɪv/ ▻ *adj* **1** favouring that which is established or traditional, with an opposition to change. **2** said of an estimate or calculation: deliberately low, for the sake of caution. **3** said of tastes, clothing, etc: restrained or modest; not flamboyant. **4** (**Conservative**) relating to a Conservative Party. ▻ *noun* **1** a traditionalist. **2** (**Conservative**) a member or supporter of a Conservative Party. ● **conservatively** *adverb*. ⓒ 14c: from Latin *conservare, conservatum* to preserve.

Conservative Party ▻ *noun* **1** in the UK: a political party on the right of the political spectrum, whose policies include support of established customs and institutions, opposition to socialism, a commitment to privatization, an emphasis on traditional family values and the advocation of free enterprise. Also called **Conservative and Unionist Party**. See also TORY. **2** in other countries: any of various right-leaning political parties.

conservatoire /kən'sɜːvətwɑː(r)/ ▻ *noun* a school specializing in the teaching of music. Also called **conservatory**. ⓒ 18c: French, from Italian *conservatorio* originally meaning 'an orphanage'.

conservatory /kən'sɜːvətrɪ/ ▻ *noun* (*conservatories*) **1 a** a greenhouse for plants; **b** a similar room used as a lounge, which is attached to and entered from, the house. **2** a conservatoire. ⓒ 17c: from Latin *conservare* to conserve.

conserve ▻ *verb* /kən'sɜːv/ (*conserved, conserving*) to keep safe from damage, deterioration, loss or undesirable change. ▻ *noun* /'kɒnsɜːv/ a type of jam, especially one containing chunks of fresh fruit. ● **conservable** *adj*. ⓒ 14c: from Latin *conservare* to save.

consider /kən'sɪdə(r)/ ▻ *verb* (*considered, considering*) **1** to go over something in one's mind. **2** to look at someone or something thoughtfully. **3** to call to mind for comparison, etc. **4** to assess with regard to employing, using, etc □ *consider someone for a job.* **5** to contemplate doing something. **6** to regard as something specified □ *He considered Neil to be his best friend.* **7** to think; to have as one's opinion. **8** to take into account; to make allowances for. **9** *intr* to think carefully. ● **all things considered** taking all the circumstances into account. ⓒ 14c: from Latin *considerare* to examine.

considerable ▻ *adj* **1** large; great. **2** having many admirable qualities; worthy □ *a considerable person.* ● **considerably** *adverb* largely; greatly. ⓒ 17c in this sense: from Latin *considerabilis* worthy to be considered.

considerate /kən'sɪdərət/ ▻ *adj* thoughtful regarding the feelings of others; kind. ● **considerately** *adverb*. ● **considerateness** *noun*. ⓒ 17c in this sense; from Latin *consideratus*, from *considerare* to examine.

consideration ▻ *noun* **1** thoughtfulness on behalf of others. **2** careful thought. **3** a fact, circumstance, etc to be taken into account. **4** a payment, reward or recompense. ● **in consideration of something a** because of it; **b** as payment for it; in return for it. ● **take something into consideration** to allow for it; to bear it in mind. ● **under consideration** being considered. ⓒ 14c: from Latin *consideratio*.

considered ▻ *adj* **1** carefully thought about □ *my considered opinion.* **2** *with an adverb* thought of or valued in a specified way □ *highly considered.*

considering ▻ *prep* in view of; when one considers. ▻ *conj* taking into account. ▻ *adverb* taking the circumstances into account □ *Her results were pretty good, considering.*

consign /kən'saɪn/ ▻ *verb* (*consigned, consigning*) **1** to hand over; to entrust. **2** to send, commit or deliver formally. **3** to send (goods). ● **consignable** *adj*. ● **consignee** *noun* someone to whom something is consigned. ● **consigner** or **consignor** *noun* someone who consigns. ⓒ 16c in this sense; from Latin *consignare* to put one's seal to, from *signum* mark.

consignment ▻ *noun* **1** a load of goods, etc sent or delivered. **2** the act of consigning. ● **on consignment** said of retail goods: to be paid for when sold.

consist /kən'sɪst, kɒn-/ ▻ *verb* (*consisted, consisting*) *intr* **1** (*always* **consist of something**) to be composed or made up of several elements or ingredients. **2** (*always* **consist in** or **of something**) to have it as an essential feature; to be contained □ *Her generosity consists in more than just her donations to charity.* ⓒ 16c: from Latin *consistere* to stand firm.

consist

See Usage Note at **comprise**.

consistency or **consistence** ▻ *noun* (*consistencies*) **1** the texture or composition of something, with regard to density, thickness, firmness, solidity, etc. **2** the quality of being consistent. **3** agreement; harmony. ⓒ 16c: from Latin *consistere* to stand firm.

consistent ▻ *adj* **1** (*usually* **consistent with something**) in agreement with it; in keeping with it. **2** reliable; regular; steady. **3** said of people or their actions: adhering to the same set of principles; not contradictory. ● **consistently** *adverb*. ⓒ 17c: from Latin *consistere* to stand firm.

consistory /kən'sɪstərɪ/ ▻ *noun* (*consistories*) *Christianity* an ecclesiastical council, especially one composed of the pope and cardinals, for conducting business. ⓒ 14c: from Latin *consistorium* meeting-place.

consolation /kɒnsə'leɪʃən/ ▻ *noun* **1** a circumstance or person that brings one comfort. **2** the act of consoling.

consolation prize ▻ *noun* a prize given to someone who has otherwise failed to win anything.

console¹ /kən'soʊl/ ▻ *verb* (*consoled, consoling*) to comfort in distress, grief or disappointment. ● **consolable** *adj*. ● **consolatory** *adj*. ● **consoler** *noun*. ⓒ 17c: from French *consoler*, from Latin *consolari*, from *solari* to soothe.

console² /'kɒnsoʊl/ ▻ *noun* **1** *music* the part of an organ with the keys, pedals and panels of stops. **2** a panel of dials, switches, etc for operating electronic equipment. **3** a freestanding cabinet for audio or video equipment. **4** an ornamental bracket for a shelf, etc. ⓒ 18c: French, apparently shortened from *consolateur* comforter or supporter.

consolidate /kən'sɒlɪdeɪt/ ▻ *verb* (*consolidated, consolidating*) *tr & intr* **1** to make or become solid or strong. **2** said of businesses, etc: to combine or merge into one. **3** *military* to rearrange and strengthen (one's position, etc). ● **consolidation** *noun*. ● **consolidator** *noun*. ⓒ 16c: from Latin *consolidare* to make firm, from *solidus* solid.

consols /ˈkɒnsɒlz, kənˈsɒlz/ ▻ *plural noun, Brit* irredeemable government securities. ⌚ 18c: shortened from CONSOLIDATED ANNUITIES.

consommé /kɒnˈsɒmeɪ, kən-/ ▻ *noun* (***consommés***) a type of thin clear soup made usually from meat stock. ⌚ 19c: French, from *consummare* to finish.

consonance /ˈkɒnsənəns/ ▻ *noun* **1** the state of agreement. **2** *music* a pleasant-sounding combination of musical notes. **3** *poetry* the repetition of sounds occupying the same position in a sequence of words.

consonant /ˈkɒnsənənt/ ▻ *noun* **a** any speech-sound produced by obstructing the passage of the breath in any of several ways; **b** a letter of the alphabet, used alone or in combination (as in *ch, ll, st,* etc), representing such a sound. Compare VOWEL. ▻ *adj* (**consonant with something**) in harmony or suitable with it. • **consonantal** *adj.* • **consonantly** *adverb.* ⌚ 14c: from Latin *consonans,* (*noun* sense *consonans litera* letter having the same sound), from *consonare* to sound together.

consort¹ ▻ *noun* /ˈkɒnsɔːt/ **1** a wife or husband, especially of a reigning sovereign. **2** *naut* an accompanying ship. ▻ *verb* /kənˈsɔːt/ (***consorted, consorting***) *intr* to agree. ⌚ 16c: from Latin *consors* sharer, from *con-* together + *sors* lot.

■ **consort with someone** (usually with unfavourable implications) to associate or keep company with them.

consort² /ˈkɒnsɔːt/ ▻ *noun* a group of singing or playing musicians, particularly specializing in early music. ⌚ 16c: erroneous variant of CONCERT.

consortium /kənˈsɔːtɪəm, -ˈsɔːʃəm/ ▻ *noun* (***consortia*** /-ə/ or ***consortiums***) **1** an association or combination of several banks, businesses, etc, usually for a specific purpose. **2** *law* the association between a husband and a wife and the right of each to enjoy the company and affection of the other. ⌚ 19c: Latin, meaning 'partnership', from CONSORT¹.

conspectus /kənˈspɛktəs/ ▻ *noun* (***conspectuses***) **1** a comprehensive survey or report. **2** a summary or synopsis. ⌚ 19c: Latin, meaning 'a view', from *conspicere, conspectum* to look at carefully.

conspicuous /kənˈspɪkjʊəs/ ▻ *adj* **1** visibly noticeable or obvious. **2** notable; striking; glaring. • **conspicuously** *adverb.* • **conspicuousness** *noun.* • **conspicuous by its absence** noticeable by the fact that it is not there. ⌚ 16c: from Latin *conspicuus* visible.

conspicuous consumption ▻ *noun* ostentatious spending on luxury goods in order to impress other people. ⌚ 20c.

conspiracy /kənˈspɪrəsɪ/ ▻ *noun* (***conspiracies***) **1** the act of plotting in secret. **2** a plot. **3** a group of conspirators. ⌚ 14c: from Latin *conspiratio* plot.

conspiracy of silence ▻ *noun* an agreement among a group of people to keep quiet about some state of affairs, usually because its disclosure could prove damaging, especially to them or their associates. ⌚ 19c.

conspirator /kənˈspɪrətə(r)/ ▻ *noun* someone who plots or joins a conspiracy. • **conspiratorial** *adj.* • **conspiratorially** *adverb.* ⌚ 15c: Latin, from *conspirare* to plot.

conspire /kənˈspaɪə(r)/ ▻ *verb* (***conspired, conspiring***) *intr* **1** to plot secretly together, especially for an unlawful purpose. **2** said of events: to seem to be working together to achieve a certain end □ *Everything conspired to make me miss my train.* ⌚ 13c: from Latin *conspirare* literally 'to breathe together'.

constable /ˈkʌnstəbəl, ˈkɒn-/ ▻ *noun* **1** a police officer of the most junior rank. **2** *historical* the chief officer of a royal household. **3** the governor of a royal castle. See also SPECIAL CONSTABLE. ⌚ 13c: from French *conestable,* from Latin *comes stabuli* count of the stable.

constabulary /kənˈstabjʊlərɪ/ ▻ *noun* (***constabularies***) the police force of a district or county. ▻ *adj* relating to constables or the police. ⌚ 19c: from Latin *constabularius,* from *constabulus* constable.

constant /ˈkɒnstənt/ ▻ *adj* **1** never stopping. **2** frequently recurring. **3** unchanging. **4** faithful; loyal. ▻ *noun, math* a symbol representing an unspecified number, which remains unchanged, unlike a VARIABLE. • **constancy** *noun.* • **constantly** *adverb.* ⌚ 14c: French, from Latin *constans,* from *constare* to stand together.

constellation /kɒnstəˈleɪʃən/ ▻ *noun* **1** *astron* **a** any of 88 regions into which the sky is conceptually divided, with each region containing a group of stars; **b** *non-technical* a group of stars. **2** a group of associated people or things. ⌚ 14c: from Latin *constellatio,* from *con-* together + *stella* star.

consternate /ˈkɒnstəneɪt/ ▻ *verb* (***consternated, consternating***) to fill with anxiety, dismay or confusion. • **consternation** *noun* dismay, alarm, anxiety or confusion. ⌚ 17c: from Latin *consternare* to dismay.

constipate /ˈkɒnstɪpeɪt/ ▻ *verb* (***constipated, constipating***) to cause constipation in (a person, etc). • **constipated** *adj* suffering from constipation. ⌚ 16c: from Latin *constipare, constipatum* to press closely together.

constipation ▻ *noun* a condition in which the faeces become hard, and bowel movements occur infrequently or with pain or difficulty.

constituency /kənˈstɪtʃʊənsɪ/ ▻ *noun* (***constituencies***) **1** the district represented by a member of parliament or other representative in a legislative body. **2** the voters in that district. ⌚ 19c: from CONSTITUENT.

constituent /kənˈstɪtʃʊənt/ ▻ *adj* **1** forming part of a whole. **2** having the power to create or alter a constitution □ *a constituent assembly.* **3** having the power to elect. ▻ *noun* **1** a necessary part; a component. **2** a resident in a constituency. ⌚ 17c: from Latin *constituens,* from *constituere* to establish.

constituent analysis ▻ *noun, linguistics* the process of analysing linguistic constructions by breaking them down into the components or constituents from which they are made, ultimately including the division of words into stems and affixes.

constitute /ˈkɒnstɪtuːt/ ▻ *verb* (***constituted, constituting***) **1** to be; to make up. **2** to establish formally. **3** to appoint □ *The board of enquiry was recently constituted.* ⌚ 15c: from Latin *constituere* to establish.

constitution /kɒnstɪˈtʃuːʃən/ ▻ *noun* **1** a set of rules governing an organization. **2** the supreme laws and rights upon which a country or state is founded, especially when it is seen as embodying the rights of its people. **3** (*often* **Constitution**) in the US, Australia, etc: the legislation which states such laws and rights. **4** a set of rules governing an organization. **5** the way in which something is formed or made up. **6** one's physical make-up, health, temperament, etc. **7** the act of forming or constituting. ⌚ 16c: from Latin *constitutio* arrangement or physical make-up, from *constitutere* to establish.

constitutional ▻ *adj* **1** legal according to a given constitution. **2** relating to, or controlled by, a constitution. **3** relating to one's physical make-up, health, etc. **4** inherent in the natural make-up or structure of a person or thing. ▻ *noun, dated* a regular walk taken for the sake of one's health. • **constitutionality** *noun.* • **constitutionally** *adverb.*

constitutionalism ▻ *noun* **1** a system of government based on a constitution. **2** adherence to the principles of the constitution.

constrain /kənˈstreɪn/ ▻ *verb* (***constrained, constraining***) **1** to force; to compel. **2** to limit the freedom, scope or range of someone. ⌚ 14c: from French *constraindre,* from Latin *constringere* to tie tightly together.

constrain, restrain

There is often confusion between **constrain** and **restrain**: **constrain** means 'to force or compel' and is usually used in the passive □ *You need not feel constrained to go*; **restrain** means 'to control or hold back' □ *He had to be restrained from hitting the man.*

constrained ▻ *adj* awkward; embarrassed; forced.

constraint ▻ *noun* **1** a limit or restriction. **2** force; compulsion. **3** awkwardness, embarrassment or inhibition.

constrict /kən'strɪkt/ ▻ *verb* (***constricted, constricting***) **1 a** to squeeze or compress; **b** to enclose tightly, especially too tightly; **c** to cause to tighten. **2** to inhibit. ● **constriction** *noun* **1** the process of constricting. **2** something that is constricted. **3** contraction; tightness. ● **constrictive** *adj* causing a constriction. ⓒ 18c: from Latin *constrictus*, from *constringere* to tie together tightly.

constrictor ▻ *noun* **1** a snake that kills by coiling around its prey and squeezing it until it suffocates. See also BOA. **2** *anatomy* any muscle that compresses an organ or narrows an opening.

construct ▻ *verb* /kən'strʌkt/ (***constructed, constructing***) **1** to build. **2** to form, compose or put together. **3** *geom* to draw (a figure). ▻ *noun* /'kɒnstrʌkt/ **1** something constructed, especially in the mind. **2** *psychol* a complex idea or thought constructed from a number of simpler ideas or thoughts. ● **constructor** or **constructer** *noun*. ● **constructable** or **constructible** *adj*. ⓒ 17c: from Latin *construere, constructum* to heap together.

construction ▻ *noun* **1** the process of building or constructing. **2** something built or constructed; a building. **3** *grammar* the arrangement of words in a particular grammatical relationship. **4** interpretation □ *put a wrong construction on someone's words.* **5** *geom* a figure drawn by following certain conditions, eg only using a ruler and compass. ● **constructional** *adj*. ● **constructionally** *adverb*.

constructive ▻ *adj* **1** helping towards progress or development; useful. **2** *law* said of facts: inferred rather than directly expressed. **3** relating to construction. ● **constructively** *adverb*. ● **constructiveness** *noun*.

constructive dismissal ▻ *noun* treatment of an employee by an employer, or an action, which leaves the employee with no alternative but to resign. ⓒ 20c.

Constructivism ▻ *noun* a Russian art movement concerned with non-representational sculpture made out of wood, plastic, etc, often suspended from the ceiling.

constructor see under CONSTRUCT

construe /kən'struː, 'kɒnstruː/ ▻ *verb* (***construed, construing***) **1** to interpret or explain. **2** *grammar* to analyse the grammatical structure of (a sentence, etc). **3** *grammar* (*often* **construe with**) to combine words grammatically. **4** *grammar, dated* to translate word for word. **5** to deduce; to infer. ⓒ 14c: from Latin *construere* to heap together.

consubstantiation /kɒnsəbstansɪ'eɪʃən, kɒnsʌb-/ ▻ *noun, Christianity* a doctrine attributed to Luther, describing the presence of Christ in the EUCHARIST as 'under and with the elements of bread and wine'. Compare TRANSUBSTANTIATION. ⓒ 16c: from Latin *consubstantiare* to identify in substance, from *con* together + *substantia* substance; modelled upon the earlier TRANSUBSTANTIATION.

consul /'kɒnsəl/ ▻ *noun* **1** an official representative of a state, stationed in a foreign country to look after its commercial interests there, the interests of its citizens living there, etc. **2** *historical* in ancient Rome: either of the two joint chief magistrates. ● **consular** /'kɒnsjʊlə(r)/ *adj*. ● **consulship** *noun*. ⓒ 14c: Latin, probably related to *consulere* to take counsel.

consulate /'kɒnsjʊlət, 'kɒnsələt/ ▻ *noun* the post or official residence of a consul (see CONSUL 1).

consult /kən'sʌlt, 'kɒnsʌlt/ ▻ *verb* (***consulted, consulting***) **1** to ask the advice of □ *consult a lawyer.* **2** to refer to (a map, book, etc). **3** to consider (wishes, feelings, etc). **4** *intr* (*often* **consult with someone**) to have discussions with them. **5** *intr* to give advice as a consultant □ *He consults on Tuesday and Friday afternoons.* ⓒ 16c: from Latin *consultare*, from *consulere* to take counsel.

consultant ▻ *noun* **1** someone who gives professional advice. **2** in a hospital or clinic: a doctor or surgeon holding the most senior post in a particular field of medicine, and accepting ultimate responsibility for the treatment and care of patients. **3** someone who seeks advice or information. ● **consultancy** *noun* (***consultancies***).

consultation /kɒnsəl'teɪʃən/ ▻ *noun* **1** the act or process of consulting. **2** a meeting for the obtaining of advice or for discussion. ● **consultative** /kən'sʌltətɪv/ *adj* available for consultation; advisory.

consulting ▻ *adj* acting as an adviser □ *a consulting architect.*

consulting room ▻ *noun* the room in which a doctor sees patients.

consume /kən'sjuːm, -'suːm/ ▻ *verb* (***consumed, comsuming***) **1** to eat or drink. **2** to use up. **3** to destroy. **4** to devour or overcome completely □ *He was consumed by jealousy.* **5** to waste away. ● **consumable** *adj*. ● **consuming** *adj* overwhelming. ⓒ 14c: from Latin *consumere* to take up completely.

consumer ▻ *noun* **1** someone who buys goods and services for personal use or need. **2** someone or something that consumes.

consumer durables ▻ *plural noun* goods that are designed to last for a relatively long time and do not need frequent replacement, eg furniture, television sets, etc.

consumer goods ▻ *plural noun* goods bought to satisfy personal needs, as distinct from those used in the production of other goods.

consumerism ▻ *noun* **1** the protection of the interests of consumers. **2** *econ* the theory that steady growth in the consumption of goods is necessary for a sound economy.

consumer protection ▻ *noun* activities devised to protect buyers of goods and services against inferior or dangerous products and misleading advertising.

consumer research ▻ *noun* the study of the needs and preferences of consumers.

consumer society ▻ *noun* the advanced stage of industrial society, in which there is a high availability and consumption of consumer goods and services. See also CONSUMER SOVEREIGNTY.

consumer sovereignty ▻ *noun, econ* the power of the consumer, as the purchaser of goods and services, to determine which goods are actually produced.

consumer terrorism ▻ *noun* the deliberate contamination of certain food products with harmful substances, usually in order to blackmail the producers or retailers of the products involved.

consummate ▻ *verb* /'kɒnsəmeɪt, 'kɒnsjʊmeɪt/ (***consummated, consummating***) **1** to finish, perfect or complete something. **2** to complete (a marriage) in its full legal sense through the act of sexual intercourse. ▻ *adj* /kən'sʌmət/ **1** supreme; very great; very skilled. **2** complete; utter □ *a consummate idiot.* ● **consummately** *adverb* perfectly; with great skill. ● **consummation** /kɒnsə'meɪʃən/ *noun* **1** the act of consummating. **2** perfection. ⓒ 16c: from Latin *consummare, consummatum* to complete or perfect.

consumption /kən'sʌmpʃən, -sʌmʃən/ ▻ *noun* **1** the act or process of consuming. **2** the amount consumed. **3** the buying and using of goods. **4** *dated* another name for

TUBERCULOSIS of the lungs. ⓒ 14c: from Latin *consumptio*, from *consumere* to consume.

consumptive /kən'sʌmptɪv, -sʌmtɪv/ ▻ *adj* **1** relating to consumption; wasteful or destructive. **2** suffering from TUBERCULOSIS of the lungs. ▻ *noun* someone suffering from tuberculosis of the lungs. ● **consumptively** *adverb*. ● **consumptiveness** or **consumptivity** /-'tɪvɪtɪ/ *noun*.

cont. ▻ *abbreviation* **1** continued. **2** contents.

contact /'kɒntakt/ ▻ *noun* **1** the condition of touching physically. **2** communication or a means of communication. **3** an acquaintance whose influence or knowledge may prove useful, especially in business. **4** in an electrical device: a connection made of a conducting material that allows the passage of a current by forming a junction with another conducting part, eg a switch that can be used to make or break a circuit. Also called **electric contact**. **5** someone who has been exposed to an infectious disease and is therefore capable of transmitting it. **6** a contact lens. ▻ *verb* (*contacted*, *contacting*) to get in touch with someone; to communicate with someone. ● **contactable** *adj*. ⓒ 17c: from Latin *contactus*, from *contingere* to touch each other.

contact lens ▻ *noun* a small lens, usually made from plastic, which is placed in direct contact with the eyeball to correct vision.

contact process ▻ *noun, chem* the process by which sulphuric acid is manufactured on an industrial scale by the oxidation of sulphur dioxide to sulphur trioxide in the presence of a catalyst.

contagion /kən'teɪdʒən/ ▻ *noun* **1** the transmission of a disease by direct physical contact with an infected person. **2** *dated* a disease that is transmitted in this way. **3** a harmful influence. **4** the transmission of an emotional state □ *contagion of excitement*. ⓒ 14c: from Latin *contagio* touching, contact, from *con* together + *tangere* to touch.

contagious /kən'teɪdʒəs/ ▻ *adj* **1** formerly used to denote a disease that can only be transmitted by direct contact. **2** denoting a disease that can be transmitted by direct contact with or close proximity to an infected individual, eg the common cold. Also called COMMUNICABLE. **3** denoting an organism that has been exposed to and is capable of transmitting such a disease. **4** said of a mood, laughter, etc: spreading easily from person to person; affecting everyone in the vicinity.

contagious

See Usage Note at **infectious**.

contain /kən'teɪn/ ▻ *verb* (*contained*, *containing*) **1** to hold or be able to hold. **2** to consist of something specified. **3** to control, limit, check or prevent the spread of something □ *The prison staff were able to contain the riot without the help of the police.* **4** to control (oneself or one's feelings). **5** to enclose or surround. **6** *math* to be divisible by (a number) without leaving a remainder. ● **containable** *adj*. ⓒ 13c: from Latin *continere* to hold together.

container ▻ *noun* **1** an object designed for holding or storing, such as a box, tin, carton, etc. **2** a huge sealed metal box of standard size and design for carrying goods by lorry or ship.

containerize or **containerise** ▻ *verb* (*containerized*, *containerizing*) **1** to put (cargo) into containers. **2** to convert so as to be able to handle containers. ● **containerization** or **containerisation** *noun*. ⓒ 20c.

container ship ▻ *noun* a cargo ship designed to carry 6m or 12m containers in pre-determined positions, largely dispensing with the loading and stowage problems associated with traditional cargo.

containment ▻ *noun* the action of preventing the expansion of a hostile power, etc.

containment building ▻ *noun* a steel or concrete structure enclosing a nuclear reactor, designed to withstand high pressure and high temperature and, in an emergency, to contain the escape of radiation.

contaminate /kən'tamɪneɪt, kɒn-/ ▻ *verb* (*contaminated*, *contaminating*) **1** to pollute or infect (a substance). **2** to make something radioactive by exposing it to radioactive material. ● **contaminable** *adj*. ● **contaminant** *noun*. ● **contamination** *noun*. ● **contaminator** *noun*. ⓒ 16c: from Latin *contaminare*, *contaminatum* to corrupt.

contd ▻ *abbreviation* continued.

contemn /kən'tɛm/ ▻ *verb* (*contemned*, *contemning*) *literary* to despise, disdain or scorn. ⓒ 15c: from Latin *contemnere*, from *temnere* to slight.

contemplate /'kɒntəmpleɪt/ ▻ *verb* (*contemplated*, *contemplating*) **1** *tr & intr* to think about; to go over something mentally; to meditate. **2** to look thoughtfully at something. **3** to consider something as a possibility. ● **contemplation** *noun*. ● **contemplator** *noun*. ⓒ 16c: from Latin *contemplari* to survey or look at carefully, from *templum* temple.

contemplative /kən'tɛmplətɪv, 'kɒntəmpleɪtɪv/ ▻ *adj* **1** thoughtful; meditative. **2** relating to religious contemplation. ▻ *noun* someone whose life is spent in religious contemplation. ● **contemplatively** *adverb*. ● **contemplativeness** *noun*.

contemporaneous /kəntɛmpə'reɪnɪəs/ ▻ *adj* (*often* **contemporaneous with something**) existing or happening at the same time or period. ● **contemporaneity** /kəntɛmpərə'niːɪtɪ, -'neɪtɪ/ *noun*. ● **contemporaneously** *adverb*. ● **contemporaneousness** *noun*. ⓒ 17c: from Latin *contemporaneus*, from *con-* same + *tempus* time.

contemporary /kən'tɛmpərərɪ/ ▻ *adj* **1** (*often* **contemporary with something**) belonging to the same period or time as something. **2** (*often* **contemporary with someone**) around the same age as them. **3** modern. ▻ *noun* (*contemporaries*) **1** someone who lives or lived at the same time as another. **2** someone of about the same age as another. ● **contemporarily** *adverb*. ⓒ 17c: from Latin *contemporarius*, from *con-* same + *tempus* time.

contemporize or **contemporise** /kən'tɛmpəraɪz/ ▻ *verb* (*contemporized*, *contemporizing*) *tr & intr* to make contemporary.

contempt /kən'tɛmpt/ ▻ *noun* **1** scorn. **2** *law* disregard of or disobedience to the rules of a court of law. ● **hold someone in contempt** to despise them. ⓒ 14c: from Latin *con-* intensive + *temnere*, *temptum* to scorn.

contemptible ▻ *adj* **1** despicable; disgusting; vile. **2** worthless; paltry. ● **contemptibility** or **contemptibleness** *noun*. ● **contemptibly** *adverb*.

contemptuous /kən'tɛmptʃʊəs/ ▻ *adj* (*often* **contemptuous of someone** or **something**) showing contempt or scorn. ● **contemptuously** *adverb*. ● **contemptuousness** *noun*. ⓒ 16c: from Latin *con-* intensive + *temnere*, *temptum* to scorn.

contend /kən'tɛnd/ ▻ *verb* (*contended*, *contending*) **1** *intr* (*often* **contend with someone** or **something**) to struggle, strive, fight or compete. **2** *intr* to argue earnestly. **3** to say, maintain or assert something. ● **contender** *noun*. ⓒ 15c: from Latin *con-* with + *tendere* to strive.

content[1] /kən'tɛnt/ ▻ *adj* (*often* **content with something**) satisfied; happy; uncomplaining. ▻ *verb* (*contented*, *contenting*) to satisfy or make (oneself or another) satisfied. ▻ *noun* peaceful satisfaction; peace of mind. ● **contentment** *noun*. ⓒ 14c: from Latin *contentus* contained, hence satisfied, from *continere* to hold together.

content[2] /'kɒntɛnt/ ▻ *noun* **1** the subject-matter of a book, speech, etc. **2** the proportion in which a particular ingredient is present in something □ *a diet with a high* *starch content.* **3** (**contents**) the items contained in something. **4** (**contents**) **a** the text of a book, divided into chapters; **b** a list of these chapters, given at the beginning of the book. ◷ 15c: from Latin *contenta* things contained, from *continere* to contain.

content analysis ▷ *noun, linguistics* the process of analysing linguistic constructions into units of independent meaning, as in the sentence *Lions eat meat*, where there are three clear units of meaning.

contented /kən'tɛntɪd/ ▷ *adj* peacefully happy or satisfied. ● **contentedly** *adverb*. ● **contentedness** *noun*.

contention /kən'tɛnʃən/ ▷ *noun* **1** a point that one asserts or maintains in an argument. **2** argument or debate. ● **bone of contention** see separate entry. ◷ 14c: from Latin *contentio* strife, controversy, from *contendere* to strive.

contentious /kən'tɛnʃəs/ ▷ *adj* **1** likely to cause argument or quarrelling. **2** quarrelsome or argumentative. ● **contentiously** *adverb*. ● **contentiousness** *noun*. ◷ 15c: from Latin *contentiosus*, from *contendere* to strive.

contentment see under CONTENT[1]

conterminous /kən'tɜːmɪnəs/ or **coterminous** /koʊ-/ ▷ *adj* having the same boundaries, duration or range. ◷ 17c: from CON- + Latin *terminus* boundary.

contest ▷ *noun* /'kɒntɛst/ **1** a competition. **2** a struggle. ▷ *verb* /kən'tɛst/ (***contested, contesting***) **1** to enter the competition or struggle for something. **2** *tr & intr* to dispute (a claim, a will, etc). ● **contestable** *adj*. ● **contestation** *noun*. ● **contested** *adj*. ● **contester** *noun*. ◷ 16c: from Latin *contestari* to call to witness.

contestant /kən'tɛstənt/ ▷ *noun* someone who takes part in a contest; a competitor.

context /'kɒntɛkst/ ▷ *noun* **1** the pieces of writing in a passage which surround a particular word, phrase, etc and which contribute to the full meaning of the word, phrase, etc in question. **2** circumstances, background or setting. ● **contextual** *adj*. ● **out of context** without regard or reference to context. ◷ 16c: from Latin *contextus* connection, from *con-* together + *texere* to weave.

contiguous /kən'tɪgjʊəs/ ▷ *adj* **1** (*often* **contiguous with** or **to something**) **a** touching; **b** neighbouring or adjacent. **2** near or next in order or time. ● **contiguity** /kɒntɪ'gjuːɪtɪ/ *noun*. ● **contiguously** *adverb*. ◷ 17c: from Latin *contiguus*, from *contingere* to touch each other.

continence /'kɒntɪnəns/ ▷ *noun* **1** the ability to control one's bowels and bladder. **2** self-control; control over one's appetites and passions. ◷ 14c: from Latin *continere* to hold together.

continent[1] /'kɒntɪnənt/ ▷ *noun* **1 a** any of the seven main land masses of the world, namely Europe, Asia, N America, S America, Africa, Australia and Antarctica; **b** the mainland portion of one of these land masses. **2** (**the Continent**) the mainland of Europe, as regarded from the British Isles. ◷ 16c: from Latin, representing the phrase *terra continens* continuous land.

continent[2] /'kɒntɪnənt/ ▷ *adj* **1** able to control one's bowels and bladder. **2** self-controlled, especially with regard to one's passions. ◷ 14c: see CONTINENCE.

continental /kɒntɪ'nɛntəl/ ▷ *adj* (*sometimes* **Continental**) **1** belonging or relating to the mainland of the continent of Europe. **2** relating to any of the continents of the world. ▷ *noun, dated* an inhabitant of the mainland of Europe.

continental breakfast ▷ *noun* a light breakfast of rolls and coffee.

continental climate ▷ *noun* the climate typical of the interior of a continent, having hot summers, cold winters and low rainfall.

continental drift ▷ *noun, geol* the theory that the continents were formed by the break-up of a single land mass, the constituent parts of which drifted apart horizontally across the Earth's surface. Sometimes shortened to **drift**.

continental quilt ▷ *noun* a DUVET.

continental shelf ▷ *noun, geol* the part of a continent that is submerged in an area of relatively shallow sea.

contingency /kən'tɪndʒənsɪ/ ▷ *noun* (***contingencies***) **1** something liable, but not certain, to occur; a chance happening. **2** something dependent on a chance future happening.

contingency plans ▷ *noun* plans made in case a certain situation should arise.

contingent /kən'tɪndʒənt/ ▷ *noun* **1** a body of troops. **2** any identifiable body of people □ *There were boos from the Welsh contingent.* ▷ *adj* **1** (*usually* **contingent on** or **upon something**) dependent on some uncertain circumstance. **2** liable but not certain to occur. **3** accidental. ◷ 14c: from Latin *contingere* to touch together.

continual /kən'tɪnjʊəl/ ▷ *adj* **1** constantly happening or done; frequent. **2** constant; never ceasing. ● **continually** *adverb*. ◷ 14c: from Latin *continualis*, from *continuus* uninterrupted.

> ***continual***
>
> See Usage Note at **continuous**.

continuance /kən'tɪnjʊəns/ ▷ *noun* **1** the act or state of continuing. **2** duration. **3** *US law* an adjournment or postponement. ◷ 14c: from Latin *continuare* to make continuous.

continuation /kəntɪnjʊ'eɪʃən, kɒn-/ ▷ *noun* **1** the act or process of continuing, often after a break or pause. **2** that which adds to something or carries it on, eg a further episode of or sequel to a story.

continue /kən'tɪnjuː, kɒn-/ ▷ *verb* (***continued, continuing***) **1** *tr & intr* to go on without stopping. **2** *tr & intr* to last or cause to last. **3** *tr & intr* to carry on or start again after a break. **4** *intr* to keep moving in the same direction. ◷ 14c: from Latin *continuare* to make continuous.

> ■ **continue with something** to persist in it; to keep on with it.

continuity /kɒntɪ'njuːɪtɪ/ ▷ *noun* **1** the state of being continuous, unbroken or consistent. **2** *TV, cinema* the arrangement of scenes so that one progresses smoothly from another, without any inconsistencies, eg in actors' clothing, etc. ◷ 16c: from Latin *continuitas*, from *continuus* uninterrupted.

continuity announcer ▷ *noun, TV* the person who speaks during the gaps between programmes, usually announcing the name of the programme which is to follow or giving information about future broadcasts.

continuity girl and **continuity man** ▷ *noun, cinema* the person responsible for ensuring the continuity of films.

continuo /kɒn'tɪnjʊoʊ/ ▷ *noun* (***continuos***) *music* **a** a bass part for a keyboard or stringed instrument; **b** the instrument or instruments playing this. Also called **thorough bass**. ◷ 18c: Italian, meaning 'continuous'.

continuous /kən'tɪnjʊəs/ ▷ *adj* **1** incessant. **2** unbroken; uninterrupted. **3** *grammar* said of a verbal aspect or tense: representing continuing action or a continuing state, in English formed with the auxiliary verb *be* and the present PARTICIPLE, as in *I am waiting, They were dancing, You will be playing tomorrow.* Also called PROGRESSIVE. ● **continuously** *adverb*. ◷ 17c: from Latin *continuus* unbroken, from *continere* to hold together.

continuous assessment ▷ *noun, education* the judging of students' progress by means of frequent tests, essays, etc throughout the year, rather than by end-of-year examinations.

continuous, continual

Note that something that is **continuous** exists or happens for a period without a break, whereas something that is **continual** exists or happens repeatedly over a period, so that *a continuous disturbance* goes on for a time without a break, whereas *continual disturbances* are several occurrences with gaps between them.

continuous creation ▷ *noun* the theory that creation is an ongoing process rather than a single act.

continuous representation ▷ *noun, art* the depiction of several consecutive stages of a story in one picture, so that the same character may well appear more than once in the same picture.

continuous stationery ▷ *noun* stationery consisting of a long sheet of paper with regular perforations.

continuum /kən'tɪnjʊəm, kɒn-/ ▷ *noun* (***continua*** /-njʊə/ or ***continuums***) a continuous sequence; an unbroken progression. ⓘ 17c: Latin, from *continuus* unbroken.

contort /kən'tɔːt/ ▷ *verb* (***contorted, contorting***) *tr & intr* to twist violently out of shape. ● **contorted** *adj*. ● **contortion** /kən'tɔːʃən/ *noun* **1** a violent twisting. **2** a deformed shape. ● **contortive** *adj*. ⓘ 16c: from Latin *contorquere, contortum* to twist.

contortionist ▷ *noun* **1** an entertainer who is able to twist their body into spectacularly unnatural positions. **2** someone who twists the meanings of words and phrases.

contour /'kɒntʊə(r), -tɔː(r)/ ▷ *noun* **1** (*often* **contours**) the distinctive outline of something. **2** a line on a map joining points of the same height or depth. Also called **contour line**. ▷ *verb* (***contoured, contouring***) **1** to shape the contour of, or shape so as to fit a contour. **2** to mark the contour lines on (a map). ⓘ 17c: French, from Italian *contornare* to draw in outline.

contra /'kɒntrə/ ▷ *noun* (*often* **Contra**) a member of a right-wing guerilla group in Central America, who attempted to overthrow the government in Nicaragua. ⓘ 1980s: shortened from Spanish *contrarrevolucionario* counter-revolutionary.

contra- /'kɒntrə/ ▷ *prefix* **1** against □ *contraception.* **2** opposite □ *contraflow.* **3** contrasting □ *contradistinction.* **4** *music* lower in pitch □ *contrabass.* ⓘ Latin.

contraband /'kɒntrəband/ ▷ *noun* **1** the smuggling of goods prohibited from being imported or exported. **2** smuggled goods. ▷ *adj* **1** prohibited from being imported or exported. **2** smuggled. ⓘ 16c: from Spanish *contrabanda*, from Latin *contra-* against + *bannum* ban.

contrabass /'kɒntrəbeɪs/ ▷ *noun* the DOUBLE BASS.

contrabassoon ▷ *noun, music* a BASSOON which sounds an octave lower than the standard instrument. Also called **double bassoon**. ⓘ 19c: from Latin *contra-* against + BASSOON.

contraception /kɒntrə'sɛpʃən/ ▷ *noun* the deliberate prevention of pregnancy by artificial or natural means. ⓘ 19c: from CONTRA- + CONCEPTION.

contraceptive /kɒntrə'sɛptɪv/ ▷ *noun* a drug or device that prevents pregnancy resulting from sexual intercourse. ▷ *adj* having the effect of preventing pregnancy.

contract ▷ *noun* /'kɒntrakt/ **1** an agreement, especially a legally binding one. **2** a document setting out the terms of such an agreement. **3** *slang* in criminal circles: an agreement to kill someone in return for a usually considerable sum of money. ▷ *verb* /kən'trakt/ (***contracted, contracting***) **1** *tr & intr* to make or become smaller. **2** *tr & intr* said of muscles: to make or become shorter, especially in order to bend a joint, etc. **3** *tr & intr* said of the brows: to draw together into a frown. **4** to catch (a disease). **5** to enter into (an alliance or marriage). **6** to incur or accumulate (a debt). **7** *tr & intr* said of a word, phrase, etc: to reduce to a short form □ *'Are not' is contracted to 'aren't'.* **8** *tr & intr* (*often* **contract with someone**) to enter a legal contract concerning them. ● **contractable** *adj* said of a disease, habit, etc: likely to be contracted. ● **contractible** *adj* said of a muscle, word, etc: capable of being contracted. ● **put a contract out on someone** to arrange to have them killed by a third party, usually for a considerable sum of money. ⓘ 14c: from Latin *contractus* agreement, from *contrahere* to draw together.

■ **contract in** or **out** to arrange to participate, or not to participate, eg in a pension scheme.

■ **contract something out** or **put something out to contract** said of a business company, etc: to arrange for part of a job to be done by another company.

contract bridge ▷ *noun* the usual form of the card game bridge, in which only tricks bid and won count in one's score. Compare AUCTION BRIDGE.

contraction /kən'trakʃən/ ▷ *noun* **1** the process of contracting or state of being contracted. **2** a decrease in length, size or volume. **3** a tightening of the muscles caused by a shortening in length of the muscle fibres. **4** (**contractions**) the regular painful spasms of the muscles of the uterus that occur during labour. **5** a shortened form of a word or phrase which includes at least the last letter of the word or phrase □ *'Aren't' is a contraction of 'are not'.* ● **contractive** *adj*.

contractor /kən'traktə(r)/ ▷ *noun* **1** a person or firm that undertakes work on contract, especially connected with building, installation of equipment or the transportation of goods. **2** something which contracts.

contractual /kən'traktʃʊəl/ ▷ *adj* relating to a contract or binding agreement. ● **contractually** *adverb*.

contradict /kɒntrə'dɪkt/ ▷ *verb* (***contradicted, contradicting***) **1** to assert the opposite of or deny (a statement, etc) made by (a person). **2** said of a statement, action, etc: to disagree or be inconsistent with another. ⓘ 16c: from Latin *contradicere, contradictum* to speak against.

contradiction ▷ *noun* **1** the act of contradicting. **2** one statement contradicting another, etc. **3** denial. **4** inconsistency. ● **contradiction in terms** a statement which contains some kind of contradiction.

contradictory ▷ *adj* **1** inconsistent. **2** denying. **3** contrary. ● **contradictorily** *adverb*. ● **contradictoriness** *noun*.

contradistinction /kɒntrədɪ'stɪŋkʃən/ ▷ *noun* a distinction made in terms of a contrast between qualities, properties, etc. ● **contradistinctive** *adj*.

contraflow /'kɒntrəfloʊ/ ▷ *noun* a form of traffic diversion whereby traffic moving in opposite directions share the same carriageway of a motorway, dual carriageway, etc. ⓘ 20c: from CONTRA- + FLOW.

contraindicate /kɒntrə'ɪndɪkeɪt/ ▷ *verb* (***contraindicated, contraindicating***) *medicine* to point to (a treatment, operation, etc) as unsuitable. ● **contraindicant** *noun*. ● **contraindication** *noun* a factor or symptom which suggests that a patient should not receive or continue to receive a particular treatment. ● **contraindicative** *adj*. ⓘ 17c: CONTRA- + INDICATE.

contralto /kən'traltoʊ, -'trɑːltoʊ/ ▷ *noun* (**contraltos** or ***contralti*** /-tiː/) **a** the female singing voice that is lowest in pitch; **b** a singer with this voice; **c** a part to be sung by this voice. ⓘ 18c: Italian, meaning, 'lower in pitch than alto'.

contraption /kən'trapʃən/ ▷ *noun, humorous, colloq* a machine or apparatus which is usually ingenious rather than effective. ⓘ 19c.

contrapuntal /kɒntrə'pʌntəl/ ▻ *adj, music* relating to or arranged as COUNTERPOINT. • **contrapuntally** *adverb*. • **contrapuntist** *noun*. ⓒ 19c: from Italian *contrappunto* counterpoint.

contrariwise /'kɒntrərɪwaɪz, kən'treərɪwaɪz/ ▻ *adverb* **1** on the other hand. **2** the opposite way round. **3** in the opposite direction.

contrary ▻ *adj* **1** /'kɒntrərɪ/ (*often* **contrary to something**) opposite; quite different; opposed. **2** /'kɒntrərɪ/ said of a wind: blowing against one; unfavourable. **3** /kən'treərɪ/ obstinate, perverse, self-willed or wayward. ▻ *noun* /'kɒntrərɪ/ (*contraries*) **1** an extreme opposite. **2** either of a pair of opposites. **3** *logic* either of two propositions that cannot both be true of the same thing, but they can both be false. • **contrariety** /kɒntrə'raɪətɪ/ or **contrariness** *noun* **1** opposition. **2** inconsistency; discrepancy. • **contrarily** *adverb*. • **on the contrary** in opposition or contrast to what has just been said. • **to the contrary** to the opposite effect; giving the contrasting position. ⓒ 14c: from Latin *contrarius*, from *contra* opposite.

contrast ▻ *noun* /'kɒntrɑːst/ **1** difference or dissimilarity between things or people that are being compared. **2** a person or thing that is strikingly different from another. **3** the degree of difference in tone between the colours, or the light and dark parts, of a photograph or television picture. ▻ *verb* /kən'trɑːst/ (*contrasted*, *contrasting*) **1** to compare so as to reveal differences. **2** (*often* **contrast with something**) to show the difference. • **contrastive** *adj*. • **in contrast to** or **with something** or **someone** as an opposite to them or something distinct from them. ⓒ 17c: from Latin *contra-* against + *stare* to stand.

contravene /kɒntrə'viːn/ ▻ *verb* (*contravened*, *contravening*) **1** to break or disobey (a law or rule, etc). **2** to dispute or challenge (a proposition, etc). • **contravention** *noun* (*often* **in contravention of something**) infringement of a law, etc. ⓒ 16c: from Latin *contravenire* to come against, oppose.

contretemps /'kɒntrətɑ̃/ ▻ *noun* (*plural* *contretemps* /-tɑ̃z/) **1** an awkward or embarrassing moment, situation, etc. **2** a slight disagreement. ⓒ 19c in this sense: French, meaning 'bad or false time'.

contribute /kən'trɪbjuːt, 'kɒntrɪbjuːt/ ▻ *verb* (*contributed*, *contributing*) (*usually* **contribute to something**) **1** *tr & intr* to give (money, time, etc) for some joint purpose. **2** *intr* to be one of the causes of something. **3** to supply (an article, etc) for publication in a magazine, etc. • **contributable** *adj*. • **contributive** *adj*. • **contributor** *noun*. ⓒ 16c: from Latin *contribuere*, *contributum* to bring together.

contribution /kɒntrɪ'bjuːʃən/ ▻ *noun* **1** the act of contributing. **2** something contributed, eg money, or an article for a magazine.

contributory /kɒn'trɪbjuːtərɪ/ ▻ *adj* **1** giving or given to a common purpose or fund. **2** having partial responsibility. **3** said of a pension scheme: involving contribution from the employee as well as the employer. ▻ *noun* (*contributories*) **1** a person or thing which makes a contribution. **2** *law* every person who is liable to contribute towards the assets of a company, in the event of the company being wound up, including past and present members.

con trick ▻ *noun, colloq* short for a CONFIDENCE TRICK.

contrite /'kɒntraɪt, kən'traɪt/ ▻ *adj* **1** sorry for something one has done. **2** resulting from a feeling of guilt □ *a contrite apology*. • **contritely** *adverb*. • **contrition** /-'trɪʃən/ *noun* **1** remorse. **2** *Christianity* deep sorrow for past sin and resolve to avoid future sin. ⓒ 14c: from Latin *contritus* crushed.

contrivance ▻ *noun* **1** the act or power of contriving. **2** a device or apparatus, especially an ingenious one. **3** a scheme; a piece of cunning.

contrive /kən'traɪv/ ▻ *verb* (*contrived*, *contriving*) **1** to manage or succeed. **2** to bring about something □ *contrive one's escape*. **3** to make or construct something, especially with difficulty. ⓒ 14c: from French *controver* to find.

contrived ▻ *adj* forced or artificial □ *a contrived ending to a play*.

control /kən'troʊl, kɒn-/ ▻ *noun* **1** authority or charge; power to influence or guide □ *take control*. **2** a means of limitation. **3** (**controls**) a device for operating, regulating, or testing (a machine, system, etc). **4** the people in control of some operation □ *mission control*. **5** the place where something is checked □ *go through passport control*. **6** (*in full* **control experiment**) a scientific experiment in which the variable being tested in a second experiment is held at a constant value, in order to establish the validity of the results of the second experiment. **7** *spiritualism* a dead person guiding a medium. ▻ *verb* (*controlled*, *controlling*) **1** to have or exercise power over someone or something. **2** to regulate. **3** to limit. **4** to operate, regulate or test (a machine, system, etc). **5** to establish the validity of (the results of a scientific experiment) by performing another experiment in which the variable being tested is held at a constant value, in order to provide a standard of comparison. • **controllability** *noun*. • **controllable** *adj*. ⓒ 15c: from French *contrerolle* duplicate account or register.

control engineering ▻ *noun* the branch of engineering concerned with the control and adjustment of systems, which need not involve a human operator.

control group ▻ *noun* a group of people, etc providing a fixed standard of comparison against which experimental results can be evaluated.

controller ▻ *noun* **1** a person or thing that controls. **2** someone in charge of the finances of an enterprise, etc. Also called **comptroller**. **3** an official in charge of public finance.

controlling interest ▻ *noun* the number of shares required to ensure control over the running of a company.

control tower ▻ *noun* a tall building at an airport providing a good view of the airport and surrounding airspace, and from which take-off and landing instructions are given to aircraft pilots by air-traffic controllers.

controversy /'kɒntrəvɜːsɪ, kən'trɒvəsɪ/ ▻ *noun* (*controversies*) a usually long-standing dispute or argument, especially one where there is a strong difference of opinion. • **controversial** *adj*. • **controversialist** *noun*. • **controversially** *adverb*. ⓒ 14c: from Latin *contra* against + *vertere* to turn.

controvert /kɒntrə'vɜːt/ ▻ *verb* (*controverted*, *controverting*) **1** to oppose or contradict. **2** to argue against something. ⓒ 17c: from Latin *controversus*; see CONTROVERSY.

contumacy /'kɒntjʊməsɪ/ ▻ *noun, formal* obstinate refusal to obey; resistance to authority. • **contumacious** /-'meɪʃəs/ *adj*. • **contumaciously** *adverb*. ⓒ 14c: from Latin *contumacia* stubbornness.

contumely /'kɒntjuːmlɪ, 'kɒntjʊmɪlɪ/ ▻ *noun* (*contumelies*) *formal* **1** scornful or insulting treatment or words. **2** a contemptuous insult. • **contumelious** /-'miːlɪəs/ *noun*. • **contumeliously** *adverb*. ⓒ 14c: from Latin *contumelia* outrage or insult.

contuse /kən'tʃuːz/ ▻ *verb* (*contused*, *contusing*) *medicine* **1** to bruise. **2** to crush. ⓒ 15c: from Latin *contundere*, *contusum* to beat or bruise.

contusion /kən'tʃuːʒən/ ▻ *noun, technical* **1** the act of bruising or the state of being bruised. **2** a bruise.

conundrum /kə'nʌndrəm/ ▻ *noun* **1** a confusing problem. **2** a riddle, especially one involving a pun.

conurbation /kɒnə'beɪʃən, kɒnɜː'beɪʃən/ ▻ *noun* an extensive cluster of towns, the outskirts of which have merged resulting in the formation of one huge urban development. ◷ 20c: from Latin *con-* together + *urbs* city.

convalesce /kɒnvə'lɛs/ ▷ *verb* (***convalesced, convalescing***) *intr* to recover one's strength after an illness, operation or injury, especially by resting. ● **convalescence** *noun* **1** the gradual recovery of health and strength. **2** the period during which this takes place. ● **convalescent** *noun, adj.* ◷ 15c: from Latin *convalescere* to grow strong.

convection /kən'vɛkʃən/ ▷ *noun* the process by which heat is transferred through a liquid or gas from a more dense region of lower temperature to a less dense region of higher temperature, as a result of movement of molecules of the fluid itself. ● **convectional** *adj.* ● **convective** *adj.* ◷ 17c: from Latin *convectio, con-* together + *vehere, vectum* to carry.

convector /kən'vɛktə(r)/ ▷ *noun* an electrical device used to heat the surrounding air in rooms, etc, by convection. ◷ 20c: from Latin *con-* together + *vehere, vectum* to carry.

convene /kən'viːn/ ▷ *verb* (***convened, convening***) *tr & intr* to assemble or summon to assemble □ ***The court shall convene at three o'clock.*** ● **convenable** *adj.* ◷ 15c: from Latin *convenire* to come together.

convener or **convenor** /kən'viːnə(r)/ ▷ *noun* someone who convenes or chairs a meeting.

convenience /kən'viːnɪəns/ ▷ *noun* **1** the quality of being convenient. **2** something useful or advantageous. **3** *Brit euphemistic* a lavatory, especially a public one. ● **at one's convenience** when and where it suits one.

convenience food ▷ *noun* any food which has been partially or entirely prepared by the manufacturer, and requires only to be cooked, eg cook-chill meals, frozen, canned or dried foods, etc.

convenience store ▷ *noun* a small grocery shop that stays open after normal hours.

convenient /kən'viːnɪənt/ ▷ *adj* **1** fitting in with one's plans, etc; not causing trouble or difficulty. **2** useful; handy; saving time and trouble. **3** available; at hand. ● **conveniently** *adverb.* ◷ 14c: from Latin *conveniens*, from *convenire* to fit or be suitable.

convent /'kɒnvənt/ ▷ *noun* **1 a** a community of nuns; **b** the building they occupy. **2** a school where the teaching is done by nuns. Also called **convent school**. ◷ 13c: from Latin *conventus* assembly.

conventicle /kən'vɛntɪkəl/ ▷ *noun, historical* **a** a secret, especially unlawful, religious meeting; **b** the building where such a meeting takes place. ◷ 14c: from Latin *conventiculum* assembly.

convention /kən'vɛnʃən/ ▷ *noun* **1** a large and formal conference or assembly. **2** a formal treaty or agreement. **3** a custom or generally accepted practice, especially in social behaviour. **4** *US politics* a meeting of delegates from one party to nominate a candidate for office. ◷ 15c: from Latin *conventio* meeting or agreement.

conventional ▷ *adj* **1** traditional; normal; customary. **2** conservative or unoriginal. **3** said of weapons or warfare: non-nuclear. ● **conventionalism** *noun.* ● **conventionally** *adj.*

conventionality ▷ *noun* (***conventionalities***) **1** the state of being conventional. **2** something which is established by use or custom.

conventionalize or **conventionalise** ▷ *verb* (***conventionalized, conventionalizing***) to make conventional. ◷ 19c.

Convention on International Trade in Endangered Species ▷ *noun* (abbreviation **CITES**) *ecol* an international convention founded in 1973 with the aim of controlling the trade in endangered plant and animal species.

converge /kən'vɜːdʒ/ ▷ *verb* (***converged, converging***) *intr* **1** (*often* **converge on** or **upon someone** or **something**) to move towards or meet at one point. **2** said eg of opinions: to tend towards one another; to coincide. **3** said of plants and animals: to undergo CONVERGENT EVOLUTION. ● **convergence** *noun.* ◷ 17c: from Latin *convergere* to incline together.

convergent ▷ *adj* **1** converging; coming together. **2** agreeing. **3** *math* said of infinite sequences, series, etc: having a limit.

convergent evolution ▷ *noun, biol* the independent development of similarities in unrelated species of plants or animals which inhabit the same environment, eg the wings of birds and insects.

converging lens ▷ *noun, physics* a lens that causes light rays to converge to a focus, eg a convex lens.

conversant /kən'vɜːsənt, 'kɒnvɜːsənt/ ▷ *adj* (*usually* **conversant with something**) having a thorough knowledge of it. ◷ 16c in this sense: from Latin *conversari* to associate with.

conversation /kɒnvə'seɪʃən/ ▷ *noun* informal talk between people; communication. ◷ 16c in this sense: from Latin *conversatio*, from *conversari* to associate with.

conversational ▷ *adj* **1** relating to conversation. **2** used in conversation rather than formal language. **3** communicative; talkative. ● **conversationalist** *noun* someone who is fond of or skilled in conversation. ● **conversationally** *adverb.*

conversation analysis ▷ *noun, linguistics* the analysis of real-life conversations and their sequential structure with the aim of understanding the strategies used to link different strands and themes, and the ways in which people interact. See also DISCOURSE ANALYSIS.

conversation piece ▷ *noun* **1** a striking object that stimulates conversation. **2** a group portrait, especially one showing members of a family engaged in characteristic activities in their usual setting.

conversation stopper ▷ *noun, colloq* a comment that kills a conversation because it is shocking, surprising, out of context, etc.

converse[1] /kən'vɜːs/ ▷ *verb* (***conversed, conversing***) *intr* (*often* **converse with someone**) *formal* **1** to hold a conversation; to talk. **2** to commune spiritually. ◷ 17c: from Latin *conversari* to associate with.

converse[2] /'kɒnvɜːs/ ▷ *adj* reverse; opposite. ▷ *noun* opposite. ● **conversely** *adverb.* ◷ 16c: from Latin *conversus* turned about, from *convertere* to transform.

conversion /kən'vɜːʃən/ ▷ *noun* **1** the act of converting. **2** something converted to another use. **3** *rugby union, rugby league, American football* the scoring of two further points after a TRY or TOUCHDOWN by kicking the ball over the goal.

convert ▷ *verb* /kən'vɜːt/ (***converted, converting***) **1** *tr & intr* to change the form or function of one thing into another. **2** *tr & intr* to win over, or be won over, to another religion, opinion, etc. **3** to change into another measuring system or currency. **4** *rugby union, rugby league, American football* to achieve a conversion after (a try or touchdown). **5** *tr & intr* to change from one state or condition into another □ ***He was given the job of converting the sugar into alcohol.*** ▷ *noun* /'kɒnvɜːt/ someone who has been converted to a new religion, practice, etc. ◷ 13c: from Latin *convertere* to transform, from *vertere* to turn.

converter or **convertor** ▷ *noun* **1** a person or thing that converts. **2** an electrical device for converting alternating current into direct current, or more rarely, direct current into alternating current. **3** a device for converting a signal from one frequency to another. **4** *computing* a device that converts coded information from one form to another. **5** a vessel in which air or oxygen is blown into a molten metal in order to refine it by oxidizing impurities.

convertible ▷ *adj* **1** capable of being converted. **2** said of a currency: capable of being freely converted into other currencies. ▷ *noun* a car with a fold-down top. ● **convertibility** *noun*. ● **convertibly** *adverb*.

convex /ˈkɒnvɛks, kɒnˈvɛks/ ▷ *adj* said of a surface or shape: outward-curving, like the surface of the eye. Compare CONCAVE. ● **convexity** *noun* **1** roundness of form on the outside. **2** a round form or figure. ⓒ 16c: from Latin *convexus* arched.

convey /kənˈveɪ/ ▷ *verb* (**conveyed**, **conveying**) **1** to carry; to transport. **2** to communicate. **3** *law* to transfer the ownership of (property). **4** said of a channel, etc: to lead or transmit. ● **conveyable** *adj*. ● **conveyer** or **conveyor** *noun*. ⓒ 14c in this sense: from French *conveier*, from Latin *via* way.

conveyance /kənˈveɪəns/ ▷ *noun* **1** the process of conveying. **2** a vehicle of any kind. **3** *law* **a** the transfer of the ownership of property; **b** the document setting out such a transfer. ● **conveyancer** *noun*. ● **conveyancing** *noun*.

conveyor belt ▷ *noun* an endless moving rubber or metal belt for the continuous transporting of articles, eg in a factory.

convict ▷ *verb* /kənˈvɪkt/ (**convicted**, **convicting**) to prove or declare someone guilty (of a crime). ▷ *noun* /ˈkɒnvɪkt/ **1** someone serving a prison sentence. **2** someone found guilty of a crime. ⓒ 14c: from Latin *convincere*, *convictum* to conquer or overcome.

conviction /kənˈvɪkʃən/ ▷ *noun* **1** the act of convicting; an instance of being convicted. **2** the state of being convinced; a strong belief. ● **carry conviction** to be convincing. ⓒ 15c: from CONVICT.

convince /kənˈvɪns/ ▷ *verb* (**convinced**, **convincing**) to persuade someone of something; to make or cause to make them believe it. ● **convinced** *adj* firm in one's belief. ● **convincing** *adj* **1** believable. **2** certain; positive. **3** said of a victory: achieved by a significant margin. ● **convincingly** *adverb*. ⓒ 17c in this sense: from Latin *convincere* to overcome wholly.

convivial /kənˈvɪvɪəl/ ▷ *adj* **1** lively, jovial, sociable and cheerful. **2** festive. ● **conviviality** *noun*. ● **convivially** *adverb*. ⓒ 17c: from Latin *convivialis*, from *convivium* feast.

convocation /kɒnvəˈkeɪʃən/ ▷ *noun* **1** the act of summoning together. **2** an assembly. **3** (**Convocation**) *C of E* a synod of either of the provinces of Canterbury or York. **4** a formal assembly of graduates of a college or university. ⓒ 14c: from Latin *convocatio* summoning together, from *convocare* to call together.

convoke /kənˈvoʊk/ ▷ *verb* (**convoked**, **convoking**) to call together; to assemble. ⓒ 16c: from Latin *convocare* to call together.

convoluted /ˈkɒnvəluːtɪd, -ljuːtɪd/ ▷ *adj* **1** coiled and twisted. **2** complicated; difficult to understand. ⓒ 19c: from Latin *convolvere*, *convolutum* to roll together.

convolution /kɒnvəˈluːʃən, -ˈljuːʃən/ ▷ *noun* **1** a twist or coil. **2** *anatomy* any of the sinuous folds of the brain. **3** a complication.

convolvulus /kɒnˈvɒlvjʊləs/ ▷ *noun* (**convolvuluses** or **convolvuli** /-laɪ/) any of a large number of trailing or twining plants native to temperate regions, with funnel-shaped flowers, eg BINDWEED. ⓒ 16c: Latin, from *convolvere* to roll up.

convoy /ˈkɒnvɔɪ, kɒnˈvɔɪ / ▷ *noun* (**convoys**) a group of vehicles or merchant ships travelling together, or under escort. ▷ *verb* (**convoyed**, **convoying**) to accompany for protection. ⓒ 14c: from French *convoier*, from Latin *con-* with + *via* way.

convulse /kənˈvʌls/ ▷ *verb* (**convulsed**, **convulsing**) *tr & intr* to jerk or distort violently by or as if by a powerful spasm. ● **convulsive** *adj* **1** causing or affected by convulsions. **2** spasmodic. ● **convulsively** *adverb*. ⓒ 17c: from Latin *convellere*, *convulsum* to pull violently.

convulsion /kənˈvʌlʃən/ ▷ *noun* **1** the state of being convulsed. **2** (*often* **convulsions**) a violent involuntary contraction of the muscles of the body, or a series of such contractions, resulting in contortion of the limbs and face and sometimes accompanied by loss of consciousness. **3** (**convulsions**) *colloq* spasms of uncontrollable laughter. ⓒ 17c: from Latin *convulsio*, from *convellere* to pull violently.

cony or **coney** /ˈkoʊnɪ/ ▷ *noun* (**conies** or **coneys**) **1** *dialect* a rabbit. **2** its fur used for clothing, etc. **3** in the Bible: a HYRAX. ⓒ 13c: from French *conil*, from Latin *cuniculus* rabbit.

coo¹ ▷ *noun* (**coos**) the soft murmuring call of a dove. ▷ *verb* (**cooed**, **cooing**) **1** *intr* to make this sound. **2** *tr & intr* to murmur affectionately. See also BILL AND COO at BILL². ⓒ 17c: imitating the sound.

coo² ▷ *exclamation*, *Brit colloq* used to express amazement. ⓒ 20c.

cooee /ˈkuːiː/ ▷ *exclamation* a usually high-pitched call used to attract attention. ▷ *verb* (**cooeed**, **cooeeing**) *intr* to make this call. ● **within a cooee of someone** or **something** *Austral*, *NZ* to be within calling distance of them. ⓒ 19c: from a signal originally used by the Aborigines which was later adopted by the colonists.

cook ▷ *verb* (**cooked**, **cooking**) **1** *tr & intr* to prepare (food) or be prepared by heating. **2** *colloq* to alter (accounts, etc) dishonestly. ▷ *noun* someone who cooks or prepares food. ● **cook the books** to falsify accounts, records, etc. ● **cook someone's goose** see under GOOSE. ● **cook with gas** or **electricity** *colloq* to be successful. ● **What's cooking?** *colloq* What's happening?; What's the plan? ⓒ Anglo-Saxon *coc*, from Latin *coquus*.

■ **cook something up** **1** *colloq* to concoct or invent it. **2** *drug-taking slang* to prepare (a drug, especially heroin) for use, by heating.

cook-chill ▷ *adj* denoting foods, especially individual meals, that are cooked, rapidly chilled, then packaged and stored in a refrigerated state, requiring reheating before being served. ▷ *noun* the process of preparing food in this way.

cooker ▷ *noun* **1** an apparatus for cooking food; a stove. **2** *Brit colloq* a COOKING APPLE.

cookery ▷ *noun* (*plural* in sense 2 only **cookeries**) **1** the art or practice of cooking food. **2** *US* a place equipped for cooking.

cookery book and **cookbook** ▷ *noun* a book of recipes.

cookie /ˈkʊkɪ/ ▷ *noun* (**cookies**) **1** *chiefly N Amer* a biscuit. **2** *Scottish* a bun. **3** *colloq* a person □ *a smart cookie*. **4** *computing* information about a user that is held on the user's hard disk and is automatically sent to a BROWSER whenever a certain page is accessed on the Internet or some other network. ● **That's the way the cookie crumbles** *N Amer colloq* That's the way it goes; That's how things usually turn out. ⓒ 18c: from Dutch *koekje*, diminutive of *koek* cake.

cooking apple and **cooker** ▷ *noun* an apple sour in taste, which is used for cooking rather than eating raw. Compare EATING APPLE.

cool ▷ *adj* **1** between cold and warm; fairly cold. **2** pleasantly fresh; free of heat □ *a cool breeze*. **3** calm; laid-back □ *He was very cool under pressure*. **4** lacking enthusiasm; unfriendly □ *a cool response*. **5** impudent; audacious; brazen. **6** said of a large sum: exact; at least □ *made a cool million*. **7** *colloq* admirable; excellent. **8** said of colours: suggestive of coolness, typically pale and containing blue. **9** sophisticated. ▷ *noun* **1** a cool part or period; coolness □ *the cool of the evening*. **2** *colloq* self-control; composure □ *keep your cool*. ▷ *verb* (**cooled**, **cooling**) *tr & intr* (*often* **cool down** or **off**) **1** to become cool. **2** to become less interested or enthusiastic □ *Martin had cooled towards Pat since her behaviour at the office* *party*. ● **coolly** *adverb* in a cool manner. ● **coolness** *noun*. ● **Cool it!** *colloq* Calm down! ● **cool one's heels** to be kept waiting. ● **play it cool** to deal with a situation calmly but warily. ⓔ Anglo-Saxon *col*.

■ **cool something down** or **off** to make it cool.

coolant /ˈkuːlənt/ ▷ *noun* **1** a liquid or gas used as a cooling agent, especially to absorb and remove heat from its source in a system such as a car radiator, nuclear reactor, etc. **2** a liquid or gas that is used to cool the edge of a cutting tool during machining.

cool box and **cool bag** ▷ *noun* an insulated container, used to keep food cool.

cooler ▷ *noun* **1** a container or device for cooling things. **2** *slang* prison. **3** a drink made from wine and fruit juice.

coolie ▷ *noun* (*coolies*) *offensive* **1** an unskilled native labourer in Eastern countries. **2** *S Afr* an Indian. ⓔ 17c: probably from Tamil *kuli* hired person.

cooling-off period ▷ *noun* an interval for reflection and negotiation before taking action.

cooling tower ▷ *noun* a tall, hollow structure in which water heated during industrial processes is cooled for re-use.

coolly and **coolness** see under COOL

coomb, **coombe**, **comb** or **combe** /kuːm/ ▷ *noun* **1** in S England: a short deep valley. **2** a deep hollow in a hillside. ⓔ Anglo-Saxon *cumb* valley.

coon ▷ *noun* **1** *offensive slang* a black person. **2** *N Amer colloq* a raccoon. ⓔ 18c: an abbreviation of RACCOON.

coop ▷ *noun* **1** a cage for hens. **2** a wicker basket. **3** any confined or restricted space. ▷ *verb* (***cooped***, ***cooping***) (*usually* **coop someone** or **something up**) to confine in a small space. ⓔ 15c: probably related to Anglo-Saxon *cypa* basket.

co-op /ˈkoʊɒp/ ▷ *noun*, *colloq* a co-operative society or a shop run by one.

cooper /ˈkuːpə(r)/ ▷ *noun* someone who makes or repairs barrels. ⓔ 14c: from Latin *cuparius*, from *cupa* cask.

co-operate ▷ *verb*, *intr* **1** (*often* **co-operate with someone**) to work together with them. **2** to be helpful, or willing to fit in with the plans of others. ● **co-operation** *noun* **1** the act of co-operating. **2** willingness to help. **3** assistance. ● **co-operator** *noun*. ⓔ 17c: from Latin *cooperari* to work together.

co-operative ▷ *adj* **1** relating to or giving co-operation. **2** helpful; willing to fit in with others' plans, etc. **3** said of a business or farm: jointly owned by workers, with profits shared equally. ▷ *noun* a co-operative business or farm. ● **co-operatively** *adverb*.

co-operative society ▷ *noun* a profit-sharing association for the cheaper purchase of goods.

co-opt /koʊˈɒpt/ ▷ *verb* said of the members of a body, etc: to elect an additional member, by the votes of the existing ones. ● **co-option** or **co-optation** *noun*. ● **co-optive** or **co-optative** *adj*. ⓔ 17c: from Latin *cooptare* to choose together.

co-ordinate ▷ *verb* (***co-ordinated***, ***co-ordinating***) **1** to integrate and adjust (a number of different parts or processes) so as to relate smoothly one to another. **2** to bring (one's limbs or bodily movements) into a smoothly functioning relationship. **3** *tr & intr* to combine harmoniously. **4** to place or classify in the same order or rank. ▷ *adj* **1** relating to or involving co-ordination or co-ordinates. **2** *grammar* said of clauses: equal in status, as when joined by *and* or *but*. ▷ *noun* **1** (*usually* **coordinate**) *math*, *geog* either of a pair of numbers taken from a vertical and horizontal axis which together establish the position of a fixed point on a map. **2** *geom* any of a set of numbers, especially either of a pair, that are used to define the position of a point, line or surface by reference to a system of axes that are usually drawn through a fixed point at right angles to each other. **3** *chem* denoting a type of covalent bond between two atoms in which both members of the shared pair of electrons are provided by one atom. **4** (**co-ordinates**) garments designed to be worn together. ● **co-ordination** *noun* **1** harmonious combination. **2** balanced or skilful movement. ● **co-ordinative** *adj*. ● **co-ordinator** *noun*.

coordinate geometry ▷ *noun*, *math* a system of geometry in which points, lines and surfaces are located in two-dimensional or three-dimensional space by means of coordinates. Also called **analytical geometry**.

co-ordinating conjunction *noun*, *grammar* a CONJUNCTION, such as *and*, *or*, *but*, *nor*, *neither*, that links clauses of equal status.

coot ▷ *noun* **1** any of 10 species of aquatic bird belonging to the rail family and closely related to the moorhen, native to Europe and Asia, with dark plumage, a characteristic white shield above the bill and large feet with lobed toes. **2** *dated*, *colloq* a fool. ⓔ 14c as *cote*.

cop[1] ▷ *noun*, *slang* **1** a policeman. **2** an arrest. ▷ *verb* (***copped***, ***copping***) **1** to catch. **2** to grab; to seize. **3** to suffer (a punishment, etc). ● **cop it** *slang* to be punished. ● **not much cop** *colloq* having little use or interest. ⓔ 18c: from French *caper* to seize.

■ **cop out** *colloq* to avoid a responsibility; to escape.

cop[2] ▷ *noun* **1** a conical ball of thread on a spindle. **2** *chiefly dialect* the summit or top of something, especially a hill. ⓔ Anglo-Saxon.

cope[1] ▷ *verb* (***coped***, ***coping***) *intr* to manage; to get by. ⓔ 14c: from French *couper* to hit.

■ **cope with something** to deal with (a difficulty or problem, etc) successfully.

cope[2] ▷ *noun* a long sleeveless cape worn by clergy on ceremonial occasions. ▷ *verb* (***coped***, ***coping***) to dress in a cope. ⓔ 13c: from Latin *capa*.

cope[3] ▷ *verb*, *building* to cut (a piece of moulding) so that it fits over another piece. ⓔ 17c: from French *couper* to cut.

Copernican system /kəˈpɜːnɪkən —/ ▷ *noun*, *astron* a model of the Solar System, proposed by Copernicus in 1543, in which the Sun is regarded as being at the centre, with the Earth and other planets moving around it, in perfectly circular orbits.

copier see under COPY

co-pilot ▷ *noun* the assistant pilot of an aircraft.

coping /ˈkoʊpɪŋ/ ▷ *noun* a capping along the top row of stones in a wall, designed to protect it from the weather. ⓔ 17c: from COPE[2].

coping saw ▷ *noun* a small saw used for cutting curves in relatively thick wood or metal. Compare FRETSAW.

coping-stone ▷ *noun* one of the stones forming the top row in a wall, etc.

copious /ˈkoʊpɪəs/ ▷ *adj* plentiful. ● **copiously** *adverb*. ● **copiousness** *noun*. ⓔ 14c: from Latin *copiosus*, from *copia* plenty.

cop-out ▷ *noun*, *colloq* an avoidance of a responsibility; an escape or withdrawal. See COP OUT at COP[1] *verb*.

copper[1] /ˈkɒpə(r)/ ▷ *noun* **1** *chem* (symbol **Cu**, atomic number 29) a soft reddish-brown metallic element that occurs both as the free metal and in various ores, especially CHALCOPYRITE, and which is an exellent conductor of heat and electricity. **2** (*usually* **coppers**) any coin of low value made of copper or bronze. **3** a large metal vessel for boiling water in. **4** a reddish-brown colour. ▷ *adj* **1** made from copper. **2** copper-coloured. ▷ *verb* (***coppered***, ***coppering***) to cover with copper. ● **coppery** *adj*. ⓔ Anglo-Saxon *coper*, from Latin *cuprum*, from *Cyprium aes* metal of Cyprus.

copper² ⊳ *noun, slang, chiefly Brit* a policeman. Often shortened to COP¹ *noun*. ⓒ 19c: from COP¹.

copper-bottomed ⊳ *adj* **1** said eg of ships or pans: having the bottom protected by a layer of copper. **2** *colloq* reliable, especially financially. ⓒ 18c.

copperhead ⊳ *noun* **1** a poisonous pit viper, native to the eastern USA, so called because the top of its head is reddish-brown. **2** a venomous snake, native to SE Australia, so called because there is a reddish-brown band at the back of its head.

copperplate ⊳ *noun* **1** *printing* **a** a copper plate used for engraving or etching; **b** a print made from it. **2** fine regular handwriting of the style formerly taught in schools and used on copperplates.

copper pyrites /— paɪəˈraɪtiːz/ ⊳ *singular noun, geol* another name for CHALCOPYRITE.

copper sulphate ⊳ *noun, chem* (formula **$CuSO_4$**) a white compound that tends to absorb moisture from the atmosphere, which is used in electroplating and as an antiseptic, pesticide and wood preservative.

coppery see under COPPER¹

coppice /ˈkɒpɪs/ ⊳ *noun, bot* an area of woodland in which trees are regularly cut back to ground level to encourage the growth of side shoots, which are then periodically harvested for firewood, fencing, etc. ⊳ *verb* (***coppiced, coppicing***) to manage woodland in this way. ⓒ 14c: from French *copeiz*.

copra /ˈkɒprə/ ⊳ *noun* the dried kernel of the coconut, rich in coconut oil. ⓒ 16c: Portuguese, from Malayalam *koppara* coconut.

coprolalia /kɒproʊˈleɪlɪə/ ⊳ *noun, psychol* the repetitive use of indecent language, which may be involuntary, eg as in TOURETTE'S SYNDROME. ⓒ 20c: from Greek *kopros* dung + -LALIA.

copse /ˈkɒps/ ⊳ *noun* a COPPICE.

Copt /ˈkɒpt/ ⊳ *noun* **1** a member of the Coptic Church. **2** an Egyptian descended from the ancient Egyptians.

Coptic /ˈkɒptɪk/ ⊳ *noun* the language of the Copts, now used only in the Coptic Church. ⊳ *adj* relating to the Copts or their language. ⓒ 17c: from Greek *Aigyptios* Egyptian.

copula /ˈkɒpjʊlə/ ⊳ *noun* (***copulas*** or ***copulae*** /-iː/) *grammar* a verb that links the subject and COMPLEMENT of a sentence, eg *is* in *She is a doctor* or *grew* in *It grew dark*. ⓒ 17c: Latin, meaning 'bond'.

copulate /ˈkɒpjʊleɪt/ ⊳ *verb* (***copulated, copulating***) *intr* to have sexual intercourse. ● **copulation** *noun*. ● **copulatory** *adj*. ⓒ 17c: from Latin *copulare* to bind or couple.

copulative ⊳ *adj* **1** serving to connect or join. **2** *grammar* said of a verb: connecting the subject and COMPLEMENT of a sentence. **3** pertaining to copulation.

copy /ˈkɒpɪ/ ⊳ *noun* (***copies***) **1** an imitation or reproduction. **2** one of the many specimens of a book or of a particular issue of a magazine, newspaper, etc. **3** written material for printing, especially as distinct from illustrations, etc. **4** the wording of an advertisement. **5** *informal* material suitable for a newspaper article. ⊳ *verb* (***copies, copied, copying***) **1** to imitate. **2** to make a copy of something; to transcribe. **3** *tr & intr* to reproduce; to photocopy. **4** *tr & intr* to make a copy of another's work, pretending that it is one's own. **5** to give a copy to someone. ● **copier** *noun* a person or machine which makes copies. ⓒ 14c: from Latin *copia* abundance.

copybook ⊳ *noun* a book of handwriting examples for copying. ⊳ *adj* **1** *derog* unoriginal. **2** faultless; perfect. ● **blot one's copybook** to spoil one's good record by misbehaviour or error.

copycat ⊳ *noun, colloq derisive* an imitator or person who copies the work of another.

copyist ⊳ *noun* **1** someone who copies (documents, etc) in writing, especially as an occupation. **2** an imitator.

copyright ⊳ *noun* the sole right, granted by law, to print, publish, translate, perform, film or record an original literary, dramatic, musical or artistic work for a certain number of years. ⊳ *adj* protected by copyright. ⊳ *verb* to secure the copyright of something. ● **copyrightable** *adj*. ⓒ 18c.

copywriter ⊳ *noun* someone who writes advertising copy.

coq au vin /kɒk oʊ ˈvan/ ⊳ *noun* a dish of chicken cooked in red wine with onions, herbs and garlic. ⓒ 1930s: French.

coquette /koʊˈkɛt, kɒ-/ ⊳ *noun* a flirtatious woman. ⊳ *verb* (***coquetted, coquetting***) *intr* **1** to flirt. **2** to dally. ● **coquetry** /ˈkoʊk-, ˈkɒk-/ *noun*. ● **coquettish** *adj*. ● **coquettishly** *adverb*. ● **coquettishness** *noun*. ⓒ 17c: French, diminutive of *coq* cock.

Cor. ⊳ *abbreviation* Book of the Bible: Corinthians. See table at BIBLE.

cor /kɔː(r)/ ⊳ *exclamation, colloq* expressing surprise or pleasure. ● **cor blimey** a form of GORBLIMEY.

cor- see CON-

coracle /ˈkɒrəkəl/ ⊳ *noun* a small oval rowing-boat made of wickerwork covered with hides or other waterproof material. ⓒ 16c: from Welsh *corwgl*.

coral /ˈkɒrəl/ ⊳ *noun* **1** a tiny invertebrate marine animal, consisting of a hollow tube with a mouth surrounded by tentacles at the top, which is found mainly in tropical seas. **2** a hard chalky substance of various colours, formed from the skeletons of this animal. **3** a pinkish-orange colour. ⊳ *adj* pinkish-orange in colour. ⓒ 14c: from Latin *coralium*, from Greek *korallion*.

coralline /ˈkɒrəlaɪn/ ⊳ *adj* consisting of, containing or like coral. ⊳ *noun* a common seaweed of a delicate pinkish or purplish colour.

coral island and **coral reef** ⊳ *noun* an area of coral containing a central lagoon that has become raised above sea level, and has then drained to form a hollow, eventually becoming colonized by plants, insects, birds, etc.

coral snake ⊳ *noun* a venomous snake native to the New World and E Asia, usually with bold alternating bands of black, yellow and red.

cor anglais /kɔː ˈrɑ̃gleɪ, kɔː ˈrɒŋgleɪ/ (***cors anglais*** /kɔːz —/) ⊳ *noun, music* a woodwind instrument similar to, but lower in pitch than, the oboe. ⓒ 19c: French, meaning 'English horn'.

corbel /ˈkɔːbəl/ ⊳ *noun, archit* a projecting piece of stone or timber, coming out from a wall and taking the weight of (eg a parapet, arch or bracket). ⊳ *verb* (***corbelled, corbelling***) (*always* **corbel out** or **off**) to project or cause to project on corbels. ● **corbelled** *adj*. ● **corbelling** *noun*. ⓒ 15c: French, from Latin *corvellum*, diminutive of *corvus* raven.

corbelling ⊳ *noun* stone or brickwork made into corbels.

corbie /ˈkɔrbɪ/ ⊳ *noun* (***corbies***) *Scots* a crow or raven. ⓒ 15c: from French *corbin*, from Latin *corvus*.

cord ⊳ *noun* **1** a thin rope or string consisting of several separate strands twisted together. **2** *anatomy* any long flexible structure resembling this ▫ *spinal cord* ▫ *umbilical cord*. **3** *N Amer* the cable of an electrical appliance. **4** a ribbed fabric, especially corduroy. **5** (**cords**) corduroy trousers. **6** a unit for measuring the volume of cut wood, equal to 128 cubic ft. (3.63 m³) ⓒ So called because it was originally determined by use of a cord or string. ⊳ *verb* (***corded, cording***) to bind with a cord. ⓒ 13c: from Latin *chorda*, from Greek *chorde* string.

cordate /ˈkɔːdeɪt/ ⊳ *adj* heart-shaped. ⓒ 17c: from Latin *cordatus*, from *cor, cordis* the heart.

corded ▷ *adj* **1** fastened with cords. **2** said of fabric: ribbed.

cordial /ˈkɔːdɪəl/ ▷ *adj* **1** warm and affectionate. **2** heartfelt; profound. ▷ *noun* a concentrated fruit-flavoured drink, which is usually diluted before being drunk. ● **cordiality** *noun*. ● **cordially** *adverb*. ◷ 14c: from Latin *cordialis*, from *cor* heart.

cordite /ˈkɔːdaɪt/ ▷ *noun* any of various smokeless explosive materials containing a mixture of cellulose nitrate and nitroglycerine, used as a propellant for guns, etc. ◷ 19c.

cordless ▷ *adj* said of an electrical appliance: operating without a flex connecting it to the mains, powered instead by an internal battery □ *cordless phone*.

cordon /ˈkɔːdɒn, -dən/ ▷ *noun* **1** a line of police or soldiers, or a system of road blocks, encircling an area so as to prevent or control passage into or out of it. **2** a ribbon bestowed as a mark of honour. **3** *hortic* a fruit tree trained to grow as a single stem. **4** a row of stones along the line of a rampart. ▷ *verb* (***cordoned***, ***cordoning***) (*often* **cordon something off**) to close off (an area) with a cordon. ◷ 15c: from French *cordon*, diminutive of *corde* cord.

cordon bleu /ˈkɔːdɔ̃ blɜː/ ▷ *adj* said of a cook or cookery: being of the highest standard. ▷ *noun* (***cordons bleus*** /ˈkɔːdɔ̃ blɜːz/) a cook of the highest standard. ◷ 19c: French, meaning 'blue ribbon'.

corduroy /ˈkɔːdərɔɪ, kɔːdəˈrɔɪ/ ▷ *noun* (***corduroys***) **1** a thick ribbed cotton fabric. **2** (**corduroys**) trousers made of corduroy. See also CORD 5. **3** *N Amer* a road made of logs lying side by side. Also called **corduroy road**. ▷ *adj* made from corduroy.

core ▷ *noun* **1** the fibrous case at the centre of some fruits, eg apples and pears, containing the seeds. **2** the innermost, central, essential or unchanging part. **3** the central region of a star or planet, especially the Earth. **4** *archaeol* the lump of stone left after flakes have been struck off it for shaping into tools. **5** the central part of a nuclear reactor, containing the fuel, where the nuclear reaction takes place. **6** *elec* a piece of magnetic material that, when placed in the centre of a wire coil through which an electric current is being passed, increases the intensity of the magnetic field and the inductance of the coil. **7** the main memory of a computer, where instructions and data are stored in such a way that they are available for immediate use. Also called **core memory**. **8** the inner part of an electric cable. **9** a cylindrical sample of rock, soil, etc, removed with a hollow tubular drill. ▷ *verb* (***cored***, ***coring***) to remove the core of (an apple, etc). ● **cored** *adj* **1** with the core removed. **2** containing a core. ◷ 14c.

core curriculum ▷ *noun, education* a basic central provision for all pupils, which usually includes mathematics, science and the student's native language.

corer /ˈkɔːrə(r)/ ▷ *noun* a knife with a hollow cylindrical blade for coring fruit.

co-respondent ▷ *noun, law* in divorce cases: someone alleged to have committed adultery with the RESPONDENT (*noun* 2).

corestone see TOR

core time ▷ *noun* in flexitime: that part of each day, usually neither early nor late, which employees must include in their working hours. ◷ 20c.

CORGI /ˈkɔːgɪ/ ▷ *abbreviation* in the UK: Confederation for Registration of Gas Installers (UK).

corgi /ˈkɔːgɪ/ ▷ *noun* (***corgis***) a sturdy short-legged breed of dog with a thick coat and fox-like head. ◷ 20c: from Welsh *cor* dwarf + *ci* dog.

coriander /kɒrɪˈandə(r)/ ▷ *noun* **1** an annual plant, native to Europe and Asia, with narrowly lobed leaves, flat-topped clusters of small white, pink or lilac flowers, and globular aromatic fruits. **2** the dried ripe fruit of this plant, used as a spice in meat products, curry powder, confectionery, tobacco, gin and liqueurs, and widely used as a flavouring in cooking. ◷ 14c: from Latin *coriandrum*.

Corinthian /kəˈrɪnθɪən/ ▷ *adj* **1** relating to ancient Corinth in Greece. **2** *archit* denoting an ORDER (noun 19) of classical architecture characterized by a style of column with a fluted shaft and a heavily carved capital having a distinctive acanthus-leaf design. Compare COMPOSITE *noun* 3, DORIC, IONIC, TUSCAN.

Coriolis effect and **Coriolis force** /kɒrɪˈoʊlɪs —/ ▷ *noun, physics* a hypothetical force, resulting from the Earth's rotation, which appears to act on objects moving across the Earth's surface, deflecting their path to the right in the northern hemisphere and to the left in the southern hemisphere. ◷ 20c: named after the French physicist Gaspard Gustave de Coriolis (1792–1843).

corium see DERMIS

cork ▷ *noun* **1** *bot* a layer of tissue that forms below the epidermis in the stems and roots of woody plants, eg trees, which is often cultivated for commercial use. **2** a piece of this used as a stopper for a bottle, etc. ▷ *verb* (***corked***, ***corking***) (*often* **cork up** or **cork something up**) **1** to stop up (a bottle, etc) with a cork. **2** to suppress (one's feelings, etc). ● **corkiness** *noun*. ● **corky** *adj*. ◷ 14c: from Arabic *qurq*, from Latin *quercus* oak.

■ **cork up** *slang* to be quiet.

corkage ▷ *noun* the fee charged by a restaurant for serving customers wine, etc that they have bought off the premises.

corked ▷ *adj* said of wine: spoiled as a result of having a faulty cork, which has affected the taste of the wine.

corker ▷ *noun, dated slang* someone or something marvellous.

cork oak ▷ *noun* an evergreen tree, native to the Mediterranean region, whose bark produces a thick cork layer which is cultivated as a commercial source of cork.

corkscrew ▷ *noun* a tool with a spiral spike for screwing into bottle corks to remove them. ▷ *verb, tr & intr* to move spirally. ◷ 18c.

corm ▷ *noun, bot* in certain plants, eg crocus: a swollen underground stem, which functions primarily as a food store between one growing season and the next, and is also involved in the production of new plants. ◷ 19c: from Greek *kormos* lopped tree trunk.

cormorant /ˈkɔːmərənt/ ▷ *noun* any of over 30 species of seabird with an upright stance, dark brown or black plumage, webbed feet, a long neck and a slender bill. ◷ 14c: from French, from Latin *corvus marinus* sea raven.

Corn. ▷ *abbreviation, English county* Cornwall.

corn¹ ▷ *noun* **1** in the UK: the most important cereal crop of a particular region, especially wheat in England, and oats in Scotland and Ireland. **2** in N America, Australia and New Zealand: MAIZE. **3** the harvested seed of cereal plants; grain. **4** *slang* something, eg a song, film, etc, trite and sentimental. ▷ *verb* (***corned***, ***corning***) to preserve with salt or brine. ● **corned** *adj* preserved in salt or brine. ◷ Anglo-Saxon.

corn² /kɔːn/ ▷ *noun* a small painful area of hard thickened skin, usually on or between the toes, which is caused by pressure or friction. ● **tread on someone's corns** *colloq* to hurt their feelings. ◷ 15c: French, from Latin *cornu* horn.

corn circle see CROP CIRCLE

corncob ▷ *noun* the woody core of an ear of maize, to which the rows of kernels are attached. See also CORN ON THE COB.

corncrake /ˈkɔːnkreɪk/ ▷ *noun* a bird belonging to the rail family, native to Europe and W Asia, which has light brown streaky plumage, chestnut wings and a barred tail. ◷ 15c: from CORN¹ + *crake*, from Norse *krakr* crow.

corn dolly ▷ *noun* a decorative plaited straw figure.

cornea /ˈkɔːnɪə/ ▷ *noun* (***corneas*** or ***corneae*** /-iː/) in vertebrates: the convex transparent membrane that covers the front of the eyeball. ● **corneal** *adj.* ⓒ 14c: Latin, short for *cornea tela* horny tissue.

corned beef ▷ *noun* beef that has been cooked, salted and then canned.

cornelian /kɔːˈniːlɪən/ or **carnelian** /kɑː-/ ▷ *noun, geol* a red and white form of agate, used as a semi-precious stone and for making seals. ⓒ 15c: from French *corneline*.

corner /ˈkɔːnə(r)/ ▷ *noun* **1 a** a point or place where lines or surface-edges meet; **b** the inside or outside of the angle so formed. **2** an intersection between roads. **3** a quiet or remote place. **4** an awkward situation □ *in a tight corner*. **5** *econ* control of a particular market gained by buying up the total stocks of a commodity, to re-sell at one's own price. **6** *boxing* either of the angles of the ring used as a base between bouts by contestants. **7** in some sports, especially football: a free kick from a corner of the field. ▷ *verb* (***cornered***, ***cornering***) **1** to force into a place or position from which escape is difficult. **2** to gain control of (a market) by obtaining a monopoly of a certain commodity or service. **3** *intr* said of a driver or vehicle: to turn a corner. ● **cut corners** to spend less money, effort, time, etc on something than one should, especially to save time. ● **take a corner** to negotiate a corner in a motor vehicle. ● **turn the corner 1** to go round a corner. **2** to get past the most dangerous stage of, eg an illness. ⓒ 13c: from French, from Latin *cornu* horn.

cornerstone ▷ *noun* **1** a stone built into the corner of the foundation of a building. **2** a crucial or indispensable part; a basis.

cornet /ˈkɔːnɪt/ ▷ *noun* **1 a** a brass musical instrument similar to the trumpet; **b** someone who plays this instrument. **2** an edible cone-shaped holder for ice cream. ● **cornetist** or **cornettist** *noun* someone who plays the cornet. ⓒ 14c: French, from Latin *cornu* horn.

cornflakes ▷ *plural noun* toasted maize flakes, usually eaten as a breakfast cereal.

cornflour ▷ *noun, cookery* a finely ground flour, usually made from maize, which is used for thickening sauces, etc. *N Amer equivalent* **cornstarch**.

cornflower ▷ *noun* an annual plant native to SE Europe, which usually has narrow hairy leaves and deep blue flowers, but can also have purple, pink or white flowers. It was formerly common as a weed in cornfields.

cornice /ˈkɔːnɪs/ ▷ *noun* **1** a decorative border of moulded plaster round a ceiling. **2** *archit* the projecting section of an ENTABLATURE. **3** *archit* a projecting moulding at the top of an external wall. **4** *art* the projecting top part of a PEDESTAL. **5** *mountaineering* an overhang formed of snow or ice. ⓒ 16c: Italian, meaning 'crow'.

Cornish ▷ *adj* belonging to Cornwall, a county in SW England, its people or language. ▷ *noun* the Celtic language once spoken in Cornwall, related to Welsh.

Cornish pasty ▷ *noun* a semicircular folded pastry case containing various fillings, eg meat, vegetables, etc.

corn on the cob ▷ *noun* a CORNCOB cooked and served as a vegetable.

corn salad ▷ *noun* any of various plants, often found growing in cornfields, whose leaves can be used in salads. Also called LAMB'S LETTUCE.

cornstarch see under CORNFLOUR

cornucopia /kɔːnjʊˈkoʊpɪə/ ▷ *noun* (***cornucopias***) **1** *art* in painting, sculpture, etc: a horn full to overflowing with fruit and other produce, used as a symbol of abundance. Also called **horn of plenty**. **2** an abundant supply. **3** an ornamental vase in the shape of a horn. ● **cornucopian** *adj.* ⓒ 16c: from Latin *cornu* horn + *copiae* abundance.

corny /ˈkɔːnɪ/ ▷ *adj* (***cornier***, ***corniest***) *colloq* **1** said of a joke: old and stale. **2** embarrassingly old-fashioned or sentimental. **3** relating to or abounding in CORN[1]. **4** relating to CORN[2]. ● **cornily** *adverb*. ● **corniness** *noun*. ⓒ 20c in senses 1 and 2, 16c in sense 3, all from CORN[1]; 18c in sense 4, from CORN[2].

corolla /kəˈrɒlə, kəˈroʊlə/ ▷ *noun* (***corollas***) *bot* the collective name for the petals of a flower. ⓒ 18c: Latin, diminutive of *corona* garland or crown.

corollary /kəˈrɒlərɪ, ˈkɒrələrɪ/ ▷ *noun* (***corollaries***) **1** something that directly follows from another thing that has been proved. **2** a natural or obvious consequence. ⓒ 14c: from Latin *corollarium* gift of money, originally for a garland, from COROLLA.

coromandel screen /kɒrəˈmandəl —/ ▷ *noun* a screen made of wood, incised with designs filled with colour or with gold and lacquered. ⓒ 19c: from the name Coromandel Coast in SE India, where the screens were imported from.

corona /kəˈroʊnə/ ▷ *noun* (***coronae*** /-iː/ or ***coronas***) **1** *astron* the outer atmosphere of the Sun, consisting of a halo of hot luminous gases that boil from its surface, visible during a total solar eclipse. **2** *astron* a circle of light which appears around the Sun or the Moon. **3** *bot* in certain plants, eg the daffodil: a trumpet-like outgrowth from the petals. **4** *physics* the glowing region produced by IONIZATION of the air surrounding a high-voltage conductor. **5** a round pendant chandelier. **6** *archit* the large flat projection of a CORNICE. ⓒ 16c: Latin, meaning 'crown'.

coronagraph see CORONOGRAPH

coronary /ˈkɒrənərɪ/ ▷ *adj, physiol* denoting vessels, nerves, etc which encircle a part or organ, especially the arteries which supply blood to the heart muscle. ▷ *noun* (***coronaries***) *pathol* a CORONARY THROMBOSIS. ⓒ 17c: from Latin *coronarius* pertaining to a crown, from CORONA.

coronary artery ▷ *noun, medicine* either of the two arteries which supply the muscle of the heart wall with blood.

coronary thrombosis ▷ *noun, pathol* the formation of a blood clot in one of the two coronary arteries, which blocks the flow of blood to the heart and usually gives rise to a heart attack.

coronation /kɒrəˈneɪʃən/ ▷ *noun* the ceremony of crowning a monarch or CONSORT[1] *noun* 1. ⓒ 14c: from French, from Latin *coronatio*, from *coronare* to crown.

coroner /ˈkɒrənə(r)/ ▷ *noun* **1** a public official whose chief responsibility is the investigation of sudden, suspicious or accidental deaths. **2** the principal officer of one of the six ancient divisions of the Isle of Man. ⓒ 14c: from French *corouner*, from *coroune* crown.

coronet /ˈkɒrənɪt, ˈkɒrənet/ ▷ *noun* **1** a small crown. **2** a circlet of jewels for the head. **3** the lowest part of a PASTERN of a horse. **4** the ring of bone at the bottom of a deer's antler. ⓒ 15c: from Old French *coronete*, diminutive of *corone* crown.

coronograph or **coronagraph** /kəˈroʊnəgrɑːf/ ▷ *noun, astron* an optical instrument that is used to observe the Sun's CORONA 1. ⓒ 19c: from CORONA + -GRAPH1.

corp. or **Corp.** ▷ *abbreviation* **1** corporal. **2** corporation.

corporal[1] /ˈkɔːpərəl/ ▷ *noun* a non-commissioned officer in the army or air force. ⓒ 16c: French, from Italian *caporale*, probably associated with *capo* head.

corporal[2] /ˈkɔːpərəl/ ▷ *adj* relating or belonging to the body. ⓒ 14c: French, from Latin *corporalis*, from *corpus* body.

corporal[3] /ˈkɔːpərəl/ ▷ *noun, Christianity* a white cloth, usually made from linen, on which the bread and wine of the EUCHARIST are laid out and with which the remains are covered. ⓒ 14c: from Latin *corporale pallium*, from *corpus* body (see also PALLIUM).

corporal punishment ▷ *noun* physical punishment such as beating or caning.

corporate /ˈkɔːpərət/ ▷ *adj* **1** shared by members of a group; joint □ *corporate membership.* **2** belonging or relating to a corporation □ *corporate finance.* **3** formed into a corporation □ *a corporate body.* • **corporately** *adverb.* ◷ 16c: from Latin *corporare* to form into one body.

corporate bond ▷ *noun, finance* a long-term fixed-interest bond offered by a corporation.

corporate raider ▷ *noun, finance* a company or individual that seeks to gain control of a business by acquiring a large proportion of its stock.

corporate state ▷ *noun, politics* a capitalist state which operates corporatism.

corporate strategy ▷ *noun, finance* the broad aims and strategies that a company wishes to follow over a period of time, especially five years.

corporation /kɔːpəˈreɪʃən/ ▷ *noun* **1** a body of people acting jointly, eg for administration or business purposes and who are recognized by law as acting as an individual. **2** the council of a town or city. **3** *informal, facetious* a paunch. ◷ 16c: from Latin *corporatio*, from *corporare* to embody.

corporation tax ▷ *noun* a tax paid by companies on the profits they make.

corporatism or **corporativism** ▷ *noun, politics* the control of a country's economy by groups of producers who have the authority to implement social and economic policies, while abiding by the principles laid down by the government.

corporeal /kɔːˈpɔːrɪəl/ ▷ *adj* **1** relating to the body as distinct from the soul; physical. **2** relating to things of a material nature. • **corporeality** or **corporeity** /-ˈriːɪtɪ/ *noun.* • **corporeally** *adverb.* ◷ 17c: from Latin *corporeus*, from *corpus* body.

corps /kɔː(r)/ ▷ *noun* (*plural* ***corps***) **1** a military body or division forming a tactical unit □ *the intelligence corps.* **2** a body of people engaged in particular work □ *the diplomatic corps.* ◷ 18c: French, from Latin *corpus* body.

corps de ballet / *French* kɔʀdəbalɛ/ ▷ *noun* a company of ballet dancers, eg at a theatre. ◷ 19c: French.

corpse /kɔːps/ ▷ *noun* the dead body of a human being. ▷ *verb* (***corpsed, corpsing***) *tr & intr, theat slang* said of an actor on stage: to laugh or cause to laugh or to forget one's lines. ◷ 19c as *verb*; 14c as *noun*: from Latin *corpus* body.

corpulent /ˈkɔːpjʊlənt/ ▷ *adj* fat; fleshy; obese. • **corpulence** or **corpulency** *noun.* ◷ 15c: French, from Latin *corpulentus*, from *corpus* body.

corpus /ˈkɔːpəs/ ▷ *noun* (***corpora*** /ˈkɔːpərə/) **1** a body of writings, eg by a particular author, on a particular topic, etc. **2** a body of written and/or spoken material for language research. **3** *anatomy* any distinct mass of body tissue that may be distinguished from its surroundings. ◷ 18c: Latin, meaning 'body'.

corpus callosum /— kəˈlɒsəm/ ▷ *noun* (***corpora callosa*** /ˈkɔːpərə kəˈlɒsə/) *anatomy* in the centre of the brain: a thick bundle of about 300m nerve fibres, that serves to connect the left and right cerebral hemispheres. ◷ 18c: Latin, meaning 'callous body'.

Corpus Christi /ˈkɔːpʊs ˈkrɪstiː, — ˈkrɪstɪ/ ▷ *noun, RC Church* a festival in honour of the Blessed Sacrament, held on the Thursday after Trinity Sunday. ◷ 14c: Latin, meaning 'the body of Christ'.

corpuscle /ˈkɔːpʌsəl, kɔːˈpʌsəl/ ▷ *noun anatomy* any small particle or cell within a tissue or organ, especially a red or white blood cell. • **corpuscular** *adj.* ◷ 17c: from Latin *corpusculum*, diminutive of *corpus* body.

corpus luteum /ˈkɔːpəs ˈluːtɪəm/ ▷ *noun* (***corpora lutea*** /ˈkɔːpərə ˈluːtiːə/) *anatomy* in the ovaries of mammals: the mass of yellowish tissue that develops from a ruptured Graafian follicle after ovulation, which secretes PROGESTERONE, thereby preparing the womb for possible implantation of a fertilized egg. ◷ 20c: from Latin *corpus* body + *luteus* yellow.

corral /kəˈrɑːl, kɒ-/ *chiefly N Amer* ▷ *noun* **1** an enclosure for driving horses or cattle into. **2** a defensive ring of wagons. ▷ *verb* (***corralled, corralling***) to herd or pen into a corral. ◷ 16c: Spanish, meaning 'courtyard'.

correct /kəˈrɛkt, kɒ-/ ▷ *verb* (***corrected, correcting***) **1** to set or put right; to remove errors from something. **2** to mark the errors in. **3** to adjust or make better. **4** *old use* to rebuke or punish. ▷ *adj* **1** free from error; accurate. **2** appropriate; conforming to accepted standards □ *very correct in his behaviour.* • **correctly** *adverb.* • **correctness** *noun.* • **corrector** *noun.* • **stand corrected** to acknowledge one's mistake. ◷ 14c: from Latin *corrigere* to make straight.

correcting fluid ▷ *noun* a usually white liquid which is used to paint over errors in writing or typing, so that when it dries, the correct version can be typed or written on top. Also called **liquid paper**.

correction /kəˈrɛkʃən/ ▷ *noun* **1** the act of correcting. **2** an alteration that improves something. **3** *old use* punishment. • **correctional** *adj.*

correction paper ▷ *noun* a small piece of paper, coated with a chalky substance on one side, which is inserted over a mistake on a type-written page, so that when the error is restruck, it becomes covered, allowing the correction to be typed over it.

corrective /kəˈrɛktɪv/ ▷ *adj* having the effect of correcting or adjusting. ▷ *noun* something that has this effect.

correlate /ˈkɒrəleɪt/ ▷ *verb* (***correlated, correlating***) **1** *tr & intr* said of two or more things: to have a connection or correspondence; to relate one to another. **2** to combine, compare or show relationships between (information, reports, etc). ▷ *noun* either of two things which are related to each other. ◷ 17c: from Latin *cor-* with + *relatum* referred.

correlation /kɒrəˈleɪʃən/ ▷ *noun* **1** a mutual relationship between two things. **2** an act of correlating. **3** *statistics* the strength of the relationship between two random variables. ◷ 16c: from Latin *correlatio*, from *cor-* together + RELATION.

correlation coefficient ▷ *noun, statistics* a number calculated to represent the degree of correlation between two variables.

correlative /kəˈrɛlətɪv/ ▷ *adj* **1** mutually linked. **2** *grammar* said of words: used as an interrelated pair, although not necessarily together, eg like *either* and *or.* ▷ *noun* a correlative word or thing.

correspond /kɒrɪˈspɒnd/ ▷ *verb* (***corresponded, corresponding***) *intr* **1** (*usually* **correspond to something**) to be similar or equivalent. **2** (*usually* **correspond with** or **to something** or **someone**) to be compatible or in agreement; to match. **3** (*usually* **correspond with someone**) to communicate, especially by letter. • **corresponding** *adj.* • **correspondingly** *adverb.* ◷ 16c: from Latin *correspondere*, from *cor-* with + *respondere* to answer.

correspondence ▷ *noun* **1** similarity; equivalence. **2** agreement. **3 a** communication by letters; **b** the letters received or sent.

correspondence course ▷ *noun* a course of study conducted by post.

correspondent ▷ *noun* **1** someone with whom one exchanges letters. **2** someone employed by a newspaper, radio station, etc to send reports from a particular part of the world or on a particular topic □ *political correspondent.*

corridor /ˈkɒrɪdɔː(r)/ ▷ *noun* **1** a passageway connecting parts of a building or off which rooms open. **2** on a train: a passageway giving access to the compartments.

3 a strip of land from a landlocked country through foreign territory, giving access eg to a port. **4** a restricted route through the air that air traffic must follow. ⓘ 17c: French, from Italian *corridore* place for running, from *correre* to run.

corridors of power ▷ *plural noun* the places where the people who make the important decisions are to be found.

corrie /ˈkɒrɪ/ ▷ *noun* (***corries***) in the Scottish Highlands: **1** a semicircular hollow on a hillside. **2** a CIRQUE. ⓘ 18c: from Gaelic *coire* cauldron.

corrigendum /kɒrɪˈdʒɛndəm, -ˈgendʊm/ ▷ *noun* (***corrigenda*** /-ə/) **1** an error for correction, eg in a book. **2** (**corrigenda**) errata (see ERRATUM). ⓘ 19c: Latin, meaning 'that which is to be corrected'.

corroborate /kəˈrɒbəreɪt/ ▷ *verb* (***corroborated, corroborating***) to confirm (eg someone's statement), especially by providing evidence. ● **corroboration** *noun*. ● **corroborative** *adj*. ● **corroborator** *noun*. ⓘ 16c: from Latin *corroborare* to strengthen.

corroboree /kəˈrɒbəriː/ ▷ *noun* (***corroborees***) *Austral* **1** a ceremonial or warlike dance. **2** a noisy gathering. ▷ *verb* (***corroboreed, corroboreeing***) *intr* to hold a corroboree. ⓘ 19c: Aboriginal.

corrode /kəˈroʊd/ ▷ *verb* (***corroded, corroding***) **1** *tr & intr* said of a material or object: to eat or be eaten away, especially by rust or chemicals. **2** to destroy gradually □ *Mutual ill feeling corroded their relationship.* ⓘ 14c: from Latin *corrodere* to gnaw away.

corrosion /kəˈroʊʒən/ ▷ *noun* **1** *chem* the gradual wearing away and eventual destruction of a metal or alloy as a result of its oxidation by air, water or chemicals, eg the rusting of iron. **2** *geol* the gradual wearing away and destruction of rock by water, etc. **3** a corroded part or patch. ⓘ 14c: French, from Latin *corrodere* to gnaw away.

corrosive /kəˈroʊsɪv, -zɪv/ ▷ *adj* **1** capable of eating away. **2** said of a substance: tending to cause corrosion. **3** said of language: hurtful, sarcastic. ▷ *noun* a corrosive thing or substance. ● **corrosively** *adverb*. ● **corrosiveness** *noun*.

corrugate /ˈkɒrəgeɪt/ ▷ *verb* (***corrugated, corrugating***) to fold into parallel ridges, so as to make stronger. ● **corrugated** *adj*. ● **corrugation** *noun* **1** an act of wrinkling. **2** a wrinkle. ⓘ 17c: from Latin *corrugare, corrugatum* to wrinkle.

corrugated iron ▷ *noun* a sheet of iron which has been bent into a wavy shape in order to strengthen it.

corrupt /kəˈrʌpt/ ▷ *verb* (***corrupted, corrupting***) **1** *tr & intr* to change for the worse, especially morally. **2** to spoil, deform or make impure. **3** to bribe. **4** *intr* to decay or deteriorate. **5** said of a text: to change it from the original, usually for the worse. **6** *computing* to introduce errors into (a program or data), either accidentally or deliberately, so that it is no longer reliable. ▷ *adj* **1** morally evil. **2** involving bribery. **3** dishonest. **4** said of a text: so full of errors and alterations as to be unreliable. **5** *computing* said of a program or data: containing errors and therefore no longer reliable, eg as a result of a fault in the hardware or software. ● **corrupter** or **corruptor** *noun*. ● **corruptive** *adj*. ● **corruptly** *adverb*. ● **corruptness** *noun*. ⓘ 13c: from Latin *corrumpere, corruptum* to spoil.

corruptible ▷ *adj* capable of being or liable to be corrupted. ● **corruptibility** *noun*.

corruption /kəˈrʌpʃən/ ▷ *noun* **1** the process of corrupting or condition of being corrupt. **2** a deformed or altered form of a word or phrase □ *'Santa Claus' is a corruption of 'Saint Nicholas'.* **3** dishonesty. **4** impurity.

corsage /kɔːˈsɑːʒ/ ▷ *noun* **1** a small spray of flowers for pinning to the bodice of a dress. **2** the bodice of a dress. ⓘ 19c in this sense: French, from *cors* body.

corsair /ˈkɔːsɛə(r)/ ▷ *noun, old use* **1** a pirate or pirate ship. **2** a privately owned warship. ⓘ 16c: from French *corsaire*, from Latin *cursarius*, from *cursus* a voyage.

corselet, **corslet** or **corselette** /ˈkɔːslɪt/ ▷ *noun* **1** *historical* a protective garment or piece of armour for the upper part of the body. **2** (*usually* **corselette**) a woman's undergarment combining girdle and bra. ⓘ 15c: French, diminutive of *cors* body or bodice.

corset /ˈkɔːsɪt/ ▷ *noun* **1 a** a tightly fitting undergarment, usually worn by women, which has been stiffened by strips of bone or plastic, and is used for shaping or controlling the figure; **b** a similar garment worn to support an injured back; **c** a laced bodice worn on the outside by women and some men during the Middle Ages; **d** in some countries: a similar garment worn by women today. **2** *commerce* government restrictions on the lending power of banks. ▷ *verb* (***corseted, corseting***) **1** to put on a corset. **2** to restrict. ● **corsetier** /kɔːsəˈtjeɪ, kɔːsəˈtɪe(r)/ or **corsetiere** /kɔːsəˈtjɛə(r)/ *noun*. ● **corsetry** *noun*. ⓘ 13c: French, diminutive of *cors* body or bodice.

cortège /kɔːˈtɛʒ, ˈkɔː-/ ▷ *noun* **1** a procession, especially at a funeral. **2** a train of attendants; entourage. ⓘ 17c: French, from Italian *corteggio* retinue.

cortex /ˈkɔːtɛks/ (***cortices*** /ˈkɔːtɪsiːz/) ▷ *noun, anatomy* the outer layer of an organ or tissue, when this differs in structure or function from the inner region, eg the CEREBRAL CORTEX. ● **cortical** *adj*. ⓘ 17c: Latin, meaning 'tree bark'.

corticosteroid /kɔːtɪkoʊˈstɪərɔɪd/ or **corticoid** /ˈkɔːtɪkɔɪd/ ▷ *noun, biochem* any steroid hormone, eg cortisone, manufactured by the ADRENAL CORTEX. ⓘ 1940s: from *cortico-*, combining form of CORTEX + STEROID.

cortisone /ˈkɔːtɪzoʊn, -soʊn/ ▷ *noun, biochem* a naturally occurring steroid hormone which, in synthetic form, is used to treat rheumatoid arthritis, certain eye and skin disorders, etc. ⓘ 20c: from *corticosteron* a hormone.

corundum /kəˈrʌndəm/ ▷ *noun, geol* a hard aluminium oxide mineral, used as an abrasive and as a constituent of emery, with its coloured crystalline forms including the gemstones ruby and sapphire. ⓘ 18c: from Tamil *kuruntam*.

coruscate /ˈkɒrəskeɪt/ ▷ *verb* (***coruscated, coruscating***) *intr* to sparkle; to give off flashes of light. ● **coruscant** /kəˈrʌskənt/ *adj*. ● **coruscating** *adj*. ● **coruscation** /kɒrəˈskeɪʃən/ *noun*. ⓘ 18c: from Latin *coruscare, coruscatum*.

corvette /kɔːˈvɛt/ ▷ *noun* **1** a small warship for escorting larger vessels. **2** *historical* a sailing warship with one tier of guns. ⓘ 17c: French, ultimately from Dutch *korf* a kind of ship.

corvine /ˈkɔːvaɪn/ ▷ *adj* pertaining to or resembling a crow. ⓘ 17c: from Latin *corvinus*, from *corvus* raven.

cos[1] /kɒs, kɒz/ and **cos lettuce** ▷ *noun* a type of lettuce with crisp slim leaves. ⓘ 17c: named after Cos, the Greek island where it originated.

cos[2] /kɒz/ ▷ *abbreviation* cosine.

'cos or **'coz** /kɒz, kəz/ ▷ *contraction, colloq* because.

cosecant /koʊˈsiːkənt/ ▷ *noun, trig* (abbreviation **cosec**) for a given angle in a right-angled triangle: a FUNCTION (*noun* 4) that is the ratio of the length of the HYPOTENUSE to the length of the side opposite the angle under consideration; the reciprocal of the sine of an angle. ⓘ 18c: from *co-*, short for COMPLEMENT 4 + SECANT.

cosh ▷ *noun* (***coshes***) a club, especially a rubber one filled with metal, used as a weapon. ▷ *verb* (***coshes, coshed, coshing***) *colloq* to hit with a cosh or something heavy. ⓘ 19c.

cosily and **cosiness** see under COSY

cosine /'koʊsaɪn/ ▻ *noun, trig* (abbreviation **cos**) in a right-angled triangle: a FUNCTION (*noun* 4), that is the ratio of the length of the side adjacent to the angle to the length of the HYPOTENUSE. ⓒ 17c: from *co-*, short for COMPLEMENT 4 + SINE.

COSLA /'kɒzlə/ ▻ *abbreviation* Convention of Scottish Local Authorities.

cosmetic /kɒz'mɛtɪk/ ▻ *adj* **1** used to beautify the face, body or hair. **2** improving superficially, for the sake of appearance only. ▻ *noun* (*often* **cosmetics**) any application intended to improve the appearance of the body, especially the face. See also MAKE-UP. ● **cosmetically** *adverb.* ⓒ 17c: from Greek *kosmetikos* relating to adornment, from *kosmein* to adorn or arrange.

cosmetic surgery ▻ *noun* surgery, eg a facelift, which is performed purely to improve the patient's appearance, rather than for any medical reason. Compare PLASTIC SURGERY.

cosmic /'kɒzmɪk/ ▻ *adj* **1** relating to the Universe; universal. **2** coming from outer space ◻ ***cosmic rays.*** **3** *colloq* large or significant. ● **cosmically** *adverb* **1** in a cosmic way. **2** said of a star rising: with the Sun. ⓒ 19c: from Greek *kosmikos*, from *kosmos* universe.

cosmic background radiation ▻ *noun, astron* short-wavelength electromagnetic radiation from outer space, consisting of heat remaining from the Big Bang.

cosmic rays and **cosmic radiation** ▻ *noun, astron* radiation which consists of streams of high-energy particles from outer space, travelling at about the speed of light, most of which are thought to originate from SUPERNOVAS.

cosmic string ▻ *noun, astron* any of the massive hypothetical filaments of matter, predicted to be an important component of the very early Universe, and which in the form of infinite lines or closed loops may have played an important role in the formation of galaxy clusters.

cosmo- /'kozmoʊ/ ▻ *combining form, indicating* the Universe. ⓒ From Greek *kosmos* world.

cosmogony /kɒz'mɒgənɪ/ ▻ *noun* (***cosmogonies***) the study of the origin and development of the Universe as a whole, or of specific celestial objects or systems, especially the Solar System. ⓒ 18c: from Greek *kosmogonia*, from *kosmos* world + *gonos* creation.

cosmological argument ▻ *noun, theol* an argument which attempts to prove that God exists by asserting that since the Universe exists and its existence cannot be explained by things in the Universe, it may therefore be supposed that there also exists a first cause, ie God.

cosmological principle ▻ *noun, astron* the principle that, at a given time, the Universe appears the same to observers in other galaxies as it does to us.

cosmology /kɒz'mɒlədʒɪ/ ▻ *noun* (***cosmologies***) **1** the scientific study of the origin, nature, structure and evolution of the Universe. **2** a particular theory or model of the origin and structure of the Universe. ● **cosmological** /kɒzmə'lɒdʒɪkəl/ *adj, noun.* ⓒ 17c: from COSMO- + -LOGY 1.

cosmologist ▻ *noun* a scientist who specializes in cosmology.

cosmonaut /'kɒzmənɔːt/ ▻ *noun* **a** *formerly* a Russian astronaut; **b** an astronaut from any of the countries of the former Soviet Union. ⓒ 20c: from COSMO- + Greek *nautes* sailor.

cosmopolitan /kɒzmə'pɒlɪtən/ ▻ *adj* **1** belonging to or representative of all parts of the world. **2** free of national prejudices; international in experience and outlook. **3** sophisticated. **4** composed of people from all different parts of the world. ▻ *noun* someone of this type; a citizen of the world. ⓒ 17c: from COSMO- + Greek *polites* citizen.

cosmos /'kɒzmɒs/ ▻ *noun* the Universe seen as an ordered system. ⓒ 17c: from Greek *kosmos* world or order.

Cossack /'kɒsak/ ▻ *noun, formerly* any member of the semi-independent communities of fugitive peasants who inhabited the steppelands of S Russia and the Ukraine and who formed an elite group of cavalrymen. ▻ *adj* belonging or relating to this people. ⓒ 16c: ultimately from Turkic *quzzaq* adventurer or guerrilla.

cosset /'kɒsɪt/ ▻ *verb* (***cosseted, cosseting***) to treat too kindly; to pamper. ▻ *noun* **1** a hand-reared animal, especially a lamb. **2** a spoiled child. ⓒ 16c.

cost ▻ *verb* (in senses 1, 2 and 4 *past tense, past participle* ***cost***, in all senses *present participle* ***costing***) **1** to be obtainable at a certain price. **2** *tr & intr* to involve the loss or sacrifice of someone or something. **3** (*past tense, past participle* ***costed***) to estimate or decide the cost of something. **4** *tr & intr, colloq* to put someone to some expense ◻ ***He would send his daughter to university, whatever it cost him.*** ▻ *noun* **1** what something costs; the price paid or required to be paid. **2** loss or sacrifice ◻ ***The war was won but the cost of human life was great.*** **3** (**costs**) *law* the expenses of a case, generally paid by the unsuccessful party. ● **at all costs** no matter what the risk or effort may be. ● **cost someone dear** to prove costly to them. ● **count the cost 1** to consider all the risks before taking action. **2** to realize the bad effects of something done. ● **to one's cost** with some loss or disadvantage. ⓒ 13c: from Latin *constare* to stand firm or cost.

costa /'kɒstə/ ▻ *noun* (***costae*** /'kɒstaɪ/) **1** *anatomy* the technical name for the RIB[1] (*noun* 1). **2** any riblike structure or part. ● **costal** *adj.* ⓒ 19c: Latin.

cost-accountant ▻ *noun, business* an accountant who analyses the costs for a product or operation, often with the aim of establishing a current standard or norm against which actual cost may be compared. See also MANAGEMENT ACCOUNTANT. ● **cost-accounting** *noun.*

co-star /'koʊstɑː(r)/ ▻ *noun* a fellow star in a film, play, etc. ▻ *verb* **1** *intr* said of an actor: to appear alongside another star. **2** said of a production: to feature as fellow stars ◻ ***The play co-starred Gielgud and Olivier.*** ⓒ 20c: CO- + STAR *noun 6, verb 1.*

Costa Rican /kɒstə'riːkən/ ▻ *adj* belonging or relating to Costa Rica, a republic in Central America, or its inhabitants. ▻ *noun* a citizen or inhabitant of, or person born in, Costa Rica.

cost-benefit analysis ▻ *noun* a type of analysis which compares the cost of a particular course of action, eg building a motorway, with the resulting benefits, taking into account the social costs and benefits as well as the strictly financial ones.

cost-effective ▻ *adj* giving acceptable financial return in relation to initial outlay.

costermonger /'kɒstəmʌŋgə(r)/ ▻ *noun, Brit* someone whose job is to sell fruit and vegetables from a barrow. Also called **coster.** ⓒ 16c: from *costard* a type of apple + -MONGER 1.

costive /'kɒstɪv/ ▻ *adj, old use* **1** constipated. **2** mean; stingy. ⓒ 14c: from French *costivé*, from Latin *constipatus* constipated.

costly /'kɒstlɪ/ ▻ *adj* (***costlier, costliest***) **1** involving much cost; expensive. **2** lavish; sumptuous. **3** involving major losses or sacrifices. ● **costliness** *noun.*

cost of living ▻ *noun* the expense to the individual of the ordinary necessities such as food, clothing, fuel, etc, required to sustain a basic standard of existence.

cost price ▻ *noun* the price paid for something by the retailer, before resale to the public at a profit.

costume /'kɒstʃuːm/ ▻ *noun* **1** a set of clothing of a special kind, especially of a particular historical period or particular country. **2** a garment or outfit for a special activity □ *a swimming-costume.* **3** *old use* a woman's suit. ▻ *verb* (***costumed***, ***costuming***) **1** to arrange or design the clothes for (a play, film, etc). **2** to dress in a costume. ⓒ 18c: Italian, meaning 'custom' or 'habit'.

costume jewellery ▻ *noun* inexpensive jewellery made from artificial materials.

costumier /kɒ'stʃuːmɪə(r)/ ▻ *noun* someone who makes or supplies costumes. ⓒ 19c: French.

cosy /'koʊzɪ/ ▻ *adj* (***cosier***, ***cosiest***) **1** warm and comfortable. **2** friendly, intimate and confidential □ *a cosy chat.* ▻ *noun* (***cosies***) a cover to keep something warm, especially a teapot or boiled egg. ▻ *verb* (***cosies***, ***cosied***, ***cosying***) to reassure or comfort, often with a hug. ● **cosily** *adverb*. ● **cosiness** *noun*. ⓒ 18c.

■ **cosy up with** or **to someone** to snuggle up to or with them.

cot¹ ▻ *noun* **1** a small bed with high, barred sides for a child. **2** a portable bed. **3** *naut* a bed like a hammock. **4** *Anglo-Indian* a light bedstead. ⓒ 17c: from Hindi *khat* bedstead.

cot² ▻ *noun* **1** *poetic* a cottage. **2** *usually in compounds* a shortened form of COTE □ *dovecot.* ⓒ Anglo-Saxon.

cot³ ▻ *abbreviation* cotangent.

cotangent /koʊ'tandʒənt/ ▻ *noun, trig* (abbreviation **cot**) for a given angle in a right-angled triangle: a FUNCTION (*noun* 4) that is the ratio of the length of the side adjacent to the angle under consideration, to the length of the side opposite it; the reciprocal of the tangent of an angle. ⓒ 17c: from *co-* short for COMPLEMENT 4 + TANGENT.

cot death see SUDDEN INFANT DEATH SYNDROME

cote /koʊt/ ▻ *noun, usually in compounds* a small shelter for birds or animals □ *dovecote.* ⓒ Anglo-Saxon.

coterie /'koʊtərɪ/ ▻ *noun* (***coteries***) a small exclusive group of people who have the same interests. ⓒ 18c: French.

coterminous see CONTERMINOUS

cotinga /koʊ'tɪŋgə/ ▻ *noun* (***cotingas***) a bird, with a broad, hooked bill, native to the New World tropics. ⓒ 18c: French, from Tupí *cutinga*.

cotoneaster /kətoʊnɪ'astə(r)/ ▻ *noun* a deciduous or evergreen shrub or small tree with clusters of white or pink flowers, followed by red or orange berries. ⓒ 18c: from Latin *cotonea* quince.

cottage /'kɒtɪdʒ/ ▻ *noun* **1** a small house, especially an old stone one, in a village or the countryside. **2** *slang* a public lavatory used for anonymous sex between men. ⓒ 13c in sense 1, 20c in sense 2: from COT².

cottage cheese ▻ *noun* a type of soft white cheese made from the curds of skimmed milk.

cottage industry ▻ *noun* a craft industry such as knitting or weaving, employing workers in their own homes.

cottage loaf ▻ *noun* a loaf consisting of a round piece of dough with a smaller round piece on top of it.

cottager ▻ *noun* someone who lives in a cottage.

cottaging ▻ *noun* the practice of using a public lavatory for anonymous sex between men.

cottar or **cotter** /'kɒtə(r)/ ▻ *noun, Scottish historical* a farm labourer occupying a cottage rent-free, in return working on the farm. ⓒ 16c: from COT².

cotton /'kɒtən/ ▻ *noun* **1 a** a shrubby plant with broad lobed leaves and egg-shaped seed pods, cultivated in tropical and subtropical regions for the creamy-white downy fibres which surround its seeds; **b** a number of these plants collectively. **2** the soft white fibre obtained from this plant, used in the production of textiles. **3** the cloth or yarn that is woven from fibres obtained from this plant. ▻ *adj* made from cotton. ▻ *verb* (***cottoned***, ***cottoning***) (*always* **cotton on to something**) *colloq* to begin to understand it. ● **cottony** *adj*. ⓒ 14c: from French *coton*, from Arabic *qutun*.

cotton candy ▻ *noun, US* CANDY FLOSS.

cotton gin ▻ *noun* a machine for separating cotton fibres from the seeds they surround.

cottongrass ▻ *noun* a variety of sedge, with long silky or cotton-like hairs around the ripened ovary.

cotton-picking or **cotton-pickin'** ▻ *adj, N Amer slang* (used to indicate annoyance) damned □ *I'll get my own back on that cotton-pickin' liar!*

cotton wool ▻ *noun* soft fluffy wadding made from cotton fibre, which is used in the treatment of injuries, application of cosmetics, etc.

cottony see under COTTON

cotyledon /kɒtɪ'liːdən/ ▻ *noun, bot* in flowering plants: one of the leaves produced by the embryo, providing the initial food source for the plant. ● **cotyledonary** *adj*. ● **cotyledonous** *adj*. ⓒ 17c: Latin, from Greek *kotyledon*, from *kotyle* cup.

couch¹ /kaʊtʃ/ ▻ *noun* (***couches***) **1** a sofa or settee. **2** a bed-like seat with a headrest, eg for patients to lie on when being examined or treated by a doctor or psychiatrist. **3** *poetic* a bed. ▻ *verb* (***couches***, ***couched***, ***couching***) **1** *tr & intr* to lie down or cause to lie down. **2** to express in words of a certain kind. ⓒ 14c: from French *coucher* to lay down.

couch² /kaʊtʃ, kuːtʃ/ and **couch grass** ▻ *noun* a perennial grass native to northern temperate regions, with rough dull green or bluish-green leaves, growing on roadsides and waste ground, and as a weed in cultivated ground. Also called **quitch**. ⓒ Anglo-Saxon *cwice*.

couchette /kuː'ʃɛt/ ▻ *noun* **a** on a ship or train: a sleeping-berth, converted from ordinary seating; **b** a railway carriage with such berths. ⓒ 20c: French, diminutive of *couche* bed.

couching /'kaʊtʃɪŋ/ ▻ *noun* **1** *surgery* an operation to remove a cataract. **2** *needlecraft* embroidery in which the surface is covered with threads and these are secured by stitches forming a pattern.

couch potato ▻ *noun, colloq* someone who spends their leisure time watching television or videos.

cougar /'kuːgə(r)/ ▻ *noun, N Amer* a PUMA. ⓒ 18c: from French *couguar*, ultimately from Guaraní *cuguaçuarana*.

cough /kɒf/ ▻ *verb* (***coughed***, ***coughing***) **1** *intr* to expel air, mucus, etc from the throat or lungs with a rough sharp noise. **2** *intr* said of an engine, etc: to make a similar noise. **3** to express with a cough. ▻ *noun* **1** an act or sound of coughing. **2** a condition of lungs or throat causing coughing.

■ **cough something up** to bring up mucus, phlegm, blood, etc by coughing.

■ **cough up** *slang* to provide (money, information, etc), especially reluctantly.

cough mixture ▻ *noun* a liquid medicine used to relieve coughing.

could /kʊd/ ▻ *verb* **1** *past tense of* CAN: □ *I found I could lift it.* **2** used to express a possibility □ *He could be exactly what we are looking for!* □ *You could be right.* **3** used to express a possible course of action □ *You could try telephoning her.* **4** used in making requests □ *Could you help me?* **5** to feel like doing something or able to do something □ *I could have strangled him* □ *I could not allow that.* ● **could be** *colloq* that may be the case □ *You think Rick's the thief? Could be!*

couldn't /'kʊdənt/ ▻ *contraction* could not.

coulis /kuːliː/ ▻ *noun* (*plural* ***coulis*** /-liːz/) a pureé of fruit, vegetables, etc often served as a sauce surrounding a meal.

coulomb /ˈkuːlɒm/ ▻ *noun* (symbol **C**) the SI unit of electric charge, equal to the amount of charge transported by a current of one ampere in one second.

council /ˈkaʊnsəl/ ▻ *noun* **1 a** a body of people whose function is to advise, administer, organize, discuss or legislate; **b** the people making up such a body. **2** the elected body of people that directs the affairs of a town, borough, district, region, etc. ⓒ 12c: from French *concile*, from Latin *concilium* assembly.

council house ▻ *noun* a house built, owned and rented out by a local council.

councillor ▻ *noun* an elected member of a council, especially of a town, etc.

councillor, counsellor

These words are often confused with each other.

council tax ▻ *noun* in the UK: a local-government tax based on and banded according to property values, which was introduced in 1993 to replace the COMMUNITY CHARGE.

counsel /ˈkaʊnsəl/ ▻ *noun* **1** advice. **2** consultation, discussion or deliberation. **3** a lawyer or group of lawyers that gives legal advice and fights cases in court. ▻ *verb* (***counselled, counselling***) to advise. ● **keep one's own counsel** to keep one's opinions and intentions to oneself. ⓒ 13c: from French *conseil*, from Latin *consilium* advice.

counsellor or *N Amer* **counselor** ▻ *noun* **1** an adviser. **2** a lawyer.

count¹ ▻ *verb* (***counted, counting***) **1** *intr* to recite numbers in ascending order □ *count to five.* **2** to find the total amount of (items), by adding up item by item. **3** to include □ *Did you remember to count Iain?* **4** *intr* to be important; to matter; to have an effect or value □ *Good contacts count in the music business.* **5** to consider □ *He counted himself lucky that he still had a job.* ▻ *noun* **1** an act of counting. **2** the number counted. **3** a charge brought against an accused person □ *He was found guilty on two counts of murder.* **4** a single response registered by a device used to detect or measure ionizing radiation. **5** the total number of responses registered by such a device. ● **countable** *adj* **1** able to be counted. **2** *grammar* said of a noun: capable of being used with *a* or *an*, or in the plural. See also COUNT NOUN. ● **count me in** or **out** I am willing, or not willing, to be included. ● **keep** or **lose count** to keep, or fail to keep, a note of the running total. ● **out for the count 1** *boxing* said of a floored boxer: unable to rise to his feet within a count of ten. **2** unconscious. **3** *facetious* fast asleep. ⓒ 14c: from French *cunter*, from Latin *computare* to calculate.

■ **count against someone** to be a disadvantage to them.

■ **count down** to count backwards from a certain number to zero, so as to indicate the time before a particular event, movement, happening, etc. See also COUNTDOWN.

■ **count someone** or **something in** to include them or it.

■ **count on someone** or **something** to rely on them or it.

■ **count someone out 1** *boxing* to declare (a floored boxer) to have lost the match if they are unable to get up within a count of ten seconds. **2** to exclude them from consideration.

■ **count something out** to lay down or present items one at a time while counting □ *counted out five pounds for each boy.*

count² ▻ *noun* a European nobleman, equal in rank to a British earl. ⓒ 16c: from French *conte*, from Latin *comes* companion.

countdown ▻ *noun* a count backwards from a certain number, with zero as the moment for action, used eg in launching a rocket. See also COUNT DOWN at COUNT1.

countenance /ˈkaʊntənəns/ ▻ *noun* **1** face; expression or appearance. **2** support; patronage. ▻ *verb* (***countenanced, countenancing***) **1** to favour or support. **2** to allow; to tolerate. ● **give countenance to something** to support it, eg a proposal, etc. ● **keep one's countenance** to remain composed, manage not to laugh, etc. ⓒ 13c: from French *contenance*, from Latin *continentia* self-control.

counter¹ /ˈkaʊntə(r)/ ▻ *noun* **1** a long flat-topped fitting in a shop, cafeteria, bank, etc over which goods are sold, food is served or business is transacted. **2** in various board games: a small flat disc used as a playing-piece, especially in board games. **3** a disc-shaped token used as a substitute coin. **4** a device for counting something □ *Geiger counter.* **5** someone who counts. ● **over the counter** by the normal method of sale in a shop, etc. ● **under the counter** by secret illegal sale, or by unlawful means. ⓒ 14c: from Latin *computare* to reckon.

counter² /ˈkaʊntə(r)/ ▻ *verb* (***countered, countering***) *tr & intr* to oppose, act against or hit back. ▻ *adverb* (*often* **counter to something**) in the opposite direction to it; in contradiction of it. ▻ *adj* contrary; opposing. ▻ *noun* **1** a return blow; an opposing move. **2** an opposite or contrary. **3** something that can be used to one's advantage in negotiating or bargaining. **4** *naut* the curved, overhanging part of a ship's stern. ● **run counter to something** to act in a way contrary to it □ *The results ran counter to our expectations.* ⓒ 14c: from French *contre*, from Latin *contra-* against.

counter- /ˈkaʊntə(r)/ ▻ *prefix, denoting* **1** opposite; against; in opposition to something □ *counter-attack.* **2** in competition or rivalry □ *counter-attraction.* **3** matching or corresponding □ *counterpart.* ⓒ From French *contre*, from Latin *contra-* against.

counteract /kaʊntəˈrakt/ ▻ *verb* to reduce or prevent the effect of something. ● **counteraction** *noun.* ● **counteractive** *adj.* ⓒ 17c.

counter-attack ▻ *noun* an attack in reply to an attack. ▻ *verb, tr & intr* to attack in return. ⓒ 20c.

counter-attraction ▻ *noun* a rival attraction. ● **counter-attractive** *adj.* ⓒ 18c.

counterbalance ▻ *noun* a weight, force or circumstance that balances another or cancels it out. ▻ *verb* to act as a counterbalance to; to neutralize or cancel out. ⓒ 17c.

counterblast ▻ *noun* a vigorous and indignant verbal or written response. ⓒ 16c.

counter-charge ▻ *noun* an accusation made in response to one made against oneself. ▻ *verb* to make an accusation against an accuser. ⓒ 17c.

counter-claim ▻ *noun* a claim or assertion made in opposition to one made by someone else. ▻ *verb* to make a counter-claim. ⓒ 18c.

counter-clockwise ▻ *adj, adverb, especially N Amer* anticlockwise.

counter-culture ▻ *noun* a culture or way of life that deliberately rejects the perceived social norm. ⓒ 20c.

counter-espionage ▻ *noun* activities undertaken to frustrate spying by an enemy or rival. Also called **counter-intelligence**.

counterfeit /ˈkaʊntəfɪt, -fiːt/ ▻ *adj* **1** made in imitation of a genuine article, especially with the purpose of deceiving; forged. **2** not genuine; insincere. ▻ *noun* an imitation, especially one designed to deceive; a forgery. ▻ *verb* (***counterfeited, counterfeiting***) **1** to copy for a dishonest purpose; to forge. **2** to pretend. ● **counterfeiter** *noun.* ⓒ 13c: from French *contrefait*, ultimately from Latin *contra-* against + *facere* to make.

counterfoil ▻ *noun* the section of a cheque, receipt, ticket, etc retained as a record by the person who issues it. ⓒ 18c: COUNTER- + FOIL².

counter-insurgency ▻ *noun* military action taken against insurgents or rebels.

counter-intelligence ▻ *noun* another name for COUNTER-ESPIONAGE. ⓒ 20c.

countermand /kaʊntəˈmɑːnd, ˈkaʊntəmɑːnd/ ▻ *verb* (***countermanded, countermanding***) **1** to cancel or revoke (an order or command). **2** to recall (a person, troops, etc). ▻ *noun* a command which cancels a previous one. ⓒ 15c: from French *contremander*, from Latin *mandare* to order.

countermarch ▻ *verb, tr & intr* to march or cause to march in the opposite direction from that previously taken. ▻ *noun* an instance of marching back in a different direction. ⓒ 16c.

counter-measure ▻ *noun* an action taken to counteract a threat, dangerous development or move. ⓒ 20c.

counter-offensive ▻ *noun* an aggressive move made in response to an initial attack. ⓒ 20c.

counterpane /ˈkaʊntəpeɪn/ ▻ *noun, dated* a bedspread. ⓒ 17c: from French *coitepoint* quilt, from Latin *culcita puncta* quilted mattress.

counterpart ▻ *noun* **1** one of two parts which form a corresponding pair. **2** a person or thing which is not exactly the same as another, but which is equivalent to it in a different place or context ▫ *The Russian ambassador triumphed at the conference, but her counterpart at the UN was not quite so successful.*

counterplot ▻ *verb* to plot against in order to frustrate another plot. ▻ *noun* a plot intended to frustrate another plot. ⓒ 16c.

counterpoint ▻ *noun, music* **1** the combining of two or more melodies sung or played simultaneously into a harmonious whole. **2** a part or melody combined with another. ▻ *verb* to set in contrast to. See also CONTRAPUNTAL. ⓒ 16c: from French *contrepoint*, from Latin *contra-* against + *punctus* musical note.

counterpoise ▻ *noun* **1** a weight which balances another weight. **2** something that counterbalances. **3** a state of equilibrium. ▻ *verb* **1** to balance with something of equal weight. **2** to bring to a state of equilibrium. ⓒ 14c: from French *contrepois*, from Latin *contra-* against + *pensum* weight.

counter-productive ▻ *adj* tending to undermine productiveness and efficiency; having the opposite effect to that intended.

counter-revolution ▻ *noun* a revolution to overthrow a system of government established by a previous revolution. ● **counter-revolutionary** *adj, noun*.

countersign ▻ *verb* to sign (a document, etc already signed by someone else) by way of confirmation. ▻ *noun* a password or signal used in response to a sentry's challenge; a sign or signal given in response to another sign or signal. ⓒ 16c: from French *contresigne*, from Italian *contrasegno* a counter-token.

counter-signature ▻ *noun* a name countersigned on a document.

countersink ▻ *verb* **1** to widen the upper part of (a screw hole) so that the top of the screw, when inserted, will be level with the surrounding surface. **2** to insert (a screw) into such a hole. ▻ *noun* **1** a tool for carrying this out. Also called **countersink bit**. **2** the enlargement made to the hole.

counter-tenor ▻ *noun, music* an adult male voice, higher than the TENOR.

countervail /kaʊntəˈveɪl/ ▻ *verb* (***countervailed, countervailing***) **1** *tr & intr* (*often* **countervail against something**) to act against something with equal effect. **2** to compensate. ⓒ 14c: from French *contrevaloir*, from Latin *contra-* against + *valere* to be strong.

counterweight ▻ *noun* a counterbalancing weight.

countess /ˈkaʊntɪs/ ▻ *noun* **1** the wife or widow of an earl or count. **2** a woman with the rank of earl or count. ⓒ 12c: from French *contesse*, from Latin *comitissa*, feminine of *comes* companion.

counties *plural of* COUNTY

countless /ˈkaʊntləs/ ▻ *adj* numerous; so many as to be impossible to count.

count noun ▻ *noun, grammar* a noun which can be qualified in the singular by the indefinite article and can also be used in the plural, eg *car* (as in *a car* or *cars*) but not *furniture*. Compare MASS NOUN.

countrified or **countryfied** /ˈkʌntrɪfaɪd/ ▻ *adj* rural; rustic in appearance or style.

country /ˈkʌntrɪ/ ▻ *noun* (***countries***) **1** an area of land distinguished from other areas by its culture, climate, inhabitants, political boundery, etc. **2** the population of such an area of land. **3** a nation or state. **4** one's native land. **5** (*often* **the country**) open land, away from the towns and cities, usually characterized by moors, woods, hills, fields, etc. **6** land having a certain character or connection ▫ *Burns country.* **7** an area of knowledge or experience ▫ *back in the familiar country of simple arithmetic.* ● **across country** not keeping to roads. ● **go to the country** *Brit* said of a government in power: to dissolve parliament and hold a general election. ⓒ 13c: from French *contrée*, from Latin *contrata terra* land lying in front of one.

country and western ▻ *noun* a style of popular music, based on the white folk music of the Southern USA, characterized by its use of instruments like banjos, fiddles and pedal steel guitar.

country bumpkin see BUMPKIN

country club ▻ *noun* a club in a rural area with facilities for sport and recreation.

country cousin ▻ *noun* a relative from the country, unaccustomed to the customs or sights in a town and, as such, prone to embarrass their town relatives.

country dance ▻ *noun* any one of many traditional British dances in which partners face each other in parallel lines or sometimes form circles. ● **country dancing** *noun*.

countryfied see COUNTRIFIED

country house and **country seat** ▻ *noun* a large house in the country, especially one belonging to a wealthy landowner.

countryman and **countrywoman** ▻ *noun* **1** someone who lives in a rural area. **2** someone belonging to a particular country, especially the same country as oneself.

country music ▻ *noun* a category of popular music, including COUNTRY AND WESTERN.

countryside ▻ *noun* rural land situated outside or away from towns.

countrywide ▻ *adj* all over the nation.

county /ˈkaʊntɪ/ ▻ *noun* (***counties***) **1** any of the geographical divisions within England, Wales and Ireland that form the larger units of local government. Compare REGION (sense 2). **2** in the USA: the main administrative subdivision within a state. ▻ *adj, derog, informal* upper class; pertaining to the landed gentry. ⓒ 15c: from French *conté*, from Latin *comes* count.

county court ▻ *noun* a local court where non-criminal cases are heard.

county town ▻ *noun* the chief town of a county, acting as its seat of administration.

coup /kuː/ ▻ *noun* **1** a successful move; a masterstroke. **2** a COUP D'ÉTAT. ⓘ 18c: French, from Latin *colaphus* blow with the fist.

coup de grâce /kuː də grɑːs; ▻ *noun* (***coups de grâce*** /kuː də grɑːs/) a final decisive blow, especially one which puts an end to suffering. ⓘ 17c: French, meaning 'blow of mercy'.

coup d'état /kuː deɪˈtɑː/ ▻ *noun* (***coups d'état*** /kuː deɪˈtɑː/) the sudden, usually violent, overthrow of a government. Often shortened to COUP. ⓘ 17c: French, meaning 'stroke of the state'.

coupe /kuːp/ ▻ *noun* **1** a dessert made with fruit and ice cream. **2** a glass bowl, designed for serving this dessert. ⓘ 19c: French, meaning 'goblet'.

coupé /ˈkuːpeɪ/ ▻ *noun* (***coupés***) **1** a car with four seats, two doors and a sloping rear. **2** a four-wheeled carriage, with two seats inside for passengers, and a seat outside for the driver. ⓘ 19c: French, from *carosse coupé* cut carriage, from *couper* to cut.

couple /ˈkʌpəl/ ▻ *noun* **1** a pair of people attached in some way, often romantically, eg a wife and husband, a man and woman, two women or two men, etc. **2** a pair of partners, eg for dancing. **3** (*usually* **a couple of**) two, or a few ▫ *I'll call you in a couple of weeks.* **4** *physics* a pair of equal but opposite forces that are applied to different points on the same object, producing a turning effect. ▻ *verb* (***coupled, coupling***) **1** to associate; to link. **2** to connect (two things). **3** *intr* to have sexual intercourse. ⓘ 13c: from French *cople*, from Latin *copula* bond or connection.

couplet /ˈkʌplət/ ▻ *noun* a pair of consecutive lines of verse, especially ones which rhyme and have the same metre. ⓘ 16c: diminutive of COUPLE.

coupling /ˈkʌplɪŋ/ ▻ *noun* **1** a link for joining things together. **2** *derog* sexual intercourse.

coupon /ˈkuːpɒn/ ▻ *noun* **1** a slip of paper entitling one to something, eg a discount. **2** a detachable order form, competition entry form, etc printed on packaging, etc. **3** a printed betting form for football pools. ⓘ 19c: French, from earlier French *colpon* piece cut off.

courage /ˈkʌrɪdʒ/ ▻ *noun* **1** bravery. **2** cheerfulness or resolution in coping with setbacks. ● **have the courage of one's convictions** to be brave enough to act in accordance with one's beliefs, no matter what the outcome. ● **pluck up courage** or **take one's courage in both hands** to become resolved to meet a challenge. ● **take courage** to be resolute or cheerful in difficult circumstances. ⓘ 14c: from French *corage*, from Latin *cor* heart.

courageous /kəˈreɪdʒəs/ ▻ *adj* having or showing courage. ● **courageously** *adverb*. ● **courageousness** *noun*.

courante /kʊˈrɑːnt/ ▻ *noun* **1** a lively dance in triple time. **2** a piece of music for it. ⓘ 16c: French, meaning 'running (dance)', from *courir* to run.

courgette /kʊəˈʒɛt, kɔːˈʒɛt/ ▻ *noun* a variety of small marrow. Also called ZUCCHINI. ⓘ 20c: French, diminutive of *courge* gourd.

courier /ˈkʊrɪə(r)/ ▻ *noun* **1** a guide who travels with and looks after, parties of tourists. **2** a messenger. ⓘ 15c: French, from Latin *currere* to run.

course /kɔːs/ ▻ *noun* **1** the path in which anyone or anything moves. **2** a direction taken or planned ▫ *go off course.* **3** the channel of a river, etc. **4** the normal progress of something. **5** the passage of a period of time ▫ *in the course of the next year.* **6** a line of action ▫ *Your best course is to wait.* **7 a** a series of lessons, etc; a curriculum; **b** the work covered in such a series. **8** a prescribed treatment, eg medicine to be taken, over a period. **9** any of the successive parts of a meal. **10** *often in compounds* the ground over which a game is played or a race run ▫ *golf course* ▫ *obstacle course.* **11** *building* a single row of bricks or stones in a wall, etc. ▻ *verb* (***coursed, coursing***) **1** *intr* to move or flow. **2** to hunt (hares, etc) using dogs. ● **coursing** *noun* the hunting of hares using dogs. ● **in the course of something** while doing it; during it. ● **in the course of time** eventually. ● **in due course** at the appropriate or expected time. ● **a matter of course** a natural or expected action or result. ● **of course 1** as expected. **2** naturally; certainly; without doubt ▫ *Am I coming to the cinema tonight? Of course!* **3** admittedly ▫ *I was annoyed that she hadn't finished the job although, of course, it was only her first day.* ● **stay the course** to endure to the end. ⓘ 13c: from French *cours*, from Latin *currere* to run.

coursebook ▻ *noun* a book to accompany a course of instruction.

courser ▻ *noun* **1 a** someone who courses hares, etc; **b** a hound used for this. **2** *poetic* a swift horse. **3** any of nine species of fast-running bird, native to Africa and S Asia, which have pale sandy plumage, a long curved bill, short strong wings, long legs and three forward-pointing toes on each foot.

court /kɔːt/ ▻ *noun* **1** the judge, law officials and members of the jury gathered to hear and decide on a legal case. **2** the room or building used for such a hearing. **3** an area marked out for a particular game or sport, or a division of this ▫ *basketball court.* **4** an open space or square surrounded by houses or by sections of a building. **5** (*often* **Court**) used in names: **a** a group of houses arranged around an open space; **b** a block of flats; **c** a country mansion. **6** the palace, household, attendants, and advisers of a sovereign. ▻ *verb* (***courted, courting***) **1** *tr & intr, old use* to try to win the love of someone. **2** to try to win the favour of someone. **3** to seek (popularity, etc). **4** to risk or invite ▫ *court danger.* ● **the ball is in his** or **your,** *etc* **court** he, you, etc must make the next move. ● **go to court** to take legal action. ● **hold court** to be surrounded by a circle of admirers. ● **out of court** without legal action being taken. ● **pay court to someone** to pay them flattering attention. ● **put** or **rule something out of court** to prevent it from being heard or considered. ● **take someone to court** to bring a legal case against them. ⓘ 12c: from French *cort*, from Latin *cohors*, shortened to *cors* yard or company of soldiers.

court bouillon /kɔːt ˈbuːjɒn/ ▻ *noun* a seasoned stock made with vegetables, wine or vinegar, etc in which fish is boiled. ⓘ 18c: French.

court card ▻ *noun* in a pack of playing cards: the king, queen or jack. Also called FACE CARD, PICTURE CARD.

courteous /ˈkɜːtɪəs, ˈkɔːtɪəs/ ▻ *adj* polite; considerate; respectful. ● **courteously** *adverb*. ● **courteousness** *noun*. ⓘ 13c: from French *corteis*, from *cort* court.

courtesan /ˈkɔːtɪzan/ ▻ *noun, historical* a prostitute with wealthy or noble clients. ⓘ 16c: from French *courtisane*, from Italian *cortigiana* woman of the court.

courtesy /ˈkɜːtəsɪ, ˈkɔːtəsɪ/ ▻ *noun* (***courtesies***) **1** courteous behaviour; politeness. **2** a courteous act. ● **by courtesy of someone 1** with their permission. **2** *colloq* from them. ⓘ 13c: from French *corteisie*, from COURTEOUS.

courtesy light ▻ *noun* in a motor vehicle: a small light usually operated by the opening and closing of the doors.

courtesy title ▻ *noun* a frequently used but legally invalid title, such as those used by the younger sons of peers.

courthouse ▻ *noun* a building in which the lawcourts are held.

courtier /ˈkɔːtɪə(r)/ ▻ *noun* **1** someone in attendance at a royal court. **2** an elegant flatterer. ⓘ 13c: ultimately from French *cortoyer* to be at or frequent the court.

courtly ▻ *adj* **1** having fine manners. **2** flattering. ● **courtliness** *noun*.

courtly love ▷ *noun* in medieval literature: a conception and tradition of love in which a knight idealizes his lady and sublimates his love for her in submission, service and devotion.

court-martial ▷ *noun* (***courts-martial*** or ***court-martials***) a military court which tries members of the armed forces for breaches of military law. ▷ *verb* (***court-martialled, court-martialling***) to try by court-martial.

Court of Appeal ▷ *noun* in England and Wales: a court with civil and criminal divisions, which hears appeals from other courts. Compare COURT OF FIRST INSTANCE.

court of first instance ▷ *noun, law* the court in which a case is first heard and where the first decision on it is made, and from which it may be referred to a higher court. Compare COURT OF APPEAL.

Court of Justice of the European Communities ▷ *noun* the court of the European Union whose jurisdiction covers the hearing of disputes on issues of EC law. Formerly called **European Court of Justice**.

court of law see LAWCOURT

Court of Session ▷ *noun* in Scotland: a court which deals with civil matters and consists of an Outer House and a more senior Inner House, similar to the High Court and the Court of Appeal respectively.

court order ▷ *noun* a direction or command of a judiciary court which, if not complied with, may lead to criminal proceedings against the offender or offenders. See also MANDAMUS.

courtroom ▷ *noun* a room in which a lawcourt is held.

courtship ▷ *noun, dated* **1** the courting or wooing of an intended spouse. **2** the period for which this lasts.

court shoe ▷ *noun* a woman's shoe in a plain low-cut style.

courtyard ▷ *noun* an open space surrounded by buildings or walls.

couscous /'kʊskʊs/ ▷ *noun* a N African dish of crushed semolina, which is steamed and served with eg vegetables, chicken, fish, etc. ⓘ 17c: French, from Arabic *kuskus*, from *kaskasa* to pound until small.

cousin /'kʌzən/ ▷ *noun* **1** a son or daughter of one's uncle or aunt. Also called **first cousin** or **cousin-german**. Compare SECOND COUSIN. **2** something kindred, especially a race or nation □ *We'd like to welcome our American cousins.* **3** a form of address used by a sovereign when addressing another. ⓘ 13c: from French *cosin*, from Latin *consobrinus* cousin on the mother's side.

cousin once removed ▷ *noun* someone one generation down from the specified cousin, ie either a son or daughter of the specified cousin (**first cousin once removed**), or the specified cousin of one's parent (**second cousin once removed**). See also REMOVED at REMOVE.

couture /kʊ'tʃʊə(r), kuː'tʊə(r)/ ▷ *noun* the designing, making and selling of fashionable clothes. ⓘ Early 20c: French, meaning 'sewing' or 'dressmaking'.

couturier /kʊ'tʃʊərɪeɪ, kuː'tʊərɪeɪ/ or **couturière** /-rɪɛə(r)/ ▷ *noun* a male, or female, fashion designer.

covalent bond /koʊ'veɪlənt —/ ▷ *noun, chem* a chemical bond in which two atoms are held together by sharing a pair of electrons between them.

covariance /koʊ'vɛərɪəns/ ▷ *noun* **1** the property of varying concomitantly. **2** *math* a statistic used to measure the agreement between two sets of random variables, which differs from CORRELATION in that it is dependent on the scale used to measure the variables.

cove¹ /koʊv/ ▷ *noun* **1** a small and usually sheltered bay or inlet on a rocky coast. **2** a small cave or cavern. ⓘ Anglo-Saxon *cofa* room.

cove² /koʊv/ ▷ *noun, Brit & Austral dated, colloq* a fellow. ⓘ 16c.

coven /'kʌvən/ ▷ *noun* **1** a gathering of witches. **2** a group of thirteen witches. ⓘ 17c in this sense; 16c in obsolete sense 'a meeting': ultimately from Latin *convenire* to meet.

covenant /'kʌvənənt/ ▷ *noun* **1** *law* a formal sealed agreement to do something, eg pay a sum of money regularly to a charity. **2** a formal binding agreement. **3** *Bible* an agreement made between God and some person or people. ▷ *verb* (***covenanted, covenanting***) *tr & intr* to agree by covenant to do something. ⓘ 13c: French, from *convenir*, from Latin *convenire* to agree.

covenanter ▷ *noun* **1** /'kʌvənəntə(r)/ a person who makes a covenant. **2** (**Covenanter**) /*also* kʌvə'nantə(r)/ *Scottish historical* an adherent of either of two 17c religious covenants defending Presbyterianism in Scotland. ⓘ 17c: from French convenir to agree, from Latin convenire.

Coventry /'kɒvəntrɪ, 'kʌv-/ ▷ *noun* (*always* **send someone to Coventry**) to refuse to speak to them or associate with them, especially as a punishment or protest. ⓘ 17c: perhaps from the imprisonment of Royalists in Coventry during the Civil War.

cover /'kʌvə(r)/ ▷ *verb* (***covered, covering***) **1** to form a layer over someone or something. **2** to protect or conceal someone or something by putting something over them or it. **3** to clothe. **4** to extend over something. **5** to strew, sprinkle, spatter, mark all over, etc. **6** (*usually* **cover with something**) to bring (a feeling, etc) upon oneself, often in an overwhelming way. **7** to deal with (a subject). **8** said of a reporter, etc: to investigate or report on (a story). **9** to have as one's area of responsibility. **10** to travel (a distance). **11** to be adequate to pay □ *He had enough money to cover the meal.* **12** to insure; to insure against something. **13** to threaten by aiming a gun at someone or something. **14** to keep (a building, its exits, etc) under armed watch. **15** to shield with a firearm at the ready or with actual fire. **16** *sport* to protect (a fellow team-member) or obstruct (an opponent). **17** said of a stallion, bull, etc: to mate with (a female). **18** said of a bird: to sit on (eggs). **19** to record a cover version of (a song, etc). **20** *intr* (*usually* **cover for someone**) to take over the duties of an absent colleague, etc. ▷ *noun* **1** something that covers. **2** a lid, top, protective casing, etc. **3** the covering of something. **4** (**covers**) the sheets and blankets on a bed. **5** the paper or board binding of a book, magazine, etc; one side of this. **6** an envelope □ *a first-day cover.* **7** shelter or protection. **8** insurance. **9** service □ *emergency cover.* **10** a pretence; a screen; a false identity □ *His cover as a salesman was blown.* **11** armed protection; protective fire. **12** *cricket* see COVER POINT. **13** in restaurants, etc: an individual place setting at table. **14** a COVER VERSION. • **under cover 1** in secret. **2** within shelter. • **under cover of something** using it as a protection or pretense. • **under plain cover** in a plain envelope without tradename, etc. • **under separate cover** in a separate envelope or parcel. ⓘ 13c: from French *covrir*, from Latin *cooperire* to cover completely.

■ **cover something up 1** to cover it entirely. **2** to conceal (a dishonest act, a mistake, etc).

coverage /'kʌvərɪdʒ/ ▷ *noun* **1** an amount covered. **2** the extent to which a news item is reported in any of the media, etc. **3** the amount of protection given by an insurance company. ⓘ 20c.

coverall /'kʌvərɔːl/ ▷ *noun, chiefly US* (*usually* **coveralls**) a one-piece protective garment worn over normal clothes. Compare OVERALLS. ▷ *adj* covering or including everything.

cover charge ▷ *noun* in a restaurant, café, etc: a service charge made per person.

cover girl ▷ *noun* a girl or woman whose photograph is shown on a magazine cover.

covering ▻ *noun* something that covers, eg a blanket, protective casing, etc.

covering letter ▻ *noun* a letter explaining the documents or goods it accompanies.

coverlet /ˈkʌvələt/ ▻ *noun* a thin top cover for a bed; a bedspread. ◷ 13c: probably from French *cuver-lit*, from *covrir* to cover + *lit* bed.

cover note ▻ *noun* a temporary certificate of insurance, giving cover until the issue of the actual policy.

cover point ▻ *noun, cricket* the fielding position forward and to the right of the batsman.

covert ▻ *adj* /ˈkʌvət, ˈkoʊvɜːt/ secret; concealed. ▻ *noun* /ˈkʌvət/ **1** a thicket or woodland providing cover for game. **2** a shelter for animals. **3** *ornithol* any of the small feathers that surround the bases of the large quill feathers of the wings and tails of a bird. • **covertly** *adverb*. ◷ 14c: French, from *covrir* to cover.

cover-up ▻ *noun* (***cover-ups***) an act of concealing or withholding information about something suspect or illicit. See COVER UP under COVER.

cover version ▻ *noun* a recording of a song, which has already been recorded by another artist.

covet /ˈkʌvɪt/ ▻ *verb* (***coveted, coveting***) to long to possess something (especially something belonging to someone else). • **covetable** *adj*. ◷ 13c: from French *coveitier*, from Latin *cupiditas* longing or greed.

covetous /ˈkʌvɪtəs/ ▻ *adj* envious; greedy. • **covetously** *adverb*. • **covetousness** *noun*.

covey /ˈkʌvɪ/ ▻ *noun* (***coveys***) **1** a small flock of game birds of one type, especially partridge or grouse. **2** a small group of people. ◷ 15c: from Old French *covée*, from *cover* to hatch.

cow[1] ▻ *noun* **1** the mature female of any bovine animal, especially domesticated cattle. See also BULL[1] *noun* 1, CALF[1]. **2** the mature female of certain other mammals, eg the elephant, whale and seal. **3** loosely used to refer to any domestic breed of cattle. **4** *derog slang* a woman. **5** *Austral & NZ slang* a distasteful person or thing. • **till the cows come home** *colloq* for an unforeseeably long time. ◷ Anglo-Saxon *cu*.

cow[2] ▻ *verb* (***cowed, cowing***) to frighten something into submission. ◷ 17c: from Norse *kuga* to subdue.

coward /ˈkaʊəd/ ▻ *noun* **1** someone easily frightened, or lacking courage to face danger or difficulty. **2** someone who acts brutally towards the weak or undefended. • **cowardice** /ˈkaʊədɪs/ *noun*. • **cowardly** *adverb*. • **cowardliness** *noun*. ◷ 13c: from French *cuard*, from Latin *cauda* tail; thought, perhaps, to refer to a frightened animal with its tail between its legs.

cowbell ▻ *noun* **1** a bell hanging from a cow's neck, which sounds when the cow moves. **2** this kind of bell, with the clapper removed, used as a percussion instrument.

cowberry /ˈkaʊbərɪ/ ▻ *noun* **1** a small evergreen shrub, native to northern temperate regions, with drooping bell-shaped pinkish-white flowers and edible red berries. **2** the berries borne by this shrub.

cowboy ▻ *noun* **1** in the western USA: a man who tends cattle, usually on horseback. **2** this kind of man as a character in films of the Wild West, especially when involved in gunfights with Indians. **3** *slang, derog* someone who undertakes building or other work without proper training or qualifications; a dishonest businessman or entrepreneur.

cowcatcher ▻ *noun, US* a concave metal fender fixed onto the front of a railway engine for clearing cattle and other obstacles from the line.

cower /kaʊə(r)/ ▻ *verb* (***cowered, cowering***) *intr* to shrink away in fear. ◷ 13c.

cowhand and **cowherd** see COWMAN

cowhide /ˈkaʊhaɪd/ ▻ *noun* the leather made from the hide of a cow.

cowl ▻ *noun* **1** a monk's large loose hood or hooded habit. **2** any large loose hood. **3** a revolving cover for a chimney-pot for improving ventilation. **4** a cowling. **5** the part of a motor vehicle to which the windscreen and bonnet are attached. ◷ Anglo-Saxon *cugele* hood.

cowlick ▻ *noun* a tuft of hair standing up stiffly from the forehead.

cowling ▻ *noun* the streamlined metal casing, usually having hinged or removable panels, that houses the engine of an aircraft or other vehicle. ◷ Early 20c: from COWL.

cowman ▻ *noun* **1** *Brit* someone assisting with cattle or having charge of them. Also called **cowhand** or **cowherd**. **2** *N Amer* a man who owns a cattle ranch.

co-worker /koʊˈwɜːkə(r), ˈkoʊwɜːkə(r)/ ▻ *noun* a fellow worker; a colleague.

cow parsley ▻ *noun* a biennial or perennial plant, native to Europe, Asia and N Africa, with small white flowers borne in UMBELs. Also called **Queen Anne's lace**.

cowpat ▻ *noun* a flat deposit of cow dung.

cowpea ▻ *noun* the BLACK-EYE BEAN.

cowpox ▻ *noun, medicine* a viral infection of the udders of cows that can be transmitted to humans by direct contact, causing mild symptoms similar to smallpox, against which it is used as a vaccine.

cowrie or **cowry** /ˈkaʊrɪ/ ▻ *noun* (***cowries***) **1** any of about 150 species of marine snail, found mainly in tropical waters. **2** the brightly coloured glossy egg-shaped shell of the animal which was formerly used in parts of Africa and S Asia as money and prized for magic qualities. ◷ 17c: from Hindi *kauri*.

cowshed and **cowhouse** ▻ *noun* a building for housing cattle; a byre.

cowslip /ˈkaʊslɪp/ ▻ *noun* a perennial plant native to Europe and Asia with a cluster of yellow sweet-smelling flowers. ◷ Anglo-Saxon *cuslyppe* cow dung.

cox ▻ *noun* (***coxes***) short for COXSWAIN. ▻ *verb* (***coxes, coxed, coxing***) *tr & intr* to act as cox of (a boat). • **coxless** *adj*.

coxcomb see COCKSCOMB

coxswain or **cockswain** /ˈkɒksən, ˈkɒksweɪn/ ▻ *noun* **1** someone who steers a small boat. Often shortened to COX. **2** a petty officer in a small ship. ◷ 15c: from *cock* ship's boat + SWAIN.

coy ▻ *adj* **1** shy; modest; affectedly bashful. **2** irritatingly uncommunicative about something. • **coyly** *adverb*. • **coyness** *noun*. ◷ 14c: from French *coi* calm, from Latin *quietus* quiet.

coyote /ˈkɔɪoʊtiː, ˈkaɪoʊt/ ▻ *noun* (***coyotes*** or ***coyote***) a small N American wolf with a pointed face, tawny fur and a black-tipped bushy tail, which was originally found mainly in deserts, prairies and open woodland, but is becoming increasingly known as an urban scavenger. Also called **prairie wolf**. ◷ 1820s: Mexican Spanish, from Nahuatl *coyotl*.

coypu /ˈkɔɪpuː, -pjuː/ ▻ *noun* (***coypus*** or ***coypu***) **1** a large rat-like aquatic rodent, native to S America and introduced elsewhere as a result of escape from captivity, which has a broad blunt muzzle and webbed hind feet. **2** the soft fur of this animal. Also called NUTRIA. ◷ 18c: from a native S American language.

CPAG ▻ *abbreviation* Child Poverty Action Group.

CPO ▻ *abbreviation* Chief Petty Officer.

CPR ▻ *abbreviation* **1** Canadian Pacific Railway. **2** cardiopulmonary resuscitation.

CPRE ▻ *abbreviation* Council for the Protection of Rural England.

CPSA ▻ *abbreviation* Civil and Public Services Association.

CPU ▻ *abbreviation, computing* central processing unit.

CR ▻ *abbreviation, IVR* Costa Rica.

Cr ▻ *abbreviation* Councillor.

Cr ▻ *symbol, chem* chromium.

crab¹ ▻ *noun* **1** any of a species of mostly marine crustaceans, with a hard flattened shell and five pairs of jointed legs, the front pair being developed into pincers. **2 a** another name for the CRAB LOUSE; **b (crabs)** infestation by this. **3 (Crab)** *astron, astrol* CANCER. ● **catch a crab** in rowing: to sink the oar too deeply or to miss the water completely, so that the rower falls backwards. Ⓒ Anglo-Saxon *crabba*.

crab² ▻ *noun* **1** short for CRAB APPLE. **2** a grumpy or irritable person. Ⓒ 15c.

crab apple ▻ *noun* **1** a large deciduous shrub or small tree, native to north temperate regions, with thorny branches, oval toothed leaves and mainly white flowers. **2** the small hard round sour fruit of this tree.

crabbed /'krabɪd, krabd/ ▻ *adj* **1** bad-tempered; grouchy. **2** said of handwriting: cramped and hard to decipher. ● **crabbedly** *adverb*. ● **crabbedness** *noun*. Ⓒ 13c: from CRAB¹; the crooked gait of the crab is said to express the contradictory nature of the people this word is applied to.

crabby ▻ *adj* (***crabbier, crabbiest***) *colloq* bad-tempered.

crab louse ▻ *noun* a crab-shaped parasitic louse which infests the hair of the human pubic area. Often shortened to CRAB (see CRAB¹ *noun* 2).

Crab nebula ▻ *noun, astron* in the constellation of Taurus: an expanding cloud of gas, consisting of the remains of a star that exploded as a SUPERNOVA in AD 1054.

crabwise ▻ *adj, adverb* moving sideways.

crack ▻ *verb* (***cracked, cracking***) **1** *tr & intr* to fracture or cause to fracture partially without falling to pieces. **2** *tr & intr* to split or make something split. **3** *tr & intr* to make or cause to make a sudden sharp noise. **4** to strike sharply. **5** *tr & intr* to give way or make someone or something give way □ *He finally cracked under the pressure.* **6** to force open (a safe). **7** to solve (a code or problem). **8** to tell (a joke). **9** *intr* said of the voice: to change pitch or tone suddenly and unintentionally. **10** *chem, tr & intr* to break down long-chain hydrocarbons produced during petroleum refining into lighter more useful short-chain products. ▻ *noun* **1** a sudden sharp sound. **2** a partial fracture in a material produced by an external force or internal stress, often originating in a defective region of the material. **3** a narrow opening. **4** a resounding blow. **5** *colloq* a joke. **6** *slang* (*in full* **crack cocaine**) a highly addictive derivative of cocaine, consisting of hard crystalline lumps that are heated and smoked. ▻ *adj, colloq* expert □ *a crack shot.* ● **at the crack of dawn** *colloq* at daybreak; very early. ● **a fair crack of the whip** a fair opportunity. ● **get cracking** *colloq* to make a prompt start with a journey, undertaking, etc. ● **have a crack at something** *colloq* to attempt it. Ⓒ Anglo-Saxon *cracian* to resound.

■ **crack down on someone** or **something** *colloq* to take firm action against them or it.

■ **crack up** *colloq* to suffer an emotional breakdown.

■ **crack something up** *colloq* to praise it extravagantly; giving the impression that it is better than it is □ *This job is not all it's cracked up to be.*

crackbrained ▻ *adj, colloq* mad; crazy.

crackdown ▻ *noun* a firm action taken against someone or something.

cracked ▻ *adj* **1** *colloq* crazy; mad. **2** said of a voice: harsh; uneven in tone. **3** damaged by splitting.

cracker ▻ *noun* **1** a thin crisp unsweetened biscuit. **2** a small, noisy firework. **3** a party toy in the form of a gaudy paper tube usually containing a paper hat, gift and motto, that pulls apart with an explosive bang. **4** *colloq* an exceptional person or thing.

crackers ▻ *adj, colloq* mad.

cracking *colloq* ▻ *adj* **1** very good □ *a cracking story.* **2** very fast □ *a cracking pace.* Also *as adverb*. ▻ *noun, chem* short for CATALYTIC CRACKING.

crackle /'krakəl/ ▻ *verb* (***crackled, crackling***) *intr* to make a faint continuous cracking or popping sound. ▻ *noun* **1** this kind of sound. **2** a type of china, characterized by tiny cracks over its surface. ● **crackly** *adj*. Ⓒ 16c: diminutive of CRACK.

crackling ▻ *noun* the crisp skin of roast pork.

cracknel /'kraknəl/ ▻ *noun* **1** a light brittle biscuit. **2** a hard nutty filling for chocolates. **3** (**cracknels**) *N Amer* crisply fried pieces of fat pork. Ⓒ 15c.

crackpot *colloq* ▻ *adj* crazy. ▻ *noun* a crazy person.

-cracy /krəsɪ/ ▻ *combining form, denoting* rule, government or domination by a particular group, etc □ *democracy* □ *autocracy* □ *bureaucracy.* Ⓒ From Greek *kratos* power.

cradle /'kreɪdəl/ ▻ *noun* **1** a cot for a small baby, especially one that can be rocked. **2** a place of origin; the home or source of something □ *the cradle of civilization.* **3** a suspended platform or cage for workmen engaged in the construction, repair or painting of a ship or building. **4** the support for the receiver on an old-style telephone. **5** a box in which sand, stones, etc are washed in order to separate them from any gold contained. ▻ *verb* (***cradled, cradling***) **1** to rock or hold gently. **2** to nurture. **3** to wash (stones, sand, etc containing gold) in a cradle. ● **from the cradle to the grave** throughout the whole of one's life. Ⓒ Anglo-Saxon *kradol*.

cradle-snatcher ▻ *noun, derog* someone who chooses a much younger person as a lover or spouse.

craft ▻ *noun* **1 a** a skill, trade or occupation, especially one requiring the use of the hands; **b** *in compounds* □ *needlecraft.*. **2** the members of a trade, as a body. **3** skilled ability. **4** cunning. **5** *often in compounds* a boat or ship, or an air or space vehicle □ *spacecraft* □ *aircraft.* ▻ *plural noun often in compounds* boats, ships, air or space vehicles collectively. ▻ *verb* (***crafted, crafting***) to make something skilfully. Ⓒ Anglo-Saxon *cræft* strength.

craftsman and **craftswoman** ▻ *noun* someone skilled at a craft.

craftsmanship ▻ *noun* the skill of a craftsman or craftswoman.

crafty ▻ *adj* (***craftier, craftiest***) clever, shrewd, cunning or sly. ● **craftily** *adverb*. ● **craftiness** *noun*.

crag ▻ *noun* a rocky peak or jagged outcrop of rock. Ⓒ 13c: Celtic.

craggy ▻ *adj* (***craggier, craggiest***) **1** full of crags. **2** rough. **3** rugged. ● **cragginess** *noun*.

cram ▻ *verb* (***crammed, cramming***) **1** to stuff full. **2** (*sometimes* **cram something in** or **together**) to push or pack it tightly □ *He crammed the box full of books.* **3** *tr & intr* to study intensively, or prepare someone rapidly, for an examination. ▻ *noun* a crush. Ⓒ Anglo-Saxon *crammian*.

cram-full ▻ *adj* full to bursting.

crammer ▻ *noun* a person or school that prepares pupils for examinations by rapid study.

cramp¹ ▻ *noun* **1** a painful involuntary prolonged contraction of a muscle or group of muscles. **2** (**cramps**) severe abdominal pain. ▻ *verb* (***cramped, cramping***) to restrict with or as with a cramp. ● **cramp someone's style** to restrict or prevent them from acting freely or creatively. Ⓒ 14c: from French *crampe*.

cramp² ▻ *noun* a piece of metal bent at both ends, used for holding stone or timbers together. Also called **cramp-iron**. ▻ *verb* (***cramped, cramping***) to fasten with a cramp. ◷ 16c: from Dutch *crampe* hook.

cramped ▻ *adj* **1** overcrowded; closed in. **2** said of handwriting: small and closely written.

crampon /ˈkrampɒn/ ▻ *noun* **1** a spiked iron attachment for climbing boots, to improve grip on ice or rock. **2** an iron bar, bent into the shape of a hook, which is used to lift heavy objects. ◷ 15c: French.

cranberry /ˈkranbərɪ/ ▻ *noun* **1** a dwarf evergreen shrub with oval pointed leaves, pink flowers and red berries. **2** the sour-tasting fruit of this plant. ◷ 17c: from German dialect *kraanbeere* crane berry.

crane ▻ *noun* **1** a machine with a long pivoted arm from which lifting gear is suspended, allowing heavy weights to be moved both horizontally and vertically. **2** a large wading bird with a long neck and long legs, found in marshlands and swamps in N America and throughout most of Europe, Asia and Africa. ▻ *verb* **1** *tr & intr* to stretch (one's neck), or lean forward, in order to see better. **2** to move with a crane. ◷ Anglo-Saxon *cran*.

cranefly ▻ *noun* a long-legged, two-winged insect. Also (*colloq*) called **daddy-long-legs**. See also LEATHER-JACKET.

cranesbill ▻ *noun* an annual or perennial plant native to temperate regions, with white, purple or blue flowers and slender beaked fruits.

cranial /ˈkreɪnɪəl/ ▻ *adj* relating to or in the region of the skull. ● **cranially** *adverb*.

cranial index ▻ *noun* **1** the CEPHALIC INDEX. **2** any of a number of other measurements of the skull, eg that measuring the height as a percentage of the breadth.

cranial nerve ▻ *noun, anatomy* in vertebrates: one of the ten to twelve pairs of nerves that arise directly from the brain.

craniosacral therapy /kreɪnɪoʊˈseɪkrəl —/ ▻ *noun* (abbreviation **CST**) *alternative medicine* a form of alternative therapy involving gentle manipulation in order to release tensions and imbalances which are said to arise in the bones and membranes of the skull, used to treat a wide range of physical and psychological symptoms. ◷ 20c: from CRANIUM + SACRUM + THERAPY.

cranium /ˈkreɪnɪəm/ ▻ *noun* (***crania*** /-ə/ or ***craniums***) **1** the dome-shaped part of the skull, consisting of several fused bones, that encloses and protects the brain. **2** the skull. ◷ 16c: Latin, from Greek *kranion*.

crank ▻ *noun* **1** a device consisting of an arm connected to and projecting at right angles from the shaft of an engine or motor, used to communicate motion to or from the shaft, or to convert reciprocating motion into rotary motion or vice versa. **2** a handle bent at right angles and incorporating such a device, used to start an engine or motor by hand. Also called **crank handle**, **starting handle**. **3** *derog* an eccentric person. **4** *N Amer derog* a bad-tempered person. ◷ Anglo-Saxon *cranc-stæf* weaving implement.

■ **crank something up 1** to rotate (a shaft) using a crank. **2** to start (an engine, a machine, etc) using a crank.

crankshaft ▻ *noun* the main shaft of an engine or other machine, bearing one or more cranks, used to transmit power from the cranks to the connecting rods to which they are attached.

cranky ▻ *adj* (***crankier, crankiest***) **1** *colloq* eccentric or faddy. **2** *N Amer* bad-tempered. ● **crankily** *adverb*. ● **crankiness** *noun*.

cranny /ˈkranɪ/ ▻ *noun* (***crannies***) **1** a narrow opening; a cleft or crevice. **2** an out-of-the-way corner. ● **crannied** *adj*. ◷ 15c: related to French *cran*.

crap¹ *coarse slang* ▻ *noun* **1** faeces. **2** nonsense. **3** rubbish. ▻ *verb* (***crapped, crapping***) *intr* to defecate. ● **crappy** *adj* (***crappier, crappiest***) rubbish; inferior. ◷ 15c: as *crappe* chaff, from Dutch *krappe*, probably from *krappen* to pluck off.

crap² ▻ *noun* **1** (*usually* **craps**) a gambling game on which the player rolls two dice. **2** a losing throw in this game. ● **shoot craps** to play craps. ◷ 19c.

crape see CRÊPE *noun* 1

crapulent /ˈkrapjʊlənt/ or **crapulous** ▻ *adj* **1** suffering from sickness caused by overdrinking. **2** relating to or resulting from intemperance. ● **crapulence** *noun*. ◷ 17c: from Latin *crapulentus*, from *crapula* intoxication.

crash ▻ *verb* (***crashes, crashed, crashing***) **1** *tr & intr* to fall or strike with a banging or smashing noise. **2** *tr & intr* (*often* **crash into something**) said of a vehicle: to collide or cause it to collide with something. **3** *intr* to make a deafening noise. **4** *intr* to move noisily. **5** *intr* said of a business or stock exchange: to collapse. **6** *intr* said of a computer or program: to fail completely, because of a malfunction or fluctuation in the power supply, etc. **7** to cause a computer system or program to break down completely. **8** *slang* to gatecrash (a party, etc). **9** (*often* **crash out**) *slang* **a** to fall asleep; **b** to sleep at someone else's place. ▻ *noun* (***crashes***) **1** a violent impact or breakage, or the sound of it. **2** a deafening noise. **3** a traffic or aircraft accident; a collision. **4** the collapse of a business or the stock exchange. **5** the failure of a computer or program. **6** *as adj* concentrated or intensive, so as to produce results in minimum time □ *a crash diet*. ◷ 14c: imitating the sound.

crash barrier ▻ *noun* a protective metal barrier along the edge of a road, carriageway, the front of a stage, etc.

crash dive ▻ *noun* **1** a rapid emergency dive by a submarine. **2** a sudden dive made by an aircraft, resulting in a crash. ▻ *verb* (**crash-dive**) *intr* **1** said of a submarine: to make a crash dive. **2** to descend quickly and suddenly before smashing into the ground.

crash helmet ▻ *noun* a protective helmet worn eg by motor-cyclists, motor-racing drivers, etc.

crashing ▻ *adj, colloq* utter; extreme □ *a crashing bore*.

crash-land ▻ *verb tr & intr* said of an aircraft: to land or cause to land in an emergency, usually without lowering the undercarriage and with the risk of crashing. ● **crash-landing** *noun*.

crass ▻ *adj* **1** gross; vulgar. **2** colossally stupid. **3** utterly tactless or insensitive. ● **crassly** *adverb*. ● **crassness** *noun*. ◷ 16c: from Latin *crassus* thick or solid.

-crat ▻ *combining form, indicating* a person who takes part in or supports government, rule or domination by a particular group □ *democrat* □ *autocrat* □ *bureaucrat*.

crate ▻ *noun* **1** a strong wooden, plastic or metal case with partitions, for storing or carrying breakable or perishable goods. **2** *derog slang* a decrepit vehicle or aircraft. ▻ *verb* (***crated, crating***) to pack in a crate. ◷ 17c in this sense; 16c in obsolete sense 'a frame of parallel cross bars': from Latin *cratis* wickerwork barrier.

crater /ˈkreɪtə(r)/ ▻ *noun* **1** the bowl-shaped mouth of a volcano or geyser. **2** a hole left in the ground where a meteorite has landed, or a bomb or mine has exploded. **3** *astron* a circular, rimmed depression in the surface of the Moon. **4** (**Crater**) *astron* a small faint constellation occurring in the southern hemisphere. ▻ *verb* (***cratered, cratering***) *tr & intr* to form craters in (a road, a surface, etc). ● **cratered** *adj*. ● **crater-like** *noun*. ● **craterous** *adj*. ◷ 17c: Latin, from Greek *krater* mixing-bowl.

-cratic /ˈkratɪk/ or **-cratical** ▻ *combining form, indicating* a person who takes part in or supports government, rule or domination by a particular group □ *democratic* □ *autocratic* □ *bureaucratic*.

craton /ˈkreɪtɒn/ ▻ *noun, geol* a relatively rigid and immobile part of the Earth's crust that has been stable for at least 1 500m years. ◷ 1940s: from Greek *kratos* strength.

cravat /krəˈvat/ ▻ *noun* a formal style of neckerchief worn chiefly by men instead of a tie. ⓒ 17c: from French *cravate*, an imitation of Serbo-Croatian *Hrvat* Croat; so called because they were worn by Croatian mercenaries in the French army during the Thirty Years War.

crave ▻ *verb* (***craved, craving***) **1** (*often* **crave for** or **after something**) to long for it; to desire it overwhelmingly. **2** *old use, formal* to ask for politely; to beg. ● **craving** *noun.* ⓒ Anglo-Saxon *crafian*.

craven /ˈkreɪvən/ ▻ *adj* cowardly; cringing. ▻ *noun* a coward. ● **cravenly** *adj.* ● **cravenness** *noun.* ⓒ 14c in this sense; 13c in obsolete sense 'vanquished'.

craw ▻ *noun* **1** the CROP (noun 6). **2** the stomach of a lower animal. ● **stick in one's craw** *colloq* to be difficult for one to swallow or accept. ⓒ 14c.

crawl ▻ *verb* (***crawled, crawling***) *intr* **1** said of insects, worms, etc: to move along the ground slowly. **2** said of a human: to move along on hands and knees, especially as a stage before learning to walk. **3** said eg of traffic: to progress very slowly. **4** to be, or feel as if, covered or overrun with something, especially insects □ *After a drugs tip-off, the club was crawling with police.* **5** (*often* **crawl to someone**) *derog colloq* to behave in a fawning way, often to someone in a senior position. ▻ *noun* **1** a crawling motion. **2** a very slow pace. **3** *swimming* a fast stroke with an alternate overarm action together with a kicking leg action. ● **crawler** *noun* **1** someone or something which crawls. **2** *derog colloq* someone who behaves in a fawning and ingratiating way, especially to those in senior positions. ⓒ 13c.

crawler lane ▻ *noun* an extra lane for slow-moving vehicles on an uphill stretch of road. ⓒ 20c.

crayfish /ˈkreɪfɪʃ/ and **crawfish** /krɔːfɪʃ/ ▻ *noun* an edible, freshwater crustacean, similar to a small lobster. ⓒ 14c: from French *crevice*, from German *krebiz* crab.

crayon /ˈkreɪən/ ▻ *noun* **1** a small pencil or stick made from coloured wax, chalk, charcoal or clay and used for drawing. **2** a drawing made using crayons. ▻ *verb* (***crayoned, crayoning***) *tr & intr* to draw or colour with a crayon. ⓒ 17c: French, from *craie*, from Latin *creta* chalk.

craze ▻ *noun* an intense but passing enthusiasm or fashion. ▻ *verb* (***crazed, crazing***) **1** to make crazy. **2** *tr & intr* said eg of a glazed or varnished surface: to develop or cause to develop a network of fine cracks. ⓒ 15c in verb sense 1; 14c in obsolete sense 'to break into pieces'.

crazy ▻ *adj* (***crazier, craziest***) **1** mad; insane. **2** foolish; absurd; foolhardy. ● **crazily** *adverb.* ● **craziness** *noun.* ● **be crazy about someone** or **something** to be madly enthusiastic about them or it. ● **like crazy** *colloq* keenly; fast and furious.

crazy paving ▻ *noun* a type of paving made up of irregularly shaped slabs of stone or concrete.

creak ▻ *noun* a shrill squeaking noise made typically by an unoiled hinge or loose floorboard. ▻ *verb* (***creaked, creaking***) *intr* to make or seem to make this noise. ● **creakily** *adverb.* ● **creakiness** *noun.* ● **creaky** *adj* (***creakier, creakiest***) **1** squeaky. **2** tending to creak. **3** badly made or performed. **4** stiff. ⓒ 16c in verb sense 1; 14c in obsolete sense, said of birds 'to utter a harsh cry'.

cream ▻ *noun* **1** the yellowish fatty substance that rises to the surface of milk, and yields butter when churned. **2** any food that resembles this substance in consistency or appearance. **3** any cosmetic substance that resembles cream in texture or consistency. **4** the best part of something; the pick. **5** a yellowish-white colour. ▻ *verb* (***creamed, creaming***) **1** to beat (eg butter and sugar) till creamy. **2** to remove the cream from (milk). **3** (*often* **cream something off**) to select or take away (the best part). **4** *colloq* to thrash or beat someone. **5** *colloq* to defeat heavily (in a sporting competition, etc). ⓒ 14c: from French *cresme*.

cream cheese ▻ *noun* a soft cheese made from soured milk or cream.

cream cracker ▻ *noun* a crisp savoury biscuit.

creamer ▻ *noun* **1** a powdered milk substitute, used in coffee. **2** *N Amer, especially US* a jug for serving cream. **3** a device for separating cream from milk.

creamery ▻ *noun* (***creameries***) a place where dairy products are made or sold.

cream of tartar ▻ *noun* a white crystalline soluble powder, used in baking powder, soft drinks, laxatives, etc. Also called **potassium hydrogen tartrate**.

cream soda and **American cream soda** ▻ *noun* a vanilla-flavoured fizzy soft drink.

creamware ▻ *noun* a hard durable type of earthenware, usually with a cream-coloured glaze, which was first produced in Staffordshire in the 18c.

creamy ▻ *adj* (***creamier, creamiest***) **1** full of cream. **2** like cream in appearance or consistency. ● **creaminess** *noun.*

crease ▻ *noun* **1** a line made by folding, pressing or crushing. **2** a wrinkle, especially on the face. **3** *cricket* a line marking the position of batsman or bowler. ▻ *verb* (***creased, creasing***) *tr & intr* **1** to make a crease or creases in (paper, fabric, etc); to develop creases. **2** to graze with a bullet. ● **creaser** *noun.* ● **creasy** *adj.* ⓒ 16c.

■ **crease up** or **crease someone up** *colloq* to be or make helpless or incapable with laughter, pain or exhaustion.

create /krɪˈeɪt/ ▻ *verb* (***created, creating***) **1** to form or produce from nothing □ *create the universe.* **2** to bring into existence; to introduce □ *create a system.* **3** to cause. **4** to produce or contrive. **5** *tr & intr* said of an artist, etc: to use one's imagination to make something. **6** *intr, Brit colloq* to make a fuss. **7** said of an actor: to be the first to play (a certain role). **8** to raise to an honourable rank □ *Sir Humphrey was created a peer.* ⓒ 14c: from Latin *creare*.

creatine or **creatin** /ˈkrɪətɪn, ˈkrɪətiːn/ ▻ *noun, biochem* an organic compound, found in muscle, whose phosphate serves as an important source of energy for muscle contraction. ⓒ 19c: from Greek *kreas, kreatos* flesh.

creation /krɪˈeɪʃən/ ▻ *noun* **1** the act of creating. **2** something created, particularly something special or striking. **3** the universe. **4** (*often* **the Creation**) *Christianity* God's act of creating the universe.

creationism ▻ *noun* the theory or belief that everything that exists was created by God, as opposed to being formed by evolution. ⓒ 19c.

creative /krɪˈeɪtɪv/ ▻ *adj* **1** having or showing the ability to create. **2** inventive or imaginative. **3** *derog* characterized by imaginative and usually dubious bending of the rules. ● **creatively** *adverb.* ● **creativity** /krɪəˈtɪvɪtɪ, kriːeɪˈtɪvɪtɪ/ *noun.*

creative accountancy ▻ *noun* the imaginative reinterpretation or dubious manipulation of certain procedures for personal benefit or ease of operation.

creator ▻ *noun* **1** someone who creates. **2** (**the Creator**) *Christianity* God.

creature /ˈkriːtʃə(r)/ ▻ *noun* **1** a bird, beast or fish. **2** something which has been created. **3** a person □ *a wretched creature.* **4** the slavish underling or puppet of someone. ⓒ 13c: from Latin *creatura* a thing created.

creature comforts ▻ *noun* material comforts or luxuries such as food, clothes, warmth, etc which add to one's physical comfort.

creature of habit ▻ *noun* **1** an animal with fixed, especially seasonal, behaviour patterns. **2** a person of unchanging routines.

crèche /krɛʃ/ ▻ *noun* **1** a nursery where babies can be left and cared for while their parents are at work, shopping, exercising, etc. **2** a model representing the scene of Christ's nativity. ⓒ 19c: French, meaning 'manger'.

cred ▷ *noun, slang* credibility □ *street cred.*

credal see under CREED

credence /ˈkriːdəns/ ▷ *noun* **1** faith or belief placed in something □ *give their claims no credence.* **2** (*also* **credence table** or **credenza** /krɪˈdɛnzə/) *Christianity* a small side-table on which the bread and wine for the Eucharist are placed, before being consecrated. ⓒ 14c: from Latin *credentia*, from *credere* to believe.

credentials /krəˈdɛnʃəlz/ ▷ *plural noun* **1** personal qualifications and achievements that can be quoted as evidence of one's trustworthiness, competence, etc. **2** documents or other evidence of these. ⓒ 17c: from Latin *credentia* belief.

credibility gap ▷ *noun* the discrepancy between what is claimed and what is actually or likely to be the case.

credible /ˈkrɛdəbəl/ ▷ *adj* **1** capable of being believed. **2** reliable; trustworthy. • **credibility** *noun*. • **credibly** *adverb*. ⓒ 14c: from Latin *credibilis*, from *credere* to believe.

credible, credulous

There is often confusion between **credible** and **credulous**: **credible** refers to things, such as statements and excuses, and means 'believable', whereas **credulous** refers to people, and means 'too ready to believe'.

credit /ˈkrɛdɪt/ ▷ *noun* **1** faith placed in something. **2** honour or a cause of honour □ *To her credit, she didn't say anything.* **3** acknowledgement, recognition or praise. **4** (**credits**) a list of acknowledgements to those who have helped in the preparation of a book or film. **5** trust given to someone promising to pay later for goods already supplied □ *buy goods on credit.* **6** one's financial reliability, especially as a basis for such trust. **7** the amount of money available to one at one's bank. **8 a** an entry in a bank account acknowledging a payment; **b** the side of an account on which such entries are made. Compare DEBIT. **9 a** a certificate of completion of a course of instruction; **b** a distinction awarded for performance on such a course. ▷ *verb* (***credited***, ***crediting***) **1** to believe; to place faith in someone or something. **2** (*often* **credit something to someone** or **someone with something**) to enter a sum as a credit on someone's account, or allow someone a sum as credit. **3** (*often* **credit someone with something**) to attribute a quality or achievement to someone □ *We credited you with more sense.* ⓒ 16c: from French *crédit*, from Latin *creditum* loan, from *credere* to believe.

creditable ▷ *adj* praiseworthy; laudable. • **creditably** *adverb*.

credit account ▷ *noun* a financial arrangement with a shop that allows one to purchase goods on credit.

credit card ▷ *noun* a card issued by a bank, finance company, etc authorizing the holder to purchase goods or services on credit. Compare DEBIT CARD.

credit insurance ▷ *noun* insurance taken out when a business sells on credit terms, with the insurer providing a safeguard against the possibility of the customer not paying.

credit note ▷ *noun* a form issued by a company or shop, stating that a particular customer is entitled to a certain sum as credit, instead of a cash refund, replacement goods, etc.

creditor ▷ *noun* a person or company to whom one owes money. Compare DEBTOR.

credit rating ▷ *noun* an assessment of a person's or company's creditworthiness.

credit squeeze ▷ *noun* restrictions on borrowing imposed by the government.

credit transfer ▷ *noun* payment made directly from one bank account to another.

credit union ▷ *noun* a co-operative and non-profit-making savings association which makes loans to its members at a low rate of interest, often for the purchase of consumer items.

creditworthy ▷ *adj* judged as deserving financial credit on the basis of earning ability, previous promptness in repaying debts, etc. • **creditworthiness** *noun*.

credo /ˈkriːdoʊ/ ▷ *noun* (***credos***) **1** a belief or set of beliefs. **2** (**Credo**) **a** the NICENE CREED or APOSTLES' CREED; **b** a musical setting of either. ⓒ 12c: Latin, meaning 'I believe'.

credulity /krəˈdʒuːlɪtɪ/ ▷ *noun* (***credulities***) a tendency to believe something without proper proof.

credulous /ˈkrɛdʒʊləs/ ▷ *adj* apt to be too ready to believe something, without sufficient evidence. • **credulously** *adverb*. • **credulousness** *noun*. ⓒ 16c: from Latin *credulus*, from *credere* to believe.

credulous

See Usage Note at **credible**.

creed /kriːd/ ▷ *noun* **1** (*often* **Creed**) a statement of the main points of Christian belief. **2** (**the Creed**) the APOSTLES' CREED. **3** any set of beliefs or principles, either personal or religious. • **credal** /ˈkriːdəl/ or **creedal** *adj*. ⓒ Anglo-Saxon *creda*.

creek ▷ *noun* **1** a small narrow inlet or bay in the shore of a lake, river, or sea. **2** *N Amer, Austral, NZ* a small natural stream or tributary, larger than a brook and smaller than a river. • **up the creek** *colloq* in desperate difficulties. ⓒ 13c: from Norse *kriki* nook.

creel ▷ *noun* **1** a large wicker basket for carrying fish. **2** a wicker basket used to trap lobsters, etc. ⓒ 15c.

creep ▷ *verb* (***crept***, ***creeping***) *intr* **1** to move slowly, with stealth or caution. **2** to move with the body close to the ground; to crawl. **3** said of a plant: to grow along the ground, up a wall, etc. **4** to enter barely noticeably □ *Anxiety crept into her voice.* **5** to develop little by little □ *Inflation was creeping slowly but surely upwards.* **6** said especially of the flesh: to have a strong tingling sensation as a response to fear or disgust. **7** to act in a fawning way. ▷ *noun* **1** an act of creeping. **2** *derog* an unpleasant person. **3** the slow deformation with time of a solid material, especially a metal, under stress, usually occuring at high temperatures. **4** the slow movement of soil, broken rock or mining ground downward under the influence of gravity. • **creeping** *adj*. • **give someone the creeps** *colloq* to disgust or frighten them. ⓒ Anglo-Saxon *creopan*.

creeper ▷ *noun* a creeping plant.

creepers ▷ *plural noun* shoes with thick quiet soles.

creepy ▷ *adj* (***creepier***, ***creepiest***) *colloq* slightly scary; spooky; eerie. • **creepily** *adverb*.

creepy-crawly ▷ *noun* (***creepy-crawlies***) *colloq* a small creeping insect. ▷ *adj* experiencing a feeling as of insects crawling over one's skin.

cremate /krəˈmeɪt, krɪˈmeɪt/ ▷ *verb* (***cremated***, ***cremating***) to burn something, especially a corpse, to ashes. • **cremation** *noun* the act or process of cremating a corpse, as an alternative to burial. ⓒ 19c: from Latin *cremare*, *crematum* to burn.

crematorium /krɛməˈtɔːrɪəm/ ▷ *noun* (***crematoria*** /-ə/ or ***crematoriums***) a place where corpses are cremated.

crematory /ˈkrɛmətərɪ/ ▷ *adj* pertaining to cremation. ▷ *noun* (***crematories***) *especially US* a crematorium.

crème /krɛm/ ▷ *noun* **1** cream, or a creamy food. **2** a liqueur with a thick syrupy consistency. ⓒ 19c: French, meaning 'cream'.

crème caramel /krɛm karəˈmɛl/ ▻ *noun* (***crème caramels***) an egg custard coated with caramel.

crème de la crème /krɛm də la krɛm/ ▻ *noun* the very best; the elite. ◷ 19c: French, literally meaning 'cream of the cream'.

crème de menthe /krɛm də ˈmɒnθ/ ▻ *noun* (***crème de menthes***) a green peppermint-flavoured liqueur.

crème fraîche /krɛm frɛʃ/ ▻ *noun* cream thickened with a culture of bacteria, used in cooking. ◷ 1990s: French, meaning 'fresh cream'.

crenel /ˈkrɛnəl/ or **crenelle** /krɪˈnɛl/ ▻ *noun, archit* an indentation in a parapet. ◷ 15c: French diminutive of *cren* notch.

crenellate /ˈkrɛnəleɪt/ ▻ *verb* (***crenellated, crenellating***) *archit* to furnish with battlements. • **crenellated** *adj.* • **crenellation** *noun.*

creole /ˈkrɪoʊl, krɪˈoʊl/ ▻ *noun* **1** a PIDGIN language that has become the accepted language of a community or region. **2** (**Creole**) the French-based creole spoken in the US states of the Caribbean Gulf. **3** (**Creole**) a native-born West Indian or Latin American of mixed European and Negro blood. **4** (**Creole**) a French or Spanish native of the US Gulf states. ◷ 17c: French, from Spanish *criollo*, from Portuguese *crioulo* slave born in one's household, from Latin *creare* to create.

creosote /ˈkrɪəsoʊt/ ▻ *noun* **1** a thick dark oily liquid with a penetrating odour, obtained by distilling coal tar, used as a wood preservative. **2** a colourless or pale yellow oily liquid with a penetrating odour, obtained by distilling wood tar, used as an antiseptic. ▻ *verb* (***creosoted, creosoting***) to treat (wood) with creosote. ◷ 19c: from Greek *kreas* flesh + *soter* saviour.

crêpe or **crepe** /kreɪp, krɛp/ ▻ *noun* **1** (*also* **crape** /kreɪp/) **a** a thin finely-wrinkled silk fabric, dyed black for mourning wear; **b** a mourning armband made of this. **2** rubber with a wrinkled surface, used for shoe soles. Also called **crêpe rubber**. **3** a thin pancake, often containing a filling. • **crêpy** or **crêpey** *adj* (***crêpier, crêpiest***) **1** like crêpe. **2** said especially of the skin: wrinkled. ◷ 19c: French, from Latin *crispus* curled.

crêpe paper ▻ *noun* a type of thin paper with a wrinkled elastic texture, used for making decorations, etc.

crêpe suzette ▻ *noun* (***crêpes suzette***) a thin pancake in a hot orange- or lemon-flavoured sauce, usually flambéed (see FLAMBÉ).

crepitate /ˈkrɛpɪteɪt/ ▻ *verb* (***crepitated, crepitating***) *intr* **1** to rattle; to crackle. **2** said of certain beetles: to discharge a pungent fluid. • **crepitant** *adj.* ◷ 17c: from Latin *crepitare, crepitatum* to crackle.

crepitation ▻ *noun* **1** a rattling sound. **2** *pathol* in certain diseases, eg pneumonia: a rattling sound heard in the lungs, which is caused either by the opening of air passages and air sacs when a patient breathes in, or by air bubbling through fluid.

crepitus /ˈkrɛpɪtəs/ ▻ *noun, anatomy* **1** a harsh grating noise produced when the ends of a fractured bone rub together or by bone rubbing on roughened cartilage, usually occurring in the movement of arthritic joints. **2** in the lungs: a similar sound heard with a stethoscope when a patient breathes in over an inflamed lung. ◷ 19c: Latin.

crept *past tense, past participle of* CREEP

crepuscular /krɪˈpʌskjʊlə(r)/ ▻ *adj* **1** relating to or like twilight; dim. **2** denoting animals that are active before sunrise or at dusk, eg bats, rabbits, deer. ◷ 17c: from Latin *crepusculum* twilight.

crêpy see under CRÊPE

Cres. ▻ *abbreviation* Crescent.

crescendo /krɛˈʃɛndoʊ/ ▻ *noun* (***crescendos***) **1** a gradual increase in loudness. **2** a musical passage of increasing loudness. **3** a high point or climax. Also *as adj* ▫ *a crescendo piece.* ▻ *verb* (***crescendoed, crescendoing***) *intr* to increase gradually in loudness. ▻ *adverb, music* played with increasing loudness. Compare DIMINUENDO. ◷ 18c: Italian, meaning 'increasing', from Latin *crescere* to grow.

crescent /ˈkrɛsənt, ˈkrɛz-/ ▻ *noun* **1** the curved shape of the Moon during its first or last quarter, when it appears less than half illuminated. **2** something similar in shape to this, eg a semicircular row of houses. **3** (*often* **Crescent**) *chiefly Brit* used in names: a street of houses arranged in a crescent shape. **4** (*often* **the Crescent**) **a** the emblem of Turkey or the Muslim faith; **b** the Turkish or Muslim power. ◷ 14c: from Latin *crescere* to grow.

cress ▻ *noun* **1** any of various plants of the cabbage family, especially a species cultivated for its edible seed leaves which are eaten raw with mustard leaves in salads, sandwiches, etc. **2** a perennial aquatic plant, commonly known as watercress, which is cultivated for its pungent-tasting leaves which are used as a garnish, and in salads, soups, etc. ◷ Anglo-Saxon *cressa*.

crest ▻ *noun* **1** a comb or a tuft of feathers or fur on top of the head of certain birds and mammals. **2** a ridge of skin along the top of the head of certain reptiles and amphibians. **3** a plume on a helmet. **4** *heraldry* the part of a coat of arms that appears above the shield. **5** the topmost ridge of a mountain. **6** the topmost part of something, especially a hill or mountain. **7** the foaming edge of a wave. ▻ *verb* (***crested, cresting***) **1** to reach the top of (a hill, mountain, etc). **2** to crown; to cap. **3** *intr* said of a wave: to rise or foam up into a crest. • **crested** *adj.* ◷ 14c: from Latin *crista* plume.

crestfallen ▻ *adj* dejected as a result of a blow to one's pride or ambitions.

cretaceous /krɪˈteɪʃəs/ ▻ *adj* **1** (**Cretaceous**) *geol* relating to the last period of the Mesozoic era, during which the first flowering plants appeared, and dinosaurs and many other reptiles became extinct. See table at GEOLOGICAL TIME SCALE. **2** (**Cretaceous**) relating to rocks formed during this period. **3** composed of or resembling chalk. ▻ (*usually* **the Cretaceous**) the Cretaceous age or rock system. ◷ 17c: from Latin *creta* chalk.

cretin /ˈkrɛtɪn/ ▻ *noun* **1** someone suffering from cretinism. **2** *loosely, offensive* an idiot. • **cretinism** *noun* a chronic condition caused by a congenital deficiency of thyroid hormone resulting in dwarfism and mental retardation. • **cretinous** *adj.* ◷ 18c: from Swiss dialect *crestin*, from Latin *christianus* Christian, human creature, emphasizing their humanity in spite of their physical and mental deformity.

cretonne /krɛˈtɒn, ˈkrɛtɒn/ ▻ *noun* a strong cotton material, usually with a printed design, used for curtains, chair-covers, etc. ◷ 19c: French, named after the village of Creton in Normandy, where the fabric probably originated.

Creutzfeldt-Jakob disease /krɔɪtsfɛlt ˈjakɒb —/ ▻ *noun, pathol* a rare and usually fatal disease caused by viral infection and characterized by dementia, sometimes accompanied by wasting of muscle tissue and various neurological abnormalities. ◷ 1960s: named after the German physicians H G Creutzfeldt (1885–1964) and A Jakob (1884–1931).

crevasse /krəˈvas, krɪˈvas/ ▻ *noun, geol* **1** a deep vertical crack in a glacier, formed by stresses that build up as different parts of the glacier move at different rates. **2** *US* a breach in the bank of the river. ▻ *verb* (***crevassed, crevassing***) to make a fissure in (a wall, a dyke, etc). ◷ 19c: from French *crevace* crevice.

crevasse, crevice

These words are sometimes confused with each other.

crevice /ˈkrɛvɪs/ ▻ *noun* **1** a narrow crack or fissure, especially in a rock. **2** a narrow opening. ⓘ 14c: from French *crevace*, from Latin *crepare* to crack.

crew¹ ▻ *noun* **1** the team of people manning a ship, aircraft, train, bus, etc. **2** a ship's company excluding the officers. **3** a team engaged in some operation □ *camera crew*. **4** *colloq, usually derog* a bunch of people □ *a strange crew*. ▻ *verb* (***crewed***, ***crewing***) *intr* to serve as a crew member on a yacht, etc. ⓘ 16c in sense 4; 15c in obsolete sense 'reinforcement of a military force': from French *creue* increase, from Latin *crescere* to increase or grow.

crew² *past tense of* CROW

crewcut ▻ *noun* a closely cropped hairstyle, originally worn by men. ⓘ 1930s: apparently first adopted by the boat crews at the universities of Harvard and Yale.

crewel /ˈkruəl/ ▻ *noun* thin loosely twisted yarn for tapestry or embroidery. ● **crewelwork** *noun*. ⓘ 15c.

crew neck ▻ *noun* a firm round neckline on a sweater. ▻ *adj* (**crew-neck**) referring or relating to such a neck.

crib ▻ *noun* **1** a baby's cot or cradle. **2** a manger. **3** a model of the nativity, with the infant Christ in a manger. **4** a literal translation of a text, used as an aid by students. **5** something copied or plagiarized from another's work. **6** *cards* the discarded cards in cribbage, used by the dealer in scoring. **7** a timber framework for a dam. **8** a timber framework used to line a mine shaft. **9** short for CRIBBAGE. ▻ *verb* (***cribbed***, ***cribbing***) **1** *tr & intr* to copy or plagiarize. **2** to put in or as if in a crib. ⓘ Anglo-Saxon *cribb* stall or manger.

cribbage /ˈkrɪbɪdʒ/ ▻ *noun* a card game for two to four players, who each try to be first to score a certain number of points. Sometimes shortened to **crib**. ⓘ 17c.

crick *colloq* ▻ *noun* a painful spasm or stiffness of the muscles, especially in the neck. ▻ *verb* (***cricked***, ***cricking***) to wrench (eg one's neck or back). ⓘ 15c: probably imitating the sound.

cricket¹ /ˈkrɪkɪt/ ▻ *noun* an outdoor game played using a ball, bats and wickets, between two sides of eleven players, the object of which is for one team to score more runs (see RUN *noun* 21) than the other by the end of play. ● **cricketer** *noun*. ● **not cricket** *colloq* unfair; unsporting. ⓘ 16c.

cricket² /ˈkrɪkɪt/ ▻ *noun* a species of mainly nocturnal insect related to the grasshopper, which has long slender antennae and whose males can produce a distinctive chirping sound by rubbing their forewings together. ⓘ 14c: imitating the sound.

cricoid /ˈkraɪkɔɪd/ *anatomy* **1** *adj* ring-shaped or resembling a ring. **2** denoting the ring-shaped cartilage in the larynx. ⓘ 18c: from Latin *cricoides*, from Greek *krikoeides* ring-shaped.

cri de coeur /kriː də ˈkɜː(r)/ ▻ *noun* (***cris de coeur*** /kriː də ˈkɜː(r)/) a heartfelt or passionate appeal. ⓘ 20c: French *cri du coeur* literally meaning 'cry of the heart'.

cried and **cries** see under CRY

crier /kraɪə(r)/ ▻ *noun, historical* an official who announces news by shouting it out in public.

crikey /ˈkraɪkɪ/ ▻ *exclamation, dated slang* an expression of astonishment. ⓘ 19c: perhaps altered from CHRIST to avoid blasphemy.

crime ▻ *noun* **1** an illegal act; an act punishable by law. **2** such acts collectively. **3** an act which is gravely wrong in a moral sense. **4** *colloq* a deplorable act; a shame. ⓘ 14c: French, from Latin *crimen* judgement or accusation.

criminal /ˈkrɪmɪnəl/ ▻ *noun* someone guilty of a crime or crimes. ▻ *adj* **1** against the law. **2** relating to crime or criminals, or their punishment. **3** *colloq* very wrong; wicked. ● **criminality** *noun*. ● **criminally** *adverb*. ⓘ 15c: from Latin *criminalis*, from *crimen* crime.

criminalize or **criminalise** ▻ *verb* (***criminalized***, ***criminalizing***) to make (an action, a practice, etc) illegal. ● **criminalization** or **criminalisation** *noun*. Compare DECRIMINALIZE. ⓘ 1950s.

criminal law ▻ *noun* the branch of law dealing with unlawful acts which are offences against the public and society generally.

criminology ▻ *noun* the scientific study of crime and criminals. ● **criminologist** *noun*. ⓘ 19c: from Latin *crimen* crime + -LOGY 1.

crimp ▻ *verb* (***crimped***, ***crimping***) **1** to press into small regular ridges; to corrugate. **2** to wave or curl (hair) with crimping-irons. **3** to roll the edge of (sheet metal). **4** to seal by pinching together. **5** *US* to thwart or hinder. ▻ *noun* a curl or wave in the hair. ● **crimped** *adj*. ● **crimper** *noun*. ⓘ Anglo-Saxon *crympan* to curl.

crimping irons and **crimpers** ▻ *plural noun* a tong-like device with two metal plates with waves cut into them, which can be heated; hair can then be placed between the plates so as to give it a crimped appearance.

Crimplene /ˈkrɪmpliːn/ ▻ *noun, trademark* **1** a thick polyester yarn. **2** a crease-resistant clothing fabric made from this.

crimson /ˈkrɪmzən/ ▻ *noun* a deep purplish red colour. ▻ *verb* (***crimsoned***, ***crimsoning***) **1** to dye crimson. **2** *intr* to become crimson; to blush. ⓘ 15c: from Spanish *cremesin*, from Arabic *qirmizi* a dye made from a Mediterranean insect.

cringe /krɪndʒ/ ▻ *verb* (***cringed***, ***cringing***) *intr* **1** to cower away in fear. **2** *derog* to behave in a submissive, over-humble way. **3** *loosely* to wince in embarrassment, etc. ▻ *noun* an act of cringing. ● **cringer** *noun*. ⓘ Anglo-Saxon *cringan* to fall in battle.

crinkle /ˈkrɪŋkəl/ ▻ *verb* (***crinkled***, ***crinkling***) *tr & intr* to wrinkle or crease. ▻ *noun* a wrinkle or crease; a wave. ⓘ related to Anglo-Saxon *crincan* to yield.

crinkly ▻ *adj* (***crinklier***, ***crinkliest***) wrinkly. ▻ *noun* (***crinklies***) *colloq* an elderly person.

crinoid /ˈkrɪnɔɪd/ ▻ *noun* a primitive ECHINODERM with a cup-shaped body and branching arms. Also *as adj*. ● **crinoidal** *adj*. Also called **feather star**.

crinoline /ˈkrɪnəlɪn, -liːn/ ▻ *noun, historical* **1** a stiff fabric made from horsehair and cotton. **2** a hooped petticoat stiffened with this fabric for making skirts stand out. **3** a hooped petticoat made from whalebone, steel wire, etc for the same purpose. ⓘ 19c: French, from Latin *crinis* hair + *linum* thread.

cripple /ˈkrɪpəl/ ▻ *verb* (***crippled***, ***crippling***) **1** to make lame; to disable. **2** to damage, weaken or undermine □ *The government introduced policies which crippled the economy.* ▻ *noun* **1** someone who is lame or badly disabled. **2** someone damaged psychologically □ *an emotional cripple.* ⓘ Anglo-Saxon *crypel*.

crisis /ˈkraɪsɪs/ ▻ *noun* (***crises*** /-iːz/) **1** a crucial or decisive moment. **2** a turning-point, eg in a disease. **3** a time of difficulty or distress. **4** an emergency. ⓘ 16c: Latin, from Greek *krisis* decision or judgement.

crisis management ▻ *noun* the practice of dealing with crises as they arise and not by any long-term strategic planning. ⓘ 1960s: the term was first used after the Cuban Missile Crisis of 1962 and implies that because the actions of others cannot always be predicted or planned for, crises have to be dealt with when they happen.

crisis theology ▻ *noun* a type of Protestant theology emphasizing the judgement of God upon all merely human, social and religious endeavours.

crisp ▻ *adj* **1** dry and brittle. **2** said of vegetables or fruit: firm and fresh. **3** said of weather: fresh; bracing. **4** said of a person's manner or speech: firm; decisive; brisk. **5** said of fabric, etc: clean; starched. **6** said of hair: springy. **7** sharp; clear. ▻ *noun, Brit* (*usually* **crisps**) thin deep-fried slices of potato, usually flavoured and sold in packets as a snack. Also called **potato crisps**. ▷ *verb* (***crisped***, ***crisping***) *tr & intr* to make or become crisp. ● **crisply** *adverb*. ● **crispness** *noun*. ● **to a crisp** *facetious* burnt till black and brittle. ⓘ Anglo-Saxon, from Latin *crispus* curled.

crispbread ▷ *noun* a brittle unsweetened biscuit made from wheat or rye.

crispy ▷ *adj* (***crispier***, ***crispiest***) **1** crisp. **2** curling; wavy. ● **crispiness** *noun*.

criss-cross /'krɪskrɒs/ ▷ *adj* **1** said of lines: crossing one another in different directions. **2** said of a pattern, etc: consisting of criss-cross lines. ▷ *adverb* in a criss-cross way or pattern. ▷ *noun* a pattern of criss-cross lines. ▷ *verb, tr & intr* to form, mark with or move in a criss-cross pattern. ⓘ 19c: from *Christ-Cross* a decorative cross introducing the alphabet in old learning-books.

criterion /kraɪ'tɪərɪən/ ▷ *noun* (***criteria*** /-ɪə/) a standard or principle on which to base a judgement. ⓘ 17c: from Greek *kriterion*, from *krites* judge.

criterion

Note that **criteria** is plural. 'A criteria' is often heard, but is not correct.

critic /'krɪtɪk/ ▷ *noun* **1** a professional reviewer of literature, art, drama, music, etc. **2** someone who finds fault with or disapproves of something. ⓘ 16c: from Latin *criticus*, from Greek *kritikos* discerning, from *krites* judge.

critical /'krɪtɪkəl/ ▷ *adj* **1** fault-finding; disapproving. **2** relating to a critic or criticism. **3** involving analysis and assessment. **4** relating to a crisis; decisive; crucial. **5** urgent; vital. **6** said of a patient: so ill or seriously injured as to be at risk of dying. **7** *physics* denoting a state, level or value at which there is a significant change in the properties of a system □ *critical mass* □ *critical temperature*. **8** *nuclear physics* said of a fissionable material, a nuclear reactor, etc: having reached the point at which a nuclear chain reaction is self-sustaining. ● **critically** *adverb*. ● **criticality** *noun*. ● **criticalness** *noun*.

critical mass ▷ *noun, physics* the smallest amount of a given fissile material, ie one that is able to undergo nuclear fission, formed into a given shape, that is needed to sustain a nuclear chain reaction, eg for a sphere of uranium-235, the critical mass is 52kg.

critical path analysis ▷ *noun* a procedure used to manage and produce a detailed schedule for a complex project so that it can be completed in the minimum time possible, often involving the use of a specially written computer package.

critical temperature ▷ *noun* **1** *physics* the temperature above which a gas cannot be liquefied by pressure alone. **2** the temperature above which a magnetic material loses its magnetic properties.

criticaster /'krɪtɪkastə(r)/ ▷ *noun, contemptuous* a petty critic. ⓘ 17c.

criticism /'krɪtɪsɪzəm/ ▷ *noun* **1** fault-finding. **2** reasoned analysis and assessment, especially of art, literature, music, drama, etc. **3** the art of such assessment. **4** a critical comment or piece of writing.

criticize or **criticise** /'krɪtɪsaɪz/ ▷ *verb* (***criticized***, ***criticizing***) *tr & intr* **1** to find fault; to express disapproval of someone or something. **2** to analyse and assess.

critique /krɪ'tiːk/ ▷ *noun* **1** a critical analysis. **2** the art of criticism. ⓘ 17c: French, from Greek *kritike*, from *krinein* to discern.

croak /kroʊk/ ▷ *noun* the harsh throaty noise typically made by a frog or crow. ▷ *verb* (***croaked***, ***croaking***) **1** *intr* to make this sound. **2** to utter with a croak. **3** *intr* to grumble or moan. **4** *intr, slang* to die. **5** *slang* to kill. ⓘ 15c: probably imitating the sound.

Croatian /kroʊ'eɪʃən/ and **Croat** /'kroʊat/ ▷ *adj* belonging or relating to Croatia, a republic in SE Europe, its inhabitants, or their language. ▷ *noun* **1** a citizen or inhabitant of, or person born in, Croatia. **2** the official language of Croatia.

crochet /'kroʊʃeɪ/ ▷ *noun* decorative work consisting of intertwined loops, made with wool or thread and a hooked needle. ▷ *verb* (***crocheted***, ***crocheting***) *tr & intr* to make this kind of work. ⓘ 19c: French, diminutive of *croche* hook.

crock[1] ▷ *noun, colloq* an old, decrepit person, vehicle, etc. ⓘ 19c in this sense: 16c meaning 'a ewe that has stopped bearing'.

crock[2] ▷ *noun* an earthenware pot. ⓘ Anglo-Saxon *crocc* pot.

crockery /'krɒkərɪ/ ▷ *noun* earthenware or china dishes collectively, especially domestic pottery, ie plates, cups, etc.

crocket /'krɒkɪt/ ▷ *noun* in Gothic architecture: a carved decoration in the shape of a stylized leaf or flower, often used as an ornamental capital on columns, and on the sloping sides of pinnacles, spires and canopies. ⓘ 17c: French, diminutive of *croc* hook.

crocodile /'krɒkədaɪl/ ▷ *noun* **1** a large aquatic reptile found in tropical regions of Africa, Asia, Australia and S and N America, with a bulky body, short legs, powerful jaws that narrow to form a long snout and a thick scaly skin. **2** leather made from its skin. **3** *colloq* a line of schoolchildren walking in twos. ⓘ 13c: from Latin *crocodilus*, from Greek *krokodeilos*.

crocodile tears ▷ *noun* a show of pretended grief. ⓘ 16c: from the belief that crocodiles wept either to allure potential victims or while eating them.

crocus /'kroʊkəs/ ▷ *noun* (***crocuses***) a small perennial plant belonging to the iris family, with yellow, purple or white flowers and an underground CORM. ⓘ 17c: Latin, from Greek *krokos* saffron.

croft ▷ *noun* especially in the Scottish Highlands: a small piece of enclosed farmland attached to a house. ● **crofter** *noun*. ● **crofting** *noun* the practice of farming such a smallholding. ⓘ Anglo-Saxon.

croissant /'kwasɑ̃, 'krwasɑ̃/ ▷ *noun* a flaky crescent-shaped bread roll, made from puff pastry or leavened dough. ⓘ 19c: French, meaning 'crescent'.

Cro-Magnon /kroʊ'magnən -'manjɑ̃/ ▷ *adj* belonging or relating to an early race of human, who lived in the late PALAEOLITHIC times and had a long skull but short face and a tall stature. ⓘ 19c: named after the place in Dordogne, France where the first skulls of this type were found.

cromlech /'krɒmlɛx, 'krɒmlɛk/ ▷ *noun, archaeol* **1** a prehistoric stone circle. **2** *loosely* a DOLMEN. ⓘ 17c: Welsh, from *crwm* curved + *llech* stone.

crone ▷ *noun, derog* an old woman. ⓘ 14c: from French *carogne*.

crony /'kroʊnɪ/ ▷ *noun* (***cronies***) a close friend. ⓘ 17c: originally university slang, from Greek *kronios* long-lasting.

crook ▷ *noun* **1** a bend or curve. **2** a shepherd's or bishop's hooked staff. **3** any of various hooked fittings, eg on woodwind instruments. **4** *colloq* a thief or swindler; a professional criminal. ▷ *adj, Austral & NZ colloq* **1** ill. **2** not working properly. **3** nasty; unpleasant. ▷ *verb* (***crooked***, ***crooking***) to bend or curve. ⓘ 13c in sense 1; 12c in obsolete sense 'trickery': from Norse *krokr* hook.

crooked /'krʊkɪd/ ▷ *adj* **1** bent, curved, angled or twisted. **2** not straight; tipped at an angle. **3** *colloq* dishonest. ● **crookedly** *adverb*. ● **crookedness** *noun*.

croon ▷ *verb* (***crooned***, ***crooning***) *tr & intr* to sing in a subdued tone and reflective or sentimental style. ▷ *noun* this style of singing. ● **crooner** *noun*. ⓘ 15c: probably from Dutch *cronen* to lament.

crop ▷ *noun* **1** *agric* a plant that is cultivated to produce food for man, fodder for animals or raw materials, eg cereals, clover, barley, etc. **2** *agric* the total yield produced by or harvested from such a plant, or from a certain area of cultivated land, such as a field. **3** a batch; a bunch □ ***this year's crop of graduates.*** **4** a very short style of haircut. **5** **a** a whip handle; **b** a horserider's short whip. **6** *zool* in the gullet of birds: the thin-walled pouch where food is stored before it is digested. Also called CRAW. ▷ *verb* (***cropped, cropping***) **1** to trim; to cut short. **2** said of animals: to feed on grass, etc. **3** to reap or harvest a cultivated crop. **4** *intr* said of land: to produce a crop. ◷ Anglo-Saxon *cropp*.

■ **crop up** *colloq* to occur or appear unexpectedly.

crop circle ▷ *noun* a flattened circle, of uncertain origin, in a field of arable crop. Also called **corn circle**. ◷ 20c.

cropper ▷ *noun* a person or thing which crops. ● **come a cropper** *colloq* **1** to fall heavily. **2** to fail disastrously.

crop rotation ▷ *noun, agric* a system of farming in which different crops are grown on the same piece of land in an ordered sequence over a number of years, thereby varying the nutrients which are removed from the soil and thus maintaining the fertility of the soil.

croquet /ˈkroʊkeɪ/ ▷ *noun* a game played on a lawn, in which the players use mallets to drive wooden balls through a sequence of hoops in a particular order, to try to be first to reach and hit a central peg. ▷ *verb* (***croqueted, croqueting***) to drive away a ball by placing it in contact with one's own and striking both with the mallet. ◷ 19c: apparently French, diminutive of *croc* hook.

croquette /kroʊˈkɛt/ ▷ *noun* a ball or round cake made from eg minced meat, fish, potato, etc which is coated in breadcrumbs and fried. ◷ 18c: French, from *croquer* to crunch.

crosier or **crozier** /ˈkroʊzɪə(r)/ ▷ *noun* a bishop's hooked staff, carried as a symbol of office. ◷ 15c in this sense; 14c in obsolete sense 'a cross-bearer': from French *crossier* one who bears a cross.

cross ▷ *noun* (***crosses***) **1** **a** a mark, structure or symbol composed of two lines, one crossing the other in the form + or ×; **b** the mark × indicating a mistake or cancellation. Compare TICK[1] *noun* 3; **c** the mark × used instead of a signature by an illiterate person; **d** the mark × used to symbolize a kiss in a letter, etc. **2** a vertical post with a shorter horizontal bar fixed to it, on which criminals were crucified in antiquity. **3** (**the Cross**) *Christianity* **a** the cross on which Christ was crucified, or a representation of it; **b** this as a symbol of Christianity. **4** a variation of this symbol, eg the ST ANDREW'S CROSS. **5** a burden or affliction □ ***have one's own cross to bear.*** **6** **a** a monument, not necessarily in the form of a cross; **b** as a place name: the site of such a monument. **7** a medal in the form of a cross. **8** a plant or animal produced by crossing two different strains, breeds or varieties of a species in order to produce an improved hybrid offspring. **9** a mixture or compromise □ ***a cross between a bedroom and a living room.*** **10** *sport, especially football* a pass of (a ball, etc) from the wing to the centre. ▷ *verb* (***crosses, crossed, crossing***) **1** *tr & intr* (*often* **cross over**) to move, pass or get across (a road, a path, etc). **2** to place one across the other □ ***cross one's legs.*** **3** *intr* to meet; to intersect. **4** *intr* said of letters between two correspondents: to be in transit simultaneously. **5** to make the sign of the Cross upon someone or on oneself, usually as a blessing □ ***He crossed himself before entering the church.*** **6** to draw a line across □ ***cross one's t's.*** **7** to make (a cheque) payable only through a bank by drawing two parallel lines across it. **8** (*usually* **cross out**, **off** or **through**) to delete or cancel something by drawing a line through it. **9** to cross-breed (two different strains, breeds or varieties of a species of animal or plant) □ ***cross a sheep with a goat.*** **10** to frustrate or thwart. **11** to cause unwanted connections between (telephone lines). **12** *sport, especially football* to pass (the ball, etc) from the wing to the centre. ▷ *adj* **1** angry; in a bad temper. **2** *in compounds* **a** across □ ***cross-Channel*** □ ***cross-country***; **b** intersecting or at right angles □ ***crossbar***; **c** contrary □ ***cross purposes***; **d** intermingling □ ***cross-breeding.*** ● **be at cross purposes** said of two or more people: to misunderstand or clash with one another. ● **cross one's fingers** or **keep one's fingers crossed** to hope for good fortune by crossing one's middle finger over one's index finger. ● **cross one's heart** to make a crossing gesture over one's heart as an indication of good faith. ● **cross one's legs** to bend one leg at the knee and rest it above the knee of the other, while sitting on a chair, etc. Compare CROSS-LEGGED. ● **cross someone's mind** to occur to them. ● **cross someone's palm** to put a coin in their hand. ● **cross someone's path** to encounter them. ● **cross swords with someone** to have a disagreement or argument with them. ◷ Anglo-Saxon *cros*, from Latin *crux*.

crossbar ▷ *noun* **1** a horizontal bar, especially between two upright posts. **2** the horizontal bar on a man's bicycle.

crossbeam ▷ *noun* a beam which stretches across from one support to another.

cross bench ▷ *noun* a seat in the House of Commons for members not belonging to the government or opposition. ● **cross bencher** *noun*. Compare BACK BENCH, FRONT BENCH.

crossbill ▷ *noun* any of various types of finch with a beak in which the points cross instead of meeting.

crossbones ▷ *plural noun* a pair of crossed femurs appearing beneath the skull in the SKULL AND CROSSBONES.

cross-border ▷ *adj* referring to international contacts and links, particularly between countries of the EU □ ***cross-border business.***

crossbow /ˈkrɒsboʊ/ ▷ *noun* a bow placed crosswise on a STOCK (*noun* 5), with a crank to pull back the bow and a trigger to release arrows.

cross-bred ▷ *adj* said of animals or plants: bred from parents belonging to different species or varieties. ▷ *noun* a cross-bred animal or plant.

cross-breed *biol* ▷ *verb* to mate (two animals or plants of different pure breeds) in order to produce offspring in which the best characteristics of both parents are combined. ▷ *noun* an animal or plant that has been bred from two different pure breeds.

cross-buttock ▷ *noun, wrestling* a particular kind of throw over the hip.

crosscheck ▷ *verb* to verify (information) from an independent source. ▷ *noun* a check of this kind.

cross-claim ▷ *noun* a claim made by the defendant against the plaintiff. ▷ *verb, tr & intr* to make a cross-claim.

cross-country ▷ *adj, adverb* across fields, etc rather than on roads.

cross-cultural ▷ *adj* relating to the differences that exist between cultures.

cross-current ▷ *noun* in a river, sea, ocean, etc: a current which flows across the main current.

cross cut ▷ *noun* a transverse or diagonal cut. ▷ *adj* cut transversely. ▷ *verb* (**cross-cut**) to cut across.

cross-cut saw ▷ *noun* a large saw worked by two people, one standing at each end, which is used to cut wood across the grain.

cross-cutting ▷ *noun, film-making* the technique of cutting between two or more different film sequences so that in the finished product, the action moves between scenes, often creating dramatic tension.

cross-dress ▷ *verb, intr* said especially of men: to dress in the clothes of the opposite sex. ● **cross-dressing** *noun*. Compare TRANSVESTITE.

crosse /krɒs/ ▷ *noun* a long stick with a netted pocket at one end, used in playing lacrosse. ◷ 19c: French.

cross-examine ▷ *verb* **1** *law* to question (especially a witness for the opposing side in a law case) so as to develop or throw doubt on his or her statement. **2** to examine very closely. ● **cross-examination** *noun*. ● **cross-examiner** *noun*.

cross-eye ▷ *noun* a turning inward of one or both eyes, towards the nose; a squint. ● **cross-eyed** *adj* **1** squinting. **2** having an abnormal condition in which one or both eyes turn inwards towards the nose.

cross-fertilization or **cross-fertilisation** ▷ *noun* **1** in animals: the fusion of male and female GAMETES from different individuals to produce an offspring. **2** in plants: another name for CROSS-POLLINATION. **3** the fruitful interaction of ideas from different cultures, etc. ● **cross-fertilize** *verb*.

crossfire ▷ *noun* **1** gunfire coming from different directions. **2** a bitter or excited exchange of opinions, arguments, etc.

cross-grained ▷ *adj* **1** said of timber: having the grain or fibres crossing or intertwined. **2** said of a person: perverse; awkward to deal with.

crosshatch ▷ *verb, tr & intr, art* to shade with intersecting sets of parallel lines.

crossing ▷ *noun* **1** the place where two or more things cross each other. **2** a place for crossing a river, road, etc. **3** a journey across something, especially the sea □ *a rough crossing*. **4** an act of cross-breeding.

crossing over ▷ *noun, genetics* in MEIOSIS: the exchange of genetic material that occurs as a result of the exchange of segments of homologous chromosomes, giving rise to genetic variation in the offspring.

cross-legged ▷ *ad, adverb* sitting, usually on the floor, with the ankles crossed and knees wide apart. See also CROSS ONE'S LEGS at CROSS.

cross-over ▷ *adj* **1** referring or relating to something moving from one side to another. **2** referring or relating to something which spans two different genres (see GENRE sense 1).

crosspatch ▷ *noun, colloq* a grumpy or bad-tempered person.

cross-ply ▷ *adj* said of a tyre: having fabric cords in the outer casing that run diagonally to stiffen and strengthen the side walls. See also RADIAL-PLY TYRE.

cross-pollination ▷ *noun, bot* the transfer of pollen from the ANTHER of one flower to the STIGMA of another flower of the same species, by wind dispersal, formation of pollen tubes, etc.

cross-purposes ▷ *plural noun* confusion in a conversation or action by misunderstanding.

cross-question ▷ *verb* to cross-examine. ▷ *noun* a question asked during a cross-examination.

cross-refer ▷ *verb, tr & intr* to direct (the reader) from one part of something, especially a text, to another.

cross-reference ▷ *noun* a reference from one part of a text to another. ▷ *verb* to supply with cross-references.

crossroads ▷ *singular noun* **1** the point where two or more roads cross or meet. **2** a point at which an important choice has to be made.

cross section ▷ *noun* **1 a** the surface revealed when a solid object is sliced through, especially at right angles to its length; **b** a diagram representing this. **2** a representative sample. ● **cross-sectional** *adj*.

cross-stitch *needlecraft* ▷ *noun* an embroidery stitch made by two stitches crossing each other. ▷ *verb* to embroider with this stitch.

crosstalk ▷ *noun* **1** unwanted interference between communication channels. **2** fast and clever conversation; repartee.

cross-training ▷ *noun* a method of exercise alternating the use of gymnasium equipment with aerobic floor exercises in the same session.

crosswind ▷ *noun* a wind blowing across the path of a vehicle or aircraft.

crosswise and **crossways** ▷ *adj, adverb* **1** lying or moving across, or so as to cross. **2** in the shape of a cross.

crossword and **crossword puzzle** ▷ *noun* a puzzle in which numbered clues are solved and their answers in words inserted into their correct places in a grid of squares that cross vertically and horizontally.

crotch ▷ *noun* (*crotches*) **1** (*also* **crutch**) **a** the place where the body or a pair of trousers forks into the two legs; **b** the human genital area. **2** the fork of a tree. ⓘ 16c: variant of CRUTCH.

crotchet /ˈkrɒtʃɪt/ ▷ *noun* **1** *music* a note equal to two QUAVERS or half a MINIM 1 in length. **2** a perverse fancy. ⓘ 15c in sense 1; 14c meaning a CROCKET: French, meaning 'hooked staff'.

crotchety ▷ *adj* **1** *colloq* irritable; peevish. **2** full of crotchets. ● **crotchetiness** *noun*.

crouch /kraʊtʃ/ ▷ *verb* (*crouches, crouched, crouching*) *intr* (*sometimes* **crouch down**) **1** to bend low or squat with one's knees and thighs against one's chest and often also with one's hands on the ground. **2** said of animals: to lie close to the ground ready to spring up. ▷ *noun* (*crouches*) a crouching position or action. ⓘ 14c.

croup[1] /kruːp/ ▷ *noun* a condition characterized by inflammation and consequent narrowing of the larynx, occurring especially in young children, the main symptoms of which are a hoarse cough, difficulty in breathing and fever. ● **croupy** *adj*. ⓘ 18c: imitating the sound.

croup[2] /kruːp/ ▷ *noun* **1** the rump or hindquarters of a horse. **2** the place behind the saddle. ⓘ 13c: from French *croupe*.

croupier /ˈkruːpɪə(r), ˈkruːpɪeɪ/ ▷ *noun* in a casino: someone who presides over a gaming-table, collecting the stakes, dealing the cards, paying the winners, etc. ⓘ 18c: French, literally meaning 'one who rides pillion on a horse'.

croûton /ˈkruːtɒn/ ▷ *noun* a small cube of fried or toasted bread, served in soup, etc. ⓘ 19c: French, diminutive of *croûte* crust.

crow /kroʊ/ ▷ *noun* **1** any of about 100 species of large black bird, including the carrion crow, rook, raven, etc, usually with a powerful black beak and shiny feathers. **2** the shrill drawn-out cry of a cock. ▷ *verb* (*past tense* ***crowed*** or ***crew*** /kruː/, *past participle* ***crowed***, *present participle* ***crowing***) *intr* **1** said of a cock: to cry shrilly. **2** said of a baby: to make happy inarticulate sounds. **3** (*usually* **crow over someone** or **something**) to triumph gleefully over them; to gloat. ● **as the crow flies** in a straight line. ● **stone the crows!** *dated, slang* an expression of amazement, horror, etc. ⓘ Anglo-Saxon *crawa*.

crowbar ▷ *noun* a heavy iron bar with a bent flattened end, used as a lever.

crowd ▷ *noun* **1** a large number of people gathered together. **2** the spectators or audience at an event. **3** (*usually* **crowds**) *colloq* a large number of people. **4** a set or group of people. **5** (**the crowd**) the general mass of people. ▷ *verb* (***crowded, crowding***) **1** *intr* to gather or move in a large, usually tightly-packed, group. **2** to fill. **3** to pack; to cram. **4** to press round, or supervise someone too closely. ● **crowded** *adj* full of people. ⓘ Anglo-Saxon *crudan* to press.

■ **crowd someone** or **something out** to overwhelm and force them out.

■ **crowd something out** to fill it completely.

crowd

● There is often uncertainty as to whether collective nouns like **crowd** should be followed by a singular or plural verb. Both are correct, and choice depends on whether the group is being thought of as a unit or as a number of individuals.

crowd pleaser ▷ *noun* something that has popular appeal, especially a product available in shops □ *The fresh nectarines proved to be a great crowd pleaser.*

crown ▷ *noun* **1** the circular, usually jewelled, gold headdress of a sovereign. **2** (**the Crown**) **a** the sovereign as head of state; **b** the authority or jurisdiction of a sovereign or of the government representing a sovereign. **3** a wreath for the head or other honour, awarded for victory or success. **4** a highest point of achievement; a summit or climax □ *the crown of one's career.* **5** the top, especially of something rounded. **6 a** the part of a tooth projecting from the gum; **b** an artificial replacement for this. **7** a representation of a royal crown used as an emblem, symbol, etc. **8** an old British coin worth 25 pence (formerly 5 shillings). **9** the junction of the root and stem of a plant. **10** a UK paper size, 385 × 505 mm. ▷ *verb* (***crowned, crowning***) **1** to place a crown ceremonially on the head of someone, thus making them a monarch. **2** to be on or round the top of someone or something. **3** to reward; to make complete or perfect □ *efforts crowned with success.* **4** to put an artificial crown on (a tooth). **5** *colloq* to hit on the head. **6** *draughts* to give (a piece) the status of king, by placing another piece on top of it. ● **to crown it all** *colloq* as the finishing touch to a series of especially unfortunate events. ⓒ 11c: from French *coroune*, from Latin *corona* wreath or crown.

crown colony ▷ *noun* a colony under the direct control of the British government.

crowning ▷ *adj* highest; greatest. ▷ *noun, obstetrics* the stage of labour when the top part of the baby's head is just passing through the vaginal opening.

crown jewels ▷ *plural noun* **1** the crown, sceptre and other ceremonial regalia of a sovereign. **2** *euphemistic* the male genitalia.

crown prince ▷ *noun* the male heir to a throne.

crown princess ▷ *noun* **1** the wife of a crown prince. **2** the female heir to a throne.

crow's feet ▷ *plural noun* the wrinkles at the outer corner of the eye.

crow's nest ▷ *noun* at the top of a ship's mast: a lookout platform.

crozier see CROSIER

CRT ▷ *abbreviation* cathode ray tube.

cruces see CRUX

crucial /ˈkruːʃəl/ ▷ *adj* **1** decisive; critical. **2** very important; essential. **3** *slang* very good; great. ● **crucially** *adverb.* ⓒ 18c meaning 'in the form of a cross' (now rare); 19c in sense 2; 20c in sense 3: French, from Latin *crux* cross.

crucible /ˈkruːsɪbəl/ ▷ *noun* **1** an earthenware pot in which to heat metals or other substances. **2** a severe test or trial. ⓒ 15c: from Latin *crucibulum* a night lamp.

crucifix /ˈkruːsɪfɪks/ ▷ *noun* a representation, especially a model, of Christ on the cross. ⓒ 13c: from Latin *crucifixus* one fixed to a cross.

crucifixion /kruːsɪˈfɪkʃən/ ▷ *noun* **1** execution by crucifying. **2** (**Crucifixion**) *Christianity* the crucifying of Christ, or a representation of this. ⓒ 17c: from Latin *crucifixio*, from *crucifigere* to crucify.

cruciform /ˈkruːsɪfɔːm/ ▷ *adj* cross-shaped. ⓒ 17c: from Latin *crux* cross + -FORM.

crucify /ˈkruːsɪfaɪ/ ▷ *verb* (***crucifies, crucified, crucifying***) **1** to put to death by fastening or nailing to a cross by the hands and feet. **2** to torment, torture or persecute someone. **3** *slang* to defeat or humiliate someone utterly. ⓒ 13c: from French *crucifier*, from Latin *crucifigere* to crucify, from *crux* cross + *figere* fix.

crud ▷ *noun* **1** *slang* dirt or filth, especially if sticky. **2** a contemptible or worthless person. **3** a disagreeable residue, especially radioactive waste. ● **cruddy** *adj.* ⓒ 20c: variant of the earlier CURD.

crude /kruːd/ ▷ *adj* **1** in its natural unrefined state. **2** rough or undeveloped □ *a crude sketch.* **3** vulgar; tasteless. ▷ *noun* short for CRUDE OIL. ● **crudely** *adverb.* ● **crudity** or **crudeness** *noun.* ⓒ 14c: from Latin *crudus* raw.

crude oil ▷ *noun* petroleum in its unrefined state. Often shortened to **crude**.

cruel /krʊəl/ ▷ *adj* (***crueller, cruellest***) **1** deliberately and pitilessly causing pain or suffering. **2** painful; distressing □ *a cruel blow.* ● **cruelly** *adverb.* ● **cruelty** *noun.* ⓒ 13c: French, from Latin *crudelis*, from *crudus* raw.

cruelty-free ▷ *adj* said of cosmetics, household products, etc: developed and produced without being tested on animals.

cruet /ˈkruːɪt/ ▷ *noun* **1** a small container which holds salt, pepper, mustard, vinegar, etc, for use at table. **2** a stand for a set of such jars. ⓒ 14c in sense 1; 13c in sense 'a vessel for holy water or wine': French, diminutive of *crue* jar.

cruise /kruːz/ ▷ *verb* (***cruised, cruising***) **1** *tr & intr* to sail about for pleasure, calling at a succession of places. **2** *intr* said eg of a vehicle or aircraft: to go at a steady comfortable speed. **3** *tr & intr* said of a warship, etc: to patrol a body of water. **4** *slang* to go around public places looking for a sexual partner. ▷ *noun* an instance of cruising, especially an ocean voyage undertaken for pleasure. ⓒ 17c: from Dutch *kruisen* to cross.

cruise control ▷ *noun* an electronic device in cars, etc that controls their cruising speed on motorways. ⓒ 20c.

cruise missile ▷ *noun* a low-flying, long-distance, computer-controlled winged missile.

cruiser ▷ *noun* **1** a large fast warship. **2** (*also* **cabin-cruiser**) a large, especially luxurious motor boat with living quarters. **3** a person or thing that cruises, especially a person in search of a sexual partner.

crumb /krʌm/ ▷ *noun* **1** a particle of dry food, especially bread. **2** a small amount □ *a crumb of comfort.* **3** the soft interior of a loaf of bread. **4** *slang* an obnoxious person. ▷ *verb* (***crumbed, crumbing***) to coat in breadcrumbs. ⓒ Anglo-Saxon *cruma.*

crumble /ˈkrʌmbəl/ ▷ *verb* (***crumbled, crumbling***) **1** *tr & intr* to break into crumbs or powdery fragments. **2** *intr* to collapse, decay or disintegrate. ▷ *noun* a baked dessert of stewed fruit covered with a crumbled mixture of sugar, butter and flour. ● **crumbly** *adj.* ⓒ 15c as *kremelen*, from Anglo-Saxon *gecrymian.*

crumbs /krʌmz/ ▷ *exclamation, colloq* an expression of mild surprise, dismay, etc. ⓒ 19c: altered form of CHRIST.

crumby /ˈkrʌmɪ/ ▷ *adj* (***crumbier, crumbiest***) **1** full of or in crumbs. **2** soft like the inside of a loaf. **3** see CRUMMY. ⓒ 18c: from CRUMB.

crummy ▷ *adj* (***crummier, crummiest***) *colloq, derog* shoddy, dingy, dirty or generally inferior. ● **crumminess** *noun.* ⓒ 19c: variant of CRUMBY.

crumpet /ˈkrʌmpɪt/ ▷ *noun* **1** a thick round cake made of soft light dough, eaten toasted and buttered. **2** *Scottish* a type of large thin pancake. **3** *offensive slang* **a** a girl; **b** female company generally.

crumple /ˈkrʌmpəl/ ▷ *verb* (***crumpled, crumpling***) **1** *tr & intr* to make or become creased or crushed. **2** *intr* said of a face or features: to pucker in distress. **3** *intr* to collapse; to give away. ⓒ From Anglo-Saxon *crump* crooked.

crumple zone ▻ *noun* part of a car, usually at the front or rear, designed to absorb the impact in a collision. ⓒ 20c.

crunch ▻ *verb* (***crunches, crunched, crunching***) **1** *tr & intr* to crush or grind noisily between the teeth or under the foot. **2** *intr* to produce a crunching sound. **3** *tr & intr, computing, colloq* to process (large quantities of data, numbers, etc) at speed. ▻ *noun* (***crunches***) **1** a crunching action or sound. **2** (**the crunch**) *colloq* the moment of decision or crisis. ▻ *adj* crucial or decisive ◻ *crunch talks*. ⓒ 19c: imitating the sound, changed from the earlier *craunch* probably through the influence of MUNCH.

crunchy ▻ *adj* (***crunchier, crunchiest***) able to be crunched; crisp. • **crunchily** *adverb*. • **crunchiness** *noun*.

crusade /kruː'seɪd/ ▻ *noun* **1** a strenuous campaign in aid of a cause. **2** (**Crusades**) *historical* any of the eight Holy Wars from 1096 onwards, which were fought to recover the Holy Land from the Muslims. ▻ *verb* (***crusaded, crusading***) *intr* to engage in a crusade; to campaign. • **crusader** *noun*. ⓒ 16c: from French *croisade*, ultimately from Latin *crux* cross.

crush ▻ *verb* (***crushes, crushed, crushing***) **1** to break, damage, bruise, injure or distort by compressing violently. **2** to grind or pound into powder, crumbs, etc. **3** *tr & intr* to crumple or crease. **4** to defeat, subdue or humiliate. ▻ *noun* (***crushes***) **1** violent compression. **2** a dense crowd. **3** a drink made from the juice of crushed fruit ◻ *orange crush*. **4** *colloq* **a** an amorous passion, usually an unsuitable one; an infatuation; **b** the object of such an infatuation. • **crushable** *adj*. • **crushed** *adj*. • **crusher** *noun*. • **crushing** *adj*. • **crushingly** *adverb*. ⓒ 14c: from French *croissir*, from Latin *cruscire* to crackle.

crush barrier ▻ *noun* a barrier for separating a crowd, eg of spectators, into sections.

crust ▻ *noun* **1 a** the hard-baked outer surface of a loaf of bread; **b** a piece of this; a dried-up piece of bread. **2** the pastry covering a pie, etc. **3** a crisp or brittle covering. **4** the dry brittle covering which forms over a skin lesion. **5** the solid outermost layer of the Earth, consisting mainly of sedimentary rocks overlying ancient igneous rocks. **6** *slang* a living or livelihood. ▻ *verb* (***crusted, crusting***) *tr & intr* to cover with or form a crust.

crustacean /krʌ'steɪʃən/ ▻ *noun, zool* in the animal kingdom: any invertebrate animal belonging to the large class **Crustacea** consisting of mainly aquatic ARTHROPODs, including crabs, lobsters, shrimps, barnacles, woodlice, etc, which typically possess two pairs of antennae and a segmented body covered by a chalky CARAPACE. ▻ *adj* relating to these creatures. ⓒ 19c: from Latin *crusta* shell.

crustie or **crusty** ▻ *noun* (***crusties***) *Brit slang* a New-Age traveller or someone with a similar outlook on life. ⓒ 1990s: from CRUST.

crusty ▻ *adj* (***crustier, crustiest***) **1** having a crisp crust. **2** irritable, snappy or cantankerous. • **crustily** *adverb* • **crustiness** *noun*.

crutch ▻ *noun* (***crutches***) **1** a stick, usually one of a pair, used as a support by a lame person, with a bar fitting under the armpit or a grip for the elbow. **2** a support, help or aid. **3** *Brit* another word for CROTCH 1. ▻ *verb* (***crutches, crutched, crutching***) **1** to support with a crutch or crutches. **2** *Austral, NZ* to cut off wool from the hindquarters of a sheep. ⓒ Anglo-Saxon *crycc*.

crux /krʌks/ ▻ *noun* (***cruces*** /'kruːsiːz/ or ***cruxes***) **1** a decisive, essential or crucial point. **2** a problem or difficulty. **3** (**Crux**) *astron, formal* the SOUTHERN CROSS. ⓒ 18c: Latin, meaning 'cross'.

cry ▻ *verb* (***cries, cried, crying***) **1** *intr* to shed tears; to weep. **2** *intr* (*often* **cry out**) to shout or shriek, eg in pain or fear, or to get attention or help. **3** (*often* **cry out**) to exclaim (words, news, etc). **4** *intr* said of an animal or bird: to utter its characteristic noise. **5** *old use* said of a street trader: to proclaim (one's wares). ▻ *noun* (***cries***) **1** a shout or shriek. **2** an excited utterance or exclamation. **3** an appeal or demand. **4** a rallying call or slogan. **5** a bout of weeping. **6** the characteristic utterance of an animal or bird. **7** a street trader's call ◻ *street cries*. • **cry blue murder** see BLUE MURDER. • **cry for the moon** to want or desire something which is impossible to get. • **cry one's eyes** or **heart out** to weep long and bitterly. • **cry over spilt milk** to cry over something which has already happened and cannot be changed. • **cry stinking fish** to belittle one's own goods. • **a crying shame** a great shame. • **a far cry 1** a great distance. **2** very different. • **For crying out loud!** *colloq* an expression of impatience or annoyance. • **in full cry** in keen pursuit of something. ⓒ 13c: from French *crier*, from Latin *quiritare* to wail.

■ **cry something down** to be critical of it; to scorn it.

■ **cry off** *colloq* to cancel an engagement or agreement.

■ **cry out for something** to be in obvious need of it.

■ **cry someone** or **something up** to praise them or it.

crybaby ▻ *noun, derog, colloq* a person, especially a child, who weeps at the slightest upset.

crying ▻ *adj* demanding urgent attention ◻ *a crying need*.

cryo- /kraɪoʊ, kraɪ'ɒ/ ▻ *combining form, denoting* frost or ice. ⓒ From Greek *kryos* frost.

cryobiology /kraɪoʊbaɪ'ɒlədʒɪ/ ▻ *noun* the branch of biology dealing with the effects of low temperatures on organisms. • **cryobiologist** *noun*. ⓒ 1960s.

cryogenics /kraɪoʊ'dʒɛnɪks/ ▻ *singular noun* the branch of physics concerned with the study of techniques for the production of very low temperatures, and of the phenomena that occur at such temperatures, eg superconductivity. ⓒ 1950s.

cryolite /'kraɪəlaɪt/ ▻ *noun, geol* a pale grey mineral, composed of sodium, aluminium and fluorine, used in the smelting of aluminium ores. ⓒ 19c: from CRYO- + Greek *lithos* stone.

cryoprecipitate ▻ *noun* a PRECIPITATE (*noun* 1) which is produced by the controlled freezing and thawing of a substance.

cryopreservation and **cryonics** /kraɪ'ɒnɪks/ ▻ *noun, biol* the preservation by freezing of living cells eg blood, human eggs, sperm, etc, especially the practice of freezing human corpses, with the idea that advances in science will enable them to be revived at a later date.

cryosurgery ▻ *noun, medicine* a type of surgery which uses instruments that produce intense cold in localized parts of the body, so as to freeze and destroy unwanted tissue.

crypt /krɪpt/ ▻ *noun* an underground chamber or vault, especially one beneath a church, often used for burials. ⓒ 18c in this sense; 15c in obsolete sense 'grotto': from Latin *crypta*, ultimately from Greek *kryptein* to hide.

cryptanalysis /krɪptə'naləsɪs/ ▻ *noun* the deciphering of coded information or messages.

cryptic /'krɪptɪk/ ▻ *adj* **1** puzzling, mysterious, obscure or enigmatic. **2** secret or hidden. **3** said of a crossword puzzle: with clues in the form of riddles, puns, anagrams, etc, rather than synonyms. • **cryptically** *adverb*. ⓒ 17c: from Greek *kryptikos*, from *kryptein* to hide.

crypto- /krɪptoʊ/ or (before a vowel) **crypt-** /krɪpt/ ▻ *combining form, denoting* **1** hidden or obscure ◻ *cryptogram*. **2** secret or undeclared ◻ *crypto-fascist*. ⓒ From Greek *kryptos*, from *kryptein* to hide.

cryptocrystalline ▻ *adj, geol* said of rocks: composed of crystals which can only be seen under a microscope.

cryptogam /'krɪptoʊgam/ ▻ *noun* **1** *bot* a general term for a plant that reproduces by means of spores, such as a seaweed, moss or fern. **2** *bot, loosely* a term often used to refer to a plant that lacks flowers. ◷ 19c: from CRYPTO- + Greek *gamos* marriage.

cryptogram /ˈkrɪptəgram/ ▻ *noun* something written in a code or cipher.

cryptography /krɪpˈtɒgrəfɪ/ ▻ *noun* the study of writing in and deciphering codes. ● **cryptographer** *noun*. ● **cryptographic** *adj*.

crystal /ˈkrɪstəl/ ▻ *noun* **1** (*also* **rock crystal**) colourless transparent quartz. **2** a CRYSTAL BALL. **3 a** a brilliant, highly transparent glass used for cut glass; **b** cut-glass articles. **4** a small piece of a solid that has a regular three-dimensional shape, and whose plane faces are arranged in a regular order and meet each other at specific angles. **5** *chem* any solid substance consisting of a regularly repeating arrangement of atoms, ions or molecules. **6** *elec* a crystalline element, made of piezoelectric or semiconductor material, that functions as a transducer, oscillator, etc in an electronic device. ▻ *adj* belonging or relating to, or made of, crystal. ● **crystal clear** as clear or obvious as can be. ◷ 11c: from Latin *crystallum*, from Greek *krystallos* ice.

crystal ball ▻ *noun* a globe of rock crystal or glass into which a fortune-teller or clairvoyant gazes, apparently seeing visions of the future.

crystal-gazing ▻ *noun* **1** a fortune-teller's practice of gazing into a crystal ball long and hard enough to apparently conjure up a vision of the future. **2** *derog* guesswork about the future. ● **crystal-gazer** *noun* a fortune-teller.

crystal healing ▻ *noun* the selection and use of crystals that are said to promote healing and well-being in humans.

crystal lattice ▻ *noun, physics* the orderly arrangement of points around which atoms or ions in a crystal are centred.

crystalline /ˈkrɪstəlaɪn, ˈkrɪstəlɪn/ ▻ *adj* **1** composed of or having the clarity and transparency of crystal. **2** *chem* displaying the properties or structure of crystals, eg with regard to the regular internal arrangement of atoms, ions, or molecules. **3** said of rocks, minerals, etc: consisting of or containing crystals.

crystalline lens see LENS (sense 2)

crystallization or **crystallisation** ▻ *noun, chem* the process whereby crystals are formed by cooling a molten mass, by allowing a solution of a crystalline solid to evaporate slowly, or by adding more of a crystalline solid to an already saturated solution.

crystallize or **crystallise** /ˈkrɪstəlaɪz/ ▻ *verb* (***crystallized, crystallizing***) **1** *tr & intr* to form crystals by the process of crystallization. **2** to coat or preserve (fruit) in sugar. **3** *tr & intr* said of plans, ideas, etc: to make or become clear and definite.

crystallography /krɪstəˈlɒgrəfɪ/ ▻ *noun* the scientific study of the structure, forms and properties of crystals. ● **crystallographer** *noun*. ● **crystallographic** *adj*.

crystalloid /ˈkrɪstəlɔɪd/ ▻ *adj* **1** relating to or resembling a substance that dissolves to form a true solution which can pass through a semi-permeable membrane. **2** resembling a crystal. ▻ *noun* a substance that dissolves to form a true solution which can pass through a semi-permeable membrane.

CS ▻ *abbreviation* **1** chartered surveyor. **2** Christian Science. **3** Civil Service. **4** Court of Session.

Cs ▻ *symbol, chem* caesium.

c/s ▻ *abbreviation* cycles per second.

CSA ▻ *abbreviation* Child Support Agency.

CSE ▻ *abbreviation, Brit* Certificate of Secondary Education, replaced in 1988 by GCSE.

CSEU ▻ *abbreviation* Confederation of Shipbuilding and Engineering Unions.

CS gas ▻ *noun* an irritant vapour which causes a burning sensation in the eyes, choking, nausea and vomiting, used as an incapacitating agent for riot control. ◷ 1928: named from the initials of its US inventors, B Carson & R Staughton.

CSP ▻ *abbreviation* Council for Scientific Policy.

CST ▻ *abbreviation* **1** *N Amer* Central Standard Time. **2** craniosacral therapy.

CSU ▻ *abbreviation* Civil Service Union.

CSV ▻ *abbreviation* community service volunteer.

CSYS ▻ *abbreviation* Certificate of Sixth Year Studies.

CT or **Ct** ▻ *abbreviation, US state* Connecticut.

Ct ▻ *abbreviation* in addresses, etc: Court.

ct ▻ *abbreviation* **1** carat. **2** cent. **3** court.

ctenophore /ˈtiːnəfɔː(r), ˈtɛ-/ ▻ *noun* any member of a class of marine organisms which move by means of rows of comblike plates. ◷ 19c: Greek *kteis, ktenos* comb + *-phoros* bearing.

CTOL ▻ *abbreviation* conventional take-off and landing.

CT scanner ▻ *noun* a CAT SCANNER.

Cu ▻ *symbol, chem* copper.

cu ▻ *abbreviation* cubic.

cub ▻ *noun* **1** the young of certain carnivorous mammals, such as the fox, wolf, lion and bear. **2** (**Cub**) a member of the junior branch of the Scout Association. Also called **Cub Scout**. See also BEAVER at BEAVER[1]. **3** *old use, derog* an impudent young man. **4** *colloq* a beginner; a novice ▫ ***a cub reporter***. ▻ *verb* (***cubbed, cubbing***) *tr & intr* to give birth to cubs. ◷ 16c.

Cuban /ˈkjuːbən/ ▻ *adj* belonging or relating to Cuba, an island republic in the Caribbean Sea, or its inhabitants. ▻ *noun* a citizen or inhabitant of, or person born in, Cuba.

cubbyhole /ˈkʌbɪhoʊl/ ▻ *noun, colloq* **1** a tiny room. **2** a cupboard, nook or recess in which to accumulate miscellaneous objects. ◷ 19c: from dialect *cub* stall or pen.

cube /kjuːb/ ▻ *noun* **1** *math* a solid figure having six square faces of equal area, in which the angle between any two adjacent sides is a right angle. **2** a block of this shape. **3** *math* the product of any number or quantity multiplied by its square, ie the third power of a number or quantity. ▻ *verb* (***cubed, cubing***) **1** to raise (a number or quantity) to the third power. **2** to form or cut into cubes. ◷ 16c: French, from Greek *kybos* a die.

cube root ▻ *noun, math* the number or quantity of which a given number or quantity is the cube, eg 3 is the cube root of 27 since $3 \times 3 \times 3 = 27$.

cubic /ˈkjuːbɪk/ ▻ *adj* **1** relating to or resembling a cube. **2** having three dimensions. **3** *math* of or involving a number or quantity that is raised to the third power, eg a cubic equation (in which the highest power of the unknown variable is three). **4** *math* said of a unit of volume: equal to that contained in a cube of specified dimensions ▫ ***a cubic metre***. ● **cubical** *adj*.

cubicle /ˈkjuːbɪkəl/ ▻ *noun* a small compartment for sleeping or undressing in, screened for privacy. ◷ 15c: from Latin *cubiculum* bedchamber, from *cubare* to lie down.

Cubism /ˈkjuːbɪzəm/ ▻ *noun, art* an early-20c movement in painting, initiated by Pablo Picasso and Georges Braque, which represented natural objects as geometrical shapes. ● **Cubist** *noun* an artist who works in the Cubist style. Also *as adj*.

cubit /ˈkjuːbɪt/ ▻ *noun* an old unit of measurement equal to the length of the forearm from the elbow to the tip of the middle finger. ◷ 14c: from Latin *cubitum* elbow, from *cubare* to lie down.

cuboid /ˈkjuːbɔɪd/ ▻ *adj* (*also* **cuboidal**) **1** resembling a cube in shape. **2** relating to the cuboid bone. ▻ *noun* **1** a cube-shaped bone in the foot. **2** *math* a solid body having six rectangular faces, the opposite faces of which are equal.

Cub Scout see CUB *noun* 2

cuckold /ˈkʌkəld, ˈkʌkoʊld/ *old use, derisive* ▻ *noun* a man whose wife is unfaithful. ▻ *verb* (***cuckolded***, ***cuckolding***) to make a cuckold of (a man). ● **cuckoldry** *noun* **1** the state of being a cuckold. **2** the act of making (a man) a cuckold. ⓘ 13c: from French *cocu* cuckoo, from the cuckoo's habit of laying her eggs in another bird's nest.

cuckoo /ˈkʊkuː/ ▻ *noun* (***cuckoos***) any of about 130 species of insectivorous birds, the common variety of which is found in Europe, Asia and America, and lays its eggs in the nests of other birds. ▻ *adj, colloq* insane; crazy. ⓘ 13c: from French *cucu*, imitating the sound of the bird's two-tone call.

cuckoo clock ▻ *noun* a clock from which a model cuckoo springs on the hour, uttering the appropriate number of cries.

cuckoo-pint see LORDS-AND-LADIES

cuckoo spit ▻ *noun* a small white frothy mass found on the leaves and stems of many plants, surrounding and secreted by the larvae of the FROG-HOPPER. Also called **frog-spit**.

cucumber /ˈkjuːkʌmbə(r)/ ▻ *noun* **1** a creeping plant cultivated for its edible fruit. **2** a long green fruit of this plant, containing juicy white flesh, which is often used raw in salads, etc. ● **cool as a cucumber** *colloq* calm and composed; unflappable. ⓘ 14c: from Latin *cucumis*.

cud ▻ *noun* in ruminant animals, eg cattle: the partially digested food that is regurgitated from the first stomach into the mouth to be chewed again. ● **chew the cud** *colloq* to meditate, ponder or reflect. ⓘ Anglo-Saxon *cwidu*.

cuddle /ˈkʌdəl/ ▻ *verb* (***cuddled***, ***cuddling***) **1** *tr & intr* to hug or embrace affectionately. **2** (*usually* **cuddle in** or **up**) to lie close and snug; to nestle. ▻ *noun* an affectionate hug. ● **cuddlesome** *adj* pleasant to cuddle. ● **cuddly** *adj* (***cuddlier***, ***cuddliest***) pleasant to cuddle; attractively soft and plump.

cudgel /ˈkʌdʒəl/ ▻ *noun* a heavy stick or club used as a weapon. ▻ *verb* (***cudgelled***, ***cudgelling***) to beat with a cudgel. ● **cudgel one's brains** to struggle to remember or solve something. ● **take up the cudgels for someone** to fight for or defend them vigorously. ⓘ Anglo-Saxon *cycgel*.

cue¹ /kjuː/ ▻ *noun* (***cues***) **1** the end of an actor's speech, or something else said or done by a performer, that serves as a prompt for another to say or do something. **2** anything that serves as a signal or hint to do something. ▻ *verb* (***cued***, ***cueing***) to give a cue to someone. ● **on cue** at precisely the right moment. ● **take one's cue from someone** to follow their lead as regards behaviour, etc. ⓘ 16c: thought to be from 'q', a contraction of Latin *quando* meaning 'when' which was formerly written in actors' scripts to show them when to begin.

cue² /kjuː/ ▻ *noun* **1** in billiards, snooker and pool: a stick tapering almost to a point, used to strike the ball. **2** *old use* a tail of hair or plait at the back of the head. ▻ *verb* (***cued***, ***cueing***) *tr & intr* to strike (a ball) with the cue. ⓘ 18c: variant of QUEUE.

cue ball ▻ *noun* in billiards, snooker and pool: the ball which is struck by the cue that in turn strikes an OBJECT BALL.

cuff¹ ▻ *noun* **1** a band or folded-back part at the lower end of a sleeve, usually at the wrist. **2** *N Amer* the turned-up part of a trouser leg. **3** (**cuffs**) *slang* handcuffs. ● **off the cuff** *colloq* without preparation or previous thought. ⓘ 15c in sense 1; 14c meaning 'mitten', now obsolete except in Canadian dialect.

cuff² ▻ *noun* a blow with the open hand. ▻ *verb* (***cuffed***, ***cuffing***) to hit with an open hand. ⓘ 16c.

cufflink ▻ *noun* one of a pair of decorative fasteners for shirt cuffs in place of buttons.

cuirass /kwɪˈras, ˈkjʊəras/ ▻ *noun, historical* a piece of armour consisting of a breastplate with a back plate attached to it. ⓘ 15c: from French *cuirasse*, from Latin *coriacea*, from *corium* leather.

cuisine /kwɪˈziːn/ ▻ *noun* **1** a style of cooking. **2** the range of food prepared and served at a restaurant, etc. ⓘ 18c: French, meaning 'kitchen'.

cul-de-sac /ˈkʌldəsak, ˈkʊl-/ ▻ *noun* (***culs-de-sac*** /ˈkʌldəsak, ˈkʊl-/ or ***cul-de-sacs***) a street closed at one end; a blind alley. ⓘ 18c: French, meaning 'sack-bottom'.

culinary /ˈkʌlɪnərɪ, ˈkjuː-/ ▻ *adj* relating to cookery or the kitchen. ⓘ 17c: from Latin *culinarius*, from *culina* kitchen.

cull /kʌl/ ▻ *verb* (***culled***, ***culling***) **1** to gather or pick up (information or ideas). **2** to select and kill (weak or surplus animals) from a group, eg seals or deer, in order to keep the population under control. **3** to gather (the best parts) from something. ▻ *noun* **1** an act of culling. **2** an inferior animal eliminated from the herd, flock, etc. ⓘ 14c: from French *cuillir* to gather.

culm¹ /kʌlm/ *bot* ▻ *noun* **1** the jointed hollow stem of a grass. **2** the solid stem of a sedge. ▻ *verb* (***culmed***, ***culming***) to form a culm. ⓘ 17c: from Latin *culmus* stalk.

culm² ▻ *noun, mining* **1** coal dust. **2** anthracite slack. ⓘ 14c.

culminate /ˈkʌlmɪneɪt/ ▻ *verb* (***culminated***, ***culminating***) **1** *tr & intr* (*often* **culminate in** or **with something**) to reach the highest point or climax. **2** *intr, astron* said of a heavenly body: to cross the meridian. **3** to bring something to its highest point. ⓘ 17c: from Latin *culminare*, from *culmen* top or summit.

culmination /kʌlmɪˈneɪʃən/ ▻ *noun* **1** the top or highest point; the climax. **2** the act or point of culminating. **3** *astron* the highest altitude attained by a heavenly body.

culottes /kjʊˈlɒts, kʊˈlɒts/ ▻ *plural noun* flared trousers for women, intended to look like a skirt. ⓘ 20c: French, meaning 'knee-breeches'.

culpable /ˈkʌlpəbəl/ ▻ *adj* deserving blame. ● **culpability** *noun*. ● **culpably** *adverb*. ⓘ 14c: from Latin *culpare* to blame.

culpable homicide ▻ *noun, Scots law* unlawful killing which lacks the evil intention which would class it as murder. Compare MANSLAUGHTER.

culprit /ˈkʌlprɪt/ ▻ *noun* **1** someone guilty of a misdeed or offence. **2** *law* someone accused of a crime. ⓘ 17c: from the fusion of French *culpable* guilty + *prest* ready, as used in *culpable: prest d'averrer notre bille*, meaning 'guilty: ready to prove our charge', the reply of the clerk of the court to a prisoner's plea of not guilty, which at a later time, after the disuse of law French, was wrongly attributed to the prisoner.

cult /kʌlt/ ▻ *noun* **1 a** a system of religious belief; **b** the sect of people following such a system. **2 a** an unorthodox or false religion; **b** the people adhering to such a system. **3** an especially extravagant admiration for a person, idea, etc. **4** something which is popular and regarded as particularly significant by a certain group of people: a fashion, craze or fad. ● **cultic** or **cultish** *adj*. ● **cultism** *noun*. ● **cultist** *noun*. ⓘ 17c: from Latin *cultus* worship, from *colere* to cultivate.

cultivar /ˈkʌltɪvɑː(r)/ ▻ *noun, hortic* (abbreviation **cv**) a variety of a plant that does not occur naturally in the wild, but has been developed and maintained by cultivation using horticultural or agricultural techniques. ⓘ 20c: a shortening of *cultivated variety*.

cultivate /ˈkʌltɪveɪt/ ▻ *verb* (***cultivated***, ***cultivating***) **1** to prepare and use (land or soil) for growing crops. **2** to grow (a crop, plant, etc). **3** to develop or improve □

cultivate a taste for literature. **4** to try to develop a friendship, a relationship, etc with (someone), especially for personal advantage. ◐ 17c: from Latin *cultivare, cultivatum*, ultimately from *colere* to till or take care of.

cultivated ▷ *adj* **1** well bred and knowledgeable. **2** said of plants: not wild; grown and cared for in a garden, etc. **3** said of soil or land: prepared for growing crops.

cultivation /kʌltɪ'veɪʃən/ ▷ *noun* **1** the act of cultivating. **2** education, breeding and culture. **3** the preparation of soil or land for growing crops.

cultivator /'kʌltɪveɪtə(r)/ ▷ *noun* **1** a tool for breaking up the surface of the ground. **2** someone or something which cultivates.

cultural ▷ *adj* **1** relating to a culture. **2** relating to the arts. ● **culturally** *adverb*.

cultural lag or **culture lag** ▷ *noun* a slower rate of cultural change found either in one part of a society compared with the whole or majority, or in a particular society compared to the world at large.

culture /'kʌltʃə(r)/ ▷ *noun* **1** the customs, ideas, values, etc of a particular civilization, society or social group, especially at a particular time. **2** appreciation of art, music, literature, etc. **3** improvement and development through care and training ◻ *beauty culture.* **4** *also in compounds* the cultivation of eg plants, trees, animals, etc, especially for commercial purposes ◻ *horticulture.* **5** *biol* a population of micro-organisms (especially bacteria), cells or tissues grown in a CULTURE MEDIUM usually for scientific study or medical diagnosis. ▷ *verb* (*cultured, culturing*) to grow (micro-organisms, cells, tissues, etc) in a CULTURE MEDIUM for study. ◐ 15c: from Latin *cultura*, from *colere* to cherish or practise.

cultured ▷ *adj* **1** well-educated; having refined tastes and manners. **2** said of micro-organisms, cells or tissues: grown in a CULTURE MEDIUM. **3** said of a pearl: formed by an oyster round a foreign body deliberately inserted into its shell.

culture medium ▷ *noun, biol* a solid or liquid nutrient medium in which micro-organisms, cells or tissues can be grown under controlled conditions in a laboratory. Sometimes shortened to **medium**.

culture shock ▷ *noun, sociol* disorientation caused by a change from a familiar environment, culture, ideology, etc, to another that is radically different or alien.

culture vulture ▷ *noun, colloq* someone who is extravangantly and, by implication, pretentiously interested in the arts.

culvert /'kʌlvət/ ▷ *noun* a covered drain or channel carrying water or electric cables underground, eg under a road or railway.

-cum- /kʌm/ ▷ *combining form* combined with; also used as ◻ *kitchen-cum-dining-room.* ◐ Latin *cum* with.

cumbersome ▷ *adj* awkward, unwieldy or unmanageable. ◐ 16c in this sense; 14c in obsolete sense 'obstructing motion': from *cumber*, short for ENCUMBER + -SOME.

cumin or **cummin** /'kʌmɪn/ ▷ *noun* **1** an umbelliferous plant of the Mediterranean region. **2** the seeds of this plant used as an aromatic herb or flavouring. ◐ Anglo-Saxon *cymen.*

cummerbund /'kʌməbʌnd/ ▷ *noun* a wide sash worn around the waist, especially one worn with a dinner jacket. ◐ 17c: from Hindi *kamarband* loin band.

cumulate ▷ *verb* /'kjuːmjʊleɪt/ (*cumulated, cumulating*) **1** *tr & intr* to heap together; to accumulate. **2** to combine (two or more things). ▷ *adj* /'kjuːmjʊlət/ heaped together. ◐ 16c: from Latin *cumulare, cumulatum*, from *cumulus* a heap.

cumulative /'kjuːmjʊlətiv/ ▷ *adj* increasing in amount, effect or strength with each successive addition. ● **cumulatively** *adverb*. ● **cumulativeness** *noun*.

cumulonimbus /kjuːmjʊloʊ'nɪmbəs/ ▷ *noun, meteorol* a type of cumulus cloud, with a dark and threatening appearance, which can rise to heights of up to 10km, and which is associated with thunderstorms and the arrival of a cold front during the passage of a depression. ◐ 19c: from CUMULUS + NIMBUS.

cumulus /'kjuːmjʊləs/ ▷ *noun* (*cumuli* /-laɪ/) *meteorol* a fluffy heaped cloud with a rounded white upper surface and a flat horizontal base, which is composed of water droplets and usually develops over a heat source, eg a volcano or hot land surface. ◐ 19c in this sense; 17c in sense 'a heap': Latin, meaning 'heap' or 'mass'.

cuneiform /'kjuːnɪfɔːm, kjʊ'niːɪfɔːm/ ▷ *adj* **1** relating to any of several ancient Middle-Eastern scripts with impressed wedge-shaped characters. **2** wedge-shaped. ▷ *noun* cuneiform writing. ◐ 17c: from Latin *cuneus* wedge + -FORM.

cunnilingus /kʌnɪ'lɪŋgəs/ or **cunnilinctus** /-'lɪŋktəs/ ▷ *noun* oral stimulation of a woman's genitals. ◐ 19c: Latin, from *cunnus* vulva + *lingere* to lick.

cunning /'kʌnɪŋ/ ▷ *adj* **1** clever, sly or crafty. **2** ingenious, skilful or subtle. ▷ *noun* **1** slyness; craftiness. **2** skill; expertise. ● **cunningly** *adverb*. ● **cunningness** *noun*. ◐ From Anglo-Saxon *cunnan* to know.

cunt ▷ *noun* **1** *taboo* the female genitals. **2** *offensive slang* a woman regarded as a sexual object. **3** *offensive slang* an abusive term for an unpleasant person. **4** *slang* a person in general. ◐ 13c.

cup ▷ *noun* **1** a small, round, open container, usually with a handle, used to drink from. **2** the amount a cup will hold, used as a measure in cookery. **3** a container or something else shaped like a cup ◻ *egg cup.* **4** an ornamental trophy awarded as a prize in sports competitions, etc. **5** a competition in which the prize is a cup. **6** a wine-based drink, with added fruit juice, etc ◻ *claret cup.* **7** *literary* something that one undergoes or experiences ◻ *one's own cup of woe.* ▷ *verb* (*cupped, cupping*) **1** to form (one's hands) into a cup shape. **2** to hold something in one's cupped hands. ● **in one's cups** *dated* drunk; under the influence of alcohol. ● **one's cup of tea** *colloq* one's personal preference. ◐ Anglo-Saxon *cuppe*, from Latin *cupa* cask.

cupboard /'kʌbəd/ ▷ *noun* a piece of furniture or a recess, fitted with doors, shelves, etc, for storing provisions or personal effects. ◐ Anglo-Saxon *cuppebord* table for crockery.

cupboard love ▷ *noun* an insincere show of affection towards someone or something in return for some kind of material gain.

cup final ▷ *noun* (*often* **the Cup Final**) the final match in a football contest or any other cup competition.

cupful ▷ *noun* (*cupfuls*) the amount a cup will hold.

cupful

● The plural is **cupfuls**. Note that this denotes an amount, whereas *cups full* (as in *several cups full of water*) refers to the cups themselves as being full.

cupid /'kjuːpɪd/ ▷ *noun* a figure of Cupid, the Roman god of love, represented in art or sculpture. ◐ 14c: from Latin *cupido* desire or love.

cupidity /kjʊ'pɪdɪtɪ/ ▷ *noun* greed for wealth and possessions. ◐ 15c: from Latin *cupiditas*, from *cupidus* eagerly desirous.

cup match ▷ *noun* a game which is not resticted to people, teams or clubs from the same league, and usually forms part of a knockout competition. Compare LEAGUE MATCH.

cupola /'kjuːpələ/ ▷ *noun* (*cupolas*) **1** a small dome or turret on a roof. **2** a domed roof or ceiling. **3** an armoured revolving gun turret. **4** a furnace used in iron foundries. ◐ 16c: Italian, from Latin *cupula*, diminutive of *cupa* cask.

cuppa /ˈkʌpə/ ▷ *noun* (***cuppas***) *Brit colloq* a cup of tea. ⓒ 20c: altered form of *cup of*.

cupping ▷ *noun, medicine* the former practice of applying heated cups to the skin, which was thought to promote healing by drawing 'harmful' blood away from diseased organs to the surface of the skin.

cupric /ˈkjuːprɪk/ ▷ *adj, chem* denoting any compound of copper in which the element has a VALENCY of two, eg cupric chloride. Compare CUPROUS. ⓒ 18c: from Latin *cuprum* copper.

cuprite /ˈkjuːpraɪt/ ▷ *noun, geol* a red oxide mineral that is an important source of copper. ⓒ 19c: from Latin *cuprum* copper.

cupro-nickel /kjuːproʊˈnɪkəl/ ▷ *noun* an alloy of copper and nickel that is resistant to corrosion, used to make silver-coloured coins in the UK.

cuprous /ˈkjuːprəs/ ▷ *adj, chem* denoting any compound of copper in which the element has a VALENCY of one, eg cuprous chloride. Compare CUPRIC. ⓒ 17c: from Latin *cuprum* copper.

cup tie ▷ *noun* a knockout match in a round of a competition for a cup.

cup-tied ▷ *adj, sport, especially football* said of a player who is ineligible to play in a cup competition having already represented another team at some previous stage in the competition.

cur ▷ *noun, derog, old use* **1** a surly mongrel dog. **2** a surly person; a scoundrel. ⓒ 13c as *curdogge*.

curable /ˈkjʊərəbəl/ ▷ *adj* capable of being cured. ● **curability** *noun*. ● **curableness** *noun*.

curacy /ˈkjʊərəsɪ/ ▷ *noun* (***curacies***) the office or benefice of a curate.

curare /kjʊˈrɑːrɪ/ ▷ *noun* (***curares***) **1** a black resin obtained from certain tropical plants in South America, which is used as a paralysing poison smeared on arrow-tips by S American Indian hunters, and which also has medicinal uses as a muscle relaxant. **2** any of the plants from which this resin is obtained. ⓒ 18c: Portuguese and Spanish, from Carib *kurari*.

curate /ˈkjʊərət/ ▷ *noun* **1** *C of E* a clergyman who acts as assistant to a vicar or rector. **2** in Ireland: an assistant barman. ⓒ 14c: from Latin *curatus*, from *cura* care.

curate's egg ▷ *noun* anything of which some parts are excellent and some parts are bad. ⓒ 1895: named after a cartoon in the magazine *Punch* depicting a modest curate who is served a bad egg, and states that 'parts of it are excellent'.

curative /ˈkjʊərətɪv/ ▷ *adj* able or tending to cure. ▷ *noun* a substance that cures. ⓒ 16c: from Latin *curativus*, from *curare* to CURE.

curator /kjʊˈreɪtə(r), ˈkjʊərətə(r)/ ▷ *noun* the custodian of a museum or other collection. ⓒ 17c in this sense; 14c in obsolete sense 'curate': from Latin *curator* overseer, from *curare* to CURE.

curb ▷ *noun* **1** something that restrains or controls. **2 a** a chain or strap passing under a horse's jaw, attached at the sides to the bit; **b** a bit with such a fitting. **3** a raised edge or border. **4** *N Amer* a kerb. ▷ *verb* (***curbed, curbing***) **1** to restrain or control. **2** to put a curb on (a horse). ⓒ 15c: from French *courb*, from Latin *curvus* curved.

curd ▷ *noun* **1** (*often* **curds**) the clotted protein substance, as opposed to the liquid component, formed when fresh milk is curdled, and used to make cheese, etc. Compare WHEY. **2** any of several substances of similar consistency. **3** the edible flowering head of cauliflower, broccoli, etc. ▷ *verb* (***curded, curding***) *tr & intr* to make or turn into curd. ⓒ 14c as *crud*.

curdle /kɜːdəl/ ▷ *verb* (***curdled, curdling***) *tr & intr* to turn into curd; to coagulate. ● **curdle someone's blood** to horrify or petrify them. ⓒ 16c.

cure /kjʊə(r)/ ▷ *verb* (***cured, curing***) **1** to restore someone to health or normality; to heal them. **2** to get rid of (an illness, harmful habit, or other evil). **3** to preserve (food, eg meat, fish, etc) by salting, smoking, etc. **4** to preserve (leather, tobacco, etc) by drying. **5** to vulcanize (rubber). ▷ *noun* **1** something that cures or remedies. **2** restoration to health. **3** a course of healing or remedial treatment. **4** *relig* the responsibility of a minister for the souls of the parishioners. ⓒ 14c: from French *curer*, from Latin *curare* to care for or heal, from *cura* care.

cure-all ▷ *noun* a universal remedy.

curettage /kjʊˈrɛtɪdʒ, kjʊərəˈtɑːʒ/ ▷ *noun* the process of using a curette. See also DILATATION AND CURETTAGE.

curette or **curet** /kjʊəˈrɛt/ ▷ *noun* (***curettes*** or ***curets***) *surgery* a spoon-shaped device used to scrape tissue from the inner surface of an organ or body cavity for diagnostic purposes, or to remove diseased tissue from such a cavity. ▷ *verb* (***curetted, curetting***) to scrape with a curette. ⓒ 18c: French, from *curer* to clean or clear.

curfew /ˈkɜːfjuː/ ▷ *noun* **1 a** an official order restricting people's movements, especially after a certain hour at night; **b** the time at which such an order applies. **2** *historical* **a** the ringing of a bell as a signal to put out fires and lights; **b** the time at which such a ringing took place; **c** the bell rung. ⓒ 13c: from French *cuevrefeu*, literally 'cover the fire'.

curie /ˈkjʊərɪ/ ▷ *noun, physics* (abbreviation **Ci**) the former unit of radioactivity, equivalent to 3.7×10^{10} disintegrations of a radioactive source per second, which has now been replaced by the BECQUEREL in SI units. ⓒ 20c: named after the French physicists Marie (1867–1934) and Pierre (1859–1906) Curie.

curio /ˈkjʊərɪoʊ/ ▷ *noun* (***curios***) an article valued for its rarity or unusualness. ⓒ 19c: shortened from CURIOSITY.

curiosity /kjʊərɪˈɒsɪtɪ/ ▷ *noun* (***curiosities***) **1** eagerness to know; inquisitiveness. **2** something strange, odd, rare, exotic or unusual. ⓒ 14c: from Latin *curiositas*; see CURIOUS.

curious /ˈkjʊərɪəs/ ▷ *adj* **1** strange; odd. **2** eager or interested. **3** inquisitive (often in an uncomplimentary sense). ● **curiously** *adverb*. ⓒ 14c: from Latin *curiosus* full of care.

curium /ˈkjʊərɪəm/ ▷ *noun, chem* (abbreviation **Cm**, atomic number 96) a radioactive element formed by bombarding plutonium-239 with alpha particles. ⓒ 20c: named after Marie and Pierre Curie; see CURIE.

curl ▷ *verb* (***curled, curling***) **1** to twist, roll or wind (hair) into coils or ringlets. **2** *intr* to grow in coils or ringlets. **3** *tr & intr* to move in or form into a spiral, coil or curve. **4** *intr* to take part in the game of curling. ▷ *noun* **1** a small coil or ringlet of hair. **2** the tendency of hair to curl. **3** a twist, spiral, coil or curve. ● **curl one's lip** to sneer. ⓒ 14c.

■ **curl up 1** to sit or lie with the legs tucked up. **2** *colloq* to writhe in embarrassment, etc.

curler ▷ *noun* **1** a type of roller for curling the hair. **2** someone who takes part in the sport of curling. **3** someone or something that curls.

curlew /ˈkɜːljuː, ˈkɜːluː/ ▷ *noun* a large wading bird, with a slender down-curved bill, long legs and a two-syllable fluting call, found on open plains, moors and marshes across Europe and Asia. ⓒ 14c: from French *corlieu*, perhaps imitating the bird's call.

curlicue /ˈkɜːlɪkjuː/ ▷ *noun* **a** a fancy twist or curl; **b** a flourish made with a pen. ⓒ 19c: from CURLY + CUE².

curling ▷ *noun* a team game played on ice with smooth heavy stones with handles, that are slid towards a circular target marked on the ice.

curling tongs ▷ *plural noun* a device made from metal which is heated up before a lock of hair is twisted around it for a short time to make a curl.

curly ▻ *adj* (*curlier*, *curliest*) **1** having curls; full of curls. **2** tending to curl. ● **curliness** *noun*.

curmudgeon /kəˈmʌdʒən, kɜː-/ ▻ *noun* a bad-tempered or mean person. ● **curmudgeonly** *adj*. ⓘ 16c.

currant /ˈkʌrənt/ ▻ *noun* **1** a small dried seedless grape. **2** any of various deciduous shrubs found in N Europe which produce a certain kind of fruit eg blackcurrant, redcurrant, etc. **3** *also in compounds* any of the small soft edible berries produced by certain of these shrubs. ⓘ 16c: shortened from French *raisins de Corinthe* grapes of Corinth, the original place of export of currants (*noun* 1).

currawong /ˈkʌrəwɒŋ/ ▻ *noun* any of several Australian songbirds, with black, grey and white feathers. ⓘ 20c: Aboriginal.

currency /ˈkʌrənsɪ/ ▻ *noun* (*currencies*) **1** the system of money, or the coins and notes, in use in a country. **2** general acceptance or popularity, especially of an idea, theory, etc. **3** the period of time during which something is current. **4** modernity. ⓘ 17c: from Latin *currere* to run.

current /ˈkʌrənt/ ▻ *adj* **1** generally accepted. **2** belonging to the present □ *current affairs.* **3** in circulation; valid. ▻ *noun* **1** the continuous steady flow of a body of water, air, heat, etc, in a particular direction. **2** the rate of flow of electric charge through a conductor per unit time. **3** an ELECTRIC CURRENT. **4** a popular trend or tendency. ● **currently** *adverb* at the present time. ⓘ 15c in *adj* sense 3; 13c in archaic sense 'flowing': from French *corant*, from Latin *currere* to run.

current account ▻ *noun* a bank account from which money or cheques can be drawn without notice, and on which little or no interest is paid.

curriculum /kəˈrɪkjələm/ ▻ *noun* (*curricula* /-ə/ or *curriculums*) **1** a course of study, especially at school or university. **2** a list of all the courses available at a school, university, etc. ● **curricular** *adj*. ⓘ 17c: Latin, from *currere* to run.

curriculum vitae /kəˈrɪkjələm ˈviːtaɪ, —ˈvaɪtiː/ ▻ *noun* (*curricula vitae* /-ə —/) (abbreviation **CV**) a written summary of one's personal details and the main events of one's education and career, produced to accompany job applications, etc. ⓘ 20c: from CURRICULUM + Latin *vita* life.

curry[1] /ˈkʌrɪ/ ▻ *noun* (*curries*) a dish, originally Indian, of meat, fish, or vegetables usually cooked with hot spices. ▻ *verb* (*curries*, *curried*, *currying*) *tr* to prepare (food) using curry powder or a curry sauce. ⓘ 16c: from Tamil *kari* sauce.

curry[2] /ˈkʌrɪ/ ▻ *verb* **1** to groom (a horse). **2** to treat (tanned leather) so as to improve its flexibility, strength and waterproof quality. **3** to beat vigorously, so as to clean. ● **curry favour with someone** to use flattery to gain their approval; to ingratiate oneself with them. ⓘ 13c: from French *correier* to make ready.

curry powder ▻ *noun* a preparation of turmeric and ground spices used to give curry its hot flavour.

curse ▻ *noun* **1** a blasphemous or obscene expression, usually of anger; an oath. **2** an appeal to God or some other divine power to harm someone. **3** the resulting harm suffered by someone □ *under a curse.* **4** an evil; a cause of harm or trouble □ *Pollution is a curse of modern life.* **5** *colloq* (**the curse**) menstruation; a woman's menstrual period. ▻ *verb* (*cursed*, *cursing*) **1** to utter a curse against; to revile with curses. **2** *intr* to use violent language; to swear. ⓘ Anglo-Saxon *curs*.

■ **be cursed with something** to be burdened or afflicted with it.

cursed /ˈkɜːsɪd, kɜːst/ ▻ *adj* **1** under a curse. **2** *old use* damnable; hateful.

cursive /ˈkɜːsɪv/ ▻ *adj* **1** said of handwriting: flowing; having letters which are joined up rather than printed separately. **2** *printing* said of a typeface: designed so as to imitate handwriting. ▻ *noun* cursive writing. ● **cursively** *adverb*. ⓘ 18c: from Latin *cursivus*, from *currere* to run.

cursor /ˈkɜːsə(r)/ ▻ *noun* **1** on the screen of a visual display unit: any of various types of special symbol or character, usually an underline character or a rectangular box, that flashes on and off and serves to indicate where the next character to be entered on the keyboard will appear. **2** the transparent movable part of a measuring device, especially a slide rule, which can be set at any point along the graduated scale. ⓘ 16c in sense 2; 13c in obsolete sense 'runner': from Latin *cursor* runner, from *currere* to run.

cursory /ˈkɜːsərɪ/ ▻ *adj* hasty; superficial; not thorough. ● **cursorily** /ˈkɜːsərəlɪ/ *adverb*. ⓘ 17c: from Latin *cursorius* pertaining to a runner, from *currere* to run.

cursus honorum /ˈkɜːsəs ɒnˈoʊrəm/ ▻ *noun, historical* in ancient Rome: the ordered career structure which was normal for anyone who aspired to high public office.

curt ▻ *adj* **1** rudely brief; dismissive; abrupt. **2** concise. ● **curtly** *adverb*. ● **curtness** *noun*. ⓘ 17c: from Latin *curtus* cut or broken.

curtail /kɜːˈteɪl, kə-/ ▻ *verb* (*curtailed*, *curtailing*) to reduce; to cut short. ● **curtailer** *noun*. ● **curtailment** *noun*. ⓘ 16c: as *curtal* something docked or shortened, from Latin *curtus* short; changed due to association with TAIL and perhaps later with French *tailler* to cut.

curtain /ˈkɜːtən/ ▻ *noun* **1** a hanging cloth over a window, round a bed, etc for privacy or to exclude light. **2** *theat* a hanging cloth in front of the stage to screen it from the auditorium. **3** *theat* (*often* **the curtain**) the rise of the curtain at the beginning, or fall of the curtain at the end, of a stage performance, act, scene, etc. **4** something resembling a curtain □ *a curtain of thick dark hair.* **5** (**curtains**) *colloq* the end; death. ▻ *verb* (*curtained*, *curtaining*) **1** (*often* **curtain something off**) to surround or enclose it with a curtain. **2** to supply (windows, etc) with curtains. ● **curtain up** the beginning of a theatre performance. ⓘ 13c: from French *courtine*, from Latin *cortina*.

curtain call ▻ *noun* an audience's demand for performers to appear in front of the curtain after it has fallen, to receive further applause.

curtain-raiser ▻ *noun* **1** *theat* a short play, etc before the main performance. **2** any introductory event.

curtain wall ▻ *noun* **1** *archit* an external wall that is not load-bearing. **2** *fortification* in medieval architecture: a wall between two towers or bastions.

curtsy or **curtsey** /ˈkɜːtsɪ/ ▻ *noun* (*curtsies* or *curtseys*) a slight bend of the knees with one leg behind the other, performed as a formal gesture of respect by women. ▻ *verb* (*curtsies*, *curtsied*, *curtsying*) *intr* to perform a curtsy. ⓘ 16c: variant of COURTESY.

curvaceous /kɜːˈveɪʃəs/ ▻ *adj, colloq* said of a woman: having a shapely figure.

curvature /ˈkɜːvətʃə(r)/ ▻ *noun* **1** an act of curving or bending. **2 a** the condition of being curved; **b** the degree of curvedness. ⓘ 17c: from Latin *curvatura*, from *curvare* to bend.

curve /kɜːv/ ▻ *noun* **1** a line no part of which is straight, or a surface no part of which is flat, eg part of a circle or sphere. **2** any smoothly arched line or shape, like part of a circle or sphere. **3** (**curves**) *colloq* the rounded contours and shapes of a woman's body. **4** any line representing measurable data, eg birth-rate on a graph. **5** *math* any line (including a straight line) representing a series of points whose co-ordinates satisfy a particular equation. ▻ *verb* (*curved*, *curving*) *tr & intr* to form or form into a curve; to move in a curve. ⓘ 16c: from Latin *curvare*, from *curvus* crooked.

curvy ▻ *adj* (*curvier*, *curviest*) **1** having many curves, or curved in shape. **2** said of a woman: having a shapely figure.

curvilinear /kɜːvɪˈlɪnɪə(r)/ ▷ *adj* consisting of or bounded by a curved line. ⓘ 18c: from CURVE + Latin *linea* line.

Cushing's syndrome /ˈkʊʃɪŋz —/ ▷ *noun, pathol* a condition characterized by obesity, raised blood pressure, acne, OSTEOPOROSIS and weakness, caused by the presence of excess amounts of CORTICOSTEROID hormones in the body. ⓘ 1932: named after the US surgeon Harvey Cushing (1869–1939) who first described it.

cushion /ˈkʊʃən/ ▷ *noun* **1** a fabric case stuffed with soft material, used for making a seat comfortable, for kneeling on, etc. **2** a thick pad or something having a similar function. **3** something that gives protection from shock, reduces unpleasant effects, etc. **4** the resilient inner rim of a billiard table. ▷ *verb* (***cushioned***, ***cushioning***) **1** to reduce the unpleasant or violent effect of something. **2** to protect from shock, injury or the extremes of distress. **3** to provide or furnish with cushions. ⓘ 14c: from French *cuissin*, ultimately from Latin *coxa* hip.

Cushitic languages /kʊˈʃɪtɪk —/ ▷ *noun* a group of about 30 Afro-Asiatic languages, spoken by c.13m people in Somalia, Kenya, Sudan and Ethiopia, the most widely spoken being Oromo (or Gassa) and Somali.

cushy /ˈkʊʃɪ/ ▷ *adj* (***cushier***, ***cushiest***) *colloq* comfortable; easy; undemanding. ● **cushiness** *noun*. ⓘ 20c: from Hindi *khush* pleasant.

cusp ▷ *noun* **1** *geom* a point formed by the meeting of two curves, corresponding to the point where the two tangents coincide. **2** *astron* either point of a crescent Moon. **3** *anatomy* a sharp raised point on the grinding surface of a molar tooth. **4** *astrol* the point of transition between one sign of the zodiac and the next. **5** *archit* a projecting point found between arcs in Gothic TRACERY. ● **cuspate** *adj*. ⓘ 16c: from Latin *cuspis* point.

cuss *old use, colloq* ▷ *noun* **1** a curse. **2** a person or animal, especially if stubborn. ▷ *verb* (***cusses***, ***cussed***, ***cussing***) *tr & intr* to curse or swear. ⓘ 19c: originally a vulgar pronunciation of CURSE.

cussed /ˈkʌsɪd/ ▷ *adj* **1** obstinate, stubborn, awkward or perverse. **2** cursed. ● **cussedly** *adverb*. ● **cussedness** *noun*.

custard /ˈkʌstəd/ ▷ *noun* **1** a sauce made with sugar, milk and cornflour. **2** (*also* **egg custard**) a baked dish or sauce of eggs and sweetened milk. ⓘ 15c: as *custade*, altered from *crustade* pie with a crust.

custard apple see PAPAW

custodial /kʌˈstoʊdɪəl/ ▷ *adj* relating to custody; involving custody.

custodian /kʌˈstoʊdɪən/ ▷ *noun* someone who has care of something, eg a public building or ancient monument; a guardian or curator. ● **custodianship** *noun*. ⓘ 18c: from Latin *custodia* watch or watchman.

custody /ˈkʌstədɪ/ ▷ *noun* (***custodies***) **1** protective care, especially the guardianship of a child, awarded to someone by a court of law. **2** the condition of being held by the police; arrest or imprisonment. ● **take someone into custody** to arrest them. ⓘ 15c: from Latin *custodia* watch, from *custos* guardian.

custom /ˈkʌstəm/ ▷ *noun* **1** a traditional activity or practice. **2** a personal habit. **3** the body of established practices of a community; convention. **4** an established practice having the force of a law. **5** the trade or business that one gives to a shop, etc by regular purchases. ▷ *adj* made to order. ⓘ 12c: from French *costume*, from Latin *consuetudo*, from *consuescere* to grow accustomed to.

customary /ˈkʌstəmərɪ/ ▷ *adj* usual; traditional; according to custom. ● **customarily** *adverb*.

custom-built and **custom-made** ▷ *adj* built or made to an individual customer's requirements □ *custom-built car*.

customer /ˈkʌstəmə(r)/ ▷ *noun* **1** someone who purchases goods from a shop, uses the services of a business, etc. **2** *colloq* someone with whom one has to deal, usually with unfavourable implications. □ *an awkward customer*.

custom house ▷ *noun* the office at a port, etc where customs duties are paid or collected.

customs ▷ *plural noun* taxes or duties paid on imports. ▷ *singular noun* **1** the government department that collects these taxes. **2** the place at a port, airport, frontier, etc where baggage is inspected for goods on which duty must be paid and illegal goods.

customs union ▷ *noun* an economic agreement by which nations adopt common excise duties, so eliminating the need for customs checks along their common frontiers and creating a free trade area.

cut ▷ *verb* (***cut***, ***cutting***) **1** *tr & intr* (*also* **cut something off** or **out**) to slit, pierce, slice or sever (a person or thing) using a sharp instrument. **2** (*often* **cut something up**) to divide something by cutting. **3** to trim (hair, nails, etc). **4** to reap or mow (corn, grass, etc). **5** to prune (flowers or plants). **6** (*sometimes* **cut something out**) to make or form it by cutting. **7** to shape the surface of (a gem) into facets, or decorate (glass) by cutting. **8** to shape the pieces of (a garment) □ *He cuts clothes so that they hang perfectly.* **9** to make (a sound recording). **10** to injure or wound with a sharp edge or instrument. **11** to hurt □ *cut someone to the heart.* **12** to reduce (eg prices, wages, interest rates, working hours, etc). **13** to shorten or abridge (eg a book or play). **14** to delete or omit. **15** to edit (a film). **16** *intr* to stop filming. **17** *intr, cinema* said of a film or camera: to change directly to another shot, etc. **18** *math* to cross or intersect. **19** to reject or renounce □ *cut one's links with one's family.* **20** *informal* to ignore or pretend not to recognize someone. **21** to stop □ *The alcoholic was told to cut his drinking or risk serious liver damage.* **22** *informal* to absent oneself from something □ *cut classes.* **23** to switch off (an engine, etc). **24** *cricket* to hit (a ball) with a slicing action, causing it to spin or swerve. **25** said of a baby: to grow (teeth). **26** *intr* (*usually* **cut across** or **through**) to go off in a certain direction; to take a short route. **27** to dilute (eg an alcoholic drink) or adulterate (a drug) □ *John cuts his whisky with ginger ale.* **28** to divide; to partition □ *a room cut in half by a bookcase.* ▷ *noun* **1** an act of cutting; a cutting movement or stroke. **2** a slit, incision or injury made by cutting. **3** a reduction. **4** a deleted passage in a play, etc. **5** the stoppage of an electricity supply, etc. **6** *slang* one's share of the profits. **7** a piece of meat cut from an animal. **8** the style in which clothes or hair are cut. **9** a sarcastic remark. **10** a refusal to recognize someone; a snub. **11** a short cut. **12** a channel, passage or canal. ● **a cut above something** *colloq* superior to it. ● **cut and dried** decided; definite; settled beforehand. ● **cut and run** *colloq* to escape smartly. ● **cut and thrust** aggressive competition; quick verbal exchange or repartee. ● **cut both ways** to have advantages and disadvantages; to bear out both sides of an argument. ● **cut someone dead** to ignore them completely. ● **cut it fine** *colloq* to have or leave barely enough time, space, etc for something. ● **cut it out** *slang* to stop doing something bad or undesirable. ● **cut out for** or **to be something** having the qualities needed for it. ● **cut something short** to reduce or shorten it. ● **cut someone short** to silence them by interrupting. ● **cut up** *colloq* distressed; upset. ● **cut up rough** *colloq* to get angry and violent. ● **cut a long story short** to come straight to the point. ● **half cut** *Brit slang* drunk. ⓘ 13c as *cutten*.

■ **cut across something** **1** to go against (normal procedure, etc). **2** said of an issue, etc: to be more important than, or transcend (the barriers or divisions between parties, etc). **3** to take a short cut through it, eg a field, etc.

■ **cut back on something** to reduce spending, etc. See also CUTBACK.

■ **cut something down** to fell a tree, etc.

■ **cut down on something** to reduce one's use of it; to do less of it.

■ **cut in 1** to interrupt. **2** said of a vehicle: to overtake and squeeze in front of another vehicle.

■ **cut something off 1** to separate or isolate it. **2** to stop (the supply of gas, electricity, etc). **3** to stop it or cut it short. See also CUT-OFF.

■ **cut someone off** to disconnect them during a telephone call.

■ **cut out 1** said of an engine, etc: to stop working. **2** said of an electrical device: to switch off or stop automatically, usually as a safety precaution. See also CUT-OUT.

■ **cut something out 1** to remove or delete it. **2** to clip pictures, etc out of a magazine, etc. **3** *colloq* to stop doing it. **4** to exclude it from consideration. **5** to block out the light or view. See also CUT-OUT.

■ **cut someone up** said of the driver of a vehicle: to drive in front of (another vehicle) in a dangerous manner.

cutaway ▷ *adj* **1** said of a diagram, etc: having outer parts omitted so as to show the interior. **2** said of a coat: with the front part cut away from below the waist. ▷ *noun, film-making* a move away from the main action of the scene.

cutback ▷ *noun* a reduction in spending, use of resources, etc. See also CUT BACK at CUT.

cute ▷ *adj, colloq* **1** attractive; pretty. **2** clever; cunning; shrewd. ● **cutely** *adverb*. ● **cuteness** *noun*. Ⓒ 18c: shortened from ACUTE.

cut glass ▷ *noun* glassware decorated with patterns cut into its surface.

cuticle /'kjuːtɪkəl/ ▷ *noun* **1** *anatomy* the EPIDERMIS, especially the outer layer of cells in hair, and the dead hardened skin at the base of fingernails and toenails. **2** *bot* the waxy, waterproof, protective layer that covers all the parts of a plant exposed to the air, except for the STOMATA. **3** *zool* the protective layer of horny non-cellular material that covers the EPIDERMIS of many invertebrates, and forms the EXOSKELETONS of ARTHROPODS. ● **cuticular** /kjuː'tɪkjʊlə(r)/ *adj*. Ⓒ 17c: from Latin *cuticula*, diminutive of *cutis* skin.

cutis /'kjuːtɪs/ ▷ *noun* the anatomical name for the skin. Ⓒ 17c: Latin.

cutlass /'kʌtləs/ ▷ *noun* (**cutlasses**) *historical* a short, broad, slightly curved sword with one cutting edge. Ⓒ 16c: from French *coutelas*, from Latin *cultellus*, diminutive of *culter* knife.

cutler /'kʌtlə(r)/ ▷ *noun* someone who manufactures and sells cutlery. Ⓒ 14c: from French *coutelier*, ultimately from Latin *culter* knife.

cutlery /'kʌtlərɪ/ ▷ *noun* **1** knives, forks and spoons used to eat food. **2** implements for cutting in general. **3** the business of a cutler.

cutlet /'kʌtlət/ ▷ *noun* **1 a** a small piece of meat with a bone attached, usually cut from a rib or the neck; **b** a piece of food in this shape, not necessarily containing meat □ *nut cutlet*. **2** a slice of veal. **3** a rissole of minced meat or flaked fish. Ⓒ 18c: from French *costelette*, diminutive of *coste* rib.

cut-off ▷ *noun* **1** the point at which something is cut off or separated. **2** a stopping of a flow or supply. **3** (**cutoffs**) *colloq* shorts which have been made by cutting jeans to above the knee, usually leaving the edges frayed. See also CUT OFF at CUT.

cut-out ▷ *noun* **1** something which has been cut out of something else, eg a newspaper clipping. **2** a safety device for breaking an electrical circuit. See also CUT OUT at CUT.

cutter[1] ▷ *noun* a person or thing that cuts.

cutter[2] ▷ *noun* **1** a small single-masted sailing ship. **2** a ship's boat, usually powered by sail or oars. **3** a motor launch, sometimes armed. Ⓒ 18c.

cut-throat ▷ *adj* **1** said of competition, etc: very keen and aggressive. **2** murderous. **3** said of a card game: played by three people. ▷ *noun* **1** a murderer. **2** (*also* **cut-throat razor**) a long-bladed razor that folds into its handle.

cutting ▷ *noun* **1** an extract, article or picture cut from a newspaper, etc. **2** *hortic* a piece cut from a plant for rooting or grafting. **3** a narrow excavation made through high ground for a road or railway. ▷ *adj* **1** hurtful; sarcastic □ *a cutting comment*. **2** said of wind: penetrating.

cutting edge ▷ *noun* a part or area (of an organization, branch of study, etc) that breaks new ground, effects change and development, etc □ *That magazine is always on the cutting edge.*

cuttlebone ▷ *noun* the internal shell of the cuttlefish, often used to supplement the diet of cagebirds, or as a polishing material, etc.

cuttlefish ▷ *noun* any of numerous species of mollusc related to the squid and octopus, which have a shield-shaped body containing an inner chalky plate, and a small head bearing eight arms and two long tentacles. Ⓒ Anglo-Saxon *cudele* + FISH.

cutwater ▷ *noun* **1** the sharp vertical front edge of a ship's prow. **2** a pointed projection at the base of a bridge support.

CV or **cv** ▷ *abbreviation* (**CVs**) curriculum vitae.

cv ▷ *abbreviation* cultivar.

CVA ▷ *abbreviation* cerebrovascular accident, such as a brain haemorrhage.

CVO ▷ *abbreviation* Commander of the (Royal) Victorian Order.

CVS ▷ *abbreviation* chorionic villus sampling.

cwm /kuːm/ ▷ *noun* **1** in Wales: a valley. **2** *geol* a CIRQUE. Ⓒ 19c: Welsh.

CWS ▷ *abbreviation* Co-operative Wholesale Society.

cwt ▷ *abbreviation* hundredweight.

CY ▷ *abbreviation, IVR* Cyprus.

cyan /'saɪən, 'saɪan/ ▷ *noun* **1** a greenish blue colour. **2** *printing* a blue ink used as a primary colour. ▷ *adj* cyan-coloured. Ⓒ 19c: from Greek *kyanos* blue.

cyanide /'saɪənaɪd/ ▷ *noun* **1** any of the poisonous salts of hydrocyanic acid, which contain the CN^- ion and smell of bitter almonds, especially potassium cyanide and sodium cyanide, which are extremely toxic and rapidly cause death. **2** the negatively charged CN^- ion, which is highly poisonous because of its ability to prevent uptake of oxygen by the respiratory pigment haemoglobin in the blood. Ⓒ 19c: CYAN + -IDE.

cyanite see KYANITE

cyano- /'saɪənoʊ, saɪ'anoʊ/ or (before a vowel) **cyan-** /saɪ'an/ ▷ *combining form, denoting* **1** blue or dark blue. **2** cyanide. **3** cyanogen. Ⓒ From Greek *kyanos* blue.

cyanobacteria ▷ *plural noun* blue-green algae. Ⓒ 1970s: CYANO- 1 + BACTERIA.

cyanocobalamin /saɪənoʊkoʊ'baləmɪn/ ▷ *noun* VITAMIN B_{12}. Ⓒ 20c: from CYANIDE + COBALT + VITAMIN.

cyanogen /saɪ'anədʒɛn/ ▷ *noun, chem* (formula NCCN) a compound of carbon and nitrogen, consisting of a colourless inflammable poisonous gas with a smell of bitter almonds. Ⓒ 19c: from French *cyanogène*.

cyanosis /saɪə'noʊsɪs/ ▷ *noun, pathol* a bluish discoloration of the skin usually caused by lack of oxygen in the blood. ● **cyanosed** *adj* said of the skin: showing symptoms typical of cyanosis. ● **cyanotic** /-'nɒtɪk/ *adj*. Ⓒ 19c.

cyber- ▷ *combining form denoting* computers or computer networks, especially the INTERNET □ *cyberspace* □ *cybercafé* □ *cyberbabble*. Ⓒ From cybernetic.

cybercafé ▷ *noun* a café equipped with Internet terminals. ⓒ 1990s.

cybernetics /saɪbəˈnɛtɪks/ ▷ *singular noun* the comparative study of communication and automatic control processes in mechanical or electronic systems, eg machines or computers, and biological systems, eg the nervous system of animals, especially humans. ● **cybernetic** *adj*. ⓒ 1940s: from Greek *kybernetes* steersman.

cyberpet ▷ *noun* an electronic device that simulates the behaviour and requirements of a pet. Also called **virtual pet.** ⓒ 1990s.

cyberpunk ▷ *noun* a genre of science fiction depicting a society rigidly controlled by computer networks and the actions of hackers who rebel against it. ⓒ 20c: from CYBER- + PUNK 1.

cybersex ▷ *noun* sexual activity or information available through computer networks. ⓒ 1990s.

cyberspace ▷ *noun* **1** the three-dimensional artificial environment of virtual reality, generated by computer, that gives the user the impression of actually being within the environment and physically interacting with it. See also VIRTUAL REALITY. **2** the space in which electronic communication takes place over computer networks. ⓒ 20c: from CYBER- + SPACE.

cycad /ˈsaɪkad/ ▷ *noun* a tropical or subtropical GYMNOSPERM, more closely resembling a palm than a conifer, with an unbranched trunk covered with the remains of old leaf bases and a crown of tough leathery leaves. ⓒ 19c: from Latin *cycas*, from Greek *kykas* a scribal error for *koikas*, from *koix* Egyptian doum-palm.

cyclamate /ˈsɪkləmeɪt, ˈsaɪ-/ ▷ *noun* (***cyclamates***) any of a number of sweet chemical compounds formerly used as sweetening agents. ⓒ 20c: from *cyclo*hexylsulph*amate*, an invented chemical name.

cyclamen /ˈsɪkləmən/ ▷ *noun* **1** a perennial plant with heart-shaped leaves growing from a corm, and white, pink or red flowers with turned-back petals. **2** a dark reddish-purple colour, characteristic of the pink or red cyclamen. ▷ *adj* cyclamen-coloured. ⓒ 16c: Latin, from Greek *kyklaminos*, probably from *kyklos* circle, in reference to the bulbous roots.

cycle /ˈsaɪkəl/ ▷ *noun* **1** a constantly repeating series of events or processes. **2** a recurring period of years; an age. **3** *physics* one of a regularly repeated set of similar changes, eg in the movement of a wave, with the duration of one cycle being equal to the PERIOD (*noun* 10) of the motion, and the rate at which a cycle is repeated per unit time being equal to its FREQUENCY (*noun* 3). **4** a series of poems, songs, plays, etc centred on a particular person or happening. **5** short for **a** BICYCLE; **b** MOTORCYCLE; **c** TRICYCLE. ▷ *verb* (***cycled***, ***cycling***) **1** *tr & intr* to ride a bicycle. **2** *intr* to happen in cycles. ⓒ 14c: from Greek *kyklos* circle.

cycle path and **cycleway** ▷ *noun, chiefly Brit* a BIKEWAY

cyclic /ˈsaɪklɪk, ˈsɪklɪk/ and **cyclical** ▷ *adj* **1** relating to, containing, or moving in a cycle. **2** recurring in cycles. **3** arranged in a ring or rings. **4** *chem* an organic chemical compound whose molecules contain one or more closed rings of atoms, eg benzene. ● **cyclically** *adverb*.

cyclist /ˈsaɪklɪst/ ▷ *noun* the rider of a bicycle, motorcycle, etc.

cyclo- /saɪkloʊ/ or (*before a vowel*) **cycl-** ▷ *combining form, denoting* **1** circle; ring; cycle □ *cyclometer*. **2** *chem* cyclic compound □ *cyclopropane*. **3** bicycle. ⓒ From Greek *kyklos* circle.

cyclo-cross ▷ *noun* a cross-country bicycle race, during which the bicycles have to be carried over natural obstacles. ⓒ 20c.

cycloid /ˈsaɪklɔɪd/ ▷ *noun, geom* the curve traced by a point on the circumference of a circle as the circle rolls along a straight line. ▷ *adj* resembling a circle. ● **cycloidal** *adj*.

cyclometer /saɪˈklɒmɪtə(r)/ ▷ *noun* a device for recording the revolutions of a wheel, used on a bicycle to measure the distance travelled. ⓒ 19c.

cyclone /ˈsaɪkloʊn/ ▷ *noun* **1** *meteorol* (*also* **depression** or **low**) an area of low atmospheric pressure, often associated with stormy weather, in which winds spiral inward towards a central low, blowing in an anticlockwise direction in the northern hemisphere and a clockwise direction in the southern hemisphere. Compare ANTICYCLONE. **2** a violent tropical storm accompanied by torrential rain and extremely strong winds, often causing widespread destruction. ● **cyclonic** /saɪˈklɒnɪk/ *adj*. ● **cyclonically** *adverb*. ⓒ 19c: from Greek *kyklon* a whirling round.

cyclopedia or **cyclopaedia** /saɪkloʊˈpiːdɪə/ ▷ *noun* (***cyclopedias***) an ENCYCLOPEDIA.

cyclopropane ▷ *noun* a colourless hydrocarbon, often used as an anaesthetic. ⓒ 19c.

cyclorama /saɪkləˈrɑːmə/ ▷ *noun* (***cycloramas***) **1** a large picture painted on to a cylindrical wall which is designed so that people viewing it from the middle ot the room see it in its natural perspective. **2** in theatre scenery: a curved background stretching along the back of the stage which is painted so as to represent the sky, thus giving the impression of distance. ⓒ 19c: from CYCLO- 1 + Greek *horama* view.

cyclostyle /ˈsaɪkloʊstaɪl/ ▷ *noun* (***cyclostyles***) **1** a pen with a small toothed wheel attached to it, which cuts holes into a specially prepared stencil. **2** a duplicating machine that reproduces copies from such a stencil. ▷ *verb* (***cyclostyled, cyclostyling***) to reproduce by means of a such a stencil. ⓒ 19c: from CYCLO-1 + Latin *stylus* writing tool.

cyclotron /ˈsaɪkloʊtrɒn/ ▷ *noun, physics* a circular type of PARTICLE ACCELERATOR. ⓒ 20c.

cyder see CIDER

cygnet /ˈsɪgnət/ ▷ *noun* a young swan. See also COB[1] (sense 2), PEN[4]. ⓒ 15c: from Latin *cygnus* swan.

Cygnus /ˈsɪgnəs/ ▷ *noun, astron* a large northern constellation that contains *Cygnus A*, a double galaxy that is one of the strongest radio sources in the sky, and *Cygnus X-1*, an intense X-ray source. Also called **the Swan**.

cylinder /ˈsɪlɪndə(r)/ ▷ *noun* **1** *geom* a solid figure of uniform circular cross-section, in which the curved surface is at right angles to the base. **2** a container, machine part or other object of this shape, eg a storage container for compressed gas. **3** *engineering* in an internal combustion engine: the tubular cylinder within which the chemical energy of the burning fuel is converted to the mechanical energy of a moving piston. ⓒ 16c: from Latin *cylindrus*, from Greek *kylindros* roller, from *kylindein* to roll.

cylindrical /sɪˈlɪndrɪkəl/ or **cylindric** ▷ *adj* shaped like a cylinder. ● **cylindrically** *adverb*.

cyma /ˈsaɪmə/ and **cymatium** /saɪˈmeɪtɪəm/ ▷ *noun* (***cymas, cymae*** /-miː/ or ***cymatiums***) in classical orders of architecture: an OGEE moulding of the cornice. ⓒ 16c: Latin, from Greek *kyma* a billow.

cymatics /saɪˈmatɪks/ ▷ *singular noun, alternative medicine* the therapeutic use of high-frequency sound waves.

cymbal /ˈsɪmbəl/ ▷ *noun* a thin plate-like brass percussion instrument, either beaten with a drumstick, or used as one of a pair that are struck together to produce a ringing clash. ● **cymbalist** *noun*. ⓒ 9c: from Latin *cymbalum*, from Greek *kymbalon*, from *kymbe* something hollow.

cymbidium /sɪmˈbɪdɪəm/ ▷ *noun* (***cybidiums***) *bot* an orchid native to tropical forests which is widely cultivated for its large showy flowers. ⓘ 19c: from Latin *cymba* boat.

cyme /saɪm/ ▷ *noun, bot* an INFLORESCENCE in which the main stem and each of its branches ends in a flower, and all subsequent flowers develop from lateral buds arising below the apical flowers. • **cymose** *adj.* ⓘ 18c: from Latin *cyma*, from Greek *kyma* wave.

Cymric /ˈkʌmrɪk, ˈkɪmrɪk/ ▷ *adj* belonging or relating to Wales, its inhabitants or their language. ⓘ 19c: from Welsh *Cymru* Wales.

cynic /ˈsɪnɪk/ ▷ *noun* **1** someone who takes a pessimistic view of human goodness or sincerity. **2** (**Cynic**) *philos* a member of a sect of ancient Greek philosophers who scorned wealth and enjoyment of life. ▷ *adj* another word for CYNICAL. ⓘ 16c: from Latin *cynicus*, from Greek *kynikos* dog-like, from *kyon, kynos* dog.

cynical /ˈsɪnɪkəl/ ▷ *adj* disinclined to believe in the goodness or sincerity of others. • **cynically** *adverb.*

cynical, sceptical

Note that a **cynical** person is suspicious of apparently good things and people, whereas a person who is **sceptical** about something is cautious about believing or accepting it.

cynicism /ˈsɪnɪsɪzəm/ ▷ *noun* **1** the attitude, beliefs or behaviour of a cynic. **2** a cynical act, remark, etc.

cynosure /ˈsaɪnəʃʊə(r)/ ▷ *noun* **1** the focus of attention; the centre of attraction. **2** something which acts as a guide. ⓘ 16c: from Greek *Kynosoura* dog's tail, ie the Ursa Minor constellation, used as a guide by sailors.

cypher see CIPHER

cypress /ˈsaɪprəs/ ▷ *noun* **1 a** a slim, dark-green coniferous tree, sometimes associated with death and mourning; **b** the wood of this tree. **2** a branch or sprig of cypress carried as a symbol of mourning at a funeral. **3** any similar kind of tree. ⓘ 13c: from French *cypres*, from Latin *cypressus*, from Greek *kyparissos*.

Cypriot /ˈsɪprɪət/ ▷ *adj* belonging or relating to Cyprus, an island republic in the NE Mediterranean, its inhabitants, or their dialect. ▷ *noun* **1** a citizen or inhabitant of, or person born in, Cyprus. **2** the dialect of Greek spoken in Cyprus.

Cyrillic /səˈrɪlɪk, sɪ-/ ▷ *adj* belonging or relating to the alphabet used for Russian, Bulgarian and other Slavonic languages. ⓘ 19c: named after St Cyril who was said to have devised it.

cyst /sɪst/ ▷ *noun* **1** *pathol* an abnormal sac that contains fluid, semi-solid material or gas. **2** *anatomy* any normal sac or closed cavity. **3** *biol* a tough outer membrane which surrounds certain organisms, eg bacteria, protozoa, etc, during the resting stage in their life cycle, thus protecting them from unfavourable environmental conditions. ⓘ 18c: from Greek *kystis* bladder or pouch.

cysteine /ˈsɪstɪiːn, -ɪn/ ▷ *noun, biochem* an amino acid found in many proteins.

cystic ▷ *adj* **1** relating to or like a cyst. **2** being enclosed within or having a cyst. **3** belonging or relating to the gall bladder or urinary bladder.

cystic fibrosis ▷ *noun, pathol* a hereditary disease in which the exocrine glands (see EXOCRINE *adj* 2) produce abnormally thick mucus that blocks the bronchi, pancreas and intestinal glands, causing recurring bronchitis and other respiratory problems.

cystine /ˈsɪstiːn/ ▷ *noun, biochem* an amino acid that is found in proteins, especially KERATIN.

cystitis /sɪˈstaɪtɪs/ ▷ *noun, pathol* inflammation of the urinary bladder which is usually caused by bacterial infection and is characterized by a desire to pass urine frequently, and pain or a burning sensation when passing urine.

-cyte /saɪt/ ▷ *combining form, denoting* a cell □ ***erythrocyte*** □ ***lymphocyte.*** ⓘ From Greek *kytos* vessel.

cyto- /ˈsaɪtoʊ/ ▷ *combining form, denoting* a cell □ *cytoplasm.* ⓘ From Greek *kytos* vessel.

cytochrome ▷ *noun, biochem* in the cells of living organisms: any of a group of substances that play an important role in the breakdown of carbohydrates to release energy. ⓘ 20c.

cytogenetics ▷ *singular noun, genetics* the scientific study of the relationship between inheritance and cell structure, especially the origin, structure and function of CHROMOSOMES, and their effects on inheritance in populations. ⓘ 20c.

cytokinesis ▷ *noun, genetics* during the last stages of MITOSIS: the division of the CYTOPLASM of the cell into two parts, resulting in the formation of two daughter cells.

cytokinin /saɪtoʊˈkaɪnɪn/ ▷ *noun, bot* KININ. ⓘ 20c.

cytology /saɪˈtɒlədʒɪ/ ▷ *noun* **1** the scientific study of the structure and function of individual cells, especially as revealed by examination with a microscope. **2** the detailed structure of a particular plant or animal tissue as revealed by examination with a microscope. • **cytological** *adj.* • **cytologist** *noun.* ⓘ 19c.

cytoplasm /ˈsaɪtoʊplazəm/ ▷ *noun, biol* the part of a living cell, excluding the NUCLEUS (sense 2), that is enclosed by the cell membrane and which contains a range of ORGANELLES. • **cytoplasmic** /-ˈplasmɪk/ *adj.* ⓘ 19c: from CYTO- + Greek *plasma* body.

cytosine /ˈsaɪtoʊsiːn/ ▷ *noun, biochem* a base, derived from PYRIMIDINE, which is one of the four bases found in NUCLEIC ACID. See also ADENINE, GUANINE, THYMINE. ⓘ 19c.

cytoskeleton ▷ *noun, biol* in the cytoplasm of a living cell: a network of protein filaments that forms the structural framework of the cell, and is also responsible for the movement of cytoplasm from one part of the cell to another.

cytosol /ˈsaɪtoʊsɒl/ ▷ *noun, biol* the soluble component of the cytoplasm.

cytotoxic ▷ *adj, biol* describing any agent, especially a drug, that destroys or prevents the division of cells, and is used in chemotherapy to treat various forms of cancer. ⓘ 20c.

cytotoxin ▷ *noun* any substance that has a destructive effect on living cells. ⓘ 20c.

czar, *etc* see TSAR, *etc*

Czech /tʃɛk/ ▷ *adj* **a** belonging or relating to the Czech Republic, a landlocked republic in E Europe, or to its inhabitants or their language; **b** *formerly, from 1918 to 1993* belonging or relating to Czechoslovakia, its inhabitants, or their language; **c** *historical* belonging or relating to Bohemia or Moravia, their inhabitants, or their language. ▷ *noun* **1 a** a citizen or inhabitant of, or person born in, the Czech Republic; **b** *formerly* a citizen or inhabitant of, or person born in, Czechoslovakia; **c** an inhabitant of, or person born in, Bohemia or Moravia. **2** the official language of the Czech Republic. ⓘ 19c: Polish.

D

D[1] or **d** /diː/ ▷ *noun* (*Ds, D's* or *d's*) **1** the fourth letter of the English alphabet. **2** (**D**) *music* **a** the second note on the scale of C major; **b** the musical key which has this note as its base. **3** (*usually* **D**) the fourth highest grade or quality, or the mark indicating this. **4** (**D**) the D-shaped mark on a billiards table.

D[2] ▷ *abbreviation* **1** *especially US* Democrat. **2** *IVR*: *Deutschland* (German), Germany. **3** *cards* diamonds. **4** *physics* electric displacement. See also 3-D (at THREE).

D[3] ▷ *symbol* **1** the Roman numeral for 500. **2** *chem* deuterium.

d ▷ *abbreviation* **1** daughter. **2** day. **3** dead. **4** deci-. **5** degree. **6** delete. **7** *denarius* (Latin), (in the UK before 1971) a penny, or pence. Compare S. **8** depth. **9** diameter. **10** died.

'd ▷ *contraction* **1** would □ ***I'd go tomorrow.*** **2** had □ ***He'd gone yesterday.*** **3** *colloq* did □ ***Where'd they go?***

DA[1] ▷ *noun* (*DAs* or *DA's*) *especially US* District Attorney.

DA[2] ▷ *abbreviation* **1** Diploma in Anaesthetics. **2** Diploma of Art.

da ▷ *abbreviation* deca-.

dab[1] ▷ *verb* (***dabbed, dabbing***) *tr & intr* (*often* **dab at something**) to touch something lightly and usually repeatedly with a cloth, etc. ▷ *noun* **1** a small amount of something creamy or liquid. **2** a light gentle touch. **3** a gentle blow. **4** (**dabs**) *slang* fingerprints. ⊙ 14c as *verb dabben*; probably imitating the sound.

■ **dab something on** or **off** to spread it on or to remove it with light touches of a cloth, etc.

dab[2] ▷ *noun* a small brown European flatfish with rough scales. ⊙ 15c: from French *dabbe*.

dab[3] ▷ *noun* (*usually* **a dab hand at** or **with something**) an expert. ⊙ 17c as *dab*; 19c as *dab hand*.

dabble /'dabəl/ ▷ *verb* (***dabbled, dabbling***) **1** *tr & intr* to move or shake (one's hand, foot, etc) about in water, especially playfully. **2** *intr* (*often* **dabble at, in** or **with something**) to do something or study something without serious effort. ▷ *noun* an act of dabbling. • **dabbler** *noun* someone who dabbles in some activity. • **dabbling** *adj, noun*. • **dabblingly** *adverb*. ⊙ 16c: from DAB[1] or Dutch *dabbelen*.

dabchick ▷ *noun* the LITTLE GREBE.

da capo /dɑː 'kɑːpoʊ/ *music* ▷ *adverb* (abbreviation **DC**) an indication to the performer to go back to the beginning of the piece. Also *as adj* □ ***the da capo sign.*** ▷ *noun* (***da capos*** or ***da capi*** /-piː/) a da capo sign, instruction or section. ⊙ 18c: Italian, meaning 'from the beginning'.

dace ▷ *noun* (*dace* or *daces*) a small European river fish. ⊙ 15c: from French *dars* dart.

dacha /'dɑːtʃə/ ▷ *noun* (*dachas*) a country house or cottage in various parts of the former Soviet Union, especially but not exclusively one provided for the use of a person of importance. ⊙ 19c: Russian, from *dach*, originally meaning 'gift', especially one from a ruler.

dachshund /'daksənd, 'dakshʊnt, 'daʃhʊnd/ ▷ *noun* (***dachshunds***) a small breed of dog with a long body and very short legs. ⊙ 19c: German, from *Dachs* badger + *Hund* dog.

dacoit or **dakoit** /də'kɔɪt/ ▷ *noun* a member of a gang of armed robbers or bandits in India or Burma, especially in the 18c and 19c. • **dacoity** *noun* violent robbery by dacoits. ⊙ 18c: from Hindi *dakait* robber.

Dacron /'dakrɒn, 'deɪ-/ ▷ *noun, US trademark* TERYLENE. ⊙ 1950s.

dactyl /'daktɪl/ ▷ *noun, poetry* a metrical foot consisting of one long or stressed syllable followed by two short or unstressed ones. • **dactylic** /dak'tɪlɪk/ *adj*. • **dactylically** *adverb*. ⊙ 14c: from Greek *daktylos* finger, from the similarity between the lengths of the syllables in a dactyl and the lengths of the bones in a finger (one long and two short).

dad ▷ *noun, colloq* father. ⊙ 16c: from the sound *da da* made by a baby.

Dada /'dɑːdɑː/ and **Dadaism** /'dɑːdɑːɪzəm/ *art & literature* ▷ *noun* a short-lived movement, from 1916 to c.1920, which aimed to abandon all form and throw off all tradition. • **Dadaist** /'dɑːdɑːɪst/ *noun*. • **Dadaistic** *adj*. ⊙ 20c: from French *dada* hobby-horse.

daddy /'dadɪ/ ▷ *noun* (***daddies***) *colloq* **1** father. **2** the oldest, biggest, best, worst, etc, example of something □ ***a real daddy of a thunderstorm.*** ⊙ 16c: from DAD.

daddy-long-legs ▷ *noun* (*plural* ***daddy-long-legs***) **1** *Brit, Austral, NZ colloq* a CRANEFLY. **2** *N Amer* a HARVESTMAN.

dado /'deɪdoʊ/ ▷ *noun* (***dadoes*** or ***dados***) **1** the lower part of the wall of a room when decorated differently from the upper part, often consisting of panelling. **2** *archit* the plain square part of the base of a column or pedestal. ⊙ 17c: Italian, meaning 'dice'.

daemon /'diːmən, 'deɪ-/ or **daimon** /'deɪ-/ ▷ *noun* **1** a spirit regarded as halfway between gods and men. **2** a spirit which guards a place or takes care of or helps a person. Also occasionally called DEMON. • **daemonic** /diː'mɒnɪk, dɪ-/ or **daimonic** /-deɪ'mɒnɪk/ *adj*. ⊙ 16c: from Greek *daimon*.

daff ▷ *noun, colloq* a DAFFODIL (senses 1, 2). ⊙ Early 20c.

daffodil /'dafədɪl/ ▷ *noun* **1** a yellow narcissus, occurring naturally in many parts of Europe, now much cultivated in many varieties varying widely in colour and shape. **2** the flower of this plant. **3** a yellow colour. ▷ *adj* yellow. ⊙ 16c: from 15c *affodille*; the initial *d* is unexplained.

daffy[1] ▷ *noun* (*daffies*) *colloq* a DAFFODIL (senses 1, 2). ⊙ 18c.

daffy[2] ▷ *adj* (***daffier, daffiest***) daft; crazy. ⊙ 19c: from obsolete English *daff* to play the fool.

DAFS ▷ *abbreviation* Department of Agriculture and Fisheries for Scotland.

daft /dɑːft/ ▷ *adj, colloq* **1** silly or foolish. **2** insane or mad. • **daftie** *noun* (*dafties*) a daft person; an imbecile. • **daftly** *adverb*. • **daftness** *noun*. • **daft about** or **on something** enthusiastic about it or keen on it. ⊙ Anglo-Saxon *gedæfte* meek or mild.

dag[1] /dag/ ▷ *noun* **1** a dirt- or dung-clotted tuft of wool on a sheep. Also called **daglock**. **2** *Austral colloq* a scruffy, untidy, slovenly person. **3** *Austral colloq* someone, especially an adolescent, who is or feels socially awkward or graceless. ▷ *verb* (***dagged, dagging***) to cut away the dags from (a sheep). ⊙ 17c.

dag[2] /dag/ ▷ *noun, Austral & NZ colloq* someone who is rather eccentric or comically entertaining. See also DAG[1]. ⊙ Early 20c: from British dialect *dag* a dare.

dagga /'dagə/ ▻ *noun* Indian hemp (also called **true dagga**), or other forms of hemp, smoked as a narcotic. ⓒ 17c: Afrikaans, from Hottentot *dagab*.

dagger ▻ *noun* **1** a knife or short sword with a pointed end, used for stabbing. **2** *printing* the symbol †, used as a reference mark. • **at daggers drawn** openly showing anger or dislike and on the point of fighting. • **look daggers at someone** to give them a fierce or angry look. ⓒ 14c: possibly from obsolete *dag* to pierce or stab; compare French *dague*, literally 'long dagger'.

daggerboard ▻ *noun, naut* a light, narrow, completely removable CENTREBOARD.

dagging *present participle of* DAG[1]

daggy /'dagɪ/ ▻ *adj* (***daggier, daggiest***) *Austral & NZ colloq* scruffy; dishevelled. ⓒ 1920s: from DAG[1].

daglock see under DAG[1]

dago /'deɪgoʊ/ ▻ *noun* (***dagoes***) *offensive* someone, usually a man, of Spanish, Portuguese, Italian or S American origin. ⓒ 19c: probably from Spanish *Diego* James.

daguerreotype /də'gɛroʊtaɪp/ ▻ *noun* **1** an early type of photography invented by Louis Daguerre (1789–1851), which used mercury vapour to develop an exposure of silver iodide on a copper plate. **2** a photograph made by this method. ⓒ 19c.

dahl see DAL

dahlia /'deɪlɪə/ ▻ *noun* (*dahlias*) *bot* a garden plant with large brightly coloured flowers, some varieties having ball-like heads with many petals. ⓒ 19c: named after the 18c Swedish botanist Anders Dahl.

Dáil /dɔɪl/ and **Dáil Éireann** / — 'ɛərən/ ▻ *noun* the lower house of the parliament of the Republic of Ireland. ⓒ Early 20c: Irish, from *Dáil* assembly + *Eireann* of Ireland.

daily ▻ *adj* **1** happening, appearing, etc every day, or every day except Sunday, or *now often* every day except Saturday and Sunday. **2** relating to a single day. ▻ *adverb* every day; every weekday. ▻ *noun* (***dailies***) **1** a newspaper published every day except Sunday. **2** *colloq* a person, usually a woman, who is paid to come in and clean and tidy a house regularly, but not necessarily every day. **3** (**dailies**) *cinematog* the RUSHES. ⓒ Anglo-Saxon *dæglic*.

daily bread ▻ *noun* the money, food, etc one needs to live; one's living.

daily double ▻ *noun, horse-racing, betting* a single bet on the winners of two races on the same day.

daily dozen ▻ *noun, old colloq* physical exercises performed every day for the sake of one's health. ⓒ Early 20c.

daimon and **daimonic** see under DAEMON

dainty /'deɪntɪ/ ▻ *adj* (***daintier, daintiest***) **1** small and pretty, and, usually, delicate. **2** small and neat. **3** said of food: particularly nice to eat. **4** *often derog* very, or excessively, careful and sensitive about what one does or says. ▻ *noun* (***dainties***) something small and nice to eat, especially a small cake or sweet. • **daintily** *adverb*. • **daintiness** *noun*. 13c as *deinte*: from French *daintie* worthiness.

daiquiri /'daɪkərɪ, 'da-/ ▻ *noun* (***daiquiris***) a drink made with rum, lime juice and sugar. ⓒ 20c: named after Daiquiri in Cuba.

dairy /'dɛərɪ/ ▻ *noun* (***dairies***) **1 a** the building on a farm where milk is cooled and temporarily stored; **b** *now rather rare* the building on a farm where butter and cheese are made. **2** a commercial processing plant or factory that processes, bottles and distributes milk, and manufactures other dairy products. **3** a company that runs such an enterprise. **4** a shop which sells milk and other dairy produce. ⓒ 13c as *deierie*, from Anglo-Saxon *dæge* dairymaid.

dairy cattle ▻ *noun, agric* cows that are kept to produce milk, and to rear calves in order to maintain a dairy herd. Compare BEEF CATTLE.

dairy farm ▻ *noun* a farm which specializes in producing milk. ⓒ 19c.

dairy farmer ▻ *noun* a farmer keeping or working a dairy farm.

dairying ▻ *noun* **1** keeping a dairy farm. **2** producing and processing dairy products. ⓒ 17c.

dairymaid ▻ *noun, historical* a MILKMAID. ⓒ 16c.

dairyman and **dairywoman** ▻ *noun* **1** someone who looks after the dairy cows on a farm. **2** someone who works in a dairy or deals in dairy products. ⓒ 18c as *-man*; 17c as *-woman*.

dairy products ▻ *plural noun* milk and its derivatives, eg butter, cheese, yoghurt.

dais /deɪs, 'deɪɪs/ ▻ *noun* (*daisies*) a raised platform in a hall, eg for speakers at a meeting. ⓒ 13c: from French *deis*, from Latin *discus* a table.

daisy /'deɪzɪ/ ▻ *noun* (***daisies***) **1** any of various common wild and cultivated flowering plants belonging to the sunflower family. **2** the common daisy, which has a flowerhead with a yellow centre consisting of many tiny flowers, surrounded by white BRACTs; a common lawn weed in Europe. • **fresh as a daisy** bright, vigorous and enthusiastic. ⓒ Anglo-Saxon *dæges eage* day's eye.

daisy-chain ▻ *noun* a string of daisies each threaded through the stem of the next. ⓒ 19c.

daisy-cutter ▻ *noun* **1** a horse that does not lift its feet high. **2** *cricket* a bowled ball that skims along the ground. ⓒ 18c in sense 1; 19c in sense 2.

daisy-wheel ▻ *noun* in a typewriter, etc: a metal disc divided into separate spokes, each with a letter of the alphabet at the end, the disc rotating so that the letter printed corresponds to the letter struck on the keyboard. ⓒ 1970s.

dal, **dahl** or **dhal** /dɑːl/ ▻ *noun* **1** any of various edible dried split pea-like seeds. **2** a cooked dish made of any of these seeds. ⓒ 17c: from Hindi *dal* to split.

dalai lama /'dalaɪ —/ ▻ *noun* the head of the Tibetan Buddhist hierarchy. ⓒ 17c: Mongolian *dalai* ocean + LAMA.

dale /deɪl/ ▻ *noun* **1** a valley, especially one in the North of England. **2** (**the Dales**) the Yorkshire Dales or other dales of the north of England. ⓒ Anglo-Saxon *dæl*.

Dalek /'dɑːlɛk/ ▻ *noun* a mobile mechanical creature with a harsh staccato voice. ⓒ 1960s: created for the BBC television series *Dr Who*.

dalesman /'deɪlzmən/ ▻ *noun* a man belonging to the dales of the north of England, especially Yorkshire. ⓒ 18c.

Dalit /'dɑːlɪt/ ▻ *noun* a member of the former UNTOUCHABLE class in India. ⓒ Hindi.

dalliance /'dalɪəns/ ▻ *noun* idle wasting of time. ⓒ 16c in this sense; 14c as *dalyaunce* with obsolete meaning 'chat' or 'conversation'.

dally /'dalɪ/ ▻ *verb* (***dallies, dallied, dallying***) *intr* **1** to waste time idly or frivolously. **2** (*often* **dally with someone**) *old use* to flirt with them. ⓒ 14c, originally meaning 'to chat, to amuse oneself with someone or something': from French *dalier* to chat.

Dalmatian /dal'meɪʃən/ ▻ *adj* belonging or relating to Dalmatia in Croatia, or its inhabitants. ▻ *noun* **1** an inhabitant of, or person born in, Dalmatia. **2** a large short-haired breed of dog, white with dark spots. ⓒ 17c as *adj*; 16c as *noun* 1; 19c as *noun* 2.

dalmatic /dal'matɪk/ ▻ *noun* a loose-fitting, wide-sleeved, ecclesiastical vestment, worn especially by deacons of the RC church, also sometimes by bishops. ⓘ 15c: from Latin *dalmatica vestis* a robe made of Dalmatian wool.

dal segno /dal 'sɛnjoʊ/ ▷ *adverb, music* (abbreviation **DS**) an indication that the performer must go back to the sign 𝄋. ⓘ 19c: Italian, meaning 'from the sign'.

dalton /'dɔːltən, 'dɒl-/ ▷ *noun, chem* ATOMIC MASS UNIT. ⓘ 1930s: named after the UK chemist John Dalton (1766–1844).

Daltonism[1] or **daltonism** /'dɔːltənɪzəm, 'dɒl-/ ▷ *noun* colour-blindness, especially confusion between red and green. ⓘ 19c: from French *daltonisme*, named after UK scientist John Dalton (1766–1844), who described his own symptoms.

Daltonism[2] /'dɔːltənɪzəm, 'dɒl-/ ▷ *noun, education* a school method by which each pupil pursues separately in their own way a course divided into monthly instalments, designed to suit each individual. Also called **the Dalton plan**. ⓘ 20c: first tried in 1920 at Dalton, Massachusetts.

Dalton's law of partial pressures ▷ *noun, chem* a law which states that, in a mixture of gases, the pressure exerted by each gas is the same as that which it would exert if it were the only gas present.

DALY ▷ *abbreviation* disability adjusted life year, a statistical measure used to calculate the number of healthy years lost in an average life-span through premature death or disability.

dam[1] ▷ *noun* **1** a barrier built to contain water and prevent flooding. **2** the water confined behind such a structure, often forming a lake or reservoir, used for irrigation, as a source of drinking water and for provision of hydroelectric power. ▷ *verb* (***dammed***, ***damming***) to hold back (water, etc) with a dam. ⓘ 14c: probably Dutch.

dam[2] ▷ *noun* said of horses, cattle and sheep: a female parent. ⓘ 14c in this sense; 13c, meaning 'DAME'.

damage /'damɪdʒ/ ▷ *noun* **1** harm or injury, or loss caused by injury. **2** (**damages**) *law* payment due for loss or injury caused by another person, organization, etc. ▷ *verb* (***damaged***, ***damaging***) to cause harm, injury or loss to someone or something. • **damageability** *noun*. • **damageable** *adj*. • **damaged** *adj* harmed; injured; broken. • **damaging** *adj* having a bad effect on a person's reputation. • **damagingly** *adverb*. ⓘ 14c: French, from Latin *damnum* loss.

damascene /'daməsiːn, -'siːn/ ▷ *noun* **1** (**Damascene**) a citizen or inhabitant of, or a person born in, Damascus in Syria. **2 a** inlay of metal, especially gold, or of other materials, on steel, etc; **b** an article of such work. **3** the structure or surface appearance of DAMASCUS STEEL. ▷ *verb* (***damascened***, ***damascening***) **1** to decorate (especially steel) by inlaying or encrusting. **2** to ornament something with the watered or wavy appearance of DAMASCUS STEEL, or in imitation of it. ⓘ 14c: from Latin *Damascenus* Damascus, famous for its steel and silk work.

Damascus steel /də'maskəs —/ ▷ *noun* a hard steel, repeatedly folded and hammered giving a wavy surface pattern.

damask /'daməsk/ ▷ *noun* **1** a type of cloth, originally silk, now usually linen, with a pattern woven into it, often used for tablecloths, curtains, etc. **2** table linen of this fabric. **3** DAMASCUS STEEL or its surface appearance. **4** the colour of a DAMASK ROSE. ▷ *adj* greyish-pink or greyish-red. ⓘ 14c: named after Damascus in Syria, where such cloth was made.

damask plum ▷ *noun* the DAMSON. ⓘ 17c.

damask rose ▷ *noun* a sweet-smelling pink or red variety of rose. ⓘ 16c.

dame ▷ *noun* **1** a woman who has been awarded the highest or second-highest class of distinction in any of four British orders of chivalry, or honours for service or merit awarded by the Queen or the Government. See also KNIGHT. **2** *N Amer slang* a woman. **3** a comic female character in a pantomime, usually played by a man. ⓘ 13c, originally meaning 'a female ruler' 'or woman of importance': French, from Latin *domina* lady.

damfool /'damfuːl/ ▷ *adj* stupid; ridiculous. ⓘ 19c: from DAMN + FOOL.

dammed and **damming** see under DAM[1]

dammit /'damɪt/ ▷ *exclamation* damn it! • **as near as dammit** see under NEAR. ⓘ 19c.

damn /dam/ ▷ *verb* (***damned*** /damd/, ***damning*** /'damɪŋ/) **1** *relig* to sentence someone to never-ending punishment in hell. **2** to declare someone or something to be useless or worthless. **3** to suggest or prove the guiltiness of someone. ▷ *exclamation* (*often* **damn it**) expressing annoyance or disappointment. ▷ *adj, colloq* used for emphasis: annoying; hateful □ *the damn cold.* ▷ *adverb, colloq* used for emphasis □ *It's damn cold.* • **damning** *adj* **1** very critical. **2** proving or suggesting guilt. • **as near as damn it** see under NEAR. • **be damned if one will do something** *colloq* to refuse to do it. • **damn all** *colloq* nothing at all. • **damn someone** or **something with faint praise** to praise them or it so unenthusiastically as to seem disapproving. • **not give a damn** *colloq* not to care at all. ⓘ 13c: from Latin *damnare* to condemn.

damnable /'damnəbəl/ ▷ *adj* **1** hateful; awful; deserving to be condemned. **2** annoying. • **damnability** or **damnableness** *noun*. • **damnably** *adverb* annoyingly; very. ⓘ 14c.

damnation /dam'neɪʃən/ ▷ *noun, relig* **1** never-ending punishment in hell. **2** the act of condemning or the state of being condemned to such punishment. ▷ *exclamation* expressing annoyance or disappointment. ⓘ 14c.

damnatory /'damnətərɪ/ ▷ *adj* bringing or incurring damnation. ⓘ 17c.

damned /damd, *poetry* 'damnɪd/ ▷ *adj* (*superlative* ***damnedest*** /'damdəst/) **1** *relig* sentenced to damnation. **2** *colloq* annoying, hateful, etc. **3** (**the damned**) those sentenced to everlasting punishment (see THE 4b). See also DAMN. ▷ *adverb, colloq* extremely; very □ *damned cold.* • **do one's damnedest** *colloq* to do one's utmost; to try as hard as possible.

damnify /'damnɪfaɪ/ *law* ▷ *verb* (***damnifies***, ***damnified***, ***damnifying***) to cause loss or damage to someone. • **damnification** /damnɪfɪ'keɪʃən/ *noun* infliction of injury or loss. ⓘ 16c: from Latin *damnificare* to injure or condemn.

damp ▷ *adj* (***damper***, ***dampest***) slightly wet. ▷ *noun* **1** slight wetness, eg in walls or the air, especially if cold and unpleasant. **2** *mining* any gas other than air. See also FIREDAMP. ▷ *verb* (***damped***, ***damping***) **1** to make something slightly wet. **2** *music* to press (the strings, or a string, of an instrument) to stop or lessen vibration. • **dampish** *adj*. • **dampishness** *noun*. • **damply** *adverb*. • **dampness** *noun*. ⓘ 16c in modern senses; 15c, meaning 'harmful vapour': from German *Dampf* steam.

■ **damp something down 1** to make (emotions, interest, etc) less strong. **2** to make (a fire) burn more slowly.

damp-course and **damp-proof course** ▷ *noun* a horizontal layer of material in a wall of a building, usually near the ground, which stops damp rising up through the wall. ⓘ 19c.

dampen ▷ *verb* (***dampened***, ***dampening***) **1** to make something slightly wet. **2** *tr & intr* (*usually* **dampen down**) said of emotions, interest, etc: to make or become less strong. • **dampener** *noun*. ⓘ 16c.

■ **dampen something down 1** to make (emotions, interest, etc) less strong. **2** to make (a fire) burn more slowly.

damper ▻ *noun* **1** something which lessens enthusiasm, interest, etc. **2** a movable plate which allows the flow of air to a fire etc, to be controlled so that the amount of heat may be altered. **3** *physics* a device for diminishing the amplitude of vibrations or oscillations. **4** *music* a MUTE (*noun* 3) on a piano. **5** *music* in a piano, harpsichord, etc: a pad which silences a note after it has been played. • **put a damper on something** to lessen enthusiasm for it or interest in it. ⓔ 18c.

damp-proof ▻ *adj* said of a material, substance, structure: not allowing wetness to get through. ▻ *verb, building* to make something damp-proof.

damp squib ▻ *noun* a disappointingly uninteresting or unsuccessful event.

damsel /ˈdamzəl/ ▻ *noun, old use or literary* a girl or young woman. ⓔ 16c in this form; 13c as *damaysel*: from French *dameisele*.

damselfish ▻ *noun* one of various small brightly coloured tropical fish.

damselfly ▻ *noun* a large predatory insect with a long body and two pairs of slender wings which are typically held together over the abdomen when at rest. ⓔ 19c.

damson /ˈdamzən/ ▻ *noun* **1** a small purple plum. **2** the tree it grows on. ⓔ 15c: from Latin *Damascenus* of Damascus in Syria.

damson cheese ▻ *noun* a solid preserve produced from damsons and sugar.

Dan. ▻ *abbreviation* **1** Book of the Bible: Daniel. See table at BIBLE. **2** Danish.

dan¹ ▻ *noun* **1** any of the ten grades of BLACK BELT awarded for particular levels of skill in judo, karate, etc. **2** someone who has achieved such a grade. ⓔ 20c: Japanese.

dan² and **dan buoy** ▻ *noun* a small sea marker-buoy. ⓔ 17c.

dance /dɑːns/ ▻ *verb* (***danced, dancing***) **1** *intr* to make a usually repeated series of rhythmic steps or movements (usually in time to music). **2** to perform (a particular series of such steps or movements) ▫ *dance a waltz.* **3** *intr* (*usually* **dance about** or **around**) to move or jump quickly up and down or from side to side. **4** to bounce (a baby), usually on one's knee. ▻ *noun* **1** a series of fixed steps, usually made in time to music. **2** a social gathering at which people dance. **3** a piece of music played for dancing. **4** *as adj* ▫ *dance-band* ▫ *dance music.* • **danceable** *adj.* • **dancer** *noun* someone who dances, especially professionally. • **dancing** *noun.* • **dance attendance on someone** *derog* to follow them closely and do whatever they want. • **dance to someone's tune** to do exactly what they want or expect. • **lead someone a merry dance** to involve them in unnecessary difficulties and exertions. ⓔ 13c: from French *danser* to dance.

dance music ▻ *noun* **1** any music that can be danced to. **2** music, such as ACID HOUSE, HIP-HOP, TECHNO, etc, created and recorded for dancing to in clubs.

D and C ▻ *abbreviation, medicine* DILATATION AND CURETTAGE.

dandelion /ˈdandɪlaɪən/ ▻ *noun* a perennial plant, widespread in most temperate regions, producing single yellow flowerheads on hollow stems containing white latex sap and having a rosette of deeply notched leaves. ⓔ 15c: from French *dent de lion* lion's tooth, referring to the leaves.

dandelion clock ▻ *noun* the round white fluffy seedhead of the dandelion.

dander /ˈdandə(r)/ ▻ *noun* (*only* **get one's** or **someone's dander up**) *colloq* to become angry, or make someone angry. ⓔ 19c.

Dandie Dinmont /ˈdandɪ ˈdɪnmənt/ ▻ *noun* a short-legged rough-coated terrier of Scottish Border origin. ⓔ 19c: from the name of the character in Sir Walter Scott's 'Guy Mannering', whose dogs are represented as the origin of the breed.

dandify /ˈdandɪfaɪ/ ▻ *verb* (***dandifies, dandified, dandifying***) to dress someone up like a dandy. ⓔ 19c: from DANDY.

dandle /ˈdandəl/ ▻ *verb* (***dandled, dandling***) to bounce or dance (usually a small child) on one's knee.

dandruff /ˈdandrəf/ ▻ *noun* thin whitish flakes of dead skin shed from the scalp. ⓔ 16c.

dandy /ˈdandɪ/ ▻ *noun* (***dandies***) **1** a man who pays a lot of attention to his appearance, dressing very fashionably or elegantly. **2** a DANDY-ROLL. ▻ *adj, colloq* (***dandier, dandiest***) good; fine. • **dandily** *adverb.* • **dandyish** *adj.* • **dandyism** *noun.*

dandy-brush ▻ *noun* a stiff-bristled brush for grooming a horse. ⓔ 19c.

dandy-roll ▻ *noun* a wire gauze cylinder that impresses the ribs and watermarks on paper. ⓔ 19c.

Dane ▻ *noun* **1** a citizen or inhabitant of, or person born in, Denmark. **2** *historical* any of the Vikings from Scandinavia who invaded Britain during the period 9c–11c. See also DANISH, GREAT DANE. ⓔ Anglo-Saxon *Dene*; later forms influenced by Norse *Danir*, Danish *Daner* Danes.

Danelaw /ˈdeɪnlɔː/ ▻ *noun* the part of England occupied by the Danes during the 9c–11c. ⓔ Anglo-Saxon *Dena lagu* Danes' law.

danger /ˈdeɪndʒə(r)/ ▻ *noun* **1** a situation or state in which someone or something may suffer harm, an injury or a loss ▫ *in danger of falling.* **2** something that may cause harm, injury or loss. **3** a possibility of something unpleasant happening. • **on the danger list** *medicine* so ill or seriously injured that there is a high risk of death. ⓔ 14c in this form; 13c as *daunger*: from French *dangier* power, therefore 'power to harm'.

danger money ▻ *noun* extra money paid to a person for doing a dangerous job.

dangerous ▻ *adj* likely or able to cause harm or injury. • **dangerously** *adverb.* • **dangerousness** *noun.* ⓔ 13c.

dangle /ˈdaŋgəl/ ▻ *verb* (***dangled, dangling***) **1** *tr & intr* to hang loosely, sometimes swinging or swaying. **2** to offer or present (an idea, a possible reward, etc) to someone. ⓔ 16c: probably originally imitative.

Danish /ˈdeɪnɪʃ/ ▻ *adj* **1** belonging or relating to a kingdom of N Europe, Denmark, its inhabitants or their language. **2** belonging or relating to the language spoken in Denmark. **3** (**the Danish**) the people of Denmark (see THE 4b). ▻ *noun* **1** the official language of Denmark. **2** *colloq* a DANISH PASTRY. See also DANE. ⓔ Anglo-Saxon *denisc*, later modified by French *daneis*.

Danish blue and **Danish blue cheese** ▻ *noun* a type of strong-tasting cheese, white with streaks of bluish mould through it.

Danish pastry ▻ *noun* a flat cake of rich light pastry, with any of various types of sweet fillings and toppings. Also (*colloq*) called DANISH. ⓔ 1920s.

dank ▻ *adj* usually said of a place: unpleasantly wet and cold. • **dankish** *adj.* • **dankness** *noun.* ⓔ 15c as *dannke*: of uncertain origin, but compare Swedish *dank* a marshy spot.

danseur /dɑ̃ˈsɜː(r)/ ▻ *noun, ballet* a male dancer. ⓔ 19c: French, from *danser* to dance.

danseuse /dɑ̃ˈsɜːz/ ▻ *noun, ballet* a female dancer; a ballerina. ⓔ 19c: French, from *danser* to dance.

Dantean /ˈdantɪən/ and **Dantesque** /danˈtɛsk/ ▻ *adj* **1** like or in the style of the Italian poet Dante Alighieri (1265–1321). **2** sublime; austere. ⓔ 18c.

dap ▻ *verb* (***dapped, dapping***) *intr* **1** *angling* to fish with a fly bounced gently on the surface of the water. **2** to dip gently into water. **3** to bounce. ▷ *noun* **1** a bounce. **2** *angling* a bait made to bounce gently on the surface. ⓒ 17c in sense 1; compare DAB.

daphne /ˈdafnɪ/ ▷ *noun* any of various evergreen shrubs that bear clusters of small flowers, eg SPURGE LAUREL. ⓒ 15c: from Greek *daphne* laurel or bay tree; according to myth, the name of a nymph who was changed into a laurel tree to escape Apollo.

daphnia /ˈdafnɪə/ ▷ *noun* a common type of water flea found in fresh water. ⓒ 19c: from Greek *daphne*; compare DAPHNE.

dapper /ˈdapə(r)/ ▷ *adj* usually said of men: neat and smart in appearance and lively in movement. • **dapperly** *adverb*. • **dapperness** *noun*. ⓒ 15c: Dutch, meaning 'brave'.

dappled /ˈdapəld/ ▷ *adj* marked with spots or rounded patches of a different, usually darker, colour. ⓒ 15c.

dapple-grey /ˈdapəl —/ ▷ *adj* said of a horse: pale-grey with darker spots. ▷ *noun* a dapple-grey horse. ⓒ 14c.

Darby and Joan /ˈdɑːbɪ ən ˈdʒoʊn/ ▷ *plural noun* an old man and old woman who have been happily married for many years. ⓒ 18c: from characters in an 18c song.

Darby and Joan club ▷ *noun* a social club for elderly men and women.

dare /dɛə(r)/ ▷ *verb* (**dared**, **daring**) **1** *intr* (also *as auxiliary verb* — see note below) to be brave enough to do something frightening, difficult or dangerous □ *He wouldn't dare to leave* □ *Dare I tell him?* **2** to challenge someone to do something frightening, difficult, dangerous, etc. **3** to be brave enough to risk facing someone or something □ *dare his father's anger*. ▷ *noun* a challenge to do something dangerous, etc. • **How dare you!** an expression of anger or indignation at something someone has said or done. • **I dare say** or **daresay** probably; I suppose □ *I dare say you're right.* ⓒ Anglo-Saxon *durran*.

> **dare**
>
> • When **dare** means 'to be brave enough to do something', it may be used either as an ordinary intransitive verb or as an auxiliary verb.
>
> • When **dare** is used as an intransitive verb, the form of the verb accompanying 'he/she/it' ends in '-s', and questions and negative statements are formed with the auxiliary verb 'do' □ *If he dares to do that, I'll just walk out* □ *I did not dare to look at him* □ *Didn't you dare to tell him?* □ *Few would have dared to predict the outcome.*
>
> As an intransitive verb, **dare** may be followed by 'to', as in the examples above, or, equally correctly, by a verb without 'to' □ *I did not dare make a noise* □ *Don't you dare say a word!* □ *Who dares contradict him?*
>
> • When **dare** is used as an auxiliary verb, the verb accompanying 'he/she/it' has no '-s' ending, questions and negative statements are formed without 'do', and there is no 'to' before the following verb □ *Dare she push her bike through the gate?* □ *I dared not look at him* □ *Daren't he tell her?*

dare-devil ▷ *noun* a person who does dangerous or adventurous things without worrying about the risks involved. ▷ *adj* said of actions, etc: daring and dangerous; reckless. ⓒ 18c.

daring /ˈdɛərɪŋ/ ▷ *adj* **1** bold, courageous or adventurous. **2** designed or intended to shock or surprise. ▷ *noun* boldness, courage. • **daringly** *adverb*.

dariole /ˈdarɪoʊl/ ▷ *noun* **1** a shell of pastry, etc, or a small round mould. **2** a dish comprising such a shell and its filling. **3** a dish prepared in such a mould. ⓒ 15c: French.

dark /dɑːk/ ▷ *adj* **1** without light. **2** said of a colour: not light or pale; closer to black than white. **3** said of a person or the colour of their skin or hair: not light or fair. **4** sad or gloomy. **5** evil or sinister □ *dark powers*. **6** mysterious and unknown □ *a dark secret*. **7** said of a theatre: closed. ▷ *noun* **1** (*usually* **the dark**) the absence of light. **2** the time of day when night begins and there is no more light □ *after dark*. **3** a dark colour. • **darkish** *adj*. • **darkness** *noun*. • **in the dark** not knowing or not aware of something. • **keep it dark** to keep something secret. ⓒ Anglo-Saxon *deorc*.

the Dark Ages ▷ *noun* the period of European history from about the 5c to the 11c, traditionally regarded as historically obscure and formerly regarded as culturally uneventful.

darken ▷ *verb* (**darkened**, **darkening**) *tr & intr* to make or become dark or darker. • **darkened** *adj*. • **darken someone's door** (*often with negative, and implying that such an arrival would be unwelcome*) to appear as a visitor.

dark horse ▷ *noun* **1** *horse-racing* a horse whose capabilities are not known. **2** someone, especially a candidate or competitor, about whom little is known, or who chooses not to reveal much about their own abilities, talents, etc.

darkie see DARKY

dark lantern ▷ *noun* a lantern with the means to dim or hide the light. ⓒ 17c.

darkly ▷ *adverb* in a mysterious, gloomy, sinister or threatening way or tone of voice. ⓒ 14c as *derkelich*.

dark matter ▷ *noun, astron* matter not visible but making up a large proportion of the mass of the universe, and sufficient to change its expansion into contraction.

dark meat ▷ *noun* said especially of poultry: the meat from the legs, etc. Compare WHITE MEAT.

darkroom ▷ *noun* a room into which no ordinary light is allowed, used for developing photographs. ⓒ 19c.

darky or **darkie** ▷ *noun* (**darkies**), *offensive* a person with black or brown skin, especially a Black. ⓒ 18c.

darling ▷ *noun* **1** often used as a term of affection: a dearly loved person. **2** a lovable person or thing. ▷ *adj* **1** well loved. **2** *colloq* delightful. ⓒ Anglo-Saxon *deorling*: see DEAR.

darn¹ ▷ *verb* (**darned**, **darning**) to mend (a hole, a garment, etc) by sewing with rows of stitches which cross each other. ▷ *noun* a darned place. • **darner** *noun* **1** someone who darns. **2** a darning-needle. • **darning** *noun* **1** the work of darning clothes, etc. **2** clothes, etc which need to be darned or which have been darned. ⓒ 17c.

darn² ▷ *exclamation* a less offensive or emphatic substitute for DAMN.

darned ▷ *adj* irritating; disliked. ⓒ 19c: from DAMNED; compare DARN².

darnel /ˈdɑːnəl/ ▷ *noun* a species of rye grass which grows as a weed in cornfields of Asia and Europe. ⓒ 14c.

darning egg and **darning mushroom** ▷ *noun* a smooth egg-shaped or mushroom-shaped object, usually wooden, for supporting material being darned.

darning-needle ▷ *noun* a long, somewhat thick needle with a large eye, suitable for darning with. ⓒ 19c.

darshan /ˈdɑːʃən/ ▷ *noun, Hinduism* a blessing conferred by seeing or touching a great or holy person. ⓒ 1920s: from Hindi *darśana* sight.

dart ▷ *noun* **1** a narrow pointed weapon that can be thrown or fired. **2** a small sharp-pointed missile used in the game of DARTS. **3** a sudden quick movement. **4** a fold sewn into a piece of clothing to make it fit more neatly. ▷ *verb* (**darted**, **darting**) **1** *intr* to move suddenly and quickly. **2** to send or give (a look or glance) quickly. ⓒ 14c: French.

darter /ˈdɑːtə(r)/ ▷ *noun* **1** a person or thing which darts. **2** a slender freshwater diving bird native to warm regions worldwide. **3** any of various small American fishes of the perch family. ◎ 19c in sense 1; 18c in sense 2; originally 16c meaning 'a person who throws darts'.

darts ▷ *singular noun* a game in which darts (see DART *noun* 2) are thrown at a **dartboard**, a circular target divided into numbered sections, with points being scored according to the section each dart hits.

Darwinian /dɑːˈwɪnɪən/ ▷ *adj, noun* a DARWINIST.

Darwinism /ˈdɑːwɪnɪzəm/ ▷ *noun, biol* the theory of evolution by NATURAL SELECTION, proposed jointly by Charles Darwin (1809–82) and Alfred Russel Wallace (1823–1913).

Darwinist ▷ *adj* belonging or relating to Charles Darwin, or to the theory of Darwinism. ▷ *noun* someone who believes in, uses or promotes the theory of Darwinism.

dash¹ ▷ *verb* (***dashes***, ***dashed***, ***dashing***) **1** *intr* to run quickly; to rush. **2** *intr* to crash or smash. **3** (*often* **dash against something**) to hit or smash it violently. **4** to destroy or put an end to (hopes, etc). ▷ *noun* (***dashes***) **1** a quick run or sudden rush. **2** a small amount of something added, especially a liquid. **3** a patch of colour. **4** a short line (-) used in writing to show a break in a sentence, etc. **5** in MORSE code: the longer of the two lengths of signal element, written as a short line. Compare DOT. **6** confidence, enthusiasm and stylishness. **7** *N Amer sport* a short race for fast runners. **8** a DASHBOARD. ◎ 14c as *dasch*; from earlier *daschen* or *dassen* to rush or strike violently.

■ **dash off** to leave abruptly.

■ **dash off something** or **dash something off** to produce or write it hastily.

dash

1. long dash —

● introduces an explanation or expansion ◻ *The film is excellent — it has slick photography, a pacy plot and lavish costumes.*

ALTERNATIVE STYLE *(more formal)*: a colon.

● It introduces an emphatic comment ◻ *He can do it — and he will!*

● In pairs, it encloses an emphatic comment ◻ *There is nothing — absolutely nothing — half so much worth doing as simply messing about in boats.*

● In pairs, it encloses an inserted comment or aside ◻ *I'm told his car — some fancy foreign job, I believe — cost over £18,000.*

ALTERNATIVE STYLES *(less informal)*: a pair of commas; *(less informal still)* a pair of round brackets.

2. short dash –

● links the limits of a range ◻ *the 1914–18 War* ◻ *pages 467–481* ◻ *volumes I–IV* ◻ *an A–Z guide to the birds of Britain.*

Don't use a dash to link items in a phrase beginning with 'between' or 'from':

✗ *between 1987–95;*

✗ *from 1918–1939;* ✓ *between 1987 and 1995;*

✓ *from 1918 to 1939.*

● It links two or more words that together modify a following word ◻ *a 3–0 win for Arsenal* ◻ *the Paris–Lyon autoroute* ◻ *the space–time continuum.*

dash² ▷ *exclamation* a milder and less offensive substitute for DAMN.

dashboard ▷ *noun* a panel with dials, switches and instruments, etc in front of the driver's seat in a motor vehicle, boat, etc. ◎ 19c: DASH¹ + BOARD; originally a board protecting the driver of a horse-drawn coach from splashes of mud.

dasheen /daˈʃiːn/ ▷ *noun* the taro plant. ◎ 19c: possibly from French *de Chine* from China.

dashiki or **dasheki** /daˈʃiːkɪ/ ▷ *noun* (***dashikis*** or ***dashekis***) a type of long, loose, brightly coloured shirt worn chiefly by Blacks in Africa, the Caribbean and the US. ◎ 20c: probably from a W African language.

dashing ▷ *adj* **1** smart; stylish. **2** lively and enthusiastic. **3** rushing. ● **dashingly** *adverb*. ◎ 18c in senses 1 and 2; 14c in sense 3: from DASH¹.

dassie /ˈdasɪ/ ▷ *noun* (***dassies***) *S Afr* the HYRAX. ◎ 18c: Afrikaans, from Dutch *dasje*, diminutive of *das* badger.

dastardly /ˈdastədlɪ/ ▷ *adj, old use* cowardly, mean and cruel. ◎ 16c: probably connected with DAZED.

DAT ▷ *abbreviation* digital audio tape.

dat. ▷ *abbreviation* dative.

data /ˈdeɪtə, ˈdɑːtə/ ▷ *noun* (originally *plural* but now generally treated as *singular*) **1** one or more pieces of information or facts, especially those obtained by scientific observation or experiment. **2** a collection of information in the form of numbers, characters, electrical signals, etc, that can be supplied to, stored in or processed by a computer. ◎ 17c: Latin, meaning 'things given'; see also DATUM.

data

When referring to collected information, especially in electronic form, **data** is increasingly treated as a singular noun, since a unified concept is often intended ◻ *The data is entered from the forms by a keyboarder.*

● When the composite nature of the information is important, the plural is often used ◻ *As more data accumulate, it may turn out that there are differences* ◻ *The data were easily converted into numerical form.* However, in these examples the singular is also possible ◻ *As more data accumulates ...* ◻ *The data was easily converted ...*

databank ▷ *noun, computing* a collection of databases, whereby integrity of DATA, organized by a database-management system (**DBMS**) program, is maintained by controlling access to the application programs by the users.

database ▷ *noun* (***databases***) *computing* a collection of computer DATA.

datable see under DATE¹

data capture ▷ *noun, computing* any process of changing information from its original form into a form which can be fed into a computer.

data communications ▷ *plural noun* the sending and receiving of computer-encoded data by means of telecommunications.

dataglove ▷ *noun* an electronically wired glove which transmits the wearer's movements to a VIRTUAL-REALITY monitor.

data processing ▷ *noun, computing* the performance of operations on data by a computer system, especially the arrangement of large amounts of data into a more useful form according to specified rules and procedures.

data protection ▷ *noun, computing* safeguards to protect the integrity, privacy and security of data.

date¹ /deɪt/ ▷ *noun* **1** the day of the month and/or the year, recorded by a number or series of numbers. **2** a statement on a letter, document, etc giving usually the day, the month and the year when it was written, sent, etc. **3** a particular period of time in history ◻ ***costumes of an earlier date.*** **4** *colloq* a planned meeting or social outing, usually with a person one is attached to. **5** *especially N Amer, colloq* a person whom one is meeting or going out with and who one usually finds attractive. **6** *colloq* an agreed time and place of performance. ▷ *verb* (***dated***, ***dating***) **1** to put a date on something. **2** to find, decide on or guess the date of something. **3** to show the age of someone or something; to make (especially a person) seem old. **4** *intr* to become old-fashioned. **5** *tr & intr, colloq* to go out with someone, especially to do so regularly. • **datable** or **dateable** *adj*. • **dated** *adj* old-fashioned. • **out of date** see under OUT. • **to date** up to the present time. • **up to date** see under UP. ⓘ 15c: French, from Latin *datum* given.

■ **date back to** or **from (a specified time)** to have begun or originated then.

date² /deɪt/ ▷ *noun* the fruit of the DATE PALM, brown, sticky and sweet-tasting when dried. ⓘ 13c: from French *datte*, from Greek *daktylos* finger or date.

date coding ▷ *noun* marking in code on a container a date after which the contents should not be used.

dateless ▷ *adj* **1** without a date or fixed limits. **2** not likely to become dated. **3** free from engagements.

dateline ▷ *noun* a line, usually at the top of a newspaper article, which gives the date and place of writing. ⓘ Late 19c.

date line see INTERNATIONAL DATE LINE

date palm ▷ *noun* a tall tree with a crown of long spreading leaves, cultivated in N Africa and the Middle East for its yellowish to reddish-brown edible fruits, which are borne in heavy clusters and have a very high sugar content.

date rape ▷ *noun* rape committed by someone known to the victim while both are on a date together.

date-stamp ▷ *noun* **1** a device, usually a rubber stamp, for printing the date on something. **2** the date printed by this. ▷ *verb* to mark something with a date-stamp.

dating agency ▷ *noun* an agency that aims to introduce people seeking personal relationships to others with similar tastes and interests. See also COMPUTER DATING.

dative /ˈdeɪtɪv/ *grammar* ▷ *noun* **1** in certain languages, eg Latin, Greek and German: the form or CASE² (*noun* 7) of a noun, pronoun or adjective which is used chiefly to show that the word is the indirect object of a verb. **2** a noun, etc in this case. ▷ *adj* belonging to or in this case. ⓘ 15c as *datif*: from Latin *dativus*, from *dare* to give.

datum /ˈdeɪtəm, ˈdɑː-/ ▷ *noun* (***data***) a piece of information. See also DATA. ⓘ 18c: Latin, meaning 'something given'.

datura /dəˈtjʊərə/ ▷ *noun* (***daturas***) **1** any plant of a group of plants including the THORN APPLE, which have strong narcotic or toxic properties. **2** the poison derived from these plants. ⓘ 16c: from Hindi *dhatura*.

dau. ▷ *abbreviation* daughter.

daub /dɔːb/ ▷ *verb* (***daubed***, ***daubing***) **1** to spread something roughly or unevenly onto or over a surface □ *daubing paint on the walls.* **2** to cover (a surface) with a soft sticky substance or liquid. **3** *tr & intr, derog* to paint carelessly or without skill. ▷ *noun* **1** soft, sticky material such as clay, often used as a covering for walls (see also WATTLE AND DAUB). **2** *derog, colloq* an unskilful or carelessly done painting. • **dauber** *noun*. ⓘ 14c: from French *dauber*, from Latin *dealbare* to whitewash.

daube /doub/ ▷ *noun* a meat stew. ⓘ 18c: French.

daughter /ˈdɔːtə(r)/ ▷ *noun* **1** a female child considered in relation to her parents. **2** a woman closely associated with, involved with or influenced by a person, thing or place □ *a faithful daughter of the Church.* ▷ *adj* **1** derived by some process from, and thought of as being like a daughter of, something □ *French is a daughter language of Latin.* **2** *biol* said of a cell: formed by division. ⓘ Anglo-Saxon *dohtor*.

daughterboard ▷ *noun, computing* a printed-circuit board, or anything similar, which plugs into a MOTHERBOARD.

daughter cell ▷ *noun, biol* either of two new cells formed as a result of cell division. ⓘ Late 19c.

daughter element ▷ *noun, physics* any of the elements produced as a result of the splitting of an atom by nuclear fission. ⓘ 1920s.

daughter-in-law ▷ *noun* (***daughters-in-law***) the wife of one's son. ⓘ 14c.

daughterly ▷ *adj* like a daughter; befitting a daughter □ *daughterly devotion.* • **daughterliness** *noun*. ⓘ 16c.

daughter nucleus ▷ *noun, biol* either of the two nuclei that are produced when the nucleus of a living cell splits into two parts during MITOSIS.

daunt /dɔːnt/ ▷ *verb* (***daunted***, ***daunting***) to frighten, worry or discourage someone. • **daunting** *adj* intimidating; discouraging. • **dauntingly** *adverb*. • **dauntless** *adj* fearless; not easily discouraged. • **dauntlessly** *adverb*. • **dauntlessness** *noun*. • **nothing daunted** not at all discouraged or less enthusiastic. ⓘ 14c: from French *danter*.

davenport /ˈdavənpɔːt/ ▷ *noun* **1** *Brit* a type of desk. **2** *N Amer* a large sofa. ⓘ 19c in sense 1; 20c in sense 2: possibly named after a certain Captain Davenport for whom early examples of such desks were made in the 18c.

davit /ˈdavɪt, ˈdeɪvɪt/ ▷ *noun* a curved device used as a crane on a ship, especially either one of a pair of such devices from which a lifeboat is hung and by means of which it can be lowered over the side of the ship. ⓘ 15c: from a form of the name *David*.

Davy /ˈdeɪvɪ/ (***Davies***) and **Davy lamp** ▷ *noun* a miner's safety-lamp. ⓘ 19c: named after the inventor Sir Humphry Davy (1778–1829).

Davy Jones's locker ▷ *noun* the bottom of the sea, especially as the place where the bodies of drowned sailors lie. ⓘ 19c: named after Davy Jones, first recorded in 18c as a sailors' name for the evil spirit of the sea.

dawdle /ˈdɔːdəl/ ▷ *verb* (***dawdled***, ***dawdling***) *intr* **1** to walk more slowly than necessary or desirable. **2** to waste time, especially by taking longer than necessary to do something. • **dawdler** *noun*.

dawn /dɔːn/ ▷ *noun* **1** the time of day when light first appears as the sun rises. **2** the beginning of (a new period of time, etc). ▷ *verb* (***dawned***, ***dawning***) said of the day: to begin; to become light. • **at the break of dawn** at the first light of day when the sun rises. ⓘ 13c first recorded as *noun dawning*; the verb first recorded 15c and the noun 16c: originally probably from Norse; related to DAY.

■ **dawn on someone** to begin to be realized by them.

dawn chorus ▷ *noun* the singing of birds at dawn. ⓘ 1920s.

dawn raid ▷ *noun* **1** a surprise attack at dawn. **2** *stock exchange* an operation in which a large proportion of a company's shares are suddenly bought at a price much higher than their prevailing market rate.

day /deɪ/ ▷ *noun* (***days***) **1 a** the period of 24 hours called the **solar day** during which the Earth rotates once on its axis with respect to the Sun; **b** *astron* a SIDEREAL DAY; **c** any period of 24 hours, especially from midnight to midnight. **2** the period of time from sunrise to sunset. **3** the period of time in any 24 hours normally spent doing something, especially working. Compare WORKING DAY. **4** (**day** or **days**) a particular period of time, usually in the past □ *one's childhood days* □ *It never happened in their day.* **5** time of recognition, success, influence, power, etc □ *Their day will come* □ *In his day he reigned supreme.* • **all in a** or **the day's work** a normal or acceptable part of one's work or routine. • **at the end of the day** when all is said and done. • **call it a day** to leave off doing something; to announce a decision to do so. • **day about** on alternate days. • **day by day** as each day passes. • **day in, day out** continuously and tediously without change. • **days of yore** see YORE. • **from day to day** concerned only with the present and not with any long-term plans. • **have had one's day** to have passed the time of one's greatest success, influence, popularity, etc. • **in this day and age** nowadays; in modern times. • **make someone's day** to satisfy or delight them. • **one day** or **one of these days** or **one of these fine days** at some time in the future. • **one of those days** a day of difficulties or misfortunes. • **that will be the day** *colloq* that is unlikely to happen. • **those were the days** that was a good or happy time. • **win** or **carry the day** to win a victory. ◷ Anglo-Saxon *dæg.*

day bed ▷ *noun* **1** a kind of couch or sofa. **2** a hospital bed for a DAY PATIENT. ◷ 16c in sense 1.

day book ▷ *noun, bookkeeping* a book for entering the transactions of each day as they are made. ◷ 16c.

day-boy, **day-girl** and **day-scholar** ▷ *noun* a pupil who attends a boarding school during school hours, but lives at home.

daybreak ▷ *noun* the time in the morning when light first appears in the sky; dawn.

day care ▷ *noun* supervision and care given by trained nurses or other staff to young children or elderly or handicapped people during the day. ◷ 1960s.

day centre and **day care centre** ▷ *noun* a place which provides supervision and care, and/or social activities, during the day for the elderly, the handicapped, people who have just left prison, etc. ◷ 1960s.

daydream ▷ *noun* pleasant thoughts which take one's attention away from what one is, or should be, doing. ▷ *verb, intr* to be engrossed in daydreams. • **daydreamer** *noun.* ◷ 19c as *verb*; 17c as *noun.*

day-girl see DAY-BOY

dayglo /ˈdeɪɡloʊ/ ▷ *adj* coloured luminously brilliant green, yellow, pink or orange. ◷ 1950s: from *Day-glo*, the trademark name of a brand of paint.

day-labour ▷ *noun* labour paid by the day. • **day-labourer** *noun.*

daylight ▷ *noun* **1** the light given by the Sun; natural light as opposed to electric light, etc. **2** the time in the morning when light first appears in the sky; dawn. • **beat** or **knock the living daylights out of someone** *colloq* to beat them severely. • **in broad daylight** said of a shocking or criminal act: **1** during the day. **2** openly, with no attempt to hide one's actions. • **scare** or **frighten the living daylights out of someone** *colloq* to frighten them greatly. • **see daylight 1** to begin to understand. **2** to realize that one has nearly completed a difficult or long task. ◷ 13c.

daylight robbery ▷ *noun, colloq* greatly overcharging for something.

daylight-saving time ▷ *noun* the time adopted, usually in summertime, usually one hour ahead of the local standard time, in order to increase the hours of daylight available at the end of the day.

day lily ▷ *noun* any of certain liliaceous plants whose flowers last for only one day. ◷ 16c.

daylong ▷ *adj* during the whole day. ◷ 19c.

day nursery ▷ *noun* a place where young children are looked after during the day, eg while their parents are at work.

day of action ▷ *noun* a day designated by an organization for industrial action, demonstrations, a strike, etc, in support of a cause.

day off ▷ *noun* a day away from school, work, etc.

Day of Atonement see YOM KIPPUR

Day of Judgement and **Last Judgement** ▷ *noun* according to some beliefs: the time when the world will end, and God will judge all humankind.

day of reckoning ▷ *noun* a time when mistakes, failures, bad deeds, etc are punished.

day-old ▷ *adj* one day old.

day out ▷ *noun* a day spent away from home for pleasure.

day patient ▷ *noun* a hospital patient who attends for treatment, eg minor surgery, and goes home on the same day.

day release ▷ *noun* a system by which employees are given time off work (usually one day a week) to study at college, etc. ◷ 1940s.

day return ▷ *noun* **1** a reduced bus or train fare for a journey to somewhere and back again on the same day. **2** a ticket for this type of journey.

day room ▷ *noun* a room used as a communal living room in a school, hospital, hostel, etc.

day-scholar see DAY-BOY

day school ▷ *noun* a school held during the day, as opposed to both a BOARDING SCHOOL and a NIGHT SCHOOL.

day shift ▷ *noun* **1** a period of working during the day. **2** the people who work during this period. See also BACK SHIFT, NIGHT SHIFT.

days of grace ▷ *plural noun* days allowed for payment of bills, etc, beyond the day named.

daytime ▷ *noun* the time when there is normally daylight, between sunrise and sunset. ◷ 16c.

day-to-day ▷ *adj* daily; routine.

day trip ▷ *noun* a trip made to somewhere and back within one day. • **day-tripper** *noun.* ◷ Early 19c.

daze /deɪz/ ▷ *verb* (***dazed, dazing***) to make someone feel confused or unable to think clearly (eg by a blow or shock). ▷ *noun* a confused, forgetful or inattentive state of mind. • **dazed** *adj* affected by a blow or shock; mentally confused. • **dazedly** /ˈdeɪzɪdlɪ/ *adverb.* • **in a daze** stunned. ◷ 14c as *dase*: from Norse *dasask* to be weary.

dazzle /ˈdazəl/ ▷ *verb* (***dazzled, dazzling***) **1** to make someone unable to see properly, with or because of a strong light. **2** to impress someone greatly by one's beauty, charm, skill, etc. • **dazzler** *noun.* ◷ 15c: from DAZE.

dazzling ▷ *adj* **1** temporarily blinding. **2** highly impressive; brilliant □ *a dazzling display.* • **dazzlingly** *adverb.*

Db ▷ *symbol, chem* dubnium.

dB ▷ *abbreviation* decibel, or decibels.

DBE ▷ *abbreviation* Dame Commander of the Order of the British Empire.

dbl. ▷ *abbreviation* double.

DBMS see under DATABANK

DBS ▷ *abbreviation* direct broadcast by satellite.

DC¹ ▷ *noun* (***DCs*** or ***DC's***) District Commissioner.

DC² ▷ *abbreviation* **1** *music* DA CAPO. **2** DIRECT CURRENT. Compare AC. **3** District of Columbia. **4** Doctor of Chiropractic.

DCC ▷ *abbreviation* digital compact cassette.

DCL ▷ *abbreviation* Doctor of Civil Law.

DCM ▷ *abbreviation* Distinguished Conduct Medal.

DCMG ▷ *abbreviation* Dame Commander of the Order of St Michael and St George.

DCVO ▷ *abbreviation* Dame Commander of the Royal Victorian Order.

DD ▷ *abbreviation: Divinitatis Doctor* (Latin), Doctor of Divinity.

dd ▷ *abbreviation* direct debit.

D-Day ▷ *noun* **1** the date of the opening day of the Allied invasion of Europe in World War II, 6 June 1944. **2** any critical day of action. ⓘ 'D' for 'unnamed *day*'.

DDR ▷ *abbreviation: Deutsche Demokratische Republik* (German), the former German Democratic Republic or East Germany.

DDS ▷ *abbreviation* **1** digital data storage. **2** Doctor of Dental Surgery.

DDT ▷ *abbreviation* dichlorodiphenyltrichloroethane /daɪˈklɔːroʊdaɪfiːnaɪltraɪklɔːroʊiːθeɪn/, a highly toxic chemical compound formerly widely used as an insecticide, but use of which is now restricted or banned in most countries due to extensive pollution of the environment resulting from its use.

de- ▷ *prefix, signifying* **1** down or away ▫ *debase*. **2** reversal or removal ▫ *decriminalize*. **3** completely ▫ *decrepitate*. ⓘ Senses 1 and 3 from Latin *de* off, from; sense 2 from French *des-*, from Latin *dis-* (see DIS-).

deacon /ˈdiːkən/ ▷ *noun* **1** a member of the lowest rank of clergy in the Roman Catholic and Anglican churches. **2** in some other churches: a member of the church with certain duties such as looking after the church's financial affairs. See also DIACONATE. ⓘ Anglo-Saxon *diacon*: from Greek *diakonos* servant.

deaconess /diːkəˈnɛs, ˈdiːkənɛs/ ▷ *noun* **1** in some churches: a woman who has similar duties to those of a deacon. **2** in some churches: a woman whose duties are similar to those of a minister and who acts as an assistant to the minister. ⓘ 16c.

deactivate /dɪˈaktɪveɪt/ ▷ *verb* to remove or lessen the capacity of (something such as a bomb) to function or work. • **deactivation** *noun*. ⓘ Early 20c.

dead /dɛd/ ▷ *adj* **1** no longer living. **2** not alive. **3** no longer in existence; extinct. **4** with nothing living or growing in or on it. **5** not, or no longer, functioning; not connected to a source of power. **6** no longer burning. **7** no longer in use for everyday communication ▫ *a dead language*. **8** no longer of interest or importance ▫ *a dead issue*. **9** having little or no excitement or activity; boring. **10** without feeling; numb. **11** complete; absolute. **12** said of a sound: dull. **13** *sport* said of a ball: in a position where it cannot be played until brought back into the game. **14** (**the dead**) dead people (see THE 4b). ▷ *adverb, slang* absolutely; quite; exactly; very ▫ *dead drunk* ▫ *dead right*. • **deadness** *noun*. • **dead against something** completely opposed to it. • **dead as a dodo** or **a doornail** or **a herring** or **mutton** absolutely dead. • **dead from the neck up** *derog colloq* very stupid or of little intelligence. • **dead on** exact; exactly ▫ *dead on time*. See also DEAD-ON. • **dead to something** incapable of understanding it; not affected by it. • **dead to the world** *colloq* fast asleep. • **I,** *etc* **wouldn't be seen dead doing something**, *colloq* I, etc would never do it. • **over my dead body** never. • **the dead of night** the middle of the night, when it is most intensely dark and still. • **the dead of winter** the middle of winter, when it is most intensely cold. ⓘ Anglo-Saxon.

dead-and-alive ▷ *adj* said of a person or place, etc: dull; uninteresting.

dead-ball line ▷ *noun, rugby* a line worked out behind the goal line at each end of the pitch, beyond which the ball is out of play.

deadbeat ▷ *noun, colloq* a useless person; a down-and-out. ⓘ 19c.

dead beat ▷ *adj, colloq* exhausted.

dead bolt ▷ *noun* a lock which is moved by turning the key or knob without the intervention of a spring. Also called **deadlock**.

dead-cat bounce ▷ *noun, stock exchange* a temporary recovery of share prices following a sharp fall, not indicative of a true upturn but merely caused by some reinvestment by speculators who had already sold shares.

dead centre ▷ *noun* **1** *engineering* in a reciprocating engine or pump: either of the positions at the top and bottom of a piston stroke, at which the CRANK and CONNECTING-ROD are in line and there is no actual turning effect. Also called **dead point**. **2** (*usually* **top** or **bottom dead centre**) the non-rotating centre in the TAILSTOCK of a lathe.

dead colour ▷ *noun, art* in painting, the first layer of paint thinly applied to the surface of a canvas or panel.

dead duck ▷ *noun, colloq* someone or something with no chance of success or survival. ⓘ 19c.

deaden /ˈdɛdən/ ▷ *verb* (***deadened***, ***deadening***) **1** to lessen, weaken or make less sharp, strong, etc. **2** to make something soundproof. • **deadener** *noun*. • **deadening** *noun, adj*. ⓘ 17c.

dead end ▷ *noun* **1** a passage, road, etc, closed off at one end. **2** a situation or activity with no possibility of further progress or movement. ▷ *adj* (**dead-end**) allowing no progress or improvement ▫ *dead-end job*.

dead-eye ▷ *noun, naut* **1** a round flattish wooden block with a rope or iron band passing around it, and pierced with three holes for a LANYARD. **2** *chiefly US* a skilled marksman.

deadfall ▷ *noun* a trap with a weight that falls on the prey when its support is removed.

deadhead ▷ *noun, chiefly N Amer* **1** someone who enjoys privileges without paying, such as free theatre tickets. **2** an ineffective unproductive person. **3** a train, etc, travelling empty. **4** a sunken or semi-submerged log in a waterway. ▷ *verb* to remove withered or dead flowers from (plants).

dead heat ▷ *noun* in a race, competition, etc: the result when two or more competitors produce equally good performances, or finish (a race) with exactly the same time. ⓘ 19c.

dead letter ▷ *noun* **1** a rule or law no longer obeyed or not in force. **2** a letter that cannot be delivered nor returned to the sender because it lacks the necessary details of direction.

dead-letter box ▷ *noun* a place where secret messages, etc, may be left for later collection.

dead light ▷ *noun, naut* a storm shutter for a porthole, etc.

deadline ▷ *noun* a time by which something must be done. ⓘ 1920s in this sense; 19c originally meaning 'a line that does not move' and *US* 'a line around a military prison beyond which an escaping prisoner could be shot'.

deadlock ▷ *noun* **1** a situation in which no further progress towards an agreement is possible. **2** a DEAD BOLT. ▷ *verb, tr & intr* to make or come to a situation of deadlock. ⓘ 18c.

dead loss ▷ *noun, colloq* someone or something that is totally useless.

deadly ▷ *adj* (***deadlier***, ***deadliest***) **1** causing or likely to cause death. **2** *colloq* very dull or uninteresting. **3** very great ▫ *in deadly earnest*. ▷ *adverb* very; absolutely. • **deadliness** *noun*.

deadly nightshade ▷ *noun* a plant with bell-shaped purple flowers and poisonous black berries from which the drug BELLADONNA is obtained. ⓘ 16c.

deadly sin see THE SEVEN DEADLY SINS

dead man's handle and **dead man's pedal** ▷ *noun* a device on a machine, eg a railway engine, which must be kept pressed down for the machine to operate and which stops the machine if the pressure is released. ⌚ Early 20c.

dead march ▷ *noun, music* a piece of solemn music played at funeral processions, especially those of soldiers.

dead men and (*Austral & NZ*) **dead marines** ▷ *plural noun, colloq* empty bottles left after a drinking session or a party.

dead-nettle ▷ *noun* any of various plants superficially like a nettle but without a sting. ⌚ 14c.

dead-on ▷ *adj, colloq* accurate; spot-on.

deadpan ▷ *adj* said of someone's expression, etc: showing no emotion or feeling, especially when joking but pretending to be serious. ⌚ 1920s.

dead point see DEAD CENTRE.

dead reckoning ▷ *noun* the estimating of the position of a ship, aircraft, etc from the distance and direction travelled, without looking at the position of the stars, Sun or Moon. ⌚ 17c.

dead ringer ▷ *noun, slang* a person who, or thing which, looks exactly like someone or something else.

dead set ▷ *noun* a complete standstill, eg the position of a gundog pointing at game. See also POINT (*verb* 4). ▷ *adj* **1** absolutely determined. **2** said of a hunting dog: pointing at game. ▷ *adverb* absolutely determined. • **dead set against something** completely opposed to it. • **dead set on something** determined or keen to do or acquire it.

dead weight ▷ *noun* **1** a heavy load. **2** *technical* (*also* **deadweight**) the difference in the displacement of a ship when unloaded and loaded. ⌚ 17c.

dead wood ▷ *noun* **1** dead trees; dead branches, etc. **2** *colloq* someone or something that is no longer useful or needed. ⌚ 18c.

deaf /dɛf/ ▷ *adj* **1** unable to hear at all or unable to hear well. **2** (*usually* **deaf to something**) not willing to listen to (advice, appeals, criticism, etc). **3** (**the deaf**) deaf people in general (see THE 4b). • **deafly** *adverb.* • **deafness** *noun* partial or total loss of hearing in one or both ears. • **turn a deaf ear to someone** or **something** to ignore or refuse to pay any attention to them. ⌚ Anglo-Saxon.

deaf aid ▷ *noun* a HEARING AID.

deaf alphabet and (*now often considered offensive*) **deaf-and-dumb alphabet** ▷ *noun* a system of representing the letters of the alphabet by signs made with the hands.

deafen /'dɛfən/ ▷ *verb* (***deafened, deafening***) to make someone deaf or temporarily unable to hear. • **deafening** *adj* **1** extremely loud. **2** causing deafness. • **deafeningly** *adverb.* ⌚ 16c.

deaf language and (*now often considered offensive*) **deaf-and-dumb language** ▷ *noun* sign language used by the deaf.

deaf-mute ▷ *noun, often considered offensive* someone who is both deaf and unable to speak. ▷ *adj* unable to hear or speak. ⌚ 19c: DEAF + MUTE, after French *sourd-muet.*

deal[1] /diːl/ ▷ *noun* **1** a bargain, agreement or arrangement, especially in business or politics. **2** a particular form of treatment or behaviour towards someone □ *a rough deal.* **3** the act or way of, or a player's turn of, sharing out cards among the players in a card game. ▷ *verb* (***dealt*** /dɛlt/, ***dealing***) *tr & intr* **1** (*also* **deal out**) to divide the cards among the players in a card game. **2** (*also* **deal out**) to give something out to a number of people, etc. • **a good** or **great deal 1** a large quantity. **2** very much or often □ *She sees them a great deal.* • **deal someone a blow** to hit, strike or distress them. ⌚ Anglo-Saxon *dæl* a part.

■ **deal in something** to buy and sell it.

■ **deal with something** or **someone 1** to take action regarding them. **2** to be concerned with them.

deal[2] /diːl/ ▷ *noun* a plank or planks of soft wood, now always fir or pine wood, used for making furniture, etc. ⌚ 15c as *dele*: from German dialect.

de-alcoholize or **de-alcoholise** /diː'alkəhəlaɪz/ ▷ *verb* (***de-alcoholized, de-alcoholizing***) to reduce the amount of alcohol in wine, beer, etc. ⌚ 19c.

dealer ▷ *noun* **1** a person or firm dealing in retail goods; a trader. **2** the player who deals in a card game. • **dealership** *noun* **1** a business which buys and sells things. **2** a business licensed to sell a particular product by its manufacturer.

dealings ▷ *plural noun* **1** one's manner of acting towards others. **2** business, etc, contacts and transactions.

dealt *past tense, past participle of* DEAL[1]

dean /diːn/ ▷ *noun* **1** a senior clergyman in an Anglican cathedral. **2** *RC Church* the chief cardinal-bishop of the College of Cardinals. **3** a senior official in a university or college, sometimes with responsibility for student discipline. **4** the head of a university or college faculty. See also RURAL DEAN. ⌚ 14c: from French *deien.*

deanery ▷ *noun* (***deaneries***) **1** the position or office of a dean. **2** the house of a dean. **3** a group of parishes for which a rural dean has responsibility. ⌚ 15c.

dear /dɪə(r)/ ▷ *adj* **1** high in price; charging high prices. **2** lovable; attractive. **3** used in addressing someone at the start of a letter. **4** (*usually* **dear to someone**) greatly loved by, or very important or precious to, them. ▷ *noun* (*also* **deary, dearie**) (***dearies***) **1** a charming or lovable person. **2** used especially as a form of address: a person one loves or likes. ▷ *exclamation* (*also* **deary, dearie**) used as an expression of dismay, etc □ *Dear, dear!* □ *Dear me!* • **dearly** *adverb* **1** very much. **2** at a high price or cost. • **dearness** *noun.* • **cost someone dear** to cause or result in a lot of trouble or suffering. • **dear knows** *colloq* no one knows. • **pay dearly** to be made to suffer. ⌚ Anglo-Saxon *deore.*

dearth /dɜːθ/ ▷ *noun* a scarceness or lack of something. ⌚ 13c as *derthe*: from DEAR + -TH[2].

deasil /'dɛʃəl,'diːəl/ ▷ *adverb, Scots* in the direction of the sun. Opposite of WITHERSHINS. ⌚ 18c: from Gaelic *deiseil*

death /dɛθ/ ▷ *noun* **1** the time, act or manner of dying, or the state of being dead. **2** *biol* the cessation of all the vital functions that are required to keep an organism alive. **3** *medicine* the cessation of the heartbeat when this is accompanied by BRAIN DEATH. **4** *often humorous* something which causes a person to die □ *His antics will be the death of me.* **5** the end or destruction of something. **6** (**Death**) the figure of a skeleton, as a symbol of death. • **deathless** *adj, often ironic* immortal; unforgettable □ *deathless prose.* • **deathlessness** *noun.* • **deathlike** *adj.* • **deathliness** *noun.* • **deathly** *adj.* • **at death's door** near death; gravely ill. • **catch one's death** or **catch one's death of cold** *colloq* to catch a very bad cold. • **do someone to death** *old use* to kill them. • **do something to death** to overuse it. • **in at the death 1** present when a hunted animal, eg a fox, is killed. **2** present at the climax, end, destruction, etc of an enterprise, undertaking, etc. • **like death warmed up** or **over** *colloq* said of someone's appearance: unhealthy; very unwell. • **like grim death** very hard or tightly. • **put someone to death** to kill them or have them killed; to execute them. • **to death** very much; to an extreme or excess □ *bored to death.* • **to the death** until dead or until one's opponent is dead; to the very end. ⌚ Anglo-Saxon.

death adder ▷ *noun* a poisonous Australian snake.

deathbed ▷ *noun* the bed in which a person dies or is about to die.

deathblow ▷ *noun* **1** a blow which causes death. **2** an action, decision, etc which puts an end to or destroys (hopes, plans, etc). ⌚ 18c.

death cap ▻ *noun* an extremely poisonous toadstool. Also called **death cup** or **death angel**.

death cell ▻ *noun* a prison cell in which a prisoner who is condemned to death is kept before the sentence is carried out.

death certificate ▻ *noun* a certificate, signed by a doctor, stating the time and cause of someone's death.

death duty ▻ *noun* (*often* **death duties**) *Brit* formerly, a tax paid on the value of property left by a person after he or she has died, replaced in 1975 by CAPITAL TRANSFER TAX.

death knell ▻ *noun* **1** the ringing of a bell when someone has died. **2** an action, announcement, etc that heralds the end or destruction of (hopes, plans, etc).

death mask ▻ *noun* a mask made from the cast of a person's face after they have died. ◷ 19c.

death penalty ▻ *noun* punishment of a crime by death. ◷ 19c.

death rate ▻ *noun* the number of deaths as a proportion of the total population, usually calculated as a percentage or rate per thousand.

death rattle ▻ *noun* a particular noise made in the throat which sometimes precedes death.

death row ▻ *noun, N Amer, especially US* the part of a prison where people who have been sentenced to death are kept.

death's-head ▻ *noun* a human skull, or a picture, mask, etc representing one.

death's-head moth ▻ *noun* a hawk-moth with pale markings on the back of the thorax somewhat like a skull.

death squad ▻ *noun* an unofficial terrorist group who murder those whose views or activities they disapprove of, often operating with the tacit or covert support of the government of the day. ◷ 1960s.

death star ▻ *noun* a small, thin, star-shaped metal plate with sharpened points, used as a missile. ◷ 1980s.

death throe ▻ *noun* (*also* **death throes**) the final struggle before death.

deathtrap ▻ *noun* a building, vehicle, place, etc which is unsafe and likely to cause serious or fatal accidents.

death warrant ▻ *noun* an official order that a death sentence is to be carried out. • **sign one's own death warrant** to do something that makes one's downfall inevitable.

deathwatch beetle ▻ *noun* a type of beetle whose wood-boring larvae can cause serious structural damage, and which makes a ticking or tapping sound that was formerly believed to be a sign that someone in the building where it was heard was going to die.

death wish ▻ *noun* a desire to die, or that someone else should die.

deb ▻ *noun, colloq* a DEBUTANTE.

debacle or **débâcle** /dɪˈbɑːkəl, deɪ-/ ▻ *noun* **1** total disorder, defeat, collapse of organization, etc. **2** a breaking up of ice on a river, sometimes resulting in flooding. **3** a sudden flood of water leaving its path strewn with debris. ◷ 19c: French.

debag /diːˈbag/ ▻ *verb, colloq* to remove the trousers from someone as a prank or punishment. ◷ Early 20c.

debar /dɪˈbɑː(r)/ ▻ *verb* to stop someone from joining, taking part in, doing, etc something. • **debarment** *noun*. ◷ 15c: from French *débarrer*.

debark /dɪˈbɑːk/ ▻ *verb* (***debarked, debarking***) *tr & intr* to DISEMBARK. ◷ 17c: from French *débarquer*.

debase /dɪˈbeɪs/ ▻ *verb* **1** to lower the value, quality, or status of something. **2** to lower the value of (a coin) by adding metal of a lower value. • **debased** *adj* lowered in value or status; spoiled. • **debasement** *noun*. • **debaser** *noun*. • **debasing** *adj*. • **debasingly** *adverb*. ◷ 16c: DE- 1 + ABASE.

debate /dɪˈbeɪt/ ▻ *noun* **1** a formal discussion, often in front of an audience, in which two or more people put forward opposing views on a particular subject. **2** any general discussion on a subject, not necessarily in one place or at one time. ▻ *verb* (***debated, debating***) *tr & intr* **1** to hold or take part in a formal discussion on a particular topic, often in front of an audience. **2** to consider the arguments for or against something. • **debatable** or **debateable** *adj* doubtful; able to be argued about; uncertain. • **debater** *noun* someone who takes part in a debate. • **debating** *noun* formal discussion of a question. • **open to debate** not certain or agreed; in doubt. ◷ 13c: from French *debatre* to discuss.

debauch /dɪˈbɔːtʃ/ ▻ *verb* (***debauches, debauched, debauching***) to corrupt someone; to cause or persuade someone to take part in immoral, especially sexual, activities or excessive drinking. ▻ *noun* a period of debauched behaviour. • **debauched** *adj* corrupted; immoral. • **debauchedly** /-ɪdlɪ/ *adverb*. • **debauchedness** /-ɪdnəs/ *noun*. • **debauchee** /dɛbɔːˈtʃiː, -ˈʃiː/ *noun* (***debauchees***) someone who likes sensual indulgence. • **debauchery** *noun* excessive sensual indulgence. ◷ 16c: from French *desbaucher* to corrupt.

debby ▻ *adj, colloq* belonging to, suitable for or like a DEBUTANTE or debutantes. ◷ 20c.

debenture /dɪˈbɛntʃə(r)/ ▻ *noun, finance* **1** a type of loan to a company or government agency which is usually made for a set period of time and carries a fixed rate of interest. **2** the document or bond acknowledging this loan. ◷ 15c: from Latin *debentur* there are due or owed.

debilitate /dɪˈbɪlɪteɪt/ ▻ *verb* (***debilitated, debilitating***) to make someone weak or weaker. • **debilitating** *adj* weakening; enervating. • **debilitation** *noun*. • **debility** *noun*. ◷ 16c: from Latin *debilis* weak.

debit /ˈdɛbɪt/ ▻ *noun* **1** an entry in an account recording what is owed or has been spent. **2** a sum taken from a bank, etc account. **3** a deduction made from a bill or account. Compare CREDIT. ▻ *verb* (***debited, debiting***) **1** to take from (an account, etc). **2** to record in a debit entry. ◷ 15c: from Latin *debitum* what is due.

debit card ▻ *noun* a card used by a purchaser by means of which money is directly transferred from his or her account to the retailers. Compare CREDIT CARD. ◷ 1970s.

debonair /dɛbəˈnɛə(r)/ ▻ *adj* said especially of a man: cheerful, charming and of elegant appearance and good manners. • **debonairly** *adverb*. ◷ 18c in this sense; 13c as *debonere* meaning 'mild, kindly, courteous': from French *de bon aire* of good manners.

debouch /dɪˈbaʊtʃ, dɪˈbuːʃ/ ▻ *verb* (***debouches, debouched, debouching***) *technical, intr* said of troops or a river, etc: to come out of a narrow place or opening into a wider or more open place. ◷ 18c: from French *déboucher*, from *de* from + *bouche* mouth.

debouchment /dɪˈbaʊtʃmənt, dɪˈbuːʃ-/ ▻ *noun* **1** coming out into an open place. **2** the outlet of a river, etc. ◷ 19c.

debrief /diːˈbriːf/ ▻ *verb* to gather information from (a diplomat, astronaut, soldier, etc) after a battle, event, mission, etc. • **debriefing** *noun* interrogation after a completed mission, etc. ◷ 1940s.

debris or **débris** /ˈdɛbriː, dəˈbriː/ ▻ *noun* **1** what remains of something crushed, smashed, destroyed, etc. **2** rubbish. **3** small pieces of rock. ◷ 18c: French.

debt /dɛt/ ▻ *noun* **1** something which is owed. See also BAD DEBT. **2** the state of owing something. • **in someone's debt** under an obligation, not necessarily financial, to them. ◷ 13c as *dete*; from 15c forms with *-b-*: from French *dette*, from Latin *debitum* what is owed.

debt of honour ▷ *noun* a debt one is morally but not legally obliged to pay.

debtor /ˈdɛtə(r)/ ▷ *noun* someone owing money. Compare CREDITOR. ⓘ 13c as *dettur*: see DEBT.

debug /diːˈbʌg/ ▷ *verb* **1** to remove secret microphones from (a room, etc). **2** to look for and remove faults in (a computer program). **3** to remove insects from someone or something. ⓘ 20c.

debunk /diːˈbʌŋk/ ▷ *verb* to show (a person's claims, good reputation, etc) to be false or unjustified. ⓘ 1920s.

debus /diːˈbʌs/ ▷ *verb, tr & intr* to unload from, or get out of, a bus or other vehicle. ⓘ Early 20c.

debut or **début** /ˈdeɪbjuː, ˈdɛbjuː/ ▷ *noun* **1** the first public appearance of a performer. **2** the formal presentation of a debutante. ⓘ 18c: French *début*.

debutante or **débutante** /ˈdɛbjʊtɑnt, ˈdeɪbjʊtɒnt/ ▷ *noun* a young woman making her first formal appearance as an adult in upper-class society, usually at a ball. ⓘ 19c: French *débutante*, from *débuter* to start off.

Dec. ▷ *abbreviation* December.

dec. ▷ *abbreviation* deceased.

deca- and (before a vowel) **dec-** ▷ *combining form, signifying* ten □ ***decagon***. ⓘ From Greek *deka* ten.

decade /ˈdɛkeɪd, dɪˈkeɪd/ ▷ *noun* **1** a period of 10 years. **2** a group or series of 10 things, etc. ⓘ 17c in sense 1; 15c in sense 2: from Greek *deka* ten.

decadence /ˈdɛkədəns/ ▷ *noun* **1** a falling from high to low standards in morals, art, etc. **2** the state of having low or immoral standards of behaviour, etc. ⓘ 16c: from French *décadence*, from Latin *de* from + *cadere* to fall.

decadent /ˈdɛkədənt/ ▷ *adj* having low moral standards. • **decadently** *adverb*.

decaff or **decaf** /ˈdiːkaf/ *colloq* ▷ *adj* decaffeinated. ▷ *noun* decaffeinated coffee.

decaffeinate /diːˈkafɪneɪt, dɪ-/ ▷ *verb* (***decaffeinated, decaffeinating***) to remove all or part of the caffeine from something. • **decaffeinated** *adj* said of coffee, etc: having all or part of the caffeine removed. ⓘ 1920s as *decaffeinated*: from DE- (sense 2) + CAFFEINE + -ATE[1].

decagon /ˈdɛkəgən, -gɒn/ ▷ *noun, geom* a polygon with 10 sides and 10 angles. • **decagonal** /dɪˈkagənəl/ *adj* having 10 sides and 10 angles. ⓘ 17c: from DECA-+ Greek *gonia* angle.

decahedron /dɛkəˈhiːdrən/ ▷ *noun* a solid figure with ten faces. • **decahedral** *adj* said of a solid figure: having 10 faces. ⓘ 19c: from DECA-+ Greek *hedra* seat.

decal /ˈdiːkal, dɪˈkal/ ▷ *noun, chiefly N Amer* a picture or design prepared for permanent transfer to glass, china, plastic, etc. ⓘ 1930s; abbreviation of DECALCOMANIA.

decalcify /diːˈkalsɪfaɪ/ ▷ *verb* to remove calcium from (bones), or deprive (bones) of calcium. • **decalcification** /-fɪˈkeɪʃən/ *noun*. • **decalcifier** *noun*. ⓘ 19c.

decalcomania /dɪkalkəˈmeɪnɪə/ ▷ *noun* the process of transferring images from specially prepared paper onto surfaces of china, glass, plastic, etc. ⓘ 19c: from French *décalcomanie*, from *décalquer* to trace or copy.

decalitre or (*N Amer*) **decaliter** /ˈdɛkəliːtə(r)/ *noun* a measure of volume equal to 10 litres.

the Decalogue /ˈdɛkəlɒg/ ▷ *noun, Bible* the Ten Commandments given by God to Moses. ⓘ 14c: from DECA-+ Greek *logos* word.

decametre or (*N Amer*) **decameter** /ˈdɛkəmiːtə(r)/ ▷ *noun* a measure of length equal to 10 metres.

decamp ▷ *verb, intr* **1** to go away suddenly, especially secretly. **2** to break camp. ⓘ 18c in sense 1; 17c in sense 2: from French *décamper*.

decanal /dɪˈkeɪnəl/ ▷ *adj, relig* **1** belonging or relating to a DEAN or DEANERY. **2** said of part of a choir: positioned on the same side of the cathedral as the dean, ie the south side. ⓘ 18c: from Latin *decanus* dean.

decant /dɪˈkant/ ▷ *verb* (***decanted, decanting***) **1** to pour (wine, etc) from one bottle or container to another, leaving any sediment behind. **2** to remove (people) from where they usually live to some other place. ⓘ 17c: from French *décanter*, from Latin *de* from + *canthus* spout.

decanter /dɪˈkantə(r)/ ▷ *noun* an ornamental bottle with a stopper, used for decanted wine, sherry, whisky, etc. ⓘ 18c: from DECANT.

decapitate /dɪˈkapɪteɪt/ ▷ *verb* (***decapitated, decapitating***) to cut off the head of someone. • **decapitation** *noun*. ⓘ 17c: from DE- 1 + Latin *caput* head.

decapod /ˈdɛkəpɒd/ ▷ *noun, zool* **1** any of various crustaceans which have 10 limbs, including pincers, eg crabs, lobsters, prawns. **2** any of various cephalopods with ten arms, eg squid, cuttlefish. ⓘ 19c: from Greek *pous, podos* foot.

decarbonize or **decarbonise** /diːˈkɑːbənaɪz/ (***decarbonized, decarbonizing***) and **decarburize** or **decarburise** /diːˈkɑːbjʊraɪz/ (***decarburized, decarburizing***) ▷ *verb* to remove carbon from (an internal-combustion engine). Also *colloq* **decoke** (***decoked, decoking***). • **decarbonization** or **decarburization** *noun*.

decathlete /dɪˈkaθliːt/ ▷ *noun* a contestant in a DECATHLON.

decathlon /dɪˈkaθlɒn/ ▷ *noun* an athletic competition (usually for men) in which competitors take part in the following 10 events over two days: 100m, long jump, shot put, high jump, 400m, 110m hurdles, discus, pole vault, javelin and 1500m. Compare HEPTATHLON, PENTATHLON. ⓘ 1912: from DECA- + Greek *athlon* contest.

decay /dɪˈkeɪ/ ▷ *verb* (***decayed, decaying***) **1** *tr & intr* to make or become rotten, ruined, weaker in health or power, etc. **2** *intr, physics* said of a radioactive substance: to break down spontaneously into one or more ISOTOPES which may or may not be radioactive. ▷ *noun* (***decays***) **1** the natural breakdown of dead organic matter. **2** *physics* the spontaneous breakdown of an unstable nucleus of a radioactive substance into one or more ISOTOPES which may or may not be radioactive, with the emission of ALPHA PARTICLES or BETA PARTICLES, or GAMMA RAYS. **3** a gradual decrease in health, power, quality, etc. **4** rotten matter in a tooth, etc. • **decayed** *adj* **1** rotten. **2** impoverished. ⓘ 15c: from French *decair*.

decease /dɪˈsiːs/ ▷ *noun, formal, law* death. ⓘ 14c: from Latin *decessus* departure or death.

deceased /dɪˈsiːst/ ▷ *adj, formal, law* **1** dead, especially recently dead. **2** (**the deceased**) the dead person or dead people in question (see THE 4b). ⓘ 15c as *adj*; 17c as *noun*.

decedent /dɪˈsiːdənt/ ▷ *noun, now chiefly US law* a deceased person. ⓘ 16c: from Latin *decedere* to die.

deceit /dɪˈsiːt/ ▷ *noun* **1** an act of deceiving or misleading. **2** dishonesty; deceitfulness; willingness to deceive. • **deceitful** *adj*. • **deceitfully** *adverb*. ⓘ 14c: French *deceite*.

deceive /dɪˈsiːv/ ▷ *verb* (***deceived, deceiving***) **1** to mislead or lie to someone. **2** to convince (oneself) that something is true when it is not. See also DECEPTION. • **deceiver** *noun*. ⓘ 13c: from Latin *decipere* to deceive.

decelerate /diːˈsɛləreɪt/ ▷ *verb* (***decelerated, decelerating***) *tr & intr* to slow down, or make something (especially a vehicle, machine, etc) slow down. • **deceleration** /diːsɛləˈreɪʃən/ *noun*. • **decelerator** *noun*. ⓘ 19c: from DE- 1 + ACCELERATE.

December /dɪˈsɛmbə(r)/ ▷ *noun* the twelfth and last month of the year, which has 31 days. ⓘ 13c: from Latin *decem* ten, because it was at one time the tenth month of the Roman year.

decency /'diːsənsɪ/ ▷ *noun* (***decencies***) **1** decent behaviour or character. **2** (**decencies**) the generally accepted rules of respectable or moral behaviour. ⓘ 16c: from DECENT.

decennial /dɪ'sɛnɪəl/ ▷ *adj* **1** happening every 10 years. **2** consisting of 10 years. ⓘ 17c: from Latin *decem* ten + *annus* year.

decent /'diːsənt/ ▷ *adj* **1** respectable; suitable; modest, not vulgar or immoral. **2** kind, tolerant or likeable. **3** fairly good; adequate □ *a decent performance.* ● **decently** *adverb.* ⓘ 16c: from Latin *decere* to be fitting.

decentralize or **decentralise** /diː'sɛntrəlaɪz/ ▷ *verb, tr & intr* said especially of a part of government, industry, etc: to alter or be altered by the transfer of organization, etc from one main central place to several smaller less central positions. ● **decentralist** or **decentralizer** *noun.* ● **decentralization** *noun.* ⓘ 19c.

deception /dɪ'sɛpʃən/ ▷ *noun* **1** an act of deceiving or the state of being deceived. **2** something which deceives or misleads. ⓘ 15c: from Latin *decipere, deceptum* to deceive.

deceptive /dɪ'sɛptɪv/ ▷ *adj* deceiving; misleading. ● **deceptively** *adverb.* ● **deceptiveness** *noun.* ⓘ 17c.

deci- /'dɛsɪ/ ▷ *combining form* (abbreviation **d**) *signifying* one-tenth □ *decilitre.* ⓘ From Latin *decimus* tenth.

decibel /'dɛsɪbɛl, -bəl/ ▷ *noun* (symbol **dB**) a unit equal to 1/10 of a BEL, used for comparing levels of power, especially sound, on a logarithmic scale.

decide /dɪ'saɪd/ ▷ *verb* (***decided, deciding***) **1** to settle something; to make the final result of something certain. **2** to make someone decide in a certain way. **3** to make a formal judgement about something. ● **decide to do something** to establish an intention of doing it. ⓘ 14c: from Latin *decidere* to cut down, settle.

■ **decide against something** to reject it as an intention or course of action.

■ **decide on** or **about something** to establish an intention or course of action regarding it.

decided ▷ *adj* **1** clear and definite; unmistakeable. **2** determined; showing no doubt. ● **decidedly** *adverb* undoubtedly; definitely □ *decidedly ugly.*

decider ▷ *noun* **1** someone or something that decides. **2** something that decides the result of something, eg the winning goal in a match.

deciduous /dɪ'sɪdjʊəs/ ▷ *adj* **1** *bot* denoting plants which shed all their leaves at a certain time of year, usually the autumn in temperate regions. Compare EVERGREEN. **2** *biol* denoting structures which are shed at maturity or after a period of growth, eg milk teeth. ● **deciduousness** *noun.* ⓘ 17c: from Latin *decidere* to fall down.

decigram or **decigramme** /'dɛsɪgram/ ▷ *noun* one tenth of a gram. ⓘ 19c.

decilitre /'dɛsɪliːtə(r)/ ▷ *noun* one tenth of a litre. ⓘ 19c.

decillion /dɪ'sɪlɪən/ ▷ *noun* **1** *Brit, France, Germany* (symbol 10^{60}) a million raised to the tenth power. **2** *chiefly N Amer* (symbol 10^{33}) a thousand raised to the eleventh power. ● **decillionth** *adj, noun.* ⓘ 18c: from Latin *decem* ten + MILLION.

decimal /'dɛsɪməl/ ▷ *adj* **1** based on the number 10; relating to powers of 10 or the base 10. **2** denoting a system of measurement, etc, with units that are related to each other by multiples of 10. ▷ *noun* a decimal fraction. ⓘ 17c: from Latin *decimalis*, from *decem* ten.

decimal classification see DEWEY DECIMAL SYSTEM

decimal currency ▷ *noun* a system of money in which each coin or note is either a tenth of or 10 times another in value.

decimal fraction ▷ *noun* a fraction in which tenths, hundredths, thousandths, etc are written in figures after a decimal point which follows the figure or figures expressing whole numbers, eg 0.5 = 5/10 or 1/2. Compare VULGAR FRACTION.

decimalize or **decimalise** /'dɛsɪməlaɪz/ ▷ *verb* (***decimalized, decimalizing***) to convert (numbers, a currency, etc) from a non-decimal to a decimal form. ● **decimalization** *noun.* ⓘ 19c.

decimal place ▷ *noun* the position of a digit to the right of the DECIMAL POINT.

decimal point ▷ *noun* the point (.) which separates the UNIT and the DECIMAL FRACTION.

decimal system ▷ *noun* **1** a system of measurement with units that are related to each other by multiples of 10. **2** the number system in common use, in which the place values of the digits in a number correspond to multiples of powers of 10. **3** see DEWEY DECIMAL SYSTEM. ⓘ 17c: from Latin *decem* ten.

decimate /'dɛsɪmeɪt/ ▷ *verb* (***decimated, decimating***) to reduce greatly in number; to destroy a large part or number of something. ● **decimation** *noun.* ● **decimator** *noun.* ⓘ 17c in this sense; 16c in historical sense 'to select by lot and execute one in every ten': from Latin *decimare* to take a tenth person or thing, from *decem* ten.

decimetre /'dɛsɪmiːtə(r)/ ▷ *noun* one tenth of a metre.

decipher /dɪ'saɪfə(r)/ ▷ *verb* (***deciphered, deciphering***) **1** to translate (a message or text in code or in an unfamiliar or strange form of writing) into ordinary understandable language. **2** to work out the meaning of something obscure or difficult to read. ● **decipherability** *noun.* ● **decipherable** *adj.* ● **decipherer** *noun.* ● **decipherment** *noun.* ⓘ 16c.

decision /dɪ'sɪʒən/ ▷ *noun* **1** the act of deciding. **2** something decided. **3** the ability to make decisions and act on them firmly □ *able to act with decision in a crisis.* ⓘ 15c: from Latin *decisio* cutting off.

decision table ▷ *noun, computing, logic* a table comprising four sections showing a number of conditions and actions to be taken if these are not met, indicating the action to be taken under any condition or set of conditions.

decisive /dɪ'saɪsɪv/ ▷ *adj* **1** putting an end to doubt or dispute. **2** willing and able to make decisions quickly and with firmness. ● **decisively** *adverb.* ● **decisiveness** *noun.*

deck[1] ▷ *noun* **1** a platform extending from one side of a ship to the other, and forming a floor or covering. **2** a floor or platform in a bus, bridge, etc. **3** *N Amer, especially US* a pack of playing-cards. **4** the part of a tape recorder or computer which contains the mechanism for operation. **5** the unit that contains the turntable and pick-up of a record player. ● **clear the decks** to clear away obstacles or deal with preliminary jobs in preparation for further activity. ● **hit the deck** *colloq* **1** to lie or fall down suddenly and quickly on the ground or floor. **2** to get out of bed. **3** to go into action. ⓘ 15c: from Dutch *dec* roof or covering.

deck[2] ▷ *verb* (***decked, decking***) **1** (*usually* **deck something out**) to decorate or embellish it. **2** to provide or fit (eg a boat) with a deck. ● **decked** *adj.* ⓘ 15c: from Dutch *dekken* to cover.

deck chair ▷ *noun* a light folding chair made of wood and a length of canvas or other heavy fabric, usually used for sitting outside in fine weather. ⓘ 19c.

-decker ▷ *adj, in compounds, signifying* having a specified number of decks or layers □ *a double-decker bus.* Also *as noun* □ *a double-decker.*

deck hand ▷ *noun* someone who does general work on the deck of a ship; an ordinary sailor.

deck house ▷ *noun* a room, house, etc erected on the deck of a ship.

decking ▷ *noun* **1** the act of adorning; adornment. **2** a platform; the materials used to build a deck. ⓘ 16c: DECK[1,2].

deckle /ˈdɛkəl/ ▷ *noun* in paper-making: **1** a device for fixing the width of a sheet. **2** a DECKLE EDGE. ◷ 18c: from German *Deckel* a lid.

deckle edge ▷ *noun* the rough edge of handmade paper, or an imitation of this.

decko see DEKKO

deck quoits ▷ *noun* the game of QUOITS as played on the deck of a ship with rope rings. ◷ Early 20c.

deck tennis ▷ *noun* a modified version of TENNIS (sense 1), suitable for playing on board ship. ◷ Early 20c.

declaim /dɪˈkleɪm/ ▷ *verb* (***declaimed, declaiming***) **1** *tr & intr* to make (a speech) in an impressive and dramatic manner. **2** *intr* (*usually* **declaim against something**) to protest about it loudly and passionately. ● **declaimer** *noun*. ◷ 14c: from Latin *declamare*.

declamation /dɛkləˈmeɪʃən/ ▷ *noun* an impressive or emotional speech, usually made in protest or condemnation. ◷ 16c: from Latin *declamare, declamatum* to declaim.

declamatory /dɪˈklamətərɪ/ ▷ *adj* said of speech: impassioned; rhetorical. ● **declamatorily** *adverb*. ◷ 16c: from Latin *declamare, declamatum* to declaim.

declarative /dɪˈklarətɪv/ ▷ *adj, grammar* making a statement. ● **declaratively** *adverb*. ◷ 17c.

declare /dɪˈklɛə(r)/ ▷ *verb* (***declared, declaring***) **1** to announce something publicly or formally □ *declare war.* **2** to say something firmly or emphatically. **3** to make known (goods on which duty must be paid, income on which tax should be paid, etc). **4** *intr, cricket* to end an innings voluntarily before 10 wickets have fallen. **5** *tr & intr, cards* to state or show that one is holding (certain cards). ● **declarable** *adj*. ● **declaration** *noun* declaring; a formal statement or announcement. ● **declaratorily** *adverb*. ● **declaratory** /dɪˈklarətərɪ/ *adj* making a statement or declaration. ● **declarer** *noun*.● ◷ 14c: from Latin *declarare*, from *clarus* clear.

■ **declare for** or **against something** to state one's support or opposition regarding it.

declassify /diːˈklasɪfaɪ/ ▷ *verb* to take (an official document, etc) off a list of secret information and allow public access to it. ● **declassification** *noun*. ◷ 19c.

declension /dɪˈklɛnʃən/ ▷ *noun, grammar* **1** in certain languages, eg Latin: any of various sets of different forms taken by nouns, adjectives or pronouns to indicate case, number and gender. **2** the act of stating these forms. See also CONJUGATION, DECLINE 4. **3** any group of nouns or adjectives showing the same pattern of forms. ◷ 16c: from French, from Latin *declinatio* bending aside.

declination /dɛklɪˈneɪʃən/ ▷ *noun* **1** *technical* the angle between TRUE NORTH and MAGNETIC NORTH, which varies according to time and geographical location. **2** *astron* the angular distance of a star or planet north or south of the celestial equator. **3** *now US* declining; a polite refusal. ◷ 16c: from Latin *declinatio* bending aside.

decline /dɪˈklaɪn/ ▷ *verb* (***declined, declining***) **1** to refuse (an invitation, etc), especially politely. **2** *intr* to become less strong or less healthy. **3** *intr* to become less in quality or quantity. **4** *grammar* to state the pattern of forms representing the various cases of (a noun, adjective or pronoun). See also CONJUGATE, DECLENSION. ▷ *noun* a lessening of strength, health, quality, quantity, etc. ● **declinable** *adj, grammar* having declensions; able to be declined. ● **on the decline** becoming less; deteriorating. ◷ 14c: from Latin *declinare* to bend aside.

declivity /dɪˈklɪvɪtɪ/ ▷ *noun* (***declivities***) *formal* a downward slope. Compare ACCLIVITY. ● **declivitous** *adj*. ◷ 17c: from Latin *declivitas*, from *clivus* sloping.

declutch /diːˈklʌtʃ/ ▷ *verb, intr* to release the clutch of (a motor vehicle). ◷ Early 20c.

decoct /dɪˈkɒkt/ ▷ *verb* (***decocted, decocting***) to extract the essence, etc of (a substance) by boiling. ◷ 15c: see DECOCTION.

decoction /dɪˈkɒkʃən/ ▷ *noun* a liquid obtained by boiling something in water, eg to extract its flavour. ◷ 14c: from Latin *decoctio*, from *coquere* to cook or boil.

decode /diːˈkoʊd/ ▷ *verb* to translate (a coded message) into ordinary language. ● **decoder** *noun* a person or device that decodes. ◷ 19c.

decoke see DECARBONIZE

decollate /diːkəˈleɪt, ˈdɛkəleɪt/ ▷ *verb* to separate (continuous stationery) into separate sheets or forms. ◷ 20c.

décolletage /deɪkɒlˈtɑːʒ/ ▷ *noun* **1** a low-cut neckline on a woman's dress, etc. **2** the exposure of the neck and shoulders in such a dress. ◷ 19c: French.

décolleté or **décolletée** /deɪˈkɒlәteɪ/ ▷ *adj* **1** said of a woman's dress, etc: having the neckline cut low at the front. **2** said of a woman: wearing such a dress, etc. ◷ 19c: from French *décolleter* to bare the neck and shoulders.

decolonize or **decolonise** /diːˈkɒlənaɪz/ ▷ *verb* to release (a state) from being a colony; to grant independence to (a colony). ● **decolonization** *noun*. ◷ 1930s; first as DECOLONIZATION.

decolour or **decolor** /diːˈkʌlə(r)/ ▷ *verb* to deprive something of colour. ◷ 19c.

decolourize or **decolourise** /diːˈkʌlәraɪz/ ▷ *verb* to DECOLOUR. Also (*US*) **decolorize** or **decolorise**.

decommission /diːkəˈmɪʃən/ ▷ *verb* to take (eg a warship or atomic reactor) out of use or operation. ● **decommissioner** *noun*. ● **decommissioning** *noun*. ◷ 1920s.

decompose /diːkəmˈpoʊz/ ▷ *verb* **1** *intr* said of a dead organism: to rot, usually as a result of the activity of fungi and bacteria. **2** *tr & intr* said of a chemical compound: to break down into simpler compounds or its constituent elements, eg as a result of heating, exposure to light or electrolysis. **3** *tr & intr, technical* to separate into smaller or simpler parts or elements. ● **decomposable** *adj*. ● **decomposer** *noun*. ◷ 18c: from French *décomposer*.

decomposition ▷ *noun* decaying; rotting; disintegration; decay.

decompress /diːkəmˈprɛs/ *technical* ▷ *verb* **1** to decrease the pressure on something. **2** to release something from pressure. ● **decompressive** *adj*. ● **decompressor** *noun*. ◷ Early 20c.

decompression ▷ *noun* reduction of air pressure. ◷ Early 20c.

decompression chamber ▷ *noun* a sealed room in which the air pressure can be varied.

decompression sickness ▷ *noun* a painful and sometimes fatal disorder that occurs when a person who has been breathing air under high pressure returns too suddenly to normal atmospheric pressure, causing nitrogen dissolved in the bloodstream to come out of solution and form bubbles that hinder or even block the circulation. Also called **the bends, caisson disease**.

decongestant /diːkənˈdʒɛstənt/ *medicine* ▷ *noun* a drug which reduces nasal mucous-membrane swelling and suppresses mucus production, thereby clearing blocked passages and sinuses. ▷ *adj* relieving congestion. ◷ 1950s.

decongestive /diːkənˈdʒɛstɪv/ ▷ *adj* reducing or relieving congestion. ◷ Early 20c.

deconsecrate /diːˈkɒnsəkreɪt/ ▷ *verb* to secularize; to transfer (a church) to secular use. ● **deconsecration** *noun*. ◷ 19c.

deconstruction /diːkənˈstrʌkʃən/ and **deconstructive criticism** /diːkənˈstrʌktɪv —/ ▷ *noun* an approach to critical analysis applied especially to literary texts which asserts that it is impossible for any text to communicate a fixed and stable meaning, and that readers should leave behind all philosophical and other concepts when approaching a text. • **deconstructionist** *noun, adj*. ◷ 1970s.

decontaminate /diːkən'tamɪneɪt/ ▻ *verb* to make something safe by removing poisons, radioactivity, etc from it. • **decontaminant** *noun*. • **decontamination** *noun*. • **decontaminative** *adj*. • **decontaminator** *noun*. ◷ 1930s.

decontrol /diːkən'troʊl/ ▻ *verb* to remove control, especially official controls or restrictions, from something. ▻ *noun* removal of control. ◷ Early 20c.

décor /'deɪkɔː(r), 'dɛk-/ ▻ *noun* **1** scenery, etc; a theatre set. **2** the style of decoration, furnishings, etc in a room or house. ◷ 19c: French, meaning 'decoration'.

decorate /'dɛkəreɪt/ ▻ *verb* (***decorated, decorating***) **1** to beautify something with ornaments, etc. **2** to put paint or wallpaper on (a wall, etc). **3** to give a medal or badge to someone as a mark of honour. • **decorator** *noun* someone who decorates buildings professionally. ◷ 16c: from Latin *decorare, decoratum* to beautify.

Decorated style ▻ *noun, archit* a style of GOTHIC architecture, elaborate and richly decorated, which prevailed until nearly the end of the 14c.

decoration /dɛkə'reɪʃən/ ▻ *noun* **1** something used to decorate. **2** the act of decorating. **3** the state of being decorated. **4** a medal or badge given as a mark of honour. ◷ 16c.

decorative /'dɛkərətɪv/ ▻ *adj* ornamental or beautiful (especially if not useful). • **decoratively** *adverb*. • **decorativeness** *noun*. ◷ 18c.

decorative arts ▻ *plural noun* the applied arts (such as ceramics, metalwork, textiles, furniture-making and calligraphy) as distinct from the FINE ARTS. In general, objects produced in the decorative arts are functional as well as ornamental. Compare FINE ART.

decorator see under DECORATE

decorous /'dɛkərəs/ ▻ *adj* said of behaviour or appearance: correct or socially acceptable; showing proper respect. • **decorously** *adverb*. ◷ 17c: from Latin *decorus* becoming or fitting.

decorum /dɪ'kɔːrəm/ ▻ *noun* correct or socially acceptable behaviour. ◷ 16c: from Latin *decorus* becoming or fitting.

decoupage or **découpage** /deɪkuː'pɑːʒ/ ▻ *noun* **1** the craft of applying decorative paper cut-outs to eg wood surfaces, practised since the 18c. **2** a picture produced in this way. ◷ 20c: French, from *découper* to cut out.

decoy ▻ *verb* /dɪ'kɔɪ, 'diːkɔɪ/ (***decoyed, decoying***) to lead or lure into a trap. ▻ *noun* /'diːkɔɪ, dɪ'kɔɪ/ (***decoys***) someone or something used to lead or lure (a person or animal) into a trap. ◷ 17c as *noun*; 16c as *verb* in Scots: probably from Dutch *de kooi* the cage.

decrease ▻ *verb* /dɪ'kriːs/ (***decreased, decreasing***) *tr & intr* to make or become less. ▻ *noun* /'diːkriːs/ (***decreases***) a lessening or loss. Opposite of INCREASE. • **decreasingly** *adverb*. ◷ 14c: from Latin *decrescere*.

decree /dɪ'kriː/ ▻ *noun* (***decrees***) **1** a formal order or ruling made by someone in high authority (eg a monarch) and which becomes law. **2** *law* a ruling made in a law court. ▻ *verb* (***decreed, decreeing***) to order or decide something formally or officially. ◷ 14c: from Latin *decretum*.

decree absolute ▻ *noun, law* a decree issued by a court in divorce proceedings which officially ends a marriage.

decree nisi /— 'naɪsaɪ/ ▻ *noun, law* a decree issued by a court in divorce proceedings which will become a DECREE ABSOLUTE after a period of time unless some reason is shown why it should not.

decrement /'dɛkrəmənt/ ▻ *noun* **1** decreasing; decrease. **2** *math* the decrease in value of a variable. **3** *physics* the ratio of each amplitude to the previous one in an oscillator. ◷ 17c: from Latin *decrementum*.

decrepit /dɪ'krɛpɪt/ ▻ *adj* **1** weak or worn out because of old age. **2** in a very poor state because of age or long use. • **decrepitude** /dɪ'krɛpɪtʃuːd/ *noun* a decrepit or worn-out state. ◷ 15c: from Latin *decrepitus* very old.

decrepitate /dɪ'krɛpɪteɪt/ *physics* ▻ *verb* (***decrepitated, decrepitating***) **1** *intr* to crackle, as salts do when heated. **2** to roast something so as to cause a continual crackling; to calcine. • **decrepitation** *noun*. ◷ 17c: from DE- 3 + Latin *crepitare* to rattle.

decrescendo /diːkrə'ʃɛndoʊ, deɪ-/ *music* ▻ *adj, adverb* becoming quieter. ▻ *noun* an instance when a piece of music becomes quieter. ◷ 19c: Italian, from *decrescere* to decrease.

decretal /dɪ'kriːtəl, 'dɛkrɪtəl/ ▻ *noun* a papal decree. ▻ *adj* belonging or relating to a decree. ◷ 15c: from Latin *decretalis* of a decree.

decriminalize or **decriminalise** /diː'krɪmɪnəlaɪz/ ▻ *verb, law* to make (a practice, etc) no longer a criminal offence; to legalize something. • **decriminalization** *noun*. Compare CRIMINALIZE. ◷ 1970s as *verb*; 1940s as *noun*.

decry /dɪ'kraɪ/ ▻ *verb* to express disapproval of someone or something; to criticize someone or something as worthless or unsuitable. • **decrial** /dɪ'kraɪəl/ *noun*. • **decrier** *noun*. ◷ 17c: from French *décrier*.

decrypt /diː'krɪpt/ ▻ *verb* (***decrypted, decrypting***) to decode something. • **decryption** /diː'krɪpʃən/ *noun*. ◷ 20c: from DE- 2 + Greek *kryptos* hidden.

decumbent /dɪ'kʌmbənt/ ▻ *adj* **1** lying down. **2** *bot, zool, anatomy* lying flat on the ground or a surface. • **decumbence** or **decumbency** *noun*. ◷ 17c: from Latin *decumbere* to lie down.

DEd ▻ *abbreviation* Doctor of Education.

dedicate /'dɛdɪkeɪt/ ▻ *verb* (***dedicated, dedicating***) (*usually* **dedicate oneself** or **something to someone** or **something**) **1** to give or devote (oneself or one's time, money, etc) wholly or chiefly to some purpose, cause, etc. **2** to devote or address (a book, piece of music, etc) to someone as a token of affection or respect. **3** to set something apart for some sacred purpose. • **dedicatee** /dɛdɪkeɪ'tiː/ *noun* (***dedicatees***) a person to whom something is dedicated. ◷ 15c: from Latin *dedicare, dedicatum* to declare or dedicate.

dedicated ▻ *adj* **1** working very hard at or spending a great deal of one's time and energy on something. **2** committed or devoted to a particular cause, etc. **3** assigned or set aside for a particular purpose □ ***a dedicated phone line***. **4** *technical* said of a computer: designed to carry out one particular function.

dedication ▻ *noun* **1** the quality of being dedicated. **2** the act of dedicating. **3** the words dedicating a book, etc to someone. • **dedicational** *adj*.

dedicator ▻ *noun* someone who makes a DEDICATION. ◷ 17c.

dedicatory /'dɛdɪkeɪtərɪ/ ▻ *adj* serving as a DEDICATION in a book, etc □ ***dedicatory remarks***. ◷ 16c.

dedifferentiation /diːdɪfərenʃɪ'eɪʃən/ ▻ *noun, biol, medicine* a change by which specialized or heterogeneous tissue reverts to a generalized or homogeneous form. ◷ Early 20c.

dedramatize or **dedramatise** /diː'dramətaɪz/ ▻ *verb* to play down the importance of something; to lessen or keep low the tension or friction caused by something.

deduce /dɪˈdʒuːs/ ▷ *verb* (***deduced, deducing***) to think out or judge on the basis of what one knows or assumes to be fact. ⓘ 15c: from DE- 1 + Latin *ducere* to lead.

deducible /dɪˈdʒuːsɪbəl/ ▷ *adj* capable of being deduced. • **deducibility** or **deducibleness** *noun*. ⓘ 17c.

deduct /dɪˈdʌkt/ ▷ *verb* (***deducted, deducting***) to take away (a number, amount, etc). • **deductible** *adj*. ⓘ 15c: from Latin *deductere, deductum*.

deduction /diːˈdʌkʃən/ ▷ *noun* **1** the act or process of deducting. **2** something, especially money, which has been or will be deducted. **3** the act or process of deducing, especially of deducing a particular fact from what one knows or thinks to be generally true. **4** something that has been deduced. Compare INDUCTION. ⓘ 15c as *deduxion*.

deductive /diːˈdʌktɪv/ ▷ *adj* said of a logical process of thought: deducing or involving deduction of particular facts from general truths. Compare INDUCTIVE. • **deductively** *adverb*. ⓘ 17c.

deed ▷ *noun* **1** something someone has done. **2** a brave action or notable achievement. **3** *law* a signed statement which records the terms of an agreement, especially about a change in ownership of a house or other property. ⓘ Anglo-Saxon *dæd* or *ded*.

deed of covenant ▷ *noun* a legal agreement in which someone promises to pay a fixed sum (to a recognized charitable organization) for an agreed time, enabling the recipient to recover the tax paid on the total payment by the person making the covenant.

deed poll ▷ *noun, law* a deed made and signed by one person only, especially when changing their name. ⓘ 16c.

deejay /ˈdiːdʒeɪ, diːˈdʒeɪ/ ▷ *noun* (***deejays***) *colloq* a DISC JOCKEY. ⓘ 1950s: from the initials DJ.

deem ▷ *verb* (***deemed, deeming***) *formal, old use* to judge, think or consider. ⓘ Anglo-Saxon *deman* to form a judgement.

de-emphasize or **de-emphasise** /diːˈemfəsaɪz/ ▷ *verb* to take the emphasis away from something; to treat or consider as of little or less importance. ⓘ 20c.

deep ▷ *adj* **1** far down from the top or surface; with a relatively great distance from the top or surface to the bottom. **2** going or being far in from the outside surface or edge. **3** *usually in compounds* going or being far down by a specified amount □ ***knee-deep in mud***. **4** in a specified number of rows or layers □ ***lined up four deep***. **5** coming from or going far down; long and full □ ***a deep sigh*** □ ***a deep breath***. **6** very great; serious □ ***deep trouble***. **7** said of a colour: strong and relatively dark; not light or pale. **8** low in pitch □ ***deep-toned***. **9** said of emotions, etc: strongly felt. **10** obscure; hard to understand □ ***deep thoughts***. **11** said of a person: mysterious; keeping secret thoughts. **12** *cricket* not close to the wickets. **13** *football* well behind one's team's front line of players. ▷ *adverb* **1** deeply. **2** far down or into. **3** late on in or well into (a period of time). ▷ *noun* **1** (**the deep**) the ocean. **2** (*also* **deeps**) *old use* a place far below the surface of the ground or the sea. See also DEPTH. • **deeply** *adverb* very greatly. • **deepness** *noun*. • **deep down** in reality, although not in appearance. • **deep in something** fully occupied or involved with it □ *deep in thought*. • **go in** or **jump in** or **dive in** or **be thrown in at the deep end** *colloq* to begin or be given a difficult undertaking with little or no experience or preparation. • **go off at** or **go off the deep end** *colloq* to lose one's temper suddenly and violently. • **in deep water** *colloq* in trouble or difficulties. ⓘ Anglo-Saxon *deop*.

deep-dyed ▷ *adj* thoroughgoing; extreme (in a bad sense).

deepen /ˈdiːpən/ ▷ *verb* (***deepened, deepening***) *tr & intr* to make or become deeper, greater, more intense, etc. ⓘ 16c.

deep-freeze ▷ *noun* a specialized refrigeration unit, or a compartment in a refrigerator, that is designed for storage of perishable material, especially food, in a frozen state at a temperature below −18°C (0°F). ▷ *verb* to preserve perishable material, especially food, by storing it in a frozen state, so as to prevent the growth and reproduction of bacteria and other micro-organisms. ⓘ 1940s.

deep-fry ▷ *verb* to fry something by completely submerging it in hot fat or oil.

deep kiss ▷ *noun* a kiss using the tongue. • **deep kissing** *noun*.

deep-laid ▷ *adj* secretly plotted or devised. ⓘ 18c.

deep litter ▷ *noun* a method of keeping hens in a henhouse with a deep layer of peat material on the floor.

deep-rooted and **deep-seated** ▷ *adj* said of ideas, habits, etc: deeply and firmly established in a person or group of people and not easily removed or changed. ⓘ 17c as *-rooted*; 18c as *-seated*.

deep-sea ▷ *adj* belonging to, for, etc, or working, etc, in the deeper parts of the sea.

deep-set ▷ *adj* said especially of the eyes: in relatively deep sockets; set deeply into the face. ⓘ 19c.

the Deep South ▷ *noun* the SE part of the USA, roughly the states of S Carolina, Georgia, Louisiana, Mississippi and Alabama.

deep space ▷ *noun* outer space, understood by some people as the area of space well outside the Earth's atmosphere or beyond the Moon's orbit, by others as the area outside the solar system.

deep structure ▷ *noun, grammar* in Chomskyan terms: the underlying grammatical or semantic concepts and relationships of words or concepts in a sentence from which its SURFACE STRUCTURE derives. ⓘ 1960s.

deep throat ▷ *noun, colloq* a highly confidential informant. ⓘ 1970s.

deer ▷ *noun* (*plural* ***deer***) any of numerous RUMINANT mammals, found throughout Europe, Asia and N and S America, and distinguished by the presence of antlers, usually branched, in the male. ⓘ Anglo-Saxon *deor* animal or deer.

deer fence ▷ *noun* a very high fence that deer should not be able to jump over. ⓘ Late 19c.

deer forest ▷ *noun* a wild tract of land, not necessarily all wooded, reserved for deer. ⓘ 19c.

deer horn ▷ *noun* a deer's antler or the material that forms it.

deerhound ▷ *noun* a large dog, developed in Scotland from Mediterranean ancestors, that has a tall slim body, shaggy grey coat, long legs and tail, and a small head with short soft ears. ⓘ Early 19c.

deer lick ▷ *noun* a patch of salty ground where deer come to lick the salt. ⓘ 18c.

deerskin ▷ *noun* the skin of deer or leather made from it. ⓘ 14c.

deerstalker ▷ *noun* **1** a kind of hat with peaks at the front and back and flaps at the side that can cover the ears. **2** a person who stalks deer. ⓘ 19c.

def. ▷ *abbreviation* **1** defendent. **2** definition.

deface /dɪˈfeɪs/ ▷ *verb* to deliberately spoil the appearance of something (eg by marking or cutting). • **defacement** *noun*. • **defacer** *noun*. • **defacingly** *adverb*. ⓘ 14c: from French *desfacier*.

de facto /diː ˈfaktoʊ, deɪ -/ ▷ *adj, adverb* actual or actually, though not necessarily legally so. Compare DE JURE. ▷ *noun* (***de factos***) *Austral* a de facto husband or wife. ⓘ 17c: Latin, meaning 'in fact'.

defalcate /ˈdiːfalkeɪt, ˈdiːfɔːl-/ *law* ▷ *verb* (***defalcated, defalcating***) *intr* to embezzle or misuse money held in trust. • **defalcation** *noun*. • **defalcator** *noun*. ◷ 16c: from Latin *defalcare*, *defalcatum*, from de away + *falcare* to cut.

defame /dɪˈfeɪm/ ▷ *verb* (***defamed***, ***defaming***) to attack the good reputation of someone by saying something unfavourable about them. • **defamation** /dɛfəˈmeɪʃən/ *noun*. • **defamatorily** *adverb*. • **defamatory** /dɪˈfamətərɪ/ *ad*. ◷ 14c: from Latin *diffamare* to spread bad reports about.

defat /diːˈfat/ ▷ *verb* (***defatted***, ***defatting***) to remove fat or fats from something. ◷ 1920s.

default /dɪˈfɔːlt, dɪˈfɒlt/ ▷ *verb*, *intr* **1** (*usually* **default on something**) to fail to do what one should do, especially to fail to pay what is due. **2** *law* to fail to appear in court when called upon. ▷ *noun* **1** a failure to do or pay what one should. **2** *computing* a preset option which will always be followed unless the operator enters a command to the contrary. • **defaulter** *noun* a person who defaults, especially in paying a debt. • **by default** because of someone's failure to do something which would have prevented or altered the situation. • **in default of something** in the absence of it; for lack of it. ◷ 16c in this form; 13c as *defaut*: from French *defaillir* to fail.

defeat /dɪˈfiːt/ ▷ *verb* (***defeated***, ***defeating***) **1** to beat or win a victory over someone, eg in a war, competition, game or argument. **2** to make (plans, etc) fail. ▷ *noun* the act of defeating or state of being defeated. ◷ 16c: from French *desfait*, from *desfaire* to ruin or undo.

defeatism ▷ *noun* a state of mind in which one too readily expects or accepts defeat or failure. • **defeatist** *adj*, *noun*. ◷ Early 20c.

defecate /ˈdɛfəkeɪt, ˈdiː-/ ▷ *verb* (***defecated***, ***defecating***) *formal*, *technical* to empty the bowels of waste matter. See also FAECES. • **defecation** *noun*. ◷ 19c in this sense; 15c, meaning to 'purify or clarify': from Latin *defaecare*, *defaecatum* to cleanse.

defect ▷ *noun* /ˈdiːfɛkt/ a flaw, fault or imperfection. ▷ *verb* /dɪˈfɛkt/ (***defected***, ***defecting***) *intr* to leave one's country, political party or group, especially to support or join an opposing one. • **defection** *noun*. • **defector** *noun*. ◷ 15c as *noun*; 16c as *verb*: from Latin *deficere*, *defectum* to fail.

defective ▷ *adj* imperfect; having a defect or defects. • **defectively** *adverb*. • **defectiveness** *noun*. ◷ 15c.

> ***defective***
>
> A word often confused with this one is **deficient**.

defence /dɪˈfɛns/ or (*US*) **defense** /ˈdiːfɛns/ *noun* **1** the act of defending against attack. **2** the method, means or equipment used to guard or protect against attack or when attacked. **3** the armed forces of a country. **4** (**defences**) fortifications. **5** a person's answer to an accusation, justifying or denying what they have been accused of. **6** (**the defence**) *law* in a court: the person or people on trial and the lawyer or lawyers acting for them. **7** (**the defence**) *sport* the players in a team whose main task is to prevent their opponents from scoring. • **defenceless** *adj*. • **defencelessly** *adverb*. • **defencelessness** *noun*. ◷ 13c: from Latin *defendere*, *defensum* to defend.

defenceman or **defenseman** *noun*, *ice-hockey*, *lacrosse* a player other than the goalkeeper who defends the goal.

defence mechanism ▷ *noun* **1** *psychol* a process, usually subconscious, of blocking out of one's mind a feeling or memory one finds painful. **2** a response by an organism in reaction to harmful organisms, predators, etc.

defend /dɪˈfɛnd/ ▷ *verb* (***defended***, ***defending***) **1** to guard or protect someone or something against attack or when attacked. **2** to explain, justify or argue in support of the actions of someone accused of doing wrong. **3** to be the lawyer acting on behalf of (the accused) in a trial. **4** *sport* to try to prevent one's opponents from scoring. **5** *sport* to take part in a contest against a challenger for (a title, medal, etc one holds). • **defendable** *adj*. • **defender** *noun* someone who defends against attack, especially in military and sporting contexts. ◷ 13c: from Latin *defendere*.

defendant ▷ *noun* someone against whom a charge is brought in a law-court. See also PLAINTIFF. ◷ 16c.

Defender of the Faith ▷ *noun* a title borne by the sovereign of England since 1521 when it was conferred by the Pope on Henry VIII in recognition of his book against Martin Luther.

defense see DEFENCE

defenseman see DEFENCEMAN

defensible /diːˈfɛnsɪbəl/ ▷ *adj* able to be defended or justified. • **defensibility** *noun*. • **defensibly** *adverb*. ◷ 14c: from Latin *defensibilis*, from *defendere* to defend.

defensive /dɪˈfɛnsɪv/ ▷ *adj* **1** defending or ready to defend. **2** attempting to justify one's actions when criticized or when expecting criticism. • **defensively** *adverb*. • **defensiveness** *noun*. • **on the defensive** defending oneself or prepared to defend oneself against attack or criticism. ◷ 15c: from Latin *defensivus*.

defer[1] /dɪˈfɜː(r)/ ▷ *verb* (***deferred***, ***deferring***) to put off something or leave it until a later time. • **deferment** *noun*. • **deferrable** or **deferable** *adj*. • **deferral** *noun*. • **deferrer** *noun*. ◷ 14c: from Latin *differre* to delay or postpone.

defer[2] /dɪˈfɜː(r)/ ▷ *verb* (***deferred***, ***deferring***) *intr* (*usually* **defer to someone**, *etc*) to yield to their wishes, opinions or orders. ◷ 15c Scots, meaning 'to submit oneself to someone': from Latin *deferre* to carry away.

deference /ˈdɛfərəns/ ▷ *noun* **1** willingness to consider or respect the wishes, etc of others. **2** the act of deferring. • **in deference to someone** or **something** deferring to them; showing recognition of or respect for them. ◷ 17c.

deferential /dɛfəˈrɛnʃəl/ ▷ *adj* showing deference or respect. • **deferentially** *adverb*. ◷ 19c.

deferred payment ▷ *noun* payment for goods one has received by small sums of money over a period of time.

deferred sentence ▷ *noun*, *law* a sentence which is delayed until after the criminal's conduct can be examined.

deferrer see under DEFER[1]

deferring *present participle of* DEFER[1,2]

defiance /dɪˈfaɪəns/ ▷ *noun* an act of defying or of open disobedience; challenging or opposition, especially in a way that shows lack of respect. ◷ 18c in this sense; 14c, meaning 'renunciation of allegiance or friendship': from DEFY.

defiant /dɪˈfaɪənt/ ▷ *adj* openly disobedient or challenging. • **defiantly** *adverb*. ◷ 16c.

defibrillation /diːfɪbrɪˈleɪʃən/ ▷ *noun*, *medicine* the application of an electric current to the heart to restore normal rhythm after FIBRILLATION has occurred. ◷ 1930s.

defibrillator /diːˈfɪbrɪleɪtə(r)/ ▷ *noun*, *medicine* a machine which applies electric current to the heart or chest during DEFIBRILLATION.

deficiency /dɪˈfɪʃənsɪ/ ▷ *noun* (***deficiencies***) **1** a shortage or lack in quality or amount. **2** the thing or amount lacking. ◷ 17c: from DEFICIENT.

deficiency disease ▷ *noun*, *medicine* any disease caused by lack of one or more specific nutrients, especially vitamins, in the diet, eg RICKETS, SCURVY, BERIBERI.

deficient /dɪˈfɪʃənt/ ▷ *adj* not good enough; not having all that is needed. • **deficiently** *adverb*. ◷ 16c: from Latin *deficere* to fail or be lacking.

deficient

A word often confused with this one is **defective**.

deficit /'dɛfɪsɪt/ ▷ *noun* the amount by which some quantity, especially a sum of money, is less than what is required, eg the amount by which expenditure is greater than income. ⓘ 18c: from Latin *deficere* to fail or be lacking.

deficit financing ▷ *noun, econ* a government policy of stimulating the economy by deliberately planning a budget deficit, where expenditure will exceed the revenue from taxes, with money being pumped into the economy to stimulate (or maintain) demand and excess spending being financed by borrowing.

defied, **defier** and **defies** see under DEFY

defile[1] /dɪ'faɪl/ ▷ *verb* (*defiled*, *defiling*) **1** to make something dirty or polluted. **2** to take away or spoil the goodness, purity, holiness, etc of something. • **defiler** *noun*. • **defilement** *noun*. ⓘ 14c: from French *defouler* to trample or violate; altered under the influence of the old word *befile*, from Anglo-Saxon *befylan* to make foul.

defile[2] ▷ *noun* /'diːfaɪl/ a narrow valley or passage between mountains. ▷ *verb* /diː'faɪl/ (*defiled*, *defiling*) *intr* to march in file. ⓘ 17c: from French *défilé*, from *défiler* to march in file.

definable /dɪ'faɪnəbəl/ ▷ *adj* capable of being defined or described precisely. • **definability** *noun*. • **definably** *adverb*. ⓘ 17c.

define /dɪ'faɪn/ ▷ *verb* (*defined*, *defining*) **1** to fix or state the exact meaning of (a word, etc). **2** to fix, describe or explain (opinions, duties, the qualities or limits of something, etc). **3** to make clear the outline or shape of something. See also DEFINITION. • **definer** *noun*. ⓘ 16c in this form; 14c as *diffyne*: from Latin *definire* to set boundaries to.

definite /'dɛfɪnət/ ▷ *adj* **1** fixed or firm; not liable to change. **2** sure; certain. **3** clear and precise. **4** having clear outlines. • **definitely** *adverb* **1** as a definite fact; certainly. **2** in a definite way. • **definiteness** *noun*. ⓘ 16c: from Latin *definire* to set boundaries to.

definite article ▷ *noun, grammar* a word, in English THE, used before a noun, or before an adjective used without a noun, to denote a specific or known example, or a defined class, as in *the dog by the door, the government, the uninitiated*. Compare INDEFINITE ARTICLE.

definition /dɛfɪ'nɪʃən/ ▷ *noun* **1** a statement of the meaning of a word or phrase. **2** the act of defining a word or phrase. **3** the quality of having clear precise limits or form. **4** the degree of clearness and preciseness of limits or form. • **by definition** because of what something or someone essentially is or does ▫ *A carpenter is by definition a craftsman.* ⓘ 16c in this form; 14c as *diffinicioun*: from Latin *definitio*.

definitive /dɪ'fɪnɪtɪv/ ▷ *adj* **1** settling a matter once and for all. **2** most complete or authoritative. ▷ *noun, grammar* an adjective used to limit the extent of meaning of a noun, eg THIS, THAT. • **definitively** *adverb*. • **definitiveness** *noun*. ⓘ 14c: from Latin *definitivus* definite.

deflagrate /'dɛfləgreɪt/ *physics, chem* ▷ *verb* (*deflagrated*, *deflagrating*) *tr & intr* to burn suddenly, generally with flame and crackling noise. • **deflagration** *noun*. ⓘ 18c: from Latin *deflagrare*, *deflagratum* to burn up.

deflate /dɪ'fleɪt, diː-/ ▷ *verb* (*deflated*, *deflating*) **1** *tr & intr* to collapse or grow smaller by letting out gas. **2** to reduce or take away the hopes, excitement, feelings of importance or self-confidence, etc of someone. **3** *tr & intr, econ* to undergo or make something undergo DEFLATION. Compare INFLATE, REFLATE. • **deflater** or **deflator** *noun*. ⓘ 19c: from DE- 2 + *-flate*, from INFLATE.

deflated ▷ *adj* **1** having the air or gas removed. **2** said of a person: deprived of confidence.

deflation /dɪ'fleɪʃən, diː-/ ▷ *noun* **1** the act of deflating or the process of being deflated. **2** the state of being or feeling deflated. **3** *econ* a reduction in the amount of money available in a country, resulting in lower levels of economic activity, industrial output and employment, and a lower rate of increase in wages and prices. See also INFLATION, REFLATION, STAGFLATION. • **deflationary** *adj*. • **deflationist** *noun, adj*. ⓘ 16c.

deflect /dɪ'flɛkt, diː-/ ▷ *verb* (*deflected*, *deflecting*) *tr & intr* to turn aside from the correct or intended course or direction. • **deflection** *noun*. • **deflective** *adj*. • **deflector** *noun*. ⓘ 16c: from Latin *deflectere* to bend aside.

deflower /dɪ'flaʊə(r), diː-/ *literary* ▷ *verb* (*deflowered*, *deflowering*) to deprive someone (especially a woman) of their virginity. • **deflowerer** *noun*. ⓘ 14c as *deflour*: from Latin *deflorare*.

defoliant /dɪ'foʊlɪənt, diː-/ ▷ *noun, technical* a type of herbicide that causes the leaves to fall off plants. ⓘ 1940s.

defoliate /dɪ'foʊlɪeɪt, diː-/ *technical* ▷ *verb* (*defoliated*, *defoliating*) to make leaves fall off (trees, etc). • **defoliation** *noun*. • **defoliator** *noun*. ⓘ 18c: from Latin *defoliare*, *defoliatum*, from *de* off + *folium* leaf.

deforest /diː'fɒrəst/ *agric* ▷ *verb* (*deforested*, *deforesting*) to cut down forest trees for commercial use, or to clear land for agriculture, without replacing them, or without allowing the natural forest to regenerate. • **deforestation** *noun*. ⓘ 16c: compare DISAFFOREST, DISFOREST.

deform /dɪ'fɔːm/ ▷ *verb* (*deformed*, *deforming*) to change the shape of something without breaking it, so that it looks ugly, unpleasant, unnatural or spoiled. • **deformed** *adj*. ⓘ 15c: from Latin *deformis* ugly.

deformity /dɪ'fɔːmɪtɪ/ ▷ *noun* (*deformities*) **1** being deformed or misshapen. **2** ugliness; disfigurement; an ugly feature. ⓘ 15c.

defraud /dɪ'frɔːd/ ▷ *verb* (*defrauded*, *defrauding*) (*usually* **defraud someone of something**) to dishonestly prevent someone getting or keeping something which belongs to them or to which they have a right. • **defrauder** *noun*. ⓘ 14c: from Latin *defraudare*.

defray /dɪ'freɪ/ ▷ *verb* (*defrayed*, *defraying*) *formal* to provide the money to pay (someone's costs or expenses). • **defrayable** *adj*. • **defrayal** or **defrayment** *noun*. • **defrayer** *noun*. ⓘ 16c: from French *deffroier* to pay costs.

defreeze /diː'friːz/ ▷ *verb* to thaw something out; to defrost (especially frozen food). ⓘ 20c.

defrock /diː'frɒk/ ▷ *verb* (*defrocked*, *defrocking*) to remove (a priest) from office, usually because of unacceptable conduct or beliefs. ⓘ 17c: from French *défroquer*.

defrost /diː'frɒst/ ▷ *verb, tr & intr* **1** to remove ice from something or have the ice removed from something; to unfreeze. **2** said of frozen food, etc: to make or become no longer frozen. • **defroster** *noun* a device for defrosting (especially a windscreen). ⓘ 19c.

deft ▷ *adj* skilful, quick and neat. • **deftly** *adverb*. • **deftness** *noun*. ⓘ Anglo-Saxon *gedæfte* meek.

defunct /dɪ'fʌŋkt/ ▷ *adj, now facetious or formal* no longer living, existing, active, usable or in use. ⓘ 16c: from Latin *defungi*, *defunctus* to finish.

defuse /dɪ'fjuːz, -diː-/ ▷ *verb* (*defused*, *defusing*) **1** to remove the fuse from (a bomb, etc). **2** to make (a situation, etc) harmless or less dangerous. ⓘ 1940s.

defy /dɪ'faɪ/ ▷ *verb* (*defies*, *defied*, *defying*) **1** to resist or disobey someone boldly and openly. **2** to dare or challenge someone. **3** *formal* to make something impossible or unsuccessful ▫ *defying explanation.* See also DEFIANCE. • **defier** *noun*. ⓘ 14c: from French *defier*, from Latin *diffidare* to renounce one's faith.

deg. ▻ *abbreviation* degree, or degrees.

degas /diːˈgas/ ▻ *verb* **1** to remove gas from something. **2** to eject or emit in the form of a gas. ⓒ Early 20c.

degaussing /diːˈgaʊsɪŋ/ ▻ *noun, physics* the process by which an object's magnetic field is neutralized by encircling it with an electric field. ⓒ 1940s: from DE- 2 + GAUSS.

degeneracy /dɪˈdʒɛnərəsɪ/ ▻ *noun* a degenerate or degraded state. ⓒ 17c.

degenerate ▻ *adj* /dɪˈdʒɛnərət/ **1** physically, morally or intellectually worse than before. **2** *biol* having lost former structure, or having changed from a complex to a simpler form. ▻ *noun* /dɪˈdʒɛnərət/ a degenerate person or animal. ▻ *verb* /dɪˈdʒɛnəreɪt/ (***degenerated, degenerating***) *intr* **1** to go from a better, more moral, etc state to a worse one. **2** *biol* to lose former structure, or change from a complex to a simpler form. • **degenerately** *adverb*. • **degenerateness** *noun*. ⓒ 15c: from Latin *degenerare, degeneratum* to become unlike one's kind.

degeneration /dɪdʒɛnəˈreɪʃən/ ▻ *noun* **1** the process or act of degenerating. **2** *biol* the breakdown, death or decay of cells, nerve fibres, etc. **3** *biol* an evolutionary change from a complex structural form to an apparently simpler form, as in the wings of flightless birds such as the emu. ⓒ 15c: from DEGENERATE.

degenerative ▻ *adj* said of a condition or disease: steadily destroying or damaging a part of the body. ⓒ 19c.

degradable /dɪˈgreɪdəbəl/ ▻ *adj, technical* capable of being broken down or destroyed chemically or biologically. See also BIODEGRADABLE, PHOTODEGRADABLE. ⓒ 19c.

degradation /dɛgrəˈdeɪʃən/ ▻ *noun* **1** moral deterioration. **2** *chem* reduction of a substance to a simpler structure. **3** being degraded; disgrace. **4** erosion. ⓒ 16c.

degrade /dɪˈgreɪd/ ▻ *verb* **1** to disgrace or humiliate someone. **2** to reduce someone or something in rank, status, etc. **3** *tr & intr, chem* to change or be converted into a substance with a simpler structure. • **degrading** *adj* humiliating; debasing. ⓒ 14c: from French *degrader*.

degrease /diːˈgriːs/ ▻ *verb* to strip or cleanse something of grease. • **degreasant** *noun* a substance which removes grease. ⓒ 19c.

degree /dɪˈgriː/ ▻ *noun* (***degrees***) **1** an amount or extent. **2** *physics* (symbol °) a unit of temperature used in the CELSIUS, FAHRENHEIT and KELVIN scales. **3** *geom* (symbol °) a unit by which angles are measured and direction is described, equal to the angle of one SECTOR of a circle that has been divided into 360 equal parts. **4** an award or title given by a university or college, either earned by examination or research, or given as a mark of honour. **5** a comparative amount of severity or seriousness (see FIRST-DEGREE, SECOND-DEGREE, THIRD-DEGREE). • **by degrees** gradually. • **to a degree 1** to a certain extent. **2** to a great extent, to extremes. ⓒ 13c as *degre*: French, from Latin *de* down + *gradus* step.

degree of freedom ▻ *noun, physics* **1** any one of the independent variables defining the state of a system, eg temperature, pressure, concentration. **2** a capability of variation.

degrees of comparison see COMPARISON

dehiscent /dɪˈhɪsənt/ ▻ *adj, bot* denoting a fruit, or the anther of a stamen, that bursts open spontaneously at maturity to release the seeds or pollen. Compare INDEHISCENT. • **dehiscence** *noun*. ⓒ 17c: from Latin *dehiscere* to gape or split open.

dehorn /diːˈhɔːn/ ▻ *verb* **1** to remove the horns from (an animal, etc). **2** to prune (a tree, etc). • **dehorner** *noun*. ⓒ 19c.

dehumanize or **dehumanise** /diːˈhjuːmənaɪz/ ▻ *verb* to remove the human qualities from someone. ⓒ 19c.

dehumidify /diːhjʊˈmɪdɪfaɪ/ ▻ *verb* to remove moisture from (the air, etc). • **dehumidification** /-fɪˈkeɪʃən/ *noun*. • **dehumidifier** *noun*. ⓒ 20c.

dehydrate /diːˈhaɪdreɪt, diːhaɪˈdreɪt/ ▻ *verb* **1** to remove water from (a substance or organism). **2** *tr & intr* to lose or make someone or something lose too much water from the body. • **dehydrated** *adj*. • **dehydrator** or **dehydrater** *noun*. ⓒ 19c: DE- 2 + Greek *hydor* water.

dehydration /diːhaɪˈdreɪʃən/ ▻ *noun* **1** the removal of water from a substance. **2** a method of preserving food by greatly reducing its moisture content. **3** *medicine* a condition in which there is insufficient water in the body, eg as a result of diarrhoea or excessive sweating. ⓒ 19c.

de-ice ▻ *verb* **1** to remove ice from (a surface). **2** to make or keep something free of ice; to prevent the formation of ice on something. • **de-icer** *noun* **1** a mechanical device for preventing the formation of ice, eg on an aircraft wing. **2** a chemical used to remove ice, eg from a car windscreen. ⓒ 1930s.

deific /deɪˈɪfɪk, diː-/ and **deifical** /-ˈɪfɪkəl/ ▻ *adj* making something or someone godlike or divine, or treating it or them as if they were godlike or divine. • **deification** *noun* /deɪɪfɪˈkeɪʃən, diː-/. ⓒ 15c.

deify /ˈdeɪɪfaɪ, ˈdiː-/ ▻ *verb* (***deifies, deified, deifying***) to regard or worship someone or something as a god. ⓒ 14c: from French *deifier*, from Latin *deus* god + *facere* to make.

deign /deɪn/ ▻ *verb* (***deigned, deigning***) *intr* to do something reluctantly and in a way that shows that one considers the matter hardly important or beneath one's dignity □ ***didn't even deign to reply***. ⓒ 16c in this form; 13c as *dein*: from French *daigner*, from Latin *dignari* to consider worthy.

deindustrialize or **deindustrialise** /diːɪnˈdʌstrɪəlaɪz/ ▻ *verb* to disperse or reduce the industrial organization and potential of a nation, area, etc. • **deindustrialization** *noun*. ⓒ 19c.

deionization /diːaɪənaɪˈzeɪʃən/ ▻ *noun, chem* an ION-EXCHANGE process that is used to purify or change the composition of a solution, especially to purify water obtained from the mains water supply.

deism /ˈdeɪɪzəm, ˈdiː-/ ▻ *noun* belief in the existence of God without acceptance of any religion or message revealed by God to man. Compare ATHEISM, THEISM, AGNOSTICISM. • **deist** *noun*. • **deistic** or **deistical** *adj*. ⓒ 17c: from Latin *deus* god + -ISM 1.

deity /ˈdeɪɪtɪ, ˈdiː-/ ▻ *noun* (***deities***) *formal* **1** a god or goddess. **2** the state of being divine. **3** (**the Deity**) God. ⓒ 14c: from Latin *deitas*, from *deus* god.

déjà vu /deɪʒɑː ˈvuː/ ▻ *noun* the feeling or illusion that one has experienced something before although one is actually experiencing it for the first time. ⓒ Early 20c: French, meaning 'already seen'.

dejected /dɪˈdʒɛktɪd/ ▻ *adj* sad; miserable. • **dejectedly** *adverb*. • **dejectedness** *noun*. ⓒ 16c from earlier verb *deject* originally meaning 'cast down': from Latin *deicere* to throw down or disappoint.

dejection /dɪˈdʒɛkʃən/ ▻ *noun* being dejected or sad.

de jure /diː ˈdʒʊərɪ, deɪ ˈjuːrɛ/ ▻ *adverb, adj, law* according to law; by right. Compare DE FACTO. ⓒ 16c: Latin, meaning 'by law'.

dekko or **decko** /ˈdɛkoʊ/ ▻ *noun* (***dekkos*** or ***deckos***) (*usually* **have** or **take a dekko**) *slang* a look. ⓒ 19c: from Hindi *dekhna* to see.

Del. ▻ *abbreviation US state* Delaware.

del see under NABLA

del ▻ *abbreviation* **1** delegate. **2** (sometimes added to the signature of the artist on a drawing) *delineavit* (Latin), he or she drew this.

delay /dɪ'leɪ/ ▻ *verb* (***delayed***, ***delaying***) **1** to slow someone or something down or make them late. **2** to put off to a later time. **3** *intr* to be slow in doing something; to linger. ▻ *noun* (***delays***) **1** the act of delaying or state of being delayed. **2** the amount of time by which someone or something is delayed. • **delayer** *noun*. ◷ 13c: from French *delaier*.

delayed action ▻ *noun* the operation of a switch, eg the shutter release on a camera or the detonator on a bomb, some time after the setting of the operating mechanism.

dele /'diːliː/ ▻ *noun* (***deles***) a direction, usually found in the margin of a manuscript or other text, to remove a letter or word, indicated by δ. ▻ verb (***deled***, ***deleing***) to mark (a text, etc) with this kind of mark. Compare SIC, STET. ◷ 18c: Latin imperative of *delere* to delete.

delectable /dɪ'lɛktəbəl/ ▻ *adj* said especially of food: delightful or enjoyable; delicious. • **delectably** *adverb*. • **delectableness** or **delectability** *noun*. ◷ 14c: from Latin *delectabilis*, from *delectare* to delight.

delectation /diːlɛk'teɪʃən/ ▻ *noun*, *formal* delight, enjoyment or amusement. ◷ 14c: from Latin *delectare*, *delectatum* to delight.

delegacy /'dɛlɪgəsɪ/ ▻ *noun* (***delegacies***) **1** a system or the process of delegating. **2** a delegate's appointment or authority. **3** a body of delegates. ◷ 16c.

delegate ▻ *verb* /'dɛlɪgeɪt/ (***delegated***, ***delegating***) **1** to give (part of one's work, power, etc) to someone else. **2** to send or name someone as a representative, as the one to do a job, etc. ▻ *noun* /'dɛlɪgət/ someone chosen to be the representative for another person or group of people eg at a conference or meeting. • **delegable** /'dɛlɪgəbəl/ *adj*. ◷ 14c: from Latin *delegare*, *delegatum*, from *de* away + *legare* to send as ambassador.

delegation /dɛlɪ'geɪʃən/ ▻ *noun* **1** a group of delegates. **2** the act of delegating or the state of being delegated. ◷ 17c.

delete /dɪ'liːt/ ▻ *verb* (***deleted***, ***deleting***) to rub out, score out or remove something, especially from something written or printed. • **deletion** /dɪ'liːʃən/ *noun* **1** a rubbing out. **2** something rubbed out or removed. ◷ 16c in this sense; 15c, meaning 'to destroy': from Latin *delere* to blot out.

deleterious /dɛlɪ'tɪərɪəs/ ▻ *adj*, *formal* harmful or destructive. • **deleteriously** *adverb*. ◷ 17c: from Greek *deleterios*.

delf or **delph** /dɛlf/, **delft** /dɛlft/ and **Delftware** ▻ *noun* a type of earthenware originally made at Delft in the Netherlands, typically with a blue design on a white background. ◷ 17c.

deli /'dɛlɪ/ ▻ *noun* (***delis***) a DELICATESSEN.

deliberate ▻ *adj* /dɪ'lɪbərət/ **1** done on purpose; not accidental. **2** slow and careful. ▻ *verb* /dɪ'lɪbəreɪt/ (***deliberated***, ***deliberating***) *tr & intr* to think about something carefully. • **deliberately** *adverb*. • **deliberateness** *noun*. • **deliberator** *noun*. ◷ 16c: from Latin *deliberare*, *deliberatum* to consider carefully.

deliberation /dɪlɪbə'reɪʃən/ ▻ *noun* **1** careful thought. **2** (**deliberations**) formal and thorough thought and discussion. **3** slowness and carefulness.

delicacy /'dɛlɪkəsɪ/ ▻ *noun* (***delicacies***) **1** the state or quality of being delicate. **2** something considered particularly delicious to eat.

delicate /'dɛlɪkət/ ▻ *adj* **1** easily damaged or broken. **2** not strong or healthy. **3** having fine texture or workmanship. **4** dainty; small and attractive. **5** small, neat and careful □ *delicate movements*. **6** requiring tact and careful handling □ *a delicate situation*. **7** careful about what one says or does, so as not to offend others. **8** said of colours, flavours, etc: light; not strong. • **delicately** *adverb*. • **delicateness** *noun*. ◷ 14c: from Latin *delicatus*.

delicatessen /dɛlɪkə'tɛsən/ ▻ *noun* **1** a shop, or part of one, selling foods prepared ready for the table, especially cheeses, cooked meats and unusual or imported foods. **2** *singular or plural noun* such foods. Often shortened to **deli**. ◷ 19c, originally in US: German, from French *délicatesse* delicacy.

delicious /dɪ'lɪʃəs/ ▻ *adj* **1** with a very pleasing taste or smell. **2** giving great pleasure. • **deliciously** *adverb*. ◷ 14c: from French *delicious*, from Latin *deliciae* delight.

delight /dɪ'laɪt/ ▻ *verb* (***delighted***, ***delighting***) **1** to please greatly. **2** *intr* (**delight in something**) to take great pleasure from it. ▻ *noun* **1** great pleasure. **2** something or someone that gives great pleasure. • **delighted** *adj* highly pleased; thrilled. • **delightedly** *adverb*. • **delightedness** *noun*. ◷ 13c as *delit*: from French *deliter*, from Latin *delectare*; modern spelling was influenced by LIGHT in 16c.

delightful /dɪ'laɪtfʊl/ ▻ *adj* giving great pleasure. • **delightfully** *adverb*. • **delightfulness** *noun*.

Delilah /dɪ'laɪlə/ ▻ *noun* a temptress; a seductive treacherous woman. ◷ 16c: named after the Philistine woman who tricked Samson (*Judges* 16).

delimit /diː'lɪmɪt, dɪ-/ ▻ *verb* to mark or fix the limits or boundaries of (powers, etc). • **delimitation** *noun*. • **delimitative** /-teɪtɪv, -tətɪv/ *adj*. ◷ 19c: from Latin *delimitare*.

delineate /dɪ'lɪnɪeɪt/ ▻ *verb* (***delineated***, ***delineating***) to show something by drawing or by describing in words. • **delineable** /dɪ'lɪnɪəbəl/ *adj*. • **delineation** *noun*. • **delineative** /-ətɪv/ *adj*. • **delineator** *noun*. ◷ 16c: from Latin *delineare*, *delineatum* to sketch out.

delinquent /dɪ'lɪŋkwənt/ ▻ *noun* someone, especially a young person, guilty of a minor criminal offence. ▻ *adj* guilty of a minor crime or misdeed. • **delinquency** *noun* (***delinquencies***) **1** minor crime, especially committed by young people. **2** delinquent nature or behaviour. • **delinquently** *adverb*. ◷ 15c: from Latin *delinquere* to fail in one's duty.

deliquesce /dɛlɪ'kwɛs/ ▻ *verb* (***deliquesced***, ***deliquescing***) *intr*, *chem* said especially of salts: to dissolve slowly in water absorbed from the air. • **deliquescence** *noun*. • **deliquescent** *adj*. ◷ 18c: from Latin *deliquescere* to dissolve.

delirious /dɪ'lɪrɪəs, dɪ'lɪərɪəs/ ▻ *adj* **1** affected by DELIRIUM, usually as a result of fever or other illness. **2** very excited or happy. • **deliriously** *adverb*. • **deliriousness** *noun*. ◷ 16c in sense 1; 18c in sense 2: from Latin *delirus*, from *delirare* to rave, originally meaning 'to go off a straight furrow', from *de* from + *lira* furrow.

delirium /dɪ'lɪrɪəm, dɪ'lɪərɪəm/ ▻ *noun* **1** a state of madness or mental confusion and excitement, often caused by fever or other illness, drugs, etc. **2** extreme excitement or joy. ◷ 16c: from Latin *delirare*; see DELIRIOUS.

delirium tremens /— 'trɛmɛnz/ ▻ *noun* (abbreviation **DTs**) delirium caused by habitual and persistent drinking of too much alcohol, inducing hallucinations, anxiety, confusion and trembling.

deliver /dɪ'lɪvə(r)/ ▻ *verb* (***delivered***, ***delivering***) **1** to carry (goods, letters, etc) to a person or place. **2** to give or make (a speech, etc). **3** to help (a woman) at the birth of (a child). **4** *tr & intr*, *colloq* to keep or fulfil (a promise or undertaking). **5** *formal* to aim or direct (a blow, criticism, etc) towards someone or something. • **deliverable** *adj*. • **deliverer** *noun*. • **deliver the goods** *colloq* to fulfil a promise or undertaking. ◷ 13c: from French *délivrer*.

■ **deliver someone from something** *formal or old use* to set them free or rescue them.

■ **deliver someone** or **something up** *formal* to hand them or it over.

deliverance ▻ *noun, formal, old use* the act of rescuing, freeing or saving from danger or harm, or the state of being rescued, freed or saved. ⓒ 13c.

delivery /dɪˈlɪvərɪ/ ▻ *noun* (***deliveries***) **1** the carrying of (goods, letters, etc) to a person or place. **2** the thing or things being delivered. **3** the process or manner of giving birth to a child. **4** the act of making, or the manner of making, a speech, etc. **5** the act or manner of throwing a ball, especially in some sports. ⓒ 15c.

dell ▻ *noun* a small valley or hollow, usually wooded. ⓒ Anglo-Saxon.

delouse /diːˈlaʊs/ ▻ *verb* (***deloused, delousing***) to free someone or something of lice. ⓒ Early 20c.

delph see under DELF

delphinium /dɛlˈfɪnɪəm/ ▻ *noun* (***delphiniums*** or ***delphinia*** /-ˈfɪnɪə/) a garden plant with tall spikes of usually blue flowers. ⓒ 17c: from Greek *delphinion* larkspur, from *delphis* dolphin (from the shape of the flowers).

Delphinus /dɛlˈfaɪnəs/ ▻ *noun, astron* the Dolphin, a small faint constellation lying just north of the celestial equator. ⓒ 17c: Latin.

delta /ˈdɛltə/ ▻ *noun* (***deltas***) **1** the fourth letter of the Greek alphabet. See table at GREEK ALPHABET. **2** at the mouth of some rivers: an area of silt, sand, gravel or clay, often roughly triangular, formed from sediment deposited by the river as it slows down on entering the relatively still waters of a sea or lake. **3** in classification systems: fourth; one of the fourth grade, the grade below GAMMA. **4** (**Delta**) *communications* in the NATO alphabet: the word used to denote the letter 'D' (see table at NATO ALPHABET). • **deltaic** /dɛlˈteɪɪk/ *adj.* ⓒ 15c in sense 1; 16c in sense 2: Greek, from Hebrew *daleth* a tent door.

delta rhythm and **delta wave** ▻ *noun, physiol* a wave representing the low-frequency activity of the brain when a person is asleep. Compare ALPHA RHYTHM, BETA RHYTHM. See also REM SLEEP.

Delta rocket ▻ *noun, astron* any of a series of increasingly powerful versions of a US rocket which was used to launch scientific and communications satellites from 1960 onward.

delta wing *aerodynamics* ▻ *noun* **1** a swept-back triangular wing. **2** a jet aeroplane with such wings. ▻ *adj* having such wings.

deltiology /dɛltɪˈɒlədʒɪ/ ▻ *noun* the study and collection of picture postcards. • **deltiologist** *noun.* ⓒ 1940s: from Greek *deltion* a small writing tablet.

deltoid /ˈdɛltɔɪd/ ▻ *adj* triangular; having the shape of the Greek capital letter delta. ▻ *noun* a DELTOID MUSCLE. ⓒ 18c: from DELTA.

deltoid muscle ▻ *noun, anatomy* the large triangular muscle of the shoulder. ⓒ 18c.

delude /dɪˈluːd, -ljuːd/ ▻ *verb* (***deluded, deluding***) to deceive or mislead. See also DELUSION. • **deludable** *adj.* • **deluder** *noun.* ⓒ 15c: from Latin *deludere* to cheat.

deluge /ˈdɛljuːdʒ, -juːʒ/ ▻ *noun* (***deluges***) **1** a flood. **2** a downpour of rain. **3** a great quantity of anything coming or pouring in. ▻ *verb* (***deluged, deluging***) *formal* to flood; to cover in water. • **be deluged with something** to be overwhelmed by it. ⓒ 16c as *verb*; 14c as *noun*: from French *deluge*, from Latin *diluvium* flood.

delusion /dɪˈluːʒən, -ˈljuːʒən/ ▻ *noun* **1** the act of deluding or the state of being deluded. **2** *psychol* a false or mistaken belief, especially because of mental illness. Compare ILLUSION, HALLUCINATION. ⓒ 15c: from Latin *delusio*.

delusions of grandeur ▻ *plural noun* a false belief in one's own importance.

delusive /dɪˈluːsɪv, -ljuːsɪv/ and **delusory** /-sərɪ/ ▻ *adj* deluding or likely to delude; deceptive. • **delusively** *adverb.* • **delusiveness** *noun.* ⓒ 17c.

de luxe or **deluxe** /də lʌks, dɪ lʊks/ ▻ *adj* **1** very luxurious or elegant. **2** with special features or qualities. ⓒ 19c: French, literally 'of luxury'.

delve /dɛlv/ ▻ *verb* (***delved, delving***) *intr* **1** (*usually* **delve into something**) to search it for information. **2** (*usually* **delve through something**) to search through it. ⓒ Anglo-Saxon *delfan* to dig.

dem. ▻ *abbreviation* democratic.

demagnetize or **demagnetise** /diːˈmagnətaɪz/ ▻ *verb* to take away the magnetic properties of something. • **demagnetization** *noun.* • **demagnetizer** *noun.* ⓒ 19c.

demagogue /ˈdɛməgɒg/ ▻ *noun* **1** *derog* someone who tries to win political power or support by appealing to people's emotions and prejudices. **2** in ancient Greece, etc: a leader of the common people. • **demagogic** /dɛməˈgɒdʒɪk, -ˈgɒgɪk/ *adj.* • **demagoguery** /ˈdɛməgɒgərɪ/ or **demagogy** /ˈdɛməgɒgɪ, -dʒɪ/ *noun.* ⓒ 17c: from Greek *demos* people + *agogos* leading.

demand /dɪˈmɑːnd/ ▻ *verb* (***demanded, demanding***) **1** to ask or ask for firmly, forcefully or urgently. **2** to require or need something. **3** to claim something as a right. ▻ *noun* **1** a forceful request or order. **2** an urgent claim for action or attention ▫ *makes great demands on one's time.* **3** people's desire or ability to buy or obtain (goods, etc). **4** *econ* the amount of any article, commodity, etc, which consumers will buy. Compare SUPPLY *noun* 6. • **demandable** *adj.* • **demander** *noun.* • **in demand** very popular; frequently asked for. • **on demand** when asked for. ⓒ 15c: from French *demander* to ask.

demand feeding ▻ *noun* the practice of feeding a baby when it wants food, rather than at set times.

demanding ▻ *adj* **1** requiring a lot of effort, ability, etc ▫ *a demanding job.* **2** needing or expecting a lot of attention ▫ *a demanding child.* ⓒ 19c.

demanning /diːˈmanɪŋ/ ▻ *noun* the deliberate reduction of the number of employees in a particular industry, etc.

demarcate /ˈdiːmɑːkeɪt/ ▻ *verb* (***demarcated, demarcating***) to mark out the limits or boundaries of something. ⓒ 19c: from DEMARCATION.

demarcation /diːmɑːˈkeɪʃən/ ▻ *noun* **1** the marking out of limits or boundaries. **2 a** the strict separation of the areas or types of work to be done by the members of the various trade unions in a factory, etc; **b** *as adj* ▫ *a demarcation dispute.* ⓒ 18c: from Spanish *demarcar* to mark the boundaries of.

démarche /ˈdeɪmɑːʃ/ ▻ *noun* a step, measure or initiative, especially in diplomatic affairs. ⓒ 17c: French, from *démarcher* to walk.

dematerialize or **dematerialise** /diːməˈtɪərɪəlaɪz/ ▻ *verb, tr & intr* to become or make someone or something become invisible; to vanish; to cease to exist. • **dematerialization** *noun.* ⓒ 19c.

deme /diːm/ ▻ *noun, biol* a group of plants or animals that are closely related and live in a single distinct locality. ⓒ 1950s: Greek *demos* a district.

demean /dɪˈmiːn/ ▻ *verb* (***demeaned, demeaning***) to lower the dignity of or lessen respect for someone, especially oneself. • **demeaning** *adj.* ⓒ 17c.

demeanour or (*US*) **demeanor** /dɪˈmiːnə(r)/ *noun* manner of behaving; behaviour towards others. ⓒ 15c: from French *demener* to treat.

demented /dɪˈmɛntɪd/ ▻ *adj* mad; out of one's mind. • **dementedly** *adverb.* • **dementedness** *noun.* ⓒ 17c, from earlier verb *dement* to drive someone mad: from Latin *de* from + *mens, mentis* mind.

dementia /dɪˈmɛnʃə/ ▻ *noun* (***dementias***) *psychol* a loss or severe lessening of normal mental ability and functioning, occurring especially in the elderly. See also SENILE DEMENTIA. ⓒ 18c: from Latin *de* from + *mens* mind.

demerara /dɛmə'rɛərə, -'rɑːrə/ and **demerara sugar** ▷ *noun* a form of crystallized brown sugar. ◷ 19c: named after Demerara in Guyana, S America, where it originally came from.

demerge /diː'mɜːdʒ/ ▷ *verb, intr* said of companies, etc: to undergo a reversal of a merger; to become separate again. • **demerger** *noun*. ◷ 1980s.

demerit /diː'mɛrɪt/ ▷ *noun* **1** *formal* a fault or failing. **2** *N Amer* a mark given for a fault or offence, especially in schools or the army, etc. ◷ 16c in sense 1; 14c, meaning 'a quality deserving reward': from Latin *demereri, demeritus* to deserve.

demersal /diː'mɜːsəl/ ▷ *adj* living underwater; found on or near the bottom of the sea, a lake etc. ◷ 19c: from DE- 1 + Latin *mergere, mersum* to plunge.

demi- /'dɛmɪ-/ ▷ *combining form, signifying* half or partly □ *demigod*. Compare SEMI-. ◷ From French *demi* half.

demigod and **demigoddess** ▷ *noun* **1** *mythol* someone who is part human and part god, especially someone believed to be the offspring of a human and a god. **2** a lesser god. **3** a person idolized like a god. ◷ 16c.

demijohn /'dɛmɪdʒɒn/ ▷ *noun* a large bottle with a short narrow neck and one or two small handles, used for storing eg wine. ◷ 18c: from French *dame-jeanne* Dame Jane, influenced by DEMI- and the name *John*.

demilitarize or **demilitarise** /diː'mɪlɪtəraɪz/ ▷ *verb* to remove armed forces from (an area) and/or not allow any military activity in it. • **demilitarization** *noun*. ◷ 19c.

demi-monde /'dɛmɪmɒnd/ ▷ *noun* **1** a class of women considered to be in an unrespectable social position, eg in the 19c, the kept mistresses of society men. **2** any group or section of a group considered to be less than completely respectable. • **demi-mondaine** /dɛmɪmɒn'dɛn/ *noun* a woman member of a demi-monde. Also *as adj*. ◷ 19c: French.

demineralize or **demineralise** ▷ *verb* (***demineralized, demineralizing***) to remove salts from (water, the body, etc). • **demineralization** *noun*. ◷ Early 20c.

demi-pension /dəmɪpɛsjθ/ ▷ *noun* HALF BOARD. ◷ 1950s: French *demi* half + *pension* boarding house.

demise /dɪ'maɪz/ ▷ *noun* **1** *formal or euphemistic* death. **2** a failure or end. ◷ 16c: from French *demise*, from *desmettre* to lay down.

demisemiquaver ▷ *noun, music* a note equal in time to half a SEMIQUAVER.

demist /diː'mɪst/ ▷ *verb* (***demisted, demisting***) to free (a vehicle's windscreen, etc) from condensation by blowing warm air over it. • **demister** *noun*. ◷ 1930s.

demitasse /'dɛmɪtas/ ▷ *noun* **1** a small cup of coffee, especially black coffee. **2 a** the quantity contained by such a cup; **b** the cup itself. ◷ 19c: French, meaning 'half-cup'.

demo /'dɛmoʊ/ ▷ *noun* (***demos***) *colloq* **1** a DEMONSTRATION, especially as in sense 2. **2** (*also* **demo tape**) a recording made as a demonstration, especially one made by as yet unsigned musicians to demonstrate their skills and style to record companies. ◷ 1930s.

demob /diː'mɒb/ *Brit colloq* ▷ *verb* (***demobbed, demobbing***) to DEMOBILIZE. ▷ *noun* DEMOBILIZATION. ◷ 1920s.

demobilize or **demobilise** /dɪ'moʊbɪlaɪz/ ▷ *verb* to release someone from service in the armed forces, eg after a war. • **demobilization** *noun* release from service in the armed forces. Often (*colloq*) shortened to **demob**. ◷ 19c.

democracy /dɪ'mɒkrəsɪ/ ▷ *noun* (***democracies***) **1** a form of government in which the people govern themselves or elect representatives to govern them. **2** a country, state or other body with such a form of government. ◷ 16c: from French *démocratie*, from Greek *demos* people + *kratos* strength.

democrat /'dɛməkrat/ ▷ *noun* **1** someone who believes in DEMOCRACY as a principle. **2** (**Democrat**) a member or supporter of the Democratic Party in the USA, or of any political party with *Democratic* in its title in any country. Compare REPUBLICAN.

democratic /dɛmə'kratɪk/ ▷ *adj* **1** concerned with or following the principles of democracy. **2** believing in or providing equal rights and privileges for all. **3** (**Democratic**) belonging or relating to the Democratic Party, one of the two chief political parties of the US. Compare REPUBLICAN. • **democratically** *adverb*. ◷ 17c.

democratize or **democratise** /dɪ'mɒkrətaɪz/ ▷ *verb* (***democratized, democratizing***) to make (a state, etc) democratic. • **democratization** *noun*. ◷ 18c.

démodé /deɪ'moʊdeɪ/ ▷ *adj* out of fashion. ◷ 19c: French.

demoded /diː'moʊdɪd/ ▷ *adj, disparaging* no longer in fashion. ◷ 19c: from DÉMODÉ.

demodulate /diː'mɒdjʊleɪt/ *radio* ▷ *verb* to perform DEMODULATION on the CARRIER WAVE of a radio broadcast. • **demodulator** *noun* a device that extracts information from the modulated carrier wave of a radio broadcast.

demodulation /diːmɒdjʊ'leɪʃən/ ▷ *noun, electronics* the inverse of MODULATION, a process by which an output wave is obtained that has the characteristics of the original modulating wave. ◷ 1920s.

demography /dɪ'mɒgrəfɪ/ ▷ *noun, technical* the scientific study of population statistics, including births, deaths, etc. • **demographer** *noun* someone who studies demography or the statistics of populations. • **demographic** /dɛmə'grafɪk/ *adj*. ◷ 19c: from Greek *demos* people + *-graphy*.

demolish /dɪ'mɒlɪʃ/ ▷ *verb* (***demolishes, demolished, demolishing***) **1** to pull or tear down (a building, etc). **2** to destroy (an argument, etc). **3** *facetious* to eat up. ◷ 16c: from Latin *demoliri* to throw down.

demolition /dɛmə'lɪʃən/ ▷ *noun* the act of demolishing. ◷ 16c.

demon /'diːmən/ ▷ *noun* **1** an evil spirit. **2** a cruel or evil person. **3** someone who has great energy, enthusiasm or skill □ *a demon at football*. **4** a good or friendly spirit; a DAEMON (sense 2). ◷ 15c: from Greek *daimon* spirit; in later Greek, eg the New Testament, 'a devil'.

demonetize or **demonetise** /diː'mʌnɪtaɪz, diː'mɒn-/ ▷ *verb* (***demonetized, demonetizing***) **1** to withdraw (a metal) from use as a monetary standard. **2** to withdraw something from use as currency. ◷ 19c.

demoniac /dɪ'moʊnɪak/ and **demoniacal** /diːmə'naɪəkəl/ ▷ *adj* **1** characteristic of, belonging to or like a demon or demons. **2** influenced, or as if influenced, by demons; frenzied or very energetic. ◷ 14c.

demonic /dɪ'mɒnɪk/ ▷ *adj* **1** characteristic of, belonging to or like a demon or demons. **2** possessed, or as if possessed, by a demon or demons; evil. • **demonically** *adverb*. ◷ 17c.

demonism /'diːmənɪzəm/ ▷ *noun* **1** a belief in or worship of demons. **2** the study of demons and belief in demons. Also called **demonology**.

demonstrable /dɪ'mɒnstrəbəl, 'dɛmən-/ ▷ *adj* capable of being demonstrated. • **demonstrably** *adverb*. • **demonstrability** or **demonstrableness** *noun*. ◷ 15c.

demonstrate /'dɛmənstreɪt/ ▷ *verb* (***demonstrated, demonstrating***) **1** to show or prove something by reasoning or providing evidence. **2** *tr & intr* to show how something is done, operates, etc. **3** *tr & intr* to show (support, opposition, etc) by protesting, marching, etc in public. ◷ 16c: from Latin *demonstrare, demonstratum* to show or indicate.

demonstration /dɛmən'streɪʃən/ ▷ *noun* **1** showing or demonstrating, especially a practical lesson, explanation or exhibition. **2** a public display of opinion on a political or moral issue. **3** *math, philos* establishing as true or evident by argument or proof. See also DEMO. ⓒ 14c.

demonstrative /dɪˈmɒnstrətɪv/ ▻ *adj* **1** showing one's feelings openly. **2** (*usually* **demonstrative of something**) showing it or proving it to be so ▫ *words demonstrative of anger.* • **demonstratively** *adverb* in a demonstrative or openly expressive way. • **demonstrativeness** *noun.* ⓒ 16c.

demonstrative pronoun and **demonstrative adjective** ▻ *noun, grammar* a word indicating which person or thing is referred to, ie THIS, THAT, THESE, THOSE.

demonstrator ▻ *noun* **1** someone who demonstrates equipment, etc, especially a teaching or marketing assistant. **2** someone who takes part in a public demonstration. **3** an example of a product or piece of merchandise, especially a vehicle, used for demonstration to customers. ⓒ 17c.

demoralize or **demoralise** /dɪˈmɒrəlaɪz/ ▻ *verb* to take away the confidence, courage or enthusiasm of someone; to dishearten them. See also MORALE. • **demoralization** *noun.* • **demoralizer** *noun.* ⓒ 19c in this sense; 18c, meaning 'to corrupt morally': from French *démoraliser.*

demo tape see under DEMO

demote /diːˈmoʊt, dɪ-/ ▻ *verb* (***demoted, demoting***) to reduce someone to a lower rank or grade. • **demotion** /-ˈmoʊʃən/ *noun.* ⓒ 19c: from DE- 2 + pro*mote.*

demotic /dɪˈmɒtɪk/ ▻ *adj* said especially of a language: used in everyday affairs; popular. ▻ *noun* **1** colloquial language. **2** (*often* **Demotic**) a form of modern Greek based on popular usage, as distinct from the formal or literary language. **3** a simplified form of ancient Egyptian writing. ⓒ 19c: from Greek *demotikos,* from *demos* people.

demulcent /dɪˈmʌlsənt/ ▻ *adj* soothing. ▻ *noun, medicine* a drug, etc, that soothes irritation. ⓒ 18c: from Latin *demulcere* to stroke caressingly.

demur /dɪˈmɜː(r)/ ▻ *verb* (***demurred, demurring***) *intr* **1** to object. **2** to show reluctance. • **demurral** *noun.* • **without demur** without objecting. ⓒ 17c in these senses; 13c, meaning 'to delay': from French *demorer* to wait.

▪ **demur at something** to object mildly to it or be reluctant to do it.

demure /dɪˈmjʊə(r)/ ▻ *adj* said of a person: quiet, modest and well-behaved. • **demurely** *adverb.* • **demureness** *noun.* ⓒ 17c in this sense; 15c, meaning 'grave' or 'reserved': from French *demorer* to wait, influenced by *meur* ripe.

demutualize or **demutualise** /diːˈmjuːtʃʊəlaɪz/ ▻ *verb, finance* said of a mutual institution such as a building society: to become a public company. • **demutualization** *noun.*

demystify /diːˈmɪstɪfaɪ/ ▻ *verb* to remove the mystery from something. • **demystification** *noun* clarification; explanation; simplifying. ⓒ 1960s.

demythologize or **demythologise** /diːmɪˈθɒlədʒaɪz/ ▻ *verb* to remove mythology from (especially the Bible or a religious statement) in order to reach or present the basic meaning. ⓒ 1950s.

den ▻ *noun* **1** a wild animal's home. **2** a centre (often secret) of illegal or immoral activity. **3** *colloq* a room in a house or a hut outside it, used as a place to work or play. ⓒ Anglo-Saxon *denn* cave or lair.

denar see DINAR

denarius /dɪˈnɛərɪəs/ ▻ *noun* (***denarii*** /-rɪaɪ, -rɪiː/) an ancient Roman silver coin. ⓒ 16c: Latin, meaning 'containing 10', because the coin was originally equal to 10 coins called *asses.*

denary /ˈdiːnərɪ/ ▻ *adj* containing or having the number 10 as a basis. ⓒ 19c: from Latin *denarius* containing ten.

denationalize or **denationalise** /diːˈnaʃənəlaɪz/ ▻ *verb* **1** to return or transfer (an industry) to private ownership from state ownership. **2** to deprive (a person, state, etc) of national rights or character. • **denationalization** *noun.* ⓒ 19c.

denaturalize or **denaturalise** /diːˈnatʃərəlaɪz/ ▻ *verb* **1** to make something unnatural. **2** to deprive (a citizen) of naturalization. • **denaturalization** *noun.* ⓒ 19c.

denature /diːˈneɪtʃə(r)/ and **denaturize** or **denaturise** ▻ *verb* (***denatured, denaturing; denaturized, denaturizing***) **1** *biol* to change the structure of (a PROTEIN, eg an ENZYME) by exposing it to high temperatures, certain chemicals or extremes of acidity and alkalinity, usually resulting in a decrease in its solubility and the loss of its biological effects. **2** *physics* to add another ISOTOPE to (a material capable of NUCLEAR FISSION), so that it is no longer suitable for use in a nuclear weapon. **3** to add a poisonous or unpalatable substance to (alcohol), so that it is unfit for human consumption. • **denaturant** /diːˈneɪtʃərənt/ *noun* a substance used to denature another. ⓒ 17c, originally meaning 'to make something unnatural'.

denazify /diːˈnɑːtsɪfaɪ/ ▻ *verb* (***denazifies, denazified, denazifying***) to free someone or something from Nazi ideology and influence. • **denazification** *noun.* ⓒ 1940s.

dendrite /ˈdɛndraɪt/ ▻ *noun* **1** *zool* any of a number of cytoplasmic projections that radiate outwards from the star-shaped cell body of a NEURONE. **2** *chem* a crystal which exhibits branched growth. • **dendritic** /dɛnˈdrɪtɪk/ *adj.* ⓒ 19c in these senses; 18c, meaning 'a stone, etc with a natural tree-like marking': from Greek *dendrites* of a tree.

dendro- /dɛndroʊ, dɛnˈdrɒ/, **dendri-** and (before a vowel) **dendr-** ▻ *combining form, signifying* tree. ⓒ 18c: from Greek *dendron* tree.

dendrochronology ▻ *noun, archaeol* the analysis of the patterns of annual growth-rings found in trees and the fixing of dates by comparative study of timber from different periods. • **dendrochronological** *adj.* • **dendrochronologist** *noun.* ⓒ 1920s.

dendroclimatology ▻ *noun* the study of growth rings in trees as evidence of climatic change. • **dendroclimatologist** *noun.* ⓒ 1950s.

dendroid /ˈdɛndrɔɪd/ ▻ *adj* tree-like; having branches. ⓒ 19c.

dendrology /dɛnˈdrɒlədʒɪ/ ▻ *noun* the scientific study of trees. • **dendrological** /-əˈlɒdʒɪkəl/ *adj.* • **dendrologist** *noun* a scientist who specializes in dendrology. ⓒ 18c.

dendron /ˈdɛndrɒn/ ▻ *noun, physiol* a DENDRITE. ⓒ 19c: Greek, meaning 'tree'.

DEng. ▻ *abbreviation* Doctor of Engineering.

dengue /ˈdɛŋgeɪ/ ▻ *noun* an acute tropical viral fever, seldom fatal, transmitted by mosquitos. ⓒ 19c: probably originally from Swahili *dinga.*

deniable /dɪˈnaɪəbəl/ ▻ *adj* able to be denied. • **deniability** *noun.* • **deniably** *adverb.* ⓒ 16c: from DENY.

denial /dɪˈnaɪəl/ ▻ *noun* **1** an act of denying or declaring something not to be true. **2** an act of refusing something to someone. **3** an act of refusing to acknowledge connections with somebody or something. • **in denial** *psychol* suffering from a condition which involves the suppression, usually at a subconscious level, of an emotion, truth, etc that is particularly painful or difficult to come to terms with ▫ *After the death of his mother, he was in denial for months.* ⓒ 16c: from DENY.

denied *past tense, past participle of* DENY

denier /ˈdɛnɪə(r), ˈdɛnɪeɪ/ ▻ *noun* the unit of weight of silk, rayon or nylon thread, usually used as a measure of the fineness of stockings or tights. ⓒ 19c; first recorded in the15c as the name of a small French coin: French, from Latin *denarius* DENARIUS.

denigrate /ˈdɛnɪgreɪt/ ▷ *verb* (***denigrated, denigrating***) to scorn or criticize someone; to attack or belittle the reputation, character or worth of someone. • **denigration** *noun*. • **denigrator** *noun*. ⓒ 16c: from Latin *denigrare, denigratum* to blacken.

denim /ˈdɛnɪm/ ▷ *noun* **1** a kind of hard-wearing, usually blue, twilled cotton cloth used for making jeans, overalls, etc. **2** (**denims**) clothing, especially jeans, made of denim. ▷ *adj* made of denim. ⓒ 17c: from French *de* of + Nîmes, a town in southern France.

denizen /ˈdɛnɪzən/ ▷ *noun* **1** *formal* an inhabitant, either human or animal. **2** *biol* a species of animal or plant which has become well established in a place to which it is not native and into which it has been introduced. **3** a naturalized foreign word or expression. **4** *Brit* someone who permanently lives in a country that is not their native country and who is accorded some rights of their adopted country. ⓒ 15c: from French *deinzein*, from *deinz* within.

den mother ▷ *noun, US* **1** an adult female leader of a Cub Scout group. **2** any adult female protective figure.

denominate /dɪˈnɒmɪneɪt/ ▷ *verb, formal* to give a specific name or title to something. ⓒ 16c: from Latin *denominare, denominatum* to name.

denomination ▷ *noun* **1** a religious group with its own particular beliefs, organization and practices. **2** a particular unit of value of a postage stamp, coin or banknote, etc. • **denominational** *adj*. ⓒ 15c.

denominator /dɪˈnɒmɪneɪtə(r)/ ▷ *noun, math* in a VULGAR FRACTION, the number shown below the line, indicating the units into which the fraction is dividing the whole, eg '5' in the fraction $^3/_5$. Compare NUMERATOR, COMMON DENOMINATOR. ⓒ 16c.

denote /dɪˈnoʊt/ ▷ *verb* **1** to mean; to be the name of or sign for something. **2** to be a sign, mark or indication of something. Compare CONNOTE. • **denotation** *noun* denoting; marking by signs or symbols. • **denotative** /dɪˈnoʊtətɪv, ˈdiːnoʊteɪtɪv/ *adj*. ⓒ 16c: from Latin *denotare* to mark out.

denouement or **dénouement** /deɪˈnuːmɑ̃/ ▷ *noun* **1** the final part of a story or plot, in which uncertainties are explained and previously unresolved problems and mysteries are resolved. **2** *loosely* any resolution. ⓒ 18c: French *dénouement*, from *dénouer* to untie a knot.

denounce /dɪˈnaʊns/ ▷ *verb* (***denounced, denouncing***) **1** to inform against or accuse someone publicly □ *denounced them as traitors*. **2** to condemn (an action, proposal, idea, etc) strongly and openly. See also DENUNCIATION. ⓒ 15c: from French *dénoncier*, from Latin *denuntiare* to announce.

de novo /diː ˈnoʊvoʊ, deɪ —/ ▷ *adverb* again; again from the beginning. ⓒ 17c: Latin.

dense ▷ *adj* **1** closely packed or crowded together. **2** thick □ *dense fog*. **3** *colloq* stupid; slow to understand. • **densely** *adverb*. • **denseness** *noun*. ⓒ 15c: from Latin *densus* thick or dense.

densimeter /dɛnˈsɪmɪtə(r)/ ▷ *noun* an instrument for measuring the relative density or the closeness of the grain of a substance. ⓒ 19c.

density /ˈdɛnsətɪ/ ▷ *noun* (***densities***) **1** the state of being dense or the degree of denseness. **2** the ratio of the mass of a substance to its volume (the SI units of density measurement being kg m^{-3}). **3** the number of items within a specific area or volume □ *population density*. **4** *computing* the number of bits (see BIT³) that can be stored on one track of a disk or within a specific area of magnetic tape, etc. ⓒ 17c: from Latin *densus* thick.

dent ▷ *noun* **1** a hollow in the surface of something, especially something hard, made by pressure or a blow. **2** a noticeable, usually bad, effect, especially a lessening (eg of resources, money, etc). ▷ *verb* (***dented, denting***) **1** to make a dent in something. **2** *intr* to become dented. **3** to injure (someone's pride, etc). ⓒ Anglo-Saxon *dynt* blow.

dental ▷ *adj* **1** concerned with or for the teeth or dentistry. **2** *phonetics* said of a speech sound: produced by putting the tongue to the teeth. ▷ *noun, phonetics* a dental sound eg *'th'* in the word *the*. ⓒ 16c: from Latin *dentalis*, from *dens* tooth.

dental alveolus see ALVEOLUS

dental caries ▷ *noun, medicine* the decay of a tooth, resulting from erosion of the enamel by acid, and the commonest cause of toothache.

dental floss ▷ *noun* a soft thread used for cleaning between the teeth.

dental formula ▷ *noun, zool* a formula that shows the number of different types of tooth present in the upper and lower jaw of a mammal.

dental surgeon ▷ *noun* a dentist.

dentate /ˈdɛnteɪt/ ▷ *adj, technical* with a tooth-like notched pattern round the edge. ⓒ 19c: from Latin *dentatus*.

dente see AL DENTE

dentifrice /ˈdɛntɪfrɪs/ ▷ *noun* paste or powder for cleaning the teeth. ⓒ 16c: French, from Latin *dens, dentis* tooth + *fricare* to rub.

dentil /ˈdɛntɪl/ ▷ *noun, archit* each of a series of small square or rectangular blocks or projections, especially those set beneath the cornice in classical orders. ⓒ 16c: from French *dentille*, from *dent* tooth, from their resemblance to a row of teeth.

dentine /ˈdɛntiːn/ or **dentin** /-tɪn/ ▷ *noun, anatomy* in vertebrates: a hard yellowish-white material, similar to bone but perforated with canals for nerve fibres and blood vessels, that forms the bulk of a tooth. ⓒ 19c: from Latin *dens* tooth.

dentist /ˈdɛntɪst/ ▷ *noun* someone who is professionally trained and qualified to practise DENTISTRY. ⓒ 18c: from French *dentiste*, from *dent* tooth.

dentistry /ˈdɛntɪstrɪ/ ▷ *noun* the branch of medicine concerned with the diagnosis, treatment and prevention of diseases of the oral cavity and teeth. ⓒ 19c.

dentition /dɛnˈtɪʃən/ ▷ *noun, technical* the number, arrangement and type of teeth in a human or animal. ⓒ 16c: from Latin *dentitio* teething.

denture /ˈdɛntʃə(r)/ ▷ *noun* a false tooth or (usually **dentures**) set of false teeth. ⓒ 19c: French, from *dent* tooth.

denuclearize or **denuclearise** /diːˈnjuːklɪəraɪz/ ▷ *verb* to remove nuclear weapons from (a country or state, etc). • **denuclearization** *noun*. ⓒ 1950s.

denudation /dɛnjʊˈdeɪʃən, diː-/ ▷ *noun* **1** denuding; making bare. **2** *geol* the process by which the surface of the land is progressively lowered as a result of weathering and erosion, so that the underlying rocks are laid bare.

denude /dɪˈnjuːd/ ▷ *verb* (***denuded, denuding***) **1** to make someone or something completely bare. **2** to strip (land). ⓒ 15c: from Latin *denudare* to lay bare or uncover.

denunciation /dɪnʌnsɪˈeɪʃən/ ▷ *noun* a public condemnation or accusation. See also DENOUNCE. ⓒ 16c: from Latin *denuntiare, denuntiatum* to announce.

Denver boot ▷ *noun, colloq* a wheel clamp. ⓒ 20c: named after Denver, US, where the device was first used.

deny /dɪˈnaɪ/ ▷ *verb* (***denies, denied, denying***) **1** to declare something not to be true. **2** to refuse to give or allow to someone. **3** to refuse to acknowledge a connection with someone or something. • **deny oneself something** to do without (things that one desires or needs). See also DENIAL. ⓒ 14c: from French *denier*.

deodar /ˈdiːoʊdɑː(r)/ ▷ *noun* **1** a cedar tree belonging to the Himalayas. **2** the hard, sweet-scented, much valued wood of this tree. ◷ 19c: Sanskrit *deva-daru* divine tree.

deodorant /dɪˈoʊdərənt/ ▷ *noun* a substance that prevents or conceals unpleasant smells, especially the smell of stale sweat on the human body. ◷ 19c.

deodorize or **deodorise** /dɪˈoʊdəraɪz/ ▷ *verb* (***deodorized***, ***deodorizing***) to remove, conceal or absorb the unpleasant smell of something. • **deodorization** *noun*. • **deodorizer** *noun*. ◷ 19c.

deontic /dɪˈɒntɪk/ ▷ *noun* (*usually* **deontics**) *philos* the study of duty and obligations. ▷ *adj* concerning duty and obligation. ◷ 19c: from Greek *deein* to be necessary.

deontology /diːɒnˈtɒlədʒɪ/ ▷ *noun* the study of duty; ethics. • **deontological** *adj*. ◷ 19c: from Greek *deein* to be necessary.

deoxidate /diːˈɒksɪdeɪt/ and **deoxidize** or **deoxidise** /diːˈɒksɪdaɪz/ ▷ *verb*, *chem* (***deoxidated***, ***deoxidating***) to remove oxygen from something or to chemically reduce it. • **deoxidation** or **deoxidization** *noun*. • **deoxidizer** *noun*.

deoxy- /diːˈɒksɪ/ ▷ *combining form*, *chem*, *signifying* less oxygen.

deoxygenate /diːˈɒksɪdʒəneɪt/ ▷ *verb*, *chem* to remove oxygen, especially free oxygen, from something.

deoxyribonucleic acid /diːˈɒksɪraɪboʊnjuːˈkleɪɪk—/ ▷ *noun*, *biochem* (abbreviation **DNA**) the nucleic acid that forms the material of which the chromosomes and genes of almost all living organisms are composed, containing coded instructions for the transmission of genetic information from one generation to the next and for the manufacture of all the proteins that are required for the growth and development of a whole new organism. ◷ 1930s.

dep. ▷ *abbreviation* **1** depart. **2** department. **3** departure. **4** deposed. **5** deposit. **6** deputy.

depart /dɪˈpɑːt/ ▷ *verb* (***departed***, ***departing***) *intr* **1** *rather formal* to leave. **2** (*usually* **depart from something**) to stop following or decline to follow a planned or usual course of action. • **departed** *adj*, *formal* **1** dead. **2** (**the departed**) a person or people recently dead (see THE 4). ◷ 13c: from French *departir*.

département /*French* departəmɑ̃/ ▷ *noun* (***départements*** /*French* -mɑ̃/) an administrative division of France. ◷ 18c: French.

department /dɪˈpɑːtmənt/ ▷ *noun* **1** a section of an organization (eg a government or other administration, a university, an office or a shop), with responsibility for one particular aspect or part of the organization's work. **2** a subject or activity which is someone's special skill or particular responsibility. ◷ 18c: from French *département*.

departmental /diːpɑːtˈmɛntə/ ▷ *adj* **1** belonging or relating to, or concerning a department or departments. **2** divided into departments. • **departmentally** *adverb*. ◷ 18c.

departmentalism ▷ *noun* excessively strict division of work among departments with too little intercommunication.

departmentalize or **departmentalise** ▷ *verb* (***departmentalized***, ***departmentalizing***) **1** to form (an organization, etc) into separate departments. **2** to deal with (a large amount of work, etc) by allotting a specific share to different departments. • **departmentalization** *noun*.

department store ▷ *noun* a large shop with many different departments selling a wide variety of goods.

departure /dɪˈpɑːtʃə(r)/ ▷ *noun* **1** an act of going away or leaving. **2** (*often* **departure from something**) a change from a planned or usual course of action. **3** (*often* **new departure**) a new activity, different from what one has been doing or normally does. **4** *naut* the distance in nautical miles travelled by a ship due East or West. ◷ 16c.

departure lounge see under LOUNGE

depend /dɪˈpɛnd/ ▷ *verb* (***depended***, ***depending***) *intr* (*usually* **depend on** or **upon someone** or **something**) **1** to rely on them or it; to be able to trust them or it. **2** to rely on financial or other support from someone. **3** to be decided by or vary according to something else. ◷ 15c: from Latin *dependere* to hang down.

dependable ▷ *adj* trustworthy or reliable. • **dependability** *noun*. • **dependably** *adverb*. ◷ 18c.

dependant ▷ *noun* a person who is kept or supported financially by another. ◷ 16c.

dependence ▷ *noun* (*usually* **dependence on** or **upon something** or **someone**) **1** the state of being dependent on them. **2** trust and reliance. ◷ 17c.

dependency ▷ *noun* (***dependencies***) **1** a country governed or controlled by another. **2** excessive dependence on someone or something, eg addiction to a drug. ◷ 16c.

dependency culture ▷ *noun* (*often derog*) a type of society which relies upon, and often expects, state benefits and other support to maintain it.

dependent ▷ *adj* (*often* **dependent on** or **upon something** or **someone**) **1** relying on it or them for financial or other support. **2** said of an issue or outcome: to be decided or influenced by them □ *Success is dependent on all our efforts.*

dependent clause ▷ *noun*, *grammar* see SUBORDINATE CLAUSE.

depersonalize or **depersonalise** /diːˈpɜːsənəlaɪz/ *psychol* ▷ *verb* to take away the characteristics or personality of someone; to make them impersonal. • **depersonalization** *noun* a condition in which a person feels unreal, or feels that the mind and body are becoming separated, which is a common symptom of severe stress, and of EPILEPSY, DEPRESSION and SCHIZOPHRENIA. ◷ 19c.

depict /dɪˈpɪkt/ ▷ *verb* (***depicted***, ***depicting***) **1** to paint or draw something. **2** to describe something, especially in detail. • **depicter** or **depictor** *noun*. • **depiction** *noun*. • **depictive** *adj*. ◷ 17c: from Latin *depingere* to paint.

depilate /ˈdɛpɪleɪt/ ▷ *verb* (***depilated***, ***depilating***) to remove hair from (a part of the body). • **depilation** *noun*. See also EPILATE. ◷ 16c: from Latin *depilatus*, from DE- + *pilare*, from *pilus* hair.

depilatory /dɪˈpɪlətərɪ/ ▷ *noun* (***depilatories***) a chemical substance used to remove unwanted hair from the body. ▷ *adj* able to remove hair. ◷ 17c: from Latin *depilare* to remove hair.

deplane /diːˈpleɪn/ ▷ *verb* (***deplaned***, ***deplaning***) *intr*, *especially N Amer* to disembark from an aeroplane.

deplete /dɪˈpliːt/ ▷ *verb* (***depleted***, ***depleting***) to reduce greatly in number, quantity, etc; to use up (supplies, money, energy, resources, etc). • **depletion** *noun*. ◷ 19c: from Latin *deplere*, *depletum* to empty.

deplorable /dɪˈplɔːrəbəl/ ▷ *adj* very bad, shocking or regrettable. • **deplorableness** or **deplorability** *noun*. • **deplorably** *adverb*. ◷ 17c.

deplore /dɪˈplɔː(r)/ ▷ *verb* (***deplored***, ***deploring***) to feel or express great disapproval of or regret for something. ◷ 16c, originally meaning 'to lament': from French *déplorer*, from Latin *deplorare* to weep for.

deploy /dɪˈplɔɪ/ ▷ *verb* (***deployed***, ***deploying***) **1** *tr & intr* to spread out and position (troops) ready for battle. **2** to organize and bring (resources, arguments, etc) into use. • **deployment** *noun*. ◷ 18c in sense 1; 15c, meaning 'to unfold or display': from French *déployer*, from Latin *displicare* to unfold.

depolarize or **depolarise** /diːˈpoʊləraɪz/ ▷ *verb* **1** *physics* to reduce or remove the POLARITY of something. **2** *physiol* to reduce the electrical potential difference across a cell membrance, especially a nerve-cell membrane. • **depolarization** *noun.*

depoliticize or **depoliticise** /diːpəˈlɪtɪsaɪz/ ▷ *verb* to remove the political nature of something or political awareness from someone or something. ⓒ 1920s.

deponent /dɪˈpoʊnənt/ ▷ *noun, law* someone who makes a deposition (see DEPOSITION 3), especially under oath, or whose written testimony is used as evidence in a court. ⓒ 16c: from Latin *deponere* to lay aside or put down.

depopulate /diːˈpɒpjʊleɪt/ ▷ *verb* to greatly reduce the number of people living in (an area, country, etc). • **depopulated** *adj.* • **depopulation** *noun.* ⓒ 16c: from Latin *depopulari, depopulatus* to lay waste, later understood as meaning 'to deprive of people'.

deport[1] /dɪˈpɔːt/ ▷ *verb* (*deported, deporting*) to legally remove or expel (a person) from a country. • **deportation** *noun.* ⓒ 17c: from Latin *deportare* to carry away.

deport[2] /dɪˈpɔːt/ ▷ *verb* (*deported, deporting*) *formal* to behave oneself (in a particular way). • **deportment** *noun* **1** the way one holds or carries oneself; one's bearing. **2** behaviour. ⓒ 16c: from Latin *deportare* to carry away.

deportee /diːpɔːˈtiː/ ▷ *noun* (*deportees*) someone who has been or is about to be expelled from a country. ⓒ 19c.

depose /dɪˈpoʊz/ ▷ *verb* (*deposed, deposing*) to remove someone from a high office or powerful position. • **deposable** *adj.* • **deposer** *noun.* ⓒ 15c: from French *deposer* to put down or away.

deposit /dɪˈpɒzɪt/ ▷ *verb* (*deposited, depositing*) **1** to put down or leave something. **2** to put (money, etc) in a bank, etc, for safekeeping or to earn interest. **3** to give (a sum of money) as the first part of the payment for something, so guaranteeing that one can complete the purchase later. **4** to pay (a sum of money) as a guarantee against loss or damage. ▷ *noun* **1** a sum of money, etc, deposited in a bank, etc. **2** a sum of money given as part payment for something or paid as a guarantee against loss or damage. **3** solid matter that has settled at the bottom of a liquid, or is left behind by a liquid. **4** *geol* a layer (of coal, oil, minerals, etc) occurring naturally in rock. ⓒ 16c: from Latin *depositum*, from *deponere* to put down.

deposit account ▷ *noun* a bank account in which money is lodged to gain interest but which cannot be used for the transfer of money to other people by eg cheque or standing order. ⓒ 19c.

depositary /dɪˈpɒzɪtərɪ/ ▷ *noun* (*depositaries*) **1** *formal* a person, etc to whom something is given for safekeeping. **2** a DEPOSITORY (sense 1). ⓒ 17c in sense 1; 18c in sense 2: from Latin *depositarius*.

deposition /diːpəˈzɪʃən, dɛ-/ ▷ *noun* **1** the act of deposing or process of being deposed. **2** the act of depositing or process of being deposited. **3** *law* a written statement made under oath and used as evidence in a court of law when the witness cannot be present. **4** *geol* the laying down on the Earth's surface of eroded material that has been transported by wind, rivers, glaciers, avalanches, etc. • **depositional** *adj.* ⓒ 14c: from Latin *depositio* putting down.

depositor /dɪˈpɒzɪtə(r)/ ▷ *noun* someone who deposits money in a bank or building society, especially in a DEPOSIT ACCOUNT.

depository /dɪˈpɒzɪtərɪ/ ▷ *noun* (*depositories*) **1** a place where anything may be left for safe-keeping, eg a furniture store. **2** a DEPOSITARY (sense 1). ⓒ 18c in sense 1; 17c in sense 2: from Latin *depositorium*.

depot /ˈdɛpoʊ; *N Amer* ˈdiːpoʊ/ ▷ *noun* (*depots*) **1** a storehouse or warehouse. **2** a place where buses, trains and certain types of vehicles are kept and repaired. **3** *N Amer* a bus or railway station. **4** a military headquarters, or a military post where stores are kept and recruits trained. ⓒ 18c: from French *dépôt*.

deprave /dɪˈpreɪv/ ▷ *verb* (*depraved, depraving*) to make someone evil or morally corrupt. • **depraved** *adj* morally corrupted. • **depravity** /dɪˈpravɪtɪ/ *noun.* ⓒ 15c, originally meaning 'to disparage; to speak ill of': from Latin *depravare* to pervert or distort.

deprecate /ˈdɛprəkeɪt/ ▷ *verb* (*deprecated, deprecating*) to express disapproval of something; to deplore something. • **deprecating** *adj.* • **deprecatingly** *adverb.* • **deprecation** *noun* the expression of disapproval. • **deprecative** or **deprecatory** *adj* **1** showing or expressing disapproval. **2** apologetic; trying to avoid disapproval. • **deprecator** *noun.* • **deprecatorily** *adverb.* ⓒ 17c, originally meaning 'to pray against evil': from Latin *deprecari, deprecatus* to try to avert.

deprecate, depreciate

• As with many confusable words, the meanings of these two overlap somewhat. Essentially, **deprecate** implies outright deploring or disapproval, whereas **depreciate** implies a more considered belittling or undervaluing □ *George made a deprecating sound, but she held up her hand to silence him* □ *He gave a tiny, self-depreciating laugh on the last word, acknowledging his inadequacy.*

depreciate /dɪˈpriːʃɪeɪt, -sɪeɪt-/ ▷ *verb* (*depreciated, depreciating*) **1** *tr & intr* to fall, or make something fall, in value. **2** to be contemptuous of the worth of something; to belittle someone or something. • **depreciatingly** *adverb.* ⓒ 15c: from Latin *depretiare, depretiatum* to lower the price of.

depreciation ▷ *noun* **1** *econ* a fall in value of a currency against the value of other currencies. **2** the reduction in the value of fixed assets such as buildings and equipment through use or age. **3** the process of depreciating. ⓒ 18c.

depreciatory ▷ *adj* belittling; contemptuous. ⓒ 19c.

depredation /dɛprəˈdeɪʃən/ ▷ *noun* (*often* **depredations**) damage, destruction or violent robbery. ⓒ 15c: from Latin *depraedatio*, from *praedari* to plunder.

depress /dɪˈprɛs/ ▷ *verb* (*depressed, depressing*) **1** to make someone sad and gloomy. **2** *formal* to make (prices, etc) lower. **3** *formal* to press down. **4** to reduce the energy or power of something: to weaken something. ⓒ 16c; 14c, meaning 'to overcome, to vanquish': from French *depresser*.

depressant /dɪˈprɛsənt/ ▷ *adj, medicine* said of a drug: able to reduce mental or physical activity. ▷ *noun* a depressant drug. See also ANTIDEPRESSANT. ⓒ 19c.

depressed ▷ *adj* **1** sad and gloomy. **2** *psychol* suffering from depression. **3** said of a region, town, etc: suffering from high unemployment and low standards of living. **4** said of trade, a market, etc: not flourishing. **5** lowered; pressed down, flattened.

depressing ▷ *adj* causing low spirits. • **depressingly** *adverb.*

depression /dɪˈprɛʃən/ ▷ *noun* **1** *psychol* a mental state, either organic or circumstantial, characterized by prolonged and disproportionate feelings of sadness, pessimism, helplessness, apathy, low self-esteem and despair. **2** a period of low business and industrial activity accompanied by a rise in unemployment. **3** (**the Depression**) the period of worldwide economic depression from 1929 to 1934. **4** *meteorol* a CYCLONE. **5** a hollow, especially in the ground.

depression of freezing point ▷ *noun, chem* the lowering of the freezing point of a liquid, achieved by dissolving a solid in it.

depressive /dɪˈprɛsɪv/ ▷ *adj* **1** depressing. **2** said of a person: suffering from frequent bouts of depression.

▷ *noun* someone who suffers frequently from depression.

depressor /dɪ'prɛsə(r)/ ▷ *noun* **1** something or someone that depresses. **2** *anatomy* a muscle that draws down the part it is connected to. **3** a surgical instrument for pressing something down.

depressurize or **depressurise** /diː'prɛʃəraɪz/ ▷ *verb* to reduce the air pressure in (eg an aircraft) especially if done suddenly. • **depressurization** *noun*. ⓒ 1940s.

deprive /dɪ'praɪv/ ▷ *verb* (***deprived, depriving***) (*usually* **deprive someone of something**) to take or keep it from them; to prevent them from using or enjoying it. • **deprivation** /dɛprɪ'veɪʃən/ *noun* **1** hardship, etc, caused by being deprived of necessities, rights, etc. **2** the act of depriving or state of being deprived. ⓒ 14c: from Latin *deprivare* to degrade.

deprived ▷ *adj* **1** said of a person: suffering from hardship through lack of money, reasonable living conditions, etc. **2** said of a district, etc: lacking good housing, schools, medical facilities, etc. **3** (**deprived of something**) having had it kept or taken away.

dept ▷ *abbreviation* department.

depth ▷ *noun* **1** deepness; the distance from the top downwards, from the front to the back or from the surface inwards. **2** said of feelings or colours: intensity or strength. **3** extensiveness □ *the depth of one's knowledge.* **4** (*usually* **the depths**) somewhere far from the surface or edge of somewhere □ *the depths of the ocean* □ *the depths of the country.* **5** (*usually* **the depths**) an extreme feeling (of despair, sadness, etc) or great degree (of deprivation, etc). **6** (*often* **the depths**) the middle and severest or most intense part (of winter, etc). **7** (**depths**) serious aspects of a person's character that are not immediately obvious. **8** said of sound: lowness of pitch. • **in depth** deeply and thoroughly. • **out of one's depth 1** in water so deep that one would be below the surface even when standing up. **2** not able to understand information or an explanation, or in a situation which is too difficult for one to deal with. ⓒ 14c: from Anglo-Saxon *deop* DEEP.

depth charge and **depth bomb** ▷ *noun* a type of bomb, usually dropped from a ship, which explodes underwater and is used to attack submarines. ⓒ Early 20c.

depth of field ▷ *noun* the distance between the nearer and further planes in an area photographed, seen through a microscope, etc, over which the image is in reasonably sharp focus.

depth of focus ▷ *noun, photog* the distance between a camera lens and the film at which the image will be clear.

depth psychology ▷ *noun, psychol* the psychology of the unconscious mind.

deputation /dɛpjʊ'teɪʃən/ ▷ *noun* a group of people appointed to represent and speak on behalf of others. ⓒ 16c in this sense; 14c, meaning 'appointment': from Latin *deputare, deputatum* to select.

depute ▷ *verb* /dɪ'pjuːt/ (***deputed, deputing***) *formal* **1** to formally appoint someone to do something. **2** (*usually* **depute something to someone**) to give (one's work, etc, or part of it) to someone else to do. ▷ *adj* /'dɛpjuːt/ in Scotland: *often following its noun* appointed deputy □ *depute headteacher* □ *sheriff-depute.* ▷ *noun* /'dɛpjuːt/ in Scotland: a deputy. ⓒ 15c: from French *deputer*, from Latin *deputare* to select.

deputize or **deputise** /'dɛpjʊtaɪz/ ▷ *verb* (***deputized, deputizing***) **1** *intr* (*often* **deputize for someone**) to act as their deputy. **2** to appoint someone as a deputy. ⓒ 18c.

deputy /'dɛpjʊtɪ/ ▷ *noun* (***deputies***) **1** a person appointed to act on behalf of, or as an assistant to, someone else. **2** in certain countries: a person elected to the lower house of parliament. ▷ *adj* in some organizations: next in rank to the head and having the authority to act on their behalf. ⓒ 16c: from French *deputer* to appoint, from Latin *deputare* to select.

der. ▷ *abbreviation* **1** derivation. **2** derivative. **3** derived.

deracialize or **deracialise** /diː'reɪʃəlaɪz/ ▷ *verb* (***deracialized, deracializing***) to remove racist characteristics from something. ⓒ 19c.

deracinate /diː'rasɪneɪt/ ▷ *verb* (***deracinated, deracinating***) *formal* to root up something; to eradicate it. • **deracination** *noun*. ⓒ 16c: from French *déraciner*, from Latin *radix* root.

derail /diː'reɪl/ ▷ *verb, tr & intr* to leave or make (a train, etc) leave the rails. • **derailment** *noun*. ⓒ 19c: from French *dérailler*.

derange /dɪ'reɪndʒ/ ▷ *verb* (***deranged, deranging***) **1** to make someone insane. **2** to disrupt or throw into disorder or confusion. • **deranged** *adj*. • **derangement** *noun*. ⓒ 18c: from French *déranger* to disturb.

derby[1] /'dɑːbɪ/ ▷ *noun* (***derbies***) **1** (**the Derby**) a horse race held annually at Epsom Downs, England. See also THE CLASSICS. **2** a race or a sports event or contest, especially a contest between teams from the same area. Also called **local derby**. ⓒ 19c: sense 1 named after the Earl of Derby, one of the founders of the race in 1780.

derby[2] /'dɜːbɪ/ ▷ *noun* (***derbies***) *N Amer* a bowler hat. ⓒ 19c: from DERBY[1].

Derby. ▷ *abbreviation* Derbyshire.

derecognize or **derecognise** ▷ *verb* to withdraw official recognition from (especially a country or trade union). • **derecognition** *noun*. ⓒ 1950s, first as the noun.

deregister ▷ *verb* to remove (a name, etc) from a register. • **deregistration** *noun*. ⓒ 1920s.

deregulate ▷ *verb* to remove controls and regulations from (a business or business activity). • **deregulation** *noun*.

derelict /'dɛrəlɪkt/ ▷ *adj* **1** abandoned. **2** said of a building: falling in ruins. ▷ *noun* **1** a tramp; someone with no home or money. **2** anything, especially a ship, forsaken or abandoned. ⓒ 18c as *noun* 1; 17c as *adj* and *noun* 2: from Latin *derelinquere, derelictum* to abandon.

dereliction /dɛrə'lɪkʃən/ ▷ *noun* **1** (*usually* **dereliction of duty**) neglect or failure. **2** the state of being abandoned.

derestrict ▷ *verb* to remove a restriction from something, especially a speed limit from (a road). • **derestriction** *noun*. ⓒ 20c.

deride /dɪ'raɪd/ ▷ *verb* (***derided, deriding***) to laugh at or make fun of someone. • **derider** *noun*. See also DERISION. ⓒ 16c: from Latin *deridere*.

de rigueur /də rɪ'gɜː(r)/ ▷ *adj* required by fashion, custom or the rules of politeness. ⓒ 19c: French, meaning 'of strictness'.

derision /dɪ'rɪʒən/ ▷ *noun* the act of deriding; scornful laughter. ⓒ 15c: from Latin *derisio*.

derisive /dɪ'raɪsɪv, -'raɪzɪv/ ▷ *adj* scornful; mocking. • **derisively** *adverb*. • **derisiveness** *noun*. ⓒ 17c: from DERISION.

derisive, derisory

• **Derisive** means 'showing derision', **derisory** means 'deserving derision' □ *A derisive note was back in Luke's voice* □ *This show in fact attracted a derisory 9000 or so paying visitors.*

derisory /dɪ'raɪsərɪ/ ▷ *adj* ridiculous and insulting, especially ridiculously small. ⓒ 20c in this sense; 17c, meaning 'scornful' or 'mocking': from Latin *derisorius* DERISIVE.

deriv. ▷ *abbreviation* **1** derivation. **2** derivative. **3** derived.

derivation /dɛrɪˈveɪʃən/ ▻ *noun* **1** the act of deriving or the state or process of being derived. **2** the source or origin (especially of a word). **3** *grammar* **a** the process of forming a word by adding one or more AFFIXes to another word; **b** a word formed in this way. • **derivational** *adj.*

derivative /dɪˈrɪvətɪv/ ▻ *adj* not original; derived from or copying something else (especially someone else's work). ▻ *noun* **1** something which is derived from something else. **2** *grammar* a word formed by adding one or more AFFIXes to another word, such as *happily* from *happy*, *decarbonize* from *carbon*. Compare COMPOUND¹ (*noun* 3). **3** *chem* a compound, usually organic, that is made from another compound. **4** *math* the result of differentiation in order to calculate the changes in one variable produced by changes in another variable. **5** *stock exchange* (**derivatives**) futures (see FUTURE *noun* 5) and options (see OPTION *noun* 4). • **derivatively** *adverb.*

derive /dɪˈraɪv/ ▻ *verb* (***derived***, ***deriving***) now only in phrases below. • **derivable** *adj.* ⓒ 14c: from French *dériver*, from Latin *derivare* to lead or draw off water.

▪ **derive from something 1** to come or arise from it; to have it as a source. **2** to trace something back to (a source or origin).

▪ **derive something from something else** to obtain or produce one thing from another.

-derm /dɜːm/ ▻ *combining form* belonging to, concerning or affecting the skin ▫ *ectoderm*. ⓒ from Greek *derma* skin.

dermal /ˈdɜːməl/ and **dermic** /dɜːmɪk/ ▻ *adj* **1** belonging or relating to skin, especially the DERMIS. **2** consisting of skin. ⓒ 19c: from Greek *derma* skin.

dermatitis /dɜːməˈtaɪtɪs/ ▻ *noun, medicine* inflammation of the skin in the absence of infection, including allergy, eczema and psoriasis, but not acne. ⓒ 19c.

dermato- /dɜːmətoʊ, dɜːməˈtɒ/ or (before a vowel) **dermat-** *combining form, denoting* the skin ▫ *dermatitis*. ⓒ From Greek *derma* skin.

dermatology ▻ *noun* the branch of medical science concerned with the study of the skin and treatment of its diseases. • **dermatological** *adj.* • **dermatologist** *noun.* ⓒ 19c.

dermis /ˈdɜːmɪs/ ▻ *noun, anatomy* the thick lower layer of the skin that lies beneath the EPIDERMIS, containing blood capillaries, nerve endings, hair follicles, sweat glands, lymph vessels and some muscle fibres. Also called **corium**. ⓒ 19c: from Greek *derma* skin.

derogate /ˈdɛrəgeɪt/ ▻ *verb* (*intr* ***derogated***, ***derogating***) now only in phrase below. • **derogation** /dɛrəˈgeɪʃən/ *noun* **1** reduction in power or authority. **2** deterioration. ⓒ 15c: from Latin *derogare*, *derogatum* to detract from.

▪ **derogate from something** *formal* to make it appear inferior; to show one's low opinion of it.

derogative /dɪˈrɒgətɪv/ ▻ *adj* derogatory. • **derogatively** *adverb.* ⓒ 15c.

derogatory /dɪˈrɒgətərɪ/ ▻ *adj* showing, or intended to show, disapproval, dislike, scorn or lack of respect. • **derogatorily** *adverb.* • **derogatoriness** *noun.* ⓒ 16c: from Latin *derogatorius*.

derrick /ˈdɛrɪk/ ▻ *noun* **1** a type of crane with a movable arm. **2** a framework built over an oil-well, used for raising and lowering the drill. ⓒ 18c, originally meaning 'a gallows': named after Derrick, a 17c hangman.

derrière /dɛrɪˈɛə(r)/ ▻ *noun* the behind; the buttocks. ⓒ 18c: French.

derring-do /dɛrɪŋˈduː/ ▻ *noun, old use, literary* daring deeds. ⓒ 16c: from a wrong understanding by Spenser, the 16c poet, of the phrase *derrynge do*, meaning 'daring to do', in the work of an earlier poet.

derringer /ˈdɛrɪndʒə(r)/ ▻ *noun* a short American pistol. ⓒ 19c: named after its inventor, Henry Deringer (1786–1868), gunsmith.

derris /ˈdɛrɪs/ ▻ *noun* **1** a tropical climbing plant related to peas and beans. **2** an insecticide made from the roots of this plant. ⓒ 19c: from Greek *derris* leather jacket, referring to the pods of the plant.

derv /dɜːv/ ▻ *noun, Brit* diesel oil used as a fuel for road vehicles. ⓒ 1940s: from *d*iesel-*e*ngine *r*oad *v*ehicle.

dervish /ˈdɜːvɪʃ/ ▻ *noun* (***dervishes***) a member of any of various Muslim religious groups who have taken vows of poverty, some of whom perform spinning dances as part of their religious ritual. ⓒ 16c: from Turkish *derviş*, from Persian *darvish* poor man or dervish.

DES ▻ *abbreviation* Department of Education and Science, replaced in 1992 by DFE.

desalinate /diːˈsalɪneɪt/ ▻ *verb, technical* to remove salt from (especially seawater). ⓒ 1940s.

desalination and **desalinization** or **desalinisation** ▻ *noun* the removal, by distillation or reverse osmosis, of salts, mainly sodium chloride, from seawater in order to produce fresh water for drinking, irrigation, etc.

descale /diːˈskeɪl/ ▻ *verb* **1** to remove scales from (especially fish). **2** to remove encrusted deposits from (a pipe, kettle, etc). ⓒ 1950s.

descant /ˈdɛskant/ *music* ▻ *noun* a melody played or harmony sung above the main tune. ▻ *adj* said of a musical instrument: having a higher pitch and register than others of the same type ▫ *descant recorder*. ⓒ 14c: French, from Latin *dis-* apart + *cantus* song.

descend /dɪˈsɛnd/ ▻ *verb* (***descended***, ***descending***) **1** *tr & intr* to go or move down from a higher to a lower place or position. **2** *intr* to lead or slope downwards. **3** *intr* (*often* **descend on** or **upon someone** or **something**) to invade or attack them or it. **4** *intr* said of titles, property, etc: to pass by inheritance from one generation to another. • **be descended from someone** to have them as an ancestor. • **would not descend to something** or **to doing something** would not demean oneself by resorting to (unworthy or immoral behaviour). ⓒ 13c: from French *descendre*.

descendant /dɪˈsɛndənt/ ▻ *adj* (*also* **descendent**) descending. ▻ *noun* a person or animal, etc that is the child, grandchild, great-grandchild, etc of another; offspring.

descender ▻ *noun* **1** someone or something that descends. **2** *printing, etc* the part of a letter such as *j* or *p* that comes below the line on which eg *x* sits.

descending ▻ *adj* **1** moving or coming down or downwards. **2** from the highest to the lowest, the greatest to the least, or the best to the worst ▫ *in descending order*.

descent /dɪˈsɛnt/ ▻ *noun* **1** the act or process of coming or going down. **2** a slope downwards. **3** family origins or ancestry; the fact of being descended from someone. **4** a sudden invasion or attack. ⓒ 14c: from French *descente*.

deschool ▻ *verb, tr & intr* to free (children) from the restrictions of traditional classroom learning and a set curriculum, and educate them in a less formal way, especially at home. • **deschooler** *noun.* • **deschooling** *noun.* ⓒ 1970s: originally as *deschooling*.

descramble ▻ *verb* **1** to convert or restore (a signal) to an understandable form. **2** to counteract the effects of, or recover, a signal deliberately transmitted in an unintelligible form.

describe /dɪˈskraɪb/ ▻ *verb* (***described***, ***describing***) **1** to say what someone or something is like. **2** *technical, geom* to draw or form something. **3** *formal* to move in the shape or pattern of something ▫ *skaters describing circles on the ice*. • **describable** *adj.* • **describer** *noun.* • **describe**

oneself as something to call oneself, or claim to be, it. ⓒ 16c: from Latin *describere*.

descried, descries see under DESCRY

description /dɪ'skrɪpʃən/ ▷ *noun* **1** the act of describing. **2** a statement of what someone or something is like. **3** *colloq* a sort, type or kind ▫ *toys of every description*. ⓒ 15c: from Latin *descriptio*.

descriptive /dɪ'skrɪptɪv/ ▷ *adj* describing, especially describing well or vividly. • **descriptively** *adverb*. • **descriptiveness** *noun*. ⓒ 18c: from Latin *descriptivus*.

descriptive geometry ▷ *noun* the study of three-dimensional figures when projected onto a two-dimensional surface.

descriptive linguistics ▷ *noun* the branch of linguistics that deals with the description of the structure of a language at any particular time, ie with no reference to its history, other languages, etc.

descriptivism ▷ *noun* **1** *grammar* on approach to language which aims to describe it in terms of the way it is actually used, without any judgements on whether or not it is correct. **2** *philos* the theory that moral statements are determined by their truth value. Compare PRESCRIPTIVISM.

descriptor /dɪ'skrɪptə(r)/ ▷ *noun, computing* **1** a symbol or form of words that identifies a particular subject in a storage system, or gives information on how particular material is stored. **2** a keyword or a heading.

descry /dɪ'skraɪ/ ▷ *verb* (*descries, descried, descrying*) *formal* **1** to see or catch sight of something. **2** to see or discover by looking carefully. ⓒ 14c: from French *descrier* to announce and *descrire* to describe.

desecrate /'dɛsəkreɪt/ ▷ *verb* (*desecrated, desecrating*) to treat or use (a sacred object) or behave in (a holy place) in a way that shows a lack of respect or causes damage. • **desecrater** or **desecrator** *noun*. • **desecration** *noun*. ⓒ 17c: from DE- 2 + CONSECRATE.

desegregate /diː'sɛgrəgeɪt/ ▷ *verb* to end segregation, especially racial segregation in (public places, schools, transport systems, etc). • **desegregation** *noun*. • **desegregationist** *noun, adj*. ⓒ 1950s.

deselect /diːsə'lɛkt/ ▷ *verb* **1** said of a branch of a political party: to reject (the existing Member of Parliament or local councillor) as a candidate for the next election. **2** said of a selection committee, etc: not to reselect (eg an athlete) for a place on a team, etc. • **deselection** *noun*.

desensitize or **desensitise** ▷ *verb* to make someone or something less sensitive to light, pain, suffering, etc. • **desensitization** *noun*. • **desensitizer** *noun*. ⓒ Early 20c.

desert[1] /dɪ'zɜːt/ ▷ *verb* (*deserted, deserting*) **1** to leave or abandon (a place or person), intending not to return. **2** *intr* to leave (especially a branch of the armed forces) without permission. **3** to take away support from (a person, cause, etc). • **deserted** *adj* said of a building, etc: empty or abandoned. • **deserter** *noun* someone who deserts from military service. • **desertion** *noun*. ⓒ 15c: from French *déserter*.

desert

There is often a spelling confusion between **desert** and **dessert**.

desert[2] /'dɛzət/ ▷ *noun* an arid area of land where rainfall is less than potential evaporation, vegetation is scarce or non-existent, and which is characterized by extremely high or low temperatures. Also *as adj*. ⓒ 13c: French, from Latin *deserere* to abandon.

desert boot ▷ *noun* a lacing suede ankle boot with a rubber sole.

desertification /dɛzɜːtɪfɪ'keɪʃən/ ▷ *noun* the process by which a new desert is formed, or an existing desert spreads across an area that was formerly moist and fertile, due to climatic changes, poor farming practices, etc. ⓒ 1970s.

desert rat ▷ *noun* **1** a JERBOA. **2** a soldier of the British 7th Armoured Division who served in N Africa during 1941–42, the divisional sign being a jerboa.

deserts /dɪ'zɜːts/ ▷ *plural noun* (*usually* **just deserts**) what one deserves, usually something unfavourable ▫ *He'll get his just deserts*. ⓒ 13c: from French *deservir* to deserve.

deserve /dɪ'zɜːv/ ▷ *verb* (*deserved, deserving*) to have earned, be entitled to or be worthy of (a reward or punishment, etc). ▷ **deservedly** /-vɪdlɪ/ *adverb*. ⓒ 13c: from French *deservir*.

deserving ▷ *adj* **1** worthy of being given support, a reward, etc. **2** *formal* (*usually* **deserving of something**) worthy of it. • **deservingly** *adverb*.

desex /diː'sɛks/ ▷ *verb* to deprive someone or something of sexual character or quality. ⓒ Early 20c.

déshabille /deɪzə'biːl/ or **dishabille** /dɪsə'biːl/ ▷ *noun* the state of being only partly dressed. ⓒ 17c: French, meaning 'undress'.

desiccant /'dɛsɪkənt/ ▷ *noun, chem* a substance that absorbs water and so can be used as a drying agent to remove water from, or prevent absorption of water by, other substances. ▷ *adj* drying; having the power of drying. ⓒ 17c.

desiccate /'dɛsɪkeɪt/ ▷ *verb* (*desiccated, desiccating*) **1** to dry or remove the moisture from something, especially from food in order to preserve it. **2** *intr* to dry up. • **desiccated** *adj*. • **desiccation** *noun*. ⓒ 16c: from Latin *desiccare, desiccatum* to dry up.

desiccator ▷ *noun, chem* a device, usually a closed glass vessel containing a DESICCANT, that is used to remove water from, or prevent the absorption of water by, other substances.

desideratum /dɪzɪdə'rɑːtəm/ ▷ *noun* (*desiderata* /-tə/) *formal* something much wanted or required. ⓒ 17c: from Latin *desiderare, desideratum* to long for.

design /dɪ'zaɪn/ ▷ *verb* (*designed, designing*) **1** to develop or prepare a plan, drawing or model of something before it is built or made. **2** *formal* to plan, intend or develop something for a particular purpose. ▷ *noun* **1** a plan, drawing or model showing how something is to be made. **2** the art or job of making such drawings, plans, etc. **3** the way in which something has been made. **4** a picture, pattern, arrangement of shapes, etc used eg as decoration. **5** a plan, purpose or intention. • **designable** *adj*. • **designedly** /-nɪdlɪ/ *adverb* intentionally; on purpose. • **designing** *adj, derog* using cunning and deceit to achieve a purpose. • **designingly** *adverb*. • **by design** intentionally. • **have designs on someone** or **something** to have plans to appropriate them or it. ⓒ 16c: from French *désigner*.

designate ▷ *verb* /'dɛzɪgneɪt/ (*designated, designating*) **1** to name, choose or specify someone or something for a particular purpose or duty. **2** to mark or indicate something. **3** to be a name or label for someone or something. ▷ *adj* /-nət/ having been appointed to some official position but not yet holding it ▫ *editor designate*. ▷ **designation** *noun*. ⓒ 18c: from Latin *designare, designatum* to plan or mark out.

design engineer ▷ *noun* a designer in engineering.

designer ▷ *noun* someone who makes designs, plans, patterns, drawings, etc, especially as a profession. ▷ *adj* **1** designed by and bearing the name of a famous fashion designer ▫ *designer dresses*. **2** especially made for a particular purpose or effect ▫ *designer drugs*. **3** *colloq, sometimes derog* following current fashion.

designer drug ▷ *noun, medicine* **1** a drug created to destroy a particular bacterium, etc. **2** any of various synthetic drugs, often narcotics, which are not controlled by law in the USA, so called because they are specifically designed by chemists to be slightly different structurally from drugs that are controlled by law (ie illegal drugs), yet chemically so similar to them that they have similar biological effects and so can be sold on the streets to drug users.

desirable ▻ *adj* **1** pleasing; worth having. **2** sexually attractive. • **desirability** *noun*. • **desirably** *adverb*.

desire /dɪ'zaɪə(r)/ ▻ *noun* **1** a longing or wish. **2** strong sexual interest and attraction. ▻ *verb* (***desired, desiring***) **1** *formal* to want. **2** to long for or feel sexual desire for someone. **3** *old use, formal* to ask or command. ⓒ 13c: from French *desirer*.

desirous /dɪ'zaɪərəs/ ▻ *adj, formal* (*usually* **desirous of something**) wanting it keenly.

> ***desirous of***
>
> ☆PLAIN ENGLISH alternatives are **wanting, wishing for, longing for**.

desist /dɪ'zɪst, -'sɪst/ ▻ *verb* (***desisted, desisting***) *intr, formal* (*often* **desist from something**) to stop. ⓒ 15c: from French *desister*.

desk ▻ *noun* **1** a sloping or flat table, often with drawers, for sitting at while writing, reading, etc. **2** a place or counter in a public building where a service is provided. **3** a section of a newspaper, etc office with responsibility for a particular subject ▫ *news desk*. **4** *music* **a** a music stand; **b** in an orchestra, especially in the string section: a seating position determined by rank. ⓒ 14c: from Latin *discus* disc or table.

desk-bound ▻ *adj* confined to a desk, doing paperwork and administration rather than active or practical work.

deskilling /diː'skɪlɪŋ/ ▻ *noun* the process of removing the element of human skill from a job, operation, process, etc, through automation, computerization, etc.

desktop ▻ *adj* small enough to fit on the top of a desk. ▻ *noun* a computer small enough to use at a desk.

desktop publishing ▻ *noun* (abbreviation **DTP**) the process of preparing and producing typeset output as a basis for published text, using a microcomputer with specialist software and high-resolution printers.

desolate ▻ *adj* /'dɛsələt/ **1** said of a place: deserted, barren and lonely. **2** said of a person: very sad; in despair. **3** lacking pleasure or comfort ▫ *a desolate life*. **4** lonely; alone. ▻ *verb* /-leɪt/ (***desolated, desolating***) **1** to overwhelm someone with sadness or grief. **2** to make somewhere deserted or barren; to lay waste (an area). • **desolated** *adj*. • **desolately** *adverb*. • **desolation** *noun*. • **desolateness** *noun*. ⓒ 14c: from Latin *desolare*, *desolatum* to forsake.

desorption /dɪ'sɔːpʃən, dɪ'zɔːp-/ ▻ *noun, chem* release from an adsorbed (see ADSORB) state. ⓒ Early 20c.

despair /dɪ'spɛə(r)/ ▻ *verb* (***despaired, despairing***) *intr* (*often* **despair of something** or **despair of doing something**) to lose or lack hope. ▻ *noun* **1** the state of having lost hope. **2** (**the despair**) someone or something that causes worry and despair ▫ *He's the despair of his parents*. • **despairing** *adj* giving up hope; involving or indicating a loss of hope ▫ *a despairing glance*. • **despairingly** *adverb*. ⓒ 14c: from French *desperer*.

despatch see DISPATCH

desperado /dɛspə'rɑːdoʊ/ ▻ *noun* (***desperados*** or ***desperadoes***) especially in 19c western USA: a bandit or outlaw. ⓒ 17c: probably a mock-Spanish word formed from DESPERATE.

desperate /'dɛspərət/ ▻ *adj* **1** extremely anxious, fearful or despairing. **2** willing to take risks fearlessly because of hopelessness and despair. **3** very serious, difficult, dangerous and almost hopeless ▫ *a desperate situation*. **4** dangerous and likely to be violent ▫ *a desperate criminal*. **5** extreme and carried out as a last resort because of the seriousness or hopelessness of the situation ▫ *desperate measures*. **6** very great ▫ *desperate need*. **7** extremely anxious or eager ▫ *desperate to go to the concert*. • **desperately** *adverb*. • **desperateness** *noun*. • **desperation** *noun*. • **desperate for something** in great or urgent need of it ▫ *desperate for supplies*. ⓒ 15c: from Latin *desperare*, *desperatum* to despair.

despicable /dɪ'spɪkəbəl/ ▻ *adj* deserving contempt; mean. • **despicably** *adverb*. ⓒ 16c: from Latin *despicabilis*.

despise /dɪ'spaɪz/ ▻ *verb* (***despised, despising***) to look down on someone or something with scorn and contempt. ⓒ 13c: from Latin *despicere*.

despite /dɪ'spaɪt/ ▻ *prep* in spite of. ⓒ 13c: French, from Latin *despicere* to despise.

despoil ▻ *verb* (***despoiled, despoiling***) *formal, literary* to rob or steal everything valuable from (a place). • **despoiler** *noun*. ⓒ 13c: from French *despoiller*, from Latin *spolium* plunder.

despoliation /dɪspoʊlɪ'eɪʃən/ ▻ *noun* plundering; robbing. ⓒ 16c.

despondency /dɪ'spɒndənsɪ/ ▻ *noun* low spirits; dejection.

despondent /dɪ'spɒndənt/ ▻ *adj* sad; dejected; in low spirits. • **despondently** *adverb*. ⓒ 17c: from Latin *despondere* to lose heart.

despot /'dɛspɒt/ ▻ *noun* someone who has very great or total power, especially if they use such power in a cruel or oppressive way. • **despotic** *adj*. • **despotically** *adverb*. ⓒ 18c; 16c, meaning 'a ruler dependent on the Turks': from Greek *despotes* master.

despotism ▻ *noun* **1** complete or absolute power. **2** a state governed by a despot. See also ABSOLUTISM, AUTOCRACY.

des res /dɛz rɛz/ ▻ *noun, colloq, facetious or property market jargon* a desirable residence. ⓒ 1980s: from *desirable residence*, originally the abbreviation used in advertisements.

dessert /dɪ'zɜːt/ ▻ *noun* **1** a sweet food served after the main course of a meal. **2** the course at or near the end of a meal, when such food is served. ⓒ 16c: French, from *desservir* to clear the table.

> ***dessert***
>
> There is often a spelling confusion between **dessert** and **desert**.

dessertspoon ▻ *noun* (abbreviation **dsp**) **1** a medium-sized spoon, about half the size of a TABLESPOON and twice the size of a TEASPOON. **2** the amount a dessertspoon will hold. Also called **dessertspoonful**.

destabilize or **destabilise** ▻ *verb* to make (a country, an economy, etc) less stable. • **destabilization** *noun*. ⓒ 1920s.

destination /dɛstɪ'neɪʃən/ ▻ *noun* the place to which someone or something is going or being sent. ⓒ 16c, originally meaning 'appointing or intending someone or something for a particular role or purpose': from Latin *destinatio* purpose.

destine /'dɛstɪn/ ▻ *verb* (***destined, destining***) *formal* (*usually* **be destined for something** or **to do something**) to have it as one's fate. ⓒ 14c: from French *destiner*.

destiny /'dɛstɪnɪ/ ▻ *noun* (***destinies***) **1** the purpose or future as arranged by fate or God. **2** (*also* **Destiny**) fate; the power which appears, or is believed, to control events. ⓒ 14c: from French *destinee*, from Latin *destinare* to appoint.

destitute /ˈdɛstɪtjuːt/ ▻ *adj* **1** lacking money, food, shelter, etc; extremely poor. **2** *formal* (**destitute of something**) completely lacking in something necessary or desirable. • **destitution** *noun* **1** poverty. **2** lack of money and food. ◷ 16c in sense 1; 15c in sense 2; 14c, meaning 'deserted': from Latin *destitutus.*

destroy /dɪˈstrɔɪ/ ▻ *verb* (***destroyed, destroying***) **1** to knock down, break into pieces, completely ruin, etc. **2** to put an end to something. **3** to defeat someone totally. **4** to ruin or seriously damage the reputation, health, financial position, etc of someone. **5** to kill (a dangerous, injured or unwanted animal). ◷ 13c: from French *destruire*, from Latin *de* down + *struere* to build.

destroyer ▻ *noun* **1** someone or something that destroys or causes destruction. **2** a type of small fast warship.

destruct /dɪˈstrʌkt/ ▻ *verb* (***destructed, destructing***) *tr & intr, chiefly N Amer* said of equipment, especially a missile in flight: to destroy or be destroyed, especially for safety reasons. ◷ 1940s in this sense; originally 17c meaning 'to destroy': from Latin *destruere, destructum.*

destructible ▻ *adj* able to be destroyed. • **destructibility** *noun.* ◷ 18c.

destruction ▻ *noun* **1** the act or process of destroying or being destroyed. **2** something that destroys. ◷ 14c: from Latin *destruere, destructum* to destroy, from *de* down + *struere* to build.

destructive ▻ *adj* **1** causing destruction or serious damage. **2** said of criticism, etc: pointing out faults, etc without suggesting improvements. • **destructively** *adverb.* • **destructiveness** *noun.* ◷ 15c.

destructive distillation ▻ *noun* the decomposition of solid substances by heating, and the subsequent collection of the volatile substances produced.

desuetude /dɪˈsjuːɪtʃuːd, ˈdɛswɪtʃuːd/ ▻ *noun* disuse; discontinuance. ◷ 17c: from Latin *desuescere, desuetum* to become unaccustomed.

desultory /ˈdɛsəltərɪ, ˈdɛzəltərɪ/ ▻ *adj* jumping from one thing to another with no plan, purpose or logical connection. • **desultorily** *adverb.* • **desultoriness** *noun.* ◷ 16c: from Latin *desultorius*, from *desultor* a circus performer who jumps from horse to horse.

Det. ▻ *abbreviation* Detective.

detach /dɪˈtatʃ/ ▻ *verb* (***detaches, detached, detaching***) **1** *tr & intr* to unfasten or separate. **2** *military* to select and separate (a group of soldiers, etc) from a larger group, especially to carry out a special task. • **detachable** *adj.* ◷ 17c in these senses; 16c, meaning 'to discharge (a weapon)': from French *destachier*, from *des-* DIS- + *atachier* to attach.

detached ▻ *adj* **1** said of a building: not joined to another on either side. Compare SEMI-DETACHED. **2** said of a person: feeling no personal or emotional involvement; showing no prejudice or bias. • **detachedly** *adverb.*

detachment ▻ *noun* **1** the state of being emotionally detached or free from prejudice. **2** a group (eg of soldiers) detached from a larger group for a special purpose. **3** the act of detaching or the state or process of being detached. ◷ 17c.

detail /ˈdiːteɪl/ ▻ *noun* **1** a small feature, fact or item. **2** something considered unimportant. **3** all the small features and parts of something considered as a whole □ ***an artist's eye for detail.*** **4** a part of a painting, map, photograph, etc considered separately, often enlarged to show small features. **5** *military* a group of eg soldiers given a special task or duty. ▻ *verb* (***detailed, detailing***) **1** to describe or list fully. **2** to appoint someone to do a particular task. • **detailed** *adj* **1** said of a list, etc: itemized. **2** said of a story, picture, etc: intricate. • **in detail** giving or looking at all the details. • **go into detail** to study, discuss, etc, a matter deeply, considering the particulars. ◷ 17c: from French *detailler* to cut up.

detain /dɪˈteɪn/ ▻ *verb* (***detained, detaining***) **1** to stop, hold back, keep waiting or delay someone or something. **2** said of the police, etc: to keep someone in a cell, prison or elsewhere, especially before trial. See also DETENTION. • **detainable** *adj.* • **detainment** *noun.* ◷ 15c in sense 2; 16c in sense 1; from French *detenir* to hold.

detainee /diːteɪˈniː/ ▻ *noun* (***detainees***) a person held under guard eg by the police, especially for political reasons. ◷ 1920s.

detect /dɪˈtɛkt/ ▻ *verb* (***detected, detecting***) **1** to see or notice. **2** to discover, and usually indicate, the presence or existence of (something which should not be there or whose presence is not obvious). • **detectable** or **detectible** *adj.* ◷ 16c; 15c, meaning 'to expose or uncover': from Latin *detegere, detectum* to uncover.

detection /dɪˈtɛkʃən/ ▻ *noun* **1** the act or process of detecting or state of being detected. **2** the work of a detective, investigating and solving crime.

detective ▻ *noun* a police officer whose job is to solve crime by observation and gathering evidence. See also PRIVATE DETECTIVE.

detective story ▻ *noun* a story whose main theme is the solving of a crime.

detector /dɪˈtɛktə(r)/ ▻ *noun* an instrument or device used for detecting the presence of something.

détente /deɪˈtɑ̃t/ ▻ *noun* (***detentes***) a lessening of tension, especially in the relationships between countries. ◷ Early 20c: French.

detention /dɪˈtɛnʃən/ ▻ *noun* **1** the act of detaining or the state of being detained, especially in prison or police custody. **2** a punishment in which a pupil is kept in school to work after the other pupils have gone home. ◷ 15c in sense 1; 19c in sense 2; from Latin *detinere, detentum* to detain.

detention centre ▻ *noun* a place where young criminals are kept for a short time by order of a court.

deter /dɪˈtɜː(r)/ ▻ *verb* (***deterred, deterring***) to discourage or prevent someone or something from doing something because of fear of unpleasant consequences. • **determent** *noun.* See also DETERRENT. ◷ 16c: from Latin *deterrere* to frighten off.

deterge /dɪˈtɜːdʒ/ ▻ *verb* (***deterged, deterging***) to cleanse (a wound, etc). ◷ 17c: from Latin *detergere*, from *de* off + *tergere* to wipe.

detergent /dɪˈtɜːdʒənt/ ▻ *noun* a SURFACE-ACTIVE cleansing agent which, unlike soaps, does not produce a scum in hard water. ▻ *adj* having the power to clean.

deteriorate /dɪˈtɪərɪəreɪt/ ▻ *verb* (***deteriorated, deteriorating***) *intr* to grow worse. • **deterioration** *noun.* ◷ 17c; 16c, meaning 'to make worse': from Latin *deterior* worse.

determinable /dɪˈtɜːmɪnəbəl/ ▻ *adj* able to be determined. • **determinably** *adverb.*

determinant /dɪˈtɜːmɪnənt/ ▻ *noun* **1** a determining factor or circumstance. **2** *math* an arrangement of elements presented as a square matrix, the determinant being the difference between the multiplied diagonal terms. **3** *biol* in an antigen molecule: a region or regions that enable it to be recognized and bound by an antibody. ▻ *adj* determining.

determinate /dɪˈtɜːmɪnət/ ▻ *adj* **1** having definite fixed limits, etc. **2** *bot* said of a plant: having the main stem and branches ending in flowers.

determination ▻ *noun* **1** firmness or strength of will, purpose or character. **2** the act of determining or process of being determined.

determinative /dɪˈtɜːmɪnətɪv/ ▻ *adj* having the power to limit or determine.

determine /dɪˈtɜːmɪn/ ▻ *verb* (***determined, determining***) **1** to fix or settle the exact limits or nature of something. **2** to find out or reach a conclusion about something by gathering facts, making measurements, etc. **3** *tr & intr* to decide or make someone decide. **4** to be the main influence on someone or something; to control someone or something. ◷ 14c: from French *determiner*, from Latin *determinare* to fix the limits of.

determined ▷ *adj* **1** (*always* **determined to do something**) firmly intending to do it. **2** having or showing a strong will. • **determinedly** /-mɪndlɪ/ *adverb*.

determiner ▷ *noun, grammar* a word that comes before a noun or before any adjectives preceding a noun, and limits the meaning of the noun in some way, eg A[1], THE, THIS, EVERY, SOME.

determinism ▷ *noun, philos* the theory that every event has a cause, and that whatever happens has to happen and could not be otherwise. • **determinist** *noun*. • **deterministic** *adj*.

deterred *past tense, past participle of* DETER

deterrent /dɪ'tɛrənt/ ▷ *noun* something which deters, especially a weapon intended to deter attack. ▷ *adj* capable of deterring. • **deterrence** *noun*. ◷ 19c.

deterring *present participle of* DETER

detest /dɪ'tɛst/ ▷ *verb* (***detested***, ***detesting***) to dislike something intensely; to hate. • **detestation** /diːtɛs'teɪʃən/ *noun*. ◷ 15c: from French *detester*.

detestable /dɪ'tɛstəbəl/ ▷ *adj* hateful. • **detestability** or **detestableness** *noun*. • **detestably** *adverb*.

dethrone /diː'θroʊn, dɪ'-/ ▷ *verb* (***dethroned***, ***dethroning***) **1** to remove (a monarch) from the throne. **2** to remove someone from a position of power, influence or authority. • **dethronement** *noun*. ◷ 17c.

detonate /'dɛtəneɪt/ ▷ *verb* (***detonated***, ***detonating***) *tr & intr* to explode or make something explode. ◷ 18c: from Latin *detonare* to thunder down.

detonation ▷ *noun* **1** detonating; explosion. **2** in an internal-combustion engine: premature combustion of part of the mixture, causing a KNOCK (*noun* 5).

detonator ▷ *noun* an explosive substance or a device used to make a bomb, etc explode.

detour /'diːtʊə(r)/ ▷ *noun* a route away from and longer than a planned or more direct route. ▷ *verb* (***detoured***, ***detouring***) *intr* to make a detour. ◷ 18c: from French *détour*.

detoxification centre ▷ *noun* a centre specializing in the treatment of drug addiction and alcoholism. Often shortened to **detox**.

detoxify /diː'tɒksɪfaɪ/ ▷ *verb* (***detoxifies***, ***detoxified***, ***detoxifying***) **1** to make (a toxic substance) harmless. **2** to remove poison, drugs or harmful substances from (a person, etc); to treat (a patient) for alcoholism or drug addiction. • **detoxification** /diːtɒksɪfɪ'keɪʃən/ *noun*. Often shortened to **detox**. ◷ 1940s: from Latin *toxicum* poison.

detract /dɪ'trakt/ ▷ *verb* (***detracted***, ***detracting***) *intr* (*chiefly* **detract from something**) to take away from it or lessen it. • **detraction** *noun*. • **detractor** *noun*. ◷ 15c: from Latin *detrahere*, *detractum* to pull away.

detrain ▷ *verb, tr & intr* to set down or get down out of a railway train. • **detrainment** *noun*. ◷ 19c.

detribalize or **detribalise** /diː'traɪbəlaɪz/ ▷ *verb* (***detribalized***, ***detribalizing***) to cause (a group) to lose tribal characteristics, customs, etc, usually in favour of an urban way of life. • **detribalization** *noun*. ◷ 1920s.

detriment /'dɛtrɪmənt/ ▷ *noun* harm or loss □ *to the detriment of her health*. • **detrimental** *adj* harmful; damaging. • **detrimentally** *adverb*. ◷ 15c: from Latin *detrimentum*.

detritus /dɪ'traɪtəs/ ▷ *noun* **1** *geol* the product of **detrition** /-trɪʃən/, the natural process of rubbing or wearing down strata by wind, water or glaciers. **2** *biol* dead plants or animals, or any debris of living organisms, eg parts that have been shed. **3** bits and pieces of rubbish left over from something. • **detrital** /dɪ'traɪtəl/ *adj*. ◷ 19c in these senses; 18c, meaning 'disintegration': from Latin *deterere*, *detritum* to rub away.

de trop /də troʊ/ ▷ *adj* not wanted; in the way. ◷ 18c: French, meaning 'too much'.

detumescence /diːtjʊ'mɛsəns/ ▷ *noun* subsidence of swelling. ◷ 17c: from Latin *detumescere* to subside from swelling.

deuce[1] /dʒuːs/ ▷ *noun* **1** *tennis* a score of forty points each in a game or five games each in a match. **2** a card, dice throw, etc, of the value two. ◷ 15c in sense 2: from French *deus* two.

deuce[2] /dʒuːs/ ▷ *noun, old use* (**the deuce**) said in exclamations: the devil □ *What the deuce is he doing?* ◷ 17c: perhaps from DEUCE[1], two being an unlucky throw in dice.

deus ex machina /'diːəs ɛks mə'ʃiːnə, 'deɪʊs — 'makɪna/ ▷ *noun* **1** in classical drama: a god lowered on to the stage by a mechanical device to resolve problems which have arisen in the course of the play or to decide the final outcome. **2** in any literary genre: someone or something introduced suddenly or unexpectedly to provide a contrived solution to a difficulty. ◷ 17c: Latin, meaning 'god out of a machine'.

Deut. ▷ *abbreviation* Book of the Bible: Deuteronomy. See table at BIBLE.

deuterium /dʒuː'tɪərɪəm/ ▷ *noun, chem* (symbol **D**) one of the three isotopes of hydrogen, being almost identical to the commonest isotope in its chemical properties, but with slightly different physical properties, eg boiling point. Also called **heavy hydrogen**. See also TRITIUM. ◷ 1930s: from Greek *deuteros* second.

deuterium oxide ▷ *noun, chem* (formula $\mathbf{D_2O}$) a compound analogous to water, consisting of DEUTERIUM and oxygen, used as a moderator to slow down neutrons in nuclear reactors. Also called **heavy water**.

deutero- /dʒuːtəroʊ/, **deuto-** or (before a vowel) **deuter-** or **deut-** ▷ *combining form, signifying* **1** second or secondary. **2** *chem* that one or more hydrogens in a compound is the DEUTERIUM isotope. ◷ 17c: Greek, from *deuteros* second.

deuteron /'dʒuːtərɒn/ ▷ *noun, physics* the nucleus of an atom of DEUTERIUM, composed of a proton and a neutron.

Deutschmark /'dɔɪtʃmɑːk/ and **Deutsche Mark** /'dɔɪtʃə-/ *noun* (abbreviation **DM** or **D-mark** /'diːmɑːk, 'deɪmɑːk/) the standard unit of currency in Germany. See also PFENNIG. ◷ 1948: German, meaning 'German mark'.

deutzia /'dʒuːtsɪə, 'dɔɪtsɪə/ ▷ *noun* (***deutzias***) any of various shrubs originally introduced from China and Japan, which flower in early summer. ◷ 19c: named after Jan van der Deutz, 18c Dutch patron of botany.

devalue and **devaluate** ▷ *verb* **1** *tr & intr* to reduce the value of (a currency) in relation to the values of other currencies. **2** to make (a person, action, etc) seem less valuable or important. • **devaluation** *noun*. ◷ 20c.

devanagari or **Devanagari** /deɪvə'nɑːgərɪ/ ▷ *noun* the script in which SANSKRIT and HINDI are usually written and printed, also used for other Indian languages. See also NAGARI. ◷ 18c: Sanskrit, meaning 'town-script of the gods', from *deva* god + *nagari* an earlier name for the script.

devastate /'dɛvəsteɪt/ ▷ *verb* (***devastated***, ***devastating***) **1** to cause great destruction in or to something. **2** to overwhelm someone with grief; to shock someone greatly. • **devastator** *noun*. ◷ 17c: from Latin *devastare*, *devastatum* to lay waste.

devastated ▷ *adj* **1** said of a person: overwhelmed with shock or grief. **2** said of an area or country: extensively harmed or damaged.

devastating ▷ *adj* **1** completely destructive. **2** shocking; overwhelming. **3** *colloq* very good or impressive; extremely attractive. ● **devastatingly** *adverb*.

devastation ▷ *noun* **1** the act of devastating. **2** the state of being devastated.

develop /dɪˈvɛləp/ ▷ *verb* (***developed***, ***developing***) **1** *tr & intr* to make or become more mature, more advanced, more complete, more organized, more detailed, etc. **2** said of a living organism, organ, tissue or cell: to become transformed from a simple structure to a much more complex one, usually by passing through a number of stages. **3** to begin to have something; to have an increasing amount of it □ *develop an interest in politics*. **4** *tr & intr* to appear and grow, or to have or suffer from something which has appeared and grown □ *developing a cold*. **5** to use chemical agents to convert an invisible image on (exposed photographic film or paper) into a visible image. **6** to bring into fuller use (the natural resources, etc of a country or region). **7** to build on (land) or prepare (land) for being built on. **8** *chess* to bring (a piece) into a position useful in attack. **9** *math* to express (an expression or function) in expanded form. **10** *geom* to unroll into a plane surface. ● **developable** *adj*. ⓒ 17c; originally meaning 'to unroll or unfurl', from French *développer*.

developer ▷ *noun* **1** a chemical used to develop photographic film. **2** someone who builds on land or improves and increases the value of buildings.

developing country ▷ *noun, econ* a country with a low income per capita of population, which is trying to improve its position through industrialization.

development ▷ *noun* **1** the act of developing or the process of being developed. **2** a new stage, event or situation. **3** a result or consequence. **4** land which has been or is being developed, or the buildings built or being built on it. **5** *math* the expression of a FUNCTION (*noun* 4) in the form of a series. **6** *music* elaboration of a theme, or that part of a MOVEMENT in which this occurs. ● **developmental** /-ˈmɛntəl/ *adj*. ● **developmentally** *adverb*.

development aid ▷ *noun, politics* financial and economic assistance given by rich industrial nations to developing countries.

developmental psychology ▷ *noun, psychol* the branch of psychology concerned with the scientific study of human mental development and behaviour from birth to maturity.

development area ▷ *noun, Brit* an area of high unemployment into which the government encourages businesses and industry to move eg by offering grants.

Devi /ˈdeɪviː/ ▷ *noun* in India: used, following her name, as a title for a married woman. ⓒ Sanskrit, meaning 'goddess'.

deviance /ˈdiːvɪəns/ and **deviancy** ▷ *noun* (***deviances***; ***deviancies***) departure from normal standards or methods. ⓒ 1940s.

deviant /ˈdiːvɪənt/ ▷ *adj* not following the normal patterns, accepted standards, etc. ▷ *noun* someone who does not behave in what is considered to be a normal or acceptable fashion, especially sexually. ⓒ 15c, but rare before 20c.

deviate ▷ *verb* /ˈdiːvɪeɪt/ (***deviated***, ***deviating***) *intr* to turn aside or move away from what is considered a correct or normal course, standard of behaviour, way of thinking, etc. ▷ *noun* /ˈdiːvɪət/ *psychol* a DEVIANT. ⓒ 17c: from Latin *deviare* to turn from the road, from *de* from + *via* road.

deviation /diːvɪˈeɪʃən/ ▷ *noun* **1** the act of deviating. **2** *geog* the existence of or the amount of a difference between north as shown on a compass and true north, caused by the magnetism of objects near the compass, etc.

deviationism ▷ *noun* a tendency to dissent from some aspects of a (usually political) belief or ideology. ● **deviationist** *noun*. ⓒ 20c.

device /dɪˈvaɪs/ ▷ *noun* **1** something made for a special purpose, eg a tool or instrument. **2** a plan or scheme for doing something, sometimes involving trickery or deceit. **3** *heraldry* a sign, pattern or symbol used eg on a crest or shield. ● **be left to one's own devices** to be left alone and without supervision or help. ⓒ 13c: from French *devis* and *devise*, from Latin *divisa* mark or device.

devil /ˈdɛvəl/ ▷ *noun* **1** (**the Devil**) *relig* the most powerful evil spirit; Satan. **2** any evil or wicked spirit. **3** *colloq* a mischievous or bad person. **4** *colloq* a person of a stated type □ *lucky devil*. **5** someone or something difficult to deal with. **6** someone who excels at something. **7** (**the devil**) used for emphasis in mild oaths and exclamations □ *What the devil is he doing?* **8** in various occupations and professions: an apprentice or junior employee expected to work on behalf of his superiors for little financial reward □ *printer's devil*. **9** *meteorol* a dust storm. **10** any of various machines used especially for tearing. ▷ *verb* (***devilled***, ***devilling***; *US* ***deviled***, ***deviling***) **1** to prepare or cook (meat, etc) with a spicy seasoning. **2** to do very menial work; to act as a drudge to someone. ● **Be a devil!** *colloq* said to encourage someone to do something they are hesitating to do. ● **between the devil and the deep blue sea** in a situation where the alternatives are equally undesirable. ● **devil take the hindmost** said to encourage one to take care of one's own success, safety, etc with no thought for others. ● **give the devil his due** to admit the good points of a person one dislikes. ● **go to the devil 1** to be ruined. **2** usually said as a command, in anger: go away. ● **like the devil** *colloq* very hard. ● **speak** or **talk of the devil** said on the arrival of someone one has just been talking about. ● **the devil to pay** serious trouble as a consequence of an action, etc. ⓒ 16c in this form; Anglo-Saxon *deofol*, from Greek *diabolos* slanderer.

devilfish ▷ *noun* **1** the giant ray of the US. **2** the octopus.

devilish ▷ *adj* **1** characteristic of or like a devil; as if from, produced by, etc a devil. **2** very wicked. **3** *colloq* very great or very difficult. ▷ *adverb, old use* very. ● **devilishly** *adverb, old use* very; terribly. ⓒ 15c.

devil-may-care ▷ *adj* cheerfully heedless of danger, consequences, etc.

devilment /ˈdɛvɪlmənt/ ▷ *noun* mischievous fun. ⓒ 18c.

devilry /ˈdɛvɪlrɪ/ ▷ *noun* (***devilries***) **1** mischievous fun. **2** wickedness or cruelty. **3** witchcraft; black magic. ⓒ 14c.

devil's advocate ▷ *noun* **1** someone who argues for or against something simply to encourage discussion or argument. **2** *RC Church* an advocate at the papal court whose duty is to propose objections against a canonization.

devil's coach-horse ▷ *noun* a large dark-coloured beetle.

devil's darning-needle ▷ *noun, colloq* a dragonfly or damselfly.

devil's food cake ▷ *noun, chiefly N Amer* a very rich kind of chocolate cake.

devils on horseback ▷ *plural noun* prunes wrapped in slices of bacon, grilled until crisp and served on toast.

devious /ˈdiːvɪəs/ ▷ *adj* **1** not totally open or honest; deceitful. **2** cunning; able to think up clever and usually deceitful ways of achieving things, etc. **3** not direct □ *came by a devious route*. ● **deviously** *adverb*. ● **deviousness** *noun*. ⓒ 17c; 16c, meaning 'remote or out of the way': from Latin *devius*, from *de* from + *via* road.

devise /dɪˈvaɪz/ ▷ *verb* (***devised***, ***devising***) **1** to invent, make up or put together (a plan, etc) in one's mind. **2** *law* to leave (property such as land or buildings) to someone in a will. See also BEQUEATH. ● **deviser** *noun* someone who devises plans, etc. • **devisor** *noun, law* someone who bequeaths property by will. ⓘ 14c: from French *deviser*, from Latin *divisa* division of goods.

devitalize or **devitalise** ▷ *verb* (***devitalized, devitalizing***) to deprive someone or something of vitality or life-giving properties. • **devitalization** *noun*. ⓘ 19c.

devoid /dɪ'vɔɪd/ ▷ *adj* (*always* **devoid of something**) free from it, lacking it or empty of it. ⓘ 15c: from French *devoidier* to take away.

devolution /diːvə'luːʃən, -'ljuːʃən, dɛ-/ ▷ *noun* the act of devolving, especially the giving of certain powers to a regional government by a central government. • **devolutionary** *adj*. • **devolutionist** *noun, adj*. ⓘ 18c in modern sense; 15c, meaning 'a transfer of a right': from Latin *devolutio*, from *devolvere* to roll down.

devolve /dɪ'vɒlv/ ▷ *verb* (***devolved, devolving***) (*usually* **devolve to** or **on** or **upon someone**) **1** *tr & intr* said of duties, power, etc: to be transferred or transfer them to someone else. **2** *intr, law* to pass by succession ◻ ***On his death, the title will devolve on his nephew.*** ⓘ 15c originally meaning 'to roll down' or 'unfurl': from Latin *devolvere, devolutum* to roll down.

Devonian /dɛ'voʊnɪən/ ▷ *adj* **1** belonging or relating to the English county of Devon. **2** *geol* **a** relating to the fourth period of the PALAEOZOIC era; **b** relating to the rocks formed during this period. See table at GEOLOGICAL TIME SCALE. ▷ *noun* **1** a person who was born in or who lives in Devon. **2** the Devonian rock system. ⓘ 17c: from Devon in SW England.

Devon minnow ▷ *noun, angling* a lure that imitates a swimming minnow.

Devonshire cream ▷ *noun* CLOTTED CREAM.

devote /dɪ'voʊt/ ▷ *verb* (***devoted, devoting***) to use or give up (a resource such as time or money) wholly to some purpose ◻ ***devoted their time to writing letters.*** ⓘ 17c in this sense; originally 16c, meaning 'to formally dedicate': from Latin *devovere, devotum* to consecrate.

devoted ▷ *adj* **1** (*usually* **devoted to someone**) loving and loyal to them. **2** (*usually* **devoted to something**) given up to it; totally occupied by it. • **devotedly** *adverb*. • **devotedness** *noun*.

devotee /dɛvoʊ'tiː, 'dɛ-/ ▷ *noun* (***devotees***) **1** a keen follower or enthusiastic supporter. **2** a keen believer in a religion or follower of a god. ⓘ 17c.

devotion /dɪ'voʊʃən/ ▷ *noun* **1** great love or loyalty; enthusiasm for or willingness to do what is required by someone. **2** devoting or being devoted. **3** religious enthusiasm and piety. **4** (**devotions**) *relig* worship and prayers. • **devotional** *adj*.

devour /dɪ'vaʊə(r)/ ▷ *verb* (***devoured, devouring***) **1** to eat up something greedily. **2** to completely destroy something. **3** to read (a book, etc) eagerly. **4** to look at something with obvious pleasure. **5** (*usually* **be devoured**) to be taken over totally ◻ ***He was devoured by guilt.*** • **devourer** *noun*. ⓘ 14c: from French *devorer*, from Latin *devorare* to gulp down.

devout /dɪ'vaʊt/ ▷ *adj* **1** sincerely religious in thought and behaviour. **2** deeply felt; earnest. • **devoutly** *adverb*. • **devoutness** *noun*. ⓘ 13c: from Latin *devovere, devotum* to consecrate.

dew /djuː, dʒuː/ ▷ *noun* **1** a form of PRECIPITATION consisting of tiny droplets of water that are deposited on objects close to the ground, eg leaves, on cool clear nights when air in contact with the ground becomes saturated. **2** anything similar, especially moisture associated with freshness. ⓘ Anglo-Saxon *deaw*.

Dewar flask or **dewar flask** and **dewar** /'djʊə(r), 'dʒ-/ ▷ *noun, physics* an insulated vessel with double walls, the inner space surrounded by a vacuum and silvered so that heat losses by convection and radiation are reduced to a minimum. ⓘ 19c: named after Sir James Dewar (1842–1923), its inventor.

dewberry ▷ *noun* **1** a trailing type of BRAMBLE, that produces fruit with a bluish dew-like bloom on the fruit. **2** the fruit of this plant.

dewclaw ▷ *noun* a small functionless toe or claw on the legs of some dogs and other animals. ⓘ 16c.

dewdrop ▷ *noun* a drop of dew.

Dewey decimal system and **classification** /'djuːɪ —/ ▷ *noun* an international library classification system, in which books are assigned to numbered classes, with further subdivision of classes shown by numbers following a decimal point. Also called **decimal classification**. ⓘ 19c: devised in 1873, by Melvil Dewey (1851–1931), US librarian.

dewfall ▷ *noun* the deposition of dew or the time that this happens.

dewier, dewiest, dewily, dewiness see DEWY

dewlap ▷ *noun* a flap of loose skin hanging down from the throat of certain cattle, dogs and other animals. ⓘ 14c: probably from DEW + Anglo-Saxon *læppa* loose hanging piece.

dew point ▷ *noun, meteorol* the temperature at which dew forms.

dew-pond ▷ *noun* a shallow pond, sometimes artificial, supplied with water by dew and mist.

dewy ▷ *adj* (***dewier, dewiest***) covered in dew. • **dewily** *adverb*. • **dewiness** *noun*.

dewy-eyed ▷ *adj, often ironic* naive and too trusting.

dexter /'dɛkstə(r)/ ▷ *adj, heraldry* **1** on the right-hand side. **2** on or belonging to that side of the shield on the right-hand side of the bearer, ie the spectator's left. Compare SINISTER. ⓘ 16c: Latin, meaning 'right'.

dexterity /dɛk'stɛrɪtɪ/ ▷ *noun* **1** skill in using one's hands. **2** quickness of mind. ⓘ 16c: from French *dextérité*, from Latin *dexter* right or skilful.

dexterous or **dextrous** /'dɛkstrəs, 'dɛkstərəs/ ▷ *adj* having, showing or done with dexterity; skilful. • **dexterously** or **dextrously** *adverb*. • **dexterousness** or **dextrousness** *noun*.

dextral /'dɛkstrəl/ ▷ *adj* **1** associated with, or located on, the right side, especially the right side of the body. **2** right-handed, or favouring the right-hand side. **3** said of flatfish: lying right side up. **4** said of the shells of some gastropod molluscs: turning in the normal manner, ie clockwise from the top. Compare SINISTRAL. • **dextrality** *noun*. • **dextrally** *adverb*. ⓘ 17c: from medieval Latin *dextralis*, from *dextra* right hand.

dextran /'dɛkstran/ ▷ *noun* a carbohydrate formed in sugar solutions, used as a substitute for blood plasma in transfusions. ⓘ 19c.

dextrin or **dextrine** /'dɛkstrɪn/ ▷ *noun, biochem* any of a group of short-chain POLYSACCHARIDES produced during the breakdown of starch or glycogen by enzymes, used as a thickener in foods and adhesives. ⓘ 19c: from French *dextrine*.

dextro- /dɛkstroʊ/ or (before a vowel) **dextr-** *combining form, signifying* to or towards the right.

dextrorotatory ▷ *adj* rotating to the right; clockwise. ⓘ 19c.

dextrorse /dɛk'strɔːs, 'dɛk-/ ▷ *adj, biol* rising spirally and turning anticlockwise. ⓘ 19c: from Latin *dextrorsus* towards the right.

dextrose /'dɛkstroʊs, -stroʊz/ ▷ *noun* a type of GLUCOSE. ⓘ 19c.

dextrous see DEXTEROUS

DF ▷ *abbreviation* Defender of the Faith.

DFC ▷ *abbreviation* Distinguished Flying Cross.

DFE ▷ *abbreviation* Department for Education which replaced the DES in 1992.

DFM ▻ *abbreviation* Distinguished Flying Medal.

DG ▻ *abbreviation* **1** *Dei gratia* (Latin), by the grace of God. **2** Director General.

dg ▻ *abbreviation* decigram, or decigrams.

dhal see DAL

dharma /'dɑːmə, 'dɜːmə/ ▻ *noun* **1** *Buddhism* truth. **2** *Hinduism* the universal laws, especially the moral laws to be followed by each individual. ⓒ 18c: Sanskrit, meaning 'decree' or 'custom'.

dhobi /'doʊbɪ/ ▻ *noun* (***dhobis***) *historical* in India, Malaya, etc: a man who does washing. ⓒ 19c: Hindi, from *dhob* washing.

dhobi itch ▻ *noun* a tropical allergic dermatitis.

dhoti /'doʊtɪ/ or **dhooti** /'duːtɪ/ ▻ *noun* (***dhotis*** or ***dhootis***) a garment worn by some Hindu men, consisting of a long strip of cloth wrapped around the waist and between the legs. ⓒ 17c: Hindi.

dhow /daʊ/ ▻ *noun* a type of LATEEN ship with one or more sails, used in countries around the Indian Ocean. ⓒ 18c: from Arabian *dawa*.

DHSS ▻ *abbreviation, Brit* Department of Health and Social Security, in 1989 split into the Department of Social Services (**DSS**) and Department of Health.

DI ▻ *abbreviation* **1** Defence Intelligence. **2** Detective Inspector. **3** *medicine* donor insemination.

di- /daɪ, dɪ/ ▻ *prefix* **1** two or double ▫ *dicotyledon*. **2** *chem* containing two atoms of the same type ▫ *dioxide*. ⓒ From Greek *dis* twice.

dia. ▻ *abbreviation* diameter.

dia- ▻ *prefix, denoting* **1** through. **2** across. **3** during. **4** composed of. ⓒ Greek.

diabetes /daɪə'biːtiːz/ ▻ *noun* any of various disorders, especially DIABETES MELLITUS, that are characterized by thirst and excessive production of urine. ⓒ 16c: Greek, meaning 'siphon'.

diabetes insipidus /— ɪn'sɪpɪdəs/ ▻ *noun, medicine* a rare disorder characterized by the excretion of large amounts of dilute urine, and constant thirst, which is caused by a deficiency of **antidiuretic hormone**, the hormone that controls reabsorption of water by the kidneys.

diabetes mellitus /— me'laɪtəs/ ▻ *noun, medicine* a common metabolic disorder in which the pancreatic hormone insulin is no longer produced in sufficient quantity or activity to control sugar metabolism.

diabetic /daɪə'betɪk/ ▻ *noun* someone suffering from diabetes. ▻ *adj* **1** relating to or suffering from diabetes. **2** especially for people who have diabetes ▫ *diabetic jam*. ⓒ 19c as *noun*; 18c as *adj*.

diablerie /dɪ'ɑːbləriː/ ▻ *noun* **1** magic, especially black magic or witchcraft. **2** knowledge of devils. **3** mischief. ⓒ 18c: from French *diable* devil.

diabolic /daɪə'bɒlɪk/ ▻ *adj* **1** characteristic of, like or belonging to a devil; devilish. **2** very wicked or cruel. ⓒ 14c: from Greek *diabolos* slanderer or devil.

diabolical /daɪə'bɒlɪkəl/ ▻ *adj, Brit colloq* very shocking, annoying, bad, difficult, etc. • **diabolically** *adverb* **1** in a diabolical way; wickedly. **2** *colloq* exceedingly; very ▫ *diabolically funny*. ⓒ 16c.

diabolism /daɪ'abəlɪzəm/ ▻ *noun* the worship of the Devil or devils; witchcraft; black magic. • **diabolist** *noun*. ⓒ 17c: from Greek *diabolos* devil + -ISM.

diabolo /dɪ'abələʊ, daɪ-/ ▻ *noun* (***diabolos***) **1** a game in which a two-headed top is spun, tossed and caught on a string attached to two sticks held one in each hand. **2** the top used in this game. ⓒ 19c: Italian.

diachronic /daɪə'krɒnɪk/ and **diachronical** /-kəl/ ▻ *adj, linguistics* concerned with the study of a language in terms of its origins and historical development. Opposite of SYNCHRONIC. ⓒ 20c in this sense; 19c, meaning 'lasting through time': DIA-1 + Greek *chronos* time +.

diacid /daɪ'asɪd/ ▻ *adj, chem* **1** having two replaceable hydrogen atoms. **2** capable of replacing two hydrogen atoms of an acid. ⓒ 19c.

diaconal /daɪ'akənəl/ ▻ *adj* belonging to or relating to a DEACON. ⓒ 17c.

diaconate /daɪ'akəneɪt, dɪ-/ ▻ *noun* **1** the position of DEACON. **2** one's period of time as a deacon. **3** deacons as a group. ⓒ 18c: from Latin *diaconus* deacon.

diacritic /daɪə'krɪtɪk/ ▻ *noun* a mark written or printed over, under or through a letter to show that that letter has a particular sound, as in *é, è, ç, ñ*. Compare ACCENT (*noun* 3). ▻ *adj* (*also* **diacritical**) functioning as a diacritic; distinguishing. ⓒ 17c: from Greek *diakritikos* able to distinguish.

diadem /'daɪədem/ ▻ *noun* **1** a crown or jewelled headband, worn by a royal person. **2** royal power or authority. ⓒ 13c: from French *diademe*.

diaeresis or (*N Amer*) **dieresis** /daɪ'erəsɪs/ ▻ *noun* (***diaereses*** /-siːz/) a mark (¨) placed over a vowel to show that it is to be pronounced separately from the vowel before it, as in **naïve**. ⓒ 17c in this sense: from Greek *diairesis* separation.

diagenesis /daɪə'dʒenəsɪs/ ▻ *noun, geol* the physical and chemical changes in a sedimentary rock after its deposition, excluding weathering and metamorphism. ⓒ 19c.

diagnose /daɪəg'noʊz, 'daɪ-/ ▻ *verb* (***diagnosed, diagnosing***) **1** to identify (an illness) from a consideration of its symptoms. **2** to identify (a fault). • **diagnosable** *adj*. ⓒ 19c: from DIAGNOSIS.

diagnosis /daɪəg'noʊsɪs/ ▻ *noun* (***diagnoses*** /-siːz/) **1** *medicine* the process whereby a disease or disorder is provisionally identified on the basis of its symptoms and the patient's medical history. **2** *biol* in taxonomy: a formal description, eg of a plant, made on the basis of its distinguishing characteristics. **3** identification of problems in other areas, eg in mechanics and computing. ⓒ 17c: Greek, from *diagignoskein* to distinguish.

diagnostic /daɪəg'nɒstɪk/ ▻ *adj* relating to or useful in diagnosis. • **diagnostician** /-'stɪʃən/ *noun*.

diagonal /daɪ'agənəl/ ▻ *adj* **1** *math* said of a straight line: joining any two non-adjacent corners of a POLYGON or any two vertices not on the same face in a POLYHEDRON. **2** sloping or slanting. ▻ *noun* a diagonal line. • **diagonally** *adverb*. ⓒ 16c: from Greek *dia* through + *gonia* angle.

diagram /'daɪəgram/ ▻ *noun* a line drawing, often labelled with text, that does not show all the visible details of an object or process, but only the most important features of its structure or the manner in which it functions. • **diagrammatic** /daɪəgrə'matɪk/ *adj*. • **diagrammatically** *adverb*. ⓒ 17c: from Greek *diagramma*, from *dia* round + *graphein* to write.

diakinesis /daɪəkaɪ'niːsɪs/ ▻ *noun, biol* during MEIOSIS: the final stage of PROPHASE, when the pairs of homologous chromosomes are almost completely separated from one another. ⓒ Early 20c: from Greek *kinesis* motion.

dial /daɪl, 'daɪəl/ ▻ *noun* **1** a disc or plate on a clock, radio, meter, etc with numbers or other scales or measurements marked on it and a movable pointer or indicator, used to indicate eg measurements of speed, time, etc or selected settings of time, temperature, radio frequency, etc. **2** the round numbered plate on some telephones and the movable disc fitted over it. ▻ *verb* (***dialled, dialling***; *US* ***dialed, dialing***) *tr & intr* to use a telephone dial or keypad to call (a number). • **dialler** or (*US*) **dialer** *noun*. ⓒ 14c: from Latin *dialis* daily, from the fact that a sundial shows the time of day from the shadow cast on it, or from its being the name for a wheel in the clockwork of medieval clocks which turned once per day.

dialect /'daɪəlɛkt/ ▷ *noun* **1** a form of a language spoken in a particular region or by a certain social group, differing from other forms in grammar, vocabulary, and in some cases pronunciation. **2** *computing* a variant form of a computer language. • **dialectal** *adj.* • **dialectally** *adverb.* Ⓒ 16c: from Greek *dialektos* manner of speech.

dialectic /daɪə'lɛktɪk/ ▷ *noun, philos* **1** (*also* **dialectics**) the art or practice of establishing truth by discussion. **2** (*also* **dialectics**) a debate which aims to resolve the conflict between two opposing theories rather than to disprove either of them. **3** the art of reasoning and arguing logically. • **dialectical** *adj.* Ⓒ 17c: from Greek *dialektike* (*techne*) (the art) of debating.

dialectology /daɪəlɛk'tɒlədʒɪ/ ▷ *noun* the study of dialect. • **dialectologist** *noun.* Ⓒ 19c.

dialling code ▷ *noun* the part of a telephone number that represents a town or area.

dialling tone and (*N Amer*) **dial tone** ▷ *noun* the continuous sound heard on picking up a telephone receiver which indicates that the equipment is functioning and ready to accept an input telephone number.

dialogue or *sometimes* (*US*) **dialog** /'daɪəlɒg/ *noun* **1** a conversation, especially a formal one. **2** the words spoken by the characters in a play, book, etc. **3** a discussion or exchange of ideas and opinions, especially between two groups, with a view to resolving conflict or achieving agreement. Ⓒ 13c as *dialoge*: French, originally from Greek *dialogos* conversation.

dialogue box ▷ *noun, computing* a small on-screen box that prompts the user to make queries, give information or enter an option.

dialyse or (*chiefly N Amer*) **dialyze** /'daɪəlaɪz/ *verb* (***dialysed, dialysing***) **1** to separate something by dialysis. **2** *intr* to use a kidney machine. • **dialysable** *adj.* • **dialyser** *noun.*

dialysis /daɪ'alɪsɪs/ ▷ *noun* (***dialyses*** /-siːz/) **1** *chem* the separation of particles of different sizes in a solution, based on the different rates at which the various substances diffuse through a semi-permeable membrane, mainly used to separate large particles such as proteins from soluble substances such as salts. **2** *medicine* the removal of toxic substances from the blood by diffusion through a semi-permeable membrane in an artificial kidney machine, used in cases of kidney failure when a transplant is not available. Also called **haemodialysis**. Ⓒ 16c: Greek, meaning 'separation'.

diam. ▷ *abbreviation* diameter.

diamagnetic /daɪəmag'nɛtɪk/ ▷ *adj* applied to any substance a rod of which, when suspended between the poles of a magnet, arranges itself across the lines of force. • **diamagnet** *noun.* • **diamagnetism** *noun.* Ⓒ 19c.

diamanté /dɪə'mɒnteɪ, -'mantɪ/ ▷ *adj* said of a fabric: decorated with small sparkling ornaments. ▷ *noun* (***diamantés***) a diamanté fabric. Ⓒ Early 20c: French, meaning 'decorated with diamonds'.

diameter /daɪ'amɪtə(r)/ ▷ *noun* **1** *geom* the length of a straight line drawn from one side of a circle to the other, and passing through its centre, equal to twice the radius of the circle. **2** the length of this line. Ⓒ 14c: from Greek *dia* across + *metron* measure.

diametric /daɪə'mɛtrɪk/ and **diametrical** ▷ *adj* **1** belonging or relating to a diameter. **2** along a diameter. **3** said of opinions, etc: directly opposed; very far apart. • **diametrically** *adverb* said in relation to opposition: completely; utterly □ *diametrically opposite opinions.*

diamond /'daɪəmənd/ ▷ *noun* **1** a crystalline ALLOTROPE of carbon, colourless when pure and the hardest known mineral, highly prized as a gemstone. **2** a piece of this substance or a synthetic form of it, used in cutting tools, etc. **3** a RHOMBUS. **4** *cards* **a** (**diamonds**) one of the four suits of playing-cards, with red rhombus-shaped symbols ♦; **b** one of the playing-cards of this suit. **5** a baseball pitch, or the part of it between the bases. ▷ *adj* **1** resembling, made of or marked with diamonds. **2** rhombus-shaped. Ⓒ 14c as *diamaunde*: from French *diamant*, from Latin and Greek *adamas* steel or diamond.

diamond anniversary ▷ *noun* a sixtieth, or occasionally a seventy-fifth, anniversary.

diamond-back ▷ *noun* **1** (*also* **diamondback terrapin** or **diamondback turtle**) any N American terrapin with diamond-shaped markings on its shell. **2** a N American rattlesnake with diamond-shaped markings.

diamond bird ▷ *noun* any of several small insectivorous Australian songbirds.

diamond dove ▷ *noun* a small Australian dove with white markings on the wings, often kept in a cage or aviary.

diamonded ▷ *adj* covered with, decorated with or wearing diamonds.

diamond jubilee ▷ *noun* a sixtieth anniversary, eg of accession, foundation, etc.

diamond snake ▷ *noun* a python with diamond-shaped markings.

diamond wedding ▷ *noun* the DIAMOND ANNIVERSARY of a marriage.

diamorphine /daɪə'mɔːfiːn/ ▷ *noun, technical* HEROIN. Ⓒ Early 20c: abbreviation of technical name *diacetylmorphine.*

dianthus /daɪ'anθəs/ ▷ *noun* (***dianthuses***) any plant of the herbaceous family of flowers to which carnations and pinks belong. Ⓒ 18c: Latin, probably from Greek *Dios anthos* Zeus's flower.

diapason /daɪə'peɪzən, -sən/ ▷ *noun, music* **1** the whole range or compass of tones. **2** a standard of pitch. **3** a full volume of various sounds in concord. **4** a foundation-stop of an organ extending through its whole compass. Ⓒ 16c: Latin, from Greek *dia pason chordon symphonia* concord through all the notes.

diapause /'daɪəpɔːz/ ▷ *noun, zool* in the life cycle of an insect: a period during which growth and development are arrested, often until environmental conditions become more favourable. Ⓒ 19c: from Greek *diapausis* pause.

diaper /'daɪəpə(r)/ ▷ *noun* **1** a type of linen or cotton cloth with a pattern of small diamond or square shapes. **2** *N Amer* a baby's nappy. Ⓒ 15c: from French *diaspre*, from Latin *dia* through + *aspros* white.

diaphanous /daɪ'afənəs/ ▷ *adj* said of cloth: light and fine, and almost transparent. • **diaphanously** *adverb.* • **diaphanousness** *noun.* Ⓒ 17c: from Greek *dia* through + *phanein* to show.

diaphoresis /daɪəfə'riːsɪs/ *medicine* ▷ *noun* perspiration. Ⓒ 17c: Greek.

diaphoretic /daɪəfə'rɛtɪk/ ▷ *adj* promoting sweating. ▷ *noun* a diaphoretic substance.

diaphragm /'daɪəfram/ ▷ *noun* **1** *anatomy* in mammals: the sheet of muscle that separates the THORAX from the ABDOMEN. **2** *optics* an opaque disc, with a central aperture of adjustable diameter, that is used to control the amount of light entering an optical instrument such as a camera or microscope. **3** a thin vibrating disc or cone that converts sound waves to electrical signals in a microphone, or electrical signals to sound waves in a loudspeaker. **4** a CAP (*noun* 10). • **diaphragmatic** /-frag'matɪk/ *adj.* Ⓒ 14c as *diafragma*: from Greek *diaphragma* partition.

diapositive /daɪə'pɒzɪtɪv/ ▷ *noun* a transparent photographic positive; a slide. Ⓒ 19c.

diarchy ▷ *noun* (***diarchies***) **1** a form of government in which two people, states or bodies are jointly vested with supreme power. **2** a government of this type. Ⓒ 19c: from DI-, modelled on *monarchy*.

diarist /'daɪərɪst/ ▷ *noun* a person who writes a diary, especially one which is published.

diarrhoea or (*N Amer*) **diarrhea** /daɪə'rɪə/ *noun* **1** *medicine* a condition in which the bowels are emptied more frequently and urgently than usual and the faeces are very soft or liquid. **2** an excessive flow of anything □ *verbal diarrhoea*. • **diarrhoeal** *adj*. • **diarrhoeic** *adj*. Ⓒ 16c: from Greek *dia* through + *rhoia* flow.

diary /'daɪərɪ/ ▷ *noun* (***diaries***) **1 a** a written record of daily events in a person's life; **b** a book containing this. **2** *Brit* a book with separate spaces or pages for each day of the year in which appointments, daily notes and reminders may be written. Ⓒ 16c: from Latin *diarium*, from *dies* day.

the Diaspora /daɪ'aspərə/ ▷ *noun* **1** the scattering of the Jewish people to various countries following their exile in Babylon in the 6c BC. **2** the new communities of Jews which arose in various countries as a result. **3** the Jews who do not live in the modern state of Israel. **4** (*also* **diaspora**) a dispersion or spreading of people originally belonging to the same nation or having the same culture. Ⓒ 19c: from Greek *dia* through + *speirein* to scatter.

diastase /'daɪəsteɪz/ ▷ *noun* the component of malt containing ß-amylase, an enzyme that converts starch into sugar, produced in germinating seeds and in pancreatic juice and used in the brewing industry. • **diastasic** /-'steɪzɪk/ or **diastatic** /-'statɪk/ *adj*. Ⓒ 19c: from Greek *diastasis* division.

diastole /daɪ'astəlɪ/ *medicine* ▷ *noun* the rhythmic expansion of the chambers of the heart during which they fill with blood. See also SYSTOLE. • **diastolic** /daɪə'stɒlɪk/ *adj*. Ⓒ 16c: from Greek *dia* apart + *stellein* to place.

diathermy /'daɪəθɜːmɪ/ ▷ *noun, medicine* the treating of internal organs with heat by passing electric currents through them. Ⓒ Early 20c: from DIA- + Greek *therme* heat.

diathesis /daɪ'aθɪsɪs/ *medicine* ▷ *noun* a particular condition or habit of body, especially one predisposing someone to certain diseases. • **diathetic** /daɪə'θetɪk/ *adj*. Ⓒ 17c: Greek, meaning 'disposition'.

diatom /'daɪətɒm/ ▷ *noun* the common name for a member of a group of microscopic one-celled algae with the cell wall composed of two overlapping valves, containing silica, that fit together like the two halves of a box. • **diatomaceous** /daɪətə'meɪʃəs/ *adj* **1** belonging to or relating to diatoms. **2** containing or consisting of diatoms or their remains. Ⓒ 19c: from Greek *diatomos* cut through.

diatomic /daɪə'tɒmɪk/ ▷ *adj, chem* denoting a molecule that consists of two identical atoms, eg O_2, H_2. Ⓒ 19c.

diatomite /daɪ'atəmaɪt, 'daɪə-/ *geol* KIESELGUHR.

diatonic /daɪə'tɒnɪk/ *music* ▷ *adj* relating to, or using notes from, the DIATONIC SCALE. See also CHROMATIC. • **diatonically** *adverb*. • **diatonicism** *noun*. Ⓒ 17c: from DIA- + Greek *tonos* tone.

diatonic scale ▷ *noun, music* a scale which consists of or involves only the basic notes proper to a particular major or minor key, with no additional sharps, flats or naturals.

diatribe /'daɪətraɪb/ ▷ *noun* a bitter or abusive critical attack in speech or writing. Ⓒ 19c in this sense; 16c, meaning 'a discourse': Greek, meaning 'a discourse'.

diazepam /daɪ'azəpam, daɪ'eɪ-/ ▷ *noun, medicine* a tranquillizing drug which relieves anxiety and acts as a muscle relaxant, but whose long-term use causes addiction. Ⓒ 1960s: from benzo*diazepine*.

diazo compound /daɪ'azoʊ —, daɪ'eɪzoʊ —/ ▷ *noun, chem* any of various organic compounds containing two adjacent nitrogen atoms, only one of which is attached to a carbon atom, these being used in the manufacture of many dyes and drugs. Ⓒ 20c: DI- + AZO-.

dibasic /daɪ'beɪsɪk/ ▷ *adj, chem* denoting an acid that contains two replaceable hydrogen atoms, eg sulphuric acid (H_2SO_4), allowing formation of two series of salts, the normal and acid salt. Ⓒ 19c.

dibble /'dɪbəl/ ▷ *noun* a short pointed hand-tool used for making holes in the ground, etc for seeds, young plants, etc. Also called **dibber** /'dɪbə(r)/. ▷ *verb* (***dibbled, dibbling***) **1** to plant (seeds, etc) with a dibble. **2** to make holes in (the ground, etc) with a dibble.

dibs /dɪbz/ ▷ *plural noun* **1** JACKS. **2** *slang* money. Ⓒ 18c in sense 1, from 17c *dibstones*.

dice /daɪs/ ▷ *noun* (*plural* ***dice***) **1** a small cube with a different number of spots, from 1 to 6, on each of its sides or faces, used in certain games of chance. **2** a game of chance played with one or more dice. See also DIE². ▷ *verb* (***diced, dicing***) **1** to cut (vegetables, etc) into small cubes. **2** *intr* to play or gamble with dice. • **dice with death** to take a great risk. • **no dice** *colloq* used to indicate a negative answer or unsuccessful outcome. Ⓒ 14c: originally the plural of DIE².

dicey /'daɪsɪ/ ▷ *adj* (***dicier, diciest***) *colloq* risky.

dichlorodiphenyltrichloroethane see DDT

dichotomy /daɪ'kɒtəmɪ, dɪ-/ ▷ *noun* (***dichotomies***) a division or separation into two groups or parts, especially when these are sharply opposed or contrasted. • **dichotomous** *adj*. • **dichotomously** *adverb*. Ⓒ 16c: from Greek *dicha* in two + *tome* cut.

dichroism /'daɪkroʊɪzəm/ *physics* ▷ *noun* a property of some crystals, that reflect certain colours when viewed from one angle, and different colours when viewed from another angle. • **dichroic** /-'kroʊɪk/ or **dichroitic** /-'ɪtɪk/ *adj*. Ⓒ 19c: from Greek *dichroos* two-coloured.

dichromatic /daɪkroʊ'matɪk/ ▷ *adj* **1** said of eg animals: having two colours or colourings. **2** able to see only two colours and combinations of these, as in red-green colour blindness when the person sees only blue and yellow. • **dichromatism** /-'kroʊmətɪzəm/ *noun*. Ⓒ 19c.

dicier and **diciest** see under DICEY.

dick ▷ *noun* **1** *coarse slang* the penis. **2** *slang* a detective. Ⓒ 18c in sense 1 from the name *Dick*.

dickens /'dɪkɪnz/ ▷ *noun, colloq* (*usually* **the dickens**) the devil, used especially for emphasis □ *What the dickens are you doing?* Ⓒ 16c: from the name *Dickon* or *Dicken*, from *Richard*.

Dickensian /dɪ'kenzɪən/ ▷ *adj* **1** resembling the 19c English social life depicted in the novels of Charles Dickens (1812–70), especially the poor living and working conditions or the odd and often grotesque characters described. **2** characteristic of or relating to the novelist Charles Dickens or to his writings.

dicker /'dɪkə(r)/ ▷ *verb* (***dickered, dickering***) *intr* to argue about the price or cost of something. ▷ *noun* **1** haggling or bargaining; barter. **2** a bargain; a deal. Ⓒ 19c: originally US.

dickhead /'dɪkhed, dɪked/ ▷ *noun, coarse slang* a stupid person; an idiot.

dicky¹ or **dickey** or **dickie** /'dɪkɪ/ ▷ *noun* (***dickies*** or ***dickeys***) **1** a false shirt front, especially when worn with evening dress. **2** a bow tie. Also called **dicky bow**. **3** a RUMBLE.

dicky² /'dɪkɪ/ ▷ *adj* (***dickier, dickiest***) *colloq* **1** shaky; unsteady. **2** not in good condition. Ⓒ 19c: possibly from *Tom and Dick*, Cockney rhyming slang for *sick*.

dicky-bird ▷ *noun* a child's word for a small bird. • **not a dicky bird** *rhyming slang* not a word. ◷ 18c: from the name *Dicky*, for *Richard*.

dicotyledon /daɪkɒtɪ'liːdən/ ▷ *noun, bot* a flowering plant with an embryo that has two COTYLEDONs, and flower parts arranged in multiples of two or five, eg potato, rose, and the hardwood trees oak and beech. Compare MONOCOTYLEDON. ◷ 18c.

dict. ▷ *abbreviation* **1** dictation. **2** dictator. **3** dictionary.

dicta see DICTUM

Dictaphone /'dɪktəfoun/ ▷ *noun, trademark* a small tape-recorder for use especially when dictating letters.

dictate ▷ *verb* /dɪk'teɪt/ (*dictated, dictating*) **1** to say or read out something for someone else to write down. **2** to state or lay down (rules, terms, etc) forcefully or with authority. **3** *tr & intr, derog* to give orders to or try to impose one's wishes on someone. ▷ *noun* /'dɪkteɪt/ (*usually* **dictates**) **1** an order or instruction. **2** a guiding principle. • **dictatory** /'dɪktətərɪ/ *adj*. ◷ 16c: from Latin *dictare*.

dictation ▷ *noun* **1** something read or spoken for another person to write down. **2** the act of dictating. **3** the words dictated.

dictator ▷ *noun* **1** a ruler with complete and unrestricted power. **2** someone who behaves in a dictatorial manner. **3** in ancient Rome: a person given complete authority in the state for a period of six months at a time of crisis. • **dictatorial** /dɪktə'tɔːrɪəl/ *adj* characteristic of, like or suggesting a dictator; fond of using one's power and authority and imposing one's wishes on or giving orders to other people. • **dictatorially** *adverb*. • **dictatorship** *noun* **1** the position of dictator. **2** a state ruled by a dictator.

diction /'dɪkʃən/ ▷ *noun* **1** the way in which one speaks. **2** one's choice or use of words to express meaning. ◷ 17c in this sense; 16c, meaning 'a word': from Latin *dicere* to say.

dictionary ▷ *noun* (*dictionaries*) **1** a book containing the words of a language arranged alphabetically with their meanings, and sometimes also their pronunciation, grammatical labels, inflections, etymologies, etc. **2** such a book giving the meanings of the words in one or more different languages. **3** *computing* a program available in some word-processing packages which will check text for spelling errors against a dictionary held on disk. **4** an alphabetically arranged book of information. ◷ 16c: from Latin *dictionarium*.

dictum /'dɪktəm/ ▷ *noun* (*dictums* or *dicta* /-tə/) **1** a formal or authoritative statement of opinion. **2** a popular saying or maxim. ◷ 16c: Latin.

did *past tense of* DO[1]

didactic /daɪ'daktɪk, dɪ-/ ▷ *adj* **1** intended to teach or instruct. **2** *derog* too eager or too obviously intended to instruct, in a way resented by the reader, listener, etc. • **didactically** *adverb*. • **didacticism** /daɪ'daktɪsɪzəm, dɪ-/ *noun*. • **didactics** *singular noun* the art or science of teaching. ◷ 17c: from Greek *didaskein* to teach.

diddle /'dɪdəl/ ▷ *verb* (*diddled, diddling*) *colloq* **1** to cheat or swindle. **2** (*usually* **diddle about** or **around**) to waste time. • **diddler** *noun, colloq* a cheat or swindler. ◷ 19c: probably from Jeremy Diddler, a character in a 19c play.

diddy /'dɪdɪ/ ▷ *adj, colloq* (*diddier, diddiest*) small; tiny.

didgeridoo /dɪdʒərɪ'duː/ ▷ *noun* (*didgeridoos*) *music* a native Australian wind instrument, consisting of a long wooden or bamboo tube which, when blown into, produces a low droning sound. ◷ Early 20c: from an Australian Aboriginal language, the name imitating the sound made.

didicoy or **diddicoy** or **didicoi** /'dɪdɪkɔɪ/ ▷ *noun* (*didicoys, diddicoys* or *didicois*) an itinerant tinker or scrap dealer, not a true gypsy. ◷ 19c: Romany.

didn't /'dɪdənt/ ▷ *contraction of* did not.

dido /'daɪdou/ ▷ *noun* (*didoes* or *didos*) *colloq, especially US* an antic or caper; an act of mischief. ◷ 19c.

didst /dɪdst/ *archaic 2nd person singular past tense of* DO[1]

didymous /'dɪdɪməs/ ▷ *adj, biol* **1** twin; twinned; growing in pairs. **2** composed of two parts slightly connected. ◷ 18c: from Greek *didymos* twin.

die[1] /daɪ/ ▷ *verb* (*dies, died, dying*) *intr* **1** to stop living; to cease to be alive. **2** to cease to exist; to come to an end or fade away. **3** said of an engine, etc: to stop working suddenly and unexpectedly. **4** (*usually* **die of something**) to suffer or be overcome by the effects of it □ *die of laughter*. • **be dying for something** or **to do something** *colloq* to have a strong desire or need for it or to do it. • **to die for** *colloq* highly desirable to the speaker's social group but perceived as being almost unobtainable □ *That new shop sells fashion accessories to die for* □ *He has a body to die for.* • **die game** to keep up one's spirit to the last. • **die hard** to be difficult to change or remove. See also DIEHARD. • **die in harness** to die while still working. • **die the death** *theat slang* to fail to get a response from an audience. • **never say die** never give up or give in. ◷ 14c as *dien*: from Norse *deyja*.

■ **die away 1** to fade away from sight or hearing until gone. **2** to become steadily weaker and finally stop. See also DIE AWAY.

■ **die back** *bot* said of a plant's soft shoots: to die or wither from the tip back to the hard wood. See also DIEBACK.

■ **die down 1** to lose strength or force. **2** said of a plant or its soft shoots: to wither back to the root without completely dying.

■ **die off** to die one after another; to die in large numbers.

■ **die out** to cease to exist anywhere; to become extinct.

die[2] /daɪ/ ▷ *noun* **1** (*plural dies*) **a** a metal tool or stamp for cutting or shaping metal or making designs on coins, etc. **b** a metal device for shaping or moulding a semisoft solid material. **2** (*plural* **dice**) a DICE. • **straight as a die 1** completely straight. **2** completely honest. • **the die is cast** a decision has been made or an action taken which cannot be changed or gone back on. ◷ 14c as *dee*: from French *de*, from Latin *datum* something given.

die-away ▷ *adj* languishing. See also DIE AWAY at DIE[1].

dieback ▷ *noun, bot* the death of young shoots of trees and shrubs, often followed by the death of larger branches and stems, due to damage, disease, or lack of water, minerals, light, etc. See also DIE BACK at DIE[1].

die casting ▷ *noun* **1** *engineering* a form of casting in which molten metal or plastic is forced under pressure into cooled dies (see DIE[2] *noun* 1) usually in order to produce large numbers of small items of a particular shape. **2** an object made in this way.

died *past tense, past participle of* DIE[1]

diehard ▷ *noun* a person who stubbornly refuses to accept new ideas or changes. Also *as adj*.

dieldrin /'diːldrɪn/ ▷ *noun* a crystalline compound, a chlorinated derivative of NAPHTHALENE, used as a contact insecticide. ◷ 1949: from the name of the German chemist O Diels (1876–1954) + ALDRIN.

dielectric /daɪɪ'lɛktrɪk/ *physics* ▷ *noun* a non-conducting material whose molecules align or polarize under the influence of applied electric fields, used as an essential component of capacitors. ▷ *adj* denoting such a material. ◷ 19c.

diene /'daɪiːn/ ▷ *noun, chem* an ALKENE containing two double bonds between carbon atoms. ◷ 1917.

dieresis an alternative *N Amer, especially US* spelling of DIAERESIS.

diesel /ˈdiːzəl/ ▷ *noun* **1** DIESEL FUEL. **2** a DIESEL ENGINE. **3** a train, etc driven by a diesel engine. ◎ 19c: named after the German engineer Rudolf Diesel (1858–1913).

diesel engine ▷ *noun* a type of internal-combustion engine in which air in the cylinder is compressed until it reaches a sufficiently high temperature to ignite the fuel.

diesel fuel and **diesel oil** ▷ *noun, engineering* a type of liquid fuel, composed mainly of hydrocarbons derived from petroleum, that is designed for use in a diesel engine.

die-sinking ▷ *noun* the engraving of dies (see DIE² *noun* 1) for embossing, etc.

diesis /ˈdaɪəsɪs/ ▷ *noun* (***dieses*** /-siːz/) **1** *printing* DOUBLE DAGGER. **2** *music* the difference between a major and a minor semitone. ◎ 16c in sense 2: Greek, meaning 'a quarter tone'.

diet¹ /daɪət/ ▷ *noun* **1** the food and drink habitually consumed by a person or animal. **2** a planned or prescribed selection of food and drink, especially one designed for weight loss, maintenance of good health or the control of a medical disorder. **3** *as adj* denoting a food or drink, often with a brand name, that contains less sugar than the standard version ☐ *diet lemonade.* Compare LOW-CAL. ▷ *verb* (***dieted, dieting***) *intr* to restrict the quantity or type of food that one eats, especially in order to lose weight. ● **dieter** *noun.* ◎ 13c: from French *diete*, from Greek *diaita* way of life.

diet² /daɪət/ ▷ *noun* **1** the legislative assembly of certain countries, eg Japan. **2** *historical* a conference held to discuss political or church affairs. ◎ 14c, originally meaning 'a day's journey': from Latin *dieta* public assembly, from Greek *diaita* way of life.

dietary /ˈdaɪətərɪ/ ▷ *adj* belonging to or concerning a DIET¹. ◎ 17c.

dietary fibre ▷ *noun* indigestible plant material, found in unrefined carbohydrate foods such as wholemeal bread and cereals, and in fruit and vegetables. Also called **roughage**.

dietetic /daɪəˈtɛtɪk/ ▷ *adj* **1** concerning or belonging to DIET¹. **2** for use in a special medical diet. ● **dietetically** *adverb.* ◎ 16c.

dietetics /daɪəˈtɛtɪks/ ▷ *singular noun* the scientific study of DIET¹ and its relation to health.

diethyl /daɪˈɛθɪl/ ▷ *adj, chem* having two ethyl groups. ◎ 19c.

diethyl ether see ETHER 2

dietician or **dietitian** /daɪəˈtɪʃən/ ▷ *noun* someone who is trained in dietetics.

diet sheet ▷ *noun* a list of permitted foods, recommended amounts, etc, for a person on a diet.

diff. ▷ *abbreviation* **1** difference. **2** different.

differ /ˈdɪfə(r)/ ▷ *verb* (***differed, differing***) *intr* **1** said of two or more people or things: to be different or unlike each other in some way. **2** (*often* **differ with someone**) to disagree. ● **agree to differ** see under AGREE. ◎ 14c: from French *differer*.

■ **differ from something** to be different from it or unlike it.

difference /ˈdɪfərəns/ ▷ *noun* **1** something that makes one thing or person unlike another. **2** the state of being unlike. **3** a change from an earlier state, etc. **4** the amount by which one quantity or number is greater or less than another. **5** a quarrel or disagreement. ● **make a** or **no**, *etc* **difference** to have some or no, etc effect on a situation. ● **with a difference** with something special; in a special way. ◎ 14c: from Latin *differentia*.

difference of opinion ▷ *noun* a disagreement.

different /ˈdɪfərənt/ ▷ *adj* **1** (*usually* **different from** or **to something** or **someone**) not the same; unlike. **2** separate; distinct; various. **3** *colloq* unusual. ● **differently** *adverb.* ◎ 15c.

different from, to, or than

● In current British English, **different** is followed more or less equally by 'from' or 'to' ☐ *He was, in fact, totally different from Keith* ☐ *James looked very different from the last time she had seen him* ☐ *This is very different to the ideal situation* ☐ *The next day was Christmas Eve, but it was no different to any other day except that the shop was very, very busy.*

● Note that the verb **differ** is never followed by 'to'.

● In American English, but much less in British English, **different** is commonly followed by 'than', especially when a clause follows ☐ AmE *It was all very different than they had imagined* ☐ BrE *It was all very different from / to what they had imagined.*

☆ RECOMMENDATION: use **different from** or **different to**; avoid **different than**, which is common in American English.

differentia /dɪfəˈrɛnʃɪə/ ▷ *noun* (***differentiae*** /-ʃiːː/) *logic* **1** that property which distinguishes one SPECIES from others. **2** a distinguishing feature. ◎ 19c.

differential /dɪfəˈrɛnʃəl/ ▷ *adj* **1** constituting, showing, relating to or based on a difference. **2** *math* an infinitesimal change in the value of one or more variables as a result of a similarly small change in another variable or variables. ▷ *noun* **1** a difference in the rate of pay between one category of worker and another in the same industry or company. Also called **wage differential**. **2** a DIFFERENTIAL GEAR. ● **differentially** *adverb.* ◎ 17c: from Latin *differentialis*.

differential calculus ▷ *noun, math* a procedure for calculating the rate of change of one variable quantity produced by changes in another variable, employing DIFFERENTIATION to determine rates of change, gradients of curves, maximum and minimum values, etc.

differential coefficient ▷ *noun, math* the ratio of the rate of change of a function to that of its independent variable.

differential equation ▷ *noun, math* an equation involving total or partial differential coefficients.

differential gear ▷ *noun* an arrangement of gears that allows the wheels on either side of a vehicle to rotate at different speeds, eg the outer wheels rotating more rapidly when the vehicle is being driven round a corner.

differential motion ▷ *noun* a mechanical movement in which the velocity of a driven part is equal to the difference of the velocities of two parts connected to it.

differentiate /dɪfəˈrɛnʃɪeɪt/ ▷ *verb* (***differentiated, differentiating***) **1** *tr & intr* (*usually* **differentiate between things**, or **one thing from another**) to establish a difference between them; to be able to distinguish one from another. **2** to constitute a difference between things, or a difference in (one thing as against another) ☐ *The shape of its mouth differentiates a crocodile from an alligator.* **3** to become different. **4** *math* to use the process of differentiation to calculate the changes in one variable quantity produced by changes in a related variable, ie to find the DERIVATIVE of a FUNCTION (*noun* 4). **5** *biol* said of an unspecialized cell or tissue: to become increasingly specialized in structure and function, eg during the development of a muscle fibre or a red blood cell. ◎ 19c: from Latin *differentiare*.

■ **differentiate between people** to treat one person, etc differently from another.

differentiation ▷ *noun* **1** the process of differentiating. **2** *math* a method used in CALCULUS to calculate the rate of change of one variable quantity produced by changes in a related variable, by finding the DERIVATIVE of a FUNCTION (*noun* 4). Compare INTEGRATION. **3** *biol* the process whereby unspecialized precursor cells or tissues develop into cells or tissues that have a highly specialized structure and function, eg the development of embryonic tissue into muscle cells, neurones, etc. **4** a change by which what is generalized or homogeneous becomes specialized or heterogeneous.

differentiator ▷ *noun* a person or thing that differentiates.

differently abled ▷ *adj, euphemistic* disabled; handicapped.

difficult /'dɪfɪkəlt/ ▷ *adj* **1** requiring great skill, intelligence or effort. **2** said of a person: not easy to please; awkward; unco-operative. **3** said of a problem, situation, etc: potentially embarrassing; hard to resolve or get out of. ⌚ 14c: from Latin *difficultas* difficulty.

difficulty /'dɪfɪkəltɪ/ ▷ *noun* (***difficulties***) **1** the state or quality of being difficult. **2** a difficult thing to do or understand. **3** a problem, obstacle or objection. **4** (*usually* **difficulties**) trouble or embarrassment, especially financial trouble.

diffident /'dɪfɪdənt/ ▷ *adj* lacking in confidence; too modest or shy. • **diffidence** *noun*. • **diffidently** *adverb*. ⌚ 15c: from Latin *diffidere* to distrust.

diffract /dɪ'frakt/ ▷ *verb* (***diffracted, diffracting***) *physics* to cause DIFFRACTION in (light, etc). ⌚ 19c: from Latin *diffringere, diffractum* to shatter.

diffraction /dɪ'frakʃən/ ▷ *noun, physics* the spreading out of waves (eg light or sound waves) as they emerge from a small opening or slit. ⌚ 19c.

diffraction grating ▷ *noun, physics* a device that contains many hundreds of slits per centimetre, used to divide a light beam into its component colours, the pattern produced being known as a SPECTRUM.

diffractive /dɪ'fraktɪv/ ▷ *adj* causing diffraction.

diffuse ▷ *verb* /dɪ'fju:z/ (***diffused, diffusing***) *tr & intr* to spread or send out in all directions. ▷ *adj* /dɪ'fju:s/ **1** widely spread; not concentrated. **2** said of a style of writing or speaking: using too many words; not concise. • **diffused** *adj* widely spread; dispersed. • **diffusely** *adverb*. • **diffuseness** *noun*. • **diffusibility** *noun*. • **diffusible** *adj*. • **diffusive** *adj* characterized by diffusion. • **diffusively** *adverb*. • **diffusiveness** or **diffusivity** *noun*. ⌚ 15c: from Latin *diffundere, diffusum* to pour in various directions.

diffused lighting ▷ *noun* lighting that is evenly distributed and so produces no glare.

diffuser /dɪ'fju:zə(r)/ ▷ *noun* **1** someone or something that diffuses. **2** an attachment for a light fitting that prevents glare. **3** a duct that as it widens out reduces the speed of an airflow or fluid. **4** an attachment for a hairdrier, which spreads the heat more evenly over the hair, giving it extra body.

diffusion /dɪ'fju:ʒən/ ▷ *noun* **1** the act of diffusing or state of being diffused. **2** *physics* the process whereby a fluid, either a liquid or gas, gradually and spontaneously disperses from a region of high concentration to one of low concentration, as a result of the random movements of its constituent atoms, molecules or ions. **3** *anthropol* the spread of cultural elements from one community, region, etc, to another.

dig ▷ *verb* (***dug, digging***) **1** *tr & intr* to turn up or move (earth, etc) especially with a spade. **2** to make (a hole, etc) by digging. **3** *tr & intr* to poke. **4** *old slang* to appreciate. **5** *tr & intr, old slang* to understand. ▷ *noun* **1** a remark intended to irritate, criticize or make fun of someone. **2** a place where archaeologists are digging, eg to uncover ancient ruins. **3** a poke. **4** an act of digging. • **dig a pit for someone** to lay a trap for them. • **dig in one's heels** or **dig one's heels in** to refuse to change one's mind. • **dig one's own grave** to be the cause of one's own failure or downfall. ⌚ 13c.

▪ **dig in 1** *colloq* to start to eat. **2** to work hard.

▪ **dig oneself in** to make a protected place for oneself; to establish oneself.

▪ **dig something in** to mix it into the soil, etc by digging.

▪ **dig into something 1** *colloq* to start eating (a meal, etc). **2** to examine or search through it for information.

▪ **dig something** or **someone out 1** to get them out by digging. **2** *colloq* to find them by extensive searching.

▪ **dig something up 1** to remove it from the ground by digging. **2** to find or reveal something buried or hidden by digging. **3** *colloq* to search for and find (information, etc).

digest[1] /dɪ'dʒɛst, daɪ-/ ▷ *verb* (***digested, digesting***) **1** to break down (food) in the stomach, intestine, etc into a form which the body can use. **2** said of food: to be broken down in this way. Compare INGEST. **3** to hear and consider the meaning and implications of (information). **4** *tr & intr, chem* to soften or disintegrate in heat and moisture. ⌚ 14c: from Latin *digerere, digestum* to dissolve.

digest[2] /'daɪdʒɛst/ ▷ *noun* **1** a collection of summaries or shortened versions of news stories or current literature, etc, usually regularly published. **2** a summary or shortened version. **3** a systematically arranged collection of laws. ⌚ 14c name given to a collection of Roman Laws: from Latin *digerere, digestum* to arrange.

digester /dɪ'dʒɛstə(r), daɪ-/ ▷ *noun* a closed vessel in which strong extracts are produced from animal and vegetable substances by means of heat and pressure. ⌚ 15c.

digestible /dɪ'dʒɛstɪbəl, daɪ-/ ▷ *adj* able to be digested. • **digestibility** *noun*.

digestion /dɪ'dʒɛstʃən, daɪ-/ ▷ *noun* **1** the process whereby complex substances in food are broken down into simpler soluble compounds by enzymes, usually in the ALIMENTARY CANAL. **2** the process of absorbing information, etc. **3** *chem* exposing to slow heat, etc. ⌚ 14c.

digestive /dɪ'dʒɛstɪv, daɪ-/ ▷ *adj* concerned with or for digestion. ▷ *noun* a type of plain slightly sweetened biscuit made from wholemeal flour. Also (*Brit*) called **digestive biscuit**.

digestive tract ▷ *noun* the ALIMENTARY CANAL.

diggable /'dɪgəbəl/ ▷ *adj* able to be dug.

digger /'dɪgə(r)/ ▷ *noun* **1** a machine used for digging and excavating. **2** someone who digs, especially a gold-miner. **3 a** *colloq* an Australian or New Zealander, especially a soldier; **b** *Austral & NZ colloq* used as a form of address.

digger-wasp ▷ *noun* a name given to various kinds of burrowing wasp.

digging *present participle of* DIG

diggings /'dɪgɪŋz/ ▷ *plural noun* **1** a place where people dig, especially for gold or precious stones. **2** *Brit old colloq* lodgings. See also DIGS.

digging stick ▷ *noun* a primitive tool for digging.

digit /'dɪdʒɪt/ ▷ *noun* **1** any of the ten figures 0 to 9. **2** *technical* a finger or toe. ⌚ 15c: from Latin *digitus* finger or toe.

digital /'dɪdʒɪtəl/ ▷ *adj* **1** showing numerical information in the form of a set of DIGITs, rather than by means of a pointer on a dial, eg as on a digital watch. **2** denoting a process or a device that operates by processing information that is supplied and stored in the form of a series of binary digits □ *digital recording* □ *digital computer*. **3** *electronics* denoting an electronic circuit that responds to and produces signals which at any given time are in one of two possible states. **4** belonging to or involving digits in any way. Compare ANALOGUE. ⌚ 15c in sense 4, but rare before 20c.

digital/analog converter ▷ *noun, computing* a device that converts digital signals into ANALOGUE signals for use by an analogue computer.

digital audio tape ▷ *noun, electronics* (abbreviation **DAT**, **Dat** or **dat**) **1** a magnetic audio tape on which sound has been recorded after it has been converted into a binary code. **2** this form of recorded sound, affording reproduction that is so like the original that the human ear cannot distinguish the difference.

digital compact cassette ▷ *noun* (abbreviation **DCC**) a DIGITAL AUDIO TAPE in standard cassette format, played via a fixed-head tape recorder.

digital compact disc ▷ *noun* a COMPACT DISC.

digitalin /dɪdʒɪ'teɪlɪn/ ▷ *noun* a GLUCOSIDE or mixture of glucosides obtained from DIGITALIS leaves, used as a heart stimulant. ◷ 19c.

digitalis /dɪdʒɪ'teɪlɪs/ ▷ *noun* **1** *bot* any plant of the genus that includes the foxglove. **2** *medicine* a collective term for drugs acting on the heart, originally obtained from the dried leaves of the foxglove, that stimulate the heart muscle by increasing contractions. They are used to treat heart failure and other cardiac disorders. ◷ 17c, originally as the Latin genus name of the foxglove.

digitate /'dɪdʒɪteɪt/ and **digitated** /-teɪtɪd/ ▷ *adj, bot* said of leaves: consisting of several finger-like sections.

digitigrade /'dɪdʒɪtɪgreɪd/ *zool* ▷ *adj* walking on the toes. ▷ *noun* a digitigrade animal, eg a cat, a horse. Compare PLANTIGRADE. ◷ 19c: from Latin *digitus* DIGIT + *gradus* walking.

digitize or **digitise** /'dɪdʒɪtaɪz/ ▷ *verb* (***digitized***, ***digitizing***) to convert (data) into BINARY form. • **digitization** *noun*. • **digitizer** *noun*. ◷ 1950s in modern sense; originally 18c meaning 'to finger' or 'to do with the fingers'.

digitizing board ▷ *noun* a device consisting of a flat surface on which diagrams, etc may be drawn with a special stylus, the co-ordinates of the position of the stylus at any given point on the diagram being digitized for storage, etc.

dignify /'dɪgnɪfaɪ/ ▷ *verb* (***dignifies***, ***dignified***, ***dignifying***) **1** to make something impressive or dignified. **2** to make something seem more important or impressive than it is. • **dignified** *adj* **1** showing or consistent with dignity. **2** stately; noble; serious. ◷ 15c: from Latin *dignus* worthy + *facere* to make.

dignitary /'dɪgnɪtərɪ/ ▷ *noun* (***dignitaries***) someone of high rank or position, especially in public life or the Church. ◷ 17c.

dignity /'dɪgnɪtɪ/ ▷ *noun* **1** stateliness, seriousness and formality of manner and appearance. **2** goodness and nobility of character. **3** calmness and self-control. **4** high rank or position. • **beneath one's dignity 1** not worthy of one's attention or time, etc. **2** degrading. • **stand on one's dignity** to demand to be treated with proper respect. ◷ 13c: from Latin *dignitas*, from *dignus* worthy.

digraph /'daɪgrɑːf/ ▷ *noun* a pair of letters that represent a single sound, eg the *ph* of *digraph*. ◷ 18c: from Greek *di-* twice + *graphe* mark or character.

digress /daɪ'grɛs/ ▷ *verb* (***digressed***, ***digressing***) *intr* to wander from the point, or from the main subject in speaking or writing. • **digression** *noun*. • **digressional** or **digressive** *adj*. • **digressively** *adverb*. ◷ 16c: from Latin *digredi*, *digressus* to move away.

digs /dɪgz/ ▷ *plural noun, Brit colloq* lodgings. See also DIGGINGS.

dihedral /daɪ'hiːdrəl/ *geom* ▷ *adj* formed or bounded by two planes. ▷ *noun* **1** the figure made by two intersecting planes. **2** the angle made by the wing of an aeroplane with the horizontal axis. Also called **dihedral angle** or **dihedron**. ◷ 18c: from Greek *di-* twice + *hedra* seat.

dik-dik /'dɪkdɪk/ ▷ *noun* a name for several very small E African antelopes. ◷ 19c: apparently the Ethiopian name.

dike see DYKE[1], DYKE[2]

diktat /'dɪktat/ ▷ *noun* **1** a forceful, sometimes unreasonable, order which must be obeyed. **2** a harsh settlement forced on the defeated or powerless. ◷ 1930s: German, meaning 'something dictated'.

dilapidated /dɪ'lapɪdeɪtɪd/ ▷ *adj* said of furniture, buildings, etc: falling to pieces because of neglect or age; in great need of repair. ◷ 16c: from Latin *dilapidare*, *dilapidatum* to demolish.

dilapidation /dɪlapɪ'deɪʃən/ ▷ *noun* a state or the process of disrepair or ruin.

dilatation /daɪlə'teɪʃən, dɪ-/ or **dilation** /daɪ'leɪʃən/ ▷ *noun* dilating; becoming or making larger.

dilatation and curettage ▷ *noun* (abbreviation **D and C**) *medicine* a minor gynaecological operation, usually performed to remove small tumours or to obtain specimens of tissue in order to diagnose various disorders, when the CERVIX (sense 1) is dilated and a CURETTE is passed through the dilated cervix into the uterus, the lining of which is gently scraped.

dilate /daɪ'leɪt, dɪ-/ ▷ *verb* (***dilated***, ***dilating***) **1** *tr & intr* said especially of an opening in the body, the pupil of the eye, etc: to make or become larger, wider or further open. **2** *intr* (*chiefly* **dilate on something**) *formal* to speak or write at great length about it. ◷ 14c: from Latin *dilatare*, *dilatatum* to spread out.

dilatory /'dɪlətərɪ/ ▷ *adj* slow in doing things; inclined to or causing delay. • **dilatorily** *adverb*. • **dilatoriness** *noun*. ◷ 15c: from Latin *dilatorius*.

dildo or **dildoe** /'dɪldoʊ/ ▷ *noun* (***dildos*** or ***dildoes***) an object shaped like an erect penis, used for sexual pleasure. ◷ 17c.

dilemma /dɪ'lɛmə, daɪ-/ ▷ *noun* (***dilemmas***) **1** a situation in which one must choose between two or more courses of action, both (or all) equally undesirable. **2** *colloq* a problem or difficult situation. ◷ 16c, originally the name given to a particular type of argument: from Greek *di-* twice + *lemma* assumption.

dilettante /dɪlə'tantɪ/ ▷ *noun* (***dilettantes*** or ***dilettanti*** /-tiː/) *often derog* someone who has an interest in a subject, especially art, literature or science, but does not study it very seriously or in depth. • **dilettantish** *adj*. • **dilettantism** *noun*. ◷ 18c: Italian, from *dilettare* to delight.

diligence /'dɪlɪdʒəns/ ▷ *noun* careful and hard-working effort.

diligent /'dɪlɪdʒənt/ ▷ *adj* **1** hard-working and careful. **2** showing or done with care and serious effort. • **diligently** *adverb*. ◷ 14c: French, from Latin *diligens* careful.

dill[1] ▷ *noun* a European herb, the fruit of which is used in flavouring, especially pickles, and to relieve wind. ◷ Anglo-Saxon *dile*.

dill[2] ▷ *noun, Austral & NZ colloq* a fool. ◷ 20c: possibly from DILLY[2].

dilly[1] ▷ *noun* (***dillies***) *colloq, especially N Amer* an excellent or very pleasing person or thing. ◷ 20c.

dilly[2] ▷ *adj* foolish; silly. ◷ 19c: probably from *daft* + *silly*.

dilly-dally /dɪlɪ'dalɪ, 'dɪlɪdalɪ/ ▷ *verb* (***dilly-dallies***, ***dilly-dallied***, ***dilly-dallying***) *intr, colloq* **1** to be slow or waste time. **2** to be unable to make up one's mind. ◷ 18c: from DALLY.

diluent /'dɪljʊənt/ ▷ *noun, chem* any solvent that is used to dilute a solution. ◷ 18c.

dilute /daɪ'luːt, -'ljuːt, dɪ-/ ▷ *verb* (***diluted***, ***diluting***) **1** to decrease the concentration of a SOLUTE in a solution by adding more SOLVENT, especially water. **2** to reduce the strength, influence or effect of something. ▷ *adj, chem* said of a solution: containing a relatively small amount of

SOLUTE compared to the amount of SOLVENT present. • **dilutable** *adj*. ◷ 16c: from Latin *diluere*, *dilutum* to wash away.

dilution ▻ *noun* the process of making a liquid thinner or weaker.

diluvial /daɪ'ljuːvɪəl, -'luːvɪəl, dɪ-/ and **diluvian** /-vɪən/ ▻ *adj* **1** concerning or pertaining to a flood, especially the Flood mentioned in the Book of Genesis in the Bible. **2** caused by a flood. ◷ 17c: from Latin *diluvium* flood.

dim ▻ *adj* **1** not bright or distinct. **2** lacking enough light to see clearly. **3** faint; not clearly remembered □ *a dim memory*. **4** *colloq* not very intelligent. **5** said of eyes: not able to see well. **6** *colloq* not good; not hopeful □ *dim prospects*. ▻ *verb* (***dimmed***, ***dimming***) *tr & intr* to make or become dim. • **dimly** *adverb*. • **take a dim view of something** *colloq* to disapprove of it. ◷ Anglo-Saxon *dimm*.

■ **dim something out** to reduce the lighting of something gradually.

dime /daɪm/ ▻ *noun* a coin of the US and Canada worth ten cents or one tenth of a dollar. ◷ 18c in this sense; 14c in obsolete or historical sense 'a tenth part' or 'tithe': from Latin *decima* tenth.

dime novel ▻ *noun*, *N Amer* a cheap popular novel.

dimension /daɪ'mɛnʃən, dɪ-/ ▻ *noun* **1** a measurement of length, width or height. **2** any directly measurable physical quantity, eg mass, length, time, charge. **3** *geom* the number of parameters that are needed to specify the size of a geometrical figure, and the location of particular points on it, eg a triangle has two dimensions, whereas a pyramid has three dimensions. **4** (*often* **dimensions**) size or extent. **5** a particular aspect of a problem, situation, etc □ *the religious dimension of the problem*. • **dimensional** *adj* **1** concerning dimension. **2** *in compounds* having a certain number of dimensions □ *two-dimensional*. ◷ 14c: from Latin *dimensio* measuring.

dimer /'daɪmə(r)/ ▻ *noun*, *chem* a chemical compound composed of two MONOMERS, which may combine during either an ADDITION REACTION or a CONDENSATION REACTION. • **dimeric** /daɪ'mɛrɪk/ *adj*. ◷ 20c.

dime store ▻ *noun*, *N Amer* a shop selling cheap goods, originally for not more than a dime.

dimin. ▻ *abbreviation* diminutive.

diminish /dɪ'mɪnɪʃ/ ▻ *verb* (***diminishes***, ***diminished***, ***diminishing***) **1** *tr & intr* to become or make something less or smaller. **2** to make someone or something seem less important, valuable or satisfactory. • **diminishable** *adj*. • **diminished** *adj* **1** having become less, smaller, less important, etc. **2** *music* reduced by a semitone. ◷ 15c: ultimately from Latin *deminuere* to make less.

diminished responsibility ▻ *noun*, *law* limitation in law of criminal responsibility on the grounds of mental weakness or abnormality, not merely of actual insanity.

diminishing returns and **law of diminishing returns** ▻ *noun*, *econ* a law or prediction that there is a point beyond which any additional input in the form of capital and labour, or additional taxation, results in progressively smaller output per unit of capital or labour, or smaller tax yields.

diminuendo /dɪmɪnjʊ'ɛndoʊ/ *music* ▻ *adj*, *adverb* with gradually lessening sound. ▻ *noun* (***diminuendos***) **1** a gradual lessening of sound. **2** a musical passage with gradually lessening sound. ▻ *verb* (***diminuendoed***, ***diminuendoing***) *intr* to lessen gradually in loudness. Compare CRESCENDO. ◷ 18c: Italian, from Latin *deminuere* to make less.

diminution /dɪmɪ'njuːʃən/ ▻ *noun* a lessening or decrease. ◷ 14c: from Latin *diminutio*.

diminutive /dɪm'ɪnjʊtɪv/ ▻ *adj* very small. ▻ *noun*, *grammar* **1** an ending added to a word to indicate smallness, eg *-let* in *booklet*. Also called **diminutive suffix**. **2** a word formed in this way. • **diminutively** *adverb*. • **diminutiveness** *noun*. ◷ 16c as *adj*; 14c as *noun*: from Latin *deminuere* to make less.

dimity /'dɪmɪtɪ/ ▻ *noun* a stout cotton fabric, woven with raised stripes or other pattern. ◷ 15c: from Greek *dimitos*, from *di-* twice + *mitos* a thread.

dimmed *past tense, past participle of* DIM

dimmer and **dimmer switch** ▻ *noun* a control used to modify the brightness of a light.

dimming *present participle of* DIM

dimmish ▻ *adj* somewhat dim.

dimness ▻ *noun* **1** being dim or faint. **2** lack of light or brightness.

dimorphism /daɪ'mɔːfɪzəm/ ▻ *noun* **1** *biol* the occurrence of two distinct forms within a species of living organism, eg the male and female in many animals. **2** *chem* the crystallization of a chemical element or compound into two different crystalline forms that have the same chemical composition. • **dimorphic** or **dimorphous** *adj*. ◷ 19c: from Greek *di-* twice + *morphe* form.

dim-out ▻ *noun* a gradual reduction in the brightness of or use of lights, especially the gradual reduction of light in the auditorium of a theatre, etc.

dimple /'dɪmpəl/ ▻ *noun* a small hollow, especially in the skin of the cheeks, chin or, especially in babies, at the knees and elbows. ▻ *verb* (***dimpled***, ***dimpling***) to show or form into dimples. • **dimpled** *adj* having dimples or slight hollows on the surface. ◷ 15c.

dim sum /dɪm 'sʌm/ ▻ *noun* a selection of Chinese foods, usually including steamed dumplings with various fillings, often served as an appetizer. ◷ 20c: Chinese.

dimwit ▻ *noun*, *colloq* a stupid person. • **dim-witted** *adj* stupid. ◷ 1920s.

DIN /dɪn/ ▻ *abbreviation*: *Deutsche Industrie-Norm* (German), German Industry Standard, a set of standards for electrical connections, paper sizes, film speed etc. ◷ 20c.

din ▻ *noun* a loud, continuous and unpleasant noise. ▻ *verb* (***dinned***, ***dinning***) (*usually* **din something into someone**) to repeat something forcefully to someone over and over again so that it will be remembered. ◷ Anglo-Saxon *dyne*.

dinar /'diːnɑː(r)/ ▻ *noun* the standard unit of currency in Bosnia-Herzegovina, Macedonia (usually in the form **denar**), Yugoslavia and several Arab countries. ◷ 19c; originally 17c, meaning any of various gold coins from the East: Arabic and Persian.

dine /daɪn/ ▻ *verb* (***dined***, ***dining***) *formal* **1** *intr* to eat dinner. **2** to give dinner to someone □ *wining and dining his girlfriend*. ◷ 13c: from French *disner*, from Latin *dis-* DIS- + *jejunare* to fast.

■ **dine off**, **on** or **upon something** to eat it for one's dinner.

■ **dine out** to have dinner somewhere other than one's own house, eg in a restaurant.

■ **dine out on something** to repeatedly tell a funny story or relate a humorous incident, in order to be amusing.

diner ▻ *noun* **1** someone who dines. **2** a restaurant car on a train. **3** *N Amer* a small cheap restaurant. ◷ 19c.

diner-out ▻ *noun* someone who is often invited and accepts invitations to dinner parties.

dinette /daɪ'nɛt/ ▻ *noun* an alcove or other small area of a room, etc, set apart for meals. ◷ 1920s.

DIng ▻ *abbreviation*: *Doctor Ingeniariae* (Latin), Doctor of Engineering.

ding ▻ *noun* a ringing sound. ▻ *verb* (***dinged, dinging***) to make a ding. ◷ 13c, originally meaning 'to knock or strike': imitating the sound.

dingbat /'dɪŋbat/ ▻ *noun, N Amer slang except sense 5* **1** something whose name one has forgotten or wishes to avoid using; a thingummy. **2** a foolish or eccentric person. **3** a tramp. **4** money. **5** *Austral & NZ colloq* (**the dingbats**) DELIRIUM TREMENS. • **dingbats** *adj, Austral & NZ colloq* daft; crazy. ◷ 19c.

ding-dong ▻ *noun* **1** the sound of bells ringing. **2** *colloq* a heated argument or fight. ▻ *adj, colloq* said of a fight, argument, etc: fierce or heated. ◷ 16c.

dinges /'dɪŋəs/ ▻ *noun, S Afr colloq* someone or something whose name one has forgotten or wishes to avoid using; thingummy. ◷ 19c: from Dutch *ding* thing.

dinghy /'dɪŋgɪ, 'dɪŋɪ/ ▻ *noun* (***dinghies***) **1** a small open boat propelled by oars, sails or an outboard motor. **2** a small collapsible rubber boat, especially one kept for use in emergencies. ◷ 19c: from Hindi *dingi* small boat.

dingle /'dɪŋgəl/ ▻ *noun* a deep wooded hollow; a dell. ◷ 17c in this sense; 13c, meaning 'abyss'.

dingo /'dɪŋgoʊ/ ▻ *noun* (***dingoes***) **1** a species of wild dog found in Australia. **2** *Austral slang* a cheat or coward. ◷ 18c: from Dharuk (Australian Aboriginal language) *dinggu*.

dingy /'dɪndʒɪ/ ▻ *adj* (***dingier, dingiest***) **1** faded and dirty-looking □ *dingy clothes.* **2** dark and rather dirty □ *a dingy room.* • **dinginess** *noun.* ◷ 18c.

dining *present participle of* DINE

dining-car see RESTAURANT CAR

dining-room ▻ *noun* a room in a house, hotel, etc, used for eating in, especially for formal meals.

dinitrogen oxide /daɪ'naɪtroʊdʒən —/ ▻ *noun, chem* NITROUS OXIDE.

dinitrogen tetroxide /daɪ'naɪtroʊdʒən tɛ'trɒksaɪd/ ▻ *noun, chem* (formula N_2O_4) a colourless or pale-yellow liquid that is used as an oxidant in rocket fuel.

dinkum /'dɪŋkəm/ *Austral & NZ colloq* ▻ *adj* real; genuine; honest. Also *as adverb.* ◷ 19c: from English dialect *dinkum* fair share of work.

Dinky /'dɪŋkɪ/ ▻ *noun* (***Dinkies***) *trademark* a proprietary name for a range of small toy model vehicles etc, especially cars. Also *as adj* □ *Dinky toys.* ◷ 1950.

dinky /'dɪŋkɪ/ ▻ *adj* (***dinkier, dinkiest***) **1** *colloq* neat; dainty. **2** *N Amer colloq* trivial; insignificant. ◷ 18c as *dinkie*: from Scots *dink* neat.

dinned *past tense, past participle of* DIN

dinner /'dɪnə(r)/ ▻ *noun* **1** the main meal of the day, eaten in the middle of the day or in the evening. **2** a formal meal, especially held in the evening, often arranged to honour a person or in celebration of an event. ◷ 13c: see DINE.

dinner-dance ▻ *noun* a social occasion consisting of a formal dinner followed by dancing. ◷ Early 20c.

dinner-jacket ▻ *noun* a jacket, usually black, worn by men at formal social gatherings, especially in the evening. Compare TUXEDO. ◷ Late 19c.

dinner lady ▻ *noun* a woman who cooks and/or serves meals in a school canteen. ◷ 1960s.

dinner party ▻ *noun* an evening party at which dinner is served. ◷ 19c.

dinner service and **dinner set** ▻ *noun* a complete set of plates and dishes for serving dinner to several people. ◷ 19c.

dinning *present participle of* DIN

dinosaur /'daɪnəsɔː(r)/ ▻ *noun* **1** any member of a large group of prehistoric reptiles that dominated life on land during the Mesozoic era, becoming extinct at the end of the Cretaceous period. **2** *often jocular* a chance survivor of a type characteristic of past times. • **dinosaurian** or **dinosauric** *adj.* ◷ 19c: from Greek *deinos* terrible + *sauros* lizard.

dint ▻ *noun* a hollow made by a blow; a dent. • **by dint of something** by means of it. ◷ Anglo-Saxon *dynt* blow.

diocese /'daɪəsɪs, -siːs/ ▻ *noun* the district over which a bishop has authority. • **diocesan** /daɪ'ɒsɪzən, -sən/ *adj.* ◷ 14c: from Greek *dioikesis* housekeeping.

diode /'daɪoʊd/ ▻ *noun, electronics* an electronic device containing two ELECTRODES, an ANODE and a CATHODE, that allows current to flow in one direction only. ◷ 19c: from Greek *di-* twice + *hodos* way.

dioecious /daɪ'iːʃəs/ ▻ *adj* **1** *bot* said of a plant: having male and female flowers on different plants. **2** *biol* with the male and female sexual organs in separate individuals or creatures. Compare MONOECIOUS. ◷ 19c: from Greek *di-* twice + *oikos* house.

dioptre or (*especially N Amer*) **diopter** /daɪ'ɒptə(r)/ *noun, optics* (abbreviation **dpt**) a unit that is used to express the power of a lens, defined as one divided by the focal length of the lens, when the focal length is measured in metres, having a positive value for a CONVERGING LENS and a negative value for a DIVERGING LENS. ◷ 19c in this sense; 16c as the name of an optical instrument: from Greek *dioptron* spyglass.

dioptrics /daɪ'ɒptrɪks/ ▻ *singular noun* the branch of OPTICS that deals with refraction. ◷ 20c.

dioxide /daɪ'ɒksaɪd/ ▻ *noun, chem* a compound formed by combining two atoms of oxygen with one atom of another element. ◷ 19c: from Greek *di-* twice + OXIDE.

dioxin /daɪ'ɒksɪn/ ▻ *noun* an AROMATIC (*adj* 2), halogenated (see HALOGENATE) hydrocarbon that is highly toxic and produced as a by-product in the manufacture of the herbicide 2,4,5-T, a tox DEFOLIANT (Agent Orange), and which has been associated with allergic skin reactions, cancer, birth defects and miscarriages. ◷ 1919.

dip ▻ *verb* (***dipped, dipping***) **1** to put something into a liquid for a short time. **2** *intr* to go briefly under the surface of a liquid. **3** *intr* to drop below a surface or level. **4** *tr & intr* to go, or push something, down briefly and then up again. **5** *intr* to slope downwards. **6** *tr & intr* to put (one's hand, etc) into a dish, container, etc and take out some of the contents. **7** to immerse (an animal) in a bath of disinfectant chemical that kills parasitic insects. **8** *Brit* to lower the beam of (a vehicle's headlights). ▻ *noun* **1** an act of dipping. **2** a downward slope or hollow (especially in a road). **3** a short swim or bathe. **4** a chemical liquid for dipping animals. **5** a type of thick sauce into which biscuits, raw vegetables, etc are dipped. ◷ Anglo-Saxon *dyppan*.

■ **dip in something** to take a share.

■ **dip into something** **1** to take or use part of it. **2** to look briefly at a book or study a subject in a casual manner.

Dip. ▻ *abbreviation* Diploma.

Dip Ed ▻ *abbreviation* Diploma in Education.

dipeptide /daɪ'pɛptaɪd/ ▻ *noun, chem* a peptide formed by the combination of two AMINO ACIDS. ◷ 20c.

diphenyl /daɪ'fiːnɪl/ ▻ *noun, chem* a hydrocarbon (formula $C_{12}H_{10}$) consisting of two PHENYL groups, used eg in dye manufacture and as a fungicide. ◷ 19c.

diphtheria /dɪp'θɪərɪə, dɪf-/ ▻ *noun, medicine* a highly contagious bacterial infection which affects the throat, causing difficulty in breathing and swallowing, and which can lead to heart failure. ◷ 19c: from French *diphthérie*, from Greek *diphthera* leather (from the leathery grey covering formed in the throat).

diphthong /'dɪpθɒŋ, 'dɪf-/ ▻ *noun* **1** two vowel sounds pronounced as one syllable, such as the sound represented by the *ou* in *sounds*. **2** a DIGRAPH. • **diphthongal** *adj*. • **diphthongally** *adverb*. ⓒ 15c: from Greek *di-* twice + *phthongos* sound.

diplodocus /dɪ'plɒdəkəs/ ▻ *noun* (***diplodocuses***) a gigantic herbivorous dinosaur that had a particularly long neck and tail. ⓒ 19c: from Greek *diplo-* twice + *dokos* bar or beam.

diploid /'dɪplɔɪd/ ▻ *adj, genetics* describing an organism, cell or nucleus in which there are two sets of chromosomes, one set being derived from each of the parents. ⓒ 19c: from Greek *diploos* double + *eidos* form.

diploma /dɪ'ploʊmə/ ▻ *noun* (***diplomas***) a document certifying that one has passed a certain examination or completed a course of study. ⓒ 17c: Latin, from Greek, meaning 'letter folded over'.

diplomacy /dɪ'ploʊməsɪ/ ▻ *noun* **1** the art or profession of making agreements, treaties, etc between countries, or of representing and looking after the affairs and interests of one's own country in a foreign country. **2** skill and tact in dealing with people. ⓒ 18c: from French *diplomatie*.

diplomat /'dɪpləmat/ ▻ *noun* **1** a government official or representative engaged in diplomacy. **2** a very tactful person. ⓒ 19c: from French *diplomate*, from Latin *diploma* official document.

diplomate /'dɪpləmeɪt/ ▻ *noun* someone who holds a DIPLOMA.

diplomatic /dɪplə'matɪk/ ▻ *adj* **1** concerning or involved in diplomacy. **2** tactful. • **diplomatically** *adverb*. ⓒ 18c.

diplomatic bag and (*US*) **diplomatic pouch** ▻ *noun* a bag or other container for official letters, packages, etc sent to and from an embassy, not subject to customs inspection. ⓒ 1950s.

diplomatic corps ▻ *noun* all the diplomats and embassy staff of all the embassies in the capital of a country. ⓒ 19c.

diplomatic immunity ▻ *noun* the privilege granted to members of the diplomatic corps by which they may not be taxed, arrested, etc by the country in which they are working. ⓒ Early 20c.

diplomatic relations ▻ *plural noun* formal relations between states marked by the presence of diplomats in each other's country.

diplomatize or **diplomatise** /dɪ'ploʊmətaɪz/ ▻ *verb* (***diplomatized, diplomatizing***) *intr* to practise diplomacy. • **diplomatist** *noun* a DIPLOMAT. ⓒ 19c: from DIPLOMAT.

dipole /'daɪpoʊl/ *physics* ▻ *noun* a separation of electric charge, in which two equal and opposite charges are separated from each other by a small distance. • **dipolar** *adj*. ⓒ Early 20c.

dipped *past tense, past participle of* DIP

dipper /'dɪpə(r)/ ▻ *noun* **1** something that dips, especially a type of ladle. **2** a small songbird which can swim under water and feeds on river-beds.

dipping *present participle of* DIP

dippy /'dɪpɪ/ ▻ *adj* (***dippier, dippiest***) *colloq* crazy; mad □ ***dippy about dogs***. ⓒ 20c.

dipsomania /dɪpsoʊ'meɪnɪə/ ▻ *noun, medicine* an extreme form of alcoholism, in which there is an insatiable craving for alcoholic drink. • **dipsomaniac** *noun*. Also called *colloq* **dipso** (***dipsos***). ⓒ 19c: from Greek *dipsa* thirst + *mania* madness.

dipstick ▻ *noun* **1** a stick used to measure the level of a liquid in a container, especially the oil in a car engine. **2** *slang* a term of abuse for a stupid person.

DipSW ▻ *abbreviation* Diploma in Social Work.

dipswitch ▻ *noun* a switch used to dip the headlights of a motor vehicle.

diptera /'dɪptərə/ ▻ *noun* any one of many two-winged insects or flies. • **dipteral** or **dipterous** *adj* two-winged. ⓒ 18c: from Greek *dipteros* two-winged.

diptych /'dɪptɪk/ ▻ *noun* a work of art, especially on a church altar, consisting of a pair of pictures painted on hinged wooden panels which can be folded together like a book. See also TRIPTYCH. ⓒ 19c: originally 17c, meaning 'something folded': from Greek *diptychos* folded together.

dir. ▻ *abbreviation* Director.

dire ▻ *adj* **1** dreadful; terrible. **2** extreme; very serious; very difficult. • **direful** *adj*. • **direfully** *adverb*. ⓒ 16c: from Latin *dirus*.

direct /dɪ'rɛkt, daɪə'rɛkt/ ▻ *adj* **1** straight; following the quickest and shortest path from beginning to end or to a destination. **2** said of a person's manner, etc: open, straightforward and honest; going straight to the point. **3** with no other factors involved □ ***the direct cause of the accident***. **4** not working or communicating through other people, organizations, etc □ ***a direct link with the chairman***. **5** exact; complete □ ***a direct opposite***. **6** forming or being part of an unbroken line of descent from parent to child to grandchild, etc □ ***a direct descendant of Sir Walter Raleigh***. ▻ *verb* (***directed, directing***) **1** to point, aim or turn something in a particular direction. **2** to show the way to someone. **3** *tr & intr* (*usually* **direct someone to do something** or **something to be done** or **that something be done**) to give orders or instructions. **4** to control or manage something; to be in charge of something. **5** *tr & intr* to plan and supervise the production of (a play or film). **6** *formal* to put a name and address on (a letter, etc). ▻ *adverb* directly; by the quickest or shortest path. ⓒ 14c, originally meaning 'to send a letter to someone': from Latin *directus*, from *dirigere* to direct or guide.

direct access ▻ *noun, computing* the ability to access data directly without having to scan any part of the storage file first.

direct action ▻ *noun* action taken in order to obtain some demand or concession from government, an employer, etc, eg strikes and civil disobedience, and the activities of terrorist organizations and other extremists.

direct current ▻ *noun* (abbreviation **DC**) electric current which flows in one direction. Compare ALTERNATING CURRENT.

direct debit ▻ *noun, finance* an order to one's bank which allows someone else to withdraw sums of money from one's account, especially in payment of bills. Compare STANDING ORDER.

direct drilling ▻ *noun, agric* the ploughing and sowing of a field in one operation.

directed energy weapon ▻ *noun, military* a weapon using advanced laser beam, particle beams, plasma beams or microwave beams, all of which travel at the speed of light and are theoretically capable of shooting down missiles in space.

direction /dɪ'rɛkʃən, daɪə-/ ▻ *noun* **1** the place or point towards which one is moving or facing. **2** the way in which someone or something is developing. **3** (*usually* **directions**) information, instructions or advice, eg on how to construct or operate a piece of equipment. **4** (**directions**) instructions about the way to go to reach a place. **5** management or supervision. **6** the act, style, etc of directing a play or film. ⓒ 16c in current senses; 15c in obsolete sense 'arrangement': from Latin *directio*.

directional ▻ *adj* relating to direction in space.

directional aerial ▻ *noun* an aerial that can receive or transmit radio waves in one direction only.

directional drilling ▻ *noun, oil industry* a method of drilling where the well is not drilled vertically, used especially in offshore sites where a number of wells may be drilled from a single platform.

direction finder ▷ *noun, engineering* a radio receiver that is used in navigation to determine the direction from which an incoming radio signal is coming, and thus to establish the location of its source.

directionless ▷ *adj* **1** not looking, moving, etc in any particular direction. **2** aimless.

directive /dɪ'rɛktɪv, daɪə-/ ▷ *noun* an official instruction issued by a higher authority, eg by the EC to the governments of member states. ▷ *adj* having the power or tendency to direct. ⓒ 17c as *noun*; 16c as *adj*: from Latin *directivus*.

directivity ▷ *noun* the property of being DIRECTIONAL.

direct labour ▷ *noun* labour employed directly, not through a contractor.

directly ▷ *adverb* **1** in a direct manner. **2** by a direct path. **3** at once; immediately. **4** very soon. **5** exactly □ ***directly opposite***. ⓒ 16c.

direct marketing and **direct selling** ▷ *noun, commerce* selling of products or services directly to the consumer without using a retail outlet.

directness ▷ *noun* a direct or straightforward manner, especially of speech or thought.

direct object ▷ *noun, grammar* the noun, phrase or pronoun which is directly affected by the action of a TRANSITIVE verb, as *the dog* in *the boy kicked the dog*. Compare INDIRECT OBJECT.

director /dɪ'rɛktə(r), daɪə-/ ▷ *noun* **1** any of the most senior managers of a business firm. **2** the person in charge of a college, organization, institution or special activity. **3** the person directing a play, film, etc. **4** *music, especially N Amer* a CONDUCTOR (sense 1). **5** part of a machine or instrument which guides the motion. • **directorial** /dɪrɛk'tɔːrɪəl, 'daɪə-/ *adj*. • **directorship** *noun*.

directorate ▷ *noun* **1** the directors of a business firm. **2** the position or office of director. ⓒ 19c.

director-general ▷ *noun* (***directors-general*** or ***director-generals***) the chief administrator of an organization, usually a non-commercial one.

director's chair ▷ *noun* a light folding chair with armrests, the seat and back made of canvas or similar material.

directory /dɪ'rɛktərɪ, daɪə-/ ▷ *noun* (***directories***) **1** a book with a (usually alphabetical) list of names and addresses of people or organizations. **2** *computing* a named grouping of files on a disk, usually with a common element, allowing a command to be applied to, or bypass, all the files it contains, etc. **3** a collection of rules or directions; a guide. ⓒ 15c: from Latin *directorium*.

directory enquiries ▷ *noun* a telephone service which supplies a customer with the relevant telephone number from the directory for any name and address specified to the operator.

directrix /dɪ'rɛktrɪks, daɪə-/ ▷ *noun* (***directrices*** /-trɪsiːz/) *geom* a straight line from which the distance to any point on a conic section is in a constant ratio to the distance between that point and a fixed point.

direct selling see DIRECT MARKETING

direct speech ▷ *noun, grammar* speech reported in the actual words of the speaker, eg *"Hello"* in the sentence *"Hello", said Henry*. Compare INDIRECT SPEECH. ⓒ 18c.

direct tax ▷ *noun* a tax paid directly to the government by a person or organization, eg INCOME TAX. Compare INDIRECT TAX.

direful and **direfully** see under DIRE

dirge /dɜːdʒ/ ▷ *noun* **1** a funeral song or hymn. **2** *sometimes derog* a slow sad song or piece of music. ⓒ 16c in sense 1: from an earlier use as the name for the OFFICE of the Dead, from Latin *dirige*, meaning 'lead', the first word sung in the Office.

dirham /'dɪəram, də'ram/ ▷ *noun* a unit of currency in various N African and Middle Eastern countries, with varying value, eg the standard unit in Morocco and the United Arab Emirates. ⓒ 18c: Arabic, from Greek *drachme*.

dirigible /'dɪrɪdʒɪbəl, dɪ'rɪdʒ-/ ▷ *noun, technical* an airship. ⓒ 19c; 16c as *adj* meaning 'able to be directed': from Latin *dirigere* to direct.

dirigisme /dɪrɪ'ʒiːzmə/ ▷ *noun* control by the State in economic and social spheres. • **dirigiste** /dɪrɪ'ʒiːst/ *adj*. ⓒ 1950s: French.

dirk /dɜːk/ ▷ *noun* a small knife or dagger. ⓒ 16c: Scots, originally as *durk*.

dirndl /'dɜːndəl/ ▷ *noun* **1** a traditional alpine peasant-woman's dress, with a tight-fitting bodice and a very full skirt. **2** a skirt that is tight at the waist and wide at the lower edge. Also called **dirndl skirt**. ⓒ 20c: German dialect, from *dirne* girl.

dirt /dɜːt/ *noun* **1** any unclean substance, eg mud or dust. **2** soil; earth. **3** a mixture of earth and cinders used to make road surfaces. **4** *euphemistic* excrement □ ***dog dirt***. **5** *colloq* obscene speech or writing. **6** *colloq* spiteful gossip; scandal □ ***journalists desperate to get some dirt on him***. • **eat dirt** to submit to humiliation. • **throw dirt** to harm someone's reputation. • **treat someone like dirt** to treat them with no consideration or respect. ⓒ 13c as *dritte*: from Norse *drit* excrement.

dirt-cheap ▷ *adj* ▷ *adverb, colloq* very cheap. ⓒ Early 19c.

dirt farmer ▷ *noun, US* someone who farms their own land, especially without hired labour. ⓒ 1920s.

dirt road ▷ *noun, Austral, NZ & US* an unmade road.

dirt track ▷ *noun* **1** a rough unsurfaced track. **2** a motorcycle racing course made of cinders, etc.

dirty /'dɜːtɪ/ ▷ *adj* (***dirtier, dirtiest***) **1** marked with dirt; soiled. **2** making one become soiled with dirt □ ***a dirty job***. **3** unfair; dishonest □ ***dirty tricks***. **4** obscene, lewd or pornographic □ ***dirty films***. **5** said of weather: rainy or stormy. **6** said of a colour: dull. **7** showing dislike or disapproval □ ***a dirty look***. **8** unsportingly rough or violent □ ***a dirty tackle***. ▷ *verb* (***dirties, dirtied, dirtying***) to make dirty. ▷ *adverb* **1** dirtily □ ***fight dirty***. **2** very □ ***dirty great stain***. • **dirtily** *adverb*. • **dirtiness** *noun*. • **do the dirty on someone** *colloq* to cheat or trick them.

dirty bomb ▷ *noun* a nuclear bomb that produces a large amount of radioactive contamination.

dirty dog ▷ *noun, colloq* a dishonest or contemptible person.

dirty linen ▷ *noun, colloq* personal problems or grievances. • **wash one's dirty linen in public** to make no secret of one's personal difficulties however embarrassing.

dirty money ▷ *noun* **1** money earned by immoral, corrupt or illegal means. **2** extra pay for handling dirty materials or working in dirty conditions.

dirty old man ▷ *noun, colloq* a man whose actions are considered lewd, with the implication that he is old enough to know better.

dirty trick ▷ *noun* a dishonest or despicable act.

dirty tricks campaign and **dirty tricks operation** ▷ *noun* a usually political intrigue intended to discredit someone, especially an opponent.

dirty word ▷ *noun* **1** an indecent or vulgar word. **2** *colloq* an unpopular concept or point of view □ ***Ambition is a dirty word***.

dirty work ▷ *noun* **1** work that makes a person or their clothing dirty. **2** *colloq* unpleasant or dishonourable duties or practices.

dis- ▷ *prefix, forming words denoting* **1** the opposite of the base word □ ***disagree*** □ ***dislike***. **2** reversal of the action of the base word □ *disassemble.* **3** removal or undoing □ *dismember* □ *disrobe.* **4** intensifying the base word □ *disgruntled.* Ⓞ Latin.

disability ▷ *noun* (*disabilities*) **1** the state of being disabled. **2** a condition, such as a physical or mental handicap, that results in partial or complete loss of a person's ability to perform social, occupational or other everyday activities. **3** *law* lack of legal power; disqualification. Ⓞ 16c.

disable ▷ *verb* **1** to deprive someone of a physical or mental ability. **2** to make (eg a machine) unable to work; to make something useless. • **disablement** *noun* **1** disabling of a person or machine. **2** the fact or state of being disabled. Ⓞ 15c.

disabled ▷ *adj* **1** said of a person: having a physical or mental handicap. **2** said of a machine, etc: made unable to work. **3** said of a device, facility, etc: designed or intended for people with physical disabilities.

disabuse /dɪsə'bjuːz/ ▷ *verb* (*always* **disabuse someone of something**) to rid them of a mistaken idea or impression. Ⓞ 17c.

disaccharide /daɪ'sakəraɪd/ ▷ *noun, biochem* a carbohydrate that consists of two MONOSACCHARIDES joined together, with the elimination of a molecule of water, eg SUCROSE, LACTOSE. Ⓞ 19c.

disadvantage ▷ *noun* **1** a difficulty, drawback or weakness. **2** an unfavourable situation. ▷ *verb* to put someone at a disadvantage. • **disadvantaged** *adj* in an unfavourable position, especially deprived of normal social or economic benefits. Ⓞ 14c as *noun*, 16c as *verb*.

disadvantageous ▷ *adj* having disadvantages or weaknesses. • **disadvantageously** *adverb.* • **disadvantageousness** *noun.*

disaffected ▷ *adj* dissatisfied and no longer loyal or committed. • **disaffectedly** *adverb.* • **disaffectedness** *noun.* Ⓞ 17c.

disaffection ▷ *noun* disloyalty; discontent. Ⓞ 17c.

disaffiliate ▷ *verb, tr & intr* (*often* **disaffiliate to** or **from someone** or **something**) to end an affiliation with them or it. • **disaffiliation** *noun.* Ⓞ 19c.

disafforest /dɪsə'fɒrəst/ and **disforest** ▷ *verb* **1** to clear (land) of forest. **2 a** to bring (land) out of the operation of forest laws; **b** *law* to take away the legal status of forest from (land). • **disafforestation** or **disafforestment** *noun.* Ⓞ 16c.

disagree ▷ *verb, intr* **1** said of two or more people: to have conflicting opinions. **2** to conflict with each other □ *The two theories disagree.* **3** *euphemistic* to quarrel. Ⓞ 15c: from French *desagréer.*

▪ **disagree with someone** **1** to have a different opinion from them. **2** said of food: to give them digestive problems.

▪ **disagree with something** to be opposed to it.

disagreeable ▷ *adj* **1** unpleasant. **2** bad-tempered; unfriendly. • **disagreeability** or **disagreeableness** *noun.* • **disagreeably** *adverb.* Ⓞ 15c.

disagreement ▷ *noun* **1** the state of disagreeing. **2** *euphemistic* a quarrel. Ⓞ 16c.

disallow ▷ *verb* **1** to formally refuse to allow or accept something. **2** to judge something to be invalid. • **disallowance** *noun.* Ⓞ 14c: from French *desalouer.*

disambiguate /dɪsam'bɪgjʊeɪt/ ▷ *verb* (*disambiguated, disambiguating*) to make something unambiguous; to remove ambiguity from it. • **disambiguation** *noun.* Ⓞ 20c.

disappear ▷ *verb* **1** *intr* to go out of sight; to vanish. **2** *intr* to cease to exist. **3** *intr* to go missing. **4** to make someone vanish, especially by imprisoning them or killing them secretly, usually for political reasons. • **disappearance** *noun.* Ⓞ 16c.

disappoint /dɪsə'pɔɪnt/ ▷ *verb* (*disappointed, disappointing*) **1** to fail to fulfil the hopes or expectations of someone. **2** *formal* to prevent (eg a plan) from being carried out. • **disappointed** *adj* having one's hopes or expectations frustrated. • **disappointing** *adj* causing disappointment; frustrating one's hopes or expectations. • **disappointment** *noun* **1** the state of being disappointed. **2** something that disappoints. Ⓞ 15c, originally meaning 'to remove someone from office': from French *desapointer.*

disapprobation /dɪsaproʊ'beɪʃən/ ▷ *noun, formal* disapproval, especially on moral grounds. Ⓞ 17c.

disapprove ▷ *verb, intr* (*usually* **disapprove of something** or **someone**) to have a low opinion of it or them; to think it or them bad or wrong. • **disapproval** *noun.* • **disapproving** *adj.* • **disapprovingly** *adverb.* Ⓞ 17c in this sense; 15c, meaning 'to disprove'.

disarm ▷ *verb* **1** to take weapons away from someone. **2** *intr* to reduce or destroy one's own military capability. **3** to take the fuse out of (a bomb). **4** to take away the anger or suspicions of someone. Ⓞ 15c: from French *desarmer.*

disarmament ▷ *noun* the reduction or destruction by a nation of its own military forces. Ⓞ 18c.

disarming ▷ *adj* taking away anger or suspicion; quickly winning confidence or affection. • **disarmingly** *adverb.*

disarrange ▷ *verb* to make something untidy or disordered. • **disarrangement** *noun.* Ⓞ 18c.

disarray ▷ *noun* a state of disorder or confusion. ▷ *verb* to throw something into disorder. Ⓞ 15c.

disassemble ▷ *verb* to take (a machine, etc) apart. • **disassembly** *noun.* Ⓞ 20c in this sense; 17c, meaning 'to separate' or 'to scatter'.

disassociate ▷ *verb, tr & intr* to DISSOCIATE. • **disassociation** *noun.* Ⓞ 17c.

disaster /dɪ'zɑːstə(r)/ ▷ *noun* **1** an event causing great damage, injury or loss of life. **2** a total failure. **3** extremely bad luck □ *Disaster struck.* • **disastrous** *adj.* • **disastrously** *adverb.* Ⓞ 16c: originally meaning 'bad influence of the stars', from French *desastre*, from *astre* star.

disaster area ▷ *noun* **1** an area where there has been a disaster such as a flood, explosion, etc requiring special official aid. **2** *colloq* any place where a misfortune has happened. **3** *colloq* any place, thing, etc which is untidy, ugly, disadvantageous, etc.

disattribution ▷ *noun* **a** the act of deciding that a work of art, etc, should no longer be considered as the product of a particular artist; **b** an instance of this.

disavow ▷ *verb, formal* to deny knowledge of, a connection with, or responsibility for something or someone. • **disavowal** *noun.* Ⓞ 14c: from French *desavouer.*

disband ▷ *verb* (*disbanded, disbanding*) *tr & intr* to stop operating as a group; to break up. • **disbandment** *noun.* Ⓞ 16c: from French *desbander* to unbind.

disbar *law* ▷ *verb* to expel someone from THE BAR (see BAR[1] *noun* 10). • **disbarment** *noun.* Ⓞ 17c.

disbelief ▷ *noun* inability or refusal to believe something □ *They looked at us in disbelief.* Ⓞ 17c.

disbelieve ▷ *verb* **1** to believe something to be false or someone to be lying. **2** *intr* to have no religious faith. • **disbeliever** *noun.* Ⓞ 17c.

disbenefit ▷ *noun* **1** a drawback, disadvantage, loss, inconvenience, etc. **2** absence or loss of benefit. Ⓞ 1960s.

disbud ▷ *verb* to remove buds from (a plant, etc). Ⓞ 18c.

disburse /dɪs'bɜːs/ ▷ *verb* (*disbursed, disbursing*) to pay out (a sum of money), especially from a fund. • **disbursement** *noun.* Ⓞ 16c: from French *desbourser.*

disc ▻ *noun* **1** a flat thin circular object. **2** any disc-shaped recording medium, such as a RECORD (*noun* 4), COMPACT DISC or VIDEO DISC. **3** *anatomy* in the spine of vertebrates: a plate of fibrous tissue between two adjacent vertebrae. See also SLIPPED DISC. **4** *computing* see DISK. • **discoid** or **discoidal** *adj* disc-shaped. ◎ 17c: from Greek *diskos*.

disc. ▻ *abbreviation* **1** discount. **2** discover.

discard ▻ *verb* /dɪs'kɑːd/ (***discarded***, ***discarding***) **1** to get rid of something as useless or unwanted. **2** *cards* to put down (a card of little value) especially when unable to follow suit. ▻ *noun* /'dɪskɑːd/ **1** something or someone that has been discarded. **2** the act of discarding. ◎ 16c as *verb*; 18c as *noun*.

disc brake ▻ *noun* a brake in which pads are pressed against a metal disc attached to the vehicle's wheel.

disc camera ▻ *noun*, *photog* a type of small camera which uses film in disc form rather than as a roll on a spool.

discern /dɪ'sɜːn/ ▻ *verb* (***discerned***, ***discerning***) to perceive, notice or make out something; to judge. • **discerning** *adj* having or showing good judgement. • **discernment** *noun* good judgement. ◎ 14c: from Latin *discernere*.

discernible /dɪ'sɜːnɪbəl/ ▻ *adj* capable of being seen or perceived □ *no discernible difference.* • **discernibly** *adverb*. ◎ 16c.

discharge ▻ *verb* /dɪs'tʃɑːdʒ/ **1** to allow someone to leave; to dismiss or send away (a person), especially from employment. **2** to perform or carry out (eg duties). **3** *tr & intr* to flow out or make something flow out or be released. **4** *law* to release someone from custody. **5** *tr & intr* to fire (a gun). **6** *law* to pay off (a debt). **7** *tr & intr* to unload (a cargo). **8** *tr & intr*, *technical* to lose, or make (a device) lose, some or all electrical charge. ▻ *noun* /'dɪstʃɑːdʒ, dɪs'tʃɑːdʒ/ **1** the act of discharging. **2** something discharged. **3** *formal*, *law* release or dismissal. **4** *physics* the flow of electric current through a gas in a discharge tube, often resulting in luminescence of the gas. **5** *elec* the release of stored electric charge from a capacitor, battery or accumulator. **6** *elec* a high-voltage spark of electricity produced when there is a large difference in electrical potential between two points, eg lightning. **7 a** an emission of a substance, liquid, etc; **b** the substance, etc emitted. • **discharger** *noun*. ◎ 14c: from French *descharger*.

discharge tube ▻ *noun*, *electronics* a tube in which a gas conducting an electric current emits light.

disc harrow ▻ *noun*, *agric* a harrow which cuts the soil by means of inclined discs.

dischuffed /dɪs'tʃʌft/ ▻ *adj*, *colloq* displeased or disappointed. ◎ 20c.

disciple /dɪ'saɪpəl/ ▻ *noun* **1** someone who believes in, and follows, the teachings of another. **2** one of the twelve close followers of Christ. • **discipleship** *noun*. ◎ Anglo-Saxon *discipul*: from Latin *discipulus*, from *discere* to learn.

discipline /'dɪsɪplɪn/ ▻ *noun* **1 a** strict training, or the enforcing of rules, intended to produce ordered and controlled behaviour in oneself or others; **b** the ordered behaviour resulting from this. **2** punishment designed to create obedience. **3** an area of learning, especially a subject of academic study. **4** a branch of sport. ▻ *verb* (***disciplined***, ***disciplining***) **1** to train or force (oneself or others) to behave in an ordered and controlled way. **2** to punish someone. • **disciplinable** *adj*. • **disciplinarian** /dɪsɪplɪ'nɛərɪən/ *noun* someone who enforces strict discipline on others. • **disciplinary** /'dɪsɪplɪnərɪ, dɪsɪ'plɪn-/ *adj* characteristic of, relating to or enforcing discipline; intended as punishment. ◎ 13c: from Latin *disciplina*.

disc jockey ▻ *noun* someone who presents a programme of recorded popular music on the radio, at a disco, in a club, etc. Also called **DJ**. ◎ 1940s.

disclaim ▻ *verb* **1** to deny (eg involvement with or knowledge of something). **2** to give up a legal claim to something. • **disclaimer** *noun* **1** a written statement denying legal responsibility. **2** a denial. ◎ 14c: from French *desclaimer*.

disclose /dɪs'kloʊz/ ▻ *verb* to make something known; to show something or make it visible. ◎ 14c: from French *desclore*.

disclosing tablet ▻ *noun* a tablet which when chewed reveals by means of coloured dye areas of plaque to be removed from the teeth.

disclosure ▻ *noun* **1** the act of disclosing or making something known. **2** the matter that is disclosed. ◎ 16c.

disco /'dɪskoʊ/ ▻ *noun* (***discos***) **1** a DISCOTHEQUE. **2** a party with dancing to recorded music. **3** the mobile hi-fi and lighting equipment used for such a party. ▻ *adj* suitable for, or designed for, discotheques. ◎ 1960s.

discography /dɪs'kɒgrəfɪ/ ▻ *noun* (***discographies***) a catalogue of sound recordings, especially those of one composer or performer. • **discographer** *noun*. ◎ 1930s.

discoid and **discoidal** see under DISC

discolour or (*US*) **discolor** /dɪs'kʌlə(r)/ ▻ *verb*, *tr & intr* to stain or dirty something; to change in colour. • **discoloration** or **discolouration** *noun*. ◎ 14c: from French *descolorer*.

discombobulate /dɪskəm'bɒbjʊleɪt/ ▻ *verb* (***discombobulated***, ***discombobulating***) *N Amer slang* to disconcert someone or to upset them. ◎ 19c.

discomfit /dɪs'kʌmfɪt/ ▻ *verb* (***discomfited***, ***discomfiting***) **1** to make someone feel embarrassed or uneasy; to perplex them. **2** to frustrate the plans of someone. • **discomfiture** *noun* frustration; humiliating disappointment. ◎ 13c: from French *desconfire*.

discomfort ▻ *noun* a slight physical pain or mental uneasiness. ▻ *verb* to make someone physically uncomfortable or mentally uneasy. ◎ 19c in these senses; 14c in obsolete senses concerned with loss of courage: from French *desconfort*.

discompose ▻ *verb* to upset, worry or agitate someone. • **discomposure** *noun* a state of upset or agitation. ◎ 15c.

disconcert /dɪskən'sɜːt/ ▻ *verb* (***disconcerted***, ***disconcerting***) to make someone feel anxious or uneasy; to fluster them. • **disconcerting** *adj* causing anxiety or unease. ◎ 17c: from obsolete French *disconcerter*.

disconnect ▻ *verb* **1** to break the connection between (especially an electrical device and a power supply). **2** to stop the supply of (eg a public service such as the gas supply or the telephone) to (a building, etc). ◎ 18c.

disconnected ▻ *adj* **1** no longer connected. **2** said especially of speech: not correctly constructed, and often not making sense. • **disconnectedly** *adverb*.

disconnection ▻ *noun* **1** a break in a connection or link. **2** the act of disconnecting or the state of being disconnected.

disconsolate /dɪs'kɒnsələt/ ▻ *adj* deeply sad or disappointed; not able to be consoled. • **disconsolately** *adverb*. • **disconsolateness** *noun*. ◎ 14c: from Latin *disconsolatus*.

discontent ▻ *noun* dissatisfaction; lack of contentment. ◎ 16c.

discontented ▻ *adj* dissatisfied; unhappy. • **discontentedly** *adverb*. • **discontentedness** *noun*. ◎ 16c.

discontinue ▻ *verb* **1** *tr & intr* to stop or cease. **2** to stop producing something □ *This model has been discontinued.* • **discontinuance** or **discontinuation** *noun*. ◎ 15c: from French *discontinuer*.

discontinuous ▻ *adj* having breaks or interruptions. • **discontinuity** *noun* (***discontinuities***). • **discontinuously** *adverb*.

discophile /ˈdɪskoufaɪl/ ▻ *noun* someone who collects and studies records (see RECORD *noun* 4) or compact discs. ⓒ 1940s.

discord /ˈdɪskɔːd/ ▻ *noun* **1** disagreement; conflict; failure to get on. **2** *music* an unpleasant-sounding combination of notes; lack of harmony. Opposite of CONCORD. **3** uproarious noise. ⓒ 13c: from Latin *discordia*.

discordant /dɪsˈkɔːdənt/ ▻ *adj* lacking harmony; disagreeing. • **discordantly** *adverb*.

discotheque /ˈdɪskətɛk/ ▻ *noun* a night-club where people dance to recorded pop music. See also DISCO. ⓒ 1950s: French *discothèque*, originally meaning 'a record library'.

discount ▻ *noun* /ˈdɪskaʊnt/ **1** an amount deducted from the normal price, eg for prompt payment. **2** the rate or percentage of the deduction granted. **3** the amount by which the price of a share or stock unit is below the par value. ▻ *verb* /dɪsˈkaʊnt/ **1** to disregard as unlikely, untrue or irrelevant. **2** to make a deduction from (a price). • **discountable** *adj*. • **discounter** *noun*. • **at a discount** **1** for less than the usual price. **2** said of shares: below par. ⓒ 17c: from French *descompter*.

discountenance ▻ *verb* **1** to refuse support to someone or something. **2** to discourage or show disapproval or someone or something. **3** to embarrass someone. ⓒ 16c.

discount house ▻ *noun* **1** a UK financial institution which buys SHORT-DATED government stocks called **Treasury Bills** with money borrowed from commercial banks for very short periods, the resulting profits being produced by the difference between the borrowing rate and the lending rate. **2** (*also* **discount store**) a shop where goods are sold at less than the usual retail price.

discount rate ▻ *noun* **1** the rate at which a discount is granted. **2** the rate at which banks can borrow funds using bills as security.

discourage /dɪsˈkʌrɪdʒ/ ▻ *verb* (***discouraged***, ***discouraging***) **1** to deprive someone of confidence, hope or the will to continue. **2** to seek to prevent (a person or an action) with advice or persuasion. • **discouragement** *noun*. • **discouraging** *adj*. • **discouragingly** *adverb*. ⓒ 15c: from French *descourager*.

discourse ▻ *noun* /ˈdɪskɔːs/ **1** a formal speech or essay on a particular subject. **2** serious conversation. ▻ *verb* /dɪsˈkɔːs/ (***discoursed***, ***discoursing***) *intr* to speak or write at length, formally or with authority. ⓒ 16c as *noun* in modern sense; 14c, meaning 'understanding'; 16c as *verb*: from Latin *discursus*.

discourse analysis ▻ *noun, linguistics* the study of continuous stretches of language to discover their structure and the features which bind sentences in a sequence. See also CONVERSATION ANALYSIS.

discourteous ▻ *adj* showing a lack of courtesy; impolite. • **discourteously** *adverb*. • **discourtesy** *noun* (***discourtesies***). ⓒ 16c.

discover /dɪsˈkʌvə(r)/ ▻ *verb* **1** to be the first person to find something or someone. **2** to find by chance, especially for the first time. **3** to learn of or become aware of for the first time. • **discoverable** *adj*. • **discoverer** *noun* someone who makes a discovery, especially of something not known before. ⓒ 16c in modern sense; 13c, meaning 'to reveal': from French *descouvrir*.

discovery ▻ *noun* (***discoveries***) **1** the act of discovering. **2** a person or thing discovered. ⓒ 16c.

discovery well ▻ *noun, oil industry* an exploratory well which proves to yield a commercially viable amount of oil.

disc parking ▻ *noun* a parking system which relies on the motorist affixing a special disc or discs to their car showing their time of arrival and the time when permitted parking ends.

disc plough ▻ *noun, agric* a plough which cuts the soil by means of inclined discs.

discredit /dɪsˈkrɛdɪt/ ▻ *noun* loss of good reputation, or the cause of it. ▻ *verb* **1** to make someone or something be disbelieved or regarded with doubt or suspicion. **2** to damage the reputation of someone. • **discreditable** *adj*. • **discreditably** *adverb*. ⓒ 16c.

discreet /dɪsˈkriːt/ ▻ *adj* **1** careful to prevent suspicion or embarrassment, especially by keeping a secret. **2** avoiding notice; inconspicuous. • **discreetly** *adverb*. • **discreetness** *noun*. See also DISCRETION. ⓒ 14c: from Latin *discretus*.

> ***discreet, discrete***
>
> These words are sometimes confused with each other.

discrepancy /dɪsˈkrɛpənsɪ/ ▻ *noun* (***discrepancies***) a failure (eg of sets of information) to correspond or be the same. • **discrepant** *adj* showing a discrepancy or failure to correspond. ⓒ 17c: from Latin *discrepare* to differ in sound.

discrete /dɪsˈkriːt/ ▻ *adj* separate; distinct. • **discretely** *adverb*. • **discreteness** *noun*. ⓒ 14c: from Latin *discretus*.

discretion /dɪsˈkrɛʃən/ ▻ *noun* **1** the quality of behaving in a discreet way. **2** the ability to make wise judgements. **3** the freedom or right to make decisions and do as one thinks best. • **discretional** or **discretionary** *adj* made, done, given, etc according to the wishes of a particular person or group; not compulsory or automatic. • **discretionally** or **discretionarily** *adverb*. • **age** or **years of discretion** the age at which one's judgement becomes mature. ⓒ 14c: from Latin *discretio*.

discriminate /dɪsˈkrɪmɪneɪt/ ▻ *verb* (***discriminated***, ***discriminating***) *intr* **1** to recognize a difference between two people or things. **2** (*usually* **discriminate in favour of** or **against someone**) to give different treatment to different people or groups in identical circumstances, especially without justification and on political or religious grounds. • **discriminating** *adj* showing good judgement; able to recognize even slight differences. • **discriminatingly** *adverb*. • **discriminator** *noun*. • **discriminatory** *adj* displaying or representing unfairly different treatment. ⓒ 17c: from Latin *discriminare*, *discriminatum* to separate.

discrimination ▻ *noun* **1** unjustifiably different treatment given to different people or groups. See also POSITIVE DISCRIMINATION. **2** the ability to draw fine distinctions; good judgement, especially in matters of taste.

discursive /dɪsˈkɜːsɪv/ ▻ *adj* **1** said of spoken or written style: wandering from the main point. **2** *philos* based on argument or reason, rather than on intuition. • **discursively** *adverb*. • **discursiveness** *noun*. ⓒ 17c: from Latin *discursus* conversation.

discus /ˈdɪskəs/ ▻ *noun* (***discuses*** /ˈdɪskəsɪz/ or ***disci*** /ˈdɪskaɪ/) **1** a heavy disc, thicker at the centre than the edge, thrown in athletic competitions. **2** (*also* **discus throw**) the competition itself. ⓒ 17c: from Greek *diskos*.

discuss /dɪsˈkʌs/ ▻ *verb* (***discussed***, ***discussing***) **1** to examine or consider something in speech or writing. **2** to talk or argue about something in conversation. • **discussable** or **discussible** *adj*. ⓒ 14c: from Latin *discutere*, *discussum* to shake to pieces.

discussion /dɪsˈkʌʃən/ ▻ *noun* **1** a conversation, debate or argument. **2** a detailed treatment in speech or writing.

disc wheel ▷ *noun* a wheel on a motor vehicle, etc in which the hub and rim are connected by a solid piece of metal rather than by spokes.

disdain /dɪs'deɪn, dɪz-/ ▷ *noun* dislike due to a feeling that something is not worthy of attention; contempt; scorn. ▷ *verb* (***disdained***, ***disdaining***) **1** to refuse or reject someone or something out of disdain. **2** to regard someone or something with disdain. ◷ 16c in modern form; 13c as *dedeyne*: from French *desdaigner*, from Latin *dignus* worthy.

disdainful ▷ *adj* showing disdain; contemptuous. • **disdainfully** *adverb*. • **disdainfulness** *noun*.

disease /dɪ'ziːz/ ▷ *noun* **1** a lack of health, a disorder or illness caused by infection rather than by an accident. **2** any one such illness with characteristic symptoms □ *immunization against diseases such as measles*. **3** any undesirable phenomenon □ *the social disease of drug addiction* . ◷ 14c: from French *desaise* unease.

diseased ▷ *adj* affected by or suffering from disease. ◷ 15c.

diseconomy /dɪsɪ'kɒnəmɪ/ ▷ *noun* (***diseconomies***) an economic disadvantage, such as lower efficiency or higher costs. ◷ 1930s.

disembark ▷ *verb, tr & intr* to take or go from a ship on to land. • **disembarkation** *noun*. ◷ 16c: from French *desembarquer*.

disembarrass ▷ *verb* (*usually* **disembarrass someone from** or **oneself of something**) to free oneself or someone else from an embarrassment, burden or complication. • **disembarrassment** *noun*. ◷ 18c.

disembodied ▷ *adj* **1** said eg of a spirit or soul: separated from the body; having no physical existence. **2** seeming not to come from, or be connected to, a body □ *a disembodied voice*. ◷ 18c.

disembowel /dɪsɪm'bɑʊəl/ ▷ *verb* (***disembowelled***, ***disembowelling***) to remove the internal organs of someone or something as a punishment, torture, etc. • **disembowelment** *noun*. ◷ 17c.

disenchant ▷ *verb* **1** to free someone from illusion. **2** to make someone dissatisfied or discontented. • **disenchanted** *adj*. • **disenchantment** *noun*. ◷ 16c: from French *desenchanter*.

disencumber ▷ *verb* to free someone from or of an encumbrance. ◷ 16c.

disenfranchise see DISFRANCHISE.

disengage ▷ *verb* **1** to release or detach someone or something from a connection. **2** *tr & intr* to withdraw (troops) from combat. ◷ 17c: from French *desengager*.

disengaged ▷ *adj* **1** free from engagement; at leisure. **2** detached; released.

disengagement ▷ *noun* release from a connection or commitment.

disentangle ▷ *verb* **1** to free something from complication, difficulty or confusion. **2** to take the knots or tangles out of (eg hair). • **disentanglement** *noun*. ◷ 16c.

disestablish ▷ *verb* to take away the official status or authority of (an organization, etc), especially to take away the national status of a church. • **disestablishment** *noun*. ◷ 16c.

disesteem ▷ *verb* to disapprove of or dislike someone or something. ▷ *noun* lack of esteem; disregard. ◷ 16c.

disfavour or (*N Amer*) **disfavor** *noun* **1** a state of being disliked, unpopular or disapproved of. **2** dislike or disapproval. ◷ 16c.

disfigure ▷ *verb* to spoil the beauty or general appearance of something. • **disfigurement** *noun*. ◷ 14c: from French *desfigurer*.

disforest see DISAFFOREST

disfranchise and **disenfranchise** ▷ *verb* to deprive someone of the right to vote or other rights and privileges of a citizen. • **disfranchisement** *noun*. ◷ 15c as *disfranchise*, 17c as *disenfranchise*.

disgorge /dɪs'gɔːdʒ/ ▷ *verb* **1** *tr & intr* to vomit. **2** to discharge or pour out something. **3** to give up or relinquish something, especially under pressure. ◷ 15c: from French *desgorger*, from *gorge* throat.

disgrace ▷ *noun* **a** shame or loss of favour or respect; **b** the cause of it; **c** an example of it. ▷ *verb* (***disgraced***, ***disgracing***) to bring shame upon someone. • **in disgrace** out of favour. ◷ 16c: from French *disgrâce*.

disgraceful ▷ *adj* bringing shame; degrading. • **disgracefully** *adverb*.

disgruntled /dɪs'grʌntəld/ ▷ *adj* annoyed and dissatisfied; in a bad mood. ◷ 17c: from DIS- 4 + obsolete *gruntle* to complain.

disguise /dɪs'gaɪz/ ▷ *verb* (***disguised***, ***disguising***) **1** to hide the identity of someone or something by a change of appearance. **2** to conceal the true nature of (eg intentions). ▷ *noun* **1** a disguised state. **2** something, especially a combination of clothes and make-up, intended to disguise. ◷ 14c: from French *desguiser*.

disgust /dɪs'gʌst/ ▷ *verb* (***disgusted***, ***disgusting***) to sicken; to provoke intense dislike or disapproval in someone. ▷ *noun* intense dislike; loathing. • **disgusted** *adj*. • **disgusting** *adj*. • **in disgust** with or because of a feeling of disgust. ◷ 16c as *noun*; 17c as *verb*: from French *desgouster*.

dish ▷ *noun* (***dishes***) **1** a shallow container in which food is served or cooked. **2** its contents, or the amount it can hold. **3** anything shaped like this. **4** a particular kind of food, especially food prepared for eating. **5** (**dishes**) the used plates and other utensils after the end of a meal □ *do the dishes*. **6** a DISH AERIAL. **7** *colloq* a physically attractive person. ▷ *verb* (***dishes, dished***, ***dishing***) **1** to put (food) into a dish for serving at table. **2** *colloq* to ruin (especially chances or hopes). ◷ Anglo-Saxon *disc* plate, bowl, table.

■ **dish something out** *colloq* **1** to distribute it. **2** to give it out. **3** (*especially* **dish it out**) to give out punishment.

■ **dish something up** *colloq* **1** to serve (food). **2** to offer or present (eg information), especially if not for the first time.

dishabille see DÉSHABILLÉ

dish aerial ▷ *noun* a large dish-shaped aerial used to receive signals in radar, radio-telescopes and satellite broadcasting. Also called **dish**, **dish antenna**, **satellite dish**.

disharmony ▷ *noun* disagreement; lack of harmony. • **disharmonious** *adj* lacking harmony; disagreeing. ◷ 17c.

dishcloth ▷ *noun* a cloth for washing, wiping or drying dishes.

dishearten ▷ *verb* to dampen the courage, hope or confidence of someone. • **disheartening** *adj*. • **disheartenment** *noun*. ◷ 16c.

dished ▷ *adj* **1** shaped like a dish; concave. **2** said of a pair of wheels on a car, etc: sloping in towards each other at the top. **3** *colloq* completely frustrated or defeated.

dishevelled /dɪ'ʃɛvəld/ ▷ *adj* said of clothes or hair: untidy; in a mess. ◷ 15c: from French *descheveler*.

dishevelment /dɪ'ʃɛvəlmənt/ ▷ *noun* a state of personal untidiness. ◷ 19c.

dishier and **dishiest** see under DISHY

dishonest ▷ *adj* not honest; likely to deceive or cheat; insincere. • **dishonestly** *adverb*. ◷ 14c: from French *deshoneste*.

dishonesty ▷ *noun* **1** lack of honesty. **2** a dishonest act. ⓒ 16c in these senses; 14c, meaning 'dishonour' or 'sexual misconduct'.

dishonorable discharge ▷ *noun, US* dismissal from the US armed forces for serious misconduct such as desertion or theft.

dishonour or (*US*) **dishonor** /dɪs'ɒnə(r)/ ▷ *noun* **a** shame or loss of honour; **b** the cause of it. ▷ *verb* **1** to bring dishonour on someone or something. **2** to treat someone or something with no respect. **3** *commerce* to refuse to honour (a cheque). • **dishonourable** *adj*. ⓒ 14c: from French *deshonneur*.

dishtowel ▷ *noun* a cloth for drying dishes. Also called TEA TOWEL.

dishwasher ▷ *noun* **1** a machine that washes and dries dishes. **2** someone employed to wash dishes, eg in a restaurant.

dishwater ▷ *noun* **1** water in which dirty dishes have been washed. **2** any liquid like it.

dishy /'dɪʃɪ/ ▷ *adj* (*dishier*, *dishiest*) *colloq* sexually attractive. ⓒ 1960s.

disillusion ▷ *verb* (*disillusioned*, *disillusioning*) to correct the mistaken beliefs or illusions of someone. ▷ *noun* (also **disillusionment**) a state of being disillusioned. ▷ **disillusioned** *adj*. ⓒ 19c as *verb* and as *noun* in this sense; 16c as *noun* meaning 'delusion'.

disincentive ▷ *noun* something that discourages or deters someone or something. ⓒ 1940s.

disinclination ▷ *noun* the state of or a feeling of being reluctant or unwilling. ⓒ 17c.

disinclined ▷ *adj* unwilling. ⓒ 17c.

disinfect ▷ *verb* to clean with a substance that kills germs. ⓒ 17c in this sense; 16c, meaning 'to rid someone or somewhere of infection'.

disinfectant ▷ *noun* a germ-killing substance. Also *as adj*. ⓒ 19c.

disinformation ▷ *noun* **a** false information intended to deceive or mislead; **b** the act of supplying it. ⓒ 1950s.

disingenuous ▷ *adj* not entirely sincere or open; creating a false impression of frankness. • **disingenuously** *adverb*. • **disingenuousness** *noun*. ⓒ 17c.

disinherit ▷ *verb* to legally deprive someone of an inheritance; to remove as one's heir. • **disinheritance** *noun* rejection of an heir; removal from inheritance. ⓒ 15c.

disintegrate /dɪs'ɪntɪgreɪt/ ▷ *verb, tr & intr* **1** to break into tiny pieces; to shatter or crumble. **2** to break up. **3** to undergo or make a substance undergo nuclear fission. ⓒ 18c.

disintegration ▷ *noun* **1** the act or state of disintegrating. **2** *physics* the breakdown of an atomic nucleus, either spontaneously by radioactive decay or as a result of bombardment with high-energy particles.

disinter ▷ *verb* **1** to dig up (especially a body from a grave). **2** to discover and make known (a fact, etc). • **disinterment** *noun* removal of a body from a grave. ⓒ 17c: from French *désenterrer*.

disinterest and **disinterestedness** ▷ *noun* **1** impartiality; objectivity. **2** lack of interest; unconcern. ⓒ 17c.

disinterested ▷ *adj* **1** not having an interest in a particular matter; impartial, objective. **2** *colloq* showing no interest; UNINTERESTED. ⓒ 17c.

disinvest ▷ *verb, intr* to remove financial investment. ⓒ 1960s.

disjointed /dɪs'dʒɔɪntɪd/ ▷ *adj* said especially of speech: not properly connected; incoherent. ⓒ 16c: from French *desjoindre*.

disjunctive /dɪs'dʒʌŋktɪv/ ▷ *adj* marked by breaks; discontinuous. ⓒ 16c: from Latin *disjunctivus*.

disk ▷ *noun* **1** *computing* a MAGNETIC DISK. See also FLOPPY DISK, HARD DISK. **2** *especially US* a DISC. ⓒ 18c: variant of DISC.

disk drive ▷ *noun, computing* a device containing the mechanisms for rotating a magnetic disk at high speed, and which also controls the movement of a **read-write head** which passes over the surfaces of the disk in order to read or write magnetic signals that represent the stored data.

diskette /dɪ'skɛt/ ▷ *noun, computing* **1** a FLOPPY DISK. **2** formerly used to refer to a 5.25in floppy disk.

disk operating system ▷ *noun* (abbreviation **DOS**) *computing* software that manages the storage and retrieval of information on disk on personal computers.

dislike ▷ *verb* to consider someone or something unpleasant or unlikeable. ▷ *noun* **1** mild hostility; aversion. **2** something disliked. • **dislikable** or **dislikeable** *adj*. ⓒ 16c.

dislocate /'dɪsləkeɪt, -loʊkeɪt/ ▷ *verb* **1** to dislodge (a bone) from its normal position in a joint. **2** to disturb the order of something; to disrupt it. ⓒ 16c: from Latin *dislocare*, *dislocatum*.

dislocation /dɪslə'keɪʃən/ ▷ *noun* the act of dislocating, especially of a bone in the body. ⓒ 15c.

dislodge ▷ *verb* **1** to force something out of a fixed or established position. **2** to drive (an enemy, etc) from a place of rest, hiding or defence. • **dislodgement** or **dislodgment** *noun*. ⓒ 15c: from French *desloger*.

disloyal ▷ *adj* not loyal or faithful. • **disloyally** *adverb*. • **disloyalty** *noun*. ⓒ 15c: from French *desloyal*.

dismal /'dɪzməl/ ▷ *adj* **1** not cheerful; causing or suggesting sadness. **2** *colloq* third-rate; of poor quality. • **dismally** *adverb*. ⓒ 16c in sense 1; originally 15c meaning 'unlucky': French, from Latin *dies mali* evil or unlucky days.

dismantle /dɪs'mantəl/ ▷ *verb* (*dismantled*, *dismantling*) **1** to take something to pieces; to demolish it. **2** to abolish or close down something, especially bit by bit. ⓒ 16c: from French *desmanteller*.

dismast ▷ *verb* (*dismasted*, *dismasting*) to topple or remove the mast or masts of (a sailing vessel). ⓒ 18c.

dismay /dɪs'meɪ/ ▷ *noun* **1** a feeling of sadness arising from deep disappointment or discouragement. **2** alarm; consternation. ▷ *verb* (*dismayed*, *dismaying*) to make someone discouraged, sad or alarmed. ⓒ 13c: from French *desmaiier*.

dismember /dɪs'mɛmbə(r)/ ▷ *verb* (*dismembered*, *dismembering*) **1** to tear or cut the limbs from (the body) ▫ *dismembering the rabbit*. **2** to divide up (especially land). • **dismemberment** *noun*. ⓒ 13c: from French *desmembrer*.

dismiss /dɪs'mɪs/ ▷ *verb* (*dismissed*, *dismissing*) **1** to refuse to consider or accept (an idea, claim, etc). **2** to put someone out of one's employment. **3** to send someone

disinterested, uninterested

• **Disinterested** used to mean the same as **uninterested**, but has developed the separate meaning given as sense 1, 'impartial'. The two words therefore relate to different senses of **interest**. The difference can be seen in the following examples ▫ *He claimed that he had been a disinterested spectator in the affair* (= not personally involved in it) ▫ *He left most of his meal, and seemed uninterested in any of the conversation she attempted* (= not interested in it or concerned about it).

• **Disinterested** is not usually followed by **in**, although **uninterested** often is.

away; to allow them to leave. **4** to close (a court case). **5** *cricket* to bowl (a batsman) out. ◷ 15c: from DIS- 3 + Latin *mittere, missum* to send.

dismissal ▷ *noun* **1** an act of dismissing, especially of a person from employment. **2** the state of being dismissed ◷ 19c.

dismissive /dɪs'mɪsɪv/ ▷ *adj* (*often* **dismissive of something** or **someone**) **1** giving no consideration or respect to someone or something. **2** showing no willingness to believe something. ◷ 17c.

dismount ▷ *verb* **1** *intr* to get off a horse, bicycle, etc. **2** to force someone off a horse, bicycle, etc. **3** to remove something from a stand or frame. ◷ 16c in sense 3: from French *desmonter*.

Disneyesque /dɪznɪ'ɛsk/ ▷ *adj* in the style of the characters, etc, appearing in the cartoon films of Walt Disney (1901–66), American cartoonist and film producer, ie fantastical, whimsical, unreal. ◷ 1930s.

Disneyfy /'dɪznɪfaɪ/ ▷ *verb* (***Disneyfies, Disneyfied, Disneyfying***) *often disparaging* to present (a site, etc) or process the history of, or facts concerning (a site, etc) in a way that may encourage tourism, but that does not encourage exposure to, and may trivialize, the actual history or real environment. • **Disneyfication** *noun*. ◷ 20c: see DISNEYESQUE.

disobedient ▷ *adj* refusing or failing to obey. • disobedience *noun*. • **disobediently** *adverb*. ◷ 15c: French.

disobey ▷ *verb* to act contrary to the orders of someone; to refuse to obey (a person, a law, etc). ◷ 14c: from French *desobeir*.

disobliging ▷ *adj* unwilling to help; disregarding, or tending to disregard, wishes or requests. ◷ 17c.

disorder ▷ *noun* **1** lack of order; confusion or disturbance. **2** unruly or riotous behaviour. **3** a disease or illness. • **disordered** *adj*. ◷ 16c: from French *desordre*.

disorderly ▷ *adj* **1** not neatly arranged; disorganized. **2** causing trouble in public.

disorderly conduct ▷ *noun, law* any of several minor infringements of the law likely to cause a BREACH OF THE PEACE.

disorganize or **disorganise** ▷ *verb* to disturb the order or arrangement of something; to throw it into confusion. • **disorganization** *noun*. ◷ 18c.

disorganized or **disorganised** ▷ *adj* **1** disordered. **2** unsystematic; inefficient. **3** muddled.

disorientate and **disorient** ▷ *verb* (***disorientated, disorientating; disoriented, disorienting***) to make someone lose all sense of position, direction or time. • **disorientation** *noun*. ◷ 18c as *disorientate*; 17c as *disorient*.

disown /dɪs'oʊn/ ▷ *verb* **1** to deny having any relationship to, or connection with, someone or something. **2** to refuse to recognize or acknowledge someone or something. • **disownment** *noun*. ◷ 17c.

disparage /dɪs'parɪdʒ/ ▷ *verb* (***disparaged, disparaging***) to speak of someone or something with contempt. • **disparagement** *noun*. ◷ 14c in this sense; originally 13c, meaning 'to marry below one's class': from French *desparager*.

disparaging ▷ *adj* contemptuous; showing disapproval. • **disparagingly** *adverb*.

disparate /'dɪspərət/ ▷ *adj* completely different; too different to be compared. ◷ 17c: from Latin *disparare, disparatum* to separate.

disparity /dɪs'parɪtɪ/ ▷ *noun* (***disparities***) great or fundamental difference; inequality. ◷ 16c: from French *disparité*.

dispassionate ▷ *adj* **1** calm; unemotional. **2** not influenced by personal feelings; impartial. • **dispassionately** *adverb*. ◷ 16c.

dispatch or **despatch** /dɪs'patʃ/ ▷ *verb* (***dispatched, dispatching; despatched, despatching***) **1** to send (mail, a person, etc) to a place for a particular reason. **2** to finish off or deal with something quickly □ *dispatch a meal*. **3** *euphemistic* to kill. ▷ *noun* **1** (*often* **dispatches**) an official (especially military or diplomatic) report. **2** a journalist's report sent to a newspaper. **3** the act of dispatching; the fact of being dispatched. **4** *old use* speed or haste. • **mentioned in despatches** as a distinction: commended in official military dispatches for bravery, etc. ◷ 16c: from French *despeechier* to set free.

dispatch box and **dispatch case** ▷ *noun* a box or case designed to carry dispatches or other valuable papers.

dispatch rider ▷ *noun* someone employed to deliver messages by motorcycle or, formerly, on horseback.

dispel /dɪ'spɛl/ ▷ *verb* (***dispelled, dispelling***) to drive away or banish (thoughts or feelings). ◷ 17c: from Latin *dispellere*.

dispensable /dɪs'pɛnsəbəl/ ▷ *adj* **1** able to be done without; expendable. **2** able to be dispensed. ◷ 16c.

dispensary /dɪs'pɛnsərɪ/ ▷ *noun* (***dispensaries***) a place where medicines are given out or dispensed, and sometimes where medical advice may be given. ◷ 17c.

dispensation /dɪspən'seɪʃən/ ▷ *noun* **1** special exemption from a rule, obligation or law (especially a religious law). **2** the act of dispensing. **3** a religious or political system regarded as the chief governing force in a nation or during a particular time. **4** *relig* God's management of human affairs. ◷ 14c.

dispense /dɪs'pɛns/ ▷ *verb* (***dispensed, dispensing***) **1** to give out (eg advice). **2** to prepare and distribute (medicine). **3** to administer (eg the law). ◷ 14c: from Latin *dispendere, dispensum* to weigh out.

■ **dispense with something** to do without it.

dispenser ▷ *noun* **1** someone who dispenses, eg a pharmacist who makes up and gives out medicines. **2** a container or machine that gives out a commodity in pre-set quantities □ *soap dispenser*. ◷ 16c.

dispensing optician see OPTICIAN 1

dispersal prison ▷ *noun* a prison designed to accommodate a certain number of particularly dangerous or high-risk prisoners in addition to other categories of detainees.

disperse /dɪs'pɜːs/ ▷ *verb* (***dispersed, dispersing***) *tr & intr* **1** to spread out over a wide area. **2** to break up, or make (a crowd) break up, and leave. **3** to vanish or make something vanish. **4** *physics* said of white light: to break up into the colours of the spectrum. **5** *physics* said of particles: to become evenly distributed thoughout a liquid or gas. • **dispersal** *noun*. • **dispersion** *noun*. ◷ 15c: from Latin *dispergere, dispersum* to scatter widely.

dispirit /dɪ'spɪrɪt/ ▷ *verb* to dishearten or discourage someone. • **dispirited** *adj* (***dispirited, dispiriting***). ◷ 17c: DIS- 2 + SPIRIT.

displace ▷ *verb* **1** to put or take something or someone out of the usual place. **2** to take the place of someone or something. **3** to remove someone from a post. ◷ 18c in senses 1 and 2; 16c in sense 3.

displaced person ▷ *noun* someone forced to leave their own country through war or persecution.

displacement ▷ *noun* **1** the act of displacing. **2** *technical* the quantity of liquid, gas, etc displaced by an immersed object, especially of water by a floating ship. ◷ 17c.

displacement activity ▷ *noun, psychol* a relatively harmless activity that is substituted for a more destructive type of behaviour, eg the release of aggression during strenuous physical exercise rather than directing it at other people.

display /dɪ'spleɪ/ ▻ *verb* (***displays***, ***displayed***, ***displaying***) **1** to put someone or something on view. **2** to show or betray (eg feelings). **3** *printing* to present (advertising copy) in an eye-catching way. ▻ *noun* (***displays***) **1** the act of displaying. **2** an exhibition; a show of talent; an arrangement of objects on view. **3** the visual display unit linked to a computer, or the digital characters of a liquid-crystal display unit used in watches, calculators, etc. **4** a pattern of animal behaviour most frequently associated with courtship or the defence of territory, usually involving stereotyped sounds, movements, colour patterns, etc, that produces a specific response in another individual, especially of the same species. **5** *printing* presentation of advertising copy, etc, in an eye-catching way, through appropriate use of typefaces, space, etc. ◷ 14c: from French *despleier*.

displease ▻ *verb* to annoy or offend someone. • **displeasure** *noun*. ◷ 14c: from French *desplaisir*.

disport /dɪ'spɔːt/ ▻ *verb* (***disported***, ***disporting***) *tr & intr, literary* to indulge (oneself) in lively amusement ▫ ***children disporting themselves on the beach***. ◷ 14c: from French *se desporter* to carry oneself away.

disposable ▻ *adj* **1** intended to be thrown away or destroyed after one use. **2** said of income or assets: remaining after tax and other commitments are paid; available for use when needed. ▻ *noun* a product intended for disposal after one use. ◷ 17c as *adj*; 1960s as *noun*.

disposal ▻ *noun* getting rid of something. • **at the disposal of someone** available for use by them. ◷ 17c.

dispose /dɪs'poʊz/ ▻ *verb* (***disposed***, ***disposing***) to place something in an arrangement or order. • **be disposed to do something** to be inclined to follow that course of action ▫ ***am not disposed to try***. • **be disposed to** or **towards someone** or **something** to have specified feelings about or towards them or it ▫ ***ill-disposed towards us***. ◷ 14c: from French *disposer* to decide.

■ **dispose of something 1** to get rid of it. **2** to deal with or settle it.

disposition /dɪspə'zɪʃən/ ▻ *noun* **1** temperament; personality; a tendency. **2** arrangement; position; distribution. **3** *law* the act of giving over (eg property). ◷ 14c.

dispossess ▻ *verb* (*always* **dispossess someone of something**) to take (especially property) away from them. • **dispossession** *noun*. ◷ 15c: from French *despossesser*.

dispossessed ▻ *adj* deprived of possessions, property, etc, especially one's home, country or rights.

disproof ▻ *noun* **1** the act of disproving. **2** something that disproves. ◷ 16c.

disproportion ▻ *noun* lack of balance or equality; failure to be in proportion. ◷ 16c.

disproportionate /dɪsprə'pɔːʃənət/ ▻ *adj* unreasonably large or small in comparison with something else. • **disproportionately** *adverb*. ◷ 16c.

disprove ▻ *verb* to prove something to be false or wrong. ◷ 14c: from French *desprover*.

disputable /dɪs'pjuːtəbəl/ ▻ *adj* liable to be disputed or argued about; not certain. • **disputably** *adverb*. ◷ 15c.

disputation /dɪspjʊ'teɪʃən/ ▻ *noun* argument; debate; discussion. ◷ 15c.

disputatious /dɪspjʊ'teɪʃəs/ ▻ *adj* said of a person: inclined to dispute or argue; contentious. ◷ 17c.

dispute ▻ *verb* /dɪs'pjuːt/ (***disputed***, ***disputing***) **1** to question or deny the accuracy or validity of (a statement, etc). **2** to quarrel over rights to or possession of something ▫ ***disputed territory***. **3** *tr & intr* to argue about something. ▻ *noun* /dɪs'pjuːt, 'dɪspjuːt/ an argument. • **in dispute** being debated or contested. ◷ 13c: from Latin *disputare* to discuss.

disqualify ▻ *verb* **1** to remove someone from a competition, especially for breaking rules. **2** to make someone or something unsuitable or ineligible. • **disqualification** *noun*. ◷ 18c.

disquiet ▻ *noun* a feeling of anxiety or uneasiness. ▻ *verb* to make someone feel anxious, uneasy, etc. • **disquieting** *adj*. • **disquietude** *noun*. ◷ 16c.

disquisition /dɪskwɪ'zɪʃən/ ▻ *noun, formal* a long and detailed discussion of a subject in speech or writing. • **disquisitional** *adj*. ◷ 15c: from Latin *disquisitio*.

disregard ▻ *verb* **1** to pay no attention to someone or something. **2** to dismiss something as unworthy of consideration. ▻ *noun* dismissive lack of attention or concern. ◷ 17c.

disremember ▻ *verb, Brit dialect* or *US colloq* to fail to remember something; to forget it. ◷ 17c.

disrepair ▻ *noun* bad condition or working order owing to a need for repair and maintenance. ◷ 18c.

disreputable ▻ *adj* suffering from, or leading to, a bad reputation; not respectable. • **disreputably** *adverb*. ◷ 18c.

disrepute ▻ *noun* the state of having a bad reputation ▫ ***bring football into disrepute***. ◷ 17c.

disrespect ▻ *noun* lack of respect; impoliteness; rudeness. • **disrespectful** *adj*. • **disrespectfully** *adverb*. ◷ 17c.

disrobe ▻ *verb, tr & intr* **1** *especially literary* to undress. **2** to take ceremonial robes off. ◷ 16c.

disrupt /dɪs'rʌpt/ ▻ *verb* (***disrupted***, ***disrupting***) to disturb the order or peaceful progress of (an activity, process, etc). ◷ 17c, but rare till 19c: from Latin *disrumpere*, *disruptum* to break into pieces.

disruption /dɪs'rʌpʃən/ ▻ *noun* disturbance to peace or order. ◷ 17c.

disruptive /dɪs'rʌptɪv/ ▻ *adj* **1** causing disturbance to peace or order. **2** unruly. • **disruptively** *adverb*. ◷ 19c.

diss ▻ *verb* (***dissed***, ***dissing***) *slang, especially US* to reject or dismiss someone with contempt; to bad mouth them. ◷ 20c rapper slang, probably from DISRESPECT.

dissatisfaction ▻ *noun* being dissatisfied; a feeling of discontent. ◷ 17c.

dissatisfy /dɪs'satɪsfaɪ/ ▻ *verb* **1** to fail to satisfy someone. **2** to make someone discontented. • **dissatisfaction** *noun*. • **dissatisfied** *adj*. ◷ 17c.

dissect /dɪ'sɛkt, daɪ-/ ▻ *verb* (***dissected***, ***dissecting***) **1** to cut open (a plant or dead body) for scientific or medical examination. **2** to examine something in minute detail, especially critically. • **dissection** *noun*. ◷ 16c: from Latin *dissecare*, *dissectum* to cut into pieces.

dissected ▻ *adj* **1** *bot* deeply cut into narrow segments. **2** *geol* cut up by valleys.

dissecting microscope ▻ *noun* a form of microscope that allows dissection of the object under examination.

dissemble /dɪ'sɛmbəl/ ▻ *verb* (***dissembled***, ***dissembling***) *tr & intr* **1** to conceal or disguise (true feelings or motives). **2** to assume a false appearance of something. • **dissemblance** *noun*. ◷ 16c: from Latin *dissimulare*.

disseminate /dɪ'sɛmɪneɪt/ ▻ *verb* (***disseminated***, ***disseminating***) to make (eg news or theories) be widely circulated or diffused. • **dissemination** *noun*. ◷ 17c: from Latin *disseminare* to sow widely.

disseminated sclerosis see MULTIPLE SCLEROSIS

dissension /dɪˈsɛnʃən/ ▷ *noun* disagreement, especially if leading to strife or violence. ⓘ 13c: French, from Latin *dissentire* to disagree.

dissent /dɪˈsɛnt/ ▷ *noun* **1** disagreement, especially open or hostile. **2** voluntary separation, especially from an established church. ▷ *verb* (***dissented, dissenting***) *intr* (*often* **dissent from someone** or **something**) **1** to differ in opinion from or to disagree with them. **2** to break away, especially from an established church. • **dissenter** *noun*. • **dissenting** *adj*. ⓘ 15c: from Latin *dissentire* to disagree.

dissentient /dɪˈsɛnʃənt/ *formal* ▷ *adj* disagreeing with a majority or established view. ▷ *noun* a dissentient person. ⓘ 17c: from DISSENT.

dissertation /dɪsəˈteɪʃən/ ▷ *noun* **1** a long essay, especially forming part of a higher education degree course. **2** a formal lecture on a particular subject. ⓘ 17c: from Latin *disserere* to discuss.

disservice ▷ *noun* a wrong; a bad turn. ⓘ 16c: from French *desservir*.

dissidence /ˈdɪsɪdəns/ ▷ *noun* open or public disagreement. ⓘ 17c: see DISSIDENT.

dissident /ˈdɪsɪdənt/ ▷ *noun* someone who disagrees publicly, especially with a government. ▷ *adj* disagreeing; dissenting. ⓘ 16c: from Latin *dissidere* to sit apart.

dissimilar ▷ *adj* (*often* **dissimilar to something**) unlike; different. • **dissimilarity** *noun*. ⓘ 16c.

dissimulate ▷ *verb, tr & intr* to hide or disguise (especially feelings). • **dissimulation** *noun*. ⓘ 17c in this sense; 16c in obsolete sense 'to pass over or ignore': from Latin *dissimulare, dissimulatum*.

dissipate /ˈdɪsɪpeɪt/ ▷ *verb* (***dissipated, dissipating***) **1** *tr & intr* to separate and scatter. **2** to use up something carelessly; to squander it. • **dissipated** *adj* over-indulging in pleasure and enjoyment; debauched. • **dissipation** *noun*. ⓘ 16c: from Latin *dissipare, dissipatum*.

dissociate /dɪˈsoʊʃɪeɪt, -sɪeɪt/ ▷ *verb* (***dissociated, dissociating***) **1** to regard something or someone as separate. **2** to declare someone or oneself to be unconnected with someone or something else. **3** *chem* said of a chemical substance: to break down into its constituent molecules, atoms or ions, eg when dissolved in water or exposed to electromagnetic radiation. • **dissociation** *noun*. ⓘ 16c: from Latin *dissociare, dissociatum*.

dissoluble /dɪˈsɒljʊbəl/ ▷ *adj* **1** able to be disconnected. **2** soluble. ⓘ 16c originally meaning 'able to be broken down': from Latin *dissolubilis*.

dissolute /ˈdɪsəluːt, -ljuːt/ ▷ *adj* indulging in pleasures considered immoral; debauched. • **dissoluteness** *noun*. ⓘ 16c in this sense; 14c meaning 'relaxed, careless': from Latin *dissolutus* lax or loose.

dissolution /dɪsəˈluːʃən, -ˈljuːʃən/ ▷ *noun* **1** the breaking up of a meeting or assembly, eg Parliament. **2** the ending of a formal or legal partnership, eg a marriage or business. **3** abolition, eg of the monarchy. **4** the process of breaking up into parts. ⓘ 14c: from Latin *dissolvere*.

dissolve /dɪˈzɒlv/ ▷ *verb* (***dissolved, dissolving***) **1** *tr & intr* to break up and merge with a liquid. **2** to bring (an assembly, eg Parliament) to a close. **3** to end (a legal partnership, eg a business). **4** *tr & intr* to disappear or make something disappear. **5** *intr* (*often* **dissolve into laughter, tears,** *etc*) to be overcome emotionally. **6** *intr, technical* said of a film or television image: to fade out as a second image fades in. ▷ *noun, technical* a fading out of one film or television image as a second is simultaneously faded in. ⓘ 14c: from Latin *dissolvere* to loosen.

dissonance /ˈdɪsənəns/ ▷ *noun* **1** *music* an unpleasant combination of sounds or notes; lack of harmony. **2** disagreement; incompatibility. ⓘ 16c: from Latin *dissonare* to be discordant.

dissonant /ˈdɪsənənt/ ▷ *adj* lacking in harmony; harsh-sounding. ⓘ 15c.

dissuade /dɪˈsweɪd/ ▷ *verb* (***dissuaded, dissuading***) (*usually* **dissuade someone from doing something**) to deter them with advice or persuasion. • **dissuasion** *noun*. • **dissuasive** *adj*. • **dissuasively** *adverb*. ⓘ 15c, originally meaning 'to advise someone against something': from Latin *dissuadere*.

dissyllable and **dissyllabic** see DISYLLABLE

dissymmetry /dɪsˈsɪmətrɪ/ ▷ *noun* **1** lack of symmetry. **2** the symmetry of an object and its mirror-image, or of the right and left hands, etc. • **dissymmetric** or **dissymmetrical** *adj*. ⓘ 19c.

distaff /ˈdɪstɑːf/ ▷ *noun* **1** the rod on which a bunch of wool, flax, etc is held ready for spinning by hand. **2** *literary* used to represent women or women's work. • **the distaff side** *old use* the wife's or mother's side of the family. ⓘ Anglo-Saxon *distæf*.

distal /ˈdɪstəl/ ▷ *adj* **1** *anatomy* farthest from the point of attachment. Compare PROXIMAL. **2** *dentistry* farthest from the centre. ⓘ 19c: formed from DISTANCE on the analogy of *central*.

Distalgesic /dɪstəlˈdʒiːzɪk/ ▷ *noun, trademark* a painkiller in tablet form, containing PARACETAMOL. ⓘ 1950s: from *Distillers' Co Ltd* + *analgesic*.

distance /ˈdɪstəns/ ▷ *noun* **1** the measured length between two points in space. **2** the fact of being apart. **3** any faraway point or place; the furthest visible area. **4** coldness of manner. **5** *horse-racing, Brit*, a point 240 yards back from the winning post. **6** *horse-racing, US* a final stretch of the course which a horse must reach during the heats before the winner reaches the finish, in order to qualify for the final heat. ▷ *adj, athletics* **1** said of races: over a long distance. **2** said of athletes: competing in longer races. ▷ *verb* (***distanced, distancing***) **1** to put someone or something at a distance. **2** (*usually* **distance oneself from someone** or **something**) to declare oneself to be unconnected or unsympathetic to something □ *distanced themselves from government policy*. • **go the distance** *colloq* said especially of someone involved in a sporting contest, especially in boxing: to last out until the end. • **keep one's distance** to stay safely away, especially refusing involvement; to avoid friendship or familiarity. ⓘ 13c: from Latin *distancia*.

distance education and **distance teaching** ▷ *noun* the provision of educational courses using means such as correspondence courses, television, etc, for students unable to attend the educational establishment concerned in person.

distance learning ▷ *noun* following courses provided in DISTANCE EDUCATION.

distant /ˈdɪstənt/ ▷ *adj* **1** far away or far apart in space or time. **2** not closely related. **3** cold and unfriendly. **4** appearing to be lost in thought. • **distantly** *adverb*. ⓘ 14c.

distaste /dɪsˈteɪst/ ▷ *noun* dislike; aversion. • **distasteful** *adj*. ⓘ 16c.

distemper[1] /dɪˈstɛmpə(r)/ ▷ *noun* any of several infectious disease of animals, especially a viral infection **canine distemper**, often fatal to dogs. ⓘ 16c, meaning a mental or physical ailment: from French *destemprer* to derange.

distemper[2] /dɪˈstɛmpə(r)/ ▷ *noun* any water-based paint, especially when mixed with glue or SIZE[2] and used eg for poster-painting or murals. ▷ *verb* (***distempered, distempering***) to paint with distemper. ⓘ 19c as *verb*, 17c as *noun*: originally from Latin *distemperare* to soak.

distend /dɪˈstɛnd/ ▷ *verb* (***distended, distending***) *tr & intr* to make or become swollen, inflated or stretched. • **distensible** *adj*. • **distension** *noun*. ⓘ 14c: from Latin *distendere*.

distil or (*N Amer*) **distill** /dɪ'stɪl/ ▻ *verb* (***distilled, distilling***) **1** to purify a liquid by the process of distillation. **2** to produce alcoholic spirits in this way. **3** to create a shortened or condensed version of something. ⓒ 14c: from Latin *destillare* to drip down.

distillate /'dɪstɪleɪt/ ▻ *noun* a concentrated extract, the product of distilling. ⓒ 19c.

distillation /dɪstɪ'leɪʃən/ ▻ *noun* **1** *chem* a method of purifying a liquid by heating it to boiling point and condensing the vapour formed to a liquid called the DISTILLATE, which is then collected. **2** the DISTILLATE.

distilled water ▻ *noun, chem* water that has been purified by distillation.

distiller ▻ *noun* a person or company that makes alcoholic spiris. ⓒ 16c.

distillery ▻ *noun* (***distilleries***) a place where alcoholic spirits are distilled.

distinct /dɪ'stɪŋkt/ ▻ *adj* **1** easily seen, heard or recognized; clear or obvious. **2** noticeably different or separate. • **distinctly** *adverb*. ⓒ 14c: from Latin *distinctus*, from *distinguere* to distinguish.

distinction /dɪ'stɪŋkʃən/ ▻ *noun* **1** exceptional ability or achievement, or an honour awarded in recognition of it. **2** the act of differentiating. **3** the state of being noticeably different. **4** a distinguishing feature. ⓒ 14c: from Latin *distinctio*.

distinctive /dɪ'stɪŋktɪv/ ▻ *adj* easily recognized because very individual. • **distinctiveness** *noun*.

distinguish /dɪ'stɪŋgwɪʃ/ ▻ *verb* (***distinguishes, distinguished, distinguishing***) **1** (*often* **distinguish one thing from another**) to mark or recognize them as different. **2** *intr* (*often* **distinguish between things** or **people**) to see the difference between them. **3** to make out or identify something. **4** (*always* **distinguish oneself**) *often ironic* to be considered outstanding because of some achievement. • **distinguishable** *adj*. • **distinguishing** *adj*. ⓒ 16c: from Latin *distinguere*.

distinguished ▻ *adj* **1** famous (and usually well respected). **2** with a noble or dignified appearance.

distort /dɪ'stɔːt/ ▻ *verb* (***distorted, distorting***) **1** to twist something out of shape. **2** to change the meaning or tone of (a statement, etc) by inaccurate retelling. **3** *radio, telecomm* to alter the quality of (a signal), eg making sound less clear. • **distortion** *noun*. ⓒ 15c: from Latin *distorquere, distortum*.

distract /dɪ'strakt/ ▻ *verb* (***distracted, distracting***) **1** (*usually* **distract someone** or **someone's attention from something**) to divert their attention from it. **2** to entertain or amuse someone. **3** to confuse, worry or anger someone. • **distracted** *adj*. • **distracting** *adj*. ⓒ 14c: from Latin *distrahere* to draw apart.

distraction ▻ *noun* **1** something that diverts the attention. **2** an amusement; recreation. **3** anxiety; anger. **4** madness. ⓒ 15c.

distrain /dɪ'streɪn/ ▻ *verb, law* to seize (eg property) as, or in order to force, payment of a debt. ⓒ 13c as *destreyn*: from French *destraindre*.

distraint /dɪ'straint/ ▻ *noun, law* seizure of property or goods in order to meet a debt or obligation. ⓒ 18c: from DISTRAIN.

distrait /dɪ'streɪ/ ▻ *adj, literary* thinking of other things. ⓒ 18c: French.

distraught /dɪ'strɔːt/ ▻ *adj* in an extremely troubled state of mind. ⓒ 14c: a form of DISTRACT.

distress /dɪ'strɛs/ ▻ *noun* **1** mental or emotional pain. **2** financial difficulty; hardship. **3** great danger; peril □ ***a ship in distress***. ▻ *verb* (***distresses, distressed, distressing***) **1** to cause distress to someone; to upset someone. **2** to give (fabric, furniture, etc) the appearance of being older than it is. • **distressed** *adj*. • **distressing** *adj*. ⓒ 13c as *destresse*: from French *destresse*.

distress signal ▻ *noun* a radio signal, flare, etc put out by a ship, etc, in danger.

distribute /dɪ'strɪbjuːt, 'dɪstrɪbjuːt/ ▻ *verb* (***distributed, distributing***) **1** to give out something. **2** to supply or deliver (goods). **3** to spread out widely; to disperse. ⓒ 15c: from Latin *distribuere, distributum*.

distribution /dɪstrɪ'bjuːʃən/ ▻ *noun* **1** the process of distributing or being distributed. **2** the location or pattern of things spread out. **3** *statistics* a set of measurements or values, together with the observed or predicted frequencies with which they occur. ⓒ 14c.

distributive ▻ *adj* **1** relating to distribution. **2** *grammar* said of a word: referring individually to all members of a group, as do the words *each, every*.

distributor ▻ *noun* **1** a person or company that distributes goods, especially someone dealing between manufacturer and retailer. **2** a device in the ignition system of a car or other motor vehicle that directs pulses of high-voltage electricity from the induction coil to the spark plugs in the cylinders of the engine.

district /'dɪstrɪkt/ ▻ *noun* an area or region, especially one forming an administrative or geographical unit. ⓒ 17c: from Latin *districtus* jurisdiction.

district attorney ▻ *noun, especially US* a lawyer employed by a district to conduct prosecutions. Often shortened to **DA**.

district court ▻ *noun, especially US* the federal court for a district.

district nurse ▻ *noun* a nurse who visits patients in their homes to give them treatment.

distrust ▻ *verb* to have no trust in someone or something; to doubt them or it. ▻ *noun* suspicion; lack of trust. See also MISTRUST. • **distrustful** *adj*. • **distrustfully** *adverb*. ⓒ 15c.

distrustful ▻ *adj* having no trust in someone or something; suspicious. ⓒ 16c.

disturb /dɪ'stɜːb/ ▻ *verb* (***disturbed, disturbing***) **1** to interrupt someone. **2** to inconvenience someone. **3** to upset the arrangement or order of something. **4** to upset the peace of mind of someone. • **disturbed** *adj, psychol* emotionally upset or confused; maladjusted. • **disturbing** *adj*. ⓒ 13c: from Latin *disturbare*.

disturbance /dɪ'stɜːbəns/ ▻ *noun* **1** an outburst of noisy or violent behaviour. **2** an interruption. **3** an act of disturbing or the process of being disturbed. ⓒ 13c.

disunite ▻ *verb* to drive (people, etc) apart; to cause disagreement or conflict between (people) or within (a group). • **disunity** *noun*. ⓒ 16c.

disuse /dɪs'juːs/ ▻ *noun* the state of no longer being used, practised or observed; neglect. • **disused** /-'juːzd/ *adj*. ⓒ 16c.

disyllable or **dissyllable** /'daɪsɪləbəl/ ▻ *noun* a word of two syllables. • **disyllabic** or **dissyllabic** /daɪsɪ'labɪk, dɪ-/ *adj*. ⓒ 16c: from Greek *di-* twice + SYLLABLE.

ditch ▻ *noun* (***ditches***) a narrow channel dug in the ground for drainage or irrigation or as a boundary. ▻ *verb* (***ditches, ditched, ditching***) **1** *slang* to get rid of someone or something; to abandon them. **2** *tr & intr, colloq* said of an aircraft or a pilot: to bring or come down in the sea. ⓒ Anglo-Saxon *dic*.

dither /'dɪðə(r)/ ▻ *verb* (***dithered, dithering***) *intr* to act in a nervously uncertain manner; to waver. ▻ *noun* a state of nervous indecision. • **ditherer** *noun*. • **dithery** *adj*. ⓒ 20c in this sense, originally 14c *didderen* to tremble or shake.

ditsy or **ditzy** /'dɪtsɪ/ ▻ *adj* (***ditsier, ditsiest***) *N Amer colloq* scatterbrained; flighty. ⓒ 20c: perhaps a mixture of DOTTY + DIZZY.

ditto ▻ *noun* (***dittos***) ▻ *noun* the same thing; the above; that which has just been said. ▻ *adverb* (abbreviation **do**) likewise; the same. ⓒ 17c: Italian, meaning 'aforesaid', from Latin *dictum* said.

ditto marks ▻ *noun* a symbol (") written immediately below a word, etc in a list to mean 'same as above'.

ditty ▻ *noun* (***ditties***) a short simple song or poem. ⓒ 14c as *ditee*: from French *dité*, from Latin *dictatum* something dictated or composed.

diuretic /daɪjʊ'rɛtɪk/ *medicine* ▻ *noun* a drug or other substance that increases the volume of urine produced and excreted. ▻ *adj* said of a substance: increasing the production and excretion of urine. ⓒ 14c: from Greek *dia* through + *ouron* urine.

diurnal /daɪ'ɜːnəl/ *formal, technical* ▻ *adj* **1** daily. **2** during the day. **3** said of animals: active during the day. **4** said of flowers: open during the day. • **diurnally** *adverb*. ⓒ 15c: from Latin *diurnus*.

div see DIVVY.

div. ▻ *abbreviation* **1** divide. **2** division. **3** divorce or divorced.

diva /'diːvə/ ▻ *noun* (***divas*** or ***dive*** /'diːveɪ/) a great female singer, especially in opera. ⓒ 19c: Latin, meaning 'goddess'.

divalent /daɪ'veɪlənt/ ▻ *adj, chem* said of an atom: able to combine with two atoms of hydrogen or the equivalent. ⓒ 19c: DI- + -VALENT.

Divali see DIWALI

divan /dɪ'van/ ▻ *noun* **1** a sofa with no back or sides. **2** a bed without a headboard or footboard. ⓒ 18c in these senses: 16c in historical sense meaning 'an oriental council': from Persian *diwan* long seat.

dive[1] /daɪv/ ▻ *verb* (***dived*** or (*N Amer*) ***dove*** /doʊv/, ***diving***) *intr* **1** to throw oneself into water, usually headfirst, or plunge down through water. **2** said of a submarine, etc: to become submerged. **3** to descend or fall steeply through the air. **4** to throw oneself to the side or to the ground □ ***The keeper had to dive to catch the ball.*** **5** to move quickly and suddenly out of sight □ ***diving behind a tree.*** ▻ *noun* **1** an act of diving. **2** *slang* any dirty or disreputable place, especially a bar or club. **3** *boxing slang* a faked knockout □ ***take a dive.*** • **diving** *noun* the activity or sport of plunging into water. ⓒ Anglo-Saxon *dyfan*.

■ **dive in** to help oneself to (food)

■ **dive into something 1** to plunge one's hands (eg into a bag). **2** to involve oneself enthusiastically in an undertaking.

dive[2] see DIVA

dive-bomb ▻ *verb* to bomb while diving in an aircraft. • **dive-bombing** *noun*.

dive-bomber ▻ *noun* an aeroplane that releases a bomb while diving.

diver /daɪvə(r)/ ▻ *noun* **1** someone who dives. **2** someone who swims or works underwater. **3** any one of various diving birds, especially one of a type of large bird, native to northern waters of the N hemisphere. ⓒ 16c.

diverge /daɪ'vɜːdʒ, dɪ-/ ▻ *verb* (***diverged, diverging***) *intr* **1** to separate and go in different directions. **2** to differ. • **divergence** *noun*. • **divergent** *adj*. ⓒ 17c: from Latin *divergere*, from *vergere* to turn.

■ **diverge from something** to depart or deviate (eg from a usual course).

diverging lens ▻ *noun, physics* a lens that causes light rays to spread out, eg a concave lens.

divers /'daɪvəz/ ▻ *adj, archaic, literary* various; many different. ⓒ 13c: from Latin *diversus*; see etymology of DIVERSE.

diverse, divers

These words are sometimes confused with each other.

diverse /daɪ'vɜːs, dɪ-/ ▻ *adj* **1** various; assorted. **2** different; dissimilar. • **diversely** *adverb*. ⓒ 13c: from Latin *diversus* turned different ways.

diversify /daɪ'vɜːsɪfaɪ, dɪ-/ ▻ *verb* (***diversifies, diversified, diversifying***) **1** *tr & intr* to become or make something diverse. **2** *intr* to engage in new and different activities; to branch out. • diversification *noun*. ⓒ 15c.

diversion /daɪ'vɜːʃən, dɪ-/ ▻ *noun* **1** the act of diverting; the state of being diverted. **2** a detour from a usual route. **3** something intended to draw attention away. **4** amusement. • **diversionary** *adj*. ⓒ 17c: from Latin *diversio*.

diversity ▻ *noun* (***diversities***) variety in kind; being varied or different. ⓒ 14c: from French *diversité*.

divert /daɪ'vɜːt, dɪ-/ ▻ *verb* (***diverted, diverting***) **1** to make someone or something change direction. **2** to draw away (especially attention). **3** to amuse someone. • **diverting** *adj*. • **divertingly** *adverb*. ⓒ 15c: from Latin *divertere* to turn aside.

diverticular /daɪvə'tɪkjʊlə(r)/ ▻ *adj* relating to or affecting diverticula. ⓒ 19c.

diverticulitis /daɪvətɪkjʊ'laɪtɪs/ ▻ *noun* inflammation of one or more diverticula. ⓒ Early 20c.

diverticulum /daɪvə'tɪkjʊləm/ ▻ *noun* (***diverticula*** /-lə/) a pouch formed at a weak point in the muscular wall of the alimentary canal, especially the colon. ⓒ 17c: Latin, originally meaning 'a byway' or 'retreat'.

divertimento /dɪvɜːtɪ'mɛntoʊ/ ▻ *noun* (***divertimenti*** /-tiː/ or ***divertimentos***) a light musical composition usually written for an orchestra or chamber ensemble and intended primarily for entertainment. ⓒ 19c: Italian, originally meaning 'entertainment' or 'amusement'.

divest /daɪ'vɛst, dɪ-/ ▻ *verb* (***divested, divesting***) (*usually* **divest someone of something**) **1** to take away or get rid of it □ ***divested himself of his peerage.*** **2** *rather formal* to undress □ ***divested herself of her jacket and scarf.*** • **divestment** *noun*. ⓒ 16c as *devest*: from Latin *de-* away from + *vestire* to clothe.

divi see DIVVY

divide /dɪ'vaɪd/ ▻ *verb* (***divided, dividing***) **1** *tr & intr* to split up or separate into parts. **2** (*also* **divide something up**) to share. **3** *math* **a** to determine how many times one number is contained in (another); **b** *intr* said of a number: to be a number of times greater or smaller than another □ ***3 divides into 9.*** **4** to bring about a disagreement among (people); to set (people) at odds. **5** to serve as a boundary between something. **6** *intr* said of an assembly, Parliament, etc: to form into groups voting for and against a motion. ▻ *noun* **1** a disagreement; a gap or split. **2** *especially US* a ridge of high land between two rivers. ⓒ 14c: from Latin *dividere* to force apart.

divided highway ▻ *noun, N Amer* a dual carriageway.

dividend /'dɪvɪdɛnd/ ▻ *noun* **1** a portion of a company's profits paid to a shareholder. **2** a benefit □ ***Meeting her would pay dividends.*** **3** *math* a number divided by another number. • **declare a dividend** to announce the sum per cent a trading concern is prepared to pay its shareholders. ⓒ 15c: from Latin *dividendum* what is to be divided.

dividers /dɪ'vaɪdəz/ ▻ *plural noun* a V-shaped device with movable arms ending in points, used in geometry, etc for measuring.

divination /dɪvɪ'neɪʃən/ ▻ *noun* **1** the practice of foretelling the future by, or as if by, supernatural means. **2** insight. **3** a guess. ⓒ 14c: from DIVINE.

divine /dɪ'vaɪn/ ▻ *adj* **1** belonging or relating to, or coming from God or a god. **2** *colloq* extremely pleasant or beautiful; excellent. ▻ *verb* (***divined***, ***divining***) **1** to foretell something. **2** to learn of something by intuition; to guess it. **3** *tr & intr* to search for (underground water) with a divining-rod. ▻ *noun* a member of the clergy who is expert in theology. • **divinely** *adverb*. • **diviner** *noun*. ◷ 14c: from Latin *divinus*, from *divus* a god.

divine office ▻ *noun, Christianity* the prayers recited daily by priests, devotees, monks, etc, which in the RC Church are those of the BREVIARY.

divine right ▻ *noun* **1** *colloq* any authority supposed to be unquestionable. **2** the concept that monarchs rule by the authority of God rather than by the consent of the people. Also called **the divine right of kings**.

diving *present participle of* DIVE[1]

divingbell ▻ *noun* a large hollow bottomless underwater container which traps air, and to which a diver without breathing apparatus returns to breathe in oxygen.

divingboard ▻ *noun* a narrow platform from which swimmers can dive into a pool, etc.

divingsuit ▻ *noun* a diver's waterproof suit, especially one with a helmet and heavy boots for walking on the sea-bottom, etc.

divining *present participle of* DIVINE

divining rod and **dowsing rod** ▻ *noun* a stick, especially of hazel, held near the ground when divining for water, which allegedly twitches when a discovery is made.

divinity /dɪ'vɪnɪtɪ/ ▻ *noun* (***divinities***) **1** theology. **2** a god. **3** the state of being God or a god. ◷ 14c: from Latin *divinitas*, from *divinus* DIVINE.

divisible /dɪ'vɪsɪbəl/ ▻ *adj* able to be divided. ◷ 16c: from Latin *divisibilis*.

division /dɪ'vɪʒən/ ▻ *noun* **1** the act of dividing; the state of being divided. **2** something that divides or separates; a gap or barrier. **3** one of the parts into which something is divided. **4** a major unit of an organization such as an army or police force. **5** *math* the process of determining how many times one number, the DIVISOR, is contained in another, the DIVIDEND. **6** a formal vote in Parliament. **7** *bot* in taxonomy: any of the major groups, eg *Bryophyta* (the mosses and liverworts), into which the plant kingdom (sense 2) is divided and which in turn is subdivided into one or more CLASSes (sense 9). It corresponds to the PHYLUM in the animal kingdom. ◷ 14c.

divisional /dɪ'vɪʒənəl/ ▻ *adj* belonging or relating to a division or section, especially of a business or organization ◻ *divisional headquarters*.

Divisional Court ▻ *noun, law* in England and Wales: a court attached to each of the three divisions of the HIGH COURT, presided over by three judges and hearing appeals from the relevant division.

Divisionism see POINTILLISM

division lobby see LOBBY

division sign ▻ *noun* the symbol ÷, representing division in calculations.

divisive /dɪ'vaɪsɪv, -zɪv/ ▻ *adj* tending to cause disagreement or conflict. • **divisively** *adverb*. • **divisiveness** *noun*. ◷ 16c: from late Latin *divisivus*.

divisor /dɪ'vaɪzə(r)/ ▻ *noun, math* a number by which another number, the DIVIDEND, is divided. ◷ 15c: Latin *divisor* divider.

divorce /dɪ'vɔːs/ ▻ *noun* **1** the legal ending of a marriage. **2** a complete separation. ▻ *verb* (***divorced***, ***divorcing***) **1** *tr & intr* to legally end marriage to someone. **2** to separate. • **divorced** *adj*. ◷ 14c: from Latin *divortere* to leave one's husband.

divorcee /dɪvɔː'siː, -'vɔːsiː/ ▻ *noun* (***divorcees***) someone who has been divorced.

divot /'dɪvət/ ▻ *noun* a clump of grass and earth removed, especially by the blade of a golf club. ◷ 19c in this sense; 16c Scots and N English, meaning 'a sod', especially one cut for roofing.

divulge /daɪ'vʌldʒ, dɪ-/ ▻ *verb* (***divulged***, ***divulging***) to make something known; to reveal (a secret, etc). • **divulgence** *noun*. ◷ 15c: from Latin *divulgare* to publish widely.

divvy[1] /'dɪvɪ/ *slang, noun* (***divvies***) a dividend or share. Also called **div** or **divi**. ▻ *verb* (***divvies***, ***divvied***, ***divvying***) (*also* **divvy up something**) to divide or share it. ◷ 19c.

divvy[2] /'dɪvɪ/ *colloq noun* (***divvies***) a stupid person; a fool. ▻ *adj* stupid; silly. ◷ 20c.

Diwali /diː'wɑːliː/ or **Divali** /-'vɑːliː/ ▻ *noun* the Hindu festival of lights, held in October or November in honour of Lakshmi, goddess of wealth and good fortune. ◷ 17c: Hindi.

dixie /'dɪksɪ/ ▻ *noun* (***dixies***) a metal cooking-pot or kettle. ◷ 19c: perhaps from Hindi *degci* a cooking-pot.

Dixieland ▻ *noun, music* an early style of jazz in New Orleans, played by small combinations of instruments. ◷ Early 20c: from the name given to the southern states of the US.

DIY ▻ *abbreviation* do-it-yourself.

dizygotic /daɪzaɪ'gɒtɪk/ ▻ *adj, biol* developed from two ZYGOTEs or fertilized eggs. Also called **fraternal**.

dizzy /'dɪzɪ/ ▻ *adj* (***dizzier***, ***dizziest***) **1** experiencing or causing a spinning sensation resulting in loss of balance ◻ *feel dizzy* ◻ *dizzy heights*. **2** *colloq* silly; not reliable or responsible ◻ *We need a trained nanny, not a dizzy teenager*. **3** *colloq* bewildered. ▻ *verb* (***dizzies***, ***dizzied***, ***dizzying***) **1** to make someone dizzy. **2** to bewilder someone. • **dizzily** *adverb*. • **dizziness** *noun*. ◷ Anglo-Saxon *dysig* foolish.

DJ ▻ *abbreviation* **1** *slang* dinner jacket. **2** disc jockey.

djinn and **djinni** see JINNI

DK ▻ *abbreviation, IVR* Denmark.

dl ▻ *abbreviation* decilitre or decilitres.

DLitt ▻ *abbreviation*: *Doctor Litterarum* (Latin), Doctor of Letters.

DM and **D-mark** /'deɪ—/ ▻ *abbreviation* Deutschmark.

DMs ▻ *abbreviation, colloq* Doc Martens.

DMus ▻ *abbreviation* Doctor of Music.

DMZ ▻ *abbreviation* demilitarized zone.

DNA /diːen'eɪ/ ▻ *abbreviation* deoxyribonucleic acid.

DNA fingerprinting ▻ *noun* GENETIC FINGERPRINTING.

DNB ▻ *abbreviation* Dictionary of National Biography.

D-notice ▻ *noun* a notice sent by the government to newspapers asking them not to publish certain information for reasons of security. ◷ 1940s: from *defence notice*.

do[1] /duː/ ▻ *verb* (***does*** /dʌz/, *past tense* ***did***, *past participle* ***done*** /dʌn/, *present participle* ***doing*** /'duːɪŋ/) **1** to carry out, perform or commit something. **2** to finish or complete something. **3** *tr & intr* to be enough or suitable ◻ *That will do for me* ◻ *That will do me*. **4** to work at or study ◻ *Are you doing maths?* **5** *intr* to be in a particular state ◻ *Business is doing well*. **6** to put in order or arrange. **7** *intr* to act or behave. **8** to provide something as a service ◻ *do lunches*. **9** to bestow (honour, etc). **10** to cause or produce. **11** to travel (a distance). **12** to travel at (a speed). **13** *colloq* to be an improvement or enhancement to something or someone ◻ *This dress doesn't do much for my figure*. **14** *colloq* to cheat someone. **15** *colloq* to copy the behaviour of someone; to mimic them. **16** to visit (a place, etc) as a tourist. **17** *colloq* to ruin something □ *Now he's done it!* **18** *colloq* to assault or injure someone □ *Tell me, or I'll do you.* **19** *colloq* to spend (time) in prison. **20** *colloq* to convict someone. **21** *intr, colloq* to happen □ *There was nothing doing.* **22** *slang* to take (drugs). ▻ *auxiliary verb* **1** used in questions and negative statements or commands, as in *Do you smoke?*, *I don't like wine* and *Don't do that!* **2** used to avoid repetition of a verb, as in *She eats as much as I do* and *She comes here every day, does she?* **3** used for emphasis, as in *She does know you've arrived.* ▻ *noun* (***dos*** or ***do's*** /duːz/) *colloq* **1** a party or other gathering. **2** something done as a rule or custom □ *dos and don'ts.* **3** a violent scene; a fracas. • **could do with something** or **someone** would benefit from having them □ We could do with Meg in our team. • **have** or **be to do with someone** or **something** **1** said of a thing, event, etc: to be related to or connected with something else □ *What has that to do with your question?* □ *It has nothing to do with me.* **2** said of a person: to be partly or wholly responsible for something □ *I had nothing to do with the arrangement.* ◷ Anglo-Saxon *don.*

■ **do away with someone** or **something** **1** to murder them. **2** to abolish (an institution, etc).

■ **do someone** or **something down** to speak of them or it as if unimportant or not very good.

■ **do for someone** *colloq* to do household cleaning for them on a regular basis.

■ **do someone in** *colloq* **1** to kill them. **2** to exhaust them.

■ **do something out** to clear out (a room, etc); to decorate it.

■ **do someone out of something** to deprive them of it, especially by trickery.

■ **do someone over** *slang* **1** to rob them. **2** to attack or injure them.

■ **do oneself up** to dress up.

■ **do something up** *colloq* **1** to repair, clean or improve the decoration of a building, etc. **2** to fasten it; to tie or wrap it up.

■ **do without something** to manage without it.

do

The use of **do** as a substitute for **have** in sentences such as *I have a more demanding job than you do* is sometimes regarded as poor style, and is best avoided in formal contexts.

do² see DOH

do. ▻ *abbreviation* ditto.

DOA ▻ *abbreviation, medicine* said especially referring to arrival at hospital: dead on arrival.

doable /'duːəbəl/ ▻ *adj* able to be done. ◷ 15c.

dob *Austral, NZ* ▻ *verb* (***dobbed***, ***dobbing***) (*often* **dob someone in**) to inform on or betray them. • **dobber** or **dobber-in** *noun.* ◷ 20c: from 19c English dialect meaning 'to put down'.

dob ▻ *abbreviation* date of birth.

Dobermann pinscher /'doʊbəmən 'pɪnʃə(r)/ or **Dobermann** ▻ *noun* a large breed of dog with a smooth black-and-tan coat. ◷ 20c: from Ludwig Dobermann, 19c German breeder's name + German *Pinscher* terrier.

DOC ▻ *abbreviation* **1** said of wine: *Denominazione di Origine Controllata* (Italian), the Italian equivalent of APPELLATION CONTRÔLLÉE. Compare DOCG. **2** District Officer Commanding.

doc ▻ *noun, colloq* a doctor.

DOCG ▻ *abbreviation*: *Denominazione di Origine Controllata* ▻ *Garantita* (Italian), a designation of wines, guaranteeing quality, strength, etc. Compare DOC.

docile /'doʊsaɪl or *N Amer* 'dɒsaɪl/ ▻ *adj* easy to manage or control; submissive. • **docilely** *adverb* in a docile or willing manner. • **docility** /doʊ'sɪlɪtɪ/ *noun* a docile manner. ◷ 15c: from Latin *docilis* easily taught.

dock¹ ▻ *noun* **1** a harbour where ships are loaded, unloaded, and repaired. **2** (**docks**) the area surrounding this. ▻ *verb* (***docked***, ***docking***) *tr & intr* **1** to bring or come into a dock. **2** said of space vehicles: to link up in space. • **in dock** **1** being repaired. **2** *colloq* said of a person: in hospital. ◷ 16c: from Dutch *docke.*

dock² ▻ *verb* (***docked***, ***docking***) **1** to cut off all or part of (an animal's tail). **2** to make deductions from (especially someone's pay). **3** to deduct (an amount). ◷ 14c as *dok.*

dock³ ▻ *noun* a weed with large broad leaves and a deep root. ◷ Anglo-Saxon *docce.*

dock⁴ *noun* the enclosure in a court of law where the accused sits or stands. • **in the dock** **1** on trial in court. **2** facing criticism. ◷ 16c: from Flemish *dok* cage or sty.

docker ▻ *noun* a labourer who loads and unloads ships. ◷ 19c.

docket /'dɒkɪt/ ▻ *noun* any label or note accompanying a parcel or package, eg detailing contents or recording receipt. ▻ *verb* (***docketed***, ***docketing***) to fix a label to something; to record the contents or delivery of something. ◷ 15c: possibly from DOCK².

dockland ▻ *noun* the district round about the docks.

dockyard ▻ *noun* a shipyard, especially a naval one.

Doc Martens /dɒk 'mɑːtɪnz/ ▻ *noun, trademark* (abbreviation **DMs**) a make of lace-up leather boots and shoes with light thick resilient soles. ◷ 1960s: named after the inventor of the sole, Klaus Maertens.

doctor /'dɒktə(r)/ ▻ *noun* **1** someone trained and qualified to practise medicine. **2** *N Amer* **a** a dentist; **b** a veterinary surgeon. **3** someone holding a DOCTORATE. **4** *angling* a type of fly. ▻ *verb* (***doctored***, ***doctoring***) **1** to falsify (eg information). **2** to tamper with something; to drug (food or drink). **3** *colloq* to sterilize or castrate (an animal). **4** *often facetious* to give medical treatment to someone. • **what the doctor ordered** *colloq* the very thing that is needed. ◷ 14c, originally meaning 'a very learned person': Latin, meaning 'teacher'.

doctoral /'dɒktərəl/ ▻ *adj* relating to a DOCTORATE □ *a doctoral thesis.*

doctorate /'dɒktərɪt/ ▻ *noun* a high academic degree, awarded especially for research. ◷ 17c.

doctoring ▻ *noun* practising as a doctor.

doctrinaire /dɒktrɪ'nɛə(r)/ ▻ *adj, derog* adhering rigidly to theories or principles, often regardless of practicalities or appropriateness. ◷ 19c: French.

doctrine /'dɒktrɪn/ ▻ *noun* a thing or things taught, especially any one of a set of religious or political beliefs, or such a set of beliefs. • **doctrinal** /dɒk'traɪnəl/ *adj.* ◷ 14c: from Latin *doctrina* teaching.

docudrama /'dɒkjʊdrɑːmə/ ▻ *noun* (***docudramas***) a play or film based on real events and characters. ◷ 1960s: a contraction of *documentary drama.*

document /'dɒkjʊmənt/ ▻ *noun* **1** any piece of writing of an official nature, eg a certificate. **2** *computing* a file of text produced and read by a computer, especially a word processor. ▻ *verb* (***documented***, ***documenting***) **1** to record something, especially in written form. **2** to provide written evidence to support or prove something. ◷ 15c: from Latin *documentum* lesson or proof.

documentary /dɒkjʊ'mɛntərɪ/ ▻ *noun* (***documentaries***) a film or television or radio programme presenting real people in real situations. ▻ *adj* **1** connected with, or consisting of, documents □ *documentary evidence.* **2** of the nature of a documentary; undramatized. • **documentarily** *adverb.* ◷ 19c as *adj* (sense 1).

documentation /dɒkjʊmɛn'teɪʃən/ ▷ *noun* **1** documents or documentary evidence. **2** the provision or collection of these. ⓒ 18c.

document reader ▷ *noun, computing* a form of optical character-reader which converts the characters into code and feeds them automatically into the computer.

dodder /'dɒdə(r)/ ▷ *verb* (***doddered, doddering***) *intr* to move in an unsteady trembling fashion, usually as a result of old age. • **dodderer** *noun.* • **doddering** *adj, derog* failing in body and mind; senile. • **doddery** *adj.* ⓒ 19c: possibly a variant of an older word *dadder.*

doddle /'dɒdəl/ ▷ *noun, colloq* something easily done or achieved. ⓒ 20c.

dodeca- ▷ *combining form, signifying* twelve. ⓒ Greek *dodeka* twelve.

dodecagon /doʊ'dɛkəgɒn/ ▷ *noun* a flat geometric figure with 12 sides and angles. ⓒ 17c: from Greek *dodekagonon,* from *dodeka* twelve + *gonia* angle.

dodecahedron /doʊdɛkə'hiːdrən/ ▷ *noun* a solid geometric figure with twelve faces. ⓒ 16c: from Greek *dodekaedron,* from *dodeka* twelve + *hedra* seat.

dodge /dɒdʒ/ ▷ *verb* (***dodged, dodging***) **1** to avoid (a blow, a person, etc) by moving quickly away, especially sideways. **2** to escape or avoid by cleverness or deceit. ▷ *noun* **1** a sudden movement aside. **2** a trick to escape or avoid something. ⓒ 16c.

Dodgems /'dɒdʒəmz/ ▷ *plural noun, trademark* a fairground amusement consisting of a rink in which drivers of small electric cars try to bump each other. ⓒ 1920s.

dodger /dɒdʒə(r)/ ▷ *noun* a shirker; a trickster.

dodgy ▷ *adj* (***dodgier, dodgiest***) *colloq* **1** difficult or risky. **2** untrustworthy; dishonest, or dishonestly obtained. **3** unstable; slightly broken. ⓒ 19c.

dodo /'doʊdoʊ/ ▷ *noun* (***dodos*** or ***dodoes***) **1** a large flightless bird of the pigeon family, about the size of a turkey, that once lived on the island of Mauritius, and became extinct around the middle of the 17c. **2** *colloq* any old-fashioned person or thing. **3** *colloq* a stupid person. • **as dead as a dodo** *colloq* **1** extinct. **2** out-of-date; obsolete. ⓒ 17c: from Portuguese *doudo* silly.

DoE ▷ *abbreviation* Department of the Environment.

doe /doʊ/ ▷ *noun* (***does*** /doʊz/ or ***doe***) an adult female rabbit, hare or small deer, eg the fallow deer. ⓒ Anglo-Saxon *da.*

doer /'duːə(r)/ ▷ *noun* **1** a person who does something. **2** a busy active person. **3** said especially of a horse: a healthy animal. ⓒ 14c.

does[1] see under DO[1]

does[2] see under DOE

doesn't /'dʌzənt/ ▷ *contraction of* does not.

doff ▷ *verb* (***doffed, doffing***) *old use, literary* **1** to lift (one's hat) in greeting. **2** to take off (a piece of clothing). ⓒ 14c: from DO[1] + OFF.

dog ▷ *noun* **1** any carnivorous mammal belonging to the family which includes the wolves, jackals and foxes. **2** any of many different breeds of a domestic species of this family. **3** the male of any such animal. **4** any of various mammals of other families, eg prairie dog. **5** a mechanical gripping device. **6** *offensive slang* an unattractive woman. **7** *colloq* a fellow or rogue. ▷ *verb* (***dogged*** /dɒgd/, ***dogging***) **1** to follow very closely; to track someone. **2** to trouble or plague someone. • **a dog's life** a life of misery. • **like a dog's dinner** *colloq, often disparaging* dressed smartly or showily. ⓒ Anglo-Saxon *docga.*

dog biscuit ▷ *noun* a hard kind of biscuit for dogs. ⓒ 19c.

dogcart ▷ *noun* a two-wheeled horse-drawn passenger carriage with seats back-to-back. ⓒ 19c in this sense; 17c, meaning 'a cart pulled by dogs'.

dog collar ▷ *noun* **1** a collar for a dog. **2** *colloq* a CLERICAL COLLAR. ⓒ 19c in sense 2; 16c in sense 1.

dog days ▷ *plural noun* the hottest period of the year, when the DOG STAR rises and sets with the sun. ⓒ 16c.

doge /doʊdʒ/ ▷ *noun* the chief magistrate in the former republics of Venice and Genoa. ⓒ 16c: Italian, meaning 'duke'.

dog-eared ▷ *adj* said of a book: with its pages turned down at the corners; shabby; scruffy. ⓒ 19c; 18c as *dog's eared.*

dog eat dog ▷ *noun* ruthless pursuit of one's own interests. Also *as adj* (**dog-eat-dog**).

dog-end ▷ *noun, slang* a cigarette end. ⓒ 1930s.

dogfight ▷ *noun* **1** a battle at close quarters between two fighter aircraft. **2** a fight between dogs. **3** any violent fight. ⓒ 17c.

dogfish ▷ *noun* any of various kinds of small shark. ⓒ 15c as *doke-fyche.*

dogged[1] /'dɒgɪd/ *adj* determined; resolute. • **doggedly** *adverb.* • **doggedness** *noun.* ⓒ 16c.

dogged[2] *past tense, past participle of* DOG

doggerel /'dɒgərəl/ ▷ *noun* **1** badly written poetry. **2** poetry with an irregular rhyming pattern for comic effect. ▷ *adj* of poor quality. ⓒ 14c, meaning 'worthless'.

doggier, doggies and **doggiest** see under DOGGY

dogging *present participle of* DOG

doggish /'dɒgɪʃ/ ▷ *adj* **1** like or characteristic of a dog. **2** churlish. ⓒ 15c.

doggo /'dɒgoʊ/ ▷ *adverb.* • **lie doggo** *rather old colloq use* to hide; to lie low. ⓒ 19c: probably from DOG.

doggone /'dɒgɒn, 'dɒggɒn/ *N Amer* ▷ *exclamation, indicating* annoyance. ▷ *adj, adverb* damned. Also **doggoned.** ⓒ 19c euphemisms *dog on, dog on it* for *God damn, God damn it.*

doggy /dɒgɪ/ ▷ *adj* (***doggier, doggiest***) *colloq* **1** belonging to, like or relating to dogs. **2** fond of dogs. ▷ *noun* (***doggies***) a child's word for a dog. Also **doggie** (***doggies***). ⓒ 17c.

doggy-bag ▷ *noun* a bag in which a customer at a restaurant can take home uneaten food. ⓒ 1960s.

doggy-paddle or **doggie-paddle** and **dog-paddle** ▷ *noun* a basic swimming stroke with short paddling movements like a dog's. ▷ *verb, intr* to swim using this stroke. ⓒ 20c.

dog-handler ▷ *noun* a person, especially a police officer, in charge of one or more specially trained dogs. ⓒ 1960s.

doghouse ▷ *noun, now chiefly N Amer* a KENNEL. • **in the doghouse** *colloq* out of favour. ⓒ 17c.

dog in the manger ▷ *noun* someone who has no need of something but refuses to let others use it. ▷ *adj* (*usually* **dog-in-the-manger**) characteristic of a dog in the manger; possessively selfish.

dogleg ▷ *noun* a sharp bend, especially on a golf course. ⓒ 19c.

dogma /'dɒgmə/ ▷ *noun* (***dogmas*** or ***dogmata*** /'dɒgmətə/) **1 a** a belief or principle laid down by an authority as unquestionably true; **b** such beliefs or principles in general. **2** *colloq* an opinion arrogantly stated. ⓒ 16c: Greek, meaning 'opinion'.

dogmatic /dɒg'matɪk/ ▷ *adj* **1** said of an opinion: forcefully and arrogantly stated as if unquestionable. **2** said of a person: tending to make such statements of opinion. • **dogmatically** *adverb.* ⓒ 17c.

dogmatism /'dɒgmətɪzəm/ ▷ *noun* the quality of being, or the tendency to be, dogmatic. • **dogmatist** *noun.*

dogmatize or **dogmatise** /ˈdɒgmətaɪz/ ▷ *verb* (***dogmatized***, ***dogmatizing***) *intr* to state one's opinions dogmatically. ⓢ 17c: from Greek *dogmatizein* to set out one's opinion.

do-gooder ▷ *noun, colloq* an enthusiastically helpful person, especially one whose help is unrealistic, impractical and not appreciated.

dog-paddle see under DOGGY-PADDLE

dog rose ▷ *noun* a European wild rose with pink or white flowers.

dogs ▷ *plural noun* (*always* **the dogs**) *colloq* greyhound racing. • **go to the dogs** *colloq* to deteriorate greatly. ⓢ 20c: DOG.

dogsbody ▷ *noun, colloq* someone who does menial tasks for someone else. Also called **hack**. ⓢ 20c: naval slang meaning 'a junior officer'.

dog's breakfast or **dinner** ▷ *noun* anything very messy or untidy.

Dog Star see SIRIUS

dog's-tongue see HOUND'S-TONGUE

dog's-tooth see HOUND'S TOOTH

dog tag ▷ *noun* a metal identity disc, etc, for a dog or *colloq* for a soldier. ⓢ 20c.

dog-tired ▷ *adj, colloq* extremely tired. ⓢ 19c.

dogtrot ▷ *noun* a gentle trotting pace.

dogwood ▷ *noun* a European shrub with small white flowers and purple berries.

doh or **do** /doʊ/ ▷ *noun, music* in sol-fa notation: the first note of the major scale. ⓢ 18c: see SOL-FA.

DoI ▷ *abbreviation* Department of Industry.

doily or **doyley** /ˈdɔɪlɪ/ ▷ *noun* (***doilies*** or ***doyleys***) a small decorative napkin of lace or lace-like paper laid on plates under sandwiches, cakes, etc. ⓢ 17c: named after Doily, a London draper.

do-in /doʊ-ˈɪn/ ▷ *noun, alternative medicine* a form of self-applied ACUPRESSURE massage that originated in China and Japan. ⓢ 1960s: Japanese, meaning 'the way of energy'.

doings /ˈduːɪŋz/ **1** *plural noun* activities; behaviour. **2** *plural noun, colloq* working parts; pieces of equipment. **3** *singular noun, colloq* something whose name cannot be remembered or is left unsaid.

do-it-yourself (abbreviation **DIY**) *noun* the practice of doing one's own household repairs, etc without professional help. ▷ *adj* designed to be built, constructed, etc by an amateur rather than a fully trained professional. ⓢ 1950s.

Dolby /ˈdɒlbɪ/ or **Dolby system** ▷ *noun* a system of noise reduction in magnetic audio tape-recording, used to reduce the background hissing sound heard during replay, and to improve the quality of stereophonic sound in cinemas. ⓢ 1960s: named after the US engineer Raymond Dolby (born 1933).

dolce /ˈdɒltʃɪ/ ▷ *adj, adverb, music* to be sung or played gently or sweetly. ⓢ 19c: Italian, meaning 'sweet'.

dolce vita /ˈdɒltʃɪ viːtə/ ▷ *noun* (*often* **la dolce vita**) a life of wealth, pleasure and self-indulgence. ⓢ 1960s: Italian.

the doldrums /ˈdɒldrəmz/ ▷ *plural noun* **1** a depressed mood; low spirits. **2** a state of inactivity. **3** (*also* **the Doldrums**) *meteorol* a hot humid region on either side of the Equator where there is generally little or no wind. ⓢ 19c: from obsolete *dold* stupid.

dole /doʊl/ ▷ *noun, colloq* (**the dole**) unemployment benefit. ▷ *verb* (***doled***, ***doling***) *intr* (*always* **dole something out**) to hand it out or give it out. • **on the dole** *colloq* unemployed; receiving a Job Seekers Allowance (formerly Unemployment Benefit), or another Social Security benefit. ⓢ Anglo-Saxon *dal* share.

dole-bludger ▷ *noun, Austral & NZ slang* someone who prefers living off state benefits to working

doleful /ˈdoʊlfʊl/ ▷ *adj* sad; expressing or suggesting sadness; mournful. • **dolefully** *adverb*. • **dolefulness** *noun*. ⓢ 13c as *deolful*: from French *doel* grief + -FUL.

dolichocephalic see CEPHALIC INDEX

doll ▷ *noun* **1** a toy in the form of a model of a human being, especially a baby. **2** *derog, colloq* a showy overdressed woman. **3** *slang, often offensive* any girl or woman, especially when considered pretty. **4** *colloq* a term of endearment, especially for a girl. ▷ *verb* (***dolled***, ***dolling***) (*always* **doll oneself up**) to dress smartly or showily. ⓢ 17c as *noun* 1; 16c, meaning a female favourite; from the name Dolly, a short form of Dorothy.

dollar /ˈdɒlə(r)/ ▷ *noun* (symbol $) the standard unit of currency in the US, Canada, Australia and numerous other countries, divided into 100 CENTS. ⓢ 18c: originally 16c name for a German *Thaler*: short for *Joachimsthaler*, the name of silver coins from Joachimsthal in Bohemia.

dollar diplomacy ▷ *noun, chiefly US* **1** diplomacy dictated by financial interests. **2** diplomacy that uses financial power to increase political power. ⓢ Early 20c.

dollarization ▷ *noun* /dɒləraɪˈzeɪʃən/ the basing of the value of a country's currency on that of the US dollar. ⓢ 20c.

dollop /ˈdɒləp/ ▷ *noun, colloq* a small shapeless mass of any semi-solid substance, especially food. ⓢ 19c; originally 16c, meaning 'a clump (of grass, etc)'.

dolly /ˈdɒlɪ/ ▷ *noun* (***dollies***) **1** *colloq* a child's name for a doll. **2** *cinema, TV* a frame with wheels on which a film or television camera is mounted for moving shots, permitting forward and sideways movement of the point of view during the action of the scene.

dolly shot ▷ *noun, cinema, TV* a scene planned to make use of a camera on a DOLLY.

dolma /ˈdɒlmə/ ▷ *noun* (***dolmas*** or ***dolmades*** /-ˈmɑːðiːz/) a vine or cabbage leaf with a savoury stuffing. ⓢ 19c: Turkish.

dolman sleeve /ˈdɒlmən —/ ▷ *noun* a kind of sleeve that tapers from a very wide armhole to a tight wrist. ⓢ 20c: from Turkish *dolaman* a robe with tight sleeves.

dolmen /ˈdɒlmən/ ▷ *noun* a simple prehistoric monument consisting of a large flat stone supported by several vertical stones. ⓢ 19c: perhaps from Breton *dol* table + *men* stone.

dolomite /ˈdɒləmaɪt/ ▷ *noun* **1** *geol* a mineral composed of calcium magnesium carbonate. **2** a sedimentary carbonate rock (**dolostone**) containing more than 50 per cent dolomite. ⓢ 18c: named after the Dolomites, the mountain range in which it is found.

doloroso /dɒləˈroʊsoʊ/ ▷ *adj, adverb, music* sorrowful or sorrowfully. ⓢ 19c: Italian.

dolorous /ˈdɒlərəs/ ▷ *adj, literary* causing, involving, or suggesting sorrow or grief. ⓢ 14c: from DOLOUR.

dolour or (*N Amer*) **dolor** /ˈdɒlə(r)/ *noun, poetic* sorrow or grief. ⓢ 14c: from Latin *dolor* pain.

dolphin /ˈdɒlfɪn/ ▷ *noun* **1** a small toothed whale found in seas almost worldwide, both in deep water and near to coasts, one species of which is the smallest marine animal. **2** a RIVER DOLPHIN. ⓢ 16c in this form; 14c as *delfyn*: from Greek *delphinos*.

dolphinarium /dɒlfɪˈnɛərɪəm/ ▷ *noun* (***dolphinaria*** or ***dolphinariums***) a large open-air aquarium in which dolphins are kept, both for study and to display to the public. ⓢ 20c: from DOLPHIN + aqu*arium*.

dolt /doʊlt/ *derog* ▷ *noun* a stupid person. • **doltish** *adj*. ⓢ Anglo-Saxon *dol* stupid.

DOM ▷ *abbreviation, IVR* Dominican Republic.

dom. ▷ *abbreviation* domestic.

-dom ▷ *suffix, forming nouns, denoting* **1** a state or rank □ ***serfdom*** □ ***dukedom***. **2** an area ruled or governed □ ***kingdom***. **3** a group of people with a specified characteristic □ ***officialdom***. ⊙ Anglo-Saxon *dom* judgement.

domain /dəˈmeɪn, doʊ-/ ▷ *noun* **1** the scope of any subject or area of interest. **2** a territory owned or ruled by one person or government. **3** *math* the set of values specified for a given mathematical function. **4** *physics* in a ferromagnetic substance, eg iron or nickel: a small region within which individual magnetic moments (see MOMENT sense 5) can be aligned, giving that substance permanent magnetic properties. **5** *Austral, NZ* a public park or recreation area. ⊙ 17c: from French *domaine*.

dome ▷ *noun* **1** a roof in the shape of a hemisphere. **2** anything of similar shape. **3** *colloq* a head. ⊙ 17c: originally 16c meaning 'a house' or 'stately building, etc': from Latin *domus* house.

domed ▷ *adj* **1** said of a building, etc: having a dome or domes. **2** dome-shaped. ⊙ 18c.

Domesday Book or **Doomsday Book** /ˈduːmzdeɪ —/ ▷ *noun* a survey of all lands in England, ordered by William the Conqueror in 1086, detailing their value, ownership, etc, so called because it was considered to be as authoritative as the Last Judgement or DOOMSDAY. ⊙ Anglo-Saxon *dom* judgement.

domestic /dəˈmɛstɪk/ ▷ *adj* **1** belonging or relating to the home, the family or private life. **2** said of animals: not wild; kept as a pet or farm animal. **3** within or relating to one's country; not foreign □ ***domestic sales and export sales***. **4** enjoying home life. ▷ *noun* **1** *colloq* a row, usually in the home, between members of a household unit. **2** a household servant. • **domestically** *adverb*. ⊙ 16c: from Latin *domesticus*, from *domus* house.

domesticate /dəˈmɛstɪkeɪt/ ▷ *verb* (***domesticated***, ***domesticating***) **1** to train (an animal) for life in the company of people. **2** *often facetious* to make someone used to home life, especially to train someone in cooking, housework, etc. • **domestication** *noun*. ⊙ 17c.

domesticity ▷ *noun* home life, or a liking for it. ⊙ 18c.

domestic science ▷ *noun* training in household skills, especially cooking; home economics.

domicile /ˈdɒmɪsaɪl/ ▷ *noun* **1** *formal* a house. **2** a legally recognized place of permanent residence. ▷ *verb* (***domiciled***, ***domiciling***) *law* to establish or be settled in a fixed residence. ⊙ 19c: from Latin *domicilium* dwelling.

domiciliary /dɒmɪˈsɪlɪərɪ/ ▷ *adj* **1** relating to people and their homes. **2** dealing with or available to people in their own homes. ⊙ 19c: from DOMICILE.

dominance /ˈdɒmɪnəns/ ▷ *noun* **1** command or influence over others. **2** being dominant. ⊙ 19c.

dominant /ˈdɒmɪnənt/ ▷ *adj* **1** most important, evident or active; foremost. **2** tending or seeking to command or influence others. **3** said of a building, etc: overlooking others from an elevated position. **4** *biol* denoting a gene, or the characteristics determined by it, whose PHENOTYPE is fully expressed in an individual whether there are two dominant ALLELES, or one dominant and one recessive ALLELE. **5** denoting a characteristic determined by such a gene. **6** *biol* denoting the most prevalent plant or animal species in a particular community or during a particular period, or describing an animal that occupies a superior position within a group of its own kind. ▷ *noun* **1** *music* the fifth note on a musical scale. **2** *biol* a dominant gene. **3** *biol* a dominant animal or plant. ⊙ 16c: from DOMINATE.

dominate /ˈdɒmɪneɪt/ ▷ *verb* (***dominated***, ***dominating***) *tr & intr* **1** to have command or influence over someone. **2** to be the most important, evident or active of (a group). **3** to enjoy an elevated position over (a place). • **dominating** *adj*. • **domination** *noun*. ⊙ 17c: from Latin *dominari*, *dominatus* to be master.

domineer /dɒmɪˈnɪə(r)/ ▷ *verb* (***domineered***, ***domineering***) *intr* to behave in an arrogantly dominant way. • **domineering** *adj* overbearing; behaving arrogantly towards others. ⊙ 16c: from Latin *dominari* to be master.

Dominican /dəˈmɪnɪkən/ ▷ *noun* a member of a Christian order of friars and nuns originally founded by St Dominic in 1215. ▷ *adj* belonging or relating to this order.

dominion /dəˈmɪnjən/ ▷ *noun* **1** rule; power; influence. **2** a territory or country governed by a single ruler or government. **3** *formerly* a self-governing colony within the British Empire. **4** in the traditional medieval hierarchy of nine ranks of angels: an angel of the fourth-highest rank. Compare SERAPH, CHERUB, THRONE, VIRTUE, POWER, PRINCIPALITY, ARCHANGEL, ANGEL. ⊙ 15c: from Latin *dominium* ownership.

domino /ˈdɒmɪnoʊ/ ▷ *noun* (***dominoes***) **1** any of a set of small rectangular tiles marked, in two halves, with varying numbers of spots, used in the game of **dominoes**. **2** (**dominoes**) a game in which these tiles are laid down, with matching halves end to end. **3** a black cloak with a hood and mask attached, worn at masked balls. ⊙ 17c: perhaps from Italian *domino!*, master!, the winner's cry in the game of dominoes.

domino effect ▷ *noun* the relation of political cause and effect implied by the DOMINO THEORY.

domino scheme ▷ *noun* a method of antenatal and postnatal care, together with hospital delivery, supervised by the mother's own midwife.

domino theory ▷ *noun* the theory that a political event can cause a series of similar events in neighbouring areas, like a falling domino causing the others in a row to fall in turn.

Don ▷ *noun* a Spanish form of address similar to Mr, which is used to indicate respect . See also DOÑA. ⊙ 16c: Spanish, from Latin *dominus* lord.

don[1] ▷ *noun* **1** a university lecturer, especially at Oxford or Cambridge. **2** *Austral & NZ colloq* an expert. • **donnish** *adj*. ⊙ 17c: etymology as for DON.

don[2] ▷ *verb* (***donned***, ***donning***) to put on (clothing). ⊙ 17c: DO 1 + ON.

Doña /ˈdɒnjə/ ▷ *noun* a Spanish form of address, similar to Madam, which is used to indicate respect. See also DON. ⊙ 17c.

donate /doʊˈneɪt/ ▷ *verb* (***donated***, ***donating***) to give, especially to charity. ⊙ 18c: from Latin *donare* to give.

donation /doʊˈneɪʃən/ ▷ *noun* a formal gift, usually of money; an amount given as a gift. ⊙ 15c: from Latin *donare*, *donatum* to give.

donder /ˈdɒnə(r)/ *S Afr slang* ▷ *verb* (***dondered***, ***dondering***) to beat up or thrash someone. ▷ *noun* a scoundrel; a rogue. ⊙ Afrikaans, from Dutch *donderen* to swear or bully.

done[1] /dʌn/ ▷ *adj* **1** finished; completed. **2** said of food: fully cooked. **3** socially acceptable. **4** used up. **5** *colloq* exhausted. ▷ *exclamation* expressing agreement or completion of a deal. • **done for** *colloq* facing ruin or death. • **done with something** or **someone** *colloq* finished with it or them; having dealt with it or them. ⊙ 14c.

done[2] *past participle of* DO[1]

doner kebab /ˈdɒnə(r), ˈdoʊnə(r) —/ ▷ *noun* thin slices cut from a block of minced and seasoned lamb grilled on a spit and eaten on unleavened bread. ⊙ 1950s: from Turkish *döner* rotating + KEBAB.

dong[1] ▷ *noun* **1** a deep ringing sound. **2** *Austral, NZ* a heavy punch; a thump. ▷ *verb* (***donged***, ***donging***) **1** to make this sound. **2** *Austral, NZ* to punch or thump someone. ⊙ 19c: imitating the sound.

dong² ▻ *noun, coarse slang* a penis.

donga /ˈdɒŋgə/ ▻ *noun* (***dongas***) *originally S Afr* a gully made by soil erosion. ◑ 19c: Zulu, meaning 'bank, side of a gully'.

doning /ˈdoʊnɪŋ/ ▻ *noun, colloq* the act of donating (especially blood).

donjon /ˈdʌndʒən, ˈdɒn-/ ▻ *noun* a heavily fortified central tower in a medieval castle. ◑ 14c: a variant of DUNGEON.

Don Juan /dɒn ˈdʒoʊən, — ˈhwɑːn/ ▻ *noun* a man who is, or claims to be, a regular seducer of women. ◑ 19c: the name of a legendary Spanish hero.

donkey /ˈdɒŋkɪ/ ▻ *noun* (***donkeys***) **1** the domestic ass, a hoofed herbivorous mammal with a large head and long ears, related to but smaller than the horse. **2** *colloq* a stupid person. ◑ 18c.

donkey jacket ▻ *noun* a heavy jacket made of a thick woollen fabric, usually black or dark blue, and with reinforced shoulders.

donkey's years ▻ *plural noun, colloq* a very long time; ages.

donkey vote ▻ *noun, Austral* **1** in a preferential system of voting: a vote accepting the order of candidates on the ballot paper. **2** such votes collectively.

donkey-work ▻ *noun* **1** heavy manual work. **2** preparation; groundwork.

Donna /ˈdɒnə/ ▻ *noun* an Italian form of address similar to Madam, which is used to indicate respect. ◑ 17c.

donned *past tense, past participle of* DON

donning *present participle of* DON²

donnish see under DON¹

donor /ˈdoʊnə(r)/ ▻ *noun* **1** someone who donates something, especially money. **2** a person or animal that provides blood, semen, living tissue or organs for medical use. **3** *electronics* an impurity in the form of a chemical element, such as antimony, that is deliberately added to a pure SEMICONDUCTOR material, such as silicon, donates electrons to the semiconductor, and so increases its conductivity. **4** *chem* an atom that donates a pair of electrons to an ACCEPTOR, resulting in the formation of a coordinate bond (see COORDINATE noun 3). ◑ 15c.

donor card ▻ *noun* a card indicating that its carrier is willing, in the event of sudden death, to have their healthy organs removed for transplant to others.

donor insemination ▻ *noun* (abbreviation **DI**) artificial insemination using semen from a donor.

don't /doʊnt/ ▻ *contraction of* do not. ▻ *noun, colloq* something that must not be done ▫ ***dos and don'ts***.

don't know ▻ *noun* **1** someone undecided, especially as to whom to vote for, or who has no definite answer to give to a question. **2** the answer given by such a person.

donut /ˈdoʊnʌt/ see DOUGHNUT

doodah /ˈduːdɑː/ and (*N Amer*) **doodad** /ˈduːdad/ ▻ *noun, colloq* a thing whose name one does not know or cannot remember. ◑ 20c.

doodle /ˈduːdəl/ ▻ *verb* (***doodled, doodling***) *intr* to scrawl or scribble aimlessly and meaninglessly. ▻ *noun* a meaningless scribble. • **doodler** *noun*. ◑ 20c in these senses: 17c, meaning 'a foolish person'.

doodlebug ▻ *noun* **1** *US* the larva of an ant-lion or other insect. **2** any device, scientific or otherwise, used by prospectors to indicate the presence of minerals. **3** *war slang* a flying bomb. ◑ 19c.

doofer /ˈduːfə(r)/ ▻ *noun, slang* a thing whose name one does not know or cannot remember. ◑ 20c: perhaps from (*It will*) *do for* (*now*).

doolally /ˈduːlalɪ/ ▻ *adj, slang* mentally unbalanced; crazy. ◑ 20c: from Deolali, a town in Bombay, where there was a sanitarium.

doom ▻ *noun* inescapable death, ruin or other unpleasant fate. ▻ *verb* (***doomed, dooming***) to condemn someone to death or some other dire fate. ◑ Anglo-Saxon *dom* judgement.

doomsday ▻ *noun* the last day of the world which in Christianity, is the day on which God will judge the human race. • **till doomsday** *colloq* for ever. ◑ Anglo-Saxon *domes dæg*.

doomwatch ▻ *noun* **1** pessimism about the contemporary situation and the future, especially of the environment. **2** observation of the environment to prevent its pollution, etc. • **doomwatcher** *noun*.

doona /ˈduːnə/ ▻ *noun* (***doonas***) *Austral* a DUVET. ◑ 20c: from a trademark.

door /dɔː(r)/ ▻ *noun* **1** a movable barrier opening and closing an entrance, eg to a room, cupboard or vehicle. **2** an entrance. **3** a house considered in relation to others ▫ ***three doors away***. **4** a means of entry; an opportunity to gain access ▫ ***opened the door to stardom***. See also WICKET DOOR at WICKET. • **close the door to something** to make it impossible. • **lay something at someone's door** to blame them for it. • **open the door to something** to make something possible. ◑ Anglo-Saxon *duru*.

doorbell ▻ *noun* a bell on or at a door, rung by visitors at the door as a sign of arrival. ◑ 19c.

door furniture ▻ *noun* handles, locks and other fittings that may be used on doors.

doorjamb /-dʒam/ and **doorpost** ▻ *noun* one of the two vertical side pieces of a door frame.

doorknocker see KNOCKER

doorman ▻ *noun* a man, usually wearing uniform, employed to guard the entrance to a hotel, restaurant, theatre, etc and give assistance to guests or customers. ◑ 19c.

doormat ▻ *noun* **1** a mat for wiping shoes on before entering. **2** *colloq* a person easily submitting to unfair treatment by others. ◑ 17c.

doorstep ▻ *noun* **1** a step positioned immediately in front of a door. **2** *slang* a thick sandwich or slice of bread. ▻ *verb* **1** said especially of politicians, their agents, etc: to go from door to door canvassing (people or an area). **2** said of journalists, etc: to pester someone by waiting at their door. • **doorstepper** *noun*. • **on one's doorstep** close to one's home, etc. ◑ 19c.

doorstop ▻ *noun* **1** a device, especially a wedge, for holding a door open. **2** a device, eg a fixed knob, for preventing a door opening too far. ◑ 19c.

door-to-door ▻ *adj, adverb* **1** going from house to house. **2** said eg of a journey time: between precise points of departure and arrival.

doorway ▻ *noun* **1** an entrance to a building or room. **2** the space where there is or might be a door.

dopa /ˈdoʊpə/ ▻ *noun, biochem* an AMINO ACID derivative that plays an important role in the production of ADRENALIN and NORADRENALIN, and of the neurotransmitter DOPAMINE, especially ***L***-dopa which is used in the treatment of PARKINSON'S DISEASE. ◑ Early 20c: from *dihydroxyphenylalanine* the chemical name for the compound.

dopamine /ˈdoʊpəmiːn/ ▻ *noun, biochem* an important chemical compound that functions as a NEUROTRANSMITTER and is also an intermediate in the manufacture of ADRENALIN and NORADRENALIN. ◑ 1950.

dope ▻ *noun* **1** *colloq* a drug taken for pleasure, especially cannabis. **2** *colloq* a drug of any kind, especially one given to athletes, dogs or horses to affect performance. **3** *colloq* a stupid person. **4** (**the dope**) *slang* information, especially when confidential. ▻ *verb* (***doped, doping***) **1** to give or apply drugs to (a person or animal), especially dishonestly or furtively. **2** *physics* to modify (a semiconductor) by DOPING. ⓘ 19c, originally meaning 'a thick liquid': from Dutch *doop* sauce.

dopey or **dopy** /'doʊpɪ/ *colloq* ▻ *adj* (***dopier, dopiest***) **1** sleepy or inactive, as if drugged. **2** stupid. • **dopily** *adverb*. • **dopiness** *noun*. ⓘ 19c.

doping /'doʊpɪŋ/ ▻ *noun, physics* the addition of very small amounts of impurities (eg antimony, arsenic) to a crystal of silicon, germanium, etc, in order to convert it into a SEMICONDUCTOR.

doppelgänger /'dɒpəlgeŋə(r)/ ▻ *noun* an apparition or double of a person. ⓘ 19c: German, meaning 'double-goer'.

Doppler effect and **Doppler shift** /'dɒplə(r) —/ ▻ *noun, physics* the change in wavelength observed when the distance between a source of waves and the observer is changing, eg the sound change perceived as an aircraft passes by. ⓘ 19c: named after the Austrian physicist Christian Doppler (1803–53).

Doric /'dɒrɪk/ ▻ *adj, archit* denoting an order of classical architecture, characterized by thick fluted columns. Compare COMPOSITE CORINTHIAN, IONIC, TUSCAN. ⓘ 16c: from Greek *Dorikos*, from Doris, in ancient Greece.

dorm ▻ *noun, colloq* a DORMITORY.

dormant /'dɔːmənt/ ▻ *adj* **1** temporarily quiet, inactive or out of use. **2** *biol* denoting a living organism or a reproductive body such as a seed, spore or cyst that is in a resting state, especially in order to survive a period of unfavourable environmental conditions. • **dormancy** *noun* (***dormancies***). ⓘ 16c, originally referring to heraldic images of sleeping animals : from Latin *dormire* to sleep.

dormer /'dɔːmə(r)/ and **dormer window** ▻ *noun* a window fitted vertically into an extension built out from a sloping roof. ⓘ 16c: from DORMITORY (sense 1), in which they were originally fitted.

dormie or **dormy** /'dɔːmɪ/ ▻ *adj, golf* as many holes up or ahead of one's opponent as there are yet to play □ *She's dormie four*. ⓘ 19c.

dormitory /'dɔːmɪtərɪ/ ▻ *noun* (***dormitories***) **1** a large bedroom for several people, nowadays especially in a school. **2** *especially US* a hall of residence in a college or university. Often shortened to **dorm**. ⓘ 15c: from Latin *dormitorium*, from *dormire* to sleep.

dormitory town and **dormitory suburb** ▻ *noun* a town or suburb from which most residents travel to work elsewhere.

Dormobile /'dɔːmoʊbiːl/ ▻ *noun, trademark* a van equipped for living and sleeping in as well as travelling. ⓘ 1950s: from DORMITORY + AUTOMOBILE.

dormouse /'dɔːmaʊs/ ▻ *noun* a small nocturnal rodent with rounded ears, large eyes, velvety fur, and a bushy tail. ⓘ 15c: associated with, but not necessarily derived from, Latin *dormire* to sleep, from its hibernating habits.

dorp /dɔːp/ ▻ *noun, now S Afr* a small town or village. ⓘ 15c: Dutch.

Dors. ▻ *abbreviation* Dorset.

dorsal /'dɔːsəl/ ▻ *adj, biol, physiol* belonging or relating to the back □ *dorsal fin*. Compare VENTRAL. ⓘ 15c: from Latin *dorsum* back.

dory[1] /'dɔːrɪ/ ▻ *noun* (***dories***) a golden-yellow fish of the mackerel family. Also called **John Dory**. ⓘ 15c as *dorre*: from French *dorée* golden.

dory[2] /'dɔrɪ/ ▻ *noun* (***dories***) *N Amer* a small flat-bottomed boat with a sharp prow and stern. ⓘ 18c.

DOS /dɒs/ ▻ *abbreviation, computing* disk-operating system, a program for handling information on a disk.

dos and **do's** see under DO[1]

dosage /'doʊsɪdʒ/ ▻ *noun* the prescribed amount of a DOSE of a medicine or drug. ⓘ 19c.

dose /doʊs/ ▻ *noun* **1** *medicine* the measured quantity of medicine, ionizing radiation such as X-rays, or some other therapeutic agent that is recommended or prescribed by a doctor to be administered to a patient at any one time, or at regular intervals over a period of time. **2** the amount of ionizing radiation to which a person is exposed over a specified period of time. **3** *colloq* a bout, especially of an illness or something unpleasant □ ***a dose of the flu***. **4** *slang* any sexually transmitted disease, especially gonorrhoea. ▻ *verb* (***dosed, dosing***) (*also* **dose someone up with something**) to give them medicine, especially in large quantities. • **like a dose of salts** *colloq* extremely quickly and effectively. ⓘ 17c: from Greek *dosis* giving.

dosh ▻ *noun, slang* money. ⓘ 20c.

dosimeter /doʊ'sɪmɪtə(r)/ ▻ *noun, physics* an instrument for measuring the absorbed dose of radiation.

doss ▻ *verb* (***dossed, dossing***) *intr, slang* (*often* **doss down**) to settle down to sleep, especially on an improvised bed. ⓘ 18c: perhaps dialect for HASSOCK.

dosser /'dɒsə(r)/ ▻ *noun, slang* **1** a homeless person sleeping on the street or in a DOSS-HOUSE. **2** a lazy person. ⓘ 19c.

doss-house ▻ *noun, slang* a very cheap lodging-house for homeless people.

dossier /'dɒsɪeɪ, 'dɒsɪə(r)/ ▻ *noun* a file of papers containing information on a person or subject. ⓘ 19c: French.

dost /dʌst/ ▻ *verb, old use* the form of DO used with THOU[1].

dot ▻ *noun* **1** a small round mark; a spot; a point. **2** in Morse code: the shorter of the two lengths of signal element, written as a point. Compare DASH. ▻ *verb* (***dotted, dotting***) **1** to put a dot on something. **2** to scatter; to cover with a scattering □ *dotted with daisies*. • **dot the i's and cross the t's 1** to pay close attention to detail. **2** to finish the last few details of something. • **on the dot** exactly on time. • **on the dot of (a time specified)** at exactly that time. • **the year dot** *colloq* a very long time ago. ⓘ Anglo-Saxon *dott* head of a boil.

dotage /'doʊtɪdʒ/ ▻ *noun* a state of feeble-mindedness owing to old age; senility. ⓘ 14c: see DOTE.

dotard /'doʊtəd/ ▻ *noun* someone in their dotage. ⓘ 14c: from DOTE.

dote /doʊt/ ▻ *verb* (***doted, doting***) *intr* to be foolish or weak-minded especially because of old age. • **doting** /'doʊtɪŋ/ *adj* foolishly or excessively fond of someone. ⓘ 15c in this sense; 13c meaning 'to act or talk foolishly': from Dutch *doten* to be silly.

■ **dote on** or **upon someone** or **something** to show a foolishly excessive fondness for them.

doth /dʌθ/ ▻ *verb* DOES (see under DO) *old use*.

dot matrix printer ▻ *noun, computing* a computer printer using arrangements of pins from a matrix or set to form the printed characters. Compare INKJET PRINTER, LASER PRINTER.

dotted *past tense, past participle of* DOT

dotted line ▻ *noun* a line composed of dots or dashes on eg a printed form, that one is instructed to sign on, tear along, etc.

dotted note and **dotted rest** ▻ *noun, music* one whose length is increased by one half by a dot placed after it.

dotting *present participle of* DOT

dotty ▻ *adj* (***dottier, dottiest***) *colloq* silly; crazy. • **dottily** *adverb*. • **dottiness** *noun*. • **dotty about someone** or **something** infatuated with them or it.

double /'dʌbəl/ ▻ *adj* **1** made up of two similar parts; paired; in pairs. **2** twice the weight, size, etc, or twice the usual weight, size, etc. **3** for two people □ *a double bed.* **4** ambiguous □ ***double meaning.*** **5** said of a musical instrument: sounding an octave lower □ ***double bass.*** ▷ *adverb* **1** twice. **2** with one half over the other □ ***folded double.*** ▷ *noun* **1** a double quantity. **2** a duplicate or lookalike. **3** an actor's stand-in, used especially in dangerous scenes. **4** a double measure of alcoholic spirit. **5** a racing bet in which any winnings from the first stake become a stake in a subsequent race. **6** a win in two events on the same racing programme. See separate entry DOUBLES. ▷ *verb* (***doubled, doubling***) **1** *tr & intr* to make or become twice as large in size, number, etc. **2** *intr* to have a second use or function □ ***The spare bed doubles as a couch.*** **3** *intr* to turn round sharply. • **at** or **on the double** very quickly. • **double or quits** in gambling: the alternative, left to chance, of doubling or cancelling payment. ⓒ 13c: from French *doble*, from Latin *duplus*.

■ **double back** to turn and go back, often by a different route.

■ **double for someone** to act as their substitute.

■ **double something over** to fold one half of it over the other.

■ **double up 1** to bend sharply at the waist, especially through pain. **2** (*also* **double up with someone**) to share a bedroom with another person.

double act ▷ *noun, theat* two entertainers working together. ⓒ 20c.

double agent ▷ *noun* a spy working for two governments with conflicting interests. ⓒ 1930s.

double axel see under AXEL

double-barrelled or (*N Amer*) **double-barreled** ▷ *adj* **1** said of a gun: having two barrels. **2** said of a surname: made up of two names □ ***Lloyd-Jones.*** **3** said eg of a compliment: ambiguous. ⓒ 18c.

double bass ▷ *noun* the largest and lowest in pitch of the orchestral stringed instruments. Also called **string bass.** ⓒ 18c.

double bassoon see CONTRABASSOON

double bill ▷ *noun* two films, plays, bands, etc presented as a single entertainment, one after the other.

double bind ▷ *noun* a situation in which conflicting cues are given so that any choice of behaviour will be considered wrong; a dilemma.

double-blind ▷ *adj* denoting a comparative experiment, trial, etc in which the identity of the CONTROL GROUP is unknown both to the experimenters and the subjects until completion of the experiment. ⓒ 1930s.

double bluff ▷ *noun* an action or statement which is meant to be seen as a bluff, but which is in fact genuine.

double boiler ▷ *noun, N Amer* a DOUBLE SAUCEPAN. ⓒ 19c.

double bond ▷ *noun, chem* a COVALENT BOND formed by the sharing of two pairs of electrons between two atoms.

double-breasted ▷ *adj* said of a coat or jacket: having overlapping front flaps. ⓒ 18c.

double-check ▷ *verb* to check twice or again. ▷ *noun* (**double check**) a second look, examination, etc. ⓒ 1950s.

double chin ▷ *noun* a chin with an area of loose flesh underneath. ⓒ 19c.

double concerto ▷ *noun, music* a concerto written for two solo instruments with orchestra.

double cream ▷ *noun* thick cream with a high fat content.

double-cross ▷ *verb* to cheat or deceive (especially a colleague or ally, or someone one is supposed to be helping). ▷ *noun* such a deceit. • **double-crosser** *noun.* ⓒ Early 20c.

double dagger ▷ *noun, printing* the symbol ‡. Also called **diesis.** ⓒ 18c.

double-dealing ▷ *noun* cheating; treachery. • **double-dealer** *noun.* ⓒ 16c.

double-decker ▷ *noun* **1** a bus with two decks. **2** *colloq* anything with two levels or layers. ⓒ 19c.

double door ▷ *singular noun* and **double doors** ▷ *plural noun* a door consisting of two parts hung on opposite posts.

double Dutch ▷ *noun, colloq* nonsense; incomprehensible jargon. ⓒ 19c.

double-edged ▷ *adj* **1** having two cutting edges. **2** having two possible meanings or purposes. ⓒ 16c.

double entendre /ˈduːbəl ɑ̃ˈtɑ̃drə/ ▷ *noun* **1** a remark having two possible meanings, one of them usually sexually suggestive. **2** the use of such remarks. ⓒ 17c: French, meaning 'double meaning'.

double-entry ▷ *noun, bookkeeping* a method by which two entries are made of each transaction. ⓒ 18c.

double exposure ▷ *noun, photog* the accidental or deliberate combination of two or more images separately exposed on a single photographic record. ⓒ Late 19c.

double fault ▷ *noun, tennis, etc* two faults (see FAULT *noun* 6) served in succession, resulting in loss of a point for the server.

double figures ▷ *plural noun* the numbers between 10 and 99 inclusive, especially the lower ones. ⓒ 19c: originally applied to cricket scores.

double first ▷ *noun* **1** a university degree with first-class honours in two different subjects. **2** someone who has gained such a degree. ⓒ 19c.

double-glazing ▷ *noun* windows constructed with two panes separated by a vacuum, providing added heat insulation. • **double-glazed** *adj.*

double helix ▷ *noun* the form of the DNA molecule, consisting of two spirals coiled around an axis. ⓒ 1950s.

double-jointed ▷ *adj* having extraordinarily flexible body joints. ⓒ 19c.

double knitting ▷ *noun, knitting* a popular weight of yarn, especially for handknitting. ⓒ 19c.

double negative ▷ *noun* an expression containing two negative words, especially where only one is logically needed □ ***He hasn't never asked me.***

double-park ▷ *verb* to park at the side of another vehicle parked alongside the kerb.

double pneumonia ▷ *noun, medicine* the popular name for PNEUMONIA affecting both lungs. ⓒ 19c.

double-quick ▷ *adj, adverb* very quick or quickly. ⓒ 19c.

doubles ▷ *singular noun* a competition in tennis, etc between two teams of two players each.

double saucepan ▷ *noun* a pair of saucepans, the top one fitting tightly into the lower one, and heated by boiling water in the lower one. ⓒ 20c.

double spacing ▷ *noun* typing with an empty line between each line of type.

double standard ▷ *noun* (*often* **double standards**) a principle or rule applied firmly to one person or group and loosely or not at all to another, especially oneself. ⓒ 1950s.

double star ▷ *noun, astron* **1** a BINARY STAR. **2** a pair of stars that appear close together when viewed through a telescope, but are in fact at very different distances from Earth, lying in very nearly the same direction from Earth. ⓒ 18c.

doublet /ˈdʌblɪt/ ▷ *noun* **1** a close-fitting man's jacket, with or without sleeves, popular from the 14c to the 17c. **2** a pair of objects of any kind, or each of these. ⓘ 14c: French.

double take ▷ *noun* an initial inattentive reaction followed swiftly by a sudden full realization, especially used as a comic device. ⓘ 1930s.

double-talk ▷ *noun* ambiguous talk, or talk that seems relevant but is really meaningless, especially as offered up by politicians. ⓘ 1930s.

doublethink ▷ *noun* simultaneous belief in, or acceptance of, two opposing ideas or principles. ⓘ 20c: originally coined by George Orwell in his novel *Nineteen Eighty-Four* (1949).

double time ▷ *noun* **1** a rate of pay equal to double the basic rate. **2** *music* a time twice as fast as that of the previous time. **3** *music* DUPLE TIME. **4** *US* a fast marching pace. ⓘ 19c.

double vision ▷ *noun* seeing two images of the one object, because of lack of co-ordination between the two eyes. ⓘ 19c.

double wedding ▷ *noun* a wedding involving two couples. ⓘ 18c.

double whammy see under WHAMMY

doubloon /dʌˈbluːn/ ▷ *noun* **1** a gold coin formerly used in Spain and S America. **2** (**doubloons**) *slang* money. ⓘ 17c in sense 1; 20c in sense 2: from Spanish *doblón*.

doubly ▷ *adverb* **1** to twice the extent; very much more. **2** in two ways. ⓘ 14c.

doubt /daʊt/ ▷ *verb* (***doubted, doubting***) **1** to feel uncertain about something; to be suspicious or show mistrust of it. **2** to be inclined to disbelieve something. ▷ *noun* **1** a feeling of uncertainty, suspicion or mistrust. **2** an inclination to disbelieve; a reservation. • **doubter** *noun*. • **beyond doubt** or **beyond a shadow of a doubt** certain; certainly. • **in doubt** not certain. • **no doubt** surely; probably. • **without a doubt** or **without doubt** certainly. ⓘ 15c in modern form; 13c as *dute*: from Latin *dubitare*.

doubtful ▷ *adj* **1** feeling doubt. **2** uncertain; able to be doubted. **3** likely not to be the case. • **doubtfully** *adverb*. ⓘ 14c as *duteful*.

> ***doubtful, dubious***
>
> • **Doubtful** means that doubt exists in someone's mind; **dubious** means that doubt is likely or justified by a situation or circumstance □ *She fixed a doubtful gaze on the whiskery young protester* □ *It was doubtful if Miss Angus liked anyone very much* □ *The story sounds dubious* □ *Everyone's position was dubious in some respect.*

doubtless ▷ *adverb* probably; certainly. • **doubtlessly** *adverb*.

douche /duːʃ/ ▷ *noun* **1** a powerful jet of water that is used to clean a body orifice, especially the vagina. **2** an apparatus for producing such a jet. ▷ *verb* (***douched, douching***) *tr & intr* to apply or make use of a douche. ⓘ 18c: French.

dough /doʊ/ ▷ *noun* **1** a mixture of flour, liquid (water or milk) and yeast, used in the preparation of bread, pastry, etc, usually referring to such a mixture that has been kneaded but not baked. **2** *slang* money. ⓘ Anglo-Saxon *dah*.

doughier, doughiest and **doughiness** see under DOUGHY

doughnut or (*especially US*) **donut** /ˈdoʊnʌt/ ▷ *noun* **1** a portion of sweetened dough fried in deep fat, sometimes made with a hole in the middle, often filled eg with cream or jam, and sometimes iced. **2** anything shaped like a doughnut. ⓘ 19c.

doughnutting ▷ *noun* the surrounding of a speaker in parliament by members of the same party, to give the impression on television of a packed House.

doughty /ˈdaʊtɪ/ *literary* ▷ *adj* (***doughtier, doughtiest***) brave; stout-hearted. • **doughtily** *adverb*. • **doughtiness** *noun* bravery. ⓘ Anglo-Saxon *dyhtig*.

doughy /ˈdoʊɪ/ ▷ *adj* (***doughier, doughiest***) like dough, or having the consistency of dough. • **doughiness** *noun*.

dour /dʊə(r), daʊə(r)/ ▷ *adj* stern; sullen. • **dourly** *adverb*. • **dourness** *noun*. ⓘ 14c; originally Scots: from Latin *durus* hard.

douse or **dowse** /daʊs/ ▷ *verb* (***doused, dousing***) **1** to throw water over something; to plunge something into water. **2** to extinguish (a light or fire). ⓘ 17c.

the Dove see COLUMBA

dove[1] *N Amer past tense of* DIVE[1]

dove[2] /dʌv/ *noun* **1** any of several members of the pigeon family, especially the smaller species. **2** *politics* a person favouring peace rather than hostility. Compare HAWK[1] (sense 3). **4** *drug-taking slang* a tablet of ECSTASY (often with a dove stamped on it). ⓘ Anglo-Saxon *dufe*.

dovecote or **dovecot** /ˈdʌvkoʊt, -kət/ ▷ *noun* a building or shed in which domestic pigeons are kept. ⓘ 15c.

Dover sole ▷ *noun* a FLATFISH, popular as a food fish, found from the Mediterranean to Norway. It has both eyes on the right side of the body, a twisted mouth with teeth on the underside only, and dorsal and anal fins that extend to the tail. Also called **European sole**.

dovetail ▷ *noun* a corner joint, especially in wood, made by fitting v-shaped pegs into corresponding slots. Also called **dovetail joint**. ▷ *verb* (***dovetailed, dovetailing***) *tr & intr* **1** to fit using one or more dovetails. **2** to fit or combine neatly. ⓘ 16c as *noun*; 17c as *verb*.

dowager /ˈdaʊədʒə(r)/ ▷ *noun* **1** a title given to a nobleman's widow, to distinguish her from the wife of her husband's heir. **2** *colloq* a grand-looking old lady. ⓘ 16c: from French *douagiere*, from Latin *dotare* to endow.

dowdy /ˈdaʊdɪ/ ▷ *adj* (***dowdier, dowdiest***) said especially of a woman or her clothing: dull, plain and unfashionable. • **dowdily** *adverb*. • **dowdiness** *noun*. ⓘ 16c: from earlier *dowd* a slut.

dowel /ˈdaʊəl/ ▷ *noun* a thin cylindrical (especially wooden) peg, especially used to join two pieces by fitting into corresponding holes in each. ⓘ 14c: from German *dovel*.

dower /ˈdaʊə(r)/ ▷ *noun* a widow's share, for life, in her deceased husband's property. ⓘ 15c: from French *douaire*, from Latin *dotare* to endow.

dower house ▷ *noun* a house smaller than, and within the grounds of, a large country house, originally one forming part of a DOWER.

Dow-Jones average and **Dow-Jones index** /ˈdaʊdʒoʊnz —/ ▷ *noun, finance* an indicator of the relative prices of stocks and shares on the New York stock exchange. ⓘ Early 20c: named after Charles H Dow (1851–1902) and Edward D Jones (1856–1920), American economists.

down[1] ▷ *adverb* **1** towards or in a low or lower position, level or state; on or to the ground. **2** from a greater to a lesser size, amount or level □ *scaled down* □ *calm down*. **3** towards or in a more southerly place. **4** in writing; on paper □ *take down notes*. **5** as a deposit □ *put down five pounds*. **6** to an end stage or finished state □ *hunt someone down* □ *grind down*. **7** from earlier to later times □ *handed down through generations*. **8** to a state of exhaustion, defeat, etc □ *worn down by illness*. **9** not vomited up □ *keep food down*. **10** in a crossword: in the vertical direction □ *5 down*. Compare ACROSS (*adverb* 10). ▷ *prep* **1** in a lower position on something. **2** along; at a further position on, by or through □ *down the road.* **3** along in the direction of the current of a river. **4** from the top to or towards the bottom. **5** *dialect* to or in (a particular place) □ *going down the town.* ▷ *adj* **1** sad; in low spirits. **2** going towards or reaching a lower position □ *a down pipe.* **3** made as a deposit □ *a down payment.* **4** reduced in price. **5** said of a computer, etc: out of action, especially temporarily. ▷ *verb* (***downed, downing***) **1** to drink something quickly, especially in one gulp. **2** to force someone to the ground. ▷ *exclamation* used as a command to animals, especially dogs: get or stay down. ▷ *noun* **1** an unsuccessful or otherwise unpleasant period □ *Life has its ups and downs.* **2** (**downs**) an area of rolling (especially treeless) hills, especially **the Downs** in southern England. • **down by** with a deficit (of something specified) □ *down by three goals.* • **down for** noted; entered in a list, etc □ *Your name is down for the hurdles.* • **down in the mouth** depressed. • **down on one's luck** in unfortunate circumstances; in a bad way. • **down to the ground** *colloq* completely; perfectly. • **down tools** *colloq* to stop working, as a protest. • **down under** *colloq* in or to Australia and/or New Zealand. • **down with ...!** let us get rid of ...! • **have a down on someone** *colloq* to be ill-disposed towards them. • **up and down** **1** to and fro. **2** alternately well and ill. ◷ Anglo-Saxon *of dune* from the hill.

down² ▷ *noun* soft fine feathers or hair. ◷ 14c: from Norse *dunn.*

down-and-out ▷ *adj* homeless and penniless, with no hope of earning a living. ▷ *noun* a down-and-out person. ◷ 19c.

down-at-heel ▷ *adj* shabby. ◷ 19c.

downbeat ▷ *adj* **1** pessimistic; cheerless. **2** calm; relaxed. ▷ *noun, music* the first beat of a bar or the movement of the conductor's baton indicating this. ◷ 19c.

downcast ▷ *adj* **1** glum; dispirited. **2** said of eyes: looking downwards. ◷ 13c.

downer ▷ *noun* **1** *colloq* a state of depression □ *He's been on a downer since his divorce.* **2** *slang* a tranquillizing or depressant drug. ◷ 1970s in sense 1; 1960s in sense 2.

downfall ▷ *noun* **1** failure or ruin, or its cause. **2** a heavy fall of rain or snow, especially a sudden one. ◷ 15c.

downgrade ▷ *verb* **1** to reduce to a lower grade. **2** to speak of someone disparagingly. ◷ 1930s.

downhearted ▷ *adj* dispirited; discouraged; dismayed. ◷ 18c.

downhill ▷ *adverb* **1** downwards. **2** to or towards a worse condition. ▷ *adj* **1** downwardly sloping. **2** becoming increasingly easier. **3** deteriorating. ▷ *noun* a ski race down a hillside. • **go downhill** to deteriorate (in health, morality or prosperity). ◷ 17c as *adverb*; 1960s as *noun.*

Downie /ˈdaʊnɪ/ ▷ *noun* (***Downies***) *trademark* a make of DUVET.

Downing Street ▷ *noun, colloq* the British Government. ◷ 18c: named after Downing Street in London, containing the official residences of the Prime Minister and the Chancellor of the Exchequer.

down-in-the-mouth ▷ *adj* unhappy; depressed.

download ▷ *verb, computing* to transfer (data) from one computer to another. ◷ 1970s.

down-market ▷ *adj* cheap, of poor quality or lacking prestige. ◷ 1970s.

down payment ▷ *noun* a deposit.

downpour ▷ *noun* a very heavy fall of rain. ◷ 19c.

downright ▷ *adj* **1** utter □ *downright idiocy.* **2** plainspoken; blunt. ▷ *adverb* utterly. ◷ 13c.

downs and **the Downs** see under DOWN¹

downside ▷ *noun* **1** the lower or under side. **2** *colloq* a negative aspect; a disadvantage.

downsizing ▷ *noun* the practice of reducing the size of a workforce, especially by redundancies. ◷ 1970s: originally *US* referring to reducing the size of cars.

Down's syndrome /ˈdaʊnz—/ ▷ *noun, pathol* a congenital disorder caused by an abnormality in chromosomes, which results in mental retardation, slow physical development, flattened facial features, and slight slanting of the eyes, which gave rise to the former name for the condition, **mongolism**. ◷ 19c: named after the UK physician John L H Down (1828–96).

downstage ▷ *adj, adverb, theat* at or towards the front of a theatre stage. ◷ 19c.

downstairs ▷ *adverb* to or towards a lower floor; down the stairs. ▷ *adj* on a lower or ground floor. ▷ *noun* a lower or ground floor. ◷ 16c.

downstream ▷ *adj, adverb* further along a river towards the sea; with the current. ◷ 18c.

downswing ▷ *noun* **1** a decline in economic activity, etc. **2** *golf* the part of the golfer's swing where the club is moving towards the ball. ◷ 19c.

downtime ▷ *noun* time during which work ceases because a machine, especially a computer, is not working. ◷ 1950s.

down-to-earth ▷ *adj* **1** sensible and practical. **2** not at all pretentious. **3** plain-speaking.

downtown ▷ *adj, adverb* in or towards either the lower part of the city or the city centre. ▷ *noun* this area of a city. ◷ 19c.

downtrodden ▷ *adj* oppressed; ruled or controlled tyrannically. ◷ 16c.

downturn ▷ *noun* a decline in economic activity. ◷ 1920s.

downward /ˈdaʊnwəd/ ▷ *adj* leading or moving down; descending; declining. ▷ *adverb* DOWNWARDS. • **downwardly** *adverb.* ◷ 13c.

downwards ▷ *adverb* to or towards a lower position or level. ◷ 15c.

downwind ▷ *adverb* **1** in or towards the direction in which the wind is blowing; with the wind blowing from behind. **2** behind in terms of wind direction; with the wind carrying one's scent away from (eg an animal one is stalking). ▷ *adj* moving with, or sheltered from, the wind. ◷ 17c.

downy ▷ *adj* (***downier, downiest***) covered with or made of down; soft like down. ◷ 16c: from DOWN².

dowry /ˈdaʊrɪ/ ▷ *noun* (***dowries***) an amount of wealth handed over by a woman's family to her husband on marriage. ◷ 15c in this sense; 14c, meaning DOWER.

dowse¹ /daʊz/ ▷ *verb* (***dowsed, dowsing***) *intr* to search for underground water with a DIVINING-ROD. • **dowser** *noun.* ◷ 17c.

dowse² see DOUSE

dowsing-rod see DIVINING-ROD

doxology /dɒkˈsɒlədʒɪ/ ▷ *noun* (***doxologies***) a Christian hymn, verse or fixed expression praising God. ◷ 17c: from Greek *doxa* glory + *logos* discourse.

doyen /ˈdɔɪən/ ▷ *noun, literary* the most senior and most respected member of a group or profession. ◷ 17c: French.

doyenne /dɔɪˈɛn/ ▷ *noun* a female DOYEN. ◷ 19c.

doyley see DOILY

doz. ▷ *abbreviation* dozen.

doze /doʊz/ ▷ *verb* (***dozed, dozing***) *intr* to sleep lightly. ▷ *noun* a brief period of light sleep. ◷ 17c: from Norse *dus* lull.

■ **doze off** to fall into a light sleep.

dozen /ˈdʌzən/ ▻ *noun* (***dozens*** or, following a number, ***dozen***) **1** a set of twelve. **2** (*often* **dozens**) *colloq* very many □ *saw dozens of them.* ◷ 13c as *dozein*: from French *dozeine*.

dozen, half a dozen

● Although **dozen** is singular, it is often followed by a plural verb, and general plurality rather than exactness of number is usually implied □ *There were a dozen or more people in the room*

● The same applies to **half a dozen**, which is similarly inexact in reference □ *Lying on the beds were half a dozen prisoners.*

dozenth ▻ *adj* **1** twelfth. **2** denoting an indeterminately high place in a sequence □ *for the dozenth time.*

dozy /ˈdoʊzɪ/ ▻ *adj* (***dozier***, ***doziest***) **1** sleepy. **2** *colloq* stupid; slow to understand; not alert. ● **dozily** *adverb*. ● **doziness** *noun*. ◷ 17c.

DP ▻ *abbreviation* **1** data processing. **2** displaced person.

DPA ▻ *abbreviation* Data Protection Authority.

DPh and **DPhil** ▻ *abbreviation* Doctor of Philosophy. See also PHD.

DPP ▻ *abbreviation* Director of Public Prosecutions.

dpt ▻ *abbreviation* **1** department. **2** *optics* dioptre.

DR ▻ *abbreviation* dry riser.

Dr ▻ *abbreviation* Doctor.

Dr. ▻ *abbreviation* in addresses: Drive.

dr. ▻ *abbreviation* drachma.

drab ▻ *adj* (***drabber***, ***drabbest***) **1** dull; dreary. **2** of a dull greenish-brown colour. ● **drably** *adverb*. ● **drabness** *noun*. ◷ 16c: perhaps from French *drap* cloth.

drachm /dram/ ▻ *noun* a measure equal to $^1/_8$ of an ounce or fluid ounce, formerly used by pharmacists. ◷ 14c: see DRACHMA.

drachma /ˈdrakmə/ ▻ *noun* (***drachmas*** or ***drachmae*** /-miː/) (abbreviation **dr.**) the standard unit of currency in Greece. ◷ 19c in this sense; 16c name for a silver coin of ancient Greece: from Greek *drakhme* handful.

draconian /drəˈkoʊnɪən, dreɪ-/ and **draconic** /drəˈkɒnɪk, dreɪ-/ ▻ *adj* said of a law, etc: harsh; severe. ◷ 19c: named after Draco, 7c Athenian lawgiver.

draft /drɑːft/ ▻ *noun* **1** a written plan; a preliminary sketch. **2** a written order requesting a bank to pay out money, especially to another bank. **3** a group of people drafted. **4** *especially US* conscription. ▻ *verb* (***drafted***, ***drafting***) **1** to set something out in preliminary sketchy form. **2** to select and send off (personnel) to perform a specific task. **3** *especially US* to conscript. ◷ 17c: a form of DRAUGHT.

draft

A word often confused with this one is **draught**.

draft-dodger ▻ *noun*, *colloq especially US* someone who avoids conscription.

drafty, **draftier** and **draftiest** alternative *N Amer* spellings of DRAUGHTY, DRAUGHTIER and DRAUGHTIEST.

drag ▻ *verb* (***dragged***, ***dragging***) **1** to pull someone or something roughly or violently; to pull them or it along slowly and with force. **2** *tr & intr* to move or make something move along scraping the ground. **3** *colloq* (*usually* **drag someone away**) to force or persuade them to come away. **4** to search (eg a lake) with a hook or dragnet. ▻ *noun* **1** an act of dragging; a dragging effect. **2** a person or thing that makes progress slow. **3** *colloq* a draw on a cigarette. **4** *colloq* a dull or tedious person or thing. **5** *colloq* women's clothes worn by a man. **6** the resistance to motion that is encountered by an object travelling through a fluid, either in the form of a liquid or gas. ● **drag one's feet** or **heels** *colloq* to delay; to be deliberately slow to take action. ◷ Anglo-Saxon *dragan*.

■ **drag by** said especially of time: to pass slowly.

■ **drag on** *colloq* to proceed or continue slowly and tediously.

■ **drag something out** *colloq* to make it last as long as possible.

■ **drag something up** *colloq* to mention an unpleasant subject long forgotten or not usually introduced.

dragée /ˈdrɑːʒeɪ/ ▻ *noun* (***dragées*** /ˈdrɑːʒeɪz/) **1** a sweet enclosing a nut or fruit. **2** a medicated sweet. **3** a chocolate drop. **4** a small silvered ball used as a cake decoration, etc. ◷ 17c: French.

draggle /ˈdragəl/ ▻ *verb* (***draggled***, ***draggling***) *tr & intr* to make or become wet and dirty through trailing along the ground or as if doing so. ◷ 16c: from DRAG.

dragnet ▻ *noun* **1** a heavy net pulled along the bottom of a river, lake, etc in a search for something. **2** a systematc police search for a wanted person ◷ 16c.

dragon /ˈdragən/ ▻ *noun* **1** a large, mythical, fire-breathing, reptile-like creature with wings and a long tail. **2** *colloq* a frighteningly domineering woman. ● **chase the dragon** see under CHASE. ◷ 13c: from Greek *drakon* serpent.

dragonfly ▻ *noun* an insect with a fairly long slender brightly coloured body often metallic in appearance, gauzy translucent wings that cannot be closed, and large eyes covering most of the head, commonly found near still or slow-moving water, and feeding on small insects caught in mid-air. ◷ 17c.

dragoon /drəˈguːn/ ▻ *noun*, *historical* still used in titles of certain British regiments: a heavily armed mounted soldier. ▻ *verb* (***dragooned***, ***dragooning***) to force or bully someone into doing something. ◷ 17c: from French *dragon*.

drag queen ▻ *noun* a man who prefers to wear women's clothes, especially a performance artist impersonating a woman.

drag race ▻ *noun* a contest in acceleration between specially designed cars or motorcycles over a short distance. See DRAGSTER.

drag-racing ▻ *noun* the activity or sport of competing in a DRAG RACE.

dragster ▻ *noun* a car designed or adapted to be used in a DRAG RACE. ◷ 1950s.

drain ▻ *verb* (***drained***, ***draining***) **1** to empty (a container) by causing or allowing liquid to escape. **2** (**drain something of liquid**) to remove liquid from it. **3** to drink the total contents of (a glass, etc). **4** to use up the strength, emotion or resources of (someone). **5** said of a river: to carry away surface water from (land). ▻ *noun* a device, especially a pipe, for carrying away liquid. ● **drainer** *noun* a device on which articles can be left to drain, or a draining board. ● **a drain on something** anything that exhausts or seriously depletes a supply. ● **down the drain** *colloq* wasted; lost. ◷ Anglo-Saxon *dreahnian*.

■ **drain away** or **drain something away** to disappear or make it disappear □ *Our support drained away after relegation.*

■ **drain from** or **off** said of liquid, etc: to escape; to flow away.

■ **drain off** or **away** to cause or allow (a liquid) to escape.

drainage ▻ *noun* the process or a method or system of draining. ◷ 17c.

drainage basin see CATCHMENT AREA

draining board ⊳ *noun* a sloping, and often channelled, surface at the side of a sink allowing water from washed dishes, etc to drain away.

drainpipe ⊳ *noun* **1** a pipe carrying waste water or rainwater, especially water from a roof into a drain below ground. **2** (**drainpipes**) *colloq* very narrow tight-fitting trousers, especially those of a style popular in the 1950s. ◷ Late 19c.

drake ⊳ *noun* a male duck. ◷ 13c.

Dralon /ˈdreɪlɒn/ ⊳ *noun, trademark* a type of acrylic fibre popular for upholstery fabrics. ◷ 1950s.

dram ⊳ *noun* **1** *colloq* a small amount of alcoholic spirit, especially whisky. **2** a measure of weight equal to $^1/_{16}$ of an ounce. ◷ 18c in sense 1; 15c in sense 2: see DRACHM.

drama /ˈdrɑːmə/ ⊳ *noun* (***dramas***) **1** a play; any work performed by actors. **2** plays in general, as an art form. **3** the art of producing, directing and acting in plays. **4** excitement and emotion; an exciting situation. ◷ 16c as *drame*: from Greek *drama*.

drama documentary see FACTION[2]

dramatherapy ⊳ *noun, psychol* a form of therapy in which drama is used as a means of acting out different responses to real-life situations, in order to aid personal development and gain insight into psychological problems and difficulties in personal relationships.

dramatic /drəˈmatɪk/ ⊳ *adj* **1** belonging or relating to plays, the theatre or acting in general. **2** exciting. **3** sudden and striking; drastic. **4** said of a person or behaviour: flamboyantly emotional. • **dramatically** *adverb*. ◷ 16c.

dramatic irony see IRONY[1]

dramatics **1** *singular noun or plural noun* activities associated with the staging and performing of plays. **2** *plural noun* exaggeratedly emotional behaviour.

dramatis personae /ˈdramətɪs pɜːˈsoʊnaɪ, ˈdrɑː--niː/ ⊳ *plural noun* (often functioning as ⊳ *singular noun*) **a**) a list of the characters in a play; **b**) these characters. ◷ 18c: Latin, meaning 'persons of the drama'.

dramatist ⊳ *noun* a writer of plays. ◷ 17c.

dramatize or **dramatise** ⊳ *verb* (***dramatized, dramatizing***) **1** to make something into a work for public performance. **2** to treat something as, or make it seem, more exciting or important. • **dramatization** *noun*. ◷ 18c.

dramaturge /ˈdramətɜːdʒ/ and **dramaturgist** ⊳ *noun* a playwright, especially a literary adviser to a theatre company. ◷ 19c.

dramaturgy /ˈdramətɜːdʒɪ/ ⊳ *noun* the principles of dramatic composition; theatrical art and techniques. • **dramaturgic** or **dramaturgical** *adj*. ◷ 19c: from DRAMA + Greek *ergon* work.

Drambuie /dramˈbjuːɪ/ ⊳ *noun, trademark* a Scotch whisky liqueur, flavoured with honey and herbs. ◷ 19c: from DRAM + Scottish Gaelic *buidhe* 'golden' or 'pleasant'.

drank *past tense of* DRINK

drape ⊳ *verb* (***draped, draping***) **1** to hang cloth loosely over something. **2** to arrange or lay (cloth, etc) loosely. ⊳ *noun, theat* or (*especially* **drapes**) *N Amer, especially US* a curtain or hanging. ◷ 19c in these senses; 15c, meaning 'to weave or make cloth': from French *draper*.

draper /ˈdreɪpə(r)/ ⊳ *noun* someone who sells fabric, and often HABERDASHERY. ◷ 14c: originally meaning 'a maker of cloth'.

drapery /ˈdreɪpərɪ/ ⊳ *noun* (***draperies***) **1** fabric; textiles. **2** curtains and other hanging fabrics. **3** *art* the representation of cloth and clothing. **4** a draper's business or shop. ◷ 13c as *draperie*.

drastic /ˈdrastɪk/ ⊳ *adj* extreme; severe. • **drastically** *adverb*. ◷ 17c: from Greek *drastikos*, from *draein* to act.

drat *colloq* ⊳ *exclamation* expressing anger or annoyance. • **dratted** *adj* □ *The dratted handle's come off.* ◷ 19c: probably an alteration of *God rot*.

draught /drɑːft/ ⊳ *noun* **1** a current of air, especially indoors. **2** a quantity of liquid swallowed in one go. **3** the amount of water required to float a ship. **4** any of the discs used in the game of DRAUGHTS. Also called **draughtsman**. **5** *colloq* draught beer. **6** the act of pulling or drawing. **7** a dose of liquid medicine. ⊳ *adj* **1** said of beer: pumped direct from the cask to the glass. **2** said of an animal: *especially in compounds* used for pulling loads. • **on draught** said of beer: stored in casks from which it is served direct. ◷ Anglo-Saxon *draht*, from *dragan* to draw.

> ***draught***
>
> A word often confused with this one is **draft**.

draughtboard ⊳ *noun* a square board marked out in two contrasting colours used for playing draughts and chess. ◷ 18c as *draftboard*.

draughts /drɑːfts/ ⊳ *singular noun* a game for two people played with 24 discs on a chequered board. ◷ 14c: plural of DRAUGHT, in earlier sense 'a move in chess'.

draughtsman ⊳ *noun* **1** someone skilled in drawing. **2** someone employed to produce accurate and detailed technical drawings. **3** see DRAUGHT *noun* 4. ◷ 18c.

draughtsmanship ⊳ *noun* skill in drawing, especially in technical drawing.

draughty /drɑːftɪ/ ⊳ *adj* (***draughtier, draughtiest***) prone to or suffering draughts of air. ◷ 19c.

Dravidian /drəˈvɪdɪən/ ⊳ *adj* **1** denoting a dark-skinned race of S India. **2** denoting a family of over 20 languages used mainly in India, SE Asia, Africa and the Pacific, including Telugu, Tamil, Kannada and Malayalam. ⊳ *noun* the languages forming this family. ◷ 19c: from Dravida, the old Sanskrit name for one province in S India.

draw /drɔː/ ⊳ *verb* (*past tense* ***drew*** /druː/, *past participle* ***drawn***, *present participle* ***drawing***) **1** *tr & intr* to make a picture of something or someone, especially with a pencil. **2** to pull out, take out or extract something □ *draw water from a well* □ *with swords drawn.* **3** *intr* to move or proceed steadily in a specified direction □ *draw nearer.* **4** to pull someone along or into a particular position □ *drawing her closer to him.* **5** to open or close (curtains). **6** to attract (eg attention or criticism). **7** *tr & intr* (*also* **draw with someone**) to end a game with neither side winning; to finish on equal terms with an opponent. **8** to choose or be given as the result of random selection. **9** to arrive at or infer (a conclusion). **10 a**) *intr* (*also* **draw on (a cigarette)**) to suck air (through a cigarette); **b** said of a chimney: to make air flow through a fire, allowing burning. **11** *technical* said of a ship: to require (a certain depth of water) to float. **12** *intr* said of tea: to brew or infuse. **13** to disembowel □ *hanged, drawn and quartered.* **14** to write (a cheque). **15** *golf* to hit (the ball) too much to the left if right-handed, or too much to the right if left-handed. **16** *bowls* **a** to deliver (a bowl) so that it moves in a curve to the point aimed for; **b** *intr* to move in a curve to the point aimed for. **17** *bridge* to force one's opponents to play (all their cards of a suit, especially trumps) by continually leading cards of that suit. **18** *billiards, etc* to hit (the cue ball) so that it recoils after striking another ball. ⊳ *noun* **1** a result in which neither side is the winner; a tie. **2 a** the making of a random selection, eg of the winners of a competition; **b** a competition with winners chosen at random. **3** the potential to attract many people, or a person or thing having this. **4** the act of drawing a gun. • **be drawn on something** to be persuaded to talk or give information □ *He refused to be drawn on his plans.* • **draw a blank** to get no result. • **draw the line** to fix a limit, eg on one's actions or tolerance. ◷ Anglo-Saxon *dragan*.

■ **draw back** to retreat; to recoil.

■ **draw back from something** to refuse to become involved in it; to avoid commitment.

■ **draw in** said of nights: to start earlier, making days shorter.

■ **draw on something** to make use of assets from a fund or source □ *draw on reserves of energy.*

■ **draw someone out** to encourage them to be less shy or reserved.

■ **draw something out** to make it last a long time or longer than necessary.

■ **draw up** to come to a halt.

■ **draw oneself up** to lift oneself into an upright position; to straighten up.

■ **draw something up** to plan and write (a contract or other document).

drawback ▷ *noun* a disadvantage. ⓒ 17c.

drawbridge ▷ *noun* a bridge that can be lifted to prevent access across or allow passage beneath. ⓒ 14c as *drawbrugge.*

drawer ▷ *noun* **1** /drɔː(r)/ a sliding lidless storage box fitted as part of a desk or other piece of furniture. **2** /'drɔːə(r)/ someone who draws. **3** (**drawers** /drɔːz/) *old use* knickers, especially when large and roomy. ● **out of the top drawer** *colloq* of the very best quality or the highest standard. ⓒ 16c in senses 1 and 3; 14c in sense 2: from DRAW.

draw hoe ▷ *noun* a hoe designed for pulling soil towards one, having a flat blade at about right angles to the handle. Compare DUTCH HOE.

drawing ▷ *noun* **1** any picture made up of lines, especially one drawn in pencil. **2** the act or art of drawing.

drawing-board ▷ *noun* a board to which paper is fixed for drawing on. ● **go back to the drawing-board** to return to the planning stage in order to find a more successful approach. ⓒ 18c.

drawing-pin ▷ *noun* a pin with a broad flat head, used especially for fastening paper to a board or wall. ⓒ 19c.

drawing-room ▷ *noun* a sitting-room or living-room. ⓒ 17c: originally 16c as *withdrawing room.*

drawl ▷ *verb* (*drawled, drawling*) *tr & intr* to speak or say in a slow lazy manner, especially with prolonged vowel sounds. ⓒ 16c: possibly connected with DRAW.

drawn¹ ▷ *adj* showing signs of mental strain or tiredness. ⓒ 19c.

drawn² ▷ *past participle of* DRAW

drawn³ ▷ *adj, in compounds* pulled by □ *horse-drawn.*

drawn-out ▷ *adj* tedious; prolonged.

drawn-thread work and **drawn work** ▷ *noun, needlecraft* ornamental work done by pulling out some of the threads of fabric.

draw-sheet ▷ *noun* in nursing: a sheet that can be removed from under a patient.

drawstring ▷ *noun* a cord sewn inside a hem eg on a bag or piece of clothing, closing up the hem when pulled. ⓒ 19c.

dray¹ ▷ *noun* a low horse-drawn cart used for heavy loads. ⓒ Anglo-Saxon *dræge*, from *dragan* to draw.

dray² see DREY

dread /drɛd/ ▷ *noun* great fear or apprehension. ▷ *verb* (*dreaded, dreading*) to look ahead to something with dread. ▷ *adj, literary* inspiring awe or great fear. ⓒ Anglo-Saxon *ondrædan.*

dreaded ▷ *adj* **1** greatly feared. **2** *loosely* much disliked.

dreadful ▷ *adj* **1** inspiring great fear; terrible. **2** *loosely* very bad, unpleasant or extreme. ● **dreadfully** *adverb* **1** terribly. **2** *colloq* extremely; very □ *It's dreadfully late.* ⓒ 13c.

dreadlocks ▷ *plural noun* thin braids of hair tied tightly all over the head, especially worn by a RASTAFARIAN. Often shortened to **dreads**. ⓒ 1960s.

dreadnought ▷ *noun* **1** a heavily armed battleship, originally built 1905–6. **2** a fearless person.

dream /driːm/ ▷ *noun* **1** a series of unconscious thoughts and mental images that are experienced during sleep. **2** a state of complete engrossment in one's own thoughts. **3** a distant ambition, especially an unattainable one. **4** *colloq* an extremely pleasing person or thing □ *He's a dream to work with.* **5** *colloq, as adj* luxurious, ideal. ▷ *verb* (*dreamed* /driːmd, drɛmt/ or *dreamt* /drɛmt/, *dreaming*) **1** *tr & intr* to have thoughts and visions during sleep. **2** (*usually* **dream of something**) **a** to have a distant ambition or hope; **b** to imagine or conceive of something. **3** *intr* to have extravagant and unrealistic thoughts or plans. **4** *intr* to be lost in thought. ● **dreamer** *noun.* ● **dreamless** *adj.* ● **like a dream** *colloq* extremely well, easily or successfully. ⓒ 13c as *dreme.*

■ **dream something up** to devise or invent something unusual or absurd.

dreamboat ▷ *noun, slang* an ideal romantic partner. ⓒ 1940s.

dreamier, dreamiest, dreamily and **dreaminess** see under DREAMY

dream ticket ▷ *noun, chiefly N Amer* an ideal or optimum list, or especially pair, of electoral candidates. ⓒ 1960s.

dream time ▷ *noun* in Aboriginal folklore: the time when the earth and patterns of life on earth took shape. Also called **alcheringa**. ⓒ 1940s.

dreamy ▷ *adj* (*dreamier, dreamiest*) **1** unreal, as if in a dream. **2** having or showing a wandering mind. **3** *colloq* lovely. ● **dreamily** *adverb.* ● **dreaminess** *noun.* ⓒ 16c.

dreary /'drɪərɪ/ ▷ *adj* (*drearier, dreariest*) **1** dull and depressing. **2** uninteresting. ● **drearily** *adverb.* ● **dreariness** *noun.* ⓒ Anglo-Saxon *dreorig* bloody or mournful.

dredge¹ /drɛdʒ/ ▷ *verb* (*dredged, dredging*) *tr & intr* to clear the bottom of or deepen (the sea or a river) by bringing up mud and waste. ▷ *noun* a machine for dredging, with a scooping or sucking action. ⓒ 15c.

■ **dredge something up** *colloq* to mention or bring up something long forgotten.

dredge² /drɛdʒ/ ▷ *verb* (*dredged, dredging*) to sprinkle (food), eg with sugar or flour. ⓒ 16c: from French *dragie* sugar-plum.

dredger¹ ▷ *noun* a barge or ship fitted with a dredge.

dredger² ▷ *noun* a container with a perforated lid for dredging (eg flour).

dregs ▷ *plural noun* **1** solid particles in a liquid that settle at the bottom. **2** worthless or contemptible elements. ⓒ 14c: from Norse *dregg.*

drench ▷ *verb* (*drenches, drenched, drenching*) **1** to make something or someone soaking wet. **2** to administer liquid medicine to (an animal). ▷ *noun* a dose of liquid medicine for an animal. ⓒ Anglo-Saxon *drencan* to cause to drink.

Dresden china, Dresden porcelain and **Dresden ware** ▷ *noun* a fine decorated china made in Saxony since 1710.

dress ▷ *verb* (*dresses, dressed, dressing*) **1** *tr & intr* to put clothes on; to wear, or make someone wear, clothes (of a certain kind). **2** to treat and bandage (wounds). **3** to prepare, or add seasoning or a sauce to (food). **4** to arrange a display in (a shop window). **5** to shape and smooth (especially stone). **6** *intr* to put on or have on formal evening wear. ▷ *noun* **1** a woman's garment with top and skirt in one piece. **2** clothing; wear □ ***in evening dress***. ▷ *adj* formal; for wear in the evenings □ ***dress jacket***. ⓘ 14c: from French *dresser* to prepare.

■ **dress someone down** to scold them.

■ **dress up 1** to put on fancy dress. **2** to dress in very smart or formal clothes.

■ **dress something up** to make it appear more pleasant or acceptable by making additions or alterations.

dressage /ˈdresɑːʒ/ ▷ *noun* the training of a horse in, or performance of, set manoeuvres signalled by the rider. ⓘ 1930s: from French.

dress circle ▷ *noun, theat* a balcony in a theatre, especially the first above the ground floor. ⓘ 19c.

dressed *past tense, past participle of* DRESS. • **get dressed** to dress.

dresser ▷ *noun* **1** a free-standing kitchen cupboard with shelves above, for storing and displaying dishes, etc. **2** *US* a chest of drawers or dressing-table. **3** a theatre assistant employed to help stage actors with their costumes. **4** a person who dresses in a particular way. **5** a tool used for dressing stone, etc. **6** a WINDOW-DRESSER.

dressier, **dressiest** and **dressily** see under DRESSY

dressing ▷ *noun* **1** *cookery* any sauce added to food, especially salad. **2** *N Amer cookery* STUFFING. **3** a covering for a wound. **4** *agric* **a** an application of fertilizer to the soil surface; **b** chemical treatment of seeds, especially those of cereal crops, before sowing in order to control fungal diseases.

dressingdown ▷ *noun* a reprimand. ⓘ 19c.

dressinggown ▷ *noun* a loose robe worn informally indoors, especially over nightclothes. ⓘ 18c.

dressingroom ▷ *noun* **1** *theat* a room backstage where a performer can change clothing, apply makeup, etc. **2** any room used when changing clothing. ⓘ 17c.

dressing station ▷ *noun* a first-aid post where the wounded are collected and given emergency treatment. ⓘ 19c.

dressingtable ▷ *noun* a piece of bedroom furniture typically with drawers and a large mirror. ⓘ 17c.

dressmaking ▷ *noun* the craft or business of making especially women's clothes. • **dressmaker** *noun*. ⓘ 19c.

dress rehearsal ▷ *noun* **1** *theat* the last rehearsal of a performance, with full costumes, lighting and other effects. **2** a practice under real conditions, or an event considered as such in relation to another more important. ⓘ 19c.

dress sense ▷ *noun* sense of style in dress; skill in choosing clothing that suits a person best.

dress shield ▷ *noun* a pad of material that protects the armpit of a dress, etc from sweat. ⓘ 19c.

dress shirt *noun* a man's formal shirt worn with a dinner-jacket.

dressy ▷ *adj* (***dressier***, ***dressiest***) **1** dressed or dressing stylishly. **2** said of clothes: for formal wear; elegant. **3** *colloq* fancy; over-decorated. • **dressily** *adverb*. ⓘ 18c.

drew *past tense of* DRAW

drey and **dray** /dreɪ/ ▷ *noun* (***dreys***; ***drays***) a squirrel's nest. ⓘ 17c.

dribble /ˈdrɪbəl/ ▷ *verb* (***dribbled***, ***dribbling***) **1** *intr* to fall or flow in drops. **2** *intr* to allow saliva to run slowly down from the mouth. **3** *tr & intr, football, hockey, etc* to move along keeping (a ball) in close control with frequent short strokes. **4** *tr & intr, basketball* to run while continuously bouncing the ball using only one hand. ▷ *noun* (***dribbles***) **1** a small quantity of liquid, especially saliva. **2** *football, hockey, etc* an act of dribbling a ball. ⓘ 16c: from obsolete *drib* to fall or let fall in drops.

driblet ▷ *noun* a very small amount, especially of liquid. ⓘ 16c, originally meaning 'a small amount of money': see DRIBBLE.

dribs and drabs ▷ *plural noun* very small quantities at a time. ⓘ 18c.

dried *past tense, past participle of* DRY

drier[1] or **dryer** /ˈdraɪə(r)/ ▷ *noun* **1** a device or substance that dries clothing, hair, paint, etc. **2** a person or thing that dries. ⓘ 16c in sense 2.

drier[2], **dries** and **driest** see under DRY

drift ▷ *noun* **1** *geol* superficial deposits of rock material that have been carried from their place of origin by glaciers. **2** *geol* CONTINENTAL DRIFT. **3** a general movement or tendency to move. **4** the movement of a stretch of sea in the direction of a prevailing wind. **5** degree of movement off course caused by wind or a current. **6** the general or essential meaning of something. ▷ *verb* (***drifted***, ***drifting***) *intr* **1** to float or be blown along or into heaps. **2** to move aimlessly or passively from one place or occupation to another. **3** to move off course. ⓘ 13c: Norse, meaning 'snowdrift'.

drifter ▷ *noun* **1** a fishing-boat that uses a DRIFT NET. **2** someone who moves from place to place, settling in none. ⓘ 19c.

drift net ▷ *noun* a large fishing net allowed to drift with the tide. ⓘ 19c.

driftwood ▷ *noun* wood floating near, or washed up on, a shore. ⓘ 17c.

drill[1] ▷ *noun* **1** a tool for boring holes. **2** a training exercise, or a session of it. **3** *colloq* correct procedure; routine. ▷ *verb* (***drilled***, ***drilling***) **1** to make (a hole) with a drill; to make a hole in something with a drill. **2** to exercise or teach through repeated practice. ⓘ 17c: probably from Dutch *drillen* to bore.

drill[2] ▷ *noun* thick strong cotton cloth. ⓘ 18c: from German *Drillich* ticking.

drill[3] ▷ *noun* **1** a shallow furrow in which seeds are sown. **2** the seeds sown or plants growing in such a row. **3** a machine for sowing seeds in rows. ▷ *verb* (***drilled***, ***drilling***) to sow (seeds) in rows. ⓘ 18c: possibly from DRILL[1].

drill[4] ▷ *noun* a W African baboon related to, but smaller than, the MANDRILL. ⓘ 17c: from a W African language.

drill bit ▷ *noun* a removable cutting and boring head in a drill.

drilling platform ▷ *noun* a floating or fixed offshore structure supporting a DRILLING RIG.

drilling rig and **drill rig** ▷ *noun* the complete apparatus and structure required for drilling an oil well. ⓘ Early 20c.

drily see under DRY

drink ▷ *verb* (***drank***, ***drunk***, ***drinking***) **1** *tr & intr* to swallow (a liquid); to consume (a liquid) by swallowing. **2** *intr* to drink alcohol; to drink alcohol to excess. **3** to get oneself into a certain state by drinking alcohol □ ***drank himself into a stupor***. ▷ *noun* **1** an act of drinking. **2** liquid suitable for or intended for drinking. **3** alcohol of any kind or the habit of drinking alcohol to excess. **4** a glass or amount of drink. **5** (**the drink**) *colloq* the sea. • **drinkable** *adj* fit to be drunk. • **drinker** *noun* someone who drinks, especially alcohol, and especially too much. • **drink someone under the table** to continue drinking and remain sober (or comparatively so) after one's companion has completely collapsed. • **drink the health of someone** or **drink to the health of someone** to drink a toast to them. ⓘ Anglo-Saxon *drincan*.

■ **drink something in 1** to listen to it eagerly. **2** to absorb it.

■ **drink to someone** or **something** to drink a toast to them.

■ **drink up 1** to finish (a drink) by drinking. **2** to finish drinking.

drink-driving ▷ *noun* the act or practice of driving while under the influence of alcohol. • **drink-driver** *noun*. ⓘ 1960s.

drinking ▷ *noun* the act or habit of drinking. ▷ *adj* fit for or intended for drinking □ *drinking water.* ⓘ 13c.

drinking fountain ▷ *noun* a device which produces a flow or jet of drinking water, especially in public places. ⓘ 19c.

drinking-up time ▷ *noun* in a public house: the few minutes allowed after official closing time for customers to finish their last drinks before leaving. ⓘ 1960s.

drip ▷ *verb* (***dripped, dripping***) **1** *tr & intr* to release or fall in drops. **2** *intr* to release a liquid in drops □ *Don't leave the tap dripping.* **3** *tr & intr, colloq* to bear or contain an impressive or excessive amount of something □ *a film dripping with sentimentality.* ▷ *noun* **1** the action or noise of dripping. **2 a** a device for passing a liquid solution slowly and continuously into a vein; **b** the act or process of introducing a liquid in this way; **c** the solution introduced in this way. Also called **drip-feed**. **3** *derog, colloq* someone who lacks spirit or character. ⓘ Anglo-Saxon *dryppan*.

drip-dry ▷ *adj* said of a garment or fabric: requiring little or no ironing if hung up to dry by dripping. ▷ *verb, tr & intr* to dry in this way. ⓘ 1950s.

drip-feed ▷ *noun* a DRIP (*noun* 2). ▷ *verb* to feed something or someone with a liquid using a drip.

dripping[1] ▷ *noun* fat from roasted meat, especially when solidified.

dripping[2] *present participle of* DRIP

drive ▷ *verb* (*past tense* ***drove***, *past participle* ***driven*** /ˈdrɪvən/ , ***driving***) **1 a** to control the movement of (a vehicle); **b** to be legally qualified to do so. **2** *intr* to travel in a vehicle. **3** to take or transport someone or something in a vehicle. **4** to urge or force someone or something to move □ *drive cattle* □ *boats driven on to the beach by the storm.* **5** to make someone or something get into a particular state or condition □ *Her chatter drives me to distraction* □ *It drove me crazy.* **6** to force by striking □ *drove the nail into the wood.* **7** to produce motion in something; to make it operate □ *machinery driven by steam.* **8** *sport* **a** in golf: to hit (a ball), especially from the tee and using a DRIVER; **b** in cricket: to hit (a ball) forward with an upright bat; **c** to hit or kick (a ball, etc) with great force. **9** to conduct or dictate □ *drive a hard bargain.* ▷ *noun* **1** a trip in a vehicle; travel by road. **2** a path for vehicles, leading from a private residence to the road outside. Also called **driveway**. **3** (**Drive**) a street title in an address. **4** energy and enthusiasm. **5** an organized campaign; a group effort □ *an economy drive.* **6** operating power, or a device supplying this. **7** a forceful strike of a ball in various sports. **8** a united movement forward, especially by a military force. **9** a meeting to play a game, especially cards. • **drivability** or **driveability** *noun*. • **drivable** or **driveable** *adj*. • **be driven by something** to be motivated by it □ *They were driven to steal by sheer hunger.* • **be driving at something** to intend or imply it as a meaning or conclusion □ *What is he driving at?* • **drive something home 1** to make it clearly understood. **2** to force (a bolt, nail, etc) completely in. ⓘ Anglo-Saxon *drifan*.

drive-in ▷ *adj* said of a cinema, restaurant, etc: providing a service or facility for customers remaining seated in vehicles. Also *as noun*. ⓘ 1930s.

drivel /ˈdrɪvəl/ ▷ *noun* nonsense. ▷ *verb* (***drivelled, drivelling***) *intr* **1** to talk nonsense. **2** to dribble or slaver. ⓘ Anglo-Saxon *dreflian* to dribble.

driver ▷ *noun* **1** someone who drives a vehicle. **2** a large-headed golf club for hitting the ball from the tee. **3** any device, etc that drives something. • **in the driver's seat** *colloq* in a controlling or commanding position.

drive-through ▷ *noun especially N Amer* a shop, restaurant, etc from a window of which drivers can be served without leaving their cars.

driveway see under DRIVE

driving /ˈdraɪvɪŋ/ ▷ *noun* the act, practice or way of driving vehicles. ▷ *adj* **1** producing or transmitting operating power □ *driving wheel.* **2** heavy and windblown □ *driving rain.* **3** providing the motive for determined hard work □ *her driving ambition.*

driving licence ▷ *noun* an official licence to drive a motor vehicle.

driving seat ▷ *noun* the seat in a vehicle in which the driver sits. • **in the driving seat** *colloq* in a controlling or commanding position.

driving test ▷ *noun* a test of ability to drive safely, especially an official or obligatory test.

drizzle /ˈdrɪzəl/ ▷ *noun* fine light rain. ▷ *verb* (***drizzled, drizzling***) *intr* to rain lightly. • **drizzly** *adj*. ⓘ Anglo-Saxon *dreosan* to fall.

drogue /droʊg/ ▷ *noun* **1** a conical canvas sleeve open at both ends, used as one form of sea-anchor, to check the way of an aircraft, etc. **2** a WINDSOCK.

droll /droʊl/ ▷ *adj* oddly amusing or comical. • **drollery** *noun*. • **drolly** /ˈdroʊllɪ/ *adverb*. ⓘ 17c: from French *drôle*.

dromedary /ˈdrɒmədərɪ, ˈdrʌ-/ ▷ *noun* (***dromedaries***) a breed of single-humped camel, capable of moving at speed across the desert, and much used as a means of transport in N Africa, the Middle East and India. Compare BACTRIAN CAMEL. ⓘ 14c: from Greek *dromados* running.

drone ▷ *verb* (***droned, droning***) *intr* to make a low humming noise. ▷ *noun* **1** a deep humming sound. **2** a male honeybee that does not contribute to the maintenance of the colony, and whose sole function is to mate with the queen. Compare QUEEN 3, WORKER. **3** a lazy person, especially one living off others. **4 a** the bass-pipe of a set of bagpipes; **b** the low sustained note it produces. ⓘ Anglo-Saxon *dran* drone (bee).

■ **drone on** to talk at length in a tedious monotonous voice.

drongo /ˈdrɒŋgoʊ/ ▷ *noun* (***drongoes*** or ***drongos***) **1** *Austral slang* an idiot; a no-hoper. **2** any member of a family of glossy-black, fork-tailed, insectivorous birds found in tropical regions of Africa, Asia and Australia. ⓘ 19c: from the Malagasay name for the bird.

drool ▷ *verb* (***drooled, drooling***) *intr* to dribble or slaver. ⓘ 19c: alteration of DRIVEL.

■ **drool over something** to show uncontrolled admiration for it or pleasure at the sight of it.

droop ▷ *verb* (***drooped, drooping***) *intr* **1** to hang loosely; to sag. **2** to be or grow weak with tiredness. ▷ *noun* a drooping state. ⓘ 14c: from Norse *drupa*.

droopy ▷ *adj* (***droopier, droopiest***) hanging loosely; drooping. • **droopily** *adverb*. • **droopiness** *noun*. ⓘ 13c.

drop ▷ *verb* (***dropped, dropping***) **1** *tr & intr* to fall or allow to fall. **2** *tr & intr* to decline or make something decline; to lower or weaken. **3** to give up or abandon (eg a friend or a habit); to stop doing something. **4** to stop discussing (a topic). **5** (*also* **drop someone** or **something off**) to set them down from a vehicle; to deliver or hand them in. **6** to leave or take out someone or something □ *They've dropped me from the team.* **7** to mention something casually □ *drop a hint.* **8** to fail to pronounce (especially a consonant) □ *drop one's h's.* **9** *colloq* to write informally □ *Drop me a line.* **10** *rugby* to score (a goal) by a DROP KICK. **11** *coarse slang except when said of an animal* to give birth to (a baby). **12** *slang* to beat to the ground. ▷ *noun* **1** a small round or pear-shaped mass of liquid, especially when falling; a small amount (of liquid). **2** a descent; a fall. **3** a vertical distance. **4** a decline or decrease. **5** any small round or pear-shaped object, eg an earring or boiled sweet. **6** (**drops**) liquid medication administered in small amounts □ *eye drops*. **7** a delivery. **8** *in compounds* (*usually* **drop-**) used of something that drops, or that is used in or for dropping. • **at the drop of a hat** *colloq* promptly; for the slightest reason. • **let something drop** to make it known inadvertently or as if inadvertently. ◷ Anglo-Saxon *droppian*.

■ **drop back** or **behind** to get left behind others in a group.

■ **drop in** or **by** to pay a brief unexpected visit.

■ **drop into something** to pass idly or passively into (a habit, etc).

■ **drop off 1** *colloq* to fall asleep. **2** to become less; to diminish; to disappear.

■ **drop out 1** to withdraw from an activity. **2** *colloq* to adopt an alternative lifestyle as a reaction against traditional social values. See also DROPOUT.

■ **drop out of something** to withdraw eg from a pre-arranged activity.

drop-dead ▷ *adj*, *slang* stunning or breathtaking, particularly in a sexual way □ *His new boyfriend is drop-dead gorgeous.*

drop forging ▷ *noun* the process of shaping metal parts by forging between two dies, one fixed to the hammer and the other to the anvil of a steam or mechanical hammer. ◷ 19c.

drop goal ▷ *noun*, *rugby* a goal secured by a DROP KICK.

drop-in ▷ *adj* said of a café, day centre, clinic, etc, especially one managed by a charity or the social services: where clients are free to attend informally and casually. ◷ 20c.

drop kick *rugby* ▷ *noun* a kick in which the ball is released from the hands and struck as it hits the ground. ▷ *verb* (**drop-kick**) to kick (a ball) in this way. ◷ 19c.

drop-leaf ▷ *adj* said of a desk or table: with a hinged leaf or leaves which can be put into horizontal position when required, but which can be stored in a vertical position. ◷ 19c.

droplet ▷ *noun* a tiny drop. ◷ 17c.

dropout ▷ *noun* **1** a student who quits before completing a course of study. **2** a person whose alternative lifestyle is a reaction against traditional social values; any unconventional person. See also DROP OUT at DROP. ◷ 20c.

drop-out ▷ *noun* **1** *telecomm* a brief loss of signal, especially in magnetic recording. **2** *computing* a patch which fails to record data on a magnetic tape.

dropper ▷ *noun* **1** a short narrow glass tube with a rubber bulb on one end, for applying liquid in drops. **2** a person or thing that drops.

droppings ▷ *plural noun* animal or bird faeces.

drop-scone ▷ *noun* a small thick pancake.

drop-shot ▷ *noun* in tennis, badminton, etc: a shot hit so that it drops low and close to the net, immediately after clearing it.

dropsy /ˈdrɒpsɪ/ ▷ *noun* the former name for OEDEMA (sense 1). • **dropsical** *adj*. ◷ 13c: from Greek *hydrops*, from *hydor* water.

drosophila /drɒˈsɒfɪlə/ ▷ *noun* (***drosophilas*** or ***drosophilae*** /-fɪleɪ/) any of various small yellow fruit flies widely used in genetic experiments. ◷ 19c: from Greek *drosos* dew or moisture + *phileein* to love.

dross ▷ *noun* **1** waste coal. **2** scum that forms on molten metal. **3** *derog colloq* rubbish; any worthless substance. • **drossy** *adj*. ◷ Anglo-Saxon *dros*.

drought /draʊt/ ▷ *noun* a prolonged lack of rainfall. ◷ Anglo-Saxon *drugath* dryness.

drove[1] *past tense of* DRIVE

drove[2] ▷ *noun* **1** a moving herd of animals, especially cattle. **2** a large moving crowd. ◷ Anglo-Saxon *draf* herd.

drover ▷ *noun*, *historical* someone employed to drive farm animals to and from market.

drown ▷ *verb* (***drowned***, ***drowning***) **1** *intr* to die by suffocation as a result of inhaling liquid, especially water, into the lungs. **2** to kill by suffocation in this way. **3** to apply an excessive amount of liquid to something; to soak or flood it. • **drown one's sorrows** *colloq* to become drunk in order to forget one's troubles. ◷ Middle English *drounen*.

■ **drown something out** to suppress the effect of one sound with a louder one.

drowse /draʊz/ ▷ *verb* (***drowsed***, ***drowsing***) *intr* to sleep lightly for a short while; to be in a pleasantly sleepy state. ◷ Anglo-Saxon *drusian* to be sluggish.

drowsy ▷ *adj* (***drowsier***, ***drowsiest***) **1** sleepy; causing sleepiness. **2** lethargic. **3** quiet and peaceful. • **drowsily** *adverb*. • **drowsiness** *noun*.

drub ▷ *verb* (***drubbed***, ***drubbing***) **1** to defeat severely. **2** to beat; to thump. • **drubbing** *noun*. ◷ 17c: from Arabic *daraba* to beat.

drudge ▷ *verb* (***drudged***, ***drudging***) *intr* to do hard, tedious or menial work. ▷ *noun* a servant; a labourer. • **drudgery** *noun*. ◷ 16c.

drug ▷ *noun* **1** any chemical substance which, when taken into the body or applied externally, has a specific effect on its functioning. **2** any such substance, especially one which is abused, habitual or addictive, and possession of which is illegal. **3** anything craved for. ▷ *verb* (***drugged***, ***drugging***) **1** to administer a drug to (a person or animal). **2** to poison or stupefy with drugs. **3** to mix or season (food) with drugs. • **a drug on the market** a commodity in plentiful supply but not in demand. ◷ 14c: from French *drogue*.

drug addict ▷ *noun* someone who has become dependent on drugs. ◷ Early 20c.

drug addiction ▷ *noun* the physical and psychological state of dependence that results from taking certain drugs habitually.

drugget /ˈdrʌɡɪt/ ▷ *noun* **1** thick coarse woollen fabric. **2** a protective cover for a floor or carpet made from this. ◷ 16c: from French *droguet* waste fabric.

druggie or **druggy** /ˈdrʌɡɪ/ ▷ *noun* (**druggies**) *colloq* a drug addict. Also *as adj*. ◷ 1960s.

druggist ▷ *noun*, *now N Amer*, *especially US* a pharmacist. ◷ 17c.

drugstore ▷ *noun*, *N Amer*, *especially US* a chemist's shop, especially one also selling refreshments.

druid or **Druid** /ˈdruːɪd/ ▷ *noun* **1** a member of a Celtic order of priests in N Europe in pre-Christian times. **2** an eisteddfod official. • **druidic** or **druidical** *adj*. • **druidism** *noun*. ◷ 16c: from Gaulish *druides*.

drum ▷ *noun* **1** a percussion instrument consisting of a hollow frame with a skin or other membrane stretched tightly across its opening, sounding when struck. **2** any object resembling this in shape, especially a cylindrical container. **3** an eardrum. ▷ *verb* (***drummed***, ***drumming***) **1** *intr* to beat a drum. **2** *tr & intr* to make or cause to make continuous tapping or thumping sounds. • **beat** or **bang the drum for something** to try to interest people in it; to publicize it. ◷ 16c: related to German *Trommel*; imitating the sound made.

■ **drum something in** or **into someone** to force it into their mind through constant repetition.

■ **drum someone out** to expel them.

■ **drum something up** *colloq* to achieve or attract it by energetic persuasion □ *managed to drum up more support.*

drum and bass or **drum'n' bass** ▷ *noun* fast rhythmic music influenced by HARDCORE, TECHNO, REGGAE and HIP-HOP, characterized by very low bass lines and complex percussion breaks (see BREAK *noun* 12). Also (*popularly*) called JUNGLE. ⓒ 1990s: originating in the UK.

drumbeat ▷ *noun* the sound made when a drum is hit.

drumhead ▷ *noun* the part of a drum that is struck; the skin. ⓒ 17c.

drumlin ▷ *noun, geol* a small elongated oval hill produced by the pressure of ice moving over glacial deposits, often found in groups. ⓒ 19c: from Scottish and Irish Gaelic *druim* back.

drum machine ▷ *noun* a SYNTHESIZER for simulating the sound of drums and other percussion instruments. ⓒ 1970s.

drum major ▷ *noun* the leader of a marching (especially military) band.

drum majorette see MAJORETTE

drummer ▷ *noun* someone who plays drums.

drum roll see ROLL *noun* 12

drumstick ▷ *noun* **1** a stick used for beating a drum. **2** the lower leg of a cooked fowl, especially a chicken. ⓒ 16c.

drunk ▷ *verb, past participle of* DRINK. ▷ *adj* lacking control in movement, speech, etc through having consumed an excess of alcohol. ▷ *noun* a drunk person, especially one regularly so. ● **drunk with something** intoxicated or overwhelmed with it □ *drunk with love.*

drunkard ▷ *noun* someone who is often drunk. ⓒ 16c.

drunken ▷ *adj* **1** drunk. **2** relating to, or brought on by, alcoholic intoxication. ● **drunkenly** *adverb*. ● **drunkenness** *noun*.

drupe /dru:p/ ▷ *noun, bot* a fleshy fruit containing one or more seeds that are surrounded by the ENDOCARP, eg plum, cherry, peach, holly. ● **drupaceous** /-'peɪʃəs/ *adj.* ⓒ 18c: from Greek *dryppa* olive.

Druze or **Druz** or **Druse** /dru:z/ *relig* ▷ *singular noun or plural noun* a people, or a member of a people, inhabiting chiefly a mountainous district in the south of Syria, whose religion is an offshoot of Islam but contains doctrines drawn from other sources, including a belief in the TRANSMIGRATION of souls. ▷ *adj* belonging or relating to this people or their religion. ⓒ 18c: perhaps from Darazi, an early exponent of the religion.

dry ▷ *adj* (***drier, driest***) **1** free from or lacking moisture or wetness. **2** with little or no rainfall. **3** from which all the water has evaporated or been taken □ *a dry well.* **4** thirsty. **5** said of an animal: no longer producing milk. **6** said of wine, etc: not sweet. **7** not buttered □ *dry toast.* **8** said of humour: expressed in a quietly sarcastic or matter-of-fact way. **9** forbidding the sale and consumption of alcohol. **10** said of eyes: without tears. **11** dull; uninteresting. **12** lacking warmth of character. **13** said of a cough: not producing catarrh. ▷ *verb* (***dries, dried, drying***) **1** *tr & intr* to make or become dry. **2** *tr* to preserve (food) by removing all moisture. ▷ *noun* (***dries*** or ***drys***) *colloq* a staunch right-wing British Conservative politician. Compare WET. ● **drily** or **dryly** *adverb*. ● **dryness** *noun*. ● **cut and dried** see under CUT. ● **high and dry** see under HIGH. ⓒ Anglo-Saxon *dryge*.

■ **dry off** to become completely dry.

■ **dry something off** to dry it completely.

■ **dry out 1** to become completely dry. **2** *colloq* to receive treatment to cure addiction to alcohol; to have one's addiction cured.

■ **dry something out** to dry it completely.

■ **dry up 1** to dry thoroughly or completely. **2** to cease to produce or be produced. **3** *colloq* said of a speaker or actor: to run out of words; to forget lines while on stage. **4** *slang* to shut up or be quiet.

■ **dry something up** to dry (dishes) after washing them.

dryad /'draɪad/ ▷ *noun, Greek mythol* a woodland nymph or fairy, often with demigod status. ⓒ 16c: from Greek *dryados.*

dry battery ▷ *noun* a battery consisting of DRY CELLS.

dry cell ▷ *noun, chem* an ELECTROLYTIC CELL in which current is passed through an electrolyte that consists of a moist paste, eg ammonium chloride, instead of a liquid, and which is used as portable energy sources in batteries for torches, radios, calculators, etc.

dry-clean ▷ *verb* to clean (especially clothes) with liquid chemicals, not with water. ● **dry-cleaner** *noun*. ● **dry-cleaning** *noun*.

dry dock ▷ *noun* a dock from which the water can be pumped out to allow work on a ship's lower parts.

dryer see DRIER

dry-fly ▷ *adj, angling* said of fishing, etc: without sinking the fly in the water.

dry hole ▷ *noun, oil industry* **1** a well which does not yield commercially viable quantities of oil or gas. **2** any unsuccessful project.

dry ice ▷ *noun* solid carbon dioxide used as a refrigerating agent and also (*theat*) for creating special effects.

dry land ▷ *noun* land as opposed to sea or other water.

dry measure ▷ *noun* a system of measurement by bulk used for grain, etc.

dry monsoon see under MONSOON

dry point ▷ *noun* a technique of engraving in INTAGLIO print-making in which the design is incised by direct pressure into the copper plate, using a strong steel or diamond-pointed tool, commonly used in combination with other engraving methods, to add tonal depth and accented line.

dry riser ▷ *noun* (abbreviation **DR**) a vertical pipe with an outside access through which water can be pumped to the individual floors of a building in the event of fire.

dry rot ▷ *noun* **1** *bot* a serious type of timber decay caused by a fungus common in damp, poorly ventilated buildings, which ultimately reduces the wood to a dry brittle mass. Compare WET ROT. **2** *bot* any of several fungal diseases of plants, eg stored potatoes, fruit.

dry run ▷ *noun* **1** a rehearsal, practice or test. **2** *military* a practice exercise.

dry-stone ▷ *adj* said of a wall: made of stones wedged together without mortar. ⓒ 18c.

DS ▷ *abbreviation, music* dal segno.

DSC ▷ *abbreviation* Distinguished Service Cross.

DSc ▷ *abbreviation* Doctor of Science.

DSM ▷ *abbreviation* Distinguished Service Medal.

DSO ▷ *abbreviation* Distinguished Service Order.

DSS ▷ *abbreviation* Department of Social Security.

DST ▷ *abbreviation* daylight saving time.

DT and **DTs** ▷ *abbreviation* delirium tremens.

DTh and **DTheol** ▷ *abbreviation* Doctor of Theology.

DTI ▷ *abbreviation* Department of Trade and Industry.

DTP ▷ *abbreviation* desktop publishing.

Du. ▷ *abbreviation* Dutch.

dual /ˈdʒʊəl ▷ *adj* **1** consisting of or representing two separate parts. **2** double; twofold. See also NUMBER (*noun* 12). ▷ *verb* (***dualled, dualling***) to upgrade (a road) by making it into a dual carriageway. ⓒ 17c: from Latin *duo* two.

dual carriageway ▷ *noun* a road on which traffic moving in opposite directions is separated by a central barrier or strip of land, usually with at least two lanes in each direction. ⓒ 1930s.

dualism ▷ *noun, philos* the belief that reality is made up of two separate parts, one spiritual and one physical, or influenced by two separate forces, one good and one bad. Compare MONISM. • **dualistic** *adj*. ⓒ 18c.

duality /dʒʊˈalɪtɪ/ ▷ *noun* the state of being double. ⓒ 15c.

dual-purpose ▷ *adj* serving or intended to serve two purposes. ⓒ Early 20c.

dub[1] ▷ *verb* (***dubbed, dubbing***) **1** to give a name, especially a nickname, to someone. **2** to confer the title of knight on someone by touching each shoulder with a sword. **3** to smear (leather) with grease. ⓒ Anglo-Saxon *dubbian* in sense 2.

dub[2] ▷ *verb* (***dubbed, dubbing***) **1** to add a new soundtrack to (eg a film), especially one in a different language. **2** to add sound effects or music to (eg a film). ▷ *noun* a type of REGGAE music in which bass, drums and the artistic arrangement are given prominence over voice and other instruments. ⓒ 20c: contraction of DOUBLE.

dubbin /ˈdʌbɪn/ ▷ *noun* a wax-like mixture of oil and tallow for softening and waterproofing leather. ⓒ 19c: from DUB[1].

dubiety /dʒʊˈbaɪɪtɪ/ ▷ *noun, formal* dubiousness; doubt. ⓒ 18c: from Latin *dubietas*.

dubious /ˈdʒuːbɪəs/ ▷ *adj* **1** feeling doubt; unsure; uncertain. **2** arousing suspicion; potentially dishonest or dishonestly obtained. • **dubiously** *adverb*. • **dubiousness** *noun*. ⓒ 16c in sense 2: from Latin *dubium* doubt.

dubious

See Usage Note at **doubtful**.

dubnium /ˈdʌbnɪəm/ ▷ *noun, chem* (symbol **Db**, atomic number 104) a name proposed for the radioactive element UNNILQUADIUM.

Dubonnet /duːˈbɒneɪ/ ▷ *noun, trademark* a type of sweet aperitif, flavoured with quinine.

ducal /ˈdʒuːkəl/ ▷ *adj* belonging or relating to a duke. ⓒ 15c: from Latin *ducalis*.

ducat /ˈdʌkət/ ▷ *noun* a former European gold or silver coin of varying value. ⓒ 13c: from Latin *ducatus* duchy.

Duchenne muscular dystrophy, Duchenne dystrophy and **Duchenne** /duˈʃɛn —/ ▷ *noun, medicine* a common and severe form of MUSCULAR DYSTROPHY which affects children under 10 years old, usually boys. ⓒ 19c: named after Guillaume Duchenne (1806–75), French physician.

duchess /ˈdʌtʃɛs, ˈdʌtʃəs/ ▷ *noun* **1** the wife or widow of a duke. **2** a woman of the same rank as a duke in her own right. ⓒ 14c: from French *duchesse*.

duchy /ˈdʌtʃɪ/ ▷ *noun* (***duchies***) the territory owned or ruled by a duke or duchess. ⓒ 14c: from French *duché*.

duck[1] ▷ *noun* **1** any wild or domesticated water bird related to the swans and geese, with short legs, webbed feet, and a large flattened beak, the females generally having a dull plumage, but the males often brightly coloured. **2** the flesh of this bird used as food. **3** the female of such a bird, as opposed to the male DRAKE. **4** *colloq* **a** a likeable person; **b** a term of endearment or (loosely) of address (*also* **ducks**). **5** *cricket* a batsman's score of zero. • **break one's duck 1** *colloq* to enjoy one's first success after several failures. **2** *cricket* to make one's first run. • **like water off a duck's back** *colloq* having no effect at all. ⓒ Anglo-Saxon *duce*.

duck[2] ▷ *verb* (***ducked, ducking***) **1** *intr* to lower the head or body suddenly, especially to avoid notice or a blow. **2** to push someone or something briefly under water. ⓒ 13c.

■ **duck out of something** *colloq* to avoid something unpleasant or unwelcome.

duck[3] ▷ *noun* hard-wearing cotton fabric, used for tents, sails, etc. ⓒ 17c: from Dutch *doek* linen cloth.

duck-billed platypus see PLATYPUS

duckboard ▷ *noun* a narrow board, slatted or with slats nailed onto it, laid across eg muddy ground or a fragile surface to form a path. ⓒ Early 19c.

duckier, duckies and **duckiest** see under DUCKY

ducking ▷ *noun* immersion of a person or animal in water.

ducking-stool ▷ *noun, historical* a chair on a long wooden pole, used for ducking offenders into water as punishment. ⓒ 16c.

duckling ▷ *noun* a young duck. ⓒ 15c.

ducks and drakes ▷ *singular noun* the game of skimming stones across the surface of water. • **play ducks and drakes with something** *colloq* to squander or waste it. ⓒ 17c.

duck soup ▷ *noun, US slang* something very easy. ⓒ Early 20c.

duckweed ▷ *noun* any of a family of plants whose broad flat leaves grow on the surface of water.

ducky /ˈdʌkɪ/ *colloq* ▷ *noun* (***duckies***) a term of endearment. ▷ *adj* (***duckier, duckiest***) excellent; attractive or pleasing. ⓒ 19c: from DUCK[1].

duct ▷ *noun* **1** *anatomy* any tube in the body, especially one for carrying glandular secretions away from a gland □ *tear duct*. **2** in a building: a casing or shaft that accommodates pipes or electrical cables, or a tube used for ventilation and air-conditioning. ⓒ 17c: from Latin *ducere, ductum* to lead.

ductile /ˈdʌktaɪl/ ▷ *adj* **1** *chem* denoting certain metals, eg copper, that can be drawn out into a thin wire or thread without breaking. **2** easily influenced by others. • **ductility** /-ˈtɪlɪtɪ/ *noun* (***ductilities***) the capacity of metal to be stretched or pressed into shape. ⓒ 17c in sense 1; originally 14c meaning 'flexible': from Latin *ductilis*, from *ducere, ductum* to lead.

dud *colloq* ▷ *noun* **1** a counterfeit article. **2** a bomb, firework, etc that fails to go off. **3** any useless or ineffectual person or thing. **4** (**duds**) clothes. ▷ *adj* **1** useless. **2** counterfeit. ⓒ 15c in sense 4.

dude /duːd, djuːd / ▷ *noun colloq N Amer, especially US, originally slang* **1** a man; a guy. **2** a city man, especially an Easterner holidaying in the West. **3** a man preoccupied with dressing smartly. ⓒ 19c.

dudgeon /ˈdʌdʒən/ ▷ *noun* (*usually* **in high dudgeon**) the condition of being very angry, resentful or indignant. ⓒ 16c.

due /dʒuː/ ▷ *adj* **1** owed; payable. **2** expected according to timetable or pre-arrangement. **3** proper. ▷ *noun* **1** what is owed; that which can be rightfully claimed or expected. **2** (**dues**) subscription fees. ▷ *adverb* directly □ *due north*. • **due to something** or **someone 1** caused by it or them. **2** because of it or them. • **give someone their due** to acknowledge their qualities or achievements, especially when disapproving in other ways. • **in due course** in the ordinary way when the time comes. 14c: from French *deü*, from *devoir* to owe.

> ***due to***
>
> ● It is sometimes argued that, because **due** is an adjective, **due to** should have a noun or pronoun that it refers back to (an antecedent), as in □ *Absence from work due to sickness has certainly not been falling* (where 'absence' is the antecedent). This argument would disallow sentences like:
> **?** *A special train service was cancelled due to operating difficulties* (where **due to** is effectively a preposition).
> ● This point of view is based on the word's behaviour in its other meanings; in this meaning it has taken on a new grammatical role that is now well established. **Due to** often refers back to a whole clause even when there is a notional antecedent, as with 'starvation' in the sentence □ *Out in the countryside, two million people are at risk of starvation, due to the failure of the harvest.*
> ☆ RECOMMENDATION: it is correct to use **due to** in both the ways shown

duel /ˈdʒʊəl, ˈdʒ-/ ▷ *noun* **1** a pre-arranged fight between two people to settle a matter of honour. **2** any serious conflict between two people or groups. ▷ *verb* (***duelled, duelling***) *intr* to fight a duel. ● **duellist** or **dueller** *noun*. ◷ 15c: from Latin *duellum*, variant of *bellum* war.

duenna /djuˈɛnə/ ▷ *noun* (***duennas***) an older woman acting as a chaperone to a girl or young woman, especially *formerly* in Spanish and Portuguese society. ◷ 17c: from Spanish *dueña*.

due process ▷ *noun, law* a principle, deriving from a clause of the Magna Carta (1215), now also embodied in the 5th and 14th amendments of the US Constitution, which provides that no person shall be arrested, imprisoned, banished, or in any way deprived of their rights, except by the lawful judgement of equals and according to the law of the land.

duet /dʒʊˈɛt/ ▷ *noun* **1** a piece of music for two singers or players. **2** a pair of musical performers. ● **duettist** *noun*. ◷ 18c: from Italian *duetto*, from Latin *duo* two.

duff[1] ▷ *noun* a heavy boiled or steamed pudding, especially one containing fruit. ◷ 19c: northern form of DOUGH.

duff[2] ▷ *adj, colloq* useless; broken. ◷ 19c: perhaps from DUFFER.

duff[3] ▷ *verb* (***duffed, duffing***) *colloq* **1** to bungle something. **2** *especially golf* to misplay or mishit (a shot). ▷ *adj* bungled. ◷ 19c: from DUFFER.

> ■ **duff someone up** *slang* to treat them violently; to beat them up.

duffel or **duffle** /ˈdʌfəl/ ▷ *noun* a thick coarse woollen fabric. ◷ 17c: Dutch, named after Duffel, a Belgian town.

duffel bag ▷ *noun* a cylindrical canvas shoulder bag with a drawstring fastening. ◷ Early 20c.

duffel coat ▷ *noun* a heavy, especially hooded, coat made of DUFFEL, typically with toggle fastenings. ◷ 17c.

duffer /ˈdʌfə(r)/ ▷ *noun, colloq* a clumsy or incompetent person. ◷ 18c.

dug[1] *past tense, past participle of* DIG

dug[2] ▷ *noun* **1** an animal's udder or nipple. **2** *coarse slang* a woman's breast. ◷ 16c.

dugong /ˈduːɡɒŋ/ ▷ *noun* a seal-like plant-eating tropical sea mammal. ◷ 19c: from Malay *duyong*.

dugout ▷ *noun* **1** a canoe made from a hollowed-out log. **2** a soldier's rough shelter dug into a slope or bank or in a trench. **3** a covered shelter at the side of a sports field, for the trainer, substitutes, etc. ◷ 19c.

duke /dʒuːk/ ▷ *noun* (***dukes***) **1** a nobleman of the highest rank outside the royal family. **2** the ruler of a small state or principality. **3** *old slang use* (*often* **dukes**) a fist. See also DUCAL, DUCHESS. ● **dukedom** *noun* the title or property of a duke. ◷ 12c: French, from Latin *dux* leader.

dulcet /ˈdʌlsɪt/ ▷ *adj, literary* said of sounds: sweet and pleasing to the ear. ◷ 15c as *doucet*: from Latin *dulcis* sweet.

dulcimer /ˈdʌlsɪmə(r)/ ▷ *noun, music* a percussion instrument consisting of a flattish box with tuned strings stretched across, struck with small hammers. ◷ 15c: from Latin *dulce melos* sweet song.

dull ▷ *adj* **1** said of colour or light: lacking brightness or clearness. **2** said of sounds: deep and low; muffled. **3** said of weather: cloudy; overcast. **4** said of pain: not sharp. **5** said of a person: slow to learn or understand. **6** uninteresting; lacking liveliness. **7** said of a blade: blunt. ▷ *verb* (***dulled, dulling***) *tr & intr* to make or become dull. ● **dullness** *noun* a dull or uninteresting state. ● **dully** /ˈdʌllɪ/ *adverb*. ◷ Anglo-Saxon *dol* stupid.

dulse /dʌls/ ▷ *noun* an edible red seaweed. ◷ 17c: from Irish Gaelic *duileasg*.

duly ▷ *adverb* **1** in the proper way. **2** at the proper time. ◷ 14c as *duelich*: from DUE.

dumb /dʌm/ ▷ *adj* **1** not having the power of speech. **2** said of animals: not having human speech. **3** temporarily deprived of the power of speech, eg by shock. **4** silent; not expressed in words. **5** *colloq, especially US* foolish; unintelligent. **6** performed without words □ *dumb show*. ● **dumbly** *adverb*. ● **dumbness** *noun*. ● **struck dumb** silenced with astonishment. ◷ Anglo-Saxon.

dumbbell /ˈdʌmbɛl/ ▷ *noun* **1** a weight usually used in pairs in muscle-developing exercises, consisting of a short metal bar with a heavy ball or disc on each end. **2** anything of that shape. **3** *colloq, chiefly N Amer* a stupid person. ◷ 18c.

dumbfound or **dumfound** /dʌmˈfaʊnd/ ▷ *verb* to astonish or confound, originally so as to leave speechless. ◷ 17c: DUMB + *found* from CONFOUND.

dumbo /ˈdʌmboʊ/ ▷ *noun* (***dumbos***) *colloq* a stupid person. ◷ 1960s: from DUMB.

dumb piano ▷ *noun, music* a soundless keyboard for practice.

dumb show ▷ *noun* gesture without words. ◷ 16c: originally part of a play.

dumbstruck ▷ *adj* silent with astonishment or shock. ◷ 19c.

dumb waiter ▷ *noun* **1** a small lift for transporting laundry, dirty dishes, etc between floors in a restaurant or hotel. **2** a movable shelved stand for food, placed near a table. **3** a revolving food tray set in the middle of a table. ◷ 18c.

dumdum /ˈdʌmdʌm/ ▷ *noun* a bullet that expands on impact, causing severe injury. ◷ 19c: named after Dum-Dum, an arsenal near Calcutta, India.

dumfound see DUMBFOUND

dummy /ˈdʌmɪ/ ▷ *noun* (***dummies***) **1** a life-size model of the human body, eg used for displaying clothes. **2** a realistic copy, especially one misleadingly substituted for the genuine article. **3** a rubber teat sucked by a baby for comfort. Also called PACIFIER. **4** *colloq, chiefly N Amer* a stupid person. **5** *sport* an act of dummying with the ball. **6** a person or company acting seemingly independently, but really the agent of another. **7** *bridge* an exposed hand of cards. ▷ *adj* false; sham; counterfeit. ▷ *verb* (***dummies, dummied, dummying***) *tr & intr, sport* **a** to make as if to move one way before sharply moving the other, in order to deceive (an opponent); **b** to do so with (a ball). ◷ 16c, originally meaning 'a person who cannot speak': from DUMB.

dummy run ▷ *noun* a practice; a try-out. ◷ Early 20c.

dump ▷ *verb* (***dumped, dumping***) **1** to put something down heavily or carelessly. **2** *tr & intr* to dispose of (rubbish), especially in an unauthorized place. **3** *slang* to break off a romantic relationship with someone. **4** *econ* to sell (goods not selling well on the domestic market) abroad at a much reduced price, either to keep the domestic price high or to eliminate competition or break into a new market. **5** *computing* to transfer (computer data) from one program to another using a dump, or to transfer a (computer program or data) onto disk or tape. ▷ *noun* **1** a place where rubbish may be dumped. **2** a military store, eg of weapons or food. **3** *computing* a printed copy of the contents of a computer's memory, used to transfer data from one program to another or to find the cause of an error in a program. **4** *colloq* a dirty or dilapidated place. • **dumping** *noun*. ⓒ 14c: possibly from Norse.

dumpbin ▷ *noun* in a shop etc: a display stand or a container for especially bargain items.

dumper ▷ *noun* **1** something or someone that dumps. **2** a DUMPER TRUCK. **3** *surfing* a wave that crashes down suddenly with great force, causing surfers to fall. ⓒ 19c.

dumper truck and **dumptruck** ▷ *noun* a lorry which can be emptied by raising one end of the carrier to allow the contents to slide out.

dumpling /'dʌmplɪŋ/ ▷ *noun* **1** a baked or boiled ball of dough served with meat. **2** a rich fruit pudding. **3** *colloq* a plump person. ⓒ 17c: from obsolete *dump* lump.

dumps ▷ *plural noun* • **down in the dumps** *colloq* in low spirits; depressed. ⓒ 16c: perhaps from German *dumpf* gloomy.

dumpy /'dʌmpɪ/ ▷ *adj* (***dumpier***, ***dumpiest***) short and plump. ⓒ 18c: perhaps from DUMPLING.

dun¹ ▷ *adj* (***dunner***, ***dunnest***) having a greyish-brown dusky colour. ▷ *noun* **1** a dun colour. **2** a horse of this colour. ⓒ Anglo-Saxon.

dun² ▷ *verb* (***dunned***, ***dunning***) to press someone persistently for payment. ▷ *noun* a demand for payment. ⓒ 17c.

dunce /dʌns/ ▷ *noun* (***dunces***) a stupid person; a slow learner. ⓒ 16c: from the *Dunses*, followers of the 13c philosopher and theologian John Duns Scotus, who in the 16c were opposed to the new classical studies.

dunderhead /'dʌndəhɛd/ ▷ *noun* a stupid person. • **dunderheaded** *adj* stupid. ⓒ 17c.

dune /dʒuːn/ ▷ *noun* a ridge or hill formed by the accumulation of windblown sand, usually on a seashore or in a hot desert. ⓒ 18c: from Dutch *duna*.

dung ▷ *noun* animal excrement. ⓒ Anglo-Saxon.

dungarees /dʌŋgə'riːz, 'dʌŋ-/ ▷ *plural noun* loose trousers with a bib and shoulder straps attached, worn as casual wear or overalls. ⓒ Late 19c: from Hindi *dungri* a coarse calico fabric.

dung-beetle ▷ *noun* a shiny dark-coloured beetle whose larvae feed on the dung of herbivorous animals, eg cattle. ⓒ 17c.

dungeon /'dʌndʒən/ ▷ *noun* a prison cell, especially underground. ⓒ 14c: from French *donjon*.

dungheap and **dunghill** ▷ *noun* **1** a pile of dung. **2** any squalid situation or place. ⓒ 14c.

dunk ▷ *verb* (***dunked***, ***dunking***) **1** to dip (eg a biscuit) into tea or a similar beverage. **2** to submerge or be submerged. **3** *basketball* to jump up and push (the ball) down through the basket. ⓒ Early 20c: originally US, from German dialect *tunke*.

dunlin /'dʌnlɪn/ ▷ *noun* a small wading bird, having mottled brown plumage with pale underparts and a slender probing bill, native to the N hemisphere and found in flocks on the shoreline or open areas near water. ⓒ 16c: a diminutive of DUN¹.

dunned *past tense, past participle of* DUN²

dunner and **dunnest** see under DUN¹

dunning *present participle of* DUN²

dunno /də'noʊ, dʌ'noʊ/ *colloq* ▷ *contraction of* I do not know.

dunnock /'dʌnək/ ▷ *noun* the hedge sparrow. ⓒ 17c: from DUN¹.

duo /'dʒuːoʊ/ ▷ *noun* (***duos***) **1** a pair of musicians or other performers. **2** any two people considered a pair. **3** *music* a duet. ⓒ 16c in sense 3; 19c in senses 1 and 2: Latin, meaning 'two'.

duodecimal ▷ *adj* **1** relating to or based on the number twelve, or multiples of it. **2** twelfth. ⓒ 17c: from Latin *duodecim* twelve.

duodenal /dʒuːoʊ'diːnəl/ ▷ *adj* relating to or affecting the DUODENUM. ⓒ 19c.

duodenal ulcer ▷ *noun, medicine* an ulcer of the DUODENUM, usually accompanied by inflammation, caused by the effect of increased levels of acid secretions from the stomach on the duodenum wall.

duodenum /dʒuːoʊ'diːnəm/ ▷ *noun* (***duodena*** /-'diːnə/ or ***duodenums***) *anatomy* the first part of the small intestine, into which food passes after leaving the stomach, where BILE from the GALL BLADDER and pancreatic juice from the PANCREAS neutralize the stomach acid and continue the digestive process. ⓒ 14c: from Latin, from *duodecim* twelve, the portion being twelve fingers' breadth in length.

duologue or (*sometimes US*) **duolog** /'dʒuːoʊlɒg/ ▷ *noun* **1** a dialogue between two actors. **2** a play for two actors. ⓒ 18c: from Latin *duo* two + Greek *logos* discourse.

duopoly /dʒʊ'ɒpəlɪ/ ▷ *noun* (***duopolies***) a situation in which two companies, etc monopolize trading in a particular commodity. • **duopolistic** /-ɒpə'lɪstɪk/ *adj*. ⓒ 1920s: from Latin *duo* two + *-poly* from MONOPOLY.

DUP ▷ *abbreviation* Democratic Unionist Party, a Protestant loyalist party in Northern Ireland.

dup. ▷ *abbreviation* duplicate.

dupe /dʒuːp/ ▷ *verb* (***duped***, ***duping***) to trick or deceive. ▷ *noun* a person who is deceived. • **dupability** *noun*. • **dupable** *adj*. ⓒ 17c: French.

duple /'dʒuːpəl/ ▷ *adj* **1** double; twofold. **2** *music* having two beats in the bar. ⓒ 16c: from Latin *duplus* double.

duple time ▷ *noun, music* musical time with two main beats to the bar.

duplex /'dʒuːplɛks/ ▷ *noun* (***duplexes***) *N Amer* **1** (*also* **duplex apartment**) a flat on two floors. **2** (*also* **duplex house**) a semi-detached house. ▷ *adj* **1** double; twofold. **2** said of a computer circuit: allowing transmission of signals in both directions simultaneously. ⓒ 1920s as *noun*; 19c as *adj*: Latin, meaning 'double'.

duplicate ▷ *adj* /'dʒuːplɪkət/ identical to another. ▷ *noun* /'dʒuːplɪkət/ **1** said especially of documents: an exact copy. **2** another of the same kind; a subsidiary or spare. ▷ *verb* /'dʒuːplɪkeɪt/ (***duplicated***, ***duplicating***) **1** to make or be an exact copy or copies of something. **2** to repeat something. • **duplication** *noun*. • **in duplicate** in the form of two exact copies. ⓒ 15c: from Latin *duplicare*, *duplicatum* to fold in two.

duplicator ▷ *noun* a machine for copying documents, etc. ⓒ Late 19c.

duplicity /dʒʊ'plɪsɪtɪ/ ▷ *noun* (***duplicities***) *formal* deception; trickery; double-dealing. • **duplicitous** *adj*. ⓒ 15c: from Latin *duplicis* double.

Dur. ▷ *abbreviation* Durham.

durable /'dʒʊərəbəl/ ▷ *adj* **1** lasting a long time without breaking; sturdy. **2** long-lasting; enduring. ▷ *noun* a durable item, especially one not frequently replaced. • **durability** *noun* (***durabilites***). • **durably** *adverb*. ⓒ 14c: from Latin *durare* to last.

dura mater /ˈdʒʊərə ˈmeɪtə(r); *Latin* ˈduːra ˈmɑːtɛr/ ▻ *noun, anatomy* the outermost and thickest of the three membranes that surround the brain and spinal cord. ◷ 15c: Latin *dura* hard + *mater* mother, a literal translation of the original Arabic name.

duration /dʒʊəˈreɪʃən/ ▻ *noun* the length of time that something lasts or continues. • **for the duration** for as long as the current situation lasts. ◷ 14c: from Latin *durare, duratum* to last.

duress /dʒʊəˈrɛs/ ▻ *noun* the influence of force or threats; coercion. ◷ 15c in modern sense; 14c, meaning 'harsh treatment': from French *duresse*, from Latin *duritia* hardness.

during /ˈdʒʊərɪŋ/ ▻ *prep* **1** throughout the time of something. **2** in the course of something. ◷ 14c: from obsolete *dure* to last, from Latin *durare*.

durum /ˈdʒʊərəm/ and **durum wheat** ▻ *noun* a kind of spring wheat whose flour is popular for making pasta. ◷ Early 20c: from Latin *durum* hard.

dusk ▻ *noun* twilight; the period of semi-darkness before night. ◷ Anglo-Saxon *dox* dark.

dusky ▻ *adj* (***duskier, duskiest***) **1** dark; shadowy. **2** dark-coloured; dark-skinned. • **duskily** *adverb*. • **duskiness** *noun*. ◷ 16c: see DUSK.

dust ▻ *noun* **1** earth, sand or household dirt in the form of a fine powder. **2** a cloud of this. **3** any substance in powder form. **4** *colloq* an angry complaint; a commotion □ *kick up a dust*. **5** *poetic* human remains; a dead body. ▻ *verb* (***dusted, dusting***) **1** to remove dust from (furniture, etc). **2** to sprinkle something with a substance in powder form. • **bite the dust** see under BITE. • **let the dust settle** *colloq* to wait until calm is restored before acting. • **not see someone for dust** not to see them again because they have gone away rapidly and suddenly. • **throw dust in someone's eyes** *colloq* to deceive them. ◷ Anglo-Saxon.

dustbin ▻ *noun* a large, usually cylindrical, lidded container for household rubbish, especially one kept outside. ◷ 19c.

dust bowl ▻ *noun* an area of land that has been farmed without protection against the effects of soil erosion, and from which the topsoil has been removed as a result of strong winds and drought. ◷ 1930s.

dustcart ▻ *noun* a vehicle in which household rubbish is collected. ◷ 18c.

dust cover ▻ *noun* **1** a DUST JACKET. **2** a DUST SHEET. **3** any cover that protects something from dust.

duster ▻ *noun* **1** a cloth for removing household dust. **2** a machine for spraying crops with fertilizer or other preparations. ◷ 16c.

dustier and **dustiest** see under DUSTY

dustily ▻ *adverb* **1** in a dusty state. **2** curtly; rudely □ *replied dustily that he didn't know*. ◷ 16c in sense 1: from DUST.

dustiness see under DUSTY

dusting powder ▻ *noun* fine powder, especially TALCUM POWDER. ◷ 1920s.

dust jacket and **dust cover** ▻ *noun* a loose protective paper cover on a book, carrying the title and other information. ◷ 1920s.

dustman ▻ *noun* someone employed to collect household rubbish. ◷ 18c.

dustpan ▻ *noun* a handled container into which dust is swept, like a flattish open-ended box with a shovel edge. ◷ 18c.

dust sheet and **dust cover** ▻ *noun* a cloth or plastic sheet used to protect unused furniture from dust or to protect furniture, carpets, etc from dust or paint when a room is being decorated. ◷ 19c.

dust storm ▻ *noun* a whirling mass of dust blown up by severe winds. ◷ 19c.

dust-up ▻ *noun, colloq* an argument or fight. ◷ 19c.

dusty ▻ *adj* (***dustier, dustiest***) **1** covered with or containing dust. **2** said of a colour: dull. **3** old-fashioned; dated. **4** lacking liveliness; flat. **5** often said of an answer: impolitely blunt: bad-tempered. **6** said of an answer: unhelpful. • **dustiness** *noun*.

Dutch ▻ *adj* belonging or referring to the Netherlands, a maritime kingdom in NW Europe, its inhabitants or their language. ▻ *noun* **1** the official language of the Netherlands. See also AFRIKAANS, FLEMISH. **2** (**the Dutch**) the people of the Netherlands (see THE 4). • **go Dutch** *colloq* each person to pay their own share of a meal, etc. ◷ 16c in modern senses; 15c, meaning 'German': from Dutch *dutsch*.

Dutch auction ▻ *noun* an auction at which the price is gradually lowered until someone agrees to buy. ◷ 19c.

Dutch barn ▻ *noun* an open-sided barn with a curved roof. ◷ 18c.

Dutch cap see CAP (*noun* 10)

Dutch courage ▻ *noun* artificial courage gained by drinking alcohol.

Dutch elm disease ▻ *noun, bot* a serious disease of elm trees, caused by a fungus, and spread by a bark beetle, resulting in wilting, yellowing of leaves and death of individual branches or whole trees.

Dutch hoe ▻ *noun* a hoe with a blade attached as in a spade. Compare DRAW HOE.

Dutchman and **Dutchwoman** ▻ *noun* a native or citizen of, or a person born in, the Netherlands.

Dutch oven ▻ *noun* **1** an open-fronted metal box for cooking food in front of a fire. **2** a lidded earthenware or iron stewpot or casserole.

Dutch treat ▻ *noun* said of dining out, attending a performance, etc: a situation in which each person pays for themselves.

Dutch uncle ▻ *noun* someone who openly criticizes or reprimands where appropriate, without sparing anyone's feelings.

duteous /ˈdʒuːtɪəs/ ▻ *adj, literary* dutiful. • **duteously** *adverb*. ◷ 16c: from DUTY + -OUS.

dutiable /ˈdʒuːtɪəbəl/ ▻ *adj* said of goods: on which duty is payable.

duty /ˈdʒuːtɪ/ ▻ *noun* (***duties***) **1** something one is or feels obliged to do; a moral or legal responsibility, or the awareness of it. **2** a task to be performed, especially in connection with a job. **3** tax on goods, especially imports. **4** respect for elders, seniors or superiors. • **dutiful** *adj*. • **dutifully** *adverb*. • **do duty for something** to serve in its place; to act as a substitute for it. • **on duty** working; liable to be called upon to go into action. • **off duty** not on duty. ◷ 13c: from French *dueté*.

duty-bound ▻ *adj* obliged by one's sense of duty. ◷ Early 20c.

duty-free ▻ *adj* said of goods, especially imports: non-taxable. ▻ *noun* (*plural* in sense 1 only ***duty-frees***) *colloq* **1** a duty-free shop. **2** an article or goods for sale at such a shop. ◷ 17c as *adj*.

duty-free shop ▻ *noun* a shop, especially at an airport or on a ship, where duty-free goods are sold.

duty officer ▻ *noun* the officer on duty at a particular time.

duvet /ˈduːveɪ, ˈdjuː-/ ▻ *noun* a thick quilt filled with feathers or man-made fibres, for use on a bed instead of a sheet and blankets. Also called **continental quilt**, DOWNIE. ◷ 18c: French.

dux /dʌks/ ▻ *noun, especially Scots* the top academic prize-winner in a school or class. ◷ 18c: Latin, meaning 'leader'.

DV ▷ *abbreviation*: *Deo volente* (Latin), God willing.

DVLA ▷ *abbreviation* Driver and Vehicle Licensing Agency (formerly known as the Driver and Vehicle Licensing Centre).

dwarf /dwɔːf/ ▷ *noun* (***dwarfs*** or *less often* ***dwarves*** /dwɔːvz/) **1** an abnormally small person, either with very short limbs and a head and body of normal size, usually due to a genetic disorder, or with fairly normal bodyshape but small proportions, usually due to a deficiency of growth hormone. Compare MIDGET. **2 a** an animal or plant that is much smaller or shorter than others of its species, usually as a result of selective breeding; **b** *as adj* □ ***Dwarf rabbits.*** **3** a mythical man-like creature with magic powers. **4** a DWARF STAR (sometimes further designated by a colour) □ ***a red dwarf.*** ▷ *verb* (***dwarfed***, ***dwarfing***) **1** to make something seem small or unimportant □ ***a church steeple dwarfed by surrounding skyscrapers.*** **2** to stunt the growth of someone or something. • **dwarfish** *adj*. • **dwarfism** *noun*. ◷ Anglo-Saxon *dweorg*.

dwarf fennel see under FINOCCHIO

dwarf star ▷ *noun, astron* a relatively small star of high density and low luminosity, eg the Sun.

dweeb ▷ *noun, especially US, derog slang* an idiot; a nerd.

dwell ▷ *verb* (***dwelt*** or ***dwelled***, ***dwelling***) *intr, formal, literary* to reside. • **dweller** *noun, often in compounds* someone who lives in a particular place or area □ ***a city-dweller.*** ◷ Anglo-Saxon *dwellan* to delay or tarry.

■ **dwell on** or **upon something** to rest attention on it; to think or speak about it obsessively.

dwelling ▷ *noun, formal, literary* a place of residence; a house. ◷ 14c.

dwindle /ˈdwɪndəl/ ▷ *verb* (***dwindled***, ***dwindling***) *intr* to shrink in size, number or intensity. ◷ Anglo-Saxon *dwinan* to fade.

DY ▷ *abbreviation, IVR* Benin.

Dy ▷ *symbol, chem* dysprosium.

dybbuk /ˈdɪbək/ ▷ *noun* (***dybbuks*** or ***dybbukim***) *Jewish folklore* an evil spirit or the soul of a dead person, which enters the body of a living person and controls their behaviour until exorcized by a religious rite. ◷ 20c: from Hebrew *dibbuq*.

dye /daɪ/ ▷ *verb* (***dyed***, ***dyeing***) *tr & intr* to colour or stain something, or undergo colouring or staining often permanently. ▷ *noun* **1** a coloured substance, either natural or synthetic, that is used in solution to impart colour to another material, eg paper, textiles, leather, hair. Compare PIGMENT. **2** the solution used for dyeing. **3** the colour produced by dyeing. • **dyable** or **dyeable** *adj*. • **dyer** *noun* someone who dyes cloth, etc, especially as a business. ◷ Anglo-Saxon *deagian*.

dyed-in-the-wool ▷ *adj* of firmly fixed opinions; out-and-out.

dyestuff ▷ *noun* a substance which can be used as a dye or from which a dye can be produced. ◷ 19c.

dying /ˈdaɪɪŋ/ ▷ *verb, present participle of* DIE[1]. ▷ *adj* **1** expressed or occurring immediately before death □ ***her dying breath.*** **2** final □ ***the dying seconds of the match.***

dyke[1] or **dike** /daɪk/ ▷ *noun* **1** a wall or embankment built to prevent flooding. **2** *geol* a vertical or semi-vertical sheet of igneous rock that cuts across the layering or bedding planes in the surrounding rock. **3** *especially Scots* a wall, eg surrounding a field. **4** *Austral & NZ slang* a lavatory. ▷ *verb* (***dyked***, ***dyking***) **1** to protect or drain with a dyke. **2** *intr* to make or build a dyke. ◷ Anglo-Saxon *dic* ditch.

dyke[2] or **dike** /daɪk/ *offensive slang* ▷ *noun* a LESBIAN. • **dykey** *adj*. ◷ 20c: now probably used positively by gay women to describe themselves.

dyn. ▷ *abbreviation* **1** dynamo. **2** dynamometer. **3** dyne.

dynamic /daɪˈnamɪk, dɪ-/ ▷ *adj* **1** full of energy, enthusiasm and new ideas. **2** relating to DYNAMICS. • **dynamically** *adverb*. ◷ 19c: from Greek *dynamis* power.

dynamics 1 *singular noun* the branch of mechanics that deals with the motion of objects and the forces that act to produce such motion. **2** *plural noun* **a** movement or change in any sphere; **b** the forces causing this □ ***political dynamics.*** **3** *plural noun, music* the signs indicating varying levels of loudness. ◷ 18c: from Greek *dynamis* power.

dynamism ▷ *noun* limitless energy and enthusiasm. ◷ 19c.

dynamite /ˈdaɪnəmaɪt/ ▷ *noun* **1** any of a group of powerful blasting explosives, formerly consisting of nitroglycerine absorbed into a porous material, but now usually containing ammonium nitrate or sodium nitrate. **2** *colloq* a thrilling or dangerous person or thing. ▷ *verb* (***dynamited***, ***dynamiting***) to explode something with dynamite. ◷ 19c: from Greek *dynamis* power.

dynamo /ˈdaɪnəmoʊ/ ▷ *noun* (***dynamos***) **1** *elec* an electric generator that converts mechanical energy into electrical energy, usually in the form of direct current. **2** *colloq* a tirelessly active person. ◷ 19c: from Greek *dynamis* power.

dynamometer /daɪnəˈmɒmətə(r)/ ▷ *noun, engineering* an instrument that is used to measure mechanical force, especially in order to determine the output power of a motor or engine. ◷ 19c.

dynastic /dɪˈnastɪk, daɪ-/ ▷ *adj* relating to or associated with a DYNASTY □ ***a dynastic marriage.***

dynasty /ˈdɪnəstɪ or (*US*) ˈdaɪnəstɪ/ ▷ *noun* (***dynasties***) **1** a succession of rulers from the same family. **2** their period of rule. **3** a succession of members of a powerful family or other connected group. ◷ 15c: from Greek *dynasteia* power or dominion.

dyne /daɪn/ ▷ *noun* (***dynes***) a unit of force, producing an acceleration of one centimetre per second every second on a mass of one gram. ◷ 19c: from Greek *dynamis* force.

dys- /dɪs/ ▷ *combining form, signifying* ill, bad or abnormal. ◷ Greek.

dysarthria /dɪsˈɑːθrɪə/ ▷ *noun, medicine* an impaired ability to enunciate speech clearly, caused by a disease or by a disorder of the tongue or other muscles associated with speech. ◷ 19c: from Greek *arthron* joint.

dysentery /ˈdɪsəntrɪ, -tərɪ/ ▷ *noun, medicine* severe infection and inflammation of the intestines caused by BACTERIA, PROTOZOA or PARASITIC worms. ◷ 14c: from Greek *dysenteria* bad bowels.

dysfunction /dɪsˈfʌŋkʃən/ ▷ *noun* impairment or abnormality of the functioning of an organ. • **dysfunctional** *adj*. ◷ Early 20c.

dysgraphia /dɪsˈgrafɪə/ ▷ *noun, psychol, medicine* inability to write, caused by disease of or damage to the brain. ◷ 1930s: from Greek *graphein* to write.

dyslexia /dɪsˈlɛksɪə/ ▷ *noun, psychol, medicine* **1** a disorder characterized by difficulty in reading and writing, and in spelling correctly, although individual letters can be recognized, and other intellectual abilities are unimpaired. **2** *popularly* a term used for difficulties in reading and writing. ◷ 19c: from DYS- + Greek *lexis* word.

dyslexic ▷ *adj* affected by dyslexia. ▷ *noun* someone affected by dyslexia.

dysmenorrhoea or **dysmenorrhea** /dɪsmɛnəˈrɪə/ ▷ *noun, medicine* pain in the lower abdomen, associated with menstruation. ◷ 19c: from DYS- + Greek *men* month + *rhoia* flow.

dyspepsia /dɪsˈpɛpsɪə/ ▷ *noun, pathol* indigestion. ◷ 18c: Greek, meaning 'difficult to digest', from *dys-* amiss + *pepsis* digestion.

dyspeptic /dɪsˈpɛptɪk/ ▷ *adj* **1** suffering from DYSPEPSIA. **2** *colloq* bad-tempered; liverish. ◷ 19c in these senses; originally 17c, meaning 'indigestible': see DYSPEPSIA.

dysphasia /dɪs'feɪzɪə/ *psychol, medicine* ▷ *noun* difficulty in expressing or understanding thought in spoken or written words, caused by brain damage. • **dysphasic** *adj, noun*. Ⓢ 19c: from Greek *phasis* speech.

dysplasia /dɪs'pleɪzɪə/ ▷ *noun, pathol* **1** abnormal development of tissue, eg skin or bone, sometimes associated with cancer. **2** an abnormal change in the size or shape of a mature cell. Ⓢ 1930s: from Greek *plasis* moulding.

dyspnoea or **dyspnea** /dɪsp'nɪə/ ▷ *noun, medicine* difficulty in breathing, often associated with serious disease of the heart or lungs, characterized by an awareness of the effort of inappropriate breathing. Ⓢ 17c: from Greek *dyspnoia*, from *dys-* amiss + *pnoe* breathing.

dysprosium /dɪs'proʊzɪəm/ ▷ *noun* (symbol **Dy**, atomic number 66) a soft, silvery-white metallic element that is one of the most magnetic substances known, and a strong absorber of neutrons. Ⓢ 19c: from Greek *dysprositos* difficult to reach.

dystrophy /'dɪstrəfɪ/ ▷ *noun* (***dystrophies***) *medicine* any of various unrelated disorders of organs or tissues, especially muscle, arising from an inadequate supply of nutrients. See also MUSCULAR DYSTROPHY. Ⓢ 19c: from DYS- + Greek *trophe* nourishment.

DZ ▷ *abbreviation, IVR* Algeria.

dz. ▷ *abbreviation* dozen.

E

E[1] or **e** /iː/ ▷ *noun* (*Es*, *E's* or *e's*) **1** the fifth letter and second vowel of the English alphabet. **2** *music* (**E**) **a** the third note in the scale of C major; **b** the musical key which has this note as its base. **4** in advertising and marketing use: a person who has no regular income, or who is dependent on state benefit due to disability, long-term illness, unemployment or old age.

E[2] ▷ *abbreviation* **1** Earl. **2** earth. **3** East. **4** Ecstasy. **5** *physics* electromotive force. **6** (*also* **e**) electronic □ *E-mail*. **7** *physics* (*also E*) energy. **8** English. **9** *IVR*: *España* (Spanish), Spain. **10** European. Also *in compounds* □ *E-number*. **11** *math* exa-.

e[1] ▷ *abbreviation* **1** electron. **2** electronic. **3** engineer. **4** engineering.

e[2] ▷ *symbol* **1** *in compounds* (with numbers) *denoting* any of a series of standard sizes of pack as set out in EC law. **2** *math* the base of the natural system of logarithms. See LOGARITHM.

ea. ▷ *abbreviation* each.

each /iːtʃ/ ▷ *adj* applied to every one of two or more people or items considered separately. ▷ *pronoun* every single one of two or more people, animals or things. ▷ *adverb* to, for or from each one □ *Give them one each*. • **each other** used as the object of a verb or preposition when an action takes place between two (or more than two) people, etc □ *They were talking to each other*. See also ONE ANOTHER at ONE. • **each way** said of a bet: winning, if the horse, dog, etc on which the bet is placed finishes first, second or third in a race. ⓘ Anglo-Saxon *ælc*, from *a* ever + *gelic* alike.

each other, one another

• There is no difference between these two expressions in current usage, regardless of the number of people or things referred to □ *Jo and I see each other every day from Monday to Thursday* □ *Everybody was arguing with each other and we had a fight* □ *Catfish tend to nip one another as they swim round the tank*.

eager /ˈiːgə(r)/ ▷ *adj* **1** (*often* **eager for something** or **to do something**) feeling or showing great desire or enthusiasm; keen to do or get something. **2** excited by desire or expectancy □ *an eager glance*. • **eagerly** *adverb*. • **eagerness** *noun*. ⓘ 13c: from French *aigre*.

eager beaver ▷ *noun*, *colloq* someone who is exceptionally enthusiastic or willing.

eagle /ˈiːgəl/ ▷ *noun* **1** any of various kinds of large birds of prey. **2** a figure of an eagle, used as a national emblem by various countries. **3** *golf* a score of two under par. ⓘ 14c: from French *aigle*, from Latin *aquila*.

eagle eye ▷ *noun* **1** exceptionally good eyesight. **2** careful supervision, with an ability to notice small details. • **eagle-eyed** *adj*.

eagle owl ▷ *noun* any one of a number of varieties of large owls with tufts of feathers on its head like horns.

eaglet /ˈiːglət/ ▷ *noun* a young eagle.

eagre /ˈeɪgə, ˈiːgə/ ▷ *noun* a sudden tidal flood in a river. ⓘ 17c.

EAK ▷ *abbreviation*, *IVR* East Africa Kenya, ie Kenya.

-ean see -AN

eaon ▷ *abbreviation* except as otherwise noted.

ear[1] /ɪə(r)/ ▷ *noun* **1** the sense organ, usually one of a pair situated on each side of the head, that is concerned with hearing and the maintenance of balance in vertebrates. **2** the external part of the ear. **3** the sense or power of hearing. **4** the ability to hear and appreciate the difference between sounds □ *an ear for music*. **5** anything like an ear in shape or position. **6** *formal or literary* attention; the act of listening □ *give ear to me*. • **eared** *adj*, *usually in compounds*. • **earless** *adj*. • **be all ears** *colloq* to listen attentively or with great interest. • **fall on deaf ears** said of a remark, etc: to be ignored. • **give someone a thick ear** to slap them on their ear, especially as a punishment. • **have** or **keep one's ear to the ground** to keep oneself well informed about what is happening around one. • **have someone's ear** to have them willing to listen or pay attention. • **in one ear and out the other** or **in at one ear and out at the other** *colloq* listened to but immediately disregarded. • **lend an ear to someone** or **something** to listen. • **make someone's ears burn** to talk, especially unpleasantly, about them in their absence. • **out on one's ear** *colloq* dismissed swiftly and without politeness. • **pin back one's ears** *colloq* to listen attentively. • **play by ear** or **play something by ear** to play (music) without the help of printed music. • **play it by ear** *colloq* to act without a fixed plan, according to the situation that arises. • **turn a deaf ear to someone** or **something** to refuse to listen. • **up to one's ears in something** *colloq* deeply involved in it or occupied with it. ⓘ Anglo-Saxon *eare*.

ear[2] /ɪə(r)/ ▷ *noun* the part of a cereal plant, such as wheat, that contains the seeds. • **eared** *adj*. ⓘ Anglo-Saxon.

earache ▷ *noun* pain or an ache in the inner part of the ear.

earbash ▷ *verb*, *tr & intr*, *slang* to pester someone with non-stop talking.

earcon /ˈɪəkɒn/ ▷ *noun*, *computing* an audio signal given by a computer, as opposed to an ICON. ⓘ 1980s: from EAR + ICON.

eardrops ▷ *plural noun* **1** medicinal drops for the ear. **2** pendant earrings.

eardrum ▷ *noun* the small thin membrane inside the ear, which transmits vibrations made by sound waves to the inner ear. *Technical equivalent* **tympanic membrane**.

eared see under EAR[1], EAR[2]

earflap ▷ *noun* one of two coverings for the ears, attached to a cap, to protect them from cold or injury.

earful ▷ *noun* (***earfuls***) *colloq* **1** a long complaint or telling-off; a rough scolding. **2** something heard. **3** as much talk or gossip as one can stand. ⓘ Early 20c.

ear-hole ▷ *noun* the aperture of the ear.

earl /ɜːl/ ▷ *noun* a male member of the British nobility ranking below a marquess and above a viscount. See also COUNTESS. • **earldom** *noun* the status or position of an earl. ⓘ Anglo-Saxon *eorl* a warrior or hero.

Earl Grey ▷ *noun* a blend of various fragrant Oriental teas flavoured and scented with oil of bergamot.

earlobe ▷ *noun* the soft, loosely hanging piece of flesh which forms the lower part of the ear.

early /ˈɜːlɪ/ ▷ *adverb*, *adj* (***earlier***, ***earliest***) **1** characteristic of or near the beginning of (a period of time, period of development, etc). **2** sooner than others, sooner than usual, or sooner than expected or intended. **3** in the near future. **4** in the distant past. ● **earliness** *noun*. ● **at the earliest** not before, and probably later than (a specified time). ● **earlier on** previously. ● **early and late** at all times. ● **early on** at or near the beginning of a period of time, etc. ● **have an early night** *colloq* to go to bed earlier than usual. ● **in the early days** during the first years of (an enterprise, marriage, reign, etc). ● **it's early days** *colloq* it is too soon to be able to judge the outcome or expect a result. ● **keep early hours** to go to bed and to get up early regularly. ◷ Anglo-Saxon *ærlice*.

early bird ▷ *noun, colloq* **1** a person who gets out of bed early. **2** a person who arrives early.

early closing ▷ *noun* **1** the shutting of local shops in a town for one afternoon each week. **2** the day on which this happens.

early day motion ▷ *noun* in Parliament: a motion for consideration on a day when business finishes early. As such days are rare, it is usually merely a means to draw attention to a matter.

Early English ▷ *adj, archit* referring or relating to the form of Gothic architecture used in England during the 12c and 13c, in which the pointed arch was first used.

early music ▷ *noun, music* music of the medieval and Renaissance periods, and sometimes including that of the baroque and early classical periods. Also (**early-music**) *as adj*.

early warning ▷ *noun* advance warning of something about to happen. ▷ *adj* (**early-warning**) belonging to or part of an EARLY WARNING SYSTEM.

early warning system ▷ *noun* a radar system designed to give the earliest possible warning of attack from enemy aircraft or missiles.

earmark ▷ *verb* **1** to set aside or intend something or someone for a particular purpose. **2** to make an identification mark on the ear of (an animal). ▷ *noun* **1** an owner's mark on an animal's ear. **2** a distinctive mark. ◷ 16c as *noun* 1.

earmuffs ▷ *plural noun* coverings worn over the ears to protect them from cold or noise.

earn /ɜːn/ ▷ *verb* (***earned, earning***) **1** *tr & intr* to gain (money, wages, one's living, etc) by working. **2** to gain. **3** to deserve. See also WELL EARNED. ● **earner** *noun* **1** a person who earns. **2** *slang* an easy and sometimes dishonest way of making money. ◷ Anglo-Saxon *earnian*.

■ **earn out** to make enough money from sales to recover costs or make a profit.

earned income ▷ *noun* income from paid employment.

earnest¹ /ˈɜːnɪst/ ▷ *adj* **1** serious or over-serious. **2** showing determination, sincerity or strong feeling. ● **earnestly** *adverb*. ● **earnestness** *noun*. ● **in earnest** **1** serious or seriously. **2** sincere. **3** not as a joke; in reality. ◷ Anglo-Saxon *eornust* seriousness.

earnest² /ˈɜːnɪst/ ▷ *noun, literary or old use* **1** a part payment made in advance, especially (*law*) one made to confirm an agreement. **2** a sign or foretaste of what is to come. ◷ 13c as *ernesse*: from French *erres* pledges.

earnings ▷ *plural noun* **1** money earned. **2** profits. **3** investment income.

earphones ▷ *plural noun* see HEADPHONES.

earpiece ▷ *noun* the part of a telephone or hearing-aid which is placed at or in the ear.

ear-piercing ▷ *adj* said of a noise: loud and sharp; shrill.

ear piercing ▷ *noun* the piercing of the earlobe in order to insert an earring.

earplug ▷ *noun* a piece of wax or rubber, etc placed in the ear as a protection against noise, cold or water.

earring ▷ *noun* a piece of jewellery worn attached to the ear, especially to the earlobe.

earshot ▷ *noun* the distance at which sound can be heard ◻ *out of earshot*.

ear-splitting ▷ *adj* said of a noise: extremely loud.

earth /ɜːθ/ ▷ *noun* **1** (*often* **the Earth**) the planet on which we live, the third planet in order of distance from the Sun. **2** the world, as opposed to heaven or hell. **3** the land and sea, as opposed to the sky. **4** dry land; the land surface; the ground. **5** soil. **6** a hole in which an animal lives, especially a badger or fox. **7** **a** an electrical connection with the ground; **b** a wire that provides this. **8** the inhabitants of the planet Earth ◻ *the whole Earth celebrated the news.* ▷ *verb* (***earthed, earthing***) *electronics* to connect to the ground. ● **come back** or **down to earth** to become aware of the realities of life again or for the first time. ● **cost the earth** *colloq* to be extremely expensive. ● **go to earth** said of an animal: to go into its hole or hiding-place. ● **on earth** used for emphasis ◻ *What on earth is that?* ● **run something to earth** **1** to chase or hunt (an animal) to its hole or hiding-place. **2** to find it after a long search. ◷ Anglo-Saxon *eorthe*.

■ **earth something up** to heap soil around the lower part of (a plant), eg as a protection against frost.

earthbound ▷ *adj* **1** attached or restricted to the earth. **2** said of a spacecraft, etc: moving towards the Earth. **3** *sometimes derog* unable to think beyond what is known or familiar; lacking imagination.

earth closet ▷ *noun* a lavatory in which earth is used to cover the excreta.

earthen /ˈɜːθən/ ▷ *adj* **1** said of a floor, etc: made of earth. **2** said of a pot, etc: made of baked clay.

earthenware ▷ *noun* pottery made of a kind of baked clay which is rather coarse to the touch.

earthier, **earthiest**, **earthily** and **earthiness** see under EARTHY

earthling /ˈɜːθlɪŋ/ ▷ *noun* in science fiction: a native of the Earth.

earthly /ˈɜːθlɪ/ ▷ *adj* (***earthlier, earthliest***) **1** *literary* referring, relating or belonging to this world; not spiritual. **2** *colloq, with negatives* used for emphasis ◻ *have no earthly chance.* ● **earthliness** *noun*. ● **not have an earthly** *colloq* **1** not to have the slightest chance of success. **2** not to have the least idea. See also UNEARTHLY.

Earthman and **Earthwoman** ▷ *noun* especially in science fiction: a male or female native of the Earth.

earth mother ▷ *noun* **1** the Earth personified as a goddess. **2** *sometimes derog or facetious* a woman whose body shape and apparent fertility seem to symbolize motherhood. ● **earth-motherly** *adj*.

earth-movement ▷ *noun, geol* elevation, subsidence or folding of the Earth's crust.

earthmover ▷ *noun* a bulldozer or other piece of mobile equipment designed to shift large quantities of soil, etc.

earthnut ▷ *noun* **1** a variety of perennial umbelliferous woodland plant. **2** the edible dark brown tubers of this plant. **3** any one of various plants that have an edible root, tuber or underground pod, eg the peanut.

earthquake ▷ *noun* a succession of vibrations that shake the Earth's surface, caused by shifting movements in the Earth's crust, volcanic activity, etc.

earth science ▷ *noun* any of the sciences broadly concerned with the Earth, eg geology and meteorology.

earth-shaking and **earth-shattering** ▷ *adj, colloq* being of great importance. ● **earth-shakingly** or **earth-shatteringly** *adverb* in a crucially important way; remarkably.

earth sign ▷ *noun, astrol* a name given to each of three signs of the zodiac, ie TAURUS, VIRGO and CAPRICORN.

earth tremor ▻ *noun* a slight earthquake.

earthward ▻ *adverb* (*also* **earthwards**) towards Earth. ▻ *adj* moving toward Earth; Earth-directed.

Earthwoman see EARTHMAN

earthwork ▻ *noun* **1** (*often* **earthworks**) *technical* excavation and embanking, eg as one process in road-building. **2** a fortification built of earth.

earthworm ▻ *noun* any of several types of worm which live in and burrow through the soil.

earthy /'ɜːθɪ/ ▻ *adj* (***earthier***, ***earthiest***) **1** consisting of, relating to, or like earth or soil. **2** coarse or crude; lacking politeness. • **earthily** *adverb*. • **earthiness** *noun*.

ear trumpet ▻ *noun* an old-fashioned HEARING AID consisting of a small trumpet held up to the ear.

earwax ▻ *noun* a waxy substance secreted by the glands of the ear. Also called **cerumen**.

earwig ▻ *noun* an insect with pincers at the end of its body. • **earwigging** *noun, colloq* a scolding. ◷ Anglo-Saxon *eare* ear + *wicga* insect: this insect was formerly thought to crawl into a person's head through the ear.

EASDAQ /'iːzdak/ ▻ *abbreviation, finance* European Association of Securities Dealers Quotation, a quotation system for European shares. Compare NASDAQ.

ease /iːz/ ▻ *noun* **1** freedom from pain or anxiety. **2** absence of difficulty. **3** freedom from embarrassment. **4** absence of restriction. **5** rest from work; leisure; relaxation. **6** wealth; freedom from the constraints of poverty. ▻ *verb* (***eased***, ***easing***) **1** to free someone from pain, trouble or anxiety. **2** to make someone comfortable. **3** to relieve or calm something. **4** to loosen something □ *ease the waistband*. **5** to make something less difficult: to assist □ *ease his progress*. **6** *intr* (*often* **ease off** or **up**) to become less intense. **7** *intr* to move gently or very gradually. • **easeful** *adj* relaxing; quiet; restful. • **at ease 1** relaxed; free from anxiety or embarrassment. **2** *military* standing with legs apart and hands clasped behind the back. • **take one's ease** *formal* to relax; to make oneself comfortable. ◷ 13c: from French *aise*.

■ **ease something in** or **out** to move (something heavy or awkward) gently or gradually in or out of position.

easel /'iːzəl/ ▻ *noun* a stand for supporting a blackboard or an artist's canvas, etc. ◷ 17c: from Dutch *ezel* ass.

easement ▻ *noun, law* the right to use something, especially land, that is not one's own, or to prevent its owner making an inconvenient use of it.

easier, easiest, **easily** and **easiness** see under EASY

east /iːst/ ▻ *noun* (abbreviation **E**) **1** the direction from which the Sun rises at the equinox. **2** one of the four CARDINAL POINTS of the compass. **3** (*also* **the east** or **the East**) any part of the Earth, a country or a town, etc lying in that direction. **4** *cards* the position at the table, or the player occupying the place, corresponding to east on a compass. **5** (**the East**) **a** the countries of Asia, east of Europe. See also THE FAR EAST, MIDDLE EAST, NEAR EAST; **b** *politics* the former communist countries of eastern Europe. **6** (**the East**) the eastern part of the US. ▻ *adj* **1** situated in the east; on the side which is on or nearest the east. **2** facing or toward the east. **3** said especially of wind: coming from the east. ▻ *adverb* in, to or towards the east. ◷ Anglo-Saxon.

eastbound ▻ *adj* going or leading towards the east.

east-by-north and **east-by-south** ▻ *noun, adj, adverb* 11 ¼ degrees north, or south, of due east.

East End ▻ *noun* in the UK: the eastern part of a town or city, especially in London, where it is traditionally associated with industry and the docks, and crowded living conditions. • **Eastender** *noun*.

Easter /'iːstə(r)/ ▻ *noun, Christianity* **1** a religious festival celebrating the resurrection of Christ, held on the Sunday after the first full moon in spring, called **Easter Day** or **Easter Sunday**. **2** the period during which the festival takes place, thought of as running from GOOD FRIDAY to the following Monday, called **Easter Monday**. ◷ Anglo-Saxon *eastre*, perhaps from *Eostre*, the name of a goddess associated with spring.

Easter egg ▻ *noun* an egg or artificial egg given as a present at Easter, traditionally a painted or dyed hard-boiled egg, but now more commonly a chocolate egg.

easterly /'iːstəlɪ/ ▻ *adj* **1** said of a wind, etc: coming from the east. **2** looking or lying, etc towards the east; situated in the east. ▻ *adverb* to or towards the east. ▻ *noun* (***easterlies***) an easterly wind.

eastern or **Eastern** /'iːstən/ ▻ *adj* situated in, directed towards or belonging to the east or the East. • **easterner** or **Easterner** *noun* a person who lives in or comes from the east, especially the eastern US.

eastern hemisphere ▻ *noun* **1** the half of the Earth containing Europe, Asia, Africa and Australia. **2** the lands within this sector, especially Asia.

easternmost ▻ *adj* situated furthest east.

Eastern Orthodox Church and **Eastern Church** see ORTHODOX CHURCH

Eastern Time and **Eastern Standard Time** ▻ *noun* (abbreviation **ET** or **EST**) the time used on the east coast of N America, which is five hours behind GMT

Easter Sunday see under EASTER

Eastertide ▻ *noun, Christianity* **1** the days around Easter. **2** *church* the fifty days from Easter to WHITSUN.

East Germanic see GERMANIC

easting /'iːstɪŋ/ ▻ *noun, nautical* the total distance travelled towards the east by a ship, etc.

east-north-east and **east-south-east** ▻ *noun, adj, adverb* 22 ½ degrees north, or south, of due east.

eastward /'iːstwəd/ ▻ *adverb* (*also* **eastwards**) towards the east. ▻ *adj* toward the east.

easy /'iːzɪ/ ▻ *adj* (***easier***, ***easiest***) **1** not difficult. **2** free from pain, trouble, anxiety, etc. **3** not strict; lenient. **4** not stiff or formal; friendly. **5** tolerant. **6** not tense or strained; leisurely. **7** *colloq* having no strong preference; ready to accept suggestions offered by others. **8** said of financial circumstances: comfortable; not straitened. **9** in plentiful supply. **10** said of clothing, etc: loose; not restricting. **11** said of exercise or speed, etc: moderate; not extreme or severe. **12** *slang* ready and willing for sexual experiences. ▻ *adverb, colloq* in a slow, calm or relaxed way □ *take it easy*. • **easily** *adverb* **1** without difficulty. **2** clearly; beyond doubt; by far. **3** very probably. • **easiness** *noun*. • **easy does it! 1** be careful! **2** in the performing of a physical task: don't strain yourself! • **easy on the eye** or **ear** pleasant to look at or listen to. • **go easy on** or **with someone** to deal with them gently or calmly. • **go easy on** or **with something** to use, take, etc not too much of it □ *Go easy on the wine*. • **stand easy** *military* to stand less stiffly than standing at ease. ◷ 12c: from French *aisie*, from *aisier* to ease.

easy-care ▻ *adj* said chiefly of fabric or clothing, etc: easy to maintain, clean or launder, etc.

easy chair ▻ *noun* a soft comfortable chair, usually one with arms.

easy game and **easy meat** ▻ *noun* someone or something that is easy to beat, fool, persuade, hit or destroy, etc.

easy-going ▻ *adj* not strict; relaxed, tolerant or placid.

easy listening ▻ *noun, music* a category of modern popular music comprising pleasant but undemanding songs and tunes. Also (**easy-listening**) *as adj*.

easy money ▻ *noun* **1** money gained without much exertion or difficulty. **2** *finance* money that can be borrowed at a low rate of interest.

easy over ▷ *adj, colloq, especially US* said of an egg: fried on both sides.

easy street or **Easy Street** ▷ *noun, colloq* a situation of comfort and financial well-being.

easy terms ▷ *plural noun* payment in instalments rather than all at once.

EAT ▷ *abbreviation, IVR* East Africa Tanganyika, ie Tanzania.

eat /iːt/ ▷ *verb* (***ate*** /ɛt, eɪt/, ***eaten, eating***) **1** to bite, chew and swallow (food). **2** *intr* to take in food; to take a meal. **3** to take something in as food. **4** to tolerate something as food. **5** to eat into something. **6** *colloq* to trouble or worry someone ◻ *What's eating you?* • **be eaten up by** or **with something**: to be greatly affected by it (usually a bad feeling) ◻ *be eaten up with jealousy.* • **eat humble pie** to lower oneself or lose dignity, eg by admitting a mistake. • **eat one's heart out** to suffer, especially in silence, from some longing or anxiety, or from envy. • **eat one's words** to admit that one was wrong. • **eat out of someone's hand** *colloq* to be very willing to follow, obey or agree with them. • **eat up the miles** said of a vehicle: to cover a distance at speed. • **What's eating you, him,** *etc?* What's wrong with you, him, etc? ⓔ Anglo-Saxon *etan*.

▪ **eat something away** or **eat away at something 1** to gnaw it. **2** to eat into it (sense 3).

▪ **eat in** to eat at home rather than in a restaurant, cafe, etc.

▪ **eat into** or **through something 1** to use it up gradually. **2** to waste it. **3** to destroy its material, substance or form, etc, especially by chemical action; to corrode it.

▪ **eat out** to eat at a restaurant, cafe, etc rather than at home.

▪ **eat up** to finish one's food.

▪ **eat something up 1** to finish (one's food). **2** to destroy it. **3** to absorb; to listen with real interest.

▪ **be eaten up with something** to be consumed by (jealousy, etc).

eatable ▷ *adj* fit to be eaten. ▷ *noun* (*usually* **eatables**) an item of food. Compare EDIBLE.

eater ▷ *noun* **1** *in compounds* a person who eats in a specified way ◻ *a noisy eater.* **2** an eating apple, or any other fruit meant to be eaten raw.

eatery /ˈiːtərɪ/ ▷ *noun* (***eateries***) *colloq* a small restaurant.

eating apple ▷ *noun* an apple for eating raw. Compare COOKING APPLE.

eating house ▷ *noun* a restaurant.

eats ▷ *plural noun, colloq* food.

EAU ▷ *abbreviation, IVR* East Africa Uganda, ie Uganda.

eau de Cologne /oʊ də ˈkəloʊn/ and **cologne** ▷ *noun* a mild type of perfume, originally made in Cologne in Germany in 1709. ⓔ Early 19c: French, literally 'water of Cologne'.

eau de nil /oʊ də niːl/ ▷ *noun* a pale green colour. Also called NILE GREEN. ⓔ French, literally 'water of the Nile'.

eau de toilette /oʊ də twɑːˈlɛt/ ▷ *noun* TOILET WATER.

eau de vie /oʊ də viː/ ▷ *noun* brandy, or sometimes other spirits. ⓔ 19c: French, literally 'water of life'.

eaves /iːvz/ ▷ *plural noun* the part of a roof that sticks out beyond the wall, or the underside of it. ⓔ Anglo-Saxon *efes* the clipped edge of thatch.

eavesdrop ▷ *verb* (***eavesdropped, eavesdropping***) (*also* **eavesdrop on someone**) *intr* to listen secretly to a private conversation. • **eavesdropper** *noun*. • **eavesdropping** *noun*. ⓔ Anglo-Saxon *yfæsdrypæ* a person who stands under the eaves to listen to conversations.

EAZ ▷ *abbreviation, IVR* East Africa Zanzibar, ie Tanzania.

ebb ▷ *verb* (***ebbed, ebbing***) *intr* **1** said of the tide: to move back from the land. **2** (*also* **ebb away**) to grow smaller or weaker. ▷ *noun* **1** the movement of the tide away from the land. **2** a decline. • **at a low ebb** in a poor or weak state, mentally or physically. • **on the ebb** in decline; failing. ⓔ Anglo-Saxon *ebba*.

ebbtide ▷ *noun* the ebbing tide. Opposite of FLOODTIDE.

EBCDIC /ˈɛbsɪdɪk/ ▷ *abbreviation, computing* extended binary-coded decimal-interchange code, a computer code for representing alphanumeric characters, the main code used in addition to ASCII.

ebony /ˈɛbənɪ/ ▷ *noun* (***ebonies***) **1** a type of extremely hard, heavy and almost black wood. **2** any of various tropical trees from which it is obtained. ▷ *adj* **1** made from this wood. **2** black ◻ *ebony skin.* • **ebonize** or **ebonise** *verb* (***ebonized, ebonizing***) to make or become like ebony. ⓔ 14c as *hebeny* f. from Latin *hebenus*.

ebonite ▷ *noun* VULCANITE.

EBU ▷ *abbreviation* European Broadcasting Union.

ebullient /ɪˈbʌlɪənt, -bʊ-/ ▷ *adj* **1** ▷ very high-spirited; full of cheerfulness or enthusiasm. **2** boiling. • **ebullience** or **ebulliency** *noun*. • **ebulliently** *adverb*. ⓔ 16c: from Latin *ebullire* to boil out.

eburnean /ɪˈbɜːnɪən/ ▷ *adj* made of or like ivory. ⓔ 17c: from Latin *eberneus*, from *ebur* ivory.

EC ▷ *abbreviation* **1** East Caribbean. **2** East Central. **3** *IVR* Ecuador. **4** European Commission. **5** European Community.

ecad /ˈiːkad/ ▷ *noun, bot, ecol* a plant form which is assumed to have adapted to its environment. ⓔ Early 20c: from ECOLOGY.

écarté /eɪˈkɑːteɪ/ ▷ *noun, ballet* a position in which the arm and leg are extended to the side. ⓔ 19c: French, meaning 'spread' or 'separated'.

eccentric /ɛkˈsɛntrɪk/ ▷ *adj* **1** said of a person or behaviour, etc: odd; unusual or unconventional. **2** *technical* said of a wheel, etc: not having the axis at the centre. **3** *geom* said of circles: not having a common centre; not concentric. **4** said of an orbit: not circular. ▷ *noun* **1** an eccentric person. **2** *technical* a device for converting rotating motion into motion backwards and forwards. • **eccentrically** *adverb*. ⓔ 16c: from Latin *eccentricus*, from Greek *ek* out of + *kentros* centre.

eccentricity /ɛksɛnˈtrɪsɪtɪ/ ▷ *noun* (***eccentricities***) **1** peculiarity of behaviour; oddness. **2** being eccentric. **3** deviation from a circular orbit, etc. **4** *geom* (symbol **e**) the constant ratio of the distance of a point on the curve from the focus to its distance from the DIRECTRIX. **5** the degree of displacement of the geometric centre of a part from the true centre, eg of the axis of rotation of a wheel.

Eccl. and **Eccles.** ▷ *abbreviation* Book of the Bible: Ecclesiastes. See table at BIBLE.

eccl. and **eccles.** ▷ *abbreviation* ecclesiastic or ecclesiastical.

Eccles cake /ˈɛkəlz —/ ▷ *noun* a small round cake of sweet pastry filled with raisins and currants, etc. ⓔ 19c: named after Eccles in Lancashire, England.

ecclesiastic /ɪkliːzɪˈastɪk/ ▷ *noun, formal* a clergyman or a member of a holy order. ▷ *adj* (*also* **ecclesiastical**) relating to the church or the clergy. • **ecclesiastically** *adverb*. • **ecclesiasticism** /-sɪzəm/ *noun* excessive regard for the rules and observances of the church. ⓔ 15c: from 15c Greek *ekklesiastikos*, meaning 'relating to the *ekklesia*' ie an assembly or gathering, and also the name given to the early church.

ecclesiology /ɪkliːzɪ'ɒlədʒɪ/ ▷ *noun* **1** the study of church forms and traditions. **2** the study of church architecture and decoration. **3** the study or knowledge of the church. • **ecclesiological** /-ə'lɒdʒɪkəl/ *adj.* • **ecclesiologist** *noun.* ◎ 19c.

eccrine /'ɛkrɪn/ *physiol* ▷ *adj* said of a gland, especially a sweat gland: secreting externally. • **eccrinology** /-'nɒlədʒɪ/ *noun* the study of the secretions of the eccrine glands. ◎ 1930s: from Greek *ek* out of + *krinein* to separate or secrete.

ecdysiast /ɛk'dɪzɪast/ ▷ *noun, facetious* a striptease performer. ◎ 1940s: coined by H L Mencken, (1880–1956), US satirist, and based on *ecdysis*.

ecdysis /'ɛkdɪsɪs/ ▷ *noun* (***ecdyses*** /'ɛkdɪsiːz/) *zool* in animals with a rigid EXOSKELETON, such as insects and crustaceans: the act of shedding the exoskeleton so that growth can occur. ◎ 19c: Latin, from Greek *ekdyein* to take off.

ECE ▷ *abbreviation* Economic Commission for Europe.

ECG ▷ *abbreviation* **1** electrocardiogram. **2** electrocardiograph.

échappé /eɪʃa'peɪ/ ▷ *noun* (***échappés***) *ballet* a double leap from two feet, starting in fifth position, landing in second or fourth, and finishing in fifth.

echelon /'ɛʃəlɒn/ ▷ *noun* **1** *formal* **a** a level or rank in an organization, etc; **b** the people at that level. **2** *technical* a roughly V-shaped formation, used by ships, planes, birds in flight, etc in which each member is in a position slightly to the outside of the one in front. ◎ 19c: French from *échelle* ladder.

echidna /ɪ'kɪdnə/ ▷ *noun* (***echidnas***) *zool* the spiny anteater, an egg-laying mammal of Australia and New Guinea, with a long snout and long claws. ◎ 19c: Greek, meaning 'viper'.

echinoderm /ɪ'kaɪnoʊdɜːm/ ▷ *noun* any sea animal of the family **Echinodermata** (/-mətə/) to which starfish and sea urchins belong, noted for having tube feet (see *tube foot*) and the body wall strengthened by calcareous plates. • **echinodermal** or **echinodermatous** *adj.* ◎ 19c: from Greek *echinos* hedgehog or sea urchin + *derma* skin.

echinoid /ɪ'kaɪnɔɪd/ *zool* ▷ *adj* like a sea urchin. ▷ *noun* a sea urchin. ◎ 19c.

echinus /ɪ'kaɪnəs/ ▷ *noun* (***echini*** /-naɪ/) **1** *zool* a type of sea urchin, eg the edible sea urchin from the Mediterranean. **2** *archit* the moulding that supports the ABACUS of a DORIC column. ◎ 14c: Latin, from Greek *echinos* hedgehog.

echo /'ɛkoʊ/ ▷ *noun* (***echoes***) **1** the repeating of a sound caused by the sound waves striking a surface and coming back. **2** a sound repeated in this way. **3** *often facetious* a person who imitates or repeats what others say or think. **4** an imitation or repetition, sometimes an accidental one. **5** (*often* ***echoes***) a trace; something which brings to mind memories or thoughts of something else. **6** a reflected radio or radar beam, or the visual signal it produces on a screen. **7** (**Echo**) *communications* in the NATO alphabet: the word used to denote the letter 'E' (see table at NATO ALPHABET). ▷ *verb* (***echoes***, ***echoed***, ***echoing***) **1** to send back an echo of something. **2** to repeat (a sound or a statement). **3** to imitate or in some way be similar to something. **4** *intr* to resound; to reverberate. • **echoic** /ɛ'koʊɪk/ *adj* **1** *formal* said of a sound: referring to or like an echo. **2** said of a word: imitating the sound it represents; onomatopoeic, eg *bump*. • **echoless** *adj.* ◎ 14c: Greek, meaning 'sound'.

■ **echo with** or **to something** to make (a sound) loudly, with an echo.

echocardiogram ▷ *noun, medicine* the record produced by **echocardiography**, the examination of the heart and its function by means of ultrasound. ◎ 1970s.

echo chamber ▷ *noun* a room where the walls reflect sound, used when making acoustic measurements or as a recording studio when an echo effect is required. ◎ 1930s.

echolalia /ɛkoʊ'leɪlɪə/ ▷ *noun, psychiatry* senseless or compulsive repetition of words heard. ◎ 19c: from ECHO + Greek *lalia* talk.

echolocation ▷ *noun* the determining of the position of objects by measuring the time taken for an echo to return from them, and the direction of the echo. ◎ 1940s.

echo-sounding ▷ *noun* a method used at sea, etc for determining the depth of water, locating shoals of fish, etc, by measuring the time taken for a signal sent out from the ship, etc to return as an echo.

echo-sounder ▷ *noun* the apparatus used in echo-sounding. See also FATHOMETER 1.

echo virus or **ECHO virus** ▷ *noun, pathol* any of a group of viruses which can cause respiratory and intestinal diseases, and meningitis. ◎ 1950s: from enteric *c*ytopathogenic *h*uman *o*rphan *virus*; 'orphan' because it was originally believed not to be related to any other disease.

echt /ɛxt/ ▷ *adj* genuine; authentic. ◎ Early 20c: German.

éclair /ɪ'klɛə(r)/ ▷ *noun* a long cake of choux pastry with a cream filling and chocolate or coffee icing. ◎ 19c: French, literally 'flash of lightning', perhaps because it is quickly eaten.

eclampsia /ɪ'klampsɪə/ ▷ *noun, pathol* a toxic condition which may develop during the last three months of pregnancy. See also PRE-ECLAMPSIA. ◎ 19c: from Greek *eklampein* to shine out.

éclat /eɪ'klɑː/ ▷ *noun, literary* **1** striking effect; showy splendour. **2** splendid success; distinction. **3** applause; praise. ◎ 17c: French, from *esclater* to break or shine.

eclectic /ɪ'klɛktɪk/ ▷ *adj* said of a style of writing or art, or a set of beliefs: selecting material or ideas from a wide range of sources or authorities. ▷ *noun* a person who adopts eclectic methods. • **eclectically** *adverb.* • **eclecticism** /-sɪzəm/ *noun.* ◎ 17c: from Greek *eklektikos*, from *ek* from + *legein* to choose.

eclipse /ɪ'klɪps/ ▷ *noun* **1** the total or partial obscuring of one planet or heavenly body by another, eg of the Sun when the Moon comes between it and the Earth (called a **solar eclipse**) or of the Moon when the Earth's shadow falls across it (called a **lunar eclipse**). **2** a loss of fame or importance. ▷ *verb* (***eclipsed***, ***eclipsing***) **1** to cause an eclipse of (a heavenly body). **2** to surpass or outshine. **3** to obscure. ◎ 14c: French, from Greek *ekleipsis* failure to appear.

ecliptic /ɪ'klɪptɪk/ ▷ *noun* (**the ecliptic**) the course which the Sun seems to follow in relation to the stars. ▷ *adj* characteristic of, belonging to or relating to an eclipse or to the ecliptic.

eclogue /'ɛklɒg/ ▷ *noun* a pastoral poem, often in the form of a dialogue. ◎ 15c: from Latin *ecloga* a short poem.

eclosion /ɪ'kloʊʒən/ ▷ *noun* emergence, especially that of an insect larva from its egg, or an adult insect from its pupal case. ◎ 19c: French *éclosion*, from Latin *excludere*, *exclusum* to shut out.

eco- /iːkoʊ, ɛkoʊ, ɪ'kɒ/ ▷ *combining form, denoting* living things in relation to their environment. ◎ From ECOLOGY.

ecocide /'iːkoʊsaɪd/ ▷ *noun* destruction of the aspects of the environment which enable it to support life. ◎ 1970s.

eco-friendly ▷ *adj* ecologically acceptable; not harmful to or threatening the environment.

ecol. ▷ *abbreviation* **1** ecological. **2** ecology.

eco-label ▷ *noun* **1** a label used by manufacturers of products claiming to be environmentally acceptable, specifying to the consumer the exact nature of their ecological soundness, eg 'contains no animal products'. **2** a label certifying that certain standards of ecological soundness have been reached, eg 'Dolphin friendly' (a label on certain brands of canned tuna). ● **eco-labelling** *noun*. ⓒ 1980s.

E. coli ▷ *abbreviation* Escherichia coli.

ecology /ɪˈkɒlədʒɪ/ ▷ *noun* **1** the relationship between living things and their surroundings. **2** the study of plants, animals, peoples and institutions, in relation to environment. ● **ecologic** /-ˈlɒdʒɪk/ or **ecological** *adj* **1** relating to, or concerned with, ecology. **2** said of policies, methods, practices or products: beneficial to the natural environment. ● **ecologically** *adverb*. ● **ecologist** *noun*. ⓒ 19c.

econ. ▷ *abbreviation* **1** economic. **2** economical. **3** economics. **4** economy.

econometrics /ɪkɒnəˈmɛtrɪks/ ▷ *singular noun* statistical analysis of economic data and their interrelations. ● **econometric** or **econometrical** *adj*. ● **econometrician** /-məˈtrɪʃən/ *noun*. ⓒ 1930s.

economic /iːkəˈnɒmɪk/ ▷ *adj* **1** relating to or concerned with economy or economics. **2** relating to industry or business. **3** said of a business practice or industry, etc: operated at, or likely to bring, a profit. **4** economical. **5** *colloq* cheap; not expensive.

> ***economic, economical***
>
> ● Although there is some overlap in meaning, **economic** is more closely associated with **economics**, and **economical** has a less specific sense related to the general sense of **economy** □ *Consultation will focus on the economic and diplomatic issues.* □ *It may be economical to use a cheaper form of fuel.*

economical /iːkəˈnɒmɪkəl/ ▷ *adj* **1** not wasting money or resources. **2** thrifty; frugal or careful. **3** economic. ● **economical with the truth** deceiving someone by not telling them some essential fact and therefore implying that something is the case when it is not; a euphemism for lying. ● **economically** *adverb*.

economic refugee ▷ *noun* someone who seeks refuge in another country because of poverty, rather than for religious or political reasons.

economics /iːkəˈnɒmɪks/ ▷ *singular noun* **1** the study of the production, distribution and consumption of money, goods and services. **2** the financial aspects of something. See also HOME ECONOMICS. ● **economist** /ɪˈkɒnəmɪst/ *noun* an expert in economics.

economize or **economise** /ɪˈkɒnəmaɪz/ ▷ *verb* (***economized***, ***economizing***) *intr* to cut down on spending or waste. ● **economization** *noun*. ● **economizer** *noun*. ⓒ 17c.

economy /ɪˈkɒnəmɪ/ ▷ *noun* (***economies***) **1** the organization of money and resources within a nation or community, etc, especially in terms of the production, distribution and consumption of goods and services. **2** a system in which these are organized in a specified way □ *a socialist economy*. **3** careful management of money or other resources, avoiding waste and cutting down on spending. **4** (*usually* **economies**) an instance of economizing; a saving. **5** efficient or sparing use of something □ *economy of movement*. **6** *as adj* **a** said of a class of travel, especially air travel: of the cheapest kind; **b** (*also* **economy-size** or **economy-sized**) said of a packet of food, etc: larger than the standard or basic size, and proportionally cheaper. ⓒ 16c: from Greek *oikos* house + *nemein* to control.

ecosphere ▷ *noun, technical* **1** the parts of the universe, especially of the Earth, in which living things can exist. **2** the BIOSPHERE. ⓒ 1950s.

écossaise /eɪkɒˈsɛz/ ▷ *noun* a lively country dance or music for it in 2/4 time. ⓒ 19c: originally the name of a dance of Scottish origin or the tune for it: feminine form of French *écossais* Scottish.

ecosystem ▷ *noun* a community of living things and their relationships to their surroundings. ⓒ 1930s.

ecotourism ▷ *noun* the careful development and management of tourism in areas of unspoiled natural beauty, so that the environment is preserved and the income from tourists contributes to its conservation.

ecotoxic ▷ *adj* poisonous to plants or animals; deleterious to the environment.

ecotoxicology ▷ *noun* the study of the destructive effect of waste materials, etc on the environment. ● **ecotoxicologist** *noun*.

ecotype ▷ *noun* a group of organisms which have adapted to a particular environment and so have become different from other groups within the species.

ecru /ˈeɪkruː/ ▷ *noun* an off-white or greyish-yellow colour; fawn. ▷ *adj* of this colour. ⓒ 19c: French *écru* the colour of unbleached linen.

ECSC ▷ *abbreviation* European Coal and Steel Community, established in 1951, a predecessor of the EEC.

Ecstasy /ˈɛkstəsɪ/ ▷ *noun, slang* (abbreviation **E**) a powerful hallucinatory drug, methylenedioxymethamphetamine.

ecstasy /ˈɛkstəsɪ/ ▷ *noun* (***ecstasies***) **1** a feeling of immense joy; rapture. **2** *psychol* a trance-like state or any similar state. ● **ecstatic** *adj* **1** relating to, showing or causing ecstasy. **2** *colloq* very happy or pleased. ● **ecstatically** *adverb*. ⓒ 14c: from French *extasie*, from Greek *ekstasis* standing outside oneself.

ECT ▷ *abbreviation* electroconvulsive therapy.

ecto- /ɛktoʊ, ɛkˈtɒ/ ▷ *combining form, signifying* outside. See also ENDO-, ENTO-, EXO-. ⓒ From Greek *ektos* outside.

ectoblast ▷ *noun* the EPIBLAST. ● **ectoblastic** *adj*. ⓒ 19c.

ectoderm and **exoderm** ▷ *noun, zool* in a multicellular animal that has two or more layers of body tissue: **a** the external germinal layer of EPIBLAST of the embryo; **b** the tissues directly derived from this layer. ● **ectodermal** or **ectodermic** *adj*. Compare ENDODERM, MESODERM. ⓒ 19c.

ectomorph ▷ *noun* a person of thin light body build. Compare ENDOMORPH, MESOMORPH. ● **ectomorphic** *adj*. ● **ectomorphy** *noun*. ⓒ 1940s; this body type has a prevalence of structures formed from *ecto*derm.

-ectomy /ɛktəmɪ/ ▷ *combining form* (***-ectomies***) *medicine, signifying* removal by surgery □ *hysterectomy*. ⓒ From Greek *ektome*, from *ektemnein* to cut out.

ectopic /ɛkˈtɒpɪk/ ▷ *adj, pathol* in an abnormal position. ⓒ 19c: from Greek *ek* out of + *topos* place.

ectopic pregnancy ▷ *noun, pathol* the development of a fetus outside the uterus, especially in a Fallopian tube.

ectoplasm /ˈɛktoʊplazəm/ ▷ *noun* **1** *biol* the outer layer of a cell's protoplasm, the material which makes up the living part. **2** the substance thought by some people to be given off by the body of a spiritualistic medium during a trance. ● **ectoplasmic** *adj*. ⓒ 19c.

ecu or **Ecu** /ˈeɪkjuː/ ▷ *noun* the **European currency unit**, a trading currency whose value is based on the combined values of several European currencies.

ecumenical or **oecumenical** /iːkjʊˈmɛnɪkəl, ɛk-/ and **ecumenic** or **oecumenic** ▷ *adj* **1** bringing together different branches of the Christian church. **2** working towards the unity of the Christian church. **3** referring to or consisting of the whole Christian church □ *an ecumenical council.* • **ecumenicalism** or **ecumenicism** /-'mɛnɪsɪzəm/ or **ecumenism** /ɪ'kjuːmənɪzəm/ *noun* the principles or practice of Christian unity. • **ecumenically** *adverb.* ⓒ 16c: from Greek *oikoumenikos* relating to the inhabited world.

ecumenical movement ▷ *noun* a movement within the Christian church towards unity on all fundamental issues of belief and worship, etc.

ecumenics *singular noun* the study of ecumenical awareness and the ecumenical movement in the Christian church.

eczema /'ɛksɪmə, ɪg'ziːmə/ ▷ *noun, pathol* a skin disorder in which red blisters form on the skin, usually causing an itching or burning sensation. • **eczematous** /ɛk'sɛmətəs, ɪg'ziː-/ *adj.* ⓒ 18c: from Greek *ekzema*, from *ek* out of + *zeein* to boil.

ed. ▷ *abbreviation* **1** edited. **2** (*plural* ***eds***) edition. **3** (*also* **Ed.**) (*plural* ***eds*** or ***Eds***) editor. **4** educated. **5** education.

-ed /ɪd, d, t/ ▷ *suffix* **1** used to form past tenses and past participles □ *walked.* **2** used to form adjectives from nouns □ *bearded* □ *bald-headed.*

Edam /'iːdam/ ▷ *noun* a type of mild yellow cheese, usually shaped into balls and covered with red wax. ⓒ 19c: from Edam, near Amsterdam, where it was originally made.

edaphic /ɪ'dafɪk/ ▷ *adj, bot, ecol* belonging or relating to the soil. • **edaphology** /ɛdə'fɒlədʒɪ/ *noun.* ⓒ 19c: from Greek *edaphos* ground.

edaphic factor ▷ *noun* any physical or chemical property of the soil that influences plants growing in it.

EDC ▷ *abbreviation* **1** ethylene dichloride. **2** European Defence Community.

eddy /'ɛdɪ/ ▷ *noun* (***eddies***) **1** a current of water running back against the main stream or current, forming a small whirlpool. **2** a movement of air, smoke or fog, etc similar to this. ▷ *verb* (***eddies, eddied, eddying***) *tr & intr* to move or make something move in this way. ⓒ 15c.

eddy current ▷ *noun* an electric current caused by varying electromotive forces which are due to varying magnetic fields, and causing heating in motors, transformers, etc. Also called **Foucault current**.

edema see OEDEMA

edelweiss /'eɪdəlvaɪs/ ▷ *noun* (*plural* ***edelweiss***) a small European mountain plant of the same family as the daisy and the dandelion, with white woolly leaves around the flower-heads. ⓒ 19c: German, from *edel* noble + *weiss* white.

Eden /'iːdən/ ▷ *noun* **1** (*also* **Garden of Eden**) the garden where, according to the Bible, the first man and woman lived after being created. **2** a beautiful region; a place of delight. • **Edenic** /iː'dɛnɪk/ *adj.* ⓒ 14c: from Hebrew *eden* delight or pleasure.

edentate /iː'dɛnteɪt/ *biol* ▷ *adj* having few or no teeth. ▷ *noun* an animal belonging to a group of mammals which have few or no teeth, but well-developed claws for digging and gripping, such as the anteater, armadillo and sloth. ⓒ 19c: from Latin *edentatus* toothless.

EDF ▷ *abbreviation* European Development Fund.

edge /ɛdʒ/ ▷ *noun* **1** the part farthest from the middle of something; a border or boundary; the rim. **2** the area beside a cliff or steep drop. **3** the cutting side of something sharp such as a knife. **4** *geom* the meeting point of two surfaces. **5** sharpness or severity □ *bread to take the edge off his hunger.* **6** bitterness □ *There was an edge to his criticism.* ▷ *verb* (***edged, edging***) **1** to form or make a border to something, edged with flowers. **2** to shape the edge or border of something. **3** (*usually* **edge forward, in** or **out**, *etc*) *tr & intr* to move gradually and carefully, especially sideways. **4** to sharpen (a knife, etc). **5** *cricket* to strike with the edge of the bat. • **edged** *adj, in compounds* **1** having an edge of a specified kind □ *sharp-edged.* **2** having a specified number of edges □ *double-edged.* • **edger** *noun* **1** a garden tool for trimming the edge of a lawn. **2** someone or something that edges. • **edging** *noun* **1** a border around something or to be applied to something, especially a decorative one. **2** the act of making an edge. **3** *as adj* used for making an edge. • **have the edge on** or **over someone** or **something 1** to have an advantage over them. **2** to be better than them. • **on edge** uneasy; nervous and irritable. • **set someone's teeth on edge** see under TOOTH. • **take the edge off something 1** to make it less unpleasant or less difficult. **2** to weaken or diminish it. ⓒ Anglo-Saxon *ecg.*

■ **edge out something** or **someone 1** to remove or get rid of it or them gradually. **2** to defeat them by a small margin.

edge tool and **edged tool** ▷ *noun* a tool with a sharp edge.

edgeways and **edgewise** ▷ *adverb* **1** sideways. **2** with the edge uppermost or forwards. **3** in the direction of the edge. • **not get a word in edgeways** to be unable to contribute to a conversation because the others are talking continuously.

edgy /'ɛdʒɪ/ ▷ *adj* (***edgier, edgiest***) *colloq* easily annoyed; anxious, nervous or tense. • **edgily** *adverb.* • **edginess** *noun.*

edible /'ɛdɪbəl/ ▷ *adj* fit to be eaten; suitable to eat. ▷ *plural noun* (**edibles**) food; things that are fit to be eaten. Compare EATABLE. • **edibility** *noun.* ⓒ 17c: from Latin *edibilis.*

edict /'iːdɪkt/ ▷ *noun* **1** an order issued by a monarch or government. **2** an order issued by any authority. • **edictal** *adj.* ⓒ 15c: from Latin *edictum*, from *edicere* to proclaim.

edifice /'ɛdɪfɪs/ ▷ *noun, formal* **1** a building, especially a large impressive one. **2** a large and complex organization. ⓒ 14c: French *édifice*, from Latin *aedificare* to build.

edify /'ɛdɪfaɪ/ ▷ *verb* (***edifies, edified, edifying***) *formal* to improve the mind or morals of someone. • **edification** *noun.* • **edifying** *adj* intellectually or morally stimulating. • **edifyingly** *adverb.* ⓒ 14c: from French *édifier*, from Latin *aedificare* to build.

edit /'ɛdɪt/ ▷ *verb* (***edited, editing***) **1** to prepare (a book, newspaper, programme, film, etc) for publication or broadcasting, especially by making corrections or alterations. **2** to be in overall charge of the process of producing (a newspaper, etc). **3** to compile (a reference work). **4** (*usually* **edit out something**) to remove (parts of a work) before printing or broadcasting, etc. **5** to prepare (a cinema film, or a TV or radio programme) by putting together material previously photographed or recorded. **6** to prepare (data) for processing by a computer. ▷ *noun* a period or instance of editing. • **edited** *adj.* ⓒ 18c: from EDITOR.

edit. ▷ *abbreviation* **1** edited. **2** edition.

edition /ɪ'dɪʃən/ ▷ *noun* **1** the total number of copies of a book, etc printed at one time, or at different times without alteration. **2** one of a series of printings of a book or periodical, etc, produced with alterations and corrections made by the author or an editor. **3** the form in which a book, etc is published □ *paperback edition.* **4** the form given to a work by its editor or publisher □ *the Cambridge edition.* ⓒ 16c.

editor /'ɛdɪtə(r)/ ▷ *noun* **1** a person who edits books, etc. **2** a person who is in charge of a newspaper or magazine, etc, or one section of it □ *letters to the editor* □ *the Arts editor.* **3** a person who is in charge of a radio or TV programme which is made up of different items, eg a news programme. **4** a person who puts together the various sections of a cinema film, etc. • **editorship** *noun.* ⓒ 17c.

editorial /ɛdɪ'tɔːrɪəl/ ▻ *adj* referring or relating to editors or editing. ▻ *noun* an article written by or on behalf of the editor of a newspaper or magazine, usually one offering an opinion on a current topic. • **editorially** *adverb*.

editorialize or **editorialise** /ɛdɪ'tɔːrɪəlaɪz/ ▻ *verb* (***editorialized, editorializing***) *intr* **1** to write an editorial. **2** *derog* in journalism: to introduce personal opinion into something meant to be factual reporting. • **editorialization** *noun*.

EDP ▻ *abbreviation* electronic data processing.

eds see ED

EDT ▻ *abbreviation, N Amer* Eastern Daylight Time.

educable /'ɛdjʊkəbəl/ ▻ *adj* capable of being educated. • **educability** *noun*.

educate /'ɛdjʊkeɪt/ ▻ *verb* (***educated, educating***) **1** to train and teach. **2** to provide school instruction for someone. **3** to train and improve (one's taste, etc). • **educatability** *noun*. • **educatable** *adj*. • **educative** /'ɛdjʊkətɪv/ *adj* **1** educating. **2** characteristic of or relating to education. • **educator** *noun* **1** a person who educates. **2** an educating experience or circumstance. • **educatory** *adj*. ◷ 15c: from Latin *educare, educatum* to bring up.

educated *adj* **1** having received an education, especially to a level higher than average. **2** produced by or suggesting an education, usually a good one. **3** based on experience or knowledge □ ***an educated guess***.

education /ɛdjʊ'keɪʃən/ ▻ *noun* **1** the process of teaching. **2** the instruction received. **3** the process of training and improving (one's taste, etc). • **educationist** *noun* an expert in methods of education.

educational ▻ *adj* **1** relating to education. **2** having the function of educating □ ***educational TV***. • **educationalist** *noun*. • **educationally** *adverb* as regards education or educating.

educe /ɪ'djuːs/ ▻ *verb* (***educed, educing***) *formal* to bring out or develop. • **educible** *adj*. • **eduction** /ɪ'dʌkʃən/ *noun*. ◷ 15c: from Latin *e* out + *ducere* to lead.

edutainment ▻ *noun* the presentation of educational material as entertainment. ◷ 1990s: from *education* + enter*tainment*.

Edwardian /ɛd'wɔːdɪən/ ▻ *adj* belonging to or characteristic of Britain in the years 1901–10, the reign of King Edward VII.

-ee /iː/ ▻ *suffix, forming nouns, signifying* **1** a person who is the object of an action of a specified verb □ ***payee*** □ ***employee***. **2** a person in a specified condition □ ***absentee*** □ ***escapee***. **3** a person with a specified association or connection □ ***bargee***. ◷ From French *-é* or *-ée*.

EEC ▻ *abbreviation* European Economic Community.

EEG ▻ *abbreviation* **1** electroencephalogram. **2** electroencephalograph.

eek ▻ *exclamation* used in children's comics, etc: representing a scream, etc.

eel ▻ *noun* **1** any of several kinds of fish with a long smooth snake-like body and very small fins. **2** any one of similar-looking animals, such as the SAND EEL or ELECTRIC EEL. **3** a devious or evasive person; a slippery character. ◷ Anglo-Saxon *æl*.

eelgrass and **eelwrack** /iːlrak/ ▻ *noun* a grasslike flowering plant of the pondweed family, which grows in seawater.

eelpout /iːlpaʊt/ ▻ *noun* **1** the BURBOT, a freshwater edible fish. **2** the BLENNY.

eelworm ▻ *noun* any of various nematode worms.

e'en /iːn/ *old use or poetic* ▻ *adverb* even. ▻ *noun* evening.

EEPROM /'iːprɒm/ ▻ *abbreviation, computing* electrically erasable programmable read-only memory. Compare EPROM.

e'er /ɛə(r)/ ▻ *adverb, old use or poetic* ever.

-eer /ɪə(r)/ ▻ *suffix* **1** *forming nouns, denoting* a person concerned with or engaged in a specified thing or activity □ ***auctioneer*** □ ***mountaineer***. **2** *forming verbs, denoting* actions or behaviour associated with a specified thing or activity □ ***electioneer***. ◷ From French *-ier*.

eerie /'ɪərɪ/ ▻ *adj* (***eerier, eeriest***) strange and disturbing or frightening. • **eerily** *adverb*. • **eeriness** *noun*. ◷ 13c: from Northern English *eri*.

EET ▻ *abbreviation* Eastern European Time.

eff *taboo, swear-word* ▻ *verb* (***effed, effing***) to fuck. • **effing** *adj* bloody; fucking. 1940s: euphemism for *fuck*.

■ **eff off** (only as command) go away!

efface /ɪ'feɪs/ ▻ *verb* (***effaced, effacing***) **1** to rub or wipe out something. **2** to block out (a memory, etc). **3** to avoid drawing attention to (oneself). See also SELF-EFFACING. **4** to surpass or outshine something. • **effaceable** *adj*. • **effacement** *noun*. • **effacer** *noun*. ◷ 15c: from French *effacer*, from Latin *ex* out + *facies* face.

effect /ɪ'fɛkt/ ▻ *noun* **1** a result. **2** an impression given or produced. **3** operation; a working state □ ***The ban comes into effect today***. **4** (*usually* **effects**) *formal* property. **5** (*usually* **effects**) devices, especially lighting and sound, used to create a particular impression in a film or on a stage, etc □ ***special effects***. ▻ *verb* (***effected, effecting***) *formal* to do something; to make something happen, or to bring it about. • **for effect** in order to make an impression on others. • **give effect to something** *formal* to do it or bring it into operation. • **in effect** in reality; practically speaking.• **take effect** to begin to work; to come into force. • **to the effect that** *formal* with the meaning or result that. • **to good** or **some**, *etc* **effect** with much or some, etc success. • **to no effect** with no success. • **to that effect** *formal* with that meaning or intended result. • **with effect from** *formal* coming into operation or becoming valid at (a specified time). • **with immediate effect** *formal* as from now. ◷ 14c as *noun*: French, from Latin *effectus*.

> ***effect***
>
> A word often confused with this one is **affect**.

effective /ɪ'fɛktɪv/ ▻ *adj* **1** having the power to produce, or producing, a desired result. **2** producing a pleasing effect. **3** impressive; striking. **4** in, or coming into, operation; working or active. **5** actual, rather than theoretical. **6** said of troops: equipped and prepared for action. ▻ *noun* a serviceman or body of servicemen equipped and prepared for action. • **effectively** *adverb* **1** in an effective way. **2** in reality; for all practical purposes. • **effectiveness** *noun*. ◷ 14c.

effector /ɪ'fɛktə(r)/ *biol* ▻ *adj* causing a response to stimulus. ▻ *noun* an organ or substance which has this property. ◷ Early 20c.

effectual /ɪ'fɛktjʊəl/ ▻ *adj* **1** producing the intended result. **2** said of a document, etc: valid. • **effectually** *adverb* with the intended result. ◷ 14c: from Latin *effectualis*.

effectuate /ɪ'fɛktjʊeɪt/ ▻ *verb* (***effectuated, effectuating***) *formal* to do; to carry out something with success. • **effectuation** *noun*. ◷ 16c: from Latin *effectuare*.

effeminate /ɪ'fɛmɪnət/ ▻ *adj, sometimes derog* said of a man: having features of behaviour or appearance more typical of a woman; not manly. • **effeminacy** /-nəsɪ/ or **effeminateness** *noun*. • **effeminately** *adverb*. ◷ 15c: from Latin *effeminare* to make in the form of a woman.

effendi /ɛ'fɛndɪ/ ▻ *noun* (***effendis***) **1** in Turkey: **a** the oral form of address equivalent to MR; **b** before 1934 a formal title for a civil official. **2** *historical* in the eastern Mediterranean: a title of respect for educated or high-ranking men. ◷ 17c in sense 2: from Turkish *efendi* master, from Greek *authentes* an absolute master.

efferent /ˈɛfərənt/ ▻ *adj, physiol* said of a nerve: carrying impulses out from the brain. Compare AFFERENT. ⓘ 19c: from Latin *efferre* to carry out, from *ferre* to carry.

effervesce /ɛfəˈvɛs/ ▻ *verb* (***effervesced, effervescing***) *intr* **1** said of a liquid: to give off bubbles of gas. **2** said of a gas: to emerge as bubbles in a liquid. **3** to behave in a lively or energetic way. • **effervescence** *noun*. • **effervescent** *adj*. ⓘ 18c: from Latin *effervescere* to boil up, from *fervere* to boil.

effete /ɪˈfiːt/ ▻ *adj, derog* **1** said of an institution or organization, etc: lacking its original power or authority. **2** said of a person: **a** lacking strength or energy; **b** decadent; **c** made weak by too much protection or refinement. **3** said of plants and animals: no longer able to reproduce. • **effetely** *adverb*. • **effeteness** *noun*. ⓘ 17c: from Latin *effetus* weakened by having given birth.

efficacious /ɛfɪˈkeɪʃəs/ *formal* ▻ *adj* producing, or certain to produce, the intended result. • **efficaciously** *adverb* with the intended result; successfully. • **efficaciousness**, **efficacity** /ɛfɪˈkasɪtɪ/ or **efficacy** /ˈɛfɪkəsɪ/ *noun* the power of producing an effect; effectiveness. ⓘ 16c: from Latin *efficax*, *efficacis* powerful.

efficient /ɪˈfɪʃənt/ ▻ *adj* **1** producing satisfactory results with an economy of effort and a minimum of waste. **2** said of a person: capable of competent work within a relatively short time. **3** *in compounds* economical in the use or consumption of a specified resource □ *energy-efficient*. • **efficiency** *noun* (***efficiencies***) **1** being efficient. **2** the ratio of a machine's output of energy to its input. • **efficiently** *adverb*. ⓘ 14c: from Latin *efficiens*, *efficientis*, from *efficere* to accomplish.

effigy /ˈɛfɪdʒɪ/ ▻ *noun* (***effigies***) **1** a crude doll or model representing a person, on which hatred of, or contempt for, the person can be expressed, eg by burning it. **2** *formal* a portrait or sculpture of a person used as an architectural ornament. • **burn** or **hang someone in effigy** to burn or hang a figure of them to express disapproval, etc of them. ⓘ 16c: from Latin *effigies*, from *fingere* to form.

effing and blinding ▻ *noun* cursing and swearing. 1950s; see EFF.

effleurage /ɛfləˈrɑːʒ/ ▻ *noun* in massage: a stroking movement. ⓘ 19c: French, meaning 'glancing' or 'grazing'.

effloresce /ɛfləˈrɛs/ ▻ *verb* (***effloresced, efflorescing***) *intr* **1** *bot* said of a plant: to produce flowers. **2** *chem* said of a chemical compound: to form an EFFLORESCENCE 2. ⓘ 18c.

efflorescence ▻ *noun* **1** the act of efflorescing. **2** *chem* a powdery substance formed as a result of crystallization or loss of water to the atmosphere. **3** *bot* the period during which a plant is producing flowers. • **efflorescent** *adj* efflorescing; producing flowers. ⓘ 17c: from Latin *efflorescere* to blossom.

effluent /ˈɛflʊənt/ ▻ *noun* **1** liquid industrial waste or sewage released into a river or the sea, etc. **2** *geog, etc* a stream or river flowing from a larger body of water. ▻ *adj, formal or technical* flowing out. • **effluence** *noun* **1** the act or process of flowing out. **2** something that flows out. ⓘ 18c: from Latin *effluere* to flow out.

effluvium /ɛˈfluːvɪəm/ ▻ *noun* (***effluvia*** /-ɪə/) *formal* an unpleasant smell or vapour given off by something, eg decaying matter. ⓘ 17c: Latin, meaning 'a flowing out'.

efflux ▻ *noun* (***effluxes***) **1** the act or process of flowing out. **2** something that flows out. ⓘ 17c: Latin, from *effluere*, *effluxum* to flow out.

effort /ˈɛfət/ ▻ *noun* **1** hard mental or physical work, or something that requires it. **2** an act of trying hard. **3** the result of an attempt; an achievement. • **effortless** *adj* done without effort or apparent effort. • **effortlessly** *adverb*. • **effortlessness** *noun*. ⓘ 15c: from French *esfort*, from Latin *fortis* strong.

effrontery /ɪˈfrʌntərɪ/ ▻ *noun* (***effronteries***) shameless rudeness; impudence. ⓘ 18c: from Latin *effrons*, *effrontis* shameless.

effulgent /ɪˈfʌldʒənt/ ▻ *adj, literary* shining brightly; brilliant. • **effulgence** *noun*. • **effulgently** *adverb*. ⓘ 18c: from Latin *effulgere* to shine out.

effuse /ɪˈfjuːz/ ▻ *verb* (***effused, effusing***) **1** to pour out. **2** to spread out. ▻ *adj* /ɪˈfjuːs/ **1** *bot* loosely spreading. **2** said of shells: with the lips separated by a groove. ⓘ 16c as *verb*: from Latin *effundere*, *effusum* to pour out.

effusion /ɪˈfjuːʒən/ ▻ *noun* **1** the act or process of pouring or flowing out. **2** something that is poured out. **3** *derog* an uncontrolled flow of speech or writing. **4 a** *pathol* an abnormal escape of blood or other fluid into tissue or a body cavity; **b** such fluid.

effusive /ɪˈfjuːsɪv/ ▻ *adj* **1** *derog* expressing feelings, especially happiness or enthusiasm, in an excessive or very showy way. **2** *geol* said of rock: volcanic. • **effusively** *adverb*. • **effusiveness** *noun*. ⓘ 17c.

E-fit ▻ *noun, trademark* a form of IDENTIKIT, the image being composed on screen and adjustable by fine degrees.

EFL ▻ *abbreviation* English as a Foreign Language.

EFTA or **Efta** /ˈɛftə/ ▻ *abbreviation* European Free Trade Association, an association with the purpose of maintaining free trade relations between its member states and members of the EC. It also has trade agreements with a number of E European states.

EFTPOS /ˈɛftpɒs/ ▻ *abbreviation* electronic funds transfer at point of sale.

EFTS ▻ *abbreviation* electronic funds transfer system.

eg ▻ *abbreviation, exempli gratia* (Latin), for example.

egalitarian /ɪgalɪˈtɛərɪən/ ▻ *adj* relating to, promoting or believing in the principle that all human beings are equal and should enjoy the same rights. ▻ *noun* a person who upholds this principle. • **egalitarianism** *noun* egalitarian principles or beliefs. ⓘ 19c: from French *égalitaire*, from *égal* equal.

egg[1] and **egg cell** ▻ *noun* **1** the reproductive cell produced by a female animal, bird, etc, from which the young one develops. Also called OVUM. **2** a reproductive cell or developing embryo produced and deposited in a hard shell by female birds, reptiles, and certain animals. **3** the hard shell of an egg. **4** a hen's egg, used as food. **5** anything with the shape of a hen's egg. • **have** or **put all one's eggs in** or **into one basket** to depend entirely on one plan, etc. • **have** or **get egg on one's face** *colloq* to be made to look foolish. ⓘ 14c: Norse.

egg[2] ▻ *verb* (***egged, egging***) (*usually* **egg someone on**) *colloq* to urge or encourage them. ⓘ Anglo-Saxon *eggian*.

egg-and-spoon race ▻ *noun* a race in which each competitor carries an egg in a spoon.

eggar see EGGER

eggbeater ▻ *noun* **1** (*also* **eggwhisk**) a utensil for beating raw eggs. **2** *colloq, especially N Amer* a helicopter.

eggbox ▻ *noun* a protective partitioned container for holding eggs, usually in multiples of six.

egg-cosy ▻ *noun* (***egg-cosies***) a cover for keeping a boiled egg hot.

eggcup ▻ *noun* a small cup-shaped container for holding a boiled egg in its shell while it is being eaten.

egg custard see CUSTARD

egger or **eggar** /ˈɛgə(r)/ ▻ *noun* any of various large brown European moths, which develop out of egg-shaped cocoons.

egghead ▻ *noun, colloq, sometimes derog* a very clever person; an intellectual. ⓘ 1950s.

eggier and **eggiest** see under EGGY

eggnog and **egg-flip** ▻ *noun* a drink made from raw eggs, milk, sugar and an alcoholic spirit, especially rum or brandy.

eggplant ▻ *noun, N Amer, especially US* an AUBERGINE.

eggs-and-bacon see BIRDSFOOT TREFOIL

eggs Benedict ▷ *singular noun, cookery* a dish consisting of a slice of ham and a poached egg placed on a slice of toast and covered with hollandaise sauce. ⓒ 1920s.

eggshell ▷ *noun* the hard thin porous CALCAREOUS covering of an egg. ▷ *adj* **1** said of paint or varnish: having a slightly glossy finish. **2** said of articles of china: very thin and fragile.

egg-slice ▷ *noun* a utensil for lifting fried eggs out of a pan.

egg-spoon ▷ *noun* a small spoon used for eating boiled eggs out of the shell.

egg-timer ▷ *noun* a device consisting of a sealed glass tube narrowed in the middle, containing sand or salt which, by trickling slowly from the top to the bottom of the tube through the narrow part, indicates the approximate time required to boil an egg.

egg tooth ▷ *noun* a temporary tooth in embryo reptiles, or a hard point on the beak of an unhatched bird, which allow them to break out of their shell.

eggwash ▷ *noun* a thin mixture of egg and milk or egg and water, used for glazing pastry.

eggwhisk see under EGGBEATER

eggy ▷ *adj* (***eggier***, ***eggiest***) **1** tasting and/or smelling of EGG[1] (sense 4). **2** marked with or covered in egg.

eglantine /ˈɛɡləntaɪn/ ▷ *noun* a fragrant species of wild rose, the sweet-brier. ⓒ 16c: French.

ego /ˈiːɡoʊ, ˈɛɡoʊ/ ▷ *noun* (***egos***) **1** personal pride. **2** *psychoanal* in Freudian theory: the part of a person that is conscious and thinks. Compare ID, SUPEREGO. **3** one's image of oneself. **4** egotism. • **massage someone's ego** *facetious* to flatter them. ⓒ 19c: Latin, meaning 'I'.

egocentric ▷ *adj, derog* interested in oneself only. • **egocentrically** *adverb*. • **egocentricity** *noun*. ⓒ Late 19c: EGO + -CENTRIC.

ego ideal ▷ *noun, psychol* **1** one's personal standards, ideals and ambitions, etc, acquired as one recognizes parental and other social standards. **2** one's idealized picture of oneself.

egoism /ˈiːɡoʊɪzəm, ˈɛɡoʊ-/ ▷ *noun* **1** *philos* the principle that self-interest is the basis of morality. **2** selfishness. **3** egotism.

egoist /ˈiːɡoʊɪst, ˈɛɡoʊ-/ ▷ *noun* a person who believes in self-interest as a moral principle. • **egoistic** or **egoistical** *adj*. • **egoistically** *adverb*.

egomania ▷ *noun, psychol* extreme self-interest which prevents one from allowing other people to come between oneself and the achievement of one's desires. • **egomaniac** *noun* a person who is governed by extreme self-interest. • **egomaniacal** *adj*. ⓒ 19c: EGO + -MANIA.

egos *plural of* EGO

egotism /ˈiːɡoʊtɪzəm, ˈɛɡoʊ-/ ▷ *noun, derog* **1** the habit of speaking too much about oneself. **2** the fact of having a very high opinion of oneself. • **egotist** *noun* a self-centred person. • **egotistic** or **egotistical** *adj*. • **egotistically** *adverb*. ⓒ 18c.

ego trip ▷ *noun, colloq* an action or actions carried out mainly to increase one's high opinion of oneself, or because one has a high opinion of oneself. • **ego tripper** *noun*. ⓒ 1960s.

egregious /ɪˈɡriːdʒəs/ *formal* ▷ *adj* outrageous; shockingly bad. • **egregiously** *adverb*. • **egregiousness** *noun*. ⓒ 16c: from Latin *egregius* standing out from the herd, from e out of + *grex, gregis* herd.

egress /ˈiːɡrɛs/ ▷ *noun* (***egresses***) *formal or law* **1** the act of leaving a building or other enclosed place. **2** an exit. **3** the power or right to depart. Opposite of INGRESS. • **egression** *noun* the act of going out; departure. ⓒ 16c: from Latin *egredi, egressus* to go out.

egret /ˈiːɡrət/ ▷ *noun* any of various white long-legged wading birds similar to herons. ⓒ 15c: from French *aigrette*.

Egyptian /ɪˈdʒɪpʃən/ ▷ *adj* belonging or relating to Egypt, a country in NE Africa, its inhabitants, or their language. ▷ *noun* **1** a citizen or inhabitant of, or person born in, Egypt. **2** the official language of Egypt. ⓒ 14c.

Egyptology /iːdʒɪpˈtɒlədʒɪ/ ▷ *noun* the study of the language, culture and history of ancient Egypt. • **Egyptologist** *noun* an expert in or student of Egyptology. ⓒ 19c.

eh /eɪ/ ▷ *exclamation* **1** used to request that a question or remark, etc be repeated. **2** added to a question, often with the implication that agreement is expected. **3** used to express surprise.

EHO ▷ *abbreviation* environmental health officer.

EIA ▷ *abbreviation* environmental impact assessment.

eider /ˈaɪdə(r)/ and **eider duck** ▷ *noun* a large sea duck from northern countries. ⓒ 18c: from Icelandic *æthr*.

eiderdown ▷ *noun* **1** the down or soft feathers of the eider. **2** a quilt filled with this or some similar material.

eidetic /aɪˈdɛtɪk/ *psychol* ▷ *adj* **1** said of a mental image: extraordinarily clear and vivid, as though actually visible. **2** said of a person or memory: reproducing or able to reproduce a vividly clear visual image of what has been previously seen. ▷ *noun* a person with this ability. • **eidetically** *adverb*. ⓒ 1920s: from Greek *eidetikos* belonging to an image.

eigen- /aɪɡən/ ▷ *combining form, signifying* proper; own. ⓒ German.

eigen-frequency ▷ *noun, physics* one of the frequencies with which a particular system may vibrate.

eigentone ▷ *noun, physics* a tone characteristic of a particular vibrating system.

eigenvalue ▷ *noun, math, physics* any of the possible values for a parameter of an equation for which the solutions will be compatible with the boundary conditions.

eight /eɪt/ ▷ *noun* **1a** the cardinal number 8; **b** the quantity that this represents, being one more than seven. **2** any symbol for this, eg **8**, **VIII**. **3** the age of eight. **4** something, especially a garment, or a person, whose size is denoted by the number 8. **5** the eighth hour after midnight or midday. □ *Come at eight* □ *8 o'clock* □ *8pm*. **6** a set or group of eight people or things. **7** *rowing* (symbol **8+**) a racing-boat manned by eight oarsmen or oarswomen; the crew of such a boat. **8** a playing-card with eight pips □ *He played his eight*. **9** a score of eight points. ▷ *adj* **1** totalling eight. **2** aged eight. • **be** or **have had one over the eight** *colloq* to be slightly drunk. ⓒ Anglo-Saxon *æhta*.

eighteen ▷ *noun* **1 a** the cardinal number 18; **b** the quantity that this represents, being one more than seventeen, or the sum of ten and eight. **2** any symbol for this, eg **18**, **XVIII**. **3** the age of eighteen. **4** something, especially a garment, or a person, whose size is denoted by the number 18. **5** a set or group of eighteen people or things. **6** (written **18**) a film classified as suitable for people aged 18 and over. **7** a score of eighteen points. ▷ *adj* **1** totalling eighteen. **2** aged eighteen. ⓒ Anglo-Saxon *æhtatene*.

eighteenth (often written **18th**) *adj* **1** in counting: **a** next after seventeenth; **b** last of 18. **2** in eighteenth position. **3** (**the eighteenth**) **a** the eighteenth day of the month; **b** *golf* the eighteenth hole. ▷ *noun* **1** one of eighteen equal parts. Also *as adj* □ *an eighteenth share*. **2** a FRACTION equal to one divided by eighteen (usually written $^1/_{18}$). **3** a person coming eighteenth, eg in a race or an exam. ▷ *adverb* eighteenthly. • **eighteenthly** *adverb* used to introduce the eighteenth point in a list. Ⓒ Anglo-Saxon; see EIGHTEEN + -TH[1]. ▷

eightfold ▷ *adj* **1** equal to eight times as much. **2** divided into or consisting of eight parts. ▷ *adverb* by eight times as much. Ⓒ Anglo-Saxon; see EIGHT + -FOLD.

eighth /eɪtθ/ (often written **8th**) ▷ *adj* **1** in counting: **a** next after seventh; **b** last of eight. **2** in eighth position. **3** (**the eighth**) **a** the eighth day of the month; **b** *golf* the eighth hole. ▷ *noun* **1** one of eight equal parts. Also *as adj* □ *an eighth share.* 2 a FRACTION equal to one divided by eight (usually written 1/8). **3** a person coming eighth, eg in a race or an exam. **4** *music* **a** an interval of an octave; **b** a note at that interval from another. ▷ *adverb* eighthly. • **eighthly** *adverb* used to introduce the eighth point in a list. Ⓒ Anglo-Saxon; see EIGHT + -TH[1].

eighth note ▷ *noun, N Amer, music* a quaver.

eighties /ˈeɪtɪz/ (often written **80s** or **80's**) ▷ *plural noun* **1** (**one's eighties**) the period of time between one's eightieth and ninetieth birthdays. **2** (**the eighties**) **a** the range of temperatures between eighty and ninety degrees □ *It must be in the eighties today*; **b** the period of time between the eightieth and ninetieth years of a century. Also *as adj* □ *an eighties hairstyle.*

eightieth (often written **80th**) ▷ *adj* **1** in counting: **a** next after seventy-ninth; **b** last of eighty. **2** in eightieth position. ▷ *noun* **1** one of eighty equal parts. Also *as adj* □ *an eightieth share.* **2** a FRACTION equal to one divided by eighty (usually written 1/80). **3** a person coming eightieth, eg in a race or an exam. Ⓒ Anglo-Saxon; see EIGHTY + -TH[1].

eightsome ▷ *noun* (*eightsomes*) **1** a set or group of eight people. **2** a game between four pairs of players. **3** an eightsome reel.

eightsome reel ▷ *noun* **1** a lively Scottish dance for eight people. **2** the music for this dance.

eighty /ˈeɪtɪ/ ▷ *noun* (*eighties*) **1 a** the cardinal number 80; **b** the quantity that this represents, being one more than seventy-nine, or the product of ten and eight. **2** any symbol for this, eg **80**, **LXXX**. Also *in compounds, forming adjectives and nouns*, with cardinal numbers between *one* and *nine* □ *eighty-two.* **3** the age of 80. **4** a set or group of 80 people or things □ *a score of eighty points.* ▷ *adj* **1** totalling eighty. Also *in compounds, forming adjectives,* with ordinal numbers beween *first* and *ninth* □ *eighty-second.* **2** aged 80. See also EIGHTIES, EIGHTIETH. Ⓒ Anglo-Saxon; see EIGHTY + -TY[2].

Einsteinian /aɪnˈstaɪnɪən/ ▷ *adj* referring or relating to Albert Einstein, or to his theories, especially that of RELATIVITY 2. Ⓒ 1920s: named after Albert Einstein (1879–1955), the German-born physicist and mathematician.

einsteinium /aɪnˈstaɪnɪəm/ ▷ *noun* (symbol **Es**, atomic number 99) an element produced artificially from plutonium. Ⓒ 1950s: named after Albert Einstein.

EIS ▷ *abbreviation* Educational Institute of Scotland, one of the trade unions of teachers.

eisteddfod /aɪˈstɛdfəd, -ˈstɛðvɒd/ ▷ *noun* (*eisteddfods* or *eisteddfodau* /aɪˈstɛðvɒdaɪ/) originally a competitive congress of Welsh BARDS and musicians, now any of several gatherings in Wales during which competitions are held to find the best Welsh poetry, drama, songs, etc, especially the **Royal National Eisteddfod**. • **eisteddfodic** *adj*. Ⓒ 19c: Welsh, literally 'a session'.

either /ˈaɪðə(r), ˈiːðə(r)/ ▷ *adj* **1** any one of two. **2** each of two □ *a garden with a fence on either side.* ▷ *pronoun* any one of two things or people, etc. ▷ *adverb, with negatives* **1** also; as well □ *I thought him rather unpleasant, and I didn't like his wife either.* **2** what is more; besides □ *He plays golf, and he's not bad, either.* • **either ... or ...** introducing two choices or possibilities □ *I need either a pen or a pencil.* • **either way** or **in either case** in both of two cases. Ⓒ Anglo-Saxon *ægther*.

ejaculate /ɪˈdʒakjʊleɪt/ ▷ *verb* (*ejaculated, ejaculating*) **1** *tr & intr* said of a man or male animal: to discharge (semen). **2** to exclaim. ▷ *noun* /-lət/ semen. • **ejaculation** *noun* **1** a sudden exclamation or cry. **2** discharge of semen. • **ejaculative** or **ejaculatory** *adj* relating to ejaculation or discharge of fluid. Ⓒ 16c: from Latin *ejaculari, ejaculatus* to throw out.

eject /ɪˈdʒɛkt/ ▷ *verb* (*ejected, ejecting*) **1** to throw out someone or something with force. **2** to force someone to leave. **3** *intr* to leave a moving aircraft using an ejector seat. • **ejection** *noun*. • **ejective** *adj*. • **ejector** *noun* a person or device that ejects something or someone. Ⓒ 16c: from Latin *ejicere, ejectum* to throw out.

ejector seat and (*US*) **ejection seat** ▷ *noun* a type of seat fitted in an aircraft, etc, designed to propel the occupant out of the aircraft at speed in case of emergency.

eke /iːk/ ▷ *verb* (*eked, eking*) (*always* **eke something out**) **1** to make (a supply) last longer, eg by adding something else to it or by careful use. **2** to manage with difficulty to make (a living, etc). Ⓒ Anglo-Saxon *eacan* to increase.

el see ELEVATED RAILROAD

elaborate ▷ *adj* /ɪˈlabərət/ **1** complicated in design; complex. **2** carefully planned or worked out. ▷ *verb* /-reɪt/ (*elaborated, elaborating*) **1** *intr* (*usually* **elaborate on** or **upon something**) to add detail to it. **2** to work out something in great detail. **3** to make something more ornate. **4** *physiol* to convert (eg food) into complex substances. • **elaborately** *adverb*. • **elaborateness** *noun*. • **elaboration** *noun*. • **elaborative** *adj*. • **elaborator** *noun*. Ⓒ 16c as *adj*: from Latin *elaborare, elaboratum*.

élan /eɪˈlan; *French* elɑ̃/ ▷ *noun, literary* impressive and energetic style. Ⓒ 19c: French.

eland /ˈiːlənd/ ▷ *noun* (*elands* or *eland*) a large African antelope with spiral horns. Ⓒ 18c: Afrikaans, from Dutch, meaning 'elk'.

elapse /ɪˈlaps/ ▷ *verb* (*elapsed, elapsing*) *intr, formal* said of time: to pass. Ⓒ 17c: from Latin *elabi, elapsus* to slide away.

elasmobranch /ɪˈlazmoʊbraŋk/ ▷ *noun* (*elasmobranchs*) any member of a class of fishes that includes sharks and skates, which have a cartilaginous skeleton and plate-like gills. Ⓒ 19c: from Greek *elasmos* a beaten-metal plate + *branchia* gills.

elastase /ɪˈlasteɪs/ ▷ *noun, physiol* an enzyme found in the pancreatic juice that decomposes ELASTIN. Ⓒ 1940s.

elastic /ɪˈlastɪk/ ▷ *adj* **1** said of a material or substance: able to return to its original shape or size after being pulled or pressed out of shape. **2** said of a force: caused by, or causing, such an ability. **3** able to be changed; flexible. **4** made of elastic. **5** said of a person or feelings: able to recover quickly from a shock or upset. ▷ *noun* stretchable cord or fabric woven with strips of rubber. • **elastically** *adverb* flexibly; so as to stretch easily. Ⓒ 17c as *adj*: from Greek *elastikos*, from *elaunein* to propel.

elasticate ▷ *verb* (*elasticated, elasticating*) to make something elastic. • **elasticated** *adj* said of a fabric: having been made elastic by being interwoven with rubber.

elastic band ▷ *noun* a thin loop of rubber for keeping papers, etc together. Also called **rubber band**.

elasticity /iːlaˈstɪsɪtɪ, ɛla-/ ▷ *noun* (*elasticities*) **1** the power of returning to original form or size after stretching, compression or deformation. **2** springiness; flexibility or stretchiness; resilience. **3** power to recover from shock, depression, etc.

elasticize or **elasticise** /ɪˈlastɪsaɪz/ ▷ *verb* (*elasticized, elasticizing*) to make something elastic.

elastic tissue ▷ *noun, physiol* tissue which has fibres with elastic quality, occurring especially in ligaments and tendons.

elastin /ɪ'lastɪn/ ▷ *noun* a protein which is the chief constituent of ELASTIC TISSUE. Ⓒ 19c.

elastomer /ɪ'lastoumə(r)/ ▷ *noun* any rubberlike substance. • **elastomeric** /-'merɪk/ *adj.* Ⓒ 1930s.

Elastoplast /ɪ'lastouplɑːst/ ▷ *noun, trademark* a dressing for a wound, consisting of gauze on a backing of adhesive tape. Ⓒ 1928.

elate /ɪ'leɪt/ ▷ *verb* (***elated, elating***) **1** to make someone intensely happy. **2** to fill someone with optimism. • **elated** *adj.* • **elatedly** *adverb.* Ⓒ 17c: from Latin *elatus* elevated or exalted.

elation /ɪ'leɪʃən/ ▷ *noun* **1** an elated state; euphoria. **2** pride resulting from success.

E-layer and **E-region** ▷ *noun, physics* in the Earth's atmosphere: a layer of the ionosphere that reflects medium-frequency radio waves, and is most effecive during the daylight hours. Also (*dated*) called **Kennelly-Heaviside layer, Heaviside layer.**

elbow /'ɛlbou/ ▷ *noun* **1** the joint where the human arm bends. **2** the part of a coat or jacket, etc which covers this joint. **3** the corresponding joint in animals. **4** a sharp turn or bend, eg in a road or pipe. ▷ *verb* (***elbowed, elbowing***) **1** to push or strike something with the elbow. **2** to make (one's way through) by pushing with the elbows. • **at one's elbow** close to one. • **bend** or **lift the elbow** *facetious* to drink alcohol, especially to excess. • **give** or **get the elbow** *slang* to dismiss or be dismissed. • **out at the elbow** or **elbows 1** said of a garment: no longer smart; worn out. **2** said of a person: wearing worn-out clothes. • **up to the elbows** completely engrossed or involved. Ⓒ Anglo-Saxon *elnboga.*

elbow-grease ▷ *noun, colloq* hard work, especially hard polishing. Ⓒ 17c.

elbow-room ▷ *noun* **1** enough space for moving or doing something. **2** freedom; lack of constraint. Ⓒ 16c.

elder[1] /'ɛldə(r)/ ▷ *adj* **1** older. **2** (**the elder**) used before or after a person's name to distinguish them from a younger person of the same name. ▷ *noun* **1** a person who is older. **2** (*often* **elders**) an older person, especially someone regarded as having authority. **3** in some tribal societies: a senior member of a tribe, who is invested with authority. **4** in some Protestant Churches: a lay person who has some responsibility for pastoral care and decision-making. Ⓒ Anglo-Saxon *eldra*, comparative of *ald* old.

elder, older

Older is the more general adjective. **Elder** is restricted in use to people, and is generally only used as an adjective in the context of family relationships, as in *an elder brother/sister.* It is always used before a noun or pronoun, or in **the elder.** **Elder** is not used in comparisons with **than**: *She is older* (not *elder*) *than me.*

elder[2] /'ɛldə(r)/ ▷ *noun* a kind of bush or small tree belonging to the same family as honeysuckle, with white flowers and purple-black or red berries. Ⓒ Anglo-Saxon *ellærn.*

elderberry ▷ *noun* the fruit of the ELDER[2].

elder hand and **eldest hand** ▷ *noun, cards* the player on the dealer's left, who leads in card-playing.

elderly /'ɛldəlɪ/ ▷ *adj* **1** rather old. **2** bordering on old age. **3** (**the elderly**) old people as a group (see THE 4b). • **elderliness** *noun.* Ⓒ 17c.

elder statesman ▷ *noun* an old and very experienced member of a group, especially a politician, whose opinions are respected.

eldest /'ɛldɪst/ ▷ *adj* oldest. ▷ *noun* someone who is the oldest of three or more.

El Dorado /ɛldə'rɑːdou/ ▷ *noun* (*plural* in sense 2 ***eldorados***) **1** the golden land or city, imagined by the Spanish explorers of America. **2** (*also* **eldorado**) any place where wealth is easy to accumulate. Ⓒ 16c: Spanish, literally 'the gilded place'.

eldritch /'ɛldrɪtʃ/ ▷ *adj, originally Scots* weird; uncanny.

elec. and **elect.** ▷ *abbreviation* **1** electric. **2** electricity.

elect /ɪ'lɛkt/ ▷ *verb* (***elected, electing***) **1** to choose someone to be an official or representative by voting. **2** to choose something by vote, in preference to other options. ▷ *adj* **1** *following its noun* elected to a position, but not yet formally occupying it □ ***president elect.*** **2** specially chosen. **3** *relig* chosen by God for salvation **4** (**the elect**) people chosen, for salvation or otherwise (see THE 4b). • **electability** *noun.* • **electable** *adj* capable of being elected, especially to political office. • **elected** *adj.* • **elect to do something** to do it by choice. Ⓒ 15c: from Latin *eligere, electum* to choose.

election /ɪ'lɛkʃən/ ▷ *noun* **1** the process or act of choosing people for office, especially political office, by taking a vote. See also GENERAL ELECTION. **2** the act of electing or choosing. **3** *theol* the exercise of God's will in the predetermination of certain people to salvation.

electioneer /ɪlɛkʃə'nɪə(r)/ ▷ *verb* (***electioneered, electioneering***) *intr* to work for the election of a candidate, especially in a political campaign. • **electioneering** *noun, adj.* Ⓒ 18c.

elective /ɪ'lɛktɪv/ ▷ *adj* **1** said of a position or office, etc: to which someone is appointed by election. **2** having the power to elect. **3** optional. ▷ *noun, medicine* an optional placement or course of study chosen by a student. • **electively** *adverb* by means of an election. • **electivity** *noun.*

elector /ɪ'lɛktə(r)/ ▷ *noun* **1** someone who has the right to vote at an election. **2** *US* a member of the ELECTORAL COLLEGE. **3** (**Elector**) *historical* a German prince or archbishop in the HOLY ROMAN EMPIRE who had the right to elect the emperor. • **electoral** *adj* **1** concerning or relating to elections or electors. **2** made up of electors. • **electorally** *adverb.*

electoral college ▷ *noun* in the US: the body of people who elect the President and Vice-President, having themselves been elected by popular vote.

electoral roll and **electoral register** ▷ *noun* the list of people in a particular area who are allowed to vote in local and general elections.

electorate /ɪ'lɛktərət/ ▷ *noun* all the electors of a city or country, etc.

Electra complex /ɪ'lɛktrə —/ ▷ *noun, psychol* the attachment of a daughter to her father, with hostility to her mother. Ⓒ Early 20c: from the Greek myth concerning Electra who helped to avenge the murder of her father by her mother.

electret /ɪ'lɛktrət/ ▷ *noun, elec* a permanently polarized dielectric material, or a piece of this. Ⓒ Late 19c: *electricity* + *magnet.*

electric /ɪ'lɛktrɪk/ ▷ *adj* **1** (*also* **electrical**) relating to, produced by, worked by or generating electricity. **2** said of a musical instrument: amplified electronically. **3** having or causing great excitement, tension or expectation. ▷ *plural noun* (**electrics**) **1** electrical appliances. **2** *colloq* wiring. • **electrically** *adverb.* Ⓒ 17c: from Greek *elektron* amber, which produces electricity when rubbed.

electrical charge see CHARGE (*noun* 7)

electrical conductivity see CONDUCTIVITY 1b

electrical conductor see CONDUCTOR 3

electrical engineering ▷ *noun* the branch of engineering concerned with the practical applications of electricity and magnetism. • **electrical engineer** *noun.*

electric arc ▷ *noun* a luminous space between electrodes when a current passes across.

electric battery ▷ *noun* a group of cells connected in series or in parallel for generating an electric current by chemical action.

electric blanket ▷ *noun* a blanket incorporating an electric element, used for warming a bed.

electric blue ▷ *noun* a vivid bright-blue colour.

electric chair ▷ *noun, US* **1** a chair used for executing criminals by sending a powerful electric current through them. **2** (*usually* **the electric chair**) execution by this means. ⓒ Late 19c.

electric charge ▷ *noun* a quantity of electricity that is either positive or negative, so that two like charges repel each other, whereas a positive charge and a negative charge attract each other.

electric contact see CONTACT 4

electric current ▷ *noun* the flow of electric charge, in the form of ELECTRONs, in the same direction through a conductor.

electric displacement ▷ *noun, physics* (abbreviation **D**) the charge per unit area that would be displaced across a layer of conductor placed across an ELECTRIC FIELD. It is measured in COULOMBS per square metre. Also called ELECTRIC FLUX DENSITY.

electric eel ▷ *noun* an eel-like fish, which is able to deliver electric shocks by means of an organ in its tail.

electric eye ▷ *noun, colloq* a PHOTOELECTRIC CELL, a light-sensitive device which, when the beam of light completing its circuit is broken, produces an electric current, eg in order to bring an alarm system into operation.

electric fence ▷ *noun* a wire fence with an electric current passing through it.

electric field ▷ *noun* a region surrounding an electrically charged particle, within which any other particles present will experience a force on them.

electric flux density see ELECTRIC DISPLACEMENT

electric guitar ▷ *noun* a guitar designed to be played through an electrical amplifier.

electrician /ɛlək'trɪʃən/ ▷ *noun* a person whose job is to install, maintain and repair electrical equipment.

electricity /ɛlək'trɪsɪtɪ/ ▷ *noun* **1** the energy which exists in a negative form in electrons and in a positive form in protons, and also as a flowing current usually of electrons. **2** an electric charge or current. **3** a supply of this energy to a household, etc, eg for heating and lighting. **4** the science or study of this energy. **5** excitement, tension or expectation. ⓒ 17c.

electric motor ▷ *noun* any device which converts electrical energy into mechanical energy.

electric organ ▷ *noun* **1** *music* an organ in which the sound is produced by electrical devices instead of wind. **2** *zool* in certain fishes: a structure that generates, stores and discharges electricity.

electric ray ▷ *noun* the TORPEDO fish.

electric shock see under SHOCK

electric shock therapy see under ELECTROCONVULSIVE THERAPY

electric storm ▷ *noun* a violent disturbance in the electric condition of the atmosphere.

electrification /ɪlɛktrɪfɪ'keɪʃən/ ▷ *noun* **1** the process of electrifying something. **2** installation of electricity.

electrify /ɪ'lɛktrɪfaɪ/ ▷ *verb* (*electrifies, electrified, electrifying*) **1** to give an electric charge to something. **2** to equip (eg a railway system) for the use of electricity as a power supply. **3** to cause great excitement in (eg a crowd). • **electrifying** *adj* extremely exciting. • **electrifyingly** *adverb*. ⓒ 18c.

electro /ɪ'lɛktroʊ/ ▷ *noun* (*electros*) *colloq* **1** an ELECTROPLATE. **2** ELECTROTYPE.

electro- /ɪlɛktroʊ, ɛlək'trɒ/ ▷ *combining form, denoting* **1** electricity. **2** ELECTROLYTIC. ⓒ From Greek *elektron* amber, which produces electricity when rubbed.

electroacoustics ▷ *plural noun* the technology of converting sound into electrical energy, and electrical energy into sound. • **electroacoustic** *adj* said of music: using both acoustic and computer-generated sound. ⓒ 1920s.

electrobiology ▷ *noun* the science of the electrical phenomena in living organisms. • **electrobiologist** *noun*. ⓒ 19c.

electrocardiogram ▷ *noun, medicine* (abbreviation **ECG**) the diagram or tracing produced by an electrocardiograph. ⓒ Early 20c.

electrocardiograph ▷ *noun, medicine* (abbreviation **ECG**) an apparatus which registers the electrical variations of the beating heart, as a diagram or tracing. • **electrocardiography** *noun*. ⓒ Early 20c.

electrochemistry ▷ *noun* the study of the relation between electricity and chemical change. • **electrochemical** *adj*. • **electrochemist** *noun*. ⓒ 19c.

electroconvulsive therapy ▷ *noun, medicine* (abbreviation **ECT**) the treatment of mental illness by passing small electric currents through the brain. Also called **electric shock therapy** or **shock therapy** or **shock treatment**. ⓒ 1940s.

electrocute /ɪ'lɛktrəkjuːt/ ▷ *verb* (*electrocuted, electrocuting*) **1** to kill someone or something by electric shock. **2** to carry out a death sentence on someone by means of electricity. • **electrocution** *noun*. ⓒ 19c: from ELECTRO-, modelled on EXECUTE.

electrode /ɪ'lɛktroʊd/ ▷ *noun, technical* either of the two conducting points by which electric current enters or leaves a battery or other electrical apparatus. ⓒ 19c.

electrodeposition ▷ *noun* deposition of a layer of metal by ELECTROLYSIS.

electrodynamics ▷ *singular noun* the study of electricity in motion, or of the interaction of currents and currents, or currents and magnets.

electrodynamometer ▷ *noun* an instrument for measuring currents by the attraction or repulsion between current-bearing coils.

electroencephalogram ▷ *noun, medicine* (abbreviation **EEG**) a diagram or tracing produced by an electroencephalograph. ⓒ 1930s.

electroencephalograph ▷ *noun, medicine* (abbreviation **EEG**) an apparatus which registers the electrical activity of the brain, as a diagram or tracing. • **electroencephalography** *noun*. ⓒ 1930s.

electrolyse and (*US*) **electrolyze** /ɪ'lɛktrəlaɪz/ ▷ *verb* (*electrolysed, electrolysing*) **1** to subject something to ELECTROLYSIS. **2** to break something up by electric means.

electrolysis /ɛlək'trɒlɪsɪs/ ▷ *noun* **1** *chem* the decomposition of a chemical in the form of a liquid or solution by passing an electric current through it. **2** the removal of tumours or hair roots by means of an electric current. ⓒ 19c.

electrolyte /ɪ'lɛktroʊlaɪt/ ▷ *noun, chem* a solution of chemical salts which can conduct electricity, eg in a battery. ⓒ 19c: from ELECTRO- + Greek *lytos* released.

electrolytic /ɪlɛktroʊ'lɪtɪk/ ▷ *adj* relating to or involving ELECTROLYSIS. • **electrolytically** *adverb*.

electrolytic cell ▷ *noun, chem* a cell in which an externally applied voltage causes a non-spontaneous change to occur, such as the breakdown of water into hydrogen and oxygen.

electromagnet *physics* ▷ *noun* a piece of soft metal, usually iron, made magnetic by the passage of an electric current through a coil of wire wrapped around the metal. • **electromagnetic** *adj* having electrical and magnetic properties. • **electromagnetism** *noun* **1** magnetic forces produced by electricity. **2** the relations between and the properties of magnetism and electric currents. **3** the science dealing with this subject. ⓒ 19c.

electromagnetic theory ▷ *noun, physics* the theory explaining light in terms of electromagnetic waves.

electromagnetic unit ▷ *noun, physics* any unit, such as the abampere or abvolt, in a cgs system of units based on the magnetic forces exerted by electric currents.

electromagnetic wave ▷ *noun, physics* a travelling disturbance in space produced by the acceleration of an electric charge.

electrometer /ɛlɛk'trɒmɪtə(r)/ ▷ *noun* an instrument for measuring difference of electric potential. • **electrometric** or **electrometrical** *adj.* • **electrometry** *noun* the science of electrical measurements. ⓒ 18c.

electromotive ▷ *adj, physics* producing or tending to produce an electric current.

electromotive force ▷ *noun, physics* the energy which forces a current to flow in an electrical circuit. Also called **electromotance**.

electron /ɪ'lɛktrɒn/ ▷ *noun, physics* a particle, present in all atoms, which has a negative electric charge and is responsible for carrying electricity in solids. ⓒ 19c.

electronegative ▷ *adj* carrying a negative charge, tending to form negative ions. • **electronegativity** *noun* **1** an electronegative state. **2** the power of an atom to attract electrons. ⓒ Early 19c.

electron gun ▷ *noun* the assembly of electrodes in a cathode ray tube which produces the electron beam. ⓒ 1930s.

electronic /ɛlək'trɒnɪk/ ▷ *adj* **1** operated by means of electrical circuits, usually several very small ones, which handle very low levels of electric current. **2** produced or operated, etc, using electronic apparatus. **3** concerned with electronics. • **electronically** *adverb.* ⓒ Early 20c.

electronic flash ▷ *noun* **1** an extremely intense and brief flash for high-speed photography, produced by passing an electric charge through a gas-filled tube. **2** the apparatus for producing this.

electronic funds transfer at point of sale ▷ *noun* (abbreviation **EFTPOS**) a retail payment system which allows the direct transfer of money from the customer's bank account to that of the retailer without the use of cash or cheques.

electronic mail see under E-MAIL

electronic mailbox ▷ *noun* a section of a central computer's memory reserved for a particular individual, into which messages can be directed.

electronic music ▷ *noun* music made by arranging sounds previously generated in the laboratory and recorded on tape.

electronic news gathering see ENG

electronic point of sale ▷ *noun* (abbreviation **EPOS**) *commerce* a computerized till system at retail checkouts which links tills that have bar-code readers to a stock control system.

electronic publishing ▷ *noun* the publishing of computer-readable texts on disk, CD-ROM, CD-I, etc. ⓒ 1970s.

electronics ▷ *singular noun* the science that deals with the study of the behaviour of electronic circuits and their applications in machines, etc. ▷ *plural noun* the electronic parts of a machine or system. ⓒ Early 20c.

electronic tagging ▷ *noun* the use of electronic tags (see TAG[1] 2).

electron microscope ▷ *noun* a microscope which operates using a beam of electrons rather than a beam of light, and is capable of very high magnification.

electron probe ▷ *noun* an X-ray device that bombards the specimen under examination with a very narrow beam of electrons, allowing non-destructive analysis.

electron tube ▷ *noun* an electronic device in which the electron conduction is in a vacuum or gas inside a gas-tight enclosure, eg a THERMIONIC VALVE.

electronvolt ▷ *noun, nuclear physics* a unit of energy equal to that acquired by an electron when accelerated by a potential of one volt.

electro-optics ▷ *singular noun* the study of the effects that an electric field has on light crossing it. • **electro-optic** or **electro-optical** *adj.*

electro-osmosis ▷ *noun* movement of liquid, under an applied electric field, through a fine tube or membrane.

electrophile ▷ *noun* an electrophilic substance. • **electrophilic** *adj* having or involving an affinity for electrons, ie negative charge, electron-seeking.

electrophoresis *chem* ▷ *noun* migration of suspended particles, such as protein macromolecules, under the influence of an electric field. • **electrophoretic** *adj.* ⓒ Early 20c.

electrophorus /ɪlɛk'trɒfərəs/ ▷ *noun* an instrument for obtaining static electricity by means of induction. ⓒ 18c.

electroplate ▷ *verb* to coat (an object) with metal, especially silver, by electrolysis. ▷ *noun* articles coated in this way. • **electroplated** *adj.* • **electroplating** *noun.* ⓒ 19c.

electroscope ▷ *noun* an instrument for detecting the presence of electricity in a body, and the nature of it. • **electroscopic** *adj.* ⓒ Early 19c.

electroshock ▷ *noun* an electric shock.

electrostatic ▷ *adj* concerning or relating to electricity at rest.

electrostatics ▷ *singular noun* the branch of science concerned with electricity at rest.

electrostatic unit ▷ *noun* any unit, such as the statvolt, in a cgs system of units based on the forces of repulsion existing between static electric charges.

electrotechnics and **electrotechnology** ▷ *singular noun* the technology of electricity.

electrotherapeutics and **electrotherapy** ▷ *noun* treatment of disease by electricity.

electrotype ▷ *noun* **1** a printing plate made by electrolytically coating a mould with copper. **2** a facsimile of a coin made by this process. ⓒ 19c.

electrovalency ▷ *noun* union within a chemical compound achieved by transfer of electrons, the resulting ions being held together by electrostatic attraction. • **electrovalent** *adj.* ⓒ 1920s.

electuary /ɪ'lɛktjʊərɪ/ ▷ *noun* (***electuaries***) a medicine mixed with honey or syrup. See also ELIXIR 3. ⓒ 14c: from Latin *electuarium*.

elegant /'ɛlɪgənt/ ▷ *adj* **1** having or showing good taste in dress or style, combined with dignity and gracefulness. **2** said of a movement: graceful. **3** said of apparatus, work in science, a plan, etc: simple and ingenious. • **elegance** *noun.* • **elegancy** *noun.* • **elegantly** *adverb.* ⓒ 16c: from Latin *elegans, elegantis*.

elegiac /ɛlə'dʒaɪək/ ▷ *adj, formal, literary* **1** mournful or thoughtful. **2** like an elegy. **3** used in elegies, especially applied to classical verse in couplets of hexameter and pentameter lines (called **elegiac couplets**) or to English verse in stanzas of four iambic pentameters rhyming alternately (called **elegiac stanzas**). ▷ *plural noun* **(elegiacs)** elegiac verse. • **elegiacal** *adj.* • **elegiacally** *adverb.*

elegize or **elegise** /'ɛlədʒaɪz/ ▷ *verb* (*elegized, elegizing*) *formal or literary* **1** *tr & intr* to write an elegy about someone or something. **2** *intr* to produce mournful or thoughtful writings or songs. ⓒ 18c.

elegy /'ɛlədʒɪ/ ▷ *noun* (*elegies*) **1** a mournful or thoughtful song or poem, especially one whose subject is death or loss. **2** a poem written in elegiac metre. • **elegist** *noun* a person who writes elegies. ⓒ 16c: from Latin *elegia*, from Greek *elegos* a lament.

element /'ɛləmənt/ ▷ *noun* **1** a part of anything; a component or feature. **2** *chem, physics* any one of 105 known substances that cannot be split by chemical means into simpler substances. **3** *sometimes derog* a person or small group within a larger group. **4** a slight amount. **5** the wire coil through which an electric current is passed to produce heat in various electrical appliances. **6** any one of the four basic substances (earth, air, fire and water) from which, according to ancient philosophy, everything is formed. **7** (**the elements**) weather conditions, especially when severe. **8** (**the elements**) basic facts or skills. **9** (**the elements**) *Christianity* bread and wine as the representation of the body and blood of Christ in the Eucharist. • **elemental** /ɛlə'mɛntəl/ *adj* **1** basic or primitive. **2** referring or relating to the forces of nature, especially the four elements (earth, air, fire and water). **3** immense; referring to the power of a force of nature. • **in one's element** in the surroundings that one finds most natural and enjoyable. ⓒ 13c: from Latin *elementum.*

elementary /ɛlə'mɛntərɪ/ ▷ *adj* **1** dealing with simple or basic facts; rudimentary. **2** belonging or relating to the elements or an element.

elementary particle ▷ *noun, chem, physics* any of the twenty or more particles (eg ELECTRONs, PROTONs and NEUTRONs) which make up an atom.

elementary school ▷ *noun, N Amer, especially US* primary school.

elemi /'ɛlɪmɪ/ ▷ *noun* a fragrant resinous substance obtained from various tropical trees, used especially in varnishes and inks. ⓒ 16c.

elephant /'ɛləfənt/ ▷ *noun* (*elephants* or *elephant*) the largest living land animal, with thick greyish skin, a nose in the form of a long hanging trunk, and two curved tusks, surviving in two species, the **African elephant** having larger ears and a flatter head than the **Asian elephant** which is usually called the **Indian elephant**. See also PINK ELEPHANT, WHITE ELEPHANT. • **elephantoid** /ɛlə'fantɔɪd/ *adj* elephant-like. ⓒ 14c as *olifans*: from Latin *elephantus*, from Greek *elephas.*

elephant cord ▷ *noun* thick wide-ribbed corduroy.

elephantiasis /ɛləfən'taɪəsɪs/ ▷ *noun, pathol* a disease, occurring mainly in the tropics, which is a complication of FILARIASIS, in which the skin becomes thicker and the limbs become greatly enlarged. ⓒ 16c.

elephantine /ɛlə'fantaɪn/ ▷ *adj* **1** belonging to, or like, an elephant. **2** huge. **3** said of memory: reliable and extensive. **4** *derog* large and awkward; not graceful. ⓒ 17c.

elephant seal ▷ *noun* either of the two largest species of seals, the males of which have large snouts.

elephant's ears or **elephant's ear** ▷ *noun, bot* any of various BEGONIAS or varieties of ornamental ARUM with heart-shaped leaves.

elevate /'ɛləveɪt/ ▷ *verb* (*elevated, elevating*) **1** to raise or lift. **2** to give a higher rank or status to someone or something. **3** to improve (a person's mind, etc) morally or intellectually. **4** to make someone more cheerful. • **elevating** *adj* improving the mind; morally uplifting. • **elevatory** *adj.* ⓒ 15c: from Latin *elevare.*

elevated ▷ *adj* **1** said of a rank or position, etc: very high; important. **2** said of thoughts or ideas, etc: intellectually advanced or very moral. **3** said of land or buildings: raised above the level of their surroundings. **4** cheerful; elated. **5** *colloq* slightly drunk. ▷ *noun, US* an ELEVATED RAILROAD.

elevated railroad ▷ *noun, US* a raised railway over a roadway. Also called **el**, **L**.

elevation ▷ *noun* **1** the act of elevating or state of being elevated. **2** *technical* height, eg of a place above sea-level. **3** *technical* a drawing or diagram of one side of a building, machine, etc. **4** *formal* a high place. **5** *ballet* a leap with apparent suspension in the air.

elevator ▷ *noun* **1** *N Amer, especially US* a LIFT (*noun* 4). **2** a person or thing that ELEVATES. **3** *chiefly N Amer, especially US* a tall building in which grain is stored. **4** a lift or machine for transporting goods to a higher level, eg bales up into a barn or corn up into a store, etc. **5** *aeronautics* a movable control surface or surfaces at the tail of an aeroplane, by which it is made to climb and dive. **6** *anatomy* a muscle which lifts part of the body.

elevatory see under ELEVATE

eleven /ɪ'lɛvən/ ▷ *noun* **1 a** the cardinal number 11; **b** the quantity that this represents, being one more than ten. **2** any symbol for this, eg **11**, **XI**. **3** the age of eleven. **4** something, eg a garment or a person, whose size is denoted by the number 11. **5** the eleventh hour after midnight or midday □ *Come at eleven* □ *11 o'clock* □ *11pm*. **6 a**) a set or group of eleven people or things; **b** *football, cricket, hockey, etc* a team of players. **7** a score of eleven points. ▷ *adj* **1** totalling eleven. **2** aged eleven. • **at the eleventh hour** at the last possible moment; only just in time. ⓒ Anglo-Saxon *endleofan.*

eleven-plus ▷ *noun, education* in the UK: an examination formerly taken at the age of 11 or 12 to determine which sort of secondary school a pupil will attend. ⓒ 1930s.

elevenses /ɪ'lɛvnzɪz/ ▷ *plural noun* (*often used with singular verb*) *colloq* a snack, usually consisting of coffee, tea, biscuits, etc, taken at about eleven o'clock in the morning. ⓒ 19c.

eleventh (often written **11th**) ▷ *adj* **1** in counting: **a** next after tenth; **b** last of eleven. **2** in eleventh position. **3** (**the eleventh**) **a** the eleventh day of the month; **b** *golf* the eleventh hole. ▷ *noun* **1** one of eleven equal parts. Also *as adj* □ *an eleventh share.* 2 a FRACTION equal to one divided by eleven (usually written $^1/_{11}$). **3** a person coming eleventh, eg in a race or an exam □ *He finished a bedraggled eleventh.* ⓒ Anglo-Saxon; see ELEVEN + -TH[1].

elf ▷ *noun* (*elves* /ɛlvz/) **1** *folklore* a tiny supernatural being with a human form, with a tendency to play tricks. **2** a mischievous child. • **elfish** or **elvish** *adj.* ⓒ Anglo-Saxon *ælf.*

elf-child ▷ *noun* a child supposed to have been left by elves in place of one stolen by them.

elfin /'ɛlfɪn/ *adj* **1** said of physical features, etc: small and delicate. **2** like an elf; small and mischievous, but charming.

elicit /ɪ'lɪsɪt/ ▷ *verb* (*elicited, eliciting*) to cause something to happen; to bring something out into the open. • **elicitation** *noun.* ⓒ 17c: from Latin *elicere, elicitum.*

■ **elicit something from someone** to succeed in getting information from them, usually with some effort or difficulty.

elide /ɪ'laɪd/ ▷ *verb* (*elided, eliding*) **1** *grammar* to omit (a vowel or syllable) at the beginning or end of a word. **2** to omit (a part of anything). See also ELISION. ⓒ 16c: from Latin *elidere* to strike out.

eligible /'ɛlɪdʒəbəl/ ▻ *adj* **1** suitable, or deserving to be chosen (for a job, as a husband, etc). **2** having a right to something □ *eligible for compensation.* • **eligibility** *noun* the status of being eligible or suitable. • **eligibly** *adverb.* ⓘ 15c: from Latin *eligere* to select.

eliminate /ɪ'lɪmɪneɪt/ ▻ *verb* (***eliminated, eliminating***) **1** to get rid of or exclude. **2** to expel (waste matter) from the body. **3** to exclude someone or something from a later part of a competition by defeat in an earlier part. **4** *slang* to kill or murder someone. • **eliminable** *adj.* • **elimination** *noun.* • **eliminator** *noun* someone or something that eliminates, eg the first round of a competition. ⓘ 16c: from Latin *eliminare* to put out of the house, from *e* from + *limen* a threshold.

elision /ɪ'lɪʒən/ ▻ *noun, grammar* the omission of a vowel or syllable, as in *I'm* and *we're*. See also ELIDE. ⓘ 16c: from Latin *elidere, elisum* to strike out.

elite or **élite** /ɛ'li:t/ ▻ *noun* **1** the best, most important or most powerful people within society. **2** the best of a group or profession. **3** in typewriting: a size of type, twelve characters per inch. ▻ *adj* best, most important or most powerful. ⓘ 18c: French, from Latin *eligere* to choose.

elitism ▻ *noun* **1** the belief in the need for a powerful social elite. **2** the belief in the natural social superiority of some people. **3** *often derog* awareness of, or pride in, belonging to an elite group in society. ⓘ 1940s.

elitist or **élitist** /ɛ'li:tɪst/ ▻ *noun* a supporter of elitism. ▻ *adj* favouring or creating an elite.

elixir /ɪ'lɪksə(r)/ ▻ *noun* **1** in medieval times: a liquid chemical preparation believed to have the power to give people everlasting life or to turn base metals into gold. **2** any medical preparation which is claimed to cure all illnesses; a panacea. **3** *pharmacol* a liquid solution containing medicine and something, especially honey or alcohol, to hide the unpleasant taste. ⓘ 14c: from Arabic *al-iksir* the philosopher's stone.

Elizabethan /ɪlɪzə'bi:θən/ ▻ *adj* relating to or typical of the reign of Queen Elizabeth, especially Queen Elizabeth I of England (1558–1603). ▻ *noun* a person living during this time.

elk ▻ *noun* (***elks*** or ***elk***) **1** in Europe and Asia: the MOOSE. **2** *N Amer* the WAPITI. ⓘ Probably Anglo-Saxon *elh*.

ellipse /ɪ'lɪps/ ▻ *noun, geom* a regular oval, as formed by a diagonal cut through a cone above the base. ⓘ 18c: from Latin *ellipsis*, from Greek *elleipsis* omission.

ellipsis /ɪ'lɪpsɪs/ ▻ *noun* (***ellipses*** /-si:z/) **1** *grammar* a figure of speech in which a word or words needed for the sense or grammar are omitted but understood. **2** in text: a set of three dots (...) that indicate the omission of a word or words, eg in a lengthy quotation. ⓘ 16c: Latin, from Greek *elleipein* to fall short.

ellipsoid /ɪ'lɪpsɔɪd/ ▻ *noun, geom* a surface or solid object of which every plane section is an ellipse or a circle. • **ellipsoidal** *adj.*

elliptical /ɪ'lɪptɪkəl/ or **elliptic** ▻ *adj* **1** *math* relating to, or having the shape of, an ELLIPSE. **2** said of speech or writing: **a** containing an ELLIPSIS; **b** so concise as to be unclear or ambiguous. • **elliptically** *adverb.* ⓘ 17c.

elm ▻ *noun* **1** (*also* **elm tree**) any of various tall deciduous trees with broad serrated leaves and clusters of small flowers which develop into winged fruits. **2** (*also* **elmwood**) the hard heavy wood of these trees. ▻ *adj* made of elm. ⓘ Anglo-Saxon.

elocution /ɛlə'kju:ʃən/ ▻ *noun* the art of speaking clearly and effectively. • **elocutionary** *adj.* • **elocutionist** *noun* a teacher of, or an expert in, elocution. ⓘ 15c: from Latin *eloqui, elocutus* to speak out.

elongate /'i:lɒŋgeɪt/ ▻ *verb* (***elongated, elongating***) to lengthen or stretch something out. • **elongated** *adj* long and narrow. • **elongation** *noun.* ⓘ 16c: from Latin *elongare*.

elope /ɪ'loʊp/ ▻ *verb* (***eloped, eloping***) *intr* to run away secretly, especially with a lover in order to get married. • **elopement** *noun.* • **eloper** *noun.* ⓘ 16c, probably as *alopen*: from French *aloper*.

eloquence /'ɛləkwəns/ ▻ *noun* **1** the art or power of using speech to impress, move or persuade. **2** persuasive, fine and effectual language. ⓘ 14c: French, from Latin *eloqui* to speak out.

eloquent /'ɛləkwənt/ ▻ *adj* having or showing eloquence. • **eloquently** *adverb.*

Elsan /'ɛlsan/ ▻ *noun, trademark* a type of portable chemical lavatory. ⓘ 1924: from *E L* Jackson, the manufacturer + *san*itation.

else /ɛls/ ▻ *adverb, adj* different from or in addition to something or someone known or already mentioned □ *I'd like something else* □ *Where else can you buy it?* • **or else 1** or if not ... ; otherwise ... □ *Hurry up, or else we'll be late.* **2** *colloq* or I will punish or harm you; or there will be trouble □ *Give me the money, or else!* ⓘ Anglo-Saxon *elles*.

elsewhere ▻ *adverb* somewhere else.

ELT ▻ *abbreviation* English Language Teaching.

eluate see under ELUTE

elucidate /ɪ'lu:sɪdeɪt/ ▻ *verb* (***elucidated, elucidating***) to make clear or explain; to shed light on something. • **elucidation** *noun.* • **elucidative** or **elucidatory** *adj.* • **elucidator** *noun.* ⓘ 16c: from Latin *elucidare*, from *lucidus* clear.

elude /ɪ'lu:d/ ▻ *verb* (***eluded, eluding***) **1** to escape or avoid something by quickness or cleverness. **2** to fail to be understood, discovered or remembered by someone. ⓘ 16c: from Latin *eludere*.

elusive /ɪ'lu:sɪv/ ▻ *adj* **1** difficult to find or catch. **2** difficult to understand or remember. **3** avoiding the issue or the question. • **elusively** *adverb.* • **elusiveness** *noun.* ⓘ 18c: from ELUDE.

elute /ɪ'lu:t/ ▻ *verb* (***eluted, eluting***) *technical* to wash out (a substance) by using a solvent. • **eluant** or **eluent** /'ɛljʊənt/ *noun* a liquid used for elution. • **eluate** /'ɛljʊeɪt/ *noun* a liquid obtained by eluting. ⓘ 18c: from Latin *eluere, elutum*, from *luere* to wash.

elutriate /ɪ'lu:trɪeɪt/ ▻ *verb* (***elutriated, elutriating***) *chem engineering* to separate something by washing it into coarser and finer portions. • **elutriation** *noun.* • **elutriator** *noun* an apparatus for elutriating. ⓘ 18c: from Latin *elutriare* to wash out.

elver /'ɛlvə(r)/ ▻ *noun* a young eel. ⓘ 17c: a variant of obsolete *eelfare*, literally 'eel journey', a reference to the migration of young eels upstream.

elves *plural of* ELF

elvish see under ELF

Elysium /ɪ'lɪzɪəm/ ▻ *noun* **1** *Greek mythol* the place where the blessed were supposed to rest after death. **2** *poetic* a state or place of perfect happiness. • **Elysian** *adj* characteristic of the happiness associated with Elysium. ⓘ 16c: Latin, from Greek *elysion*.

elytron /'ɛlɪtrən/ and **elytrum** /-trəm/ ▻ *noun* (*plural* ***elytra***) *zool* a beetle's forewing modified to form a case for the hindwing. ⓘ 18c: Greek, meaning 'a sheath'.

em /ɛm/ ▻ *noun, printing* the unit of measurement, based on the 12-point lower-case 'm', used in spacing material, and in estimating dimensions of pages. ⓘ Early 19c.

em- /ɛm, ɪm/ ▻ *prefix* a form of EN- used before *b, m* and *p*.

'em /əm/ ▻ *pronoun, colloq* them. ⓘ Anglo-Saxon *hem* them.

emaciate /ɪ'meɪsɪət/ ▻ *verb* (***emaciated, emaciating***) to make (a person or animal) extremely thin, especially through illness or starvation, etc. • **emaciated** *adj.* • **emaciation** *noun* extreme leanness or wasting of the body caused by malnutrition, parasitic infestation or disease. ⓒ 17c: from Latin *emaciare*, from *maciare* to make lean.

e-mail, **email** or **E-mail** /ˈiː—/ ▷ *noun* (*in full* **electronic mail**) **1** a system for transmitting messages and computer files electronically from one computer to another, eg within an office computer network, over THE INTERNET, etc. **2** correspondence sent in this way. ▷ *verb* (***e-mailed***, ***e-mailing***) to send someone an electronic message.

emanate /ˈɛmәneɪt/ ▷ *verb* (***emanated***, ***emanating***) *intr* **1** said of an idea, etc: to emerge or originate. **2** said of light or gas, etc: to flow; to issue. ⓒ 18c: from Latin *emanare*, *emanatum* to flow out.

emanation ▷ *noun* **1** the process of emanating or originating from something else. **2** something that issues or proceeds from something else. **3** radon.

emancipate /ɪˈmansɪpeɪt/ ▷ *verb* (***emancipated***, ***emancipating***) to set someone free from slavery, or from some other social or political restraint. • **emancipated** *adj*. • **emancipation** *noun*. • **emancipator** *noun*. ⓒ 17c: from Latin *emancipare*, *emancipatum* to give independence to (one's child or wife), from *mancipare* to transfer property.

emasculate /ɪˈmaskjʊleɪt/ ▷ *verb* (***emasculated***, ***emasculating***) **1** to reduce the force, strength or effectiveness of someone or something. **2** to castrate (a man or male animal). • **emasculated** *adj*. • **emasculation** *noun*. ⓒ 17c: from Latin *e-* away + *masculus*, diminutive of *mas* male.

embalm /ɛmˈbɑːm/ ▷ *verb* (***embalmed***, ***embalming***) **1** to preserve (a dead body) from decay, originally with oils and spices, but now by treatment with chemicals or drugs. **2** to preserve something unchanged; to keep (eg a memory) from obscurity. **3** to impregnate with balm; to perfume. • **embalmer** *noun*. • **embalmment** *noun*. ⓒ 14c as *enbaume*: from French *embaumer*, from *basme* balm.

embankment /ɪmˈbaŋkmәnt/ ▷ *noun* **1** a bank or wall of earth made to enclose a waterway. **2** a mound built to carry a road or railway over a low-lying place. **3** a slope of grass, earth, etc on either side of a road or railway.

embargo /ɛmˈbɑːgoʊ/ ▷ *noun* (***embargoes***) **1** an official order forbidding something, especially trade with another country. **2** the resulting stoppage, especially of trade. **3** any restriction or prohibition. ▷ *verb* (***embargoes***, ***embargoed***, ***embargoing***) **1** to place something under an embargo. **2** to take something for use by the state. ⓒ 16c: from Spanish *embargar* to impede or restrain.

embark /ɛmˈbɑːk/ ▷ *verb* (***embarked***, ***embarking***) *tr & intr* to go or put on board ship or an aircraft □ *embark for America*. • **embarkation** *noun*. ⓒ 16c as *embarque*: from French *embarquer*.

■ **embark on** or **upon something** to begin (a task, especially a lengthy one).

embarrass /ɪmˈbarәs/ ▷ *verb* (***embarrasses***, ***embarrassed***, ***embarrassing***) **1** *tr & intr* to make someone feel, or become anxious, self-conscious or ashamed. **2** to confuse or perplex. • **embarrassed** *adj*. • **be embarrassed** to be in financial difficulties. ⓒ 17c, meaning 'to impede': from French *embarrasser*.

embarrassing ▷ *adj* said of an incident or remark, etc: causing awkwardness or self-consciousness. • **embarrassingly** *adverb*.

embarrassment ▷ *noun* **1** self-conscious awkwardness. **2** something which causes embarrassment □ *He's an embarrassment to all of us*. **3** difficulties in money matters. **4** a confusing amount □ *an embarrassment of riches to choose from*.

embassy /ˈɛmbәsɪ/ ▷ *noun* (***embassies***) **1** the official residence of an ambassador. **2** an ambassador and their staff. **3** a diplomatic mission to a foreign country. ⓒ 16c: from French *ambassee*.

embattled /ɪmˈbatәld/ ▷ *adj* **1** troubled by problems or difficulties; engaged in a struggle. **2** prepared for battle. ⓒ 15c in sense 2: from French *embataillier* to prepare or arm for battle.

embed or **imbed** /ɪmˈbɛd/ ▷ *verb* (***embedded***, ***embedding***; ***imbedded***, ***imbedding***) to set or fix something firmly and deeply. ⓒ 18c.

embellish /ɪmˈbɛlɪʃ/ ▷ *verb* (***embellishes***, ***embellished***, ***embellishing***) **1** to make (a story, etc) more interesting by adding details which may not be true. **2** to beautify something with decoration. • **embellished** *adj*. • **embellishment** *noun*. ⓒ 14c: from French *embellir* to make beautiful.

ember /ˈɛmbә(r)/ ▷ *noun* **1** a piece of glowing or smouldering coal or wood. **2** (**embers**) red-hot ash; the smouldering remains of a fire. **3** (**embers**) *literary* what remains of a once-strong feeling. ⓒ Anglo-Saxon *æmerge*.

embezzle /ɪmˈbɛzәl/ ▷ *verb* (***embezzled***, ***embezzling***) to take or use dishonestly (money or property with which one has been entrusted). • **embezzlement** *noun*. • **embezzler** *noun*. ⓒ 15c: from French *embesiler* to make away with.

embitter /ɪmˈbɪtә(r)/ ▷ *verb* (***embittered***, ***embittering***) **1** to make someone feel bitter. **2** to make someone more bitter or a difficult situation worse. • **embittered** *adj*. • **embitterment** *noun*. ⓒ 17c.

emblazon /ɪmˈbleɪzәn/ ▷ *verb* (***emblazoned***, ***emblazoning***) **1** to decorate with a coat of arms or some other bright design. **2** to display in a very obvious or striking way. • **emblazonment** *noun* decoration or display, especially heraldic. ⓒ 16c: from French *blason* shield.

emblem /ˈɛmblәm/ ▷ *noun* an object chosen to represent an idea, a quality, a country, etc. • **emblematic** *adj* **1** in the nature of an emblem. **2** serving as an emblem. • **emblematically** *adverb*. ⓒ 15c: from Greek *emblema* something inserted.

embodiment /ɪmˈbɒdɪmәnt/ ▷ *noun* **1** a typical example or representative of something □ *the embodiment of evil*. **2** something in which something else is embodied. **3** the act of embodying.

embody ▷ *verb* (***embodies***, ***embodied***, ***embodying***) **1** to be an expression or a representation of something in words, actions or form; to typify or personify. **2** to include or incorporate. ⓒ 16c, meaning 'to put into a body'.

embolden /ɪmˈboʊldәn/ ▷ *verb* (***emboldened***, ***emboldening***) **1** to make someone bold; to encourage. **2** *printing* to set in bold type. ⓒ 15c.

embolism /ˈɛmbәlɪzәm/ ▷ *noun*, *pathol* the blocking of a blood vessel by an air bubble, a blood clot or a fragment of tissue, etc. ⓒ 14c: from Greek *embolismos*, from *emballein* to insert.

embolus /ˈɛmbәlәs/ ▷ *noun* (*plural* ***emboli*** /-laɪ/) *pathol* any obstruction in a blood vessel, especially a blood clot. ⓒ 19c: from Greek *embolos* a stopper.

emboss /ɪmˈbɒs/ ▷ *verb* (***embosses***, ***embossed***, ***embossing***) to carve or mould a raised design on (a surface). ⓒ 14c: from French *embocer*, from *boce* a BOSS².

embossed ▷ *adj* **1** carved or moulded with a raised design. **2** *bot* having a protuberance in the centre.

embouchure /ɒmbuːˈʃʊә(r)/ ▷ *noun* **1** the mouth of a river. **2** *music* **a** the positioning of the lips and tongue when playing a wind instrument; **b** the mouthpiece of a wind instrument. ⓒ 18c: French, from *bouche* mouth.

embrace /ɪmˈbreɪs/ ▷ *verb* (***embraced***, ***embracing***) **1** to hold someone closely in the arms, affectionately or as a greeting. **2** *intr* said of two people: to hold each other closely in the arms, affectionately or as a greeting. **3** to take (eg an opportunity) eagerly, or accept (eg a religion) wholeheartedly. **4** to include. ▷ *noun* **1** an act of embracing. **2** a loving hug. ⓘ 14c: from French *embracer*, from Latin *bracchium* arm.

embrasure /ɛm'breɪʒə(r)/ ▷ *noun* **1** an opening in the wall of a castle, etc for shooting through. **2** an opening in a thick wall for a door or window, with angled sides which make it narrower on the outside. **3** the sloping of these sides. ⓘ 18c: from French *embraser* to splay.

embrocation /ɛmbroʊ'keɪʃən/ ▷ *noun* **1** a lotion for rubbing into the skin, eg as a treatment for sore or pulled muscles. **2** the act of rubbing in such lotion. ⓘ 16c in sense 2: from Greek *embroche* lotion.

embroider /ɪm'brɔɪdə(r)/ ▷ *verb* (***embroidered***, ***embroidering***) **1** to decorate (cloth) with sewn designs. **2** to make (a story, etc) more interesting by adding details, usually untrue ones. • **embroiderer** *noun*. ⓘ 15c: from French *embroder*.

embroidery ▷ *noun* (***embroideries***) **1** the art or practice of sewing designs on to cloth. **2** decorative needlework. **3** articles decorated with this work. **4** *derog* gaudy decoration. **5** the addition of details, usually false ones, to a story, etc.

embroil /ɪm'brɔɪl/ ▷ *verb* (***embroiled***, ***embroiling***) **1** to involve in a dispute or argument. **2** to throw into a state of confusion. • **embroilment** *noun* embroiling; uproar; commotion. ⓘ 17c: from French *embrouiller* to throw into confusion.

■ **embroil someone in something** to involve them in (a quarrel or a difficult situation).

embryo /'ɛmbrɪoʊ/ ▷ *noun* (***embryos***) *biol* **1** in animals: the developing young organism until hatching or birth. **2** in humans: the developing young organism during the first seven weeks after conception (compare FETUS). **3** a plant in its earliest stages of development between fertilization and germination. **4** anything in its earliest stages. ⓘ 16c: from Greek *embryon*, from *bryein* to swell.

embryology ▷ *noun* the science which studies the formation and development of embryos. • **embryological** *adj*. • **embryologist** *noun*. ⓘ 19c.

embryonic /ɛmbrɪ'ɒnɪk/ ▷ *adj* in an early stage of development; rudimentary.

embryo transfer ▷ *noun* (abbreviation **ET**) surgical transfer of the young embryo into the uterus, a technique used in the treatment of infertility.

embus /ɛm'bʌs/ ▷ *verb* (***embusses***, ***embussed***, ***embussing***) **1** to put (troops) onto a bus. **2** *intr* to board a bus. ⓘ Early 20c.

emcee /ɛm'siː/ ▷ *noun* (***emcees***) a master of ceremonies. ▷ *verb* (***emceed***, ***emceeing***) *tr & intr* (*also* **emcee for** or **at something**) to act as master of ceremonies (at (an event). ⓘ 1930s: phonetic representation of MC.

emend /ɪ'mɛnd/ ▷ *verb* (***emended***, ***emending***) to edit (a text), removing errors and making improvements. Compare AMEND. • **emendation** *noun* **1** a change or correction, especially to a text. **2** making a correction or changes to a text. ⓘ 18c; 15c in obsolete sense 'to free a person from faults': from Latin *emendare*, from *e* out + *mendum* a fault.

emend

See Usage Note at **amend**.

emerald /'ɛmərəld/ ▷ *noun* **1** a deep green variety of BERYL, highly valued as a gemstone. **2** (*also* **emerald green**) its colour. ⓘ 13c as *emeraude*: from French *esmeralde*, from Greek *smaragdos*.

emerge /ɪ'mɜːdʒ/ ▷ *verb* (***emerged***, ***emerging***) *intr* **1** to come out from hiding or into view. **2** to become known or apparent. **3** to survive a difficult or dangerous situation. • **emergence** *noun* emerging; first appearance. • **emergent** *adj* emerging; developing. ⓘ 17c: from Latin *emergere* to rise up from, from *e* out of + *mergere* to plunge.

emergency /ɪ'mɜːdʒənsɪ/ ▷ *noun* (***emergencies***) **1** an unexpected and serious happening which calls for immediate and determined action. **2 a** a serious injury needing immediate medical treatment; **b** a patient suffering such an injury. See also STATE OF EMERGENCY.

emergency exit ▷ *noun* an exit to be used in an emergency, eg in case of fire.

emerging market ▷ *noun, finance* a developing country that recognizes and is acquiring the benefits of outside funding and investment.

emeritus /ɪ'mɛrɪtəs/ ▷ *adj, often following its noun* retired or honourably discharged from office, but retaining a former title as an honour □ ***emeritus professor*** □ ***professor emeritus***. ⓘ 19c: Latin, meaning 'having served one's term', from Latin *mereri* to deserve.

emersion /ɪ'mɜːʃən/ ▷ *noun, astron* the reappearance of a celestial body after an ECLIPSE or OCCULTATION. ⓘ 17c: from Latin *emergere*, *emersum* to rise up from.

emery /'ɛmərɪ/ ▷ *noun* (***emeries***) a very hard mineral, a variety of CORUNDUM, usually used in powder form, for polishing or abrading. ⓘ 15c: from French *esmeril*, from Greek *smyris* polishing powder.

emery board ▷ *noun* a small flat strip of wood or card coated with emery powder or some other abrasive, used for filing one's nails.

emery paper and **emery cloth** ▷ *noun* paper or cloth coated with emery, used for cleaning or polishing metal.

emetic /ɪ'mɛtɪk/ ▷ *adj, medicine* making one vomit. ▷ *noun* an emetic medicine. ⓘ 17c: from Greek *emeein* to vomit.

EMF ▷ *abbreviation* **1** (*also* **emf**) electromotive force. **2** European Monetary Fund.

emigrant /'ɛmɪgrənt/ ▷ *noun* someone who emigrates or who has emigrated. ▷ *adj* **a** belonging or relating to emigrants; **b** emigrating or having recently emigrated. Compare IMMIGRANT.

emigrate /'ɛmɪgreɪt/ ▷ *verb* (***emigrated***, ***emigrating***) *intr* to leave one's native country and settle in another. Compare IMMIGRATE. • **emigration** *noun*. ⓘ 18c: from Latin *emigrare*, *emigratum* to move from a place.

emigrate

A related word often confused with this one is **immigrate**.

émigré /'ɛmɪgreɪ/ ▷ *noun* (***émigrés*** /-greɪz/) a person who has emigrated, usually for political reasons. ⓘ 18c: French.

eminence /'ɛmɪnəns/ ▷ *noun* **1** honour, distinction or prestige. **2** an area of high ground. • **Your** or **His Eminence** (***Your*** or ***Their Eminences***) or **Your** or **His Eminency** (***Your*** or ***Their Eminencies***) a title of honour used in speaking to or about a cardinal. ⓘ 17c: from Latin *eminere* to stand out.

éminence grise /*French* eminɑ̃s griz/ ▷ *noun* (***éminences grises*** /eminɑ̃s griz/) a person who has great influence over a ruler or government, etc, without occupying an official position of power. ⓘ 17c: French, literally 'grey eminence', first applied to Père Joseph, private secretary to Cardinal Richelieu (1585–1642).

eminent /'ɛmɪnənt/ ▷ *adj* **1** famous and admired. **2** distinguished; outstanding. • **eminently** *adverb* **1** very. **2** obviously. ⓘ 15c: from Latin *eminere* to stand out.

eminent domain ▷ *noun, law* the right by which the state may appropriate an individual's property for public use.

emir /ɛ'mɪə(r)/ ▷ *noun* **1** a title given to various Muslim rulers, especially in the Middle East or W Africa. **2** a title given to the supposed descendants of Muhammad through his daughter Fatima. Also written **amir**. • **emirate** *noun* the position or authority of, or the territory ruled by, an emir. ◷ 17c: French, from Arabic *amir* ruler.

emissary /'ɛmɪsərɪ/ ▷ *noun* (***emissaries***) **1** a person sent on a mission, especially on behalf of a government. **2** a person sent with a message. ◷ 17c: from Latin *emissarius*.

emission /ɪ'mɪʃən/ ▷ *noun* **1** the act of emitting. **2** something emitted, especially heat, light or gas. **3** the discharge of semen or other fluid from the body. **4** *physics* the release of electrons from parent atoms on absorption of energy which exceeds the average. • **emissive** *adj*. ◷ 17c: from Latin *emissio* a sending out.

emit /ɪ'mɪt/ ▷ *verb* (***emitted, emitting***) to give out (light, heat, a sound or smell, etc). ◷ 17c: from Latin *emittere* to send out.

Emmental or **Emmenthal** /'ɛməntɑːl/ ▷ *noun* a mild hard Swiss cheese with holes in it. ◷ Early 20c: from Emmenthal, a valley in Switzerland.

Emmy /'ɛmɪ/ ▷ *noun* (***Emmies*** or ***Emmys***) one of a set of trophies awarded annually by the American Academy of Television Arts and Sciences. Compare OSCAR. ◷ 1940s.

emollient /ɪ'mɒlɪənt/ ▷ *adj* **1** *medicine* softening or soothing the skin. **2** *formal* advocating a calmer, more peaceful attitude. ▷ *noun, medicine* a substance which softens or soothes the skin. ◷ 17c: from Latin *emolliens*, from *emollire* to soften.

emolument /ɪ'mɒljumənt/ ▷ *noun, formal* (*often* **emoluments**) any money earned or otherwise gained through a job or position, eg salary or fees. • **emolumentary** *adj*. ◷ 15c: from Latin *emolumentum* a corn-grinder's fee, from *molere* to grind.

emote /ɪ'mout/ ▷ *verb* (***emoted, emoting***) *intr, derog colloq* to display exaggerated or insincere emotion. ◷ Early 20c: back-formation from EMOTION.

emotion /ɪ'mouʃən/ ▷ *noun* a strong feeling. • **emotionless** *adj*. • **emotionlessly** *adverb*. ◷ 16c: from Latin *emovere*, *emotum* to stir up or disturb.

emotional ▷ *adj* **1** referring or relating to the emotions. **2** causing or expressing emotion. **3** said of a person: tending to express emotions easily or excessively. **4** *often derog* based on emotions, rather than rational thought □ *an emotional response*. • **emotionally** *adverb*.

emotionalism ▷ *noun, often derog* the tendency to be too easily affected or excited by the emotions. • **emotionalist** *noun*. • **emotionalistic** *adj*.

emotive /ɪ'moutɪv/ ▷ *adj* tending or designed to excite emotion. • **emotively** *adverb* so as to excite emotion □ *talks emotively about her childhood*. ◷ 19c; 18c in obsolete sense 'causing movement'.

empanel /ɪm'panəl/ ▷ *verb* (***empanelled, empanelling***; *US* ***empaneled, empaneling***) **1** to enter (the names of prospective jurors) on a list. **2** to select (a jury) from such a list. • **empanelment** *noun*. ◷ 15c.

empathize or **empathise** /'ɛmpəθaɪz/ ▷ *verb* (***empathized, empathizing***) *intr* (*usually* **empathize with someone**) to share their feelings; to feel empathy. ◷ 1920s.

empathy /'ɛmpəθɪ/ ▷ *noun* **1** the ability to share, understand and feel another person's feelings. **2** the power of entering into the feeling or spirit of something, especially a work of art, and so appreciating it fully. • **empathetic** /ɛmpə'θɛtɪk/ or **empathic** /ɛm'paθɪk/ *adj* able to share others' feelings. ◷ Early 20c: from Greek *empatheia* passion or affection.

empennage /ɛm'pɛnɪdʒ/ ▷ *noun, aeronautics* an aeroplane's tail unit, including elevator, rudder and fin. ◷ Early 20c: French, meaning 'feathering of an arrow', from Latin *penna* feather or wing.

emperor /'ɛmpərə(r)/ ▷ *noun* the male ruler of an empire or of a country which was once the centre of an empire. See also EMPRESS. ◷ 13c: from French *emperere*, from Latin *imperator* commander.

emperor moth ▷ *noun, zool* a large broad-winged moth found in Europe, N America and Asia.

emperor penguin ▷ *noun* the largest species of penguin, found in the Antarctic.

emphasis /'ɛmfəsɪs/ ▷ *noun* (***emphases*** /-siːz/) **1** (*usually* **emphasis on something**) special importance or attention given to it. **2** greater force or loudness on certain words or parts of words to show that they are important or have a special meaning. **3** force or firmness of expression. ◷ 16c: Greek, meaning 'outward appearance' or 'implied meaning'.

emphasize or **emphasise** /'ɛmfəsaɪz/ ▷ *verb* (***emphasized, emphasizing***) to put emphasis on something. ◷ 19c.

emphatic /ɪm'fatɪk/ ▷ *adj* **1** expressed with or expressing emphasis. **2** said of a person: speaking firmly and forcefully. • **emphatically** *adverb*. ◷ 18c: from Greek *emphatikos*.

emphysema /ɛmfɪ'siːmə/ ▷ *noun, pathol* the presence of air in the body tissues. See also PULMONARY EMPHYSEMA. • **emphysemic** *noun* a sufferer from emphysema. ◷ 17c: Latin, from Greek *emphysaein* to swell.

empire /'ɛmpaɪə(r)/ ▷ *noun* **1** a group of nations or states under the control of a single ruler or ruling power, especially an emperor or empress. **2** the period of time during which such control is exercised. **3** a large commercial or industrial organization which controls many separate firms, especially one headed by one person. **4** *often facetious* that part of an organization or company, etc under the management of a particular person. **5** *formal or literary* supreme control or power. See also EMPEROR, EMPRESS. ▷ *adj* (*usually* **Empire**) referring especially to dress or furniture: relating to, or in the style of, the first French Empire (1804–14). ◷ 13c: French, from Latin *imperium* command or power.

empire-builder ▷ *noun, colloq, often derog* someone who seeks to acquire extra personal authority or responsibility, etc, within an organization, usually by expanding personnel and resources. • **empire-building** *noun*.

empirical /ɪm'pɪrɪkəl/ and **empiric** ▷ *adj* **1** based on experiment, observation or experience, rather than on theory. **2** regarding experiment and observation as more important than scientific law. • **empirically** *adverb* by means of experiment rather than theory. ◷ 16c: from Latin *empiricus*, from Greek *empeiria* experience.

empirical formula ▷ *noun, chem* a chemical formula which shows the simplest possible ratio of atoms in a molecule.

empiricism /ɪm'pɪrɪsɪzəm/ ▷ *noun* **1** *philos* the theory or philosophy stating that knowledge can only be gained through experiment and observation. **2** the application of empirical methods, eg to science. • **empiricist** *noun* someone who believes in experiment as a basis of knowledge. ◷ 17c.

emplace ▷ *verb* (***emplaced, emplacing***) to put something in place. ◷ 19c: back-formation from EMPLACEMENT.

emplacement /ɪm'pleɪsmənt/ ▷ *noun* **1** *military* a strongly defended position from which a field gun may be fired. **2** *formal* the act of putting, or the state of having been put, into place. ◷ 19c: French.

employ /ɪm'plɔɪ/ ▷ *verb* (***employed, employing***) **1** to give work, usually paid work, to someone. **2** to use. • **employable** *adj* said of a person: suitable or able to be employed. • **employed** *adj* having a job; working. • **employer** *noun* a person or company that employs workers. • **be employed in something** to have one's time and attention devoted to it. • **be in someone's**

employ *formal* to be employed by them. ◷ 15c: from French *employer*, from Latin *implicare* to enfold.

employee /ɪm'plɔiː, -'iː/ ▷ *noun* (***employees***) a person who works for another in return for payment.

employment ▷ *noun* **1** the act of employing or the state of being employed. **2** an occupation, especially regular paid work. Compare UNEMPLOYMENT.

employment agency ▷ *noun* an organization which finds jobs for people, and workers for companies seeking them.

employment exchange ▷ *noun* the former name for a JOB CENTRE.

employment office ▷ *noun, formal* a JOB CENTRE.

emporium /ɛm'pɔːrɪəm/ ▷ *noun* (***emporiums*** or ***emporia***) *formal* a shop, especially a large one that sells a wide variety of goods. ◷ 16c: from Greek *emporion* trading station.

empower /ɪm'paʊə(r)/ ▷ *verb* (*usually* **empower someone to do something**) to give them authority or official permission to do it. • **empowerment** *noun*. ◷ 17c.

empress /'ɛmprəs/ ▷ *noun* (***empresses***) **1** the female ruler of an empire or of a country which was once the centre of an empire. **2** the wife or widow of an emperor. ◷ 12c as *emperice*: from French *emperesse*.

empty /'ɛmptɪ/ ▷ *adj* (***emptier***, ***emptiest***) **1** having nothing inside. **2** not occupied, inhabited or furnished. **3** not likely to be satisfied or carried out ▫ *empty promises*. **4** (*usually* **empty of something**) completely without it ▫ *a life empty of meaning*. ▷ *verb* (***empties***, ***emptied***, ***emptying***) *tr & intr* **1** to make or become empty. **2** to tip, pour or fall out of a container. ▷ *noun* (***empties***) *colloq* an empty container, especially a bottle. • **emptily** *adverb*. • **emptiness** *noun*. ◷ Anglo-Saxon *æmetig* unoccupied.

empty-handed ▷ *adj* **1** carrying nothing. **2** having gained or achieved nothing.

empty-headed ▷ *adj* foolish or frivolous; having no capacity for serious thought.

empty-nester ▷ *noun* a parent whose children have grown up and left the family home. ◷ 1970s.

empyema /ɛmpaɪ'iːmə/ ▷ *noun* (***empyemata*** /-'iːmətə/ or ***empyemas***) *pathol* a collection of pus in any cavity, especially the PLEURA. ◷ 17c: Latin, from Greek *pyon* pus.

empyrean /ɛmpɪ'rɪən/ *poetic* ▷ *noun* (*usually* **the empyrean**) the heavens; the sky. Also *as adj*. • **empyreal** *adj*. ◷ 17c: from Latin *empyreus*, from Greek *empyros* fiery.

EMS ▷ *abbreviation* European Monetary System.

EMU ▷ *abbreviation* **1** Economic and Monetary Union (between EU countries). **2** (*also* **emu**) electromagnetic unit.

emu /'iːmjuː/ ▷ *noun* (***emus***) a large flightless but swift-running bird, almost 2m (6ft 6in) tall with coarse brown plumage, found in deserts, plains and forests in Australia. ◷ 17c: from Portuguese *ema* ostrich.

emulate /'ɛmjʊleɪt/ ▷ *verb* (***emulated***, ***emulating***) **1** to try hard to equal or be better than someone or something. **2** to imitate. **3** *tr & intr* said of a computer or a program: to behave or make a computer or program behave as if it were (a different computer or program). • **emulation** *noun*. ◷ 16c: from Latin *aemulari* to rival.

emulous /'ɛmjʊləs/ ▷ *adj* (*often* **emulous of someone**) keen to achieve the same success or excellence as them. • **emulously** *adverb*. • **emulousness** *noun*. ◷ 14c: from Latin *aemulus* competing with.

emulsifier and **emulsifying agent** ▷ *noun* a chemical substance that coats the surface of droplets of one liquid so that they can remain dispersed throughout a second liquid (eg margarine or ice cream) forming a stable emulsion.

emulsify /ɪ'mʌlsɪfaɪ/ ▷ *verb* (***emulsifies***, ***emulsified***, ***emulsifying***) *tr & intr* to make or become an emulsion. • **emulsification** *noun*. ◷ 19c.

emulsion /ɪ'mʌlʃən/ ▷ *noun* **1** *chem* a COLLOID consisting of a stable mixture of two IMMISCIBLE liquids (such as oil and water), in which small droplets of one liquid are dispersed uniformly throughout the other, eg salad cream and low-fat spreads. **2** *photog* the light-sensitive material that is used to coat photographic film and paper, etc. **3** emulsion paint. **4** a liquid mixture containing globules of fat, such as milk, or of resinous or bituminous material. ▷ *verb* (***emulsioned***, ***emulsioning***) *colloq* to apply emulsion paint to something. ◷ 17c: from Latin *emulgere*, *emulsum*, from *mulgere* to milk.

emulsion paint ▷ *noun* water-based paint.

EN ▷ *abbreviation* Enrolled Nurse.

en ▷ *noun, printing* half of an EM. ◷ 18c.

en- /ɪn, ɛn/ ▷ *prefix, forming verbs, signifying* **1** to put into, on or onto a specified thing ▫ *entrust* ▫ *enthrone*. **2** to cause someone or something to be a specified thing ▫ *enrich* ▫ *enfeeble*. **3** intensifying the meaning of the base verb ▫ *entangle* ▫ *enliven*. See also EM-.

-en /n, ən/ ▷ *suffix* **1** *forming verbs, signifying* **a** to make or become a specified thing, or make or become more so ▫ *deepen* ▫ *sadden*; **b** to give or endow with a specified thing ▫ *strengthen*. **2** *forming adjectives, signifying* made or consisting of a specified thing ▫ *wooden*. Compare -ENT.

enable /ɪn'eɪbəl/ ▷ *verb* (***enabled***, ***enabling***) **1** to make someone able; to give them the necessary means, power or authority (to do something). **2** to make something possible. • **enabler** *noun*. ◷ 15c.

enabling act, **enabling bill** and **enabling resolution** ▷ *noun* an act, bill or resolution giving or proposing to give someone power to act.

enact /ɪn'akt/ ▷ *verb* (***enacted***, ***enacting***) **1** to act or perform something on stage or in real life. **2** to establish by law. ◷ 15c.

enactment ▷ *noun, formal* **1** the act of passing, or the passing of, a parliamentary bill into law. **2** that which is enacted; a law.

enamel /ɪ'naməl/ ▷ *noun* **1** a hardened coloured glass-like substance applied as a decorative or protective covering to metal or glass. **2** any paint or varnish which gives a finish similar to this. **3** the hard white covering of the teeth. ▷ *verb* (***enamelled***, ***enamelling***; *US* ***enameled***, ***enameling***) to cover or decorate something with enamel. ◷ 15c: from French *enameler*, from *esmail* enamel.

enamoured or (*US*) **enamored** /ɪ'naməd/ ▷ *adj* **1** (*usually* **enamoured with someone**) *formal or literary* in love with them. **2** (*usually* **enamoured of something**) very fond of it, pleased with it, or enthusiastic about it. ◷ 14c as *verb enamour*: from French *amour* love.

en bloc / *French* ɑ̃blɔk/ ▷ *adverb* all together; as one unit. ◷ 19c: French, meaning 'in a block'.

enc. ▷ *abbreviation* **1** enclosed. **2** enclosure.

encamp /ɪŋ'kamp/ ▷ *verb, tr & intr* to settle in a camp. • **encampment** *noun*. ◷ 16c.

encapsulate or **encapsulate** /ɪŋ'kapsjʊleɪt/ ▷ *verb* (***encapsulated***, ***encapsulating***; ***incapsulated***, ***incapsulating***) **1** to express concisely the main points or ideas of something, or capture the essence of it. **2** to enclose something in, or as if in, a capsule. • **encapsulation** *noun*. ◷ Early 20c.

encase /ɪŋ'keɪs/ ▷ *verb* **1** to enclose something in, or as if in, a case. **2** to surround or cover. • **encasement** *noun*. ◷ 17c.

encash /ɪŋ'kaʃ/ ▷ *verb* (***encashes***, ***encashed***, ***encashing***) to convert something into cash; to cash. • **encashment** *noun*. ◷ 19c.

encaustic /ɪŋ'kɒstɪk/ ▻ *adj* said of ceramics: decorated by any process that burns in colours, especially using pigments melted in wax and burnt into the clay. ▻ *noun* **1** the technique which uses pigments in this way. **2** a piece of pottery or any other article decorated using this technique. • **encaustically** *adverb*. Ⓒ 17c: from Greek *enkaustikos*, from *enkaiein* to burn in.

-ence /əns/ ▻ *suffix*, forming nouns corresponding to adjectives in -ENT, *signifying* **1** a state or quality, or an action, etc which shows a state or quality □ *confidence* □ *diligence*. **2** an action □ *reference*. Ⓒ French, from Latin *-entia*.

encephalic /ɛnsə'falɪk, ɛŋkə-/ ▻ *adj* concerning or relating to the brain. Ⓒ 19c.

encephalitis /ɛnsɛfə'laɪtɪs, ɛŋkɛ-/ ▻ *noun, pathol* inflammation of the brain. Ⓒ 19c.

encephalitis lethargica /— lə'θɑːdʒɪkə/ ▻ *noun, technical* SLEEPING SICKNESS.

encephalo- /ɛnsɛfəloʊ, ɛnsɛfə'lɒ, ɛŋkɛ-/ or (before a vowel) **encephal-** *combining form, anatomy signifying* relating to the brain. Ⓒ From Greek *enkephalos* brain, from *en* in + *kephale* head.

encephalogram see ELECTROENCEPHALOGRAM

encephalograph see ELECTROENCEPHALOGRAPH

encephalon /ɛŋ'kɛfəlɒn/ ▻ *noun* (**encephala** /-lə/) *anatomy* the brain. Ⓒ 18c: Latin, from Greek *enkephalos*.

enchain /ɪn'tʃeɪn/ ▻ *verb, literary* **1** to put in chains. **2** to hold or fix (attention, etc). • **enchainment** *noun*. Ⓒ 15c: from French *enchaîner*.

enchant /ɪn'tʃɑːnt/ ▻ *verb* (**enchanted**, **enchanting**) **1** to charm or delight. **2** to put a magic spell on someone or something. • **enchanted** *adj*. • **enchanter** *noun*. Ⓒ 14c: from French *enchanter*, from Latin *incantare* to sing a magic spell over.

enchanting ▻ *adj* charming; delightful. • **enchantingly** *adverb*.

enchantment ▻ *noun* **1** the act of enchanting or the state of being enchanted. **2** a magic spell. **3** charm; attraction.

enchantress ▻ *noun* (**enchantresses**) **1** a female ENCHANTER. **2** a charming woman or girl, especially one who sets out to be so. Ⓒ 16c: from French *enchâsser* to enshrine, from *châsse* case.

enchase ▻ *verb* **1** to set (gold, silver, etc) with jewels. **2** to engrave. **3** to adorn with raised or embossed work.

enchilada /ɛntʃɪ'lɑːdə/ ▻ *noun* (**enchiladas**) *cookery* a Mexican dish consisting of a flour tortilla with a meat filling, served with a chilli-flavoured sauce. Ⓒ 19c: from Spanish *enchilar* to season with chilli.

encipher /ɪn'saɪfə(r)/ ▻ *verb* (**enciphered**, **enciphering**) to put something into cipher or code. Ⓒ 16c.

encircle /ɪn'sɜːkəl/ ▻ *verb* to surround or form a circle round, something. • **encirclement** *noun* encircling, especially of territory. Ⓒ 16c.

encl. ▻ *abbreviation* **1** enclosed. **2** enclosure.

enclave /'ɛŋkleɪv, 'ɒŋ-/ ▻ *noun* **1** a small country or state entirely surrounded by foreign territory. **2** a distinct racial or cultural group isolated within a country. Ⓒ 19c: French, from Latin *inclavare* to lock up.

enclitic /ɪŋ'klɪtɪk/ ▻ *adj, grammar* said of a word or especially a particle: without stress; treated as if part of the previous word. ▻ *noun* a word or particle which always follows another word, and is enclitic to it. Ⓒ 17c: from Greek *enklitikos*, from *en* in + *klinein* to lean.

enclose or **inclose** /ɪŋ'kloʊz/ ▻ *verb* **1** to put something inside a letter or in its envelope. **2** to shut in or surround. • **enclosed** *adj* **1** placed inside something, especially an envelope. **2** (**the enclosed**) something enclosed within a letter. Ⓒ 14c as *verb* 2.

enclosed order ▻ *noun* a Christian religious order that leads a contemplative life, not going out into the world to work.

enclosure or **inclosure** /ɪŋ'kloʊʒə(r)/ ▻ *noun* **1** the process of enclosing or being enclosed, especially with reference to common land. **2** land surrounded by a fence or wall. **3** an enclosed space at a sporting event. **4** an additional paper or other item included with a letter. Ⓒ 16c.

encode /ɪŋ'koʊd/ ▻ *verb* to express something in, or convert it into, code. • **encoder** *noun*. Ⓒ Early 20c.

encomium /ɪŋ'koʊmɪəm/ ▻ *noun* (**encomiums** or **encomia** /ɪŋ'koʊmɪə/) *formal* a formal speech or piece of writing praising someone. • **encomiastic** *adj*. • **encomiastically** *adverb*. Ⓒ 16c: Latin, from Greek *enkomion* song of praise.

encompass /ɪŋ'kʌmpəs/ ▻ *verb* (**encompasses**, **encompassed**, **encompassing**) **1** to include or contain something, especially to contain a wide range or coverage of something. **2** to surround something. **3** to cause something or bring it about. • **encompassment** *noun*. Ⓒ 16c.

encore /'ɒŋkɔː(r), ɒŋ'kɔː(r)/ ▻ *noun* a repetition of a performance, or an additional performed item, after the end of a concert, etc. ▻ *exclamation* an enthusiastic call from the audience for such a performance. ▻ *verb* (**encored**, **encoring**) to call for an extra performance of something or from someone. Ⓒ 18c: French, meaning 'again'.

encounter /ɪŋ'kaʊntə(r)/ ▻ *verb* (**encountered**, **encountering**) **1** to meet someone or something, especially unexpectedly. **2** to meet with (difficulties, etc). **3** to meet someone in battle or conflict. ▻ *noun* **1** a chance meeting. **2** a fight or battle. Ⓒ 13c: from French *encontrer*, from Latin *contra* against.

encounter group ▻ *noun, psychol* a group of people formed to discuss personal problems and feelings openly, in order to arrive at a better understanding of themselves and others.

encourage /ɪŋ'kʌrɪdʒ/ ▻ *verb* (**encouraged**, **encouraging**) **1** to give support, confidence or hope to someone. **2** to urge someone to do something. **3** to promote or recommend something or someone. • **encouragement** *noun* support; a source of increased confidence. • **encouraging** *adj*. • **encouragingly** *adverb*. Ⓒ 15c: from French *encourager*, from *corage* courage.

encroach /ɪŋ'kroʊtʃ/ ▻ *verb* (**encroaches**, **encroached**, **encroaching**) *intr* (*usually* **encroach on someone or something**) **1** to intrude or extend gradually or stealthily (on someone else's land, etc). **2** to go beyond the fair limits of a right, etc. **3** to overstep proper or agreed limits. • **encroacher** *noun*. • **encroachment** *noun*. Ⓒ 14c: from French *encrochier* to seize, from *croc* a hook.

encrust or **incrust** /ɪŋ'krʌst/ ▻ *verb* to cover something with a thick hard coating, eg of jewels or ice. • **encrustation** *noun*. Ⓒ 17c: from Latin *incrustare*, from *crusta* crust.

encrypt /ɪŋ'krɪpt/ ▻ *verb* (**encrypted**, **encrypting**) to put information (eg computer data or TV signals) into a coded form. Ⓒ 1940s.

encumber /ɪŋ'kʌmbə(r)/ ▻ *verb* (**encumbered**, **encumbering**) **1** to prevent the free and easy movement of someone or something; to hamper or impede. **2** to burden someone or something with a load or debt. Ⓒ 14c: from French *encombrer* to block.

encumbrance or **incumbrance** ▻ *noun* an impediment, hindrance or burden.

ency., **encyc.** and **encycl.** ▻ *abbreviation* **1** encyclopedia. **2** encyclopedic.

-ency /ənsɪ/ ▻ *suffix, forming nouns, indicating* a state or quality, or something which shows a state or quality □ *efficiency* □ *inconsistency*. Ⓒ From Latin *-entia*.

encyclical /ɛn'sɪklɪkəl/ ▷ *noun, RC Church* a letter sent by the Pope to all Roman Catholic bishops. ▷ *adj* (*also* **encyclic**) *formal* said of a letter: for general or wide circulation. ◷ 17c: from Greek *enkyklios*, from *en* in + *kyklos* circle.

encyclopedia or **encyclopaedia** /ɪnsaɪklə'piːdɪə/ ▷ *noun* (***encyclopedias***) a reference work containing information on every branch of knowledge, or on one particular branch, usually arranged in alphabetical order. • **encyclopedic** *adj* **1** said of knowledge: full and detailed. **2** relating to, belonging to, or like an encyclopedia. • **encyclopedist** *noun* a compiler of encyclopedias. ◷ 16c: from Greek *enkyklios paideia* general education.

encyst /ɛn'sɪst/ ▷ *verb* (***encysted, encysting***) *tr & intr, biol* to enclose or become enclosed in a CYST or VESICLE. • **encysted** *adj*. ◷ 19c.

end ▷ *noun* **1** the point or part farthest from the beginning, or either of the points or parts farthest from the middle, where something stops. **2** a finish or conclusion. **3** (**the end**) *colloq* the last straw; the limit. **4** a piece left over □ *a cigarette end.* **5** death or destruction □ *meet one's end.* **6** an object or purpose □ *The end justifies the means.* **7** *sport* one of the two halves of a pitch or court defended by a team or player, etc. **8** the part of a project, etc for which one is responsible □ *had a few problems at their end.* ▷ *verb* (***ended, ending***) *tr & intr* **1** to finish or cause something to finish. **2** *intr* to reach a conclusion or cease to exist. • **ended** *adj* **1** brought to an end. **2** *in compounds* having ends of a specified kind. • **at a loose end** with nothing to do. • **at an end** terminated, discontinued or exhausted. • **at the end of one's tether** exasperated; at the limit of one's endurance. • **at the end of the day** *colloq* when everything has been taken into account. • **be the end of someone** *colloq* to bring about their death. • **end it all** *colloq* to kill oneself. • **end of story** *colloq* that's that. • **end on 1** (**also end to end**) with ends touching. **2** with the end pointing towards one. • **get hold of the wrong end of the stick** to misunderstand. • **get** or **have one's end away** *slang* to have sexual intercourse. • **in the end** finally; after much discussion or work, etc. • **keep** or **hold one's end up** *colloq* to fulfil one's promises or obligations in spite of difficulties. • **make ends meet** to live within one's income and avoid debts. • **no end** *colloq* very much □ *His visit pleased her no end.* • **no end of people** or **things** very many; a lot. • **on end 1** vertical; standing straight up. **2** continuously; without a pause. • **put an end to something** to make it stop, usually completely and permanently. • **the end of the road** the point beyond which one cannot continue or survive. ◷ Anglo-Saxon *ende*.

▪ **end up** *colloq* **1** to arrive or find oneself eventually or finally □ *We ended up in Manchester.* **2** to finish.

▪ **end up as something** to become (a specified thing) finally.

end- see under ENDO-

endanger ▷ *verb* (***endangered, endangering***) to put someone or something in danger; to expose them to possible loss or injury. ◷ 16c.

endangered species ▷ *noun* any plant or animal species that is in danger of extinction in the near future, either because its populations have fallen to very low levels, or because it only occurs naturally in a few restricted areas.

endear /ɪn'dɪə(r)/ ▷ *verb* (***endeared, endearing***) (*usually* **endear someone to someone else**) to make them beloved or liked. ◷ 16c in obsolete sense 'to make more valuable'.

endearing ▷ *adj* arousing feelings of affection. • **endearingly** *adverb* with an endearing or affectionate manner.

endearment ▷ *noun* **1** a word or phrase expressing affection. **2** a caress.

endeavour or (*US*) **endeavor** /ɪn'dɛvə(r)/ ▷ *verb* (***endeavoured, endeavouring***) (*usually* **endeavour to do something**) to try to do it, especially seriously and with effort. ▷ *noun* a determined attempt or effort. ◷ 14c as *endeveren* to exert oneself: from French *devoir* duty.

> ***endeavour***
>
> ☆ PLAIN ENGLISH alternatives are **try, attempt, strive**. Note that **endeavour** and **strive** have connotations of personal commitment that are lacking in the more neutral words **try** and **attempt**.

ended and **ending** see under END

endemic /ɛn'dɛmɪk/ ▷ *adj* **1** said of a disease, etc: regularly occurring in a particular area or among a particular group of people. **2** *biol* said of a plant or animal: native to, or restricted to, a particular area. • **endemically** *adverb*. ◷ 18c: from Greek *endemios* native.

endermic /ɛn'dɜːmɪk/ ▷ *adj* said of a medicine, etc: that acts through, or is applied directly to, the skin. ◷ 19c: from Greek *en* in + *derma* skin.

endgame ▷ *noun* **1** the final stage in a game of chess, or certain other games. **2** the way in which one plays the endgame. ◷ Late 19c.

ending ▷ *noun* **1** the end, especially of a story or poem, etc. **2** *grammar* the end part of a word, especially an INFLECTION.

endive /'ɛndɪv/ ▷ *noun* **1** a plant, related to chicory, whose crisp curly or broad leaves are used in salads. **2** *loosely, especially US* chicory. ◷ 15c: French.

endless ▷ *adj* having no end, or seeming to have no end. • **endlessly** *adverb*. • **endlessness** *noun*.

endmost ▷ *adj* farthest; nearest the end.

endo- /ɛndoʊ, ɛn'dɒ/ or (before a vowel) **end-** *combining form, signifying* internal; inside. See also ECTO-, ENTO-, EXO-. ◷ From Greek *endon* within.

endocarditis ▷ *noun, pathol* inflammation of the **endocardium**, the delicate membrane that lines the heart and the valves of the heart. ◷ 19c.

endocarp ▷ *noun, bot* the inner layer of the PERICARP of a fruit, usually hard, eg a plum stone. ◷ 19c.

endocrine /'ɛndoʊkraɪn, -krɪn/ ▷ *adj* **1** *physiol* relating to internal secretions, or to a pathway or structure that secretes internally. **2** said of a gland: ductless, and producing and secreting one or more hormones directly into the bloodstream. See also EXOCRINE. ▷ *noun* an endocrine gland. • **endocrinal** /-'kraɪnəl/ or **endocrinic** /-'krɪnɪk/ *adj*. ◷ Early 20c: from Greek *krinein* to separate.

endocrinology /ɛndoʊkrɪ'nɒlədʒɪ/ ▷ *noun, physiol* the scientific study of the ENDOCRINE glands, that produce and secrete hormones, and of the hormones themselves. ◷ Early 20c.

endoderm ▷ *noun, zool* in a multicellular animal that has two or more layers of body tissue: **a** the innermost layer of cells of the embryo, which develops into the digestive system of the adult, also forming the yolk sac and ALLANTOIS in birds and mammals; **b** the tissues directly derived from this layer. Compare ECTODERM, MESODERM. ◷ 19c.

endodontics ▷ *noun, medicine* the branch of dentistry concerned with the diagnosis, treatment and prevention of disorders of the tooth pulp, including root canal treatment. ◷ 1940s.

endogamy /ɛn'dɒgəmɪ/ ▷ *noun, anthropol* the practice or rule of marrying only within one's own group. ◷ 19c.

endogenous /ɛn'dɒdʒənəs/ ▷ *adj* said of depression: with no external cause. ◷ 19c.

endometriosis /ɛndoumiːtrɪ'ousɪs/ ▷ *noun, anatomy* the presence of tissue similar to the ENDOMETRIUM at other sites in the pelvic cavity. ◷ 1920s.

endometritis /ɛndoumə'traɪtɪs/ ▻ *noun, pathol* inflammation of the ENDOMETRIUM. ⓒ 19c.

endometrium /ɛndou'miːtrɪəm/ ▻ *noun, anatomy* the mucous membrane which lines the UTERUS. ⓒ 19c: from Greek *metra* womb.

endomorph ▻ *noun* **1** a person of rounded or plump build, sometimes said to be associated with a calm easy-going personality. Compare ECTOMORPH, MESOMORPH. **2** a mineral that occurs enclosed within another. • **endomorphic** *adj.* ⓒ 1940s; 19c in sense 2.

endophyte /'ɛndoufaɪt/ ▻ *noun, bot* a plant living within another, whether parasitically or not. • **endophytic** /-'fɪtɪk/ *adj.* ⓒ 19c.

endoplasm ▻ *noun, biol* the central portion of the CYTOPLASM of a cell. ⓒ 19c.

end organ ▻ *noun, anatomy* a specialized sensory or motor structure at a nerve-end.

endorphin /ɛn'dɔːfɪn/ ▻ *noun, biochem* any of a group of chemical compounds that occur naturally in the brain and have similar pain-relieving properties to morphine, thought to be involved in the control of emotional responses. ⓒ 1970s: from *endo-* + m*orphine*.

endorse or **indorse** /ɪn'dɔːs/ ▻ *verb* (***endorsed, endorsing***) **1** to write one's signature on the back of (a document), especially on the back of (a cheque) to specify oneself or another person as payee. **2** to make a note of an offence on (a driving licence). **3** to state one's approval of or support for something. • **endorser** or **endorsor** *noun.* • **endorsee** *noun* (***endorsees***). ⓒ 15c: from Latin *in* on + *dorsum* back.

endorsement ▻ *noun* **1** an act of endorsing or confirming. **2** a signature or other mark endorsing a document. **3** a record of a conviction entered on a driving licence.

endoscope ▻ *noun, medicine* a long thin flexible instrument containing bundles of optical fibres and having a light at one end, used for viewing internal body cavities and organs. Compare FIBRESCOPE. • **endoscopic** *adj.* • **endoscopy** /ɛn'dɒskəpɪ/ *noun* examination of the internal organs by means of an endoscope. ⓒ 19c.

endoskeleton ▻ *noun, zool* in vertebrates: an internal skeleton made of bone or cartilage. • **endoskeletal** *adj.* ⓒ 19c.

endosperm ▻ *noun, biol* nutritive tissue within the seed of some plants. • **endospermic** *adj.* ⓒ 19c.

endothelium /ɛndou'θiːlɪəm/ ▻ *noun* (***endothelia*** /-θiːlɪə/) *zool* a single layer of cells that lines the internal surfaces of the heart, blood vessels, and lymph vessels. ⓒ 19c: Latin, from ENDO- + Greek *thele* nipple + -IUM.

endothermic reaction ▻ *noun, chem* any process, especially a chemical reaction, that involves the absorption of heat. ⓒ 19c.

endow /ɪn'daʊ/ ▻ *verb* (***endowed, endowing***) **1** to provide a source of income for (a hospital or place of learning, etc), often by a bequest. **2** (*often* **be endowed with something**) to have a quality or ability, etc □ *endowed with common sense.* ⓒ 14c: from French *endouer*, from Latin *dos* dowry.

endowment ▻ *noun* **1** the act of endowing. **2** a sum endowed. **3** a quality or skill, etc with which a person is endowed.

endowment assurance or **endowment insurance** ▻ *noun* a form of insurance in which a set sum is paid at a certain date, or earlier in the event of death.

endpaper ▻ *noun, publishing, etc* one of the two leaves at the front or back of a hardback book, fixed with paste to the inside of the cover, to give strength to the binding.

end product ▻ *noun* the final product of a series of operations, especially industrial processes. Compare BY-PRODUCT.

end result ▻ *noun* the final result or outcome.

endue or **indue** /ɪn'djuː/ ▻ *verb* (***endued, enduing***) (*usually* **endue someone with something**) to provide them with (a specified quality). ⓒ 15c: from French *enduire*, from Latin *inducere* to lead in.

endurable ▻ *adj* capable of being endured. • **endurably** *adverb.*

endurance ▻ *noun* **1** the capacity for, or the state of, patient toleration. **2** the ability to withstand physical hardship or strain.

endure /ɪn'djʊə(r)/ ▻ *verb* (***endured, enduring***) **1** to bear something patiently; to put up with it. **2** *intr, formal* to continue to exist; to last. • **enduring** *adj.* • **enduringly** *adverb.* ⓒ 14c: from French *endurer*, from Latin *indurare* to harden.

end user ▻ *noun* a person, company or nation, etc that will buy and use a product that is being sold.

endways and (*especially N Amer*) **endwise** ▻ *adverb* **1** with the end forward or upward. **2** end to end.

end zone ▻ *noun, Amer football* the area in front of the goal posts to which the ball must be brought, or in which it must be caught, for a TOUCHDOWN to be awarded.

ENE ▻ *abbreviation* east-north-east.

-ene /iːn/ ▻ *combining form, chem, signifying* an unsaturated hydrocarbon containing a double bond □ *benzene* □ *acetylene.*

enema /'ɛnəmə/ ▻ *noun* (***enemas*** or ***enemata*** /ɛ'nɛmətə/) *medicine* **1** the injection of a liquid into the rectum, eg to clean it out or to introduce medication. **2** the liquid injected. ⓒ 15c: Latin, from Greek *enienai* to send in.

enemy /'ɛnəmɪ/ ▻ *noun* (***enemies***) **1** a person who is actively opposed to someone else. **2** a hostile nation or force, or a member of it. **3** an opponent or adversary. **4** a person or thing that opposes or acts against someone or something □ *Cleanliness is the enemy of disease.* ▻ *adj* hostile; belonging to a hostile nation or force. ⓒ 13c: from French *enemi*, from Latin *inimicus*, from *in-* not + *amicus* a friend.

energetic /ɛnə'dʒɛtɪk/ ▻ *adj* having or displaying energy; forceful or vigorous. • **energetically** *adverb.* ⓒ 18c: from Greek *energetikos.*

energize or **energise** /'ɛnədʒaɪz/ ▻ *verb* (***energized, energizing***) **1** to stimulate, invigorate or enliven. **2** to provide energy for the operation of (a machine, etc). • **energizer** *noun.* ⓒ 18c.

energy /'ɛnədʒɪ/ ▻ *noun* (***energies***) **1** the capacity for vigorous activity; liveliness or vitality. **2** force or forcefulness. **3** *physics* the capacity to do work. ⓒ 16c: from Greek *energeia*, from *en* in + *ergon* work.

energy conservation ▻ *noun, ecol* the reduction or avoidance of energy loss or wastage by various means.

energy gap ▻ *noun* the amount by which energy requirements exceed the energy supply.

energy level ▻ *noun, physics* one of the fixed amounts of energy that an electron in an atom can possess at any given time.

enervate /'ɛnəveɪt/ ▻ *verb* (***enervated, enervating***) **1** to take energy or strength from something. **2** to deprive someone of moral or mental vigour. • **enervating** *adj.* • **enervation** *noun.* ⓒ 17c: from Latin *enervare, enervatum* to weaken, from *e* out of + *nervus* a nerve.

en famille /*French* ɑ̃famij/ ▻ *adverb* **1** amongst the family; as if at a family gathering. **2** informally. ⓒ 18c: French.

enfant terrible /*French* ɑ̃fɑ̃tɛʀibl/ ▻ *noun* (***enfants terribles*** / *French* ɑ̃fɑ̃tɛʀibl/) a person with a reputation for rude or embarrassing behaviour in public. ⓒ 19c: French, meaning 'dreadful child'.

enfeeble /ɪn'fiːbl/ ▻ *verb* (***enfeebled, enfeebling***) *formal* to make someone weak. • **enfeebled** *adj.* • **enfeeblement** *noun.* ⓒ 14c.

en fête /*French* ɑ̃fɛt/ ▻ *adverb* **1** in festive mood; celebrating. **2** dressed up for a celebration or holiday, etc. ⓒ 19c: French.

enfilade /ɛnfɪ'leɪd/ *military* ▻ *noun* a continuous burst of gunfire sweeping from end to end across a line of enemy soldiers. ▷ *verb* (***enfiladed, enfilading***) to direct an enfilade at someone or something. ⓒ 18c: French, from *enfiler* to thread on a string.

enfold or **infold** /ɪn'foʊld/ ▷ *verb* **1** to wrap up or enclose. **2** to embrace. ⓒ 16c.

enforce /ɪn'fɔːs/ ▷ *verb* **1** to cause (a law or decision) to be carried out. **2** to press (an argument). **3** to persist in (a demand). • **enforceable** *adj*. • **enforced** *adj* not voluntary or optional. • **enforcedly** /ɪnfɔːsɪdlɪ/ *adverb*. • **enforcement** *noun*. ⓒ 16c in sense 1; 14c in obsolete senses: from French *enforcer*.

▪ **enforce something on someone** to impose (one's will, etc) on them.

enfranchise /ɪn'frantʃaɪz/ ▷ *verb* (***enfranchised, enfranchising***) *formal* **1** to give someone the right to vote in elections. **2** to set someone free, especially from slavery. **3** to give (a town) the right to be represented in parliament. • **enfranchisement** /-tʃɪzmənt/ *noun* the conferring of rights, especially to vote in elections. ⓒ 16c: from French *enfranchir* to set free, from *franc* free.

ENG ▷ *abbreviation* electronic news gathering, TV news reports put together on location, using the most up-to-date video equipment.

Eng. ▷ *abbreviation* **1** England. **2** English.

eng. ▷ *abbreviation* **1** engineer. **2** engineering. **3** engraver. **4** engraving.

engage /ɪŋ'geɪdʒ/ ▷ *verb* (***engaged, engaging***) **1** to take someone on as a worker. **2** to book or reserve (eg a table or room). **3** *tr & intr, military* to come or bring something into battle ▫ *engage with the enemy*. **4** *tr & intr* to cause part of a machine (eg the gears) to fit into and lock with another part. ⓒ 15c: from French *engager*, from *en gage* in pledge.

▪ **engage someone in something** to involve or occupy them in it ▫ *She engaged me in small talk.*

engagé /*French* ɑ̃ga'ʒeɪ/ ▷ *adj* having or showing a political or moral commitment. ⓒ 1940s: French, literally 'engaged'.

engaged ▷ *adj* **1** (*usually* **engaged to someone**) bound by a promise to marry them. **2** said of a room or a telephone line, etc: not free or vacant; occupied; in use. **3** geared together; interlocked. • **engaged in something** busy or occupied with it.

engagement ▷ *noun* **1** the act of engaging or state of being engaged. **2** a firm agreement between two people to marry. **3** an arrangement made in advance; an appointment. **4** *military* a battle.

engaging ▷ *adj* charming; attractive. • **engagingly** *adverb*.

en garde /*French* ɑ̃gaʀd/ ▷ *exclamation, fencing* a warning to one's opponent to take up a defensive position.

engender /ɪn'dʒɛndə(r)/ ▷ *verb* (***engendered, engendering***) to produce or cause (especially feelings or emotions). ⓒ 14c: from French *engendrer*, from Latin *generare* to generate.

engine /'ɛndʒɪn/ ▷ *noun* **1** a machine that is used to convert some form of energy into mechanical energy that can be used to perform useful work. **2** a railway locomotive. **3** *formal* a device or instrument ▫ *an engine of destruction*. ⓒ 13c: from French *engin*, from Latin *ingenium* device.

engine-driver ▷ *noun* a person who drives a railway locomotive.

engineer /ɛndʒɪ'nɪə(r)/ ▷ *noun* **1** someone who designs, makes, or works with machinery, including electrical equipment. **2** (*also* **civil engineer**) someone who designs or constructs roads, railways, bridges, etc. **3** an officer in charge of a ship's engines. **4** *N Amer* the driver of a locomotive. **5** someone who contrives to bring something about ▫ *the engineer of the scheme*. **6** a person, especially a member of the armed forces, who designs and builds military apparatus and is trained in construction work. ▷ *verb* (***engineered, engineering***) **1** *often derog* to arrange or bring something about by skill or deviousness. **2** to design or construct something as an engineer. ⓒ 14c as *engyneour*: from French *engignier* to contrive, from Latin *ingeniare*.

engineering ▷ *noun* the application of scientific knowledge, especially that concerned with matter and energy, to the practical problems of design, construction, operation and maintenance of devices encountered in everyday life. See also CHEMICAL ENGINEERING, CIVIL ENGINEERING, ELECTRICAL ENGINEERING, ELECTRONIC ENGINEERING, MECHANICAL ENGINEERING.

engine room ▷ *noun* **1** the room in an industrial plant or a ship, etc that houses the engines. **2** the source of strength and power.

English /'ɪŋglɪʃ/ ▷ *adj* **1** belonging or relating to England or its inhabitants. **2** relating to English (*noun* 2), the language. ▷ *noun* **1** (**the English**) the citizens or inhabitants of, or people born in, England, considered as a group. See also BRITON. **2** the native language of Britain, N America, much of the British Commonwealth and some other countries. • **in plain English** in clear simple language. ⓒ Anglo-Saxon *Englisc*, from *Engle* the Angles.

English horn ▷ *noun* a COR ANGLAIS.

Englishman and **Englishwoman** ▷ *noun* a male or female citizen, or person born in, England.

engorged /ɪŋ'gɔːdʒd/ ▷ *adj* **1** crammed full. **2** *pathol* congested with blood. • **engorgement** *noun*. ⓒ 16c: from 15c *engorge* to gorge.

engraft or **ingraft** /ɪŋ'grɑːft/ ▷ *verb* (***engrafted, engrafting***) **1** to graft (a shoot, etc) on to a stock. **2** to insert; to fix deeply. • **engraftation** or **engraftment** *noun*. ⓒ 16c.

engrain see INGRAIN

engrained see INGRAINED

engrave /ɪŋ'greɪv/ ▷ *verb* (***engraved, engraving***) **1** to carve (letters or designs) on stone, wood or metal, etc. **2** to decorate (stone, etc) in this way. **3** to fix or impress something deeply on the mind, etc. • **engraver** *noun* a person who engraves letters or designs, especially as their profession. ⓒ 16c, from obsolete *grave* to carve.

engraving ▷ *noun* **1** the art or process of carving or incising designs on wood or metal, etc, especially for the purpose of printing impressions from them. In metal the lines to be printed are sunk or incised, in wood they appear in relief, the wood between them being cut away. **2** a print taken from an engraved metal plate, etc. **3** a piece of stone, etc decorated with carving.

engross /ɪŋ'groʊs/ ▷ *verb* (***engrosses, engrossed, engrossing***) to take up someone's attention and interest completely. • **engrossed** *adj*. • **engrossing** *adj* engaging one's full attention; highly interesting. ⓒ 17c: from French *engrosser*, from *en gros* completely.

engulf /ɪŋ'gʌlf/ ▷ *verb* (***engulfed, engulfing***) **1** to swallow something up completely. **2** to overwhelm. • **engulfment** *noun*. ⓒ 16c.

enhance /ɪn'hɑːns/ ▷ *verb* (***enhanced, enhancing***) to improve or increase the value, quality or intensity of something (especially something already good). • **enhancement** *noun*. ⓒ 14c: from French *enhauncer*, from Latin *in* in + *altus* high.

enhanced radiation weapon ▷ *noun* (abbreviation **ERW**) a more precise term for a NEUTRON BOMB.

enharmonic /ɛnhɑː'mɒnɪk/ ▷ *adj, music* **1** referring to music constructed on a scale containing intervals less than a semitone. **2** having a minute pitch difference, eg between F♯ and G♭, not identifiable in a scale of EQUAL TEMPERAMENT. • **enharmonically** *adverb*. ⓒ 16c: from Greek *en* in + *harmonia* harmony.

enigma /ɪ'nɪgmə/ ▷ *noun* (***enigmas***) **1** a puzzle or riddle. **2** a mysterious person, thing or situation. ⓒ 16c: Latin, from Greek *ainigma*, from *ainos* a fable.

enigmatic /ɛnɪg'matɪk/ ▷ *adj* obscure, ambiguous or puzzling. • **enigmatically** *adverb*.

Differences between British and American English

There are many differences of meaning, pronunciation, spelling and syntax between British and American English. Some of the commoner differences in meaning in typical usage are listed below. The increasing influence of American usage on British English is having the effect of blurring distinctions. It should also be remembered that practice differs widely within the USA; and it is becoming increasingly difficult to establish linguistic boundaries between the language used in the USA and the language used in Canada.

There are also a number of general spelling differences between British and American English. Others are less distinct, because both varieties permit variants of form and inflections (for example, the forms **acknowledgement** and **acknowledgment** are found in both American and British English).

	British		American
-ae-	as in anaesthetic	-e-	as in anesthetic
-oe-	as in oestrogen	-e-	as in estrogen
-ence	as in defence, licence (noun)	-ense	as in defense, license (noun)
-re	as in centre	-er	as in center
-our	as in flavour	-or	s in flavor
-ogue	as in catalogue	-og	as in catalog
-ou-	as in mould	-o-	as in mold
-l-	as in instil, instalment, skilful	-ll-	as in instill, installment, skillful
-ll-	as in traveller	-l-	as in traveler

British	American
aeroplane	airplane
aluminium	aluminum
anticlockwise	counterclockwise
aubergine	eggplant
autumn	fall
back garden	yard
banknote	bill
bath	tub
biscuit (savoury)	cracker
biscuit (sweet)	cookie
bonnet (of a car)	hood (of a car)
braces	suspenders
brooch	pin
camp-bed	cot
caretaker	janitor
chemist's shop	drugstore
cheque	check
chips	french fries
cinema (building)	movie theater
city centre	downtown
coffin	casket
cornflour	cornstarch
cotton reel	spool
courgette	zucchini
crisps	potato chips
cupboard	closet
current account (bank)	checking account
curriculum vitae	résumé
curtains	drapes
draughts (game)	checkers
drawing pin	thumb tack
driving licence	driver's license
dual carriageway	divided highway
dustbin	garbage can
engine driver	engineer
estate agent	realtor
first floor	second floor
flag day	tag day
flat	apartment
frying pan	skillet
grill	broil
ground floor	first floor
handbag	purse, pocketbook
hoarding	billboard
icing	frosting
insect	bug
ironmonger	hardware store
kerb	curb
knickers	underpants
lavatory	washroom
lawyer	attorney
lift	elevator

British	American
lorry	truck
loud-hailer	bull-horn
main road	highway
murder	homicide
motorway	expressway
number plate (of a vehicle)	license plate (of a vehicle)
nappy	diaper
pavement	sidewalk
pedestrian crossing	crosswalk
petrol	gasoline (gas)
pig	hog
plot (of ground)	lot
pram	baby carriage
queue	line
railway	railroad
return ticket	round-trip ticket
reverse charge (telephone) call	collect call
rise (in salary)	raise
roundabout (traffic)	rotary
rowing-boat	rowboat
rubber	eraser
rubbish	trash
scone	biscuit
season ticket	commutation ticket
shoelace	shoestring
shop assistant	clerk
silencer (car)	muffler (car)
spring onions	green onions
sweets	candy
tap	faucet
tart	pie
terraced house	row house
tights	pantihose
timber	lumber
traffic jam	gridlock
tram	streetcar
trolley (at supermarket, etc)	cart
trousers	pants
turn-up (trousers)	cuff (pants)
tyre	tire
underground	subway
undertaker	mortician
verandah	porch
vest	undershirt
waistcoat	vest
wallet	billfold
windscreen	windshield
wing (of a car)	fender (of a car)
zip	zipper

enjambment /ɪn'dʒammənt; *French* ɑ̃ʒɑ̃bmɑ̃/ ▻ *noun* in verse: the continuation of the sense without a pause beyond the end of the line. 🕓 Early 19c: from French *enjambement*, from *enjamber* to stride or encroach.

enjoin ▻ *verb* (***enjoined***, ***enjoining***) *formal* to order or command someone to do something. 🕓 17c: from French *enjoindre*, from Latin *jungere* to join.

■ **enjoin someone from something** *law* to forbid them to do it, by means of an injunction.

■ **enjoin something on someone** to demand behaviour of a certain kind from them □ *enjoin politeness on one's children.*

enjoy /ɪn'dʒɔɪ/ ▻ *verb* (***enjoyed***, ***enjoying***) **1** to find pleasure in something. **2** to have, experience or have the benefit of something good □ *The room enjoys sunlight all day.* • **enjoy oneself** to experience pleasure or happiness. 🕓 14c: from French *enjoir*, see JOY.

enjoyable ▻ *adj* capable of being enjoyed; offering pleasure. • **enjoyably** *adverb*.

enjoyment ▻ *noun* **1** enjoying; deriving pleasure. **2** the possession of something that gives pleasure. **3** happinesss.

enkephalin /ɛŋ'kɛfəlɪn/ ▻ *noun, biochem* either of two chemical compounds that occur naturally in the brain and spinal cord, but which can be produced synthetically. They have pain-relieving properties similar to those of morphine and other opiates. 🕓 1970s: from Greek *enkephalos* brain + -IN.

enlace ▻ *verb* **1** to encircle something with, or as if with, laces; to bind. **2** to entwine. 🕓 14c.

enlarge ▻ *verb* (***enlarged***, ***enlarging***) **1** *tr & intr* to make or become larger. **2** to reproduce (a photograph, etc) in a larger form. 🕓 14c.

■ **enlarge on** or **upon something** to speak or write about it at greater length or in greater detail.

enlargement ▻ *noun* **1** something enlarged, especially a photographic print larger than the standard or original print. **2** the act of enlarging or the state of being enlarged. **3** the process of admitting new member countries to the European Union.

enlarger ▻ *noun, photog* an apparatus with a lens, used for enlarging photographs.

enlighten ▻ *verb* (***enlightened***, ***enlightening***) **1** to give more information to someone. **2** to free someone from ignorance or superstition. **3** to make someone aware or uplift them by knowledge or religion. • **enlightened** *adj*. • **enlightening** *adj*. 🕓 Anglo-Saxon *inlihtan*, from *lihtan* to light.

enlightenment ▻ *noun* **1** the act of enlightening or the state of being enlightened. **2** freedom from ignorance or superstition. **3** (**the Enlightenment**) the philosophical movement originating in 18c France, with a belief in reason and human progress, and a questioning of tradition and authority.

enlist ▻ *verb* **1** *intr* to join one of the armed forces. **2** to obtain the support and help of someone; to obtain (support and help). • **enlistment** *noun*. 🕓 16c.

enlisted man and **enlisted woman** ▻ *noun, N Amer, especially US* a member of the armed forces below the rank of officer.

enliven /ɪn'laɪvən/ ▻ *verb* (***enlivened***, ***enlivening***) to make active or more active, lively or cheerful. • **enlivener** *noun*. • **enlivenment** *noun*. 🕓 17c.

en masse / *French* ɑ̃mas/ ▻ *adverb* all together; as a mass or group. 🕓 18c: French, literally 'in a body'.

enmesh /ɪn'mɛʃ/ ▻ *verb* (***enmeshes***, ***enmeshed***, ***enmeshing***) to catch or trap something in a net, or as if in a net; to entangle. 🕓 17c.

enmity /'ɛnmɪtɪ/ ▻ *noun* (***enmities***) **1** the state or quality of being an enemy. **2** ill-will; hostility. 🕓 13c: from French *enemistie*, from Latin *inimicus* enemy.

ennoble /ɪ'noʊbəl/ ▻ *verb* (***ennobled***, ***ennobling***) **1** to make something noble or dignified. **2** to make someone a member of the nobility. • **ennoblement** *noun*. 🕓 15c.

ennui /ɒ'nwiː; *French* ɑ̃nɥi/ ▻ *noun, literary* boredom or discontent caused by a lack of activity or excitement. 🕓 18c: French.

ENO ▻ *abbreviation* English National Opera.

eno- see OENO-

enormity /ɪ'nɔːmɪtɪ/ ▻ *noun* (***enormities***) **1** outrageousness or wickedness. **2** an outrageous or wicked act. **3** immenseness or vastness. 🕓 15c: from Latin *enormitas*.

enormity, enormousness

• Strictly, **enormity** should not be used in a neutral sense (see sense 3) to mean 'very great size or scale':

✗ *He was clearly exhausted by the enormity of the task he had set himself.*

• You will come across this usage quite often, because the alternative **enormousness** is awkward.

☆ RECOMMENDATION: if the meaning is neutral, use another word or expression such as **hugeness, great size/scale, greatness, immensity, vastness.**

enormous /ɪ'nɔːməs/ ▻ *adj* extremely large; huge. • **enormously** *adverb* to a large extent; hugely □ *enormously helpful.* • **enormousness** *noun*. 🕓 16c: from Latin *enormis* unusual.

enough /ɪ'nʌf/ ▻ *adj* in the number or quantity needed; sufficient □ *enough food to eat.* ▻ *adverb* **1** to the necessary degree or extent. **2** fairly □ *She's pretty enough, I suppose.* **3** quite □ *Oddly enough, I can't remember.* ▻ *pronoun* the amount needed. • **have had enough of something** to be able to tolerate no more of it. 🕓 Anglo-Saxon *genoh*.

en papillotte /*French* ɑ̃papijɔt/ ▻ *adverb* said of cooking and serving food: in an envelope of oiled paper or foil. 🕓 French, literally 'in a curlpaper'.

en passant / *French* ɑ̃pasɑ̃/ ▻ *adverb* **1** in passing; by the way. **2** *chess* applied to the taking of a pawn that has just moved two squares as if it had moved only one. 🕓 17c: French, literally 'in passing'.

en pension / *French* ɑ̃pɑ̃sjɔ̃/ ▻ *adverb* at a fixed rate for board and lodging. 🕓 French.

en primeur / *French* ɑ̃prɪmœr/ ▻ *adverb* said of tasting, buying or investing in wine: when the wine is new. 🕓 French, literally 'in newness'.

enprint /'ɛnprɪnt/ ▻ *noun, photog* a standard size of photographic print produced from a negative, usually approximately 12.7cm x 9cm. 🕓 20c: both '*en*velope-sized *print*' and '*en*larged *print*' have been suggested as the origin.

enquire see INQUIRE

enquiring see INQUIRING

enquiry see INQUIRY

enrage /ɪn'reɪdʒ/ ▻ *verb* to make someone extremely angry. • **enraged** *adj*. 🕓 15c: from French *enrager* to become enraged; see RAGE.

en rapport /*French* ɑ̃rapɔr/ ▻ *adverb* in close touch or harmony. 🕓 19c: French.

enrapture /ɪn'raptʃə(r)/ ▻ *verb* (***enraptured***, ***enrapturing***) to give intense pleasure or joy to someone.

• **enraptured** or **enrapt** *adj* intensely pleased or delighted. ⓒ 18c.

enrich ▻ *verb* (***enriches, enriched, enriching***) **1** to make something rich or richer, especially better or stronger in quality, value or flavour, etc. **2** to make wealthy or wealthier. **3** to fertilize (soil, etc). **4** *physics* to increase the proportion of one or more particular isotopes in a mixture of the isotopes of an element. • **enriched** *adj*. • **enrichment** *noun*. ⓒ 14c.

enrol or (*US*) **enroll** /ɪn'roʊl/ ▻ *verb* (***enrolled, enrolling***) **1** to add the name of (a person) to a list or roll, eg of members or pupils. **2** to secure the membership or participation of someone. **3** *intr* to add one's own name to such a list; to become a member. • **enrolment** *noun*. ⓒ 14c: from French *enroller*, from *rolle* a roll or register.

en route /ɒn 'ruːt/ ▻ *adverb* on the way □ *stop en route for a meal* □ *en route for Leeds*. ⓒ 18c: French.

ENSA /'ɛnsə/ ▻ *abbreviation*, *historical* Entertainments National Service Association.

ensconce /ɪn'skɒns/ ▻ *verb* (***ensconced, ensconcing***) *literary or humorous* (*often* **be ensconced**) **1** to settle comfortably or safely. **2** to hide safely. ⓒ 16c: from *sconce* a small fort.

ensemble /ɒn'sɒmbəl; *French* ɑ̃sɑ̃bl/ ▻ *noun* **1** a small group of (usually classical) musicians who regularly perform together. **2** a passage in opera or ballet, etc performed by all the singers, musicians or dancers together. **3** a set of items of clothing worn together; an outfit. **4** all the parts of a thing considered as a whole. ⓒ 15c: French, literally 'together'.

enshrine ▻ *verb* (***enshrined, enshrining***) **1** to enter and protect (a right or idea, etc) in the laws or constitution of a state, constitution of an organization, etc. **2** to place something in a shrine. ⓒ 16c in sense 2.

enshroud ▻ *verb* **1** to cover something completely; to hide something by covering it up. **2** to cover something or someone in a shroud. ⓒ 16c.

ensign /'ɛnsaɪn, (in senses 1 and 2 *also* 'ɛnsən/) ▻ *noun* **1** the flag of a nation or regiment. **2** a coloured flag with a smaller union flag in one corner, especially the **White Ensign**, the flag of the Royal Navy and the Royal Yacht Squadron, the **Red Ensign**, the flag of the Merchant Navy, or the **Blue Ensign**, now the flag of naval auxiliary vessels. **3** *historical* the lowest rank of officer in the infantry, or an officer of this rank. **4** *N Amer, especially US* **a** the lowest rank in the navy; **b** an officer of this rank. ⓒ 14c: from Latin *insignia*, from *signum* sign.

ensilage /'ɛnsɪlɪdʒ/ ▻ *noun* **1** the process of making SILAGE. **2** silage. ⓒ 19c: French, from Spanish *ensilar* to make silage.

ensile /ɛn'saɪl, 'ɛnsaɪl/ ▻ *verb* (***ensiled, ensiling***) **1** to turn (fodder) into silage. **2** to store (fodder) as silage. ⓒ 19c: French.

enslave ▻ *verb* (***enslaved, enslaving***) **1** to make someone into a slave. **2** to subject to a dominating influence. • **enslavement** *noun*. ⓒ 17c.

ensnare ▻ *verb* (***ensnared, ensnaring***) to catch something or someone in, or as if in, a trap; to trick or lead them dishonestly (into doing something). ⓒ 16c.

ensue /ɪn'sjuː/ ▻ *verb* (***ensued, ensuing***) (*usually* **ensue from something**) *intr* **1** to follow it; to happen after it. **2** to result from it. • **ensuing** *adj*. ⓒ 14c: from French *ensuer*, from Latin *sequi* to follow.

en suite /ʃ swiːt/ ▻ *adverb* ▻ *adj* forming, or attached as part of, a single unit or set. ▻ *noun*, *colloq* an en suite bathroom. ⓒ 1960s as *adj*; 19c as *adverb*: French, literally 'in sequence'.

ensure /ɪn'ʃʊə(r), ɪn'ʃɔː(r)/ *verb* (***ensured, ensuring***) **1** to make something certain; to assure or guarantee it. **2** to make (a thing or person) safe and secure. See also INSURE. ⓒ 14c: from French *enseurer*, from Latin *securus* safe.

ENT ▻ *abbreviation*, *medicine* ear, nose and throat.

ent., **entom.** and **entomol.** ▻ *abbreviation* entomology.

ent- see ENTO-

-ent /ənt/ ▻ *suffix* **1** forming adjectives corresponding to nouns in -ENCE, *signifying* acting, causing an action, or existing in a certain state □ *resident* □ *different*. **2** *forming nouns, signifying* an agent. Compare -EN. ⓒ From Latin *-ens*, *-entis*, present participle inflection of 2nd (and 3rd, as *-ient*) conjugation verbs; compare -ANT.

entablature /ɛn'tablətʃə(r)/ ▻ *noun*, *archit* in classical architecture: the part of a building directly supported by the columns, usually with a frieze and a CORNICE. ⓒ 17c: French, from Italian *in* on + *tavola* a board.

entail /ɛn'teɪl/ ▻ *verb* (***entailed, entailing***) **1** to have something as a necessary result or requirement. **2** (*usually* **entail something on someone**) *law* to bequeath (property) to one's descendants, not allowing them the option to sell it. ▻ *noun*, *law* **1** the practice of entailing (property). **2** property which has been entailed. **3** the successive heirs to property. • **entailment** *noun*. ⓒ 14c: from TAIL².

entangle ▻ *verb* **1** to cause something to get caught in some obstacle, eg a net. **2** to involve someone or something in difficulties. **3** to make something complicated or confused. • **entanglement** *noun*. ⓒ 17c.

entasis /'ɛntəsɪs/ ▻ *noun* (***entases*** /-siːz/) *archit* the slightly bulging outline of a column or similar structure, intended to counteract the illusion of concavity that an absolutely straight column would create. ⓒ 18c: Greek, from *en* in + *tasis* a stretch.

entente /ɑ̃'tɑ̃t/ ▻ *noun* **1** an ENTENTE CORDIALE. **2** those who are collectively party to an ENTENTE CORDIALE. ⓒ 19c: French, literally 'intent' or 'understanding'.

entente cordiale /ɑ̃'tɑ̃t kɔːdɪ'ɑːl/ ▻ *noun* (***entente cordiales***) a friendly agreement or relationship between nations or states. ⓒ 19c: French.

enter /'ɛntə(r)/ ▻ *verb* (***entered, entering***) **1** *tr & intr* to go or come in or into (eg a room). **2** *tr & intr* to register (another person, oneself, one's work, etc) in a competition. **3** to record something in a book, diary, etc. **4** to join (a profession or society, etc). **5** to submit or present something □ *enter a complaint*. **6** *intr*, *theat* to come on to the stage. • **enterable** *adj*. • **enterer** *noun*. ⓒ 13c: from French *entrer*, from Latin *intrare*, from *intra* within.

■ **enter into something 1** to begin to take part in it. **2** to become involved in it; to participate actively or enthusiastically in it. **3** to agree to be associated in or bound by (eg an agreement).

■ **enter on** or **upon something** to begin (an undertaking, especially a lengthy one) □ *enter upon a new stage of life*.

enter- see under ENTERO-

enterectomy /ɛntə'rɛktəmɪ/ ▻ *noun* (***enterectomies***) *surgery* the removal of part of the bowel. ⓒ 19c.

enteric /ɛn'tɛrɪk/ ▻ *adj*, *anatomy* intestinal. ▻ *noun* (*also* **enteric fever**) TYPHOID FEVER. ⓒ 19c: from Greek *enteron* intestine.

enteric-coated ▻ *adj*, *pharmacol* (abbreviation **ec**) said of a capsule or tablet: coated in a substance that prevents the release of the contents until after passing through the stomach into the intestine.

enteritis /ɛntə'raɪtɪs/ ▻ *noun*, *pathol* inflammation of the intestines, especially the small intestine. ⓒ Early 19c.

entero- /ɛntəroʊ, ɛntə'rɒ/ or (before a vowel) **enter-** *combining form, signifying* intestine. ⓒ From Greek *enteron* intestine.

enterovirus ▻ *noun*, *pathol* any of several VIRUSes occurring in and infecting the intestine. ⓒ 1950s.

enterprise /ˈɛntəpraɪz/ ▷ *noun* **1** a project or undertaking. **2** a project that requires boldness and initiative. **3** boldness and initiative. **4** a business firm. ◎ 15c: from French *entreprise*, from *entreprendre* to undertake.

enterprise culture ▷ *noun, econ* a culture based on an economic policy that encourages commercial initiative and audacious imaginative planning.

enterprise zone ▷ *noun* in the UK: an area of the country, eg an inner city district, or an area where the traditional industries have gone, which is designated by government as a site where industrial and commercial renewal is to be encouraged by financial and other incentives.

enterprising ▷ *adj* showing boldness and initiative; adventurous; imaginative. • **enterprisingly** *adverb*.

entertain /ɛntəˈteɪn/ ▷ *verb* (***entertained***, ***entertaining***) **1** to provide amusement or recreation for someone. **2** *tr & intr* to give hospitality to (a guest), especially in the form of a meal. **3** to consider or be willing to adopt (an idea or suggestion, etc). • **entertainer** *noun* a person who provides amusement, especially one who does so as their profession. ◎ 15c: from French *entretenir* to maintain or hold together.

entertaining ▷ *adj* interesting and amusing; giving entertainment. ▷ *noun* provision of entertainment. • **entertainingly** *adverb*.

entertainment ▷ *noun* **1** something that entertains, eg a theatrical show. **2** the act of ENTERTAINing. **3** amusement or recreation.

enthalpy /ɛnˈθalpɪ, ˈɛnθəlpɪ/ ▷ *noun, chem* the amount of heat energy possessed by a substance, expressed per unit mass. ◎ 1920s: from Greek *enthalpein* to warm.

enthral or (*especially US*) **enthrall** /ɪnˈθrɔːl/ ▷ *verb* (***enthralled***, ***enthralling***) to fascinate; to hold the attention or grip the imagination of someone. • **enthralled** *adj*. • **enthralling** *adj*. • **enthralment** *noun*. ◎ 16c.

enthrone ▷ *verb* (***enthroned***, ***enthroning***) to place someone on a throne. • **enthronement** *noun* enthroning, especially as the ceremony of installing a monarch on the throne. ◎ 17c.

enthuse /ɪnˈθjuːz, -θuːz/ ▷ *verb* (***enthused***, ***enthusing***) *tr & intr* to be enthusiastic, or make someone enthusiastic. ◎ 19c.

enthusiasm /ɪnˈθjuːzɪazəm, -ˈθuː-/ ▷ *noun* lively or passionate interest or eagerness. ◎ 17c: from Greek *enthousiasmos* zeal inspired by a god, from *en* in + *theos* god.

enthusiast ▷ *noun* someone filled with enthusiasm, especially for a particular subject; a fan or devotee.

enthusiastic /-ɪˈastɪk/ ▷ *adj* showing lively interest; extremely keen. • **enthusiastically** *adverb*.

entice /ɪnˈtaɪs/ ▷ *verb* (***enticed***, ***enticing***) to tempt or persuade, by arousing hopes or desires or by promising a reward. • **enticeable** *adj*. • **enticement** *noun*. • **enticer** *noun*. ◎ 13c: from French *enticier* to provoke.

enticing ▷ *adj* alluring; fascinating. • **enticingly** *adverb*.

entire /ɪnˈtaɪə(r)/ ▷ *adj* **1** whole or complete. **2** absolute or total. **3** *bot* said of leaves and petals: with an untoothed and unlobed margin. **4** said especially of a horse: not castrated. ▷ *noun* **1** a stallion. **2** *philately* a used or unused stamped envelope. • **entirely** *adverb* **1** fully or absolutely. **2** solely. ◎ 14c: from French *entier*, from Latin *integer* whole.

entirety /ɪnˈtaɪərətɪ/ ▷ *noun* (***entireties***) completeness; wholeness; the whole. • **in its entirety** totally; taken as a whole. ◎ 16c.

entitle ▷ *verb* (***entitled***, ***entitling***) to give a title or name to (a book, etc). • **entitlement** *noun* having a right to something. ◎ 14c.

■ **entitle someone to something** to give them a right to have or to do it.

entity /ˈɛntɪtɪ/ ▷ *noun* (***entities***) **1** something that has a physical existence, as opposed to a quality or mood. **2** the essential nature of something. **3** *philos* the fact or quality of existing. ◎ 16c: from Latin *entitas*, from *ens* thing that exists.

ento- /ɛntoʊ, ɛnˈtɒ/ or (before a vowel) **ent-** *combining form, signifying* inside. See also ECTO-, ENDO-, EXO-. ◎ From Greek *entos* within.

entom. see ENT.

entomb ▷ *verb* (***entombed***, ***entombing***) **1** to put (a body) in a tomb. **2** to cover, bury or hide someone or something as if in a tomb. • **entombment** *noun*. ◎ 16c.

entomo- /ˈɛntəmoʊ/ ▷ *combining form, signifying* insect, or insects. ◎ From Greek *entomon* insect.

entomol. see ENT.

entomology /ɛntəˈmɒlədʒɪ/ ▷ *noun* the scientific study of insects. • **entomological** /-məˈlɒdʒɪkəl/ *adj*. • **entomologically** *adverb*. • **entomologist** *noun*. ◎ 18c: from Greek *entomon* insect, from *entomos* cut into sections.

entourage /ˈɒntʊərɑːʒ ˈɑ̃-/ ▷ *noun* a group of followers or assistants, especially one accompanying a famous or important person. ◎ 19c: French, from *entourer* to surround.

entr'acte /ˈɒntrakt, ˈɑ̃-/ ▷ *noun* (***entr'actes***) **1** an interval between the acts of a play. **2** entertainment formerly provided during this interval. ◎ 19c: French, from *entre* between + *acte* act.

entrails /ˈɛntreɪlz/ ▷ *plural noun* **1** the internal organs of a person or animal. **2** *literary* the inner parts of anything. ◎ 13c: from French *entrailles*, from Latin *intralia*, from *inter* within.

entrain ▷ *verb* (***entrained***, ***entraining***) *tr & intr* to board or put someone on board a train. ◎ 19c.

entrance¹ /ˈɛntrəns/ ▷ *noun* **1** a way in, eg a door. **2** *formal* the act of entering. **3** the right to enter. ◎ 16c: French, from *entrer* to enter.

entrance² /ɪnˈtrɑːns/ ▷ *verb* (***entranced***, ***entrancing***) **1** to grip or captivate someone's attention and imagination. **2** to put someone into a trance. • **entrancement** *noun*. • **entrancing** *adj* gripping the imagination; fascinating; delightful. ◎ 16c.

entrance fee ▷ *noun* the money paid on entering a club, society or show, etc.

entrant /ˈɛntrənt/ ▷ *noun* someone who enters something, especially an examination, a competition or a profession. ◎ 17c.

entrap ▷ *verb* **1** to catch something in a trap. **2** to trick someone into doing something. • **entrapper** *noun*. ◎ 16c.

entrapment ▷ *noun* **1** the act of entrapping or process of being entrapped. **2** *law* the act or process of deliberately inducing someone to commit a crime in order to provide a reason for arresting and prosecuting them.

entreat ▷ *verb, tr & intr* to ask passionately or desperately; to beg. ◎ 15c: from French *entraiter*.

entreaty /ɪnˈtriːtɪ/ ▷ *noun* (***entreaties***) a passionate or desperate request.

entrechat /ˈɑ̃trəʃɑː/ ▷ *noun* (***entrechats***) *ballet* a leap in which the dancer crosses their feet and beats their heels together. ◎ 18c: from French, originally from Italian *capriola intrecciata* complicated caper.

entrecôte /'ɒntrəkoʊt/ ▻ *noun, cookery* a boneless steak cut from between two ribs. ⓒ 19c: French, from *entre* between + *côte* rib.

entrée /'ɒntreɪ/ ▻ *noun* (***entrées***) **1** a small dish served after the fish course and before the main course at a formal dinner. **2** *chiefly US* a main course. **3** *formal* the right of admission or entry □ ***entrée into polite society***. ⓒ 18c: French, literally 'entrance'.

entrench or **intrench** ▻ *verb* **1** to fix or establish something firmly, often too firmly □ ***deeply entrenched ideas***. **2** to fortify something with trenches dug around. ● **entrenchment** *noun*. ⓒ 16c.

entrepot or **entrepôt** /'ɒntrəpoʊ/ ▻ *noun* a port through which goods are imported and exported, especially one from which goods are re-exported without duty being paid on them. ⓒ 18c: French, meaning 'warehouse'.

entrepreneur /ɒntrəprə'nɜː(r)/ ▻ *noun* someone who engages in business enterprises, often with some personal financial risk. ● **entrepreneurial** *adj* acting as an entrepreneur; undertaking business enterprises. ● **entrepreneurship** *noun*. ⓒ 19c: French, literally 'someone who undertakes'.

entrepreneuse /ɒntrəprə'nɜːz/ ▻ *noun* a female ENTREPRENEUR.

entropy /'ɛntrəpɪ/ ▻ *noun* (***entropies***) *physics* a measure of the amount of disorder in a system, or of the unavailability of energy for doing work. ● **entropic** /ɪn'trɒpɪk/ *adj*. ⓒ 19c: from German *Entropie*, from Greek *en* in + *tropos* turn or change.

entrust or **intrust** ▻ *verb* (*usually* **entrust something to someone**, or **someone with something**) to give it to them to take care of or deal with. ⓒ 17c.

entry /'ɛntrɪ/ ▻ *noun* (***entries***) **1** the act of coming or going in. **2** the right to enter. **3** a place of entering such as a door or doorway. **4** a person, or the total number of people, entered for a competition, etc. **5** an item written on a list or in a book, etc, or the act of recording an item or items in this way. ⓒ 14c as *entre*: from French *entrée*, from *entrer*, from Latin *intrare* to go into.

entryism ▻ *noun, derog* the practice of joining a political party in large enough numbers to gain power and change the party's policies. ● **entryist** *noun, derog* someone who engages in political entryism. ⓒ 1960s as *entrism*.

Entryphone ▻ *noun, trademark* an intercom system fitted at the entrance to a building, especially a block of flats, by which visitors can identify themselves to specific occupants before being admitted to the building. ⓒ 1960s.

entwine ▻ *verb* **1** to wind or twist (two or more things) together. **2** to make something by winding or twisting materials together. ⓒ 16c.

E-number ▻ *noun* any of various identification codes, consisting of the letter E (for European) followed by a number, that are used to denote all food additives, except flavourings, that have been approved by the European Union. ⓒ 1970s.

enumerate /ɪ'njuːməreɪt/ ▻ *verb* (***enumerated, enumerating***) **1** to list one by one. **2** to count. ● **enumeration** *noun*. ⓒ 17c: from Latin *enumerare* to count up.

enumerator ▻ *noun* **1** someone who, or something which, enumerates. **2** someone who issues and then collects census forms. ⓒ 19c.

enunciate /ɪ'nʌnsɪeɪt/ ▻ *verb* (***enunciated, enunciating***) **1** *tr & intr* to pronounce words clearly. **2** to state something formally. ● **enunciable** *adj*. ● **enunciator** *noun*. ● **enunciation** *noun* clear pronunciation of words. ⓒ 17c: from Latin *enuntiare* to announce.

enure see INURE

enuresis /ɛnjʊə'riːsɪs/ ▻ *noun, pathol* involuntary urination, especially during sleep. ● **enuretic** /ɛnjʊ'rɛtɪk/ *adj*. ⓒ 19c: from Greek *en* in + *ouresis* urination.

envelop /ɪn'vɛləp/ ▻ *verb* (***enveloped, enveloping***) **1** to cover or wrap something or someone completely. **2** to obscure or conceal □ ***an event enveloped in mystery***. ● **envelopment** *noun*. ⓒ 14c: from French *envoloper*, from *voloper* to wrap.

envelope /'ɛnvəloʊp, 'ɒn-/ ▻ *noun* **1** a thin flat sealable paper packet or cover, especially for a letter. **2** a cover or wrapper of any kind. **3** *biol* a plant or animal structure that contains or encloses something, eg the **nuclear envelope**, consisting of a double membrane that surrounds the nucleus of a cell. **4** *technical* the glass casing that surrounds an incandescent lamp. ⓒ 18c: from French *enveloppe*; related to ENVELOP.

enviable /'ɛnvɪəbəl/ ▻ *adj* likely to cause envy; highly desirable. ● **enviably** *adverb*. ⓒ 17c.

envious /'ɛnvɪəs/ ▻ *adj* feeling or showing envy □ ***am so envious of your house***. Compare JEALOUS. ● **enviously** *adverb*. ● **enviousness** *noun*. ⓒ 14c.

environ /ɪn'vaɪərən/ ▻ *verb* (***environed, environing***) to surround or encircle. ⓒ 14c: from French *environner*, from *virer* to turn around.

environment /ɪn'vaɪərənmənt/ ▻ *noun* **1** the surroundings or conditions within which something or someone exists. **2** (*usually* **the environment**) the combination of external conditions that surround and influence a living organism. **3** *computing* a program, set of programs or an operating system that allows a particular application to be employed. ● **environmental** /-'mɛntəl/ *adj* □ ***environmental issues***. ● **environmentally** *adverb*. ⓒ 17c: from French *environnement*, from *environner* to surround.

environmental health officer ▻ *noun* (abbreviation **EHO**) a person whose job is to enforce regulations regarding eg hygiene in food-handling shops, maintenance of clean water supplies and waste disposal. See also SANITARY INSPECTOR

environmentalism ▻ *noun* concern about the natural environment and its protection from pollution and other harmful effects of human activity.

environmentalist ▻ *noun* someone who is concerned about the harmful effects of human activity on the environment. ▻ *adj* used to describe a group or organization whose aims are to protect the environment and to increase public awareness of environmental issues. ⓒ Early 20c.

environmentally friendly ▻ *adj* said eg of a detergent or non-aerosol spray: not harmful to the environment, eg referring to certain detergents and non-aerosol sprays.

environmental studies ▻ *noun* the science which studies the interaction between man and the environment, emphasizing the links between different subjects related to this issue, including ECOLOGY, ECONOMICS, GEOGRAPHY, GEOLOGY, METEOROLOGY, POLITICS and SOCIOLOGY.

environs /ɪn'vaɪərənz/ ▻ *plural noun* surrounding areas, especially the outskirts of a town or city. ⓒ 17c: from French *environ* around.

envisage /ɪn'vɪzɪdʒ/ ▻ *verb* (***envisaged, envisaging***) **1** to picture something in the mind. **2** to consider as likely in the future □ ***We envisage a pay rise in the autumn***. ⓒ 19c: from French *envisager*, from *visage* face.

envoy[1] /'ɛnvɔɪ/ ▻ *noun* **1** a diplomat ranking next below an ambassador. **2** a messenger or agent, especially on a diplomatic mission. ⓒ 17c: from French *envoyer* to send.

envoy[2] or **envoi** /'ɛnvɔɪ/ ▻ *noun* the concluding part of a poem or book, eg the short concluding verse at the end of a ballad. ⓒ 14c: from French *envoye*.

envy /'ɛnvɪ/ ▻ *noun* (***envies***) **1** a feeling of resentment or regretful desire for another person's qualities, better fortune or success. **2** anything that arouses envy □ *She is the envy of his friends.* ▻ *verb* (***envies, envied, envying***) **1** feel envy towards someone. **2** to covet; to wish to have something. **3** (**envy someone something**) to feel envy towards them on account of (their fortune or success, etc) □ *envied him his good luck.* ◷ 14c: from French *envie.*

Enzed /ɛn'zɛd/ ▻ *noun, Austral, NZ* **1** New Zealand. **2** (*also* **Enzedder**) a New Zealander. ◷ Early 20c: reproducing pronunciation of NZ.

enzootic /ɛnzoʊ'ɒtɪk/ ▻ *adj* said of a disease: prevalent in a particular district or at a particular season. ▻ *noun* a disease of this type. ◷ 19c: from Greek *zoion* animal.

enzyme /'ɛnzaɪm/ ▻ *noun, biochem* a specialized protein molecule that acts as a catalyst for the biochemical reactions that occur in living cells. • **enzymatic** or **enzymic** /-'zaɪmɪk/ *adj.* ◷ 19c: from Greek *zyme* leaven.

enzymology ▻ *noun* the scientific study of ENZYMES. • **enzymologist** *noun.* ◷ Early 20c.

EOC ▻ *abbreviation* Equal Opportunities Commission.

Eocene /'iːoʊsiːn/ ▻ *noun, geol* the second epoch of the TERTIARY period, lasting from about 54 million to 38 million years ago. ▻ *adj* **1** relating to this epoch. **2** relating to rocks formed during this epoch. See table at GEOLOGICAL TIME SCALE. ◷ 19c: from Greek *eos* dawn + *kainos* new.

EOKA /eɪ'oʊkə/ ▻ *abbreviation, Ethnike Organosis Kypriakou Agonos* (Greek), National Organization for the Cypriot Struggle.

eolian harp see as AEOLIAN HARP

eolithic or **Eolithic** /iːoʊ'lɪθɪk/ ▻ *adj, archaeol* belonging to the early part of the Stone Age, when crude stone implements were first used by man. ◷ 19c: from Greek *eos* dawn + *lithos* stone.

eon or **aeon** /'iːɒn/ ▻ *noun* **1** a long period of time; an endless or immeasurable period of time. **2** (*usually* **eon**) *geol* the largest unit of geological time, consisting of a number of ERAs. See table at GEOLOGICAL TIME SCALE. **3** *astron* a period of a thousand million years. ◷ 17c: from Greek *aion.*

eonism /'iənɪzəm/ ▻ *noun, psychiatry* the practice of TRANSVESTISM. ◷ 1920s: from the name of Chevalier d'Eon (died 1810), the French diplomat who chose female dress as a disguise.

eosin /'iːoʊsɪn/ ▻ *noun, biol* a red acidic dye. ◷ 19c: from Greek *eos* dawn, referring to the rosy colour of the sky.

-eous /ɪəs/ ▻ *suffix, forming adjectives, signifying* relating to, or of the nature of a specified thing. ◷ From Latin *-eus.*

EP[1] ▻ *noun* an extended-play RECORD (*noun* 4).

EP[2] ▻ *abbreviation* **1** electroplated. **2** European Parliament. **3** said of gramophone records: extended-play.

ep- see EPI-

EPA ▻ *abbreviation, US* Environmental Protection Agency.

epact /'iːpakt/ ▻ *noun* **1** the Moon's age at the beginning of the calendar year. **2** the excess of the calendar month or solar year over the lunar. ◷ 16c: from Greek *epaktos* brought on.

eparch /'ɛpɑːk/ ▻ *noun* **1** *Greek church* a bishop or METROPOLITAN in the ORTHODOX CHURCH. **2** the governor of a modern Greek province. ◷ 17c: from Greek *eparchos,* from *epi* upon + *arche* dominion.

epaulette or (*chiefly US*) **epaulet** /ɛpə'lɛt/ ▻ *noun* a decoration on the shoulder of a coat or jacket, especially of a military uniform. ◷ 18c: from French *épaulette,* from *épaule* shoulder.

épée /'eɪpeɪ/ ▻ *noun* (***épées***) a sword with a narrow flexible blade, formerly used in duelling, now, with a blunted end, used in fencing. ◷ 19c: French.

epeirogenesis /ɛpaɪəroʊ'dʒɛnəsɪs/ and **epeirogeny** /-'rɒdʒənɪ/ *geol* ▻ *noun* the building of continents by movement of the Earth's crust. • **epeirogenic** or **epeirogenetic** *adj.* ◷ 19c: from Greek *epeiros* mainland.

Eph. ▻ *abbreviation* Book of the Bible: Ephesians. See table at BIBLE.

ephedrine /'ɛfədrɪn/ ▻ *noun, pharmacol* an alkaloid drug, with similar effects to adrenaline, now mainly used as a nasal decongestant. ◷ 19c: from Greek *ephedra* horsetail (the plant).

ephemera[1] /ɪ'fɛmərə, ɪ'fiː-/ ▻ *noun* (***ephemeras*** or ***ephemerae*** /-riː/) **1** a mayfly. **2** something that lasts or is useful for only a short time; an EPHEMERON (sense 1). ◷ 17c: from Latin *ephemerus* lasting only a day, from Greek *ephemeros.*

ephemera[2] *plural of* EPHEMERON

ephemeral ▻ *adj* **1** lasting a short time. **2** *biol* denoting a plant or animal that completes its life cycle within weeks, days or even hours, eg the mayfly and many desert plants. ▻ *noun, biol* such a plant or animal. • **ephemerality** *noun* (***ephemeralities***). ◷ 16c.

ephemeris /ɪ'fɛmərɪs/ ▻ *noun* (***ephemerides*** /ɛfɪ'mɛrɪdiːz/) *astron* **1** a table that shows the predicted future positions of celestial bodies such as the Sun, Moon, planets, certain stars and comets. **2** a book, usually published annually, containing a collection of such tables, together with other relevant information about predictable astronomical phenomena such as eclipses. ◷ 16c: from Greek *ephemeris* diary or calendar.

ephemeron /ɪ'fɛmərən/ ▻ *noun* (***ephemera*** /-mərə/) **1** (**ephemera**) things that are valid or useful only for a short time, especially printed items such as tickets and posters. **2** an insect which lives for one day only. ◷ 16c: from Greek *ephemeros* living for a day.

epi- /ɛpɪ, ɪ'pɪ/ or (before a vowel) **ep-** or (combined with *h*) **eph-** /ɛf/ *combining form, signifying* **1** above, over or upon □ *epicentre* □ *epidural.* **2** in addition □ *epiphenomenon.* **3** after □ *epilogue.* **4** close to; near □ *epicalyx.* ◷ From Greek *epi* on or over.

epiblast /'ɛpɪblɑːst/ ▻ *noun, zool* the ECTODERM. Also called **ectoblast**. • **epiblastic** *adj.* ◷ 19c.

epic /'ɛpɪk/ ▻ *noun* **1** a long narrative poem telling of heroic acts, the birth and death of nations, etc. **2** a long adventure story or film, etc. ▻ *adj* referring to or like an epic, especially in being large-scale and imposing. ◷ 16c: from Greek *epikos,* from *epos* word or song.

epicalyx ▻ *noun, bot* an apparent accessory calyx outside the true calyx, composed of bracts or of fused stipules of sepals. ◷ 19c.

epicanthus /ɛpɪ'kanθəs/ ▻ *noun, anatomy* a fold of skin that covers the inner angle of the eye, characteristic of the MONGOLIAN race. • **epicanthic** *adj.* ◷ 19c.

epicarp ▻ *noun, bot* the outermost layer of the PERICARP of fruit; the skin. ◷ 19c.

epicene /'ɛpɪsiːn/ ▻ *adj* **1** having characteristics of both sexes, or of neither sex. **2** relating to, or for use by, both sexes. **3** effeminate. **4** *grammar* said of a noun: referring to people or animals of either sex (eg *driver,* as opposed to *waiter* and *waitress*). ◷ 15c: from Latin *epicoenus* of both genders, from Greek *epikoinos* common to many.

epicentre or (*US*) **epicenter** /'ɛpɪsɛntə(r)/ ▻ *noun* the point on the Earth's surface which is directly above the FOCUS (sense 4) of an earthquake, or directly above or below a nuclear explosion. • **epicentral** *adj.* ◷ 19c.

epicure /'ɛpɪkjʊə(r)/ ▻ *noun* someone who has refined taste, especially one who enjoys good food and drink. •

epicurism *noun* **1** the pursuit of pleasure, especially as found in good food and drink. **2** the tendency to be critical and hard to please in matters of luxury. ⓘ 16c: from Epicurus (341–270 BC), the ancient Greek philosopher who believed that the greatest good is pleasure.

epicurean /ɛpɪkjʊə'rɪən/ **1** *noun* someone who likes pleasure and good living; an epicure. **2** (**Epicurean**) a follower of Epicurus or his philosophy. ▷ *adj* **1** given to luxury or to the tastes of an epicure. **2** (**Epicurean**) referring or relating to Epicurus or his philosophy. • **Epicureanism** *noun* the philosophical system of Epicurus.

epicycle ▷ *noun, math* a circle whose centre rolls around the circumference of another fixed circle. • **epicyclic** *adj.* ⓘ 14c.

epideictic /ɛpɪ'daɪktɪk/ and **epideictical** ▷ *adj* done for show or display. ⓘ 18c: from Greek *deiknynai* to show.

epidemic /ɛpɪ'dɛmɪk/ ▷ *noun* **1** a sudden outbreak of infectious disease which spreads rapidly and affects a large number of people, animals or plants in a particular area for a limited period of time. **2** a sudden and extensive spread of anything undesirable. ▷ *adj* referring to or like an epidemic, sometimes also used to describe a non-infectious condition such as malnutrition. See also ENDEMIC. • **epidemically** *adverb.* ⓘ 17c: ultimately from Greek *epi* among + *demos* the people.

epidemiology /ɛpɪdiːmɪ'ɒlədʒɪ/ ▷ *noun, biol* the study of the distribution, effects and causes of diseases in populations, and the means by which they may be treated or prevented, not only including infectious diseases, but also conditions such as heart disease and cancer. • **epidemiological** /-ə'lɒdʒɪkəl/ *adj.* • **epidemiologist** *noun.* ⓘ 19c.

epidermis /ɛpɪ'dɜːmɪs/ ▷ *noun, biol* the outermost layer of a plant or animal, which serves to protect the underlying tissues from infection, injury and water loss. • **epidermal** *adj.* ⓘ 17c: Latin, from Greek *derma* the skin.

epididymis /ɛpɪ'dɪdɪmɪs/ ▷ *noun* (*epididymides* /-dɪ'dɪmɪdiːz/) *anatomy, zool* a long narrow highly coiled tube in the testis of mammals, birds and reptiles, that stores and conveys sperm to the VAS DEFERENS. ⓘ 17c: Greek, from *didymos* a twin or testicle.

epidural /ɛpɪ'djʊərəl/ *medicine* ▷ *adj* situated on, or administered into, the DURA MATER. ▷ *noun* (*in full* **epidural anaesthetic**) the epidural injection of an anaesthetic to remove all sensation below the waist, used especially during childbirth. ⓘ 19c as *adj.*

epigene /'ɛpɪdʒiːn/ ▷ *adj, geol* acting, formed or taking place at the Earth's surface. Compare HYPOGENE. ⓘ 19c: EPI- + -GENE.

epiglottis /ɛpɪ'glɒtɪs/ ▷ *noun* (*epiglottises* or *epiglottides* /-ɪdiːz/) *anatomy* in mammals: a movable flap of cartilage hanging at the back of the tongue, which closes the opening of the larynx when food or drink is being swallowed. • **epiglottal** *adj.* ⓘ 17c: Greek; see GLOTTIS.

epigram /'ɛpɪgram/ ▷ *noun* **1** a witty or sarcastic saying. **2** a short poem with such an ending. • **epigrammatic** /-grə'matɪk/ *adj.* ⓘ 18c; 16c in sense 2: from Greek *epigramma*, from *gramma* writing.

epigraph /'ɛpɪgrɑːf/ ▷ *noun* **1** a quotation or motto at the beginning of a book or chapter. **2** an inscription on a building. ⓘ 16c: from Greek *epigraphe*, from *graphein* to write.

epigraphic /ɛpɪ'grafɪk/ *adj.* • **epigraphy** /ɪ'pɪgrəfɪ/ *noun* **1** the study of inscriptions, especially those left by earlier civilizations. **2** epigrams. ⓘ 19c.

epilate /'ɛpɪleɪt/ ▷ *verb* (*epilated*, *epilating*) to remove (hair) by any method. • **epilation** *noun.* • **epilator** *noun.* ⓘ 19c: from French *épiler*, modelled on DEPILATE.

epilepsy /'ɛpɪlɛpsɪ/ ▷ *noun, pathol* any of a group of disorders of the nervous system characterized by recurring attacks that involve impairment, or sudden loss, of consciousness. See also GRAND MAL, PETIT MAL. ⓘ 16c: from Greek *epilepsia*, from *epilambanein* to seize.

epileptic /ɛpɪ'lɛptɪk/ *adj* **1** referring or relating to, or like epilepsy. **2** suffering from epilepsy. ▷ *noun* someone who suffers from epilepsy.

epilogue or (*US*) **epilog** /'ɛpɪlɒg/ ▷ *noun* **1** the closing section of a book or programme, etc. **2 a** a speech addressed to the audience at the end of a play; **b** the actor making this speech. **3** the concluding, and often religious, item of a day's radio or TV programmes. ⓘ 15c: from Greek *epilogos*, from *logos* speech.

epinasty /'ɛpɪnastɪ/ ▷ *noun, bot* an active growth on the upper side of an organ of a plant, causing a downward bend. Compare HYPONASTY.

epinephrine or **epinephrin** /ɛpɪ'nɛfrɪn, -friːn/ ▷ *noun, especially US* ADRENALINE. ⓘ 19c: from Greek *nephros* kidney.

epiphany /ɪ'pɪfənɪ/ ▷ *noun* (*epiphanies*) **1** (*usually* **Epiphany**) *Christianity* a festival on 6 January which, in the western churches, commemorates the showing of Christ to the three wise men, and, in the Orthodox and other eastern Churches, the baptism of Christ. **2** the sudden appearance of a god. **3** *literary* a sudden revelation or insight. ⓘ 14c: from Greek *epiphaneia* manifestation, from *phainein* to show.

epiphenomenon ▷ *noun* (*plural* *epiphenomena*) **1** an accompanying phenomenon; a fortuitous, less important or irrelevant by-product. **2** *pathol* a secondary symptom of a disease. ⓘ 17c.

epiphysis /ɪ'pɪfɪsɪs/ ▷ *noun* (*epiphyses* /-siːz/) *anatomy* **1** the growing end of a long bone. **2** the PINEAL GLAND. • **epiphyseal** /ɛpɪ'fɪzɪəl/ *adj.* ⓘ 17c: Greek, meaning 'excrescence', from *phyesthai* to grow.

epiphyte /'ɛpɪfaɪt/ ▷ *noun, bot* a plant that grows on another plant for support, but which is not a parasite. ⓘ 19c.

Epis. ▷ *abbreviation* **1** (*also* **Episc.**) Episcopal. **2** (*also* **Ep.**) *Bible* Epistle.

episcopacy /ɪ'pɪskəpəsɪ/ ▷ *noun* (*episcopacies*) **1** the government of the church by bishops. **2** bishops as a group. **3** the position or period of office of a bishop. ⓘ 17c: from Greek *episkopos* overseer.

episcopal /ɪ'pɪskəpəl/ ▷ *adj* **1** belonging or relating to bishops. **2** said of a church: governed by bishops.

episcopalian /ɪpɪskə'peɪlɪən/ ▷ *adj* **1** belonging or relating to an episcopal church. **2** advocating church government by bishops. ▷ *noun* a member of an episcopal church, especially the Anglican Church. • **episcopalianism** *noun.*

episcopate /ɪ'pɪskəpət/ ▷ *noun* **1** the position or period of office of a bishop. **2** bishops as a group. **3** an area under the care of a bishop; a diocese or bishopric.

episiotomy /ɪpɪzɪ'ɒtəmɪ/ ▷ *noun* (*episiotomies*) *medicine* a surgical cut made at the opening of the vagina during childbirth, to assist the delivery of the baby. ⓘ 19c: from Greek *epision* pubic area + -TOMY.

episode /'ɛpɪsoʊd/ ▷ *noun* **1** one of several events or distinct periods making up a longer sequence. **2** one of the separate parts in which a radio or TV serial is broadcast, or a serialized novel, etc is published. **3** any scene or incident forming part of a novel or narrative poem, often one providing a digression from the main story. • **episodic** /-'sɒdɪk/ *adj* **1** consisting of several distinct periods. **2** occurring at intervals; sporadic. • **episodically** *adverb.* ⓘ 17c: from Greek *epeisodion*, from *eisodos* a coming in.

epistemics /ɛpɪ'stiːmɪks/ ▷ *singular noun* the scientific study of knowledge, its acquisition and its communication. ⓒ 1960s: from Greek *episteme* knowledge.

epistemology /ɪpɪstəˈmɒlədʒɪ/ ▷ *noun* the philosophical theory of knowledge. • **epistemological** /-məˈlɒdʒɪkəl/ *adj*. • **epistemologist** *noun*. ⓒ 19c: from Greek *episteme* knowledge.

epistle /ɪˈpɪsəl/ ▷ *noun* **1** *literary* a letter, especially a long one, dealing with important matters. **2** a novel or poem written in the form of letters. **3** (*usually* **Epistle**) *Christianity* **a** each of the letters written by Christ's Apostles, which form part of the New Testament; **b** a reading from one of the Epistles as part of a religious service. • **epistolary** /ɪˈpɪstələrɪ/ *adj, formal* relating to or consisting of letters. ⓒ Anglo-Saxon *epistol*.

epistolary novel ▷ *noun* a type of novel in which the story is told entirely through an exchange of letters between the characters.

epistyle /ˈɛpɪstaɪl/ ▷ *noun, archit* an ARCHITRAVE. ⓒ 19c: from Greek *stylos* a pillar.

epitaph /ˈɛpɪtɑːf/ ▷ *noun* **1** an inscription on a gravestone. **2** a short commemorative speech or piece of writing in a similar style. ⓒ 14c: from Greek *epitaphion*, from *taphos* tomb.

epitaxy /ˈɛpɪtaksɪ/ ▷ *noun, crystallog* the growth of a thin layer of crystals on another crystal, so that they have the same structure. • **epitaxial** /-ˈtaksɪəl/ *adj*. ⓒ 1930s.

epithelium /ɛpɪˈθiːlɪəm/ ▷ *noun* (*plural* ***epithelia***) *anatomy* the layer of tissue that covers all external surfaces of a multicellular animal, and lines all hollow structures except for blood vessels and lymph vessels. • **epithelial** *adj*. ⓒ 18c: from Greek *thele* nipple.

epithet /ˈɛpɪθɛt/ ▷ *noun* an adjective or short descriptive phrase which captures the particular quality of the person or thing it describes. • **epithetic** *adj*. ⓒ 16c: from Greek *epitheton*, from *tithenai* to place.

epitome /ɪˈpɪtəmɪ/ ▷ *noun* (***epitomes***) **1** a miniature representation of a larger or wider idea, issue, etc. **2** a person or thing that is the embodiment or a perfect example (of a quality, etc). **3** a summary of a written work. ⓒ 16c: from Greek *tome* a cut.

epitomize or **epitomise** /ɪˈpɪtəmaɪz/ ▷ *verb* (***epitomized, epitomizing***) **1** to typify or personify. **2** to make an epitome of something; to shorten. • **epitomizer** or **epitomist** *noun* someone who abridges something. ⓒ 16c.

epizoon /ɛpɪˈzoʊɒn/ ▷ *noun* (*plural* ***epizoa***) *zool* an animal that lives on the surface of another animal, either parasitically or commensally. • **epizoan** *adj, noun*. • **epizoic** *adj* **1** living on an animal. **2** having seeds dispersed by animals. ⓒ 19c: from Greek *zoion* animal.

epizootic /ɛpɪzoʊˈɒtɪk/ *adj* **1** belonging or referring to epizoa. **2** affecting animals as an epidemic affects humans. ▷ *noun* an epizootic disease.

epizootics ▷ *singular noun* the study of epidemic animal diseases.

EPNS ▷ *abbreviation* electroplated nickel silver.

EPO ▷ *abbreviation* European Patent Office.

epoch /ˈiːpɒk/ ▷ *noun* **1** a major division or period of history, or of a person's life, etc, usually marked by some important event. **2** *geol* an interval of geological time representing a subdivision of a period, and during which a particular series of rocks was formed. See table at GEOLOGICAL TIME SCALE. • **epochal** /ˈɛpɒkəl, ˈiː-/ *adj* relating to, or lasting for, an epoch. ⓒ 17c: from Greek *epoche* fixed point.

epoch-making ▷ *adj* highly significant or decisive.

eponym /ˈɛpənɪm/ ▷ *noun* **1** the name of a person after whom something is named, especially the main character in a play or novel, etc whose name provides its title. **2** a name derived from a person's name, eg *Hamlet*, *Gettysburg*. • **eponymous** /ɪˈpɒnɪməs/ *adj* said of a character in a story, etc: having the name which is used as the title. ⓒ 19c: from Greek *onyma* a name.

EPOS /iːpɒs/ ▷ *abbreviation* electronic point of sale.

epoxy /ɪˈpɒksɪ/ *chem* ▷ *adj* consisting of an oxygen atom bonded to two carbon atoms. ▷ *noun* (***epoxies***) (*also* **epoxy resin**) any of a group of synthetic thermosetting resins, that are tough, resistant to abrasion and chemical attack, and form strong adhesive bonds. ⓒ Early 20c: from EPI- 1 + OXYGEN.

EPP ▷ *abbreviation* European People's Party.

EPROM /ˈiːprɒm/ ▷ *abbreviation, computing* erasable programmable read-only memory, a read-only memory in which stored data can be erased by ultraviolet light, etc and reprogrammed.

EPS or **eps** ▷ *abbreviation, stock exchange* earnings per share.

epsilon /ɛpˈsaɪlən, ˈɛpsɪlɒn/ ▷ *noun* the fifth letter of the Greek alphabet. See table at GREEK ALPHABET. ⓒ 14c: Greek *e psilon* bare, or mere, e.

Epsom salts /ˈɛpsəm —/ ▷ *singular or plural noun* a bitter white powder, a preparation of magnesium sulphate, used as a medicine, eg for clearing the bowels. ⓒ 18c: from Epsom in Surrey, where it occurs naturally in spring water.

EPSRC ▷ *abbreviation* Engineering and Physical Sciences Research Council.

Epstein-Barr virus /ɛpstaɪnˈbɑː(r) —/ ▷ *noun* a virus which causes GLANDULAR FEVER and is associated with various human cancers, eg Burkitt's lymphoma. ⓒ 1960s: from M A Epstein and Y M Barr, British virologists, who first isolated the virus in 1964.

equable /ˈɛkwəbəl/ ▷ *adj* **1** said of a climate: never showing very great variations or extremes. **2** said of a person: even-tempered. • **equability** *noun*. • **equably** *adverb*. ⓒ 17c: from Latin *aequabilis*, from *aequus* equal.

equal /ˈiːkwəl/ ▷ *adj* **1** the same in size, amount or value, etc. **2** evenly balanced; displaying no advantage or bias. **3** having the same status; having or entitled to the same rights. ▷ *noun* a person or thing of the same age, rank, ability or worth, etc. ▷ *verb* (***equalled, equalling***) **1** to be the same in amount, value or size, etc as someone or something. **2** to be as good as someone or something; to match. **3** to achieve something which matches (a previous achievement or achiever). • **equality** /ɪˈkwɒlɪtɪ/ *noun* (***equalities***). • **equally** *adverb*. • **equal to something** having the necessary ability for it. • **equal to the occasion** fit or able to cope with an emergency or an unexpected situation, etc. ⓒ 14c: from Latin *aequalis*, from *aequus* level or equal.

equalize or **equalise** /ˈiːkwəlaɪz/ ▷ *verb* (***equalized, equalizing***) **1** *tr & intr* to make or become equal. **2** *intr* to reach the same score as an opponent, after being behind. • **equalization** *noun*. • **equalizer** *noun* a person or thing that equalizes, especially a goal or point scored which makes one equal to one's opponent. See also GRAPHIC EQUALIZER. ⓒ 17c.

equal opportunities ▷ *plural noun* the principle of equal treatment of all employees or candidates for employment, irrespective of race, religion or sex, etc.

equal sign or **equals sign** ▷ *noun, math* the symbol written =, which indicates that two numerical values are equal.

equanimity /ɛkwəˈnɪmɪtɪ/ ▷ *noun* calmness of temper; composure. ⓒ 17c: from Latin *aequanimitas*, from *aequus* equal + *animus* mind.

equate /ɪˈkweɪt/ ▷ *verb* (***equated, equating***) (*usually* **equate with something**) to be equivalent to it. ⓒ 19c; 15c in obsolete sense 'to make something equal': from Latin *aequare*.

■ **equate one thing to** or **with another** to consider them as equivalent.

equation /ɪ'kweɪʒən/ ▷ *noun* **1** *math* a mathematical statement of the equality between two expressions involving constants and/or variables. **2** *chem* a CHEMICAL EQUATION. **3** the act of equating. **4** the state of being equal or balanced equally.

equator /ɪ'kweɪtə(r)/ ▷ *noun* **1** (*often* **the Equator**) *geog* the imaginary great circle that passes around the Earth at latitude 0 at an equal distance from the North and South Poles, and divides the Earth's surface into the northern and southern hemispheres. **2** *astron* the CELESTIAL EQUATOR. **3** a circle dividing a spherical body into two equal parts. ◷ 14c: from Latin *aequator* equalizer (of day and night).

equatorial /ɛkwə'tɔːrɪəl/ *adj* **1** belonging to, or near, the equator. **2** said of a telescope: mounted on an axis capable of moving parallel to the equator. ▷ *noun* an equatorial telescope. ● **equatorially** *adverb* so as to have motion or direction parallel to the equator.

equerry /'ɛkwərɪ, ɪ'kwɛrɪ/ ▷ *noun* (*equerries*) an official who serves as a personal attendant to a member of a royal family. ◷ 16c as *esquiry*: from French *esquierie* company of squires, from *esquier* squire.

equestrian /ɪ'kwɛstrɪən/ ▷ *adj* **1** belonging or relating to horse-riding or horses. **2** on horseback. ▷ *noun* a rider or performer on horseback. ● **equestrianism** *noun* horsemanship. ◷ 17c: from Latin *equestris* relating to horsemen.

equestrienne /ɪkwɛstrɪ'ɛn/ ▷ *noun* a female EQUESTRIAN. ◷ 19c: modelled on feminine nouns ending *-enne*.

equi- /ɛkwɪ, iːkwɪ, ɪ'kwɪ/ ▷ *combining form, signifying* equal or equally □ *equidistant*. ◷ From Latin *aequus* equal.

equiangular ▷ *adj* having equal angles. ● **equiangularity** *noun*. ◷ 17c.

equidistant ▷ *adj* equally distant. ● **equidistance** *noun*. ● **equidistantly** *adverb*. ◷ 16c.

equilateral ▷ *adj* having all sides of equal length. ◷ 16c: from Latin *latus* side.

equilibrium /ɛkwɪ'lɪbrɪəm/ ▷ *noun* (*equilibria* or *equilibriums*) **1** *physics* a state in which the various forces acting on an object or objects in a system balance each other, so that there is no tendency for any part of the system to move. **2** *chem* a reversible chemical reaction in which the rate of forward and backward reactions is the same, so that the concentrations of reactants and products remain unchanged. **3** a calm and composed state of mind. **4** a state of balance. ◷ 17c: from Latin *aequi librium*, from *aequus* equal + *libra* balance.

equilibrate /ɪ'kwɪlɪbreɪt, iːkwɪ'laɪbreɪt/ *verb* (*equilibrated, equilibrating*) to balance. ● **equilibrator** *noun* a balancing or stabilizing device, especially an aeroplane fin. ◷ 17c.

equilibrist /ɪ'kwɪlɪbrɪst/ ▷ *noun* someone who does balancing tricks.

equine /'ɛkwaɪn/ ▷ *adj, formal* belonging or relating to, or like, a horse or horses. ◷ 18c: from Latin *equinus*, from *equus* horse.

equinoctial /ɛkwɪ'nɒkʃəl/ *adj* happening on or near an equinox. ▷ *noun* **1** a storm or gale occurring about the time of an equinox. **2** (*also* **equinoctial line**) *astron* the CELESTIAL EQUATOR. ● **equinoctially** *adverb* in the direction of the equinox.

equinoctial point ▷ *noun, astron* either of the two points in the heavens where the EQUINOCTIAL LINE cuts the ECLIPTIC.

equinoctial year see SOLAR YEAR

equinox /'ɛkwɪnɒks, 'iːk-/ ▷ *noun* (*equinoxes*) either of the two occasions on which the Sun crosses the equator, making night and day equal in length, the **spring equinox** occurring about 21 March and the **autumnal equinox** occurring about 23 September. ◷ 14c: from Latin *aequi noctium*, from *aequus* equal + *nox* night.

equip /ɪ'kwɪp/ ▷ *verb* (*equipped, equipping*) to fit out or provide someone or something with the necessary tools, supplies, abilities, etc. ● **equipment** *noun* **1** the clothes, machines, tools or instruments, etc necessary for a particular kind of work or activity. **2** *formal* the act of equipping. ◷ 16c: from French *équiper*, from earlier French *eschiper* to fit out a ship.

equipage /'ɛkwɪpɪdʒ/ *noun* **1** a horse-drawn carriage with its footmen. **2** *formerly* the equipment carried by a military unit. ◷ 16c.

équipe / *French* ekip/ ▷ *noun, sport* a team, especially a motor-racing team. ◷ 1930s: French.

equipoise /'ɛkwɪpɔɪz/ ▷ *noun, formal* **1** a state of balance. **2** a counterbalancing weight. ▷ *verb* (*equipoised, equipoising*) to balance; to counterpoise. ◷ 17c.

equitable /'ɛkwɪtəbəl/ ▷ *adj* **1** fair and just. **2** *law* relating to, or valid according to, the concept of natural justice, or equity, as opposed to common law or statute law. ● **equitableness** *noun*. ● **equitably** *adverb*. ◷ 16c: from French *équitable*.

equitation /ɛkwɪ'teɪʃən/ ▷ *noun, formal* the art of riding a horse. ◷ 16c: from Latin *equitare, equitatum* to ride.

equity /'ɛkwɪtɪ/ ▷ *noun* (*equities*) **1** fair or just conditions or treatment. **2** *law* the concept of natural justice, as opposed to common law or statute law, often invoked to support an interpretation, or the complete waiving, of a law. **3** the excess in value of a property over the mortgage and other charges held on it. Compare NEGATIVE EQUITY. **4** (*usually* **equities**) an ordinary share in a company. **5** (**Equity**) the trade union for actors. ◷ 14c: from Latin *aequitas* equality.

equivalent /ɪ'kwɪvələnt/ ▷ *adj* equal in value, power or meaning, etc. ▷ *noun* an equivalent thing or amount, etc. ● **equivalence** *noun*. ● **equivalently** *adverb*. ◷ 15c: from Latin *aequus* equal + *valere* to be worth.

equivalent weight ▷ *noun, chem* the quantity of one which reacts chemically with a given amount of a standard.

equivocal /ɪ'kwɪvəkəl/ ▷ *adj* **1** ambiguous; of doubtful meaning. **2** of an uncertain nature. **3** questionable, suspicious or mysterious. ● **equivocally** *adverb*. ● **equivocate** *verb* (*equivocated, equivocating*) *intr* to use ambiguous words in order to deceive or to avoid answering a question. ● **equivocation** *noun* evasive ambiguity. ◷ 16c: from Latin *aequus* equal + *vox, vocis* voice or word.

ER ▷ *abbreviation* **1** *Elizabeth Regina* (Latin), Queen Elizabeth. **2** *Edwardus Rex* (Latin), King Edward.

Er ▷ *symbol, chem* erbium.

er /ɜː/ used to represent a sound made while hesitating in speech.

-er[1] /ə(r)/ ▷ *suffix* used to form the comparative of adjectives and adverbs □ *happier* □ *sooner*. ◷ Anglo-Saxon *-ra* for adjectives and *-or* for adverbs.

-er[2] /ə(r)/ ▷ *suffix, forming nouns, signifying* **1** the person or thing performing the action of the verb □ *driver* □ *heater*. **2** a person from a specified town or city □ *Londoner* □ *New Yorker*. ◷ Anglo-Saxon *-ere*.

ERA ▷ *abbreviation* Equal Rights Amendment.

era /'ɪərə/ ▷ *noun* (*eras*) **1** a distinct period in history marked by or beginning at an important event. **2** *geol* the second largest unit of geological time, representing a subdivision of an EON. See table at GEOLOGICAL TIME SCALE. ◷ 17c: from Latin *aera* number.

eradicate /ɪ'radɪkeɪt/ ▷ *verb* (*eradicated, eradicating*) to get rid of something completely. ● **eradicable** /-kəbəl/

adj. • **eradication** *noun*. • **eradicative** /-kətɪv/ *adj*. • **eradicator** *noun*. ⓘ 16c: from Latin *eradicare, eradicatum* to root out.

erase /ɪˈreɪz/ ▷ *verb* (***erased, erasing***) **1** to rub out (pencil marks, etc). **2** to remove all trace of something. **3** to destroy (a recording) on audio or video tape. • **erasable** *adj*. • **eraser** *noun* something that erases, especially a rubber for removing pencil or ink marks. • **erasure** *noun* **1** the act of rubbing out. **2** a place where something written has been erased. ⓘ 17c: from Latin *eradere, erasum* to scratch out.

erbium /ˈɜːbɪəm/ ▷ *noun, chem* (symbol **Er**, atomic number 68) a soft silvery metallic element, that absorbs neutrons and has a high electrical resistivity. ⓘ 19c: from the name Ytterby in Sweden, where it was first discovered.

ere /ɛə(r)/ ▷ *prep, conj, now only poetic* before. ⓘ Anglo-Saxon *ær*.

erect /ɪˈrɛkt/ ▷ *adj* **1** upright; not bent or leaning. **2** *physiol* said of the penis, clitoris or nipples: enlarged and rigid through being filled with blood, usually as a result of sexual excitement. ▷ *verb* (***erected, erecting***) **1** to put up or to build something. **2** to set or put (a pole or flag, etc) in a vertical position. **3** to set up or establish something. • **erecter** or **erector** *noun*. • **erectly** *adverb*. • **erectness** *noun*. ⓘ 14c: from Latin *erigere, erectum* to set upright.

erectile /ɪˈrɛktaɪl/ *adj, physiol* **1** said of an organ, etc: capable of becoming erect. **2** capable of being erected. ⓘ 19c.

erection /ɪˈrɛkʃən/ *noun* **1** the act of erecting or the state of being erected. **2** *sometimes derog* a building or structure. **3** said of a sexual organ, especially the penis: the process of becoming erect or the state of being erect. **4** an erect sexual organ, especially an erect penis. ⓘ 16c.

E-region see E-LAYER

erepsin /ɪˈrɛpsɪn/ ▷ *noun* an enzyme in the small intestine. ⓘ Early 20c: from Latin *eripere, ereptum* to snatch.

erf /ɜːf/ ▷ *noun* (*plural* ***erven*** /ɜːvən/) *chiefly S Afr* a garden plot or small piece of ground. ⓘ 17c: Dutch.

erg¹ /ɜːg/ ▷ *noun, physics* in the cgs system: a unit of work or energy defined as the amount of work done when a force of one DYNE moves through a distance of one centimetre. ⓘ 19c: from Greek *ergon* work.

erg² /ɜːg/ ▷ *noun* (***areg*** /ˈarɛg/ or ***ergs***) an area of shifting sand dunes, especially in the Sahara Desert. ⓘ 19c: French, from Arabic *'irj*.

ergo /ˈɜːgoʊ/ ▷ *adverb, formal or logic* therefore. ⓘ 14c: Latin.

ergonomics /ɜːgəˈnɒmɪks/ ▷ *singular noun* the study of the relationship between people and their working environment, including machinery, computer sytems, etc. • **ergonomic** *adj*. • **ergonomically** *adverb* in relation to people and their work environment. • **ergonomist** /ɜːˈgɒnəmɪst/ *noun*. ⓘ 1940s: from Greek *ergon* work, modelled on ECONOMICS.

ergot /ˈɜːgɒt/ ▷ *noun* **1** a disease of rye and other cereals caused by a fungus. **2** (**ergots**) the hard purple structures characteristic of this disease. **3** the fungus that produces this disease, now an important source of alkaloid drugs. ⓘ 17c: French, from earlier French *argot* cock's spur, because of its appearance.

ergotism /ˈɜːgətɪzəm/ *noun, pathol* poisoning caused by the consumption of bread made from rye infected with ergot.

erica /ˈɛrɪkə/ ▷ *noun* (***ericas***) any plant of the heath genus. • **ericaceous** /ɛrɪˈkeɪʃəs/ *adj* belonging or relating to the family of plants which includes azalea, rhododendron and heather. ⓘ 17c: from Greek *ereike* heath.

Erinys /ɛˈrɪnɪs/ ▷ *noun* (***Erinyes*** /ɛˈrɪnɪiːz/) *Greek mythol* any of THE FURIES.

ERM ▷ *abbreviation* Exchange Rate Mechanism.

ermine /ˈɜːmɪn/ ▷ *noun* (***ermine*** or ***ermines***) **1** the stoat in its winter phase, when its fur has turned white except for the tip of the tail, which remains dark. **2** the fur of this animal, highly prized by the fur trade, and formerly reserved for royalty. ⓘ 12c: from French *hermine*, from Latin *Armenius mus* Armenian mouse.

Ernie /ˈɜːnɪ/ ▷ *noun, Brit* the computer which applies the laws of chance to pick the prize-winning numbers of PREMIUM BONDS. ⓘ 1950s: electronic *r*andom *n*umber *i*ndicator equipment.

erode /ɪˈroʊd/ ▷ *verb* (***eroded, eroding***) *tr & intr* to wear away, destroy or be destroyed gradually. • **erodible** *adj*. ⓘ 17c; see EROSION.

erogenous /ɪˈrɒdʒənəs/ and **erogenic** /ɛroʊˈdʒɛnɪk/ ▷ *adj* said of areas of the body, usually called **erogenous zones**: sensitive to sexual stimulation. ⓘ Late 19c: from Greek *eros* love.

-erooney see -AROONEY

erosion /ɪˈroʊʒən/ *noun* the loosening, fragmentation and transport from one place to another of rock material by water, wind, ice, gravity or living organisms, including human activity. • **erosive** *adj* causing erosion. ⓘ 16c: from Latin *erodere, erosum* to gnaw away.

erotic /ɪˈrɒtɪk/ ▷ *adj* arousing; referring or relating to sexual desire, or giving sexual pleasure. • **erotically** *adverb*. ⓘ 17c: from Greek *erotikos*, from *eros* love.

erotica /ɪˈrɒtɪkə/ ▷ *plural noun* erotic literature or pictures, etc. ⓘ 19c.

eroticism /ɪˈrɒtɪsɪzm/ *noun* **1** the erotic quality of a piece of writing or a picture, etc. **2** interest in, or pursuit of, sexual sensations. **3** the use of erotic images and symbols in art and literature, etc.

err /ɜː(r)/ ▷ *verb* (***erred, erring*** /ˈɜːrɪŋ, ˈɛərɪŋ/) *intr* **1** to make a mistake, be wrong or do wrong. **2** to sin. • **err on the side of something** to run the risk of (a particular fault) in order to avoid an opposite and greater fault □ *Err on the side of caution*. ⓘ 14c: from Latin *errare* to stray.

errand /ˈɛrənd/ ▷ *noun* **1** a short journey made in order to get or do something, especially for someone else. **2** the purpose of such a journey. • **run an errand** or **run errands** to perform small pieces of business, deliver messages, etc. ⓘ Anglo-Saxon *ærende* verbal message.

errant /ˈɛrənt/ ▷ *adj, literary* **1** doing wrong; erring. **2** wandering in search of adventure □ *a knight errant*. • **errantry** /ˈɛrəntrɪ/ *noun*. ⓘ 14c: from French *errer*, in sense 1 from Latin *errare* to stray, and in sense 2 from Latin *itinerare* to make a journey.

erratic /ɪˈratɪk/ ▷ *adj* **1** irregular; having no fixed pattern or course. **2** unpredictable in behaviour. ▷ *noun, geol* a mass of rock transported by ice and deposited at a distance. Also called **erratic block** or **boulder**. • **erratically** *adverb*. ⓘ 14c: from Latin *errare* to stray.

erratum /ɛˈrɑːtəm/ ▷ *noun* (***errata***) *formal* an error in writing or printing. ⓘ 16c: past participle of Latin *errare* to stray.

erred and **erring** see under ERR

erroneous /ɪˈroʊnɪəs/ ▷ *adj* wrong or mistaken. • **erroneously** *adverb* in error; by mistake. • **erroneousness** *noun*. ⓘ 14c, meaning 'straying from what is right': from Latin *erroneus* straying.

error /ˈɛrə(r)/ ▷ *noun* **1** a mistake, inaccuracy or misapprehension. **2** the state of being mistaken. **3** the possible discrepancy between an estimate and an actual value or amount □ *a margin of error*. ⓘ 14c: Latin, also meaning 'a wandering or straying'.

error message ▷ *noun, computing* a message to help a user correct an error, eg an incorrect filename.

ersatz /'ɜːzats, 'ɛə-/ *derog* ▻ *adj* substitute; imitation. ▻ *noun* (*ersatzes*) a cheaper substitute, often used because the genuine article is unavailable. ⓘ Late 19c: German.

Erse /ɜːs, ɛəs/ ▻ *noun* the name formerly used by lowland Scots for Scottish GAELIC; now also applied to Irish Gaelic. ▻ *adj* relating to, or spoken or written in, these languages. ⓘ 15c: Lowland Scots *Erisch* Irish.

erstwhile /'ɜːstwaɪl/ ▻ *adj, formal or archaic* former; previous. ⓘ Anglo-Saxon *ærest* earliest, from *ær* before.

eructation /iːrʌk'teɪʃən/ ▻ *noun, formal* a belch or the act of belching. ⓘ 16c: from Latin *eructare, eructatum* to belch out.

erudite /'ɛrʊdaɪt, 'ɛrjʊ-/ ▻ *adj* showing or having a great deal of knowledge; learned. • **eruditely** *adverb* in an erudite or learned manner. • **erudition** /-'dɪʃən/ *noun*. ⓘ 15c: from Latin *erudire, eruditum* to instruct.

erupt /ɪ'rʌpt/ ▻ *verb* (*erupted, erupting*) *intr* **1** said of a volcano: to throw out lava, ash and gases. **2** to break out suddenly and violently. **3** said of a skin blemish or rash: to appear suddenly and in a severe form. **4** said of a tooth: to emerge through the gum. • **eruption** *noun* **1** the process of erupting, especially by a volcano. **2** a sudden or violent breaking out. • **eruptive** *adj*. ⓘ 17c: from Latin *erumpere, eruptum* to break out.

erven *plural of* ERF

ERW ▻ *abbreviation* enhanced radiation weapon.

-ery /ərɪ/ or **-ry** ▻ *suffix, forming nouns, indicating* **1** a place where work or an activity of the specified kind is carried out □ *brewery*. **2** a class, group or type of the specified kind □ *greenery* □ *weaponry*. **3** an art, skill or practice of the specified kind □ *dentistry*. **4** behaviour of the specified kind □ *bravery*. **5** anything connected with the specified person or thing □ *popery*. ⓘ From French *-erie*, from Latin *-arius*.

erysipelas /ɛrɪ'sɪpɪləs/ ▻ *noun, pathol* an infectious disease of the skin, especially of the face, which produces deep red sore patches, accompanied by fever. ⓘ 16c: Latin, perhaps from Greek *erythros* red + *pella* skin.

erythema /ɛrɪ'θiːmə/ ▻ *noun, pathol* redness of the skin, caused by dilation of the blood capillaries. ⓘ 18c: Latin, from Greek, from *erythros* red.

erythro- /ɛrɪθroʊ/ or (before a vowel) **erythr-** *combining form, denoting* red. ⓘ From Greek *erythros*.

erythrocyte ▻ *noun* a red blood corpuscle. ⓘ Late 19c.

erythromycin ▻ *noun, medicine* an antibiotic used to treat a wide range of bacterial infections, especially in patients who are allergic to penicillin. ⓘ 1950s.

ES ▻ *abbreviation, IVR* El Salvador.

Es ▻ *symbol, chem* einsteinium.

-es see -S[1], -S[2]

ESA ▻ *abbreviation* **1** Environmentally Sensitive Area. **2** European Space Agency.

Esc. ▻ *abbreviation* escudo, or escudos, the Portuguese currency unit.

escalate /'ɛskəleɪt/ ▻ *verb* (*escalated, escalating*) *tr & intr* to increase or be increased rapidly in scale or degree, etc. • **escalation** *noun*. • **escalatory** *adj*. ⓘ 1940s: from ESCALATOR.

escalator /'ɛskəleɪtə(r)/ ▻ *noun* a type of conveyor belt which forms a continuous moving staircase. ⓘ 1900: originally a trademark, modelled on ELEVATOR, probably from Spanish *escalada*, from Latin *scala* ladder.

escalator clause and **escalation clause** ▻ *noun* a clause in an agreement allowing for adjustment up or down according to changes in circumstances, eg changes in costs of materials.

escallonia /ɛskə'loʊnɪə/ ▻ *noun* (*escallonias*) any plant belonging to an American branch of the saxifrage family. ⓘ 19c: from Escallon, the 18c Spanish traveller who discovered the plants.

escallop see SCALLOP

> ***escallop, escalope***
>
> These words are sometimes confused with each other.

escalope /'ɛskəlɒp/ ▻ *noun, cookery* a thin slice of boneless meat, especially veal. ⓘ 19c: French, originally meaning 'shell'.

escapade /ɛskə'peɪd, 'ɛskəpeɪd/ ▻ *noun* a daring, adventurous or unlawful act. ⓘ 17c, meaning 'escape': French.

escape /ɪ'skeɪp/ ▻ *verb* (*escaped, escaping*) **1** *intr* to gain freedom. **2** to manage to avoid (punishment or disease, etc). **3** not to be noticed or remembered by someone □ *Nothing escapes his notice.* **4** *intr* said of a gas or liquid, etc: to leak out or get out. **5** said of words, etc: to be uttered unintentionally by someone. ▻ *noun* **1** an act of escaping. **2** a means of escape. **3** the avoidance of danger or harm □ *a narrow escape*. **4** a leak or release. **5** something providing a break or distraction. **6** something which has escaped, especially a plant originally cultivated as a garden plant but now growing in the wild. • **escapable** *adj*. • **escaper** *noun*. ⓘ 14c: from French *escaper*, probably from Latin *excappare* to remove one's cape.

escape clause ▻ *noun* a clause in a contract stating the conditions under which the contract may be broken.

escapee *noun* (*escapees*) someone who has escaped, especially from prison. ⓘ 19c.

escape key ▻ *noun, computing* a key that usually cancels a previous action.

escapement ▻ *noun* **1** the mechanism in a clock or watch which connects the moving parts to the balance. **2** the mechanism in a piano which allows the hammers to move away after striking the strings while the keys are held down. ⓘ 18c: from French *échappement*.

escape road ▻ *noun* a short track leading off a road on a steep hill or sharp bend, etc, which allows the driver to stop if the vehicle malfunctions or goes out of control, etc.

escape velocity ▻ *noun, physics* the minimum velocity required for an object to escape from the pull of the gravitational field of the Earth, or of another planet or celestial body.

escapism *noun* the means of escaping, or the tendency to escape, from unpleasant reality into day-dreams or fantasy. • **escapist** *adj* characterized by escapism. ▻ *noun* someone who indulges in escapism. ⓘ 1930s.

escapologist /ɛskə'pɒlədʒɪst/ *noun* someone who practises escapology, especially as their profession. • **escapology** *noun* the art or practice of freeing oneself from chains and other constraints, especially as theatrical entertainment. ⓘ 1920s.

escargot /ɪ'skɑːgoʊ; *French* ɛskaʀgo/ ▻ *noun* an edible snail. ⓘ 19c: French.

escarpment /ɪ'skɑːpmənt/ ▻ *noun, geol* a more or less continuous line of very steep slopes, formed by faulting or erosion, especially around the margins of a plateau. ⓘ 19c: from French *escarper* to cut steeply.

eschatology /ɛskə'tɒlədʒɪ/ ▻ *noun* the branch of theology dealing with final things, eg death, divine judgement and life after death. • **eschatological** /-'lɒdʒɪkəl/ *adj*. • **eschatologist** *noun*. ⓘ 19c: from Greek *eschatos* last.

escheat /ɪs'tʃiːt/ *law* ▻ *noun* **1** *formerly* the handing over of property to the state or a feudal lord in the absence of a legal heir. **2** property handed over in this way. ▻ *verb* (*escheated, escheating*) **1** *intr* said of property: to be handed over in this way. **2** to confiscate (property). ⓒ 14c: from French *eschete*, from *escheoir* to fall to someone.

Escherichia coli /ɛʃəˈrɪkɪə ˈkoʊlaɪ/ ▷ *noun, biol* (abbreviation **E. coli**) a species of bacterium that occurs naturally in the intestines of vertebrates including humans, and which sometimes causes disease. ⓒ 19c: named after the German physician T Escherich (died 1911).

eschew /ɪsˈtʃuː/ ▷ *verb* (***eschewed, eschewing***) *formal* to avoid, keep away from, or abstain from something. • **eschewal** *noun*. ⓒ 14c: from French *eschever*.

eschscholtzia or **eschscholzia** /ɛˈʃɒltsɪə/ ▷ *noun* (***eschscholtzias***) any plant of the poppy family, especially the **Californian poppy**, a showy garden annual. ⓒ 19c: from J F von Eschscholtz (1793–1831), a member of the expedition which discovered the poppy in 1821.

escort ▷ *noun* /ˈɛskɔːt/ **1** one or more people or vehicles, etc accompanying another or others for protection, guidance, or as a mark of honour. **2** someone of the opposite sex asked or hired to accompany another at a social event. ▷ *verb* /ɪˈskɔːt/ (***escorted, escorting***) to accompany someone or something as an escort. ⓒ 16c: from French *escorte*.

escritoire /ɛskrɪˈtwɑː(r)/ ▷ *noun* a writing-desk, usually ornamented and with drawers and compartments, etc. ⓒ 16c: French, from Latin *scriptorium* writing-room.

escudo /ɛˈskuːdoʊ/ ▷ *noun* (***escudos***) (abbreviation **Esc.**) the standard unit of currency of Portugal. ⓒ 19c: Portuguese and Spanish, from Latin *scutum* shield.

esculent /ˈɛskjʊlənt/ *formal* ▷ *adj* edible. ▷ *noun* any edible substance. ⓒ 17c: from Latin *esculentus* eatable, from *esca* food.

escutcheon /ɪˈskʌtʃən/ ▷ *noun* **1** a shield decorated with a coat of arms. **2** a small metal plate around a keyhole or doorknob. • **a blot on the escutcheon** *facetious* a stain on one's good reputation. ⓒ 15c: from French *escuchon*, from Latin *scutum* shield.

Esd. ▷ *abbreviation* Book of the Bible: Esdras (in the Apocrypha). See table at BIBLE.

ESE ▷ *abbreviation* east-south-east.

-ese /iːz/ ▷ *suffix, forming nouns and adjectives* **1** relating to a specified country or place □ ***Japanese*** □ ***Vietnamese***. **2** indicating the people or language of a specified country □ ***Chinese***. **3** *often derog* the typical style or language of a particular group or profession □ ***journalese***. ⓒ From French *-eis* (modern French equivalents *-ois, -ais*), from Latin *-ensis*.

esker /ˈɛskə(r)/ ▷ *noun, geol* a long narrow hill of gravel and sand which may wind for long distances along a valley floor, and is thought to be formed by water flowing in tunnels underneath glaciers. ⓒ 19c: from Irish *eiscir* ridge.

Eskimo /ˈɛskɪmoʊ/ *now often offensive* ▷ *noun* (***Eskimos*** or ***Eskimo***) INUIT. ▷ *adj* INUIT. ⓒ 16c: from French *Esquimaux*, from Native N American *esquimantsic* eaters of raw flesh.

Eskimo, Inuit

Although **Eskimo** is the established English name for this people, the people themselves prefer the name **Inuit**.

Eskimo dog ▷ *noun* a powerful breed of dog used by the INUIT to pull sledges.

ESL ▷ *abbreviation* English as a second language.

ESN ▷ *abbreviation* educationally subnormal.

esophagus the *N Amer* spelling of OESOPHAGUS.

esoteric /ɛsoʊˈtɛrɪk, iːsoʊ-/ ▷ *adj* understood only by those few people who have the necessary special knowledge; secret or mysterious. • **esoterically** *adverb*. • **esotericism** /-ˈtɛrɪsɪzəm/ *noun*. ⓒ 17c: from Greek *esoterikos*, from *eso* within.

ESP ▷ *abbreviation* **1** English for special purposes. **2** extrasensory perception.

esp. or **espec.** ▷ *abbreviation* especially.

espadrille /ɛspəˈdrɪl/ ▷ *noun* a light canvas shoe with a sole made of rope or other plaited fibre. ⓒ 19c: French, from Provençal *espardillo*, from *espart* esparto grass.

espalier /ɪˈspalɪə(r)/ ▷ *noun* **1** a trellis or arrangement of wires against which a shrub or fruit tree is trained to grow flat, eg against a wall. **2** such a shrub or tree. ⓒ 17c: French.

esparto /ɛˈspɑːtoʊ/ and **esparto grass** ▷ *noun* (***espartos*** or ***esparto grasses***) a tough coarse grass native to Spain and N Africa, used to make rope, etc. ⓒ 19c: Spanish, from Greek *sparton* kind of rope.

especial /ɪˈspɛʃəl/ ▷ *adj* special. • **especially** *adverb* principally; more than in other cases. ⓒ 14c: French, from Latin *specialis* individual.

especially

See Usage Note at **specially**.

Esperanto /ɛspəˈrantoʊ/ ▷ *noun* a language invented for international use, based on European languages, and published in 1887. Also *as adj*. • **Esperantist** *noun*. ⓒ 19c: originally the pseudonym of its inventor, Dr Zamenhof, meaning 'the one who hopes'.

espied *past tense, past participle of* ESPY

espionage /ˈɛspɪənɑːʒ/ ▷ *noun* the activity of spying, or the use of spies to gather information. ⓒ 18c: from French *espionnage*, from *espion* spy.

esplanade /ɛspləˈneɪd/ ▷ *noun* **1** a long wide pavement next to a beach. **2** a level open area between a fortified place and the nearest houses. ⓒ 17c: French, from Spanish *esplanar* make level.

espouse /ɪˈspaʊz/ ▷ *verb* (***espoused, espousing***) **1** *formal* to adopt or give one's support to (a cause, etc). **2** *old use* to marry, or to give (eg a daughter) in marriage. • **espousal** *noun* **1** *formal* the act of espousing (a cause, etc). **2** *old use* a marriage or engagement. ⓒ 15c: from French *espouser* to marry.

espresso /ɛˈsprɛsoʊ/ or **expresso** /ɛk-/ ▷ *noun* (***espressos*** or ***expressos***) **1** coffee made by forcing steam or boiling water through ground coffee beans. **2** the machine for making this. ⓒ 1940s: Italian, literally 'pressed out'.

esprit / *French* ɛspri/ ▷ *noun, formal or literary* liveliness or wit. ⓒ 16c: French, literally 'spirit'.

esprit de corps /ɛsˈpriː də kɔː(r)/ ▷ *noun* loyalty to, or concern for the honour of, a group or body to which one belongs. ⓒ 18c: French, literally 'spirit of the group'.

espy /ɪˈspaɪ/ ▷ *verb, literary* to catch sight of someone or something; to observe. ⓒ 14c: from French *espier* to spy.

Esq. or **esq.** ▷ *abbreviation* esquire.

-esque /ɛsk/ ▷ *suffix, signifying* **1** in the style or fashion of the specified person or thing □ ***Byronesque***. **2** like or similar to the specified thing □ ***picturesque***. ⓒ French, from Italian *-esco*.

esquire /ɪˈskwaɪə(r)/ ▷ *noun* (*plural* in sense 2 only ***esquires***) **1** (abbreviation **Esq.** or **esq.**) a title used after a man's name when no other form of address is used, especially when addressing letters. **2** *now chiefly historical* a squire. ⓒ 15c in sense 2: from French *esquier* squire.

ESRC ▷ *abbreviation* Economic and Social Research Council.

-ess /ɛs, ɪs, əs/ ▷ *suffix, forming noun, signifying* a female of the specified type or class □ ***lioness*** □ ***duchess***. ⓒ From French *-esse*, from Latin *-issa*.

essay /ˈɛseɪ/ ▻ *noun* (***essays***) **1** a short formal piece of writing, usually one dealing with a single subject. **2** *formal* an attempt. ▻ *verb* /ɛˈseɪ/ (***essayed, essaying***) *formal* to attempt. • **essayist** /ˈɛseɪɪst/ *noun* a writer of literary essays. ⓒ 16c: from French *essayer* to try.

essence /ˈɛsəns/ ▻ *noun* **1** the basic distinctive part or quality of something, which determines its nature or character. **2** a liquid obtained from a plant or drug, etc, which has its properties in concentrated form. • **in essence** basically or fundamentally. • **of the essence** absolutely necessary or extremely important. ⓒ 14c: French, from Latin *essentia*, from *esse* to be.

essential /ɪˈsɛnʃəl/ ▻ *adj* **1** absolutely necessary. **2** relating to the basic or inner nature of something or its essence. ▻ *noun* **1** something necessary. **2** (*often* **the essentials**) a basic or fundamental element, principle or piece of information. • **essentially** *adverb*. ⓒ 14c.

essential oil ▻ *noun, bot* a mixture of volatile oils which have distinctive and characteristic odours, obtained from certain aromatic plants. ⓒ 17c.

Esso /ˈɛsoʊ/ ▻ *abbreviation* Standard Oil (the initials represented phonetically).

EST ▻ *abbreviation* **1** *N Amer* Eastern Standard Time. **2** electric shock treatment.

est. ▻ *abbreviation* **1** established. **2** estimated.

-est /əst, ɪst/ ▻ *suffix* forming the superlative of adjectives and some adverbs □ ***quickest*** □ ***soonest***. ⓒ Anglo-Saxon *-est* and *-ost*.

establish /ɪˈstablɪʃ/ ▻ *verb* (***establishes, established, establishing***) **1** to settle someone firmly in a position, place or job, etc. **2** to set up (eg a university or a business). **3** to find, show or prove something. **4** to cause people to accept (eg a custom or a claim). • **established** *adj* **1** settled or accepted. **2** said of a church: recognized as the official church of a country. • **establishment** *noun* **1** the act of establishing. **2** a business, its premises or its staff. **3** a public or government institution □ ***a research establishment***. **4** (**the Establishment**) the group of people in a country, society or community who hold power and exercise authority, and are regarded as being opposed to change. ⓒ 14c: from French *establir*.

estate /ɪˈsteɪt/ ▻ *noun* **1** a large piece of land owned by a person or group of people. **2** an area of land on which development of a particular kind has taken place, eg houses on a HOUSING ESTATE or factories on an INDUSTRIAL ESTATE. **3** *law* a person's total possessions (property or money, etc), especially at death. **4** an ESTATE CAR. **5** *historical* any of various groups or classes within the social structure of society, eg the **first estate** or **Lords Spiritual** (ie bishops and archbishops), the **second estate** or **Lords Temporal** (ie the nobility) and the **third estate** (the common people). **6** *formal or old use* a condition or state □ ***the holy estate of matrimony***. **7** a plantation. ⓒ 13c: from French *estat*.

estate agent ▻ *noun* **1** a person whose job is the buying, selling, leasing and valuation of houses and other property. **2** the manager of a private estate.

estate car ▻ *noun* a car with a large area behind the rear seats for luggage, etc, and a rear door. Often shortened to **estate**.

estate duty ▻ *noun* DEATH DUTY.

esteem /ɪˈstiːm/ ▻ *verb* (***esteemed, esteeming***) **1** to value, respect or think highly of someone or something. **2** *formal* to consider someone to be a specified thing. ▻ *noun* high regard or respect. • **esteemed** *adj* **1** respected. **2** *especially formerly* in commercial correspondence: a colourless complimentary word. ⓒ 15c: from French *estimer*, from Latin *aestimare* to estimate the value of something.

ester /ˈɛstə(r)/ ▻ *noun, chem* an organic chemical compound formed by the reaction of an alcohol with an organic acid, with the loss of a water molecule. ⓒ 19c: probably a contraction of German *Essigäther* acetic ether.

esterify /ɪˈstɛrɪfaɪ/ *verb* (***esterifies, esterified, esterifying***) to make something into an ester. • **esterification** *noun*. ⓒ Early 20c.

Esth. ▻ *abbreviation* Book of the Bible: Esther. See table at BIBLE.

esthete the *US* spelling of AESTHETE

esthetic the *US* spelling of AESTHETIC

Esthonian see ESTONIAN

estimable /ˈɛstɪməbəl/ ▻ *adj* highly respected; worthy of respect. • **estimably** *adverb*.

estimate ▻ *verb* /ˈɛstɪmeɪt/ (***estimated, estimating***) **1** to judge or calculate (size, amount or value, etc) roughly or without measuring. **2** to have or form an opinion (that ...); to think. **3** to submit to a possible client a statement of (the likely cost) of carrying out a job. ▻ *noun* /ˈɛstɪmət/ **1** a rough assessment (of size, etc). **2** a calculation of the probable cost of a job. **3** (**the estimates**) accounts laid before parliament, etc showing the probable expenditure for the year. • **estimation** *noun* **1** judgement; opinion. **2** the act of estimating. • **estimator** *noun*. • **hold someone** or **something in estimation** to esteem them or it highly. ⓒ 16c: from Latin *aestimare, aestimatum* to estimate the value of something.

estival the *US* spelling of AESTIVAL

estivate the *US* spelling of AESTIVATE

estivation the *US* spelling of AESTIVATION

Estonian or **Esthonian** /ɛˈstoʊnɪən/ ▻ *adj* belonging or relating to Estonia, a republic in E Europe, its inhabitants, or their language. ▻ *noun* **1** a citizen or inhabitant of, or person born in, Estonia. **2** the official language of the Estonia. ⓒ 18c.

estrange /ɪˈstreɪndʒ/ ▻ *verb* (***estranged, estranging***) to cause someone to break away from a previously friendly state or relationship. • **estranged** *adj* no longer friendly or supportive; alienated □ ***his estranged wife***. • **estrangement** *noun*. ⓒ 15c: from French *estranger*, from Latin *extraneare* to treat as a stranger.

estradiol the *N Amer* spelling of OESTRADIOL.

estrogen the *N Amer* spelling of OESTROGEN.

estrus the *N Amer* spelling of OESTRUS.

estuary /ˈɛstjʊərɪ/ ▻ *noun* (***estuaries***) the broad mouth of a river that flows into the sea, where fresh water mixes with tidal sea water. • **estuarial** /ɛstjʊˈɛərɪəl/ *adj*. • **estuarine** /ˈɛstjʊəraɪn/ *adj*. ⓒ 16c: from Latin *aestus* commotion or tide.

ESU ▻ *abbreviation* English-Speaking Union.

ET ▻ *abbreviation* **1** *IVR* Egypt. **2** EXTRATERRESTRIAL.

ETA ▻ *abbreviation* **1** estimated time of arrival. **2** /ˈɛtə/ *Euzkadi ta Askatasuna*, a militant Basque separatist organization.

eta /ˈiːtə/ ▻ *noun* the seventh letter of the Greek alphabet. See table at GREEK ALPHABET.

et al. /ɛt al/ ▻ *abbreviation* **1** *et alia* (Latin), and other things. **2** *et alii* (Latin), and other people. **3** *et alibi* (Latin), and in other places.

etalon /ˈeɪtəlɒn/ ▻ *noun, physics* an INTERFEROMETER used to measure wavelengths. ⓒ Early 20c: French *étalon*, from earlier *estalon* standard of weights and measures.

et cetera or **etcetera** /ɛt ˈsɛtərə/ ▻ *adverb* (abbreviation **etc.** or **&c**) **1** and the rest; and so on. **2** and/or something similar. ⓒ 15c: Latin.

etceteras /ɛtˈsɛtərəz/ ▻ *plural noun* additional things or people; extras.

etch /ɛtʃ/ ▻ *verb* (***etches, etched, etching***) **1** *tr & intr* to make designs on (metal or glass, etc) using an acid to eat out the lines. **2** to make a deep or irremovable impression. • **etcher** *noun* a person who etches, especially as their profession. • **etching** *noun* **1** the act or art of making etched designs. **2** a print made from an etched plate. ◷ 17c: from German *ätzen* to etch or eat away with acid.

ETD ▻ *abbreviation* estimated time of departure.

eternal /ɪ'tɜːnəl/ ▻ *adj* **1** without beginning or end; everlasting. **2** unchanging; valid for all time. **3** *colloq* frequent or endless. **4** (**the Eternal**) a name for God. • **eternally** *adverb* for ever; without end or constantly. ◷ 14c: from French *éternel*, from Latin *aeternalis*.

eternalize or **eternalise** /ɪ'tɜːnəlaɪz/ ▻ *verb* (***eternalized***, ***eternalizing***) **1** to make someone or something eternal. **2** to make someone or something eternally famous. • **eternalization** *noun*.

eternal triangle ▻ *noun* a relationship involving love and jealousy between two men and a woman, or two women and a man.

eternity /ɪ'tɜːnɪtɪ/ ▻ *noun* (***eternities***) **1** time regarded as having no end. **2** the state of being eternal. **3** *relig* a timeless existence after death. **4** *colloq* an extremely long time. ◷ 14c: from French *éternité*, from Latin *aeternitas*.

eternity ring ▻ *noun* a ring given as a symbol of lasting love, especially one set with stones all round the band.

etesian /ɪ'tiːzɪən/ ▻ *adj* said especially of NW winds in the E Mediterranean in the summer: recurring annually. ◷ 17c: from Greek *etesios* annual.

ETH ▻ *abbreviation, IVR* Ethiopia.

ethane /'iːθeɪn, 'ɛθeɪn/ ▻ *noun, chem* (formula C_2H_6) a colourless odourless flammable gas belonging to the alkane series of hydrocarbons, and found in natural gas. ◷ 19c: from ETHER + -ANE.

ethanediol /'iːθeɪndaɪɒl/ ▻ *noun* ethylene glycol.

ethanedioic acid /iːθeɪndaɪ'oʊɪk —/ ▻ *noun* OXALIC ACID.

ethanoate see ACETATE sense 1

ethanoic acid see ACETIC ACID

ethanol /'ɛθənɒl/ ▻ *noun, chem* (formula C_2H_5OH) a colourless volatile flammable alcohol that is produced by fermentation of the sugar in fruit or cereals, and is used as an intoxicant in alcoholic beverages, and as a fuel. Also called **ethyl alcohol**.

ethene /'ɛθiːn/ ▻ *noun, chem* ETHYLENE.

ether /'iːθə(r)/ ▻ *noun* **1** any of a group of organic chemical compounds formed by the dehydration of alcohols, that are volatile and highly flammable, and contain two hydrocarbon groups linked by an oxygen atom. **2** (*also* **diethyl ether**) (formula $C_2H_5OHC_2H_5$) the commonest ether, widely used as a solvent, and formerly employed as an anaesthetic. **3** (*also* **aether**) *physics* a hypothetical medium formerly believed to be necessary for the transmission of electromagnetic radiation, a concept abandoned when the theory of relativity was accepted. **4** (*also* **aether**) *poetic* the clear upper air or a clear sky. ◷ 17c: from Greek *aither* the heavens.

ethereal /ɪ'θɪərɪəl/ ▻ *adj* **1** having an unreal lightness or delicateness; fairy-like. **2** heavenly or spiritual. • **ethereally** *adverb*. ◷ 16c: from ETHER.

Ethernet /'iːθənɛt/ ▻ *noun, trademark, computing* a type of LOCAL AREA NETWORK. ◷ 20c: ETHER 3 + *network*.

ethic /'ɛθɪk/ ▻ *noun* the moral system or set of principles particular to a certain person, community or group, etc. • **ethical** *adj* **1** relating to or concerning morals, justice or duty. **2** morally right. **3** said of a medicine or drug: not advertised to the general public, and available only on prescription. • **ethicality** *noun*. • **ethically** *adverb*. ◷ 15c: from Greek *ethikos* moral, from *ethos* custom or character.

ethics /'ɛθɪks/ ▻ *singular noun* the study or the science of morals. ▻ *plural noun* rules or principles of behaviour □ *medical ethics*.

Ethiopian /iːθɪ'oʊpɪən/ ▻ *adj* belonging or relating to Ethiopia, a country in NE Africa, its inhabitants, or their group of Semitic languages which includes Amharic. ▻ *noun* **1** a citizen or inhabitant of, or person born in, Ethiopia. **2** *archaic* a black person. ◷ 16c: ultimately from Greek *Aithiops*, literally 'burnt-face', from *aithein* to burn + *ops* face.

Ethiopic /iːθɪ'ɒpɪk/ ▻ *adj* belonging to Ethiopia, to the Ethiopian Church or to the group of Semitic languages including Amharic. ▻ *noun* the ancient Semitic language of Ethiopia.

ethnic /'ɛθnɪk/ ▻ *adj* **1** relating to or having a common race or cultural tradition □ *an ethnic group*. **2** associated with or resembling an exotic, especially non-European, racial or tribal group □ *ethnic clothes*. **3** seen from the point of view of race, rather than nationality □ *ethnic Asians*. **4** between or involving different racial groups □ *ethnic violence*. ▻ *noun, especially US* a member of a particular racial group or cult, especially a minority one. • **ethnically** *adverb*. • **ethnicity** /ɛθ'nɪsɪtɪ/ *noun* (***ethnicities***) racial status or distinctiveness. ◷ 14c as *noun* and 15c as *adj* meaning 'heathen': from Greek *ethnos* nation.

ethnic cleansing ▻ *noun* GENOCIDE or forced removal inflicted by one ethnic group on all others in a particular area.

ethno- /ɛθnoʊ, ɛθ'nɒ/ ▻ *combining form, signifying* race; people or culture. ◷ From Greek *ethnos* race.

ethnocentric ▻ *adj* relating to or holding the belief that one's own cultural tradition or racial group is superior to all others. • **ethnocentricity** /-sɛn'trɪsɪtɪ/ or **ethnocentrism** *noun* (***ethnocentricities***) the policy or practice of being ethnocentric. ◷ 20c.

ethnography /ɛθ'nɒgrəfɪ/ ▻ *noun* (***ethnographies***) a detailed description of the culture of a particular society based on fieldwork and participation in the life of the society. • **ethnographer** *noun*. • **ethnographic** /-'grafɪk/ or **ethnographical** *adj*. ◷ 19c.

ethnolinguistics ▻ *singular noun* the study of the relationship between language and cultural behaviour. • **ethnolinguist** *noun*. • **ethnolinguistic** *adj*. ◷ 1940s.

ethnology /ɛθ'nɒlədʒɪ/ ▻ *noun* the scientific study of different races and cultural traditions, and their relations with each other. • **ethnological** *adj*. • **ethnologically** *adverb*. • **ethnologist** *noun* a person who studies ethnology or race. ◷ 19c.

ethnomusicology ▻ *noun* the study of music in its racial, cultural and social contexts. • **ethnomusicologist** *noun*. ◷ 1950s.

ethnoscience ▻ *noun* **1** a branch of social and cultural anthropology which investigates folk beliefs or ideologies that correspond to such fields of Western science as medicine, astronomy and zoology. **2** ethnography. ◷ 1960s.

ethology /iː'θɒlədʒɪ/ ▻ *noun, zool* the study of animal behaviour, especially by direct observation and monitoring of animals in their natural habitats. ◷ 19c; 17c in obsolete sense 'to portray character by mimicry'.

ethos /'iːθɒs/ ▻ *noun* (***ethoses***) the typical spirit, character or attitudes (of a group or community, etc). ◷ 19c: Greek, meaning 'custom' or 'culture'.

ethyl /'iːθaɪl, 'ɛθɪl/ ▻ *noun, chem* in organic chemical compounds: the (C_2H_5-) group, as for example in ethylamine ($C_2H_5NH_2$). ◷ 19c.

ethyl alcohol see under ETHANOL

ethylene /'ɛθɪliːn/ ▻ *noun, chem* (formula C_2H_4) a colourless flammable gas with a sweet smell, belonging to the ALKENE series of hydrocarbons. ◷ 19c.

ethylene glycol ▷ *noun, chem* a thick liquid alcohol used as an antifreeze. Also called ETHANEDIOL.

ethyne /ˈiːθaɪn, ˈɛθaɪn/ ▷ *noun, chem* ACETYLENE.

etiolated /ˈiːtɪouleɪtɪd/ ▷ *adj* **1** *bot* said of a plant: having foliage that has become yellow through lack of sunlight. **2** *formal or literary* said of a person: pale and weak in appearance. ⓒ 18c: from French *étioler* to become pale.

etiolation ▷ *noun, bot* the abnormal appearance of plants grown in darkness or severely reduced light, where the leaves appear yellow due to lack of chlorophyll and the stems are long and spindly.

etiology the *US* spelling of AETIOLOGY.

etiquette /ˈɛtɪkɛt/ ▷ *noun* **1** conventions of correct or polite social behaviour. **2** rules, usually unwritten ones, regarding the behaviour of members of a particular profession, etc towards each other. ⓒ 18c: from French *étiquette* a label.

Eton crop /ˈiːtən —/ ▷ *noun* a short sleek haircut fashionable among women in the 1920s.

Etonian /ɪˈtounɪən/ ▷ *noun* a person educated at Eton College, an English public school. Also *as adj.*

-ette /ɛt/ ▷ *suffix, forming nouns, indicating* **1** a female of the specified type ◻ ***usherette***. **2** a small thing of the specified type ◻ ***cigarette*** ◻ ***kitchenette***. **3** an imitation of something specified ◻ ***leatherette***. ⓒ French.

étude /eɪˈtjuːd/ ▷ *noun, music* a short piece written for a single instrument, intended as an exercise or a means of showing talent. ⓒ 19c: French, literally 'study'.

ety. or **etym.** ▷ *abbreviation* etymology.

etymology /ɛtɪˈmɒlədʒɪ/ ▷ *noun* (***etymologies***) **1** the study of the origin and development of words and their meanings. **2** an explanation of the history of a particular word. • **etymological** /-məˈlɒdʒɪkəl/ *adj.* • **etymologically** *adverb.* • **etymologist** *noun.* ⓒ 15c: from Latin *etymologia*, from Greek *etymon* the literal sense of a word, from *etymos* true.

etymon /ˈɛtɪmɒn/ ▷ *noun* (*plural* ***etyma***) the earliest recorded form, or reconstructed earliest form, of a word. ⓒ 16c: Latin, from Greek *etymos* true.

EU ▷ *abbreviation* European Union.

Eu ▷ *symbol, chem* europium.

eu- /juː/ ▷ *combining form, signifying* **1** good; well. **2** *medicine* normal. ⓒ From Greek *eu* well.

eucalyptus /juːkəˈlɪptəs/ ▷ *noun* (***eucalyptuses*** or ***eucalypti*** /-taɪ/) **1** any of various trees belonging to the myrtle family, native to Australia, planted for timber, their oil or their ornamental appearance. **2** the hard durable wood of this tree. **3** eucalyptus oil. ⓒ 19c: from Greek *eu* well + *kalyptos* covered.

Eucharist /ˈjuːkərɪst/ ▷ *noun, Christianity* **1** the sacrament of THE LAST SUPPER. **2** THE LORD'S SUPPER. **3** the elements of the sacrament, the bread and wine. • **Eucharistic** *adj.* ⓒ 14c: from Greek *eucharistia* giving of thanks.

euchre /ˈjuːkə(r)/ ▷ *noun* **1** a N American card-game for two, three or four players, played with 32 cards. **2** an instance of euchring or being euchred. ▷ *verb* (***euchred***, ***euchring***) **1** to prevent (a player) from winning three tricks. **2** (*usually* **euchre someone out of something**) *N Amer, Austral, NZ* to cheat or outwit them. ⓒ 19c.

Euclidean or **Euclidian** /juːˈklɪdɪən/ ▷ *adj* referring or relating to or based on the geometrical system devised by Euclid, a Greek mathematician who lived in c.300 BC.

eudiometer /juːdɪˈɒmɪtə(r)/ ▷ *noun, chem* an apparatus for analysing gas. ⓒ 18c: from Greek *eudios* clear or fine (as of weather).

eugenics /juːˈdʒɛnɪks/ ▷ *singular noun* **1** the science concerned with the detection and elimination of human hereditary diseases and disorders by genetic counselling of parents who may be carriers of such conditions. **2** the principle or practice, now largely discredited, of improving the human race by selective breeding from individuals who are regarded as strong, healthy, intelligent, etc. • **eugenic** *adj.* • **eugenically** *adverb.* ⓒ 19c: from Greek *eugenes* well-born or of good stock.

euglena /juːˈgliːnə/ ▷ *noun* (***euglenas***) a single-celled organism found in fresh water, with a long FLAGELLUM at its front end which is used to propel it through the water. ⓒ 19c: from Greek *glene* eyeball.

eukaryote or **eucaryote** /juːˈkarɪout/ ▷ *noun, biol* an organism in which the cells have a distinct nucleus containing the genetic material and separated from the cytoplasm by a nuclear membrane. • **eukaryotic** *adj.* ⓒ 1940s: from Greek *karyon* kernel; see also PROKARYOTE.

eulogize or **eulogise** /ˈjuːlədʒaɪz/ ▷ *verb* (***eulogized***, ***eulogizing***) to praise highly. • **eulogistic** *adj.* • **eulogistically** *adverb.* ⓒ 19c.

eulogy /ˈjuːlədʒɪ/ ▷ *noun* (***eulogies***) **1** a speech or piece of writing in praise of someone or something. **2** high praise. ⓒ 16c: from Latin *eulogium*, from Greek *eu* well + *logos* discourse.

eunuch /ˈjuːnək/ ▷ *noun* **1 a** a man who has been castrated; **b** *especially formerly* such a man employed as a guard of a harem. **2** *derog* a person who lacks power or effectiveness in some respect. ⓒ 15c: from Greek *eunouchos*, from *eune* bed + *echein* to have charge of.

eupepsy /juːˈpɛpsɪ/ and **eupepsia** /-sɪə/ ▷ *noun* good digestion. • **eupeptic** *adj.* ⓒ 18c: Greek *eupepsia*, from *pepsis* digestion.

euphemism /ˈjuːfəmɪzəm/ ▷ *noun* **1** a mild or inoffensive term used in place of one considered offensive or unpleasantly direct. **2** the use of such terms. • **euphemistic** *adj.* • **euphemistically** *adverb.* ⓒ 17c: from Greek *euphemismos*, from *phanai* to speak.

euphenics /juːˈfɛnɪks/ ▷ *singular noun* the science concerned with the physical improvement of human beings by modifying their development after birth. Compare EUGENICS. ⓒ 1960s: from PHENOTYPE, modelled on EUGENICS.

euphonium /juːˈfounɪəm/ ▷ *noun* a four-valved brass instrument of the tuba family usually found in brass and military bands. ⓒ 19c: from Greek *euphonos* sweet-sounding, modelled on HARMONIUM.

euphony /ˈjuːfənɪ/ ▷ *noun* (***euphonies***) **1** a pleasing sound, especially in speech. **2** pleasantness of sound, especially of pronunciation. • **euphonious** /-ˈfounɪəs/ or **euphonic** /-ˈfɒnɪk/ *adj* pleasing to the ear. • **euphoniously** *adverb.* ⓒ 17c: from Greek *euphonia*, from *phone* sound.

euphoria /juːˈfɔːrɪə/ ▷ *noun* (***euphorias***) a feeling of wild happiness and well-being. • **euphoric** /-ˈfɒrɪk/ *adj.* • **euphorically** *adverb.* ⓒ 19c: Greek, meaning 'ability to endure well'.

euphrasy /ˈjuːfrəsɪ/ ▷ *noun* (***euphrasies***) *bot* any plant of the figwort family, especially EYEBRIGHT. ⓒ 18c: from Greek *euphrasia* delight.

euphuism /ˈjuːfjuɪzəm/ ▷ *noun* a pompous and affected style of writing. • **euphuistic** /-ˈɪstɪk/ *adj.* • **euphuistically** *adverb.* ⓒ 16c: from the style of John Lyly's romance *Euphues* (1578–80); from Greek *euphyes* graceful.

Eur. ▷ *abbreviation* Europe.

Eur- see EURO-

Eurasian /juəˈreɪʒən/ ▷ *adj* **1** of mixed European and Asian descent. **2** belonging, referring or relating to Europe and Asia. ▷ *noun* a person of mixed European and Asian descent. ⓒ 19c.

Euratom /ˈjuəratəm/ ▷ *abbreviation* European Atomic Energy Community.

eureka /jʊə'riːkə/ ▻ *exclamation* expressing triumph at finding something or solving a problem, etc. ◷ 17c: from Greek *heureka* I have found it, traditionally believed to have been said by Archimedes when he realized he could work out the proportion of base metal in a golden crown by means of what is now known as specific gravity.

eurhythmic ▻ *adj* **1** *archit* in harmonious proportion. **2** relating to eurhythmics. ◷ 19c.

eurhythmics ▻ *singular noun* the art or a system of rhythmic movement, specifically the system of musical training devised by the Swiss composer and teacher Emile Jaques-Dalcroze (1865–1950). • **eurhythmist** *noun*. ◷ Early 20c.

eurhythmy or **eurythmy** /jʊə'rɪðmɪ/ ▻ *noun* **1** harmony of proportion. **2** (*usually* **Eurhythmy**) an artistic, therapeutic and educational system based on rhythmic body movement correlated to music or poetry, etc, created by Rudolph Steiner (1861–1925).

Euro /'jʊəroʊ/ ▻ *noun* (***Euros***) a EUROPEAN (*noun* senses 1 and 2). ◷ 1980s.

euro /'jʊəroʊ/ ▻ *noun* (***euros***) *finance* **1** a proposed common system of currency for countries in the European Union. **2** the basic monetary unit in this system. ◷ 1990s: from *Europe*.

Euro- /jʊəroʊ, jʊə'rɒ/ or (before a vowel) **Eur-** *combining form, denoting* Europe; European; relating to the EC or EU □ *Europhile* □ *Euromyth*.

Eurobond ▻ *noun* a bond issued in Eurocurrency. ◷ 1960s.

Eurocentric ▻ *adj* centred, or concentrating, on Europe. ◷ 1960s.

Eurocheque ▻ *noun* a cheque which may be drawn on the user's own account and exchanged for cash, goods or services in a number of European as well as non-European countries. ◷ 1960s.

Eurocrat /'jʊəroʊkrat/ ▻ *noun, sometimes derog* an official involved in the administration of any organization in the EC or EU. ◷ 1960s.

Eurocurrency and **Euromoney** ▻ *noun* convertible currencies, including pounds sterling, French and Swiss francs, Deutschmarks and US dollars, held in banks in W Europe outside the country of origin, which can be borrowed by commercial undertakings for trade. ◷ 1960s.

Eurodollars ▻ *plural noun* US currency held in European banks to assist trade. ◷ 1960s.

Euro-MP ▻ *noun* a member of the European Parliament.

European /jʊərə'pɪən/ ▻ *adj* **1** belonging or relating to Europe. **2** showing or favouring a spirit of co-operation between the countries of Europe, especially those of the EU. ▻ *noun* **1** a citizen or inhabitant of Europe. **2** a person who favours close political and economic contact between the countries of Europe, especially those of the EU. ◷ 17c.

European Commission ▻ *noun* an executive body composed of members of the European Union countries (or *formerly* the EEC or EC countries), which is responsible for the formulation of community policy, and initiates and drafts most community legislation.

European Community ▻ *noun* (abbreviation **EC**) an economic and political association of W European states formed by the merging of the EEC, ECSC and EURATOM (known officially as **the European Communities**). It consists of the 12 member states of the EEC in 1995 extended to include Austria, Finland and Sweden. It was renamed **European Union** (abbreviation **EU**) by the coming into force of the Maastricht Treaty in 1993, which extended its remit to include areas of foreign and security policy and justice and home affairs. Technically EC is used to refer to legislation of the EU but it can also be used to refer to the Union itself.

European currency unit see ECU

European Economic Community ▻ *noun* (abbreviation **EEC**) the economic association formed (by the Treaty of Rome in 1957) by France, W Germany, Italy, Belgium, the Netherlands and Luxembourg. In 1973 it extended to include the United Kingdom, Denmark and the Republic of Ireland, in 1981 Greece, and in 1986 Spain and Portugal. Also (*informal*) called **the Common Market**. Now officially renamed **European Community**.

European Free Trade Association see EFTA

Europeanize or **Europeanise** /jʊərə'pɪənaɪz/ ▻ *verb* (***Europeanized***, ***Europeanizing***) **1** to assimilate or convert to European character or ways. **2** to integrate into the European Union. • **Europeanism** *noun*. • **Europeanist** *noun* a person who favours the European Union and seeks to uphold or develop it. • **Europeanization** *noun*. ◷ 19c.

European Parliament ▻ *noun* the legislative assembly of the European Union.

European plan ▻ *noun, US* in hotels: the system of charging for lodgings and service without including meals. Compare AMERICAN PLAN.

European sole see DOVER SOLE

European Union see under EUROPEAN COMMUNITY

europium /jʊə'roʊpɪəm/ ▻ *noun, chem* (symbol **Eu**, atomic number 63) a soft silvery metallic element belonging to the LANTHANIDE series. ◷ 19c: Latin, named after Europe.

Euro-rebel ▻ *noun, politics* someone who does not have the same belief in the benefit of the EU as their political party professes.

Eurosceptic ▻ *noun* someone, particularly a politician, who is not in favour of the UK's continuing political and economic integration with other states of the EU. • **Euroscepticism** *noun*.

Eurotunnel ▻ *noun* the CHANNEL TUNNEL.

eurythmics an alternative (*especially N Amer*) spelling of EURHYTHMICS.

eurythmy see EURHYTHMY

Eustachian tube /juː'steɪʃən —/ ▻ *noun, anatomy* either of the two tubes which connect the MIDDLE EAR to the PHARYNX, serving to equalize the pressure on the two sides of the eardrum. ◷ 18c: named after the Italian anatomist B Eustachio (died 1574).

eustasy /'juːstəsɪ/ ▻ *noun, geol* worldwide change in sea-level caused by advancing or receding polar ice caps. • **eustatic** /juː'statɪk/ *adj*. • **eustatically** *adverb*. ◷ 1940s; *adj* early 20c: from EU- + Greek *stasis* standing.

euthanasia /juːθə'neɪzɪə/ ▻ *noun* the act or practice of ending the life of a person who is suffering from an incurable and often painful or distressing illness. ◷ 19c; 17c meaning 'a gentle and easy death': Greek, from *eu-* good + *thanatos* death.

eutrophic /juː'trɒfɪk/ ▻ *adj, ecol* said of a body of water: suffering from eutrophication.

eutrophication ▻ *noun* the process whereby a body of water becomes over-enriched with nutrients, from sewage disposal and run-off of agricultural fertilizers, etc, which results in overgrowth of algae and depleted oxygen levels in the water, leading to the death of aquatic animals. ◷ 1940s: from Greek *eutrophia*.

evacuate /ɪ'vakjʊeɪt/ ▻ *verb* (***evacuated***, ***evacuating***) **1** to leave (a place), especially because of danger. **2** to make (people) evacuate a place. **3** *technical* to empty (the bowels). **4** *physics* to create a vacuum in (a vessel). • **evacuee** /ɪvakjʊ'iː/ *noun* (***evacuees***) an evacuated person. • **evacuation** *noun*. ◷ 16c: from Latin *evacuare*, *evacuatum* to empty out.

evade /ɪˈveɪd/ ▷ *verb* (*evaded, evading*) **1** to escape or avoid something or someone by trickery or skill. **2** to avoid answering (a question). See also EVASION. ◷ 16c: from Latin *evadere* to go out.

> ***evade***
>
> See Usage Note at **avoid**.

evaginate /ɪˈvadʒɪneɪt/ ▷ *verb* (*evaginated, evaginating*) *medicine* to turn an organ inside out. • **evagination** *noun*. ◷ 17c: from Latin *evaginare* to unsheath.

evaluate /ɪˈvaljʊeɪt/ ▷ *verb* (*evaluated, evaluating*) **1** to form an idea or judgement about the worth of something. **2** *math* to calculate the value of something. • **evaluation** *noun*. • **evaluative** /ɪˈvaljʊətɪv/ *adj*. ◷ 19c; 18c as *evaluation*.

evanesce /ɛvəˈnɛs/ ▷ *verb* (*evanesced, evanescing*) *intr, literary* said of smoke or mist, etc: to disappear gradually; to fade from sight. • **evanescence** /ɛvəˈnɛsəns/ *noun*. • **evanescent** *adj* **1** quickly fading. **2** short-lived; transitory. ◷ 19c: from Latin *evanescere* to vanish.

evangelical /iːvanˈdʒɛlɪkəl/ ▷ *adj* **1** based on the Gospels. **2** referring or relating to, or denoting any of various groups within the Protestant church stressing the authority of the Bible and claiming that personal acceptance of Christ as saviour is the only way to salvation. **3** enthusiastically advocating a particular cause, etc. ▷ *noun* a member of an evangelical movement, or a supporter of evangelical beliefs. • **evangelicalism** *noun*. • **evangelically** *adverb*. ◷ 16c.

evangelism /ɪˈvandʒəlɪzəm/ ▷ *noun* **1** the act or practice of evangelizing. **2** evangelicalism. ◷ 17c in sense 1.

evangelist /ɪˈvandʒəlɪst/ ▷ *noun* **1** a person who preaches Christianity, especially at large public meetings. **2** (*usually* **Evangelist**) any of the writers of the four Biblical Gospels: Matthew, Mark, Luke or John. • **evangelistic** *adj*. ◷ 14c; 12c in sense 2: from Greek *euangelistes*, from *eu* well + *angellein* to bring news.

evangelize or **evangelise** /ɪˈvandʒəlaɪz/ ▷ *verb* (*evangelized, evangelizing*) **1** *tr & intr* to attempt to persuade someone to adopt Christianity. **2** *intr* to preach Christianity, especially travelling from place to place to do so. **3** *tr & intr, often facetious* to attempt to persuade someone to adopt a particular principle or cause. • **evangelization** *noun*. ◷ 14c.

evaporate /ɪˈvapəreɪt/ ▷ *verb* (*evaporated, evaporating*) *tr & intr* **1** to change or cause something to change from a liquid into a vapour at a temperature below the boiling point of the liquid. **2** to disappear or make disappear. • **evaporable** *adj*. • **evaporation** *noun* the process of evaporating; disappearance. • **evaporative** /-ətɪv/ *adj*. • **evaporator** *noun*. ◷ 16c: from Latin *evaporare, evaporatum*, from *e* from + *vapor* steam or vapour.

evaporated milk ▷ *noun* unsweetened milk that has been concentrated by evaporation.

evaporite /ɪˈvapəraɪt/ *noun, geol* a mineral deposit formed as a result of the evaporation of all or most of the water from a saline solution such as sea water.

evapotranspiration /ɪvapoutranspɪˈreɪʃən/ ▷ *noun, ecol* the loss of water from the Earth's surface as a result of both evaporation from the surface of soil, rocks and bodies of water, and TRANSPIRATION from plants. ◷ 1930s.

evasion /ɪˈveɪʒən/ ▷ *noun* **1** the act of evading, especially evading a commitment or responsibility. **2** a trick or excuse used to evade (a question, etc). ◷ 15c in sense 2: from Latin *evasio*, from *evadere, evasum* to go out.

evasive /ɪˈveɪsɪv/ ▷ *adj* **1** intending or intended to evade something, especially trouble or danger. **2** not honest or open ▫ *an evasive answer*. • **evasively** *adverb*. • **evasiveness** *noun*. • **take evasive action** to move or act in such a way as to avoid an object or consequence.

eve /iːv/ ▷ *noun* **1** *especially in compounds* the evening or day before some notable event ▫ *New Year's Eve*. **2** the period immediately before ▫ *the eve of war*. ◷ 13c: from EVEN[2].

even[1] /ˈiːvən/ ▷ *adj* **1** smooth and flat. **2** constant or regular ▫ *travelling at an even 50mph*. **3** said of a number: divisible by 2, with nothing left over. **4** designated or marked by an even number ▫ *the even houses in the street*. **5** (*usually* **even with something**) level, on the same plane or at the same height as it. **6** (*often* **even with someone**) having no advantage over or owing no debt to them. **7** said of temper or character, etc: calm. **8** equal ▫ *an even chance*. ▷ *adverb* **1** used with a comparative to emphasize a comparison with something else ▫ *He's good, but she's even better*. **2** used with an expression stronger than a previous one ▫ *He looked sad, even depressed*. **3** used to introduce a surprising piece of information ▫ *Even John was there!* **4** used to indicate a lower extreme in an implied comparison ▫ *Even a child would have known that!* ▷ *verb* (*evened, evening*) (*often* **even something up**) to make it equal. ▷ *noun* **1** (*usually* **evens**) an even number, or something designated by one. **2** (**evens**) same as EVEN MONEY. • **evenly** *adverb* **1** in an even way; uniformly. **2** in equal parts or shares ▫ *evenly divided*. • **evenness** *noun*. • **even as** at that, or this, very moment when something specified happened or happens ▫ *Even as we speak the result is announced*. • **even if, even so** or **even though** used to emphasize that whether or not something is or might be true, the following or preceding statement is or would remain true ▫ *He'd be unhappy even if he did get the job* ▫ *He got the job but, even so, he's still unhappy*. • **even now** still; after all that has happened. • **even then** after all that had happened, will have happened, or would have happened. • **get even with someone** to be revenged on them. • **on an even keel 1** balanced; not tilting to either side. **2** said eg of business affairs: well organized; running smoothly. **3** said of a person: not in an unstable state of mind. ◷ Anglo-Saxon *efen*.

> ■ **even out** to become level or regular.
>
> ■ **even something out** or **up** to make it smooth or level.

even[2] /ˈiːvən/ ▷ *noun, old use or poetic* evening. ◷ Anglo-Saxon *æfen*.

even-handed ▷ *adj* fair; impartial. • **even-handedly** *adverb*. • **even-handedness** *noun*. ◷ 17c.

evening /ˈiːvnɪŋ/ ▷ *noun* **1** the last part of the day, usually from late afternoon until bedtime. **2** *often in compounds* a party or other social gathering held at this time ▫ *a poetry evening*. **3** *poetic* the latter part of something ▫ *the evening of her life*. ▷ *adj* referring to or during the evening. • **evenings** *adverb, especially N Amer* in the evening; in the evening on a number of occasions. ◷ Anglo-Saxon *æfnung*.

evening class ▷ *noun* a class held in the evening, often for people who are at work during the day.

evening dress ▷ *noun* clothes worn on formal occasions in the evening.

evening primrose ▷ *noun, bot* any of about 200 species of a biennial plant with large scented yellow flowers that open at dusk.

evening primrose oil ▷ *noun* oil produced from the seeds of the evening primrose, much used in alternative medicine.

evening star ▷ *noun* a planet, especially Venus, clearly visible in the west just after sunset. See also MORNING STAR.

Evenki /ɪwɛŋkiː, -vɛŋkiː/ *noun* (***Evenki*** or ***Evenkis***) TUNGUS. ◷ Russian, from the Evenki name for themselves.

evenly see under EVEN[1]

even money ▷ *noun* gambling odds with the potential to win the same as the amount gambled.

evenness see under EVEN[1]

evensong ▷ *noun, C of E* the service of evening prayer. Compare MATINS. ◷ Anglo-Saxon *æfensang* evening song.

event /ɪ'vɛnt/ ▷ *noun* **1** something that occurs or happens; an incident, especially a significant one. **2** an item in a programme of sports, etc. • **at all events** or **in any event** in any case; whatever happens. • **in either event** no matter which (of two things or possibilities, etc) happens. • **in the event** in the end; as it happened, happens or may happen. • **in the event of** or **that something** if it occurs □ *in the event of a power cut* □ *in the event that power fails.* • **in that event** if that occurs. ◷ 16c: from Latin *eventus* result or event.

even-tempered ▷ *adj* placid; calm.

eventer ▷ *noun* a person or horse that takes part in EVENTING.

eventful /ɪ'vɛntfʊl/ *adj* full of important or characterized by important or significant events. • **eventfully** *adverb.*

event horizon ▷ *noun, astron* the boundary of a black hole.

eventide /'iːvəntaɪd/ ▷ *noun, poetic or old use* evening. ◷ Anglo-Saxon *æfentid.*

eventide home ▷ *noun, euphemistic* a home for old people.

eventing *noun* the practice of taking part in horse-riding events, especially the THREE-DAY EVENT.

eventual /ɪ'vɛntʃʊəl/ ▷ *adj* happening after or at the end of a period of time or a process, etc. • **eventuality** *noun* (**eventualities**) a possible happening or result □ *plan for every eventuality.* • **eventually** *adverb* after an indefinite period of time; in the end. ◷ 17c: from French *éventuel*, from Latin *eventus* result or event.

eventuate /ɪ'vɛntʃʊeɪt/ ▷ *verb* (**eventuated, eventuating**) *intr, formal* to result; to turn out. ◷ 18c.

ever /'ɛvə(r)/ ▷ *adverb* **1** at any time. **2 a** *formal* always; continually; **b** *in compounds* □ *ever-hopeful.* **3** *colloq* used for emphasis □ *She's ever so beautiful!* • **ever such a ...** *colloq* a very ... □ *ever such a good boy.* • **for ever 1** always. **2** *colloq* for a long time. ◷ Anglo-Saxon *æfre.*

everglade /'ɛvəgleɪd/ ▷ *noun* **1** a large shallow lake or marsh. **2** (**the Everglades**) a large expanse of these in S Florida in the USA. ◷ 19c.

evergreen ▷ *adj* **1** *bot* denoting plants that bear leaves all the year round, eg pines or firs. **2** always popular. **3** always fresh, vigorous or interesting, etc. ▷ *noun* an evergreen tree or shrub. Compare DECIDUOUS. ◷ 17c.

everlasting ▷ *adj* **1** without end; continual. **2** lasting a long time, especially so long as to become tiresome. ▷ *noun* **1** any of several kinds of flower that keep their shape and colour when dried. **2** eternity. • **everlastingly** *adverb.* ◷ 13c.

evermore ▷ *adverb* (*often* **for evermore**) for all time to come; eternally. ◷ 13c.

evert /ɪ'vɜːt/ ▷ *verb* (**everted, everting**) *physiol* to turn (an eyelid or other organ) outwards or inside out. • **eversible** *adj.* • **eversion** *noun.* ◷ 16c: from Latin *evertere* to overthrow, from *vertere* to turn.

every /'ɛvrɪ/ ▷ *adj* **1** each one or single of a number or collection; omitting none. **2** the greatest or best possible □ *making every effort.* ▷ *adverb* at, in, or at the end of, each stated period of time or distance, etc □ *every fourth week* □ *every six inches.* • **every bit** or **whit** the whole; all of it; quite or entirely. • **every last** (used for emphasis) every. • **every man Jack** or **every mother's son** everyone without exception. • **every now and then** or **every now and again** or **every so often** occasionally; from time to time. • **every other ...** or **every second ...** one out of every two (things) repeatedly (the first, third, fifth, etc or second, fourth, sixth, etc) □ *comes every other day.* • **every which way** *US* **1** in every direction. **2** by method. **3** in disorder. • **have everything** *colloq* to be well endowed with possessions, good looks, etc. ◷ Anglo-Saxon *æfre ælc* ever each.

everybody ▷ *pronoun* every person.

everyday ▷ *adj* **1** happening, done or used, etc daily, or on ordinary days, rather than on special occasions. **2** common or usual □ *an everyday occurrence.* ◷ 17c.

Everyman ▷ *noun* (*also* **everyman**) the ordinary or common person; anybody; mankind. ◷ Early 20c: from the name of the hero of a medieval morality play.

everyone ▷ *pronoun* every person.

every-place ▷ *adverb, US* everywhere.

everything ▷ *pronoun* **1** all things; all. **2** the most important thing □ *Fitness is everything in sport.*

everywhere ▷ *adverb* in or to every place.

evict /ɪ'vɪkt/ ▷ *verb* (**evicted, evicting**) to put someone out of a house, etc or off land by force of law. • **eviction** /ɪ'vɪkʃən/ *noun* the process of evicting people, especially from a building. ◷ 15c: from Latin *evincere, evictum* to overcome.

eviction order ▷ *noun* a court order by which a person may be evicted.

evidence /'ɛvɪdəns/ ▷ *noun* **1** information, etc that gives grounds for belief; that which points to, reveals or suggests something. **2** written or spoken testimony used in a court of law. ▷ *verb* (**evidenced, evidencing**) *formal* to be evidence of something; to prove. • **in evidence** easily seen; clearly displayed. • **turn Queen's** or **King's evidence** or (*US*) **turn state's evidence** to give evidence for the prosecution against an accomplice in a crime. ◷ 14c: from Latin *evidentia* clearness of speech.

evident /'ɛvɪdənt/ ▷ *adj* clear to see or understand; obvious or apparent. • **evidently** *adverb* **1** obviously; apparently □ *He is evidently drunk.* **2** as it appears; so it seems □ *Evidently they don't believe us.*

evidential /ɛvɪ'dɛnʃəl/ *adj, formal* relating to, based on or providing evidence. • **evidentially** *adverb* in terms of evidence; as based on evidence.

evil /'iːvɪl/ ▷ *adj* **1** morally bad or offensive. **2** harmful. **3** *colloq* very unpleasant □ *an evil stench.* ▷ *noun* **1** wickedness or moral offensiveness, or the source of it. **2** harm, or a cause of harm; a harmful influence. **3** anything bad or unpleasant, eg crime or disease. • **evilly** *adverb.* • **evilness** *noun.* • **speak evil of someone** to slander them. ◷ Anglo-Saxon *yfel.*

evildoer ▷ *noun* a person who does evil things.

the evil eye ▷ *noun* **1** the supposed power of causing harm by a look. **2** a glare, superstitiously thought to cause harm.

evil-minded ▷ *adj* **1** inclined to evil. **2** malicious; wicked.

evil-tempered ▷ *adj* bad-tempered; unpleasant or spiteful.

evince /ɪ'vɪns/ ▷ *verb* (**evinced, evincing**) *formal* to show or display something (usually a personal quality) clearly. • **evincible** *adj.* ◷ 17c: from Latin *evincere* to overcome.

eviscerate /ɪ'vɪsəreɪt/ ▷ *verb* (**eviscerated, eviscerating**) *formal* **1** to tear out the bowels of someone or something; to gut. **2** to take away the essential quality or meaning of something. • **evisceration** *noun, formal* disembowelling. ◷ 17c: from Latin *eviscerare* to disembowel, from *e* out + *viscera* the bowels.

evoke /ɪ'voʊk/ ▷ *verb* (**evoked, evoking**) **1** to cause or produce (a response or reaction, etc). **2** to bring (a memory or emotion, etc) into the mind. • **evocation** /iːvə'keɪʃən/ *noun*. • **evocative** /ɪ'vɒkətɪv/ *adj* bringing a feeling vividly to mind. ⓒ 17c: from Latin *evocare* to call out.

evolute /'iːvəluːt, -ljuːt/ ▷ *noun, geom* the original curve from which the INVOLUTE is described. ⓒ 18c: from Latin *evolutus*, from *evolvere* to EVOLVE.

evolution /iːvə'luːʃən, -'ljuː-/ ▷ *noun* **1** the process of evolving. **2** a gradual development. **3** *biol* the cumulative changes in the characteristics of living organisms or populations of organisms from generation to generation, resulting in the development of new types of organism over long periods of time. **4** *chem* the giving off of a gas. • **evolutionary** *adj* relating to, or as a part of, evolution. • **evolutionism** *noun, anthropol, biol* the theory of evolution. • **evolutionist** *noun* a person who believes in the theory of evolution. ⓒ 17c: from Latin *evolutio* unrolling.

evolve /ɪ'vɒlv/ ▷ *verb* (***evolved, evolving***) **1** *tr & intr* to develop or produce gradually. **2** *intr* to develop from a primitive into a more complex or advanced form. **3** *chem* to give off (heat, etc). ⓒ 17c: from Latin *evolvere* to roll out or unroll.

ewe /juː/ ▷ *noun* a female sheep. ⓒ Anglo-Saxon *eowu*.

> ***ewe***
>
> There is sometimes a spelling confusion between **ewe** and **yew**.

ewer /'juːə(r)/ ▷ *noun* a large water-jug with a wide mouth. ⓒ 14c: from French *eviere*, from Latin *aquarius* of water.

Ex. ▷ *abbreviation* Book of the Bible: Exodus. See table at BIBLE.

ex[1] ▷ *noun* (***ex's*** or ***exes***) *colloq* a person who is no longer what he or she was, especially a former husband, wife or lover. ⓒ 19c: from words formed with EX-[1].

ex[2] ▷ *prep, commerce* **1** direct from somewhere □ *ex warehouse*. **2** excluding something □ *ex VAT*. ⓒ 19c: Latin, meaning 'out of'.

ex-[1] ▷ *prefix, signifying* **1** former □ *ex-wife* □ *ex-president*. **2** outside □ *ex-directory*. ⓒ From Latin *ex*, meaning 'out of'.

ex-[2] see under EXO-

exa- /ɛksə/ ▷ *prefix, math* (symbol **E**) *signifying* 10^{18}.

exacerbate /ɪg'zasəbeɪt/ ▷ *verb* (***exacerbated, exacerbating***) to make (a bad situation, anger or pain, etc) worse or more severe. • **exacerbation** *noun*. ⓒ 17c: from Latin *exacerbare, exacerbatum* to irritate, from *acerbus* bitter.

exact /ɪg'zakt/ ▷ *adj* **1** absolutely accurate or correct. **2** insisting on accuracy or precision in even the smallest details. **3** dealing with measurable quantities or values □ *Psychology is not an exact science*. ▷ *verb* (***exacted, exacting***) **1** (*usually* **exact something from** or **of someone**) to demand (payment, etc) from them. **2** to insist on (a right, etc). • **exacting** *adj* making difficult or excessive demands. • **exactingly** *adverb*. • **exaction** *noun, formal* **1** the act of demanding payment, or the payment demanded. **2** illegal demands for money; extortion. • **exactitude** *noun, formal* accuracy or correctness. • **exactness** *noun*. ⓒ 15c: from Latin *exigere, exactum* to demand.

exactly *adverb* **1** just; quite, precisely or absolutely. **2** with accuracy; with attention to detail. **3** said in reply: you are quite right. • **not exactly** **1** not altogether. **2** *colloq, ironic* not at all.

exaggerate /ɪg'zadʒəreɪt/ ▷ *verb* (***exaggerated, exaggerating***) **1** *tr & intr* to regard or describe something as being greater or better than it really is. **2** to emphasize something or make it more noticeable. **3** to do something in an excessive or affected way. • **exaggeration** *noun*. • **exaggerator** *noun*. ⓒ 16c: from Latin *exaggerare, exaggeratum* to heap up, from *agger* a heap.

exalt /ɪg'zɔːlt/ ▷ *verb* (***exalted, exalting***) **1** to praise (eg God) highly. **2** to fill someone with great joy. **3** to give a higher rank or position to someone or something. • **exaltation** /ɛgzɔːl'teɪʃən/ *noun* **1** the act of exalting or state of being exalted. **2** a strong feeling of happiness. • **exalted** *adj* **1** noble; very moral. **2** exaggerated; too high. • **exaltedly** *adverb*. ⓒ 15c: from Latin *exaltare* to raise.

exam /ɪg'zam/ ▷ *noun, colloq* an EXAMINATION (sense 1).

examination /ɪgzamɪ'neɪʃən/ *noun* **1** a set of tasks, especially in written form, designed to test knowledge or ability. **2** an inspection of a person's state of health, carried out by a doctor. **3** the act of examining, or process of being examined. **4** *law* formal questioning in a court of law.

examination-in-chief ▷ *noun, law* questioning of one's own witness.

examine /ɪg'zamɪn/ ▷ *verb* (***examined, examining***) **1** to inspect, consider or look into something closely. **2** to check the health of someone. **3** to test the knowledge or ability of (a person), especially in a formal examination. **4** *law* to question formally in a court of law. • **examinability** *noun*. • **examinable** *adj*. • **examinee** *noun* (***examinees***) a candidate in an examination. • **examiner** *noun* someone who sets an examination. • **need one's head examined** *colloq* to be crazy or stupid, etc. ⓒ 14c: from French *examiner*, from Latin *examinare* to weigh or test, from *examen* the pointer on a set of scales.

example /ɪg'zɑːmpəl/ ▷ *noun* **1** someone or something that is a typical specimen. **2** something that illustrates a fact or rule. **3** a person or pattern of behaviour, etc as a model to be, or not to be, copied □ *set a good example*. **4** a punishment given, or the person punished, as a warning to others □ *make an example of someone*. • **for example** as an example or illustration. ⓒ 14c: French, from Latin *exemplum*.

exanthema /ɛksan'θiːmə/ ▷ *noun* (***exanthemata*** /-mətə/ or ***exanthemas***) *pathol* **1** a rash or other skin eruption, symptomatic of a febrile disease. **2** a disease characterized by such a symptom. ⓒ 17c: Greek, from *exanthein* to burst out, from *anthein* to blossom.

exasperate /ɪg'zɑːspəreɪt/ ▷ *verb* (***exasperated, exasperating***) to make someone annoyed and frustrated; to anger them. • **exasperating** *adj*. • **exasperatingly** *adverb*. • **exasperation** *noun* a feeling of angry frustration. ⓒ 16c: from Latin *exasperare, exasperatum* to make rough.

Exc. ▷ *abbreviation* Excellency.

ex cathedra /ɛks kə'θiːdrə, —'kaθɛdrɑː/ ▷ *adverb* with authority, especially the full authority of the Pope. ▷ *adj* (*usually* **ex-cathedra**) **1** said of a papal pronouncement: stating an infallible doctrine. **2** made with, or as if with, authority. ⓒ 17c: Latin, literally 'from the chair'.

excavate /'ɛkskəveɪt/ ▷ *verb* (***excavated, excavating***) **1** to dig up or uncover something (especially historical remains). **2** to dig up (a piece of ground, etc); to make (a hole) by doing this. • **excavation** *noun* **1** *especially archaeol* the process of excavating or digging up ground. **2** an excavated area or site. • **excavator** *noun* **1** someone who excavates or digs up ground. **2** a machine for digging. ⓒ 16c: from Latin *excavare, excavatum* to make hollow.

exceed /ɪk'siːd/ ▷ *verb* (***exceeded, exceeding***) **1** to be greater than someone or something. **2** to go beyond; to do more than is required by something. • **exceedingly** *adverb* very; extremely. ⓒ 14c: from French *exceder*.

excel /ɪk'sɛl/ ▷ *verb* (***excelled, excelling***) **1** (*usually* **excel in** or **at something**) *intr* to be exceptionally good at it. **2** to be better than someone or something. • **excel oneself** *often ironic* to do better than usual or previously. ⓒ 15c: from Latin *excellere* to rise up.

excellence /'ɛksələns/ ▻ *noun* great worth; very high or exceptional quality. • **excellent** *adj* of very high quality; extremely good. • **excellently** *adverb*. ⓒ 14c: French, from Latin *excellentia*.

Excellency /'ɛksələnsɪ/ ▻ *noun* (***Excellencies***) (*usually* **His, Her** or **Your Excellency** or **Your** or **Their Excellencies**) a title of honour given to certain people of high rank, eg ambassadors. ⓒ 16c.

excentric see ECCENTRIC (senses 2 to 4)

except /ɪk'sɛpt/ ▻ *prep* leaving out; not including. ▻ *verb* (***excepted, excepting***) to leave out or exclude □ *present company excepted.* • **excepting** *prep* leaving out; not including or counting. • **except for something** apart from it; not including or counting. ⓒ 14c: from Latin *excipere, exceptum* to take out.

exception /ɪk'sɛpʃən/ ▻ *noun* **1** someone or something not included. **2** someone or something that does not, or is allowed not to, follow a general rule □ *make an exception.* **3** an act of excluding. • **exceptionable** *adj* **1** likely to cause disapproval, offence or dislike. **2** open to objection. • **exceptionably** *adverb*. • **take exception to something** to object to it; to be offended by it. • **the exception proves the rule** the existence of an exception to a supposed rule proves the general truth of the rule (often used in argument when no such conclusion is justified). ⓒ 14c.

exceptional ▻ *adj* **1** remarkable or outstanding. **2** being or making an exception. • **exceptionally** *adverb* in an exceptional way; to an exceptional or unusual degree.

excerpt ▻ *noun* /'ɛksɜːpt/ a short passage or part taken from a book, film or musical work, etc. ▻ *verb* /ɪk'sɜːpt/ (***excerpted, excerpting***) to select extracts from (a book, etc). • **excerption** *noun*. • **excerptor** *noun*. ⓒ 17c: from Latin *excerptum*, from *excerpere* to pick out.

excess /ɪk'sɛs/ ▻ *noun* (***excesses***) **1** the act of going, or the state of being, beyond normal or suitable limits. **2** an amount or extent greater than is usual, necessary or wise. **3** the amount by which one quantity, etc exceeds another; an amount left over. **4** (*usually* **excesses**) an outrageous or offensive act. ▻ *adj* /'ɛksɛs/ **1** greater than is usual, necessary or permitted. **2** additional; required to make up for an amount lacking □ *excess postage* □ *excess fare.* • **excessive** /ɪk'sɛsɪv/ *adj* too great; beyond what is usual, right or appropriate. • **excessively** *adverb* to an excessive degree. • **in excess of something** going beyond (a specified amount); more than it □ *in excess of 5 million.* ⓒ 14c: from French *exces*, from Latin *excessus* departure or going beyond.

excess

A word often confused with this one is **access**.

excess baggage and **excess luggage** ▻ *noun* luggage which exceeds the limits on weight, size or number of items that will be carried free by an airline, etc.

excess profits tax ▻ *noun* a tax levied on a company's profits above a specified level.

exch. ▻ *abbreviation* **1** exchange. **2** exchequer.

exchange /ɪks'tʃeɪndʒ/ ▻ *verb* (***exchanged, exchanging***) **1** (*usually* **exchange one thing for another**) to give, or give up, something, in return for something else. **2** to give and receive in return □ *The two leaders exchanged gifts.* ▻ *noun* **1** the giving and taking of one thing for another. **2** a thing exchanged. **3** a giving and receiving in return. **4** a conversation or argument, especially a brief one. **5** the act of exchanging the currency of one country for that of another. **6** a place where shares are traded, or international financial deals carried out. **7** (*also* **telephone exchange**) a central telephone system where lines are connected, or the building housing this. • **exchangeability** *noun*. • **exchangeable** *adj*. • **exchanger** *noun* a person who exchanges money or goods, etc, especially as a profession. • **exchange blows** or **words** to quarrel verbally or physically. • **in exchange for something** in return for it. ⓒ 14c: from French *eschangier*, from Latin *ex* from + *cambiare* to barter.

exchange control ▻ *noun* the official control of the level of a country's foreign exchange transactions so as to regulate its holding of foreign currency.

exchange rate and **rate of exchange** ▻ *noun* the value of the currency of one country in relation to that of another country or countries.

Exchange Rate Mechanism ▻ *noun* (abbreviation **ERM**) an arrangement set up to regulate exchange rate fluctuations between participating currencies in the European Monetary System, by fixing their rates, and limiting fluctuation against the ECU.

exchange student and **exchange teacher** ▻ *noun* a student or teacher spending some time at a school, etc in a foreign country, while one from that country attends their own school in their place.

exchequer /ɪks'tʃɛkə(r)/ ▻ *noun* **1** (*often* **Exchequer**) the government department in charge of the financial affairs of a nation. **2** *informal* one's personal finances or funds. ⓒ 14c as *eschekere*: from French *eschequier*, from Latin *scaccarium* chessboard, from the practice of keeping accounts on a chequered cloth.

excise¹ ▻ *noun* /'ɛksaɪz/ the tax or duty payable on goods, etc produced and sold within a country, and on certain trading licences □ *excise duty.* ▻ *verb* /ɪk'saɪz/ (***excised, excising***) **1** to charge excise on (goods, etc). **2** to force someone to pay excise. • **excisable** *adj* liable to excise duty. ⓒ 15c as *excys*: from Dutch *excijs*, from French *acceis* tax.

excise² /ɪk'saɪz/ ▻ *verb* (***excised, excising***) **1** to remove (eg a passage from a text). **2** to cut out something, or cut off something by surgery. • **excision** /ɪk'sɪʒən/ *noun*. ⓒ 16c: from Latin *excidere, excisum* to cut out.

exciseman /ɪk'saɪzmən/ ▻ *noun, formerly* an officer whose job was to collect excise duty and prevent smuggling. ⓒ 17c.

excitable /ɪk'saɪtəbəl/ ▻ *adj* **1** easily made excited, flustered, frantic, etc. **2** said of a nerve, etc: responsive to a stimulus. • **excitability** *noun*. • **excitableness** *noun*. • **excitably** *adverb*.

excitant /'ɛksɪtənt, ɪk'saɪtənt/ ▻ *noun* **1** *medicine* something which stimulates the vital activity of the body; a stimulant. **2** *physics* the electrolyte in an electric cell. ▻ *adj* exciting or stimulating. • **excitancy** /'ɛksɪtənsɪ/ *noun*. ⓒ 17c.

excite /ɪk'saɪt/ ▻ *verb* (***excited, exciting***) **1** to make someone feel lively expectation or a pleasant tension and thrill. **2** to arouse (feelings, emotions or sensations, etc). **3** to provoke (eg action). **4** to arouse someone sexually. **5** *physics* to raise (a nucleus, atom or molecule) from the GROUND state to a higher level. **6** *physics* to produce electric or magnetic activity in something. • **excitation** /ɛksɪ'teɪʃən/ *noun*. • **excitative** /ɪk'saɪtətɪv/ or **excitatory** /-tərɪ/ *adj* tending to excite. ⓒ 14c: from French *exciter*.

excited ▻ *adj* **1** emotionally or sexually aroused; thrilled. **2** in a state of great activity. **3** *physics* having energy higher than that of the GROUND state. • **excitedly** *adverb*.

excitement ▻ *noun* **1** the state of being excited. **2** objects and events that produce such a state, or the quality they have which produces it. **3** behaviour or a happening, etc which displays excitement.

exciter ▻ *noun* **1** a person or thing that excites. **2** an auxiliary machine that supplies current for another machine. **3** a sparking apparatus for producing electric waves.

exciting ▷ *adj* arousing a lively expectation or a pleasant tension and thrill. • **excitingly** *adverb.*

exciton /ɪk'saɪtɒn, 'ɛksɪtɒn/ ▷ *noun, physics* a bound pair comprising an electron and a hole. ⓒ 1930s.

excitor /ɪk'saɪtə(r)/ ▷ *noun* **1** an EXCITER 1. **2** *anatomy* a nerve that brings impulses to the brain which stimulate a part of the body.

exclaim /ɪks'kleɪm/ ▷ *verb* (***exclaimed, exclaiming***) *tr & intr* to call or cry out suddenly and loudly, eg in surprise or anger. ⓒ 16c: from Latin *exclamare.*

exclamation /ɛksklə'meɪʃən/ ▷ *noun* **1** a word or expression uttered suddenly and loudly. **2** the act of exclaiming. ⓒ 14c: from Latin *exclamatio.*

exclamation mark and (*US*) **exclamation point** ▷ *noun* the punctuation mark (!), used to indicate an exclamation.

exclamation mark

An **exclamation mark**

• is used, in place of a full stop, to indicate emphasis or strong emotion □ *Good heavens! What are you doing here?* □ *What a lovely garden!* □ *Don't you dare say that to me again!* □ *Help!*
Sentences that are questions in form but exclamations in meaning can take an exclamation mark □ *Wasn't that a marvellous film!* □ *Isn't she a despicable person!*
Commands don't always take an exclamation mark, only when they are said with particularly strong emphasis □ *'Sit down, all of you.'* □ *'Sit down when I tell you!', he shouted.*

• It indicates that what has been said should not be taken seriously □ *At this rate, we'll be seeing little green men next!*

• It draws attention to something the writer finds surprising □ *Although he said he enjoyed (!) being ill, he was clearly depressed that morning.*

exclamatory /ɛks'klamətərɪ/ ▷ *adj* containing or expressing exclamation. ⓒ 16c.

exclave /'ɛkskleɪv/ ▷ *noun* a part of a country or province etc, separated from the main part and enclosed in foreign territory. ⓒ 19c: from *ex-*, modelled on ENCLAVE.

exclude /ɪks'kluːd/ ▷ *verb* (***excluded, excluding***) **1** to prevent someone from sharing or taking part. **2** to shut someone or something out, or to keep them out. **3** to omit someone or something or leave them out of consideration. **4** to make something impossible. Opposite of INCLUDE. • **excludable** or **excludible** *adj.* • **excluding** *prep* not counting; without including. ⓒ 14c: from Latin *excludere* to shut out.

exclusion /ɪks'kluːʒən/ ▷ *noun* the act of excluding, or the state of being excluded. • **exclusionary** *adj.* • **to the exclusion of someone** or **something** so as to leave out or make no time or room for them or it. ⓒ 17c: from Latin *exclusio.*

exclusion order *law* ▷ *noun* **1** an order prohibiting the presence in, or entry into, the UK, of any person known to be concerned in acts of terrorism. **2** an order prohibiting a man guilty of battering his wife from returning to their home.

exclusion zone ▷ *noun* a zone into which entry is forbidden, eg an area of territorial waters where foreign exploitation is banned.

exclusive /ɪks'kluːsɪv/ ▷ *adj* **1** involving the rejection or denial of something else or everything else. **2** (**exclusive to someone** or **something**) limited to, given to, found in, etc only that place, group or person. **3** (**exclusive of someone** or **something**) not including a specified thing. **4** not readily accepting others into the group, especially because of a feeling of superiority □ *an exclusive club.* **5** fashionable and expensive □ *an exclusive restaurant.* ▷ *noun* a report or story published in only one newspaper or magazine. • **exclusively** *adverb.* • **exclusiveness** or **exclusivity** /ɛkskluː'sɪvɪtɪ/ *noun.* ⓒ 16c: from Latin *exclusivus.*

exclusive reckoning ▷ *noun* the usual modern method of counting, in which either the first or the last term is counted, but not both. Compare INCLUSIVE RECKONING.

excommunicate /ɛkskə'mjuːnɪkeɪt/ ▷ *verb, Christianity* to exclude someone from membership of a church. • **excommunication** *noun.* • **excommunicator** *noun.* ⓒ 15c: from Latin *excommunicare* to exclude from the community, from *communis* common.

excoriate /ɛks'kɔːrɪeɪt/ ▷ *verb* (***excoriated, excoriating***) **1** *technical* to strip the skin from (a person or animal). **2** to criticize someone severely. • **excoriation** *noun.* ⓒ 15c: from Latin *excoriare*, from *corium* skin.

excrement /'ɛkskrəmənt/ ▷ *noun* waste matter passed out of the body, especially faeces. • **excremental** *adj.* ⓒ 16c: from Latin *excrementum*, from *ex-* out + *cernere* to sift.

excrescence /ɪks'krɛsəns/ ▷ *noun* **1** an abnormal, especially an ugly, growth on a part of the body or a plant. **2** an unsightly addition. • **excrescent 1** growing abnormally; forming an excrescence; superfluous. **2** said of a sound or letter in a word: added to the word without etymological justification. ⓒ 16c: from Latin *excrescere* to grow up.

excreta /ɪks'kriːtə/ *plural noun, formal* excreted matter; faeces or urine.

excrete /ɪks'kriːt/ ▷ *verb* (***excreted, excreting***) said of a plant or animal: to eliminate (waste products). • **excretion** *noun, biol* in plants and animals: the removal of excess waste, or harmful material produced by the organism. • **excretive** or **excretory** *adj.* ⓒ 17c: from Latin *excernere* to sift out.

excruciating /ɪks'kruːʃɪeɪtɪŋ/ ▷ *adj* **1** causing great physical or mental pain. **2** *colloq* extremely bad or irritating. • **excrutiatingly** *adverb.* ⓒ 16c: from Latin *excruciare* to torture, from *cruciare, cruciatum* to crucify.

exculpate /'ɛkskʌlpeɪt, ɪks'kʌlpeɪt/ ▷ *verb* (***exculpated, exculpating***) *formal* to free someone from guilt or blame; to absolve or vindicate. Compare INCULPATE. • **exculpation** *noun.* • **exculpatory** *adj* freeing from the charge of a fault or crime. ⓒ 17c: from Latin *ex* from + *culpa* fault or blame.

excursion /ɪks'kɜːʃən, -ʒən/ ▷ *noun* **1** a short trip, usually one made for pleasure. **2** a brief change from the usual course or pattern. ⓒ 17c: from Latin *excurrere, excursum* to run out.

excursive ▷ *adj, formal* tending to wander from the main point. • **excursively** *adverb.* • **excursiveness** *noun.* ⓒ 17c.

excuse ▷ *verb* /ɪk'skjuːz/ (***excused, excusing***) **1** to pardon or forgive someone. **2** to offer justification for (a wrongdoing). **3** to free someone from (an obligation or duty, etc). **4** to allow someone to leave a room, etc, eg in order to go to the lavatory. ▷ *noun* /ɪk'skjuːs/ **1** an explanation for a wrongdoing, offered as an apology or justification. **2** *derog* a very poor example □ *You'll never sell this excuse for a painting!* • **excusable** *adj.* • **excusably** *adverb.* • **excuse me** an expression of apology, or one used to attract attention. • **excuse oneself** to leave after apologizing or asking permission. • **make one's excuses** to apologize for leaving or for not attending. ⓒ 14c: from Latin *excusare*, from *ex* from + *causa* cause or accusation.

excuse-me ▷ *noun* (***excuse-mes***) a dance during which one may exchange partners.

ex-directory ▷ *adj* **1** said of a telephone number: not included in the directory at the request of the subscriber. **2** said of a telephone subscriber: having such a number.

ex dividend ▷ *adverb* (abbreviation **ex div.**) referring to shares: without the next dividend.

exeat /ˈɛksɪat/ ▷ *noun* **1** formal leave of absence from a college or boarding school, etc eg for a weekend. **2** a permission granted by a bishop to a priest to move on to another diocese. 🕓 18c: Latin, meaning 'let him go out'.

exec /ɪgˈzɛk/ ▷ *noun* (*execs*) *colloq* short form of EXECUTIVE.

exec. ▷ *abbreviation* **1** executive. 2 executor.

execrable /ˈɛksəkrəbəl/ ▷ *adj* **1** detestable. **2** dreadful; of very poor quality. • **execrably** *adverb*. 🕓 14c: from Latin *exsecrabilis* detestable.

execrate /ˈɛksəkreɪt/ ▷ *verb* (***execrated***, ***execrating***) *formal* **1** to feel or express hatred or loathing of something. **2** to curse. • **execration** *noun* an expression of loathing; cursing. • **execrative** or **execratory** *adj*. 🕓 16c: from Latin *exsecrari*, *exsecratus* to curse.

executant /ɪgˈzɛkjʊtənt/ ▷ *noun* someone who carries out or performs something, especially a technically accomplished musician. 🕓 19c.

execute /ˈɛksəkjuːt/ ▷ *verb* (***executed***, ***executing***) **1** to put someone to death by order of the law. **2** to perform or carry out something. **3** to produce something, especially according to a design. **4** *law* to make something valid by signing. **5** *law* to carry out instructions contained in (a will or contract). • **executable** *adj*. • **executer** *noun* someone who carries out (a plan, etc) or puts (a law, etc) into effect. Compare EXECUTOR. 🕓 14c: from Latin *exsequi*, *exsecutus* to follow up or carry out.

execution ▷ *noun* **1** the act, or an instance, of putting someone to death by law. **2** the act or skill of carrying something out; an instance or the process of carrying something out. • **executioner** *noun* a person who carries out a sentence of death. 🕓 14c.

executive /ɪgˈzɛkjʊtɪv/ ▷ *adj* **1** in a business organization, etc: concerned with management or administration. **2** for the use of managers and senior staff. **3** *colloq* expensive and sophisticated □ *executive cars*. **4** *law*, *politics* relating to the carrying out of laws □ *executive powers*. ▷ *noun* **1** someone in an organization, etc who has power to direct or manage. **2** (**the executive**) *law*, *politics* the branch of government that puts laws into effect. • **executively** *adverb*. 🕓 17c.

Executive Council ▷ *noun*, *Austral*, *NZ* a ministerial council headed by the Governor or Governor-General.

executive program ▷ *noun*, *computing* a program which controls the use of a computer and of other programs.

executive session ▷ *noun*, *US* **1** a meeting of the Senate for executive business, usually held in private. **2** any meeting held in private.

executive toy ▷ *noun* a gadget or object with little practical use, intended primarily as a diversion for executives.

executor /ɪgˈzɛkjʊtə(r)/ ▷ *noun*, *law* a male or female person appointed to carry out instructions stated in a will. • **executorial** *adj*. • **executorship** *noun*. 🕓 13c.

executory /ɪgˈzɛkjʊtərɪ/ *adj* **1** relating to the carrying out of laws or orders. **2** designed to be carried into effect.

executrix /ɪgˈzɛkjʊtrɪks/ ▷ *noun* (***executrices*** /-trɪsiːz/ or ***executrixes***) *law* a female EXECUTOR. 🕓 15c.

exegesis /ɛksəˈdʒiːsɪs/ ▷ *noun* (*exegeses* /-siːz/) a critical explanation of a text, especially of the Bible. • **exegetic** /-ˈdʒɛtɪk/ or **exegetical** *adj* critically explaining a text. • **exegetically** *adverb*. 🕓 17c: Greek, meaning 'explanation'.

exemplar /ɪgˈzɛmplɑː(r)/ ▷ *noun* **1** a person or thing worth copying; a model. **2** a typical example. 🕓 14c: from Latin *exemplum* example.

exemplary /ɪgˈzɛmplərɪ/ *adj* **1** worth following as an example. **2** serving as an illustration or warning. • **exemplarily** *adverb*. • **exemplariness** *noun*. 🕓 16c.

exemplary damages ▷ *plural noun*, *law* damages in excess of the value needed to compensate the plaintiff, awarded as a punishment to the offender.

exemplify /ɪgˈzɛmplɪfaɪ/ ▷ *verb* (***exemplifies***, ***exemplified***, ***exemplifying***) **1** to be an example of something. **2** to show an example of something, or show it by means of an example. • **exemplifiable** *adj*. • **exemplification** *noun*. 🕓 15c.

exempt /ɪgˈzɛmt/ ▷ *verb* (***exempted***, ***exempting***) to free someone from a duty or obligation that applies to others. ▷ *adj* free from some obligation; not liable. • **exemption** *noun*. 🕓 14c: from Latin *eximere*, *exemptum* to take out.

exequies /ˈɛksəkwɪz/ ▷ *plural noun*, *formal* funeral rites. • **exequial** /ɛkˈsiːkwɪəl/ *adj*. 🕓 14c: from Latin *exequiae*, from *exsequi* to follow to the end.

exercise /ˈɛksəsaɪz/ ▷ *noun* **1** physical training or exertion for health or pleasure. **2** an activity intended to develop a skill. **3** a task designed to test ability. **4** a piece of written work intended as practice for learners. **5** *formal* the act of putting something into practice or carrying it out □ *the exercise of one's duty*. **6** (*usually* **exercises**) *military* training and practice for soldiers. ▷ *verb* (***exercised***, ***exercising***) **1** *tr & intr* to give exercise to (oneself, or someone or something else). **2** to use something or bring it into use □ *exercised his right to appeal*. **3** to trouble, concern, or occupy someone's thoughts. • **exercisable** *adj*. • **exerciser** *noun*. • **the object of the exercise** the purpose of a particular operation or activity. 🕓 14c: from French *exercice*, from Latin *exercere* to keep busy.

exercise bike, **exercise bicycle** or **exercise cycle** ▷ *noun* a stationary machine which is pedalled like a bicycle against adjustable resistance.

exercise book ▷ *noun* **1** a notebook for writing exercises in. **2** a book containing exercises to practise.

exert /ɪgˈzɜːt/ ▷ *verb* (***exerted***, ***exerting***) **1** to bring something into use or action forcefully □ *exert one's authority*. **2** (**exert oneself**) to force oneself to make a strenuous, especially physical, effort. • **exertion** *noun*. 🕓 17c: from Latin *exserere*, *exsertum* to thrust out.

exes[1] /ˈɛksɪz/ ▷ *plural noun*, *colloq* expenses. 🕓 19c.

exes[2] see under EX[1]

exeunt /ˈɛksɪʌnt, -ʊnt/ ▷ *verb*, *theat* as a stage direction: leave the stage; they leave the stage. • **exeunt omnes** all leave the stage. See also EXIT. 🕓 15c: Latin, meaning 'they go out', from *exire* to go out + *omnis* all or every.

exfoliate /ɛksˈfoʊlɪeɪt/ ▷ *verb* (***exfoliated***, ***exfoliating***) *tr & intr* said of bark, rocks or skin, etc: to shed or peel off in flakes or layers. • **exfoliation** *noun*. • **exfoliative** /-ətɪv/ *adj*. 🕓 17c: from Latin *exfoliare*, *exfoliatum* to strip of leaves.

ex gratia /ɛks ˈgreɪʃɪə/ ▷ *adverb*, *adj* given as a favour, not in recognition of any obligation, especially a legal one. 🕓 18c: Latin, meaning 'as a favour'.

exhale /ɛksˈheɪl/ ▷ *verb* (***exhaled***, ***exhaling***) *tr & intr* **1** to breathe out. **2** to give off or be given off. Compare INHALE. • **exhalation** /ɛkshəˈleɪʃən/ *noun*. 🕓 14c: from French *exhaler*, from Latin *ex* out + *halare* to breathe.

exhaust /ɪgˈzɔːst/ ▷ *verb* (***exhausted***, ***exhausting***) **1** to make (a person or animal) very tired. **2** to use something up completely. **3** to say all that can be said about (a subject, etc). **4** *engineering* to empty (a container) or draw off (gas). ▷ *noun* **1** the escape of waste gases from an engine, etc. **2** the gases themselves. **3** the part or parts of an engine, etc through which the waste gases escape. • **exhausted** *adj*. • **exhaustible** *adj*. • **exhausting** *adj*. • **exhaustion** *noun*. 🕓 16c: from Latin *exhaurire*, *exhaustum* to draw off or drain away.

exhaustive /ɪg'zɔːstɪv/ *adj* complete; comprehensive or very thorough. • **exhaustively** *adverb.* ⓒ 18c.

exhibit /ɪg'zɪbɪt/ ▷ *verb* (***exhibited***, ***exhibiting***) **1** to present or display something for public appreciation. **2** to show or manifest (a quality, etc). ▷ *noun* **1** an object displayed publicly, eg in a museum. **2** *law* an object or article produced in court as part of the evidence. • **exhibitor** *noun* a person who provides an exhibit for a public display. ⓒ 15c: from Latin *exhibere, exhibitum* to produce or show.

exhibition /ɛksɪ'bɪʃən/ ▷ *noun* **1** a display, eg of works of art, to the public. **2** the act or an instance of showing something, eg a quality. **3** a scholarship awarded by a college or university. • **exhibitioner** *noun* a student receiving an educational exhibition. • **make an exhibition of oneself** to behave foolishly in public. ⓒ 15c.

exhibitionism ▷ *noun* **1** *derog* the tendency to behave so as to attract attention to oneself. **2** *psychol* the compulsive desire to expose one's sexual organs publicly. • **exhibitionist** *noun.* • **exhibitionistic** *adj.*

exhilarate /ɪg'zɪləreɪt/ ▷ *verb* (***exhilarated***, ***exhilarating***) to fill someone with a lively cheerfulness. • **exhilarating** *adj.* • **exhilaratingly** *adverb.* • **exhilaration** *noun* a feeling of extreme cheerfulness. • **exhilarative** /-rətɪv/ *adj.* ⓒ 16c: from Latin *exhilarare, exhilaratum,* from *hilaris* cheerful.

exhort /ɪg'zɔːt/ ▷ *verb* (***exhorted***, ***exhorting***) to urge or advise someone strongly and sincerely. • **exhortation** *noun* a strong appeal or urging. • **exhortative** /-tətɪv/ or **exhortatory** /-tətərɪ/ *adj.* ⓒ 14c: from Latin *exhortari* to encourage, from *hortari* to urge.

exhume /ɪg'zjuːm/ ▷ *verb* (***exhumed***, ***exhuming***) *formal* **1** to dig up (a body) from a grave. **2** to reveal; to bring something up or mention it again. • **exhumation** /ɛkshjʊ'meɪʃən/ *noun* the digging up of a body from a grave. ⓒ 18c: from Latin *ex* out of + *humus* the ground.

exigency /'ɛksɪdʒənsɪ, ɪg'zɪdʒənsɪ/ ▷ *noun* (***exigencies***) *formal* **1** (*usually* **exigencies**) urgent need. **2** an emergency. ⓒ 16c: from Latin *exigere* to drive out.

exigent /'ɛksɪdʒənt/ ▷ *adj, formal* **1** pressing; urgent. **2** demanding. ⓒ 15c: from Latin *exigens, exigentis.*

exiguous /ɪg'zɪgjʊəs/ *formal* ▷ *adj* scarce or meagre; insufficient. • **exiguousness** or **exiguity** /ɛksɪ'gjuːɪtɪ/ *noun.* • **exiguously** *adverb.* ⓒ 17c: from Latin *exiguus* small or meagre.

exile /'ɛksaɪl, 'ɛgzaɪl/ ▷ *noun* **1** enforced or regretted absence from one's country or town, especially for a long time and often as a punishment. **2** someone who suffers such absence. ▷ *verb* (***exiled***, ***exiling***) to send someone into exile. ⓒ 13c: from Latin *exsilium* banishment, from *ex* out of + *salire* to leap.

ex int. ▷ *abbreviation, finance* without interest.

exist /ɪg'zɪst/ ▷ *verb* (***existed***, ***existing***) *intr* **1** to be, especially to be present in the real world or universe rather than in story or imagination. **2** to occur or be found. **3** to manage to stay alive; to live with only the most basic necessities of life. ⓒ 17c: from Latin *exsistere* to stand out.

existence ▷ *noun* **1** the state of existing. **2** a life, or a way of living. **3** everything that exists. • **existent** *adj* having an actual being; existing. ⓒ 14c meaning 'actuality' 'reality'.

existential /ɛgzɪ'stɛnʃəl/ ▷ *adj* **1** relating to human existence. **2** *philos* relating to existentialism. ⓒ 17c.

existentialism ▷ *noun* a philosophy that emphasizes freedom of choice and personal responsibility for one's own actions, which create one's own moral values and determine one's future. • **existentialist** *adj, noun.* ⓒ 1940s: from German *Existentialismus.*

exit /'ɛksɪt, 'ɛgzɪt/ ▷ *noun* **1** a way out of a building, etc. **2** going out or departing. **3** an actor's departure from the stage. **4** a place where vehicles can leave a motorway or main road. **5** *computing* the last instruction of a subroutine. ▷ *verb* (***exited***, ***exiting***) *intr* **1** *formal* to go out, leave or depart. **2** *theat* **a** to leave the stage; **b** as a stage direction: (**exit**) he or she leaves the stage. See also EXEUNT. **3** *computing* to leave (a program or system, etc). ⓒ 16c: from Latin *exire, exitum* to go out.

exit poll ▷ *noun* a poll of a sample of voters in an election, taken as they leave a polling-station, and used to give an early indication of voting trends in a particular election.

exo- /ɛksoʊ, ɛk'sɒ/ or (before a vowel) **ex-** ▷ *combining form* out or outside. See also ECTO-, ENDO-, ENTO-. ⓒ From Greek *exo* outside.

exobiology ▷ *noun, astron* the study of living organisms that may exist elsewhere in the universe, methods of detecting them, and the possible effects of extraterrestrial conditions on terrestrial life forms. • **exobiological** *adj.* • **exobiologist** *noun.* ⓒ 1960s.

exocarp ▷ *noun, bot* the outer layer of the EPICARP. ⓒ 19c.

Exocet /'ɛksoʊsɛt/ ▷ *noun, trademark* a subsonic tactical missile, launched from a ship, aircraft or submarine and travelling at low altitude. ⓒ 1970: French, from Latin *Exocoetus volitans* the flying fish.

exocrine /'ɛksoʊkraɪn, -krɪn/ *physiol* ▷ *adj* **1** relating to external secretions, or to a pathway or structure that secretes externally. **2** said of a gland, such as the sweat gland or salivary gland: discharging its secretions through a duct which opens onto an epithelial surface. See also ENDOCRINE. ▷ *noun* an exocrine gland. ⓒ Early 20c: from EXO- + Greek *krinein* to separate.

Exod or **Exod.** ▷ *abbreviation* Book of the Bible: Exodus. See table at BIBLE.

exoderm see ECTODERM

exodus /'ɛksədəs/ ▷ *noun* (***exoduses***) **1** a mass departure of people. **2** (**Exodus**) the departure of the Israelites from Egypt, probably in the 13c BC. ⓒ 17c; Anglo-Saxon in sense 2: Latin, from Greek *exodos,* from *ex* out + *hodos* way.

ex officio /ɛks ə'fɪʃɪoʊ/ ▷ *adverb, adj* by virtue of one's official position. ⓒ 16c: Latin.

exogamy /ɛk'sɒgəmɪ/ ▷ *noun* **1** *anthropol* the practice of marrying only outside of one's own group. **2** *biol* the union of GAMETEs from unrelated individuals. • **exogamic** or **exogamous** *adj.* ⓒ 19c.

exogenous /ɛk'sɒdʒənəs/ ▷ *adj, biol* **1** originating outside a cell, organ or organism. **2** growing from near the surface of a living organism. ⓒ 19c.

exon /'ɛksɒn/ ▷ *noun, genetics* any segment of DNA in a gene that is transcribed into MESSENGER RNA and then into protein. See also INTRON. ⓒ 1970s.

exonerate /ɪg'zɒnəreɪt/ ▷ *verb* (***exonerated***, ***exonerating***) to free someone from blame, or acquit them of a criminal charge. • **exoneration** *noun.* • **exonerative** /-rətɪv/ *adj.* ⓒ 16c: from Latin *exonerare, exoneratum,* from *ex* from + *onus* burden.

exophthalmia /ɛksɒf'θalmɪə/, **exophthalmos** and **exophthalmus** /-'θalməs/ ▷ *noun, pathol* protrusion of the eyeballs. • **exophthalmic** *adj.* ⓒ Late 19c: from Greek *ex* out + *opthalmos* eye.

exophthalmic goitre ▷ *noun, pathol* a form of hyperthyroidism marked by exophthalmia and swelling of the thyroid gland.

exor ▷ *abbreviation, law* executor.

exorbitant /ɪg'zɔːbɪtənt/ ▷ *adj* said of prices or demands: very high, excessive or unfair. • **exorbitance** *noun.* • **exorbitantly** *adverb.* ⓒ 15c: from Latin *exorbitare* to go out of the track, from *ex* out of + *orbita* track.

exorcize or **exorcise** /'ɛksɔːsaɪz/ ▻ *verb* (***exorcized, exorcizing***) in some beliefs: **1** to drive away (an evil spirit or influence) with prayer or holy words. **2** to free (a person or place) from the influence of an evil spirit in this way. • **exorcism** /-sɪzəm/ *noun*. • **exorcist** *noun*. ⓒ 17c; 16c in sense 2: from Greek *exorkizein*, from *ex-* out + *horkos* an oath.

exoskeleton ▻ *noun, zool* in some invertebrates: an external skeleton forming a rigid covering that is external to the body. • **exoskeletal** *adj*. ⓒ 19c.

exosphere ▻ *noun, astron* the outermost layer of the Earth's atmosphere, which starts at an altitude of about 500km. • **exospheric** /-'sfɛrɪk/ or **exospherical** *adj*. ⓒ 1940s: from EXO-, modelled on ATMOSPHERE.

exothermic reaction ▻ *noun, chem* any process, especially a chemical reaction, that involves the release of heat. ⓒ 19c.

exotic /ɪg'zɒtɪk/ ▻ *adj* **1** introduced from a foreign country, especially a distant and tropical country ▫ *exotic plants*. **2** interestingly different or strange, especially colourful and rich, and suggestive of a distant land. ▻ *noun* an exotic person or thing. • **exotically** *adverb*. • **exoticism** *noun*. ⓒ 16c: from Greek *exotikos*, from *exo* outside.

exotica /ɪg'zɒtɪkə/ ▻ *plural noun* strange or rare objects. ⓒ 19c: Latin, neuter plural of *exoticus* EXOTIC.

exotic dancer ▻ *noun* a striptease dancer or belly-dancer.

expand /ɪk'spand/ ▻ *verb* (***expanded, expanding***) **1** *tr & intr* to make or become greater in size, extent or importance. **2** *intr, formal* to become more at ease or more open and talkative. **3** *tr & intr, formal* to fold out flat or spread out. **4** to write something out in full. **5** *math* to multiply out (terms in brackets). • **expandable** *adj*. ⓒ 15c: from Latin *expandere*, *expansum* to spread out.

■ **expand on** or **upon something** to give additional information; to enlarge on (a description, etc).

expanded *adj* said of plastic: combined with a gas during manufacture to produce a lightweight insulating or packaging material ▫ *expanded polystyrene*.

expanded metal ▻ *noun* steel, etc stretched to form a mesh, used for reinforcing concrete, etc.

expander *noun* **1** a device used for exercising and developing muscles. **2** *electronics* a device which increases the range of amplitude variations in a transmission system.

expanding universe theory ▻ *noun, astron* the theory that the whole universe is constantly expanding and the galaxies are moving away from each other.

expanse /ɪk'spans/ ▻ *noun* a wide area or space. ⓒ 17c: from Latin *expansum*.

expansible ▻ *adj* able to expand or be expanded. • **expansibility** *noun*. • **expansible** *adverb*. ⓒ 17c.

expansion ▻ *noun* **1** the act or state of expanding. **2** the amount by which something expands. **3** *math* the result of expanding terms in brackets. • **expansionary** *adj*. ⓒ 15c.

expansion board and **expansion card** ▻ *noun, computing* a printed circuit board which can be inserted into an **expansion slot**, a connector in a computer which allows extra facilities to be added either temporarily or permanently.

expansion bolt ▻ *noun* a bolt that expands within a hole or crack, etc to provide a firm support.

expansionism *noun* the act or practice of increasing territory or political influence or authority, usually at the expense of other nations or bodies. • **expansionist** *noun, adj*.

expansion joint ▻ *noun, engineering* a gap left at a joint, eg between lengths of rail or sections of concrete, to allow for heat expansion.

expansive /ɪk'spansɪv/ ▻ *adj* **1** ready or eager to talk; open or effusive. **2** wide-ranging. **3** able or tending to expand. • **expansively** *adverb*. • **expansiveness** *noun*.

expat /ɛks'pat/ ▻ *noun, colloq* an EXPATRIATE. ⓒ 1960s.

expatiate /ɛk'speɪʃɪeɪt/ ▻ *verb* (***expatiated, expatiating***) *intr, formal* to talk or write at length or in detail. • **expatiation** *noun*. ⓒ 17c: from Latin *exspatiari* to digress, from *ex* out of + *spatium* course.

expatriate ▻ *adj* /ɛk'spatrɪət, -'peɪt-/ **1** living abroad, especially for a long but limited period. **2** exiled. ▻ *noun* a person living or working abroad. ▻ *verb* /-eɪt/ **1** to banish or exile. **2** to deprive someone of citizenship. • **expatriation** *noun*. ⓒ 18c: from Latin *ex* out of + *patria* native land.

expect /ɪk'spɛkt/ ▻ *verb* (***expected, expecting***) **1** to think of something as likely to happen or come. **2** *colloq* to suppose ▫ *I expect you're tired*. • **expectable** *adj*. • **expectably** *adverb*. • **be expecting** *colloq* to be pregnant. ⓒ 16c: from Latin *exspectare* to look out for.

■ **expect something from** or **of someone** to require it of them; to regard it as normal or reasonable.

expectancy *noun* (***expectancies***) **1** the act or state of expecting. **2** a future chance or probability. Also *in compounds* ▫ *life expectancy*.

expectant *adj* **1** eagerly waiting; hopeful. **2** not yet, but expecting to be something (especially a mother or father). • **expectantly** *adverb*.

expectation *noun* **1** the state, or an attitude, of expecting. **2** (*often* **expectations**) something expected, whether good or bad. **3** (*usually* **expectations**) money or property, etc that one expects to gain, especially by inheritance.

expectation of life see LIFE EXPECTANCY

expectorant *medicine, adj* causing the coughing up of phlegm. ▻ *noun* an expectorant medicine.

expectorate /ɪk'spɛktəreɪt/ ▻ *verb* (***expectorated, expectorating***) *tr & intr, medicine* to cough up and spit out (phlegm). ⓒ 17c: from Latin *expectorare*, from *ex* from + *pectus* the chest.

expectoration *noun* **1** the act of expectorating. **2** the matter coughed up; spittle or phlegm.

expedient /ɪk'spiːdɪənt/ ▻ *adj* **1** suitable or appropriate. **2** practical or advantageous, rather than morally correct. ▻ *noun* a suitable method or solution, especially one quickly thought of to meet an urgent need. • **expediency** or **expedience** *noun* (***expediencies*** or ***expediences***) **1** suitability or convenience. **2** practical advantage or self-interest, especially as opposed to moral correctness. • **expediently** *adverb*. ⓒ 14c: from Latin *expediens* setting free.

expedite /'ɛkspədaɪt/ ▻ *verb* (***expedited, expediting***) **1** to speed up, or assist the progress of something. **2** to carry something out quickly. ⓒ 15c in sense 2: from Latin *expedire* set free, literally 'free the feet'.

expedition /ɛkspə'dɪʃən/ ▻ *noun* **1** an organized journey with a specific purpose. **2** a group making such a journey. **3** *formal* speed or promptness. • **expeditionary** *adj* relating to, forming, or for use on, an expedition. ⓒ 15c: from Latin *expeditio*.

expeditious /ɛkspə'dɪʃəs/ ▻ *adj, formal* carried out with speed and efficiency. • **expeditiously** *adverb*. ⓒ 15c.

expel /ɪk'spɛl/ ▻ *verb* (***expelled, expelling***) **1** to dismiss from or deprive someone of membership of (a club or school, etc), usually permanently as punishment for misconduct. **2** to get rid of something; to force it out. • **expellable** *adj*. • **expellee** *noun* (***expellees***) a person who is expelled. ⓒ 14c: from Latin *expellere* to drive out.

expend /ɪk'spɛnd/ ▻ *verb* (***expended, expending***) to use or spend (time, supplies or effort, etc). ⓒ 15c: from Latin *expendere* to weigh out.

expendable *adj* **1** that may be given up or sacrificed for some purpose or cause. **2** not valuable enough to be worth preserving. • **expendability** *noun*.

expendable launch vehicle ▷ *noun, space flight* a launch vehicle made up of throwaway stages with no recoverable parts.

expenditure *noun* **1** the act of expending. **2** an amount expended, especially of money.

expense /ɪk'spɛns/ ▷ *noun* **1** the act of spending money, or the amount of money spent. **2** something on which money is spent. **3** (**expenses**) a sum of one's own money spent doing one's job, or this sum of money or an allowance paid by one's employer to make up for this. • **at the expense of something** or **someone 1** with the loss or sacrifice of them. **2** causing damage to their pride or reputation □ *a joke at my expense*. **3** with the cost paid by them. ⓒ 14c: from Latin *expensa*, from *expendere* to weigh out.

expense account ▷ *noun* **1** an arrangement by which expenses incurred during the performance of an employee's duties are reimbursed by the employer. **2** a statement of such incurred expenses.

expensive ▷ *adj* involving much expense; costing a great deal. • **expensively** *adverb*. • **expensiveness** *noun*. ⓒ 17c.

experience /ɪk'spɪərɪəns/ ▷ *noun* **1** practice in an activity. **2** knowledge or skill gained through practice. **3** wisdom gained through long and varied observation of life. **4** an event which affects or involves one. ▷ *verb* (***experienced***, ***experiencing***) **1** to have practical acquaintance with someone or something. **2** to feel or undergo. • **experienced** *adj*. ⓒ 14c: from Latin *experientia*, from *experiri* to try.

experiential /ɪkspɪərɪ'ɛnʃəl/ *philos* ▷ *adj* said of knowledge or learning: based on direct experience, as distinct from theoretical knowledge. • **experientialism** *noun* the doctrine that all knowledge comes from experience. • **experientialist** *noun*. • **experientially** *adverb* in terms of direct experience. ⓒ 19c.

experiment /ɪk'spɛrɪmənt/ ▷ *noun* **1** a trial carried out in order to test a theory, a machine's performance, etc or to discover something unknown. **2** the carrying out of such trials. **3** an attempt at something original. ▷ *verb* (***experimented***, ***experimenting***) *intr* (*usually* **experiment on** or **with something**) to carry out an experiment. • **experimentation** *noun* the process of experimenting; experimental procedure. • **experimenter** *noun*. ⓒ 14c.

experimental /ɪkspɛrɪ'mɛntəl/ ▷ *adj* **1** consisting of or like an experiment. **2** relating to, or used in, experiments. **3** trying out new styles and techniques. • **experimentally** *adverb*. • **experimentalism** *noun* use of, or reliance on, experiment. • **experimentalist** *noun*. • **experimentally** *adverb*. ⓒ 15c.

expert /'ɛkspɜːt/ ▷ *noun* someone with great skill in, or extensive knowledge of, a particular subject. ▷ *adj* **1** highly skilled or extremely knowledgeable. **2** relating to or done by an expert or experts. • **expertly** *adverb*. ⓒ 14c as *adj*, 19c as *noun*: from Latin *expertus*, from *experiri* to try.

expertise /ɛkspɜː'tiːz/ *noun* special skill or knowledge. ⓒ 19c.

expert system ▷ *noun, computing* a program that is designed to solve problems by utilizing both knowledge and reasoning derived from human expertise in a particular field. ⓒ 1980s.

expiate /'ɛkspɪeɪt/ ▷ *verb* (***expiated***, ***expiating***) to make amends for (a wrong). • **expiable** *adj* capable of being atoned for or done away with. • **expiation** *noun*. • **expiator** *noun*. • **expiatory** *adj*. ⓒ 16c: from Latin *expiare*, *expiatum* to atone for.

expire /ɪk'spaɪə(r)/ ▷ *verb* (***expired***, ***expiring***) *intr* **1** to come to an end or cease to be valid. **2** to breathe out. **3** to die. • **expiration** /ɛkspɪ'reɪʃən/ *noun, formal* **1** expiry. **2** the act or process of breathing out. ⓒ 15c: from Latin *exspirare* to breathe out.

expiry /ɪk'spaɪərɪ/ *noun* (***expiries***) the ending of the duration or validity of something. ⓒ 18c.

explain /ɪk'spleɪn/ ▷ *verb* (***explained***, ***explaining***) *tr & intr* **1** to make something clear or easy to understand. **2** to give, or be, a reason for or account for. **3** (**explain oneself**) **a** to justify (oneself or one's actions); **b** to clarify one's meaning or intention. • **explainable** *adj*. ⓒ 15c: from Latin *explanare* to make flat.

■ **explain something away** to dismiss it or lessen its importance by explanation.

explanation /ɛksplə'neɪʃən/ *noun* **1** the act or process of explaining. **2** a statement or fact that explains.

explanatory /ɪk'splanətərɪ/ *adj* serving to explain.

explantation /ɛksplɑːn'teɪʃən/ ▷ *noun, biol* the process of culturing a part or organ removed from a living individual in an artificial medium. ⓒ Early 20c: from Latin *explantare*, from *ex* out + *plantare* to plant.

expletive /ɪk'spliːtɪv/ ▷ *noun* **1** a swear-word or curse. **2** a word added to fill a gap, eg in poetry. **3** a meaningless exclamation. ▷ *adj* (*also* **expletory** /-tərɪ/) being, or like, such a word or exclamation. ⓒ 17c: from Latin *explere*, *expletum* to fill up.

explicable /ɪk'splɪkəbəl, 'ɛks-/ ▷ *adj* able to be explained. ⓒ 16c.

explicate /'ɛksplɪkeɪt/ ▷ *verb* (***explicated***, ***explicating***) **1** to explain (especially a literary work) in depth, with close analysis of particular points. **2** to unfold or develop (an idea or theory, etc). • **explication** *noun*. ⓒ 17c: from Latin *explicare*, *explicatum* to fold out.

explicit /ɪk'splɪsɪt/ ▷ *adj* **1** stated or shown fully and clearly. **2** speaking plainly and openly. • **explicitly** *adverb*. • **explicitness** *noun*. ⓒ 17c: from Latin *explicitus* straightforward.

explode /ɪk'sploʊd/ ▷ *verb* (***exploded***, ***exploding***) **1** *intr* said of a substance: to undergo an explosion. **2** to cause something to undergo an explosion. **3** *intr* to undergo a violent explosion as a result of a chemical or nuclear reaction. **4** *intr* to suddenly show a strong or violent emotion, especially anger. **5** to disprove (a theory, etc) with vigour. **6** *intr* said especially of population: to increase rapidly. ⓒ 17c; 16c in obsolete sense 'to reject scornfully': from Latin *explodere* to force off stage by clapping, from *plaudere* to clap the hands.

exploded ▷ *adj* **1** blown up. **2** said of a theory, etc: no longer accepted; proved false. **3** said of a diagram: showing the different parts of something relative to, but slightly separated from, each other.

exploding star ▷ *noun, astron* a star that flares up, such as a NOVA or SUPERNOVA.

exploit ▷ *noun* /'ɛksplɔɪt/ (*usually* **exploits**) an act or feat, especially a bold or daring one. ▷ *verb* /ɪk'splɔɪt/ (***exploited***, ***exploiting***) **1** to take unfair advantage of something or someone so as to achieve one's own aims. **2** to make good use of something. • **exploitable** *adj*. • **exploitation** /ɛksplɔɪ'teɪʃən/ *noun*. • **exploitative** /ɪk'splɔɪtətɪv/ or **exploitive** *adj*. • **exploiter** *noun*. ⓒ 14c *noun*, meaning 'progress' or 'success': from Latin *explicitum* unfolded.

exploratory /ɪk'splɒrətərɪ/ ▷ *adj* **1** said of talks, etc: serving to establish procedures or ground rules. **2** said of surgery: aiming to establish the nature of a complaint rather than treat it.

explore /ɪk'splɔː(r)/ ▷ *verb* (***explored***, ***exploring***) **1** to search or travel through (a place) for the purpose of discovery. **2** to examine something carefully □ *explore every possibility*. • **exploration** /ɛksplə'reɪʃən/ *noun*. • **explorative** /ɪk'splɒrətɪv/ *adj*. ⓒ 16c: from Latin *explorare* to search out.

explorer *noun* a person who explores unfamiliar territory, especially as a profession or habitually.

Explorer spacecraft ▷ *noun, astron* a series of US satellites.

explosion /ɪk'sploʊʒən/ ▷ *noun* **1** *chem* a sudden and violent increase in pressure, which generates large amounts of heat and destructive shock waves that travel outward from the point of explosion and are heard as a loud bang. **2** the sudden loud noise that accompanies such a reaction. **3** a sudden display of strong feelings, etc. **4** a sudden great increase. ⓒ 17c: from Latin *explodere, explosum.*

explosion welding ▷ *noun* the welding of metals with very different melting points by means of pressure produced by an explosion.

explosive /ɪk'sploʊsɪv/ ▷ *adj* **1** likely, tending or able to explode. **2** likely to become marked by physical violence or emotional outbursts. **3** likely to result in violence or an outburst of feeling □ *an explosive situation.* ▷ *noun* any substance that is capable of producing an explosion, especially one created to do so. • **explosively** *adverb.* • **explosiveness** *noun.*

expo /'ɛkspoʊ/ ▷ *noun* (**expos**) *colloq* a large public exhibition. ⓒ Early 20c: from EXPOSITION.

exponent /ɪks'poʊnənt/ ▷ *noun* **1** someone able to perform some art or activity, especially skilfully. **2** someone who explains and promotes (a theory or belief, etc). **3** *math* a number that indicates how many times a given quantity, called the **base**, is to be multiplied by itself, usually denoted by a superscript number or symbol immediately after the quantity concerned, eg $6^4 = 6 \times 6 \times 6 \times 6$. Also called **power**, **index**. ⓒ 16c: from Latin *exponere* to set out.

exponential /ɛkspə'nɛnʃəl/ *math, adj* **1** denoting a function that varies according to the power of another quantity, ie a function in which the variable quantity is an EXPONENT, eg if $y = a^x$, then y varies exponentially with x. **2** denoting a logarithmic increase or decrease in numbers of a population, eg exponential growth of bacteria or an exponential decay of radioactive isotopes. ▷ *noun* (*also* **exponential function**) the function e^x, where e is a constant with a value of approximately 2.718. • **exponentially** *adverb* on an exponential basis; very rapidly. ⓒ 18c.

exponential curve ▷ *noun, math* a curve expressed by an **exponential equation** in which the variable occurs in the EXPONENT of one or more terms.

export ▷ *verb* /ɪk'spɔːt/ (**exported**, **exporting**) to send or take (goods, etc) to another country, especially for sale. ▷ *noun* /'ɛkspɔːt/ **1** the act or business of exporting. **2** something exported. • **exportable** *adj.* • **exportability** *noun.* • **exportation** *noun* the exporting of goods. • **exporter** *noun* a person or business that exports goods commercially. ⓒ 17c; 15c meaning 'to take away': from Latin *exportare* to carry away.

export reject ▷ *noun* a manufactured article that is flawed in some way and so not passed for export, often sold at a reduced price on the home market.

expose /ɪk'spoʊz/ ▷ *verb* (**exposed**, **exposing**) **1** to remove cover, protection or shelter from something, or to allow this to be the case □ *exposed to the wind* □ *exposed to criticism.* **2** to discover something (eg a criminal or crime) or make it known. **3** to allow light to fall on (a photographic film or paper) when taking or printing a photograph. • **exposal** *noun* **1** exposure. **2** exposition. • **expose oneself** to display one's sexual organs in public. ⓒ 15c: from French *exposer* to set out.

■ **expose someone to something** to cause or allow them to have experience of it.

exposé /ɛk'spoʊzeɪ/ ▷ *noun* **1** a formal statement of facts, especially one that introduces an argument. **2** an article or programme which exposes a public scandal or crime, etc. ⓒ 19c: French, literally 'set out' or 'exposed'.

exposition /ɛkspə'zɪʃən/ ▷ *noun* **1** an in-depth explanation or account (of a subject). **2** the act of presenting such an explanation, or a viewpoint. **3** a large public exhibition. **4** *music* the part of a sonata, fugue, etc, in which themes are presented. • **expositional** *adj.* ⓒ 14c: from Latin *expositio* a setting out.

expository /ɪk'spɒzɪtərɪ/ *adj* explanatory; serving as, or like, an explanation.

ex post facto /ɛks poʊst 'faktoʊ/ ▷ *adj* retrospective. ▷ *adverb* retrospectively. ⓒ 17c: Latin, meaning 'from what is done or enacted after'.

expostulate /ɪks'pɒstjʊleɪt/ ▷ *verb* (**expostulated**, **expostulating**) *intr* (*usually* **expostulate with someone about something**) to argue or reason with them, especially in protest or so as to dissuade them. • **expostulation** *noun.* • **expostulative** /-lətɪv/ or **expostulatory** /-lətərɪ/ *adj.* • **expostulator** *noun.* ⓒ 16c: from Latin *expostulare* to demand.

exposure /ɪk'spoʊʒə(r)/ ▷ *noun* **1** the act of exposing or the state of being exposed. **2** the harmful effects on the body of extreme cold. **3** the number or regularity of someone's appearances in public, eg on TV. **4** the act of exposing photographic film or paper to light. **5** the amount of light to which a film or paper is exposed, or the length of time for which it is exposed. **6** the amount of film exposed or to be exposed in order to produce one photograph.

exposure meter ▷ *noun, photog* a device, now often incorporated in the camera, for measuring the light falling on, or reflected by, a photographic subject.

expound /ɪk'spaʊnd/ ▷ *verb* (**expounded**, **expounding**) **1** to explain something in depth. **2** (*often* **expound on something**) *intr* to talk at length about it. • **expounder** *noun.* ⓒ 14c as *expoun*: from Latin *exponere* to set out.

express /ɪk'sprɛs/ ▷ *verb* (**expresses**, **expressed**, **expressing**) **1** to put something into words. **2** to indicate or represent something with looks, actions, symbols, etc. **3** to show or reveal. **4** to press or squeeze out something. **5** to send something by fast delivery service. ▷ *adj* **1** said of a train, etc: travelling especially fast, with few stops. **2** belonging or referring to, or sent by, a fast delivery service. **3** clearly stated □ *his express wish.* **4** particular; clear □ *with the express purpose of insulting him.* ▷ *noun* (**expresses**) **1** an express train. **2** an express delivery service. ▷ *adverb* by express delivery service. • **expressible** *adj.* • **expressly** *adverb* **1** clearly and definitely. **2** particularly or specifically. • **express oneself** to put one's thoughts into words. ⓒ 14c: from Latin *exprimere, expressum* to press out.

express delivery ▷ *noun* **1** immediate delivery by special messenger. **2** delivery by an agency offering this service.

expression /ɪk'sprɛʃən/ ▷ *noun* **1** the act of expressing. **2** a look on the face that displays feelings. **3** a word or phrase. **4** the indication of feeling, eg in a manner of speaking or a way of playing music. **5** *math* a symbol or combination of symbols. • **expressionless** *adj* said of a face or voice: showing no feeling. ⓒ 15c.

Expressionism or **expressionism** ▷ *noun* a movement in art, architecture and literature which aims to communicate the internal emotional realities of a situation, rather than its external 'realistic' aspect. • **Expressionist** *noun* a person, especially a painter, who practises Expressionism. Also *as adj.* • **expressionistic** *adj.* ⓒ Early 20c.

expression mark ▷ *noun* a direction marked on a piece of music, usually in Italian.

expressive /ɪk'sprɛsɪv/ ▷ *adj* **1** showing meaning or feeling in a clear or lively way. **2** (*always* **expressive of something**) expressing a feeling or emotion □ *words* *expressive of anger.* • **expressively** *adverb.* • **expressiveness** *noun.*

expressly see under EXPRESS

expresso see ESPRESSO

express train ▷ *noun* a railway train which travels at high speed, making few or no scheduled stops before its final destination.

expressway ▷ *noun, N Amer* a motorway.

expropriate /ɪks'proupriert/ ▷ *verb* (***expropriated, expropriating***) *formal or law* said especially of the state: to take (property, etc) from its owner for some special use. • **expropriation** *noun.* • **expropriator** *noun.* ⓒ 17c: from Latin *expropriare*, from *proprium* property.

expulsion /ɪk'spʌlʃən/ ▷ *noun* **1** the act of expelling from school or a club, etc. **2** the act of forcing or driving out. ⓒ 14c: from Latin *expulsio* a forcing out.

expulsive /ɪk'spʌlsɪv/ *adj* having the power to expel or drive out.

expunge /ɪk'spʌndʒ/ ▷ *verb* (***expunged, expunging***) **1** to cross out or delete something (eg a passage from a book). **2** to cancel out or destroy something. • **expunction** /ɪk'spʌŋkʃən/ *noun.* • **expunger** *noun.* ⓒ 17c: from Latin *expungere* to mark for deletion by a row of dots, from *pungere* to prick.

expurgate /'ɛkspəgeɪt/ ▷ *verb* (***expurgated, expurgating***) **1** to revise (a book) by removing objectionable or offensive words or passages. **2** to remove (such words or passages). • **expurgation** *noun.* • **expurgator** *noun.* ⓒ 17c: from Latin *expurgare* to purify.

exquisite /ɪk'skwɪzɪt, 'ɛkskwɪzɪt/ ▷ *adj* **1** extremely beautiful or skilfully produced. **2** able to exercise sensitive judgement; discriminating □ *exquisite taste.* **3** said of pain or pleasure, etc: extreme. • **exquisitely** *adverb.* • **exquisiteness** *noun.* ⓒ 15c: from Latin *exquisitus*, from *exquirere* to search out.

ex's see under EX[1]

ex-serviceman and **ex-servicewoman** ▷ *noun* a former male or female member of the armed forces.

ext. ▷ *abbreviation* **1** extension. **2** exterior. **3** external or externally.

extant /'ɛkstant/ ▷ *adj* still existing; surviving. ⓒ 16c: from Latin *extans, extantis*, from *exstare* to stand out.

extempore /ɪk'stɛmpərɪ/ ▷ *adverb, adj* without planning or preparation; off the cuff. • **extemporaneous** /-'reɪnɪəs/ or **extemporary** *adj* **1** spoken or done, etc without preparation; impromptu. **2** makeshift or improvised. • **extemporaneously** or **extemporarily** *adverb.* • **extemporaneousness** or **extemporariness** *noun.* ⓒ 16c: Latin *ex tempore* on the spur of the moment.

extemporize or **extemporise** /ɪk'stɛmpəraɪz/ ▷ *verb* (***extemporized, extemporizing***) *tr & intr* to speak or perform without preparation. • **extemporization** *noun.* ⓒ 17c.

extend /ɪk'stɛnd/ ▷ *verb* (***extended, extending***) **1** to make something longer or larger. **2** *tr & intr* to reach or stretch in space or time. **3** to hold out or stretch out (a hand, etc). **4** to offer (kindness or greetings, etc) to someone. **5** to increase something in scope. **6** (*always* **extend to something**) *intr* to include or go as far as it □ *Their kindness did not extend to lending money.* **7** to exert someone to their physical or mental limit □ *extend oneself.* • **extendability**, **extendibility** or **extensibility** *noun.* • **extendable**, **extendible**, **extensible** or **extensile** *adj.* ⓒ 14c: from Latin *extendere, extensum* to stretch out.

extended family ▷ *noun* the family as a unit including all relatives. Compare NUCLEAR FAMILY.

extended-play ▷ *adj* (abbreviation **EP**) said of a gramophone RECORD (*noun* 4): with each side playing for about twice the length of a single. ⓒ 1950s.

extensification ▷ *noun, agric* a policy within the European Community by which land is farmed less intensively, with savings in expenditure balancing the loss of income from lower production. Compare EXTENSIVE FARMING, INTENSIVE FARMING, FACTORY FARMING at FACTORY FARM.

extension /ɪk'stɛnʃən/ ▷ *noun* **1** the process of extending something, or the state of being extended. **2** an added part, that makes the original larger or longer. **3** a subsidiary or extra telephone, connected to the main line. **4** an extra period beyond an original time limit. **5** a scheme by which services, eg those of a university or library, are made available to non-members □ *an extension course.* **6** range or extent. **7** *logic* the extent of the application of a term or the number of objects included under it. Opposite of INTENSION. ⓒ 14c.

extensive /ɪk'stɛnsɪv/ ▷ *adj* large in area, amount, range or effect. • **extensively** *adverb* to an extensive degree; widely. • **extensiveness** *noun.* ⓒ 17c.

extensive farming ▷ *noun, agric* farming in which a relatively small crop is produced in return for a relatively low level of expenditure. Compare EXTENSIFICATION, INTENSIVE FARMING, FACTORY FARMING at FACTORY FARM.

extensor /ɪk'stɛnsə(r)/ ▷ *noun, physiol* any of various muscles that straighten out parts of the body. Compare FLEXOR. ⓒ 18c: from Latin *extendere, extensum* to stretch out.

extent /ɪk'stɛnt/ ▷ *noun* **1** the area over which something extends. **2** amount, scope or degree. ⓒ 15c.

extenuate /ɪk'stɛnjʊeɪt/ ▷ *verb* (***extenuated, extenuating***) to reduce the seriousness of (an offence) by giving an explanation that partly excuses it. • **extenuating** *adj* said especially of a circumstance: reducing the seriousness of an offence by partially excusing it. • **extenuatingly** *adverb.* • **extenuation** *noun.* ⓒ 16c; 15c in obsolete sense 'to emaciate': from Latin *extenuare* to make thin or to lessen.

exterior /ɪk'stɪərɪə(r)/ ▷ *adj* **1** on, from, or for use on the outside. **2** foreign, or dealing with foreign nations. **3** *cinematog* outdoor. ▷ *noun* **1** an outside part or surface. **2** an outward appearance, especially when intended to conceal or deceive. **3** an outdoor scene in a film, etc. ⓒ 16c: Latin, from *exterus* on the outside.

exterior angle ▷ *noun, math* the angle between any extended side and the adjacent side of a polygon.

exteriorize or **exteriorise** /ɪk'stɪərɪəraɪz/ ▷ *verb* (***exteriorized, exteriorizing***) **1** to externalize. **2** *surgery* to bring an internal organ or part of one outside the body temporarily. • **exteriorization** *noun.* ⓒ 19c.

exterminate /ɪk'stɜːmɪneɪt/ ▷ *verb* (***exterminated, exterminating***) to get rid of or completely destroy (something living). • **extermination** *noun* the total destruction of something living. • **exterminator** *noun* a person or thing that destroys something living. ⓒ 16c meaning 'to banish': from Latin *exterminare* to drive away, from *ex* out + *terminus* boundary.

external /ɪk'stɜːnəl/ ▷ *adj* **1** belonging to, for, from or on the outside. **2** being of the world, as opposed to the mind □ *external realities.* **3** foreign; involving foreign nations □ *external affairs.* **4** said of a medicine: to be applied on the outside of the body, not swallowed, etc. **5** taking place, or coming from, outside one's school or university, etc □ *an external examination.* ▷ *noun* **1** (*often* **externals**) an outward appearance or feature, especially when superficial or insignificant. **2** *colloq* an external examination or examiner. • **externally** *adverb.* ⓒ 15c: from Latin *externus*, from *exterus* on the outside.

externalize or **externalise** ▷ *verb* (***externalized, externalizing***) **1** to express (thoughts, feelings or ideas, etc) in words. **2** *psychol* to assign (one's feelings) to things outside oneself. **3** to ascribe something to causes outside oneself. • **externalization** *noun.* ⓒ 19c.

exteroceptor /'ɛkstərousɛptə(r)/ ▻ *noun, zool* a sensory organ, eg the eye, receiving stimuli from outside the body. Ⓒ Early 20c: modelled on RECEPTOR, with *exter-* from EXTERIOR or EXTERNAL.

extinct /ɪk'stɪŋkt/ ▻ *adj* **1** said of a species of animal, etc: no longer in existence. **2** said of a volcano: no longer active. **3** *formal* said of an emotion, etc: no longer felt; dead. • **extinction** *noun* **1** the process of making or becoming extinct; elimination or disappearance. **2** *biol* the total elimination or dying out of any plant or animal species, or a whole group of species, worldwide. Ⓒ 15c: from Latin *exstinguere, exstinctum* to EXTINGUISH.

extinguish /ɪk'stɪŋgwɪʃ/ ▻ *verb* (***extinguishes, extinguished, extinguishing***) **1** to put out (a fire, etc). **2** *formal* to kill off or destroy (eg passion). **3** *law* to pay off (a debt). • **extinguishable** *adj.* • **extinguisher** *noun* **1** a person or thing that extinguishes. **2** a FIRE EXTINGUISHER. Ⓒ 16c: from Latin *exstinguere*.

extirpate /'ɛkstəpeɪt/ ▻ *verb* (***extirpated, extirpating***) **1** *formal* to destroy completely. **2** *formal* to uproot. **3** *surgery* to remove completely. • **extirpation** *noun.* • **extirpator** *noun.* • **extirpatory** *adj.* Ⓒ 16c: from Latin *exstirpare* to tear up by the roots, from *stirps* root or stock.

extol /ɪk'stoul/ ▻ *verb* (***extolled, extolling***) *rather formal* to praise enthusiastically. • **extoller** *noun.* • **extolment** *noun.* Ⓒ 15c: from Latin *extollere* to lift or raise up.

extort /ɪk'stɔːt/ ▻ *verb* (***extorted, extorting***) to obtain (money or information, etc) by threats or violence. • **extortion** *noun.* Ⓒ 16c: from Latin *extorquere, extortum* to twist or wrench out.

extortionate /ɪk'stɔːʃənət/ *adj* **1** said of a price or demand, etc: unreasonably high or great. **2** using extortion. • **extortionately** *adverb.*

extra /'ɛkstrə/ ▻ *adj* **1** additional; more than is usual, necessary or expected. **2** for which an additional charge is made. ▻ *noun* (***extras***) **1** an additional or unexpected thing. **2 a** an extra charge; **b** an item for which this is made. **3** an actor employed temporarily in a small, usually non-speaking, part in a film. **4** a special edition of a newspaper containing later news. **5** *cricket* a run scored other than by hitting the ball with the bat. ▻ *adverb* unusually or exceptionally. Ⓒ 17c: probably a shortening of EXTRAORDINARY.

extra- /ɛkstrə/ ▻ *prefix, signifying* outside or beyond ▫ *extra-curricular.* Ⓒ From Latin *extra* outside.

extracellular ▻ *adj, biol* located or taking place outside a cell. Ⓒ 19c.

extracorporeal ▻ *adj* outside the body. Ⓒ 19c.

extra cover ▻ *noun, cricket* **1** a fielding position between COVER and MID-OFF (see under MID-ON). **2** the person in this position.

extract ▻ *verb* /ɪk'strakt/ (***extracted, extracting***) **1** to pull or draw something out, especially by force or with effort. **2** to separate (a substance) from a liquid or solid mixture. **3** to derive (pleasure, etc). **4** to obtain (money, etc) by threats or violence. **5** to select (passages from a book, etc). ▻ *noun* /'ɛkstrakt/ **1** a passage selected from a book, etc. **2** *chem* a substance that is separated from a liquid or solid mixture by using heat, solvents or distillation, etc. • **extractable** *adj.* • **extractability** *noun.* • **extractor** *noun* **1** a person or thing that extracts. **2** an extractor fan. Ⓒ 15c: from Latin *extrahere, extractum* to draw out.

extraction ▻ *noun* **1** the act of extracting. **2** the process whereby a metal is obtained from its ore. **3** the removal of a tooth from its socket. **4** the use of a solvent to separate a substance from a liquid or solid mixture. **5** family origin; descent ▫ *of Dutch extraction.*

extractor fan and **extraction fan** ▻ *noun* an electric device for ventilating a room or building, etc.

extra-curricular ▻ *adj* **1** not belonging to, or offered in addition to, the subjects studied in the main teaching curriculum of a school or college, etc. **2** additional to ordinary responsibilities or routine, etc.

extradite /'ɛkstrədaɪt/ ▻ *verb* (***extradited, extraditing***) to return (a person accused of a crime) for trial in the country where the crime was committed. • **extraditable** *adj* said of a crime: rendering the perpetrator liable to be extradited. Ⓒ 19c: from EXTRADITION.

extradition /ɛkstrə'dɪʃən/ ▻ *noun* the procedure of returning a person accused of a crime to the country where it was committed. Ⓒ 19c: from Latin *ex* from + *traditio, traditionis* a handing over.

extrados /ɛk'streɪdɒs/ ▻ *noun* (***extrados*** /-douz/ or ***extradoses***) *archit* the outer or upper curve of an arch. Ⓒ 18c: French, from Latin *extra* outside + French *dos* back.

extragalactic ▻ *adj* outside the GALAXY. Ⓒ 19c.

extramarital ▻ *adj* said especially of sexual relations: taking place outside marriage. Ⓒ 1920s.

extramural /ɛkstrə'mjuərəl/ ▻ *adj* **1** said of courses, etc: for people who are not full-time students at a college, etc. **2** outside the scope of normal studies. Ⓒ 19c: from Latin *murus* wall.

extraneous /ɪk'streɪnɪəs/ ▻ *adj* **1** not belonging; not relevant or related. **2** coming from outside. • **extraneously** *adverb.* • **extraneousness** *noun.* Ⓒ 17c: from Latin *extraneus* external.

extraordinary /ɪk'strɔːdɪnərɪ/ ▻ *adj* **1** unusual; surprising or remarkable. **2** additional; not part of the regular pattern or routine ▫ *extraordinary meeting.* **3** (*often following its noun*) *formal* employed to do additional work, or for a particular occasion ▫ *ambassador extraordinary.* • **extraordinarily** *adverb.* • **extraordinariness** *noun.* Ⓒ 15c: from Latin *extra ordinem* outside the usual order.

extrapolate /ɪk'strapəleɪt/ ▻ *verb* (***extrapolated, extrapolating***) *tr & intr* **1** *math* to estimate (a value that lies outside a known range of values), on the basis of those values and usually by means of a graph. **2** to make (estimates) or draw (conclusions) from known facts. • **extrapolation** *noun.* • **extrapolative** or **extrapolatory** *adj.* • **extrapolator** *noun.* Ⓒ 19c: from EXTRA-, modelled on INTERPOLATE.

extrasensory ▻ *adj* achieved using means other than the ordinary senses of sight, hearing, touch, taste and smell ▫ *extrasensory perception.* Ⓒ 1930s.

extraterrestrial ▻ *adj* (abbreviation **ET**) said of a being or creature, etc: coming from outside the Earth or its atmosphere. ▻ *noun* an extraterrestrial being. Ⓒ 19c.

extra time ▻ *noun, football, etc* additional time allowed at the end of a match because of time lost through injury, or in order to achieve a decisive result.

extravagant /ɪk'stravəgənt/ ▻ *adj* **1** using, spending or costing too much. **2** unreasonably or unbelievably great ▫ *extravagant praise.* • **extravagance** *noun.* • **extravagantly** *adverb.* Ⓒ 14c: from Latin *vagari* to wander.

extravaganza /ɪkstravə'ganzə/ ▻ *noun* (***extravaganza***) a spectacular display, performance or production. Ⓒ 18c, originally meaning 'extravagant language or behaviour': from Italian *estravaganza* extravagance.

extravasate /ɪk'stravəseɪt/ ▻ *verb* (***extravasated, extravasating***) **1** *pathol* to let or force (blood or other fluid) out of the vessel that should contain it. **2** to pour out (lava). • **extravasation** *noun.* Ⓒ 17c: from Latin *vas* a vessel.

extravehicular ▻ *adj, space flight* situated, used or happening outside a spacecraft. Ⓒ 1960s.

extraversion see EXTROVERSION

extravert see EXTROVERT

extra virgin ▻ *adj* said of olive oil: of the best quality; extracted by pressing not by chemical processes.

extreme /ɪk'striːm/ ▷ *adj* (***extremer, extremest***) **1** very high, or highest, in degree or intensity. **2** very far, or furthest, in any direction, especially out from the centre. **3** very violent or strong. **4** not moderate; severe □ *extreme measures*. ▷ *noun* **1** either of two people or things as far, or as different, as possible from each other. **2** the highest limit; the greatest degree of any state or condition. • **extremely** *adverb* to an extreme degree. • **go to extremes** to take action beyond what is thought to be reasonable. • **in the extreme** to the highest degree. ◷ 15c: from Latin *extremus*, from *exterus* on the outside.

extreme unction ▷ *noun, RC Church* former name for SACRAMENT OF THE SICK.

extremist *noun* someone who has extreme opinions, especially in politics. ▷ *adj* relating to, or favouring, extreme measures. • **extremism** *noun*. ◷ 19c.

extremity /ɪk'strɛmɪtɪ/ ▷ *noun* (***extremities***) **1** the furthest point. **2** an extreme degree; the quality of being extreme. **3** a situation of great danger. **4** (**extremities**) the hands and feet. ◷ 14c: from Latin *extremitas* end or farthest point.

extricable /'ɛkstrɪkəbəl, ɪk'strɪk-/ ▷ *adj* capable of being extricated or disentangled. ◷ 17c.

extricate /'ɛkstrɪkeɪt/ ▷ *verb* (***extricated, extricating***) to free someone or something from difficulties; to disentangle. • **extrication** *noun*. ◷ 17c: from Latin *extricare*, from *ex* from + *tricae* hindrances.

extrinsic /ɛks'trɪnsɪk/ ▷ *adj* **1** external. **2** operating from outside. • **extrinsically** *adverb*. ◷ 16c: from Latin *extrinsecus* outwardly.

extroversion or **extraversion** /ɛkstrə'vɜːʃən/ ▷ *noun, psychol* a personality trait characterized by a tendency to be more concerned with the outside world and social relationships than with one's inner thoughts and feelings. Compare INTROVERSION.

extrovert or **extravert** /'ɛkstrəvɜːt/ ▷ *noun* **1** *psychol* someone who is more concerned with the outside world and social relationships than with their inner thoughts and feelings. **2** someone who is sociable, outgoing and talkative. ▷ *adj* having the temperament of an extrovert; sociable or outgoing. Compare INTROVERT. • **extroverted** *adj*. ◷ Early 20c: from *extro-*, a variant of EXTRA- + Latin *vertere* to turn.

extrude /ɪk'struːd/ ▷ *verb* (***extruded, extruding***) **1** to squeeze something or force it out. **2** to force or press (a semisoft solid material) through a DIE[2] (sense 1b) in order to mould it into a continuous length of product. • **extruder** *noun*. • **extrusion** *noun* **1** *engineering* the act or process of extruding. **2** *geol* an EXTRUSIVE ROCK. ◷ 16c: from Latin *extrudere* to push out.

extrusive rock ▷ *noun, geol* igneous rock formed from molten rock material, such as magma or volcanic lava, that has poured out on to the Earth's surface and then solidified, eg basalt.

exuberant /ɪg'zuːbərənt/ ▷ *adj* **1** in very high spirits. **2** enthusiastic and energetic. **3** said of health, etc: excellent. **4** said of plants, etc: growing abundantly. • **exuberance** *noun* high spirits; enthusiasm. • **exuberantly** *adverb*. ◷ 15c: from Latin *exuberans*, from *uber* rich.

exudate /'ɛksjʊdeɪt/ ▷ *noun* **1** *biol* any substance released from an organ or cell of a plant or animal to the exterior through a gland, pore, or membrane, eg resin and sweat. **2** *pathol* the fluid containing proteins and white blood cells that is discharged through small pores in membranes, usually as a result of inflammation. ◷ 19c; see EXUDE.

exude /ɪg'zjuːd/ ▷ *verb* (***exuded, exuding***) **1** to give off or give out (an odour or sweat). **2** to show or convey (a quality or characteristic, etc) by one's behaviour. **3** *intr* to ooze out. • **exudation** *noun*. ◷ 16c: from Latin *exsudare*, *exsudatum* to sweat out.

exult /ɪg'zʌlt/ ▷ *verb* (***exulted, exulting***) *intr* **1** (*often* **exult in** or **at something**) to be intensely joyful about it. **2** (*often* **exult over something**) to show or enjoy a feeling of triumph. • **exultant** *adj* joyfully or triumphantly elated. • **exultantly** *adverb*. • **exultation** *noun* a feeling or state of joyful elation. ◷ 16c: from Latin *exsultare* to jump up and down, from *saltare* to leap.

exurb /ɛks'ɜːb/ ▷ *noun, originally US* a prosperous residential area outside the suburbs of a town. • **exurban** *adj*. • **exurbanite** *adj, noun*. • **exurbia** *noun* exurbs collectively. ◷ 1950s: from EX-, modelled on SUBURB.

exuviae /ɪg'zjuːviː/ ▷ *plural noun* **1** cast-off skins, shells, or other coverings of animals. **2** *geol* fossil remains of animals. • **exuvial** *adj*. ◷ 17c: Latin, meaning 'skins of animals' or 'clothing stripped off', from *exuere* to strip off.

ex works ▷ *adverb, adj* excluding any costs, eg delivery charges, retailer's profit, incurred after an item leaves the factory.

-ey see -Y[2]

eye /aɪ/ ▷ *noun* **1** the organ of vision, usually one of a pair. **2** the area of the face around the eye. **3** (*often* **eyes**) sight; vision □ *Surgeons need good eyes*. **4** attention, gaze or observation □ *catch someone's eye* □ *in the public eye*. **5** the ability to appreciate and judge □ *an eye for beauty*. **6** a look or expression □ *a hostile eye*. **7** *bot* the bud of a tuber such as a potato. **8** an area of calm and low pressure at the centre of a tornado, etc. **9** any rounded thing, especially when hollow, eg the hole in a needle or the small wire loop that a hook fits into. ▷ *verb* (***eyed, eyeing*** or ***eying***) to look at something carefully. • **eyed** *adj, especially in compounds* **1** having eyes of the specified kind. **2** spotted. • **eyeless** *adj*. • **an eye for an eye** retaliation; justice enacted in the same way or to the same degree as the crime. • **be all eyes** *colloq* to be vigilant. • **cast** or **run an eye over something** to examine it cursorily. • **clap, lay** or **set eyes on someone** or **something** *colloq, usually with negatives* to see them or it □ *I never want to set eyes on you again*. • **close** or **shut one's eyes to something** to ignore or disregard it. • **eyes down** the command at the start of a game of bingo or other non-physical contest. • **get** or **keep one's eye in** to become or remain familiar with the way in which a game or sport is played. • **give an eye to something** *colloq* to attend to it. • **give someone the eye** or **the glad eye** *colloq* to look at them in a sexually inviting way. • **have an eye to something** to have it as a purpose or intention. • **have eyes for someone** to be interested in them. • **have one's eye on something** to be eager to acquire it. • **in one's mind's eye** in one's imagination. • **in the eyes of someone** in their estimation or opinion. • **in the wind's eye** against the wind. • **keep an eye on someone** or **something** *colloq* to keep them or it under observation. • **keep one's eyes skinned** or **peeled** *colloq* to watch or look out. • **make eyes at someone** *colloq* to look at them with sexual interest or admiration, or in a sexually inviting way. • **more than meets the eye** more complicated or difficult, etc than appearances suggest. • **my eye!** *colloq* nonsense! • **one in the eye for someone** *colloq* a harsh disappointment or rebuff for them. • **see eye to eye with someone** to be in agreement with them; to think alike. • **under the eye of someone** under their observation. • **be up to the** or **one's eyes in something** to be busy or deeply involved in (work, a commitment, etc). • **with an eye to something** having it as a purpose or intention. • **with one's eyes open** with full awareness of what one is doing. ◷ Anglo-Saxon *eage*.

■ **eye someone** or **something up** *colloq* to assess their worth or attractiveness.

eyeball ▷ *noun* the nearly spherical body of the eye. ▷ *verb, colloq* **1** to face someone; to confront them. **2** to examine something closely. **3** to glance over (a page, etc). • **eyeball to eyeball** *colloq* **1** said of people: face to face and close together in a threatening confrontation. **2** said of discussion or diplomacy, etc: dealing with matters very frankly and firmly.

eyebath and (*especially US*) **eye-cup** ▻ *noun* a small vessel for holding and applying medication or cleansing solution, etc to the eye.

eye-black ▻ *noun* mascara.

eyebolt ▻ *noun* a bolt with an EYE (*noun* 9) instead of the normal head, used for lifting or fastening. ⓘ 18c.

eyebright ▻ *noun* a small annual plant with white flowers marked with purple, used in herbal medicine to treat sore eyes. ⓘ 16c.

eyebrow /'aɪbrɑʊ/ ▻ *noun* the arch of hair on the bony ridge above each eye. • **raise an eyebrow** or **one's eyebrows** to show surprise, interest or disbelief. ⓘ 15c.

eyecatching ▻ *adj* drawing attention, especially by being strikingly attractive. • **eye-catcher** *noun* a strikingly attractive person or thing.

eye contact ▻ *noun* a direct look between two people.

eye-cup see EYEBATH

eye-drops ▻ *plural noun* medicine administered to the eye in drops.

eyeful ▻ *noun, colloq* **1** an interesting or beautiful sight. **2** *slang* an attractive woman. **3** a look or view. ⓘ 19c.

eyeglass ▻ *noun* **1** a single lens in a frame, to assist weak sight. **2** (**eyeglasses**) *chiefly US* spectacles. ⓘ 17c.

eyehole ▻ *noun* **1** an eyelet. **2** an eye socket. **3** a peep-hole. ⓘ 17c.

eyelash ▻ *noun* any of the short protective hairs that grow from the edge of the upper and lower eyelids. Often shortened to **lash**. ⓘ 18c.

eye-legible ▻ *adj* said of headings on microfilm, etc: able to be read by the naked eye, without any aid.

eyelet /'aɪlət/ ▻ *noun* **1** a small hole in fabric, etc through which a lace, etc is passed. **2** the metal, etc ring reinforcing such a hole. **3** *needlecraft* a small hole bound with stitching. **4** a small or narrow opening to peep through. ⓘ 14c: from French *oillet*, diminutive of *oil* eye.

eye-level ▻ *adj* at the same height above ground as a person's, or the average person's, eyes. ▻ *noun* (**eye level**) the height of the eyes.

eyelid ▻ *noun* in many animals, including humans: a protective fold of skin and muscle, lined with a membrane, that can be moved to cover or uncover the front of the eyeball. ⓘ 13c.

eyeliner ▻ *noun* a cosmetic used to outline the eye. See also KOHL.

eye-opener ▻ *noun* **1** *colloq* a surprising or revealing sight or experience, etc. **2** *N Amer* a drink of alcohol taken early in the morning.

eyepiece ▻ *noun, optics* the lens or group of lenses in an optical instrument that is nearest to the eye of the observer.

eye-rhyme ▻ *noun* a similarity of spelling but not pronunciation between words, as with *come* and *home*.

eyeshade ▻ *noun* a VISOR.

eyeshadow ▻ *noun* a coloured cosmetic for the eyelids.

eyeshot ▻ *noun* the reach or range of sight of the eye. ⓘ 16c.

eyesight ▻ *noun* the ability to see; power of vision.

eye socket ▻ *noun* either of the two recesses in the skull in which the eyeballs are situated.

eyesore ▻ *noun, derog* an ugly thing, especially a building. ⓘ 16c.

eyestrain ▻ *noun* tiredness or irritation of the eyes.

Eyetie or **Eyeti** or **Eytie** /'aɪtaɪ/ ▻ *noun* (***Eyeties*** or ***Eyties***) *offensive slang* an Italian. ⓘ 1920s.

eye tooth ▻ *noun* a CANINE TOOTH. • **give one's eye teeth for something** to go to any lengths to obtain it.

eyewash ▻ *noun* **1** liquid for soothing sore eyes. **2** *colloq, derog* nonsense; insincere or deceptive talk.

eyewitness ▻ *noun* someone who sees something happen, especially a crime.

eyrie or **aerie** /'ɪərɪ, 'aɪərɪ/ ▻ *noun* (*eyries*) **1** the nest of an eagle or other bird of prey, built in a high inaccessible place. **2** any house or fortified place, etc perched high up. ⓘ 15c: from French *aire*, from Latin *area* open ground.

Ez. and **Ezr.** ▻ *abbreviation* Book of the Bible: Ezra. See table at BIBLE.

Ezek. ▻ *abbreviation* Book of the Bible: Ezekiel. See table at BIBLE.

EZT ▻ *abbreviation, finance* Enterprise Zone Trust, a high-risk tax-avoidance scheme with potentially high rewards.

F

F¹ or **f** /ɛf/ ▷ *noun* (*Fs*, *F's* or *f's*) **1** the sixth letter of the English alphabet. **2** (**F**) *music* **a** the fourth note in the scale of C major; **b** the musical key which has this note as its base.

F² ▷ *abbreviation* **1** Fahrenheit. **2** farad. 3 Fellow (of a society, etc). **4** said of pencil leads: fine. **5** *physics* force. **6** franc. **7** *IVR* France.

F³ ▷ *symbol* **1** *chem* fluorine. **2** *genetics* filial generation, where $\mathbf{F_1}$ is the first filial generation, etc.

F ▷ *abbreviation* faraday.

f ▷ *abbreviation* **1** fathom. **2** female. **3** feminine. **4** focal length. **5** (*plural ff.*) folio. **6** (*plural ff.*) following (page). **7** *music* forte. **8** frequency.

FA ▷ *abbreviation* **1** Football Association. **2** Faculty of Actuaries. **3** FANNY ADAMS.

Fa ▷ *abbreviation*, *US state* Florida.

fa see FAH

fab /fab/ ▷ *adj*, *colloq* short for FABULOUS. ◷ 1960s.

Fabian /ˈfeɪbɪən/ ▷ *adj* **1** cautious; inclined to use delaying tactics. **2** relating to the **Fabian Society**, a body founded in 1884 for the gradual establishment of socialism. ▷ *noun* a member of this society. ● **Fabianism** *noun*. ● **Fabianist** *noun*. ◷ 18c: named after Q Fabius Maximus, the Roman general who wore down Hannibal by a cautious strategy of avoiding a pitched battle.

fable /ˈfeɪbəl/ ▷ *noun* **1** a story with a moral, usually with animals as characters. **2** a lie; a false story. **3** **a** a tale of wonder; **b** myths and legends generally. ▷ *verb* (***fabled***, ***fabling***) **1** *intr*, *old use* to tell fictitious tales. **2** to invent; to relate something as if it were true. ● **fabler** *noun*. ◷ 13c: from Latin *fabula* story.

fabled ▷ *adj* **1** made famous by legend. **2** made-up; feigned.

Fablon /ˈfablɒn/ ▷ *noun*, *trademark* a flexible plastic material with an adhesive backing, used to cover shelves, tabletops, etc.

fabric /ˈfabrɪk/ ▷ *noun* **1** woven, knitted or felted cloth. **2** quality; texture. **3** the walls, floor and roof of a building. **4** orderly structure □ *the fabric of society*. **5** a type or method of construction. ◷ 15c: from Latin *fabrica* craft.

fabricate /ˈfabrikeɪt/ ▷ *verb* (***fabricated***, ***fabricating***) **1** to invent or make up (a story, evidence, etc). **2** to make something, especially from whatever materials are available. **3** to forge (a document, signature, etc). ● **fabrication** *noun*. ● **fabricator** *noun*. ◷ 16c: from Latin *fabricari* to construct.

fabric conditioner and **fabric softener** ▷ *noun* a liquid to be added to laundry while it is being washed, to make it soft to the touch and usually sweet-smelling.

fabulist /ˈfabjʊlɪst/ ▷ *noun* someone who invents fables.

fabulous /ˈfabjʊləs/ ▷ *adj* **1** **a** *colloq* marvellous; wonderful; excellent; **b** immense; amazing. Often shortened to FAB. **2** legendary; mythical. ● **fabulously** *adverb*. ● **fabulousness** *noun*. ◷ 16c: from Latin *fabulosus*.

façade or **facade** /fəˈsɑːd/ ▷ *noun* **1** the front of a building. **2** a false appearance that hides the reality. ◷ 17c: French, from Italian *facciata*, from *faccia* FACE.

face /feɪs/ ▷ *noun* **1** the front part of the head, from forehead to chin. **2** the features or facial expression. **3** a surface or side, eg of a mountain, gem, geometrical figure, etc. **4** the important or working side, eg of a golf-club head. **5** **a** in a mine or quarry: the exposed surface from which coal, etc is mined; **b** on a cliff: the exposed surface, usually vertical; **c** *in compounds* □ *coalface* □ *cliff-face*. **6** the dial of a clock, watch, etc. **7** the side of a playing card that is marked with numbers, symbols, etc. **8** general look or appearance □ *The face of the landscape remains the same*. **9** an aspect. **10** impudence; cheek. **11** *literary* someone's presence □ *stand before his face*. **12** *printing* a typeface. ▷ *verb* (***faced***, ***facing***) **1** *tr & intr* to be opposite to something or someone; to turn to look at or look in some direction. **2** to have something unpleasant before one □ *face ruin*. **3** to confront, brave or cope with (problems, difficulties, etc). **4** to accept (the unpleasant truth, etc). **5** to present itself to someone □ *the scene that faced us*. **6** to cover with a surface □ *bricks were faced with plaster*. ● **face the music** *colloq* to accept the unpleasant consequences at their worst; to brave a trying situation, hostile reception, etc. ● **face to face** **1** in the presence of each other □ *met face to face for the first time*. **2** facing or confronting each other. Also *as adj* □ *a face-to-face meeting*. ● **face up to something** or **someone** to recognize the facts and prepare to endure the consequences, or to act bravely. ● **in your face** or (*often*) **in yer face** **1** right in front of someone. **2** dealing with an issue in a direct and often provocative way. Also *as adj* □ *an in-your-face film*. ● **in the face of something** in spite of a known circumstance, etc. ● **look someone in the face** to look directly at them without shame or embarrassment. ● **lose face** see under LOSE. ● **make** or **pull a face** to grimace, scowl, frown, etc. ● **on the face of it** superficially; at first glance. ● **put a good** or **brave face on something** to try to hide disappointment, fear, etc concerning it. ● **put one's face on** *colloq* to apply make-up to one's face. ● **save one's face** to preserve one's reputation, etc in difficult circumstances, while avoiding humiliation or the appearance of giving in or climbing down. ● **set one's face against something** to oppose an idea, course of action, etc, firmly. ● **show one's face** *often with negatives* to make an appearance □ *didn't dare show his face*. ● **to someone's face** directly; openly, in someone's presence. See also FACIAL. ◷ 13c: from Latin *facies* face.

■ **face someone down** to confront them boldly until they give way from embarrassment, shame, etc.

■ **face up to something** or **someone** to accept an unpleasant fact, etc; to deal with it or them bravely.

face-ache ▷ *noun* **1** neuralgia. **2** *slang* an ugly or gloomy-looking person.

face card see COURT CARD

face cloth ▷ *noun* a small square of cloth, usually towelling, for washing with. See also FLANNEL, WASHCLOTH.

face cream ▷ *noun* a cosmetic cream for the face.

faced ▷ *adj* **1** **a** having a face; **b** *in compounds* having a face of a specified kind □ *long-faced*. **2** having the outer surface dressed, eg of a building, with the front covered with a different material from that for the main body.

faceless ▷ *adj* **1** without a face. **2** of a person or people: with identity concealed; anonymous. **3** said especially of bureaucratic officials: robot-like; impersonal.

facelift ▻ *noun* **1** a surgical operation to remove facial wrinkles by tightening the skin. **2** a procedure for improving the appearance of something, eg the outside of a building.

face-off ▻ *noun* **1** *ice-hockey* the dropping of the puck by the referee between two players to start the game. **2** a confrontation in which each side tries to make the other give way, from embarrassment, shame, etc.

face pack and **face mask** ▻ *noun* a liquid cosmetic preparation for cleaning the face, that hardens on the skin and is peeled or washed off.

face-painting ▻ *noun* the art or practice of applying paint to the face, especially in decorative or symbolic patterns.

facer ▻ *noun* **1** a tool for smoothing or facing a surface. **2** *slang* a severe blow on the face. **3** *colloq* an affront. **4** *colloq* anything that staggers one.

face-saving ▻ *noun, adj* preserving one's reputation, credibility, etc, in difficult circumstances, while avoiding humiliation or the appearance of climbing down.

face-saver *noun* a face-saving course of action.

facet /'fasɪt, 'fasɛt/ ▻ *noun* **1** any of the faces of a cut jewel. **2** an aspect, eg of a problem, topic or someone's personality. ▻ *verb* (***faceted***, ***faceting***) to cut a facet on (a jewel). ◷ 17c: from French *facette* small face.

facetious /fə'siːʃəs/ ▻ *adj* said of a person or remark, etc: intending or intended to be amusing or witty, especially unsuitably so. • **facetiously** *adverb*. • **facetiousness** *noun*. ◷ 16c: from Latin *facetus* witty.

face value ▻ *noun* **1** the stated value on a coin, stamp, etc. **2** the apparent meaning or implication, eg of a statement, which may not be the same as its real meaning.

facia see FASCIA

facial /'feɪʃəl/ ▻ *adj* belonging or relating to the face ▫ *facial hair*. See also under FASCIA. ▻ *noun* a beauty treatment for the face. • **facially** *adverb*. ◷ 17c: from Latin *facies* face.

facies /'feɪʃiiːz/ ▻ *noun* (*plural* ***facies***) **1** the general form and appearance, especially of plant, animal or geological species or formations. **2** *medicine* the facial appearance or expression of a patient, especially when it is characteristic of a disease or condition.

facile /'fasaɪl/ ▻ *adj* **1** *derog* said of success, etc: too easily achieved. **2** *derog* said of remarks, opinions, etc: over-simple; showing a lack of careful thought. **3** speaking or performing with fluency and ease. • **facilely** *adverb*. • **facileness** *noun*. ◷ 15c: from Latin *facilis* easy.

facilitate /fə'sɪlɪteɪt/ ▻ *verb* (***facilitated***, ***facilitating***) to make something easy or easier to do or achieve. • **facilitation** *noun*. • **facilitator** *noun*. ◷ 17c: from French *faciliter*, from Latin *facilis* easy.

facility /fə'sɪlɪtɪ/ ▻ *noun* (***facilities***) **1** skill, talent or ability. **2** fluency; ease. **3** an arrangement, feature, attachment, etc that enables someone to do something. **4** (*chiefly* **facilities**) a building, service or piece of equipment for a particular activity ▫ ***sports facilities***. **5** (**facilities**) *euphemistic* a lavatory. **6** *econ* an agreed amount of money made available for borrowing ▫ ***overdraft facility***. ◷ 16c: from Latin *facilitas* ease.

facing /'feɪsɪŋ/ ▻ *noun* **1** an outer layer, eg of stone covering a brick wall. **2** a piece of material used to back and strengthen part of a garment. **3** (**facings**) the collar and cuffs of a jacket, etc, especially if in a contrasting colour.

facsimile /fak'sɪmɪlɪ/ ▻ *noun* (***facsimilies***) **1** an exact copy made, eg of a manuscript, picture, etc. **2** electronic copying of a document and the transmission of it by telephone line. Usually called FAX. **3** a copy made by facsimile. ▻ *verb* (***facsimiled***, ***facsimileing***) to make an exact copy of something. ◷ 17c: from Latin *fac simile* make the same.

facsimile edition ▻ *noun* an edition of a book, etc, that is an exact reproduction of an earlier edition.

fact /fakt/ ▻ *noun* **1** a thing known to be true, to exist or to have happened. **2** truth or reality, as distinct from mere statement or belief. **3** a piece of information. • **after** or **before the fact** after, or before, a crime is committed. • **as a matter of fact** or **in actual fact** or **in fact** or **in point of fact** in reality; actually. • **fact of life** see separate entry. • **for a fact** with complete certainty. • **the fact of the matter** the plain truth about the subject in question. See also FACTUAL. ◷ 16c: from Latin *factum* something done, from *facere* to do.

fact-finding ▻ *adj* with the task of ascertaining all the facts of a situation ▫ *fact-finding mission*.

faction¹ /'fakʃən/ ▻ *noun* **1** an active or trouble-making group within a larger organization. **2** argument and fighting between members of a group. **3** dissension. • **factional** *adj*. • **factionalism** *noun*. ◷ 16c: from Latin *factio* party or side.

faction² /'fakʃən/ ▻ *noun* **1** a play, programme, piece of writing, etc that is a mixture of fact and fiction. **2** this type of writing, etc. Also called **drama documentary** or **news fiction**. Compare DOCUDRAMA. ◷ 1960s: from FACT + FICTION.

factious /'fakʃəs/ ▻ *adj* **1** turbulent; quarrelsome. **2** dissident; disruptive; seditious. • **factiously** *adverb*.

factitious /fak'tɪʃəs/ ▻ *adj* **1** deliberately contrived rather than developing naturally. **2** insincere; false ▫ *factitious respect*. • **factitiously** *adverb*. • **factitiousness** *noun*. ◷ 17c: from Latin *facticius*.

factitive /'faktɪtɪv/ ▻ *adj, grammar* denoting a verb which can take both a direct object and a complement, eg the verb *made* in *made him president*. ◷ 19c: from Latin *factitivus*, from *facere* to make.

fact of life ▻ *noun* **1** an unavoidable truth, especially if unpleasant. **2** (**the facts of life**) basic information on sexual matters and reproduction.

factoid /'faktɔɪd/ ▻ *noun* a statement which is not (or may not be) true but has achieved acceptance by its appearance or frequent repetition in print. ◷ 1970s: FACT + -OID.

factor /'faktə(r)/ ▻ *noun* **1** a circumstance that contributes to a result. **2** *math* one of two or more numbers that, when multiplied together, produce a given number ▫ *4 is a factor of 12*. **3** in Scotland: **a** the manager of an estate; **b** an agent responsible for renting property for an absent owner. ▻ *verb* (***factored***, ***factoring***) *intr* to act as a factor (on someone's behalf). • **safety factor** see separate entry. ◷ 15c: Latin, meaning 'a person who acts'.

factor 8 or **factor VIII** ▻ *noun* one of the proteins which form the clotting agent in blood, absent in haemophiliacs.

factorial /fak'tɔːrɪəl/ ▻ *noun, math* (symbol **!**) the number resulting when a whole number and all whole numbers below it are multiplied together eg, 5! is 5 × 4 × 3 × 2 × 1 = 120. ▻ *adj* relating to a factor or factorial. • **factorially** *adverb*.

factorize or **factorise** /'faktəraɪz/ ▻ *verb* (***factorized***, ***factorizing***) *math* to find the factors of (a number). • **factorization** *noun*.

factory /'faktərɪ/ ▻ *noun* (***factories***) a building or buildings with equipment for the large-scale manufacture of goods. ◷ 16c: from Latin *factoria*, from FACTOR.

factory farm ▻ *noun* a farm carrying out **factory farming**, in which animals are reared usually with a minimum of space to move and which uses highly industrialized machinery, etc.

factory ship ▻ *noun* **1** a whaling-ship on which whales are processed. **2** a ship which processes the catch of a fishing fleet.

factory shop ▷ *noun* a shop in which goods manufactured in a factory are sold directly to the public at a reduced price.

factotum /fak'toutəm/ ▷ *noun* (***factotums***) a person employed to do a large number of different jobs. ◷ 16c: from Latin *fac totum* do all.

fact sheet ▷ *noun* a paper setting out relevant information on a particular subject, particularly relating to items covered in a TV or radio programme.

factual /'faktʃuəl/ ▷ *adj* **1** concerned with, or based on, facts. **2** actual. • **factually** *adverb*. • **factualness** or **factuality** (***factualities***) *noun*.

facultative /'fakəltətɪv/ ▷ *adj* **1** optional. **2** incidental. **3** relating to a faculty. **4** conferring privilege, permission or authority. **5** *biol* able to live under different conditions. • **facultatively** *adverb*.

faculty /'fakəltɪ/ ▷ *noun* (***faculties***) **1** any of the range of mental or physical powers. **2** a particular talent or aptitude for something. **3 a** a section of a university, comprising a number of departments □ ***the Faculty of Science***; **b** the professors and lecturers belonging to such a section. **4** *N Amer* the staff of a college, school or university. **5** the members of a professional body. ◷ 14c: from Latin *facultas* power or ability; related to *facilis* easy.

FA Cup ▷ *noun, football* **1** in England and Wales: an annual football competition organized by the Football Association. **2** the trophy awarded each year to the winning team.

fad /fad/ ▷ *noun, colloq* **1** a shortlived fashion; a craze. **2** any seemingly unimportant belief or practice that is too strongly advocated, usually with regard to food. • **faddiness** or **faddishness** *noun*. • **faddy** (***faddier***, ***faddiest***) or **faddish** *adj*. ◷ 19c.

fade /feɪd/ ▷ *verb* (***faded***, ***fading***) (*often* **fade away**) **1** *tr & intr* to lose or cause to lose strength, freshness or colour. **2** *intr* said of a sound or image: to disappear gradually. **3** *golf* to strike the ball so that it curves to the right, but less so than an ordinary SLICE (*noun* 5). ▷ *noun, golf* a slight, delayed SLICE (*noun* 5), often deliberate. ◷ 13c: French, meaning 'dull' or 'pale'.

■ **fade something in** or **out** *cinematog, broadcasting* to cause (a sound or picture) to become gradually louder and more distinct, or gradually fainter and disappear.

fade-in ▷ *noun, cinematog, broadcasting* the process of fading in a picture or sound.

fade-out ▷ *noun, cinematog, broadcasting* the process of fading out a picture or sound.

faeces or (*N Amer*) **feces** /'fiːsiːz/ *plural noun* the solid waste matter discharged from the body through the anus. • **faecal** or **fecal** /'fiːkəl/ *adj*. ◷ 17c in this sense; 15c meaning 'sediment' or 'dregs': plural of Latin *faex* dregs.

faff /faf/ ▷ *verb* (***faffed***, ***faffing***) *intr, colloq* (*also* **faff about**) to act in a fussy, uncertain way, not achieving very much; to dither. ◷ 19c.

fag¹ /fag/ ▷ *noun* **1** *colloq* a cigarette. **2** *colloq* a piece of drudgery; a bore. **3** in some schools, especially public schools: a young schoolboy who runs errands and does jobs for an older one. ▷ *verb* (***fagged***, ***fagging***) **1** to tire someone out; to exhaust someone. **2** *intr* said of a schoolboy: to act as fag for an older boy. **3** *intr* to work hard; to toil. • **fagged out** very tired; exhausted. ◷ 19c in noun sense 1, shortened from FAG-END; 18c in noun senses 2 and 3; 15c, meaning 'something that hangs loose or flaps'; originally probably related to FLAG.

fag² /fag/ ▷ *noun, slang, sometimes derog* a gay man. • **faggy** *adj*. ◷ 1920s: short for FAGGOT².

fag end ▷ *noun, colloq* **1** the butt or end of a cigarette. **2** the last part of something, after the best has been used. ◷ 1850s in sense 1; 18c originally referring to the last part of a piece of cloth.

faggot¹ or (*N Amer*) **fagot** /'fagət/ ▷ *noun* **1** *cookery* a ball or roll of chopped pork and liver mixed with breadcrumbs and herbs, and eaten fried or baked. **2** a bundle of sticks, twigs, etc, used for fuel, fascines, etc. • **faggoting** or (*N Amer*) **fagoting** a kind of embroidery in which some of the cross threads are drawn together in the middle. ◷ 19c in sense 1; 16c in sense 3; 13c in sense 2: from French *fagot* bundle of sticks.

faggot² /'fagət/ ▷ *noun, slang, sometimes derog* a gay man. Also shortened to **fag**. • **faggoty** *adj*. ◷ Early 20c: originally used offensively and probably as an extension of FAGGOT¹ sense 3.

fag hag ▷ *noun, slang, sometimes derog* a heterosexual woman who enjoys spending a lot of time in the company of gay men.

fah or **fa** /fɑː/ ▷ *noun, music* in sol-fa notation: the fourth note of the major scale. ◷ 14c; see SOL-FA.

Fahrenheit /'farənhaɪt, 'fɑː-/ ▷ *noun* a scale of temperature on which water boils at 212° and freezes at 32° under standard atmospheric pressure. ▷ *adj* (abbreviation **F**) on or relating to this scale. Compare CELSIUS. ◷ 18c: named after G D Fahrenheit (1686–1736), German physicist.

faience or **faïence** /faɪ'ɑ̃s, feɪ-/ ▷ *noun* glazed decorated pottery. ◷ 18c: from French *faïence*, from *Faenza* in Italy, the place of manufacture.

fail /feɪl/ ▷ *verb* (***failed***, ***failing***) **1** *tr & intr* (*often* **fail in something**) not to succeed; to be unsuccessful in (an undertaking). **2** to judge (a candidate) not good enough to pass a test, etc. **3** *intr* said of machinery, a bodily organ, etc: to stop working or functioning. **4** *intr* not to manage (to do something) □ ***failed to pay the bill in time.*** **5** not to bother (doing something). **6** to let (someone) down; to disappoint. **7** said of courage, strength, etc: to desert (one) at the time of need. **8** *intr* to become gradually weaker. **9** *intr* said of a business, etc: to collapse; to become insolvent or bankrupt. ▷ *noun* a failure, especially in an exam. • **fail to see** to be unable to understand. • **without fail** for certain; with complete regularity and reliability. ◷ 13c: from Latin *fallere* to deceive or disappoint.

failing ▷ *noun* a fault; a weakness □ ***one of his failings.*** ▷ *adj* referring to something that is in the process of failing □ ***a failing business.*** ▷ *prep* if … is impossible or does not happen □ ***Failing an agreement today, the issue will be referred for arbitration.***

fail-safe ▷ *adj* **1** said of a mechanism: ensuring a return to a safe condition when something goes wrong. **2** said of a machine or system: returning to a safe condition when something goes wrong.

failure /'feɪljə(r)/ ▷ *noun* **1** the act of failing; lack of success. **2** someone or something that is unsuccessful. **3** a stoppage in functioning, eg of a computer, machine, system, etc. **4** a poor result. **5** the non-doing of something □ ***failure to turn up.***

fain /feɪn/ *old use* ▷ *adj* glad or joyful. ▷ *adverb* gladly; willingly. ◷ Anglo-Saxon *fægen*.

faint /feɪnt/ ▷ *adj* (***fainter***, ***faintest***) **1** pale; dim; indistinct; slight. **2** physically weak; on the verge of losing consciousness. **3** feeble; timid; unenthusiastic. ▷ *verb* (***fainted***, ***fainting***) *intr* to lose consciousness; to collapse. ▷ *noun* a sudden loss of consciousness. • **faintly** *adverb*. • **faintness** *noun*. ◷ 13c: from French *faindre* to feign.

faint-hearted ▷ *adj* timid; cowardly; spiritless. • **faint-heartedly** *adverb*. • **faint-heartedness** *noun*.

fair¹ /fɛə(r)/ ▷ *adj* (***fairer***, ***fairest***) **1** just; not using dishonest methods or discrimination. **2** in accordance with the rules. **3 a** said of hair and skin: light-coloured; **b** said of someone: having light-coloured hair and skin. **4** *old use* beautiful. **5** quite good; reasonable. **6** sizeable;

considerable. **7** said of weather: fine. **8** said of the wind: favourable. **9** said of words: insincerely encouraging. ▷ *adverb* **1** in a fair way. **2** *dialect* completely. • **fairly** see separate entry. • **fairness** *noun*. • **be fair game** to deserve to be attacked or criticized. • **by fair means or foul** using any possible means, even if dishonest. • **fair-and-square 1** absolutely; exactly. **2** honest and open. • **fair crack at the whip** just treatment. • **fair enough** all right. • **in all fairness** or **to be fair** one ought to remember or take into consideration, if one is fair; being scrupulously fair. • **stand fair with someone** to be in favour with them. ⓔ Anglo-Saxon *fæger* beautiful.

fair² and (*nostalgic*) **fayre** /fɛə(r)/ ▷ *noun* (*fairs* or *fayres*) **1** a collection of sideshows and amusements, often set up temporarily on open ground and travelling from place to place. **2** *historical* a market for the sale of produce, livestock, etc, with or without sideshows. **3** (*only* **fair**) an indoor exhibition of goods from different countries, firms, etc, held to promote trade. **4** a sale of goods to raise money for charity, etc. ⓔ 14c: from French *feire*, from Latin *feria* holiday.

fair copy ▷ *noun* a neat finished copy of a piece of writing, after corrections have been made.

fair dinkum ▷ *adj, adverb, Austral* honest or honestly.

fair dos or **fair do's** /fɛə'duːz/ ▷ *plural noun, colloq* an expression appealing for, or agreeing to, equal treatment for everyone, strict honesty, etc.

fairground ▷ *noun* the piece of land on which sideshows and amusements are set up for a fair. Also *as adj* □ *fairground attractions.*

fair-haired ▷ *adj* having light-coloured hair.

fairies *plural of* FAIRY

fairing /'fɛərɪŋ/ ▷ *noun* an external structure fitted to an aircraft, vessel or other vehicle to improve streamlining and reduce drag. ⓔ 1860s: from *fair* to make smooth or to streamline.

Fair Isle ▷ *noun* **1** a complex multicoloured type of knitting pattern. **2** an article of clothing, usually a jumper, knitted with such a pattern □ *put on his Fair Isle and went fishing.* ▷ *adj* referring to or decorated with such a pattern □ *Fair Isle jumper.* ⓔ 1850s: named after one of the Shetland Islands, where the designs were first developed.

fairly ▷ *adverb* **1** justly; honestly. **2** quite; rather. **3** *colloq* absolutely.

fair-minded ▷ *adj* making fair judgements.

fair play ▷ *noun* honourable behaviour; just treatment.

the fair sex ▷ *noun, facetious* women.

fair-spoken ▷ *adj* bland and civil in language and address.

fairway ▷ *noun* **1** *golf* a broad strip of short grass extending from the tee to the green, distinguished from the uncut rough, and from hazards. **2** a navigable deep-water channel in a river, etc, used by shipping.

fair-weather friend ▷ *noun* a friend who deserts one when one is in trouble.

fairy /'fɛərɪ/ ▷ *noun* (*fairies*) **1** *mythol* any of various supernatural beings with magical powers, generally of diminutive and graceful human form, common in folklore. **2** *slang, sometimes derog* a gay man. ▷ *adj* like a fairy; fanciful or whimsical; delicate. • **fairylike** *adj, adverb*. ⓔ 14c: from French *faerie*, from *fae* FAY; related to Latin *fata* the FATES.

fairy godmother ▷ *noun* someone who comes unexpectedly or magically to a person's aid, and whose identity often remains unknown.

fairyland ▷ *noun* **1** *mythol* the home of fairies. **2** an entrancing place.

fairy lights ▷ *plural noun* a string of small coloured lights used for decoration, especially on a Christmas tree.

fairy ring ▷ *noun* a ring of darker grass marking the outer edge of an underground growth of fungi, traditionally attributed to the dancing of fairies.

fairy tale and **fairy story** ▷ *noun* **1** a story about fairies, magic and other supernatural things. **2** a fantastical tale. **3** *euphemistic, colloq* a lie. **4** *as adj* (**fairy-tale**) beautiful; fanciful; elaborate; marvellous, etc □ *a fairy-tale castle.*

fait accompli /feɪt ə'kɒmpliː—/ ▷ *noun* (*faits accomplis* /-pliː/) something done and unalterable; an established fact. ⓔ 19c: French, meaning 'accomplished fact'.

faith /feɪθ/ ▷ *noun* **1** trust or confidence. **2** strong belief, eg in God. **3** a specified religion □ *the Jewish faith.* **4** any set or system of beliefs. **5** loyalty to a promise, etc; trust □ *break faith with someone.* • **bad faith** dishonest; treachery. • **in good faith** from good or sincere motives. ⓔ 13c: from French *feid*.

faithful ▷ *adj* **1** having or showing faith. **2** loyal and true. **3** accurate. **4** loyal to a sexual partner. **5** reliable; constant. ▷ *plural noun* (**the Faithful**) **a** the believers in a particular religion, especially Islam; **b** loyal supporters. • **faithfully** *adverb*. • **faithfulness** *noun*. • **Yours faithfully** formal wording for ending a letter.

faith healing ▷ *noun* the curing of illness through religious faith rather than medical treatment. • **faith healer** *noun*.

faithless ▷ *adj* **1** disloyal; treacherous. **2** having no religious faith. • **faithlessly** *adj*. • **faithlessness** *noun*.

fake /feɪk/ ▷ *noun* someone or something, or an act that is not genuine. ▷ *adj* not genuine; false; counterfeit. ▷ *verb* (*faked, faking*) **1** to alter something dishonestly; to falsify something or make something up. **2** *tr & intr* to pretend to feel (an emotion) or have (an illness). • **fakery** *noun* (*fakeries*) the act of faking. ⓔ 18c.

fakir /'feɪkɪə(r), fɑː-/ ▷ *noun* **1** a wandering Hindu or Muslim holy man depending on begging for survival. **2** a member of any Muslim religious order. ⓔ 17c: from Arabic *faqir* poor man.

falafel see FELAFEL

falcate /'falkeɪt/ and **falciform** /'falsɪfɔːm/ ▷ *adj, anatomy, zool* shaped like a sickle. ⓔ 18c: from Latin *falcatus*, from *falx* sickle.

falcon /'fɔːlkən, 'fɔːkən/ ▷ *noun* **1** a type of long-winged bird of prey that can be trained to hunt small birds and animals. **2** among falconers: the female falcon, especially the PEREGRINE. See also TERCEL. ⓔ 13c: from Latin *falco* hawk.

falconer ▷ *noun* someone who sports with, or breeds and trains, falcons or hawks for hunting small birds and animals. **2** the sport that involves the use of falcons hunting prey. ⓔ 14c.

falconry /'fɔːlkənrɪ/ ▷ *noun* **1** the art or practice of breeding and training falcons for hunting. **2** the sport that involves the use of falcons hunting prey. ⓔ 16c.

falderal /'faldəral/ or **folderol** /'fɒldərɒl/ ▷ *noun* **1** a meaningless refrain in songs. **2** any kind of flippant nonsense. ⓔ 18c.

faldstool /'fɔːldstuːl/ ▷ *noun* **1** a bishop's armless seat, used when officiating at their own church away from their throne, or at another church. **2** a foldable stool or desk at which worshippers kneel during certain parts of a church service. **3** a small desk in churches in England, at which litany is sung or said. **4** a coronation stool. ⓔ 11c: as *fyldestol*, from Latin *faldistolium* folding chair.

the Fall ▷ *noun, Bible* the sinning of Adam and Eve when they disobeyed God by eating from the tree of knowledge, resulting in a state of sinfulness marking the human condition.

fall /fɔːl/ ▷ *verb* (***fell***, ***fallen*** /fɔːlən/, ***falling***) *intr* **1** to descend or drop freely and involuntarily, especially accidentally, by force of gravity. **2** (*also* **fall over** or **down**) said of someone, or something upright: to drop to the ground after losing balance. **3** said of a building, bridge, etc: to collapse. **4** said of rain, snow, etc: to come down from the sky; to precipitate. **5** said eg of hair: to hang down. **6** (*usually* **fall on something**) said of a blow, glance, shadow, light, etc: to land □ *The blow fell sharply on his jaw* □ *The light of the moon fell on the trees.* **7** to go naturally or easily into position □ *fell open at page 69.* **8** said of a government, leader, etc: to lose power; to be no longer able to govern. **9** said of a stronghold: to be captured. **10** said of defences or barriers: to be lowered or broken down. **11** to die or be badly wounded in battle, etc. **12** to give in to temptation; to sin. **13** said eg of value, temperature, etc: to become less. **14** said of sound: to diminish. **15** said eg of silence: to intervene. **16** said of darkness or night: to arrive. **17** to pass into a certain state; to begin to be in that state □ *fall asleep* □ *fall in love* □ *fall unconscious.* **18** to be grouped or classified in a certain way □ *falls into two categories.* **19** to occur at a certain time or place □ *The accent falls on the first syllable.* **20** said of someone's face: to show disappointment. ▷ *noun* **1** an act or way of falling. **2** something, or an amount, that falls. **3** (*often* **falls**) a waterfall. **4** a drop in eg quality, quantity, value, temperature, etc □ *A fall in interest rates was announced.* **5** a defeat or collapse. **6** (*also* **Fall**) *N Amer* autumn. **7** *wrestling* a manoeuvre by which one pins one's opponent's shoulders to the ground. • **break someone's fall** to stop them landing with the full impact of a free fall; to cushion their fall. • **fall between two stools 1** to be neither one thing nor the other. **2** to succeed in neither of two alternatives. • **fall flat on one's face** to come to grief; to fail dismally. • **fall from grace** said of a person: to lose standing. • **fall foul of someone** or **something** to get into trouble or conflict with them or it. • **fall head over heels** to fall hopelessly (in love). • **fall on one's feet 1** to come out of a difficult situation advantageously. **2** to gain an unexpectedly good fortune. • **fall over oneself** or **fall over backwards** *colloq* to be strenuously or noticeably eager to please or help. • **fall short** or **fall short of something 1** to turn out not to be enough; to be insufficient. **2** to fail to attain or reach what is aimed at. See also SHORTFALL. • **fall to pieces** or **bits 1** said of something: to break up; to disintegrate. **2** said of someone: to be unable to carry on or function normally, especially because of overwhelming grief, etc □ *fell to pieces when his wife died.* ⓘ Anglo-Saxon *feallan.*

■ **fall about** *colloq* to be helpless with laughter.

■ **fall apart 1** to break in pieces. **2** to fail; to collapse.

■ **fall away 1** said of land: to slope downwards. **2** to become fewer or less. **3** to disappear.

■ **fall back** to move back; to retreat.

■ **fall back on something** to make use of it in an emergency. See also FALL-BACK.

■ **fall behind** or **fall behind with something 1** to fail to keep up with someone, with one's work, etc. **2** to be late in paying instalments, rent, etc.

■ **fall down** said of an argument, etc: to be shown to be invalid.

■ **fall down on something** to fail in a task; to do it unsatisfactorily, especially a particular part of a larger task.

■ **fall for someone** to become infatuated with them, or fall in love with them.

■ **fall for something** to be deceived or taken in by it; to be conned by it.

■ **fall in 1** said eg of a roof: to collapse. **2** said of a soldier, etc: to take his or her place in a parade.

■ **fall into something** to become involved in it, especially by chance or without having put much effort into getting there.

■ **fall in with someone** to chance to meet or coincide with them.

■ **fall in with something** to agree to it; to support it.

■ **fall off** to decline in quality or quantity; to become less.

■ **fall on** or **upon someone 1** to attack them. **2** to embrace them passionately.

■ **fall out 1** said of soldiers: to come out of military formation. See also FALL-OUT. **2** to happen in the end; to turn out.

■ **fall out with someone** to quarrel with them, and then not talk to them or have contact with them for a period of time. See also FALL-OUT.

■ **fall through** said of a plan, etc: to fail; to come to nothing.

■ **fall to someone** to become their job or duty □ *It falls to me to deal with the matter.*

fallacious /fəˈleɪʃəs/ ▷ *adj* having the nature of a fallacy; deceptive; misleading. • **fallaciously** *adverb.* • **fallaciousness** *noun.*

fallacy /ˈfaləsɪ/ ▷ *noun* (***fallacies*** /-sɪz/) **1** a mistaken notion. **2** a mistake in reasoning that spoils a whole argument. See also LOGIC, SYLLOGISM. ⓘ 15c: from Latin *fallax* deceptive.

fall-back ▷ *noun* a retreat or resource especially money, for use in case of emergency. Also *as adj* □ *fall-back plans.* See also FALLBACK at FALL.

fallen /ˈfɔːlən/ ▷ *adj* **1** *old use* having lost one's virtue, honour or reputation □ *fallen woman.* **2** killed in battle. **3** having dropped or overturned.

fall guy ▷ *noun, colloq* **1** someone who is easily cheated; a dupe. **2** someone who is left to take the blame for something; a scapegoat.

fallibility ▷ *noun* (***fallibilities***) capacity or tendency to make mistakes.

fallible /ˈfalɪbəl/ ▷ *adj* capable of making mistakes. • **fallibly** *adverb.* ⓘ 15c: from Latin *fallere* to deceive.

falling-off ▷ *noun* a decline in quality or quantity.

falling star ▷ *noun* a meteor.

Fallopian tube /fəˈloʊpɪən — / ▷ *noun, anatomy, zool* in female mammals: either of the two long slender tubes through which the egg cells pass from either of the ovaries to the uterus. ⓘ 18c: named after G Fallopius (1523–62), the Italian anatomist who is reputed to have discovered them.

fallout ▷ *noun* **1** a cloud of radioactive dust caused by a nuclear explosion. **2** (**fall-out**) a quarrel. **3** (**fall-out**) the act of leaving a military formation or parade. See also FALL OUT, FALL OUT WITH SOMEONE at FALL.

fallow /ˈfaloʊ/ ▷ *adj* said of land: left unplanted after ploughing, to recover its natural fertility. ▷ *noun* land that has been left for a year or more unsown after having been ploughed. ▷ *verb* (***fallowed***, ***fallowing***) to plough land without seeding. ⓘ Anglo-Saxon *fealga.*

fallow deer ▷ *noun* a small reddish-brown deer, white-spotted in summer, with broad flat antlers. ⓘ Anglo-Saxon *fealu* tawny.

false /fɔːls, fɒls/ ▷ *adj* **1** said of a statement, etc: untrue. **2** said of an idea, etc: mistaken. **3** artificial; not genuine. **4** said of words, promises, etc: insincere. **5** treacherous; disloyal. **6** *bot* said of a plant: resembling, but wrongly so called □ *false acacia.* ▷ *adverb* in a false manner;

incorrectly; dishonestly. • **falsely** *adj*. • **falseness** *noun*. • **play someone false** to cheat or deceive them. • **under false pretences** by giving a deliberately misleading impression. ⓘ 12c: from Latin *falsus*, from *fallere* to deceive.

false alarm ▻ *noun* an alarm given unnecessarily.

false bottom ▻ *noun* a partition that disguises a space between it and the true bottom, eg of a suitcase.

false dawn ▻ *noun* the first light appearing in the sky in the morning before sunrise.

false-hearted ▻ *adj* treacherous; deceitful.

falsehood ▻ *noun* **1** dishonesty. **2** a lie; an untrue statement.

false imprisonment ▻ *noun* illegal detention of someone by force.

false move ▻ *noun* a careless or unwise action.

false pregnancy ▻ *noun, medicine* a psychological disorder in which some of the physical symptoms of pregnancy, eg abdominal swelling, weight gain, morning sickness and cessation of menstruation, occur in a woman who is not pregnant. Also called **pseudocyesis**.

false rib ▻ *noun* any of the lower five pairs of ribs in humans which are not directly attached to the breastbone. Compare FLOATING RIB, TRUE RIB.

false start ▻ *noun* **1** a failed attempt to begin something. **2** an invalid start to a race, in which one or more competitors begin before the signal is given.

false teeth ▻ *plural noun* artificial teeth; dentures.

falsetto /fɔːl'sɛtoʊ/ ▻ *noun* (***falsettos***) **1** an artificially high voice, especially produced by a tenor above his normal range. **2** someone who uses such a voice. **3** a false or strained sentiment. ⓘ 18c: Italian.

falsies /fɔːlsɪz/ ▻ *plural noun* pads of rubber or other material inserted into a bra to exaggerate the size of the breasts. ⓘ 1940s.

falsify /'fɔːlsɪfaɪ, 'fɒl-/ ▻ *verb* (***falsifies***, ***falsified***, ***falsifying***) to alter something dishonestly or make something up, in order to deceive or mislead. • **falsifiable** *adj*. • **falsifiability** *noun*. • **falsification** /-fɪ'keɪʃən/ *noun*. • **falsifier** *noun*. ⓘ 15c: from French *falsifier*, from Latin *falsus* false.

falsity /'fɔːlsɪtɪ/ ▻ *noun* (***falsities***) the quality of being false; a false assertion.

falter /'fɔːltə(r)/ ▻ *verb* (***faltered***, ***faltering***) **1** *intr* to move unsteadily; to stumble. **2** *intr* to start functioning unreliably. **3** *intr* to lose strength or conviction; to hesitate or break down in speaking. **4** to say something hesitantly. • **falteringly** *adverb*. ⓘ 14c.

fame /feɪm/ ▻ *noun* **1** the condition of being famous; celebrity. **2** *old use* repute. • **famed** *adj* famous; renowned. • **house of ill fame** *euphemistic, archaic* a brothel. ⓘ 13c: from Latin *fama* report or rumour.

familial /fə'mɪlɪəl/ ▻ *adj* belonging to, typical of, or occurring in, a family.

familiar /fə'mɪlɪə(r)/ ▻ *adj* **1** well known or recognizable. **2** frequently met with. **3** (**familiar with something**) well acquainted with it; having a thorough knowledge of it. **4** friendly; close. **5** over-friendly; excessively informal. ▻ *noun* **1** a close friend. **2** a demon or spirit, especially one in the shape of an animal, that serves a witch. • **familiarity** *noun*. • **familiarly** *adverb*. ⓘ 14c: from Latin *familiaris* domestic or intimate.

familiarize or **familiarise** /fə'mɪlɪəraɪz/ ▻ *verb* (***familiarized***, ***familiarizing***) **1** (*usually* **familiarize someone** or **oneself with something**) to make them or oneself familiar with it. **2** to make something well known or familiar. • **familiarization** *noun*.

family /'famɪlɪ/ ▻ *noun* (***families***) **1** a group consisting of a set of parents and children. Compare NUCLEAR FAMILY. **2** a group of people related to one another by blood or marriage. Compare EXTENDED FAMILY. **3** a person's children. **4** a household of people. **5** all those descended from a common ancestor. **6** a related group, eg of races, languages, etc. **7** *biol* in taxonomy: any of the groups, eg *Canidae* (dogs, wolves, etc), into which an ORDER (sense 11) is divided and which in turn is subdivided into one or more genera (see GENUS sense 1). **8** *math* a collection of curves in the equations of which different values are given to the parameters. **9** *as adj*: **a** belonging to or specially for a family □ *family car* □ *family get-together*; **b** concerning the family □ *family matters*; **c** suitable for the whole family, or for children as well as parents □ *family pub* □ *family viewing*. • **in the family way** *colloq* pregnant. ⓘ 14c: from Latin *familia* household, from *famulus* servant.

family allowance ▻ *noun, old use* CHILD BENEFIT.

family Bible ▻ *noun* a large Bible for family worship, with a page for recording family events.

family credit ▻ *noun* an allowance paid by the state to families whose income from employment is below a certain level.

family doctor ▻ *noun* a general practitioner.

family man ▻ *noun* **1** a married man with children, especially one fond of home life. **2** a domesticated man.

family name ▻ *noun* **1** a surname. **2** the family honour □ *a stain on the family name*.

family planning ▻ *noun* BIRTH CONTROL.

family tree ▻ *noun* the relationships within a family throughout the generations, or a diagram showing these. Compare GENEALOGY.

famine /'famɪn/ ▻ *noun* **1** a severe general shortage of food, usually caused by a population explosion or failure of food crops. **2** the period during which this shortage occurs. **3** extreme hunger; starvation. ⓘ 14c: French, from Latin *fames* hunger.

famished /'famɪʃt/ ▻ *adj* **1** very hungry; starving □ *famished children*. **2** (*also* **famishing**) feeling very hungry □ *I'm famishing*. ⓘ 14c: from Latin *fames* hunger.

famous /'feɪməs/ ▻ *adj* **1** well known; celebrated; renowned. **2** great; glorious □ *a famous victory*. • **famously** *adverb*. • **famousness** *noun*. • **famous last words** a remark or prediction likely to be proved wrong by events. • **get on famously** to be on excellent terms (with someone). ⓘ 14c: from Latin *famosus*, from *fama* report or fame.

fan[1] /fan/ ▻ *noun* **1** a hand-held device made of paper, silk, etc, usually semicircular and folding flat when not in use, for creating a current of air to cool the face. **2 a** something of a similar shape, ie a semicircle or a smaller sector of a circle; **b** any structure that can be spread into the shape of a fan, eg a bird's wing or tail. **3** a machine with revolving blades, for producing a current of air. **4** a device for winnowing grain. ▻ *verb* (***fanned***, ***fanning***) **1** to cool something or someone by blowing a current of air onto it, with or as if with a fan. **2** to kindle something or stir something up, with or as if with a current of air. **3** to agitate (air), with or as if with a fan. **4** to winnow (grain). ⓘ Anglo-Saxon *fann*.

■ **fan out** to spread out, or cause to spread out, in the shape of a fan □ *The peacock's feathers fanned out giving a beautiful display*.

fan[2] /fan/ ▻ *noun* an enthusiastic supporter or devoted admirer of something, eg a pop group, a football team, a sport, etc. ⓘ 17c: from FANATIC.

Fanagalo /fanəgə'loʊ/ ▻ *noun* a Zulu-based English pidgin, spoken mainly by African mineworkers around Johannesburg, in Zimbabwe, and in Namibia. ⓘ 1940s: from Fanagalo *fana ga lo*, meaning 'like this'.

fanatic /fə'natɪk/ ▻ *noun* someone with an extreme or excessive enthusiasm for something, especially a religion, or religious issues. ▻ *adj* FANATICAL. ● **fanaticism** *noun*. Ⓒ 16c: from Latin *fanaticus* filled with a god or frenzied.

fanatical ▻ *adj* excessively enthusiastic about something. ● **fanatically** *adverb*.

fan belt ▻ *noun* in a vehicle engine: the rubber belt that drives the cooling fan.

fancier /'fansıə(r)/ ▻ *noun, especially in compounds* someone with a special interest in something, especially a breeder of a certain kind of bird or animal, or a grower of a certain kind of plant □ *pigeon fancier.*

fanciful /'fansıful/ ▻ *adj* **1** indulging in fancies; imaginative or over-imaginative. **2** existing in fancy only; imaginary. **3** designed in a curious or fantastic way. ● **fancifully** *adverb*. ● **fancifulness** *noun*.

fan club ▻ *noun* a club of admirers of a movie or pop star, etc.

fancy /'fansı/ ▻ *noun* (*fancies*) **1** the imagination. **2** an image, idea or whim. **3** a sudden liking or desire for something. ▻ *adj* (*fancier, fanciest*) **1** elaborate. **2** *colloq* special, unusual or superior, especially in quality. **3** *colloq, facetious* said of prices: too high. ▻ *verb* (*fancies, fancied, fancying*) **1** to think or believe something. **2** to have a desire for something. **3** *colloq* to be physically attracted to someone. **4** to consider likely to win or do well. **5** *tr & intr* to take in mentally; to imagine □ *Fancy him getting married at last!* **6** *colloq* to think too highly of (oneself). ▻ *exclamation* (*also* **fancy that!**) expressing surprise. ● **fanciable** *adj*. ● **fancily** *adverb*. ● **take a fancy to someone** or **something** to become fond of them or it. ● **take** or **tickle the fancy of someone** to appeal to them; to intrigue or attract them. Ⓒ 15c: shortened from FANTASY.

fancy dress ▻ *noun* clothes one dresses up in for fun, usually representing a historical, fictional, popular, etc character, especially for a **fancy-dress ball** or **fancy-dress party**.

fancy-free ▻ *adj* **1** not in love. **2** free to do as one pleases; carefree □ *footloose and fancy-free.*

fancy goods ▻ *plural noun* small gifts, souvenirs, etc.

fancy man ▻ *noun, old use, colloq* **1** a lover. **2** a pimp.

fancy woman ▻ *noun, old use, colloq* **1** a lover. **2** a prostitute.

fancywork ▻ *noun* fine decorative needlework.

fan dance ▻ *noun* a solo dance in the nude, or semi-nude, in which the performer partially reveals their nakedness by tantalisingly manipulating fans or a bunch of ostrich plumes.

fandangle /fan'daŋgəl/ ▻ *noun* elaborate ornament; nonsense. Ⓒ 1830s: possibly from FANDANGO.

fandango /fan'daŋgoʊ/ ▻ *noun* (*fandangos*) **1** an energetic Spanish dance. **2** the music for it, in 3/4 time. Ⓒ 18c: Spanish.

fanfare /'fanfɛə(r)/ ▻ *noun* (*fanfares*) a short piece of music played on trumpets to announce an important event or arrival. Ⓒ 18c: French, probably imitating the sound.

fanfold ▻ *adj* said of paper: scored or perforated so as to fall flat in sections, one sheet on top of the other, used for computer print-outs.

fang /faŋ/ ▻ *noun* **1** the pointed canine tooth of a carnivorous animal. **2** the tooth of a poisonous snake. **3** any large pointed tooth. **4** the root of a tooth or one of its prongs. ● **fanged** *adj*. ● **fangless** *adj*. Ⓒ Anglo-Saxon, meaning 'something caught', ie plunder or booty, etc.

fan heater ▻ *noun* a type of heater in which an internal fan drives air over an element.

fan-jet ▻ *noun* **1** an aeroplane engine in which air is taken in through a fan and some of it, bypassing compressors, combustion chamber and turbines, mixes with the jet formed by the rest of the air. **2** a plane with a fan-jet engine.

fanlight ▻ *noun* a semicircular window over a door or window, usually found in Georgian and Regency buildings.

fan mail ▻ *noun* the admiring letters received by a celebrity from their fans.

fannings ▻ *plural noun* the siftings of tea.

fanny /'fanı/ ▻ *noun* (*fannies*) **1** *Brit taboo slang* a woman's genitals. **2** *N Amer slang* the buttocks. Ⓒ 19c.

Fanny Adams see SWEET FANNY ADAMS

fan oven see CIRCOTHERM OVEN

fan-shaped ▻ *adj* forming a sector of a circle.

fantail ▻ *noun* **1** a tail shaped like a fan. **2** a variety of domestic pigeon with tail feathers that can be spread out like a fan. **3** any of various small insectivorous birds native to Australia, New Zealand and SE Asia, with tail feathers that can be spread out like a fan.

fantasia /fan'teızıə/ ▻ *noun* (*fantasias*) **1** a musical composition that is free and unconventional in form. **2** a piece of music based on a selection of popular tunes. Ⓒ 18c: Italian, meaning 'imagination'; compare FANTASY.

fantasize or **fantasise** /'fantəsaız/ ▻ *verb* (*fantasized, fantasizing*) *intr* (*often* **fantasize about something**) to indulge in pleasurable fantasies or daydreams.

fantastic /fan'tastık/ and **fantastical** ▻ *adj* **1** *colloq* splendid; excellent. **2** *colloq* enormous; amazing. **3** said of a story: absurd; unlikely; incredible. **4** fanciful; capricious. **5** strange; weird. **6** unrealistic □ *fantastic idea.* ● **fantastically** *adverb*. Ⓒ 15c in sense 4: from Greek *phantastikos* presenting to the mind.

fantasy or **phantasy** /'fantəsı/ ▻ *noun* (*fantasies* or *phantasies*) **1** a pleasant daydream; something longed-for but unlikely to happen. **2** a mistaken notion. **3** imaginings. **4** the activity of imagining. **5** a product of the imagination; a fanciful piece of writing, music, film-making, etc. ● **fantasist** *noun*. Ⓒ 14c, in the sense 'delusive imagination': from Greek *phantasia* image in the mind, imagination.

fantasy football ▻ *noun* a system, usually in the form of a competition run by newspapers, etc, whereby participants choose 11 players from a specified league, eg The Scottish First Division, the English Premiership, etc, to make up their own composite team, and receive or lose points based on the performance of those players throughout the season.

fanzine /'fanziːn/ ▻ *noun* **1** a magazine written, published and distributed by and for supporters of football, or amateur enthusiasts of science fiction, pop music, etc. **2** a TV programme in magazine format for football fans. Ⓒ 1940s: FAN[2] + MAGAZINE.

FAO ▻ *abbreviation* Food and Agriculture Organization of the United Nations.

FAQ ▻ *abbreviation, computing* Frequently Asked Questions, a list of such questions, and their answers, on the Internet. Ⓒ 1990s.

f.a.q. ▻ *abbreviation* **1** *commerce* fair average quality. **2** free alongside quay.

far /fɑː(r)/ (*farther, farthest* or *further, furthest*) ▻ *adverb* **1** at, to or from a great distance. **2** to or by a great extent □ *My guess wasn't far out.* **3** at or to a distant time. ▻ *adj* **1** distant; remote. **2** the more distant of two things. **3** extreme □ *the far Right of the party.* ● **farness** *noun*. ● **as far as** up to a certain place or point. ● **as** or **so far as** to the extent that. ● **as** or **so far as I'm, you're,** *etc* **concerned** in my, your, etc opinion. ● **as** or **so far as it goes** in its own limited way. ● **as** or **so far as that goes** or **is concerned** concerning that, etc in particular. ● **by far** or **far and away** by a considerable amount; very much □ *It's far and away the most expensive model* □ *by far the* *most expensive item.* • **far and wide** extensively; everywhere. • **far be it from me to do something** I am reluctant to do it □ *Far be it from me to criticize.* • **a far cry from something** greatly different from it □ *His ideas are a far cry from mine.* • **far from** the opposite of; not at all □ *That is far from the truth.* • **far from** or **so far from** not only not □ *So far from winning, they finished last.* • **far gone** in an advanced state, eg of illness or drunkenness. • **go far** to achieve great things. • **go so far** or **as far as to do something** to be prepared to do it; to go to the extent of doing it. • **go too far** to behave, speak, etc unreasonably. • **in so far as** to the extent that. See also FARTHER, FURTHER. ⓔ Anglo-Saxon *feorr*.

farad /ˈfarəd, ˈfarad/ ▷ *noun, electronics* (abbreviation **F**) the SI unit of electrical CAPACITANCE, defined as the capacitance of a capacitor in which a charge of one COULOMB produces a potential difference of one VOLT[1] between its terminals. ⓔ 19c: see FARADAY.

faraday /ˈfarədeɪ/ ▷ *noun, physics* (abbreviation **F**) a unit of electrical charge, defined as the charge on a MOLE[4] (6.02 x 10^{23}) of electrons, which is equal to 9.65 x 10^{4} COULOMBS. ⓔ Early 20c: named after M Faraday (1791–1867), British physicist.

faradic /fəˈradɪk/ or **faradaic** /farəˈdeɪɪk/ ▷ *adj* referring or relating to the laws or theories of Michael Faraday. ⓔ 19c: see FARADAY.

farandole /farənˈdoʊl/ ▷ *noun* **1** a Provençal folk dance, usually in 6/8 time. **2** the music that goes with this dance or its rhythm. ⓔ 19c: from Provençal *farandoulo*, from Spanish *farandula* troop of travelling comedians.

faraway ▷ *adj* **1** distant. **2** said of a look or expression: dreamy; abstracted; absent-minded.

farce /fɑːs/ ▷ *noun* **1 a** a comedy involving a series of ridiculously unlikely turns of events; **b** comedies of this type. **2** an absurd situation; something ludicrously badly organized. **3** forcemeat; stuffing. • **farcical** *adj.* • **farcically** *adverb.* ⓔ 16c in sense 1; 14c in sense 3: French, meaning 'stuffing'.

farceur /fɑːˈsɜː(r)/ and **farceuse** /-ˈsɜːz/ ▷ *noun* **1** a male or female joker respectively. **2** a person who writes, or acts in, farces. ⓔ 18c: French.

fare /fɛə(r)/ ▷ *noun* (*fares*) **1** the price paid by a passenger to travel on a bus, train, etc. **2** a taxi passenger. **3** *old use, formal* food or the provision of food □ *great Scottish fare.* ▷ *verb* (*fared, faring*) *intr, formal* **1** to get on (in a specified way) □ *She fared well.* **2** *archaic, poetic* to travel. • **farer** *noun.* ⓔ Anglo-Saxon *faran* to go.

the Far East ▷ *noun* a loosely-used term for the countries of E and SE Asia, especially China, Japan, North and South Korea, and sometimes also including the Philippines, Vietnam, Laos, Kampuchea, Thailand, Burma (Myanmar), Malaysia, Singapore and Indonesia.

Far-Eastern *adj* belonging or referring to the countries of the Far East.

fare stage ▷ *noun* **1** each of the sections into which a bus route is divided, and for which a standard fare is charged. **2** a bus stop marking a fare stage.

farewell /fɛəˈwɛl/ ▷ *exclamation, old use* goodbye! ▷ *noun* an act of saying goodbye; an act of departure. ▷ *adj* parting; valedictory; final □ *a farewell party.* ⓔ 14c: FARE + WELL[1].

far-fetched ▷ *adj* said of an idea: unlikely; unconvincing.

far-flung ▷ *adj* **1** extensive. **2** distant □ *the far-flung corners of the world.*

farina /fəˈriːnə, fəˈraɪnə/ ▷ *noun* flour; meal. ⓔ 14c: Latin, from *far* corn.

farinaceous /farɪˈneɪʃəs/ ▷ *adj* **1** like or containing flour or starch. **2** having a soft mealy texture. ⓔ 17c.

farm /fɑːm/ ▷ *noun* **1** a piece of land with its buildings, used for growing crops or breeding and keeping livestock. **2** a farmer's house and the buildings round it. **3** a place specializing in the rearing or growing of specified animals, fish, vegetables or fruit □ *pig farm* □ *salmon farm* □ *fish farm.* ▷ *verb* (*farmed, farming*) **1** *tr & intr* to prepare and use (land) for crop-growing, animal-rearing, etc; to be a farmer. **2** to collect and keep the proceeds from (taxes, etc) in return for a fixed sum. ⓔ 14c: from French *ferme* rented land, from Latin *firma* fixed payment, from *firmus* FIRM.

■ **farm someone out** to hand over (children) temporarily to a carer.

■ **farm something out** to give (work) to others to do.

farmer ▷ *noun* someone who earns a living by managing or operating a farm, either as owner or tenant.

farmer's lung ▷ *noun, medicine* a lung disease caused by an allergy to fungal spores that develop in hay baled while it is still damp.

farm hand, **farm labourer** and **farm worker** ▷ *noun* a person whose job is to work on a farm.

farmhouse ▷ *noun* the farmer's house on a farm.

farming ▷ *noun* the business of running a farm by growing crops and/or raising livestock for sale.

farmost ▷ *adj* most distant or most remote.

farmstead ▷ *noun* a farmhouse and the buildings round it.

farmyard ▷ *noun* the central yard at a farm, surrounded by farm buildings.

farness see under FAR

the Far North ▷ *noun* the Arctic regions of the world.

faro /ˈfɛəroʊ/ ▷ *noun, cards* a game of chance played by betting on the order of appearance of certain cards taken singly from the top of the pack. ⓔ 18c: from PHARAOH.

far-off ▷ *adj, adverb* distant; remote.

farouche /fəˈruːʃ, faˈruːʃ/ ▷ *adj* **1** shy. **2** sullen or unsociable. ⓔ 18c: French, meaning 'wild' or 'shy' or 'savage'.

far-out ▷ *adj, colloq* **1** strange; weird; outlandish. **2** excellent.

farrago /fəˈrɑːgoʊ, fəˈreɪgoʊ/ ▷ *noun* (*farragos* or *farragoes*) a confused mixture; a hotchpotch. ⓔ 17c: Latin, meaning 'mixed fodder'.

far-reaching ▷ *adj* having wide validity, scope or influence □ *far-reaching consequences.*

farrier /ˈfarɪə(r)/ ▷ *noun* **1** a person who shoes horses. **2** *old use* a VETERINARY SURGEON. **3** *old use* a person in charge of cavalry horses. • **farriery** *noun* (*farrieries*) **1** the art or work of a farrier. **2** the place where a farrier works. ⓔ 16c: from French *ferrier*, from Latin *ferrarius* smith, from *ferrum* iron.

farrow /ˈfaroʊ/ ▷ *noun* a sow's litter of piglets. ▷ *verb* (*farrowed, farrowing*) *tr & intr* said of a sow: to give birth to (piglets). ⓔ Anglo-Saxon *fearh*.

Farsi /ˈfɑːsiː/ ▷ *noun* modern PERSIAN, the official language of Iran and first language of 20-30 million people in Iran, Afghanistan, Iraq and Tadzhikistan, belonging to the INDO-IRANIAN branch of the INDO-EUROPEAN languages. ⓔ 19c: from Arabic *Fars*, the name of a province in SW Iran.

far-sighted ▷ *adj* **1** (*also* **far-seeing**) wise; prudent; forward-looking. **2** long-sighted. • **far-sightedly** *adverb.* • **far-sightedness** *noun.*

the Far South ▷ *noun* the Antarctic regions of the world.

fart /fɑːt/ *coarse slang* ▷ *verb* (*farted, farting*) *intr* to emit wind formed by flatulence from the anus. ▷ *noun* **1** an act of farting. **2** *slang* a term of abuse for a person □ *He is such a boring old fart.* □ *You fart!* ⓔ 19c in sense 2; 13c as *verten*.

■ **fart about** or **around** *slang* to fool about, waste time, etc.

farther /ˈfɑːðə(r)/ ▷ *adj, adverb* FURTHER (with reference to physical distance). See also FAR.

farther, further

• Use either **farther** or **further** when there is an actual physical distance involved □ *I can't walk any farther / further.*

• Use **further** when the meaning is 'additional' or 'beyond this point' □ *I would like to make one further point.*

farthest /ˈfɑːðɛst/ ▷ *adj, adverb* FURTHEST (with reference to physical distance).

farthing /ˈfɑːðɪŋ/ ▷ *noun, formerly* **1 a** one quarter of an old British penny; **b** a coin of this value, eg one which was legal tender in Britain until 1961. **2** something very small. ◷ Anglo-Saxon *feortha* quarter.

fartlek /ˈfɑːtlɛk/ ▷ *noun, athletics* alternate fast and slow running, done as training for marathons and other long-distance races. ◷ 1950s: Swedish, from *fart* speed + *lek* play.

FAS ▷ *abbreviation* fetal alcohol syndrome.

f.a.s. ▷ *abbreviation* free alongside ship.

fasces /ˈfasiːz/ ▷ *plural noun, Roman hist* a bundle of rods with an axe in the middle, carried before magistrates as a symbol of authority. ◷ 16c: from Latin *fascis* bundle.

fascia or **facia** /ˈfeɪʃɪə/ (*fasciae* /-ʃɪiː/ or *fascias*) ▷ *noun* **1** the board above a shop entrance, bearing the shop name and logo, etc. **2** *Brit* the dashboard of a motor vehicle. **3** *archit* a long flat band or surface. **4** /ˈfaʃɪə/ *anatomy* connective tissue sheathing a muscle or organ. **5** any bandlike structure. • **fascial** or **facial** *adj.* ◷ 16c: from Latin *fascia* band.

fascicule /ˈfasɪkjuːl/ or **fascicle** /ˈfasɪkəl/ ▷ *noun* one part of a book published in separate parts. ◷ 17c: from Latin *fasciculus*, diminutive of FASCES.

fascinate /ˈfasɪneɪt/ ▷ *verb* (*fascinated*, *fascinating*) **1** to interest strongly; to intrigue. **2** said of a snake: to make (an animal or person) unable to move, from fright. **3** to hold spellbound; to enchant irresistibly. • **fascination** *noun.* ◷ 17c: from Latin *fascinare* to bewitch.

fascinating ▷ *adj* **1** intriguing; deeply interesting. **2** charming; compelling; irresistible. • **fascinatingly** *adverb.*

fascine /faˈsiːn/ ▷ *noun, old military use* (*usually* **fascines**) a brushwood faggot, used to fill ditches or trenches, protect a shore, etc, in order to hold back an attack. ◷ 17c: French, from Latin *fascina*, from *fascis* a bundle.

fascioliasis /fasɪəˈlaɪəsɪs/ ▷ *noun, medicine* an infection of the intestines caused by a liver fluke and characterized by fever, jaundice, diarrhoea and abdominal pain. ◷ 19c: Latin *fasciola* small bandage.

fascism /ˈfaʃɪzəm/ ▷ *noun* **1** a political movement or system characterized mainly by a belief in the supremacy of the chosen national group over all others, and in which there is, typically, state control of all aspects of society, a supreme dictator, suppression of democratic bodies such as trade unions and emphasis on nationalism and militarism. **2** (**Fascism**) this system in force in Italy from 1922 to 1943. **3** any system or doctrine characterized by a belief in the supremacy of a particular way of viewing things, usually an idealization of what is considered perfect □ *body fascism*. Compare NAZISM at NAZI, NEO-NAZISM at NEO-NAZI. ◷ 1920s: from Italian *fascismo*, from Italian *Fasci* groups of men organized politically, from Latin *fascis* bundle or group.

fascist /ˈfaʃɪst/ ▷ *noun* **1** an exponent or supporter of Fascism or (loosely) anyone with extreme right-wing nationalistic, etc views. **2** (**Fascist**) a member of the ruling party in Italy from 1922-43, or a similar party elsewhere, in particular the NAZI party in Germany. ▷ *adj* belonging or relating to Fascism. • **fascistic** *adj.*

fashion /ˈfaʃən/ ▷ *noun* **1** style, especially the latest style, in clothes, music, lifetyle, etc, particularly that which prevails among those whose lead is accepted. **2** a currently popular style or practice; a trend. **3** a manner of doing something □ *in a dramatic fashion.* **4** the way something is made or constructed. **5** sort, type or kind. **6** *dated* high society. Also *as adj* □ *fashion house* □ *fashion victim.* ▷ *verb* (*fashioned*, *fashioning*) **1** to form or make something into a particular shape, especially with the hands. **2** to mould or influence something. • **fashioner** *noun.* • **after a fashion** in a rather clumsy or inexpert way. • **do something as if it were going out of fashion** *colloq* to do it with great vigour and enthusiasm as though for the last time. • **in fashion** currently fashionable. • **out of fashion** no longer fashionable; passé. ◷ 14c: from French *fachon*, from Latin *factio*, from *facere* to make.

fashionable /ˈfaʃənəbəl/ ▷ *adj* **1** said of clothes, people, etc: following the latest fashion. **2** used by or popular with fashionable people. **3** *dated* moving in high society. • **fashionably** *adj.* • **fashionableness** *noun.*

fashion house ▷ *noun* an establishment in which fashionable clothes are designed, made and sold.

fashion plate ▷ *noun* **1** an illustration showing the latest style in dress. **2** a well-groomed, fashionably dressed person.

fashion victim ▷ *noun, colloq* a person who slavishly follows the latest fashions.

fast[1] /fɑːst/ ▷ *adj* (*faster*, *fastest*) **1** moving, or able to move, quickly. **2** taking a relatively short time. **3** said of a clock, etc: showing a time in advance of the correct time. **4** allowing or intended for rapid movement □ *the fast lane.* **5** said of a photographic film: requiring only brief exposure. **6** *colloq* tending to make sexual advances on rather brief acquaintance. **7** firmly fixed or caught; steadfast. **8** said of friends: firm; close. **9** said of fabric colours: not liable to run or fade. ▷ *adverb* **1** quickly; rapidly. **2** in quick succession □ *coming thick and fast.* **3** firmly; tight □ *The glue held fast.* **4** deeply; thoroughly □ *fast asleep.* • **fastish** *adj.* • **fast and furious** fast and lively; frenzied or frantic in pace. • **live life in the fast lane** *colloq* to have a lifestyle full of high excitement, expensive enjoyment and glamour. • **play fast and loose** to behave irresponsibly or unreliably. • **pull a fast one** *colloq* to cheat or deceive. ◷ Anglo-Saxon *fæst* fixed or firm.

fast[2] /fɑːst/ ▷ *verb* (*fasted*, *fasting*) *intr* to go without food, or restrict one's diet, especially as a religious discipline. ▷ *noun* a period of fasting. See LENT, RAMADAN, YOM KIPPUR. • **fast-day** *noun.* • **faster** *noun.* • **fasting** *noun.* ◷ Anglo-Saxon *fæstan.*

fastback ▷ *noun* a type of car whose roof slopes smoothly down towards the rear, giving a streamlined effect.

fastball ▷ *noun, baseball* a high-speed, rising delivery of the ball from the pitcher.

fast bowling ▷ *noun, cricket* bowling of a ball which is delivered fast; pace-bowling.

fast bowler *noun, cricket* a bowler skilled in FAST BOWLING.

fast-breeder reactor ▷ *noun* (abbreviation **FBR**) a type of nuclear reactor in which the neutrons produced during nuclear fission are not slowed down by a moderator, but are used to produce more of the same nuclear fuel, with at least as much fuel being produced as is consumed by the reactor. Compare BREEDER REACTOR.

fasten /ˈfɑːsən/ ▷ *verb* (*fastened*, *fastening*) **1** (*also* **fasten up**) to make something firmly closed or fixed. **2** to attach something to something else □ *fastened the rope to the mast.* **3** *intr* to become fastened. **4** to be capable of being fastened. ● **fastener** or **fastening** *noun* a device that fastens something; a clasp or catch. ⓒ Anglo-Saxon *fæstnian.*

■ **fasten on** or **upon something 1** to concentrate on it eagerly; to dwell on it. **2** to focus (the eyes) on someone or something in a fixed or penetrating way.

fast food ▷ *noun* ready-prepared food, such as hamburgers, fried fish, chips, etc, which is served quickly to customers, to be either eaten in the establishment or taken away. Also *as adj* □ *fast-food outlet.*

fast-forward ▷ *noun* the facility provided in a video player, CD player, cassette player, etc, for winding a tape quickly forward, or moving quickly to a later part of the CD, etc. ▷ *verb* to advance a tape, CD, etc quickly by this means.

fastidious /fa'stɪdɪəs/ ▷ *adj* **1** particular in matters of taste and detail, especially excessively so. **2** easily disgusted. **3** said of bacteria: having highly specific requirements for growth. ● **fastidiously** *adverb.* ● **fastidiousness** *noun.* ⓒ 15c in the obsolete sense 'full of pride': from Latin *fastidium* disgust.

fastigiate /fa'stɪdʒɪeɪt/ or **fastigiated** ▷ *adj* **1** pointed; sloping to a point or edge; conical. **2** *bot* with branches which taper at the ends. ⓒ 17c: from Latin *fastigium* the gable end of a roof.

fastness /'fɑːstnəs/ ▷ *noun* **1** the quality of being firmly fixed or, with reference to fabric colours, fast. **2** *old use* a stronghold.

fast neutron ▷ *noun, physics* a neutron produced by nuclear fission, which has a very high energy content, travels too fast to cause further fission, and which is used to sustain nuclear chain reactions.

fast stream ▷ *noun* a category of personnel in an organization, particularly the civil service, who are advanced swiftly into high positions.

fast-talk ▷ *verb* to persuade with rapid talk and plausible arguments.

fast-track *colloq* ▷ *noun* **1** a routine for accelerating a proposal, etc through its formalities. **2** a quick but competitive route to advancement. ▷ *verb* to process or promote someone or something speedily. ● **fast-tracker** *noun.*

fat ▷ *noun* **1** any of a group of organic compounds that occur naturally in animals and plants, are solid at room temperature, and are insoluble in water. **2 a** in mammals: a layer of white or yellowish tissue that lies beneath the skin and between various organs, and which serves both as a thermal insulator and as a means of storing energy; **b** an excess of this. **3** *chem* any member of a group of naturally occurring substances consisting of the GLYCERIDEs of higher fatty acids, eg palmitic acid, stearic acid, oleic acid. ▷ *adj* (*fatter, fattest*) **1** having too much fat on the body; plump; overweight. **2** containing a lot of fat. **3** thick or wide. **4** *colloq* said of a fee, profit, etc: large. **5** fertile; profitable □ *a fat land.* **6** *facetious, slang* none at all □ *a fat lot of good* □ *a fat chance.* ▷ *verb* (*fatted, fatting*) *old use* to fatten something. ● **fatless** *adj.* ● **fatly** *adverb.* ● **fatness** *noun.* ● **fattish** *adj.* ● **The fat's in the fire** said in expectation of disastrous consequences from something just said or done: that's done it; now there'll be trouble. ● **grow fat on something** to grow wealthy from the profits of something. ● **kill the fatted calf** to prepare a feast for someone's homecoming after a long absence. ● **live off the fat of the land** to live in luxury. ⓒ Anglo-Saxon *fætt* fatted.

fatal /'feɪtəl/ ▷ *adj* **1** causing death; deadly □ *a fatal injury.* **2** bringing ruin; disastrous. **3** decisive; critical. **4** destined; unavoidable. ● **fatally** *adverb.* ⓒ 14c in the sense 'alloted or decreed by fate': from Latin *fatalis,* from *fatum* FATE.

fatalism /'feɪtəlɪzəm/ ▷ *noun* **1** the philosophical doctrine that all events are controlled by fate, and happen by unavoidable necessity, so that humans cannot control them. **2** the acceptance of or surrender to this doctrine. **3** lack of effort in the face of threatened difficulty or disaster. ● **fatalist** *noun.* ● **fatalistic** *adj.* ● **fatalistically** *adverb.* ⓒ 17c: FATAL + -ISM.

fatality /fə'talɪtɪ, feɪ-/ ▷ *noun* (***fatalities***) **1** an accidental or violent death. **2** a person who has been killed in an accident, etc. **3** the quality of being fatal. **4** the quality of being controlled by fate.

fat cat ▷ *noun, slang* a rich, prosperous person.

fate /feɪt/ ▷ *noun* **1** (*also* **Fate**) the apparent power that determines the course of events, over which humans have no control. **2** the individual destiny or fortune of a person or thing; what happens to someone or something. **3** ultimate outcome. **4** death, downfall, destruction or doom. ● **a fate worse than death** *facetious* a gruesome or unpleasant situation. ⓒ 14c: from Latin *fatum* that which has been spoken, ie by an oracle.

fated /'feɪtɪd/ ▷ *adj* **1** destined or intended by fate. **2** doomed.

fateful ▷ *adj* **1** said of a remark, etc: prophetic. **2** decisive; critical; having significant results. **3** bringing calamity or disaster. ● **fatefully** *adverb.* ● **fatefulness** *noun.*

the Fates ▷ *plural noun, mythol* the three goddesses who determine the birth, life and death of humans, who are supposed to appear on the third night after a child's birth to decide upon the course of its life. Compare PARCAE, MOIRAI.

fat-free ▷ *adj* said of food, especially dairy products: having virtually all the fat removed. Compare FULL-FAT, LOW-FAT.

fathead /'fathɛd/ ▷ *noun, colloq, offensive* a fool; a stupid person. ● **fat-headed** *adj.*

father /'fɑːðə(r)/ ▷ *noun* **1** a male parent. **2** (**fathers**) one's ancestors. **3** a founder, inventor, originator, pioneer or early leader. **4** (**Father**) a title or form of address for a priest. **5** (**Father**) *Christianity* **a** God; **b** the first person of the Trinity (see TRINITY); God. **6** (**fathers**) the leading or senior men of a city, etc. **7** the oldest member or member of longest standing of a profession or body. **8** (**Father**) used as a title in personifying something ancient or venerable □ *Father Time.* **9** one of a group of ecclesiastical writers of the early centuries, usually ending with Ambrose, Jerome and Augustine. ▷ *verb* (***fathered, fathering***) **1** to be the father of (a child); to beget (offspring); to procreate. **2** to invent or originate (an idea). ● **fatherhood** *noun.* ● **fatherless** *adj* not having a living father. ● **fatherlike** *adj.* ● **how's your father** see under HOW. ● **like father like son** said on remarking that someone is like his father in some way. ● **the father and mother of something** a very extreme (especially bad) example of something □ *There'll be the father and mother of a row if the boss sees this!* ⓒ Anglo-Saxon *fæder.*

■ **father something on** or **upon someone 1** to claim that they are the father of something. **2** to assign it as their responsibility.

Father Christmas see SANTA CLAUS

father figure ▷ *noun* an older man who is respected and admired, who people turn to for help, support, advice, etc.

fatherhood see under FATHER

father-in-law ▷ *noun* (***fathers-in-law***) the father of one's wife or husband.

fatherland ▷ *noun* **1** said especially of Germany: one's native country. **2** the country of one's ancestors.

fatherless and **fatherlike** see under FATHER

fatherly /ˈfɑːðəlɪ/ ▷ *adj* benevolent, protective and encouraging, as a father ideally is to a child. ● **fatherliness**.

Father's Day ▷ *noun* a day on which children offer gifts of thanks to fathers, which in the UK is the third Sunday in June. ◷ Early 20c: the idea originates in the US, in imitation of MOTHER'S DAY.

fathom /ˈfaðəm/ ▷ *noun* in the imperial system: a unit of measurement of the depth of water, equal to 6ft (1.8m). ▷ *verb* (***fathomed***, ***fathoming***) (*also* **fathom something out**) **1** to work out a problem; to get to the bottom of a mystery. **2** to measure the depth of water. ● **fathomable** *adj*. ● **fathomless** *adj* unfathomable. ◷ Anglo-Saxon *fæthm*.

fathometer /fəˈðɒmɪtə(r)/ ▷ *noun* **1** a sonic device for measuring the depth of water. Also called ECHO SOUNDER. **2** (**Fathometer**) *trademark* a specific brand of echo sounder.

fathom line ▷ *noun* a line with a lead weight attached to the end used by sailors for taking soundings.

fatigue /fəˈtiːg/ ▷ *noun* (*plural* in senses 4 and 5 only ***fatigues***) **1** tiredness after work or effort, either mental or physical; exhaustion. **2** *physiol* a decreased power of response to stimulus, resulting from work or effort. **3** weakness, especially in metals, caused by variations in stress. **4** *military* fatigue-duty. **5** (**fatigues**) uniform worn by soldiers in battle or for domestic tasks. ▷ *verb* (***fatigued***, ***fatiguing***) *tr & intr* to exhaust or become exhausted. ● **fatigable** or **fatiguable** *adj*. ◷ 17c: French, from Latin *fatigare* to weary.

fatigue-dress ▷ *noun* clothes worn by a soldier on fatigue-duty.

fatigue-duty ▷ *noun* the part of a soldier's work distinct from work when arms are used.

fatless, fatly, fatness see under FAT

fatsia /ˈfatsɪə/ ▷ *noun* (***fatsias***) an evergreen spreading shrub of the ivy family, with leathery leaves and clusters of white flowers in the form of umbels.

fatso /ˈfatsoʊ/ ▷ *noun* (***fatsos*** or ***fatsoes***) *derog, slang* a fat person. ◷ 1940s.

fatten /ˈfatən/ ▷ *verb* (***fattened***, ***fattening***) **1** *tr & intr* (*also* **fatten up** or **fatten someone** or **something up**) to make or become fat. **2** to enrich (the soil). ● **fattener** *noun*. ● **fattening** *adj, noun*.

fattish see under FAT

fatty /ˈfatɪ/ ▷ *adj* (***fattier***, ***fattiest***) **1** containing fat. **2** greasy; oily. **3** said of an acid: occurring in, derived from or chemically related to animal or vegetable fats. ▷ *noun* (***fatties***) *derog, colloq* a fat person. ● **fattiness** *noun*.

fatty acid ▷ *noun* any of a group of acids, obtained from animal and vegetable fats, that are used in soaps and detergents, as lubricants, etc.

fatuity /fəˈtʃuːɪtɪ/ ▷ *noun* (*plural* in sense 2 only ***fatuities***) **1** foolishness; stupidity. **2** something fatuous, eg an inappropriate remark, a stupid action. ● **fatuitous** *adj*.

fatuous /ˈfatʃʊəs/ ▷ *adj* foolish, especially in a self-satisfied way; empty-headed; inane. ● **fatuously** *adverb*. ● **fatuousness** *noun*. ◷ 17c: from Latin *fatuus*.

fatwa or **fatwah** /ˈfatwə/ or **fetwa** /ˈfɛtwə/ ▷ *noun* (***fatwas***, ***fatwahs*** or ***fetwas***) a formal legal opinion or decree issued by a Muslim authority. ◷ 17c as *fetfa*: Arabic, meaning 'a legal decision'.

faubourg /ˈfoʊbʊəg; *French* fobuʀ/ ▷ *noun* a suburb just beyond the city walls, or a district recently included within a city.

fauces /ˈfɔːsiːz/ ▷ *noun* (*plural* ***fauces*** /ˈfɔːsiːz/) *anatomy* the upper part of the throat between the back of the mouth and the pharynx. ◷ 16c: Latin.

faucet /ˈfɔːsɪt/ ▷ *noun* **1** a TAP² fitted to a barrel. **2** *N Amer* a TAP² on a washbasin, etc. ◷ 15c in sense 1: from French *fausset* peg.

fault /fɔːlt/ ▷ *noun* **1** a weakness or failing in character. **2** a flaw or defect in an object or structure. **3** a misdeed or slight offence. **4** responsibility for something wrong ▫ *all my fault*. **5** *geol* a break or crack in the Earth's crust, resulting in the slippage of a rock mass. **6** *tennis, etc* an incorrectly placed or delivered serve. **7** *showjumping* a penalty for refusing or failing to clear a fence. ▷ *verb* (***faulted***, ***faulting***) **1** *intr* to commit a fault. **2** to blame someone. ● **at fault 1** culpable; to blame. **2** said of dogs: unable to find the scent. ● **find fault with something** or **someone** to criticize it or them, especially excessively or unfairly; to complain about it or them. ● **to a fault** to too great an extent. ◷ 14c in *noun* 2: from French *faute*.

fault-finding ▷ *noun* **1** criticism; captiousness. **2** detection and investigation of faults and malfunctions in electronic equipment. ▷ *adj* tending to find fault.

fault-finder ▷ *noun* someone who tends to find fault.

faultless ▷ *adj* perfect; without fault or defect. ● **faultlessly** *adverb*. ● **faultlessness** *noun*.

fault plane ▷ *noun, geol* the surface along which two rock masses on either side of a fault rub against each other.

faulty /ˈfɔːltɪ/ ▷ *adj* (***faultier***, ***faultiest***) **1** having a fault or faults. **2** said particularly of a machine or instrument: not working correctly. ● **faultily** *adverb*. ● **faultiness** *noun*.

faun /fɔːn/ ▷ *noun, Roman mythol* a mythical creature with a man's head and body and a goat's horns, hind legs and tail. ◷ 14c: from Latin *Faunus* a rural deity worshipped by shepherds and farmers.

fauna /ˈfɔːnə/ ▷ *noun* (***faunas*** or ***faunae*** /-niː/) **1** the wild animals of a particular region, country, or time period. **2** a book or list giving descriptions of such animals. Compare FLORA. ● **faunal** *adj*. ◷ 18c: Latin *Fauna* goddess of living creatures, sister of Faunus (see FAUN).

fauteuil /ˈfoʊtɜːɪ/ ▷ *noun* **1** an armchair. **2** a theatre seat. ◷ 18c: French, from Latin *faldistolium* FALDSTOOL.

Fauvism /ˈfoʊvɪzəm/ ▷ *noun, art* a painting style adopted by a group of Expressionists, including Matisse, who regarded a painting as essentially a two-dimensional decoration in colour for communicating emotion, and not necessarily imitating nature. ● **Fauvist** *noun, adj*. ◷ Early 20c: from French *fauve* wild beast.

faux ami / *French* fozami/ ▷ *noun* (***faux amis***) a word in a foreign language that looks similar to one in one's own language, but has a rather different meaning, eg *prétendre* is French meaning 'claim' or 'assert', not 'pretend'.

faux pas /foʊ pɑː/ ▷ *noun* (*plural* ***faux pas*** /foʊ pɑː/) an embarrassing blunder, especially a social blunder. ◷ 17c: French, meaning 'false step'.

favela /fɑːˈveɪlə/ ▷ *noun* (***favelas***) especially in Brazil: a shanty town. ◷ 1960s: Portuguese.

favour or (*N Amer*) **favor** /ˈfeɪvə(r)/ *noun* **1** a kind or helpful action performed out of goodwill. **2** the liking, approval or goodwill of someone. **3** unfair preference. **4** a knot of ribbons worn as a badge of support for a particular team, political party, etc. **5** *historical* something given or worn as a token of affection. **6** (**favours**) *euphemistic old use* a woman's consent to lovemaking or sexual liberties. ▷ *verb* (***favoured***, ***favouring***) **1** to regard someone or something with goodwill. **2** to treat someone or something with preference, or over-indulgently. **3** to prefer; to support. **4** said of circumstances: to give an advantage to someone or something. **5** *old use* to look like (eg one's mother or father). **6** *affected* to be wearing (a colour, etc). ● **favourer** *noun*. ● **in favour of something** or **someone 1** having a preference for it or them. **2** to their benefit. **3** in support or approval of them. ● **in** or **out**

of favour with someone having gained, or lost, their approval. ⓘ 14c: from Latin *favor*, from *favere* to favour.

favourable or (*N Amer*) **favorable** ▻ *adj* **1** showing or giving agreement or consent. **2** pleasing; likely to win approval. **3** (**favourable to someone**) advantageous or helpful to them; suitable. **4** said of a wind: following. • **favourableness** *noun*. • **favourably** *adverb*.

favoured or (*N Amer*) **favored** ▻ *adj* **1** enjoying favour or preferential treatment. **2** having a certain appearance □ *ill-favoured* □ *well-favoured*.

favourite or (*US*) **favorite** /ˈfeɪvərɪt/ ▻ *adj* best-liked; preferred. ▻ *noun* **1** a favourite person or thing. **2** someone unfairly preferred or particularly indulged □ *He's the boss's favourite.* **3** *sport* a horse or competitor expected to win. ⓘ 16c: from French *favorit*.

favouritism or (*US*) **favoritism** /ˈfeɪvərɪtɪzəm/ ▻ *noun* the practice of giving unfair preference, help or support to someone or something.

fawn¹ /fɔːn/ ▻ *noun* **1** a young deer of either sex. **2** beige; the colour of a fawn. ▻ *adj* having this colour □ *a fawn coat.* ▻ *verb* (***fawned, fawning***) *intr* said of deer: to give birth to young. ⓘ 14c: from French *faon*.

fawn² /fɔːn/ ▻ *verb* (***fawned, fawning***) *intr* (*often* **fawn on** or **upon someone**) **1** said of a dog: to show affection for someone by licking, nuzzling, etc. **2** to flatter or behave over-humbly towards someone, in order to win approval. • **fawner** *noun*. • **fawning** *noun, adj*. • **fawningly** *adverb*. ⓘ Anglo-Saxon *fagnian*.

fax /faks/ ▻ *noun* (***faxes***) **1** a machine that scans documents electronically and transmits a photographic image of the contents to a receiving machine by telephone line. **2 a** a document received by such a machine □ *Has a fax arrived for me this morning?* **b** *loosely* a document sent by a fax machine □ *Please send this fax by noon.* **3** Also *as adj* □ *fax number* □ *fax machine.* ▻ *verb* (***faxes, faxed, faxing***) **1** to transmit a photographic image of (a document) by this means. **2** to send a communication to someone by fax □ *Please fax me by noon.* • **faxable** *adj*. ⓘ Fax machines have become commonplace since the 1980s, but *fax* was first used in the 1940s referring to an early type of fax transmitted by radio: contraction and respelling of FACSIMILE.

fay /feɪ/ ▻ *noun* (***fays***) *poetic* a fairy. ⓘ 14c: from French *fae*, from Latin *fata* the FATES.

fayre /fɛə(r)/ ▻ *noun* a nostalgic spelling of FAIR².

faze /feɪz/ ▻ *verb* (***fazed, fazing***) *colloq* to disturb, worry or fluster □ *He wasn't fazed by the adverse publicity he received.* □ *That film completely fazed me.* ⓘ 19c: variant of the dialect word *feeze* to beat off.

fazenda /faˈzɛndə/ ▻ *noun* (***fazendas***) especially in Brazil: a large estate, plantation or cattle ranch. • **fazendeiro** /-ˈdɛərou/ *noun* (***fazendeiros***) someone who owns or runs such a property. ⓘ 19c: Portuguese, same as Spanish HACIENDA, from Latin *facienda* things to be done.

FBA ▻ *abbreviation* Fellow of the British Academy.

FBI ▻ *abbreviation* Federal Bureau of Investigation, a special police department in the US that investigates political or other activities that are thought to threaten state security. Compare CIA.

FBR ▻ *abbreviation* fast-breeder reactor or fast-breeder reactors.

FC ▻ *abbreviation* **1** football club. **2** Free Church.

F-clef see BASS CLEF

FCO ▻ *abbreviation* Foreign and Commonwealth Office.

FD ▻ *abbreviation* used on British coins: *Fidei Defensor* (Latin), DEFENDER OF THE FAITH.

Fe ▻ *symbol, chem* iron. ⓘ 19c: from Latin *ferrum* iron.

fealty /ˈfɪəltɪ/ ▻ *noun* (***fealties***) *feudalism* the loyalty sworn by a vassal or tenant to his feudal lord. ⓘ 14c: from French *fealte*, from Latin *fidelitas* loyalty.

fear /fɪə(r)/ ▻ *noun* **1** anxiety and distress caused by the awareness of danger or expectation of pain. **2** a cause of this feeling. **3** *relig* reverence, awe or dread. ▻ *verb* (***feared, fearing***) **1** to be afraid of someone or something. **2** to think or expect something with dread. **3** to regret something; to be sorry to say something. • **for fear of ...** or **for fear that ...** because of the danger of something or that something will happen. • **in fear of something** or **someone** frightened of it or them. • **no fear** *colloq* no chance; definitely not □ *no fear of winning* □ *No fear!* • **put the fear of God into someone** *colloq* to terrify them. • **without fear or favour** completely impartially. ⓘ Anglo-Saxon *fær* calamity.

■ **fear for something** to be frightened or anxious about it □ *feared for their lives.*

fearful ▻ *adj* **1** afraid. **2** frightening. **3** *colloq* very bad. • **fearfully** *adj*. • **fearfulness** *noun*.

fearless ▻ *adj* without fear; brave. • **fearlessly** *adverb*. • **fearlessness** *noun*.

fearsome ▻ *adj* **1** causing fear. **2** frightening. • **fearsomely** *adverb*.

feasibility study ▻ *noun* an investigation to determine whether a proposed project, system, etc would be desirable, cost effective, etc to develop or put into operation.

feasible /ˈfiːzɪbəl/ ▻ *adj* **1** capable of being done or achieved; possible. **2** *loosely* probable; likely. • **feasibility** *noun*. • **feasibly** *adverb*. ⓘ 15c: from French *faisible* that can be done, from Latin *facere* to do.

feast /fiːst/ ▻ *noun* **1** a large rich meal, eg to celebrate some occasion. **2** a pleasurable abundance of something. **3** *relig* a regularly occurring celebration commemorating a person or event. ▻ *verb* (***feasted, feasting***) **1** *intr* to take part in a feast, ie to eat and drink a lot. **2** *old use* to provide a feast for someone; to entertain someone sumptuously. • **feaster** *noun*. • **feasting** *noun*. • **feast one's eyes on** or **upon something** to gaze at it with pleasure. • **movable feast** see under MOVABLE. ⓘ 13c: from French *feste*, from Latin *festum* a holiday.

■ **feast on** or **upon something** to eat or experience it with enjoyment.

Feast of Tabernacles see under SUKKOTH

feat /fiːt/ ▻ *noun* a deed or achievement, especially a remarkable one requiring extraordinary strength, skill or courage. ⓘ 15c: from French *fait*, from Latin *factum*; compare FACT.

feather /ˈfɛðə(r)/ ▻ *noun* **1** any of the light growths that form the soft covering of a bird. **2** something with a featherlike appearance. **3** plumage. **4** condition; spirits □ *in fine feather.* **5** something of little importance. **6** the feathered end of an arrow. **7** *rowing* the action of feathering an oar. ▻ *verb* (***feathered, feathering***) **1** to provide, cover or line with feathers. **2** to turn (one's oar) parallel to the water to lessen air resistance. • **featheriness** *noun*. • **feathering** *noun*. • **feathery** *adj*. • **a feather in one's cap** something one can be proud of. • **feather one's own nest** to accumulate money for oneself, especially dishonestly. • **birds of a feather** see under BIRD. • **in full** or **high feather** greatly elated or in high spirits. • **make the feathers fly** *colloq* to cause a commotion. • **ruffle someone's feathers** to upset or offend someone. • **show the white feather** to show signs of cowardice ⓘ A white feather in a gamecock's tail being considered as a sign of inferior breeding. • **You could have knocked me down with a feather** I was astonished. ⓘ Anglo-Saxon.

feather bed ▻ *noun* a mattress stuffed with feathers. ▻ *verb* (**featherbed**) **1** to spoil or pamper someone. **2** to protect (an industry, workers, etc) by practices such as overmanning in order to save or create jobs. **3** *colloq* to give financial inducements to someone.

featherbrain ▻ *noun, derog* a frivolous, feckless person; an empty-headed person.

feather-brained ▻ *adj, derog* silly; empty-headed.

feather duster ▻ *noun* a stick with a head made of feathers, used for dusting.

feathered ▻ *adj* covered or fitted with feathers or something featherlike.

feathered friend ▻ *noun, jocular* a bird.

feather star see under CRINOID

feather stitch ▻ *noun, needlework* a zigzag stitch in embroidery.

featherweight ▻ *noun* **1** a class for boxers, wrestlers and weightlifters of not more than a specified weight, which is 57kg (126 lb) in professional boxing, and similar weights in the other sports. **2** a boxer, etc of this weight. **3** someone who weighs very little. **4** *derog* someone of little importance or influence.

feature /ˈfiːtʃə(r)/ ▻ *noun* **1** any of the parts of the face, eg eyes, nose, mouth, etc. **2** (**features**) the face. **3** a characteristic. **4** a noticeable part or quality of something. **5** an extended article in a newspaper, discussing a particular issue □ *a feature on coalmining in Britain.* **6** an article or item appearing regularly in a newspaper. **7** a FEATURE FILM. ▻ *verb* (***featured, featuring***) **1** to have as a feature or make a feature of something. **2** to give prominence to (an actor, a well-known event, etc) in a film □ *The film features the French Revolution.* • **featureless** *adj* dull; with no points of interest. Ⓢ 14c in the sense 'bodily form': from French *faiture*.

■ **feature in something** to play an important part or role in (a film, documentary, etc).

featured ▻ *adj* **1** said of an actor, etc: prominent in a particular film, etc. **2** *in compounds* having features of a specified type □ *sharp-featured.*

feature film ▻ *noun* a film, usually of about 1½ to 3 hours in length, that forms the main part of a cinema programme, as opposed to a SHORT, TRAILERS or advertising, etc.

feature-length ▻ *adj* said of films: comparable in length to a feature film.

Feb. ▻ *abbreviation* February.

febrifuge /ˈfɛbrɪfjuːdʒ, ˈfiː-/ ▻ *noun, medicine* a medicine, treatment, etc that reduces fever. • **febrifugal** /fɪˈbrɪfjʊgəl, fɛbrɪˈfjuːgəl/ *adj.* Ⓢ 17c: from Latin *febrifugia* FEVERFEW.

febrile /ˈfiːbraɪl, ˈfɛ-/ ▻ *adj* relating to fever; feverish. Ⓢ 17c: from Latin *febris* fever.

February /ˈfɛbrʊərɪ, ˈfɛbjʊərɪ/ ▻ *noun* (***Februaries***) (abbreviation **Feb.**) the second month of the year, which follows January and comes before March, and has 28 days, except in LEAP YEARS when it has 29. Ⓢ 13c: from Latin *Februarius* month of expiation, from *februa* the Roman festival of purification.

fec. ▻ *abbreviation*: *fecit* (Latin), he or she made or did this.

fecal the *N Amer* spelling of FAECAL.

feces the *N Amer* spelling of FAECES.

feckless /ˈfɛkləs/ ▻ *adj* **1** helpless; clueless. **2** irresponsible; aimless. • **fecklessly** *adj.* • **fecklessness** *noun.* Ⓢ 16c: from Scots *feck* effect.

feculent /ˈfɛkjʊlənt/ ▻ *adj* containing or consisting of faeces or sediment; foul; turbid. • **feculence** *noun.* Ⓢ 15c: from Latin *faeculentus* full of dregs.

fecund /ˈfiːkənd, ˈfɛk-/ ▻ *adj* fruitful; fertile; richly productive. • **fecundity** *noun.* Ⓢ 15c: from Latin *fecundus*.

fecundate /ˈfiːkəndeɪt, ˈfɛkəndeɪt/ ▻ *verb* (***fecundated, fecundating***) to make something fruitful or fertile; to impregnate. • **fecundation** *noun.* Ⓢ 17c: from Latin *fecundare* to fertilize.

Fed. *US* ▻ *abbreviation* **1** Federal Reserve Board. **2** Federal Reserve System. ▻ *noun, slang* an agent of the FBI.

fed *past tense, past participle of* FEED. See also FED UP.

fedayee /fəˈdɑːjiː/ (***fedayeen*** /-jiːn/) *noun* an Arab commando or guerilla fighter, especially one involved in the conflict against Israel, trained by organizations such as the PLO. Ⓢ 1950s: from Arabic *fida'i* one who sacrifices himself or herself.

federal /ˈfɛdərəl/ ▻ *adj* **1** belonging or relating to a country consisting of a group of states independent in local matters but united under a central government for other purposes, eg defence, foreign policy □ *the Federal Republic of Germany.* **2** relating to the central government of a group of federated states. **3** (**Federal**) *historical* supporting the union government during the American Civil War. Ⓢ 17c: from Latin *foedus* treaty.

Federal Bureau of Investigation see under FBI

federalism ▻ *noun, politics* the principles and practice of federal government, especially a system in which constitutional powers are devolved to national and regional governments. Ⓢ 18c.

federalist ▻ *noun* someone who advocates or supports a federal constitution or union.

federalize or **federalise** ▻ *verb* (***federalized, federalizing***) **1** *tr & intr* to bring together as a federal union or federation. **2** to subject to federal control. • **federalization** *noun.*

Federal Republic of Germany ▻ *noun* the official name of Germany, and of West Germany before unification in 1990 with East Germany.

Federal Reserve Board ▻ *noun* the board of governors in charge of the **Federal Reserve System**, which acts as the CENTRAL BANK in the US, and comprises twelve **Federal Reserve Banks**.

federate ▻ *verb* /ˈfɛdəreɪt/ (***federated, federating***) *tr & intr* to unite to form a federation. ▻ *adj* /ˈfɛdərɪt/ united by a federal union; federated. Ⓢ 19c: from Latin *foedus* treaty.

federation /fɛdəˈreɪʃən/ ▻ *noun* **1** a FEDERAL union of states, ie a group of states united politically by a treaty. Compare CONFEDERATION. **2** a union of business organizations, institutions, etc. **3** the act of uniting in a league.

federative /ˈfɛdərətɪv/ ▻ *adj* relating to or constituted as a federation.

fedora /fɪˈdɔːrə/ ▻ *noun* (***fedoras***) a brimmed felt hat, dented lengthways. Ⓢ Late 19c: said to be from *Fédora*, the title of a play by Vitorien Sardou (1831–1908).

fed up ▻ *adj* (*also* **fed up with** or (*colloq*) **of something**) bored; irritated. • **fed up to the back teeth** or **fed up to the back teeth with** or **of something** *colloq* bored, tired and annoyed by something, and impatient for a solution.

fee /fiː/ ▻ *noun* (***fees***) **1** a charge made for professional services, eg by a doctor or lawyer. **2** a charge for eg membership of a society, sitting an examination, entrance to a museum, etc. **3** (*usually* **fees**) a payment for school or college education, or for a course of instruction. **4** a payment made to a football club for the transfer of one of its players. **5** *law* an estate in the form of land that is inheritable with either restricted rights (**fee tail**) or unrestricted rights (**fee simple**). ▻ *verb* (***fees, feed, feeing***) to pay a fee to someone. Ⓢ 13c: partly from Anglo-Saxon *feoh* cattle or property; partly from French *fie* fee, which is probably from the same Germanic origin.

feeble /ˈfiːbəl/ ▻ *adj* (***feebler, feeblest***) **1** lacking strength; weak. **2** said of a joke, an excuse, etc: lacking power, influence or effectiveness; unconvincing. **3** easily influenced. • **feebleness** *noun.* • **feebly** *adverb.* Ⓢ 12c: from French *foible*.

feeble-minded ▷ *adj* **1** unable to make a decision; lacking resolve. **2** stupid; considered to lack intelligence. • **feeble-mindedly** *adverb*. • **feeble-mindedness** *noun*.

feed[1] /fiːd/ ▷ *verb* (**fed**, **feeding**) *verb* **1** to give or supply food to (animals, etc). **2** to give something as food (to animals, etc) □ *fed biscuits to his dog.* **3** to administer food (to an infant, young animal) □ *to feed the baby.* **4** *in compounds* to administer food to someone in a specified way □ *breast-feed* □ *bottle-feed* □ *force-feed.* **5** *intr* said of animals: to eat food □ *Sheep feed all day.* **6** to supply a machine, etc with fuel or other material required for continued operation or processing. **7** *theat* to provide (an actor, especially a comedian) with material or a cue to achieve an effect, often a comic effect. **8** *sport* to pass the ball to (a team-mate). ▷ *noun* **1** an act or session of feeding. **2** an allowance of food for animals, eg cattle or babies. **3** food for livestock, etc. **4** *colloq* a meal, especially a hearty one □ *a good feed.* **5** the channel or mechanism by which a machine is supplied with fuel, etc. **6** the material supplied progressively for any operation. **7** the rate of supply of material to a machine; the rate of progress of a tool. **8** *theat* an actor who feeds or cues another one; a stooge. • **feedable** *adj.* ⓒ Anglo-Saxon *fedan*.

■ **feed on something 1** said especially of animals: to eat it, especially as a regular diet □ *The cattle fed on hay.* **2** said of an emotion, etc: to be fuelled by something; to be strengthened or encouraged.

■ **feed** (**animals**, *etc*) **on something** to give them it as food, especially as a regular diet □ *The farmer fed the cattle on hay.*

■ **feed someone up** to fatten them up with nourishing food.

feed[2] *past tense, past participle of* FEE

feedback ▷ *noun* **1** responses and reactions to an inquiry or report, etc that provide guidelines for adjustment and development. **2** the process by which part of the output of a system or device, or of a component of a living organism, is returned to the input, in order to regulate or modify subsequent output. **3** in a public-address system, etc: the partial return to the microphone of the sound output, producing high-pitched whistle or howl. **4** the whistling noise so produced. **5** used in relation to biological, etc, self-adjusting systems.

feeder ▷ *noun* **1** a person, especially a baby or animal, with particular eating habits □ *a poor feeder* □ *a big feeder.* **2** a person who feeds another. **3** a child's feeding bottle. **4** a child's bib. **5** a stream that runs into a river; a tributary. **6** a minor road, railway line, etc leading to a main one; any channel of supply to a main system. **7** a power line with large current-carrying capacity, used to transmit electric power between a generating station and a distribution network.

feeding ▷ *noun* the act of giving food □ *The feeding took two hours.* • **feeding time** a particular time of each day, etc when a feed is given.

feeding bottle ▷ *noun* a bottle with a rubber teat used for feeding liquid food, especially to a human infant.

fee-faw-fum see FE FI FO FUM

feedstock ▷ *noun* raw material used in an industrial process or machine.

feel /fiːl/ ▷ *verb* (**felt**, **feeling**) **1** to become aware of something through the sense of touch. **2** *tr & intr* to have a physical or emotional sensation of something; to sense. **3** *tr & intr* to find out or investigate with the hands, etc. **4** *tr & intr* to have (an emotion). **5** *tr & intr* to react emotionally to something or be emotionally affected by something □ *feels the loss very deeply.* **6** *intr* to give the impression of being (soft, hard, rough, etc) when touched. **7** *intr* to be or seem (well, ill, happy, etc). **8** to instinctively believe in something □ *She feels that this is a good idea.* **9** to seem to oneself to be □ *feel a fool.* ▷ *noun* **1** a sensation or impression produced by touching. **2** an impression or atmosphere created by something. **3** an act of feeling with the fingers, etc. **4** an instinct, touch or knack. • **feel oneself** to feel as well as normal □ *felt herself again after a good sleep.* • **feel one's feet** to get used to a new situation, job etc. • **feel one's way** to make one's way cautiously. • **get the feel of something** to become familiar with it or used to it. • **have a feel for something** have a natural ability for or understanding of (an activity, etc). ⓒ Anglo-Saxon *felan*.

■ **feel around for something** to search for it with the fingers, etc.

■ **feel for someone** to have sympathy or compassion for them.

■ **feel for something** to try to find it by feeling.

■ **feel like something 1** to seem to oneself to be like something, to perceive oneself as something □ *feel like an idiot* □ *feel like a fool.* **2** to have an inclination or desire for it □ *feel like a walk* □ *I feel like going to the cinema tonight.*

■ **feel someone up** *slang* to move one's hands over their sexual organs.

■ **feel up to something** *usually with negatives or in questions* to feel fit enough for it □ *I don't feel up to a late night out.*

feel-bad ▷ *adj, colloq* associated with feelings of discontentment and unease with the economy, society, etc. □ *feel-bad factor.*

feeler ▷ *noun* **1** a tentacle. **2** either of a pair of long slender jointed structures, sensitive to touch, on the head of certain invertebrate animals, especially insects or crustaceans. Also called ANTENNA. • **put out feelers** to sound out the opinion of others on a particular subject before taking action.

feelgood ▷ *adj, colloq* reinforcing or associated with pleasant feelings of comfort, security, etc □ *the feelgood factor* □ *the ultimate feelgood film.*

feeling ▷ *noun* **1** the sense of touch, a sensation or emotion. **2** emotion as distinct from reason. **3** strong emotion □ *speak with feeling.* **4** a belief or opinion. **5** (*usually* **a feeling for something**) a natural ability for, or understanding of, an activity, etc. **6** affection. **7** mutual interactive emotion between two people, such as **bad feeling** (resentment), **good feeling** (friendliness), **ill feeling** (hostility), etc. **8** (*often* **feeling for something**) an instinctive grasp or appreciation of it. **9** (**feelings**) one's attitude to something □ *have strong feelings* □ *have mixed feelings.* **10** (**feelings**) one's sensibilities; delicately balanced emotional attitude □ *hurt someone's feelings.* ▷ *adj* sensitive; sympathetic. • **feelingless** *adj.* • **feelingly** *adverb* with sincerity resulting from experience. • **feelings are running high** there is a general feeling of anger, strong emotion, etc. • **no hard feelings** no offence taken. ⓒ Anglo-Saxon *felan* to feel.

feet /fiːt/ ▷ *noun, plural of* FOOT. • **at someone's feet** or **at the feet of someone** under their spell; totally devoted to them; in a position of submission, homage, etc. • **drag one's feet** see under DRAG. • **fall on one's feet** to be unexpectedly or undeservedly lucky. • **get** or **rise to one's feet** to stand up. • **have one's feet on the ground** to have plenty of common sense. • **have the ball at one's feet** to be in control of things, with many opportunities ahead. • **put one's feet up** to take a rest. • **under one's feet** in one's way; hindering one □ *She got nothing done all day; the toddler just kept getting under her feet.* See also under FOOT.

fe fi fo fum /ˈfiːˈfaɪˈfoʊˈfʌm/ and **fee-faw-fum** /ˈfiːˈfɔːˈfʌm/ ▷ *exclamation* **1** the first phrase spoken by the giant in the nursery tale 'Jack the giant killer' when he discovers the presence of Jack. The giant continues by saying *I smell the blood of an Englishman.* **2** used in fun to frighten children. **3** expressive of bloodthirstiness or murderous intent. ⓘ From aural storytelling tradition.

feign /feɪn/ ▷ *verb* (*feigned*, *feigning*) to pretend to have (eg an illness) or feel (an emotion, etc); to invent. • **feigning** *noun*. ⓘ 13c: from Latin *fingere* to contrive.

feigned ▷ *adj* **1** pretended. **2** simulated. **3** imagined.

feint¹ /feɪnt/ ▷ *noun* **1** said in boxing, fencing or other sports: a mock attack; a movement intended to deceive or distract one's opponent. **2** a misleading action or appearance. ▷ *verb* (*feinted*, *feinting*) *intr* to make a feint, eg a mock attack. ⓘ 17c: from French *feinte* to feign.

feint² /feɪnt/ ▷ *adj* said of paper: ruled with pale, fine horizontal lines to guide writing. ⓘ 19c: variant of FAINT.

feisty /ˈfaɪstɪ/ ▷ *adj* (*feistier*, *feistiest*) *colloq* **1** spirited; lively. **2** irritable; quarrelsome. ⓘ Late 19c: US dialect *fist* an aggressive small dog.

felafel or **falafel** /fəˈlafəl, fəˈlɑː-/ ▷ *noun* a deep-fried ball of ground chick-peas, with onions, peppers, etc and spices, usually served in a roll or a round of pitta bread. ⓘ 1950s: from Arabic *falafil*.

feldspar /ˈfɛldspɑː(r)/ or **felspar** /ˈfɛlspɑː(r)/ ▷ *noun*, *geol* any of a large group of rock-forming minerals, mainly aluminium silicates, found in most igneous and many metamorphic rocks, eg orthoclase, plagioclase. • **feldspathic** or **felspathic** *adj*. ⓘ 18c: from German *Feld* field + *Spat* spar.

felicia /ˈfəlɪʃɑ/ ▷ *noun* (*felicias*) any member of a S African genus of the daisy family, with blue or lilac flowers. ⓘ 20c: from Latin *felix* happy.

felicitate /fəˈlɪsɪteɪt/ ▷ *verb* (*felicitates*, *felicitated*, *felicitating*) to congratulate someone. • **felicitation** *noun* **1** the act of congratulating. **2** (**felicitations**) congratulations. ⓘ 17c: from Latin *felicitas* happiness.

felicitous /fəˈlɪsɪtəs/ ▷ *adj* **1** said of wording: elegantly apt; well-chosen; appropriate. **2** pleasant; happy. • **felicitously** *adverb*. • **felicitousness** *noun*.

felicity /fəˈlɪsɪtɪ/ ▷ *noun* (*felicities*) **1** happiness. **2** a cause of happiness. **3** elegance or aptness of wording; an appropriate expression. ⓘ 14c: from Latin *felicitas* happiness.

feline /ˈfiːlaɪn/ ▷ *adj* **1** relating to the cat or cat family, eg cats, lions, leopards, cheetahs. **2** like a cat, especially in terms of its movement, eg in stealth or elegance. ▷ *noun* any animal of the cat family; a cat. ⓘ 17c: from Latin *felis* cat.

fell¹ ▷ *verb* (*felled*, *felling*) **1** to cut down (a tree). **2** to knock down someone or something; to make them fall. **3** *needlecraft* to turn under and stitch down the edges of, eg a seam. ▷ *noun* **1** a quantity of timber felled at one time. **2** *needlecraft* a felled seam. • **fellable** *adj*. • **feller** *noun*. ⓘ Anglo-Saxon *fyllan* to make something fall.

fell² ▷ *noun* (*often* **fells**) *Scottish & Northern English* **1** a hill or moor. **2** an upland tract of waste, pasture or moorland. ⓘ 14c: from Norse *fjall*.

fell³ ▷ *adj*, *old use* destructive; deadly. • **at** or **in one fell swoop** at a single deadly blow; in one quick operation. ⓘ 13c: from French *fel* cruel.

fell⁴ ▷ *noun* **1** an animal skin. **2** a covering of rough hair. ⓘ Anglo-Saxon.

fell⁵ *past tense of* FALL¹

fellah /ˈfɛlə/ ▷ *noun* (*fellahs* or *fellaheen* or *fellahin* /fɛləˈhiːn/) a peasant in Arabic-speaking countries, especially in Egypt. ⓘ 18c: Arabic, meaning 'someone who cultivates the soil'.

fellatio /fɛˈleɪʃɪoʊ/ ▷ *noun* sexual stimulation of the penis by sucking or licking. ⓘ 19c: from Latin *fellare* to suck.

feller see under FELL², FELLOW

fellow /ˈfɛloʊ/ ▷ *noun* **1** a companion or equal. **2** (*also colloq* **fella** or **fellah** or **feller**) **a** a man or boy, sometimes used dismissively; **b** *colloq* a boyfriend. **3** a senior member of a college or university; a member of the governing body of a college or university. **4** a postgraduate research student financed by a fellowship. **5** (**Fellow**) a member of any of many learned societies ▫ *Fellow of the Royal Society of Edinburgh*. **6** one of a pair ▫ *one sock on the chair, its fellow on the floor*. **7** *as adj* relating to a person in the same situation or condition as oneself, or having the same status, etc ▫ *a fellow citizen* ▫ *a fellow worker* ▫ *a fellow countryman*. ⓘ Anglo-Saxon *feolaga* partner.

fellow feeling ▷ *noun* sympathy for someone with experiences similar to one's own.

fellowship ▷ *noun* **1** friendly companionship. **2** commonness or similarity of interests between people, often common religious interests ▫ *Christian fellowship*. **3** a society or association. **4** the status of a fellow of a college, society, etc. **5** a salary paid to a research fellow, often from a college or university endowment fund.

fellow traveller ▷ *noun* **1** someone who sympathizes with a political party, especially the Communist Party, without actually joining it. **2** a person travelling in the same train, bus, etc as oneself.

fell-running ▷ *noun* the sport of running over fells (see FELL²), sometimes competitively. • **fell-runner** *noun*.

fell-walking ▷ *noun* the pastime of walking over fells (see FELL²). • **fell-walker** *noun*.

felon¹ /ˈfɛlən/ ▷ *noun*, *law* a person guilty of FELONY. ⓘ 13c.

felon² /ˈfɛlən/ ▷ *noun* an inflamed sore. ⓘ 14c.

felonious /fəˈloʊnɪəs/ ▷ *adj*, *law* involving or constituting FELONY. • **feloniously** *adverb*. • **feloniousness** *noun*.

felony /ˈfɛlənɪ/ ▷ *noun* (*felonies*) *law* a serious crime. ⓘ 13c: from Latin *fello* traitor.

felspar see FELDSPAR

felt¹ ▷ *noun* a fabric formed by matting or pressing together wool fibres, rather than by weaving, using the natural tendency of the fibres to cling together. ▷ *verb* (*felted*, *felting*) **1** *tr & intr* to make into felt; to mat. **2** to cover with felt. **3** *intr* to become felted or matted. ⓘ Anglo-Saxon.

felt² *past tense, part participle of* FEEL

felting ▷ *noun* **1** the art or process of making felt or matting fibres together. **2** heavy tar-covered material used to waterproof an outhouse, shed, garage, etc ▫ *roof felting*.

felt pen, **felt-tip pen** and **felt tip** ▷ *noun* a pen with a nib made of felt, often one of a set of felt pens of various colours used for artwork, etc. ⓘ 1960s: originally *felt-tipped (marking) pen*.

fem see FEMME

fem. ▷ *abbreviation* feminine.

female /ˈfiːmeɪl/ ▷ *adj* **1** belonging or relating to the sex that gives birth to young, produces eggs, etc. **2** denoting the reproductive structure of a plant that contains an egg cell, such as the pistil of flowering plants. **3** belonging or relating to, or characteristic of, a woman. **4** *engineering* said of a piece of machinery, etc: having a hole or holes into which another part (the MALE *adj* 5) fits. ▷ *noun* **1** *sometimes derog* a woman or girl. **2** a female animal or plant. • **femaleness** *noun*. ⓘ 14c: from Latin *femella* young woman, with spelling influenced by association with *male*.

female circumcision ▷ *noun* surgical mutilation or removal of external female genital organs, especially involving CLITORIDECTOMY and INFIBULATION.

female condom ▷ *noun* a form of contraception consisting of a thin polyurethane pouch that fits inside the vagina. ⓘ 1992.

female, feminine

There is often confusion between **female** and **feminine**: **female** classifies living things, and (for people) refers to the fact of being a woman □ *Nearly everyone, female as well as male, can shed surplus fat.* **Feminine** describes and refers to characteristics that are typical of women □ *We took it for granted that washing regularly was an exclusively feminine pursuit.*

female screw ▷ *noun* a cylindrical hole with a thread or groove cut on the inward surface.

feminine /'fɛmɪnɪn/ ▷ *adj* **1** typically belonging or relating to, or characteristic of, a woman. **2** having or reflecting qualities considered typical of a woman, effeminate. **3** *grammar* (abbreviation **f.** or **fem.**) in some languages: belonging or relating to the GENDER into which most words for human and animal females fall, along with many other nouns. Compare COMMON GENDER, MASCULINE, NEUTER. ▷ *noun, grammar* **1** the feminine gender. **2** a word belonging to this gender. • **femininely** *adverb*. • **femininity** *noun*. ⓒ 14c: from Latin *feminina*, diminutive of *femina* woman.

feminism ▷ *noun* a belief or movement advocating the cause of women's rights and opportunities, particularly equal rights with men, by challenging inequalities between the sexes in society. ⓒ Late 19c: from Latin *femina* woman.

feminist ▷ *noun* a person who adheres to the tenets of feminism. ▷ *adj* relating to feminism □ *the feminist cause.*

feminize or **feminise** ▷ *verb* (*feminized, feminizing*) *tr & intr* **1** to make or become feminine. **2** to make (a male animal) develop female characteristics.

femme or **fem** /fɛm/ *informal* ▷ *noun* **1** someone who is dressed up in a particularly feminine way. **2** someone, usually a lesbian or gay man, who takes on a passive role in sex. ▷ *adj* said especially of lesbians: dressed in a particularly feminine way □ *She's looking very femme today.* Compare BUTCH. ⓒ 20c in these senses: French, meaning 'woman'.

femme fatale /fam fə'tɑːl/ ▷ *noun* (*femmes fatales* /fam fə'tɑːl/) a woman with an irresistible charm and fascination, often bringing those who love her (usually men) into despair and disaster. ⓒ Early 19c: French, meaning 'fatal woman'.

femoral see under FEMUR

femto- /fɛmtoʊ/ ▷ *combining form* a thousand million millionth (10^{-15}). ⓒ From Danish or Norwegian *femten* fifteen.

femur /'fiːmə(r)/ ▷ *noun* (*femurs* or *femora* /'fɛmərə/) **1** the longest and largest bone of the human skeleton, the upper end of which articulates with the hip joint, and the lower end with the knee joint. Also called thigh bone. **2** the corresponding bone in the hind limb of four-limbed vertebrates. **3** the segment of an insect's leg that is closest to its body. • **femoral** /'fɛmərəl/ *adj* belonging or relating to, or in the region of, the femur or the thigh. ⓒ 18c: Latin, meaning 'thigh'.

fen ▷ *noun* a waterlogged area of lowland dominated by grasses, sedges and rushes, having an alkaline soil. Also called **fenland**. Compare THE FENS. • **fenny** *adj*. ⓒ Anglo-Saxon *fenn*.

fence /fɛns/ ▷ *noun* **1** a barrier eg of wood or wire, for enclosing or protecting land. **2** a barrier of various designs for a horse to jump. **3** *slang* someone who receives and disposes of stolen goods. **4** a guard to limit motion in a piece of machinery. **5** a guiding device on a circular saw or plane. ▷ *verb* (*fenced, fencing*) **1** (*also* **fence something in** or **off**) to enclose or separate it with a fence, or as if with a fence. **2** *intr* to practise the art or sport of fencing. **3** to build fences. **4** (*usually* **fence with words**) *intr* to avoid answering directly. **5** *intr, slang* to be a receiver or purchaser of stolen goods. • **fenceless** *adj*. • **mend one's fences** to improve or restore one's relations, reputation or popularity, especially in politics. • **sit on the fence** to be unable or unwilling to support either side in a dispute, etc. ⓒ 14c: as *fens*, shortened from DEFENCE.

fencer ▷ *noun* **1** someone who builds fences. **2** someone who practices the art or sport of fencing.

fencible /'fɛnsɪbəl/ ▷ *noun, historical* a volunteer enlisted to defend their country.

fencing /'fɛnsɪŋ/ ▷ *noun* **1** the art, act or sport of attack and defence with a foil, épée or sabre. **2** material used for constructing fences. **3** fences collectively.

fencing-master ▷ *noun* someone who has mastered and/or teaches the art of fencing.

fend /fɛnd/ ▷ *verb* (*fended, fending*) **1** (*usually* **fend something** or **someone off**) to defend oneself from (blows, questions, etc). **2** *intr* (*especially* **fend for someone**) to provide for, especially oneself. ⓒ 14c: shortened from DEFEND.

fender /'fɛndə(r)/ ▷ *noun* **1** a low guard fitted round a fireplace to keep ash, coals, etc within the hearth. **2** *N Amer* the wing or mudguard of a car. **3** a bundle of rope, tyres, etc hanging from a ship's side to protect it when in contact with piers, etc. **4** any structure serving as a guard against contact or impact.

fenestra /fə'nɛstrə/ ▷ *noun* (*fenestrae* /-striː/) **1** *archit* a window or other wall opening. **2** *biol* a small opening, especially between the middle and inner ear. **3** *zool* a translucent spot, eg one found on a moth's wing. • **fenestral** *adj*. ⓒ 19c: Latin.

fenestra ovalis see OVAL WINDOW

fenestra rotunda see ROUND WINDOW

fenestrated /fə'nɛstreɪtɪd, 'fɛnə-/ and **fenestrate** ▷ *adj* **1** *archit* having windows. **2** *biol* perforated; pierced; having translucent spots.

fenestration /fɛnə'streɪʃən/ ▷ *noun* **1** *archit* the arrangement of windows in a building. **2** *surgery* the operation of making an artificial fenestra in bone, especially in the ear to restore hearing.

feng shui /'fɛŋʃuiː, 'fʌŋ-/ ▷ *noun* the process of making the correct decision about the siting of a building, placing of furniture, etc in a building, room, etc so as to ensure the optimum happiness for the occupants, based on the notion that the natural elements (water, earth, etc) and YIN and YANG influence the cosmic currents of a locality. ⓒ 18c: Chinese, meaning 'wind and water'.

feni or **fenny** /'fɛnɪ/ ▷ *noun* (*fenis* or *fennies*) an alcoholic spirit produced in Goa from coconuts or cashew nuts.

Fenian /'fiːnɪən/ ▷ *noun* **1** a member of an association of Irishmen founded in New York in 1857 for the overthrow of the British government in Ireland. **2** *especially Irish, offensive* Catholic. ▷ *adj* **1** belonging to the modern Fenians. **2** *offensive* Catholic. • **Fenianism** *noun*. ⓒ 19c: from Irish Gaelic *Féne*, one of the names of the ancient population of Ireland, confused in modern times with *fiann* the militia of Finn and other ancient Irish kings.

fenks /fɛŋks/ ▷ *plural noun* the fibrous parts of the blubber of a whale, forming the refuse when the oil has been melted out. ⓒ 19c.

fenland see under FEN

fenman ▷ *noun* someone who lives in fen country.

fennec /'fɛnək/ ▷ *noun* a little African fox with large ears. ⓒ 18c: from Arabic *fenek* fox.

fennel /'fɛnəl/ ▷ *noun* a strong-smelling, yellow-flowered, umbelliferous plant, whose seeds and leaves are used in cooking. See also FINOCCHIO. ⓒ Anglo-Saxon *finul*, from Latin *fenum* hay.

fenny see under FEN, FENI

the Fens ⊳ *plural noun* a flat low-lying region around the Wash in Eastern England, which was a marsh area until reclaimed between the 17th and 19th centuries. Compare FEN.

fenugreek /ˈfɛnjʊgriːk/ ⊳ *noun* a white-flowered leguminous plant with strong-smelling seeds, native to SW Asia and the Mediterranean region and widely cultivated in India, grown as animal fodder and also used in curries and salads. ◷ Anglo-Saxon *fenograecum*, from Latin *fenum graecum* Greek hay.

feoff /fiːf, fɛf/ ⊳ *verb* (***feoffed***, ***feoffing***) *feudalism* to grant possession (of a fief or property) in land. Compare FIEF, and also FEE which is in current usage. • **feoffee** *noun* (***feoffees***) the person invested with the fief. • **feoffer** or **feoffor** *noun* the person who grants the fief. • **feoffment** *noun* the gift of a fief. ◷ 13c: from French *feoffer* or *fiefer*, from French *fief*.

feral /ˈfɛrəl, ˈfɪərəl/ ⊳ *adj* **1** said of animals normally found in a domestic situation or in captivity: wild; fending for itself ▫ ***feral cats***. **2** said of a plant: uncultivated; having run wild. ◷ 17c: from Latin *fera* wild beast.

fer-de-lance /fɛədəˈlɑːns/ ⊳ *noun* (***fers-de-lance*** or ***fer-de-lances***) either of two tropical American species of PIT VIPER. ◷ 19c: French, meaning 'head (literally 'iron') of a lance'.

feretory /ˈfɛrətərɪ/ ⊳ *noun* (***feretories***) *RC Church* **1** a shrine for relics of saints, often carried in processions. **2** a chapel attached to an abbey or church in which shrines are kept. ◷ 14c: from Latin *feretrum*, from Greek *pherein* to bear.

ferial /ˈfɪərɪəl/ ⊳ *adj, RC Church* relating to any day of the week which is neither a fast nor a festival. ◷ 14c: from Latin *feria* a holiday.

fermata /fɜːˈmɑːtə/ ⊳ *noun* (***fermatas*** or ***fermate*** /-eɪ/) *music* a pause. ◷ 19c: Italian.

ferment ⊳ *noun* /ˈfɜːmɛnt/ **1** a substance that causes fermentation, such as a bacterium, yeast or mould. **2** fermentation. **3** a state of agitation or excitement. ⊳ *verb* /fəˈmɛnt/ (***fermented***, ***fermenting***) **1** *tr & intr* to undergo or make something undergo fermentation. **2** to be or make something be in a state of excitement or instability. • **fermentability** *noun*. • **fermentable** *adj*. • **fermented** *adj*. ◷ 15c: from Latin *fermentum* yeast, from *fervere* to boil.

fermentation /fɜːmɛnˈteɪʃən/ ⊳ *noun, chem* a biochemical process in which micro-organisms such as bacteria, yeasts, moulds or enzymes are used to break down an organic compound, usually a carbohydrate, in the absence of oxygen, eg the conversion of sugar into alcohol. • **fermentative** *adj*.

fermi /fɜːmɪ/ ⊳ *noun* (***fermis***) *nuclear physics* a unit of length equal to 10^{-5} angstrom, or 10^{-15} metres. ◷ Early 20c: named after E Fermi (1901–54), Italian physicist.

fermion ⊳ *noun* one of a group of subatomic particles, such as protons, electrons and neutrons, having half-integral spin and obeying the exclusion principle. ◷ 20c: see FERMI.

fermium /fɜːmɪəm/ ⊳ *noun, chem* (symbol **Fm**, atomic number 100) an artificially produced metallic radioactive element. ◷ 20c: see FERMI.

fern /fɜːn/ ⊳ *noun* any of several thousand species of flowerless feathery-leaved plants that reproduce by spores (forming on the leaves or fronds) rather than seeds. • **ferny** *adj* (***fernier***, ***ferniest***) **1** belonging or relating to, or resembling, a fern. **2** covered with or full of ferns. ◷ Anglo-Saxon *fearn*.

fernbird ⊳ *noun* a small brown and white New Zealand bird with fern-like tail feathers.

ferocious /fəˈroʊʃəs/ ⊳ *adj* savagely fierce; cruel; savage. • **ferociously** *adverb*. • **ferociousness** *noun*. ◷ 17c: from Latin *ferox* wild.

ferocity /fəˈrɒsɪtɪ/ ⊳ *noun* (***ferocities***) a fierce or cruel temperament.

-ferous /fərəs/ ⊳ *combining form, signifying* bearing or containing ▫ ***carboniferous*** ▫ ***umbelliferous***. ◷ From Latin *ferre* to carry + -OUS.

ferrate /ˈfɛreɪt/ ⊳ *noun* a salt of ferric acid. ◷ Late 19c: from Latin *ferrum* iron.

ferrel see FERRULE

ferret /ˈfɛrɪt/ ⊳ *noun* **1** a small, half-tame, albino type of polecat, used for driving rabbits and rats from their holes. **2** an inquisitive and persistent investigator. ⊳ *verb* (***ferreted***, ***ferreting***) *tr & intr* to hunt (rabbits, etc) with a ferret. • **ferreter** *noun* someone who ferrets. • **ferrety** *adj* like a ferret. ◷ 14c: from French *furet*, from Latin *fur* thief.

▪ **ferret about** or **around** to search busily; to rummage.

▪ **ferret something out** **1** to drive (an animal, etc) out of a hiding place. **2** to find it out through persistent investigation.

ferri- /fɛrɪ-/ ⊳ *combining form, chem, denoting* a compound that contains iron in its higher degree of valency, usually trivalent ▫ *ferricyanide*. Compare FERRIC and FERRO- sense 2. ◷ From Latin *ferrum* iron.

ferriage /ˈfɛrɪɪdʒ/ ⊳ *noun* **1** transportation by ferry. **2** the fare paid for a ferry crossing.

ferric /ˈfɛrɪk/ ⊳ *adj* **1** referring or relating to iron. **2** *chem* denoting a compound that contains iron in its trivalent state. ◷ 18c: from Latin *ferrum* iron.

ferric oxide ⊳ *noun* (formula $\mathbf{Fe_2O_3}$) a reddish-brown or black solid, occurring naturally as HAEMATITE, used in magnetic tapes and as a catalyst and pigment. Also called **iron oxide**.

ferries *plural of* FERRY

Ferris wheel /ˈfɛrɪs —/ ⊳ *noun* a giant fairground wheel that turns vertically, with seats hanging from its rim. ◷ Late 19c: named after G W G Ferris (1859–96), US engineer.

ferrite /ˈfɛraɪt/ ⊳ *noun, chem* any of a class of ceramic materials composed of oxides of iron and some other metal, eg copper, nickel, etc, that have magnetic properties and a low electrical conductivity, and are used in loudspeaker magnets, tape-recorder heads, etc.

ferro- /fɛroʊ/ ⊳ *combining form* **1** relating to or containing iron ▫ *ferroalloy* ▫ *ferromagnetism*. **2** *chem* denoting a compound that contains iron in its divalent state ▫ *ferrocyanide*. Compare FERRI- and FERROUS. ◷ From Latin *ferrum* iron.

ferroconcrete ⊳ *noun* reinforced concrete.

ferromagnetism ⊳ *noun* a phenomenon displayed by certain metals and alloys, in which the magnetic moments of atoms are capable of spontaneous magnetic polarization. • **ferromagnetic** *adj*.

ferrous /ˈfɛrəs/ ⊳ *adj, chem* **1** belonging or relating to iron. **2** denoting a chemical compound that contains iron in its divalent state. ◷ 19c: from Latin *ferrum* iron.

ferruginous /fɛˈruːdʒɪnəs/ ⊳ *adj* **1** rust-coloured; reddish-brown. **2** containing iron. ◷ 17c: from Latin *ferrugo*, *ferruginis* iron rust.

ferrule /ˈfɛruːl, ˈfɛrjuːl/ ⊳ *noun* **1** a metal ring or cap for protecting the tip of a walking-stick or umbrella. **2** a cylindrical fitting, threaded internally like a screw, for joining pipes, etc together. ◷ 15c: from Latin *viriola* little bracelet.

ferry /ˈfɛrɪ/ ⊳ *noun* (***ferries***) **1** (*also* **ferryboat**) a boat that carries passengers and often cars across a river or strip of water, especially as a regular service. **2** the service thus provided. **3** the place or route where a ferryboat runs. **4** the right to provide a ferry service. ▷ *verb* (***ferries***, ***ferried***, ***ferrying***) **1** *tr & intr* (*sometimes* **ferry across**) to transport or go by ferry. **2** to convey (passengers, goods, etc) in a vehicle ◻ ***He ferried them to school each day.*** **3** to deliver (an aircraft coming from a factory) to its destination under its own power. ◷ Anglo-Saxon *ferian* to convey.

ferryman ▷ *noun* someone who conveys passengers by ferry.

fertile /ˈfɜːtaɪl, *N Amer* ˈfɜːtəl/ ▷ *adj* **1** said of land, soil, etc: containing the nutrients required to support an abundant growth of crops, plants, etc. **2** producing or capable of producing babies, young or fruit. **3** said of an egg or seed: capable of developing into a new individual. **4** said of the mind: rich in ideas; very productive. **5** providing a wealth of possibilities ◻ ***fertile ground for research.*** **6** producing many offspring; prolific. **7** *physics* said of a chemical substance: capable of being converted into a fissile or fissionable material. • **fertilely** *adverb*. ◷ 15c: from Latin *fertilis*, from *ferre* to bear.

Fertile Crescent ▷ *noun* a crescent-shaped region stretching from Armenia to Arabia, formerly fertile but now mainly desert, considered to be the cradle of civilization.

fertility /fɜːˈtɪlɪtɪ, fə-/ ▷ *noun* **1** fruitfulness; richness; abundance. **2** the state of being fertile. **3** the ability of a living organism to produce offspring or large numbers of offspring. **4** the ability of soil or land to support an abundant growth of crops or other plants. **5** *ecol* the number of eggs produced by a species or individual that develop into living young. Compare FECUNDITY.

fertility drug ▷ *noun, medicine* a drug that is used to treat infertility in women by inducing ovulation.

fertilization or **fertilisation** /fɜːtɪlaɪˈzeɪʃən/ ▷ *noun* the act or process of fertilizing.

fertilize or **fertilise** /ˈfɜːtɪlaɪz/ ▷ *verb* (***fertilized***, ***fertilizing***) **1** said of a male gamete, especially a sperm cell: to fuse with (a female gamete, especially an egg cell) to form a ZYGOTE. **2** said of a male animal: to inseminate or impregnate (a female animal). **3** said of flowering and conebearing plants: to transfer (pollen) by the process of POLLINATION. **4** to supply (soil or land) with extra nutrients in order to increase its fertility and improve the growth of crops or other plants on it.

fertilizer or **fertiliser** ▷ *noun* **1** any natural or chemical substance, especially nitrogen, potassium salts or phosphates, that is added to or dug into soil to improve the yield, size or quality of plants, especially food crops. **2** someone or something that fertilizes an animal or plant.

ferule /ˈfɛruːl, ˈfɛrjuːl/ ▷ *noun* a cane or rod formerly used for punishment (in some schools). ◷ 16c: from Latin *ferula* giant fennel.

fervent /ˈfɜːvənt/ ▷ *adj* enthusiastic; earnest or ardent. • **fervency** *noun*. • **fervently** *adverb*. ◷ 14c: from Latin *fervere* to boil or to glow.

fervid /ˈfɜːvɪd/ ▷ *adj* fervent; full of fiery passion or zeal. • **fervidity** and **fervidness** *noun*. • **fervidly** *adverb*. ◷ 16c: from Latin *fervidus* fiery, from *fervere* to boil or to glow.

fervour or (*N Amer*) **fervor** /ˈfɜːvə(r)/ ▷ *noun* passionate enthusiasm; intense eagerness or sincerity. ◷ 15c: from Latin *fervor* violent heat.

fescue /ˈfɛskjuː/ and **fescue grass** ▷ *noun* a tufted grass with inrolled bristle-like leaves, which forms much of the turf on chalk downs. ◷ 14c: from French *festu*, from Latin *festuca* a straw.

fess ▷ *verb* (*fesses, fessed, fessing*) (*always* **fess up**) *US colloq* to confess to having committed a crime.

fesse or **fess** /fɛs/ ▷ *noun* (***fesses***) *heraldry* one of the simple heraldic forms consisting of a band between two horizontal lines over the middle of an ESCUTCHEON, usually covering one third of it. ◷ 15c: from Latin *fascia* band.

fest ▷ *noun, in compounds* **1** a party, gathering or festival for a specified activity ◻ ***songfest*** ◻ ***filmfest*** ◻ ***thrill fest.*** **2** an indulgent spree or concentration over a period of time on a specified activity or theme ◻ ***newsfest*** ◻ ***sleaze-fest.*** ◷ 19c: German, meaning 'festival'.

fester /ˈfɛstə(r)/ ▷ *verb* (***festered***, ***festering***) **1** *intr* said of a wound: to form or discharge pus. **2** said of an evil: to continue unchecked or get worse. **3** *intr* to rot or decay. **4** *intr* said of resentment or anger: to smoulder; to become more bitter, usually over an extended period of time. **5** *intr* to be a continuing source of resentment; to rankle. **6** *old* to make something fester. ▷ *noun* a small sore discharging pus. ◷ 14c: from Latin *fistula* a kind of ulcer.

festival /ˈfɛstɪvəl/ ▷ *noun* **1** a day or period of celebration, especially one kept traditionally. **2** *relig* a feast or saint's day. **3** a season or series of performances (of musical, theatrical or other cultural events). ▷ *adj* belonging or relating to a festival. ▷ *verb* (***festivaled***, ***festivaling***) *intr* to attend performances at a festival; to participate in festival activities ◻ ***He has been festivaling all week.*** ◷ 15c: from Latin *festivalis*, from *festum* feast.

Festival of Dedication and **Festival of Lights** CHANUKKAH

festive /ˈfɛstɪv/ ▷ *adj* **1** relating to a festival or holiday. **2** celebratory; joyous; lively; cheerful. • **festively** *adverb*. ◷ 17c: from Latin *festivus*, from *festus* feast.

festivity /fɛˈstɪvɪtɪ/ ▷ *noun* (***festivities***) **1** a lighthearted event; celebration, merrymaking. **2** (**festivities**) festive activities; celebrations ◻ ***The festivities continued into the early hours.***

festoon /fɛˈstuːn/ ▷ *noun* **1** a decorative chain of flowers, ribbons, etc looped between two points. **2** *archit* a carved or moulded ornament representing this. ▷ *verb* (***festooned***, ***festooning***) to hang or decorate with festoons. ◷ 17c: from Italian *festone* decoration for a feast.

festoon blind ▷ *noun* a window blind pleated and hung to fall in festoon-like folds.

festschrift /ˈfɛstʃrɪft/ ▷ *noun* (***festschrifts*** or ***festschriften***) a celebratory publication, usually a collection of writings presented by the authors and published in honour of someone. ◷ 19c: German, literally 'festival writing'.

feta or **fetta** /ˈfɛtə/ ▷ *noun* a crumbly salty white low-fat cheese originating in Greece and the Middle East, traditionally made from goat's or ewe's milk, and now sometimes from cow's milk. ◷ 1950s: Modern Greek *pheta* a slice (ie of cheese), from Italian *fetta*.

fetal or **foetal** /ˈfiːtəl/ ▷ *adj* belonging or relating to, or resembling, a fetus.

fetal alcohol syndrome ▷ *noun* (abbreviation **FAS**) a condition characterized by mental retardation in a newborn baby, caused by excessive alcohol intake by its mother during pregnancy.

fetch /fɛtʃ/ ▷ *verb* (***fetched***, ***fetching***) **1** to go and get something, and bring it back ◻ ***John fetched help.*** ◻ ***The dog fetched the bone.*** **2** to be sold for (a certain price). **3** *informal* to deal someone (a blow, slap, etc). **4** *old use* to utter (a sigh or groan). **5** to bring forth (tears or blood). ▷ *noun* **1** an act of bringing. **2** a trick or dodge. • **fetch and carry** to act as servant; to perform menial tasks. ◷ Anglo-Saxon *feccan*.

■ **fetch up** *colloq* to arrive; to turn up; to end up.

■ **fetch something up** *informal* to vomit (food, etc).

fetching ▷ *adj, colloq, jocular* said of appearance: attractive, charming. • **fetchingly** *adverb*.

fête or **fete** /feɪt, fɛt/ ▷ *noun* **1** an outdoor event with entertainment, competitions, stalls, etc, usually to raise money for a charity. **2** a festival or holiday, especially to mark the feast day of a saint. ▷ *verb* (*fêtes*, *fêted*, *fêting*) to entertain or honour someone lavishly. ⓒ 18c: French.

fetid or **foetid** /ˈfiːtɪd, ˈfɛtɪd/ ▷ *adj* having a strong disgusting smell. • **fetidly** *adverb*. • **fetidness** *noun*. ⓒ 16c: from Latin *fetere* to stink.

fetish /ˈfɛtɪʃ/ ▷ *noun* (*fetishes*) **1** in primitive societies: an object worshipped for its perceived magical powers. **2** a procedure or ritual followed obsessively, or an object of obsessive devotion. **3 a** an object other than the sexual organs that is handled or visualized as an aid to sexual stimulation; **b** a person's attachment to such an object. • **fetishism** *noun*. • **fetishist** *noun*. • **fetishistic** *adj*. ⓒ 17c: from French *fétiche*, from Portuguese *feitiço* magic; a name given by the Portuguese to the gods of W Africa, from Portuguese *feitiço* artificial, from Latin *facere* to make.

fetishize or **fetishise** ▷ *verb* (*fetishized*, *fetishizing*) to make a fetish of someone or something.

fetlock /ˈfɛtlɒk/ ▷ *noun* **1** the thick projection at the back of a horse's leg just above the hoof. **2** the tuft of hair growing on this. ⓒ 14c as *fetlak*.

fetoscopy or **foetoscopy** /fiːˈtɒskəpɪ/ ▷ *noun* a procedure for viewing the fetus directly, within the uterus, or for taking a sample of fetal blood from the placenta, by inserting a hollow needle through the abdomen into the uterus, in order to determine if there are any disorders.

fetta see FETA

fetter /ˈfɛtə(r)/ ▷ *noun* **1** (*usually* **fetters**) a chain or shackle fastened to a prisoner's ankle. Compare MANACLE. **2** (**fetters**) tiresome restrictions. ▷ *verb* (*fettered*, *fettering*) **1** to put someone in fetters. **2** to restrict someone. ⓒ Anglo-Saxon *fetor*.

fettle /ˈfɛtəl/ ▷ *verb* (*fettled*, *fettling*) **1** *pottery* to knock or rub excess material off the edges of (a casting or piece of pottery) with **fettling tools**; to remove visible seams, casting marks, etc. **2** *dialect* to get ready or put in order; prepare something or oneself. **3** to line or repair (a furnace) with REFRACTORY. ▷ *noun* spirits; condition; state of health. • **fettler** *noun*. • **in fine fettle** in good form; in good spirits. ⓒ Anglo-Saxon *fetel* belt.

fettuccine or **fettucine** or **fettucini** /fɛtʊˈtʃiːnɪ/ ▷ *noun* pasta made in long ribbons. Also called TAGLIATELLE. ⓒ 1920: Italian, from *fettucia* slice or ribbon.

fetus or (*non-technical*) **foetus** /ˈfiːtəs/ ▷ *noun* (*fetuses* or *foetuses*) **1** the embryo of a VIVIPAROUS mammal during the later stages of development in the uterus, when it has started to resemble the fully-formed animal. **2** the human embryo from the end of the eighth week after conception until birth. ⓒ 14c: from Latin *fetus* offspring, incorrectly written *foetus* from the 16c to the late 1980s, and still often seen as *foetus* in non-technical contexts.

fetwa see FATWA

feu /fjuː/ ▷ *noun* (*feus*) **1** *often as adj* **a** *legal hist, feudalism* a tenure of land where the VASSAL makes a return in grain or in money, in place of military service; **b** in modern use: a perpetual lease for a fixed rent □ *feu-farm*; **c** a piece of land so held. **2** *Scots law* a right to the use of land, houses, etc in return for payment of **feu-duty**, a fixed annual payment. ▷ *verb* to grant (land, etc) on such terms. ⓒ 15c: French, variant of FEE.

feud¹ /fjuːd/ ▷ *noun* **1** a long-drawn-out bitter quarrel between families, individuals or clans. **2** a persistent state of private enmity. ▷ *verb* (*feuded*, *feuding*) *intr* (*often* **feud with someone**) to carry on a feud with them. • **feuding** *noun, adj*. • **right of feud** the right to protect oneself and one's family, and to punish those who do one wrong. ⓒ 13c as *fede*: from French *feide* feud; see also FOE.

feud² /fjuːd/ ▷ *noun*, a fief or land held on condition of service. ⓒ 17c: from Latin *feudum*.

feudal /ˈfjuːdəl/ ▷ *adj* **1** relating to FEUD². **2** relating to feudalism. **3** relating to a FEU. **4** *disparaging* old-fashioned. ⓒ 17c.

feudalism and **feudal system** ▷ *noun* a system of social and political organization prevalent in W Europe in the Middle Ages, in which powerful land-owning lords granted degrees of privilege and protection to lesser subjects holding a range of positions within a rigid social hierarchy. See also FIEF, LIEGE, VASSAL. • **feudalist** *noun*. • **feudalistic** *adj*. ⓒ 19c: FEUDAL + -ISM.

feudalize or **feudalise** ▷ *verb* (*feudalized*, *feudalizing*) to create a feudal system. • **feudalization** *noun*. ⓒ 19c.

feudist /ˈfjuːdɪst/ ▷ *noun* **1** a writer on feuds (see FEUD²). **2** a person knowledgeable in the laws of feudal tenure.

feu-duty see under FEU

feuilleté /*French* fœjte/ ▷ *noun* puff-pastry. ⓒ French.

fever /ˈfiːvə(r)/ ▷ *noun* **1** in humans: any rise in body temperature above the normal level (37°C or 98.6°F), usually accompanied by shivering, thirst and headache. **2** any of many diseases which are usually infectious, in which this is a marked symptom, eg scarlet fever, yellow fever. **3** an extreme state of agitation or excitement. ▷ *verb* (*fevered*, *fevering*) to put into a fever. ⓒ Anglo-Saxon *fefor*, from Latin *febris*.

fevered /ˈfiːvəd/ ▷ *adj* **1** affected with fever. **2** highly excited.

feverfew /ˈfiːvəfjuː/ ▷ *noun* a perennial plant of the daisy family, closely related to camomile, reputed to relieve the symptoms of migraine. ⓒ Anglo-Saxon *feferfuge*, from Latin *febris* fever and *fugare* to put to flight.

feverish /ˈfiːvərɪʃ/ and **feverous** ▷ *adj* **1** suffering from, or showing symptoms of, fever. **2** agitated or restless. • **feverishly** *adverb*. • **feverishness** *noun*.

fever pitch ▷ *noun* a state of high excitement □ *The crowd was at fever pitch.*

fever therapy ▷ *noun* cure by inducement of fever.

few /fjuː/ (*fewer*, *fewest*) ▷ *adj* not many; a small number; hardly any □ *She had few books on the shelf.* ▷ *pronoun* (used as a plural) hardly any things, people, etc □ *There were few today, but many yesterday.* • **a few** a small number; some □ *He took a few into the garden* □ *He had a few rabbits in the hat.* • **as few as** no more than (a stated number). • **every few** (**hours**, **days**, *etc*) at intervals of a few hours, days, etc. • **few and far between** *colloq* rare; scarce. • **a good few** or **quite a few** *informal* a fairly large number; several. • **have had a few** *colloq* to have drunk sufficient alcohol to affect one's behaviour. • **no fewer than** as many as (a stated number). • **precious few** *colloq* hardly any at all. • **the few** the minority of discerning people, as distinct from *the many*. ⓒ Anglo-Saxon *feawe*.

fewer

See Usage Note at **less**.

fey /feɪ/ ▷ *adj* **1** strangely fanciful; whimsical. **2** able to foresee future events; clairvoyant. **3** *chiefly Scots* doomed to die early. **4** *chiefly Scots* in a state of high spirits. • **feyness** *noun*. ⓒ Anglo-Saxon *fæge* doomed to die.

fez /fɛz/ ▷ *noun* (*fezzes* or *fezes*) a hat shaped like a flat-topped cone, with a tassel, worn by some Muslim men. Also called TARBOOSH. ⓒ 19c: from Turkish *fes*, named after Fez, a city in Morocco.

FF ▷ *abbreviation* French franc or French francs.

ff ▷ *abbreviation* **1** *music* fortissimo. **2** and the following (pages, etc). **3** folios.

fiacre /fɪˈakrə/ ▷ *noun* (*fiacres*) a hackney coach; a cab. ⓒ 17c: French, named after the Hôtel de St Fiacre in Paris, where these were first used.

fiancé or **fiancée** /fɪ'ɑ̃seɪ, fɪ'ɒnseɪ/ ⊳ *noun* (***fiancés*** or ***fiancées***) respectively, a man or woman to whom one is engaged to be married. ⓒ 19c: from French *fiancer* to betroth.

fianchetto /fɪaŋ'kɛtoʊ/ ⊳ *noun* (***fianchetti*** /-kɛtiː/) *chess* the early movement of a knight's pawn to allow the movement of a bishop on a long diagonal. ⓒ 19c: Italian diminutive of *fianco* flank.

fiar /'fɪə(r)/ ⊳ *noun, Scots law* the owner of the **fee simple** (ie the right to unconditional inheritance) of a property (contrasted with a LIFE-RENTER of a property). ⓒ 16c: related to FEE.

fiasco /fɪ'askoʊ/ ⊳ *noun* (***fiascos*** or ***fiascoes*** /-oʊz/) **1** originally referring to a musical performance: a ludicrous or humiliating failure. **2** a bizarre or ludicrous happening □ *What a fiasco!* ⓒ 19c: Italian, meaning 'flask'.

fiat /'fiːat, 'faɪat/ ⊳ *noun* **1** an official command; a decree. **2** a formal authorization for some procedure. ⓒ 17c: Latin, meaning 'let it be done'.

fiat currency see under FIDUCIARY ISSUE

fib *colloq* ⊳ *noun* a trivial lie. ⊳ *verb* (***fibbed***, ***fibbing***) *intr* to tell fibs. ⓒ 17c: possibly shortened from *fible-fable* nonsense, from FABLE.

fibber ⊳ *noun* someone who fibs.

fiber see FIBRE

Fibonacci numbers, sequence and **series** /fiːboʊ'nɑːtʃi —/ ⊳ *noun, math* the infinite series of numbers (0, 1, 1, 2, 3, 5, 8, etc) in which each term is the sum of the preceding two terms. ⓒ 19c: named after Leonardo Fibonacci of Pisa (c.1170–c.1230).

fibre or (*N Amer*) **fiber** /'faɪbə(r)/ ⊳ *noun* (***fibres*** or ***fibers***) **1** a fine thread or thread-like cell of a natural or artificial substance, eg cellulose, nylon. **2** a material composed of fibres. **3** any fibrous material which can be made into textile fabrics. **4** *bot* in the stems of woody plants: a long, narrow, thick-walled cell that provides mechanical support for the plant. **5** the indigestible parts of edible plants or seeds, that help to move food quickly through the body □ *dietary fibre.* **6** strength of character; stamina □ *moral fibre.* ● **fibred** *adj.* ● **fibreless** *adj.* ● **to the very fibre of one's being** deeply; fundamentally. ⓒ 14c: from Latin *fibra* thread or fibre.

fibreboard or (*N Amer*) **fiberboard** ⊳ *noun* strong board made from compressed wood chips or other organic fibres.

fibreglass or (*N Amer*) **fiberglass** ⊳ *noun* **1** a strong light plastic strengthened with glass fibres, which is resistant to heat, fire and corrosion, and is used for boat-building, car bodies, etc. **2** material consisting of fine, tangled fibres of glass, used for insulation.

fibre-optic or (*N Amer*) **fiber-optic** ⊳ *adj* containing or using FIBRE OPTICS.

fibre optics or (*N Amer*) **fiber optics** ⊳ *singular noun* the technique of using flexible strands of glass or plastic (OPTICAL FIBRES) to carry information in the form of light signals.

fibrescope or (*N Amer*) **fiberscope** ⊳ *noun, optics* an optical device consisting of a flexible bundle of optical fibres, an eyepiece and an objective lens, capable of transmitting a clear image of objects that would not otherwise be directly visible. Compare ENDOSCOPE. ⓒ 1950s: FIBRE + -SCOPE.

fibril /'faɪbrɪl/ ⊳ *noun* **1** a small fibre or part of a fibre. **2** a root hair. ● **fibrillar** or **fibrillous** *adj.* ⓒ From Latin *fibrilla* small fibre.

fibrillate /'faɪbrɪleɪt, 'fɪ-/ ⊳ *verb* (***fibrillated***, ***fibrillating***) *intr, medicine* said of the muscle fibres of the heart: to contract spontaneously, rapidly, and irregularly. ⓒ 19c..

fibrillation ⊳ *noun* **1** *medicine* the spontaneous, rapid and irregular contraction of the individual muscle fibres in the muscular walls of the chambers of the heart. **2** the production or formation of fibrils or fibres. **3** a mass or bundle of fibres. ⓒ 19c.

fibrillose /'faɪbrɪloʊs, 'fɪ-/ ⊳ *adj* having small fibres, covered with small fibres, or having the appearance of being covered with them. ⓒ 19c.

fibrin /'faɪbrɪn, 'fɪb-/ ⊳ *noun, biochem* an insoluble protein produced from fibrinogen during the blood-clotting process. It forms a network of fibres which trap red blood cells and platelets to seal off the ruptured bood vessel. ⓒ 19c: see FIBRE.

fibrinogen /faɪ'brɪnədʒən, fɪ-/ ⊳ *noun, biochem* a soluble blood plasma protein which the enzyme THROMBIN converts into fibrin during the blood-clotting process. ⓒ 19c: from FIBRIN.

fibrinolysin /faɪbrɪ'nɒlɪsɪn, fɪ-/ ⊳ *noun* **1** *biochem* an enzyme in the blood which causes the breakdown of fibrin in blood clots. **2** a drug having the same effect. ⓒ Early 20c.

fibro /'faɪbroʊ/ ⊳ *noun* (***fibros***) *Austral* **1** a board for lining walls made from a compressed asbestos and cement mixture. Also called **fibrocement**. **2** a house built with such materials.

fibroid /'faɪbrɔɪd/ ⊳ *adj* fibrous. ⊳ *noun, pathol* a benign tumour consisting of fibrous tissue, one or more of which may develop in the muscular walls of the uterus. ⓒ 19c.

fibrosis /faɪ'broʊsɪs/ ⊳ *noun, pathol* the formation of an abnormal amount of fibrous connective tissue over the surface of or in place of normal tissue of an organ or body part, usually as a result of inflammation or injury. See also CYSTIC FIBROSIS. ⓒ 19c..

fibrositis /faɪbroʊ'saɪtɪs/ ⊳ *noun* inflammation of fibrous connective tissue, especially that sheathing the muscles of the back, causing pain and stiffness.

fibrous /'faɪbrəs/ ⊳ *adj* consisting of, containing or like fibre.

fibula /'fɪbjʊlə/ ⊳ *noun* (***fibulae*** /-iː/or ***fibulas***) **1** in the human skeleton: the outer and narrower of the two bones in the lower leg, between the knee and the ankle. Compare TIBIA. **2** the corresponding bone in the hind limb of four-limbed vertebrates. **3** a brooch in the shape of a safety pin. ● **fibular** *adj.* ⓒ 16c: Latin, meaning 'brooch'.

-fic /fɪk/ ⊳ *combining form, forming adjectives* causing, making or producing □ *horrific* □ *scientific.* ⓒ From Latin *-ficus*, from *facere* to do.

fiche /fiːʃ/ ⊳ *noun* short form of MICROFICHE.

fickle /'fɪkəl/ ⊳ *adj* inconstant or changeable in affections, loyalties or intentions. ● **fickleness** *noun.* ⓒ Anglo-Saxon *ficol* deceitful.

fictile /'fɪktaɪl/ ⊳ *adj* **1** capable of being moulded, especially in clay. **2** relating to pottery. ⓒ 17c: from Latin *fictilis*, from *fingere* to mould.

fiction /'fɪkʃən/ ⊳ *noun* **1** literature concerning imaginary characters or events, eg a novel or story. **2** a pretence; a lie. **3** *law* a misrepresentation of the truth, accepted for convenience. ● **fictional** *adj* occurring in or created for fiction. ● **fictionally** *adverb.* ⓒ 14c: from Latin *fictio*, from *fingere* to mould.

fictional, fictitious

These words are often confused with each other.

fictionalize or **fictionalise** ⊳ *verb* (***fictionalized***, ***fictionalizing***) to give a fictional character to (a narrative dealing with real facts); to make into fiction. ● **fictionalization** *noun.* ● **fictionalized** *adj.* ⓒ 19c.

fictitious /fɪk'tɪʃəs/ ⊳ *adj* imagined; invented; not real. ● **fictitiously** *adverb.* ⓒ 17c.

fid ⊳ *noun, naut* **1** a conical pin of hard wood used to open the strands of rope in splicing. **2** a square bar with a shoulder used to support the weight of the topmast. ◎ 17c.

fiddle /ˈfɪdəl/ ▷ *noun* **1 a** a violin, especially when used to play folk music or jazz; **b** *colloq, often disparaging* any violin. **2** *colloq* a dishonest arrangement; a fraud. **3** a raised rim round a table to keep dishes from sliding off it. **4** a manually delicate or tricky operation. ▷ *verb* (***fiddled, fiddling***) **1** *intr* (*often* **fiddle with something**) to play about aimlessly with it; to tinker, toy or meddle with it □ *He was fiddling all the time* □ *She was always fiddling with her hair.* **2** *tr & intr* to falsify (accounts, etc); to manage or manipulate dishonestly □ *to fiddle the cash till.* **3** *tr & intr* to play a violin or fiddle; to play (a tune) on one. • **as fit as a fiddle** in excellent health. • **fiddle while Rome burns** to be preoccupied with trifles in a crisis. • **on the fiddle** *colloq* making money dishonestly □ *He was always on the fiddle.* • **play second fiddle to someone** to be subordinate to them. ◎ Anglo-Saxon *fithele*; compare VIOL.

■ **fiddle around** or **about** to waste time □ *kept fiddling about and got nothing done.*

fiddle-de-dee! ▷ *exclamation, old use* nonsense!

fiddler ▷ *noun* **1** a person who plays the fiddle. **2** a swindler. **3** (*also* **fiddler crab**) any of various small burrowing crabs, so called because the movements of an enlarged pincer-like claw in the male resemble those of a fiddler.

fiddlestick ▷ *noun* **1** a trifle. **2** *old use* a violin bow.

fiddlesticks! ▷ *exclamation* expressing annoyance or disagreement.

fiddling ▷ *adj* unimportant; trifling.

fiddly ▷ *adj* (***fiddlier, fiddliest***) awkward to handle or do, especially if the task requires delicate finger movements.

FIDE ▷ *abbreviation*: *Fédération Internationale des Echecs* (French), the International Chess Federation.

fidei defensor see FD

fidelity /fɪˈdɛlɪtɪ/ ▷ *noun* (***fidelities***) **1** faithfulness; loyalty or devotion (often to a sexual partner). **2** accuracy in reporting, describing or copying something. **3** precision in sound reproduction. ◎ 16c: from Latin *fidelitas*.

fidget /ˈfɪdʒɪt/ ▷ *verb* (***fidgeted, fidgeting***) **1** *intr* to move about restlessly and aimlessly □ *The little boy wouldn't stop fidgeting.* **2** (*often* **fidget with something**) to touch and handle it aimlessly. ▷ *noun* **1** a person who fidgets. **2** (**the fidgets**) nervous restlessness □ *He's got the fidgets.* • **fidgetiness** *noun*. • **fidgety** *adj*. ◎ 17c: from earlier *fidge* to twitch.

fiducial /fɪˈdjuːʃəl/ ▷ *adj* **1** *physics, surveying* applied to a point or line: serving as a standard basis of measuring. **2** showing confidence or reliance. **3** relating to or based on trust or faith. • **fiducially** *adverb*. ◎ 17c: from Latin *fiducia* confidence, from *fidere* to trust.

fiduciary /fɪˈdjuːʃərɪ/ *law* ▷ *noun* (***fiduciaries***) someone who holds anything in trust; a trustee. ▷ *adj* **1** held or given in trust. **2** like a trust; relating to a trust or trustee. **3** depending on public confidence. ◎ 17c: from Latin *fiducia* trust.

fiduciary issue ▷ *noun* an issue of banknotes not backed by gold. Also called **fiat currency**.

fie /faɪ/ ▷ *exclamation, facetious or old use* expressing disapproval or disgust, real or feigned. ◎ 13c: imitating the sound made on perceiving a disagreeable smell.

fief /fiːf/ ▷ *noun* **1** ▷ *feudalism* land granted to a VASSAL by his lord in return for military service, or on other conditions. **2** a person's own area of operation or control. Compare FEOFF. ◎ 17c: from French *fie* or *fief* fee; see FEE.

fiefdom ▷ *noun, feudalism* **1** a piece of land held as a fief. **2** any area of influence autocratically controlled by an individual or organization.

field /fiːld/ ▷ *noun* **1** a piece of land enclosed for crop-growing or pasturing animals. **2** a piece of open grassland. **3** an area marked off as a ground for a sport, etc. **4** *in compounds* an area rich in a specified mineral, etc □ *coalfield* □ *oilfield.* **5** *in compounds* an expanse of something specified, usually from the natural world □ *snowfields* □ *poppy fields.* **6** an area of knowledge, interest or study; speciality. **7** *physics* a region of space in which one object exerts force on another □ *force field.* **8** the area included in something; the range over which a force, etc extends; the area visible to an observer at any one time □ *field of vision.* **9 a** the contestants in a race, competition, etc; **b** all contestants except for the favourite; the rivals of a particular contestant. **10 a** a battlefield □ *fell on the field*; **b** the battle itself. **11** *sport, especially cricket* the fielders collectively. **12** any place away from the classroom, office, etc, eg a **field centre**, where practical experience is gained. See also FIELDWORK. **13** the background to the design on a flag, coin, heraldic shield, etc. **14** (**the field**) the people taking part in a hunt. **15** *math* a system or collection of elements upon which binary operations of addition, subtraction, multiplication and division can be performed excluding division by 0. **16** *computing* a set of characters comprising a unit of information. ▷ *verb* (***fielded, fielding***) **1** *tr & intr, sport, especially cricket* **a** said of a team: to be the team whose turn it is to retrieve balls hit by the batting team; **b** *tr & intr* said of a player: to retrieve the ball from the field; **c** *intr* said of a player: to play in the field. **2** to put forward as (a team or player) for a match. **3** to enter someone in a competition □ *Each group fielded a candidate.* **4** to deal with a succession of (inquiries, etc) □ *to field questions.* • **hold the field** to remain supreme. • **lead the field** to be in the foremost or winning position. • **play the field** *colloq* to try out the range of possibilities before making a choice. • **take the field 1** said of a team: to go on to the pitch ready for a match. **2** to go into battle; to begin a campaign. ◎ Anglo-Saxon *feld*.

field ambulance ▷ *noun* a medical unit on the battlefield.

field artillery ▷ *noun* mobile military equipment for active operations in the battlefield.

field book ▷ *noun* the notebook used by a surveyor or fieldworker.

field colours ▷ *plural noun, military* small flags used for marking the position for companies and regiments in the battlefield; hence, any regimental headquarters' flags.

field day ▷ *noun* **1** a day spent on some specific outdoor activity, such as a nature study. **2** *informal* any period of exciting activity. **3** *military* a day of exercises and manoeuvres.

fielder ▷ *noun, sport, particularly cricket* a player in the field; a member of the fielding side, as distinct from the batting side.

field event ▷ *noun, athletics* a contest involving jumping, throwing, etc, as distinct from a TRACK EVENT.

fieldfare ▷ *noun* a species of thrush, having a reddish-yellow throat and breast spotted with black. ◎ Anglo-Saxon *feldefare*.

field glasses ▷ *plural noun* binoculars.

field goal ▷ *noun, Amer football, basketball* a goal scored from normal play.

field hand ▷ *noun* an outdoor farm labourer.

field hockey ▷ *noun, N Amer* hockey played on grass, as distinct from ice hockey.

field hospital ▷ *noun* a temporary hospital near the scene of battle, for emergency treatment.

field ice ▷ *noun* ice formed in the polar seas as large surfaces, as distinguished from icebergs.

field marshal ▷ *noun* an army officer of high rank. See table at RANK.

fieldmouse ▻ *noun* any of various species of small mouse, native to Europe, non-tropical Asia and S America, with yellowish-brown fur, prominent ears, large beady eyes and a long tail, that live among dense vegetation and feed mainly on seeds, but also eat berries, roots, insects and grubs, and can cause serious damage to tree seedlings.

field officer ▻ *noun* a general term for an army officer between the ranks of captain and general.

field of view and **field of vision** ▻ *noun* what is visible to someone at any given moment.

fieldsman ▻ *noun, cricket, baseball* a fielder.

field mushroom see under AGARIC

field sports ▻ *plural noun* sports carried out in the countryside, such as hunting, shooting, line-fishing, etc.

field trial ▻ *noun, often in plural* a test in practice, as distinct from one under laboratory conditions.

field trip ▻ *noun* an expedition, especially by students, to observe and study something at its location.

fieldwork ▻ *noun* practical work or research done at a site away from the laboratory or place of study.

fieldworker *noun* a person who carries out fieldwork; a practical researcher.

fiend /fiːnd/ ▻ *noun* **1** a devil; an evil spirit. **2** *colloq* a spiteful person. **3** *colloq* an enthusiast for something specified □ ***dope fiend*** □ ***sun fiend.*** ◎ Anglo-Saxon *feond* enemy.

fiendish ▻ *adj* **1** like a fiend. **2** devilishly cruel. **3** extremely difficult or unpleasant. • **fiendishly** *adverb*. • **fiendishness** *noun*.

fierce /fɪəs/ ▻ *adj* (*fiercer, fiercest*) **1** violent and aggressive □ ***a fierce dog.*** **2** intense; strong □ ***fierce competition.*** **3** severe; extreme □ ***a fierce storm.*** **4** *informal* very unpleasant. • **fiercely** *adverb*. • **fierceness** *noun*. ◎ 13c: from French *fers*, from Latin *ferus* savage.

fiery /ˈfaɪərɪ/ ▻ *adj* (*fierier, fieriest*) **1** consisting of fire; like fire. **2** easily enraged □ ***a fiery temper.*** **3** passionate; spirited; vigorous □ ***fiery oratory.*** **4** said of food: hot-tasting; causing a burning sensation. • **fierily** *adverb*. • **fieriness** *noun*. ◎ 13c: FIRE + -Y.

fiesta /fɪˈɛstə/ ▻ *noun* (*fiestas*) **1** especially in Spain and Latin America: a religious festival with dancing, singing, etc. **2** any carnival, festivity or holiday. ◎ 19c: Spanish, meaning 'feast'.

FIFA /ˈfiːfə/ ▻ *abbreviation*: *Fédération Internationale de Football Association* (French), International Federation of Association Football, the world governing body of Association Football, which stages its World Cup tournament every four years.

fife /faɪf/ ▻ *noun* a small type of flute played in military bands □ ***with his musket, fife and drum.*** ▻ *verb* (*fifed, fifing*) *intr* to play on the fife. • **fifer** *noun* a fife player. ◎ 15c: from German *pfifa* pipe or French *fifre* fifer, both from Latin *pipare* to cheep.

FIFO ▻ *abbreviation* first in, first out, a method of pricing goods, controlling stock or storing data in a computer. Compare LIFO.

fifteen /fɪfˈtiːn/ ▻ *noun* **1 a** the cardinal number 15; **b** the quantity that this represents, being one more than fourteen or the sum of ten and five. **2** any symbol for this, eg **15** or **XV**. **3** the age of fifteen. **4** something, especially a garment, or a person, whose size is denoted by the number 15. **5 a** a set or group of fifteen people or things; **b** *rugby union* a team of players. **6** a score of fifteen points. **7** (**15**) *Brit* a film classified as suitable for people aged 15 and over. **8** (**the Fifteen**) the Jacobite rebellion of 1715. ▻ *adj* **1** totalling fifteen. **2** aged fifteen. ◎ Anglo-Saxon *fiftene*; see FIVE and -TEEN.

fifteenth (often written **15th**) ▻ *adj* **1** in counting: **a** next after fourteenth; **b** last of fifteen; **c** in fifteenth position. **2** (**the fifteenth**) **a** the fifteenth day of the month; **b** *golf* the fifteenth hole. ▻ *noun* **1** one of fifteen equal parts. Also *as adj* □ ***a fifteenth share.*** **2** a FRACTION equal to one divided by fifteen (usually written $^1/_{15}$). **3** the position in a series corresponding to fifteen in a sequence of numbers. **4** *music* a double octave. **5** an organ stop sounding two octaves above the DIAPASON.

fifth /fɪfθ, fɪftθ/ (often written **5th**) ▻ *adj* **1** in counting: **a** next after fourth; **b** last of five. **2** in fifth position. **3** (**the fifth**) **a** the fifth day of the month; **b** *golf* the fifth hole. ▻ *noun* **1** one of five equal parts. Also *as adj* □ ***a fifth share.*** **2** a FRACTION equal to one divided by five (usually written $^1/_5$). **3** the position in a series corresponding to five in a sequence of numbers. **4** a person coming fifth, eg in a race or exam □ ***He finished a comfortable fifth.*** **5** *music* **a** an interval consisting of 3 whole tones and a semitone; an interval of four diatonic degrees; **b** a note at that interval from another. ▻ *adverb* fifthly. • **fifthly** *adverb* used to introduce the fifth point in a list. ◎ Anglo-Saxon *fifta*.

the Fifth Amendment ▻ *noun* (*often* **the Fifth**) an amendment to the US constitution which allows a person on trial not to testify against himself or herself and forbids a second trial if a person has been acquitted in a first □ ***take the Fifth Amendment*** □ ***invoked the Fifth.***

fifth column ▻ *noun* **1** a body of citizens prepared to co-operate with an invading enemy. **2** a group of Franco sympathizers in Madrid during the Spanish Civil War who were prepared to betray the city by fighting with the four columns marching on the city. • **fifth columnist** *noun*. ◎ 1936, originally in sense 2.

fifth-generation see under COMPUTER GENERATIONS

fifth wheel ▻ *noun* **1** the spare wheel of a four-wheeled vehicle. **2** a superfluous or useless person or thing.

fifties /ˈfɪftɪz/ (often written **50s** or **50's**) ▻ *plural noun* **1** (**one's fifties**) the period of time between one's fiftieth and sixtieth birthdays □ ***David is in his fifties.*** **2** (**the fifties**) the range of temperatures between fifty and sixty degrees □ ***It must be in the fifties today.*** **3** the period of time between the fiftieth and sixtieth years of a century □ ***born in the 50s.*** Also *as adj* □ ***a fifties hairstyle.***

fiftieth (often written **50th**) ▻ *adj* in counting: **1** next after forty-ninth. **2** last of fifty. **3** in fiftieth position. ▻ *noun* **1** one of fifty equal parts. Also *as adj* □ ***a fiftieth share.*** **2** a FRACTION equal to one divided by fifty (usually written $^1/_{50}$). **3** a person coming fiftieth, eg in a race or exam □ ***He finished a bedraggled fiftieth.*** ◎ Anglo-Saxon; see FIFTY and -TH.

fifty /ˈfɪftɪ/ ▻ *noun* (*fifties*) **1 a** the cardinal number 50; **b** the quantity that this represents, being one more than forty-nine, or the product of ten and five. **2** any symbol for this, eg **50** or **L**. Also *in compounds, forming adjectives and nouns*, with cardinal numbers between *one* and *nine* □ ***fifty-six.*** **3** the age of fifty. **4** something, especially a garment, or a person, whose size is denoted by the number 50. **5** a set or group of fifty people or things. **6** a score of fifty points. ▻ *adj* **1** totalling fifty. Also *in compounds, forming adjectives*, with ordinal numbers between *first* and *ninth* □ ***fifty-fourth.*** **2** aged fifty. See also FIFTIES, FIFTIETH. ◎ Anglo-Saxon *fiftig*; see FIVE + -TY.

fifty-fifty ▻ *adj* **1** said of a chance: equal either way. **2** half-and-half. ▻ *adverb* divided equally between two; half-and-half.

fiftyish ▻ *adj* **1** about fifty years old. **2** about fifty.

fig ▻ *noun* **1** any of a group of tropical and sub-tropical trees and shrubs of the mulberry family bearing a soft pear-shaped fruit full of tiny seeds. **2** the green, brown or purple pear-shaped fleshy fruit produced by a fig tree, eaten fresh or dried. • **not give** or **care a fig** *colloq* not to care in the least. ◎ 13c: from Latin *ficus* fig or fig tree.

fig. ▻ *abbreviation* **1** ▻ figurative or figuratively. **2** figure, ie a diagram, illustration.

fight /faɪt/ ▷ *verb* (***fought*** /fɔːt/, ***fighting***) **1** *tr & intr* to attack or engage (an enemy, army, etc) in combat. **2** to take part in or conduct (a battle, campaign, etc). **3** *tr & intr* (*sometimes* **fight against something** or **someone**) to oppose them (eg an enemy, a person, an illness, a cause, etc) vigorously. **4** *intr* to quarrel; to disagree, sometimes coming to blows ◻ *They fought all evening.* **5** *intr* (*often* **fight for something** or **someone**) to struggle or campaign on its or their behalf; to struggle or campaign in an attempt to achieve or maintain it ◻ *fight for the right to remain silent.* **6** *intr* to make (one's way) with a struggle. ▷ *noun* **1** a battle; a physically violent struggle. **2** a quarrel; a dispute; a contest. **3** resistance. **4** the will or strength to resist ◻ *lost all his fight.* **5** a boxing-match. **6** a campaign or crusade ◻ *the fight for freedom.* • **fight a losing battle** to continue trying for something when there is little chance of succeeding ◻ *She was fighting a losing battle against the illness.* • **fighting fit** *colloq* in vigorous health. • **fight it out** to fight over something until one side wins. • **fight shy of something** to avoid it. • **fight to the finish** to fight until completely exhausted. Ⓒ Anglo-Saxon *feohtan.*

■ **fight back** to resist an attacker; to counter an attack.

■ **fight something back** or **down** to try not to show one's emotions, etc.

■ **fight someone off** to repulse them (especially an attacker).

■ **fight something off** to get rid of or resist (an illness).

fighter ▷ *noun* **1** a person who fights, especially a professional boxer. **2** a person with determination. **3** (*also* **fighter plane**) an aircraft equipped to attack other aircraft.

fighting ▷ *adj* engaged in, or eager or fit for, war or combat. ▷ *noun* the act of fighting or contending.

fighting chance ▷ *noun* a chance to succeed dependent chiefly on determination.

fighting cock ▷ *noun* **1** a gamecock. **2** a pugnacious person.

fighting fish ▷ *noun* a small freshwater fish, native to Thailand, that is renowned for its aggressive behaviour, and commonly held in captivity for staged fights.

fighting fit ▷ *adj* in good physical condition; at the peak of one's fitness.

fighting talk and **fighting words** ▷ *plural noun* spirited words demonstrating an inclination to fight.

fig leaf ▷ *noun* **1** the leaf of a fig tree. **2** *art* the traditional representation of a fig leaf covering the genitals of a statue or picture, etc of a nude figure. **3** any device used to cover up something considered embarrassing.

figment /ˈfɪgmənt/ ▷ *noun* something imagined or invented ◻ *a figment of the imagination.* Ⓒ 15c: from Latin *figmentum* a fiction.

figurant /ˈfɪgjʊrənt/ ▷ *noun* a ballet dancer or actor who is one of a group forming background for the solo dancers. Ⓒ 18c: French, meaning 'a ballet dancer', from *figurer* to figure.

figuration /fɪgəˈreɪʃən, fɪgjʊˈreɪʃən/ ▷ *noun* **1** the act of giving figure or form. **2** representation by, or in, figures or shapes. **3** ornamentation with a design. **4** *music* **a** consistent use of particular melodic or harmonic series of notes; **b** florid treatment.

figurative ▷ *adj* **1** metaphorical; not literal. **2** said of writing, etc: full of figures of speech, especially metaphor. **3** representing a figure; representing using an emblem or symbol, etc. **4** said of art: not abstract; showing things as they look; representational; pictorial. Compare ABSTRACT *adj* 3. • **figuratively** *adverb.* • **figurativeness** *noun.*

figure /ˈfɪgə(r), ˈfɪgjʊə(r); *N Amer* ˈfɪgjər/ ▷ *noun* **1** the form of anything in outline. **2** a symbol representing a number; a numeral. **3** a number representing an amount; a cost or price ◻ *He quoted a figure of £50 to do the job.* **4** an indistinctly seen or unidentified person ◻ *He saw a figure coming through the mist.* **5** a representation of the human form, especially in painting or sculpture. **6** (**figures**) arithmetical calculations; statistics. **7** a well-known person ◻ *a public figure.* **8** a specified impression that one makes by one's behaviour ◻ *He cut a lonely figure walking down the street.* **9** a diagram or illustration, especially in a text. **10** the shape of one's body ◻ *to have a good figure.* **11** an image, design or pattern. **12** a geometrical shape, formed from a combination of points, lines, curves or surfaces. **13** *music* a short distinctive series of notes in music. **14** *dancing, sport, etc* a set pattern of steps or movements. Compare FIGURE SKATING. **15** a FIGURE OF SPEECH. ▷ *verb* (***figured***, ***figuring***) **1** *N Amer* to think; to reckon. **2** to imagine; to envisage. **3** *intr, colloq* to be probable or predictable; to make sense ◻ *That figures!* **4** to decorate (a surface) with a design; to add elaborations to (music). • **keep one's figure** to remain slim. • **lose one's figure** to become fat. Ⓒ 13c: from Latin *figura*, from *fingere* to mould.

■ **figure in something** to play a part in a story, incident, etc.

■ **figure on something** to intend to do it.

■ **figure someone out** to understand how they are thinking or what their motivation is for something ◻ *At last I've figured him out.*

■ **figure something out** to work it out; to begin to understand it.

figured ▷ *adj* **1** marked or decorated with figures. **2** in the form of figures.

figured bass ▷ *noun, music* a musical shorthand indicating a bass or THOROUGH BASS part, with numerals written below notes to indicate harmonies to be played above it.

figurehead ▷ *noun* **1** a leader in name only, without real power. **2** *historical* a carved wooden figure fixed to a ship's prow.

figure-hugging ▷ *adj* referring or relating to a tight piece of clothing which reveals the contours of the body ◻ *wore a figure-hugging dress.*

figure of eight ▷ *noun* a pattern, movement, etc in the shape of the number eight ◻ *The skater did a series of figures of eight.*

figure of fun ▷ *noun* someone who is ridiculed by others.

figure of speech ▷ *noun* any of many devices such as METAPHORS, SIMILES, etc that enliven language.

figure skating ▷ *noun* skating in which a skater sketches out prescribed patterns on ice.

figure skater *noun* a skater who specializes in figure skating.

figurework ▷ *noun* counting or calculation using numbers.

figurine /ˈfɪgjʊriːn, ˈfɪgə-/ ▷ *noun* a small carved or moulded figure, usually representing a human form. Ⓒ 19c: French, from Italian *figurina* small figure.

filagree see FILIGREE

filament /ˈfɪləmənt/ ▷ *noun* **1** a fine thread or fibre. **2** *elec* in electrical equipment: a fine wire with a high resistance that emits heat and light when an electric current is passed through it, eg in a light bulb, toaster, etc. **3** *bot* the stalk of a stamen, which bears the anther. **4** *bot* a long strand of cells joined end to end, as in certain algae and fungi. • **filamentary** *adj.* • **filamentous** *adj.* Ⓒ 16c: from Latin *filare* to spin, from *filum* thread.

filar /ˈfaɪlə(r)/ ▷ *adj, optics* having threads or wires. Ⓒ 19c: from Latin *filum* thread + -AR.

filaria /fɪˈlɛərɪə/ (***filariae*** /-iː/) ▷ *noun* any worm of the genus **Filaria** of nematode worms, introduced into the blood of vertebrates by mosquitoes. • **filarial** *adj*. ◷ 19c: from Latin *filum* thread.

filariasis /fɪləˈraɪəsɪs/ ▷ *noun* a disease caused by the presence of filariae in the blood, and characterized by inflammation of the lymphatic vessels.

filbert /ˈfɪlbət/ ▷ *noun* **1** the nut of the cultivated hazel. **2** (*also* **filbert tree**) the tree bearing the nut. ◷ 14c: probably named after St Philibert, whose feast day (August 22) fell in the nutting season.

filch /fɪltʃ/ ▷ *verb* (***filched, filching***) to steal something small or trivial. ◷ 16c, meaning 'to take as booty'.

file¹ /faɪl/ ▷ *noun* **1** a folder or box in which to keep loose papers. **2** a collection of papers so kept, especially dealing with a particular subject. **3** *computing* an organized collection of data that is stored in the external memory of a computer, and can be accessed and manipulated as a single named unit. **4** a line of people or things, especially soldiers, positioned or moving one behind the other □ *single file*. **5** *chess* any of the eight lines of squares extending across the chessboard from player to player. Compare RANK¹. ▷ *verb* (***filed, filing***) **1** (*often* **file something away**) to put (papers, etc) into a file. **2** (*often* **file for something**) to make a formal application to a law court on (a specified matter) □ *file a complaint* □ *file for divorce*. **3** to place (a document) on official or public record. **4** *intr* to march or move along one behind the other □ *The soldiers filed onto the square*. **5** said of a reporter: to submit (a story) to a newspaper. • **filer** *noun*. • **filed** *adj*. • **on file** retained in a file (*noun* 1 or 3 above) for reference; on record. ◷ 16c: from Latin *filum* a thread, originally referring to a string or wire on which papers were hung.

file² /faɪl/ ▷ *noun* **1** a steel hand tool with a rough surface consisting of fine parallel grooves with sharp cutting edges, used to smooth or rub away wood, metal, etc. **2** a small object of metal or emeryboard used for smoothing or shaping fingernails or toenails. Also called a **nailfile**. ▷ *verb* (***filed, filing***) to smooth or shape (a surface) using a file. • **filer** *noun*. • **filed** *adj*. ◷ Anglo-Saxon *fyl*.

file copy ▷ *noun* a copy, often a photocopy, of a document which is kept on file for reference.

filefish ▷ *noun* a tropical fish, with skin granulated like a FILE². ◷ 18c.

filename ▷ *noun, computing* any name or reference used to specify a file stored in a computer.

file server ▷ *noun, computing* a central database of computer files available to all the terminals which are linked to one system.

filet /ˈfiːleɪ/ ▷ *noun* French for FILLET¹ □ *filet de boeuf*. ◷ 19c.

filet mignon /ˈfiːleɪ miːnˈjɔ̃/ ▷ *noun* (***filets mignons***) a thin slice, usually of beef, cut from the centre of the fillet. ◷ 19c: French, meaning 'dainty fillet'.

filial /ˈfɪlɪəl/ ▷ *adj* **1** belonging or relating to, or resembling, a son or daughter □ *filial duties*. **2** *biol, genetics* denoting any successive generation following a parental generation (abbreviation $\mathbf{F_1}$, $\mathbf{F_2}$, etc). ◷ 14c: from Latin *filia* daughter, and *filius* son.

filibeg or **philibeg** /ˈfɪlɪbɛg/ ▷ *noun* a kilt. ◷ 18c: from Scottish Gaelic *feileahbeag*, from *feileadh* pleat or fold + *beag* little.

filibuster /ˈfɪlɪbʌstə(r)/ ▷ *noun* **1** especially in the US Senate: **a** the practice of making long speeches, often continuing for a number of hours, to delay the passing of laws; **b** a member of a law-making assembly who does this. Compare OBSTRUCTIONISM. **2** a freebooter or military adventurer. ▷ *verb* (***filibustered, filibustering***) *intr* **1** especially in the US Senate: to obstruct legislation by making long speeches. **2** *intr* to engage in unlawful military action. • **filibusterer** *noun*. ◷ 19c in sense 1; 16c in sense 2: from Spanish *filibustero*, probably from Dutch *vrijbuiter*, from *vrij* free and *buit* booty; compare FREEBOOTER.

filicide /ˈfɪlɪsaɪd/ ▷ *noun* someone who murders their own child. ◷ 19c: from Latin *filia, filius* daughter or son, + -CIDE.

filigree /ˈfɪlɪgriː/ or **filagree** ▷ *noun* (***filigrees*** or only in sense 2 ***filagrees***) **1** delicate work in gold or silver wire, twisted into convoluted forms and soldered together, used in jewellery, etc. **2** any delicate ornamentation □ *a pastry filigree*. ▷ *adj* made of, or as if with, filigree. ◷ 17c: from French *filigrane*, from Latin *filum* thread + *granum* grain.

filing cabinet ▷ *noun* a set of drawers, usually metal, for holding collections of papers and documents, ie for holding files (see FILE¹).

filings ▷ *plural noun* particles or shavings rubbed off with a FILE².

fill ▷ *verb* (***filled, filling***) **1** (*also* **fill something up**) to make it full □ *fill the bath with water*. **2** *intr* (*also* **fill up**) to become full □ *The petrol tank filled up quickly*. **3** to take up all the space in something. **4** to satisfy (a need); to perform (a role) satisfactorily. **5** (*sometimes* **fill up**) to occupy (time). **6** (*also* **fill something in** or **up**) to put material into (a hole, cavity, etc) to level the surface. **7** to appoint someone to (a position or post of employment). **8** **a** to take up (a position or post of employment); **b** to work in (a job), sometimes temporarily □ *She filled the post for six months*. **9** *intr* said of a sail: to billow out in the wind. ▷ *noun* **1** anything used to fill something. **2** *sometimes in compounds* material such as stones, gravel, etc used to fill a space to a required level □ *rock-fill*. • **be filled with feelings** to be profoundly affected by them. • **eat one's fill** to consume enough to satisfy. • **fill the bill** to be perfectly suited for something. • **to have had one's fill of something** or **someone** to have received or experienced more of it or them than one can tolerate. ◷ Anglo-Saxon *fyllan*.

■ **fill someone in** to inform them fully; to brief them.

■ **fill something in 1** to write information as required on to (a form, etc). **2** said of a drawing: to complete it.

■ **fill in for someone** to take over their work temporarily. See also FILL-IN.

■ **fill out** to put on weight and become fatter or plumper.

■ **fill something out 1** to enlarge it satisfactorily; to amplify it. **2** *chiefly N Amer* to fill in (a form, etc).

■ **fill something up 1** to fill in (a form, etc). **2** to make it full.

filler ▷ *noun* **1** a person or thing that fills. **2** a paste-like substance used for filling cracks or holes, usually in walls of buildings. **3** a material or substance used to add bulk or weight to something, or to fill a gap or space, etc □ *Duck down was used as a filler for the duvet*. **4** an article, photograph, clip, etc used to fill a gap between main features in a newspaper, or a TV or radio programme.

fillet /ˈfɪlɪt/ ▷ *noun* **1 a** a piece of meat without bone, taken as an undercut of the SIRLOIN, or the fleshy part of the thigh □ *pork fillet*; **b** (*in full* **fillet steak**) the most highly valued cut of beef, cut from the lowest part of the LOIN; **c** the flesh of a fish without its bone □ *salmon fillet*. **2** a thin narrow strip of wood, metal or other material. **3** a ribbon, band, strip of lace, etc worn in the hair or round the neck. **4** *archit* a narrow flat band, often between mouldings. ▷ *verb* (***filleted, filleting***) **1 a** to cut fillets from (meat or fish); **b** to remove the bones from (a fish); **c** to prepare (meat) as fillets, often by beating or rolling it. **2** to decorate with or as if with a fillet. ◷ 14c: from Latin *filum* thread.

fill-in ▷ *noun* someone who temporarily takes the place of another; a substitute. See also FILL IN FOR SOMEONE at FILL.

filling ▻ *noun* **1** *dentistry* a specially prepared substance, such as amalgam, gold or composite resin, that is inserted into a cavity that has been drilled in a decaying tooth. **2** food put inside a pie, sandwich, etc. ▻ *adj* said of food, a meal, etc: substantial and satisfying.

filling-station ▻ *noun, originally US* a place where motorists can buy petrol and other supplies; a petrol station. ⓒ 1920s.

fillip /ˈfɪlɪp/ ▻ *noun* **1** something that has a stimulating or brightening effect; a boost. **2** a movement of a finger when it is engaged under the thumb and then suddenly released away from the hand. ▻ *verb* (***filliped, filliping***) **1** to excite or stimulate. **2** to put into motion by a fillip; to flick. ⓒ 16c as *philippe*.

filly /ˈfɪlɪ/ ▻ *noun* (***fillies***) **1** a young female horse or pony. **2** *colloq* a young girl or woman. ⓒ 15c: probably from Norse *fylja*.

film /fɪlm/ ▻ *noun* **1** a strip of thin flexible plastic or other substance, coated so as to be light-sensitive and exposed inside a camera to produce still or moving pictures. **2** a series of images, often of moving objects, recorded and edited to tell a story, present a subject, etc, and shown in the cinema (also called **motion picture**, **cinema film**, **movie**), or shown on TV or video (also called **TV movie**). **3** a fine skin, membrane, or coating over something. **4** *sometimes in compounds* a thin sheet of plastic used for wrapping □ *clingfilm*. ▻ *verb* (***filmed, filming***) **1** *tr & intr* to record any series of images, usually moving objects, using a TV camera, cine camera, video camera, camcorder, etc. **2** *intr* the overall activity of setting up a film set, directing actors and recording material on camera to be edited at a later stage. ⓒ 19c in modern senses: Anglo-Saxon *filmen* membrane.

■ **film over** to become covered with a FILM *noun* 3.

filmable ▻ *adj* particularly suited to being made into a film.

film fiction ▻ *noun* FACTION[2].

filmgoer ▻ *noun* a person who regularly attends films, and is usually particularly knowledgeable about cinema. Also called **cinema-goer**. ⓒ Early 20c.

filmic ▻ *adj* referring or relating to the cinema, film or cinematography. • **filmically** *adverb*.

film noir /— nwɑː(r)/ ▻ *noun, cinema* a style of cinema film popular in American cinema in the 1940s and 1950s, in which the darker side of human nature is presented, in a bleak and often starkly urban setting. ⓒ 20c: French, meaning 'black film'.

filmography ▻ *noun* (***filmographies***) **1** a list of films of a particular actor or director. **2** a list of films or articles about cinema or films, referred to in a particular essay or article. ⓒ 1960s: modelled on BIBLIOGRAPHY.

filmset ▻ *verb, printing* to set (text, etc) by filmsetting.

film set ▻ *noun* the scenery, furniture, etc arranged for the scene of a cinema film.

filmsetting ▻ *noun, printing* typesetting by exposing text on to film which is then transferred to printing plates. Also called **photocomposition**. ⓒ 1950s.

film speed ▻ *noun* the sensitivity of a film or paper to light, measured by an ASA or DIN index, which assigns low numbers to slow film and higher numbers to faster film.

film star ▻ *noun* a celebrated film actor or actress.

film strip ▻ *noun* a series of photographs on a strip of film, for separate projection as slides.

filmy ▻ *adj* (***filmier, filmiest***) said of a fabric: thin, light and transparent.

filo or **phyllo** /ˈfiːloʊ/ ▻ *noun* (*in full* **filo pastry**) a type of Greek flaky pastry made in thin sheets. ⓒ 1940s: from Modern Greek *phyllon* leaf.

Filofax /ˈfaɪloʊfaks/ ▻ *noun, trademark* (*often* **filofax**) a small loose-leaf personal filing system containing a diary and a variable selection of other information, eg addresses or maps, to help the user organize their affairs. Compare PERSONAL ORGANIZER. ⓒ 1920s: representing the colloquial pronunciation of *file of facts*, originating in the 1920s but not widely used until the 1980s.

filter /ˈfɪltə(r)/ ▻ *noun* **1** a porous substance that allows liquid, gas, smoke, etc through, but traps solid matter, impurities, etc. **2** a device containing this. **3** a fibrous pad at the unlit end of a cigarette, and some types of cigars, that traps some of the smoke's impurities, such as tar. **4** a transparent tinted disc used to reduce the strength of certain colour frequencies in the light entering a camera or emitted by a lamp. **5** *elec, radio* a device for suppressing the waves of unwanted frequencies. **6** *Brit* a traffic signal at traffic lights that allows vehicles going in some directions to proceed while others are stopped □ *The pedestrian failed to notice the filter for traffic turning left.* ▻ *verb* (***filtered, filtering***) **1** *tr & intr* to pass something through a filter, often to remove impurities, particles, etc. **2** *intr* to go past little by little. **3** *intr, Brit* said of vehicles: to proceed with one of the streams of traffic at a filter. See also FILTRATE. ⓒ 16c as *filtre*: from Latin *filtrum* felt used as a filter.

■ **filter something out** to remove (impurities, etc) from (liquids, gases, etc) by filtering.

■ **filter through** or **out** *intr* said of news: to leak out, often gradually.

filterable or **filtrable** ▻ *adj* able to pass through a filter; capable of being filtered.

filter bed ▻ *noun* a layer of sand, gravel, clinker, etc used for filtering water or sewage.

filter coffee ▻ *noun* coffee made by allowing water to pass through a filter paper which contains ground coffee.

filter paper ▻ *noun* a porous paper through which a liquid can be passed in order to separate out any solid particles suspended in it.

filter tip ▻ *noun* **1** a FILTER *noun* 3. **2** a cigarette with a filter □ *She smokes filter tips.* • **filter-tipped** *adj* □ *filter-tipped cigarettes.*

filth /fɪlθ/ ▻ *noun* **1** repulsive dirt; any foul matter □ *dog filth.* **2** anything that is perceived as physically or morally obscene □ *That magazine is absolute filth!* **3** (**the filth**) *slang, derog* the police. • **filthily** *adverb*. • **filthiness** *noun*. ⓒ Anglo-Saxon *fylth*, from *ful* foul.

filthy ▻ *adj* (***filthier, filthiest***) **1** extremely dirty. **2** obscenely vulgar □ *filthy language.* **3** offensive or vicious □ *a filthy lie.* **4** *informal or dialect* extremely unpleasant □ *filthy weather.* ▻ *verb* (***filthied, filthying***) to make filthy □ *He filthied his shirt playing football.* ▻ *adverb, colloq* used for emphasis, especially showing disapproval □ *filthy rich.*

filthy lucre ▻ *noun, humorous* money, profit. ⓒ 16c: from Titus 1.11 *aischron kerdos*, literally 'dishonourable gain'.

filtrate /ˈfɪltreɪt/ *chem* ▻ *noun* the clear liquid obtained after filtration. ▻ *verb* (***filtrated, filtrating***) *tr & intr* to filter. • **filtration** *noun*. ⓒ 17c: from Latin *filtrare* to filter.

filtration /fɪlˈtreɪʃən/ ▻ *noun* act or process of filtering.

fin ▻ *noun* **1** a thin wing-like projection on a fish's body consisting of a thin fold of skin supported by bone or cartilage, used for propelling the fish through the water, balancing, steering, display and in some cases protection. **2** anything that resembles a fin in appearance or function, eg the vertical projection in the tail of an aircraft, a blade projecting from the hull of a ship, a swimmer's flipper, attachments on 1950s cars. ▻ *verb* (***finned, finning***) **1** to provide something with fins. **2** to cut off the fins from a fish. • **finless** *adj*. • **finned** *adj*. • **finny** *adj*. ⓒ Anglo-Saxon *finn*; Latin *pinna* feather or fin is probably the same word.

finable or **fineable** /ˈfaɪnəbəl/ ▻ *adj* liable to a fine.

finagle /fɪˈneɪgəl/ ▻ *verb* (***finagled, finagling***) **1** *tr & intr* to obtain by guile or swindling, to wangle. **2** (*often* **finagle someone out of something**) to cheat someone (out of something). ⓘ 1920s: from an English dialect form *fainaigue* cheat.

final /ˈfaɪnəl/ ▻ *adj* **1** occurring at the end; last in a series, after all the others. **2** completed; finished. **3** said of a decision, etc: definite; not to be altered; conclusive. ▻ *noun* **1 a** the last part of a competition at which the winner is decided; **b** (**finals**) the last round or group of contests resulting in a winner ☐ *Our team has made it to the finals.* **2** (**finals**) the examinations held at the end of a degree course, etc. **3** *music* **a** the keynote or tonic; **b** the lowest note in the AUTHENTIC modes; **c** a fourth above it in the PLAGAL. **4** the final edition of a newspaper ☐ *Have you bought the final yet?* ⓘ 14c: from Latin *finalis* pertaining to an end, from *finis* end.

final demand ▻ *noun* a last bill or reminder sent to someone before legal action is taken to recover an unpaid debt.

finale /fɪˈnɑːlɪ/ ▻ *noun* (*finales* /-lɪz/) **1** the grand conclusion to a show, etc. **2** the last or closing movement of a symphony or other piece of music. ⓘ 18c: Italian, from Latin *finis* end.

finalist /ˈfaɪnəlɪst/ ▻ *noun* someone who reaches the final round in a competition.

finality /faɪˈnalɪtɪ/ ▻ *noun* **1** the state of being final or concluded. **2** a final or conclusive act.

finalize or **finalise** /ˈfaɪnəlaɪz/ ▻ *verb* (***finalized, finalizing***) **1** to sign (especially a commercial agreement), taking into account the concluding stages of discussion and negotiation. **2** to decide on or finally agree to something; to settle on (a particular plan or formula). • **finalization** *noun.*

finally /ˈfaɪnəlɪ/ ▻ *adverb* **1** at last; in the end; eventually ☐ *He finally arrived.* **2** lastly. **3** irrevocably; decisively ☐ *The city was finally destroyed.* **4** at the end of a speech, etc: as the last point or conclusion ☐ *And finally, the vote of thanks.*

finals see under FINAL

the final solution ▻ *noun, historical* the German Nazi policy and process, from 1941, of exterminating European Jews. ⓘ 1940s: English version of the German *Endlösung.*

finance ▻ *noun* /ˈfaɪnans, faɪˈnans, fɪ-/ **1** money affairs and the management of them ☐ *Government finance.* **2** the money or funds needed or used to pay for something. **3** (**finances**) one's financial state. ▻ *verb* /faɪˈnans, fɪ-/ (***financed, financing***) to provide funds for something. ⓘ 14c: from French *finer* to settle, from Latin *finis* an end.

finance company and **finance house** ▻ *noun* a firm whose main activity is lending money, usually to enable the borrower to make a specific purchase.

financial ▻ *adj* **1** relating to finance or finances. **2** *Austral & NZ slang* having money; financially solvent. • **financially** *adverb.*

financial year ▻ *noun* **1** any annual period for which accounts are made up. **2** *chiefly Brit* the twelve-month period, in Britain starting 6 April, used in accounting, annual taxation, etc, over which the Government's financial policies and estimates are made. Compare FISCAL YEAR.

financier /fɪˈnansɪə(r), faɪ-/ ▻ *noun* someone engaged in large financial transactions. ⓘ 17c: French.

finback see FIN WHALE

finch /fɪntʃ/ ▻ *noun* (***finches***) any of several small songbirds with short stout conical beaks adapted for cracking seeds, eg sparrow, canary, chaffinch, goldfinch. ⓘ Anglo-Saxon *finc.*

find /faɪnd/ ▻ *verb* (***found*** /faʊnd/, ***finding***) **1** to discover through search, enquiry, mental effort or chance. **2** to seek out and provide something ☐ *I'll find you a plumber.* **3** to realize or discover something. **4** to experience something as being (easy, difficult, etc) ☐ *find it hard to express oneself.* **5** to consider; to think. **6** to get or experience ☐ *find pleasure in reading.* **7** to become aware of something or someone ☐ *found her beside him.* **8** to succeed in getting (time, courage, money, etc for something). **9** to see or come across ☐ *a bird found only in Madagascar.* **10** to reach ☐ *find one's best form.* **11** *tr & intr, law* said of a jury or court, etc: to decide on and deliver a specified verdict about (an accused person) ☐ *found the accused innocent* ☐ *found that the accused was guilty* ☐ *found a verdict of guilty.* ▻ *noun* something or someone that is found; an important discovery. • **all found** with food and housing provided. • **find it in oneself** or **in one's heart** to be prepared (to do something hurtful, etc). • **find oneself** to find the role, etc that satisfies one. • **find oneself doing something** to discover or realize that one is doing it ☐ *found themselves agreeing.* • **find one's feet** to establish oneself confidently in a new situation. ⓘ Anglo-Saxon *findan.*

■ **find out about something** to discover or get information about it.

■ **find someone out** to detect them in wrongdoing; to discover the truth about them.

finder ▻ *noun* **1** someone who finds something. **2** *astrol* a small telescope attached to a larger one for finding the required object and setting it in the centre of the field. **3** short for VIEWFINDER. • **finders keepers** *colloq* used especially by children: a saying meaning that someone who finds something is entitled to keep it.

fin de siècle /fɛ̃ də sɪˈɛklə/ *noun* **1** the end of the 19th century. **2** the end of the 20th century. ▻ *adj* (***fin-de-siècle***) **1 a** characteristic of the ideas of the late 19th century, particularly of the Modernist movement and a decadent society; **b** decadent. **2** referring or relating to the late 20th century ☐ *fin-de-siècle angst.* ⓘ 19c: French, meaning 'end of century or era'.

finding /ˈfaɪndɪŋ/ ▻ *noun* **1** a thing that is found or discovered. **2** the event of discovering something. **3** *law* a decision or verdict reached as the result of a judicial inquiry. **4** (*usually* **findings**) conclusions reached as the result of some research or investigation.

find the lady see THREE-CARD TRICK

fine¹ /faɪn/ ▻ *adj* **1** of high quality; excellent; splendid. **2** beautiful; handsome. **3** *facetious* grand; superior ☐ *her fine relations.* **4** said of weather: bright; not rainy. **5** well; healthy. **6** quite satisfactory ☐ *That's fine by me.* **7** pure; refined. **8** thin; delicate. **9** close-set in texture or arrangement. **10** consisting of tiny particles. **11** intricately detailed ☐ *fine embroidery.* **12** slight; subtle ☐ *fine adjustments.* ▻ *adverb* **1** *colloq* satisfactorily. **2** finely; into fine pieces. • **finely** *adverb.* • **fineness** *noun.* • **cut** or **run it fine** *colloq* to leave barely enough time for something. • **fine and dandy** working or doing well; OK now; in order after there has been a problem. • **get something down to a fine art** to find the most efficient way of doing it. • **not to put too fine a point on it** used as an introductory expression before speaking honestly or bluntly. ⓘ 13c: from French *fin* end, in the sense of 'boundary or limit'.

fine² /faɪn/ ▻ *noun* an amount of money to be paid as a penalty, constituting a punishment for breaking a regulation or law. ▻ *verb* (***fined, fining***) to impose a fine on someone. • **in fine** in total; to sum up. ⓘ 12c: from French *fin* end, settlement or ending a dispute.

fineable see FINABLE

fine art ▻ *noun* **1** art produced mainly for its aesthetic value. **2** as the name of a college or university course: a course combining art history and sometimes practical art tuition. **3** (*usually* **fine arts**) painting, drawing, sculpture and architecture; the arts that appeal to the sense of beauty.

fine leg ▷ *noun, cricket* **1** a position in fielding between LONG LEG and SQUARE LEG. **2** a fielder in this position.

finery[1] /'faɪnərɪ/ ▷ *noun* splendour; very ornate and showy clothes, jewellery, etc. ⓒ 17c.

finery[2] /'faɪnərɪ/ ▷ *noun* (***fineries***) a furnace for making iron malleable. ⓒ 17c: from French *finerie*, from *finer* to refine; compare FINE[1].

fines herbes /*French* finzɛʀb/ *plural noun, cookery* a mixture of herbs for use in cooking, often in phrases □ *omelette aux fines herbes.* ⓒ 19c: French, meaning 'fine herbs'.

finespun ▷ *adj* delicate; over-subtle.

finesse /fɪ'nɛs/ ▷ *noun* (*plural* ***finesses*** in sense 3 only) **1** skilful elegance or expertise. **2** tact and poise in handling situations. **3** *cards* an attempt by a player holding a high card to win a trick with a lower one. ▷ *verb* (***finessed, finessing***) to attempt to win a trick by finesse. ⓒ 15c: French, meaning 'fineness'.

fine-tooth comb or **fine-toothed comb** ▷ *noun* a comb with narrow close-set teeth. • **go over** or **through something with a fine-tooth comb** to search or examine it very thoroughly or exhaustively.

fine-tune ▷ *verb* to make slight adjustments to something to obtain optimum performance.

finger /'fɪŋgə(r)/ ▷ *noun* **1 a** one of the five jointed extremities of the hand; **b** any of the four of these other than the thumb; **c** *as adj* □ *finger buffet*; **d** *in compounds* □ *fingerprint.* **2** the part of a glove that fits over a finger. **3** anything resembling or similar to a finger in shape. **4** a measure or quantity of alcoholic spirits in a glass, filling it to a depth which is equal to the width of a finger. ▷ *verb* (***fingered, fingering***) **1** to touch or feel something with the fingers, often affectionately or lovingly; to caress □ *He fingered the velvet.* **2** *music* to indicate (on a part or composition) the choice and configuration of fingers to be used for a piece of music. **3** *slang* (*also* **fingerfuck**) to stimulate someone sexually by inserting the finger into an orifice, usually the vulva or anus. **4** *slang* to identify (a criminal) to the police, etc. **5** *colloq* used by computer users: to call up a file showing information about another computer user, eg whether they are logged-on, where their office is located, etc. • **fingerless** *adj* □ *fingerless gloves.* • **be all fingers and thumbs** *colloq* to be clumsy in handling or holding things. • **get one's fingers burnt** *colloq* to suffer for one's over-boldness or mistakes. • **have a finger in every pie** *colloq, often derog* to have an interest, or be involved, in many different things. • **not lay a finger on someone** not to touch or harm them. • **lift a finger** or **hand** see under LIFT. • **point the finger at someone** *colloq* to blame or accuse them. • **pull** or **get one's finger out** *slang* to make an effort to start working more efficiently. • **put the finger on someone** *slang* to finger (*verb* 4) (a criminal, etc). • **slip through someone's fingers** to manage to escape from them. • **wrap** or **twist someone round one's little finger** *colloq* to be able to get what one wants from them. ⓒ Anglo-Saxon.

fingerboard ▷ *noun* the part of a violin, guitar, etc against which the strings are pressed by the fingers to change the note.

fingerbowl ▷ *noun* a small bowl of water for cleaning one's fingers at the table.

finger buffet ▷ *noun* a buffet meal consisting of food which may be eaten with the fingers, such as small sandwiches, cocktail sausage rolls, canapés, etc (*sometimes* called **finger food**), without any need for a knife and fork.

finger-dry ▷ *verb* to dry (hair) without using a hairdrier or brush by repeatedly running one's fingers through it.

fingered ▷ *adj* **1** soiled or dirtied by a lot of touching. **2** *usually in compounds* having or using a finger or fingers of a specified kind or number.

fingerfuck see under FINGER

fingering /'fɪŋgərɪŋ/ ▷ *noun* **1** the correct positioning of the fingers for playing a particular musical instrument or piece of music. **2** the written or printed notation indicating this. **3** touching with the fingers.

fingerling ▷ *noun* a fish no bigger than a finger, especially a salmon parr or young trout less than a year old.

fingermark ▷ *noun* a mark left on a surface by dirty or greasy fingers.

fingernail ▷ *noun* the nail at the tip of one's finger.

fingerprint ▷ *noun* **1** the print or inked impression made by the pattern of minute swirling ridges on the surface of the end joints of the fingers and thumbs, which is unique to each person, and can be used as a means of identification, especially of criminals. **2** any accurate and unique identifying feature or characteristic, especially that produced by analysis of a sample of a person's DNA, using a technique known as **DNA fingerprinting** or GENETIC FINGERPRINTING. ▷ *verb* **1** to make an impression of someone's fingerprints. **2** to take a sample of someone's DNA.

fingerstall ▷ *noun* a covering for protecting the finger, especially after an injury.

fingertip ▷ *noun* the end or tip of one's finger. • **have something at one's fingertips** to know a subject thoroughly and have information readily available.

finicky /'fɪnɪkɪ/ and **finickety** /fɪ'nɪkɪtɪ/ ▷ *adj* **1** too concerned with detail. **2** said of a task: intricate; tricky. **3** fussy; faddy. ⓒ 19c: probably derived from FINE[1].

finish /'fɪnɪʃ/ ▷ *verb* (***finished, finishing***) (*often* **finish off** or **up**) **1** *tr & intr* to bring something to an end, or come to an end; to reach a natural conclusion. **2** to complete or perfect something. **3** to use, eat, drink, etc the last of something □ *I've finished the coffee.* **4** *intr* to reach or end up in a certain position or situation. **5** to give a particular treatment to the surface of (cloth, wood, etc). ▷ *noun* **1** the last stage; the end. **2** the last part of a race, etc. **3** perfecting touches put to a product. **4** the surface texture given to cloth, wood, etc. • **finisher** *noun.* • **fight to the finish** to fight till one party is dead or so severely disabled that they are unable to continue. ⓒ 14c as *fenys*: from Latin *finire* to end.

■ **finish someone** or **something off 1** *colloq* to exhaust them emotionally or physically □ *His emotional blackmailing really finished me off last night.* **2** *colloq* to defeat or kill them □ *The lion finished the buffalo off.*

■ **finish with someone 1** to end a relationship with them. **2** to stop dealing with or needing them.

■ **finish with something** to stop using or needing it.

finished ▷ *adj* **1** *colloq* no longer useful, productive, creative, wanted or popular. **2** said of a performer: accomplished.

finishing post ▷ *noun* the post marking the end of a race, especially for horses.

finishing-school ▷ *noun* a private school where girls are taught social skills and graces. ⓒ Early 19c.

finishing touches ▷ *plural noun* the last minor improvements needed to achieve perfection □ *put the finishing touches to the flower arrangement.*

finite /'faɪnaɪt/ ▷ *adj* **1** having an end or limit. **2** *math* having a fixed, countable number of elements. **3** *grammar* said of a verb: being in a form that reflects person, number, tense, etc, as distinct from being an infinitive or participle. Compare INFINITIVE. • **finitely** *adverb.* • **finiteness** or **finitude** /'fɪnɪtʃuːd, 'faɪn-/ *noun.* ⓒ 15c: from Latin *finitus* limited, from *finire* to end or limit.

Finlandization or **Finlandisation** /fɪnləndaɪ'zeɪʃən/ ▷ *noun, politics* the tendency of a small state to shape its foreign policy so as to accommodate a much more powerful neighbour. ⓘ 1960s: based on the conciliatory rather than confrontational development of the relationship between Finland and the Soviet Union after 1944.

Finn ▷ *noun* a native or citizen of Finland. ⓘ Anglo-Saxon *Finnas* Finns.

finnan /'fɪnən/ and **finnan haddock** ▷ *noun* haddock cured in the smoke from peat, turf or green wood. ⓘ 18c: probably named after Findhorn or Findon in NE Scotland.

Finnish ▷ *adj* belonging or relating to Finland, a republic in Scandinavia, its inhabitants or their language. ▷ *noun* the official language of Finland.

Finno-Ugric /fɪnoʊ'juːgrɪk, -'uːgrɪk/ and **Finno-Ugrian** /-grɪən/ ▷ *noun* a family of languages spoken in Scandinavia (eg FINNISH and ESTONIAN), Central Europe (HUNGARIAN) and W Asia, belonging to the north-western group of the URAL-ALTAIC languages.

finocchio /fɪ'nɒkɪoʊ/ ▷ *noun* (*finocchios*) a dwarf variety of fennel. Also called **dwarf fennel** and **Florence fennel**. ⓘ 18c: Italian, from Latin *feniculum* fennel.

fin whale and **finback** ▷ *noun* a rorqual.

fiord see FJORD

fioritura /fjɒrɪ'tʊərə/ ▷ *noun* (*fioriture* /-'riː, -'reɪ/) *music* a florid embellishment to a piece of music, especially by the performer. ⓘ 19c: Italian, meaning 'flowering'.

fipple /'fɪpəl/ ▷ *noun, music* the piece of wood, etc that plugs the mouthpiece of a recorder or other similar wind instrument, with a narrow slit through which the player blows. ⓘ 17c: probably from the dialectal sense 'loose lower lip' or 'pouting lip'; compare Icelandic *flipi* lip of a horse.

fir /fɜː(r)/ ▷ *noun* **1** any of various coniferous evergreen trees native to north temperate regions and Central America, and usually having silvery or bluish foliage, with leathery needle-like leaves. **2** any of various related trees, eg the Douglas fir. **3** the wood of these trees. ⓘ Anglo-Saxon *fyrh*.

fire /faɪə(r)/ ▷ *noun* (*plural* ***fires*** in senses 2, 3 and 4 only) **1** flames coming from something that is burning. **2** an occurrence of destructive burning of something □ *a warehouse fire* □ *a forest fire*. **3** mainly in homes: a mass of burning wood, coal or other fuel, usually in a grate, etc, used for warmth or cooking □ *log fire* □ *peat fire*. Also called **open fire**. **4** a gas or electric room-heater □ *gas fire* □ *electric fire*. **5** the discharge of firearms. **6** the launching of a missile. **7** heat and light produced by something burning or some other source. **8** enthusiasm; passion; ardour. **9** fever; a burning sensation from inflammation, etc. **10** sparkle; brilliance (eg of a gem). **11** *astrol* **a** *as adj* relating to a group of three signs of the zodiac, ie Aries, Leo and Sagittarius □ *the fire signs*; **b** one of four elements in the zodiac. ▷ *verb* (***fired***, ***firing***) **1** *tr & intr* to discharge (a gun); to send off (a bullet or other missile) from a gun, catapult, bow, etc □ *fired the gun*. **2** to launch (a rocket, missile, etc). **3** to detonate (an explosive). **4** said of a gun, missile, etc: to be discharged, launched, etc □ *The gun fired*. **5** to direct (eg questions) in quick succession at someone. **6** *colloq* to dismiss someone from employment, usually because of bad discipline □ *You're fired!* **7** *intr* said of a vehicle engine, boiler, etc: to start working when a spark causes the fuel to burn □ *The motor fired*. **8** to put fuel into (a furnace, etc). **9** to inspire or stimulate someone. **10** *pottery* to bake (pottery, bricks, etc) in a kiln, usually at a very high temperature. ▷ *exclamation* **1** a cry, warning others of a fire. **2** the order to start firing weapons, etc. • **fireless** *adj*. • **between two fires** under attack from two sides. • **draw someone's fire** to deliberately divert their gunfire, criticism, etc towards oneself. • **fire away** *colloq* an expression inviting someone to start saying what they have to say, especially to begin asking questions. • **go through fire and water for someone** or **something** to suffer or undergo danger for their sake. • **hold one's fire** to stop shooting. • **in the line of fire 1** between the guns and the target, and therefore in danger of being hit. **2** exposed to questioning or verbal attack from an opponent. • **on fire 1** burning. **2** filled with enthusiasm, love, etc. • **open fire on someone** or **something** to begin shooting at them, with a gun, artillery, etc. • **play with fire** *colloq* to take risks; to act recklessly. • **pull something out of the fire** to rescue the situation at the last minute. • **return someone's fire** to shoot back at them. • **set fire to something** or **set something on fire** to make it burn; to set light to it. • **set someone on fire** to fill them with enthusiasm, love, etc. • **under fire 1** being shot at. **2** being criticized or blamed. See also CATCH FIRE at CATCH, CEASEFIRE. ⓘ Anglo-Saxon *fyr*.

■ **fire at** or **on someone** to discharge a gun, etc at them.

■ **fire someone up** to make them highly excited or agitated about something □ *fired him up with enthusiasm*.

■ **fire up** to catch light and produce a lively flame □ *The coal fired up well*.

fire alarm ▷ *noun* a bell or other device activated to warn people of fire.

fire and brimstone ▷ *noun* the supposed condition or torment of hell; eternal damnation.

firearm ▷ *noun* (*often* **firearms**) a gun, pistol, revolver or rifle, carried and used by an individual.

fireball ▷ *noun* **1** ball lightning. **2** a mass of hot gases at the centre of a nuclear explosion. **3** *colloq* a lively energetic person. **4** *astron* a large bright meteor.

firebomb ▷ *noun* an incendiary bomb. ▷ *verb* to attack or destroy something with one or more firebombs. ⓘ 19c.

firebrand ▷ *noun* **1** a piece of burning wood. **2** someone who stirs up unrest; a troublemaker.

firebreak ▷ *noun* a strip of land in a forest which is cleared to stop the spread of fire.

firebrick ▷ *noun* a heat-resistant brick made from fire clay used to line furnaces, fireplaces, etc.

fire brigade ▷ *noun, chiefly Brit* an organized team of people trained and employed to prevent and extinguish fires, and to perform other dangerous duties such as rescuing people, etc. *N Amer equivalent* **fire department**. See also FIREFIGHTER.

firebug ▷ *noun, colloq* an arsonist.

fire clay ▷ *noun* a type of clay that contains large amounts of hydrous aluminium silicates and can withstand high temperatures, used for making fire-resistant pottery, firebricks, etc.

firecracker ▷ *noun* a small firework that bangs repeatedly.

fired ▷ *adj* **1** *pottery* referring to ceramics which have been baked in a kiln □ *high fired*. **2** *usually in compounds* affected or having the appearance of having been affected in a specified way by fire □ *I prefer well-fired rolls*. **3** *in compounds* powered by a specified type of fuel □ *gas-fired central heating*. ▷ *verb, past tense, past participle of* FIRE.

firedamp ▷ *noun* an explosive mixture of methane gas and air, formed in coalmines by the decomposition of coal. See also AFTERDAMP.

fire department see under FIRE BRIGADE

firedog ▷ *noun* an ANDIRON.

fire door ▷ *noun* **1** a fire-resistant door between two parts of a building to prevent the spread of fire within the building, which should be kept closed when not in use. **2**

a door leading out of a building which can be easily opened from the inside, used as an emergency exit.

fire drill ▷ *noun* the routine of evacuating and checking a building, etc, to be followed in case of fire, or a practice of this routine.

fire-eater ▷ *noun* **1** a performer who pretends to swallow fire from flaming torches. **2** an aggressive or quarrelsome person.

fire engine ▷ *noun* a vehicle which carries firefighters and firefighting equipment to the scene of a fire.

fire escape ▷ *noun* an external metal staircase or other device by which people can escape from a burning building.

fire extinguisher ▷ *noun* a portable device containing water, liquid carbon dioxide under pressure, foam, etc, for spraying on to a fire to put it out, either by cooling it or by excluding oxygen.

firefighter ▷ *noun* a person who is trained to put out large fires and rescuing those endangered by them, usually as part of a FIRE BRIGADE.

firefighting *noun* the act, process or occupation of fighting fire. Also *as adj*.

firefly ▷ *noun* (***fireflies***) any of a number of species of small winged nocturnal beetles, found mainly in tropical regions, that emit light in a series of brief flashes.

fireguard ▷ *noun* a metal or wire-mesh screen for putting round an open fire to protect against sparks or falling coal, logs, etc.

fire hose ▷ *noun* a hose supplying water for extinguishing fires, usually attached to a hydrant.

fire hydrant ▷ *noun* a HYDRANT.

fire insurance ▷ *noun* insurance against loss of property, etc by fire.

fire irons ▷ *plural noun* a set of tools for looking after a household fire, usually including a poker, tongs, brush and shovel. Also called COMPANION SET.

firelighter ▷ *noun* a block of flammable material placed underneath the fuel to help light a fire.

fireman ▷ *noun* **1** a male member of a FIRE BRIGADE, officially called a FIREFIGHTER. **2** on steam trains: the person who stokes the fire. **3** a stoker, eg of a furnace, on a steamboat, etc. **4** *mining* a miner responsible for safety measures, checking for firedamp, supervising blasts, etc.

fireman's lift ▷ *noun* a method of carrying someone by putting them face down over one's shoulder, used especially by firefighters in rescuing unconscious or injured people.

fireplace ▷ *noun* mainly in homes: the recess of an open fire in a room and its surrounding area which has an opening to a chimney above it.

fire-power ▷ *noun, military* the destructive capacity of an artillery unit.

fireproof ▷ *adj* resistant to fire and fierce heat. ▷ *verb* to make something resistant to fire.

firer ▷ *noun* a person who fires (a gun, ceramics, a furnace, etc).

fire-raiser ▷ *noun* someone who deliberately sets fire to buildings, etc. Compare ARSONIST at ARSON.

fire-raising ▷ *noun, Scots law* ARSON.

firescreen ▷ *noun* a decorative screen put on the fireplace when there is no fire.

fireship ▷ *noun* **1** a ship which carries firefighters and firefighting equipment, for putting out fires on ships, oil rigs, etc. **2** *historical* a ship carrying combustible materials, set alight and sent to float freely amongst enemy ships in order to destroy them.

fireside ▷ *noun* the area round a fireplace, especially as a symbol of home. ▷ *adj* domestic; familiar.

fire station ▷ *noun* a building where fire engines and equipment are housed and firefighters are stationed.

fire-storm ▷ *noun* a huge blaze which fans its own flames by creating its own draught, especially as a result of heavy bombing.

firethorn ▷ *noun* PYRACANTHA.

firetrap ▷ *noun* **1** a building without adequate escape routes in case of fire. **2** a building likely to burn easily.

fire-water ▷ *noun, colloq* any strong alcoholic spirit, especially whisky.

fireweed ▷ *noun* rose-bay willow-herb, often the first vegetation to spring up on burned ground.

firewood ▷ *noun* wood for burning as fuel.

firework ▷ *noun* **1** a device containing combustible chemicals, designed to produce spectacular coloured sparks, flares, etc, often with accompanying loud bangs, when ignited. **2** (**fireworks** or **firework display**) a show at which such devices are let off for entertainment, usually to mark a special event. **3** (**fireworks**) *colloq* a show of anger or bad temper.

firing ▷ *noun* **1** a discharge of guns, etc. **2** the process of baking ceramics, etc in a kiln. **3** the act of fuelling a furnace, etc. **4** the ignition of a boiler, etc. **5** *bell-ringing* the simultaneous ringing of a peal of bells.

firing line ▷ *noun* the position from which gunfire, etc is delivered, especially the front line of battle.

firing squad ▷ *noun* a detachment of soldiers with the job of shooting a condemned person.

firkin /ˈfɜːkɪn/ ▷ *noun* **1** *brewing* a measure equal to 9 gallons (c. 40 l). **2** a small container with a capacity equal to quarter of a barrel, varying in amount depending on the commodity. ◷ 15c as *ferdekyn*: from Dutch *vierde* fourth + -KIN.

firm[1] /fɜːm/ ▷ *adj* **1** strong; compact; steady. **2** solid; not soft or yielding. **3** definite □ ***a firm offer.*** **4** said of prices, markets, etc: steady or stable, with a slight upward trend. **5** determined; resolute. **6** said of a mouth or chin: suggesting determination. ▷ *adverb* in a determined and unyielding manner; with resolution □ ***hold firm to one's promise.*** ▷ *verb* (***firmed***, ***firming***) to make something firm or secure □ ***He firmed the soil around the plant.*** ● **firmness** *noun*. ◷ 14c as *ferme*: from Latin *firmus* firm or solid.

■ **firm up** said of prices, markets, etc: to become more stable, usually with a slight upward trend □ ***Prices were firming up.***

■ **firm something up** to discuss (ideas, plans, etc) and make them clearer and more definite □ ***Can we firm up the plans for your visit?***

firm[2] /fɜːm/ ▷ *noun* **1** any organization or individual engaged in economic activity with the aim of producing goods or services for sale to others; a business or company. **2** a business partnership. ◷ 18c in sense 2; 16c, meaning 'one's signature': from Italian *firma* signature, from Latin *firmare* to confirm, to ratify by one's signature, from *firmus* firm or solid.

firmament /ˈfɜːməmənt/ ▷ *noun, literary, old use* the sky; heaven. ◷ 13c: from Latin *firmamentum*, from *firmus* firm or solid; relating to the earlier belief that the position of the stars was fixed.

firmly ▷ *adverb* in a firm way; earnestly, sincerely □ ***He shook his friend's hand firmly.***

firmware ▷ *noun, computing* a software program which cannot be altered and is held in a computer's read-only memory, eg the operating system. ◷ 1960s: from FIRM[1], modelled on SOFTWARE.

first /fɜːst/ (often written **1st**) ▷ *adj* **1** in counting: before all others; before the second and following ones. **2** earliest in time or order; the starting object of a series of objects. **3** (**the first**) **a** the first day of the month; **b** *golf* the first hole. **4** the most important; foremost in importance □ *first prize.* **5** basic; fundamental □ *first principles.* **6** *music* **a** having the higher part □ *the first violins;* **b** being the principal player □ *the first clarinet.* ▻ *adverb* **1** before anything or anyone else. **2** foremost □ *got in feet first.* **3** before doing anything else □ *first make sure of the facts.* **4** for the first time □ *since he first saw him.* **5** preferably; rather □ *I'd die first.* **6** firstly. ▻ *noun* **1** a person or thing coming first, eg in a race or exam. **2** *colloq* a first occurrence of something; something never done before □ *That's a first for me!* **3** the beginning; the start □ *from first to last.* **4** denoting the first or lowest forward GEAR (sense 2) in a motor vehicle □ *She changed from first to second.* **5** (**a first**) *education, chiefly Brit* first-class honours in a university degree; a degree of the highest class. • **at first** at the start of something; early on in the course of something. • **at first hand** directly from the original source □ *to obtain information at first hand.* • **first and last** essentially; on the whole. • **first come, first served** those who respond before others to an offer have priority over them. • **first thing** *colloq* early; before anything else; as the first action of the day □ *I'll do it first thing in the morning.* • **first things first** an expression suggesting that one should organize oneself by doing the most important things before other things. • **get to** or **make first base** to complete the first stage of a process. • **in the first place** from the start; to begin with □ *He didn't want to go in the first place.* • **not have the first idea** or **not know the first thing about something** *colloq* to be completely ignorant about it; to know nothing about it. ⏲ Anglo-Saxon *fyrest.*

first aid ▻ *noun* immediate emergency treatment given to an injured or ill person.

first-born *literary or old use* ▻ *noun* the eldest child in a family. ▻ *adj* eldest.

first-class ▻ *adj* **1** referring to the best or highest grade in terms of value, performance or quality. **2** excellent. **3** referring to the most comfortable grade of accommodation in a train, plane, etc □ *He took a first-class ticket from Edinburgh to Aberdeen.* **4** *chiefly Brit* the category of mail most speedily delivered. Also *as noun.* ▻ *adverb* (**first class**) by first-class mail, transport, etc □ *to send it first class.* □ *to travel first class* ⏲ 18c.

first cousin see COUSIN

first cousin once removed see COUSIN ONCE REMOVED

first-day cover ▻ *noun, philately* an envelope bearing a newly-issued stamp postmarked with the stamp's date of issue.

first-degree ▻ *adj* **1** *medicine* denoting the least severe type of burn in which only the outer layer of the skin is damaged, characterized by pain and reddening of the skin surface □ *first-degree burn.* **2** *N Amer law* denoting the most serious of the two levels of murder, ie unlawful killing with intent and premeditation.

first estate see under ESTATE 5

first finger ▻ *noun* the finger next to the thumb.

first floor ▻ *noun* **1** the floor directly above the ground floor. **2** *US* the ground floor.

first foot *Scottish* ▻ *noun* (*also* **first-footer**) the first person to enter one's house in the New Year. ▻ *verb* (**first-foot**) to enter someone's house as a first foot. • **first-footing** *noun* the activity of going to first-foot neighbours, friends, etc, usually taking gifts of food and drink.

first fruits ▻ *plural noun* **1** the first produce of the season. **2** the first results or proceeds from a new enterprise.

first-generation ▻ *adj* **1** denoting the first or earliest stage in technological development □ *a first-generation missile.* **2** *computing* see under COMPUTER GENERATION.

first-hand ▻ *adj, adverb* direct; from the original source; without an intermediary.

first in, first out see FIFO

first lady ▻ *noun, N Amer, chiefly US* (*often* **First Lady**) **1** the wife or partner of the governor of a city, state or country, especially of the US President. **2** a woman who is highly regarded in a particular field or activity, such as music, fashion, etc □ *Vivienne Westwood is often considered the first lady of fashion.*

first language see under LANGUAGE

first lieutenant an officer in the US army, air force and marine corps. See table at RANK.

first light ▻ *noun* the time in the morning when daylight first appears in the sky; dawn.

first love ▻ *noun* **1 a** the emotion felt by someone when they fall in love for the first time; **b** the person who someone feels this emotion for. **2** someone's favourite activity, hobby, etc □ *Cycling is his first love.*

firstly ▻ *adverb* used to introduce a list of things: before all others; in the first place; to begin with.

first name ▻ *noun* one's personal name as distinct from one's family name or surname. Compare CHRISTIAN NAME, FORENAME. • **be on first-name terms** to be friendly enough to address one another by first names.

first night ▻ *noun* the first public performance of a play, film, etc at a particular venue; opening night.

first offender ▻ *noun* a person found guilty of a crime who has no previous conviction.

first-past-the-post ▻ *adj* referring or relating to an election system in which voters have one vote only and whoever gets most votes wins, without necessarily gaining an ABSOLUTE MAJORITY, often contrasted with a system of PROPORTIONAL REPRESENTATION.

first person see under PERSON

the first post ▻ *noun, military* the first bugle call of a series that denotes that it is time to retire at night. Compare THE LAST POST.

first quartile see under QUARTILE

first-rate ▻ *adj* **1** being of the highest quality, as opposed to SECOND-RATE, etc. **2** excellent; fine.

first refusal ▻ *noun* an agreement allowing a prospective customer to buy goods, etc before they are offered to others □ *We'll give you first refusal on this offer.*

first school ▻ *noun* a primary school.

first strike ▻ *noun, military, politics* a pre-emptive attack on an enemy, intended to destroy their nuclear weapons before they can be brought into use. Also *as adj* □ *first-strike capability.*

first-time buyer ▻ *noun* someone buying a property who has not previously owned a home, and therefore does not have one to sell.

First World ▻ *noun* the richest and technologically most developed countries of the world, used in contrast to THIRD WORLD.

First World War see WORLD WAR I

firth /fɜːθ/ ▻ *noun* especially in Scotland: a river estuary or an inlet. ⏲ 15c: from Norse *fjörthr* fjord.

fiscal /ˈfɪskəl/ ▻ *adj* **1** belonging or relating to government finances or revenue. **2** belonging or relating to financial matters generally. ▻ *noun, Scottish* a PROCURATOR FISCAL. • **fiscally** *adverb.* ⏲ 16c: from Latin *fiscus* rush-basket or purse.

fiscal drag ▻ *noun, econ* the effect of inflation on tax revenues if tax allowances are not kept in line with inflation, and individuals therefore pay relatively higher amounts of tax reducing their net income, thereby reducing demand for goods and services.

fiscal year ▷ *noun, chiefly N Amer* the twelve-month period, in the US starting 1 July, used in accounting, annual taxation, etc, over which the Government's financial policies and estimates are made. Compare FINANCIAL YEAR.

fish ▷ *noun* (***fish*** or ***fishes***) **1** any cold-blooded aquatic vertebrate that has no legs, and typically possesses paired fins, breathes by means of gills, and has a bony or cartilaginous skeleton and a body covered with scales. **2** *in compounds* any of various water-inhabiting creatures □ ***shellfish*** □ ***jellyfish***. **3** the flesh of fish used as food. Compare FLESH *noun* 2. **4** *derog, colloq* a person □ ***an odd fish*** □ ***a cold fish***. **5** (**the Fish**) *astron, astrol* PISCES. ▷ *verb* (***fished***, ***fishing***) **1** *intr* to catch or try to catch fish □ ***She was fishing all day.*** **2** to catch or try to catch fish in (a river, lake, etc) □ ***fish a river.*** **3** *intr* to search or grope □ ***fished in his bag for a pen.*** **4** *intr* (*usually* **fish for something**) to seek information, compliments, etc by indirect means. • **drink like a fish** *colloq* to be in the habit of drinking a lot of alcohol. • **a fish out of water** someone in an unaccustomed, unsuitable situation which makes them ill at ease. • **have other fish to fry** *colloq* to have other, more important, things to do. ◷ Anglo-Saxon *fisc*.

■ **fish something out** to retrieve it.

fish and chips and (*Scottish*) **fish supper** ▷ *noun* a meal consisting of a fillet of fish deep-fried in batter, served with potato chips, and traditionally bought ready cooked at a **fish and chip shop** or **chip shop**. ◷ 19c.

fishcake ▷ *noun* cooked fish and mashed potato made into a round flat shape, coated in breadcrumbs and fried or grilled.

fisher ▷ *noun* **1** any animal that catches fish for food. **2** a PEKAN. **3** *old use* a fisherman.

fisherman ▷ *noun* a person who fishes as a job or hobby.

fishery ▷ *noun* (***fisheries***) **1** an area of water where fishing takes place, particularly sea waters; a fishing ground. **2** the business or industry of catching, processing and selling fish.

fish-eye lens ▷ *noun, image tech* a convex camera lens with an extremely wide angle and a small focal length, giving a scope of nearly 180°.

fish face ▷ *noun, derog* a term of abuse, sometimes used in a friendly way.

fish farm ▷ *noun* a place where fish are bred and reared in a confined area as a business.

fish farmer ▷ *noun* a person who owns, manages or runs a fish farm. • **fish farming** *noun*.

fish finger ▷ *noun* an oblong piece of filleted or minced fish coated in breadcrumbs.

fishgig see FIZGIG *noun* 3

fish-hawk ▷ *noun* an osprey.

fish hook ▷ *noun* a hook with barbs for gripping the jaw of a fish taking the bait.

fishing ▷ *noun* **1** the sport or business of catching fish. **2** a fishing ground.

fishing ground ▷ *noun* an area of water that is good for fishing.

fishing-line ▷ *noun* a strong line, usually made of nylon, with a fish hook attached.

fishing-rod ▷ *noun* a long flexible rod to which a fishing-line, and usually a reel, is attached.

fishing tackle ▷ *noun* nets, lines, rods, hooks and other equipment used for fishing.

fish knife ▷ *noun* a specially-shaped and usually decorated knife with a broad, blunt-edged blade used for eating fish.

fish-ladder ▷ *noun* a series of small steps built on a river at a waterfall or dam to enable fish to ascend and swim upstream.

fishmonger ▷ *noun* a retailer of fish. ◷ 15c.

fishnet ▷ *noun* **1** a net for catching fish. **2** *as adj* said of clothes: having an open mesh, like netting □ ***fishnet tights***.

fish slice ▷ *noun* a kitchen utensil with a flat slotted head, for lifting and turning food in a frying-pan, etc.

fish supper see FISH AND CHIPS

fishtail ▷ *adj* shaped like the tail of a fish. ▷ *verb* (***fishtailed***, ***fishtailing***) *intr* **1** said of an aircraft: to swing the aircraft's tail from side to side, to reduce speed while gliding downward. **2** said of a car, vehicle, etc: to skid when the back of the vehicle swings from side to side.

fishwife ▷ *noun derog* a loud-voiced, coarse-mannered woman.

fishy ▷ *adj* (***fishier***, ***fishiest***) **1 a** relating to fish; like a fish □ ***smell very fishy***; **b** consisting of fish □ ***I fancy something fishy for dinner.*** **2** *colloq* dubious; questionable. • **fishiness** *noun*.

fissile /ˈfɪsaɪl/ ▷ *adj* **1** *geol* said of certain rocks, eg shale: tending to split or capable of being split. **2** *nuclear physics* capable of undergoing nuclear fission. ◷ 17c: from Latin *fissilis* that can be split.

fission /ˈfɪʃən/ ▷ *noun* **1** a splitting or division into pieces. **2** *biol* the division of a cell or a single-celled organism into two or more new cells or organisms as a means of asexual reproduction. **3** *nuclear physics* see NUCLEAR FISSION. • **fissive** *adj*. ◷ 19c: from Latin *fissio* splitting; compare FISSURE.

fissionable ▷ *adj, nuclear physics* capable of nuclear fission. ◷ 1940s.

fissiparous /fɪˈsɪpərəs/ ▷ *adj, biol* reproducing by fission. ◷ 19c: from Latin *fissus* split + *parere* to bring forth.

fissure /ˈfɪʃə(r)/ ▷ *noun* **1** *geol* a long narrow crack or fracture especially in a body of rock, the Earth's surface or a volcano. **2** *anatomy* a natural narrow cleft or groove that divides an organ such as the brain into lobes. ▷ *verb* (***fissured***, ***fissuring***) *tr & intr* to crack, split or divide. ◷ 14c: from Latin *fissura* split, from *findere* to split.

fist /fɪst/ ▷ *noun* **1** a tightly closed or clenched hand with the fingers and thumb doubled back into the palm. **2** *old use* a hand. **3** *old use, informal* a person's handwriting. **4** *printing* a mark, shaped like a pointing hand, used to direct the reader to a reference note, different section, etc. Also called **index**. ▷ *verb* (***fisted***, ***fisting***) to strike or hit with the fist. ◷ Anglo-Saxon *fyst*.

fistful ▷ *noun* (***fistfuls***) an amount that can be held in a closed hand; a handful. ◷ 17c.

fisticuffs /ˈfɪstɪkʌfs/ ▷ *plural noun, humorous* fighting with fists. ◷ 17c: from FIST + CUFF.

fistula /ˈfɪstjʊlə/ ▷ *noun* (***fistulas*** or ***fistulae*** /-liː/) *pathol* an abnormal connection between two internal organs or body cavities, or between an internal organ or body cavity and the surface of the skin, usually caused by infection or injury. • **fistular** or **fistulous** *adj*. ◷ 14c: Latin, meaning 'tube' or 'pipe'.

fit[1] ▷ *verb* (***fitted*** or (*N Amer*) ***fit***, ***fitting***) **1** *tr & intr* to be the right shape or size for something or someone □ ***Fortunately the new car fitted into the garage*** □ ***The jeans fitted him well.*** **2** to be suitable or appropriate for something □ ***a punishment that fits the crime.*** **3** *tr & intr* to be consistent or compatible with something □ ***a theory that fits the facts.*** **4** to install or put something new in place □ ***fit the new kitchen sink.*** **5** to equip □ ***Warning! This car is fitted with an alarm.*** **6** (*often* **fit someone for something**) to make them suitable □ ***qualities that fit her for the job.*** **7** to try clothes on someone to see where adjustment is needed □ *The tailor fitted the suit by pinning the seams.* ▷ *noun* the way something fits according to its shape or size □ *a good fit* □ *a tight fit.* ▷ *adj* (*fitter*, *fittest*) **1 a** healthy; feeling good □ *Are you fit today?* **b** healthy, especially because of exercise □ *He's the fittest of all.* **2** about to do something, or apparently so □ *looked fit to drop.* ▷ *adverb* enough to do something □ *laughed fit to burst.* • **fitly** *adverb.* • **fitness** *noun.* • **fit for something** suited to it; good enough for it. • **fit like a glove** to fit perfectly. • **fit the bill** to be perfectly suited to something; to be just right. • **see** or **think fit** to choose to do something. ⓒ 15c.

■ **fit in 1** said of someone in a social situation: to behave in a suitable or accepted way □ *She never quite fitted in.* **2** to be appropriate or to conform to certain arrangements □ *The dates of the flight fitted in with my plans.*

■ **fit in** or **into something** to be small or few enough to be contained in it □ *Five people fitted into the car.*

■ **fit someone** or **something in** to find time to deal with them or it □ *I can't fit you in before Friday.*

■ **fit something out** to furnish or equip it with all necessary things for its particular purpose □ *fit out the ship.*

■ **fit something together** or **fit something in** to insert or place it in position.

■ **fit someone up** *colloq* to incriminate them; to frame them.

■ **fit something up** to install it by putting it up and making it work □ *fitted up the satellite dish.*

fit[2] ▷ *noun* **1** a sudden attack of one or more symptoms, usually of an involuntary and relatively violent nature, eg convulsions in grand mal epilepsy, eg *epileptic fit*, or paroxysms of coughing, eg *coughing fit*. **2** a burst, spell or bout □ *a fit of giggles.* • **by** or **in fits and starts** in irregular spells; spasmodically. • **in fits** *colloq* laughing uncontrollably. • **have** or **throw a fit** to become very angry. ⓒ Anglo-Saxon *fitt* struggle.

fitch /fɪtʃ/ ▷ *noun* **1** a polecat. **2** the fur of the polecat. ⓒ 16c: from Dutch *visse*, *fisse*, from French *fissel*.

fitful ▷ *adj* irregular, spasmodic or intermittent; not continuous. • **fitfully** *adverb.* • **fitfulness** *noun.* ⓒ 17c.

fitment /ˈfɪtmənt/ ▷ *noun* a piece of equipment or furniture which is fixed to a wall, floor, etc.

fitted ▷ *adj* **1** made to fit closely □ *fitted sheets.* **2** said of a carpet: covering the floor entirely. **3** fixed; built-in □ *fitted cupboards.* **4** said of a kitchen, etc: with built-in shelves, cupboards, etc, usually of matching style.

fitter ▷ *noun* a person who installs, adjusts or repairs machinery, equipment, etc.

fitting ▷ *adj* suitable; appropriate. ▷ *noun* **1** an accessory or part □ *a light fitting.* **2** (**fittings**) fitted furniture or equipment. **3** an act or an occasion of trying on a specially made piece of clothing, to see where adjustment is necessary. • **fittingly** *adverb.*

fitting-room ▷ *noun* a designated area in a clothes shop where customers can try on clothes before deciding whether or not to buy them. Also called **changing-room**.

five /faɪv/ ▷ *noun* **1 a** the cardinal number 5; **b** the quantity that this represents, being one more than four. **2** any symbol for this number, eg **5** or **V**. **3** the age of five. **4** something, especially a garment, or a person, whose size is denoted by the number 5. **5** the fifth hour after midnight or midday □ *The meeting starts at five* □ *5 o'clock* □ *5am.* **6** a set or group of five people or things. **7** a playing-card with 5 pips □ *He had a run of fives.* **8** a score of five points. ▷ *adj* **1** totalling five. **2** aged five. • **bunch of fives** *slang* the fist. • **gimme five** *slang* a greeting or a congratulation where two people slap their right palms together in the air. ⓒ Anglo-Saxon *fif*.

five-day week ▷ *noun* a week which consists of working for five days, usually from Monday to Friday, with the following two days off □ *She works a five-day week.*

fivefold ▷ *adj* **1** equal to five times as much or many. **2** divided into, or consisting of, five parts. ▷ *adverb* by five times as much. ⓒ Anglo-Saxon *fiffeald*; see FIVE + -FOLD.

the five K's ▷ *plural noun* the five symbolic articles worn by baptized Sikhs (KHALSA), namely KACCHA, KANGHA, KARA, KESH and KIRPAN.

five-o'clock shadow ▷ *noun, colloq* the new growth of hair that becomes noticeable on a man's face in the late afternoon, if he has shaved in the morning.

fivepins ▷ *singular noun* a bowling game using five skittles, similar to ninepins and tenpins.

fiver /ˈfaɪvə(r)/ ▷ *noun, colloq* **a** *Brit* a five-pound note; **b** *N Amer* a five-dollar bill □ *Can you lend me a fiver?* ⓒ 19c.

fives ▷ *singular noun* a game like squash played in a walled court, in which a gloved hand or a bat is used to hit the ball.

fix ▷ *verb* (**fixed**, **fixing**) **1** to attach or place something firmly □ *fixed it to the wall* □ *fixed the blame on him.* **2** to mend or repair something □ *fixed the brakes on the bike.* **3** to direct; to concentrate □ *fixed his eyes on her.* **4** to transfix someone □ *fixed him with a stare.* **5** to arrange or agree (a time, etc) □ *Let's fix a meeting for Monday.* **6** to establish (the time of an occurrence). **7** *colloq* to arrange (the result of a race, trial, etc) dishonestly □ *They fixed the verdict.* **8** *colloq* to bribe or threaten someone into agreement. **9** *colloq* to thwart, punish or kill someone. **10** *photog* to make (the image in a photograph) permanent by the use of chemicals which dissolve unexposed silver halides. **11** *colloq* to prepare (a meal, etc) □ *I'll fix breakfast.* **12** *N Amer* to tidy something. See also FIXED. ▷ *noun* (**fixes**) **1** *colloq* a situation which is difficult to escape from; a predicament □ *She got herself in a real fix.* **2** *slang* **a** an act of injecting a narcotic drug, etc, usually by drug addicts; **b** the quantity injected or to be injected in this way □ *Give us a fix!* **3** a calculation of the position of a ship, etc, by radar, etc. ⓒ 15c: from Latin *fixare*.

■ **fix on something** to choose it; to single it out.

■ **fix something up 1** to arrange it (eg a meeting). **2** to get a place ready for some purpose. **3** to set it up, especially temporarily.

■ **fix someone up** with something to provide them with what is needed □ *She can fix you up with a flat.*

fixate /fɪkˈseɪt, ˈfɪkseɪt/ ▷ *verb* (**fixated**, **fixating**) *tr & intr* to become or make something (eg the eyes) become fixed on something □ *Her eyes fixated on the pendulum.* ⓒ 19c: from Latin *fixus* fixed.

fixated ▷ *adj* **1** *psychoanal* affected by or engaged in FIXATION. □ *He is fixated on his mother.* **2** obsessed; obsessively attached.

fixation ▷ *noun* **1** the act of fixing or state of being fixated. **2** an (often abnormal) attachment, preoccupation or obsession. **3** *psychol* a strong attachment of a person to another person, an object or a particular means of gratification during childhood. **4** *biol* the procedure whereby cells or tissues are killed, hardened and their shape and structure preserved with suitable chemical agents, before they are stained and examined under a microscope. **5** *chem* the conversion of a chemical substance into a form that does not evaporate, ie a non-volatile or solid form. **6** *psychol* inability to change a particular way of thinking or acting, which has become habitual as a result of repeated reinforcement or frustration.

fixative /ˈfɪksətɪv/ ▷ *noun* **1** a liquid sprayed on a drawing, painting or photograph to preserve and protect it. **2** a liquid used to hold eg dentures in place. **3** a substance added to perfume to stop it evaporating.

fixed /fɪkst/ ▻ *adj* **1** fastened; immovable. **2** unvarying; unchanging; set or established □ *fixed ideas.* **3** said of a gaze or expression: steady; concentrated; rigid. **4** said of a point: stationary. **5** permanent □ *a fixed address.* • **fixedly** /'fɪksɪdlɪ/ *adverb.* • **fixedness** *noun.* • **fixed for something** *colloq* supplied with, especially financially □ *How are you fixed for cash?*

fixed assets ▻ *plural noun, econ* items bought by a company for long-term use, such as buildings, machinery, equipment, etc, whose value is calculated as cost minus DEPRECIATION from year to year.

fixed costs ▻ *plural noun, econ* overheads such as rent and rates which do not vary with the volume of business done.

fixed penalty ▻ *noun* a fine of a certain amount of money which is invariable and obligatory. ▻ *adj* (**fixed-penalty**) said of an offence, such as illegal parking: automatically liable to such a fine.

fixed-rate ▻ *adj* having a set and invariable rate of interest □ *fixed-rate mortgage.*

fixed satellite ▻ *noun* a satellite that orbits the Earth in time with the Earth's rotation, ie circling it once every 24 hours, so that it remains above the same point on the Earth's surface. Also called **geostationary satellite**.

fixed star ▻ *noun, astron* a former name for a distant star whose position appears to be stationary with respect to other stars because of its distance from Earth.

fixed-wing aircraft ▻ *noun* an aircraft which has wings attached to the fuselage, in contrast eg to helicopters with rotating propellers or 'wings'.

fixer ▻ *noun* **1** *photog* a chemical solution that FIXes photographic images. **2** *slang* a person who arranges things, especially illegally.

fixity ▻ *noun* the quality of being fixed, steady, unchanging, unmoving or immovable.

fixture ▻ *noun* **1** a permanently fixed piece of furniture or equipment □ *Fixtures and fittings are included in the house price.* **2 a** a match, horse-race or other event in a sports calendar; **b** the date for such an event. **3** someone or something permanently established in a place or position. ⓘ 16c: from Latin *fixura* a fastening, modelled on MIXTURE.

fizgig ▻ *noun* **1** a giddy or flirtatious girl. **2** a firework. **3** (*also* **fishgig**) a harpoon. ⓘ 16c: probably from obsolete *fise* fart + *gig* frivolous person; sense 3 from Spanish *fisga* harpoon.

fizz ▻ *verb* (**fizzed, fizzing**) *intr* **1** said of a liquid: to give off bubbles of carbon dioxide with a hissing sound. **2** to hiss. ▻ *noun* **1** a hiss or spluttering sound; fizziness. **2** vivacity; high spirits. **3** the bubbly quality of a drink; effervescence □ *The champagne had a good fizz to it.* **4** any effervescent drink □ *Do you want some fizz?* • **fizzer** *noun.* • **fizziness** *noun.* • **fizzy** *adj.* ⓘ 17c: imitating the sound.

fizzle /'fɪzəl/ ▻ *verb* (**fizzled, fizzling**) *intr* to make a faint hiss. ▻ *noun* a faint hissing sound. ⓘ 16c: from *fysel* to fart.

▪ **fizzle out 1** to come to a feeble end; to come to nothing, especially after an enthusiastic start. **2** to go out with a spluttering sound.

fjord or **fiord** /'fiːɔːd, fjɔːd/ ▻ *noun* a long narrow steep-sided inlet of the sea in a mountainous coast, eg in Norway, Greenland or New Zealand, formed by the flooding of a previously glaciated valley. ⓘ 17c: Norwegian, from Norse *fjörthr.*

FL ▻ *abbreviation* **1** *US state* Florida. Also written **Fla. 2** *IVR: Fürstentum Liechtenstein* (German), Liechtenstein.

fl. ▻ *abbreviation* **1** florin. **2** floruit. **3** fluid.

flab ▻ *noun, colloq* excess flesh or fat on the body. ⓘ 1920s: back-formation from FLABBY.

flabbergast /'flabəgɑːst/ ▻ *verb* (**flabbergasted, flabbergasting**) *colloq* to amaze; to astonish □ *I was flabbergasted at their impudence.* ⓘ 18c.

flabby /'flabɪ/ ▻ *adj* (**flabbier, flabbiest**) *derog* **1 a** said of flesh: sagging, not firm; **b** said of a person: having excess or sagging flesh. **2** lacking vigour; feeble; ineffective. • **flabbily** *adverb.* • **flabbiness** *noun.* ⓘ 17c: altered form of FLAPPY.

flaccid /'flaksɪd, 'flasɪd/ ▻ *adj* limp and soft; not firm. • **flaccidity** *noun.* • **flaccidly** *adverb.* ⓘ 17c: from Latin *flaccidus*, from *flaccus* feeble.

flacon /*French* flakɔ̃/ ▻ *noun* a small bottle with a stopper, especially for perfume. ⓘ 19c: French; compare FLAGON.

flag¹ ▻ *noun* **1** a piece of cloth, usually rectangular in shape, with a distinctive design, flown from a pole to represent a country, political party, etc, or used for signalling. **2** national identity represented by a flag. **3** any kind of marker used to indicate and draw special attention to something, eg a code placed at a particular position in a computer program, a paper marker pinned onto a map, etc. **4** *obsolete* an adjustable plate in a taxi, raised to show that the taxi is for hire. ▻ *verb* (**flagged, flagging**) **1** to mark something with a flag, tag or symbol. **2** to signal (a message) using flags. • **dip the flag** to lower a flag and then hoist it again as a token of respect. • **fly the flag** or **keep the flag flying** to maintain a show of support for one's country or other affiliation. • **lower the flag** to indicate surrender, relinquishment of command or respect, etc □ *The flag was finally lowered on the Empire.* • **with flags flying** with flying colours; triumphantly. ⓘ 16c.

▪ **flag someone** or **something down** to signal, usually with a hand, to a vehicle or driver to stop □ *The police flagged us down.*

flag² ▻ *verb* (**flagged, flagging**) *intr* to grow weak or tired after a period of intense work or activity. ⓘ 16c: probably derived from FLAP, in the sense of 'hang down' or 'droop'.

flag³ ▻ *noun* **1** (*also* **flagstone**) a large flat stone for paving. **2** a flat slab of any fine-grained rock which can be split into flagstones. ▻ *verb* (**flagged, flagging**) to pave (a floor, street, etc) with flagstones. ⓘ 15c: from Norse *flaga* slab.

flag⁴ ▻ *noun* any of several plants of the iris family, with long blade-like leaves, especially those with yellow flowers. ⓘ 14c.

flag-captain ▻ *noun* the captain of a flagship.

flag day ▻ *noun, Brit* a day chosen by a charity for stationing collectors in the street who distribute stickers in return for donations. ⓘ Early 20c: small paper flags with a pin have now been replaced by stickers.

flagella see under FLAGELLUM

flagellant /'fladʒələnt/ and **flagellator** /-leɪtə(r)/ ▻ *noun* someone who whips themselves or others either as a religious penance or for sexual stimulation. ⓘ 16c: from Latin *flagellare* to whip.

flagellate ▻ *verb* /fladʒə'leɪt/ (**flagellated, flagellating**) to whip someone or oneself, for the purposes either of religious penance or for sexual stimulation. ▻ *adj* /'fladʒələt/ **1** *biol* having or relating to a flagellum or flagella. **2** whiplike. ▻ *noun* any of a group of single-celled protozoan animals, including free-living marine and freshwater species, as well as parasitic species, characterized by the possession of one or more flagella. ⓘ 17c: from Latin *flagellare* to whip.

flagellation ▻ *noun* the act of whipping, for religious or sexual purposes.

flagellum /flə'dʒɛləm/ ▻ *noun* (**flagella** /-lə/) **1** *biol* the long whip-like structure that projects from the cell surface of sperm, and certain bacteria, unicellular algae and protozoans, used to propel the cell through a liquid medium. **2** *bot* a long thin runner or creeping shoot. ⓒ 19c: Latin, meaning 'a small whip', from *flagrum* a whip.

flageolet[1] /fladʒoʊ'lɛt, -'leɪ/ ▷ *noun* a small pale green bean which is a type of kidney bean. ⓒ 19c: French from Latin *faseolus* bean.

flageolet[2] /fladʒoʊ'lɛt, -'leɪ/ ▷ *noun* a high-pitched woodwind instrument similar to the recorder. ⓒ 17c: French, from *flajol* pipe.

flag of convenience ▷ *noun* the flag of a foreign country in which a ship is registered to avoid taxation, etc in its real country of origin.

flag of distress ▷ *noun* a flag displayed as a signal of distress, usually upside down or at half-mast.

flag of truce ▷ *noun* a white flag flown to show willingness to stop fighting.

flagon /'flagən/ ▷ *noun* a large bottle or jug with a narrow neck, usually with a spout and handle. ⓒ 15c: French, from Latin *flasconum* flask.

flagpole and **flagstaff** ▷ *noun* a pole from which a flag is flown.

flagrant /'fleɪgrənt/ ▷ *adj* said of something bad: undisguised; blatant; outrageous; brazen or barefaced □ *a flagrant lie.* • **flagrancy** *noun.* • **flagrantly** *adj.* ⓒ 16c: from Latin *flagrare* to blaze.

flagrante delicto see IN FLAGRANTE DELICTO.

flagship ▷ *noun* **1** the ship that carries and flies the flag of the fleet commander. **2** the leading ship in a shipping-line. **3 a** a commercial company's leading product, model, etc; the product considered most important; **b** *as adj* □ *The newly refurbished shop is now their flagship branch.*

flagstone see FLAG[3]

flag-waving ▷ *noun* an excessive show of patriotic feeling.

flail /fleɪl/ ▷ *noun* a threshing tool consisting of a long handle with a free-swinging wooden or metal bar attached to the end. ▷ *verb* (***flailed, flailing***) to beat with or as if with a flail. ⓒ Anglo-Saxon *fligel.*

■ **flail about** or **around** to wave or move about violently like a flail.

flair /flɛə(r)/ ▷ *noun* **1** (*often* **flair for something**) a natural ability or talent for something □ *She has a flair for maths.* **2** stylishness; elegance □ *He always dresses with flair.* ⓒ 19c: French, meaning 'sense of smell', from Latin *flagrare*, altered from *fragrare* to smell sweet; compare FRAGRANT.

flak ▷ *noun* **1** anti-aircraft fire. **2** *colloq* unfriendly or adverse criticism □ *You take too much flak from her.* ⓒ 1930s: acronym from German *Fliegerabwehrkanone* anti-aircraft gun, literally 'pilot defence gun'.

flake ▷ *noun, often in compounds* **1** a small flat particle which has broken away or is breaking away from a larger object □ *flakes of plaster.* **2** a small piece or particle □ *snowflake* □ *cornflake.* ▷ *verb* (***flaked, flaking***) **1** *intr* to come off in flakes □ *The paint was flaking off the wall.* **2** to break (eg cooked fish) into flakes. ⓒ 14c: possibly related to Norse *floke* flock of wool.

■ **flake out** *slang* to collapse or fall asleep from exhaustion.

flak jacket ▷ *noun* a metal-reinforced jacket worn by police, soldiers, etc for protection from gunfire, shrapnel, etc.

flaky /'fleɪkɪ/ ▷ *adj* (***flakier, flakiest***) **1** made of flakes or tending to form flakes □ *flaky pastry.* **2** *chiefly US colloq* crazy; eccentric. • **flakiness** *noun.* • **flakily** *adverb.*

flambé /'flɒmbeɪ/ ▷ *adj* said of food: soaked in spirit, usually brandy, and set alight before serving. ▷ *verb* (***flambéed, flambéing***) to serve (food) in this way. ⓒ 19c: from French *flamber* to expose to flame.

flambeau /'flamboʊ/ ▷ *noun* (***flambeaux*** /-boʊz/ or ***flambeaus*** /-boʊz/) a pole dipped in wax and set alight as a flaming torch, used in processions at festivals, etc. ⓒ 17c: French, meaning 'a small flame', from Latin *flamma* flame.

flamboyant /flam'bɔɪənt/ ▷ *adj* **1** said of a person or behaviour: colourful, exuberant, and showy. **2** said of clothing or colouring: bright, bold and striking. • **flamboyance** or **flamboyancy** *noun.* • **flamboyantly** *adverb.* ⓒ 19c: French, meaning 'blazing'.

flame ▷ *noun* **1 a** a hot, luminous and flickering tongue shape of burning gases coming from something that is on fire □ *The cigarette lighter produced a very small flame*; **b** (*often* **flames**) a mass of these □ *burst into flames* □ *go up in flames.* **2** a strong passion or affection □ *the flame of love.* **3** *as adj* (*also* **flame-coloured**) a bright reddish-orange colour □ *She wore a flame party dress.* ▷ *verb* (***flamed, flaming***) **1** *intr* to burn with flames; to blaze. **2** *intr* to shine brightly. **3** *intr* to explode with anger. **4** *intr* to get red and hot □ *Her cheeks flamed with anger.* **5** to apply a flame to (an object or substance). • **fan the flames** or **add fuel to the flames** to stir up an already existing emotion or unrest. • **an old flame 1** a feeling of passion or affection for someone from one's past. **2** a person who excites such feelings. ⓒ 14c: from Latin *flamma.*

flamenco /flə'mɛŋkoʊ/ ▷ *noun* (***flamencos***) **1** a rhythmical, emotionally stirring type of Spanish gypsy music, usually played on the guitar, originally from the S Spanish region of Andalusia. **2** the dance performed to it. ⓒ 19c: Spanish, meaning 'flamingo'.

flame-proof ▷ *verb* to make something resistant to burning or damage by high temparatures. ▷ *adj* not easily damaged by fire or high temparatures.

flame retardant ▷ *noun* a material that burns very slowly if at all, and is used to make clothing, etc.

flame-thrower ▷ *noun* a gun that discharges a stream of burning liquid, used as a weapon in war.

flame tree ▷ *noun* **1** a thick-stemmed Australian tree with glossy leaves and scarlet bell-shaped flowers. **2** any of various tropical trees with flame-coloured flowers.

flaming ▷ *adj* **1** blazing. **2** bright; glowing, particularly a brilliant red. **3** *colloq* very angry; furious; violent. **4** *colloq* damned □ *That flaming dog!*

flamingo /flə'mɪŋgoʊ/ ▷ *noun* (***flamingos*** or ***flamingoes***) any of several large wading birds, found in flocks of many thousands on lakes and lagoons in tropical regions, with white or pinkish plumage, a long neck and long legs, webbed feet, and a broad down-curving bill. ⓒ 16c: from Portuguese *flamengo*, from Provençal *flamenc* flaming.

flammable /'flaməbəl/ ▷ *adj* liable to catch fire; inflammable. Opposite of NON-FLAMMABLE. • **flammability** *noun.* ⓒ 19c: from Latin *flammare* to blaze.

flammable, inflammable

These mean the same thing; **inflammable** is not the opposite of **flammable**, it is simply a version of it preferred in everyday, non-technical contexts.

flan ▷ *noun* **1** an open pastry or sponge case with a savoury or fruit filling, usually round in shape. Compare QUICHE. **2** a flat metal base on which a design is stamped in producing coins. ⓒ 19c: French, from Latin *flado* a flat cake.

flange /flandʒ/ ▷ *noun* a broad flat projecting rim, eg round a wheel, added for strength or for connecting with another object or part. ▷ *verb* (***flanged, flanging***) to put a flange on something. • **flanged** *adj.* • **flangeless** *adj.* ⓒ 17c: from French *flanc* flank.

flank /flaŋk/ ▷ *noun* **1 a** the side of an animal, between the ribs and hip; **b** the corresponding part of the human body. **2** a cut of beef from the flank, consisting of the abdominal muscles. **3** the side of anything, eg a mountain, building, etc. **4** said of a body of things, especially of troops or a fleet drawn up in formation: the left or right extremities of that formation, eg a line of soldiers. ▻ *verb* (***flanked***, ***flanking***) **1 a** to be on the edge of (an object, a body of things, etc); **b** to move around the sides of a body of things. **2** *military* **a** to guard on or beside the flank of a formation; **b** to move into a position in the flanks or beside the flanks of a formation. ⓒ 12c: from French *flanc*, of Germanic origin.

flanker ▻ *noun* **1** *military* **a** one of a detachment of soldiers responsible for guarding the flanks; **b** a fortification used to protect a flank. **2** *rugby union* one of the two outside players on either side of the second row of the scrum. Also called **flank forward** or **wing forward**. • **do** or **pull a flanker** *slang* to trick or deceive someone.

flannel /'flanəl/ ▻ *noun* **1** soft woollen cloth with a slight nap used to make clothes. **2** (*also* **face flannel**) *Brit except Scotland* a small square of towelling for washing with. Compare FACE CLOTH. **3** *colloq* flattery or meaningless talk intended to hide one's ignorance or true intentions. **4** (**flannels**) **a** *dated* trousers made of flannel; **b** white trousers, originally made of flannel, worn by cricketers. ▻ *verb* (***flannelled***, ***flannelling***; *N Amer* ***flanneled***, ***flanneling***) **1** *tr & intr* to flatter or persuade by flattery, or to talk flannel. **2** to rub with a flannel. ⓒ 16c: possibly from Welsh *gwlanen*, from *gwlan* wool.

flannelette ▻ *noun* a cotton imitation of flannel, with a soft brushed surface.

flap ▻ *verb* (***flapped***, ***flapping***) **1** *tr & intr* to wave something up and down, or backwards and forwards ▫ *He was flapping his arms all over the place.* **2** *tr & intr* said of a bird: to move (the wings) up and down; to fly with pronounced wing movements. **3** *intr, colloq* (*often* **flap about** or **around**) to get into or be in a panic or flustered state ▫ *She was always flapping about her work.* ▻ *noun* **1** a broad piece or part of something attached along one edge and hanging loosely, usually as a cover to an opening ▫ *pocket flaps.* **2** an act, sound or impact of flapping. **3** *colloq* a panic; a flustered state ▫ *She was always in a flap about her work.* **4** a hinged section on an aircraft wing adjusted to control speed. **5** *phonetics* a sound produced by a rapid single light tap of the tongue against the alveolar ridge or uvula as the tip is lowered, eg *r* in some pronunciations of *very*. • **flappable** *adj* easily perturbed, agitated, irritated, flustered, etc. Opposite of the much commoner UNFLAPPABLE. • **flappy** *adj*. ⓒ 14c: probably imitative.

flapjack ▻ *noun* **1** a thick biscuit made with oats and syrup. **2** *N Amer* a pancake. ⓒ 16c.

flapper ▻ *noun* **1** a fashionable and frivolous young woman of the 1920s. **2** something or someone that flaps.

flare /flɛə(r)/ ▻ *verb* (***flared***, ***flaring***) **1** *intr* to burn with sudden brightness. **2** *intr* to explode into anger. **3** *tr & intr* to widen towards the edge. ▻ *noun* **1** a sudden blaze of bright light. **2** a device composed of combustible material that produces a sudden blaze of intense light, and is activated to give warning, emergency illumination (eg on an airfield), or a distress signal (eg at sea). **3** in chemical plants and oil refineries: a device for burning off superfluous combustible gas or oil, in order to ensure its safe disposal. **4** short for SOLAR FLARE. **5 a** a widening out towards the edges ▫ *sleeves with a wide flare*; **b** a flared edge. ⓒ 16c.

▪ **flare up 1** to explode into anger. **2** to burst into a blaze suddenly.

flare path ▻ *noun, aeronautics* the line of lights marking out the length of a runway to enable an aircraft to land or take off when natural visibility is insufficient.

flares ▻ *plural noun, colloq, fashion* trousers with legs which are very tight around the thigh and widen greatly below the knee, popular in the late 1960s and early 1970s, and revived as fashion items in the late 1980s; flared trousers.

flare stack ▻ *noun, chem eng* a tall chimney with an automatic igniter at the top, for the safe disposal by burning of superfluous gas, oil, etc.

flare star ▻ *noun* a class of stars which have brief and unpredictable outbursts of energy, and therefore brightness, over their surface area.

flare-up ▻ *noun* **1** *colloq* a sudden explosion of emotion or violence ▫ *Harry couldn't help his constant flare-ups.* **2** a sudden burst into flames.

flash /flaʃ/ ▻ *noun* **1** a sudden brief blaze of light. **2** an instant; a very short length of time. **3** a brief but intense occurrence ▫ *a flash of inspiration.* **4** a fleeting look on a face or in the eyes ▫ *a flash of joy.* **5** *photog* **a** a bulb or electronic device attached to a camera which produces a momentary bright light as a picture is taken ▫ *camera with built-in flash*; **b** the bright light produced by it ▫ *The flash made her blink.* **6** an emblem on a military uniform, etc indicating one's unit. **7** a sudden rush of water down a river. **8** a sudden and temporary increase in brightness and temperature of an evolving star. ▻ *verb* (***flashes***, ***flashed***, ***flashing***) **1** *tr & intr* to shine briefly or intermittently. **2** *tr & intr* to appear or cause to appear briefly; to move or pass quickly ▫ *The car flashed past the window.* **3** *intr* said of the eyes: to brighten with anger, etc. **4** to give (a smile or look) briefly ▫ *He flashed a smile.* **5** to display briefly; to flourish, brandish, or flaunt. **6** *tr & intr* to send (a message) by radio, satellite, etc ▫ *The news flashed around the network.* **7** *tr & intr* to operate (a light) as a signal. **8** *intr, colloq* (*usually* **flash at someone**) said of a man: to expose his genitals in a public place as an exhibitionist, often directed at an individual, usually a woman. ▻ *adj* **1** sudden and severe ▫ *flash floods.* **2** quick ▫ *flash freezing.* **3** *colloq* smart and expensive ▫ *That's a flash restaurant.* • **a flash in the pan** *colloq* an impressive but untypical success, unlikely to be repeated.

flashback ▻ *noun* especially in a film, novel, etc: a scene depicting events which happened before the current ones. ▻ *verb* (**flash back**) to shift to a scene which happened before the current one ▫ *The next scene flashed back to his childhood.*

flash blindness ▻ *noun* temporary inability to see after exposure to an intensely bright light due to inactivation of the photopigments.

flashbulb ▻ *noun, photog* a small light bulb used to produce a brief bright light in photography.

flash burn ▻ *noun* a burn sustained by exposure to intense heat for a short time, caused by the explosion of gases or from an electrical discharge, etc.

flash card ▻ *noun, education* used as an aid to learning: a card on which a picture or word is printed and is shown briefly to a child who then identifies the picture or reads the word, with the intention of developing the child's verbal skills.

flasher ▻ *noun* **1 a** a light that flashes; **b** a device causing a light to do this. **2** *colloq* a man who flashes (see FLASH *verb* 8).

flash flood ▻ *noun* a sudden, severe and brief flood caused by a heavy rainstorm. • **flash flooding** *noun*.

flashforward ▻ *noun* especially in a film, novel, etc: a scene depicting events which happen after the current ones.

flashgun ▻ *noun* **1** a device with an electronic flash or a flashbulb that produces a momentary bright illumination for indoor or night photography. **2** a device that holds and operates an electronic flash or a flashbulb, sometimes with an attachment so that it can be fixed onto the camera.

flash Harry ▻ *noun* (***flash Harries***) *colloq* a pretentiously flashy person. Also *as adj* ▫ *a flash-Harry tie.* ⓒ 14c.

flashlight ▻ *noun* **1** *N Amer* a torch. **2** *photog* the momentary bright light emitted from an electronic flash or a flashbulb as a photograph is taken. Usually shortened to FLASH.

flash-over ▻ *noun* **1** *elec engineering* an electric discharge over the surface of an insulator. **2** in a burning building, etc: instant combustion of material that has reached a high temperature as soon as oxygen reaches it.

flash point ▻ *noun* **1** a stage in a tense situation at which people lose their tempers and become angry or violent. **2** an area in the world of political unrest where violence is liable to break out. **3** *chem* the lowest temperature at which the vapour in the air above a volatile liquid, eg petrol or oil, will ignite momentarily on application of a small flame.

flashy ▻ *adj* (***flashier***, ***flashiest***) *colloq* ostentatiously smart and showy, often in a superficial way. • **flashily** *adverb*. • **flashiness** *noun*.

flask /flɑːsk/ ▻ *noun* **1** (*also* **hip flask**) a small flat pocket bottle for alcoholic spirits. **2** a VACUUM FLASK. **3** a narrow-necked bottle used in chemical experiments, etc. **4** a wooden, iron or steel box used to hold the mould in which a casting is made. ⓒ 16c: from Latin *flasco*, possibly of Germanic origin.

flat[1] ▻ *adj* (***flatter***, ***flattest***) **1** level; horizontal; even. **2** without hollows or prominences. **3** lacking the usual prominence □ ***a flat nose.*** **4** not bent or crumpled. **5** said of feet: having little or no arch to the instep of the foot, so that the sole lies flat against the ground. **6** said of shoes: not having a raised heel. **7** bored; depressed. **8** dull; not lively. **9** toneless and expressionless. **10** *colloq* definite; downright; emphatic □ ***a flat refusal.*** **11** *music* **a** said of an instrument, voice, etc: lower than the correct PITCH; **b** *following its noun* that lowers the specified note by a SEMITONE □ ***C flat*** □ ***C♭***. Compare SHARP *adj* 13. **12** said of a tyre: having too little air in it □ ***The tyre went flat.*** **13** said of a drink: having lost its fizziness. **14** said of a battery: having little or no electrical charge remaining. **15** said of a price, rate, economic indicator, etc: fixed; unvarying. **16** said of a business, company, etc: commercially inactive. **17** said of paint: matt, not glossy. ▻ *adverb* **1** stretched out rather than curled up, crumpled, etc. **2** into a flat compact shape □ ***folds flat for storage.*** **3** exactly □ ***in two minutes flat.*** **4** bluntly and emphatically □ ***I can tell you flat.*** **5** *music* at lower than the correct pitch □ ***He sang flat.*** ▻ *noun* **1** something flat; a flat surface or part. **2** (**flats**) **a** an area of flat land; **b** a mud bank exposed at low tide. **3** *colloq* a punctured tyre on a vehicle □ ***Oh no! We've got another flat.*** **4** *music* **a** a sign (♭) that lowers a note by a SEMITONE from the note that it refers to; **b** a note lowered in this way. **5** a flat upright section of stage scenery slid or lowered onto the stage. **6** (**the flat**) *horse-racing* **a** FLAT RACING; **b** the season of flat racing, from March to November. • **flatly** *adverb* emphatically □ ***she flatly refused to go.*** • **flatness** *noun*. • **flattish** *adj*. • **fall flat** *colloq* to fail to achieve the hoped-for effect □ ***The joke fell flat.*** • **fall flat on one's face** *colloq* to fail at something in a humiliating way. • **flat broke** *colloq* completely without money. • **flat out** *colloq* with maximum speed and energy □ ***They were all working flat out.*** • **that's flat** *colloq* that's certain or final. ⓒ 14c: from Norse *flatr* flat.

flat[2] ▻ *noun* **1** a set of rooms for living in as a self-contained unit, in a building or tenement with a number of such units. *N Amer equivalent* APARTMENT. **2** *in compounds* □ ***flat-hunting*** □ ***flat-dweller*** □ ***studio flat.*** ⓒ 19c in this sense; originally Anglo-Saxon *flett* floor, house.

flatback ▻ *noun* a pottery figure with a flat surface at the back of it, designed to stand on a mantelpiece, hang on a wall, etc.

flatbed lorry ▻ *noun* a lorry with a flat sideless platform for carrying loads.

flatfish ▻ *noun* any of about 500 species of fish with a body that is flat horizontally rather than vertically, with both eyes on the upper surface of the body, eg sole, plaice, halibut, flounder, etc. They live mainly on the sea bed and are an important source of food.

flat-footed ▻ *adj* **1** having flat feet. **2** *derog* clumsy or tactless. • **flat-footedly** *adverb*. • **flat-footedness** *noun*. • **catch someone flat-footed** to take them unawares or off guard.

flatiron ▻ *noun, historical* a clothes-pressing iron heated on the fire or stove.

flatlet ▻ *noun* a small FLAT[2].

flatmate ▻ *noun* someone one shares a FLAT[2] with.

flat playing field see LEVEL PLAYING FIELD

flat race ▻ *noun* a horse race over a course without any obstacles. See FLAT RACING.

flat racing ▻ *noun, horse-racing* the sport of racing horses on courses with no obstacles for the horses to jump. Compare HURDLING at HURDLE, STEEPLECHASING at STEEPLECHASE.

flat rate ▻ *noun, finance* a fixed uniform rate.

flat spin ▻ *noun* **1** uncontrolled rotation of an aircraft or projectile in a horizontal plane around a vertical axis. **2** *colloq* a state of agitated confusion; dither.

flatsquare ▻ *adj* said of a television screen: flat rather than convex, eliminating the distortion produced by convex screens.

flatten ▻ *verb* (***flattened***, ***flattening***) **1** *tr & intr* to make or become flat or flatter. **2** *colloq* **a** to knock someone to the ground in a fight; **b** to overcome, crush or subdue someone utterly. **3** *music* to lower the pitch of (a note) by one semitone.

■ **flatten something out 1** to make something flat or flatter. **2** to bring (an aeroplane) into a horizontal flying position.

flatter /ˈflatə(r)/ ▻ *verb* (***flattered***, ***flattering***) **1** to compliment someone excessively or insincerely, especially in order to win a favour from them. **2** said of a picture or description: to represent someone or something over-favourably. **3** to show something off well □ ***a dress that flatters the figure.*** **4** to make someone feel honoured; to gratify. • **flatterable** *adj*. • **flatterer** *noun*. • **flattering** *adj*. • **flatteringly** *adverb*. • **flatter oneself** to feel pleased, usually smugly and unjustifiably, about something concerning oneself. ⓒ 13c.

flattery ▻ *noun* (***flatteries***) **1** the act of flattering. **2** excessive or insincere praise.

flattish see under FLAT

flat top ▻ *noun* a style of haircut with the hair cut short on top so that it sticks up and appears flat from the crown to the forehead.

flatulence /ˈflatjʊləns/ or **flatulency** /-lənsɪ/ ▻ *noun* **1** an accumulation of gas formed during digestion in the stomach or intestines, causing discomfort. **2** pretentiousness. ⓒ 18c: from Latin *flatus* blowing.

flatulent /ˈflatjʊlənt/ ▻ *adj* **1** suffering from or caused by flatulence. **2** causing flatulence. • **flatulently** *adverb*.

flatus /ˈfleɪtəs/ ▻ *noun* (***flatuses*** /-sɪz/) gas generated in the sotmach or intestines. ⓒ 17c: Latin *flatus* blowing, from *flare* to blow.

flatworm ▻ *noun* a type of worm (distinct from eg ROUNDWORMS) with a flattened body, a definite head but no true body cavity, eg the TAPEWORM[2] and FLUKE.

flaunt /flɔːnt/ ▻ *verb* (***flaunted***, ***flaunting***) to display or parade oneself or something, especially one's clothes, in an ostentatious way, in the hope of being admired. • **flaunter** *noun*. • **flaunting** *adj*. • **flaunty** *adverb*. • **flauntingly** *adverb*. ⓒ 16c.

flaunt

A word often confused with this one is **flout**.

flautist /ˈflɔːtɪst/ and (*chiefly N Amer*) **flutist** /ˈfluːtɪst/ ▷ *noun* someone skilled in playing the flute. ⓒ 19c: from Italian *flautista*, from *flauto* flute.

flavescent /fleˈvɛsənt/ ▷ *adj* yellowish; turning yellow. ⓒ 19c: from Latin *flavescens* becoming yellow, from *flavus* yellow.

flavonoid /ˈfleɪvənɔɪd/ ▷ *noun, biochem* any of a group of organic compounds including numerous water-soluble plant pigments, which are responsible for most of the red, pink and purple colours found in higher plants. ⓒ 20c: from Latin *flavus* yellow.

flavour or (*N Amer*) **flavor** /ˈfleɪvə(r)/ *noun* **1** a sensation perceived when eating or drinking which is a combination of taste and smell. **2** any substance added to food, etc to give it a particular taste. **3** a characteristic quality or atmosphere. **4** *physics* an index which denotes different types of QUARK[1]. ▷ *verb* (***flavoured, flavouring***) to add something (usually to food) to give it a particular flavour or quality. • **flavourful** *adj.* • **flavourless** *adj.* • **flavourous** *adj.* • **flavoursome** *adj.* • **flavour of the week, month,** *etc* the favourite person or thing for someone for a period of time, chosen on a whim ⓒ originally used in the 1940s in the US to promote different flavours of ice cream. ⓒ 14c: from French *flaour*.

flavour enhancer ▷ *noun* any substance that enhances the natural flavour of a food when added to it, without contributing any taste of its own, eg monosodium glutamate, small quantities of sugar and salt.

flavouring or (*N Amer*) **flavoring** *noun* any substance added to food, etc to give it a particular taste.

flaw /flɔː/ ▷ *noun* **1** a fault, defect, imperfection or blemish. **2** a mistake, eg in an argument. • **flawed** *adj* having flaws; imperfect □ ***That argument is flawed.*** • **flawless** *adj.* • **flawlessly** *adverb*. ⓒ 14c: probably from Norse *flaga* stone flag.

flax /flaks/ ▷ *noun* (***flaxes***) **1** a slender herbaceous plant that usually has blue flowers and is cultivated in many parts of the world for the fibre of its stem and for its seeds (FLAXSEEDS). **2** the fibre of this plant, used to make thread and woven into LINEN fabrics. ⓒ Anglo-Saxon *fleax*.

flax-bush and **flax-lily** ▷ *noun* a plant of the lily family native to New Zealand, producing a valuable fibre. Also called **New Zealand flax**.

flaxen /ˈflaksən/ ▷ *adj* **1** said of hair: very fair. **2** made of or resembling flax. ⓒ 16c.

flaxseed ▷ *noun* LINSEED.

flay /fleɪ/ ▷ *verb* (***flayed, flaying***) **1** to strip the skin from (an animal or a person). **2** to whip or beat violently. **3** to criticize harshly. • **flayer** *noun*. ⓒ Anglo-Saxon *flean*.

F-layer ▷ *noun, physics* in the Earth's atmosphere: an ionized region that reflects radio waves, widely used for radio transmission around the curved surface of the Earth. Also called APPLETON LAYER. Compare E-LAYER.

flea /fliː/ ▷ *noun* (***fleas***) **1** any of about 1 800 species of wingless, blood-sucking, jumping insects, that live as parasites on mammals (including humans) and some birds. **2** *in compounds* referring to small CRUSTACEANS which leap like fleas □ ***sand flea*** □ ***water flea.*** • **a flea in one's ear** *colloq* a reply that is unwelcome or surprisingly sharp; a severe scolding. ⓒ Anglo-Saxon *fleah*.

flea-bag ▷ *noun, slang* **1 a** an unpleasant or shabby building, especially lodgings; **b** a shabby or unkempt person. **2** a sleeping bag.

fleabane ▷ *noun* a leafy perennial plant, native to marshes in Europe, N Africa and Asia Minor, that has lance-shaped leaves with wavy margins, and yellow daisy-like flowers, and whose strong smell is said to drive away fleas. ⓒ 16c.

flea-bite ▷ *noun* **1** the bite of a flea, or an itchy swelling caused by it. **2** a trivial inconvenience. ⓒ 15c.

flea-bitten ▷ *adj* **1** bitten or infested with fleas. **2** dingy; squalid.

flea circus ▷ *noun* a side-show at a fair in which fleas allegedly perform tricks like riding chariots across blotting paper, jumping through hoops, etc. ⓒ 1920s: originating in the US.

flea collar ▷ *noun* a collar for a dog or a cat impregnated with a chemical which kills fleas. ⓒ 1950s.

flea market ▷ *noun, colloq* a street market that sells second-hand goods or clothes. ⓒ 1920s.

flea-pit ▷ *noun, colloq* a drab cinema or other public building. ⓒ 1930s.

fleawort ▷ *noun* any of several biennial or perennial European plants with clusters of small daisy-like flower heads. It usually grows in damp places. ⓒ Anglo-Saxon *fleawyrt*.

flèche /flɛʃ, fleɪʃ/ ▷ *noun* **1** *archit* a small slender spire rising from the ridge of a church roof in some large churches, usually from the intersection of the nave and transepts. **2** *backgammon* one of the 24 points on a backgammon board. **3** *fencing* a running attack. ⓒ 18c: French, meaning 'arrow'.

fléchette /fleɪˈʃɛt/ ▷ *noun* a steel dart dropped or thrown from an aeroplane during World War I. ⓒ Early 20c: French, meaning 'little arrow'.

fleck ▷ *noun* **1** a spot or marking □ ***a white coat with flecks of gray.*** **2** a speck or small bit □ ***a fleck of dirt.*** ▷ *verb* (*also* **flecker**) (***flecked, flecking; fleckered, fleckering***) to spot or speckle. ⓒ 16c: from Norse *flekkr* speck or spot.

flecked ▷ *adj* spotted; dappled.

fled *past tense, past participle of* FLEE

fledged /flɛdʒd/ ▷ *adj* **1** said of a young bird: able to fly because the feathers are fully developed. **2** qualified; trained □ ***a fully-fledged doctor.*** ⓒ Anglo-Saxon *flycge*.

fledgling or **fledgeling** ▷ *noun* **1** a young bird that has just grown its feathers and is still unable to fly. **2** an inexperienced person new to a situation; a recently formed organization. Also *as adj* □ ***a fledgling company.*** ⓒ 19c: from *fledge* ready to fly.

flee /fliː/ ▷ *verb* (***flees, fled, fleeing***) **1** *intr* to run away quickly. **2** to hurriedly run away from or escape from (danger or a dangerous place). • **fleer** *noun* someone who is fleeing. ⓒ Anglo-Saxon *fleon*.

fleece /fliːs/ ▷ *noun* **1** a sheep's woolly coat. **2** a sheep's wool cut from it at one shearing. **3** sheepskin or a fluffy fabric for lining garments, etc. **4** a garment made of fluffy acrylic thermal fabric and used like a jacket or pullover. ▷ *verb* (***fleeced, fleecing***) **1** to cut wool from (sheep); to shear (sheep). **2** *slang* to rob, swindle or overcharge. • **fleeceless** *adj.* • **fleecer** *noun*. ⓒ Anglo-Saxon *flies*.

fleecy /ˈfliːsɪ/ ▷ *adj* (***fleecier, fleeciest***) woolly, like a fleece. • **fleecily** *adverb*.

fleer[1] /ˈfliːə(r)/ ▷ *old use, verb* (***fleered, fleering***) *intr* to make wry faces in contempt; to jeer. ▷ *noun* a mocking look or glance; a gibe. ⓒ 14c: compare Norwegian *flira* to titter.

fleer[2] see under FLEE

fleet[1] /fliːt/ ▷ *noun* **1** a number of ships under one command and organized as a tactical unit. **2** a navy; all the ships of a nation. **3** a number of buses, taxis, aircraft, etc operating under the same ownership or management □ ***a fleet of taxis.*** ⓒ Anglo-Saxon *fleot* ship, from *fleotan* to float.

fleet[2] /fliːt/ ▷ *verb* (***fleeted, fleeting***) *intr* to flit or pass swiftly □ ***The clouds were fleeting across the sky.*** ▷ *adj, poetic* swift; rapid □ ***fleet of foot.*** • **fleetness** *noun*. ⓒ Anglo-Saxon *fleotan* to float.

fleeting ▷ *adj* passing swiftly; brief; short-lived □ ***a fleeting smile.*** • **fleetingly** *adverb*.

Fleet Street ▻ *noun* British newspapers or journalism collectively. ⓘ Late 19c: named after the street in London where many newspapers were formerly produced and published.

Fleming ▻ *noun* a native of Flanders (a region in northern Europe comprising NW Belgium, part of northern France and a western part of the Netherlands) or of the Flemish-speaking part of Belgium. ⓘ 15c as *flemmyng*.

Flemish /'flɛmɪʃ/ ▻ *adj* belonging or relating to Flanders, or to the Flemings or their language. ▻ *noun* the language of the Flemings, one of the two official languages of Belgium, which is virtually identical to Dutch. ⓘ 15c as *Flemis*; compare WALLOON.

flench /flɛntʃ/ , **flense** /'flɛns, flɛnz/ and **flinch** /'flɪntʃ/ ▻ *verb* (***flenched, flenching; flensed, flensing; flinched, flinching***) **1** to cut the blubber from (a whale, seal, etc) and slice it up. **2** to flay or skin (a seal, etc). ⓘ 19c: from Danish *flense*.

flesh /flɛʃ/ ▻ *noun* **1** in animals: the soft tissues covering the bones, consisting chiefly of muscle. **2** the meat of animals, as distinct from that of fish, used as food; sometimes the meat of birds, used as food. Compare FISH *noun* 2, FOWL *noun* 2. **3** the pulp of a fruit or vegetable. **4** the body as distinct from the soul or spirit; bodily needs. **5** *poetic* humankind. **6** excess fat; plumpness. **7** a yellowish-pink colour. ▻ *verb* (***fleshed, fleshing***) to train (eg dogs) for hunting by giving them raw meat. • **fleshless** *adj*. • **flesh and blood** bodily or human nature. • **one's flesh and blood** one's family or relations. • **in the flesh** in person; actually present. ⓘ Anglo-Saxon *flæsc*.

■ **flesh something out** to add descriptive detail to it.

flesh-coloured ▻ *adj* yellowish pink. ⓘ 17c: referring to the perceived colour of the flesh of a Caucasian.

fleshings ▻ *plural noun* flesh-coloured tights.

fleshly ▻ *adj* relating to the body as distinct from the soul; worldly.

fleshpots ▻ *plural noun, facetious* **1** luxurious living. **2** a place where bodily desires or lusts can be gratified.

flesh wound ▻ *noun* a superficial wound, not deep enough to damage bone or a bodily organ.

fleshy ▻ *adj* (***fleshier, fleshiest***) **1** plump. **2** relating to or like flesh. **3** said of leaves, etc: thick and pulpy. • **fleshiness** *noun*.

fletcher /'flɛtʃər/ ▻ *noun, old use* a person whose job is to make arrows. ⓘ 14c: from French *flecher* arrow maker, from *flèche* arrow.

fleur-de-lis or **fleur-de-lys** /flɜːdə'li, flɜːdə'liːs/ ▻ *noun* (***fleurs-de-lis, fleurs-de-lys*** /flɜːdə'li, flɜːdə'liːs/) a stylized three-petal representation of a lily or iris, used as a heraldic design. ⓘ 14c: from French *flour de lis* lily flower.

flew *past tense of* FLY[2]

flews /'fluːz/ ▻ *plural noun* the pendulous upper lips of a bloodhound or similar dog. ⓘ 16c.

flex[1] /flɛks/ ▻ *verb* (***flexed, flexing***) **1** to bend (a limb or joint). **2** to contract or tighten (a muscle) so as to bend a joint. • **flex one's muscles 1** to display the muscles of the arms and shoulders, etc by contracting them, prior to a trial of strength, etc □ *As he went into the boxing ring, he flexed his muscles.* **2** to refer to one's authority as a warning that it might be used. ⓘ 16c: from Latin *flectere* to bend.

flex[2] /flɛks/ ▻ *noun* flexible insulated electrical cable. ⓘ Early 20c: from FLEXIBLE.

flexible ▻ *adj* **1** bending easily; pliable. **2** readily adaptable to suit circumstances. • **flexibility** *noun*. • **flexibly** *adverb*. ⓘ 16c: from Latin *flexibilis*.

flexile /'flɛksaɪl/ ▻ *adj* flexible.

flexion /'flɛkʃən/ ▻ *noun* **1** the bending of a limb or joint, especially a flexor muscle. **2** a fold or bend.

flexitime /'flɛksɪtaɪm/ ▻ *noun* a system of flexible working hours operated in some organizations whereby employees may choose their time of arrival and departure, provided they work the agreed number of hours, usually including certain hours (**core time**) each day when everyone must be at work. ⓘ 1970s: from *flex*ible + TIME.

flexor /'flɛksɔː(r)/ ▻ *noun, anatomy* any muscle that causes bending of a limb or other body part. Compare EXTENSOR. ⓘ 17c: from FLEX[1].

flexuous /'flɛksjuəs/ ▻ *adj* **1** full of bends or curves. **2** undulating; bending in a zigzag manner.

flexure /'flɛkʃə(r), -sjuə(r)/ ▻ *noun* **1** a bend or turning. **2** *math* the curving of a line or surface. **3** *building* the bending of leaded beams. • **flexural** *adj*.

flibbertigibbet /'flɪbətɪdʒɪbɪt/ ▻ *noun* a frivolous or over-talkative person. • **flibberty-gibberty** *adj* flighty; frivolous. ⓘ 16c: imitating fast talking.

flic /flik/ ▻ *noun* a French policeman. ⓘ 19c: French slang.

flick /flɪk/ ▻ *verb* (***flicked, flicking***) **1** to move or touch something with a quick light movement □ *He flicked his hair back wih a jerk of his head.* **2** to move the hand or finger quickly and jerkily against something small, eg a speck of dust, crumbs, etc, in order to remove it □ *She flicked the crumbs off the table.* ▻ *noun* a flicking action. ⓘ 15c: imitating the sound; compare French *flicflac* the cracking of a whip.

■ **flick through something** to glance quickly through (a book, a video, etc), in order to get a rough impression of it.

flicker /'flɪkə(r)/ ▻ *verb* (***flickered, flickering***) **1** *intr* to burn or shine unsteadily by alternately flashing bright and dying away again □ *The flames were flickering brightly* □ *There was thunder, and then the lights started to flicker.* **2** *intr* to move lightly to and fro; to flutter. **3** to cause something to flicker. ▻ *noun* **1** a brief or unsteady light □ *He glimpsed a flicker of light at the end of the tunnel.* **2** a fleeting appearance or occurrence □ *a flicker of hope.* • **flickering** *noun*. • **flickeringly** *adverb*. ⓘ Anglo-Saxon *flicorian* to flutter.

flick knife ▻ *noun* a knife whose blade is concealed in its handle and springs out at the touch of a button. ⓘ 1950s.

the flicks ▻ *plural noun, colloq* the cinema □ *Do you fancy going to the flicks tonight?* ⓘ 1920s: from FLICKER.

flier or **flyer** /flaɪə(r)/ ▻ *noun* **1** a leaflet used to advertise a product, promote an organization, etc, usually distributed on street corners or as an insert in a newspaper, etc. **2** an aviator or pilot. **3** *colloq* a FLYING START. **4** someone or something that flies or moves fast. **5** *informal* a risky or speculative business transaction. **6** each of the rectangular steps making up a straight flight of stairs. Compare WINDER *noun*. ⓘ 15c as *flyer*.

flies see under FLY[1], FLY[2]

flight[1] /flaɪt/ ▻ *noun* **1** the art or the act of flying with wings or in an aeroplane or other vehicle. **2** the movement of eg a vehicle, bird or projectile through the air, supported by aerodynamic forces. **3** a flock of birds flying together. **4** a regular air journey, numbered and at a fixed time, made by an aircraft. **5** a journey of a spacecraft. **6** a group of aircraft involved in a joint mission. **7** a set of steps or stairs leading straight up or down □ *a flight of stairs.* **8** a feather or something similar attached to the end of a dart or arrow. ▻ *verb* (***flighted, flighting***) **1** *sport* to impart a deceptive trajectory or a deceptively slow speed to (eg, a cricket ball). **2** to shoot (a bird) in flight. • **a flight of fancy** *sometimes derog* a free use of the imagination. • **in the first** or **top flight** in the highest class. • **in flight** flying. ⓘ Anglo-Saxon *flyht*.

flight² /flaɪt/ ▷ *noun* the act of fleeing; escape. • **put someone to flight** to cause them to flee. • **take flight** or **take to flight** to run away. ⓘ 12c.

flight attendant ▷ *noun* a member of the CABIN CREW on a passenger aircraft. Also called STEWARDESS, STEWARD.

flight crew ▷ *noun* the members of an aircraft crew whose responsibility is operation and navigation, ie the pilot, engineer, navigator, etc. Compare CABIN CREW.

flight deck ▷ *noun* **1** the forward part of an aeroplane where the pilot and flight crew sit. **2** the upper deck of an AIRCRAFT CARRIER where planes take off or land.

flight-feather ▷ *noun* one of the wing feathers of a bird.

flightless ▷ *adj* said of certain birds or insects: unable to fly.

flight lieutenant ▷ *noun* an officer in the British air force. See table at RANK.

flight path ▷ *noun* the course taken, or intended to be taken, by an aircraft, rocket, spacecraft, etc.

flight plan ▷ *noun* a statement of the proposed schedule of an aircraft flight.

flight recorder ▷ *noun* an electronic device fitted to an aircraft, recording information about its performance in flight, prevailing weather conditions, etc, often used in determining the cause of an air crash. Also called **black box**. ⓘ 1940s.

flighty ▷ *adj* (*flightier*, *flightiest*) irresponsible; frivolous; flirtatious. • **flightily** *adverb*. • **flightiness** *noun*.

flimflam ▷ *noun* **1** a trick or deception. **2** idle, meaningless talk; nonsense. ⓘ 16c: reduplication of *flam*, possibly from Norse *flimska* mockery.

flimsy /ˈflɪmzɪ/ ▷ *adj* (*flimsier*, *flimsiest*) **1** said of clothing, etc: light and thin. **2** said of a structure: insubstantially made; frail. **3** said of an excuse, etc: inadequate or unconvincing. • **flimsily** *adverb*. • **flimsiness** *noun*. ⓘ 18c: perhaps from FILM.

flinch¹ /flɪntʃ/ ▷ *verb* (*flinched*, *flinching*) *intr* to start or jump in pain, fright, surprise, etc. • **flincher** *noun*. • **flinchingly** *adverb*. ⓘ 16c: probably connected with French *flechir* to bend.

▪ **flinch from something** to shrink back from or avoid something difficult such as a task, duty, etc.

flinch² see FLENCH

fling ▷ *verb* (*flung*, *flinging*) **1** to throw something, especially violently or vigorously. **2** *sometimes intr* to throw oneself or one's body about. ▷ *noun* **1** the act of flinging. **2** *colloq* a sexual relationship with someone for a short period of time. **3** *colloq* a spell of enjoyable self-indulgence. **4** a lively reel ▫ *the Highland fling*. • **fling something open** to throw (a door, a window, etc) open, usually angrily. • **full fling** at the utmost speed; recklessly. • **have a fling at something** to attempt it; have a try at it. ⓘ 13c: probably related to Norse *flengja* and Swedish *flänga* to flog.

▪ **fling off** or **out** to rush angrily.

▪ **fling someone out** to get rid of them.

▪ **fling something out** to throw it away or reject it.

flint ▷ *noun* **1** *geol* a crystalline form of quartz, found in chalk and limestone, consisting of hard dark-grey or black nodules encrusted with white, and used as an abrasive. **2** *archaeol* a trimmed piece of this used as a tool. **3** a piece of a hard metal alloy from which a spark can be struck, eg in a cigarette-lighter. ⓘ Anglo-Saxon.

flint glass ▷ *noun* a very fine and pure lead glass, originally made of calcined flints.

flintlock ▷ *noun, historical* a gun in which the powder was lit by a spark from a flint.

flinty ▷ *adj* (*flintier*, *flintiest*) **1** made of or containing flint. **2** like flint. **3** hard or cruel; obdurate. • **flintily** *adverb*. • **flintiness** *noun*.

flip ▷ *verb* (*flipped*, *flipping*) **1** to toss (eg a coin) so that it turns over in mid-air. **2** *intr, colloq* (*also* **flip one's lid**) to become suddenly wild with anger; to suddenly go crazy or lose one's temper. ▷ *noun* **1** a flipping action. **2** a somersault, especially performed in mid-air. **3** an alcoholic drink made with beaten egg. **4** *colloq* a short air trip. ▷ *adj, colloq* flippant; over-smart. ⓘ 17c: probably imitating the sound.

▪ **flip something over** to toss or turn it with a light flick.

▪ **flip through something** to look quickly through it (eg a magazine or book).

flip chart ▷ *noun* a large blank pad of paper mounted on legs, on which information, data, graphs, etc can be displayed during a meeting, presentation, etc. ⓘ 1950s.

flip-flop ▷ *noun* **1** *colloq* a rubber or plastic sandal consisting of a sole held on to the foot by a thong that separates the big toe from the other toes. **2** *elec, computing* an electronic circuit that remains in one of two stable states until it receives a suitable electric pulse, which causes it to switch to the other state, widely used to store data in the form of binary digits in the integrated circuits of computers. Also called **bistable**. **3** a kind of backwards somersault in which the performer jumps over onto their hands and then over onto their feet, often repeatedly. Also called **flip-flap**. ▷ *verb, chiefly intr* **1** to move with a flapping sound. **2** *politics, chiefly US* to reverse a policy; to do a U-turn. ⓘ 1970s as *noun* 1; 1930s as *noun* 2; 16c: reduplication of FLIP indicating the repetition of the movement.

flippant /ˈflɪpənt/ ▷ *adj* not serious enough about grave matters; disrespectful; irreverent; frivolous. • **flippancy** *noun*. • **flippantly** *adverb*. ⓘ 17c: probably from FLIP.

flipper ▷ *noun* **1** a limb adapted for swimming, eg in the whale, seal, penguin, etc. **2** a rubber foot-covering imitating an animal flipper, worn for underwater swimming. ⓘ 19c.

flipping ▷ *adj, adverb, colloq* used to express annoyance ▫ *that flipping cat!* ▫ *He's flipping done it again!* ⓘ Early 20c: used as a euphemism for FUCKING.

flip side ▷ *noun, colloq* **1** *dated* a B-SIDE. **2** said of a coin: the reverse; tails. **3** a less familiar aspect of something. **4** a different (and sometimes opposite) aspect of something.

flirt /flɜːt/ ▷ *verb* (*flirted*, *flirting*) *intr* (*usually* **flirt with someone**) to behave in a playful sexual manner towards them. ▷ *noun* someone who flirts. • **flirtation** *noun*. • **flirtingly** *adverb*. • **flirty** *adj*. ⓘ 16c: compare FLICK, FLIP.

▪ **flirt with something** **1** to take a fleeting interest in it; to consider it briefly. **2** to treat (death, danger, etc) lightly; to play riskily with it.

flirtatious /flɜːˈteɪʃəs/ ▷ *adj* **1** given to flirting. **2** said of a remark, glance, etc: conveying a playful sexual invitation. • **flirtatiously** *adverb*.

flit /flɪt/ ▷ *verb* (*flitted*, *flitting*) *intr* **1 a** to move about lightly and quickly from place to place; **b** to fly silently or quickly from place to place. **2** *Scottish & N Eng* to move house. **3** *Brit colloq* to move house stealthily to avoid paying debts. ▷ *noun* an act of flitting. • **flitter** *noun*. ⓘ 12c: from Norse *flytja* to carry.

flitch /flɪtʃ/ ▷ *noun* a salted and cured side of pork. ⓘ Anglo-Saxon *flicce*.

flitter /ˈflɪtə(r)/ ▷ *verb* (*flittered*, *flittering*) *intr* to flutter. ⓘ 16c: from FLIT.

float /floʊt/ ▷ *verb* (*floated*, *floating*) **1** *tr & intr* to rest or move, or make something rest or move, on the surface of a liquid. **2** *intr* to drift about or hover in the air. **3** *intr* to move about in an aimless or disorganized way ▫ *The*

manager was floating about the shop floor. **4** to start up or launch (a company, scheme, etc). **5** to offer (stocks) for sale □ ***51 per cent of the shares were floated on the stock market.*** **6** *finance* to allow (a currency) to vary in value in relation to other currencies □ ***The rouble was floated on the international money market.*** ▷ *noun* **1** something that floats or is designed to keep something afloat. **2** *angling* a floating device fixed to a fishing-line, that moves to indicate a bite. **3** a low-powered delivery vehicle □ ***milk float.*** **4** a vehicle decorated as an exhibit in a street parade. **5** an amount of money set aside each day for giving change, etc in a shop at the start of business □ ***We always keep a float of £20.*** **6** a blade in a paddle-wheel or water-wheel. **7** a plasterer's trowel. • **floatable** *adj.* ⓒ Anglo-Saxon *flotian*; compare FLEET[2].

floatage see FLOTAGE

floatarium /floʊ'teɪrɪəm/ ▷ *noun* (***floatariums***) a place where FLOATATION THERAPY can be experienced.

floatation see FLOTATION

floatation therapy ▷ *noun* an alternative therapy for relieving stress, in which the client floats for about an hour in a sealed capsule (a **floatation tank** or **float tank**) filled with salt water and minerals while listening to new-age music. ⓒ 1980s.

floatel see FLOTEL

floater ▷ *noun* **1** someone or something that floats. **2** someone who drifts from job to job, or allegiance to allegiance. **3** a dark speck that appears to float before the eyes, caused by dead cells and fragments of cells in the lens and vitreous humour.

float glass ▷ *noun* flat glass hardened while floating on the surface of a liquid.

floating ▷ *adj* **1** not fixed; moving about □ ***a floating population.*** **2** said of a voter: not committed to supporting any one party. **3** said of a currency: free to vary in value in relation to other currencies. **4** said of a bodily organ, eg a kidney: moving about abnormally. • **floatingly** *adverb.* • **floaty** *adj.*

floating capital ▷ *noun* goods, money, etc not permanently invested in FIXED ASSETS; working capital.

floating dock ▷ *noun* a floating structure that can be sunk by letting water into the air chambers, and raised again to carry a vessel to be repaired in dry dock.

floating island ▷ *noun* **1** a floating collection of driftwood or a mass of vegetation. **2** *cookery* a dessert consisting of custard with whipped and cooked egg whites floating on top.

floating-point notation ▷ *noun, computing* the expressing of numbers in the general form $a \times b^n$, eg 2.3×10^5 instead of 230 000, or 4.7×10^{-2} instead of 0.047.

floating rib ▷ *noun* any of the lower two pairs of ribs in humans which do not reach the breastbone at all. Compare FALSE RIB, TRUE RIB.

floats ▷ *plural noun, theat* floodlights.

float-stone ▷ *noun* **1** a porous spongelike variety of silica, so light that it floats for a while on water. **2** a bricklayer's smoothing tool.

float tank see under FLOATATION THERAPY

floccinaucinihilipilification /'flɒksɪnɔːsɪ'naɪɪlɪpɪlɪfɪ'keɪʃən/ ▷ *noun, facetious* setting at little or no value. ⓒ 18c: from Latin *flocci* and *nauci* 'at a trifle', *nihili* 'at nothing', *pili* 'at a hair' + -FICATION.

floccose /'flɒkoʊs/ ▷ *adj, bot* said of plant structures: covered in small hairs giving a downlike appearance.

flocculate /'flɒkjʊleɪt/ ▷ *verb* (***flocculated, flocculating***) to cluster together or be clustered together in a flocculent mass. • **flocculation** *noun.*

flocculent /'flɒkjʊlənt/ ▷ *adj* **1** woolly; fleecy. **2** *chem* said of a precipitate: aggregated in woolly cloudlike masses. **3** *bot* covered with tufts or flakes. • **flocculence** *noun.* ⓒ 18c: from FLOCCUS.

flocculus /'flɒkjʊləs/ ▷ *noun* (***flocculi*** /-laɪ/) **1** *astron* a light or dark cloudy patch on the sun's surface caused by calcium or hydrogen vapour and usually appearing near sun spots. **2** *anatomy* a small outgrowth of the cerebellum.

floccus /'flɒkəs/ ▷ *noun* (***flocci*** /'flɒksaɪ/) **1** *bot* a tuft of woolly hair. **2** the covering of unfledged birds. ⓒ 19c: Latin, meaning 'tuft of wool'.

flock[1] ▷ *noun* **1** a group of creatures, especially birds or sheep □ ***flock of sheep.*** **2** a crowd of people. **3** a body of people under the spiritual charge of a priest or minister. ▷ *verb* (***flocked, flocking***) *intr* to gather or move in a group or a crowd □ ***The sheep flocked down the hillside*** □ ***People flocked to the first day of the spring sales.*** ⓒ Anglo-Saxon *flocc*.

flock[2] ▷ *noun* **1** a tuft of wool, etc. **2** (*also* **flocks**) waste wool or cotton used for stuffing mattresses, etc. **3** fine particles of wool or nylon fibre applied to paper or cloth to give a velvety surface, especially wallpaper called **flock-paper**. ⓒ 14c: from French *floc* tuft of wool, from Latin *floccus*.

floe /floʊ/ ▷ *noun* (***floes***) a sheet of ice other than the edge of an ice shelf or glacier, floating in the sea. ⓒ 19c: from Norwegian *flo* layer.

flog ▷ *verb* (***flogged, flogging***) **1** to beat; to whip repeatedly, particularly as a form of punishment. **2** *colloq* to sell something, especially when it is said to be a bargain □ ***She flogged her car for £3 000.*** • **flog a dead horse** *colloq* to waste time and energy trying to do something that is impossible or a lost cause. • **flog something to death** *colloq* to over-use (an idea, expression, etc) so that it becomes tedious, often resulting in the opposite effect from the desired one. • **flogger** *noun.* ⓒ 17c: probably from Latin *flagellare*; see FLAGELLANT.

flokati /flɒ'kɑːtɪ/ ▷ *noun* (***flokatis***) a hand-woven Greek rug with a thick shaggy wool pile. ⓒ 1960s: from modern Greek *phlokate* a blanket or sleeveless cape of shaggy cloth.

flong /flɒŋ/ ▷ *noun, printing* in stereotyping: papier-mâché for making moulds . ⓒ 19c: from French *flan* (see FLAN *noun* 2).

the Flood ▷ *noun, Bible* in the Old Testament (Genesis 6.8): a worldwide flood that God caused in Noah's time to destroy all living beings, except Noah, his family, and selected animals, because the people were sinful.

flood /flʌd/ ▷ *noun* **1** an overflow of water from rivers, lakes or the sea on to dry land. **2** any overwhelming flow or quantity of something. **3** the rising of the tide. **4** *colloq* a floodlight. ▷ *verb* (***flooded, flooding***) **1** to overflow or submerge (land) with water. **2** to fill something too full or to overflowing. **3** (*usually* **flood someone out**) to force them to leave a building, etc because of floods. **4** *intr* to become flooded, especially frequently. **5** *intr* to move in a great mass □ ***Crowds were flooding through the gates.*** **6** *intr* to flow or surge. **7** *intr* to bleed profusely from the uterus, eg sometimes after childbirth. **8** to supply (a market) with too much of a certain kind of commodity. **9** to supply (an engine) with too much petrol so that it cannot start. • **in flood** overflowing. ⓒ Anglo-Saxon *flod.*

floodgate ▷ *noun* a gate for controlling the flow of a large amount of water. • **open the floodgates** to remove all restraints or controls.

floodlight ▷ *noun* (*also* **floodlamp**) a powerful light used to illuminate extensive areas, especially sports grounds or the outside of buildings. ▷ *verb* (***floodlit, floodlighting***) to illuminate with floodlights. • **floodlighting** *noun.*

flood plain ▷ *noun, geol* an extensive level area beside a river, corresponding to that part of the river valley which becomes covered with water when the river floods.

floodtide ▷ *noun* the rising tide. Opposite of EBBTIDE.

floodwall ▷ *noun* a wall built as protection against floods from the sea, a river, etc.

floodway ▷ *noun* an artificial passage to direct floodwater away from an endangered area, eg an overflowing dam, a town, etc.

floor /flɔː(r)/ ▷ *noun* **1** the lower interior surface of a room or vehicle. **2** all the rooms on the same level in a building; the storey of a building □ *ground floor* □ *first floor*. **3** *usually in compounds* the lowest surface of some open areas, eg the ground in a forest or cave, the bed of the sea, etc □ *the sea floor*. **4** the debating area in a parliamentary assembly or the open area of a stock exchange as opposed to the viewing gallery. **5** the right to speak in a parliamentary assembly □ *have the floor* □ *be given the floor*. ▷ *verb* (***floored***, ***flooring***) **1** to construct the floor of (a room, etc). **2** *colloq* to knock someone down. **3** *colloq* to baffle someone completely. • **floored** *adj* said of lofts, attics, etc: having flat floor-covering rather than exposed beams, etc □ *a floored loft*. • **cross the floor** said of a member of parliament, etc: to change one's allegiance from one party to another. • **hold the floor** to be the person who is talking while others listen, sometimes a person who is dominating a debate by a lot of speaking. • **take the floor 1** to rise to speak in a debate, etc. **2** to start dancing at a dance, etc □ *The orchestra played and the bridal couple took the floor*. **3** to start a performance on stage □ *The comedian took the floor*. • **wipe the floor with someone** *slang* to defeat them ignominiously; to humiliate them. ⓘ Anglo-Saxon *flor*.

floorboard ▷ *noun* one of the narrow boards that form a wooden floor.

floorcloth ▷ *noun* a cloth for washing floors.

flooring ▷ *noun* **1** material for constructing floors. **2** a platform.

floor plan ▷ *noun* a diagram showing the layout of rooms, etc on one storey of a building.

floor price see RESERVE PRICE

floor show ▷ *noun* a series of performances such as singing and dancing at a nightclub or restaurant.

floor-walker ▷ *noun, dated* a supervisor of a section of a department store who attends to customers' complaints, etc.

floor work ▷ *noun* a set of exercises carried out while lying on the floor, usually as a warm-up or to cool down during a work-out, aerobics session, etc.

floosie, floozie or **floozy** /ˈfluːzɪ/ ▷ *noun* (***floosies*** or ***floozies***) *colloq, often facetious* a woman or girl, especially a disreputable or immodestly dressed one. ⓘ Early 20c.

flop ▷ *verb* (***flopped***, ***flopping***) **1** *intr* to fall, drop, move or sit limply and heavily. **2** *intr* said of eg hair: to hang or sway about loosely. **3** *intr, colloq* said of a play, project, business, etc: to fail dismally. **4** *intr, slang* (*usually* **flop out**) to fall asleep, especially because of exhaustion. ▷ *noun* **1** a flopping movement or sound. **2** *colloq* a complete failure. **3** *N Amer colloq* a place to sleep; temporary lodgings. ▷ *adverb* with a flop □ *Business went flop* □ *He fell flop into the swimming pool*. ⓘ 17c: variant of FLAP.

floppy ▷ *adj* (***floppier***, ***floppiest***) tending to flop; loose and insecure. ▷ *noun* (***floppies***) *wordprocessing, computing* a floppy disk. • **floppily** *adverb*. • **floppiness** *noun*.

floppy disk ▷ *noun, wordprocessing, computing* a portable flexible plastic disc, coated with magnetic material and enclosed in a hard rectangular plastic casing, which is used to store data. Compare HARD DISK. ⓘ 1970s.

flor /flɔː(r)/ ▷ *noun* a yeasty growth which is allowed to form on the surface of sherries after fermentation and which gives them a nutty taste. ⓘ 19c: Spanish, meaning 'flower', from Latin *flos, floris*.

flor. ▷ *abbreviation* floruit.

flora /ˈflɔːrə/ ▷ *noun* (***floras*** or ***florae*** /-riː/) *bot* **1** the wild plants of a particular region, country or time period. **2** a book or list giving descriptions of such plants. Compare FAUNA. ⓘ 16c: named after Flora, Roman goddess of flowers, from Latin *flos, floris* flower.

floral ▷ *adj* **1** consisting of or relating to flowers □ *a floral tribute*. **2** patterned with flowers □ *floral curtains*. • **florally** *adverb*. ⓘ 17c: from Latin *floralis*.

Florence fennel see under FINOCCHIO

Florentine /ˈflɒrəntaɪn/ ▷ *adj* **1** belonging or relating to Florence, a city in Tuscany, Italy, or its inhabitants. **2** (*sometimes* **florentine**) *usually following its noun* said of a cooked dish: containing or served with spinach □ *eggs florentine*. ▷ *noun* (***Florentines***) **1** a citizen or inhabitant of, or person born in, Florence. **2** (*sometimes* **florentine**) a biscuit on a chocolate base, the top being covered with preserved fruit and nuts. ⓘ 16c.

florescence /flɔːˈrɛsəns, flə-/ ▷ *noun, bot* the process, state or period of flowering. ⓘ 18c: from Latin *florescere* to begin to blossom.

floret /ˈflɒrɪt/ ▷ *noun, bot* **1** a small flower; one of the single flowers in the head of a composite flower, such as a daisy or sunflower. **2** each of the branches in the head of a cauliflower or of broccoli. ⓘ 17c: from French *florete*, from Latin *flos, floris* flower.

floriated or **floreated** /ˈflɒrɪeɪtɪd/ ▷ *adj, archit* decorated with floral ornament. ⓘ 19c.

floribunda /flɒrɪˈbʌndə, flɔː-/ ▷ *noun* (***floribundas***) a plant, especially a rose, whose flowers grow in clusters. ⓘ 19c: from Latin *floribundus* flowering freely.

florid /ˈflɒrɪd/ ▷ *adj* **1** over-elaborate □ *a florid speech*. **2** pink or ruddy in complexion. • **floridity** *noun*. • **floridly** *adverb*. • **floridness** *noun*. ⓘ 17c: from Latin *floridus* blooming.

floriferous /flɒˈrɪfərəs/ ▷ *adj* bearing or producing flowers. ⓘ 17c.

floriform /ˈflɒrɪfɔːm/ ▷ *adj* flower-shaped. ⓘ 19c.

florin /ˈflɒrɪn/ ▷ *noun* **1** a name for the coin worth two shillings or 24 old British pence, minted from 1849 and worth 10 new pence when currency was DECIMALIZED in 1971. **2** (abbreviation **fl.**) another name for the Dutch GUILDER 1. ⓘ 14c: French, from Italian *fiorino*, from *fiore* a flower. The first coin bearing the name carried a flower on one side.

florist /ˈflɒrɪst/ ▷ *noun* someone who sells or arranges flowers; *sometimes* someone who also grows flowers. • **floristic** *adj*. ⓘ 17c: from Latin *flos, floris* flower.

floristry ▷ *noun* **1** the profession of selling flowers. **2** the art of arranging them. ⓘ 19c.

floruit /ˈflɔːruɪt, ˈflɒ-/ ▷ *noun* (abbreviation **fl.** or **flor.**) a period during which someone was most active, produced most works, etc, used especially when exact birth and death dates are unknown. ⓘ 19c: Latin, meaning 'he or she flourished', from *florere* to flourish.

floss ▷ *noun* (***flosses***) **1** loose strands of fine silk which are not twisted together, used in embroidery, for tooth-cleaning (**dental floss**), etc. **2** the rough silk on the outside of a silkworm's cocoon. **3** any fine silky plant substance. ▷ *verb* (***flosses***, ***flossed***, ***flossing***) *tr & intr* to clean the teeth with dental floss □ *He flosses every evening*. ⓘ 18c: probably from French *flosche* down.

flossy ▷ *adj* (***flossier***, ***flossiest***) made of or like floss.

flotage or **floatage** /ˈfloʊtɪdʒ/ ▷ *noun* **1** buoyancy; the capacity for floating. **2** the state of floating. **3** flotsam. **4** the part of a ship above the waterline. ⓘ 17c.

flotation or **floatation** /floʊˈteɪʃən/ ▷ *noun* **1** the launching of a commercial company with a sale of shares to raise money. **2** the act of floating. **3** the science of floating objects. ⓘ 19c.

flotel or **floatel** /floʊˈtɛl/ ▷ *noun* **1** a rig or boat containing the sleeping accommodation and eating, leisure, etc facilities for workers on oil-rigs. **2** a floating hotel, or a hotel built over water. ◷ 1950s: from FLOAT, modelled on HOTEL.

flotilla /flə'tɪlə/ ▻ *noun* (***flotillas***) a small fleet, or a fleet of small ships. ◷ 18c: Spanish, meaning 'little fleet'.

flotsam /'flɒtsəm/ ▻ *noun* goods lost by shipwreck and found floating on the sea. Compare JETSAM. • **flotsam and jetsam** odds and ends. ◷ 16c: from French *floteson* something floating.

flounce[1] /flaʊns/ ▻ *verb* (***flounced, flouncing***) *intr* to move in a way expressive of impatience or indignation. ▻ *noun* a flouncing movement. ◷ 16c: possibly related to Norse *flunsa* to hurry.

flounce[2] /flaʊns/ ▻ *noun* a deep frill on a dress, etc. • **flouncing** *noun* material for flounces. • **flouncy** *adj* decorated with flounces. ◷ 18c: altered from *frounce* plait or curl.

flounder[1] /'flaʊndə(r)/ ▻ *verb* (***floundered, floundering***) *intr* **1** to thrash about helplessly, as when caught in a bog. **2** to stumble helplessly in thinking or speaking, struggling to find the appropriate words, etc. ▻ *noun* the act of floundering. ◷ 16c: partly imitating the action, partly a blend of FOUNDER[2] + BLUNDER.

flounder[2] /'flaʊndə(r)/ *noun* a type of European FLATFISH with greyish-brown mottled skin with orange spots, used as food. ◷ 15c: from French *flondre*.

flour /flaʊə(r)/ ▻ *noun* **1** the finely ground meal of wheat or any other cereal grain. **2** a dried powdered form of any other vegetable material □ ***potato flour***. ▻ *verb* (***floured, flouring***) to cover or sprinkle something with flour. • **floury** *adj*. ◷ 13c: a specific use of FLOWER, best part of the MEAL[2].

flourish /'flʌrɪʃ/ ▻ *verb* (***flourishes, flourished, flourishing***) **1** *intr* to be strong and healthy; to grow well. **2** *intr* to do well; to develop and prosper. **3** *intr* to be at one's most productive, or at one's peak. **4** to adorn with flourishes or ornaments. **5** to wave or brandish something. ▻ *noun* (***flourishes***) **1** a decorative twirl in handwriting. **2** an elegant sweep of the hand. **3** a showy piece of music; a fanfare. **4** a piece of fancy language. • **flourished** *adj*. • **a flourish of trumpets 1** a fanfare heralding an important person or people. **2** any ostentatious introduction. • **flourishing** *adj*. • **flourishingly** *adverb*. ◷ 13c: from French *florir* to flower.

flout /flaʊt/ ▻ *verb* (***flouted, flouting***) **1** to defy (an order, convention, etc) openly; to disrespect (authority, etc). **2** (*usually* **flout at**) *intr* to jeer; to mock. • **floutingly** *adverb*. ◷ 16c, meaning 'to play the flute'.

flout

A word often confused with this one is **flaunt**.

flow /floʊ/ ▻ *verb* (***flowed, flowing***) *intr* **1** to move along like water. **2** said of blood or electricity: to circulate. **3** to keep moving steadily □ ***Traffic was not flowing well through the city centre.*** **4** said of hair: to hang or ripple in a loose shining mass. **5** said of words or ideas: to come readily to mind or in speech or writing. **6** to be present in abundance. **7** said of the tide: to advance or rise. Compare EBB *verb* 1. ▻ *noun* **1** the action of flowing. **2** the rate of flowing. **3** a continuous stream or outpouring. **4** the rising of the tide. **5** *old use, euphemistic* menstruation. • **in full flow** speaking energetically. ◷ Anglo-Saxon.

flow chart and **flow sheet** ▻ *noun* a diagram representing the nature and sequence of operations to be carried out, especially in a computer program or an industrial process.

flower /flaʊə(r)/ ▻ *noun* **1** in a flowering plant: the structure that bears the reproductive organs, which consists of a leafy shoot in which the leaves are modified to form sepals, petals, etc. **2** a plant that bears flowers, especially if cultivated for them. **3** the best part; the cream. **4** the most distinguished person or thing. **5** a term of endearment. **6** *pharmacol* (*usually* **flowers**) a sublimate □ ***flowers of sulphur***. ▻ *verb* (***flowered, flowering***) *intr* **1** to produce flowers; to bloom. **2** *intr* to reach a peak; to develop to full maturity. **3** *intr* to adorn or decorate with flowers or a floral design. • **floweriness** *noun*. • **flowering** *noun, adj*. • **flowerless** *adj*. • **in flower** blooming or blossoming; with flowers fully out. ◷ 13c: from French *flour*, from Latin *flos, floris* flower.

flower-bed ▻ *noun* a garden bed planted with flowering plants.

flower-bud ▻ *noun* the bud of a flower which is unopened.

flowerer ▻ *noun* a plant that flowers.

flower girl ▻ *noun* **1** a young girl who forms part of the bride's retinue at a wedding ceremony. **2** *old* a woman or girl who sells flowers in the street.

flower-head ▻ *noun* a close INFLORESCENCE in which all the florets grow together at the tip of the stem, rather than on separated stalks.

flowerpecker ▻ *noun* a name loosely applied to many small woodland birds found from India to Australia, which have a tube-like tongue and which feed on nectar and berries, especially mistletoe.

flower people ▻ *noun* members of the FLOWER POWER movement.

flowerpot ▻ *noun* a clay or plastic container for growing plants in.

flower power ▻ *noun* a popular movement in the 1960s, which rejected materialism and advocated peace and universal love.

flower show ▻ *noun* a competition and/or exhibition of flowers, flower arrangements and sometimes also plant displays □ ***a church flower show***.

flower-stalk ▻ *noun* the stem that supports the flower.

flowery /'flaʊərɪ/ ▻ *adj* **1** decorated or patterned with flowers □ ***a flowery dress***. **2** said of language or gestures: excessively elegant or elaborate.

flowing /'floʊɪŋ/ ▻ *adj* **1** moving as a fluid. **2** smooth and continuous; fluent. **3** falling or hanging in folds or waves □ ***a flowing dress*** □ ***flowing locks***. • **flowingly** *adverb*.

flow-meter ▻ *noun* a device for measuring the rate of flow of liquids or gases in a pipe.

flown *past participle of* FLY[2]

flow sheet see under FLOWCHART

fl. oz. ▻ *abbreviation* fluid ounce or fluid ounces.

flu /fluː/ ▻ *noun, colloq* (*often* **the flu**) influenza □ ***She's in bed with the flu***. ◷ 19c: shortened form of INFLUENZA.

flub *N Amer colloq* ▻ *verb* (***flubbed, flubbing***) *tr & intr* to make a mess of something; to botch it. ▻ *noun* **1** a gaffe; a mistake. **2** someone who tends to make mistakes. ◷ 1920s.

fluctuate /'flʌktʃueɪt/ ▻ *verb* (***fluctuated, fluctuating***) *intr* to vary in amount, value, level, etc; to rise and fall □ ***Stock prices fluctuated dramatically over the day***. • **fluctuant** *adj*. • **fluctuation** *noun*. ◷ 17c: from Latin *fluctuare, fluctuatum* to undulate, from *fluere* to flow.

flue /fluː/ ▻ *noun* (***flues***) **1** an outlet for smoke or gas, eg through a chimney. **2** a pipe or duct for conveying heat. **3** *music* a flue pipe. **4** the opening by which the air escapes from the foot of a FLUE PIPE. ◷ 16c.

flue-cure ▻ *verb* to prepare (tobacco) by heat introduced through flues. • **flue-cured** *adj*.

fluent /'fluənt/ ▻ *adj* **1** having full command of a foreign language □ ***fluent in French***. **2** spoken or written with ease □ ***speaks fluent Russian***. **3** speaking or writing in an easy flowing style. **4** said of a movement: smooth, easy or graceful. • **fluency** *noun*. • **fluently** *adverb*. ◷ 17c: from Latin *fluere* to flow.

flue pipe ▷ *noun* an organ pipe in which the sound is produced by air passing across a small aperture or flue. Compare REED PIPE.

fluff ▷ *noun* **1** small bits of soft woolly or downy material. **2** *colloq* a mistake, eg in speaking or reading aloud. **3** *colloq* a DUFFed stroke at golf, etc. ▷ *verb* (***fluffed***, ***fluffing***) **1** (*usually* **fluff something out** or **up**) to shake or arrange it into a soft mass. **2** *tr & intr* said eg of an actor: to make a mistake in (their lines, etc); to bungle something. • **a bit of fluff** *slang* a young woman, often used to refer to someone's girlfriend □ *Harry's bit of fluff.* ⓘ 18c: from earlier *flue* a downy substance.

fluffy ▷ *adj* (***fluffier***, ***fluffiest***) **1** consisting of or resembling fluff. **2** covered with fluff or something similar. • **fluffily** *adverb.* • **fluffiness** *noun.*

flugelhorn or **flügelhorn** /'fluːgəlhɔːn/ ▷ *noun* a brass musical instrument, like a cornet but with a larger bell, which is a standard instrument in British brass bands, is occasionally used by jazz musicians, but is rarely found in orchestras. ⓘ Late 19c: German from *Flügel* wing + *Horn* horn.

fluid /'fluːɪd/ ▷ *noun* a substance, such as a liquid or gas, which can move about with freedom and has no fixed shape. ▷ *adj* **1** able to flow like a liquid; unsolidified. **2** said eg of movements: smooth and graceful. **3** altering easily; adaptable. • **fluidity** /flʊ'ɪdɪtɪ/ or **fluidness** *noun.* ⓘ 17c: from Latin *fluidus* flowing.

fluidics /flʊ'ɪdɪks/ ▷ *singular noun, physics* the study and use of systems based on the movement of jets of fluid in pipes, used as an alternative to electronic devices to control instruments, industrial processes, etc. • **fluidic** *adj.*

fluidize or **fluidise** ▷ *verb* (***fluidized***, ***fluidizing***) **1** to make something fluid. **2** to make (fine particles or other solids) move as a fluid, eg by passing a gas or vapour through them. • **fluidization** *noun.*

fluid ounce ▷ *noun* (abbreviation **fl. oz.**) **1** in the UK: a unit of liquid measurement, equal to one twentieth of a British or imperial pint (28.41cm^3). **2** in the US: a unit of liquid measurement, equal to one sixteenth of a US pint (29.6cm^3).

fluke[1] ▷ *noun* a success achieved by accident or chance. ▷ *verb* (***fluked***, ***fluking***) to make, score or achieve something by a fluke. • **flukey** or **fluky** *adj.* • **flukiness** *noun.* ⓘ 19c: originally referring to a successful stroke made by chance in billiards.

fluke[2] ▷ *noun* **1** any of thousands of species of parasitic flatworm, having a complex life cycle which may involve several different hosts including sheep, cattle and humans, so called because of its resemblance to a miniature flounder. **2** a FLOUNDER[2]. ⓘ Anglo-Saxon *floc* plaice.

fluke[3] ▷ *noun* **1** one of the triangular plates of iron on each arm of an anchor. **2** a barb, eg of an arrow, harpoon, etc. **3** a lobe of a whale's tail. ⓘ 16c: probably a special use of FLUKE[2].

flume ▷ *noun* **1 a** a descending chute with flowing water at a swimming pool, used for riding or sliding down; a water-slide; **b** a ride at an amusement park with small boats which move through water-filled channels. **2** an artificial channel for water, used in industry, eg for transporting logs. ⓘ 1970s as *noun* 1; 18c as *noun* 2; 12c in obsolete sense 'a river or stream': from Latin *flumen* river.

flummery /'flʌmərɪ/ ▷ *noun* (***flummeries***) **1** a jelly made with oatmeal, milk, egg and honey. **2** pompous nonsense; empty flattery. ⓘ 17c: from Welsh *llymru.*

flummox /'flʌməks/ ▷ *verb* (***flummoxed***, ***flummoxing***) *colloq* to confuse someone; to bewilder someone □ *That flummoxed him* □ *He was flummoxed by that.* ⓘ 19c.

flump ▷ *verb* (***flumped***, ***flumping***) *colloq* **1** to throw something down heavily. **2** *intr* to fall or move heavily with flop or thud. ▷ *noun* the dull sound produced by this action. ⓘ 19c: imitating the sound.

flung *past tense, past participle of* FLING

flunk ▷ *verb* (***flunked***, ***flunking***) *especially N Amer colloq* **1** *tr & intr* to fail (a test, examination, etc) □ *Bill flunked the exam again.* **2** said eg of an examiner: to fail (a candidate) □ *The professor flunked Bill.* ⓘ 19c.

■ **flunk out** *intr* to be dismissed from a school or university for failing examinations.

flunkey or **flunky** /'flʌŋkɪ/ ▷ *noun* (***flunkeys*** or ***flunkies***) **1** a uniformed manservant, eg a footman. **2** *derog* a slavish follower. **3** *N Amer* a person doing a humble or menial job. ⓘ 18c: possibly from *flanker* someone who runs alongside.

Fluon /'fluːɒn/ ▷ *noun, trademark* polytetrafluoroethylene.

fluor /'fluːɔː(r)/ ▷ *noun* **1** a material that absorbs electrons or radiation, especially ultraviolet light, and converts these into radiation of a different wavelength, usually visible light, which it then emits. **2** FLUORSPAR.

fluoresce /flʊə'rɛs/ ▷ *verb* (***fluoresced***, ***fluorescing***) *intr* to demonstrate fluorescence. ⓘ 19c: from FLUORESCENCE.

fluorescence ▷ *noun, physics* **1** the emission of light and other radiation by an object after it has absorbed electrons or radiation of a different wavelength, especially ultraviolet light. **2** the radiation emitted as a result of fluorescence. Compare LUMINESCENCE, PHOSPHORESCENCE. • **fluorescent** *adj.* ⓘ 19c: from FLUORSPAR, modelled on opalescence; see OPALESCENT.

fluorescent brightener ▷ *noun* any of various chemical compounds frequently incorporated in detergents, that are used to increase the brightness of the colours of textiles, paper, etc, and counteract their natural yellowness by converting invisible ultraviolet light into visible blue light.

fluorescent light and **fluorescent lamp** ▷ *noun, elec* a type of electric light consisting of a glass discharge tube containing mercury vapour or a chemically inert gas, the inner part of which is coated with phosphors that absorb ultraviolet radiation and emit visible light by the process of fluorescence. Also called STRIP LIGHT.

fluoridate and **fluoridize** or **fluoridise** ▷ *verb* (***fluoridated***, ***fluoridating***; ***fluoridized***, ***fluoridizing***) to subject (water) to **fluoridation**, the addition of small amounts (about one part per million) of fluoride salts to drinking water supplies to help prevent tooth decay, a policy adopted by certain water authorities. ⓘ 1940s.

fluoride /'flʊəraɪd, 'flɔː-/ ▷ *noun, chem* **1** any chemical compound consisting of fluorine and another element, especially sodium fluoride, which is added to drinking water supplies and toothpaste to prevent tooth decay in children. **2** a salt of hydrofluoric acid in which the fluorine atom is in the -1 oxidation state. ⓘ 19c: from FLUORINE.

fluorine /'flʊəriːn/ ▷ *noun, chem* (symbol **F**, atomic number 9) a highly corrosive poisonous yellow gas (one of the HALOGENs) that is the most electronegative and reactive chemical element. It has been used as a rocket fuel and in the manufacture of organic compounds such as fluorocarbons. ⓘ 19c: from Latin *fluor* flow.

fluorite see FLUORSPAR

fluorocarbon ▷ *noun, chem* any of various compounds of carbon and fluorine that are highly resistant to heat and chemical action, and very stable over long periods, formerly widely used as aerosol propellants and refrigerants until recent concern about their damaging effect on the ozone layer. See also CHLOROFLUOROCARBON. ⓘ 1930s: from FLUORINE + CARBON, modelled on HYDROCARBON.

fluoroscope ▷ *noun* an instrument for X-ray examination by means of a fluorescent screen. • **fluoroscopic** *adj.* ⓘ 19c.

fluoroscopy /flʊəˈrɒskəpɪ, flɔː-/ ▻ *noun* examination of a person or thing by means of a fluoroscope.

fluorspar /ˈflʊəspɑː, ˈflɔː-/, **fluorite** and **fluor** ▻ *noun, geol* calcium fluoride, a mineral that is transparent when pure, but commonly occurs as blue or purple crystals. It is used in glass and some cements, and in the manufacture of hydrofluoric acid for the plastic industry. ◷ 18c: from Latin *fluor* flow (from the use of fluorspar as a flux) + SPAR[2].

flurry /ˈflʌrɪ/ ▻ *noun* (***flurries***) **1** a sudden commotion; a sudden bustle or rush ▫ ***a flurry of activity.*** **2** a sudden gust; a brief shower of rain, snow, etc ▫ ***a flurry of snowflakes.*** ▻ *verb* (***flurries, flurried, flurrying***) **1** to agitate, confuse or bewilder someone. **2** said of a bird: to fluff up (its feathers). ◷ 17c: imitating the sound.

flush[1] ▻ *verb* (***flushes, flushed, flushing***) **1** *usually intr* to blush or make someone blush or go red. **2** to clean out (especially a lavatory pan) with a rush of water, usually by operating a handle, pressing a button, etc. ▻ *noun* (***flushes***) **1** a redness or rosiness, especially of the cheeks or face; a blush. **2** a rush of water that cleans a lavatory pan, or the mechanism that controls it. **3** high spirits ▫ ***in the first flush of enthusiasm.*** **4** freshness; bloom; vigour ▫ ***the flush of youth.*** • **flushed** *adj* suffused with a rosy colour; excited or elated. • **be flushed with pride,** *etc* to be visibly affected by it, eg by blushing. ◷ 16c: possibly influenced by FLASH, BLUSH and FLUSH[4].

▪ **flush something away** to wash it down the lavatory.

flush[2] ▻ *adj* **1** (*often* **flush with something**) level or even with an adjacent surface. **2** *colloq* having plenty of money ▫ ***Are you flush this week?*** **3** abundant or plentiful. **4** full to the brim. ▻ *adverb* so as to be level with an adjacent surface ▫ ***fixed it flush with the wall.*** ▻ *verb* (***flushes, flushed, flushing***) **1** to make something level with adjacent surfaces. **2** (*often* **flush something up**) to fill up to the level of a surface. ◷ 17c: perhaps from FLUSH[1].

flush[3] ▻ *noun* (***flushes***) *cards* a hand made up of cards from a single suit. ◷ 16c: from Latin *fluxus* flow, influenced by FLUSH[1].

flush[4] ▻ *verb* (***flushes, flushed, flushing***) *hunting* to startle (game birds) so that they rise from the ground. ◷ 13c: probably imitating the sound.

▪ **flush someone** or **something out** to drive them out of a hiding-place.

fluster /ˈflʌstə(r)/ ▻ *verb* (***flustered, flustering***) to agitate, confuse or upset someone; to make them hot and flurried. ▻ *noun* a state of confused agitation. • **flustery** *adj* confused and agitated. ◷ 15c: related to Norse *flaustr* hurry.

flute ▻ *noun* **1** a wind instrument consisting of a wooden or metal tube with holes stopped by the fingertips or by keys, which is held horizontally and played by directing the breath across the EMBOUCHURE. See also FLAUTIST. **2** *archit* a rounded concave groove or furrow in wood or stone, eg running vertically down a pillar. **3** a tall narrow wineglass, used especially for sparkling wine and champagne. Also called **flute-glass**. ▻ *verb* (***fluted, fluting***) **1** to produce or utter (sounds) like the high shrill tones of a flute. **2** *archit* to make long narrow grooves or furrows in (wood or stone). ◷ 14c: from French *flahute*.

fluted ▻ *adj* ornamented with flutes (see FLUTE sense 2).

fluting ▻ *noun* a series of parallel grooves cut into wood or stone.

flutist ▻ *noun, N Amer* a FLAUTIST.

flutter /ˈflʌtə(r)/ ▻ *verb* (***fluttered, fluttering***) **1** *tr & intr* said of a bird, etc: to flap (its wings) lightly and rapidly; to fly with a rapid wing movement. **2** *intr* said of a flag, etc: to flap repeatedly in the air. **3** *intr* drift with a twirling motion ▫ ***Leaves fluttered to the ground.*** **4** *intr* to move about in a restless, aimless way. **5** *intr* said of the heart: to race, from excitement or some medical disorder. **6** *old use* to cause agitation in (someone's heart). ▻ *noun* **1** a quick flapping or vibrating motion. **2** agitation; excitement ▫ ***flutter of excitement.*** **3** *colloq* a small bet; a speculation. **4** *music* in wind-instrument playing: rapid movement of the tongue as for a rolled *r*. Also called **flutter-tonguing**. **5** in a hi-fi system, etc: a regularly recurring variation in loudness and pitch. • **flutterer** *noun*. ◷ Anglo-Saxon *floterian*.

fluty ▻ *adj* (***flutier, flutiest***) like a flute in tone.

fluvial /ˈfluːvɪəl/ ▻ *adj* relating to or found in rivers. ◷ 14c: from Latin *fluvialis*.

flux /flʌks/ ▻ *noun* (***fluxes***) **1** a flow of matter; the act of flowing. **2** constant change; instability. **3** any substance added to another in order to aid the process of melting. **4** in the smelting of metal ores: any substance that is added so that it will combine with impurities which can then be removed as a flowing mass of slag. **5** any substance, such as a resin, that is used to remove oxides from the surfaces of metals that are to be soldered, welded or brazed. **6** *physics* the rate of flow of particles, energy, mass or some other quantity per unit cross-sectional area per unit time. See also LUMINOUS FLUX and MAGNETIC FLUX. **7** *pathol* an excessive discharge of fluid from the body. ▻ *verb* (***fluxes, fluxed, fluxing***) **1** to apply flux to (a metal, etc) when soldering. **2** *tr & intr* to make or become fluid. • **be in a state of flux** to be in an unsettled state or a state of indecision. ◷ 14c: from Latin *fluxus* flow.

fly[1] ▻ *noun* (***flies***) **1** a two-winged insect, especially the common housefly. **2** *in compounds* any of various other flying insects ▫ ***mayfly*** ▫ ***dragonfly*** ▫ ***butterfly.*** **3** *angling* a fish hook tied with colourful feathers to look like a fly, used in fly-fishing. • **drop like flies** *colloq* to fall ill or die in large numbers. • **a fly in the ointment** a drawback or disadvantage to an otherwise satisfactory state of affairs. • **a fly on the wall** the invisible observer, usually at a meeting or in a social situation, that one would like to be on certain occasions to find out what is happening without having to take part. • **no flies on someone** *colloq* referring to someone who is cunning and not easily fooled ▫ ***There are no flies on Harry.*** • **they,** *etc* **wouldn't harm a fly** they, etc have a gentle nature. ◷ Anglo-Saxon *fleoge*.

fly[2] ▻ *verb* (*3rd person present tense* ***flies***, *past tense* ***flew*** /fluː/, *past participle* ***flown*** /floun/, *present participle* ***flying***) **1** *intr* **a** said of birds, bats, insects and certain other animals: to move through the air using wings or structures resembling wings; **b** said of an aircraft or spacecraft: to travel through the air or through space. **2** *tr & intr* to travel or convey in an aircraft ▫ ***They flew to Moscow*** ▫ ***The company flew them to Moscow.*** **3** to operate and control (an aircraft, kite, etc); to cause it to fly ▫ ***The pilot flew the plane competently.*** **4** to cross (an area of land or water) in an aircraft ▫ ***They flew the Atlantic to New York.*** **5** **a** to raise (a flag) ▫ ***fly the flag on St George's day***; **b** *intr* said of a flag: to blow or flutter in the wind. **6** *intr* to move or pass rapidly ▫ ***fly into a temper*** ▫ ***rumours flying around.*** **7** *intr, colloq* to depart quickly; to dash off ▫ ***I must fly.*** **8** *tr & intr* to escape; to flee (a country, a war zone, etc). ▻ *noun* (***flies***) **1** (*chiefly* **flies**) a zip or set of buttons fastening a trouser front, or the flap covering these. **2** a flap covering the entrance to a tent. **3** (**flies**) the space above a stage, concealed from the audience's view, from which scenery is lowered. **4** short for FLYWHEEL. • **do something on the fly** to work something out immediately without any preparation. • **fly by the seat of one's pants** to do a job instinctively or by feel when one doesn't know the usual procedure. • **fly high 1** to be ambitious. **2** to prosper or flourish. • **fly in the face of something** to oppose it; to be at variance with it. • **fly a kite** to release information about an idea, proposal, etc to find out what people's opinion might be about it. • **fly off the handle** to lose one's temper. • **fly open** said of a door, window, etc: to open suddenly or violently, due to a gust of wind, someone's abrupt entry, etc. • **let fly** to loose one's temper (with someone) ▫ ***Suddenly, Paul let***

fly at Mark. • **let something fly** to shoot or throw something. • **send someone** or **something flying** to knock them down or knock them over with considerable force. Ⓒ Anglo-Saxon *fleogan.*

■ **fly at** or **out at someone** *intr* to attack them angrily and suddenly.

fly³ ▻ *adj, colloq* cunning; smart. Ⓒ 19c.

fly agaric ▻ *noun* a mushroom with a flattened scarlet cap covered with concentric rings of small white scales, and a white stem with a swollen base, containing poisonous (though not deadly) substances and mild hallucinogens. Ⓒ 18c: so called because of the custom of using the cap crumbled in milk to kill flies, and its use on flypaper.

fly ash ▻ *noun* fine particles of ash released into the air during eg the burning of fossil fuels in power stations. Ⓒ 1930s.

flyblown ▻ *adj* **1** said of food: covered with blowfly eggs, and therefore unfit to eat; contaminated. **2** shabby, dirty or dingy. Ⓒ 16c.

flyboat ▻ *noun* a long narrow boat used on canals which is faster than a conventional canal boat.

flybook ▻ *noun* a small case or wallet used by anglers for holding fishing-flies.

fly-by ▻ *noun* (***fly-bys***) a flight, at low altitude or close range, past a place, target, etc, for observation, especially the close approach of a spacecraft to a planet, etc.

fly-by-night ▻ *adj, derog* said of a business, etc: not reliable or trustworthy. ▻ *noun* an absconding debtor, especially one who disappears overnight. Ⓒ 18c.

fly-by-wire ▻ *adj* said of the control systems of an aircraft: electronically operated with the aid of a computer, and not mechanically operated. Ⓒ 1980s.

flycatcher ▻ *noun* **1** a name applied to birds of three distinct groups, New World or tyrant flycatchers, Old World flycatchers, and silky flycatchers, all of which usually eat insects caught in flight. **2** any of various birds of other families. Ⓒ 16c.

fly-dressing ▻ *noun* FLY-TYING.

flyer see FLIER

fly-fish ▻ *verb, intr, angling* to fish using artificial flies as bait. • **fly-fishing** *noun.*

fly half ▻ *noun, rugby* a STAND-OFF HALF (see STAND-OFF 2).

flying ▻ *adj* **1** hasty; brief □ *a flying visit.* **2** designed or organized for fast movement. **3** that flies; able to fly, or to glide for long distances. **4** said eg of hair or a flag: streaming; fluttering. ▻ *noun* **1** flight. **2** the activity of piloting, or travelling in, an aircraft. Also *as adj.* • **not give a flying fuck** *taboo slang* not to care about something; not to give a damn about something.

flying boat ▻ *noun* a seaplane whose fuselage is shaped like a boat hull.

flying buttress ▻ *noun, archit* a support structure forming an arch or half-arch built against the outside wall of a large building, especially a church, in order to resist the outward thrust of the wall. Ⓒ 17c.

flying colours ▻ *plural noun* triumphant success □ *She passed the exam with flying colours.* Ⓒ 18c.

flying doctor ▻ *noun* especially in the remote parts of Australia: a doctor who can be called by radio and who travels by light aircraft to visit patients.

flying dragon see FLYING LIZARD

flying fish ▻ *noun* any of various small surface-living fishes, native to tropical and warm temperate seas, with stiff, greatly enlarged pectoral fins superficially resembling wings, that enable the fish to leap from the water and glide for considerable distances above the surface at speeds of up to 50km per hour.

flying fox ▻ *noun* any of many species of large fruit-eating bat which does not employ ECHO LOCATION for navigation but relies on their excellent eyesight. Ⓒ 18c: so called because some species have a fox-like head.

flying jib ▻ *noun* in a vessel with more than one jib: the one set furthest forward.

flying leap and **flying jump** ▻ *noun* a jump taken from a running start.

flying lemur see COLUGO

flying lizard ▻ *noun* a species of lizard native to SE Asia that is able to glide between trees by using a semicircular membrane, which is supported by movable ribs on either side of its body. Also called **flying dragon**.

flying machine ▻ *noun, dated* an early power-driven aircraft. Ⓒ 18c: referring to contrivances used in the theatre to suspend actors from, and also to describe aircraft before any were successfully invented.

flying officer *noun,* an officer in the air force. See table at RANK.

flying phalanger ▻ *noun* a nocturnal squirrel-like marsupial, native to Australia and New Guinea, that has a gliding membrane between its front and hind limbs, and can glide for distances of up to 114m (125yd).

flying picket ▻ *noun* a picket travelling from place to place to support local pickets during any strike.

flying saucer ▻ *noun* any unidentified circular flying object reported in the sky from time to time, believed by some to be craft from outer space.

flying snake ▻ *noun* a snake from SE Asia that glides between trees by launching itself in the air and then flattening its body and forming several S-shaped curves.

flying spot scanner ▻ *noun, telecomm* a device for producing television picture signals from photographic transparencies or motion picture film, by scanning the picture area with a spot of light, generated on the screen of a cathode-ray tube.

flying squad ▻ *noun* a body of police specially trained for quick response and fast action, and available for duty wherever the need arises.

flying squirrel ▻ *noun* any of various species of squirrel, most of which are found in SE Asia, with a large flap of skin between the front and hind legs, which they use to glide between trees for distances of up to 450m (492yd).

flying start ▻ *noun, sport* **1** a start to a race in which the contestants are already travelling at full speed when they cross the starting-line. **2** a start by a competitor in a race which anticipates the starting signal. • **get off to a flying start** said of a task, project, etc or of a person: to begin promisingly or with a special advantage.

flying suit ▻ *noun* **1** a pilot's one-piece suit. **2** a similar fashion garment, worn especially in the 1980s.

flyleaf ▻ *noun* a blank page at the beginning or end of a book.

Flymo /'flaɪmoʊ/ ▻ *noun* (***Flymos***) *trademark* a type of lawnmower which hovers on a cushion of air.

flyover ▻ *noun* a bridge that takes a road or railway over another. *N Amer equivalent* **overpass**.

flypaper ▻ *noun* a strip of paper with a sticky poisonous coating that attracts, traps and kills flies.

flypast ▻ *noun* a ceremonial flight of military aircraft over a particular place, where a crowd sometimes including royalty is gathered for an event like a festival or fête.

flypitch ▻ *noun, colloq* a market stall for which the operator does not have a licence.

flypitcher ▻ *noun, colloq* the operator of an unlicensed market stall.

flyposting ▻ *noun* the putting up of advertising or political posters, etc illegally.

flysheet ▻ *noun* **1** a protective outer sheet for a tent which is fitted over the main body. **2** a single-sheet leaflet.

flyspray ▻ *noun* a liquid poisonous to flies, sprayed from an aerosol can.

fly-tipping ▻ *noun* unauthorized disposal of waste.

flytrap ▻ *noun* **1** a device for catching flies. **2** *bot* any of various plants that trap flies and digest them, eg the VENUS FLYTRAP.

fly-tying ▻ *noun* making artificial flies for angling.

flyway ▻ *noun* a migration route of birds.

flyweight ▻ *noun* **1** a class of boxers, wrestlers and weight-lifters of not more than a specified weight (51kg or 112 lb in professional boxing, similar weights in the other sports). **2** a boxer, etc weighing not more than the specified amount for their category. See also MINI-FLYWEIGHT, LIGHT-FLYWEIGHT, SUPER FLYWEIGHT.

flywheel ▻ *noun* a heavy wheel on a revolving shaft that stores kinetic energy and regulates the action of a machine by maintaining a constant speed of roation over the whole cycle.

FM ▻ *abbreviation* **1** Field Marshal. **2** frequency modulation.

Fm ▻ *symbol, chem* fermium.

f-number ▻ *noun, photog* the numerical value of the relative aperture of a camera lens, expressing the diameter of the lens diaphragm as a fraction of its focal length, eg if the relative aperture is f/8, f:8 or f8, then the f-number is 8.

FO ▻ *abbreviation* **1** Field Officer. **2** Flying Officer. **3** *historical* Foreign Office (now FCO).

fo or **fol.** ▻ *abbreviation* folio.

foal ▻ *noun* the young of a horse or of a related animal. See also STALLION, MARE. ▻ *verb* (***foaled***, ***foaling***) *intr* to give birth to a foal. • **in foal** or **with foal** said of a mare: pregnant. ◷ Anglo-Saxon *fola*.

foam ▻ *noun* **1** a mass of tiny bubbles forming on the surface of liquids. **2** a substance composed of tiny bubbles formed by passing gas through it. **3** frothy saliva or perspiration. **4** any of many light cellular materials used for packaging, insulation, etc, produced by passing gas through, and then solidifying, a liquid. **5** a colloid consisting of gas bubbles dispersed evenly throughout a liquid □ ***shaving foam***. **6** *poetic* the sea. **7** Also *as adj* □ ***foam rubber***. ▻ *verb* (***foamed***, ***foaming***) *tr & intr* (*sometimes* **foam up**) to produce or make something produce foam. • **foaming** *noun, adj*. • **foamless** *adj*. • **foam at the mouth 1** *colloq* to be furiously angry. **2** to produce and expel frothy saliva at the mouth, eg as a rabid animal does. ◷ Anglo-Saxon *fam*.

foamy ▻ *adj* (***foamier***, ***foamiest***) **1** said of a liquid: covered with foam; with foam floating on the top of it. **2** resembling foam; frothy. • **foaminess** *noun*.

fob¹ ▻ *verb* (***fobbed***, ***fobbing***) now only in phrases below. ◷ 16c: related to German *foppen* to delude.

▪ **fob someone off** to dismiss or ignore them □ ***tried to fob off his critics***.

▪ **fob someone off with something** to provide them with something inferior (eg a poor substitute, or an inadequate explanation), usually in the hope that they will be satisfied.

▪ **fob something off on someone** to manage to sell or pass off something inferior to someone.

fob² ▻ *noun* **1** a chain attached to a watch. **2** a decorative attachment to a key ring or watch chain. **3** *historical* a small watch pocket in a waistcoat or trouser waistband, for holding a **fob watch**. ◷ 17c: perhaps related to German dialect *fuppe* pocket.

f.o.b. ▻ *abbreviation* free on board.

FOC ▻ *abbreviation* in a trade union: father of the chapel.

foc ▻ *abbreviation* free of charge.

focaccia /fəˈkatʃə/ ▻ *noun* (***focaccias***) a flat round of Italian bread topped with olive oil and herbs or spices. ◷ 20c: Italian.

focal /ˈfoʊkəl/ ▻ *adj* relating to, or at, a focus. ◷ 18c.

focal distance and **focal length** ▻ *noun* the distance between the surface of a mirror or centre of a lens and its focal point.

focalize or **focalise** /ˈfoʊkəlaɪz/ ▻ *verb* (***focalized***, ***focalizing***) *tr & intr, technical* to focus something. • **focalization** *noun*.

focal point ▻ *noun* **1** *optics* the point at which rays of light which are initially parallel to the axis of a lens or mirror converge, or appear to diverge, having been reflected or refracted. Also called **focus**. **2** a centre of attraction of some event or activity.

focimeter /foʊˈsɪmɪtə(r)/ ▻ *noun* an instrument for measuring the focal length of a lens.

fo'c'sle /ˈfoʊksəl/ ▻ *noun, naut* a spelling of FORECASTLE suggested by its pronunciation.

focus /ˈfoʊkəs/ ▻ *noun* (***focuses*** or ***foci*** /ˈfoʊsaɪ/) **1** the point at which rays of light or sound waves converge or appear to diverge. **2** *optics* FOCAL POINT 1. **3 a** the condition in which an image is sharp □ ***The picture is in focus***; **b** the state of an instrument producing this image □ ***The telescope is in focus*** □ ***These binoculars are out of focus***. **4** *geol* in seismology: the location of the centre of an earthquake, where the subterranean fracture takes place and from which the elastic waves radiate outward. See also EPICENTRE. **5** a centre of interest or attention. **6** special attention paid to something □ ***a shift of focus***. **7** *pathol* the main site of an infection. **8** *geom* a point associated with a CONIC SECTION where the distance between it and any point on the curve is a fixed ratio (the ECCENTRICITY 4) to the distance between that point and a line (the DIRECTRIX). ▻ *verb* (***focused***, ***focusing***; ***focussed***, ***focussing***) **1** *tr & intr* to bring or be brought into focus; to meet or make something meet or converge at a focus. **2** to adjust the thickness of the lens of (the eye) or to move the lens of (an optical instrument) so as to obtain the sharpest possible image of a particular object. **3** to cause (electron beams) to converge or diverge by varying the voltage or current that controls the magnetic or electric fields through which they pass. **4** (*often* **focus something on something**) *tr & intr* to concentrate (one's attention, etc) on it □ ***focused her energies on the problem*** □ ***focused on the problem***. ◷ 17c: Latin, meaning 'hearth or fireplace'; probably referring to the 'burning point of a lens or mirror'.

focus group ▻ *noun* a small group of people brought together to discuss some topic in a relaxed conversational way so that others may get their insights or opinions about the topic concerned. ◷ 1990s.

fodder /ˈfɒdə(r)/ ▻ *noun* **1** any bulk feed, especially hay and straw, for cattle and other animal livestock. **2** *colloq* something that is constantly made use of by someone (eg newspaper editors) to feed an ongoing need (eg for copy) □ ***Stories about royalty are fodder for the popular press***. See also CANNON FODDER. ▻ *verb* (***foddered***, ***foddering***) to supply (livestock) with fodder. ◷ Anglo-Saxon *fodor*.

FOE or **FoE** ▻ *abbreviation* Friends of the Earth.

foe ▻ *noun, literary, old use* an enemy. ◷ Anglo-Saxon *fah* hostile.

foehn see FÖHN

foetal see FETAL

foetid see FETID

foetoscopy see FETOSCOPY

foetus see FETUS

fog¹ ▻ *noun* **1** a suspension of tiny water droplets or ice crystals forming a cloud close to the ground surface and reducing visibility to less than 1 km; thick mist. **2** *photog* a blurred patch on a negative, print or transparency, which can be caused by excess light, chemical impurities, aged materials, etc. **3** a blur; cloudiness. **4** a state of confusion or bewilderment. ▷ *verb* (***fogged***, ***fogging***) **1** *tr & intr* (*often* **fog over** or **up**) to obscure or become obscured with, or as if with, fog or condensation. **2** to confuse or perplex. **3** *photog* to be affected by fog. • **fogless** *adj.* ◷ 16c: derived from *foggy* boggy or marshy, from FOG².

fog² and **foggage** ▷ *noun* the grass that grows after the hay is cut. ◷ 14c.

fog bank ▷ *noun* a distant and well-defined mass of dense fog, especially at sea.

fogbound ▷ *adj* usually said eg of an airport: brought to a standstill by fog.

fogey or **fogy** /ˈfoʊgɪ/ ▷ *noun* (***fogeys*** or ***fogies***) *noun, derog* someone with boring, old-fashioned and usually conservative ideas and attitudes, often called **old fogey**, also sometimes **young fogey** if the person with these characteristics seems particularly young to have such staid attitudes. • **fogeyish** or **fogyish** *adj.* ◷ 18c: probably from *foggy* moss-grown; *young fogey* used particularly since the 1980s.

foggy ▷ *adj* (***foggier***, ***foggiest***) **1** covered with or thick with fog¹; misty, damp. **2** not clear; confused. • **fogginess** *noun.* • **not have the foggiest** or **not have the foggiest idea** *colloq* not to know at all.

foghorn ▷ *noun* **1** a horn that sounds at regular intervals to ships in fog as a warning of some danger or obstruction, eg land, other vessels, etc. **2** *colloq* a deep, loud and penetrating voice. ◷ 19c.

fog lamp and **fog light** ▷ *noun* a powerful lamp used by vehicles in fog.

föhn or **foehn** /fɜːn/ ▷ *noun* a hot dry wind which blows to the lee of a mountain range, especially down the valleys to the north side of the Alps. ◷ 19c: German, from Romansch *favugn*, from Latin *Favonius* a west wind and a warming wind.

foible /ˈfɔɪbəl/ ▷ *noun* a slight personal weakness or eccentricity in someone. ◷ 17c: French, variant of *faible* feeble or week.

foie gras /fwɑː grɑː/ ▷ *noun* a pâté made of specially fattened goose liver. Also called **pâté de foie gras**. ◷ 19c: French, meaning '(pâté of) fat liver'.

foil¹ ▷ *verb* (***foiled***, ***foiling***) to prevent, thwart or frustrate someone or something. ◷ 16c: from French *fuler* to trample.

foil² ▷ *noun* **1 a** metal beaten or rolled out into thin sheets; **b** *also in compounds* □ *tinfoil* □ *gold foil.* **2** a thin metallic coating (usually mercury or a mercury-alloy) on a piece of glass which produces a reflection, forming the backing of a mirror. **3** a thin leaf of metal put under a precious stone to show it to advantage. **4** someone or something that acts as a contrast to, and brings out, the superior or different qualities of another. **5** *archit* in tracery, particularly of Gothic architecture: a small leaf-shaped curve or arc, forming a CUSP where two foils meet. **6** a hydrofoil or an aerofoil. • **foilborne** said of a craft: lifted up from the water or travelling along the water on hydrofoils. ◷ 14c: from French *foil* leaf, from Latin *folium*.

foil³ /fɔɪl/ ▷ *noun, fencing* a long slender sword with a blunt edge and a point protected by a button. ◷ 16c.

foist /fɔɪst/ ▷ *verb* (***foisted***, ***foisting***) now only in phrases below. ◷ 16c: perhaps from Dutch dialect *vuisten* to take in hand, from *vuist* fist.

■ **foist something in** or **into something** to insert it wrongly.

■ **foist something on someone** **1** to inflict or impose something unwanted on them □ *foisted the baby on her for the day.* **2** to sell or pass on something inferior to them, while suggesting that it has value or is genuine; to palm something off on someone.

fol. ▷ *abbreviation* **1** folio. **2** following.

folate /ˈfoʊleɪt, ˈfɒ-/ ▷ *adj* relating to folic acid. ▷ *noun* **1** a salt of folic acid. **2** folic acid.

fold¹ /foʊld/ ▷ *verb* (***folded***, ***folding***) **1** (*also* **fold something over, back, up**, *etc*) to double it over so that one part lies on top of another. **2** *intr* (*also* **fold away**) to be able to be folded, or closed up so that it takes up less space, usually making it flat □ *The chair folds away for storage.* **3** said of an insect, etc: to bring in (wings) close to its body. **4** (*often* **fold something up**) to arrange (clothes, etc) tidily for storage by laying them flat and doubling each piece of clothing over on itself □ *folded the jumpers up and put them in the drawer.* **5** *intr* said of flower petals: to close. **6** to clasp someone in one's arms, etc. **7** (*also* **fold up**) *colloq* said of a business, etc: to collapse; to fail □ *The shop folded after 1 year.* ▷ *noun* **1** a doubling of one layer over another. **2** a rounded or sharp bend made by this, particularly the inside part of it; a crease. **3** a hollow in the landscape. **4** *geol* a buckling, bending or contortion of stratified rocks as a result of movements of the Earth's crust, the most common types of which are arch-shaped (ANTICLINES) and trough-shaped (SYNCLINES). • **foldable** *adj.* • **foldaway** *adj* referring to something that can be folded and put away. • **fold one's arms** to cross over and intertwine (one's arms) across one's chest. ◷ Anglo-Saxon *faldan* to fold.

■ **fold something in** *cookery* to add and stir (an ingredient) gently into a mixture with an action like folding.

fold² /foʊld/ ▷ *noun* **1** a walled or fenced enclosure or pen for sheep or cattle. **2** the body of believers within the protection of a church □ *They were invited into the fold.* ◷ Anglo-Saxon *falod*.

-fold ▷ *suffix, forming adverbs and adjectives* **1** multiplied by a specified number □ *The chairman's salary increased threefold.* **2** *adj* having a specified number of parts □ *a twofold benefit.* ◷ Anglo-Saxon *-feald*.

folder /ˈfoʊldə(r)/ ▷ *noun* a cardboard or plastic cover in which to keep loose papers. ◷ Early 20c in this sense.

folderol see FALDERAL

folding ▷ *adj* referring to something that can be folded away so that it takes up less space, particularly for storage □ *a folding chair* □ *a folding bed.* ▷ *noun* **1** a fold or plait. **2** *geol* the bending of strata, usually as the result of compression.

folding money ▷ *noun, colloq* paper money.

foldout ▷ *noun* a large page, eg containing a diagram or illustration, which is folded to fit into a book, and is unfolded when used. Also called **gatefold**.

foliaceous /foʊlɪˈeɪʃəs/ ▷ *adj* **1** consisting of or resembling leaves; leaflike. **2** *geol* composed of thin leaflike or platelike layers of minerals. ◷ 17c: from Latin *foliaceus*, from *folium* leaf.

foliage /ˈfoʊlɪɪdʒ/ ▷ *noun* **1** the green leaves on a tree or plant. **2** sprays of leaves used for decoration. ◷ 15c: from French *feuillage*, from *feuille* leaf; influenced by Latin *folium* leaf.

foliage plant ▷ *noun* a plant grown for the beauty of its foliage.

foliate /ˈfoʊlɪeɪt/ ▷ *adj* leaflike or having leaves. ▷ *verb* (***foliated***, ***foliating***) **1** to cover with leaf-metal or foils. **2** to hammer (metal) into thin sheets. **3** to mark the leaves or folios (not pages) of a book, etc with consecutive numbers. Compare PAGINATE. **4** *intr* said of a plant: to grow leaves. **5** to decorate (*especially* Gothic architecture) with ornamental leaf carving. ◷ 17c: from Latin *foliatus* leafy.

folic acid /ˈfoʊlɪk —, ˈfɒlɪk —/ ▷ *noun, biochem* a member of the VITAMIN B COMPLEX found in many foods, especially liver and green leafy vegetables, which is required for the manufacture of DNA and RNA and the formation of red blood cells, deficiency of which causes anaemia and retarded growth. ⓒ 1940s: from Latin *folium* leaf (because of its presence in green leaves).

folie à deux /*French* fɒli a 'dø/ *noun, pathol* a form of mental illness in which two people, generally close to one another, share the same delusion. ⓒ 19c: French.

folie de grandeur /*French* fɒli də gʀɑ̃dœʀ/ *noun, pathol* a form of mental illness characterized by a delusion that one possesses wealth, beauty or irresistible charms. ⓒ 20c: French.

folio /'foulɪou/ ▷ *noun* (**folios**) **1** a leaf of a manuscript, etc, numbered on one side. **2** *printing* a page number in a book. **3 a** a body of written work, etc, submitted as part of an examination □ *Your English folio must be completed by March.* **b** *as adj* □ *Folio pieces must be handwritten.* **4** *historical* **a** a sheet of paper folded once to make two leaves for a book; **b** a book of the largest size, composed of such sheets. **5** *old use* a folder. Also *as adj* □ *a folio edition.* ⓒ 16c: from Latin *folium* leaf.

foliole ▷ *noun* **1** *bot* a leaflet of a compound leaf. **2** a small leaflike structure.

folk /fouk/ ▷ *plural noun* **1** people in general. **2** (*also colloq* **folks**) one's family □ *Her folk are from Edinburgh* □ *going to visit the folks.* **3** people belonging to a particular group, nation or tribe □ *country folk.* ▷ *singular noun, colloq* folk music □ *Folk is popular at the Royal Oak.* ▷ *adj* traditional among, or originating from, a particular group of people or nation □ *folk music* □ *a folksong* □ *folk art.* ⓒ Anglo-Saxon *folc.*

folk art ▷ *noun* traditional handicrafts, especially pottery, wood-carvings, textiles and basketware, produced by local craftsmen with no formal training, usually employing techniques, patterns and designs that have been handed down from generation to generation.

folk etymology ▷ *noun* an etymology in which popular ideas about the origin of words or phrases leads to an erroneous analysis, with direct relations being drawn with other words which have a similar form or meaning, eg when 'asparagus' is referred to as 'sparrow-grass'.

folk hero ▷ *noun* a hero in the eyes of a particular group of people.

folkie /'foukɪ/ ▷ *noun, colloq* **1** someone who enjoys listening to folk music. **2** someone who enjoys playing or singing folk music; a folk musician. ⓒ 1960s.

folklore ▷ *noun* **1** the customs, beliefs, stories, traditions, etc of a particular group of people, usually passed down through the oral tradition. **2** the study of these. • **folkloric** *adj.* • **folklorist** *noun* someone who studies folklore. ⓒ 19c.

folk-memory ▷ *noun* a memory of an event that survives in a community through many generations.

folk music ▷ *noun* **1** music which is played on traditional instruments or sung in the tradition style, handed down from generation to generation, and relating to the music of a particular area or group of people. **2** contemporary music of a similar style.

folk song ▷ *noun* any song or ballad originating among the people and traditionally handed down from generation to generation through the oral tradition.

folksy ▷ *adj* (**folksier**, **folksiest**) **1** simple and homely, especially in an over-sweet or twee way. **2** everyday; friendly; sociable; unpretentious. • **folksiness** *noun.* ⓒ 19c: originally US.

folk tale and **folk story** ▷ *noun* a popular story handed down by oral tradition from generation to generation, and whose origin is often unknown.

folk-weave ▷ *noun* a loosely woven fabric.

follicle /'fɒlɪkəl/ ▷ *noun* **1** *anatomy* a small cavity or sac within a tissue or organ, eg the pit surrounding the root of a hair □ *hair follicle* □ *Graafian follicle.* **2** *bot* a fruit formed from a single carpel, containing several seeds, which splits along one side when mature, eg columbine fruit. • **follicular** or **folliculose** *adj.* ⓒ 17c: from Latin *folliculus* a small bag or sack, diminutive of *follis* bellows.

follicle-stimulating hormone ▷ *noun* (abbreviation **FSH**) *physiol* a hormone, secreted by the pituitary gland in vertebrates, which in mammals stimulates the growth of the OVARIAN FOLLICLES (in females) and the production of SPERM (in males).

follow /'fɒlou/ ▷ *verb* (**followed**, **following**) **1** *tr & intr* (*also* **follow after someone**) to go or come after them, either immediately or shortly afterwards. **2** to accompany someone; to go with them. **3** to secretly go after someone to find out what they are doing; to pursue stealthily. **4** to accept someone as leader or authority. **5** *intr* (*sometimes* **follow from something**) to result from it; to be a consequence of it □ *It follows that John will arrive around 2pm.* **6** to go along (a road, etc), alongside (a river, etc) or on the path marked by (signs). **7** to watch someone or something as they or it move □ *His eyes followed her up the street.* **8** to do something in a particular way; to practise it □ *follow a life of self-denial* □ *follow a trade.* **9** to conform to something □ *follows a familiar pattern.* **10** to obey (advice, etc). **11** *tr & intr* to copy □ *follow her example* □ *followed unthinkingly.* **12** *tr & intr* to understand □ *Do you follow me?* **13** to read (a piece of writing or music) while listening to a performance of it. **14** to take a keen interest in (a sport, etc) □ *Fiona avidly follows football.* • **as follows** as announced immediately after this, or shown in the text below. • **followed by something** and then; after which □ *Sweet, followed by coffee* □ *a trailer followed by the main feature film.* • **follow suit 1** *cards* to play a card of the same suit as the one which is leading for that hand. **2** to do what someone else has done without thinking much about it □ *Paul always simply follows suit.* ⓒ Anglo-Saxon *folgian.*

■ **follow on** *intr* **1** to continue; to take something up where someone else has left off □ *I'll follow on after you.* **2** *cricket* said of a side: to play a FOLLOW-ON.

■ **follow something out** to carry out (eg instructions) fully, or to their required conclusion.

■ **follow through** or **follow something through** *tennis, golf* to continue the action of (a stroke) after hitting the ball. See also FOLLOW-THROUGH.

■ **follow something through** or **up** to pursue (an idea, a project, etc) beyond its early stages, and often to fruition; to investigate or test it.

■ **follow something up** to take the next step after a particular procedure □ *followed up their investigations with a detailed report.* See also FOLLOW-UP.

follower ▷ *noun* **1** someone or something that follows or comes after others. **2** someone who copies. **3** an avid supporter or devotee, eg of a particular sport, celebrity, etc. **4** a disciple. **5** an attendant; someone who is part of someone's entourage. **6** a part of a machine driven by another part.

following ▷ *noun* a body of supporters, devotees, etc □ *Thomas has a big following.* ▷ *adj* **1** coming after; next. **2** about to be mentioned □ *need to deal with the following points.* **3** said of a wind, currents, etc: blowing in the direction in which a ship, etc is travelling. ▷ *prep* after.

follow-on ▷ *noun, cricket* a second innings batted immediately after the first, as a result of a team having scored a particular number of runs less than the competing team. See FOLLOW ON at FOLLOW.

follow-through ▷ *noun* **1** *tennis, golf* the continuation of the swing of a stroke after hitting the ball. **2** *billiards* a shot that causes the ball to follow the one it has struck. **3** following through; further investigation or testing. See FOLLOW THROUGH at FOLLOW.

follow-up ▷ *noun* **1 a** continuing something that is not completed; further action or investigation; **b** *as adj* □ ***follow-up questions.*** **2** an examination of a patient after treatment to check what progress they have made □ ***Come back on Monday for a follow-up.*** See also FOLLOW SOMETHING UP at FOLLOW.

folly /ˈfɒlɪ/ ▷ *noun* (*follies*) **1** foolishness; a foolish act. **2** a mock temple, castle, ruin, etc built eg as a romantic addition to a view. ◷ 13c: from French *folie* madness.

foment /foʊˈmɛnt/ ▷ *verb* (*fomented*, *fomenting*) to encourage or foster (ill-feeling, etc). ● **fomentation** *noun*. ● **fomenter** *noun*. ◷ 17c: from Latin *fomentum*, from *fovere* to cherish or warm.

fond ▷ *adj* **1** loving; tender □ ***fond glances.*** **2** happy □ ***fond memories.*** **3** said of desire, hopes, etc: foolishly impractical □ ***He harboured a fond hope that sparks would fly between them again.*** ● **fondly** *adverb*. ● **fondness** *noun*. ● **fond of someone** or **something** having a liking for them or it □ ***fond of her cat.*** ◷ 14c as *fonned*; from *fonnen* to act foolishly.

fondant /ˈfɒndənt/ ▷ *noun* a soft sweet or paste made with sugar and water, often flavoured and used for the fillings of chocolates, or as icing. ◷ 19c: French, from *fondre* to melt.

fondle /ˈfɒndəl/ ▷ *verb* (*fondled*, *fondling*) to touch, stroke or caress someone or something lovingly, affectionately or lustfully. ● **fondler** *noun*. ● **fondling** *noun*. ◷ 17c: from FOND showing fondness or affection for something.

fondue /ˈfɒnduː, ˈfɒndjuː/ ▷ *noun* (*fondues*) *cookery* **1** a dish, originally Swiss, consisting of hot cheese sauce into which bits of bread are dipped. **2** a steak dish in which pieces of meat are cooked at the table by dipping them briefly into hot oil. Also called **fondue bourguignonne** /— bʊəgiːnˈjɒn/). ◷ 19c: from French *fondu* melted.

font¹ /fɒnt/ ▷ *noun, church* the basin in a church that holds water for baptisms. ● **fontal** *adj*. ◷ Anglo-Saxon *fant*, from Latin *fons, fontis* fountain.

font² see FOUNT¹

fontanelle or (*chiefly US*) **fontanel** /fɒntəˈnɛl/ *noun, anatomy* a soft membrane-covered gap between the immature bones of the skull of a fetus or young infant, or of a young animal. ◷ 16c: from French *fontanele*.

food /fuːd/ ▷ *noun* **1** a substance taken in by a living organism that provides it with energy and materials for growth, maintenance and repair of tissues. **2** solid as distinct from liquid nourishment □ ***food and drink.*** **3** something that provides stimulation □ ***food for thought.*** ◷ Anglo-Saxon *foda*.

food additive ▷ *noun* any naturally occurring or artificially manufactured chemical compound that is added in small quantities to a food product, eg to improve its flavour, nutritional value or visual appeal, or to prolong its shelf-life, including preservatives, flavourings and colourings. ◷ 1950s.

food canal ▷ *noun* the alimentary canal.

food chain ▷ *noun, ecol* a sequence of organisms arranged in such a way that each feeds on the organism below it in the chain, and serves as a source of food for the organism above it.

food court ▷ *noun* an area in a shopping mall with a variety of fast-food booths and an area with communal seating and tables for the customers.

food-fish ▷ *noun* a fish used as food by humans.

foodie ▷ *noun, colloq* a person who is greatly or excessively interested in the preparation and eating of food, especially wholefoods and additive-free foods. ● **foodism** *noun* great interest in, or concern over, food. ◷ 1980s.

food poisoning ▷ *noun* any of various illnesses that result from eating food or drinking water containing toxins or micro-organisms, especially species of the SALMONELLA bacterium.

food processor ▷ *noun* an electrical domestic apparatus for chopping and blending food. ◷ 1970s.

foodstuff ▷ *noun* a substance used as food. ◷ 19c.

food technology ▷ *noun* the application of scientific methods and engineering technology to the commercial processing, preparation, packaging, storage and distribution of foodstuffs.

food value ▷ *noun* the nutritional value of a particular food, expressed in terms of its protein, carbohydrate, fat, fibre and energy content.

food web ▷ *noun, ecol* the interlocking patterns formed by a series of interconnected FOOD CHAINS.

fool¹ /fuːl/ ▷ *noun* **1** someone who lacks common sense or intelligence. **2** someone made to appear ridiculous. **3** *historical* a person employed by kings, nobles, etc to amuse them; a jester. ▷ *verb* (*fooled*, *fooling*) to deceive someone so that they appear foolish or ridiculous. ● **make a fool of oneself** to act in a way that makes one appear foolish. ● **make a fool of someone** to trick them or make them appear ridiculous; to humiliate them. ● **nobody's fool** someone too wary to be tricked or deceived; astute □ ***Bill is nobody's fool.*** ● **play** or **act the fool** deliberately to act in a comically foolish manner. ◷ 13c: from French *fol*.

▪ **fool someone into** or **out of something** to persuade them by deception to do something or not to do it.

▪ **fool about** or **around** to behave stupidly or playfully.

▪ **fool with something** to meddle with it irresponsibly or thoughtlessly.

fool² /fuːl/ ▷ *noun* a dessert of puréed fruit mixed with cream or custard □ ***gooseberry fool.*** ◷ 16c.

foolery ▷ *noun* (*fooleries*) stupid or ridiculous behaviour. ◷ 16c.

foolhardy ▷ *adj* taking foolish risks; rash; reckless. ● **foolhardiness** *noun*. ◷ 13c: from French *fol hardi*, literally 'foolish-bold'.

foolish ▷ *adj* **1** unwise; senseless. **2** ridiculous; silly; comical. ● **foolishly** *adverb*. ● **foolishness** *noun*.

foolproof ▷ *adj* **1** said of a plan, etc: designed so that it is easy to follow and very unlikely to go wrong; unable to go wrong. **2** said of a machine, etc: simple to use; unable to be misunderstood or misused, or easy to correct if a mistake is made.

foolscap /ˈfuːlskap/ ▷ *noun* a large size of printing- or writing-paper, measuring 17 × 13½ in (432 × 343mm). ◷ 17c: from *fool's cap*, referring to the jester's cap which was used as a watermark in the 18c.

fool's cap ▷ *noun* a jester's hat, usually a coxcomb hood with bells. ◷ 17c.

fool's errand ▷ *noun* a pointless or unprofitable task or venture; a futile journey.

fool's gold see under PYRITE

fool's paradise ▷ *noun* a state of confidence based on false expectations. ◷ 15c.

foot /fʊt/ ▷ *noun* (*plural usually* ***feet*** but see sense 7) **1** the part of the leg on which a human being or animal stands or walks. **2** in molluscs: a muscular organ used for locomotion, which can be retracted into the animal's shell. **3** the part of a sock, stocking, etc that fits over the foot. **4** the bottom or lower part of something □ ***the foot of a mountain.*** **5** the part on which something stands; anything functioning as or resembling a foot. **6** the end of a bed where the feet go, as opposed to the head. **7** (*plural* ***feet*** or *often* ***foot***) (abbreviation **ft** or ′, eg 6ft or 6′) in the imperial system: a unit of length equal to 12in (30.48cm) □

The room is sixteen foot by ten. **8** *prosody* a unit of rhythm in verse containing any of various combinations of stressed and unstressed syllables. **9** a part of a sewing machine that holds the fabric in position. **10** *plural, old use* infantry. **11** *as adj & in compounds* □ *foot soldier* □ *footlights.* • **footless** *adj.* • **foot it 1** *colloq* to walk. **2** *old use* to dance. • **foot the bill** to pay the bill. • **get a foot in the door** to gain entry into, or get accepted for the first time in, an organization, profession, etc. • **get off on the wrong foot** to make a bad start. • **have a foot in both camps** to be connected with both of two opposed parties. • **have one foot in the grave** *colloq* to be very old or near death. • **my foot!** *exclamation, colloq* used to express derisive disbelief. • **not put a foot right** to make many mistakes. • **not put a foot wrong** to make no mistakes. • **on foot** walking. • **put one's best foot forward** to set off with determination. • **put one's foot down** to be firm about something. • **put one's foot in it** *colloq* to cause offence or embarrassment. • **set foot in** or **on something** to arrive in or on it. • **under foot** beneath one's feet; on the ground □ *It was very wet under foot.* See also under FEET. ◷ Anglo-Saxon *fot.*

footage ▻ *noun* **1** measurement or payment by the foot. **2 a** the length of exposed cine film measured in feet; **b** a clip from a film used, eg in a TV programme, documentary, etc, to depict events relevant to the programme, usually historical events □ *archive footage.*

foot-and-mouth disease ▻ *noun, vet medicine* a notifiable and highly contagious viral disease of sheep, cattle, pigs and goats, characterized by the development of blisters in the mouth and around the hooves, by weight loss, and in dairy cattle by a decline in milk yield.

football ▻ *noun* **1** any of several team games played with a large ball that players try to kick or head into the opposing team's goal or carry across their opponents' goal line. Also called **Association Football**. Sometimes called **soccer**. **2** the ball used in the game. **3** (**the football**) a football match, usually an official game between clubs in a league □ *Fiona is going to the football on Saturday.* See also AMERICAN FOOTBALL, AUSTRALIAN RULES FOOTBALL, GAELIC FOOTBALL, RUGBY.

football colours ▻ *plural noun* scarves, caps, banners, etc that show someone's affiliation to a particular football club.

footballer ▻ *noun* a football player.

football hooligan ▻ *noun* someone who attends football matches with the intention to cause violence, and may or may not be a supporter of one of the teams playing.

football match ▻ *noun* **1** a game of football, played at a stadium, often viewed by spectators and sometimes as part of a league. **2** any game of football played by a group, often spontaneously, eg on a piece of waste ground, on the beach, in a field, etc.

foot brake ▻ *noun* a brake, eg in a car, operated by the foot.

footbridge ▻ *noun* a bridge for pedestrians.

footed ▻ *adj* **1** provided with a foot or feet. **2** *in compounds* **a** having a specified number or type of feet □ *four-footed*; **b** having a specified manner of walking □ *light-footed.*

footer ▻ *noun* **1** *slang* football. **2** *colloq* a kick of a football. **3** *in compounds* something, eg a person, boat, etc, of the specified height or length in feet □ *six-footer* □ *That boat's an eighteen-footer.*

footfall ▻ *noun* the sound of a footstep.

footfault ▻ *noun, tennis* a fault that makes the stroke invalid, caused by stepping over the BASELINE when serving.

foothill ▻ *noun* (*usually* **foothills**) a lower hill on the approach to a high mountain or mountain range.

foothold ▻ *noun* **1** a place to put one's foot when climbing. **2** a firm starting position.

footie or **footy** ▻ *noun, colloq* football.

footing ▻ *noun* **1** the stability of one's feet on the ground □ *lose one's footing.* **2** basis or status; position or rank. **3** relationship □ *on a friendly footing.* **4** the lower part of a column or wall, immediately above the foundation.

footle /ˈfuːtəl/ ▻ *verb* (*footled, footling*) *intr* (*often* **footle about** or **around**) to waste time, potter, wander aimlessly. ▻ *noun* silly nonsense. • **footling** *adj.* ◷ 19c.

footlights ▻ *plural noun, theat* **1** a row of lights set along the front edge of a stage to illuminate it. Also called **foots**. **2** the theatre in general, as a profession.

footloose ▻ *adj* free to go where, or do as, one likes; not hampered by any ties □ *footloose and fancy-free.* ◷ 19c in this sense.

footman ▻ *noun, old use* a uniformed male attendant. ◷ 18c in this sense.

footmark see under FOOTPRINT

footnote ▻ *noun* a comment at the bottom of a page, often preceded by a numbered mark or asterisk, etc which relates the comment to a particular part of the main text. ◷ 19c.

footpath ▻ *noun* **1** a path or track for walkers, usually in the countryside, eg alongside fields, through a wood, etc □ *public footpath.* **2** a pavement.

footplate ▻ *noun, old use* in a steam train: a platform for the driver and fireman, who are known as the **footplatemen**.

foot-pound and **foot-pound force** ▻ *noun* the energy needed to raise a mass of one pound through a height of one foot.

footprint ▻ *noun* **1** the mark or impression of a foot or shoe left eg in sand, in soft ground, etc. Also called **footmark**. **2** *computing* the amount of space taken up by a computer and its hardware on a desk, etc.

footpump ▻ *noun* a pump held or operated by the foot.

footrest ▻ *noun* a support for the feet, such as a stool or rail, used when sitting down.

footrope ▻ *noun, naut* **1** a rope stretching along under a ship's YARD[1] (sense 2) for the crew to stand on when furling the sail. **2** the rope to which the lower edge of a sail is attached.

foot rot ▻ *noun, vet medicine* a contagious infection of the feet in sheep or cattle.

foots see under FOOTLIGHTS

Footsie /ˈfʊtsɪ/ ▻ *noun, informal* the *Financial Times* Stock Exchange 100-Share Index. See under FT INDEX.

footsie ▻ *noun, colloq* • **play footsie** or **play footsie with someone 1** to rub one's foot or leg against someone else's, as a way of indicating attraction to them or sexual interest, usually done surreptitiously under the table eg at a dinner party. **2** to make furtively flirtatious advances towards them, eg by making comments, by eye contact, etc.

footslog ▻ *verb, intr* to go on foot; to trudge.

foot soldier ▻ *noun* a soldier serving on foot; an infantry soldier or infantryman.

footsore ▻ *adj* having sore and tired feet from prolonged walking.

footstalk ▻ *noun, bot* the stalk or petiole of a leaf.

footstep ▻ *noun* **1** the sound of a step in walking. **2** a footprint. • **follow in the footsteps of someone** to do as was done earlier by them; to copy or succeed them □ *He followed in his sister's footsteps and became a top barrister.*

footstool ▻ *noun* a low stool for supporting the feet while sitting.

foot-tapping ▻ *adj* said of music: having a beat that makes one tap, or want to tap, one's feet in time with it.

footway ▻ *noun* a passage for pedestrians.

footwear *singular noun* shoes, boots, socks, etc.

footwork ▻ *noun* the agile use of the feet in dancing or sport.

fop ▻ *noun* a man who is very consciously elegant in his dress and manners; a dandy. • **foppery** *noun*. • **foppish** *adj*. • **foppishness** *noun*. ◷ 17c.

for /fɔː(r), fə(r)/ ▻ *prep* **1** intended to be given or sent to someone □ *This is for you.* **2** towards □ *heading for home.* **3** throughout (a time or distance) □ *was writing for half an hour.* **4** in order to have, get, etc □ *meet for a chat* □ *fight for freedom.* **5** at a cost of something □ *said he'd do it for £10.* **6** as reward, payment or penalty appropriate to something □ *got seven months for stealing* □ *charge for one's work.* **7** with a view to something □ *train for the race.* **8** representing; on behalf of someone □ *the MP for Greenfield* □ *speaking for myself.* **9** to the benefit of someone or something □ *What can I do for you?* **10** in favour of someone □ *for or against the proposal.* **11** proposing to oneself □ *I'm for bed.* **12** because of something □ *couldn't see for tears.* **13** on account of something □ *famous for its confectionery.* **14** suitable to the needs of something □ *books for children.* **15** having as function or purpose □ *scissors for cutting hair.* **16** on the occasion of something □ *got it for my birthday.* **17** meaning □ *The German word for 'help' is 'helfen'.* **18** in place of; in exchange with something □ *replacements for the breakages* □ *translated word for word.* **19** in proportion to something □ *one woman for every five men.* **20** up to someone □ *It's for him to decide.* **21** as being □ *took you for someone else* □ *know for a fact.* **22** with regard to something □ *can't beat that for quality.* **23** considering what one would expect □ *serious for his age* □ *warm for winter.* **24** about; aimed at □ *proposals for peace* □ *a desire for revenge.* **25** in spite of something □ *quite nice for all his faults.* **26** available to be disposed of or dealt with by □ *not for sale.* **27** with reference to time: **a** at or on □ *an appointment for 12 noon on Friday*; **b** so as to be starting by □ *7.30 for 8.00*; **c** throughout (a time) □ *in jail for 15 years.* ▻ *conj, archaic* because; as □ *He left, for it was late.* • **as for** as far as concerns. • **be for it** or **be in for it** *colloq* to be about to receive a punishment, etc □ *You're for it now that he knows.* • **if it hadn't been for someone** or **something** had they not intervened or had it not happened, then (some other course of events would have unfolded). • **O for** if only I had □ *O for a pot of gold!* ◷ Anglo-Saxon.

f.o.r. ▻ *abbreviation* free on rail.

fora see FORUM

forage /ˈfɒrɪdʒ/ ▻ *noun* (**forages**) **1** (*also* **forage crop**) *agric* a crop grown for consumption by livestock, eg grass, kale, swede, which may be either grazed directly or harvested and stored for later use. **2** the activity of searching around for food or provisions. ▻ *verb* (**foraged**, **foraging**) **1** *intr* to search around, especially for food. **2** to gather food or provisions from (an area), especially forcibly; to plunder (an area). **3** to rummage about for what one wants. • **forager** *noun*. ◷ 14c: from French *fourrage*; compare FODDER.

forage cap ▻ *noun* the undress cap worn by infantry soldiers.

foramen /fəˈreɪmən/ (**foramina** /fəˈramɪnə/ or **foramens**) *noun, zool, anatomy* a naturally occurring small opening, particularly in the bone. • **foraminal** *adj*. • **foraminated** or **foraminous** *adj* pierced with small holes; porous. ◷ 17c: from Latin, from *forare* to pierce.

forasmuch as ▻ *conj, old use, law* since; seeing that.

foray /ˈfɒreɪ/ ▻ *noun* (**forays**) **1** a raid or attack. **2** a venture; an attempt. ▻ *verb* (**forayed**, **foraying**) *tr & intr* to raid; to pillage; to forage. • **forayer** *noun*. ◷ 14c as *forrayen*: to pillage, from FORAGE.

forbade or **forbad** *past tense of* FORBID

forbear¹ /fɔːˈbɛə(r)/ ▻ *verb* (*past tense* **forbore** /-ˈbɔː/, *past participle* **forborne** /-bɔːn/, *present participle* **forbearing**) **1** *archaic* to tolerate something. **2** *intr* (*usually* **forbear from something** or **forbear to do something**) to stop oneself going as far as that; to refrain from it □ *forbear from answering* □ *forbear to mention it.* ◷ Anglo-Saxon *forberan*.

forbear² see FOREBEAR

forbearance /fɔːˈbɛərəns/ ▻ *noun* patience and self-control. ◷ 16c.

forbearing ▻ *adj* long-suffering; patient and tolerant. • **forbearingly** *adverb*.

forbid /fəˈbɪd/ ▻ *verb* (*past tense* **forbade** /-ˈbad, -ˈbeɪd/ or **forbad** /-ˈbad/, *past participle* **forbidden** or **forbid**, *present participle* **forbidding**) **1** to order someone not to do something. **2** to prohibit someone from doing something. **3** to refuse someone access to somewhere □ *had forbidden them the orchard.* **4** *tr & intr* to prevent or not allow. ◷ Anglo-Saxon *forbeodan*.

forbidden ▻ *adj* **1** prohibited; not allowed; not permitted, eg access to somewhere □ *forbidden territory* □ *Smoking is forbidden.* **2** *computing* said of a combination of symbols: not permitted because the combination will cause a fault, eg the corruption of data, or the system to reboot.

forbidden degrees ▻ *plural noun* the degrees of blood relationship within which marriage is not allowed.

forbidden fruit ▻ *noun* **1** *Bible* the fruit forbidden to Adam by God (Genesis 2.17). **2** anything tempting but prohibited.

forbidding ▻ *adj* **1** threatening; grim. **2** uninviting; sinister; unprepossessing. • **forbiddingly** *adverb*. • **forbiddingness** *noun*.

forbore and **forborne** see under FORBEAR

force¹ /fɔːs/ ▻ *noun* **1** strength; power; impact or impetus. **2** compulsion, especially with threats or violence. **3** military power. **4** passion or earnestness. **5** strength or validity □ *the force of her argument* □ *come into force.* **6** meaning. **7** influence □ *by force of habit.* **8** a person or thing seen as an influence □ *a force for good.* **9** *physics* (SI unit NEWTON) (abbreviation **F**) **a** any external agent that produces a change in the speed or direction of a moving object, or that makes a stationary object move □ *the force of gravity*; **b** any external agent that produces a strain on a static object. **10** any irresistible power or agency □ *the forces of nature.* **11** the term used in specifying an index between 0 and 12 on the BEAUFORT SCALE, each of which corresponds to a different wind speed □ *a gale of force 8* □ *a force-10 gale.* **12 a** a military body; **b** (**the forces**) a nation's armed services. **13** any organized body or workers, etc. **14** (**the force**) the police force. ▻ *verb* (**forced**, **forcing**) **1** to make or compel someone to do something. **2** to obtain something by effort, strength, threats, violence, etc □ *forced an admission from them.* **3** to produce something with an effort. **4** to inflict, eg views, opinions etc (on someone) □ *force one's opinions on people.* **5** to make (a plant) grow or (fruit) ripen unnaturally quickly or early so that it can appear on the market out of its normal season □ *Nowadays, tomatoes are often forced.* **6** to strain □ *force one's voice.* **7** *cards* to induce or make someone play a particular suit or in a particular way. • **forceless** *adj*. • **forcer** *noun*. • **force one's way** to make progress by effort or ruthless determination. • **force someone's hand** to compel them to act in a certain way. • **in force 1** said of a law, etc: valid; effective. **2** in large numbers □ *Protestors arrived in force.* • **join forces** to come together or unite for a purpose. ◷ 13c: from Latin *fortia* strength.

■ **force someone** or **something back** or **out** to drive them back or out, especially meeting resistance.

force² /fɔːs/ ▷ *noun, N Eng* a waterfall. ◷ 16c: from Norse *fors*.

forced ▷ *adj* **1** said of a smile, laugh, etc: unnatural; unspontaneous. **2** done or provided under compulsion □ *forced labour*. **3** carried out as an emergency □ *a forced landing*. **4** done with great and long effort □ *forced marches*. ● **forcedly** /ˈfɔːsɪdlɪ/ *adverb*. ● **forcedness** /ˈfɔːsɪdnəs/ *noun*.

force-feed ▷ *verb* to feed (a person or animal) forcibly, especially by passing liquid food through a soft rubber tube into the stomach via the mouth or nostril.

forceful ▷ *adj* powerful; effective; influential. ● **forcefully** *adverb*. ● **forcefulness** *noun*.

force majeure /fɔːs maˈʒɜː(r)/ ▷ *noun, law* an unforeseeable or uncontrollable course of events which will excuse a party from fulfilling its part of a contract. ◷ 19c: French, meaning 'superior force'.

forcemeat ▷ *noun, cookery* a mixture of chopped or minced ingredients, eg vegetables, or sausage meat, herbs, etc, used as stuffing. ◷ 17c: from FARCE + MEAT, influenced by *force*.

forceps /ˈfɔːsɛps/ ▷ *singular noun* (*plural* ***forceps***) *biol, medicine, etc* an instrument like pincers, for gripping firmly, used especially in surgery and dentistry. ◷ 16c: said to be from Latin *formus* warm + *capere* to take.

forcible /ˈfɔːsəbəl/ ▷ *adj* **1** done by or involving force □ *forcible entry*. **2** powerful □ *a forcible reminder*. ● **forcibleness** or **forcibility** *noun*. ● **forcibly** *adverb*. ◷ 15c: French, from 16-18c sometimes spelt *forceable*.

ford /fɔːd/ ▷ *noun* a crossing-place in a river, where a road or track crosses by passing through shallow water. ▷ *verb* (***forded***, ***fording***) to ride, drive or wade across (a stream, river, etc) by passing through shallow water. ● **fordable** *adj*. ◷ Anglo-Saxon.

fore¹ /fɔː(r)/ ▷ *adj, usually in compounds* towards the front. ▷ *noun* **1** the front part. **2** *naut* the foremast. ● **to the fore** at or to the front; prominent; conspicuous. ◷ Anglo-Saxon *fore*.

fore² /fɔː(r)/ ▷ *exclamation, golf* ball coming!; a warning shout to anybody who may be in the ball's path. ◷ 19c: probably a short form of BEFORE.

fore- ▷ *prefix* **1** before or beforehand □ *forewarn*. **2** in front □ *foreleg*. ◷ Anglo-Saxon *fore*.

fore-and-aft ▷ *adj, naut* **1** at the front and rear of a vessel □ *fore-and-aft rig*. **2** set lengthways, pointing to the bow and stern.

fore-and-after ▷ *noun* a schooner or any other vessel with a fore-and-aft rig.

forearm ▷ *noun* /ˈfɔːrɑːm/ the lower part of the arm between wrist and elbow. ▷ *verb* /fɔːrˈɑːm/ (***forearmed***, ***forearming***) to prepare someone or arm someone beforehand. ◷ 18c.

forebear or **forbear** /ˈfɔːbɛə(r)/ ▷ *noun* an ancestor, usually more remote than grandfather or grandmother. ◷ 15c.

forebode ▷ *verb* (***foreboded***, ***foreboding***) *tr & intr, old use* **1** to foretell; to prophesy. **2** to have a premonition of something, or that something will happen, especially something bad. ● **foreboding** *noun* a feeling of approaching trouble □ *She had a foreboding that the journey would be difficult*. ◷ 17c: FORE- + BODE¹.

forebrain ▷ *noun, anatomy* the largest part of the brain in vertebrates, consisting of the left and right cerebral hemispheres, the thalamus and the hypothalamus.

forecast ▷ *verb* (***forecast*** or *sometimes* ***forecasted***, ***forecasting***) *tr & intr* **1** to give warning of something; to predict something. **2** to gauge or estimate (weather, statistics, etc) in advance. *They forecast snow for tonight*. ▷ *noun* **1** a warning, prediction or advance estimate. **2** a weather forecast □ *The forecast is good for skiers*. ● **forecaster** *noun*. ◷ 14c.

forecastle /ˈfoʊksəl, ˈfɔːkɑːsəl/ ▷ *noun* **1** a short raised deck at the front of a vessel. **2** the bow section of a ship under the main deck, formerly the crew's quarters. Often shortened to **fo'c'sle**. ◷ 14c.

foreclose ▷ *verb* **1** said of a mortgager, bank, etc: to repossess a property because of failure on the part of the mortgagee to repay agreed amounts of the loan. **2** to prevent or hinder. ● **foreclosure** *noun*. ◷ 15c.

forecourt ▷ *noun* **1** a courtyard or paved area in front of a building, eg a filling-station. **2** the part of a tennis court, badminton court, etc between the net and the service line. ◷ 16c.

foredate ▷ *verb* to mark something with a date that is prior to the current date.

forefather ▷ *noun* an ancestor.

forefinger ▷ *noun* the INDEX FINGER. ◷ 15c.

forefoot ▷ *noun* either of the two front feet of a four-legged animal.

forefront ▷ *noun* **1** the very front. **2** the most prominent or active position.

foregather see FORGATHER

forego¹ /fɔːˈgoʊ, fəˈgoʊ/ ▷ *verb* (***foregoes***, ***forewent***, ***foregone***, ***foregoing***) *tr & intr* to precede, either in position or time. ◷ Anglo-Saxon *foregan*.

forego² see FORGO

foregoing ▷ *adj* just mentioned. ▷ *noun* the thing or person just mentioned. ◷ 15c.

foregone conclusion ▷ *noun* an inevitable or predictable result or conclusion. ◷ 17c.

foreground ▷ *noun* **1** the part of a picture or field of view perceived as being nearest to the observer, as opposed to the BACKGROUND. **2** a position where one is noticeable. ▷ *verb* (***foregrounded***, ***foregrounding***) to spotlight or emphasize something. ◷ 19c.

forehand ▷ *adj* **1** *tennis, squash, etc* said of a stroke: with the palm in front, as opposed to BACKHAND. **2** done beforehand. ▷ *noun* **1** *tennis, squash, etc* **a** a stroke made with the palm facing forward; **b** the part of the court to the right of a right-handed player or to the left of a left-handed player. **2** the part of a horse that is in front of its rider. ▷ *adverb* with the hand in forehand position.

forehanded ▷ *adj, US* **1** planning ahead, with thought or provision for the future. **2** well-off.

forehead /ˈfɔːhɛd, ˈfɒrɪd/ ▷ *noun* the part of the face between the eyebrows and hairline; the brow. ◷ Anglo-Saxon *forheafod*.

foreign /ˈfɒrɪn, ˈfɒrən/ ▷ *adj* **1** belonging or relating to, or coming from another country. **2** concerned with relations with other countries □ *foreign affairs*. **3** not belonging where found □ *a piece of grit or other foreign body in the eye*. ● **foreign to someone** **1** unfamiliar □ *the technique was foreign to them*. **2** uncharacteristic □ *Envy was foreign to his nature*. ● **foreignness** *noun*.

foreign aid ▷ *noun, politics* financial or other aid given by richer to poorer nations.

foreign correspondent ▷ *noun* a newspaper or broadcasting correspondent working in a foreign country in order to report news, etc.

foreigner ▷ *noun* **1** a person from another country. **2** an unfamiliar person; a person who isn't normally part of a situation and therefore doesn't seem to belong.

foreign exchange ▷ *noun, commerce* the amount of currency of foreign origin held in a country, derived from exporting and from overseas investment.

foreign minister and **foreign secretary** ▷ *noun* the government minister responsible for a country's relationships with other countries, and the head of the FOREIGN OFFICE. *US equivalent* **secretary of state**.

foreign office ▷ *noun* (abbreviation **FO**) the department or ministry of a government dealing with foreign or external affairs, officially called the **Foreign and Commonwealth Office** (abbreviation **FCO**). *US equivalent* **State Department**.

forejudge[1] ▷ *verb* to pass judgement before hearing the facts and proof. ⓒ 16c.

forejudge[2] see FORJUDGE

foreknow ▷ *verb* (***foreknown***, ***foreknowing***) to know something before it happens; to foresee something. • **foreknowable** *adj*. • **foreknowledge** *noun*. ⓒ 15c.

foreland ▷ *noun* a point of land running forward into the sea; a headland.

foreleg ▷ *noun* either of the two front legs of a four-legged animal.

forelock ▷ *noun* a lock of hair growing or falling over the brow. • **pull, touch** or **tug the forelock** to raise one's hand to the forehead as a sign of respect or subservience to someone. ⓒ 17c.

foreman, **forewoman** and **foreperson** ▷ *noun* **1** someone in charge of a department or group of workers, who usually also has a role as worker as well as carrying out a supervisory role. **2** *law* the principal juror who presides over the deliberations of the jury and communicates their verdict to the court; the chairperson or spokesperson of a jury. ⓒ 15c as *foreman*; *forewoman* and *foreperson* have been used since the 1970s.

foremast ▷ *noun, naut* the mast that is nearest to the bow of a ship. Compare MAINMAST.

forementioned ▷ *adj* mentioned beforehand or earlier in writing or discussion.

foremost ▷ *adj* leading; best. ▷ *adverb* leading; coming first. • **first and foremost** essentially; most importantly. ⓒ Anglo-Saxon *formest*, from *forma* first.

forename ▷ *noun* used on official forms, etc: one's personal name as distinct from one's family name or surname. Compare CHRISTIAN NAME, FIRST NAME.

forenamed ▷ *adj* mentioned before.

forenoon /ˈfɔːnuːn/ ▷ *noun, Scots* the morning. ▷ *adj* referring to this time. ⓒ 16c.

forensic /fəˈrɛnsɪk, -zɪk/ ▷ *adj* **1** belonging or relating to courts of law, or to the work of a lawyer in court. **2** concerned with the scientific side of legal investigations □ *forensic laboratory*. • **forensically** *adverb*. ⓒ 17c: from Latin *forensis*, belonging to the *forum*, where law courts were held in Rome.

forensic linguistics ▷ *noun* the use of linguistic techniques to investigate crime and to examine evidence relating to a crime.

forensic medicine ▷ *noun* the branch of medicine concerned with the production of evidence in order to determine the cause of a death, the identity of a criminal, etc, used in civil or criminal law cases. Also called **medical jurisprudence**.

foreordain ▷ *verb* to determine (events, etc) in advance; to destine. ⓒ 15c.

forepart ▷ *noun* the front; the early part.

forepayment ▷ *noun* payment for something in advance or before receiving the goods or services.

foreperson see under FOREMAN

foreplay ▷ *noun* sexual stimulation, often leading up to sexual intercourse. ⓒ 1920s.

forequarter ▷ *noun* **1** the front portion of a side of meat, including the leg. **2** (**forequarters**) said of an animal, especially a horse: the forelegs and shoulders, and the body area adjoining them.

forerunner ▷ *noun* **1** a person or thing that goes before; an earlier type or version; a predecessor. **2** a sign of what is to come. **3** an advance messenger or herald.

foresaid ▷ *adj* already mentioned.

foresee ▷ *verb* to see that something will happen in advance, or know in advance, often by circumstantial evidence.

foreseeable ▷ *adj* **1** capable of being foreseen. **2** referring to a time as long as one can envisage given the current circumstances □ *for the foreseeable future*.

foreshadow ▷ *verb* to give or have some indication of something in advance.

foreshore ▷ *noun* the area on the shore between the positions that the high and low tides reach, regularly covered and uncovered by the tide. ⓒ 18c.

foreshorten ▷ *verb* in photographic or artistic perspective: to give a shortening effect to something, in order to give it a realistic-looking perspective □ *foreshortened limbs*. • **foreshortening** *noun*. ⓒ 17c.

foresight ▷ *noun* **1** the ability to foresee. **2** wise forethought; prudence. **3** consideration taken or provision made for the future. **4** the front sight on a gun. • **foresighted** *adj*.

foreskin ▷ *noun, anatomy* the retractable fold of skin that covers the end of the penis. *Technical equivalent* PREPUCE. ⓒ 16c.

forest /ˈfɒrəst/ ▷ *noun* **1** *bot* a plant community extending over a large area and dominated by trees, the crowns of which form an unbroken covering layer or canopy. **2** a tract of country formerly owned, and used for hunting, by a sovereign. **3** a dense arrangement of objects. ▷ *adj* relating to or consisting of a forest. ▷ *verb* (***forested***, ***foresting***) to cover (an area) with trees; to cover (an area) thickly with tall, upright objects. • **forested** *adj*. ⓒ 13c: French, from Latin *forestis silva* unfenced woodland, from *foris* outside.

forestall ▷ *verb* **1** to prevent something by acting in advance □ *issue an announcement to forestall the inevitable questions*. **2** to buy something up before it reaches the market, so as to sell it again at higher prices. • **forestaller** *noun*. • **forestalling** *noun*. ⓒ 15c, meaning 'to waylay'.

forester ▷ *noun* **1** a person whose job is to manage a forest; someone trained in forestry. **2** a person or animal that lives in a forest. **3** (**Forester**) a member of the Ancient Order of Foresters.

forestry ▷ *noun* the management of forest and woodland for the commercial production of timber, including the growing and maintenance of trees, the felling of mature trees, etc.

foretaste ▷ *noun* a brief experience of what is to come.

foretell ▷ *verb* to tell about something beforehand; to predict or prophesy something. ⓒ 13c.

forethought ▷ *noun* consideration taken or provision made for the future.

foretop ▷ *noun, naut* the platform at the top or head of the foremast.

forever ▷ *adverb* (*also* **for ever**) **1** always; eternally; for all time. **2** continually □ *forever whining*. **3** *informal* for a very long time. ▷ *noun* **1** an endless or indefinite length of time. **2** a very long time.

forevermore ▷ *adverb* a more emphatic term for FOREVER.

forewarn ▷ *verb* to warn beforehand; to give previous notice.

forewent *past participle of* FOREGO

forewoman see FOREMAN

foreword ▻ *noun* an introduction to a book, often by a writer other than the author; preface. ◷ 19c.

forfeit /ˈfɔːfɪt/ ▻ *noun* **1** something that one must surrender as a penalty. **2** a penalty or fine for a crime. **3** (*especially* **forfeits**) a game in which a player surrenders an item (a **forfeit**) which can be won back only by performing a task, or fulfilling a challenge, set for them. ▻ *adj* surrendered or liable to be surrendered as a penalty. ▻ *verb* (***forfeited***, ***forfeiting***) **1** to hand over as a penalty □ *forfeit his passport.* **2** to give up or do without voluntarily. • **forfeitable** *adj.* ◷ 14c: from French *forfait*, from Latin *forisfactum* penalty.

forfeiture ▻ *noun* **1** the act of forfeiting. **2** the state of being forfeited. **3** something that is forfeited. ◷ 14c.

forgather or **foregather** ▻ *verb, intr* to meet together; to assemble. ◷ 16c.

forgave *past tense of* FORGIVE

forge¹ /fɔːdʒ/ ▻ *noun* **1** a special furnace for heating metal, especially iron, prior to shaping it. **2** the workshop of a blacksmith, where metal is heated and shaped into horseshoes, tools, etc. ▻ *verb* (***forged***, ***forging***) **1** to shape metal by heating and hammering, or by heating and applying pressure more gradually. **2** to make an imitation of (a signature, document, banknote, etc) for a dishonest or fraudulent purpose. • **forgeable** *adj.* • **forger** *noun.* ◷ 13c: French, from Latin *fabrica* workshop.

forge² /fɔːdʒ/ ▻ *verb* (***forged***, ***forging***) *intr* to progress swiftly and steadily □ *forged through the forest at breakneck speed.* ◷ 18c.

■ **forge ahead** **1** to forge. **2** to take the lead.

forgery ▻ *noun* (***forgeries***) **1** imitating pictures, documents, signatures, etc for a fraudulent purpose. **2** a copy made for a fraudulent purpose. ◷ 17c.

forget /fəˈɡɛt/ ▻ *verb* (***forgot***, ***forgotten***, ***forgetting***) *tr & intr* (*usually* **forget something** or **forget about something**) **1** (*also* **forget to do something**) to fail to remember it or be unable to remember it. **2** to stop being aware of something □ *forgot his headache in the excitement.* **3** to neglect or overlook something. **4** to leave something behind accidentally. **5** *colloq* to dismiss something from one's mind □ *You can forget your proposed skiing trip.* **6** to lose control over (oneself). • **forget it** *colloq* it doesn't matter. • **not forgetting ...** and also ...; including ... ◷ Anglo-Saxon *forgietan*.

forgetful ▻ *adj* inclined to forget. • **forgetfully** *adj.* • **forgetfulness** *noun.*

forget-me-not ▻ *noun* a low-growing annual or perennial plant, native to temperate regions, with clusters of small flowers, often pink in bud and turning blue as they open, and sometimes having a yellow or white eye as a HONEY GUIDE. ◷ 16c: a translation of French *ne m'oubliez mye*.

forgive ▻ *verb* (***forgave***, ***forgiven***, ***forgiving***) **1** to stop being angry with (someone who has done something wrong) or about (an offence). **2** to pardon someone. **3** to spare someone the paying of (a debt). • **forgivable** *adj.* • **forgivably** *adverb.* • **forgiver** *noun.* ◷ Anglo-Saxon *forgiefan*.

forgiveness ▻ *noun* **1** the act of forgiving or state of being forgiven. **2** readiness to forgive.

forgiving ▻ *adj* ready to forgive; patient and tolerant.

forgo or **forego** /fɔːˈɡoʊ, fəˈɡoʊ/ ▻ *verb* (***forgoes***, ***forwent***, ***forgone***, ***forgoing***) to do without something; to sacrifice something or give it up □ *I'll forgo that for you.* Compare FOREGO¹. ◷ Anglo-Saxon *forgan*.

forgot and **forgotten** see under FORGET

forint /ˈfɒrɪnt/ ▻ *noun* the standard unit of currency of Hungary since 1946. ◷ 1940s: Hungarian, from Italian *fiorino* florin.

forjudge and **forejudge** ▻ *verb, law* to deprive someone of a right, etc, by a judgement. Compare also FOREJUDGE¹. ◷ 13c.

fork /fɔːk/ ▻ *noun* **1** an eating or cooking implement with prongs (usually three), for spearing and lifting food. **2** a pronged digging or lifting tool. **3 a** the division of a road, etc into two branches; **b** one such branch □ *take the left fork.* **4** something that divides similarly into two parts, eg the wheel support of a bicycle. **5** *in compounds* □ *fish fork* □ *hayfork.* ▻ *verb* (***forked***, ***forking***) **1** *intr* said of a road, etc: to divide into two branches. **2** *intr* said of a person or vehicle: to follow one such branch □ *fork left at the church.* **3** to lift or move with a fork. **4** *chess* to simultaneously put two of one's opponent's pieces under attack with one of one's own pieces. • **forker** *noun.* ◷ Anglo-Saxon *forca*, from Latin *furca* a fork for hay.

■ **fork out something for something** *colloq* to pay for it, under pressure rather than voluntarily.

forked ▻ *adj* **1** dividing into two branches or parts; shaped like a fork. **2** said of lightning: forming zigzagged lines of light.

forkful ▻ *noun* (***forkfuls***) the amount which can be held on a fork.

fork-lift truck ▻ *noun* a small vehicle equipped with two horizontal prongs that can be raised and lowered to move or stack goods, used in particular in warehouses.

forlorn /fəˈlɔːn/ ▻ *adj* **1** exceedingly unhappy; miserable. **2** deserted; forsaken. **3** desperate. • **forlornly** *adverb.* • **forlornness** *noun.* ◷ Anglo-Saxon *forloren*.

forlorn hope ▻ *noun* **1** a desperate but impractical hope. **2** a hopeless undertaking, with little chance of success. ◷ 16c: from Dutch *verloren hoop* literally 'lost troop', originally referring to a body of soldiers dispatched to begin an attack.

form¹ /fɔːm/ ▻ *noun* **1** shape. **2** figure or outward appearance. **3** kind, type, variety or manifestation. **4** a document with printed text and spaces for the insertion of information. **5** a way, especially the correct way, of doing or saying something. **6** structure and organization in a piece of writing or work of art. **7** one's potential level of performance, eg in sport □ *soon find your form again.* **8** any of the ways that a word can be spelt or grammatically inflected □ *the past tense form.* **9** a school class. **10** a bench. **11** *slang* a criminal record. **12** a hare's burrow. ▻ *verb* (***formed***, ***forming***) **1** to organize or set something up. **2** *intr* to come into existence; to take shape. **3** to shape; to make (a shape). **4** to take on the shape or function of something. **5** to make up; to constitute. **6** to develop □ *form a relationship.* **7** to influence or mould someone or something □ *the environment that formed him.* **8** to construct, inflect grammatically or pronounce (a word). • **formable** *adj.* • **forming** *noun.* • **good** or **bad form** polite or impolite social behaviour □ *That really is bad form.* • **in good form** in good spirits or health. • **a matter of form** a case of a procedure being gone through for the sake of legality or convention. • **on** or **off form** performing well or badly. • **take form** to come into existence; to begin to have shape. • **true to form** in the usual, typical or characteristic way. ◷ 13c: from Latin *forma* shape or model.

form² see FORME

-form ▻ *combining form* **1** having the specified appearance or structure □ *cuneiform* □ *cruciform* □ *fusiform.* **2** in the specified number of forms or varieties □ *multiform* □ *uniform.* ◷ From Latin *-formis*, from *forma* shape.

formal ▻ *adj* **1** relating to or involving etiquette, ceremony or conventional procedure generally □ *formal dress.* **2** stiffly polite rather than relaxed and friendly. **3** valid; official; explicit □ *a formal agreement* □ *formal proof.* **4** said of language: strictly correct with regard to grammar, style and choice of words, as distinct from conversational. **5** organized and methodical □ *the formal approach to teaching.* **6** precise and symmetrical in design □ *a formal garden.* **7** relating to outward form as distinct from content. • **formally** *adverb* in a formal way.

formaldehyde /fɔːˈmaldɪhaɪd/ ▻ *noun, chem* (formula **HCHO**) a colourless pungent gas, the simplest of the aldehydes, widely used as a disinfectant and preservative for biological specimens, and also used in the manufacture of synthetic resins, eg Bakelite. Also called **methanal**. ◷ 19c: from FORMIC + ALDEHYDE.

formalin /ˈfɔːməlɪn/ ▻ *noun, chem* a clear solution of formaldehyde in water used as a preservative, antiseptic and disinfectant. ◷ 19c: from FORMALDEHYDE.

formalism ▻ *noun* **1** concern, especially excessive concern, with outward form, to the exclusion of content. **2** *math* the mathematical or logical structure of a scientific argument, consisting of formal rules and symbols which are intrinsically meaningless. **3** *literary theory* concern with literary technique and analysis to the exclusion of social and historical content ◷ referring in particular to a Russian literary group of the early 20c that promoted this approach to literary analysis. • **formalist** *noun*. • **formalistic** *adj*. ◷ 19c.

formality ▻ *noun* (***formalities***) **1** a procedure gone through as a requirement of etiquette, ceremony, the law, etc. **2** a procedure gone through merely for the sake of correctness or legality □ *The interview was a formality, as she had already been promised the job.* **3** strict attention to the rules of social behaviour.

formalize or **formalise** ▻ *verb* (***formalized***, ***formalizing***) **1** to make something precise; to give a clear statement of something. **2** to make something official, eg by putting it in writing, etc; to give definite or legal form to something. • **formalization** *noun*.

formally see under FORMAL

formal verdict ▻ *noun* **1** *law* a verdict in which the jury follows the judge's directions. **2** *Scots law* in a fatal accident inquiry: a finding of death by misadventure with no apportioning of blame.

formant /ˈfɔːmənt/ ▻ *noun, acoustics, phonetics* the dominant component or components which determine the particular sound quality of all vowels and some consonants, being peaks of acoustic energy which reflect the principal points of resonance in the vocal tract. ◷ 19c: from German *Formant*, from Latin *formare* to form.

format /ˈfɔːmat/ ▻ *noun* **1** the size and shape of something, especially a book or magazine. **2** the style in which a television programme, radio programme, etc is organized and presented. **3** *computing* a specific arrangement of data in tracks and sectors on a disk. ▻ *verb* (***formatted***, ***formatting***) **1** to design, shape or organize in a particular way. **2** to organize (data) for input into a particular computer. **3** to prepare a new disk for use by marking out the surface into tracks and sectors, so that it is capable of receiving data. • **formatter** *noun* a program for formatting a disk, tape, etc. ◷ 19c: French, from Latin *liber formatus* a book formed or shaped in a certain way.

formation /fɔːˈmeɪʃən/ ▻ *noun* **1** the process of forming, making, developing or establishing something. **2 a** a particular arrangement, pattern or order, particularly of troops, aircraft, players of a game, etc □ *flew in formation over the showground*; **b** a shape or structure; **c** *as adj* □ *formation dancing* □ *formation flying.* **3** *geol* a mass or area of rocks which have common characteristics. ◷ 15c: from Latin *formatio* shape.

formative ▻ *adj* **1** relating to development or growth □ *the formative years.* **2** having an effect on development. ◷ 15c: from French *formatif*.

forme or (*US*) **form** /fɔːm/ ▻ *noun, printing* the type and blocks assembled in a CHASE[3], ready for printing. ◷ 15c: variant of FORM[1].

former ▻ *adj* **1** belonging to an earlier time □ *in former years* □ *the former prime minister.* **2** said of two people or things: mentioned, considered, etc first. **3** previous; earlier. • **the former** said of two people or things: the first one mentioned, considered, etc. Compare LATTER. ◷ Anglo-Saxon *formere*, the comparative of *forma* first or earliest.

> ***former***
>
> • **Former** contrasts with **latter**; unlike **latter** it is invariably used to refer to one of only two things. This is not for any grammatical reason but because it would be awkward to refer back across several things in reference to the first of them.

formerly ▻ *adverb* previously; in the past; before this time. ◷ 16c.

formic /ˈfɔːmɪk/ ▻ *adj* **1** relating to or derived from ants. **2** containing or derived from formic acid. ◷ 18c: from Latin *formica* ant.

Formica /fɔːˈmaɪkə/ ▻ *noun, trademark* a hard heat-resistant plastic, used for making easy-to-clean work surfaces in kitchens, laboratories, etc. ◷ 1920s.

formic acid ▻ *noun, chem* (formula **HCOOH**) a colourless pungent liquid that is toxic and corrosive, and is largely responsible for the stinging sensation produced by ant bites and stinging nettles. It is also used in the dyeing of textiles, and as a fumigant and insecticide. Also called **methanoic acid**. ◷ 18c: from Latin *formica* ant.

formidable /ˈfɔːmɪdəbəl, fəˈmɪ-/ ▻ *adj* **1** awesomely impressive. **2** said of problems, etc: enormous; difficult to overcome. • **formidability** *noun*. • **formidableness** *noun*. • **formidably** *adverb*. ◷ 16c: from Latin *formidabilis* causing fear, from *formido* fear.

formless ▻ *adj* lacking a clear shape or structure. • **formlessly** *adverb*. • **formlessness** *noun*.

form letter ▻ *noun* a letter with a fixed form and contents, used especially when writing to a number of people about the same or similar matters.

form of address ▻ *noun* **1** the word or words used as a title before a person's name. **2** the form of words used in speaking to someone on a formal or ceremonial occasion.

formula /ˈfɔːmjʊlə/ ▻ *noun* (***formulae*** /-liː, -laɪ/ or ***formulas***) **1** the combination of ingredients used in a product, etc. **2** a method or rule of procedure, especially a successful one. **3** *chem* a combination of chemical symbols that represents the chemical composition of a particular substance. **4** *math, physics* a mathematical equation or expression, or a physical law, that represents the relationship between various quantities, and is usually expressed in numerical figures and letters, eg $E=mc^2$. **5** an established piece of wording used by convention eg in religious ceremonies or legal proceedings. **6** a term used for classifying racing cars acccording to engine size □ *Formula One racing.* **7** *N Amer* powdered milk for babies. • **formulaic** /fɔːmjʊˈleɪɪk/ *adj*. ◷ 16c: Latin diminutive of *forma* form.

formularize or **formularise** /ˈfɔːmjʊləraɪz/ ▻ *verb* (***formularized***, ***formularizing***) to FORMULATE (senses 1 and 2).

formulary /ˈfɔːmjʊlərɪ/ ▻ *noun* (***formularies***) a book or collection of formulas, especially legal or religious ones. ◷ 16c: from French *formulaire*.

formulate /ˈfɔːmjʊleɪt/ ▻ *verb* (***formulated***, ***formulating***) **1** to express something in terms of a formula. **2** to express something in systematic terms. **3** to express something precisely and clearly □ *formulated the idea carefully.* • **formulation** *noun*. ◷ 19c.

fornicate /ˈfɔːnɪkeɪt/ ▻ *verb* (***fornicated***, ***fornicating***) *intr* to have sexual intercourse outside marriage. • **fornicator** *noun*. ◷ 16c: from Latin *fornicari*, *fornicatus*.

fornication /fɔːnɪˈkeɪʃən/ ▻ *noun* **1** voluntary sexual intercourse outside marriage. **2** *Bible* sexual immorality in general.

forsake /fə'seɪk, fɔː-/ ▷ *verb* (***forsook***, ***forsaken***, ***forsaking***) to desert; to abandon. ◷ Anglo-Saxon *forsacan*, from *sacan* to strive.

forsaken ▷ *adj* completely abandoned; forlorn. • **forsakenly** *adverb*. • **forsakenness** *noun*.

forswear /fɔː'swɛə(r), fə-/ ▷ *verb* (***forswore***, ***forsworn***, ***forswearing***) *old use* **1** to give up or renounce (one's foolish ways, etc). **2** to perjure (oneself). ◷ Anglo-Saxon *forswerian* to swear falsely.

forsythia /fɔː'saɪθɪə/ ▷ *noun* (***forsythias***) a deciduous shrub cultivated for its bright yellow flowers that appear before the leaves. ◷ 19c: named after the British botanist W Forsyth (1737–1804).

fort /fɔːt/ ▷ *noun* a fortified military building, enclosure or position. • **hold the fort** to keep things running in the absence of the person normally in charge. ◷ 16c: from Latin *fortis* strong.

forte¹ /'fɔːteɪ/ ▷ *noun* something one is good at; a strong point. ◷ 17c: from French *fort* strong.

forte² /'fɔːteɪ/ ▷ (abbreviation **f**) *music, adverb* in a loud manner. ▷ *adj* loud. See also FORTISSIMO. ◷ 18c: Italian.

forte-piano /'fɔːtɪpɪ'anoʊ/ (abbreviation **fp**) *music* ▷ *adj, adverb* loud and then immediately soft . ▷ *noun* (***forte-pianos***) an early type of piano. ◷ 18c: Italian.

forth /fɔːθ/ ▷ *adverb, old use* except in phrases **1** into existence or view □ *bring forth children.* **2** forwards □ *swing back and forth.* **3** out □ *set forth on a journey.* **4** onwards □ *from this day forth.* • **and so forth** and so on; et cetera. • **hold forth** to speak, especially at length. ◷ Anglo-Saxon.

> ***forth***
>
> There is often a spelling confusion between **forth** and **fourth**.

forthcoming ▷ *adj* **1** happening or appearing soon. **2** said of a person: willing to talk; communicative. **3** available on request.

forthright /'fɔːθraɪt, fɔːθ'raɪt/ ▷ *adj* firm, frank, straightforward and decisive. • **forthrightly** *adverb*. • **forthrightness** *noun*. ◷ Anglo-Saxon *forthriht*.

forthwith /fɔːθ'wɪθ, -wɪð/ ▷ *adverb* immediately; at once.

the Forties ▷ *plural noun* the sea area lying between NE Scotland and SW Norway, with a minimum depth of 40 fathoms.

forties /'fɔːtɪz/ (often written **40s** or **40's**) ▷ *plural noun* **1** (**one's forties**) the period of time between one's fortieth and fiftieth birthdays □ *Gill is in her forties.* **2** (**the forties**) **a** the range of temperatures between forty and fifty degrees □ *It must be in the forties today*; **b** the period of time between the fortieth and fiftieth years of a century □ *died in the 40s.* **3** *as adj* □ *forties music.* • **the roaring forties** the area of stormy west winds south of latitude 40°S, or north of latitude 40°N in the Atlantic.

fortieth (often written **40th**) ▷ *adj* **1** in counting: **a** next after thirty-ninth; **b** last of forty. **2** in fortieth position. ▷ *noun* **1** one of forty equal parts. Also *as adj* □ *a fortieth share.* **2** a FRACTION equal to one divided by forty (usually written 1/40). **3** a person coming fortieth, eg in a race or exam □ *He came fortieth in a class of ninety.* ◷ Anglo-Saxon; see FORTY + -TH.

fortification /fɔːtɪfɪ'keɪʃən/ ▷ *noun* **1** the process of fortifying. **2** (**fortifications**) walls and other defensive structures built in preparation for an attack.

fortify /'fɔːtɪfaɪ/ ▷ *verb* (***fortifies***, ***fortified***, ***fortifying***) **1** to strengthen (a building, city, etc) in preparation for an attack. **2** to add extra alcohol to (wine) in the course of production, in order to produce sherry, port, etc. **3** to confirm. • **fortifiable** *adj*. • **fortifier** *noun*. ◷ 15c: ultimately from Latin *fortis* strong + -FY.

fortis /'fɔːtɪs/ *phonetics* ▷ *adj* articulated with considerable muscular effort and pressure of breath. ▷ *noun* (*plural* ***fortes*** /-tiːz/) a consonant that is produced in this way. Compare LENIS. ◷ Early 20c: Latin, meaning 'strong'.

fortissimo /fɔː'tɪsɪmoʊ/ *music* (abbreviation **ff**) ▷ *adverb* in a very loud manner. ▷ *adj* very loud. See also FORTE². ◷ 18c: Italian superlative of *forte* (see FORTE²).

fortitude /'fɔːtɪtʃuːd/ ▷ *noun* uncomplaining courage in pain or misfortune. ◷ 16c: from Latin *fortitudo* strength.

fortnight /'fɔːtnaɪt/ ▷ *noun* a period of 14 days; two weeks. ◷ Anglo-Saxon *feowertiene niht* fourteen nights.

fortnightly ▷ *adj* occurring, appearing, etc once every fortnight; bi-monthly. ▷ *adverb* once a fortnight. ▷ *noun* (***fortnightlies***) a publication which comes out every two weeks.

FORTRAN /'fɔːtran/ ▷ *noun, computing* a high-level programming language widely used for mathematical, scientific and engineering programs in the 1950s and 1960s. ◷ 1950s: from *formula translation*.

fortress /'fɔːtrəs/ ▷ *noun* a fortified town, or large fort or castle. ◷ 13c: from French *forteresse* strength or a strong place.

fortress Europe ▷ *noun* the idea that as economic and political internal borders within the European Union are abolished, external barriers on trade and immigration will be strengthened, threatening free world trade and increasing prejudice against things non-European.

fortuitous /fɔː'tʃuːɪtəs/ ▷ *adj* happening by chance; accidental. • **fortuitously** *adverb*. • **fortuitousness** *noun*. • **fortuity** *noun* (***fortuities***). ◷ 17c: from Latin *fortuitus*, from *forte* by chance, from *fors* chance.

> ***fortuitous, fortunate***
>
> • You will occasionally find **fortuitous** used to mean **fortunate**, a use that is encouraged when both meanings are possible or intended in a particular sentence □ *It was fortuitous that they arrived as we were leaving.*
>
> ☆ RECOMMENDATION: use **fortunate** if that is what you mean.

fortunate ▷ *adj* **1** lucky; favoured by fate. **2** timely; opportune. • **fortunately** *adverb*. ◷ 14c: from Latin *fortunatus*; see also FORTUNE, FORTUITOUS.

fortune /'fɔːtʃən/ ▷ *noun* **1** chance as a force in human affairs; fate. **2** luck. **3** (**fortunes**) unpredictable happenings that swing affairs this way or that □ *the fortunes of war.* **4** (**fortunes**) the state of one's luck. **5** one's destiny. **6** a large sum of money. • **make one's fortune** to become prosperous. • **a small fortune** a large amount of money. • **tell someone's fortune** to tell them what their destiny is. ◷ 13c: from Latin *fortuna*.

fortune cookie ▷ *noun* dough wrapped and cooked around a piece of paper which has a maxim or (supposed) fortune on it, served especially in Chinese homes and restaurants.

fortune-hunter ▷ *noun* someone who seeks marriage with a wealthy partner in order to secure a large amount of money.

fortune-teller ▷ *noun* a person who claims to be able to tell people their destinies. • **fortune-telling** *noun, adj*.

forty /'fɔːtɪ/ ▷ *noun* (***forties***) **1 a** the cardinal number 40; **b** the quantity that this represents, being one more than thirty-nine, or the product of ten and four. **2** any symbol for this, eg **40** or **XL**. Also *in compounds, forming adjectives and nouns* with cardinal numbers between *one* and *nine* □ *forty-three.* **3** the age of forty. **4** something, especially a garment or a person, whose size is denoted by the number 40. **5** a set or group of forty people or things. **6** a score of forty points. ▷ *adj* **1** totalling forty. Also *in* *compounds forming adjectives and nouns*, with ordinal numbers between *first* and *ninth* □ *forty-third*. **2** aged forty. See also FORTIES, FORTIETH. ◎ Anglo-Saxon *feowertig*, see FOUR + -TY.

forty-five ▷ *noun, dated* a RECORD (*noun* 4), usually 7 inches in diameter, played at a speed of 45 revolutions per minute. Compare TWELVE-INCH, LP, SEVENTY-EIGHT.

the Forty-Five ▷ *noun* the Jacobite rebellion of 1745–6.

fortyish ▷ *adj* **1** about forty years old. **2** about forty in number. ◎ 19c.

forty winks ▷ *plural noun, colloq* a short sleep; a nap.

forum /ˈfɔːrəm/ ▷ *noun* (***forums*** or (*rare*) ***fora*** /ˈfɔːrə/) **1** *historical* a public square or market place, especially that in ancient Rome where public business was conducted and law courts held. **2** a meeting to discuss topics of public concern. **3** a place, programme or publication where opinions can be expressed and openly discussed. ◎ 15c: Latin.

forward /ˈfɔːwəd/ ▷ *adverb* **1** (*also* **forwards**) in the direction in front or ahead of one. **2** (*also* **forwards**) progressing from first to last. **3** on or onward; to a later time □ *put the clocks forward*. **4** to an earlier time □ *bring the wedding forward a month*. **5** into view or public attention □ *put forward suggestions*. **6** /ˈfɒrəd/ *naut* towards the front or bow of an aircraft or ship. ▷ *adj* **1** in the direction in front or ahead. **2** at the front. **3** advanced in development □ *How far forward are the plans?* **4** concerning the future □ *forward planning*. **5** *derog* inclined to push oneself forward; over-bold in offering one's opinions. ▷ *noun, sport* a player whose task is to attack rather than defend. Compare BACK *noun* 6. ▷ *verb* (***forwarded, forwarding***) **1** to send (mail) on to another address from the one to which it arrived. **2** to help the progress of something. ● **forwardly** *adverb*. ● **forwardness** *noun*. ◎ Anglo-Saxon *foreweard*.

forward-looking ▷ *adj* planning ahead; progressive, enterprising or go-ahead.

forwent *past tense of* FORGO

Fosbury flop /ˈfɒzbərɪ —/ ▷ *noun* a method of high-jumping in which the athlete goes over the bar horizontally on their back. ◎ 20c: named after R Fosbury, born 1947, US athlete.

fossa /ˈfɒsə/ ▷ *noun* (***fossae*** /-siː/) *anatomy* a pit or depression, or hollow area. ◎ 19c: Latin, meaning 'ditch', from *fodere, fossum* to dig.

fosse or **foss** /fɒs/ ▷ *noun* (***fosses***) a ditch, moat, trench or canal. ◎ 14c: French, from Latin *fossa* ditch.

fossil /ˈfɒsɪl/ ▷ *noun* **1** *geol* the petrified remains, impression or cast of an animal or plant preserved within a rock. **2** a relic of the past. **3** *colloq* a curiously antiquated person. **4** *as adj* **a** like or in the form of a fossil; **b** formed naturally through the decomposition of organic matter, and dug or otherwise got from the earth □ *fossil fuels*. ◎ 17c: from Latin *fossilis* dug up.

fossil-fired ▷ *adj* said of a power station, etc: burning fossil fuel.

fossil fuel ▷ *noun* any fuel derived from the fossilized remains of plants and animals, such as coal, petroleum and natural gas, often contrasted with sources of NUCLEAR ENERGY and RENEWABLE RESOURCES. ◎ Early 19c.

fossiliferous /fɒsɪˈlɪfərəs/ ▷ *adj, geol* said of rocks, etc: containing fossils.

fossilize or **fossilise** ▷ *verb* (***fossilized, fossilizing***) *tr & intr* **1** to change or be changed into a fossil. **2** to become or make someone or something old-fashioned, inflexible, etc. ● **fossilization** *noun*.

fossil water ▷ *noun* water which has been trapped in an underground reservoir since a previous geological age.

fossorial /fɒˈsɔːrɪəl/ ▷ *adj, zool* adapted for digging. ◎ 19c: from Latin *fodere, fossum* to dig.

foster /ˈfɒstə(r)/ ▷ *verb* (***fostered, fostering***) **1** *tr & intr* to bring up (a child that is not one's own). **2** to put (a child) into the care of someone who is not its parent, usually for a temporary period of time. **3** to encourage the development of (ideas, feelings, etc). **4** *as adj* **a** concerned with or offering fostering □ *foster home*; **b** in a specified family relationship through fostering rather than by birth □ *foster mother* □ *foster parent* □ *foster brother*. Compare ADOPT. ● **fosterer** *noun*. ● **fostering** *noun*. ◎ Anglo-Saxon *fostrian* to feed.

Foucault current see under EDDY CURRENT

Foucault's pendulum /ˈfuːkouz —/ ▷ *noun, astron* an instrument consisting of a heavy metal ball suspended by a very long fine wire, devised in 1851 to demonstrate the rotation of the Earth, and often seen in shopping malls as a clock. ◎ 19c: named after its inventor J B L Foucault (1819–68), French physicist.

fouetté / *French* fwete/ ▷ *noun* (***fouettés***) *ballet* a step in which the foot makes a sideways whiplike movement. ◎ 19c: French, meaning 'whipped'.

fought *past tense, past participle of* FIGHT

foul /faʊl/ ▷ *adj* **1** disgusting □ *a foul smell*. **2** soiled; filthy. **3** contaminated □ *foul air*. **4** *colloq* very unkind or unpleasant. **5** said of language: offensive or obscene. **6** unfair or treacherous □ *by fair means or foul*. **7** said of weather: stormy. **8** clogged. **9** entangled. ▷ *noun, sport* a breach of the rules. ▷ *verb* (***fouled, fouling***) **1** *tr & intr, sport* to commit an act against (an opponent) which breaches the rules. **2** to make something dirty or polluted. **3** to contaminate or pollute something. **4** *tr & intr* **a** (*also* **foul up**) to become entangled; **b** to become entangled with something so as to hinder its movement or functioning. ▷ *adverb* in a foul manner; unfairly. ● **foully** *adverb*. ● **foulness** *noun*. ● **fall foul of someone** or **something** see under FALL. ● **foul one's nest** to do something harmful or dishonourable to oneself or one's family. ◎ Anglo-Saxon *ful*.

■ **foul something up** **1** to clog it. **2** *colloq* to mess it up; to bungle it.

foulard /fuːˈlɑːd, fuːˈlɑː(r)/ ▷ *noun* a soft untwilled silk fabric. ◎ 19c: French.

foul-mouthed and **foul-spoken** ▷ *adj* said of a person: using offensive or obscene language. ● **foul-mouthedness** and **foul-spokenness** *noun*.

foul play ▷ *noun* **1** treachery or criminal violence, especially murder. **2** *sport* a breach of the rules.

foul-up ▷ *noun, colloq* a bungled situation; a failure or disaster.

found¹ /faʊnd/ ▷ *verb* (***founded, founding***) **1** to start or establish (an organization, institution, city, etc), often with a provision for future funding. **2** to lay the foundation of (a building). ◎ 13c: from Latin *fundare*, from *fundus* bottom or foundation.

found² /faʊnd/ ▷ *verb* (***founded, founding***) **1** to cast (metal or glass) by melting and pouring it into a mould. **2** to produce (articles) by this method. ● **founding** *noun*. See also FOUNDRY. ◎ 14c: from Latin *fundere* to pour.

found³ *past tense, past participle of* FIND. ● **all found** see under ALL.

foundation /faʊnˈdeɪʃən/ ▷ *noun* **1** **a** the act of founding or establishing an institution, etc; **b** the institution, etc founded or the fund providing for it □ *Paul was awarded a grant from the Smith Foundation*. **2** (*usually* **foundations**) the underground structure on which a building is supported and built. **3** the basis on which a theory, etc rests or depends. ● **foundational** *adj*. ◎ 14c.

foundation course ▷ *noun* (*also* **foundation**) an introductory course, usually taken as a preparation for more advanced studies □ *He's taking a foundation course at art college* □ *He's on foundation this year*.

foundation cream ▷ *noun* (*usually* **foundation**) a cream, lotion, etc smoothed into the skin as a base for additional cosmetics.

foundation garment ▷ *noun* a woman's undergarment for supporting or controlling the figure, eg a corset, girdle, etc.

foundation stone ▷ *noun* a stone laid ceremonially as part of the foundations of a new building, often with an inscription on it.

founder[1] /ˈfaʊndə(r)/ ▷ *noun* someone who founds or endows an institution, etc. ◷ 14c: from FOUND[1].

founder[2] /ˈfaʊndə(r)/ ▷ *verb* (***foundered***, ***foundering***) *intr* **1** said of a ship: to sink. **2** said of a vehicle, etc: to get stuck in mud, etc. **3** said of a horse: to go lame. **4** said of a business, scheme, etc: to fail. ◷ 14c: from French *fondrer* to plunge to the bottom.

founder[3] /ˈfaʊndə(r)/ ▷ *noun* a person whose job is to make metal castings □ ***bell-founder***. ◷ 15c: from FOUND[2].

founder member ▷ *noun* one of the members of a society, organization, etc who was instrumental in its foundation.

founding father ▷ *noun* someone who founds or establishes an institution, organization, etc.

foundling ▷ *noun* an abandoned child of unknown parents. ◷ 13c: from FOUND[3].

found object ▷ *noun, art* **1** a term used by the Dadaists and Surrealists for any everyday object incorporated in a picture. **2** any object, such as a piece of driftwood or a length of rope, picked up and exhibited as a work of art, displayed either on its own or in a composition. Also called **objet trouvé**. ◷ 1920s.

foundry /ˈfaʊndrɪ/ ▷ *noun* (***foundries***) **1** a place where metal or glass is melted and cast. **2** the art of founding or casting of metal or glass. ◷ 17c: from French *fonderie*; see FOUND[2].

fount[1] /faʊnt/ or **font** /fɒnt/ ▷ *noun, printing* a set of printing type of the same design and size. ◷ 17c: from French *fonte* casting.

fount[2] /faʊnt/ ▷ *noun* **1** a spring or fountain. **2** a source of inspiration, etc. ◷ 16c: from FOUNTAIN.

fountain /ˈfaʊntɪn/ ▷ *noun* **1 a** a jet or jets of water for ornamental effect; **b** a structure supporting this, consisting of a basin and statues, etc. **2** a jet of water for drinking □ ***drinking fountain***. **3** a spring of water. **4** a source of wisdom, etc. ◷ 15c: from French *fontaine*, from Latin *fons* fountain.

fountainhead ▷ *noun* **1** a spring from which a stream flows. **2** the principal source of something.

fountain pen ▷ *noun* a metal-nibbed pen equipped with a cartridge or reservoir of ink.

four /fɔː(r)/ ▷ *noun* **1 a** the cardinal number 4; **b** the quantity that this represents, being one more than three. **2** any symbol for this, eg **4** or **IV**. **3** the age of four. **4** something, especially a garment, or a person, whose size is denoted by the number 4. **5** the fourth hour after midnight or midday □ ***Tea's at four*** □ ***4 o'clock*** □ ***4pm***. **6** a set or group of four people or things. **7 a** the crew of a rowing boat with four sweep oars; **b** such a boat. **8** a playing-card with four pips. **9** a score of four points. **10** *cricket* a score of four runs awarded if the ball reaches the boundary having hit the ground. ▷ *adj* **1** totalling four. **2** aged four. • **on all fours** on hands and knees. ◷ Anglo-Saxon *feower*.

four-by-four ▷ *noun* a vehicle in which the driving power is transmitted to all four wheels, as opposed to the front two or back two wheels. Also called **four-wheel drive** (abbreviation **4WD**). Compare FRONT-WHEEL DRIVE, REAR-WHEEL DRIVE.

four-colour process ▷ *noun, photog, printing* a technique for reproducing a full-colour image using only four colours of ink.

four-eyed fish see ANABLEPS

four-figure number ▷ *noun* a number consisting of four figures, ie one between 1 000 and 9 999.

fourfold ▷ *adj* **1** equal to four times as much. **2** divided into or consisting of four parts. ▷ *adverb* by four times as much. ◷ Anglo-Saxon; see FOUR + -FOLD.

four-foot ▷ *adj* measuring four feet (ie 48 inches) in width, length, etc □ ***a four-foot table*** □ ***four-foot square***.

four-footed ▷ *adj* referring to an animal, etc with four feet.

the Four Freedoms ▷ *plural noun* four basic human rights proclaimed by President Roosevelt in his annual message to Congress (1941), ie freedom of speech and worship, and freedom from want and fear.

four-handed ▷ *adj* **1** *cards* referring to a game with four players. **2** having four hands.

four-in-hand ▷ *noun* a coach drawn by four horses and driven by one driver.

four-leaf clover ▷ *noun* a clover with four leaflets, rather than the normal three, which is supposed to bring good luck to the finder.

four-letter word ▷ *noun* **1** any of several short English words referring to sex or excretion, such as *fuck*, *shit* and *cunt*, often used as expletives, usually considered offensive, and sometimes written with some of the letters replaced by asterisks. **2** any word which would be considered offensive or frustrating to someone with certain ambitions or principles □ ***He's on a diet, so chocolate is a four-letter word.***

fourpenny one ▷ *noun, slang* a blow or punch.

four-poster ▷ *noun* a large bed with a post at each corner to support curtains and a canopy. Also called **four-poster bed**. ◷ 19c.

fourscore ▷ *adj, noun, archaic* eighty. ◷ 13c.

foursome ▷ *noun* **1** a set or group of four people. **2** *golf* a game between two pairs of players. Also *as adj* □ ***foursome match***. ◷ 16c.

four-square ▷ *adj* **1** strong; steady; solidly based. **2** said of a building: square and solid-looking. ▷ *adverb* steadily; squarely.

four-stroke ▷ *adj* referring to an internal-combustion engine in which the piston makes a recurring cycle of two pairs of in-out strokes for each explosion.

fourteen ▷ *noun* **1 a** the cardinal number 14; **b** the quantity that this represents, being one more than thirteen, or the sum of ten and four. **2** any symbol for this, eg **14** or **XIV**. **3** the age of fourteen. **4** something, especially a garment, or a person, whose size is denoted by the number 14. **5** a set or group of fourteen people or things. **6** a score of fourteen points. ▷ *adj* **1** totalling fourteen. **2** aged fourteen. ◷ Anglo-Saxon *feowertiene*; see FOUR + -TEEN.

fourteenth (often written **14th**) ▷ *adj* **1** in counting: **a** next after thirteenth; **b** last of fourteen. **2** in fourteenth position. **3** (**the fourteenth**) **a** the fourteenth day of the month; **b** (*golf*) the fourteenth hole. ▷ *noun* **1** one of fourteen equal parts. Also *as adj* □ ***a fourteenth share***. **2** a FRACTION equal to one divided by fourteen (usually written $^1/_{14}$). **3** a person coming fourteenth, eg in a race or exam. ▷ *adverb* in the fourteenth place. ◷ Anglo-Saxon; see FOURTEEN + -TH.

fourth (often written **4th**) ▷ *adj* **1** in counting: **a** next after third; **b** last of four. **2** in fourth position. **3** (**the fourth**) **a** the fourth day of the month; **b** (*golf*) the fourth hole. ▷ *noun* **1** one of four equal parts. Usually called QUARTER. Also *as adj* □ ***a fourth share***. **2** a FRACTION equal to one divided by four (usually written $^1/_4$). Usually called QUARTER. **3** a person coming fourth, eg in a race or exam □ ***a good fourth***. **4** *music* **a** an interval of three diatonic degrees; **b** a tone at that interval from another, or a combination of two tones separated by that interval. ▷ *adverb* fourthly. • **fourthly** *adverb* used to introduce the fourth point in a list. ◎ Anglo-Saxon; see FOUR + -TH.

fourth

There is often a spelling confusion between **fourth** and **forth**.

fourth dimension ▷ *noun* **1** time regarded as a dimension complementing the three dimensions of space (length, width and depth). **2 a** a dimension, such as parallel universes, which may exist in addition to the three dimensions of space; **b** anything which is beyond ordinary experience.

the Fourth Estate ▷ *noun* the Press regarded as a political force. ◎ Coined in 1828 by Macaulay, who described the gallery of the house of Commons in which the reporters sit as 'the fourth estate of the realm'; see ESTATE *noun* 5.

the Fourth of July ▷ *noun* a public holiday in the USA, commemorating the adoption of the Declaration of Independence in 1776.

fourth-rate ▷ *adj* inferior to something else, particularly something considered FIRST-RATE, SECOND-RATE, etc.

the Fourth World ▷ *noun* **1** the poorest and technologically least developed countries of the world, ie the poorest countries of the THIRD WORLD. **2** the poorest people in developed countries. ◎ 1970s.

4WD ▷ *abbreviation* four-wheel-drive.

four-wheel drive see under FOUR-BY-FOUR

fousty /'fuːstɪ/ ▷ *adj, Scots* **1** mouldy or damp. **2** having a musty smell; fusty. ◎ 19c.

fovea /'foʊvɪə/ ▷ *noun* (***foveae*** /-viiː/) **1** *anatomy* a shallow depression in the retina at the back of the eye in birds, lizards and primates where vision is sharpest. Also called **yellow spot**. **2** any small hollow or depression in a body structure. • **foveal** *adj*. • **foveate** *adj* pitted. ◎ 19c: Latin, meaning 'small pit'.

fowl /faʊl/ ▷ *noun* (***fowls*** or ***fowl***) **1** a farmyard bird, eg a chicken or turkey. **2** the flesh or meat of fowl used as food. Compare FLESH *noun* 2. **3** *old use, in compounds* any bird, especially if eaten as meat or hunted as game □ *wildfowl*. ▷ *verb* (***fowled, fowling***) *intr* to hunt or trap wild birds. • **fowler** *noun*. • **fowling** *noun*. ◎ Anglo-Saxon *fugel* bird.

fox ▷ *noun* (***foxes***) **1** any of various carnivorous mammals belonging to the dog family, found in most parts of the world, with a pointed muzzle, large pointed ears and a long bushy tail. **2** the fur of this animal. **3** *colloq* a cunning person. See also VIXEN. **4** *N Amer* an attractive and usually young man or woman. ▷ *verb* (***foxed, foxing***) **1** to puzzle, confuse or baffle someone. **2** to deceive, trick or outwit someone □ *She was completely foxed by his behaviour*. See also OUTFOX. **3** *tr & intr* said of paper: to become or make it become discoloured with brown spots. • **foxlike** *adj*. ◎ Anglo-Saxon.

fox-bat ▷ *noun* a flying fox; a fruit bat.

foxed ▷ *adj* **1** baffled; bamboozled. **2** said of books: discoloured.

foxglove ▷ *noun* a biennial or perennial plant, that produces tall spikes with many thimble-shaped purple or white flowers, and whose leaves are a source of DIGITALIS. ◎ Anglo-Saxon.

foxhole ▷ *noun, military* a hole in the ground from which a soldier may shoot while protected from the enemy's guns. ◎ Anglo-Saxon *foxhol*.

foxhound ▷ *noun* a breed of dog bred and trained to chase foxes.

fox hunt ▷ *noun* **1** a hunt for a fox. **2** a group of people who meet to hunt foxes. • **foxhunter** *noun*. • **fox-hunting** *noun* the bloodsport in which mounted huntsmen pursue foxes with a pack of foxhounds.

foxing ▷ *noun* discoloration in the form of brownish marks on paper that has been allowed to become damp.

fox terrier ▷ *noun* a breed of small dog originally trained to drive foxes out of their holes.

foxtrot /'fɒkstrɒt/ ▷ *noun* **1** a ballroom dance with gliding steps, alternating between quick and slow. **2** the music for this dance. **3** (**Foxtrot**) *communications* in the NATO alphabet: the word used to represent the letter 'F' (see table at NATO ALPHABET). ▷ *verb, intr* to perform this dance.

foxy ▷ *adj* (***foxier, foxiest***) **1** referring to foxes; foxlike. **2** cunning; sly. **3** reddish brown in colour. **4** *slang* said of a woman: sexually attractive. • **foxily** *adverb*. • **foxiness** *noun*.

foyer /'fɔɪeɪ, fɔɪə(r)/ ▷ *noun* **1** the entrance hall of a theatre, hotel, etc. **2** *N Amer* the hallway of a house or apartment. ◎ 19c: French, meaning 'fireplace', from Latin *focus* hearth.

FP ▷ *abbreviation* **1** former pupil. **2** Free Presbyterian.

fp ▷ *abbreviation* **1** forte-piano. **2** freezing point.

FPA ▷ *abbreviation* Family Planning Association.

Fr[1] ▷ *abbreviation* **1** Father, the title of a priest. **2** (**Fr.**) France. **3** (**Fr.**) French. **4** (**Fr.**) Friday.

Fr[2] ▷ *symbol, chem* francium.

fr. ▷ *abbreviation* **1** fragment. **2** (**fr**) franc. **3** frequently.

frabjous /'frabdʒəs/ ▷ *adj* joyous; wonderful. • **frabjously** *adverb*. ◎ Late 19c: invented by Lewis Carroll (1832–98).

fracas /'frakɑː/ ▷ *noun* (***fracas***) a noisy quarrel; a fight or brawl. ◎ 18c: French, from Italian *fracassare* to make an uproar.

fractal /'fraktəl/ ▷ *noun, math* an irregular curve or surface produced by repeated subdivision, eg a *snowflake curve* (resembling a snowflake in outline), produced by repeatedly dividing the sides of an equilateral triangle into three segments and adding another triangle to the middle section. Also *as adj* □ *fractal geometry*. ◎ 1970s: from Latin *frangere, fractum* to break.

fraction /'frakʃən/ ▷ *noun* **1** *math* an expression that indicates one or more equal parts of a whole, usually represented by a pair of numbers separated by a horizontal or diagonal line, where the upper number (the NUMERATOR) represents the number of parts selected and the lower number (the DENOMINATOR) the total number of parts. Compare INTEGER. **2** a portion; a small part of something. **3** *Christianity* the breaking of the bread in the Eucharist. **4** *chem* a group of chemical compounds whose boiling points fall within a very narrow range, the components of which can be separated by FRACTIONAL DISTILLATION. ◎ 14c: from Latin *fractio* breaking.

fractional ▷ *adj* **1** referring to a fraction or fractions. **2** referring to the nature of a fraction. **3** tiny; insignificant. • **fractionally** *adverb*.

fractional distillation ▷ *noun, chem* the separation by distillation of the various constituents of a mixture of liquids with different boiling points.

fractionalize or **fractionalise** ▷ *verb* (***fractionalized, fractionalizing***) to break something up into parts. • **fractionalization** *noun*.

fractionate ▷ *verb* (***fractionated, fractionating***) **1** to break something up into smaller units. **2** to separate the components of (a liquid) by distillation, particularly FRACTIONAL DISTILLATION. • **fractionation** *noun*.

fractionator ▷ *noun* a plant for carrying out FRACTIONAL DISTILLATION.

fractious /'frakʃəs/ ▷ *adj* cross and quarrelsome; inclined to quarrel and complain. • **fractiously** *adverb*. •

fractiousness *noun*. ⓘ 18c: modelled on FRACTION, in an earlier sense of 'dispute' or 'quarrel'.

fractography /frak'tɒgrəfɪ/ ▷ *noun* the study of microscopic fractures in metal surfaces.

fracture /'fraktʃə(r)/ ▷ *noun* **1** the breaking or cracking of anything hard, especially bone, rock or mineral. **2** the medical condition resulting from this, different types of which are SIMPLE FRACTURE, COMPOUND FRACTURE, IMPACTED FRACTURE, GREENSTICK FRACTURE, COLLES' FRACTURE, POTT'S FRACTURE, etc. **3** said of freshly broken mineral rock: the appearance of the surface. ▷ *verb* (***fractured***, ***fracturing***) **1** to break or crack something, especially a bone. **2** *intr* said of a bone, etc: to break or crack. ⓘ 16c: French, from Latin *fractura* a break.

fraena and **fraenum** see under FRENUM.

fragile /'fradʒaɪl; *US* 'fradʒəl/ ▷ *adj* **1** easily broken; liable to break. **2** easily damaged or destroyed. **3** delicate □ *fragile beauty*. **4** in a weakened state of health □ *She's feeling very fragile today*. • **fragilely** *adverb*. • **fragility** /frə'dʒɪlɪtɪ/. ⓘ 17c: from Latin *fragilis* breakable.

fragment ▷ *noun* /'fragmənt/ **1** a piece broken off; a small piece of something that has broken. **2** something incomplete; a small part remaining. ▷ *verb* /frag'mɛnt/ (***fragmented***, ***fragmenting***) **1** *tr & intr* to break into pieces. **2** *intr*, *computing* said of a file: to be stored in sections on different parts of a floppy disk, making access slower. ⓘ 16c: from Latin *fragmentum*, from *frangere* to break.

fragmental /frag'mɛntəl/ ▷ *adj* **1** *geol* CLASTIC. **2** in fragments.

fragmentary /'fragməntərɪ, frag'mɛn-/ and **fragmented** /frag'mɛntɪd/ ▷ *adj* **1** consisting of small pieces, not usually amounting to a complete whole; in fragments. **2** existing or operating in separate parts, not forming a harmonious unity. • **fragmentarily** *adverb*. • **fragmentariness** *noun*.

fragmentation /fragmən'teɪʃən/ ▷ *noun* division into fragments.

fragmentation bomb and **fragmentation grenade** ▷ *noun* a bomb or grenade designed to shatter into small pieces on explosion, increasing its destructiveness.

fragrance /'freɪgrəns/ and **fragrancy** ▷ *noun* (***fragrances*** or ***fragrancies***) **1** sweetness of smell. **2** a sweet smell or odour. • **fragrant** *adj*. • **fragrantly** *adverb*. ⓘ 15c: from Latin *fragrare* to give out a smell.

frail /freɪl/ ▷ *adj* **1** easily broken or destroyed; delicate; fragile. **2** in poor health; weak. **3** morally weak; easily tempted. • **frailly** *adverb*. • **frailness** *noun*. • **frailty** *noun* (***frailties***). ⓘ 14c: from French *fraile*, from Latin *fragilis* fragile.

framboesia or (*US*) **frambesia** /fram'biːzɪə/ *noun*, *pathol* the YAWS. ⓘ 19c: from French *framboise* raspberry, from its raspberry-like excrescences.

frame ▷ *noun* **1** a hard main structure or basis to something, round which something is built or to which other parts are added. **2** a structure that surrounds and supports something □ *put the picture in a frame*. **3** something that surrounds □ *her face with its frame of dark hair*. **4** a body, especially a human one, as a structure of a certain size and shape □ *eased his tall frame into the chair*. **5** one of the pictures that make up a strip of film. **6** a single television picture, eg a still picture seen when the pause button on a video player is pressed. **7** one of the pictures in a comic strip. **8** a low glass or semi-glazed structure for protecting young plants growing out of doors, which is smaller than a greenhouse. Also called **cold frame**. **9** a framework of bars, eg in a playground for children to play on □ *climbing frame*. **10** *snooker, etc* **a** a triangular structure for confining the balls for the BREAK (*noun* 8) at the start of a round; **b** each of the rounds of play, a pre-determined number of which constitute the entire match. **11** the rigid part of a bicycle, usually made of metal tubes. ▷ *verb* (***framed***, ***framing***) **1** to put a frame round something □ *Pauline framed the picture*. **2** to be a frame for something. **3** to compose or design something □ *He framed the question with simple words*. **4** to shape or direct (one's thoughts, actions, etc) for a particular purpose. **5** *colloq* to dishonestly direct suspicion for a crime, etc at (an innocent person). See also FRAME-UP. • **frameless** *adj*. • **framer** *noun*. • **framing** *noun*. ⓘ Anglo-Saxon *framian* to benefit.

frame of mind ▷ *noun* (***frames of mind***) a mood; state of mind; attitude towards something.

frame of reference ▷ *noun* (***frames of reference***) **1** a set of facts, beliefs or principles that serves as the context within which specific actions, events or behaviour patterns can be analysed or described, or on the basis of which opinions can be formed and decisions made. **2** *math* a set of points, lines or planes, especially three geometrical axes, used to define and locate the position of a point in space.

frame-saw ▷ *noun* a saw with a thin blade stretched in a frame.

frame-up ▷ *noun*, *colloq* a plot or set-up to make an innocent person appear guilty. ⓘ Early 20c: originally US.

framework ▷ *noun* **1** a basic supporting structure. **2** a basic plan or system. **3** a structure composed of horizontal and vertical bars or shafts.

franc /fraŋk/ ▷ *noun* the standard unit of currency of various countries, including France, Belgium, Switzerland, and several other French-speaking countries. ⓘ 14c: from French *Francorum rex* king of the Franks, the inscription on the first such coins.

franchise /'frantʃaɪz/ ▷ *noun* **1** the right to vote, especially in a parliamentary election. **2** a right, privilege, exemption from a duty, etc, granted to a person or organization. **3** **a** an agreement by which a business company gives someone the right to market its products in an area; **b** the area concerned. **4** a concession granted by a public authority to a TV, radio, etc company to broadcast in a certain area. ▷ *verb* (***franchised***, ***franchising***) to grant a franchise to (a person, a company, etc). ⓘ 13c: from French *franchir* to set free.

franchisee /frantʃaɪ'ziː/ ▷ *noun* (***franchisees***) someone to whom a franchise is granted.

franchiser /'frantʃaɪzə(r)/ ▷ *noun* **1** a firm, an authority, etc which grants a commercial concession. **2** a voter.

Franciscan /fran'sɪskən/ ▷ *noun* a member of a Christian order of nuns and friars founded by St Francis of Assisi in 1209. ▷ *adj* belonging or relating to the Franciscans □ *a Franciscan monastery*. ⓘ 16c: from Latin *Franciscus* Francis.

francium /'fransɪəm/ ▷ *noun*, *chem* (symbol **Fr**, atomic number 87) a radioactive metallic element, the heaviest of the alkali metals, obtained by bombarding thorium with protons. ⓘ 1940s: from *France*, the country where it was discovered.

Franco- ▷ *combining form*, *signifying* France or the French, together with some other specified group □ *Franco-Russian* □ *Franco-Canadians*. ⓘ 18c: from Latin *Francus* the Franks or the French.

francolin /'fraŋkoulɪn/ ▷ *noun* a partridge native to Africa and S Asia. ⓘ 17c.

francophone /'fraŋkoufoun/ ▷ *noun* (*sometimes* **Francophone**) a French-speaking person, especially in a country where other languages are spoken. ▷ *adj* **1** speaking French as a native language. **2** using French as a second mother-tongue or lingua franca. ⓘ Late 19c.

frangipane /'frandʒɪpeɪn/ ▷ *noun* **1** a cream made with crushed almonds, used in the preparation of various desserts, sweets, cakes, etc. **2** FRANGIPANI (sense 2). ⓘ 17c: from FRANGIPANI.

frangipani /frandʒɪˈpɑːnɪ/ ⊳ *noun* (***frangipanis***) **1** a shrub or small tree native to tropical America, which grows up to 6m (20ft) tall, and has oval leaves and large clusters of highly fragrant white, yellow or pink flowers. **2** (*also* **frangipane**) a perfume made from this, or imitating it. ◷ 17c: named after the Italian nobleman Frangipani, who invented a perfume based on bitter almonds for scenting gloves.

franglais /ˈfrɒŋgleɪ/ ⊳ *noun, usually humorous* informal French with many English words and forms. ◷ 1960s: French, from *français* French + *anglais* English.

Frank ⊳ *noun* a member of a W Germanic people that invaded Gaul (an ancient region of W Europe) in the late 5c AD, and founded France. • **Frankish** *adj*. ◷ Anglo-Saxon *Franca*, probably from *franca* javelin.

frank ⊳ *adj* (***franker***, ***frankest***) **1** open and honest in speech or manner; candid. **2** bluntly outspoken. **3** undisguised; openly visible. ⊳ *verb* (***franked***, ***franking***) to mark (a letter), either cancelling the stamp or, in place of a stamp, to show that postage has been paid. ⊳ *noun* a franking mark on a letter. • **frankly** *adverb*. • **frankness** *noun*. ◷ 13c: from Latin *francus* free.

Frankenstein /ˈfraŋkənstaɪn/ and **Frankenstein's monster** ⊳ *noun* a name for a creation or creature that destroys its creator. ◷ 19c: named after such a creature in Mary Shelley's Gothic novel *Frankenstein* (1818).

frankfurter /ˈfraŋkfɜːtə(r)/ ⊳ *noun* a type of spicy smoked sausage, originally made in Frankfurt am Main. ◷ Late 19c: short for German *Frankfurter Wurst* Frankfurt sausage.

frankincense /ˈfraŋkɪnsɛns/ ⊳ *noun* an aromatic gum resin obtained from certain E African or Arabian trees, burnt to produce a sweet smell, especially during religious ceremonies. Also called OLIBANUM. ◷ 14c: from French *franc encens* pure incense.

frantic /ˈfrantɪk/ ⊳ *adj* **1** desperate, eg with fear or anxiety. **2** hurried; rushed □ *a frantic rush to meet the deadline*. • **frantically** *adverb*. ◷ 14c: from French *frenetique*; compare FRENETIC.

frappé /ˈfrapeɪ/ ⊳ *adj* iced; artificially cooled. ⊳ *noun* (***frappés***) an iced drink. ◷ 19c: French, meaning 'iced drink', from *frapper* to strike.

Frascati /frasˈkɑːtɪ/ ⊳ *noun* (*also* **frascati**) an Italian wine, usually white. ◷ 20c: named after Frascati, a district in S Italy where it is produced.

fraternal /frəˈtɜːnəl/ ⊳ *adj* **1** concerning a brother; brotherly. **2** said of twins: DIZYGOTIC. Compare IDENTICAL[2]. • **fraternally** *adverb*. ◷ 15c: from Latin *fraternus*, from *frater* brother.

fraternity /frəˈtɜːnɪtɪ/ ⊳ *noun* (***fraternities***) **1** a religious brotherhood. **2** a group of people with common interests. **3** the fact of being brothers; brotherly feeling. **4** *N Amer* a social club for male students. Compare SORORITY. ◷ 14c: from Latin *fraternitas*, from *frater* brother.

fraternize or **fraternise** /ˈfratənaɪz/ ⊳ *verb* (***fraternized***, ***fraternizing***) *intr* (*often* **fraternize with someone**) to meet or associate together as friends. • **fraternization** or **fraternisation** *noun*. ◷ 17c: from Latin *fraternus* brotherly.

fratricide /ˈfratrɪsaɪd, ˈfreɪtrɪ-/ ⊳ *noun* **1** the murder of a brother. **2** someone who murders their brother. • **fratricidal** *adj*. ◷ 15c: from Latin *frater* brother + -CIDE.

Frau /fraʊ/ ⊳ *noun* (***Fraus*** /-z/ or ***Frauen*** /-ən/) usually said of a German woman: a woman or wife, usually used as a title equivalent to MRS or MS. ◷ 19c: German, meaning 'woman' or 'wife'.

fraud /frɔːd/ ⊳ *noun* **1** an act of deliberate deception, with the intention of gaining some benefit. **2** *colloq* someone who dishonestly pretends to be something they are not; a cheat □ *She turned out to be a fraud*. ◷ 14c: from Latin *fraus*, *fraudis* trick.

fraudster ⊳ *noun* a cheat; a swindler.

fraudulent /ˈfrɔːdjʊlənt/ ⊳ *adj* involving deliberate deception; intended to deceive □ *fraudulent behaviour*. • **fraudulence** or **fraudulency** *noun*. • **fraudulently** *adverb*. ◷ 15c.

fraught /frɔːt/ ⊳ *adj, colloq* causing or feeling anxiety or worry □ *Jenny has been fraught since the vote went against her*. • **fraught with danger**, *etc* full of or laden down with danger, difficulties, problems, etc. ◷ 14c: from Dutch *vracht* freight.

Fräulein /ˈfrɔɪlaɪn, ˈfraʊ-/ ⊳ *noun, dated* a title often given to a German governess in Britain. ◷ 17c: German, meaning 'young woman', and also formerly used as a title equivalent to *Miss* for an unmarried woman.

Fraunhofer lines /ˈfraʊnhoʊfə(r) —/ ⊳ *plural noun* a set of dark lines which appear in the stellar and solar spectra. ◷ 19c: named after Joseph von Fraunhofer (1787–1826), Bavarian physicist.

fray[1] /freɪ/ ⊳ *verb* (***frayed***, ***fraying***) *tr & intr* **1** said of cloth or rope: to wear away along an edge or at a point of friction, so that individual threads come loose □ *The rope frayed over a number of months, and was badly frayed when it broke*. **2** said of tempers, nerves, etc: to make or become edgy and strained □ *Tempers started fraying just before midnight*. ◷ 18c in this sense; 15c in obsolete sense referring to deer rubbing velvet off their antlers: from French *frayer*, from Latin *fricare* to rub.

fray[2] /freɪ/ ⊳ *noun* (***frays***) **1** a fight, quarrel or argument. **2** any scene of lively action. ◷ 14c: short for AFFRAY.

frazil /ˈfrazɪl, ˈfreɪzɪl/ ⊳ *noun* ice formed in small spikes and plates in rapidly-moving streams. ◷ 19c: from Canadian French *frasil*, probably from French *fraisil* cinders.

frazzle /ˈfrazəl/ ⊳ *noun* **1** a state of nervous and physical exhaustion. **2** a scorched and brittle state □ *burnt to a frazzle*. ⊳ *verb* (***frazzled***, ***frazzling***) to tire out physically and emotionally. ◷ 19c: probably related to FRAY[1].

FRCP ⊳ *abbreviation* Fellow of the Royal College of Physicians.

FRCS ⊳ *abbreviation* Fellow of the Royal College of Surgeons.

freak /friːk/ ⊳ *noun* **1** a person, animal or plant of abnormal shape or form. **2** someone or something odd or unusual. **3** *especially in compounds* someone highly enthusiastic about the specified thing □ *health freak* □ *film freak*. **4** a drug addict □ *an acid freak*. **5** a whim or caprice □ *a freak of fancy*. ⊳ *adj* abnormal □ *a freak storm*. ⊳ *verb* (***freaked***, ***freaking***) *tr & intr* (*also* **freak out** or **freak someone out**) *colloq* **1 a** to become or make someone mentally or emotionally over-excited □ *The film really freaked him*; **b** to become or make someone so by means of hallucinatory drugs □ *The LSD really freaked them out*. **2** to become or make someone angry □ *He freaked when he heard the news*. • **freakish** *adj*. ◷ 16c: possibly related to Anglo-Saxon *frician* to dance.

freak-out ⊳ *noun, slang* a hallucinatory or wildly exciting unconventional experience or occurrence, often drug-induced.

freaky ⊳ *adj* (***freakier***, ***freakiest***) odd; strange; unusual; eccentric; way-out. • **freakily** *adverb*. • **freakiness** *noun*.

freckle /ˈfrɛkəl/ ⊳ *noun* a small yellowish-brown benign mark on the skin, especially of fair-skinned people, which sometimes appears in large numbers, usually becoming darker and more prominent with exposure to the sun. ⊳ *verb* (***freckled***, ***freckling***) *tr & intr* to mark, or become marked, with freckles. • **freckled** or **freckly** *adj*. ◷ 14c as *frecken*: from Norse *freknur* freckles.

free ⊳ *adj* (***freer*** /ˈfriːə(r)/, ***freest*** /friːɪst/) **1** allowed to move as one pleases; not shut in. **2** not tied or fastened. **3** allowed to do as one pleases; not restricted, controlled or enslaved. **4** said of a country: independent. **5** costing nothing. **6** open or available to all. **7** not working, busy, engaged or having another appointment. **8** not occupied; not being used. **9** said of a translation: not precisely literal. **10** smooth and easy □ *free and relaxed body movement.* **11** without obstruction □ *given free passage.* **12** *derog* said of a person's manner: disrespectful, over-familiar or presumptuous. **13** *chem* not combined with another chemical element. **14** *in compounds* **a** not containing the specified ingredient, substance, factor, etc (which is usually considered to be undesirable) □ *sugar-free* □ *milk-free* □ *nuclear-free*; **b** free from, or not affected or troubled by, the specified thing □ *trouble-free meeting* □ *stress-free weekend* □ *carefree*; **c** not paying or exempt from the specified thing □ *rent-free* □ *tax-free* ⓒ 17c and particularly since the 1970s in sense 14a; 16c in sense 14b; Anglo-Saxon in sense 14c. ▻ *adverb* **1** without payment □ *free of charge.* **2** freely; without restriction □ *wander free.* ▻ *verb* (***frees***, ***freed***, ***freeing***) to allow someone to move without restriction after a period in captivity, prison, etc; to set or make someone free; to liberate someone. • **freely** *adverb.* • **freeness** *noun.* • **feel free** *colloq* you have permission (to do something) □ *Feel free to borrow my bike anytime.* • **for free** *colloq* without payment. • **free and easy** cheerfully casual or tolerant. • **a free hand** scope to choose how best to act. • **free of** or **from something** without; not or no longer having or suffering (especially something harmful, unpleasant or not wanted) □ *free of fear* □ *finally free from the aching pain.* • **free with something** open, generous, lavish or liberal □ *free with her money* □ *free with his body.* • **it's a free country** *colloq* there's no objection to acting in the way mentioned. • **make free with something** to make too much, or unacceptable, use of something not one's own. ⓒ Anglo-Saxon *freo.*

■ **free someone of something 1** to make them free from it; to release them. **2** to rid or relieve them of it.

free alongside ship ▻ *adj* (abbreviation **f.a.s.**) said of a shipment of goods: delivered to the quayside free of charge, but exclusive of the cost of loading onto the ship. Compare FREE ON BOARD.

free association ▻ *noun, psychoanal* a technique based either on the first thought coming to mind in response to a series of words, or based on a train of thought suggested by a single word, used in therapy for exploring someone's unconscious.

freebase *drug-taking slang* ▻ *noun* cocaine refined for smoking by being heated with ether. ▻ *verb* **1** to purify cocaine in this way. **2** to smoke the residue produced by freebasing. ⓒ 1980s: originally US.

freebie or **freebee** or **freeby** /ˈfriːbɪ/ ▻ *noun* (***freebies*** or ***freebees***) *colloq* something given or provided without charge, particularly as a sales promotion.

freeboard ▻ *noun, naut* the distance between the top edge of the side of a boat and the surface of the water.

freebooter ▻ *noun, historical* a pirate. ⓒ 17c: from Dutch *vrijbuiter*, from *vrij* free + *buit* booty; compare FILIBUSTER.

freeborn ▻ *adj* born as a free citizen, not a slave.

freeby see FREEBIE

freecall see FREEPHONE

Free Church ▻ *noun* **1** *Scottish church history* **a** that branch of the Presbyterians in Scotland which left the Established Church at the Disruption of 1843; **b** the small minority of that group who refused to combine with the United Presbyterians in the United Free Church. **2** *chiefly Brit* a Protestant Church other than an Established Church.

free collective bargaining ▻ *noun* bargaining without government-imposed or other restrictions.

freed *past tense, past participle of* FREE

freedman or **freedwoman** ▻ *noun* a man or woman who has been a slave and has been emancipated.

freedom ▻ *noun* **1** the condition of being free to act, move, etc without restriction. **2** personal liberty or independence, eg from slavery, serfdom, etc. **3** a right or liberty □ *freedom of speech* □ *freedom to demonstrate.* **4** (*often* **freedom from something**) the state of being without or exempt from something □ *freedom from pain.* **5** autonomy, self-government or independence, eg of a state or republic. **6** unrestricted access to or use of something □ *give someone the freedom of one's house.* **7** honorary citizenship of a place, entitling one to certain privileges □ *was granted freedom of the town of Rochester.* **8** frankness; candour. **9** over-familiarity; presumptuous behaviour. ⓒ Anglo-Saxon *freodom.*

freedom fighter ▻ *noun* someone who fights in an armed movement for the liberation of a nation, etc from a government considered unjust, tyrannical, etc.

freedom of conscience ▻ *noun* the right to hold religious or other beliefs without persecution.

freedwoman see under FREEDMAN

free enterprise ▻ *noun* business carried out between companies, firms, etc without interference or control by the government, particularly where supply and demand determine the allocation of resources without regulation, pursued in a MARKET ECONOMY or MIXED ECONOMY.

free fall ▻ *noun* **1** the fall of something acted on by gravity alone. **2** the part of a descent by parachute before the parachute opens.

free flight ▻ *noun* the movement or flight of a rocket, missile, etc when its motor is no longer producing thrust.

freefone see FREEPHONE

free-for-all ▻ *noun* a fight, argument, or discussion in which everybody present feels free to join.

free-form ▻ *adj* freely flowing; spontaneous.

free gift ▻ *noun* something given free of charge with a product as an incentive to buy.

freehand ▻ *adj, adverb* said of a drawing, etc: done without the help of a ruler, compass, etc.

free hand ▻ *noun* complete freedom of action. • **give someone a free hand** to put them in control, eg of a project or venture, and allow them to deal with any issues that arise.

free-handed ▻ *adj* liberal or generous. • **free-handedness** *noun.*

freehold ▻ *adj* said of land, property, etc: belonging to the owner by FEE SIMPLE, FEE TAIL, or for life and without limitations. ▻ *noun* ownership of such land, property, etc. Compare LEASEHOLD.

freeholder ▻ *noun* an owner of freehold property.

free house ▻ *noun* a hotel or bar not owned by a particular beer-producer and therefore free to sell a variety of beers.

free kick ▻ *noun, football* a kick allowed to one side with no tackling from the other, as a penalty imposed on the latter for infringing the rules.

freelance ▻ *noun* **1** a self-employed person offering their services where needed, not under contract to any single employer. Also called **freelancer**. **2** *as adj* □ *freelance journalist.* ▻ *adverb* as a freelance □ *She works freelance now.* ▻ *verb* (***freelanced***, ***freelancing***) *intr* to work as a freelance. ⓒ 19c, meaning 'a medieval mercenary soldier', coined by Sir Walter Scott, but now referring to any kind of work.

free-living ▻ *adj, biol* not parasitic or symbiotic.

freeload ▻ *verb, intr, colloq* to eat, live, enjoy oneself, etc at someone else's expense. • **freeloader** *noun.* ⓒ 1960s: originally US.

free love ▷ *noun* the practice of having sexual relations with people regardless of marriage or fidelity to a single partner, especially referring to those who advocated and practised this in the 1960s. ⓒ 19c.

free lunch ▷ *noun* something that seems to be free but is not because one is expected to return the favour. ⓒ 1970s: from the expression *there's no such thing as a free lunch.*

freeman /ˈfriːmən/ and **freewoman** ▷ *noun* **1** a man or woman who is free or enjoys liberty. **2** a respected man or woman who has been granted the freedom of a city.

Freemason and **Mason** ▷ *noun* a member of an international secret male society, organized into LODGES, having among its purposes mutual help and brotherly fellowship. • **Freemasonic** *adj.* ⓒ 17c in this sense; 14c in obsolete sense referring to skilled craftsmen working in stone, who travelled where large buildings were being constructed.

Freemasonry ▷ *noun* **1** the institutions of the Freemasons. **2** (*usually* **freemasonry**) instinctive understanding and sympathy, usually among like-minded people rather than a formal group.

free on board ▷ *adj* (abbreviation **f.o.b.**) said of a shipment of goods: delivered to a vessel or other carrier and loaded onto it without charge to the buyer. Compare FREE ALONGSIDE SHIP.

free on rail ▷ *adj* (abbreviation **f.o.r.**) said of a shipment of goods: delivered to a railway station and loaded onto a train without charge to the buyer.

free pardon ▷ *noun* an unconditional pardon given, eg as a result of fresh evidence, to someone previously convicted of a crime.

freephone or **freefone** and **freecall** ▷ *noun, trademark* (also with capital) a telephone service whereby calls made to a business or organization are charged to that organization rather than to the caller, eg those with a number starting 0500 or 0800. Also *as adj* □ ***freephone number.*** *N Amer equivalent* **toll-free**. Compare LO-CALL. ⓒ 1950s.

free port ▷ *noun* **1** a port open on equal terms to all traders. **2** a port, or a free-trade zone adjacent to a port or airport, where goods may be imported free of tax or import duties, provided they are re-exported or used to make goods to be re-exported.

Freepost or **freepost** ▷ *noun, trademark* a Royal Mail service whereby postage costs for letters sent to a business or organization are charged to that organization rather than being prepaid by the sender. ⓒ 1970s.

freer /ˈfrɪə(r)/ ▷ *noun* a liberator. See also under FREE.

free radical ▷ *noun, chem* a group of atoms, containing at least one unpaired electron, that is capable of initiating a wide range of chemical reactions.

free-range ▷ *adj* **1** said of animal livestock, especially poultry: allowed some freedom to move about and graze or feed naturally; not kept in a BATTERY. **2** said of eggs: laid by free-range poultry.

freesheet ▷ *noun* a newspaper, available or distributed without charge, financed by its advertisements.

freesia /ˈfriːzɪə, ˈfriːʒə/ ▷ *noun* a plant of southern Africa belonging to the iris family, which has an underground bulb and is widely cultivated for its fragrant trumpet-shaped white, yellow, purple or crimson flowers. ⓒ 19c: named after F H T Freese or H Th Frees, German physicians, or according to some, E M Fries, Swedish botanist.

free skating ▷ *noun* competitive FIGURE SKATING in which the skater selects movements from an officially approved list of jumps, spins, etc.

free speech ▷ *noun* the right to express any opinion freely, particularly in public.

free-spoken ▷ *adj* accustomed to speaking openly and frankly without reserve. • **free-spokenness** *noun.*

freest see under FREE

free-standing ▷ *adj* not attached to or supported by a wall or other structure.

freestone ▷ *noun* **1 a** any fine-grained stone, eg sandstone or limestone, that can be shaped easily for building without a tendency to split in layers; **b** a slab of such stone. **2** a freestone fruit. ▷ *adj* said of certain types of eg peaches and nectarines: having a stone from which the flesh comes away easily when ripe. Compare CLINGSTONE.

freestyle ▷ *adj, sport* **1 a** applied to a competition or race in which competitors are allowed to choose their own style or programme; **b** *swimming* applied to the front crawl stroke, as being the fastest. **2** applied to ALL-IN WRESTLING. **3** said of a competitor: taking part in freestyle competitions, etc. ▷ *noun, sport* a freestyle competition or race. • **freestyler** *noun.*

freethinker ▷ *noun* someone who forms their own ideas, especially religious ones, rather than accepting the view of an authority. ⓒ 18c.

freethinking ▷ *noun* freedom of thought. ▷ *adj* independently minded, especially with regard to religious doctrine.

free trade ▷ *noun* trade between or amongst countries without protective tariffs, such as customs, taxes, etc.

free verse ▷ *noun* poetry with no regular pattern of rhyme, rhythm or line length.

free vote ▷ *noun* a parliamentary vote left to the individual choice of the voter, and not subject to party discipline or whip.

freeware ▷ *noun, computing* software which is in the public domain, allowing it to be copied legally and at no charge, but not resold commercially.

freeway ▷ *noun, N Amer* a toll-free highway. Compare TURNPIKE.

freewheel ▷ *noun* the mechanism on a bicycle by which the back wheel can run free from the gear mechanism with the pedals stationary. ▷ *verb, intr* **1** to travel, usually downhill, on a bicycle, in a car, etc without using mechanical power. **2** to act or drift about unhampered by responsibilities.

free will ▷ *noun* **1 a** the power of making choices without the constraint of fate or some other uncontrollable force, regarded as a human characteristic; **b** the philosophical doctrine that this human characteristic is not illusory. Compare DETERMINISM. **2** a person's independent choice.

freewoman see under FREEMAN

the Free World ▷ *noun* a name used by countries pursuing capitalist policies to refer to themselves, especially used during the Soviet era by non-communist countries to contrast themselves with the countries of the Soviet bloc.

freeze ▷ *verb* (***freezes***, ***froze***, ***frozen*** /ˈfroʊzən/, ***freezing***) **1** *tr & intr* to change (a liquid) into a solid by cooling it to below its freezing point, eg to change water into ice. **2** said of a liquid: to change into a solid when it is cooled to below its freezing point. **3** *tr & intr* (*often* **freeze together**) to stick or cause to stick together by frost. **4** *intr* said of the weather, temperature, etc: to be at or below the freezing-point of water □ ***It's freezing today.*** **5** *tr & intr, colloq* to be or make very cold. **6** *intr* to die of cold □ ***The sheep froze in the drifts.*** **7** *tr & intr* said of food: to preserve, or be suitable for preserving, by refrigeration at below freezing-point. **8** *tr & intr* to make or become motionless or unable to move, because of fear, etc. **9** to fix (prices, wages, etc) at a certain level. **10** to prevent (money, shares, assets, etc) from being used □ ***froze the bank account.*** **11** to stop (a video, a moving film, etc) at a certain frame. **12** *intr* said of a computer program, system, etc: to stop working, usually so as to require the machine that the program is running on to be rebooted. **13** to stop (a process) at some point in its development to assess progress made. **14** to anaesthetize (a part of the body). ▻ *noun* **1** a period of very cold weather with temperatures below freezing-point. See also FREEZE-UP. **2** a period of control of wages, prices, etc. ▻ *exclamation, chiefly US* a command to stop instantly or risk being shot. • **freezable** *adj*. ⓘ Anglo-Saxon *freosan*.

■ **freeze over** or **freeze something over** to become covered or cover with ice.

■ **freeze someone out** to exclude them from an activity, conversation, etc by persistent unfriendliness or unresponsiveness.

■ **freeze up** or **freeze something up** to become blocked up or stop operating because of frost or ice. See also FREEZE-UP.

freeze-dry ▻ *verb* to preserve (perishable material, especially food and medicines) by rapidly freezing it and then drying it under high-vacuum conditions.

freeze-frame ▻ *noun* **1** a single frame of film that is isolated and then repeated as a continuous series in order to give an effect like a still photograph. **2** a facility on a video recorder allowing the stopping of a videotape while being played to give a still view of a particular image. ▻ *verb, intr* to use the freeze-frame facility; to stop a videotape in order to view a still. ⓘ 1980s in this sense; 1960s in cinematography: from the phrase *freeze the frame*.

freezer ▻ *noun* a refrigerated cabinet or compartment in which to preserve food at a temperature below freezing-point. Compare DEEP-FREEZE, FRIDGE-FREEZER. ⓘ 19c.

freeze-thaw ▻ *noun, geol* the alternate freezing and thawing of water resulting in erosion of rock.

freeze-up ▻ *noun* the period when ice forms on lakes, rivers, etc at the onset of winter, often preventing travel by water. See also FREEZE *noun* 1, FREEZE UP under FREEZE.

freezing point ▻ *noun* (abbreviation **fp**) **1** the temperature at which the liquid form of a particular substance turns into a solid. **2** (*also* **freezing**) the freezing point of water (0°C at sea level).

F region see APPLETON LAYER

freight /freɪt/ ▻ *noun* **1** transport of goods by rail, road, sea or air. **2** the goods transported in this way. **3** the cost of such transport. ▻ *verb* (***freighted***, ***freighting***) **1** to transport (goods) by rail, road, sea or air. **2** to load (a vehicle, etc) with goods for transport. ⓘ 16c in this sense; 15c referring to the hire of a vessel for transporting goods: from Dutch *vrecht*.

freightage ▻ *noun* money paid for transporting freight.

freighter ▻ *noun* **1** a ship or aircraft that carries cargo rather than passengers. **2** someone who loads a ship with freight.

freightliner ▻ *noun* a train with specially designed rolling-stock for containers which can be lifted on to lorries or ships.

freight-train ▻ *noun* a train carrying goods or cargo rather than passengers.

frena see under FRENUM

French /frentʃ/ ▻ *adj* belonging or relating to France, a republic in NW Europe, its inhabitants or their language. ▻ *noun* **1** (**the French**) the people of France. **2** the official language of France. **3** one of the official languages of Belgium, Canada, Luxembourg, Switzerland, etc. **4** a language spoken in many former French colonies in Africa, the Caribbean and Oceania. • **pardon** or **excuse my French** *colloq* usually said after swearing: please excuse my bad language. ⓘ Anglo-Saxon *frencisc*, from FRANK.

Pronunciation of French in English

• In the dictionary we give an anglicized pronunciation of French for words which are in common use in English. The main difference between an Anglicized and a real French pronunciation is the exact quality of the vowels. In the examples below we give pronunciations as they are in the dictionary, ie usually Anglicized, but occasionally real French. The latter are marked *French*.

• With nasalized vowels, as in **vin blanc** and **aide-de-camp**, try to match the French pronunciation as closely as possible.

• **u** is pronounced /y/, rather like the common Scottish pronunciation of the vowel in words such as **you** and **book**.

• **ch** is pronounced /ʃ/, not /tʃ/, as in French loan words such as **brochure**, **champagne**, **chic** and **echelon**.

• Final **s, x** and **z** are usually not pronounced in French, as in **faux pas** /foʊ pɑː/. However they are pronounced before a following vowel, as in **faux ami** (/*French* fozami/ or **vous avez** /*French* vuzave/).

• **gn** is pronounced /nj /, as in the French pronunciation of **bourgignon** /*French* buʀginjɔ̃/.

• **ll** after an **i** may be either silent (or /*French* j/), as in **ratatouille**, or /l/, as in **mille**. Note that the name of the cream-and-pastry cake **millefeuille** is therefore pronounced /*French* milfœj/.

French bean ▻ *noun* a widely cultivated species of bean plant whose edible seeds together with the pods, can be cooked and eaten as a vegetable while unripe and still in the pod. Alternatively they can be left to ripen on the plant, and the mature seeds, known as haricot beans or HARICOTs, can be dried or processed to form baked beans, etc.

French bread, **French loaf** and **French stick** ▻ *noun* white bread in the form of long narrow loaves with tapered ends and a thick crisp crust. See also BAGUETTE.

French Canadian ▻ *noun* a native of the French-speaking part of Canada. ▻ *adj* (**French-Canadian**) relating to French Canadians or their language.

French chalk ▻ *noun* a form of the mineral talc used to mark cloth or remove grease marks. See also SOAPSTONE.

French cricket ▻ *noun* a game resembling cricket, in which the batsman's legs serve as the wicket, played especially by children.

French curve ▻ *noun* a thin template with the outlines of various curves cut on it, used for drawing curves.

French doors see FRENCH WINDOWS

French dressing ▻ *noun* a salad dressing made from oil, spices, herbs, and lemon juice or vinegar; vinaigrette.

French fries and **fries** ▻ *plural noun, chiefly N Amer & Brit informal* long thin strips of potato deep-fried in oil, usually longer and thinner than chips (see CHIP *noun* 3). Also (*Brit formal*) called **French fried potatoes**.

French horn ▻ *noun* an orchestral HORN.

Frenchify ▻ *verb* (***Frenchifies***, ***Frenchified***, ***Frenchifying***) *informal* to make something French or Frenchlike in appearance, character, etc. ⓘ 16c.

French kiss ▻ *noun* a kiss in which two people press their lips together and either or both insert their tongue into each other's mouth. ▻ *verb* (**French-kiss**) *tr & intr* to kiss in this way.

French knickers ▻ *plural noun* a type of wide-legged knickers, normally made from silk or a silky material.

French leave ▻ *noun* (*often* **take French leave**) leave taken without permission from work or duty.

French letter ▻ *noun, slang* a condom.

French Words and Phrases Used in English

à deux for two; (of a dinner or conversation) romantic, intimate
affaire liaison, intrigue; an incident arousing speculation and scandal
agent provocateur provocative agent; someone employed to lead others in illegal acts for which they will be punished
aide-de-camp assistant in the field; an officer in the armed forces who acts as assistant to a senior officer
aide-mémoire help-memory; something that helps one to remember something; a reminder
à la carte on the menu; with each dish individually priced and ordered separately
à la mode in fashion; fashionable
ambiance surroundings, atmosphere
amour-propre own love, self-love; self-esteem
ancien régime old regime; a superseded and outdated political system or ruling elite
à point into the right condition; to a nicety, precisely
appellation contrôlée certified name; used in the labelling of French wines, a guarantee of specified conditions of origin, strength, etc
après-ski after ski; evening social activities after a day's skiing
au contraire on the contrary
au fait to the point; highly skilled; knowledgeable or familiar with something
au naturel in the natural state; naked; cooked plainly, raw, or without dressing
au pair on an equal basis; a young person from abroad who lives with a family and helps with housework, looking after children, etc, in return for board and lodging
avant-garde front guard; using or supporting the most modern and advanced ideas in literature, art, music, etc
bain-marie bath of Mary; a pan of hot water in which a container of food can be cooked gently or kept warm
beau geste beautiful gesture; a generous or unselfish act
belle époque fine period; the time of gracious living for the well-to-do immediately preceding World War I
belles-lettres beautiful letters; works of literature valued for their style rather than their content
bête noire black beast; someone or something that bothers, annoys or frightens one more than anything else
blasé cloyed; bored through over-familiarity
bon mot good word; a short, clever remark
bon vivant good living (person); someone who lives well, particularly enjoying good food and wine
bon voyage good journey; have a safe and pleasant journey
bourgeois citizen; a member of the middle class; conventional, conservative
canard duck; an untrue report; a false rumour
carte blanche blank sheet of paper; freedom to do or organize things as one thinks best
cause célèbre famous case; a matter that attracts attention and causes much controversy
c'est la vie that's life; denotes fatalistic resignation
chacun à son goût each to his own taste; implies surprise at or acceptance of another's choice
chambré put into a room; (of red wine) at room temperature
chargé-d'affaires in charge of business; an ambassador's deputy or substitute
chef d'oeuvre chief work; an artist's or writer's masterpiece
cinéma-vérité truth cinema; realism in films usually sought by photographic scenes of real life
cliché; stereotype printing block; a phrase that has become stale and feeble through repetition
comme il faut as is necessary; correct; genteel
cordon bleu; blue ribbon; (of a cook or cookery) of the highest standard
coup de foudre flash of lightning; a sudden and astonishing happening; love at first sight
coup de grâce blow of mercy; a final decisive blow
coup d'état; blow of state; the sudden, usually violent, overthrow of a government
coupé cut; a four-seated, two-door car with a sloping rear
crème de la crème cream of the cream; the very best
cuisine minceur slenderness cooking; a style of cooking characterized by imaginative use of light, simple, low-fat ingredients
cul-de-sac bottom of the bag; a street closed at one end
décolleté with bared neck and shoulders; (of a dress) low-cut; wearing a low-cut dress
déjà vu already seen; the feeling or illusion of having experienced something before
de rigueur of strictness; compulsory; strictly required
derrière behind; the buttocks
déshabillé undressed; only partially or casually dressed
de trop of too much; not wanted, in the way
distingué distinguished; with a noble or dignified appearance; striking
double entendre double meaning; a remark with two possible meanings, one of which is sexually suggestive
doyen dean; the most senior and most respected member of a profession, etc
droit de seigneur the lord's right; originally the alleged right of a feudal superior to take the virginity of a vassal's bride; an excessive claim imposed on a subordinate
élan dash, rush, bound; impressive and energetic style
embarras de richesse embarrassment of wealth; a disconcerting amount of wealth or an abundance of any kind
embonpoint *en bon point* in fine form; well-fed, stout, plump; plumpness, etc

French loaf see FRENCH BREAD

Frenchman and **Frenchwoman** ▷ *noun* a man or woman of French nationality.

French polish ▷ *noun* a varnish for furniture, consisting of shellac dissolved in alcohol. ▷ *verb* (**French-polish**) to varnish (furniture, etc) with French polish. • **French polisher** *noun*.

French stick see FRENCH BREAD

French toast ▷ *noun* slices of bread dipped in beaten egg (sometimes mixed with milk), and fried.

French windows and (*N Amer*) **French doors** ▷ *plural noun* a pair of glass doors that open on to a garden, balcony, etc.

Frenchwoman see FRENCHMAN

Frenchy ▷ *noun* (***Frenchies***) a contemptuous name for a French person.

frenetic or (*rare*) **phrenetic** /frəˈnɛtɪk/ *adj* frantic, distracted, hectic or wildly energetic. • **frenetically** or (*rare*) **phrenetically** *adverb*. ◷ 14c: from French *frenetique*, from Greek *phrenitis* delirium, from *phren* heart or mind; compare FRANTIC, FRENZY.

frenum or **fraenum** /ˈfriːnəm/ (*plural* ***frena*** or ***fraena*** /-nə/) *noun* a ligament restraining the motion of a part of the body, such as the ligament under the tongue. ◷ 18c: Latin, meaning 'bridle'.

frenzy /ˈfrɛnzɪ/ ▷ *noun* (***frenzies***) **1** wild agitation or excitement. **2** a frantic burst of activity. **3** a state of violent mental disturbance. • **frenzied** *adj*. ◷ 14c: from French *frenesie*, from Latin, from Greek *phrenesis* madness; compare FRENETIC.

Freon or **freon** /ˈfriːɒn/ ▷ *noun, trademark* any of the family of chemicals containing fluorine, used as refrigerants, etc. ◷ 1930s.

frequency /ˈfriːkwənsɪ/ ▷ *noun* (***frequencies***) **1** the condition of happening often. **2** the rate at which a happening, phenomenon, etc, recurs. **3** *physics* (SI unit HERTZ; abbreviation **f**) a measure of the rate at which a complete cycle of wave motion is repeated per unit time. **4** *radio* the rate of sound waves per second at which a particular radio signal is sent out. See under VERY HIGH

French Words and Phrases Used in English contd.

éminence grise grey eminence; someone who has great influence without actually occupying an official position of power
enfant terrible terrible child; someone with a reputation for rude or embarrassing behaviour in public
ennui boredom or discontent caused by a lack of activity or excitement
en passant in passing; by the way, incidentally
en route on the way, on the road
entente understanding; a friendly agreement between nations
épater les bourgeois to shock the middle class; to disconcert the prim and proper, eg by an artistic production which defies convention
fait accompli accomplished fact; something done and unalterable; an established fact
faute de mieux for lack of anything better
faux ami false friend; a word in a foreign language that does not mean what it appears to
faux pas false step; a social blunder
femme fatale fatal woman; a woman whose irresistible charms fascinate and destroy others, especially men
film noir black film; style of film depicting the dark side of human nature, using stark lighting and often urban settings, etc
fin de siècle end of the century; of the end of the 19c in Western culture or of an era
force majeure superior force; an unforeseeable or uncontrollable course of events, excusing one from fulfilling a legal contract
grand mal great illness; a violently convulsive form of epilepsy
grand prix great prize; any of a series of international motor races held to decide the world championship; a competition of similar importance in other sports
haute couture high tailoring; the most expensive and fashionable clothes available; the leading fashion designers or their products
haut monde high world; high society, fashionable society
idée fixe a fixed idea; an obsession
laissez-faire let do; a policy of not interfering in what others are doing
lèse-majesté injured majesty; treason
ménage à trois household of three; a household comprising a husband and wife and the lover of one of them
mot juste exact word; the word which fits the context exactly
négociant merchant, trader
noblesse oblige nobility obliges; rank imposes obligations
nostalgie de la boue hankering for mud; a craving for a debased physical life without civilized refinements
nouveau riche new rich; someone who has recently acquired wealth but lacks the good taste or social graces to go with it
nouvelle cuisine new cooking; a simple style of cookery characterized by much use of fresh produce and elegant presentation
nouvelle vague new wave; a movement in French cinema aiming at imaginative quality films
outré gone to excess; beyond what is customary or proper; eccentric
pied-à-terre foot on the ground; a flat, small house, etc kept for temporary or occasional accommodation
plus ça change abbreviated form of **plus ça change, plus c'est la même chose** the more things change, the more they stay the same
pour encourager les autres to encourage the others (Voltaire *Candide*, on the execution of Admiral Byng); said of exemplary punishment
premier cru first vintage; wine of the highest quality in a system of classification
prêt-à-porter ready to wear; (of clothes) made in standard sizes rather than being made-to-measure
prix fixe fixed price; (of a meal) offered at a set price for a restricted choice
raison d'être reason for existence
recherché sought out; particularly choice; rare or exotic
reculer pour mieux sauter to move backwards in order to jump better; referring to a strategic withdrawal to wait for a better opportunity
répondez, s'il vous plaît reply, please; used in its abbreviated form, **RSVP**, on invitations
revenons à nos moutons let us return to our sheep; let us get back to our subject
risqué risky, hazardous; bordering on the rude or indecent
sang froid cold blood; self-possession; coolness under stress
savoir faire knowing what to do; expertise; tact
succès de scandale success of scandal; a book, film, etc that is successful because of its connection with a scandal rather than on merit
table d'hôte host's table; denoting a set meal at a fixed price
touché touched; used to acknowledge a hit made in fencing, or a point scored in an argument
tour de force turning movement; a feat of strength or skill
trompe l'oeil deceives the eye; a painting or decoration which gives a convincing illusion of reality
vin de pays wine of the country; a locally produced wine for everyday consumption
vis-à-vis face to face; in relation to; with regard to
volte-face turn-face; a sudden and complete change in opinion or in views expressed

FREQUENCY. **5** *statistics* the number of items, values, etc, that occur within a specified category, eg the number of students with a score of 90 to 100 in a class test may be five, so for that category the frequency is five. ⓒ 17c in sense 1; 16c in obsolete sense 'being crowded': from Latin *frequens* happening often.

frequency distribution ▷ *noun, statistics* a set of data that includes numerical values for the frequencies of different scores or results, ie the number of times that each particular score or result occurs.

frequency modulation ▷ *noun, radio* (abbreviation **FM**) a method of radio transmission in which the frequency of the carrier wave (the signal-carrying wave) increases or decreases instantaneously in response to changes in the amplitude of the signal being transmitted, giving a better signal-to-noise ratio than AMPLITUDE MODULATION.

frequent ▷ *adj* /'friːkwənt/ **1** recurring at short intervals. **2** habitual. ▷ *verb* /frɪ'kwɛnt/ (***frequented, frequenting***) to visit or attend (a place, an event, etc) often. • **frequenter** *noun*. • **frequently** *adverb*.

frequentative /frɪ'kwɛntətɪv/ *grammar* ▷ *adj* denoting the ASPECT (sense 6) of verbs used to express the frequent repetition or habitual occurrence of an action. ▷ *noun* a verb or affix expressing frequentative aspect, such as -LE in English *wrestle, wriggle*, etc.

fresco /'frɛskoʊ/ ▷ *noun* (***frescoes*** or ***frescos***) a picture painted on a wall, usually while the plaster is still damp. • **frescoed** *adj*. • **frescoer** or **frescoist** *noun*. ⓒ 17c: Italian, meaning 'cool' or 'fresh'.

fresh /frɛʃ/ ▷ *adj* **1** newly made, gathered, etc. **2** having just arrived from somewhere, just finished doing something or just had some experience, etc □ ***fresh from university.*** **3** other or another; different; clean □ ***a fresh sheet of paper.*** **4** new; additional □ ***fresh supplies.*** **5** original □ ***a fresh approach.*** **6** said of fruit or vegetables: not tinned, frozen, dried, salted or otherwise preserved. **7** not tired; bright and alert. **8** cool; refreshing □ ***a fresh breeze.*** **9** said of water: not salty. **10** said of air: cool and uncontaminated; invigorating. **11** said of the face or complexion: youthfully healthy; ruddy. **12** not worn or faded. **13** *colloq* said of behaviour: offensively informal;

cheeky. ▷ *adverb* in a fresh way ◻ ***Milk keeps fresh in the fridge.*** • **freshly** *adverb*. • **freshness** *noun*. Ⓒ Anglo-Saxon *fersc* not salt.

freshen /ˈfrɛʃən/ ▷ *verb* (***freshened***, ***freshening***) **1** to make something fresh or fresher. **2** *tr & intr* (*also* **freshen up** or **freshen oneself** or **someone up**) to get washed and tidy; to wash and tidy (oneself or someone). **3** *intr* said of a wind: to become stronger.

fresher or (*N Amer*) **freshman** *noun* a student in their first year at university or college.

freshet /ˈfrɛʃɪt/ ▷ *noun* **1** a stream of fresh water flowing into the sea. **2** the sudden overflow of a river. Ⓒ 16c: a diminutive of FRESH.

freshwater ▷ *adj* **1** referring to, consisting of or living in fresh as opposed to salt water ◻ ***freshwater lake*** ◻ ***freshwater fish.*** **2** *technical* denoting water that contains less than 0.2% dissolved salts, such as that found in most rivers and lakes.

Fresnal lens /freɪˈnɛl —/ ▷ *noun* an optical lens consisting of a number of concentric circles, which is thinner and flatter than a conventional lens. Ⓒ 19c: named after A J Fresnel (1788–1827), French physicist.

fret[1] /frɛt/ ▷ *verb* (***fretted***, ***fretting***) **1** *intr* (*also* **fret about** or **over something**) to worry, especially unnecessarily; to show or express anxiety. **2** to wear something away or consume something by rubbing or erosion. Ⓒ Anglo-Saxon *fretan* to gnaw, from *etan* to eat.

fret[2] /frɛt/ ▷ *noun* any of the narrow metal ridges across the neck of a guitar or similar musical instrument, onto which the strings are pressed in producing the various notes. Ⓒ 16c: probably from FRET[3].

fret[3] /frɛt/ ▷ *noun* a type of decoration for a cornice, border, etc, consisting of lines which (usually) meet at right angles, the pattern being repeated to form a continuous band. ▷ *verb* (***fretted***, ***fretting***) to decorate something with a fret, or carve with fretwork. Ⓒ 14c: from French *frete* interlaced design, probably influenced by Anglo-Saxon *fraetwa* ornament.

fret[4] /frɛt/ ▷ *noun*, *NE Eng dialect* a cold sea mist or fog off the North Sea. Also called HAAR.

fretful ▷ *adj* anxious and unhappy; tending to fret; peevish. • **fretfully** *adverb*. • **fretfulness** *noun*.

fretsaw ▷ *noun* a narrow-bladed saw for cutting designs in wood or metal. Compare COPING SAW. Ⓒ 19c.

fretwork ▷ *noun* decorative carved openwork in wood or metal. Ⓒ 16c.

Freudian /ˈfrɔɪdɪən/ ▷ *adj* relating to or suggestive of the ideas of the Austrian neurologist, Sigmund Freud (1856–1939), especially in regard to sexuality as a factor in human character and behaviour, or his method of psychoanalysis. • **Freudianism** *noun*. Ⓒ Early 20c.

Freudian slip ▷ *noun* an error or unintentional action, especially a slip of the tongue, taken as revealing an unexpressed or unconscious thought.

FRG ▷ *abbreviation* Federal Republic of Germany.

Fri. ▷ *abbreviation* Friday.

friable /ˈfraɪəbəl/ ▷ *adj* easily broken; easily reduced to powder. • **friability** *noun*. • **friableness** *noun*. Ⓒ 16c: from Latin *friare* to crumble.

friar /fraɪə(r)/ ▷ *noun* a member of any of various religious orders of the Roman Catholic Church who, especially formerly, worked as teachers of the Christian religion and lived by begging, often named according to the order they belong to, such as the FRANCISCANS, DOMINICANS, CARMELITES, AUGUSTINIANS, etc. Ⓒ 13c: from French *frere*, from Latin *frater* brother.

friarbird ▷ *noun* an Australian honey-eating bird with a featherless head.

friar's balsam ▷ *noun* a strong-smelling compound of benzoin, storax, tolu and aloes that is mixed with hot water and used as an inhalant.

friary /ˈfraɪərɪ/ ▷ *noun* (***friaries***) *historical* **1** a building inhabited by a community of friars. **2** the community itself.

fricadel see FRIKKADEL

fricandeau /frɪkənˈdoʊ, ˈfrɪkəndoʊ/ ▷ *noun* (*plural* ***fricandeaux*** /-doʊz/) a thick slice of veal, etc which is larded and then braised, roasted or fried. Ⓒ 18c: French.

fricassee /frɪkəˈsiː, ˈfrɪkəsiː/ ▷ *noun* (***fricassees***) a cooked dish, usually of pieces of meat or chicken served in a sauce. ▷ *verb* (***fricasseed***, ***fricasseeing***) to prepare meat as a fricassee. Ⓒ 16c: from French *fricasser* to cook chopped food in its own juice.

fricative /ˈfrɪkətɪv/ *phonetics* ▷ *adj* said of a sound: produced partly by friction, the breath being forced through a narrowed opening. ▷ *noun* a fricative consonant, eg *sh*, *f* and *th*. Ⓒ 19c: from Latin *fricare*, *fricatum* to rub.

friction /ˈfrɪkʃən/ ▷ *noun* **1** the rubbing of one thing against another. **2** *physics* the force that opposes the relative motion of two bodies or surfaces that are in contact with each other. **3** quarrelling; disagreement; conflict. • **frictional** *adj*. • **frictionless** *adj*. Ⓒ 16c: from Latin *frictio*, from *fricare* to rub.

Friday /ˈfraɪdɪ, ˈfraɪdeɪ/ ▷ *noun* (abbreviation **Fri.**) the sixth day of the week, counting from Sunday; the fifth day of the working week. See also GIRL FRIDAY, GOOD FRIDAY, MAN FRIDAY. Ⓒ Anglo-Saxon *Frigedæg*, the day of the Norse goddess Frig.

Friday the thirteenth ▷ *noun* any Friday which falls on the thirteenth day of a month, which is considered by some to be a day of bad luck.

fridge /frɪdʒ/ ▷ *noun*, *colloq* a refrigerator, especially a household refrigerator. Ⓒ 1920s.

fridge-freezer ▷ *noun* a fridge with a self-contained and often smaller freezer constructed as a single unit of furniture. Ⓒ 1970s.

fried *past tense, past participle of* FRY[1]

friend /frɛnd/ ▷ *noun* **1** someone whom one knows and likes, and to whom one shows loyalty and affection; a close or intimate acquaintance. **2** someone who gives support or help ◻ ***a friend of the poor.*** **3** an ally as distinct from an enemy or foe. **4** someone or something already encountered or mentioned ◻ ***our old friend the woodworm.*** **5** (**Friend**) a Quaker; a member of the RELIGIOUS SOCIETY OF FRIENDS. **6** a member of an organization which gives voluntary financial or other support to an institution, etc ◻ ***Friends of the National Gallery.*** **7** *euphemistic* a lover. • **friendless** *adj*. • **be** or **make friends with someone** to be or become their friend. • **have a friend at court** to have a friend in a position where their influence is likely to prove useful. Ⓒ Anglo-Saxon *freond*.

friendly ▷ *adj* (***friendlier***, ***friendliest***) **1** kind; behaving as a friend. **2** (**friendly with someone**) on close or affectionate terms with them. **3** relating to, or typical of, a friend. **4** being a colleague, helper, partner, etc rather than an enemy ◻ ***friendly nations.*** **5** *sport* said of a match, etc: played for enjoyment or practice and not as part of a formal competition. **6** *in compounds, forming adjectives* **a** denoting things that are made easy or convenient for those for whom they are intended ◻ ***user-friendly*** ◻ ***reader-friendly***; **b** indicating that something causes little harm to something, particularly something related to the environment ◻ ***eco-friendly*** ◻ ***planet-friendly*** Ⓒ 1970s: originating from the term USER-FRIENDLY which initially referred only to computer systems, but the metaphor was extended in the 1980s to other themes, particularly the environmental one. ▷ *noun* (***friendlies***) *sport* a friendly match. • **friendlily** *adverb*. • **friendliness** *noun*.

friendly fire ▻ *noun, military* accidental firing on one's own or one's allies' forces instead of the enemy.

friendly society ▻ *noun, Brit* an organization which gives support to members in sickness, old age, widowhood, etc, in return for regular financial contributions. Also called **benefit society**.

friendship ▻ *noun* **1** the having and keeping of friends. **2** a particular relationship that two friends have.

Friends of the Earth ▻ *noun* a charitable organization of conservationists and environmentalists.

frier see FRYER

fries¹ see under FRY¹

fries² see FRENCH FRIES

Friesian /'friːʒən/ ▻ *noun* **1** *agric* a breed of black-and-white dairy cattle, originating in the Netherlands, and now the most important dairy breed in the UK on account of its very high milk yields. **2** FRISIAN. ◷ 1920s: a variant of FRISIAN.

frieze¹ /friːz/ ▻ *noun* **1** a decorative strip running along a wall. **2** *archit* **a** a horizontal band between the cornice and capitals of a classical temple; **b** the sculpture which fills this space. ◷ 16c: from French *frise*, probably related to Italian *fregio*, from Latin *Phrygium* a piece of Phrygian work, Phrygia being famous for embroidered garments.

frieze² /friːz/ ▻ *noun* a rough heavy woollen cloth. ◷ 15c: from French *frise*.

frig /frɪg/ ▻ *verb* (***frigged, frigging***) *taboo, slang* **1** *intr* to masturbate. **2** *loosely* to have penetrative sex with someone. **3** (*often* **frig about** or **around**) to mess about. ▻ *noun* **1** masturbation. **2** an expression of emphasis, displeasure, etc, as a euphemism for *fuck* ▫ ***I don't give a frig about that.*** ◷ 15c as *friggen*: possibly from Latin *fricare* to rub.

frigate /'frɪgət/ ▻ *noun* **1** a naval escort vessel, smaller than a destroyer. **2** *historical* a small fast-moving sailing warship. ◷ 16c: from French *fregate*.

frigate bird ▻ *noun* a large bird, native to tropical seas, the male having an inflatable coloured pouch on the throat and very long wings.

frigging *taboo slang* ▻ *noun* masturbation. ▻ *adj* ▻ *adverb* expressing emphasis, displeasure, etc, as a euphemism for *fucking* ▫ ***That's a frigging lie.***

fright /fraɪt/ ▻ *noun* **1** sudden fear; a shock. **2** *colloq* a person or thing of ludicrous appearance. • **take fright** to become scared. ◷ Anglo-Saxon *fyrhto*.

frighten ▻ *verb* (***frightened, frightening***) to make someone afraid; to alarm them. • **frightened** *adj*. • **frightening** *adj*. • **frighteningly** *adverb*. ◷ 17c.

▪ **frighten someone away** or **off** to scare them away.

▪ **frighten someone into** or **out of something** to persuade or dissuade them by threats.

frightful ▻ *adj* **1** ghastly; frightening. **2** *colloq* bad; awful. **3** *colloq* great; extreme. • **frightfully** *adverb*. • **frightfulness** *noun*.

frigid /'frɪdʒɪd/ ▻ *adj* **1** cold and unfriendly; without spirit or feeling. **2** said usually of a woman: not sexually responsive. **3** *geog* intensely cold. • **frigidity** *noun*. • **frigidly** *adverb*. ◷ 17c: from Latin *frigidus* cold.

frigid zones ▻ *plural noun* the parts of the earth's surface within the polar circles.

frijol /friː'hoʊl/ ▻ *noun* (***frijoles*** /-'hoʊlz/) the kidney bean. ◷ 16c: Spanish *frijol*.

frikkadel or **fricadel** /'frɪkədɛl/ ▻ *noun, S Afr* a fried ball of minced meat. ◷ 19c: Afrikaans, from French.

frill ▻ *noun* **1** a gathered or pleated strip of cloth attached along one edge to a garment, etc as a trimming. **2** (*usually* **frills**) something extra serving no very useful purpose. • **without frills** straightforward; clear; with no superfluous additions.

frilled lizard ▻ *noun* a large Australian lizard with an erectile frill around its neck.

frillies ▻ *plural noun* women's underwear with lacey frills.

frilly ▻ *adj* (***frillier, frilliest***) with frills.

fringe /frɪndʒ/ ▻ *noun* **1** a border of loose threads on a carpet, tablecloth, garment, etc. **2** hair cut to hang down over the forehead but above the eyeline. **3** the outer area; the edge; the part farthest from the main area or centre. **4** *as adj* **a** bordering, or just outside, the recognized or orthodox form, group, etc ▫ ***fringe medicine***; **b** unofficial, not part of the main event ▫ ***fringe meeting*** ▫ ***fringe festival***; **c** less important or less popular ▫ ***fringe sports***. ▻ *verb* (***fringed, fringing***) **1** to decorate something with a fringe. **2** to form a fringe round something. ◷ 14c: from French *frenge*, from Latin *fimbriae* threads or fringe.

fringe benefits ▻ *plural noun* things that one gets from one's employer in addition to wages or salary, eg a cheap mortgage, a car, etc.

fringe-dweller ▻ *noun, Austral* someone, especially an Aborigine, who lives on the edge of a town or community, usually in poverty and squalor.

frippery /'frɪpərɪ/ ▻ *noun* (***fripperies***) **1** showy and unnecessary finery or adornment. **2** trifles; trivia. ◷ 16c: from French *freperie*, from *frepe* a rag.

Frisbee /'frɪzbɪ/ ▻ *noun* (***Frisbees***) *trademark* (*usually* **frisbee**) a light, concave, plastic, saucer-shaped object that spins when thrown, used for recreation, usually in a park, on the beach, etc, and also for competitive sport. ◷ 1950s: based on the name of the Frisbie bakery in Bridgeport, Connecticut, whose pie tins presumably inspired its invention; the name was altered by the Frisbee's inventor, Fred Morrison.

Frisian /'frɪzɪən/ or **Friesian** /'friːʒən/ ▻ *adj* belonging or relating to Friesland, a province in N Netherlands, its inhabitants or their language. ▻ *noun* **1** a citizen or inhabitant of, or person born in, Friesland. **2** the language of Friesland. See also FRIESIAN. ◷ 16c: from Latin *Frisii* a tribe of NW Germany.

frisk /frɪsk/ ▻ *verb* (***frisked, frisking***) **1** *intr* (*also* **frisk about**) to jump or run about happily and playfully. **2** *slang* to search someone for concealed weapons, drugs, etc. ▻ *noun* **1** a frolic; spell of prancing or jumping about. **2** *slang* an act of searching a person for weapons, etc. • **frisker** *noun*. ◷ 18c as *verb* 2; 16c as *verb* 1: originally from French *frisque* lively.

frisky ▻ *adj* (***friskier, friskiest***) lively; playful; high-spirited; frolicsome. • **friskily** *adverb*. • **friskiness** *noun*.

frisson /'friːsɒn/ ▻ *noun* a shiver of fear or excitement. ◷ 18c: French *frisson*.

frit ▻ *noun* the mixed materials for making glass, glazes for ceramics, etc. ▻ *verb* (***fritted, fritting***) to fuse (substances) partially in the process of making frit. ◷ 17c: from French *fritte*, from Italian *fritta*, from Latin *frigere* to roast.

fritillary /frɪ'tɪlərɪ, 'frɪtɪlərɪ/ ▻ *noun* (***fritallaries***) **1** *bot* a perennial plant, widespread in central Europe, with narrow greyish-green leaves and a drooping head bearing a single bell-shaped flower, chequered pink and dull purple. **2** *zool* any of many species of a colourful butterfly having yellowish-brown wings with black markings, and only four fully-developed legs, the front pair of legs being short and brush-like, especially in the male. ◷ 17c: from Latin *fritillus* dice-box.

fritter¹ /'frɪtə(r)/ ▻ *noun* a piece of meat, fruit, etc coated in batter and fried ▫ ***spam fritter*** ▫ ***banana fritter***. ◷ 15c: from French *friture*.

fritter² /'frɪtə(r)/ ▻ *verb* (***frittered, frittering***) (*chiefly* **fritter something away**) to waste (time, money, energy, etc) on unimportant things; to squander something □ *had frittered his inheritance away within two years.* • **fritterer** *noun*. ◎ 18c: from *fitter* fragment.

fritto misto /'frɪtoʊ 'mɪstoʊ/ ▻ *noun* (***fritto mistos***) a mixed dish of fried food. ◎ Early 20c: Italian, meaning 'mixed fry'.

Friulian see RHAETIAN

frivolity /frɪ'vɒlɪtɪ/ ▻ *noun* (***frivolities***) frivolous behaviour; being frivolous.

frivolous /'frɪvələs/ ▻ *adj* **1** silly; not sufficiently serious. **2** trifling or unimportant; not useful and sensible. • **frivolously** *adverb*. ◎ 16c: from Latin *frivolus* worthless or empty.

frizz ▻ *noun* said mainly of hair: a mass of tight curls. ▻ *verb* (***frizzed***, ***frizzing***) *tr & intr* (*also* **frizz something up**) to form or make something form a frizz. ◎ 17c: French *friser* to curl.

frizzante /frɪ'zæntɪ/ ▻ *adj* said of wine: sparkling. ◎ 20c: Italian, from *frizzare* to sparkle.

frizzle¹ /'frɪzəl/ ▻ *verb* (***frizzled***, ***frizzling***) *tr & intr* said of food: to fry till scorched and brittle. ◎ 19c: possibly imitating the sound.

frizzle² /'frɪzəl/ ▻ *verb* (***frizzled***, ***frizzling***) to frizz (hair). ▻ *noun* **1** a curl. **2** a frizz. ◎ 16c: appearing earlier than and therefore not derived from FRIZZ; possibly related to *frieze*, meaning 'to cover cotton with a nap'.

frizzy ▻ *adj* (***frizzier***, ***frizziest***) tightly curled.

fro see TO AND FRO at TO

frock /frɒk/ ▻ *noun* **1** a woman's or girl's dress. **2** a priest's or monk's long garment, with large open sleeves. **3** a loose smock. ◎ 16c in sense 1; 14c in sense 2: from French *froc* monk's garment.

frock-coat ▻ *noun, historical* a man's double-breasted coat, close-fitting round the waist and extending to the knees both at the front and the back. ◎ 19c.

Frog /frɒg/ and **Froggy** (***Frogs*** or ***Froggies***) *noun, Brit, offensive slang* a French person. ◎ 19c: from the reputation of the French of eating frogs' legs.

frog¹ /frɒg/ ▻ *noun* **1** a tailless amphibian, found worldwide except in Arctic and Antarctic regions, with a moist smooth skin, protruding eyes, powerful hind legs for swimming and leaping, and webbed feet. **2** the block by which hair is attached to the heel of eg a violin bow. • **froggy** *adj*. • **a frog in one's throat** an accumulation of phlegm on the vocal cords that temporarily interferes with one's speech; hoarseness. ◎ Anglo-Saxon *frogga*.

frog² /frɒg/ ▻ *noun* **1** an attachment to a belt for carrying a weapon. **2** a decorative looped fastener on a garment. • **frogging** *noun* a set of such fasteners, especially on a military uniform. ◎ 18c.

frog³ /frɒg/ ▻ *noun* a triangular horny pad in a horse's hoof. ◎ 17c.

frog-hopper ▻ *noun* a small hopping insect that feeds by sucking the sap of plants, whose larvae surround themselves with CUCKOO SPIT.

frogman ▻ *noun* an underwater swimmer wearing a protective rubber suit and using breathing equipment.

frogmarch ▻ *verb* **1** to force someone forward, holding them firmly by the arms □ *The lager lout was frogmarched out of the pub.* **2** to carry someone horizontally in a face-downward position between four people, each holding one limb. ▻ *noun* the act or process of frogmarching. ◎ 19c.

frogspawn ▻ *noun* a mass of frogs' eggs encased in protective nutrient jelly. ◎ 17c: from *frogs'* SPAWN (*noun* 1a).

frog-spit see CUCKOO SPIT

frolic /'frɒlɪk/ ▻ *verb* (***frolicked***, ***frolicking***) *intr* to frisk or run about playfully; to gambol about. ▻ *noun* **1** a spell of happy playing or frisking; a gambol. **2** something silly done as a joke; a prank. ◎ 16c: from Dutch *vrolijk* merry.

frolicsome ▻ *adj* playful; full of fun.

from /frɒm, frəm/ ▻ *prep, indicating* **1** a starting-point in place or time □ *from London to Glasgow* □ *crippled from birth.* **2** a lower limit □ *tickets from £12 upwards.* **3** repeated progression □ *trail from shop to shop.* **4** movement out of □ *took a letter from the drawer.* **5** distance away □ *16 miles from Dover.* **6** a viewpoint □ *can see the house from here.* **7** separation; removal □ *took it away from her.* **8** point of attachment □ *hanging from a nail.* **9** exclusion □ *omitted from the sample.* **10** source or origin □ *made from an old curtain.* **11** change of condition □ *translate from French into English* □ *From being an intimate lover, he turned very hostile.* **12** cause □ *ill from overwork.* **13** deduction as a result of observation □ *see from her face she's angry.* **14** distinction □ *can't tell one twin from the other.* **15** prevention, protection, exemption, immunity, release, escape, etc □ *safe from harm* □ *excused from attending* □ *exempted from tax* □ *released from prison.* ◎ Anglo-Saxon *fram*.

fromage frais /'frɒmɑːʒ 'freɪ/ ▻ *noun* a creamy low-fat cheese originating in France with the consistency of whipped cream, often used for desserts, similar to QUARK². ◎ 1980s: French, meaning 'fresh cheese'.

frond /frɒnd/ ▻ *noun, bot* a large compound leaf, especially of a fern or palm. ◎ 18c: from Latin *frons*.

front /frʌnt/ ▻ *noun* **1** the side or part of anything that is furthest forward or nearest to the viewer; the most important side or part, eg the side of a building where the main door is. **2** any side of a large or historic building. **3** the part of a vehicle, etc that faces or is closest to, the direction in which it moves. **4** *theat* the auditorium of a theatre, etc. See also FRONT OF HOUSE. **5** the cover or first pages of a book. **6** a road or promenade in a town that runs beside the sea, or large lake, etc; sea front. **7** in war, particularly when fought on the ground: the area where the soldiers are nearest to the enemy □ *eastern front.* See also FRONT LINE. **8** a matter of concern or interest □ *no progress on the job front.* **9** *meteorol* the boundary between two air masses that have different temperatures, eg a WARM FRONT is the leading edge of a mass of warm air. Also compare COLD FRONT. **10** an outward appearance. **11** (*usually* **Front**) a name given to some political movements, particularly when a number of organizations come together as a unified force against opponents. **12** *slang* an organization or job used to hide illegal or secret activity □ *The corner shop was just a front for drug dealing.* **13** *archaic* the forehead; the face. ▻ *verb* (***fronted***, ***fronting***) **1** *tr & intr* said of a building: to have its front facing or beside something specified □ *The house fronts on to the main road.* **2** to be the leader or representative of (a group, etc). **3** to be the presenter of (a radio or television programme). **4** to cover the front of (a building, etc) □ *The house was fronted with grey stone.* ▻ *adj* **1** relating to, or situated at or in the front. **2** *phonetics* said of a vowel: articulated with the front of the tongue in a forward position. • **frontless** *adj*. • **in front 1** on the forward-facing side. **2** ahead. • **in front of someone** or **something 1** at or to a position in advance of them. **2** to a place towards which a vehicle, etc is moving □ *ran in front of a car.* **3** ahead of them □ *pushed in front of her.* **4** facing or confronting them □ *stood up in front of an audience.* **5** in their presence □ *dare not say so in front of my mother.* • **out front** *colloq* in the audience, from the performer's standpoint. • **up front** *colloq* said of money: paid before work is done or goods received, etc □ *Can you pay that up front?* ◎ 13c: French, from Latin *frons, frontis* forehead.

■ **front for something** to provide a cover or excuse for an illegal activity, etc.

frontage /'frʌntɪdʒ/ ▻ *noun* the front of a building, especially in relation to the street, etc along which it extends. • **frontager** *noun, law* someone who owns or occupies property along a road, river, shore, etc.

frontal /ˈfrʌntəl/ ▷ *adj* **1** relating to the front. **2** aimed at the front; direct □ ***a frontal assault.*** **3** *anatomy* relating to the forehead. **4** *meteorol* relating to a FRONT *noun* 9 □ ***frontal system.*** ▷ *noun* **1** the façade of a building. **2** something worn on the forehead or face. **3** an embroidered hanging of silk, satin, etc, for the front of an altar, now usually covering only the top. Ⓒ 17c.

front bench ▷ *noun* **1** the bench on either side of the House of Commons closest to the centre of the House, occupied on one side by Government ministers and on the other by leading members of the Opposition. **2** the corresponding benches in the House of Lords, occupied by ex-ministers and former leading members of the Opposition. **3** the leadership of the government or opposition in various legislative assemblies, eg in Australia. Also *as adj* □ ***front-bench spokesman.*** • **frontbencher** *noun* someone who sits on one of the front benches, ie a minister or leading member of the Opposition. Compare BACKBENCH, CROSS BENCH. Ⓒ 19c.

fronted /ˈfrʌntəd/ ▷ *adj* **1** formed with a front. **2** *phonetics* changed into or towards a FRONT (*adj* 2) sound.

front end ▷ *noun* **1** the part of a vehicle that is furthest forward □ ***front end of a car.*** **2** *computing* **a** any of the terminals of a computing network where information is inputted or processed, which are backed-up by larger, more powerful computers □ ***the front end of the information network***; **b** *as adj* □ ***front-end processor*** □ ***front-end computer.*** **3** *as adj*, *finance* **a** referring to an initial charge to cover costs and commission, which is made to someone taking on a long-term savings or investment plan; **b** referring to any similar deductions during the early stages of a financial transaction or accounting period □ ***front-end load*** □ ***front-end fee.***

frontier /ˈfrʌntɪə(r), frʌnˈtɪə(r)/ ▷ *noun* **1 a** the part of a country bordering onto another country; **b** a line, barrier, etc marking the boundary between two countries. **2** (**frontiers**) limits □ ***the frontiers of knowledge.*** **3** *N Amer history* the furthest edge of civilization, habitation or cultivation, beyond which the country is wild and thought to be deserted. Ⓒ 15c: French, from *front* FRONT.

frontiersman and **frontierswoman** ▷ *noun* someone who lives on the frontier of a country, particularly on the outlying edges of a settled society. Ⓒ 18c.

frontispiece /ˈfrʌntɪspiːs/ ▷ *noun* **1** a picture at the beginning of a book, facing the title page. **2** *archit* the decorated pediment over a door, gate, etc. **3** *archit* the main front or façade of a building. Ⓒ 16c: from Latin *frons, frontis* front + *specere* to see, influenced by PIECE.

frontlet /ˈfrʌntlɪt/ ▷ *noun* **1** *Judaism* a PHYLACTERY attached to the forehead. **2** something worn on the forehead. Ⓒ 16c: from French *frontelet* a small FRONTAL.

front line ▷ *noun* **1** in a war, particularly when fought on the ground: **a** the area of a FRONT (*noun* 7) where soldiers are physically closest to the enemy; **b** *as adj* belonging or relating to the front line □ ***front-line soldiers.*** **2** that area in any concern where the important pioneering work is going on. **3** *as adj* (**front-line**) relating to a state bordering on another state in which there is an armed conflict, and often inevitably involved in that conflict.

front man ▷ *noun* **1** the nominal leader or representative of an organization. **2** the presenter of a radio or television programme.

front of house ▷ *noun* in a theatre: the collective activities carried out in direct contact with the public, such as box-office activity, programme selling, ushering, etc. Also *as adj* □ ***front-of-house staff.*** Ⓒ 19c: originally *front of the house*.

frontogenesis /frʌntoʊˈdʒɛnɪsɪs/ ▷ *noun*, *meteorol* the formation or intensification of a front. Ⓒ 1930s: from FRONT + -GENESIS.

frontolysis /frʌnˈtɒlɪsɪs/ ▷ *noun*, *meteorol* the weakening or disappearance of a front. Ⓒ 1930s: from FRONT + -LYSIS.

fronton /ˈfrʌntən/ ▷ *noun*, *archit* a pediment crowning a window or other small opening.

front-page ▷ *adj* suitable or important enough for publication on the first or front page of a newspaper □ ***front-page news.***

front projection ▷ *noun*, *cinema* the projection of an image on to an opaque screen to be viewed from the same side as the projector; the normal practice for cinema and audio-visual presentation.

front-runner ▷ *noun* **1** the person most likely or most favoured to win a competition, election, etc. **2** in a race: someone who runs best when they are in the lead, or someone who sets the pace for the rest of the runners.

front-running ▷ *noun*, *stock exchange* a practice whereby traders buy or sell stocks for themselves before placing big orders for customers that may affect the share price, and which is a type of INSIDER DEALING. Also *as adj* □ ***front-running ring.***

frontward and **frontwards** ▷ *adverb* towards the front.

front-wheel drive ▷ *noun* a system in which the driving power is transmitted to the front wheels of a vehicle, as opposed to the rear wheels. Compare REAR-WHEEL DRIVE, FOUR-BY-FOUR.

frost /frɒst/ ▷ *noun* **1** a white feathery or powdery deposit of ice crystals formed when water vapour comes into contact with a surface whose temperature is below the freezing point of water. **2** an air temperature below freezing-point □ ***12 degrees of frost.*** ▷ *verb* (***frosted, frosting***) **1** *tr & intr* (*also* **frost up** or **over**) to cover or become covered with frost. **2** to damage (plants) with frost. • **frostless** *adj*. • **frostlike** *adj*. Ⓒ Anglo-Saxon.

frostbite ▷ *noun* damage to the body tissues, usually of the extremities, especially fingers or toes, caused by exposure to very low temperatures, with the affected parts becoming pale and numb as a result of lack of oxygen due to narrowing of the blood vessels.

frostbitten ▷ *adj* suffering from frostbite; affected by frost.

frosted ▷ *adj* **1** covered by frost. **2** damaged by frost. **3** said of glass: patterned or roughened as though with frost, so as to be difficult to see through.

frosting ▷ *noun* **1** *N Amer* cake icing. **2** a rough or matt finish on glass, silver, etc.

frostwork ▷ *noun* **1** tracery made by frost, eg on windows. **2** on glass, silver, etc: work resembling frost tracery, etc.

frosty ▷ *adj* (***frostier, frostiest***) **1** covered with frost. **2** cold enough for frost to form. **3** said of a person's behaviour or attitude: cold; unfriendly; unwelcoming. • **frostily** *adverb*. • **frostiness** *noun*.

froth /frɒθ/ ▷ *noun* **1** a mass of tiny bubbles forming eg on the surface of a liquid, or round the mouth in certain diseases. **2** writing, talk, etc that has no serious content or purpose. **3** showy glamour; something frivolous or trivial. ▷ *verb* (***frothed, frothing***) *tr & intr* to produce or make something produce froth. Ⓒ 14c: from Norse *frotha*.

froth-fly and **froth-hopper** ▷ *noun* a FROG-HOPPER.

frothy ▷ *adj* (***frothier, frothiest***) **1** full of or like froth. **2** insubstantial. • **frothily** *adverb*. • **frothiness** *noun*. • **frothless** *adj*.

frottage /frɒˈtɑːʒ/ ▷ *noun* **1** *art* a technique, analogous to brass-rubbing, in which paper is placed over a textured surface such as wood or fabric and rubbed with a soft pencil or crayon to produce an impression. **2** a type of sexual activity in which sexual pleasure and often orgasm is obtained by rubbing one's clothed body against someone or something. ⓒ 1930s in both senses: French, meaning 'rubbing' or 'friction'.

frown /fraʊn/ ▷ *verb* (***frowned, frowning***) *intr* to wrinkle one's forehead and draw one's eyebrows together in worry, disapproval, deep thought, etc. ▷ *noun* **1** the act of frowning. **2** a disapproving expression or glance. • **frowner** *noun*. • **frowningly** *adverb*. ⓒ 14c: from French *froignier*.

▪ **frown on** or **at something** to disapprove of it.

frowst /fraʊst/ ▷ *noun* hot stuffy fustiness. • **frowsty** *adj* (***frowstier, frowstiest***) stuffy; stale-smelling. • **frowst** *noun*. • **frowstiness** *noun*. ⓒ 19c.

frowsy or **frowzy** /'fraʊzɪ/ ▷ *adj* (***frowsier, frowsiest***) **1** said of someone's appearance: untidy, dishevelled or slovenly. **2** said of an atmosphere: stuffy; stale-smelling. • **frowsiness** *noun*. ⓒ 17c.

froze *past tense of* FREEZE

frozen¹ /'froʊzən/ ▷ *adj* **1** preserved by keeping at a temperature below freezing point. **2** very cold. **3** stiff and unfriendly.

frozen² *past participle of* FREEZE

frozen shoulder ▷ *noun* a shoulder joint which has become stiff owing to injury or a period of enforced immobilization.

FRS ▷ *abbreviation* Fellow of the Royal Society.

FRSE ▷ *abbreviation* Fellow of the Royal Society of Edinburgh.

fructiferous /frʌk'tɪfərəs/ ▷ *adj* bearing fruit. ⓒ 17c.

fructification /frʌktɪfɪ'keɪʃən/ ▷ *noun, bot* **1** the fruit of a plant or the spore-producing structure of a fungus. **2** the process of forming a fruit or spore-producing structure. ⓒ 17c: from Latin *fructus* fruit + *facere* to make.

fructivorous /frʌk'tɪvərəs/ ▷ *adj* eating or feeding on fruit. ⓒ 17c: from Latin *fructus* fruit + *-vorus* eating.

fructose /'frʌktoʊs, 'frʊk-/ ▷ *noun, biochem* a six-carbon sugar found in fruit, honey and combined with GLUCOSE in SUCROSE, whose derivatives, in the form of fructose phosphates, play an important role in the chemical reactions that take place in living cells. Also called **fruit sugar**. ⓒ 19c: from Latin *fructus* fruit.

frugal /'fruːgəl/ ▷ *adj* **1** thrifty; economical; not generous; careful, particularly in financial matters. **2** not large; costing little ▫ ***a frugal meal.*** • **frugality** /-'galɪtɪ/ *noun*. • **frugally** *adverb*. ⓒ 16c: from Latin *frugalis* economical or useful, from *frux, frugis* profit or fruit.

fruit /fruːt/ ▷ *noun* **1** the fully ripened ovary of a flowering plant, containing one or more seeds that have developed from fertilized OVULEs, and sometimes including associated structures such as the RECEPTACLE. **2** an edible part of a plant that is generally sweet and juicy, especially the ovary containing one or more seeds, but sometimes extended to include other parts, eg the leaf stalk in rhubarb. See also BERRY, SOFT FRUIT. **3** plant products generally ▫ ***the fruits of the land.*** **4** (*also* **fruits**) whatever is gained as a result of hard work, etc ▫ ***the fruit of his labour.*** **5** *colloq* a gay man. **6** *old use, colloq* a person ▫ ***old fruit.*** **7** *rare* offspring; young ▫ ***the fruit of her womb.*** ▷ *verb* (***fruited, fruiting***) *intr* to produce fruit. • **bear fruit** **1** to produce fruit. **2** to produce good results. • **in fruit** said of a tree: bearing fruit. ⓒ 12c: from French *fruict*, from Latin *fructus* fruit, enjoyment.

fruit bat ▷ *noun* a large fructivorous bat of the Old World.

fruit cage ▷ *noun* an enclosure with mesh sides and roof to protect growing fruit and vegetables from birds, etc.

fruitcake ▷ *noun* **1** a cake containing dried fruit, nuts, etc. **2** *colloq* a slightly mad person.

fruiter ▷ *noun* **1** a tree, etc that bears fruit ▫ ***a good fruiter.*** **2** a person whose job is to grow fruit; a fruit-grower. ⓒ 15c.

fruiterer /'fruːtərə(r)/ ▷ *noun* a person whose job is to sell fruit. ⓒ 15c: FRUITER + -ER.

fruit fly ▷ *noun* any of various tiny brown or yellowish flies with red eyes, mainly found in tropical regions, which feed on sap and fermenting fruit, and can be a minor pest of orchards and stored fruit.

fruitful ▷ *adj* producing good or useful results; productive; worthwhile. • **fruitfully** *adverb*. • **fruitfulness** *noun*.

fruition /frʊ'ɪʃən/ ▷ *noun* **1** the achievement of something that has been aimed at and worked for ▫ ***The project finally came to fruition.*** **2** the bearing of fruit. ⓒ 15c: French, from Latin *frui* to enjoy.

fruitless ▷ *adj* **1** useless; unsuccessful; done in vain. **2** not producing fruit. • **fruitlessly** *adverb*. • **fruitlessness** *noun*.

fruit machine ▷ *noun* a coin-operated gambling-machine with symbols originally and still usually in the form of fruits, that may be made to appear in winning combinations, found in amusement arcades, pubs, etc. ⓒ Early 20c.

fruit salad ▷ *noun* a dish of mixed chopped fruits, usually eaten as a dessert, and often with fresh cream.

fruit sugar ▷ *noun* FRUCTOSE.

fruit tree ▷ *noun* any tree bearing edible fruit.

fruity ▷ *adj* (***fruitier, fruitiest***) **1** full of fruit; having the taste or appearance of fruit. **2** said of a voice: deep and rich in tone. **3** *colloq* said of a story, etc: containing humorous and slightly risqué references to sexual matters. **4** *colloq* referring to a gay man. **5** *colloq* sexually aroused. • **fruitily** *adverb*. • **fruitiness** *noun*.

frump ▷ *noun, derog, colloq* a woman who dresses in a dowdy, old-fashioned way. ⓒ Early 19c in this sense; 16c in obsolete sense 'a sneer' or 'jeer'.

frumpish and **frumpy** ▷ *adj* (***frumpier, frumpiest***) dressed in a dowdy unattractive way.

frustrate /frʌ'streɪt/ ▷ *verb* (***frustrated, frustrating***) **1** to prevent someone from doing or getting something; to thwart or foil (a plan, attempt, etc). **2** to make (someone) feel disappointed, useless, lacking a purpose in life, etc. • **frustrating** *adj*. • **frustratingly** *adverb*. ⓒ 15c: from Latin *frustrari, frustratus* to deceive or disappoint.

frustrated ▷ *adj* **1** a feeling of agitation and helplessness at not being able to do something. **2** disappointed; unhappy; dissatisfied. **3** unfulfilled in one's ambitions for oneself. **4** not sexually satisfied.

frustration ▷ *noun* **1** being frustrated. **2** *law* a term used in contract law whereby a contract ends, through no fault of any party to the contract, because it has become impossible to perform or illegal.

frustum /'frʌstəm/ ▷ *noun* (***frustums*** or ***frusta*** /-tə/) **1** a slice of a solid body. **2** the part of a cone or pyramid between the base and a parallel plane, or between two planes. ⓒ 17c: Latin, meaning 'a bit'.

fry¹ /fraɪ/ ▷ *verb* (***fries, fried, frying***) *tr & intr* to cook (food) in hot oil or fat, either in a frying-pan, or by deep-frying (see DEEP-FRY). ▷ *noun* (***fries***) **1** a dish of anything fried, eg the offal of a pig or lamb. **2** a FRY-UP. **3** (**fries**) FRENCH FRIES. ⓒ 14c: from French *frire*, from Latin *frigere* to roast or fry.

fry² /fraɪ/ ▷ *plural noun* **1** young or newly spawned fish. **2** salmon in their second year. ⓒ 14c: from French *frai* seed, offspring.

fryer or **frier** ▷ *noun* **1** a frying pan. **2** a chicken or fish suitable for frying. **3** someone who fries something (especially fish).

frying-pan ▷ *noun* a shallow long-handled pan for frying food in. ● **out of the frying-pan into the fire** from a bad situation into a worse one.

fry-up ▷ *noun* (***fry-ups***) **1** a mixture of fried foods. **2** the cooking of these. Sometimes shortened to **fry**.

FSB ▷ *abbreviation*: *Federalnaya sluzhba bezopasnosti* (Russian), Federal Security Service, responsible for Russian state security, created in 1995 as a successor agency of the FSK and KGB.

FSH ▷ *abbreviation* follicle-stimulating hormone.

FSK ▷ *abbreviation*: *Federalnaya sluzhba kontrapazvedki* (Russian), Federal Counter-Intelligence Service, a successor agency of the KGB from 1991 to 1995 when it was renamed FSB.

f-stop see STOP *noun* 8

FT ▷ *abbreviation*: *the Financial Times*, a British daily newspaper.

ft ▷ *abbreviation* referring to the measure of length: foot or feet.

fth. or **fthm** ▷ *abbreviation* fathom.

FT Index ▷ *abbreviation* **1** Financial Times Industrial Ordinary Share Index, an index produced daily to show the general trend in share prices on the London stock exchange. **2** Financial Times Stock Exchange 100-Share Index, which records the share prices of the top 100 UK public companies, giving an indication of movements in share prices. Also called **FT-SE** /'fʊtsɪ/ or **FT-SE Index**. **3** a term referring to other, similar indices, such as **FT-SE 250 Index**, **FT-SE All Share Index**. See also FOOTSIE.

FTP ▷ *abbreviation* file-transfer protocol, a means of transferring data from one computer to another over the INTERNET.

fuchsia /'fjuːʃə/ ▷ *noun* (***fuchsias***) a shrub with purple, red or white hanging flowers. Ⓒ 18c: named after Leonard Fuchs (1501–66), German botanist.

fuchsine /'fuːksiːn/ ▷ *noun* dark-green crystals which, when dissolved in water, form a purplish-red solution, used as a disinfectant, a clothes dye, etc. Also called **magenta**. Ⓒ 19c: named after the flower FUCHSIA, because of its colour.

fuck *taboo slang* (*sometimes* **f**k**, **f*****, *etc*) ▷ *verb* (***fucked***, ***fucking***) *tr & intr* to have penetrative sex (with someone). ▷ *noun* **1** an act of sexual intercourse. **2** a sexual partner. ▷ *exclamation* an expression of anger, frustration, etc □ *Fuck him!* ● **fuck all** nothing □ *He knows fuck all about sailing.* ● **not give a fuck** not to care at all. ● **the fuck** used for emphasis □ *What the fuck are you doing?* See also THE F-WORD. Ⓒ 16c: of unknown origin.

■ **fuck about** or **around** to behave foolishly or waste time.

■ **fuck someone about** or **around** to annoy them or waste their time, especially by behaving foolishly or inconsiderately.

■ **fuck off** *offensive* to go away. Also *as exclamation* used in frustration or anger: demanding someone leaves you alone.

■ **fuck up** or **fuck something up** to ruin or spoil it. See also FUCK-UP.

fucked ▷ *adj* **1** confused; in trouble. **2** exhausted.

fucker ▷ *noun, taboo slang* **1** someone or something that is difficult or awkward □ *What a fucker!* **2** a term of abuse □ *You stingy fucker!* **3** a person; fellow □ *a fashionable fucker.* **4** someone who fucks.

fuckhead and **fuckwit** ▷ *noun, taboo slang* a fool; an idiot.

fucking ▷ *adj, taboo slang* **1** expressing annoyance, frustration, etc; damned; bloody □ *a fucking bore.* **2** expressing emphasis □ *a fucking great film.* Also *as infix* □ *im-fucking-possible.*

fuck-up ▷ *noun, taboo slang* a bungled or spoilt situation; a mess. See also FUCK UP at FUCK.

fuddle /'fʌdəl/ ▷ *verb* (***fuddled***, ***fuddling***) to muddle the wits of; to confuse or stupefy. ▷ *noun* a state of confusion or intoxication. Ⓒ 16c.

fuddy-duddy /'fʌdɪdʌdɪ/ *colloq* ▷ *adj* quaintly old-fashioned or prim. ▷ *noun* (***fuddy-duddies***) a fuddy-duddy person; an old fogey. Ⓒ Early 20c.

fudge¹ ▷ *noun* a soft toffee made from butter, sugar and milk. ▷ *exclamation, colloq* **1** expressing annoyance or frustration: damn. **2** rubbish; nonsense. Ⓒ 19c as *noun*; 18c as *exclamation* sense 2: probably related partly to FUDGE².

fudge² ▷ *verb* (***fudged***, ***fudging***) *colloq* **1** to invent or concoct (an excuse, etc). **2** to distort or deliberately obscure (figures, an argument, etc), to cover up problems, mistakes, etc. **3** to dodge or evade something. **4** *intr* to avoid stating a clear opinion. ▷ *noun* the action of obscuring, distorting an issue, etc. Ⓒ 17c: perhaps from earlier *fadge* to succeed or turn out.

fuel /fjʊəl/ ▷ *noun* **1** any material that releases energy when it is burned, which can be used as a source of heat or power. **2** fissile material that is used to release energy by nuclear fission in a nuclear reactor. **3** food, as a source of energy and a means of maintaining bodily processes. **4** something that feeds or inflames passions, etc. ▷ *verb* (***fuelled***, ***fuelling***) **1** to fill or feed with fuel. **2** *intr* to take on or get fuel. **3** to inflame (anger or other passions). ● **fueller** *noun*. ● **add fuel to the fire** to make an angry person, situation, etc angrier; to make a heated discussion more heated, etc. Ⓒ 14c: from French *feuaile*, from Latin *focus* hearth.

fuel cell ▷ *noun, chem* a device in which chemical energy released by the oxidation of a liquid or gaseous fuel, eg methanol, is converted directly into electrical energy.

fuel injection ▷ *noun* in an internal-combustion engine: a system that injects pure fuel under pressure directly into the cylinder, the timing and amount of fuel injected being under electronic control, eliminating the need for a carburettor and producing improved running performance.

fug ▷ *noun* a stale-smelling stuffy atmosphere, often very hot, close and airless. ● **fuggy** (***fuggier***, ***fuggiest***) *adj*. ● **fugginess** *noun*.

fugal and **fugally** see under FUGUE

fugato /fjʊ'gɑːtoʊ/ ▷ *adj, adverb* in the manner of a FUGUE, without strictly being a fugue.

-fuge ▷ *combining form, forming adjectives and nouns, denoting* **1** dispelling or expelling □ *centrifuge.* **2** *bot* disliking or hating □ *calcifuge.* Ⓒ From Latin *fugare* to put to flight and *fugere* to flee.

fugitive /'fjuːdʒɪtɪv/ ▷ *noun* a person who is fleeing someone or something, usual some kind of authority, such as the law, an army, a political system, etc. ▷ *adj* **1** fleeing away. **2** lasting only briefly; fleeting □ *a fugitive smile.* Ⓒ 17c: French, from Latin *fugitivus*.

fugue /fjuːg/ ▷ *noun, music* a style of composition in which a theme is introduced in one part and developed as successive parts take it up. ● **fugal** *adj*. ● **fugally** *adverb*. Ⓒ 16c: from French *fugue*, from Italian *fuga* flight.

Führer /'fjʊərə(r)/ ▷ *noun* **1** the title taken by Hitler as dictator of Nazi Germany. **2** (**führer**) any autocratic dictator or boss. Ⓒ 1930s: German, meaning 'leader'.

-ful ▷ *suffix* **1** *forming nouns* denoting an amount held by a container, or something thought of as one □ *an armful of books* □ *two mugfuls of coffee.* **2** *forming adjectives* **a** full of something specified □ *meaningful* □ *eventful*; **b** characterized by something specified □ *merciful* □ *graceful*; **c** having the qualities of something specified □ *youthful*; **d** in accordance with something specified □

lawful; **e** showing an inclination to do something □ *forgetful*. ⓒ Anglo-Saxon, as in *handful*.

-ful

● Nouns ending in **-ful** which denote an amount form plurals ending in **-fuls**: □ *armfuls, cupfuls, fistfuls, forkfuls, handfuls, lungfuls, mouthfuls, sackfuls, shovelfuls, spoonfuls, trunkfuls*, etc. Note that *cupfuls, handfuls*, etc, denote an amount or contents, whereas *cups full* (as in *several cups full of water*) denote the container or thing holding the contents.

fulcrum /ˈfʊlkrəm, ˈfʌl-/ ▻ *noun* (**fulcrums**, **fulcra** /-krə/) **1** *technical* the point on which a LEVER turns, balances or is supported. **2** a support; a means to an end. ⓒ 17c: Latin, meaning 'prop'.

fulfil or (*N Amer*) **fulfill** /fʊlˈfɪl/ *verb* (**fulfilled**, **fulfilling**) **1** to carry out or perform (a task, promise, etc). **2** to satisfy (requirements). **3** to achieve (an aim, ambition, etc). ● **fulfilment** *noun*. ● **fulfil oneself** to realize one's potential through the full use of one's talents. ⓒ Anglo-Saxon *fullfyllan*.

fulgent /ˈfʌldʒənt/ ▻ *adj* shining; bright. ● **fulgency** *noun*. ⓒ 15c: from Latin *fulgens* shining, from *fulgere* to shine.

fuliginous /fjʊˈlɪdʒɪnəs/ ▻ *adj* **1** sooty. **2** soot-coloured; dusky. ⓒ 17c: from Latin *fuligo* soot.

full[1] /fʊl/ ▻ *adj* (**fuller**, **fullest**) **1** (*also* **full of something**) holding, containing or having as much as possible, or a large quantity. **2** complete □ *do a full day's work*. **3** detailed; thorough; including everything necessary □ *a full report*. **4** occupied □ *My hands are full*. **5** having eaten till one wants no more. **6** plump; fleshy □ *the fuller figure* □ *full lips*. **7** said of clothes: made with a large amount of material □ *a full skirt*. **8** rich and strong □ *This wine is very full*. **9** rich and varied □ *a full life*. **10** having all possible rights, privileges, etc □ *a full member*. **11** said of the Moon: at the stage when it is seen as a fully-illuminated disc. **12 a**) said of a brother or sister: having the same parents as oneself (compare HALF-BROTHER, HALF-SISTER); **b** said of a cousin: see FIRST COUSIN. ▻ *adverb* **1** completely; at maximum capacity □ *Is the radiator full on?* **2** exactly; directly □ *hit him full on the nose*. ▻ *verb* (**fulled**, **fulling**) *needlecraft* to make something with gathers or puckers. ● **be full up 1** to be full to the limit. **2** to have had enough to eat. ● **full of something** unable to talk about anything but it; engrossed in it □ *full of her holidays*. ● **full of oneself** having too good an opinion of oneself and one's importance. ● **full of years** *literary or old use* old; aged. ● **full well** perfectly well. ● **in full 1** completely. **2** at length; in detail □ *reported in full*. ● **in full rig** with the maximum number of masts and sails. ● **in full swing** at the height of activity. ● **to the full** to the greatest possible extent. ⓒ Anglo-Saxon.

full[2] /fʊl/ ▻ *verb* (**fulled**, **fulling**) to shrink and beat (cloth) to thicken it. ● **fuller** *noun* someone who fulls cloth. ⓒ 14c: from French *fuler*, from Latin *fullo* fuller.

fullback ▻ *noun, hockey, football, rugby* a defence player positioned towards the back of the field to protect the goal.

full beam ▻ *noun* (*usually* **at full beam**) said of a vehicle's headlights: the strongest, undipped, setting.

full-blast ▻ *adverb* with maximum energy and fluency.

full-blooded ▻ *adj* **1** of pure breed; thoroughbred; not mixed blood. **2** enthusiastic; whole-hearted. ● **full-bloodedness** *noun*.

full-blown ▻ *adj* **1** having all the features of the specified thing □ *a full-blown war* □ *full-blown AIDS*. **2** said of a rose, etc: completely open.

full board ▻ *noun* accommodation at a hotel, guesthouse, etc including the provision of all meals, etc. Also called *US* AMERICAN PLAN. Compare HALF BOARD.

full-bodied ▻ *adj* having a rich flavour or quality □ *a full-bodied wine*.

full-circle ▻ *adverb* **1** round in a complete revolution. **2** back to the original starting position.

full complement see COMPLEMENT *noun* 2

full dress ▻ *noun* the style of dress to be worn on formal or ceremonial occasions. Also *as adj* □ *a full-dress occasion*.

full employment ▻ *noun* a situation in which all those seeking work in a community or country are able to find suitable work fairly readily, and in which the number of unfilled vacancies exceeds the number of people seeking work.

fuller[1] and **fullest** see FULL[1]

fuller[2] see under FULL[2]

fuller's earth ▻ *noun, geol* a green, blue or yellowish-brown clay with a high adsorptive capacity, used to decolour fats and oils, to remove grease from fabrics, as a filter and as a base for paper and cosmetics.

full-face or **full-faced** ▻ *adj* **1** facing straight towards the viewer. **2** having a full or broad face.

full-fat ▻ *adj* said of food, usually dairy products: containing all the original fat with none of it removed. Compare LOW-FAT, FAT-FREE.

full-frontal ▻ *adj* **1** referring to the front view of a completely naked man or woman. **2** unrestrained; with no detail left unrevealed.

full house ▻ *noun* **1** a performance at a theatre, cinema, etc, at which every seat is taken. **2** *cards, especially poker* a set of five cards consisting of three cards of one kind and two of another. Also called **full hand**. **3** in bingo: having all the numbers needed to win. **4** a complete set of anything.

full-length ▻ *adj* **1** complete; of the usual or standard length. **2** showing the whole body □ *a full-length mirror*. **3** of maximum length; long □ *a full-length skirt*.

full moon ▻ *noun* **1** one of the four phases of the Moon, when the whole of it is illuminated and it is seen as a complete disc. Compare NEW MOON. **2** the time when the Moon is full.

full nelson same as NELSON

fullness or (*N Amer or dated*) **fulness** ▻ *noun* the condition of being full or complete. ● **in the fullness of time** when the proper time or the time allowed for something has elapsed.

full-out ▻ *adj* at full power; total.

full-page ▻ *adj* occupying a whole page □ *full-page spread*.

full-pelt, **full-speed** and **full-tilt** ▻ *adj, adverb* with highest speed and impetus.

full-rigged ▻ *adj* having three or more masts square-rigged.

full-sailed ▻ *adj* **1** having all sails set; having sails filled with wind. **2** advancing with speed and momentum.

full-scale ▻ *adj* **1** said of a drawing, etc: the same size as the subject. **2** using all possible resources, means, etc; complete or exhaustive □ *a full-scale search for the missing climbers*.

full-speed see under FULL-PELT

full stop ▻ *noun* a punctuation mark (.) used to indicate the end of a sentence or to mark an abbreviation. Also (*especially Scottish and N Amer*) called PERIOD.

full-tilt see under FULL-PELT

full time ▻ *noun* the end of the time normally allowed for a sports match, etc.

full-time ▻ *adj* occupied for or extending over the whole of the working week. ▻ *adverb* (**full time**) □

full stop

A **full stop**

- marks the end of a sentence □ *John is coming.* □ *Two and two makes four.*

In direct speech, the full stop is replaced by a comma if the quoted speech is followed by a verb of saying, wondering, etc □ *'I have no complaints,' she said with a smile.* □ *'Let's just forget it,' replied the girl.*

- It can be used to mark the end of an abbreviation □ *Wood St.* □ *Wm. Shakespeare* □ *John Brown and Co.*

There is an increasing tendency to write abbreviations without full stops, particularly those that include the final letter of the word, such as *Dr* and *Mr*, and abbreviations of countries and organizations, such as *USA*, *UN* and *EC*.

- Three full stops, sometimes called 'an ellipsis' or 'omission marks', indicate that something has been left out □ *She lay in her cabin, weeping, weeping ...* □ *As Evan Daniel has said, '... it is in the language itself, not in books, that these facts are primarily to be sought'.* □ *What the ... does he think he's doing?*

working full time. • **full-timer** someone who works full time. Compare PART-TIME.

fully ▷ *adverb* **1** to the greatest possible extent. **2** completely □ *fully qualified.* **3** in detail □ *deal with it more fully next week.* **4** at least □ *stayed for fully one hour.*

fully-fashioned ▷ *adj* said of knitwear or stockings: seamed and shaped so as to give a close fit. Ⓒ 1940s.

fully-fledged ▷ *adj* **1** said of a person: completely trained or qualified. **2** said of a bird: old enough to have grown feathers.

fulmar /'fʊlmɑː(r), -mə(r)/ ▷ *noun* a gull-like sea bird found in Arctic and sub-Arctic regions. Ⓒ 17c: originally a dialect word from the Hebrides, probably from Icelandic *ful* foul or stinking + *mar* gull.

fulminate /'fʌlmɪneɪt, 'fʊl-/ ▷ *verb* (***fulminated***, ***fulminating***) *intr* to utter angry criticism or condemnation. • **fulminant** *adj*, *pathol* developing suddenly or rapidly. • **fulmination** *noun*. • **fulminatory** *adj*. Ⓒ 15c: from Latin *fulminare*, *fulminatum* to hurl lightning.

fulness see FULLNESS

fulsome /'fʊlsəm/ ▷ *adj* said of praise, compliments, etc: so overdone as to be distasteful. • **fulsomely** *adverb*. • **fulsomeness** *noun*. Ⓒ 13c.

fulvous /'fʌlvəs/ ▷ *adj* dull yellow; yellowish-brown; tawny. Ⓒ 17c: from Latin *fulvus* tawny.

fumarole /'fjuːməroʊl/ ▷ *noun* a hole from which gases issue in a volcano or volcanic region. Ⓒ 19c: from French *fumerolle* or Italian *fumaruola*, from Latin *fumus* smoke.

fumble /'fʌmbəl/ ▷ *verb* (***fumbled***, ***fumbling***) **1** *intr* (*also* **fumble for something**) to handle it, or grope, clumsily □ *fumbled in his pockets for the change.* **2** to say or do something awkwardly. **3** to fail to manage, because of clumsy handling □ *The fielder fumbled the catch.* ▷ *noun* **1** an act of fumbling. **2** in ball sports: a dropped or fumbled ball. • **fumbler** *noun*. • **fumblingly** *adverb*.

■ **fumble with** or **fumble about with something** to toy with or finger something (eg documents) in a distracted and aimless way.

fume /fjuːm/ ▷ *noun* **1** (*often* **fumes**) smoke, gases or vapour, especially if strong-smelling or toxic, emanating from heated materials, operating engines or machinery, etc. **2** the pungent toxic vapours given off by solvents or concentrated acids. **3** a rage; fretful excitement. ▷ *verb* (***fumed***, ***fuming***) **1** *intr* to be furious; to fret angrily. **2** *intr* to give off smoke, gases or vapours. **3** *intr* said of gases or vapours: to come off in fumes, especially during a chemical reaction. **4** to treat (eg wood) with fumes. • **fumous** or **fumey** *adj*. • **fumingly** *adverb*. Ⓒ 16c: from Latin *fumus* smoke.

fumed ▷ *adj* said of wood, especially oak: darkened by ammonia fumes.

fumigant /'fjuːmɪgənt/ ▷ *noun* a gaseous form of a chemical compound that is used to fumigate a place.

fumigate /'fjuːmɪgeɪt/ ▷ *verb* (***fumigated***, ***fumigating***) to disinfect (a room, a building, etc) with fumes, in order to destroy pests, especially insects and their larvae. • **fumigation** *noun*. • **fumigator** *noun* an apparatus used to fumigate a place. Ⓒ 18c: from Latin *fumigare*, *fumigatum* to smoke, from Latin *fumus* smoke.

fuming sulphuric acid see under OLEUM

fumitory /'fjuːmɪtərɪ/ ▷ *noun* (***fumitories***) an annual plant with slender stems, bluish-green leaves and flowers with four pink petals with blackish-purple tips, found as a common weed on cultivated ground. Ⓒ 14c: from French *fume-terre*, from Latin *fumus* smoke + *terra* earth, so named because it grows so rapidly that its spread was compared to the spread of fire.

fun ▷ *noun* **1** enjoyment; merriment. **2** a source of amusement or entertainment. ▷ *adj*, *colloq* intended for amusement, enjoyment, etc. • **for fun** as a joke; for amusement. • **in fun** as a joke; not seriously. • **make fun of** or **poke fun at someone** or **something** to laugh at them or it, especially unkindly; to tease or ridicule them or it. Ⓒ 17c, from earlier *fon* to make a fool of.

funambulist /fjʊ'nambjʊlɪst/ ▷ *noun* someone who performs on ropes, eg walking a tightrope, dancing on ropes, etc. Ⓒ 18c: from Latin *funambulus*, from *funis* rope + *ambulare* to walk.

fun and games ▷ *noun* **1** amusement; excitement. **2** *ironic* trouble □ *There'll be fun and games when Phil sees this mess!*

function /'fʌŋkʃən, 'fʌŋʃən/ ▷ *noun* **1** the special purpose or task of a machine, person, bodily part, etc. **2 a** an organized event such as a party, reception, meeting, etc; **b** Also *as adj* □ *function room.* **3** a duty particular to someone in a particular job. **4** *math*, *logic* a mathematical procedure that relates one or more variables to one or more other variables, eg in the algebraic expression $y = x + 4$, the variable y is a function of the variable x, usually written as $y = f(x)$, and a change in x will produce a change in y. **5** *computing* any of the basic operations of a computer, usually corresponding to a single operation. ▷ *verb* (***functioned***, ***functioning***) *intr* **1** to work; to operate □ *The washing-machine functions well.* **2** to fulfil a function; to perform one's duty. **3** to serve or act as something □ *a torch that functions as a screwdriver.* • **functionless** *adj*. Ⓒ 16c: French, from Latin *functio*, from *fungi*, *functus* to perform.

functional ▷ *adj* **1** said of buildings, machines, etc: designed for efficiency rather than decorativeness; plain rather than elaborate. **2** in working order; operational. **3** referring to or performed by functions. • **functionally** *adverb*.

functional group ▷ *noun*, *chem* in a molecule of a substance: a combination of two or more atoms that are bonded together and tend to act as a single unit in chemical reactions, eg the hydroxyl (-OH) group.

functionalism ▷ *noun* **1** the policy or practice of the practical application of ideas. **2** *art*, *archit* the theory that beauty is to be identified with functional efficiency. **3** *anthropol*, *sociol* the theory which develops a picture of society as a self-regulating organism in which social institutions, customs and beliefs all have a part to play in maintaining a single, integrated social system. • **functionalist** *noun*.

functionality ▷ *noun* the capacity that a thing, idea, etc has to be functional or practical.

functionary ▷ *noun* (***functionaries***) *derog* someone who works as a minor official in the government, etc.

function key ▷ *noun, computing* **1** any of the keys marked with an 'F' and a following numeral on a keyboard, pressed alone or in combination with other keys to perform a specific task within a program. **2** any key used in combination with the 'control' key for the same purpose.

function word ▷ *noun, linguistics* a word, such as an ARTICLE 4 or AUXILIARY 3, which expresses a grammatical concept, such as definiteness (see DEFINITE ARTICLE) or TENSE[1], and has little or no meaning apart from this.

fund ▷ *noun* **1** a sum of money on which some enterprise is founded or on which the expenses of a project are supported. **2** a large store or supply □ *a fund of jokes.* **3** (**funds**) *colloq* money available for spending. **4** (**funds**) British government securities paying fixed interest, which finance the NATIONAL DEBT. ▷ *verb* (***funded, funding***) **1** to provide money for a particular purpose □ *fund the project.* **2** to make (a debt) permanent, with fixed interest. • **funded** *adj* **1** invested in public funds. **2** existing in the form of bonds. • **funder** *noun* a financial backer. • **in funds** *colloq* having plenty of cash. ◷ 17c: from Latin *fundus* bottom.

fundament /ˈfʌndəmənt/ ▷ *noun, euphemistic* the buttocks or anus. ◷ 13c.

fundamental /fʌndəˈmɛntəl/ ▷ *adj* **1** basic; underlying □ *fundamental rules of physics* □ *her fundamental honesty.* **2** large; important □ *fundamental differences.* **3** essential; necessary. ▷ *noun* **1** (*usually* **fundamentals**) a basic principle or rule. **2** *music* the lowest note of a chord. • **fundamentality** *noun.* • **fundamentally** *adverb.* ◷ 15c: from Latin *fundamentum* foundation, from *fundare* to FOUND[1].

fundamentalism ▷ *noun* in religion, politics, etc: strict adherence to the traditional teachings of a particular religion or political doctrine. • **fundamentalist** *noun.* ◷ 1920s: the term was originally used of the conservative US Protestant movement, which was characterized by a literal interpretation of the Bible. It was revived to describe conservative Christian and Islamic movements in the late 20c.

fundamental particle ▷ *noun, physics* an elementary particle.

fundamental unit ▷ *noun, physics* each of the arbitrarily defined units in a system of measurement from which all other units are derived, eg in the SI system, the metre, kilogram and second are, respectively, the fundamental units of length, mass and time.

funded and **funder** see under FUND

fundholder ▷ *noun* a general practitioner who controls the budget allocated to their practice. • **fundholding** *noun, adj.*

fundi /ˈfʊndiː/ ▷ *noun* (***fundis***) *S Afr* an expert. ◷ 19c: from Nguni (a South African language) *umfundisi* a teacher.

funding ▷ *noun* **1** financial backing; funds. **2** the action of providing money for a project, etc. ▷ *adj* providing funds; relating to funding.

fundraiser ▷ *noun* **1** someone engaged in fundraising for a charity, organization, etc. **2** an event held to raise money for a cause.

fundraising ▷ *noun* the raising of money for an organization, project, etc. ▷ *adj* for the purpose of, or relating to, fundraising.

funds see under FUND

fundus /ˈfʌndəs/ ▷ *noun* (***fundi*** /ˈfʌndaɪ/) *anatomy* the rounded bottom of a hollow organ. ◷ 18c: Latin, meaning 'bottom'.

funeral /ˈfjuːnərəl/ ▷ *noun* **1** the ceremonial burial or cremation of a dead person. **2** *colloq* one's own problem, affair, etc □ *That's his funeral.* ▷ *adj* relating to funerals. ◷ 19c as US slang in noun sense 2; 14c in sense 1: from Latin *funeralia* funeral rites.

funeral director ▷ *noun* an undertaker.

funeral parlour ▷ *noun* **1** an undertaker's place of business. **2** a room that can be hired for funeral ceremonies.

funerary /ˈfjuːnərərɪ/ ▷ *adj* belonging to or used for funerals. ◷ 17c: from Latin *funerarius.*

funereal /fjʊˈnɪərɪəl/ ▷ *adj* **1** associated with or suitable for funerals. **2** mournful; dismal. **3** extremely slow. • **funereally** *adverb.* ◷ 18c: from Latin *funereus.*

funfair ▷ *noun* a collection of sideshows, amusements, rides, etc, often set up temporarily on open ground and moving from town to town. ◷ 1920s.

fungal and **fungi** see FUNGUS

fungibles /ˈfʌndʒɪbəlz/ ▷ *plural noun, Scots law* perishable goods which may be estimated by weight, number and measure and which are consumed in use. ◷ 18c: from Latin *fungi* to perform.

fungicide /ˈfʌndʒɪsaɪd, ˈfʌŋgɪ-/ ▷ *noun* a chemical that kills or limits the growth of fungi. • **fungicidal** *adj.* ◷ 19c: FUNGUS + -CIDE.

fungoid /ˈfʌŋgɔɪd/ ▷ *adj, bot* resembling a fungus in nature or consistency; fungus-like. ◷ 19c: FUNGUS + -OID.

fungus /ˈfʌŋgəs/ ▷ *noun* (***fungi*** /-giː, -gaɪ, -dʒaɪ/ or ***funguses*** /-gəsɪz/) any organism that superficially resembles a plant, but does not have leaves and roots, and lacks CHLOROPHYLL, so that it must obtain its nutrients from other organisms, by living either as a parasite on living organisms, or as a SAPROPHYTE on dead organic matter. • **fungal** /-gəl/ *adj.* • **fungous** /-gəs/ *adj.* ◷ 16c: Latin, meaning 'mushroom' or 'fungus'.

funicular /fjʊˈnɪkjʊlə(r)/ ▷ *adj* said of a mountain railway: operating by a machine-driven cable, with two cars, one of which descends while the other ascends. ▷ *noun* a funicular railway. ◷ Early 20c in these senses.

funk[1] ▷ *noun* **1** *colloq* jazz or rock music with a strong rhythm and repeating bass pattern, with a down-to-earth bluesy feel. **2** *in compounds* a mix of the specified types of music, containing elements from both traditions □ *disco-funk* □ *jazz-funk* □ *techno-funk.* ◷ 1950s in sense 1 as a back-formation from FUNKY; 17c in obsolete sense (except *US dialect*) of 'a strong, unpleasant smell': from French dialect *funquer* to give off smoke.

funk[2] ▷ *noun, colloq* **1 a** (*also* **blue funk**) a state of fear or panic; **b** shrinking back or shirking because of a loss of courage. **2** a coward. ▷ *verb* (***funked, funking***) to avoid doing something from panic; to balk at something or shirk from fear. ◷ 18c: possibly from Flemish *fonck.*

funkhole ▷ *noun, slang, originally military* **1** a place of refuge; a dug-out. **2** a place to which one can retreat for shelter, etc. **3** a job that enables one to avoid military service. ◷ Early 20c.

funky ▷ *adj* (***funkier, funkiest***) *colloq* **1** said of jazz or rock music: strongly rhythmical and emotionally stirring. **2** trendy; good □ *What funky socks you've got on!* **3** earthy; smelly.

funnel /ˈfʌnəl/ ▷ *noun* **1** a tube with a cone-shaped opening through which liquid, etc can be poured into a narrow-necked container. **2** a vertical exhaust pipe on a steamship or steam engine through which smoke escapes. ▷ *verb* (***funnelled, funnelling***; (*US*) ***funneled, funneling***) **1** *intr* to rush through a narrow space □ *wind funnelling through the streets.* **2** to transfer (liquid, etc) from one container to another using a funnel. • ***funnelled*** *adj* with a funnel; funnel-shaped. ◷ 15c: from Provençal *fonil,* from Latin *infundere* to pour in.

funnel-web or **funnel-web spider** ▷ *noun* a venomous spider of E Australia which constructs a tube-shaped or funnel-shaped lair.

funny /'fʌnɪ/ ▷ *adj* (***funnier***, ***funniest***) **1** amusing; causing laughter. Also (*colloq*) called **funny-ha-ha**. **2** strange; odd; mysterious. Also (*colloq*) called **funny-peculiar**. ◷ 1930s: to distinguish from sense 1. **3** *colloq* dishonest; shady; involving trickery. **4** *colloq* ill □ *feeling funny*. **5** *colloq* slightly crazy. ▷ *noun* (***funnies***) *colloq* **1** a joke. **2** (**funnies**) *N Amer* comic strips, or the comic section of a newspaper. • **funnily** *adverb*. • **funniness** *noun*. ◷ 18c.

funny bone ▷ *noun* a place in the elbow joint where the ulnar nerve passes close to the skin, is comparatively unprotected, and when struck shoots a tingling sensation down the forearm to the fingers.

funny farm ▷ *noun, dated colloq* a mental hospital.

funny money ▷ *noun, colloq* any currency, or unit of account, considered in some way less real or trustworthy than 'ordinary' money.

fun run ▷ *noun* a long-distance race that people run in for amusement, to raise money for a charity, etc.

fur /fɜː(r)/ ▷ *noun* **1** the thick fine soft coat of a hairy animal. **2 a** the skin of such an animal with the hair attached, used to make, line or trim garments; **b** a synthetic imitation of this. **3** a coat, cape or jacket made of fur or an imitation of it. **4** a whitish coating on the tongue, generally a sign of illness. **5** a whitish coating that forms on the inside of water pipes and kettles in hard-water regions. ▷ *verb* (***furred***, ***furring***) **1** *tr & intr* (*often* **fur up** or **fur something up**) to coat or become coated with a fur-like deposit. **2** to cover, trim or line with fur. • **furring** or **furry** see separate entries. • **make the fur fly** *colloq* to cause a commotion; to upset people. ◷ 14c: from French *fuerre* sheath or case.

fur. ▷ *abbreviation* furlong.

furbelow /'fɜːbəloʊ/ ▷ *noun* **1** a dress trimming in the form of a ruched or pleated strip, ruffle or flounce. **2** (**furbelows**) fussy ornamentation. ◷ 18c: from French and Italian *falbala*.

furbish /'fɜːbɪʃ/ ▷ *verb* (**furbishes**, **furbished**, ***furbishing***) (*also* **furbish something up**) to restore, decorate or clean it; to rub it up until it is bright. • **furbisher** *noun*. • **furbishment** *noun*. ◷ 14c: from French *fourbir* to polish.

furcate /'fɜːkeɪt, fɜː'keɪt/ ▷ *verb* (***furcated***, ***furcating***) *intr* to fork or divide; to branch like a fork. ▷ *adj* /fɜːˈkeɪt, 'fɜːkət/ forked. ◷ Early 19c: from Latin *furca* fork.

furcation /fɜː'keɪʃən/ ▷ *noun* a forking; a fork-like division.

furcula /'fɜːkjʊlə/ ▷ *noun* (***furculas***) the united clavicles of a bird; the wishbone. ◷ 1850s: Latin, meaning 'small fork'.

fur fabric ▷ *noun* a fabric with a fur-like pile.

furfur /'fɜːfɜː(r), 'fɜːfə(r)/ ▷ *noun* dandruff; scurf. • **furfuraceous** /fɜːfjʊ'reɪʃəs/ *adj* branny; scaly; scurfy. ◷ 17c: Latin, meaning 'bran'.

the Furies ▷ *plural noun* the three spirits of vengeance, known in Greek mythology as the Erinyes (see ERINYS).

furioso /fjʊərɪ'oʊsoʊ, fʊərɪ-/ *music* ▷ *adverb* in a vigorous manner. ▷ *adj* vigorous. ◷ 19c: Italian.

furious /'fjʊərɪəs/ ▷ *adj* **1** violently or intensely angry. **2** raging; stormy □ *furious winds*. **3** frenzied; frantic □ *furious activity*. • **furiously** *adverb*. • **furiousness** *noun*. • **fast and furious** see under FAST. ◷ 14c: from Latin *furiosus*.

furl /fɜːl/ ▷ *verb* (***furled***, ***furling***) *tr & intr* said of flags, sails or umbrellas: to roll up. ◷ 16c: from French *ferlier*, from *fer* FIRM + *lier* to bind.

furlong /'fɜːlɒŋ/ ▷ *noun* (abbreviation **fr.**) a measure of distance now used mainly in horse-racing, equal to one eighth of a mile, or 220 yards (201.2m). ◷ Anglo-Saxon *furlang*, from *furh* furrow + *lang* long.

furlough /'fɜːloʊ/ ▷ *noun* leave of absence, especially from military duty abroad. ◷ 17c: from Dutch *verlof*.

furnace /'fɜːnɪs/ ▷ *noun* **1 a** an enclosed chamber in which heat is produced, eg for smelting metal, heating water or burning rubbish; **b** a BLAST FURNACE. **2** *colloq* a very hot place. ◷ 13c: from Latin *fornax*, *fornacis* kiln or oven.

furnish /'fɜːnɪʃ/ ▷ *verb* (***furnishes***, ***furnished***, ***furnishing***) **1** to provide (a house, etc) with furniture. **2** to supply (what is necessary). • **furnished** *adj* usually said of a house, flat, etc: stocked with furniture □ *The flat she is renting is fully furnished.* ◷ 15c: from French *furnir* to provide.

■ **furnish someone with something** to supply or equip them with what they require (eg information, documents).

furnishings ▷ *plural noun* articles of furniture, fittings, carpets, curtains, etc.

furniture /'fɜːnɪtʃə(r)/ ▷ *noun* **1** movable household equipment such as tables, chairs, beds, etc. **2** the equipment needed on board ship or in a factory. **3** door fittings such as locks and handles. ◷ 16c: from French *fourniture*, from *fournir* to provide.

furniture van ▷ *noun* a long, high-sided van for transporting furniture and other fittings from a house, etc, eg when moving house.

furore /fjʊ'rɔːrɪ/ or (*especially N Amer*) **furor** /fʊə'rɔː(r)/ *noun* (***furores***) a general outburst of excitement or indignation in reaction to something. ◷ 18c: Italian, from Latin *furor* frenzy.

furrier /'fʌrɪə(r)/ ▷ *noun* someone whose job is to make or sell furs. ◷ 16c.

furring /'fɜːrɪŋ/ ▷ *noun* **1** fur trimmings. **2** a coating on the tongue. **3** strips of wood fastened to joists or to a wall onto which floorboards or plasterboard are fixed.

furrow /'fʌroʊ/ ▷ *noun* **1** a groove or trench cut into the earth by a plough; a rut. **2** a wrinkle, eg in the forehead. ▷ *verb* (***furrowed***, ***furrowing***) **1** to plough (land) into furrows. **2** *intr* to become wrinkled. ◷ Anglo-Saxon *furh*.

furry /'fɜːrɪ/ ▷ *adj* (***furrier***, ***furriest***) **1** covered with fur. **2** made of, or like, fur. • **furrily** *adverb*. • **furriness** *noun*.

further /'fɜːðə(r)/ ▷ *adj* **1** more distant or remote (than something else). **2** more extended than was originally expected □ *further delay*. **3** additional □ *no further clues*. ▷ *adverb* **1** at or to a greater distance or more distant point. **2** to or at a more advanced point □ *further developed*. **3** to a greater extent or degree □ *modified even further*. **4** moreover; furthermore. ▷ *verb* (***furthered***, ***furthering***) to help the progress of something. • **further to ...** following on from (our telephone conversation, your letter, etc). See also FAR. ◷ Anglo-Saxon *furthra*.

further

See Usage Note at **farther**.

furtherance /'fɜːðərəns/ ▷ *noun* the furthering, advancement or continuation of something.

further education ▷ *noun, Brit* formal education at a college, usually on a vocational course, for school-leavers or mature students. Compare HIGHER EDUCATION.

furthermore /fɜːðə'mɔː(r)/ ▷ *adverb* in addition to what has already been said; moreover.

furthermost ▷ *adj* most distant or remote; farthest.

further outlook ▷ *noun, meteorol* a general weather forecast given for a longer and more distant period than that given for the immediate future by a more detailed forecast.

furthest /ˈfɜːðəst/ ▻ *adj* most distant or remote. ▻ *adverb* **1** at or to the greatest distance or most distant point. **2** at or to the most advanced point; to the greatest extent or degree. Compare FARTHEST.

furtive /ˈfɜːtɪv/ ▻ *adj* secretive; stealthy; sly ▫ ***a furtive glance.*** • **furtively** *adverb.* • **furtiveness** *noun.* ◷ 15c: from Latin *furtivus* stolen, clandestine.

furuncle /ˈfjʊərʌŋkəl/ ▻ *noun, pathol* a boil. • **furuncular** or **furunculous** *adj.* ◷ 17c: from Latin *furunculus* a little thief.

fury /ˈfjʊərɪ/ ▻ *noun* (*furies*) **1** violent or frenzied anger; an outburst of this. **2** violence ▫ ***the fury of the wind.*** **3** a frenzy ▫ ***a fury of activity.*** • **like fury** *colloq* fast; eagerly; powerfully; like mad; furiously. ◷ 14c: from French *furie*, from Latin *furere* to rage. See also THE FURIES.

furze /fɜːz/ ▻ *noun* GORSE. ◷ Anglo-Saxon *fyrs*.

fuse[1] /fjuːz/ ▻ *noun, elec* a safety device consisting of a length of wire which melts when the current exceeds a certain value, thereby breaking the circuit. It is designed to prevent damage to electrical equipment and reduce the risk of fire. See also BLOW[1] (*verb* 8). ▻ *verb* (*fused*, *fusing*) *tr & intr* **1** to melt as a result of the application of heat. **2** (*also* **fuse together**) to join by, or as if by, melting together. **3** said of an electric circuit or appliance: to cease to function as a result of the melting of a fuse. • **blow a fuse** *colloq* to lose one's temper. ◷ 16c: from Latin *fundere*, *fusum* to melt.

fuse[2] or (*US*) **fuze** /fjuːz/ ▻ *noun* a cord or cable containing combustible material, used for detonating a bomb or explosive charge. ▻ *verb* (*fused*, *fusing*) to fit with such a device. • **have a short fuse** or **burn on a short fuse** to be quick-tempered. ◷ 17c: from Latin *fusus* spindle.

fuse box ▻ *noun* a box containing the switches and fuses (usually encased in a small glass or ceramic tube with metal ends) which lead into an electrical system serving eg a whole building or part of it.

fuselage /ˈfjuːzəlɑːʒ, -ɪdʒ/ ▻ *noun* the main body of an aircraft, which carries crew and passengers, and to which the wings and tail unit are attached. ◷ Early 20c: from French *fuselé* spindle-shaped.

fusel-oil /ˈfjuːzəlɔɪl/ ▻ *noun* a nauseous mixture of alcohols in spirits distilled from potatoes, grain, etc. ◷ 19c: from German *Fusel* bad spirits.

fusible /ˈfjuːzɪbəl/ ▻ *adj* able to be fused; easily fused. • **fusibility** *noun.*

fusiform /ˈfjuːzɪfɔːm/ ▻ *adj* spindle-shaped; tapering from the middle towards each end. ◷ 18c: from Latin *fusus* spindle + -FORM.

fusilier /fjuːzɪˈlɪə(r)/ ▻ *noun* **1** *historical* an infantryman armed with a **fusil**, which is a light musket. **2** a member of any of several British regiments formerly armed with these. ◷ 17c: from French *fusilier*, from *fuisil* a musket with a flintlock.

fusillade /fjuːsɪˈleɪd, -zɪˈlɑːd/ ▻ *noun* **1** a simultaneous or continuous discharge of firearms. **2** an onslaught, eg of criticism. ◷ 19c: from French *fusillade*, from *fusiller* to shoot, from *fuisil*; see FUSILIER.

fusilli /fjuːˈziːliː/ ▻ *singular or plural noun* pasta shaped into short thick spirals. ◷ 20c: Italian.

fusion /ˈfjuːʒən/ ▻ *noun* **1** *chem* the process of melting, whereby a substance changes from a solid to a liquid. **2** the act of joining together. **3** *nuclear physics* see under NUCLEAR FUSION. ◷ 16c: from Latin *fusio* melting.

fusion bomb ▻ *noun* a bomb deriving its energy from NUCLEAR FUSION, such as the HYDROGEN BOMB.

fusion reactor ▻ *noun* a NUCLEAR REACTOR operating by NUCLEAR FUSION.

fuss ▻ *noun* (*fusses*) **1** agitation and excitement, especially over something trivial. **2** a commotion, disturbance or bustle. **3** a show of fond affection. ▻ *verb* (*fusses*, *fussed*, *fussing*) *intr* (*also* **fuss over** or **about something**) **1** to worry needlessly. **2** to concern oneself too much with trivial matters. **3** to agitate. • **fusser** *noun.* • **make a fuss** or **make a fuss about something** to complain about it. • **make a fuss of someone** *colloq* to give them a lot of affectionate or amicable attention. ◷ 18c.

fusspot ▻ *noun, derog, colloq* someone who worries excessively, especially over trifles; a fusser.

fussy ▻ *adj* (*fussier*, *fussiest*) **1** choosy; discriminating. **2** over-concerned with details or trifles; finicky. **3** bustling and officious. **4** said of clothes, etc: over-elaborate. • **fussily** *adverb.* • **fussiness** *noun.*

fustanella /fʌstəˈnɛlə/ ▻ *noun* (*fustanellas*) a white kilt sometimes worn by Greek and Albanian men. ◷ 19c: Italian diminutive of FUSTIAN (in its original sense), which is used to make the garment.

fustian /ˈfʌstɪən/ ▻ *noun* **1** a kind of coarse twilled cotton fabric with a nap, including moleskin, velveteen, corduroy, etc. **2** a pompous and unnatural style of writing or speaking; bombast. ▻ *adj* **1** made of fustian. **2** bombastic. ◷ 12c: from French *fustaigne*, probably named after El-Fustat (Old Cairo) where the original coarse cloth of cotton and flax may have been made.

fustic /ˈfʌstɪk/ ▻ *noun* **1** the wood of a tropical American tree. Also called **old fustic**. **2** the yellow dye obtained from the old fustic or the YOUNG FUSTIC. ◷ 16c: from French *fustoc*, through Spanish from Arabic *fustuq*, from Greek *pistake* PISTACHIO.

fusty /ˈfʌstɪ/ ▻ *adj* (*fustier*, *fustiest*) **1** stale-smelling; old and musty. **2** old-fashioned. • **fustily** *adverb.* • **fustiness** *noun.* ◷ 14c: from French *fusté* smelling of the cask, from *fust* wine cask.

futhark /ˈfuːθɑːk/ or **futhork** /ˈfuːθɔːk/ ▻ *noun* the runic alphabet. ◷ 19c: derived from the first six symbols of the alphabet: *f, u, þ* (*th*), *a* or *o, r, k*.

futile /ˈfjuːtaɪl; *US* -təl/ ▻ *adj* unproductive, unavailing, foolish, vain or pointless. • **futilely** *adverb.* ◷ 16c: from Latin *futilis* 'easily pouring out' or 'leaky', and therefore also meaning 'unreliable'.

futility /fjuːˈtɪlɪtɪ/ ▻ *noun* uselessness. ◷ 17c: from French *futilité*.

futon /ˈfuːtɒn, fuːˈtɒn/ ▻ *noun* a thin cloth-filled mattress designed to be used on the floor, and meant to be rolled up when not in use. ◷ 19c in descriptions of Japanese life, but more common since the 1970s when futons started becoming popular in Britain.

futtock /ˈfʌtək/ ▻ *noun, naut* one of the crooked timbers of a wooden ship. ◷ 17c.

future /ˈfjuːtʃə(r)/ ▻ *noun* **1** the time to come; events that are still to occur. **2** *grammar* **a** the future tense; **b**) a verb in the future tense. **3** prospects ▫ ***must think about one's future.*** **4** likelihood of success ▫ ***no future in that.*** **5** (**futures**) *stock exchange* commodities bought or sold at an agreed price, to be delivered at a later date, the price of which remains the same whether the market price of the particular commodity has fallen or risen in the meantime. ▻ *adj* **1** yet to come or happen. **2** about to become ▫ ***my future wife.*** **3** *grammar* said of the tense of a verb: indicating actions or events yet to happen, in English formed with the auxiliary verb *will* and infinitive without *to*, as in *She will see him tomorrow*. Compare PAST, PRESENT, PERFECT, PLUPERFECT, IMPERFECT. • **futureless** *adj* without prospects. • **for future reference** so that you will know the correct procedure when you do this again. • **in future** from now on. ◷ 14c: from Latin *futurus* about to be.

future perfect see under PERFECT

futurism ▻ *noun* a movement founded in Italy in 1909 by the poet Marinetti, concerned with expressing the motion and movement of machines in all art forms. It reflects the dynamism of modern technology. • **futurist** *noun*. Ⓒ Early 20c.

futuristic ▻ *adj* **1** said of design, etc: so modern or original as to seem appropriate to the future, or considered likely to be fashionable in the future. **2** relating to futurism. • **futuristically** *adverb*.

futurity /fjʊ'tjʊərɪtɪ/ ▻ *noun* (***futurities***) **1** the future. **2** a future event.

futurology /fjuːtʃə'rɒlədʒɪ/ ▻ *noun* the forecasting of future events from present tendencies. • **futurologist**.

fu yung or **fu yong** /fuː jʊŋ/ ▻ *noun* a Chinese sauce of eggs mixed and cooked with bean sprouts, onion, meat, etc. Ⓒ 20c: Chinese, meaning 'hibiscus'.

fuze an alternative *US* spelling of FUSE[2]

fuzz ▻ *noun* (***fuzzes***) **1** a mass of fine fibres or hair, usually curly. **2** a blur. ▻ *verb* (***fuzzes, fuzzed, fuzzing***) (*also* **fuzz something up**) to make or become fuzzy. Ⓒ 17c.

the fuzz ▻ *noun, slang* the police. Ⓒ 1920s.

fuzz box ▻ *noun* an electronic device that changes the characteristics of the sound of eg an electric guitar.

fuzzy ▻ *adj* (***fuzzier, fuzziest***) **1** covered with fuzz. **2** forming a mass of tight curls. **3** indistinct; blurred. • **fuzzily** *adverb*. • **fuzziness** *noun*.

fuzzy logic ▻ *noun, computing* a form of logic or reasoning that is a central part of artificial intelligence, and resembles human thinking in that it is used to process information that cannot be defined precisely because it is dependent on its context.

fwd ▻ *abbreviation* forward.

the f-word or **F-word** ▻ *noun* a euphemistic way of referring to the word FUCK.

FX ▻ *noun* short for SPECIAL EFFECTS.

-fy *combining form, forming verbs* to make or become □ *gentrify*. Ⓒ From French *-fier*, from Latin *-ficare*, from *-ficus*; compare -FIC.

fyi ▻ *abbreviation* for your information.

fz. ▻ *abbreviation, music* forzando, a variant of sforzando.

G

G[1] or **g** /dʒiː/ ▻ *noun* (***Gs, G's*** or ***g's***) **1** the seventh letter of the English alphabet. **2** (**G**) *music* **a** the fifth note on the scale of C major; **b** the musical key which has this note as its base.

G[2] ▻ *abbreviation* **1** German. **2** *N Amer slang* a grand, 1000 dollars.

g ▻ *abbreviation* **1** gallon. **2** gram or gramme. **3** gravity, or acceleration due to gravity.

GA ▻ *abbreviation, US state* Georgia. Also written **Ga.**

Ga ▻ *symbol, chem* gallium.

G&T or **G and T** ▻ *noun* a gin and tonic.

gab *colloq* ▻ *noun* idle talk; chat. ▻ *verb* (***gabbed, gabbing***) *intr* (*also* **gab on** or **away**) to talk idly, especially at length. • **the gift of the gab** *colloq* the ability to speak with ease, especially persuasively. ◷ 18c: probably from Irish Gaelic *gob* beak or mouth.

gabardine see GABERDINE

gabble /ˈgabəl/ ▻ *verb* (***gabbled, gabbling***) *tr & intr* to talk or say something quickly and unclearly. ▻ *noun* fast indistinct talk. • **gabbling** *noun*. ◷ 16c: from Dutch *gabbelen*.

gabbro /ˈgabroʊ/ ▻ *noun* (***gabbros***) *geol* a coarse-grained crystalline igneous rock with a low silica content. ◷ 19c: Italian.

gabby ▻ *adj* (***gabbier, gabbiest***) garrulous; gossipy.

gaberdine or **gabardine** /gabəˈdiːn, ˈgab-/ ▻ *noun* (*plural* ***gabardines*** or ***gaberdines*** in sense 2) **1** a closely woven twill fabric, especially one made of wool or cotton. **2** a coat or loose cloak made from this. ◷ 16c, meaning 'a loose garment': from French *gauvardine* a pilgrim's garment.

gabfest ▻ *noun, slang, chiefly N Amer* **1** a gathering characterized by gossipy conversation. **2** a lengthy chat or discussion. ◷ 19c: from GAB + German *Fest* festival.

gabian /ˈgeɪbɪən/ ▻ *noun* a metal or wicker cylindrical basket that can be filled with stones, earth, etc, used in the construction industry. ◷ 16c: French, from Italian *gabbia* a cage.

gable /ˈgeɪbəl/ ▻ *noun* (***gables***) **1** the triangular upper part of a side wall between the sloping parts of a roof. **2** a triangular canopy above a door or window. • **gabled** *adj* having a gable or gables. ◷ 14c: from Norse *gafl*.

Gad see GAD[2]

gad[1] ▻ *verb* (***gadded, gadding***) *intr, colloq* (*usually* **gad about** or **around**) to go from place to place busily, especially in the hope of finding amusement or pleasure. ◷ 15c: back-formation from Anglo-Saxon *gædeling* companion.

gad[2] or **Gad** ▻ *exclamation, old use* (*also* **by Gad**) expressing surprise or affirmation. ◷ 17c: a form of *God*.

gadabout ▻ *noun, colloq, derog, often humorous* a person who gads about.

Gadarene /ˈgadəriːn/ ▻ *adj* applied to those who panic and rush headlong towards disaster. ◷ 19c: from the swine of Gadara in Matthew 8.28.

gadfly ▻ *noun* (***gadflies***) **1** any of various large flies that suck the blood of cattle and other animal livestock, inflicting painful bites. **2** *derog, old use* a person who deliberately and persistently annoys others. ◷ 16c: from Anglo-Saxon *gad* goad.

gadget /ˈgadʒɪt/ ▻ *noun* any small device or appliance, especially one more ingenious than necessary. • **gadgetry** /-trɪ/ *noun* **1** gadgets. **2** the use or application of gadgets in a particular instance. ◷ 19c.

gadoid /ˈgeɪdɔɪd, ˈga-/ ▻ *noun, zool* any fish (including cod and hake) that belongs to the family **Gadidae** /ˈgadɪdiː/ of marine fishes, with small scales, and pectoral and pelvic fins situated close together. ▻ *adj* said of a fish: belonging to this order. ◷ 19c: ultimately from Greek *gados* cod.

gadolinium /gadəˈlɪnɪəm/ ▻ *noun, chem* (symbol **Gd**, atomic number 64) a soft silvery-white metallic element, belonging to the LANTHANIDE series, which is highly magnetic at low temperatures, and also behaves as a superconductor. ◷ 19c: named after Johan Gadolin (1760–1852), Finnish mineralogist.

gadroon or **godroon** /gəˈdruːn/ ▻ *noun* an embossed, cable-like decoration used as an edging on silverware, etc. • **gadrooned** *adj*. • **gadrooning** *noun*. ◷ 18c: from French *godron*.

gadwall /ˈgadwɔːl/ ▻ *noun* a dabbling duck related to the mallard, native to northern inland waters. ◷ 17c.

Gaea see GAIA

Gael /geɪl/ ▻ *noun* a person from the Scottish Highlands and Islands, Ireland or the Isle of Man, especially one who speaks Gaelic. ◷ 19c: from Gaelic *Gaidheal*.

Gaeldom ▻ *noun* **1** the Gaels. **2** Gaelic civilization and culture. **3** the territory inhabited by the Gaels.

Gaelic ▻ *noun* any of the closely related Celtic languages spoken in the Scottish Highlands and Islands /ˈgɑːlɪk/, or Ireland or the Isle of Man /ˈgeɪlɪk/. ▻ *adj* **1** relating to these languages or the people who speak them, or to their customs. **2** relating to sports, eg HURLING and SHINTY, played especially in, or originating in, Ireland and the Scottish Highlands. Compare GOIDELIC.

Gaelic coffee see IRISH COFFEE

Gaelic football ▻ *noun* a kind of football played mainly in Ireland between teams of 15 players, using a round ball which may be kicked, bounced or punched, but not thrown or run with.

Gaeltacht /ˈgeɪltəxt/ ▻ *noun* **1** any of the Gaelic-speaking districts of Ireland or Scotland. **2** these districts thought of collectively. ◷ 1920s: Irish Gaelic.

gaff[1] ▻ *noun* **1** a long pole with a hook, for landing large fish. **2** *naut* a vertical spar to which the tops of certain types of sail are attached. ▻ *verb* (***gaffed, gaffing***) to catch (a fish) with a gaff. ◷ 13c: from Provençal *gaf* a boathook.

gaff[2] *slang* ▻ *noun* nonsense. • **blow the gaff** *Brit* to give away a secret.

gaffe /gaf/ ▻ *noun* a socially embarrassing action or remark. ◷ 19c: French.

gaffer /ˈgafə(r)/ ▻ *noun* **1** *colloq* a boss or foreman. **2** *cinema & TV* the senior electrician in a production crew. **3** *dialect* often as a form of address: an old man. ◷ 16c in sense 3; 19c in sense 1; 1950s in sense 2: perhaps from GODFATHER or GRANDFATHER.

gag[1] ▻ *verb* (***gagged, gagging***) **1** to silence someone by putting something in or over their mouth. **2** to deprive someone of free speech. **3** *intr* to retch. **4** *intr* to choke. ▷ *noun* **1** something put into or over a person's mouth to prevent them from making any sound. **2** any suppression of free speech. **3** a CLOSURE (*noun* 3) applied to a parliamentary debate. ◷ 15c in obsolete sense 'to suffocate'.

gag[2] *colloq* ▷ *noun* a joke or trick, especially as used by a professional comic. ▷ *verb* (***gagged***, ***gagging***) *intr* to tell jokes. ◷ 19c.

gaga /ˈɡɑːɡɑː/ ▷ *adj*, *colloq* **1** weak-minded through old age; senile. **2** silly; foolish. **3** (*usually* **gaga about** or **over someone** or **something**) wildly enthusiastic. ◷ 20c: French.

gage[1] /ɡeɪdʒ/ ▷ *noun* **1** an object given as security or a pledge. **2** *historical* something thrown down to signal a challenge, eg a glove. ◷ 14c: from French *guage*.

gage[2] /ɡeɪdʒ/ ▷ *noun* a GREENGAGE.

gage[3] see GAUGE

gaggle /ˈɡaɡəl/ ▷ *noun* **1** a flock of geese. **2** *colloq* a group of noisy people. ▷ *verb* (***gaggled***, ***gaggling***) *intr* said of geese: to cackle. ◷ 14c as verb: imitating the sound.

Gaia or **Gaea** /ˈɡaɪə/ ▷ *noun* the Earth considered as a living entity within the solar system. ◷ Late 20c: in Greek mythology Gaia was the goddess of the Earth.

gaiety /ˈɡeɪətɪ/ ▷ *noun* **1** the state of being merry or bright. **2** attractively bright appearance. **3** fun; merrymaking. ◷ 17c: from French *gaieté*.

gaily /ˈɡeɪlɪ/ ▷ *adverb* **1** in a light-hearted, merry way. **2** brightly; colourfully. ◷ 14c: from GAY.

gain /ɡeɪn/ ▷ *verb* (***gained***, ***gaining***) **1** to get, obtain or earn (something desirable). **2** to win (especially a victory or prize). **3** to have or experience an increase in something □ ***gain speed***. **4** *tr & intr* said of a clock, etc: to go too fast by (a specified amount of time). **5** to reach (a place), especially after difficulties. ▷ *noun* **1** (*often* **gains**) something gained, eg profit. **2** an increase, eg in weight. **3** an instance of gaining. **4** *telecomm* the ratio of output to input voltage in an amplifier, usually expressed in decibels. • **gain ground** to make progress or win an advantage. • **gain time** to get extra time for something through a delay or postponement. ◷ 15c: from French *gaaignier* to earn, gain or till (land).

▪ **gain by** or **from something** to benefit or profit from it.

▪ **gain on someone** or **something** to come closer to them or it; to catch them up.

gainful ▷ *adj* **1** profitable. **2** said of employment: paid. • **gainfully** *adverb*.

gainsay /ˈɡeɪnseɪ, ɡeɪnˈseɪ/ ▷ *verb* (***gainsays***, ***gainsaid***, ***gainsaying***) *formal* to deny or contradict. • **gainsayer** *noun*. ◷ 13c: from Anglo-Saxon *gean* against + *sayen* to say.

gainst or **'gainst** /ɡɛnst, ɡeɪnst/ ▷ *prep*, *poetic* against. ◷ 16c.

gait /ɡeɪt/ ▷ *noun* **1** a way of walking. **2** an animal's leg-movements at a specified speed, eg trotting. • **gaited** *adj*, *in compounds* having a specified gait □ ***slow-gaited***. ◷ 16c: variant of obsolete *gate* manner of doing.

gaiter /ˈɡeɪtə(r)/ ▷ *noun* a leather or cloth covering for the lower leg and ankle, often with a strap fitting under the shoe. ◷ 18c: from French *guêtre*.

gal[1] ▷ *noun*, *colloq*, *old use* a girl.

gal[2] or **Gal** ▷ *noun*, *physics* a unit of gravitational acceleration, equal to one centimetre per second per second, used in geological surveying. Also called **galileo** /ɡalɪˈleɪoʊ/. ◷ 20c: named after Galileo Galilei, Italian astronomer and mathematician (1564–1642).

gal. ▷ *abbreviation* gallon.

gala /ˈɡɑːlə, ˈɡeɪlə/ ▷ *noun* (***galas***) **1 a** an occasion of special entertainment or a public festivity of some kind, eg a carnival □ ***miners' gala***; **b** *as adj* □ ***gala night at the theatre***. **2** a meeting for sports competitions, especially swimming. ◷ 17c: French, from *galer* to make merry.

galactic /ɡəˈlaktɪk/ ▷ *adj* **1** relating to a galaxy or the Galaxy. **2** *medicine* relating to or obtained from milk. ◷ 19c: from Greek *gala*, *galaktos* milk; see also GALAXY.

galactic halo ▷ *noun*, *astron* an almost spherical aggregation of stars, globular clusters, dust and gas surrounding a galaxy.

galactic plane ▷ *noun*, *astron* the plane that passes through the spiral arms of the Milky Way galaxy. See also SPIRAL GALAXY.

galactose /ɡəˈlaktoʊs/ ▷ *noun*, *biochem* (formula $C_6H_{12}O_6$) a sugar obtained by hydrolysis from LACTOSE.

galah /ɡəˈlɑː/ ▷ *noun* **1** an Australian cockatoo with grey wings and back and pink underparts. **2** *Austral slang* a fool; an idiot. ◷ 19c: Aboriginal.

Galahad /ˈɡaləhad/ ▷ *noun* someone of outstanding integrity and nobility of character. ◷ 19c: named after Sir Galahad, the noblest knight of King Arthur's Round Table.

galantine /ˈɡaləntiːn/ ▷ *noun*, *cookery* boneless cooked white meat or fish served cold in aspic. ◷ 18c: French, from *galatine*, a sauce for fish.

galaxy /ˈɡaləksɪ/ ▷ *noun* (***galaxies***) **1** a huge collection of stars, dust and gas held together by mutual gravitational attraction. **2** (**the Galaxy**) the vast spiral arrangement of stars to which our solar system belongs, known as the Milky Way. **3** a fabulous gathering or array, eg of famous people. ◷ 14c as *the Galaxy*: from Greek *galaxias* the Milky Way, from *gala*, *galaktos* milk; compare GALACTIC.

gale ▷ *noun* **1 a** *loosely* any very strong wind; **b** *technical* a wind that blows with a speed of 51.5 to 101.4km per hour, corresponding to force 7 to 10 on the BEAUFORT SCALE. Also *as adj* □ ***gale warning*** □ ***gale force winds***. **2** (*usually* **gales**) a sudden loud burst, eg of laughter. ◷ 16c.

galena /ɡəˈliːnə/ ▷ *noun* the most important ore of LEAD[2] (*noun* 1) which occurs as compact masses of very dense dark grey crystals consisting mainly of lead sulphide. Also called **galenite** /-naɪt/. ◷ 16c: Latin, meaning 'lead ore'.

galette /ɡaˈlɛt/ ▷ *noun* a round flat sweet or savoury cake, pastry or pancake. ◷ 18c: French; the variations originate in different parts of France.

Galilean[1] /galɪˈlɪən/ ▷ *adj* relating to Galilee, one of the Roman divisions of Palestine. ▷ *noun* a native or inhabitant of Galilee. ◷ 17c.

Galilean[2] /galɪˈlɪən/ ▷ *adj* belonging or relating to Galileo Galilei, Italian astronomer and mathematician (1564–1642). ◷ 18c.

Galileo see under GAL[2]

gall[1] /ɡɔːl/ ▷ *noun* **1** *colloq* impudence; cheek. **2** bitterness or spitefulness. **3** something unpleasant. **4** *medicine*, *old use* bile. ◷ Anglo-Saxon *gealla* bile.

gall[2] /ɡɔːl/ ▷ *noun* a small round abnormal growth on the stem or leaf of a plant, usually caused by invading parasitic fungi or bacteria, or by insects, eg gall wasps. ◷ 14c: from Latin *galla* the oak apple.

gall[3] /ɡɔːl/ ▷ *noun* **1** a sore or painful swelling on the skin, especially of horses, caused by chafing. **2** something annoying or irritating. **3** a state of being annoyed. ▷ *verb* (***galled***, ***galling***) **1** to annoy. **2** to chafe (skin). ◷ 14c as *gealla* a sore on a horse.

gall. ▷ *abbreviation* gallon or gallons.

gallant /ˈɡalənt/ *also* /ɡəˈlant/ ▷ *adj* **1** brave. **2** *literary or old use* splendid, grand or fine. **3** /ɡəˈlant/ said of a man:

courteous and attentive to women. ▷ *noun, old use* **1** / *also* gə'lant/ a woman's lover. **2** a handsome young man who pursues women. • **gallantly** *adverb*. ◷ 15c: from French *galant*, from *galer* to make merry.

gallantry /'galəntrɪ/ ▷ *noun* (*plural* ***gallantries*** in sense 2b) **1** bravery. **2** *old use* **a** politeness and attentiveness to women; **b** an action or phrase demonstrating this.

gall bladder ▷ *noun, anatomy* a small muscular pear-shaped sac that usually lies beneath the right lobe of the liver. Its function is to store bile produced by the liver.

galleon /'galɪən/ ▷ *noun, historical* a large Spanish ship, usually with three masts, used for war or trade from 15c to 18c. ◷ 16c: from Spanish *galeón*.

galleria /galəri:ə/ ▷ *noun* (***gallerias***) a collection of small shops under one roof. ◷ Early 20c: Italian, related to gallery.

gallery /'galərɪ/ ▷ *noun* (***galleries***) **1** a room or building used to display works of art. **2** a balcony along an inside upper wall, eg of a church or hall, providing extra seating or reserved for musicians, etc □ ***minstrels' gallery***. **3 a** the upper floor in a theatre, usually containing the cheapest seats; **b** the part of the audience seated there. **4** a long narrow room or corridor. **5** an underground passage in a mine or cave. **6** a covered walkway open on one or both sides. **7** the spectators in the stand at a golf, tennis or other tournament. **8** in a TV studio: a soundproof room overlooking the action, for the director or lighting engineer. • **galleried** *adj* **1** having a gallery. **2** made in the form of a gallery or arcade. • **play to the gallery** to seek mass approval or favour by appealing to popular taste. ◷ 15c: from French *galerie*, from Latin *galeria* a covered walkway.

galley /'galɪ/ ▷ *noun* **1** *historical* a long single-deck ship propelled by sails and oars. **2** *historical* a Greek or Roman warship. **3** *historical* a large open rowing boat. **4** *naut* the kitchen on a ship. **5** *printing, publishing* **a** a rectangular tray holding metal pieces of type arranged as text, from which a GALLEY PROOF is made; **b** a galley proof. ◷ 13c: from French *galie*, from Greek *galaia* a low flat boat.

galley proof ▷ *noun* a preliminary PROOF (*noun* 7) of part of a book, etc (taken after the text has been typeset and before it is made up into pages), on which corrections are marked.

galley slave ▷ *noun* **1** *historical* a slave forced to row a galley. **2** *colloq* someone who is given menial tasks; a drudge.

gallfly ▷ *noun* any of various small insects, the larva of which often produces galls in plant tissues (see GALL[2]).

galliard /'galɪəd, -ɑːd/ ▷ *noun* a lively dance for couples, in triple time, popular in 16c and 17c. ◷ 16c in this sense: from French *gaillard* valiant.

Gallic /'galɪk/ ▷ *adj* **1** typically or characteristically French. **2** *historical* relating to ancient Gaul or the Gauls. ◷ 17c: from Latin *gallicus* Gaulish.

gallic acid /'galɪk —/ ▷ *noun, chem* (formula $C_6H_2(OH)_3COOH$) a colourless crystalline compound, obtained from tannins derived from nut-like galls, used in photography, tanning, ink, dyes, antioxidants and pharmaceutical products. ◷ 18c: from GALL[2].

Gallicism /'galɪsɪzəm/ ▷ *noun* a French word or idiom used in another language. ◷ 17c.

Gallicize or **Gallicise** /'galɪsaɪz/ ▷ *verb* (***Gallicized, Gallicizing***) *tr & intr* to assimilate or conform to French attitudes, habits, etc. ◷ 18c.

gallinaceous /galɪ'neɪʃəs/ ▷ *adj, biol* belonging, relating or referring to the order of birds that includes domestic fowl, turkeys, pheasants, grouse, etc. ◷ 18c: from Latin *gallina* hen.

galling ▷ *adj* irritating. • **gallingly** *adverb*. ◷ 17c: from GALL[3].

gallium /'galɪəm/ ▷ *noun* (symbol **Ga**, atomic number 31) a soft silvery metallic element found in zinc blende, bauxite and kaolin, used in alloys with low melting points and in luminous paints. ◷ 19c: from Latin *gallus* cock, from the name of its French discoverer, Lecoq de Boisbaudran (1838–1912).

gallivant /'galɪvant/ ▷ *verb* (***gallivanted, gallivanting***) *intr, humorous or derog, colloq* to go out looking for entertainment or amusement. ◷ 19c: perhaps based on GALLANT.

gallnut /gɔːl—/ ▷ *noun* any round nutlike abnormal growth on the stem or leaf of a plant.

Gallo- /galoʊ/ ▷ *combining form, denoting* **1** France, French, or French people. **2** *historical* Gaul, Gaulish or Gauls. ◷ From Latin *Gallus* a Gaul.

Gallomania ▷ *noun* a passion for all things French. ◷ 19c; see -MANIA.

gallon /'galən/ ▷ *noun* (abbreviation **gal.**) in the imperial system: a unit of liquid measurement equal to four quarts or eight pints, equivalent to 4.546 litres (an **imperial gallon**) in the UK, and 3.785 litres in the USA. • **gallons of something** *colloq* a large amount of it (not always something liquid). ◷ 13c: from French *galon*, from Latin *galletta* a measure of wine.

gallonage /'galənɪdʒ/ ▷ *noun* **1** an amount in gallons. **2** the rate of use in gallons. ◷ 20c.

gallop /'galəp/ ▷ *verb* (***galloped, galloping***) **1** *intr* said of a horse or similar animal: to move at a gallop. **2** *intr* to ride a horse, etc at a gallop. **3 a** to read, talk or do something quickly; **b** to make (a horse, etc) move at a gallop. **4** *intr, colloq* to move, progress or increase very quickly □ ***inflation is galloping out of control***. ▷ *noun* **1** the fastest pace at which a horse or similar animal moves, during which all four legs are off the ground together. **2** a period of riding at this pace. **3** an unusually fast speed. • **galloper** *noun*. • **galloping** *noun, adj*. ◷ 16c: from French *galoper*.

Gallophile /'galoʊfaɪl/ or **Gallophil** /-fɪl/ ▷ *noun* someone who loves all things French. ◷ 19c: GALLO- + -PHILE.

Gallophobia /galoʊ'foʊbɪə/ ▷ *noun* a dislike or fear of all things French. • **Gallophobe** *noun* someone who dislikes or fears all things French. ◷ 19c: GALLO- + -PHOBIA.

Galloway or **galloway** /'galəweɪ/ ▷ *noun* **1 a** a breed of large black hornless cattle; **b** an animal of this breed. **2 a** a breed of small strong horse; **b** an animal of this breed or any small riding horse; **c** *as adj* □ ***a galloway mare***. ◷ 16c: both types of animal were originally from Galloway in SW Scotland.

gallows /'galoʊz/ ▷ *singular noun* **1** a wooden frame on which criminals are put to death by hanging. **2** a similar frame for suspending things. **3** (**the gallows**) death by hanging. ◷ Anglo-Saxon *gealga*.

gallows humour ▷ *noun* humour derived from unpleasant subjects like death and illness; black humour.

gallows tree ▷ *noun, old use* a GALLOWS (sense 1).

gallstone ▷ *noun, pathol* a small hard mass, usually consisting of cholesterol crystals, bile pigments, and calcium salts, that is formed in the gall bladder or one of its ducts.

Gallup poll /'galəp poʊl/ ▷ *noun* a survey of the views of a representative group of people, used to assess overall public opinion, especially with regard to voting intentions. ◷ 1930s: named after G H Gallup (1901–84), US statistician.

galoot /gə'luːt/ ▷ *noun, slang, especially US* a clumsy person. ◷ 19c: originally nautical slang meaning 'a soldier' or 'an inexperienced sailor'.

galop /gə'lɒp, 'galəp/ ▷ *noun, historical* **1** a lively 19c dance for couples. **2** a piece of music for this dance. ◷ 19c: from GALLOP.

galore /gə'lɔː(r)/ ▷ *adverb* (placed after the noun) in large amounts or numbers ▫ *I read books galore.* ◷ 17c: from Irish Gaelic *go leór* to sufficiency, though its use in modern English may be due to Sir Walter Scott, who probably took it from Scottish Gaelic.

galosh or **golosh** /gə'lɒʃ/ ▷ *noun, usually in plural* (***galoshes***) a waterproof overshoe. ◷ 14c, meaning 'wooden clog': from French *galoche*, from Latin *gallicula* a small Gaulish shoe.

galumph /gə'lʌmf/ ▷ *verb* (***galumphed, galumphing***) *intr, colloq* **1** to stride along triumphantly. **2** to walk in a heavy ungainly manner. ◷ 19c: coined by Lewis Carroll, perhaps from GALLOP + TRIUMPH.

galvanic /gal'vanɪk/ ▷ *adj* **1** *physics* **a** relating to or producing an electric current, especially a direct current, by chemical means; **b** said of an electric current, especially a direct current: produced by chemical means. **2** said of behaviour, etc: sudden, or startlingly energetic, as if the result of an electric shock. • **galvanically** *adverb*. ◷ 18c: from GALVANISM.

galvanism /'galvənɪzəm/ ▷ *noun* **1** *medicine, historical* any form of medical treatment involving the application of pulses of electric current to body tissues. **2** *elec, old use* electric current produced by chemical means, eg by means of a cell or battery. ◷ 18c: named after Luigi Galvani (1738–98), Italian scientist.

galvanize or **galvanise** /'galvənaɪz/ ▷ *verb* (***galvanized, galvanizing***) **1** *technical* to coat (a metallic surface, usually iron or steel) with a thin layer of zinc, in order to protect it from corrosion. **2** to stimulate by applying an electric current. • **galvanization** *noun*.

▪ **galvanize someone into something** to stimulate or rouse them to action.

galvanized or **galvanised** ▷ *adj* **1** said of a metallic surface, usually iron or steel: coated with a thin layer of zinc. **2** coated with metal by using GALVANISM.

galvanometer /galvə'nɒmətə(r)/ ▷ *noun* an instrument for detecting or measuring small electric currents by measuring the mechanical movements that result from the electromagnetic forces produced by the current. ◷ 19c: from GALVANISM + -METER.

gam[1] ▷ *noun* a school (of whales).

gam[2] ▷ *noun, slang, chiefly old use* a leg, especially a woman's. ◷ 18c: perhaps from French dialect *gambe* a leg.

gambier or **gambir** /'gambɪə(r)/ ▷ *noun* an astringent substance prepared from the leaves of a climbing shrub of SE Asia, used in tanning and dyeing. ◷ 19c: Malay *gambir* the name of the plant.

gambit /'gambɪt/ ▷ *noun* **1** *chess* a chess move made early in a game, in which a pawn or other piece is sacrificed in order to gain an overall advantage. **2** an initial action or remark inviting a response or establishing a point of view. **3** a piece of trickery; a stratagem. ◷ 17c: from Italian *gambetto* a tripping up.

gamble /'gambəl/ ▷ *verb* (***gambled, gambling***) **1** *tr & intr* to bet (usually money) on the result of a card game, horse race, etc. **2** (*also* **gamble something away**) to lose (money or other assets) through gambling. ▷ *noun* **1** an act of gambling; a bet. **2** a risk or a situation involving risk ▫ *take a gamble.* • **gambler** *noun*. ◷ 18c: from Anglo-Saxon *gamen* to play.

▪ **gamble on something** to take a chance or risk on it ▫ *gamble on the weather being fine.*

gambling ▷ *noun* **1** making a bet. **2** playing a game of chance. **3** taking a risk.

gamboge /gam'boudʒ, -'buːdʒ/ ▷ *noun* **1** a gum resin obtained from various tropical Asian trees, used as a source of a yellow pigment or as a laxative. **2** the yellow pigment derived from this gum resin. ◷ 18c: from scientific Latin *gambogium*, derived from Cambodia, the name of a country in in SE Asia.

gambol /'gambəl/ ▷ *verb* (***gambolled, gambolling***; *US also* ***gamboled, gamboling***) *intr* to jump around playfully. ▷ *noun* jumping around playfully; a frolic. ◷ 16c: from Italian *gamba* leg.

gambrel /'gambrəl/ ▷ *noun* **1** the hock of a horse. **2** (*also* **gambrel roof**) *archit* **a** *Brit* a hipped roof in which the upper parts of the hipped ends take the form of a small vertical gable end; **b** *N Amer* a roof with the lower part at a steeper pitch than the upper. ◷ 16c: from French *gamberel*.

game[1] ▷ *noun* **1** an amusement or pastime. **2** the equipment used for this, eg a board, cards, dice, etc. **3** a competitive activity with rules, involving some form of skill. **4** an occasion on which individuals or teams compete at such an activity; a match. **5** in some sports, eg tennis: a division of a match. **6** (**games**) an event consisting of competitions in various activities, especially sporting ones ▫ *the Commonwealth games.* **7** *colloq, often derog* a type of activity, profession, or business ▫ *the game of politics.* **8** a person's playing ability or style ▫ *her backhand game.* **9** *derog* an activity undertaken light-heartedly ▫ *War is just a game to him.* **10** **a** certain birds and animals which are killed for sport; **b** the flesh of such creatures. **11** *derog, colloq* a scheme, trick or intention ▫ *give the game away* ▫ *What's your game?* ▷ *adj* (***gamer, gamest***) *colloq* **1** (*also* **game for something**) ready and willing to undertake it ▫ *game for a try.* **2** *old use* having plenty of fighting spirit; plucky. ▷ *verb* (***gamed, gaming***) *intr* to gamble. • **gamely** *adverb* bravely, sportingly. • **gameness** *noun*. • **be on the game** *slang* to be a prostitute. • **give the game away** to reveal the truth. • **make game of someone** *old use* to make fun of or laugh at them. • **play the game** to behave fairly. • **the game is up** the plan or trick has failed or has been found out. ◷ Anglo-Saxon *gamen* amusement.

game[2] ▷ *adj, old use* lame. See also GAMMY. ◷ 18c: perhaps from Irish Gaelic *cam* crooked.

Game Boy ▷ *noun, trademark* a hand-held battery-operated device for playing computer games. It has a small screen, direction and function buttons and a slot where various game cartridges can be inserted. See also NINTENDO. ◷ 1980s.

game chips ▷ *plural noun* thinly cut potato chips served with GAME (*noun* 10b).

gamecock ▷ *noun* a cock that is bred and trained for cock-fighting.

game dealer ▷ *noun* a retailer that sells GAME[1] (*noun* 10a) to the public.

gamekeeper ▷ *noun* a person employed to look after and manage the GAME[1] (*noun* 10a) on a country estate.

game laws ▷ *plural noun* laws relating to the protection of GAME[1] (*noun* 10a).

game plan ▷ *noun* strategy or tactics, especially in business or politics.

game point ▷ *noun* the stage in a game at which the next point wins the game.

game preserve ▷ *noun* an area of land stocked with protected wild animals or with game preserved for sport.

gamer see GAME[1] *adj*

game show ▷ *noun* a TV quiz or other game, usually with prizes, and sometimes with celebrities as competitors.

gamesmanship ▷ *noun, derog* the art, practice or process of winning games by trying to disturb or upset one's opponent.

gamest see GAME[1] *adj*

gamester /'geɪmstə(r)/ ▷ *noun* a gambler. ◷ 16c: from GAME[1].

gamete /ˈgamiːt/ ▻ *noun* (***gametes***) *biol* in sexually reproducing organisms: a specialized sex cell, especially an OVUM or SPERM, which fuses with another gamete of the opposite type during fertilization. See also GIFT. • **gametic** /gəˈmɛtɪk/ *adj.* ◷ 19c: from Greek *gameein* to marry.

game theory ▻ *noun, math* the branch of mathematics that is concerned with the analysis of choices and strategies available in a range of activities involving decision-making, eg chess, roulette, military strategies.

gametophyte /gəˈmiːtoʊfaɪt, ˈgamətoʊfaɪt/ ▻ *noun, bot* in plants whose life cycle shows ALTERNATION OF GENERATIONS: a plant of the generation that produces gametes and reproduces sexually. See also SPOROPHYTE. ◷ 19c: GAMETE + -PHYTE.

game warden ▻ *noun* a person who looks after GAME[1] (*noun* 10a) especially in a GAME PRESERVE.

gamey see GAMY

gameyness see under GAMY

gamier and **gamiest** see under GAMY

gamin /ˈgamɪn; *French* gamɛ̃/ ▻ *noun* **1** a cheeky and mischievous little boy. **2** a street urchin. ▻ *adj* **1** said of a little boy: precocious, impish and mischievous. **2** typical of this kind of little boy □ ***gamin features.*** ◷ 19c: French, meaning 'mischievous, playful'.

gamine /ˈgamiːn/ ▻ *noun* a girl or young woman with a mischievous, boyish appearance. ▻ *adj* said of a girl or young woman: boyish and mischievous in appearance. ◷ 19c: French, literally 'a female urchin'.

gaminess see GAMY

gaming ▻ *noun* gambling. Also *as adj and in compounds* □ ***gaming-house*** □ ***gaming-table.*** ◷ 16c: from GAME[1] *verb.*

gamma /ˈgamə/ ▻ *noun* (***gammas***) **1** the third letter of the Greek alphabet. See table at GREEK ALPHABET. **2** a mark indicating the third highest grade or quality. **3** the third element, etc in a series. Compare ALPHA, BETA.

gamma camera ▻ *noun, technical* an imaging device that detects gamma rays and which is used to take photographs of parts of the body into which radioactive compounds have been introduced as TRACERs (sense 3).

gammadion /gaˈmeɪdɪən/ ▻ *noun* (***gammadia*** /-dɪə/) a figure composed of Greek capital gammas, especially a swastika.

gamma globulin /— ˈglɒbjʊlɪn/ ▻ *noun, biol* any of various proteins in blood plasma that confer passive immunity to certain diseases, as well as to disorders resulting from blood incompatibility.

gamma rays ▻ *plural noun, physics* electromagnetic radiation of very high frequency, consisting of high-energy PHOTONs, often produced during radioactive decay. Also called **gamma radiation**.

gammon¹ /ˈgamən/ ▻ *noun* **1** cured meat from the upper leg and hindquarters of a pig, usually cut into thick slices. **2** the back part of a side of bacon including the whole back leg and hindquarters. ◷ 15c: from French *gambon*, from *gambe* leg.

gammon² /ˈgamən/ ▻ *noun, backgammon* a win in which a player removes all their men before their opponent removes any, and which collects a double score. ▻ *verb* (***gammoned***, ***gammoning***) to defeat by a gammon. ◷ 18c.

gammon³ /ˈgamən/ ▻ *noun* **1** *criminal slang* patter; chatter. **2** humbug or nonsense. ▻ *verb* (***gammoned***, ***gammoning***) **1** to pretend. **2** to hoax or deceive. ◷ 18c.

gammy /ˈgamɪ/ ▻ *adj* (***gammier***, ***gammiest***) *colloq, old use* lame with a permanent injury. ◷ 19c: related to GAME[2].

gamo- /gamoʊ, gaˈmɒ/ ▻ *combining form, signifying* **1** reproduction; fertilization. **2** fusion; union. ◷ From Greek *gamos* marriage.

gamopetalous /gamoʊˈpɛtələs/ ▻ *noun, bot* said of a flower: having the petals united at their edges.

-gamous /gəməs/ ▻ *combining form, forming adjectives* **1** having a specified number of marriage partners □ ***bigamous.*** **2** having a specified means of fertilization or reproduction □ ***allogamous.*** ◷ From Greek *gamos* marriage.

gamp ▻ *noun, colloq* an umbrella. ◷ 19c: named after Mrs Gamp, a character in Dickens's novel *Martin Chuzzlewit.*

gamut /ˈgamət/ ▻ *noun* **1** the whole range of anything, eg a person's emotions. **2** *music, historical* **a** a scale of notes; **b** the range of notes produced by a voice or instrument. ◷ 14c: from *gamma* the lowest note on a medieval six-note scale + *ut* the first note (now called DOH) of an early sol-fa notation system.

gamy or **gamey** /ˈgeɪmɪ/ ▻ *adj* (***gamier***, ***gamiest***) **1** said of meat: having the strong taste or smell of game which has been kept for a long time. **2** *colloq* spirited or lively. **3** sensational or scandalous. • **gaminess** or **gameyness** *noun.*

-gamy /gəmɪ/ ▻ *combining form, forming nouns, signifying* **1** marriage to a specified number of partners □ ***bigamy.*** **2** a specified means of fertilization or reproduction □ ***allogamy.*** ◷ From Greek *gamos* marriage.

gander /ˈgandə(r)/ ▻ *noun* **1** a male goose. **2** *colloq* a look □ ***have a gander.*** ◷ Anglo-Saxon *gandra.*

gang¹ ▻ *noun* **1** a group, especially one of criminals or troublemakers. **2** a group of friends, especially children. **3** an organized group of workers. **4** a set of tools arranged so as to be used together. ▻ *verb* (***ganged***, ***ganging***) to arrange (tools) for simultaneous use. ◷ 17c in senses 1 to 3; 14c in sense 4; from Anglo-Saxon *gong* a journeying.

■ **gang up on** or **against someone** to act as a group against them.

■ **gang up with someone** to join in or form a gang with them.

gang² see GANGUE

gang-bang or **gangbang** *slang* ▻ *noun* an instance of sexual intercourse with one woman, usually against her will, by several men in succession. ▻ *verb* (***gang-banged***, ***gang-banging***) to subject (a woman) to a gang-bang. ◷ 1950s.

ganger /ˈgaŋə(r)/ ▻ *noun, colloq* the foreman of a group of workers.

gangland ▻ *noun* the world of organized crime.

gangling /ˈgaŋglɪŋ/ and **gangly** /ˈgaŋglɪ/ ▻ *adj* (***ganglier***, ***gangliest***) tall and thin, and usually awkward in movement. ◷ 19c: from Anglo-Saxon *gangan* to go.

ganglion /ˈgaŋglɪən/ ▻ *noun* (***ganglia*** or ***ganglions***) **1** *anatomy* in the central nervous system: a group of nerve cell bodies, usually enclosed by a sheath or capsule. **2** *pathol* a cyst or swelling that forms on the tissue surrounding a tendon, eg on the back of the hand. **3** *literary* a centre of energy or activity. • **gangliar** *adj.* ◷ 17c: Greek, meaning 'cystic tumour'.

gangplank ▻ *noun* a movable plank, usually with projecting crosspieces fixed to it, serving as a gangway for a ship.

gang plug ▻ *noun* an electrical adaptor with a row of sockets.

gang-rape ▻ *verb* said of a group of males: to rape (a single victim) one after another on a single occasion. ▻ *noun* (*also* **gang rape**) an act or instance or the process of doing this. ◷ 1960s.

gangrene /ˈgaŋgriːn/ ▻ *noun, pathol* the death and subsequent decay of part of the body due to some failure of the blood supply to that region as a result of disease, injury, frostbite, etc. • **gangrenous** /ˈgaŋgrɪnəs/ *adj* **1** affected with gangrene. **2** like gangrene. ◷ 16c: from Greek *gangraina.*

gang saw ▷ *noun* a saw with several blades in a single frame, used in a mill to cut logs into planks.

gangsta /'gaŋstə/ ▷ *noun* **1** a style of RAP MUSIC with violent, and often misogynistic, lyrics or subject matter. **2** a rapper who performs in this style. ⓒ 1990s; representing the pronunciation of GANGSTER.

gangster /'gaŋstə(r)/ ▷ *noun* a member of a gang of violent criminals. • **gangsterism** *noun*. ⓒ 19c.

gangue or **gang** /gaŋ/ ▷ *noun, mining* any of the mainly non-metallic minerals associated with an ore deposit that are not considered to be economically valuable. ⓒ 19c: from German *Gang* a vein of ore.

gangway ▷ *noun* **1 a** a small movable bridge used for getting on and off a ship; **b** the opening on the side of a ship into which this fits. **2** a passage between rows of seats, eg on a plane or in a theatre. ▷ *exclamation* make way!

ganister or **gannister** /'ganɪstə(r)/ ▷ *noun, geol* a hard sedimentary rock containing silica, found beneath coal seams. ⓒ 19c: perhaps named after the quarry at Gannister, Cheshire.

ganja /'gandʒə/ ▷ *noun* marijuana. ⓒ 19c: from Hindi *ganjha* hemp, especially the tops of unfertilized female plants.

gannet /'ganɪt/ ▷ *noun* **1** any of several large seabirds which have a heavy body, white plumage with dark wing tips, a long straight conical bill and webbed feet. **2** *colloq* a greedy person. • **gannetry** *noun* a breeding-place for gannets. ⓒ Anglo-Saxon *ganot*: related to Dutch *gent* gander.

gannister see GANISTER

ganoid /'ganɔɪd/ ▷ *adj, zool* **1** said of the scales of certain primitive fish: rhomboid-shaped with a hard shiny enamel-like outer layer. **2** said of fish: having such scales. ⓒ 19c: from Greek *ganos* brightness; see also -OID.

gansey /'ganzɪ/ ▷ *noun* (***ganseys*** or ***gansies***) a woollen sweater; a JERSEY (sense 1). ⓒ 19c: named after Guernsey, one of the Channel Islands.

gantry /'gantrɪ/ ▷ *noun* (***gantries***) **1** a large metal supporting framework, eg serving as a bridge for a travelling crane, overhead for railway signals, or used at the side of a rocket's launch pad. **2** a stand for barrels. **3** the racks behind a bar in which bottles of alcoholic drink are kept. ⓒ 16c: from Latin *cantherius* a trellis.

gaol and **gaoler** see JAIL

gaolbird see JAILBIRD

gaolbreak see JAILBREAK

gap ▷ *noun* **1** a break or open space, eg in a fence, etc. **2** a break in time; an interval. **3** a difference or disparity □ *the generation gap.* **4** a ravine or gorge. **5** *electronics* **a** a SPARK GAP; **b** a break in a magnetic circuit. • **bridge, close, fill** or **stop a gap** to make good a deficiency. ⓒ 14c: Norse, meaning 'a chasm'.

gape /geɪp/ ▷ *verb* (***gaped, gaping***) *intr* **1** to stare with the mouth open, especially in surprise or wonder. **2** to be or become wide open. **3** to open the mouth wide. ▷ *noun* (***gapes***) **1** a wide opening. **2** an open-mouthed stare. **3** the extent to which the mouth can be opened. • **gaping** *adj* **1** wide open □ *a gaping hole.* **2** astonished. • **gapingly** *adverb*. ⓒ 13c: from Norse *gapa* to open the mouth.

gaper /'geɪpə(r)/ ▷ *noun* **1** *cricket* an easy catch. **2** a bivalve mollusc with a shell open at one end. **3** someone who gapes.

gappy ▷ *adj* (***gappier, gappiest***) full of gaps.

gap site ▷ *noun* in a built-up area: a piece of land lying empty because the building which once stood on it has been demolished.

gap-toothed ▷ *adj* having teeth with noticeable spaces between them.

gar /gɑː(r)/ ▷ *noun* a GARFISH.

garage /'garɑːʒ, 'garɪdʒ, gə'rɑːʒ/ ▷ *noun* **1** a building in which motor vehicles are kept. **2** an establishment where motor vehicles are bought, sold and repaired, often also selling petrol, etc. **3** a filling station. **4** (*in full* **garage music**) a style of pop music played in a loud, energetic and unpolished style (see also GARAGE BAND). • **garagey** *adj* applied to music in the garage style. ▷ *verb* (***garaged, garaging***) to put or keep (a car, etc) in a garage. • **garaging** *noun* accommodation for vehicles. ⓒ 20c: from French *garer* to shelter.

garage band ▷ *noun* an unsophisticated rock group. See also GARAGE 4.

garage sale ▷ *noun* a sale of personal or household items held on the seller's premises, especially in the garage.

garam masala /'garəm mə'sɑːlə, 'gɑːrəm —/ ▷ *noun, cookery* a mixture of spices used in Indian cookery. ⓒ 20c: Hindi, meaning 'hot mixture'.

garb /gɑːb/ *literary* ▷ *noun* **1** clothing, especially as worn by people in a particular job or position □ *priestly garb.* **2** outward appearance. ▷ *verb* (***garbed, garbing***) to dress or clothe. ⓒ 16c: from Italian *garbo* grace.

garbage /'gɑːbɪdʒ/ ▷ *noun* **1** *N Amer, especially US* domestic waste; refuse. *Brit equivalent* RUBBISH. **2** *derog* worthless or poor quality articles or matter. **3** *derog* nonsense. **4** *computing* erroneous, irrelevant or meaningless data, especially data which cannot be recognized by a computer program. **5** any object or objects, discarded from a spacecraft, orbiting in space. ⓒ 15c.

garbage can ▷ *noun, N Amer* **1** a bin for food waste. **2** a rubbish bin. Also called TRASHCAN. *Brit equivalent* DUSTBIN.

garbageman ▷ *noun, N Amer* a dustman or refuse collector.

garble /'gɑːbəl/ ▷ *verb* (***garbled, garbling***) **1** to mix up the details of something unintentionally. **2** to deliberately distort the meaning of something, eg by making important omissions. • **garbled** *adj* said of a report or account: muddled. ⓒ 15c: from Arabic *ghirbal* a sieve.

garbo /'gɑːboʊ/ ▷ *noun* (***garbos***) *Austral colloq* a dustman or refuse collector. ⓒ 20c: from GARBAGE.

garbologist /gɑː'bɒlədʒɪst/ ▷ *noun* **1** *US facetious* a dustman or refuse collector. **2** someone who studies a society's waste materials in order to comment on its people's lifestyle, etc. ⓒ 20c: from GARBAGE.

garbology ▷ *noun, social science* the investigation of the refuse discarded by a society as part of the study of that society. ⓒ 1970s: from GARBAGE.

garçon /'gɑːsɔ̃; *French* garsɔ̃/ ▷ *noun* a waiter, especially a French one, in a restaurant or café. ▷ *exclamation* a call to attract a waiter's attention. ⓒ 19c: French, meaning 'boy'.

garda /'gɑːdə/ ▷ *noun* (***gardaí*** /-diː/) a member of the **Garda Síochána** /— ʃɪə'xɔːnə/, the Police Force in the Irish Republic. ⓒ 20c: Irish Gaelic, literally 'guard'.

garden /'gɑːdən/ ▷ *noun* **1** an area of land, usually one adjoining a house, where grass, trees, ornamental plants, fruit, vegetables, etc, are grown. **2** (*usually* **gardens**) such an area of land, usually of considerable size, with flower beds, lawns, trees, walks, etc, laid out for enjoyment by the public □ *botanical gardens.* **3** a similar smaller place where food and drinks are served outdoors □ *tea garden.* **4** a fertile region □ *Kent is the garden of England.* **5** (**Gardens**, abbreviation Gdns) used in street names. ▷ *adj* **1** said of a plant: cultivated, not wild. **2** belonging to or for use in a garden, or in gardening □ *garden fork.* ▷ *verb* (***gardened, gardening***) *intr* to cultivate, work in or take care of a garden, especially as a hobby. • **gardener** *noun* **1** someone who gardens; someone skilled in gardening. **2** someone whose job is to tend a garden. •

gardening *noun* the laying out and cultivation of gardens. • **everything in the garden is lovely** or **rosy** *colloq* everything is, or seems to be, fine. • **lead someone up the garden path** *colloq* to mislead or deceive them deliberately. ◎ 14c: from French *gardin*, variant of *jardin*.

garden centre ▷ *noun* a place where plants, seeds, garden tools, etc are sold.

garden city ▷ *noun* a spacious modern town designed with trees, private gardens and numerous public parks.

gardenia /gɑːˈdiːnɪə/ ▷ *noun* (***gardenias***) **1** an evergreen shrub or small tree, native to tropical and subtropical regions, with glossy leaves and flattened rosettes of large, usually white, fragrant flowers. **2** the flower produced by this plant. ◎ 18c: named after Dr Alexander Garden (1730–91), US botanist.

garden leave and **gardening leave** ▷ *noun, colloq* compulsory paid leave between the time someone gives or is given notice that they are leaving a post of employment and the day on which they do leave it.

Garden of Eden see EDEN 1

garden party ▷ *noun* a formal party held in a large private garden.

garden suburb ▷ *noun* a residential area on the outskirts of a town or city, that has plenty of open spaces, parks, etc.

garfish /ˈgɑːfɪʃ/ and **garpike** ▷ *noun* any of various slim fast-swimming fishes with a long beak-like mouth containing many sharp teeth.

gargantuan or **Gargantuan** /gɑːˈgantjʊən/ ▷ *adj* enormous; colossal. ◎ 16c: named after *Gargantua*, the greedy giant in Rabelais's novel *Gargantua and Pantagruel* (1534).

gargle /ˈgɑːgəl/ ▷ *verb* (***gargled, gargling***) *tr & intr* to cleanse, treat or freshen the mouth and throat by breathing out through (a medicinal liquid) that is held there for a while before spitting it out. ▷ *noun* (***gargles***) **1** an act of gargling or the sound produced while gargling. **2** the liquid used. ◎ 16c: from French *gargouille* throat.

gargoyle /ˈgɑːgɔɪl/ ▷ *noun* **1** a grotesque carved open-mouthed head or figure acting as a rainwater spout from a roof-gutter, especially on a church. **2** any grotesque figure or person. ◎ 15c: from French *gargouille* throat.

garial see GHARIAL

garibaldi or **Garibaldi** /garɪˈbɔːldɪ, -ˈbɒldɪ/ ▷ *noun* (***garibaldis***) (*in full* **garibaldi biscuit**) *Brit* a kind of flat, oblong biscuit containing currants. ◎ 19c: named after G Garibaldi (1807–82), Italian patriot, apparently arbitrarily.

garish /ˈgɛərɪʃ/ ▷ *adj, derog* unpleasantly bright or colourful; very gaudy. • **garishly** *adverb*. • **garishness** *noun*. ◎ 16c: from obsolete *gaurish*, from *gaure* to stare.

garland /ˈgɑːlənd/ ▷ *noun* **1** a circular arrangement of flowers or leaves worn round the head or neck, or hung up as a decoration. **2** a collection of short poems or pieces of prose. ▷ *verb* (***garlanded, garlanding***) to decorate something or someone with a garland. ◎ 14c: from French *garlande*.

garlic /ˈgɑːlɪk/ ▷ *noun* **1** a perennial plant of the onion family, widely cultivated for its underground bulb, which is divided into segments known as cloves. **2** the bulb of this plant, which contains a pungent oil and is widely used as a flavouring in cooking. • **garlicky** *adj* smelling or tasting of garlic. ◎ Anglo-Saxon *garleac*, from *gar* spear + *leac* leek.

garment /ˈgɑːmənt/ ▷ *noun, now rather formal* an article of clothing. ◎ 14c: from French *garniment*, from *garnir* to supply.

garner /ˈgɑːnə(r)/ ▷ *verb* (***garnered, garnering***) *formal or literary* to collect and usually store (information, knowledge, etc). ◎ 12c: from Latin *granarium* granary.

garnet /ˈgɑːnɪt/ ▷ *noun* any of various silicate minerals found mainly in metamorphic rocks, especially a deep red variety used as a semi-precious stone. ◎ 13c: from Latin *granatum* pomegranate.

garni /ˈgɑːniː; *French* garni/ ▷ *adj, following its noun, cookery* with a garnish.

garnish /ˈgɑːnɪʃ/ ▷ *verb* (***garnishes, garnished, garnishing***) **1** to decorate (especially food to be served). **2** *law* **a** to ATTACH (sense 4) (a debt) with a GARNISHMENT; **b** to serve someone with a GARNISHMENT. ▷ *noun* (***garnishes***) a decoration, especially one added to food. ◎ 14c: from French *garnir* to supply.

garnishee order ▷ *noun, law* a court order which requires a party A not to pay money owed by them to B, but instead to give it to C, because B owes money to C and it is C who has obtained the order.

garnishment ▷ *noun* **1** *literary* a decoration or adornment. **2** *law* a legal warning, often to ATTACH (sense 4) a debt.

garniture /ˈgɑːnɪtʃə(r)/ ▷ *noun usually formal or literary* decorations, embellishments or accessories. ◎ 16c: French.

garotte see GARROTTE

garpike see GARFISH

garran see GARRON

garret /ˈgarət/ ▷ *noun* an attic room, often a dingy one. ◎ 14c, meaning 'watchtower': from French *garite* refuge.

garrison /ˈgarɪsən/ ▷ *noun* **1** a body of soldiers stationed in a town or fortress in order to defend it. **2** the building or fortress they occupy. ◎ 13c: from French *garison*, from *garir* to protect.

garron or **garran** /ˈgarən/ ▷ *noun* a small horse, used especially in Ireland and Scotland. ◎ 16c: from Irish *gearran*.

garrotte or **garotte** or (*US*) **garrote** /gəˈrɒt/ ▷ *noun* **1** a wire loop or metal collar that can be tightened around the neck to cause strangulation. **2** this method of execution. ▷ *verb* (***garrotted, garrotting***) **1** to execute or kill with a garrotte. **2** to make someone unconscious by semi-strangulation in order to rob them. • **garrotter** *noun*. • **garrotting** *noun*. ◎ 17c: from Spanish *garrote*.

garrulous /ˈgarʊləs, ˈgarjʊləs/ ▷ *adj* **1** said of a person: tending to talk a lot, especially about trivial things. **2** *derog* said of a speech, etc: long and wordy. • **garrulousness** or **garrulity** /gəˈruːlɪtɪ, gəˈrjuː-/ *noun*. ◎ 17c: from Latin *garrulus*, from *garrire* to chatter.

garryowen /garɪˈoʊɪn/ ▷ *noun, rugby* a high kick forward that the kicker follows up with a rush towards the landing-place of the ball. Also called **up-and-under**. ◎ 1960s: named after Garryowen rugby club in Limerick.

garter /ˈgɑːtə(r)/ ▷ *noun* **1** a band of tight material, usually elastic, worn on the leg to hold up a stocking or sock. **2** (**the Garter**) **a** the highest order of British knighthood; **b** membership of the order; **c** the emblem of the order, a blue garter. **3** (**Garter**) short form of **Garter King of Arms**, the chief herald of the English COLLEGE OF ARMS. ◎ 14c: from French *gartier*, from *garet* the bend of the knee.

garter snake ▷ *noun* any of several non-venomous snakes found in N and C America, that have stripes running along the length of their bodies.

garter stitch ▷ *noun* **1** a plain stitch in knitting. **2** horizontally ribbed knitting made by knitting in plain stitch only.

gas ▷ *noun* (***gases***) **1** a form of matter that has no fixed shape, is easily compressed, and which will expand to occupy all the space available because its molecules are in constant rapid motion and can move about freely and independently of each other. **2** a substance or mixture of substances which is in this state at ordinary temperatures, eg hydrogen, air. **3 a** NATURAL GAS used as a source of fuel for heating, lighting or cooking; **b** *as adj* □ *gas cooker.* **4** a gas, especially nitrous oxide, used as an anaesthetic. **5** FIREDAMP, explosive in contact with air. **6** a poisonous gas used as a weapon in war. **7** *N Amer, Austral, NZ colloq* gasoline; petrol. **8** *colloq, especially N Amer* an amusing or entertaining event, situation or person □ *The film was a real gas!* **9** *derog colloq* foolish talk; boasting. ▷ *verb* (*gasses, gassed, gassing*) **1** to poison or kill (people or animals) with gas. **2** *intr, derog colloq* to chat, especially at length, boastfully or about trivial things. ⓒ 17c: coined by J B van Helmont, Belgian chemist (1577–1644), after Greek *chaos* atmosphere.

gasbag ▷ *noun, derog, colloq* someone who talks a lot or too much.

gas chamber ▷ *noun* a sealed room which can be filled with poisonous gas and used for killing people or animals.

gas chromatography ▷ *noun* a form of CHROMATOGRAPHY that is used to identify the components of a mixture of gases and which is often also used to separate them.

gaseous /'gasɪəs, 'geɪʃəs/ ▷ *adj* in the form of, or like, gas. • **gaseousness** *noun.*

gasfield ▷ *noun* a region that is rich in economically valuable NATURAL GAS.

gas fitter ▷ *noun* someone whose job is to fit the pipes, etc for gas appliances.

gas gangrene ▷ *noun, pathol* a form of GANGRENE in which gas accumulates within the injured tissue.

gas guzzler ▷ *noun, slang, originally US* a car that uses large amounts of petrol.

gash ▷ *noun* (*gashes*) a deep open cut or wound. ▷ *verb* (*gashes, gashed, gashing*) to make a gash in something. ⓒ 16c: from French *garser* to scratch or wound.

gas holder ▷ *noun* a GASOMETER.

gasify /'gasɪfaɪ/ ▷ *verb* (*gasifies, gasified, gasifying*) to convert something into gas, especially to convert coal into a gaseous hydrocarbon fuel. • **gasification** *noun.*

gas jar ▷ *noun* a tall narrow cylindrical glass container for collecting and holding gas in chemical experiments.

gas jet ▷ *noun* **1** the perforated part of a gas appliance where the gas issues and is burned. **2** a gas flame.

gasket /'gaskɪt/ ▷ *noun* **1** a compressible ring or sheet made of rubber, paper or asbestos that fits tightly in the join between two metal surfaces to form an airtight seal. **2** *naut* a cord or band for securing a furled sail to the yard. • **blow a gasket** *colloq* to become extremely angry. ⓒ 17c in sense 2.

gaslight ▷ *noun* **1** a lamp powered by gas. **2** the light from such a lamp.

gas main ▷ *noun* a principal pipe conveying gas from the gasworks.

gas man ▷ *noun* a man whose job is to install gas appliances and deal with gas repairs, leaks and meter-reading for domestic customers.

gas mantle ▷ *noun* a MANTLE (*noun* 4) for use in a gas lamp.

gas mask ▷ *noun* a type of mask that is used in warfare and certain industries to filter out any poisonous gases.

gas meter ▷ *noun* a device that measures and records the amount of gas used, eg by a domestic customer.

gasohol /'gasəhɒl/ ▷ *noun* a mixture of petrol and a small amount of alcohol, used as fuel.

gasoline /'gasəliːn/ ▷ *noun, N Amer* petrol. Often shortened to GAS.

gasometer /ga'sɒmɪtə(r)/ ▷ *noun* **1** a large metal tank, the top section of which can move freely up and down, used for storing COAL GAS or NATURAL GAS before it is distributed to customers. Also called **gas holder**. **2** any container that is used for holding and measuring gas, especially for the purpose of chemical analysis, eg to measure the volume of gas evolved during a chemical reaction.

gasp /gɑːsp/ ▷ *verb* (*gasped, gasping*) **1** *intr* to take a sharp breath in, through surprise, sudden pain, etc. **2** *intr* to breathe in with difficulty, eg because of illness, exhaustion, etc. **3** (*also* **gasp something out**) to say it breathlessly. ▷ *noun* a sharp intake of breath. • **at the last gasp** **1** at the point just before death. **2** at the last minute. ⓒ 14c: from Norse *geispa* to yawn.

■ **be gasping for something** *colloq* to want or need it very much □ *gasping for a cuppa.*

gasper ▷ *noun* **1** *slang* a cheap cigarette. **2** someone who gasps.

gas-permeable ▷ *adj* said of hard contact lenses: allowing oxygen to penetrate through to the eye.

gas plasma display ▷ *noun, computing* a kind of screen display used on portable computers in which electronic signals form illuminated characters on a flat screen.

gas poker ▷ *noun* a poker-shaped gas appliance with GAS JETs that can be inserted into fuel to kindle a flame.

gas ring ▷ *noun* a hollow ring with perforations that serve as GAS JETS.

gasses see under GAS

gassy ▷ *adj* (*gassier, gassiest*) **1** like gas; full of gas. **2** *derog, colloq* talking a lot, especially about unimportant things. • **gassiness** *noun.*

Gastarbeiter or **gastarbeiter** /'gastɑːbaɪtə(r)/ ▷ *noun* an immigrant worker, especially one who does menial work, originally and especially in Germany. ⓒ 20c: German, meaning 'guest-worker'.

gasteropod see GASTROPOD

gastr- see GASTRO-

gastric /'gastrɪk/ ▷ *adj, medicine, etc* relating to or affecting the stomach. ⓒ 17c: from Greek *gaster* belly.

gastric flu ▷ *noun, colloq* a popular term for any of several disorders of the stomach and intestinal tract, the main symptoms of which are nausea, diarrhoea, abdominal cramps and fever.

gastric juice ▷ *noun, biochem* a strongly acidic fluid produced by the gastric glands of the stomach wall during the digestion of food.

gastritis /ga'straɪtɪs/ ▷ *noun, medicine* inflammation of the lining of the stomach. ⓒ Early 19c: GASTR- + -ITIS.

gastro- /gastroʊ, ga'strɒ/ or (before a vowel) **gastr-** ▷ *combining form, signifying* the stomach. ⓒ From Greek *gaster* belly.

gastroenteritis ▷ *noun, medicine* inflammation of the lining of the stomach and intestine, usually caused by bacterial or viral infection, food poisoning, or excessive alcohol consumption. ⓒ 19c.

gastronome /'gastrənoʊm/ or **gastronomist** /ga'strɒnəmɪst/ ▷ *noun* a person who enjoys, and has developed a taste for, good food and wine. ⓒ 19c: from GASTRO- + Greek *nomos* law.

gastronomy /ga'strɒnəmɪ/ ▷ *noun* **1** the appreciation and enjoyment of good food and wine. **2** (**gastronomics**) the style of cooking typical of a particular country or region. • **gastronomic** /gastrə'nɒmɪk/ *adj.*

gastropod or **gasteropod** /'gastəroʊpɒd/ ▷ *noun, biol* any member of a class of invertebrate animals which typically possess a large flattened muscular foot and often have a single spirally coiled shell, eg snail, slug, whelk, winkle. ⓒ 19c: GASTRO- + -POD.

gastroscope ▻ *noun* (***gastroscopes***) *medicine* an instrument for inspecting the interior of the stomach. Ⓒ 19c.

gas turbine ▻ *noun* an engine that passes the products of combustion of a mixture of fuel and air over the blades of a turbine which, in turn, drives an air compressor that provides the energy for the combustion process.

gasworks ▻ *singular noun* a place where gas is manufactured from coal.

gat[1] /gɑːt/ ▻ *noun* in Indian music: the second and usually final section of a RAGA. Ⓒ 20c: from Sanskrit *gath*.

gat[2] /gat/ ▻ *verb, archaic past tense of* GET

gate /geɪt/ ▻ *noun* **1 a** a door or barrier, usually a hinged one, which is moved in order to open or close an entrance in a wall, fence, etc leading eg into a garden, field or city; **b** the entrance itself. **2** at an airport: any of the numbered exits from which passengers can board or leave a plane. **3** the total number of people attending a sports event or other entertainment. **4** (*also* **gate money**) the total money paid in admission fees to an entertainment. **5** *skiing* any of the pairs of posts that a slalom skier passes through. **6** *technical* an electronic circuit whose output is controlled by the combination of signals at the input terminals. **7** *mech* the H-shaped slotted frame which controls the movement of the gear lever in a gearbox. ▻ *verb* (***gated***, ***gating***) to confine (pupils) to school after hours. • **gating** *noun* **a** confinement of pupils to school after hours; **b** an instance of this. Ⓒ Anglo-Saxon *geat* a way.

-gate /geɪt/ ▻ *suffix* (attached to the name of a person or place) *signifying* a scandal connected with them or it ▫ *Camillagate* ▫ *Irangate*. Ⓒ 20c: modelled on *Watergate*.

gateau or **gâteau** /ˈgatoʊ/ ▻ *noun* (***gateaux***, ***gâteaux*** or ***gateaus*** /-toʊz/) a large rich cake, especially one filled with cream and decorated with fruit, nuts, etc. Ⓒ 20c in this sense: French *gâteau* a cake.

gatecrash ▻ *verb, tr & intr, colloq* to join or attend (a party, meeting, etc) uninvited or without paying. • **gatecrasher** *noun*.

gated ▻ *adj* **1** having a gate or gates. **2** said of a pupil, etc: punished by GATING (see under GATE).

gatefold ▻ *noun* a FOLDOUT.

gatehouse ▻ *noun* a building at or above the gateway to a city, castle, etc, often occupied by the person who guards it.

gateleg table ▻ *noun* a table that has a hinged and framed leg or legs that can be swung out to support a leaf or leaves in order to make the table bigger.

gate money see under GATE *noun* 4

gatepost ▻ *noun* either of the posts on each side of a gate.

gateway ▻ *noun* **1** an entrance, especially to a city, park, etc, with a gate across it. **2** *computing, etc* a connection between computer networks, or between a computer network and a telephone line. • **gateway to somewhere** or **something 1** a way to or into it ▫ *Stirling, the gateway to the Highlands*. **2** a means of acquiring it ▫ *the gateway to success*.

gather /ˈgaðə(r)/ ▻ *verb* (***gathered***, ***gathering***) **1** *tr & intr* (*also* **gather together**) to bring or come together in one place. **2** (*also* **gather something in**) to collect, pick or harvest it. **3** to pick something up. **4** to increase in (speed or force). **5** to accumulate or become covered with (eg dust). **6** to learn or understand something from information received. **7** to pull (material) into small folds, usually by sewing it with one or more threads and then pulling the cloth over these. **8** to pull (a garment) closely round the body. **9** to pull someone or something close to oneself ▫ *She gathered the child into her arms*. **10** to wrinkle (the brow). **11** to draw together or muster (strength, courage, etc) in preparation for something. **12** *intr* said of a boil, etc: to form a head. ▻ *noun* a small fold in material, often stitched. Ⓒ Anglo-Saxon *gaderian*.

■ **gather oneself together** to prepare for action.

gathering ▻ *noun* **1** a meeting or assembly. **2** a series of gathers in material.

gating see under GATE

gatling gun or **gatling** /gatlɪŋ —/ ▻ *noun* a type of machine gun with a cluster of rotating barrels which are automatically loaded. It was first used during the American Civil War. Ⓒ 19c: named after its inventor Dr R J Gatling (1818–1903).

GATT /gat/ ▻ *abbreviation* General Agreement on Tariffs and Trade, an international treaty to promote trade and economic benefits, signed in 1947.

gauche /goʊʃ/ ▻ *adj* (***gaucher***, ***gauchest***) ill-at-ease, awkward in social situations. • **gauchely** *adverb*. • **gaucheness** *noun*. Ⓒ 18c: French, meaning 'left, left-handed, awkward'.

gaucherie /ˈgoʊʃərɪ/ ▻ *noun* **1** social awkwardness. **2** an instance of this. Ⓒ 18c: French.

gaucho /ˈgaʊtʃoʊ/ ▻ *noun* **1** a modern cowboy of the S American plains. **2** (**gauchos**) women's knee-length wide trousers. Ⓒ 19c: American Spanish.

gaud /gɔːd/ ▻ *noun, dated* **1** a showy ornament. **2** *usually derog* a piece of finery. Ⓒ 16c; 14c in old sense 'a prank': from Latin *gaudere* to rejoice.

gaudy[1] /ˈgɔːdɪ/ ▻ *adj* (***gaudier***, ***gaudiest***) *derog* coarsely and brightly coloured or decorated. • **gaudily** *adverb*. • **gaudiness** *noun*. Ⓒ 16c: from GAUD.

gaudy[2] /ˈgɔːdɪ/ (***gaudies***) ▻ *noun, Brit* in some schools and colleges: an entertainment or feast. Ⓒ 16c: from Latin *gaudere* to rejoice.

gauge or (*US*) **gage** /geɪdʒ/ ▻ *verb* (***gauged***, ***gauging***; *US* ***gaged***, ***gaging***) **1** to measure something accurately. **2** to estimate or guess (a measurement, size, etc). **3** to judge or appraise. **4** to adjust something so as to match a standard. ▻ *noun* **1** any of various instruments that are used to measure a quantity such as weight, volume, pressure, etc ▫ *pressure gauge*. **2** each of the standard sizes used in measuring articles (especially by diameter) such as wire, bullets or knitting needles. **3** on a railway: **a** the distance between the inner faces of the rails on a line, in Britain **standard gauge** and **broad gauge** being broader and narrower respectively than the **narrow gauge** of 56.5in (1.435m); **b** the distance between wheels on an axle. **4** the width of film or magnetic tape. **5** a standard against which other things are measured or judged. • **gaugeable** or (*US*) **gageable** *adj*. Ⓒ 15c: French.

Gaul /gɔːl/ ▻ *noun, historical* an inhabitant of, or a person born in, ancient Gaul, which consisted of what is now France, Belgium and adjacent parts of Italy, Germany and the Netherlands. See also GALLIC. Ⓒ 17c: from Latin *Gallus*.

gauleiter /ˈgaʊlaɪtə(r)/ ▻ *noun* **1** *historical* under the Nazi regime: a chief official of a district. **2** an overbearing wielder of petty authority. Ⓒ 20c: German *Gauleiter* in sense 1, from *Gau* district + *Leiter* leader.

Gaulish *historical* ▻ *noun* the language of the Gauls. ▻ *adj* belonging or relating to the Gauls or their language.

Gaullist /ˈgɔːlɪst, ˈgoʊ-/ ▻ *noun* a follower of the French soldier and statesman General Charles de Gaulle, President of the Fifth Republic 1958–69. Also *as adj*. • **Gaullism** *noun*.

gaunt /gɔːnt/ ▻ *adj* **1** thin or thin-faced; lean, haggard. **2** said of a place: barren and desolate. • **gauntly** *adverb*. • **gauntness** *noun*. Ⓒ 15c.

gauntlet[1] /ˈgɔːntlət/ ▻ *noun* **1** *historical* a metal or metal-plated glove worn by medieval soldiers. **2** a heavy protective leather glove loosely covering the wrist. • **take**

up the gauntlet to accept a challenge. • **throw down the gauntlet** to make a challenge. ⓘ 15c: from French *gantelet*, diminutive of *gant* glove; the idioms are derived from the former practice of throwing a gauntlet on the ground when issuing a challenge to a duel and picking it up when accepting such a challenge.

gauntlet² /'gɔːntlət/ ▻ *noun* • **run the gauntlet 1** to expose oneself to hostile treatment or criticism. **2** *historical* to suffer the military punishment of having to scramble along between two rows of men while receiving hard blows from them. ⓘ 17c: altered (under the influence of GAUNTLET¹) from obsolete *gantlope*, from Swedish *gatlopp* passageway.

gauss /gɑʊs/ ▻ *noun* (**gauss**) *physics* the cgs unit of magnetic flux density, which in the SI system has been replaced by the TESLA. ⓘ 19c: named after J K F Gauss (1777–1855), German mathematician and physicist.

Gaussian /'gɑʊsɪən/ ▻ *adj* **1** *physics* discovered by, relating to or named after Gauss (see GAUSS). **2** *statistics* referring or relating to a normal distribution.

gauze /gɔːz/ ▻ *noun* **1** thin transparent fabric, especially cotton muslin as used to dress wounds. **2** thin wire mesh. • **gauzy** *adj* (**gauzier**, **gauziest**). • **gauzily** *adverb*. • **gauziness** *noun*. ⓘ 16c: from French *gaze*.

gave *past tense of* GIVE

gavel /'gavəl/ ▻ *noun* a small hammer used by a judge, auctioneer, etc to call attention. ⓘ 19c.

gavial /'geɪvɪəl/ ▻ *noun* see GHARIAL.

gavotte /gə'vɒt/ ▻ *noun* **1** a lively French country dance that was popular during the 18c. **2** a piece of music for this or in this rhythm. ⓘ 17c: French, meaning 'the dance of the Gavots or Alpine people'.

gawk /gɔːk/ *colloq* ▻ *verb* (**gawked**, **gawking**) *intr* to stare blankly or stupidly; to gawp. ▻ *noun, derog* an awkward, clumsy or stupid person. ⓘ 18c: perhaps from obsolete *gaw* to stare.

gawky /'gɔːkɪ/ ▻ *adj* (**gawkier**, **gawkiest**) *colloq, derog* awkward-looking, ungainly, and usually tall and thin. • **gawkily** *adverb*. • **gawkiness** *noun*.

gawp /gɔːp/ ▻ *verb* (**gawped**, **gawping**) *intr, colloq* to stare stupidly, especially open-mouthed; to gape. ⓘ 14c as *galpen* to yawn.

gay /geɪ/ ▻ *adj* (**gayer**, **gayest**) **1** homosexual; relating to, frequented by, or intended for, homosexuals ▫ *a gay bar*. ⓘ first attested in the 1930s, though it may have been in use earlier; now the principal sense, so much so that to use *gay* in any other sense causes raised eyebrows or a titter. Compare QUEER *adj* 1. **2** happily carefree. **3** bright and attractive. **4** fun-loving or pleasure-seeking. ▻ *noun* a homosexual. • **gayness** *noun* the state of being gay, especially in the sense 'homosexual'. ⓘ 14c in senses 3 and 4: from French *gai*.

gay plague ▻ *noun, dated offensive slang,* AIDS. ⓘ 1980s: from the disease's early epidemiology in the US, among the homosexual population.

gazar /ga'zɑː(r)/ ▻ *noun* a silk fabric of loose construction with a stiff finish. ⓘ 1990s: French, from *gaze* GAUZE.

gaze /geɪz/ ▻ *verb* (**gazed**, **gazing**) *intr* (*especially* **gaze at something** or **someone**) to stare fixedly, usually for a long time. ▻ *noun* a fixed stare. ⓘ 14c as *gasen*.

gazebo /gə'ziːboʊ/ ▻ *noun* (**gazebos** or **gazeboes**) a small summerhouse or open hut, especially in a garden, and usually situated in a place that offers pleasant views. ⓘ 18c: perhaps coined from GAZE.

gazelle /gə'zɛl/ ▻ *noun* (**gazelles** or **gazelle**) a fawn-coloured antelope with a white rump and belly, and black-and-white face markings, found in arid plains of Africa and Asia. ⓘ 17c: French, from Arabic *ghazal* wild goat.

gazette /gə'zɛt/ ▻ *noun* **1** an official newspaper giving lists of government, military and legal notices. **2** *often facetious* a newspaper. ▻ *verb* (**gazetted**, **gazetting**) *formal* to announce or publish something in an official gazette. ⓘ 17c: from Venetian dialect *gazeta*, from *gazet* a small coin or the cost of an early news-sheet.

gazetteer /gazə'tɪə(r)/ ▻ *noun* a book or part of a book which lists place names and describes the places. ⓘ 18c in this sense: from GAZETTE.

gazpacho /gəz'patʃoʊ/ ▻ *noun* (**gazpachos**) a spicy Spanish vegetable soup, served cold. ⓘ 19c: Spanish.

gazump /gə'zʌmp/ ▻ *verb* (**gazumped**, **gazumping**) *colloq* said of someone selling a property: to raise the price that has already been verbally agreed with (a prospective buyer), usually because someone else has offered a higher price. • **gazumper** *noun*. • **gazumping** *noun*. ⓘ 1970s in this sense; 1920s as *gazoomph*, meaning 'swindle': from Yiddish *gezumph* to swindle.

gazunder /gə'zʌndə(r)/ ▻ *verb* (**gazundered**, **gazundering**) said of a buyer: to lower the sum offered to (a seller of property) just before contracts are due to be signed. ⓘ 1980s: humorously based on GAZUMP and UNDER.

GB ▻ *abbreviation* Great Britain.

GBA ▻ *abbreviation, IVR* Great Britain, Alderney (ie Alderney, Channel Islands).

GBE ▻ *abbreviation* **1** Grand Cross of the British Empire. **2** Knight or Dame Grand Cross of the British Empire.

GBG ▻ *abbreviation, IVR* Great Britain, Guernsey (ie Guernsey, Channel Islands).

GBH or **gbh** ▻ *abbreviation* grievous bodily harm.

GBJ ▻ *abbreviation, IVR* Great Britain, Jersey (ie Jersey, Channel Islands).

GBM ▻ *abbreviation, IVR* Great Britain, Man (ie Isle of Man).

GBZ ▻ *abbreviation, IVR* Great Britain, Zakak (ie Gibraltar). From the Arabic name for the Strait of Gibraltar, *Bab al Zakak*.

GC ▻ *abbreviation* GEORGE CROSS

GCA ▻ *abbreviation* **1** *aeronautics* **a** ground control apparatus; **b** ground control approach system; **c** ground controlled approach system. **2** *IVR* Guatemala, Central America.

GCB ▻ *abbreviation* **1** Grand Cross of the Order of the Bath. **2** Knight or Dame Grand Cross of the Order of the Bath.

GCE ▻ *abbreviation* GENERAL CERTIFICATE OF EDUCATION. ▻ *noun* (**GCEs**) **1** a subject in which an examination is taken at this level. **2** an examination pass or a certificate gained at this level.

GCHQ ▻ *abbreviation, Brit* Government Communication Headquarters.

G-clef ▻ *noun, music* the TREBLE CLEF.

GCMG ▻ *abbreviation* **1** Grand Cross of the Order of St Michael and St George. **2** Knight or Dame Grand Cross of the Order of St Michael and St George.

GCSE ▻ *abbreviation* GENERAL CERTIFICATE OF SECONDARY EDUCATION. ▻ *noun* (**GCSEs**) **1** a subject in which an examination is taken at this level. **2** an examination pass or a certificate gained at this level.

GCVO ▻ *abbreviation* **1** Grand Cross of the Royal Victorian Order. **2** Knight or Dame Grand Cross of the Royal Victorian Order.

Gd ▻ *symbol, chem* gadolinium.

g'day /gə'deɪ/ ▻ *exclamation, Austral colloq* the usual greeting at any time of day. ⓘ 19c as *good day*.

Gdns ▻ *abbreviation* especially in street names: Gardens.

GDP ▻ *abbreviation* gross domestic product.

GDR ▻ *abbreviation* German Democratic Republic, the former republic of East Germany.

Ge ▻ *symbol, chem* germanium.

gean /giːn/ ▻ *noun* the European wild cherry. © 16c: from French *guigne*.

gear /gɪə(r)/ ▻ *noun* **1** (*also* **gearwheel**) a toothed wheel or disc that engages with another wheel or disc having a different number of teeth, and turns it, so transmitting motion from one rotating shaft to another. **2** the specific combination of such wheels or discs that is being used □ *second gear* □ *low gear* □ *to change gear.* **3** *colloq* the equipment or tools needed for a particular job, sport, etc. **4** *aeronautics* landing gear. **5** *colloq* personal belongings. **6** *colloq* clothes, especially young people's current fashion. **7** *slang* drugs. ▻ *verb* (***geared***, ***gearing***) to supply something with, or connect it by, gears. ● **in gear** said especially of a motor vehicle: with a gear selected. ● **out of gear 1** said of a motor vehicle: with no gear selected. **2** not working properly. © 13c as *gere* in obsolete sense 'arms' or 'equipment': from Norse *gervi*.

■ **gear something to** or **towards something else** to adapt or design it to suit (a particular need).

■ **gear oneself up** to become or make oneself ready or prepared.

■ **gear something up** *finance* to raise the GEARING of (a company).

gearbox ▻ *noun* **1** especially in a motor vehicle: the set or system of gears that transmits power from the engine to the road wheels, allowing the road speed to be varied while maintaining the engine speed at a constant high level. **2** the metal casing that encloses such a set or system of gears.

gearing ▻ *noun* **1** a set of gearwheels as a means of transmission of motion. **2** the arrangement of gears on a particular machine or device. **3** *finance* **a** the ratio of a company's ordinary shares to shares with fixed interest; **b** the ratio of a company's equity to its debts.

gear lever and **gear stick** and (*N Amer*) **gearshift** ▻ *noun* a lever or similar device for engaging and disengaging gears, especially in a motor vehicle, by moving the gearwheels in relation to each other.

gear ratio ▻ *noun* **1** the ratio of the number of teeth on two engaged gearwheels. **2** in a motor vehicle: the number of revolutions made by the engine per revolution made by the rear wheels.

gearshift see GEAR LEVER

gearwheel see under GEAR

GEC ▻ *abbreviation, Brit* General Electric Company.

gecko /ˈgɛkoʊ/ ▻ *noun* (***geckos*** or ***geckoes***) any of numerous mainly nocturnal lizards found in warm countries, known for their chirping or barking calls and for the ease with which some species can climb smooth vertical surfaces. © 18c: from Malay *gekoq*, imitating the sound it makes.

gee[1] /dʒiː/ ▻ *exclamation* (*usually* **gee up**) used to encourage a horse to move, or to go faster. ▻ *verb* (***geed***, ***geeing***) to encourage (a horse, etc) to move or move faster.

■ **gee someone up** *colloq* to encourage them to work or perform better, more quickly, etc.

gee[2] /dʒiː/ ▻ *exclamation, colloq* expressing surprise, admiration or enthusiasm. Also **gee whiz**. © 20c: from *Jesus*.

gee-gee /ˈdʒiːdʒiː/ ▻ *noun* (***gee-gees***) *colloq* **1** used especially to or by small children: a horse. **2** (**the gee-gees**) used especially in relation to betting on horse-racing: the horses. © 19c.

geek /giːk/ *N Amer slang* ▻ *noun* **1** a circus freak or sideshow performer. **2** a strange or eccentric person. **3** a creep or misfit. ● **geeky** *adj*. © 16c as *geke*: from Dutch *geck* a fool.

geep /giːp/ ▻ *noun* a creature produced by artificially combining DNA from a *g*oat and a sh*eep*. © 1980s.

geese *plural of* GOOSE

gee-string see G-STRING

gee up see under GEE[1]

gee whiz see under GEE[2]

geezer /ˈgiːzə(r)/ ▻ *noun, colloq* a man, especially an old man, often one who is odd in some way. © 19c: from a dialect pronunciation of *guiser* a masked actor in mime.

gefilte fish or **gefüllte fish** /gəˈfɪltə —/ ▻ *noun, Jewish cookery* **a** a cooked mixture of fish, eggs, seasoning and breadcrumbs or matzo meal, served as balls or cakes; **b** a fish stuffed with this. © 20c: from Yiddish *gefüllte fisch* stuffed fish.

Geiger counter /ˈgaɪgə —/ ▻ *noun, physics* an instrument that is used to detect and measure the intensity of IONIZING RADIATION by counting the number of electrical pulses generated by electrons released from ionized gas atoms. © 1920s: named after Hans Geiger (1882–1945), German physicist.

geisha /ˈgeɪʃə/ ▻ *noun* (***geisha*** or ***geishas***) **1** a Japanese girl or woman who is trained to entertain men with music, dancing and the art of conversation. Also called **geisha girl**. **2** *loosely* in Japan: a prostitute. © 19c: from Japanese *gei* art + *sha* person.

Geissler tube /ˈgaɪslə —/ ▻ *noun, chem* an early form of glass discharge tube, containing gas at low pressure which glows when an electric discharge is passed through the gas between two electrodes. © 1860s: named after Heinrich Geissler (1814–79), its inventor.

gel /dʒɛl/ ▻ *noun* **1** a COLLOID consisting of a solid and a liquid that are dispersed evenly throughout a material and have set to form a jellylike mass, eg gelatine. **2** (*also* **hair gel**) such a substance used in styling the hair or fixing it in place. **3** in theatre and photographic lighting: a translucent coloured substance, or a sheet of this, used to produce light of different colours. ▻ *verb* (***gelled***, ***gelling***) **1** *tr & intr* to become or cause something to become a gel. **2** to style (hair) using gel. **3** to JELL. © 19c: from GELATINE.

gelatine /ˈdʒɛlətiːn/ or (*technical*) **gelatin** /-tɪn/ ▻ *noun* a clear tasteless protein extracted from animal bones and hides that forms a stiff jelly when dissolved in water. It is used in food thickenings, adhesives, photographic materials, etc. © 19c: from French *gélatine* jelly.

gelatinize or **gelatinise** /dʒəˈlatɪnaɪz/ ▻ *verb* (***gelatinized***, ***gelatinizing***) **1** *tr & intr, technical* to make (a substance) gelatinous. **2** *photog* to coat (paper, glass, etc) with gelatine or jelly. **3** *intr* said of a substance: to become gelatinous. ● **gelatinization** *noun*.

gelatinous /dʒəˈlatɪnəs/ ▻ *adj* like gelatine or jelly.

gelation[1] /dʒəˈleɪʃən/ ▻ *noun, technical or formal* a solidification by cooling. © 19c: from Latin *gelatio*, from *gelare* to freeze.

gelation[2] /dʒəˈleɪʃən/ ▻ *noun, chem* formation of a GEL from a SOL[2]. © 20c.

geld /gɛld/ ▻ *verb* (***gelded***, ***gelding***) to castrate (a male animal, especially a horse) by removing its testicles. ● **gelding** *noun* a castrated male animal, especially a horse. © 13c: from Norse *geldr* barren.

gelid /ˈdʒɛlɪd/ *formal or humorous* ▻ *adj* **1** icy cold; frosty. **2** chilly; chill. © 17c: from Latin *gelidus* icy.

gelignite /ˈdʒɛlɪgnaɪt/ ▻ *noun* a powerful explosive, used especially in mining, made from a mixture of nitroglycerine, cellulose nitrate, sodium nitrate and wood pulp. © 19c: from GELATINE + Latin *ignis* fire.

gelly /'dʒɛlɪ/ ▻ *noun, colloq* gelignite.

gem /dʒɛm/ ▻ *noun* **1** (*also* **gemstone**) a precious or semi-precious stone or crystal, especially one that has been cut and polished for use in jewellery or other ornaments, eg a diamond or ruby. **2** *colloq* someone or something that is highly valued, admired, etc. ⓒ Anglo-Saxon as *gim*: from Latin *gemma* a bud or precious stone.

geminate /'dʒɛmɪneɪt/ *technical* ▻ *adj* **1** doubled. **2** said especially of leaves: arranged in pairs. ▻ *verb* (***geminated, geminating***) **1** to double. **2** to arrange something in pairs. • **geminated** *adj* doubled or arranged in pairs. • **gemination** *noun* doubling; repetition. ⓒ 16c: from Latin *geminus* a twin.

Gemini /'dʒɛmɪnaɪ, -ni/ ▻ *singular noun* (*plural* in sense 2b ***Geminis***) **1** *astron* a conspicuous zodiacal constellation that lies to the north-east of Orion. Also called **the Twins**. **2** *astrol* **a** the third sign of the zodiac; **b** a person born between 21 May and 20 June, under this sign. ⓒ 14c: Latin, meaning 'twins'.

Geminian ▻ *noun, astrol* a person born under the sign Gemini. ▻ *adj* belonging or relating to this sign.

gemma /'dʒɛmə/ ▻ *noun* (***gemmae*** /-miː/) **1** *bot* **a** a leaf bud; **b** in mosses, etc: a small multicellular body capable of separating and becoming a new individual. **2** *zool* a bud or protuberance that becomes a new individual. • **gemmation** *noun, bot, zool* the formation of gemmae. ⓒ 18c: Latin, meaning 'a bud'.

gemmiparous /dʒɛ'mɪpərəs/ ▻ *adj, bot, zool* reproducing by means of gemmae. ⓒ 18c: from GEMMA.

Gems /dʒɛmz/ ▻ *abbreviation* Global Environment Monitoring System, set up by the United Nations Environment Programme.

gemsbok /'gɛmzbɒk; *S Afr* 'xɛmz-/ ▻ *noun* a large S African antelope of the ORYX family with long straight horns and distinctive markings on its face and underparts. ⓒ 18c: Dutch, meaning 'male chamois'.

gemstone see under GEM

gemütlich /*German* gə'myːtlɪç/ *adj* **1** amiable; kindly. **2** cosy; comfortable. • ***Gemütlichkeit*** /-kaɪt/ **1** kindness. **2** cosiness; comfort. ⓒ 19c: German, meaning 'comfortable'.

gen /dʒɛn/ ▻ *noun, colloq* (*especially* **the gen**) the required or relevant information ▫ *got all the gen on working abroad.* ⓒ 1940s: from *gen*eral information.

■ **gen up on something** (***genned up, genning up***) to obtain the relevant information, etc, and become familiar with it.

Gen. ▻ *abbreviation* **1** General. **2** Book of the Bible: Genesis. See table at BIBLE.

gen. ▻ *abbreviation* **1 a** general; **b** generally. **2** genitive. **3** genus.

-gen /dʒən/ *chiefly scientific* ▻ *combining form, forming nouns, signifying* **1** something that causes or produces (a specified effect) ▫ *carcinogen.* **2** growth at a specified point or of a specified kind ▫ *endogen.* ⓒ From Greek -*genes* born.

gendarme /'ʒɒndɑːm, 'ʒɑ̃-/ ▻ *noun* a member of an armed police force in France and other French-speaking countries. • **gendarmerie** /-'dɑːməriː/ *noun* **1** an armed police force in France, etc. **2** a police station or barracks in France, etc. ⓒ 18c; 16c in historical sense 'a mounted soldier': French, from *gens d'armes* armed people.

gender /'dʒɛndə(r)/ ▻ *noun* **1** the condition of being male or female; one's sex. **2** *grammar* **a** in many languages: a system of dividing nouns and pronouns into different classes, often, but not necessarily, related to the sex of the persons and things denoted; **b** any of these classes, usually two or three in European languages (see COMMON GENDER, FEMININE, MASCULINE and NEUTER) . ⓒ 14c: from Latin *genus, generis* kind or sort.

gender-bender *colloq* ▻ *noun* someone who adopts a sexually ambiguous public image, eg by wearing androgynous clothes, hairstyle, makeup, etc. • **gender-bending** *noun.* ⓒ 1980s.

gender-specific ▻ *adj* belonging to or limited to either males or females.

gene /dʒiːn/ ▻ *noun* the basic unit of inheritance, consisting of a sequence of DNA that occupies a specific position on a CHROMOSOME. It is the means by which one or more specific characteristics are passed on from parents to offspring. • **genetic** *adj* see separate entry. ⓒ 20c: from German *Gen*, from Greek -*genes* born.

-gene /dʒiːn/ ▻ *combining form, scientific* a less common and usually older variant of -GEN.

genealogy /dʒiːnɪ'alədʒɪ/ ▻ *noun* (***genealogies***) **1 a** a person's direct line of descent from an ancestor; **b** a diagram or scheme showing this. Compare FAMILY TREE. **2** the study of the history and lineage of families. **3** the study of the development of plants and animals into present-day forms. • **genealogical** /-ə'lɒdʒɪkəl/ *adj* relating to or tracing genealogy. • **genealogically** *adverb.* • **genealogist** *noun* someone who studies or traces genealogies. ⓒ 13c: from Greek *genealogia*, from *genea* race + *logos* discourse.

gene amplification see under AMPLIFICATION

gene bank ▻ *noun* a collection of genetic material in the form of cloned DNA fragments, stored for subsequent use in plant and animal breeding programmes, genetic engineering, etc.

genera *plural of* GENUS

general /'dʒɛnərəl/ ▻ *adj* **1** relating to, involving or applying to all or most parts, people or things; widespread, not specific, limited, or localized ▫ *the general opinion* ▫ *as a general rule.* **2** not detailed or definite; rough; vague ▫ *general description* ▫ *in general terms.* **3** not specialized ▫ *general knowledge.* **4** (**the general**) generalized non-specific ideas ▫ *turn from the general to the particular.* **5** (especially before or after a job title) chief ▫ *general manager* ▫ *director-general.* ▻ *noun* **1** an officer in the army. See table at RANK[1]. **2** the commander of a whole army. **3** any leader, especially when regarded as a competent one. **4** the head of a religious order, eg the Jesuits. • **in general** usually; mostly. ⓒ 13c: from Latin *generalis* meaning 'applying to the whole group', from *genus* race or kind.

general anaesthetic ▻ *noun, medicine* a drug that causes a complete loss of consciousness. Compare LOCAL ANAESTHETIC.

General Assembly ▻ *noun* **1** the deliberative body of the entire membership of the United Nations. **2** the highest deliberative body of Presbyterian and some other Churches.

General Certificate of Education ▻ *noun* (abbreviation **GCE**) in England and Wales: a qualification obtainable for various school subjects by passing an examination at Advanced (or A) level and Special (or S) level and, also formerly, at Ordinary (or O) level.

General Certificate of Secondary Education ▻ *noun* (abbreviation **GCSE**) in England and Wales: a school-leaving qualification in one or more subjects, which replaced the GCE Ordinary level and CSE qualifications in 1988.

general election ▻ *noun* a national election in which the voters of every constituency in the country elect a member of parliament. Compare BY-ELECTION.

general hospital ▻ *noun* a hospital that treats patients of any age and either sex, who are suffering from any disease, illness or infirmity.

generalise see GENERALIZE

generalissimo ▻ *noun* (***generalissimos***) a supreme commander of the combined armed forces in some countries, who often also has political power. ◐ 17c: Italian, superlative of *generale* general.

generalist ▻ *noun* usually in reference to someone's occupation: someone whose knowledge and skills are not restricted to one particular field. Opposite of SPECIALIST.

generality /dʒɛnəˈralɪtɪ/ ▻ *noun* (*plural* in sense 2 ***generalities***) **1** the quality or fact of being general. **2** a general rule or principle. **3** (**the generality**) the majority.

generalize or **generalise** ▻ *verb* (***generalized, generalizing***) **1** *intr* to speak in general terms or form general opinions, especially ones that are too general to be applied to all individual cases. **2** to make something more general, especially to make it applicable to a wider variety of cases. • **generalization** *noun* an act or example, or the process, of generalizing.

general ledger ▻ *noun, bookkeeping* a book that contains NOMINAL ACCOUNTS.

generally ▻ *adverb* **1** usually. **2** without considering details; broadly. **3** as a whole; collectively.

general meeting ▻ *noun* a meeting of members of a company, association, etc whose decisions are legally binding on the organization. See also ANNUAL GENERAL MEETING.

general post office or **General Post Office** ▻ *noun* (abbreviation **GPO**) the head post office of a town or district.

general practice ▻ *noun, medicine* the area and type of work that is done by a GENERAL PRACTITIONER.

general practitioner ▻ *noun* (abbreviation **GP**) a community doctor who treats most illnesses and complaints, and refers appropriate cases to specialists.

general principle ▻ *noun* a principle to which there are no exceptions within its range of application.

general-purpose ▻ *adj* **1** useful for a wide range of purposes □ *general-purpose cleaner*. **2** not restricted to a particular function □ *general-purpose committee*.

generalship ▻ *noun* **1** the art or position of being a military commander. **2** tactical management and leadership in general.

general staff ▻ *noun* military officers who advise senior officers on policy, administration, etc.

general strike ▻ *noun* a strike by workers in all or most of the industries in a country at the same time.

generate /ˈdʒɛnəreɪt/ ▻ *verb* (***generated, generating***) to produce or create something. ◐ 16c: from Latin *generare*, from *genus* a kind.

generation /dʒɛnəˈreɪʃən/ ▻ *noun* **1** the act or process of producing something, eg electricity or ideas. **2** *biol* said of living organisms: the act or process of producing offspring. **3** all the individuals produced at a particular stage in the natural descent of humans or animals □ *the younger generation*. **4** the average period between the birth of a person or animal and the birth of their offspring, which, in humans, is usually considered to be about 30 years □ *three generations ago*. **5 a** a single stage in a person's descent; **b** *as adj and in compounds* □ *second-generation American*. **6** a COMPUTER GENERATION. • **generational** *adj*.

generation gap ▻ *noun* the extent to which two, usually successive, generations differ, eg in lifestyles, ideas, values, etc and the lack of mutual understanding that results from these differences.

Generation X ▻ *noun* a term variously applied to sections of society that share a common scepticism about the value of traditionally held beliefs, lifestyles, etc, especially those pertaining to work, the family, etc. ◐ 1960s: first coined as the title of a collection of interviews with young Mods (see MOD[1] *noun*) and ROCKERS (*noun* 5).

generative /ˈdʒɛnərətɪv/ ▻ *adj, formal* **1** able to produce or generate. **2** relating to production or creation.

generative grammar ▻ *noun, linguistics* a description of a language as a finite set of grammatical rules able to generate an infinite number of grammatical sentences. ◐ 1950s: first coined by the US linguist, Noam Chomsky (born 1928).

generator /ˈdʒɛnəreɪtə(r)/ ▻ *noun, elec* a machine that converts mechanical energy into electrical energy, eg a DYNAMO.

generic /dʒəˈnɛrɪk/ ▻ *adj* **1** belonging, referring or relating to any member of a general class or group. **2 a** said especially of a drug: not protected by a trademark and sold as a specific brand; non-proprietary □ *generic aspirin*; **b** applied to supermarket products: sold without a brand-name. **3** applied to a product name that was originally a trademark, eg HOOVER, BIRO, etc: now used as the general name for the product. **4** *biol* belonging, referring or relating to a GENUS. **5** said of computers, computer sofware, etc: belonging to the same family; interchangeable. ▻ *noun* **1** a generic drug. **2** a supermarket product sold without a brand-name, in plain packaging, and without advertising. ◐ 17c: from GENUS.

generic name ▻ *noun* **1** *biol* in taxonomy: the name of the genus, placed first in naming a species. **2** the name of a generic drug (see GENERIC *adj* 2a).

generous /ˈdʒɛnərəs/ ▻ *adj* **1** giving or willing to give or help unselfishly. **2** said eg of a donation: large and given unselfishly. **3** large; ample; plentiful □ *generous portions*. **4** kind; willing to forgive □ *of generous spirit*. **5** said of wine: rich; invigorating. • **generosity** /-ˈrɒsɪtɪ/ *noun* (*plural* in sense 2 ***generosities***) **1** the quality of being generous. **2** a generous act. • **generously** *adverb*. • **generousness** *noun*. ◐ 16c: from Latin *generosus* of noble birth.

genesis /ˈdʒɛnəsɪs/ ▻ *noun* (***geneses*** /-siːz/) **1** a beginning or origin. **2** (**Genesis**) the title of the first book in the Old Testament which describes the creation of the world. See table at BIBLE. ◐ 17c; Anglo-Saxon in sense 2: Greek, meaning 'origin' or 'creation'.

-genesis /ˈdʒɛnəsɪs/ ▻ *combining form, signifying* origin or generation □ *parthenogenesis* □ *pathogenesis*. ◐ Greek.

genet[1] /ˈdʒɛnɪt/ or **genette** /dʒəˈnɛt/ ▻ *noun* **1** a carnivore related to the civet. **2** its fur or an imitation of it. ◐ 15c: French *genette*, from Arabic *jarnait*.

genet[2] see JENNET

gene therapy ▻ *noun* the application of GENETIC ENGINEERING techniques to alter or replace a defective gene or genes. The procedures are still at the experimental stage, but it is hoped that they could lead to the prevention of hereditary diseases such as haemophilia.

genetic /dʒəˈnɛtɪk/ or (*less commonly*) **genetical** ▻ *adj* **1** referring or relating to GENES or GENETICS; inherited □ *a genetic defect*. **2** belonging or relating to origin. • **genetically** *adverb*. ◐ 19c: from GENE.

-genetic /dʒəˈnɛtɪk/ ▻ *combining form* (forming adjectives corresponding to nouns in -GENESIS) *signifying* productive of a specified thing.

genetic code ▻ *noun, genetics* the form in which genetic instructions for the manufacture of proteins in the cells of living organisms are encoded.

genetic counselling ▻ *noun* advice given to prospective parents by a genetics specialist, in cases where there is some likelihood that they could conceive children with hereditary disorders.

genetic engineering ▻ *noun* a form of BIOTECHNOLOGY in which the genes of an organism are deliberately altered by a method other than conventional breeding in order to change one or more characteristics of the organism.

genetic fingerprinting ▻ *noun, genetics* the process of analyzing samples of DNA from body tissues or fluids such as blood, saliva or semen in order to establish a person's identity in criminal investigations, paternity disputes, etc. Also called **DNA fingerprinting**.

genetic parents ▻ *noun* the parents whose genetic material has produced the child.

genetics /dʒəˈnɛtɪks/ ▻ *singular noun* the scientific study of heredity and of the mechanisms by which characteristics are transmitted from one generation to the next. ▻ *plural noun* the genetic makeup of an organism or group. • **geneticist** /dʒəˈnɛtɪsɪst/ *noun*.

genetic screening ▻ *noun, medicine* the systematic testing of high-risk sections of the population for signs of hereditary diseases, eg the testing of women whose close relatives have had breast cancer for early signs of the disease.

genette see GENET[1]

Geneva bands ▻ *plural noun* the two strips of white linen that hang down from the neck of some clerical robes. ◔ 19c: named after the Swiss city of Geneva and so called because they were first worn by Swiss Calvinists.

Geneva Bible ▻ *noun* a version of the Bible in English produced by English Protestant exiles at Geneva in 1560.

Geneva Convention ▻ *noun* an international agreement that regulates the status and treatment in wartime of the sick and wounded, prisoners of war, etc. ◔ 19c: named after the Swiss city of Geneva where the first agreement was ratified and signed in 1864. There have been subsequent revisions, notably one in 1906, also held in Geneva, which is now the significant agreement.

Geneva cross ▻ *noun* a red cross on a white background, displayed for protection in war of people serving in hospitals, etc. See also RED CROSS.

Geneva gown ▻ *noun* the long dark preaching gown worn by the early Protestant reformers and still the common form of pulpit-gown among Presbyterians.

Genevan /dʒəˈniːvən/ and **Genevese** /dʒɛnəˈviːz/ ▻ *adj* belonging or relating to the city of Geneva in Switzerland. ▻ *noun* **1** a citizen or inhabitant of, or person born in, Geneva. **2** *Christianity* a believer in Calvinist theology.

genial[1] /ˈdʒiːnɪəl/ ▻ *adj* **1** cheerful; friendly; sociable. **2** said of climate: pleasantly warm or mild. • **geniality** /-ˈalɪtɪ/ *noun*. • **genially** *adverb*. ◔ 16c: from Latin *genialis*, from *genius* guardian spirit or deity.

genial[2] /ˈdʒiːnɪəl/ ▻ *adj, anatomy* relating to the chin. ◔ 19c: from Greek *geneion* chin.

genic /ˈdʒiːnɪk/ ▻ *adj* relating to a GENE.

-genic /ˈdʒɛnɪk/ ▻ *combining form, signifying* **1** causing or producing a specified thing ▫ ***carcinogenic*** ▫ ***pathogenic***. **2** ideal or suitable for a specified thing ▫ ***photogenic***. **3** caused by a specified thing ▫ ***iatrogenic***. ◔ Based on -GEN.

genie /ˈdʒiːnɪ/ ▻ *noun* (***genies*** or ***genii*** /ˈdʒiːnɪaɪ/) in folk or fairy stories: a spirit with the power to grant wishes. ◔ 18c: from French *génie*, influenced by Arabic *jinni* a demon.

genii *plural of* GENIE, GENIUS

genista /dʒəˈnɪstə/ ▻ *noun, technical* the plant BROOM. ◔ 17c: Latin.

genital /ˈdʒɛnɪtəl/ ▻ *adj* **1 a** relating to or affecting the GENITALS; **b** in the region of the genitals. **2** connected with or relating to reproduction. **3** *psychol* relating to the stage of mature psychosexual development. ◔ 14c.

genitals or **genitalia** /dʒɛnɪˈteɪlɪə/ ▻ *plural noun* the external sexual organs. ◔ 14c: from Latin *genitalis*, from *gignere* to beget.

genitive /ˈdʒɛnɪtɪv/ *grammar* ▻ *noun* (abbreviation **gen.**) **1** in certain languages, eg Latin, Greek and German: the form or CASE of a noun, pronoun or adjective which shows possession or association. **2** a noun, etc in this case. ▻ *adj* belonging to or in this case. • **genitival** /-ˈtaɪvəl/ *adj*. • **genitivally** *adverb*. ◔ 14c: from Latin *genitivus*.

genito-urinary /dʒɛnɪtoʊˈjʊərɪnərɪ/ ▻ *adj* relating to both the GENITAL and the URINARY organs and functions.

genius /ˈdʒiːnɪəs/ ▻ *noun* (***geniuses*** or in sense 5 ***genii*** /ˈdʒiːnɪaɪ/) **1** someone who has outstanding creative or intellectual ability. **2** such ability. **3** a person who exerts a powerful influence on another (whether good or bad). **4** *Roman mythol* a guardian spirit. **5** *formal* a quality or attitude with which something (eg a country or a period of time) is identified or typically associated ▫ ***Rational inquiry was the genius of the century.*** ◔ 16c: Latin, meaning 'guardian spirit' or 'deity'.

genoa /ˈdʒɛnoʊə, dʒəˈnoʊə/ ▻ *noun* (***genoas***) *naut* a large jib sail. ◔ 20c: named after Genoa in Italy.

Genoa cake ▻ *noun* a rich fruit cake with almonds on top.

genocide /ˈdʒɛnəsaɪd/ ▻ *noun* the deliberate killing of a whole nation or people. • **genocidal** *adj*. ◔ 20c: from Greek *genos* race + -CIDE.

Genoese /dʒɛnoʊˈiːz/ and **Genovese** /dʒɛnoʊˈviːz/ ▻ *adj* relating or belonging to *Genoa* in NW Italy or its inhabitants. ▻ *noun* a citizen or inhabitant of, or a person born in, Genoa.

genome /ˈdʒiːnoʊm/ ▻ *noun genetics* the complete set of genetic material in the cell of a living organism. ◔ 1930s: from German *genom*.

genotype /ˈdʒɛnoʊtaɪp/ ▻ *noun, genetics* the particular set of genes possessed by an organism, which interacts with environmental factors to determine the organism's PHENOTYPE. • **genotypic** /-ˈtɪpɪk/ or **genotypical** *adj*. • **genotypically** *adverb*. ◔ 20c: from GENE + TYPE.

-genous /dʒɪnəs/ ▻ *combining form, forming adjectives, denoting* producing ▫ ***erogenous***.

Genovese see GENOESE

genre /ˈʒɑ̃rə, ˈʒɒnrə/ ▻ *noun* (***genres***) **1** a particular type or kind of literature, music or other artistic work. **2** (*in full* **genre painting**) *art* a type of painting featuring scenes from everyday life. ◔ 19c: French, literally 'kind' or 'type'.

gent /dʒɛnt/ ▻ *noun, colloq* a gentleman. See also GENTS.

genteel /dʒɛnˈtiːl/ ▻ *adj* (***genteeler***, ***genteelest***) **1** *derog* polite or refined in an artificial, affected way approaching snobbishness. **2** well-mannered. **3** *old use, facetious* referring to or suitable for the upper classes. • **genteelly** *adverb*. • **genteelness** *noun*. ◔ 16c, meaning 'fashionably stylish': from French *gentil* well-bred.

genteelism ▻ *noun* a word or phrase used instead of an ordinary one which is felt by the speaker to be coarse or vulgar. ◔ 20c.

gentian /ˈdʒɛnʃən/ ▻ *noun* **1** any of numerous mostly low-growing perennial plants with opposite leaves and erect funnel-shaped or bell-shaped flowers, often deep blue in colour. **2** the root and rhizome of the yellow gentian, used as a tonic. ◔ 14c: from Latin *gentiana*.

gentian violet ▻ *noun* **1** in the British pharmacopeia: an antiseptic dye, used especially in the treatment of burns. **2** *sometimes* METHYL VIOLET. **3** *sometimes* a mixture of the two.

gentile /ˈdʒɛntaɪl/ ▻ *noun* (*often* **Gentile**; *plural* ***gentiles*** or ***Gentiles***) **a** used especially by Jews: a person who is not Jewish; **b** used especially by Mormons: a person who is not Mormon. ▻ *adj* **1** (*often* **Gentile**) **a** used especially by Jews: not Jewish; **b** used especially by Mormons: not Mormon. **2** *now rare* relating to a nation or tribe. ◔ 15c: from Latin *gentilis* belonging to the same *gens* or clan.

gentility /dʒɛnˈtɪlɪtɪ/ ▻ *noun* **1** good manners and respectability. **2** *derog* artificial politeness. **3** *old use* **a** noble birth; **b** people of the upper classes. ◐ 14c: from French *gentilité*.

gentle /ˈdʒɛntəl/ ▷ *adj* (*gentler*, *gentlest*) **1** mild-mannered, not stern, coarse or violent. **2** light and soft; not harsh, loud, strong, etc □ *a gentle caress* □ *a gentle breeze*. **3** moderate; mild □ *a gentle reprimand*. **4** said of hills, etc: rising gradually. **5** *old use* noble; of the upper classes. ▷ *noun* (*gentles*) **1** a soft maggot used as bait by anglers. **2** (**gentles**) *old use* gentlefolk. • **gentleness** *noun*. • **gently** *adverb*. ◐ 13c in sense 5; 16c and 17c in the other senses: from French *gentil* well-bred.

gentlefolk ▷ *plural noun, old use* (though until 19c (later in dialect) the form used is **gentlefolks**) people of good breeding; members of the upper classes.

gentleman ▷ *noun* **1** (especially as a term of reference or address) a polite name for a man □ *Ask that gentleman* □ *Good afternoon, gentlemen*. **2** a polite, well-mannered, respectable man. **3** a man from the upper classes, especially one with enough private wealth to live on without working.

gentleman-at-arms ▷ *noun* a member of the group of men who guard the king or queen on important occasions.

gentleman farmer ▷ *noun* (*gentlemen farmers* or *gentleman farmers*) **1** a landowner who lives on his own estate supervising the cultivation of his own land. **2** a gentleman who owns a farm and employs a farm manager and other staff to work it on his behalf.

gentlemanly /ˈdʒɛntəlmənlɪ/ ▷ *adj* **1** said of a man or boy: polite and well-mannered. **2** suitable for or typical of a gentleman. • **gentlemanliness** *noun*.

gentleman's gentleman *rather dated* ▷ *noun* the VALET or personal servant of a gentleman.

Gentleman's Relish ▷ *noun, trademark* a savoury paste made from anchovies, for spreading on sandwiches, etc.

gentlemen's agreement or **gentleman's agreement** ▷ *noun* an agreement based on honour rather than on a formal contract and thus not legally binding.

gentleness, **gentler**, **gentles** and **gentlest** see under GENTLE

gentlewoman ▷ *noun* **1** *dated* a woman from the upper classes. **2** *old use* her female servant or attendant.

gently see under GENTLE

gentoo /ˈdʒɛntuː/ or **gentoo penguin** ▷ *noun* a species of long-tailed penguin that is common in the Falkland Islands. ◐ 19c: perhaps from Portuguese *gentio* a Gentile.

gentrify /ˈdʒɛntrɪfaɪ/ ▷ *verb* (*gentrifies*, *gentrified*, *gentrifying*) **1** to convert or renovate (housing) to conform to middle-class taste. **2** to make (an area) middle-class. • **gentrification** *noun, derog* the change in the character of a traditionally working-class area following an influx of new middle-class residents. ◐ 1970s: from GENTRY.

gentry /ˈdʒɛntrɪ/ ▷ *plural noun* **1** (*especially* **the gentry**) people belonging to the class directly below the nobility □ *the landed gentry*. **2** *sometimes colloq* people (with their class or characteristics specified) □ *ignorant gentry* □ *idle gentry*. ◐ 14c, meaning 'high rank' or 'good breeding': from French *genterise* nobility.

gents /dʒɛnts/ ▷ *singular noun* (*often* **the gents**) a men's public toilet.

genuflect /ˈdʒɛnjʊflɛkt/ ▷ *verb* (*genuflected*, *genuflecting*) *intr* to bend one's knee in worship or as a sign of respect. • **genuflection** or **genuflexion** *noun*. ◐ 17c: from Latin *genu* knee + *flectere* to bend.

genuine /ˈdʒɛnjʊɪn/ ▷ *adj* **1** authentic, not artificial or fake. **2** honest; sincere. • **genuinely** *adverb*. • **genuineness** *noun*. ◐ 17c; 16c in obsolete sense 'natural': from Latin *genuinus* natural.

genus /ˈdʒiːnəs, ˈdʒɛnəs/ ▷ *noun* (*genera* /ˈdʒɛnərə/ or *genuses*) **1** *biol* in taxonomy: any of the groups, eg CANIS (the dogs), into which a FAMILY (sense 7) is divided and which in turn is subdivided into one or more SPECIES (sense 1). **2** a class divided into several subordinate classes. ◐ 16c: Latin, meaning 'race' or 'kind'.

Geo. ▷ *abbreviation* George.

geo- /dʒiːoʊ, dʒɪˈɒ/ ▷ *combining form, signifying* **1** the Earth. **2** geography or geographical. ◐ From Greek *ge* earth.

geocentric ▷ *adj* **1** said of a system, especially the universe or the solar system: having the Earth as its centre. **2** measured from the centre of the Earth. • **geocentrically** *adverb*. ◐ 17c.

geocentricism /dʒiːoʊˈsɛntrɪsɪzəm/ ▷ *noun* the belief that the Earth is the centre of the universe.

geochemistry ▷ *noun, geol* the branch of geology concerned with the scientific study of the chemical composition of the Earth. • **geochemical** *adj*. • **geochemically** *adverb*. • **geochemist** *noun*. ◐ Early 20c.

geochronology ▷ *noun* the science of measuring geological time. • **geochronological** *adj*. • **geochronologist** *noun*. ◐ 19c.

geode /ˈdʒiːoʊd/ ▷ *noun, geol* a hollow rock cavity that is lined with crystals which point inward towards its centre. ◐ 17c: from Greek *geodes* earthy.

geodemographics ▷ *singular noun* a system of analysis of demographic data in terms of geographical area, used eg for market research sampling. See DEMOGRAPHY. ◐ 1990s.

geodesic /dʒiːoʊˈdɛsɪk, -ˈdiːsɪk/ and **geodetic** /-ˈdɛtɪk/ ▷ *adj* **1** relating to or determined by GEODESY. **2** denoting an artificial structure composed of a large number of identical components, especially a dome. See also GEODESIC DOME. ▷ *noun* a geodesic line. ◐ 19c.

geodesic dome ▷ *noun* a dome whose surface is composed of a large number of identical small triangles. ◐ 1950s.

geodesic line ▷ *noun, math, surveying, etc* a line on a plane or curved surface that represents the shortest distance between two points.

geodesy /dʒiːˈɒdəsɪ/ ▷ *noun* the scientific study of the Earth's surface by surveying (especially by satellite) and mapping in order to determine its exact shape and size, and to measure its gravitational field. ◐ 16c: from Greek *geodaisia*, from *ge* earth + *daisis* division.

geodetic see GEODESIC

geog. ▷ *abbreviation* **1** geographical. **2** geography.

geography /dʒɪˈɒgrəfɪ/ ▷ *noun* (*geographies*) **1** the scientific study of the Earth's surface, especially its physical features, climate, resources, population, etc. **2** *colloq* the layout of a place. • **geographer** *noun* someone who studies or is an expert in geography. • **geographical** /dʒiːoʊˈgrafɪkəl/ *adj*. • **geographically** *adverb*. ◐ 16c.

geoid /ˈdʒiːɔɪd/ ▷ *noun, surveying* the shape of the Earth, ie a slightly flattened sphere, taken as the reference for geodesic measurement.

geol. ▷ *abbreviation* **1** geological. **2** geology.

geological survey ▷ *noun* a survey of the geology of a particular area, especially in order to locate economically important rocks and minerals, eg coal and oil.

geological time ▷ *noun* a time scale in which the Earth's history is subdivided into units known as EONS, which are further subdivided into ERAS, PERIODS, and EPOCHS.

geologize or **geologise** ▷ *verb* (*geologized*, *geologizing*) **1** *tr* to study the geology of (a specified area, etc). **2** *intr* to carry out geological researches.

geology /dʒɪˈɒlədʒɪ/ ▷ *noun* **1** the scientific study of the origins and structure, composition, etc of the Earth, especially its rocks. **2** a similar scientific study applied to other planets. **3** the distinctive geological features of an area, country, planet, etc. • **geological** *adj.* • **geologically** *adverb.* • **geologist** *noun.* ◷ 18c.

geomagnetism ▷ *noun* **1** the Earth's magnetic field. **2** the scientific study of this. • **geomagnetic** *adj.* • **geomagnetically** *adverb.* ◷ 20c.

geometric /dʒɪəˈmɛtrɪk/ or **geometrical** ▷ *adj* **1** relating to or using the principles of GEOMETRY. **2** said of a pattern, design, style of architecture, etc: using or consisting of lines, points, or simple geometrical figures such as circles or triangles. • **geometrically** *adverb.*

geometric mean see under MEAN[3]

geometric progression ▷ *noun, math* a sequence of numbers in which the ratio between one term and the next remains constant, eg 1, 2, 4, 8..., where each successive term is obtained by multiplying its predecessor by 2.

geometrid see under LOOPER

geometry /dʒɪˈɒmɪtrɪ/ ▷ *noun* the branch of mathematics dealing with lines, angles, shapes, etc and their relationships. • **geometer** or **geometrician** *noun.* ◷ 14c: from Greek *geometria*; see GEO- + -METRY.

geomorphology ▷ *noun, geol* the scientific study of the nature and history of the landforms on the surface of the Earth and other planets, and of the processes that create them. • **geomorphological** *adj* • **geomorphologist** *noun.* ◷ 1890s.

Geological Time Scale

Eon	Era	Period	Epoch	Million years before present
Phanerozoic	Cenozoic	Quaternary	Holocene	0.01–
			Pleistocene	2–0.01
		Tertiary	Pliocene	7–2
			Miocene	25–7
			Oligocene	38–25
			Eocene	54–38
			Palaeocene	65–54
	Mesozoic	Cretaceous		140–65
		Jurassic		210–140
		Triassic	Late Middle Early	250–210
	Palaeozoic	Permian	Late Early	290–250
		Carboniferous	Pennsylvanian Mississippian	360–290
		Devonian		410–360
		Silurian		440–410
		Ordovician		505–440
		Cambrian		580–505
Proterozoic	Precambrian			4 500–580

geophysics ▷ *singular noun* the scientific study of the physical properties of the Earth and the physical processes that determine its structure. • **geophysical** *adj.* • **geophysicist** *noun.* ◷ 1880s.

geopolitics ▷ *singular noun* **1** the study of those political problems which are affected by the geographical environment, eg frontiers. **2** worldwide politics. ▷ *plural noun* the combination of geographical and political aspects in a particular state or area. • **geopolitical** *adj.* • **geopolitically** *adverb.* ◷ Early 20c.

Geordie /ˈdʒɔːdɪ/ *colloq* ▷ *noun* **1** someone who was born on or who lives on Tyneside. **2** the Tyneside dialect. ▷ *adj* belonging or relating to Tyneside, its people,or their dialect. ◷ 19c: diminutive of the name *George*.

George /dʒɔːdʒ/ ▷ *noun, airmen's slang* the automatic pilot of an aircraft.

George Cross ▷ *noun* (abbreviation **GC**) in the UK: an award for bravery, usually given to civilians. ◷ 1940s: named after King *George* VI, who instituted it.

George Medal ▷ *noun* (abbreviation **GM**) in the UK: an award for bravery given to civilians and to members of the armed forces.

georgette /dʒɔːˈdʒɛt/ ▷ *noun* (*georgettes*) a kind of thin silk material. ◷ 20c: named after *Georgette* de la Plante, French dressmaker.

Georgian /ˈdʒɔːdʒən/ ▷ *adj* **1** said of architecture, painting, antiques, etc: belonging to or typical of the reigns of King George I, II, III and IV, ie the period 1714–1830. **2** said of literature: typical of the kind that was written during the reign of King George V, especially the period 1910–20. **3** relating to the Caucasian republic of Georgia, its people or their language. **4** relating to the US state of Georgia or its people. ▷ *noun* **1 a** a citizen or inhabitant of, or a person born in, the Caucasian republic of Georgia; **b** its official language. **2** a citizen or inhabitant of, or a person born in, the US state of Georgia.

geosphere ▷ *noun* **1** the non-living part of the Earth, including the LITHOSPHERE, HYDROSPHERE and ATMOSPHERE. **2** the solid part of the Earth, as opposed to the atmosphere and hydrosphere. ◷ 19c.

geostationary ▷ *adj, technical* denoting the orbit of an artificial satellite above the Earth's equator, at an altitude of 35 900km, at which distance it takes exactly 24 hours to complete one orbit and so appears to remain stationary above a fixed point on the Earth's surface. ◷ 20c.

geostationary satellite see FIXED SATELLITE

geostrophic /dʒiːoʊˈstrɒfɪk/ ▷ *adj, meteorol, etc* applied to the CORIOLIS FORCE, especially as it affects the direction and strength of a wind or current. ◷ 20c: from GEO- + Greek *strophe* a turning.

geosyncline ▷ *noun, geol* an extensive SYNCLINE. ◷ 1890s.

geothermal ▷ *adj, technical* **1** relating to the internal heat of the Earth. **2** relating to or using the energy that can be extracted from this heat. ◷ 19c.

geothermal energy ▷ *noun* the energy that can be extracted from the internal heat of the Earth, produced as a result of radioactive decay within rocks and the slow cooling of the planet with time.

geotropism ▷ *noun, bot* the growth of the roots or shoots of plants in response to gravity, eg roots show *positive geotropism*, because they grow in the direction of gravity. • **geotropic** *adj.* ◷ 19c: from German *geotropisms*; see GEO- + TROPISM.

Ger. ▷ *abbreviation* German.

geranium /dʒəˈreɪnɪəm/ ▷ *noun* **1** *loosely* any of several plants of the PELARGONIUM family widely cultivated as houseplants. **2** *bot* any of numerous herbaceous plants or shrubs such as the CRANESBILL that have divided leaves and large flowers with five pink or purplish petals. ◷ 16c: from Greek *geranos* crane.

gerbil /ˈdʒɜːbɪl/ ⊳ *noun* any of numerous small burrowing rodents with long hind legs and a long furry tail. They are native to desert and semi-desert regions of Asia and Africa, and are often kept as children's pets. ◷ 19c: from Latin *gerbillus* little jerboa.

gerfalcon see GYRFALCON

geriatric /dʒɛrɪˈatrɪk/ ⊳ *adj* **1** for or dealing with old people; relating to GERIATRICS □ *geriatric medicine.* **2** *derog, colloq* very old. ⊳ *noun* an old person.

geriatrician /dʒɛrɪəˈtrɪʃən/ ⊳ *noun* a specialist in geriatrics.

geriatrics /dʒɛrɪˈatrɪks/ ⊳ *singular noun* the branch of medicine concerned with the care of the elderly, and with the diagnosis and treatment of diseases and disorders associated with ageing. ◷ 20c: from Greek *geras* old age + -IATRICS.

germ /dʒɜːm/ ⊳ *noun* **1** an imprecise term for any micro-organism, especially a bacterium or virus that causes disease. Also *as adj* □ *germ warfare.* **2** the embryo of a plant, especially of wheat. **3** an origin or beginning □ *the germ of a plan.* **4** *formerly* any living structure that is capable of developing into a complete organism, eg a seed or a fertilized egg. ◷ 17c: from Latin *germen* bud or sprout.

German /ˈdʒɜːmən/ ⊳ *adj* (abbreviation **Ger.**) **1 a** belonging or relating to Germany, a federal republic in central Europe formed by the unification of West Germany and East Germany in 1990; **b** belonging or relating to its inhabitants or their language. **2** *historical* belonging or relating to the country, state or republic of Germany in any of its various historical forms. ⊳ *noun* **1** a citizen or inhabitant of, or person born in, Germany. **2** the official language of Germany and Austria, and one of the official languages of Switzerland. ◷ 16c: from Latin *Germanus.*

german /ˈdʒɜːmən/ ⊳ *adj, following its noun* **1** characterized by having both parents the same □ *brother german.* **2** characterized by having both grandparents the same on one side of the family □ *cousin german.* ◷ 14c: from Latin *germanus* having the same parents.

germane /dʒɜːˈmeɪn/ ⊳ *adj* said of ideas, remarks, etc: relevant; closely related (to the topic under discussion). • **germanely** *adverb.* • **germaneness** *noun.* ◷ 19c development of GERMAN.

Germanic /dʒɜːˈmanɪk, dʒə-/ ⊳ *noun* a branch of the Indo-European family of languages that includes both the modern and historical varieties and which is divided into **East Germanic** (Gothic and other extinct languages), **North Germanic** (Norwegian, Danish, Swedish, Icelandic) and **West Germanic** (English, Frisian, Dutch, Low German, High German). ⊳ *adj* **1** relating to these languages or to the people speaking them. **2** typical of Germany or the Germans. ◷ 17c, meaning 'German'.

Pronunciation of German in English

1. consonants

- **ch** is pronounced /x/, as in **Bach** and the Scots pronunciation of **loch**; after **i** and **e**, it is pronounced with a sound between /x/ and /ʃ/.
- **sch** is pronounced /ʃ/, as in **Schumacher**.
- **j** is pronounced /j/, as in the name of the psychologist **Jung**.
- **w** is pronounced /v/, as in **auf Wiedersehen**.
- **z** is pronounced /ts/, as in **Mozart**.

2. vowels

- **ie** is pronounced /iː/, as in **auf Wiedersehen** (so **Riesling** is /ˈriːslɪŋ/, not /ˈraɪs-/).
- **ei** is pronounced /aɪ/, as in **Eine Kleine Nachtmusik**.
- **au** is pronounced /aʊ/, as in **Strauss**.
- **äu** is pronounced /ɔɪ/, so the first vowel in **fräulein** rhymes with the English vowel in **coy**, not in **cow**.
- **eu** is also pronounced /ɔɪ/, as in **Deutschland**.
- **ö**, sometimes written **oe**, is pronounced /ɜː/, as in **Goethe**.
- **ü**, like the French **u**, is pronounced /y/, close to the common Scottish pronunciation of the vowel in words such as **you** and **book**.
- **u** is close to the Standard English pronunciations of the vowel in words such as **you** and **book**.

germanium /dʒɜːˈmeɪnɪəm/ ⊳ *noun, chem* (symbol **Ge**, atomic number 32) a hard greyish-white metalloid element, widely used as a semiconductor in electronic devices. ◷ 19c: named after Germany, the native country of its discoverer, C A Winkler (1838–1904).

German measles ⊳ *singular noun* RUBELLA.

Germano- /dʒɜːˈmanoʊ/ ⊳ *combining form, signifying* Germany, German, or Germans.

German Words Used in English

angst anxiety; a feeling of anxiety caused by the uncertainties of human existence

Anschluss joining together; union, especially the political union of German and Austria in 1938

Bildungsroman education novel; a novel depicting a character's early spiritual and emotional development and education

blitzkrieg lightning war; a sudden strong attack, especially from the air

doppelgänger double-goer; a ghostly duplicate of a living person; someone who looks exactly like someone else

dummkopf dumb-head; a blockhead, an idiot

echt real, genuine; authentic, typical

ersatz replacement, substitute; a second-rate or cheaper substitute; substitute, imitation

führer leader, guide; someone who bossily asserts their authority

Gastarbeiter guest worker; an immigrant worker, especially one who does menial work

gauleiter district leader; a chief official of a district under the Nazi regime; an overbearing wielder of petty authority

gemütlich amiable, comfortable, cosy

gestalt form, shape; a whole pattern or structure perceived as more than the sum of its parts

Gesundheit health; your health, said to someone who has just sneezed

götterdämmerung twilight of the gods; the downfall of any once powerful system

kaput broken, destroyed

kitsch rubbish; sentimental or vulgar tastelessness in art, design, etc

Lebensraum life space; room to live; used by Hitler to justify his acquisition of land for Germany

leitmotiv leading motif; a recurrent theme associated with a particular person or thing in a piece of music, etc

putsch thrust; a sudden attempt to remove a government from power

realpolitik politics of realism; politics based on the practical needs of life, rather than moral or ethical ideas

schadenfreude hurt-joy; pleasure in others' misfortunes

Übermensch over-person; a superman

weltanschauung world perception; a particular philosophy of life

weltschmerz world pain; sympathy with universal misery; thoroughgoing pessimism

wunderkind wonder-child; a child prodigy, someone who shows great talent and/or achieves great success at an early age

Zeitgeist time-spirit; the spirit of the age.

German shepherd dog ▷ *noun* a large dog with a thick coat, a long pointed muzzle, and pointed ears, widely used by police and security officers. Also called **Alsatian**.

germicide /ˈdʒɜːmɪsaɪd/ ▷ *noun* (***germicides***) any agent that destroys disease-causing micro-organisms such as bacteria and viruses. • **germicidal** *adj.* ◷ 19c: GERM + -CIDE.

germinal /ˈdʒɜːmɪnəl/ ▷ *adj* **1** *technical* relating to or similar to a GERM or germs. **2** in the earliest stage of development. **3** seminal, productive of new and original ideas. • **germinally** *adverb*. ◷ 19c: from Latin *germen* bud or sprout.

germinate /ˈdʒɜːmɪneɪt/ ▷ *verb* (***germinated***, ***germinating***) **1** *intr, biol* said of a seed or spore: to show the first signs of development into a new individual. **2 a** to make (a seed, an idea, etc) begin to grow; **b** *intr* to come into being or existence. • **germination** *noun* the first stages in the development of an embryo into a seedling, involving the emergence of the RADICLE (sense 1) and PLUMULE (sense 1) from the seed. ◷ 17c: from Latin *germinare, germinatum*.

germ warfare ▷ *noun* the use of bacteria to inflict disease on an enemy in war.

gerontocracy /dʒɛrɒnˈtɒkrəsɪ/ ▷ *noun* **1** government by old people. **2** a state, country, society, etc that has this form of government. • **gerontocratic** /-təˈkratɪk/ *adj* relating to, or characteristic of, a gerontocracy. • **gerontocrat** *noun*. ◷ 19c: from Greek *geron* old man + -CRACY.

gerontology /dʒɛrɒnˈtɒlədʒɪ/ ▷ *noun* the scientific study of old age, the ageing process and the problems of elderly people. • **gerontological** /-təˈlɒdʒɪkl/ *adj* relating to gerontology. • **gerontologist** *noun* someone who studies, or is expert in, gerontology. ◷ Early 20c: from Greek *geron, gerontos* old man + -LOGY 1.

gerrymander /ˈdʒɛrɪmandə(r)/ *derog* ▷ *verb* (***gerrymandered***, ***gerrymandering***) **1** to arrange or change the boundaries of (one or more electoral constituencies) so as to favour one political party. **2** to manipulate (eg data, a situation, etc) unfairly. ▷ *noun* a rearrangement or manipulation of this sort. • **gerrymandering** *noun*. ◷ 19c: named after Massachusetts Governor Elbridge Gerry (1744–1814) and SALAMANDER, from the shape on the map of one of his electoral districts after manipulation.

gerund /ˈdʒɛrənd/ ▷ *noun, grammar* a noun that is formed from a verb and which describes an action. In English it ends in *-ing*, eg 'the *baking* of bread' and '*Smoking* damages your health'. • **gerundial** *adj*. ◷ 16c: from Latin *gerundium*, from *gerere* to carry.

gerundive /dʒəˈrʌndɪv/ ▷ *noun, Latin grammar* an adjectival form of a verb, used to indicate that something deserves or requires to be done, as in *agenda* 'requiring to be done' (see AGENDA). ◷ Early 18c; 15c in original sense meaning GERUND.

gesso /ˈdʒɛsoʊ/ ▷ *noun* (***gessoes***) plaster for sculpting with or painting on. ◷ 16c: Italian, from Latin *gypsum*; see GYPSUM.

gestalt /gəˈʃtalt, gəˈʃtɑːlt/ ▷ *noun* (***gestalts*** or ***gestalten***) *psychol* a whole pattern or structure perceived as something greater than simply the sum of its separate parts. ◷ 20c: from German *Gestalt* form or shape.

Gestalt psychology ▷ *noun* a school of psychology based on the concept that the whole is greater than the sum of its parts.

Gestapo /gəˈstɑːpoʊ/ ▷ *noun* (*plural* in sense 2 ***gestapos***) **1** *historical* the secret police in Nazi Germany, known for its brutality. **2** (**gestapos**) *derog* any similar secret police organization. ◷ 1930s: from German *Geheime Staatspolizei*, secret state police.

gestate /dʒɛˈsteɪt/ ▷ *verb* (***gestated***, ***gestating***) *tr & intr* **1** *zool* said of a mammal that bears live young: to carry (young) or be carried in the uterus, and to undergo physical development, during the period between fertilization and birth. **2** to develop (an idea, etc) slowly in the mind. ◷ 19c: from Latin *gestare, gestatum* to carry.

gestation /dʒɛˈsteɪʃən/ ▷ *noun, zool* in mammals that bear live young: the period between fertilization of the egg and birth, during which the embryo develops in the uterus of the mother. ◷ 17c; 16c in general sense of 'an act of carrying': from Latin *gestatio* from *gestare* to carry.

gesticulate /dʒəˈstɪkjʊleɪt/ ▷ *verb* (***gesticulated***, ***gesticulating***) **1** *intr* to make gestures, especially when speaking. **2** to express (eg feelings) by means of gestures. • **gesticulation** *noun* the act, an instance or the process of gesticulating. ◷ 17c: from Latin *gesticulare*, from *gestus* gesture.

gestural /ˈdʒɛstʃərəl/ ▷ *adj* **1** relating to gesture. **2** by or using gestures.

gesture /ˈdʒɛstʃə(r)/ ▷ *noun* **1** a movement of a part of the body as an expression of meaning, especially when speaking. **2** something done to communicate feelings or intentions, especially when these are friendly. **3** *derog* something done simply as a formality ▫ ***Asking our opinion was merely a gesture.*** ▷ *verb* (***gestured***, ***gesturing***) **1** *intr* to make gestures. **2** to express (eg feelings) with gestures. ◷ 15c, meaning 'bearing or deportment': from Latin *gestus*.

Gesundheit / *German* gəˈzʊnthaɪt/ *exclamation* said to someone who sneezes: bless you! ◷ 20c: German, literally 'good health'.

get ▷ *verb* (***got***, *past participle* ***got*** or (*US*) ***gotten***, ***getting***) **1** to receive or obtain. **2** to have or possess. **3** *tr & intr* (*also* **get across** or **get someone across** or **away, to, through**, *etc*) to go or make them go, move, travel or arrive as specified ▫ ***tried to get past him*** ▫ ***Will you get him to bed at 8?*** ▫ ***got to Paris on Friday.*** **4** (*often* **get something down, in, out**, *etc*) to fetch, take, or bring it as specified ▫ ***Get it down from the shelf.*** **5** to put into a particular state or condition ▫ ***Don't get it wet*** ▫ ***got him into trouble.*** **6** *intr* to become ▫ ***I got angry.*** **7** to catch (a disease, etc) ▫ ***She got measles and couldn't come.*** **8** to order or persuade ▫ ***Get him to help us.*** **9** *colloq* to receive (a broadcast, etc) ▫ ***unable to get the World Service.*** **10** *colloq* to make contact with someone, especially by telephone ▫ ***never get him at home.*** **11** *colloq* to arrive at (a number, etc) by calculation. **12** *intr, colloq* to receive permission (to do something) ▫ ***Can you get to stay out late?*** **13** *colloq* to prepare (a meal). **14** *colloq* to buy or pay for something ▫ ***got her some flowers for her birthday.*** **15** *colloq* to suffer ▫ ***got a broken arm.*** **16** *colloq* to receive something as punishment ▫ ***got ten years for armed robbery.*** **17** *colloq* to attack, punish, or otherwise cause harm to them ▫ ***I'll get you for that!*** **18** *colloq* to annoy someone. **19** *colloq* to understand something. **20** *colloq* to hear something ▫ ***I didn't quite get his name.*** **21** *colloq* to affect someone emotionally. ▫ ***The sight of the starving children really got to me.*** **22** *colloq* to baffle someone ▫ ***You've got me there.*** See also have got to below. ▷ *noun, derog slang* a stupid or contemptible person; a git. ▷ *exclamation* clear off! get lost! • **be getting on 1** said of a person: to grow old. **2** said of time, etc: to grow late. • **be getting on for ...** *colloq* to be approaching (a certain time or age). • **get along with you!** *colloq* **1** go away! **2** an expression of disbelief. • **get it** *slang* to be punished. • **get it together** *colloq* to use one's energies and abilities effectively. • **get it up** *slang* to succeed in having an erection. • **get nowhere** *colloq* to make no progress or produce no results. • **get one's own back** *colloq* to have one's revenge. • **get somewhere** *colloq* to make progress. • **get there** *colloq* to make progress towards or achieve one's final aim. • **have got** to have; to be in the state of having ▫ ***I've got a headache*** ▫ ***Have you got a drink?*** • **have got into someone** *colloq* to have affected or taken control of their behaviour ▫ ***What's got into him?*** • **have got to** to have to, to be required to do something ▫ ***I've got to write to her at once.*** • **tell someone where to get off** *colloq* to deal with someone rudely and dismissively. ◷ 13c: from Norse *geta* to obtain or beget.

■ **get about** or **around** *colloq* **1** to travel; to go from place to place. **2** said of a rumour, etc: to circulate.

■ **get something across** to make it understood.

■ **get ahead** to make progress; to be successful.

■ **get along with someone** *colloq* to be on friendly terms with them. See also *get along with you!* above.

■ **get at someone** *colloq* **1** to criticize or victimize them persistently. **2** *colloq* to influence them by dishonest means, eg bribery.

■ **get at something 1** to reach or take hold of it. **2** *colloq* to suggest or imply it □ *What are you getting at?*

■ **get away 1** to leave or be free to leave. **2** to escape. **3** *colloq* as an exclamation: used to express disbelief, shock, etc.

■ **get away with something** to commit (an offence or wrongdoing, etc) without being caught or punished.

■ **get back at someone** or **get someone back** *colloq* to take revenge on them.

■ **get by 1** *colloq* to manage to live. **2** *colloq* to be just about acceptable.

■ **get someone down** *colloq* to make them sad or depressed.

■ **get something down 1** to manage to swallow it. **2** to write it down.

■ **get down to something** to apply oneself to (a task or piece of work).

■ **get in 1** said of a political party: to be elected to power. **2** to be accepted for entry or membership.

■ **get something in 1** to gather or harvest it. **2** *colloq* to succeed in doing or making it before something else occurs □ *tried to get some work in before dinner.*

■ **get in on something** *colloq* to take part in it or share in it.

■ **get into something** *colloq* to develop a liking or enthusiasm for it. See also *have got into someone* above.

■ **get in with someone** *colloq* to become friendly with them, often for selfish reasons.

■ **get off** or **get someone off** *colloq* **1** to escape, or cause them to escape, with no punishment or with only the stated punishment □ *was charged but got off* □ *managed to get him off with a warning.* **2** to fall asleep or send (eg a child) to sleep.

■ **get off something** *colloq* to stop discussing or dealing with (a subject).

■ **get off on something** *colloq* to derive excitement from it.

■ **get off with someone** *colloq* to begin a casual sexual relationship with them.

■ **get on** *colloq* to make progress; to be successful. See also be getting on above.

■ **get on at** or **to someone** *colloq* to pester or criticize them continually.

■ **get on to someone 1** to make contact with them. **2** to begin dealing with them.

■ **get on to something 1** to find out the truth about it. **2** to start dealing with a matter.

■ **get on with someone** to have a friendly relationship with them.

■ **get on with something** to continue working on it or dealing or progressing with it.

■ **get out** said of information: to become known.

■ **get something out 1** to manage to say it, usually with difficulty. **2** to publish it.

■ **get out of something** to avoid having to do it.

■ **get over someone** or **something** to be no longer emotionally affected by them or it.

■ **get over something** to recover from (an illness, disappointment, etc).

■ **get something over** to explain it successfully; to make it understood.

■ **get something over with** to deal with (something unpleasant) as quickly as possible.

■ **get round** *colloq* said of information, a rumour, etc: to become generally known.

■ **get round someone** *colloq* to persuade them or win their approval or permission.

■ **get round something** to successfully pass by or negotiate (a problem, etc).

■ **get round to something** or **someone** to deal with it or them eventually.

■ **get through something 1** to complete (a task, piece of work, etc). **2** to use it steadily until it is finished □ *got through a bottle of whisky every day.* **3** *colloq* to pass (a test, etc).

■ **get someone through** to help someone pass (a test, etc).

■ **get through to someone 1** to make contact with them by telephone. **2** to make them understand □ *We can't get through to him how important this is.*

■ **get to someone** *colloq* to annoy them □ *You shouldn't let him get to you.*

■ **get up 1** to get out of bed. **2** to stand up. **3** said of the wind, etc: to become strong. See also GET IT UP above.

■ **get oneself up** to get dressed up.

■ **get something up 1** to arrange, organize or prepare it □ *decided to get up a celebration.* **2** to learn it by deliberate effort. **3** to increase and maintain (speed).

■ **get someone up** to make them get out of bed.

■ **get together** to assemble, especially for a specified purpose □ *got together for a drink* □ *got together to discuss the pay freeze.* See also GET-TOGETHER.

■ **get up to something** *colloq* to do or be involved in it, especially when it is bad, unwelcome or not approved of □ *He's forever getting up to no good.*

geta /ˈgeɪtə, ˈgɛtə/ ▷ *noun* (*plural* **geta** or **getas**) a Japanese wooden sandal with a thong between the big toe and the other toes. ⓒ 19c: Japanese.

get-at-able /gɛtˈatəbəl/ ▷ *adj, colloq* able to be easily reached, achieved, etc.

getaway ▷ *noun* an escape, especially after committing a crime. Also *as adj* □ *getaway car.*

get-out ▷ *noun* **1 a** a means or instance of escape; **b** *as adj* □ *a get-out clause.* **2** *theat* **a** the dismantling and removal of all scenery, props, lighting, etc at the end of a run; **b** the total weekly cost of a production. • **as all get-out** *colloq* (emphasizing the preceding adjective) as can be □ *as drunk as all get-out.*

get-rich-quick ▷ *adj, colloq* applied to those who attempt or wish to make money rapidly, and often by dubious means.

getter ▷ *noun, electronics* any of various substances used for removing the residual gas from the vacuum in valves. Also *as adj* and *in compounds* □ *a getter metal.* See also GO-GETTER. ⓒ 20c in this sense; 15c as agent noun of GET.

get-together ▷ *noun, colloq* an informal meeting.

get-up ▷ *noun, colloq* an outfit or clothes, especially when considered strange or remarkable.

get-up-and-go ▷ *noun, colloq* energy.

geum /'dʒiːəm/ ▷ *noun* a perennial plant with lobed leaves and brilliant yellow, orange or scarlet flowers, often grown in rock gardens. ⓒ 16c: scientific Latin.

GeV ▷ *abbreviation* giga-electron-volt, a unit of energy, equal to 10^9 electron volts, used in high-energy physics.

gewgaw /'gjuːgɔː, 'guː-/ ▷ *noun, derog, old use* a flashy trinket. ⓒ 13c as *giuegoue*.

geyser /'giːzə(r), 'gaɪzə(r)/ ▷ *noun* **1** *geol* in an area of volcanic activity: a type of hot spring that intermittently spouts hot water and steam into the air, used as a source of GEOTHERMAL ENERGY in some parts of the world. **2** a domestic appliance for heating water rapidly. ⓒ 18c: from Icelandic *Geysir*, the name of a famous hot spring, from Norse *geysa* to gush.

G5 or **G-5** ▷ *abbreviation* GROUP OF FIVE.

GH ▷ *abbreviation*, **1** *IVR* Ghana. **2** growth hormone.

Ghanaian /gɑː'neɪən/ ▷ *adj* belonging or relating to Ghana a W African republic or its inhabitants. ▷ *noun* a citizen or inhabitant of, or person born in, Ghana.

gharial or **garial** /'gʌrɪəl/ ▷ *noun* a large narrow-snouted Indian crocodile which, although considered sacred by the Hindus, is now an endangered species. Also called GAVIAL. ⓒ 19c: from Hindustani *ghariyal*.

ghastly /'gɑːstlɪ, 'gɑːslɪ/ ▷ *adj* (*ghastlier*, *ghastliest*) **1** extremely frightening, hideous or horrific. **2** *colloq* very bad. **3** *colloq* very ill. ▷ *adverb, colloq* extremely; unhealthily □ *ghastly pale*. • **ghastliness** *noun*. ⓒ 14c as *gastlich* in sense 1, from obsolete *gast* to terrify.

ghat /gɔːt/ ▷ *noun, Indian subcontinent* **1** a mountain pass. **2** a set of steps leading down to a river. **3** (in full **burning ghat**) the site of a Hindu funeral pyre at the top of a river ghat. ⓒ 17c: Hindi, meaning 'descent'.

ghee or **ghi** /giː/ ▷ *noun* in Indian cookery: clarified butter made from cow's or buffalo's milk and used as a cooking oil. ⓒ 17c: from Hindi *ghi*, from Sanskrit *ghri* to sprinkle.

gherkin /'gɜːkɪn/ ▷ *noun* **1** a variety of cucumber that bears very small fruits. **2** a small or immature fruit of any of various varieties of cucumber, used for pickling. ⓒ 17c: from Dutch *augurkje*.

ghetto /'gɛtoʊ/ ▷ *noun* (*ghettos* or *ghettoes*) **1** *derog* a poor area densely populated by people from a deprived social group, especially a racial minority. **2** *historical* a part of a European city to which Jews were formerly restricted. ⓒ 17c: perhaps from Italian *ghetto* foundry, after one on the site of the first Jewish ghetto in Venice.

ghetto-blaster ▷ *noun, colloq* a large portable radio-cassette recorder, especially one used to play pop music at high volume. ⓒ 1980s, originally US.

ghettoize or **ghettoise** /'gɛtoʊaɪz/ ▷ *verb* (*ghettoized*, *ghettoizing*) to think of (a group of people or things) as being confined to a specific restricted function or area of activity; to pigeonhole. • **ghettoization** *noun*.

ghi see GHEE

ghillie see GILLIE

ghost /goʊst/ ▷ *noun* **1** the spirit of a dead person when it is visible in some form to a living person. See also SPECTRE. **2** a suggestion, hint or trace. **3** a faint shadow attached to the image on a television screen. ▷ *verb* (*ghosted*, *ghosting*) *tr & intr* to be a GHOST WRITER for a person or of (some written work).• **not a ghost of a chance** no chance at all. • **give up the ghost** see under GIVE. ⓒ Anglo-Saxon *gast*.

ghostbuster ▷ *noun* someone who claims to be able to rid a haunted house, etc of its ghosts.

ghostly ▷ *adj* **1** belonging to or like a ghost or ghosts. **2** relating to or suggesting the presence of ghosts. • **ghostliness** *noun*.

ghost town ▷ *noun* a deserted town, especially one that was formerly thriving.

ghost word ▷ *noun* a word found in dictionaries that never existed in real life, but arose from a mistake, eg when a manuscript was transcribed or a page was set up in print.

ghost writer ▷ *noun* someone who writes books, speeches, etc on behalf of another person who is credited as their author.

ghoul /guːl/ ▷ *noun* **1** someone who is interested in morbid or disgusting things. **2 a** in Arab mythology: a demon that robs graves and eats dead bodies; **b** an evil spirit or presence. ⓒ 18c: from Arabic *ghul*.

ghoulish ▷ *adj* like or typical of a ghoul. • **ghoulishly** *adverb*. • **ghoulishness** *noun*.

GHQ ▷ *abbreviation, military* General Headquarters.

ghyll see GILL[3]

GHz ▷ *abbreviation* gigahertz (see GIGA-).

GI ▷ *noun* (*GIs*) *colloq* a soldier in the US army, especially during World War II. ⓒ 20c: from *G*overnment *I*ssue.

giant /dʒaɪənt/ ▷ *noun* **1** in stories: a huge, extremely strong, often cruel creature of human form. **2** *colloq* an unusually large person or animal. **3** a person, group, etc of exceptional ability, importance or size □ *corporate giants*. ▷ *adj* **1** *colloq* huge □ *giant portions*. **2** belonging to a particularly large species, in implied contrast to smaller ones □ *giant tortoise*. • **giantess** *noun* a female giant. ⓒ 13c: from Greek *gigas*.

giant panda ▷ *noun* a large bear-like mammal, native to Tibet and south-west China, which has thick white fur and black legs, shoulders, ears, and patches round the eyes. It is now an endangered species.

giant slalom ▷ *noun, skiing* a type of slalom in which the distance from one GATE (sense 5) to the next is farther, and the course longer, than in ordinary slalom.

giardiasis /dʒiːɑː'daɪəsɪs/ ▷ *noun, medicine* an intestinal infection caused by ingesting a flagellate protozoan, usually from water that contains the faeces of infected animals. The symptoms are prolonged diarrhoea and abdominal pain. ⓒ Early 20c: named after A Giard (died 1908), the French biologist who identified the protozoan that causes the infection.

giant star ▷ *noun, astron* a highly luminous star that is much larger than the Sun, and is reaching the end of its life.

gib /dʒɪb/ ▷ *noun* a small metal or wooden wedge used for keeping a machine part in place. ▷ *verb* (*gibbed*, *gibbing*) *tr* to secure with a gib. ⓒ 18c.

Gib /dʒɪb/ ▷ *noun, colloq* Gibraltar, a British colony located on a rocky peninsula off the coast of SW Spain.

gibber /'dʒɪbə(r)/ ▷ *verb* (*gibbered*, *gibbering*) *intr* **1** to talk so fast that one cannot be understood. **2** *derog* to talk foolishly. **3** said of monkeys, apes, etc: to make their usual chattering sound. • **gibbering** *adj*. ⓒ 17c: imitating the sound.

gibberellin /dʒɪbə'relɪn/ ▷ *noun, bot* any of a group of plant hormones that stimulate rapid growth by the elongation of cells as opposed to cell division. ⓒ 20c: from *Gibberella* (the generic name of a type of fungus in which it was first found) + -IN.

gibberish ▷ *noun* **1** speech that is meaning less or difficult to understand. **2** utter nonsense. ⓒ 16c.

gibbet /'dʒɪbɪt/ ▷ *noun, historical* **1** a gallows-like frame on which the bodies of executed criminals were hung as a public warning. **2** a gallows. ▷ *verb* (*gibbeted*, *gibbeting*) **1** *historical* to hang someone on a gibbet. **2** to expose someone to public ridicule. ◎ 13c: from French *gibet* gallows.

gibbon /ˈgɪbən/ ▷ *noun* the smallest of the apes, with very long arms, and the only ape to walk upright habitually, found in SE Asia. ◎ 18c: French.

gibbous /ˈgɪbəs/ ▷ *adj, technical* **1** said of the moon or a planet: not fully illuminated but more than half illuminated. **2** humpbacked. **3** swollen; bulging. • **gibbosity** /gɪˈbɒsɪtɪ/ *noun*. ◎ 17c in senses 1 and 2; 15c, meaning 'convex': from Latin *gibbus* hump.

gibe¹ or **jibe** /dʒaɪb/ ▷ *verb* (***gibed***, ***gibing***) *intr* to mock, scoff or jeer. ▷ *noun* a jeer. • **giber** *noun*. • **gibing** *adj, noun*. • **gibingly** *adverb*. ◎ 16c: from French *giber* to treat roughly.

gibe² see GYBE

giblets /ˈdʒɪbləts/ ▷ *plural noun* the heart, liver and other edible internal organs of a chicken or other fowl. ◎ 15c as singular: from French *gibelet* game stew, from *gibier* game.

giddy /ˈgɪdɪ/ ▷ *adj* (***giddier***, ***giddiest***) **1** suffering an unbalancing spinning sensation. **2** causing such a sensation. **3** *literary* overwhelmed by feelings of excitement or pleasure. **4** light-hearted and carefree; frivolous. • **giddily** *adverb*. • **giddiness** *noun*. ◎ Anglo-Saxon *gidig* insane.

GIFT /gɪft/ ▷ *abbreviation* gamete intrafallopian transfer, an infertility treatment involving direct transfer of eggs and sperm into the woman's FALLOPIAN TUBES, where conception may occur. Compare IN-VITRO FERTILIZATION, ZIFT.

gift ▷ *noun* **1** something given; a present. **2** a natural ability. **3** the act or process of giving □ *the gift of a book.* **4** *colloq* something easily obtained, made easily available or simply easy □ *The first exam question was a gift.* ▷ *verb* (***gifted***, ***gifting***) *formal* to give something as a present to someone. • **in someone's gift** *formal* able to be given away by someone if they wish. • **look a gift horse in the mouth** *usually with negatives* to find fault with or quibble over a gift or unexpected opportunity. • **gift of the gab** see under GAB. ◎ 13c: from Norse *gipt*.

gifted ▷ *adj* having a great natural ability. • **giftedness** *noun*.

gift shop ▷ *noun* a shop selling articles suitable for presents.

gift token and **gift voucher** ▷ *noun, Brit* a voucher given in place of a present, which allows the person receiving it to buy something of their choice.

gift-wrap ▷ *verb* to wrap something attractively, especially for giving as a present.

gig¹ /gɪg/ ▷ *noun* **1** *historical* a small open two-wheeled horse-drawn carriage. **2** a small rowing boat carried on a ship. ◎ 18c: probably from earlier *gigge* a whirling thing.

gig² /gɪg/ *colloq* ▷ *noun* **1** a pop, jazz or folk concert. **2** a musician's booking to perform, especially for one night only. ▷ *verb* (***gigged***, ***gigging***) *intr* to play a gig or gigs.

giga see GIGUE

giga- /ˈgaɪgə, gɪgə, dʒɪgə/ ▷ *prefix, denoting* **1** in the metric system: ten to the power of nine (10^9), ie one thousand million □ *gigahertz.* **2** *computing* two to the power of thirty (2^{30}) □ *gigabyte.* ◎ 1940s: from Greek *gigas* giant.

gigantesque /dʒaɪganˈtɛsk/ ▷ *adj* suitable for or like a giant.

gigantic /dʒaɪˈgantɪk/ ▷ *adj* huge; enormous. • **gigantically** *adverb*. ◎ 17c: from Greek *gigantikos*, from *gigas* giant.

gigantism /dʒaɪˈgantɪzəm/ ▷ *noun, biol* **1** excessive overgrowth of the whole human body, usually owing to overactivity of the PITUITARY GLAND. **2** excessive size in plants. ◎ 19c.

giggle /ˈgɪgəl/ ▷ *verb* (***giggled***, ***giggling***) *intr* to laugh quietly in short bursts or in a nervous or silly way. ▷ *noun* **1** such a laugh. **2** (**the giggles**) a fit of giggling. **3** *colloq* a funny person, situation, thing, activity, etc □ *the film was a right giggle.* • **giggler** *noun*. • **giggling** *noun, adj*. ◎ 16c: imitating the sound.

giggly (***gigglier***, ***giggliest***) ▷ *adj* giggling or likely to giggle.

GIGO /ˈgaɪgoʊ/ ▷ *abbreviation, computing* garbage in, garbage out, ie bad input results in bad output.

gigolo /ˈdʒɪgəloʊ/ ▷ *noun* **1** *derog* a young, and usually attractive, man who is paid by an older woman to be her companion, escort and, sometimes, lover. **2** a hired professional dancing partner or escort. ◎ 1920s: French.

gigot /ˈdʒɪgət, ˈʒɪgoʊ/ ▷ *noun* a leg of lamb or mutton. ◎ 16c: French.

gigue /ʒiːg/ and **giga** /ˈdʒiːgə/ ▷ *noun* (***gigues*** or ***gigas***) the music for a lively dance, usually in 6/8 time, in two repeated sections. It was often used to complete 18c dance suites. ◎ 17c: the two forms are French and Italian respectively, literally meaning 'fiddle' or 'lute'.

gila monster /hiːlə —/ and **gila** ▷ *noun* a venomous lizard with dark colouring and yellow mottling, bead-like scales, a blunt head and a thick tail, found in the SW states of the US.

gild¹ /gɪld/ ▷ *verb* (***gilded*** or ***gilt***, ***gilding***) **1** to cover something with a thin coating of gold or something similar. **2** to give something a falsely attractive or valuable appearance. • **gild the lily** to try to improve something which is already beautiful enough, often spoiling it in the process. ◎ Anglo-Saxon, from *gyldan* gold.

gild² see GUILD

gilder see GUILDER

gilet /ˈʒiːleɪ/ ▷ *noun* **1** a garment like a waistcoat. **2** a quilted sleeveless jacket. ◎ 19c: French.

gill¹ /gɪl/ ▷ *noun* **1** in all fishes and many other aquatic animals: a respiratory organ that extracts dissolved oxygen from the surrounding water. **2** see LAMELLA sense 3. **3** (**gills**) *colloq* the flesh around the jaw. • **green about the gills** see under GREEN. ◎ 14c: perhaps from Scandinavian.

gill² /dʒɪl/ ▷ *noun* **1** in the UK: a unit of liquid measure equal to 142.1ml or a quarter of a pint. **2** *colloq* an alcoholic drink. ◎ 13c: from French *gelle*.

gill³ or **ghyll** (the latter spelling apparently invented by Wordsworth) /gɪl/ ▷ *noun* **1** a deep wooded ravine. **2** a mountain stream. ◎ 15c: from Norse *gil*.

gill⁴ /dʒɪl/ ▷ *noun, Brit* a female feret, weasel or polecat. ◎ 19c in this sense; 15c used a contemptuous term for a woman: a shortened form of the female name *Gillian*.

gillyflower /ˈdʒɪlɪʃlaʊə(r)/ ▷ *noun* **1** (*in full* **clove gillyflower**) a PINK that smells of CLOVES (see CLOVE¹ *noun* 2). **2** a name applied to various other garden flowers, eg WALLFLOWER and STOCK (sense 11). ◎ 14c: from French *gilofre* clove.

gillie or **ghillie** /ˈgɪlɪ/ ▷ *noun* (***gillies*** or ***ghillies***) a guide or assistant to a game-hunter or fisherman, especially in Scotland. ◎ 19c: from Gaelic *gille* boy.

gilt¹ /gɪlt/ ▷ *adj* covered with a thin coating of gold or apparently so covered; gilded. ▷ *noun* **1** gold or a gold-like substance used in gilding. **2** (**gilts**) gilt-edged securities. **3** glitter; superficial attractiveness; glamour. ▷ verb *past tense, past participle of* GILD¹. • **take the gilt off the gingerbread** to destroy the glamour or illusion. ◎ 14c.

gilt² /gɪlt/ ▷ *noun* a young female pig, especially one that has not produced a litter. ◎ 15c: from Norse *gyltr*.

gilt-edged ▷ *adj* **1** said of a book: having pages with gilded edges. **2** of the highest quality. **3** said of government securities with a fixed rate of interest: able to be sold at face value. See also GILTS at GILT[1].

gimbals /'dʒɪmbəlz/ ▷ *plural noun* a device that allows a navigation instrument mounted on it to rotate freely about two perpendicular axes, and so to remain in a horizontal position at sea or in the air. ⓒ 18c: from French *gemel* a double ring for a finger.

gimcrack /'dʒɪmkrak/ *derog* ▷ *adj* cheap, showy and badly made. ▷ *noun* a cheap and showy article. ⓒ 18c in this sense; from 14c *gibecrake* fancy woodwork.

gimlet /'gɪmlət/ ▷ *noun* **1** a T-shaped hand-tool for boring holes in wood. **2** a cocktail made of lime juice and gin or vodka. ⓒ 15c: from French *guimbelet*.

gimlet-eyed ▷ *adj* having a piercing look or stare.

gimme /'gɪmɪ/ ▷ *contraction* give me. ▷ *noun* (***gimmes***) *golf* **1** *colloq* a short putt that a player is willing to accept as successfully played by their opponent without it actually being played. **2** (**the gimmes**) *US slang* greed; acquisitiveness. ⓒ 19c; 20c as *noun*.

gimmick /'gɪmɪk/ ▷ *noun, derog* a scheme or object used to attract attention or publicity, especially to bring in customers. • **gimmickry** *noun* gimmicks, or the use of gimmicks. • **gimmicky** /'gɪmɪkɪ/ *adj* **1** relating to a gimmick or gimmicks. **2** designed to catch attention. **3** insignificant. ⓒ 20c.

gimp /gɪmp/ ▷ *noun* a strip of silk or other fabric with a core of wire or cord, used as a decoration in dressmaking, etc. ⓒ 17c.

gin[1] /dʒɪn/ ▷ *noun* an alcoholic spirit made from barley, rye or maize and flavoured with juniper berries. ⓒ 18c: from Dutch *genever* juniper.

gin[2] /dʒɪn/ ▷ *noun* **1** (*also* **gin trap**) a wire noose laid as a snare or trap for catching game. **2** a COTTON GIN. **3** the building in which a cotton gin is housed. **4** a hoisting machine, especially one equipped with a windlass, pulleys and ropes. ▷ *verb* (***ginned***, ***ginning***) **1** to snare or trap (game) in a gin. **2** to remove (the seeds) from raw cotton using a cotton gin. ⓒ 13c: from French *engin* engine or ingenuity.

gin[3] /dʒɪn/ ▷ *noun* an Australian Aboriginal woman. ⓒ 19c: from Aboriginal *diyin* a woman or wife.

gin[4] see GIN RUMMY

gin and it ▷ *noun* a drink consisting of GIN1 and Italian vermouth.

ginger /'dʒɪndʒə(r)/ ▷ *noun* **1** an aromatic spicy swollen root or rhizome, often dried and ground to a yellow powder and widely used as a flavouring in biscuits, cakes, curries, etc or preserved in syrup. **2** the perennial tropical plant from which this root is obtained. **3** a reddish-brown colour. **4** *colloq* energy; liveliness. ▷ *adj* **1** flavoured with ginger. **2 a** said of hair: reddish-orange in colour; **b** reddish-brown in colour. ▷ *verb* (***gingered***, ***gingering***) (*usually* **ginger up**) *colloq* to urge, persuade or force someone or something to become more lively, active, interesting or efficient. • **gingerly** *adj* see separate entry. ⓒ Anglo-Saxon *ingifer*, from Latin *ingiber*, from Sanskrit *srnga* horn + *vera* body (from the shape of the root).

ginger ale and **ginger beer** ▷ *noun* a non-alcoholic fizzy drink flavoured with ginger.

ginger beer plant ▷ *noun* a symbiotic association of a yeast and a bacterium, used to ferment a sugary liquid also containing ginger, which, after the alcohol has been removed, is used to produce GINGER BEER. Also called **Californian bees**.

gingerbread ▷ *noun* **1** a cake flavoured with treacle and ginger. **2** *Brit* (**Gingerbread**) a self-help support organization for single parents. • **take the gilt off the gingerbread** see under GILT.

ginger group ▷ *noun* especially in politics: a small group within a larger one (such as a political party) which urges stronger or more radical action.

gingerly /'dʒɪndʒəlɪ/ ▷ *adverb* with delicate caution. ▷ *adj* very cautious or wary. ⓒ 17c; 16c in the sense 'daintily': perhaps from French *gensor* delicate.

ginger nut and **ginger snap** ▷ *noun* a ginger-flavoured biscuit.

ginger wine ▷ *noun* an alcoholic drink made by fermenting sugar and water, and flavoured with various spices, chiefly ginger.

gingery ▷ *adj* **1** tasting of, flavoured with, coloured like, etc ginger. **2** said of remarks: critical.

gingham /'gɪŋəm/ ▷ *noun* striped or checked cotton cloth. Also *as adj* □ ***a gingham frock.*** ⓒ 17c: from Malay *ginggang* striped.

gingili /'dʒɪndʒɪlɪ/ ▷ *noun* **1** the plant SESAME. **2** the oil obtained from its seeds. ⓒ 18c: from Hindi *jinjali*.

gingival /dʒɪn'dʒaɪvəl, -dʒɪvəl/ ▷ *adj, medicine, dentistry, etc* relating to the gums. ⓒ 17c: from Latin *gingiva* gum.

gingivitis /dʒɪndʒɪ'vaɪtɪs/ ▷ *noun, medicine, dentistry, etc* inflammation of the gums, usually caused by the accumulation of PLAQUE (sense 3) in the region where the gums meet the teeth. ⓒ 19c.

gingko see GINKGO

ginglymus /'dʒɪŋglɪməs, 'gɪŋ-/ ▷ *noun* (***ginglymi*** /-maɪ/) *anatomy* a joint, such as the knee or elbow, that permits movement in one plane only; a hinge joint. ⓒ 17c: from Greek *ginglymos* a hinge.

gink /gɪŋk/ ▷ *noun, slang* (*originally US & often disparaging*) someone, especially a man, who is considered a bit odd.

ginkgo /'gɪŋkgoʊ/ or **gingko** ▷ *noun* (***ginkgoes*** or ***gingkoes***) a deciduous cone-bearing tree, native to China and Japan, which has fan-shaped leaves similar to those of the maidenhair fern. Also called **maidenhair tree**. ⓒ 18c: from Japanese *ginkyo*, from Chinese *yin* silver + *hing* apricot.

ginormous /dʒaɪ'nɔːməs/ ▷ *adj, colloq* exceptionally huge. ⓒ 1940s: from GIGANTIC + ENORMOUS.

gin rummy and **gin** ▷ *noun, cards* a type of RUMMY in which players have the option of ending the round at any time when their unmatched cards count ten or less, though they may decide not to do so for tactical reasons.

ginseng /'dʒɪnseŋ/ ▷ *noun* **1 a** a plant cultivated in China for its roots; **b** a similar American species of this plant. **2** the aromatic root of either of these plants. **3** a preparation derived from the root of either or these plants, widely used as a tonic, stimulant and aphrodisiac. ⓒ 17c: Chinese *ren-shen*, perhaps 'image of man', from the shape of the root.

gin sling ▷ *noun* an iced drink of sweetened gin.

gin trap see under GIN[2]

giocoso /dʒɒ'koʊsoʊ/ *music* ▷ *adverb* in a lively or humorous manner. ▷ *adj* lively or humorous. ⓒ 19c: Italian.

gip same as GYP

gippy tummy or **gyppy tummy** /'dʒɪpɪ —/ ▷ *noun, colloq* a severe stomach upset with diarrhoea, especially as suffered by visitors to hot countries. ⓒ 20c: from *gippy*, earlier form of GYPPO, meaning 'Egyptian'.

Gipsy see GYPSY

giraffe /dʒɪ'rɑːf/ ▷ *noun* (***giraffes*** or ***giraffe***) a very tall African mammal with an extremely long neck and legs, a small head, large eyes and a pale buff coat boldly marked with irregular chestnut or dark brown blotches. ⓒ 17c: from Arabic *zarafah*.

girandole /'dʒɪrəndoʊl/ ▷ *noun* **1** a branched wall-bracket for candles. **2** a piece of jewellery with a large central stone surrounded by a circle of small stones. **3** a rotating firework. ⓒ 17c: French, from Greek *gyrus* a circle.

girasol or **girasole** /ˈdʒɪrəsɒl, -soʊl/ ▻ *noun* an opal that seems to send a fire-like glow from within in certain lights. ⓒ 16c: Italian *girasole*, from *girare* to turn + *sole* the sun.

gird /gɜːd/ ▻ *verb* (***girded*** or ***girt*** /gɜːt/, ***girding***) *literary* to encircle or fasten something (especially part of the body) with a belt or something similar. • **gird oneself 1** to tuck up loose garments under one's belt (so as to be able to move more quickly). **2** to prepare oneself for action. • **gird** or **gird up one's loins** to prepare oneself for action. ⓒ Anglo-Saxon *gyrdan*.

girder /ˈgɜːdə(r)/ ▻ *noun* a large beam of wood, iron or steel used to support a floor, wall, road or bridge. ⓒ 17c: from GIRD.

girdle¹ /ˈgɜːdəl/ ▻ *noun* **1** a woman's close-fitting elasticated undergarment that covers the area from waist to thigh. **2** *old use* a belt or cord worn round the waist. **3** a surrounding part, especially such a part of the body □ *pelvic girdle*. ▻ *verb* (***girdled***, ***girdling***) **1** to put a girdle on someone or something. **2** *literary* to surround something. ⓒ Anglo-Saxon *gyrdel*, from GIRD.

girdle² see GRIDDLE

girl /gɜːl/ ▻ *noun* **1** a female child. **2** a daughter. **3** *often offensive* a young woman, especially an unmarried one. **4** *often offensive* a woman of any age. **5** *colloq* a woman's female friend or colleague. **6** *colloq* a sweetheart □ *Dave is bringing his girl home for tea.* 7 a female employee, especially (*formerly*) as a maid. ⓒ 13c *gerle*, *girle* and *gurle* a child.

girl Friday ▻ *noun* (***girl Fridays***) a young woman who does general office work. See also MAN FRIDAY. ⓒ 1940s: modelled on *Man Friday*, Crusoe's servant and companion in Defoe's *Robinson Crusoe*.

girlfriend ▻ *noun* **1** a female sexual or romantic partner. **2** a female friend, especially of a woman. **3** *US* used especially by young black women: a close female friend, especially one who shares the speaker's fierce and streetwise sense of independence.

Girl Guide ▻ *noun*, *old use* GUIDE *noun* 4.

girlhood ▻ *noun* the state or time of being a girl.

girlie or **girly** ▻ *adj* ▻ *noun*, *colloq* **1** said of a magazine, picture, etc: featuring naked or nearly naked young women in erotic poses. **2** *derog* girlish, especially in being overly or stereotypically feminine □ *wearing a pink fluffy girly jumper*. ▻ *noun* **1** a girl, especially used as an endearment. **2** *derog* a young woman who dresses, behaves, etc in an overly or stereotypically feminine way.

girlish ▻ *adj* like a girl. • **girlishly** *adverb*. • **girlishness** *noun*.

girl power ▻ *noun*, *colloq* the social and economic importance and influence of young women.

Girl Scout see under GUIDE *noun* 4.

girner /ˈgɜːnə(r)/ ▻ *noun* someone who makes grotesque faces as an entertainment at country fairs, etc. ⓒ 20c: from *girn*, a northern dialect variant of GRIN, with a range of meanings including 'to screw up the face'.

giro /ˈdʒaɪəroʊ/ ▻ *noun* (***giros***) **1** a banking system by which money can be transferred from one account directly to another. **2** *Brit colloq* a social security benefit received in the form of a cheque that can be cashed at a Post Office or paid into a bank or building society. ⓒ 19c: Italian, meaning 'turn' or 'transfer'.

girt *past tense, past participle of* GIRD

girth /gɜːθ/ ▻ *noun* **1** the distance round something such as a tree or a person's waist. **2** the strap round a horse's belly that holds a saddle in place. ▻ *verb* (***girthed***, ***girthing***) to put a girth on (a horse). ⓒ 14c in sense 2: from Norse *gjörth* belt.

gism see JISM

gismo or **gizmo** /ˈgɪzmoʊ/ ▻ *noun* (***gismos*** or ***gizmos***) *colloq* a gadget, a thingummyjig. ⓒ 1940s: US.

gismology or **gizmology** /gɪzˈmɒlədʒɪ/ ▻ *noun* gadgetry; technology involving gadgetry, especially strange or baffling examples of it.

gist /dʒɪst/ ▻ *noun* the general meaning or main point of something said or written. ⓒ 18c: French, 3rd person of *gesir (en)* to consist (in), used in the Anglo-French legal phrase *cest action gist* this action lies.

git ▻ *noun*, *derog slang* a stupid or contemptible person. ⓒ 20c: variant of GET, and now the commoner form.

gite or **gîte** /ʒiːt/ ▻ *noun* (***gites*** or ***gîtes***) in France: a self-catering holiday cottage. ⓒ 20c: French, from *giste* a resting place.

give /gɪv/ ▻ *verb* (***gave***, ***given***, ***giving***) **1** to transfer ownership of something; to transfer possession of something temporarily □ *gave him my watch* □ *Give me your bags.* **2** to provide or administer □ *give advice* □ *give medicine.* **3** to produce □ *Cows give milk.* **4** to perform (an action, service, etc) □ *give a smile* □ *She gave a lecture on beetles.* **5** to pay □ *gave £20 for it.* **6** *intr* to make a donation □ *Please give generously.* **7** (*also* **give something up**) to sacrifice it □ *give one's life* □ *gave up his day off to finish the job on time.* **8** to be the cause or source of something □ *gives me pain.* **9** *intr* to yield or break □ *give under pressure.* **10** to organize something at one's own expense □ *give a party.* **11** to have something as a result □ *four into twenty gives five.* **12** to reward or punish with something □ *was given 20 years.* **13** *colloq* to agree to or admit something; to concede □ *I'll give you that.* **14** to offer a toast to someone or something. **15** *sport* to declare someone to be a specified thing □ *He was given offside.* ▻ *noun* capacity to yield; flexibility □ *a board with plenty of give.* • **give and take** to make mutual concessions. • **give as good as one gets** *colloq* to respond to an attack with equal energy, force and effect. • **give me** *colloq* I prefer □ *Give me jazz any day.* • **give or take something** *colloq* allowing for a (specified) margin of error □ *We have all the money, give or take a pound.* • **give someone to believe that ...** to make someone think that or to give the impression that ... • **give someone up for dead** or **lost**, *etc* to assume that they are dead or lost, etc, after abandoning hope. • **give up the ghost** *colloq* to die. • **give way 1** to allow priority. **2** to collapse under pressure. • **give way to something** to allow oneself to be affected by it □ *give way to tears.* • **what gives?** what is happening, the matter, etc? For many other idioms containing *give*, see under the next significant word in the idiom. ⓒ Anglo-Saxon *gefan*.

■ **give someone away 1** to betray them. **2** to present (the bride) to the bridegroom at a wedding ceremony.

■ **give something away 1** to hand it over as a gift. **2** to sell it at an incredibly low price. **3** to allow (a piece of information) to become known, usually by accident.

■ **give in to someone** or **something** to yield to them; to admit defeat.

■ **give something off** to produce or emit (eg a smell).

■ **give on to** or **into something** said of a passage, etc: to lead or be an opening to it □ *a terrace giving on to the lawn.*

■ **give out** *colloq* to break down or come to an end □ *Their resistance gave out.*

■ **give something out 1** to announce or distribute it. **2** to emit (a sound, smell, etc).

■ **give over** or **give over doing something** *colloq* usually as a command: to stop (doing it) □ *Give over shouting!*

■ **give something over 1** to transfer it. **2** to set it aside or devote it to some purpose □ *The morning was given over to discussing the budgets.*

■ **give up** to admit defeat.

■ **give oneself up** to surrender.

■ **give oneself up to something** to devote oneself to (a cause, etc).

■ **give someone** or **something up** to surrender or hand over (a wanted person, a weapon, etc).

■ **give something up** **1** to renounce or quit (a habit, etc) □ *give up smoking.* **2** to resign from or leave (a job, etc).

■ **give up doing something** to stop making the effort to achieve it □ *gave up trying to talk sense to them.*

give-and-take ▻ *noun* **1** mutual willingness to accept the other's point of view. **2** a useful exchange of views.

giveaway or **giveaway** *colloq* ▻ *noun* **1** an act of accidentally revealing secrets, etc. **2** something obtained extremely easily or cheaply □ *That goal was a giveaway.* **3** a free gift. ▻ *adj* **1** extremely cheap □ *giveaway price.* **2** free.

given /ˈɡɪvən/ ▻ *adj* **1** stated or specified. **2** admitted, assumed or accepted as true. ● **given to something** prone to it; having it as a habit □ *given to biting his nails.* ▻ *prep, conj* accepting (a specified thing) as a basis for discussion; assuming □ *given his illegitimacy* □ *given that he is illegitimate.* ▻ *noun* something that is admitted, assumed or accepted as true □ *His illegitimacy is a given.* ▻ *verb, past participle of* GIVE.

given name ▻ *noun* someone's first or Christian name, especially when contrasted with their SURNAME.

giving /ˈɡɪvɪŋ/ ▻ *adj* generous; liberal. ⓘ 20c: present participle of GIVE.

gizmo see GISMO

gizmology see GISMOLOGY

gizzard /ˈɡɪzəd/ ▻ *noun* **1** in birds, earthworms and certain other animals: a muscular chamber specialized for grinding up indigestible food. **2** *colloq* the stomach. ● **stick in one's gizzard** *colloq* to be distasteful or objectionable. ⓘ 14c: from French *guisier* fowl's liver.

Gk ▻ *abbreviation* Greek.

glabella /ɡləˈbɛlə/ ▻ *noun* (**gabellae** /-liː/) *anatomy* the part of the forehead between the eyebrows and just above. ⓘ 19c: from Latin *glaber* hairless.

glabrous /ˈɡleɪbrəs/ ▻ *adj, scientific* smooth; hairless. ⓘ 17c: from Latin *glaber* hairless, smooth.

glacé /ˈɡlɑseɪ/ ▻ *adj* **1** coated with a sugary glaze; candied □ *glacé cherries.* **2** applied to the icing on cakes, etc: made with icing sugar and liquid □ *fairy cakes with glacé icing.* **3** applied to drinks, etc: frozen or served with ice □ *mousse glacée.* **4** applied especially to thin silk and kid leather: glossy, shiny. ▻ *verb* (**glacéed**, **glacéing**) **1** to crystallize (fruit, etc). **2** to ice (cake, etc) with glacé icing. ⓘ 19c: French.

glacial /ˈɡleɪʃəl, -sɪəl/ ▻ *adj* **1** *geol, geog* **a** relating to or resembling a glacier; **b** caused by the action of a glacier. **2** referring or relating to ice or its effects. **3** said of a geological time period, etc: characterized by the presence of glaciers or large masses of ice. **4** *chem* said of a chemical compound: tending to form crystals that resemble ice □ *glacial acetic acid.* **5** *now colloq* extremely cold. **6** hostile □ *a glacial stare.* ▻ *noun* a glacial period; an ice age. ● **glacially** *adverb.* ⓘ 17c in sense 2: from Latin *glacialis* icy.

glacial acetic acid ▻ *noun* almost pure ACETIC ACID.

glacial period ▻ *noun* **1** any interval of geological time during which a large part of the earth's surface was covered with ice. **2** (**the Glacial Period**) the Ice Age (the Pleistocene epoch) or any other ice age.

glaciate /ˈɡleɪsɪeɪt/ ▻ *verb* (**glaciated**, **glaciating**) *geol, geog* **1** said of land, etc: to become covered with glaciers or ice sheets. **2** to subject (land, etc) to the eroding action of moving glaciers or ice sheets. **3** to polish (rock, etc) by the action of ice. ● **glaciation** *noun.* ⓘ 19c in this sense: from Latin *glaciare, glaciatum* to freeze.

glacier /ˈɡlasɪə(r), ˈɡleɪ-/ ▻ *noun* a large body of ice, formed by the compaction of snow, that slowly moves either down a gradient or outward in all directions until it reaches a point where it melts or breaks up into icebergs. ⓘ 18c: French, from *glace* ice.

glad¹ ▻ *adj* (**gladder**, **gladdest**) **1** (*sometimes* **glad about something**) happy or pleased □ *I'm glad you liked your present.* **2** (**glad of something**) grateful for it □ *I was glad of your support.* **3** very willing □ *We are glad to help.* **4** *old use* bringing happiness □ *glad tidings.* ● **gladly** *adverb.* ● **gladness** *noun.* ⓘ Anglo-Saxon *glæd.*

glad² ▻ *contraction, colloq* a gladiolus.

gladden ▻ *verb* (**gladdened**, **gladdening**) to make someone (or their heart, etc) happy or pleased.

glade /ɡleɪd/ ▻ *noun, literary* an open space in a wood or forest. ⓘ 16c.

glad eye ▻ *noun* (*usually* **give someone the glad eye**) *old use* to glance amorously or in a sexually inviting way at them. ⓘ Early 20c.

glad hand ▻ *noun* (*usually* **the glad hand**) *US, often ironic* a handshake of welcome or of effusive greeting (generally to a stranger or a group of strangers). ▻ *verb* (**glad-hand**) to extend the glad hand to someone. ● **glad-hander** *noun.* ● **glad-handing** *noun.* ⓘ 19c.

gladiator /ˈɡladɪeɪtə(r)/ ▻ *noun* **1** in ancient Rome: a man trained to fight against other men or animals in an arena. **2** a contestant in a TV show where participants take part in trials of strength, fitness, stamina, etc. ⓘ 16c: Latin, meaning 'swordsman'.

gladiatorial /gladɪəˈtɔːrɪəl/ ▻ *adj* **1** relating to gladiators. **2** said of arguments or debates: contentious.

gladiolus /gladɪˈoʊləs/ ▻ *noun* (**gladioli** /-laɪ/ or **gladioluses**) **1** a perennial plant with upright sword-shaped leaves borne in flat fans and one-sided spikes of brightly coloured funnel-shaped flowers. **2** any of the one-sided spikes of flowers produced by this plant. Sometimes (*colloq*) shortened to **glad**. ⓘ 16c: Latin diminutive of *gladius* sword.

glad rags ▻ *plural noun, colloq* one's best clothes, worn for special occasions; party clothes.

Gladstone bag ▻ *noun* a piece of luggage which opens out flat. ⓘ 19c: named after the statesman, W E Gladstone (1809–98).

Glagolitic /glagoʊˈlɪtɪk/ ▻ *adj* **1** relating to the ancient Slavonic alphabet, which was replaced in almost all contexts by the Cyrillic, but retained in the service books of the Roman Catholics of the Slavonic rite. **2** referring or relating to such Roman Catholics. ⓘ 19c: from Slavonic *glagolu* a word.

glair /ɡlɛə(r)/ ▻ *noun* egg-white, or a similar substance, used as a glaze or an adhesive. ▻ *verb* (**glaired**, **glairing**) to apply glair to something. ⓘ 14c: from French *glaire.*

glam *slang* ▻ *adj* glamorous. ▻ *noun* **1** glamour. **2** GLAM ROCK. ▻ *verb* (**glammed**, **glamming**) (*often* **glam someone** or **something up**) to glamorize. ⓘ 20c shortening.

glamorize or **glamorise** ▻ *verb* (**glamorized**, **glamorizing**) **1** to make someone or something glamorous. **2** to romanticize. ● **glamorization** *noun.*

glamorous ▻ *adj* full of glamour. ● **glamorously** *adverb.*

glamour /ˈɡlamə(r)/ ▻ *noun* **1** the quality of being fascinatingly, if perhaps falsely, attractive. **2** great beauty or sexual charm, especially when created by make-up, clothes, etc. ⓘ 18c Scots variant of *gramarye*, an older variant of GRAMMAR, meaning 'a spell', from the medieval association of magic with learning; introduced into literary English by Sir Walter Scott.

glamour boy and **glamour girl** ▷ *noun, often derog or ironic* a man or woman considered to be very glamorous.

glamourpuss ▷ *noun, colloq* a glamorous person, especially a woman.

glam rock ▷ *noun, pop music* a type of rock music that was popular in Britain in the early 70s and which is remembered more for the outrageous clothes, hairstyles and make-up of artistes like Marc Bolan than for the music.

glance /glɑːns/ ▷ *verb* (***glanced***, ***glancing***) *usually intr* **1** (*often* **glance at something** or **someone**) to look quickly or indirectly at it or them. **2** *tr & intr* (*often* **glance off**) **a** said of a blow or weapon: to be deflected; to hit (a target) obliquely; **b** said of light: to shine or reflect in flashes; to glint □ *The sunlight glanced off the table.* ▷ *noun* **1** a brief (and often indirect) look. **2** a deflection. **3** *literary* a brief flash of light. • **glancing** *adj, noun* • **glancingly** *adverb*. • **at a glance** at once; from one brief look □ *could see at a glance that it was wrong.* ⓒ 15c.

■ **glance at** or **over something** to read or look at it cursorily.

gland[1] ▷ *noun* **1** *zool* in humans and animals: an organ that produces a specific chemical substance (eg a hormone) for use inside the body. **2** *bot* in plants: a specialized cell or group of cells involved in the secretion of plant products such as nectar, oils and resins. ⓒ 17c: from Latin *glans* acorn.

gland[2] ▷ *noun, engineering* a device for preventing leakage at the point where a rotating or reciprocating shaft emerges from a vessel containing fluid under pressure. ⓒ 19c.

glanders /ˈglandəz/ ▷ *singular noun, vet medicine, pathol* a highly infectious bacterial disease of horses, donkeys and mules, sometimes transmitted to humans, which causes inflammation and ulceration of the skin and lymph glands and fever. ⓒ 16c: from Latin *glans* acorn.

glandes *plural of* GLANS.

glandular /ˈglandjʊlə(r)/ ▷ *adj, zool, bot, etc* relating to, containing or affecting a gland or glands. ⓒ 18c: from French *glandulaire*.

glandular fever ▷ *noun, non-technical* INFECTIOUS MONONUCLEOSIS.

glans /glanz/ ▷ *noun* (***glandes*** /ˈglandiːz/) *anatomy* an acorn-shaped part of the body, especially the **glans penis**, the end of the penis.

glare /gleə(r)/ ▷ *verb* (***glared***, ***glaring***) **1** *intr* to stare angrily. **2** *intr* to be unpleasantly bright or shiny. **3** to express something with a glare. ▷ *noun* **1** an angry stare. **2** dazzling light. **3** *computing* excessive luminance emitted from a VDU screen or from light reflecting off a terminal. **4** brash colour or decoration. ⓒ 13c: from Dutch *glaren* to gleam.

glaring ▷ *adj* **1** unpleasantly bright. **2** obvious. • **glaringly** *adverb*.

glasnost /ˈglaznɒst, ˈglas-/ ▷ *noun* a policy of openness and willingness to provide information on the part of governments, especially the Soviet government under Mikhail Gorbachev (President 1988–91). ⓒ 20c: Russian, meaning 'speaking aloud, openness'.

glass /glɑːs/ ▷ *noun* (***glasses***) **1 a** a hard brittle non-crystalline material that is usually transparent or translucent, used to make windows, bottles and other containers, cooking utensils, lenses, etc. **2** an article made from this, eg a mirror, a lens or, especially, a drinking cup. **3** (*also* **glassful**) the amount held by a drinking glass. **4** (*also* **glassware**) articles made of glass □ *a collection of glass.* **5** (**glasses**) spectacles. ▷ *verb* (***glassed***, ***glassing***) to supply or cover something with glass. ⓒ Anglo-Saxon *glæs*.

glass-blower ▷ *noun* someone who is skilled at glass-blowing.

glass-blowing ▷ *noun* the process of shaping molten glass by blowing air into it through a tube.

glass case ▷ *noun* a case made at least partly of glass, used to display objects, etc.

glass ceiling ▷ *noun* an invisible but unmistakable barrier on the career ladder that certain categories of employees (especially women) find they can see through but which they cannot progress beyond. ⓒ 1990s.

glass cloth ▷ *noun* **1** a cloth for drying glasses. **2** a material woven from glass threads. **3** a polishing cloth covered with powdered glass.

glass eye ▷ *noun* an artificial eye made of glass.

glass fibre ▷ *noun* glass that has been melted and then drawn out into extremely fine fibres, often set in plastic resin and used to make strong lightweight materials.

glassful see under GLASS

glasshouse ▷ *noun* **1** a building with walls and roof constructed mainly or entirely of glass, and with the internal temperature maintained at a constant predetermined level, used for growing plants which need special protection or conditions. **2** *slang* a military prison.

glassine /glɑːˈsiːn/ ▷ *noun* a glossy, translucent, greaseproof paper.

glasspaper ▷ *noun* paper coated with finely ground glass, used as an abrasive.

glassware see under GLASS

glass wool ▷ *noun* glass that has been spun into fine thread-like fibres, forming a wool-like mass, used in air filters, insulation, fibreglass, etc.

glasswort ▷ *noun* a marsh plant that yields soda, formerly used in making glass.

glassy ▷ *adj* (***glassier***, ***glassiest***) **1** like glass. **2** expressionless □ *glassy eyes.*

Glaswegian /glɑːzˈwiːdʒən, glaz-, -s-/ ▷ *noun* a citizen or inhabitant of, or person born in, Glasgow, the largest city in Scotland. ▷ *adj* belonging or relating to Glasgow, its inhabitants or its distinctive dialect. ⓒ 19c: modelled on *Galwegian* a native of Galloway, itself modelled on *Norwegian*.

Glauber's salt /ˈglaʊbəz —/ or **Glauber salt** ▷ *noun* hydrated sodium sulphate, used for storing thermal energy in solar heating systems and air conditioning systems, and also used in textile dyeing and in medicine. ⓒ 18c: discovered by the German chemist Johann Rudolf *Glauber* (1604–68).

glaucoma /glɔːˈkoʊmə, glaʊ-/ *medicine, opthalmol, etc* ▷ *noun* any of various eye diseases in which increased pressure within the eyeball causes impaired vision and which, if left untreated, can lead to blindness. • **glaucomatous** /-mətəs/ *adj*. ⓒ 17c: from Greek *glaukoma* cataract.

glaucous /ˈglɔːkəs/ ▷ *adj* **1** having a dull green or blue colour. **2** *bot* having a pale bluish-green waxy coating that can be rubbed off, eg the bloom of grapes. ⓒ 17c: from Greek *glaukos* bluish-green or grey.

glaze /gleɪz/ ▷ *verb* (***glazed***, ***glazing***) **1** to fit glass panes into (a window, door, etc). **2** to achieve a glaze on or apply a glaze to (pottery). **3** in painting: to apply a glaze to something. **4** *intr* (*usually* **glaze over**) said of the eyes: to become fixed and expressionless. **5** to achieve a glaze on or apply a glaze to (eg pastry). ▷ *noun* **1** a hard glassy coating on pottery or the material for this coating before it is applied or fired. **2** in painting: a thin coat of semi-transparent colour. **3 a** a shiny coating of milk, eggs or sugar on food; **b** the material for this coating before it is applied or baked. • **glazing** *noun*. ⓒ 14c as *glase*: originally a variant of GLASS.

glazed ▻ *adj* **1** fitted or covered with glass. **2** covered with a glaze. **3** stupefied □ *a glazed look.*

glazier /ˈgleɪzɪə(r)/ ▻ *noun* someone whose job is to fit glass in windows, doors, etc.

glazing see under GLAZE

GLC ▻ *abbreviation* Greater London Council, abolished in 1986.

gleam /gliːm/ ▻ *noun* **1** a gentle glow. **2** a brief flash of light, especially reflected light. **3** a brief appearance or sign □ *a gleam of excitement in his eyes.* ▻ *verb* (***gleamed***, ***gleaming***) *intr* **1** to glow gently. **2** to shine with brief flashes of light. **3** said of an emotion, etc: to be shown briefly. • **gleaming** *adj.* Ⓢ Anglo-Saxon *glæm.*

glean /gliːn/ ▻ *verb* (***gleaned***, ***gleaning***) **1** to collect (information, etc) bit by bit, often with difficulty. **2** *tr & intr* to collect (loose grain and other useful remnants of a crop left in a field) after harvesting. • **gleaner** *noun.* • **gleanings** *plural noun* things which have been or may be gleaned, especially bits of information. Ⓢ 14c: from French *glener* in sense 2.

glebe /gliːb/ ▻ *noun* **1** a piece of church-owned land providing income in rent, etc for the resident minister. **2** *poetic* land; a field. Ⓢ 14c: from Latin *gleba* clod.

glee ▻ *noun* (*plural* in sense 2 ***glees***) **1** great delight; joy. **2** a song with different parts for three or four unaccompanied voices, especially male voices. Ⓢ Anglo-Saxon *glio* mirth or jesting.

glee club ▻ *noun* especially in the US: a choral society or choir, usually one that sings short pieces.

gleeful ▻ *adj* joyful; merry. • **gleefully** *adverb.* • **gleefulness** *noun.*

glei see GLEY

glen ▻ *noun* especially in Scotland: a long narrow valley. Ⓢ 15c: from Gaelic *gleann.*

glengarry /glɛŋˈgarɪ, glɛnˈgarɪ/ ▻ *noun* (***glengarries***) a narrow brimless cap creased in the middle from front to back and usually with two ribbons hanging at the back, worn eg by some Scottish regiments. Compare BALMORAL. Ⓢ 19c: named after Glengarry in Inverness-shire.

gley or **glei** /gleɪ/ ▻ *noun, soil science* a bluish-grey sticky clay found under some types of very damp soil. • **gleyed** *adj* turned into a gley. • **gleying** *noun* the formation of a gley. Ⓢ 1920s: from Ukrainian *glei.*

glia /glaɪə, gliə/ ▻ *noun, anatomy* the supporting tissue of the brain and spinal cord. Also called **neuroglia**. • **glial** *adj.* Ⓢ 19c: Greek, meaning 'glue'.

glib ▻ *adj* (***glibber***, ***glibbest***) *derog* speaking or spoken readily and persuasively, but neither sincere nor reliable □ *glib politicians* □ *glib explanations.* • **glibly** *adverb.* • **glibness** *noun.* Ⓢ 16c: compare Dutch *glibberig* slippery.

glide /glaɪd/ ▻ *verb* (***glided***, ***gliding***) *intr* **1** to move smoothly and often without any visible effort □ *glide along the ice.* **2** said of a bird: to travel through the air without beating its wings. **3** said of an aircraft: to travel through the air or to land without engine power. **4** to travel through the air by glider. **5** to pass gradually □ *glide into sleep.* ▻ *noun* **1** a gliding movement. **2** the controlled descent of an aircraft without engine power. **3** in ballroom dancing: **a** a smooth sliding step; **b** a dance containing such steps. **4** *music* movement from one note to another with no break in sound; portamento. **5** *phonetics* a sound produced at the transition from one speech sound to the next. • **gliding** *adj.* • **glidingly** *adverb.* Ⓢ Anglo-Saxon *glidan* to slip.

glide path ▻ *noun* the sloping path adopted by aircraft when landing.

glider /ˈglaɪdə(r)/ ▻ *noun* **1** a fixed-wing aircraft that is designed to glide and soar in air currents without using any form of engine power. **2** any of various small Australian marsupials that are capable of gliding through the air for long distances by extending a membrane of skin attached to the sides of the body. **3** a curtain RUNNER. • **gliding** *noun* the sport of flying in a glider. See also under GLIDE.

glimmer /ˈglɪmə(r)/ ▻ *verb* (***glimmered***, ***glimmering***) *intr* to glow faintly. ▻ *noun* **1** a faint glow; a twinkle. **2** a hint or trace □ *a glimmer of hope.* • **glimmering** *noun, adj.* • **glimmeringly** *adverb.* Ⓢ 14c as *glemern.*

glimpse /glɪmps/ ▻ *noun* a very brief look. ▻ *verb* (***glimpsed***, ***glimpsing***) to see something or someone momentarily. Ⓢ 14c as *glymsen.*

glint /glɪnt/ ▻ *verb* (***glinted***, ***glinting***) *intr* to give off tiny flashes of bright light. ▻ *noun* a brief flash of light. Ⓢ 15c as *glent*, probably from Scandinavian.

glioma /glaɪˈoʊmə, glɪˈoʊmə/ ▻ *noun* (***gliomas*** or ***gliomata*** /-mətə/) *pathol* a tumour of glial cells. • **gliomatous** *adj.* Ⓢ 19c: GLIA + -OMA.

gliomatosis /glaɪoʊməˈtoʊsɪs, glɪoʊməˈtoʊsɪs/ ▻ *noun, pathol* diffuse gliomatous proliferation of cells. Ⓢ 19c: GLIOMA + -OSIS.

gliosis /glaɪˈoʊsɪs, glɪˈoʊsɪs/ ▻ *noun, pathol* excessive growth of fibrous tissue in the GLIA. Ⓢ 1890s: GLIA + -OSIS.

glissade /glɪˈseɪd, glɪˈsɑːd/ ▻ *noun* **1** a sliding ballet step. **2** *mountaineering* an act of sliding down a snowy or icy slope in a standing or squatting position, often with the aid of an ice axe. ▻ *verb* (***glissaded***, ***glissading***) *intr* to perform a glissade. Ⓢ 19c: French, from *glisser* to slide.

glissando /glɪˈsandoʊ/ ▻ *noun* (***glissandos*** or ***glissandi*** /-diː/) *music* **1** the effect produced by sliding the finger along a keyboard or a string. **2** a similar effect produced on the trombone. Also *adj, adverb.* Ⓢ 19c: Italian.

glisten /ˈglɪsən/ ▻ *verb* (***glistened***, ***glistening***) *intr* often said of something wet or icy: to shine or sparkle. • **glistening** *adj.* Ⓢ Anglo-Saxon *glisnian.*

glister /ˈglɪstə(r)/ ▻ *verb* (***glistered***, ***glistering***) *intr, archaic* to glitter □ *All that glisters is not gold.* Ⓢ 14c: related to Dutch *glisteren.*

glitch /glɪtʃ/ ▻ *noun* (***glitches***) *colloq* a sudden brief irregularity or failure to function, especially in electronic equipment. Ⓢ 1960s.

glitter /ˈglɪtə(r)/ ▻ *verb* (***glittered***, ***glittering***) *intr* **1** to shine with bright flashes of light; to sparkle. **2** *colloq* to be sparklingly attractive or resplendent □ *a party glittering with famous film stars.* ▻ *noun* **1** sparkle. **2** *colloq* bright attractiveness, often superficial. **3** tiny pieces of shiny material, especially silvery paper, used for decoration. • **glittery** *adj.* Ⓢ 14c as *gliteren.*

glitterati /glɪtəˈrɑːtiː/ ▻ *plural noun, colloq* famous, fashionable and beautiful people. Ⓢ 1950s: from GLITTER, modelled on LITERATI.

glittering ▻ *adj* brightly shining. • **glitteringly** *adverb.* • **glittering generality** *US* a cliché or platitude.

glitz /glɪts/ ▻ *noun* showiness; garishness. Ⓢ 1970s: a back-formation from GLITZY.

glitzy /ˈglɪtsɪ/ ▻ *adj* (***glitzier***, ***glitziest***) *derog slang* extravagantly showy; flashy. Ⓢ 1960s: perhaps from German *glitzern* to glitter.

gloaming /ˈgloʊmɪŋ/ ▻ *noun, poetic or Scottish* dusk; twilight. Ⓢ Anglo-Saxon *glomung.*

gloat /gloʊt/ ▻ *verb* (***gloated***, ***gloating***) *intr* (*often* **gloat over something**) to feel or show smug or vindictive satisfaction, especially in one's own success or in another's misfortune. ▻ *noun* an act of gloating. Ⓢ 16c, meaning 'to look furtively or sidelong': perhaps from Norse *glotta* to grin.

glob ▻ *noun, colloq* a small amount of thick liquid; a blob or dollop. Ⓢ 20c.

global /ˈgloʊbəl/ ▻ *adj* **1** affecting the whole world. **2** total; including everything. **3** *computing* affecting or applying to a whole program or file □ *made a global exchange.* • **globally** *adverb.* Ⓒ 17c, meaning 'globe-shaped'.

globalist ▻ *noun* someone who thinks in terms of the well-being of the world as a whole or promotes sensitivity to global political issues in others.

global village ▻ *noun* the world perceived as shrunk to the size of a village, both because of mass communication and also in relation to the way in which changes in one area are likely to affect the rest of the world. Ⓒ 1960s.

global warming ▻ *noun, ecol* a gradual increase in the average temperature of the Earth's surface and its atmosphere which has been attributed to the GREENHOUSE effect. Ⓒ 1970s.

globe /gloʊb/ ▻ *noun* **1** (**the globe**) the Earth. **2** a sphere with a map of the world on it. **3** any approximately ball-shaped object, eg a goldfish bowl. **4** *Scottish, Austral, NZ* a light-bulb. Ⓒ 16c: from Latin *globus.*

globe artichoke ▻ *noun* **1** a tall perennial plant with deeply divided leaves and large purplish-blue flowers. **2** the fleshy base of the immature flower-head of this plant, eaten as a vegetable.

globeflower ▻ *noun* a poisonous perennial plant that has almost-spherical flowers on long stalks, with broad overlapping pale-yellow sepals curving in at the top and concealing the yellow petals.

globetrotter ▻ *noun, colloq* someone who travels all over the world, especially as a tourist. • **globetrotting** *noun.*

globigerina /gloʊbɪdʒə'raɪnə/ ▻ *noun* (*globigerinae* /-niː/) *zool* a minute marine invertebrate whose shell consists of globe-shaped chambers arranged in a spiral. Ⓒ 19c: Latin.

globin /'gloʊbɪn/ ▻ *noun, biochem* in animals: any of a group of soluble proteins that are present in the iron-containing pigments HAEMOGLOBIN (in red blood cells) and MYOGLOBIN (in muscle cells). Ⓒ 19c: see -IN1.

globular /'glɒbjʊlə(r)/ ▻ *adj* **1** shaped like a globe or globule. **2** consisting of globules.

globular cluster ▻ *noun, astron* a symmetrical cluster into which many thousands of stars are gathered. Compare OPEN CLUSTER.

globule /'glɒbjuːl/ ▻ *noun* a small drop, especially of liquid. Ⓒ 17c: from Latin *globulus,* diminutive of *globus* globe.

glockenspiel /'glɒkənspiːl, -ʃpiːl/ ▻ *noun* a musical instrument consisting of tuned metal plates held in a frame, played with two small hammers. Ⓒ 19c: German, from *Glocke* bell + *Spiel* play.

glomerate /'glɒməreɪt/ ▻ *adj, bot* clustered into a head or heads. Ⓒ 18c: from Latin *glomerare* to form into a ball.

gloom /gluːm/ ▻ *noun* **1** near-darkness. **2** sadness or despair. ▻ *verb* (*gloomed, glooming*) *intr* **1** said of the sky: to be dark and threatening. **2** to behave in a sad or depressed way. Ⓒ 14c as *gloumbe.*

gloomy ▻ *adj* (*gloomier, gloomiest*) **1** dark; dimly lit. **2** causing gloom. **3** sad or depressed. • **gloomily** *adverb.* • **gloominess** *noun.*

glop ▻ *noun, slang, especially N Amer* a mushy mess of something, especially of unappetizing food. Ⓒ 20c.

gloria /'glɔːrɪə/ ▻ *noun* (*glorias*) **a** a DOXOLOGY beginning with the word 'gloria'; **b** a musical setting of one. Ⓒ 15c: Latin, meaning 'glory', as in 'Glory be to the Father' and 'Glory be to God on high'.

glorified ▻ *adj, derog* given a fancy name or appearance □ *a glorified skivvy.*

glorify /'glɔːrɪfaɪ/ ▻ *verb* (*glorified, glorifying*) **1** to exaggerate the beauty, importance, etc of something or someone. **2** to praise or worship (God). **3** to make someone or something glorious. • **glorification** *noun.* Ⓒ 14c in sense 3: from Latin *glorificare,* from *gloria* glory + *facere* to make.

glorious /'glɔːrɪəs/ ▻ *adj* **1** having or bringing glory. **2** splendidly beautiful. **3** *colloq* excellent. **4** *humorous, colloq* very bad □ *glorious mess.* • **gloriously** *adverb.* • **gloriousness** *noun.* Ⓒ 14c: Anglo-French.

the glorious twelfth ▻ *noun, Brit* 12 August, the opening day of the grouse-shooting season.

glory /'glɔːrɪ/ ▻ *noun* (*glories*) **1** great honour and prestige. **2** great beauty or splendour. **3** praise and thanks given to God. **4** a greatly-admired asset □ *Patience is her crowning glory.* **5** a halo eg round a saint's head in a painting. **6** the splendour and blessedness of heaven. ▻ *verb* (*glories, gloried, glorying*) *intr* (*usually* **glory in something**) to feel or show great delight or pride in it. ▻ *exclamation* (*also* **glory be**) *rather dated* expressing surprise or amazement. Ⓒ 14c: from Latin *gloria.*

glory box ▻ *noun, Austral, NZ, rather dated* a woman's BOTTOM DRAWER.

glory hole ▻ *noun, colloq* a room, cupboard, drawer, etc where odds and ends are kept, especially in a disorganized way. Ⓒ 19c: perhaps related to 15c *glory* to defile.

Glos. ▻ *abbreviation, English county* Gloucestershire.

gloss[1] ▻ *noun* (*glosses*) **1** shiny brightness on a surface. **2** a superficial pleasantness or attractiveness. **3** (*in full* **gloss paint**) paint which produces a shiny finish. **4** a substance which adds shine □ *lip gloss.* ▻ *verb* (*glosses, glossed, glossing*) **1** to give a shiny finish to something. **2** to paint (a surface, etc) with gloss. Ⓒ 16c.

■ **gloss over something** to disguise or mask (a deficiency, mistake, etc), especially by treating a subject briefly and dismissively. Compare GLOSS SOMETHING OVER at GLOSS[2].

gloss[2] ▻ *noun* (*glosses*) **1** a short explanation of a difficult word, phrase, etc in a text, eg in the margin of a manuscript. **2** an intentionally misleading explanation. ▻ *verb* (*glossed, glossing*) **1** to provide a gloss of (a word, etc) or add glosses to (a text). **2** (*also* **gloss something over** or **away**) to explain it away; to give a different or false interpretation of it. Compare GLOSS OVER SOMETHING at GLOSS[1]. Ⓒ 16c: from Latin *glossa* a word requiring explanation.

gloss- or (before a consonant) **glosso-** ▻ *combining form, denoting* **1** the tongue. **2** a tongue or language. **3** a GLOSS[2] (sense 1). Ⓒ From Greek *glossa* tongue.

glossary /glɒsərɪ/ ▻ *noun* (*glossaries*) a list of glosses (GLOSS[2] *noun* 1), often at the end of a book. Ⓒ 14c: from Latin *glossarium.*

glossier and **glossiest** see under GLOSSY

glosso- see GLOSS-

glossolalia /glɒsoʊ'leɪlɪə/ ▻ *noun* unintelligible utterances, thought to form part of unknown languages, spoken while under the influence of religious excitement, and believed by Christian groups of various periods to be a sign of GRACE (sense 7). Compare XENOGLOSSIA. Ⓒ 19c: from Greek *glossa* tongue + *lalia* speech.

gloss paint see under GLOSS[1]

glossy ▻ *adj* (*glossier, glossiest*) **1** smooth and shiny. **2** superficially attractive. **3** said of a magazine: printed on glossy paper. ▻ *noun* (*glossies*) *colloq* such a magazine. • **glossily** *adverb.* • **glossiness** *noun.*

-glot ▻ *combining form, denoting* speaking, or written in, a specified number of languages □ *polygot.* Ⓒ From Greek *glotta* tongue or language.

glottal /'glɒtəl/ ▻ *adj, technical* relating to or produced by the GLOTTIS.

glottal stop ▻ *noun, linguistics* a sound produced when the glottis is closed and then opened sharply, eg used in German before syllables beginning with a vowel, or in some pronunciations of English substituted for a 't' in words such as 'bottle'.

glottis /'glɒtɪs/ ▻ *noun* (***glottises*** or (*anatomy*) ***glottides*** /-tɪdiːz/) the opening through which air passes from the pharynx to the trachea, including the space between the vocal cords. ⓘ 16c: Latin, from Greek *glotta* tongue.

glottochronology ▻ *noun, linguistics* the statistical study of the vocabulary of two or more languages that are related, or thought to be related, in order to determine the extent to which their vocabulary can be said to be shared or similar and also to chart the chronology of their independent development. ⓘ 1950s: from Greek *glotta* tongue or language + CHRONOLOGY.

glove /glʌv/ ▻ *noun* (***gloves***) **1** a covering for the hand which usually has individual casings for each finger. **2** a similar padded hand covering used in sports such as boxing, baseball, etc. ▻ *verb* (***gloved***, ***gloving***) to cover something with a glove or gloves. • **fit like a glove** see under FIT[1]. • **the gloves are off** *colloq* the serious argument, fight, etc is about to begin. See also KID GLOVE. ⓘ Anglo-Saxon *glof.*

glove box ▻ *noun* **1** a GLOVE COMPARTMENT. **2** *nuclear engineering* a closed compartment in which radioactive or toxic material may be manipulated by the use of gloves attached to the walls.

glove compartment ▻ *noun* a small compartment in the front of a car, usually part of the dashboard where small articles can be kept.

glove puppet ▻ *noun* a puppet worn on the hand like a glove and manipulated by the fingers.

glover /'glʌvə(r)/ ▻ *noun* a glove-maker.

glow /gloʊ/ ▻ *verb* (***glowed***, ***glowing***) *intr* **1** to give out a steady heat or light without flames. **2** to shine brightly, as if very hot. **3** to feel or communicate a sensation of intense contentment or well-being □ *glow with pride.* **4** said of the complexion: to be well-coloured (either rosy or tanned) and healthy-looking □ *cheeks glowing with health.* ▻ *noun* **1** a steady flameless heat or light. **2** bright, shiny appearance. **3** intensity of feeling, especially pleasant feeling. **4** a healthy colour of complexion. ⓘ Anglo-Saxon *glowan.*

glow discharge ▻ *noun, electronics* a luminous electrical discharge in gas at low pressure.

glower /glaʊə(r)/ ▻ *verb* (***glowered***, ***glowering***) *intr* to stare angrily. ▻ *noun* an angry stare; a scowl. ⓘ 16c as *glowr* or *glowir.*

glowing ▻ *adj* commendatory; full of praise □ *glowing report.* ▻ *verb, present participle of* GLOW. • **glowingly** *adverb.*

glow plug ▻ *noun* **1** an electric plug fitted in a diesel engine to make starting easier in cold weather. **2** a similar device for re-igniting the flame in a gas turbine automatically.

glow-worm ▻ *noun* **1** a small nocturnal beetle, the wingless female of which attracts the male by giving out a bright greenish light from special organs on the underside of her abdomen. **2** *N Amer* any of various luminous insect larvae. ⓘ 14c.

gloxinia /glɒk'sɪnɪə/ ▻ *noun* (***gloxinias***) any of various plants, native to Brazil, with large velvety funnel-shaped white, pink, red or purple flowers.

glucagon /'gluːkəgɒn/ ▻ *noun biochem* a polypeptide hormone secreted by the islets of Langerhans in the pancreas, which accelerates glycogen breakdown in the liver, so increasing blood sugar levels. ⓘ 20c: from GLUCOSE + Greek *agein* to lead.

glucose /'gluːkoʊs, -koʊz/ ▻ *noun* **1** *biochem* (formula $C_6H_{12}O_6$) the most common six-carbon MONOSACCHARIDE in living cells, and in animals the main form in which energy derived from carbohydrates is transported around the bloodstream. **2** (*usually* **glucose syrup**) a concentrated solution of the products of breakdown of starch, used in the confectionery industry, for canning fruit, etc. ⓘ 19c: from Greek *glykys* sweet + -OSE[2].

glucoside /'gluːkoʊsaɪd/ ▻ *noun, biochem* any of various derivatives of glucose in which the first hydroxyl group is replaced by another group, and which yields glucose when treated with enzymes or acids. ⓘ 19c.

glue /gluː/ ▻ *noun* **1** any adhesive obtained by extracting natural substances, especially from bone, in boiling water. **2** any adhesive made by dissolving synthetic substances such as rubber or plastic in a suitable solvent. ▻ *verb* (***glued***, ***glueing*** or ***gluing***) to use such an adhesive to stick (two materials or parts) together. ⓘ 14c: from Latin *glus.*

▪ **glue something to something** *colloq* (*usually* **be glued to something**) to fix (especially the eyes) on it □ *eyes glued to the TV.*

▪ **glue oneself to something** or **be glued to something** *colloq* to stay very close to it □ *The toddler was glued to its mother's side.*

glue ear ▻ *noun* deafness and discharge from the ear caused by a build-up of fluid in the middle ear.

glue-sniffing ▻ *noun* the practice or process of breathing in fumes from some types of glue to produce hallucinatory or intoxicating effects. • **glue-sniffer** *noun.*

gluey /'gluːɪ/ (***gluier***, ***gluiest***) ▻ *adj* containing glue; like glue; sticky. • **glueyness** *noun.*

glug /glʌg/ ▻ *noun* (*often* **glug-glug**) the sound of liquid being poured, eg from a bottle or down someone's throat. ▻ *exclamation* representing this sound. ▻ *verb* (***glugged***, ***glugging***) **1** *intr* to make such a sound. **2** to swallow something in big gulps. ⓘ 18c: imitating the sound.

glühwein or **Glühwein** / *German* 'glyːvaɪn/ ▻ *noun* mulled wine, especially as prepared in Germany, Austria, etc. ⓘ 19c: German, from *glühen* to glow + *Wein* wine.

gluing *present participle of* GLUE

glum ▻ *adj* (***glummer***, ***glummest***) in low spirits; sullen. • **glumly** *adverb.* • **glumness** *noun.* ⓘ 16c: related to GLOOM.

glumaceous /glʊ'meɪʃəs/ ▻ *adj, bot* like a GLUME, ie thin, brownish and papery.

glume /gluːm/ ▻ *noun bot* in grasses and sedges: an outer sterile BRACT which, alone or with others, encloses the SPIKELET. ⓘ 18c: from Latin *gluma* husk of grain.

gluon /'gluːɒn/ ▻ *noun, physics* a hypothetical particle with no mass, the carrier of the force that is believed to hold quarks (see QUARK[1]) together. ⓘ 1970s: from GLUE + -ON.

glut ▻ *noun* **1** an excessive supply of goods, etc. **2** an act or instance of glutting. ▻ *verb* (***glutted***, ***glutting***) **1** to feed or supply something to excess. **2** to block or choke up. ⓘ 14c: from Latin *glutire* to swallow.

glutamate /'gluːtəmeɪt/ ▻ *noun, chem* a salt of glutamic acid.

glutamic acid /gluː'tamɪk —/ ▻ *noun, biochem* an important amino-acid, found in many proteins. ⓘ 19c: from GLUTEN + AMINE.

gluten /'gluːtən/ ▻ *noun, biochem* a mixture of two plant storage proteins occurring in wheat flour that gives bread dough elastic properties and is responsible for the condition known as COELIAC DISEASE in people who are abnormally sensitive to it. • **glutenous** *adj* consisting of or containing gluten. ⓘ 16c, meaning FIBRIN: Latin, meaning 'glue'.

gluteus /'gluːtɪəs, glʊ'tɪəs/ ▻ *noun, anatomy* any of the three large muscles in the human buttock. • **gluteal** *adj.* ⓘ 17c: Latin, from Greek *gloutos* the rump.

gluteus maximus ▷ *noun* **1** *anatomy* the outermost of the three muscles of the human buttock. **2** *jocular* the buttocks.

glutinous /ˈgluːtɪnəs/ ▷ *adj* like glue; sticky. ● **glutinously** *adverb*. ● **glutinousness** *noun*. ⓘ 16c: from Latin *gluten* glue.

glutton¹ /ˈglʌtən/ ▷ *noun* **1** *derog* someone who eats too much. **2** someone whose behaviour suggests an eagerness (for something unpleasant) □ *a glutton for hard work*. ● **gluttonous** *adj* greedy. ● **gluttony** *noun, derog* the habit or practice of eating too much. ● **a glutton for punishment** someone who is eager to undertake difficult or arduous tasks. ⓘ 13c: from Latin *gluttire* to swallow.

glutton² /ˈglʌtən/ ▷ *noun* a WOLVERINE.

glyceride /ˈglɪsəraɪd/ ▷ *noun* an ESTER of glycerol.

glycerine /ˈglɪsəriːn/ or **glycerin** /-rɪn/ ▷ *noun, non-technical* GLYCEROL. ⓘ 19c: from Greek *glykeros* sweet + -INE or -IN.

glycerol /ˈglɪsərɒl/ ▷ *noun, chem* (formula **$CH_2OHCHOHCH_2OH$**) a colourless viscous sweet-tasting liquid that is soluble in water and alcohol. It is a by-product in the manufacture of soap from naturally-occurring fats and is widely used in various foodstuffs and medicines. ⓘ 19c: from Greek *glykeros* sweet + -OL.

glyco- /glaɪkoʊ, glaɪˈkɒ/ ▷ *combining form, denoting* **1** sugar. **2** glycogen. ⓘ From Greek *glykys* sweet.

glycogen ▷ *noun, biochem* a highly branched chain of glucose molecules, the main form in which carbohydrate is stored (especially in the liver and muscles) in vertebrates. ● **glycogenic** /-ˈdʒenɪk/ *adj*. ⓘ 19c: GLYCO- + -GEN.

glycol /ˈglaɪkɒl/ ▷ *noun, chem* any of a class of compounds with two hydroxyl groups on adjacent carbon atoms, and so intermediate between *glyc*erine and alcoh*ol*. ⓘ 19c.

glycolysis /glaɪˈkɒlɪsɪs/ ▷ *noun, biochem* during respiration in the cells of living organisms: the conversion of glucose to pyruvic acid, accompanied by the release of energy in the form of ATP. ⓘ 19c: GLYCO- + -LYSIS.

glycoside /ˈglaɪkoʊsaɪd/ ▷ *noun, chem* any of a group of compounds derived from simple sugars by replacing the hydroxyl group with another group. ● **glycosidic** /-ˈsɪdɪk/ *adj*. ⓘ 1930s in this sense; in 19c used as a variant of GLUCOSIDE.

glyph /glɪf/ ▷ *noun, archit* an ornamental channel or fluting, usually vertical. ⓘ 18c: from Greek *glyphe* carving.

glyptic /ˈglɪptɪk/ ▷ *adj* relating to carving or engraving, especially gem-carving. ⓘ 19c: from Greek *glyptikos* relating to carving.

glyptography /glɪpˈtɒgrəfɪ/ ▷ *noun* the art of gem-carving. ⓘ 18c.

GM ▷ *abbreviation* **1** general manager. **2** General Motors. **3** George Medal. **4** Grand Master. **5** grant-maintained □ *GM school*.

gm ▷ *abbreviation* gram or gramme; grams or grammes.

G-man ▷ *noun* **1** *US slang* an FBI agent. **2** *Irish* a political detective. ⓘ 1917 in Ireland; 1930s in US: probably from GOVERNMENT + MAN.

GMB ▷ *abbreviation* General, Municipal and Boilermakers' Union.

GmbH ▷ *abbreviation*: *Gesellschaft mit beschränkter Haftung* (German), a limited company.

GMC ▷ *abbreviation* General Medical Council.

Gmc ▷ *contraction* Germanic.

GMT ▷ *abbreviation* Greenwich Mean Time.

GMWU ▷ *abbreviation* General and Municipal Workers Union.

gnarled /nɑːld/ and **gnarly** ▷ *adj* (*gnarlier*, *gnarliest*) said of tree trunks, branches, human hands, etc: twisted, with knotty swellings, usually as a result of age. ⓘ 17c: from 14c *knarre* a knob-like protuberance.

gnash /naʃ/ ▷ *verb* (*gnashed*, *gnashing*) *tr & intr* to grind (the teeth) together, especially in anger or pain. ● **gnashing** *noun*. ⓘ 15c: from 13c *gnasten*.

gnashers ▷ *plural noun, humorous colloq* teeth, especially false ones.

gnat /nat/ ▷ *noun* **1** any of various small fragile biting flies. **2** (**winter gnat**) a small delicate fly, particularly noticeable when the males dance up and down in conspicuous swarms low over water or in woodland clearings. ⓘ Anglo-Saxon *gnætt*.

gnathic /ˈnaθɪk/ and **gnathal** /ˈnaθəl, ˈneɪθəl/ ▷ *adj, anatomy* relating to the jaw. ⓘ 19c: from Greek *gnathos* jaw.

gnaw /nɔː/ ▷ *verb* (*gnawed*, *past participle* ***gnawed*** or ***gnawn***, *present participle* ***gnawing***) **1** (*also* **gnaw at** or **gnaw away at something**) to bite it with a scraping action, causing a gradual wearing away. **2** to make (eg a hole) in this way. **3** *tr & intr* (*also* **gnaw at someone**) said of pain, anxiety, etc: to trouble them persistently □ *He is gnawed by guilt*. ● **gnawing** *adj*. ⓘ Anglo-Saxon *gnagan*.

gneiss /naɪs/ ▷ *noun, geol* a coarse-grained metamorphic rock that contains bands of quartz and feldspar alternating with bands of mica. ● **gneissose** *adj*. ⓘ 18c: from German *Gneis*.

gnocchi /ˈnɒkiː, ˈnjɒkiː/ ▷ *plural noun, cookery* small dumplings made from flour, semolina or potato and served in a sauce. ⓘ 19c: Italian, from *gnocco*, from *nocchio* a knot in wood.

gnomae *plural of* GNOME²

gnome¹ /noʊm/ ▷ *noun* (*gnomes*) **1** a fairy-tale creature, usually in the form of a small misshapen old man, who lives underground, often guarding treasure. **2** a statue of such a creature taking part in various activities such as fishing, digging, etc and used especially as a garden ornament. **3** *colloq* a person with secret financial influence □ *gnomes of Zurich*. ● **gnomish** *adj*. ⓘ 18c: from Latin *gnomus* dwarf, coined by Paracelsus in the 16c.

gnome² /noʊm, ˈnoʊmiː/ ▷ *noun* (*gnomes* or *gnomae* /-miː/) a pithy aphorism, usually in verse, that embodies some moral sentiment or precept. ⓘ 16c: Greek.

gnomic /ˈnoʊmɪk/ ▷ *adj, formal* said of speech or writing: **1** expressed in gnomes (see GNOME²). **2** *often derog* moralizing. ⓘ 19c: from Greek *gnomikos*.

gnomish see under GNOME¹

gnomon /ˈnoʊmɒn/ ▷ *noun* **1** on a sundial: the raised arm that casts the shadow which points to the hour. **2** *math* the remainder of a parallelogram after a similar parallelogram has been removed from one corner. ⓘ 16c: Greek, in sense 1.

gnostic /ˈnɒstɪk/ ▷ *adj* **1** relating to knowledge, especially mystical or religious knowledge. **2** (**Gnostic**) relating to Gnosticism. ▷ *noun* (**Gnostic**) an early Christian heretic believing in redemption of the soul from the world of matter through special religious knowledge. ⓘ 16c as *noun*: from Greek *gnostikos* relating to knowledge.

Gnosticism /ˈnɒstɪsɪzəm/ ▷ *noun* the doctrines of the GNOSTICS.

GNP ▷ *abbreviation, econ* gross national product.

gnu /nuː or (*humorous*) gəˈnuː/ ▷ *noun* (*gnus* or *gnu*) either of two species of large African antelope with a stocky body, a large bull-like head, horns in both sexes, a long mane and tufts of hair growing from the muzzle, throat and chest. Also called WILDEBEEST. ⓘ 18c: from Hottentot.

GNVQ ▷ *abbreviation* General National Vocational Qualification, a two-year vocational course for those who are 16 and over.

go[1] /goʊ/ ▷ *verb* (**goes**, **went**, **gone**, **going**) *usually intr* **1** (*often* **go about** or **by** or **down**, *etc*) to walk, move or travel in the direction specified. **2** to lead or extend □ *a path that goes across the field* □ *The road goes all the way to the farm.* **3** (*usually* **go to somewhere**) to visit or attend it, once or regularly □ *go to the cinema* □ *go to school.* **4 a** to leave or move away; **b** (*only as exclamation*) said by someone signalling the start of a race: begin the race! **5** to be destroyed or taken away; to disappear □ *The old door had to go* □ *The peaceful atmosphere has gone.* **6** to proceed or fare □ *The scheme is going well.* **7** to be used up □ *All his money went on drink.* **8** to be given or sold for a stated amount □ *went for £20.* **9** to leave or set out for a stated purpose □ *go for a ride* □ *go on holiday* □ *gone fishing.* **10** *tr & intr* to perform (an action) or produce (a sound) □ *go like this* □ *go bang.* **11** *colloq* to break, break down, or fail □ *The old TV finally went* □ *His eyes have gone.* **12** to work or be in working order □ *get it going.* **13** to become; to pass into a certain condition □ *go mad.* **14** to belong; to be placed correctly □ *Where does this go?* **15** to fit, or be contained □ *My foot won't go into the shoe* □ *Four into three won't go.* **16** to be or continue in a certain state □ *go hungry.* **17** said of time: to pass. **18** said of a story or tune: to run □ *How does it go?* **19** (*often* **go for someone** or **something**) to apply to them; to be valid or accepted for them □ *The same goes for you* □ *In this office, anything goes.* **20** *colloq* to carry authority □ *What she says goes.* **21** (*often* **go with something**) said of colours, etc: to match or blend. **22** to subject oneself □ *go to much trouble.* **23** to adopt a specified system □ *go metric.* **24** *tr* to bet (a specified amount), especially at cards □ *went five pounds.* **25** *colloq* to be in general, for the purpose of comparison □ *As girls go, she's quite naughty.* **26** to exist or be on offer □ *the best offer going at the moment.* **27** *very colloq* to say □ *She goes, 'No, you didn't!' and I goes, 'Oh, yes I did!'.* ▷ *noun* (*plural* **goes**) **1** a turn or spell □ *It's my go.* **2** energy; liveliness □ *She lacks go.* **3** *colloq* busy activity □ *It's all go.* **4** *colloq* a success □ *make a go of it.* • **be going on for something** *colloq* to be approaching (a specified age) □ *She's going on for 60.* • **from the word go** from the very beginning. • **give it a go** *colloq* to make an attempt at something. • **go all out for something** to make a great effort to obtain or achieve it. • **go and ...** to be so unwise or unfortunate as to ... □ *They've gone and got lost.* • **go great guns** see under GUN. • **go it alone** *colloq* to manage or try to manage without help, especially when in difficulties. • **go native** to assimilate oneself to an alien culture or to the way of life of a foreign country. • **go slow** to work slowly so as to encourage an employer to negotiate or meet a demand. See also GO-SLOW. • **have a go** *colloq* to try; to make an attempt. • **have a go at someone** to attack them verbally. • **have something going for one** *colloq* to have it as an attribute or advantage □ *You have a lot going for you.* • **I could go something** *very colloq* I would like it; I could do with it; I need it □ *I could really go a pint of cold beer.* • **no go** *colloq* not possible. • **on the go** *colloq* busily active. • **to be going on with** *colloq* for the moment □ *enough to be going on with.* ◎ Anglo-Saxon *gan*.

■ **go about 1** to circulate □ *a rumour going about.* **2** *naut* to change course.

■ **go about something 1** to busy oneself with it. **2** to attempt or tackle it □ *how to go about doing this.*

■ **go against someone** to be decided unfavourably for them □ *The court case went against him.*

■ **go against something** to be contrary to it.

■ **go ahead** to proceed.

■ **go along with someone** or **something** to agree with and support them or it.

■ **go back on something** to break (an agreement, etc).

■ **go by something** to be guided by it or act in accordance with it □ *Don't go by what he says.*

■ **go down 1** to decrease. **2** *colloq* to be accepted or received □ *The joke went down well.*

■ **go down on someone** *taboo slang* to perform fellatio or cunnilingus on them.

■ **go down with something** to contract an illness.

■ **go for someone** or **something** *colloq* **1** to attack them. **2** to be attracted by them. **3** to choose them □ *went for the red shoes instead.* **4** (*usually* **go for it**) *colloq* to try very hard to achieve something.

■ **go in for something** *colloq* **1** to take up (a profession). **2** to enter (a contest). **3** to be interested or attracted by something, as a rule □ *don't usually go in for films with subtitles.*

■ **go into something 1** to take up or join (a profession). **2** to discuss or investigate something □ *cannot go into that now.*

■ **go off 1** to explode. **2** *colloq* said of perishables, eg food: to become rotten. **3** to proceed or pass off □ *The party went off well.*

■ **go off someone** or **something** *colloq* to stop liking them or it.

■ **go on 1** to continue or proceed. **2** *colloq* to talk too much. **3** (*only as exclamation*) *colloq* expressing disbelief.

■ **go on at someone** *colloq* to criticize them or complain to them persistently.

■ **go out 1** said of a fire or light: to become extinguished. **2** to be broadcast. **3** to no longer be fashionable.

■ **go out to someone** said of someone's heart: be in sympathy with them □ *My heart goes out to the victim's family.*

■ **go out with someone** to spend time with someone socially or (especially) romantically.

■ **go over** to pass off or be received □ *The play went over well.*

■ **go over something 1** to examine it. **2** to revise or rehearse it.

■ **go over to** to transfer support or allegiance □ *go over to the enemy.*

■ **go round** to be enough for all.

■ **go through** to be approved.

■ **go through something 1** to use it up. **2** to revise or rehearse it. **3** to examine it. **4** to suffer it □ *went through hell.* **5** to search it □ *went through all our bags.*

■ **go through with something** to carry it out to the end.

■ **go under** *colloq* to fail or be ruined.

■ **go up 1** to increase. **2** said of a building, etc: to be erected. **3** *colloq* to be destroyed by fire or explosion.

■ **go with someone** *colloq* to have a close romantic friendship with them.

■ **go with something 1** to co-exist with it □ *Goodness doesn't always go with beauty.* **2** to agree with or support it. 3 to be a good match with it.

■ **go without something** to suffer a lack of it.

go[2] ▷ *noun* a Japanese board game for two players, played with black and white pieces, the object being to capture one's opponent's pieces and control the larger part of the board. ◷ 19c: Japanese.

goa /goʊə/ ▻ *noun* (**goas**) a grey-brown Tibetan gazelle, with backward-curving horns. ◷ 19c: from Tibetan *dgoba*.

Goa trance /goʊə —/ ▻ *noun* TRANCE MUSIC with various ethnic influences, originating in Goa, a state on the W coast of India. ◷ 1990s: from TRANCE (sense 5).

goad /goʊd/ ▻ *verb* (**goaded**, **goading**) (*usually* **goad someone into something** or **to do something**) to urge or provoke them to action. ▻ *noun* **1** a sharp-pointed stick used for driving cattle, etc. **2** anything that provokes or incites. ◷ Anglo-Saxon *gad*.

go-ahead *colloq* ▻ *adj* energetically ambitious and far-sighted. ▻ *noun* (**the go-ahead**) permission to start □ *got the go ahead to install the new computers.*

goal /'goʊl/ ▻ *noun* **1 a** in various sports, especially football: a set of posts with a crossbar, through which the ball is struck to score points; **b** the area in which the goal stands. **2 a** an act of scoring in this way; **b** the point or points scored. **3** an aim or purpose □ *You really should have a goal in life.* **4** a destination, etc □ *Paris was our goal.* • **goalless** *adj*. • **in goal** playing in the position of goalkeeper. ◷ 16c: perhaps from 14c *gol* boundary.

goal average ▻ *noun* the number of goals scored by a team in comparison with the number of goals conceded over a specified period.

goal difference ▻ *noun* the difference between the number of goals scored for and against a team over a specified period.

goalie /'goʊlɪ/ ▻ *noun* (**goalies**) *colloq* a goalkeeper.

goalkeeper ▻ *noun* in various sports: the player who guards the goal and tries to prevent the opposition from scoring.

goal kick ▻ *noun* **1** *football* a free kick awarded to defending team when their opponents have put the ball out of play over the GOAL LINE but a goal has not been scored. **2** *rugby* an attempt to kick a goal, eg after a try has been awarded.

goal kicker ▻ *noun* **1** a player who kicks a goal. **2** a player who kicks a goal kick. • **goal-kicking** *noun*.

goalless see under GOAL

goal line ▻ *noun* in various sports: the line marking each end of the field of play.

goalmouth ▻ *noun* in various sports: the area around the goal.

goalpost ▻ *noun* in various sports: each of two upright posts forming the goal. • **move the goalposts** to change the accepted rules or aims of an activity during its course in order to accommodate new conditions.

go-as-you-please ▻ *adj* not restricted by rules; informal.

goat /goʊt/ ▻ *noun* **1** any of numerous species of herbivorous mammal, noted for its physical agility and sure-footedness. The males have tufty beards on their lower jaws. Domesticated goats are kept for their milk and meat. See also BILLY GOAT, NANNY GOAT, KID[1] *noun* 2, CAPRINE. **2** *derog colloq* a man, especially an old one, who makes unwanted sexual advances to women. **3** *derog, colloq* a foolish person. **4** (**the Goat**) the constellation and sign of the zodiac CAPRICORN. • **get someone's goat** *colloq* to annoy or irritate them. ◷ Anglo-Saxon *gat*.

goatee /goʊ'tiː/ ▻ *noun* (**goatees**) a pointed beard growing on the front of the chin only. ◷ 19c.

goatherd /'goʊthɜːd/ ▻ *noun* someone who looks after goats out in the pastures.

goatish ▻ *adj* **1** like a goat. **2** stupid. **3** lustful. • **goatishly** *adverb*.

gob ▻ *noun* **1** *coarse slang* the mouth. **2** a soft wet lump. **3** *coarse slang* spit. ▻ *verb* (**gobbed**, **gobbing**) *intr, coarse slang* to spit. • **gobbing** *noun* **1** spitting. **2** communal spitting, often done by fans attending PUNK (*adj* 1) gigs. ◷ 14c, meaning 'a lump': from French *gobe* a lump or mouthful.

gobbet /'gɒbɪt/ ▻ *noun* **1** a lump or chunk. **2** *colloq* an extract from a text. ◷ 14c: from French *gobet*, diminutive of *gobe* mouthful.

gobble[1] /'gɒbəl/ ▻ *verb* (**gobbled**, **gobbling**) *tr & intr* (*usually* **gobble something up** or **down**) to eat hurriedly and noisily. ◷ 17c: from French *gober* to gulp down.

gobble[2] /'gɒbəl/ ▻ *verb* (**gobbled**, **gobbling**) *intr* said of a male turkey: to make a loud gurgling sound in the throat. ▻ *noun* (**gobbles**) the loud gurgling sound made by a male turkey. ◷ 17c: imitating the sound.

gobbledygook or **gobbledegook** /gɒbəldɪ'guːk/ ▻ *noun, colloq, usually derog* **1** official jargon, meaningless to ordinary people. **2** nonsense; rubbish. ◷ 1940s: imitating the sound and based on GOBBLE.

gobbler ▻ *noun, N Amer, especially US* a male turkey.

go-between ▻ *noun* (**go-betweens**) a messenger between two people or sides; an intermediary.

goblet /'gɒblət/ ▻ *noun* **1** a drinking-cup with a base and stem but no handles, often made from metal or glass. **2** the tall bowl of a LIQUIDIZER. ◷ 14c: from French *gobelet*, diminutive of *gobel* cup.

goblin /'gɒblɪn/ ▻ *noun* in folk-tales: an evil or mischievous spirit in the form of a small man. ◷ 14c: from French *gobelin*, perhaps from Greek *kobalos* mischievous spirit.

gobshite /'gɒbʃaɪt/ ▻ *noun, coarse slang* a stupid person. ◷ 20c: GOB *noun* 3 + SHITE.

gobsmacked ▻ *adj, colloq* astonished; dumbfounded. ◷ From the action of clapping a hand to one's mouth in surprise.

gobstopper ▻ *noun, colloq* a very large round sweet for lengthy sucking.

goby /'goʊbɪ/ ▻ *noun* (**gobies**) any of numerous small, usually colourful, marine fishes with large eyes, fleshy lips, and the pelvic fins fused together to form a disc-shaped sucker. ◷ 18c: from Latin *gobius* gudgeon.

go-by ▻ *noun* • **give someone the go-by** *colloq* to ignore or snub them.

go-cart see GO-KART

god ▻ *noun* **1** (**God**) in the Christian and other monotheistic religions: the unique supreme being, creator and ruler of the universe. **2** in other religions: a superhuman male being with power over nature and humanity; a male object of worship. Compare GODDESS. **3** a man greatly admired, especially for his fine physique or wide influence. **4** *often derog* an object of excessive worship or influence □ *He made money his god.* **5** (**the gods**) superhuman beings collectively, both male and female. **6** (**the gods**) **a** the area of the balcony or upper circle in a theatre; **b** the theatregoers in this area. ▻ *exclamation* (**God!** or **my God!**) expressing amazement, anger, etc. • **godlike** *adj*. • **for God's sake 1** expressing pleading. **2** expressing irritation, disgust, etc. • **God knows 1** God is my (or his, etc) witness. **2** *ironic* it is beyond human understanding. • **God willing** (abbreviation **DV**) if circumstances allow. ◷ Anglo-Saxon.

god-awful ▻ *adj, colloq* **1** very bad. **2** unpleasant, distasteful.

godchild ▻ *noun* a child that a godparent is responsible for.

goddam /'gɒdɑ̃m/ or **god-damned** /'gɒdamd/ ▻ *adj* (*usually* used as an intensifier) **1** damned, accursed. **2** utter, complete □ *a goddam fool.* ◷ 20c: from exclamations *god damn* (19c) and *god damn me* (17c), originally an oath.

goddaughter ▷ *noun* a female godchild.

goddess /ˈgɒdɛs/ ▷ *noun* (***goddesses***) **1** a superhuman female being who has power over nature and humanity; a female object of worship. Compare GOD. **2** a woman greatly admired for her beauty.

Gödel's theorem /ˈgɜːdəlz —/ ▷ *noun* the theorem which states that it is impossible to prove the consistency of a logical or mathematical system from within that system. ⓘ 1930s: named after the Austrian-born American logician Kurt Gödel (1906–78).

godetia /goʊˈdiːʃə/ ▷ *noun* (***godetias***) a highly-prized garden plant valued for its showy red or purplish-red flowers and closely related to the evening primrose. ⓘ 19c: named after the Swiss botanist C H Godet (died 1879).

godfather ▷ *noun* **1** a male godparent. **2** the head of a criminal group, especially in the Mafia.

God-fearing ▷ *adj* respectful of God's laws; pious.

godforsaken (also **Godforsaken**) ▷ *adj* **1** *derog* said of a place: remote and desolate. **2** said of a person: depraved.

Godhead ▷ *noun* **1** the divine state attributed to God or a god. **2** (**the Godhead**) God. ⓘ 13c.

godless ▷ *adj* **1** not religious; not believing in God. **2** having no god. **3** wicked; immoral. • **godlessness** *noun*.

godly /ˈgɒdlɪ/ ▷ *adj* (***godlier***, ***godliest***) religious; pious. • **godliness** *noun*.

godmother ▷ *noun* a female godparent.

godown /goʊˈdaʊn/ ▷ *noun* in Eastern countries: a warehouse or storeroom. ⓘ 16c as *godon*: from Malay *godong*.

godparent ▷ *noun* someone who takes on the responsibility of the religious education of another, especially a child and who, in the case of a child, agrees to supervise its upbringing in the event of the death of its parents.

godroon see GADROON

godsend /ˈgɒdsɛnd/ ▷ *noun* someone or something whose arrival is unexpected but very welcome.

God squad ▷ *noun*, *derog* any religious group, especially a Christian one, that is considered to be overly zealous, evangelical or pious.

God slot ▷ *noun*, *colloq* a regular time for religious programmes in a broadcasting schedule.

godson ▷ *noun* a male godchild.

God's own country ▷ *noun* an especially well-favoured and, in particular, scenically beautiful region.

Godspeed ▷ *exclamation*, *old use* expressing good wishes for a person's safety on a journey.

God's gift ▷ *noun*, *facetious* an absolute godsend □ *thinks he's God's gift to women.*

God's truth ▷ *noun*, *colloq* (*usually* **the God's truth** or **the God's honest truth**) (used for emphasis) the absolute truth.

godwit /ˈgɒdwɪt/ ▷ *noun* any of various wading birds which have a long straight or slightly upcurved bill, long legs and greyish-brown plumage in winter with bright chestnut markings in summer. ⓘ 16c.

goer /ˈgoʊə(r)/ ▷ *noun* **1** *in compounds* someone who makes visits, especially regular ones, to a specified place □ *cinema-goer.* **2** *colloq* a sexually energetic person, especially a woman. **3** *colloq* something that travels fast or makes fast progress.

goes see under GO *verb* and *noun*

gofer /ˈgoʊfə(r)/ ▷ *noun*, *originally N Amer, especially US* in an office or on a film set: a junior employee who runs errands. ⓘ 1960s: from *go for*.

goffer /ˈgɒfə(r)/ ▷ *verb* (***goffered***, ***goffering***) to crimp (paper or material) or make it wavy. ⓘ 18c as *gowpher*: from French *gaufrer* (*à la paille*).

go-getter /ˈgoʊgɛtə(r)/ ▷ *noun*, *colloq* an ambitious enterprising person. • **go-getting** *adj*.

goggle /ˈgɒgəl/ ▷ *verb* (***goggled***, ***goggling***) **1** *intr* to look with wide staring eyes. **2** to roll (the eyes). **3** *intr* said of the eyes: to stick out. ▷ *noun* a wide-eyed stare. See also GOGGLES. ⓘ 14c, meaning 'to turn the eyes to one side'.

goggle-box ▷ *noun* (*usually* **the goggle-box**) *colloq* the TV.

goggle-eyed ▷ *adj* having bulging, staring or rolling eyes.

goggles ▷ *plural noun* **1** protective spectacles with edges that fit closely against the face. They were formerly used by pilots, motorists, etc and are now chiefly used in industry and when swimming. **2** *colloq* spectacles. See also GOGGLE.

go-go dancer ▷ *noun* a female erotic dancer, especially in a club or bar. ⓘ 1960s: from French *à gogo* galore or aplenty.

Goidel /ˈgɔɪdəl/ ▷ *noun* **1** a Gael. **2** someone who can speak any of the Goidelic languages. ⓘ 19c: Irish.

Goidelic /gɔɪˈdɛlɪk/ ▷ *noun*, *linguistics* the Gaelic or Q-Celtic branch of the Celtic language family. ▷ *adj* relating to the Gaels or especially to their language-group. Compare GAELIC. ⓘ 19c: from Irish *Goidel* a Gael.

going /ˈgoʊɪŋ/ ▷ *noun* **1** leaving; a departure □ *comings and goings of the lodgers.* **2** *horse-racing* the condition of the track. **3** progress □ *made good going.* **4** *colloq* general situation or conditions □ *when the going gets tough.* **5** *in compounds* the act or practice of making visits, especially regular ones, to specified places □ *theatre-going.* ▷ *verb, present participle of* GO **1** about or intending (to do something). **2** *in compounds* in the habit of visiting specified places □ *the cinema-going public.* ▷ *adj* **1** flourishing, successful □ *a going concern.* **2** usual or accepted □ *the going rate.* **3** in existence; currently available □ *These are the cheapest ones going.* • **be tough** or **hard going** to be difficult to do. • **going on** or **going on for something** approaching (a certain age or period of time) □ *going on for sixteen.* • **going strong** flourishing; fully operational.

going-away dress and **going-away outfit**, etc ▷ *noun* the dress, outfit, etc that a newly-married woman wears when leaving on her honeymoon.

going-over ▷ *noun* (***goings-over***) *colloq* **1** a beating. **2** a close inspection.

goings-on ▷ *plural noun*, *colloq* events or happenings, especially if they are strange or disapproved of.

goitre and (*US*) **goiter** /ˈgɔɪtə(r)/ ▷ *noun*, *pathol* an abnormal enlargement of the THYROID gland which often results in a large visible swelling in the neck. ⓘ 17c: French *goître*, from Latin *guttur* throat.

go-kart or **go-cart** ▷ *noun* **1** a low racing vehicle consisting of a frame with wheels, engine and steering gear. **2** a children's homemade vehicle for riding on.

gold /goʊld/ ▷ *noun* **1** (symbol **Au**, atomic number 79) a soft yellow precious metallic element used for making jewellery, coins, etc. **2** articles made from it, especially jewellery and coins. **3** its value, used as a standard for the value of currency. **4** its deep yellow colour. **5** *colloq* a gold medal. **6** precious or noble quality □ *heart of gold.* **7** monetary wealth. ▷ *adj* **1** made of gold. **2** gold-coloured. ⓘ Anglo-Saxon.

gold card ▷ *noun* a special-privilege credit card available only to people in the higher-income bracket.

goldcrest ▷ *noun* a small European and Asian woodland bird with a yellow or orange crest on its head.

gold-digger ▻ *noun* **1** *derog colloq* someone who starts love affairs with rich people in order to get at their money. **2** someone who digs for gold.

gold disc ▻ *noun, pop music* **1** an album that has sold 250 000 (*Brit*) or 500 000 (*US*) copies. **2** a single that has sold 500 000 (*Brit*) or one million (*US*) copies.

gold dust ▻ *noun* gold in the form of a very fine powder.

golden /'gouldən/ ▻ *adj* **1** gold-coloured. **2** made of or containing gold. **3** happy; prosperous or thriving □ *golden years* □ *golden age*. **4** excellent; extremely valuable □ *golden opportunity*. **5** greatly admired or favoured □ *golden girl*. **6** denoting a 50th anniversary □ *golden wedding*.

golden age ▻ *noun* **1** an imaginary past time of innocence and happiness. **2** the period of highest achievement in any sphere.

Golden Delicious or **golden delicious** ▻ *noun* a variety of eating apple with a sweet flavour and a yellowish-green skin.

golden eagle ▻ *noun* a large eagle with dark brown plumage and a golden nape, which lives in mountainous regions of the N hemisphere.

golden-eye ▻ *noun* a variety of northern sea-duck.

golden fleece ▻ *noun, Greek mythol* the fleece that Jason and the Argonauts set out on an expedition to recover.

golden goose and **the goose that lays the golden eggs** ▻ *noun* a source of profit, especially if it is in danger of being destroyed by over-exploitation. ◷ 19c in this figurative sense, independently of the fable (known in England in the 15c but Greek in origin) of the goose that laid a golden egg every day until its greedy owner killed it to get all the eggs at once.

golden handcuffs ▻ *noun, colloq* a substantial financial incentive offered to a valued employee to persuade them to remain with the company.

golden handshake ▻ *noun, colloq* a large sum received from an employer on retirement or in compensation for compulsory redundancy.

golden hello ▻ *noun* a large sum given to a new employee as an inducement to join a company.

golden jubilee ▻ *noun* a 50th anniversary.

golden mean ▻ *noun* **1** the midpoint between two extremes. **2** the GOLDEN SECTION.

golden oldie ▻ *noun, colloq* a song, recording, film, etc first issued years ago and still popular or well-known.

golden oriole see under ORIOLE

golden parachute ▻ *noun, colloq* a lavish cash payment made to senior executives of companies if they are dismissed after a takeover.

golden pheasant ▻ *noun* a golden-crested Chinese pheasant.

golden plover ▻ *noun* a plover with yellow-speckled feathers.

golden retriever ▻ *noun* a type of RETRIEVER with a thick wavy golden-yellow coat.

goldenrod ▻ *noun* a late-flowering perennial garden plant with long pointed lance-shaped leaves and numerous spikes of tiny golden-yellow flowers, originally native to N America.

golden rule ▻ *noun* **1** any essential principle or rule. **2** Christ's instruction to treat others as one would wish to be treated by them.

golden section ▻ *noun, math* the division of a line so that the proportion of the whole to the larger section is the same as that of the larger to the smaller section.

golden share ▻ *noun* a controlling share in a company, held by an institution or by a government in order to prevent takeover, especially such a share held by the UK government in newly-privatized companies.

golden syrup ▻ *noun* light-golden-coloured treacle.

golden wattle ▻ *noun* any of various kinds of yellow-flowered Australian acacia.

gold export point see under GOLD POINT

goldfield ▻ *noun* an area where gold is mined.

goldfinch ▻ *noun* any of numerous species of European and Asian finch that are distinguished by having a broad yellow bar across each wing.

goldfish ▻ *noun* any of numerous yellow, orange or golden-red varieties of a freshwater fish belonging to the CARP[1] family, which are often kept as pets or used to stock aquariums and artificial ponds.

goldfish bowl ▻ *noun* **1** a spherical glass aquarium for ornamental fish. **2** a situation entirely lacking in privacy.

gold foil ▻ *noun* gold beaten into thin sheets, but not as thin as gold leaf.

goldilocks ▻ *noun, often patronizing or derisive* a term of address for a person with fair hair. ◷ 16c (the fairy-tale character has this name only since 20c).

gold import point see under GOLD POINT

gold leaf ▻ *noun* gold that is rolled or beaten into very thin sheets and used to decorate books, crockery, etc.

gold medal ▻ *noun* a medal awarded to the winner of a sporting contest, or in recognition of excellence, eg of a wine. Often shortened to GOLD.

gold mine or **goldmine** ▻ *noun* **1** a place where gold is mined. **2** *colloq* a source of great wealth □ *the cybercafé turned out to be a real goldmine*.

gold plate ▻ *noun* **1** a thin coating of gold, especially on silver. **2** articles such as spoons and dishes made of gold. ▻ *verb* (**gold-plate**) to coat (another metal) with gold. • **gold-plated** *adj*.

gold point ▻ *noun* in international financial transactions: an exchange rate at which it becomes advisable to export (**gold export point**) or import (**gold import point**) gold bullion rather than settle an account by bills of exchange.

gold reserve ▻ *noun* the stock of gold held by a country's central bank, to finance any calls that may be made from overseas creditors for the settlement of debt.

gold rush ▻ *noun* a frantic scramble by large numbers of people to prospect in a newly-discovered goldfield.

goldsmith ▻ *noun* someone who makes articles out of gold.

gold standard ▻ *noun* a monetary system in which the unit of currency is assigned a value relative to gold.

golf /gɒlf/ ▻ *noun* **1** a game played on a golf course, the object being to hit a small ball into each of a series of nine or eighteen holes using a set of long-handled clubs, taking as few strokes as possible. **2** (**Golf**) *communications* in the NATO alphabet: the word used to denote the letter 'G' (see table at NATO ALPHABET). ▻ *verb* (***golfed, golfing***) *intr* to play this game. ◷ 15c Scots: perhaps from Dutch *colf* club.

golf bag ▻ *noun* a bag for carrying golf clubs.

golf ball ▻ *noun* **1** a small ball used in golf, made of tightly wound rubber strands and a cover of GUTTA-PERCHA. **2** in some electric typewriters and printers: a small detachable metal sphere or hemisphere with the type characters moulded on to its surface.

golf club ▻ *noun* **1** any of the set of long-handled clubs used to play golf. **2 a** an association of players of golf; **b** its premises with a golf course attached.

golf course ▻ *noun* an area of specially prepared ground on which golf is played. This is often landscaped, and contains features such as tees (see TEE²), GREENs and HAZARDS (*noun* 3).

golfer ▻ *noun* someone who plays golf.

golfiana /gɒlfɪˈɑːnə/ ▻ *plural noun* a collector's or dealer's term for items of golfing interest.

golf links ▻ *plural noun* a golf course, especially one by the sea, typically open and undulating.

goliath or **Goliath** ▻ *noun, colloq* **1** an unusually large or tall person. **2** a person or organization of great importance or influence. ⓒ 16c as *Golias*: from *Goliath*, the Old Testament Philistine giant killed by David (1 Samuel 17).

golliwog or **gollywog** /ˈgɒlɪwɒg/ ▻ *noun* **1** *old use* a child's cloth or knitted doll with a black face, bristling hair and bright clothes. **2** *taboo* a person with fuzzy or bristling hair. Often shortened to GOLLY². ⓒ Late 19c: from *Golliwogg*, the name of a doll character in children's books in the US, published from 1895.

gollop /ˈgɒləp/ ▻ *verb* (***golloped, golloping***) *tr & intr, colloq* to gulp greedily or hastily. ⓒ 19c.

golly¹ /ˈgɒlɪ/ ▻ *exclamation, old use* expressing surprise or admiration. ⓒ 18c: a euphemistic form of *God*.

golly² /ˈgɒlɪ/ ▻ *noun* (***gollies***) *colloq* short form of GOLLIWOG.

golosh see GALOSH

GOM ▻ *abbreviation* Grand Old Man, used of an elderly and venerated person, especially in a specific field. ⓒ 19c: originally applied to the British statesman, W E Gladstone (1809–98), who was Prime Minister four times.

-gon /gɒn/ ▻ *combining form, math, forming nouns, signifying* a two-dimensional figure with a specified number of angles ▫ ***polygon***. ⓒ From Greek *gonia* angle.

gonad /ˈgoʊnad, ˈgɒ-/ ▻ *noun, biol* an organ in which eggs or sperm are produced, especially the OVARY or TESTIS. ⓒ 19c: from Greek *gone* generation.

gonadotrophic hormone ▻ *noun, physiol* any of various hormones that stimulate the ovary and testis and are responsible for the production of sex hormones, the onset of sexual maturity and the control of the menstrual cycle.

gonadotrophin /goʊnadoʊˈtroʊfɪn, gɒ-/ ▻ *noun, physiol* gonadotrophic hormone. • **gonadotrophic** /-ˈtroʊfɪk/ *adj* that stimulates the gonads. ⓒ 1930s: from GONAD.

gondola /ˈgɒndələ/ ▻ *noun* (***gondolas***) **1** a long narrow flat-bottomed boat with pointed upturned ends, used to transport passengers on the canals of Venice. **2** the passenger cabin suspended from an airship, balloon or cable-railway. **3** a free-standing shelved unit for displaying goods in a supermarket. • **gondolier** /gɒndəˈlɪə(r)/ *noun* someone who propels a gondola in Venice. ⓒ 16c: a Venetian dialect word, meaning 'to rock'.

Gondwanaland /gɒnˈdwɑːnəland/ and **Gondwana** ▻ *noun* an ancient continent believed to have connected India with S Africa, S America, Antarctica and Australia from Carboniferous to Jurassic times.

gone /gɒn/ ▻ *verb, past participle of* GO. ▻ *adj* **1** departed. **2** *colloq* said of time: past ▫ ***gone six***. **3** used up. **4** lost. **5** dead. **6** *colloq* pregnant ▫ ***four months gone***. **7** *colloq* in an exalted state, eg from drugs. • **gone on someone** or **something** *colloq* infatuated or obsessed with them.

goner /ˈgɒnə(r)/ ▻ *noun, colloq* someone or something that is considered beyond hope of recovery. ⓒ 19c.

gonfalon /ˈgɒnfəlɒn/ ▻ *noun* a banner hung from a horizontal bar, especially one used in some medieval Italian republics. • **gonfalonier** /-nɪə(r)/ *noun* a standard-bearer. ⓒ 16c: from Italian *gonfalone*, from German *gund* battle + *fano* flag.

gong /gɒŋ/ ▻ *noun* **1** a hanging metal plate that makes a resonant sound when struck ▫ ***a dinner gong***. **2** *slang* a medal. **3** an orchestral percussion instrument, usually of definite pitch, that consists of a flattened metal disc played by striking it with a softly padded mallet. ⓒ 17c: from Malay.

goniometer /goʊnɪˈɒmɪtə(r), gɒnɪ-/ ▻ *noun* **1** an instrument for measuring angles, especially between crystal faces. **2** a direction-finding instrument, used especially to trace radio signals. ⓒ 18c: from Greek *gonia* an angle.

gonna /ˈgɒnə, ˈgənə/ ▻ *contraction, colloq, especially N Amer* going to.

gonococcus /gɒnoʊˈkɒkəs/ ▻ *noun* (***gonococci*** /-ˈkɒksaɪ/) *medicine* the bacterium that causes gonorrhoea. • **gonococcal** *adj*. ⓒ 19c: from Greek *gonos* seed + COCCUS.

gonorrhoea or (*N Amer*) **gonorrhea** /gɒnəˈrɪə/ ▻ *noun, pathol* a sexually transmitted disease, caused by infection with the GONOCOCCUS bacterium which, if left untreated, may cause sterility, arthritis and inflammation of the heart. • **gonorrhoeal** *adj*. ⓒ 16c as *gomory*: from Greek *gonos* seed or semen + *rhoia* a flowing, from a misunderstanding of the symptoms.

gonzo /ˈgɒnzoʊ/ ▻ *adj, slang, especially N Amer* applied especially to eccentric subjective journalism: bizarre; weird. ⓒ Coined by the US writer Hunter S Thompson in *Rolling Stone* magazine in 1971.

goo ▻ *noun* (*plural* in sense 1 ***goos***) *colloq* **1** any sticky substance. **2** *derog* excessive sentimentality. • **gooey** ***see separate entry***. ⓒ 20c.

good /gʊd/ ▻ *adj* (***better, best***) **1 a** having desirable or necessary (positive) qualities; admirable; **b** *patronizing* used when addressing or referring to someone ▫ ***my good man*** ▫ ***your good lady***. **2 a** morally correct; virtuous; **b** (**the good**) virtuous people in general (see THE 4). **3** kind and generous. **4** bringing happiness or pleasure ▫ ***good news***. **5** well-behaved. **6** wise; advisable ▫ ***a good buy***. **7** thorough. **8** finest compared with others ▫ ***my good china***. **9** adequate; satisfactory ▫ ***a good supply***. **10** enjoyable ▫ ***having a good time***. **11** valid. **12** well-respected. **13** sound; giving use; serviceable ▫ ***The roof is good for another winter***. **14** financially sound ▫ ***a good investment***. **15** considerable; at least ▫ ***waited a good while*** ▫ ***lasted a good month***. **16** certain to provide the desired result ▫ ***good for a laugh***. **17** used to introduce exclamations expressing surprise, dismay, or exasperation ▫ ***good heavens*** ▫ ***good grief*** ▫ ***good golly***. ▻ *noun* **1** moral correctness; virtue. **2** benefit; advantage ▫ ***do you good*** ▫ ***£20 to the good*** ▫ ***It turned out all to the good***. ▻ *exclamation* expressing approval or satisfaction. ▻ *adverb, colloq* very well ▫ ***The boy Linneker done good***. • **as good as ...** almost ... ; virtually ... . • **as good as gold** or **good as gold** said especially of children: extremely well-behaved. • **be as good as one's word** to carry out one's promises. • **for good** or **for good and all** for ever; permanently. • **good and ...** *colloq* very ... ; completely or absolutely ... ▫ ***good and ready***. • **good at something** competent at it; talented in that area. • **good for someone** or **something** beneficial to them or it. • **good for you**, *etc*! or (*Austral, NZ colloq*) or **good on you**, *etc*! **1** an expression of approval or congratulation. **2** an expression of snide resentment. • **good morning** or **good afternoon** or **good evening** traditional expressions used when either meeting or parting from someone at the specified time of day. • **good night** a traditional expression used when parting from someone at night or well on in the day. • **in someone's good books** in favour with someone. • **make good** to be successful. • **make something good 1** to repair it. **2** to carry it out or fulfil it. • **no good 1** useless. **2** worthless. • **to the good** on the credit side. ⓒ Anglo-Saxon *god*.

the Good Book ▻ *noun* the Bible.

goodbye /ɡʊdbaɪ/ ▻ *exclamation* used when parting from someone. ▻ *noun* (***goodbyes***) an act or instance of saying goodbye □ *said our goodbyes.* ⓒ 16c as *God be wy you* God be with you.

good day ▻ *exclamation, Brit, rather formal* a traditional expression used when either meeting or parting from someone. Compare G'DAY.

good evening see under GOOD MORNING at GOOD

good feeling ▻ *noun* friendly feeling; amicable relations.

good-for-nothing ▻ *adj* lazy and irresponsible. ▻ *noun* a lazy and irresponsible person.

Good Friday ▻ *noun* a Christian festival on the Friday before Easter, in memory of Christ's crucifixion. ⓒ 13c: from GOOD in the sense 'holy'.

good humour ▻ *noun* a cheerful, tolerant mood or disposition. • **good-humoured** *adj.* • **good-humouredly** *adverb.* • **good-humouredness** *noun.*

goodies /ˈɡʊdɪz/ *plural noun, colloq* things considered pleasant or desirable □ *a table laden with goodies* □ *A new company car was just one of the goodies that came with the job.* See also GOODY.

good looks ▻ *plural noun* attractive appearance. • **good-looker** *noun, colloq.* • **good-looking** *adj.*

goodly /ˈɡʊdlɪ/ ▻ *adj* (***goodlier***, ***goodliest***) *old use or jocular* **1** quite large □ *a goodly measure of the amber nectar.* **2** physically attractive; fine. • **goodliness** *noun.* ⓒ 13c in obsolete sense 'beautifully'.

good nature ▻ *noun* natural goodness and mildness of disposition. • **good-natured** *adj.* • **good-naturedly** *adverb.* • **good-naturedness** *noun.*

goodness ▻ *noun* **1** the state or quality of being good; generosity; kindness; moral correctness. **2** *euphemistic* used in exclamations: God □ *goodness knows.* **3** nourishing quality □ *all the goodness of the grain.* ▻ *exclamation* expressing surprise or relief □ *Goodness! What a mess!*

good night see under GOOD

goods ▻ *plural noun* **1** articles for sale; merchandise. **2** freight. Often *as adj* □ *goods train.* **3** *colloq* the required result □ *deliver the goods.* **4** *old use* personal possessions. • **have the goods on someone** *colloq* to have proof of wrongdoings or crimes committed by them.

goodwill ▻ *noun* **1** a feeling of kindness towards others. **2** the good reputation of an established business, seen as having an actual value.

goody /ˈɡʊdɪ/ ▻ *noun* (***goodies***) *colloq* a hero in a film, book, etc. See also GOODIES.

goody-goody /ˈɡʊdɪɡʊdɪ/ *colloq* ▻ *adj* virtuous in an ostentatious or self-satisfied way. ▻ *noun* (***goody-goodies***) an ostentatiously virtuous person.

gooey /ˈɡuːɪ/ (***gooier***, ***gooiest***) *colloq* ▻ *adj* sticky. • **gooily** *adverb.* • **gooiness** *noun.* ⓒ 20c: from GOO.

goof /ɡuːf/ *chiefly N Amer colloq* ▻ *noun* **1** a silly or foolish person. **2** a stupid mistake. ▻ *verb* (***goofed***, ***goofing***) *intr* (*sometimes* **goof up**) to make a stupid mistake. ⓒ 20c.

▪ **goof about** or **around** *N Amer* to mess about or behave in a silly way.

▪ **goof off** *N Amer* to spend time idly when one should be working or acting responsibly; to evade work, school, college, etc; to skive off.

goof-ball ▻ *noun, N Amer slang* **1** a barbiturate sleeping tablet. **2** a goofy person.

goofy ▻ *adj* (***goofier***, ***goofiest***) *colloq* **1** silly; crazy. **2** said of teeth: protruding.

googly /ˈɡuːɡlɪ/ ▻ *noun* (***googlies***) *cricket* a ball bowled so that it changes direction unexpectedly after bouncing.

googol /ˈɡuːɡɒl/ ▻ *noun* a fanciful term for ten to the power of 100. ⓒ 1940s.

gook /ɡuːk/ ▻ *noun* **1** *US offensive slang* someone of Asiatic race, especially a Japanese, Korean or Vietnamese soldier. **2** *especially formerly* in Rhodesia: a guerrilla or terrorist. ⓒ 1930s.

gooly, **gooley** and **goolie** /ˈɡuːlɪ/ ▻ *noun* (***goolies***) **1** (*usually* **goolies**) *slang* a testicle. **2** *Austral colloq* a small stone. ⓒ 1930s: perhaps from Hindi *goli* a bullet or ball.

goombah /ˈɡuːmbə/ ▻ *noun, US slang* **1** someone who belongs to a criminal gang, especially one that has links with the Mafia. **2** a close friend or associate. ⓒ 20c: from Italian *compare* a godfather.

goon ▻ *noun* **1** *colloq* a silly person. **2** *slang* a hired thug. ⓒ 1920s: from US cartoon character Alice the Goon, created by E C Segar (1894–1938).

goop ▻ *noun* **1** *N Amer* a rude, ill-mannered person. **2** a stupid person. • **goopy** stupid. ⓒ Early 20c: compare GOOF.

goosander /ɡuːˈsandə(r)/ ▻ *noun* a large duck with a bulky body, a large dark head bearing a stiff double crest, and a long slender pointed red bill, native to Europe and N America. ⓒ 17c: perhaps from GOOSE + Norse *ander* (plural of *önd* duck).

goose /ɡuːs/ ▻ *noun* (***geese*** in senses 1 to 4, ***gooses*** in sense 5) **1** any of numerous large wild or domesticated waterfowl, related to ducks and swans, with a stout body, long neck, webbed feet and a broad flat bill. **2** the female of this, as opposed to the male (the GANDER). **3** the flesh of a goose cooked as food. **4** *colloq, old use* a silly person. **5** *colloq* a poke or pinch on the buttocks. ▻ *verb* (***goosed***, ***goosing***) *colloq* to poke or pinch someone on the buttocks. • **cook someone's goose** *colloq* to ruin their plans or chances. See also GOSLING. ⓒ Anglo-Saxon *gos.*

gooseberry /ˈɡʊzbərɪ/ ▻ *noun* (***gooseberries***) **1** a low-growing deciduous shrub with spiny stems, lobed leaves and greenish flowers on short drooping stalks. **2** one of the small sour-tasting yellowish-green or reddish berries produced by this plant, used to make jam, pies, etc. • **play gooseberry** *colloq* to be an unwanted third person, especially in the company of an amorous couple.

goose bumps and **goose flesh** see under GOOSE PIMPLES.

goosefoot ▻ *noun* (***goosefoots***) a plant of various species in the beet family, with a leaf shaped like a goose's foot.

goosegog /ˈɡʊsɡɒɡ/ ▻ *noun, colloq or dialect* a gooseberry.

goosegrass ▻ *noun* **1** CLEAVERS. **2** SILVERWEED.

goose pimples and **goose bumps** ▻ *plural noun* and **goose flesh** ▻ *singular noun* a condition of the skin caused by cold or fear, in which the body hairs become erect, pimples appear and there is a bristling feeling.

goose-step ▻ *noun* a military marching step in which the legs are kept rigid and swung very high. ▻ *verb, intr* to march with this step.

the goose that lays the golden eggs see GOLDEN GOOSE

gopak /ˈɡoupak/ ▻ *noun* a high-leaping Ukrainian folk-dance for men. ⓒ 20c: Russian.

gopher[1] /ˈɡoufə(r)/ ▻ *noun* **1** a small burrowing N American rodent with a stocky body, short legs, large chisel-like incisor teeth and two large external fur-lined cheek pouches. **2** a GROUND SQUIRREL. **3** *N Amer* any of various other burrowing animals, eg a burrowing tortoise, a burrowing snake and certain salamanders. ▻ *verb* (***gophered***, ***gophering***) *intr, US* to carry on small-scale mining. ⓒ 19c.

gopher² /ˈgoʊfə(r)/ ▻ *noun, Bible* the unidentified tree which was the source of the wood that Noah used to build his ark. ⌚ 17c: Hebrew.

gorblimey or **gorblimy** /gɔːˈblaɪmɪ/ ▻ *exclamation* expressing surprise. ▻ *adj* **1** vulgar. **2** relating to the ordinary population. ▻ *noun* (*in full* **gorblimey cap**) a type of flat army cap. ⌚ 19c: representing a Cockney pronunciation of *God blind me*.

Gordian knot /ˈgɔːdɪən —/ ▻ *noun* a difficult problem or dilemma. • **cut the Gordian knot** to resolve a difficulty by decisive and often evasive action. ⌚ 16c: named after Gordius, king of ancient Phrygia in Asia Minor, who tied a complicated knot that no-one could untie; Alexander the Great solved the problem by cutting the knot with a sword.

Gordon Bennett /ˈgɔːdən ˈbɛnɪt/ ▻ *exclamation* expressing mild surprise or annoyance. ⌚ Late 19c euphemism for GOD; referring to James *Gordon Bennett* (1841–1918), US journalist and flamboyant figure of the day.

Gordon setter ▻ *noun* a SETTER with a black and tan coat, bred as a gun dog. ⌚ 19c: popularized by Alexander Gordon (1743–1827), Scottish nobleman.

gore¹ /gɔː(r)/ ▻ *noun* blood from a wound, especially when clotted. ⌚ Anglo-Saxon *gor* filth.

gore² /gɔː(r)/ ▻ *verb* (***gored, goring***) to pierce something or someone with horn or tusk. ⌚ Anglo-Saxon *gar* spear.

gore³ /gɔː(r)/ ▻ *noun* a triangular piece of material, eg a section of an umbrella or a tapering piece in a garment, glove, etc. ▻ *verb* (***gored, goring***) to construct something from, or shape it with, gores. • **gored** *adj* made with gores. ⌚ Anglo-Saxon *gara* a triangular piece of land.

gorge /gɔːdʒ/ ▻ *noun* **1** a deep narrow valley, usually containing a river. **2** the contents of the stomach. **3** a spell of greedy eating. **4** *old use* the throat or gullet. ▻ *verb* (***gorged, gorging***) **1** *tr & intr* to eat or swallow greedily. **2** (*usually* **gorge oneself**) to stuff oneself with food. • **make someone's gorge rise 1** to disgust or sicken them. **2** to fill them with resentment. ⌚ 14c: French, meaning 'throat'.

gorgeous /ˈgɔːdʒəs/ ▻ *adj* **1** extremely beautiful or attractive; magnificent. **2** *colloq* excellent; extremely pleasant. • **gorgeously** *adverb*. • **gorgeousness** *noun*. ⌚ 15c: from French *gorgias* fine or elegant.

gorget /ˈgɔːdʒɪt/ ▻ *noun, historical* **1** a piece of armour for the throat. **2** a WIMPLE. ⌚ 15c: from French *gorgete*.

gorgio /ˈgɔːdʒɪoʊ/ ▻ *noun* a gypsy word for a non-gypsy. ⌚ 19c: Romany.

gorgon /ˈgɔːgən/ ▻ *noun* **1** (**Gorgon**) *mythol* any of the three female monsters which had live snakes for hair and were capable of turning people to stone. **2** *derog, colloq* a fierce, frightening or very ugly woman. ⌚ 14c: from Greek *gorgos* terrible.

Gorgonzola /gɔːgənˈzoʊlə/ ▻ *noun* a blue-veined Italian cheese with a sharp flavour. ⌚ 19c: named after the town near Milan where it was first made.

gorilla /gəˈrɪlə/ ▻ *noun* (***gorillas***) **1** the largest of the apes, native to African rainforests, which has a heavily built body, broad chest, strong hands and feet and jet black skin covered with dense fur. **2** *colloq* a brutal-looking man, especially a hired thug. ⌚ 19c: from Greek *Gorillai* the hairy females supposedly seen on a voyage to Africa in the 6c BC.

gorily and **goriness** see under GORY

gormandize or **gormandise** /ˈgɔːməndaɪz/ ▻ *verb* (***gormandized, gormandizing***) *tr & intr* to eat greedily; to guzzle. • **gormandizer** *noun*. • **gormandizing** *noun*. ⌚ 16c: from GOURMANDISE.

gormless /ˈgɔːmləs/ *derog colloq* ▻ *adj* stupid; dim. • **gormlessly** *adverb*. • **gormlessness** *noun*. ⌚ 19c: variant of obsolete *gaumless*, from *gaum* understanding.

gorse /gɔːs/ ▻ *noun* (***gorses***) a highly branched evergreen shrub with leaves reduced to very sharp deeply furrowed spines and bright yellow flowers. It grows along hedgerows and on heath and grassland. Also called **furze** and **whin**. • **gorsy** *adj*. ⌚ Anglo-Saxon *gors*.

gory /ˈgɔːrɪ/ ▻ *adj* (***gorier, goriest***) **1** causing or involving bloodshed. **2** *colloq* unpleasant ▫ ***gory details***. **3** covered in GORE. • **gorily** *adverb*. • **goriness** *noun*. ⌚ 15c.

gosh /gɒʃ/ ▻ *exclamation, colloq* expressing mild surprise. ⌚ 18c: euphemistic form of GOD.

goshawk /ˈgɒshɔːk/ ▻ *noun* a large hawk with bluish-grey plumage with paler underparts, short rounded wings and a long tail. It is used in falconry. ⌚ Anglo-Saxon *goshafoc*, from *gos* goose + *hafoc* hawk.

gosling /ˈgɒzlɪŋ/ ▻ *noun* a young goose. ⌚ 15c: from Anglo-Saxon *gos* goose + -LING 1.

go-slow ▻ *noun* an instance or the process of deliberately working slowly so as to encourage an employer to negotiate. See also GO SLOW at GO¹.

gospel /ˈgɒspəl/ ▻ *noun* **1** the life and teachings of Christ ▫ ***preach the gospel***. **2** (**Gospel**) each of the New Testament books ascribed to Matthew, Mark, Luke and John. **3** a passage from one of these read at a religious service. **4** (*also* **gospel truth**) *colloq* the absolute truth. **5** a set of closely followed principles or rules. **6** (*also* **gospel music**) lively religious music of Black American origin. ⌚ Anglo-Saxon *godspel*, from *god* good + *spel* story.

gossamer /ˈgɒsəmə(r)/ ▻ *noun* **1** fine filmy spider-woven threads seen on hedges or floating in the air. **2** any soft fine material. • **gossamery** *adj*. ⌚ 14c as *gossomer* in sense 1, but perhaps originally meaning 'goose summer', ie a period in November when goose was traditionally eaten and these cobwebs were often seen.

gossip /ˈgɒsɪp/ ▻ *noun* **1** *derog* talk or writing about the private affairs of others, often spiteful and untrue. **2** *derog* someone who engages in or spreads such talk. **3** casual and friendly talk. ▻ *verb* (***gossiped, gossiping***) *intr* **1** to engage in, or pass on, malicious gossip. **2** to chat. • **gossiping** *noun, adj*. • **gossipy** *adj*. ⌚ Anglo-Saxon *godsibb* godparent, hence a familiar friend one chats to.

gossip column ▻ *noun* a newspaper column about the lives and loves of well-known people. • **gossip columnist** *noun*.

got *past tense & past participle of* GET

Goth /gɒθ/ ▻ *noun* **1** *historical* a member of an East Germanic people (see under GERMANIC) who invaded various parts of the Roman Empire between the third and fifth centuries. **2** a rude or uncivilized person. **3** (**goth**) someone who dresses mainly in black, often having dyed black or purple hair and stark black and white make-up, and who identifies with GOTHIC ROCK music. ⌚ Anglo-Saxon plural *Gotan*.

Gothamite /ˈgɒθəmaɪt, ˈgoʊ-/ ▻ *noun* **1** a foolish or simple-minded person. **2** a New Yorker. ⌚ 19c: from *Gotham*, a village in Nottinghamshire, traditionally (since the 15c) renowned for the foolishness of its inhabitants; the name was applied to New York in the 19c.

Gothic /ˈgɒθɪk/ ▻ *adj* **1** belonging or relating to the Goths or their language. **2** belonging or relating to a style of architecture featuring high pointed arches, popular in Europe between the 12c and 16c. **3** belonging or relating to a type of literature dealing with mysterious or supernatural events in an eerie setting, popular in the 18c. **4** (*also* **gothick**) belonging or relating to a modern style of literature, films, etc which imitates this. **5** *printing* relating to various styles of heavy type with elaborate angular features. ▻ *noun* **1** Gothic architecture or literature. **2** Gothic lettering. **3** the extinct Germanic language of the Goths. ⌚ 17c.

Gothic Rock ▻ *noun* a style of rock music derived from PUNK (noun 1) and characterized by guitar-based music, dark lyrics and occult iconography.

gotta /ˈgɒtə, ˈgɒɾə/ ▷ *contraction, very informal* **1** got to; must □ *gotta get there before it shuts.* **2** got a □ *gotta really sore head.*

gotten *US past participle of* GET

gouache /guˈɑːʃ, gwɑːʃ/ ▷ *noun* **1** a painting technique using a blend of watercolour and a glue-like substance, giving an opaque matt surface. **2** a painting done in this way. ◷ 19c: French.

Gouda /ˈgaʊdə/ ▷ *noun* (***Goudas***) a flat round mild Dutch cheese. ◷ 19c: named after the town in Holland where it originated.

gouge /gaʊdʒ/ ▷ *noun* **1** a chisel with a rounded hollow blade, used for cutting grooves or holes in wood. **2** a groove or hole made using, or as if using, this. ▷ *verb* (***gouged***, ***gouging***) to cut something out with or as if with a gouge. ◷ 15c: French, from Latin *gubia* chisel.

■ **gouge something out** **1** to use a gouge on it. **2** to force or press it out of position □ *gouged his eye out.*

gougère /guːˈdʒɛə(r)/ ▷ *noun, cookery* a kind of choux pastry that has grated cheese added to it before baking. ◷ 20c: French.

goujons /ˈguːdʒɒnz; *French* guʒɔ̃/ ▷ *plural noun, cookery* strips of fish or meat coated in flour, batter or breadcrumbs and deep-fried. ◷ 1940s: French.

goulash /ˈguːlaʃ/ ▷ *noun* (***goulashes***), *cookery* **1** a thick meat stew heavily seasoned with paprika, originally from Hungary. **2** *bridge* a re-deal of cards in blocks of up to five at once, without reshuffling after the first deal. ◷ 19c: from Hungarian *gulyas hus* herdsman's meat.

gourd /gʊəd, gɔːd/ ▷ *noun* **1 a** any of various mostly climbing plants related to the cucumber, that produce a large fruit with a hard woody outer shell; **b** the large usually pear-shaped or bottle-shaped fruit of this plant. **2** the hard durable shell of this fruit, often hollowed out, dried, and used as an ornament, cup, bowl, etc. ◷ 14c: from French *gourde*.

gourmand /ˈgʊəmənd, ˈgɔː-/ ▷ *noun* **1** a greedy eater; a glutton. **2** a gourmet. ◷ 15c: French.

gourmandise /gɔːmənˈdiːz/ and **gourmandism** ▷ *noun* **1** indulgence in good eating. **2** discerning appreciation of good food and wines. ◷ 15c: French.

gourmet /ˈgʊəmeɪ, ˈgɔː-/ ▷ *noun* someone who has expert knowledge of, and a passion for, good food and wine. ◷ 19c: French, originally meaning 'a wine-merchant's assistant'.

gout /gaʊt/ ▷ *noun, medicine, pathol* a disease in which excess URIC ACID accumulates in the bloodstream and is deposited as crystals in the joints, causing acute ARTHRITIS, especially of the big toe. • **goutiness** *noun*. • **gouty** *adj* afflicted with gout. ◷ 13c: from French *goute* a drop, the disease having formerly been thought of as being caused by drops of humours.

Gov. or **gov.** ▷ *abbreviation* **1** government. **2** governor.

govern /ˈgʌvən/ ▷ *verb* (***governed***, ***governing***) **1** *tr & intr* to control and direct the affairs of (a country, state, or organization). **2** to guide or influence; to control or restrain □ *govern his temper.* **3** *grammar* said of a word or part of speech: to dictate the CASE² (sense 7), MOOD² (sense 1) or inflectional ending of another, closely associated word □ *prepositions that govern the accusative.* • **governable** *adj*. • **governing** *adj*. ◷ 13c: from Latin *gubernare*, from Greek *kybernaein* to steer.

governance ▷ *noun, formal* **1** the act or state of governing. **2** the system of government. **3** authority or control. ◷ 14c.

governess ▷ *noun* (***governesses***) *chiefly formerly* a woman employed to teach, and perhaps look after, children, usually while living in their home. ◷ 18c; 15c as 'a woman who governs'.

government /ˈgʌvəmənt, ˈgʌvən-/ ▷ *noun* **1** (*often* **the Government**) a body of people, usually elected, with the power to control the affairs of a country or state. **2 a** the way in which this is done; **b** the particular system used. **3** the act or practice of ruling; control. **4** *grammar* the power of one word to determine the form, CASE2 (sense 7) or MOOD² (sense 1) of another. • **governmental** /-ˈmentəl/ *adj*. ◷ 16c in senses 2 and 3.

governor /ˈgʌvənə(r), ˈgʌvnə(r)/ ▷ *noun* **1** (*also* **Governor**) the elected head of a US state. **2** the head of an institution, eg a prison. **3** a member of a governing body of a school, hospital, college, etc. **4** (*also* **Governor**) the head of a colony or province, especially the monarch's representative. See also GUBERNATORIAL. **5** *mech* a regulator or other device for maintaining uniform speed in an engine. **6** (*also* **guvnor** or **guv'nor**) *colloq* **a** (*often* **the governor**) a boss or father; **b** (*often* **guv**) a respectful, though now often ironical, form of address to a man, eg from a workman. • **governorship** *noun*. ◷ 13c.

Governor-General ▷ *noun* (***Governors-General*** or ***Governor-Generals***) the official representative of the British monarch in a Commonwealth country or British colony.

Govt ▷ *abbreviation* Government.

gown /gaʊn/ ▷ *noun* **1** a woman's long formal dress. **2** an official robe worn by clergymen, lawyers and academics. See also TOWN AND GOWN. **3** a protective overall worn eg by surgeons, patients, hairdressers' clients, etc. ◷ 14c: from Latin *gunna* a garment made of fur or leather.

goy /gɔɪ/ ▷ *noun* (***goys*** or ***goyim*** /gɔɪɪm/) *slang* a Jewish word for a non-Jewish person. • **goyish** or **goyisch** *adj* Gentile. ◷ 19c: from Hebrew *goy* people or nation.

GP ▷ *abbreviation* **1** Gallup poll. **2** general practitioner.

GPO ▷ *abbreviation* General Post Office.

GR ▷ *abbreviation* **1** *Georgius Rex* (Latin), King George. **2** *IVR* Greece.

Gr. ▷ *abbreviation* Greek.

gr. ▷ *abbreviation* **1** grain or grains. **2** gram or gramme, grams or grammes. **3** gross.

Graafian follicle /grɑːfɪən —/ ▷ *noun, anatomy* in the ovary of female mammals: one of many small spherical sacs within which an egg cell develops prior to ovulation. ◷ 19c: named after Regnier de Graaf (1641–73), the Dutch anatomist who discovered these.

grab ▷ *verb* (***grabbed***, ***grabbing***) **1** *tr & intr* (*also* **grab at something**) to seize suddenly and often with violence. **2** to take something greedily. **3** to take something hurriedly or without hesitation □ *grab a snack* □ *grab an opportunity.* **4** *colloq* to impress or interest someone □ *How does that grab you?* ▷ *noun* **1** an act or an instance of grabbing something. **2** a mechanical device with scooping jaws, used eg for excavation. • **up for grabs** *colloq* available, especially easily or cheaply. ◷ 16c: from German dialect or Dutch *grabben*.

GRACE ▷ *abbreviation, telecomm* group routing and charging equipment, an automatic telephone system by which all calls can be dialled directly by subscribers and by which all STD calls are charged. ◷ 1990s.

grace /greɪs/ ▷ *noun* **1** elegance and beauty of form or movement. **2** decency; politeness □ *had the grace to offer.* **3** a short prayer of thanks to God said before or after a meal. **4** a delay allowed, especially to a debtor, as a favour □ *gave us two days' grace.* **5** a pleasing or attractive characteristic □ *completely lacking in social graces* □ *a saving grace.* **6 a** *relig* the mercy and favour shown by God to mankind; **b** *relig* the condition of a person's soul when they have been made free from sin and evil by God. **8** (**His** or **Her Grace** or **Your Grace** (*plural* ***Their*** or ***Your Graces***)) a title used of or to a duke, duchess or archbishop. See also separate entry THE GRACES. ▷ *verb* (***graced***, ***gracing***) **1** *often facetious* to honour (an occasion, person, etc), eg with one's presence. **2** to add beauty or charm to something. • **with a good** or

bad grace willingly or unwillingly. ◷ 12c: from Latin *gratia* favour.

grace-and-favour ⊳ *adj, Brit* said of a house or flat: owned by the British sovereign and let rent-free in gratitude for services to the nation.

graceful ⊳ *adj* having or showing elegance and beauty of form or movement. • **gracefully** *adverb*. • **gracefulness** *noun*.

graceless ⊳ *adj* **1** awkward in form or movement. **2** bad-mannered. • **gracelessly** *adverb*. • **gracelessness** *noun*.

grace note ⊳ *noun, music* a note introduced as an embellishment and not essential to the melody or harmony.

the Graces ⊳ *plural noun, Greek mythol* the three sister goddesses who have the power to grant beauty, charm and happiness. ◷ 16c: from Latin *Gratiae*; see GRACE.

gracing *present participle of* GRACE

gracious /ˈgreɪʃəs/ ⊳ *adj* **1** kind and polite. **2** said of God: merciful. **3** having qualities of luxury, elegance, comfort and leisure □ ***gracious living***. **4** *formal* used out of polite custom to describe a royal person or their actions □ ***Her Gracious Majesty***. ⊳ *exclamation* (*also* **gracious me!**) expressing surprise. • **graciously** *adverb*. • **graciousness** *noun*. ◷ 14c: from Latin *gratiosus*.

gradate /grəˈdeɪt/ ⊳ *verb* (***gradated***, ***gradating***) **1** *intr* to shade off; to change imperceptibly. **2** to arrange something according to grades. ◷ 18c: from GRADATION.

gradation /grəˈdeɪʃən/ ⊳ *noun* **1 a** a series of gradual and successive stages or degrees; **b** one step in this. **2** the act or process of forming grades or stages. **3** the gradual change or movement from one state, musical note, colour, etc to another. **4** *linguistics* ABLAUT. • **gradational** *adj*. ◷ 16c: from GRADE.

grade /greɪd/ ⊳ *noun* **1** a stage or level on a scale of quality, rank, size, etc. **2** a mark indicating this. **3** *N Amer, especially US* **a** a particular class or year in school; **b** the level of work taught in it; **c** *as adj* □ ***grade school***. **4** a slope or gradient. **5** in stock-breeding: **a** an improved variety of animal produced by crossing usually a native animal with one of purer breed; **b** *as adj* □ ***grade lambs***. ⊳ *verb* (***graded***, ***grading***) **1** to arrange (things or people) in different grades. **2** to award a mark indicating grade, eg on a piece of written work, essay, etc. **3** to produce a gradual blending or merging of (especially colours). **4** to adjust the gradients of (a road or railway). **5** *intr* to pass gradually from one grade, level, value, etc to another. • **make the grade** *colloq* to succeed; to reach the required or expected standard. ◷ 16c in obsolete mathematical sense 'degree': from Latin *gradus* step.

grade crossing ⊳ *noun, N Amer* a LEVEL CROSSING.

grade post ⊳ *noun, educ* in British schools: a post with some special responsibility and extra payment.

grader /ˈgreɪdə(r)/ ⊳ *noun* **1** a machine that makes a smooth surface for road-building. **2** *in compounds, N Amer* a school pupil in a specified grade □ ***sixthgrader***. **3** someone or something that grades.

grade school ⊳ *noun, N Amer* elementary or primary school.

gradient /ˈgreɪdɪənt/ ⊳ *noun* **1** the steepness of a slope. **2** *formal* a slope. **3** *math* the slope of a line or the slope of a tangent to a curve at a particular point. **4** *physics* the rate of change of a variable quantity over a specified distance. ◷ 19c: from Latin *gradiens* stepping.

gradual /ˈgradʒʊəl/ ⊳ *adj* **1** developing or happening slowly, by degrees. **2** said of a slope: not steep; gentle. ⊳ *noun, RC Church* **1** an ANTIPHON sung between the epistle and the gospel ◷ because it was formerly always sung from the altar steps. **2** a book containing the music and words for the sung parts of the mass. • **graduality** or **gradualness** *noun*. • **gradually** *adverb*. ◷ 16c: from Latin *gradualis*, from *gradus* step.

gradualism /ˈgradʒʊəlɪzəm/ ⊳ *noun* the process of, or support for, gradual progress or change, especially in politics. • **gradualist** *noun, adj*.

graduand /ˈgradʒʊənd/ ⊳ *noun, especially Scottish* someone who is about to be awarded a higher-education degree. ◷ 19c: from Latin *graduare* to take a degree.

graduate ⊳ *verb* /ˈgradʒʊeɪt/ (***graduated***, ***graduating***) **1** *intr* or (*N Amer*) *sometimes* **be graduated** to receive an academic degree from a higher-education institution. **2** *intr, N Amer* to receive a diploma at the end of a course of study at high school. **3** *intr* to move up from a lower to a higher level, often in stages. **4** to mark (eg a thermometer) with units of measurement or other divisions. **5** to arrange something into regular groups, according to size, type, etc. ⊳ *noun* /-ɪt/ someone who has a higher-education degree or (*N Amer*) a high-school diploma. ◷ 15c: from Latin *graduari*, *graduatus* to take a degree, from *gradus* step.

graduated pension scheme ⊳ *noun* a British government pension scheme in addition to the basic OLD AGE PENSION, to which both employees and employers contribute in proportion to the employees' earnings.

graduation /gradʒʊˈeɪʃən/ ⊳ *noun* **1** the act of receiving a higher-education degree or (*N Amer*) a high-school diploma. **2** the ceremony marking this. **3 a** a unit of measurement or other division marked on a ruler, thermometer, etc; **b** the process of making or marking such divisions.

Graeco- or **Greco-** /ˈgriːkoʊ/ ⊳ *combining form, denoting* relating to Greece; Greek □ ***Graeco-Roman***. ◷ From Latin *Graecus* Greek.

graffiti /grəˈfiːtɪ/ ⊳ *plural noun*, sometimes used as *singular* (*singular also **graffito***) words or drawings, usually humorous, political or rude, scratched, sprayed or painted on walls, etc in public places. ◷ 19c: Italian, literally 'little scratches or scribbles'.

graft¹ /grɑːft/ ⊳ *noun* **1** *hortic* a piece of plant tissue that is inserted into a cut in the outer stem of another plant, resulting in fusion of the tissues and growth of a single plant. **2** *surgery* the transfer or transplantation of an organ or tissue from one individual to another, or to a different site within the same individual, usually to replace diseased or damaged tissue □ ***skin graft***. **3** a transplanted organ. Compare IMPLANT. ⊳ *verb* (***grafted***, ***grafting***) **1** (*also* **graft in** or **into** or **on** or **together**) **a** to attach a graft in something or someone; **b** to attach something as a graft. **2** *intr* to attach grafts. ◷ 15c: from French *graffe*, from Greek *graphein* to write.

graft² /grɑːft/ ⊳ *noun* **1** *colloq* hard work. **2** *slang* **a** the use of illegal or unfair means to gain profit or advantage, especially by politicians or officials; **b** the profit or advantage gained. ⊳ *verb* (***grafted***, ***grafting***) *intr* **1** *colloq* to work hard. **2** *slang* to practise graft. ◷ 19c, originally US.

grafter ⊳ *noun, colloq* **1** a hard worker. **2** someone who practises graft. **3** a corrupt politician or official.

Grail /greɪl/ ⊳ *noun* (*in full* **Holy Grail**) **1** in medieval legend: the platter or cup used by Christ at the Last Supper, in which Joseph of Arimathea caught his blood at the Crucifixion and which became the object of quests by medieval knights. **2** a cherished ambition or goal. ◷ 14c: from Latin *gradalis* a flat dish.

grain /greɪn/ ⊳ *noun* **1** a single small hard fruit, resembling a seed, produced by a cereal plant or other grass. **2** such fruits referred to collectively. **3** any of the cereal plants that produce such fruits, eg wheat, corn. **4** a small hard particle of anything. **5** a very small amount □ ***a grain of truth***. **6 a** the arrangement, size and direction of the fibres or layers in wood, leather, etc **b** the pattern formed as a result of this arrangement. **7** the main direction of the fibres in paper or the threads in a woven fabric. **8** any of the small particles of metallic silver that form the dark areas of the image on a developed photograph. **9** in the avoirdupois system: the smallest unit of weight, equal to 0.065 grams, formerly said to be the average weight of a grain of wheat (7 000 grains being equivalent to one pound avoirdupois). **10** in the troy system: a similar unit of weight (5 760 grains being equivalent to one pound troy). ▻ *verb* (***grained***, ***graining***) **1** *tr & intr* to form into grains. **2** to give a rough appearance or texture to something. **3** to paint or stain something with a pattern like the grain of wood or leather. • **grained** *adj*. • **graining** *noun*. • **go against the grain** to be against someone's principles or natural character. ◷ 13c: from Latin *granum* seed.

grain alcohol ▻ *noun* alcohol made by the fermentation of grain.

grainy ▻ *adj* (***grainier***, ***grainiest***) said of a photograph, TV picture, etc: having a large grain size (see GRAIN ▻ *noun* 8), and therefore not sharp or distinct.

gram or **gramme** /gram/ ▻ *noun* (abbreviation **g** or **gr**) in the metric system: the basic unit of mass, equal to one thousandth of a kilogram (0.035oz). ◷ 18c: from Greek *gramma* a small weight.

gram. ▻ *abbreviation* **1** grammar. **2** grammatical.

-gram /gram/ ▻ *combining form, forming nouns, denoting* something written, recorded or drawn □ ***pentagram*** □ ***telegram***. ◷ From Greek *gramma* letter.

graminaceous /gramɪ'neɪʃəs/ and **gramineous** /grə'mɪnɪəs/ ▻ *adj, bot* referring or relating to the large family of flowering plants that consists of the grasses. ◷ 17c: from Latin *gramen* grass; see also -EOUS, -ACEOUS.

graminivorous /gramɪ'nɪvərəs/ ▻ *adj* said of animals: feeding on grass or cereals. ◷ 18c: from Latin *gramen* grass.

grammar /'gramə(r)/ ▻ *noun* **1** the accepted rules by which words are formed and combined into sentences. **2** the branch of language study dealing with these. **3 a** a description of these rules as applied to a particular language; **b** a book containing this. **4** a person's understanding of or ability to use these rules □ ***bad grammar***. ◷ 14c: from Greek *gramma* something written.

grammarian /grə'mɛərɪən/ ▻ *noun* an expert on grammar.

grammar school ▻ *noun, Brit, especially formerly* a secondary school which emphasizes the study of academic rather than technical subjects. Compare SECONDARY SCHOOL. See also COMPREHENSIVE.

grammatical /grə'matɪkəl/ ▻ *adj* **1** relating to grammar. **2** correct according to the rules of grammar. • **grammaticality** /-'kalɪtɪ/ *noun*. • **grammatically** *adverb*. ◷ 16c: from Greek *grammatikos*, from *gramma* something written.

grammatical gender ▻ *noun* in various languages: a distinction which marks eg nouns, adjectives and determiners as either masculine, feminine or (in some languages) neuter. Natural gender corresponds to this in some but not all instances. See also GENDER.

gramme see GRAM

Gram-negative and **Gram-positive** ▻ *adj, biol* said of a bacterium: respectively staining red or deep purple when subjected to GRAM'S STAIN, because of differences in cell wall structure. ◷ 20c: named after H J C Gram (1853–1938), a Danish physician who devised the technique as a means of distinguishing the two types of bacteria.

gramophone /'graməfoun/ ▻ *noun* (***gramophones***) *dated* a record-player, especially an old-fashioned one. See RECORD *noun* 4. Also *as adj* □ ***gramophone record***. *N Amer equivalent* PHONOGRAPH. • **gramophonic** /-'fɒnɪk/ *adj*. • **gramophonically** *adverb*. ◷ Greek *gramma* something written + -PHONE.

grampus /'grampəs/ ▻ *noun* (***grampuses***) **1** a large grey dolphin with a bulbous forehead, no beak, an extensively scarred body, relatively short flippers and a tall fin. Also called **Risso's dolphin**. **2** a killer whale. **3** someone who breathes heavily. ◷ 16c: from French *graspois*, from *gras* fat + *pois* fish.

Gram's stain ▻ *noun, biol* an important staining procedure used to distinguish between two major groups of bacteria. See GRAM-NEGATIVE.

gran ▻ *noun, colloq* short form of GRANNY.

granary /'granərɪ/ ▻ *noun* (***granaries***) **1** a building where grain is stored. **2** a region that produces large quantities of grain. **3** (**Granary**) *trademark* a make of bread containing malted wheat flour, which gives it a special nutty flavour. ▻ *adj, loosely* said of bread: containing whole grains of wheat. ◷ 16c: from Latin *granarium*, from *granum* grain.

grand ▻ *adj* (***grander***, ***grandest***) **1** large or impressive in size, appearance or style. **2** *sometimes derog* dignified; self-important. **3** intended to impress or gain attention □ ***a grand gesture***. **4** complete; in full □ ***grand total***. **5** *colloq* very pleasant; excellent. **6** greatest; highest ranking □ ***Grand Master***. **7** highly respected □ ***grand old man***. **8** main; principal □ ***the grand entrance***. **9** *in compounds* indicating a family relationship that is one generation more remote than that of the base word □ ***grandson***. See also GREAT *adj* 4. ▻ *noun* (*plural* in sense 1 ***grand***) **1** *slang* a thousand dollars or pounds. **2** *colloq* a grand piano. • **grandly** *adverb*. • **grandness** *noun*. ◷ 16c: French, from Latin *grandis* great.

grandad or **granddad** /'grandad/ ▻ *noun, colloq* **1** a grandfather. **2** *offensive* an old man.

grandad collar ▻ *noun* a round shirt-collar without a folded-over band or points, originally intended to take a detachable stud-fastened collar.

grandaddy ▻ *noun, colloq* **1** a grandfather. **2** something considered the biggest, oldest, first, etc of its kind □ ***the grandaddy of them all***.

grandad shirt ▻ *noun* a shirt with a GRANDAD COLLAR.

grand-aunt ▻ *noun* a great-aunt.

grandchild ▻ *noun* a child of one's son or daughter.

grand cru / *French* grɑ̃kry/ ▻ *adj* said of a wine: produced by a famous vineyard or group of vineyards.

granddad see GRANDAD

granddaughter ▻ *noun* a daughter of one's son or daughter.

grand duchess ▻ *noun* **1** the wife or widow of a grand duke. **2** a high-ranking noblewoman who rules a grand duchy in her own right.

grand duchy ▻ *noun* in the modern period in imperial Germany and Russia: a small European country or territory which has a grand duke or grand duchess as its ruler.

grand duke ▻ *noun* a high-ranking nobleman who rules a grand duchy.

grande dame / *French* grɑ̃ddam/ ▻ *noun* (***grandes dames*** / *French* grɑ̃ddam/) an aristocratic or socially important lady; a woman highly revered in her particular profession or field.

grandee /gran'diː/ ▻ *noun* (***grandees***) **1** a Spanish or Portuguese nobleman of the highest rank. **2** any well-respected or high-ranking person. ◷ 16c: from Spanish *grande*.

grandeur /'grandjə(r)/ ▻ *noun* **1** greatness of character, especially dignity or nobility. **2** impressive beauty; magnificence. **3** *derog* self-importance; pretentiousness. ◷ 15c: French.

grandfather ▻ *noun* the father of one's father or mother.

grandfather clock ▻ *noun* a clock driven by a system of weights and a pendulum contained in a tall free-standing wooden case.

grandfatherly ▻ *adj* kindly.

grandiloquent /granˈdɪləkwənt/ ▻ *adj, derog* speaking, or spoken or written, in a pompous, self-important style. • **grandiloquence** *noun.* • **grandiloquently** *adverb.* ⓒ 16c: from Latin *grandis* great + *loqui* to speak.

grandiose /ˈgrandɪoʊs, -oʊz/ ▻ *adj* **1** *derog* exaggeratedly impressive or imposing, especially on a ridiculously large scale. **2** splendid; magnificent; impressive. • **grandiosely** *adverb.* • **grandiosity** /-ˈɒsɪtɪ/ *noun.* ⓒ 19c: from Italian *grandioso*, from *grande* great.

grand jury ▻ *noun* in the US: a jury which decides whether there is enough evidence for a person to be brought to trial. • **grand juror** *noun.*

grandma /ˈgranmɑː/ *colloq* and (*old use*) **grandmamma** /ˈgranməmɑː/ ▻ *noun* a grandmother.

grand mal / *French* ɡʀɑ̃mal/ ▻ *noun, medicine* a serious form of EPILEPSY in which there is sudden loss of consciousness followed by convulsions. Compare PETIT MAL. ⓒ 19c: French, meaning 'great illness'.

grandmaster ▻ *noun, chess* the title given to an extremely skilled player, originally only to the winner of a major international tournament.

Grand Master ▻ *noun* the head of the freemasons, or of a religious order of chivalry such as the Templars.

grandmother ▻ *noun* the mother of one's father or mother.

grandmother clock ▻ *noun* a clock that is similar to a GRANDFATHER CLOCK, but in a smaller case.

grandmotherly ▻ *adj* fussy, over-anxious.

grand Mufti /— mʌftɪ/ ▻ *noun* **1** the head of the Muslim community in Jerusalem. **2** the former head of the Turkish state religion.

the Grand National ▻ *noun, Brit horse-racing* a steeplechase held annually at Aintree racecourse in Liverpool, famous for its high and difficult fences.

grand-nephew ▻ *noun* a great-nephew.

grand-niece ▻ *noun* a great-niece.

grand opera ▻ *noun* serious opera of the 19c, based on grand themes and using choruses, elaborate staging, spectacular costumes, etc, and with all the dialogue usually sung.

grandpa /ˈgranpɑː/ *colloq* and (*old use*) **grandpapa** /ˈgranpəpɑː/ ▻ *noun* a grandfather.

grandparent ▻ *noun* either parent of one's father or mother.

grand piano ▻ *noun* a large, harp-shaped piano that has its strings arranged horizontally.

grand prix /grɑ̃ priː/ ▻ *noun* (*plural* ***grands prix*** /grɑ̃priː/) **1** any of a series of races held annually in various countries to decide the motor racing championship of the world. **2** in other sports: any competition of similar importance. ⓒ 19c: French, literally 'great prize'.

grand slam ▻ *noun* **1** *sport, eg tennis, rugby* the winning in one season of every part of a competition or of all major competitions. **2** *cards, especially bridge* the winning of all thirteen tricks by one player or side, or the contract to do so.

grandson ▻ *noun* a son of one's son or daughter.

grandstand ▻ *noun* a large covered sports-ground stand that has tiered seating and which provides a good view for spectators. Also *as adj* □ ***a grandstand view.***

grand tour see TOUR (*noun* 1b)

grand-uncle ▻ *noun* a great-uncle.

grange /greɪndʒ/ ▻ *noun* a country house with attached farm buildings. ⓒ 13c: French, meaning 'barn'.

granite /ˈgranɪt/ ▻ *noun* a hard coarse-grained igneous rock, consisting mainly of quartz, feldspar and mica, widely used in the construction of buildings and roads. • **granitic** /grəˈnɪtɪk/ *adj.* ⓒ 17c: from Italian *granito*, literally 'grained'.

the Granite City ▻ *noun* a name for Aberdeen, a city in NE Scotland famous for its sparkling grey granite buildings.

granny or **grannie** /ˈgranɪ/ ▻ *noun* (***grannies***) *colloq* a grandmother.

granny bonds ▻ *noun, Brit* a former name of index-linked National Savings Certificates, before 1981 only available to people of over 50.

granny flat ▻ *noun, colloq* a flat built on to or contained in a house, which allows an elderly parent or relative to live nearby while remaining independent.

granny glasses ▻ *noun* small, round, gold- or steel-rimmed spectacles.

granny knot ▻ *noun* a reef knot with the ends crossed the wrong way, allowing it to slip or undo easily.

Granny Smith ▻ *noun* a crisp green variety of eating apple, originally Australian.

granola /grəˈnoʊlə/ ▻ *noun, N Amer* a mixture of oats, dried fruit, nuts and brown sugar, usually eaten with milk for breakfast. ⓒ 1970s: originally a trademark.

grant /grɑːnt/ ▻ *verb* (***granted, granting***) **1** to give, allow or fulfil. **2** to admit something to be true. ▻ *noun* **1** something granted, especially an amount of money from a public fund for a specific purpose. **2** *law* the transfer of property by deed. ⓒ 13c: from French *granter* or *greanter*, variant of *creanter* to promise.

granted ▻ *verb, past participle of* GRANT (used as a sentence substitute) an admission that something is true or valid □ ***She's a good writer. — Granted. But rather limited.*** ▻ *conj* though it is admitted that □ ***granted you gave it back later.*** ▻ *prep* though (a specified thing) is admitted □ ***Granted his arrogance, still he gets results.*** • **take someone for granted** to treat them casually and without appreciation. • **take something for granted** to assume it to be true or valid; to accept it without question.

grantee /grɑːnˈtiː/ ▻ *noun, law* the person to whom a GRANT is made.

Granth /grʌnt/ and **Granth Sahib** ▻ *noun* the sacred scripture of the Sikh religion. Also called **Adi Granth** /ʌˈdɪ —/. ⓒ 18c: Hindi *granth* book.

grant-in-aid ▻ *noun* (***grants-in-aid***) an official grant of money for a particular purpose, especially from the Treasury to a government department or local authority.

grant-maintained ▻ *adj* (abbreviation **GM**) said of an educational establishment, especially a school: funded by central rather than local government, and self-governing.

grantor /ˈgrɑːntɔː(r)/ ▻ *noun, law* the person who makes a GRANT.

granular /ˈgranjʊlə(r)/ ▻ *adj, technical* **1** made of or containing tiny particles or granules. **2** said of appearance or texture: rough. • **granularity** /-ˈlarɪtɪ/ *noun.* ⓒ 18c: from GRANULE.

granulate /ˈgranjʊleɪt/ ▻ *verb* (***granulated, granulating***) **1** *tr & intr* to break down into small particles or granules. **2** to give a rough appearance or texture to something. • **granulation** *noun.* ⓒ 17c.

granulated sugar ▻ *noun* white sugar in fairly coarse grains.

granule /ˈgranjuːl/ ▷ *noun* a small particle or grain. ◎ 17c: from Latin *granulum*, diminutive of *granum* grain.

granulocyte /ˈgranjʊləsaɪt/ ▷ *noun, medicine* any white blood cell that has granules in its cytoplasm.

granuloma /granjʊˈloʊmə/ ▷ *noun* (***granulomas*** or ***granulomata***) *pathol* a small localized tumour composed of growing connective tissue and caused by infection or invasion by a foreign body. ◎ 19c: from GRANULE.

grape /greɪp/ ▷ *noun* **1** a pale green or purplish-black juicy edible berry which may be eaten fresh, pressed to make wine or dried to form currants, raisins, etc. **2** any species of perennial climbing vine that bears this fruit. **3** (**the grape**) *affected or literary* wine. • **grapey** or **grapy** *adj.* ◎ 13c: French, meaning 'bunch of grapes'.

grapefruit ▷ *noun* (***grapefruit*** or ***grapefruits***) **1** an evergreen tree, native to tropical and warm temperate regions, widely cultivated for its large edible fruits. **2** the round fruit produced by this tree which has acidic pale yellow or pink flesh surrounded by a thin yellow rind. ◎ 19c: GRAPE (because the fruit grow in clusters) + FRUIT.

grape hyacinth ▷ *noun* a plant of the lily family with grass-like leaves and dense spikes of small drooping blue flowers.

grapeshot ▷ *noun* ammunition in the form of small iron balls which scatter when fired in clusters from a cannon.

grape sugar ▷ *noun* glucose or dextrose.

grapevine ▷ *noun* **1** a vine on which grapes grow. **2** (**the grapevine**) *colloq* an informal means of spreading information through casual conversation □ ***I heard on the grapevine that you're leaving.***

graph /grɑːf/ ▷ *noun* **1** a diagram that illustrates the way in which one quantity varies in relation to another, usually consisting of horizontal and vertical axes (see AXIS sense 3) which cross each other at a point called the ORIGIN. **2** a symbolic diagram. ▷ *verb* (***graphed***, ***graphing***) to represent something with or as a graph. ◎ 19c: short for the earlier *graphic formula*, from Greek *graphein* to write.

-graph /grɑːf/ ▷ *combining form, forming nouns, denoting* **1** an instrument for writing or recording information □ ***telegraph***. **2** information written, drawn or recorded by such an instrument □ ***cardiograph***. ◎ From Greek *graphein* to write.

grapheme /ˈgrafiːm/ *linguistics* ▷ *noun* (***graphemes***) all the letters or combinations of letters that may be used to represent a single PHONEME. • **graphemic** /-fiːmɪk/ *adj.* ◎ 1930s: from Greek *graphema* a letter.

graphic /ˈgrafɪk/ and **graphical** ▷ *adj* **1** described or shown vividly and in detail. **2** referring to or composed in a written medium □ ***the graphic representation of a dog's bark as 'woof'***. **3** referring to the **graphic arts**, ie those concerned with drawing, printing and lettering □ ***graphic design***. **4** relating to graphs; shown by means of a graph. • **graphically** *adverb*.

-graphic /grafɪk/ or **-graphical** ▷ *combining form* forming adjectives corresponding to nouns in *-graph* and *-graphy* □ ***telegraphic*** □ ***geographical***.

graphic equalizer ▷ *noun, electronics* in a sound system: a type of sliding control that enables the listener to regulate the tone by adjusting the output signal in each of a series of specific frequency bands.

graphic formula ▷ *noun* a chemical formula in which the symbols for single atoms are joined by lines representing valency bonds.

graphic novel ▷ *noun* an adult novel in comic-book form.

graphics ▷ *singular noun* the art or science of drawing according to mathematical principles, especially the drawing of three-dimensional objects on a two-dimensional surface. ▷ *plural noun* **1** the photographs and illustrations used in a magazine. **2** the non-acted visual parts of a film or television programme, eg the credits. **3** *computing* **a** the use of computers to display and manipulate information in graphical or pictorial form, either on a visual-display unit or via a printer or plotter; **b** the images that are produced by this.

graphics character ▷ *noun, computing* a pictorial character that appears on the screen. Compare ALPHANUMERIC.

graphics tablet ▷ *noun, computing* an input device which translates the movements of a pen over a sensitive pad into a corresponding pattern on the screen of a visual-display unit.

graphite /ˈgrafaɪt/ ▷ *noun* a soft black ALLOTROPE of carbon that is used as a lubricant and electrical contact, and is mixed with clay to form the 'lead' in pencils. • **graphitic** /graˈfɪtɪk/ *adj.* • **graphitize** or **graphitise** *verb* (***graphitized***, ***graphitizing***). ◎ 18c: from Greek *graphein* to write + -ITE.

graphology /graˈfɒlədʒɪ/ ▷ *noun* **1** the study of handwriting, especially as a way of analysing the writer's character. **2** *linguistics* the study of the systems and conventions of writing. • **graphologic** /grafəˈlɒdʒɪk/ or **graphological** *adj.* • **graphologist** *noun.* ◎ 19c: from Greek *graphein* to write + -LOGY 1.

graph paper ▷ *noun* paper covered in small squares, used for drawing graphs.

-graphy /grəfɪ/ ▷ *combining form, forming nouns, signifying* **1** a method of recording or representing something in graphic form □ ***calligraphy*** □ ***photography*** □ ***lithography***. **2** a descriptive science or art □ ***biography*** □ ***geography*** □ ***choreography***. ◎ From French *-graphie*, Latin *-graphia*, from Greek *graphein* to write.

grapnel /ˈgrapnəl/ ▷ *noun* **1** a large multi-pointed hook on one end of a rope, used for securing a heavy object on the other end. **2** a light anchor for small boats. ◎ 14c: from French *grapin*, diminutive of *grape* hook.

GRAPO or **Grapo** /ˈgrɑːpoʊ/ ▷ *abbreviation* First of October Anti-Fascist Resistance Groups, a left-wing Spanish terrorist organization.

grappa /ˈgrapə/ ▷ *noun* (***grappas***) a brandy (originally from Italy) distilled from what is left after the grapes have been pressed for wine-making. ◎ 19c: Italian, literally 'grape-stalk'.

grapple /ˈgrapəl/ ▷ *verb* (***grappled***, ***grappling***) **1** struggle and fight, especially at close quarters, eg in hand-to-hand combat. **2** to secure something with a hook, etc. ▷ *noun* **1** a hook or other device for securing. **2** an act of gripping, as in wrestling; a way of gripping. ◎ 16c: from French *grappelle*, diminutive of *grape* hook.

■ **grapple with someone** to grasp and struggle or fight with them.

■ **grapple with something** to struggle mentally with (a difficult problem).

grappling-iron and **grappling-hook** ▷ *noun* a GRAPNEL.

graptolite /ˈgraptəlaɪt/ ▷ *noun* **1** any of a group of extinct marine animals that were common in the Palaeozoic era, thought to be related to present-day jellyfish and corals. **2** any of the fossilized skeletons of these animals, often used to date rocks of the Ordovician and Silurian periods. ◎ 19c: from Greek *graptos* written, because on hard shale the fossils look like writing.

grapy see under GRAPE

GRAS ▷ *abbreviation, US* generally recognized as safe, used to designate an officially approved food additive.

grasp /grɑːsp/ ▷ *verb* (***grasped***, ***grasping***) **1** to take a firm hold of something or someone; to clutch. **2** (*often* **grasp at** or **after something**) to make a movement as if to seize it. **3** to understand. ▷ *noun* **1** a grip or hold. **2** power or control; ability to reach, achieve or obtain □ *felt the promotion was within her grasp.* **3** ability to understand □ *beyond their grasp.* • **grasp at straws** see under CLUTCH. • **grasp the nettle** see under NETTLE. ⓘ 14c as *graspen*.

grasping ▷ *adj, derog* greedy, especially for wealth. • **graspingly** *adverb.* • **graspingness** *noun.*

grass /grɑːs/ ▷ *noun* (***grasses***) **1** any of a family of flowering plants (eg cereals, bamboos, etc) that typically have long narrow leaves with parallel veins, a jointed upright hollow stem and flowers (with no petals) borne alternately on both sides of an axis. **2** an area planted with or growing such plants, eg a lawn or meadow. **3** lawn or pasture. **4** *slang* marijuana. **5** *slang* someone who betrays someone else, especially to the police. ▷ *verb* (***grassed, grassing***) **1** to plant something with grass or turf. **2** to feed (animals) with grass; to provide pasture for them. **3** *intr, slang* (*often* **grass on someone** or **grass someone up**) to inform on them, especially to the police. • **let the grass grow under one's feet** to delay or waste time. • **put (an animal or a person) out to grass 1** to give a life of grazing to (eg an old racehorse). **2** *colloq* to put (eg a worker) into retirement. ⓘ Anglo-Saxon *gærs, græs.*

grass box ▷ *noun* a container attached to some lawnmowers to catch the grass cuttings.

grass court ▷ *noun* a grass-covered tennis court.

grass-cutter ▷ *noun* a mowing machine.

grasshopper ▷ *noun* a large brown or green jumping insect, related to the cricket, the male of which produces a characteristic chirping sound by rubbing its hind legs against its wings.

grasshopper mind ▷ *noun* a mind that is unable to concentrate on any one subject for long.

grassier, **grassiest** and **grassiness** see under GRASSY.

grassland ▷ *noun* permanent pasture.

grass roots ▷ *plural noun* **1** *especially politics* ordinary people, as opposed to those in a position of power. **2** bare essentials; fundamental principles. **3** *as adj* □ *opinion at grass-roots level.*

grass snake ▷ *noun* **1** a small non-venomous greenish-grey to olive-brown snake with black and yellow patches on the back of its neck, native to Europe, Asia and N Africa. **2** any of various related European snakes.

grass widow and **grass widower** ▷ *noun* someone whose partner is absent from home for long periods of time.

grassy ▷ *adj* (***grassier, grassiest***) covered with, or like, grass. • **grassiness** *noun.*

grat see under GREET[2]

grate[1] /greɪt/ ▷ *verb* (***grated, grating***) **1** to cut (eg vegetables or cheese) into shreds by rubbing them against a rough or perforated surface. **2** *tr & intr* to make, or cause something to make, a harsh grinding sound by rubbing. ⓘ 15c: from French *grater* to scrape.

■ **grate on someone** to irritate or annoy them.

grate[2] /greɪt/ ▷ *noun* **1** a framework of iron bars for holding coal, etc in a fireplace or furnace. **2** the fireplace or furnace itself. ⓘ 15c: from Latin *grata*.

grateful ▷ *adj* **1 a** feeling thankful; **b** showing or giving thanks. **2** *formal* pleasant and welcome □ *grateful sleep.* • **gratefully** *adverb.* • **gratefulness** *noun.* ⓘ 16c: from Latin *gratus* pleasing or thankful.

grater ▷ *noun* a device with a rough surface, and usually with sharpened perforations, for grating food.

graticulation /grətɪkjʊ'leɪʃən/ ▷ *noun, technical* the division of a design into squares for convenience in making a larger or smaller copy. ⓘ 18c.

graticule /'gratɪkjuːl/ ▷ *noun, technical* (***graticules***) a ruled grid for the identification of points on a map or the field of a telescope, etc. ⓘ 20c in this sense: French, from Latin *craticula* gridiron.

gratify /'gratɪfaɪ/ ▷ *verb* (***gratified, gratifying***) **1** to please someone. **2** to satisfy or indulge (eg a desire). • **gratification** /-fɪ'keɪʃən/ *noun.* • **gratifying** *adj.* • **gratifyingly** *adverb.* ⓘ 16c: from Latin *gratus* pleasing or thankful + *facere* to make.

gratin see AU GRATIN

gratiné or **gratinée** /'gratɪneɪ/ ▷ *adj, cookery* said of a dish: cooked or served AU GRATIN. ⓘ 20c: French, from *grater* to grate.

grating[1] /'greɪtɪŋ/ ▷ *noun* a framework of metal bars fixed into a wall (eg over a window) or into a pavement (eg over a drain). ⓘ 17c in sense 'an openwork cover made of wood': from GRATE[1].

grating[2] /'greɪtɪŋ/ ▷ *adj* **1** said of sounds, etc: harsh. **2** irritating. ▷ *noun* a grating sound.

gratis /'gratɪs, 'greɪ-/ ▷ *adverb, adj* free; without charge. ⓘ 15c: Latin, from *gratia* favour.

gratitude /'gratɪtjuːd/ ▷ *noun* the state or feeling of being grateful; thankfulness. ⓘ 16c: from Latin *gratus* thankful.

gratuitous /grə'tjuːɪtəs/ ▷ *adj* **1** done without good reason; unnecessary or unjustified □ *gratuitous violence.* **2** given or received without charge; voluntary. • **gratuitously** *adverb.* • **gratuitousness** *noun.* ⓘ 17c: from Latin *gratuitas*, from *gratia* favour.

gratuity /grə'tjuːɪtɪ/ ▷ *noun* (***gratuities***) **1** a sum of money given as a reward for good service; a tip. **2** a sum of money given to a soldier, etc on retirement, in recognition of long service. ⓘ 16c: from Latin *gratus* thankful.

gravadlax see GRAVLAX

gravamen /grə'veɪmen/ ▷ *noun* (***gravamina*** /-mɪnə/) *law* the principal ground of a complaint or accusation. ⓘ 19c in this sense: Latin, meaning 'grievance'.

grave[1] /greɪv/ ▷ *noun* **1** a deep trench dug in the ground for burying a dead body. **2** the site of an individual burial. **3** (**the grave**) *literary* death. • **dig one's own grave** see under DIG. • **turn in one's grave** see under TURN. ⓘ Anglo-Saxon *græf* grave or trench, from *grafan* to dig.

grave[2] /greɪv/ ▷ *adj* (***graver, gravest***) **1** giving cause for great concern; very dangerous. **2** very important; serious. **3** solemn and serious in manner. • **gravely** *adverb.* • **graveness** *noun* (more commonly GRAVITY sense 2). ⓘ 16c: from Latin *gravis*.

grave[3] /grɑːv/ and **grave accent** ▷ *noun* a sign placed above a vowel in some languages, eg *à* and *è* in French, to indicate a particular pronunciation or extended length of the vowel. ⓘ 17c: French.

grave[4] /grɑːveɪ/ ▷ *adverb, music* in a solemn manner. ▷ *adj* slow and solemn. ⓘ 17c: Italian.

grave clothes ▷ *plural noun* the clothes or other wrappings in which a corpse is buried.

grave goods ▷ *plural noun, archaeol* the objects buried along with a corpse.

gravel /'gravəl/ ▷ *noun* **1** a mixture of small loose rock fragments and pebbles, coarser than sand, found on beaches and in the beds of rivers, streams and lakes. **2** *pathol* small stones formed in the kidney or bladder, often causing severe pain. ▷ *verb* (***gravelled, gravelling***; *US* ***graveled, graveling***) **1** to cover (eg a path) with gravel. **2** to puzzle or perplex someone. **3** *colloq* to irritate or annoy someone. ⓘ 13c: from French *gravele*.

gravelly ▷ *adj* **1** full of, or containing, small stones. **2** said of a voice: rough and deep.

gravel pit ▷ *noun* a pit from which gravel is dug.

gravely see under GRAVE[2]

graven /ˈɡreɪvən/ ▻ *adj* **1** *old use* carved or engraved. **2** firmly fixed in the mind. ⓒ 14c: from old word *grave* to carve or engrave.

graveness see under GRAVE[2]

graven image ▻ *noun* a carved idol used in worship.

graver /ˈɡreɪvə(r)/ ▻ *noun* an engraving tool, eg a BURIN. ⓒ 17c in this sense: from old word *grave* to carve or engrave.

Graves /ɡrɑːv/ ▻ *noun* **1** a white or red table wine from the Graves district, near Bordeaux in France. **2** *loosely* any dry or medium-dry white wine.

gravestone ▻ *noun* a stone marking a grave, usually having the dead person's name and dates of birth and death engraved on it. Also called TOMBSTONE, **headstone**.

graveyard ▻ *noun* a burial place; a cemetery.

gravid /ˈɡravɪd/ ▻ *adj, medicine* pregnant. ⓒ 16c: from Latin *gravis* heavy.

gravies *plural of* GRAVY

gravimeter /ɡrəˈvɪmɪtə(r)/ ▻ *noun* an instrument for measuring variations in the magnitude of the gravitational field at different points on the Earth's surface, used to prospect for mineral deposits, etc. ⓒ 1790s: from Latin *gravis* heavy.

gravimetry /ɡrəˈvɪmətrɪ/ ▻ *noun, technical* **1** the scientific measurement of the Earth's gravitational field at different points on its surface, especially in order to map structures beneath the surface. **2** the chemical analysis of substances by separating their constituents and determining their relative proportions by weight. • **gravimetric** /ɡravɪˈmɛtrɪk/ *adj* relating to measurement by weight. ⓒ 18c.

gravitas /ˈɡravɪtɑːs/ ▻ *noun* seriousness of manner; solemnity, authoritativeness; weight. ⓒ 20c: Latin.

gravitate /ˈɡravɪteɪt/ ▻ *verb* (***gravitated, gravitating***) *intr* **1** to fall or be drawn under the force of gravity. **2** to move or be drawn gradually, as if attracted by some force □ *gravitated towards a life of crime.* ⓒ 17c: from GRAVITY1.

gravitation /ɡravɪˈteɪʃən/ ▻ *noun* **1** *physics* the force of attraction that exists between any two bodies on account of their mass. **2** the process of moving or being drawn, either by this force or some other attracting influence. • **gravitational** *adj.* • **gravitationally** *adverb.*

gravitational field ▻ *noun, physics* that region of space in which one object, by virtue of its mass, exerts a force of attraction on another object.

gravity /ˈɡravɪtɪ/ ▻ *noun* **1** the observed effect of the force of attraction that exists between two massive bodies. **2** the name commonly used to refer to the force of attraction between any object situated within the Earth's gravitational field, and the Earth itself, on account of which objects feel heavy and are pulled down towards the ground. **3** seriousness; dangerous nature. **4** serious attitude; solemnity. ⓒ 17c in senses 1 and 2; 16c in senses 3 and 4: from Latin *gravitas* heaviness or seriousness.

gravity platform ▻ *noun* in the oil industry: a concrete and steel drilling platform whose weight allows it to rest on the sea bed.

gravity wave ▻ *noun, physics* a surface wave in a liquid controlled by gravity and not by surface tension.

gravlax /ˈɡravlaks/ and **gravadlax** /ˈɡravadlaks/ ▻ *noun* a dish originating in Scandinavia, of salmon dry-cured with spice, sugar, salt and pepper. ⓒ 1960s: Swedish *gravlax*, Norwegian *gravlaks*, literally 'buried salmon'.

gravure /ɡrəˈvjʊə(r)/ ▻ *noun* **1** any process of making an INTAGLIO (sense 3) printing plate, including PHOTOGRAVURE. **2** the printing plate made in this way. **3** any impression from such a printing plate. ⓒ 19c: French, meaning 'engraving'.

gravy /ˈɡreɪvɪ/ ▻ *noun* (***gravies***) **1** the juices released by meat as it is cooking. **2 a** a sauce made by thickening and seasoning these juices; **b** a similar sauce made with an artificial substitute. **3** *slang* easily obtained money. ⓒ 14c: perhaps from French *gravé*, a mistaken reading of *grané* cooking spice.

gravy boat ▻ *noun* a small boat-shaped container with a handle, for serving gravy and other sauces.

gravy train ▻ *noun, slang* a job or scheme from which a lot of money is gained for little effort.

gray[1] /ɡreɪ/ ▻ *noun* (symbol **Gy**) the SI unit of absorbed dose of ionizing radiation, equivalent to one joule per kilogram. ⓒ 1970s: named after L H Gray (1905-65), British radiobiologist.

gray[2] see GREY

grayling /ˈɡreɪlɪŋ/ ▻ *noun* (***grayling*** or ***graylings***) **1** any of various freshwater fishes, related to the salmon, that have silvery scales with a greenish-gold sheen, dark zigzag lines along the length of the body and a large purplish spiny dorsal fin. **2** any of various European butterflies with grey or greyish-brown wings with eyespots, and front legs reduced to small brush-like appendages. ⓒ 15c: GREY + -LING 1.

graze[1] /ɡreɪz/ ▻ *verb* (***grazed, grazing***) **1** *tr & intr* said of animals: to eat grass. **2 a** to feed (animals) on grass; **b** to feed animals on (an area of pasture). **3** *intr, colloq* to snack. **4** *intr, colloq* to pilfer and immediately eat food off supermarket shelves. **5** *tr & intr, colloq* to browse through TV channels, etc. • **grazer** *noun.* • **grazing** *noun* **1** the act or practice of grazing. **2** pasture. ⓒ Anglo-Saxon *grasian*, from *græs* grass.

graze[2] /ɡreɪz/ ▻ *verb* (***grazed, grazing***) **1** to suffer a break in (the skin of eg a limb), through scraping against a hard rough surface. **2** to brush against something lightly in passing. ▻ *noun* **1** an area of grazed skin. **2** the action of grazing skin. ⓒ 17c.

grease /ɡriːs, ɡriːz/ ▻ *noun* **1** animal fat softened by melting or cooking. **2** any thick oily substance, especially a lubricant for the moving parts of machinery. ▻ *verb* (***greased, greasing***) to lubricate or dirty something with grease. • **grease someone's palm** or **hand** *colloq* to bribe them. • **grease the wheels** *colloq* to make progress easier. • **like greased lightning** very quickly. ⓒ 13c: from French *graisse*.

grease gun ▻ *noun* a lubricating pump.

grease monkey ▻ *noun, slang* a mechanic.

greasepaint ▻ *noun* waxy make-up used by actors.

greaseproof ▻ *adj* resistant or impermeable to grease.

greaser /ˈɡriːsə(r), ˈɡriːzə(r)/ ▻ *noun* **1** someone whose job is to grease machinery. **2** a ship's engineer. **3** *colloq* a long-haired member of a gang of motorcyclists. **4** *N Amer offensive slang* a Mexican or Spanish American.

greasy /ˈɡriːsɪ, ˈɡriːzɪ/ ▻ *adj* (***greasier, greasiest***) **1** containing, or covered in, grease. **2** having an oily appearance or texture. **3** slippery, as if covered in grease. **4** *colloq* insincerely friendly or flattering. • **greasily** *adverb.* • **greasiness** *noun.*

greasy spoon and **greasy spoon restaurant** ▻ *noun* a cheap café that serves very basic meals, eg egg and chips, beans on toast, etc.

great /ɡreɪt/ ▻ *adj* (***greater, greatest***) **1** outstandingly talented and much admired and respected. **2** very large in size, quantity, intensity or extent. **3** (**greater**) (added to the name of a large city) indicating the wider area surrounding the city, sometimes including other boroughs, etc, as well as the city itself □ *Greater Glasgow* □ *Greater Manchester.* **4** (*also* **greater**) *biol* larger in size than others of the same kind, species, etc □ *great tit.* **5** *in* *compounds* indicating a family relationship that is one generation more remote than that of the base word □ ***great-grandmother*** □ ***great-great-grandson.*** **6** *colloq* very enjoyable; excellent or splendid. **7** (*also* **great at something**) *colloq* clever; talented. **8** (*also* **great for something**) *colloq* very suitable or useful. **9** most important □ ***the great advantage of it.*** **10** enthusiastic; keen □ ***a great reader.*** **11** *colloq* used to emphasize other adjectives describing size, especially *big* □ ***a great big dog.*** **12** (**the Great**) in names and titles: indicating an importance or reputation of the highest degree □ ***Alexander the Great.*** **13** (**the greatest**) *colloq* **a** the best in their field; **b** a marvellous person or thing. **14** *old use* used in various expressions of surprise □ ***Great Scott!*** ▷ *noun* **1** a person who has achieved lasting fame, deservedly or not □ ***one of the all-time greats.*** **2** (**Greats**) **a** the final honours School of Classics and Philosophy or of Modern Philosophy at Oxford University; **b** the final examination in these courses. ▷ *adverb, colloq* very well. • **greatly** *adverb.* • **greatness** *noun.* ◷ Anglo-Saxon.

great ape ▷ *noun* any of the larger anthropoid apes, a chimpanzee, gibbon, gorilla or orang-utan.

great auk ▷ *noun* a large flightless auk once common in the North Atlantic areas, but now extinct.

great-aunt ▷ *noun* an aunt of one's father or mother.

the Great Barrier Reef ▷ *noun* a 2000km (1243ml) coral reef off the coast of NE Australia.

the Great Bear ▷ *noun* Ursa Major, a constellation of stars in the Northern hemisphere, whose seven brightest stars form the PLOUGH.

Great Britain ▷ *noun* the largest island in Europe, containing England, Wales and Scotland, and forming, together with Northern Ireland, the UNITED KINGDOM.

great circle ▷ *noun* a circle on the surface of a sphere, whose centre is the centre of the sphere.

greatcoat ▷ *noun* a heavy overcoat.

Great Dane ▷ *noun* a very large dog with a smooth coat, usually pale brown in colour with dark flecks, long powerful legs, a deep muzzle and short erect ears.

the Great Lakes ▷ *plural noun* a group of five interconnected lakes (Superior, Huron, Erie, Ontario and Michigan) which separate Eastern Canada from the USA.

great-nephew ▷ *noun* a son of one's nephew or niece.

great-niece ▷ *noun* a daughter of one's nephew or niece.

Great Seal ▷ *noun, Brit* a seal kept by the Lord Chancellor or Lord Keeper and used on the most important state papers. ◷ 14c.

great-uncle ▷ *noun* an uncle of one's father or mother.

the Great War ▷ *noun* WORLD WAR I (1914–18).

greave /griːv/ ▷ *noun* (*usually as* **greaves**) armour for the legs below the knee. ◷ 14c: from French *greve* shin.

grebe /griːb/ ▷ *noun* (***grebes***) any of various waterfowl with short wings, a pointed bill, almost no tail and, in most species, colourful plumes on the head. ◷ 18c: from French *grèbe*.

Grecian /ˈgriːʃən/ ▷ *adj* said of a design, etc: in the style of ancient Greece. ▷ *noun* a Greek scholar. ◷ 16c: from Latin *Graecus* Greek.

Grecian nose ▷ *noun* an uncurved nose forming a straight line with the forehead.

Greco- see GRAECO-

greed ▷ *noun* **1** an excessive desire for, or consumption of, food. **2** selfish desire in general, eg for money. ◷ 17c: back-formation from GREEDY.

greedy /ˈgriːdɪ/ ▷ *adj* (***greedier, greediest***) filled with greed. • **greedily** *adverb.* • **greediness** *noun.* • **greedy for something** anxious or intensely keen to achieve or get (power, praise, etc). ◷ Anglo-Saxon *grædig*.

greegree see GRISGRIS

Greek ▷ *adj* **1** belonging or relating to Greece, a republic in SE Europe, its inhabitants or their language. **2** belonging or relating to ancient Greece, its inhabitants or their language. ▷ *noun* **1** a citizen or inhabitant of, or person born in, Greece. **2 a** the official language of Greece (**Modern Greek**); **b** the language of the ancient Greeks (**Ancient Greek**), dating from the second millenium BC and chiefly written in the Greek alphabet (see table at GREEK ALPHABET). See also LINEAR B. **3** *colloq* any language, jargon or subject one cannot understand. ◷ Anglo-Saxon plural *Grecas*: from Latin *Graecus*.

Greek architecture ▷ *noun* the style of architecture developed in ancient Greece, consisting of the DORIC, IONIC and CORINTHIAN orders.

Greek Church and **Greek Orthodox Church** see ORTHODOX CHURCH

Greek cross ▷ *noun* an upright cross with arms of equal length.

Greek gift ▷ *noun* a gift given with intent to harm. ◷ 19c: from the story of the Trojan horse in Virgil's *Aeneid* 2, especially line 49, 'I fear the Greeks, even when they bring gifts'.

Greek god ▷ *noun* an outstanding example of male good looks.

Greek key ▷ *noun* a fret pattern.

green ▷ *adj* (***greener, greenest***) **1** like the colour of the leaves of most plants, between yellow and blue in the spectrum. **2** covered with grass, bushes, etc □ ***green areas of the city.*** **3** consisting mainly of leaves □ ***green salad.*** **4** said of fruit: not yet ripe. **5** *colloq* said of a person: young, inexperienced or easily fooled. **6** showing concern for, or designed to be harmless to, the environment. **7** said of someone's face: pale; showing signs of nausea. **8** not dried or dry □ ***green bacon*** □ ***green timber.*** **9** extremely jealous or envious. **10** healthy, vigorous, or flourishing □ ***green old age.*** **11** applied to the currency values in which EU farm prices are expressed □ ***green pound*** □ ***green franc.*** ▷ *noun* **1** the colour of the leaves of most plants, between yellow and blue in the spectrum. **2** something of this colour. **3** an area of grass, especially one in a public place □ ***the village green.*** **4** an area of specially prepared turf □ ***bowling green*** □ ***putting green.*** **5** (**greens**) vegetables with edible green leaves and stems. **6** (*sometimes* **Green**) someone who supports actions or policies designed to protect or benefit the environment, especially someone belonging to or supporting a political party that is concerned about such issues. ▷ *verb* (***greened, greening***) *tr & intr* to make or become green. • **greenish** *adj.* • **greenness** *noun.* • **greeny** *adj.* • **green about the gills** *colloq* looking or feeling sick. ◷ Anglo-Saxon *grene*.

The Greek Alphabet

Letter	Name	Usual trans-literation	Letter	Name	Usual trans-literation
Α α	alpha	a	Ν ν	nu	n
Β β	beta	b	Ξ ξ	xi	x
Γ γ	gamma	g	Ο ο	omicron	o
Δ δ	delta	d	Π π	pi	p
Ε ε	epsilon	e	Ρ ρ	rho	r
Ζ ζ	zeta	z	Σ σ,ς	sigma	s
Η η	eta	e, ē	Τ τ	tau	t
Θ θ	theta	th	Υ υ	upsilon	y
Ι ι	iota	i	Φ φ	phi	ph
Κ κ	kappa	k	Χ χ	chi	ch, kh
Λ λ	lambda	l	Ψ ψ	psi	ps
Μ μ	mu	m	Ω ω	omega	o, ō

green audit ▷ *noun, business* an assessment of and investigation into a company's claims, methods and policies in relation to environmental issues.

greenback ▷ *noun, colloq* a US currency note, a dollar bill. Often shortened to **greens**.

green bean ▷ *noun* any variety of bean, such as the French bean, string bean, etc, of which the narrow green unripe pod and contents can be eaten whole.

green belt ▷ *noun* open land surrounding a town or city, where building or development is strictly controlled.

Green Beret ▷ *noun, colloq* a British or American commando.

green card ▷ *noun* **1** an international motorists' insurance document. **2** an official US work and residence permit issued to foreign nationals.

Green Cross Code ▷ *noun, Brit* a code of road-safety rules for children.

greenery /'griːnərɪ/ ▷ *noun* green plants or their leaves, either when growing or when cut for decorative use.

green-eyed ▷ *adj, colloq* jealous or envious.

the green-eyed monster ▷ *noun* jealousy. ◷ 16c: coined by Shakespeare in *Othello* (1604).

greenfield site ▷ *noun* a site, separate from existing developments, which is to be developed for the first time.

green fingers ▷ *plural noun, colloq* natural skill at growing plants successfully.

greenfly ▷ *noun* (***greenfly*** or ***greenflies***) any of various species of APHID. ◷ 18c: so called because the female has a greenish body.

greengage ▷ *noun* **1** any of several cultivated varieties of tree, sometimes regarded as a subspecies of the plum. **2** the small round plum-like edible fruit produced by this tree, which has greenish-brown flesh enclosed by greenish-yellow skin. Sometimes shortened to GAGE.

Green Goddess ▷ *noun, Brit* a type of fire engine operated by the army in civil emergencies, etc.

greengrocer ▷ *noun* a person or shop that sells fruit and vegetables. • **greengrocery** *noun* the produce sold by a greengrocer.

greenhorn ▷ *noun, colloq* an inexperienced person; a novice.

greenhouse ▷ *noun* a GLASSHOUSE, especially one with little or no artificial heating, used for growing plants which need special protection or conditions.

greenhouse effect ▷ *noun, meteorol, ecol, etc* the warming of the Earth's surface as a result of the trapping of long-wave radiation by carbon dioxide, ozone, and certain other gases in the Earth's atmosphere.

greenhouse gas ▷ *noun* any of various gases, eg carbon dioxide or chlorofluorocarbons, which are present in the atmosphere and act like a pane of glass in a greenhouse, redirecting solar radiation reflected from the Earth's surface back towards the Earth.

greening ▷ *noun* **1** becoming or making green. **2** a deliberate policy of planting, especially as part of a project of urban renewal. **3** the process of becoming or making politically green, ecologically or environmentally conscious, or conservationist.

greenish see under GREEN

greenkeeper ▷ *noun* someone who is responsible for the maintenance of a golf course or bowling green.

green light ▷ *noun* **1** a signal to drivers of cars, trains, etc that they can move forward. **2** (**the green light**) *colloq* permission to proceed □ *We've got the green light on the project.*

greenmail ▷ *noun, especially US* a form of business blackmail in which a company buys a strategically significant block of shares in another company, sufficient to threaten takeover, and thus forces the company to buy back its shares at an inflated price. ◷ 1980s: from GREENS (see under GREENBACK) and modelled on BLACKMAIL.

the green man ▷ *noun, Brit colloq* **1** the illuminated green walking figure that indicates the pedestrians' turn to cross at a PELICAN CROSSING. **2** a PELICAN CROSSING.

green monkey ▷ *noun* a W African long-tailed monkey with greenish-grey fur on its back and a yellowish tail.

green paper ▷ *noun* (*often* **Green Paper**) *politics* in the UK: a written statement of the Government's proposed policy on a particular issue which is put forward for discussion. Compare COMMAND PAPER, WHITE PAPER.

green party or **Green Party** ▷ *noun* a political party concerned with promoting policies for the protection and benefit of the environment.

Greenpeace ▷ *noun* an international environmental PRESSURE GROUP that campaigns against commercial whaling and seal culling, the dumping of toxic and radioactive waste at sea, the testing of nuclear weapons, etc.

green pepper ▷ *noun* a green unripe sweet pepper, eaten as a vegetable. Compare RED PEPPER.

green pound ▷ *noun* the pound's value compared with that of the other European currencies used in trading EC farm produce.

greenroom ▷ *noun* a backstage room in a theatre, etc where actors, musicians, etc can relax and receive visitors. ◷ Early 18c: so called because these rooms were originally painted a restful green.

greens see GREEN *noun* 5, GREENBACK

greenstick fracture ▷ *noun* a fracture, especially in the limbs of children, where the bone is partly broken and partly bent.

green tea ▷ *noun* a sharp-tasting light-coloured tea made from leaves that have been dried quickly without fermenting.

green-wellie ▷ *adj, Brit colloq* belonging or referring to the British upper-class country-dwelling set □ *the green-wellie brigade.* ◷ 1980s: so called because they are represented stereotypically as wearing a certain kind of heavy green wellingtons.

Greenwich Mean Time /'grɛnɪtʃ, 'grɛnɪdʒ or 'grɪnɪdʒ —/ ▷ *noun* (abbreviation **GMT**) the local time at the line of 0° longitude, which passes through Greenwich in England, used to calculate times in most other parts of the world.

greet[1] ▷ *verb* (***greeted***, ***greeting***) **1** to address or welcome someone, especially in a friendly way. **2** to receive or respond to something in a specified way □ *His remarks were greeted with dismay.* **3** to be immediately noticeable to someone □ *smells of cooking greeted me.* ◷ Anglo-Saxon *gretan* to greet or accost.

greet[2] *Scots, N Eng dialect* ▷ *verb* (*past tense* ***grat***, *past participle* ***grat*** or ***grutten***, *present participle* ***greeting***) *intr* to weep or cry. ▷ *noun* a spell of crying. • **greeting** *adj* miserable □ *a greeting face.* ◷ Anglo-Saxon *greotan* to weep.

greeting ▷ *noun* **1** a friendly expression or gesture used on meeting or welcoming someone. **2** (**greetings**) a good or fond wish; a friendly message. ◷ Anglo-Saxon.

greetings card ▷ *noun* a decorated card used to send greetings.

gregarious /grə'gɛərɪəs/ ▷ *adj* **1** liking the company of other people; sociable. **2** said of animals: living in groups. • **gregariously** *adverb*. • **gregariousness** *noun*. ◷ 17c: from Latin *gregarius*, from *grex*, *gregis* flock.

Gregorian calendar /grɪgɔːrɪən —/ ▷ *noun* the system introduced by Pope *Gregory* XIII in 1582, and still widely in use, in which an ordinary year is divided into twelve months or 365 days, with a leap year of 366 days every four years. See also JULIAN CALENDAR.

Gregorian chant /ɡrɪɡɔːrɪən —/ ▷ *noun* a type of PLAINSONG used in Roman Catholic religious ceremonies, introduced in the 6c by Pope Gregory I.

gremial /ˈɡriːmɪəl/ ▷ *noun* a cloth laid on a bishop's knees to keep the vestments clean during Mass or ordination. ⓘ 19c in this sense; 17c in obsolete *adj* sense 'relating to the lap': from Latin *gremium* lap.

gremlin /ˈɡrɛmlɪn/ ▷ *noun* an imaginary mischievous creature blamed for faults in machinery or electronic equipment. ⓘ 1940s: originally RAF slang, modelled on GOBLIN.

grenade /ɡrəˈneɪd/ ▷ *noun* **1** a small bomb thrown by hand or fired from a rifle. **2** a glass projectile containing chemicals, eg for putting out fires, testing drains, dispensing poison gas or tear gas, etc. ⓘ 16c as *granade*: from Spanish *granada* pomegranate.

grenadier /ɡrɛnəˈdɪə(r)/ ▷ *noun* a member of a regiment of soldiers formerly trained in the use of grenades.

grenadine /ˈɡrɛnədiːn/ ▷ *noun* a syrup made from pomegranate juice, used to flavour drinks, especially alcoholic ones. ⓘ 19c: related to GRENADE.

grew *past tense of* GROW

grey or (*especially N Amer*) **gray** /ɡreɪ/ ▷ *adj* (***greyer***, ***greyest***) **1** of a colour between black and white, the colour of ash and slate. **2** said of the weather: dull and cloudy. **3 a** said of a someone's hair: turning white; **b** said of a person: having grey hair. **4** *derog* anonymous or uninteresting; having no distinguishing features □ ***a grey character***. **5** *literary* aged, mature or experienced. **6** *colloq* referring or relating to elderly or retired people □ ***the grey population***. ▷ *noun* (***greys***) **1** a colour between black and white. **2** grey material or clothes □ ***dressed in grey***. **3** dull light. **4** an animal, especially a horse, that is grey or whitish in colour. ▷ *verb* (***greyed***, ***greying***) *tr & intr* to make or become grey. • **greyish** *adj*. • **greyly** *adverb*. • **greyness** *noun*. ⓘ Anglo-Saxon *grei*.

grey area ▷ *noun* an unclear situation or subject, often with no distinct limits, guiding principles or identifiable characteristics.

greybeard ▷ *noun* an old man.

Grey Friar ▷ *noun* a Franciscan friar.

grey hen ▷ *noun* the female of the BLACK GROUSE.

greyhound ▷ *noun* a tall dog with a slender body, short coat, arched back, long powerful legs and a long tail, renowned for its speed and raced for sport. ⓘ Anglo-Saxon *grighund*.

greying ▷ *noun* **1** the process of becoming GREY. **2** the process or phenomenon of having an increasing elderly or retired sector in the population.

greyish see under GREY

greylag ▷ *noun* the largest of the grey geese, native to Europe and Asia, which has greyish-brown plumage, a large pale head and neck and a large blunt orange bill. Also called **greylag goose**.

grey literature ▷ *noun* literature published non-commercially, eg government reports.

greyly see under GREY

grey matter ▷ *noun* **1** *anatomy* the tissue of the brain and spinal cord that appears grey in colour, especially the cerebral cortex of the brain. Compare WHITE MATTER. **2** *colloq* intelligence or common sense.

greyness see under GREY

grey seal ▷ *noun* a type of seal common in N Atlantic coastal waters.

grey squirrel ▷ *noun* a species of squirrel with fine grey hair and a bushy tail with light-coloured fringes, which has replaced the native RED SQUIRREL in most parts of the UK.

grey wolf ▷ *noun* the N American TIMBER WOLF.

grid ▷ *noun* **1** a network of evenly spaced horizontal and vertical lines that can be superimposed on a map, chart, etc, especially in order to locate specific points. **2** such a network used for constructing a chart. **3** (**the grid** or **the national grid**) the network of power transmission lines, consisting of overhead wires and underground cables, by means of which electricity is distributed from power stations across a region or country. **4** a network of underground pipes by which gas, water, etc is distributed across a region or country. **5** a framework of metal bars, especially one covering the opening to a drain. See also GRATING. **6** an arrangement of lines marking the starting-points on a motor-racing track. **7** *electronics* an electrode, usually consisting of a perforated wire screen or a spiral of wire, that controls the flow of electrons from the cathode to the anode of a thermionic valve or vacuum tube. ⓘ 19c: back-formation from GRIDIRON.

griddle /ˈɡrɪdəl/ or (*Scottish*) **girdle** /ˈɡʌrdəl/ ▷ *noun* a flat iron plate that is heated for baking or frying, either set into the top of a stove or separate, and which looks like a flat pan with a handle. ⓘ 13c: from French *gridil*.

gridiron /ˈɡrɪdaɪən/ ▷ *noun* **1** a frame of iron bars used for grilling food over a fire. **2** *Amer football* the field of play. ⓘ 13c as *gredire*.

gridlock ▷ *noun* **1** a severe traffic jam in which no vehicles are able to move. **2** a jammed-up situation, in which no progress is possible. • **gridlocked** *adj*. ⓘ 1980s.

grief /ɡriːf/ ▷ *noun* **1 a** great sorrow and unhappiness, especially at someone's death; **b** an event that is the source of this. **3** *colloq* trouble or bother □ ***was getting grief from her parents for staying out late***. • **come to grief** *colloq* **1** to end in failure. **2** to have an accident. • **Good Grief!** an exclamation expressing shock, surprise, fear, etc. ⓘ 13c: from French *grever* to grieve.

grief-stricken ▷ *adj* crushed with sorrow.

grievance /ˈɡriːvəns/ ▷ *noun* **1** a real or perceived cause for complaint, especially unfair treatment at work. **2** a formal complaint, especially one made in the workplace. ⓘ 15c in sense 1; 13c, meaning 'injury' or 'trouble': from French *grevance*.

grieve[1] /ɡriːv/ ▷ *verb* (***grieved***, ***grieving***) **1** *intr* **a** to feel grief, especially at a death; **b** to mourn. **2** to upset or distress someone □ ***It grieves me to learn that he's still on drugs***. ⓘ 13c: from French *grever* to grieve, from Latin *gravare* to burden.

grieve[2] /ɡriːv/ ▷ *noun, Scots* **1** a farm bailiff. **2** a manager or overseer of workers, especially farm labourers or miners.

grievous /ɡriːvəs/ ▷ *adj* **1** very severe or painful. **2** causing or likely to cause grief. **3** showing grief. **4** said of a fault, etc: extremely serious. • **grievously** *adverb*. • **grievousness** *noun*. ⓘ 13c: from French *grevos*.

grievous bodily harm ▷ *noun* (abbreviation **GBH**) *law* **1** severe injury caused by a physical attack. **2** the criminal charge of causing such injury. Compare ACTUAL BODILY HARM.

griffin /ˈɡrɪfɪn/ or **gryphon** /ˈɡrɪfən/ ▷ *noun, mythol* a winged monster with an eagle's head and a lion's body. ⓘ 14c: from French *grifon*, from Greek *gryps*.

griffon /ˈɡrɪfən/ ▷ *noun* **1** any of various small dogs with a square body, a rounded head, a short muzzle and a coarse wiry blackish or black and tan coat. **2** a large vulture with a heavy body, brownish-black wings and a bald head with a neck ruff. ⓘ 17c: French, meaning 'griffin'.

grill ▷ *verb* (***grilled***, ***grilling***) **1** to cook over or, more usually, under radiated heat. See also BROIL. **2** *colloq* to interrogate someone, especially at length. **3** *intr* said usually of someone out in the sun: to suffer extreme heat. ▷ *noun* **1** a device on a cooker which radiates heat downwards. **2** a metal frame for cooking food over a fire; a gridiron. **3** a dish of grilled food □ *mixed grill.* **4** (*also* **grillroom**) a restaurant or part of a restaurant which specializes in grilled food. • **grilling** *noun.* ◷ 17c: from French *griller* to grill.

grille or **grill** /grɪl/ ▷ *noun* a protective framework of metal bars or wires, eg over a window or a car radiator. ◷ 17c: French.

grilse /grɪls/ ▷ *noun* (***grilse*** or ***grilses***) a young salmon returning from the sea to fresh water for the first time.

grim ▷ *adj* (***grimmer, grimmest***) **1** stern and unsmiling. **2** terrible; horrifying. **3** resolute; dogged □ *grim determination.* **4** depressing; gloomy. **5** *colloq* unpleasant. **6** *colloq* ill. • **grimly** *adverb.* • **grimness** *noun.* ◷ Anglo-Saxon.

grimace /ˈgrɪməs, grɪˈmeɪs/ ▷ *noun* an ugly twisting of the face that expresses pain or disgust, or that is pulled for amusement. ▷ *verb* (***grimaced, grimacing***) *intr* to make a grimace. ◷ 17c: French.

grime /graɪm/ ▷ *noun* thick ingrained dirt or soot. ▷ *verb* (***grimed, griming***) to soil something heavily; to make something filthy. ◷ 15c: from Flemish *grijm.*

grimier, grimiest, grimily and **griminess** see under GRIMY

grimy /ˈgraɪmɪ/ ▷ *adj* (***grimier, grimiest***) covered with grime; dirty. • **grimily** *adverb.* • **griminess** *noun.*

grin /grɪn/ ▷ *verb* (***grinned, grinning***) **1** *intr* to smile broadly, showing the teeth. **2** to express (eg pleasure) in this way. ▷ *noun* a broad smile, showing the teeth. • **grinning** *adj, noun* • **grinningly** *adverb.* • **grin and bear it** *colloq* to endure something unpleasant without complaining. ◷ Anglo-Saxon *grennian.*

grind /graɪnd/ ▷ *verb* (***ground, grinding***) **1** to crush something into small particles or powder between two hard surfaces. **2** to sharpen, smooth or polish something by rubbing against a hard surface. **3** *tr & intr* to rub something together with a jarring noise. **4** to press something hard with a twisting action □ *ground his heel into the dirt.* **5** to operate something by turning a handle □ *grinding his barrel-organ.* ▷ *noun* **1** *colloq* steady, dull and laborious routine. **2** the act or sound of grinding. **3** a specified size or texture of crushed particles □ *fine grind.* **4** *colloq* in dancing: an erotic circling movement of the hips. • **grind to a halt** to stop completely, especially after a spell of trying to keep going. ◷ Anglo-Saxon *grindan.*

■ **grind away** to work on doggedly, especially at something tedious.

■ **grind someone down** to crush their spirit; to oppress them.

■ **grind something out 1** to produce it mechanically or routinely. **2** to say it in a grating voice.

grinder ▷ *noun* **1** a person or machine that grinds. **2** a molar tooth.

grinding ▷ *adj* crushing; oppressive □ *grinding poverty.* • **grindingly** *adverb* □ *grindingly poor.*

grindstone ▷ *noun* a revolving stone wheel used for sharpening and polishing. • **have** or **keep one's nose to the grindstone** *colloq* to work hard and with perseverance. ◷ 13c.

gringo /ˈgrɪŋgoʊ/ ▷ *noun, derog* in Latin America, especially Mexico: an English-speaking foreigner. ◷ 19c: Spanish, from *griego* a Greek or a foreigner.

grinned, grinning and **grinningly** see under GRIN

grip ▷ *verb* (***gripped, gripping***) **1** to take or keep a firm hold of something. **2** to capture the imagination or attention of a person. ▷ *noun* **1** a firm hold; the action of taking a firm hold. **2** a way of gripping. **3** a handle or part that can be gripped. **4** a U-shaped wire pin for keeping the hair in place. **5** *N Amer, especially US* a holdall. **6** *colloq* understanding. **7** *colloq* control; mastery □ *lose one's grip of the situation.* **8** *theat* a stagehand who moves scenery. **9** *cinema, TV* someone who manoeuvres a film camera. • **gripper** *noun.* • **get to grips with something** to begin to deal successfully with it. ◷ Anglo-Saxon *gripe* a grasp.

gripe /graɪp/ ▷ *verb* (***griped, griping***) **1** *intr, colloq* to complain persistently. **2** *tr & intr* to feel, or cause someone to feel, intense stomach pain. ▷ *noun* (***gripes***) **1** *colloq* a complaint. **2** (*usually* **gripes**) *old use, colloq* a severe stomach pain. ◷ Anglo-Saxon *gripan.*

gripe water or **Gripe Water** ▷ *noun, trademark* medicine given to babies to relieve colic and stomach complaints.

gripping ▷ *adj* holding the attention; exciting. • **grippingly** *adverb.*

grisaille /grɪˈzeɪəl; *French* grizɑj/ ▷ *noun, art* a style of painting in greyish tints in imitation of BAS-RELIEF, eg on ceilings or on pottery. ◷ 19c: French, from *gris* grey.

griseofulvin /grɪzɪoʊˈfʊlvɪn/ ▷ *noun, pharmacol* an antibiotic administered by mouth as a treatment for fungal infections of the skin, hair, and nails. ◷ 1930s: from Latin *griseus* grey + *fulvus* reddish-yellow, a descriptive term used to identify a species of penicillin mould.

grisette /grɪˈzɛt/ ▷ *noun* (***grisettes***) *especially formerly* a young French working girl. ◷ 18c: French, also meaning the grey fabric in which they dressed.

grisgris or **greegree** /ˈgriːgriː/ ▷ *noun* (***grisgris*** /ˈgriːgriː/ or ***greegrees***) an African charm or fetish. ◷ 17c: French, probably of African origin.

grisly /ˈgrɪzlɪ/ ▷ *adj* (***grislier, grisliest***) horrible; ghastly; gruesome. • **grisliness** *noun.* ◷ 12c *grislic.*

grissino /grɪˈsiːnoʊ/ ▷ *noun* (*plural* ***grissini*** /-niː/) a BREADSTICK. ◷ 19c: Italian.

grist ▷ *noun* grain that is to be, or that has been, ground into flour. • **grist to the mill** anything useful or profitable; a useful contribution. ◷ Anglo-Saxon.

gristle /ˈgrɪsəl/ ▷ *noun* cartilage, especially in meat. • **gristliness** *noun.* • **gristly** *adj.* ◷ Anglo-Saxon.

grit ▷ *noun* **1** small particles of a hard material, especially of stone or sand. **2** *colloq* courage and determination. ▷ *verb* (***gritted, gritting***) **1** to spread grit on (icy roads, etc). **2** to clench (the teeth), eg to overcome pain. ◷ Anglo-Saxon *greot.*

grit blasting ▷ *noun, engineering* a process used in preparation for metal spraying which cleans the surface and gives it the roughness required to retain the sprayed metal particles.

grits ▷ *plural noun* coarsely ground grain, especially oats, with the husks removed. ▷ *singular noun* a dish of this, boiled and eaten for breakfast in the southern US. ◷ 16c as *greyts* in sense 1; Anglo-Saxon as *grytt* meaning 'bran'; related to GROATS.

gritter ▷ *noun* a vehicle for spreading grit (on icy roads, etc).

gritty ▷ *adj* (***grittier, grittiest***) **1** full of or covered with grit. **2** like grit. **3** determined; dogged.

grizzle /ˈgrɪzəl/ ▷ *verb* (***grizzled, grizzling***) *intr, colloq* **1** said especially of a young child: to cry fretfully. **2** to sulk or complain. ◷ 19c; 18c in old sense 'to show one's teeth'.

grizzled /ˈgrɪzəld/ ▷ *adj* **1** said of the hair or a beard: grey or greying. **2** said of a person: having such hair. ◷ 15c as *griseld*: from French *gris* grey.

grizzly /ˈgrɪzlɪ/ ▷ *adj* (***grizzlier, grizzliest***) grey or greying; grizzled. ▷ *noun* (***grizzlies***) *colloq* a grizzly bear. ◷ 16c as *gristelly*: see GRIZZLED.

grizzly bear ▷ *noun* the largest of the bears, so called because its dark brown fur is frosted with white.

groan ▻ *verb* (***groaned, groaning***) **1** *intr* to make a long deep sound in the back of the throat, expressing pain, distress, disapproval, etc. **2** to utter or express something with or by means of a groan. **3** *intr* to creak loudly. **4** *intr* to be weighed down or almost breaking □ ***tables groaning with masses of food*** □ ***a system groaning under inefficiency.*** ▻ *noun* an act, or the sound, of groaning. • **groaner** *noun*. • **groaning** *noun, adj*. • **groaningly** *adverb*. Ⓒ Anglo-Saxon *granian*.

groat ▻ *noun* an obsolete British silver coin worth four old pennies. Ⓒ 14c as *grote*: from Dutch *groot* thick.

groats ▻ *plural noun* crushed grain, especially oats, with the husks removed. Ⓒ Anglo-Saxon *grotan*, from *grot* particle; related to GRITS.

grocer /ˈɡrousə(r)/ ▻ *noun* **1** someone whose job is selling food and general household goods. **2** a grocer's shop. Ⓒ 15c as *grosser* wholesale merchant, from French *grossier*, see GROSS.

grocery /ˈɡrousərɪ/ ▻ *noun* (***groceries***) **1** the trade or premises of a grocer. **2** (**groceries**) merchandise, especially food, sold in a grocer's shop. Ⓒ 15c.

grockle /ˈɡrɒkəl/ ▻ *noun, Brit, colloq, derog* a tourist or holidaymaker, especially in SW England. Ⓒ 20c.

grog ▻ *noun* **1** a mixture of alcoholic spirit (especially rum) and water, as formerly drunk by sailors. **2** *Austral & NZ colloq* any alcoholic drink. Ⓒ 18c: from Old Grog, the nickname (probably deriving from his habit of wearing a GROGRAM cloak) of British admiral Edward Vernon, who in 1740 ordered the naval ration of rum to be diluted with water.

groggy ▻ *adj* (***groggier, groggiest***) *colloq* weak, dizzy and unsteady on the feet, eg from the effects of illness or alcohol. • **groggily** *adverb*. • **grogginess** *noun*. Ⓒ 18c in old sense 'intoxicated'.

grogram /ˈɡrɒɡrəm/ ▻ *noun* a coarse fabric made from a mix of silk and wool or mohair. Ⓒ 16c: from French *gros grain* coarse grain.

groin /ɡrɔɪn/ ▻ *noun* **1** the part of the body where the lower abdomen joins the upper thigh. **2** *euphemistic* the male sex organs. **3** *archit* the edge formed by the joining of two vaults in a roof; the rib covering the intersection. ▻ *verb* (***groined, groining***) *archit* to build (a vault, etc) with groins. • **groined** *adj*. • **groining** *noun*. Ⓒ 15c as *grynde*.

grommet or **grummet** /ˈɡrɒmɪt/ ▻ *noun* **1** a rubber or plastic ring around a hole in metal, to protect a tube or insulate a wire passing through. **2 a** a metal ring lining an eyelet; **b** the eyelet itself. **3** *medicine* a small tube passed through the eardrum to drain the middle ear. **4** (**grommet**) *slang* a novice surfer or skateboarder. Ⓒ 17c, meaning a small ring made of rope, used for attaching a sail to its stay: perhaps from French *grommette* the curb on a bridle.

groom /ɡruːm, ɡrʊm/ ▻ *noun* **1** someone who looks after horses and cleans stables. **2** a bridegroom. **3** a title given to various officers in a royal household. ▻ *verb* (***groomed, grooming***) **1** to clean, brush and generally smarten (animals, especially horses). **2** to keep (a person) clean and neat, especially regarding clothes and hair. **3** to train or prepare someone for a specified office, stardom or success in any sphere. Ⓒ 13c as *grom* boy, man, or manservant.

groomsman ▻ *noun* an attendant on a bridegroom, either alone (as BEST MAN) or one of a group.

groove /ɡruːv/ ▻ *noun* **1** a long narrow channel, especially one cut with a tool. **2** the continuous track cut into the surface of a RECORD (*noun* 4), along which the STYLUS moves. **3** *colloq* a set routine, especially a monotonous one. **4** repetitive, rhythmic, musical patterns used in creating DANCE MUSIC for clubs. ▻ *verb* (***grooved, grooving***) **1** to cut a groove in something. **2** *intr, dated slang* to enjoy oneself. • **in the groove** *colloq* in top form □ ***The champion is really in the groove.*** Ⓒ 14c as *grofe*: from Dutch *groeve* a furrow.

groovy ▻ *adj* (***groovier, grooviest***) *slang* excellent, attractive or fashionable. Ⓒ 20c; 19c in original sense, 'relating to a groove'.

grope /ɡroup/ ▻ *verb* (***groped, groping***) **1** *intr* to search by feeling about with the hands, eg in the dark. **2** *intr* to search uncertainly or with difficulty □ ***groping for answers.*** **3** to find (one's way) by feeling. **4** *colloq* to touch or fondle someone sexually. ▻ *noun, colloq* an act of sexual fondling. • **groping** *adj, noun*. • **gropingly** *adverb*. Ⓒ Anglo-Saxon *grapian*.

groper see GROUPER

grosbeak /ˈɡrousbiːk, ˈɡrɒs-/ ▻ *noun* **1** any of various finches with a stout conical beak, found mainly in N America. **2** any of various unrelated birds with a stout conical beak, eg certain weavers. Ⓒ 17c: from French *grosbec* thick beak.

groschen /ˈɡrouʃən/ ▻ *noun* (*plural* **groschen**) **1** an Austrian coin, a 100th part of a schilling. **2** a German coin, a 10-pfennig piece. **3** *formerly* in N Germany: a small silver coin. Ⓒ 17c: German.

grosgrain /ˈɡrouɡreɪn/ ▻ *noun* a heavy corded silk used especially for ribbons and hat bands. Ⓒ 19c: French, meaning 'coarse grain'.

gros point /ɡrou pɔɪnt/ ▻ *noun, needlecraft* **1** a large cross-stitch. **2** embroidery in this stitch. Ⓒ 20c: French.

gross /ɡrous/ ▻ *adj* (***grosser, grossest***, except in sense 1) **1** total, with no deductions □ ***gross weight.*** Opposite of NET[2]. **2** very great; flagrant; glaring □ ***gross negligence.*** **3** *derog* vulgar; coarse. **4** *derog* unattractively fat. **5** *colloq, derog* very unpleasant. **6** dense; lush □ ***gross vegetation.*** **7** *derog* dull; lacking sensitivity or judgement. **8** solid; tangible; concrete; not spiritual or abstract. ▻ *noun* **1** (*plural* **gross**) twelve dozen, 144. **2** (*plural* **grosses**) the total amount or weight, without deductions. ▻ *verb* (***grossed, grossing***) to earn (a specified sum) as a gross income or profit, before tax is deducted. • **grossly** *adverb*. • **grossness** *noun*. Ⓒ 14c: from French *gros* large or fat.

▪ **gross someone out** *slang* to disgust or offend them.

▪ **gross something up** to convert (a net figure) into a gross one, eg for the purpose of calculating tax.

gross domestic product ▻ *noun* (abbreviation **GDP**) *econ* the total value of all goods produced and all services provided by a nation in one year.

gross national product ▻ *noun* (abbreviation **GNP**) *econ* gross domestic product plus the value of income from investments abroad.

grot /ɡrɒt/ *slang* ▻ *noun* rubbish. ▻ *adj* dirty; worthless. Ⓒ 1960s: a back-formation from GROTTY.

grotesque /ɡrouˈtɛsk/ ▻ *adj* (***grotesquer, grotesquest***) **1** very unnatural or strange-looking, so as to cause fear or laughter. **2** exaggerated; ridiculous; absurd. ▻ *noun* **1** (**the grotesque**) a 16c style in art which features animals, plants and people mixed together in a strange or fantastic manner. **2** a work of art in this style. • **grotesquely** *adverb*. • **grotesqueness** *noun*. • **grotesquery** or **grotesquerie** *noun* **1** grotesque objects collectively. **2** grotesqueness. Ⓒ 16c as *crotesque*: from Italian *pittura grottesca* cave painting, from *grotta* cave.

grotto /ˈɡrɒtou/ ▻ *noun* (***grottos*** or ***grottoes***) **1** a cave, especially a small and picturesque one. **2** a man-made cave-like structure, especially in a garden or park. Ⓒ 17c: from Italian *grotta* cave.

grotty /ˈɡrɒtɪ/ ▻ *adj* (***grottier, grottiest***) *colloq* **1** *derog* unpleasantly dirty or shabby. **2** ill. • **grottiness** *noun*. Ⓒ 1960s: short form of GROTESQUE.

grouch /ɡrautʃ/ *colloq* ▻ *verb* (***grouched, grouching***) *intr* to grumble or complain. ▻ *noun* (***grouches***) **1** a complaining person. **2** **a** a bad-tempered complaint; **b** the cause of it. ◎ 19c US variant of obsolete *grutch* grudge: from French *groucher* to complain.

grouchy /ˈgraʊtʃɪ/ (***grouchier***, ***grouchiest***) ▷ *adj* bad-tempered; tending to grumble. • **grouchily** *adverb*. • **grouchiness** *noun*.

ground¹ /graʊnd/ ▷ *noun* **1** the solid surface of the Earth, or any part of it; soil; land. **2** (*often* **grounds**) an area of land, usually extensive, attached to or surrounding a building. **3** an area of land used for a specified purpose □ *football ground*. **4** distance covered or to be covered. **5** the substance of discussion □ *cover a lot of ground*. **6** a position or standpoint, eg in an argument □ *stand or shift one's ground*. **7** progress relative to that made by an opponent; advantage □ *lose or gain ground*. **8** (*usually* **grounds**) a reason or justification. **9** *art* **a** the background in a painting; **b** a surface prepared specially before paint is applied. **10** *N Amer, elec* EARTH (*noun* 7). **11** (**grounds**) sediment or dregs, especially of coffee. **12** the bottom of the sea or a river. ▷ *verb* (***grounded***, ***grounding***) **1** *tr & intr* to hit or cause (a ship) to hit the seabed or shore and remain stuck. **2** to refuse to allow (a pilot or aeroplane) to fly. **3** to forbid (eg teenagers) to go out socially as a punishment □ *Jane's been grounded for coming in late*. **4** to lay (eg weapons) on the ground. **5** *N Amer, elec* to EARTH (*verb* 1). ▷ *adj* on or relating to the ground □ *ground forces*. • **cut** or **take the ground from under someone's feet** to act in anticipation of someone's plan, etc, destroying its effect. • **down to the ground** *colloq* absolutely; completely □ *suits me down to the ground*. • **give ground** to give way; to retreat. • **go to ground 1** said of an animal: to go into a burrow to escape from hunters. **2** to go into hiding, eg from the police. • **into the ground** to the point of exhaustion; to a position of total defeat. • **off the ground** started; under way □ *still can't get the project off the ground*. • **on firm** or **shaky ground** in a strong or weak position. • **on the ground** amongst ordinary people □ *opinion on the ground*. • **on the ground floor** on the same terms as the original promoters, or at the start (eg of a business venture). ◎ Anglo-Saxon as *grund*, in sense 12.

■ **ground someone in something** to give them basic instruction in (a subject).

■ **ground something on something else** to base (an argument, complaint, etc) on it □ *an argument grounded on logic*.

ground² /graʊnd/ *past tense, past participle of* GRIND

ground bait ▷ *noun* bait which is dropped on to the river bed to attract fish to a general area.

ground bass /— beɪs/ ▷ *noun, music* a short bass part constantly repeated while the melody or harmony changes.

groundbreaking ▷ *adj* innovative.

ground control ▷ *noun* **1** the control and monitoring from the ground of the flight of aircraft or spacecraft, especially by continuous transmission of radio instructions. **2** at an airport: the personnel and equipment by means of which air traffic controllers monitor the progress of approaching aircraft and issue detailed instructions to pilots.

ground cover ▷ *noun* low-growing plants that cover the surface of the ground.

ground crew ▷ *noun* a team of mechanics whose job is to maintain aircraft.

ground elder ▷ *noun* a perennial plant and persistent weed, with white flowers and creeping underground stems that send up shoots some distance from the parent plant.

ground floor ▷ *noun, Brit* the floor of a building that is at street level. *US equivalent* FIRST FLOOR. • **get in on the ground floor** to be involved, eg in a project, business, etc right from the start and so have some kind of advantage.

ground frost ▷ *noun, meteorol* a temperature of 0°C or less, registered on a horizontal thermometer in contact with the shorn grass tips of a turf surface.

ground glass ▷ *noun* glass fogged by grinding, sandblasting or etching.

groundhog ▷ *noun* the WOODCHUCK.

grounding ▷ *noun* a foundation of basic knowledge or instruction.

ground ivy ▷ *noun* a creeping herbaceous plant, with leaves which look like ivy when the edges curl.

groundless ▷ *adj* having no reason or justification. • **groundlessly** *adverb*. • **groundlessness** *noun*.

groundling ▷ *noun* **1** any of various small freshwater fishes, especially loaches, that live close to the bottom of a river or lake. **2** a low-growing or creeping plant. **3** *colloq* someone on the ground as opposed to one in an aircraft. **4** *historical* someone standing in the pit (ie the cheapest area) of an Elizabethan theatre. **5** *derog* someone of inferior tastes. ◎ Early 17c in senses 1 and 4.

groundnut ▷ *noun* **1** **a** any of various N American climbing plants of the pulse family that produce small edible underground tubers, seed pods, etc, eg the PEANUT plant; **b** one of the underground tubers produced by such a plant. **2** *N Amer* a peanut.

ground plan ▷ *noun* **1** a plan of the ground floor of a building. **2** any general, undetailed plan.

ground rent ▷ *noun* rent paid to the owner of land leased for building purposes.

ground rule ▷ *noun* a basic principle.

groundsel /ˈgraʊnsəl, ˈgraʊndsəl/ ▷ *noun* an annual plant and common weed with irregularly toothed oblong leaves and numerous small cylindrical flower-heads consisting of clusters of yellow florets. ◎ Anglo-Saxon *gundæswelgiæ*, from *gund* pus + *swelgan* to swallow, so called because of its use in poultices.

groundsheet ▷ *noun* a waterproof sheet spread on the ground, eg in a tent, to give protection against damp.

groundsman ▷ *noun* someone whose job is to maintain a sports field.

ground squirrel ▷ *noun* any of various species of burrowing rodent, mostly native to N America, including certain marmots, chipmunks and gophers.

ground staff ▷ *noun* **1** GROUND CREW. **2** a team of people whose job is to maintain a sports field.

ground state ▷ *noun, physics* the lowest energy state of an atom.

ground stroke ▷ *noun, tennis* a return shot played after the ball has bounced.

groundswell ▷ *noun* **1** a broad high swell of the sea, increasing in height rapidly as it passes through the water, often caused by a distant storm or earthquake. **2** a rapidly growing indication of public or political feeling.

groundwater ▷ *noun, geol* water which occurs in the rocks beneath the surface of the Earth and which can surface in springs.

group /gruːp/ ▷ *noun* **1** a number of people or things gathered, placed or classed together. **2** (*sometimes* **Group**) a number of business companies under single ownership and central control. **3** a band of musicians and singers, especially one that plays pop music. **4** **a** a division of an air force consisting of two or more WINGS; **b** a division of the US air force subordinate to a WING; **c** a division of the US army consisting of two or more BATTALIONS. **5** *chem* in the periodic table: a vertical column representing a series of chemical elements with similar chemical properties. **6** *chem* a combination of two or more atoms that are bonded together and tend to act as a single unit in chemical reactions. ▷ *verb* (***grouped***, ***grouping***) *tr & intr* to form (things or people) into a group. ◎ 17c: from French *groupe*.

group nouns

See Usage Note at **collective nouns**.

group captain ▻ *noun* an officer in the air force. See table at RANK.

group dynamics ▻ *singular noun, psychol* the way in which people in small, usually face-to-face, groups interact and the processes and principles involved in this.

grouper *Southern US* /'gruːpə(r)/ or (*Austral, NZ*) **groper** /'groʊpə(r)/ ▻ *noun* a name given to various fishes, especially ones resembling BASS². ⓘ 17c: from Portuguese *garupa*, probably from some S American Indian name.

groupie ▻ *noun, colloq* **1** *often derog* an ardent follower of a touring pop star or group, often a young woman seeking a sexual relationship with them. **2** *loosely* someone who follows a specified activity, sport, pastime, etc □ *a religious groupie.*

Group of Five (abbreviation **G5** or **G-5**) and **Group of Seven** (abbreviation **G7** or **G-7**) and **Group of Ten** (abbreviation **G10** or **G-10**) *noun, econ* a series of joint committees formed to deal with aspects of common economic interest to various groups of countries since the 1960s, the Five consisting of the US, Japan, West Germany, the UK and France, the Seven being these plus Italy and Canada, and the Ten being the main industrial members of the International Monetary Fund.

Group of Three ▻ *noun* the US, Japan and Germany, the wealthiest western-style industrialized nations.

group practice ▻ *noun* a medical practice in which several doctors work together as partners.

group theory ▻ *noun, math* the study of the properties of mathematical groups.

group therapy ▻ *noun* a form of psychotherapy that involves the joint participation of several people, under the guidance of a trained therapist, who discuss their problems and possible ways of overcoming them.

groupware ▻ *noun, computing* software that is designed for use on several computers, workstations, etc at the same time.

grouse¹ /graʊs/ ▻ *noun* (*plural* **grouse**) any of various mainly ground-living gamebirds with a plump body, feathered legs and a short curved bill, found in cold northern regions. See THE GLORIOUS TWELFTH.

grouse² /graʊs/ *colloq* ▻ *verb* (**groused, grousing**) *intr* to complain. ▻ *noun* **1** a complaint or spell of complaining. **2** a querulous person; a moaner. • **grouser** *noun*. ⓘ 19c as *verb* (originally army slang).

grouse³ /graʊs/ *adj* ▻ *Austral, NZ slang* very good; excellent. ⓘ 20c.

grouse moor ▻ *noun* a tract of moorland on which grouse live, breed and are shot for sport.

grout /graʊt/ ▻ *noun* thin mortar applied to the joints between bricks or especially ceramic tiles, as a decorative finish. ▻ *verb* (**grouted, grouting**) to apply grout to the joints of something. • **grouting** *noun* **1** filling up or finishing with grout. **2** grout. ⓘ 17c as *growt*.

grove /groʊv/ ▻ *noun* (**groves**) **1** a small group of trees, often planted for shade or ornament. **2** an area planted with fruit trees, especially citrus and olive. **3** an avenue of trees. **4** (**Grove**) used in street names. ⓘ Anglo-Saxon as *graf*.

grovel /'grɒvəl, 'grʌvəl/ ▻ *verb* (**grovelled, grovelling**; (*US*) **groveled, groveling**) *intr* **1** to act with exaggerated (and usually insincere) respect or humility, especially to gain the favour of a superior. **2** to lie or crawl face down, in fear or respect. • **groveller** *noun*. • **grovelling** *adj*. ⓘ 16c back-formation from *groveling* (first appears in 14c) face down, from Norse *a grufa* face down.

grow /groʊ/ ▻ *verb* (**grew, grown, growing**) **1** *intr* said of a living thing: to develop into a larger more mature form. **2** *tr & intr* to increase, or allow (hair, nails, etc) to increase, in length. **3** *intr* **a** to increase in size, intensity or extent; **b** to increase in size in a specified direction □ *grow upwards towards the light.* **4** to cultivate (plants). **5 a** to become ... gradually □ *Over the years they grew very lazy;* **b** (*usually* **grow to ...**) to come gradually to (have a specified feeling) □ *grew to hate him.* • **grow like Topsy 1** simply to grow, apparently from nothing ⓘ as Topsy in Harriet Beecher Stowe's *Uncle Tom's Cabin* thought she did.. **2** to grow in a random, indiscriminate, or unplanned way. ⓘ Anglo-Saxon *growan*.

▪ **grow from something** to originate in it □ *The scheme grew from an idea they had at school.*

▪ **grow into something 1** to develop and become (a specified form) □ *Tadpoles grow into frogs* □ *grew into a talented writer.* **2** to become big enough to wear (clothes that were originally too large).

▪ **grow on someone** to gradually come to be liked by them.

▪ **grow out of something 1** to become too big to wear (clothes that were originally the right size). **2** to lose a liking for it, or the habit of doing it, with age □ *grew out of reading comics.* **3** to originate in it □ *The plan grew out of an idea of mine.*

▪ **grow together** to become united by growth.

▪ **grow up 1** to become, or be in the process of becoming, an adult. **2** to behave in an adult way. **3** to come into existence; to develop.

grow bag ▻ *noun* a large plastic bag containing a sterile growing medium in which seeds can be germinated and plants grown to full size. ⓘ 20c: from *Gro-bag*, trademark of the first ones to be sold.

growing pains ▻ *plural noun* **1** muscular pains, especially in the legs, sometimes experienced by growing children. **2** temporary problems or difficulties encountered in the early stages of a project, business or enterprise.

growl /graʊl/ ▻ *verb* (**growled, growling**) **1** *intr* said of animals: to make a deep rough sound in the throat, showing hostility. **2** *tr & intr* said of people: to make a similar sound showing anger or displeasure; to speak or say something angrily. ▻ *noun* an act or the sound of growling. • **growling** *adj, noun* • **growlingly** *adverb*. • **growly** *adj*. ⓘ 14c, meaning 'to rumble'.

growler ▻ *noun* **1** someone or something that growls. **2** a small iceberg. **3** *old slang* a four-wheeled horse-drawn cab.

grown /groʊn/ ▻ *adj* **1** mature □ *a grown woman.* **2** *in compounds* developed to a specified degree □ *fully grown.*

grown-up *colloq* ▻ *adj* adult. ▻ *noun* an adult.

growth /groʊθ/ ▻ *noun* **1 a** the process or rate of growing; **b** the increase in size, weight and complexity of a living organism that takes place as it develops to maturity. **2** an increase. **3** *econ* an increase in economic activity or profitability. **4** *medicine* a benign or malignant tumour formed as a result of the uncontrolled multiplication of cells.

growth hormone ▻ *noun, physiol* **1** a hormone, secreted by the anterior lobe of the PITUITARY GLAND, that controls growth and development in vertebrates. **2** any artificially manufactured substance used for the same purpose.

growth industry ▻ *noun* an industry or branch of industry that is developing and expanding.

growth market ▻ *noun, econ* a market in which demand for a product is greatly increasing.

groyne /grɔɪn/ ▻ *noun* (**groynes**) a BREAKWATER built to check land erosion. ⓘ 16c: from French *groign* snout or promontory.

grub ▷ *noun* **1** the worm-like larva of an insect, especially a beetle. **2** food. ▷ *verb* (***grubbed, grubbing***) **1** *intr* (*usually* **grub about**) to dig or search in the soil. **2** *intr* (*usually* **grub around**) to search or rummage. **3** *intr* (*especially* **grub away** or **along**) to toil or slog away. **4** (*especially* **grub up**) to dig up (roots and stumps). **5** to clear (ground). ◷ 13c as *grube* (verb).

grubby ▷ *adj* (***grubbier, grubbiest***) *colloq* dirty. • **grubbily** *adverb*. • **grubbiness** *noun*. ◷ 19c: from GRUB.

grub kick ▷ *noun, rugby* a kick where the ball moves along the ground.

grub screw ▷ *noun* a small headless screw.

grubstake *N Amer* ▷ *noun* supplies or money given to a prospector in return for a share in any finds. ▷ *verb* (***grubstaked, grubstaking***) to provide someone with such supplies. ◷ 19c.

Grub Street ▷ *noun, slang* **a** the profession, lifestyle or standards of writers of low-grade literature; **b** *as adj* □ *Grub-street hack*. ◷ 17c: formerly the name of a London street frequented by such writers.

grudge /grʌdʒ/ ▷ *noun* a long-standing feeling of resentment □ *bear a grudge*. ▷ *verb* (***grudged, grudging***) **1** (*especially* **grudge doing something**) to be unwilling to do it; to do it unwillingly. **2** (**to grudge someone something**) **a** to be unwilling to give them it; to give them it unwillingly; **b** to feel envy or resentment at their good fortune. ◷ 15c: from French *grouchier* to grumble.

grudge fight ▷ *noun* a fight to settle a grudge.

grudging ▷ *adj* **1** resentful. **2** unwilling. • **grudgingly** *adverb*.

gruel /grʊəl/ ▷ *noun* thin porridge. ◷ 14c: French, meaning 'groats'.

gruelling or (*US*) **grueling** /ˈgrʊəlɪŋ/ ▷ *adj* exhausting; punishing. ◷ 19c: from GRUEL in old sense 'to punish'.

gruesome /ˈgruːsəm/ ▷ *adj* inspiring horror or disgust; sickening; macabre. • **gruesomely** *adverb*. • **gruesomeness** *noun*. ◷ 16c as *growsome*: from dialect *grue* to shiver or shudder + -SOME.

gruff ▷ *adj* (***gruffer, gruffest***) **1** said of a voice: deep and rough. **2** rough, unfriendly or surly in manner. • **gruffly** *adverb*. • **gruffness** *noun*. ◷ 16c Scots as *groiff*, meaning 'coarse': from Dutch *grof* coarse.

grumble /ˈgrʌmbəl/ ▷ *verb* (***grumbled, grumbling***) *intr* **1** to complain in a bad-tempered way. **2** to make a low rumbling sound. ▷ *noun* **1** a complaint. **2** a rumbling sound. • **grumbler** *noun*. • **grumbling** *noun, adj*. • **grumblingly** *adverb*. • **grumbly** *adj*. ◷ 16c: from Dutch *grommelen*.

grumbling appendix ▷ *noun, non-technical* a condition in which the appendix is intermittently painful but where appendicitis proper has not developed.

grummet see GROMMET

grump ▷ *noun, colloq* **1** a grumpy person. **2** (**the grumps**) a fit of bad temper or sulking. ◷ 18c, meaning 'a cause of ill humour': an imitation of a snort of displeasure.

grumpy /ˈgrʌmpɪ/ ▷ *adj* (***grumpier, grumpiest***) bad-tempered; surly. • **grumpily** *adverb*. • **grumpiness** *noun*. ◷ 18c.

grunge /grʌndʒ/ ▷ *noun, slang, originally US* **1** dirt; rubbish; trash. **2** (*in full* **grunge rock**) a style of music in which a strident discordant guitar-based sound is combined with a deliberately understated and sometimes apathetic delivery. It is heavily influenced by PUNK. **3** thrift-shop fashion. **4** the designer equivalent of this. ◷ 1960s in sense 1; 1990s otherwise.

grungy /ˈgrʌndʒɪ/ ▷ *adj, slang* (***grungier, grungiest***) **1** dirty; messy. **2** unattractive; unappealing.

grunt ▷ *verb* (***grunted, grunting***) **1** *intr* said of animals, especially pigs: to make a low rough sound in the back of the throat. **2** *intr* said of people: to make a similar sound, eg indicating disgust or unwillingness to speak fully. **3** to express or utter something with this sound. ▷ *noun* an act or the sound of grunting. • **grunter** *noun*. • **grunting** *noun, adj*. ◷ Anglo-Saxon *grunnettan*.

grutten *past participle of* GREET[2]

Gruyère /gruːˈjɛə(r)/ ▷ *noun* a pale yellow holey cheese, originally made in Gruyère, in Switzerland. ◷ 19c.

gr. wt. ▷ *abbreviation* gross weight.

gryphon see GRIFFIN

GS ▷ *abbreviation* **1** General Secretary. **2** General Staff.

gs ▷ *abbreviation* gauss.

G7 or **G-7** ▷ *abbreviation* Group of Seven (see under GROUP OF FIVE).

g-spot (*in full* **Gräfenberg spot** /ˈgrɛfənbɜːg —, ˈgra- —/) ▷ *noun* an EROGENOUS zone in women, reputedly lying on the front wall of the vagina, behind the pubic bone. ◷ 1980s: named after the German-born gynaecologist, Ernst Gräfenberg (1881–1957).

G-string ▷ *noun* **1** (*also* **gee-string**) a garment which barely covers the pubic area, consisting of a strip of cloth attached to a narrow waistband. **2** *music* a string (eg for a violin) tuned or intended to be tuned to G.

g-suit or **G-suit** ▷ *noun* a close-fitting inflatable garment worn by astronauts and the pilots of high-speed aircraft to prevent blackout caused by accumulation of blood below the chest under conditions of high acceleration. ◷ 1940s: abbreviation of *gravity suit*.

GT ▷ *noun* a name given to certain fast but comfortable sports cars. ◷ 20c: abbreviation of Italian *gran turismo* grand touring.

Gt ▷ *abbreviation* in place names: Great.

GTi ▷ *noun* a name given to a high-performance car with a fuel-injection engine. ◷ 20c: from GT + *injection*.

G10 or **G-10** ▷ *abbreviation* Group of Ten (see under GROUP OF FIVE).

guacamole /gwakəˈmoʊlɪ, gwɑːkəˈmoʊlɪ/ ▷ *noun* a traditional Mexican dish of mashed avocado mixed with spicy seasoning, tomatoes and onions, eaten cold, eg as a dip. ◷ 1920s: American Spanish, from Aztec *ahuacatl* avocado + *molli* sauce.

guanine /ˈgwɑːnɪn, -niːn/ ▷ *noun biochem* a base, derived from purine, which is one of the four bases found in NUCLEIC ACID. See also ADENINE, CYTOSINE, THYMINE. ◷ 19c: from GUANO.

guano /ˈgwɑːnoʊ/ ▷ *noun* (***guanos***) **1** the accumulated droppings of large colonies of bats, fish-eating seabirds or seals. It is rich in nitrogen and is used as a fertilizer. **2** any fertilizer resembling this. ◷ 17c: Spanish, from Quechua *huanu* dung.

guarantee /garənˈtiː/ ▷ *noun* **1 a** a formal agreement, usually in writing, that a product, service, etc will conform to specified standards for a particular period of time; **b** a document that records this kind of agreement. **2** an assurance that something will have a specified outcome, condition, etc □ *no guarantee that there wouldn't be more pay cuts*. **3** *law* an agreement, usually backed up by some kind of collateral, under which one person, the GUARANTOR, becomes liable for the debt or default of another. **4** someone who agrees to give a guarantee. ▷ *verb* (***guaranteed, guaranteeing***) **1** to provide (eg a product, service, etc) with a guarantee. **2** to ensure something □ *Their reputation guarantees their success*. **3** to assure or promise □ *I guarantee the script will be finished tomorrow*. **4** to act as a GUARANTOR for something. • **guaranteed** *adj*. See also WARRANTY. ◷ 17c.

guarantor /garənˈtɔː(r)/ ▷ *noun* someone who gives a guarantee.

guaranty /ˈgarəntɪ/ ⊳ *noun* (***guaranties***) a GUARANTEE (sense 3). ◷ 16c: from French *guarantie* and related to WARRANTY.

guard /gɑːd/ ⊳ *verb* (***guarded, guarding***) **1** to protect someone or something from danger or attack. **2** to watch over someone in order to prevent their escape. **3** to control or check □ *guard your tongue*. **4** to control passage through (eg a doorway). **5** *tr & intr, curling, bowls* to protect a stone or bowl by placing another in the line of a potential attack. ⊳ *noun* **1** a person or group whose job is to provide protection, eg from danger or attack, or to prevent escape. **2** *Brit* a person in charge of a railway train. **3** a state of readiness to give protection or prevent escape □ *keep guard*. **4** *boxing, cricket, etc* a defensive posture. **5** *basketball, Amer football, etc* a defensive player or their position. **6** *especially in compounds* anything that gives protection from or to something □ *fireguard* □ *shinguard*. **7** the act or duty of protecting. **8** (*often* **Guard**) a soldier in any of certain army regiments originally formed to protect the sovereign. • **mount guard** to go on sentry duty. • **mount guard over someone or something** to protect or defend them or it. • **off guard** or **off one's guard** not on the alert; unwary about what one says or does □ *caught you off guard*. • **on guard 1** on sentry duty. **2** (*also* **on one's guard**) on the alert; wary about what one says or does □ *be on your guard against thieves*. • **stand guard** to act as a guard or sentry. ◷ 15c: from French *garder* to protect.

■ **guard against something** to take precautions to prevent it.

guard cell ⊳ *noun, bot* on the aerial parts of a plant, especially the under surface of the leaves: either of two semicircular cells that surround each of the specialized pores or STOMATA.

guard dog ⊳ *noun* a watch dog.

guarded /ˈgɑːdɪd/ ⊳ *adj* cautious. • **guardedly** *adverb*. • **guardedness** *noun*.

guardhouse and **guardroom** ⊳ *noun* a building or room for guards on duty, especially at the gate of a military camp, often also housing prisoners.

guardian /ˈgɑːdɪən/ ⊳ *noun* **1** someone who is legally responsible for the care of another, especially an orphaned child. **2** a guard, defender or protector □ *the Church's role as guardian of public morals*. • **guardianship** *noun*. ◷ 15c: from Anglo-French *gardein*.

guardian angel ⊳ *noun* **1** an angel believed to watch over a particular person. **2** someone who is specially devoted to the interests of another. **3** (**Guardian Angels**) vigilantes who patrol public places such as New York's subway to prevent crimes of violence.

guard of honour ⊳ *noun* (***guards of honour***) a body of soldiers serving as a ceremonial escort.

guardrail ⊳ *noun* **1** a rail, eg on a ship or train, which acts as a safety barrier. **2** on a railway: an additional rail fitted on a track to improve a train's stability.

guard ring ⊳ *noun* a ring worn on the finger to prevent another from slipping off. Also called **keeper ring**.

guardroom see GUARDHOUSE

guardsman ⊳ *noun* **1** *Brit* a member of a regiment of Guards. **2** *US* a member of the National Guard.

Guarnerius /gwɑːˈnɛərɪəs/ and **Guarneri** /-riː/ ⊳ *noun* (***Guarneriuses*** or ***Guarneris***) a violin made by a member of the *Guarneri* family, violin-makers in 17c and 18c Cremona, Italy. ◷ 19c.

guava /ˈgwɑːvə/ ⊳ *noun* (***guavas***) **1** any of various small tropical trees cultivated for their edible fruits, especially a species native to Central America. **2** its yellow pear-shaped fruit which has sweet juicy pink, white, or yellow edible pulp. ◷ 16c as *guiava*: from Spanish *guayaba*.

gubbins /ˈgʌbɪnz/ *colloq* ⊳ *singular noun* **1** *derog* a worthless object. **2** a device or gadget. **3** *derog* a silly person. ⊳ *singular or plural noun* rubbish. ◷ 16c: related to GOB and GOBBET.

gubernatorial /gʌbənəˈtɔːrɪəl/ ⊳ *adj, formal, especially US* referring or relating to a GOVERNOR (in senses 1-4, especially sense1). ◷ 18c: from Latin *gubernator* steersman.

gudgeon[1] /ˈgʌdʒən/ ⊳ *noun* **1** a small freshwater fish related to the carp, which has a blackish or greenish back with dark spots, a silvery underside and a pair of sensory feelers or BARBELS (sense 2) at the corners of its mouth. **2** *colloq* a gullible person. ◷ 15c: from French *goujon*.

gudgeon[2] /ˈgʌdʒən/ ⊳ *noun* **1** a pivot or pin of any kind. **2** the socket part of a hinge or rudder that the pin part fits into. ◷ 15c: from French *goujon* pin of a pulley.

guelder rose /ˈgɛldə —/ ⊳ *noun* a deciduous shrub belonging to the honeysuckle family, which has white flowers. Also called SNOWBALL TREE. ◷ 16c: from *Gelder*land, a province in the Netherlands.

guenon /ˈgɛnən, gəˈnɔ̃/ ⊳ *noun* any of several species of long-tailed African monkeys. ◷ 19c: French.

guerilla see GUERRILLA

guernsey /ˈgɜːnzɪ/ ⊳ *noun* **1** a hand-knitted woollen pullover, originally one worn by sailors. **2** *Austral* a sleeveless football jersey worn by Australian rules players. **3** (**Guernsey**) a breed of dairy cattle that has a golden-red coat, often with distinct white markings, and which produces high yields of rich creamy milk that is widely used for butter-making. • **get a guernsey** *Austral* **1** to be selected for a team. **2** to win recognition or approval. ◷ 19c: *Guernsey* in the Channel Islands; compare GANSEY and JERSEY.

guerrilla or **guerilla** /gəˈrɪlə/ ⊳ *noun* a member of a small, independent, often politically motivated armed force making surprise attacks, eg against government troops. Also *as adj* □ *guerrilla warfare*. ◷ 19c: Spanish diminutive of *guerra* war.

guess /gɛs/ ⊳ *verb* (***guessed, guessing***) **1** *tr & intr* to make an estimate or form an opinion about something, based on little or no information. **2** to estimate something correctly. **3** to think or suppose □ *I guess we could go*. ⊳ *noun* (***guesses***) an estimate based on guessing. • **guessable** *adj*. • **guesser** *noun*. • **guessing** *noun, adj*. • **anybody's guess** *colloq* something impossible to know or determine. ◷ 14c as *gess*: from Dutch *gissen*.

guesstimate *colloq* ⊳ *noun* /ˈgɛstɪmət/ a very rough estimate, based on guesswork. ⊳ *verb* /-meɪt/ (***guesstimated, guesstimating***) to estimate something using a rough guess. ◷ 1930s: GUESS + ESTIMATE.

guesswork ⊳ *noun* the process or result of guessing.

guest /gɛst/ ⊳ *noun* **1** someone who receives hospitality in the home of, or at the expense of, another. **2** someone who stays at a hotel, boarding-house, etc. **3** a person specially invited to take part □ *guest star* □ *guest speaker*. ⊳ *verb* (***guested, guesting***) *intr* to appear as a guest, eg on a television show. ◷ Anglo-Saxon *gest*.

guesthouse ⊳ *noun* a private home that offers accommodation to paying guests; a boarding-house.

guest room ⊳ *noun* a room for a guest.

guest worker ⊳ *noun* a GASTARBEITER.

guff ⊳ *noun, colloq, derog* nonsense. ◷ 19c: originally as PUFF, meaning 'a blow of air'.

guffaw /gʌˈfɔː/ ⊳ *noun* a loud coarse laugh. ⊳ *verb* (***guffawed, guffawing***) *intr* to laugh in this way. ◷ 19c: imitating the sound.

GUI /ˈguːɪ/ ⊳ *abbreviation, computing* Graphical User Interface, an on-screen interface incorporating graphics.

guidance /ˈgaɪdəns/ ⊳ *noun* **1** help, advice or counselling; the act or process of guiding. **2** direction or leadership. **3** *as adj* □ *guidance teacher*.

guide /gaɪd/ ▷ *verb* (***guided***, ***guiding***) **1** to lead, direct or show the way to someone. **2** to control or direct the movement or course of something. **3** to advise or influence □ *be guided by your parents*. ▷ *noun* **1** someone who leads the way for eg tourists or mountaineers. **2** any device used to direct movement. **3** a GUIDEBOOK. **4** (**Guide**) a member of a worldwide youth organization for girls. *US equivalent* **Girl Scout**. **5** someone or something, especially a quality, which influences another person's decisions or behaviour □ *Let truth be your guide*. ⓘ 14c: from French *guider*.

guidebook ▷ *noun* a book containing information about a particular place or instructions for a practical activity.

guided missile ▷ *noun* a jet- or rocket-propelled projectile that carryies a warhead and which can be electronically directed to its target by remote control for all or part of the way.

guide dog ▷ *noun* a dog specially trained to guide a blind person safely.

guideline ▷ *noun* (*often* **guidelines**) an indication of what future action is required or recommended.

guiding light and **guiding star** ▷ *noun* someone or something that is adopted as a guide or model.

guild or **gild** /gɪld/ ▷ *noun* **1** a medieval association of merchants or craftsmen for maintaining standards and providing mutual support. **2** a name used by various modern societies, clubs and associations □ *the Townswomen's Guild*. ⓘ Anglo-Saxon *gield*.

guilder or **gilder** /ˈgɪldə(r)/ ▷ *noun* **1** (*plural* ***guilder*** or ***guilders***) the standard unit of currency of the Netherlands. **2** (*plural* ***guilders***) an old German and Dutch gold coin. ⓘ 15c as *guldren*: from Dutch *gulden*; compare GULDEN.

guildhall ▷ *noun* **1** a hall where members of a guild or other association meet. **2** a town hall.

guile /gaɪl/ ▷ *noun* **1** the ability to deceive or trick. **2** craftiness or cunning. • **guileful** *adj*. • **guilefully** *adverb*. • **guilefulness** *noun*. • **guileless** *adj*. • **guilelessly** *adverb*. • **guilelessness** *noun*. ⓘ 13c as *gile*: French, meaning 'deceit'.

guillemot /ˈgɪlɪmɒt/ ▷ *noun* any of various seabirds of the AUK family, with black and white plumage, a long narrow bill and short narrow wings. ⓘ 17c.

guillotine /ˈgɪlətiːn/ ▷ *noun* (***guillotines***) **1** an instrument for beheading, consisting of a large heavy blade that slides rapidly down between two upright posts. **2** a device with a large blade moved by a lever, for cutting paper or metal. **3** *surgery* an instrument for excising the tonsils. **4** *politics* a time limit set to speed up discussion of, and voting on, a parliamentary bill. ▷ *verb* (***guillotined***, ***guillotining***) to use a guillotine in any of the senses above, eg to behead someone, to cut or cut out something, or to speed up the progress of something. ⓘ 18c: named after French physician Joseph Guillotin (1738–1814), who proposed beheading by guillotine in the French Revolution.

guilt /gɪlt/ ▷ *noun* **1** a feeling of shame or remorse resulting from a sense of having done wrong. **2** the state of having done wrong or having broken a law. **3** blame. **4** *law* liability to a penalty. ⓘ Anglo-Saxon *gylt*.

guiltless ▷ *adj* innocent. • **guiltlessly** *adverb*. • **guiltlessness** *noun*.

guilty /ˈgɪltɪ/ ▷ *adj* (***guiltier***, ***guiltiest***) (*often* **guilty of something**) **1** responsible for a crime or wrongdoing, or judged to be so. Compare INNOCENT 2, NOT PROVEN. **2** feeling, showing or involving guilt □ *a guilty look*. **3** able to be justly accused of something □ *guilty of working too hard*. • **guiltily** *adverb*. • **guiltiness** *noun*.

guinea /ˈgɪnɪ/ ▷ *noun* (***guineas***) **1** an obsolete British gold coin worth 21 shillings (£1.05). **2** its value, still used as a monetary unit in some professions, especially horse-racing. ⓘ 17c, meaning a coin worth 20 shillings: named after Guinea, W Africa, where the gold for the coin was originally mined.

guinea fowl ▷ *noun* (*plural* ***guinea fowl***) any of various ground-living birds related to pheasants and chickens, with a naked head and greyish plumage speckled with white. ⓘ 18c: it was imported from *Guinea*, W Africa, in the 16c.

guinea hen ▷ *noun* a guinea fowl, especially a female.

guinea pig ▷ *noun* **1** any of numerous varieties of a domesticated species of CAVY, widely kept as a domestic pet and also used as a laboratory animal. **2** (*also* **human guinea pig**) a person used as the subject of an experiment. ⓘ 17c.

guipure /gɪˈpjʊə(r), giːˈpʊə(r)/ ▷ *noun* heavy lace which has a large open pattern with no background. ⓘ 19c: French, from *guiper* to cover with cloth.

guise /gaɪz/ ▷ *noun* **1** assumed appearance; pretence □ *under the guise of friendship*. **2** external appearance in general. **3** *archaic* style of dress. ⓘ 13c in sense 3: French.

guiser /ˈgaɪzə(r)/ ▷ *noun*, *Scottish* someone, especially a child, who goes from house to house in disguise, especially at Hallowe'en, entertaining with songs, etc and receiving small gifts in return. ⓘ 15c as *gysar*: from GUISE.

guitar /gɪˈtɑː(r)/ ▷ *noun* a musical instrument with a body generally shaped like a figure eight, a long fretted neck and usually six strings that are plucked or strummed. • **guitarist** *noun*. ⓘ 17c as *guitarra*: from Spanish *guitarra*.

gulag /ˈguːlag/ ▷ *noun* **1 a** a network of political prisons or labour camps that formerly existed in the Soviet Union; **b** one of these prisons or camps; **c** the government department responsible for their administration. **2** any system in which dissidents are oppressed. **3** any place that dissidents, especially political ones, may be sent to. ⓘ 1940s: Russian acronym, from *glavnoe upravlenie ispravitelno-trudovykh lagerei* main administration for corrective labour camps, made familiar by the writer A Solzhenitsyn (born 1918) in *The Gulag Archipelago*.

gulch /gʌltʃ/ ▷ *noun* (***gulches***) *N Amer, especially US* a narrow rocky ravine with a fast-flowing stream running through it. ⓘ 19c.

gulden /ˈguːldən/ ▷ *noun* (***gulden*** or ***guldens***) same as GUILDER. ⓘ 16c: German and Dutch, literally 'golden'.

gules /gjuːlz/ ▷ *noun*, *heraldry* red. ⓘ 14c as *goulez*: from French *goules* ermine dyed red.

gulf ▷ *noun* **1** a very large inlet of the sea extending far into the land, much more deeply indented and more enclosed than a BAY[1]. **2** a vast difference or separation, eg between points of view, etc. **3** a deep hollow in the ground; a chasm. **4** (**the Gulf**) **a** the region around the Persian Gulf in the Middle East; **b** the area around the Gulf of Mexico in Central America. ⓘ 14c: from French *golfe*, from Greek *kolpos*, also meaning 'bosom'.

Gulf States ▷ *plural noun* **1** the oil-producing countries around the Persian Gulf, ie Iran, Iraq, Kuwait, Bahrain, Saudi Arabia, Oman, Qatar and the United Arab Emirates. **2** the US states around the Gulf of Mexico, ie Florida, Texas, Alabama, Mississippi and Louisiana.

Gulf Stream ▷ *noun* a warm ocean current which flows out of the Gulf of Mexico, past Florida and along the east coast of the USA, and then deflected north-east across the Atlantic Ocean towards NW Europe. Also called **North Atlantic Drift**.

gull[1] ▷ *noun* any of various omnivorous seabirds with a stout body, predominantly white or greyish plumage, a hooked bill, long pointed wings and webbed feet. ⓘ 15c.

gull[2] *old use* ▷ *verb* (***gulled***, ***gulling***) to cheat or deceive. ▷ *noun* an easily fooled person. ⓘ 16c.

gullery /'gʌlərɪ/ ▻ *noun* (***gulleries***) a place where gulls breed.

gullet /'gʌlɪt/ ▻ *noun* the OESOPHAGUS or throat. ⓒ 14c as *golet*: French diminutive of *goule* throat, from Latin *gula*.

gullible /'gʌləbəl/ ▻ *adj* easily tricked or fooled. • **gullibility** *noun*. ⓒ 18c: from GULL².

gully or **gulley** /'gʌlɪ/ ▻ *noun* (***gullies*** or ***gulleys***) **1** a small channel or cutting with steep sides formed by running water especially during heavy rainstorms in tropical and semi-arid regions. **2** *cricket* **a** a fielding position between point and slips; **b** a fielder in this position.

gulp ▻ *verb* (***gulped, gulping***) **1** *tr & intr* (*also* **gulp down**) to swallow (food, drink, etc) eagerly or in large mouthfuls. **2** *intr* to make a swallowing motion, eg because of fear. ▻ *noun* **1** a swallowing motion. **2** an amount swallowed at once; a mouthful. ⓒ 15c: from Dutch *gulpen*.

■ **gulp something back** or **down** to stifle (tears, etc).

gum¹ ▻ *noun* the firm fibrous flesh surrounding the roots of the teeth. ⓒ Anglo-Saxon *goma* palate.

gum² ▻ *noun* **1** any of various substances found in certain plants, especially trees, that produce a sticky solution or gel when added to water, used in confectionery, gummed envelopes, etc. **2** this or any similar substance used as glue. **3** a gumdrop. **4** *colloq* chewing-gum. ▻ *verb* (***gummed, gumming***) to smear, glue or unite something with gum. ⓒ 13c: from French *gomme*, from Latin *gummi*.

■ **gum something up 1** to stick something to itself so that it no longer functions properly. **2** (*often* **gum up the works** *colloq*) to prevent (a machine, scheme, etc) from working properly.

gum arabic ▻ *noun* a thick sticky water-soluble gum exuded by certain acacia trees. It is used as an adhesive and emulsifier, and in inks, food-thickening agents and pharmaceutical products. ⓒ 16c.

gumbo /'gʌmboʊ/ ▻ *noun* (***gumbos***) **1** a thick soup or stew made from meat or fish and thickened with okra. **2** OKRA or its pods. ⓒ 19c: from Louisiana French *gombo*.

gumboil ▻ *noun* a small abscess on the gum.

gumboot ▻ *noun* a WELLINGTON BOOT.

gumdrop ▻ *noun* a sweet made from transparent hard jelly.

gummy¹ ▻ *adj* (***gummier, gummiest***) toothless. • **gummily** *adverb*. ⓒ Early 20c: from GUM¹.

gummy² ▻ *adj* (***gummier, gummiest***) **1** sticky. **2** producing gum. • **gumminess** *noun*. ⓒ 14c: from GUM².

gumption /'gʌmʃən, 'gʌmpʃən/ ▻ *noun, colloq* **1** common sense; initiative. **2** courage. ⓒ 18c.

gumshield ▻ *noun, sport* a flexible pad worn in the mouth to protect the teeth.

gumshoe ▻ *noun* **1** a rubber overshoe; a galosh. **2** *slang* a detective, especially a private detective.

gum tree ▻ *noun* the common name for any of various evergreen trees that yield gum (see GUM²), especially species of eucalyptus. • **up a gum tree** *colloq* in a difficult position, especially with no chance of escape.

gun ▻ *noun* **1** any weapon which fires bullets or shells from a metal tube. **2** any instrument which forces something out under pressure □ *spray gun*. **3** *colloq* a gunman □ *a hired gun*. **4** a member of a party of hunters. **5** the signal to start a race, etc. ▻ *verb* (***gunned, gunning***) *colloq* to rev up (a car engine) noisily. • **go great guns** *colloq* to function or be performed with great speed or success. • **jump the gun** see under JUMP. • **stick to one's guns** see under STICK². ⓒ 14c as *gonne*: probably from the Scandinavian female name *Gunnhildr*, both parts of which mean 'war', from the medieval habit of giving large engines of war female names.

■ **be gunning for someone** to be searching determinedly for them, usually with hostile intent.

■ **be gunning for something** to try to obtain it □ *were gunning for a pay rise*.

■ **gun someone** or **something down** to shoot them or it with a gun.

gunboat ▻ *noun* a small warship with large mounted guns.

gunboat diplomacy ▻ *noun* negotiation, usually in international politics, that involves threats of force.

gun carriage ▻ *noun* a wheeled support on which a gun is mounted.

gun cotton ▻ *noun* any of various highly explosive materials formed by treating clean cotton with nitric acid and sulphuric acid, used mainly in propellants and smokeless gunpowder.

gun dog ▻ *noun* **1** any dog specially trained to FLUSH⁴ birds or small mammals and to retrieve them when they have been shot by a gamekeeper or hunter. **2** any dog that is used for this type of work.

gunfight ▻ *noun* a fight involving two or more people with guns, especially formerly in the American West. • **gunfighter** *noun*.

gunfire ▻ *noun* **1** the act of firing guns. **2** the bullets fired. **3** the sound of firing. See also GUNSHOT.

gunge /gʌndʒ/ *colloq* ▻ *noun* any messy, slimy or sticky substance. ▻ *verb* (***gunged, gunging***) (*usually* **be gunged up**) to be covered or blocked with gunge. • **gungy** *adj*. ⓒ 1960s.

gung-ho /gʌŋ'hoʊ/ ▻ *adj, derog, colloq* excessively or foolishly eager, especially to attack an enemy. ⓒ 1940s, originally US: from Chinese *gong* work + *he* together.

gunk /gʌŋk/ ▻ *noun, colloq* any slimy or oily semi-solid substance. ⓒ 1930s: originally a US trademark of a grease-solvent.

gunlock ▻ *noun* the mechanism in some guns that causes the charge to explode.

gunman /'gʌnmən/ ▻ *noun* **1** an armed criminal. **2** an assassin. **3** a terrorist.

gunmetal ▻ *noun* **1** any of several dark-grey alloys, composed mainly of copper with small amounts of tin and zinc, formerly used to make cannons. **2** any of various other alloys that are used to make guns. **3** a dark-grey colour, especially if metallic. ▻ *adj* dark-grey.

gunnel¹ /'gʌnl/ ▻ *noun* a small eel-like coastal fish of the BLENNY family. ⓒ 18c.

gunnel² see GUNWALE

gunner ▻ *noun* **1** any member of an armed force who operates a heavy gun. **2** a soldier in an artillery regiment.

gunnery ▻ *noun* **1** the use of guns. **2** the science of designing guns.

gunny /'gʌnɪ/ ▻ *noun* (***gunnies***) **1** thick coarse jute cloth, used especially for sacking. **2** a sack made from this. ⓒ 18c: from Hindi *goni*.

gunplay ▻ *noun* the use of guns, especially in a fight or display of skill.

gunpoint ▻ *noun* (*only* **at gunpoint**) threatening, or being threatened, with a gun.

gunpowder ▻ *noun* the oldest known explosive, consisting of a mixture of potassium nitrate, sulphur and charcoal, still used in fireworks and for quarry blasting.

Gunpowder Plot see under GUY FAWKES DAY

gunroom ▻ *noun* **1** a room where guns are kept. **2** on board ship: a mess-room for junior officers.

gunrunning ▻ *noun* the act of smuggling arms into a country, often to help terrorists, etc. • **gunrunner** *noun*.

gunshot ▷ *noun* **1** bullets fired from a gun. **2** the distance over which a gun can fire a bullet □ *within gunshot.* **3** a sound of firing. See also GUNFIRE.

gun-shy ▷ *adj* said originally of gun dogs: frightened by guns or the sound of guns.

gunslinger /ˈɡʌnslɪŋə(r)/ ▷ *noun, colloq* an armed fighter in the lawless days of the American West.

gunsmith ▷ *noun* someone whose job is to make and/or repair firearms.

gunwale or **gunnel** /ˈɡʌnəl/ ▷ *noun* the upper edge of a ship's side. ● **full** or **packed to the gunwales** completely full. ⓒ 15c as *gonne walle*: from GUN + WALE.

gunyah /ˈɡʌnjə/ ▷ *noun, Austral* a temporary or improvised shelter, originally an Aboriginal hut. ⓒ 19c: from Aboriginal *guni* a hut.

Guo yu see under PUTONGHUA

guppy /ˈɡʌpɪ/ ▷ *noun* (*guppies*) a small brightly coloured freshwater fish that varies widely in form and colour, breeds prolifically, and is a popular aquarium fish. ⓒ 1940s: named after R J L Guppy, who sent the first specimens to the British Museum in the 19c.

gurdwara /ɡɜːˈdwɑːrə/ ▷ *noun* (*gurdwaras*) a Sikh place of worship. ⓒ Early 20c: from Punjabi *gurduara*, from Sanskrit *guru* teacher + *dvara* door.

gurgle /ˈɡɜːɡəl/ ▷ *verb* (*gurgled, gurgling*) **1** *intr* said of water: to make a bubbling noise when flowing. **2** *intr* to make a bubbling noise in the throat. **3** to utter something with a gurgle. ▷ *noun* the sound of gurgling. ⓒ 16c as *gurgull*: from Latin *gurgulare*.

Gurkha /ˈɡɜːkə/ ▷ *noun* (*Gurkhas*) **1** a member of a Hindu people of Nepal. **2** a member of a regiment of Gurkhas in the British or Indian armies.

Gurkhali /ɡɜːˈkɑːlɪ/ ▷ *noun* the Indo-European language spoken by Gurkhas.

guru /ˈɡʊəruː/ ▷ *noun* (*gurus*) **1** a Hindu or Sikh spiritual leader or teacher. See also MAHARISHI, SWAMI. **2** *sometimes facetious* any greatly respected and influential leader or adviser. ⓒ 17c: Hindi; from Sanskrit, meaning 'venerable'.

gush ▷ *verb* (*gushed, gushing*) **1** *tr & intr* said of a liquid: to flood out or make it flood out suddenly and violently. **2** *intr, derog, colloq* to speak or act with affected and exaggerated emotion or enthusiasm. ▷ *noun* (*gushes*) **1** a sudden violent flooding-out. **2** *derog, colloq* exaggerated emotion or enthusiasm. ● **gushing** *adj, noun.* ● **gushingly** *adverb.* ● **gushy** *adj* effusively sentimental. ⓒ 14c as *gosshe* or *gusche*: imitating the sound.

gusher ▷ *noun* **1** an oil well that oil flows from without the use of pumps. **2** someone who talks or behaves in a gushing way.

gusset /ˈɡʌsɪt/ ▷ *noun, dressmaking* a piece of material sewn into a garment for added strength or to allow for freedom of movement, eg at the crotch. ● **gussetting** *noun.* ⓒ 15c: from French *gousset*.

gust ▷ *noun* **1** a sudden blast or rush, eg of wind or smoke. **2** an emotional outburst. ▷ *verb* (*gusted, gusting*) *intr* said of the wind: to blow in gusts. ⓒ 16c: from Norse *gustr* blast.

gusto /ˈɡʌstoʊ/ ▷ *noun* enthusiastic enjoyment; zest □ *plays the piano with great gusto.* ⓒ 17c: Italian, meaning 'taste', from Latin *gustus*.

gusty ▷ *adj* (*gustier, gustiest*) **1** blowing in gusts; stormy. **2** fitfully irritable or upset. ● **gustily** *adverb.* ● **gustiness** *noun.*

gut ▷ *noun* **1** *anatomy* the alimentary canal or part of it. **2** (**guts**) *colloq* the insides of a person or animal. **3** *colloq* the stomach or abdomen. **4** *colloq* a fat stomach; a paunch. **5** (**guts**) *colloq* courage or determination. **6** (**guts**) *colloq* the inner or essential parts □ *the guts of the scheme.* **7 a** CATGUT; **b** a fibre obtained from silkworms, used for fishing tackle. ▷ *verb* (*gutted, gutting*) **1** to take the guts out of (an animal, especially fish). **2** to destroy the insides of something; to reduce to a shell □ *Fire gutted the building.* ▷ *adj, colloq* **1** based on instinct and emotion, not reason □ *a gut reaction.* **2** essential; basic □ *the gut problem.* ● **hate someone's guts** see under HATE. ● **have someone's guts for garters** *colloq* especially used as a threat: to punish them severely. ● **work** or **sweat** or **slave one's guts out** *colloq* to work extremely hard. ⓒ Anglo-Saxon *gutt*.

gutless ▷ *adj, derog* cowardly; lacking determination. ● **gutlessly** *adverb.* ● **gutlessness** *noun.*

gutrot ▷ *noun, colloq* **1** ROTGUT. **2** a stomach upset.

guts ▷ *verb* (*gutsed, gutsing*) *tr & intr, colloq* to eat greedily. ⓒ Early 20c.

gutsy ▷ *adj* (*gutsier, gutsiest*) *colloq* **1** courageous and determined. **2** gluttonous. ● **gutsily** *adverb.* ● **gutsiness** *noun.*

gutta-percha /ɡʌtəˈpɜːtʃə/ ▷ *noun* a whitish rubbery substance, obtained from the latex of certain Malaysian trees, used in dentistry to form the core of root fillings and also used in electrical insulation, etc. ⓒ 19c: from Malay *getah* gum + *percha* the tree which produces it.

gutted¹ ▷ *adj, colloq* extremely shocked or disappointed.

gutted² *past tense, past participle of* GUT

gutter /ˈɡʌtə(r)/ ▷ *noun* **1** a channel for carrying away rainwater, fixed to the edge of a roof or built between a pavement and a road. **2** *ten-pin bowling* either of the channels at the sides of a lane. **3** (**the gutter**) a state of poverty and social deprivation or of coarse and degraded living. **4** *printing* the inner margins between two facing pages. ▷ *verb* (*guttered, guttering*) **1** *intr* said of a candle: to have its melted wax, etc suddenly pour down a channel which forms on its side. **2** said of a flame: to flicker and threaten to go out. **3** to wear away channels in something. **4** *intr* to trickle. ⓒ 13c: from French *goutiere*, from *goute* drop.

guttering ▷ *noun* **1** gutters collectively. **2** material for making roof-gutters.

gutter press ▷ *noun, derog* newspapers which specialize in sensationalistic journalism that deals largely with scandal and gossip.

guttersnipe ▷ *noun, derog old use* a raggedly dressed or ill-mannered person, especially a child.

guttural /ˈɡʌtərəl/ ▷ *adj* **1** *non-technical* said of sounds: produced in the throat or the back of the mouth. Compare VELAR. **2** said of a language or style of speech: having or using such sounds; harsh-sounding. ▷ *noun, non-technical* a sound produced in the throat or the back of the mouth. ● **gutturalize** or **gutturalise** *verb* (*gutturalized, gutturalizing*). ● **gutturally** *adverb.* ⓒ 16c: from Latin *guttur* throat.

guv, **guvnor** and **guv'nor** see under GOVERNOR

GUY ▷ *abbreviation, IVR* Guyana.

guy¹ /ɡaɪ/ ▷ *noun* **1** *colloq* a man or boy. **2** *colloq, originally US* **a** a person; **b** (**guys**) used to address or refer to a group of people □ *What do you guys think?* **3** a crude model of Guy Fawkes that is burnt on a bonfire on GUY FAWKES DAY. **4** someone who is eccentrically dressed. ▷ *verb* (*guyed, guying*) to make fun of someone. ⓒ 19c: named after Guy Fawkes; see GUY FAWKES DAY.

guy² /ɡaɪ/ ▷ *noun* (*in full* **guy rope**) a rope or wire used to hold something, especially a tent, firm or steady. ▷ *verb* (*guyed, guying*) to secure something with guys. ⓒ 17c; 14c, meaning 'guide': from French *guie* guide.

Guy Fawkes Day /— fɔːks —/ ▷ *noun* 5 November, the anniversary of the discovery of the **Gunpowder Plot**, a plot to blow up Parliament in 1605 of which Guy Fawkes was the leader. It is celebrated with firework displays and the burning of an effigy of Guy Fawkes on a bonfire.

guzzle /'gʌzəl/ ▻ *verb* (***guzzled***, ***guzzling***) *tr & intr* to eat or drink greedily. • **guzzler** *noun*. ⓘ 16c as *gossel*.

gybe, **gibe** or **jibe** /dʒaɪb/ ▻ *verb* (***gybed***, ***gybing***) *tr & intr, naut* **1** said of a sail: to swing, or make it swing, over from one side of a boat to the other. **2** said of a boat: to change or make it change course in this way. ▻ *noun* an act of gybing. ⓘ 17c.

gym /dʒɪm/ ▻ *noun, colloq* **1** GYMNASTICS; **2** GYMNASIUM. ⓘ 19c colloquial abbreviation.

gymkhana /dʒɪm'kɑːnə/ ▻ *noun* (***gymkhanas***) **1** a local public event consisting of competitions in various sports, especially horse-riding. **2** *formerly* in India under British rule: **a** an athletics meeting; **b** a public place providing athletics facilities. ⓘ 19c: from Hindi *gend-khana* racket-court, remodelled on GYMNASIUM.

gymnasium ▻ *noun* **1** /dʒɪm'neɪzɪəm/ (*plural* ***gymnasiums*** or ***gymnasia*** /-zɪə/) a building or room with equipment for physical exercise. **2** /gɪm'nɑːzɪʊm/ (*plural also* ***gymnasien*** /-zɪən/) in various European countries: a top-grade secondary school which prepares pupils for university. ⓘ 16c: from Greek *gymnasion* school for physical training, and hence school in general, from *gymnazein* to exercise naked.

gymnast /'dʒɪmnast/ ▻ *noun* someone who is skilled in gymnastics. ⓘ 16c: from Greek *gymnastes* trainer of athletes.

gymnastic /dʒɪm'nastɪk/ ▻ *adj* **1** relating to gymnastics. **2** athletic; agile. • **gymnastically** *adverb*. ⓘ 16c: from Greek *gymnastikos*.

gymnastics ▻ *singular noun* physical training designed to strengthen the body and improve agility, usually using special equipment. ▻ *plural noun* **1** feats of agility. **2** difficult exercises that test or demonstrate ability of any kind □ *mental gymnastics*.

gymnosperm ▻ *noun, bot* any member of a division of plants that includes the conifers and cycads. They produce seeds that are usually borne on the surface of overlapping scale-like leaves in cones. Compare ANGIOSPERM. ⓘ 19c: from Latin *gymnospermus*, from Greek *gymnos* naked + *sperma* seed, because the seeds are not enclosed in any ovary.

gym shoe ▻ *noun* a PLIMSOLL.

gym slip ▻ *noun* a belted PINAFORE DRESS worn (*especially formerly*) by schoolgirls as part of their uniform.

gyn- see GYNO-

gynaecium or **gynoecium** /gaɪ'niːsɪəm, dzaɪ-/ ▻ *noun* (***gynaecia*** or ***gynoecia***) *bot* the female reproductive parts of a flower. ⓘ 17c: from Greek *gynaikeion* women's apartments.

gynaeco- or (*US*) **gyneco-** /gaɪnəkoʊ, -'kɒ/ ▻ *combining form, signifying* female; woman; women □ *gynaecology*. ⓘ From Greek *gyne, gynaikos* woman.

gynaecology or (*US*) **gynecology** /gaɪnə'kɒlədʒɪ/ ▻ *noun* the branch of medicine concerned with the diagnosis and treatment of diseases and disorders that affect the reproductive organs of the female body. • **gynaecological** *adj*. • **gynaecologically** *adverb*. • **gynaecologist** *noun*. ⓘ 19c: GYNAECO- + -LOGY 1.

gyno- /gaɪnoʊ, gaɪ'nɒ/ or (before a vowel) **gyn-** ▻ *combining form, denoting* **1** female; woman; women. **2** *biol* referring or relating to a female reproductive organ. ⓘ From Greek *gyne, gynaikos* woman.

-gyny /dʒɪnɪ/ ▻ *combining form, forming nouns, denoting* **1** female; woman; women □ *misogyny*. **2** *biol* referring or relating to female organs □ *androgyny*. • **-gynous** *combining form, forming adjectives*. ⓘ from Greek *gyne, gynaikos* woman.

gyp[1] /dʒɪp/ ▻ *noun* • **give someone gyp** *colloq* to cause them pain or discomfort □ *My tooth's been giving me gyp*. ⓘ 19c: possibly a contraction of GEE UP.

gyp[2] /dʒɪp/ ▻ *verb* (***gypped***, ***gypping***) to cheat or swindle someone. ▻ *noun* someone who cheats. ⓘ 19c: back-formation from GYPSY.

Gyppo /'dʒɪpoʊ/ *derog slang* ▻ *noun* (***Gyppos***) an Egyptian. ▻ *adj* Egyptian.

gyppy tummy see GIPPY TUMMY

gypsophila /dʒɪp'sɒfɪlə/ ▻ *noun, bot* an annual or perennial plant with dainty branching heads of small white, pink or crimson flowers, widely used by florists. ⓘ 18c: from Greek *gypsos* chalk + *philos* loving.

gypsum /'dʒɪpsəm/ ▻ *noun* a soft mineral composed of calcium sulphate, used to make plaster of Paris, cement, rubber and paper. ⓘ 17c: Latin, from Greek *gypsos* chalk.

Gypsy or **Gipsy** /'dʒɪpsɪ/ ▻ *noun* (***Gypsies*** or ***Gipsies***) **1** (also without capital) a member of a dark-skinned travelling people, originally from NW India, now scattered throughout Europe and N America. Also called **Romany**. **2** (without capital) someone who resembles or lives like a Gypsy. Also *as adj*. ⓘ 17c; 16c as *gipsen*: from *Egyptian*, because they were originally thought to have come from Egypt.

gyrate /dʒaɪə'reɪt/ ▻ *verb* (***gyrated***, ***gyrating***) *intr* to move with a circular or spiralling motion. ⓘ 19c: from Greek *gyros* circle.

gyration ▻ *noun* **1** a whirling motion. **2** a whirl, a twist. **3** a whorl.

gyre /dʒaɪə(r)/ ▻ *noun* **1** a vortex. **2** a rotating ocean current. ▻ *verb* (***gyred***, ***gyring***) to whirl. ⓘ 16c in literary sense 'a whirl or spiralling turn': from Latin *gyrus* circle.

gyrfalcon or **gerfalcon** /'dʒɜːfɔːkən/ ▻ *noun* the largest of all the falcons, with plumage ranging from dark greyish-brown to almost white. ⓘ 14c as *gerfauk*: from French *gerfaucon*.

gyro- /dʒaɪroʊ/ ▻ *combining form, denoting* **1** circular; spiral. **2** referring or relating to a GYROSCOPE. **3** with gyrating or rotating motion □ *gyrocompass*. ⓘ From Greek *gyros* circle.

gyrocompass ▻ *noun* a non-magnetic compass, widely used for navigation, operated by means of a spinning disc like a gyroscope powered by an electric motor. ⓘ 20c.

gyromagnetic ▻ *adj* belonging or relating to, or caused by, magnetic properties of rotating electric charges. • **gyromagnetism** *noun*.

gyroscope ▻ *noun* a device consisting of a small flywheel with a heavy rim, mounted so that once in motion it resists any changes in the direction of motion, used in ship stabilizers and in the automatic steering systems of aircraft, missiles, etc. • **gyroscopic** *adj* **1** relating to or like a gyroscope. **2** rotatory. • **gyroscopically** *adverb*. ⓘ 19c.

gyrus /'dʒaɪrəs/ ▻ *noun* (***gyri*** /-raɪ/) a convoluted fold, eg of the brain. ⓘ 19c: Latin, meaning 'a circle'.

H

H[1] /eɪtʃ/ ▷ *noun* (*Hs, H's* or *h's*) **1** the eighth letter of the English alphabet. **2** the speech sound represented by this letter, an aspirate. **3** something shaped like an H. Also *in compounds* □ *H-beam*.

H[2] ▷ *abbreviation* **1** on pencils: hard. **2** height. **3** *slang* heroin. **4** hospital. **5** *IVR* Hungary. **6** hydrant.

H[3] ▷ *symbol* **1** *chem* hydrogen. **2** *physics* magnetic field strength. **3** *electronics* henry.

h[1] ▷ *abbreviation* **1** harbour. **2** hecto-. **3** height. **4** high. **5** hour. **6** hundred. **7** husband.

h[2] ▷ *symbol, physics* Planck's constant.

Ha ▷ *symbol, chem* hahnium.

ha or **hah** /hɑː/ ▷ *exclamation* expressing surprise, happiness, triumph, etc. See also HA-HA[1].

ha ▷ *abbreviation* hectare or hectares.

haar /hɑː(r)/ ▷ *noun, Scot & NE Eng dialect* a cold mist or fog off the North Sea. ◷ 17c: from Dutch *hare* bitter cold.

Hab. ▷ *abbreviation* Book of the Bible: Habakkuk. See table at BIBLE.

habanera /haba'nɛərə/ ▷ *noun* (***habaneras***) **1** a slow Cuban dance in 2-4 time. **2** a piece of music for this dance. ◷ 19c: from Spanish *danza habanera* dance from Havana.

habdabs /'habdabz/ and **abdabs** ▷ *plural noun, colloq* (*especially* **the screaming habdabs**) a state of extreme nervousness.

habeas corpus /'heɪbɪəs 'kɔːpəs/ ▷ *noun, law* a writ requiring a prisoner to be brought into court for a judge to decide if their imprisonment is legal. ◷ 15c: Latin, meaning 'have the body (brought before the judge)'.

haberdasher /'habədaʃə(r)/ ▷ *noun* **1** *Brit* a person or shop that deals in small items used for sewing, such as ribbons, needles, buttons, etc. **2** *N Amer* a men's oufitter. ◷ 14c: from French *hapertas*.

haberdashery /'habədaʃərɪ/ ▷ *noun* (***haberdasheries***) **1** a haberdasher's shop, business or department. **2** the ribbons, etc sold by a haberdasher.

habit /'habɪt/ ▷ *noun* **1** a tendency to behave or act in a specific way. **2** a usual practice or custom. **3** a practice which is hard to give up; an addiction □ ***smoking soon becomes a habit.*** **4** mental attitude or constitution □ ***a good habit of mind.*** **5** a long loose garment worn by monks and nuns. **6** *psychol* a learned behavioural response to particular circumstances. **7** *bot, zool* characteristic type of development, growth or existence; general appearance. **8** the geometric form taken by a crystal. **9** (*especially* **riding habit**) a woman's riding dress. ▷ *verb, archaic* (***habited, habiting***) **1** to clothe. **2** to inhabit. ◷ 14c: from Latin *habitus* practice.

habitable /'habɪtəbəl/ ▷ *adj* (*also* **inhabitable**) suitable for living in. See also ● **habitability** or **habitableness** *noun*. ● **habitably** *adverb*. ◷ 14c: from Latin *habitabilis*.

habitat /'habɪtat/ ▷ *noun* **1** *biol* the natural home of an animal or plant. **2** the place where a person, group, class, etc can usually be found. ◷ 18c: Latin, meaning 'it inhabits', from *habitare* to dwell.

habitation /habɪ'teɪʃən/ ▷ *noun* **1** the act of living in a particular dwelling place. **2** a house or home. ◷ 14c: from Latin *habitatio*.

habit-forming ▷ *adj* said of a drug, activity, etc: likely to become a habit or addiction.

habitual /hə'bɪtʃʊəl/ ▷ *adj* **1** seen, done, etc regularly and repeatedly □ ***the habitual evening stroll.*** **2** done, or doing something, by habit □ ***The English are habitual tea-drinkers.*** **3** customary; usual. ● **habitually** *adverb*. ● **habitualness** *noun*. ◷ 16c: from Latin *habitualis*.

habituate /hə'bɪtʃʊeɪt/ ▷ *verb* (***habituated, habituating***) **1** (*usually* **habituate someone to something**) to make them accustomed or used to it. **2** *N Amer archaic* to frequent. ● **habituation** *noun*. ◷ 16c: from Latin *habituare*.

habitué /hə'bɪtʃʊeɪ/ ▷ *noun* a regular or frequent visitor to a place, eg a restaurant. ◷ 19c: from French *habituer* to frequent.

háček /'hatʃɛk/ ▷ *noun* a diacritic (ˇ) placed over a consonant in some Slavonic languages, eg Czech, to modify the sound, eg (č) pronounced /tʃ/.

hachure /ha'ʃʊə(r)/ ▷ *noun* **1** (**hachures**) a system of parallel lines on a map to show the contours of hills, in which the closeness of the lines indicates steepness. **2** any of these lines. ▷ *verb* to shade with hachures. ◷ 19c: from French *hacher* to chop up.

hacienda /hasɪ'ɛndə/ ▷ *noun* in Spain and Spanish-speaking countries: **1** a ranch or large estate with a main dwelling-house on it. **2** this house. **3** any important manufacturing establishment. ◷ 18c: Spanish.

hack[1] ▷ *verb* (***hacked, hacking***) **1** (*often* **hack something down, away**, *etc*) to cut or chop it roughly. **2** (*often* **hack something out**) to cut (a path, etc) eg through undergrowth. **3** *intr, colloq* (*often* **hack into something**) to use a computer with skill, especially to obtain unauthorized access to (someone else's computer files). **4** *with negatives and in questions, slang* to be able to bear or suffer someone or something □ ***He can't hack it.*** **5** *intr* to cough in short dry spasms. **6** *football, rugby* to kick an opponent on the shins. **7** to cut (a story, article, etc) in a damaging way. ▷ *noun* **1** a kick on the shins. **2** a wound or rough cut, especially from a kick. **3** a MATTOCK or miner's PICK[2]. **4** a short dry cough. **5** a chop or blow. ◷ Anglo-Saxon *tohaccian*; 1970s in *verb* sense 3.

hack[2] ▷ *noun* **1** a horse kept for general riding, especially one for hire. **2** a ride on horseback. **3** an old or worn-out horse. **4** a writer who produces dull, mediocre or routine work. **5** a DOGSBODY. **6** *US informal* **a** a taxi; **b** a cab driver. ▷ *verb* (***hacked, hacking***) **1** *tr & intr* to ride a horse at a leisurely pace, usually for pleasure. **2** to write (an article, etc) in a mediocre or tedious manner. **3** *intr* to work as a hack. ▷ *adj* mediocre, banal or commonplace □ ***hack writer.*** ◷ 17c: short form of HACKNEY.

hackamore /'hakəmɔː(r)/ ▷ *noun* **1** a halter used in breaking in foals. **2** a bridle without a bit, which exerts pressure on the horse's muzzle rather than its mouth. ◷ 19c: from Spanish *jáquima* headstall.

hackberry see under HAGBERRY

hacker /'hakə(r)/ ▷ *noun* **1** someone or something that hacks. **2** *colloq* someone skilled in using computers, particularly in programming them. ◷ 17c; 1970s in sense 2.

hackery /'hakərɪ/ ▷ *noun* **1** an ox-drawn cart used in India for transporting goods. **2** *ironic* poor journalism or HACKWORK. **3** HACKING[2].

hackette ▷ *noun, derog slang* a woman journalist. ◷ 20c: from HACK[2] *noun* 4.

hacking[1] ▻ *adj* said of a cough: rough and dry.

hacking[2] ▻ *noun, colloq* the act or practice of gaining unauthorized access to computer files.

hacking[3] ▻ *noun* the sport of riding on horseback for pleasure.

hacking jacket ▻ *noun* a tweed jacket with slits at the sides, worn when hacking (see HACK[2]).

hackle /'hakəl/ ▻ *noun* **1** any of the long shining feathers on the neck of certain birds, eg cocks. **2** one of these worn in a cap, eg in the headdress of some Highland regiments. **3** *angling* an artificial fly made from hackle feathers. **4** a comb for FLAX (sense 2) or HEMP. ▻ *verb* (***hackled, hackling***) to comb flax or hemp with a hackle. • **hackly** *adj* rough, broken or jagged. • **hackler** *noun*. ⓘ 15c.

hackles ▻ *plural noun* the hairs or feathers on the back of the neck of some animals and birds, which are raised when they are angry. • **make someone's hackles rise** to make them very angry. ⓘ 15c.

hackney /'haknı/ ▻ *noun* **1** a HACK[2]. **2** a horse with a high-stepping trot, bred to draw light carriages. **3** a vehicle that is for hire. ⓘ 14c: named after Hackney, a borough in East London, where horses were formerly pastured.

hackney cab and **hackney carriage** ▻ *noun* **1** *historical* a horse-drawn carriage for public hire. **2** *formal* a taxi.

hackneyed /'haknıd/ ▻ *adj* **1** said of a word, phrase, etc: meaningless and trite through too much use. **2** used too frequently; commonplace or banal. ⓘ 18c.

hacksaw ▻ *noun* a saw for cutting metals.

hackwork ▻ *noun* poor quality literary work produced to order. ⓘ 19c.

had *past tense, past participle of* HAVE

haddock /'hadək/ ▻ *noun* (***haddock*** or ***haddocks***) a commercially important N Atlantic sea-fish similar to but smaller than the cod. ⓘ 14c.

hade /heıd/ *geol* ▻ *noun* the angle between the plane of a fault, etc and a vertical plane. ▻ *verb* (***haded, hading***) *intr* to incline from the vertical. ⓘ 17c.

Hades /'heıdiːz/ ▻ *noun, Greek mythol* **1** the underworld, where the souls of the dead live. **2** Pluto, the god of the underworld. **3** (*often* **hades**) hell. ⓘ 16c: from Greek *Haides*.

Hadith /'hadıθ, hɑː'diːθ/ ▻ *noun* the body of traditions about Mohammed which form a supplement to the Koran. ⓘ 19c: Arabic.

hadj see HAJJ

hadji see HAJJI

hadn't /'hadənt/ ▻ *contraction* had not.

hadron /'hadrɒn/ ▻ *noun, physics* one of a class of subatomic particles, comprising BARYONs and MESONs, that interact strongly with other subatomic particles. • **hadronic** *adj*. ⓘ 1960s: from Greek *hadros* heavy + -ON.

hadst /'hadst/ ▻ *verb, archaic* the form of the past tense of the verb HAVE used with the pronoun THOU 1.

haem or (*US*) **heme** /hiːm/ ▻ *noun, biochem* the iron compound which combines with the protein GLOBIN to form the respiratory pigment HAEMOGLOBIN, and which gives the red blood cells their colour. ⓘ 1920s: from Greek *haima* blood.

haem- and **haema-** see HAEMO-

haemal or **hemal** /'hiːməl/ ▻ *adj, medicine* **1** relating to the blood or blood-vessels. **2** *old use* denoting or situated towards the region of the body which contains the heart. ⓘ 19c.

haemat- see HAEMATO-

haematemisis or (*US*) **hematemisis** /hiːmə'tɛmısıs/ ▻ *noun, medicine* vomiting blood from the stomach, especially because of a bleeding ulcer. ⓘ 19c: from HAEMATO- + Greek *emisis* vomiting.

haematic or (*US*) **hematic** /hiː'matık/ ▻ *adj, medicine* **1** referring or relating to blood. **2** containing or having the colour of blood. ⓘ 19c.

haematin or (*US*) **hematin** /'hiːmətın, hɛ-/ ▻ *noun, medicine* a bluish or brownish derivative of HAEMOGLOBIN after removal of the protein and oxidation of the HAEM. ⓘ 19c.

haematite or **hematite** /'hiːmətaıt, 'hɛ-/ ▻ *noun, geol* a dense and relatively hard mineral containing ferric oxide, the most important ore of iron, used as a pigment (red ochre) and as a polishing agent. ⓘ 17c; 16c as *ematites*.

haemato- or (*US*) **hemato-** /hiːmətoʊ, hɛ-'tɒ/ or (before a vowel) **haemat-** or (*US*) **hemat-** ▻ *combining form, medicine, denoting* blood □ ***haematology***. ⓘ 19c: from Greek *haima* blood.

haematocrit or (*US*) **hematocrit** /'hiːmətoʊkrıt, 'hɛ-/ ▻ *noun, medicine* **1** a centrifuge for determining the ratio of the volume occupied by blood cells, especially ERYTHROCYTEs, to the total volume of blood. **2** this ratio expressed as a percentage. ⓘ 20c: HAEMATO- + Greek *krites* judge.

haematology or (*US*) **hematology** /hiːmə'tɒlədʒı/ ▻ *noun, medicine* the branch of medicine concerned with the diagnosis and treatment of diseases of the blood, and of the tissues in which the blood cells are formed. • **haematologic** /-tə'lɒdʒık/ or **haematological** *adj*. • **haematologist** *noun*. ⓘ 19c.

haematolysis see HAEMOLYSIS

haematoma or **hematoma** /hiːmə'toʊmə, hɛ-/ (***haematomas*** or ***haematomata*** /-mətə/) *noun, medicine* a swelling resulting from bleeding into tissues. ⓘ 19c: HAEMAT- + -OMA.

haematuria or **hematuria** /hiːmə'tjʊərıə, hɛ-/ ▻ *noun, medicine* the presence of blood in the urine. ⓘ 19c: HAEMAT- + -URIA.

-haemia see -AEMIA

haemic /'hiːmık/ ▻ *adj, medicine* haematic.

haemo-, (*US*) **hemo-** /hiːmoʊ, hɛmoʊ, hı'mɒ/ or **haema-**, (*US*) **hema-** or (before a vowel) **haem-**, (*US*) **hem-** ▻ *combining form, medicine, denoting* blood. ⓘ From Greek *haima* blood.

haemocyanin or (*US*) **hemocyanin** /hiːmoʊ'saıənın/ ▻ *noun, biol* a blue pigment in the circulatory fluid of crustaceans and molluscs that transports oxygen and carbon dioxide.

haemocyte or (*US*) **hemocyte** /'hiːmoʊsaıt, 'hɛ-/ ▻ *noun, medicine, rare* a blood cell, especially an ERYTHROCYTE. ⓘ 19c.

haemocytometer or (*US*) **hemocytometer** /hiːmoʊsaı'tɒmıtə(r)/ ▻ *noun, medicine* a device for counting the number of cells in a volume of blood.

haemodialysis or (*US*) **hemodialysis** ▻ *noun* (***haemodialyses*** /-siːz/) *medicine* DIALYSIS (sense 2).

haemoglobin or **hemoglobin** /hiːmə'gloʊbın/ ▻ *noun, biochem* the pigment in red blood cells that carries oxygen round the body and gives these cells their characteristic colour. ⓘ 19c.

haemolysis or (*US*) **hemolysis** /hı'mɒlısıs/ and **haematolysis** or (*US*) **hematolysis** /hiːmə'tɒlısıs/ ▻ *noun* (***haemolyses*** /-siːz/ or ***haematolyses*** /-siːz/) *medicine* the abnormal disintegration of the red blood cells accompanied by the release of HAEMOGLOBIN. • **haemolytic** /hiːmoʊ'lıtık/ *adj*.

haemophilia or (*US*) **hemophilia** /hiːmə'fılıə/ ▻ *noun, medicine* a hereditary disease, usually only affecting males, in which the normal clotting ability of blood is lost or impaired due to a deficiency of factor 8. • **haemophiliac** *noun, adj*. • **haemophilic** *noun, adj*. ⓘ 19c.

haemoptysis or (*US*) **hemoptysis** /hɪˈmɒptɪsɪs/ ▻ *noun* (***haemoptyses*** /-siːz/) *medicine* spitting or coughing up of blood, especially from the lungs, as in tuberculosis. ◷ 17c: from HAEMO- + Greek *ptysis* spitting, from *ptyein* to spit.

haemorrhage or **hemorrhage** /ˈhɛmərɪdʒ/ ▻ *noun* **1** *medicine* the escape of profuse amounts of blood, especially from a ruptured blood vessel. **2** persistent or severe loss or depletion of resources, staff, etc. ▻ *verb* (***haemorrhaged***, ***haemorrhaging***) *intr* to lose copious amounts of blood. ◷ 17c: from HAEMO- + Greek *rhegnynai* to burst.

haemorrhoids or (*US*) **hemorrhoids** /ˈhɛmərɔɪdz/ ▻ *plural noun, medicine* swollen veins in the anus. Also called PILES. • **haemorrhoidal** *adj*. ◷ 14c: from HAEMO- + Greek *rheein* to flow.

haemostasis or (*US*) **hemostasis** /hiːmoʊˈsteɪsɪs, hɛˈ-/ ▻ *noun, medicine* the stoppage of the flow of blood, in a pathological condition or as in a surgical operation. • **haemostatic** *adj*. ◷ 18c.

haemostat or (*US*) **hemostat** /ˈhiːmoʊstat, hɛˈ-/ ▻ *noun, medicine* a chemical substance or surgical device that stops bleeding.

haeremai /ˈhaɪrəmaɪ/ *NZ* ▻ *exclamation* welcome! ▻ *noun* the act of saying ‘haeremai!’. ◷ 18c: Maori, literally ‘come hither’.

hafiz /ˈhɑːfɪz/ ▻ *noun, Islam* **1** someone who knows the Koran by heart. **2** the guardian of a mosque. ◷ 17c: from Arabic *hafiza* to guard.

hafnium /ˈhafnɪəm/ ▻ *noun, chem* (symbol **Hf**, atomic number 72) a metallic element found mainly in zirconium minerals and used in electrodes. ◷ 1920s: from Latin *Hafnia* Copenhagen, where it was discovered.

haft /hɑːft/ ▻ *noun* a handle of a knife, sword, axe, etc. ▻ *verb* (***hafted***, ***hafting***) to fit with a haft. ◷ Anglo-Saxon *hæft*.

hag[1] ▻ *noun* **1** *offensive* an ugly old woman. **2** a witch. **3** short form of HAGFISH. • **haggish** *adj* old and ugly like a hag. • **haggishly** *adverb*. ◷ Anglo-Saxon *hægtes*.

hag[2] ▻ *noun, Scottish & N Eng dialect* **1** an area of firm ground in a bog. **2** a piece of soft bog in a moor. ◷ 13c: from Norse *högg*.

Hag. ▻ *abbreviation* Book of the Bible: Haggai. See table at BIBLE.

hagberry ▻ *noun* **1** an American tree related to the elm. **2** its purple edible fruit. Also called **hackberry**. ◷ 16c: from Norse *heggr* bird-cherry.

hagfish ▻ *noun* an eel-like marine vertebrate related to the lamprey, which feeds on the tissues of other animals and on dead organic material. ◷ 17c.

Haggadah or **Haggadoh** /həˈgɑːdə/ ▻ *noun* (***Haggadahs*** or ***Haggadas*** or ***Haggadoth*** /hagəˈdoʊt/) *Judaism* **1** the book which contains the text recited at the SEDER on the first two nights of the Passover. **2** the narrative of the Exodus from Egypt which constitutes the main part of the Passover service. • **Haggadic** *adj*. ◷ 18c: from Hebrew *hagged* to tell.

haggard /ˈhagəd/ ▻ *adj* **1** looking very tired and thin-faced, because of pain, worry, etc. **2** wild or intractable. **3** said of a hawk: untamed, having matured in the wild before being caught. ▻ *noun, falconry* an untamed hawk, or one caught when adult, especially a female. • **haggardly** *adverb*. • **haggardness** *noun*. ◷ 16c: from French *hagard* wild.

haggis /ˈhagɪs/ ▻ *noun* a Scottish dish made from sheep's or calf's offal mixed with suet, oatmeal and seasonings and then boiled in a bag traditionally made from the animal's stomach. ◷ 16c: Scots.

haggish and **haggishly** see under HAG[1]

haggle /ˈhagəl/ ▻ *verb* (***haggled***, ***haggling***) *intr* (*often* **haggle over** or **about something**) to bargain over or argue about (a price, etc). • **haggler** *noun*. ◷ 16c: from Norse *heggra* to hew.

hagio- /hagɪə, hagɪˈɒ/ or (before a vowel) **hagi-** ▻ *combining form, signifying* a saint; saints; holiness. ◷ 18c: from Greek *hagios* holy.

Hagiographa /hagɪˈɒgrəfə/ ▻ *plural noun* the third of the three main books which, together with the LAW OF MOSES and the PROPHETS, comprise the Old Testament in Jewish tradition. ◷ 16c: from Greek *hagios* holy + *-grapha* writings.

hagiographer /hagɪˈɒgrəfə(r)/ and **hagiographist** ▻ *noun* **1** someone who writes hagiography. **2** one of the writers of the Hagiographa.

hagiography /hagɪˈɒgrəfɪ/ ▻ *noun* (***hagiographies***) **1** the writing of the stories of saints' lives. **2** a biography that idealizes or overpraises its subject. • **hagiographic** or **hagiographical** *adj*. ◷ 19c; 16c as *hagiographical*.

hagiolatry /hagɪˈɒlətrɪ/ ▻ *noun* worship or reverence of saints. ◷ 19c.

hagiology /hagɪˈɒlədʒɪ/ ▻ *noun* (***hagiologies***) literature about the lives and legends of saints. • **hagiological** or **hagiologic** *adj*. • **hagiologist** *noun*. ◷ 19c.

hag-ridden ▻ *adj* tormented; mentally oppressed. ◷ 17c: ie as if possessed by a witch.

hah see HA

ha-ha[1] /hɑːˈhɑː/ or **haw-haw** /hɔːˈhɔː/ ▻ *exclamation* **1** a conventional way of representing the sound of laughter. **2** expressing triumph, mockery, scorn, etc.

ha-ha[2] /ˈhɑːhɑː/ or **haw-haw** /ˈhɔːhɔː/ ▻ *noun* a wall or a fence separating areas of land in a large garden or park, but placed in a ditch so as not to interrupt the view. ◷ 18c: French, possibly from the supposed cry made when discovering one.

hahnium /ˈhɑːnɪəm/ ▻ *noun, chem* (symbol **Ha**) a name proposed for the radioactive elements of atomic number 105 (see UNNILPENTIUM) and 108 (see UNNILOCTIUM). ◷ 1970s: named after the German physicist Otto Hahn (1879–1968).

haik /haɪk/ ▻ *noun* an oblong cloth which Arabs wrap round the head and body as an outer garment. ◷ 17c: from Arabic *hayk*.

haiku /ˈhaɪkuː/ and **hokku** /ˈhɒkuː/ ▻ *noun* (*plural* ***haiku*** or ***hokku***) **1** a Japanese poem which consists of three lines of five, seven and five syllables, is usually comical or epigrammatic, and often incorporates a word or phrase that symbolizes one of the seasons. **2** an English imitation of this, such as *Letters fluttering, over a garden of verbs, dictionary my spring*. ◷ 19c: Japanese, from *hai* amusement + *ku* verse.

hail[1] /heɪl/ ▻ *noun* **1** grains of ice which fall from the clouds when there are strong rising air currents. **2** a large quantity (of words, questions, missiles, etc) directed at someone or something with force □ ***a hail of criticism***. ▻ *verb* (***hailed***, ***hailing***) **1** *intr* said of hail: to fall from the clouds □ ***It's hailing***. **2** *tr & intr* to shower someone or something with words, questions, missiles, etc or come down on them or it in great numbers. ◷ Anglo-Saxon *hagol*.

hail[2] /heɪl/ ▻ *verb* **1** to attract attention by shouting or making gestures, eg to signal (especially a taxi) to stop. **2** to greet someone, especially enthusiatically. **3** to recognize or describe someone as being or representing something □ ***He was hailed a hero***. ▻ *exclamation, old use* an expression of greeting. ▻ *noun* the act or an instance of hailing. • **within hail** or **within hailing distance** close enough to hear when called to. ◷ 13c: from Norse *heill* healthy.

■ **hail from somewhere** to come from or belong to (a place) □ ***he hails from Manchester***.

hail-fellow-well-met ▻ *adj* friendly and familiar, especially in an overpowering or offensive way.

hail Mary ▷ *noun* (***hail Marys***) **1** a prayer to the Virgin Mary, the English version of the Ave Maria (see AVE[2]). **2** *Amer football slang* a long high pass into the end area, made in the final seconds of a game or of the first half.

hailstone ▷ *noun* a single grain of hail.

hailstorm ▷ *noun* a storm during which hail falls heavily.

hair /hɛə(r)/ ▷ *noun* **1** each of many long thread-like structures that grow from follicles beneath the skin of animals. **2** a mass or growth of such strands, especially on a person's head. **3** a fabric made from such strands. **4** *bot* any thread-like cell growing from the surface of a plant. **5** a hair's-breadth □ ***she won by a hair.*** **6** a locking spring or other safety mechanism on a firearm. • **hairless** *adj.* • **hairlessness** *noun.* • **hairlike** *adj.* • **hairy** see separate entry. • **get in someone's hair** *colloq* to annoy them incessantly. • **a hair of the dog (that bit one)** *colloq* an alcoholic drink taken as a cure for a hangover. • **by the short hairs** in a powerless situation or at someone's mercy. • **keep your hair on!** *colloq* keep calm and don't get angry. • **let one's hair down** *colloq* to enjoy oneself or behave without restraint. • **make someone's hair curl** *colloq* to shock them. • **make someone's hair stand on end** *colloq* to frighten them. • **not turn a hair** to remain calm and show no surprise, anger, etc. • **split hairs** to make unnecessary petty distinctions or quibbles. • **tear one's hair out** to show extreme irritation or anxiety. • **to a hair** exactly. ⓒ Anglo-Saxon *hær.*

hair-brained see HARE-BRAINED

hairbrush ▷ *noun* a brush for smoothing and arranging one's hair.

haircare ▷ *noun* the care of the hair. Also *as adj* □ ***haircare products.***

haircloth ▷ *noun* a coarse cloth made from woven horsehair, used (*especially formerly*) in upholstery.

haircut ▷ *noun* **1** the cutting of someone's hair. **2** the shape or style in which it is cut.

hairdo ▷ *noun* (***hairdos***) *colloq* a woman's haircut, especially after styling and setting.

hairdresser ▷ *noun* **1** a person whose job is washing, cutting, styling, etc hair. **2** the shop where this takes place. • **hairdressing** *noun.*

hairdryer or **hairdrier** ▷ *noun* a piece of electrical equipment which dries hair by blowing hot air over it.

haired ▷ *adj, in compounds* having a specified kind of hair □ ***a white-haired rabbit.***

hair gel see GEL

hairgrip ▷ *noun, chiefly Brit* a small wire clasp for holding the hair in place. *N Amer, Austral & NZ equivalent* BOBBY PIN.

hairier see under HAIRY

hairline ▷ *noun* **1** the line along the forehead where the hair begins to grow. **2 a** a very fine line; **b** *as adj* said of a crack, etc: very thin.

hairnet ▷ *noun* any kind of netting, usually worn by women, to keep the hair in place.

hairpiece ▷ *noun* **1** a wig or piece of false hair worn over a bald area on the head. **2** an arrangement of hair that a woman attaches to her own hair to add length or volume to it.

hairpin ▷ *noun* a thin flat U-shaped piece of wire for keeping the hair in place.

hairpin bend ▷ *noun* a sharp and often U-shaped bend, especially on a mountain road.

hair-raising ▷ *adj* extremely frightening or disturbing.

hair restorer ▷ *noun* a product which is claimed to make hair grow on bald places.

hair's-breadth ▷ *noun* a very small distance or margin. Also *as adj* □ ***a hair's-breadth victory.***

hair shirt ▷ *noun* **1** a shirt made of HAIRCLOTH worn by religious people as a penance. **2** a secret worry or affliction.

hair-slide ▷ *noun* a small metal or plastic clip, used to keep the hair in place.

hair-splitting ▷ *noun* an insistance of petty distinctions. ▷ *adj* based on or preoccupied with petty distinctions. • **hair-splitter** *noun.*

hairspray ▷ *noun* lacquer sprayed from a can or bottle onto the hair to hold it in place.

hairspring ▷ *noun* a very small spiral spring which regulates a watch in conjunction with the BALANCE WHEEL.

hairstreak ▷ *noun* a small butterfly whose wings have narrow white streaks on the underside.

hairstyle ▷ *noun* the way in which someone's hair is cut or shaped. • **hair-stylist** *noun.*

hair trigger ▷ *noun* **1** a device in a firearm that responds to very light pressure and releases the HAIR 6. **2** *informal* any apparatus, reaction, etc, set in operation by the slightest stimulus. Also *as adj* □ ***hair-trigger reaction.***

hairy /ˈhɛərɪ/ ▷ *adj* (***hairier, hairiest***) **1** covered in hair. **2** *colloq* **a** dangerous, frightening or exciting; **b** difficult or tricky. • **hairiness** *noun.*

Haitian /ˈheɪʃən, hɑːˈiːʃən/ ▷ *noun* **1** a native or inhabitant of Haiti, a republic situated in the W part of the island of Hispaniola in the Caribbean Sea. **2** the creolized form of French spoken in Haiti. ▷ *adj* belonging or relating to Haiti, its inhabitants, or the creolized form of French they speak.

hajj or **hadj** /hɑːdʒ, hadʒ/ ▷ *noun* (***hajjes*** or ***hadjes***) the pilgrimage to Mecca that every Muslim is supposed to make at least once in their lifetime. ⓒ 17c: from Arabic *hajj* pilgrimage.

hajji or **haji** or **hadji** /ˈhɑːdʒɪ, ˈhadʒɪ/ ▷ *noun* (***hajjis*** or ***hajis*** or ***hadjis***) **1** a Muslim who has been on pilgrimage to Mecca. **2** a Christian who has visited Jerusalem.

haka /ˈhɑːkɑː/ ▷ *noun, NZ* **1** a Maori war-dance accompanied by chanting. **2** a similar ceremony performed by the All-Blacks before a rugby match, etc. ⓒ 19c: Maori.

hake /heɪk/ ▷ *noun* (***hake*** or ***hakes***) **1** a sea-fish that resembles cod, used for food. **2** a similar fish found on the coast of N America. ⓒ 15c: from Norse *haki* hook.

hakeem or **hakim** /hɑːˈkiːm/ ▷ *noun* **1** a Muslim physician. **2** a Muslim judge, governor or official. ⓒ 16c: Arabic *hakim.*

Halakah or **Halacha** /hɑːˈlɑːkɑː/ ▷ *noun, Judaism* the complete body of Jewish religious law as contrasted with the HAGGADAH. • **Halakic** /həˈlakɪk/ *adj.* ⓒ 19c: Hebrew, from *halak* to walk.

halal /ˈhalal, hɑːˈlɑːl/ ▷ *noun* meat from an animal which has been killed according to Muslim holy law. Also *as adj* □ ***halal butcher.*** ▷ *verb* (***halalled, halalling***) to slaughter (an animal) according to Muslim holy law. ⓒ 19c: from Arabic *halal* lawful.

halation /həˈleɪʃən/ ▷ *noun* blurring in a photograph, usually seen as a bright ring surrounding a source of light. ⓒ 19c: from HALO.

halberd /ˈhalbəd/ and **halbert** /ˈhalbət/ ▷ *noun, historical* a long spear with an axe-blade and a pick at one end. • **halberdier** /halbəˈdɪə(r)/ *noun.* ⓒ 15c: from German *helm* handle + *barde* hatchet.

halcyon /ˈhalsɪən/ ▷ *adj* peaceful, calm and happy □ ***halcyon days.*** ▷ *noun, Greek mythol* a bird which charmed the sea at the time of the winter solstice, usually identified with the KINGFISHER. ⓒ 14c: from Greek *halkyon* kingfisher.

hale /heɪl/ ▷ *adj* (*especially* **hale and hearty**) strong and healthy. • **haleness** *noun.* ⓒ Anglo-Saxon *hál* whole.

half /hɑːf/ ▻ *noun* (***halves*** /hɑːvz/) **1 a** one of two equal parts which together form a whole; **b** a quantity which equals such a part □ *half a bar of chocolate.* **2** the FRACTION equal to one divided by two (usually written 1/2). **3** *colloq* a half pint, especially of beer. **4** *Scottish* a measure of spirits, especially whisky. **5** one of two equal periods of play in a match. **6** *football, hockey, etc* the half of the pitch considered to belong to one team. **7** *golf* an equal score with an opponent. **8** a HALF-HOUR. **9** *sport* a HALFBACK. **10** a half-price ticket, especially for a child. ▻ *adj* **1** forming or equal to half of something □ *a half chicken.* **2** not perfect or complete □ *We don't want any half measures.* ▻ *adverb* **1** to the extent or amount of one half □ *half finished.* **2** almost; partly; to some extent □ *half dead with exhaustion.* **3** thirty minutes past the hour stated □ *half three.* • **a ... and a half** *colloq* a very good ... □ *She's a singer and a half.* • **by half** *colloq* excessively □ *He's too clever by half.* • **by halves** without being thorough □ *They never do things by halves.* • **go halves** or **go halves on something** to share the cost or expenses of something □ *let's go halves on a pizza.* • **have half a mind to do something** to have a strong desire to do it. • **how the other half lives** *facetious* other people's way of life, especially if they are richer or poorer. • **not half** *colloq* **1** very □ *It isn't half cold.* **2** not nearly □ *I'm not half fit enough.* **3** yes, indeed. • **one's other** or **better half** *colloq* one's husband, wife or partner. ◷ Anglo-Saxon *healf.*

half- ▻ *prefix* **1** one of two equal parts □ *half-day.* **2** having only one parent in common □ *half-sister.* **3** partly; not completely or thoroughly □ *a half-baked idea.*

half-and-half ▻ *adverb, adj* in equal parts; in part one thing, in part another. ▻ *noun* **1** a mixture of two things in equal proportion. **2** a drink that consists of equal parts of two different alcohols, traditionally beer or stout and ale.

halfback ▻ *noun* **1** *football, hockey, etc* a player or position immediately behind the forwards and in front of the fullbacks. **2** *rugby* either the STAND-OFF HALF (see STAND-OFF 2) or the SCRUM HALF.

half-baked ▻ *adj* **1** *colloq* said of an idea, scheme, etc: **a** not properly or completely thought out; **b** unrealistic or foolish. **2** not properly baked.

halfbeak ▻ *noun* a marine and freshwater fish with a spearlike lower jaw.

half-binding ▻ *noun* a type of bookbinding in which the spine is bound in a different material from the sides.

half-blood ▻ *noun* **1** the relationship between individuals who have only one parent in common. **2** same as HALF-BREED. • **half-blooded** *adj.*

half-board ▻ *noun, Brit* the provision of bed, breakfast and one other meal in a hotel or boarding house. Also called **demi-pension**.

half-boot ▻ *noun* a boot that reaches to the mid-calf.

half-breed ▻ *noun, often offensive* someone with parents of different races, especially one a White person and the other a Native American.

half-brother ▻ *noun* a brother with whom one has only one parent in common.

half-butt ▻ *noun, snooker* a cue that is longer than an ordinary one, but shorter than a long butt.

half-caste ▻ *noun, often offensive* a person who has parents of different races, especially an Indian mother and a European father.

half-cock ▻ *noun* the position of a firearm's HAMMER when it cocks the trigger and therefore cannot reach the PRIMER² (sense 3) to fire the weapon. • **to go off half-cocked** or **at half-cock** to fail due to insufficient preparation or premature starting.

half-crown and **half-a-crown** ▻ *noun* a former British coin worth two shillings and sixpence (12½p), since 1970 no longer legal tender.

half-cut ▻ *adj, slang* drunk.

half-day ▻ *noun* a day on which someone only works, etc in the morning or in the afternoon.

half-dozen ▻ *noun* six, or roughly six.

half-hardy ▻ *adj* said of a cultivated plant: able to grow outdoors except during severe winter weather.

half-hearted ▻ *adj* not eager; without enthusiasm. • **half-heartedly** *adverb.* • **half-heartedness** *noun.*

half-hitch ▻ *noun* a simple knot or noose formed by passing the end of a piece of rope around the rope and through the loop made in the process.

half-hour ▻ *noun* **1** a period of thirty minutes. Also *as adj* □ *a half-hour lesson.* **2** the moment that is thirty minutes after the start of an hour □ *Buses run on the hour and on the half-hour.*

half-hourly ▻ *adj, adverb* done, occurring, etc every half-hour.

half-hunter ▻ *noun* a watch with a metal case in which a small circular opening or glass allows the time to be read. Compare HUNTER 4.

half-inch ▻ *noun* a unit of length equal to half an inch. ▻ *verb, rhyming slang* to pinch or steal.

half-landing ▻ *noun* a small landing at the bend of a staircase.

half-life ▻ *noun, physics* the period of time required for half the original number of atoms of a radioactive substance to undergo spontaneous radioactive decay.

half-light ▻ *noun* dull light, especially at dawn or dusk.

half-marathon ▻ *noun* a foot-race half the length of a marathon, usually 21.243km (13ml 352yd).

half mast ▻ *noun* the lower-than-normal position at which a flag flies as a sign of mourning.

half measures ▻ *plural noun* actions or means which are not sufficient or thorough enough to deal with a problem.

half-moon ▻ *noun* **1** the Moon when only half of it can be seen from the Earth. **2** the time when this occurs. **3** anything shaped like a half-moon. **4** *non-technical* the LUNULA.

half nelson ▻ *noun, wrestling* a hold in which a wrestler puts an arm under one of their opponent's arms from behind, and pushes on the back of their neck. Compare NELSON.

half-note ▻ *noun, N Amer* a MINIM 1.

halfpenny or **ha'penny** /ˈheɪpnɪ/ (***halfpennies*** or ***halfpence***) *noun* **1** *formerly* a small British coin worth half a new penny, withdrawn from circulation in 1985. **2** *historical* an old British coin worth half an old penny. ▻ *adj* **1** valued at a halfpenny □ *a halfpenny loaf.* **2** referring to something of negligible value □ *a halfpenny matter.*

halfpennyworth or **ha'pennyworth** or **hap'orth** /ˈheɪpəθ/ ▻ *noun, Brit* **1** *historical* an amount of something costing a halfpenny. **2** *colloq* a very small amount □ *not make a hap'orth of difference.*

half-pie ▻ *adj, NZ slang* **1** badly planned or thought out □ *half-pie tactics.* **2** imperfect; mediocre □ *a half-pie officer.* ◷ 1920s: from Maori *pai* good.

half-pint ▻ *noun, slang* a small or nondescript person.

half-plate and **half-print** ▻ *noun, photog* a size of plate measuring 16.5cm by 10.8cm.

half-price ▻ *adj, adverb* at half the usual price.

half-seas-over ▻ *adj, dated Brit colloq* drunk. ◷ 18c.

half-section ▻ *noun, engineering* a scale drawing of a cross-section of a symmetrical object that shows only half the object.

half-sister ▻ *noun* a sister with whom one only has one parent in common.

half-size ▻ *noun* any size in clothes, shoes, etc that is halfway between two full sizes.

half-sole ▻ *noun* the part of the sole of a shoe from the instep to the toe.

half-step ▻ *noun, N Amer* a SEMITONE.

half-term ▻ *noun, Brit education* a short holiday halfway through an academic term.

half-timbered and **half-timber** ▻ *adj* said of a building, especially one in Tudor style: having a visible timber framework filled with brick, stone or plaster. • **half-timbering** *noun*.

half-time ▻ *noun, sport* an interval between the two halves of a match. Also *as adj* □ *the half-time whistle.*

half-title ▻ *noun* **1** a short title on the right-hand page of a book which precedes the title page. **2** a title on a page of a book which precedes a section of the book.

half-tone ▻ *noun* **1** a photographic process in which tones are broken up by a fine screen into dots of different sizes to produce varying shades. **2** the illustration obtained. **3** *N Amer* a SEMITONE.

half-track ▻ *noun* a vehicle, usually a military one, with wheels in front and caterpillar tracks behind.

half-truth ▻ *noun* a statement which is only partly true and is intended to mislead.

half volley ▻ *noun, sport* a stroke in which the ball is hit immediately after it bounces or as it bounces.

halfway ▻ *adj* ▻ *adverb* **1** at, to or referring to a point equally far from two others □ *halfway between France and England.* **2** in an incomplete manner. • **meet someone halfway** to come to a compromise with them.

halfway house ▻ *noun* **1** *historical* a place, often an inn, where one can take a rest during a journey. **2** *colloq* something which is between two extremes, and which has some features of each. **3** a home where former prisoners or mental patients stay temporarily so that they may readjust to life outside the prison or hospital.

halfwit ▻ *noun* a foolish or stupid person. • **halfwitted** *adj*. • **halfwittedly** *adverb*.

half-yearly ▻ *adj, adverb* done, occurring, etc every six months. ▻

halibut /'halɪbət/ ▻ *noun* (***halibut*** or ***halibuts***) either of two species of very large commercially important flatfish found in the N Atlantic and N Pacific. ⓒ 15c: Anglo Saxon *halybutte*, from *haly* holy + *butt* flatfish, so called because it was eaten on holy days.

halide /'heɪlaɪd/ ▻ *noun, chem* a binary compound (eg sodium chloride) formed by a HALOGEN and a metal or radical. ⓒ 19c: from Greek *hals* salt.

halite /'halaɪt/ ▻ *noun* a mineral which consists of sodium chloride in cubic crystalline form and occurs in sedimentary beds and dried salt lakes, a major source of table salt. Also called ROCK SALT. ⓒ 19c: from Greek *hals* salt.

halitosis /halɪ'toʊsɪs/ ▻ *noun* unpleasant-smelling breath. ⓒ 19c: from Latin *halitus* breath + -OSIS.

hall /hɔːl/ ▻ *noun* **1** a room or passage just inside the entrance to a house, which usually allows access to other rooms and the stairs. **2** a building or large room, used for concerts, public meetings, assemblies, etc. **3** (*usually* **Hall**) a large country house or manor. **4** *Brit* (*in full* **hall of residence**) a building where university or college students live. **5** *Brit* **a** the dining-room in a college or university; **b** the dinner in such a room. **6** the main room of a great house, castle, etc. **7** *especially N Amer* a corridor onto which rooms open. **8** (*often* **halls**) *informal* MUSIC HALL. ⓒ Anglo-Saxon *heall*.

hallelujah or **halleluia** /halɪ'luːjə/ and **alleluia** /alɪ-/ ▻ *exclamation* expressing praise to God. ▻ *noun* (***hallelujahs*** or ***halleluias*** or ***alleluias***) **1** the exclamation of 'hallelujah'. **2** a musical composition based on the word 'Hallelujah'. ⓒ 16c: from Hebrew *hallelu* praise ye + *jah* Jehova.

halliard see HALYARD

hallmark ▻ *noun* **1** an official series of marks stamped on gold, silver and platinum articles to guarantee their authenticity. **2** any mark of genuineness or excellence. **3** a typical or distinctive feature, especially of quality. ▻ *verb* (***hallmarked, hallmarking***) to stamp with a hallmark. ⓒ 18c: named after Goldsmiths' Hall in London where articles were originally classed and stamped.

hallo see HELLO

halloo /hə'luː/ or **hallo** /hə'loʊ/ or **halloa** /hə'loʊ/ ▻ *noun* (***halloos*** or ***hallos*** or ***halloas***) ▻ *exclamation* **1** a cry to encourage hunting dogs or call for attention. **2** a shout of 'halloo'. ▻ *verb* (***hallooed, hallooing***) *intr* **1** to cry 'halloo', especially to dogs at a hunt. **2** to urge on hunting dogs with shouts. ⓒ 16c.

halloumi /ha'luːmɪ/ ▻ *noun* a Greek dish of fried goat's cheese, eaten as a starter.

hallow /'haloʊ/ ▻ *verb* (***hallowed, hallowing***) **1** to make or regard as holy. **2** to consecrate or set apart as being sacred. • **hallowed** *adj*. ⓒ Anglo-Saxon *halgian*, from *halig* holy.

Hallowe'en or **Halloween** /haloʊ'iːn/ ▻ *noun* the evening of 31 October, the eve of All Saints' Day. Also called **All Hallows Eve**. ⓒ 18c: from *All-Hallow-Even* All Saints' Eve.

hall stand and (*especially US*) **hall-tree** ▻ *noun* a piece of furniture, usually in the hall of a house, for hanging outdoor clothing on.

Hallstatt /'halʃtat/ ▻ *adj, archaeol* relating to a European culture which extended from central Europe to Britain and lasted from the Bronze Age to the Iron Age. ⓒ 19c: named after Hallstatt, a village in Upper Austria where remains were found.

hallucinate /hə'luːsɪneɪt/ ▻ *verb* (***hallucinated, hallucinating***) *intr* to experience HALLUCINATION. • **hallucinator** *noun*. • **hallucinatory** *adj*. ⓒ 17c: from Latin *(h)allucinari* to wander in the mind.

hallucination ▻ *noun* the apparent observation of something which is not actually present or may not even exist. ▻

hallucinogen /hə'luːsɪnədʒən/ ▻ *noun* a drug that causes HALLUCINATION. • **hallucinogenic** *adj*.

hallux /'haləks/ ▻ *noun* (***halluces*** /'haljʊsiːz/) **1** the innermost digit of the hind foot of a bird, mammal, reptile or amphibian. **2** the big toe of humans. ⓒ 19c: from Latin *allex* big toe.

hallway ▻ *noun* an entrance hall or corridor.

halma /'halmə/ ▻ *noun* a board game in which players try to reach their opponents' bases. ⓒ 19c: from Greek *halma* leap, so called because the characteristic move is a leap or series of leaps over any man in an adjacent square to an empty square beyond.

halo /'heɪloʊ/ ▻ *noun* (***halos*** or ***haloes***) **1** in paintings etc: a ring of light around the head of a saint, angel, etc. **2** the glory or glamour that is attached to a famous or admired person or thing. **3** a ring of light that can be seen around the sun or moon, caused by the refraction of light by ice crystals. ▻ *verb* (***haloes, haloed, haloing***) to put a halo round someone or something. ⓒ 16c: from Greek *halos* circular threshing floor.

halocarbon /haloʊ'kɑːbən/ ▻ *noun, chem* a compound which consists of carbon and one or more HALOGENS.

halo effect ▻ *noun, psychol* the tendency to judge someone favourably on the basis of one or only a few positive characteristics.

halogen /'halədʒɛn/ ▻ *noun, chem* any of the non-metallic elements fluorine, chlorine, bromine, iodine and astatine which form salts when in union with metals. • **halogenous** /həˈlɒdʒənəs/ *adj.* ◷ 19c: from Greek *hals*, *halos* salt.

halogenate /həˈlɒdʒəneɪt/ ▷ *verb* (***halogenated***, ***halogenating***) *chem* to treat or combine with a HALOGEN. • **halogenation** *noun*.

haloid /ˈhalɔɪd, ˈheɪ-/ *chem* ▷ *noun* a HALIDE. ▷ *adj* having the composition of a HALIDE □ *a haloid salt*.

halon /ˈhalɒn, ˈheɪ-/ ▷ *noun* any of a class of organic chemical compounds containing bromine combined with other HALOGENs (eg bromotrifluoromethane) used in fire extinguishers, being very potent destroyers of the OZONE LAYER.

halophile /ˈhaloʊfaɪl, ˈheɪ-, -fɪl/ ▷ *noun* an organism that thrives in or can tolerate very salty conditions.

halt[1] /hɔːlt, hɒlt/ ▷ *noun* **1** an interruption or stop to movement, progression or growth. **2** *Brit* a small railway station without a building. ▷ *verb* (***halted***, ***halting***) *tr & intr* to come or bring to a halt. ▷ *exclamation* a command to halt, especially one given as an order when marching. • **call a halt to something** to put an end to it or stop it. ◷ 17c: from German *Halt* stoppage.

halt[2] /hɔːlt, hɒlt/ ▷ *verb* (***halted***, ***halting***) *intr* **1** to be unsure or in doubt; to hesitate. **2** especially of verse: to be defective. **3** *archaic* to be lame. ▷ *adj*, *archaic* lame or crippled. ◷ Anglo-Saxon *healt* lame.

halter /ˈhɔːltə(r), ˈhɒl-/ ▷ *noun* **1** a rope or strap for holding and leading a horse by its head. **2** a rope with a noose for hanging a person. **3** a HALTERNECK. ▷ *verb* (***haltered***, ***haltering***) **1** to put a halter on (a horse, etc). **2** to hang someone with a halter. ◷ Anglo-Saxon *hælfter*.

halteres /halˈtɪəriːz/ ▷ *plural noun* the pair of modified hindwings of flies that are used to maintain balance during flight. ◷ 19c: from Greek *halteres* weights held in the hands to give impetus when leaping.

halterneck ▷ *noun* a style of woman's top or dress held in place by a strap which goes round her neck, leaving the shoulders and back bare.

halting ▷ *adj* **1** pausing frequently; hesitant □ *in halting French*. **2** lame. • **haltingly** *adverb*.

halva /ˈhalvə/ ▷ *noun* an Eastern delicacy which contains sesame seeds, nuts, honey and saffron. ◷ 19c: Yiddish, originally from Arabic *halwa*.

halve /hɑːv/ ▷ *verb* (***halved***, ***halving***) **1** to divide into two equal parts or halves. **2** to share equally. **3** *tr & intr* said of costs, problems, etc: to reduce by half. **4** *golf* to draw a hole or match with one's opponent. ◷ Anglo-Saxon *halfen*.

halves *plural of* HALF

halyard or **halliard** /ˈhaljəd/ ▷ *noun* a rope for raising or lowering a sail or flag on a ship. ◷ 14c: *halier* from French *haler* to haul in + YARD[1].

ham[1] ▷ *noun* **1** the top part of the back leg of a pig. **2** the meat from this part, salted and smoked and used as food. **3** *informal* the back of the thigh. ◷ Anglo-Saxon *hamm*.

ham[2] ▷ *noun*, *colloq* **1** *theat* **a** a bad actor, especially one who overacts or exaggerates; **b** inexpert or clumsy acting. Also *as adj* □ *a ham actor*. **2** an amateur radio operator. ▷ *verb* (***hammed***, ***hamming***) *tr & intr* (*also* **ham something up**) to overact or exaggerate. ◷ 19c: perhaps from *hamfatter* a third-rate minstrel.

hamadryad /haməˈdraɪad/ ▷ *noun* (***hamadryads*** or ***hamadrayades*** /-diːz/) **1** *Greek & Roman mythol* a nymph who lives in a tree and dies when it dies. **2** a KING COBRA. **3** (*also* **hamadryas**) a large baboon of Arabia and NE Africa. ◷ 14c: from Greek *Hamadryades* tree nymphs, from *hama* at the same time (as) + *drys* oak tree.

hamburger ▷ *noun* a flat round cake of finely chopped beef, usually fried and served in a soft bread roll. ◷ 1930s: originally called *Hamburger steak*, from Hamburg a city in N Germany.

hame /heɪm/ ▷ *noun* either of the two curved bars attached to the collar of a draught animal. ◷ 14c: from Dutch *haam*.

ham-fisted and **ham-handed** ▷ *adj*, *colloq* clumsy; lacking skill or grace.

Hamitic /haˈmɪtɪk/ ▷ *noun* a group of N African languages related to SEMITIC. ▷ *adj* **1** referring or relating to this group of languages. **2** belonging to or characteristic of the **Hamites**, a race of N Africa. ◷ 19c: named after Ham, one of Noah's sons and the supposed founder of this race, which includes the ancient Egyptians.

hamlet /ˈhamlət, -lɪt/ ▷ *noun* a small village, especially and originally one without a church. ◷ 14c: from French *hamelet*.

hammer /ˈhamə(r)/ ▷ *noun* **1** a tool with a heavy metal head on the end of a handle, used for driving nails into wood, breaking hard substances, etc. **2** the part of a bell, piano, clock, etc that hits against some other part, making a noise. **3** the part of a gun that strikes the PRIMER[2] or PERCUSSION CAP when the trigger is pulled and causes the bullet to be fired. **4** *sport* **a** a metal ball on a long flexible steel chain, that is thrown in competitions; **b** the sport of throwing this. **5** the mallet with which an auctioneer announces that an article is sold. **6** *anatomy* a small bone of the ear, the MALLEUS. ▷ *verb* (***hammered***, ***hammering***) **1** *tr & intr* to strike or hit with or as if with a hammer. **2** *intr* to make a noise as of a hammer. **3** *Brit colloq* to criticize or beat severely. **4** *colloq* to defeat. **5** *stock exchange* **a** to declare a member a defaulter; **b** to cause a fall in prices of securities, the market, etc. • **hammering** *noun*, *Brit colloq* a severe beating. • **hammer-like** *adj*. • **come** or **go under the hammer** to be sold at auction. • **hammer and tongs** *colloq* with a lot of noise or effort. • **hammer something home to someone** to impress (a fact, etc) strongly and effectively on them. • **on someone's hammer** *Austral* & *NZ slang* following closely on someone's trail. ◷ Anglo-Saxon *hamor*.

■ **hammer at** or **away at something** to work constantly at it □ *he hammered away at the problem*.

■ **hammer at** or **on something** to strike it loudly and repeatedly.

■ **hammer something in 1** to drive or force something in with, or as if with, a hammer. **2** to force (facts, etc) into someone through constant repetition.

■ **hammer something out 1** to shape or remove it with, or as if with, a hammer. **2** to reconcile or settle (problems, differences, etc) after a great deal of effort and discussion.

hammer and sickle ▷ *noun* the sign of a hammer and a sickle laid across each other, symbolic of labour, used as the emblem of the Soviet Union and as a symbol of communism. ◷ 1920s.

hammer beam ▷ *noun* either one of a pair of beams that project horizontally from opposite walls to support arched frameworks.

hammer drill ▷ *noun* a drill where the DRILL BIT makes a hammering action as well as rotating.

hammerhead ▷ *noun* **1** a shark with a hammer-shaped head. **2** an African wading bird with a backward-pointing crest and long thick bill. **3** a large African fruit bat with a hammer-shaped muzzle. • **hammerheaded** *adj*.

hammerlock ▷ *noun*, *wrestling* a hold in which a wrestler twists the opponent's arm upwards behind their back.

hammer-toe ▷ *noun* a deformity in which a toe is permanently bent.

hammock /ˈhamək/ ▷ *noun* a piece of canvas or net hung by the corners and used as a bed. ◷ 16c: from Spanish *hamaca*.

hammy /ˈhamɪ/ ▷ *adj* (***hammier***, ***hammiest***) *informal* **1** said of an actor: inclined to overact. **2** said of a play, performance, etc: overacted or exaggerated.

hamper¹ /ˈhampə(r)/ ▷ *verb* (***hampered, hampering***) to hinder the progress or movement of someone or something. ▷ *noun, naut* essential but often cumbersome equipment aboard a vessel. ◷ 14c.

hamper² /ˈhampə(r)/ ▷ *noun* **1** a large basket with a lid, used especially for carrying food. **2** *Brit* the food and drink packed in such a basket. ◷ 14c: from *hanypere* wicker basket.

hamster /ˈhamstə(r)/ ▷ *noun* a small nocturnal Eurasian rodent with a short tail and pouches in its mouth for storing food, often kept as a pet. ◷ 17c: from German *hamustro*.

hamstring ▷ *noun* **1** in humans: one of the tendons at the back of the knee that are attached to muscles in the thigh. **2** in horses: the large tendon at the back of the hind leg. ▷ *verb* (***hamstringed*** or ***hamstrung, hamstringing***) **1** to make powerless or hinder. **2** to lame by cutting the hamstring. ◷ 17c: from HAM¹ + STRING.

hamulus /ˈhamjʊləs/ ▷ *noun* (***hamuli*** /-laɪ/) the hook or hook-shaped apparatus between the fore and hind wings of a bee. ◷ 18c: from Latin *hamus* hook.

hand ▷ *noun* **1** in humans: the extremity of the arm below the wrist, consisting of a thumb, four fingers and a palm. **2** any corresponding part in the higher vertebrates. **3** something that resembles this in form or function. **4** *as adj* **a** relating to or involving the hand ▫ *hand grenade*; **b** worn on, for or carried in the hand ▫ *hand lotion*; **c** operated by hand ▫ *hand saw*. **5** *in compounds* made by hand rather than by a machine ▫ *hand-knitted*. **6** control, agency or influence ▫ *the hand of fate*. **7** (**a hand**) help; assistance ▫ *He gave us a hand*. **8** a part or influence in an activity ▫ *They had a hand in the victory*. **9** a needle or pointer on a clock, watch or gauge. **10** *colloq* a round of applause ▫ *He got a big hand*. **11** a manual worker or assistant, especially in a factory, on a farm or on board ship ▫ *All hands on deck!* **12** someone who is skilful at some specified activity ▫ *a dab hand at baking*. **13** a specified way of doing something ▫ *She has a light hand at pastry*. **14** *cards* **a** the cards dealt to a player in one round of a game; **b** a player holding such cards; **c** one round of a card game. **15 a**) a specified position in relation to an object or onlooker ▫ *on the right hand*; **b** *in compounds* a specified position in relation to a point in time ▫ *behindhand with the work*. **16** a source of information considered in terms of closeness to the original source ▫ *hear the news at first hand*. **17** an opposing aspect, point of view, etc ▫ *on the other hand*. **18** someone's handwriting or style of handwriting. **19** a promise or acceptance of partnership, especially to marry ▫ *He asked for her hand*. **20** in measuring the height of horses: a unit of measurement equal to 4in (about 10cm). **21** a bunch of bananas. **22** (**hands**) *football* the offence of touching the ball with the hand or arm. Also called **handling**. ▷ *verb* (***handed, handing***) **1** (*often* **hand something back** or **in** or **out** or **round**, *etc*) to deliver or give it using the hand or hands. **2** to lead, help or escort in a specified direction with the hand or hands ▫ *He handed her into the carriage*. **3** *naut* to furl (a sail). • **a free hand** freedom to do as desired. • **a hand's turn** *usually with negatives* the least amount of work ▫ *He didn't do a hand's turn all day*. • **a heavy hand** tyranny or oppression ▫ *to rule with a heavy hand*. • **a high hand** a dictatorial manner. • **at first hand** directly from the source. • **at hand** near by; about to happen. • **at someone's hand** by them. • **by hand 1** using the hands or tools held in the hand rather than by mechanical means. **2** delivered by messenger, not by post. • **change hands** to pass to other ownership or custody. • **come to hand** to arrive; to be received. • **force someone's hand** to force them to act. • **live from hand to mouth 1** to live with only enough money and food for immediate needs. **2** to live without preparation or planning. • **get one's hand in 1** to get control of the play so as to turn one's cards to good use. **2** to get into the way or knack of something. • **get one's hands on someone** or **something** *colloq* **1** to catch or find them or it. **2** to obtain it. • **hand and foot** completely; in every possible way ▫ *Servants wait on him hand and foot*. • **hand in glove** very closely associated. • **hand in hand 1** with hands mutually clasped. **2** in close association. • **hand it to someone** *colloq* to give them credit. • **hand of God** an unforeseen or unavoidable accident, such as lightning or a storm. • **hand over fist** *colloq* in large amounts and very quickly ▫ *They're making money hand over fist*. • **hands down** without effort; easily ▫ *She won the race hands down*. • **hands off!** keep off!; do not touch! • **hands up!** hold your hands up above your head. • **have one's hands full** *colloq* **1** to be very busy. **2** to be plagued with problems. • **have one's hands tied** to be unable to act, usually because of instructions from a higher authority. • **in good hands** in good keeping; in the care of someone who may be trusted. • **in hand 1** under control. **2** being done or prepared. **3** available in reserve ▫ *with half an hour in hand*. **4** with deferred payment ▫ *They work a week in hand*. • **in someone's hands** in their power or keeping ▫ *Their fate is in our hands*. • **keep one's hand in** *colloq* to continue to have some involvement in an activity so as to remain proficient at it. • **lay hands on** or **upon something** or **someone 1** to obtain or find it. **2** to beat up or assault them. **3** *Christianity* to bless or ordain them by touching them with the hand or hands. • **lend a hand** to give assistance. • **lift a hand** *usually with negatives* to make the least effort ▫ *He didn't lift a hand to help us*. • **off one's hands** *colloq* no longer one's responsibility. • **on hand** near; available if required. • **on one's hands 1** *colloq* left over; not sold or used; to spare ▫ *too much time on my hands*. **2** remaining as one's responsibility ▫ *Her position as manager means she has a lot on her hands*. • **on one's hands and knees 1** with one's hands, knees and feet on the ground. **2** begging. • **on the one hand... on the other hand** from one point of view... from another point of view. • **out of hand 1** beyond control. **2** immediately and without thinking ▫ *I'm inclined to dismiss it out of hand*. • **raise one's hand to someone** *often with negatives* to strike or behave violently towards them. • **show of hands** a vote by holding up hands. • **show one's hand** to reveal one's opinion, stance or purpose. • **sit on one's hands** to take no action. • **stand one's hand** *colloq* to buy someone else a drink. • **take something** or **someone in hand 1** to undertake it. **2** to take charge of them in order to discipline, educate, etc them. • **take something off someone's hands** to relieve them of it. • **throw in one's hand** to give up a venture or plan; to concede defeat. • **to hand** within reach. • **try one's hand at something** to attempt to do it. • **the upper hand** the power or advantage ▫ *The strikers have the upper hand*. • **wash one's hands of something** or **someone** to cease to be involved with or be responsible for them or it. ◷ Anglo-Saxon.

▪ **hand something down 1** to pass on (an heirloom, tradition, etc) to the next generation. **2** to pass on (an outgrown item of clothing) to a younger member of a family. **3** *N Amer law* to pronounce (a verdict).

▪ **hand something in** to return or submit (an examination paper, etc).

▪ **hand something on** to give it to the next person in succession.

▪ **hand something out** to pass it by hand or distribute it to individuals. See also HANDOUT.

▪ **hand something over** to transfer it or give possession of it to someone else. See also HANDOVER.

handbag ▷ *noun* **1** a woman's small bag, often with a strap, for carrying personal articles. Also called BAG. *N Amer equivalent* PURSE. **2** a light travelling-bag that can be carried by hand. **3** (*in full* **handbag music**) a commercial form of HOUSE MUSIC with long piano breaks (see BREAK *noun* 12) and diva-style vocals.

handball ▷ *noun* **1** a game in which two or four players hit a small ball against a wall with their hands. **2** the small hard rubber ball used in this game. **3** a game between goals in which the ball is struck with the palm of the hand. **4** *football* the offence a player other than a goalkeeper in their own penalty area commits if they touch the ball with their hand.

hand-barrow ▻ *noun* a flat tray with handles for transporting loads, usually carried by two people.

handbell ▻ *noun* a small bell with a handle, rung by hand.

handbill ▻ *noun* a small printed notice or advertisement distributed by hand.

handbook ▻ *noun* **1** a manual that gives guidelines on maintenance or repair, eg of a car. **2** a guidebook that lists brief facts on a subject or place.

handbrake ▻ *noun* **1** a brake on a motor vehicle, operated by a lever. **2** the lever that operates the handbreak.

handbreadth or **hand's breadth** ▻ *noun* the breadth of a hand used to measure length.

h and c or **h & c** ▻ *abbreviation* hot and cold (water).

handcart ▻ *noun* a small light cart which can be pushed or pulled by hand.

handclap ▻ *noun* a clap of the hands.

handcraft ▻ *noun* handicraft. ▻ *verb* to make something by handicraft. • **handcrafted** *adj.*

handcuff ▻ *noun* (**handcuffs**) a pair of steel rings, joined by a short chain, for locking round the wrists eg of prisoners, etc. ▻ *verb* (***handcuffed, handcuffing***) to put handcuffs on someone. ⓒ 18c.

handed ▻ *adj, in compounds* **1** using one hand in preference to the other ▫ *left-handed.* **2** having or using a hand or hands as specified ▫ *one-handed.*

handful ▻ *noun* (***handfuls***) **1** the amount or number that can be held in one hand. **2** a small amount or number. **3** *colloq* **a** someone who is difficult to control; **b** a difficult task.

hand gallop ▻ *noun* an easy gallop, restrained by the bridle-hand.

hand glass ▻ *noun* a mirror or magnifying-glass with a handle.

hand grenade ▻ *noun* a grenade to be thrown by hand.

hand grip ▻ *noun* something for the hand to grasp.

handgun ▻ *noun* a firearm that can be held and fired in one hand, eg a revolver.

handicap /ˈhandɪkap/ ▻ *noun* **1** a physical or mental disability that results in partial or total inability to perform social, occupational or other normal everyday activities. **2** something that impedes or hinders. **3** **a** a disadvantage imposed on a superior competitor in a contest, race, etc, or an advantage given to an inferior one, so that everyone has an equal chance of winning; **b** a race or competition in which competitors are given a handicap. **4** the number of strokes by which a golfer's averaged score exceeds par for the course. ▻ *verb* (***handicapped, handicapping***) **1** to impede or hamper someone. **2** to impose special disadvantages or advantages on (a player or players) in order to make a better contest. **3** to organize (a race, etc) by handicapping. • **handicapper** *noun* in some sports: an official who fixes the handicaps of competitors. ⓒ 17c: probably from *hand i' cap* an old lottery game in which money was deposited in a cap and forfeits were drawn from it.

handicapped /ˈhandɪkapt/ ▻ *adj* **1** physically or mentally disabled. **2** (**the handicapped**) handicapped people in general (see THE 4B). **2** said of a competitor: given a handicap.

handicraft /ˈhandɪkrɑːft/ ▻ *noun* **1** an activity which requires skilful use of the hands, eg pottery or model-making. **2** (*usually* **handicrafts**) the work produced by this activity. • **handicraftsman** or **handicraftswoman** *noun.* See also HANDCRAFT. ⓒ 15c: changed from HANDCRAFT through the influence of HANDIWORK.

handier, handiest, *etc* see under HANDY

handiwork /ˈhandɪwɜːk/ ▻ *noun* **1** work, especially skilful work, produced by hand. **2** *often derog* the outcome of the action or efforts of someone or something. ⓒ Anglo-Saxon *handgeweorc*, from HAND + *ge-*, collective prefix, + *woerc* work.

handkerchief /ˈhaŋkətʃɪf, -ʃiːf/ ▻ *noun* (***handkerchiefs*** or ***handkerchieves*** /-ʃiːvz/) a small, usually square, piece of cloth or soft paper used for wiping the nose, face, etc.

hand-knit ▻ *noun* a garment knitted by hand. ▻ *verb* to knit by hand.

handle /ˈhandəl/ ▻ *noun* **1** the part of a utensil, door, etc by which it is held so that it may be used, moved or picked up. **2** an opportunity or excuse for doing something ▫ *Her shyness served as a handle for their bullying.* **3** *slang* a person's name or title. **4** *slang* the CALL SIGN of a CB radio user. **5** said of textiles, etc: the quality which is appreciated by touching or handling. **6** *NZ* a glass beer mug with a handle. ▻ *verb* (***handled, handling***) **1** to touch, hold, move or operate with the hands. **2** to deal with, control or manage, especially successfully or in the correct way ▫ *The inquest was handled tactfully* ▫ *She handles all the accounts.* **3** to buy, sell or deal in (specific merchandise). **4** to write about or discuss (a theme, subject, etc). **5** *intr* to respond in a specified way to being operated ▫ *This car handles very smoothly.* • **handled** *adj, in compounds* having handles of a specified type or number. • **handling** *noun.* • **fly off the handle** *colloq* to become suddenly very angry. ⓒ Anglo-Saxon.

handlebar moustache ▻ *noun* a wide thick moustache which curls up at the ends.

handlebars ▻ *plural noun, sometimes singular* a metal bar with curved ends which form handles, for steering a bicycle, motorcycle, etc.

handler ▻ *noun* **1** someone who trains and controls an animal, especially a police dog. **2** *in compounds* someone who handles something specified ▫ *a baggage handler.* **3** *boxing* a trainer or second.

handless ▻ *adj* **1** without a handle or handles. **2** *dialect* awkward; clumsy.

hand-line ▻ *noun* a fishing-line used without a rod. ▻ *verb* to fish with such a line.

handling see under HANDLE and HAND *noun* 22

hand-list ▻ *noun* a list without detail, for handy reference.

handmade ▻ *adj* made by a person's hands or with tools held in the hands, not by machine.

handmaiden and **handmaid** ▻ *noun* **1** *old use* a female servant. **2** someone or something that serves a useful but ancillary purpose.

hand-me-down ▻ *noun, colloq* something, especially a second-hand garment, passed down from one person to another.

hand organ ▻ *noun* a BARREL ORGAN.

handout ▻ *noun* **1** money, food, etc given to people who need it. **2** a leaflet, free sample, etc, given out as publicity for something. **3** a statement given to the press, students, etc as a supplement to or substitute for an oral address.

handover ▻ *noun* the transfer of power from one person or group of people to another.

hand-pick ▻ *verb* to choose carefully, especially for a particular purpose ▫ *hand-picked the grapes* ▫ *hand-picked the team.* • **hand-picked** *adj.*

handrail ▻ *noun* a narrow rail running alongside a stairway, etc for support.

hand saw ▻ *noun* a saw worked with one hand.

hand's breadth see HANDBREADTH

handsel /'hansəl/ *archaic* ▻ *noun* a good-luck present given at the start of a new year, new undertaking, etc. ▻ *verb* (***handselled***, ***handselling***; (*US*) ***handseled***, ***handseling***) **1** to give a handsel to someone. **2** to inaugurate someone. ⓒ Anglo-Saxon *handselen* giving into the hands.

handset ▻ *noun* a telephone mouthpiece and earpiece together in a single unit.

handshake ▻ *noun* the act of holding or shaking a person's hand, especially as a greeting or when concluding a deal.

hands-off ▻ *adj* **1** said of a machine, etc: not touched or operated by the hands. **2** said of a strategy, policy, etc: deliberately avoiding involvement.

handsome /'hansəm/ ▻ *adj* **1** said of a man: good-looking. **2** said of a woman: attractive in a strong, dignified, imposing way. **3** said of a building, room, etc: well-proportioned; impressive. **4** substantial or generous □ *a handsome donation.* **5** liberal or noble □ *a handsome gesture.* • **handsomely** *adverb*. • **handsomeness** *noun*. ⓒ 16c in these senses; 15c, meaning 'easy to handle': from HAND + -SOME.

hands-on ▻ *adj* involving practical experience rather than just information or theory □ *hands-on training in computer technology.*

handspring ▻ *noun* a somersault or cartwheel in which one lands first on one's hands and then on one's feet.

handstand ▻ *noun* the act of balancing one's body on one's hands with one's legs in the air.

hand-to-hand ▻ *adj* said of fighting: involving direct physical contact with the enemy.

hand-to-mouth ▻ *adj*, *adverb* with just enough money or food for immediate needs only □ *has always lived hand-to-mouth.*

handwriting ▻ *noun* **1** writing with a pen or pencil rather than by typing or printing. **2** the characteristic way a person writes.

handwritten *adj* written by hand, not typed or printed.

handy ▻ *adj* (***handier***, ***handiest***) **1** ready to use and conveniently placed. **2** easy to use or handle. **3** clever with one's hands. • **handily** *adverb*. • **handiness** *noun*.

handyman ▻ *noun* a man skilled at, or employed to do, odd jobs around the house.

hanepoot /'hɑːnəpuːt/ ▻ *noun*, *S Afr* a kind of grape for eating and wine-making. ⓒ 18c: Afrikaans, from Dutch *haan* cock + *poot* foot.

hang /haŋ/ ▻ *verb* (***hung*** or (in sense 3) ***hanged***, ***hanging***) **1** *tr & intr* to fasten or be fastened from above, especially with the lower part free. **2** *tr & intr* said of a door, etc: to fasten or be fastened with hinges so that it can move freely. **3** *tr & intr* to suspend or be suspended by a rope or something similar around the neck until dead. **4** (*sometimes* **hang over**) to be suspended or hover, especially in the air or in a threatening way □ *The smell of paint hung in the air* □ *The fear of redundancy hung over me.* **5** *tr & intr* to droop or make something droop □ *hang one's head in shame.* **6** to fix (wallpaper) to a wall. **7** *tr & intr* said of a painting, etc: to place or be placed in an exhibition. **8** to decorate (a room, wall, etc) with pictures or other hangings. **9** *tr & intr*, *colloq* to damn or be damned □ *Hang the expense.* **10** *intr* said of a piece of clothing: to sit in a specified way when worn □ *a coat which hangs well.* **11** to suspend game from a hook to allow it to decompose slightly and become more flavoursome. **12** to prevent (a jury) from reaching a verdict. **13** *computing* said of a computer or a program: to stop functioning. ▻ *noun* **1** the way something hangs, falls or droops. **2** *usually with negatives*, *colloq* a damn □ *I couldn't give a hang.* See also HANGING. • **get the hang of something** *colloq* to learn or begin to understand how to do it. • **hang a left** or **right** *US colloq* to turn left or right, especially when driving. • **hang by a thread** to depend upon very precarious conditions, a slim chance, etc. • **hang fire 1** to delay taking action. **2** to cease to develop or progress. • **hang in the balance** to be uncertain or in doubt. • **hang loose** *N Amer colloq* **1** to do nothing. **2** to be relaxed and unperturbed by one's surroundings, etc. • **hang on in there** *colloq* keep trying; don't give up. • **hang one's head** to look ashamed or sheepish. • **hang on someone's lips** or **words** to give close admiring attention to someone. • **let it all hang out** *chiefly US colloq* **1** to be totally uninhibited and relaxed. **2** to act or speak freely. ⓒ Anglo-Saxon *hangian*.

■ **hang about** or **around** *colloq* **1** to waste time; to stand around doing nothing. **2** to stay or remain.

■ **hang about** or **around with someone** to spend a lot of time in their company.

■ **hang back** to be unwilling or reluctant to do something.

■ **hang on** *colloq* **1** to wait □ *I'll hang on for a bit.* **2** to carry on bravely, in spite of problems or difficulties.

■ **hang on something 1** to depend on it □ *It all hangs on the weather.* **2** to listen closely to it □ *hanging on her every word.*

■ **hang something on someone** *colloq* to blame them for it.

■ **hang on to something** to keep a hold or control of it.

■ **hang out 1** to lean or bend out (eg of a window, etc). **2** said of clothes: to hang up outside to dry. **3** *colloq* to frequent a place □ *He hangs out in local bars.* See also HANG-OUT.

■ **hang something out** to hang up (washing) outside to dry.

■ **hang out for something** to insist on it and wait until one gets it.

■ **hang over someone** said of an unresolved problem, decision, etc: to overshadow or threaten them.

■ **hang over something** to project over or lean out from it.

■ **hang together 1** said of two people: to be united and support each other. **2** said of ideas, etc: to be consistent.

■ **hang up** to finish a telephone conversation by replacing the receiver.

■ **hang something up** to hang something on a hook, hanger, etc.

hanged, hung

• The normal past tense and past participle of the verb **hang** is **hung** □ *She hung the apron over the back of a chair* □ *They hung on as the plane made an emergency dive.* □ *Curtains could be hung from a pole across the wall*

• When the verb refers to killing by hanging, the correct form of the past tense and past participle is **hanged** □ *He was later hanged for his part in a bomb plot* □ *An unidentified man has hanged himself in his cell.* **Hung** is increasingly used in this sense also, but in formal English it is better to use **hanged**.

hangar /'haŋə(r)/ ▻ *noun* a large shed or building in which aircraft are kept. ⓒ 19c: French.

hangdog ▷ *adj* said of someone's appearance or manner: ashamed, guilty or downcast.

hanger /'haŋə(r)/ ▷ *noun* **1** a metal, wooden or plastic frame on which jackets, dresses, etc are hung up to keep their shape. **2 a** someone who hangs something; **b** *in compounds* a person or contraption that hangs the specified thing □ *paper-hanger.* **3** *Brit* a wood on a steep hillside.

hanger-on ▷ *noun* (***hangers-on***) a dependant or follower, especially one who is not wanted.

hang-glider ▷ *noun* **1** a large light metal frame with cloth stretched across it and a harness hanging below it for the pilot, which flies using air currents. **2** the pilot of this. • **hang-gliding** *noun.*

hangi /'haŋɪ/ ▷ *noun* (***hangis***) *NZ* **1** an open-air cooking pit. **2** the food cooked in it. **3** the social get-together at the ensuing meal. ◷ 19c: Maori.

hanging ▷ *noun* **1 a** the execution of someone by suspending their body by the neck; **b** *as adj* □ *a hanging offence.* **2** (*usually* **hangings**) curtains, tapestries, etc hung on walls for decoration. ▷ *adj* **1** suspended; not fixed below; overhanging. **2** undecided □ *a hanging question.* **3** situated on a steep slope.

hanging valley ▷ *noun, geog* a tributary valley which enters a main valley at a much higher level owing to overdeepening of the main valley, especially by glacial erosion.

hangman ▷ *noun* an official who carries out executions by hanging.

hangnail ▷ *noun* a piece of loose skin that has been partly torn away from the base or side of a fingernail. ◷ 17c: from Anglo-Saxon *angnail*, from *ange* painful + *nægl* nail.

hang-out ▷ *noun, colloq* a place where one lives or spends much time □ *This bar is his usual hang-out.*

hangover ▷ *noun* **1** a collection of unpleasant physical symptoms that may follow a period of heavy drinking. See also BE HUNG OVER at HUNG. **2** someone or something left over from or influenced by an earlier time.

hang-up ▷ *noun, colloq* **1** an emotional or psychological problem or preoccupation. **2** a continual source of annoyance. See also BE HUNG UP at HUNG.

hank /haŋk/ ▷ *noun* **1** a coil, loop or skein of wool, string, rope, etc. **2** said of cloth, yarn, etc: a unit of measurement which varies with the type of material, eg a length of 840 yards (767m) of cotton or 560 yards (512m) of worsted yarn. **3** *naut* a ring for attaching a luff to a sail. ◷ 13c: from Norse *hanki* a hasp.

hanker /'haŋkə(r)/ ▷ *verb* (***hankered, hankering***) *intr* (*usually* **hanker after** or **for something**) to have a longing or craving for it. • **hankering** *noun.* ◷ 17c: perhaps from Dutch dialect *hankeren*.

hankie or **hanky** /'haŋkɪ/ ▷ *noun* (***hankies***) *colloq* a handkerchief.

hanky-panky /haŋkɪ'paŋkɪ/ ▷ *noun, colloq* **1** slightly improper sexual behaviour. **2** dubious or foolish conduct. ◷ 19c: probably a variant of HOCUS-POCUS.

Hanoverian /hanə'vɪərɪən, -'vɛərɪən/ ▷ *adj* applied to British sovereigns from George I (1714) to Victoria (1901). ▷ *noun* a member of this dynasty. ◷ 18c: from George I's being also the Elector of Hanover in N Germany.

Hansard /'hansɑːd/ ▷ *noun* an official printed daily report of what has happened in the British parliament. ◷ 19c: named after Luke Hansard (1752–1828), the first compiler and printer of such reports.

Hanseatic League /hansɪ'atɪk —/ ▷ *noun* an organization of N German commercial cities, formed in the 14c to protect trade. ◷ 17c: from German *hansa* a band of men.

hansom /'hansəm/ and **hansom cab** ▷ *noun, historical* a small two-wheeled horse-drawn carriage with a fixed roof and the driver's seat high up at the back, used as a taxi. ◷ 19c: named after its inventor J A Hansom (1803–82).

Hants /hants/ ▷ *abbreviation, English county* Hampshire.

Hanukkah see CHANUKKAH

hap *dated* ▷ *noun* **1** luck; chance. **2** an occurrence. ▷ *verb* (***happed, happing***) *intr* to happen. ◷ 13c: from Norse *happ* good luck.

ha'penny see HALFPENNY

ha'pennyworth see HALFPENNYWORTH

haphazard /hap'hazəd/ ▷ *adj* **1** careless. **2** random. ▷ *adverb* at random. • **haphazardly** *adverb.* • **haphazardness** *noun.* ◷ 16c.

hapless /'hapləs/ ▷ *adj* unlucky; unfortunate. • **haplessly** *adverb.* • **haplessness** *noun.* ◷ 16c.

haplo- /haploʊ, hap'lɒ/ ▷ *combining form, signifying* single. ◷ 19c: from Greek *haplous* single.

haplography /hap'lɒgrəfɪ/ ▷ *noun* (***haplographies***) in writing: the unintentional omission of a recurring syllable or letter, eg in writing *haplogy* instead of *haplology*. ◷ 19c.

haploid /'haplɔɪd/ *biol* ▷ *adj* said of a cell nucleus: having a single set of unpaired chromosomes. ▷ *noun* a haploid cell or organism. • **haploidy** *noun.* ◷ 20c.

haplology /hap'lɒlədʒɪ/ ▷ *noun* the omission of a recurring sound or syllable in fluent speech, as in pronouncing *deteriorate* as *deteriate*. ◷ 19c.

hap'orth see HALFPENNYWORTH

happed and **happing** see under HAP

happen /'hapən/ ▷ *verb* (***happened, happening***) *intr* **1** to take place or occur. **2** to have the good or bad luck (to do something) □ *I happened to meet him on the way.* ▷ *adverb, N Eng dialect* perhaps. ◷ 14c: from Norse *happ* good luck.

■ **happen on** or **upon something** to discover or encounter it, especially by chance.

■ **happen to someone** said of some unforeseen event, especially an unwelcome one: to be done to them, or be experienced by them.

happening /'hapənɪŋ/ ▷ *noun* **1** an event. **2** a performance, especially one which takes place in the street, which has not been fully planned, and in which the audience is invited to take part. ▷ *adj* fashionable and up to the minute. ◷ 1970s as adjective; 1950s in sense 2; 16c.

happenstance /'hapənstans/ ▷ *noun, N Amer* something that happens by chance. ◷ 19c: *happen* + circum*stance*.

happily /'hapɪlɪ/ ▷ *adverb* **1** in a happy way. **2** luckily.

happy /'hapɪ/ ▷ *adj* (***happier, happiest***) **1** feeling or showing pleasure or contentment □ *a happy smile.* **2** causing pleasure □ *a happy day for the company.* **3** suitable; fortunate □ *a happy coincidence.* **4** suitably expressed; appropriate □ *a happy reply.* **5** *colloq* slightly drunk. **6** *in compounds* overcome with the thing specified, usually implying irresponsibility □ *power-happy* □ *bomb-happy.* • **happiness** *noun.* • **happy as Larry** *colloq* completely happy. ◷ 14c: from HAP.

happy event ▷ *noun, euphemistic* the birth of a child.

happy-go-lucky ▷ *adj* carefree or easy-going.

happy hour ▷ *noun* in bars, restaurants, etc: a period of time, usually in the early evening, when drinks, meals, etc are sold at reduced prices.

happy hunting ground ▷ *noun* **1** the Paradise of the Native Americans. **2** a lucrative area worth exploring □ *French flea markets can be happy hunting grounds.*

happy medium ▷ *noun* a reasonable middle course between two extreme positions.

haptic /'haptɪk/ ▷ *adj* relating to or based on the sense of touch. ▷ *singular noun* (**haptics**) the study of data obtained by means of touch. ⓘ 19c: from Greek *haptein* to fasten.

hara-kiri /harə'kɪrɪ/ or **hari-kari** /harɪ'kɑːrɪ/ ▷ *noun* ritual suicide by cutting one's belly open with a sword, formerly practised in Japan to avoid dishonour. Also called SEPPUKU. ⓘ 19c: from Japanese *hara* belly + *kiri* cut.

harambee /hə'rambiː, hɑːrɑːm'beɪ/ ▷ *noun, exclamation* a rallying-cry used in Kenya. ⓘ 1960s: Swahili, meaning 'let's organize together'.

harangue /hə'raŋ/ ▷ *noun* a loud forceful speech either to attack people or to try to persuade them to do something. ▷ *verb* (***harangued***, ***haranguing***) to address such a speech to someone or to a crowd of people. ⓘ 15c: from Italian *aringa* public speech.

harass /'harəs, hə'ras/ ▷ *verb* (***harasses***, ***harassed***, ***harassing***) **1** to pester, torment or trouble someone by continually questioning or attacking them. **2** to make frequent sudden attacks on an enemy. • **harassed** *adj.* • **harassment** *noun*. ⓘ 17c: from French *harasser* to HARRY, perhaps a derivative form of *harer* to set a dog on.

harbinger /'hɑːbɪndʒə(r)/ ▷ *noun* a person or thing that announces or predicts something to come; a forerunner. ▷ *verb* (***harbingered***, ***harbingering***) to announce the approach or arrival of something. ⓘ 12c as *harbeger*: from French *herbergere* host.

harbour or (*N Amer*) **harbor** /'hɑːbə(r)/ ▷ *noun* **1** a place of shelter for ships. **2** a refuge or safe place. ▷ *verb* (***harboured***, ***harbouring***; (*N Amer*) ***harbored***, ***harboring***) **1** to give shelter or protection to someone, especially to a criminal. **2** to have (an idea or feeling) in one's head □ *harbour a grudge*. **3** to shelter (a vessel) in a harbour. **4** *intr* to take shelter. ⓘ Anglo-Saxon *herebeorg* from *here* army + *beorg* protection.

harbourage or (*N Amer*) **harborage** /'hɑːbərɪdʒ/ ▷ *noun* **1** shelter or refuge, as for a ship. **2** the act of harbouring.

harbour dues ▷ *plural noun* charges for the use of a harbour.

harbour master ▷ *noun* a person officially in charge of a harbour.

hard /hɑːd/ ▷ *adj* **1** said of a substance: resistant to scratching or indentation; firm; solid. **2** toughened; not soft or smooth □ *hard skin*. **3** difficult to do, understand, solve or explain. **4** using, needing or done with a great deal of effort. **5** demanding □ *a hard master*. **6** harsh; cruel. **7** tough or violent □ *a hard man*. **8** said of weather: severe. **9** forceful □ *a hard knock*. **10** cool or uncompromising □ *The managers took a long hard look at sales figures*. **11** causing hardship, pain or sorrow □ *hard times*. **12** harsh and unpleasant to the senses □ *a hard light*. **13** said of information, etc: proven and reliable □ *hard facts*. **14** shrewd or calculating □ *a hard businesswoman*. **15** said of water: containing calcium or magnesium salts, and tending to produce an insoluble scum instead of a lather with soap. **16** said of a drug: highly addictive. **17** said of an alcoholic drink: very strong, especially one which is a spirit rather than a beer or wine, etc. **18** politically extreme □ *hard right* □ *hard left*. **19** *phonetics, non-technical* said of the sounds of certain consonants: produced as a stop rather than a fricative, as eg the *c* in *cat* and the *g* in *got*. Compare SOFT. **20** said of currency: in strong demand due to having a stable value and exchange rate. **21** said of credit: difficult to obtain. **22** said of pornography: sexually explicit. **23** as a classification of pencil leads: indicating durable quality and faintness in use. **24** said of photographic paper: giving a high degree of image contrast. **25** said of radiation: having high energy and the ability to penetrate solids. **26** *chiefly US* said of goods: durable. **27** said of nuclear missiles: located underground. ▷ *adverb* **1** with great effort or energy □ *She works hard*. **2** *in compounds* achieved in the specified way with difficulty or as a result of great effort □ *a hard-won victory* □ *hard-earned results*. **3** earnestly or intently □ *He thought hard to find a solution*. **4** with great intensity □ *The news hit us hard*. ▷ *noun* **1** a firm beach or foreshore. **2** *colloq* hard labour. • **hardness** *noun*. • **be hard going** to be difficult to do. • **be hard put to do something** to have difficulty doing it. • **go hard with someone** to be unpleasant or difficult for them. • **hard after** or **by** or **on** or **upon someone** or **something** close or near them or it. • **hard as nails** said of a person: very hard; callous, very tough. • **hard at it** working hard; very busy. • **hard by** close by. • **hard done by** *colloq* unfairly treated. • **hard hit** severely affected by a problem, trouble, etc or by love. • **hard of hearing** partially deaf. • **hard on someone's heels** following immediately after them. • **hard up** *colloq* in need of money. • **hard up for something** *colloq* in great need of it □ *hard up for new ideas*. • **no hard feelings** said as a result of a defeat, etc: no offence taken, no animosity. • **the hard way** through personal endeavours or difficulties. ⓘ Anglo-Saxon *heard*.

hard-and-fast ▷ *adj* said of a rule or principle: permanent or absolute; that can never be changed. • **hard-and-fastness** *noun*.

hardback ▷ *noun* a book with a hard cover. Also *as adj* □ *hardback sales*.

hardball ▷ *noun* no-nonsense tough tactics, used especially for political gain.

hard-bitten ▷ *adj, colloq* said of a person: tough and ruthless.

hardboard ▷ *noun* light strong board made by compressing wood pulp.

hard-boiled ▷ *adj* **1** said of eggs: boiled until the yolk is solid. **2** *colloq* said of a person: tough; cynical.

hard card ▷ *noun* a hard disk, mounted on a card, that can be added to a personal computer.

hard case ▷ *noun, colloq* a tough, often violent, person who is difficult to reform.

hard cash ▷ *noun* coins and bank-notes, as opposed to cheques and credit cards.

hard cheese ▷ *exclamation, colloq, often insincere or ironic* bad luck! ⓘ 19c.

hard coal see under ANTHRACITE

hard copy ▷ *noun* information from a computer printed on paper, as opposed to machine-readable output such as magnetic tape. ⓘ 1960s.

hardcore ▷ *noun* **1** pieces of broken brick, stone, etc used as a base for a road. **2** (*also* **hard core**) the central, most important group within an organization, resistant to change. **3** (*originally* **hard-core punk**) a type of rock music consisting of short fast songs with minimal melody and aggressive delivery. **4** a form of fast rhythmic DANCE MUSIC developed in the UK in the early 1990s. ▷ *adj* (*often* **hard-core**) **1** said of pornography: describing or depicting sexual acts in explicit detail. **2** having long-lasting, strong and unchanging beliefs □ *hard-core revolutionaries*.

hard court ▷ *noun* a tennis court laid with asphalt, concrete, etc, rather than grass.

hard disk or **hard disc** ▷ *noun, computing* a rigid aluminium disk, coated with magnetic material and normally permanently sealed within a disk drive, that is used to store data and has a higher recording density than a floppy disk. Compare FLOPPY DISK.

hard drinker ▷ *noun* a person who drinks persistently and heavily.

hard-earned ▷ *adj* having taken a great deal of hard work to achieve or acquire.

harden /ˈhɑːdən/ ▷ *verb* (***hardened***, ***hardening***) **1** *tr & intr* to make or become hard or harder. **2** *tr & intr* to become or make less sympathetic or understanding ◻ *He hardened his heart to her tears.* **3** to make or become stronger or firmer. **4** *intr, commerce* **a** said of prices, a market, etc: to stop fluctuating; **b** said of prices: to rise. • **hardened** *adj* **1** rigidly set, eg in a behavioural pattern. **2** toughened through experience and not likely to change ◻ *a hardened criminal.* • **hardener** *noun.*

■ **harden something off** to accustom (a plant) to cold, frost, etc by gradually exposing it to outdoor conditions.

hardening of the arteries ▷ *noun* ARTERIOSCLEROSIS.

hard-favoured and **hard-featured** ▷ *adj* with coarse features.

hard-fought ▷ *adj* strongly contested.

hard hat ▷ *noun* **1** a protective helmet worn especially by building workers. **2** *chiefly US colloq* a construction worker. **3** *chiefly US colloq* a person with conservative or reactionary views.

hard-headed ▷ *adj* **1** tough, realistic or shrewd. **2** not influenced by emotion.

hard-hearted ▷ *adj* feeling no pity or kindness; intolerant. • **hard-heartedly** *adverb.* • **hard-heartedness** *noun.*

hard-hit ▷ *adj* **1** affected very severely by something, eg the loss of money, the death of a loved one, etc. **2** deeply smitten with love.

hard-hitting ▷ *adj* direct; frankly critical.

hardier, **hardiest**, **hardily** and **hardiness** see under HARDY

hardihood /ˈhɑːdɪhʊd/ ▷ *noun* courage or daring.

hard labour ▷ *noun, law, formerly* the punishment of obligatory physical work, eg breaking rocks, imposed on prisoners in addition to a sentence of imprisonment.

hard landing ▷ *noun* **1** a landing made by a spacecraft, etc in which the craft is destroyed on impact. **2** a solution to a problem, especially an economic one, that involves hardship.

hard line ▷ *noun* an uncompromising course, opinion, decision or policy. Also *as adj* ◻ *hardline attitude.* • **hardliner** *noun.*

hard lines! ▷ *exclamation* bad luck!

hardly ▷ *adverb* **1** barely; scarcely ◻ *I hardly knew the man.* **2** only just ◻ *She could hardly keep her eyes open.* **3** *often ironic* certainly not ◻ *They'll hardly come now.* **4** with difficulty ◻ *I can hardly believe it.* **5** *rare* harshly.

hard-nosed ▷ *adj, colloq* **1** tough and shrewd. **2** influenced by reason, not emotion.

hard nut ▷ *noun, colloq* a person or thing that is tough or difficult to deal with. • **a hard nut to crack 1** a person not easily won over. **2** a thing not easily done or understood.

hard-on ▷ *noun, coarse slang* an erection of the penis.

hardpad ▷ *noun* a symptom of DISTEMPER[1] in dogs, which causes hardness of the pads of the feet.

hard palate ▷ *noun* the bony front part of the palate, which separates the mouth from the nasal cavities.

hard paste ▷ *noun* a porcelain of Chinese origin made in Europe from the early 18c.

hard porn and **hard pornography** *noun, colloq* HARD-CORE pornography in which sexual acts are described or depicted explicitly.

hard-pressed and **hard-pushed** ▷ *adj* **1** having problems; in difficulties. **2** threatened by severe competition or attack. **3** closely pursued.

hard rock ▷ *noun* very loud but rhythmically simple rock music.

hard sauce ▷ *noun* BRANDY BUTTER.

hard science ▷ *noun* any of the physical or natural sciences, especially those involving quantitative empirical research, such as physics, chemistry, biology, geology or astronomy. Compare SOFT SCIENCE, PSEUDOSCIENCE. • **hard scientist** *noun.*

hard-sectored ▷ *adj, computing* said of a floppy disk: formatted by a set of holes punched near the hub of the disk, each hole marking the start of a sector.

the hard sell ▷ *noun* an aggressive and insistent way of promoting, selling or advertising.

hard-shell and **hard-shelled** ▷ *adj* **1** *zool* with a shell that is thick, heavy or hard. **2** *US* strictly orthodox.

hardship ▷ *noun* **1** living conditions that are difficult to endure. **2** severe suffering or pain, or a cause of this.

hard shoulder ▷ *noun, Brit* a hard verge along the side of a motorway, on which vehicles can stop if in trouble.

hard-standing ▷ *noun* a concrete or other hard surface on which cars, aircraft, etc, may be parked.

hard stuff ▷ *noun, colloq* **1** strong alcohol or spirits. **2** important information.

hardtack ▷ *noun* a kind of hard biscuit, formerly given to sailors as food on long journeys.

hardware ▷ *noun* **1** metal goods such as pots, cutlery, tools, etc. **2** *computing* the electronic, electrical, magnetic and mechanical components of a computer system, as opposed to the programs that form the SOFTWARE. See also LIVEWARE. **3** heavy military equipment, eg tanks and missiles. **4** mechanical equipment, components, etc. **5** *colloq* a gun.

hard-wearing ▷ *adj* indicating something that will last a long time and stay in good condition despite regular use.

hard wheat ▷ *noun* wheat that has a hard kernel with a high gluten content.

hard-wired ▷ *adj* said of computers: having functions that are controlled by hardware and cannot be altered by software programmes.

hardwood ▷ *noun* **1** the wood of a slow-growing deciduous tree, such as the oak, mahogany or teak. **2** any tree that produces such wood.

hardy /ˈhɑːdɪ/ ▷ *adj* (***hardier***, ***hardiest***) **1** tough; strong; able to bear difficult conditions. **2** said of a plant: able to survive outdoors in winter. **3** bold; courageous. **4** foolhardy; rash. • **hardily** *adverb.* • **hardiness** *noun.* ◷ 13c: from French *hardi*, from *hardir* to become bold.

hardy annual ▷ *noun* **1** a plant that lives for up to a year and which can withstand severe climatic conditions. **2** *facetious* a story or topic of conversation that comes up regularly.

hare /hɛə(r)/ ▷ *noun* a herbivorous mammal like a rabbit but slightly larger and with longer legs and ears, which lives in a FORM (*noun* 12) and whose young are called LEVERETS. ▷ *verb* (***hared***, ***haring***) *intr* (*often* **hare off** or **hare after something**) *colloq* to run very fast or wildly. • **harelike** *adj.* • **first catch your hare** make sure you have a thing first before you decide what to do with it. • **raise** or **start a hare** to introduce a topic of conversation, line of inquiry, etc. • **run with the hare and hunt with the hounds** to be on good terms with both sides at the same time. ◷ Anglo-Saxon *hara.*

hare and hounds ▷ *singular noun* a cross-country paper chase in which certain players (known as HARES) run scattering pieces of paper that the other players (known as HOUNDS) follow in an attempt to catch the hares.

harebell ▷ *noun* a wild plant with violet-blue bell-shaped flowers. In Scotland called BLUEBELL.

hare-brained or **hair-brained** ▷ *adj* said of people, actions, etc: foolish; rash; heedless.

harelip ▷ *noun* a deformity of the upper lip, present from birth, in which there is a cleft on one or both sides of the centre, often occurring with a CLEFT PALATE. • **harelipped** *adj*.

harem or **hareem** /'hɑːriːm, hɑː'riːm/ ▷ *noun* **1** a separate part of a traditional Muslim house in which wives, concubines, etc live. **2** the women living in this. **3** a group of female animals that are the mates of a single male. ◷ 17c: from Arabic *harim* forbidden.

hare's foot and **hare's foot trefoil** ▷ *noun* a plant that grows on sandy soils in Europe and NW Asia and has long soft fluffy heads.

haricot /'harɪkoʊ/ and **haricot bean** ▷ *noun* a small white dried bean, used as food. ◷ French.

hari-kari see HARA-KIRI

hark /hɑːk/ ▷ *verb* (***harked***, ***harking***) *intr*, *literary & dialect* (*usually* **hark at something** or **someone**) to listen to it or to them attentively. ◷ Anglo-Saxon, from *heorcnian* to hearken.

▪ **hark back to something** to refer to or remind one of (past experiences) □ *hark back to one's childhood.*

harken see HEARKEN

harl[1] /hɑːl/ or **herl** /hɜːl/ ▷ *noun* **1** a fibre of flax, etc. **2** *angling* **a** the barb or barbs of a feather used in making an artificial fly for fishing; **b** an artificial fly made with such barbs. ◷ 15c: from German *herle*.

harl[2] /harl, hɑːl/ *Scots* ▷ *verb* (***harled***, ***harling***) to roughcast (eg a wall). ▷ *noun* roughcast. • **harling** *noun*. ◷ 18c.

harlequin /'hɑːləkwɪn/ ▷ *noun* **1** (*also* **Harlequin**) *theat* a humorous character from traditional Italian plays who wears a black mask and a brightly coloured, diamond-patterned costume. **2** a clown or buffoon. ▷ *adj* in varied bright colours. ◷ 16c: from French *arlequin*, from *Hellequin* leader of a troop of demon horsemen.

harlequinade /hɑːləkwɪ'neɪd/ ▷ *noun* **1** (*also* **Harlequinade**) *theat* a play in which a harlequin has a leading role. **2** buffoonery. ◷ 18c: from French *arlequinade*.

harlot /'hɑːlət/ ▷ *noun*, *old use* a prostitute. • **harlotry** *noun*. ◷ 13c: from French *herlot* rascal.

harm /hɑːm/ ▷ *noun* physical, mental or moral injury or damage. ▷ *verb* (***harmed***, ***harming***) to injure physically, mentally or morally □ *didn't want to harm the children* □ *CFCs continue to harm the environment.* • **out of harm's way** in a safe place, not able to be harmed or cause harm. ◷ Anglo-Saxon *hearm*.

harmful ▷ *adj* causing or tending to cause harm. • **harmfully** *adverb*. • **harmfulness** *noun*.

harmless ▷ *adj* not able or likely to cause harm. • **harmlessly** *adverb*. • **harmlessness** *noun*.

harmonic /hɑː'mɒnɪk/ ▷ *adj* **1** relating or referring to, or producing, harmony; harmonious. **2** *music* relating or belonging to harmony. **3** *math* **a** able to be expressed in the form of SINE[1] and COSINE functions; **b** relating or referring to numbers whose reciprocals form an arithmetic progression; **c** (*physics*) relating to, or concerned with, a harmonic or harmonics. ▷ *noun* **1** *music* an overtone of a fundamental note, produced on a stringed instrument by touching one of the strings lightly at one of the points which divide the string into exact fractions. **2** *physics* a component of a sound whose frequency is an integral multiple of the base frequency. **3** one of the components of what the ear hears as a single sound. **4** in television broadcasting: a reflected signal received on a different channel from that on which the main signal is received. • **harmonically** *adverb*. ◷ 16c: from Latin *harmonicus* relating to HARMONY.

harmonica /hɑː'mɒnɪkə/ ▷ *noun* (***harmonicas***) a small rectangular wind instrument with metal reeds along one side, played by being held against the mouth, blown or sucked, and moved from side to side to change the notes. Also called **mouth organ**. ◷ 18c: from Latin *harmonicus* relating to HARMONY.

harmonic analysis ▷ *noun* the representation of a periodic function by means of the SUMMATION and INTEGRATION (sense 2) of simple trigonometric functions.

harmonic mean ▷ *noun* the reciprocal of the arithmetic mean of the reciprocals of a set of specified numbers.

harmonic minor scale ▷ *noun*, *music* a minor musical scale altered from the natural by the sharpening of the seventh degree.

harmonic motion ▷ *noun* (*in full* **simple harmonic motion**) a periodic motion in which the restoring influence acting towards the rest position is proportional to the displacement from the rest, as in a pendulum undergoing small swings.

harmonic progression ▷ *noun*, *math* a series of terms in which there is a constant difference between the RECIPROCALs of the terms, eg 1, $^1/_2$, $^1/_3$, $^1/_4$, ...

harmonics /hɑː'mɒnɪks/ ▷ *singular noun* the science of musical sounds and their acoustic properties.

harmonic series ▷ *noun* **1** *math* HARMONIC PROGRESSION. **2** *music* the combination or series of notes produced when a string or column of air is vibrated.

harmonious /hɑː'moʊnɪəs/ ▷ *adj* **1** pleasant-sounding and tuneful. **2** forming a pleasing whole □ *a harmonious arrangement of colours.* **3** without disagreement or bad feeling. • **harmoniously** *adverb*. • **harmoniousness** *noun*. ◷ 16c.

harmonist /'hɑːmənɪst/ ▷ *noun* **1** someone skilled in the theory or composition of harmony. **2** someone who merges and collates parallel narratives. **3** someone who seeks to reconcile apparent inconsistencies.

harmonium /hɑː'moʊnɪəm/ ▷ *noun* a musical instrument with a keyboard, in which air from bellows pumped by the feet makes the reeds vibrate to produce sound. ◷ 19c: French, from *harmonie* harmony.

harmonize or **harmonise** /'hɑːmənaɪz/ ▷ *verb* (***harmonized***, ***harmonizing***) **1** *tr & intr* to be in or bring into musical harmony. **2** *tr & intr* to form or be made to form a pleasing whole. **3** to add notes to (a simple tune) to form harmonies. **4** *intr* to sing in harmony, eg with other singers. **5** to reconcile (conflicting accounts). • **harmonization** *noun*.

harmony /'hɑːmənɪ/ ▷ *noun* (***harmonies***) **1** *music* **a** a pleasing combination of notes or sounds produced simultaneously; **b** the whole chordal structure of a piece as distinguished from its MELODY or its RHYTHM; **c** the art or science concerned with combinations of chords. **2** a pleasing arrangement of parts or things □ *a harmony of colour.* **3** agreement in opinions, actions, feelings, etc. **4** a reconciliation of conflicting accounts, especially of the four Gospels. ◷ 14c: from Latin *harmonia* concord of sounds, from Greek *harmos* a joint.

harness /'hɑːnɪs/ ▷ *noun* **1** a set of leather straps used to attach a cart to a horse, and to control the horse's movements. **2** a similar set of straps for attaching to a person's body, eg to hold a child who is just learning to walk. **3** *weaving* the part of a loom that raises and lowers the warp threads. **4** the wiring system of a car, etc when built separately for installing as a unit. ▷ *verb* (***harnesses***, ***harnessed***, ***harnessing***) **1** to put a harness on (a horse, person, etc). **2** (*usually* **harness something to something**) to attach a draught animal to a cart, etc. **3** to control (resources, especially natural ones) so as to make use of the potential energy or power they contain. • **harnesser** *noun*. • **in harness** occupied with one's daily work or routine. ◷ 13c: from French *herneis* equipment.

harness race ▷ *noun*, *horse-racing* a trotting or pacing race in which horses pull sulkies (see SULKY *noun*).

harp /hɑːp/ ▷ *noun* a large three-sided musical instrument with a series of strings stretched vertically across it, played by plucking the strings with the fingers. ▷ *verb* (***harped***, ***harping***) *intr* to play the harp. • **harpist** or (*archaic*) **harper** *noun*. ⓒ Anglo-Saxon *hearpe*.

■ **harp on about something** *colloq* to talk or write repeatedly and tediously about it.

harpoon /hɑːˈpuːn/ ▷ *noun* a barbed spear fastened to a rope, used for catching whales. Also *as adj* □ *harpoon gun*. ▷ *verb* (***harpooned***, ***harpooning***) to strike (a whale, etc) with a harpoon. • **harpooner** or **harpooneer** *noun*. ⓒ 17c: from French *harpon* clamp.

harp-seal ▷ *noun* a brownish-grey seal with a dark harp-shaped mark on its back, found in N Atlantic and Arctic regions.

harpsichord /ˈhɑːpsɪkɔːd/ ▷ *noun* a triangular-shaped keyboard instrument in which the strings are plucked mechanically by pivoted plectra mounted on jacks when the player presses the keys. • **harpsichordist** *noun*. ⓒ 17c: from Latin *harpa* harp + *chorda* string.

harpy /ˈhɑːpɪ/ ▷ *noun* (***harpies***) **1** *Greek mythol* an evil creature with the head and body of a woman and the wings and feet of a bird. **2** a cruel, grasping woman. **3** (*also* **harpy eagle**) a large S American eagle. ⓒ 16c: from Greek *harpyia* snatcher, from *harpazein* to seize.

harquebus see ARQUEBUS

harridan /ˈharɪdən/ ▷ *noun* a bad-tempered, scolding old woman; a nag. ⓒ 17c: probably from French *haridelle*, literally 'broken-down horse'.

harrier[1] /ˈharɪə(r)/ ▷ *noun* **1** a cross-country runner. **2** a hound used originally for hunting hares. ⓒ 15c: from HARE + *-er*, influenced by HARRIER[2].

harrier[2] /ˈharɪə(r)/ ▷ *noun* **1** a diurnal bird of prey with broad wings and long legs. **2** any person or thing that harries (see HARRY). ⓒ 16c: from HARRY.

harrow /ˈharoʊ/ ▷ *noun* a heavy metal framed farm implement with spikes or teeth, used to break up clods of soil and cover seed. ▷ *verb* (***harrowed***, ***harrowing***) **1** to pull a harrow over (land). **2** (*usually* **be harrowing**) to distress greatly; to vex. • **harrower** *noun*. • **harrowing** *adj* acutely distressing. • **harrowingly** *adverb*. ⓒ Anglo-Saxon *haerwe*.

harry /ˈharɪ/ ▷ *verb* (***harries***, ***harried***, ***harrying***) **1** to ravage or destroy (a town, etc), especially in war. **2** to annoy or worry someone. See also HARRIER[2]. ⓒ Anglo-Saxon *hergian*, related to *here* army.

harsh /hɑːʃ/ ▷ *adj* **1** rough; grating; unpleasant to the senses. **2** strict, cruel or severe. • **harshly** *adverb*. • **harshness** *noun*. ⓒ 13c.

hart /hɑːt/ ▷ *noun* a male deer, especially one over five years old, when the antlers begin to appear. ⓒ Anglo-Saxon *heorot*.

hartal /ˈhɑːtal, ˈhɜːtɑːl/ ▷ *noun* in India: a stoppage of work in protest or boycott. ⓒ 1920s: Hindi.

hartebeest /ˈhɑːtəbiːst/ and **hartbeest** /ˈhɑːtbiːst/ ▷ *noun* either of the two large African antelopes with an elongated muzzle, curved horns and a fawn-coloured coat. ⓒ 18c: Afrikaans, from Dutch *hert* HART + *beest* BEAST.

hartshorn /ˈhɑːtshɔːn/ ▷ *noun, obsolete* SAL VOLATILE. ⓒ Anglo-Saxon *heortes horn* hart's horn, formerly a chief source of ammonia.

hart's tongue ▷ *noun* an evergreen Eurasian fern with bright-green strap-shaped undivided fronds.

harum-scarum /hɛərəmˈskɛərəm/ ▷ *adj* wild and thoughtless; reckless. ▷ *adverb* recklessly. ▷ *noun* someone who is wild, impetuous or rash. ⓒ 17c: from *hare* in obsolete sense 'harass' + SCARE.

haruspex /həˈrʌspɛks/ ▷ *noun* (***haruspices*** /-spɪsiːz/) in ancient Rome: someone who foretold events, especially by examining the entrails of animals. • **haruspicy** /-spɪsɪ/ *noun*. ⓒ 16c: Latin.

harvest /ˈhɑːvɪst/ ▷ *noun* **1** the gathering in of ripened crops, usually in late summer or early autumn. **2** the season when this takes place. **3** the crop or crops gathered. **4** the product or result of some action, effort, etc. ▷ *verb* (***harvested***, ***harvesting***) **1** *tr & intr* to gather (a ripened crop) from the place where it has grown. **2** to receive or reap (benefits, consequences, etc). • **harvesting** *noun*. ⓒ Anglo-Saxon *hærfest*.

harvester /ˈhɑːvɪstə(r)/ ▷ *noun* **1** someone who harvests. **2** a machine that harvests a crop, eg a combine harvester or potato lifter.

harvest festival and **harvest thanksgiving** ▷ *noun* a Christian religious service to thank God for the crops gathered in the harvest.

harvest home ▷ *noun* **1** the bringing in of the harvest. **2** *chiefly Brit* a celebration of this.

harvestman ▷ *noun* a type of arachnid with very long legs. Also called (*US*) **daddy-long-legs**.

harvest mite see CHIGGER

harvest moon ▷ *noun* the full moon nearest to the autumnal equinox, usually 22 or 23 September.

harvest mouse ▷ *noun* a very small reddish-brown mouse that nests in cornfields.

has see HAVE

has-been ▷ *noun* (***has-beens***) *colloq* someone or something that is no longer successful, important or influential although they or it used to be such. ⓒ 17c.

hash[1] /haʃ/ ▷ *noun* (***hashes***) **1** a dish of cooked meat and vegetables chopped up together and recooked. **2** a re-using of old material. **3** *colloq* a mess □ *He'll make a hash of it*. ▷ *verb* (***hashes***, ***hashed***, ***hashing***) **1** to chop up into small pieces. **2** to mess up. • **settle someone's hash** *colloq* to silence or subdue them. ⓒ 17c: from French *hacher* to chop, from *hache* hatchet.

hash[2] /haʃ/ ▷ *noun, slang* hashish.

hash browns and **hash brown potatoes** ▷ *plural noun* a dish of potato (sometimes mixed with onion) cut into thin strips, fried to form a flat browned cake, and eaten hot.

hashish or **hasheesh** /ˈhaʃɪʃ, ˈhaʃiːʃ/ ▷ *noun* CANNABIS. ⓒ 16c: from Arabic *hashish* dry leaves of hemp.

Hasid or **Hassid** /ˈhasɪd/ ▷ *noun* (***Hasidim***) a member of any of a number of extremely devout and often mystical Jewish sects existing at various times throughout history. Also called **Chassid**. • **Hasidic** *adj*. • **Hasidism** *noun*. • **Hasidist** *noun*.

haslet /ˈhazlət/ and **harselet** /ˈhɑːzlət/ ▷ *noun* a loaf of cooked minced pig's offal, eaten cold. ⓒ 14c: from French *hastelet* piece of roasted meat, from *haste* spit.

hasn't /ˈhazənt/ ▷ *contraction* has not.

hasp /hɑːsp/ ▷ *noun* a metal fastening for a door, box, etc consisting of a flat metal strip with a narrow slit in it, which fits over a small curved metal bar and is secured by a pin or padlock. ▷ *verb* (***hasped***, ***hasping***) to secure (a door, window, etc) with a hasp. ⓒ Anglo-Saxon *hæpse*.

hassle /ˈhasəl/ *colloq* ▷ *noun* **1** trouble, annoyance or inconvenience, or a cause of this. **2** a fight or argument. ▷ *verb* (***hassled***, ***hassling***) **1** to annoy or bother someone, especially repeatedly; to harass. **2** *intr* to argue or fight. ⓒ 1940s.

hassock /ˈhasək/ ▷ *noun* **1** a firm cushion for kneeling on, especially in church. **2** a tuft of grass. ⓒ Anglo-Saxon *hassuc*.

hast /hast/ ▷ *verb, old use* the form of the present tense of the verb HAVE used with THOU 1.

hastate /ˈhasteɪt/ ▷ *adj* said of a leaf: with a pointed tip and two outward-pointing lobes at the base. ⓒ 19c: from Latin *hastatus*, from *hasta* spear.

haste /ˈheɪst/ ▷ *noun* **1** speed, especially speed in an action. **2** urgency of movement; necessity for hurrying. **3** the act of hurrying in a careless fashion. ▷ *verb* (***hasted, hasting***) to hasten. ● **in haste** in a hurry; quickly. ● **make haste** to hurry. ◷ 14c: French.

hasten /ˈheɪsən/ ▷ *verb* **1** *tr & intr* to hurry or cause to hurry. **2** (*always* **hasten to do something**) to do it eagerly and promptly □ *He hastened to admit we were right.* ◷ 16c: from HASTE.

hasty /ˈheɪstɪ/ ▷ *adj* (***hastier, hastiest***) **1** hurried; swift; quick. **2** without enough thought or preparation; rash. **3** short-tempered. **4** conveying irritation or anger □ *hasty words*. ● **hastily** *adverb*. ● **hastiness** *noun*.

hat ▷ *noun* **1** a covering for the head, usually worn out of doors. **2** *colloq* a role or capacity □ *wearing her vet's hat*. ▷ *verb* (***hatted, hatting***) to provide someone with a hat or put a hat on someone. ● **hatless** *adj*. ● **a bad hat** *colloq* an unscrupulous person. ● **at the drop of a hat** see under DROP. ● **keep something under one's hat** *colloq* to keep it secret. ● **my hat!** an exclamation expressing surprise or disbelief. ● **old hat** *colloq* so well known, familiar, etc as to be tedious and uninteresting. ● **pass** or **send the hat round** to collect money for a cause. ● **take one's hat off to someone** *colloq* to admire or praise them, especially for some particular achievement. ● **talk through one's hat** *colloq* **1** to talk nonsense. **2** to deceive or bluff. ● **throw one's hat into the ring** see under RING[1]. ● **wear several hats** or **another hat**, *etc* to act in several roles or capacities. ◷ Anglo-Saxon *hæt*.

hatband ▷ *noun* a band of cloth or ribbon around a hat just above the brim.

hatbox ▷ *noun* a large rounded box or case for storing or carrying hats.

hatch[1] /hatʃ/ ▷ *noun* (***hatches***) **1** a door covering an opening in a ship's deck. **2** a hatchway. **3** a door in an aircraft or spacecraft. **4** (*also* **serving hatch**) an opening in a wall between a kitchen and dining-room, used especially for serving food. **5** the lower half of a divided door. **6** a flood-gate or sluice. ● **down the hatch** *colloq* said as a toast: drink up! ● **under hatches 1** below decks. **2** out of sight. **3** dead. ◷ Anglo-Saxon *hæc*.

hatch[2] /hatʃ/ ▷ *verb* (***hatches, hatched, hatching***) **1** *intr* (*also* **hatch out**) said of an animal or bird: to break out of an egg. **2** *intr* said of an egg: to break open, allowing young animals or birds to be born. **3** to produce (young animals or birds) from eggs. **4** (*often* **hatch something up**) to plan or devise (a plot, scheme, etc), especially in secret. ▷ *noun* (***hatches***) **1** the act or process of hatching. **2** a brood of newly hatched animals. ● **count one's chickens before they are hatched** *usually with negatives* to rely too much on some uncertain future event. ◷ 13c.

hatch[3] /hatʃ/ ▷ *verb* (***hatches, hatched, hatching***) said of the surface of a map, drawing, engraving, etc: to shade with close parallel or crossed lines. ● **hatching** *noun*. ◷ 15c: from French *hacher* to chop, from *hache* hatchet.

hatchback ▷ *noun* **1** a sloping rear end of a car with a single door which opens upwards, allowing access to the compartment inside. **2** a car with such a rear end.

hatchery /ˈhatʃərɪ/ ▷ *noun* (***hatcheries***) a place where eggs, especially fish eggs, are hatched under artificial conditions.

hatchet /ˈhatʃɪt/ ▷ *noun* **1** a small axe held in one hand. **2** a tomahawk. ● **bury the hatchet** to end hostilities and become reconciled. ◷ 14c: from French *hachette*, from *hache* axe.

hatchet-faced ▷ *adj* with a long thin face and sharp profile.

hatchet job ▷ *noun*, *colloq* a severe critical attack on someone or their good reputation.

hatchet man ▷ *noun*, *colloq* **1** a person employed to carry out illegal, unpleasant or destructive assignments. **2** a severely critical or malicious journalist.

hatchment /ˈhatʃmənt/ ▷ *noun*, *heraldry* a diamond-shaped tablet displaying the coat of arms of a dead person, fixed to the front of their former home. ◷ 16c: altered from *achievement* in this sense.

hatchway ▷ *noun* **1** an opening in a ship's deck for loading cargo through. **2** a similar opening in a wall, ceiling, floor, etc.

hate ▷ *verb* (***hated, hating***) **1** to dislike intensely. **2** *colloq* to regret □ *I hate to bother you.* ▷ *noun* **1** an intense dislike. **2** (*especially* **pet hate**) *colloq* an intensely disliked person or thing. **3** *as adj* expressing or conveying hatred □ *hate mail*. ● **hatable** or **hateable** *adj*. ● **hate someone's guts** *colloq* to dislike them intensely. ◷ Anglo-Saxon *hatian*.

hateful ▷ *adj* causing or deserving great dislike; loathsome; detestable. ● **hatefully** *adverb*. ● **hatefulness** *noun*.

hate mail ▷ *noun* correspondence containing an abusive or threatening message, especially sent to a celebrity or person in the news.

hath /haθ/ ▷ *verb*, *archaic* the form of the present tense of HAVE, used where we would now use HAS.

hatpin ▷ *noun* a long metal pin, often decorated, pushed through a woman's hat and hair to keep the hat in place.

hatred /ˈheɪtrɪd/ ▷ *noun* intense dislike; enmity; ill-will.

hatstand and (*especially US*) **hat tree** ▷ *noun* a piece of furniture with pegs for hanging hats, coats, umbrellas, etc on.

hatter /ˈhatə(r)/ ▷ *noun* someone who makes or sells hats. ● **mad as a hatter** extremely mad or eccentric.

hat trick ▷ *noun* **1** *cricket* the taking of three wickets with three successive balls. **2** the scoring of three points, goals, etc in a single period of time or match. **3** the winning of three victories in a row. ◷ 19c: in sense 1, probably because the cricketer would be entitled to receive a new hat or other prize for achieving this.

hauberk /ˈhɔːbək/ ▷ *noun*, *historical* a long coat of chain-mail. ◷ 13c: from French *hauberc*.

haughty /ˈhɔːtɪ/ ▷ *adj* (***haughtier, haughtiest***) very proud; arrogant or contemptuous. ● **haughtily** *adverb*. ● **haughtiness** *noun*. ◷ 16c: from French *haut* lofty, from Latin *altus* high.

haul /hɔːl/ ▷ *verb* (***hauled, hauling***) **1** *tr & intr* to pull with great effort or difficulty. **2** to transport by road, eg in a lorry. **3** *naut* to alter the course of a vessel, especially so as to sail closer to the wind. **4** *intr*, *naut* said of the wind: to blow from a direction nearer the bow of a vessel. ▷ *noun* **1** the distance to be travelled □ *Just a short haul now over the mountains* □ *It's a long haul to Sydney.* **2** the act of dragging something with effort or difficulty. **3** the amount gained at any one time, eg the amount of fish caught in a single net or of something stolen. **4** something that is hauled. **5** the amount of contraband seized at any one time □ *drugs haul*. ● **hauler** *noun*. ● **haul someone over the coals** see under COAL. ● **long haul** see separate entry. ◷ 16c: from French *haler* to drag.

■ **haul up** to sail a vessel closer to the wind.

■ **haul someone up** *colloq* to call them to account (before a court, judge, etc).

haulage ▷ *noun* **1** the act or labour of hauling. **2 a** the business of transporting goods by road, especially in lorries; **b** the money charged for this.

haulier /ˈhɔːlɪə(r)/ ▷ *noun* **1** a person or company that transports goods by road, especially in lorries. **2** a mine worker who conveys coal from the workings to the foot of the shaft.

haulm or **halm** /hɔːm/ ▷ *noun*, *bot* **1** the stalks or stems of potatoes, peas, beans or grasses, collectively. **2** one such stalk or stem. ◷ Anglo-Saxon *healm*.

haunch /hɔːntʃ/ ▻ *noun* (***haunches***) **1** the fleshy part of the buttock or thigh. **2** the leg and loin, especially of a deer, as a cut of meat □ *a haunch of venison.* **3** *archit* the side or flank of an arch between the top and start of its curve. ⓒ 13c: from French *hanche*.

haunch bone ▻ *noun* the ILIUM.

haunt /hɔːnt/ ▻ *verb* (***haunted, haunting***) **1** said of a ghost or spirit: to be present in (a place) or visit (a person or place) regularly. **2** said of unpleasant thoughts, etc: to keep coming back to someone's mind □ *She was haunted by the memory of his death.* **3** to visit (a place) frequently. **4** to associate with someone frequently. ▻ *noun* **1** (*often* **haunts**) a place visited frequently. **2** the habitation or usual feeding-ground of deer, game, fowls, etc. • **haunted** *adj* **1** frequented or visited by ghosts or spirits. **2** constantly worried or obsessed. ⓒ 13c: from French *hanter*.

haunting ▻ *adj* said of a place, memory, piece of music, etc: making a very strong and moving impression; poignant. • **hauntingly** *adverb*.

Hausa /ˈhaʊsə, -zə/ ▻ *noun* (***Hausas*** or ***Hausa***) **1** a Negroid people of W Africa, living mainly in N Nigeria. **2** a member of this people. **3** the language of this people, widely used in commerce throughout W Africa.

hausfrau /ˈhaʊsfraʊ/ ▻ *noun* (***hausfraus***) a German housewife, especially one exclusively interested in domestic matters. ⓒ 18c: German, from *Haus* house + *Frau* woman or wife.

hautboy /ˈoʊbɔɪ, ˈhoʊbɔɪ/ ▻ *noun* **1** *old use* an oboe. **2** (*also* **hautbois**) a large kind of strawberry. ⓒ 16c: French, from *haut* high + *bois* wood.

haute couture /oʊt kʊˈtjʊə(r)/ ▻ *noun* **1** the most expensive and fashionable clothes available. **2** the leading fashion designers or their products, collectively. ⓒ Early 20c: French, literally 'high dressmaking'.

haute cuisine /oʊt kwɪˈziːn/ ▻ *noun*, cookery, especially French cookery, of a very high standard. ⓒ 1920s: French, literally 'high cooking'.

hauteur /oʊˈtɜː(r)/ ▻ *noun* haughtiness; arrogance. ⓒ 17c: French, from *haut* high.

have /hav, həv/ ▻ *verb* (***has*** /haz, həz/, ***had*** /had, həz/, ***having***) **1** to possess or own □ *They have a big house.* **2** to possess as a characteristic or quality □ *He has brown eyes.* **3** to receive, obtain or take □ *I'll have a drink* □ *He had a look.* **4** to think of or hold in the mind □ *I have an idea.* **5** to experience, enjoy or suffer □ *You'll have a good time* □ *I have a headache* □ *I had my car stolen.* **6** to be in a specified state □ *The book has a page missing.* **7** to arrange or hold □ *I'm having a party.* **8** to take part in something □ *We had a conversation.* **9** to cause, order or invite someone to do something or something to be done □ *You should have your hair cut* □ *They had him fired.* **10** to state or assert □ *Rumour has it that they've only just met.* **11** to place □ *I'll have the fridge in this corner.* **12** to eat or drink □ *I had beans and chips.* **13** to gain an advantage over or control of someone □ *You have me on that point.* **14** *colloq* to cheat or deceive □ *You've been had.* **15** to show or feel □ *I have no pity for them* □ *She had the goodness to leave.* **16** *with negatives* to accept or tolerate □ *I won't have any of that!* **17** to receive as a guest □ *We're having people to dinner.* **18** to be pregnant with or give birth to (a baby, etc) □ *She had a boy.* **19** *coarse slang* to have sexual intercourse with someone. **20** to possess a knowledge of something □ *I have some French.* ▻ *auxiliary verb* used with a past PARTICIPLE to show that the action or actions described have been completed, as in *I have made the cake* and *She has been there many times.* ▻ *noun* **1** (**haves** /havz/) *colloq* people who have wealth and the security it brings □ *the haves and the have-nots.* **2** *slang* a trick or swindle. • **had better** or **best** ... would do best to ... □ *I had better be off.* • **had rather** or **sooner** ... would consider preferable that ... □ *I had rather you didn't bother.* • **have had it** *colloq* **1** to be dead, ruined or exhausted. **2** to have missed one's opportunity. **3** to become unfashionable. • **have it coming** *colloq* to deserve the bad luck, punishment, etc that one will get. • **have it in for someone** *colloq* to feel hostile towards them and wish to cause them unpleasantness. • **have it in one** to have the courage or ability within oneself (to do something). • **have it off** or **away with someone** *Brit coarse slang* to have sexual intercourse with them. • **have it out** to settle a disagreement by arguing or discussing it frankly. • **have it so good** *usually with negatives* to have very many material benefits. • **have to be** to surely be □ *That has to be the reason.* • **have to be** or **do something** to be required to be or do it □ *He had to run fast* □ *We had to be gentle.* • **have to do with someone** to have dealings with them. • **have to do with something** to be of relevance to it. • **have what it takes** *colloq* to have the required qualities or ability. • **I have it!** or **I've got it!** I have found the answer, solution, etc. • **let someone have it** *colloq* to launch an attack on them, either physical or verbal. • **not be having any of that** to be unwilling to accept or tolerate the thing mentioned. ⓒ Anglo-Saxon *habban*.

■ **have at someone** *archaic* to make an opening attack on them, especially in fencing.

■ **have someone on** *colloq* to trick or tease them.

■ **have something on 1** to be wearing it. **2** to have an engagement or appointment.

■ **have something on someone** to have information about them, especially adverse or incriminating information.

■ **have something out** to have (a tooth, etc) extracted or removed.

■ **have someone up for something** *Brit colloq* to bring them to court to answer (a charge) □ *He was had up for robbery.*

> ***have***
>
> A common error is the insertion of an extra **have** after **had** in sentences such as:
>
> ✗ *If he had have done it, I would have been very angry.*
>
> ✗ *If they'd have told me earlier, I would have been able to prevent it.*

have-a-go ▻ *adj, colloq* said of members of the public at the scene of a crime, etc: willing to intervene in an attempt to catch or obstruct a criminal, especially one carrying a weapon.

havelock /ˈhavlək/ ▻ *noun* a white cover for a military cap with a flap hanging over the back of the neck to protect the head and neck from the sun. ⓒ 19c: named after the English general in India Sir Henry Havelock (1795–1857).

haven /ˈheɪvən/ ▻ *noun* **1** a place of safety or rest. **2** a harbour or other sheltered spot for ships. ⓒ Anglo-Saxon *hæfen*.

have-nots ▻ *plural noun* people with relatively little material wealth.

haven't /havənt/ ▻ *contraction* have not.

haver /ˈheɪvə(r)/ *especially Scottish & N Eng*, ▻ *verb* (***havered, havering***) *intr* **1** to babble; to talk nonsense. **2** to be slow or hesitant in making a decision. ▻ *noun* (*usually* **havers**) foolish talk; nonsense. ⓒ 18c.

haversack /ˈhavəsak/ ▻ *noun* a canvas bag carried over one shoulder or on the back. ⓒ 18c: from German *Habersack*, literally 'oat-bag'.

haversine /ˈhavəsaɪn/ ▻ *noun, math* half the value of the versed sine. ⓒ 19c: from *half* + *versed* + *sine*.

havildar /ˈhavɪldɑː(r)/ ▻ *noun* a non-commissioned officer in the Indian army, equivalent in rank to sergeant. ⓒ 17c: from Persian *hawaldar* one in charge.

having *past participle of* HAVE

havoc /'havək/ ▷ *noun* **1** great destruction or damage. **2** *colloq* chaos; confusion. • **cry havoc** *archaic* to give the signal for pillage and destruction. • **play havoc with something** to cause a great deal of damage or confusion to it. ⓘ 15c: from French *havot* plunder.

haw¹ see HUM AND HAW at HUM

haw² /hɔː/ ▷ *noun* **1** a hawthorn berry. **2** the hawthorn. ⓘ Anglo-Saxon *haga*.

haw³ /hɔː/ ▷ *noun* the nictitating membrane or 'third eyelid' of a horse, dog, etc. ⓘ 15c.

hawfinch ▷ *noun* a type of European finch with a stout beak.

haw-haw see HA-HA¹, HA-HA²

hawk¹ /hɔːk/ ▷ *noun* **1** a relatively small diurnal bird of prey with short rounded wings and very good eyesight which hunts by pouncing on small birds and mammals. **2** in the USA: any of various falcons. **3** *politics* a person favouring force and aggression rather than peaceful means of settling disputes. Compare DOVE² (sense 2). **4** a ruthless or grasping person. ▷ *verb* (***hawked, hawking***) **1** *intr* to hunt with a hawk. **2** *intr* said of falcons or hawks: to fly in search of prey. **3** to pursue or attack on the wing, as a hawk does. • **hawking** *noun*. • **hawkish** like a hawk. • **hawklike** *adj*. • **know a hawk from a handsaw** to be able to judge between things pretty well. • **watch someone like a hawk** to watch them closely. ⓘ Anglo-Saxon *hafoc*.

hawk² /hɔːk/ ▷ *verb* (***hawked, hawking***) **1** to carry (goods) round, usually from door to door, trying to sell them. **2** (*often* **hawk about**) to spread news, gossip, etc. ⓘ 16c: a back-formation from HAWKER².

hawk³ /hɔːk/ ▷ *verb* (***hawked, hawking***) **1** *intr* to clear the throat noisily. **2** to bring phlegm up from the throat. ▷ *noun* the act or an instance of doing one of the above. ⓘ 16c.

hawk⁴ /hɔːk/ ▷ *noun* a MORTARBOARD 1.

hawker¹ /'hɔːkə(r)/ ▷ *noun* someone who hunts with a hawk. ⓘ Anglo-Saxon *hafocere*.

hawker² /'hɔːkə(r)/ *noun* someone who goes from place to place offering goods for sale. ⓘ 16c: probably from German *haker* retail dealer.

hawk-eyed ▷ *adj* **1** having very keen eyesight. **2** watchful; observant.

hawk moth ▷ *noun* any of various moths with long triangular wings, able to fly fast and hover over flowers to suck the nectar.

hawksbill turtle and **hawksbill** ▷ *noun* a small tropical turtle with a hook-like mouth, from which tortoiseshell is derived.

hawkweed ▷ *noun, bot* a perennial plant which has leaves arranged spirally around the stem, or forming a rosette at the base, and yellow flower heads that may be solitary or in loose clusters.

hawse /hɔːz/ ▷ *noun, naut* **1** the part of a vessel's bow in which the hawseholes are cut. **2** a hawsehole. **3** a hawsepipe. **4** the distance between the head of an anchored vessel and the anchor itself. **5** the position of the port and starboard anchor ropes when a vessel is moored with two anchors. ⓘ 15c: originally *halse*, probably from Norse *háls* neck or ship's bow.

hawsehole ▷ *noun, naut* a hole in the bow or stem of a vessel through which an anchor cable passes.

hawsepipe ▷ *noun, naut* a strong metal pipe fitted into a hawsehole through which an anchor cable passes.

hawser /'hɔːzə(r)/ ▷ *noun, naut* a thick rope or steel cable for tying ships to the quayside. ⓘ 14c: from French *haucier* to hoist.

hawthorn ▷ *noun* a thorny tree or shrub with pink or white flowers and red berries (see HAW² sense 1). Also called MAY², MAY TREE, MAYFLOWER, **quickthorn**, **whitethorn**. ⓘ Anglo-Saxon *haguthorn*, from *haga* hedge + THORN.

hay ▷ *noun* grass, clover, etc that has been cut and allowed to dry in the field before being baled and stored for use as winter fodder for animal livestock. ▷ *verb* (***hayed, haying***) *tr & intr* to cut, dry and store (grass, clover, etc) as fodder. • **hit the hay** *colloq* to go to bed. • **make hay of something** to throw it into confusion. • **make hay while the sun shines** to take advantage of an opportunity while one has the chance. ⓘ Anglo-Saxon *hieg*.

haybox ▷ *noun* an airtight box full of hay used to continue the cooking of preheated food by placing it within the hay which acts as a heat insulator.

haycock ▷ *noun* a small cone-shaped pile of hay in a field.

hay fever ▷ *noun, non-technical* allergic RHINITIS, an allergic response to pollen characterized by itching and watering of the eyes, dilation of nasal blood vessels and increased nasal mucus, due to the body's release of histamine.

hayfork ▷ *noun* a long-handled, long-pronged fork for tossing and lifting hay.

haymaker ▷ *noun* **1** a person employed in making hay, especially one who lifts, tosses and spreads the hay after it is cut. **2** either of two types of machine for shaking up and breaking hay to cause it to dry more rapidly and evenly. **3** *boxing* a wild swinging punch. • **haymaking** *noun, adj*.

haymow ▷ *noun* **1** the part of a barn where hay is stored. **2** the pile of hay stored.

hayseed ▷ *noun* **1** seeds or small pieces of grass or straw. **2** *US, Austral & NZ derog, colloq* a yokel.

haystack and **hayrick** ▷ *noun* a large firm stack of hay built in an open field and protected by plastic sheets or thatching. • **look for a needle in a haystack** to try to find something which is lost or hidden in a pile of things and so is almost impossible to find.

haywire ▷ *adj, colloq* (*often* **go haywire**) **1** said of things: out of order; not working properly. **2** said of people: crazy or erratic. ⓘ 1920s: originally US.

hazard /'hazəd/ ▷ *noun* **1** a risk of harm or danger. **2** something which is likely to cause harm or danger. **3** *golf* an obstacle on a golf course, such as water, a bunker, etc. **4** chance; accident. **5** a game played with two dice. **6** *real tennis* **a** the side of the court into which the ball is served; **b** each of the winning openings in a tennis court. **7** *billiards* a scoring stroke in which either the striker pockets a ball other than his own (a winning hazard), or his own cue ball is pocketed (a losing hazard). ▷ *verb* (***hazarded, hazarding***) **1** to put forward (a guess, suggestion, etc). **2** to risk. **3** to expose to danger. ⓘ 13c: from French *hasard*.

hazard lights and **hazard warning lights** ▷ *plural noun* the orange direction indicators on a motor vehicle when they all flash at once to indicate that the vehicle is stationary and temporarily obstructing traffic.

hazardous /'hazədəs/ ▷ *adj* **1** very risky; dangerous. **2** depending on chance; uncertain. • **hazardously** *adverb*. • **hazardousness** *noun*.

hazardous substance ▷ *noun* any chemical substance that is potentially damaging to health and can cause pollution of the environment.

hazard pay ▷ *noun, US* danger money.

haze¹ /heɪz/ ▷ *noun* **1** *meteorol* a thin mist, vapour or shimmer in the atmosphere which obscures visibility. **2** a feeling of confusion or of not understanding. ▷ *verb* (***hazed, hazing***) *tr & intr* to make or become hazy. ⓘ 17c: a back-formation from HAZY.

■ **haze over** to become covered in a thin mist.

haze² /heɪz/ ▷ *verb* (*hazed, hazing*) **1** *chiefly N Amer* to subject (fellow students) to abuse or bullying. **2** *naut* to punish or harass someone with humiliating work. • **hazer** *noun*. • **hazing** *noun*. ◷ 17c: from French *haser* to annoy.

hazel /ˈheɪzəl/ ▷ *noun* **1** a small deciduous shrub or tree with edible nuts that is widespread in Europe. **2** its wood. **3** a hazelnut. **4** a greenish-brown colour. ▷ *adj* greenish-brown in colour. ◷ Anglo-Saxon *hæsel*.

hazelnut ▷ *noun* the edible nut of the hazel tree, with a smooth hard shiny shell.

hazy /ˈheɪzɪ/ ▷ *adj* (*hazier, haziest*) **1** misty □ *was hazy over the lake.* **2** vague; not clear □ *hazy sunshine.* • **hazily** *adverb*. • **haziness** *noun*. ◷ 17c.

HB ▷ *abbreviation* on pencils: hard black.

Hb ▷ *abbreviation* haemoglobin.

HBC ▷ *abbreviation* Hudson's Bay Company.

HBM ▷ *abbreviation, Brit* His or Her Britannic Majesty.

H-bomb see HYDROGEN BOMB

HC ▷ *abbreviation* **1** Heralds' College. **2** Holy Communion. **3** *Brit* House of Commons.

HCF ▷ *abbreviation* **1** (*also* **hcf**) highest common factor. **2** Honorary Chaplain to the Forces.

HCG ▷ *abbreviation* human chorionic gonadotrophin.

HCM ▷ *abbreviation* His or Her Catholic Majesty.

hcp ▷ *abbreviation* handicap.

HD ▷ *abbreviation* heavy duty.

hdqrs ▷ *abbreviation* headquarters.

HDTV ▷ *abbreviation* high-definition television, an advanced TV system in which the image is formed by a much greater number of scanning lines than in standard TV, giving a much improved picture quality. ◷ 1980s.

HE ▷ *abbreviation* **1** high explosive. **2** His Eminence. **3** His or Her Excellency.

He ▷ *symbol, chem* helium.

he /hiː, hɪ/ ▷ *pronoun* **1** a male person or animal already referred to. **2** a person or animal of unknown or unstated sex, especially after pronouns such as 'someone' or 'whoever' □ *A student may attend as he feels necessary* □ *A teacher should do whatever he thinks best.* ▷ *noun* **1** a male person or animal. Also *in compounds* □ *he-goat.* **2** in children's games: same as TAG² *noun*, IT¹ *noun* 1. ◷ Anglo-Saxon *he*.

head /hɛd/ ▷ *noun* **1** the uppermost or foremost part of an animal's body, containing the brain and the organs of sight, smell, hearing and taste. **2** the head thought of as the seat of intelligence, imagination, ability, etc □ *Use your head* □ *You need a good head for heights.* **3** something like a head in form or function, eg the top of a tool. **4** the person with the most authority in an organization, country, etc. **5** the position of being in charge. **6** *colloq* a head teacher or principal teacher. **7** the top or upper part of something, eg a table or bed. **8** the highest point of something □ *the head of the pass.* **9** the front or forward part of something, eg a queue. **10** the foam on top of a glass of beer, lager, etc. **11** the top part of a plant which produces leaves or flowers. **12** a culmination or crisis □ *Things came to a head.* **13** the pus-filled top of a boil or spot. **14** (*plural* *head*) a person, animal or individual considered as a unit □ *600 head of cattle* □ *The meal cost £10 a head.* **15** *colloq* a headache. **16** the source of a river, lake, etc. **17** the height or length of a head, used as a measurement □ *He won by a head* □ *She's a head taller than her brother.* **18** a headland □ *Beachy Head.* **19 a**) the height of the surface of a liquid above a specific point, especially as a measure of the pressure at that point □ *a head of six metres*; **b** water pressure, due to height or velocity, measured in terms of a vertical column of water; **c** any pressure □ *a full head of steam.* **20** an electromagnetic device in a tape recorder, video recorder, computer, etc for converting electrical signals into the recorded form on tapes or disks, or vice versa, or for erasing recorded material. **21** (**heads**) the side of a coin bearing the head of a monarch, etc. Compare TAILS at TAIL *noun* 7. **22** (*often* **heads**) a headline or heading. **23** a main point of an argument, discourse, etc. **24** (*often* **heads**) *naut slang* a ship's toilet. **25** the taut membrane of a tambourine, drum, etc. **26** *colloq* a drug-user, especially one who takes LSD or cannabis. Usually *in compounds* □ *acid head* □ *smack head.* **27** *mining* an underground passage for working the coal. **28** the final point of a route. Also *in compounds* □ *railhead.* **29** *as adj* **a** for or belonging to the head □ *headband* □ *head cold*; **b** chief; principal □ *head gardener*; **c** at, or coming from, the front □ *head wind.* ▷ *verb* (*headed, heading*) **1** to be at the front of or top of something □ *to head the queue.* **2** (*often* **head up something**) to be in charge of it, or in the most important position. **3** *tr & intr* (*often* **head for somewhere**) to move or cause to move in a certain direction □ *They are heading for home.* **4** *tr & intr* to turn or steer (a vessel) in a particular direction □ *They headed into the wind.* **5** to provide with or be (a headline or heading) at the beginning of a chapter, top of a letter, etc. **6** *football* to hit (the ball) with one's head. **7 a** to chop off the top branches or shoots of a plant, etc; **b** *intr* said of a plant, etc: to form a head. **8** *intr* said of streams, rivers, etc: to originate or rise. • **above** or **over one's head** too difficult for one to understand. • **against the head** said of the ball in a rugby scrum, or of the scrum itself: won by the team not putting the ball in. • **bang one's head against a brick wall** to try in vain to make someone understand something, agree with your point of view, etc • **bite** or **snap someone's head off** to speak sharply to them. • **bring** or **come to a head** to reach or cause to reach a climax or crisis. • **give a horse its head** to let it go where, and as quickly as, it chooses. • **give head** *coarse slang* to perform oral sex. • **give someone his** or **her head** to allow them to act freely and without restraint. • **go to one's head 1** said of alcoholic drink: to make one slightly intoxicated. **2** said of praise, success, etc: to make one conceited. • **have**

he or she

• There is no pronoun in English that stands neutrally for male and female. In order to achieve neutrality of gender, many people use **he or she**, as in:

✓ *There is a limit on what an individual teacher can achieve if he or she is not working in harmony with the rest of the school.*

• This becomes awkward if it has to be sustained in longer sentences, eg if you want to say □ *... if he or she is not working in harmony with his or her colleagues.*

The result is often inconsistency:

✗ *The aim is to find the child a substitute home until such time as he or she can return to their own home.*

• Other devices such as **s/he** are not widely accepted. An alternative is to put the whole sentence in the plural:

✓ *There is a limit on what individual teachers can achieve if they are not working in harmony with their colleagues.*

• Because of these difficulties, it is common to use **they** and **their** as gender-neutral pronouns, especially in less formal contexts:

✓ *If anyone has lost an umbrella, will they let me know.*

☆ RECOMMENDATION: use **they** and **their** in more informal English, but avoid it if you are talking to someone who is likely to be precise about the use of language.

a good head on one's shoulders to be sensible, have ability, etc. • **have one's head in the clouds 1** to be inattentive to what is said. **2** to have impractical or unrealistic thoughts, ideas, etc. • **have one's head screwed on (the right way)** to be sensible, bright, etc. • **head and shoulders** by a considerable amount; to a considerable degree □ *He's head and shoulders above his competitors.* • **headfirst 1** moving especially quickly with one's head in front or bent forward. **2** without thinking; rashly. • **head over heels 1** rolling over completely with the head first. **2** completely □ *He's head over heels in love.* • **hold up one's head** to be unashamed. • **keep one's head** to remain calm and sensible in a crisis. • **keep one's head above water** to manage to cope with problems, especially financial ones. • **lose one's head** to become angry, excited or act foolishly, particularly in a crisis. • **not get it into one's head** to be unable to come to terms with or understand something. • **not make head or tail of something** to not understand it. • **off one's head** *colloq* mad; crazy. • **off one's (own) head** at one's (own) risk or responsibility. • **off the top of one's head** *colloq* without much thought or calculation. • **on your,** *etc* **own head be it** you, etc will bear the full responsibility for your, etc actions. • **out of one's head 1** *colloq* mad, crazy. **2** of one's own invention. • **over someone's head 1** without considering the obvious candidate □ *He was promoted over the head of his supervisor.* **2** referring to a higher authority without consulting the person in the obvious position □ *She complained to the director, over the head of the managing editor.* **3** too difficult for them to understand □ *Her jokes are always over my head.* • **put one's head on the block** to stick one's neck out, running the risk of censure, etc. • **put our** or **your** or **their heads together** to consult together. • **take** or **get it into one's head 1** to decide to do something, usually foolishly. **2** to come to believe something, usually wrongly. • **turn someone's head 1** to make them vain and conceited. **2** to attract their attention □ *Those rubber shorts will turn a few heads.* ⓒ Anglo-Saxon *heafod.*

■ **head off** to leave □ *I want to head off before it gets too dark.*

■ **head someone off** to get ahead of them so as to intercept them and force them to turn back □ *We managed to head off the rams.*

■ **head something off** to prevent or hinder it □ *We wish to head off possible unrest.*

headache ▷ *noun* **1** any continuous pain felt deep inside the head. **2** *colloq* someone or something that causes worry or annoyance. • **headachy** *adj.*

headband ▷ *noun* **1** a band worn round the head, especially for decoration. **2** a narrow band of cloth attached to the top of the spine of a book for protection or decoration.

headbang ▷ *verb, intr, colloq* to shake one's head violently to the beat of heavy-metal rock music. • **headbanger** *noun, colloq* **1** a fan of heavy-metal or rock music. **2** a stupid or fanatical person.

headboard ▷ *noun* a board at the top end of a bed.

head-butt ▷ *verb* to strike someone deliberately and violently with the head. ▷ *noun* such a blow.

head case ▷ *noun, colloq* **1** someone who behaves in a wild or irrational way. **2** a mentally ill person.

head cold ▷ *noun* a cold which affects one's eyes, nose and head, rather than one's throat and chest.

head count ▷ *noun* a count of people present.

headdress ▷ *noun* a covering for the head, especially one which is highly decorative and is used in ceremonies.

headed ▷ *adj* **1** having a heading □ *headed notepaper.* **2** *in compounds* □ *two-headed* □ *clear-headed.*

header /ˈhɛdə(r)/ ▷ *noun* **1** *colloq* a fall or dive forwards. **2** *football* the hitting of the ball with the head. **3** *building* a brick or stone laid across a wall so that the shorter side shows on the wall surface. Compare STRETCHER. **4** a heading for a chapter, article, etc. **5 a** a machine that removes the heads from castings, etc, or supplies heads, eg to wire to make nails; **b** someone who operates such a machine. **6** *computing* an optional piece of coded information preceding a collection of data, giving details about the data. **7** *marketing* a card attached to the top of a dumpbin giving information on the books displayed. **8** (*also* **header tank**) a reservoir that maintains a gravity feed or a static fluid pressure in an apparatus.

headgear ▷ *noun* **1** anything worn on the head. **2** any part of a horse's harness that is worn about the head. **3** the hoisting apparatus at the pithead of a mine.

headguard ▷ *noun* a lightweight helmet worn to protect the head in some sports.

headhunt ▷ *verb* to practice HEADHUNTING (sense 2).

headhunting ▷ *noun* **1** *anthropol* the practice in certain societies of taking the heads of one's dead enemies as trophies. **2** the practice of trying to attract people in senior positions or specialist fields away from their present jobs to work for one's own or a client's company. **3** *US colloq* the practice of destroying or neutralizing one's political opponents. • **headhunter** *noun.*

headier, **headiest**, *etc* see under HEADY

heading ▷ *noun* **1** a title at the top of a page, letter, section of a report, etc. **2** a main division, eg in a speech. **3** *mining* **a** a horizontal tunnel in a mine; **b** the end of such a tunnel. **4** *football* the act of striking the ball with the head. **5** the angle between the course of an aircraft and a specified meridian, often due north. **6** the compass direction parallel to the keel of a vessel.

headland ▷ *noun* **1** /ˈhɛdlənd/ a strip of land which sticks out into a sea or other expanse of water. **2** /ˈhɛdland/ a strip of land along the edge of an arable field left unploughed to allow space for the plough to turn.

headless ▷ *adj* lacking a head.

headlight and **headlamp** ▷ *noun* a powerful light on the front of a vehicle.

headline ▷ *noun* **1 a** the title or heading of a newspaper article, written above the article in large letters; **b** a line at the top of a page, indicating the page number, title, etc. **2** (**headlines**) the most important points in a television or radio news broadcast, read out before the full broadcast. ▷ *verb* **1** to provide (an article or page) with a headline. **2** *tr & intr* to have top billing in (a show, etc). • **hit the headlines** *colloq* to be an important or dramatic item of news.

headlong ▷ *adj, adverb* **1** moving especially quickly with one's head in front or bent forward. **2** quickly, and usually without thinking.

headman ▷ *noun* **1** *anthropol* a tribal chief or leader. **2** a foreman or supervisor.

headmaster and **headmistress** see under HEAD TEACHER

head on ▷ *adverb* **1** head to head; with the front of one vehicle hitting the front of another. **2** in direct confrontation. Also *as adj* □ *a head-on crash* □ *The government had a head-on collision with the unions.*

headphones ▷ *plural noun* a device consisting of two small sound receivers, either held over the ears by a metal strap passed over the head, or inserted into the ear (also called **earphones**), for listening to a radio, CD player, personal stereo, etc.

headpin ▷ *noun, ten-pin bowling* the front pin in the triangular arrangement of the ten pins.

headquarters ▷ *singular or plural noun* (abbreviation **HQ, hq**) **1** the centre of an organization or group, eg in the police, from which activities are controlled. **2** *military* the residence of the commander-in-chief, from where orders are issued.

headrace ▷ *noun* the channel leading to a waterwheel, turbine, etc.

head register see HEAD VOICE

headrest ▷ *noun* a cushion which supports the head, fitted to the top of a car seat, etc.

head restraint ▷ *noun* an adjustable cushioned frame fitted to the top of a car seat to prevent the head from jerking back in a collision or sudden stop.

headroom ▷ *noun* **1** the space between the top of a vehicle and the underside of a bridge. **2** any space overhead, below an obstacle, etc. Also called HEADWAY.

headscarf ▷ *noun* a scarf worn over the head and tied under the chin.

headset ▷ *noun* a pair of headphones, often with a microphone attached.

headship ▷ *noun* the position of, or time of being, head or leader of an organization, especially a school.

headshrinker ▷ *noun* **1** *colloq* a psychiatrist. Often shortened to SHRINK. **2** *anthropol* a headhunter who shrinks the heads of his victims (see HEADHUNTING sense 1).

headsman ▷ *noun, formerly* an executioner who beheaded condemned persons.

headstall ▷ *noun* the part of a bridle which fits round a horse's head.

head start ▷ *noun* an initial advantage in a race or competition.

headstock ▷ *noun* a device for supporting the end or head of a part of a machine.

headstone ▷ *noun* **1** a GRAVESTONE. **2** *archit* a keystone.

headstream ▷ *noun* the stream forming the highest or remotest source of a river.

headstrong ▷ *adj* **1** said of a person: difficult to persuade; determined; obstinate. **2** said of an action: heedless; rash.

head teacher ▷ *noun* the principal teacher in charge of a school. Also called (*old use*) **headmaster** and **headmistress**.

head to head ▷ *adverb, informal* in direct competition. Also *as adj* □ ***a head-to-head clash.*** ▷ *noun* a competition involving two people, teams, etc.

head-up display ▷ *noun* a projection of readings from instruments onto a windscreen directly in front of a pilot's or driver's eyes.

head voice and **head register** ▷ *noun* one of the high registers of the human voice in singing or speaking, in which the vibrations are felt in the head.

headwaters ▷ *plural noun* the tributary streams of a river, which flow from the area in which it rises.

headway ▷ *noun* **1** progress □ ***I'm not making much headway with the backlog.*** **2** a ship's movement forwards. **3** headroom. **4** the interval between consecutive trains, buses, etc, on the same route in the same direction.

headwind ▷ *noun* a wind which is blowing towards a person, ship or aircraft, in the opposite direction to the chosen course of travel.

headword ▷ *noun* a word forming a heading, especially for a dictionary or an encyclopedia entry.

headwork ▷ *noun* **1** mental work. **2** the decoration of the keystone of an arch.

heady /ˈhɛdɪ/ ▷ *adj* (***headier, headiest***) **1** said of alcoholic drinks: tending to make one drunk quickly. **2** very exciting. **3** rash; impetuous. ● **headily** *adverb*. ● **headiness** *noun*.

heal /hiːl/ ▷ *verb* (***healed, healing***) **1** to cause (a person, wound, etc) to become healthy again. **2** *intr* (*also* **heal up** or **over**) said of a wound: to become healthy again by natural processes, eg by scar formation. **3** to make (sorrow) less painful. **4** *tr & intr* to settle (disputes, etc) and restore friendly relations, harmony, etc. ● **healer** *noun*. ● **healing** *noun, adj*. ⓒ Anglo-Saxon *hælan*.

health /hɛlθ/ ▷ *noun* **1** a state of physical, mental and social well-being accompanied by freedom from illness or pain. **2** a person's general mental or physical condition □ ***He's in poor health.*** **3** the soundness, especially financial soundness, of an organization, country, etc □ ***the economic health of the nation.*** **4** a toast drunk in a person's honour. **5** *as adj* **a** referring or relating to produce considered to be beneficial to health □ ***health food***; **b** referring or relating to health □ ***health care.*** ⓒ Anglo-Saxon *hælth*.

health camp ▷ *noun, NZ* a camp for children, intended to improve the physical and emotional condition of those who attend it.

health centre ▷ *noun, Brit* a centre where a group of doctors and nurses provide health care for a community.

health education ▷ *noun* teaching, advice and the provision of information on healthy living.

health farm ▷ *noun* a place, usually in the country, where people go to improve their health through diet and exercise.

health food ▷ *noun* any food that is considered to be natural, free of additives and particularly beneficial to one's health, eg whole-grain cereals, honey, organically grown fruit and vegetables.

healthful ▷ *adj* causing or bringing good health.

health salts ▷ *plural noun* salts, especially magnesium sulphate, taken as a mild laxative.

health screening ▷ *noun, medicine* the performance of various tests on large populations to identify certain diseases which may be preventable.

health service ▷ *noun* a public service providing medical care, usually without charge.

health stamp ▷ *noun, NZ* a postage stamp, part of the revenue from which goes to supporting HEALTH CAMPS.

health visitor ▷ *noun* a nurse trained in health education, who is responsible for visiting individuals susceptible to health problems on a regular basis.

healthy /ˈhɛlθɪ/ ▷ *adj* (***healthier, healthiest***) **1** having or showing good health. **2** causing good health. **3** in a good state □ ***a healthy economy.*** **4** wise □ ***a healthy respect for authority.*** **5** signifying soundness of body or mind □ ***a healthy appetite.*** **6** *colloq* considerable □ ***a healthy sum.*** ● **healthily** *adverb*. ● **healthiness** *noun*.

heap /hiːp/ ▷ *noun* **1** a collection of things in an untidy pile or mass. **2** (*usually* **heaps**) *colloq* a large amount or number □ ***heaps of time.*** **3** *colloq* something, especially a motor vehicle, that is very old and not working properly. ▷ *verb* (***heaped, heaping***) *tr & intr* (*also* **heap something up** or **heap up**) to collect or be collected together in a heap. ▷ *adverb* (**heaps**) *colloq* very much □ ***I'm heaps better.*** ● **heaped** *adj* denoting a spoonful that forms a rounded heap on the spoon. ⓒ Anglo-Saxon *héap*.

■ **heap something on someone** or **heap someone with something** to give them it in large amounts □ ***He heaped insults on his ex-wife*** □ ***They were heaped with riches.***

hear /hɪə(r)/ ▷ *verb* (***heard*** /hɜːd/, ***hearing***) **1** *tr & intr* to perceive (sounds) with the ear. **2** to listen to something □ ***Did you hear what he said?*** **3** *intr* (*usually* **hear about** or **of something**) to be told about it or informed of it. **4** *intr* (*usually* **hear from someone**) to be contacted by them, especially by letter or telephone. **5** *law* to listen to and judge (a case). • **hearer** *noun*. • **hear! hear!** an expression of agreement or approval. • **hear tell** or **hear tell of something** *dialect* to be told about it. • **not hear of something** not to allow it to happen □ *They would not hear of it.* ⓒ Anglo-Saxon *hieran*.

■ **hear someone out** to listen to them until they have said all they wish to say.

hearing ▷ *noun* **1** the sense that involves the perception of sound. **2** the distance within which something can be heard □ *within hearing.* **3** an opportunity to state one's case □ *We gave him a hearing.* **4** a judicial investigation and listening to evidence and arguments, especially without a jury.

hearing aid ▷ *noun* (*also* **deaf aid**) a small electronic device consisting of a miniature sound receiver, an amplifier and a power source, worn in or behind the ear by a partially deaf person to help them hear more clearly.

hearing dog ▷ *noun* a dog that has been specially trained to alert deaf or partially deaf people to sounds such as an alarm, a doorbell, etc.

hearken or (*sometimes US*) **harken** /ˈhɑːkən/ ▷ *verb* (***hearkened***, ***hearkening***) *intr* (*often* **hearken to something** or **someone**) *old use* to listen or pay attention to it or them. ⓒ Anglo-Saxon *heorcnian*.

hearsay /ˈhɪəseɪ/ ▷ *noun* rumour; gossip.

hearsay evidence ▷ *noun*, *law* evidence based on what has been reported to a witness by others rather than what they themselves saw.

hearse /hɜːs/ ▷ *noun* a vehicle used for carrying a coffin at a funeral. ⓒ 14c: from Latin *hirpex* harrow.

heart /hɑːt/ ▷ *noun* **1** in vertebrates: the hollow muscular organ that contracts and pumps blood through the blood vessels of the body. **2** the corresponding organ or organs that pump circulatory fluid in invertebrates. **3** this organ considered as the centre of a person's thoughts, emotions, conscience, etc. **4** emotional mood □ *a change of heart.* **5** ability to feel tenderness or pity □ *You have no heart.* **6** courage and enthusiasm □ *take heart* □ *lose heart.* **7** the most central part □ *the heart of the old town.* **8** the most important part □ *the heart of the problem.* **9** the breast □ *She held the child to her heart.* **10** the compact inner part of some vegetables, eg cabbages and lettuces. **11** a symbol (♥), usually red in colour, representing the heart, with two rounded lobes at the top curving down to meet in a point at the bottom. **12** *cards* **a** (**hearts**) one of the four suits of playing-cards, with the heart-shaped (♥) symbols on them; **b** one of the playing-cards of this suit **13** a term of affection or compassion □ *dearest heart.* ▷ *verb* (***hearted***, ***hearting***) *intr* said of vegetables: to form a compact head or inner mass. • **after one's own heart** exactly to one's own liking. • **at heart** really; basically. • **break someone's heart** to cause them great sorrow, because one does not reciprocate their love. • **by heart** by or from memory. • **cross one's heart** to emphasize the truth of a statement (often literally, by making the sign of the cross over one's heart). • **dear** or **near to one's heart** of great interest and concern to one. • **find it in one's heart** to be able to bring oneself (to do something). • **from the bottom of one's heart** most sincerely. • **have a change of heart** to alter one's former opinion, attitude, etc. • **have a heart** to show pity or kindness. • **have someone** or **something at heart** to cherish them or it as a matter of deep interest. • **have one's heart in it** *usually with negatives* to have enthusiasm for what one is doing. • **have one's heart in one's boots** to feel a sinking of the spirit. • **have one's heart in one's mouth** or **throat** to be very frightened, worried, anxious or excited. • **have one's heart in the right place** to be basically kind, thoughtful or generous. • **have one's heart set on something** to desire it earnestly. • **have the heart** *usually with negatives* to have the will, callousness, etc, required (to do something) □ *I didn't have the heart to refuse.* • **heart and soul** completely; with all one's attention and energy. • **one's heart of hearts** one's innermost feelings or convictions; one's deepest affections. • **heart of oak** a brave resolute person. • **in good heart 1** said of land: in fertile condition. **2** said of a person: in good spirits. • **lose heart** to become discouraged or disillusioned over something. • **lose one's heart to someone** to fall in love with them. • **set one's heart on** or **upon something** to want it very much. • **set someone's heart at rest** to reassure them or set their mind at ease. • **take heart** to become encouraged or more confident. • **take something to heart** to pay great attention to it or be very affected by it. • **take someone to one's heart** to form an affection for them. • **to one's heart's content** as much as one wants. • **wear one's heart on one's sleeve** to show one's deepest feelings openly. • **with all one's heart** very willingly or sincerely. ⓒ Anglo-Saxon *heorte*.

heartache ▷ *noun* great sadness or mental suffering.

heart attack ▷ *noun*, *non-technical* a sudden severe chest pain caused by failure of part of the heart muscle to function. See also CORONARY THROMBOSIS.

heartbeat ▷ *noun* **1** the pulsation of the heart, produced by the alternate contraction and relaxation of the heart muscle as it pumps blood around the body. **2** a single pumping action of the heart.

heart block ▷ *noun* defective electrical conduction of the heart muscle, resulting in impaired co-ordination between the heart chambers.

heartbreak ▷ *noun* very great sorrow or grief, especially due to disappointment in love. • **heartbreaker** *noun*. • **heartbreaking** *adj*. • **heartbroken** *adj*.

heartburn ▷ *noun* a feeling of burning in the chest caused by indigestion.

heart disease ▷ *noun* any morbid condition of the heart.

hearted ▷ *adj*, *in compounds* having a heart or character as specified □ *warm-hearted* □ *kind-hearted.*

hearten /ˈhɑːtən/ ▷ *verb* (***heartened***, ***heartening***) *tr & intr* to make or become happier, more cheerful or encouraged. • **heartening** *adj*. • **hearteningly** *adverb*.

heart failure ▷ *noun* a condition in which the ventricles of the heart fail to pump outgoing arterial blood at a rate sufficient to clear incoming venous blood, resulting in increased venous pressure and body tissue damage.

heartfelt ▷ *adj* sincerely and deeply felt.

hearth /hɑːθ/ ▷ *noun* **1** the floor of a fireplace, or the area surrounding it. **2** the home. **3** the lowest part of a blast-furnace, in which the molten metal is produced or contained. ⓒ Anglo-Saxon *heorth*.

hearth rug ▷ *noun* a rug placed on the floor in front of the hearth.

hearthstone ▷ *noun* **1** a stone forming a hearth. **2** a soft stone formerly used for cleaning and whitening hearths, doorsteps, etc.

heartier, **heartiest**, *etc* see under HEARTY

heartland ▷ *noun* a central or vitally important area or region.

heartless ▷ *adj* cruel; very unkind. • **heartlessly** *adverb*. • **heartlessness** *noun*.

heart-lung machine ▷ *noun* a machine that replaces the mechanical functions of the heart and lungs.

heart murmur see MURMUR *noun* 4

heart-rending ▷ *adj* causing great sorrow or pity. • **heart-rendingly** *adverb*.

hearts ▷ *singular noun* a card game in which the aim is to avoid winning tricks containing hearts (see HEART *noun* 12) or the queen of spades. Also called **Black Maria**.

heart's blood ▷ *noun* **1** the blood of the heart. **2** life; essence.

heart-searching ▷ *noun* the close examination of one's deepest feelings and conscience.

heartsease or **heart's-ease** ▷ *noun* **1** an annual, biennial or perennial plant native to Europe, with tufted stems, heart-shaped to lance-shaped leaves, and multicoloured flowers. Also called **wild pansy**. **2** peace of mind.

heartsick ▷ *adj* very sad or disappointed. • **heart-sickness** *noun*.

heart-sore ▷ *adj* greatly distressed; very sad.

heartstrings ▷ *plural noun, often facetious* deepest feelings of love, sympathy or pity □ *The music tugged at her heartstrings.* ⓒ 15c: from old notions of anatomy, in which the tendons or nerves were thought to support the heart.

heart-throb ▷ *noun* **1** *colloq* someone whom a lot of people find very attractive, especially a male actor or singer. **2** a heartbeat.

heart-to-heart ▷ *adj* said of a conversation: intimate, sincere and candid. ▷ *noun* an intimate and candid conversation.

heart-warming ▷ *adj* gratifying; pleasing; emotionally moving.

heartwood ▷ *noun, bot* the dark, hard wood at the centre of a tree trunk or branch, consisting of dead cells containing oils, gums and resins. *Technical equivalent* **duramen** /djʊ'reɪmen/.

hearty /'hɑːtɪ/ ▷ *adj* (***heartier, heartiest***) **1** very friendly and warm in manner. **2** strong, vigorous or enthusiastic □ *hale and hearty.* **3** heartfelt □ *a hearty dislike of examinations.* **4** said of a meal, or an appetite: large. ▷ *noun* (***hearties***) *colloq* **1** a hearty person, especially one who is very keen on sports. **2** a comrade, especially a sailor. • **heartily** *adverb*. • **heartiness** *noun*.

heat /hiːt/ ▷ *noun* **1** a form of energy that is stored as the energy of vibration or motion (kinetic energy) of the atoms or molecules of a material. **2** a high temperature; warmth; the state of being hot. **3** hot weather. **4** intensity of feeling, especially anger or excitement □ *the heat of the argument.* **5** the most intense part □ *in the heat of the battle.* **6** *sport* **a** a preliminary race or contest which eliminates some competitors; **b** a single section in a contest. **7** oestrus, a period of sexual receptivity in some female mammals. **8** redness of the skin, especially when sore, with a feeling of heat □ *prickly heat.* **9** *colloq* police investigation following a crime □ *The heat is on.* **10** *colloq, chiefly US* criticism or abuse. ▷ *verb* (***heated, heating***) *tr & intr* **1** to make or become hot or warm. **2** to make or become intense or excited. • **in** or **on heat** said of some female mammals: ready to mate. See also OESTRUS. • **in the heat of the moment** without pausing to think. • **take the heat out of something** to lessen the vehemence or acrimony of (a situation, etc). • **turn on the heat** *colloq* to use brutal treatment in order to coerce. ⓒ Anglo-Saxon *hætu*.

heat barrier ▷ *noun* an obstacle to flight at high speeds caused by a thin envelope of hot air which develops round an aircraft and causes structural and other problems. Also called THERMAL BARRIER.

heat capacity and **specific heat capacity** ▷ *noun, physics* the ratio of the heat supplied to a unit mass of a substance to the resulting rise in temperature.

heat death ▷ *noun, thermodynamics* the final state of the Universe, if it is a closed system, when it has no available energy remaining.

heated ▷ *adj* **1** having been made hot or warm. **2** angry or excited. • **heatedly** *adverb*. • **heatedness** *noun*.

heat engine ▷ *noun, engineering* any device that transforms heat energy into useful mechanical work.

heater ▷ *noun* **1** an apparatus for heating a room, building, water in a tank, etc. **2** *US slang* a pistol. **3** *electronics* a conductor carrying a current that indirectly heats the cathode in some types of valve.

heat exchanger ▷ *noun, physics* a device that transfers heat from one stream of fluid (gas or liquid) to another, without allowing the two fluids to come into contact, eg a car radiator.

heat exhaustion ▷ *noun* a condition caused by exposure to intense heat, characterized by dizziness, abdominal pain and fatigue.

heath /hiːθ/ ▷ *noun* **1** an area of open land, usually with dry sandy acidic soil, dominated by low-growing evergreen shrubs, especially heathers. **2** any low evergreen shrub found in northern and alpine regions, especially on open moors and heaths with acid soil. • **heathlike** *adj*. • **heathy** *adj*. ⓒ Anglo-Saxon *hæth*.

heathen /'hiːðən/ ▷ *noun* (***heathens*** or ***heathen***) **1** someone who is not a Christian, Jew or Muslim, but who follows another religion, especially one with many gods; a pagan. **2** *colloq* an ignorant or uncivilized person. **3** (**the heathen**) heathens as a group (see THE 4b). ▷ *adj* **1** having no religion; pagan. **2** *colloq* ignorant; uncivilized. **3** referring or relating to heathen peoples or their beliefs or traditions. ⓒ Anglo-Saxon *hæthen*.

heathenize or **heathenise** ▷ *verb* (***heathenized, heathenizing***) *tr & intr* to make or become heathen.

heather /'hɛðə(r)/ ▷ *noun* **1** a low evergreen shrub with many side shoots with small scale-like leaves and small pink or purple bell-shaped flowers, found in northern and alpine regions, and usually the predominant plant on open moors and heaths with acid soil. Also called **ling**. **2** HEATH (sense 2). **3** a purplish-pink colour. ▷ *adj* **1** having a heather colour. **2** composed of or from heather. **3** said of fabrics, etc: with interwoven yarns of speckled colours thought to resemble heather □ *heather mixture.* ⓒ 14c: *hathir*.

Heath-Robinson /hiːθ'rɒbɪnsən/ ▷ *adj* said of a machine or device: peculiarly or ludicrously complicated and impractical in design, especially in relation to its function. ⓒ 19c: named after William Heath Robinson (1872–1944), the cartoonist who drew such machines.

heating ▷ *noun* **1** any of various systems for maintaining the temperature inside a room or building at a level higher than that of the surroundings. **2** the heat generated by such a system.

heat pump ▷ *noun, engineering* a device used to transfer heat from a cooler object or space to a warmer one, ie in the opposite direction to the natural flow of heat, so that an input of energy is required.

heat-seeking ▷ *adj* said of a missile, etc: able to detect heat from its target and use this as a guide to hitting it. • **heat-seeker** *noun*.

heat shield ▷ *noun* an apparatus or substance which protects a spacecraft from the extreme heat it experiences when returning to the Earth's atmosphere.

heatstroke ▷ *noun* a sometimes fatal condition due to continuous exposure to unaccustomed heat, characterized by progressively severe symptoms of lassitude, fainting and high fever. Also called SUNSTROKE.

heatwave ▷ *noun* **1** a prolonged period of unusually hot dry weather. **2** an extensive mass of hot air in the atmosphere, especially one passing from one place to another.

heave /hiːv/ ▷ *verb* (***heaved*** or (in sense 6 and for *heave into sight* and *heave to*) ***hove, heaving***) **1** to lift or pull with great effort. **2** *colloq* to throw something heavy. **3** *intr* to rise and fall heavily or rhythmically. **4** to make something rise and fall heavily or rhythmically. **5** *intr, colloq* to retch or vomit. **6** *geol* to displace (a vein or stratum) in a horizontal direction. ▷ *noun* **1** an act of heaving. **2** *geol* a horizontal displacement of a vein or stratum at a fault. •

heaver *noun*. • **get the heave** *colloq* to be dismissed or rejected. • **give someone the heave** *colloq* to dismiss or reject them. • **heave a sigh** to sigh heavily or with effort. • **heave into sight** *especially naut* to move in a particular direction. • **heave ho!** a sailors' call to exertion, as in heaving the anchor. ◷ Anglo-Saxon *hebban*.

■ **heave to** said of a ship: to stop or make it stop at sea.

heaven /ˈhɛvən/ ▻ *noun* **1** the place believed to be the abode of God, angels and the righteous after death. **2** (*usually* **the heavens**) the sky. **3** a place or the state of great happiness or bliss. **4** often used in exclamations: God or Providence □ *heaven forbid*. See also HEAVENS. ◷ Anglo-Saxon *heofon*.

heavenly ▻ *adj* **1** *colloq* very pleasant; beautiful. **2** situated in or coming from heaven or the sky □ *heavenly body*. **3** holy. • **heavenliness** *noun*.

heavenly bodies ▻ *plural noun* the Sun, Moon, planets, stars, etc.

the heavenly host ▻ *noun, Bible* the massed angels and archangels.

heavens ▻ *exclamation* expressing surprise, anger, dismay, etc.

heaven-sent ▻ *adj* very lucky or convenient; timely.

heaves ▻ *singular or plural noun, vet medicine* a chronic respiratory disease of horses. Also called **broken wind**. ◷ 19c.

Heaviside layer see E-LAYER

heavy /ˈhɛvɪ/ ▻ *adj* (***heavier***, ***heaviest***) **1** having great weight. **2** said of breathing: loud, because of excitement, exhaustion, etc. **3** great in amount, size, power, etc □ *heavy traffic* □ *a heavy crop*. **4** great in amount, frequency, etc □ *a heavy drinker*. **5** considerable □ *heavy emphasis*. **6** hard to bear, endure or fulfil □ *a heavy fate*. **7** ungraceful and coarse □ *heavy features*. **8** severe, intense or excessive □ *heavy fighting*. **9** sad or dejected □ *with a heavy heart* □ *heavy-hearted*. **10** said of food: difficult to digest □ *a heavy meal*. **11** having a great or relatively high density □ *a heavy metal*. Compare HEAVY METAL. **12** striking or falling with force; powerful □ *heavy rain*. **13** forceful or powerful □ *a heavy sea*. **14** intense or deep □ *a heavy sleep*. **15** said of the sky: dark and cloudy. **16** needing a lot of physical or mental effort. **17** said of literature, music, etc: **a** serious in tone and content; **b** not immediately accessible or appealing. **18** physically and mentally slow. **19** fat; solid. **20** said of soil: wet and soft due to its high clay content. **21** *colloq* strict; severe □ *Don't be heavy on him*. **22** *military* **a** equipped with powerful weapons, armour, etc; **b** said of guns: large and powerful. **23** said of cakes and bread: dense through not having risen enough. ▻ *noun* (***heavies***) **1** *slang* a large, violent and usually not very intelligent man. **2** a villain in a play, film, etc. **3** *Scottish* a beer like bitter but darker in colour and gassier. **4** (*usually* **the heavies**) serious newspapers. ▻ *adverb* **1** heavily □ *Time hangs heavy on my hands*. **2** with a heavy burden □ *heavy-laden*. • **heavily** *adverb* **1** in a heavy way; with or as if with weight. **2** intensely, severely or violently. • **heaviness** *noun*. • **make heavy weather of something** to experience great difficulty in doing something, or exaggerate the difficulties involved in it. ◷ Anglo-Saxon *hefig*.

heavy-armed ▻ *adj* with heavy armour or weapons.

heavy breathing ▻ *noun* deep, quickened, audible breathing resulting from exertion (especially sexual) or sexual excitement.

heavy-duty ▻ *adj* made to resist or withstand very hard wear or use.

heavy going ▻ *noun* difficult or slow progress. ▻ *adj* (***heavy-going***) difficult to deal with or to get further with.

heavy-handed ▻ *adj* **1** clumsy and awkward. **2** too severe or strict; oppressive. • **heavy-handedly** *adverb*. • **heavy-handedness** *noun*.

heavy hydrogen ▻ *noun* DEUTERIUM.

heavy industry ▻ *noun* a factory or factories involving the use of large or heavy equipment, eg coal-mining, ship-building, etc.

heavy metal ▻ *noun* **1** loud repetitive rock music with a strong beat. **2** large guns. Compare HEAVY *adj* 11.

heavy particle ▻ *noun* a baryon.

heavy petting ▻ *noun* sexual embracing and fondling, distinct from FOREPLAY in that it does not lead to intercourse.

heavy spar ▻ *noun* barytes.

heavy water ▻ *noun* DEUTERIUM OXIDE.

heavyweight ▻ *noun* **1** in boxing, wrestling and weight-lifting: **a** the class for the heaviest competitors. See table at WEIGHT; **b** *as adj* □ *heavyweight bout*. **2** a boxer, etc of this weight. **3** *colloq* an important, powerful or influential person. **4** a person who is heavier than average.

hebdomadal /hɛbˈdɒmədəl/ ▻ *adj* weekly. • **hebdomadally** *adverb*. ◷ 18c: from Greek *hebdomas* week.

hebetate /ˈhɛbəteɪt/ ▻ *adj* blunt or soft-pointed; dull. ▻ *verb* (***hebetated***, ***hebetating***) to make or become dull or blunt. ◷ 16c: from Latin *hebes* blunt.

Hebraic /hɪˈbreɪɪk/ ▻ *adj* referring or relating to the Hebrews or the Hebrew language. ◷ Anglo-Saxon: from Greek *hebraikos*.

Hebrew /ˈhiːbruː/ ▻ *noun* **1** the ancient Semitic language of the Hebrews, revived and spoken in a modern form and as the formal language by Jews in Israel. **2** a member of an ancient Semitic people, originally based in Palestine, and claiming descent from Abraham, an Israelite. ▻ *adj* relating or referring to the Hebrew language or people. ◷ 13c: from Greek *Hebraios*, from Aramaic *Ibhraij* someone from the other side of the river.

Hebridean /hɛbrɪˈdɪən/ ▻ *adj* referring to the Hebrides, islands off the W coast of Scotland. ▻ *noun* a native of the Hebrides. ◷ 17c: due to a misprint of Latin *Hebudes*.

hecatomb /ˈhɛkətuːm, -tɒm/ ▻ *noun* **1** a great public sacrifice, originally of oxen. **2** a large number of victims. ◷ 16c: from Greek *hekaton* one hundred + *bous* ox.

heck ▻ *exclamation, colloq* mildly expressing anger, annoyance, surprise, etc. ◷ 19c: alteration of HELL.

heckelphone /ˈhɛkəlfoʊn/ ▻ *noun* a musical instrument belonging to the oboe family whose pitch ranges between that of the BASSOON and the COR ANGLAIS. ◷ 20c: named after its inventor W Heckel (1856–1909).

heckle /ˈhɛkəl/ ▻ *verb* (***heckled***, ***heckling***) *tr & intr* to interrupt (a speaker) with critical or abusive shouts and jeers, especially at a public meeting. • **heckler** *noun*. ◷ 15c as *hekelen*.

hectare /ˈhɛktɛə(r), -tɑː(r)/ ▻ *noun* (abbreviation **ha**) in the metric system: a metric unit of land measurement, equivalent to 100 ares (see ARE[2]), or 10 000 square metres (2.471 acres). ◷ 19c: from HECTO- + ARE[2].

hectic /ˈhɛktɪk/ ▻ *adj* agitated; very excited, flustered or rushed. • **hectically** *adverb*. ◷ 14c: from Greek *hektikos* habitual.

hecto- /ˈhɛktoʊ, ˈhɛktə/ or (before a vowel) **hect-** ▻ *combining form, signifying* one hundred times □ *hectometre*. ◷ French, contraction of Greek *hekaton* a hundred.

hectogram or **hectogramme** ▻ *noun* one hundred grammes.

hectograph ▻ *noun* a gelatine pad used for printing multiple copies. ▻ *verb* to reproduce (copies) using this method. • **hectographic** *adj*.

hectolitre ▻ *noun* one hundred litres.

hectometre ▻ *noun* one hundred metres.

hector /ˈhɛktə(r)/ ▻ *verb* (***hectored***, ***hectoring***) *tr & intr* to bully, intimidate or threaten. ▻ *noun* a bully or tormentor. ◐ 17c: named after Hektor, the Trojan hero in Homer's *Iliad*.

he'd /hiːd, hɪd/ ▻ *contraction* **1** he had. **2** he would.

heddle /ˈhɛdəl/ ▻ *noun, weaving* a series of vertical cords or wires, each with a loop in the middle to receive the warp thread. ◐ Anglo-Saxon *hefeld* chain.

hedge /hɛdʒ/ ▻ *noun* **1** a boundary formed by bushes and shrubs planted close together, especially between fields. **2** a barrier or protection against (especially financial) loss, criticism, etc. ▻ *verb* (***hedged***, ***hedging***) **1** to enclose or surround (an area of land) with a hedge. **2** to avoid making a decision or giving a clear answer. **3** to protect oneself from possible loss or criticism eg in (a bet or argument) by backing both sides □ *hedge one's bets*. **4** *intr* to make hedges. **5** *intr* to be evasive or shifty, eg in an argument. **6** *intr* to buy or sell something as a financial hedge. • **hedged** *adj*. • **hedger** *noun*. ◐ Anglo-Saxon *hecg*.

hedge fund ▻ *noun, finance* any of a number of types of investment fund, generally designed to minimize risk and produce profits under all circumstances, but sometimes employing investment strategies aimed at high gains but equally risking high losses. ◐ 1960s.

hedgehog ▻ *noun* **1** a small, prickly-backed insectivorous mammal with a short tail and a hoglike snout, that lives in bushes and hedges. **2** *military slang* a small, strongly fortified, defensive position.

hedge-hop ▻ *verb, intr* to fly at a very low altitude as if hopping over hedges, eg when crop-spraying. ◐ 1920s.

hedgerow ▻ *noun* a row of bushes, hedges or trees forming a boundary.

hedge sparrow ▻ *noun* a small grey-brown songbird, similar to the sparrow, but with a slimmer beak. Also called DUNNOCK.

hedonics /hiːˈdɒnɪks, hɛ-/ *singular noun* the part of ethics or psychology that deals with pleasure. • **hedonic** *adj*.

hedonism /ˈhiːdənɪzəm, ˈhɛ-/ ▻ *noun, ethics* **1** the belief that pleasure is the most important achievement or the highest good in life. **2** the pursuit of and devotion to pleasure. **3** a lifestyle devoted to seeking pleasure. • **hedonist** *noun*. • **hedonistic** *adj*. ◐ 19c: from Greek *hedone* pleasure.

-hedron /ˈhiːdrən/ (***-hedra*** /-drə/ or ***-hedrons***) ▻ *combining form, geom, signifying* face, referring to a geometric solid with the specified number of faces or surfaces □ *dodecahedron* □ *polyhedron*. ◐ From Greek *hedra* base.

the heebie-jeebies /-hiːbɪˈdʒiːbɪz/ ▻ *plural noun, slang* feelings or fits of nervousness or anxiety. ◐ Early 20c: coinage by W De Beck (1890–1942), American cartoonist.

heed /hiːd/ ▻ *verb* (***heeded***, ***heeding***) **1** to pay attention to or take notice of something, especially advice or a warning, etc. **2** *intr* to mind or care. ▻ *noun* careful attention; notice □ *Take heed of what she says*. • **heedful** *adj* (*often* **heedful of someone** or **something**) attentive or cautious. • **heedfully** *adverb*. • **heedfulness** *noun*. ◐ Anglo-Saxon *hedan*.

heedless ▻ *adj* (*often* **heedless of someone** or **something**) taking no care; careless. • **heedlessly** *adverb*. • **heedlessness** *noun*.

hee-haw /ˈhiːhɔː/ ▻ *noun* the bray of a donkey, or an imitation of this sound. ▻ *verb* (***hee-hawed***, ***hee-hawing***) *intr* to bray. ◐ 19c: imitating the sound.

heel[1] ▻ *noun* **1** the rounded back part of the foot below the ankle. **2** the part of a sock, stocking and tights that covers the heel. **3** the part of a shoe, boot and other such footwear which supports the heel. **4** anything shaped or functioning like the heel, eg that part of the palm near the wrist. **5** a heel-like bend, as on a golf club. **6** the end of a loaf. **7** *slang* a despicable person; someone who is untrustworthy or who lets others down. ▻ *verb* (***heeled***, ***heeling***) **1** to execute or perform with the heel. **2** to strike using the heel. **3** to repair or fit a new heel on (a shoe, etc). **4** *intr* to move one's heels in time to a dance rhythm. **5** *intr, rugby* to kick the ball backwards out of the scrum with the heel. **6** *intr* said of a dog: to walk at, or go to, someone's side. • **heeled** *adj* **1** having a heel or heels. **2** *in compounds* referring to shoes with a specified type of heel □ *high-heeled*. • **at, on** or **upon someone's heels** following closely behind them. • **cool** or **kick one's heels** to be kept waiting indefinitely. • **dig one's heels in** to behave stubbornly. • **down at heel** untidy; in poor condition or circumstances. • **heel and toe** with a strict walking pace, as opposed to running. • **kick up one's heels** to frisk or gambol. • **lay** or **set someone by the heels** *old use, colloq* to put them in prison or confinement. • **show a clean pair of heels** to run away. • **take to one's heels** to run away; to abscond. • **to heel 1** said especially of a dog: walking obediently at the heels of the person in charge of it. **2** under control; subject to discipline; submissive. • **turn on one's heel** to turn round suddenly or sharply. • **under the heel** crushed; ruled over tyrannically. ◐ Anglo-Saxon *hela*.

heel[2] /hiːl/ ▻ *verb* (***heeled***, ***heeling***) **1** *intr* (*often* **heel over**) said of a vessel: to lean over to one side; to list. **2** to cause (a vessel) to tilt. ◐ Anglo-Saxon *hieldan* to slope.

heel[3] ▻ *verb* (***heeled***, ***heeling***) (*usually* **heel something in**) to temporarily cover (the roots of a plant) with soil to keep them moist. ◐ Anglo-Saxon *helian*, a combination of *hellan* and *helan*, both meaning 'to hide'.

heelball ▻ *noun* a black waxy substance used for blacking and polishing the heels and soles of shoes and boots, and for doing brass rubbings. ◐ 19c.

heeltap ▻ *noun* **1** a layer of material in a shoe-heel. **2** a small quantity of alcohol or liquor left in a glass after drinking. ◐ 17c in sense 1; 18c in sense 2.

hefty /ˈhɛftɪ/ ▻ *adj* (***heftier***, ***heftiest***) *colloq* **1** said of a person: strong, robust or muscular. **2** said of an object, blow, etc: large, heavy or powerful; vigorous. **3** large or considerable in amount □ *a hefty sum of money*. • **heftily** *adverb*. • **heftiness** *noun*. ◐ 19c: from HEAVE.

Hegelian /hɪˈgeɪlɪən/ ▻ *adj* referring or relating to the German philosopher Wilhelm Friedrich Hegel (1770–1831) or his philosophy. ▻ *noun* a follower of Hegel. • **Hegelianism** *noun*.

hegemony /hɪˈgɛmənɪ, hɪˈdʒɛ-/ ▻ *noun* (***hegemonies***) authority or control, especially of one state over another within a confederation. ◐ 16c: from Greek *hegemonia* leadership.

Hegira or **Hejira** /ˈhɛdʒɪrə, hɪˈdʒaɪərə/ ▻ *noun, relig* the flight of the Prophet Muhammad from Mecca to Yathrib (Medina) in AD 622, marking the beginning of the Muslim era. ◐ 16c: Arabic *hejira* flight.

he-he /hiːhiː/ ▻ *exclamation* imitating or representing a high-pitched or gleeful laugh. ▻ *noun* (***he-hes***) such a laugh. ▻ *verb* (***he-he'd***, ***he-heing***) *intr* to laugh in this way. ◐ 19c.

heifer /ˈhɛfə(r)/ ▻ *noun* a female cow over one year old that has either not calved, or has calved only once. ◐ Anglo-Saxon *heahfore*.

heigh /heɪ, haɪ/ ▻ *exclamation* expressing enquiry, encouragement or exultation. • **heigh-ho** *exclamation* expressing weariness. ◐ 16c.

height /haɪt/ ▻ *noun* **1** the condition of being high, or the distance from the base of something to the top. **2** the distance above the ground from a recognized point, especially above sea level. **3** relatively high altitude. **4** a high place or location. **5** the highest point of elevation; the summit. **6** the most intense part or climax □ *the height of battle*. **7** an extremely good, bad or serious example □ *the height of stupidity*. • **heighten** *verb* (***heightened***, ***heightening***) to make higher, greater, stronger, etc. ◐ Anglo-Saxon *hiehthu*.

heil! /haɪl/ ▷ *exclamation, German* hail!

heinous /ˈheɪnəs, ˈhiː-/ ▷ *adj* extremely wicked or evil; odious. • **heinously** *adverb*. • **heinousness** *noun*. ⓘ 14c: from French *haineus*, from *hair* to hate.

heir /ɛə(r)/ ▷ *noun* **1** someone who by law receives or is entitled to receive wealth, a title, etc when the previous owner or holder dies. **2** someone who is successor to a position, eg leadership, or who continues a convention or tradition. • **heirless** *adj*. • **fall heir to something** to inherit it. ⓘ 13c: from Latin *heres*.

heir apparent ▷ *noun* (***heirs apparent***) **1** *law* an heir whose claim to an inheritance cannot be challenged, even by the birth of another heir. **2** *colloq* someone expected to succeed the leader of an organization, especially a political party.

heiress /ˈɛərɛs/ *noun* a female heir, especially a woman who has inherited or will inherit considerable wealth.

heirloom /ˈɛəluːm/ ▷ *noun* **1** a personal article or piece of property which descends to the legal heir by means of a will or special custom. **2** an object that has been handed down through a family over many generations. ⓘ 15c: HEIR + *lome* tool.

heir presumptive ▷ *noun* (***heirs presumptive***) *law* an heir whose claim to an inheritance may be challenged by the birth of another heir more closely related to the holder.

Heisenberg uncertainty principle see UNCERTAINTY PRINCIPLE

heist /haɪst/ ▷ *noun, N Amer slang* a robbery. ▷ *verb* (***heisted, heisting***) to steal or rob in a heist. • **heister** *noun*. ⓘ 1920s: variant of HOIST.

hejab or **hijab** /hɪˈdʒab, hɛˈdʒɑːb/ ▷ *noun* a covering for a Muslim woman's face and head, sometimes reaching to the ground. ⓘ Arabic and Persian.

Hejira see HEGIRA

held *past tense, past participle of* HOLD

heli-[1] /ˈhɛlɪ/ ▷ *combining form, signifying* helicopter. ⓘ From Greek *helix, helikos* screw or spiral.

heli-[2] see HELIO-

heliacal /hɪˈlaɪəkəl/ ▷ *adj, astron* solar or relating to the Sun, especially to the rising and setting of stars which coincide with those of the Sun. • **heliacally** *adverb*. • **heliacal rising** the emergence of a star from the light of the Sun. • **heliacal setting** a star's disappearance into the Sun's light. ⓘ 17c: from Greek *heliakos*.

helianthus /hiːlɪˈanθəs/ ▷ *noun* a plant of the sunflower genus. ⓘ 18c: HELIO- + *anthos* flower.

helical /ˈhɛlɪkəl/ ▷ *adj* relating to or like a helix; coiled. ⓘ 17c.

helical scan ▷ *noun, electronics* a system of magnetic tape recording in which the tape is wrapped in a partial helix around a drum carrying two or more rotating heads which trace a series of tracks diagonally across its width, thus allowing very high frequencies to be recorded economically.

helicopter /ˈhɛlɪkɒptə(r)/ ▷ *noun* an aircraft that is lifted and propelled by rotating blades, which also allow it to take off and land vertically, hover, and fly horizontally in any direction. ⓘ 1880s: from Greek *helix, helikos* screw + *pteron* wing.

helideck ▷ *noun* a landing deck for helicopters on a ship. ⓘ 1960s.

helio- /hiːlɪoʊ, hiːlɪˈɒ/ or (before a vowel) **heli-** ▷ *combining form, signifying* the Sun ◻ *heliograph*. ⓘ from Greek *helios* the Sun.

heliocentric *astron* ▷ *adj* denoting a system with the Sun at its centre. • **heliocentrically** *adverb*. ⓘ 17c.

heliograph ▷ *noun* **1** an instrument which uses mirrors to reflect light from the Sun in flashes as a way of sending messages in Morse code. **2** *photog* an engraving obtained photographically. **3** an apparatus used to photograph the Sun. **4** a device to measure the intensity of sunlight. • **heliographic** or **heliographical** *adj*. • **heliographically** *adverb*. • **heliography** *noun*. ⓘ 19c.

heliogravure /hiːlɪoʊgrəˈvjʊə(r)/ ▷ *noun* a photo-engraving. ⓘ 19c.

heliometer /hiːlɪˈɒmɪtə(r)/ ▷ *noun, astron* a device used to measure angular distances, eg. the Sun's diameter, or more commonly the angular distances between stars. ⓘ 18c.

heliosphere /ˈhiːlɪoʊsfɪə(r)/ ▷ *noun, astron* the spherical area of space surrounding the Sun, whose outer boundary (the **heliopause**), beyond which the Sun's influence is negligible, is thought to lie about 100 ASTRONOMICAL UNITS from the Sun. ⓘ 1970s.

heliostat /ˈhiːlɪoʊstat/ ▷ *noun, astron* a device where a mirror is used to reflect a beam of sunlight in a fixed direction either for studying the Sun or for signalling purposes. ⓘ 18c.

heliotherapy /hiːlɪoʊˈθɛrəpɪ/ ▷ *noun* medical treatment for an illness by exposing the patient to the Sun. ⓘ 19c.

heliotrope /ˈhiːlɪətroʊp, ˈhɛ-/ ▷ *noun* **1** a garden plant of the borage family, with small fragrant lilac-blue flowers which grow towards the Sun. **2** the colour of these flowers. • **heliotropic** or **heliotropical** *adj*. • **heliotropically** *adverb*. ⓘ 17c: HELIO- + Greek *trepein* to turn.

heliotropism /hiːlɪˈɒtrəpɪzəm/ and **heliotropy** /ˈtrəpɪ/ ▷ *noun* the tendency of the stems and leaves of plants to grow towards (**positive heliotropism**) and of the roots to grow away from (**negative heliotropism**) the light. Compare HYDROTROPISM.

heliotypy /ˈhiːlɪoʊtaɪpɪ/ *photog* ▷ *noun* the photo-mechanical process where the imprint is taken from the gelatine relief itself. • **heliotype** *noun* photography by heliotypy. • **heliotypic** /-ˈtɪpɪk/ *adj*. ⓘ 19c.

helipad ▷ *noun* a landing place for a helicopter, usually a square marked with a large H. ⓘ 1960s: HELI-[1] + PAD[1].

heliport ▷ *noun* a place where helicopters take off and land, usually for commercial purposes. ⓘ 1940s: HELI-[1] + air*port*.

helium /ˈhiːlɪəm/ ▷ *noun* (symbol **He**, atomic number 2) *chem* a colourless odourless inert gas found in natural gas deposits, also formed in stars by nuclear fusion. ⓘ 19c: from Greek *helios* Sun, so called because it was first identified in the Sun's atmosphere.

helix /ˈhiːlɪks/ ▷ *noun* (***helices*** /-siːz/ or ***helixes***) **1** a spiral or coiled structure, eg the thread of a screw. **2** *geom* a spiral-shaped curve that lies on the lateral surface of a cylinder or cone, and becomes a straight line if unrolled into a plane. **3** the folds in the external part of the ear. ⓘ 16c: Greek.

hell ▷ *noun* **1** the place or state of infinite punishment for the wicked after death. **2** the abode of the dead and evil spirits. **3** any place or state which causes extensive pain, misery and discomfort. ▷ *exclamation, colloq* **1** expressing annoyance or exasperation. **2** (**the hell**) an expression of strong disagreement or refusal ◻ *The hell I will!* • **a hell of a …** or **one hell of a …** or **helluva** or **hellova …** *colloq* a very great or significant … ◻ *one hell of a row*. • **all hell breaks** or **is let loose** there is chaos and uproar. • **as hell** absolutely; extremely ◻ *He's as mad as hell*. • **beat** or **knock the hell out of someone** *colloq* to beat them severely and violently. • **come hell or high water** *colloq* no matter what problems or difficulties may arise. • **for the hell of it** *colloq* for the fun or sake of it. • **from hell** considered to be the most awful ever example of its kind ◻ *boyfriend from hell* ◻ *anorak from hell*. • **give someone hell** *colloq* **1** to punish or rebuke them severely. **2** to make things extremely difficult for them. • **hell for**

leather *colloq* at an extremely fast pace ◻ *drove hell for leather to the airport.* • **hell to pay** serious trouble or consequences. • **like hell** very much; very hard or fast ◻ *Like hell* ◻ *ran like hell* • **not to have a cat in hell's chance** see under CAT. • **not to have a hope in hell** to have absolutely no chance or hope at all. • **play hell with** see under PLAY. • **raise hell** see under RAISE. • **to hell with someone** or **something 1** an expression of angry disagreement with them or it. **2** an intention to ignore or reject them or it. • **what the hell 1** what does it matter?; who cares? **2** an expression of surprise and amazement ◻ *what the hell are you doing?* ⓒ Anglo-Saxon *hel.*

he'll ▻ *contraction* **1** he will. **2** he shall.

Helladic /hɛ'ladɪk/ ▻ *adj* referring or relating to the Greek mainland Bronze Age which occurred from 2900 to 1100 BC. ⓒ 18c: from Greek *Helladikos* Greek, from *Hellas* Greece.

hellbender ▻ *noun* **1** a large American salamander. **2** a debauched, corrupt or reckless person. ⓒ 19c.

hellbent ▻ *adj* (*usually* **hellbent on something**) *colloq* recklessly determined or intent about it.

hellcat ▻ *noun* a malignant or violent-tempered woman.

hellebore /'hɛlɪbɔː(r)/ ▻ *noun* **1** any plant of the buttercup or lily family, with white, greenish-white or purplish flowers. **2** the winter aconite. **3** the roots and rhizome of these, used as a treatment for heart disease. ⓒ 14c: from Greek *helleboros.*

Hellene /'hɛliːn/ ▻ *noun* a Greek. ⓒ 17c: from Greek *Hellen.*

Hellenic /hɛ'liːnɪk, hɛ'lɛnɪk/ ▻ *adj* relating to the Greeks and their language.

Hellenism /'hɛlənɪzm/ ▻ *noun* **1** a Greek idiom, especially one used in another language. **2** the nationality or spirit of Greece. **3** conformity to the Greek character, language and culture, especially that of ancient Greece.

Hellenist /'hɛlənɪst/ ▻ *noun* **1** a person who is interested and skilled in the Greek language and culture. **2** a person, especially a Jew, who has adopted the Greek customs and language.

Hellenistic /hɛlə'nɪstɪk/ and **Hellenistical** ▻ *adj* **1** relating or referring to Hellenists. **2** referring or relating to the Greek culture after the time of Alexander the Great, which was greatly affected by the foreign influences. • **Hellenistically** *adverb.*

Hellenize or **Hellenise** ▻ *verb* (**Hellenized**, **Hellenizing**) **1** to make Greek. **2** *intr* to conform, or have a tendency to conform, to Greek usages.

hellfire ▻ *noun* **1** the fire of hell. **2** the punishment suffered in hell. Also *as adj* ◻ *hellfire preacher.*

hellhole ▻ *noun* **1** the pit of hell. **2** a disgusting, evil and frightening place.

hellhound ▻ *noun* a hound or agent of hell.

hellion /'hɛljən/ ▻ *noun, especially US colloq* a troublesome or mischievous child or person.

hellish /'hɛlɪʃ/ ▻ *adj* **1** relating to or resembling hell. **2** *colloq* very unpleasant or horrifying. • **hellishly** *adverb.* • **hellishness** *noun.*

hello, hallo or **hullo** /hə'loʊ/ ▻ *exclamation* **1** used as a greeting, to attract attention or to start a telephone conversation. **2** expressing surprise or discovery.

hellova see under HELL

hellraiser ▻ *noun, colloq* a boisterously debauched person.

hell's angel ▻ *noun* (*also* **Hell's Angel**) a member of a gang of young motorcyclists, especially one whose behaviour is violent and anti-social. ⓒ 1950s.

hell's bells and **hell's teeth** ▻ *exclamation, colloq* expressing irritation, exasperation, surprise, etc.

helluva see under HELL

helm /hɛlm/ ▻ *noun, naut* the steering apparatus of a boat or ship, such as a wheel or tiller. • **at the helm** in a controlling position; in charge. ⓒ Anglo-Saxon *helma.*

helmet /'hɛlmɪt/ ▻ *noun* **1** an armoured and protective covering for the head, worn by police officers, firefighters, soldiers, motorcyclists, bicyclists, etc. **2** any similar covering for the head. **3** anything resembling a helmet, such as a cloud on a mountain top or the hooded upper lip of certain flowers. • **helmeted** *adj.* ⓒ Anglo-Saxon *helm.*

helminth /'hɛlmɪnθ/ ▻ *noun* a worm. • **helminthiasis** /-'θaɪəsɪs/ *noun* an infestation with worms. ⓒ 19c: from Greek *helmins, helminthos* parasitic worm.

helmsman ▻ *noun* someone who steers a boat or ship.

helot /'hɛlət/ ▻ *noun* a member of the serf class, especially in ancient Sparta, who was bound to the state. ⓒ 16c: from Greek *Heilotes* inhabitants of Helos, a town in ancient Laconia, the area around Sparta.

help /hɛlp/ ▻ *verb* (**helped, helping**) **1** to contribute towards the success of something; to assist or aid. **2** to give the means to do something. **3** to relieve a difficult situation or burden; to improve or lighten (a predicament). **4** to provide or supply with a portion; to deal out. **5** to remedy; to mitigate or alleviate. **6** to refrain from something ◻ *I couldn't help laughing.* **7** to prevent or control ◻ *I can't help the bad weather.* **8** *intr* to give assistance. **9** *intr* to contribute. ▻ *noun* **1** an act of helping. **2** means or strength given to another for a particular purpose. **3** someone who is employed to help, especially a domestic help. **4** a remedy or relief. ▻ *adj* giving help, aid or support. • **helpable** *adj.* • **helper** *noun* someone who helps; an assistant. • **cannot help oneself** is not able to refrain from or resist doing something. • **more than one can help** more than is necessary. • **so help me** or **so help me God** a form of solemn oath; on my word. ⓒ Anglo-Saxon *helpan.*

■ **help someone off with something** to assist them in taking it off or disposing of it.

■ **help someone on with something** to help them to put it on.

■ **help out** or **help someone out** to offer help, usually for a short time, and especially by sharing a burden or the cost of something.

■ **help oneself to something 1** to take (food, etc) for oneself without being served. **2** to take it without authority or permission.

■ **help someone to something** to serve them with it ◻ *help him to potatoes.*

help

When **help** is followed by another verb, the 'to' is often omitted, because 'help' is a semi-modal verb like 'may' and 'dare' ◻ *Will you help me look for my glasses?* ◻ *Your book helped me put my life back together.*

helpful ▻ *adj* giving help or aid; being useful. • **helpfully** *adverb.* • **helpfulness** *noun.*

helping ▻ *noun* a single portion of food served at a meal.

helping hand ▻ *noun* **1** help or assistance ◻ *He gave a helping hand.* **2** a long-handled device used to reach and grip objects that cannot be reached by hand.

helpless ▻ *adj* **1** unable or unfit to do anything for oneself. **2** weak and defenceless; needing assistance. • **helplessly** *adverb.* • **helplessness** *noun.*

helpline ▻ *noun* a telephone line which may be used (often free of charge) by people with specific problems in order to contact advisers and counsellors who are specifically qualified to deal with them.

helpmate ▷ *noun* a friend or partner, especially a husband or wife.

helter-skelter /hɛltə'skɛltə(r)/ ▷ *adj* careless, confused and disorderly. ▷ *adverb* in a careless and disorientated manner; tumultuously. ▷ *noun, Brit* a spiral slide down the outside of a tower in a fairground or playground. ⓒ 16c: a rhyming compound based on 14c *skelten* to hurry.

helve /hɛlv/ ▷ *noun* the handle of an axe or other similar tool. ▷ *verb* (***helved, helving***) to provide with a handle. ⓒ Anglo-Saxon *helfe* a handle.

Helvetic /hɛl'vɛtɪk/ and **Helvetian** /hɛl'viːʃən/ ▷ *adj* Swiss. ⓒ 16c: from Latin *Helvetia* Switzerland.

hem¹ /hɛm/ ▷ *noun* a bottom edge or border of a piece of cloth that is folded over and sewn down. ▷ *verb* (***hemmed, hemming***) *tr & intr* to form a border or edge on a piece of cloth. ⓒ Anglo-Saxon *hemm*.

■ **hem something** or **someone in** to surround them closely, preventing movement.

hem² /həm, əm/ ▷ *exclamation* a slight clearing of the throat or cough to show hesitation or to draw attention. ▷ *noun* such a sound. ▷ *verb* (***hemmed, hemming***) *intr* to utter this kind of cough or sound. ⓒ 16c: imitating the sound.

hem- and **hema-** see HAEMO-

he-man ▷ *noun* (***he-men***) *colloq* a man of exaggerated or extreme strength, stamina and virility.

hemat- see HAEMATO-

hematite see HAEMATITE

hemato- see HAEMATO-

heme see HAEM

hemeralopia /hɛmərə'loʊpɪə/ ▷ *noun* day blindness; the inability to see clearly or at all in bright light. • **hemeralopic** *adj*. ⓒ 18c: from Greek *hemera* day + *alaos* blind + *ops* eye.

hemi- /hɛmɪ/ ▷ *combining form, signifying* half □ *hemisphere*. ⓒ Greek *hemi*.

-hemia see -AEMIA

hemicellulose ▷ *noun, bot* a type of polysaccharide, found in plant cell walls, which is broken down more easily than cellulose, the main component of the cell walls.

hemidemisemiquaver ▷ *noun, music* a note equal in time to half a DEMISEMIQUAVER.

hemiplegia /hɛmɪ'pliːdʒɪə/ ▷ *noun, pathol* paralysis of one side of the body only. Compare MONOPLEGIA, PARAPLEGIA, QUADRIPLEGIA. • **hemiplegic** *adj, noun*. ⓒ 17c.

hemipterous /hɛ'mɪptərəs/ ▷ *adj, zool* referring or relating to insects belonging to the order **Hemiptera**, members of which have an oval flattened body, wings which (if present) are membranous and half leathery, and mouthparts that are modified for piercing and sucking. ⓒ 19c.

hemisphere ▷ *noun* **1** one half of a sphere. **2** each half of the Earth's sphere, divided by the equator into the northern and southern hemispheres, and by a meridian into the eastern and western hemispheres. • **hemispheric** or **hemispherical** *adj*. ⓒ 14c.

hemline ▷ *noun* the height or level of the hem on a dress or skirt, etc.

hemlock /'hɛmlɒk/ ▷ *noun* **1** a poisonous umbelliferous plant with small white flowers and a spotted stem. **2** the poison extracted from this plant. **3** (*also* **hemlock spruce**) a North American tree whose branches are thought to resemble hemlock leaves. ⓒ Anglo-Saxon *hymlic*.

hemo- see HAEMO-

hemp /hɛmp/ ▷ *noun* **1** (*in full* **Indian hemp**) a tall annual plant which is native to Asia and grown commercially for its stem fibres, a drug and an oil. **2** any drug obtained from this plant, eg cannabis or marijuana. **3** the coarse fibre obtained from the stem of this plant, used to make rope, cord, tough cloth, etc. • **hempen** *adj* made of hemp. ⓒ Anglo-Saxon *hænep*.

hemstitch ▷ *noun* a decorative finishing stitch used on the inner side of a hem, achieved by stitching the cross threads into small groups.

hen ▷ *noun* **1** a female bird of any kind, especially the domestic fowl. **2** the female of certain fishes and crustaceans. ⓒ Anglo-Saxon *henn*.

henbane ▷ *noun* a poisonous wild plant of the nightshade family, with hairy leaves, light-green flowers, and an unpleasant smell. ⓒ 13c: HEN + BANE, so called because it is especially poisonous to domestic fowl.

hence /hɛns/ ▷ *adverb* **1** for this reason or cause. **2** from this time onwards. **3** *old use* from this place or origin. ⓒ 13c as *hennes*, from Anglo-Saxon *heonan*.

henceforth and **henceforward** ▷ *adverb* from now on.

henceforth

☆ PLAIN ENGLISH alternative is **from now on**.

henchman /'hɛntʃmən/ ▷ *noun* a faithful supporter or right-hand man, especially one who obeys and assists without question. ⓒ Anglo-Saxon *hengest* a horse + *man*.

hen coop ▷ *noun* a small enclosure or cage for hens.

hendeca- /hɛn'dɛkə, 'hɛn-/ ▷ *combining form, signifying* eleven. ⓒ Greek.

hendecagon /hɛn'dɛkəgɒn/ ▷ *noun* a plane figure with eleven sides and eleven angles. • **hendecagonal** /hɛndɪ'kagənəl/ *adj*. ⓒ 17c: HENDECA- + -GON.

hendecasyllable ▷ *noun* a metrical line containing eleven syllables. • **hendecasyllabic** *adj*. ⓒ 18c.

hendiadys /hɛn'daɪədɪs/ ▷ *noun* a rhetorical figure in which a notion, normally expressible by an adjective and a noun, is instead expressed by two nouns linked by a conjunction, as in *clad in cloth and green*. ⓒ 16c: from Greek *hen dia dyoin* one by means of two.

henequen, henequin or **heniquin** /'hɛnəkən/ ▷ *noun* **1** a Mexican agave. **2** the leaf fibre from this plant, sisal hemp, used for making rope. ⓒ 19c: American Spanish.

henge /hɛndʒ/ ▷ *noun, archaeol* **1** a circular or oval area surrounded by a bank and ditch, often containing burial chambers. **2** a circular, oval or horseshoe-shaped monument consisting of large upright stones or wooden posts and dating from prehistoric times. ⓒ 18c: a back-formation from *Stonehenge*, a famous stone circle in S England.

hen harrier ▷ *noun* a bird of prey or hawk; the common harrier.

hen house ▷ *noun* a house or coop for fowl.

henna /'hɛnə/ ▷ *noun* **1** a small Asian and N African shrub of the loosestrife family with fragrant white flowers. **2** reddish-brown dye obtained from the leaves of this shrub, used for colouring the hair and decorating the skin. ▷ *verb* (***hennaed, hennaing***) to dye or stain using henna. ⓒ 16c: from Arabic *hinna*.

henotheism /'hɛnoʊθiːɪzəm/ ▷ *noun, relig* the belief in one particular god (out of several in a specific belief system) as the god of the tribe, household, etc. • **henotheist** *noun*. • **henotheistic** *adj*. ⓒ 19c: from Greek *heis, henos* one + *theos* god.

hen party and **hen night** ▷ *noun* a party attended by women only, especially one to celebrate the future marriage of one woman in the group.

henpecked ▻ *adj, colloq* usually said of a man: constantly harassed, criticized and dominated by a woman, especially a wife, girlfriend, etc. • **henpecker** *noun*.

hen roost ▻ *noun* a roosting place for fowl.

hen run ▻ *noun* an enclosure or pen for fowl.

henry /ˈhɛnrɪ/ ▻ *noun* (***henry, henrys*** or ***henries***) (symbol **H**) in the SI system: the unit of electrical inductance, defined as the inductance that produces an electromotive force of one volt when the electric current in a closed circuit changes at the rate of one ampere per second. ⓘ 19c: named after Joseph Henry (1797–1878), the US physicist.

hep ▻ *adj, slang* an old-fashioned variant of HIP[4], used especially in relation to jazz.

heparin /ˈhɛpərɪn/ ▻ *noun, biochem* **1** a chemical substance formed in most tissues of the body (eg liver, lung, etc) that prevents the clotting of the blood. **2** an extracted and purified form of this used as an anticoagulant drug in medicine for the treatment of thrombosis. ⓘ 1920s: from Greek *hepar* liver.

hepatic /hɪˈpatɪk/ ▻ *adj* **1** relating or referring to the liver. **2** liver-coloured. ▻ *noun* **1** a liverwort. **2** a hepatic medicine. ⓘ 15c: from Greek *hepar* liver.

hepatica /hɪˈpatɪkə/ ▻ *noun* (***hepaticas***) a plant with three-lobed leaves, and white, pink or purple flowers. ⓘ 16c: Latin, from the shape of the leaves.

hepatitis /hɛpəˈtaɪtɪs/ ▻ *noun* inflammation of the liver, caused either by a viral infection, or as a reaction to toxic substances such as alcohol or drugs, the symptoms of which include jaundice, fever and nausea. ⓘ 18c: from Greek *hepar, hepatos* liver + -ITIS.

hepatitis A ▻ *noun* a form of viral hepatitis transmitted by contaminated food and drink.

hepatitis B ▻ *noun* a form of viral hepatitis transmitted by contaminated blood products or hypodermic syringes, etc.

hepatologist /hɛpəˈtɒlədʒɪst/ ▻ *noun* a scientist who specializes in liver diseases. • **hepatology** *noun*.

Hepplewhite /ˈhɛpəlwaɪt/ ▻ *adj* relating or referring to the elegant school of furniture design which favoured the use of curves, especially seen in shield-shaped chairbacks. ⓘ 18c: named after George Hepplewhite (died 1786), the English furniture maker and designer.

hepta- /hɛptə/ or (before a vowel) **hept-** *combining form, signifying* seven. ⓘ Greek.

heptachord ▻ *noun* **1** *Greek music* a diatonic series of seven tones, comprising five whole steps and one half step. **2** an instrument with seven strings. **3** an interval of a seventh. ⓘ 18c.

heptad ▻ *noun* a group of seven.

heptagon ▻ *noun* a plane figure with seven angles and sides. • **heptagonal** *adj* heptagon-shaped. ⓘ 16c: HEPTA- + -GON.

heptameter /hɛpˈtamɪtə(r)/ ▻ *noun* a verse line containing seven measures or feet. ⓘ 19c.

heptane /ˈhɛpteɪn/ ▻ *noun, chem* a hydrocarbon which is seventh of the methane series.

heptarchy /ˈhɛptɑːkɪ/ ▻ *noun* (***heptarchies***) **1** government by a group of seven leaders, or a country ruled in this way. **2** *historical* the seven kingdoms into which Anglo-Saxon England was allegedly divided: Wessex, Sussex, Kent, Essex, East Anglia, Mercia and Northumbria. • **heptarch** *noun* the ruler of a heptarchy. • **heptarchic** *adj*. ⓘ 16c.

heptasyllable ▻ *noun* a word or line containing seven syllables. • **heptasyllabic** *adj*. ⓘ 18c.

heptathlon /hɛpˈtaθlɒn/ ▻ *noun* an athletic contest introduced in 1984 consisting of seven events: 100 metres hurdles, shot put, javelin, high jump, long jump and races over 200 and 800 metres. Compare DECATHLON, PENTATHLON. ⓘ 1980s.

her /hɜː(r)/ ▻ *pronoun* **1** the form of SHE used as the object of a verb or preposition □ *We all like her* □ *send it to her.* **2** the possessive form of SHE □ *Her car is outside.* ▻ *adj* referring to a female person or animal, or something personified or thought of as female, eg a ship □ *went to her house* □ *gave the cat her milk.* ⓘ Anglo-Saxon *hire*.

her. ▻ *abbreviation* heraldry. ⓘ 13c.

herald /ˈhɛrəld/ ▻ *noun* **1** in ancient and medieval societies: a person who announces important news, or an officer whose task it is to make public proclamations and arrange ceremonies. **2** someone or something that is a sign of what is to come; a forerunner. **3** an officer responsible for keeping a record of the genealogies and coats of arms of noble families. **4** (**Herald**) a name given to several newspapers. ▻ *verb* (***heralded, heralding***) to be a sign of the approach of something; to proclaim or usher it in □ *dark clouds heralding a storm.* • **heraldic** /həˈraldɪk/ *adj*. • **heraldically** *adverb*. ⓘ 14c: from French *herault*.

heraldry /ˈhɛrəldrɪ/ ▻ *noun* **1** the art of recording genealogies, and blazoning coats of arms. **2** the office or duty of a herald. ⓘ 14c.

herb /hɜːb; (*US*) ɜːb / ▻ *noun* **1** *hortic* a flowering plant which, unlike a shrub or tree, has no woody stem above the ground. **2** any of the aromatic plants such as rosemary, mint and parsley, used in cookery or in herbal medicine. ⓘ 13c: from Latin *herba* grass or green plant.

herbaceous /hɜːˈbeɪʃəs/ ▻ *adj* said of a plant: relating to or having the characteristics of herbs, especially the tall plants which die down in winter and survive underground. ⓘ 17c: from Latin *herbaceus* relating to grass or green plants.

herbaceous border ▻ *noun* a garden border containing mainly perennial plants and flowers.

herbage /ˈhɜːbɪdʒ/ ▻ *noun* herbs collectively; herbaceous vegetation covering a large area, especially for use as pasture. ⓘ 13c.

herbal ▻ *adj, hortic* composed of or relating to herbs. ▻ *noun, bot* a book describing the use of plants, or substances extracted from them, for medicinal purposes. ⓘ 16c: from Latin *herbalis* belonging to grass or herbs.

herbalism *noun, medicine* the use of herbs for medicinal purposes.

herbalist and **herbist** ▻ *noun* **1** a person who researches, collects and sells herbs and plants. **2** a person who practises herbalism. **3** an early botanist.

herbarium /hɜːˈbɛərɪəm/ ▻ *noun* (***herbaria*** /-ˈrɪə/ or ***herbariums***) **1** *bot* a classified collection of preserved plants (in a room or building, etc). **2** the room or building used to house such a collection.

herb bennet /— ˈbɛnɪt/ ▻ *noun* an aromatic plant with yellow flowers. ⓘ 18c: from Latin *herba benedicta* blessed herb.

herb garden ▻ *noun* a garden used primarily for the culture of herbs.

herbicide /ˈhɜːbɪsaɪd/ ▻ *noun, agric* a substance used to kill weeds, etc, especially when used as a selective weedkiller. • **herbicidal** *adj*. ⓘ 19c.

herbivore /ˈhɜːbɪvɔː(r)/ ▻ *noun* an animal, especially an ungulate that feeds on grass, herbage or other vegetation. ⓘ 19c: from Latin *herba* grass or green plant + *vorare* to swallow.

herbivorous /hɜːˈbɪvərəs/ ▻ *adj* feeding on grass and other plants. • **herbivory** *noun*. ⓘ 17c.

herb Paris ▻ *noun* a plant of the lily family, comprising four leaves and a single yellow flower. ⓘ 16c: from Latin *herba paris* herb of a pair, so called because the four leaves resemble a lover's knot.

herb Robert ▻ *noun* the common cranesbill or geranium, a plant with small reddish-purple flowers. ⓘ 13c: from Latin *herba Roberti* herb of Robert.

herb tea and **herbal tea** ▻ *noun* a tea made by brewing aromatic herbs, eg camomile.

Herculean /hɜːkjʊ'lɪən, hɜː'kjuːlɪən/ ▻ *adj* **1** relating or referring to Hercules, the mythical Greek hero famous for his great strength. **2** (**herculean**) **a** extremely difficult or dangerous; **b** requiring an enormous effort ▫ ***a herculean task.*** ⓘ 17c: from *Hercules*, Latin form of *Heracles*, the hero's Greek name.

Hercules /'hɜːkjʊliːz/ ▻ *noun, astron* the fifth largest constellation, which is situated in the N hemisphere, but contains no prominent stars.

Hercules beetle ▻ *noun* an enormous S American beetle, growing to over 6 inches in length, the male of which has a long horn on the thorax and a smaller one on its head.

herd¹ /hɜːd/ ▻ *noun* **1** a company of animals, especially large ones, that habitually remain together. **2** a collection of livestock or domestic animals, especially cows or pigs. **3** a person who looks after a herd. **4** a large crowd of people, especially when behaving in a contagious manner that is noisy and often antisocial. **5** (**the herd**) a mass of people in general when seen as behaving in an unimaginative and conventional way. ▻ *verb* (***herded, herding***) **1** *intr* to associate as if in a herd; to gather together in a crowd like an animal in a herd. **2** to look after or tend a herd of (animals). **3** to group (animals) together. ⓘ Anglo-Saxon *heord*.

herd² /hɜːd/ ▻ *noun, combining form* the keeper of a herd, flock or group of particular animals ▫ ***goatherd*** ▫ ***swineherd***. ⓘ Anglo-Saxon *hirde, hierde*.

herd instinct ▻ *noun* the instinct that causes people or animals to act on joint impulses, or to follow the behaviour of the herd.

herdsman ▻ *noun* **1** the keeper of a herd of animals. **2** someone who tends the herd.

here /hɪə(r)/ ▻ *adverb* **1** at, in or to this place. **2** in the present life or state; at this point, stage or time. **3** used with *this, these*, etc for emphasis: **a** after a noun ▫ ***this chair here***; **b** *colloq, dialect* between a noun and *this, that*, etc ▫ ***this here chair.*** ▻ *noun* this place or location. ▻ *exclamation* **1** calling for attention. **2** calling attention to one's own presence, or to something one is about to say. • **here and now** the present moment; straight away. • **here and there** in various places; irregularly or thinly. • **here goes!** an exclamation indicating that the speaker is about to proceed with something, often with apprehension. • **here's to someone** or **something** used when proposing a toast to them or it ▫ ***Here's to the President*** ▫ ***Here's to gambling.*** • **here today, gone tomorrow** a comment on the ephemeral or transient nature of something. • **here we are** *colloq* **1** this is what we are looking for. **2** now we have arrived. • **here we go again** *colloq* a phrase said on the recurrence of an undesirable situation. • **here you are** *colloq* **1** this is what you are after. **2** this is something for you. **3** do it this way. • **neither here nor there** of no particular importance or relevance. • **the here and now** the present time. ⓘ Anglo-Saxon *her*.

hereabouts or **hereabout** ▻ *adverb* around or near this place; within this area.

hereafter ▻ *adverb, formal* **1** after this time; in a future time, life or state. **2** in a legal document or case: from this point on. • **the hereafter** a future stage or phase; the after-life.

hereat /hɪə'rat/ ▻ *adverb, archaic* because of or by reason of this.

hereby ▻ *adverb, formal* **1** not far off. **2** as a result of this or by this.

hereditable /hə'rɛdɪtəbəl/ ▻ *adj* referring to something that may be inherited. • **hereditability** *noun*. ⓘ 15c: from Latin *hereditas* inheritance.

hereditament /hɛrə'dɪtəmənt/ ▻ *noun, law* any type of property that may be passed down to an heir.

hereditarian /hərɛdɪ'tɛərɪən/ and **hereditarianist** ▻ *noun* an adherent of **hereditarianism**, the opinion that heredity is the main factor in influencing human and animal behaviour.

hereditary /hə'rɛdɪtərɪ/ ▻ *adj* **1** descending or acquiring by inheritance. **2** passed down or transmitted genetically to offspring ▫ ***a hereditary disease.*** **3** succeeding to a title or position, etc by inheritance. **4** passed down according to inheritance. • **hereditarily** *adverb*. • **hereditariness** *noun*. ⓘ 16c: from Latin *hereditas* inheritance.

heredity /hə'rɛdɪtɪ/ ▻ *noun* (***heredities***) **1** the transmission of recognizable and genetically based characteristics from one generation to the next. **2** the total quantity of such characteristics inherited. Also called **inheritance**. • **hereditist** *noun* a hereditarian. ⓘ 16c.

Hereford cattle /'hɛrəfəd —/ ▻ *noun* a breed of beef cattle with a white face and a reddish-brown coat, originating in Herefordshire.

herein /hɪə'rɪn/ ▻ *adverb* **1** *formal* in this case or respect. **2** *law & formal* contained within this letter or document, etc.

hereinafter ▻ *adverb, law & formal* later in this document or form, etc.

hereof /hɪə'rɒv/ ▻ *adverb, law & formal* relating to or concerning this.

hereon /hɪə'rɒn/ ▻ *adverb, formal* on, upon or to this point.

heresy /'hɛrəsɪ/ ▻ *noun* (***heresies***) **1** an opinion or belief contrary to the authorized teaching of the religious community to which one ostensibly belongs. **2** an opinion opposed to the conventional or traditional belief; heterodoxy. ⓘ 13c: from Greek *hairesis* choice.

heretic /'hɛrətɪk/ ▻ *noun* **1** someone who believes in and endorses heresy. **2** someone who has views and opinions that conflict with those of the majority. • **heretical** *adj*. • **heretically** *adverb*. ⓘ 14c: from Greek *hairein* to choose.

hereto /hɪə'tuː/ ▻ *adverb, law & formal* to this place or document. **2** for this purpose.

heretofore /hɪətʊ'fɔː(r)/ ▻ *adverb, law & formal* before or up to this time; formerly.

hereunder /hɪə'rʌndə(r)/ ▻ *adverb, law & formal* **1** in a document: below; following. **2** by or under the authority of this document, case, etc.

hereunto /hɪə'rʌntuː, -'tuː/ ▻ *adverb, law & formal* to this point in time; to this place or matter.

hereupon /hɪərə'pɒn/ ▻ *adverb, law & formal* **1** on this. **2** immediately after or as a result of this.

herewith /hɪə'wɪð, -'wɪθ/ ▻ *adverb, law & formal* with this; enclosed or together with this letter, etc.

Her Highness see under HIGHNESS sense 1

Her Honour see under HONOUR

heritable /'hɛrɪtəbəl/ ▻ *adj* **1** said of property: able to be inherited or passed down. **2** said of people: able or in a position to inherit property. • **heritability** *noun*. • **heritably** *adverb*. ⓘ 14c: from French *heriter* to inherit.

heritage /'hɛrɪtɪdʒ/ ▻ *noun* **1** something that is inherited. **2** the characteristics, qualities, property, etc that one inherits at birth. **3** a nation's mark of history, such as stately buildings, countryside, cultural traditions, etc seen as the nation's wealth to be inherited by future generations. ⓒ 13c: French.

heritor /ˈhɛrɪtə(r)/ ▻ *noun, law* a person who inherits, either legally or by tradition. ⓒ 14c: from French *heriter* to inherit.

herl see HARL[1]

hermaphrodite /hɜːˈmafrədaɪt/ ▻ *noun* **1** a human being, plant or animal that, either normally or abnormally, possesses both male and female reproductive organs, eg the earthworm and many plants. **2** a compound of opposite qualities. ▻ *adj* combining the characteristics of both sexes or opposite qualities. • **hermaphroditic** /-ˈdɪtɪk/ and **hermaphroditical** *adj* **1** belonging to or having characteristics typical of a hermaphrodite. **2** combining two opposites. • **hermaphroditically** *adverb*. • **hermaphroditism** *noun* the union of the two sexes in one body. ⓒ 15c: named after Hermaphroditos, in Greek mythology the son of Hermes and Aphrodite, who grew into one person with the nymph *Salmacis*.

hermeneutic /hɜːməˈnjuːtɪk/ and **hermeneutical** ▻ *adj* concerned with or relating to interpretation, especially that of Scripture. • **hermeneutically** *adverb*. ⓒ 19c.

hermeneutics ▻ *singular noun* **1** the science of the interpretation and understanding of texts, especially of Scriptures. **2** *psychol* the method used to understand and study human beings in society. ⓒ 18c: from Greek *hermeneutikos* interpreting, from *hermeneus* an interpreter.

hermetic /hɜːˈmɛtɪk/ and **hermetical** ▻ *adj* **1** perfectly closed or sealed so as to be airtight. **2** belonging or relating to magic or alchemy. **3** obscure or abstruse. • **hermetically** *adverb*. • **hermeticity** /hɜːməˈtɪsɪtɪ/ *noun*. ⓒ 17c: named after Hermes Trismegistos, supposedly the Greek author of texts on magic and alchemy, and also the inventor of a magic seal.

hermetically sealed ▻ *adj* said of a container: **1** closed or sealed completely. **2** made airtight by melting the glass at the neck.

hermetics /hɜːˈmɛtɪks/ ▻ *singular noun* esoteric or obscure science; alchemy.

hermit /ˈhɜːmɪt/ ▻ *noun* **1** an ascetic who leads an isolated life for religious reasons. **2** someone who lives a solitary life. ⓒ 13c: from Greek *eremos* solitary.

hermitage /ˈhɜːmɪtɪdʒ/ ▻ *noun* **1** the dwelling-place of a hermit. **2** a secluded place or abode; a retreat.

hermit crab ▻ *noun* a soft-bodied crustacean that protects itself by inhabiting the shells of other molluscs and only allowing the hard front end of its body to protrude.

hernia /ˈhɜːnɪə/ ▻ *noun* (***hernias***) the protrusion of an organ (especially part of the viscera) through an opening or weak spot in the wall of its surroundings. *Non-technical equivalent* RUPTURE (*noun* 3). • **hernial** *adj*. • **herniated** *adj*. ⓒ 14c: Latin.

hero /ˈhɪəroʊ/ ▻ *noun* (***heroes***) **1** a man of distinguished bravery and strength; any illustrious person. **2** a person who is venerated and idealized. **3** in fiction, a play, film, etc: the principal male character or the one whose life is the theme of the story. **4** *originally* a man of superhuman powers; a demigod. See also HEROINE. ⓒ 14c: from Greek *heros*.

heroic /hɪˈroʊɪk/ ▻ *adj* **1** supremely courageous and brave. **2** befitting or suited to a hero. **3** relating to or concerning heroes or heroines. **4** using extreme and elaborate means to obtain a desired result, such as the preserving of life. **5** on a superhuman scale or larger-than-life. • **heroically** *adverb*.

heroic age ▻ *noun* a semi-mythical period when heroes and demigods were represented as living among men.

heroic couplet ▻ *noun, poetry* a pair of rhymed 10-syllable lines usually in IAMBIC PENTAMETERS, one of the commonest metrical forms in English poetry.

heroics ▻ *noun* **1** over-dramatic or extravagant speech. **2** excessively bold behaviour. ⓒ 16c: from Greek *heroikos* relating to a hero.

heroic verse ▻ *noun* the form of verse in which the exploits of heroes are celebrated (in classical poetry, the HEXAMETER; in English, the IAMBIC PENTAMETER, especially in couplets; in French, the ALEXANDRINE).

heroin /ˈhɛroʊɪn/ ▻ *noun* a powerful drug produced from MORPHINE, used medicinally to lessen pain, and illegally for pleasure, but with continued use likely to lead to dependence and addiction. *Technical equivalent* DIAMORPHINE. ⓒ 19c: from German *Heroin*, from Greek *heros* hero, perhaps from the initial feeling of euphoria produced.

heroin, heroine

There is sometimes a spelling confusion between **heroin** and **heroine**.

heroine /ˈhɛroʊɪn/ ▻ *noun* **1** a woman with heroic characteristics. **2** a woman admired and idealized for her qualities of bravery, courage, noble abilities, etc. **3** in fiction, a play, film, etc: the principal female character or the one whose life is the theme of the story. See also HERO. ⓒ 17c: from Greek *heros*.

heroism /ˈhɛroʊɪzəm/ ▻ *noun* the qualities of a hero; courage, boldness and strength.

heron /ˈhɛrən/ ▻ *noun* **1** a large wading bird with a long neck and legs, and commonly grey or white in colour. **2** any of a number of related wading birds. • **heronry** /ˈhɛrənrɪ/ *noun* a place where herons breed. ⓒ 14c: from French *hairon*.

hero-worship ▻ *noun* **1** an excessive fondness and admiration for someone. **2** the worship of heroes in antiquity. ▻ *verb* to idealize or to have a great admiration for someone.

herpes /ˈhɜːpiːz/ ▻ *noun* any of various contagious skin diseases caused by a virus which gives rise to watery blisters, especially **herpes simplex**, a sexually transmitted disease, and **herpes zoster** or SHINGLES. • **herpetic** /hɜːˈpɛtɪk/ *adj* **1** relating to or resembling herpes. **2** creeping. ⓒ 17c: from Greek *herpein* to creep.

herpetology /hɜːpəˈtɒlədʒɪ/ ▻ *noun* the study of reptiles and amphibians. • **herpetologist** *noun*. ⓒ 19c: from Greek *herpeton* a creeping animal.

Herrenvolk / *German* ˈhɛrənfɔlk/ ▻ *noun* a race that believes itself to be fitted and entitled by its superior qualities to rule the world. ⓒ 1920s: German, literally 'master race'.

herring /ˈhɛrɪŋ/ ▻ *noun* (***herring*** or ***herrings***) a small silvery sea-fish of considerable commercial value, found in large shoals in northern waters, and eaten either fresh or cured. ⓒ Anglo-Saxon *hæring*.

herringbone ▻ *noun* **1** a zigzag pattern, like the spine of a herring, woven into cloth. **2** *skiing* a technique used to scale slopes by climbing with the skis pointing outwards while pressing one's weight down on the inner edges. ⓒ 17c.

herring gull ▻ *noun* a large gull with white feathers and black-tipped grey wings.

hers /hɜːz/ ▻ *pronoun* the one or ones belonging to HER. • **of hers** relating to or belonging to HER.

herself /hɜːˈsɛlf, hə-/ ▻ *pronoun* **1** the reflexive form of HER and SHE □ *She made herself a dress.* **2** used for emphasis □ *She did it herself.* **3** her normal self or true character □ *She isn't feeling herself.* **4** (*also* **by herself**) alone; without help. ⓒ Anglo-Saxon *hire self*.

Herts. /hɑːts/ ▻ *abbreviation, English county* Hertfordshire.

hertz /hɜːts/ ▻ *noun* (*plural* ***hertz***) (abbreviation **Hz**) in the SI system: the unit of frequency, equal to one cycle per second. Compare KILOHERTZ, MEGAHERTZ. ⓘ 1920s: named after Heinrich Hertz (1857–1894), the German physicist.

Her Worship see WORSHIP *noun* 3

he's /hiːz, hɪz/ ▻ *contraction* **1** he is. **2** he has.

hesitant /ˈhɛzɪtənt/ ▻ *adj* uncertain; holding back; doubtful. • **hesitantly** *adverb*. • **hesitance** and **hesitancy** *noun* wavering, doubt, delay, etc.

hesitate /ˈhɛzɪteɪt/ ▻ *verb* (***hesitated, hesitating***) *intr* **1** to falter or delay in speaking, acting or making a decision; to be in doubt. **2** to be unwilling to do or say something, often because one is uncertain if it is right. • **hesitatingly** *adverb*. • **hesitation** *noun*. ⓘ 17c: from Latin *haesitare* to remain stuck.

Hesperian /hɛˈspɪərɪən/ ▻ *adj, poetic* western. ⓘ 16c: from Greek *hesperios*.

hesperidium /hɛspəˈrɪdɪəm/ ▻ *noun, bot* a fruit similar to an orange. ⓘ 19c: Latin, named after the mythological fruit guarded by the nymphs the Hesperides.

Hesperus /ˈhɛspərəs/ ▻ *noun, poetry* the evening star. ⓘ 14c: from Greek *hesperos*.

hessian /ˈhɛsɪən/ ▻ *noun* a coarse cloth made from jute, similar to sacking. ⓘ 18c: from *Hesse*, a state in central Germany.

Hessian fly ▻ *noun* a midge whose larva infests wheat stems in America, originally believed to have been introduced in straw for the mercenary Hessian troops used by the British army in the American War of Independence.

het ▻ *noun, adj, slang, usually derog* short form of HETEROSEXUAL.

hetaera or **hetaira** /hɛˈtɪərə, hɛˈtaɪərə/ ▻ *noun* (***hetaeras*** or ***hetaerae*** /-riː/ or ***hetairai*** /-raɪ/) in ancient Greece: a prostitute, especially a COURTESAN. ⓘ 19c: Greek *hetaira*, feminine form of *hetairos* companion.

hetero /ˈhɛtəroʊ/ ▻ *noun* (**heteros**), *adj, colloq, usually derog* short form of HETEROSEXUAL.

hetero- /hɛtəroʊ, hɛtəˈrɒ/ or (before a vowel) **heter-** *combining form, signifying* **1** the other ▫ *heterodox*. **2** different ▫ *heterogeneous*. **3** one or the other ▫ *heterogamy*. Compare HOMO-, AUTO-. ⓘ From Greek *heteros* other.

heterochromatic and **heterochromous** /hɛtəroʊˈkroʊməs/ ▻ *adj, chem, physics* having different or varying colours. ⓘ 19c.

heterocyclic ▻ *adj, chem* said of a compound: having a closed chain of atoms where at least one is not the same as the others. Compare HOMOCYCLIC. ⓘ 19c.

heterodoxy /ˈhɛtəroʊdɒksɪ/ ▻ *noun* a belief, especially a religious one, that is different from the one most commonly accepted. • **heterodox** *adj*. ⓘ 17c.

heterodyne /ˈhɛtəroʊdaɪn/ ▻ *adj, electronics* in radio communication: superimposing one wave on another continuous wave of slightly different wavelength, creating beats. ⓘ Early 20c: from Greek *dynamis* power.

heterogamy /hɛtəˈrɒgəmɪ/ ▻ *noun* **1** *genetics* reproduction from unlike reproductive cells. **2** *bot* the presence of different kinds of flowers (eg male, female, hermaphrodite, neuter) in the same inflorescence. **3** *bot* CROSS-POLLINATION. • **heterogamous** *adj*. ⓘ 1830s.

heterogeneity /hɛtəroʊdʒəˈniːɪtɪ, -ˈneɪɪtɪ/ ▻ *noun* **1** being heterogeneous. **2** something which is heterogeneous.

heterogeneous /hɛtəroʊˈdʒiːnɪəs/ ▻ *adj* composed of parts, people, things, etc that are not related to each other, or are of different kinds. • **heterogeneously** *adverb*. • **heterogeneousness** *noun*. ⓘ 17c: from Greek *genos* a kind.

heterogenesis /hɛtəroʊˈdʒɛnɪsɪs/ ▻ *noun, biol* **1** ALTERNATION OF GENERATIONS. **2** spontaneous generation, the idea (now rejected) that living organisms can develop from inanimate material. • **heterogenetic** *adj*. ⓘ 19c: from Greek *genesis* generation.

heterogony /hɛtəˈrɒgənɪ/ ▻ *noun* **1** *bot* said of flowers: the condition of having stamens of different lengths. **2** *biol* ALTERNATION OF GENERATIONS. • **heterogonous** *adj*. ⓘ 19c: from Greek *gonos* offspring.

heterograft ▻ *noun* a graft of tissue from a member of one species to a member of a different species. ⓘ Early 20c.

heterology /hɛtəˈrɒlədʒɪ/ ▻ *noun, pathol* a lack of correspondence between apparently similar structures owing to a different origin. • **heterologous** *adj* not homologous; different in form and origin; abnormal. ⓘ 19c.

heteromerous /hɛtəˈrɒmərəs/ ▻ *adj* **1** *bot* containing different numbers of parts in different whorls. **2** *bot* said of lichens: containing the algal cells in a layer. **3** *zool* containing segments not related to each other. ⓘ 19c: from Greek *meros* part.

heteromorphic /hɛtəroʊˈmɔːfɪk/ and **heteromorphous** ▻ *adj, biol* **1** changing or differing in form from a given type. **2** said of insects: experiencing changes in form at varying stages of life. • **heteromorphism** or **heteromorphy** *noun*. ⓘ 19c.

heteronomous /hɛtəˈrɒnɪməs/ ▻ *adj* subject to different laws; subject to external or outside rules or laws. Opposite of AUTONOMOUS. • **heteronomy** *noun*. ⓘ 19c: HETERO- + Greek *nomos* law.

heteronym /ˈhɛtərənɪm/ ▻ *noun, grammar* a word which has the same spelling as another, but has a different pronunciation and meaning, such as lead (see LEAD[1] and LEAD[2]). ⓘ 17c: HETERO- + Greek *onyma* name.

heterophyllous /hɛtəroʊˈfɪləs/ ▻ *adj* said of a plant: having different types of foliage leaf. • **heterophylly** /ˈhɛtərəfɪlɪ/ *noun*. ⓘ 19c: from Greek *phyllon* leaf.

heteroplasia /hɛtəroʊˈpleɪzɪə/ ▻ *noun, pathol* the development of abnormal tissue, or the growth of tissue in an abnormal place. ⓘ 19c: from Greek *plasis* a forming or moulding.

heteroplasty /ˈhɛtəroʊplastɪ/ ▻ *noun, surgery* a repair to damaged tissue by grafting tissue from another person. • **heteroplastic** *adj*. ⓘ 19c.

Heteroptera /hɛtəˈrɒptərə/ ▻ *plural noun, entomol* a suborder of the insect group HEMIPTERA, including insects in which fore and hind wings (when present) are markedly different. • **heteropterous** *adj*. ⓘ 19c.

heterosexism ▻ *noun* the belief and opinion that homosexuality is a perversion, used as grounds for discrimination against homosexuals. • **heterosexist** *noun* someone who discriminates against homosexuals. ⓘ 19c.

heterosexual ▻ *adj* **1** having a sexual attraction to people of the opposite sex. **2** said of a relationship: between a man and a woman. ▻ *noun* a heterosexual person. Sometimes shortened to HET, HETERO. • **heterosexuality** *noun*.

heterosis see under HYBRID VIGOUR

heterotaxis /hɛtəroʊˈtaksɪs/ and **heterotaxy** ▻ *noun, anatomy* an anomalous and disproportionate arrangement eg of parts of the body. • **heterotactic** *adj*.

heterotrophy /hɛtəˈrɒtrəfɪ/ ▻ *noun, biol* a dependence, either immediate or ultimate, on the part of animals and some plants, on green plants, and on organic compounds generally, as a source of food. • **heterotroph**

/ˈhɛtəroʊtrɒf/ *noun* a heterotrophic organism. • **heterotrophic** *adj.* ◷ 19c: from Greek *trophe* livelihood.

heterozygote ▷ *noun, genetics* a zygote or individual containing two different alleles, one dominant and one recessive, for a particular gene, and which may therefore produce offspring that differ from the parent with respect to that gene. ◷ Early 20c.

heterozygous /hɛtəroʊˈzaɪɡəs/ ▷ *adj, genetics* describing an individual that has different DNA segments for a particular gene and produces offspring that are not always identical to the parent with respect to that gene. ◷ Early 20c.

hetman ▷ *noun* (***hetmans***) *historical* a Polish or Cossack military commander. ◷ 18c: from German *Hauptmann* captain.

het up ▷ *adj, colloq* angry; agitated. ◷ 19c: originally British and N American dialect past participle of HEAT, meaning 'heated'.

heuristic /hjʊəˈrɪstɪk/ ▷ *adj* **1** serving or leading to discover or find out. **2** said of a teaching method: encouraging a desire in learners to find their own solutions. **3** *computing* using a method of trial and error to solve a problem. ▷ *noun* (***heuristics***) the principles used to make decisions when all possibilities cannot be explored. • **heuristically** *adverb.* ◷ 19c: from Greek *heuriskein* to find.

hew /hjuː/ ▷ *verb* (***hewed, hewn*** /hjuːn/, ***hewing***) **1** to cut, fell or sever something using a cutting instrument, eg axe, sword, etc. **2** to carve or shape something from wood or stone. **3** *intr* to deal out blows with a cutting instrument. ◷ Anglo-Saxon *heawan.*

hex ▷ *noun* (***hexes***) *N Amer informal* **1** a witch, wizard or wicked spell. **2** anything that brings bad luck. ▷ *verb* (***hexed, hexing***) to bring misfortune; to bewitch. ◷ 19c: from German *Hexe* witch.

hexa- /hɛksə/ or (before a vowel) **hex-** *combining form, signifying* six. ◷ From Greek *hex.*

hexachlorophene /hɛksəˈklɔːrəfiːn/ ▷ *noun* a bactericide used in antiseptic soaps, deodorants, toothpastes, etc. ◷ 1940s.

hexachord ▷ *noun, music* **1** a diatonic series of six notes, with a semitone between the third and fourth notes. **2** an interval of a sixth. ◷ 17c: from Greek *hexachordos* having six strings.

hexad /ˈhɛksad/ ▷ *noun* **1** a series of six items. **2** a sequence of six numbers. **3** *chem* an atom, element or radical with a combined power of six units.

hexadecane see CETANE

hexadecimal ▷ *adj, computing* relating to or being a number system with a base of 16 (see BASE[1] sense 8). ▷ *noun* **1** such a system. **2** the notation used in the system. **3** a number expressed using the system. ◷ 1950s.

hexagon /ˈhɛksəɡən/ ▷ *noun* a plane figure with six sides and angles. • **hexagonal** /hɛkˈsaɡənəl/ *adj.* ◷ 16c: HEXA- + -GON.

hexagram ▷ *noun* a star-shaped figure created by extending the lines of a uniform hexagon until they meet at six points. ◷ 19c.

hexahedron /hɛksəˈhiːdrən, -drɒn/ ▷ *noun* (***hexahedrons*** or ***hexahedra*** /-drə/) a solid figure with six sides or faces, eg a cube. • **hexahedral** *adj.* ◷ 16c.

hexamerous /hɛkˈsamərəs/ ▷ *adj* comprising six parts, or parts divided into sixes. ◷ 19c: from Greek *meros* part.

hexameter /hekˈsamɪtə(r)/ ▷ *noun, poetry* **1** a line or verse with six measures or feet. **2** in Greek and Latin poetry: a line of verse with six feet where the first four are dactyls or spondees, the fifth usually a dactyl, and the sixth a spondee or a trochee. ◷ 16c.

hexane /ˈhɛkseɪn/ ▷ *noun, chem* (formula C_6H_{14}) a hydrocarbon that is a toxic flammable liquid, and the sixth member of the methane series. ◷ 19c.

hexapod /ˈhɛksəpɒd/ ▷ *noun* an animal with six legs, ie an insect. ◷ 17c.

hexastyle /ˈhɛksəstaɪl/ ▷ *adj* said of a temple or façade of a building: having six columns. ◷ 18c: from Greek *stylos* a pillar.

Hexateuch /ˈhɛksətjuːk/ ▷ *noun* the first six books of the Old Testament. • **hexateuchal** *adj.* ◷ 19c: from Greek *teuchos* tool, later meaning a book.

hexose /ˈhɛksoʊs, -soʊz/ ▷ *noun, chem* a monosaccharide carbohydrate with six carbon atoms in each molecule.

hey /heɪ/ ▷ *exclamation, colloq* **1** a shout expressing joy, surprise, interrogation or dismay. **2** a call to attract attention. • **hey presto!** a conjuror's expression, usually used at the successful finale of a trick. ◷ 13c: as *hei.*

heyday /ˈheɪdeɪ/ ▷ *noun* the period or climax of the most success, power, prosperity, popularity, etc. ◷ 16c: from German *heida* hey there.

HF ▷ *abbreviation* high frequency.

Hf ▷ *symbol, chem* hafnium.

hf ▷ *abbreviation* half.

HG ▷ *abbreviation* **1** High German. **2** His or Her Grace.

Hg ▷ *symbol, chem* mercury.

HGH ▷ *abbreviation* human growth hormone. Also called GH.

HGV ▷ *abbreviation, Brit* heavy goods vehicle.

HH ▷ *abbreviation* **1** His or Her Highness. **2** His Holiness. **3** on pencils: very hard.

HI ▷ *abbreviation* Hawaii; Hawaiian Islands.

hi /haɪ/ ▷ *exclamation, colloq* **1** a casual form of greeting. **2** a word used to attract attention. ◷ 19c: from HEY.

hiatus /haɪˈeɪtəs/ ▷ *noun* (***hiatus*** or ***hiatuses***) **1** an opening or gap; a break in something which should be continuous. **2** *grammar* the use of two consecutive vowels in adjacent syllables without any intervening consonant. ◷ 16c: Latin, from *hiare* to gape.

hiatus hernia ▷ *noun* a hernia in which part of the stomach protrudes through an opening in the diaphragm intended for the oesophagus.

hibernal /haɪˈbɜːnəl/ ▷ *adj* referring or belonging to the winter; wintry.

hibernate /ˈhaɪbəneɪt/ ▷ *verb* (***hibernated, hibernating***) *intr* said of certain animals: to pass the winter in a dormant state; to be completely inactive. • **hibernation** *noun.* ◷ 19c: from Latin *hibernare* to spend the winter, from *hibernus* wintry.

Hibernian /haɪˈbɜːnɪən, hi-/ *poetry* ▷ *adj* relating to Ireland. ▷ *noun* a native of Ireland. • **Hibernicism** /-nɪsɪzəm/ *noun* an Irish expression, idiom or peculiarity. ◷ 17c: from Latin *Hibernia* Ireland.

hibiscus /hɪˈbɪskəs/ ▷ *noun* (***hibiscuses***) a tree or shrub, usually from tropical climes, with large brightly coloured flowers. ◷ 18c: from Greek *ibiskos* marsh-mallow.

hiccup and **hiccough** /ˈhɪkʌp/ ▷ *noun* **1 a** an involuntary inhalation of air caused by a spasm in the diaphragm; **b** the sound caused by this. **2** (**hiccups** or **the hiccups**) the state of having these spasms at intervals of a few seconds. **3** *colloq* a temporary and usually minor setback, difficulty or interruption. ▷ *verb* (***hiccuped, hiccuping; hiccoughed, hiccoughing***) **1** *intr* to produce a hiccup or hiccups. **2** *intr* to falter, hesitate or malfunction. **3** to say something with a hiccup. ◷ 16c: an alteration of French *hocquet* an abrupt interruption; the spelling *hiccough* is a result of confusion with *cough.*

hic iacet or ***hic jacet*** /hɪk'jakɛt, hɪk'ɔ 'dʒakɛt/ ▻ *noun* usually preceding the name of the deceased on older grave monuments: here lies. ⓒ 17c: Latin.

hick ▻ *noun, chiefly N Amer derog* **1** someone from the country. **2** any unsophisticated, uncultured or ignorant person. ⓒ 16c: a familiar form of *Richard*.

hickey or **hickie** /'hɪkɪ/ ▻ *noun* (***hickeys*** or ***hickies***) *N Amer* a LOVE BITE.

hickory /'hɪkərɪ/ ▻ *noun* (***hickories***) a N American tree of the walnut family, with edible nuts and heavy strong tenacious wood. ⓒ 17c: from a Native American language.

hide[1] /haɪd/ ▻ *verb* (***hid, hidden*** /'hɪdən/, ***hiding*** /'haɪdɪŋ/) **1** to conceal someone or something from sight; to keep something secret. **2** *intr* to conceal oneself; to go into or stay in concealment. **3** to make something difficult to view; to obscure □ ***trees hiding the house.*** ▻ *noun* a concealed shelter used for observing birds and wild animals. • **hidden** *adj.* See also HIDING[1]. ⓒ Anglo-Saxon *hydan*.

hide[2] /haɪd/ ▻ *noun* **1** the skin of an animal, especially a large one, either raw or treated. **2** *colloq* the human skin. • **not** or **neither hide nor hair of someone** or **something** not the slightest trace of them or it. ⓒ Anglo-Saxon *hyd*.

hide-and-seek and (*N Amer*) **hide-and-go-seek** ▻ *noun* a game in which one person seeks the others who have hidden themselves. ⓒ 18c.

hideaway /'haɪdəweɪ/ and **hideout** ▻ *noun* a refuge or retreat; concealment.

hidebound /'haɪdbaʊnd/ ▻ *adj* **1** *derog* reluctant to accept new ideas or opinions, especially because of a petty, stubborn or conservative outlook. **2** said of livestock: having skin attached closely to the back and ribs due to poor feeding. ⓒ 17c in sense 1; 16c in sense 2.

hideous /'hɪdɪəs/ ▻ *adj* **1** said of a person or thing: dreadful; revolting; extremely ugly. **2** frightening; horrific; ghastly. • **hideously** *adverb*. • **hideousness** *noun*. ⓒ 13c: from French *hisdos*.

hiding[1] /'haɪdɪŋ/ ▻ *noun* **1** the state of being hidden or concealed. **2** concealment; a secret location. ▻ *verb, present participle of* HIDE[1].

hiding[2] /'haɪdɪŋ/ ▻ *noun, colloq* a severe beating. • **be on a hiding to nothing** *colloq* to be in a situation in which a favourable outcome is impossible. ⓒ 19c: from HIDE[2].

hiding-place ▻ *noun* a place of concealment; a hidden location.

hie /haɪ/ ▻ *verb* (***hied, hieing*** or ***hying***) *archaic* **1** *intr* to hasten or hurry. **2** to urge. ⓒ Anglo-Saxon *higian*.

hierarch /'haɪərɑːk/ ▻ *noun* **1** a holy ruler; a chief priest. **2** someone in a high position in a hierarchy. ⓒ 14c: from Greek *hieros* sacred + *archein* to rule.

hierarchy /'haɪərɑːkɪ/ ▻ *noun* (***hierarchies***) **1** an organization or body that classifies people or things in order of rank or importance. **2** the people who control such an organization. **3** *relig* the graded organization of priests or ministers. **4** the organization or classification of a particular group, eg plants. • **hierarchical** or **hierarchic** *adj* relating to or involving a hierarchy. • **hierarchically** *adverb*. • **hierarchism** *noun*. ⓒ 16c.

hieroglyph /'haɪərəglɪf/ and **hieroglyphic** /-fɪk/ ▻ *noun* a character or symbol representing a word, syllable, sound or idea, especially in ancient Egyptian. • **hieroglyphic** or **hieroglyphical** *adj*. • **hieroglyphically** *adverb*. ⓒ 16c: from Greek *hieros* sacred + *glyphein* to carve.

hieroglyphics /haɪərə'glɪfɪks/ ▻ *singular noun* **1** the system of writing using hieroglyphs, or representative symbols, used in ancient Egypt. **2** *colloq* writing that is difficult or impossible to read or decipher.

hierophant /'haɪəroʊfant/ ▻ *noun* in ancient Greece: someone who reveals or deciphers sacred mysteries. • **hierophantic**. ⓒ 17c: from Greek *hieros* sacred + *phainein* to show.

hi-fi /'haɪfaɪ/ ▻ *adj* being of high fidelity. ▻ *noun* (***hi-fis***) a set of equipment, usually consisting of an amplifier, tape deck, CD player, record player, etc, for sound reproduction that has such a high quality that it is virtually indistinguishable from the original sound. ⓒ 1940s: a shortening of HIGH FIDELITY.

higgledy-piggledy /'hɪgəldɪ'pɪgəldɪ/ ▻ *adverb, adj, colloq* haphazard; in confusion; disorderly. ⓒ 16c.

high /haɪ/ ▻ *adj* (***higher, highest***) **1** elevated; tall; towering □ ***high buildings.*** **2** being a specific height □ ***a hundred feet high.*** **3** far up from a base point, such as the ground or sea level □ ***a high branch*** □ ***a high mountain.*** **4** intense or advanced; more forceful than normal □ ***a high wind.*** **5** at the peak or climax □ ***high summer*** □ ***high season.*** **6** (*also* **High**,) said of a period or era: at the height of its development □ ***High Renaissance.*** **7** significant; exalted or revered □ ***high art.*** **8** said of sound: acute in pitch. **9** fully developed in terms of emotions and content □ ***high drama.*** **10** said of meat: partially decomposed or tainted. **11** elated or euphoric; over-excited. **12** *colloq* under the influence of drugs or alcohol □ ***was high on E.*** **13** taller or bigger than average □ ***a high-necked sweater.*** ▻ *adverb* at or to a height; in or into an elevated position □ ***The plane flew high.*** ▻ *noun* **1** a high point or level. **2** the maximum or highest level. **3** *colloq* a state of ecstasy and euphoria, often produced by drugs or alcohol □ ***on a high.*** **4** *meteorol* an ANTICYCLONE. • **a high old time** a period of exuberance and enthusiasm. • **high and dry 1** stranded or helpless; defenceless. **2** said of boats: out of the water. • **high and low 1** up and down; everywhere. **2** said of people: rich and poor alike. • **high and mighty** arrogant; pompous. • **high as a kite** *colloq* **1** over-excited or ecstatic. **2** under the influence of drugs or alcohol. • **hit the high spots** to continue to excess; to reach a high level. • **on high** above or aloft; in heaven. • **on one's high horse** *colloq* **1** having an attitude of arrogance and imagined superiority. **2** having a condescending or disdainful manner. ⓒ Anglo-Saxon *heah*.

highball ▻ *noun, chiefly N Amer* an alcoholic drink of spirits and soda served with ice in a long glass. ⓒ 19c.

high-born ▻ *adj* being of noble birth. ⓒ 13c.

highbrow *often derog* ▻ *noun* an intellectual or learned person. ▻ *adj* said of art, literature, etc: intellectual; cultured. Compare MIDDLEBROW, LOWBROW. • **high-browism** *adj*. ⓒ 19c.

high-chair ▻ *noun* a tall chair with a small attached table for babies or young children, used especially at mealtimes. ⓒ 19c.

High Church ▻ *noun* a section within the Church of England which places great importance on holy ceremony and priestly authority. ⓒ 17c.

high-class ▻ *adj* **1** being of very high quality. **2** superior and distinguished; typical of or relating to the upper class. ⓒ 19c.

high-coloured ▻ *adj* **1** having a very strong and brilliant colour. **2** said of a complexion: ruddy; flushed or glowing. ⓒ 1920s.

high comedy ▻ *noun* comedy set in a refined sophisticated society, characterized more by complex plot, amusing and witty dialogue, and skilful characterization than by comical activities and situations. ⓒ 19c.

High Commission ▻ *noun* an embassy representing one member country of the British Commonwealth in another country. • **High Commissioner** *noun* the senior diplomat at the head of such an embassy. ⓒ 19c.

high court ▻ *noun* **1** a supreme court. **2** (**the High Court**) the supreme court for civil cases in England and Wales. ⓒ 13c.

high-definition television see HDTV

high-density ▷ *adj, computing* said of a disk: having a very compact data-storage capacity. ⓘ 1950s.

Higher *noun, Scottish* an examination generally taken at the end of the fifth year of secondary education, more advanced than STANDARD GRADE. Compare A LEVEL.

higher education ▷ *noun, Brit* education beyond secondary school level, ie at university or college, usually studying for a degree. Compare FURTHER EDUCATION. ⓘ 19c.

higher-up ▷ *noun* (***higher-ups***) *colloq* someone who holds an upper position; a superior.

highest see under HIGH

high explosive ▷ *noun* **1** a detonating explosive of immense power and extremely rapid action, eg dynamite, TNT, etc. **2** *as adj* exploding with a huge effect □ *a high-explosive bomb.* ⓘ 19c.

highfalutin and **highfaluting** /haɪfə'luːtɪn/ ▷ *adj, informal* ostentatious; pompous or affected. ⓘ 19c: HIGH + *falutin,* variation of *fluting,* present participle of FLUTE.

high fidelity ▷ *noun* an accurate and high quality reproduction of sound. See also HI-FI. ⓘ 1930s.

high-five ▷ *noun, especially N Amer* a sign of greeting or celebration, involving the slapping together of raised palms.

high-flier or **high-flyer** ▷ *noun* **1** an ambitious person, likely to achieve their goals. **2** someone naturally skilled and competent in their career. • **high-flying** *adj.* ⓘ 17c.

high-flown ▷ *adj* often said of language: sounding grand but lacking real substance; rhetorical; extravagant.

high frequency ▷ *noun* a radio frequency between 3 and 30 megahertz. ⓘ 19c.

high gear ▷ *noun* a gear set to give a high number of revolutions of the driven part relative to the driving part.

High German ▷ *noun* the standard form of the German language as spoken and written by the educated population. See also LOW GERMAN. ⓘ 18c.

high-handed ▷ *adj* overbearing and arrogant; arbitrary. • **high-handedness** *noun.* • **high-handedly** *adverb.* ⓘ 17c.

high-hat or **hi-hat** ▷ *noun, colloq* **1** *formerly* the wearer of a top hat. **2** a snob or aristocrat; someone who affects airs. **3** a pair of cymbals on a stand. ▷ *adj* affectedly superior. ▷ *verb* **1** *intr* to put on airs. **2** to assume a superior attitude towards someone or something; to ignore them socially. ⓘ Early 20c.

highjack see HIJACK

high jump ▷ *noun* **1** an athletic event where competitors jump over a high bar which is raised higher after each successful jump. **2** *colloq* a severe punishment or reproof □ *He's for the high jump.* ⓘ 19c.

high-key ▷ *adj* said of paintings and photographs: containing pale tones and very little contrast. ⓘ Early 20c.

high kick ▷ *noun* a dancer's high kick, usually while keeping the leg straight.

highland /'haɪlənd/ ▷ *noun* **1** (*often* **highlands**) a mountainous area of land. **2** (**the Highlands**) the mountainous area of northern and western Scotland. ▷ *adj* referring to or characteristic of highland regions or the Scottish Highlands. ⓘ Anglo-Saxon.

Highland cattle ▷ *noun* a Scottish breed of small cattle with a long-haired shaggy coat and long horns.

Highland dress ▷ *noun* the traditional outfit of the Highland soldiers, comprising a kilt, plaid and sporran.

highlander /'haɪləndə(r)/ ▷ *noun* a native or inhabitant of highland regions, especially the Scottish Highlands.

Highland fling ▷ *noun* a lively solo dance from the Scottish Highlands.

high-level ▷ *adj* conducted by or involving people at a high level, eg management of a company, ministers of a government, etc □ *high-level discussions.* ⓘ 19c.

high-level language ▷ *noun, computing* a programming language which allows users to employ instructions that more closely resemble their own language, rather than machine code. See also LOW-LEVEL LANGUAGE. ⓘ 1960s.

high life ▷ *noun* **1** the life of fashionable society. **2** the people of this society. ⓘ 18c.

highlight ▷ *noun* **1** the most memorable or outstanding feature, event, experience, etc. **2** (**highlights**) patches or streaks in one's hair, often achieved artificially, that are lighter than the rest of the hair. ▷ *verb* (***highlighted, highlighting***) **1** to draw attention to or emphasize something. **2** to overlay sections of (a text) with a bright colour for special attention. **3** to put highlights in (someone's hair). ⓘ 19c; 1940s as *noun* 2.

highlighter ▷ *noun* (*in full* **highlighter pen**) a broad-tipped felt pen used to highlight parts of a text, etc. ⓘ 1960s.

highly ▷ *adverb* **1** very; extremely □ *highly gratified.* **2** with approval □ *speak highly of her.* **3** at or to a high degree; in a high position □ *He is rated highly in his office.*

highly-strung ▷ *adj* excitable; extremely nervous; easily upset or sensitive. ⓘ 18c.

High Mass ▷ *noun, RC Church* an especially elaborate form of the mass involving music, ceremonies and incense. ⓘ 12c.

high-minded ▷ *adj* having or showing noble and moral ideas and principles, etc. • **high-mindedly** *adverb.* • **high-mindedness** *noun.* ⓘ 15c.

highness /'haɪnɪs/ ▷ *noun* **1** (**Highness**) an address used for royalty, usually as **Her Highness, His Highness** and **Your Highness**. **2** the state of being high.

high noon ▷ *noun* **1** exactly at noon. **2** the peak or culmination of something. ⓘ 14c.

high-octane ▷ *adj* said of petrol: having a high OCTANE NUMBER.

high-pitched ▷ *adj* **1** said of sounds, voices, etc: high or acute in tone. **2** said of a roof: steeply angled. ⓘ 16c.

high places ▷ *noun* positions of importance and influence.

high point ▷ *noun* the most memorable, pleasurable, successful, etc moment or occasion; a high spot.

high-powered ▷ *adj* **1** very powerful or energetic. **2** very important or responsible. ⓘ Early 20c.

high-pressure ▷ *adj* **1** having, using or allowing the use of air, water, etc at a pressure higher than that of the atmosphere □ *high-pressure water reactor.* **2** *colloq* forceful and persuasive □ *high-pressure negotiations.* **3** involving considerable stress or intense activity □ *a high-pressure job.* ⓘ Early 19c.

high priest and **high priestess** ▷ *noun* the chief priest or priestess of a cult. ⓘ 14c.

high relief ▷ *noun* a sculpture in which the relief figures project well above the surface. Also called **alto-relievo**. Compare BAS-RELIEF.

high-rise ▷ *adj* said of a building: having many storeys □ *high-rise flats.* ▷ *noun* (***high-rises***) *colloq* a building with many storeys; a tower block. ⓘ 1950s.

high-risk ▷ *adj* potentially very dangerous; particularly vulnerable to danger □ *high-risk sports.*

high road ▷ *noun* a public or main road; a road for general traffic. ⓘ 18c.

high school ▷ *noun* a secondary school in the UK, formerly often called GRAMMAR SCHOOL. ⓘ Early 19c.

high seas ▻ *noun* the open ocean not under the control of any country. ⓒ Anglo Saxon *heah sae*.

high season ▻ *noun* the busiest time of year at a holiday resort, tourist town, etc; the peak tourist period.

high society ▻ *noun* fashionable wealthy society; the upper classes.

high-sounding ▻ *adj* pretentious; pompous; imposing. ⓒ 16c.

high-speed ▻ *adj* working, functioning or having the capacity to work or function, at a great speed. ⓒ 19c.

high-spirited ▻ *adj* daring or bold; naturally cheerful and vivacious. ⓒ 17c.

high spirits ▻ *noun* a positive, happy and exhilarated frame of mind.

high spot ▻ *noun* an outstanding feature, moment, location, etc.

high street ▻ *noun* **1** (*also* **High Street**) the main shopping street of a town. **2** (**the high street**) **a** shops generally; the retail trade; **b** the public, when regarded as consumers.

high table ▻ *noun* the dons' table in a college dining hall. ⓒ 14c.

hightail ▻ *verb* (*usually* **hightail it**) *N Amer colloq* to hurry away.

high tea ▻ *noun, Brit* a meal served in the late afternoon, usually consisting of a cooked dish, with bread, cakes and tea. ⓒ 19c.

high tech or **hi-tech** or **hi-tec** /haɪˈtɛk/ ▻ *noun* **1** an advanced and sophisticated technology within a specific field, eg electronics, also involving high investment into research and development. **2** a style of interior decoration, designs, etc based on styles or equipment found in industry. Also *as adj* □ ***a high-tech industry.*** ⓒ 1960s: a shortening of *high technology*.

high-tension ▻ *adj* carrying high-voltage electrical currents. ⓒ Early 20c.

high tide ▻ *noun* the time when the tide is at its highest level, between the flood and ebb tides. Also called **high water**. ⓒ Anglo Saxon *heahtid*.

high time ▻ *adverb, colloq* the right or latest time by which something ought to have been done □ ***It's high time you went home.***

high-toned ▻ *adj* **1** high in pitch. **2** morally or socially elevated. **3** superior; fashionable. ⓒ 18c.

high treason ▻ *noun* treason or betrayal against one's sovereign or country. ⓒ 14c.

high-up ▻ *noun* (***high-ups***) *colloq* someone in a high or advanced position. ⓒ 19c.

high-voltage ▻ *adj* having or concerning a voltage large enough to cause damage or injury. ⓒ 1960s.

high water ▻ *noun* HIGH TIDE. ⓒ 16c.

high-water mark ▻ *noun* **1 a** the highest level reached by a tide, river, etc; **b** a mark indicating this. **2** the highest point reached by anything. ⓒ 16c.

highway /ˈhaɪweɪ/ ▻ *noun, chiefly N Amer* **1** a public road that everyone has the right to use. **2** the main or normal way or route. ⓒ Anglo-Saxon *heiweg*.

Highway Code ▻ *noun, Brit* an official booklet containing rules and guidance on the correct procedure for road-users.

highwayman ▻ *noun, historical* a robber, usually on horseback, who attacks and robs people travelling on public roads. ⓒ 17c.

high wire ▻ *noun* a tightrope stretched high above the ground for performing. ⓒ 19c.

high words ▻ *noun* angry and heated arguing or altercation.

HIH ▻ *abbreviation* His or Her Imperial Highness.

hi-hat see HIGH-HAT

hijab see HEJAB

hijack or **highjack** /ˈhaɪdʒak/ ▻ *verb* (***hijacked, hijacking***) **1** to take control of a vehicle, especially an aircraft, and force it to go to an unscheduled destination, often taking any passengers present as hostages. **2** to stop and rob (a vehicle). **3** to steal (goods) in transit. • **hijacker** *noun*. • **hijacking** *noun*. ⓒ 1920s.

hike /haɪk/ ▻ *noun* a long walk or tour, often for recreation, and usually in the country. ▻ *verb* (***hiked, hiking***) **1** *intr* to go on or for a hike. **2** (*often* **hike something up**) to pull up, raise or lift it with a jerk. **3** to increase (prices) suddenly. • **hiker** *noun*. ⓒ 18c: formerly a dialect word for HITCH.

hilarious /hɪˈlɛərɪəs/ ▻ *adj* extravagantly funny or humorous; merry. • **hilariously** *adverb* □ ***The joke was hilariously funny.*** • **hilariousness** *noun* being hilarious. ⓒ 19c: from Greek *hilaros* cheerful.

hilarity /hɪˈlarɪtɪ/ ▻ *noun* merriment; laughter; elation. ⓒ 16c: from French *hilarité*.

hill ▻ *noun* **1** a raised area of land or mound, smaller than a mountain. **2** an incline on a road. • **hilliness** *noun*. • **hilly** *adj*. • **old as the hills** *colloq* immeasurably old. • **over the hill** *colloq* past one's peak or best; becoming too old for something. • **up hill and down dale** with vigour and persistence. ⓒ Anglo-Saxon *hyll*.

hillbilly /ˈhɪlbɪlɪ/ ▻ *noun* (***hillbillies***) *especially US* **1** *derog* any unsophisticated person, particularly from a remote, mountainous or rustic area. **2 a** country and western music; **b** *as adj* □ ***hillbilly blues.*** ⓒ Early 20c: HILL + dialect *billy* a fellow.

hillock /ˈhɪlək/ ▻ *noun* **1** a small hill. **2** a small heap or pile. • **hillocked** or **hillocky** *adj*. ⓒ 14c: English *hilloc*.

hillside ▻ *noun* the sloping side of a hill. ⓒ 15c.

hill station ▻ *noun* especially in N India: a government station or office situated in the hills. ⓒ 19c.

hilltop ▻ *noun* the summit of a hill.

hillwalking ▻ *noun* the activity of walking in hilly or mountainous country. • **hillwalker** *noun*.

hilt ▻ *noun* the handle, especially of a sword, dagger, knife, etc. • **up to the hilt** completely; thoroughly. ⓒ Anglo-Saxon *hilte*.

hilum /ˈhaɪləm/ ▻ *noun* (***hila*** /-lə/) *bot* a scar on the seed of a plant indicating where it was attached to its stalk. ⓒ 17c: Latin *hilum* a little thing.

HIM ▻ *abbreviation* His or Her Imperial Majesty.

him ▻ *pronoun* a male person or animal, the object form of HE □ ***We saw him*** □ ***We gave it to him.*** ⓒ Anglo-Saxon *him*.

himself /hɪmˈsɛlf/ ▻ *pronoun* **1** the reflexive form of HIM and HE □ ***He made himself a drink.*** **2** used for emphasis □ ***He did it himself.*** **3** his normal self □ ***He's still not feeling himself after the operation.*** **4** (*also* **by himself**) alone; without help. ⓒ Anglo-Saxon *him selfum*.

Hinayana /hɪnəˈjɑːnə/ ▻ *noun* the form of Buddhism, found in former Ceylon and SE Asia, that holds more conservatively to the original teachings of Buddha and the practices of the original Buddhist communities than MAHAYANA. Also *as adj* □ ***Hinayana Buddhism.*** Compare ZEN. • **Hinayanist** *noun*. ⓒ 19c: Sanskrit, meaning 'lesser vehicle'.

hind[1] /haɪnd/ ▻ *adj* **1** at the back; referring to the area behind □ ***hind legs.*** **2** backward. • **hindmost** *adj* the furthest behind. • **hindforemost** *adverb* having the hind area situated in the front place. ⓒ Anglo-Saxon *hindan*.

hind[2] /haɪnd/ ▻ *noun* (***hind*** or ***hinds***) a female red deer, usually older than three years of age. ⓒ Anglo-Saxon *hind*.

hindbrain ▷ *noun, anatomy* the lowest part of the brain containing the CEREBELLUM and the MEDULLA OBLONGATA.

hinder¹ /ˈhɪndə(r)/ ▷ *verb* (***hindered, hindering***) **1** to delay or hold back; to prevent the progress of something. **2** *intr* to be an obstacle; to obstruct. • **hinderer** *noun*. • **hinderingly** *adverb*. Ⓒ Anglo-Saxon *hindrian*.

hinder² /ˈhaɪndə(r)/ ▷ *adj* **1** placed at the back. **2** further back □ *the hinder region*. • **hindermost** hindmost.

Hindi /ˈhɪndɪ/ ▷ *noun* **1** one of the official languages of India, a literary form of HINDUSTANI, and including terms from SANSKRIT. **2** a group of Indo-European languages spoken in N India, including HINDUSTANI. ▷ *adj* relating or referring to any of these languages. Ⓒ 18c: from Persian *Hind* India.

hindquarters ▷ *plural noun* the rear parts of an animal, especially a four-legged one. Ⓒ 19c.

hindrance /ˈhɪndrəns/ ▷ *noun* **1** someone or something that hinders; an obstacle or prevention. **2** the act of hindering. Ⓒ 15c, meaning 'damage or loss': from HINDER¹.

hindsight /ˈhaɪndsaɪt/ ▷ *noun* wisdom or knowledge after an event. • **with the benefit of hindsight** realizing or knowing after the event what could or should have been done. Ⓒ 19c.

Hindu /ˈhɪnduː, hɪnˈduː/ ▷ *noun* **1** someone who practises HINDUISM. **2** a native or citizen of Hindustan or India. ▷ *adj* relating or referring to Hindus or Hinduism. Ⓒ 17c: from Persian *Hind* India.

Hinduism ▷ *noun* the main religion of India, that includes the worship of several gods, a belief in reincarnation, and the arrangement of society into a caste system.

Hindustani /hɪnduˈstɑːnɪ/ ▷ *noun* a form of Hindi with elements from Arabic and Persian, used as a lingua franca in much of India and Pakistan. ▷ *adj* relating to, spoken or written in Hindustani.

hinge /hɪndʒ/ ▷ *noun* **1** the movable hook or joint by which a door is fastened to a door-frame or a lid is fastened to a box, etc and also on which they turn when opened or closed. **2** *biol* the pivoting point from which a BIVALVE opens and closes. **3** *philately* (*in full* **stamp hinge**) a small piece of gummed paper used for attaching stamps to the page of an album. **4** a principle or fact on which anything depends or turns. ▷ *verb* (***hinged, hinging***) **1** to provide a hinge or hinges for something. Ⓒ 14c as *henge*.

▪ **hinge on something 1** to hang or turn on it. **2** to depend on it □ *Everything hinges on their decision.*

hinge joint ▷ *noun, anatomy* in vertebrates: a joint that allows movement in one plane only, eg the elbow or knee joint. Ⓒ 18c.

hinny /ˈhɪnɪ/ ▷ *noun* (***hinnies***) the offspring of a stallion and a female donkey or ass. Ⓒ 17c: from Greek *hinnos* mule.

hint ▷ *noun* **1** a distant or indirect indication or allusion; an insinuation or implication. **2** a helpful suggestion or tip. **3** a small amount; a slight impression or suggestion of something □ *a hint of perfume*. ▷ *verb* (***hinted, hinting***) **1** to indicate something indirectly. **2** *intr* to give a hint or hints. • **take** or **get the hint** *colloq* to understand and act on what a person is hinting at. Ⓒ Anglo-Saxon *hentan* to seize.

▪ **hint at something** to suggest or imply it, especially indirectly.

hinterland /ˈhɪntəland/ ▷ *noun* **1** the region lying inland from the coast or the banks of a river. **2** an area dependent on a nearby port, commercial site, or any centre of influence. Ⓒ 19c: German, from *hinter* behind + *Land* land.

hip¹ ▷ *noun* **1** the haunch or upper fleshy part of the thigh just below the waist. **2** the joint between the thigh bone and the pelvis. **3** *archit* the external angle created when the sloping end of a roof meets the sloping sides. • **hipped** *adj* **1** possessing a hip or hips. **2** said of a specific type of roof: sloping at the end in addition to the sides. • **hippy** *adj* having large hips. • **have** or **catch someone on the hip** to get an advantage over them. Ⓒ 16c: a metaphor taken from wrestling. • **shoot** or **fire from the hip** to speak bluntly and directly; to deal with someone assertively. Ⓒ Anglo-Saxon *hype*.

hip² ▷ *noun* the large red fruit of the dog-rose, or any other rose. Ⓒ Anglo-Saxon *heope*.

hip³ ▷ *exclamation* used to encourage a united cheer □ *Hip, hip, hooray!* Ⓒ 18c.

hip⁴ ▷ *adj* (***hipper, hippest***) *colloq* informed about, knowledgeable of, or following, current fashions in music, fashion, political ideas, etc. Ⓒ Early 20c.

hip bath ▷ *noun* a bath for sitting in.

hip bone ▷ *noun* the INNOMINATE BONE. Ⓒ 14c.

hip flask ▷ *noun* a small flask, especially for alcoholic drink, carried in the hip pocket.

hip-hop ▷ *noun* **1** a popular culture movement originating in the US in the early 1980s, incorporating rap music, breakdancing and graffiti art, and the wearing of baggy clothing and loosely tied or untied training shoes or boots. **2** the music associated with this movement, especially RAP MUSIC. *As adj* □ *hip-hop music*. Ⓒ 1980s: from HIP⁴.

hip joint ▷ *noun* the articulation of the head of the thigh bone with the INNOMINATE BONE. Ⓒ 18c.

hipped see under HIP¹

hipper and **hippest** see under HIP⁴

hippie or **hippy** /ˈhɪpɪ/ ▷ *noun* (***hippies***) *colloq* especially in the 1960s: someone, typically young, with long hair and wearing brightly-coloured clothes, stressing the importance of self-expression and love, and rebelling against the more conservative standards and values of society.

hippo /ˈhɪpoʊ/ ▷ *noun* (***hippos***) *colloq* short for HIPPOPOTAMUS.

hippo- /ˈhɪpoʊ, hɪpə/ or (before a vowel) **hipp-** *combining form, signifying* a horse. Ⓒ 19c: from Greek *hippos*.

hippocampus /hɪpoʊˈkampəs/ ▷ *noun* (***hippocampi*** /-paɪ/) **1** *mythol* a fish-tailed sea monster with a horse-like head and neck. **2** a genus of small fishes with a horse-like head and neck. Also called SEA HORSE. **3** *anatomy* a structure in the vertebrate brain consisting of two curved ridges across the ventricles, associated with emotional responses. Ⓒ 16c: from Greek *hippos* horse + *kampos* sea-monster.

hip pocket ▷ *noun* a small trouser pocket behind the hip.

Hippocratic oath /hɪpəˈkratɪk —/ ▷ *noun* the oath taken by doctors obligating them to observe the code of medical ethics contained within it. Ⓒ 18c: named after Hippocrates (c.460–c.377 BC), the Greek physician who devised it.

hippodrome /ˈhɪpədroʊm/ ▷ *noun* **1** a variety theatre or circus. **2** ancient Greece and Rome: a racecourse for horses and chariots. Ⓒ 16c: from Greek *hippos* horse + *dromos* course.

hippopotamus /hɪpəˈpɒtəməs/ ▷ *noun* (***hippopotamuses*** or ***hippopotami*** /-maɪ/) a hoofed mammal with a thick skin, large head and muzzle, and short stout legs, found in rivers and lakes in parts of Africa. Ⓒ 16c: from Greek *hippos* horse + *potamos* river.

hippy¹ see HIPPIE

hippy² see under HIP¹

hipsters /ˈhɪpstəz/ ▷ *plural noun* trousers which hang from the hips rather than the waist. Ⓒ 1960s.

hire /ˈhaɪə(r)/ ▷ *verb* (***hired, hiring***) **1** to procure the temporary use of something belonging to someone else in exchange for payment. **2** to employ or engage someone for wages. ▷ *noun* **1** payment for the use or hire of something. **2** wages paid for services. **3** the act of hiring. **4** the arrangement where one is hired. ● **for hire** ready for hiring. ● **on hire** hired out. ● **hirable** or **hireable** *adj.* ◷ Anglo-Saxon *hyr.*

▪ **hire something out** to grant the temporary use of it for payment.

hireling /ˈhaɪəlɪŋ/ ▷ *noun, derog* **1** a hired servant. **2** someone whose work is motivated solely by money. ◷ Anglo-Saxon *hyrling.*

hire-purchase ▷ *noun, Brit* (abbreviation **HP** or **hp**) a system where a hired article becomes owned by the hirer after a specified number of payments.

hirsute /ˈhɜːsjuːt, hɜːˈsjuːt/ ▷ *adj* **1** hairy; shaggy. **2** said of plants: having long stiffish hairs. ● **hirsuteness** *noun.* ◷ 17c: from Latin *hirsutus* shaggy.

his /hɪz/ ▷ *adj* referring or belonging to a male person or animal. ▷ *pronoun* the one or ones belonging to HIM. ● **of his** relating or belonging to HIM. ◷ Anglo-Saxon.

His Highness see under HIGHNESS sense 1

His Holiness see under HOLINESS sense 2

His Honour see under HONOUR

Hispanic /hɪˈspanɪk/ ▷ *adj* relating to or deriving from Spain, the Spanish or other Spanish-speaking countries or peoples. ▷ *noun, N Amer, especially US* a Spanish-speaking American of Latin-American descent. ◷ 16c: from Latin *Hispania* Spain.

hispanicism /hɪˈspanɪsɪzəm/ ▷ *noun* a Spanish phrase or saying.

hispid /ˈhɪspɪd/ ▷ *adj, bot, zool* covered with strong hairs and bristles. ● **hispidity** *noun.* ◷ 17c: from Latin *hispidus.*

hiss /hɪs/ ▷ *noun* a sharp sibilant sound like a sustained *s*. ▷ *verb* (***hisses, hissed, hissing***) **1** *intr* said of an animal, such as a snake or goose, or a person: to make such a sound, especially as a sign of disapproval or anger. **2** *tr* to show one's disapproval of someone or something by hissing. ◷ 14c: imitating the sound.

hist ▷ *exclamation* a demand for silence and attention.

hist. *abbreviation* **1** histology. **2** historian. **3** history.

histamine /ˈhɪstəmiːn, -mɪn/ ▷ *noun, biochem* a chemical compound released by body tissues during allergic reactions, causing discomfort. ◷ Early 20c.

histidine /ˈhɪstɪdiːn/ ▷ *noun, biochem* an amino acid obtained from proteins. ◷ 19c.

histo- /hɪsˈtɒ, hɪstoʊ, hɪstə/ or (before a vowel) **hist-** *combining form, signifying* animal or plant tissue. ◷ From Greek *histos* web.

histogenesis and **histogeny** /hɪˈstɒdʒɪnɪ/ ▷ *noun, biol* the development and differentiation of tissues. ● **histogenetic** or **histogenic** *adj.* ● **histogenetically** or **histogenically** *adverb.* ◷ 19c.

histogram /ˈhɪstəgram/ ▷ *noun* a statistical graph in which vertical rectangles of differing heights are used to represent a frequency distribution. ◷ 19c.

histology /hɪˈstɒlədʒɪ/ ▷ *noun* the study of the microscopic structure of cells and tissues of living organisms. ● **histologic** /hɪstəˈlɒdʒɪk/ or **histological** *adj.* ● **histologically** *adverb.* ● **histologist** /hɪˈstɒlədʒɪst/ *noun* a scientist who specializes in HISTOLOGY. ◷ 19c.

histolysis /hɪˈstɒlɪsɪs/ ▷ *noun* the breakdown of organic tissues. ● **histolytic** /hɪstəˈlɪtɪk/ *adj.* ● **histolytically** *adverb.* ◷ 19c.

historian /hɪˈstɔːrɪən/ ▷ *noun* a person who studies or writes about history, often an expert or specialist. ◷ 15c.

historic /hɪˈstɒrɪk/ ▷ *adj* famous, important or significant in history. ◷ 17c: from Greek *historikos.*

historic, historical

● These words do not mean quite the same.
Historic refers to fame or importance in history □ *Today will be remembered as a historic day in boxing* □ *the conversion of historic barns into houses.*
Historical is a less judgemental word that refers to something as a fact or to its connection with history □ *The historical fact is that the settlement of 1688–1701 failed to settle everything* □ *Some people think of Sherlock Holmes as being an historical figure.*
● Note that you can use either **a** or **an** before both words; **a** is now more usual.

historical /hɪˈstɒrɪkəl/ ▷ *adj* **1** relevant to or about history. **2** relevant to or about people or events in history. **3** said of the study of a subject: based on its development over a period of time. **4** referring to something that actually existed or took place; authentic. ● **historically** *adverb.* ◷ 14c: from Latin *historicus.*

historical novel ▷ *noun* a novel with a period in history as its setting, which includes historical events and characters. ◷ 19c.

historicism /hɪˈstɒrɪsɪzəm/ ▷ *noun* **1** the idea that historical events are determined by natural laws. **2** the theory that sociological circumstances are historically determined. **3** a strong or excessive involvement with and respect for the institutions of the past. ● **historicist** *noun, adj.* ◷ 19c: HISTORIC + -ISM.

historicity /hɪstəˈrɪsɪtɪ/ ▷ *noun* historical truth or actuality.

historiographer /hɪstɒrɪˈɒgrəfə(r)/ ▷ *noun* a writer of history, especially an official historian. ◷ 15c: from Greek *historiographos.*

historiography /hɪstɒrɪˈɒgrəfɪ/ ▷ *noun* the art or employment of writing history. ● **historiographic** or **historiographical** *adj.* ● **historiographically** *adverb.* ◷ 16c: from Greek *historiographia.*

history /ˈhɪstərɪ/ ▷ *noun* (***histories***) **1** an account of past events and developments. **2** a methodical account of the origin and progress of a nation, institution, the world, etc. **3** the knowledge of past events associated with a particular nation, the world, a person, etc. **4** the academic discipline of understanding and interpreting past events. **5** a past full of events of more than common interest □ *a building with a fascinating history.* **6** a play or drama representing historical events. ● **be history** *colloq* to be finished, over, dead, etc □ *He's history.* ● **make history** to do something significant or memorable, especially to be the first person to do so, often with an influence on the future. ◷ 15c: from Greek *historia*, from *histor* knowing.

histrionic /hɪstrɪˈɒnɪk/ ▷ *adj* **1** said of behaviour, etc: theatrical; melodramatic; expressing too much emotion. **2** *formerly* referring or relating to actors or acting. ● **histrionically** *adverb.* ▷ *noun* (**histrionics**) theatrical or dramatic behaviour expressing excessive emotion and insincerity. ◷ 17c: from Latin *histrionicus*, from *histrio* actor.

His Worship see WORSHIP *noun* 3

hit ▷ *verb* (*past tense, past participle* ***hit****, present participle* ***hitting***) **1** to strike someone or something. **2** to come into forceful contact with something. **3** to reach a target with a blow, missile, etc. **4** to knock something (eg oneself or part of oneself) against something, especially hard or violently □ *hit one's head on the door.* **5** to affect suddenly and severely □ *The sad news hit her hard.* **6** *intr* to strike or direct a blow. **7** *colloq* to find or attain something, especially an answer, by chance □ *You've hit it!* **8** to reach or arrive at something □ *hit an all-time low.* **9** *sport* to drive (the ball) with a stroke of the bat. **10** *colloq* to reach a place or location □ *We'll hit the city tomorrow.* ▻ *noun* **1** a stroke or blow. **2** *sport* a successful stroke or shot. **3** *colloq* something of extreme popularity or success □ *The new cinema is a real hit.* **4** an effective remark, eg a sarcasm or witticism. **5** *slang* a murder, especially one by organized gangs. **6** *drug-taking slang* a shot of a hard drug. • **hard hit** see under HARD. • **hit it off with someone** to get on well with them. • **hit it up** *drug-taking slang* to inject a drug. • **hit the bottle** see under BOTTLE. • **hit the ceiling** or **roof** to be extremely angry. • **hit the hay** or **sack** *slang* to go to bed. • **hit the nail on the head** see under NAIL. • **hit the road** to leave or depart. • **make** or **score a hit with someone** to be successful or popular with them. ⓘ Anglo-Saxon *hittan*.

■ **hit at someone** to direct a blow, sarcasm, jibe, attack, etc at them.

■ **hit back** to retaliate.

■ **hit someone** or **something off** to imitate, mimic, or aptly describe them or it.

■ **hit on** or **upon someone 1** (*also* **hit upon something**) to come upon or discover them or it; to single them or it out. **2** to make sexual advances towards them.

■ **hit out at** or **against someone** or **something** to attack them or it physically or verbally.

hit-and-miss or **hit-or-miss** ▻ *adj, colloq* without any order or planning; random. ⓘ 19c.

hit-and-run ▻ *adj* **1** said of the driver in a vehicle accident (and of the accident itself): causing injury, and then fleeing the scene without stopping, reporting the accident or helping the victim. **2** said of an air raid, assault, etc: having a very short duration. ⓘ 1920s in sense 1; 19c as a baseball term.

hitch /hɪtʃ/ ▻ *verb* (***hitches, hitched, hitching***) **1** to move something jerkily. **2** to move or lift something with a jerk into a specified position. **3** (*also* **hitch something up**) to pull it up with a jerk □ *He hitched up his trousers.* **4** *intr* to move jerkily. **5** *intr* to falter, hobble or limp. **6** to hook, fasten or tether. **7** to catch on an obstacle. **8** (*also* **hitch something up**) to attach something to a vehicle □ *The caravan was hitched to the car.* **9 a** *intr* to hitchhike; **b** to obtain (a lift) as a hitchhiker. • **to get hitched** or **get hitched up** *slang* to get married. ▻ *noun* (***hitches***) **1** a small temporary setback or difficulty. **2** a jerk; a sudden movement. **3** a knot for attaching two pieces of rope together. • **hitcher** *noun*. ⓘ 15c.

hitchhike /ˈhɪtʃhaɪk/ ▻ *verb* (***hitchhiked, hitchhiking***) *intr* to travel, especially long distances, by obtaining free lifts from passing vehicles. • **hitchhiker** *noun*. ⓘ 1920s.

hitching post ▻ *noun* a post to which a horse's reins can be tied. ⓘ 1830s.

hi-tec and **hi-tech** see HIGH TECH

hither /ˈhɪðə(r)/ ▻ *adverb, old use* to this place. ▻ *adj, archaic* nearer of usually two things. • **hither and thither** in different directions; this way and that. ⓘ Anglo-Saxon *hider*.

hithermost /ˈhɪðəmoʊst/ ▻ *adj* the nearest in this direction. ⓘ 16c.

hitherto /ˈhɪðətuː/ ▻ *adverb* up to this or that time. ⓘ 13c.

Hitler /ˈhɪtlə(r)/ ▻ *noun* a person similar in character to Adolf Hitler (1889–1945), the German Nazi dictator; an overbearing and domineering person.

hit list ▻ *noun, colloq* a list of people, organizations, etc to be killed or eliminated by gangsters or terrorists; a list of targeted victims. ⓘ 1970s.

hit man ▻ *noun, colloq* someone hired to assassinate or attack others. ⓘ 1960s.

hit parade ▻ *noun* **1** *formerly* a list of the best-selling records. **2** a list of the most popular things of any type. ⓘ 1930s.

HIV ▻ *abbreviation* human immunodeficiency virus, a virus which breaks down the human body's natural immune system, often leading to AIDS. ▻ *adj, colloq* HIV-positive.

hive /haɪv/ ▻ *noun* **1** a box or basket for housing bees. **2** the colony of bees living in such a place. **3** a scene of extreme animation, eg where people are working busily □ *a hive of activity.* ▻ *verb* (***hived, hiving***) **1** to gather or collect into a hive. **2** (*usually* **hive away** or **up**) to lay up or store. **3** *intr* said of bees: to enter or occupy a hive. **4** *intr* to take shelter or reside together. ⓘ Anglo-Saxon *hyf*.

■ **hive off** to gather together as if in a swarm.

■ **hive something off 1** to separate (a company, etc) from a larger organization. **2** to divert (assets or sectors of an industrial organization) to other organizations, especially private ones. **3** to assign (work) to a subsidiary company.

hives /haɪvz/ ▻ *plural noun, non-technical* URTICARIA. ⓘ 16c.

HIV-positive ▻ *adj, medicine* denoting a person who has tested positively for the presence of HIV, and who may therefore be assumed to be carrying the virus.

hiya /ˈhaɪjə/ ▻ *exclamation, slang* a familiar greeting. ⓘ 1940s: a contraction of *how are you?*.

hl ▻ *abbreviation* hectolitres.

HM ▻ *abbreviation* used in the titles of some British government organizations: Her or His Majesty or Majesty's.

hm ▻ *abbreviation* hectometre.

HMG ▻ *abbreviation* Her or His Majesty's Government.

HMI ▻ *abbreviation* Her or His Majesty's Inspector or Inspectorate.

HMS ▻ *abbreviation* Her or His Majesty's Service or Ship.

HMSO ▻ *abbreviation* Her or His Majesty's Stationery Office.

HNC ▻ *abbreviation* Higher National Certificate, a qualification in a technical subject recognized by many professional establishments.

HND ▻ *abbreviation* Higher National Diploma, a qualification in a technical subject recognized by many professional establishments as equivalent to the first two years of a degree.

Ho ▻ *abbreviation, chem* holmium.

ho or **hoh** /hoʊ/ ▻ *exclamation* **1** a call or shout to attract attention or indicate direction or destination. **2** (*especially* **ho-ho**) representation of laughter. ⓘ 13c.

hoactzin see HOATZIN

hoar /hɔː(r)/ ▻ *adj, especially poetic* white or greyish-white, especially with age or frost. ⓘ Anglo-Saxon *har*.

hoard /hɔːd/ ▻ *noun* a store of money, food or treasure, usually one hidden away for use in the future. ▻ *verb* (***hoarded, hoarding***) *tr & intr* to store or gather (food, money or treasure), often secretly, and especially for use in the future. • **hoarder** *noun* someone who hoards. ⓘ Anglo-Saxon *hord*.

hoard

There is sometimes a spelling confusion between **hoard** and **horde**.

hoarding /ˈhɔːdɪŋ/ ▻ *noun* **1** a screen of light boards, especially round a building site. **2** a similar wooden surface for displaying advertisements, posters, etc. *N Amer equivalent* BILLBOARD. ⓘ 19c: from French *hourd* palisade.

hoarfrost ▻ *noun* the white frost on grass, leaves, etc in the morning formed by freezing dew after a cold night. Also called **white frost**. ⓘ 13c.

hoarse /hɔːs/ ▷ *adj* **1** said of the voice: rough and husky, especially because of a sore throat or excessive shouting. **2** said of a person: having a hoarse voice. • **hoarsely** *adverb*. • **hoarsen** *verb* (***hoarsened, hoarsening***) *tr & intr* to make or become hoarse • **hoarseness** *noun*. ⓘ Anglo-Saxon *has*.

hoary /ˈhɔːrɪ/ ▷ *adj* (***hoarier, hoariest***) **1** white or grey with age. **2** ancient. **3** *bot, entomol* covered with short, thick, whitish hairs. • **hoariness** *noun*. ⓘ 16c.

hoatzin or **hoactzin** /hoʊˈatsɪn/ ▷ *noun* a S American bird with a large crop and, while young, a temporary claw used for climbing trees and swimming. Also called **stink bird**. ⓘ 17c: from Nahuatl *huactzin* or *huahtzin* pheasant.

hoax /hoʊks/ ▷ *noun* (***hoaxes***) a deceptive trick played either humorously or maliciously. Also *as adj* □ *hoax call*. ▷ *verb* (***hoaxes, hoaxed, hoaxing***) to trick or deceive with a hoax. • **hoaxer**. ⓘ 18c: perhaps from *hocus* to trick; see HOCUS-POCUS.

hob¹ ▷ *noun* **1** the flat surface on which pots are heated, either on top of a cooker or as a separate piece of equipment. **2** a small shelf next to a fireplace on which anything may be placed to keep hot. ⓘ 16c: a variant of HUB.

hob² ▷ *noun* **1** a goblin, elf or fairy. **2** a male ferret. ⓘ 14c: a variant of *Rob*, short for *Robert*.

hobbies plural of HOBBY

hobbit /ˈhɒbɪt/ ▷ *noun* one of an imaginary race of people, half the size of humans and hairy-footed, living below the ground. ⓘ Created by J R R Tolkien (died 1973) in his novel *The Hobbit* (1937).

hobble /ˈhɒbəl/ ▷ *verb* (***hobbled, hobbling***) **1** *intr* to walk awkwardly and unsteadily by taking short unsteady steps. **2** to loosely tie the legs of (a horse) together, to inhibit its movement. **3** to hamper or impede. ▷ *noun* **1** an awkward and irregular gait. **2** any object used to hamper an animal's feet. ⓘ 14c.

hobbledehoy /ˈhɒbəldɪhɔɪ/ ▷ *noun* an awkward youth, between the age of a boy and man. • **hobbledehoyhood** *noun*. • **hobbledehoyish** *adj*. ⓘ 16c.

hobble skirt ▷ *noun* a narrow skirt that restricts walking.

hobby¹ /ˈhɒbɪ/ ▷ *noun* (***hobbies***) an activity or occupation carried out in one's spare time for amusement or relaxation. ⓘ 14c as *hobyn*, meaning 'a small horse', and also a variant of *Robin*, often used as a pet name for a horse, therefore also applied to a HOBBY-HORSE.

hobby² ▷ *noun* (***hobbies***) a small species of falcon. ⓘ 15c: from French *hobe* falcon.

hobby-horse ▷ *noun* **1** a child's toy consisting of a long stick with a horse's head at one end that they prance about with as if riding a horse. **2** a figure of a horse used in Morris dancing. **3** a subject which a person talks about frequently.

hobgoblin /hɒbˈgɒblɪn/ ▷ *noun* a mischievous or evil spirit; a frightful apparition. ⓘ 16c: HOB² + GOBLIN.

hobnail ▷ *noun* a short nail with a large strong head for protecting the soles of boots, shoes and horseshoes. Also *as adj* □ *hobnail boots*. • **hobnailed** *adj*. ⓘ 16c: from an old meaning of HOB¹, meaning 'peg or pin'.

hobnob /ˈhɒbnɒb/ ▷ *verb* (***hobnobbed, hobnobbing***) *intr* (*usually* **hobnob with someone**) to associate or spend time with them socially; to talk informally with them. ⓘ 18c: from the phrase *hab or nab* have or have not.

hobo /ˈhoʊboʊ/ ▷ *noun* (***hobos*** or ***hoboes***) *N Amer* **1** a tramp. **2** an itinerant worker, especially an unskilled one. ⓘ 19c.

Hobson's choice /ˈhɒbsənz —/ ▷ *noun* the choice of taking the thing offered, or nothing at all. ⓘ 17c: named after Thomas Hobson (1544–1631), a Cambridge carrier who hired out the horse nearest the door or none at all.

hock¹ ▷ *noun* **1** the joint on the hindleg of horses and other hoofed mammals, corresponding to the ankle-joint on a human leg. Also called HAMSTRING. **2** a piece of meat extending upwards from the hock-joint. ▷ *verb* (***hocked, hocking***) to hamstring. ⓘ 16c: a contraction of *hockshin*, from Anglo-Saxon *hohsinu* heel sinew.

hock² ▷ *noun* a white wine, originally only one made in Hochheim, on the River Main, in Germany, but now applied to all white wines from the Rhine valley. ⓘ 17c: from German *Hochheimer* of Hochheim.

hock³ ▷ *verb* (***hocked, hocking***) *colloq* to pawn. ▷ *noun* (*always* **in hock**) *colloq* **1** in debt. **2** in prison. **3** in pawn; having been pawned. ⓘ 19c: from Dutch *hok* prison, hovel or debt.

hockey /ˈhɒkɪ/ ▷ *noun* **1** a ball game played by two teams of eleven players with long clubs curved at one end, each team attempting to score goals. **2** *N Amer* short for ICE HOCKEY. **3** (also **hockey line**) see OCHE. ⓘ 16c: from French *hoquet* a crook or staff.

hocus-pocus /hoʊkəsˈpoʊkəs/ ▷ *noun, colloq* **1** the skill of trickery or deception. **2** a conjurer's chant while performing a magic trick. ⓘ 17c: sham Latin, once believed to be a corruption of *hoc est corpus* this is my body, Christ's words spoken in the communion service at the consecration of the bread.

hod ▷ *noun* **1** an open V-shaped box on a pole, used for carrying bricks on one's shoulder. **2** a coal-scuttle, usually kept near a fireplace. ⓘ 16c, from *hott* basket: from French *hotte* pannier.

hodgepodge see HOTCHPOTCH

Hodgkin's disease /ˈhɒdʒkɪnz —/ and **Hodgkin's lymphoma** ▷ *noun, pathol* a malignant disease in which the lymph nodes, spleen and liver become enlarged, the main symptoms being anaemia, fever and fatigue. ⓘ 19c: named after Thomas Hodgkin, (1798–1866), the British physician who first described the disease.

hodograph /ˈhɒdəgrɑːf/ ▷ *noun, math* a curve whose radius vector represents the velocity of a moving point. ⓘ 19c: from Greek *hodos* way + GRAPH.

hodometer see ODOMETER

hoe /hoʊ/ ▷ *noun* (***hoes***) a long-handled tool with a narrow blade at one end, used for loosening soil, digging out and controlling weeds, etc. ▷ *verb* (***hoed, hoeing***) **1** to dig, loosen, clean or weed (the ground, etc) using a hoe. **2** *intr* to use a hoe. ⓘ 14c: from French *houe*.

hoedown /ˈhoʊdaʊn/ ▷ *noun, especially US* **1** a country dance, especially a square dance. **2** a gathering for performing such dances. ⓘ 19c: HOE + DOWN¹.

hog ▷ *noun* **1** *N Amer, especially US* a general name for PIG. **2** a castrated boar. **3** a pig reared specifically for slaughter. **4** *colloq* a greedy, inconsiderate and often coarse person. **5** (*also* **hogg**) a young sheep or yearling, yet to be shorn. ▷ *verb* (***hogged, hogging***) **1** *colloq* to take, use or occupy something selfishly. **2** to cut short like a hog's mane. **3** *tr & intr* to eat in a hoggish manner. **4** *tr & intr* especially said of the hull of a ship: to arch or hump like a hog's back. • **hoggish** *adj*. • **hoggishly** *adverb*. • **hoggishness** *noun*. • **go the whole hog** to carry out or do something completely. • **hog it** *slang* **1** to eat greedily. **2** to live in an unkempt and slovenly manner. ⓘ Anglo-Saxon *hogg*.

hogback and **hog's-back** ▷ *noun* an object, eg a hill-ridge, shaped like a hog's back, by having sides with a sharp crest but gentle end slopes. ⓘ 17c.

hogfish ▷ *noun* a fish with bristles on its head, living in the N Atlantic. ⓘ 16c.

hogget /ˈhɒgɪt/ ▷ *noun* a yearling sheep or colt. ⓘ 14c.

Hogmanay /hɒgməˈneɪ, ˈhɒgməneɪ/ ▷ *noun* (***Hogmanays***) *Scottish* New Year's Eve, the last day of the year, when children traditionally demanded gifts. ⓘ 17c: from French *aguillaneuf* a gift at New Year.

hognose /ˈhɒgnoʊz/ ▻ *noun* a N American non-poisonous snake with a flattened nose. ⓘ 18c.

hogshead /ˈhɒgzhɛd/ ▻ *noun* **1** a large cask for liquids. **2** a measure of capacity (usually about 63 gallons or 238 litres), usually used for alcohol. ⓘ 14c.

hogtie ▻ *verb* **1** to tie someone up so that they are unable to move their arms and legs. **2** to frustrate, obstruct or impede. ⓘ Late 19c.

hogwash ▻ *noun, colloq* **1** the refuse from a kitchen, brewery, etc given to pigs; pigswill. **2** any worthless nonsense. ⓘ Early 20c in sense 2; 15c in sense 1.

hogweed ▻ *noun* a robust perennial plant with ribbed hairy stems, large coarse leaves, and white or pinkish flowers; the cow-parsnip. ⓘ 18c.

hoh see HO

hoi see HOY²

hoick or **hoik** /hɔɪk/ ▻ *verb* (***hoicked, hoicking***) *colloq* to lift up sharply; to heave up. ⓘ 19c.

hoi polloi /hɔɪ pəˈlɔɪ/ ▻ *plural noun* (*usually* **the hoi polloi**) the masses; the common people. ⓘ Early 19c: Greek, meaning 'the many'.

hoist /hɔɪst/ ▻ *verb* (***hoisted, hoisting***) **1** to lift or heave something up (especially something heavy). **2** to raise or heave up using lifting equipment. ▻ *noun* **1** *colloq* the act of hoisting. **2** equipment for hoisting heavy articles. **3** the height of a sail. • **hoister** *noun* someone or something that lifts. • **hoist with one's own petard** caught in one's own trap or ruse. ⓘ 16c: past tense of obsolete verb *hoise*.

hoity-toity /hɔɪtɪˈtɔɪtɪ/ ▻ *adj, colloq* arrogant; superciliously haughty. ▻ *exclamation* expressing surprise, disapproval or contempt. ⓘ 17c: rhyming compound from obsolete *hoit* to romp.

hokey cokey /ˈhoʊkɪˈkoʊkɪ/ ▻ *noun* a Cockney song with lyrics dictating the pattern of accompanying dance movements, performed by a large group of people in a circle, especially at parties.

hokum /ˈhoʊkəm/ ▻ *noun, N Amer slang* **1** an action done for the sake of pleasing an audience. **2** nonsense or claptrap. **3** pretentious or over-sentimental material in a play, film, etc. ⓘ 20c: probably from HOCUS-POCUS, modelled on BUNKUM.

hold¹ /hoʊld/ ▻ *verb* (***held*** /hɛld/, ***holding***) **1** to have or keep something in one's hand or hands; to grasp. **2** to have something in one's possession. **3** to think or believe. **4** to retain or reserve ▫ *They can hold reserved seats for a week.* **5** *tr & intr* to keep or stay in a specified state or position ▫ *hold firm.* **6** *intr* to remain perfectly in position, especially when under pressure ▫ *The bridge can't hold any longer.* **7** to detain or restrain ▫ *They held him at the airport for two hours.* **8** to contain or be able to contain ▫ *This bottle holds three pints.* **9** to conduct or carry on ▫ *hold a conversation* ▫ *hold a meeting.* **10** to have (a position of responsibility, a job, etc) ▫ *held office for two years* ▫ *held a good job.* **11** to have or possess ▫ *holds the world record.* **12** to keep or sustain (a person's attention). **13** to affirm or allege ▫ *He holds that he is right.* **14** to maintain one's composure and awareness, and not suffer any bad effects, even after large amounts of (alcohol) ▫ *She can hold her drink.* **15** *intr* said of good weather: to continue. **16** to consider to be; to think or believe. **17** *intr* to continue to be valid or apply ▫ *That attitude doesn't hold any more* ▫ *The law still holds.* **18** to defend from the enemy. **19** to cease or stop ▫ *hold fire.* **20** *music* to continue (a note or pause). **21** *intr* said of a telephone caller: to wait without hanging up while the person being called comes on the line. **22** said of the future, regarded as a force: to have in store or readiness ▫ *Who knows what the future holds?* ▻ *noun* **1** the act of holding; a grasp. **2** a power or influence ▫ *They have a hold over him.* **3** a way of holding someone, especially in certain sports, eg judo. **4** a place of confinement; a prison cell. **5** an object to hold on to. • **get hold of someone** *colloq* to manage to find and speak to them. • **get hold of something** to find, obtain or buy it. • **hold good** or **hold true** to remain true or valid; to apply. • **hold one's own** said of someone who is ill: to maintain a stable condition. • **hold one's peace** or **tongue** to remain silent. • **keep hold of someone** or **something** to continue to hold on to them or it. • **no holds barred** not observing any fair rules; having no restrictions. • **on hold** in a state of suspension; temporarily postponed ▫ *She put the trip on hold.* ⓘ Anglo-Saxon *healdan*.

▪ **hold back** to hesitate; to restrain oneself.

▪ **hold someone back** to restrain them from doing something.

▪ **hold something back 1** to keep it in reserve. **2** to hesitate.

▪ **hold someone down** to control their freedom; to restrain them.

▪ **hold something down** to manage to keep it ▫ *hold down a job.*

▪ **hold forth** to put forward one's opinions about something, usually loudly and at great length.

▪ **hold something in** to restrain or check it.

▪ **hold off** or **hold off doing something** to delay or not begin to do it; to refrain from doing it ▫ *I hope the rain holds off* ▫ *hold off making a start.*

▪ **hold someone off** to keep an attacker at a distance.

▪ **hold on** *colloq* to wait, especially during a telephone conversation.

▪ **hold on!** an exclamation requesting the other person to wait.

▪ **hold on to something 1** to keep or maintain it in one's possession. **2** to keep a strong hold or grip on it.

▪ **hold out 1** to stand firm, especially resisting difficulties ▫ *held out against the enemy.* **2** to endure or last.

▪ **hold something out** to offer it, especially as a promise or inducement ▫ *held out the prospect of a pay rise.*

▪ **hold out for something** to wait persistently for something one wants or has demanded.

▪ **hold out on someone** *colloq* to keep back money, information, etc from them.

▪ **hold something over** to postpone or delay it.

▪ **hold someone** or **something up as something** to exhibit them or it as an example of some quality, attribute, etc ▫ *held them up as models of integrity.*

▪ **hold someone up 1** to delay or hinder them. **2** to stop and rob them.

▪ **hold something up 1** to support it. **2** to delay or hinder it. See also HOLD-UP.

▪ **hold with something** *with negatives and in questions* to endorse or approve of it.

hold² /hoʊld/ ▻ *noun* the interior cavity for storing cargo in ships and aeroplanes. ⓘ 16c: variant of HOLE.

holdall /ˈhoʊldɔːl/ ▻ *noun* a large strong bag for carrying miscellaneous articles, especially clothes when travelling. ⓘ 19c.

holder /ˈhoʊldə(r)/ ▻ *noun* **1** someone or something that holds or grips. **2** *law* someone who has ownership or control of something, eg shareholder. ⓘ 14c.

holdfast ▻ *noun* **1** something that holds fast or firmly. **2** a device for fixing or holding something together, eg a long nail or a hook. **3** the attaching organ of a plant other than a root, eg as found in many sea plants. Ⓒ 16c.

holding /'hoʊldɪŋ/ ▷ *noun* **1** land held by lease. **2** an amount of land, shares, etc owned by a person or company. Ⓒ 12c.

holding company ▷ *noun* an industrial company which owns and controls all or part of at least one other company, usually without being directly involved in production. Ⓒ Early 20c.

holding operation ▷ *noun* a procedure or course of action designed to preserve the status quo.

holding pattern ▷ *noun* a specific course which aircraft are instructed to follow while waiting to land. Ⓒ 1950s.

holdover ▷ *noun, N Amer* something or someone held over from a previous era; a relic. Ⓒ 19c.

hold-up ▷ *noun* **1** a delay or setback. **2** an attack with a view to robbery. Ⓒ Early 19c.

hole /hoʊl/ ▷ *noun* **1** a hollow area or cavity in something solid. **2** an aperture or gap in or through something ◻ *a hole in the wall.* **3** an animal's refuge or excavation. **4** *colloq* an unpleasant or contemptible place. **5** *colloq* an awkward or difficult situation. **6** *colloq* a fault or error ◻ *a hole in the argument.* **7** *golf* **a** a cylindrical hollow in the middle of each green, into which the ball is hit; **b** each section of a golf course extending from the tee to the green. **8** *electronics* an energy deficit caused by the removal of an electron, which leaves a positive charge. ▷ *verb* (***holed, holing***) **1** to make a hole in something. **2** to hit or play (a ball, etc) into a hole. • **holey** see separate entry. • **make a hole in something** *colloq* to use up a large amount of it, eg money. • **in holes** full of holes. • **pick holes in something** to find fault with it. • **toad in the hole** a dish comprising sausages cooked in batter. Ⓒ Anglo-Saxon *hol.*

■ **hole up** *colloq* to go to earth; to hide.

■ **hole out** *golf* to play the ball into the hole.

hole-and-corner ▷ *adj* secret; underhand.

hole card ▷ *noun* in stud poker: the card dealt face down in the first round.

hole in one ▷ *noun, golf* a shot of the ball played directly into the hole from the tee, therefore completing the hole with a single stroke.

hole in the heart ▷ *noun* a congenital condition of the heart, resulting in imperfect separation of the left and right sides.

hole in the wall ▷ *noun, colloq* **1 a** a small and insignificant place; **b** *as adj* (**hole-in-the-wall**) small, insignificant, difficult to find. **2** *colloq* a cash machine outside a bank, etc.

holey /'hoʊlɪ/ ▷ *adj* (***holier, holiest***) full of holes.

Holi /'hoʊliː/ ▷ *noun* the Hindu 'Festival of Fire' in honour of Krishna, held in February or March over several days, and characterized by boisterous revelry, including the throwing of coloured water over people, and, among Sikhs, by sports competitions. Ⓒ Early 20c: from Sanskrit *holika*, a mythological female demon.

holiday /'hɒlɪdeɪ, -dɪ/ ▷ *noun* (***holidays***) **1** (*often* **holidays**) a period of recreational time spent away from work, study or general routine. Sometimes (*old use* or *facetious*) shortened to HOLS. **2** a day when one does not have to work, originally a religious festival. **3** *as adj* befitting a holiday; cheerful or light-spirited ◻ *a holiday atmosphere.* ▷ *verb* (***holidayed, holidaying***) *intr* to spend or go away for a holiday in a specified place or at a specified time ◻ *They holiday every year in Cornwall.* Ⓒ Anglo-Saxon *haligdæg* holy day.

holiday camp ▷ *noun* a place, often near the sea, where activities and entertainment are organized for the people staying there on holiday in hotels, chalets, etc.

holidaymaker ▷ *noun* someone on holiday away from home; a tourist. Ⓒ 19c.

holier-than-thou ▷ *adj, derog* believing oneself to be morally superior; sanctimonious, often patronizingly so.

holier[1] and **holiest**[1] see under HOLEY

holier[2], **holiest**[2] and **holily** see under HOLY

holiness /'hoʊlɪnəs/ ▷ *noun* **1** the state of being holy; sanctity. **2** (**Holiness**) a title of the Pope and other specific religious leaders, in the form of **Your Holiness** and **His Holiness**.

holing see under HOLE

holism /'hɒlɪzəm, 'hoʊ-/ ▷ *noun, philos* **1** the theory stating that a complex entity or system is more than merely the sum of its parts or elements. **2** the theory that the basic principle of the Universe is the creation of whole entities, ie the evolution of the atom and the cell to complex, complete and self-contained forms of life and mind. • **holist** *noun.* • **holistic** *adj.* • **holistically** *adverb.* Coined in 1926 by General J C Smuts in his book *Evolution and Holism*: from Greek *holos* whole.

holistic medicine ▷ *noun* a form of medicine involving the consideration of a person as a whole, physically and psychologically, rather than merely targeting the diseased area. Ⓒ 1920s.

holland /'hɒlənd/ ▷ *noun* a smooth, hard-wearing linen fabric, either unbleached or dyed brown, often used for covering furniture, etc. Ⓒ 15c: originally made in Holland.

hollandaise sauce /'hɒləndeɪz —, hɒlən'deɪz —/ ▷ *noun* a sauce made from the yolk of an egg, melted butter, and lemon juice or vinegar. Ⓒ Early 20c: French.

holler /'hɒlə(r)/ ▷ *verb* (***hollered, hollering***) *tr & intr, colloq* to shout or yell. ▷ *noun* a HOLLO. Ⓒ 16c: from French *holà* stop!

hollo /'hɒloʊ/ and **holla** /'hɒlə/ ▷ *noun* (***hollos*** or ***holloes***; ***hollas***) *exclamation* an encouraging shout or a call for attention. ▷ *verb* (***holloed, holloing***) *tr & intr* to shout. Ⓒ 16c: French.

hollow /'hɒloʊ/ ▷ *adj* **1** containing an empty space within or below; not solid. **2** sunken or depressed ◻ *hollow cheeks.* **3** said of a sound: echoing as if made in a hollow place. **4** said of a voice: dull or stifled. **5** worthless; insincere ◻ *a hollow statement.* ▷ *noun* **1** a hole or cavity in something. **2** a valley or depression in the land. ▷ *adverb, colloq* completely ◻ *beat someone hollow.* ▷ *verb* (***hollowed, hollowing***) (*usually* **hollow something out**) to make a hollow in it; to form it by making a hollow. • **hollowly** *adverb.* • **hollowness** *noun.* Ⓒ Anglo-Saxon *holh.*

hollow-eyed ▷ *adj* having sunken eyes, usually because of tiredness. Ⓒ 16c.

holly /'hɒlɪ/ ▷ *noun* (***hollies***) an evergreen tree or shrub with dark shiny prickly leaves and red berries, usually used for Christmas decorations. Ⓒ Anglo-Saxon *holen.*

hollyhock /'hɒlɪhɒk/ ▷ *noun* a tall garden plant of the mallow family, with thick hairy stalks and colourful flowers, brought into Europe from the Holy Land. Ⓒ 13c: from *holi* holy + *hoc* mallow.

holly-oak see under HOLM-OAK

holm[1] /hoʊm/ ▷ *noun* **1** in placenames: a small island, especially in a river. **2** the rich flat land beside a river or stretch of water. Ⓒ Anglo-Saxon.

holm[2] /hoʊm/ ▷ *noun* a regional term for HOLLY. Ⓒ 14c.

holmium /'hoʊlmɪəm/ ▷ *noun* (symbol **Ho**, atomic number 67) a soft silver-white metallic element with no apparent uses, though its compounds are highly magnetic. Ⓒ 19c: from Latin *Holmia* Stockholm, since many minerals with this element were found there.

holm-oak ▷ *noun* the evergreen oak, with leaves similar to holly. Also called **holly-oak** or **ilex**. Ⓒ 14c.

holo- /hɒloʊ, hɒ'lɒ, hɒlə/ or (before a vowel) **hol-** *combining form, signifying* whole or wholly. ⓒ From Greek *holos*.

holocaust /'hɒləkɔːst/ ▷ *noun* **1** a large-scale slaughter or destruction of life, often by fire. **2** (**the Holocaust**) the mass murder of Jews by the German Nazis during World War II. ⓒ 13c: HOLO- + Greek *kaustos* burnt.

Holocene /'hɒləsiːn/ ▷ *noun, geol* the most recent geological period, during which modern human beings appeared and civilization began. See table at GEOLOGICAL TIME SCALE. ⓒ 19c.

hologram /'hɒləgram/ ▷ *noun, photog* a photograph produced without a lens, by the interference between two split laser beams which, when suitably illuminated, shows a three-dimensional image. ⓒ 1940s.

holograph /'hɒləgrɑːf/ ▷ *adj* said of a document: completely in the handwriting of the author. ▷ *noun* a holograph document. ▷ *verb* to make a hologram of something. ⓒ 17c.

holographic /hɒlə'grafɪk/ ▷ *adj* relating to or concerning HOLOGRAPHY or HOLOGRAPH documents. • **holographically** *adverb*.

holography /hɒ'lɒgrəfɪ/ ▷ *noun, photog* the process or technique of producing or using holograms.

holohedron /hɒlə'hiːdrən/ ▷ *noun* a geometrical shape with all the planes needed for the symmetry of a crystal system. • **holohedral** *adj, math* said of a crystal: holohedron-shaped. • **holohedrism** *noun*. ⓒ 19c.

holophrase ▷ *noun* a one-word utterance used by young children in the earliest stages of language-learning to express meaning which in more mature speech would normally be contained in more complex grammatical structure, such as a phrase or sentence. ⓒ 19c.

holophytic /hɒloʊ'fɪtɪk/ ▷ *adj* said of certain organisms, especially green plants: able to obtain their nutrients by generating them from inorganic matter, eg by photosynthesis. • **holophytism** *noun*. • **holophyte** /'hɒləfaɪt/ *noun*. ⓒ 19c.

holothurian /hɒloʊ'θjuərɪən/ ▷ *noun* any member of a class of unarmoured echinoderms with soft elongated bodies and tentacles round the mouth area, eg sea cucumber. ⓒ 19c: from Greek *holothourion* a type of sea animal.

hols /hɒlz/ ▷ *plural noun, old use or facetious* short form of HOLIDAYS.

holster /'hoʊlstə(r)/ ▷ *noun* a leather pistol-case, usually hung on a saddle or on a belt round a person's hips. ⓒ 17c: Dutch.

holt /hoʊlt/ *noun* an animal's den, especially that of an otter. ⓒ Anglo-Saxon: from HOLD[1].

holus-bolus /hoʊləs'boʊləs/ ▷ *adverb* altogether; all at once. ⓒ 19c: sham Latin, based on *whole bolus*.

holy /'hoʊlɪ/ ▷ *adj* (***holier, holiest***) **1** associated with God or gods; religious or sacred. **2** *often ironic* morally pure and perfect; saintly or sanctimonious. • **holily** *adverb*. • **holiness** see separate entry. ⓒ Anglo-Saxon *halig*.

the Holy City ▷ *noun* **1** a particular city regarded as sacred, varying according to the religion, eg Jerusalem, Rome, Mecca, etc. **2** *Christianity* heaven. ⓒ 14c.

Holy Communion see COMMUNION 3

holy day ▷ *noun* a religious festival. See also HOLIDAY.

the Holy Father ▷ *noun, RC Church* the Pope. ⓒ 14c.

the Holy Ghost, the Holy Spirit and **the Spirit** ▷ *noun, Christianity* the third person in the Trinity.

the Holy Grail see under GRAIL

the Holy Land ▷ *noun, Christianity* Palestine, especially Judea, the scene of Christ's ministry in the New Testament.

holy of holies ▷ *noun* any place or thing regarded as especially sacred.

holy orders ▷ *noun, Christianity* **1** a sacrament in the Roman and Greek Churches whereby a person is ordained as a religious minister. **2** the office of an ordained member of the clergy □ ***take holy orders***. ⓒ 14c.

Holy Roman Empire ▷ *noun* the empire held by the **Holy Roman Emperors** in Italy and central Europe, strictly from the 12c, but more generally so called from the reign of Charlemagne, King of the Franks, in the 9c, until its abandonment by Francis II in 1806.

holy rood ▷ *noun, Christianity* **1** *especially RC Church* a cross above the entrance to a church's chancel. **2** (*especially* **the Holy Rood**) the cross on which Christ was crucified. ⓒ Anglo-Saxon.

the Holy See ▷ *noun, RC Church* the see or office of the pope in Rome. ⓒ 18c.

Holy Thursday see ASCENSION DAY

holy war ▷ *noun* a war waged for the elimination of heresy or a rival religion; a Crusade. ⓒ 17c.

holy water ▷ *noun* water blessed for use in religious ceremonies. ⓒ Anglo-Saxon *haligwæter*.

Holy Week ▷ *noun, Christianity* the week before Easter Sunday, which includes MAUNDY THURSDAY and GOOD FRIDAY. ⓒ 18c.

Holy Writ ▷ *noun* a collection of holy or religious writings, especially the Bible. ⓒ Anglo-Saxon *halige writu*.

homage /'hɒmɪdʒ/ ▷ *noun* **1** a display of great respect towards someone or something; an acknowledgement of their superiority. **2** *historical* a vassal's acknowledgement of being his feudal lord's servant. ⓒ 13c: French.

Homburg /'hɒmbɜːg/ ▷ *noun* a man's soft felt hat, with a narrow brim and a depression in the crown. ⓒ 1890s: named after Homburg, a town in western Germany, where it was first made and worn.

home /hoʊm/ ▷ *noun* **1** the place where one lives, often with one's family. **2** the country or area one originally comes from, either a birthplace or where one grew up. **3** a place where something first occurred, or was first invented. **4** an institution for people who need care or rest, eg the elderly, orphans, etc. **5** a match played by a team on their own ground. **6** the den, base or finishing point in some games and races. ▷ *adj* **1** being at or belonging to one's home, country, family, sports ground, etc. **2** made or done at home or in one's own country □ ***home baking***. ▷ *adverb* **1** to or at one's home. **2** to the target place, position, etc □ ***hit the point home***. **3** to the furthest or final point; as far as possible □ ***hammer the nail home***. **4** said of a sporting event: on one's own ground, etc. ▷ *verb* (***homed, homing***) *intr* **1** to go or find the way home. **2** said of an animal, especially a bird: to return home safely. • **at home 1** in one's home, country, sports ground, etc. **2** feeling at ease or familiar with a place or situation. **3** prepared to receive a visitor or visitors. • **bring something home to someone** to make it clear or obvious to them, so that there is no avoiding the conclusion. • **eat someone out of house and home** *colloq* to eat vast amounts of food at their expense. • **go** or **strike home 1** said of a remark, etc: to make an effective impression on the mind of the person addressed. **2** said of a blow: to hit its target. • **home and dry** having arrived home or achieved one's goal. • **home from home** a place where one feels completely comfortable, relaxed, and happy, as if at home. • **make oneself at home** to be relaxed and unrestrained as if in one's own home. • **not at home** not at one's house, or not willing to receive visitors. • **nothing to write home about** *colloq* something that is not particularly exciting or attractive. ⓒ Anglo-Saxon *ham*.

■ **home in on something** to identify (a target or destination) and focus on attempting to reach it.

home banking ▻ *noun* a banking service allowing customers to access information about their account, transfer funds, pay bills, etc using a computer or telephone link from their home or office to the bank's system.

home-brew ▻ *noun* a beverage, usually alcoholic, brewed at home or for home use. ▻ *verb* to produce a beverage at home. ◷ 19c.

homebuyer ▻ *noun* someone in the process of arranging to buy their own home. ◷ 1960s.

homecoming ▻ *noun* an arrival home, usually of someone who has been away for a long time. ◷ 14c: *homcomyng*.

home counties ▻ *plural noun* (*also* **Home Counties**) the counties around London, including Essex, Kent, Surrey and Hertfordshire.

home economics ▻ *noun* the study of domestic science, household skills and management. • **home economist** *noun*. ◷ 19c.

home farm ▻ *noun, Brit, historical* a farm, usually one of several on a large estate, set aside to produce food, etc for the owner of the estate.

the Home Guard ▻ *noun, Brit* a volunteer army formed to defend Britain from invasion during World War II. ◷ When first formed in May 1940, the force was known as the *Local Defence Volunteers*, but this was later changed at Winston Churchill's demand; it was disbanded in December 1945.

home guard ▻ *noun* a member of any volunteer force for the defence of a country. ◷ 18c.

home help ▻ *noun, Brit* a person who is hired, often by the local authority, to help sick, handicapped or aged people with domestic chores.

homeland ▻ *noun* **1** one's native country; the country of one's ancestors. **2** in South Africa: an area of land formerly reserved by the government for the Black African population. ◷ 17c.

homeless /ˈhoʊmləs/ ▻ *adj* **1** referring to people without a home, who therefore live and sleep in public places or squats. **2** (**the homeless**) people without a place to live (see THE 4b). • **homelessness** *noun*.

home loan ▻ *noun* a loan of money to buy a home; a mortgage.

homely /ˈhoʊmlɪ/ ▻ *adj* (***homelier***, ***homeliest***) **1** relating to home; familiar. **2** making someone feel at home. **3** said of people: honest and unpretentious; pleasant. **4** *N Amer* said of people: plain and unattractive. ◷ 14c.

home-made ▻ *adj* **1** said of food, clothes, etc: made at home. **2** made in one's native country. ◷ 17c.

home maker ▻ *noun* someone whose main activity is managing the household, especially someone who makes the home more pleasant. ◷ 19c.

home market ▻ *noun* the market for goods in the country where they were produced.

home movie ▻ *noun* a motion picture made by an amateur, usually using a portable cine camera or camcorder, often intended for domestic viewing.

homeo-, **homoeo-** or **homoio-** /ˈhoʊmɪoʊ, hoʊmɪˈɒ, hɒ-/ ▻ *combining form, signifying* like or similar. ◷ From Greek *homoios*.

the Home Office ▻ *noun, Brit* the government department concerned with the domestic civil affairs of the country.

homeopath or **homoeopath** /ˈhoʊmɪəpaθ/ ▻ *noun* someone who believes in or practises HOMEOPATHY. Also called **homeopathist**. /-ˈɒpəθɪst/. • **homeopathic** *adj*. • **homeopathically** *adverb*.

homeopathy or **homoeopathy** /hoʊmɪˈɒpəθɪ, hɒmɪ-/ ▻ *noun* a system of alternative medicine where a disease is treated by prescribing small doses of drugs which produce symptoms similar to those of the disease itself. ◷ 19c.

homeostasis or **homoeostasis** /hoʊmɪˈɒstəsɪs, hɒmɪ-/ ▻ *noun, biol* the tendency of an animal or organism to maintain a constant internal environment regardless of varying external conditions. ◷ 1920s.

home owner ▻ *noun* someone who owns rather than rents their own home. ◷ 1940s.

home page ▻ *noun, computing* the first or main page of an Internet WEBSITE. ◷ 1990s.

home plate ▻ *noun, US baseball* the final point reached by a batter in order to score a run. ◷ 1870s.

homer /ˈhoʊmə(r)/ ▻ *noun* **1** a breed of pigeon that can be trained to return home from a distance. **2** *baseball* a home run. **3** an out-of-hours job illicitly done by a tradesman for cash-in-hand payment.

Homeric /hoʊˈmɛrɪk/ ▻ *adj* **1** relating to the c.8c BC Greek poet Homer or the poems attributed to him. **2** relating to Bronze Age Greece. ◷ 18c.

home rule ▻ *noun* **1** the government of a country and its internal affairs by its own citizens. **2** (**Home Rule**) the form of self-government claimed by Irish, Scottish and Welsh Nationalists, including a separate government to manage internal affairs. ◷ 19c.

the Home Secretary ▻ *noun, Brit* the government minister who is the official head of the HOME OFFICE. ◷ Late 18c.

homesick ▻ *adj* pining for one's home and family when away from them, with resulting sadness and depression. • **homesickness** *noun*.

homespun ▻ *adj* **1** said of character, advice, thinking, etc: artless, simple and straightforward. **2** *old use* said of cloth: woven at home. ▻ *noun* a cloth produced at home.

homestead /ˈhoʊmstɛd/ ▻ *noun* **1** a dwelling-house and its surrounding land and buildings. **2** any such estate where one lives. **3** *N Amer, especially US* an area of land (usually about 65ha) granted to a settler for development as a farm. ◷ Anglo-Saxon *hamstede*.

home straight and **home stretch** ▻ *noun* **1** the last part of a racecourse just before the finish. **2** the final or winning stage of anything.

home town ▻ *noun* the town where one lives or lived; the place of one's birth.

home truth ▻ *noun* (*usually* **home truths**) a true but unwelcome fact told directly to someone about themselves.

home unit ▻ *noun, Austral* a flat or apartment.

home video ▻ *noun* a home movie made with a video camera.

homeward /ˈhoʊmwəd/ ▻ *adj* going home. ▻ *adverb* (*also* **homewards**) towards home. ◷ Anglo-Saxon *hamweard*.

homework ▻ *noun* **1** work or study done at home, especially for school. **2** paid work, especially work paid for according to quantity rather than time, done at home. • **do one's homework** *colloq* to be well prepared for, eg a discussion, by being acquainted with relevant facts. ◷ 17c.

home worker ▻ *noun* someone who works at home, but under similar terms and conditions to a worker in a conventional office, and linked to an office by a computer. • **homeworking** *noun*.

homey or **homy** /ˈhoʊmɪ/ ▻ *adj* (***homier***, ***homiest***) homelike; homely.

homicidal /hɒmɪˈsaɪdəl/ ▻ *adj* **1** referring or pertaining to HOMICIDE. **2** said of a person: psychologically disposed to commit murder. • **homicidally** *adverb*.

homicide /ˈhɒmɪsaɪd/ ▷ *noun* **1** the murder or manslaughter of one person by another. **2** a person who kills another person. ⓘ 14c: from Latin *homo* man + -CIDE.

homiletic /hɒmɪˈlɛtɪk/ and **homiletical** ▷ *adj* **1** relating to or involving a homily or sermon. **2** relating to or involving the art of writing or giving sermons. ⓘ 17c.

homiletics ▷ *singular noun* the art of preaching. ⓘ 19c.

homily /ˈhɒmɪlɪ/ ▷ *noun* (***homilies***) **1** a sermon, based more on practical than religious teachings. **2** a long and often tedious talk, giving moral advice and encouragement. ⓘ 14c: from Greek *homilia*.

homing /ˈhoʊmɪŋ/ ▷ *verb, present participle of* HOME. ▷ *adj* **1** said of animals, especially pigeons: trained to return home, usually from a distance. **2** guiding home. **3** said of navigational devices on missiles, crafts, etc: guiding itself towards a target.

homing instinct ▷ *noun, biol* the navigational behaviour occurring in several animal species, which ranges from returning home after daily foraging and other excursions, to the more complex navigational task involved in large migrations.

hominid /ˈhɒmɪnɪd/ ▷ *noun* a primate belonging to the family which includes modern man and his fossil ancestors. ⓘ 19c: from Latin *homo, hominis* man.

hominoid /ˈhɒmɪnɔɪd/ ▷ *adj* resembling man; manlike. ▷ *noun* any member of the primate family, comprising man, the modern apes and their fossil ancestors. ⓘ 1920s: from Latin *homo, hominis* man + -OID.

hominy /ˈhɒmɪnɪ/ ▷ *noun, N Amer, especially US* coarsely ground maize boiled with milk or water to make a porridge. ⓘ 17c: a Native American word.

homo[1] or (*zool*) **Homo** /ˈhoʊmoʊ/ ▷ *noun* the generic name for modern man and his ancestors. See HOMO SAPIENS. ⓘ 16c: Latin.

homo[2] /ˈhoʊmoʊ/ ▷ *noun* (***homos***), *adj, colloq, usually derog* short form of HOMOSEXUAL.

homo- /ˈhoʊmoʊ, hoʊˈmɒ, hɒ-/ ▷ *combining form, signifying* same ▫ *homogeneous* ▫ *homomorph* ▫ *homosexual*. ⓘ From Greek *homos*.

homocyclic ▷ *adj, chem* said of a compound: having a closed chain of similar atoms. Compare HETEROCYCLIC. ⓘ Early 20c: from Greek *kyklos* a ring.

homoeopath see HOMEOPATH

homoeopathic see HOMEOPATHIC

homoeopathy see HOMEOPATHY

homoeostasis see HOMEOSTASIS

homoeothermic or **homoiothermic** and **homoeothermal** or **homoiothermal** ▷ *adj, zool* said of an animal: capable of maintaining its internal body temperature at a relatively constant level, independent of fluctuations in the temperature of its environment. Also called **warm-blooded**. ⓘ 19c.

homogamy /həˈmɒgəmɪ/ ▷ *noun* **1** *bot* a condition in which all the flowers on the same axis or of an inflorescence are sexually alike. **2** *bot* the simultaneous ripening of the stamens and stigmas. ● **homogamous** *adj*. ⓘ 19c.

homogeneous /hɒməˈdʒiːnɪəs, hoʊ-/ ▷ *adj* **1** made up of parts or elements that are all of the same kind or nature. **2** made up of similar parts or elements. **3** *math* having the same degree or dimensions throughout in every term. ● **homogeneously** *adverb*. ● **homogeneousness** or **homogeneity** /hɒmoʊdʒəˈniːɪtɪ, hoʊ-/ *noun*. ⓘ 17c: from Greek *genos* kind.

homogenize or **homogenise** /həˈmɒdʒənaɪz/ ▷ *verb* (***homogenized, homogenizing***) **1** to make or become homogeneous. **2** to break up the fat droplets of (a liquid, especially milk) into smaller particles so that they are evenly distributed throughout the liquid. ⓘ 19c: from Greek *genos* kind.

homogeny /həˈmɒdʒənɪ/ ▷ *noun, biol* a similarity owing to common descent or origin. ● **homogenous** *adj*. ⓘ 17c: from Greek *homogeneia* similarity of origin.

homograph ▷ *noun* a word with the same spelling as another, but with a different meaning, origin, and sometimes a different pronunciation, eg *like* (similar) and *like* (be fond of), and *entrance* (/ˈɛntrəns/ a way in) and *entrance* (/ɪnˈtrɑːns/ to charm or delight). ⓘ 19c.

homoiothermic and **homoiothermal** see HOMOEOTHERMIC

homologate /həˈmɒləgeɪt/ ▷ *verb* (***homologated, homologating***) to approve or consent to something; to confirm. ● **homologation** /hɒmələˈgeɪʃən/ *noun*. ⓘ 17c: from Latin *homologare, homologatum* to agree to.

homologize or **homologise** /həˈmɒlədʒaɪz/ ▷ *verb* (***homologized, homologizing***) *tr & intr* to be, seem or make homologous. ⓘ 18c.

homologous /həˈmɒləgəs/ ▷ *adj* **1** having a related or similar function or position. **2** *biol* said of plant or animal structures: having a common origin, but having evolved in such a way that they no longer perform the same functions or resemble each other, eg a human arm and a bird's wing. Compare ANALOGOUS. **3** *genetics* said of two chromosomes in a cell, usually of the same size and shape: pairing during meiosis, and containing genes for the same set of characteristics, but derived from different parents. ⓘ 17c.

homologous series ▷ *noun, chem* a series of organic compounds in which each successive member has one more of a chemical group in its molecule than the preceding member.

homologue or (*US*) **homolog** /ˈhɒmәlɒg/ ▷ *noun* anything which is homologous to something else, such as a human arm and a bird's wing. ⓘ 19c.

homology /həˈmɒlədʒɪ/ ▷ *noun* (***homologies***) **1** the state of being homologous. **2** a similarity in structure and origin, apart from form or use. ⓘ 17c: from Greek *homologia* agreement.

homomorph ▷ *noun* something that has the same form as something else. ● **homomorphism** *noun*. ⓘ 19c.

homomorphic and **homomorphous** ▷ *adj* similar in form, especially if different otherwise.

homonym /ˈhɒmənɪm/ ▷ *noun* a word with the same sound and spelling as another, but with a different meaning, eg *kind* (helpful) and *kind* (sort). ⓘ 17c: from Greek *onoma* name.

homophobe ▷ *noun* a person with a strong aversion to or hatred of homosexuals. ● **homophobia** *noun*. ● **homophobic** *adj*. ⓘ 1950s: HOMO[2] + -PHOBE.

homophone ▷ *noun, linguistics* **1** a word which sounds the same as another word but is different in spelling and/or meaning, eg *bear* and *bare*. **2** a character or characters that represent the same sound as another, eg *f* and *ph*. ⓘ 17c.

homophonic /hɒməˈfɒnɪk, hoʊmə-/ ▷ *adj, music* **1** sounding the same or alike. **2** relating to or concerning homophony. ⓘ 19c.

homophony /həˈmɒfənɪ/ ▷ *noun, music* a style of composition in which one part or voice carries the melody, and other parts or voices add texture with simple accompaniment. Compare POLYPHONY. ⓘ 19c.

homopterous /hoʊˈmɒptərəs/ ▷ *adj* relating or referring to the order of insects **Homoptera**, belonging to the group HEMIPTERA, which have wings of a uniform texture. ● **homopteran** *noun*. ⓘ 19c: from Greek *pteron* wing.

Homo sapiens /ˈhoʊmoʊ ˈsapɪɛnz/ ▷ *noun* the species to which modern man belongs, and the only member of the Homo genus still in existence. ⓘ 18c: Latin, meaning 'wise man'.

homosexual /hɒmə'sɛkʃʊəl/ ▷ *noun* a person who is sexually attracted to people of the same sex. ▷ *adj* **1** having a sexual attraction to people of the same sex. **2** relating to or concerning a homosexual or homosexuals. ⓘ 1890s.

homosexuality ▷ *noun* **1** the state of being homosexual. **2** a homosexual character or nature. **3** homosexual activity or behaviour. ⓘ 1890s.

homozygote ▷ *noun, genetics* a ZYGOTE produced by the union of two identical gametes. ⓘ Early 20c.

homozygous ▷ *adj, genetics* describing an individual that has two identical DNA segments for a particular gene, and produces offspring that are identical to the parent with respect to that gene. Compare HETEROZYGOUS. ⓘ Early 20c.

homunculus /hə'mʌŋkjʊləs, hoʊ-/ and **homuncule** /hə'mʌnkjuːl/ ▷ *noun* (***homunculi*** /-laɪ/) a small man; a dwarf. • **homuncular** *adj.* ⓘ 17c: Latin diminutive of HOMO[1].

homy see HOMEY

Hon. ▷ *abbreviation* **1** Honourable. **2** Honorary.

honcho /'hɒntʃoʊ/ ▷ *noun* (***honchos***) *N Amer colloq* an important person, especially someone in charge; a big shot. ⓘ 1940s: from Japanese *han* squad + *cho* head or chief.

hone /hoʊn/ ▷ *noun* a smooth stone used for sharpening tools. ▷ *verb* (***honed, honing***) to sharpen with or as if with a hone. ⓘ Anglo-Saxon *han*.

honest /'ɒnɪst/ ▷ *adj* **1** not inclined to steal, cheat or lie; truthful and trustworthy. **2** fair or justified ▫ *an honest wage.* **3** sincere and respectable ▫ *an honest attempt.* **4** ordinary and undistinguished; unremarkable ▫ *an honest wine.* ▷ *adverb, colloq* honestly ▫ *I do like it, honest.* • **honest-to-God** or **honest-to-goodness** *adj* genuine or real; true. ⓘ 13c: from Latin *honestus*.

honest broker ▷ *noun* an impartial and objective mediator in a dispute. ⓘ 19c.

honestly /'ɒnɪstlɪ/ ▷ *adverb* **1** in an honest way. **2** in truth. **3** used for emphasis ▫ *I honestly don't know.* ▷ *exclamation* **1** expressing annoyance. **2** expressing disbelief.

honesty /'ɒnɪstɪ/ ▷ *noun* **1** the state of being honest and truthful. **2** integrity and candour. **3** *hortic* a common garden plant with silvery leaf-like pods. ⓘ 14c: from Latin *honestus*.

honey /'hʌnɪ/ ▷ *noun* (***honeys***) **1** a sweet viscous fluid made by bees from the nectar of flowers, and stored in honeycombs, used as a food and sweetener. **2** a dark dull-yellow or golden-brown colour resembling that of honey. **3** anything sweet or pleasant like honey. **4** *N Amer colloq* a term of endearment used to address a person one loves. **5** *colloq* someone or something which is excellent of its kind. ▷ *verb* (***honeyed, honeying***) **1** to sweeten. **2** to make agreeable. ⓘ Anglo-Saxon *hunig*.

honey badger ▷ *noun* a badger-like animal, related to the WOLVERINE, native to India and Africa. Also called **ratel**.

honey bear see KINKAJOU, SUNBEAR

honey bee ▷ *noun* a species of bee that has been semi-domesticated in most parts of the world as a source of honey.

honey buzzard ▷ *noun* a European hawk that feeds on the larvae and honey of bees and wasps.

honeycomb ▷ *noun* **1** the structure made up of rows of hexagonal wax cells in which bees store their eggs and honey. **2** anything like a honeycomb. **3** a bewildering maze of cavities, rooms, passages, etc. ▷ *verb* **1** to form like a honeycomb. **2** to spread or pervade. ⓘ Anglo-Saxon *hunigcamb*.

honeydew /'hʌnɪdjuː/ ▷ *noun* a sugar secretion from aphids and plants, originally associated with dew. ⓘ 16c.

honeydew melon ▷ *noun* a type of sweet melon with a smooth green or orange skin. ⓘ Early 20c.

honey-eater ▷ *noun* an Australian bird with a long beak that feeds on the nectar of flowers. ⓘ 18c.

honeyed or **honied** /'hʌnɪd/ ▷ *adj* said of a voice, words, etc: sweet, flattering or soothing. ⓘ 14c.

honey guide ▷ *noun* **1** a species of bird, native to Africa, that guides the way to honey bees' nests by hopping from tree to tree with a distinctive call. **2** *bot* a marking on the petal of a flower said to show the way to the NECTARY. ⓘ 18c.

honeymoon ▷ *noun* **1** the first weeks after marriage, often spent on holiday, before settling down to the normal routine of life. **2** a period of unusual or temporary goodwill, enthusiasm and harmony at the start eg of a new business relationship. ▷ *verb* (***honeymooned, honeymooning***) *intr* to spend time on a honeymoon, usually on holiday. ⓘ 16c: so called because the feelings of the couple were thought to wax and wane like the moon phases.

honeymooner ▷ *noun* a person taking a honeymoon; a newly married person. ⓘ 1840s.

honeysuckle /'hʌnɪsʌkəl/ ▷ *noun* a climbing garden shrub with sweet-scented white, pale-yellow or pink flowers. ⓘ Anglo-Saxon *hunigsuce*, so called because honey is easily sucked from the flower by long-tongued insects.

honing *present participle of* HONE

honk ▷ *noun* **1** the cry of a wild goose. **2** the sound made by a car horn. ▷ *verb* (***honked, honking***) **1** *tr & intr* to make or cause something to make a honking noise. **2** *intr, slang* to smell badly or unpleasantly. **3** *intr, Brit slang* to vomit. ⓘ 19c: imitating the sound.

honky or **honkie** /'hɒŋkɪ/ ▷ *noun* (***honkies***) *N Amer, derog Black slang* a white person. ⓘ 1940s.

honky-tonk /'hɒŋkɪtɒŋk/ ▷ *noun, colloq* **1** a style of jangly popular piano music based on RAGTIME. **2** *N Amer slang* a cheap seedy nightclub. Also *as adj* ▫ *honky-tonk music.* ⓘ 1890s: a rhyming compound derived from HONK.

honorand /'ɒnərand/ ▷ *noun* someone who receives an award, especially an honorary degree. ⓘ 1940s: from Latin *honorandus*, honouring, from *honorare* to honour.

honorarium /ɒnə'rɛərɪəm/ ▷ *noun* (***honorariums*** or ***honoraria*** /-rɪə/) a fee paid to a professional person in return for services carried out on a voluntary basis. ⓘ 17c: Latin.

honorary /'ɒnərərɪ/ ▷ *adj* **1** conferring or bestowing honour. **2** given to a person as a mark of respect, and without the usual functions, dues, etc. **3** said of an official position: receiving no payment. ⓘ 17c: from Latin *honorarius*.

honorific /ɒnə'rɪfɪk/ ▷ *adj* showing or giving honour or respect. ▷ *noun* a form of title, address or mention. • **honorifically** *adverb.* ⓘ 17c: from Latin *honorificus*.

Honour /ɒnə(r)/ ▷ *noun* a title of respect given to judges, mayors, etc, in the form of **Your Honour**, **His Honour** and **Her Honour**.

honour or (*US*) **honor** /'ɒnə(r)/ ▷ *noun* **1** the esteem or respect earned by or paid to a worthy person. **2** great respect or public regard. **3** a source of credit, such as fame, glory or distinction (for one's country, etc). **4** a scrupulous sense of what is right; a high standard of moral behaviour or integrity. **5** a pleasure or privilege. **6** *old use* a woman's chastity or virginity, or her reputation for this. ▷ *verb* (***honoured, honouring***) **1** to respect or venerate; to hold in high esteem. **2** to confer an award, title or honour on someone as a mark of respect for an ability, achievement, etc. **3** to pay (a bill, debt, etc) when it falls due. **4** to keep or meet (a promise or agreement). ● **do the honours** *colloq* to perform or carry out a task, especially that of a host. ● **in honour of someone** or **something** to do something out of respect for or in celebration of them or it. ● **on one's honour** under a moral obligation. ⌚ 12c: from Latin *honor*.

honourable or (*US*) **honorable** /ˈɒnərəbəl/ ▻ *adj* **1** deserving or worthy of honour. **2** having high moral principles. **3** (**Honourable**) a prefix to the names of certain people as a courtesy title. See also RIGHT HONOURABLE. ● **honourableness** *noun*. ● **honourably** *adverb*. ⌚ 14c.

honour-bound ▻ *adj* (*also* **in honour bound**) obliged to do something by duty or by moral considerations.

honour bright ▻ *noun, school slang* an oath or appeal to one's honour.

honour-guard ▻ *noun, US* a guard of honour.

honours /ˈɒnəz/ ▻ *plural noun* **1** said of a university degree: a higher grade of distinction for specialized or advanced work. **2** a mark of civility or respect, especially at a funeral. **3** in some card games: any of the top four or five cards. **4** *golf* the right to play first from the tee.

honours list ▻ *noun* a list of people who have received or are about to receive a knighthood, order, etc from the monarch.

honours of war ▻ *noun, military* the privileges granted to the surrendering force by the victors of marching out with their flags flying, arms, etc.

hooch or **hootch** /huːtʃ/ ▻ *noun, N Amer colloq* any strong alcoholic drink, such as whisky, especially when distilled or obtained illegally. ⌚ 19c: a shortening of *Hoochinoo*, the Native American people who originally made the drink.

hood[1] /hʊd/ ▻ *noun* **1** a flexible covering for the whole head and back of the neck, often attached to a coat at the collar. **2** a folding and often removable roof or cover on a car, push-chair, etc. **3** *N Amer* a car bonnet. **4** an ornamental loop of material worn as part of academic dress, specifically coloured according to the university and degree obtained. **5** a covering for a hawk's head. **6** any projecting or protective covering. **7** the expanding section of a cobra's neck. ▻ *verb* (***hooded, hooding***) to cover with a hood; to blind. ⌚ Anglo-Saxon *hod*.

hood[2] /hʊd/ ▻ *noun, slang* a hoodlum.

-hood /hʊd/ ▻ *suffix, forming nouns, denoting* **1** a state or condition of being the specified thing □ *manhood* □ *motherhood*. **2** a collection or group of people □ *priesthood*. ⌚ Anglo-Saxon *-had*.

hooded /ˈhʊdɪd/ ▻ *adj* having, covered with, or shaped like a hood.

hooded crow ▻ *noun* a crow with a grey body and black head. Also called **hoodie crow**.

hoodlum /ˈhuːdləm/ ▻ *noun* **1** *N Amer* a small-time criminal. **2** a violent, destructive or badly behaved youth. ⌚ 19c: from German *Hudellump* a sloppy or careless person.

hoodoo /ˈhuːduː/ ▻ *noun* (***hoodoos***) **1** voodoo. **2** a jinx or bad luck. **3** the thing or person that brings such. ▻ *verb* (***hoodoos, hoodooed, hoodooing***) to bring bad luck to someone. ⌚ 19c variant of VOODOO.

hoodwink ▻ *verb* (*often* **hoodwink someone into something**) to trick or deceive them into doing it. ⌚ 16c, meaning 'to blindfold', from HOOD[1] + WINK.

hooey /ˈhuːɪ/ ▻ *noun, slang* nonsense.

hoof /huːf, hʊf/ ▻ *noun* (***hoofs*** or ***hooves*** /-huːvz/) the horny structure that grows beneath and covers the ends of the digits in the feet of certain mammals, eg horses. ▻ *verb* (***hoofs, hoofed, hoofing***) to kick or strike with a hoof. ● **on the hoof** said of cattle, horses, etc: alive. ● **hoof it** *slang* **1** to go on foot. **2** to dance. ⌚ Anglo-Saxon *hof*.

hoofer ▻ *noun, slang* a professional dancer.

hoo-ha or **hoo-hah** /ˈhuːhɑː/ ▻ *noun* (***hoo-has*** or ***hoohahs***) *colloq* excited and noisy talk; a commotion. ⌚ 1930s: probably from Yiddish *hu-ha* uproar.

hook /hʊk/ ▻ *noun* **1** a curved piece of metal or similar material, used for catching or holding things. **2** a snare, trap, attraction, etc. **3** a curved tool used for cutting grain, branches, etc. **4** a sharp bend or curve, eg in land or a river. **5** *boxing* a swinging punch with the elbow bent. **6** *sport* a method of striking the ball causing it to curve in the air. **7** *cricket, golf* a shot that causes the ball to curve in the direction of the swing. **8** *pop music* a catchy or easily memorized phrase. ▻ *verb* (***hooked, hooking***) **1** to catch, fasten or hold with or as if with a hook. **2** to form into or with a hook. **3** to ensnare, trap, attract, etc. **4 a** *golf, cricket* to hit (the ball) out round the other side of one's body, to the left if the player is right-handed, and vice versa; **b** said of the ball: to curve in this direction. **5** in a rugby scrum: to catch (the ball) with the foot and kick it backwards. **6** *tr & intr* to bend or curve. **7** *tr & intr* to pull abruptly. ● **by hook or by crook** by some means or other. ● **hook and eye** a device used to fasten clothes by means of a hook that catches in a loop or eye. ● **hook, line and sinker** *colloq* completely. ● **off the hook 1** *colloq* out of trouble or difficulty; excused of the blame for something. **2** said of a telephone receiver: not on its rest, and so not able to receive incoming calls. ⌚ Anglo-Saxon *hoc*.

■ **hook up** or **hook something up** to fasten or be fastened to something else by means of a hook or hooks.

hookah or **hooka** /ˈhʊkə/ ▻ *noun* (***hookahs*** or ***hookas***) a tobacco-pipe used by Turks, Arabs, etc consisting of a tube which passes through water, used to cool the smoke before it is inhaled. ⌚ 18c: from Arabic *huqqah* bowl.

hooked /hʊkt/ ▻ *adj* **1** curved like a hook. **2** *colloq* physically or mentally dependent. ● **hooked on something 1** addicted to (a drug, activity or indulgence). **2** obsessively interested or involved in it.

hooker /ˈhʊkə(r)/ *noun* **1** someone or something that hooks. **2** *colloq* a prostitute. **3** *rugby* the forward whose job is to hook the ball out of a scrum.

Hooke's law /hʊks —/ ▻ *noun physics* the law which states that, for an elastic material within its elastic limit, the extension produced by stretching the material is proportional to the force that is producing the extension. Above the elastic limit permanent deformation of the material occurs. ⌚ 19c: named after the English physicist Robert Hooke (1635–1703).

hookey or **hooky** /ˈhʊkɪ/ ▻ *noun* (*always* **play hookey**) *N Amer colloq* to be absent from school without permission; to play truant. ⌚ 19c.

hook-up ▻ *noun* a temporary link-up of different broadcasting stations, especially the radio and a television channel, for a special transmission. ⌚ Early 20c.

hookworm ▻ *noun* a parasitic worm with hook-like parts in its mouth, which lives in the intestines of animals and humans, causing mild anaemia. ⌚ Early 20c.

hooligan /ˈhuːlɪgən/ ▻ *noun* a violent, destructive or badly-behaved youth. ● **hooliganism** *noun*. ⌚ 19c: from *Houlihan* an Irish surname.

hoop /huːp/ ▻ *noun* **1** a thin ring of metal, wood, etc, especially those used round casks. **2** anything similar to this in shape. **3** a large ring made of light wood or plastic, used for amusement, eg rolled along the ground, whirled round the body, or used by circus performers, etc to jump through. **4** an iron arch through which the ball is hit in croquet. **5** a ring for holding a skirt wide. **6** a horizontal band of colour running round a sportsperson's shirt. ▻ *verb* (***hooped, hooping***) to bind or surround with a hoop or hoops. ● **go** or **be put through the hoops** *colloq* to undergo or suffer a thorough and difficult test or ordeal. ◷ Anglo-Saxon *hop*.

hoop-la /ˈhuːplɑː/ ▻ *noun* (***hoop-las***) **1** *Brit* a fairground game in which small rings are thrown at objects, with the thrower winning any objects hooked by the rings. **2** *US slang* pointless activity or nonsense; a nuisance. ◷ Early 20c: from French *houp la!* an order for someone to move.

hoopoe /ˈhuːpuː/ ▻ *noun* (***hoopoes***) a crested bird with salmon-coloured feathers and black-and-white striped wings, occasionally seen in Britain. ◷ 17c: from Latin *upupa*, imitating its cry.

hoorah and **hooray** see under HURRAH

Hooray Henry /ˈhureɪ ˈhenrɪ/ ▻ *noun* (***Hooray Henrys*** or ***Hooray Henries***) *slang* a young middle- or upper-class man with a loud voice and an ineffectual manner.

hoosegow or **hoosgow** /ˈhuːsgaʊ/ ▻ *noun, US slang* a prison or jail. ◷ Early 20c: from Spanish *jusgado* prison.

hoot /huːt/ ▻ *noun* **1** the call of an owl, or a similar sound. **2** the sound of a car horn, siren, steam whistle, etc, or a similar sound. **3** a loud shout of laughter, scorn or disapproval. **4** *colloq* a hilarious person, event or thing. ▻ *verb* (***hooted, hooting***) **1** *intr* said of an owl: to make a hoot. **2** to sound (a car horn, etc). **3** *intr* said of a person: to shout or laugh loudly, often expressing disapproval, scorn, etc. **4** to force (a performer) offstage by hooting. ● **not care** or **give a hoot** or **two hoots** *colloq* not to care at all. ◷ 13c: probably imitating the sound.

hootch see HOOCH

hootenanny or **hootnanny** /ˈhuːtnanɪ, ˌhʊt-/ ▻ *noun* (***hootenannies*** or ***hootnannies***) *US colloq* an informal concert of folk music. ◷ Early 20c.

hooter /ˈhuːtə(r)/ ▻ *noun* **1** a person or thing that makes a hooting sound. **2** *Brit colloq* a nose.

Hoover /ˈhuːvə(r)/ ▻ *noun, trademark* (*also* **hoover**) a VACUUM CLEANER. ▻ *verb* (**hoover**) (***hoovered, hoovering***) *tr & intr* to clean (a carpet, etc) with or as if with a vacuum cleaner. ◷ Early 20c: named after William Henry Hoover (1849–1932), the US industrialist who patented it.

hooves see HOOF

hop[1] /hɒp/ ▻ *verb* (***hopped, hopping***) **1** *intr* said of a person: to jump up and down on one leg, especially forwards as a form of movement. **2** *intr* said of certain small birds, animals and insects: to move by jumping on both or all legs simultaneously. **3** to walk lame; limp. **4** to jump over something. **5** *intr* (*usually* **hop in, out**, *etc*) *colloq* to move in a lively or agile way in the specified direction. **6** (*usually* **hop over**) *colloq* to make a short journey, especially by air. ▻ *noun* **1** an act of hopping; a jump on one leg. **2** *colloq* a distance travelled in an aeroplane without stopping; a short journey by air. **3** *old use, colloq* an informal dance. ● **catch someone on the hop** *colloq* to catch them unawares or by surprise. ● **hop it** *Brit slang* to take oneself off; to leave. ● **hopping mad** *colloq* very angry or furious. ● **hop, skip** (or **step**) **and jump 1** a jump on one leg, a skip, and a leap with both legs. 2 as an athletic event: the former name for the triple jump. ● **keep someone on the hop** to keep someone busy, active or alert. ● **on the hop** in a state of restless activity. ◷ Anglo-Saxon *hoppian* to dance.

hop[2] /hɒp/ ▻ *noun* **1** a tall perennial climbing plant or vine of the mulberry family, grown for its green cone-shaped female flowers, which are used to give a bitter flavour to beer. **2** (*usually* **hops**) **a** the female flower of this plant, which contains the bitter flavours used in brewing and in medicine; **b** *US slang* any narcotic drug, especially opium. ▻ *verb* (***hopped, hopping***) **1** *intr* to pick or gather hops. **2** to flavour (beer) with hops. ● **hopper** *noun* a person or machine that picks or gathers hops. ● **hopping** *noun* the time of the hop harvest. ● **hoppy** *adj* smelling or tasting of hops. ◷ 15c as *hoppe*, from Dutch.

hope /hoʊp/ ▻ *noun* **1** a desire for something, with some confidence or expectation of success. **2** a person, thing or event that gives one good reason for hope. **3** a reason for justifying the belief that the thing desired will still occur. **4** something desired or hoped for □ *His hope is that he will pass his exams.* ▻ *verb* (***hoped, hoping***) **1** (*also* **hope for something**) to wish or desire that something may happen, especially with some reason to believe or expect that it will. **2** *intr* to have confidence. ● **hope against hope** to continue hoping when all reason for it has gone; to hope in vain. ● **Some hope!** or **what a hope!** or **not a hope!** *colloq* there's no chance at all that what has been said will happen. ◷ Anglo-Saxon *hopa*.

hope chest ▻ *noun, N Amer* a place, often a trunk or chest, for a woman to store her things for her marriage; a bottom drawer. ◷ Early 20c.

hopeful ▻ *adj* **1** feeling, or full of, hope. **2** having qualities that excite hope. **3** likely to succeed; promising. ▻ *noun* a person, especially a young one, who is ambitious or expected to succeed. ● **hopefulness** *noun*.

hopefully ▻ *adverb* **1** in a hopeful way. **2** *colloq* it is to be hoped, if all goes according to plan.

hopefully

● In sense 2, **hopefully** is called a 'sentence adverb', because it qualifies the whole sentence and not just one word or phrase in it □ *Hopefully, it was all over now and he'd be able to take a spot of leave.* There are many sentence adverbs, eg **clearly, honestly, really, thankfully, undoubtedly, usually**, etc, as you will see in these examples □ *Clearly, fact and fiction became intermingled* □ *I've honestly no idea* □ *Well, it isn't a lot, really* □ *Thankfully, at weekends Clare felt almost normal again.*

● Most of these uses pass unnoticed, but for some reason many people dislike this use of **hopefully**. It may have something to do with its meaning (with its suggestion of likely disappointment) and the fact that it is originally North American. It is not usually ambiguous, except in rare cases like the following (where intonation usually clarifies) □ *They were hopefully attempting a reconciliation.*

☆ RECOMMENDATION: avoid it if you are talking to someone who is likely to be precise about the use of language.

hopeless ▻ *adj* **1** without hope. **2** having no reason or cause to expect a good outcome or success. **3** *colloq* having no ability; incompetent □ *He is hopeless at maths.* **4** said of a disease, etc: incurable. **5** said of a problem: unresolvable. ● **hopelessly** *adverb*. ● **hopelessness** *noun*.

hophead ▻ *noun, derog, slang* a drug addict.

hopper[1] ▻ *noun* **1** a person, animal or insect that hops. **2** *especially US* a grasshopper. **3** *especially agric* a funnel-like device used to feed material into a container below it, or on to the ground. **4** a barge with an opening in the bottom for discharging refuse. **5** an open railway wagon with an opening in the bottom for discharging its cargo. **6** a container in which seed-corn is carried for sowing. **7** *computing, formerly* a device for holding and passing on punched cards to a feed mechanism which then interprets them.

hopper[2] see under HOP[2]

hopsack and **hopsacking** ▻ *noun* **1** a coarse fabric made from hemp and jute, used to make sacking for hops. **2** a woollen or cotton fabric with a roughened surface, used to make clothing. ◷ 19c.

hopscotch ▻ *noun* a children's game in which players take turns at throwing a stone into one of a series of squares marked on the ground, and hopping in the others around it in order to fetch it. ◷ Early 19c: HOP[1] + SCOTCH[1].

Horatian /həˈreɪʃən/ ▻ *adj* referring or relating to Horace, the Latin poet (65–8 BC), or to his verse or its style.

horde /hɔːd/ ▻ *noun* **1** *often derog* a huge crowd or multitude, especially a noisy one. **2** a group of nomads; a migratory tribe. ▻ *verb* (***horded***, ***hording***) *intr* **1** to come together to form a horde. **2** to live together as a horde. ⓒ 16c: from Turkish *ordu* camp.

horde

There is sometimes a spelling confusion between **horde** and **hoard**.

horizon /həˈraɪzən/ ▻ *noun* **1** the line at which the Earth and the sky seem to meet. Also called **sensible horizon**, **apparent horizon** or **visible horizon**. **2** the plane through the Earth's centre parallel to the sensible horizon. Also called **rational horizon**. **3** *astron* the large circle in which the rational horizon meets the heavens. **4** a level of strata characterized by: **a** *geol* some particular fossil or fossils; **b** *soil science* different physical properties of the soil; **c** *archaeol* artefacts from a particular culture or period. **5** the limit of a person's knowledge, interests or experience. ⓒ 14c: from Greek *horizon kyklos* limiting circle, from *horizein* to limit.

horizontal /hɒrɪˈzɒntəl/ ▻ *adj* **1** at right angles to vertical. **2** relating to or parallel to the horizon; level or flat. **3** measured in the plane of the horizon. **4** applying equally to all members of a group or aspects of a situation. ▻ *noun* a horizontal line, position or object. • **horizontally** *adverb*. ⓒ 16c: French.

horizontal bar ▻ *noun, gymnastics* a raised steel bar used for swinging and vaulting exercises.

hormonal /hɔːˈmoʊnəl/ ▻ *adj* **1** relating to or involving hormones. **2** referring to something that is or behaves as a hormone.

hormone /ˈhɔːmoʊn/ ▻ *noun* **1** a substance secreted by an endocrine gland, and carried in the bloodstream to organs and tissues located elsewhere in the body, where it performs a specific physiological action. **2** an artificially manufactured chemical compound which has the same function as such a substance. **3** a substance in plants which influences their growth and development. ⓒ Early 20c: from Greek *horman* to stimulate.

hormone replacement therapy ▻ *noun, medicine* (abbreviation **HRT**) a treatment whereby an imbalance in levels of any endogenous hormone is rectified by administering an exogenous agent, but especially for post-menopausal women lacking oestrogenic hormones. ⓒ 20c.

horn /hɔːn/ ▻ *noun* **1** one of a pair of hard hollow outgrowths, usually pointed, on the heads of many ruminant animals, such as cattle, sheep, etc. **2** any similar structure growing on the head of another animal, such as the growth on the snout of a rhinoceros, a male deer's antlers, or a snail's tentacle. **3** the bony substance (KERATIN) of which horns are made. **4** something resembling a horn in shape. **5** a horn-shaped area of land or sea. **6** an object made of horn, or an equivalent of horn, eg a drinking vessel. **7** *music* a wind instrument originally made from horn, now usually made of brass, specifically: **a** *Brit* a FRENCH HORN; **b** *jazz* any wind instrument. **8** an apparatus for making a warning sound, especially on motor vehicles. **9** one of a pair of outgrowths believed to spring from a cuckold's forehead. **10** *Brit slang* an erection of the penis. **11** *US slang* a telephone. ▻ *verb* (***horned***, ***horning***) **1** to fit with a horn or horns. **2** to injure or gore with a horn or horns. ▻ *adj* made of horn. • **on the horns of a dilemma** having to make a choice between two equally undesirable alternatives. • **pull** or **draw in one's horns 1** to control one's strong emotions. **2** to restrict or confine one's activities, especially spending, etc. ⓒ Anglo-Saxon.

■ **horn in** *slang* to interrupt or butt in.

hornbeam ▻ *noun* a tree similar to a beech, with hard tough wood. ⓒ 16c: so called because of its hard wood.

hornbill ▻ *noun* a tropical bird with a horn-like growth on its beak. ⓒ 18c.

hornblende /ˈhɔːnblɛnd/ ▻ *noun, geol* a dark green or black mineral that is a major component of many metamorphic and igneous rocks, including granite, and consists primarily of calcium, magnesium and iron. • **hornblendic** *adj*. ⓒ 18c: German, from *Horn* horn + BLENDE sense 1.

hornbook ▻ *noun, historical* a first book for children, consisting of a single page of basic information, such as the alphabet and numbers, and covered with a thin plate of semitransparent horn for protection. ⓒ 16c.

horned /hɔːnd, ˈhɔːnɪd/ ▻ *adj* having a horn or horns, or something shaped like a horn.

horned toad ▻ *noun* **1** a spiny American lizard that lives in desert areas. **2** a S American toad with a bony shield on its back.

hornet /ˈhɔːnɪt/ ▻ *noun* any of several large social wasps, with a brown and yellow striped body, and a more acute sting. • **stir up a hornet's** or **hornets' nest** to do something that causes a strong or hostile reaction. ⓒ Anglo-Saxon *hyrnet*.

hornfels /ˈhɔːnfɛls/ ▻ *noun, geol* any of various hard fine-grained rocks that are formed from sedimentary rocks under heat and/or pressure. ⓒ 19c: German, from *Horn* horn + *Fels* rock.

horn of plenty see CORNUCOPIA 1

hornpipe ▻ *noun* **1** an old Welsh musical instrument, often with a mouthpiece or bell made from horn. **2 a** a lively solo jig, conventionally regarded as popular amongst sailors; **b** the music for this dance. ⓒ 14c.

hornswoggle /ˈhɔːnswɒgəl/ ▻ *verb* (***hornswoggled***, ***hornswoggling***) *originally US slang* to trick, deceive or cheat. ⓒ 19c.

horny /ˈhɔːnɪ/ ▻ *adj* (***hornier***, ***horniest***) **1** relating to or resembling horn, especially in hardness. **2** *slang* sexually excited.

horologic /hɒrəˈlɒdʒɪk/ and **horological** ▻ *adj* **1** relating or referring to horology. **2** measuring time. ⓒ 16c.

horologist /hɒˈrɒlədʒɪst/ and **horologer** ▻ *noun* **1** an expert in horology. **2** a maker of clocks and watches.

horology /hɒˈrɒlədʒɪ/ ▻ *noun* the art of measuring time or of making clocks and watches. ⓒ 19c: from Greek *hora* hour.

horoscope /ˈhɒrəskoʊp/ ▻ *noun* **1** an astrologer's prediction of someone's future based on the position of the stars and planets at the time of their birth. **2** a map or diagram showing the positions of the stars and planets at a particular moment in time, eg at the time of someone's birth. • **horoscopic** *adj*. ⓒ 16c in this form and sense 2; Anglo-Saxon in its Latin form *horoscopus*, meaning 'ASCENDENT': from Greek *hora* hour + *skopos* observer.

horoscopy /hɒˈrɒskəpɪ/ ▻ *noun* **1** the art of predicting someone's future from their horoscope. **2** the aspect of the stars and planets at a particular moment in time, eg at the time of someone's birth. ⓒ 17c.

horrendous /hɒˈrɛndəs/ ▻ *adj* causing great shock, fear or terror; dreadful or horrifying. • **horrendously** *adverb*. • **horrendousness** *noun*. ⓒ 17c: from Latin *horrendus*, shuddering, from *horrere* to shudder.

horrible /ˈhɒrɪbəl/ ▻ *adj* **1** causing horror, dread or fear. **2** *colloq* unpleasant, detestable or foul. • **horribleness** *noun*. ⓒ 14c: from Latin *horribilis*.

horribly /ˈhɒrɪblɪ/ ▻ *adverb* **1** in a horrible way. **2** badly; very or extremely □ *The plot went horribly wrong.*

horrid /ˈhɒrɪd/ ▻ *adj* **1** revolting; detestable or nasty. **2** *colloq* unpleasant; distasteful. **3** spiteful or inconsiderate. • **horridly** *adverb*. • **horridness** *noun*. ⓒ 16c: from Latin *horridus*.

horrific /həˈrɪfɪk/ ▻ *adj* **1** causing horror; terrible or frightful. **2** *colloq* very bad; awful. • **horrifically** *adverb*. ⓒ 17c: from Latin *horror* horror + *facere* to make.

horrify /ˈhɒrɪfaɪ/ ▻ *verb* (***horrified, horrifying***) to shock greatly; to cause a reaction of horror. • **horrified** *adj*. • **horrifying** *adj* causing horror. • **horrifyingly** *adverb*. ⓒ 18c: from Latin *horror* HORROR + *facere* to make.

horripilation /hɒrɪpɪˈleɪʃən/ ▻ *noun* a contraction of the skin muscles, often induced by cold, horror, etc, causing the erection of hairs and gooseflesh. • **horripilant** /hɒˈrɪpɪlənt/ *adj*. ⓒ 17c: from Latin *horripilatio*, from *horrere* to bristle and *pilus* a hair.

horror /ˈhɒrə(r)/ ▻ *noun* **1** intense fear, loathing or disgust. **2** intense dislike or hostility. **3** someone or something causing horror. **4** *colloq* a bad, distasteful or ridiculous person or thing. **5** *as adj* said of literature, films, etc: based on horrifying, frightening or bloodcurdling themes □ *a horror film*. • **the horrors** *colloq* a fit of extreme anxiety and fear. ⓒ 14c: Latin, meaning 'a shudder with fear'.

horror-stricken and **horror-struck** ▻ *adj* shocked, horrified or dismayed.

hors de combat / *French* ɔrdəkɔba/ ▻ *adverb* unfit to fight; disabled. ⓒ 18c: French, literally 'out of the fight'.

hors d'oeuvre /ɔː ˈdɜːvr/ ▻ *noun* (*plural* ***hor d'oeuvres*** or ***hors d'oeuvres***) a savoury appetizer, usually served at the beginning of a meal, to whet the appetite. ⓒ 18c: French, literally 'out of the work'.

horse /hɔːs/ ▻ *noun* **1** a large hoofed mammal, with a slender head, a long neck, a mane and long legs, used in many countries for pulling and carrying loads, and for riding. **2** an adult male of this species. See also MARE1, FOAL. **3** cavalry. **4** *gymnastics* a piece of apparatus used for vaulting over, etc. **5** *in compounds* any of various types of supporting apparatus □ *clothes-horse* □ *saw-horse*. **6** *mining* a barren area of land interrupting a lode. **7** *slang* heroin. ▻ *verb* (***horsed, horsing***) **1** to mount or put someone on, or as if on, a horse. **2** to provide with a horse. **3** *intr* to climb or travel on horseback. • **flog a dead horse** see under FLOG. • **gift horse** see under GIFT. • **high horse** see under HIGH. • **hold your horses** wait a moment; not so fast or hasty. • **horse of a different colour** a person or matter of a different kind □ *Most of her friends are quiet, but he's a horse of a different colour*. • **horses for courses** a phrase literally indicating that a racehorse will perform best on a racecourse particularly suited to it, but applied figuratively to people. • **put the cart before the horse** see under CART. • **straight from the horse's mouth** directly from a well-informed and reliable source. • **willing horse** a willing and obliging worker. ⓒ Anglo-Saxon as *hors*.

■ **horse about** or **around** *colloq* to fool about.

horseback ▻ *noun* the back of a horse, *especially* **on horseback**.

horse block ▻ *noun* a block or stage, often made from stone or wood, used for mounting and dismounting horses.

horse-box ▻ *noun* **1** a closed trailer pulled by a car or train, designed to carry horses. **2** *facetious* a church pew with high sides.

horse brass ▻ *noun* a brass ornament, originally used for securing the harness to the horse.

horse chestnut see under CHESTNUT

horseflesh ▻ *noun* **1** the edible flesh or meat of a horse. **2** horses as a group.

horsefly ▻ *noun* any of several large flies that bite horses and cattle. Also called **cleg**.

horsehair ▻ *noun* **1** a hair or mass of hairs taken from a horse's mane or tail. **2** a fabric woven from horsehair. ▻ *adj* made of or filled with horsehair □ *a horsehair mattress*.

Horsehead Nebula ▻ *noun, astron* a dark thick cloud of dust and gas in the constellation of Orion, resembling a horse's head and neck, being conspicuous because of its much brighter background.

horse latitudes ▻ *plural noun, naut* either or both of the two zones in the Atlantic Ocean, at 30°N and 30°S noted for their long calm periods of weather.

horse laugh ▻ *noun* a loud coarse laugh.

horseleech ▻ *noun* a large type of freshwater leech. ⓒ 15c: *horsleych*.

horse mackerel ▻ *noun* **1** the SCAD. **2** the tuna, or various related fish.

horseman and **horsewoman** ▻ *noun* **1** a horse rider. **2** a person skilled in riding and managing horses. • **horsemanship** *noun*.

horse mushroom ▻ *noun* a type of large edible mushroom.

horseplay ▻ *noun* rough boisterous play.

horsepower ▻ *noun* (abbreviation **HP** or **hp**) **1** the power exerted by a horse. **2** in the imperial system: the unit of power, replaced in the SI system by the watt, with one horsepower equal to 745.7 watts.

horse-race ▻ *noun* a race of horses against each other, each ridden by a jockey. • **horse-racing** *noun*.

horseradish ▻ *noun* a plant with a long white pungent root, which is crushed and used to make a savoury sauce that is usually eaten with beef.

horse sense ▻ *noun, colloq* plain common sense.

horseshoe ▻ *noun* **1** a piece of curved iron nailed to the bottom of a horse's hoof to protect the foot. **2** anything shaped like a horseshoe, especially as a symbol of good luck.

horseshoe crab ▻ *noun, zool* a marine invertebrate, not a true crab, with a heavily armoured horseshoe-shaped body and a long pointed tail. Also called **king crab**.

horsetail ▻ *noun* **1** the tail of a horse. **2** a plant with hollow jointed stems, with whorls of small, scale-like leaves at regular intervals.

horse-trading ▻ *noun* hard bargaining.

horse trials ▻ *noun* a training competition combining the three main equestrian disciplines: dressage, showjumping and cross-country.

horsewhip ▻ *noun* a long whip, used for driving or managing horses. ▻ *verb* to beat, especially severely, with a horsewhip.

horsewoman see HORSEMAN

horsey or **horsy** /ˈhɔːsɪ/ ▻ *adj* (***horsier, horsiest***) **1** referring or relating to horses. **2** *often derog* said of people: like a horse, especially in appearance. **3** *Brit colloq* very interested in or devoted to horses, horse-racing or -breeding. • **horsiness** *noun*.

horst /hɔːst/ ▻ *noun, geol* a block of the Earth's crust that has remained in position while the ground around it has subsided, due to one or more faults in the surrounding area. ⓒ 19c: German, meaning 'thicket'.

hortative /ˈhɔːtətɪv/ and **hortatory** /ˈhɔːtətərɪ, hɔːˈteɪtərɪ/ ▻ *adj* giving advice or encouragement. • **hortatively** or **hortatorily** *adverb*. • **hortation** *noun*. ⓒ 16c: from Latin *hortari* to incite to action.

horticulture /ˈhɔːtɪkʌltʃə(r)/ ▻ *noun* **1** the intensive cultivation of fruit, vegetables, flowers and ornamental shrubs. **2** the art of gardening or cultivation. •

horticultural *adj.* • **horticulturist** *noun.* ⓒ 17c: from Latin *hortus* garden + *cultura* cultivation.

Hos. ▷ *abbreviation* Book of the Bible: Hosea. See table at BIBLE.

hosanna /hoʊ'zanə/ ▷ *noun* (***hosannas***) ▷ *exclamation* a shout of adoration and praise to God. ⓒ Anglo-Saxon *osanna*: from Hebrew *hoshiah nna* save now, I pray.

hose[1] /hoʊz/ ▷ *noun* (*also* **hosepipe**) a flexible tube for conveying water, eg for watering plants. ▷ *verb* (***hosed***, ***hosing***) (*often* **hose something down**) to direct water at it or clean it with a hose. ⓒ Anglo-Saxon *hosa*.

hose[2] /hoʊz/ ▷ *noun* (***hose*** or (*archaic*) ***hosen***) a covering for the legs and feet, such as stockings, socks and tights. ⓒ Anglo-Saxon *hosa*.

hose reel ▷ *noun* a large revolving drum for storing a hose.

hosier /'hoʊzɪə(r)/ ▷ *noun* a person who makes or deals in hosiery. ⓒ 15c.

hosiery /'hoʊzɪərɪ/ ▷ *noun* **1** stockings, socks and tights collectively. **2** knitted underwear. ⓒ 18c.

hospice /'hɒspɪs/ ▷ *noun* **1** a home or institution that specializes in the care of the terminally ill, and provides support for their families. **2** *historical* a HOSPITAL (sense 3). ⓒ 19c: from Latin *hospes* guest.

hospitable /hɒ'spɪtəbəl, 'hɒspɪtəbəl/ ▷ *adj* **1** generous and welcoming towards guests. **2** showing kindness to strangers. • **hospitableness** *noun.* • **hospitably** *adverb.* ⓒ 16c: from Latin *hospitare* to receive as a guest, from *hospes* guest.

hospital /'hɒspɪtəl/ ▷ *noun* **1** an institution, staffed by doctors and nurses, for the treatment and care of people who are sick or injured. **2** *archaic* a charitable institution providing shelter for the old and destitute, and education for the young. **3** *historical* a hostel offering lodging and entertainment for travellers, especially one kept by monks or a religious order. ⓒ 13c: from Latin *hospitale* a place for receiving guests, from *hospes* guest.

hospitality /hɒspɪ'talɪtɪ/ ▷ *noun* (***hospitalities***) the friendly welcome and entertainment of guests or strangers, which usually includes offering them food and drink. ⓒ 14c: from Latin *hospitalitas*, from *hospes* guest.

hospitalize or **hospitalise** /'hɒspɪtəlaɪz/ ▷ *verb* (***hospitalized***, ***hospitalizing***) **1** to take or admit someone to hospital for treatment. **2** to injure someone so badly that hospital treatment is necessary. • **hospitalization** *noun* **1** being hospitalized. **2** the period during which someone is in hospital. ⓒ Early 20c.

hospitaller or (*US*) **hospitaler** /'hɒspɪtələ(r)/ ▷ *noun* **1** a member of a religious order which does charity work, especially for the sick in hospitals. **2** (**Hospitaller**) a member of the Knights of St John, an order founded when it built a hospital for pilgrims in Jerusalem in the 11c. ⓒ 14c: from Latin *hospitale*, from *hospes* guest.

host[1] /hoʊst/ ▷ *noun* **1** someone who entertains guests or strangers in his or her own home. **2** *old use* an innkeeper or publican. **3** someone who introduces performers and participants, chairs discussions and debates, etc on a TV or radio show. **4** a place acting as a venue for an event or organization, usually with the implication of its involvement with the event and its welcoming of the participants. **5** *biol* a plant or animal on which a parasite lives and feeds, whether causing harm or not, for all or part of its life. **6** *medicine* the recipient of a tissue graft or organ transplant. ▷ *verb* (***hosted***, ***hosting***) to be the host of (an event, programme, show, etc). ⓒ 13c: from French *hoste*, from Latin *hospes* guest.

host[2] /hoʊst/ ▷ *noun* **1** a very large number; a multitude. **2** *old use* an army. ⓒ 13c: from French *hoste*, from Latin *hostis* enemy.

host[3] /hoʊst/ ▷ *noun* (*often* **the Host**) *RC Church* the consecrated bread of the Eucharist, used in a Holy Communion service. ⓒ 14c: from French *oiste*, from Latin *hostia* victim.

hosta /'hɒstə/ ▷ *noun* (***hostas***) a perennial plant native to China and Japan, grown for its decorative ribbed leaves and spikes of tubular white or violet flowers. ⓒ 19c: named after Nicolaus Thomas Host (1761–1834), the Austrian botanist.

hostage /'hɒstɪdʒ/ ▷ *noun* **1** someone who is held prisoner as a guarantee or security that the captor's demands and conditions are carried out and fulfilled. **2** the condition of being a hostage. **3** any guarantee or security. • **hostages to fortune** the people and things most valued by someone, the loss of which would be particularly painful. ⓒ 13c: from French *otâge*, from Latin *obses*.

host computer ▷ *noun* a computer attached to and in control of a multi-terminal computer system, or one attached to a multi-computer network and able eg to provide access to a number of databases.

hostel /'hɒstəl/ ▷ *noun* **1** a residence providing shelter for the homeless, especially one run for charitable rather than for profitable purposes. **2** a residence for students or nurses, outside the confines of the college. **3** a YOUTH HOSTEL. ⓒ 13c: French, from Latin *hospes* guest.

hosteller or (*US*) **hosteler** /'hɒstələ(r)/ ▷ *noun* **1** someone who lives in or regularly uses a hostel, especially a youth hostel. **2** *archaic* the keeper of a hostel or inn. ⓒ 13c: from French *hostelier*.

hostelling ▷ *noun* the use of youth hostels when on holiday.

hostelry /'hɒstəlrɪ/ ▷ *noun* (***hostelries***) *old use, now facetious* an inn or public house. ⓒ 14c: as *hostelrye*, a variant of French *hostellerie*.

hostess /hoʊ'stɛs, 'hoʊstəs/ ▷ *noun* **1** a female host. **2** a woman employed as a man's companion for the evening at a night club, dance hall, etc. **3** *euphemistic* a prostitute. **4** an AIR HOSTESS. ⓒ 13c: from French *ostesse*.

hostess trolley ▷ *noun* a TROLLEY (sense 2) with electrically heated compartments so that a meal can be kept warm while it is brought to the dining table. ⓒ 1960s.

hostile /'hɒstaɪl; *US* 'hɑːstəl/ ▷ *adj* **1** expressing enmity, aggression or angry opposition. **2** relating or belonging to an enemy. **3** resistant or strongly opposed to something. **4** said of a place, conditions, atmosphere, etc: harsh, forbidding or inhospitable. **5** relating to or engaged in hostilities. • **hostilely** *adverb.* ⓒ 16c: from Latin *hostilis*, from *hostis* enemy.

hostility /hɒ'stɪlɪtɪ/ ▷ *noun* (***hostilities***) **1** enmity, aggression or angry opposition. **2** (**hostilities**) acts of warfare; battles. ⓒ 14c: from Latin *hostilitas*.

hot ▷ *adj* (***hotter***, ***hottest***) **1** having or producing a great deal of heat; having a high temperature. **2** having a higher temperature than is normal or desirable. **3** said of food: spicy or fiery. **4** easily made angry; excitable or passionate ◻ ***a hot temper.*** **5** *slang* sexually excited or lustful. **6** said of a contest or fight: intense and animated. **7** said of news: recent, fresh and of particular interest. **8** strongly favoured ◻ ***a hot favourite.*** **9** said of jazz music: having strong and exciting rhythms, with complex improvisations. **10** said of a colour: bright and fiery. **11** *slang* said of goods: recently stolen or illegally acquired. **12** said of a scent in hunting: fresh and strong, suggesting the quarry is not far ahead. **13** *slang* said of information: up-to-date and reliable ◻ ***a hot tip.*** **14** *colloq* said of a situation: difficult, unpleasant, or dangerous ◻ ***make life hot for him.*** **15** *slang* highly radioactive. **16** in certain games, etc: very close to guessing the answer or finding the person or thing sought. ▷ *adverb* in a hot way; hotly ◻ ***a dish served hot.*** • **hotly** *adverb* **1** with great heat. **2** excitedly or passionately. ▷ *verb* (***hotted***, ***hotting***) *colloq* to heat something. • **go** or **sell like hot cakes** to sell or disappear rapidly; to be extremely popular. • **have** or **get the hots for someone** *slang* to have a strong sexual desire or attraction for them. • **hot and bothered** *colloq* anxious and confused; agitated. • **hot on something** interested in, skilled at or well-informed about it. • **hot on the heels of someone** *colloq* following or pursuing them closely. • **hot under the collar** *colloq* indignant or annoyed; uncomfortable. • **in hot pursuit** chasing as fast or as closely as one can. • **hotness** *noun*. ⌚ Anglo-Saxon *hat*.

▪ **hot up** or **hot something up** to increase in excitement, energy, danger, etc.

hot air ▷ *noun, colloq* empty, unsubstantial or boastful talk.

hotbed ▷ *noun* **1** a glass-covered bed of earth heated by a layer of fermenting manure, to encourage rapid plant growth. **2** a place which has conditions allowing the rapid growth of something, especially something bad □ *a hotbed of discontent*.

hot-blooded ▷ *adj* having strong and passionate feelings; high-spirited.

hot chocolate see CHOCOLATE sense 3

hotchpotch /ˈhɒtʃpɒtʃ/ and **hodgepodge** /ˈhɒdʒpɒdʒ/ ▷ *noun* **1** a confused mass or jumble. **2** a mutton broth or stew, containing many different vegetables. ⌚ 15c: from French *hochepot*, from *hocher* to shake + POT.

hot cross bun ▷ *noun* a fruit bun marked with a pastry cross on top, customarily eaten on Good Friday.

hot date ▷ *noun* a planned social meeting, usually for the first time, especially with someone to whom one is sexually attracted.

hot dog ▷ *noun* a sausage in a long soft bread roll.

hot-dog ▷ *verb, intr chiefly US colloq* to perform clever manoeuvres such as spins and turns while skiing, surfing or skate-boarding. • **hot dogger** *noun* a person who performs such tricks. ⌚ 1960s.

hotel /hoʊˈtɛl, oʊˈtɛl/ ▷ *noun* **1** a commercial building providing accommodation, meals and other services to visitors for payment. **2** /hoʊˈtɛl/ (**Hotel**) *communications* in the NATO alphabet: the word used to denote the letter 'H' (see table at NATO ALPHABET). ⌚ 17c: from French *hostel*, from Latin *hospes* guest.

hotelier /hoʊˈtɛlɪeɪ/ ▷ *noun* a person who owns or manages a hotel.

hotfoot *colloq* ▷ *adverb* in haste; as fast as possible. ▷ *verb* (*usually* **hotfoot it**) to rush or hasten.

hot gospeller ▷ *noun* a loud and dynamic proclaimer of a strongly interactive religious faith. • **hot gospelling** *noun*.

hothead ▷ *noun* **1** an easily angered or agitated person. **2** an impetuous or headstrong person. • **hotheaded** *adj*. • **hotheadedness** *noun*.

hothouse ▷ *noun* **1** a greenhouse which is kept warm for growing tender or tropical plants. **2** any type of heated room used for drying something, especially one where pottery is placed before going into the kiln. **3** any establishment promoting a rapid development of skills, ideas, etc. **4** *as adj* said of a plant: suitable only for growing in a greenhouse; too delicate to exist in normal outdoor or indoor conditions.

hot key *computing* ▷ *noun* a key which activates a program when pressed, either alone or in combination with other keys.

hot line ▷ *noun* **1** a direct and exclusive telephone link between political leaders of governments, allowing prompt communication in an emergency. **2** an emergency telephone number for inquiries about a particular incident or accident.

hotly see under HOT

hot melt ▷ *noun* an adhesive that is applied while hot, and which sets as it cools. Also *as adj* □ *hot-melt glue*.

hot money ▷ *noun* funds or money transferred suddenly from one country to another to profit from better exchange rates and trading conditions.

HOTOL ▷ *abbreviation* horizontal take-off and landing. Compare VTOL.

hotplate ▷ *noun* **1** the flat top surface of a cooker on which food is cooked. **2** a portable heated surface for keeping food, dishes, etc hot.

hotpot ▷ *noun* chopped meat and vegetables, seasoned and covered with sliced potatoes, and cooked slowly in a sealed pot.

hot potato ▷ *noun, colloq* a difficult or controversial problem or situation.

hot rod ▷ *noun* a motor car modified for extra speed by removing non-essential items and increasing the engine power.

the hot seat ▷ *noun* **1** *colloq* an uncomfortable or difficult situation. **2** *N Amer slang* the electric chair.

hotshot ▷ *noun, chiefly US* a person who is, often boastfully or pretentiously, successful or skilful.

hot spot ▷ *noun* **1** an area of too high a temperature in an engine, etc. **2** *geol* an area of the earth where there is evidence of isolated volcanic activity due to hot material rising up through the mantle. **3** *colloq* a popular or trendy nightclub. **4** an area of potential trouble or conflict, especially political or military conflict. **5** an area of very high local radioactivity.

hot spring ▷ *noun, geol* a spring of water heated naturally underground, particularly in volcanic regions.

hot stuff ▷ *noun, colloq* **1** a person, object or performance of outstanding ability, excellence or importance. **2** a person who is sexually attractive or exciting.

hot-tempered ▷ *adj* easily angered or provoked.

Hottentot /ˈhɒtəntɒt/ ▷ *noun* (***Hottentots*** or ***Hottentot***) **1** a member of a pale-brown-skinned nomad people of SW Africa, now almost extinct. **2** the language spoken by this race of people. ⌚ 17c: Afrikaans.

hotted, **hotter** and **hottest** see under HOT

hotting ▷ *verb, present participle of* HOT. ▷ *noun, slang* the performing of stunts and skilful manoeuvres at high speed in a stolen car.

hot water ▷ *noun, colloq* trouble; bother □ *get into hot water*.

hot-water bottle ▷ *noun* a container, usually made of rubber, filled with hot water and used to warm beds, or sometimes parts of the body. ⌚ 19c.

hot-wire ▷ *verb, colloq* to start (a vehicle engine) by touching electrical wires together, rather than using the ignition switch.

hoummos and **houmus** see HUMMUS

hound /haʊnd/ ▷ *noun* **1** *colloq* a dog. **2** a type of dog used in hunting. **3** an assiduous hunter, tracker or seeker of anything. **4** *colloq* a despicable or contemptible man. **5** *often in compounds* **a** a hunting-dog □ *foxhound*; **b** an addict or devotee □ *news-hound*. **6** (**the hounds**) a pack of foxhounds. ▷ *verb* (***hounded***, ***hounding***) **1** to chase or bother relentlessly. **2** to set or urge on in chase. • **ride to hounds** to hunt foxes (on horseback). ⌚ Anglo-Saxon *hund*.

hound's-tongue ▷ *noun* a plant of the borage family, with tough tongue-shaped leaves. Also called **dog's-tongue**. ⌚ Anglo-Saxon *hundestunge*.

hound's-tooth ▷ *noun* a textile pattern of small broken checks. Also called **dog's-tooth**.

hour /ˈaʊə(r)/ ▷ *noun* **1** sixty minutes, or the twenty-fourth part of a day. **2** the time indicated by a clock or watch. **3** an occasion or a point in time □ *an early hour.* **4** a special occasion or point in time □ *his finest hour.* **5** (**hours**) the time allowed or fixed for a specified activity □ *office hours.* **6** the distance travelled in an hour □ *two hours away from the airport.* **7** a time for action □ *The hour has come.* **8** (**hours**) **a)** CANONICAL HOURS; **b)** BOOK OF HOURS. • **after hours** after CLOSING-TIME. • **at all hours** at irregular times, especially late at night. • **at the eleventh hour** at the last or latest moment. • **keep good hours** to lead a calm and regular life; to go to bed and rise early. • **on the hour** at exactly one, two, etc, o'clock □ *The train departs on the hour.* • **out of hours** before or after usual working hours. ⓘ 13c: from Greek *hora.*

hour-circle ▻ *noun, astron* a great circle passing through the celestial poles and through a specific object; the equivalent of a meridian.

hourglass ▻ *noun* **1** an instrument that measures time, consisting of a glass container on top of and connected to another by a narrow glass tube, and filled with sand that takes a certain amount of time, not necessarily an hour, to pass from one container to the other. **2** *as adj* curving in at the waist or middle like an hourglass □ *an hourglass figure.*

hour hand ▻ *noun* the hand on a clock or watch that indicates the hour.

houri /'hʊərɪ, 'haʊərɪ/ ▻ *noun* **1** a nymph in the Muslim Paradise. **2** any voluptuous and beautiful young woman. ⓘ 18c: from Arabic *hur*, plural of *haura* gazelle-eyed.

hourly /'aʊəlɪ/ ▻ *adj* **1** happening or done every hour. **2** measured by the hour □ *an hourly wage.* **3** frequent or constant □ *live in hourly fear of discovery.* ▻ *adverb* **1** every hour. **2** at any hour □ *expect news hourly.* **3** by the hour. **4** frequently.

house ▻ *noun* /haʊs/ **1** a building in which people, especially a single family, live. **2** the people living in such a building. **3** an inn or public house. **4** *in compounds* a building used for a specified purpose □ *an opera-house.* **5** **a** a business firm □ *a publishing house*; **b** *as adj* □ *the house journal.* **6** the audience in a theatre, a theatre itself or a performance given there. **7** (*often* **the House**) the legislative body that governs a country, especially either chamber in a bicameral system □ *the House of Commons* □ *the House of Lords.* **8** (**the House**) **a** in Oxford: Christ Church College; **b** in London: the Stock Exchange; **c** in London: the Houses of Parliament. **9** (**House**) a family, especially a noble or royal one □ *the House of Hanover.* **10** *astrol* one of the twelve divisions of the heavens. **11** *Brit* one of several divisions of pupils at a large school. **12** **a** a college or university building in which students live; **b** a building at a boarding-school in which pupils live. **13** a building in which members of a religious community live; a convent. **14** HOUSE MUSIC. ▻ *verb* /haʊz/ (***housed, housing***) **1** to provide with a house or similar shelter. **2** to store. **3** to protect by covering. • **bring the house down** *colloq* to evoke loud applause in a theatre; to be a great success. • **keep house** to manage a household. • **keep open house** to be hospitable or provide entertainment for all visitors. • **like a house on fire** *colloq* **1** very well □ *They get on like a house on fire.* **2** very quickly. • **on the house** said of food, drink, etc: at the expense of the manager or owner; free of charge. • **put** or **set one's house in order** to organize or settle one's affairs. • **safe as houses** see under SAFE. • **set up house** to begin one's own domestic life. ⓘ Anglo-Saxon *hus.*

house agent ▻ *noun* a person who arranges the buying, selling and leasing of houses.

house arrest ▻ *noun* confinement in one's own home, a hospital or other public place, instead of imprisonment.

houseboat ▻ *noun* a barge or boat, usually stationary, with a deck-cabin designed and built for living in.

housebound ▻ *adj* confined to one's house because of illness, responsibility to young children, etc.

housebreaker ▻ *noun* **1** a person who commits housebreaking. **2** a person whose job is demolishing old buildings.

housebreaking ▻ *noun* the act or process of unlawful breaking into and entering a house or building with the intention to steal.

housecoat ▻ *noun* a woman's long loose garment similar to a dressing-gown, worn in the home.

housecraft ▻ *noun* skill in domestic or household activities.

housefly ▻ *noun* a common fly often found in houses.

house guest ▻ *noun* a guest staying in a private house, usually for several nights.

household ▻ *noun* **1** the people who live together in a house, making up a family. **2** (**the Household**) the royal domestic establishment or household. ▻ *adj* relating to the house or family living there; domestic.

householder ▻ *noun* **1** the owner or tenant of a house. **2** the head of a family or household.

household name and **household word** ▻ *noun* a familiar name, word or saying.

house-hunt ▻ *verb, intr* to look for a house to live in, either to rent or to buy. • **house-hunter** *noun.* • **house-hunting** *noun*

house husband ▻ *noun* a man who looks after the house, his wife or partner, and the family instead of having a paid job. ⓘ 1950s: originally US.

housekeeper ▻ *noun* a person who is paid to manage a household's domestic arrangements.

housekeeping ▻ *noun* **1** the management of a household's domestic arrangements. **2** money set aside to pay for this. **3** *computing* operations carried out on or within a computer program or system ensuring its efficient functioning.

house leek ▻ *noun* a plant of the stonecrop family with succulent leaves and pink flowers, often found growing on roofs. ⓘ 14c as *howsleke.*

house lights ▻ *plural noun* the lights that illuminate the auditorium of a cinema, theatre, etc.

housemaid ▻ *noun* a maid employed to keep a house clean and tidy.

housemaid's knee ▻ *noun* inflammation of the sac between the kneecap and the skin, caused by prolonged kneeling.

houseman ▻ *noun* a recently qualified doctor holding a junior resident post in a hospital to complete their training.

house martin ▻ *noun* a type of black and white swallow with a short forked tail, that often builds nests on house walls.

housemaster and **housemistress** ▻ *noun* in Britain: a male or female teacher in charge of a house in a school, especially a boarding-school.

house music ▻ *noun* (*often* **House music**) a style of DANCE MUSIC that has developed from 1980s disco music, is produced electronically and often incorporates edited fragments of other recordings. ⓘ 1980s: from ACID HOUSE.. Often shortened to HOUSE.

the House of Commons ▻ *noun* in the UK and Canada: the lower elected assembly in parliament, or the building where this meets.

house of correction ▻ *noun, formerly* a jail for those guilty of minor crimes.

house of God, **house of prayer** and **house of worship** ▻ *noun* a place used specifically for holy worship and prayer.

house of ill repute ▻ *noun* a brothel.

the House of Keys ▻ *noun* in the Isle of Man: the elected chamber of the Manx parliament; the Tynwald.

the House of Lords ▻ *noun* in the UK: the non-elected upper assembly in parliament, made up of peers and bishops (see PEER[1]), and also constituting the highest court in the UK. Also called **the Lords**.

the House of Representatives ▻ *noun* **1** in the US: the lower assembly of the United States Congress, whose members are elected every two years by the population. **2** similar assembly elsewhere.

house-parent ▻ *noun* a man or woman in charge of children in an institution.

house party ▻ *noun* a group of guests staying in a private house for several days, especially in the country.

houseplant ▻ *noun* a plant that may be grown indoors as decoration.

house-proud ▻ *adj* taking an often excessive amount of pride in the condition and appearance of one's house.

houseroom ▻ *noun* room in one's house for accommodating someone or something.

house-sit ▻ *verb, intr* to look after someone's house by living in it while they are away on holiday, etc. • **house-sitting** *noun*.

housetop ▻ *noun* (*usually* **housetops**) the roof of a house, especially seen in a row against the skyline. • **shout something from the housetops** to announce it loudly and publicly.

housetrain ▻ *verb* to train (a pet, particularly a young one) to urinate and defecate outside or in a special tray, etc. • **housetrained** *adj*.

house-warming ▻ *noun* a party given to celebrate moving into a new house.

housewife /'haʊswaɪf/ ▻ *noun* **1** a woman who looks after the house, her husband or partner, and the family, and who often does not have a paid job outside the home. **2** /'hʌzɪf/ a pocket sewing-kit. • **housewifely** *adj* **1** thrifty; neat and tidy. **2** like or suitable for a housewife. • **housewifery** /haʊs'wɪfərɪ/ *noun* the management of domestic affairs. ⌚ 13c.

housework ▻ *noun* the work involved in keeping a house clean and tidy.

housey-housey /haʊzɪ'haʊzɪ/ ▻ *noun* BINGO.

housing[1] /'haʊzɪŋ/ ▻ *verb, present participle of* HOUSE. ▻ *noun* **1** houses and accommodation collectively. **2** the act, or process of providing housing for people. **3** anything designed to cover, contain or protect machinery.

housing[2] ▻ *noun* **1** an ornamental covering or saddle-cloth for a horse. **2** (**housings**) the ornaments or trappings of a horse. ⌚ 14c: from French *houce* a mantle.

housing estate ▻ *noun* a planned residential estate, especially one built by a local authority, usually with its own shopping facilities.

housing scheme ▻ *noun* **1** the plan, especially by a local authority, to design, build and provide housing. **2** *Scottish* a local-authority housing estate.

hove see HEAVE

hovel /'hɒvəl/ ▻ *noun* **1** a small, dirty and dismal dwelling. **2** a shed, usually used for housing livestock. ⌚ 15c.

hover /'hɒvə(r)/ ▻ *verb* (**hovered**, **hovering**) *intr* **1 a** said of a bird, helicopter, etc: to remain in the air without moving in any direction; **b** *in compounds, describing* a vehicle or object which moves or rests on a cushion of air □ *hovercraft* □ *hovertrain*. **2** to linger, especially anxiously or nervously, near someone or something. **3** to be or remain undecided (usually between two options). ▻ *noun* **1** an act or state of hovering. **2** a condition of uncertainty or indecision. ⌚ 14c: from English *hoveren*.

hovercraft ▻ *noun* a vehicle which is able to move over land or water, supported by a cushion of down-driven air.

hoverfly ▻ *noun* a wasp-like fly that hovers and feeds on pollen and nectar.

hoverport ▻ *noun* a port for hovercraft.

how /haʊ/ ▻ *adverb* **1** in what way; by what means □ *How did it happen?* **2** to what extent □ *How old is he?* □ *How far is it?* **3** in what condition, especially of health □ *How is she feeling now?* **4** to what extent or degree is something good, successful, etc □ *How was your holiday?* **5** for what cause or reason; why □ *How can you behave like that?* **6** using whatever means are necessary □ *Do it how best you can.* ▻ *conj* **1** *colloq* that □ *He told me how he'd done it on his own.* **2** in which manner or condition □ *I don't care how you get there.* ▻ *noun* a manner or means of doing something □ *The hows and whys of it.* • **and how!** *originally N Amer colloq* very much indeed; definitely. • **how about ...?** would you like ...? what do you think of ...? □ *How about another piece of cake?* □ *How about going to see a film?* • **how are you?** a conventional greeting to someone, sometimes referring specifically to their state of health. • **how come?** *colloq* for what reason? how does that come about? □ *How come you're not going tomorrow?* • **how do you do?** a formal greeting to a person one is meeting for the first time. • **how now** or **how so?** what is this? how is this so? • **how's that? 1** what is your opinion of that? **2** *cricket* an appeal to the umpire to give the batsman out. Also written **howzat**. • **how's your father** *facetious* **1** amorous play; sexual intercourse. **2** ridiculous or foolish activity; nonsense. • **the how and why** the method, or manner, and the cause. ⌚ Anglo-Saxon *hu*, probably an adverbial form of *hwa* who.

howbeit /haʊ'biːɪt/ ▻ *conj, adv, archaic* **1** be it how it may; however. **2** notwithstanding; although.

howdah or **houdah** /'haʊdə/ ▻ *noun* a seat, usually one with a sun-shade, used for riding on an elephant's back. ⌚ 18c: from Arabic *haudaj*.

howdy /'haʊdɪ/ ▻ *exclamation, N Amer colloq* hello. ⌚ 16c: a colloquial form of *how do you do?*

how-d'ye-do and **howdy-do** ▻ *noun* (***how-d'ye-dos*** or ***howdy-dos***) a difficult or troublesome state of affairs.

however /haʊ'ɛvə(r)/ ▻ *adverb, conj* **1** in spite of that; nevertheless. **2** *colloq* especially implying surprise: in what way; by what means □ *However did you do that?* **3** by whatever means □ *Do it however you like.* **4** to no matter what extent □ *You must finish this however long it takes.* ⌚ 14c.

howitzer /'haʊɪtsə(r)/ ▻ *noun* a short heavy gun which fires shells high in the air and at a steep angle, especially used in trench warfare. ⌚ 17c: from Czech *houfnice* sling, catapult.

howl /haʊl/ ▻ *noun* **1** a long mournful cry of a wolf or dog. **2** a long, loud cry made eg by the wind. **3** a prolonged cry of pain or distress. **4** a loud peal of laughter. **5** *electronics* a vibrant sound made by loud speakers caused by feedback. ▻ *verb* (***howled***, ***howling***) **1** *intr* to make a long, mournful cry or similar wailing noise. **2** *intr* to laugh or cry loudly. **3** to shout or shriek (instructions, orders, etc). • **howling** *adj, colloq* very great; tremendous □ *a howling success.* ⌚ 14c.

■ **howl someone down** to prevent (a speaker) from being heard by shouting loudly and angrily.

howler /'haʊlə(r)/ ▻ *noun* **1** someone or something that howls. **2** (*also* **howler monkey**) the largest of the S American monkeys, with black, brown or reddish fur. **3** *colloq* an outrageous and amusing blunder.

howsoever ▻ *adverb* in whatever way; to whatever extent.

howzat see HOW'S THAT at HOW

hoy[1] /hɔɪ/ ▻ *noun* a large one-decked boat, usually rigged as a sloop. ⌚ 15c: from Dutch *hoei*.

hoy² or **hoi** /hɔɪ/ ▻ *exclamation* a word used to attract someone's attention. ⓒ 14c variant of HEY.

hoyden /'hɔɪdən/ ▻ *noun* a wild lively girl; a tomboy. • **hoydenism** *noun*. • **hoydenish** *adj* boisterous. ⓒ 16c: from Dutch *heyden* boor.

HP or **hp** ▻ *abbreviation* **1** high pressure. **2** *Brit* hire-purchase. **3** horsepower.

HQ or **hq** ▻ *abbreviation* headquarters.

hr ▻ *abbreviation* hour.

HRE ▻ *abbreviation* Holy Roman Emperor or Empire.

HRH ▻ *abbreviation* His or Her Royal Highness.

HRT ▻ *abbreviation* hormone replacement therapy.

HS ▻ *abbreviation* **1** High School. **2** Home Secretary.

HSE ▻ *abbreviation* Health and Safety Executive.

Hse ▻ *abbreviation* in addresses and place names: House.

HSH ▻ *abbreviation* His or Her Serene Highness.

HSM ▻ *abbreviation* His or Her Serene Majesty.

HT ▻ *abbreviation* high tension.

ht ▻ *abbreviation* height.

HTLV ▻ *abbreviation* human T-cell lymphotrophic virus.

http ▻ *abbreviation* in Web addresses: hypertext transfer protocol.

hub ▻ *noun* **1** the centre of a wheel; a nave. **2** the focal point of activity, interest, discussion, etc. ⓒ 17c: perhaps a variant of HOB¹.

hubble-bubble /'hʌbəlbʌbəl/ ▻ *noun* **1** a bubbling sound. **2** a simple kind of HOOKAH. ⓒ 17c: a rhyming elaboration of BUBBLE.

Hubble's constant /'hʌbəlz —/ or **Hubble constant** ▻ *noun, astron* a constant that describes the rate at which the universe is expanding by relating the speed at which a galaxy is moving away from us to its distance. ⓒ 1950s: named after Edwin Hubble, (1889–1953), the American astronomer.

Hubble's law ▻ *noun, astron* the law which states that the speed at which a galaxy is moving away increases as it becomes more distant (as measured by the REDSHIFT), due to the uniform expansion of the universe. ⓒ 1930s.

Hubble space telescope ▻ *noun, astron* an optical telescope launched into orbit around the Earth in 1990 in the space shuttle *Discovery*, allowing observation of a volume of the universe 350 times as large as that observable from Earth and detecting objects seven times further away than was previously possible.

hubbub /'hʌbʌb/ ▻ *noun* **1** a confused noise of many sounds, especially voices. **2** uproar; commotion. ⓒ 16c: perhaps Irish; compare Scottish Gaelic *ub! ub!* an exclamation expressing contempt.

hubby /'hʌbɪ/ ▻ *noun* (***hubbies***) *colloq* an affectionate contraction of HUSBAND. ⓒ 17c.

hub-cap ▻ *noun* the metal covering over the hub of a wheel.

hubris /'hjuːbrɪs/ ▻ *noun* arrogance or over-confidence, especially when likely to result in disaster or ruin. • **hubristic** /hjʊ'brɪstɪk/ *adj*. • **hubristically** *adverb*. ⓒ 19c: from Greek *hybris*.

huckaback /'hʌkəbak/ ▻ *noun* a coarse linen or cotton fabric with alternately woven threads forming a raised surface, used for towels, etc. ⓒ 17c.

huckleberry /'hʌkəlbərɪ/ ▻ *noun* **1** a species of plant native to woodlands and swamps of eastern N America. **2** the fruit of this plant, which is either dark-blue or black, depending on the species. ⓒ 17c: probably a variant of American *hurtleberry* whortleberry.

huckster /'hʌkstə(r)/ ▻ *noun* **1** *old use* a street trader; a hawker or pedlar. **2** an aggressive seller. **3** a mercenary person. ▻ *verb* (***huckstered, huckstering***) **1** *intr* to hawk or peddle (goods, etc). **2** to sell aggressively. **3** *intr* to haggle meanly. ⓒ 12c as *huccstere*, from Dutch *hoekster*.

huddle /'hʌdəl/ ▻ *verb* (***huddled, huddling***) **1** *tr & intr* (*usually* **huddle together** or **up**) to heap or crowd together closely, eg because of cold. **2** *intr* to sit curled up. **3** to curl oneself up. **4** *chiefly Brit* to drive, draw, throw or crowd together in a disorderly way. **5** to hustle. **6** *intr, Amer football* to form or gather into a huddle. ▻ *noun* **1** a confused mass or crowd. **2** *colloq* a secret or private conference ◻ *go into a huddle.* **3** *Amer football* a gathering together of the players during a game, in order to receive instructions, etc. • **huddled** *adj* **1** crouching or curled up. **2** gathered or crowded together. ⓒ 16c: from *hoder* to wrap up, probably related to HIDE¹.

hue /hjuː/ *noun* **1** a colour, tint or shade. **2** the feature of a colour that distinguishes it from other colours. **3** a view or aspect. • **hued** *adj, in compounds* having a hue of a specified kind ◻ *dark-hued.* • **hueless** *adj*. ⓒ Anglo-Saxon *hiw*.

hue and cry ▻ *noun* **1** a loud public protest or uproar. **2** an outcry calling for the pursuit of someone who is to be imprisoned. **3** *historical* a publication or proclamation to the same effect. ⓒ 16c.

huff ▻ *noun* a fit of anger, annoyance or offended dignity ◻ *in a huff.* ▻ *verb* (***huffed, huffing***) **1** *intr* to blow or puff loudly. **2** *tr & intr* to give or take offence. **3** *draughts* to remove an opponent's piece for failing to capture one's own piece. • **huffing and puffing** loud empty threats or objections. ⓒ 16c: imitating the sound of blowing or puffing loudly.

huffy /'hʌfɪ/ and **huffish** ▻ *adj* (***huffier, huffiest***) **1** offended. **2** easily offended; touchy. • **huffily** or **huffishly** *adverb*. • **huffiness** *noun*.

hug ▻ *verb* (***hugged, hugging***) **1** *tr & intr* to hold tightly in one's arms, especially to show love. **2** to keep close to something ◻ *The ship was hugging the shore.* **3** to hold or cherish (a belief, etc) very firmly. ▻ *noun* **1** a tight grasp with the arms; a close embrace. **2** *wrestling* a particular type of grip. • **huggable** *adj*. ⓒ 16c: perhaps from Norse *hugga* to soothe.

huge /hjuːdʒ/ ▻ *adj* very large or enormous. • **hugely** *adj* very; very much ◻ *The film was hugely popular.* • **hugeness** *noun*. ⓒ 13c: from French *ahuge*.

hugger-mugger /'hʌgəmʌgə(r)/ ▻ *noun* **1** confusion or disorder. **2** secrecy. ▻ *adj, adverb* **1** secret; in secret. **2** confused; in confusion or disorder. ⓒ 16c: from *mokeren* to hoard.

Huguenot /'hjuːgənoʊ, -nɒt/ ▻ *noun* a French Protestant, especially of the 16c or 17c. ▻ *adj* relating or belonging to the Huguenots. ⓒ 16c: perhaps from *Hugues* a Genevan political leader + French *eidgenot*, from Swiss German *Eidgenoss* confederate.

huh /hʌ, hʌh/ ▻ *exclamation, colloq* expressing disgust, disbelief or inquiry. ⓒ 17c.

hula /'huːlə/ (***hulas***) and **hula-hula** ▻ *noun* a Hawaiian dance in which the dancer, usually a woman, sways their hips and moves their arms gracefully. ⓒ 19c: Hawaiian.

hula hoop ▻ *noun* a light hoop, usually made of plastic, which is kept spinning round the waist by a swinging movement of the hips, similar to that of the dance.

hula skirt ▻ *noun* a grass skirt worn by hula dancers.

hulk /hʌlk/ ▻ *noun* **1** the dismantled body of an old ship. **2** a ship which is or looks unwieldy or difficult to steer. **3** *derog, colloq* a large, awkward and ungainly person or thing. **4** (**the hulks**) *historical* the body of an old ship used as a prison. ⓒ Anglo-Saxon *hulc*.

hulking /'hʌlkɪŋ/ ▻ *adj, colloq* big and clumsy.

hull¹ /hʌl/ ▻ *noun* **1** the frame or body of a ship or airship. **2** the armoured body of a tank, missile, rocket, etc. ▻ *verb* (***hulled, hulling***) to pierce the hull of (a ship, etc). ⓒ 14c: probably from HULL².

hull² /hʌl/ ▻ *noun* **1** the outer covering or husk of certain fruit and seeds, especially the pods of beans and peas. **2**

the calyx at the bottom of a strawberry, raspberry, etc. ▷ *verb* (***hulled***, ***hulling***) to remove from the hulls; to husk (fruit and seeds). ⓒ Anglo-Saxon *hulu* husk.

hullabaloo /hʌləbəˈluː/ ▷ *noun* (***hullabaloos***) *colloq* an uproar or clamour. ⓒ 18c: a rhyming compound derived from Scottish *baloo* lullaby.

hullo see HELLO

hum ▷ *verb* (***hummed***, ***humming***) **1** *intr* to make a low, steady murmuring sound similar to that made by a bee. **2** *tr & intr* to sing (a tune) with closed lips. **3** *intr* to speak indistinctly or stammer, especially through embarrassment or hesitation. **4** *intr, colloq* to be full of activity □ *The whole building was humming.* **5** *intr, slang* to have an unpleasant smell or odour. ▷ *noun* **1** a humming sound. **2** an inarticulate sound or murmur. **3** *slang* a bad smell. ▷ *exclamation* expressing embarrassment or hesitation. • **hummable** *adj.* • **hum and haw** or **ha** or **hah** /hʌm ən ˈhɔː, — ˈhɑː/ to make inarticulate sounds expressing doubt, uncertainty or hesitation; to hesitate □ *He hummed and hahed for hours before making a decision.* • **make things hum** to set things going; to stir up some activity. ⓒ 14c: imitating the sound.

human /ˈhjuːmən/ ▷ *adj* **1** referring or belonging to people □ *human weakness.* **2** having or showing the qualities and limitations of people, especially the weaknesses, as opposed to God, animals or machines. **3** having or showing the better qualities of people, eg in being kind, thoughtful, etc. ▷ *noun* a human being. • **humanness** *noun.* See also HUMANITY. ⓒ 14c as *humayne*; 17c as *human*: from French *humain*, from Latin *humanus*, from *homo* man; by 18c the forms *human* and *humane* began to be differentiated and restricted to the senses in which they are now formed.

human being ▷ *noun* a member of the human race; a person.

human chorionic gonadotrophin ▷ *noun* (abbreviation **HCG**) a CHORIONIC GONADOTROPHIN.

humane /hjʊˈmeɪn/ ▷ *adj* **1** kind and sympathetic. **2** said of a killing: done with as little pain and suffering as possible. **3** said of a branch of learning: aiming to civilize and make more elegant and polite. • **humanely** *adverb.* • **humaneness** *noun.* See HUMAN.

human guinea pig see under GUINEA PIG

human immunodeficiency virus see HIV

human interest ▷ *noun* in newspaper articles, broadcasts, etc: references to people's lives and their emotions.

humanism /ˈhjuːmənɪzəm/ ▷ *noun* **1** a system of thought which rejects the supernatural, any belief in a god, etc, but holds that human interests and the human mind are paramount, that humans are capable of solving the problems of the world and deciding what is or is not correct moral behaviour. **2** (*often* **Humanism**) a cultural movement of the Renaissance period which promoted classical studies.

humanist /ˈhjuːmənɪst/ ▷ *noun* **1** a follower of HUMANISM (sense 1 or 2). **2** a student of human nature.

humanistic /hjuːməˈnɪstɪk/ ▷ *adj* **1** relating to or involving humanism or humanists. **2** *psychol* emphasizing the observation of one's feelings and reactions to other people as a basis for a greater understanding of oneself.

humanitarian /hjʊmanɪˈtɛərɪən/ ▷ *adj* concerned with improving people's lives and welfare □ *humanitarian aid for the war-zone.* ▷ *noun* a person who tries to improve the quality of people's lives by means of reform, charity, etc; a philanthropist. • **humanitarianism** *noun* humanitarian principles, systems or practices. ⓒ 19c.

humanity /hjʊˈmanɪtɪ/ ▷ *noun* (***humanities***) **1** the human race; mankind. **2** the nature peculiar to human beings. **3** the qualities of human beings, especially in being kind or merciful; humaneness. **4** in some Scottish Universities: the study of Latin language and literature. **5** (**humanities**) the subjects involving the study of human culture, especially language, literature, philosophy, and Latin and Greek. ⓒ 14c: from French *humanité*, from Latin *humanitas.*

humanize or **humanise** /ˈhjuːmənaɪz/ ▷ *verb* (***humanized***, ***humanizing***) **1** to render, make or become human. **2** to make more caring, more thoughtful, etc; to make humane. • **humanization** *noun.* ⓒ 17c.

humankind ▷ *noun* **1** the human species. **2** people generally or collectively.

humanly /ˈhjuːmənlɪ/ ▷ *adverb* **1** in a human or humane way. **2** by human agency or means. **3** with regard to human limitations □ *Is it humanly possible to foresee events?*

human nature ▷ *noun* **1** the nature of man, often with reference to the weaker aspects of character. **2** the qualities that distinguish man from other species.

humanoid /ˈhjuːmənɔɪd/ ▷ *noun* **1** any of the ancestors from which modern humankind is descended and to which they are immediately related, more closely than to ANTHROPOIDS. **2** an animal or machine with human characteristics. ⓒ Early 20c: from HUMAN + -OID.

human resources ▷ *plural noun* **1** people collectively in terms of their skills, training, knowledge, etc in the work place. **2** the workforce of an organization. • **human-resource** *adj* referring or relating to human resources □ *human-resource management.* Compare PERSONNEL.

human rights ▷ *noun* the rights every person has to justice and freedom.

human shield ▷ *noun, military* a person or group of people purposely deployed in strategic sites during hostilities, in order to deter enemy attack on those sites.

humble /ˈhʌmbəl/ ▷ *adj* (***humbler***, ***humblest***) **1** having a low opinion of oneself and one's abilities, etc. **2** having a low position in society. **3** lowly, modest or unpretentious. ▷ *verb* (***humbled***, ***humbling***) **1** to make humble or modest. **2** to abase or degrade. • **humbleness** *noun.* • **humbling** *adj.* • **humbly** *adverb.* ⓒ 13c: from Latin *humilis* low, from *humus* the ground.

humble-bee ▷ *noun* a BUMBLE-BEE. ⓒ 15c: from German *homelbe*, from Dutch *hommel.*

humble pie and **umble pie** ▷ *noun* a pie made from the umbles or entrails of a deer. • **eat humble pie** to be forced to humble or abase oneself, or to make a humble apology. ⓒ 17c: ultimately from 14c *numbles* the offal of a deer.

humbug /ˈhʌmbʌɡ/ ▷ *noun* **1** a trick or deception. **2** nonsense or rubbish. **3** an impostor or fraud. **4** *Brit* a hard, peppermint-flavoured sweet. ▷ *verb* (***humbugged***, ***humbugging***) **1** to deceive or hoax. **2** to cajole. ▷ *exclamation* expressing annoyance or irritation. • **humbuggery** *noun.* ⓒ 18c.

humdinger /hʌmˈdɪŋə(r)/ ▷ *noun, slang* an exceptionally good person or thing. ⓒ 19c.

humdrum /ˈhʌmdrʌm/ ▷ *adj* dull or monotonous; ordinary. ▷ *noun* **1** a dull or stupid person. **2** tedious or monotonous talk or routine. ⓒ 16c: a rhyming compound derived from HUM.

humectant /hjuːˈmɛktənt/ ▷ *adj* moistening; dampening. ▷ *noun* a substance used to retain moisture or prevent moisture loss in another substance. ⓒ 17c: from Latin *umectare* to moisten.

humerus /ˈhjuːmərəs/ ▷ *noun* (***humeri*** /-raɪ/) *anatomy* the bone in the upper arm. • **humeral** /ˈhjuːmərəl/ *adj* relating to or in the region of the humerus or shoulders. ⓒ 17c: from Latin *umerus* shoulder.

humic see under HUMUS

humid /'hjuːmɪd/ ▷ *adj* damp; moist. • **humidly** *adverb*. • **humidness** *noun*. See also HUMIDITY. ◎ 16c: from Latin *umidus*.

humidifier ▷ *noun* a device for increasing or maintaining the humidity of a room, etc. ◎ 19c.

humidify /hjʊ'mɪdɪfaɪ/ ▷ *verb* (***humidifies, humidified, humidifying***) to make something damp or humid (eg the air or atmosphere). • **humidification** *noun*. ◎ 19c.

humidity /hjʊ'mɪdɪtɪ/ ▷ *noun* **1** *meteorol* the amount of water vapour in the atmosphere, usually expressed as a percentage. **2** moisture; dampness. ◎ 15c: from Latin *umiditas*.

humidor /'hjuːmɪdɔː(r)/ ▷ *noun* a box or room for keeping cigars or tobacco moist. ◎ Early 20c.

humify /'hjuːmɪfaɪ/ ▷ *verb* (***humifies, humified, humifying***) *tr & intr* to make or turn into HUMUS. • **humification** *noun*.

humiliate /hjʊ'mɪlɪeɪt/ ▷ *verb* (***humiliated, humiliating***) to injure someone's pride, or make them feel ashamed or look foolish, especially in the presence of others. • **humiliating** *adj* □ *a humiliating experience*. • **humiliatingly** *adverb*. • **humiliation** *noun*. ◎ 16c: from Latin *humiliatus*, from *humilis* humble.

humility /hjʊ'mɪlɪtɪ/ ▷ *noun* (***humilities***) **1** the quality or state of being humble. **2** a lowly self-opinion; modesty or meekness. ◎ 13c: from French *humilité*, from Latin *humilis* humble.

hummingbird /'hʌmɪŋbɜːd/ ▷ *noun* a small S American bird with brilliant plumage. ◎ 17c: so called because its wings beat so rapidly that they produce a low humming sound.

humming-top ▷ *noun* a spinning top (see TOP²) that makes a humming sound as it spins.

hummock /'hʌmək/ ▷ *noun* **1** a low hill; a hillock. **2** a ridge of ice. • **hummocky** *adj*. ◎ 16c.

hummus or **hoummos** or **houmus** /'hʊməs, 'hʌ-/ ▷ *noun* a Middle-Eastern hors d'oeuvre or dip containing puréed cooked chickpeas and tahini, flavoured with lemon juice and garlic. ◎ 1950s: Arabic, meaning 'chickpeas'.

humongous or **humungous** /hjuː'mʌŋgəs/ ▷ *adj, colloq* huge or enormous. ◎ 1960s: perhaps from *huge* + *monstrous*.

humoral /'hjuːmərəl/ ▷ *adj, medicine* referring or relating to body fluid. ◎ 16c: from HUMOUR *noun* 5.

humoresque /hjuːmə'rɛsk/ ▷ *noun* a humorous piece of music; a musical caprice. ◎ 19c: from German *humoreske*, from Latin *humor*.

humorist /'hjuːmərɪst/ ▷ *noun* someone with a talent for talking, behaving or writing humorously. ◎ 16c: from French *humoriste*.

humorous /'hjuːmərəs/ ▷ *adj* **1** containing humour; funny or amusing. **2** said of a person, joke, etc: having the ability or quality to cause humour □ *a humorous play*. • **humorously** *adverb*. • **humorousness** *noun*. ◎ 16c.

humour or (*US*) **humor** /'hjuːmə(r)/ ▷ *noun* **1** the quality of being amusing. **2** the ability to appreciate and enjoy something amusing. **3** a specified temperament or state of mind □ *He is in good humour today*. **4** writings, plays, speeches, etc that are amusing or funny. **5** a specified type of fluid in the body □ *aqueous humour*. **6** *old physiol* any of the four bodily fluids (BLOOD senses 1,5, CHOLER, MELANCHOLY and PHLEGM) formerly believed to determine a person's physical health and character. ▷ *verb* (***humoured, humouring***) **1** to please or gratify someone by doing what they wish. **2** to adapt to eg the mood or ideas of someone else. • **out of humour** displeased or disgruntled; in a bad mood. • **humourless** *adj*. ◎ 14c: from Latin *humor* liquid.

humous see under HUMUS

hump /hʌmp/ ▷ *noun* **1** a large rounded lump of fat on the back of a camel that serves as an energy store when food is scarce. **2** an abnormal curvature of the spine that gives the back a hunched appearance, due to spinal deformity. **3** a rounded lump on a road. **4** *Brit colloq* a feeling of despondency or annoyance. ▷ *verb* (***humped, humping***) **1** to hunch or bend in a hump. **2** (*usually* **hump something about** or **around**) to shoulder or carry (especially something awkward or heavy) with difficulty. **3** to strain or exert oneself. **4** *tr & intr, coarse slang* to have sexual intercourse with someone. • **humpy** *adj, colloq* **1** having a hump or humps. **2** sulky or irritable. • **have** or **give someone the hump** to be in, or put someone in, a bad mood or sulk. • **over the hump** *colloq* past the crisis; over the worst. ◎ 18c.

humpback ▷ *noun* **1** a back with a hump or hunch. **2** someone whose back has a hump; a hunchback. **3** a whale with a fin on its back which forms a hump. • **humpbacked** *adj* **1** rising and falling in the shape of a hump. **2** having a humpback. ◎ 17c.

humpback bridge ▷ *noun, Brit* a bridge, usually narrow, with steep slopes on either side.

humph /hʌmf/ ▷ *exclamation* expressing doubt, displeasure or hesitation. ◎ 17c: imitating a snorting sound.

humpty-dumpty /'hʌmptɪ 'dʌmptɪ/ ▷ *noun* a short stout person. ◎ 18c: from the name of the egg-shaped nursery rhyme character.

humungous see HUMONGOUS

humus /'hjuːməs/ ▷ *noun* dark-brown organic material produced in the topmost layer of soil due to the decomposition of plant and animal matter. • **humic** or **humous** *adj*. ◎ 18c: Latin.

Hun ▷ *noun* (***Huns*** or ***Hun***) **1** *historical* a member of a powerful, warlike and nomadic people from Asia who, led by Attila, invaded and controlled Europe in the 4c and 5c. **2** *offensive colloq* a German. **3** a barbarian or vandal. ◎ Anglo-Saxon *Hune*.

hunch /hʌntʃ/ ▷ *noun* **1** an idea, guess or belief based on feelings, suspicions or intuition rather than on actual evidence. **2** a hump. ▷ *verb* (***hunched, hunching***) **1** to bend or arch; to hump. **2** *intr* (*also* **hunch up**) to sit with the body hunched or curled up. ◎ 16c.

hunchback ▷ *noun* someone with a large rounded lump on their back, due to spinal deformity. • **hunchbacked** *adj*. ◎ 18c as *hunchback*, 16c as *hunchbacked*.

hundred /'hʌndrəd/ ▷ *noun* (***hundreds*** or, after a number, ***hundred***) **1** the number which is ten times ten. **2** a numeral, figure or symbol representing this, eg **100** or **C**. **3** a set of 100 people or things □ *one hundred pounds*. **4** a score of a 100 points. **5** (**hundreds**) *colloq* a large but indefinite number □ *hundreds of people*. **6** (**hundreds**) *in compounds* the 100 years of a specified century □ *the thirteen-hundreds*. **7** *historical* a division of an English county originally meant to contain a hundred families. ▷ *adj* **1** totalling or to the number of 100. **2** *colloq* very many □ *I've told you a hundred times to stop*. • **great** or **long hundred** 120. • **not a hundred miles from something** *colloq* very near it. • **not a hundred per cent** not in perfect health. • **one, two,** *etc* **hundred hours** one, two, etc o'clock ◎ from the style of writing hours and minutes as 0100, 0200, ... 1400, 1500, etc. ◎ Anglo-Saxon, from *hund* a hundred + suffix *-red* a reckoning.

hundredfold ▷ *adj* **1** equal to 100 times as much. **2** divided into or consisting of 100 parts. ▷ *adverb* by 100 times as much.

hundreds and thousands ▷ *plural noun* tiny balls of coloured sugar used for decorating cakes.

hundredth /'hʌndrədθ/ ▷ *adj* **1** the last of 100 people or things. **2** the next after the 99th. **3** the 100th position in a sequence of numbers. ▻ *noun* **1** one of 100 equal parts. **2** someone or something in 100th position.

hundredweight ▻ *noun* (***hundredweight*** or ***hundredweights***) (abbreviation **cwt**) *Brit* a measure of weight equal to 112 pounds (50.8kg). Also called **long hundredweight**. • **short hundredweight** *N Amer* a measure of weight equal to 100 pounds (45.4kg). • **metric hundredweight** a metric measure of weight equal to 50kg.

hung ▻ *verb, past tense, past participle of* HANG. ▻ *adj* said of a parliament or jury: with neither side having a majority. • **be hung over** *colloq* to be suffering from a hangover. • **be hung up on** or **about someone** or **something** *colloq* **1** to be extremely anxious or upset about it **2** to be obsessed with them or it □ *She is completely hung up on him.* See also HANG-UP.

hung

See Usage Note at **hang**.

Hung. ▻ *abbreviation* **1** Hungarian. **2** Hungary.

Hungarian /hʌŋˈɡɛərɪən/ ▻ *adj* **1** belonging or relating to Hungary, a republic in central Europe, or its inhabitants. **2** belonging or relating to the official language of Hungary, also spoken in parts of Romania, belonging to the Finno-Ugric language family. ▻ *noun* **1** a citizen or inhabitant of, or person born in, Hungary. **2** the Magyar or Hungarian language. See also MAGYAR.

hunger /ˈhʌŋɡə(r)/ ▻ *noun* **1** the desire or need for food. **2** a strong desire for anything □ *He has a hunger for affection.* ▻ *verb* (***hungered, hungering***) *intr* **1** to crave or long for food. **2** (*usually* **hunger for** or **after something**) to have a strong desire for it. ⓒ Anglo-Saxon *hungor*.

hunger march ▻ *noun* a procession of the unemployed or others in need, as a demonstration. • **hunger-marcher** *noun*.

hunger strike ▻ *noun* a prolonged refusal to eat, especially by a prisoner, as a form of protest or as an attempt to ensure release. • **hunger-striker** *noun*.

hungry /ˈhʌŋɡrɪ/ ▻ *adj* (***hungrier, hungriest***) **1** having a need or craving for food. **2** (*usually* **hungry for something**) having a great desire for it □ *He is hungry for success.* **3** eager; greedy □ *hungry eyes.* • **hungrily** *adverb*. • **hungriness** *noun*. • **go hungry** to remain without food. ⓒ Anglo-Saxon *hungrig*.

hunk /hʌŋk/ ▻ *noun* **1** a lump or piece, sometimes broken or cut off from a larger piece. **2** *colloq* a strong, muscular, sexually attractive man. ⓒ 19c: from Flemish *hunke*.

hunky¹ /ˈhʌŋkɪ/ ▻ *adj* (***hunkier, hunkiest***) *colloq* said of a man: strong, muscular and sexually attractive.

hunky² /ˈhʌŋkɪ/ ▻ *noun* (***hunkies***) *N Amer, derog* someone of E European descent, especially an unskilled worker.

hunky-dory /hʌŋkɪˈdɔːrɪ/ ▻ *adj, colloq* said of a situation, condition, etc: fine; excellent. ⓒ 19c.

hunt /hʌnt/ ▻ *verb* (***hunted, hunting***) **1** *tr & intr* to chase and kill (animals) for food or sport. **2** *intr, Brit* to hunt animals, especially foxes, using hounds, and on horseback. **3** to seek out and pursue game over (a certain area). **4** to hound or drive with force. **5** *mech* to oscillate around a middle point, or to vary in speed. ▻ *noun* **1** the act of hunting. **2** a group of people meeting together on horses to hunt animals, especially foxes. **3** the area where such a group of people hunts. **4** a pack of hunting hounds. **5** a search. • **good hunting!** *colloq* good luck! ⓒ Anglo-Saxon *huntian*.

■ **hunt after** or **for something** or **someone** to search for it or them □ *hunt for a new house.*

■ **hunt someone** or **something down** **1** to pursue and capture them or it. **2** to persecute them or it out of existence.

■ **hunt someone** or **something out** or **up** to search or seek something out.

■ **hunt up** or **down** *bell-ringing* to ring (a bell) progressively earlier or later respectively in a sequence. See also HUNTING².

hunt ball ▻ *noun* a ball given by the members of a hunt.

hunter /ˈhʌntə(r)/ ▻ *noun* **1 a** someone who hunts; **b** *especially in compounds* someone who seeks something out □ *bounty hunter.* **2** an animal that hunts (usually other animals) for food. **3** a horse used in hunting, especially fox-hunting. **4** a watch with a hinged metal cover to protect the glass over its face. Compare HALF-HUNTER.

hunter-gatherer ▻ *noun, anthropol* a member of a society which lives by hunting animals from the land and sea, and by gathering wild fruit.

hunter-killer ▻ *adj* said of a surface craft or submarine: designed to hunt down and destroy enemy vessels, especially submarines. ▻ *noun* a vessel designed to carry out such a task.

hunter's moon ▻ *noun* the next full moon after the harvest moon.

hunting¹ ▻ *noun* the activity or sport of pursuing, capturing or killing wild animals.

hunting² *noun, bell-ringing* the shift in the order of ringing a bell through a set of CHANGES (*noun* 9) achieved by **hunting up** and **hunting down** (see HUNT UP OR DOWN at HUNT).

hunting-box, **hunting-lodge** and **hunting-seat** ▻ *noun* temporary accommodation reserved for huntsmen during the hunting season.

hunting-horn ▻ *noun* a horn or bugle used for giving signals in hunts.

hunting spider ▻ *noun* a WOLF SPIDER.

Huntington's chorea /ˈhʌntɪŋtənz kəˈrɪə/ and **Huntington's disease** ▻ *noun, medicine* a hereditary brain disorder which usually appears in the fourth decade of life, characterized by progressive dementia, uncontrolled jerking and writhing movements, and speech problems. ⓒ 19c: named after the US physician George Summer Huntington (1851–1916) who described it.

huntress /ˈhʌntrɪs/ ▻ *noun* a female hunter, especially applied to the goddess Diana.

hunt saboteur ▻ *noun* someone who is opposed to all blood sports, especially fox-hunting, and who often participates in activities intended to thwart the hunters, usually as part of an organized group.

huntsman ▻ *noun* **1** someone who hunts. **2** an official who manages the hounds during a fox-hunt.

hurdle /ˈhɜːdəl/ ▻ *noun* **1** *athletics, horse-racing* one of a series of portable frames, hedges or barriers to be jumped in a race. **2** an obstacle, problem or difficulty to be overcome. **3** (**hurdles**) a race with hurdles □ *She won the 200m hurdles.* **4** a light frame with bars or wire across it, used as a temporary fence. **5** *historical* a basic sledge on which criminals were dragged to their execution. ▻ *verb* (***hurdled, hurdling***) **1** *tr & intr* to jump over (a hurdle in a race, an obstacle, etc). **2** to enclose with hurdles. • **hurdler** *noun* **1** a person or horse that runs hurdle races. **2** someone who makes hurdles. • **hurdling** *noun* racing over hurdles. ⓒ Anglo-Saxon *hyrdel*.

hurdy-gurdy /hɜːdɪˈɡɜːdɪ/ ▻ *noun* (***hurdy-gurdies***) a musical instrument whose strings make a droning sound when a wheel is turned by a handle. Also called BARREL ORGAN. ⓒ 18c: a variant of Scots *hirdy-girdy* uproar.

hurl /hɜːl/ ▻ *verb* (***hurled, hurling***) **1** to fling violently. **2** to utter with force and spite □ *hurl abuse.* **3** *intr* to play the game of HURLING. ▻ *noun* an act of hurling. ⓒ 13c.

hurling and **hurley** ▻ *noun* a traditional Irish game resembling hockey, played by two teams of 15, with curved broad-bladed sticks or **hurleys**, and a hide-covered cork ball. ⓒ 16c: from HURL.

hurly-burly /hɜːlɪˈbɜːlɪ/ ▷ *noun* the noisy activity of crowds of people; confusion or uproar. ⓒ 16c: from *hurling* and *burling*, a rhyming compound based on *hurling* in its obsolete meaning 'uproar'.

hurrah or **hoorah** /həˈrɑː/ ▷ *exclamation* a shout of joy, enthusiasm or victory. ▷ *noun* such a shout. ▷ *verb* (***hurrahed, hurrahing***) to shout or cheer 'hurrah'. Also **hooray** and **hurray** /hʊˈreɪ/. ⓒ 17c: from German *hurra*.

hurricane /ˈhʌrɪkən, -keɪn/ ▷ *noun* **1** an intense, often devastating, cyclonic tropical storm with average wind speeds exceeding 118kph, or force 12 on the BEAUFORT SCALE. **2** a wind or storm of extreme violence. **3** (**Hurricane**) a type of fighter aeroplane used in World War II. ⓒ 16c: from West Indian *huracán*.

hurricane lamp ▷ *noun* an oil lamp whose flame is enclosed in glass to protect it from the wind.

hurried /ˈhʌrɪd/ ▷ *adj* carried out or forced to act quickly, especially too quickly. • **hurriedly** *adverb*. • **hurriedness** *noun*.

hurry /ˈhʌrɪ/ ▷ *verb* (***hurries, hurried, hurrying***) **1** to urge forward or hasten; to make someone or something move or act quickly. **2** *intr* to move or act with haste, especially with excessive speed. ▷ *noun* **1** great haste or speed; a driving forward. **2** the necessity for haste or speed. **3** flurried or excessive haste. **4** commotion or confusion. **5** eagerness. • **in a hurry 1** rushed; in haste ◻ *They were in a hurry because they left late.* **2** readily; willingly ◻ *I won't do that again in a hurry.* ⓒ 16c: from English *horyen*.

■ **hurry someone up** or **along** to encourage them to move or act more quickly.

hurt /hɜːt/ ▷ *verb* (***hurt, hurting***) **1** to injure or cause physical pain to someone. **2** to cause mental or emotional pain to someone. **3** *intr* to be painful ◻ *The wound hurts.* **4** *intr* to be injured. ▷ *noun* **1** an injury or wound. **2** mental or emotional pain or suffering. ▷ *adj* **1** injured ◻ *He had a hurt leg.* **2** aggrieved; upset ◻ *She had a hurt expression.* ⓒ 12c: from French *hurter* to knock against something.

hurtful ▷ *adj* causing mental pain; emotionally harmful. • **hurtfully** *adverb*. • **hurtfulness** *noun*.

hurtle /ˈhɜːtəl/ ▷ *verb* (***hurtled, hurtling***) *tr & intr* to move or throw very quickly or noisily ◻ *The car hurtled down the road* ◻ *He was hurtling towards disaster.* ⓒ 13c: *hurtlen*, from French *hurtler* to knock against.

husband /ˈhʌzbənd/ ▷ *noun* a man to whom a woman is married. ▷ *verb* (***husbanded, husbanding***) to manage (money, resources, etc) wisely and economically. ⓒ Anglo-Saxon *husbonda*, from Old Norse *husbondi*, from *hus* a house and *buandi* inhabiting.

husbandry /ˈhʌzbəndrɪ/ ▷ *noun* **1** the farming business. **2** the economical and wise management of money and resources. ⓒ 14c: from English *housebondrie*.

hush /hʌʃ/ ▷ *exclamation* silence!; be still! ▷ *noun* silence or calm, especially after noise. ▷ *verb* (***hushes, hushed, hushing***) *tr & intr* to make or become silent, calm or still. • **hushed** *adj* silent; very quiet or calm. ⓒ 16c: from the obsolete adjective *husht*, whose final *-t* was thought to indicate a past participle.

■ **hush something up** to stifle or suppress it; to keep it secret.

hushaby /ˈhʌʃəbaɪ/ ▷ *noun* (***hushabies***) a lullaby used to soothe or lull babies to sleep. ▷ *verb* (***hushabies, hushabied, hushabying***) to soothe or lull to sleep.

hush-hush ▷ *adj, colloq* secret or private.

hushkit ▷ *noun, colloq* a device fitted to the jet engine of an aircraft to reduce noise.

hush money ▷ *noun, colloq* money paid to someone to guarantee that something remains secret and confidential.

husk /hʌsk/ ▷ *noun* **1** the thin dry covering of certain fruits and seeds. **2** a case, shell or covering, especially one that is worthless. ▷ *verb* (***husked, husking***) to remove the husk of (a fruit, etc). ⓒ 14c.

husky[1] /ˈhʌskɪ/ ▷ *adj* (***huskier, huskiest***) **1** said of a voice: rough and dry in sound. **2** *colloq* usually said of a man: big, tough and strong. **3** resembling or full of husks. • **huskily** *adverb*. • **huskiness** *noun*. ⓒ 19c: from HUSK.

husky[2] /ˈhʌskɪ/ ▷ *noun* (***huskies***) an Inuit dog with a thick coat and curled tail, used as a sledge-dog in the Arctic. ⓒ 19c: perhaps an alteration and contraction of ESKIMO.

hussar /həˈzɑː(r), hʊ-/ ▷ *noun* **1** a soldier in a cavalry regiment who carries only light weapons. **2** a soldier in the national cavalry of Hungary in the 15c. ⓒ 15c: from Hungarian *huszar*.

Hussite /ˈhʌsaɪt, ʲhʊ-/ ▷ *noun* a follower of the principles of the Bohemian reformer John Hus, martyred in 1415. • **Hussitism** *noun*.

hussy /ˈhʌsɪ/ ▷ *noun* (***hussies***) *derog* an immoral or promiscuous girl or woman. ⓒ 16c: a contraction of *hussif* housewife.

hustings /ˈhʌstɪŋz/ ▷ *singular or plural noun* **1** the platform, etc from which speeches are given by candidates during a political election campaign. **2** the speeches, etc made by candidates during an election campaign. **3** *formerly* the booths where the votes were taken at an election of an MP. ⓒ Anglo-Saxon *husting* tribunal, from *hus* house + *thing* assembly.

hustle /ˈhʌsəl/ ▷ *verb* (***hustled, hustling***) **1 a** to push or shove quickly and roughly; to jostle; **b** to push or shove in a specified direction or into a specified position ◻ *He hustled her out of the room.* **2** to act hurriedly or hastily. **3** *colloq* to coerce or pressure someone to act or deal with something quickly ◻ *They hustled us into agreeing.* **4** to earn money or one's living illicitly. **5** *intr* to act strenuously or aggressively. **6** *intr, slang* to work as a prostitute. ▷ *noun* **1** lively or frenzied activity. **2** *slang* a swindle or fraud. **3** a type of lively disco dance with a variety of steps. ⓒ 17c: from Dutch *husselen* to shake.

hustler /ˈhʌslə(r)/ ▷ *noun, slang* **1** a lively or energetic person. **2** a swindler. **3** a prostitute.

hut /hʌt/ ▷ *noun* **1** a small and crudely built house, usually made of wood. **2** a small temporary dwelling. ▷ *verb* (***hutted, hutting***) **1** to quarter (troops) in a hut or huts. **2** to provide or furnish with a hut or huts. **3** *intr* to lodge or dwell in a hut or huts. ⓒ 17c: from German *hutta*.

hutch /hʌtʃ/ ▷ *noun* (***hutches***) **1** a box, usually made of wood and with a wire-netting front, in which small animals, eg rabbits, are kept. **2** *colloq* a small cramped house. **3** a trough used with some ore-dressing machines. **4** *mining* a low wagon used for pulling coal up from a pit. ⓒ 14c: from French *huche*.

hutment ▷ *noun, chiefly military* an encampment of huts.

HV or **hv** ▷ *abbreviation* high voltage.

HWM ▷ *abbreviation* high water mark.

hyacinth /ˈhaɪəsɪnθ/ ▷ *noun* **1** a plant of the lily family, which grows from a bulb, and has sweet-smelling clusters of purple, pink or white flowers. **2** see JACINTH 2. **3** in the ancient world: a blue gemstone, perhaps a sapphire. • **hyacinthine** *adj* having the colour of a hyacinth. ⓒ 16c: named after Greek *Hyakinthos*, in Greek mythology a youth from whose blood a blue flower sprang when he was killed by Apollo.

Hyades /ˈhaɪədiːz/ and **Hyads** /ˈhaɪadz/ ▷ *plural noun* **1** *astron* a cluster of five stars in the constellation Taurus, near the Pleiades. **2** *Greek mythol* a group of seven nymphs, the sisters of the Pleiades, placed in the heavens as stars by Zeus. ⓒ 14c: Greek, from *hyein* to rain, because the stars were believed to bring rain when they rose with the sun.

hyaena see HYENA

hyaline /ˈhaɪəlɪn, -laɪn/ ▻ *adj* referring to or like glass; clear or transparent. ◷ 17c: from Latin *hyalinus*, from Greek *hyalos* glass.

hyaline cartilage ▻ *noun, anatomy* the common, translucent, bluish-white cartilage, especially found covering bones at points of articulation. ◷ 19c.

hyalinize or **hyalinise** /ˈhaɪələnaɪz/ ▻ *verb* (***hyalinized, hyalinizing***) *tr & intr, biol* said of tissue: to change into a firm, glassy consistency. • **hyalinization** *noun*. ◷ Early 20c.

hyalite /ˈhaɪəlaɪt/ ▻ *noun* a transparent colourless opal.

hyaloid /ˈhaɪəlɔɪd/ ▻ *adj, anatomy* clear and transparent; hyaline.

hyaloid membrane ▻ *noun, anatomy* the transparent membrane enclosing the vitreous humour of the eye. ◷ 19c.

hybrid /ˈhaɪbrɪd/ ▻ *noun* **1** an animal or plant produced by crossing two different species, varieties, races or breeds; a mongrel. **2** *linguistics* a word whose elements are taken from different languages, eg BICYCLE. **3** anything produced by combining elements from different sources. ▻ *adj* being produced by combining elements from different sources; mongrel. • **hybridism** or **hybridity** *noun* /haɪˈbrɪdɪtɪ/. ◷ 17c: from Latin *hibrida* the offspring of a tame sow and wild boar.

hybrid computer ▻ *noun* one which combines the features of digital and analog computers. ◷ 1960s.

hybridize or **hybridise** /ˈhaɪbrɪdaɪz/ ▻ *verb* (***hybridized, hybridizing***) **1** to cause different species, etc to breed together or interbreed. **2** *intr* to produce hybrids; to interbreed. • **hybridizable** *adj*. • **hybridization** *noun* the production of hybrids; cross-breeding. ◷ 19c.

hybridoma /haɪbrɪˈdoʊmə/ ▻ *noun* (***hybridomas***) *biol* a hybrid cell formed by combining a cancer cell with an antibody-producing cell. ◷ 1970s.

hybrid vigour ▻ *noun, biol* the increased size and vigour of a hybrid relative to its parents. Also called **heterosis**.

hydatid /ˈhaɪdətɪd/ ▻ *noun* **1** a watery cyst or vesicle formed in the body of an animal, especially one containing a tapeworm larva. **2** the larva that causes such a cyst. ▻ *adj* containing or resembling a hydatid. ◷ 17c: from Greek *hydatis, hydatidos* watery cyst, from *hydor* water.

hydatid disease ▻ *noun* an infection in the organs of animals, especially the liver, caused by tapeworm larvae, resulting in the development of cysts.

hydr- see HYDRO-

hydra /ˈhaɪdrə/ ▻ *noun* (***hydras*** or ***hydrae*** /ˈhaɪdriː/) **1** a freshwater polyp with a tube-like body and tentacles round the mouth, remarkable for its ability to multiply when cut or divided. **2** any manifold or persistent evil. **3** (**Hydra**) *Greek mythol* a water-monster with many heads, each of which when cut off was immediately replaced by two more. **4** (**Hydra**) *astron* a large southern constellation. ◷ 14c: from Greek *hydor* water.

hydrangea /haɪˈdreɪndʒə/ ▻ *noun* (***hydrangeas***) a garden shrub, native to China and Japan, that has large clusters of white, pink or blue flowers. ◷ 18c: from Greek *hydor* water + *angeion* vessel.

hydrant /ˈhaɪdrənt/ ▻ *noun* a pipe connected to the main water supply, especially in a street, with a nozzle for attaching a hose when fighting fires. ◷ 19c: HYDR- + -ANT.

hydrate *chem* ▻ *noun* /ˈhaɪdreɪt/ a compound containing water which is chemically combined, and which may be expelled without affecting the composition of the other substance. ▻ *verb* /haɪˈdreɪt/ (***hydrated, hydrating***) **1** to form (such a compound) by combining with water. **2** to cause something to absorb water. ◷ 19c: HYDR- + -ATE.

hydration ▻ *noun, chem* the process whereby water molecules become attached to the constituent ions of a SOLUTE as it is being dissolved in water.

hydraulic /haɪˈdrɔːlɪk, -ˈdrɒlɪk/ ▻ *adj* **1** relating to hydraulics. **2** worked by the pressure of water or other fluid carried in pipes □ *hydraulic brakes*. **3** referring to something that sets in water □ *hydraulic cement*. • **hydraulically** *adverb*. ◷ 17c: from Greek *hydor* water + *aulos* pipe.

hydraulic brake ▻ *noun, engineering* a brake in which the force is transmitted by means of compressed fluid.

hydraulic press ▻ *noun, engineering* a press that enables a small force on a small piston to exert a greater force on a larger piston by means of compressed water.

hydraulic ram ▻ *noun* **1** the larger piston in a hydraulic press system. **2** a device whereby the pressure head of moving water brought to rest in one compartment delivers water under pressure from a second compartment of a HYDRAULIC PRESS.

hydraulics ▻ *singular noun, engineering* the science of hydrodynamics, or the mechanical properties of fluids, especially water, at rest or in motion, and their practical applications, eg to water pipes.

hydraulic suspension and **hydroelastic suspension** ▻ *noun* in a motor vehicle: a system of suspension using hydraulic units, where a fluid provides the interconnection between the front and rear suspension units.

hydrazoic acid see under AZIDE

hydric /ˈhaɪdrɪk/ ▻ *adj* **1** relating to or containing hydrogen. **2** having or using an abundance of moisture. ◷ Early 20c.

hydride /ˈhaɪdraɪd/ ▻ *noun* a chemical compound of hydrogen with another element or radical. ◷ 19c.

hydriodic acid /haɪdrɪˈɒdɪk —/ ▻ *noun* the aqueous solution of hydrogen iodide.

hydro¹ /ˈhaɪdroʊ/ *noun* hydroelectric power. ◷ Early 20c.

hydro² /ˈhaɪdroʊ/ *noun* (***hydros***) *Brit old use* a hotel or clinic, often situated near a spa, providing hydropathic treatment. ◷ 1880s.

hydro- /haɪdroʊ, haɪdrə, haɪˈdrɒ/ or (before a vowel) **hydr-** *combining form, signifying* **1** water □ *hydroelectricity*. **2** hydrogen. ◷ From Greek *hydor* water.

hydrobromic acid /haɪdroʊˈbroʊmɪk —/ ▻ *noun, chem* an aqueous solution of hydrogen and bromide.

hydrocarbon ▻ *noun, chem* any of a large group of organic chemical compounds that contain only carbon and hydrogen, occurring notably in oil, natural gas and coal. ◷ 19c.

hydrocele /ˈhaɪdroʊsiːl/ ▻ *noun, medicine* a swelling containing serous fluid, often in the scrotum. ◷ 16c: from Greek *kele* swelling.

hydrocephalus /haɪdroʊˈsɛfələs, -ˈkɛfələs/ ▻ *noun, medicine* an accumulation of serous fluid within the ventricles or cavities of the brain, usually occurring in young children. It causes enlargement of the head, and, if unimpeded, deterioration of the brain and its faculties. • **hydrocephalic** /-ˈfalɪk/ or **hydrocephalous** *adj*. ◷ 17c: from Greek *kephale* head.

hydrochloric acid ▻ *noun, chem* (formula **HCl**) a strong corrosive acid, formed by dissolving hydrogen and chlorine in water, and widely used in laboratories and industries. ◷ 19c.

hydrodynamics ▻ *singular noun* the science of the movement, equilibrium and power of liquids. See also HYDROKINETICS, HYDROSTATICS. • **hydrodynamicist** *noun* a specialist in or student of hydrodynamics. • **hydrodynamic** or **hydrodynamical** *adj.* ◷ 18c.

hydroelectricity and **hydroelectric power** ▷ *noun* electricity generated by turbines that are driven by the force of falling water. • **hydroelectric** *adj* electricity generated using this system. • **hydroelectrically** *adverb.* ◷ 19c.

hydrofluoric acid /haɪdroʊflʊ'ɒrɪk —/ ▷ *noun* an acid composed of hydrogen and fluorine.

hydrofoil /'haɪdrəfɔɪl/ ▷ *noun* **1** a device on a boat which raises it out of the water as it accelerates. **2** a boat fitted with such a device. ◷ Early 20c: modelled on AEROFOIL.

hydrogen /'haɪdrədʒən/ ▷ *noun* (symbol **H**, atomic number 1) a flammable colourless odourless gas which is the lightest of all known substances and by far the most abundant element in the universe. ◷ 18c: from French *hydrogène*, from HYDRO- + Greek *gennaein* to produce.

hydrogenate /'haɪdrədʒəneɪt, haɪ'drɒ-/ ▷ *verb* (***hydrogenated***, ***hydrogenating***) to undergo or cause to undergo hydrogenation.

hydrogenation ▷ *noun, chem* any chemical reaction where hydrogen is combined with another substance. ◷ Early 19c.

hydrogen bomb and **H-bomb** ▷ *noun, military* a bomb which releases vast amounts of energy as a result of hydrogen nuclei being converted into helium nuclei by fusion, a process started by a fission bomb. Also called **thermonuclear bomb**.

hydrogen bond ▷ *noun, chem* a weak chemical bond between an electronegative atom with a lone pair of electrons (eg oxygen, nitrogen, fluorine) and covalently bonded hydrogen atoms.

hydrogen carbonate ▷ *noun, chem* an acid salt of carbonic acid. Also called **bicarbonate**.

hydrogen chloride ▷ *noun, chem* (formula **HCl**) a poisonous colourless and corrosive gas prepared by treating sodium chloride with concentrated sulphuric acid.

hydrogen cyanide ▷ *noun, chem* (formula **HCN**) a toxic gas which when dissolved in water forms **hydrocyanic acid** (a dilute form of which is called PRUSSIC ACID).

hydrogen iodide ▷ *noun, chem* (formula **HI**) a heavy, colourless, poisonous gas formed by the direct combination of hydrogen and iodine.

hydrogen ion ▷ *noun, chem* a hydrogen atom or molecule carrying a positive charge, especially one formed in a solution of acid in water. Also called PROTON.

hydrogenize or **hydrogenise** /'haɪdrədʒɪnaɪz, haɪ'drɒ-/ ▷ *verb* (***hydrogenized***, ***hydrogenizing***) to hydrogenate.

hydrogenous /haɪ'drɒdʒənəs/ ▷ *adj* relating to or consisting of hydrogen. ◷ 18c.

hydrogen peroxide ▷ *noun, chem* (formula $\mathbf{H_2O_2}$) an unstable colourless viscous liquid that is a strong oxidizing agent, is soluble in water and is used as an oxidant in rocket fuel and a bleach for hair and textiles. Also called PEROXIDE.

hydrogensulphate ▷ *noun, chem* a salt or ester of sulphuric acid containing the ion HSO_4. Also called **bisulphate**.

hydrogen sulphide ▷ *noun, chem* (formula $\mathbf{H_2S}$) a colourless, toxic gas composed of hydrogen and sulphur with a characteristic smell of bad eggs, produced by decaying organic matter, and also found in natural gas and volcanic emissions.

hydrography /haɪ'drɒgrəfɪ/ ▷ *noun* the science of charting and mapping seas, rivers and lakes, and of studying tides, currents, winds, etc. • **hydrographer** *noun.* • **hydrographic** *adj.* ◷ 16c.

hydroid /'haɪdrɔɪd/ *zool* ▷ *adj* belonging, referring or similar to a hydra; polypoid. ▷ *noun* a type of COELENTERATE which reproduces asexually; a polyp.

hydrokinetics ▷ *singular noun* the branch of hydrodynamics which deals with fluids in motion. Compare HYDROSTATICS. • **hydrokinetic** *adj* **1** referring or relating to hydrokinetics or to the movement of fluids. **2** operated or operating by the movement of fluids. ◷ 19c.

hydrology /haɪ'drɒlədʒɪ/ ▷ *noun* the scientific study of the occurrence, movement and properties of water on the Earth's surface, and in the atmosphere. • **hydrologic** or **hydrological** *adj.* • **hydrologically** *adverb.* • **hydrologist** *noun.* ◷ 18c.

hydrolyse or **hydrolyze** /'haɪdrəlaɪz/ ▷ *verb* (***hydrolysed***, ***hydrolysing***) to subject to or occur by hydrolysis.

hydrolysis /haɪ'drɒlɪsɪs/ ▷ *noun* the chemical decomposition of organic compounds caused by the action of water. • **hydrolytic** /haɪdrə'lɪtɪk/ *adj.* ◷ 19c.

hydrolyte /'haɪdrəlaɪt/ ▷ *noun* a body subjected to hydrolysis.

hydromel /'haɪdroʊmɛl/ ▷ *noun* MEAD[1]. ◷ 15c: from Greek *meli* honey.

hydrometer /haɪ'drɒmɪtə(r)/ ▷ *noun, physics* a floating device used to measure the density of a liquid, indicated by the depth of immersion of a weighted glass bulb with a calibrated stem. • **hydrometric** or **hydrometrical** *adj.* • **hydrometry** *noun.* ◷ 17c.

hydropathy /haɪ'drɒpəθɪ/ ▷ *noun* the treatment of disease or illness using large amounts of water both internally and externally. • **hydropathic** /haɪdroʊ'paθɪk/ *adj.* • **hydropathically** *adverb.* • **hydropathist** *noun* a person who practises hydropathy. ◷ 19c.

hydrophilic /haɪdroʊ'fɪlɪk/ ▷ *adj, chem* referring to a substance that absorbs, attracts or has an affinity for water. • **hydrophile** /-faɪl/ *noun.* ◷ Early 20c.

hydrophobia ▷ *noun* **1** a fear or horror of water. **2** the inability to swallow water, especially as a symptom of rabies. **3** rabies. • **hydrophobe** *noun.* ◷ 16c.

hydrophobic ▷ *adj* **1** *chem* referring to a substance that repels or does not absorb water. **2** relating to or suffering from hydrophobia. • **hydrophobicity** *noun.*

hydrophone ▷ *noun* a device for listening to sounds conveyed by water. ◷ 19c.

hydrophylic /haɪdroʊ'fɪlɪk/ ▷ *adj, chem* referring to a substance that readily absorbs water or is easily wetted by water.

hydrophyte /'haɪdroʊfaɪt/ ▷ *noun, bot* a plant which grows in water or very moist conditions. • **hydrophytic** /-'fɪtɪk/ *adj.* ◷ 19c.

hydroplane ▷ *noun* **1** a light motorboat with a flat bottom or hydrofoils which, at high speeds, skims along the surface of the water. **2** a fin-like device attached to a submarine allowing it to rise and fall in the water. **3** a seaplane. ▷ *verb, intr* **1** said of a boat: to skim on the surface of the water like a hydroplane. **2** said of a road vehicle: to skid on a wet surface; to aquaplane. ◷ Early 20c.

hydroponics /haɪdroʊ'pɒnɪks/ ▷ *singular noun, bot* the practice or technique of growing plants without using soil, by immersing the roots in a chemical solution that contains essential nutrients, and using sand or gravel as support. • **hydroponic** *adj.* • **hydroponically** *adverb.* ◷ 1930s: from Greek *ponos* work or toil.

hydropower ▷ *noun* hydroelectric power.

hydroquinone /haɪdrə'kwɪnoʊn/ ▷ *noun, photog* a white crystalline substance that is used as a reducing agent and as a photographic developer. Also called **quinol**.

hydrosphere ▷ *noun* the water, such as seas and rivers, on the surface of the earth. ⓒ 19c.

hydrostatics ▷ *singular noun* the branch of hydrodynamics which deals with the behaviour and power of fluids which are not in motion. • **hydrostatic** or **hydrostatical** *adj*. Compare HYDROKINETICS. ⓒ 17c.

hydrotherapy ▷ *noun, medicine* the treatment of diseases and disorders by the external use of water, especially the treatment of disability by developing movement in water. • **hydrotherapeutic** *adj*. • **hydrotherapeutics** *singular noun* the area of medicine concerned with hydrotherapy. ⓒ 19c.

hydrotropism /haɪˈdrɒtrəpɪzəm/ ▷ *noun* the tendency of the roots of a plant to turn towards (**positive hydrotropism**) or away from (**negative hydrotropism**) moisture. Compare HELIOTROPISM. ⓒ 19c.

hydrous /ˈhaɪdrəs/ ▷ *adj* said of a substance: containing water. ⓒ 19c.

hydroxide /haɪˈdrɒksaɪd/ ▷ *noun, chem* a chemical compound containing one or more hydroxyl groups.

hydroxy- /haɪˈdrɒksɪ/ ▷ *combining form, chem, signifying* that it contains one or more hydroxyl groups.

hydroxyl /haɪˈdrɒksɪl/ ▷ *noun, chem* a compound radical containing one oxygen atom and one hydrogen atom. ⓒ 19c: from *hydrogen* + *oxygen* + -YL.

hydrozoan /haɪdroʊˈzoʊən/ ▷ *noun* (***hydrozoa***) a coelenterate of the mainly marine class **Hydrozoa,** in which alternation of generations typically occurs, eg the zoophytes. • **hydrozoan** *noun, adj*. ⓒ 19c: from HYDRO- + Greek *zoon*, plural *zoa* animal.

hyena or **hyaena** /haɪˈiːnə/ ▷ *noun* (***hyenas*** or ***hyaenas***) any of various kinds of carrion-feeding doglike mammals native to Africa and Asia, which have a long thick neck, coarse mane, and a sloping body, and known for their howls which resemble hysterical laughter. ⓒ 14c: from Greek *hyaina*, from *hys* pig.

hygiene /ˈhaɪdʒiːn/ ▷ *noun* **1** the practice or study of preserving one's health and preventing the spread of disease, especially by keeping oneself and one's surroundings clean. **2** sanitary principles and practices. ⓒ 16c: from Greek *hygieia* health.

hygienic /haɪˈdʒiːnɪk/ ▷ *adj* promoting and preserving health; sanitary. • **hygienically** *adverb*. ⓒ 19c.

hygienics /haɪˈdʒiːnɪks/ ▷ *singular noun* the principles of HYGIENE (sense 1).

hygienist /ˈhaɪdʒiːnɪst/ ▷ *noun* a person skilled in the practice of hygiene.

hygro- /haɪgroʊ, haɪˈgrɒ, haɪgrə/ or (before a vowel) **hygr-** *combining form, signifying* wet, moist.

hygrology /haɪˈgrɒlədʒɪ/ ▷ *noun* the study of humidity in gases, especially the atmosphere. ⓒ 18c.

hygrometer /haɪˈgrɒmɪtə(r)/ ▷ *noun, meteorol* a device for measuring the humidity of gases or of the air, ie the amount of water vapour in the atmosphere. ⓒ 17c.

hygrometry /haɪˈgrɒmɪtrɪ/ ▷ *noun* a measurement of the humidity of the air or of other gases. • **hygrometric** or **hygrometrical** *adj*.

hygrophyte /ˈhaɪgroʊfaɪt/ ▷ *noun, bot* a plant adapted for living in moist conditions. • **hygrophytic** /-ˈfɪtɪk/ *adj*. ⓒ Early 20c.

hygroscope /ˈhaɪgrəskoʊp/ ▷ *noun* a device which indicates changes in air humidity without measuring it. ⓒ 17c.

hygroscopic /haɪgrəˈskɒpɪk/ and **hygroscopical** ▷ *adj* **1** relating to the hygroscope. **2** said of a substance: able to absorb moisture from the air. **3** said eg of some movements of plants: indicating or caused by absorption or loss of moisture. • **hygroscopically** *adverb*. • **hygroscopicity** /-skɒˈpɪsɪtɪ/ *noun*. ⓒ 18c.

hying see under HIE

hymen /ˈhaɪmɛn, -mən/ ▷ *noun, anatomy* a thin membrane that covers the opening of the vagina, and may be broken the first time a woman has sexual intercourse, but is usually at least partially ruptured before puberty. • **hymenal** *adj*. ⓒ 17c: Greek.

hymenopteran /haɪməˈnɒptərən/ ▷ *noun* an insect belonging to the diverse order **Hymenoptera**, members of which often but not always have four membranous wings, including ants, bees, wasps and sawflies. • **hymenopterous** *adj*. ⓒ 18c: from Greek *hymen* membrane + -PTERA.

hymn /hɪm/ ▷ *noun* a song of praise, especially to God, but also to a nation, etc. ▷ *verb* (***hymned***, ***hymning***) **1** to celebrate in song or worship by hymns. **2** *intr* to sing in adoration. ⓒ Anglo-Saxon: from Greek *hymnos*.

hymnal /ˈhɪmnəl/ ▷ *noun* (*also* **hymnary**) a book containing hymns. ▷ *adj* (*also* **hymnic**) referring or relating to hymns. ⓒ 17c.

hymn-book ▷ *noun* a book or collection of hymns.

hymnody /ˈhɪmnədɪ/ ▷ *noun* (***hymnodies***) **1** the writing or singing of hymns. **2** hymns as a group. • **hymnodist** or **hymnist** *noun* someone who composes hymns. ⓒ 18c.

hymnology /hɪmˈnɒlədʒɪ/ ▷ *noun* the study or composition of hymns. • **hymnologist** *noun*. ⓒ 17c.

hyoid /ˈhaɪɔɪd/ ▷ *adj* referring to the **hyoid bone**, a curved bone at the base of the tongue.

hyoscine /ˈhaɪoʊsiːn/ ▷ *noun* an alkaloid drug obtained from certain plants, eg henbane, with actions on the intestines and nervous system, given for travel sickness, used as a truth drug, etc. Also called **scopolamine**. ⓒ 19c.

hyoscyamine /haɪəˈsaɪəmiːn/ ▷ *noun* a poisonous alkaloid similar to atropine, extracted from henbane. ⓒ 19c: from Greek *hyoskyamos*, from *hys* pig + *kyamos* bean.

hyp. ▷ *abbreviation* **1** hypotenuse. **2** hypothesis. **3** hypothetical.

hypaethral /hɪˈpiːθrəl, haɪ-/ ▷ *adj* said especially of a classical building: open to the sky; roofless. ⓒ 18c: from Greek *hypo* beneath + *aither* air or sky.

hypallage /haɪˈpalədʒiː, hɪ-/ ▷ *noun, rhetoric* a figure of speech where the standard relations of words are mutually interchanged. ⓒ 16c: Greek, literally 'interchange', from *hypo* under + *allassein* to exchange.

hype¹ /haɪp/ *colloq, noun* **1** intensive, exaggerated or artificially induced excitement about, or enthusiasm for, something or someone. **2** exaggerated and usually misleading publicity or advertising; a sales gimmick. **3** a publicity stunt, or the person or thing promoted by such a stunt. **4** a deception. ▷ *verb* (***hyped***, ***hyping***) to promote or advertise something intensively. ⓒ Early 20c.

■ **hype someone** or **something up** to attempt to induce excessive excitement or enthusiasm for them or it □ *The film was hyped up too much.*

hype² /haɪp/ *slang, noun* **1** a hypodermic needle. **2** a drug addict. **3** something which artificially stimulates, especially a drug. ▷ *verb* (***hyped***, ***hyping***) *intr, slang* (*usually* **hype up**) to inject oneself with a drug. See also HYPO¹. ⓒ 1920s: short form of HYPODERMIC.

hyped up ▷ *adj, slang* **1** artificially stimulated or highly excited, eg with drugs. **2** artificial; false or fake.

hyper /ˈhaɪpə(r)/ ▷ *adj, colloq* said of a person: over-excited; over-stimulated. ⓒ 1940s: short form of HYPERACTIVE.

hyper- /haɪˈpɜː, haɪpə(r)/ ▷ *combining form, signifying* over, excessive, more than normal □ *hyperactive*. ⓒ Greek, meaning 'over'.

hyperacidity ▻ *noun* an excessive level of acidity, especially in the stomach. ⓒ 19c.

hyperactive ▻ *adj* said especially of a child: abnormally or pathologically active. ⓒ 19c.

hyperactivity ▻ *noun, psychol* a condition characterized by overactive, poorly controlled behaviour and lack of concentration, most frequently seen in children.

hyperaemia or (*N Amer*) **hyperemia** /haɪpər'iːmɪə/ ▻ *noun, pathol* an excess or congestion of blood in any part or organ of the body. See also HYPOSTASIS 3. • **hyperaemic** *adj*. ⓒ 19c.

hyperaesthesia or (*N Amer*) **hyperesthesia** /haɪpəriːs'θiːzɪə/ ▻ *noun, pathol* abnormal or excessive sensitivity to stimulation. • **hyperaesthetic** or **hyperesthetic** abnormally sensitive. ⓒ 19c.

hyperbaton /haɪ'pɜːbətən/ ▻ *noun* (***hyperbatons*** or ***hyperbata*** /-tə/) *rhetoric* a figure of speech where the customary order of words is reversed, especially for emphasis. ⓒ 16c: Greek, literally 'overstepping', from *hyper* over + *bainein* to walk, step.

hyperbola /haɪ'pɜːbələ/ ▻ *noun* (***hyperbolas, hyperbolae*** /-liː/) *geom* the curve produced when a PLANE^2 cuts through a cone so that the angle between the base of the cone and the plane is greater than the angle between the base and the sloping side of the cone. ⓒ 17c: Latin, from Greek *hyperbole*, from *hyper* over + *ballein* to throw.

hyperbole /haɪ'pɜːbəlɪ/ ▻ *noun, rhetoric* the use of an overstatement or exaggeration for effect. ⓒ 16c: Greek, literally 'exaggeration'.

hyperbolic /haɪpə'bɒlɪk/ ▻ *adj* **1** *geom* relating to or in the form of a hyperbola. **2** *rhetoric* involving hyperbole. • **hyperbolically** *adverb*. ⓒ 17c.

hyperbolic function ▻ *noun, math* any of a set of six functions (sinh, cosh, tanh, etc) analogous to the trigonometrical functions.

hyperbolize or **hyperbolise** /haɪ'pɜːbəlaɪz/ ▻ *verb* (***hyperbolized, hyperbolizing***) **1** to represent with hyperbole. **2** *intr* to speak using hyperbole; to exaggerate. • **hyperbolism** *noun*. ⓒ 16c.

hypercritical ▻ *adj* over-critical, especially of small faults. • **hypercritically** *adverb*. ⓒ 17c.

hyperemia see HYPERAEMIA

hyperesthesia and **hyperesthetic** see HYPERAESTHESIA

hyperglycaemia or (*N Amer*) **hyperglycemia** /haɪpəglaɪ'siːmɪə/ ▻ *noun, pathol* a condition in which the sugar concentration in the blood is abnormally high. Compare HYPOGLYCAEMIA. ⓒ 20c.

hyperlink ▻ *noun, computing* a link between pieces of information within HYPERMEDIA.

hypermarket ▻ *noun, Brit* a very large supermarket with a wide range of goods, usually on the edge of a town. ⓒ 1960s: a translation of French *hypermarché*.

hypermedia ▻ *noun, computing* a computer file and related software which identifies and links information in various media, such as text, graphics, sound, video clips, etc, so that, for example, an encyclopedia entry might have a video clip of Nelson Mandella accessible from a text entry by a simple click or double click on the mouse. ⓒ 1990s: from *hyper*text + multi*media*.

hypermetropia /haɪpəmə'troupɪə/ ▻ *noun, pathol* a condition where rays of light entering the eye are focused behind the retina so near objects are blurred; long-sightedness. Also called **hyperopia** /-'oupɪə/. ⓒ 19c: from HYPER- + Greek *metron* measure + *ops* eye.

hyperon /'haɪpərɒn/ ▻ *noun, physics* any of a class of elementary particles with masses greater than that of a neutron.

hyperphysical ▻ *adj* beyond physical laws; supernatural. • **hyperphysically** *adverb*. ⓒ 17c.

hypersensitive ▻ *adj* excessively sensitive; more sensitive than normal. • **hypersensitiveness** or **hypersensitivity** *noun*. ⓒ 19c.

hypersonic ▻ *adj* **1** said of speeds: being greater than Mach number 5 (about five times the speed of sound in the same medium and in the same environment). **2** *aeronautics* said of an aircraft or rocket: capable of flying at such speeds. **3** said of sound waves: having a frequency greater than 1 000 million hertz. • **hypersonics** *plural noun*. ⓒ 1930s.

hypertension ▻ *noun* **1** *pathol* a condition in which the blood pressure is abnormally high. **2** a state of great emotional tension. • **hypertensive** *adj, noun*. ⓒ 19c.

hypertext ▻ *noun, computing* computer-readable text in which cross-reference links (HYPERLINKS) have been inserted, enabling the user to call up relevant data from other files, or parts of the same file, by clicking on a coded word or symbol, etc.

hyperthermia ▻ *noun, pathol* a condition where the body temperature becomes abnormally and sometimes dangerously high. • **hyperthermal** *adj*. Compare HYPOTHERMIA. ⓒ 19c: from Greek *therme* heat.

hyperthyroidism ▻ *noun* **1** overproduction of thyroid hormones by the thyroid gland. **2** the condition resulting from this, including weight loss, insomnia, rapid heartbeat and increased appetite. • **hyperthyroid** *adj* suffering, or resulting, from this condition. Compare HYPOTHYROIDISM. ⓒ Early 20c.

hypertonic ▻ *adj* **1** *pathol* said of muscles: having excessive tone, or tensed to an abnormally high degree. **2** *chem* said of a solution: having a higher osmotic pressure than another solution with which it is being compared. • **hypertonia** *noun* a hypertonic condition. Compare HYPOTONIC. ⓒ 19c.

hypertrophy /haɪ'pɜːtrəfɪ/ ▻ *noun* (***hypertrophies***) *biol* an abnormal increase in the size of an organ as a result of overnourishment. ▻ *verb* (***hypertrophied, hypertrophying***) to subject or be subjected to hypertrophy. • **hypertrophic** or **hypertrophied** *adj*. ⓒ 19c.

hyperventilation ▻ *noun* a condition in which the speed and depth of breathing becomes abnormally rapid, causing dizziness, a feeling of suffocation and sometimes unconsciousness. ⓒ 1920s.

hypha /'haɪfə/ ▻ *noun* (***hyphae*** /-fiː/) *biol* in multicellular fungi: any of many thread-like filaments that form the MYCELIUM. • **hyphal** *adj*. ⓒ 19c: from Greek *hyphe* web.

hyphen /'haɪfən/ ▻ *noun* a punctuation mark (-) used to join two words to form a compound (eg, *booby-trap, double-barrelled*) or, in texts, to split a word between the end of one line and the beginning of the next. ▻ *verb* (***hyphened, hyphening***) to hyphenate. ⓒ 19c: from Greek *hypo* under + *hen* one.

hyphenate /'haɪfəneɪt/ ▻ *verb* (***hyphenated, hyphenating***) to join or separate two words or parts of words with a hyphen. • **hyphenated** *adj* **1** containing a hyphen. **2** *N Amer* of mixed nationality ⓒ1890s: because such people have their nationality expressed in a hyphenated word such as *Irish-American*. • **hyphenation** *noun*. ⓒ 19c.

hypno- /'hɪpnou, hɪpnə/ or (before a vowel) **hypn-** *combining form, signifying* **1** sleep. **2** hypnosis. ⓒ From Greek *hypnos* sleep.

hypnoid /'hɪpnɔɪd/ and **hypnoidal** ▻ *adj, psychol* in a state like or similar to sleep or hypnosis. ⓒ 19c.

hypnology /hɪp'nɒlədʒɪ/ ▻ *noun, psychol* the scientific study of sleep and hypnosis. ⓒ 19c.

hypnopaedia /hɪpnou'piːdɪə/ ▻ *noun* the learning of something, or conditioning of someone by the repetition

hyphen

A **hyphen** should be used for

1. linking words

● It links elements of a multi-word phrase that describes a following noun □ *a never-to-be-forgotten experience* □ *a balance-of-payments problem* □ *her absurd caught-in-at-the-knees skirt* □ *an up-to-date timetable.*

Note that hyphens are not normally needed when the phrase describes a preceding noun, as in *It was an experience never to be forgotten*, although where there is an intervening modifying adverb, hyphens are usually retained, as in *This timetable is thoroughly up-to-date.*

● It links elements of a multi-word phrase that functions as a noun □ *his mother-in-law* □ *a bunch of forget-me-nots* □ *a man-about-town* □ *a jack-in-the-box.*

● It links elements of a multi-word phrase that has a suffix added to make it function as a single unit □ *Esmond was being very Justice-of-the-Peace-y* □ *The aunts raised their eyebrows with a good deal of To-what-are-we-indebted-for-the-honour-of-this-visitness.*

● It links elements of numbers from 21 to 99, and elements of fractions □ *twenty-three* □ *three-quarters.*

● It links elements of a two-word adjective that describes a following noun □ *a half-open door* □ *a repertoire of all-time favourites* □ *a next-door neighbour* □ *a well-known writer* □ *one of its best-loved characters.*

Note that there are categories of two-word adjectives that retain their hyphens when they describe a preceding noun:

(1) a combination of adjective + participle, or word ending in *-ed*, as in *We are dreadfully short-staffed here* and *The toll of job losses seems never-ending*;

(2) a combination of adjective + noun, as in *I thought the performance was pretty second-rate*;

(3) a combination of noun + adjective, as in *The path was ankle-deep in weeds.*

Note that adverbs ending in *-ly* are not linked to a following word, except in cases where the two are felt to function as a single unit of meaning, so *a beautifully illustrated book*, but *a mentally-handicapped child.*

● It links elements of nouns formed from phrasal verbs □ *line-up* □ *drive-in fly-past.*

● It links elements of adjectives formed from phrasal verbs when the adjective describes a following noun □ *an unhoped-for success* □ *a hung-up young man.*

2. splitting words

● A hyphen marks a break in a word at the end of a line of print, where part of the word has been taken over to the next line.

Take care to split the word into logical or unambiguous units: *mis-/shapen*, not *miss-/hapen*; *re-/install*, not *rein-/stall*; and, *ther-/apist*, not *the-/rapist.*

● It marks a break in a word whose second element is implied but not shown, as in *a four- or fivefold increase.*

of recorded sound during sleep or semi-wakefulness. Ⓒ 1930s: from Greek *paideia* education.

hypnopompic /hɪpnoʊ'pɒmpɪk/ ▷ *adj* relating to the state between sleep and wakefulness. Ⓒ Early 20c: from Greek *pompe* sending away.

hypnosis /hɪp'noʊsɪs/ ▷ *noun* (***hypnoses*** /-siːz/) an induced sleeplike state in which a person is deeply relaxed, and in which the mind responds to external suggestion and can recover memories of events thought to have been forgotten. Ⓒ 19c: from Greek *hypnos* sleep.

hypnotherapy ▷ *noun* the treatment of illness or altering of habits, eg smoking, by hypnosis. Ⓒ 19c.

hypnotic /hɪp'nɒtɪk/ ▷ *adj* **1** relating to, causing or caused by, hypnosis. **2** causing sleepiness; soporific. ▷ *noun* **1** a drug that produces sleep. **2** someone who is subject to hypnosis. **3** someone in a state of hypnosis. ● **hypnotically** *adverb*. Ⓒ 17c.

hypnotism /'hɪpnətɪzəm/ ▷ *noun* **1** the science or practice of hypnosis. **2** the art or practice of inducing hypnosis. Ⓒ 19c: a shortening of *neuro-hypnotism*, a term introduced by James Braid (1795–1860), a British surgeon.

hypnotist /'hɪpnətɪst/ ▷ *noun* a person who practises or is skilled in hypnotism. Ⓒ 19c.

hypnotize or **hypnotise** /'hɪpnətaɪz/ ▷ *verb* (***hypnotized, hypnotizing***) **1** to put someone in a state of hypnosis. **2** to fascinate, captivate or bewitch. ● **hypnotizable** *adj*. ● **hypnotizability** *noun*. ● **hypnotization** *noun*. Ⓒ 19c.

hypo¹ /'haɪpoʊ/ ▷ *noun* (***hypos***) *colloq* a hypodermic syringe or injection. See also HYPE². Ⓒ Early 20c: short form of HYPODERMIC.

hypo² /'haɪpoʊ/ ▷ *noun, photog* short form of HYPOSULPHITE.

hypo- /haɪpoʊ, haɪpə/ or (before a vowel) **hyp-** *combining form, signifying* **1** under. **2** inadequate. **3** defective. Ⓒ Greek, meaning 'under'.

hypoblast /'haɪpoʊblast, -blɑːst/ ▷ *noun, biol* the inner layer of the gastrula. ● **hypoblastic** *adj*. Ⓒ 19c.

hypocaust /'haɪpoʊkɔːst/ ▷ *noun* in ancient Rome: a form of heating system in which hot air was passed through a hollow space between the walls and under the floor. Ⓒ 17c: from Latin *hypocaustum*, from Greek *hypo-* under *kaiein* to burn.

hypochlorite /haɪpoʊ'klɔːraɪt/ ▷ *noun, chem* a salt of HYPOCHLOROUS ACID. Ⓒ 19c.

hypochlorous acid /haɪpoʊ'klɔːrəs —/ ▷ *noun, chem* (formula **HClO**) a weak acid that is only stable in solution, and is used as a disinfectant and bleach. Ⓒ 19c.

hypochondria /haɪpə'kɒndrɪə/ and **hypochondriasis** /-'draɪəsɪs/ ▷ *noun* a condition, often associated with anxiety or depression, characterized by excessive or morbid concern over one's health and sometimes belief in the existence of a serious illness. Ⓒ 17c: from Greek *hypochondrion* abdomen, formerly believed to be the source of melancholy.

hypochondriac /haɪpə'kɒndrɪak/ ▷ *noun* someone suffering from hypochondria. ▷ *adj* **1** relating to hypochondria or hypochondriacs. **2** affected with hypochondria. ● **hypochondriacal** /-'draɪəkəl/ *adj*. Ⓒ 17c.

hypochondrium /haɪpə'kɒndrɪəm/ ▷ *noun* (***hypochondria*** /-drɪə/) *anatom* the right and left sides of the abdomen, under the costal cartilages and short ribs. Ⓒ 17c: from Greek *hypochondrion* abdomen.

hypocorism /haɪ'pɒkərɪzəm, hɪ-/ ▷ *noun* a pet-name; a diminutive or abbreviated name, eg 'Libby' as one hypocorism for 'Elizabeth'. ● **hypocoristic** /haɪpəkə'rɪstɪk/ or **hypocoristical** *adj* having the nature of a pet-name. ● **hypocoristically** *adverb*. Ⓒ 19c: from Greek *hypokorisma*, from *hypokorizesthai* to use child-talk, from *koros* boy, *kore* girl.

hypocrisy /hɪ'pɒkrɪsɪ/ ▷ *noun* (***hypocrisies***) **1** the act of pretending to have feelings, beliefs or principles which one does not actually have. **2** the act of concealing one's true character. Ⓒ 13c: from Greek *hypokrisis* play-acting.

hypocrite /ˈhɪpəkrɪt/ ▷ *noun* a person who practises hypocrisy. • **hypocritical** *adj.* • **hypocritically** *adverb.* ⓒ 13c: from Greek *hypokrites* an actor.

hypocycloid /haɪpəˈsaɪklɔɪd/ ▷ *adj* a curve formed by a point on the circumference of a circle which rolls on the inside of another circle. • **hypocycloidal** *adj.* ⓒ 19c.

hypodermic /haɪpəˈdɜːmɪk/ ▷ *adj* **1** referring or relating to the hypodermis. **2** said of a drug: for injecting under the skin or subcutaneously. ▷ *noun* **1** a hypodermic syringe. **2** an injection of a drug under the skin. • **hypodermically** *adverb.* ⓒ 19c: from Greek *hypo* under + *derma* skin.

hypodermic syringe ▷ *noun* a syringe with a fine hollow needle, used for injecting drugs under the skin or taking blood samples.

hypodermis /haɪpəˈdɜːmɪs/ and **hypoderma** ▷ *noun, bot, anatomy* the tissue beneath the epidermis or surface. ⓒ 19c.

hypogastric /haɪpoʊˈgastrɪk/ ▷ *adj, anatomy* belonging or referring to the lower central part of the abdomen, the **hypogastrium**. ⓒ 17c: from Greek *hypogastrion* lower belly, from *hypo* under + *gaster* stomach.

hypogeal /haɪpoʊˈdʒɪəl/ , **hypogean** and **hypogeous** ▷ *adj, bot* existing or growing underground. ⓒ 19c: from Greek *hypogeios*, from *hypo-* under + *ge* earth, the ground.

hypogene /ˈhaɪpoʊdʒiːn/ ▷ *adj, geol* formed beneath the Earth's surface; plutonic. Compare EPIGENE. • **hypogenic** *adj.* ⓒ 19c: HYPO- + Greek *gennaein* to engender or generate.

hypogeum /haɪpoʊˈdʒɪəm/ ▷ *noun* (***hypogea*** /-dʒɪə/) an underground or subterranean chamber, especially for use as a tomb. ⓒ 18c: Latin, from Greek *hypo* under + *ge* earth.

hypoglycaemia or **hypoglycemia** /haɪpoʊglaɪˈsiːmɪə/ ▷ *noun, pathol* a condition in which the sugar content of the blood is abnormally low, usually occurring in diabetics after an insulin overdose. • **hypoglycaemic** *adj.* ⓒ 19c: HYPO- + GLYCO- + -AEMIA.

hypoid /ˈhaɪpɔɪd/ ▷ *adj* a type of bevel gear in which the axes of the driving and driven shafts are at right angles but not in the same plane. ⓒ 1920s.

hyponasty /ˈhaɪpoʊnastɪ/ ▷ *noun, bot* an increased growth on the lower side of an organ of a plant, causing an upward bend. Compare EPINASTY. • **hyponastic** *adj.* ⓒ 19c: from Greek *nastos* pressed close.

hyponym /ˈhaɪpoʊnɪm/ ▷ *noun, linguistics* any of a group of specific terms whose meanings are included in a more general term, eg *oak* and *cedar* are hyponyms of *tree* and also of *wood*, and *spaniel* and *terrier* are hyponyms of *dog*. • **hyponymy** /haɪˈpɒnɪmɪ/ *noun.* ⓒ Early 20c: from HYPO- + Greek *onyma* a name.

hypophosphite /haɪpoʊˈfɒsfaɪt/ ▷ *noun, chem* a salt of HYPOPHOSPHOROUS ACID. ⓒ 19c.

hypophosphorous acid /haɪpoʊˈfɒsfərəs —/ ▷ *noun, chem* (formula H_3PO_2) a monobasic, water-soluble acid, used as a reducing agent.

hypophysis /haɪˈpɒfɪsɪs, hɪ-/ ▷ *noun* (***hypophyses*** /-siːz/) *anatomy* the pituitary gland. • **hypophysial** or **hypophyseal** /haɪpəˈfɪzɪəl, haɪpɒfɪˈsɪəl/ *adj.* ⓒ 18c: Greek, meaning 'outgrowth', from *phyein* to grow.

hypostasis /haɪˈpɒstəsɪs, hɪ-/ ▷ *noun* (***hypostases*** /-siːz/) **1** *metaphysics* **a** the underlying essence of a substance; **b** the foundation or basis of a substance. **2** *theol* **a** the essence or personal subsistence or substance of each of the three divisions of the Trinity; **b** Christ as the union of human and divine qualities. **3** *medicine* HYPERAEMIA caused by bad circulation. • **hypostatic** /haɪpoʊˈstatɪk/ or **hypostatical** *adj.* • **hypostatically** *adverb.* ⓒ 16c: Greek, meaning 'foundation' or 'substance'.

hypostyle /ˈhaɪpoʊstaɪl/ *archit* ▷ *adj* having the roof supported by pillars. ▷ *noun* a hypostyle construction. ⓒ 19c: from Greek *hypo* under + *stylos* pillar.

hyposulphite /haɪpoʊˈsʌlfaɪt/ ▷ *noun, photog* a substance used as a fixer. Also called HYPO². ⓒ 19c.

hypotension ▷ *noun, pathol* an abnormally low level of blood-pressure. Compare HYPERTENSION. • **hypotensive** *adj* someone with low blood-pressure. ⓒ 19c.

hypotenuse /haɪˈpɒtənjuːz/ ▷ *noun, math* (abbreviation **hyp.**) the longest side of a right-angled triangle, opposite to the right angle. ⓒ 16c: from Greek *hypoteinousa* subtending or stretching under.

hypothalamus /haɪpoʊˈθaləməs/ ▷ *noun* (***hypothalami*** /-maɪ/) *anatomy* the region of the brain situated below the thalamus and above the pituitary gland, which acts as a centre of control of the autonomic nervous system and hormonal activity. It is involved in the regulation of involuntary functions, such as body temperature. • **hypothalamic** *adj.* ⓒ 19c.

hypothec /ˈhaɪpoʊθɛk, ˈhɪ-/ ▷ *noun, Roman & Scots law* a lien or security, rather than possession, over goods or property in respect of a debt due by the owner of the goods or property. ⓒ 16c: from Greek *hypotheke* a pledge, from *hypotithenai* to deposit as a pledge.

hypothecate /haɪˈpɒθɪkeɪt/ ▷ *verb* (***hypothecated***, ***hypothecating***) *law* to place or assign as security under an arrangement; to mortgage. ⓒ 17c.

hypothermia /haɪpəˈθɜːmɪə/ ▷ *noun* **1** *pathol* a condition in which the body temperature falls below normal as a result of prolonged exposure to extremely cold temperatures. **2** *medicine* a decrease in body temperature that is deliberately induced, eg to reduce a patient's oxygen requirements during heart surgery. Compare HYPERTHERMIA. ⓒ 19c: from Greek *therme* heat.

hypothesis /haɪˈpɒθəsɪs/ ▷ *noun* (***hypotheses*** /-siːz/) **1** a statement or proposition assumed to be true for the sake of argument. **2** a statement or theory to be proved or disproved by reference to evidence or facts. **3** a provisional explanation of anything. ⓒ 16c: Greek.

hypothesize or **hypothesise** /haɪˈpɒθəsaɪz/ ▷ *verb* (***hypothesized***, ***hypothesizing***) **1** *intr* to form a hypothesis. **2** to assume as a hypothesis.

hypothetical /haɪpəˈθɛtɪkəl/ and **hypothetic** ▷ *adj* based on or involving hypothesis; assumed. • **hypothetically** *adverb.*

hypothyroidism /haɪpoʊˈθaɪrɔɪdɪzəm/ ▷ *noun, medicine* **1** an insufficient production of thyroid hormones by the thyroid gland. **2** a condition resulting from this, such as CRETINISM or MYXOEDEMA. • **hypothyroid** *adj* referring to or affected by hypothyroidism. Compare HYPERTHYROIDISM. ⓒ Early 20c.

hypotonic /haɪpəˈtɒnɪk/ ▷ *adj* **1** *pathol* said of muscles: lacking normal tone. **2** *chem* said of a solution: having a lower osmotic pressure than another solution with which it is being compared. • **hypotonia** *noun* a hypotonic condition. Compare HYPERTONIC. ⓒ 19c.

hypoxia /haɪˈpɒksɪə/ ▷ *noun, pathol* a deficiency of oxygen reaching the body tissues. • **hypoxic** *adj.* ⓒ 20c.

hypso- /hɪpsoʊ, hɪpˈsɒ/ or (before a vowel) **hyps-** *combining form, signifying* height. ⓒ From Greek *hypsos*.

hypsography /hɪpˈsɒgrəfɪ/ ▷ *noun* **1** the branch of geography dealing with the measurement and mapping of heights, or topography, above sea level. **2** a map displaying topographical relief. ⓒ 19c.

hypsometer /hɪpˈsɒmɪtə(r)/ ▷ *noun* a device for measuring the heights of positions on the Earth's surface by observing the effect of altitude on the boiling point of water, because this decreases with increasing altitude. ⓒ 19c.

hypsometry /hɪpˈsɒmɪtrɪ/ ▷ *noun* the science of measuring heights of positions on the earth's surface. • **hypsometric** *adj.* ⓒ 16c.

hyrax /'haɪraks/ ▻ *noun* (***hyraxes*** or ***hyraces*** /'haɪrəsiːz/) any of a group of mammals, native to Africa and Arabia, related to the elephant, which superficially resemble a large guinea pig, with a pointed muzzle, round ears, and short legs and tail. ⓘ 19c: Greek, meaning 'shrew'.

hyssop /'hɪsəp/ ▻ *noun* **1** a small shrubby aromatic plant, native to S Europe and W Asia, with narrow leaves and clusters of long blue flowers, formerly cultivated as a medicinal herb. **2** in the Bible: a plant used as a ceremonial sprinkler. **3** a holy water sprinkler. ⓘ Anglo-Saxon: from Greek *hyssopos*.

hyster- see HYSTERO-

hysterectomy /hɪstə'rɛktəmɪ/ ▻ *noun* (***hysterectomies***) the surgical removal of the uterus or womb. ⓘ 19c.

hysteresis /hɪstə'riːsɪs/ ▻ *noun, physics* the delay or lag between the cause of an effect, and the effect itself, eg when a magnetic material becomes magnetized. • **hysteretic** /-'rɛtɪk/ *adj*. ⓘ 19c: Greek, meaning 'deficiency', from *hysteros* later.

hysteria /hɪ'stɪərɪə/ ▻ *noun* (***hysterias***) **1** *psychol* a psychoneurosis characterized by mental and physical symptoms such as hallucinations, convulsions, amnesia or paralysis. **2** any state of emotional instability caused by acute stress or a traumatic experience. **3** any extreme emotional state, such as laughter or weeping. ⓘ 19c: from Greek *hystera* womb, from the former belief that disturbances in the womb caused emotional imbalance.

hysteric /hɪ'stɛrɪk/ ▻ *noun* someone suffering from hysteria. ⓘ 17c.

hysterical /hɪ'stɛrɪkəl/ ▻ *adj* **1** relating to or suffering from hysteria. **2** characterized by hysteria □ *a hysterical laugh*. **3** *colloq* extremely funny or amusing □ *a hysterical joke*. • **hysterically** *adverb*. ⓘ 17c.

hysterics /hɪ'stɛrɪks/ ▻ *plural noun* **1** a fit of hysteria. **2** *colloq* fits of uncontrollable laughter □ *She was in hysterics when she heard the joke*. ⓘ 18c.

hystero- /hɪstərou, -rɒ/ or (before a vowel) **hyster-** *combining form, signifying* womb. ⓘ From Greek *hystera*.

hysteron proteron /'hɪstərɒn 'prɒtərɒn/ ▻ *noun, rhetoric* a figure of speech where there is an inversion of the usual order of words, phrases, etc. ⓘ 16c: Greek, literally 'latter former'.

Hz ▻ *abbreviation* hertz.

I

I[1] or **i** /aɪ/ ▷ *noun* (***Is***, ***I's*** or ***i's***) **1** the ninth letter of the English alphabet. **2** an object or figure shaped like an I. See also I-BEAM.

I[2] /aɪ/ ▷ *pronoun* used by the speaker or writer to refer to himself or herself, as the subject of an actual or implied verb. Compare ME[1]. ◷ Anglo-Saxon *ic*.

> ***I, me***
>
> After prepositions, the object form **me** should always be used:
>
> ✓ *between you and me*
>
> ✗ *between you and I*
>
> ✓ *for John and me*
>
> ✗ *for John and I.*
>
> If in doubt, try the phrase without the *you*, and you will see that *for I* and *with I* are not right.

I[3] ▷ *abbreviation* **1** Independent. **2** Institute, or Institution. **3** International. **4** Island, or Isle. **5** *IVR* Italy.

I[4] ▷ *symbol* **1** *chem* iodine. **2** as a Roman numeral: one. See table at NUMBER SYSTEMS.

I ▷ *symbol, physics* electric current.

IA ▷ *abbreviation, US state* Iowa. Also written **Ia**.

-ia[1] /ɪə/ *suffix, forming nouns, signifying* **1** *medicine* a diseased or pathological condition □ ***anaemia*** □ ***pneumonia***. See also -IASIS. **2** *biol* a genus or class of plants or animals □ ***Magnolia***. **3** a state or type of society or world □ ***utopia*** □ ***suburbia***. **4** the name of a country or place □ ***Australia***. ◷ Latin and Greek feminine noun suffix.

-ia[2] /ɪə/ *suffix, forming plural and collective nouns, signifying* **1** *biol* a taxonomic DIVISION (sense 7) □ ***Mammalia***. **2** items belonging or relating to, or derived from, a specified thing □ ***militaria*** □ ***regalia***. See also -ANA. **3** used in the plural form of certain nouns of Latin and Greek origin (see etymology) □ ***effluvia*** □ ***genitalia*** □ ***media***. ◷ Latin and Greek neuter plural ending for adjectives in *-ius* and -ios and nouns in *-ium* and -ion respectively.

IAAF ▷ *abbreviation* International Amateur Athletic Federation.

IAEA ▷ *abbreviation* International Atomic Energy Agency.

-ial /ɪəl/ ▷ *suffix* **1** *forming adjectives, signifying* belonging or relating to a specified thing □ ***managerial***. **2** *forming nouns, signifying* the action of a specified thing □ ***tutorial***. See also -AL. ◷ From Latin *-ialis*.

iambic /aɪ'ambɪk/ ▷ *adj* in verse: relating to, or using, IAMBUSes □ ***iambic pentameters***. ▷ *noun* **1** an iambus. **2** (*usually* **iambics**) iambic verse.

iambic pentameter ▷ *noun, poetry* a verse form comprising lines each of five feet, each foot containing two syllables, used in HEROIC VERSE or HEROIC COUPLETs in English.

iambus /aɪ'ambəs/ and **iamb** /'aɪamb/ ▷ *noun* (***iambuses***, ***iambi*** /-baɪ/) in verse: a metrical foot containing one short or unstressed syllable followed by one long or stressed one, the most common measure in English verse. ◷ 19c as *iamb*; 16c: Latin, from Greek *iambos*, from *iaptein* to lampoon (because this verse form was first used by satirists).

-ian or **-ean** /ɪən/ and **-an** /ən, an/ ▷ *suffix* **1** *forming adjectives, signifying* relating to or similar to a specified thing, person, etc □ ***Dickensian***. **2** *forming nouns, signifying* someone interested or skilled in a specified thing □ ***grammarian***. ◷ From Latin *-ianus*.

-iana see -ANA

-iasis /aɪəsɪs/ or (*sometimes*) **-asis** *medicine* ▷ *combining form, forming nouns, denoting* a diseased condition □ ***psoriasis***. ◷ From Greek suffix denoting 'state or condition'.

IATA /aɪ'ɑːtə/ ▷ *abbreviation* International Air Transport Association.

-iatric /ɪatrɪk/ *medicine* ▷ *combining form, forming adjectives, denoting* relating to care or treatment within a particular specialty □ ***paediatric*** □ ***psychiatric***. ● **-iatrics** *combining form, forming singular nouns* □ ***paediatrics***. ● **-iatry** /aɪətrɪ/ *combining form, forming nouns* □ ***psychiatry***. ◷ From Greek *iatros* physician.

iatrogenic /aɪatroʊ'dʒɛnɪk/ ▷ *adj, medicine* said of a disease or symptom in a patient: brought about unintentionally by the treatment, action or comments of a physician. ◷ 20c: from Greek *iatros* physician + -GENIC 3.

ib. and ***ibid.*** /ɪbɪd/ ▷ *abbreviation*: *ibidem*.

IBA ▷ *abbreviation, Brit* Independent Broadcasting Authority, the former name of the ITC.

I-beam ▷ *noun, engineering, building* a metal girder which is I-shaped in cross-section.

Iberian /aɪ'bɪərɪən/ ▷ *adj* relating to the Iberian Peninsula, a region of Europe lying SW of the Pyrenees comprising Portugal and Spain, to its inhabitants or to their languages or culture. ▷ *noun* an inhabitant of, or person born in, the Iberian Peninsula; a Spaniard or Portuguese. ◷ 17c: from Latin *Iberia*, the region.

ibex /'aɪbɛks/ ▷ *noun* (***ibex***, ***ibexes*** or ***ibices*** /'aɪbɪsiːz/) any of various species of wild mountain goat with large ridged backward-curving horns, found in precipitous mountain regions of Europe, N Africa and Asia. ◷ 17c: Latin.

ibidem /'ɪbɪdəm, ɪ'baɪdəm/ ▷ *adverb* (abbreviation ***ib.*** or ***ibid.***) in the same book, article, passage, etc as was previously mentioned or cited. Compare IDEM. ◷ 17c: Latin, meaning 'in the same place'.

ibis /'aɪbɪs/ ▷ *noun* (***ibis*** or ***ibises***) any of various large wading birds with a long slender downward-curving beak, found in warm temperate and tropical regions. ◷ 14c: Latin, from Greek, from Egyptian.

-ible /ɪbəl/ ▷ *suffix, forming adjectives, signifying* that may be or is capable of being dealt with as specified □ ***expressible*** □ ***possible***. See also -ABLE. ● **-ibility** /ɪbɪlɪtɪ/ *suffix* (***-ibilities***) *forming nouns* □ ***possibility***. ● **-ibly** *suffix, forming adverbs* □ ***inexpressibly***. ◷ From Latin *-ibilis*.

IBRD ▷ *abbreviation* International Bank for Reconstruction and Development. See also WORLD BANK.

IBS ▷ *abbreviation, medicine* irritable bowel syndrome.

ibuprofen /aɪbjʊ'proʊfən/ ▷ *noun, medicine* a non-steroidal anti-inflammatory drug used to relieve rheumatic and arthritic pain, headache, etc. ◷ 1960s: from its full name *isobutylphenylpropionic acid*.

i/c ▷ *abbreviation* **1** in charge or command of. **2** internal combustion.

-ic ▷ *suffix, forming adjectives, signifying* **1** (*also* **-ical**, often with some difference in meaning) belonging or relating to, or in terms of, a specified thing □ ***historic*** □ ***historical*** □ ***photographic*** □ ***political***. **2** *chem* formed with an element in its higher VALENCY □ ***sulphuric***. Compare -OUS. See also -ICS. ▷ *suffix*, forming nouns, especially corresponding to adjectives in -IC □ ***cosmetic*** □ ***lunatic***. See also -AHOLIC. ● **-ically** *suffix, forming adverbs* □ ***historically*** □ ***graphically***. ⓔ From French *-ique*.

ICA ▷ *abbreviation, Brit* **1** Institute of Contemporary Arts, in London. **2** Invalid Care Allowance.

-ical /ɪkəl/ ▷ *suffix, forming adjectives* often, but not always, the same as -IC (compare ECONOMIC and ECONOMICAL).● **-ically** see under -IC.

ICAO ▷ *abbreviation* International Civil Aviation Organization.

ICBM ▷ *abbreviation* intercontinental ballistic missile.

ICD ▷ *abbreviation* interactive compact disc. See CD-I.

ice ▷ *noun* **1** water in its solid frozen state. **2** a sheet of frozen water, eg on the surface of a road. **3** ICE CREAM or WATER ICE or a portion of this. **4** *slang* diamonds. **5** *slang* an illicit drug, a highly synthesized form of METHAMPHETAMINE. **6** coldness of manner; reserve. ▷ *verb* (***iced***, ***icing***) **1** to cover (a cake) with icing. **2** *intr* (*usually* **ice over** or **up**) to become covered with ice; to freeze. **3** to cool or mix something with ice. ● **be on thin ice** see under SKATE[1]. ● **break the ice** see under BREAK. ● **on ice** in readiness or reserve, either to be used later or awaiting further attention. ⓔ Anglo-Saxon *is*.

ice age ▷ *noun, geol* **1** any of several periods in the Earth's history when the average temperature of the atmosphere decreased to such an extent that ice sheets and glaciers covered large areas of the Earth that previously had a temperate climate. **2** (**the Ice Age**) a popular name for the PLEISTOCENE epoch.

ice axe ▷ *noun* an axe used by mountaineers to cut holes or steps in the ice for their hands and feet.

iceberg ▷ *noun* **1** a huge mass of ice broken off from a glacier or polar ice sheet and floating in the sea, with only a small part of it projecting above the surface of the sea. Sometimes shortened to **berg**. **2** an iceberg lettuce. **3** *colloq, especially US* a cold and unemotional person. ● **the tip of the iceberg** see separate entry. ⓔ 19c; 18c in the obsolete sense 'an Arctic glacier': from Scandinavian or Dutch (see BERG[1]).

iceberg lettuce ▷ *noun* a type of lettuce with crisp, tightly packed, pale-green leaves.

iceblink ▷ *noun* a glare reflected in the sky from the distant masses of ice.

icebound ▷ *adj* said of a ship, etc: covered, surrounded or immobilized by ice.

icebox ▷ *noun* **1** a refrigerator compartment where food is kept frozen and ice is made and stored. **2** a container packed with ice for keeping food and drink, etc cold. **3** *N Amer* a refrigerator.

icebreaker ▷ *noun* **1** a ship designed to cut channels through floating ice. **2** *especially US* something or someone that breaks down reserve, shyness or formality, especially between strangers (see BREAK THE ICE at BREAK). **3** any implement for breaking ice. ● **ice-breaking** *adj, noun*.

ice bucket ▷ *noun* **1** a small bucket that ice cubes can be kept in before they are served in drinks. **2** a small bucket, sometimes on a stand, that is filled with ice and used for keeping wine at the table cool.

icecap ▷ *noun, geog* a thick permanent covering of ice, eg on top of a mountain or at the North or South Pole. Compare ICE FIELD, ICE SHEET.

ice-cold ▷ *adj* extremely cold, like ice.

ice cream ▷ *noun* a sweet creamy frozen dessert, made either from cream or a substitute and flavoured. ⓔ 18c.

ice cube ▷ *noun* a small block of ice used for cooling drinks, etc.

iced /aɪst/ ▷ *adj* **1** covered or cooled with, or affected by, ice □ ***iced coffee***. **2** said of a cake, etc: covered with icing □ ***an iced bun***.

ice dance and **ice dancing** ▷ *noun* a form of ICE-SKATING based on the movements of ballroom dancing. ● **ice dancer** *noun*.

ice field ▷ *noun* **1** a large flat area of land covered with ice; an ice sheet. **2** an area of sea covered with floating ice; a large ice floe.

ice floe ▷ *noun* a sheet of ice floating on the sea. Compare ICE FIELD, ICE SHEET.

ice hockey ▷ *noun* a form of hockey played on ice by two teams of six skaters (plus substitutes), and with a PUCK instead of a ball.

Icelander /ˈaɪsləndə(r), -landə(r)/ ▷ *noun* a citizen or inhabitant of, or person born in, Iceland. See also ICELANDIC.

Icelandic /aɪsˈlandɪk/ ▷ *adj* belonging or relating to the Republic of Iceland, an island state lying between the N Atlantic and the Arctic Ocean, to its inhabitants or to their language. ▷ *noun* the official language of Iceland. See also NORSE.

Iceland spar ▷ *noun, geol* a pure transparent form of CALCITE, noted for its ability to split a single incident ray of light into two refracted rays.

ice lolly ▷ *noun, Brit colloq* a portion of flavoured water or ice cream, frozen on a small stick. Often shortened to **lolly**.

ice pack ▷ *noun* **1** *medicine* a bag packed with crushed ice, used eg to reduce a swelling or to reduce a patient's temperature. **2** *geog* an area of PACK ICE. **3** a gel-filled pack that stays frozen for long periods, used in a COOL BOX, etc.

ice pick ▷ *noun* **1** a tool with a pointed end used by rock- and mountain-climbers for splitting ice. **2** a similar smaller tool for breaking ice into small pieces for drinks.

ice rink see RINK 1

ice sheet ▷ *noun* a layer of ice covering a whole region. See also ICECAP, ICE FIELD. Compare ICE FLOE.

ice skate ▷ *noun* a SKATE[1] with a metal blade, used for skating on ice. ▷ *verb* (**ice-skate**) *intr* to skate on ice, wearing ice skates. ● **ice-skater** *noun*. ● **ice-skating** *noun*. See also FIGURE SKATING.

ice track ▷ *noun* a frozen track used in the sport of SPEED SKATING.

ICFTU ▷ *abbreviation* International Confederation of Free Trade Unions.

IChemE ▷ *abbreviation*, *Brit* Institute of Chemical Engineers.

I Ching /aɪ tʃɪŋ, iː —, — dʒɪŋ/ ▷ *noun, Chinese philos* **1** an ancient Chinese system of divination, consisting of a set of symbols. **2** the text containing and supplementing this, used to interpret the symbols, and including the notion of YIN and YANG. ⓔ 19c: Chinese, literally 'book of changes'.

ichneumon /ɪkˈnjuːmən/ ▷ *noun* **1** (*also* **ichneumon fly**) any of thousands of species of small winged insects which lay their larvae in or on the larvae of other insects, especially in caterpillars. **2** a large mongoose, native to Africa and S Europe, with greyish-brown fur and a long tail. ⓔ 17c in sense 1; 16c in sense 2: Greek, literally 'tracker'.

ichthyoid /ˈɪkθɪɔɪd/ ▷ *adj* belonging or relating to a fish; fishlike. ▷ *noun* a fishlike vertebrate. ⓔ 19c: from Greek *ichthys* fish.

ichthyology /ɪkθɪ'ɒlədʒɪ/ ▻ *noun* the study of fishes. • **ichthyological** /-ə'lɒdʒɪkəl/ *adj.* • **ichthyologist** *noun.* 🕓 17c: from Greek *ichthys* fish + -LOGY1.

ichthyosaur /'ɪkθɪəsɔː(r)/ or **ichthyosaurus** /-sɔːrəs/ ▻ *noun* (***ichthyosaurs***, ***ichthyosauruses*** or ***ichthyosauri*** /-raɪ/) *palaeontol* a gigantic sharklike extinct marine reptile of the Mesozoic period, with a long snout and four paddle-like limbs. 🕓 19c: from Greek *ichthys* fish + -SAUR.

ichthyosis /ɪkθɪ'oʊsɪs/ ▻ *noun, pathol* an inherited disease in which the skin becomes dry, thickened, scaly and darkened. • **ichthyotic** /-'ɒtɪk/ *adj.* 🕓 19c: from Greek *ichthys* fish + -OSIS.

ICI ▻ *abbreviation* Imperial Chemical Industries.

-ician /ɪʃən/ ▻ *suffix, forming nouns* (especially based on nouns ending in *-ic* or *-ics*) *denoting* someone who is skilled or trained in a specified area or activity ▫ ***beautician*** ▫ ***technician***. See also -IC, -IAN. 🕓 From French *-icien*.

icicle /'aɪsɪkəl/ ▻ *noun* a long hanging spike of ice, formed by water freezing as it drips. 🕓 Anglo-Saxon *ises gicel*, from *is* ice + *gicel* icicle.

-icide see -CIDE

icily and **iciness** see under ICY

icing ▻ *noun* **1** any of various sugar-based coatings for cakes, etc. *N Amer equivalent* **frosting**. **2** the formation of ice on a ship, aircraft, road, etc. • **the icing on the cake** *colloq* a desirable but unnecessary addition to something which is already satisfactory.

icing sugar ▻ *noun* sugar in the form of a very fine powder, used to make icing, sweets, etc. Also (*especially US*) called **confectioners' sugar**.

-icist, **-icism**, **-icity** and **-icize** same as -IST, -ISM, *etc* (used in words formed from others ending in *-ic* or -ics). ▫ ***physicist*** ▫ ***fanaticism***.

icky /'ɪkɪ/ ▻ *adj* (***ickier***, ***ickiest***) *colloq* **1** sickly; cloying or sticky. **2** repulsive, nasty or unpleasant. 🕓 1930s.

ICL ▻ *abbreviation* International Computers Ltd.

icon or (*sometimes*) **ikon** /'aɪkɒn/ ▻ *noun* **1** *relig art* especially in the Orthodox Church: an image of Christ, the Virgin Mary or a saint, usually painted on wood or done as a mosaic. **2** a person or thing that is uncritically adored, revered or admired, or is regarded as a symbol of a particular culture or sphere, etc; an idol. **3** *computing* a picture or symbol displayed on a computer screen, which represents a function, facility, file, etc, available to the user, and which may be selected using the cursor or a mouse rather than a typed command. Compare EARCON. **4** a picture, image or representation. • **iconic** /aɪ'kɒnɪk/ *adj.* 🕓 16c: from Greek *eikon* image.

iconoclast /aɪ'kɒnəklast/ ▻ *noun* **1** *especially church history* someone who destroys religious images and is opposed to their use in worship. **2** someone who is opposed to, and attacks, traditional and cherished beliefs and superstitions. • **iconoclasm** /-klazəm/ *noun.* • **iconoclastic** /-'klastɪk/ *adj.* 🕓 17c: from Latin *iconoclastes*, from Greek *eikon* image + *klastes* breaker.

iconography ▻ *noun, art hist* **1** the branch of study concerned with the form and representation of the subject; the science of description of subject-matter and symbolism in the figurative arts. **2** a generally recognized set of objects that are considered to symbolize a particular movement, genre, etc. **3** until the mid-19c: the branch of study concerned with the identification or collective representation of portraits, eg those on coins. • **iconographer** *noun.* • **iconographic** /aɪkɒnə'grafɪk/ or **iconographical** *adj.* 🕓 17c.

iconology ▻ *noun* **1** *art hist* a development of ICONOGRAPHY, involving the historical study of the social, political and religious meanings of works of art. **2 a** the study of icons; **b** icons or symbols collectively. 🕓 20c in sense 1, first used by German art historian Edwin Panofsky (1892–1968); 18c in sense 2: from Greek *eikon* image + -LOGY1.

iconostasis /aɪkə'nɒstəsɪs/ ▻ *noun* (***iconostases*** /-siːz/) *church archit* in a Greek Orthodox or Byzantine church: a screen dividing the sanctuary from the main part of the church, usually covered with icons arranged in rows. 🕓 19c: Latin, from Greek *eikonostasis*, from *eikon* image + *stasis* placing.

icosahedron /aɪkɒsə'hiːdrən, -drɒn/ ▻ *noun* (***icosahedrons*** or ***icosahedra*** /-drə/) *geom* a solid figure with twenty faces. 🕓 16c: Greek, from *eikosi* twenty + *hedra* seat.

ICR ▻ *abbreviation, computing* intelligent character recognition, a system that uses context and dictionaries to assist in the recognition of characters. Compare OCR.

-ics ▻ *suffix, usually forming singular nouns, denoting* a subject or subjects of study, a specific activity, art or science ▫ ***acoustics*** ▫ ***athletics*** ▫ ***mathematics*** ▫ ***politics***. 🕓 From French *-iques*, from Greek *-ika* (neuter plural word-ending).

ictus /'ɪktəs/ ▻ *noun* (***ictus*** or ***ictuses***) **1** in verse: rhythmic or metrical stress. **2** *medicine* a stroke, seizure or fit. 🕓 18c: Latin, from *ictere* to strike.

ICU ▻ *abbreviation, medicine* intensive-care unit.

icy /'aɪsɪ/ ▻ *adj* (***icier***, ***iciest***) **1** very cold ▫ ***icy wind***. **2** covered with ice ▫ ***icy roads***. **3** said of someone's manner, behaviour, etc: unfriendly; hostile ▫ ***an icy stare***. • **icily** *adverb.* • **iciness** *noun.*

ID ▻ *abbreviation* **1** *US state* Idaho. Also written **Id.** **2** identification, or identity ▫ ***ID card***. **3** *medicine* infectious diseases. **4** *medicine* intradermal, or intradermally. Also written **i.d.**

id ▻ *noun, psychoanal* in Freudian theory: the part of the unconscious mind that is regarded as the source of primitive biological instincts and urges for survival and reproduction. Compare EGO, SUPEREGO. 🕓 1920s: Latin, meaning 'it'.

id. ▻ *abbreviation: idem.*

I'd /aɪd/ ▻ *contraction* **1** I had. **2** I would ▫ ***I'd love to come***.

-id¹ ▻ *suffix, forming nouns, denoting* **1** *biol* a member of a particular zoological or racial group ▫ ***arachnid*** ▫ ***hominid***. **2** a member of a particular dynastic line ▫ ***Fatimid***. **3** *astron* a meteor that has come from a particular constellation ▫ ***Perseid***. 🕓 From scientific Latin family names ending in *-idae*, from Greek *-ides* son of ….

-id² ▻ *suffix, forming nouns* **1** *technical* used in the names of bodies, formations, particles, etc ▫ ***hydatid***. **2** *bot* used in the names of plants belonging to family whose scientific Latin name ends in *-aceae* ▫ ***orchid***. **3** used in the names of some classical epic poems based on a personal or place name ▫ ***Aeneid***. 🕓 From French *-ide*.

-id³ see -IDE

IDA ▻ *abbreviation* International Development Association, an agency of the IBRD.

'Id-al-Adha /ɪd al aːd'haː/ ▻ *noun, Islam* a festival that celebrates the faith of Abraham, who was willing to sacrifice his son Isaac at Allah's request. At the festival sheep and goats are killed as a reminder of the sheep Allah provided as a substitute for the boy, the meat being shared with the poor. 🕓 Arabic, literally 'Feast of Sacrifice'.

'Id-al-Fitr /ɪd al 'fɪtə(r)/ ▻ *noun, Islam* a festival that is celebrated on the first day after RAMADAN, by having festive meals, wearing new clothes and giving gifts to charity. 🕓 18c: Arabic, literally 'Feast of Breaking Fast'.

IDD ▻ *abbreviation, telecomm* International Direct Dialling.

-ide /aɪd/ and (*especially US*) **-id** *chem* ▻ *suffix, forming nouns, denoting* a compound of an element with some other element □ *chloride*. Compare -ATE, -ITE. ⓒ First used in OXIDE (as a compound of oxygen).

idea /aɪˈdɪə/ ▷ *noun* (*ideas*) **1** a thought, image, notion or concept formed by the mind. **2** a plan or intention. **3** a main aim, purpose or feature □ *The idea of the game is to win as many cards as possible.* **4** an opinion or belief □ *He's got the idea that no one likes him.* **5** *especially with negatives* a vague notion or fancy □ *had no idea what to do.* **6** someone's conception of what is a good example of something □ *not my idea of fun.* **7** *philos* in Plato: a universal model of which all existing examples are imperfect copies. • **get ideas** *colloq* to have ideas which are over-ambitious or undesirable □ *He got ideas above his station* □ *You should have known she'd get ideas if you went out with her.* • **put ideas into someone's head** to give them over-ambitious or impractical ideas. • **that's an idea** *colloq* that plan is worth considering. • **the very idea** *colloq* the mere thought □ *shuddered at the very idea of it.* • **the very idea!** or **what an idea!** *colloq* that's absurd! that's outrageous! • **what's the big idea** *ironic slang* what do you think you're doing. ⓒ 16c, originally in sense 7: Latin and Greek, meaning 'form' or 'pattern'.

ideal /aɪˈdɪəl/ ▷ *adj* **1** perfect; highest and best possible or conceivable. **2** existing only in the mind; imaginary; visionary. **3** theoretical; conforming absolutely to theory. ▷ *noun* **1** the highest standard of behaviour, perfection, beauty, etc. **2** someone or something that is considered to be perfect. **3** something that exists only in the imagination. • **ideally** *adverb* **1** in an ideal way. **2** in ideal circumstances. ⓒ 17c: from French *idéal*, from Latin *idealis*, from *idea* IDEA.

ideal gas ▷ *noun, physics* a hypothetical gas in which atoms do not interact with one another. Also called **perfect gas**.

idealism /aɪˈdɪəlɪəm/ ▷ *noun* **1** a tendency to show or present things in an ideal or idealized form rather than as they really are. **2** the practice of forming, and living according to, ideals. **3** impracticality. **4** *philos* the theory that material objects and the external world do not really exist but are products of the mind. Compare REALISM. • **idealist** *noun* **1** someone who lives or tries to live according to ideals. **2** an impractical person. **3** *philos* a believer in idealism. • **idealistic** *adj*. • **idealistically** *adverb*.

idealize or **idealise** /aɪˈdɪəlaɪz/ ▷ *verb* (*idealized, idealizing*) **1** to regard or treat someone or something as perfect or ideal. **2** *intr* to form ideas, concepts or an ideal. • **idealization** *noun*. • **idealizer** *noun*.

idée fixe /iːdeɪˈfiːks/ ▷ *noun* (*idées fixes* /iːdeɪˈfiːks/) an idea which dominates the mind; an obsession. ⓒ 19c: French, literally 'fixed idea'.

idem /ˈaɪdɛm, ˈɪ-/ (abbreviation **id.**) *pronoun* the same author, place, etc as previously mentioned. ▷ *adverb* in the same place as previously mentioned. Compare IBIDEM. ⓒ 14c: Latin, meaning 'the same'.

identical /aɪˈdɛntɪkəl/ ▷ *adj* **1** said of two different items: exactly similar in every respect □ *Her coat was identical to mine.* **2** said of the same item on two or more different occasions: the very same □ *It wasn't just any copy, it was the identical copy I'd given her.* **3** said of twins: developed from a single fertilized egg which subsequently divided into equal halves to give two separate fetuses, the twins being always of the same sex and closely resembling each other both physically and mentally. *Technical equivalent* **monozygotic**. Compare FRATERNAL 2. • **identically** *adverb*. • **identicalness** *noun*. ⓒ 17c: from Latin *identicus*, from *idem* the same.

identification /aɪdɛntɪfɪˈkeɪʃən/ ▷ *noun* **1** an act or the process of identifying or of being identified. **2** something which allows a person or thing to be identified. **3** *psychol* the mental process of establishing a close bond or link between oneself and a person, people or group that one admires or feels sympathy or understanding towards.

identification parade ▷ *noun, Brit* a line of people containing one person who is suspected of a crime and others who are innocent of it, from which a witness is asked to try and identify the criminal. Also called **identity parade**.

identify /aɪˈdɛntɪfaɪ/ ▷ *verb* (*identifies, identified, identifying*) **1** to recognize someone or something as being a particular person or thing; to establish their or its identity. **2** *technical* to assign (a plant or animal, etc) to a particular species; to classify. **3** to associate (one person, thing or group) closely with another. **4** to see clearly or pinpoint (a problem, method, solution, etc). • **identifiable** *adj*. ⓒ 17c: from Latin *identificare*.

■ **identify with someone** **1** to feel sympathy and understanding for (a real or fictional person) because of shared personal characteristics or experiences. **2** *psychol* to link oneself to them by a process of IDENTIFICATION (sense 3).

Identikit /aɪˈdɛntɪkɪt/ ▷ *noun, trademark* (*often* **identikit**) **1** a series of transparent strips, each one showing a different typical facial feature, from which it is possible to put together an impression or rough picture of a criminal or suspect from witnesses' descriptions. **2** *as adj* **a** composed from Identikit □ *an Identikit picture*; **b** as though put together using, or resembling something put together from, Identikit; artificial, without any true identity □ *just another identikit teenage pop star.* See also PHOTOFIT. ⓒ 1950s: invented by H C McDonald (born 1913).

identity /aɪˈdɛntɪtɪ/ ▷ *noun* (*identities*) **1** the state or quality of being a specified person or thing; who or what a person or thing is □ *The winner's identity is not yet known.* **2** *as adj* serving to identify someone (eg the wearer or holder) or to give necessary information about them □ *identity bracelet.* **3** the individual characteristics by which a person or thing can be identified; individuality; personality. **4** *now formal* the state of being exactly the same □ *Having no identity of interests, the two sides cannot agree.* **5** *Austral & NZ colloq* an established or well-known character in a place. **6** *math* **a** IDENTITY ELEMENT; **b** an equation that is valid for all possible values of the unknown variables involved, often indicated by the symbol ≡, eg $7x \equiv 3x + 4x$. ⓒ 16c in sense 3: from French *identité*, from Latin *identitas*, from *idem* the same.

identity card ▷ *noun* a card bearing information about, and often a photograph of, the holder, used as proof of their identity.

identity crisis ▷ *noun, psychol* a mental conflict, with symptoms of withdrawal or rebelliousness, etc, involving the loss of a person's sense of self, and inability to accept or adopt the role they believe is expected of them by society.

identity element ▷ *noun, math* an element or member of a set that, when combined with another element or member x, leaves x unchanged. The identity element for the multiplication of numbers is1, because $x.1 = 1.x = x$ in all cases. Also shortened to **identity**.

identity parade see under IDENTIFICATION PARADE

ideogram /ˈɪdɪoʊgram, ˈaɪdɪoʊ-/ ▷ *noun* on a sign or label, etc: a written symbol designed to convey an abstract concept, or one which stands for a real object without being a direct representation of it. Also called **ideograph**. Compare LOGOGRAPH, PICTOGRAPH. ⓒ 19c: from Greek *idea* idea + -GRAM.

ideograph /ˈɪdɪoʊgrɑːf, ˈaɪdɪoʊ-/ ▷ *noun* an IDEOGRAM. • **ideographic** *adj*. • **ideographically** *adverb*. • **ideography** *noun*. ⓒ 19c: from Greek *idea* idea + -GRAPH sense 2.

ideological and **ideologically** see under IDEOLOGY

ideologist /aɪdɪˈɒlədʒɪst, ɪdɪ-/ ▻ *noun* **1** someone who supports a particular ideology. Compare IDEOLOGUE. **2** a theorist. **3** someone who studies or is an expert in ideologies.

ideologue /ˈaɪdɪəlɒg, ɪdɪ-/ ▻ *noun, usually derog* someone who supports a particular ideology very rigidly, often when it is not appropriate or practical. ⓒ 19c: from French *idéologue*, from Greek *idea* idea + -LOGUE 3.

ideology /aɪdɪˈɒlədʒɪ, ɪdɪˈ-/ ▻ *noun* (***ideologies***) **1** the body of ideas and beliefs which form the basis for a social, economic or political system. **2** the opinions, beliefs and way of thinking characteristic of a particular person, group of people or nation. **3** abstract or visionary speculation. ● **ideological** /-əˈlɒdʒɪkəl/ *adj.* ● **ideologically** *adverb.* ⓒ 18c, meaning 'the science of ideas': from French *idéologie*, from Greek *idea* idea + -LOGY 1.

Ides /aɪdz/ ▻ *plural or singular noun* (*also* **ides**) in the ancient Roman calendar: the fifteenth day of March, May, July and October, and the thirteenth day of the other months. ⓒ 14c: French, from Latin *idus*.

idiocy /ˈɪdɪəsɪ/ ▻ *noun* (***idiocies***) **1** a foolish action or foolish behaviour. **2** *non-technical* the state of being an idiot or extremely retarded mentally.

idiolect /ˈɪdɪoulɛkt/ ▻ *noun, linguistics* the individual and distinctive way a particular person has of speaking. ⓒ 1940s: from Greek *idios* own, modelled on DIALECT.

idiom /ˈɪdɪəm/ ▻ *noun* **1** an expression with a meaning which cannot be guessed at or derived from the meanings of the individual words which form it □ *The idiom 'to have a chip on one's shoulder' is of US origin.* **2** the syntax, grammar and forms of expression peculiar to a language or a variety of language. **3** the language, vocabulary, forms of expression, etc used by a particular person or group of people. **4** the characteristic style or forms of expression of a particular artist, musician, artistic or musical school, etc. ● **idiomatic** /ɪdɪəˈmatɪk/ *adj* **1** characteristic of a particular language. **2** tending to use idioms; using idioms correctly □ *fluent idiomatic French.* ● **idiomatically** *adverb.* ⓒ 16c: from French *idiome*, from Latin *idioma*, from Greek *idios* own.

idiosyncrasy /ɪdɪouˈsɪŋkrəsɪ/ ▻ *noun* (***idiosyncrasies***) **1** any personal way of behaving, reacting or thinking; a personal peculiarity or eccentricity. **2** *medicine* hypersensitivity of an individual to a particular food, drug, etc. ● **idiosyncratic** /-sɪŋˈkratɪk/ *adj.* ● **idiosyncratically** *adverb.* ⓒ 17c: from Greek *idiosynkrasis*, from *idios* own, *syn* together + *krasis* mixing.

idiot /ˈɪdɪət/ ▻ *noun* **1** *colloq* a foolish or stupid person. **2** *non-technical* someone who is severely mentally retarded. ● **idiotic** /ɪdɪˈɒtɪk/ *adj.* ● **idiotically** *adverb.* ⓒ 14c: French, from Greek *idiotes* a person lacking skill or expertise.

idiot board ▻ *noun, colloq* in TV production: **1** a board or card on which script or a cue is written, held up out of camera-shot for eg a presenter to read from. **2** an AUTOCUE.

idiot light ▻ *noun, US colloq* on a car dashboard: a light which comes on to indicate that there is a fault or imminent problem, eg that the engine needs more oil.

idiot savant /ˈɪdɪət ˈsavənt; *French* idjosavɑ̃/ ▻ *noun* (***idiot savants*** /ˈɪdɪət ˈsavənts/ or ***idiots savants*** /idjosavɑ̃/) *psychol* someone with a mental disability who nevertheless shows a remarkable talent in some specific respect, such as memorizing or rapid calculation. ⓒ 1920s: French, literally 'clever idiot'.

idle /ˈaɪdəl/ ▻ *adj* (***idler, idlest***) **1** not in use; not being used; unoccupied. **2** not wanting to work; lazy; indolent. **3** having no purpose or value □ *idle chatter.* **4** without cause, basis or good reason; unnecessary □ *an idle rumour.* **5** having no effect or result; not taken seriously □ *an idle threat.* ▻ *verb* (***idled, idling***) **1** (*usually* **idle away time**, *etc*) to spend time doing nothing or being idle. **2** *intr* to do nothing or be idle. **3** *intr* said of an engine, machinery, etc: to run gently while out of gear or without doing any work. **4** to make (an engine, etc) idle. ● **idleness** *noun.* ● **idler** *noun.* ● **idly** *adverb.* ⓒ Anglo-Saxon *idel*, meaning 'empty' or 'worthless'.

idle time ▻ *noun, computing* a period or periods when a computer is able to function properly but is not being used for productive work or program testing.

idol /ˈaɪdəl/ ▻ *noun* **1** an image or symbol, especially an image of a god, used as an object of worship. **2** an object of excessive love, honour or devotion. ⓒ 14c: from Latin *idolum*, from Greek *eidolon*.

idolater /aɪˈdɒlətə(r)/ and (*now rare*) **idolatress** ▻ *noun* **1** someone who worships idols. **2** someone who is a passionate and devoted admirer of someone or something. ⓒ 14c as *idolatrer*: see IDOLATRY.

idolatry /aɪˈdɒlətrɪ/ ▻ *noun* (***idolatries***) **1** the worship of idols. **2** excessive, love, honour, admiration or devotion. ● **idolatrous** *adj.* ● **idolatrously** *adverb.* ⓒ 13c: from Latin *idololatria*, from Greek *eidolon* idol + *latreuein* to worship.

idolize or **idolise** /ˈaɪdəlaɪz/ ▻ *verb* (***idolized, idolizing***) **1** to love, honour, admire, etc someone or something too much. **2** to make an idol of someone or something. ● **idolization** *noun.* ● **idolizer** *noun.* ⓒ 16c in sense 2.

IDP ▻ *abbreviation, computing* integrated data processing.

idyll or (*US, sometimes*) **idyl** /ˈɪdɪl/ ▻ *noun* **1** a short poem or prose work describing a simple, pleasant, usually rural or pastoral scene. **2** a story, episode or scene suitable for such a work, eg one of happy innocence or love. **3** a work of this character in another art form, especially music. ● **idyllic** /ɪˈdɪlɪk/ *adj* **1** relating to or typical of an idyll. **2** charming; picturesque. ● **idyllically** *adverb.* ⓒ 17c: from Latin *idyllium*, from Greek *eidyllion*, diminutive of *eidos* an image.

ie or **i.e.** ▻ *abbreviation*: *id est* (Latin), that is; that is to say.

-ie /ɪ/ ▻ *suffix, forming nouns* a variant of -Y² □ *hippie* □ *nightie* □ *movie.*

if ▻ *conj* **1** in the event that; on condition that; supposing that □ *I'll go if he asks me to.* **2** although; even though □ *It was very enjoyable, if overpriced.* **3** whenever □ *She jumps if the phone rings.* **4** whether □ *I wonder if he knows.* **5** (*usually* **if only**) used to express a wish □ *If only it would stop raining!* **6** used to make a polite request or suggestion □ *if you wouldn't mind stopping just a minute.* **7** used in exclamations, to express surprise or annoyance □ *Well, if it isn't that book I'd thought I'd lost!* ▻ *noun* **1** a condition or supposition □ *too many ifs and buts.* **2** an uncertainty. ● **if anything** perhaps; on the contrary. ● **if only** see sense 5 above. ● **if only to do something** if for no other reason than to do it □ *I'll be there, if only to give her moral support.* ● **if you like 1** to say it another way. **2** if you want or approve. ⓒ Anglo-Saxon *gif.*

IFAD ▻ *abbreviation* International Fund for Agricultural Development.

IFC ▻ *abbreviation* International Finance Corporation.

iffy /ˈɪfɪ/ ▻ *adj* (***iffier, iffiest***) *colloq* uncertain; doubtful; dubious. ⓒ 1930s.

IFP ▻ *abbreviation, S Afr* Inkatha Freedom Party.

IGC ▻ *abbreviation, especially* in the EU: intergovernmental conference.

igloo /ˈɪgluː/ ▻ *noun* (***igloos***) a dome-shaped Inuit house built with blocks of snow and ice. ⓒ 19c: from Inuit *iglu* house.

igneous /ˈɪgnɪəs/ ▻ *adj* **1** belonging or relating to, or like, fire. **2** *geol* said of a rock: formed by the solidification of molten MAGMA, either beneath the Earth's surface (eg GRANITE) or after it has been forced to the surface (eg BASALT). Compare METAMORPHIC, SEDIMENTARY. ⓒ 17c: from Latin *igneus*, from *ignis* fire.

ignis fatuus /ˈɪɡnɪs ˈfatjʊəs/ ▷ *noun* (***ignes fatui*** /ˈɪɡniːz ˈfatjʊaɪ/) WILL-O'-THE-WISP 1. ⓒ 16c: Latin, literally 'foolish fire'.

ignite /ɪɡˈnaɪt/ ▷ *verb* (***ignited***, ***igniting***) **1** to set fire to something. **2** *intr* to catch fire. **3** to heat something to the point at which combustion occurs. **4** to excite (feelings, emotions, etc). ● **ignitable** or **ignitible** *adj*. ● **igniter** *noun*. ⓒ 17c: from Latin *ignire* to set on fire, from *ignis* fire.

ignition /ɪɡˈnɪʃən/ ▷ *noun* **1** *chem* the point at which combustion of a chemical substance begins. **2** (*usually* **the ignition**) *engineering* a system that initiates such combustion, especially by producing a spark which ignites an explosive mixture of fuel and air in an INTERNAL-COMBUSTION ENGINE. **3** an act or the means or process of igniting something.

ignition key ▷ *noun* in a motor vehicle: the key which is turned in order to operate the ignition system.

ignition temperature ▷ *noun, chem* the temperature to which a substance must be heated before it will burn in air.

ignoble /ɪɡˈnoʊbəl/ ▷ *adj* **1** said of an action, etc: causing shame; dishonourable; mean. **2** said of a person, etc: of humble or low birth; not noble. ● **ignobility** or **ignobleness** *noun*. ● **ignobly** *adverb*. ⓒ 15c: French, from Latin *ignobilis*.

ignominious /ɪɡnəˈmɪnɪəs/ ▷ *adj* causing shame or dishonour; humiliating. ● **ignominiously** *adverb*. ● **ignominiousness** *noun*. ⓒ 16c: from Latin *ignominiosus*; see IGNOMINY.

ignominy /ˈɪɡnəmɪnɪ/ ▷ *noun* (***ignominies***) **1** public shame, disgrace or dishonour. **2** dishonourable conduct. ⓒ 16c: from Latin *ignominia*, from *in-* not + *nomen* name or reputation.

ignoramus /ɪɡnəˈreɪməs/ ▷ *noun* (***ignoramuses***) an ignorant or uneducated person. ⓒ 17c, after *Ignoramus*, a foolish lawyer in a farce of the same name by the English playwright George Ruggle (1575–1622); 16c in obsolete legal use, meaning 'we ignore or take no notice': from Latin *ignoramus* we do not know.

ignorance ▷ *noun* **1** lack of knowledge or awareness. **2** the state of being ignorant.

ignorant /ˈɪɡnərənt/ ▷ *adj* **1** knowing very little; uneducated. **2** (*usually* **ignorant of something**) knowing little or nothing about it □ *ignorant of the facts*. **3** rude; ill-mannered. ● **ignorantly** *adverb*. ⓒ 14c: French, from Latin *ignorare* not to know.

ignore /ɪɡˈnɔː(r)/ ▷ *verb* (***ignored***, ***ignoring***) to deliberately take no notice of someone or something. ● **ignorer** *noun*. ⓒ 19c in this sense: 17c in obsolete sense 'to be ignorant of something': from Latin *ignorare* not to know.

iguana /ɪˈɡwɑːnə/ ▷ *noun* (***iguanas*** or ***iguana***) any member of a family of large insectivorous lizards with a crest of spines along their back, including the **common iguana** which is green and lives in tree branches in tropical Central and S America. ⓒ 16c: Spanish, from Carib (S American Indian language) *iwana*.

iguanodon /ɪˈɡwɑːnədɒn/ ▷ *noun* a large bipedal herbivorous dinosaur of the Jurassic and Cretaceous periods, with teeth like those of the iguana. ⓒ 19c: IGUANA + Greek *odous*, *odontos* tooth.

IHS ▷ *abbreviation* used as a Christian symbol or monogram: *Iesous* (Greek), Jesus. ⓒ Taken from the capital IOTA, capital ETA and capital SIGMA, ie the first two and the last letters of the name.

ikat /ˈɪkat/ ▷ *noun* a technique of TIE-DYEING yarn before weaving it, resulting in a fabric with a geometric pattern of colours. ⓒ 1930s: from Malay-Indonesian *mengikat* to tie.

ikebana /iːkɪˈbɑːnə, ɪkɪ-/ ▷ *noun* the Japanese art of flower-arranging, in which blooms (or a single bloom), leaves and other materials are arranged in a formal and carefully balanced way. ⓒ Early 20c: Japanese, from *ikeru* to arrange + *hana* flower.

ikon see ICON

IL ▷ *abbreviation, US state* Illinois. Also written **Ill.**

il- ▷ *prefix* a form of IN- (see IN-^{1}, IN-^{2}) used before words beginning in *l* □ ***illegible*** □ ***illuminate***.

ilea and **ileac** see under ILEUM

ileostomy /ɪlɪˈɒstəmɪ/ ▷ *noun* (***ileostomies***) *surgery* an operation in which the ILEUM is brought through a permanent artificial opening in the abdominal wall, so that its contents can be discharged directly to the outside of the body, bypassing the colon. ⓒ 19c: see -STOMY.

ileum /ˈɪlɪəm, ˈaɪlɪəm/ ▷ *noun* (***ilea***) *anatomy* in mammals: the lowest part of the small intestine, lying between the JEJUNUM and the CAECUM, whose main function is the digestion and absorption of food. ● **ileac** *adj*. ⓒ 17c: from Latin *ilia* groin or guts.

ilex /ˈaɪlɛks/ ▷ *noun* (***ilexes***) **1** *bot* a shrub or tree of the genus that includes HOLLY. **2** the HOLM-OAK. ⓒ 14c in sense 2: Latin.

ilium /ˈɪlɪəm, ˈaɪlɪəm/ ▷ *noun* (***ilia***) *anatomy* the largest of the three bones that form the upper part of each side of the pelvis. *Non-technical equivalent* **haunch bone**. See also INNOMINATE BONE. ● **iliac** *adj*. See also SACROILIAC. ⓒ 18c; 14c in obsolete sense meaning ILEUM: from Latin *ilia* groin or guts.

ilk ▷ *noun* type; kind; class □ ***I had never met anyone of his ilk.*** ▷ *adj, Scottish* same. ● **of that ilk 1** of that type or kind. **2** *Scottish* of the estate or place of the same name as the person's family name, eg *Macdonald of that ilk* (ie Macdonald of Macdonald). ⓒ Anglo-Saxon *ilca*.

ill ▷ *adj* (***worse***, ***worst***; *colloq* ***iller***, ***illest***) **1** not in good health; sick or unwell. **2** said of health: not good. **3** bad or harmful □ ***ill effects*** □ ***ill-treatment***. **4** hostile; unfriendly □ ***ill will*** □ ***ill feeling***. **5** causing or heralding bad luck □ ***an ill omen***. **6** said of manners: incorrect; improper. ▷ *adverb* (***worse***, ***worst***) (rather *formal or archaic* in senses 3–5) **1** badly; wrongly □ ***ill-matched*** □ ***ill-fitting***. **2** harshly □ ***speak ill of someone***. **3** hardly; scarcely □ ***be ill able to afford the money***. **4** unfavourably □ ***It went ill with them*** □ ***think ill of him***. **5** not easily; with difficulty □ ***can ill spare the time***. ▷ *noun* **1** evil; harm; trouble □ ***one of the ills of modern society***. **2** an injury, ailment or misfortune. ● **go ill with someone** *chiefly old use* to end in danger or misfortune for them. ● **ill at ease** uneasy; uncomfortable; embarrassed. ● **ill become someone** *rather formal or old use* to do them no credit; not to be to their advantage. ● **speak ill of someone** or **something** see under SPEAK. ● **take something ill** *chiefly old use* to be offended by it. ● **with an ill grace** ungraciously. ⓒ 15c in sense 1; 12c in the sense 'wicked' or 'immoral': from Norse *illr*.

Ill. see under IL

I'll /aɪl/ ▷ *contraction* I will or I shall.

ill-advised ▷ *adj* foolish; done, or doing things, with little thought or consideration. ● **ill-advisedly** *adverb*.

ill-assorted ▷ *adj* badly matched; not going well together.

ill blood see under ILL FEELING

ill-bred ▷ *adj* badly brought up or educated; rude. ● **ill-breeding** *noun*.

ill-considered ▷ *adj* badly thought out; not well planned.

ill-defined ▷ *adj* vague or imprecise; without any clear outline.

ill-disposed ▷ *adj* (*especially* **ill-disposed towards someone** or **something**) unfriendly; unsympathetic; unwilling to be supportive or helpful.

illegal ▷ *adj* **1** against the law; not legal. Also called UNLAWFUL. **2** not authorized by law or by specific rules which apply □ *an illegal immigrant.* Compare ILLEGITIMATE, ILLICIT. ● **illegality** /ɪlɪ'galɪtɪ/ *noun* (*illegalities*). ● **illegally** *adverb.* ⓘ 17c: from Latin *illegalis.*

illegible ▻ *adj* difficult or impossible to read. ● **illegibility** *noun.* ● **illegibly** *adverb.* ⓘ 17c.

illegitimate ▻ *adj* **1** said of a person: born of parents who were not married to each other at the time of the birth. See also BASTARD. **2** said of a birth: happening outside marriage. **3** unacceptable or not allowed, especially illegal. **4** *logic* not properly inferred or reasoned. **5** improper. ● **illegitimacy** *noun.* ● **illegitimately** *adverb.* ⓘ 16c: from Latin *illegitimus.*

ill-equipped ▻ *adj* poorly provided with the necessary tools, skills, etc.

ill fame ▻ *noun* a bad reputation; notoriety.

ill-fated ▻ *adj* ending in or bringing bad luck or ruin; doomed.

ill-favoured ▻ *adj* not attractive, especially in appearance; objectionable.

ill feeling and **ill blood** ▻ *noun* bad or hostile feeling; animosity.

ill-founded ▻ *adj* said of an argument, theory, suspicion, etc: without sound basis or reason.

ill-gotten ▻ *adj* obtained dishonestly □ *ill-gotten gains.*

ill-humoured ▻ *adj* bad-tempered or sullen. ● **ill-humouredly** *adverb.*

illiberal ▻ *adj* **1** having strict opinions about morality, behaviour, etc; narrow-minded; prejudiced. **2** not generous; mean. **3** uncultured; unrefined. ● **illiberality** *noun.* ● **illiberally** *adverb.* ⓘ 16c: from Latin *illiberalis* mean or ignoble.

illicit /ɪ'lɪsɪt/ ▻ *adj* not permitted by law, rule or social custom. ● **illicitly** *adverb.* ● **illicitness** *noun.* ⓘ 17c: from Latin *illicitus.*

illimitable ▻ *adj* limitless; infinite. ● **illimitableness** *noun.* ● **illimitably** *adverb.* ⓘ 16c.

ill-informed ▻ *adj* **1** said of a person: lacking knowledge or information. **2** said of a decision, etc: made without access to the relevant or necessary information.

illiterate ▻ *adj* **1** unable to read and write. **2** uneducated or ignorant, especially in a particular field or subject □ *He left an illiterate note* □ *I am mathematically illiterate.* ▻ *noun* an illiterate person. ● **illiteracy** *noun.* ● **illiterately** *adverb.* ⓘ 16c: from Latin *illiteratus.*

ill-judged ▻ *adj* poorly advised; done without proper consideration.

ill-mannered ▻ *adj* rude; uncouth.

ill-natured ▻ *adj* spiteful; mean; surly. ● **ill-naturedly** *adverb.*

illness ▻ *noun* (*illnesses*) **1** a disease. **2** the state of being ill or unwell.

illocution /ɪlə'kjuːʃən/ *noun, philos* a speech act that involves warning, promising, ordering, etc. Compare PERLOCUTION. ⓘ 1950s: IL- + LOCUTION.

illogical ▻ *adj* **1** not based on careful thinking or reason. **2** contrary to, or not following, the principles of logic. ● **illogicality** *noun.* ● **illogically** *adverb.* ⓘ 16c: see LOGIC.

ill-omened and **ill-starred** ▻ *adj* said of a plan, course of action, etc: likely to end badly; unlucky or doomed.

ill temper ▻ *noun* bad temper; surliness. ● **ill-tempered** *adj.* ● **ill-temperedly** *adverb.*

ill-timed ▻ *adj* said or done at an unsuitable time; inopportune.

ill-treat ▻ *verb* to abuse; to MALTREAT. ● **ill-treatment** *noun.*

illuminance /ɪ'luːmɪnəns, ɪ'ljuː-/ ▻ *noun, physics* (SI unit LUX) the luminous FLUX incident on a given surface per unit area. Also called **illumination**.

illuminant /ɪ'luːmɪnənt, ɪ'ljuː-/ ▻ *noun* something that gives off light. ▻ *adj* giving off light. ⓘ 17c: from Latin *illuminare*, see ILLUMINATE.

illuminate /ɪ'luːmɪneɪt, ɪ'ljuː-/ ▻ *verb* (*illuminated, illuminating*) **1** to light something up or make it bright. **2** to decorate something with lights. **3** to decorate (a manuscript) with elaborate designs and initial letters in gold, silver or bright colours. **4** to make something clearer and more easily understood. **5** to enlighten someone spiritually or intellectually. ● **illuminating** *adj.* ● **illuminative** /ɪ'luːmɪnətɪv, ɪ'ljuː-/ *adj.* ● **illuminator** *noun.* ⓘ 16c: from Latin *illuminare, illuminatum*, from IL- + *lumen* light.

illuminati /ɪluːmɪ'nɑːtiː/ ▻ *plural noun* **1** people who claim to have some kind of special or enlightened knowledge on a particular subject, especially in philosophy or religion. **2** (**Illuminati**) *historical* any of various groups or movements of illuminati. ⓘ 16c: from Latin *illuminatus* enlightened.

illumination /ɪluːmɪ'neɪʃən, ɪljuː-/ ▻ *noun* **1** the act or process of illuminating or the state of being illuminated. **2** any source of light; lighting. **3** (*usually* **illuminations**) decorative lights hung in streets and towns, eg at times of celebration. **4** the art or skill of decorating manuscripts with elaborate designs and initial letters in gold, silver and bright colours. **5** such a design or initial letter in a manuscript. **6** *physics* ILLUMINANCE. **7** intellectual enlightenment or spiritual inspiration.

illumine /ɪ'luːmɪn, ɪ'ljuː-/ ▻ *verb* (*illumined, illumining*) *poetic, literary* to illuminate. ⓘ 14c: from French *illuminer.*

illusion /ɪ'luːʒən, ɪ'ljuː-/ ▻ *noun* **1** a deceptive or misleading appearance □ *A mirage is an optical illusion.* **2** a false or misleading impression, idea, belief or understanding □ *was under the illusion he worked here.* **3** *psychol* a false perception of an object or experience due to the mind misinterpreting the evidence relayed to it by the senses. Compare DELUSION, HALLUCINATION. ⓘ 14c: from Latin *illusio* irony, mocking or deceit, from *illudere* to mock or make fun of someone.

illusionism ▻ *noun* **1** *art* the use of perspective, foreshortening, light and shade, and other pictorial devices to produce an illusion of reality. **2** *philos* the doctrine that the external world is actually an illusion.

illusionist ▻ *noun* **1** a conjurer who plays tricks, performs optical illusions, etc. **2** *art* someone who practises illusionism. **3** *philos* a believer in illusionism.

illusive /ɪ'luːsɪv, ɪ'ljuːsɪv/ and **illusory** /ɪ'luːsərɪ, ɪ'ljuː-/ ▻ *adj* **1** seeming to be, or having the characteristics of, an illusion. **2** deceptive; unreal. ● **illusively** or **illusorily** *adverb.* ● **illusiveness** or **illusoriness** *noun.* ⓘ 17c.

illustrate /'ɪləstreɪt/ ▻ *verb* (*illustrated, illustrating*) **1** to provide or create pictures and/or diagrams for (a book, text, lecture, etc). **2** to make (a statement, etc) clearer, especially by providing examples. **3** to be an example of, or an analogy for, something □ *That illustrates my point exactly.* ● **illustrated** *adj.* ● **illustrative** *adj.* ● **illustratively** *adverb.* ● **illustrator** *noun.* ⓘ 17c; 16c in obsolete senses 'to enlighten (the mind)', 'to beautify' or 'to throw light or distinction on someone': from Latin *illustrare, illustratum* to light up.

illustration /ɪlə'streɪʃən/ ▻ *noun* **1** a picture or diagram that is used for clarifying or decorating a text, book, lecture, etc. **2** an example □ *The essay was an illustration of her brilliance.* **3** the act or process of illustrating or the state of being illustrated.

illustrious /ɪ'lʌstrɪəs/ ▻ *adj, rather formal* distinguished; renowned; celebrated; noble. ● **illustriously**

adverb. • **illustriousness** *noun.* ⌚ 16c: from Latin *illustris* bright or lustrous.

ill will ▷ *noun* bad or unfriendly feeling; the urge or wish to do harm ▫ *I bear him no ill will.*

ilmenite /ˈɪlmənaɪt/ ▷ *noun, geol* a black or dark-brown mineral composed of iron, titanium and oxygen, found in igneous rocks, and in metamorphic rocks such as GNEISS and SCHIST. ⌚ 19c: named after the Ilmen Mountains in the Urals.

ILO ▷ *abbreviation* International Labour Organization.

IM ▷ *abbreviation, medicine* intramuscular, or intramuscularly. Also written **i.m.**

im- ▷ *prefix* a form of IN- (see IN-[1], IN-[2]) used before words beginning in *b*, *m* and *p* ▫ *immature* ▫ *implode.*

I'm /aɪm/ ▷ *contraction* I am.

image /ˈɪmɪdʒ/ ▷ *noun* **1** a likeness of a person or thing, especially in the form of a portrait or statue. **2** someone or something that resembles another person or thing closely ▫ *He's the image of his father.* See also SPITTING IMAGE. **3** (*also* **mental image**) an idea or picture in the mind. **4** the visual display reproduced by a television receiver. **5** (*also* **public image**) the impression that people in general have of someone's character, behaviour, etc. **6** in literature, etc: a simile or metaphor. **7** *optics* an optical reproduction of a physical object formed by light reflected in a mirror or refracted through a lens ▫ *The light rays are focused to form an image on the retina.* **8** *physics* any reproduction of a physical object formed by sound waves or electromagnetic radiation originating from or reflected by the object, eg an ULTRASOUND SCAN or an X-RAY photograph. **9** *psychol* a mental picture or representation resulting from thought or memory rather than from sensory perception. See also IMAGO. **10** a typical example or embodiment of something. ▷ *verb* (*imaged*, *imaging*) **1** to form a likeness or image of something or someone. **2** *medicine* to produce a pictorial representation of (a body part) for diagnostic purposes, using eg X-ray, ultrasound or CT scanning, etc. **3** to form a mental image of something or someone; to imagine. **4** to mirror, or form an optical image of, something. **5** to portray. **6** to be a typical example of something. • **imaging** *noun.* ⌚ 13c: from Latin *imago* a likeness.

image converter and **image converter tube** ▷ *noun, physics* an electronic instrument which converts infrared or other invisible images into visible images.

image enhancement ▷ *noun* a method used to enhance the definition of an image, eg one obtained from a surveillance camera, microscope, etc. It uses a computer program to convert shades of grey into either black or white depending on their relative values.

image intensifier ▷ *noun, radiol* an electronic device which increases the brightness of an optical image, eg in X-ray examinations.

image maker ▷ *noun* a person whose job is to create or enhance the public image of someone, especially a politician.

imagery /ˈɪmɪdʒərɪ, ˈɪmɪdʒrɪ/ ▷ *noun* (*imageries*) **1** figures of speech in writing, literature, etc that produce a specified effect ▫ *Heaney's use of agricultural imagery.* **2** the making of images, especially in the mind. **3** mental images. **4** images in general or collectively. **5** statues, carvings, etc.

imaginary /ɪˈmadʒɪnərɪ/ ▷ *adj* **1** existing only in the mind or imagination; not real. **2** *math* consisting of or containing an IMAGINARY NUMBER. • **imaginarily** *adverb.*

imaginary number ▷ *noun, math* the square root of a negative number.

imagination ▷ *noun* **1** the ability to form, or the process of forming, mental images of things, people, events, etc that one has not seen or of which one has no direct perception or knowledge. **2** the creative ability of the mind. **3** the ability to cope resourcefully with unexpected events or problems.

imaginative /ɪˈmadʒɪnətɪv/ ▷ *adj* **1** showing, done with or created by imagination. **2** said of a person: having a lively imagination. • **imaginatively** *adverb.* • **imaginativeness** *noun.*

imagine /ɪˈmadʒɪn/ ▷ *verb* (*imagined*, *imagining*) **1** to form a mental picture of something ▫ *I can't imagine her wearing a hat.* **2** to see, hear, believe, etc something which is not true or does not exist ▫ *When you're alone a lot, you start to imagine things.* **3** to think, suppose or guess ▫ *I can't imagine where she's got to.* **4** *intr* to use the imagination. **5** used as an exclamation of surprise ▫ *Imagine that!* • **imaginable** *adj.* • **imaginably** *adverb.* • **imaginer** *noun* ⌚ 14c: from Latin *imaginari*, from *imago* a likeness.

imaginings ▷ *plural noun* things seen or heard which do not exist; fancies or fantasies.

imago /ɪˈmeɪgoʊ, ɪˈmɑː-/ ▷ *noun* (*imagos* or *imagines* /-dʒɪniːz/) **1** *entomol* the final stage in the life cycle of an insect, when it is a sexually mature adult. **2** *psychol* a mental, often idealized, view of another person, formed in childhood (eg a child's image of its mother), that persists in a person's subconscious and influences their adult life. ⌚ 18c; early 20c in sense 2: Latin, meaning 'image' or 'likeness'.

imam /ɪˈmɑːm/ *Islam* ▷ *noun* **1** a leader of prayers in a mosque. **2** (**Imam**) a title given to various Muslim leaders, eg a Shiite religious leader believed to be a direct successor of the prophet Muhammad or a learned Muslim theologian. • **imamate** *noun* **1** the territory governed by an imam. **2** the office, or period of office, of an imam. ⌚ 17c: Arabic, meaning 'chief' or 'leader', from *amma* to precede.

Imari /iːˈmɑːrɪ/ ▷ *noun* a type of Japanese porcelain, richly decorated in red, green and blue. Also *as adj* ▫ *Imari bowl.* ⌚ 19c: named after Imari, the Japanese seaport from where it was exported.

IMAX or **Imax** /ˈaɪmaks/ ▷ *noun, trademark, cinematog* a system of large wide-screen motion-picture presentation using 70mm film running horizontally with a frame size 70 × 46mm, projected on to a large screen situated comparatively close to the audience so that the picture fills their field of vision. ⌚ 1960s: from *image* + *maximum*.

imbalance ▷ *noun* a lack of balance or proportion; inequality.

imbecile /ˈɪmbəsiːl, -saɪl/ ▷ *noun* (*imbeciles*) **1** *old use* someone of very low intelligence, especially someone who is capable of keeping out of danger and of performing simple tasks only if someone else is supervising. **2** *colloq* a stupid person; a fool. ▷ *adj* (*also* **imbecilic** /-ˈsɪlɪk/) mentally weak; stupid; foolish. • **imbecility** /-ˈsɪlɪtɪ/ *noun* (*imbecilities*). ⌚ 16c: from Latin adjective *imbecillus* feeble or fragile.

imbed a less usual spelling of EMBED

imbibe /ɪmˈbaɪb/ ▷ *verb* (*imbibed*, *imbibing*) **1** *now facetious or formal* to drink, especially alcoholic drinks. **2** *formal or literary* to take in or absorb something (eg ideas), as if drinking them in or soaking them up. • **imbiber** *noun.* ⌚ 14c in obsolete sense 'to soak something in liquid': from Latin *imbibere*, from *bibere* to drink.

imbricate ▷ *adj* /ˈɪmbrɪkət, -keɪt/ *biol* said of fish scales, leaves, layers of tissue, teeth, etc: overlapping like roof tiles. ▷ *verb* /-keɪt/ (*imbricated*, *imbricating*) *tr & intr* to overlap or be overlapping like roof tiles. ⌚ 17c: from Latin *imbricatus*, from *imbricare* to cover with overlapping tiles.

imbroglio /ɪmˈbroʊlɪoʊ/ ▷ *noun* (*imbroglios*) **1** a confused and complicated situation. **2** a misunderstanding or disagreement. **3** a confused mass or heap. ⌚ 18c: Italian, from *imbrogliare* to confuse or entangle.

imbue /ɪm'bjuː/ ▷ *verb* (***imbued***, ***imbuing***) **1** (*especially* **imbue someone with something**) to fill or inspire, especially with ideals or principles. **2** to soak or saturate something, especially with dye. ⓒ 16c: from Latin *imbuere* to saturate.

IMF ▷ *abbreviation* International Monetary Fund.

imit. ▷ *abbreviation* **1** imitation. **2** imitative.

imitable /'ɪmɪtəbəl/ ▷ *adj* capable of being imitated. • **imitability** *noun*. Compare INIMITABLE. ⓒ 16c: French, from Latin *imitabilis*; see IMITATE.

imitate /'ɪmɪteɪt/ ▷ *verb* (***imitated***, ***imitating***) **1** to copy the behaviour, manners, appearance, etc of someone; to use them as a model. **2** to mimic or try to be like someone. **3** to make a copy of something; to reproduce or duplicate it. • **imitator** *noun*. ⓒ 16c: from Latin *imitari, imitatus*, from *imago* a likeness.

imitation /ɪmɪ'teɪʃən/ ▷ *noun* **1** an act of imitating. **2** something which is produced by imitating; a copy or counterfeit. **3** *music* the repeating of a passage, phrase, theme, etc which has already been heard, often at a different pitch or in a different voice. **4** *as adj* cheaply made to look or function like something which is more expensive; sham or artificial □ *imitation leather*.

imitative /'ɪmɪtətɪv, -teɪtɪv/ ▷ *adj* **1** imitating, copying or mimicking. **2** copying a more expensive or superior-quality original. **3** tending to imitate. **4** said of a word: that imitates the sound (eg *sizzle*) or tries to represent the appearance, movement or general impression (eg *flash*) of a thing or action. Also called ONOMATOPOEIC. • **imitatively** *adverb*. • **imitativeness** *noun*.

immaculate /ɪ'makjʊlət/ ▷ *adj* **1** perfectly clean and neat; perfectly groomed □ *immaculate clothes*. **2** free from blemish, flaw or error □ *an immaculate performance*. **3** pure; free from any moral stain or sin. • **immaculacy** or **immaculateness** *noun*. • **immaculately** *adverb*. ⓒ 15c: from Latin *immaculatus*, from *macula* a spot or stain.

Immaculate Conception ▷ *noun*, *Christianity* the belief that the Virgin Mary was free from ORIGINAL SIN from the moment of her conception. Compare VIRGIN BIRTH.

immanence /'ɪmənəns/ and **immanency** ▷ *noun* (***immanences*** or ***immanencies***) *philos* the concept of an IMMANENT Supreme Being. ⓒ 19c.

immanent /'ɪmənənt/ ▷ *adj* **1** existing or remaining within something; inherent. **2** said of a Supreme Being or power: permanently present throughout the universe everywhere. ⓒ 16c: from medieval Latin *immanere*, from *im-* + *manere* to remain.

immaterial /ɪmə'tɪərɪəl/ ▷ *adj* **1** not important or relevant. **2** not formed of matter; incorporeal. ⓒ 14c: from Latin *immaterialis*.

immature ▷ *adj* **1** not fully grown or developed; not mature or ripe. **2** not fully developed emotionally or intellectually and therefore childish. • **immaturely** *adverb*. • **immaturity** *noun*. ⓒ 16c: from Latin *immaturus*; see MATURE.

immeasurable ▷ *adj* too great to be measured; very great; immense. • **immeasurably** *adverb*. ⓒ 15c; see MEASURE.

immediacy /ɪ'miːdɪəsɪ/ ▷ *noun* (***immediacies***) **1** the quality of being immediate or appealing directly to the emotions, understanding, etc. Also called **immediateness**. **2** an immediate problem, requirement or necessity.

immediate /ɪ'miːdɪət/ ▷ *adj* **1** happening or done at once and without delay □ *my immediate reaction*. **2** nearest or next in space, time, relationship, etc □ *the immediate family* □ *the immediate vicinity*. **3** belonging to the current time; urgent □ *deal with the immediate problems first*. **4** having a direct effect and without anything coming in between □ *the immediate cause of death*. ⓒ 16c: from Latin *immediatus*, from *mediare* to be in the middle.

immediately /ɪ'miːdɪətlɪ/ ▷ *adverb* **1** at once or without delay. **2** directly, without anything coming in between □ *sitting immediately next to me*. ▷ *conj* as soon as □ *Immediately he arrived, the meeting began*.

immemorial /ɪmə'mɔːrɪəl/ ▷ *adj* extending far back in time, beyond anyone's memory or written records □ *a custom since time immemorial*. • **immemorially** *adverb*. ⓒ 17c: from Latin *immemorialis*.

immense /ɪ'mɛns/ ▷ *adj* **1** very or unusually large or great. **2** *dated colloq* very good; splendid. • **immensely** *adverb*. • **immenseness** or **immensity** *noun* (***immensities***). ⓒ 15c: French, from Latin *immensus* immeasurable.

immerse /ɪ'mɜːs/ ▷ *verb* (***immersed***, ***immersing***) (*especially* **immerse something** or **someone in something**) **1** to dip it or them into or under the surface of a liquid completely. **2** to baptize them by submerging their whole body in water. • **be immersed in something** to be occupied or involved deeply in it; to be absorbed □ *soon became immersed in the book*. • **immersible** *adj*. ⓒ 17c: from Latin *immergere* to dip.

immersion /ɪ'mɜːʃən, -ʒən/ *noun* **1** immersing or being immersed. **2** baptism. **3** *colloq* an IMMERSION HEATER. **4** *education* a method of teaching a foreign language by giving the student intensive practice in a situation where only that language is used.

immersion heater ▷ *noun* an electric heater with an element that is immersed directly in a tank of water and controlled by a thermostat, used to provide a domestic hot water supply. Often shortened to **immersion**.

immigrant /'ɪmɪgrənt/ ▷ *noun* **1** someone who immigrates or has immigrated. **2** *biol* an animal or plant which becomes established in an area where it was previously not found. ▷ *adj* **1** belonging or relating to immigrants. **2** immigrating or having recently immigrated. Compare EMIGRANT.

immigrate /'ɪmɪgreɪt/ ▷ *verb* (***immigrated***, ***immigrating***) *intr* to come to a foreign country with the intention of settling in it. Compare EMIGRATE. • **immigration** *noun* **1 a** the process of immigrating; settling in a foreign country; **b** *as adj* □ *immigration control*. **2** *colloq* **a** the immigration checkpoint at an airport, seaport, etc that all travellers entering a country pass through □ *They walked straight through immigration unchallenged*; **b** the immigration authorities. ⓒ 17c: from Latin *immigrare*; see MIGRATE.

> ***immigrate***
>
> A related word often confused with this one is **emigrate**.

imminent /'ɪmɪnənt/ ▷ *adj* likely to happen in the near future; looming or impending □ *looks as though divorce is imminent*. • **imminence** *noun*. • **imminently** *adverb*. ⓒ 16c: from Latin *imminere* to project over something.

immiscible /ɪ'mɪsɪbəl/ ▷ *adj*, *chem* said of two or more liquids: forming separate layers and not mixing when shaken together, eg oil and water. • **immiscibly** *adverb*. ⓒ 17c: from Latin *immiscibilis*, from *miscere* to mix.

immobile /ɪ'moʊbaɪl, -bɪl/ ▷ *adj* **1** not able to move or be moved. **2** motionless. • **immobility** /ɪmoʊ'bɪlɪtɪ/ *noun*. ⓒ 14c: French, from Latin *immobilis*.

immobilize or **immobilise** ▷ *verb* (***immobilized***, ***immobilizing***) **1** to make or keep something or someone immobile. **2** to put or keep something or someone out of action or circulation. • **immobilization** *noun*. ⓒ 19c.

immoderate ▷ *adj* going far beyond normal or reasonable limits; excessive or extreme. • **immoderacy** *noun*. • **immoderately** *adverb*. • **immoderateness** or **immoderation** *noun*. ⓒ 14c: from Latin *immoderatus*.

immodest ▷ *adj* **1** shameful; indecent; improper. **2** boastful and conceited; forward. • **immodestly** *adverb*. • **immodesty** *noun*. ◎ 16c: from Latin *immodestus*.

immolate /ˈɪməleɪt/ ▷ *verb* (***immolated, immolating***) **1** to kill or offer as a sacrifice. **2** *literary* to give up (something highly prized or valued). • **immolation** *noun* **1** an act of immolating. **2** something that is sacrificed. • **immolator** *noun*. ◎ 16c: from Latin *immolare* to sprinkle (the sacrificial victim) with meal before sacrificing it.

immoral ▷ *adj* **1** morally wrong or bad; evil. **2** not conforming to the sexual standards of society; promiscuous. **3** unscrupulous; unethical. Compare AMORAL. • **immorality** *noun*. • **immorally** *adverb*. ◎ 17c.

> ***immoral***
>
> See Usage Note at **amoral**.

immortal ▷ *adj* **1** living forever and never dying. **2** lasting forever; perpetual. **3** to be remembered forever. ▷ *noun* **1** someone who will live forever, or who will always be remembered. **2** someone, eg an author, whose greatness or genius will be remembered forever. **3** (**the immortals**) the ancient Greek and Roman gods. • **immortality** *noun*. • **immortally** *adverb*. ◎ 14c: from Latin *immortalis*.

immortalize or **immortalise** ▷ *verb* (***immortalized, immortalizing***) **1** to make (a person, event, etc) famous for ever, especially by including them or it in a work of art or literature. **2** to make someone immortal. • **immortalization** *noun*.

immovable or **immoveable** ▷ *adj* **1** impossible to move; not meant to be moved. **2** steadfast; unyielding. **3** incapable of feeling or showing emotion, especially sorrow or pity. **4** *law* said of property: not liable to be removed; consisting of land or houses. **5** said of a religious festival: not movable (see MOVABLE sense 2). • **immovability** *noun*. • **immovably** *adverb*. ◎ 14c.

immune /ɪˈmjuːn/ ▷ *adj* **1** (*especially* **immune to something**) having a natural resistance to or protected by INOCULATION from (a particular disease) □ *She is immune to German measles.* **2** (*especially* **immune from something**) free, exempt or protected from it □ *I was immune from prosecution.* **3** (*especially* **immune to something**) unaffected by or not susceptible to it □ *immune to criticism.* **4** *physiol* relating to or concerned with producing immunity. • **immunity** *noun*. See also ACTIVE IMMUNITY, PASSIVE IMMUNITY. ◎ 15c in sense 2: from Latin *immunis*, from *munis* ready to be of service.

> ***immunity***
>
> A word sometimes confused with this one is **impunity**.

immune body ▷ *noun* an ANTIBODY

immune response ▷ *noun, physiol* the response of the body to the introduction of an ANTIGEN, especially by the formation of antibodies.

immune system ▷ *noun, physiol* the tissues and cells of the body that recognize and attack the ANTIGENS associated with different diseases.

immunize or **immunise** /ˈɪmjʊnaɪz/ ▷ *verb* (***immunized, immunizing***) *medicine* to produce artificial immunity to a disease in someone by injecting them with an antiserum or a treated antigen. See also ACTIVE IMMUNITY, PASSIVE IMMUNITY. • **immunization** *noun*.

immuno- /ˈɪmjʊnoʊ, ɪˈmjuːnoʊ/ ▷ *combining form, denoting* **1** immunity. **2** immune.

immunoassay ▷ *noun, biochem* a BIOASSAY in which the reaction of suspected antigens in a sample, usually a serum, with specific known antibodies, allows a quantitative assessment. See TITRE.

immunodeficiency ▷ *noun, physiol, medicine* a deficiency or breakdown in the body's ability to fight infection.

immunoglobulin ▷ *noun, biochem* one of a group of proteins found in blood plasma, that act as antibodies.

immunology /ɪmjʊˈnɒlədʒɪ/ ▷ *noun* the scientific study of immunity and the defence mechanisms that the body uses to resist infection and disease. • **immunological** *adj*. • **immunologically** *adverb*. • **immunologist** *noun*. ◎ Early 20c.

immunosuppressive and **immunosuppressant** ▷ *noun, medicine* a drug or other agent that suppresses the body's normal IMMUNE RESPONSE and so lowers its resistance to infection. It is used to counteract the body's natural response to reject transplanted organs, tissue, etc. Also *as adj* □ *immunosuppressive drugs.* • **immunosuppression** *noun*.

immunotherapy ▷ *noun* the treatment of disease, especially cancer, by antigens which stimulate the patient's own natural immunity.

immure /ɪˈmjʊə(r)/ ▷ *verb* (***immured, immuring***) **1** to enclose or imprison within, or as if within, walls. **2** to shut away. ◎ 16c: from Latin *immurare*, from *murus* wall.

immutable /ɪˈmjuːtəbəl/ ▷ *adj* **1** unable to be changed. **2** not susceptible to change. • **immutability** *noun*. • **immutably** *adverb*. ◎ 15c: from Latin *immutabilis*.

imp ▷ *noun* **1** a small mischievous or evil spirit. **2** a mischievous or annoying child. See also IMPISH. ◎ Anglo-Saxon *impa* a shoot, slip or offspring.

impact ▷ *noun* /ˈɪmpakt/ **1** the act of an object hitting or colliding with another object; a collision. **2** the force of such a collision. **3** a strong effect or impression. ▷ *verb* /ɪmˈpakt/ (***impacted, impacting***) **1 a** to press (two objects) together with force; **b** to force (one object) into (another). **2** *intr* to come forcefully into contact with another body or surface, etc. **3** *intr* to have an impact or effect on. • **impaction** /ɪmˈpakʃən/ *noun*. ◎ 17c: from Latin *impingere, impactum* to strike against.

impacted ▷ *adj* said of a tooth, especially a wisdom tooth: unable to erupt through the gum into a normal position because it is firmly wedged between the jawbone and another tooth.

impacted fracture ▷ *noun* a fracture with the jagged broken ends of the bone driven into each other.

impair /ɪmˈpɛə(r)/ ▷ *verb* (***impaired, impairing***) to damage or weaken something, especially in terms of its quality or strength □ *His health is much impaired* □ *visually-impaired.* • **impairment** *noun*. ◎ 14c: from French *empeirer*, from Latin *pejorare* to make worse.

impala /ɪmˈpɑːlə/ ▷ *noun* (***impalas*** or ***impala***) ▷ *noun* an antelope of S and E Africa, distinguished by the long high elegant leaps it takes when running. The male has lyre-shaped horns. ◎ 19c: from Zulu *i-mpala*.

impale /ɪmˈpeɪl/ ▷ *verb* (***impaled, impaling***) **1 a** to pierce with, or as if with, a long, pointed object or weapon; **b** to put someone to death by this method. **2** *heraldry* to put (two coats-of-arms) on a shield divided vertically into two. • **impalement** *noun*. ◎ 16c: from Latin *impaler*, from *palus* a stake.

impalpable ▷ *adj* **1** not able to be felt or perceived by touch. **2** difficult to understand or grasp. • **impalpability** *noun*. • **impalpably** *adverb*. ◎ 16c: French, from Latin *impalpabilis*, from *palpare* to touch gently.

impanel see EMPANEL

impart /ɪmˈpɑːt/ ▷ *verb* (***imparted, imparting***) **1** to make (information, knowledge, etc) known; to communicate (news, etc). **2** to give or transmit (a particular quality) □ *The bay leaf imparts a special flavour to the soup.* • **impartation** or **impartment** *noun*. ◎ 15c: from Latin *impartire*, from *pars, partis* a part.

impartial ▷ *adj* not favouring one person, etc more than another; fair and unbiased. • **impartiality** *noun*. • **impartially** *adverb*. ⓒ 16c.

impassable ▷ *adj* said of a road, path, etc: not able to be passed through or travelled along. • **impassability** or **impassableness** *noun*. • **impassably** *adverb*. ⓒ 16c.

impasse /'ɪmpas, am'pas; *French*; ɛ̃pas/ ▷ *noun* a situation in which progress is impossible and from which there is no way out; a deadlock. ⓒ 19c: French, from *passer* to pass.

impassion /ɪm'paʃən/ ▷ *verb* (***impassioned***, ***impassioning***) to fill with passion; to rouse emotionally. ⓒ 16c: from Italian *impassionare*; see PASSION.

impassioned ▷ *adj* **1** fervent, zealous or animated □ *an impassioned plea for help.* **2** deeply moved by emotion. • **impassionedly** *adverb*. • **impassionedness** *noun*.

impassive /ɪm'pasɪv/ ▷ *adj* **1** incapable of feeling and expressing emotion. **2** showing no feeling or emotion. • **impassively** *adverb*. • **impassiveness** or **impassivity** /ɪmpa'sɪvɪtɪ/ *noun*. ⓒ 17c: from Latin *passivus* susceptible to pain.

impasto /ɪm'pastoʊ, -'pɑːstoʊ/ ▷ *noun, art* in painting and pottery: **a** the technique of laying paint or pigment on thickly; **b** paint applied thickly, with clearly visible brushwork. • **impastoed** or **impasto'd** *adj*. ⓒ 18c: Italian, from Latin *impastare*, from *pasta* paste.

impatiens /ɪm'peɪʃɪenz, ɪm'patɪ-/ ▷ *noun* (*plural* ***impatiens***) any of numerous annual or perennial plants with translucent stems, oval-toothed leaves and flowers that hang from a slender stalk. Varieties include the TOUCH-ME-NOT and the popular ornamental hybrids commonly known as BUSY LIZZIE. ⓒ 19c: Latin, meaning 'impatient', because the fruit capsules explode as if impatient to scatter their seeds.

impatient ▷ *adj* **1** unwilling or lacking the patience to wait or delay. **2** (*usually* **impatient of** or **with something** or **someone**) intolerant; showing a lack of patience □ *impatient of fools* □ *impatient with bureaucracy.* **3** (*often* **impatient to do** or **for something**) restlessly eager and anxious □ *impatient for change* □ *impatient to get started.* • **impatience** *noun*. • **impatiently** *adverb*. ⓒ 14c: French, from Latin *impatiens*, from *patiens* suffering or enduring.

impeach /ɪm'piːtʃ/ ▷ *verb* (***impeaches***, ***impeached***, ***impeaching***) **1** *Brit law* to charge someone with a serious crime, especially a crime against the state or treason. **2** *N Amer* to accuse (a public or government official) of misconduct while in office. **3** to call something into question; to cast doubt upon (eg a person's honesty). • **impeachable** *adj*. ⓒ 14c: from French *empecher* to hinder or impede, from Latin *impedicare* to fetter.

impeachment ▷ *noun, politics* the legal process of removing an undesirable person from office.

impeccable /ɪm'pɛkəbəl/ ▷ *adj* **1** free from fault or error; perfectly executed or flawless. **2** said of a person: not susceptible to sin. • **impeccability** *noun*. • **impeccably** *adverb*. ⓒ 16c: from Latin *impeccabilis*, from *peccare* to sin.

impecunious /ɪmpɪ'kjuːnɪəs/ ▷ *adj* having little or no money; poor; penniless. • **impecuniously** *adverb*. • **impecuniousness** *noun*. ⓒ 16c: from Latin *pecunia* money, from *pecu* cattle.

impedance /ɪm'piːdəns/ ▷ *noun* **1** *elec* (SI unit OHM) (symbol **Z**) the effective RESISTANCE (sense 4) of an electric circuit or circuit component to the passage of an electric current. Compare REACTANCE. **2** anything that impedes.

impede /ɪm'piːd/ ▷ *verb* (***impeded***, ***impeding***) to prevent or delay the start or progress of (an activity, etc); to obstruct or hinder something or someone. • **impeding** *adj*. • **impedingly** *adverb*. ⓒ 17c: from Latin *impedire*, literally 'to snare the foot'.

impediment /ɪm'pɛdɪmənt/ ▷ *noun* **1** someone or something that delays or prevents the start or progress of something; an obstacle or hindrance. **2** (*also* **speech impediment**) a defect in a person's speech, eg a lisp or stutter. • **impedimental** /-'mɛntəl/ *adj*. ⓒ 14c: see IMPEDE.

impedimenta /ɪmpɛdɪ'mɛntə/ ▷ *plural noun* any objects which impede progress or movement, eg military baggage and equipment, legal obstructions, etc. ⓒ 16c: Latin, the plural of *impedimentum* a hindrance.

impel /ɪm'pɛl/ ▷ *verb* (***impelled***, ***impelling***) **1** to push, drive or urge something forward; to propel. **2** to force or urge someone into action. • **impellent** *adj*. • **impeller** *noun*. ⓒ 15c: from Latin *impellare*.

impend /ɪm'pɛnd/ ▷ *verb* (***impended***, ***impending***) *intr* **1** to be about to happen. **2** said of a danger, etc: to threaten; to hover threateningly. • **impending** *adj*. ⓒ 16c in sense 2: from Latin *impendere* to hang over.

impenetrable ▷ *adj* **1** incapable of being entered or passed through □ *an impenetrable jungle.* **2** not capable of being understood or explained; unfathomable or inscrutable □ *I found his argument completely impenetrable.* **3** not capable of receiving or being touched by intellectual ideas and influences □ *impenetrable ignorance.* **4** unable to be seen through; gloomy □ *sank into impenetrable despair.* • **impenetrability** *noun*. • **impenetrably** *adverb*. ⓒ 15c: from Latin *impenetrabilis*.

impenitent ▷ *adj* not sorry for having done something wrong; unrepentant. ▷ *noun* an unrepentant person; a hardened sinner. • **impenitence** *noun*. • **impenitently** *adverb*. ⓒ 16c: from Latin *impaenitens*, from *paenitere* to repent.

imperative /ɪm'pɛrətɪv/ ▷ *adj* **1** absolutely essential; urgent □ *It is imperative that we act at once.* **2** having or showing authority; commanding □ *At meetings his manner is imperative, never conciliatory.* **3** *grammar* (abbreviation **imper.**) said of the MOOD² of a verb: used for giving orders. ▷ *noun* **1** *grammar* a set of verb forms, or mood, used for giving orders, eg '*Listen* to me' and '*Do* as I say!'. Compare INDICATIVE, CONDITIONAL, SUBJUNCTIVE. **2** a verb form of this kind. **3** something which is imperative, especially a command or order. • **imperatively** *adverb*. ⓒ 16c: from Latin *imperativus*, from *imperare* to command.

imperceptible ▷ *adj* **1** too small, slight or gradual to be seen, heard, noticed, etc. **2** not able to be perceived by the senses. • **imperceptibility** *noun*. • **imperceptibly** *adverb*. ⓒ 16c.

imperceptive and **impercipient** ▷ *adj* having no power to perceive; lacking perception. • **imperceptively** or **impercipiently** *adverb*. • **imperceptiveness** or **impercipience** *noun*. ⓒ 17c as *imperceptive*; 19c as *impercipient*.

imperfect ▷ *adj* **1** having faults; spoilt. **2** lacking the full number of parts; incomplete or unfinished. **3** *grammar* (abbreviation **imperf.**) said of the tense of a verb: expressing a continuing state or incomplete action in the past. **4** *music* said of a chord, interval, etc: diminished (see under DIMINISH); reduced by a semitone. Compare PERFECT. ▷ *noun, grammar* **a** the imperfect tense; **b** a verb in the imperfect tense. Compare PAST, PRESENT, PERFECT, PLUPERFECT, FUTURE. • **imperfection** /ɪmpə'fɛkʃən/ *noun*. • **imperfectly** *adverb*. ⓒ 14c: from French *imparfait*, from Latin *imperfectus*.

imperial /ɪm'pɪərɪəl/ ▷ *adj* **1** belonging to or suitable for an empire, emperor or empress. **2** having supreme authority. **3** commanding; august. **4** regal; magnificent. **5** *Brit* said of a non-metric measure or weight, or of the non-metric system: conforming to standards fixed by parliament. **6** said of a product, etc: of superior quality or size. ▷ *noun* **1** a traditional paper size, in Britain 22 × 30in (559 × 762mm) or in USA 23 × 33in (584 × 838mm). **2** a small beard or tuft of hair under the lower lip, as popularized by Napoleon III. **3** an emperor, empress or member of an imperial family. • **imperially** *adverb*. ◎ 14c: from Latin *imperialis*, from *imperium* command or sovereignty.

imperial gallon see GALLON

imperialism /ɪm'pɪərɪəlɪzəm/ ▷ *noun* **1** the power of, or rule by, an emperor or empress. **2** the policy or principle of having and extending control over the territory of other nations, of creating or maintaining an empire, or of extending one's country's influence through trade and diplomacy, etc. Compare COLONIALISM. **3** *derog* an attempt by a developed country to interfere in the affairs of an underdeveloped country or countries. **4** the spirit, character, motivation, etc of empire. ◎ 19c.

imperialist ▷ *noun* a believer in or supporter of imperialism. ▷ *adj* relating to or characterized by imperialism. • **imperialistic** *adj* **1** involving imperialism. **2** according to an imperial system. • **imperialistically** *adverb*.

imperil /ɪm'perɪl/ ▷ *verb* (***imperilled***, ***imperilling***; *US* ***imperiled***, ***imperiling***) to put in peril or danger; to endanger. • **imperilment** *noun*. ◎ 16c.

imperious /ɪm'pɪərɪəs/ ▷ *adj* arrogant, haughty and domineering. • **imperiously** *adverb*. • **imperiousness** *noun*. ◎ 16c: from Latin *imperiosus*, from *imperium* command or sovereignty.

imperishable ▷ *adj* subject or liable to decay; lasting forever. • **imperishability** *noun*. • **imperishably** *adverb*. ◎ 17c.

impermanent ▷ *adj* not lasting or remaining; transient. • **impermanence** or **impermanency** *noun* lack of permanence. • **impermanently** *adverb*. ◎ 17c.

impermeable ▷ *adj* said of a material, etc: not allowing substances, especially liquids, to pass through or penetrate it. • **impermeability** *noun*. • **impermeably** *adverb*. ◎ 17c: from Latin *impermeabilis*.

impermissible ▷ *adj* not allowed. • **impermissibility** *noun*. • **impermissibly** *adverb*. ◎ 19c.

impersonal ▷ *adj* **1** having no reference to any particular person; objective. **2** without or unaffected by personal or human feelings, warmth, sympathy, etc; cold. **3** without personality. **4** *grammar* (abbreviation **impers.**) said of a verb: used without a subject or with a purely formal one (in English usually *it*, as in *It's snowing*). **5** *grammar* (abbreviation **impers.**) said of a pronoun: not referring to a particular person; indefinite. • **impersonality** *noun*. • **impersonally** *adverb*. ◎ 16c: from Latin *impersonalis*.

impersonalize or **impersonalise** ▷ *verb* (***impersonalized***, ***impersonalizing***) to make something impersonal, especially to take away its personal and human aspects, warmth, etc. • **impersonalized** *adj* □ *working for a large impersonalized organization*. • **impersonalization** *noun*.

impersonate /ɪm'pɜːsəneɪt/ ▷ *verb* (***impersonated***, ***impersonating***) to pretend to be, or copy the behaviour and appearance of, someone, especially in order to entertain or deceive other people □ *was arrested for impersonating a police officer*. • **impersonation** *noun*. • **impersonator** *noun*. ◎ 18c; 17c in archaic and obsolete senses 'to embody' and 'to personify': from Latin *persona* person.

impertinent ▷ *adj* **1** rude; not showing respect where it is due; impudent. **2** *old use or law* not relevant or pertinent. • **impertinence** *noun*. • **impertinently** *adverb*. ◎ 14c: from Latin *impertinens*.

imperturbable ▷ *adj* not liable to become, or not capable of being, easily worried or upset; always calm and unruffled. • **imperturbability** *noun*. • **imperturbably** *adverb*. ◎ 15c: from Latin *imperturbabilis*.

impervious ▷ *adj* (*usually* **impervious to something**) **1** said of a substance or material, etc: not allowing (eg water) to pass through or penetrate it; impermeable. **2** not influenced or affected by it □ *They seem impervious to criticism*. • **imperviously** *adverb*. • **imperviousness** *noun*. ◎ 17c: from Latin *impervius*, from *via* way.

impetigo /ɪmpɪ'taɪgoʊ/ ▷ *noun*, *pathol* a highly contagious skin disease, most common in babies and young children, characterized by the development of pustules and yellow crusty sores. • **impetiginous** /ɪmpɪ'tɪdʒɪnəs/ *adj*. ◎ 14c: Latin, from *impetere* to attack or force.

impetuous /ɪm'pɛtjʊəs/ ▷ *adj* **1** acting or done hurriedly and without thinking; rash. **2** moving or acting forcefully or with great energy. • **impetuosity** /ɪmpɛtjʊ'ɒsɪtɪ/ or **impetuousness** *noun*. • **impetuously** *adverb*. ◎ 14c: from Latin *impetuosus*, from *impetus* attack or force.

impetus /'ɪmpətəs/ ▷ *noun* (***impetuses***) **1** the force or energy with which something moves; momentum. **2** a driving force. **3** an incentive or encouragement. ◎ 17c: Latin, meaning 'attack' or 'force'.

impiety /ɪm'paɪətɪ/ ▷ *noun* (***impieties***) **1** lack of piety or devotion. **2** an impious act □ *committed many impieties*. ◎ 14c (16c in sense 2): from French *impieté*, from Latin *impietas*.

impinge /ɪm'pɪndʒ/ ▷ *verb* (***impinged***, ***impinging***) *intr* (*usually* **impinge against** or **on something** or **someone**) **1** to interfere with or encroach on it or them. **2** to come into contact or collide with it or them. **3** to make an impression on it or them. • **impingement** *noun*. ◎ 17c: from Latin *impingere* to force, thrust or drive violently.

impious /ɪm'paɪəs/ ▷ *adj* lacking respect or proper reverence, especially for a divine being. • **impiously** *adverb*. • **impiousness** *noun*. ◎ 16c: from Latin *impius*.

impish ▷ *adj* like an imp; mischievous. • **impishly** *adverb*. • **impishness** *noun*. ◎ 17c.

implacable /ɪm'plakəbəl/ ▷ *adj* not able to be calmed, satisfied or placated. • **implacability** or **implacableness** *noun*. • **implacably** *adverb*. ◎ 16c: French, from Latin *implacabilis*, from *placare* to appease.

implant ▷ *verb* /ɪm'plɑːnt, 'ɪmplɑːnt/ (***implanted***, ***implanting***) **1** to fix or plant something securely; to embed. **2** to fix or instil (ideas, beliefs, etc) in someone's mind. **3** *surgery* to insert or graft (an object, tissue, substance, etc) permanently into the body. ▷ *noun* /'ɪmplɑːnt/ *surgery* any object, tissue, substance, etc implanted in the body, eg silicone breast implants, hormones, etc. Compare GRAFT[1]. • **implantation** *noun*. ◎ 16c: from French *implanter* to implant or engraft.

implausible ▷ *adj* not easy to believe; not likely to be true. • **implausibility** *noun*. • **implausibly** *adverb*. ◎ 17c.

implement ▷ *noun* /'ɪmpləmənt/ **1** a tool or utensil. **2** something which is required in order to fulfil a purpose. ▷ *verb* /'ɪmpləmɛnt/ (***implemented***, ***implementing***) to carry out, fulfil or perform. • **implemental** /-'mɛntəl/ *adj*. • **implementation** /ɪmpləmən'teɪʃən, -mɛn'teɪʃən/ *noun*. ◎ 15c: from Latin *implementum*, from *implere* to fill.

implicate /'ɪmplɪkeɪt/ ▷ *verb* (***implicated***, ***implicating***) **1** to show or suggest that someone is involved or took part in something, especially in a crime □ *There is very strong evidence implicating him in the raid*. **2** to imply. • **implicative** /ɪm'plɪkətɪv, 'ɪmplɪkeɪtɪv/ *adj*. • **implicatively** *adverb*. ◎ 16c: from Latin *implicare* to interweave.

implication /ɪmplɪ'keɪʃən/ ▷ *noun* **1** the act or process of implicating someone, or the state of being implicated. **2** the act of implying something, or the state of being implied. **3** something that is implied □ *Have you considered the long-term implications of this plan?* • **by implication** by suggestion, without being stated directly.

implicit /ɪm'plɪsɪt/ ▷ *adj* **1** implied or meant, although not stated directly □ *His consent is implicit in the statement.* **2** present, although not explicit or immediately discernible □ *There was disappointment implicit in her words.* **3** unquestioning; complete □ *has implicit faith in her.* • **implicitly** *adverb.* • **implicitness** *noun.* ◷ 16c: from Latin *implicitus* involved or interwoven.

implode /ɪm'ploʊd/ ▷ *verb* (***imploded, imploding***) *tr & intr* to collapse or make something collapse inwards, especially suddenly or violently. ◷ 19c: modelled on EXPLODE.

implore /ɪm'plɔː(r)/ ▷ *verb* (***implored, imploring***) **1** to entreat or beg someone. **2** (*usually* **implore someone for** or **to do something**) to beg them earnestly for it or to do it □ *I implored him to reconsider.* • **imploration** *noun.* • **imploratory** /ɪm'plɒrətərɪ/ *adj.* • **imploring** *adj.* • **imploringly** *adverb.* ◷ 16c: from Latin *implorare*, from *plorare* to weep.

implosion /ɪm'ploʊʒən/ ▷ *noun, physics, etc* a violent collapse or bursting inward, eg when the seal of a vacuum-filled glass vessel is broken or when material capable of nuclear fission is compressed by ordinary explosives in a nuclear weapon. • **implosive** /ɪm'ploʊsɪv, -zɪv/ *adj.*

imply /ɪm'plaɪ/ ▷ *verb* (***implies, implied, implying***) **1** to suggest or express something indirectly; to hint at it □ *Are you implying that it was my fault?* **2** to suggest or involve something as a necessary result or consequence □ *These privileges imply a heavy responsibility.* • **implied** *adj.* ◷ 14c: from French *emplier*, from Latin *implicare* to interweave.

imply

See Usage Note at **infer**.

impolite ▷ *adj* rude, disrespectful. • **impolitely** *adverb.* • **impoliteness** *noun.* ◷ 17c: from Latin *impolitus*, from *politus* polished.

impolitic ▷ *adj* unwise; not to be advised. • **impoliticly** *adverb.* ◷ 16c.

imponderable ▷ *adj* having an influence or importance which cannot be measured, counted, assessed or determined. ▷ *noun* something that is imponderable. • **imponderably** *adverb.* ◷ 18c, meaning 'having no weight': from Latin *imponderabilis*, from *pondus, ponderis* weight.

import ▷ *verb* /'ɪmpɔːt, ɪm'pɔːt/ (***imported, importing***) **1** to bring (goods, etc) in to a country from another country. **2** to bring something in from another, external source. **3** *computing* to load (a file, text, data, etc) prepared with one program into another program. **4** *formal or old use* to signify, imply or portend. ▷ *noun* /'ɪmpɔːt/ **1** a commodity, article, etc that has been imported. **2** the act or business of importing goods. **3** *as adj* □ *import duty.* **4** *formal* importance □ *a matter of great import.* **5** *formal or old use* meaning. • **importable** *adj.* • **importation** /ɪmpɔː'teɪʃən/ *noun* **1** the act or process of importing. **2** something that is imported. • **importer** *noun.* ◷ 15c: from Latin *importare*, from *portare* to carry away.

important /ɪm'pɔːtənt/ ▷ *adj* **1** having great value, influence, significance or effect □ *an important day.* **2** of great significance or value □ *Your happiness is important to me.* **3** said of a person: having high social rank or status; eminent □ *an important woman in her field.* **4** *rather formal or literary* pompous or pretentious. • **importance** *noun.* See also SELF-IMPORTANT. • **importantly** *adverb.* ◷ 16c: French, from Latin *importare* to be of consequence.

importunate /ɪm'pɔːtʃʊnət/ ▷ *adj, formal* **1** persistent or excessively demanding. **2** extremely urgent or pressing. • **importunately** *adverb.* ◷ 15c: from Latin *importunus* inconvenient.

importune /ɪmpə'tʃuːn, ɪm'pɔːtʃuːn/ ▷ *verb* (***importuned, importuning***) *tr & intr, formal* **1** to make persistent and usually annoying requests of someone. **2** to solicit for immoral purposes, eg prostitution. • **importunely** *adverb.* • **importuner** *noun.* • **importunity** /ɪmpə'tʃuːnɪtɪ/ (***importunities***) *noun.* ◷ 15c: from Latin *importunus* inconvenient.

impose /ɪm'poʊz/ ▷ *verb* (***imposed, imposing***) **1** (*usually* **impose something on** or **upon someone**) to make payment of (a tax, fine, etc) or performance of (a duty) compulsory; to enforce it. **2** (*especially* **impose oneself on** or **upon someone**) to force oneself, one's opinions or company, etc on them. **3** (*especially* **impose on** or **upon someone** or **something**) *intr* to take advantage of them or it; to set unreasonable burdens or tasks on them □ *We mustn't impose on your good nature* □ *I wouldn't dream of imposing.* **4** (*usually* **impose something on** or **upon someone**) to palm it off on them surreptitiously or dishonestly. **5** *printing, publishing* to arrange (pages) in the proper order for printing. ◷ 17c: from French *imposer.*

imposing ▷ *adj* impressive, especially in size, dignity, handsome appearance, etc. • **imposingly** *adverb.*

imposition /ɪmpə'zɪʃən/ ▷ *noun* **1** the act or process of imposing. **2** an unfair or excessive demand, burden or requirement. **3** a tax or duty. **4** *printing, publishing* the assembling of pages in the proper order for printing. ◷ 14c: see IMPOSE.

impossibility ▷ *noun* **1** the state or quality of being impossible. **2** something that has no likelihood of happening, existing, etc □ *A holiday is a complete impossibility on my salary.*

impossible ▷ *adj* **1** not capable of happening, being done, etc □ *It is impossible to get there in an hour.* **2** not capable of being true; difficult to believe □ *an impossible story.* **3** *colloq* unacceptable, unsuitable or difficult to bear; intolerable □ *His conduct has put me in an impossible position* □ *That child is quite impossible!* • **impossibly** *adverb* □ *This is impossibly hard.* ◷ 14c: from Latin *impossibilis.*

impost[1] /'ɪmpoʊst/ ▷ *noun* **1** *chiefly old use* a tax, especially one on imports. **2** *colloq* the weight carried by a horse in a handicap race (see HANDICAP *noun* 3). ◷ 16c: French, from Latin *imponere*; see IMPOSE.

impost[2] /'ɪmpoʊst/ ▷ *noun, archit* the upper part of a pillar, where the weight of the arch, vault, etc rests. ◷ 17c: from French *imposte*, from Italian *imposta*, from Latin *impositus* imposed or placed on.

impostor or **imposter** /ɪm'pɒstə(r)/ ▷ *noun* someone who pretends to be someone else in order to deceive others. Compare IMPERSONATOR. ◷ 16c: from French *imposteur*, from Latin *imponere* to impose.

imposture /ɪm'pɒstʃə(r)/ ▷ *noun* an act, instance or the process of deceiving, especially by pretending to be someone else. ◷ 16c: French.

impotent /'ɪmpətənt/ ▷ *adj* **1** powerless; lacking the necessary strength. **2** said of an adult male: **a** unable to maintain a sexual erection and therefore unable to perform sexual intercourse; **b** unable to have an orgasm. • **impotence** *noun.* • **impotently** *adverb.* ◷ 15c: French, from Latin *impotentia* lack of self-control.

impound /ɪm'paʊnd/ ▷ *verb* (***impounded, impounding***) **1** to shut (eg an animal) up in, or as if in, a POUND[2]; to confine. **2** to take legal possession of something; to confiscate it □ *Police impounded the illegally-parked car.* **3** said of a reservoir, dam, etc: to collect and hold (water). • **impoundable** *adj.* • **impoundage** *noun.* • **impounder** *noun* ◷ 16c.

impoverish /ɪm'pɒvərɪʃ/ ▷ *verb* (***impoverished, impoverishing***) **1** to make poor or poorer. **2** to reduce the quality, richness or fertility of something (eg soil). • **impoverished** *adj.* • **impoverishment** *noun.* ◷ 15c: from French *empovrir*, from Latin *pauper* poor.

impracticable /ɪm'praktɪkəbəl/ ▷ *adj* **1** not able to be done, put into practice, used, etc. **2** said eg of a road: not in a suitable condition for vehicles to use it. • **impracticability** *noun.* • **impracticably** *adverb.* ◷ 17c: see PRACTICE.

impractical /ɪmˈpraktɪkəl/ ▷ *adj* **1** not effective in actual use. **2** said of a person, plan, etc: lacking common sense. Compare UNPRACTICAL. • **impracticality** *noun* (***impracticalities***). • **impractically** *adverb.* ◷ 19c.

imprecate /ˈɪmprəkeɪt/ ▷ *verb* (***imprecated, imprecating***) *formal or old use* **1** to call (eg an evil curse) down. **2** *tr & intr, now rare* to curse. • **imprecation** *noun.* • **imprecatory** /ˈɪmprəkeɪtərɪ, -kətərɪ, ɪmˈprɛk-/ *adj.* ◷ 17c: from Latin *imprecari, imprecatus* to pray to or for something.

imprecise ▷ *adj* inaccurate. • **imprecisely** *adverb.* • **imprecision** /ɪmprəˈsɪʒən/ *noun.* ◷ 19c.

impregnable /ɪmˈprɛgnəbəl/ ▷ *adj* **1** said of a city, fortress, etc: not able to be seized, defeated or taken by force. **2** not able to be affected or shaken by criticism, doubts, etc. • **impregnability** *noun.* • **impregnably** *adverb.* ◷ 15c: from French *imprenable.*

impregnate /ˈɪmprɛgneɪt, ɪmˈprɛg-/ ▷ *verb* (***impregnated, impregnating***) **1** to make (a woman or female animal) pregnant; to fertilize (eg a female cell or plant). **2** to permeate something completely; to saturate it □ *The pads have been impregnated with soap.* **3** to fill or imbue something. • **impregnation** *noun.* ◷ 16c: from Latin *impraegnare* to fertilize.

impresario /ɪmprəˈsɑːrɪoʊ/ ▷ *noun* (***impresarios***) **1** someone who organizes public entertainments such as concerts. **2** the manager of an opera or theatre company. ◷ 18c: Italian, meaning 'someone who undertakes (business)', from *impresa* an enterprise or undertaking.

impress ▷ *verb* /ɪmˈprɛs/ (***impressed, impressing***) **1** to produce a strong, lasting, and usually favourable impression on someone □ *You impressed my family with your knowledge* □ *He was dressed to impress.* **2** (*especially* **impress something on** or **upon someone**) to make it very clear or emphasize it to them □ *I impressed on them the need for silence.* **3** to make or stamp (a mark, pattern, etc) on something by applying pressure. **4** (*often* **impress something on** or **upon someone**) to fix (a fact, belief, etc) firmly or deeply in their mind or memory □ *He impressed his socialist values on me.* ▷ *noun* /ˈɪmprɛs/ **1** the act or process of impressing. **2** something (eg a mark or impression) made by impressing or by being impressed. • **impressible** *adj.* ◷ 14c: from Latin *imprimere, impressum* to press into or on.

impression /ɪmˈprɛʃən/ ▷ *noun* **1** an idea or effect, especially a favourable one, produced in the mind or made on the senses □ *It is vital to create a good impression.* **2** a vague or uncertain idea, notion or belief □ *I got the impression he was lying.* **3** an act or the process of impressing (see IMPRESS[1]). **4** a mark or stamp produced by, or as if by, impressing or pressure. **5** an imitation, especially a caricature, of a person, or an imitation of a sound, done for entertainment □ *He does impressions of pop stars.* **6** the number of copies of a book, newspaper, etc printed at one time. **7** *printing* **a** the pressing of a prepared inked plate or type on to the paper, etc being printed; **b** a copy made in this way. • **be under the impression that ...** to think, feel or believe (especially wrongly) that ... □ *I was under the impression that you were paying for this meal.* ◷ 14c.

impressionable /ɪmˈprɛʃənəbəl/ ▷ *adj* easily impressed or influenced. • **impressionability** *noun.* • **impressionably** *adverb.* ◷ 19c: see IMPRESS.

Impressionism ▷ *noun* (*sometimes* **impressionism**) in art, music or literature: a 19c style which aims to give a general impression of feelings and events rather than a formal or structural treatment of them: **a** in art: a movement begun in France in the 1860s by artists who rejected the dark tones of 19c studio painting, set up their easels out-of-doors (see PLEIN AIR) and used bright natural colours to build up an impression of the actual effects of light rather than a detailed firmly-outlined image; **b** in literature: the conveying of a subjective impression of the world rather than its objective appearance, as in the work of symbolist (see SYMBOLISM) poets and the STREAM-OF-CONSCIOUSNESS novel; **c** in music: a style of harmony and instrumentation which blurs the edges of TONALITY, aiming for veiled suggestion and understatement rather than a detailed picture. ◷ 19c: the name, coined by a hostile critic, was taken from Claude Monet's picture *Impression: soleil levant* (Impression: Rising Sun, 1872).

impressionist ▷ *noun* **1** (*usually* **Impressionist**) a painter, writer or composer in the style of Impressionism. **2** someone who imitates, or performs impressions of, other people. ▷ *adj* (*usually* **Impressionist**) relating to or characteristic of Impressionism.

impressionistic ▷ *adj* based on impressions or personal observation as distinct from definite facts or particular knowledge. • **impressionistically** *adverb.* ◷ 19c.

impressive /ɪmˈprɛsɪv/ ▷ *adj* **1** capable of making a deep impression on a person's mind, feelings, etc. **2** producing admiration, wonder or approval. • **impressively** *adverb.* • **impressiveness** *noun.* ◷ 16c.

imprest /ˈɪmprɛst, ɪmˈprɛst/ ▷ *noun* **1** a loan or advance of money, especially one from government funds for some public purpose. **2** (*usually* **imprest system**) *bookkeeping, commerce, etc* a method of maintaining a cash fund (eg petty cash) for incidental expenses, in which a fixed FLOAT (*noun* 5) is regularly topped up from central funds. ◷ 16c: from Latin *praestare* to offer.

imprimatur /ɪmprɪˈmeɪtə(r), -mɑːtə(r)/ ▷ *noun* **1** a licence or permission to print or publish a book, now especially one granted by the Roman Catholic church. **2** approval; permission. ◷ 17c: Latin, meaning 'let it be printed'.

imprint ▷ *noun* /ˈɪmprɪnt/ **1** a mark or impression made by pressure. **2** a permanent effect, eg on the mind, produced by some experience or event. **3** *printing, publishing* **a** the publisher's name and address, and the date and place of publication, printed at the bottom of a book's title page; **b** the printer's name and address, printed on the back of a book's title page, or on the last page. ▷ *verb* /ɪmˈprɪnt/ (***imprinted, imprinting***) (*usually* **imprint something on something**) **1** to mark or print an impression of it on (eg a surface). **2** to fix it firmly in (the mind, etc) □ *The incident is imprinted on my memory in every detail.* **3** *zool* to cause (a young animal) to undergo IMPRINTING □ *The chicks were imprinted on Jane from birth and think she is their mother.* ◷ 15c: see PRINT.

imprinting ▷ *noun, zool* the process by which animals rapidly learn the appearance, sound or smell of significant individual members of their own species (eg parents, offspring, suitable mates).

imprison /ɪmˈprɪzən/ ▷ *verb* (***imprisoned, imprisoning***) **1** to put in prison. **2** to confine or restrain as if in a prison. • **imprisonment** *noun.* ◷ 13c: from French *emprisoner.*

improbable ▷ *adj* **1** unlikely to happen or exist. **2** hard to believe. • **improbability** *noun* (***improbabilities***). • **improbably** *adverb.* ◷ 16c: from Latin *improbabilis.*

improbity /ɪmˈproʊbɪtɪ/ ▷ *noun* (***improbities***) dishonesty; wickedness. ◷ 16c: from Latin *improbitas.*

impromptu /ɪmˈprɒmptʃuː/ ▷ *adj* made or done without preparation or rehearsal; improvised; spontaneous. ▷ *adverb* without preparation; spontaneously. ▷ *noun* (***impromptus***) **1** something that is impromptu, eg a spontaneous speech or composition. **2** a piece of music which suggests improvisation. ◷ 17c: from Latin *in promptu* in readiness.

improper ▷ *adj* **1** not conforming to accepted standards of modesty and moral behaviour; unseemly; indecent □

made an improper suggestion to a female officer. **2** not correct; wrong □ *improper use of funds.* **3** not suitable □ *We consider jeans improper dress for the occasion.* • **improperly** *adverb.* 16c: from Latin *improprius.*

improper fraction ▷ *noun, math* a fraction in which the NUMERATOR has a value which is equal to or higher than that of the DENOMINATOR, eg 5/4, and which therefore is always equal to or greater than 1. Compare PROPER FRACTION.

impropriety /ɪmprəˈpraɪətɪ/ ▷ *noun* (***improprieties***) **1** an improper act. **2** the state of being improper; indecency. 17c: from Latin *improprietas.*

improve /ɪmˈpruːv/ ▷ *verb* (***improved, improving***) **1** *tr & intr* to make or become better or of higher quality or value; to make or cause something to make progress □ *must improve his appearance if he wants this job* □ *Her health has improved lately.* **2** (*especially* **improve on something**) to produce something better, or of higher quality or value, than a previous example □ *has improved on the world record by one second.* **3** to increase the value or beauty of (land or property) by cultivation, laying out gardens, building, etc. • **improvable** *adj.* • **improver** *noun.* • **improving** see separate entry. 17c: from French *emprower,* from *en-* into + *prou* profit.

improvement *noun* **1** the act or process of improving; the state of being improved. **2** something that has been improved or that is considered better than a previous example □ *He's a definite improvement on her last boyfriend.* **3** something that improves, especially by adding value, beauty, quality, etc □ *Their home improvements are very tastefully done.*

improvident ▷ *adj* **1** not considering or providing for likely future needs; lacking foresight. **2** careless; thoughtless; rash. • **improvidence** *noun.* • **improvidently** *adverb.* 16c.

improving ▷ *adj* **1** tending to cause improvement. **2** uplifting or instructive, especially in regard to someone's morals □ *should sit down with an improving book* □ *think improving thoughts.* ▷ *noun* an act or the process of making something better □ *Improving the decor added to the value of the house.* • **improvingly** *adverb.*

improvisation /ɪmprəvaɪˈzeɪʃən/ ▷ *noun* **1** the act or process of improvising. **2** an instance of improvising, eg an improvised performance or creation. • **improvisational** *adj.*

improvise /ˈɪmprəvaɪz/ ▷ *verb* (***improvised, improvising***) **1** *tr & intr* to compose, recite or perform (music, verse, etc) without preparing it in advance. **2** to make or provide something quickly, without preparing it in advance and using whatever materials are to hand. • **improvisatorial** /-vɪzəˈtɔːrɪəl/ or **improvisatory** /-ˈvaɪzətərɪ, -ˈvɪzətərɪ, -vaɪˈzeɪtərɪ/. • **improviser** *noun.* 19c: from French *improviser,* from Latin *provisus* foreseen.

imprudent ▷ *adj* said of a person, act, etc: lacking in good sense or caution; rash; heedless. • **imprudence** *noun.* • **imprudently** *adverb.* 14c: from Latin *imprudens,* from *providere* to see ahead.

impudent /ˈɪmpjʊdənt/ ▷ *adj* rude, insolent or impertinent. • **impudence** *noun* **1** being impudent. **2** an instance of impudent behaviour or language. • **impudently** *adverb.* 14c: from Latin *impudens,* from *pudens* being ashamed.

impugn /ɪmˈpjuːn/ ▷ *verb* (***impugned, impugning***) to call into question or raise doubts about (the honesty, integrity, etc of someone or something); to criticize or challenge. • **impugnable** *adj.* • **impugnment** *noun.* 14c: from French *impugner,* from Latin *impugnare* to attack.

impulse /ˈɪmpʌls/ ▷ *noun* **1** a sudden push forwards; a force producing sudden movement forwards; a thrust. **2** the motion or movement produced by such a force or push. **3** a sudden desire or urge to do something without thinking of the consequences □ *bought the dress on impulse.* **4** an instinctive or natural tendency. **5** *physiol* an electrical signal that travels along a nerve fibre, and in turn causes excitation of other nerve, muscle or gland cells, so relaying information throughout the nervous system. Also called NERVE IMPULSE. **6** *physics* for two objects that briefly collide with each other: the product of the force produced and the time for which it acts. • **impulsion, impulsive,** *etc* see separate entries. 17c: from Latin *impulsus* pressure.

impulse buy ▷ *noun* something bought on impulse, especially something that was not really necessary. • **impulse buyer** *noun.* • **impulse buying** *noun.*

impulsion /ɪmˈpʌlʃən/ ▷ *noun* **1** an act of urging, forcing or pushing forwards, into motion or into action, or the state of being so urged. **2** a force which urges, etc forwards, into motion, etc. **3** a sudden desire or urge.

impulsive ▷ *adj* **1** said of a person: tending or likely to act suddenly and without considering the consequences. **2** said of an action: done without such consideration; reckless; spontaneous. **3** having the power to urge or push forwards, into motion or into action. **4** not continuous; acting or actuated by impulse. • **impulsively** *adverb.* • **impulsiveness** *noun.*

impunity /ɪmˈpjuːnɪtɪ/ ▷ *noun* freedom or exemption from punishment, injury, loss or other bad consequences. • **with impunity** without having to suffer the normal consequences □ *thinks he can break the rules with impunity.* 16c: from Latin *impunitas,* from *impunis* unpunished.

impunity

A word often confused with this one is **immunity**.

impure ▷ *adj* (***impurer, impurest***) **1** mixed with something else; adulterated or tainted. **2** dirty. **3** immoral; not chaste. **4** *relig* ritually unclean. • **impurely** *adverb.* • **impureness** *noun.* • **impurity** *noun* (***impurities***) **1** the state of being impure. **2** an impure or unclean thing or constituent. 16c: from Latin *impurus.*

impute /ɪmˈpjuːt/ ▷ *verb* (***imputed, imputing***) (*usually* **impute something to someone** or **something**) **1** to regard (something unfavourable or unwelcome) as being brought about by them. **2** to believe it to be caused by them or it; to attribute □ *imputed his failure to laziness.* • **imputable** *adj.* • **imputation** /ɪmpjʊˈteɪʃən/ *noun.* 14c: from French *imputer,* from Latin *imputare.*

IMRO /ˈɪmroʊ/ ▷ *abbreviation, Brit* Investment Management Regulatory Organization.

IMunE ▷ *abbreviation, Brit* Institution of Municipal Engineers.

IN ▷ *abbreviation, US state* Indiana. Also written **Ind.**

In ▷ *symbol, chem* indium.

in ▷ *prep* **1** used to express the position of someone or something with regard to what encloses, surrounds or includes them or it; within □ *Stay in bed* □ *They are in the park* □ *She's in the sixth form.* **2** into □ *get in the car* □ *I put it in my bag.* **3** after (a period of time) □ *Come back in an hour* □ *It will be ready in one minute.* **4** during; while □ *lost in transit* □ *In running for the bus, she tripped.* **5** used to express arrangement or shape □ *in a square* □ *in alphabetical order.* **6** from; out of something □ *two in every eight.* **7** by the medium or means of, or using, something □ *sung in Italian* □ *written in code.* **8** wearing something □ *the lady in red* □ *a man in a fur hat.* **9** used to describe a state or manner □ *in a hurry* □ *in a daze.* **10** used to state an occupation □ *She's in banking* □ *a job in local government.* **11** used to state a purpose □ *a party in his honour* □ *built in memory of his wife.* **12** said of some animals: pregnant with (young) □ *in calf.* ▷ *adverb* **1** to or towards the inside; indoors □ *Do come in.* **2** at home or work □ *Is John in?* **3** so as to be added or included □ *beat in the eggs.* **4** so as to enclose or conceal, or be enclosed or concealed □ *The fireplace was bricked in.* **5** in or into political power or office. **6** in or into fashion. **7** in a good position; in favour □ *trying to keep in with the boss.* **8** in certain games: batting. **9** into a proper, required or efficient state □ *run a new car in.* **10** said of the tide: at its highest point; as close to the shore as it gets. **11** *in compounds* expressing prolonged activity, especially by large numbers of people gathered in one room or building, originally as a form of organized protest □ *a sit-in* □ *a work-in* □ *a teach-in.* ▷ *adj* **1** inside; internal; inwards □ *Never go out of the in door.* See also INNER, INMOST. **2** fashionable □ *Orange was the in colour last summer* □ *the in thing to do.* **3** in power or office □ *when the Tories were in.* **4** *especially in compounds* used for receiving things coming in □ *an in-tray.* **5** *also in compounds* shared by a group of people □ *an in-joke.* • **be in for it** or **something** *colloq* to be likely to experience some trouble or difficulty □ *We'll be in for it when we get home* □ *He's in for a rough ride.* • **have it in for someone** *colloq* to make trouble for them, especially because of disliking them. • **have it in her, him, one,** *etc* to be capable of (doing something) □ *I was amazed at Jo's high dive; I didn't think she had it in her.* • **in as far as** or **in so far as** ... to the degree that ... (sometimes written **insofar as** ...) • **in as much as ...** or **inasmuch as ...** because ... ; considering that ... • **in itself** intrinsically; essentially; considered on its own □ *It's not much of a job in itself, but the prospects and perks are good.* • **in on something** *colloq* knowing about it and sharing in it □ *Were you in on the secret?* • **ins and outs** the complex and detailed facts of a matter; intricacies. Also called OUTS AND INS. • **insomuch that** or **insomuch as 1** in as much as. **2** to such an extent that. • **in that ...** for the reason that ... • **in with someone** *colloq* friendly with them or in favour with them. ◷ Anglo-Saxon.

in. ▷ *abbreviation* inch, or inches.

in-[1] ▷ *prefix* (*also* **il-** before words beginning in *l*, **im-** before words beginning in *b*, *m* and *p*, and **ir-** before words beginning in *r*) *signifying* the negative or opposite of the root word or a lack of the quality implied by the root word; not; lacking □ *inhospitable* □ *illogical* □ *immaturity* □ *irrelevance.* Compare NON-, UN-. ◷ Latin.

in-[2] ▷ *prefix* (*also* **il-** before words beginning with *l*, **im-** before words beginning with *b*, *m* and *p*, and **ir-** before words beginning with *r*) *signifying* **1** in, on or towards □ *immigrant* □ *imprison* □ *intrude.* **2** used to add emphasis or force, or sometimes with almost no meaning □ *intumesce.* ◷ Latin *in-* and French *en-* in or into.

-in ▷ *suffix, chem, forming nouns, denoting* **1** a neutral substance such as a protein, fat or glycoside □ *albumin* □ *insulin.* **2** an antibiotic or other pharmaceutical drug □ *penicillin* □ *aspirin.* **3** any of certain enzymes □ *pepsin* □ *thrombin.* ◷ A variant of -INE[2].

-ina /iːnə/ ▷ *suffix, denoting* a feminized form of a male name, title, etc □ *Christina* □ *tsarina.* ◷ Italian, Spanish or Latin, modelled on such words as BALLERINA.

inability ▷ *noun* the lack of sufficient power, means or ability. ◷ 15c.

in absentia /ɪn abˈsɛnʃə, — abˈsɛntɪɑː/ ▷ *adverb* in his, her or their absence □ *Her degree was conferred in absentia.* ◷ 19c: Latin, literally 'in absence'.

inaccessible ▷ *adj* **1** difficult or impossible to approach, reach or obtain □ *The garden is inaccessible from the road.* **2** said of a person: difficult to understand or influence; unapproachable. • **inaccessibility** *noun.* • **inaccessibly** *adverb.* ◷ 16c.

inaccurate ▷ *adj* containing errors; not correct or accurate. • **inaccuracy** *noun* (*inaccuracies*). • **inaccurately** *adverb.*

inaction ▷ *noun* lack of action; sluggishness; inactivity.

inactive ▷ *adj* **1** taking little or no exercise; idle or sluggish. **2** no longer operating or functioning. **3** said of members of a group, especially members of the armed forces: not taking part in or available for eg military duties. **4** *chem* said of a substance: showing little or no chemical reactivity. • **inactively** *adverb.* • **inactivity** *noun.* ◷ 18c.

inadequate ▷ *adj* **1** not sufficient or adequate. **2** said of someone: not able to cope; not competent or capable. • **inadequacy** *noun* (*inadequacies*) • **inadequately** *adverb.*

inadmissible ▷ *adj* not allowable or able to be accepted □ *inadmissible evidence.* • **inadmissibility** *noun.* • **inadmissibly** *adverb.*

inadvertent /ɪnədˈvɜːtənt/ ▷ *adj* **1** said of an act: not done deliberately; unintentional. **2** not paying proper attention; heedless. • **inadvertence** or **inadvertency** *noun.* • **inadvertently** *adverb.* ◷ 17c: from Latin *advertere* to direct attention to something.

inadvisable ▷ *adj* not wise; not advisable. • **inadvisability** *noun.*

inalienable /ɪnˈeɪlɪənəbəl/ ▷ *adj* not capable of being taken or given away, eg to another person □ *an inalienable right.* • **inalienability** *noun.* • **inalienably** *adverb.* ◷ 17c.

inalterable ▷ *adj* UNALTERABLE. • **inalterability** or **inalterableness** *noun.* • **inalterably** *adverb.*

inamorata /ɪnaməˈrɑːtə/ ▷ *noun* (*inamoratas*) *chiefly literary, formal or old use* a woman who is in love or who is beloved; a girlfriend. ◷ 17c: Italian, from *innamorare* to inflame with love.

inamorato /ɪnaməˈrɑːtoʊ/ ▷ *noun* (*inamoratos*) a man who is in love or who is beloved; a male lover or sweetheart. ◷ 16c: see INAMORATA.

inane /ɪˈneɪn/ ▷ *adj* (*inaner, inanest*) **1** without meaning or point. **2** silly or senseless. • **inanely** *adverb.* See also INANITY. ◷ 19c in this sense; 17c, meaning 'empty': from Latin *inanis* empty.

inanimate ▷ *adj* **1** without life; not living □ *inanimate objects.* **2** dull; spiritless. • **inanimately** *adverb.* • **inanimation** *noun.* ◷ 16c.

inanition /ɪnəˈnɪʃən/ ▷ *noun, formal* emptiness or exhaustion, especially of a physical kind, due to lack of nutrients in the blood resulting from starvation or some intestinal disease. ◷ 15c: from Latin *inanitio* (see INANE).

inanity /ɪˈnanɪtɪ/ ▷ *noun* (*inanities*) **1** an inane remark or action, etc. **2** the state of being inane; silliness or senselessness. ◷ 17c: from Latin *inanitas* emptiness.

inapplicable ▷ *adj* not applicable or suitable. • **inapplicability** *noun.* • **inapplicably** *adverb.*

inapposite ▷ *adj, rather formal* not suitable or apposite; out of place. • **inappositely** *adverb.* • **inappositeness** *noun.*

inappreciable ▷ *adj* too small or slight to be noticed or to be important □ *an inappreciable difference in quality.* • **inappreciably** *adverb.* ◷ 19c; 18c in obsolete sense 'invaluable'.

inappropriate ▷ *adj* not suitable or appropriate. • **inappropriately** *adverb.* • **inappropriateness** *noun.*

inapt /ɪnˈapt/ ▷ *adj* **1** not apt or appropriate. **2** lacking skill; unqualified. • **inaptly** *adverb.* • **inaptitude** or **inaptness** *noun.*

inapt

See Usage Note at **inept**.

inarticulate ▷ *adj* **1** unable to express oneself clearly or to speak distinctly. **2** badly expressed; not spoken or pronounced clearly. **3** not jointed or hinged. •

inarticulately *adverb*. • **inarticulateness** *noun*. ⓒ 17c in senses 2 and 3: from Latin *inarticulatus*.

inartistic ▷ *adj* **1** not following the rules or principles of art; not artistic. **2** not able to appreciate art. **3** not artistically talented. • **inartistically** *adverb*.

inasmuch as see under IN

inattentive ▷ *adj* not paying proper attention; neglectful; not attentive. • **inattention** or **inattentiveness** *noun*. • **inattentively** *adverb*.

inaudible ▷ *adj* not audible; not loud enough to be heard. • **inaudibility** *noun*. • **inaudibly** *adverb*.

inaugural /ɪn'ɔːgjʊrəl/ ▷ *adj* **1** relating to or describing a ceremony that officially marks the beginning of something. **2** said of a speech, lecture, etc: given by someone on taking office or at their inauguration ceremony. ▷ *noun* an inaugural speech or lecture. ⓒ 17c: from Latin *inaugurare* to inaugurate.

inaugurate /ɪn'ɔːgjʊreɪt/ ▷ *verb* (***inaugurated, inaugurating***) **1** to place (a person) in office with a formal ceremony. Compare INDUCT. **2** to mark the beginning of (some activity) with a formal ceremony or dedication, etc. **3** to mark the opening of (a new building or service), especially by being the first person to try it out. • **inauguration** *noun*. • **inaugurator** *noun*. ⓒ 17c: from Latin *inaugurare*, literally 'to take omens'; see AUGUR.

inauspicious ▷ *adj* not promising future success; not auspicious; unlucky. • **inauspiciously** *adverb*. • **inauspiciousness** *noun*.

in-between ▷ *adj* coming between two things in space, time, style, etc; neither one thing nor the other. ▷ *noun* any thing or person that is in-between.

inboard ▷ *adj, adverb* **1** said especially of a boat's motor or engine: situated inside the hull. **2** said especially of an aircraft's engine: situated between the wingtip and the fuselage. Compare OUTBOARD.

inborn ▷ *adj* said of a human attribute or characteristic: possessed or apparently possessed from birth; innate or hereditary. *Technical equivalent* CONGENITAL. ⓒ 16c.

inbound ▷ *adj* said of a vehicle, flight, carriageway, etc: coming towards its destination; arriving. Opposite of OUTBOUND.

inbred ▷ *adj* **1** INBORN. **2** *biol* said of a plant or animal: produced by inbreeding.

inbreed ▷ *verb* (***inbred, inbreeding***) **1 a** *biol* to allow reproduction between closely related individuals of a species, especially over several generations; **b** *intr* said of closely related individuals: to reproduce, especially over several generations. **2** to create within; to engender.

inbreeding *noun, biol* breeding within a closely-related group, which eventually results in an increased frequency of abnormalities, eg certain mental defects in humans. See also OUTBREEDING.

in-built ▷ *adj* integral; built-in.

Inc. ▷ *abbreviation, especially US* Incorporated.

inc. see INCL.

Inca /ɪŋkə/ ▷ *noun, historical* **1** a member of an indigenous S American people living in Peru before the Spanish conquest in the 16c, who had a complex civilization and empire. **2 a** a king or emperor of the Incas; **b** a member of the Incan royal family. **3** the language of the Incas; QUECHUA. ▷ *adj* belonging or relating to this people or their language. • **Incan** *adj*. ⓒ 16c: Spanish, from Quechua *inka* ruler or king.

incalculable /ɪŋ'kalkjʊləbəl, ɪn-/ ▷ *adj* **1** not able to be estimated or reckoned in advance; unpredictable. **2** too great to be measured. • **incalculability** *noun*. • **incalculably** *adverb*. ⓒ 18c.

in camera ▷ *adverb* **1** *law* said of a hearing, etc: in a judge's private room, as distinct from in OPEN COURT. **2** in secret; in private. ⓒ 19c: Latin, meaning 'in a chamber'.

incandesce /ɪŋkan'dɛs, ɪn-/ ▷ *verb* (***incandesced, incandescing***) *tr & intr* to become or make something become incandescent. ⓒ 19c.

incandescent /ɪŋkən'dɛsənt, ɪn-/ ▷ *adj* **1** white-hot or glowing with intense heat. **2** shining brightly; luminous. **3** said of a substance: emitting light as a result of being heated to a high temperature. **4** belonging or relating to, or consisting of, light produced by heating a substance to a high temperature. • **incandescence** *noun*. • **incandescently** *adverb*. ⓒ 18c: from Latin *incandescere*, from *candescere* to glow or become white.

incandescent lamp ▷ *noun* an electric lamp with a glass bulb containing an inert gas and a filament of highly resistive wire that becomes white hot and emits light when a current passes through it.

incantation /ɪŋkan'teɪʃən, ɪn-/ ▷ *noun* **1** words said or sung as a spell; a magical formula. **2** the use of spells and magical formulae. • **incantatory** /ɪŋkan'teɪtərɪ, ɪŋ'kantətərɪ, ɪn-/ *adj*. ⓒ 14c: French, from Latin *incantare* to put a spell on.

incapable ▷ *adj* (*especially* **incapable of something**) **1** lacking the necessary ability, power, character, etc to do it; not capable. **2** unable or unfit to do it, especially to look after one's own affairs. • **incapability** *noun*. • **incapably** *adverb*. ⓒ 17c: from Latin *incapabilis*.

incapacitate /ɪŋkə'pasɪteɪt, ɪn-/ ▷ *verb* (***incapacitated, incapacitating***) (*often* **incapacitate someone for something**) **1** to take away strength, power or ability; to make unfit (eg for work). **2** to disqualify someone legally. • **incapacitated** *adj*. • **incapacitation** *noun*. ⓒ 17c: from INCAPACITY.

incapacity ▷ *noun* (***incapacities***) **1** a lack of the necessary strength, power, ability, etc; inability or disability □ *an incapacity to think straight*. **2** legal disqualification. ⓒ 17c: from French *incapacité*.

incapsulate see ENCAPSULATE

incapsulating language ▷ *noun* POLYSYNTHETIC LANGUAGE.

in-car ▷ *adj* said of a music system, etc: situated inside a car □ *fully equipped with in-car stereo*.

incarcerate /ɪŋ'kɑːsəreɪt, ɪn-/ ▷ *verb* (***incarcerated, incarcerating***) to shut in or keep in prison. • **incarceration** *noun*. ⓒ 16c: from Latin *incarcerare*, from *carcer* prison.

incarnate /ɪŋ'kɑːnət, ɪn-/ ▷ *adj* (usually placed immmediately after its noun) **1** in bodily, especially human, form □ *God incarnate*. **2** personified; typified □ *She is laziness incarnate*. ▷ *verb* /-neɪt/ (***incarnated, incarnating***) **1** to give bodily, especially human, form to (a spirit or god). **2** to personify or typify something. ⓒ 16c as *adjective* (16c as *verb*): from Latin *incarnatus* made flesh, from *carnis* flesh.

incarnation /ɪŋkɑː'neɪʃən, ɪn-/ ▷ *noun* **1** the bodily form, especially human form, taken by a spirit or god. **2** someone or something that typifies a quality or idea; an embodiment. **3 a** the act or process of taking bodily form, especially human form, by a spirit or god; **b** (**the Incarnation**) *Christianity* God becoming human, in the person of Jesus Christ. **4** any of a succession of periods spent in a particular bodily form or state.

incautious ▷ *adj* acting or done without thinking; heedless. • **incautiously** *adverb*. • **incautiousness** *noun*. ⓒ 18c.

incendiary /ɪn'sɛndɪərɪ/ ▷ *adj* **1** belonging or relating to the deliberate and illegal burning of property or goods. **2** said of a substance: capable of catching fire and burning readily. **3** causing, or likely to cause, trouble or violence. See also INFLAMMATORY. ▷ *noun* (***incendiaries***) **1** someone who deliberately and illegally sets fire to buildings or property; an arsonist. **2** (*also* **incendiary bomb**) a device containing a highly inflammable substance, designed to burst into flames on striking its target. **3** someone who stirs up trouble or violence. • **incendiarism** *noun.* ⓒ 17c: from Latin *incendiarius*, from *incendere* to kindle or set on fire.

incense[1] /ˈɪnsɛns/ ▷ *noun* **1** a spice or other substance which gives off a pleasant smell when burned, used especially during religious services. **2** the smell or smoke given off by burning spices, etc. ▷ *verb* (***incensed***, ***incensing***) **1** to offer incense to (a god). **2** to perfume or fumigate something with incense. ⓒ 13c: from Latin *incensum* a thing burnt.

incense[2] /ɪnˈsɛns/ ▷ *verb* (***incensed***, ***incensing***) to make very angry; to enrage □ ***was incensed by the article in the paper.*** ⓒ 15c: from Latin *incendere, incensum* to set on fire.

incentive /ɪnˈsɛntɪv/ ▷ *noun* **1** something that motivates or encourages an action, work, etc, such as extra money paid to workers to increase output. See also CARROT (sense 3). **2** *as adj* serving to motivate or encourage □ ***an incentive scheme.*** ⓒ 15c: from Latin *incentivus*, from *incinere* to blow on an instrument.

inception /ɪnˈsɛpʃən/ ▷ *noun* beginning; outset □ ***The business was corrupt from its inception.*** • **inceptive** *adj.* ⓒ 15c: from Latin *incipere, inceptum* to begin.

incertitude /ɪnˈsɜːtɪtʃuːd/ ▷ *noun, formal* uncertainty; doubt. ⓒ 17c: French.

incessant /ɪnˈsɛsənt/ ▷ *adj* going on without stopping; continual. • **incessancy** *noun.* • **incessantly** *adverb.* • **incessantness** *noun.* ⓒ 16c: French, from Latin *cessare* to cease.

incest /ˈɪnsɛst/ ▷ *noun* sexual intercourse between people who are too closely related to be allowed to marry, eg between brother and sister. ⓒ 13c: from Latin *incestum*, from *castus* chaste.

incestuous /ɪnˈsɛstʃʊəs/ ▷ *adj* **1** relating to, guilty of or involving INCEST. **2** said of a relationship or group of people: closed to outside influences or other people; excessively or unhealthily close-knit. • **incestuously** *adverb.* • **incestuousness** *noun.*

inch[1] /ɪntʃ/ ▷ *noun* (***inches***) **1** in the imperial system: a unit of length equal to 2.54cm or one twelfth of a foot. **2** *meteorol, especially formerly* the amount of rain or snow that will cover a surface to the depth of one inch, now usually measured in millimetres. **3** *meteorol, especially formerly* a unit of pressure equal to the amount of atmospheric pressure required to balance the weight of a column of mercury one inch high, now usually measured in millibars. **4** (*also* **inches**) a small amount or distance □ ***It wouldn't budge an inch*** □ ***The ball only missed me by inches.*** **5** (**inches**) stature. **6** *in compounds* □ ***inch-tape.*** ▷ *verb* (***inched***, ***inching***) *tr & intr* (*especially* **inch along, forward, out**, *etc*) to move or be moved slowly, carefully and by small degrees □ ***inched forward to see if any cars were coming.*** See also *inch something out* below. • **every inch** completely; in every way □ ***He's every inch a gentleman.*** • **inch by inch** or **by inches** gradually; by small degrees. • **within an inch of something** very close to or almost as far as it. • **within an inch of one's life** almost to the point of death; very thoroughly □ ***beat him within an inch of his life.*** ⓒ Anglo-Saxon *ynce*, from Latin *uncia* a twelfth part; see also OUNCE.

■ **inch someone out** to outdo or defeat them by a very small amount.

■ **inch something out** to measure out or dispense it very cautiously or in tiny amounts.

inch[2] /ɪntʃ/ ▷ *noun, especially Scots* often in place names: a small island. ⓒ 15c: from Gaelic *innis* an island or land next to a river.

-in-chief ▷ *combining form, forming nouns, denoting* highest in rank; supreme □ ***commander-in-chief.***

inchoate /ɪŋˈkoʊeɪt, ɪn-, -ət, ˈɪŋ-, ˈɪn-/ *formal or technical* ▷ *adj* **1** at the earliest stage of development; just beginning. **2** not fully developed; unfinished; rudimentary. ▷ *verb* (***inchoated***, ***inchoating***) to begin. • **inchoately** *adverb* so as to be inchoate. • **inchoateness** *noun.* ⓒ 16c: from Latin *inchoare* or *incohare* to begin, from *cohum* thong of a yoke.

inchoative /ɪŋˈkoʊətɪv, ɪn-/ ▷ *adj, grammar* said of a verb: denoting the beginning of an action. ▷ *noun* an inchoative verb.

inchworm ▷ *noun* a type of caterpillar, the LOOPER. Also called **measuring-worm**.

incidence /ˈɪnsɪdəns/ ▷ *noun* **1** the frequency with which something happens or the extent of its influence. **2** *physics* the way in which something moving in a line (eg a ray of light) comes into contact with a surface or plane. See also ANGLE OF INCIDENCE. **3** the fact or manner of falling on, striking or affecting something. ⓒ 15c.

incident /ˈɪnsɪdənt/ ▷ *noun* **1** an event or occurrence. **2** an event or occurrence which is dependent on, related to or a consequence of something else. **3** a relatively minor event or occurrence which might have serious consequences. **4** a brief violent conflict or disturbance, eg a bomb explosion. ▷ *adj* **1** (*especially* **incident to something**) belonging naturally to it or being a natural consequence of it. **2** *law* (*usually* **incident to something**) dependent on it. **3** *physics* said of light rays, particles, etc: falling on or striking a surface, etc. ⓒ 15c: French, from Latin *incidens*, from *cadere* to fall.

incidental /ɪnsɪˈdɛntəl/ ▷ *adj* **1** happening, etc by chance in connection with something else, and of secondary or minor importance □ ***incidental expenses.*** **2** (*usually* **incidental to something**) occurring or likely to occur as a minor consequence of it. **3** (*usually* **incidental on** or **upon something**) following or depending upon it, or caused by it, as a minor consequence. ▷ *noun* **1** anything that occurs incidentally. **2** (**incidentals**) minor expenses, details, items, etc. • **incidentally** *adverb* **1** by the way, parenthetically — often used to introduce a sentence or phrase describing something which is, or might seem to be, a secondary or minor but related matter. **2** in an incidental manner. ⓒ 17c: see INCIDENT.

incidental music ▷ *noun* music which accompanies the action of a film, play, etc.

incinerate /ɪnˈsɪnəreɪt/ ▷ *verb* (***incinerated***, ***incinerating***) *tr & intr* to burn to ashes. • **incineration** *noun.* ⓒ 16c: from Latin *incinerare, incineratum* to reduce to ashes.

incinerator /ɪnˈsɪnəreɪtə(r)/ ▷ *noun* a furnace or machine for burning rubbish, etc to ashes.

incipient /ɪnˈsɪpɪənt/ ▷ *adj* beginning to exist; in an early stage. • **incipience** or **incipiency** *noun.* • **incipiently** *adverb.* ⓒ 17c: from Latin *incipere* to begin.

incise /ɪnˈsaɪz/ ▷ *verb* (***incised***, ***incising***) *especially technical* **1** to cut into, especially precisely and with a specialized sharp tool. **2** to engrave (an inscription, stone, etc). ⓒ 16c: from French *inciser.*

incision /ɪnˈsɪʒən/ ▷ *noun* **1** a cut, especially one made by a surgeon. **2** an act of cutting, especially by a surgeon. **3** forcefulness or sharpness, eg in speech or action.

incisive /ɪnˈsaɪsɪv/ ▷ *adj* clear and sharp; to the point; acute. • **incisively** *adverb.* • **incisiveness** *noun.* ⓒ 16c: see INCISE.

incisor /ɪnˈsaɪzə(r)/ ▷ *noun* in mammals: a sharp chisel-edged tooth in the front of the mouth, used for biting and nibbling. Compare CANINE TOOTH, MOLAR[1].

incite /ɪnˈsaɪt/ ▷ *verb* (***incited***, ***inciting***) (*especially* **incite someone to something**) to stir up or provoke to action, etc. • **incitement** or **incitation** *noun.* • **inciter** *noun.* • **incitingly** *adverb.* ⓒ 15c: from Latin *incitare*, from *citare* to set in rapid motion.

incivility ▷ *noun* **1** rudeness; lack of civility. **2** a rude or uncivil act or remark. ⓒ 17c.

incl. or (*sometimes*) **inc.** ▷ *abbreviation* **1** included. **2** including. **3** inclusive.

inclement /ɪŋ'klɛmənt, ɪn-/ ▷ *adj, formal* said of weather: stormy or severe; harsh. • **inclemency** *noun* (***inclemencies***). • **inclemently** *adverb*. ⓒ 17c: from Latin *inclemens*, from *clemens* mild.

inclination /ɪŋklɪ'neɪʃən, ɪn-/ ▷ *noun* **1** (*often* **an inclination for** or **towards something** or **to do something**) a particular tendency or disposition, especially a liking, interest or preference □ *My own inclination is to wait till tomorrow* □ *had an inclination for chocolate ice-cream.* **2** the degree at which an object slopes away from a horizontal or vertical line or plane. **3** see INCLINE *noun*. **4** an act of inclining or bowing (the head, etc); a bow or nod. **5** the act of inclining; being inclined.

incline /ɪŋ'klaɪn, ɪn-/ ▷ *verb* (***inclined, inclining***) **1** *tr & intr* (*especially* **incline to** or **towards something**) to lean or make someone lean towards (a particular opinion or conduct); to be, or make someone, disposed towards it □ *I incline to agree* □ *He inclined towards the radical approach.* **2** *tr & intr* to slope or make something slope from a horizontal or vertical line or direction; to slant. **3** to bow or bend (the head, one's body, etc) forwards or downwards. ▷ *noun* /'ɪŋklaɪn, 'ɪn-/ a slope; an inclined plane. Also called **inclination**. • **inclined** *adj* **1** sloping or bent. **2** having a tendency; disposed. ⓒ 14c: from Latin *inclinare* to bend towards.

inclined plane ▷ *noun, mech, etc* a plane surface at an angle to a horizontal surface, used especially as a mechanism for lessening the force needed to raise or lower heavy objects.

inclose see ENCLOSE

inclosure see ENCLOSURE

include /ɪŋ'kluːd, ɪn-/ ▷ *verb* (***included, including***) **1** to take in or consider something or someone along with other things or people, as part of a group □ *I don't include him among my friends* □ *He has five pairs, if you include the blue ones.* **2** to contain or be made up of something, or to have it as parts of its contents □ *The price includes postage and packing.* Opposite of EXCLUDE. • **includable** or **includible** *adj*. • **including** *prep* which includes. • **include me out** *colloq, originally & especially US* do not include me; count me out. ⓒ 15c: from Latin *includere* to shut in.

inclusion /ɪŋ'kluːʒən, ɪn-/ ▷ *noun* **1** the act or process of including; the state of being included. **2** something that is included. **3** a small amount of liquid or gas that is encapsulated in a mineral.

inclusive /ɪŋ'kluːsɪv, ɪn-/ ▷ *adj* **1** (*usually* **inclusive of something**) incorporating it; taking it in □ *inclusive of VAT.* **2** counting the specified limits □ *pages 13 to 27 inclusive.* See also INCLUSIVE RECKONING. **3** comprehensive; all-embracing. • **inclusively** *adverb*. • **inclusiveness** *noun*.

inclusive reckoning ▷ *noun* a method of counting in which both the first and the last term is counted □ *by inclusive reckoning, Easter Sunday is the third day after Good Friday.* Compare EXCLUSIVE RECKONING.

incognito /ɪŋkɒg'niːtoʊ, ɪn-/ ▷ *adj, adverb* keeping one's identity a secret, eg by using a disguise and a false name. ▷ *noun* (***incognitos***) **1** the disguise and false name of a person who wishes to keep their identity secret. **2** someone who is incognito. ⓒ 17c: Italian (adjective and adverb), meaning 'unknown', from Latin *incognitus* unknown.

incognizant or **incognisant** ▷ *adj, formal* (*especially* **incognizant of something**) not aware of it; not knowing. • **incognizance** *noun*. ⓒ 19c: see COGNIZANT.

incoherent ▷ *adj* **1** said of speech or writing: not expressed clearly or logically; difficult to understand and follow. **2** said of a person: unable to speak clearly and logically. • **incoherence** *noun* **1** being incoherent. **2** lack of clarity in speech or writing. **3** difficulty in expressing oneself. • **incoherently** *adverb*. ⓒ 17c.

incombustible ▷ *adj* incapable of being set alight or burned. ⓒ 15c.

income /'ɪŋkʌm, -kəm, ɪn-/ ▷ *noun* money received over a period of time as payment for work, etc or as interest or profit from shares or investment. See also REVENUE. ⓒ 17c in this sense; 14c, meaning 'an arrival' or 'a coming in'.

incomer ▷ *noun* someone who comes to live in a place, not having been born there.

incomes policy ▷ *noun, econ* a government policy designed to curb inflation by controlling wages.

income support ▷ *noun, Brit* a state benefit paid to people on low incomes and to the unemployed, and which replaced SUPPLEMENTARY BENEFIT in 1988, itself being replaced in October 1996 by JOB SEEKERS ALLOWANCE.

income tax ▷ *noun* a personal tax levied on income, often set as a fixed percentage of income, with increasing percentages being levied on higher levels of income.

incoming ▷ *adj* **1** coming in; approaching □ *the incoming train.* **2** next or following. **3** said of an official, politician, etc: coming in to office □ *the incoming president.* **4** said of interest, etc: accruing. Opposite of OUTGOING.

incommensurable ▷ *adj* (*especially* **incommensurable with something**) **1** having no common standard or basis and not able to be compared with it. **2** *math* said of a quantity or magnitude: having no common factor with another. • **incommensurability** *noun*. ⓒ 16c: from Latin *incommensurabilis*; see COMMENSURABLE.

incommensurate ▷ *adj* **1** (*especially* **incommensurate with** or **to something**) out of proportion to it; inadequate for it. **2** INCOMMENSURABLE. • **incommensurately** *adverb*. • **incommensurateness** *noun*. ⓒ 17c: see COMMENSURATE.

incommode /ɪŋkə'moʊd, ɪn-/ ▷ *verb* (***incommoded, incommoding***) *formal or old use* to cause bother, trouble or inconvenience to someone. ⓒ 16c: from French *incommoder*, from Latin *incommodare*.

incommodious ▷ *adj, formal* said eg of accommodation: inconvenient or uncomfortable, especially because too small. • **incommodiously** *adverb*. • **incommodiousness** *noun*. ⓒ 16c: see COMMODIOUS.

incommunicado /ɪŋkəmjuːnɪ'kɑːdoʊ, ɪn-/ ▷ *adverb, adj* said of a person: not able or allowed to communicate with other people, especially when held in solitary confinement □ *He will be strictly incommunicado for a month.* ⓒ 19c: Spanish.

incomparable ▷ *adj* **1** having no equal; above comparison. **2** not comparable; having no common properties or other basis by which to make a comparison. • **incomparability** or **incomparableness** *noun*. • **incomparably** *adverb*. ⓒ 15c.

incompatible ▷ *adj* **1** said of people: unable to live, work or get on together in harmony. **2** (*often* **incompatible with something**) said of statements, etc: not in agreement; inconsistent. **3** said eg of drugs: not able to be combined; mutually intolerant. **4** said eg of machines, computer software or hardware, etc: incapable of functioning together; not able to operate in combination. • **incompatibility** *noun*. • **incompatibly** *adverb*. ⓒ 16c.

incompetent /ɪn'kɒmpɪtənt/ ▷ *adj* **1** lacking the necessary skill, ability or qualifications, especially for a job. **2** not legally qualified or COMPETENT. ▷ *noun* an incompetent person. • **incompetence** *noun*. • **incompetently** *adverb*. ⓒ 16c.

incomplete ▷ *adj* not complete or finished. • **incompletely** *adverb*. • **incompleteness** *noun*. ⓒ 14c.

incomprehensible ▻ *adj* difficult or impossible to understand; not comprehensible. • **incomprehensibility** *noun*. • **incomprehensibly** *adverb*. • **incomprehension** *noun*. ⓘ 14c.

inconceivable ▻ *adj* **1** unable to be imagined, believed or conceived by the mind. **2** *colloq* stretching a person's powers of belief or imagination. • **inconceivability** *noun*. • **inconceivably** *adverb*. ⓘ 17c.

inconclusive ▻ *adj* not leading to a definite conclusion, result or decision. • **inconclusively** *adverb*. • **inconclusiveness** *noun*. ⓘ 17c.

incongruous ▻ *adj* **1** out of place; unsuitable; inappropriate. **2** (*often* **incongruous with** or **to something**) incompatible or out of keeping with it. • **incongruity** *noun* (***incongruities***). • **incongruously** *adverb*. • **incongruousness** *noun*. ⓘ 17c: from Latin *incongruus*; see CONGRUOUS.

inconsequent ▻ *adj* **1** not following logically or reasonably; illogical. **2** irrelevant. **3** (also **inconsequential**) not connected or related. • **inconsequently** *adverb*. ⓘ 16c: from Latin *inconsequens*; see CONSEQUENT.

inconsequential ▻ *adj* **1** of no importance, value or CONSEQUENCE. **2** INCONSEQUENT. • **inconsequentiality** *noun*. • **inconsequentially** *adverb*. ⓘ 17c: from Latin *inconsequens*; see CONSEQUENT.

inconsiderable ▻ *adj, often with negatives* not worth considering; small in amount, value, etc; insignificant □ *lent her a not inconsiderable sum.* • **inconsiderably** *adverb*. ⓘ 17c.

inconsiderate ▻ *adj* thoughtless, especially in not considering the feelings, rights, etc of others. • **inconsiderately** *adverb*. • **inconsiderateness** or **inconsideration** *noun*. ⓘ 15c.

inconsistent ▻ *adj* **1** (*especially* **inconsistent with something**) not in agreement or accordance with it. **2** said of a single thing: having contradictory or incompatible elements in it. **3** said of a person: not always thinking, speaking, behaving, etc in accordance with the same principles; not consistent in thought, speech, behaviour, etc; changeable. • **inconsistency** *noun* **1** lack of consistency. **2** an instance of this. • **inconsistently** *adverb*. ⓘ 17c.

inconsolable ▻ *adj* not able to be comforted; not consolable. • **inconsolably** *adverb*. ⓘ 16c.

inconsonant /ɪŋ'kɒnsənənt, ɪn-/ ▻ *adj* (*especially* **inconsonant with something**) not agreeing with it or in harmony with it. • **inconsonantly** *adverb*. ⓘ 17c: see CONSONANT.

inconspicuous ▻ *adj* not easily noticed or conspicuous; attracting little attention. • **inconspicuously** *adverb*. • **inconspicuousness** *noun*. ⓘ 17c.

inconstant ▻ *adj* **1** *formal or literary* said of a person: having feelings which change frequently; fickle; unfaithful. **2** subject to frequent change; variable. • **inconstancy** *noun* changeability. • **inconstantly** *adverb*. ⓘ 15c.

incontestable ▻ *adj* too clear or definite to be disputed; not contestable; undeniable. • **incontestability** *noun*. • **incontestably** *adverb*. ⓘ 17c.

incontinent ▻ *adj* **1** unable to control one's bowels or bladder or both. **2** *formal or old use* unable to control oneself, especially one's sexual desires. **3** *medicine* (*usually* **incontinent of something**) lacking control over it. • **incontinence** or **incontinency** *noun*. ⓘ 14c: French, from Latin *incontinens*; see CONTINENT[2].

incontrovertible ▻ *adj* not able to be disputed or doubted. • **incontrovertibility** *noun*. • **incontrovertibly** *adverb*. ⓘ 17c.

inconvenience ▻ *noun* **1** trouble or difficulty □ *I'm sorry to put you to any inconvenience.* **2** something that causes trouble or difficulty □ *He clearly saw my visit as a major inconvenience.* ▻ *verb* (***inconvenienced, inconveniencing***) to cause trouble or difficulty to someone. ⓘ 16c.

inconvenient ▻ *adj* not convenient, especially causing trouble or difficulty. • **inconveniently** *adverb*.

incorporate ▻ *verb* /ɪŋ'kɔːpəreɪt, ɪn-/ (***incorporated, incorporating***) **1** to contain something as part of a whole. **2** *tr & intr* to include something, or be included, as part of a whole. **3** *tr & intr* to combine something, or be united thoroughly, in a single mass. **4** to admit someone to membership of a legal corporation. **5** to form (a company or other body) into a legal corporation. **6** *intr* to form a legal corporation. ▻ *adj* /ɪŋ'kɔːpərət, ɪn-/ (*also* **incorporated**) **1** united in one body or as a single whole. **2** said of a company, etc: forming or formed into a legal corporation. • **incorporation** *noun*. ⓘ 14c: from Latin *incorporare*, from *corpus* a body.

incorporating language *noun* POLYSYNTHETIC LANGUAGE.

incorporeal /ɪŋkɔː'pɔːrɪəl, ɪn-/ ▻ *adj* **1** without bodily or material form or substance. **2** *law* having no material existence or value in itself, but attached as a right or profit to something else. **3** spiritual. • **incorporeally** *adverb*. • **incorporeality** or **incorporeity** /ɪŋkɔːpə'riːɪtɪ, ɪn-/ *noun*. ⓘ 16c.

incorrect ▻ *adj* **1** not accurate; containing errors or faults. **2** said of behaviour, etc: not in accordance with normal or accepted standards; improper. • **incorrectly** *adverb*. • **incorrectness** *noun*. ⓘ 15c.

incorrigible /ɪŋ'kɒrɪdʒɪbəl, ɪn-/ ▻ *adj* said of a person, behaviour or habit: not able to be improved, corrected or reformed, usually because the habit is too bad or too well established □ *an incorrigible flirt.* • **incorrigibility** /-ɪ'bɪlɪtɪ/ *noun*. • **incorrigibly** *adverb*. ⓘ 14c.

incorruptible ▻ *adj* **1** incapable of being bribed or morally corrupted. **2** not able to decay. • **incorruptibility** /-'bɪlɪtɪ/ *noun*. • **incorruptibly** *adverb*. ⓘ 14c.

increase ▻ *verb* /ɪŋ'kriːs, ɪn-/ (***increased, increasing***) *tr & intr* to make or become greater in size, intensity or number. ▻ *noun* /'ɪŋkriːs, 'ɪn-/ **1** the act or process of increasing or becoming increased; growth. **2** the amount by which something increases or is increased. Opposite of DECREASE. • **on the increase** increasing in number, size or frequency □ *Violent crime is on the increase.* • **increasable** *adj*. ⓘ 14c: from French *encresser*, from Latin *increscere* to grow.

increasing ▻ *adj, noun* growing in size, number, or frequency, etc. • **increasingly** *adverb*.

incredible ▻ *adj* **1** difficult or impossible to believe; unbelievable. **2** *colloq* amazing; unusually good. • **incredibility** /-'bɪlɪtɪ/ or **incredibleness** *noun*. • **incredibly** *adverb* **1** in an incredible way, or so as to be incredible. **2** *colloq* extremely □ *I'm incredibly grateful.* ⓘ 15c.

> ***incredible, incredulous***
>
> These words are often confused with each other.

incredulity ▻ *noun* **1** the state of being incredulous. **2** disbelief. ⓘ 15c.

incredulous ▻ *adj* **1** showing or expressing disbelief. **2** (*often* **incredulous of something**) unwilling to believe or accept that it is true. • **incredulously** *adverb*. • **incredulousness** *noun*. ⓘ 16c.

increment /'ɪŋkrəmənt, 'ɪn-/ ▻ *noun* **1** an increase, especially of one point or level on a fixed scale, eg a regular increase in salary. **2** the amount by which something is increased. **3** *math* a small positive or negative change in the value of a variable x, often written Δx, so the new value is $x + \Delta x$. • **incremental** *adj*. • **incrementally**

adverb. ◷ 15c: from Latin *incrementum*, from *increscere* to increase.

incremental plotter ▷ *noun, computing* a device that represents computer output on paper in the form of line images, eg graphs.

incriminate /ɪŋ'krɪmɪneɪt, ɪn-/ ▷ *verb* (***incriminated, incriminating***) **1** (*sometimes* **incriminate someone in something**) **a** to show that they were involved in it (especially in a crime) □ *The witnesses' evidence incriminated him*; **b** to involve or implicate them (especially in a crime) □ *tried to incriminate me in the theft*. **2** to charge someone with a crime or fault. • **incriminating** or **incriminatory** *adj*. • **incrimination** *noun*. ◷ 18c: from Latin *incriminare, incriminatum* to accuse someone of a crime.

incrust see under ENCRUST

incubate /'ɪŋkjʊbeɪt, 'ɪn-/ ▷ *verb* (***incubated, incubating***) **1** *tr & intr* said of birds: to hatch (eggs) by sitting on them to keep them warm. **2** to encourage (germs, bacteria, etc) to develop by creating favourable and controlled conditions, eg in a culture medium in a laboratory. **3** *intr* said of germs, etc: to remain inactive in a living organism before the first signs and symptoms of disease appear. **4** to maintain (a substance or a mixture of substances) at a constant temperature over a period of time in order to study chemical or biochemical reactions. **5** *tr & intr* to develop slowly or gradually. **6** said of embryos, premature babies, etc: to develop under favourable or controlled conditions, eg in an incubator. ◷ 17c: from Latin *incubare* to lie on.

incubation /ɪŋkjʊ'beɪʃən, ɪn-/ ▷ *noun* **1** an act or process of incubating. **2** (*also* **incubation period**) the period between infection with germs, etc and the appearance of the actual disease they cause □ *Measles has an incubation period of 7 to 14 days*. Also called **latent period**. • **incubative** *adj*.

incubator /'ɪŋkjʊbeɪtə(r), 'ɪn-/ ▷ *noun* **1** *medicine* a transparent boxlike container in which a prematurely born baby can be nurtured under controlled conditions and protected from infection. **2** a cabinet or room that can be maintained at a constant preset temperature, used for culturing bacteria and other micro-organisms, hatching eggs, etc. **3** an animal, etc that incubates.

incubus /'ɪŋkjʊbəs, 'ɪn-/ ▷ *noun* (***incubuses, incubi*** /-baɪ/) **1** *folklore* an evil male spirit which is supposed to have sexual intercourse with sleeping women. Compare SUCCUBUS. **2** something which oppresses or weighs heavily upon one, especially a nightmare. ◷ 13c: Latin, meaning 'nightmare'.

incudes *plural of* INCUS

inculcate /'ɪŋkʌlkeɪt, 'ɪn-/ ▷ *verb* (***inculcated, inculcating***) (*especially* **inculcate something in** or **into** or **upon someone**) *rather formal* to teach or fix (ideas, habits, a warning, etc) firmly in their mind by constant repetition. • **inculcation** *noun*. • **inculcator** *noun*. ◷ 16c: from Latin *inculcare* to tread something in.

inculpate /'ɪŋkʌlpeɪt, 'ɪn-/ ▷ *verb* (***inculpated, inculpating***) *formal* to blame someone or show them to be guilty of a crime; to incriminate. Compare EXCULPATE. • **inculpation** *noun*. • **inculpatory** /-'kʌlpətərɪ/ *adj* ◷ 18c: from Latin *inculpare* to blame.

incumbency ▷ *noun* (***incumbencies***) **1** the period during which an incumbent holds office. **2 a** the office or duty of an incumbent; **b** an ecclesiastical benefice. **3** the state of fact of being incumbent or an incumbent.

incumbent /ɪŋ'kʌmbənt, ɪn-/ ▷ *adj, rather formal* **1** (*especially* **incumbent on** or **upon someone**) imposed as a duty or heavy responsibility on them □ *feel it incumbent upon me to defend him*. **2** currently occupying a specified position or office □ *the incumbent bishop*. ▷ *noun* a holder of an office, especially a church office or benefice. ◷ 15c: from Latin *incumbere* to lie, lean or press on.

incumbrance see ENCUMBRANCE

incunabulum /ɪŋkjʊ'nabjʊləm, ɪn-/ ▷ *noun* (*plural* ***incunabula***) *historical* or *technical* an early printed book, especially one printed before 1501. ◷ 19c: Latin, meaning 'swaddling-clothes'.

incur /ɪŋ'kɜː(r), ɪn-/ ▷ *verb* (***incurred, incurring***) **1** to bring (something unpleasant) upon oneself. **2** to become liable for (debts, etc) □ *She incurred a £500 fine*. • **incurrable** *adj*. ◷ 16c: from Latin *incurrere* to run into.

incurable ▷ *adj* **1** said eg of a condition or disease: unable to be corrected or put right by treatment; not curable. **2** said of a person: incapable of changing a specified aspect of their character, disposition, etc □ *an incurable romantic* □ *an incurable optimist*. ▷ *noun* an incurable person or thing. • **incurability** *noun*. • **incurably** *adverb*. ◷ 14c.

incurious ▷ *adj* showing no interest; lacking a normal curiosity; indifferent. • **incuriously** *adverb*. • **incuriousness** or (*sometimes*) **incuriosity** *noun*. ◷ 16c.

incurrable see under INCUR

incursion /ɪŋ'kɜːʃən, ɪn-/ ▷ *noun* **1** a brief or sudden attack made into enemy territory. **2** a damaging invasion into or using up of something □ *unexpected expenses which made an incursion into their savings*. See also INROAD. **3** the action of leaking or running into something. • **incursive** *adj* making incursions; aggressive; invasive. ◷ 15c: from Latin *incursio*, from *incurrere* to incur or run into.

incus /'ɪŋkəs/ ▷ *noun* (*plural* ***incudes*** /'ɪŋkjʊdiːz, ɪn-/) *anatomy* a small, anvil-shaped bone in the middle ear which, together with two other bones, the MALLEUS and STAPES, transmits sound waves from the eardrum to the inner ear. Also called **anvil**. ◷ 17c: Latin, meaning 'anvil'.

IND ▷ *abbreviation, IVR* India.

Ind. ▷ *abbreviation* **1** Independent. **2** India or Indian. **3** see under IN.

indaba /ɪn'dɑːbə/ ▷ *noun* (***indabas***) *S Afr* **1 a** an important conference or discussion between members of different tribes; **b** *more loosely* a meeting or conference, etc between different political parties or other bodies, leaders, etc. Compare POWWOW. **2** *colloq* a concern or problem for discussion. ◷ 19c: Zulu *in-daba*, meaning 'affair' or 'business'.

indebted /ɪn'dɛtɪd/ ▷ *adj* (*usually* **indebted to someone**) **1** having reason to be grateful or obliged to them. **2** owing them money. • **indebtedness** *noun*. ◷ 14c: from French *endetter* to involve someone in debt.

indecent ▷ *adj* **1** offensive to accepted standards of morality or sexual behaviour; revolting or shocking. **2** in bad taste; improper; unseemly □ *He remarried with indecent haste*. • **indecency** *noun* (***indecencies***). • **indecently** *adverb*. ◷ 16c.

indecent assault ▷ *noun, law* a sexual attack which falls short of RAPE, eg touching or attempting to touch someone's genitals without their consent.

indecent exposure ▷ *noun, law* the offence of indecently showing parts of the body, especially the sexual organs, in public.

indecipherable ▷ *adj* unable to be DECIPHERed or understood; illegible. • **indecipherability** *noun*. • **indecipherably** *adverb*.

indecision ▷ *noun* the state of not being able to decide; uncertainty or hesitation. Also called INDECISIVENESS. ◷ 18c.

indecisive ▷ *adj* **1** not producing a clear or definite decision or result; unconclusive. **2** said of a person: unable to make a firm decision; hesitating. • **indecisively** *adverb*. • **indecisiveness** see under INDECISION. ◷ 18c.

indecorous ▷ *adj, euphemistic or formal* in bad taste; improper or unseemly. • **indecorously** *adverb*. • **indecorousness** *noun*. ◷ 17c.

indecorum ▻ *noun* improper or unseemly behaviour; lack of decorum. Ⓒ 16c.

indeed /ɪn'diːd/ ▻ *adverb, now slightly formal* except in sense 3 **1** without any question; in truth □ *This is indeed a sad day.* **2** in fact; actually □ *He did well; indeed he came top of the class.* **3** used for emphasis □ *very wet indeed* □ *enjoyed it very much indeed.* ▻ *exclamation* expressing irony, surprise, disbelief, disapproval, etc, or simple acknowledgement of a previous remark □ *I'm going whether you like it or not. Are you indeed?* □ *Why did he wait so long before telling you? Why indeed?* □ *He's from Peru. Indeed!* Ⓒ 14c: IN + DEED.

indef. see under INDEFINITE

indefatigable /ɪndɪ'fatɪgəbəl/ ▻ *adj* **1** without ever becoming tired; unflagging. **2** never stopping; unremitting. • **indefatigableness** *noun.* • **indefatigably** *adverb.* Ⓒ 16c: French, from Latin *indefatigabilis*, from *defatigare* to wear out.

indefeasible /ɪndɪ'fiːzɪbəl/ ▻ *adj, formal, literary* or *law* not to be annulled or forfeited. • **indefeasibility** *noun.* • **indefeasibly** *adverb.* Ⓒ 16c: from French *desfaire* to undo; related to DEFEAT.

indefensible ▻ *adj* **1** unable to be excused or justified □ *Her rudeness was indefensible.* **2** said of an opinion, position, etc: untenable; unable to be defended. **3** *literally* not possible to defend (against enemy attack). • **indefensibility** *noun.* • **indefensibly** *adverb.* Ⓒ 16c.

indefinable ▻ *adj* unable to be clearly, fully or exactly defined or described. • **indefinably** *adverb.* Ⓒ 19c.

indefinite ▻ *adj* **1** without fixed or exact limits or clearly marked outlines □ *off sick for an indefinite period.* **2** uncertain; vague; imprecise □ *was very indefinite about her plans.* **3** *grammar* (abbreviation **indef.**) not referring to a particular person or thing. See also INDEFINITE ARTICLE. • **indefinitely** *adverb.* • **indefiniteness** *noun.* Ⓒ 16c.

indefinite article ▻ *noun, grammar* a word (*a or an* in English) used before a noun to refer to an example that is not a definite or specific one, as in *a cat in the garden, a new government, half a pound* . Compare DEFINITE ARTICLE.

indehiscent /ɪndɪ'hɪsənt/ ▻ *adj, bot* said of a fruit: characterized by not splitting open to scatter its seeds when mature. Compare DEHISCENT. • **indehiscence** *noun.*

indelible /ɪn'dɛlɪbəl/ ▻ *adj* **1** said eg of a mark or writing, or of a memory, etc: unable to be removed or rubbed out. **2** said of a pen, pencil, ink, etc: designed to make an indelible mark. • **indelibly** *adverb.* Ⓒ 16c: from Latin *indelebilis*, from *delere* to destroy.

indelicate ▻ *adj* **1** tending to embarrass or offend; in poor taste; immodest. **2** slightly coarse; rough. • **indelicacy** *noun* (***indelicacies***). • **indelicately** *adverb.* Ⓒ 18c.

indemnify /ɪn'dɛmnɪfaɪ/ ▻ *verb* (***indemnifies, indemnified, indemnifying***) **1** (*especially* **indemnify someone against** or **from something**) to provide them with security or protection against (loss or misfortune). **2** (*usually* **indemnify someone for something**) to pay them money in compensation for (especially loss or damage); to reimburse them for it. • **indemnification** *noun.* Ⓒ 17c: from Latin *indemnis* unharmed or without loss.

indemnity /ɪn'dɛmnɪtɪ/ ▻ *noun* (***indemnities***) **1 a** compensation for loss or damage; **b** money paid in compensation. **2** security or protection from loss or damage; insurance. **3** legal exemption from liabilities or penalties incurred. Ⓒ 15c; see INDEMNIFY.

indent[1] ▻ *verb* /ɪn'dɛnt/ **1** *printing, typing* to begin (a line or paragraph) further in from the margin than the main body of text. **2** to divide (a document drawn up in duplicate in two columns) along a zigzag line. **3** to draw up (a document, deed, etc) in duplicate. **4** *tr & intr, Brit, commerce* to make out a written order (especially for foreign goods). **5** to indenture someone as an apprentice. **6** to make a notch or notches in something (eg a border). ▻ *noun* /'ɪndɛnt, -'dɛnt/ **1** *Brit, commerce* **a** a written order for goods, especially foreign goods; **b** an official requisition for goods. **2** *printing, typing* an indented line or paragraph. **3** a notch. **4** an indenture. Ⓒ 14c: from French *endenter*, from Latin *indentare* to make toothlike notches in something, from *dens, dentis* tooth.

indent[2] ▻ *verb* /ɪn'dɛnt/ (***indented, indenting***) to form a dent in something or mark it with dents. ▻ *noun* /'ɪndɛnt, -'dɛnt/ a hollow, depression or dent. Ⓒ 14c, meaning 'to inlay'.

indentation ▻ *noun* **1** a cut or notch, often one of a series. **2** a deep, inward curve or recess, eg in a coastline. **3** the act or process of indenting. **4** a less common word for INDENTION.

indention ▻ *noun, printing, typing* **1** the indenting of a line or paragraph. **2** the blank space at the beginning of a line caused by indenting a line or paragraph.

indenture /ɪn'dɛntʃə(r)/ ▻ *noun* **1** (*usually* **indentures**) a contract binding an apprentice to a master. **2** an indented document, agreement or contract between two or more parties (see INDENT[1] *verb* 2, 3). ▻ *verb* (***indentured, indenturing***) *chiefly old use* **1** to bind (eg an apprentice) by indentures. **2** to bind (eg another party) by an indented contract or agreement. Ⓒ 14c; see INDENT[1].

independence ▻ *noun* the state, condition, quality or process of being independent.

Independence Day ▻ *noun* a public holiday when the anniversary of a country's declaration of independence from the control of another country is celebrated, eg 4 July in the US.

independency ▻ *noun* (***independencies***) **1** a territory or state that is politically independent. Also called **sovereign state**. **2** independence.

independent ▻ *adj* (*sometimes* **independent of something** or **someone**) **1 a** not under the control or authority of others; **b** said especially of a country or state: completely self-governing. **2** not relying on others for financial support, care, help or guidance. **3** thinking and acting for oneself and not under an obligation to others. **4** *math, etc* not dependent on something else for value, purpose or function. **5** said of two or more people or things: not related to or affected by the others. **6** said of private income or resources: large enough to make having to work for a living unnecessary □ *a man of independent means.* **7** not belonging to a political party. **8** said of a school or broadcasting company: not paid for with public money; not belonging to the state system. ▻ *noun* **1** a politician, etc who is not a member of any party. **2** an independent person or thing. • **independently** *adverb.* See also INDIE. Ⓒ 17c.

independent clause ▻ *noun, grammar* a MAIN CLAUSE.

in-depth ▻ *adj* thorough; exhaustive □ *an in-depth study of the problem.*

indescribable ▻ *adj* said eg of an experience, sensation or emotion: unable to be put into words, especially because it is (or was) too extreme, too difficult, too vague, too exciting, etc. • **indescribably** *adverb.* Ⓒ 18c.

indestructible ▻ *adj* not able to be destroyed. • **indestructibility** *noun.* • **indestructibly** *adverb.* Ⓒ 17c.

indeterminable /ɪndɪ'tɜːmɪnəbəl/ ▻ *adj* **1** not able to be fixed, decided or measured. **2** said of an argument, etc: unable to be settled. • **indeterminably** *adverb.* Ⓒ 17c: from Latin *indeterminabilis*.

indeterminate /ɪndɪ'tɜːmɪnət/ ▻ *adj* **1** not precisely or exactly fixed, determined or settled □ *an indeterminate number of guests.* **2** doubtful; vague □ *an indeterminate outlook.* **3** *math* said of an equation: having more than one variable and an infinite number of possible solutions. **4** *math, denoting* an expression that has no defined or fixed value, or that has no quantitative meaning, eg 0/0. **5** *bot, denoting* growth of a plant that continues indefinitely. • **indeterminacy** /-nəsɪ/ *noun*. • **indeterminately** *adverb*. • **indeterminateness** *noun* **1** being indeterminate. **2** lack of determination. **3** absence of direction. ◷ 17c: from Latin *indeterminatus*.

index /ˈɪndɛks/ ▷ *noun* (*indexes* or *technical* ***indices*** /ˈɪndɪsiːz/) **1** an alphabetical list of names, subjects, etc dealt with in a book, usually given at the end of that book, and with the page numbers on which each item appears. Compare THUMB INDEX. **2** in a library, etc: a catalogue or set of reference cards which lists each book, magazine, etc alphabetically, usually by author or title, and gives details of where it is shelved. **3** anything which points to, identifies or highlights a particular trend or condition. **4** a scale of numbers which shows changes in price, wages, rates of interest, etc □ *retail price index*. **5** *math* an EXPONENT (sense 3). **6** *physics* a numerical quantity, usually one lacking units, that indicates the magnitude of a particular physical effect □ *refractive index*. **7** *geol* a fossil or mineral that characterizes a particular type of rock. **8** (**Index**) *RC Church* an official list of prohibited books. **9** *printing* a FIST (noun 4). **10** *now rare* a hand or pointer on a dial or scale. ▷ *verb* (***indexed***, ***indexing***) **1** to provide (a book, etc) with an index. **2** to list something in an index. **3** to relate (prices, wages, etc) to an index (see *index noun* 4 above), so that they may rise or fall accordingly; to make something INDEX-LINKED. ◷ 16c; 14c: from Latin, meaning 'informer' or 'forefinger'.

indexation, **indexing** and **index-linking** ▷ *noun* the linking of prices, wages, rates of interest, etc to changes in an INDEX (*noun* 4).

indexer ▷ *noun* someone who compiles an INDEX (*noun* 1), or whose job is to compile indexes.

index finger ▷ *noun* the finger next to the thumb. Also called **forefinger**.

index-linked ▷ *adj, econ* said of prices, wages, rates of interest, etc: calculated so as to rise or fall by the same amount as the cost of living.

index number ▷ *noun, econ* a number which, by varying around a value of 100 (taken as a standard), enables a straightforward comparison over time in the average value of a set of items.

India /ˈɪndɪə/ ▷ *noun, communications* in the NATO alphabet: the word used to denote the letter 'I' (see table at NATO ALPHABET).

Indiaman /ˈɪndɪəmən/ ▷ *noun* (***Indiamen***) *historical* a merchant ship used for trading with India or the East Indies.

Indian /ˈɪndɪən/ ▷ *adj* **1** belonging or relating to India, a federal republic in S Asia, or to the Indian subcontinent (India, Bangladesh and Pakistan), its inhabitants, languages or culture. **2** *chiefly old use* belonging or relating to the indigenous peoples of America, their languages or culture. Now NATIVE AMERICAN. ▷ *noun* **1** a citizen or inhabitant of, or person born in, India, or the Indian subcontinent. **2** *S Afr, etc* someone belonging to the Asian racial group, who was born, or whose ancestors were born, in India. **3** *chiefly old use* a NATIVE AMERICAN or someone belonging to one of the indigenous peoples of Central and S America. See also AMERICAN INDIAN, RED INDIAN. Compare WEST INDIAN. **4** *chiefly old use* any of the Native American languages. **5** *colloq* **a** a restaurant that specializes in Asian food, especially curries; **b** a meal in, or a takeaway from, this type of restaurant □ *went out for an Indian*. ◷ 15c as *noun*: from Greek *India*, from *Indos* the Indus river.

Indian buffalo see BUFFALO

Indian club ▷ *noun* one of a pair of heavy bottle-shaped clubs swung to develop the arm muscles.

Indian corn see under MAIZE

Indian elephant see ELEPHANT

Indian file see SINGLE FILE

Indian hemp see HEMP

Indian ink or (*N Amer*) **India ink** ▷ *noun* black ink made from LAMPBLACK.

Indian meal ▷ *noun* ground maize.

Indian rope-trick ▷ *noun* the supposed Indian trick of climbing up a rope that is not attached to anything at the top.

Indian summer ▷ *noun* **1** a period of unusually warm dry weather in late autumn. **2** a period of happiness and success towards the end of someone's life, or towards the end of an era, etc. ◷ 18c.

India paper ▷ *noun* **1** a type of thin soft absorbent paper originally made in China and Japan. **2** a very thin strong opaque paper, used eg for printing Bibles.

India rubber ▷ *noun* a RUBBER[1] 2.

Indic /ˈɪndɪk/ ▷ *adj* belonging or relating to the Indian branch of the Indo-European languages, which comprises Sanskrit and its modern descendants, Hindi, Gujarati, Urdu, Bengali, Punjabi, Romany, etc. ▷ *noun* approximately 500 languages that form this group. Also called **Indo-Aryan**. ◷ 19c: from Latin *Indicus*, from Greek *Indikos* Indian.

indic. see under INDICATIVE

indicate /ˈɪndɪkeɪt/ ▷ *verb* (***indicated***, ***indicating***) **1** to point out or show □ *An arrow indicates the way.* **2** to be a sign or symptom of something □ *Such behaviour often indicates trouble at home.* **3** said of a gauge, dial, etc: to show something as a reading. **4** to state something briefly □ *He indicated his consent.* **5** *medicine, etc* (especially in the passive) to point to something as a suitable treatment or desirable or required course □ *A course of steroids was indicated for her condition.* **6** *intr* to use the INDICATOR (sense 2) or indicators when driving a motor vehicle □ *Remember to indicate before pulling out.* ◷ 17c: from Latin *indicare*, *indicatum* to proclaim or make known.

indication ▷ *noun* **1** something which serves to indicate; a sign or symptom. **2** something which is indicated. **3** a reading on a gauge, dial, etc. **4** an act of indicating.

indicative /ɪnˈdɪkətɪv/ ▷ *adj* **1** (*also* **indicatory** /ɪnˈdɪkətərɪ/) (*usually* **indicative of something**) serving as a sign or indication of it □ *Irritability is often indicative of stress.* **2** *grammar* (abbreviation **indic.**) **a** said of the MOOD[2] of a verb used to state facts, describe events or ask questions; **b** said of a verb, tense, etc: in this mood. ▷ *noun, grammar* **1** a MOOD[2] used to state facts, describe events or ask questions. Compare IMPERATIVE, SUBJUNCTIVE, CONDITIONAL. **2** a verb form of this kind. • **indicatively** *adverb*.

indicator ▷ *noun* **1 a** an instrument or gauge that shows the level of temperature, fuel, pressure, etc; **b** a needle or pointer on such a device. **2** any of the flashing lights on a motor vehicle which show that the vehicle is about to change direction. Sometimes called **blinker**. **3** any sign, condition, situation, etc which shows or indicates something □ *The result is a good indicator of current opinion* □ *an economic indicator.* **4** a board or diagram giving information, eg in a railway station. **5** *chem* a substance (eg LITMUS) that changes colour reversibly depending on the pH of a solution, and that indicates when a chemical reaction is complete. **6** *biol* (*also* **indicator species**) a plant or animal species whose presence or absence indicates the levels of a particular environmental factor in an area.

indices see INDEX

indict /ɪnˈdaɪt/ ▷ *verb* (***indicted***, ***indicting***) *law* to accuse someone of, or charge them formally with, a crime, especially in writing. • **indictable** *adj* **1** said of a person: liable to be indicted for a crime. **2** said of a crime: liable to cause a person to be indicted. • **indictee** *noun* someone who is indicted. • **indicter** *noun*. ⓘ 14c: from French *enditer*, with spelling later influenced by Latin *indicere*, *indictum* to announce.

indictable offence *noun*, *law* any serious common-law offence such as rape, murder, etc that must be tried before a jury in the Crown Court. Compare SUMMARY OFFENCE.

indictment ▷ *noun* **1** a formal written accusation or charge. **2** an act of indicting someone. **3** something which deserves severe criticism or censure, or which serves to criticize or condemn something or someone □ *Such poverty is a terrible indictment against our 'civilized' society.*

indie /'ɪndɪ/ ▷ *noun* (***indies***) *colloq* **1** a small independent and usually non-commercial record or film company. **2** *as adj* produced by small independent companies; not mainstream or commercial □ *indie music.* **3** a type of music produced predominantly by indie labels, particularly music that is melodic and guitar-based. ⓘ 1940s, originally in the US film industry; abbreviation of INDEPENDENT.

indifference ▷ *noun* **1** lack of interest, concern, etc. **2** lack of quality. **3** lack of importance. ⓘ 16c.

indifferent ▷ *adj* **1** (*especially* **indifferent to** or **towards something** or **someone**) showing no interest in or concern for it or them. **2** neither good nor bad; average; mediocre. **3** fairly bad; inferior. **4** unimportant. **5** neutral. • **indifferently** *adverb*. ⓘ 14c: from Latin *indifferens* not differing, of medium quality.

indigenous /ɪn'dɪdʒənəs/ ▷ *adj* **1** *biol* said of plants or animals: belonging naturally to or occurring naturally in a country or area; native. **2** said of a person: born in a region, area, country, etc. • **indigenously** *adverb*. ⓘ 17c: from Latin *indigenus*, from *indigena* an original inhabitant.

indigent /'ɪndɪdʒənt/ ▷ *adj, formal* very poor; needy. • **indigence** *noun* poverty. • **indigently** *adverb*. ⓘ 15c: French, from Latin *indigens*, from *indigere* to lack.

indigestible ▷ *adj* **1** said of food: difficult or impossible to digest. **2** said of text, information, etc: not easily understood; complicated. • **indigestibility** *noun*. • **indigestibly** *adverb*. ⓘ 16c: from Latin *indigestibilis*; see DIGEST[1].

indigestion ▷ *noun* discomfort or pain in the abdomen or lower region of the chest, especially after eating, caused by difficulty in digesting or inability to digest food. See also HEARTBURN. ⓘ 15c: French.

indignant /ɪn'dɪgnənt/ ▷ *adj* feeling or showing anger or a sense of having been treated unjustly or wrongly. • **indignantly** *adverb*. ⓘ 16c: from Latin *indignans*, from *indignari* to consider something or someone unworthy.

indignation /ɪndɪg'neɪʃən/ *noun* anger caused by something felt to be unjust, unfair, etc. ⓘ 14c: from Latin *indignatio*.

indignity ▷ *noun* (***indignities***) **1** any act or treatment which causes someone to feel shame or humiliation; disgrace or dishonour. **2** a feeling of shame, disgrace or dishonour. ⓘ 16c: from Latin *indignitas*; see INDIGNANT.

indigo /'ɪndɪgoʊ/ ▷ *noun* (***indigos*** or ***indigoes***) **1** a violet-blue dye either obtained naturally from a plant or made synthetically. **2** any of several leguminous plants whose leaves yield a violet-blue dye. **3** the deep violet-blue colour of this dye. ▷ *adj* violet-blue. ⓘ 16c: Spanish *indigo* or *indico*, from Greek *Indikon* Indian substance (ie dye).

indirect ▷ *adj* **1** said of a route, course, line, etc: not direct or straight. **2** not going straight to the point; not straightforward or honest; devious. **3** not directly aimed at or intended □ *indirect consequences.* • **indirectly** *adverb*. • **indirectness** *noun*. ⓘ 15c.

indirect lighting ▷ *noun* a system of lighting in which the light is reflected upwards, or diffused, from concealed fittings.

indirect object ▷ *noun, grammar* a noun, phrase or pronoun which is affected indirectly by the action of a verb, usually standing for the person or thing to whom something is given or for whom something is done, eg *the dog* in *Give the dog a bone*. Compare DIRECT OBJECT.

indirect question ▷ *noun* a sentence which has a SUBORDINATE CLAUSE expressing an implied question, or the subordinate clause itself, as in *Tell me who you are* (which means *Tell me: 'Who are you?'*).

indirect speech ▷ *noun, grammar* a speaker's words reported by another person with change of person and tense, eg *We will come* becomes *They said they would come* in indirect speech. Also called REPORTED SPEECH. Compare DIRECT SPEECH.

indirect tax ▷ *noun* a tax levied on goods and services when they are purchased, eg VAT. Compare DIRECT TAX.

indiscernible ▷ *adj* unable to be noticed or recognized as being distinct, especially because too small □ *indiscernible differences.* • **indiscernibly** *adverb*. ⓘ 17c.

indiscipline ▷ *noun* lack of discipline. • **indisciplined** *adj*. ⓘ 18c.

indiscreet ▷ *adj* **1** giving away too many secrets or too much information; not discreet. **2** not wise or cautious; injudicious. • **indiscreetly** *adverb*. ⓘ 15c.

indiscrete ▷ *adj, chiefly technical or formal* not separated into parts; homogeneous or indivisible. • **indiscretely** *adverb*. ⓘ 17c.

indiscretion ▷ *noun* **1** lack of discretion or caution; rashness. **2** an act or remark showing this. ⓘ 14c.

indiscriminate ▷ *adj* **1** making no distinctions; not making or showing careful choice and discrimination; chosen at random. **2** confused; not differentiated. • **indiscriminately** *adverb*. • **indiscriminateness** *noun*. ⓘ 17c.

indispensable ▷ *adj* necessary; essential. • **indispensability** *noun*. • **indispensably** *adverb*. ⓘ 17c.

indisposed ▷ *adj, rather formal* **1** slightly ill. **2** (*especially* **indisposed to do something**) reluctant or unwilling to do it. • **indisposition** *noun*. ⓘ 15c, meaning 'not organized or properly arranged'.

indisputable ▷ *adj* certainly true; beyond doubt; not disputable. • **indisputableness** *noun*. • **indisputably** *adverb*. ⓘ 16c.

indissoluble ▷ *adj* incapable of being dissolved or broken; permanent; lasting. Compare INSOLUBLE. • **indissolubility** *noun*. • **indissolubly** *adverb*. ⓘ 16c.

indistinct ▷ *adj* not clear to a person's eye, ear or mind; confused; dim. • **indistinctly** *adverb*. • **indistinctness** *noun*. ⓘ 16c.

indistinguishable ▷ *adj* not able to be distinguished or told apart from it or them □ *This spread is indistinguishable from butter.* • **indistinguishably** *adverb*. ⓘ 17c.

indium /'ɪndɪəm/ ▷ *noun, chem* (symbol **In**, atomic number 49) a soft, silvery-white metallic element used in the manufacture of mirrors, semiconductor devices, metal bearings and certain alloys. ⓘ 19c: from Latin *indicium* INDIGO (because of the indigo-coloured lines in its spectrum) and modelled on SODIUM.

individual /ɪndɪ'vɪdʒʊəl/ ▷ *adj* **1** intended for or relating to a single person or thing □ *jam served in individual portions* □ *unable to give students individual attention.* **2** particular to one person; showing or having a particular person's unique qualities or characteristics □ *The room reflects her individual taste* □ *has a very individual talent.* **3** separate; single □ *checks every individual item for quality.* ▷ *noun* **1** a particular person, animal or thing, especially in contrast to the group to which it belongs □ *The lions select the weakest* *individual as their prey* □ *a society which respects the rights of the individual.* **2** *colloq* a person □ *What an offensive individual!* • **individually** *adverb*. Ⓒ 15c: from Latin *individualis*, from *individuus* indivisible.

individualism ▻ *noun* **1 a** behaviour governed by the belief that individual people should lead their lives as they want and should be independent; **b** behaviour governed by this belief. See also LAISSEZ-FAIRE. **2** the theory that the state should in no way control the actions of the individual. Compare SOCIALISM, COLLECTIVISM at COLLECTIVIZE. **3** self-centredness; egoism. Ⓒ 19c.

individualist ▻ *noun* **1** someone who thinks and acts with independence or great individuality, sometimes for the sake of being different. **2** someone who supports individualism. ▻ *adj* (*also* **individualistic**) belonging or relating to individualists or individualism. • **individualistically** *adverb*.

individuality /ɪndɪvɪdʒʊ'alɪtɪ/ ▻ *noun* (***individualities***) **1** the qualities and character which distinguish one person or thing from others. **2** a separate and distinct existence or identity. Ⓒ 17c.

individualize or **individualise** ▻ *verb* (***individualized***, ***individualizing***) **1** to make something suitable for a particular person, thing or situation. **2** to give someone or something a distinctive character or personality. Also **individuate**. • **individualization** *noun*. Ⓒ 17c.

individuate /ɪndɪ'vɪdʒʊeɪt/ ▻ *verb* (***individuated***, ***individuating***) **1** to INDIVIDUALIZE 2. **2** to form something into an individual. • **individuation** *noun*. Ⓒ 17c.

indivisible ▻ *adj* **1** not able to be divided or separated. **2** *math* said of a number: incapable of being divided (by a given number) without leaving a remainder. ▻ *noun*, *math* an indefinitely small quantity. • **indivisibility** *noun*. • **indivisibly** *adverb*. Ⓒ 14c.

Indo- /'ɪndoʊ/ ▻ *combining form, denoting* Indian, or India □ *Indo-European*. Ⓒ From Greek *Indos* Indian.

Indo-Aryan ▻ *noun* ▻ *adj*, *linguistics* INDIC.

Indo-Chinese ▻ *adj*, *chiefly historical* belonging or relating to Indo-China, the south-eastern peninsula of Asia which comprises Myanmar (formerly called Burma), Laos, Vietnam, Thailand, Cambodia and Malaysia. ▻ *noun* a citizen or inhabitant of, or a person born in, this region.

indoctrinate /ɪn'dɒktrɪneɪt/ ▻ *verb* (***indoctrinated***, ***indoctrinating***) to teach (an individual or group) to accept and believe a particular set of beliefs, etc uncritically. • **indoctrination** *noun*. • **indoctrinator** *noun*. Ⓒ 17c: from Latin *doctrinare* to teach.

Indo-European ▻ *adj*, *linguistics* belonging or relating to the family of languages that are spoken throughout Europe and in many parts of Asia, including most European and many Asian languages such as Hindi and Persian. ▻ *noun* **1** the languages that form this family. **2** (*also* **Proto-Indo-European**) the hypothetical language which all of the languages in the Indo-European family come from.

Indo-Iranian ▻ *adj*, *linguistics* belonging or relating to the easternmost branch of the INDO-EUROPEAN family of languages, made up of two major subgroups: the Indo-Aryan (or INDIC) languages and the Iranian languages. ▻ *noun* the languages that form this branch.

indolent /'ɪndələnt/ ▻ *adj* **1** said of a person: lazy; disliking and avoiding work and exercise. **2** *medicine* said of a tumour, etc: causing little or no pain. **3** *medicine* said of ulcers, etc: persistent; slow to heal. • **indolence** *noun* laziness; idleness. • **indolently** *adverb*. Ⓒ 17c: from Latin *indolens* not suffering pain.

indomitable /ɪn'dɒmɪtəbəl/ ▻ *adj* unable to be conquered or defeated □ *Despite her illness, she has an indomitable spirit.* • **indomitability** or **indomitableness** *noun*. • **indomitably** *adverb*. Ⓒ 17c.

Indonesian /ɪndə'niːʒən/ ▻ *adj* belonging or relating to Indonesia, a republic in SE Asia comprising the world's largest island group, or to its inhabitants, their languages or culture. ▻ *noun* **1** a citizen or inhabitant of, or person born in, Indonesia. **2** the languages spoken in the Malay archipelago, especially the official language (**Bahasa Indonesia**) of the Republic of Indonesia. Ⓒ 19c: from INDO- + Greek *nesos* island.

indoor ▻ *adj* used, belonging, done, happening, etc inside a building □ *indoor football*. Ⓒ 18c: from earlier *within-door*.

indoors ▻ *adverb* in or into a building □ *We hurried indoors.* • **her indoors** *colloq* someone's wife or partner □ *I'll have to consult her indoors first.* Ⓒ 19c: see INDOOR.

Indo-Pacific ▻ *adj*, *linguistics* belonging, referring or relating to a group of around 700 languages spoken in New Guinea, nearby islands to the West and East, and Tasmania. ▻ *noun* the languages that form this group. Ⓒ 19c.

indorse see ENDORSE

indraught or **indraft** /'ɪndrɑːft/ ▻ *noun* **1** an inward flow (eg of air) or current (eg of water). **2** an act of drawing in. Ⓒ 16c: see DRAUGHT.

indrawn ▻ *adj* **1** said especially of the breath: drawn or pulled in. **2** said of a person: aloof or introspective. See also WITHDRAWN. Ⓒ 18c: see DRAW.

indri /'ɪndrɪ/ and **indris** /'ɪndrɪs/ ▻ *noun* (***indris***) a rare type of LEMUR that lives in tree tops feeding on leaves, and has a dark coat with white legs and hindquarters, fluffy round ears, a very short tail and a loud far-reaching cry. Ⓒ 19c: from Malagasy *indry!* look!; the exclamation was mistaken for the animal's name.

indubitable /ɪn'dʒuːbɪtəbəl/ ▻ *adj* unable to be doubted; certain. • **indubitability** or **indubitableness** *noun*. • **indubitably** *adverb*. Ⓒ 17c: from Latin *indubitabilis*, from *dubitare* to doubt.

induce /ɪn'djuːs/ ▻ *verb* (***induced***, ***inducing***) **1** to persuade, influence or cause someone to do something □ *tried to induce her to move back home.* **2** *obstetrics* to initiate or hasten (labour) by artificial means, especially by administering a drug to stimulate contractions of the womb. **3** to make something happen or appear. **4** to produce or transmit (an electromotive force) by INDUCTION. **5** *biol* to cause (an embryonic non-specialized cell) to become specialized. **6** to activate (a virus or a gene) in response to a specific stimulus. **7** to cause the synthesis of enzymes in response to a specific molecule. **8** *logic* to infer or come to (eg a general conclusion) from particular cases. • **inducible** *adj*. Ⓒ 14c: from Latin *inducere* to lead in.

induced abortion see ABORTION sense 1

inducement ▻ *noun* **1** something that induces, especially something that is persuasive or that influences or encourages certain behaviour; an incentive or motive □ *gave him a car as an inducement to stay with the firm.* **2** *law* a statement of facts that introduces other important facts.

induct /ɪn'dʌkt/ ▻ *verb* (***inducted***, ***inducting***) **1** to place (eg a priest) formally and often ceremonially in an official position; to install. **2** to initiate someone as a member of eg a society or profession. **3** *N Amer* to enrol someone for military service or training. **4** to induce. Ⓒ 14c: from Latin *inducere* to lead in.

inductance ▻ *noun*, *physics* the property of an electric circuit or circuit component that causes an ELECTROMOTIVE FORCE to be generated in it when a changing current is present.

induction /ɪn'dʌkʃən/ ▻ *noun* **1** the act or process of inducting or being inducted, especially into office; installation, initiation or enrolment. **2** *obstetrics* the initiation of labour by artificial means, often involving the use of drugs. **3** *elec* the production of an electric current in a conductor as a result of its close proximity to a varying magnetic field. **4** *elec* the production of magnetization in an unmagnetized material as a result of its close proximity either to a magnetic field or to the electromagnetic field of a current-carrying conductor. **5** *engineering* the process of drawing in steam or an explosive mixture of fuel and air into the cylinder of an engine. **6** *logic, etc* the process of forming or coming to a general conclusion from particular cases. Compare DEDUCTION. • **inductional** *adj.*

induction coil ▻ *noun, physics* a type of TRANSFORMER that can produce a high-voltage alternating current from a low-voltage direct current source, used to produce short bursts of high voltages, eg across the terminals of a SPARK PLUG in a motor vehicle.

induction course ▻ *noun* a course of formal instruction given to a new employee, appointee, etc, eg in order to familiarize them with the ways in which the company operates, etc.

induction heating ▻ *noun, elec engineering* the heating of a conductive material by means of an induced current (see INDUCE 4) passing through it.

induction loop system ▻ *noun* in public buildings, churches, places of entertainment, etc: a method of sound distribution in which signals fed into a wire loop are received via headphones or hearing-aids by those people sitting inside the area enclosed by the loop.

induction motor ▻ *noun, engineering* an alternating-current motor in which an electric current is supplied to a stationary coil, which creates a magnetic field and induces an electric current in a moving coil (known as the ROTOR).

inductive ▻ *adj* **1** *logic, etc* relating to or using INDUCTION. **2** *elec* belonging or relating to electric or magnetic INDUCTION. Compare DEDUCTIVE. • **inductively** *adverb.*

inductor ▻ *noun* **1** *elec* a component of an electrical circuit that shows the property of INDUCTANCE. **2** *chem* any substance that accelerates a reaction between two or more chemical substances by reacting rapidly with one of them. **3** someone or something that inducts. ◷ 17c: see INDUCT.

indue see ENDUE

indulge /ɪn'dʌldʒ/ ▻ *verb* (***indulged, indulging***) **1** *tr & intr* (*especially* **indulge in something** or **indulge someone in something**) to allow oneself or someone else pleasure or the pleasure of (a specified thing) □ *I'm going to indulge in some new gloves.* **2** to allow someone to have anything they want; to pamper or spoil them □ *My mother indulges the children dreadfully.* **3** to give into (a desire, taste, wish, etc) without restraint. **4** *intr, colloq* to eat or drink, usually freely or without restraint □ *No, I won't indulge, I'm driving.* ◷ 17c: from Latin *indulgere* to be kind or indulgent.

indulgence /ɪn'dʌldʒəns/ ▻ *noun* **1** the state of being indulgent; generosity; favourable or tolerant treatment. **2** an act or the process of indulging a person, desire, etc. **3** a pleasure that is indulged in. **4** *RC Church* a special grant of remission from the punishment which remains due for a sin after it has been absolved. ◷ 14c: French.

indulgent /ɪn'dʌldʒənt/ ▻ *adj* quick or too quick to overlook or forgive faults or gratify the wishes of others; too tolerant or generous. • **indulgently** *adverb.* ◷ 16c: from Latin *indulgere*; see INDULGE.

industrial /ɪn'dʌstrɪəl/ ▻ *adj* **1** relating to, concerned with or suitable for industry □ *an industrial dispute* □ *industrial machinery.* **2** used in industry □ *industrial labour.* **3** said of a country, city, etc: having highly developed industry. • **industrially** *adverb.*

industrial action ▻ *noun, Brit* action taken by workers as a protest, eg a STRIKE (*noun* 2), GO-SLOW or WORK TO RULE.

industrial archaeology ▻ *noun* the study of industrial machines and buildings of the past.

industrial democracy ▻ *noun, business* a form of industrial management in which workers' representatives are appointed to the board of a company or actively participate in the management in some other capacity.

industrial design ▻ *noun* **1** the art of incorporating aesthetic details into manufactured goods. **2** the process of doing this. • **industrial designer** *noun.* ◷ 1930s.

industrial diamond ▻ *noun* a small diamond, not of gemstone quality and often made synthetically from carbon, used in abrasive grinding, drilling boreholes in rock, etc.

industrial disease ▻ *noun* a disease or condition caused by the nature of the sufferer's employment or by substances that they have been exposed to in the workplace, etc, eg PNEUMOCONIOSIS in coalminers. Also called OCCUPATIONAL DISEASE.

industrial espionage ▻ *noun* the practice of obtaining or attempting to obtain TRADE SECRETs or other confidential information about a company's activities by underhand or dishonest means, eg in order to destroy a company's competitive advantage.

industrial estate ▻ *noun* an area in a town which is developed for industry and business. Also called **trading estate.** *N Amer equivalent* **industrial park.**

industrialism ▻ *noun* a social system in which industry (rather than agriculture) is dominant and forms the basis of commerce and the economy.

industrialist ▻ *noun* someone who owns a large industrial organization or who is involved in its management at a senior level.

industrialize or **industrialise** ▻ *verb* (***industrialized, industrializing***) *tr & intr* to make or become industrially developed; to introduce industry or have industry introduced in (a place, region, country, etc). • **industrialization** *noun.*

industrial relations ▻ *plural noun* relations between management and workers, especially in manufacturing industries.

industrial revolution ▻ *noun* **1** (*sometimes* **Industrial Revolution**) the rapid development of a country's industry, characterized by a change from small-scale production to increased mechanization and mass production in factories. **2** (**the Industrial Revolution**) *historical* in Britain from the last quarter of the 18c: this process, initiated by the mechanization of the cotton and woollen industries of Lancashire, etc, resulting in a concentration of cotton and woollen mills in towns, and hugely increased rates of URBANIZATION.

industrial-strength ▻ *adj, sometimes humorous* very powerful; suitable for use in industry □ *industrial-strength adhesive* □ *industrial-strength coffee.*

industrial tribunal ▻ *noun, business, law* a tribunal set up to hear complaints and make judgements in disputes between employers and employees on matters such as INDUSTRIAL RELATIONS and alleged unfair dismissal.

industrious /ɪn'dʌstrɪəs/ ▻ *adj* busy and hard-working; diligent. • **industriously** *adverb.* • **industriousness** *noun.* ◷ 16c: from Latin *industriosus* diligent.

industry /'ɪndəstrɪ/ ▻ *noun* (***industries***) **1** the business of producing goods; all branches of manufacturing and trade. See also HEAVY INDUSTRY, LIGHT INDUSTRY. **2** a branch of manufacturing and trade which produces a particular product □ *the coal industry.* **3** organized commercial exploitation or use of natural or national assets, such as historical buildings, famous people, etc □ *the tourist industry.* **4** hard work or effort; diligence. ◷ 15c: from Latin *industria* diligence.

Indy ▷ *noun* **1** (*in full* **Indy 500** or **Indianapolis 500**) a high-speed motor race where drivers cover a distance of 500 miles by doing circuits of an oval track in rear-engine cars which must conform to certain specifications. **2** high speed motor racing of this kind. Also *as adj* □ *Indy racing.* ◷ 20c: named after Indianapolis, the state capital of Indiana, USA, where the major race of the year is held.

Indycar ▷ *noun* a car that has been modified to meet the specifications for taking part in Indy racing. Also *as adj* □ *Indycar champion.*

-ine[1] /aɪn/ *suffix, forming adjectives, signifying* **1** belonging or relating to the specified thing □ *Alpine.* **2** like, similar to or consisting of the specified thing □ *crystalline.* ◷ From Latin adjectival ending *-inus.*

-ine[2] /iːn, aɪn/ *suffix, chem, forming nouns, denoting* **1** a basic organic compound containing nitrogen, such as an amino acid or alkaloid □ *glutamine.* **2** a HALOGEN □ *chlorine* □ *fluorine.* **3** a mixture of compounds □ *kerosine* □ *benzine.* **4** a feminized form □ *heroine.* ◷ French, from Latin feminine adjectival ending *-ina.*

inebriate ▷ *verb* /ɪn'iːbrɪeɪt/ (***inebriated, inebriating***) **1** to make someone drunk; to intoxicate. **2** to exhilarate someone greatly. ▷ *adj* /ɪn'iːbrɪət/ (*now usually* **inebriated**) drunk, especially habitually drunk. ▷ *noun* /ɪn'iːbrɪət/ *formal* someone who is drunk, especially on a regular basis. • **inebriation** or **inebriety** /-'braɪətɪ/ *noun.* ◷ 16c: from Latin *inebriare*, from *ebrius* drunk.

inedible ▷ *adj* said of food: not fit or suitable to be eaten, eg because it is poisonous or indigestible, or it has gone off. • **inedibility** *noun.* ◷ 19c.

ineducable /ɪn'ɛdʒukəbəl/ ▷ *adj* said of a person: not capable of being educated, especially because of some form of learning difficulty, brain injury, emotional trauma, etc. • **ineducability** *noun.* ◷ 19c.

ineffable /ɪn'ɛfəbəl/ ▷ *adj, especially literary or formal* **1** unable to be described or expressed in words, especially because of size, magnificence, etc □ *the ineffable love of God.* **2** not supposed or not allowed to be said, especially because of being perceived as too sacred. • **ineffability** or **ineffableness** *noun.* • **ineffably** *adverb.* ◷ 15c: French, from Latin *ineffabilis.*

ineffective ▷ *adj* **1** having no effect; not able or likely to produce a result, or the result or effect intended □ *ineffective policies.* **2** said of a person: not capable of achieving results; inefficient or incompetent. • **ineffectively** *adverb.* • **ineffectiveness** *noun.* ◷ 17c.

ineffectual ▷ *adj* **1** not producing any result or the intended result. **2** said of a person: lacking the ability and confidence needed to achieve results; weak or impotent. • **ineffectually** *adverb.* • **ineffectuality** or **ineffectualness** *noun.* ◷ 15c.

inefficacious ▷ *adj* said of a medicine or medical treatment: not having the desired or intended effect. • **inefficaciously** *adverb.* • **inefficacy** *noun.* ◷ 17c.

inefficient ▷ *adj* lacking the power or skill to do or produce something in the best, most satisfactory or economical, etc way. • **inefficiency** *noun.* • **inefficiently** *adverb.* ◷ 18c.

inelegant ▷ *adj* lacking grace or refinement. • **inelegance** *noun.* • **inelegantly** *adverb.* ◷ 16c.

ineligible ▷ *adj* **1** said of a person: not qualified to stand for election. **2** not suitable to be chosen. • **ineligibility** *noun.* • **ineligibly** *adverb.* ◷ 18c.

ineluctable /ɪnɪ'lʌktəbəl/ ▷ *adj, especially literary* or *formal* not able to be avoided, resisted or escaped from. • **ineluctably** *adverb.* ◷ 17c: from Latin *ineluctabilis*, from *eluctari* to struggle out.

inept /ɪn'ɛpt/ ▷ *adj* **1** awkward; done without, or not having, skill. **2** not suitable or fitting; out of place. **3** silly; foolish. • **ineptly** *adverb.* • **ineptness** *noun.* ◷ 17c: from Latin *ineptus* unsuited.

> ***inept, inapt***
>
> Note that **inept** is a great deal more judgemental and depreciatory than **inapt**, and tends to describe general attributes or characteristics rather than the circumstances of a particular instance or occurrence.

ineptitude /ɪn'ɛptɪtʃuːd/ ▷ *noun* **1** awkwardness; incapacity. **2** silliness. ◷ 17c: from Latin *ineptitudo* the quality of being inept.

inequable ▷ *adj* **1** not fair or just. **2** changeable; not even or uniform. ◷ 18c.

inequality ▷ *noun* (***inequalities***) **1** a lack of equality, fairness or evenness. **2** an instance of this; a dissimilarity or disparity, especially in social or economic terms. **3** *math* a statement that the values of two numerical quantities, algebraic expressions, functions, etc are not equal. **4** *astron* any departure from uniform orbital motion of an object. ◷ 15c.

inequitable ▷ *adj, rather formal* not fair or just. • **inequitably** *adverb.* ◷ 17c.

inequity ▷ *noun* (***inequities***) *rather formal* **1** an unjust action. **2** lack of fairness or equity. ◷ 16c.

ineradicable ▷ *adj* not able to be removed completely or rooted out (now especially from a person's mind, heart, memory, etc). • **ineradicably** *adverb.* ◷ 19c: from Latin *eradicare* to root out.

inert /ɪ'nɜːt/ ▷ *adj* (***inerter, inertest***) **1** tending to remain in a state of rest or uniform motion in a straight line unless acted upon by an external force. **2** not wanting to move, act or think; indolent; sluggish. **3** *chem* unreactive or showing only a limited ability to react with other chemical elements. Compare LABILE. • **inertly** *adverb.* • **inertness** *noun.* ◷ 17c: from Latin *iners, inertis* unskilled or idle.

inert gas see NOBLE GAS

inertia /ɪ'nɜːʃə/ ▷ *noun* **1** *physics* the tendency of an object to remain at rest, or to continue to move in the same direction at constant speed, unless it is acted on by an external force. **2** the state of not wanting to move, act or think; indolence; sluggishness. • **inertial** *adj.* ◷ 18c: from Latin *iners* (see INERT).

inertial control guidance, inertial guidance and **inertial navigation** ▷ *noun* an automatic guidance system for aircraft, submarines, missiles, etc, which depends on inertia (see INERTIA sense 1), and works without a magnetic compass, independently of ground-based radio aids.

inertia-reel seat belt ▷ *noun* in a vehicle: a seat belt on a reel which allows the wearer to move freely in normal conditions but which locks tight under impact or sudden movement.

inertia selling ▷ *noun, Brit* the illegal practice of sending unrequested goods to people followed by a bill if the goods are not returned.

inescapable ▷ *adj* inevitable; unable to be avoided. • **inescapably** *adverb.* ◷ 18c.

inessential ▷ *adj* not necessary. ▷ *noun* an inessential thing. ◷ 17c.

inestimable ▷ *adj, rather formal* too great, or of too great a value, to be estimated, measured or fully appreciated. • **inestimably** *adverb.* ◷ 14c.

inevitable /ɪn'ɛvɪtəbəl/ ▷ *adj* **1** unable to be avoided; certain to happen. **2** *colloq* tiresomely regular or predictable. ▷ *noun* (*especially* **the inevitable**) something that is certain to happen and is unavoidable. • **inevitability** /-'bɪlɪtɪ/ *noun.* • **inevitably** *adverb.* ◷ 15c: from Latin *inevitabilis.*

inexact ▷ *adj* not quite correct or true. • **inexactitude** or **inexactness** *noun.* • **inexactly** *adverb.* ◷ 19c.

inexcusable ▻ *adj* said eg of behaviour: too bad to be excused, justified or tolerated. • **inexcusably** *adverb*. ◷ 16c.

inexhaustible ▻ *adj* **1** said eg of a supply or commodity: incapable of being used up. **2** tireless; never failing or giving up. • **inexhaustibility** *noun*. • **inexhaustibly** *adverb*. ◷ 17c.

inexorable /ɪnˈɛksərəbəl/ ▻ *adj* **1** incapable of being made to change position or course of action, etc by entreaty or persuasion; unrelenting. **2** unable to be altered or avoided. • **inexorability** *noun*. • **inexorably** *adverb*. ◷ 16c: from Latin *inexorabilis*, from *exorare* to prevail upon.

inexpedient ▻ *adj* not wise, suitable or appropriate. • **inexpedience** or **inexpediency** *noun*. • **inexpediently** *adverb*. ◷ 17c.

inexpensive ▻ *adj* cheap or reasonable in price. • **inexpensively** *adverb*. • **inexpensiveness** *noun*. ◷ 19c.

inexperience ▻ *noun* lack of skill or knowledge gained from experience. • **inexperienced** *adj*. ◷ 16c.

inexpert ▻ *adj* (*often* **inexpert at** or **in something**) unskilled at it. • **inexpertly** *adverb*. ◷ 15c.

inexplicable /ɪnɪkˈsplɪk-, ɪnˈɛksplɪkəbəl/ ▻ *adj* impossible to explain, understand or account for. • **inexplicability** *noun*. • **inexplicably** *adverb*. ◷ 16c.

inexplicit ▻ *adj* not clearly and exactly stated. • **inexplicitly** *adverb*. ◷ 19c.

inexpressible ▻ *adj* unable to be expressed or described. • **inexpressibly** *adverb*. ◷ 17c.

inexpressive ▻ *adj* said especially of a person's face: expressing little or no emotion. ◷ 17c.

inextinguishable ▻ *adj* incapable of being put out or destroyed. ◷ 16c.

in extremis /ɪn ɪkˈstriːmɪs/ ▻ *adverb* **1** at, or as if at, the point of death or ultimate failure. **2** in desperate or extreme circumstances; in serious difficulties. ◷ 16c: Latin, meaning 'in the last things'.

inextricable /ɪnɪkˈstrɪkəbəl, ɪnˈɛk-/ ▻ *adj* **1** said of a situation, etc: unable to be escaped from. **2** said of a knot, dilemma, etc: unable to be disentangled or untied. • **inextricably** *adverb*. ◷ 16c.

inf. ▻ *abbreviation* **1** infantry. **2** inferior. **3** infinitive. **4** information. See also INFO. **5** informal.

infallible ▻ *adj* **1** said of a person: never liable to make a mistake; incapable of error. **2** *RC Church* said of the Pope: unable to err when pronouncing officially on dogma. **3** said of a plan, method, etc: sure; always, or bound to be, successful or effective. • **infallibility** *noun*. • **infallibly** *adverb*. ◷ 15c.

infamous /ˈɪnfəməs/ ▻ *adj* **1** having a very bad reputation; notoriously bad. **2** *formal* evil; vile; disgraceful. • **infamously** *adverb*. ◷ 14c: from Latin *infamosus* (see FAMOUS).

infamy /ˈɪnfəmɪ/ ▻ *noun* (***infamies***) **1** bad reputation; notoriety; shame. **2** *formal* an infamous act or happening. ◷ 15c: from French *infamie*, from Latin *infamis* infamous.

infancy /ˈɪnfənsɪ/ ▻ *noun* (***infancies***) **1** the state or time of being an infant. **2** an early period of existence, growth and development ▫ *when television was still in its infancy*. **3** *law* MINORITY (sense 4). ◷ 15c.

infant /ˈɪnfənt/ ▻ *noun* **1** a very young child in the first period of life; a baby. **2** *Brit* a schoolchild under the age of seven or eight. **3** *law* a MINOR (*noun* 1). **4** *as adj* ▫ *infant mortality* ▫ *infant teacher*. ▻ *adj* at an early stage of development ▫ *an infant colony*. ◷ 14c: from French *enfant*, from Latin *infans* a child or someone who cannot speak, from *fari* to speak.

infanta /ɪnˈfantə/ ▻ *noun* (***infantas***) *historical* (*often* **Infanta**) **1** a daughter of the reigning monarch of Spain or Portugal who is not heir to the throne, especially the eldest daughter. **2** the wife of an INFANTE. ◷ 17c: Spanish and Portuguese, from Latin *infans* INFANT.

infante /ɪnˈfanteɪ, -tɪ/ ▻ *noun* (***infantes***) *historical* (*often* **Infante**) a son of the king of Spain or Portugal who is not heir to the throne, especially the second son. ◷ 16c: Spanish and Portuguese, from Latin *infans* INFANT.

infanticide /ɪnˈfantɪsaɪd/ ▻ *noun* **1** the murder of a young child or infant. **2** someone who murders a young child or infant. **3** the practice of killing newborn children. • **infanticidal** *adj*. ◷ 17c.

infantile /ˈɪnfəntaɪl/ ▻ *adj* **1** belonging or relating to infants or infancy. **2** very childish; puerile; immature. ◷ 17c: from Latin *infantilis*.

infantile paralysis ▻ *noun, medicine, old use* POLIOMYELITIS.

infantilism /ɪnˈfantɪlɪzəm/ ▻ *noun, technical, psychol, etc* the presence of childish characteristics in an adult or older child. ◷ 19c.

infantry /ˈɪnfəntrɪ/ ▻ *noun* (***infantries***) a body of soldiers trained and equipped to fight on foot. Also *as adj* ▫ *infantry regiment*. Compare CAVALRY. ◷ 16c: from French *infanterie*, from Italian *infanteria*, from *infante* a foot-soldier, from Latin *infans* a youth.

infantryman ▻ *noun* a soldier in the infantry.

infant school ▻ *noun, Brit* a school for children between five and seven or eight years old. *N Amer equivalent* ELEMENTARY SCHOOL. See also PRIMARY SCHOOL.

infarction /ɪnˈfɑːkʃən/ ▻ *noun, pathol* the death of a localized area of tissue as a result of the blocking of its blood supply, usually by a blood clot, air bubble or fragment of tissue, etc. See also MYOCARDIAL INFARCTION. ◷ 17c: from Latin *infarcire*, *infarctum* to stuff or block off.

infatuate /ɪnˈfatjʊeɪt/ ▻ *verb* (***infatuated, infatuating***) to inspire someone with, or make them feel, passionate, foolish, intense, etc love or admiration. • **infatuated** *adj* (*especially* **infatuated with someone** or **something**) filled with passion for them or it; besotted with them or it. • **infatuation** *noun* **1** the state of being infatuated. **2** someone or something one is infatuated with ▫ *DIY is an infatuation with him*. ◷ 16c: from Latin *infatuare*, *infatuatum* to make a fool of.

infect /ɪnˈfɛkt/ ▻ *verb* (***infected, infecting***) (*often* **infect something** or **someone with something**) **1** *biol, medicine, etc* to contaminate (a living organism) with a PATHOGEN, such as a bacterium, virus or fungus, and thereby cause disease. **2** to taint or contaminate (especially water, food or air) with a bacterium, pollutant, etc. **3** to pass a feeling or opinion, especially an adverse or negative one, to someone. **4** *computing* to inflict or become inflicted with a VIRUS (sense 5). ◷ 14c: from Latin *inficere*, *infectum* to spoil or impregnate.

infection /ɪnˈfɛkʃən/ ▻ *noun* **1** the process of infecting or state of being infected. **2** *biol, medicine, etc* the invasion of a human, animal or plant by disease-causing micro-organisms, such as bacteria, viruses, fungi or protozoa, which then multiply rapidly and usually cause symptoms of disease. Compare INCUBATION. **3** an infectious disease, caused by such a micro-organism. **4** the passing on of feelings, opinions, etc, especially negative ones.

infectious /ɪnˈfɛkʃəs/ ▻ *adj* **1** said of a disease: caused by bacteria, viruses or other micro-organisms, and therefore capable of being transmitted through air, water, etc. **2** said eg of a person: capable of infecting others; causing infection ▫ *The children are no longer infectious, even though their spots are not healed*. **3** said of an emotion, opinion, etc: likely to be passed on to others ▫ *Laughter is very infectious*. • **infectiously** *adverb*. • **infectiousness** *noun*.

infectious mononucleosis ▻ *noun, pathol* an infectious disease, mainly affecting adolescents, caused by the EPSTEIN-BARR VIRUS. The symptoms include swollen lymph nodes, fever, a sore throat and headache

infectious, contagious

There is often confusion between **infectious** and **contagious**: an **infectious** disease is spread through the air, while a **contagious** disease is spread by touch, although when used figuratively, of laughter for example, they mean the same thing.

and they can persist over several weeks, often followed by fatigue and depression. Also called **glandular fever**.

infective ▷ *adj* **1** INFECTIOUS (sense 1). **2** *rare* or *old use* INFECTIOUS (in other senses). • **infectively** *adverb*. • **infectiveness** *noun*. ⓒ Late 14c.

infelicitous ▷ *adj* **1** not happy, fortunate or lucky. **2** not suitable, fitting or apt. ⓒ 19c.

infer /ɪn'fɜː(r)/ ▷ *verb* (***inferred***, ***inferring***) **1** *tr & intr* to conclude or judge from facts, observation and deduction. **2** *colloq* to imply or suggest. • **inferable** /ɪn'fɜːrəbəl, 'infə-/ or **inferrable** *adj*. ⓒ 16c: from Latin *inferre* to bring in.

infer

The meaning given in sense 2 is common, but is still subject to disapproval.

☆ RECOMMENDATION: avoid it if you are talking or writing to someone who is likely to be precise about the use of language. Use **imply** or **suggest**.

inference /'ɪnfərəns/ ▷ *noun* **1** an act of inferring, especially of reaching a conclusion from facts, observation and careful thought. **2** something which is inferred, especially a conclusion.

inferential /ɪnfə'rɛnʃəl/ ▷ *adj* relating to or based on inference. • **inferentially** *adverb*.

inferior /ɪn'fɪərɪə(r)/ ▷ *adj* (*often* **inferior to something** or **someone**) **1** poor or poorer in quality. **2** low or lower in value, rank or status. **3** low or lower in position. **4** said of letters or figures: printed or written slightly below the line. **5** said of a planet: revolving within the Earth's orbit; nearer the Sun than the Earth is. ▷ *noun* someone or something which is inferior. • **inferiority** /-'ɒrɪtɪ/ *noun* the state of being inferior. ⓒ 15c: Latin, meaning 'lower'.

inferior

Remember that **inferior** does not behave like *better*, *worse* and the other comparative adjectives. It is followed by **to** not **than**.

inferiority complex ▷ *noun* **1** *psychol* a disorder that arises from the conflict between the desire to be noticed and the fear of being shown to be inadequate, characterized by aggressive behaviour or withdrawal. **2** *loosely* a general feeling of inadequacy or worthlessness. Compare SUPERIORITY COMPLEX.

infernal /ɪn'fɜːnəl/ ▷ *adj* **1** belonging or relating to the underworld. **2** belonging or relating to hell. **3** wicked; evil; hellish. **4** *colloq* extremely annoying, unpleasant, burdensome, etc. • **infernally** *adverb*. ⓒ 14c: French, from Latin *infernalis*, from *inferus* low.

inferno /ɪn'fɜːnoʊ/ ▷ *noun* (***infernos***) **1** (*often* **the Inferno**) hell. **2** a place or situation of horror and confusion. **3** a raging fire. ⓒ 19c: Italian, from Latin *infernus* hell.

infertile ▷ *adj* **1** said of soil, etc: lacking the nutrients required to support an abundant growth of crops or other plants; barren. **2** said of a person or animal: unable to produce offspring; sterile. • **infertility** *noun*. ⓒ 16c.

infest /ɪn'fɛst/ ▷ *verb* (***infested***, ***infesting***) **1** said of parasites such as fleas, lice and certain fungi: to invade and occupy another animal or plant. **2** said of someone or something harmful or unpleasant: to exist in large numbers or quantities ▫ *Heroin-dealers infested the poorer parts of the city*. • **infestation** *noun*. ⓒ 15c: from Latin *infestare* to assail or molest.

infibulation /ɪnfɪbjʊ'leɪʃən/ ▷ *noun* the act of stitching or clasping together the labia, often after a CLITORIDECTOMY, to prevent sexual intercourse. See also FEMALE CIRCUMCISION. ⓒ 17c: from Latin *infibulare* to fasten the prepuce with a clasp.

infidel /'ɪnfɪdəl, -dɛl/ ▷ *noun* **1** someone who rejects a particular religion, especially Christianity or Islam. **2** someone who rejects all religions; an unbeliever. **3** someone who rejects a theory. ▷ *adj* relating to unbelievers; unbelieving. ⓒ 15c: from Latin *infidelis* unfaithful.

infidelity /ɪnfɪ'dɛlɪtɪ/ ▷ *noun* (***infidelities***) **1** unfaithfulness, especially of a sexual nature. **2** an instance of this. **3** lack of belief or faith in a religion. ⓒ 16c: from Latin *infidelitas* unfaithfulness.

infield ▷ *noun* **1** *cricket* **a** the area of the field close to the wicket; **b** the players positioned there. **2** *baseball* **a** the diamond-shaped area of the pitch enclosed by the four bases; **b** the players positioned there. **3** the land belonging to a farm which is closest to the farm bulidings. Compare OUTFIELD. • **infielder** *noun* a player who stands in the infield.

in-fighting ▷ *noun* **1** fighting or competition between members of the same group, company, organization, etc. **2** *boxing* fighting at close quarters. • **in-fighter** *noun*.

infill /'ɪnfɪl/ ▷ *noun* (*also* **infilling**) **1** the act of filling or closing gaps, holes, etc. **2** the material used to fill a gap, hole, etc. ▷ *verb* to fill in (a gap, hole, etc). ⓒ 19c.

infiltrate /'ɪnfɪltreɪt/ ▷ *verb* (***infiltrated***, ***infiltrating***) **1** said of troops, agents, etc: to pass into (territory or an organization held by the enemy or rivals) secretly, to gain influence, control or information. **2** to filter slowly (eg liquid or gas) through the pores (of a substance). **3** *intr* said eg of liquid or gas: to filter in. **4** said of mineral matter dissolved in water: to become deposited among (the pores or grains of a rock). ▷ *noun* any substance that permeates a solid and becomes deposited within it. • **infiltration** *noun*. • **infiltrator** *noun*. ⓒ 18c.

infinite /'ɪnfɪnət/ ▷ *adj* **1** having no boundaries or limits in size, extent, time or space. **2** too great to be measured or counted. **3** very great; vast. **4** *math* said of a number, a series, etc: having an unlimited number of elements, digits or terms. **5** all-encompassing; complete ▫ *God in his infinite wisdom*. ▷ *noun* **1** anything which has no limits, boundaries, etc. **2** (**the Infinite**) God. • **infinitely** *adverb*. • **infiniteness** *noun*. ⓒ 14c: see FINITE.

infinitesimal /ɪnfɪnɪ'tɛsɪməl/ ▷ *adj* **1** infinitely small; with a value too close to zero to be measured. **2** *colloq* extremely small. ▷ *noun* an infinitesimal amount. • **infinitesimally** *adverb*. ⓒ 19c: from Latin *infinitesimus* 'infiniteth' (modelled on *centesimus* hundredth, etc), from *infinitus* infinite.

infinitive /ɪn'fɪnɪtɪv/ ▷ *noun*, *grammar* (abbreviation **inf.**) a verb form which expresses an action but which does not refer to a particular subject or time, in English often used with *to* (eg *Tell him to go*), but used without *to* after certain verbs (eg *Let her go*). See also SPLIT INFINITIVE. ▷ *adj* said of a verb: having this form. Compare FINITE. • **infinitival** /-'taɪvəl/ *adj*. ⓒ 16c: from Latin *infinitivus* unlimited or indefinite.

infinitude /ɪn'fɪnɪtjuːd/ ▷ *noun* **1** the state or quality of being infinite. **2** something infinite, especially an infinite quantity, degree or amount. ⓒ 17c: from INFINITE, modelled on MAGNITUDE, etc.

infinity /ɪn'fɪnətɪ/ ▷ *noun* (***infinities***) **1** space, time, distance or quantity that is without limit or boundaries. **2** *loosely* a quantity, space, time or distance that is too great to be measured. **3** *math* (symbol ∞) **a** a number that is larger than any FINITE value, that can be approached but never reached, because the sequence of NATURAL NUMBERS continues indefinitely; **b** the RECIPROCAL of zero, ie 1/0. **4** the quality or state of being infinite. ⓒ 14c: from Latin *infinitas*.

infirm /ɪnˈfɜːm/ ▷ *adj* (***infirmer***, ***infirmest***) **1** weak or ill, especially from old age. **2** (**the infirm**) weak or ill people as a group (see THE 4b). ⓒ 14c: from Latin *infirmus* weak, fragile, frail.

infirmary /ɪnˈfɜːmərɪ/ ▷ *noun* (***infirmaries***) **1** a hospital. **2** a room or ward, eg in a boarding school, monastery, etc, where the sick and injured are treated. ⓒ 17c: from Latin *infirmaria*, from *infirmus* infirm.

infirmity ▷ *noun* (***infirmities***) **1** the state or quality of being sick, weak or infirm. **2** a disease or illness. ⓒ 14c.

infix ▷ *verb* /ɪnˈfɪks, ˈɪnfɪks/ (***infixed***, ***infixing***) **1** to fix something firmly in (eg the mind). **2** *grammar* to insert (an AFFIX) into the middle of a word as opposed to adding it as a prefix or suffix. ▷ *noun* /ˈɪnfɪks/ (***infixes***) an affix inserted into the middle of a word. Compare PREFIX, SUFFIX. • **infixation** *noun*. ⓒ 16c: from Latin *infigere*, *infixum*.

in flagrante delicto /ɪn fləˈgrantɪ dɪˈlɪktoʊ/ ▷ *adverb* **1** *originally & especially law* in the very act of committing a crime; red-handed. **2** *colloq, often jocular* said of someone's spouse or partner: in the act of committing adulterous sexual intercourse. Sometimes shortened to **in flagrante**. ⓒ 18c: Latin, literally 'with the crime blazing'.

inflame /ɪnˈfleɪm/ ▷ *verb* **1** to arouse strong or violent emotion in someone or something ▫ *Desire inflamed my heart* ▫ *His strong words inflamed the crowd with anger.* **2** to make something more heated or intense; to exacerbate ▫ *The police action only inflamed the situation.* **3 a** to make (part of the body) become red, heated, swollen and painful; **b** *intr* said of part of the body: to become affected by inflammation. **4** *tr & intr* to burst, or make something burst, into flames. • **inflamed** *adj*. ⓒ 14c: from French *enflammer*, from Latin *inflammare* to kindle.

inflammable ▷ *adj* **1** easily set on fire. See also FLAMMABLE. **2** easily excited or angered. ▷ *noun* an inflammable substance or thing. • **inflammability** *noun*. • **inflammably** *adverb*. ⓒ 17c.

inflammable

See Usage Note at **flammable**.

inflammation /ɪnfləˈmeɪʃən/ ▷ *noun* **1** *pathol* a protective response of the body tissues to disease, injury, infection or the presence of an ALLERGEN, in which the affected part becomes red, heated, swollen and painful. **2** an act or the process of inflaming or state of being inflamed. ⓒ 16c.

inflammatory /ɪnˈflamətərɪ/ ▷ *adj* **1** likely to cause strong or violent emotion, especially anger ▫ *inflammatory language.* **2** *pathol* belonging or relating to, causing, or caused by, inflammation of part of the body. ⓒ 18c.

inflatable /ɪnˈfleɪtəbəl/ ▷ *adj* said of a cushion, ball, boat, etc: able to be inflated with air for use. ▷ *noun* an inflatable object.

inflate /ɪnˈfleɪt/ ▷ *verb* (***inflated***, ***inflating***) **1** *tr & intr* to swell or cause something to swell or expand with air or gas. **2** *econ* **a** to increase (prices generally) by artificial means; **b** to increase (the volume of money in circulation). Compare DEFLATE, REFLATE. **3** to exaggerate the importance or value of something. **4** to raise (the spirits, etc); to elate. • **inflated** *adj* **1** said of prices: artificially increased to a high level. **2** said especially of language or opinions: showing too great a sense of the speaker's importance; pompous. **3** blown up or filled with air or gas; distended. ⓒ 16c: from Latin *inflare*, *inflatum* to blow into.

inflation /ɪnˈfleɪʃən/ ▷ *noun* **1** *econ* a general increase in the level of prices accompanied by a fall in the purchasing power of money, caused by an increase in the amount of money in circulation and credit available. See also DEFLATION, REFLATION, STAGFLATION. **2** *loosely* the rate at which the general level of prices is rising. **3** the process of inflating or being inflated. • **inflationary** *adj* relating to or involving inflation.

inflationism ▷ *noun* the policy or concept of creating INFLATION by increasing the money supply. • **inflationist** *noun, adj*.

inflect /ɪnˈflɛkt/ ▷ *verb* (***inflected***, ***inflecting***) **1 a** *grammar* to change the form of (a word) to show eg tense, number, gender or grammatical case; **b** *intr* said of a word, language, etc: to change, or to be able to be changed, to show (or AGREE in) tense, number, gender, grammatical case, etc. See note at INFLECTION. **2** to vary the tone or pitch of (the voice, a note, etc); to modulate. **3** to bend inwards. ⓒ 15c in sense 4: from Latin *inflectere* to curve.

inflection or **inflexion** /ɪnˈflɛkʃən/ ▷ *noun* **1** *grammar* **a** the change in the form of a word which shows tense, number, gender, grammatical case, etc; **b** an inflected form of a word; **c** a suffix which is added to a word to form an inflected form, eg *-s*, *-ing*. See also ENDING. **2** a change in the tone, pitch, etc of the voice. See also INTONATION. **3** *geom* a change in a curve from being CONVEX to CONCAVE, or vice versa. **4** an act of inflecting or state of being inflected. • **inflectional** *adj, grammar* relating to or involving inflection. • **inflective** *adj, grammar* tending to inflect or subject to inflection. ⓒ 16c.

inflexible /ɪnˈflɛksɪbəl/ ▷ *adj* **1** incapable of being bent; rigid; not flexible. **2** *derog* said of a person: never giving way; unyielding; obstinate. **3** unable to be changed; fixed. • **inflexibility** or **inflexibleness** *noun*. • **inflexibly** *adverb*. ⓒ 15c.

inflict /ɪnˈflɪkt/ ▷ *verb* (***inflicted***, ***inflicting***) (*especially* **inflict something on someone**) to impose (something unpleasant, eg a blow, defeat or pain) on them, or make them suffer it ▫ *ordered twenty lashes to be inflicted on the prisoner* ▫ *could not inflict my rowdy family on you.* • **inflictable** *adj*. • **inflicter** or **inflictor** *noun*. • **infliction** *noun* **1** an act of inflicting. **2** something that is inflicted. ⓒ 16c: from Latin *infligere*, *inflictum* to strike against.

inflict

A word sometimes confused with this one is **afflict**.

in-flight ▷ *adj* available or provided during an aircraft flight ▫ *the in-flight movie.*

inflorescence /ɪnfləˈrɛsəns, ɪnflɔː-/ ▷ *noun, bot* **1** the complete flower-head of a flowering plant, including the stem. **2** any of a number of different arrangements of the flowers on the main stem of a flowering plant. ⓒ 18c: from Latin *inflorescere* to begin to blossom.

inflow /ˈɪnfloʊ/ ▷ *noun* **1** the act or process of flowing in. **2** something that flows in. • **inflowing** *noun, adj*.

influence /ˈɪnflʊəns/ ▷ *noun* **1** (*especially* **influence on** or **over someone** or **something**) the power that one person or thing has to affect another. **2** a person or thing that has such a power ▫ *be a good influence on him.* **3** power resulting from political or social position, wealth, ability, standards of behaviour, etc ▫ *a man of some influence* ▫ *Couldn't you use your influence to get me a ticket?* ▷ *verb* (***influenced***, ***influencing***) **1** to have an effect, especially an indirect or unnoticed one, on (a person or their work, or events, etc) ▫ *Rock and roll influenced his music greatly.* **2** to exert influence on someone or something; to persuade ▫ *Her encouraging letter influenced me to stay.* • **under the influence** *colloq* affected by alcohol; drunk. ⓒ 14c in an astrological sense, referring to a substance thought to flow out from the stars and exert power over human destinies, etc: French, from Latin *influere* to flow into.

influential /ɪnflʊ'ɛnʃəl/ ▻ *adj* **1** having influence or power. **2** (*especially* **influential in something**) making an important contribution to it. • **influentially** *adverb*.

influenza /ɪnflʊ'ɛnzə/ ▻ *noun, pathol* a highly infectious viral infection, with symptoms including headache, fever, a sore throat, catarrh and muscular aches and pains. Commonly shortened to **flu**. • **influenzal** *adj*. ⓒ 18c: Italian, literally 'influence' (from the belief that the stars caused epidemics generally).

influx /'ɪnflʌks/ ▻ *noun* (*influxes*) **1** a continual stream or arrival of large numbers of people or things. **2** a flowing in or inflow. ⓒ 17c: from Latin *influere, influxum* to flow in.

info /'ɪnfoʊ/ ▻ *noun, colloq* information. ⓒ Early 20c shortening.

infobahn see under THE INTERNET

infold see ENFOLD

infomercial /ɪnfoʊ'mɜːʃəl/ ▻ *noun, TV* a short informational film promoted for commercial purposes. Compare ADVERTORIAL, INFOTAINMENT. ⓒ 1981: from *information* + *commercial*.

inform /ɪn'fɔːm/ ▻ *verb* (*informed, informing*) **1** *tr & intr*, (*especially* **inform someone about** or **of something**) to give them knowledge or information about it; to tell them about it. **2** *literary or formal* to animate, inspire, or give life to something. **3** *formal* to give an essential quality to something. ⓒ 14c: from Latin *informare* to give form to or describe.

■ **inform against** or **on someone** to give incriminating evidence about them to the authorities. See also GRASS (*verb* 3), SHOP (*verb* 2).

informal ▻ *adj* **1** without ceremony or formality; relaxed and friendly. **2** said of language, clothes, etc: suitable for and used in relaxed, everyday situations. **3** *Austral, NZ* said of a vote, ballot, etc: not valid. • **informality** *noun* (*informalities*) **1** lack of formality. **2** an instance of this. • **informally** *adverb*. ⓒ 17c.

informant /ɪn'fɔːmənt/ ▻ *noun* someone who informs, eg against another person, or who gives information. Compare INFORMER. ⓒ 17c.

informatics ▻ *noun* INFORMATION SCIENCE (sense 1).

information /ɪnfə'meɪʃən/ ▻ *noun* **1** knowledge gained or given; facts; news. Often shortened to **info**. **2** the communicating or receiving of knowledge. Also *as adj* □ *information desk* □ *information centre*. **3** *especially N Amer* DIRECTORY ENQUIRIES. **4** *especially telecomm, computing* a signal or character which represents data. **5** *law* an accusation made before a court or magistrate. • **informational** *adj*. ⓒ 14c: from Latin *informatio* conception of an idea.

information retrieval ▻ *noun* **1** the process of obtaining selected information from data stored in a database. **2** the storage, categorization and subsequent tracing of (especially computerized) information in the form of large blocks of data.

information science ▻ *noun* **1** the processing and communication of data, especially by means of computerized systems. **2** the study of this subject. • **information scientist** *noun*.

information superhighway see under SUPERHIGHWAY

information technology ▻ *noun, computing* (abbreviation **IT**) the use, study or production of a range of technologies (especially computer systems, digital electronics and telecommunications) to store, process and transmit information.

information theory ▻ *noun, math* analysis of the efficiency of communication channels, especially with regard to the coding and transmission of information in computers and telecommunication systems, using statistical methods.

informative /ɪn'fɔːmətɪv/ ▻ *adj* giving useful or interesting information; instructive. • **informatively** *adverb*. • **informativeness** *noun*.

informed ▻ *adj* **1** said especially of a person: having or showing knowledge, especially in being educated and intelligent. **2** said of eg a newspaper article, a guess or estimate, opinion, etc: based on sound information; showing knowledge or experience; educated. Also *in compounds* □ *well-informed*.

informer ▻ *noun* someone who informs against another, especially to the police and usually for money or some other reward. Compare INFORMANT.

infotainment /ɪnfoʊ'teɪnmənt/ ▻ *noun, chiefly TV* the presentation of serious subjects or current affairs as entertainment. Compare ADVERTORIAL, INFOMERCIAL. ⓒ Late 20c: from *information* + *entertainment*.

infra /'ɪnfrə/ ▻ *adverb* in books, texts, etc: below; lower down on the page or further on in the book. ⓒ 18c: Latin, meaning 'below'.

infra- /'ɪnfrə/ ▻ *prefix, chiefly technical, forming adjectives and nouns, denoting* below, or beneath, a specified thing □ *infra-molecular* □ *infrared*. ⓒ 17c: Latin, meaning 'below'.

infraction /ɪn'frakʃən/ ▻ *noun, formal* the breaking of a law, rule, etc; violation. ⓒ 17c: from Latin *infractio*.

infra dig ▻ *adj, colloq* beneath one's dignity. ⓒ 19c: abbreviation of Latin *infra dignitatem*.

infrared or (*sometimes*) **infra-red** ▻ *adj* **1** said of electromagnetic radiation: with a wavelength between the red end of the visible spectrum and microwaves and radio waves. **2** belonging or relating to, using, producing or sensitive to, radiation of this sort □ *infrared camera*. Compare ULTRAVIOLET. ▻ *noun* **1** infrared radiation. **2** the infrared part of the spectrum. ⓒ 19c.

infrared astronomy ▻ *noun, astron* the study of infrared radiation produced by celestial bodies or by gas or dust in space, as a means of detecting comets, star formation in galaxies, dust clouds, etc.

infrared photography ▻ *noun* photography using film that is specially sensitized to infrared radiation, useful especially in conditions where there is little or no visible light.

infrasonic ▻ *adj* relating to or having a frequency or frequencies below the range which can normally be heard by the human ear. Compare SUBSONIC, SUPERSONIC, ULTRASONIC. ⓒ 1920s.

infrasound ▻ *noun, physics* sound waves which have a frequency of less than 20Hz and cannot be heard by humans, but may be felt as vibrations. Compare ULTRASOUND. ⓒ 1930s.

infrastructure ▻ *noun* **1** the basic inner structure of a society, organization, or system. **2** the permanent services and equipment, eg the roads, railways, bridges, factories and schools, needed for a country to be able to function properly. **3** the permanent services and equipment, eg roads, railways and bridges, needed for military purposes. ⓒ 1920s.

infrequent ▻ *adj* occurring rarely or only occasionally. • **infrequency** *noun*. • **infrequently** *adverb*. ⓒ 16c.

infringe /ɪn'frɪndʒ/ ▻ *verb* (*infringed, infringing*) **1** to break or violate (eg a law or oath) □ *You are infringing the copyright by using that material.* **2** *intr* (*especially* **infringe on** or **upon something**) to encroach or trespass; to affect (a person's rights, freedom, etc) in such a way as to limit or reduce them. **3** to interfere with (a person's rights). • **infringement** *noun*. ⓒ 16c: from Latin *infringere* to break.

infuriate /ɪn'fjʊərɪeɪt/ ▻ *verb* (*infuriated, infuriating*) to make someone very angry. ⓒ 17c: from Latin *infuriare, infuriatum*.

infuriating ▻ *adj* maddening; causing great anger or annoyance. • **infuriatingly** *adverb*.

infuse /ɪn'fjuːz/ ▻ *verb* (***infused, infusing***) **1** *tr & intr* to soak, or cause (an organic substance, eg herbs or tea) to be soaked, in hot water to release flavour or other qualities. **2** (*especially* **infuse someone with something** or **infuse something into someone**) to inspire them with (a positive feeling, quality, etc); to imbue or instil it in them. • **infusible** *adj*. • **infusive** *adj*. ⓒ 15c: from Latin *infundere* to pour in.

infusion /ɪn'fjuːʒən/ ▻ *noun* **1** an act or the process of infusing something. **2** a solution produced by infusing eg herbs or tea. **3** something poured in or introduced, eg an **intravenous infusion** administered to a patient.

-ing[1] ▻ *suffix, forming nouns* **1** formed from a verb: usually expressing the action of that verb, its result, product or something relating to it, etc □ *building* □ *driving* □ *lining* □ *washing*. **2** formed from a noun: describing something made of, used in, etc the specified thing □ *guttering* □ *roofing* □ *bedding*. **3** formed from an adverb: □ *offing* □ *outing*. ⓒ Anglo-Saxon *-ing* or *-ung*.

-ing[2] ▻ *suffix* used to form **1** the present participle of verbs, as in *I was only asking* and *saw you walking in the park*. **2** adjectives derived from present participles, eg *charming, terrifying*. ⓒ Anglo-Saxon as *-ende*.

-ing[3] ▻ *suffix* (no longer productive), *forming nouns, signifying* one belonging to a specified kind, etc or one of the same kind of quality, character, etc □ *gelding* □ *whiting*. Also used formerly as a diminutive, etc (compare -LING) □ *farthing*. ⓒ Anglo-Saxon.

ingenious /ɪn'dʒiːnɪəs/ ▻ *adj* marked by, showing or having skill, originality and inventive cleverness □ *an ingenious plan*. • **ingeniously** *adverb*. • **ingeniousness** *noun* (see also INGENUITY). ⓒ 15c: from Latin *ingenium* common sense or cleverness.

ingénue / *French* ɛ̃ʒeny/ ▻ *noun* (***ingénues***) **1** a naïve and unsophisticated young woman. **2** an actress playing the role of an ingénue. ⓒ 19c: French feminine of *ingénu* ingenuous.

ingenuity /ɪndʒə'njuːɪtɪ/ ▻ *noun* inventive cleverness, skill or originality; ingeniousness. ⓒ 16c in obsolete sense 'ingenuousness' (from Latin *ingenuitas*); the current meaning (influenced by INGENIOUS) dates from the 17c.

ingenuous /ɪn'dʒɛnjʊəs/ ▻ *adj* innocent and childlike, especially in being frank, honest and incapable of deception. • **ingenuously** *adverb*. • **ingenuousness** *noun*. ⓒ 16c: from Latin *ingenuus* native or freeborn.

ingest /ɪn'dʒɛst/ ▻ *verb* (***ingested, ingesting***) *technical* to take (eg food or liquid) into the body. Compare DIGEST. • **ingestible** *adj*. • **ingestion** *noun*. ⓒ 17c: from Latin *ingerere, ingestum* to carry something in.

inglenook /'ɪŋgəlnʊk/ ▻ *noun* a corner or alcove in a large open fireplace. ⓒ 18c: from Scottish Gaelic *aingeal* fire + NOOK.

inglorious ▻ *adj* **1** bringing shame. **2** *chiefly old use* ordinary; not glorious or noble. • **ingloriously** *adverb*. • **ingloriousness** *noun*. ⓒ 16c.

ingoing ▻ *adj* going in; entering □ *ingoing vehicles*.

ingot /'ɪŋgət, -gɒt/ ▻ *noun* a brick-shaped block of metal, especially one of gold or silver. ⓒ 14c, meaning 'a mould for casting metal in'.

ingraft see ENGRAFT

ingrain /ɪn'greɪn/ ▻ *verb* (***ingrained, ingraining***) **1** to dye something in a lasting colour. **2** to fix (a dye) firmly in. **3** to firmly instil (a habit or attitude). ⓒ 18c.

ingrained /ɪŋ'greɪnd/ ▻ *adj* **1** difficult to remove or wipe off or out. **2** fixed firmly; instilled or rooted deeply. • **ingrainedly** /-'greɪndlɪ, -'greɪnɪdlɪ/ *adverb*. • **ingrainedness** *noun*. ⓒ 16c: from the phrase *in grain* or *dyed in grain* thorough, indelible, dyed in the yarn or thread (before manufacture).

ingrate /'ɪŋgreɪt/ *formal or old use* ▻ *noun* an ungrateful person. ▻ *adj* ungrateful. ⓒ 14c: from Latin *ingratus* ungrateful or unkind.

ingratiate /ɪŋ'greɪʃɪeɪt/ ▻ *verb* (***ingratiated, ingratiating***) (*especially* **ingratiate oneself with someone**) to gain or try to gain their favour or approval. ⓒ 17c: from Italian *ingratiarsi*.

ingratiating ▻ *adj* trying to gain favour. • **ingratiatingly** *adverb*.

ingratitude ▻ *noun* lack of due gratitude. ⓒ 14c: from Latin *ingratitudo*.

ingredient /ɪŋ'griːdɪənt/ ▻ *noun* a component of a mixture or compound, especially one added to a mixture in cooking. ⓒ 15c: from Latin *ingrediens* going into, from *gradi* to step.

ingress /'ɪŋgrɛs/ ▻ *noun* (***ingresses***) *formal* **1** the act of going in or entering. **2** the power or right to go in or enter somewhere or something. Opposite of EGRESS. • **ingression** *noun*. ⓒ 16c: from Latin *ingredior, ingressus* to go in.

ingrowing ▻ *adj* **1** growing inwards, in or into something. **2** said especially of a toenail: growing abnormally so that it becomes embedded in the flesh. • **ingrown** *adj*.

inguinal /'ɪŋgwɪnəl/ ▻ *adj, medicine, anatomy* belonging or relating to, or situated in the area of, the groin □ *an inguinal hernia*. ⓒ 17c: from Latin *inguinalis*.

inhabit /ɪn'habɪt/ ▻ *verb* (***inhabited, inhabiting***) to live in or occupy (a place). • **inhabitable** *adj* HABITABLE. • **inhabitant** *noun* a person or animal that lives permanently in a place. See also RESIDENT. • **inhabitation** *noun*. ⓒ 14c: from Latin *inhabitare* to live in.

inhabitance ▻ *noun* **1** a dwelling place. **2** (*also* **inhabitancy**) a period of residence.

inhalant /ɪn'heɪlənt/ ▻ *noun* a medicinal preparation, especially a drug in the form of a gas, vapour or aerosol, inhaled via the nose for its therapeutic effect, especially in the treatment of respiratory disorders. ▻ *adj* **1** inhaling; drawing in. **2** said of a medicinal preparation: inhaled via the nose in order to relieve congestion, treat a respiratory disorder, etc.

inhale /ɪn'heɪl/ ▻ *verb* (***inhaled, inhaling***) to draw (air or other substances, eg tobacco smoke) into the lungs; to breathe in □ *smoked pot but didn't inhale*. Compare EXHALE. • **inhalation** /ɪnhə'leɪʃən/ *noun*. ⓒ 18c: from Latin *inhalare*, from *halare* to breathe out.

inhaler ▻ *noun* **1** *medicine* a small, portable device used for inhaling certain medicinal preparations, eg in the treatment of asthma. See also NEBULIZER. **2** someone who inhales, especially a smoker who fully inhales tobacco smoke. **3** a respirator or gas mask.

inharmonious ▻ *adj* **1** not sounding well together. **2** not agreeing or going well together; not compatible. • **inharmoniously** *adverb*. • **inharmoniousness** *noun*. ⓒ 18c: see HARMONY.

inhere /ɪn'hɪə(r)/ ▻ *verb* (***inhered, inhering***) *formal* or *technical, intr* said of character, a quality, etc: to be an essential or permanent part of it or them. ⓒ 16c: from Latin *inhaerere* to stick in.

inherent /ɪn'hɪərənt/ ▻ *adj* said of a quality, etc: existing as an essential, natural or permanent part. • **inherently** *adverb*. ⓒ 16c: see INHERE.

inherit /ɪn'hɛrɪt/ ▻ *verb* (***inherited, inheriting***) **1** to receive (money, property, a title, position, etc) after someone's death or through legal descent from a predecessor; to succeed to something. **2** to receive (genetically transmitted characteristics, eg eye colour) from the previous generation. **3** *colloq* to receive something secondhand from someone. • **inheritable** *adj* **1** capable of being passed by heredity from one generation to another. **2** capable of being inherited. •

inheritor *noun*. ⓘ 14c: from French *enheriter*, from Latin *inhereditare*.

inheritance ▷ *noun* **1** something (eg money, property, a title, a physical or mental characteristic) that is or may be inherited. **2** the legal right to inherit something. **3** HEREDITY. **4** the act of inheriting.

inheritance tax ▷ *noun* in the UK: a tax levied on a bequest over a certain amount (other than one to a charity or spouse), or on a taxable gift made within the seven years prior to the death of the donor, which replaced CAPITAL TRANSFER TAX in 1986.

inhibit /ɪn'hɪbɪt/ ▷ *verb* (***inhibited, inhibiting***) **1** to make someone feel nervous or frightened about acting freely or spontaneously, eg by causing them to doubt their abilities. **2** to hold back, restrain or prevent (an action, desire, progress, etc). **3** to prohibit or forbid someone from doing something. **4** *chem* to decrease the rate of (a chemical reaction), or to stop it altogether, by means of an INHIBITOR (sense 1). • **inhibitive** *adj.* • **inhibitory** *adj.* ⓘ 15c in sense 3: from Latin *inhibere, inhibitum* to keep back.

inhibited ▷ *adj* said of a person or their disposition, actions, thinking, etc: restrained; held in check. • **inhibitedly** *adverb*.

inhibition /ɪnhɪ'bɪʃən/ ▷ *noun* **1** a feeling of fear or embarrassment, caused by emotional or psychological factors which prevents one from acting, thinking, etc freely or spontaneously in some way □ *sexual inhibitions*. **2** an act of inhibiting or process of being inhibited. **3** something which inhibits, prevents progress, holds back or forbids, etc. **4** *chem* a decrease in the rate of a chemical reaction, or of a biochemical reaction in living cells, brought about by an INHIBITOR (sense 1).

inhibitor or **inhibiter** ▷ *noun* **1** *chem* a substance that interferes with a chemical or biological process. **2** something that inhibits.

inhospitable ▷ *adj* **1** said of a person: not friendly or welcoming to others, especially in not offering them food, drink, and other home comforts. **2** said of a place: offering little shelter, eg from harsh weather; bleak or barren. • **inhospitably** *adverb*. ⓘ 16c.

in-house ▷ *adverb, adj* within a particular company, organization, etc, as opposed to outside or separate from it □ *The work was done by two in-house editors and one freelance.*

inhuman ▷ *adj* **1** without human feeling; cruel and unfeeling; brutal. **2** said of eg an intelligence or form: not human. • **inhumanly** *adverb*. ⓘ 15c.

inhuman, inhumane

Inhuman and **inhumane** overlap in meaning to such an extent that it is impossible to sustain a distinction in their use. In general, **inhuman** refers to the characteristic of a person or action, whereas **inhumane** considers the same characteristic rather more in relation to the effect or consequences of the action on the sufferer.

inhumane ▷ *adj* showing no kindness, sympathy or compassion; cruel; unfeeling. • **inhumanely** *adverb*. ⓘ 16c.

inhumanity ▷ *noun* (***inhumanities***) **1** brutality; cruelty; lack of feeling or pity. **2** an action that is inhuman, inhumane, cruel, etc.

inimical /ɪn'ɪmɪkəl/ ▷ *adj, formal* **1** tending to discourage; unfavourable. **2** not friendly; hostile or in opposition. • **inimically** *adverb*. ⓘ 17c: from Latin *inimicalis*, from *inimicus* enemy.

inimitable /ɪn'ɪmɪtəbəl/ ▷ *adj* too good, skilful, etc to be satisfactorily imitated by others; unique. • **inimitability** or **inimitableness** *noun*. • **inimitably** *adverb*. ⓘ 16c.

iniquitous /ɪ'nɪkwətəs/ ▷ *adj* **1** grossly unjust or unreasonable. **2** wicked. • **iniquitously** *adverb*. ⓘ 18c: see INIQUITY.

iniquity /ɪ'nɪkwɪtɪ/ ▷ *noun* (***iniquities***) **1** an unfair, unjust, wicked or sinful act. **2** wickedness; sinfulness □ *That club is just a den of iniquity.* ⓘ 14c: from Latin *iniquitas*.

initial /ɪ'nɪʃəl/ ▷ *adj* belonging or relating to, or at, the beginning □ *in the initial phase of the project* □ *My initial reaction was anger.* ▷ *noun* the first letter of a word, especially the first letter of a personal or proper name □ *Write your initials at the bottom.* ▷ *verb* (***initialled, initialling***; (*N Amer*) ***initialed, initialing***) to mark or sign something with the initials of one's name, especially as a sign of approval □ *He hasn't initialled this memo.* ⓘ 16c: from Latin *initialis*, from *initium* a beginning.

initialism ▷ *noun* **1** *Brit* a set of initial, usually capital, letters used as an abbreviation, especially of an organization, where each letter is given its own separate pronunciation, eg 'BBC' for British Broadcasting Corporation or 'FBI' for Federal Bureau of Investigation. **2** *US* an ACRONYM.

initialize or **initialise** ▷ *verb* (***initialized, initializing***) *computing* **1** to assign initial values to (variables, eg in a computer program). **2** to return (a device, eg a computer or printer) to its initial state.

initially ▷ *adverb* **1** at first □ *I had some doubts initially.* **2** as a beginning □ *We plan initially to draw up a proposal.*

Initial Teaching Alphabet ▷ *noun* (abbreviation **i.t.a.** or **ITA**) an alphabet of 44 characters that was developed for teaching reading and writing. Each character corresponds to a single sound (or PHONEME) in English. ⓘ 1960s: devised in 1959 by James Pitman (1901–85).

initiate ▷ *verb* /ɪ'nɪʃɪeɪt/ (***initiated, initiating***) **1** to make something begin (eg a relationship, project, conversation, etc). **2** (*usually* **initiate someone into something**) to accept (a new member) into a society, organization, etc, especially with secret ceremonies. **3** (*usually* **initiate someone in something**) to give them instruction in the basics or rudiments of a skill, science, etc. ▷ *noun* /ɪ'nɪʃɪət/ someone who has recently been or is soon to be initiated. ▷ *adj* /ɪ'nɪʃɪət/ having been recently initiated or soon to be initiated. ⓘ 17c: from Latin *initiare* to begin.

initiation ▷ *noun* **1** the act or process of initiating or being initiated. **2** the formal introduction of a new member into an organization or society, etc.

initiation rites ▷ *plural noun, anthropol* ceremonies that bring about or mark a transition from one social condition or role to another, especially the transition from childhood to adulthood. See also RITE OF PASSAGE.

initiative /ɪ'nɪʃətɪv, -ʃɪətɪv/ ▷ *noun* **1** the ability or skill to initiate things, take decisions or act resourcefully. **2** (*especially in* **take the initiative**) a first step or move towards an end or aim. **3** (*especially* **the initiative**) the right or power to begin something. **4** the right of voters, eg in Switzerland and certain US states, to originate legislation. ▷ *adj* serving to begin; introductory. • **on one's own initiative** as a result of one's own action; without needing to be prompted by others. ⓘ 17c.

initiator ▷ *noun* **1** someone who initiates. **2** *chem* a substance which starts a chain reaction. **3** a highly sensitive explosive used in a detonator.

inject /ɪn'dʒɛkt/ ▷ *verb* (***injected, injecting***) **1** to introduce (a liquid, eg medicine) into the body of a person or animal using a hypodermic syringe □ *was injected as a local anaesthetic.* **2** to force (fuel) into an engine, eg of a motor vehicle. **3** to introduce (a quality, element, etc) □ *inject a note of optimism.* • **injectable** *adj.* ⓘ 17c: from Latin *injicere, injectum* to throw in.

injection /ɪn'dʒɛkʃən/ ▷ *noun* **1 a** the act or process of introducing a liquid, eg medicine into the body with a hypodermic syringe; **b** the liquid that is used for this. **2 a** the process of spraying vaporized liquid fuel under pressure directly into the cylinder of an internal-combustion engine, so dispensing with the need for a carburettor; **b** *as adj* □ ***injection pump***. See also FUEL INJECTION. **3** *geol* the magma injected under pressure into a crack, cleft or fissure in an existing rock.

injection moulding ▷ *noun, engineering* in the manufacture of plastics: a process in which plastic is heated until it is soft enough to inject through a nozzle into a mould in the shape of the desired article.

in-joke ▷ *noun* a joke that can only be appreciated fully by members of a particular group.

injudicious ▷ *adj* not wise; showing poor judgement or lack of perception. • **injudiciously** *adverb*. • **injudiciousness** *noun*. ◷ 17c: see JUDICIOUS.

injunction /ɪnˈdʒʌŋkʃən/ ▷ *noun* **1** *law* an official court order that forbids something or commands that something should be done □ ***Mick took out an injunction to prevent Jenny from harassing him.*** Also called (*Scots law*) **interdict**. **2** any authoritative order or warning. **3** the act of commanding or enjoining. • **injunctive** *adj* serving to command or enjoin. ◷ 16c: from Latin *injungere* to enjoin.

injure /ˈɪndʒə(r)/ ▷ *verb* (***injured***, ***injuring***) **1** to do physical harm or damage to someone □ ***injured his knee when he fell off his bike.*** **2** to harm, spoil or weaken something □ ***His pride was injured.*** **3** to do an injustice or wrong to someone. ◷ 16c: back-formation from INJURY.

injurious /ɪnˈdʒʊərɪəs/ ▷ *adj* causing injury or damage; harmful. • **injuriously** *adverb*. • **injuriousness** *noun*.

injury /ˈɪndʒərɪ/ ▷ *noun* (***injuries***) **1 a** physical harm or damage □ ***Did the passengers suffer any injury?*** **b** an instance of this □ ***did herself an injury playing squash.*** **2** a wound □ ***has a serious head injury.*** **3** something that harms, spoils or hurts something □ ***a cruel injury to her feelings.*** **4** *now chiefly law* a wrong or injustice. ◷ 14c: from Latin *injuria* a wrong, from *jus* right.

injury time ▷ *noun, sport, chiefly football & rugby* playing time that is added on to the end of each half of a match to make up for time taken to treat injured players during the match.

injustice ▷ *noun* **1** unfairness or lack of justice. **2** an unfair or unjust act. • **do someone an injustice** to judge them unfairly. ◷ 14c.

ink /ɪŋk/ ▷ *noun* **1** a liquid, or sometimes a paste or powder, consisting of a PIGMENT or a DYE, used for writing, drawing or printing on paper and other materials. See also INDIAN INK. **2** *biol* a dark liquid ejected by certain CEPHALOPODS, such as octopus and squid, to confuse predators by decreasing visibility. ▷ *verb* (***inked***, ***inking***) **1** to mark something with ink. **2** to cover (a surface to be printed) with ink. ◷ 13c: from French *enque*, from Latin *encaustum* a purplish-red ink used by Roman emperors.

■ **ink something in** to write it in over a rough design or draft in pencil, using ink.

Inkatha /ɪnˈkɑːtə/ ▷ *noun* (*in full* **Inkatha Freedom Party** (abbreviation **IFP**)) a S African Zulu cultural and political movement, originally a paramilitary organization, which, before the end of apartheid, sought a multiracial democracy and liberation from white minority rule. ◷ 20c: from the Zulu word for a plaited grass coil used for carrying loads on the head.

inkblot test see RORSCHACH TEST

ink-cap ▷ *noun* a mushroom-like fungus which produces a black, ink-like fluid when the gills (see GILL[1] sense 2) on its cap liquefy after the SPOREs mature.

inkier, **inkiest** and **inkiness** see under INKY

inkjet printer ▷ *noun, computing* a printer which produces characters on paper by spraying a fine jet of ink which is vibrated, electrically charged and deflected by electrostatic fields. Compare DOT MATRIX PRINTER, LASER PRINTER.

inkling /ˈɪŋklɪŋ/ ▷ *noun* a hint; a vague or slight idea or suspicion. ◷ 15c: from obsolete *inkle* to utter in a whisper.

inkpad ▷ *noun* a pad of inked cloth inside a box, used for putting ink on rubber stamps.

inkstand ▷ *noun* a small rack for ink bottles and pens on a desk.

inkwell ▷ *noun* a small container for ink, especially one which fits into a hole in a desk.

inky ▷ *adj* (***inkier***, ***inkiest***) **1** covered with ink. **2** like ink, especially in being black or very dark. • **inkiness** *noun*.

INLA ▷ *abbreviation* Irish National Liberation Army.

inlaid ▷ *adj* **1** said of a design, etc: set into a surface. **2** said of an object: having a design set into its surface □ ***a table inlaid with mother-of-pearl.*** ◷ 16c: past participle of INLAY.

inland ▷ *adj* **1** belonging or relating to, or in, that part of a country which is not beside the sea □ ***inland waterways.*** **2** *especially Brit* done, operating, etc inside one country and not abroad; domestic. ▷ *noun* that part of a country that is not beside the sea. ▷ *adverb* in or towards the inner regions of a country away from the sea □ ***travelling inland.*** See also LANDWARD. ◷ Anglo-Saxon.

Inland Revenue ▷ *noun, Brit* the government department responsible for assessing and collecting taxes. *US equivalent* IRS.

in-laws /ˈɪnlɔːz/ ▷ *plural noun, colloq* relatives by marriage, especially someone's mother- and father-in-law. ◷ 19c.

inlay ▷ *verb* (***inlaid***, ***inlaying***) **1** to set or embed (eg pieces of wood, metal, etc) in another material in such a way that the surfaces are flat. **2** to decorate (eg a piece of furniture) by setting flat pieces of different coloured wood, ivory, metal, etc in the surface. ▷ *noun* (***inlays***) **1** a decoration or design made by inlaying. Compare MARQUETRY. **2** the pieces used to create an inlaid design. **3** *dentistry* a filling shaped to fit a cavity in a tooth. ◷ 16c: see LAY[1].

inlaying ▷ *noun* a method of decorating furniture and other wooden objects by cutting away part of the surface of the solid material and replacing it with a thin sheet of wood in another colour or texture, or occasionally a sliver of ivory, bone, shell, etc.

inlet /ˈɪnlət/ ▷ *noun* **1** *geog* a narrow arm of water running inland from a sea coast or lake shore, or forming a passage between two islands. See also FJORD. **2** a narrow opening or valve through which a substance, especially a fluid such as air or fuel, enters the cylinder of an engine, pump, compressor or other device. Opposite of OUTLET. **3** *dressmaking* an extra piece of material sewn into a garment to make it larger. ◷ 13c: meaning 'letting in'.

in loco parentis /ɪn ˈloʊkoʊ pəˈrɛntɪs/ ▷ *adverb* said of those responsible for children: in the role or position of a parent. ◷ 19c: Latin, literally 'in the place of a parent'.

inmate ▷ *noun* any of the people living in or confined to an institution, especially a prison or a hospital. ◷ 16c, originally meaning a person living in the same house as others.

in medias res /ɪnˈmiːdɪəs reɪz/ ▷ *adverb* in the middle of the story; without any kind of introduction. ◷ 18c: Latin, meaning 'into the middle of things'.

in memoriam /ɪn məˈmɔːrɪam/ ▷ *preposition* on gravestones or in obituaries, epitaphs, etc: in memory of (the specified person). ◷ 19c: Latin.

inmost ▷ *adj* INNERMOST. ◷ Anglo-Saxon as *innemest*.

inn ▷ *noun, especially Brit* a PUBLIC HOUSE or small hotel providing food and accommodation, especially (*formerly*) one for travellers. ◷ 15c; Anglo-Saxon in obsolete sense 'a dwelling'.

innards /ˈɪnədz/ ▷ *plural noun, colloq* **1** the inner organs of a person or animal, especially the stomach and intestines. **2** the inner workings of a machine. ◎ 19c: a dialect variant of INWARDS.

innate /ɪˈneɪt/ ▷ *adj* **1** belonging to or existing from birth; inherent. **2** natural or instinctive, rather than learnt or acquired. • **innately** *adverb*. • **innateness** *noun*. ◎ 15c: from Latin *innatus* inborn.

inner /ˈɪnə(r)/ ▷ *adj* **1** further in; situated inside, close or closer to the centre ▫ *built with an inner courtyard* ▫ *one of his inner circle of friends*. **2** said of thoughts, feelings, etc: secret, hidden and profound, or more secret, profound, etc ▫ *look for the inner meaning*. ◎ Anglo-Saxon *innera*.

inner city ▷ *noun* the central area of a city, referring especially to one that is densely populated and very poor, with bad housing, roads, etc. Also *as adj* ▫ *inner-city housing*.

inner ear ▷ *noun, anatomy* in vertebrates: the innermost part of the ear, located in a bony cavity in the skull, containing the COCHLEA and the SEMICIRCULAR CANAL. Compare MIDDLE EAR.

inner man and **inner woman** ▷ *noun* **1** the mind or soul. **2** *humorous* the stomach.

innermost and **inmost** ▷ *adj* **1** furthest within; closest to the centre. **2** most secret or hidden ▫ *my innermost thoughts*. ◎ 15c.

inner tube ▷ *noun* an inflatable rubber tube inside a tyre.

inning /ˈɪnɪŋ/ ▷ *noun, N Amer* in a baseball or softball game: any one of the nine divisions per game in which each team has an opportunity to bat. See also INNINGS.

innings ▷ *noun* **1** *cricket* **a** a team's or a player's turn at batting; **b** the runs scored during such a turn; **c** the quality of batting during it. **2** *Brit* a period during which someone has an opportunity for action or achievement. • **have had a good innings** *colloq* to have lived a long and eventful life. See also INNING. ◎ 18c; Anglo-Saxon as *innung*, meaning 'contents', ie what is put in.

innkeeper ▷ *noun, old use* someone who owns or manages an INN. See also LANDLORD, LANDLADY, PUBLICAN.

innocent /ˈɪnəsənt/ ▷ *adj* **1** free from sin; pure. **2** not guilty, eg of a crime. Compare GUILTY 1, NOT PROVEN. **3** not intending to cause harm, or not causing it; inoffensive ▫ *an innocent remark*. **4** simple and trusting; guileless; artless. **5** lacking, free or deprived of something ▫ *innocent of all knowledge of the event*. **6** *medicine* said of a tumour, etc: not malignant or cancerous; benign. ▷ *noun* an innocent person, especially a young child or simple and trusting adult. • **innocence** *noun*. • **innocently** *adverb*. ◎ 14c: French, from Latin *innocens*, from *nocere* to hurt harmless.

innocuous /ɪˈnɒkjʊəs/ ▷ *adj* harmless; inoffensive. • **innocuously** *adverb*. • **innocuousness** *noun*. ◎ 16c: from Latin *innocuus*, from *nocere* to hurt.

Inn of Court ▷ *noun, Brit law* **1** any of the four voluntary, unincorporated societies in London, or the one in Belfast, with the exclusive right to 'call lawyers to the bar' (see BAR[1] *noun* 10) in England, Wales and N Ireland. See also BENCHER. **2** any of the sets of buildings that these societies occupy. ◎ 14c, referring to any of the four Inns in London (*Middle Temple, Inner Temple, Lincoln's Inn*, and *Gray's Inn*); the Inn of Court in Belfast dates from 1926.

innominate bone /ɪˈnɒmɪnət —/ ▷ *noun, anatomy, etc* either of the two bones which form each side of the pelvis, being a fusion of the ISCHIUM, ILIUM and PUBIS. Also called **hip bone**. ◎ 18c: from Latin *innominatus* unnamed.

innovate /ˈɪnəveɪt/ ▷ *verb* (***innovated***, ***innovating***) *intr* to make changes; to introduce new ideas, methods, etc. • **innovative** /-veɪtɪv, -vətɪv/ or **innovatory** /-veɪtərɪ, -vətərɪ/ *adj*. • **innovator** *noun*. ◎ 16c: from Latin *innovare, innovatum* to renew.

innovation ▷ *noun* **1** something new which is introduced, eg a new idea or method. **2** an act of innovating. • **innovational** *adj*. • **innovationist** *noun*.

innuendo /ɪnjʊˈɛndoʊ/ ▷ *noun* (***innuendos*** or ***innuendoes***) **1 a** a remark that indirectly conveys some unpleasant, critical or spiteful meaning, etc, especially about someone's reputation or character; **b** an oblique allusion, suggestion or insinuation, often of a rude or smutty nature. **2** the act or practice of making such remarks. ◎ 17c in these senses; 16c as a legal term meaning 'that is to say' or 'indicating': Latin, meaning 'by nodding at'.

Innuit see INUIT

innumerable /ɪˈnjuːmərəbəl/ ▷ *adj* too many to be counted; a great many. • **innumerability** or **innumerableness** *noun*. • **innumerably** *adverb*. ◎ 14c: from Latin *innumerabilis*.

innumerate /ɪˈnjuːmərət/ ▷ *adj* having no knowledge or understanding of mathematics or science. • **innumeracy** *noun*. ◎ 1950s: modelled on ILLITERATE.

inoculate /ɪˈnɒkjʊleɪt/ ▷ *verb* (***inoculated***, ***inoculating***) **1** *medicine* to produce a mild form of a particular infectious disease in (a person or animal), and thereby create IMMUNITY by injecting a harmless form of an ANTIGEN which stimulates the body to produce its own antibodies ▫ *They were inoculated against smallpox*. Compare IMMUNIZE, VACCINATE. **2** *biol, etc* to introduce a micro-organism, eg a bacterium or virus, into (a sterile medium) in order to start a CULTURE, or into another organism, eg a rabbit, in order to produce ANTIBODIES to that micro-organism. **3** *literary or old use* to imbue or instil someone, eg with ideas or feelings. • **inoculation** *noun*. • **inoculative** /ɪˈnɒkjʊlətɪv, -leɪtɪv/ *adj*. • **inoculator** *noun*. ◎ 15c: from Latin *inoculare* to implant.

in-off ▷ *noun* in snooker: **1** the act of striking the cue ball in such a way that it goes into the pocket after contacting the OBJECT BALL, which counts as a foul shot. **2** a shot in which this happens. • **go in-off** to pocket the cue ball after hitting the object ball.

inoffensive ▷ *adj* harmless; not objectionable or provocative. • **inoffensively** *adverb*. • **inoffensiveness** *noun*. ◎ 16c.

inoperable ▷ *adj* **1** *medicine* said of a disease or condition: not able to be removed by surgery or operated on successfully. **2** said of a plan, idea, etc: not workable. • **inoperability** /-əˈbɪlɪtɪ/ or **inoperableness** *noun*. • **inoperably** *adverb*. ◎ 19c.

inoperative ▷ *adj* **1** said of a machine, etc: not working or functioning. **2** said of rule, etc: having no effect. ◎ 17c.

inopportune ▷ *adj* not suitable or convenient; badly-timed ▫ *We arrived at an inopportune moment*. • **inopportunely** *adverb*. • **inopportuneness** *noun* ◎ 16c: from Latin *inopportunus*.

inordinate /ɪnˈɔːdɪnət/ ▷ *adj* greater than is reasonable; beyond acceptable limits; excessive ▫ *It took an inordinate amount of time*. • **inordinately** *adverb*. • **inordinateness** *noun*. ◎ 14c: from Latin *inordinatus* disorderly or unrestrained.

inorganic ▷ *adj* **1** not composed of material that has or formerly had the structure and characteristics of living organisms. **2** not caused by natural growth. **3** not produced or developed naturally. **4** *chem* belonging or relating to compounds which do not contain chains or rings of carbon atoms. • **inorganically** *adverb*. ◎ 18c.

inorganic chemistry ▷ *noun* the branch of chemistry concerned with the properties and reactions of the elements, and of compounds (mainly of mineral origin) that do not contain chains or rings of carbon atoms, therefore including only the simpler carbon compounds. Compare ORGANIC CHEMISTRY.

inorganic fertilizer ▷ *noun, agric* a fertilizer containing a mixture of chemical compounds that are added to the soil in order to improve its fertility, but which can be harmful to the environment if used in large amounts.

inpatient ▷ *noun* a patient temporarily living in hospital while receiving treatment there. Compare OUTPATIENT. Also *as adj* □ *inpatient treatment.*

in personam /ɪn pə'soʊnam/ ▷ *adj, law* said of a proceeding or action, etc: taken or instituted against a specific person or organization. Compare IN REM. Also *as adverb*. ⓒ 19c: Latin, meaning 'against the person'.

input ▷ *noun* **1** *computing* the data that is transferred from a disk, tape or INPUT DEVICE into the main memory of a computer. **2** something which is put or taken in, eg a contribution to a discussion □ *Your input would be valuable at the meeting.* **3** the money, power, materials, labour, etc required to produce something, especially the power or electrical current put into a machine. **4** an act or process of putting something in. Also *as adj*. ▷ *verb* to transfer (data) from a disk, tape or input device into the main memory of a computer. Compare OUTPUT. ● **inputter** *noun*. ⓒ 18c, meaning 'a contribution', ie a sum of money put in; 14c as *verb*, meaning 'to impose'.

input device ▷ *noun, computing* any piece of equipment used to transfer data into memory, such as a KEYBOARD, MOUSE or LIGHT PEN.

input-output analysis ▷ *noun, econ* an analysis which demonstrates how materials and goods flow between industries, and identifies where additional value is created.

input/output system ▷ *noun* (abbreviation **I/O system**) *computing* the software and hardware involved in the flow of data into and out of a computer.

inquest /'ɪŋkwɛst, 'ɪn-/ ▷ *noun* **1** an official investigation into an incident, especially an inquiry into a sudden and unexpected death, held in a CORONER's court before a jury. **2** *colloq, especially facetious* any discussion after an event, game, etc, especially one which analyses the result and discusses mistakes made. ⓒ 13c: from French *enqueste*, from Latin *inquirere* to inquire.

inquietude /ɪŋ'kwaɪətʃuːd, ɪn-/ ▷ *noun, formal or literary* physical or mental restlessness or uneasiness. ⓒ 15c: from Latin *inquietudo*.

inquire or **enquire** /ɪŋ'kwaɪə(r), ɪn-/ ▷ *verb* (***inquired, inquiring***) *tr & intr* to seek or ask for information □ *I inquired how long it would take* □ *Go and inquire at the desk* ● **inquirer** *noun* someone who inquires; an investigator or questioner. ⓒ 13c: from Latin *inquirere, inquisitum*.

■ **inquire after someone** to ask about their health or happiness.

■ **inquire into something** to try to discover the facts of (a crime, etc) especially formally.

inquire, enquire

Inquire and **enquire** are to a great extent interchangeable variants. **Inquire** is used more than **enquire**, especially in formal writing such as reports, with reference to formal or systematic investigating. The distinction is more apparent in the nouns **enquiry** and **inquiry**.

inquiring or **enquiring** ▷ *adj* **1** eager to discover or learn things □ *He has an inquiring mind.* **2** said especially of a look: appearing to be asking a question. ● **inquiringly** *adverb*.

inquiry or **enquiry** /ɪŋ'kwaɪərɪ, ɪn-; *chiefly N Amer* 'ɪŋkwɪrɪ/ ▷ *noun* (***inquiries***) **1** an act or the process of asking for information. **2** (*often* **an inquiry into something**) an investigation, especially a formal one.

inquiry, enquiry

Inquiry and **enquiry** are interchangeable variants in the more general sense 1. **Inquiry** and not **enquiry** is used in the more formal and specific sense 2.

inquisition /ɪŋkwɪ'zɪʃən, ɪn-/ ▷ *noun* **1** a searching or intensive inquiry or investigation. **2** an official or judicial inquiry. **3** (**the Inquisition**) *historical* in the RC Church between the 13c and 19c: a papal tribunal responsible for discovering, suppressing and punishing heresy and unbelief, etc. ● **inquisitional** *adj* relating to or in the nature of inquiry or the Inquisition. ⓒ 14c: French, from Latin *inquisitio*.

inquisitive /ɪŋ'kwɪzɪtɪv, ɪn-/ ▷ *adj* **1** *rather derog* over-eager to find out things, especially about other people's affairs. **2** eager for knowledge or information; curious. ● **inquisitively** *adverb*. ● **inquisitiveness** *noun*. ⓒ 15c: from Latin *inquisitivus*; see INQUIRE.

inquisitor /ɪŋ'kwɪzɪtə(r), ɪn-/ ▷ *noun* **1** *usually derog* someone who carries out an inquisition or inquiry, especially harshly or intensively. **2** (*usually* **Inquisitor**) *historical* a member of the Inquisition tribunal or often specifically the Spanish Inquisition. ⓒ 16c: Latin; see INQUIRE.

inquisitorial /ɪŋkwɪzɪ'tɔːrɪəl, ɪn-/ ▷ *adj* **1** belonging or relating to, or like, an inquisitor or inquisition. **2** *derog* unnecessarily or offensively curious about other people's affairs. **3** *law* **a** said of a trial or legal system: having a judge who is also the prosecutor; **b** said of a trial or legal procedure: held in secret. Compare ACCUSATORIAL. ● **inquisitorially** *adverb*. ● **inquisitorialness** *noun*.

inquorate /ɪŋ'kwɔːrət, ɪn-/ ▷ *adj, formal* said of a meeting, etc: not making up a QUORUM.

in re /ɪn riː, ɪn reː/ ▷ *prep, formal, business, etc* in the matter of; about. ⓒ 17c: Latin, meaning 'in the matter'.

in rem /ɪn rɛm/ ▷ *adj, law* said of a proceeding or action, etc: taken or instituted against a thing, eg a property or right, rather than against a person. Compare IN PERSONAM. Also *as adverb*. ⓒ 19c: Latin, meaning 'against the thing'.

INRI ▷ *abbreviation Iesus Nazarenus Rex Iudaeorum* (Latin), Jesus of Nazareth, King of the Jews.

inro /'ɪnroʊ/ ▷ *noun* (*plural* ***inro***) *antiq* a small set of decorative, usually lacquer, nested containers for pills, ink, seals, etc, once hung from the OBI by a silk cord, as part of traditional Japanese dress. See also NETSUKE. ⓒ 17c: Japanese, meaning 'seal-box'.

inroad ▷ *noun* **1** (*usually* **inroads into something**) a large or significant using up or consumption of it, or encroachment on it □ *This will make inroads into my savings.* **2** a hostile attack or raid. ⓒ 16c.

inrush ▷ *noun* a sudden crowding or rushing in; an influx. ● **inrushing** *adj, noun*.

INS ▷ *abbreviation, US* Immigration and Naturalization Service.

ins. ▷ *abbreviation* **1** (or **in.**) inches. **2** insurance.

insalubrious ▷ *adj* usually said of a place or conditions: unhealthy; sordid. ● **insalubriously** *adverb*. ● **insalubrity** *noun*. ⓒ 17c: from Latin *insalubris*.

ins and outs see under IN

insane ▷ *adj* (***insaner, insanest***) **1** said of a person: not of sound mind; mentally ill. **2** *colloq* said especially of actions: extremely foolish; stupid. **3** belonging or relating to, or for, the mentally ill □ *an insane asylum.* **4** (**the insane**) insane people as a group (see THE 4b). ● **insanely** *adverb*. ⓒ 16c: from Latin *insanus*.

insanitary ▷ *adj* so dirty as to be dangerous to health. ● **insanitariness** *noun*. ⓒ 16c.

insanity ▷ *noun* (***insanities***) **1** the state of being insane. **2** extreme folly or stupidity, or an instance of this. **3** *law* the state or condition of having a mental illness so severe that the affected individual cannot be held responsible for their actions under law.

insatiable /ɪnˈseɪʃəbəl/ ▻ *adj* not able to be satisfied; extremely greedy □ ***an insatiable desire for power*** □ ***an insatiable appetite for trashy fiction.*** • **insatiability** *noun.* • **insatiably** *adverb.* ⓘ 15c: from Latin *insatiabilis.*

insatiety /ɪnsəˈtaɪətɪ/ *noun, rare* the state of not being satisfied, or of being incapable of being so. ⓘ 16c: from Latin *insatietas.*

inscribe /ɪnˈskraɪb/ ▻ *verb* (***inscribed, inscribing***) **1** to write, print or engrave (words) on (paper, metal, stone, etc), often as a lasting record. **2** to enter (a name) on a list or in a book; to enrol. **3** (*often* **inscribe something to someone**) to dedicate or address (a book, etc) to them, usually by writing in the front of it. **4** *geom* to draw (a figure) within another figure so as to touch all or some of its sides or faces. Compare CIRCUMSCRIBE. • **inscriber** *noun.* ⓘ 16c: from Latin *scribere* to write in.

inscription /ɪnˈskrɪpʃən/ ▻ *noun* **1** words written, printed or engraved, eg as a dedication in the front of a book or as an epitaph on a gravestone. **2** the act of inscribing, especially of writing a dedication in the front of a book or of entering a name on a list. • **inscriptional** or **inscriptive** *adj.* ⓘ 15c: from Latin *inscriptio.*

inscrutable /ɪnˈskruːtəbəl/ ▻ *adj* hard to understand or explain; mysterious; enigmatic. • **inscrutability** *noun.* • **inscrutably** *adverb.* ⓘ 15c: from Latin *inscrutabilis*, from *scrutare* to search thoroughly.

insect /ˈɪnsɛkt/ ▻ *noun* **1** *zool* an invertebrate animal, such as the fly, beetle, ant and bee, belonging to the class INSECTA, typically having a segmented body and two pairs of wings. See also ENTOMOLOGY. **2** *loosely* any other small invertebrate, eg a spider. **3** *derog* an insignificant or worthless person. ⓘ Early 17c: from Latin *insectum*, meaning 'cut' or 'notched' (animal), from *secare* to cut.

Insecta /ɪnˈsɛktə/ ▻ *plural noun, zool* in the animal kingdom: the largest and most diverse class of living organisms, containing more than a million identified species of insect; a division of the ARTHROPODS. ⓘ 17c: Latin plural of *insectum* insect.

insecticide /ɪnˈsɛktɪsaɪd/ ▻ *noun* any naturally occurring or artificially manufactured substance that is used to kill insects. • **insecticidal** *adj.* ⓘ 19c.

insectivore /ɪnˈsɛktɪvɔː(r)/ ▻ *noun* **1** a living organism that feeds mainly or exclusively on insects, eg the anteater. **2** *zool* an animal belonging to an order of small placental mammals (eg the mole and hedgehog) that feed mainly on insects. **3** a plant such as the Venus flytrap, sundew, etc, that supplements its supply of nitrogen by trapping and digesting insects. • **insectivorous** /ɪnsɛkˈtɪvərəs/ *adj.* ⓘ 19c: French, from Latin *insectivorus* insect-eating.

insecure ▻ *adj* **1** not firmly fixed; unstable. **2** said of a person or their disposition: lacking confidence; anxious about possible loss or danger. **3** under threat or in danger or likely to be so □ ***insecure jobs.*** • **insecurely** *adverb.* • **insecurity** *noun* (***insecurities***). ⓘ 17c: from Latin *insecurus.*

inselberg /ˈɪnzəlbɜːg, ˈɪnsəl-/ ▻ *noun* (***inselberge*** /-bɜːgə/) *geol* a steep-sided hill rising from a plain, often found in semi-arid regions of tropical countries. ⓘ Early 20c: German, meaning 'hill-island'.

inseminate /ɪnˈsɛmɪneɪt/ ▻ *verb* (***inseminated, inseminating***) **1** to introduce SEMEN into (a female) by a natural or artificial method. **2** *now rather formal or literary* to sow (seeds, ideas, attitudes, etc). • **insemination** *noun.* • **inseminator** *noun.* ⓘ 17c: from Latin *inseminare, inseminatum* to implant or impregnate.

insensate /ɪnˈsɛnseɪt, -sət/ ▻ *adj, formal or literary* **1** not able to perceive physical sensations or experience consciousness; inanimate. **2** insensitive and unfeeling. **3** having little or no good sense; stupid. • **insensately** *adverb.* • **insensateness** *noun.* ⓘ 16c.

insensible /ɪnˈsɛnsɪbəl/ ▻ *adj, formal or literary* **1** not able to feel pain or experience consciousness; unconscious. **2** (*usually* **insensible of** or **to something**) unaware of it; not caring about it. **3** not capable of feeling emotion; callous; indifferent. **4** too small or slight to be noticed; imperceptible. • **insensibility** *noun.* • **insensibly** *adverb.* ⓘ 14c.

insensitive ▻ *adj* **1** not aware of, or not capable of responding sympathetically or thoughtfully to something, eg other people's feelings, etc. **2** not feeling or reacting to (stimulation, eg touch or light). • **insensitively** *adverb.* • **insensitivity** *noun.* ⓘ 17c.

inseparable ▻ *adj* **1** incapable of being separated. **2** said of friends, siblings, etc: unwilling to be apart; constantly together. **3** *grammar* said of a prefix, etc: not able to be used as a separate word. • **inseparability** *noun.* • **inseparably** *adverb.* ⓘ 14c.

insert ▻ *verb* /ɪnˈsɜːt/ (***inserted, inserting***) **1** to put or fit something inside something else □ ***could not insert the key.*** **2** to introduce (text, words, etc) into the body of other text, words, etc □ ***inserted a whole new paragraph into my article.*** ▻ *noun* /ˈɪnsɜːt/ **1** something inserted, especially a loose sheet in a book or magazine, or piece of material in a garment. **2** (*in full* **insert mode**) *computing* a facility that allows characters to be added to a text as opposed to OVERWRITE which replaces existing characters. It is usual to be able to TOGGLE (*verb* 2b) between the two. • **inserter** *noun.* ⓘ 16c: from Latin *inserere, insertum.*

insertion /ɪnˈsɜːʃən/ ▻ *noun* **1** an act of inserting. **2** something inserted, especially a piece of lace or embroidery inserted in a garment, or an advertisement, leaflet, etc inserted in a newspaper. **3** *medicine* **a** the place where a muscle is attached to a bone; **b** the way in which it is attached. • **insertional** *adj.*

in-service ▻ *adj* carried on while a person is employed □ ***in-service training.***

INSET /ˈɪnsɛt/ ▻ *abbreviation, Brit, education* in-service training □ ***an INSET day.***

inset ▻ *noun* /ˈɪnsɛt/ **1** something set in or inserted, eg a piece of lace or cloth set into a garment, or a page or pages set into a book. **2** a small map or picture put in the corner of a larger one. ▻ *verb* /ɪnˈsɛt/ (***inset, insetting***) to put in, add or insert something. ⓘ Anglo-Saxon, meaning 'to institute'; 19c in current noun senses.

inshallah /ɪnˈʃɑːlɑː/ ▻ *exclamation, Islam* if Allah wills. ⓘ 19c: from Arabic *in sha'llah.*

inshore ▻ *adverb, adj* in or on the water, but near or towards the shore □ ***inshore shipping.*** Compare OFFSHORE.

inside ▻ *noun* **1** the inner side, surface or part of something. Opposite of OUTSIDE. **2** the side of a road nearest to the buildings, pavement, etc (as opposed to the other lane or lanes of traffic) □ ***tried to overtake on the inside.*** **3** the part of a pavement or path away from the road □ ***Children should walk on the inside.*** **4** *sport* **a** *athletics* the INSIDE TRACK; **b** the equivalent part of any racetrack. **5** (**insides**) *colloq* the inner organs, especially the stomach and bowels. **6** *colloq* a position which gains one the confidence of and otherwise secret information from people in authority □ ***Those on the inside knew that he planned to resign.*** ▻ *adj* **1 a** being on, near, towards or from the inside □ ***the inside walls of the house;*** **b** indoor □ ***without an inside toilet.*** **2** *colloq* coming from, concerned with, provided by or planned by a person or people within a specific organization or circle □ ***The robbery was an inside job*** □ ***inside knowledge.*** ▻ *adverb* **1** to, in or on the inside or interior □ ***He smashed the window and climbed inside.*** **2** indoors □ ***Come inside for tea.*** **3** *colloq* in or into prison □ ***spent three years inside.*** ▻ *prep* **1** to or on the interior or inner side of something; within. **2** in less than (a specified time) □ ***be back inside an hour.*** ⓘ 16c.

insider ▷ *noun* a recognized or accepted member of an organization or group who has access to confidential or exclusive information about it.

insider dealing and **insider trading** ▷ *noun, finance* the illegal buying and selling of shares by people, eg those who work on the STOCK EXCHANGE, based on their having access to information which has not been made public.

inside out ▷ *adverb* **1** (*also colloq* **outside in**) with the inside surface turned out □ *wearing his shirt inside out.* **2** *colloq* thoroughly; completely □ *I know this story inside out.*

inside track ▷ *noun* **1** *athletics* the lane on the inside of a race track (ie nearest the centre), slightly shorter than the other lanes because of the curve. **2** *especially US* a position of strength, power or advantage.

insidious /ɪnˈsɪdɪəs/ ▷ *adj* **1** developing gradually without being noticed but causing very great harm. **2** attractive but harmful; treacherous. • **insidiously** *adverb.* • **insidiousness** *noun.* ⓒ 16c: from Latin *insidiosus* cunning.

insight ▷ *noun* **1** the ability to gain a relatively rapid, clear and deep understanding of the real, often hidden and usually complex nature of a situation, problem, etc. **2** an instance or example of this. **3** *psychol* awareness of one's own mental or psychological condition, processes, etc. • **insightful** *adj.* ⓒ 13c, meaning 'inner sight' or 'discernment'.

insignia /ɪnˈsɪɡnɪə/ ▷ *singular or plural noun* (***insignia*** or ***insignias***) **1** badges or emblems of office, honour or membership. **2** *loosely* the distinguishing marks by which something is known. ⓒ 17c: Latin, meaning 'badges'.

insignificant ▷ *adj* **1** of little or no meaning, value or importance. **2** relatively small in size or amount. • **insignificance** *noun.* • **insignificantly** *adverb.* ⓒ 17c.

insincere ▷ *adj* not genuine; false; hypocritical. • **insincerely** *adverb.* • **insincerity** /-ˈserɪtɪ/ *noun* (***insincerities***). ⓒ 17c.

insinuate /ɪnˈsɪnjʊeɪt/ ▷ *verb* (***insinuated, insinuating***) **1** to suggest or hint (something unpleasant) in an indirect way □ *Are you insinuating that I am lying?* **2** to introduce (eg an idea) in an indirect, subtle or devious way □ *somehow insinuated his original design into the project.* • **insinuation** *noun.* • **insinuative** /-eɪtɪv, -ətɪv/ *adj.* • **insinuator** *noun.* • **insinuatory** /-ətərɪ/ *adj.* ⓒ 16c: from Latin *insinuare, insinuatum.*

■ **insinuate oneself into something** to succeed in gaining (eg acceptance or favour) by gradual, careful and often cunning means □ *insinuated himself into the boss's good books.*

insinuating ▷ *adj* **1** said of a person: wheedling, or acting in a subtle, cunning or devious way. **2** said of a remark, etc: indirectly hinting at something. • **insinuatingly** *adverb.*

insipid /ɪnˈsɪpɪd/ ▷ *adj* **1** having little or no interest or liveliness; boring. **2** having little or no taste or flavour. • **insipidly** *adverb.* • **insipidness** or **insipidity** /-ˈpɪdɪtɪ/ *noun.* ⓒ 17c: from Latin *insipidus.*

insist /ɪnˈsɪst/ ▷ *verb* (***insisted, insisting***) **1** *tr & intr* to maintain, state or assert something firmly □ *insisted that we were right* □ *I only came because he insisted.* **2** (*usually* **insist on** or **upon something**) to demand it firmly □ *insisted on a fair hearing* □ *insisted on paying the bill.* ⓒ 16c: from Latin *insistere* to persist.

insistent /ɪnˈsɪstənt/ ▷ *adj* **1** making continual forceful demands; insisting. **2** demanding attention; compelling. • **insistence** or **insistency** *noun.* • **insistently** *adverb.*

in situ /ɪn ˈsɪtjuː, ɪn ˈsɪtuː/ ▷ *adverb* in the natural or original position. ▷ *adj* (placed before its noun) done or carried out, etc while remaining in place. ⓒ 18c: Latin, meaning 'in the place'.

insofar as see under IN

insole /ˈɪnsoʊl/ ▷ *noun* **1** a loose inner sole which can be put in a shoe or boot for extra warmth or to make it slightly smaller. **2** in a shoe or boot: a fixed inner sole. ⓒ 19c.

insolent /ˈɪnsələnt/ ▷ *adj* rude or insulting; showing a lack of respect. • **insolence** *noun.* • **insolently** *adverb.* ⓒ 14c: from Latin *insolens,* literally 'departing from custom'.

insoluble /ɪnˈsɒljʊbəl/ ▷ *adj* **1** said of a substance: not able to be dissolved in a particular solvent (especially water) to form a solution. **2** said of a problem or difficulty: not able to be solved or resolved. • **insolubility** *noun.* • **insolubly** *adverb.* ⓒ 14c.

insolvent ▷ *adj* **1** not having enough money to pay debts, creditors, etc. **2** belonging or relating to insolvent people or to the state of being insolvent. ▷ *noun* an insolvent person. • **insolvency** *noun.* ⓒ 16c.

insomnia /ɪnˈsɒmnɪə/ ▷ *noun* the chronic and habitual inability to fall asleep or remain asleep for an adequate length of time. • **insomniac** /-ak/ *noun* someone who suffers from insomnia. ▷ *adj* **1** suffering from insomnia. **2** causing or caused by insomnia. ⓒ 18c: Latin.

insomuch see under IN

insouciant /ɪnˈsuːsɪənt; *French* ɛsusjɑ̃/ ▷ *adj, rather formal or literary* without cares or worries; light-hearted; unconcerned. • **insouciance** *noun.* • **insouciantly** *adverb.* ⓒ 19c: French.

inspect /ɪnˈspɛkt/ ▷ *verb* (***inspected, inspecting***) **1** to look at or examine closely, often to find faults or mistakes. **2** to look at or examine (a body of soldiers, etc) officially or ceremonially. • **inspection** *noun.* ⓒ 17c: from Latin *inspicere, inspectum* to look into.

inspector ▷ *noun* **1** someone whose job is to inspect something, especially officially □ *tax inspector* □ *school inspector.* Also *in compounds* □ *Inspector General.* **2** (*often* **Inspector**) *Brit* a police officer below a superintendent and above a sergeant in rank. Also *in compounds* □ *Deputy Chief Inspector.* • **inspectorial** /-ˈtɔːrɪəl/ *adj.*

inspectorate /ɪnˈspɛktərət/ ▷ *noun* **1** a body of inspectors. **2** the office or post of inspector. Also called **inspectorship**. **3** a district under the charge of an inspector.

inspiration /ɪnspɪˈreɪʃən/ ▷ *noun* **1** a supposed power which stimulates the mind, especially to artistic activity or creativity. **2** someone or something that inspires, or the state of being inspired. **3** a brilliant or inspired idea. **4** *relig* a supposed divine power or influence which leads to the writing of Scripture. **5** *physiol* **a** the act of drawing breath into the lungs; **b** a breath taken in this way. • **inspirational** *adj.* • **inspirationally** *adverb.*

inspiratory /ɪnˈspɪrətərɪ, ˈɪnspɪreɪtərɪ/ ▷ *adj* belonging or relating to or aiding inspiration or inhalation.

inspire /ɪnˈspaɪə(r)/ ▷ *verb* (***inspired, inspiring***) **1** (*often* **inspire someone to something** or **to do something**) to stimulate them into activity, especially into artistic or creative activity. **2** to fill someone with a feeling of confidence, encouragement and exaltation. **3** (*especially* **inspire someone with something** or **inspire something into someone**) to create (a particular feeling) in them. **4** to be the origin or source of (a poem, piece of music, etc). **5** *relig* said of supposed divine power or influence: to guide or instruct someone. **6** *tr & intr* to breathe in (air, etc); to inhale. • **inspired** *adj* so good, skilful, accurate, etc as to seem to be the result of inspiration, especially divine inspiration. • **inspirer** *noun.* ⓒ 14c: from Latin *inspirare* to breathe into.

inspiring ▷ *adj* said of something or someone: providing inspiration; stimulating, encouraging, guiding, etc. • **inspiringly** *adverb.*

Inst. ▷ *abbreviation* **1** Institute. **2** Institution.

inst. ▷ *abbreviation* instant, ie of or in the current month (see INSTANT *adj* 4). □ ***my letter of the 14th inst.***

instability ▷ *noun* lack of physical or mental steadiness or stability. • **instable** *adj* unstable. ◷ 15c: from Latin *instabilitas*.

install or (*sometimes*) **instal** /ɪn'stɔːl/ ▷ *verb* (***installed, installing***) **1** to put (equipment, machinery, etc) in place and make it ready for use □ ***installed a new drinks machine in the canteen*** **2** to place (a person) in office with a formal ceremony □ ***The new chancellor was installed with great pomp.*** **3** to place (something, oneself, etc) in a particular position, condition or place □ ***quickly installed herself in the best seat.*** ◷ 16c: from Latin *installare*.

installation /ɪnstə'leɪʃən/ ▷ *noun* **1** the act or process of installing. **2** a piece of equipment, machinery, etc, or a complete system, that has been installed ready for use. **3** a military base.

instalment or (*US*) **installment** /ɪn'stɔːlmənt/ ▷ *noun* **1** one of a series of parts into which a debt is divided for payment □ ***to be paid in six monthly instalments.*** **2** one of several parts published, issued, broadcast, etc at regular intervals □ ***Don't miss the second exciting instalment next week.*** ◷ 18c: from French *estaler* to fix or set, probably influenced by INSTALL.

instalment plan ▷ *noun, N Amer* payment for goods purchased by instalments; HIRE-PURCHASE.

instance /'ɪnstəns/ ▷ *noun* **1** an example, especially one of a particular condition or circumstance □ ***a prime instance.*** **2** a particular stage in a process or a particular situation □ ***in the first instance.*** **3** *formal* request; urging □ ***at the instance of your partner.*** **4** *law* a process or suit. • **for instance** for example. ◷ 14c: from Latin *instantia*, from *instare* to be present.

instant /'ɪnstənt/ ▷ *adj* **1** immediate □ ***instant success.*** **2** said of food and drink, etc: quickly and easily prepared, especially by reheating or the addition of boiling water □ ***instant coffee.*** **3** present; current. **4** (abbreviation **inst.**) relating to or occurring in the current month. **5** *rather formal* or *old use* urgent; pressing. ▷ *noun* **1** a particular moment in time, especially the present □ ***cannot speak to him at this instant*** □ ***At that same instant she walked in.*** **2** a very brief period of time □ ***I'll be there in an instant.*** **3** *colloq* an instant drink, especially instant coffee □ ***We only drink instant as a rule.*** • **instantly** *adverb* at once; immediately □ ***I'll be there instantly.*** Also **this instant** and (*formal* or *old use*) **on the instant** □ ***Come here this instant!*** □ ***The carriage arrived on the instant.*** ◷ 14c: French, from Latin *instare* to be present.

instantaneous /ɪnstən'teɪnɪəs/ ▷ *adj* done, happening or occurring at once, very quickly or in an instant; immediate □ ***The poison has an instantaneous effect.*** • **instantaneously** *adverb.* • **instantaneousness** or **instantaneity** /-tə'niːɪtɪ/ *noun.* ◷ 17c: from Latin *instantaneus*, from *instare* to be present.

instant replay see ACTION REPLAY

Instants /'ɪnstənts/ ▷ *singular noun* a SCRATCHCARD available from shops, post offices, etc, issued by the UK National Lottery organizers.

instar /'ɪnstɑː(r)/ ▷ *noun, zool* the form of an insect at any stage of its physical development between two successive MOULTs, before it has become fully mature. ◷ 19c: Latin, meaning 'an image' or 'form'.

instate /ɪn'steɪt/ ▷ *verb* (***instated, instating***) to install someone (in an official position, etc). See also REINSTATE. • **instatement** *noun.* ◷ 17c.

instead /ɪn'stɛd/ ▷ *adverb* as a substitute or alternative; in place of something or someone □ ***She is too busy; can I go instead?*** • **instead of** in place of, or as an alternative □ ***I used yoghurt instead of cream.*** ◷ 13c as *in stude*; 17c as *in stead*, meaning 'in place' (see STEAD).

instep /'ɪnstɛp/ ▷ *noun* **1** the prominent arched middle section of the human foot, between the ankle and the toes. **2** the part of a shoe, sock, etc that covers this. ◷ 16c: see STEP.

instigate /'ɪnstɪgeɪt/ ▷ *verb* (***instigated, instigating***) **1** to urge someone on or incite them, especially to do something wrong or evil. **2** to set in motion or initiate (eg an inquiry). • **instigation** *noun.* • **instigative** /'ɪnstɪgeɪtɪv/ *adj.* • **instigator** *noun.* ◷ 16c: from Latin *instigare, instigatum* to goad or urge on.

instil or (*US*) **instill** /ɪn'stɪl/ ▷ *verb* (***instilled, instilling***) **1** (*especially* **instil something in** or **into someone**) to impress, fix or plant (ideas, feelings, etc) slowly or gradually in their mind □ ***Father instilled in us a strong sense of fair play.*** **2** *rare or technical* to pour (a liquid) into something drop by drop. • **instillation** or **instilment** *noun.* • **instiller** *noun.* ◷ 16c: from Latin *instillare* to drip into.

instinct /'ɪnstɪŋkt/ ▷ *noun* **1** in animal behaviour: an inherited and usually fixed pattern of response to a particular stimulus, common to all members of a species, and not learned but based on a biological need, especially for survival or reproduction. **2** in humans: a basic natural drive that urges a person towards a specific goal, such as survival or reproduction. **3** intuition □ ***Instinct told me not to believe him.*** ◷ 16c: from Latin *instinctus* prompting.

instinctive /ɪn'stɪŋktɪv/ ▷ *adj* **1** prompted by instinct or intuition. **2** involuntary; automatic. • **instinctively** *adverb.*

institute /'ɪnstɪtʃuːt/ ▷ *noun* **1** a society or organization which promotes research, education or a particular cause. **2** a building or group of buildings used by an institute. **3** an established law, principle, rule or custom. **4** (**institutes**) a book of laws or principles. ▷ *verb* (***instituted, instituting***) *rather formal* **1** to set up, establish or organize something □ ***instituted a trust fund.*** **2** to initiate something or cause it to begin □ ***to institute legal proceedings.*** **3** to appoint someone to, or install them in, a position or office. • **institutor** or **instituter** *noun.* ◷ 14c: from Latin *instituere, institutum* to establish.

institution /ɪnstɪ'tʃuːʃən/ ▷ *noun* **1** an organization or public body founded for a special purpose, especially for a charitable or educational purpose or as a hospital. **2** a hospital, old people's home, etc, regarded as an impersonal or bureaucratic organization. **3** a custom or tradition; something which is well-established □ ***the institution of marriage.*** **4** *colloq* a familiar and well-known object or person. **5** the act of instituting or process of being instituted. • **institutional** *adj* **1** belonging or relating to, like or typical of an institution, especially in being dull or regimented □ ***typical institutional food.*** **2** depending on, or originating in, an institution. ◷ 15c: see INSTITUTE.

institutionalism ▷ *noun* **1** the characteristics or system of institutions or of life in institutions. **2** belief in the merits of such a system. • **institutionalist** *noun.* ◷ 19c.

institutionalize or **institutionalise** /ɪnstɪ'tʃuːʃənəlaɪz/ ▷ *verb* (***institutionalized, institutionalizing***) **1** to place someone in an institution. **2** to make someone lose their individuality and ability to cope with life by keeping them in an institution (eg a long-stay hospital or prison) for too long □ ***After so long in prison, she was completely institutionalized.*** **3** to make something into an institution. • **institutionalization** *noun.* ◷ 19c.

in-store ▷ *adj* provided or located within a shop □ ***an in-store crèche facility.***

instruct /ɪn'strʌkt/ ▷ *verb* (***instructed, instructing***) **1 a** to teach or train someone in a subject or skill; **b** (*usually* **instruct someone in something**) to give them information about or practical knowledge of it. **2** to direct or order, eg someone to do something. **3** *law* to give (a lawyer) the facts concerning a case. **4** *law* to engage (a lawyer) to act in a case. ◷ 15c: from Latin *instruere, instructum* to equip or train.

instruction /ɪn'strʌkʃən/ ▻ *noun* **1** (*often* **instructions**) a direction, order or command □ *She's always issuing instructions.* **2** teaching; the act or process of instructing. **3** *computing* an element in a computer program or language, consisting of a coded command, that activates a specific operation. **4** (**instructions**) a set of detailed guidelines, eg on how to operate a machine or piece of equipment □ *Read the instructions before you use it.* **5** (**instructions**) *law* the information, details, etc of a case, given to a lawyer □ *I have not yet taken instructions from my client or his solicitor.* • **instructional** *adj.* ⓘ 15c.

instructive ▻ *adj* giving knowledge or information; serving to instruct others. • **instructively** *adverb.* • **instructiveness** *noun.*

instructor ▻ *noun* **1** someone who gives instruction □ *driving instructor.* **2** *N Amer* a college or university teacher ranking below a professor or assistant professor. Compare LECTURER, READER, TUTOR. • **instructorship** *noun.*

instrument ▻ *noun* /'ɪnstrəmənt/ **1** a tool, especially one used for delicate scientific work or measurement. Also *as adj* □ *instrument case.* **2** (*also* **musical instrument**) any of several devices which are used to produce musical sounds. See also WIND INSTRUMENT, PERCUSSION 2, STRING 3. **3** inside a vehicle or aircraft: any of several devices which measure, show and control speed, temperature, direction, etc. Also *as adj* □ *instrument panel.* **4** someone or something that is seen as a means of achieving or doing something □ *She was the instrument of his downfall.* **5** a formal or official legal document. ▻ *verb* /'ɪnstrəmɛnt, -'mɛnt/ (*instrumented, instrumenting*) **1** to arrange, orchestrate or score (music). **2** to equip something with instruments for measuring, etc. ⓘ 13c: from Latin *instrumentum* equipment or tool.

instrumental /ɪnstrə'mɛntəl/ ▻ *adj* **1** (*often* **instrumental in** or **to something**) being responsible for it or an important factor in it □ *She was instrumental in catching the culprit.* **2** said of music: performed by, or written or arranged for, musical instruments only. Compare VOCAL, CHORAL. **3** relating to or done with an instrument or tool. **4** *grammar* belonging to or in the instrumental case. ▻ *noun* **1** a piece of music performed by or written or arranged for musical instruments only, ie with no vocal part. **2** *grammar* (abbreviation **instr.**) in some languages, eg Russian: **a** the form or CASE[2] (sense 7) of a noun, pronoun or adjective that shows primarily how or by what means an action is performed; **b** a noun, etc in this case. • **instrumentality** /-mɛn'talɪtɪ/ *noun.* • **instrumentally** *adverb.* ⓘ 14c: French.

instrumentalist ▻ *noun* someone who plays a musical instrument. Compare VOCALIST. ⓘ 19c.

instrumentation /ɪnstrəmɛn'teɪʃən, -mən'teɪʃən/ ▻ *noun* **1** the particular way in which a piece of music is written or arranged to be played by instruments; orchestration. **2** the instruments used to play a particular piece of music. **3** the use, design or provision of instruments or tools.

instrument flying and **instrument landing** ▻ *noun, aeronautics* navigation or landing of an aircraft by means of instruments and ground radio devices, radar, etc only, used when visibility is poor.

instrument panel and **instrument board** ▻ *noun* the area in a car, plane, boat, etc where the information dials, measuring gauges, etc are mounted.

insubordinate ▻ *adj,* disobedient; refusing to take orders or submit to authority. • **insubordinately** *adverb.* • **insubordination** *noun.* ⓘ 19c.

insubstantial ▻ *adj* **1** not solid, strong or satisfying; flimsy; tenuous □ *The evidence against them was too insubstantial to pursue the case.* **2** not made up of solid material; not real. • **insubstantiality** /-'alɪtɪ/ *noun.* • **insubstantially** *adverb.* ⓘ 17c.

insufferable /ɪn'sʌfərəbəl/ ▻ *adj* too unpleasant, annoying, etc to bear; intolerable. • **insufferably** *adverb.* ⓘ 16c.

insufficiency ▻ *noun* **1** the state or quality of being insufficient. **2** *pathol* the failure of an organ to function.

insufficient ▻ *adj* not enough or not adequate. • **insufficiently** *adverb.* ⓘ 14c: from Latin *insufficiens*; see SUFFICIENT.

insular /'ɪnsjʊlə(r)/ ▻ *adj* **1** belonging or relating to an island, or to the inhabitants of an island. **2** said of someone or their opinions, etc: not influenced by or responsive to contact with other people, cultures, etc; narrow-minded; prejudiced. • **insularity** /-'larɪtɪ/ *noun.* ⓘ 17c: from Latin *insularis*, from *insula* island.

insulate /'ɪnsjʊleɪt/ ▻ *verb* (*insulated, insulating*) **1** to surround (a body, device or space) with a material that prevents or slows down the flow of heat, electricity or sound. **2** to remove or set someone or something apart; to isolate. ⓘ 16c: from Latin *insula* island.

insulating tape ▻ *noun* adhesive tape used to cover bare or exposed electrical wires to protect people from electric shocks.

insulation ▻ *noun* **1** material used in insulating, especially material which does not conduct heat or electricity. **2** the process of insulating or being insulated.

insulator *noun* **1** any material that is a poor conductor of heat or electricity, eg plastics, glass or ceramics. **2** a device made of such material.

insulin /'ɪnsjʊlɪn/ ▻ *noun* a HORMONE (sense 1) secreted by the ISLETS OF LANGERHANS in the PANCREAS, which controls the concentration of sugar in the blood. A lack of it causes DIABETES. ⓘ Early 20c: from Latin *insula* island.

insult ▻ *verb* /ɪn'sʌlt/ (*insulted, insulting*) **1** to speak rudely or offensively to or about someone or something. **2** to behave in a way that offends or affronts. ▻ *noun* /'ɪnsʌlt/ **1** a rude or offensive remark or action. **2** an affront □ *The film was an insult to the intelligence.* **3** *medicine* **a** injury or damage to the body; **b** a cause of this. • **insulting** *adj.* • **insultingly** *adverb.* • **add insult to injury 1** to treat someone who has already been hurt, offended, etc with further discourtesy. **2** to make matters worse □ *And then, to add insult to injury, we ran out of petrol!* ⓘ 16c: French: from Latin *insultare* to leap on, to assail.

insuperable /ɪn'suːpərəbəl, ɪn'sjuː-/ ▻ *adj* too difficult to be overcome, defeated or dealt with successfully. • **insuperability** *noun.* • **insuperably** *adverb.* ⓘ 14c.

insupportable /ɪnsə'pɔːtəbəl/ ▻ *adj* **1** too unpleasant, severe, annoying, etc to be tolerated. **2** not justifiable. ⓘ 16c.

insurance ▻ *noun* **1** an agreement by which one party promises to pay another party money in the event of loss, theft or damage to property, personal injury or death, etc. **2** the contract for such an agreement. Also called **insurance policy**. **3** the protection offered by such a contract. **4** money, usually paid regularly, in return for such a contract; an insurance PREMIUM. **5** the sum which will be paid in the event of loss, theft or damage to property, personal injury or death, etc. **6** the business of providing such contracts for clients. **7** anything done, any measure taken, etc to try to prevent possible loss, disappointment, problems, etc. **8** an act or instance of insuring. **9** *as adj* □ *insurance company.* ⓘ 17c.

insurance

See Usage Note at **assurance**.

insure /ɪn'ʃʊə(r), ɪn'ʃɔː(r)/ ▻ *verb* (*insured, insuring*) **1** *tr & intr* to arrange for the payment of an amount of money in the event of the loss or theft of or damage to (property) or injury to or the death of (a person), etc by paying regular amounts of money to an insurance company. **2** to take measures to try to prevent (an event leading to loss, damage, difficulties, etc). **3** *intr, chiefly N Amer* to provide insurance; to underwrite. • **insurable** *adj*. ⓒ 15c variant of ENSURE.

insured ▷ *adj* **1** covered by insurance. **2** (**the insured**) *law, etc* a person whose life, health or property is covered by insurance (see THE 4b).

insurer ▷ *noun* (*especially* **the insurer**) *law, etc* a person or company that provides insurance.

insurgence /ɪn'sɜːdʒəns/ or **insurgency** ▷ *noun* (***insurgences*** or ***insurgencies***) an uprising or rebellion.

insurgent /ɪn'sɜːdʒənt/ ▷ *adj* opposed to and fighting against the government of the country; rebellious. ▷ *noun* a rebel. ⓒ 18c: from Latin *insurgere* to rise up.

insurmountable /ɪnsɜː'maʊntəbəl/ ▷ *adj* too difficult to be dealt with successfully; impossible to overcome. • **insurmountability** *noun*. ⓒ 17c.

insurrection /ɪnsə'rɛkʃən/ ▷ *noun* an act of rebellion against authority. • **insurrectionist** *noun* someone who takes part in or supports an insurrection. ⓒ 15c: French, from Latin *insurgere, insurrectum* to rise up.

in-swinger ▷ *noun* **1** *cricket* a ball bowled so as to swerve to the leg of the batsman. **2** *football* a ball kicked so as to swing in towards the goal or to the centre of the pitch. ⓒ 20c.

int. ▷ *abbreviation* **1** interior. **2** internal. **3** (*also* **Int.**) international.

intact /ɪn'takt/ ▷ *adj* whole; not broken or damaged; untouched. ⓒ 15c: from Latin *intactus*.

intaglio /ɪn'tɑːlɪoʊ/ ▷ *noun* (***intaglios***) **1** a stone or gem which has a design engraved in its surface. Compare CAMEO (sense 1). **2 a** the art or process of engraving designs into the surface of objects, especially jewellery; **b** an engraved design. **3** in printmaking: a technique in which a design is incised into a metal plate, ink is forced into the cut lines and wiped off the rest of the surface, damp paper is laid on top and both plate and paper are rolled through a press. ⓒ 17c: Italian, from *intagliare* to cut into.

intake /'ɪnteɪk/ ▷ *noun* **1** a thing or quantity taken in or accepted. **2 a** a number or the amount taken in, eg in an academic year; **b** the people, etc involved in this. **3** an opening through which liquid or gas enters a pipe, engine, etc. **4** an act of taking in. **5** an airway in a mine.

intangible /ɪn'tandʒɪbəl/ ▷ *adj* **1** not able to be felt or perceived by touch. **2** difficult to understand or for the mind to grasp. **3** said of part of a business, eg an asset: not having a solid physical existence, but having some value or worth. ▷ *noun* something intangible. • **intangibility** *noun*. • **intangibly** *adverb*. ⓒ 17c: from Latin *intangibilis*.

intarsia /ɪn'tɑːsɪə/ ▷ *noun* **1** decorative wood inlay work. **2** *knitting* **a** a highly intricate method of creating patterns using a number of different coloured or textured wools or threads; **b** a pattern that is produced using this method. Also *as adj* □ ***a beautiful intarsia sweater***. ⓒ 19c: from Italian *intarsio*, from *tarsia* marquetry or inlaid work.

integer /'ɪntɪdʒə(r)/ ▷ *noun* **1** *math* any of the positive or negative whole numbers or zero, eg 0, 8, –12. Compare FRACTION 1. **2** any whole or complete entity. ⓒ 16c: Latin, meaning 'entire' or 'untouched'.

integral /'ɪntɪgrəl or (in all senses except *math*) ɪn'tɛgrəl/ ▷ *adj* **1** being a necessary part of a whole. **2** forming a whole; supplied or fitted as part of a whole. **3** whole; complete. **4** *math, denoting* a number that is an INTEGER. ▷ *noun, math* the result of integrating a function. ⓒ 16c: from Latin *integralis*, from *integer* (see INTEGER).

integral calculus ▷ *noun, math* the branch of CALCULUS concerned with INTEGRATION (*noun* 2), used eg to solve DIFFERENTIAL EQUATIONS, to calculate the area enclosed by a curve, etc.

integrand /'ɪntəgrand/ ▷ *noun, math* a function that is to be integrated. ⓒ 19c: from Latin *integrandus*, from *integrare* to integrate.

integrate /'ɪntəgreɪt/ ▷ *verb* (***integrated, integrating***) **1** to fit (parts) together to form a whole. **2** *tr & intr* to mix (people) or cause (people) to mix freely with other groups in society, etc. **3** to end racial segregation in something. **4** *math* **a** to find the integral of (a function or equation); **b** to find the total or mean value of (a variable). ⓒ 17c: from Latin *integrare* to renew or make whole.

integrated circuit ▷ *noun, electronics* a miniature solid-state circuit formed on a single paper-thin chip of semiconductor material, usually silicon, and ranging in size from about one millimetre to one centimetre square.

integration /ɪntə'greɪʃən/ ▷ *noun* **1** the process of integrating. **2** *math* a method used in CALCULUS to sum the effects of a continuously varying quantity or function, by treating it as a very large number of infinitely small quantities that represent the difference between two values of a given function. Compare DIFFERENTIATION.

integrity /ɪn'tɛgrɪtɪ/ ▷ *noun* **1** strict adherence to moral values and principles; uprightness. **2** the quality or state of being whole and unimpaired. ⓒ 15c: from Latin *integritas* wholeness.

integument /ɪn'tɛgjʊmənt/ ▷ *noun* **1** *zool* any protective outer layer of tissue covering a body part, organ, etc, eg the epidermis of the skin in vertebrates or the cuticle or exoskeleton of insects. **2** *bot* either of the two protective outer coats that surrounds the OVULE in ANGIOSPERMS or the one outer coat that surrounds the ovule in GYMNOSPERMS. • **integumental** or **integumentary** *adj*. ⓒ 17c: from Latin *integumentum*, from *integere* to cover.

intellect /'ɪntəlɛkt/ ▷ *noun* **1** the part of the mind that uses both memory and intelligence in order to think, reason creatively and understand concepts. **2** the capacity to use this part of this mind. **3** someone who has a highly developed intellect and great mental ability. ⓒ 14c: from Latin *intelligere* to understand.

intellectual /ɪntə'lɛktʃʊəl/ ▷ *adj* **1** involving or appealing to the intellect. **2** having a highly developed ability to think, reason and understand. ▷ *noun* someone who has a highly developed intellect and great mental ability. • **intellectually** *adverb*.

intellectualize or **intellectualise** /ɪntə'lɛktʃʊəlaɪz/ ▷ *verb* (***intellectualized, intellectualizing***) **1** to think about or analyse (eg a problem) intellectually or rationally. **2** *intr* to think rationally or intellectually; to philosophize.

intellectual property ▷ *noun, law* property, such as copyright, trademarks, etc, that has no tangible form but represents the product of creative work or invention.

intelligence /ɪn'tɛlɪdʒəns/ ▷ *noun* **1** the ability to use memory, knowledge, experience, understanding, reasoning, imagination and judgement in order to solve problems and adapt to new situations. **2** news or information. **3** the gathering of secret information about an enemy. **4** the government department or group of people, eg in the army, responsible for gathering such information. ⓒ 14c: from Latin *intelligentia*, from *intelligere* to understand.

intelligence quotient ▷ *noun* (abbreviation **IQ**) a measure of a person's intellectual ability, expressed as the ratio of mental age to actual age, multiplied by 100, and is based on the scores achieved in an intelligence test.

intelligence test ▷ *noun, psychol* any standardized assessment procedure to determine an individual's intellectual ability, or the age at which their ability would be normal, with the score achieved usually expressed as an intelligence quotient.

intelligent /ɪn'tɛlɪdʒənt/ ▷ *adj* **1** having or showing highly developed mental ability; clever. **2** said of a machine, computer, weapon, etc: able to vary its behaviour according to the situation. • **intelligently** *adverb*.

intelligentsia /ɪntɛlɪ'dʒɛntsɪə/ ▻ *noun* (*usually* **the intelligentsia**) the most highly educated and cultured people in a society, especially when considered as a political class. ◷ Early 20c: from Russian *intelligentsiya*, from Latin *intelligentia* intelligence.

intelligible /ɪn'tɛlɪdʒɪbəl/ ▻ *adj* **1** able to be understood; clear. **2** *philos* only able to be understood by the intellect and not by the senses or feelings. • **intelligibility** *noun*. • **intelligibly** *adverb*. ◷ 14c: from Latin *intelligibilis*, from *intellegere* to understand.

Intelsat ▻ *noun* a worldwide satellite service dealing with commercial (ie non-military) communications. ◷ 20c: from *Int*ernational *Tel*ecommunications *Sat*ellite Consortium.

intemperate ▻ *adj* **1** going beyond reasonable limits; not controlled or restrained. **2** habitually drinking too much alcohol. **3** said of a climate or region: having extreme and severe temperatures. Compare TEMPERATE. • **intemperance** *noun*. • **intemperately** *adj*. ◷ 15c.

intend /ɪn'tɛnd/ ▻ *verb* (***intended***, ***intending***) **1** to plan or have in mind as one's purpose or aim. **2** (**intend something for someone** or **something**) to set it aside or destine it to some specified person or thing. **3** to mean. ◷ 14c: from French *entendre*, from Latin *intendere* to stretch towards.

intended ▻ *adj* meant; done on purpose or planned. ▻ *noun, colloq* someone's future husband or wife.

intense ▻ *adj* **1** very great or extreme. **2** feeling or expressing emotion deeply. **3** very deeply felt □ *intense happiness*. • **intensely** *adverb*. ◷ 14c: French, from Latin *intendere*, *intensum* to stretch towards.

intensifier ▻ *noun, grammar* an adverb or adjective which adds emphasis to or intensifies the word or phrase which follows it, eg *very*. Also called **intensive**.

intensify ▻ *verb* (***intensifies***, ***intensified***, ***intensifying***) *tr & intr* to make or become intense or more intense. • **intensification** *noun*.

intension /ɪn'tɛnʃən/ ▻ *noun, logic* the set of qualities by which a general name is determined. Opposite of EXTENSION.

intensity ▻ *noun* (***intensities***) **1** the quality or state of being intense. **2** *physics* the rate at which power or radiant energy is transmitted per unit area by a wave or in the form of radiation, eg the loudness of sound or the brightness of light. **3** *chem* the concentration of a solution. **4** *physics* the power per unit area transmitted by a wave. ◷ 17c.

intensive ▻ *adj* **1** *often in compounds* using, done with or requiring considerable amounts of thought, effort, time, etc within a relatively short period □ *labour-intensive*. **2** thorough; intense; concentrated. **3** using large amounts of capital and labour (rather than more land or raw materials) to increase production. **4** *grammar* said of an adverb or adjective: adding force or emphasis, eg *extremely*, *quite*. See INTENSIFIER. ▻ *noun, grammar* an INTENSIFIER. • **intensively** *adverb*. • **intensiveness** *noun*. ◷ 16c: from Latin *intensivus*; see INTENSE.

intensive care ▻ *noun* **1** the care of critically ill patients who require continuous attention, eg following severe injury or major surgery. **2** (*in full* **intensive-care unit**) a hospital unit that provides such intensive care.

intensive farming ▻ *noun, agric* a method of farming that uses large amounts of capital or labour to obtain the maximum yield from a limited area of land. Compare EXTENSIFICATION, EXTENSIVE FARMING, FACTORY FARMING at FACTORY FARM.

intent /ɪn'tɛnt/ ▻ *noun* **1** something which is aimed at or intended; a purpose. **2** *law* the purpose of committing a crime □ *loitering with intent*. ▻ *adj* **1** (*usually* **intent on** or **upon something**) firmly determined to do it. **2** (*usually* **intent on something**) having one's attention firmly fixed on it; concentrating hard on it. **3** showing concentration; absorbed □ *an intent look*. • **intently** *adverb*. • **intentness** *noun*. • **to all intents and purposes** in every important respect; virtually. ◷ 13c: from Latin *intentus*, from *intendere* to stretch towards.

intention /ɪn'tɛnʃən/ ▻ *noun* **1** something that someone plans or intends to do; an aim or purpose. **2** (**intentions**) *colloq* someone's, especially a man's, purpose with regard to marriage to a particular woman. **3** *RC Church* (*also* **special** or **particular intention**) the purpose or reason for prayers being said or mass celebrated. ◷ 14c: from Latin *intendere* to stretch towards.

intentional ▻ *adj* said, done, etc on purpose; deliberate. • **intentionally** *adverb*.

inter /ɪn'tɜː(r)/ ▻ *verb* (***interred***, ***interring***) to bury (a dead person, etc) in the earth or a tomb. ◷ 14c: from Latin *interrare*, from *terra* earth.

inter- /'ɪntə(r)/ ▻ *prefix, denoting* **1** between or among □ *intermingle*. **2** mutual or reciprocal. ◷ Latin, meaning 'among'.

interact /ɪntə'rakt/ ▻ *verb, intr* to act with or on one another. ◷ 18c.

interaction ▻ *noun* action or influence of people or things on each other.

interactive ▻ *adj* **1** characterized by the interaction of people, things, etc. **2** involving or allowing a continuous exchange of information between a computer and its user. • **interactively** *adverb*.

interactive compact disc ▻ *noun* a CD-I.

inter alia /ɪntə'reɪlɪə' *Latin* 'ɪnter 'alɪa/ ▻ *adverb* among other things. ◷ 17c: Latin.

interbreed ▻ *verb, tr & intr* **1** to breed within a single family or strain so as to control the appearance of certain characteristics in the offspring. **2** to cross-breed. • **interbreeding** *noun*.

intercalary /ɪn'tɜːkələrɪ, ɪntə'kalərɪ/ ▻ *adj* **1** said of a day: added to a calendar month to make the calendar year match the solar year, eg the day added to February every leap year. **2** said of a year: containing such a day or days. **3** coming between two layers; intervening. **4** *biol* inserted or located between other structures or parts. ◷ 17c: from Latin *intercalarius*.

intercalate /ɪn'tɜːkəleɪt/ ▻ *verb* (***intercalated***, ***intercalating***) **1** to insert (a day in the calendar) between others. **2** to insert or introduce. • **intercalation** *noun*. ◷ 17c: from Latin *intercalare*.

intercede /ɪntə'siːd/ ▻ *verb* (***interceded***, ***interceding***) *intr* **1** to act as a peacemaker between (two parties, countries, etc). **2** (*usually* **intercede for someone**) to plead or make an appeal on their behalf. See also INTERCESSION. ◷ 17c: from Latin *intercedere* to intervene.

intercellular ▻ *adj, biol* situated or occurring between cells.

intercept ▻ *verb* /ɪntə'sɛpt/ (***intercepted***, ***intercepting***) **1 a** to stop or catch (eg a person, missile, aircraft, etc) on their or its way from one place to another; **b** to prevent (a missile, etc) from arriving at its destination, often by destroying it. **2** *math* to mark or cut off (a line, plane, curve, etc) with another another line, plane, etc that crosses it. ▻ *noun* /'ɪntəsɛpt/ *math* **1** the part of a line or plane that is cut off by another line or plane crossing it, especially the distance from the origin to the point where a straight line or a curve crosses one of the axes of a coordinate system. **2** the point at which two figures intersect, that part of a line that is intercepted. • **interception** *noun*. • **interceptive** *adj*. ◷ 16c: from Latin *intercipere*, *interceptum*.

interceptor ▷ *noun* someone or something that intercepts, especially a small light aircraft used to intercept approaching enemy aircraft.

intercession /ɪntəˈsɛʃən/ ▷ *noun* **1** an act of interceding or making an appeal on behalf of another. **2** *Christianity* a prayer or request to God on behalf of someone else. • **intercessional** or **intercessory** *adj.* • **intercessor** *noun.* • **intercessorial** /-sɛˈsɔːrɪəl/ *adj.* ⓒ 16c: from Latin *intercessio*, from *intercedere* to intercede.

interchange /ɪntəˈtʃeɪndʒ/ ▷ *verb, tr & intr* to change or cause to change places with something or someone. ▷ *noun* /ˈɪntətʃeɪndʒ/ **1** an act of interchanging; an exchange. **2** a road junction, especially leading to or from a motorway, consisting of a series of roads and bridges designed to prevent streams of traffic from directly crossing one another. • **interchangeability** *noun.* • **interchangeable** *adj.* • **interchangeably** *adverb.* ⓒ 14c.

intercity /ɪntəˈsɪtɪ/ ▷ *adj, Brit* (*also* **Intercity**) said of rail transport: denoting an express service between major cities. ▷ *noun* (***intercities***) an intercity train.

intercom /ˈɪntəkɒm/ ▷ *noun* an internal system which allows communication within a building, aircraft, ship, etc. ⓒ 1940s: abbreviation of **intercommunication**.

intercommunicate ▷ *verb, intr* **1** to communicate mutually or together. **2** said of adjoining rooms: to have a connecting door; to interconnect. • **intercommunication** *noun.* ⓒ 16c.

interconnect ▷ *verb, tr & intr* to connect (two things) or be connected together or with one another. • **interconnection** *noun.* ⓒ 19c.

intercontinental ▷ *adj* travelling between or connecting different continents. ⓒ 19c.

intercontinental ballistic missile ▷ *noun* (abbreviation **ICBM**) a ballistic missile which can travel distances of over 5500km and which can therefore be fired at a target in another continent.

intercostal /ɪntəˈkɒstəl/ ▷ *adj, anatomy* between the ribs. ⓒ 16c: from Latin *costa* rib.

intercourse /ˈɪntəkɔːs/ ▷ *noun* **1** SEXUAL INTERCOURSE. **2** communication, connection or dealings between people, groups of people, countries, etc. **3** communion, eg between people and God. ⓒ 15c: from French *entrecours* commerce.

intercropping ▷ *noun, agric* the practice of growing two or more crops in a field at the same time, in alternate rows. Compare CATCH CROP.

intercurrent ▷ *adj* **1** occurring between or during something. **2** *pathol* said of a disease: occurring and intervening in the course of another disease. • **intercurrence** *noun.*

intercut ▷ *verb, cinematog* to alternate (contrasting shots) within a sequence by cutting.

interdenominational ▷ *adj* happening between or involving (members of) different religious denominations.

interdepartmental ▷ *adj* happening between or involving (members of) different departments within a single organization, etc.

interdependent ▷ *adj* depending on one another. • **interdependence** *noun.* • **interdependently** *adverb.*

interdict ▷ *noun* /ˈɪntədɪkt/ **1** an official order forbidding someone to do something. **2** *RC Church* a sentence or punishment removing the right to most sacraments (including burial but not communion) from the people of a place or district. **3** *Scots law* an INJUNCTION (sense 1). ▷ *verb* /ɪntəˈdɪkt/ (***interdicted***, ***interdicting***) to place under an interdict; to forbid or prohibit. • **interdiction** *noun.* • **interdictory** *adj.* ⓒ 13c: from Latin *interdictum* prohibition.

interdisciplinary ▷ *adj* involving two or more subjects of study.

interest /ˈɪntərəst/ ▷ *noun* **1** the desire to learn or know about someone or something; curiosity. **2** the power to attract attention and curiosity. **3** something which arouses attention and curiosity; a hobby or pastime. **4** money paid as a charge for borrowing money or using credit, usually in the form of a percentage of what is borrowed or owed. **5** (*often* **interests**) advantage, benefit or profit, especially financial □ ***It is in your own interests to be truthful.*** **6** a share or claim in a business and its profits, or a legal right to property. **7** (*also* **interest group**) a group of people or organizations with common, especially financial, aims and concerns □ ***the banking interest.*** ▷ *verb* (***interested***, ***interesting***) **1** to attract the attention and curiosity of someone. **2** (*often* **interest someone in something**) to cause them to take a part in or be concerned about some activity. • **in the interest** or **interests of something** in order to achieve or contribute to an objective □ ***in the interests of good industrial relations.*** ⓒ 15c: from Latin *interest* it concerns.

interested ▷ *adj* **1** showing or having a concern or interest. **2** personally involved and therefore not impartial or disinterested. Compare DISINTERESTED, UNINTERESTED. • **interestedly** *adverb.*

interesting ▷ *adj* attracting interest; holding the attention. • **interestingly** *adverb.*

interest rate ▷ *noun, finance* a charge made on borrowed money.

interface /ˈɪntəfeɪs/ ▷ *noun* **1** a surface forming a common boundary between two regions, things, etc which cannot be mixed, eg oil and water. **2** a common boundary or meeting-point between two different systems or processes. **3** *physics* the boundary between two adjacent PHASES, ie between gas and liquid, gas and solid, liquid and liquid, etc. **4** *computing* a device, consisting of hardware together with software programs to drive it, that links a computer to a peripheral device such as a printer. **5** *computing* the physical connection between a computer and the user. ▷ *verb, tr & intr* to connect (a piece of equipment, etc) with another so as to make them compatible. • **interfacial** *adj.* ⓒ 19c.

interfacing ▷ *noun* a piece of stiff fabric sewn between two layers of material to give shape and firmness.

interfere /ɪntəˈfɪə(r)/ ▷ *verb* (***interfered***, ***interfering***) *intr* **1** (*often* **interfere with** or **in something**) **a** said of a person: to be involved in or meddle with something not considered their business □ ***Her mother is always interfering in the children's upbringing;*** **b** said of a thing: to hinder or adversely affect something else □ ***The weather is interfering with picture reception.*** **2** *physics* said of sound waves, rays of light, etc: to combine together to cause disturbance or interference. **3** said of a horse: to strike a foot against the opposite leg in walking. • **interfering** *adj.* ⓒ 16c: from French *s'entreferir* to strike each other.

■ **interfere with someone** *euphemistic* to assault or molest them sexually.

interference ▷ *noun* **1** the act or process of interfering. **2** *physics* the interaction between two or more waves of the same frequency, which will combine to give a larger wave if their peaks arrive at the same point together, but will cancel each other out if a peak of one wave coincides with a trough of the other. **3** *telecomm* the distortion of transmitted radio or television signals by an external power source, eg machinery near to the receiver.

interferometer /ɪntəfɪəˈrɒmɪtə(r)/ ▷ *noun, physics* an instrument which, by splitting a beam of light into two or more parts which are then recombined to form an INTERFERENCE pattern, is used to measure wavelengths, to test optical surfaces and to measure accurately small angles and distances.

interferon /ɪntəˈfɪərɒn/ ▷ *noun, biochem* any of various proteins, secreted by animal cells that have been infected with a virus, which are capable of preventing the multiplication of that virus in non-infected cells. ⓒ 1950s: from INTERFERE.

interfuse /ɪntəˈfjuːz/ ▻ *verb* **1** to mix (with something). **2** *tr & intr* to blend or fuse together. • **interfusion** *noun*. ⓒ 16c: from Latin *interfundere, interfusum* to pour between.

intergalactic ▻ *adj* happening or situated between different galaxies.

interim /ˈɪntərɪm/ ▻ *adj* not intended to be final or to last; provisional, temporary. • **in the interim** in the time between two events; in the meantime. ⓒ 16c: Latin, meaning 'meanwhile'.

interior /ɪnˈtɪərɪə(r)/ ▻ *adj* **1** on, of, suitable for, happening or acting in, or coming from the inside; inner □ *interior design*. **2** away from the shore or frontier; inland. **3** concerning the domestic or internal, rather than foreign, affairs of a country. **4** belonging to or existing in the mind or spirit; belonging to the mental or spiritual life. ▻ *noun* **1** an internal or inner part; the inside. **2** the part of a country or continent that is furthest from the coast. **3** the internal or home affairs of a country. **4** a picture or representation of the inside of a room or building, especially with reference to its decoration or style □ *a typical southern French interior*. ⓒ 15c: Latin, comparative of *inter* inward.

interior angle ▻ *noun* an angle between two adjacent sides of a polygon.

interior decoration and **interior design** ▻ *noun* **1** the decoration, design and furnishings of a room or building. **2** the art or job of designing the insides of rooms, including selecting colours and furnishings. • **interior decorator** or **interior designer** someone whose job is interior decoration or design.

interj ▻ *abbreviation* interjection.

interject /ɪntəˈdʒɛkt/ ▻ *verb* (***interjected, interjecting***) to say or add abruptly; to interrupt with something. ⓒ 16c: from Latin *intericere, interiectum* to insert.

interjection ▻ *noun* **1** a word, phrase or sound used as an exclamation to express surprise, sudden disappointment, pain, etc. **2** an act of interjecting. • **interjectional** *adj*.

interlace ▻ *verb* **1** *tr & intr* to join by lacing or by crossing over. **2** to mix or blend with something □ *a story interlaced with graphic descriptions*. • **interlacement** *noun*. ⓒ 14c.

interlard ▻ *verb* to add foreign words, quotations, unusual phrases, etc to (a speech or piece of writing), especially to do so excessively. ⓒ 16c.

interlay ▻ *verb* to lay (eg layers) between; to interpose. ⓒ 17c.

interleaf ▻ *noun* (***interleaves***) a leaf of paper, usually a blank one, inserted between any two leaves of a book.

interleave /ɪntəˈliːv/ ▻ *verb* (***interleaved, interleaving***) to insert interleaves between the pages of a book.

interleukin /ɪntəˈljuːkɪn/ ▻ *noun* any of a group of soluble protein factors, produced by white blood cells, which play an important role in fighting infection. ⓒ 1980s: see LEUCOCYTE.

interline[1] ▻ *verb* to insert (words) between the lines of (a document, book, etc). • **interlineation** /ɪntəlɪnɪˈeɪʃən/ *noun*. ⓒ 15c.

interline[2] ▻ *verb* to put an extra lining between the first lining and the fabric (of a garment), especially for stiffness. ⓒ 15c.

interlinear /ɪntəˈlɪnɪə(r)/ ▻ *adj* said of words: inserted between the lines of a document, book, etc.

interlining ▻ *noun* a piece of material used as an extra lining.

interlink ▻ *verb, tr & intr* to join or connect together. ⓒ 16c.

interlock ▻ *verb* /ɪntəˈlɒk/ *tr & intr* to fit, fasten or connect together, especially by the means of teeth or parts which fit into each other. ▻ *noun* /ˈɪntə-/ a device or mechanism that connects and co-ordinates the functions of the parts or components of eg a machine. ▻ *adj* said of a fabric or garment: knitted with closely locking stitches. • **interlocking** *adj*. ⓒ 17c.

interlocutor /ɪntəˈlɒkjʊtə(r)/ ▻ *noun* **1** someone who takes part in a conversation or dialogue. **2** *Scots law* **a** *strictly* a judgement coming just short of the final decree; **b** *loosely* any order of the court. • **interlocution** /ɪntələˈkjuːʃən/ *noun*. ⓒ 16c: from Latin *interloqui* to speak between.

interlocutory /ɪntəˈlɒkjʊtərɪ/ ▻ *adj* **1** relating or belonging to conversation or dialogue. **2** *law* said of a decree: given during legal proceedings and only provisional.

interloper /ˈɪntəloupə(r)/ ▻ *noun* someone who meddles in or interferes with other people's affairs, or goes to places where they have no right to be; an intruder. ⓒ 17c: from Dutch *loopen* to leap.

interlude /ˈɪntəluːd, -ljuːd/ ▻ *noun* **1** a short period of time between two events or a short period of a different activity; a brief distraction. **2** a short break between the acts of a play or opera or between items of music. **3** a short piece of music, or short item of entertainment, played during such a break. **4** a short dramatic or comic piece, formerly often performed during this interval. ⓒ 14c: from Latin *interludium*, from *ludus* play.

intermarry ▻ *verb, intr* **1** said of different races, social or religious groups, etc: to become connected by marriage. **2** to marry someone from one's own family. • **intermarriage** *noun*.

intermediary /ɪntəˈmiːdɪərɪ/ ▻ *noun* (***intermediaries***) **1** someone who mediates between two people or groups, often to try to settle a dispute between them or bring them into agreement. **2** any intermediate person or thing. ▻ *adj* **1** acting as intermediary. **2** intermediate.

intermediate /ɪntəˈmiːdɪət/ ▻ *adj* in the middle; placed between two points, stages or extremes in place or time or skill. ▻ *noun* **1** an intermediate thing. **2** *chem* a short-lived chemical compound formed during one of the middle stages of a complex series of chemical reactions. **3** *chem* a chemical compound that is the precursor of a particular end-product, eg a dye, and which must undergo a number of chemical changes to give the finished product. ▻ *verb* /ɪntəˈmiːdɪeɪt/ *intr* to act as an intermediary. • **intermediation** *noun*. ⓒ 17c: from Latin *intermediatus*, from *medius* middle.

intermediate technology ▻ *noun* technology involving the adaptation of sophisticated scientific inventions and techniques for use in developing countries using local materials and methods of manufacture in order to reduce overhead costs, increase self-sufficiency and minimize environmental damage.

interment /ɪnˈtɜːmənt/ ▻ *noun* burial, especially with appropriate ceremony. ⓒ 14c.

interment

A word often confused with this one is **internment**.

intermezzo /ɪntəˈmɛtsou, -ˈmɛdzou/ ▻ *noun* (***intermezzi*** /-tsiː/ or ***intermezzos***) *music* a short instrumental piece usually performed between the sections of a symphonic work, opera or other dramatic musical entertainment. ⓒ 18c: Italian, from Latin *intermedium* intervening place.

interminable /ɪnˈtɜːmɪnəbəl/ ▻ *adj* without or seemingly without an end, especially because of being extremely dull and tedious. • **interminableness** *noun*. • **interminably** *adverb*. ⓒ 14c: from Latin *interminabilis*.

intermingle ▻ *verb, tr & intr* to mingle or mix together. ⓒ 15c.

intermission /ɪntəˈmɪʃən/ ▻ *noun* **1** a short period of time between two things, eg two parts of a film, play, etc. **2** the act of intermitting. ⓒ 16c: from Latin *intermissio* interruption.

intermit /ɪntəˈmɪt/ ▻ *verb* (***intermitted, intermitting***) *tr & intr* to suspend or cause to suspend; to stop for a while. ⓒ 16c: from Latin *intermittere*.

intermittent ▻ *adj* happening occasionally; stopping for a while and then starting again; not continuous. • **intermittence** *noun*. • **intermittently** *adverb*.

intern ▻ *verb* (***interned, interning***) **1** /ɪnˈtɜːn/ to confine within a country, restricted area or prison, especially during a war. **2** /ˈɪntɜːn/ *intr, chiefly US* to train or work as an intern. ▻ *noun* (*also* **interne**, *plural* ***internes***) /ˈɪntɜːn/ **1** *chiefly US* an advanced student or graduate who gains practical experience by working, especially in a hospital or medical centre. **2** an inmate. • **internee**, **internment** see separate entries. • **internship** *noun*. ⓒ 19c: from French *interne*, from Latin *internus* inward.

internal /ɪnˈtɜːnəl/ ▻ *adj* **1** on, in, belonging to or suitable for the inside; inner. **2** on, in, belonging to or suitable for the inside of the body. **3** relating to a nation's domestic affairs as opposed to its relations with foreign countries. **4** for, belonging to or coming from within an organization. **5** relating to the inner nature or feelings or of the mind or soul. • **internally** *adverb*. ⓒ 16c: from Latin *internalis*, from *internus* inward.

internal-combustion engine ▻ *noun* an engine that produces power by the burning of a mixture of fuel and air within an enclosed space inside the engine, with the hot gas produced being used to drive a moving piston, rotor or turbine.

internalize or **internalise** ▻ *verb* (***internalized, internalizing***) **1** to make (a type of behaviour, characteristic, etc) part of one's personality. **2** to keep (an emotion, etc) inside oneself rather than express it. • **internalization** *noun*.

international ▻ *adj* involving, affecting, used by or carried on between two or more nations. ▻ *noun* **1** a sports match or competition between two national teams. **2** (*also* **internationalist**) someone who takes part in, or has taken part in, such a match or competition □ *The Dutch internationalist injured his leg in a reckless tackle.* • **internationality** *noun*. • **internationally** *adverb*.

International Atomic Energy Agency ▻ *noun* (abbreviation **IAEA**) an international agency which promotes research into and development of the non-military uses of nuclear energy, and oversees a system of safeguards and controls that restrict the use of nuclear materials for military purposes. ⓒ 1957.

International Date Line ▻ *noun* an imaginary line on the Earth's surface running N to S across the middle of the Pacific Ocean, the date in countries to the West of it being one day ahead of the date in countries to the East.

internationalism ▻ *noun* the view that the nations of the world should co-operate politically, economically, culturally, etc and work towards greater mutual understanding.

internationalist ▻ *noun* **1** someone who favours internationalism. **2** an INTERNATIONAL (*noun* 2).

internationalize or **internationalise** ▻ *verb* to make international, especially to bring under the control of two or more countries. • **internationalization** *noun*.

international law ▻ *noun* the law that governs relationships between states (**public international law**), or the law that determines which nation's law shall, in any particular case, govern the relations of private persons (**private international law**).

International Monetary Fund ▻ *noun* (abbreviation **IMF**) an international financial organization set up to promote trade by keeping currencies stable and having a fund of money from which member states may borrow.

International Phonetic Alphabet ▻ *noun* (abbreviation **IPA**) a conventionalized system of letters and symbols used to represent or record all the speech sounds of every language.

interne see INTERN *noun*

internecine /ɪntəˈniːsaɪn/ ▻ *adj* **1** said of a fight, war, etc: destructive and damaging to both sides. **2** involving or consisting of a conflict or struggle within a group or organization □ *an internecine feud.* ⓒ 17c: from Latin *internecinus* murderous, from *necare* to kill.

internee /ɪntɜːˈniː/ ▻ *noun* (***internees***) someone who is interned.

the Internet ▻ *noun* a global computer communications network providing almost instant transfer of electronic data from one computer to another, linking business, academic and private users. Also *as adj* □ *an Internet connection* □ *Internet cafés.* Often shortened to **the net**. Also called **infobahn** /ˈɪnfoʊbɑːn/. See also WORLD WIDE WEB, SUPERHIGHWAY. ⓒ 1990s: originally referring to any computer network linking several other networks.

internist /ɪnˈtɜːnɪst/ ▻ *noun* a specialist in internal diseases.

internment /ɪnˈtɜːnmənt/ ▻ *noun* the act or process of interning or the state of being interned.

> ***internment***
>
> A word often confused with this one is **interment**.

internode ▻ *noun* **1** *bot* the part of a plant stem that lies between two successive nodes (see NODE 2). **2** *anatomy* a slender part situated between two nodes (see NODE 1). ⓒ 17c: from Latin *internodium*, from *nodus* knot.

internship see under INTERN

interpellate /ɪnˈtɜːpəleɪt, ɪntəˈpeleɪt/ ▻ *verb* (***interpellated, interpellating***) to question (eg a government minister) about policy during the course of, and as an interruption to, a debate. Compare INTERPOLATE. • **interpellation** *noun*. • **interpellator** *noun*. ⓒ 16c: from Latin *interpellare*, *interpellatum* to disturb by speaking.

interpenetrate ▻ *verb* **1** to penetrate thoroughly. **2** *intr* to penetrate mutually. • **interpenetration** *noun*. • **interpenetrative** *adj*.

interpersonal /ɪntəˈpɜːsənəl/ ▻ *adj* concerning or involving relationships between people.

interphase ▻ *noun, biol* the period between successive divisions by MITOSIS of a living cell.

interplanetary ▻ *adj* **1** relating to the solar system. **2** happening or existing in the space between the planets.

interplanetary matter ▻ *noun, astron* matter in the solar system other than the planets and their satellites, including dust particles and gas that flow continuously outward from the Sun in the solar wind.

interplay /ˈɪntəpleɪ/ ▻ *noun* the action and influence of two or more things on each other.

Interpol /ˈɪntəpɒl/ ▻ *noun* an international organization that allows police forces in different countries to communicate and co-operate with each other in fighting crime. ⓒ 1950s: from *Inte*rnational Criminal *Pol*ice Organization.

interpolate /ɪnˈtɜːpəleɪt/ ▻ *verb* (***interpolated, interpolating***) **1** to add (words) to a book or manuscript, especially in order to make the text misleading or corrupt. **2** to alter (a text) in this way. **3** to interrupt a conversation, a person speaking, etc with (a remark or comment). **4** *math* to estimate (the value of a function) at a point between values that are already known. • **interpolation** *noun*. ⓒ 17c: from Latin *interpolare*, *interpolatum* to refurbish.

interpose /ɪntə'poʊz/ ▻ *verb* **1** *tr & intr* to put something, or come, between two other things. **2** to interrupt a conversation or argument with (a remark, comment, etc). **3** *intr* to act as mediator; to intervene. • **interposition** *noun*. ⓒ 16c: from French *interposer*, from Latin *interponere*.

interpret /ɪn'tɜːprɪt/ ▻ *verb* (***interpreted***, ***interpreting***) **1** to explain the meaning of (a foreign word, dream, etc). **2** *intr* to act as an interpreter. **3** to consider or understand (behaviour, a remark, etc) ▫ *Interpret her silence as disapproval.* **4** to convey one's idea of the meaning of (eg a dramatic role, piece of music) in one's performance. • **interpretability** *noun*. • **interpretable** *adj*. • **interpretative** or **interpretive** *adj*. • **interpretatively** or **interpretively** *adverb*. ⓒ 14c: from Latin *interpretari*, from *interpres* explainer.

interpretation /ɪntɜːprə'teɪʃən/ ▻ *noun* **1** an act of interpreting or the sense given as a result. **2** the representing of one's idea of the meaning of a dramatic role, piece of music, etc in one's performance.

interpreter ▻ *noun* **1** someone who translates foreign speech as the words are spoken and relays the translation orally. **2** *computing* a program that translates a statement written in a high-level language into machine code and then executes it, and continues to read, translate and execute one source program at a time. **3** a machine that senses a punched card which is fed into it and prints out the data contained in the patterns of holes in the card. • **interpretership** *noun*.

interproximal /ɪntə'prɒksɪməl/ ▻ *adj, dentistry* belonging or relating to the surfaces of the teeth where they adjoin.

interracial /ɪntə'reɪʃəl/ ▻ *adj* between different races of people. • **interracially** *adverb*.

interregnum /ɪntə'rɛgnəm/ ▻ *noun* (***interregnums*** or ***interregna***) **1** the period of time between two reigns when the throne is unoccupied, eg between the death of one monarch and the coronation of the next. **2** the period of time between the end of rule by one government and the beginning of rule by the next. **3** any interval or pause in a continuous sequence of events. ⓒ 16c: from Latin *regnum* reign.

interrelate /ɪntərɪ'eɪt/ ▻ *verb, tr & intr* to be in or be brought into a mutually dependent or reciprocal relationship. • **interrelated** *adj*. • **interrelation** *noun*. • **interrelationship** *noun*.

interrogate /ɪn'tɛrəgeɪt/ ▻ *verb* (***interrogated***, ***interrogating***) **1** to question closely and thoroughly, or examine by asking questions, sometimes threateningly. **2** said of a radar set, etc: to send out signals to (a radio beacon) to work out a position. • **interrogation** *noun*. • **interrogator** *noun* **1** someone who interrogates. **2** a transmitter used to send out interrogating signals. ⓒ 15c: from Latin *interrogare*, *interrogatum*, from *rogare* to ask.

interrogation mark and **interrogation point** less common terms for QUESTION MARK

interrogative /ɪntə'rɒgətɪv/ ▻ *adj* **1** like a question; asking or seeming to ask a question. **2** *grammar* said of an adjective or pronoun: used to introduce a question, eg *what*, *whom*, etc. ▻ *noun* an interrogative word, sentence or construction. • **interrogatively** *adverb*. ⓒ 16c.

interrogatory /ɪntə'rɒgətərɪ/ ▻ *adj* involving or expressing a question. ▻ *noun* (***interrogatories***) *especially law* a question or inquiry. ⓒ 16c.

interrupt /ɪntə'rʌpt/ ▻ *verb* (***interrupted***, ***interrupting***) **1** *tr & intr* to break into (a conversation or monologue) by asking a question or making a comment. **2** to make a break in the continuous activity of (an event), or to disturb someone from some action ▫ *We interrupt this broadcast to bring you an important message* ▫ *I'm not interrupting, am I?* **3** to destroy (a view, eg of a clear sweep of land) by getting in the way. • **interrupter** or **interruptor** *noun* **1** someone who interrupts. **2** *electronics* an electrical, electronic or mechanical device for opening and closing an electric circuit at set intervals in order to interrupt the flow of electric current and so produce pulses. • **interruptive** *adj*. • **interruptively** *noun*. ⓒ 15c: from Latin *interrumpere*, *interruptum* to break apart.

interruption ▻ *noun* **1** the act or process of interrupting or state of being interrupted. **2** something that interrupts, such as a question or remark. **3** a short pause or break.

interscapular ▻ *adj, anatomy* between the shoulder blades. ⓒ 18c: see SCAPULA.

interscholastic ▻ *adj* involving competition or co-operation between schools. ⓒ 1870s.

intersect /ɪntə'sɛkt/ ▻ *verb* (***intersected***, ***intersecting***) **1** to divide (lines, an area, etc) by passing or cutting through or across. **2** *intr* said especially of lines, roads, etc: to run through or cut across each other. ⓒ 17c: from Latin *intersecare*, *intersectum* to cut through.

intersection ▻ *noun* **1** a place where things meet or intersect, especially a road junction. **2** the act of intersecting. **3** *geom* the point or set of points where two or more lines or plane surfaces cross each other. **4** *geom* a set of points common to two or more geometrical figures. **5** *math* the set of elements formed by the elements common to two or more other sets. • **intersectional** *adj*.

intersex ▻ *noun, biol* an individual that has characteristics of both sexes. ⓒ Early 20c.

intersexual ▻ *noun* **1** belonging or relating to both sexes. **2** relating or belonging to an intersex.

interspace ▻ *noun* /'ɪntəspeɪs/ a space between two things; an interval. ▻ *verb* /ɪntə'speɪs/ to put a space or spaces between. ⓒ 15c.

intersperse /ɪntə'spɜːs/ ▻ *verb* (***interspersed***, ***interspersing***) **1** to scatter or insert something here and there. **2** *intr* to diversify or change slightly with scattered things. • **interspersion** *noun*. ⓒ 16c: from Latin *interspergere*, *interspersum*.

interstate ▻ *adj* between two or more states, especially in the USA or Australia. ▻ *noun, especially US* a major road that crosses a state boundary. ⓒ 19c.

interstellar ▻ *adj* happening or existing in the space between individual stars within galaxies. ⓒ 17c.

interstice /ɪn'tɜːsɪs/ ▻ *noun* **1** a very small gap or space between two things. **2** *physics* any of the spaces between atoms in a crystal. ⓒ 17c: from Latin *interstitium*.

intertextual ▻ *adj, literary criticism* said of a text, play, film, work of art, etc: making use of references or allusions to another work or works, usually to a specified degree ▫ *Eliot's 'The Waste Land' is a highly intertextual poem.*

intertextuality ▻ *noun, literary criticism* **1** the extent to which particular text, play, film, work of art, etc makes use of references or allusions to another work or works. **2** the use of this technique by an author, director, artist, text, etc. ⓒ 1980s.

intertextualize or **intertextualise** ▻ *verb* (***intertextualized***, ***intertextualizing***) said of an author, director, artist, text, etc: to make use of references or allusions to another work or works in (the work under discussion).

intertrigo /ɪntə'traɪgoʊ/ ▻ *noun* (***intertrigos***) *medicine* an inflammation of the skin from chafing or rubbing. ⓒ 18c: from *terere* to rub.

intertwine ▻ *verb, tr & intr* to twist or be twisted together. ⓒ 17c.

interurban ▻ *adj* between cities. ⓒ 19c.

interval /'ɪntəvəl/ ▻ *noun* **1** a period of time between two events. **2** a space or distance between two things. **3** *Brit* a short break between the acts of a play or opera, or between parts of a concert or long film. **4** *music* the difference in pitch between two notes or tones. ● **at intervals 1** here and there; now and then. **2** with a stated distance in time or space between □ ***at intervals of ten minutes.*** ⓒ 13c: from Latin *intervallum* space between pallisades.

intervene /ɪntə'viːn/ ▷ *verb* (***intervened, intervening***) *intr* **1** (*often* **intervene in something**) to involve oneself in something which is happening in order to affect the outcome. **2** (*often* **intervene in something** or **between people**) to involve oneself or interfere in a dispute between other people in order to settle it or prevent more serious conflict. **3** to come or occur between two things in place or time. **4** *law* to become involved in a lawsuit as a third party. ⓒ 16c: from Latin *intervenire* to come between.

intervention /ɪntə'vɛnʃən/ ▷ *noun* an act of intervening, especially in the affairs of other people or other countries.

interventionism ▷ *noun* the belief that the government of a country should be allowed to interfere, or should interfere, in the economic affairs of the country, or in the internal affairs of other countries or states. ● **interventionist** *noun, adj.*

interview /'ɪntəvjuː/ ▷ *noun* **1** a formal meeting and discussion with someone, especially one at which an employer meets and judges a prospective employee. **2** a conversation or discussion which aims at obtaining information, especially one in which a journalist asks questions of a famous or important person and which is broadcast or published. ▷ *verb* to hold an interview. ● **interviewer** *noun.* ● **interviewee** /ɪntəvjuː'iː/ *noun.* ⓒ 16c: from French *entrevue*, from *entrevoir* to glimpse.

interweave /ɪntə'wiːv/ ▷ *verb, tr & intr* to weave or be woven together. ⓒ 16c.

intestate /ɪn'tɛsteɪt, -stət/ *law* ▷ *adj* said of a person: not having made a valid will before their death. ▷ *noun* someone who dies without making a valid will. ● **intestacy** /-stəsɪ/ *noun.* ⓒ 14c: from Latin *intestatus*, from *testari* to make a will.

intestine /ɪn'tɛstɪn/ ▷ *noun* the muscular tube-like part of the alimentary canal leading from the stomach to the anus, divided into the LARGE INTESTINE and the SMALL INTESTINE. ● **intestinal** /ɪn'tɛstɪnəl, ɪntɛ'staɪnəl/ *adj.* ⓒ 16c: from Latin *intestinus* internal.

intimacy /'ɪntɪməsɪ/ ▷ *noun* (***intimacies***) **1** warm close personal friendship. **2** an intimate or personal remark. **3** *euphemistic* sexual intercourse. **4** the state or quality of being intimate.

intimate¹ /'ɪntɪmət/ ▷ *adj* **1** marked by or sharing a close and affectionate friendship. **2** very private or personal. **3** said of a place: small and quiet with a warm, friendly atmosphere. **4** (*often* **intimate with someone**) sharing a sexual relationship with them. **5** said of knowledge: deep and thorough. ▷ *noun* a close friend. ● **intimately** *adverb.* ⓒ 17c: from Latin *intimus* innermost.

intimate² /'ɪntɪmeɪt/ ▷ *verb* (***intimated, intimating***) **1** to announce or make known. **2** to hint or suggest indirectly. ● **intimation** *noun.* ⓒ 16c: from Latin *intimare, intimatum.*

intimidate /ɪn'tɪmɪdeɪt/ ▷ *verb* (***intimidated, intimidating***) **1** to coerce, especially with threats. **2** to frighten, scare or overawe. ● **intimidating** *adj.* ● **intimidation** *noun.* ⓒ 17c: from Latin *intimidare*, from *timidus* frightened.

intimisme or **intimism** /'ɪntɪmɪzəm/ ▷ *noun, art* a genre of French Impressionist painting characterized by the representation of everyday subjects, such as domestic interiors, portrayal of close family members and friends in their home.

into /'ɪntuː, 'ɪntə/ ▷ *prep* **1** to or towards the inside or middle of something □ ***Go into the room.*** **2** against; into contact or collision with something or someone. **3** used to express a change of state or condition: □ ***change into a suit*** □ ***get into difficulties*** □ ***form into groups.*** **4** having reached a certain period of time □ ***We were into extra time before Booth scored the winner.*** **5** *math* used to express division □ ***four into twenty makes five.*** **6** *colloq* involved with, interested in or enthusiastic about □ ***She's into Nirvana in a big way.*** ⓒ Anglo-Saxon.

intolerable /ɪn'tɒlərəbəl/ ▷ *adj* too bad, difficult, painful, etc to be put up with. ● **intolerability** or **intolerableness** *noun.* ● **intolerably** *adverb.* ⓒ 15c.

intolerant /ɪn'tɒlərənt/ ▷ *adj* (*often* **intolerant of something**) refusing or unwilling to accept ideas, beliefs, behaviour, etc different from one's own. ● **intolerance** *noun.* ● **intolerantly** *adverb.* ⓒ 18c: from Latin *intolerans*, from *tolerare* to endure.

intonate /'ɪntəneɪt/ ▷ *verb* (***intonated, intonating***) *tr & intr* to intone. ⓒ 18c: see INTONE.

intonation /ɪntə'neɪʃən/ ▷ *noun* **1** the rise and fall of the pitch of the voice in speech. **2** the opening phrase of a plainsong melody. **3** an act of intoning. **4** the correct pitching of musical notes.

intone /ɪn'toʊn/ ▷ *verb* (***intoned, intoning***) *tr & intr* **1** to recite (a prayer, etc) in a solemn monotonous voice or in singing tones. **2** to say something with a particular intonation or tone. **3** to sing the opening phrase of a PLAINSONG. ⓒ 15c: from Latin *intonare, intonatum* to thunder.

in toto /ɪn 'toʊtoʊ/ ▷ *adverb* totally, completely; in sum. ⓒ 18c: Latin.

intoxicant /ɪn'tɒksɪkənt/ ▷ *noun* something that causes intoxication, especially an alcoholic drink. ▷ *adj* intoxicating. ⓒ 19c.

intoxicate /ɪn'tɒksɪkeɪt/ ▷ *verb* (***intoxicated, intoxicating***) **1** to make drunk. **2** to excite or elate. ● **intoxicating** *adj.* ⓒ 16c: from *intoxicare* to poison.

intoxication ▷ *noun* a condition in which certain centres in the brain are affected by alcohol (or other drugs), gases, heavy metals or other toxic substances. It is characterized by impaired intellectual ability, confusion, unsteady walking, etc.

intra- /'ɪntrə/ ▷ *prefix, denoting* within; inside; on the inside. ⓒ Latin, meaning 'within'.

intracellular /ɪntrə'sɛljələ(r)/ ▷ *adj, biol* situated or occurring within cells. ⓒ 19c.

intractable /ɪn'traktəbəl/ ▷ *adj* **1** said of a person: difficult to control or influence; obstinate. **2** said of a problem, illness, etc: difficult to solve, cure or deal with. ● **intractability** *noun.* ● **intractably** *adverb.* ⓒ 16c: from Latin *intractabilis*, from *tractare* to handle.

intradermal ▷ *adj* (abbreviation **ID** or **i.d.**) *medicine* **1** within the DERMIS. **2** said of an injection, etc: administered just below the surface of the skin, eg to test for an allergy. Compare SUBCUTANEOUS. ⓒ 19c.

intramural /ɪntrə'mjʊərəl/ ▷ *adj* **1** within or amongst the people in an institution, especially a school, college or university. **2** within the scope of normal studies. **3** situated within walls. ● **intramurally** *adverb.* ⓒ 19c: from Latin *murus* wall.

intramuscular ▷ *adj* (abbreviation **Im** or **i.m.**) *medicine* located within or introduced into a muscle or muscles. ⓒ 19c.

intransigent /ɪn'transɪdʒənt, -zɪdʒənt/ ▷ *adj* holding firmly to one's (often extreme) beliefs and refusing to change or compromise; stubborn. ▷ *noun* an intransigent person. ● **intransigence** *noun.* ● **intransigently** *adverb.* ⓒ 18c: from Spanish *intransigente*, from Latin *transigere* to come to an agreement.

intransitive /ɪn'transɪtɪv, -zɪtɪv/ ▷ *adj, grammar* said of a verb: not taking or having a direct object, such as *run* in the phrase *run as fast as you can.* ▷ *noun* such a verb.

Compare ABSOLUTE, TRANSITIVE. • **intransitively** *adverb.* 🕒 17c: from Latin *intransitivus* not passing over.

intrapreneur ▷ *noun* someone who initiates commercial ventures within a large organization. 🕒 1970s: from INTRA-, modelled on ENTREPRENEUR.

intrauterine /ɪntrə'juːtəraɪn/ ▷ *adj* (abbreviation **IU** or **i.u.**) *medicine* located or occurring within the uterus. 🕒 19c.

intrauterine device and **intrauterine contraceptive device** ▷ *noun* (abbreviation **IUD** or **IUCD**) a contraceptive device consisting of a plastic or metal coil, loop or other shape that is inserted into the womb to prevent implantation of a fertilized egg (and thus pregnancy) by causing mild inflammation of the lining of the uterus. Also called **coil**. 🕒 1960s.

intravenous /ɪntrə'viːnəs/ ▷ *adj* (abbreviation **IV** or **i.v.**) *medicine* located within or introduced into a vein or veins. • **intravenously** *adverb.* 🕒 19c.

intravenous infusion see INFUSION 3

in-tray ▷ *noun, Brit* a tray, eg in an office, on a desk, etc, that incoming mail, etc is put in before it is dealt with.

intrench see ENTRENCH

intrepid /ɪn'trepɪd/ ▷ *adj* bold and daring; fearless; brave. • **intrepidity** *noun.* • **intrepidly** *adj.* 🕒 17c: from Latin *intrepidus.*

intricate /'ɪntrɪkət/ ▷ *adj* full of complicated, interrelating or tangled details or parts and therefore difficult to understand, analyse or sort out. • **intricacy** *noun* (***intricacies***). • **intricately** *adverb.* 🕒 16c: from Latin *intricare, intricatum* to perplex.

intrigue ▷ *noun* /'ɪntriːg/ (***intrigues***) **1** secret plotting or underhand scheming. **2** a secret plot or plan. **3** a secret illicit love affair. ▷ *verb* /ɪn'triːg/ (***intrigued, intriguing***) **1** to arouse the curiosity or interest of someone; to fascinate. **2** *intr* to plot secretly. **3** (*usually* **intrigue with someone**) to carry on a secret love affair with them. • **intriguing** *adj.* • **intriguingly** *adverb.* 🕒 17c: French, from Latin *intricare* to perplex.

intrinsic /ɪn'trɪnsɪk/ ▷ *adj* **1** belonging to something or someone as an inherent and essential part of their nature. **2** *anatomy* denoting a muscle that is entirely contained within the organ or body part on which it acts, eg the muscles of the tongue. • **intrinsically** *adverb.* 🕒 17c in sense 1; 15c, meaning 'internal': from Latin *intrinsecus* inwardly.

intro /'ɪntroʊ/ ▷ *noun* (***intros***) *colloq* an introduction, especially to a piece of music. 🕒 1920s.

intro- /ɪntroʊ/ ▷ *prefix, denoting* within; into; inwards □ *introspection.* 🕒 Latin, meaning 'to the inside'.

introduce /ɪntrə'dʒuːs/ ▷ *verb* (***introduced, introducing***) **1** (*usually* **introduce someone to someone else**) to make them known by name to each other, especially formally □ *I'll introduce you to Joe tonight.* **2** to announce or present (eg a radio or television programme) to an audience. **3** to bring (especially something new) into a place, situation, etc for the first time □ *introduced flexitime.* **4** to bring into operation, practice or use. **5** to put forward or propose (a possible law or bill) for attention, consideration or approval. **6** (*usually* **introduce someone to something**) to cause someone to experience or discover something for the first time □ *I introduced Nick to the delights of Graham Greene.* **7** to start or preface □ *Introduce the play with a brief analysis of the plot.* **8** (*usually* **introduce one thing into another**) to insert or put something into something else. • **introducible** *adj.* 🕒 16c: from Latin *introducere* to lead in.

introduction /ɪntrə'dʌkʃən/ ▷ *noun* **1** the act or process of introducing or process of being introduced. **2** a presentation of one person to another or others. **3** a section at the beginning of a book which explains briefly what it is about, why it was written, etc. **4** a book which outlines the basic principles of a subject, suitable for beginners. **5** a short passage of music beginning a piece or song, or leading up to a movement. **6** something which has been introduced.

introductory ▷ *adj* giving or serving as an introduction; preliminary □ *a special introductory price.* • **introductorily** *adverb.*

introit /'ɪntrɔɪt/ ▷ *noun, Christianity* a hymn, psalm or anthem sung at the beginning of a service or, in the RC Church, as the priest approaches the altar to celebrate Mass. 🕒 15c: from Latin *introitus* entrance.

intron /'ɪntrɒn/ ▷ *noun, genetics* any segment of DNA in a gene that does not carry coded instructions for the manufacture of a protein. Also called **intervening sequence**. See also EXON. 🕒 1970s.

introspection /ɪntrə'spɛkʃən/ ▷ *noun* the examination of one's own thoughts, feelings and intuitions, etc, sometimes with the tendency of obsession. • **introspective** *adj.* • **introspectively** *adverb.* 🕒 17c: from Latin *introspicere* to look within.

introversion /ɪntrə'vɜːʃən, -ʒən/ ▷ *noun, psychol* a personality trait characterized by a tendency to be more interested in the self and inner feelings than in the outside world and social relationships. Compare EXTROVERSION.

introvert /'ɪntrəvɜːt/ ▷ *noun* **1** *psychol* someone who is more concerned with their thoughts and inner feelings than with the outside world and social relationships. **2** someone who tends not to socialize and who is uncommunicative and withdrawn. ▷ *adj* (*also* **introverted**) concerned more with one's own thoughts and feelings than with other people and outside events. ▷ *verb* /ɪntrə'vɜːt/ (***introverted, introverting***) **1** to turn (one's thoughts) inward to concentrate on oneself. **2** to withdraw (eg a part of the body) into the main part, eg as a tortoise can withdraw its head into its shell. Compare EXTROVERT. 🕒 17c: from Latin *vertere* to turn.

intrude /ɪn'truːd/ ▷ *verb* (***intruded, intruding***) *tr & intr* (*often* **intrude into** or **on someone** or **something**) to force or impose (oneself, one's presence or something) without welcome or invitation. 🕒 16c: from Latin *intrudere* to thrust in.

intruder ▷ *noun* someone who enters premises secretly or by force, especially in order to commit a crime.

intrusion /ɪn'truːʒən/ ▷ *noun* **1** an act or process of intruding, especially on someone else's property. **2** *geol* the forcing of molten magma under pressure into pre-existing rock. **3** a mass of igneous rock formed by the solidification of molten magma beneath the Earth's surface, after it has been forced into pre-existing rock. 🕒 14c: from Latin *intrusio*, from *intrudere* to thrust in.

intrusive /ɪn'truːsɪv, -zɪv/ ▷ *adj* **1** tending to intrude. **2** said of rock: formed by INTRUSION (sense 3). **3** said of a speech sound: introduced into a piece of connected speech for a phonetic reason and without etymological justification. • **intrusively** *adverb.* • **intrusiveness** *noun.*

intrusive rock ▷ *noun, geol* igneous rock formed by the cooling and solidification of magma beneath the Earth's surface, eg granite.

intrust see ENTRUST

intubate /'ɪntʃʊbeɪt/ ▷ *verb* (***intubated, intubating***) *medicine* to insert a tube into (a hollow body part such as the trachea to assist breathing during anaesthesia. 🕒 19c: from Latin *tuba* tube.

intuit /ɪn'tʃuːɪt/ ▷ *verb* (***intuited, intuiting***) to know or become aware of something by intuition. • **intuitable** *adj.*

intuition /ɪntʃʊ'ɪʃən/ ▷ *noun* **1** the power of understanding or realizing something without conscious rational thought or analysis. **2** something understood or realized in this way. **3** immediate instinctive understanding or belief. 🕒 16c in sense 1; 15c in obsolete sense 'a view': from Latin *intuitio*, from *tueri* to look.

intuitive /ɪn'tʃuːɪtɪv/ ▻ *adj* having, showing or based on intuition. • **intuitively** *adverb*. • **intuitiveness** *noun*.

intumesce /ɪntʃʊ'mɛs/ ▻ *verb* (***intumesced***, ***intumescing***) *intr* to swell up. • **intumescent** *adj*. • **intumescence** *noun*. ⓒ 18c: from Latin *intumescere*, from *tumere* to swell.

intussusception /ɪntəsə'sɛpʃən/ ▻ *noun* **1** *medicine* the pushing down of one part of the intestine into the part below it. **2** *biol* the insertion of new material into the thickness of an existing cell wall. ⓒ 18c: from Latin *intus* within + *susceptio* a taking up.

Inuit or **Innuit** /'ɪnʊɪt/ ▻ *noun* (*plural* ***Inuit*** or ***Innuit***) an individual belonging to a group of peoples of the Arctic and sub-Arctic regions of Canada, Greenland and Alaska. **2** their language. ▻ *adj* belonging or relating to this group or their language. ⓒ 19c: Inuit, plural of *inuk* person.

Inuit

See Usage Note at **Eskimo**.

Inuktitut /ɪ'nʊktɪtʊt/ ▻ *noun* the form of the Inuit language spoken in the Canadian Arctic. ⓒ 20c: Inuit, meaning 'the Eskimo way', the title of a periodical.

inulin /'ɪnjəlɪn/ ▻ *noun*, *biochem* a water-soluble carbohydrate stored as a food reserve in the roots and tubers of certain plants, eg dahlia. ⓒ 19c: from Latin *Inula* a genus of plants.

inunction /ɪn'ʌŋkʃən/ ▻ *noun* **1** the application of ointment or liniment to the skin by rubbing or smearing. **2** the act of anointing. **3** the ointment or liniment used. ⓒ 15c: from Latin *inungere* to anoint.

inundate /'ɪnʌndeɪt/ ▻ *verb* (***inundated***, ***inundating***) **1** to overwhelm with water. **2** to swamp □ *was inundated with applications for the job.* • **inundation** *noun* **1** a flood. **2** an act of inundating. ⓒ 17c: from Latin *inundare*, *inundatum* to flow over.

inure or **enure** /ɪn'jʊə(r)/ ▻ *verb* (***inured***, ***inuring***) **1** (*often* **inure someone to something**) to accustom them to something unpleasant or unwelcome. **2** *law* to come into use or effect. • **inurement** *noun*. ⓒ 15c: from French *en ure* in use.

in utero /ɪn 'juːtəroʊ/ ▻ *adverb*, *adj* in the womb. ⓒ 18c: Latin.

invade /ɪn'veɪd/ ▻ *verb* (***invaded***, ***invading***) **1** *tr & intr* to enter (a country) by force with an army. **2** *tr & intr* to attack or overrun □ *Angry supporters invaded the pitch.* **3** to interfere with (a person's rights, privacy, etc). See also INVASION. • **invader** *noun*. ⓒ 15c: from Latin *invadere*.

invaginate /ɪn'vadʒɪneɪt/ ▻ *verb* (***invaginated***, ***invaginating***) **1** *pathol* to push back (a tubular organ) so that it becomes introverted. **2** *intr* to become invaginated. • **invagination** *noun*. ⓒ 17c: from Latin *invaginare*, *invaginatum*, from *vagina* sheath.

invalid¹ /'ɪnvəlɪd/ ▻ *noun* someone who is constantly ill or who is disabled. ▻ *adj* suitable for or being an invalid. ▻ *verb* (***invalided***, ***invaliding***) **1 a** (*usually* **invalid someone out**) to discharge (a soldier, etc) from service because of illness; **b** (*usually* **invalid someone home**) to send (a soldier, etc) home because of illness. □ *served in Gallipoli before being invalided back home.* **2** to affect with disease. • **invalidity** *noun*. ⓒ 17c: from French, from Latin *invalidus* weak.

invalid² /ɪn'valɪd/ ▻ *adj* **1** said of a document, agreement, etc: having no legal force. **2** said of an argument, reasoning, etc: based on false reasoning or a mistake and therefore not valid, correct or reliable. • **invalidity** *noun*. • **invalidly** *adverb*. ⓒ 17c: from Latin *invalidus* weak.

invalidate /ɪn'valɪdeɪt/ ▻ *verb* to make (a document, agreement, argument, etc) invalid. • **invalidation** *noun*. ⓒ 17c.

invalidity benefit ▻ *noun*, *Brit* (abbreviation **IVB**) a government allowance paid to someone who has been unable to work because of illness, for more than half a year.

invaluable /ɪn'valjʊəbəl/ ▻ *adj* having a value that is too great to be measured. • **invaluableness** *noun*. • **invaluably** *adverb*.

Invar /'ɪnvɑː(r), ɪn'vɑː(r)/ ▻ *noun*, *trademark* an alloy of iron, nickel and carbon which is expanded only very slightly by heat, and is used in the manufacture of scientific instruments. ⓒ Early 20c: from *invariable*.

invariable ▻ *adj* not prone to change or alteration; constant. ⓒ 17c: from Latin *invariabilis*.

invariably ▻ *adverb* **1** always; without exception □ *Dave is invariably late.* **2** in an invariable way.

invariant /ɪn'vɛərɪənt/ ▻ *noun*, *math* a property of a mathematical equation, geometric figure, etc, that is unaltered by a particular procedure. ▻ *adj* invariable.

invasion /ɪn'veɪʒən/ ▻ *noun* **1** an act of invading or process of being invaded, eg by a hostile country or by something harmful. **2** an encroachment or violation. **3** *pathol* the spread of a disease from its place of origin to other places in the living organism affected by it. **4** *ecol* the spread of a species of plant to an area where it previously did not grow. • **invasive** /ɪn'veɪsɪv/ *adj*. ⓒ 16c: from Latin *invasio*, from *invadere* to invade.

invective /ɪn'vɛktɪv/ ▻ *noun* **1** severe or bitter accusation or denunciation, using sarcastic or abusive language. **2** an attack using such words. ▻ *adj* characterized by such an attack. ⓒ 15c: from Latin *invectivus* abusive; see INVEIGH.

inveigh /ɪn'veɪ/ ▻ *verb* (***inveighed***, ***inveighing***) *intr* (*usually* **inveigh against someone** or **something**) to speak strongly or passionately against them or it, especially in criticism or protest. ⓒ 16c in this sense; 15c in obsolete sense 'to introduce': from Latin *invehi*, *invectus* to attack with words.

inveigle /ɪn'viːgəl, ɪn'veɪ-/ ▻ *verb* (***inveigled***, ***inveigling***) (*usually* **inveigle someone into something**) to trick, deceive or persuade them into doing it. • **inveiglement** *noun*. ⓒ 16c: from French *enveogler* to blind, from Latin *ab* without + *oculus* eye.

invent /ɪn'vɛnt/ ▻ *verb* (***invented***, ***inventing***) **1** to be the first person to make or use (a machine, game, method, etc). **2** to think or make up (an excuse, false story, etc). • **inventor** *noun* someone who invents, especially as an occupation. ⓒ 16c: from Latin *invenire*, *inventum* to find.

invention ▻ *noun* **1** something invented, especially a device, machine, etc. **2** the act of inventing. **3** the ability to create and invent things; inventiveness. **4** *colloq* a lie. **5** *music* a short piece of keyboard music based on a single, simple idea.

inventive ▻ *adj* **1** skilled at inventing; creative; resourceful. **2** characterized by invention. • **inventively** *adverb*. • **inventiveness** *noun*.

inventory /'ɪnvəntərɪ/ ▻ *noun* (***inventories***) **1** a formal and complete list of the articles, goods, etc found in a particular place, eg of goods for sale in a shop, or of furniture and possessions in a house. **2** the items included in such a list. ▻ *verb* (***inventories***, ***inventoried***, ***inventorying***) to make an inventory of items; to list in an inventory. ⓒ 16c: from Latin *inventorium* a list of things that have been found, from *invenire* to find.

inverse /'ɪnvɜːs, ɪn'vɜːs/ ▻ *adj* opposite or reverse in order, sequence, direction, effect, etc. ▻ *noun* **1** a direct opposite. **2** the state of being directly opposite or reversed. **3** *math* a mathematical function that is opposite in effect or nature to another function. • **inversely** *adverb*. ⓒ 17c: from Latin *inversus*, from *invertere* to invert.

inversion /ɪn'vɜːʃən, -ʒən/ ▻ *noun* **1** the act of turning upside down or inside out, or otherwise inverting. **2** the state of being turned upside down, inside out or otherwise inverted. **3** a reversal of position, order, direction, form, effect, etc. **4** something achieved by inverting. **5** *grammar* the reversal of the word order of normal subject followed by verb, as in *up popped the toast*. Also called **anastrophe**. ⓘ 16c: from Latin *inversio*.

invert /ɪnˈvɜːt/ ▷ *verb* (***inverted***, ***inverting***) **1** to turn upside down or inside out. **2** to reverse in order, sequence, direction, effect, etc. **3** *music* to change (eg a chord) by placing the lowest note an octave higher. ⓘ 17c: from Latin *invertere*.

invertase /ˈɪnvəteɪs, ɪnˈvɜːteɪs/ ▷ *noun, biochem* an enzyme found in yeasts that breaks down SUCROSE to form GLUCOSE and FRUCTOSE.

invertebrate /ɪnˈvɜːtəbrət, -breɪt/ ▷ *noun, zool* any animal that does not possess a backbone, such as an insect, worm, snail or jellyfish. ▷ *adj* (*also* **invertebral**) **1** relating to an animal that does not possess a backbone. **2** having no strength of character. ⓘ 19c: from Latin *vertebra* spinal joint.

inverted comma see QUOTATION MARK

inverted snob ▷ *noun* someone who makes a point of practising, approving, etc things that a snobbish person would find objectionable.

invert sugar /ˈɪnvɜːt—/ ▷ *noun, biochem* a mixture of GLUCOSE and FRUCTOSE, found in many fruits, and formed as a result of the breakdown of SUCROSE by INVERTASE.

invest /ɪnˈvɛst/ ▷ *verb* (***invested***, ***investing***) **1** *tr & intr* to put (money) into a company or business, eg by buying shares in it, in order to make a profit. **2** *tr & intr* to devote (time, effort, energy, etc) to something □ *They invested all their energies in animal welfare.* **3** (*often* **invest someone with something**) to give them the symbols of power, rights, rank, etc officially. See also INVESTITURE. **4** (*usually* **invest something in someone**) to place power, rank, a quality or feeling, etc in someone. **5** to clothe or adorn. **6** *military* to besiege (a stronghold). • **investor** *noun*. ⓘ 16c: from Latin *investire* to clothe.

■ **invest in something** *colloq* to buy it □ *I decided to invest in some new socks.*

investigate /ɪnˈvɛstɪgeɪt/ ▷ *verb* (***investigated***, ***investigating***) *tr & intr* to carry out a thorough, detailed and often official inquiry into, or examination of, something or someone. • **investigation** *noun*. • **investigative** /ɪnˈvɛstɪgətɪv, -geɪtɪv/ or **investigatory** /ɪnˈvɛstɪgeɪtərɪ, -gətərɪ/ *adj*. • **investigator** *noun*. ⓘ 16c: from Latin *investigare*, *investigatum* to track down.

investigative journalism ▷ *noun* journalism involving the investigation and exposure of corruption, crime, inefficiency, etc.

investiture /ɪnˈvɛstɪtʃə(r)/ ▷ *noun* a formal ceremony giving a rank or office to someone. See also INVEST. ⓘ 14c: from Latin *investitura*.

investment ▷ *noun* **1** a sum of money invested. **2** something, such as a business, house, etc in which one invests money, time, effort, etc. **3** the act of investing.

investment bank ▷ *noun* a US bank that handles new share issues, often in a syndicate with others. Compare MERCHANT BANK.

investment company and **investment trust** ▷ *noun* a company which, on behalf of its members, holds a portfolio of shares in other companies, aimed at obtaining a reasonable dividend yield, growth and balanced risk.

investor see under INVEST

inveterate /ɪnˈvɛtərət/ ▷ *adj* **1** said of a habit, practice, etc: firmly established. **2** said of a person: firmly fixed in a habit by long practice. • **inveterately** *adverb*. ⓘ 16c: from Latin *inveteratus* long continued.

invidious /ɪnˈvɪdɪəs/ ▷ *adj* likely to cause envy, resentment or indignation, especially by being or seeming to be unfair. • **invidiously** *adverb*. • **invidiousness** *noun*. ⓘ 17c: from Latin *invidiosus*, from *invidia* envy.

invigilate /ɪnˈvɪdʒɪleɪt/ ▷ *verb* (***invigilated***, ***invigilating***) *tr & intr, Brit* to keep watch over people sitting an examination, especially to prevent cheating. • **invigilation** *noun*. • **invigilator** *noun*. ⓘ 16c: from Latin *invigilare*, *invigilatum* to keep watch over.

invigorate /ɪnˈvɪgəreɪt/ ▷ *verb* (***invigorated***, ***invigorating***) to give fresh life, energy and health to something or someone; to strengthen or animate. • **invigorating** *adj*. • **invigoration** *noun*. ⓘ 17c: from Latin *vigor* strength.

invincible /ɪnˈvɪnsɪbəl/ ▷ *adj* indestructible; unable to be defeated. • **invincibility** *noun*. • **invincibly** *adverb*. ⓘ 15c: from Latin *invincibilis*, from *vincere* to defeat.

inviolable /ɪnˈvaɪələbəl/ ▷ *adj* not to be broken or violated; sacred. • **inviolability** *noun*. • **inviolably** *adverb*. ⓘ 16c: from Latin *inviolabilis*.

inviolate /ɪnˈvaɪələt, -leɪt/ ▷ *adj* not broken, violated or injured. ⓘ 15c: from Latin *inviolatus* unhurt.

invisible ▷ *adj* **1** not able to be seen. **2** unseen. **3** *econ* relating to services (eg insurance, tourism) rather than goods □ *invisible earnings* □ *invisible exports*. **4** not shown in regular statements □ *invisible assets*. ▷ *noun* an invisible item of trade. • **invisibility** *noun*. • **invisibly** *adverb*. ⓘ 14c.

invisible ink ▷ *noun* a kind of ink that cannot be seen on the paper until it is heated, subjected to ultraviolet light, treated with chemicals, etc.

invitation /ɪnvɪˈteɪʃən/ ▷ *noun* **1** a request to a person to come or go somewhere, eg to a party, meal, etc. **2** the form such a request takes, either verbally or written on a card, etc. **3** an act of inviting. **4** encouragement; enticement; inducement.

invite ▷ *verb* /ɪnˈvaɪt/ (***invited***, ***inviting***) **1** to request the presence of someone at one's house, at a party, etc, especially formally or politely. **2** to ask politely or formally for (eg comments, advice, etc). **3** to bring on or encourage (something unwanted or undesirable). **4** to attract or tempt. ▷ *noun* /ˈɪnvaɪt/ *colloq* an invitation. ⓘ 16c: from Latin *invitare*.

inviting /ɪnˈvaɪtɪŋ/ ▷ *adj* attractive or tempting. • **invitingly** *adverb*.

in vitro /ɪn ˈviːtroʊ/ ▷ *adj, adverb, biol* said of biological techniques or processes: performed outside a living organism in an artificial environment created by means of scientific equipment, eg in a test-tube. Compare IN VIVO. ⓘ 19c: Latin, meaning 'in the glass'.

in-vitro fertilization ▷ *noun* (abbreviation **IVF**) a technique whereby a human embryo is conceived outside the mother's body, by removing a mature OVUM from her ovary, placing it in a culture medium in a laboratory and fertilizing it with SPERM from the father. It is then re-implanted in the mother's womb and the pregnancy proceeds normally. Compare GIFT.

in vivo /ɪn ˈviːvoʊ/ ▷ *adj, adverb, biol* said of biological techniques or processes: performed within a living organism. Compare IN VITRO. ⓘ Early 20c: Latin, meaning 'in a living thing'.

invocation /ɪnvəˈkeɪʃən/ ▷ *noun* **1** an act or the process of invoking. **2** a prayer calling on God, a saint, etc for blessing or help. **3** an opening prayer at the beginning of a public service or sermon. **4** any appeal to supernatural beings, spirits, etc, such as an appeal to a Muse for inspiration at the beginning of a poem. • **invocatory** /ɪnˈvɒkətərɪ/ *adj*. ⓘ 14c: from Latin *invocatio*.

invoice /ˈɪnvɔɪs/ ▷ *noun* a list of goods supplied, delivered with the goods and giving details of price and quantity, usually treated as a request for payment. ▷ *verb* (***invoiced***, ***invoicing***) **1** to send an invoice to (a customer). **2** to provide an invoice for (goods). ⓘ 16c: from French *envoyer* to send.

invoke /ɪn'voʊk/ ▻ *verb* (***invoked, invoking***) **1** to make an appeal to (God, some deity, a Muse, authority, etc) for help, support or inspiration. **2** to appeal to (a law, principle, etc) as an authority or reason for eg one's behaviour. **3** to make an earnest appeal for (help, support, inspiration, etc). **4** to conjure up (a spirit) by reciting a spell. **5** to put (a law, decision, etc) into effect. See also INVOCATION. ◷ 15c: from Latin *invocare* to call upon, from *vocare* to call.

involucre /'ɪnvəluːkə(r), -ljuːkə(r)/ ▻ *noun* **1** *anatomy* an enveloping membrane. **2** *bot* a ring or crowd of BRACTs around an INFLORESCENCE. • **involucral** *adj*. • **involucrate** *adj*. ◷ 16c: French, from Latin *involucrum* something that envelops.

involuntary /ɪn'vɒləntərɪ/ ▻ *adj* said of an action, movement, muscle action, etc: done without being controlled by the will; not able to be controlled by the will; unintentional. • **involuntarily** *adverb*. ◷ 16c.

involuntary muscle ▻ *noun, anatomy* muscle that is not under conscious control, eg muscle of the heart, blood vessels, stomach and intestines. Also called **smooth muscle**.

involute /'ɪnvəluːt, -ljuːt/ ▻ *adj* **1** entangled; intricate. **2** *bot* said of petals, etc: rolled in at the edges. **3** said of shells: curled up in a spiral shape, so that the axis is concealed. ▻ *noun, geom* the curve traced out by the different points on a piece of string unwinding from the curve. Compare EVOLUTE. ▻ *verb* /ɪnvə'luːt, -ljuːt/ (***involuted, involuting***) *intr* to become involute or undergo involution. ◷ 17c: from Latin *involvere*, *involutum* to INVOLVE.

involution /ɪnvə'luːʃən/ ▻ *noun* **1** the act of involving or the state of being involved or entangled. **2** *zool* degeneration. **3** *physiol* the shrinking in size of an organ, eg the womb, after its purpose has been served or as a result of ageing. **4** *math* raising to a power.

involve /ɪn'vɒlv/ ▻ *verb* (***involved, involving***) **1** to require as a necessary part. **2** (*usually* **involve someone in something**) to cause them to take part or be implicated in it. **3** to have an effect on someone or something. **4** (*often* **involve oneself in something**) to become emotionally concerned in it. • **involved** *adj* **1** concerned, implicated. **2** complicated. • **involvement** *noun*. ◷ 14c: from Latin *involvere* to roll up.

invulnerable /ɪn'vʌlnərəbəl/ ▻ *adj* incapable of being hurt, damaged or attacked. • **invulnerability** *noun*. • **invulnerably** *adj*. ◷ 16c.

inward /'ɪnwəd/ ▻ *adj* **1** placed or being within. **2** moving towards the inside. **3** relating or belonging to the mind or soul. ▻ *adverb* (*also* **inwards**) **1** towards the inside or the centre. **2** into the mind, inner thoughts or soul. ◷ Anglo-Saxon *inweard*.

inwardly ▻ *adverb* **1** on the inside; internally. **2** in one's private thoughts; secretly.

inwards see INWARD

in-your-face see under FACE

I/O ▻ *abbreviation, computing* input/output □ ***I/O system***.

IOB ▻ *abbreviation* Institute of Building.

IOC ▻ *abbreviation* International Olympic Committee.

iodide /'aɪədaɪd, 'aɪoʊdaɪd/ ▻ *noun* **1** a chemical compound containing iodine and another element or radical, eg potassium iodide, methyl iodide. **2** a salt of HYDRIODIC ACID.

iodine /'aɪədiːn, 'aɪoʊ-, -daɪn/ ▻ *noun* **1** *chem* (abbreviation **I**, atomic number 53) a non-metallic element consisting of dark-violet crystals that SUBLIME to a violet vapour when heated, and which is used as an antiseptic, in the production of dyes, and as a catalyst and chemical reagent. **2** (*also* **tincture of iodine**) *medicine* a solution of iodine in ethanol, used as an antiseptic. ◷ 19c: from Greek *ioeides* violet-coloured.

iodize or **iodise** /'aɪədaɪz/ ▻ *verb* (***iodized, iodizing***) to treat something with iodine, especially common salt so as to provide iodine as a nutritional supplement.

IoJ ▻ *abbreviation* Institute of Journalists.

IOM ▻ *abbreviation* Isle of Man.

ion /'aɪən, 'aɪɒn/ ▻ *noun, chem* an atom or group of atoms that has acquired a net positive charge as a result of losing one or more electrons, or a net negative charge as a result of gaining one or more electrons. ◷ 19c: Greek, meaning 'going', from *ienai* to go.

-ion /ən/ ▻ *suffix, forming nouns, denoting* a process, state, result, etc □ ***completion*** □ ***contrition*** □ ***pollution***. See also -ATION. ◷ French, from Latin *-io*, *-ionis*.

ion engine ▻ *noun, engineering* an engine, used to propel spacecraft or satellites, in which the thrust is produced by a stream of charged particles.

ion exchange ▻ *noun, chem* a chemical reaction in which ions which have the same charge are exchanged between a solution and a porous granular solid, such as a synthetic resin, in contact with the solution.

Ionic /aɪ'ɒnɪk/ ▻ *adj* **1** *archit, denoting* an ORDER (*noun* 19) of classical architecture, characterized by a style of column with slim and usually fluted shafts and capitals with spiral scrolls known as **volute**. Compare COMPOSITE, CORINTHIAN, DORIC, TUSCAN. **2** belonging or relating to Ionia, an ancient region of the W coast of Asia Minor, its inhabitants or their dialect of Ancient Greek. ▻ *noun* one of the four main dialects of Ancient Greek, spoken in Ionia. ◷ 16c: from Greek *Ionikos*.

ionic /aɪ'ɒnɪk/ ▻ *adj* **1** belonging or relating to or using ions. **2** *denoting* a chemical compound that occurs in the form of ions.

ionic bond ▻ *noun, chem* a chemical bond formed by the transfer of one or more electrons from one atom to another, resulting in the conversion of electrically neutral atoms to positively and negatively charged ions.

ion implantation ▻ *noun, electronics* the introduction of impurities into a semiconductor crystal, in order to modify its electronic properties, by directing a beam of ions at its surface.

ionization or **ionisation** ▻ *noun, chem, physics* the formation of ions from atoms as a result of chemical reactions, dissociation of atoms of a molecule in solution, electrolysis, exposure to ionizing radiation or short-wavelength electromagnetic radiation, passage through a discharge tube or very high temperatures.

ionize or **ionise** /'aɪənaɪz/ ▻ *verb* (***ionized, ionizing***) *tr & intr, chem* to produce or make something produce ions.

ionizer or **ioniser** ▻ *noun* a device that produces negatively charged ions, considered to relieve headaches, fatigue and other symptoms which are said to be caused by the accumulation of positive ions in rooms and buildings where electrical machinery, computers, etc, are in frequent use.

ionizing radiation ▻ *noun, physics* any radiation that can cause ionization.

ionomer /aɪ'ɒnəmə(r)/ ▻ *noun, chem* a resilient and highly transparent thermoplastic which has both organic and inorganic components, and is used to make goggles, shields, bottles, refrigerator trays, toys and electrical parts.

ionosphere /aɪ'ɒnəsfɪə(r)/ ▻ *noun, meteorol* the layer of the Earth's atmosphere that extends from about 50km to about 70 to 80km above the Earth's surface to an indefinite height, and which contains many ions and free electrons produced by the ionizing effects of solar radiation. • **ionospheric** *adj*. ◷ 1920s: from ION + SPHERE.

iota /aɪ'oʊtə/ ▻ *noun* **1** the ninth letter of the Greek alphabet. See table at GREEK ALPHABET. **2** (***iotas***) a very small amount; a jot □ ***Nothing she said seemed to make an iota of difference***. ◷ 17c: Greek.

IOU /aɪoʊ'juː/ ▻ *noun* (*IOUs, IOU's* /aɪoʊ'juːz/) *colloq* a written and signed note that serves as an acknowledgement of a debt. ◷ 17c: pronunciation of *I owe you.*

IOW ▻ *abbreviation* Isle of Wight.

IPA ▻ *abbreviation* International Phonetic Alphabet.

IPC ▻ *abbreviation* International Publishing Corporation.

IPCC ▻ *abbreviation* Intergovernmental Panel on Climate Change.

IPCS ▻ *abbreviation* Institution of Professional Civil Servants.

ipecacuanha /ɪpɪkakjʊ'anə, -'ɑːnə/ or **ipecac** /'ɪpɪkak/ ▻ *noun* (*ipecacuanhas* or *ipecacs*) **1** a small Latin American shrub. **2** the dried root of this plant prepared as a tincture or syrup, which is used in small doses as an expectorant or as a purgative or emetic. ◷ 17c: Portuguese, from Tupí (S American Indian language) *ipekaaguene*, from *ipeh* low + *kaa* leaves + *guene* vomit.

IPM ▻ *abbreviation* Institute of Personnel Management.

IPPF ▻ *abbreviation* International Planned Parenthood Federation.

ipse dixit /'ɪpsɪ 'dɪksɪt/ ▻ *noun* an unsupported or dogmatic statement. ◷ 16c: Latin, meaning 'he himself said it'.

ipso facto /'ɪpsoʊ 'faktoʊ/ ▻ *adverb* by or because of that very fact; thereby. ◷ 16c: Latin.

IQ ▻ *abbreviation* (*IQs, IQ's*) intelligence quotient.

IR ▻ *abbreviation* **1** Inland Revenue. **2** *IVR* Iran.

Ir ▻ *symbol, chem* iridium.

Ir. ▻ *abbreviation* **1** Ireland. **2** Irish.

ir- ▻ *prefix* a form of IN-[1] or IN-[2] used before words beginning in *r* ▫ *irrelevant.*

IRA ▻ *abbreviation* Irish Republican Army.

Iranian /ɪ'reɪnɪən; *N Amer* aɪ'reɪnɪən/ ▻ *adj* **1** belonging or relating to Iran, a republic in SW Asia formerly called Persia, or its inhabitants. **2** belonging or relating to the language subgroup called Iranian. ▻ *noun* **1** a citizen or inhabitant of, or person born in, Iran. **2** a subgroup of the Indo-European family of languages. **3** the modern Persian language. Also called **Farsi**.

Iranian languages ▻ *plural noun* a subgroup of the Indo-Iranian branch of the Indo-European family of languages, spoken in the area of present-day Afghanistan and Iran, and which includes Farsi, Tadzhik, Pashto, Kurdish and Baluchi.

Iraqi /ɪ'rɑːkɪ, ɪ'rakɪ/ ▻ *adj* belonging or relating to Iraq, a republic in SW Asia, or its inhabitants. ▻ *noun* (*Iraqis*) a citizen or inhabitant of, or person born in, Iraq.

irascible /ɪ'rasɪbəl/ ▻ *adj* **1** easily made angry; irritable. **2** characterized by irritability ▫ *irascible nature.* • **irascibility** *noun.* • **irascibly** *adverb.* ◷ 16c: from Latin *irascibilis*, from *ira* anger.

irate /aɪə'reɪt/ ▻ *adj* very angry; enraged. • **irately** *adverb.* • **irateness** *noun.* ◷ 19c: from Latin *iratus*, from *ira* anger.

IRBM ▻ *abbreviation* intermediate range ballistic missile.

ire /aɪə(r)/ ▻ *noun, literary* anger. • **ireful** *adj.* ◷ 13c: from Latin *ira* anger.

irenic /aɪə'riːnɪk, -'rɛnɪk/ or **irenical** ▻ *adj* tending to create peace. ◷ 19c: from Greek *eirene* peace.

iridescent /ɪrɪ'dɛsənt/ ▻ *adj* having many bright rainbow-like colours which seem to shimmer and change constantly. • **iridescence** *noun.* • **iridescently** *adverb.* ◷ 18c: from Greek *iris* rainbow.

iridium /ɪ'rɪdɪəm, aɪə'rɪdɪəm/ ▻ *noun, chem* (abbreviation **Ir**, atomic number 77) a silvery metallic element that is resistant to corrosion, and is mainly used in hard alloys with platinum or osmium to make surgical instruments, pen nibs, bearings, electrical contacts and crucibles. ◷ 19c: from Greek *iris* rainbow, from the colourful appearance of some solutions of its salts.

iris /'aɪərɪs/ ▻ *noun* **1** (*irises, technical* ***irides*** /'aɪərɪdiːz, 'ɪr-/) a perennial plant that arises from a RHIZOME or a CORM, and has flattened sword-shaped leaves and large brilliantly coloured flowers, consisting of equal numbers of upright and hanging petals. **2** *anatomy* an adjustable pigmented ring of muscle lying in front of the lens of the eye, surrounding the pupil, and which, through contraction or relaxation of its muscle fibres, increases or decreases the size of the pupil, thereby controlling the amount of light entering the eye. **3** (*in full* **iris diaphragm**) a device consisting of a series of thin overlapping crescent-shaped plates surrounding a central circular aperture, used to control the amount of light entering an optical instrument. ◷ 14c: Greek, meaning 'rainbow'.

Irish /'aɪərɪʃ/ ▻ *adj* **1** belonging or relating to Ireland, an island on the NW fringe of Europe divided into the Irish Republic and Northern Ireland, to its inhabitants, or to their Celtic language or their dialect of English. **2** (**the Irish**) the people of Ireland (see THE 4). **3** *colloq* amusingly contradictory or inconsistent; illogical. ▻ *noun* **1** (*in full* **Irish Gaelic**) the Celtic language of Ireland. **2** whiskey made in Ireland. ◷ Anglo-Saxon *Iras* people of Ireland.

Irish coffee ▻ *noun* coffee mixed with a dash of Irish whiskey and served with cream on top. Also called **Gaelic coffee**.

Irish elk ▻ *noun* a giant fossil deer that ranged through open woodland from Ireland to Siberia and China during the Pleistocene epoch.

Irishman and **Irishwoman** ▻ *noun* someone who is Irish by birth or descent.

Irish moss see CARRAGEEN

Irish stew ▻ *noun* a stew made from mutton, potatoes and onions.

Irish wolfhound ▻ *noun* a tall dog with a long, usually grey, coat and soft ears.

irk /ɜːk/ ▻ *verb* (*irked, irking*) to annoy or irritate, especially persistently. ◷ 16c in this sense; 13c, meaning 'to grow weary'.

irksome ▻ *adj* annoying, irritating or boring. • **irksomely** *adverb.* • **irksomeness** *noun.*

IRL ▻ *abbreviation, IVR* Ireland.

IRO ▻ *abbreviation* Inland Revenue Office.

iron /aɪən/ ▻ *noun* **1** (symbol **Fe**, atomic number 26) a strong hard silvery-white metallic element that is naturally magnetic, and is thought to be the main component of the Earth's core. See also FERRIC, FERROUS. **2** a tool, weapon or other implement made of iron. **3** a triangular, flat-bottomed, now usually electrical, household tool used for smoothing out creases and pressing clothes. **4** *golf* any of various clubs with an angled iron head, used for shorter distance shots of about 100–200 yards. Compare PUTTER 1, WEDGE 4, WOOD 5. **5** a BRAND (sense 4). **6** great physical or mental strength. **7** (**irons**) chains; fetters. **8** (**irons**) supports for a weak or lame leg or legs. ▻ *adj* **1** made of iron. **2** like iron, especially in being very strong, inflexible, unyielding, etc ▫ *iron determination* ▫ *the iron man of British rugby.* ▻ *verb* (*ironed, ironing*) **1** to smooth the creases out of or press (eg clothes) with an iron. **2** *intr* said of clothing or fabric: to react or respond in the way specified to being ironed ▫ *shiny material which irons badly.* • **have several** or **too many irons in the fire** to have several or too many commitments at the same time. • **strike while the iron is hot** to act while the situation is to one's advantage. ◷ Anglo-Saxon *isen*.

▪ **iron something out 1** to remove or put right (difficulties, problems, etc) so that progress becomes easier. **2** to remove creases in it by ironing.

Iron Age ▷ *noun* the period in history following the Bronze Age and beginning about 1200 BC, when weapons and tools were made of iron.

ironclad ▷ *adj* **1** covered with protective iron plates. **2** inflexible; set firm. ▷ *noun, historical* a 19c warship covered with protective iron plates.

Iron Curtain ▷ *noun* **a** from 1945 to 1989, a notional barrier between countries in W Europe and the communist countries of E Europe, which hindered trade and communications; **b** *as adj* □ *Iron Curtain nations.* ⓒ First used by Nazi propaganda minister Goebbels in 1945, it became widely known after Winston Churchill used it in a speech in 1946.

iron-grey ▷ *noun* a dark-grey colour. ▷ *adj* iron-grey in colour.

iron hand ▷ *noun* strict despotic control. See also VELVET GLOVE.

ironic /aɪə'rɒnɪk/ and **ironical** ▷ *adj* **1** containing, characterized by or expressing irony. **2** said of a person: given to frequent use of irony. • **ironically** *adverb.*

ironing ▷ *noun* **1** clothes and household linen, etc which need to be or have just been ironed. **2** the act or process of ironing.

ironing board ▷ *noun* a collapsible narrow wooden or metal table usually with a thick fitted cover, on which to iron clothes.

iron lung ▷ *noun* an type of respirator consisting of an airtight metal chamber which covers the body up to the neck and which, by means of rhythmically varying air pressure, helps the person in it to breathe.

iron maiden ▷ *noun* a medieval method of torture in which a person was placed inside a hinged case lined with protruding metal spikes, with the door closed in on them.

ironmaster ▷ *noun* the owner of an ironworks.

ironmonger ▷ *noun, Brit* a dealer in articles made of metal, eg tools, locks, etc, and other household hardware. • **ironmongery** *noun.* ⓒ 14c.

iron-on ▷ *adj* said of a motif, repair material, etc: designed to be applied by using a hot iron.

iron oxide see FERRIC OXIDE

iron pyrites see PYRITE

iron rations ▷ *plural noun* small quantities of food with a high energy value, carried for emergencies by climbers, walkers, military personnel, etc.

Ironsides ▷ *plural noun, historical* Oliver Cromwell's cavalry during the English Civil War (1642–9).

ironstone ▷ *noun* **1** *geol* a sedimentary rock, at least 15 per cent of which comprises iron minerals such as haematite and pyrite. **2** hard, white earthenware.

ironware ▷ *noun* things made of iron, especially household hardware.

ironwork ▷ *noun* **1** articles made of iron, especially iron which has been specially shaped for decoration, such as gates and railings. **2** (**ironworks**) a factory where iron is smelted and made into goods.

irony[1] /'aɪərənɪ/ ▷ *noun* (*ironies*) **1** a linguistic device or form of humour that takes its effect from stating or implying the opposite of what is the case or what is intended, eg saying 'You've made a really good job of that, haven't you', when someone has done something badly. **2** a dramatic device by which information is given to the audience that is not known to all the characters in the drama, or in which the same words are meant to convey different meanings to the audience and to the characters. Also called **dramatic irony**. **3** awkward or perverse circumstances applying to a situation that is in itself satisfactory or desirable. **4** SOCRATIC IRONY. ⓒ 16c: from Latin *ironia*, from Greek *eironeia* dissimulation.

irony[2] /'aɪərənɪ/ ▷ *adj* belonging or relating to, or containing, IRON.

Iroquoian /ɪrə'kwɔɪən/ ▷ *adj* belonging or relating to the Iroquois, a confederacy of Native American people, or their language. ▷ *noun* **1** an individual belonging to this group. **2** their language.

IRQ ▷ *abbreviation, IVR* Iraq.

irradiate /ɪ'reɪdɪeɪt/ ▷ *verb* (*irradiated, irradiating*) **1** *medicine* to expose (a part of the body) to IRRADIATION (sense 1). **2** to preserve food by exposing it to IRRADIATION (sense 3). **3** to shed light on something; to light up. **4** to make bright or clear intellectually or spiritually. ⓒ 17c: from Latin *irradiare, irradiatum* to shine forth.

irradiation ▷ *noun* **1** *medicine* exposure of part of the body to electromagnetic radiation or a radioactive source, for diagnostic or therapeutic purposes. **2** *optics* an optical illusion that causes bright objects to appear larger than their actual size when viewed against a dark background. **3** a method of preserving food by exposing it to either ultraviolet radiation or ionizing radiation from radioactive isotopes. **4** the use of microwaves to heat food.

irrational /ɪ'raʃənəl/ ▷ *adj* **1** not the result of clear, logical thought. **2** unable to think logically and clearly. **3** *math* said of a root, expression, etc: involving irrational numbers. **4** *math* not commensurable with natural numbers. ▷ *noun* an irrational number. • **irrationality** *noun.* • **irrationally** *adverb.* ⓒ 15c.

irrational number ▷ *noun, math* a real number that cannot be expressed as a fraction in the form *m/n*, where *m* and *n* are integers, eg π; and surds such as √2. Compare RATIONAL NUMBER.

irreclaimable ▷ *adj* not able to be claimed back, brought into cultivation or reformed. • **irreclaimably** *adverb.*

irreconcilable ▷ *adj* **1** not agreeing or able to be brought into agreement; inconsistent; incompatible. **2** hostile and opposed; unwilling to be friendly. ▷ *noun* **1** a hostile or obstinate opponent. **2** any of various opinions, ideas, etc that cannot be brought into agreement. • **irreconcilability** *noun.* • **irreconcilably** *adverb.*

irrecoverable ▷ *adj* **1** not able to be recovered or regained. **2** not able to be corrected. • **irrecoverably** *adverb.*

irrecusable /ɪrɪ'kjuːzəbəl/ ▷ *adj* incapable of being rejected. • **irrecusably** *adverb.* ⓒ 18c: from Latin *irrecusabilis*, from *recusare* to refuse.

irredeemable ▷ *adj* **1** said of a person: too evil to be saved; beyond help. **2** incapable of being recovered, repaired or cured. **3** said of shares, etc: unable to be bought back from the shareholder by the issuing company for the sum originally paid. **4** said of paper money: unable to be exchanged for coin. • **irredeemably** *adverb.*

irredentist /ɪrə'dentɪst/ ▷ *noun* a person, especially in 19c Italy, who is in favour of his or her country recovering territory which belonged to it in the past. • **irredentism** *noun.* ⓒ 19c: from Italian *irredentista*, from (*Italia*) *irredenta* unredeemed (Italy).

irreducible ▷ *adj* **1** unable to be reduced or made simpler. **2** unable to be brought from one state into another, usually desired, state. • **irreducibly** *adverb.*

irrefragable /ɪ'refrəgəbəl/ ▷ *adj* not able to be refuted. • **irrefragability** or **irrefragableness** *noun.* • **irrefragably** *adverb.* ⓒ 16c: from Latin *irrefragabilis*, from *refragari* to resist.

irrefutable /ɪrɪ'fjuːtəbəl, ɪ'ref-/ ▷ *adj* not able to be denied or proved false. • **irrefutability** *noun.* • **irrefutably** *adverb.* ⓒ 17c.

irregular /ɪ'regjʊlə(r)/ ▷ *adj* **1** not happening or occurring at regular or equal intervals. **2** not smooth, even or balanced. **3** not conforming to rules, custom, accepted or normal behaviour, or to routine. **4** *grammar* said of a word, especially a verb or noun: not changing its form (eg to show tenses or plurals) according to the usual patterns in the language. **5** said of troops: not belonging to the regular army. ▷ *noun* an irregular soldier. • **irregularity** *noun*. • **irregularly** *adverb*. ◎ 14c.

irrelevant /ɪ'rɛləvənt/ ▷ *adj* not connected with or applying to the subject in hand; not relevant. • **irrelevance** *noun*. • **irrelevantly** *adverb*. ◎ 18c.

irreligion ▷ *noun* **1** lack of religion. **2** lack of respect for or opposition or hostility towards religion. • **irreligious** *adj*. ◎ 16c.

irremediable ▷ *adj* unable to be cured, corrected or made better. • **irremediably** *adverb*. ◎ 16c.

irremissible /ɪrɪ'mɪsɪbəl/ ▷ *adj* not able to be forgiven. • **irremissibility** or **irremissibleness** *noun*. • **irremissibly** *adverb*. ◎ 15c.

irremovable ▷ *adj* not able to be removed. • **irremovability** *noun*. • **irremovably** *adverb*. ◎ 16c.

irreparable /ɪ'rɛpərəbəl/ ▷ *adj* not able to be restored or put right. • **irreparability** *noun*. • **irreparably** *adverb*. ◎ 15c.

irreplaceable ▷ *adj* not able to be replaced, especially because too rare or valuable or because the sentimental value is so great. • **irreplaceably** *adverb*. ◎ 19c.

irrepressible ▷ *adj* not able to be controlled, restrained or repressed, especially because of being too lively and full of energy or strength. • **irrepressibility** *noun*. • **irrepressibly** *adverb*. ◎ 19c.

irreproachable ▷ *adj* said especially of behaviour: free from faults; blameless. • **irreproachability** *noun*. • **irreproachably** *adverb*. ◎ 17c.

irresistible ▷ *adj* **1** too strong to be resisted; overpowering. **2** very attractive or enticing; fascinating. • **irresistibility** or **irresistibleness** *noun*. • **irresistibly** *adverb*. ◎ 16c: from Latin *irresistibilis*.

irresolute ▷ *adj* hesitating or doubtful; not able to take firm decisions. • **irresolutely** *adverb*. • **irresoluteness** or **irresolution** *noun*. ◎ 16c.

irrespective ▷ *adj* (*always* **irrespective of something**) without considering or taking it into account. ▷ *adverb, colloq* without consideration ◻ *Although it rained, the garden party continued irrespective.* • **irrespectively** *adverb*. ◎ 17c.

irresponsible ▷ *adj* **1** done without, or showing no, concern for the consequences; reckless; careless. **2** not able to bear responsibility; not reliable or trustworthy. • **irresponsibility** *noun*. • **irresponsibly** *adverb*. ◎ 17c.

irretrievable ▷ *adj* not able to be recovered or put right. • **irretrievability** *noun*. • **irretrievably** *adverb*.

irreverent ▷ *adj* lacking respect or reverence (eg for things considered sacred or for important people). • **irreverence** *noun*. • **irreverential** *adj*. • **irreverently** *adverb*. ◎ 15c.

irreversible ▷ *adj* **1** not able to be changed back to a former or original state; permanent. **2** not able to be recalled or annulled. • **irreversibility** or **irreversibleness** *noun*. • **irreversibly** *adverb*. ◎ 17c.

irreversible reaction ▷ *noun, chem* a chemical reaction which takes place in one direction only, and therefore proceeds to completion.

irrevocable /ɪ'rɛvəkəbəl/ ▷ *adj* unable to be changed, stopped, or undone. • **irrevocability** *noun*. • **irrevocably** *adj*. ◎ 14c.

irrigate /'ɪrɪgeɪt/ ▷ *verb* (***irrigated, irrigating***) **1** said of a river, etc: to provide (land) with a supply of water. **2** to supply water to (agricultural land) by channels or other artificial means, especially so as to enable crops to be grown in dry regions. **3** *medicine* to wash out (the eye, a wound, body cavity, or hollow organ, eg the colon), with a continuous flow of water or antiseptic solution. • **irrigable** /'ɪrɪgəbəl/ *adj*. • **irrigation** *noun*. ◎ 17c: from Latin *irrigare, irrigatum*, from *rigare* to moisten.

irritable /'ɪrɪtəbəl/ ▷ *adj* **1** easily annoyed, angered or excited. **2** extremely or excessively sensitive. **3** *biol* denoting a living organism that is capable of responding to an external stimulus, such as light, heat or touch. • **irritability** or **irritableness** *noun*. • **irritably** *adverb*. ◎ 17c: see IRRITATE.

irritable bowel syndrome ▷ *noun* (abbreviation **IBS**) *medicine* a condition in which the mucous membrane lining the colon becomes inflamed, causing abdominal pain, with constipation or diarrhoea, in otherwise healthy individuals.

irritant /'ɪrɪtənt/ ▷ *noun* **1** any chemical, physical or biological agent that causes irritation of a tissue, especially inflammation of the skin or eyes. **2** something or someone that causes physical or mental irritation. ▷ *adj* irritating.

irritate /'ɪrɪteɪt/ ▷ *verb* (***irritated, irritating***) **1** to make someone angry or annoyed. **2** to make (part of the body, an organ, etc) sore and swollen or itchy. **3** *biol* to stimulate (eg an organ) to respond in a characteristic manner. • **irritating** *adj*. • **irritatingly** *adverb*. • **irritative** /-teɪtɪv/ *adj*. ◎ 16c: from Latin *irritare, irritatum* to incite, provoke or irritate.

irritation ▷ *noun* **1** something that irritates. **2** the act of irritating. **3** the state of being irritated.

irrupt /ɪ'rʌpt/ ▷ *verb* (***irrupted, irrupting***) *intr* to burst into or enter (a place, etc) suddenly with speed and violence. • **irruption** *noun*. • **irruptive** *adj*. ◎ 19c: from Latin *irrumpere, irruptum* to break in.

IRS ▷ *abbreviation, US* Internal Revenue Service. Compare INLAND REVENUE.

IS ▷ *abbreviation, IVR* Iceland.

is *present tense of* BE

isagogic /aɪsə'gɒdʒɪk, -'gɒgɪk/ ▷ *adj* introductory. ▷ *noun* (**isagogics**) introductory studies, especially in theology. ◎ 19c: from Latin *isagogicus* from Greek *eisagogikos* introductory.

ISBN ▷ *abbreviation* International Standard Book Number.

ischaemia or **ischemia** /ɪ'skiːmɪə/ ▷ *noun, medicine* an inadequate flow of blood to a part of the body, caused by blockage or constriction of a blood vessel. ◎ 19c: from Greek *ischein* to restrain + *haima* blood.

ischium /'ɪskɪəm/ ▷ *noun* (***ischia*** /'ɪskɪə/) a posterior bone in the pelvic girdle. ◎ 17c: Latin, from Greek *ischion*.

-ise[1] /aɪz, iːz/ ▷ *suffix, forming abstract nouns, denoting* a specified quality, state, function, etc ◻ *exercise* ◻ *expertise*. ◎ French.

-ise[2] see -IZE

-ise

See Usage Note at **-ize**.

-ish /ɪʃ/ ▷ *suffix, forming adjectives, signifying* **1** slightly; fairly; having a trace of something specified ◻ *reddish*. **2** like; having the qualities of something specified ◻ *childish*. **3** having as a nationality ◻ *Swedish*. **4** approximately; about; roughly ◻ *fiftyish*. ◎ Anglo-Saxon *-isc*.

isinglass /'aɪzɪŋglɑːs/ ▷ *noun* **1** the purest form of animal gelatine, made from the dried SWIM BLADDERS of certain fish, eg sturgeon, which has strong adhesive properties, and is used in glues, cements and printing inks. **2** thin transparent sheets of MICA used in furnace and stove doors. ◎ 16c.

ISIS ▻ *abbreviation* Independent Schools Information Service.

Islam /'ɪzlɑːm, 'ɪslɑːm, -'lɑːm/ ▻ *noun* **1** the religion of the MUSLIMS, which teaches that individuals, societies and governments should all be obedient to the Will of Allah as set forth in the KORAN. **2 a** all Muslims collectively; **b** all the parts of the world in which Islam is the main or recognized religion. • **Islamic** /ɪz'lamɪk, -'lɑːmɪk, ɪs-/ *adj.* ⓘ 19c in these senses; 17c in obsolete sense 'an orthodox Muslim': Arabic, meaning 'surrendering', from *aslama* to surrender (to God).

Islamicist /ɪz'lamɪsɪst, -'lɑːmɪsɪst, ɪs-/ ▻ *noun* someone who studies Islam, Islamic law or Islamic culture.

Islamicize or **Islamicise** ▻ *verb* to Islamize. • **Islamicization** *noun*.

Islamize or **Islamise** /'ɪzləmaɪz/ ▻ *verb* (***Islamized, Islamizing***) to make someone become a follower of or conform to Islam. • **Islamization** *noun*.

island /'aɪlənd/ ▻ *noun* **1** a piece of land, smaller than a continent, which is completely surrounded by water, eg Britain, Cyprus, Greenland, etc. **2** anything which is like an island, especially in being isolated or detached. **3** (*in full* **traffic island**) a small raised traffic-free area in the middle of a street on which people may stand when crossing the road. **4** *anatomy* a group of cells or a region of tissue detached and clearly differing from surrounding cells or tissues. ⓘ Anglo-Saxon *iegland*, with spelling influenced by *isle*.

island arc ▻ *noun, geol* a curved chain of oceanic islands, eg the islands of Japan, that usually contain active volcanoes.

islander ▻ *noun* someone who lives on an island.

island-hop ▻ *verb, intr* to travel around a group of islands on holiday, usually only staying for a short time on each. • **island-hopper** *noun*. • **island-hopping** *noun, adj.*

isle /aɪl/ ▻ *noun* an island, especially a small one. ⓘ 13c: French, from Latin *insula*.

> ***isle***
>
> There is sometimes a spelling confusion between **isle** and **aisle**.

islet /'aɪlət/ ▻ *noun* **1** a small island. **2** any small group of cells which has a different nature and structure to the cells surrounding it.

islets of Langerhans /— 'lɑːŋəhɑːns/ ▻ *plural noun, anatomy* in vertebrates: small groups of specialized cells scattered throughout the pancreas, which control the level of GLUCOSE in the blood by secreting the hormones INSULIN and GLUCAGON. ⓘ 19c: named after the German anatomist Paul Langerhans who, in 1869, was the first person to describe them.

ism /'ɪzəm/ ▻ *noun, colloq, often derog* a distinctive and formal set of ideas, principles or beliefs. ⓘ 17c: from -ISM, regarded as a separate word.

-ism /ɪzəm/ ▻ *suffix, forming nouns, denoting* **1** a formal set of beliefs, ideas, principles, etc □ *feminism.* **2** a quality or state □ *heroism.* **3** an activity or practice or its result □ *criticism.* **4** discrimination or prejudice on the grounds of

Isms

Most of the words included here denote beliefs and practices. Some, however, denote aspects of discrimination; these include **ageism** and **sexism**.

ageism discrimination on the grounds of age
agnosticism belief in the impossibility of knowing God
alcoholism addiction to alcohol
altruism unselfish concern for the welfare of others
atavism reversion to an earlier type
atheism belief that God does not exist
barbarism state of being coarse or uncivilized
behaviourism a psychological theory based on behaviour of people and animals
cannibalism practice of eating human flesh
capitalism economic system based on the private ownership of wealth and resources
communism political and economic system based on collective ownership of wealth and resources
conservatism inclination to preserve the status quo
consumerism economic policy of encouraging spending and consuming
Cubism artistic movement using geometrical shapes to represent objects
cynicism belief in the worst in others
defeatism belief in the inevitability of defeat
dogmatism tendency to present statements of opinion as if unquestionable
dynamism state of having limitless energy and enthusiasm
egoism principle that self-interest is the basis of morality
elitism belief in the natural superiority of some people
empiricism theory that knowledge can only be gained through experiment and observation
environmentalism concern to protect the natural environment
escapism tendency to escape from unpleasant reality into fantasy
evangelism practice of trying to persuade someone to adopt a particular belief or cause
exhibitionism tendency to behave so as to attract attention to oneself
existentialism philosophy emphasizing freedom of choice and personal responsibility for one's actions
Expressionism artistic movement emphasizing expression of emotions over representation of external reality
extremism adherence to fanatical or extreme opinions
fanaticism excessive enthusiasm for something
fatalism belief that fate is predetermined and unalterable
fascism political system based on dictatorial rule and suppression of democracy
favouritism practice of giving unfair preference to a person or group
feminism advocacy of equal rights and opportunities for women
feudalism social system based on tenants' allegiance to a lord
functionalism theory that the intended use of something should determine its design
hedonism belief in the importance of pleasure above all else
heroism quality of showing great courage in one's actions
holism theory that any complex being or system is more than the sum of its parts
humanism philosophy emphasizing human responsibility for moral behaviour
hypnotism practice of inducing a hypnotic state in others
idealism practice of living according to ideals
imperialism principle of extending control over other nations' territory
Impressionism artistic movement emphasizing artists' impressions of nature
individualism belief in individual freedom and self-reliance
liberalism belief in tolerance of different opinions or attitudes
magnetism state of possessing magnetic attraction
mannerism excessive use of an individual artistic style
Marxism philosophy that political change is brought about by struggle between social classes

some specified quality □ ***ageism***. **5** an illness caused by, causing resemblance to or named after something or someone specified □ ***alcoholism*** □ ***dwarfism***. **6** a characteristic of a specified language or variety of language □ ***regionalism*** □ ***Americanism***. ⓘ From Greek *-ismos* or *-isma*.

isn't /'ɪzənt/ ▷ *contraction* is not.

ISO ▷ *abbreviation* **1** Imperial Service Order. **2** International Standards Organization.

iso- /aɪsoʊ/ ▷ *combining form, denoting* **1** same; equal. **2** *chem* an isomeric substance. ⓘ From Greek *isos* equal.

isobar /'aɪsoʊbɑː(r)/ ▷ *noun* **1** a line drawn on a weather chart connecting points that have the same atmospheric pressure at a given time. **2** *physics* either of two atoms which have the same mass number but different atomic numbers and chemical properties. • **isobaric** /-'barɪk/ *adj*. ⓘ 19c: from Greek *isobares* of equal weight.

isochronal /aɪ'sɒkrənəl/ and **isochronous** /aɪ'sɒkrənəs/ ▷ *adj* **1** having the same length of time. **2** performed or happening at the same time. **3** happening at equal or regular intervals. ⓘ 17c: from Greek *isochronos* equal in age or time.

isoclinal /aɪsoʊ'klaɪnəl/ ▷ *adj* **1** *geol* folded with the same or nearly the same dip in each limb. **2** in terrestrial magnetism: having the same magnetic dip. ▷ *noun* (*also* **isocline**) a contour line which connects points on the surface of the earth which have the same magnetic dip. ⓘ 19c: from ISO- + Greek *klinein* to bend.

isocracy /aɪ'sɒkrəsɪ/ ▷ *noun* **1** equality of political power. **2** (***isocracies***) a system of government in which all the people have equal political power. • **isocratic** /aɪsoʊ'kratɪk/ *adj*. ⓘ 17c.

isocyclic /aɪsoʊ'saɪklɪk/ ▷ *adj* HOMOCYCLIC.

isodiametric and **isodiametrical** ▷ *adj* having equal diameters. ⓘ 19c.

isodimorphism ▷ *noun, crystallog* ISOMORPHISM between each of the two forms of a dimorphous (see DIMORPHISM sense 2) substance and the corresponding forms of another dimorphous substance. • **isodimorphic** or **isodimorphous** *adj*.

isodynamic ▷ *adj* **1** having equal strength. **2** relating to an imaginary line on the surface of the earth, which connects points of equal magnetic intensity. ▷ *noun* an isodynamic line. ⓘ 19c.

isogloss /'aɪsoʊglɒs/ ▷ *noun* a line drawn on a map, which marks the boundaries of areas which manifest particular linguistic features. ⓘ 1920s.

isohel /'aɪsoʊhel/ ▷ *noun* a line drawn on a weather map connecting places with equal periods of sunshine. ⓘ Early 20c: from ISO- + Greek *helios* sun.

isohyet /aɪsoʊ'haɪət/ ▷ *noun* a line drawn on a weather map connecting places with equal amounts of rainfall. ⓘ 19c: from ISO- + Greek *hyetos* rain.

isolate /'aɪsəleɪt/ ▷ *verb* (***isolated***, ***isolating***) **1** to separate from others; to cause to be alone. **2** to place in quarantine. **3** to separate or detach, especially to allow closer examination □ ***isolate the problem***. **4** to separate so as to obtain in a pure or uncombined form. ▷ *noun* someone or something that is isolated. • **isolation** *noun*. ⓘ 19c: from ISOLATED.

Isms contd.

masochism derivation of pleasure from one's own pain or suffering
materialism excessive interest in material possessions and financial success
monarchism support of the institution of monarchy
monetarism economic theory emphasizing the control of a country's money supply
mysticism practice of gaining direct communication with a deity through prayer and meditation
narcissism excessive admiration for oneself or one's appearance
nationalism advocacy of national unity or independence
naturalism realistic and non-idealistic representation of objects
nihilism rejection of moral and religious principles
objectivism tendency to emphasize what is objective
opportunism practice of taking advantage of opportunities regardless of principles
optimism tendency to expect the best possible outcome
pacifism belief that violence and war are unjustified
paganism belief in a religion which worships many gods
pantheism doctrine that equates all natural forces and matter with God
parochialism practice of being narrow or provincial in outlook
paternalism practice of benevolent but over-protective management or government
patriotism devotion to one's country
pessimism tendency to expect the worst possible outcome
plagiarism practice of stealing an idea from another's work and presenting it as one's own
pluralism co-existence of several ethnic and religious groups in a society
Pointillism artistic movement using small dabs of unmixed colour to suggest shapes
polytheism belief in more than one god
pragmatism practical, matter-of-fact approach to dealing with problems
professionalism practice of showing professional competence and conduct
racism *or* **racialism** discrimination on the grounds of ethnic origin
realism tendency to present things as they really are
regionalism devotion to or advocacy of one's own region
sadism derivation of pleasure from inflicting pain on others
Satanism belief in and worship of the devil
scepticism tendency to question widely-accepted beliefs
sexism discrimination on the grounds of sex
socialism doctrine that a country's wealth belongs to the people as a whole
spiritualism practice of communicating with the spirits of the dead through a medium
stoicism tendency to accept misfortune or suffering without complaint
Surrealism artistic movement emphasizing use of images from the unconscious
symbolism use of symbols to express ideas or emotions
terrorism practice of using violence to achieve political ends
Thatcherism political system based on privatization and monetarism advocated by Margaret Thatcher
tokenism practice of doing something once or with minimum effort, while appearing to comply with a law or principle
tourism practice of travelling to and visiting places for pleasure and relaxation
vandalism practice of inflicting indiscriminate damage on others' property
vegetarianism practice of not eating meat or animal products
ventriloquism making one's voice appear to come from another source
voyeurism practice of watching private actions of others for pleasure or sexual gratification

isolated ▷ *adj* **1** placed or standing alone or apart. **2** separate. **3** solitary. ⓘ 18c: from Italian *isolato*, from Latin *insula* island.

isolationism ▷ *noun* the policy of not joining with other countries in international political and economic affairs. • **isolationist** *noun, adj.*

isoleucine ▷ *noun, biochem* an essential amino acid found in proteins. ⓘ Early 20c: from ISO- 2 + LEUCINE.

isomer /ˈaɪsəmə(r)/ ▷ *noun* **1** *chem* one of two or more chemical compounds that have the same chemical formula, ie the same molecular composition, but different three-dimensional structures. **2** *physics* one of two or more atomic nuclei with the same atomic number and mass number, but with different energy states and radioactive properties, eg different half-lives. • **isomeric** /aɪsəˈmɛrɪk/ *adj.* ⓘ 19c: from Greek *isomeres* having equal parts.

isometric ▷ *adj* **1** having equal size or measurements. **2** *physiol* belonging or relating to muscular contraction that generates tension but does not produce shortening of the muscle fibres. **3** said of a three-dimensional drawing: having all three axes equally inclined to the surface of the drawing and all lines drawn to scale. **4** *denoting* a system of exercises for increasing fitness, strengthening the muscles and toning up the body, especially by pushing one or more limbs against a stationary object. ⓘ 19c.

isometrics ▷ *singular or plural noun* a system of physical exercises for strengthening and toning the body in which the muscles are pushed either together or against an immovable object and are not contracted, flexed or made to bend limbs.

isomorph ▷ *noun* **1** any object that is similar or identical in structure or shape to another object. **2** *chem* any of two or more substances having the same crystalline structure but differing in chemical composition. **3** *biol* any of two or more individuals that appear similar in form, although they belong to different races or species.

isomorphism ▷ *noun* **1** *biol* the apparent similarity of form between individuals belonging to different races or species. **2** *chem* the existence of two or more chemical compounds with the same crystal structure. **3** *math* a one-to-one correspondence between the elements of two or more sets and between the sums or products of the elements of one set and those of the equivalent elements of the other set or sets. • **isomorphic** or **isomorphous** *adj.* ⓘ 19c.

isonomy /aɪˈsɒnəmɪ/ ▷ *noun* equal law, rights or privileges. ⓘ 17c.

isoprene /ˈaɪsoʊpriːn/ ▷ *noun, chem* (formula C_5H_8) a colourless liquid hydrocarbon that is the basic unit of natural rubber, and can be POLYMERIZEd to form synthetic rubber. ⓘ 19c: from ISO- 2 + *propyl* + *-ene*.

isosceles /aɪˈsɒsəliːz/ ▷ *adj* said of a triangle: having two sides of equal length. ⓘ 16c: from ISO- + Greek *skelos* leg.

isoseismal /aɪsoʊˈsaɪzməl/ ▷ *adj* belonging or relating to equal intensity of earthquake shock. ▷ *noun* a curve or line on a map connecting points at which an earthquake shock is felt with equal intensity. • **isoseismic** *adj.* ⓘ 19c: from ISO- + Greek *seismos* a shaking.

isostasy /aɪˈsɒstəsɪ/ ▷ *noun, geol* a theoretical state of equilibrium in which the Earth's crust, which is considered to consist of relatively low density material, floats on the surface of the much denser semi-solid material of the Earth's mantle. ⓘ 19c: from ISO- + Greek *stasis* setting.

isothere /ˈaɪsoʊθɪə(r)/ ▷ *noun* a line on a weather map connecting places where the mean summer temperature is the same. ⓘ 19c: from ISO- + Greek *theros* summer.

isotherm /ˈaɪsoʊθɜːm/ ▷ *noun* **1** a line on a weather map connecting places where the temperature is the same at a particular time or for a particular period of time. **2** *physics* a line on a graph linking all places or points that having a certain temperature. **3** *physics* a curve representing the relationship between two variables, especially volume and pressure, when the temperature is maintained at a constant level. ⓘ 19c: from ISO- + Greek *therme* heat.

isotonic ▷ *adj, chem denoting* a solution that has the same OSMOTIC PRESSURE as another solution with which it is being compared. ⓘ 19c.

isotope /ˈaɪsətoʊp/ ▷ *noun, chem* one of two or more atoms of the same chemical element that contain the same number of protons but different numbers of neutrons in their nuclei and therefore have the same atomic number and chemical properties, but different mass numbers and physical properties. • **isotopic** /-ˈtɒpɪk/ *adj.* • **isotopically** *adverb.* • **isotopy** /aɪˈsɒtəpɪ/ *noun.* ⓘ Early 20c: from ISO- + Greek *topos* place (ie on the periodic table).

isotropic /aɪsoʊˈtrɒpɪk/ ▷ *adj* **1** said of a substance, material, etc: having physical properties that are identical in all directions. **2** tending to show equal growth in all directions. • **isotropy** /aɪˈsɒtrəpɪ/ *noun.* ⓘ 19c: from ISO- + Greek *tropos* turn.

I-spy /aɪˈspaɪ/ ▷ *noun* a game in which someone chooses an object in view and the other players have to guess which object it is, with only its initial letter as a clue. ⓘ 18c.

Israeli /ɪzˈreɪliː/ ▷ *adj* belonging or relating to Israel, a modern state in the Middle East, or its inhabitants. ▷ *noun* (***Israelis***) a citizen or inhabitant of, or person born in, Israel. ⓘ 1948.

Israelite /ˈɪzrəlaɪt, ˈɪzrɪə-/ ▷ *noun* **1** *Bible, historical* someone born or living in the ancient kingdom of Israel (922–721 BC), especially a Jew claiming descent from Jacob. **2** a member of any of various Christian sects who proclaim themselves as one of God's chosen people. ▷ *adj* belonging or relating to the ancient kingdom of Israel or its inhabitants.

issue /ˈɪʃuː, ˈɪsjuː/ ▷ *noun* **1** the giving out, publishing or making available of something, eg stamps, a magazine, etc. **2** something given out, published or made available, eg stamps, a magazine, book, etc. **3** one item in a regular series □ ***the December issue of the magazine.*** **4** a subject for discussion or argument. **5** a result or consequence. **6** *formal* children; offspring. **7** an act of going or flowing out. **8** a way out, outlet or outflow, eg where a stream begins. ▷ *verb* (***issued, issuing***) **1** to give or send out, distribute, publish or make available, especially officially or formally. **2** (*usually* **issue someone with something**) to supply them with the required item, eg an official document. **3** *intr* (*often* **issue forth** or **out**) to flow or come out, especially in large quantities. **4** (*usually* **issue in something**) to end or result in it. **5** *intr* (*often* **issue from someone** or **something**) to come or descend from them or it; to be produced or caused by them or it. • **at issue 1** in dispute or disagreement. **2** under discussion. • **force the issue** to act so as to force a decision to be taken. • **join** or **take issue with someone** to disagree with them. • **make an issue of something** to make it the explicit subject of an argument or disagreement. ⓘ 13c: French, from Latin *exitus* exit.

issuing house ▷ *noun* a merchant bank which specializes in the issue of shares and bonds on the stock market.

-ist /ɪst/ ▷ *suffix, denoting* **1** a believer in some formal system of ideas, principles or beliefs □ ***feminist*** □ ***realist.*** **2** someone who carries out some activity or practises some art or profession □ ***novelist*** □ ***guitarist*** □ ***dentist.*** ⓘ From Greek *-istes*.

isthmus /ˈɪsməs, ˈɪsθməs/ ▷ *noun* (***isthmuses***) **1** a narrow strip of land, bounded by water on both sides, that joins two larger areas of land. **2** *anatomy* a narrow or constricted region of an organ or tissue. ⓒ 16c: Latin, from Greek *isthmos*.

-istic /ɪstɪk/ ▷ *suffix, forming adjectives and some nouns* corresponding to words formed by -IST and -ISM.

istle or **ixtle** /ˈɪstlɪ/ ▷ *noun* a valuable fibre obtained from various tropical trees such as the agave and yucca and which is used for cords, carpets, etc. ⓒ 19c: from Mexican Spanish *ixtli*.

IT ▷ *abbreviation* information technology.

it¹ ▷ *pronoun* **1** the thing, animal, small baby or group already mentioned. **2** the person in question ▫ ***Who is it?*** **3** used as the subject with impersonal verbs and when describing the weather or distance or telling the time ▫ ***It's a bit blustery today.*** **4** used as the grammatical subject of a sentence when the real subject comes later, eg *It's not a very good idea running away* (which means *Running away is not a very good idea*). **5** used to refer to a general situation or state of affairs ▫ ***How's it going?*** **6** used to emphasize a certain word or phrase in a sentence ▫ ***When is it that her train is due to arrive?*** **7** exactly what is needed, suitable or available ▫ ***That's it!*** **8** used with many verbs and prepositions as an object with little meaning ▫ ***run for it.*** ▷ *noun* **1** the person in a children's game who has to oppose all the others, eg by trying to catch them. See also TAG² **2** *old use, colloq* sex appeal. **3** *colloq* sexual intercourse. ⓒ Anglo-Saxon *hit*.

it² see GIN AND IT

ITA ▷ *abbreviation, Brit* Independent Television Authority, the former name of the IBA, and now replaced by the ITC.

ITA or **i.t.a.** ▷ *abbreviation* Initial Teaching Alphabet.

Ital. ▷ *abbreviation* **1** Italian. **2** Italy.

ital. ▷ *abbreviation* italic.

Italian /ɪˈtaljən/ ▷ *adj* belonging or relating to Italy, a republic in S Europe, its inhabitants or their language. ▷ *noun* **1** a citizen or inhabitant of, or person born in, Italy. **2** the official language of Italy, also spoken in parts of Switzerland, San Marino, the Vatican City, Sardinia and some urban parts of the US. **3** *colloq* **a** a restaurant that serves Italian food, eg pizzas, pasta dishes, etc; **b** a meal in one of these restaurants ▫ ***went out for an Italian.*** ⓒ 15c: from Latin *Italianus*, from *Italia* Italy.

Pronunciation of Italian in English

- **gl** should strictly be pronounced /lj/, close to its Italian pronunciation, eg in **zabaglione**, but it is increasingly being pronounced /gl/ in English, eg especially in **tagliatelle, Modigliani**.
- **gh** is pronounced /g/, as in **spaghetti**.
- **gn** is pronounced /nj/, as in **gnocchi**.
- **g** before **e** or **i** is pronounced /dʒ/, as in **arpeggio**.
- **ch** is pronounced /k/, as in **Chianti**.
- **c** before **e** or **i** is pronounced /tʃ/, as in **ciao**.
- **z** at the beginning of a word is pronounced /z/, but within a word is pronounced /ts/ or /dz/, as in **scherzo** and **intermezzo**.

Italianate /ɪˈtaljəneɪt/ ▷ *adj* said especially of decoration, architecture or art: done in an Italian style.

italic /ɪˈtalɪk/ ▷ *adj* **1** said of a typeface: containing characters which slope upwards to the right. **2** (**Italic**) belonging or relating to ancient Italy. **3** (**Italic**) denoting a group of Indo-European languages spoken in ancient Italy, including Latin. ▷ *noun* **1** (*usually* **italics**) a typeface with characters which slope upwards to the right, usually used to show emphasis, foreign words, etc. **2** a character written or printed in this typeface. Compare ROMAN. **3** the Italic languages. ⓒ 16c: from Greek *Italikos*, from Latin *Italia* Italy.

italicize or **italicise** /ɪˈtalɪsaɪz/ ▷ *verb* (***italicized, italicizing***) to print or write in italics; to change (characters, words, etc in normal typeface) to italics. • **italicization** *noun*.

Italo- /ɪˈtaloʊ, ˈɪtəloʊ/ ▷ *combining form, signifying* Italy or the Italians, etc ▫ ***Italo-Celtic.***

ITAR-Tass or **Itar-Tass** /ɪtɑːˈtas/ ▷ *noun* the official news agency of Russian. ⓒ 1992: acronym of Russian *Informatsionnoe telegrafnoe agentsvo Rossii* Information Telegraph Agency of Russia + TASS.

ITC ▷ *abbreviation* Independent Television Commission. Compare ITA.

itch /ɪtʃ/ ▷ *noun* **1** an unpleasant or ticklish irritation on the surface of the skin which makes one want to scratch. **2** *colloq* a strong or restless desire. **3** a skin disease or condition which causes a constant unpleasant irritation, especially scabies. ▷ *verb* (***itched, itching***) **1** *intr* to have an itch and want to scratch. **2** *tr & intr* to cause someone to feel an itch. **3** *intr, colloq* to feel a strong or restless desire. ⓒ Anglo-Saxon *giccan*.

itchy ▷ *adj* (***itchier, itchiest***) causing or affected with an itch or itching. • **itchiness** *noun*.

itchy feet ▷ *noun, colloq* the strong desire to leave, move or travel.

itchy palm and **itching palm** ▷ *noun* greed for money.

it'd /ˈɪtəd/ ▷ *contraction* **1** it had. **2** it would.

-ite /aɪt/ ▷ *suffix, forming nouns, signifying* **1** a national, regional, tribal, etc group ▫ ***Canaanite*** ▫ ***Semite.*** **2** a follower of or believer in something; a member of a group or faction ▫ ***Shiite*** ▫ ***pre-Raphaelite*** ▫ ***anti-semite.*** **3** a fossil ▫ ***trilobite.*** **4** a mineral ▫ ***graphite.*** **5** a salt of a certain formula ▫ ***nitrite.*** Compare -ATE, -IDE. **6** any of various manufactured substances ▫ ***Bakelite*** ▫ ***dynamite.*** ⓒ From Greek *-ites*.

item /ˈaɪtəm/ ▷ *noun* 1 a separate object or unit, especially one on a list. **1** a separate piece of information or news. **2** *informal* a couple regarded as having a romantic or sexual relationship. ⓒ 16c: Latin, meaning 'likewise'.

itemize or **itemise** ▷ *verb* (***itemized, itemizing***) to list (things) separately, eg on a bill. • **itemization** *noun*. • **itemizer** *noun*. ⓒ 19c.

iterate /ˈɪtəreɪt/ ▷ *verb* (***iterated, iterating***) to say or do again; to repeat. • **iteration** *noun*. • **iterative** /ˈɪtərətɪv/ *adj*. ⓒ 16c: from Latin *iterare*, *iteratum*, from *iterum* again.

itinerant /ɪˈtɪnərənt, aɪˈtɪn-/ ▷ *adj* travelling from place to place, eg on business ▫ ***works as an itinerant music teacher.*** ▷ *noun* an itinerant person, especialy one whose work involves going from place to place or one who has no fixed address. • **itinerantly** *adverb*. ⓒ 16c: from Latin *itinerare* to travel.

itinerary /aɪˈtɪnərərɪ/ ▷ *noun* (***itineraries***) **1** a planned route for a journey or trip, especially one that gives details of the expected stops, visits, etc. **2** a diary or record of a journey. **3** a guidebook. ▷ *adj* belonging or relating to journeys. ⓒ 15c: ultimately from Latin *iter* journey.

-itis /aɪtɪs/ ▷ *combining form, denoting* **1** in the names of diseases: inflammation ▫ ***appendicitis.*** **2** *colloq* in one-off formations: a condition of distress or suffering caused by an excess of a specified thing ▫ ***footballitis*** ▫ ***Nintendoitis.*** ⓒ From Greek *-itis*.

it'll /ˈɪtəl/ ▷ *contraction* **1** it will. **2** it shall.

ITN ▷ *abbreviation* Independent Television News.

ITO ▷ *abbreviation* International Trade Organization.

its ▷ *adj* belonging to it ▫ ***its big cheesy grin.*** ▷ *pronoun* the one or ones belonging to it ▫ ***Its has gone missing.***

its, it's

Confusion between **its** and **it's** is still the most common error in the English language.

Its = belonging to it, **it's** = 'it is' or in informal use, 'it has'.

it's ▷ *contraction* **1** it is. **2** *informal* it has.

itself /ɪt'sɛlf/ ▷ *pronoun* **1** the reflexive form of IT. **2** used for emphasis □ ***His behaviour itself wasn't enough for me to leave.*** **3** its usual or normal state □ ***After some treatment at the vet's, the puppy was soon back to itself.*** **4** (*also* **by itself**) alone; without help.

itsy-bitsy /'ɪtsɪ'bɪtsɪ/ and **itty-bitty** /'ɪtɪ'bɪtɪ/ ▷ *adj, colloq* very small. ⓔ 1930s: a childish rhyming compound based on *little bit*.

ITT ▷ *abbreviation* International Telephone and Telegraph Corporation.

ITU ▷ *abbreviation* International Telecommunication Union.

ITV ▷ *abbreviation, Brit* Independent Television.

-ity /ɪtɪ/ ▷ *suffix, forming nouns, denoting* a state or quality, or an instance of it □ ***irregularity*** □ ***confidentiality.*** ⓔ From French *-ité*, from Latin *-itas*.

IU or **i.u.** ▷ *abbreviation, medicine* intrauterine.

IUCD ▷ *abbreviation* intrauterine contraceptive device.

IUD ▷ *abbreviation* intrauterine device.

-ium /ɪəm/ ▷ *suffix, forming nouns, signifying* **1** (*also* **-um**) a metallic element □ ***plutonium.*** **2** a group forming positive ions. **3** a biological structure. ⓔ Latin, from Greek *-ion*.

IV or **i.v.** ▷ *abbreviation, medicine* intravenous, or intravenously.

I've /aɪv/ ▷ *contraction* I have.

-ive /ɪv/ ▷ *suffix, forming adjectives, signifying* a quality, action, tendency, etc □ ***creative*** □ ***emotive.*** ⓔ From French *-if*.

IVF ▷ *abbreviation* in-vitro fertilization.

ivory /'aɪvərɪ/ ▷ *noun* (***ivories***) **1 a** a hard white material that forms the tusks of the elephant, walrus, etc, formerly used to make ornaments, art objects and piano keys; **b** *as adj* □ ***ivory statuette.*** **2** the creamy-white colour of this substance. **3** an article made from this substance. **4** (**ivories**) *colloq* the keys on a piano. ▷ *adj* ivory-coloured, often with the implication of smoothness □ ***ivory skin.*** ⓔ 13c: from French *ivoire*, from Latin *ebur*.

ivory tower ▷ *noun* a hypothetical place where the unpleasant realities of life can be ignored. ● **live in an ivory tower** said especially of academics: to exist in a secluded world, ignoring everyday reality.

IVR ▷ *abbreviation* International Vehicle Registration.

ivy /'aɪvɪ/ ▷ *noun* (***ivies***) **1** a woody evergreen climbing or trailing plant, with dark glossy leaves with five points and black berry-like fruits. **2** any of several other climbing plants, such as poison ivy. ⓔ Anglo-Saxon *ifig*.

ixia /'ɪksɪə/ ▷ *noun* (***ixias***) a plant of the iris family with large showy flowers, originally found in S Africa. ⓔ 18c: from Greek *ixos* mistletoe.

ixtle see ISTLE

-ize or **-ise** /aɪz/ ▷ *suffix, forming verbs, signifying* **1** to make or become something specified □ ***equalize.*** **2** to treat or react to in a specified way □ ***criticize.*** **3** to engage in a specified activity □ ***theorize.*** ● **-ization** *suffix, forming nouns* □ ***familiarization.*** ⓔ From Latin *-izare*.

-ize, -ise

Although **-ize** is common in American English, it is not an Americanism. It is common also in British English, although **-ise** is also common. Note that some verbs require **-ise** because it is part of an invariable element such as **-cise, -prise** or **-vise**, eg *supervise* and *comprise*.

J

J[1] or **j** /dʒeɪ/ ▻ *noun* (*Js, J's* or *j's*) the tenth letter of the English alphabet. See also JAY[2].

J[2] ▻ *abbreviation* **1** *IVR* Japan. **2** joule. **3** (*plural JJ*) Judge. **4** (plural *JJ*) Justice.

JA ▻ *abbreviation, IVR* Jamaica.

jab ▻ *verb* (*jabbed, jabbing*) (*also* **jab at something**) **1** to poke or prod it. **2** to strike with a short quick punch. ▻ *noun* **1** a poke or prod. **2** *colloq* an injection or inoculation □ ***a tetanus jab.*** **3** *boxing* a short straight punch. Ⓒ 19c: variant of Scots *job* to stab or pierce.

jabber /ˈdʒabə(r)/ ▻ *verb* (*jabbered, jabbering*) *tr & intr* to talk or utter rapidly and indistinctly. ▻ *noun* rapid indistinct speech. • **jabberer** *noun*. • **jabbering** *noun, adj.* • **jabberingly** *adverb*. Ⓒ 15c: imitating the sound.

jabberwocky /ˈdʒabəwɒkɪ/ ▻ *noun* nonsensical writing, speech or behaviour, especially when intended for comic effect. Ⓒ 19c: first coined by Lewis Carroll as the title of a poem in *Through the Looking Glass*.

jabot /ˈʒaboʊ/ ▻ *noun* a lace ruffle for a shirt front, especially one worn with full Highland dress. Ⓒ 19c: French.

jacaranda /dʒakəˈrandə/ ▻ *noun* (*jacarandas*) **1** a tropical tree with lilac-coloured flowers and fern-like leaves. **2** the fragrant hard wood of this tree. Ⓒ 18c: Tupí.

jacinth /ˈdʒasɪnθ, ˈdʒeɪ-/ ▻ *noun* **1** *originally* a blue gemstone, perhaps sapphire. **2** *mineralogy* a reddish-orange variety of transparent zircon. Also called **hyacinth**. **3** a variety of garnet, topaz, quartz or other stone. **4** a reddish-orange colour. **5** a slaty-blue fancy pigeon. Ⓒ 13c as *iacinct*: see HYACINTH.

jack ▻ *noun* **1** a machine or device which originally took the place of a servant, eg a BOOT-JACK. **2** a device for raising a heavy weight, such as a car, off the ground. **3** a winch. **4** *elec, telecomm, etc* a socket with two or more terminals into which a **jackplug** can be inserted in order to make or break a circuit or circuits. **5** the male of certain animals, especially the ass or donkey. See also JACKASS, JACK-RABBIT, JACKDAW. **6** *naut* a small flag indicating nationality, flown by a ship. **7** *cards* the court card of least value, bearing a picture of a page (see PAGE[2] *noun* 2). Also called KNAVE. **8** *bowls* the small white ball that the players aim at. **9** a small national flag flown at the bows of a ship. **10** one of the playing-pieces used in the game of JACKS. **11** *in compounds* man □ ***steeplejack*** □ ***lumberjack.*** ▻ *verb* (*jacked, jacking*) **1** (*often* **jack something up**) to raise it with a jack. • **every man jack** everybody. Ⓒ 16c; 14c as *Iacke* for the man's name *Jack*.

■ **jack something in** or **up** *slang* to give it up, or abandon it.

■ **jack off** *coarse slang* to masturbate.

■ **jack up** *drug-taking slang* to inject oneself; to take a fix.

■ **jack something up 1** to increase (prices, etc). **2** *Austral slang* to refuse it; to resist it.

jackal /ˈdʒakɔːl, -kəl/ ▻ *noun* **1** a mainly nocturnal, carnivorous, scavenging mammal, closely related to the dog and wolf, that lives in deserts, grassland and woodland in Asia and Africa. **2** a person who does someone else's dirty work. Ⓒ 17c: from Persian *shagal*.

jackaroo or **jackeroo** /dʒakəˈruː/ ▻ *noun* (*jackaroos* or *jackeroos*) *Austral colloq* a newcomer, or novice, on a sheep- or cattle-station. ▻ *verb* (*jackarooed, jackarooing*) *intr* to be a jackaroo. See also JILLAROO. Ⓒ 19c: from JACK (see sense 11) + ending of *kangaroo*.

jackass /ˈdʒakas/ ▻ *noun* **1** a male ass or donkey. **2** *colloq* a foolish person. Ⓒ 18c.

jackboot ▻ *noun* **1** a tall leather knee-high military boot. **2** such a boot as a symbol of oppressive military rule. Ⓒ 17c in sense 1; 18c in sense 2.

jackdaw /ˈdʒakdɔː/ ▻ *noun* a bird of the crow family with black plumage shot with blue on the back and head, and a reputation for stealing bright objects. Ⓒ 16c: from JACK + old word *daw* jackdaw.

jacket /ˈdʒakɪt/ ▻ *noun* **1** a short coat, especially a long-sleeved, hip-length one. **2** something worn over the top half of the body □ ***life jacket.*** **3** a DUST JACKET. **4 a** an outer casing for a boiler, etc, for preventing heat loss; **b** any protective casing. **5** the skin of a potato that has been cooked without being peeled. Ⓒ 15c: from French *jaquet*.

Jack Frost ▻ *noun* a personification of frost.

jackhammer ▻ *noun* a hand-held compressed-air HAMMER DRILL for rock-drilling.

jack-in-office ▻ *noun* (*jack-in-offices*) *Brit derog* a self-important minor official.

jack-in-the-box ▻ *noun* (*jack-in-the-boxes*) a box containing a doll attached to a spring, which jumps out when the lid is opened. Ⓒ 18c.

jackknife ▻ *noun* **1** a large pocket knife with a folding blade. **2** a dive in which the body is bent double and then straightened before entering the water. ▻ *verb, intr* **1** said of an articulated vehicle: to go out of control in such a way that the trailer swings round against the cab. **2** said of a diver: to perform a jackknife. Ⓒ 18c in sense 1.

jack-of-all-trades ▻ *noun* (*jacks-of-all-trades*) someone who turns their hand to a variety of different jobs.

jack-o'-lantern ▻ *noun* a lantern made from a hollowed-out pumpkin, turnip, etc, with holes cut to resemble eyes, mouth and nose.

jack plug see under JACK 4

jackpot ▻ *noun* the maximum win, to be made in a lottery, card game, etc, especially one consisting of the accumulated stakes. • **hit the jackpot** *colloq* to have a remarkable financial win or stroke of luck. Ⓒ 20c.

jack rabbit ▻ *noun* a large N American hare with a brown coat, long hind legs and large ears with black tips. Ⓒ 19c: shortened from *jackass-rabbit*, an animal so called because of its long ears.

Jack Robinson ▻ *noun* • **before you could say Jack Robinson** *colloq* very suddenly or quickly; in a trice. Ⓒ 18c.

Jack Russell and **Jack Russell terrier** ▻ *noun* a small terrier, usually white with brown, tan or black markings. Ⓒ 19c: named after John Russell (1795–1883), the English clergyman who introduced them.

jacks and **jackstones** ▻ *noun* a game in which playing-pieces (originally small bones or pebbles) are tossed and caught on the back of the hand. Also called **dibs**. Ⓒ 19c.

jacksie or **jacksy** /ˈdʒaksɪ/ ▻ *noun* (*jacksies*) *slang* **1** the buttocks or bottom. **2** the anus. Ⓒ 19c.

Jack tar ▻ *noun* (***Jack tars***) *old use* a sailor. ⓒ 18c.

Jack the Lad ▻ *noun, colloq* a flashy, cocksure young man. ⓒ 18c: from the nickname of Jack Sheppard, an 18c thief.

Jacobean /dʒakə'biən/ ▻ *adj* **1** belonging or relating to the reign of James I of England (1603-25) (also VI of Scotland). **2** said of furniture, drama, etc: typical of the style current in his reign. **3** denoting a style of English and Scottish architecture characterized by a symmetry of façades, large windows and, in manor houses, often E- or H-shaped plans. ▻ *noun* someone who lived during the reign of James I & VI. ⓒ 18c: from Latin *Jacobus* James.

Jacobite /'dʒakəbaɪt/ *Brit historical* ▻ *noun* an adherent of the **Jacobites**, supporters of James II, his son or grandson, the Stuart claimants to the British throne. ▻ *adj* relating to the Jacobites. ⓒ 17c: from Latin *Jacobus* James.

Jacob's ladder /'dʒeɪkəbz —/ ▻ *noun* **1** a ladder with metal or wooden rungs held in a rope or chain framework. **2** a perennial wild or garden plant with purplish-blue flowers and leaves arranged like the rungs of a ladder. ⓒ 19c in sense 1; 18c in sense 2: from Genesis 28.12 where Jacob has a vision of a ladder reaching up to heaven.

Jacob's staff /'dʒeɪkəbz —/ ▻ *noun* **1** a surveyor's rod. **2** any of several different surveying instruments of different periods. ⓒ 16c: apparently named after the pilgrim's staff, one of the emblems of St James (*Jacobus* in Latin).

jaconet /'dʒakənɪt/ ▻ *noun* a type of cotton fabric, especially one with a waterproof backing and used for medical dressings. ⓒ 18c: from Urdu *jagannathi*, named after Jagannathpuri, the town in India where it was first made.

jacquard /'dʒakɑːd/ ▻ *noun* **1** a piece of equipment consisting of a set of coded perforated cards that can be fitted to a loom to produce a fabric with an intricate woven pattern. **2** (*in full* **jacquard loom**) a loom with this kind of device fitted to it. **3** fabric produced on this kind of loom. ⓒ 19c: named after the French inventor of the device, Joseph Marie Jacquard (1752–1834).

jactitation /dʒaktɪ'teɪʃən/ ▻ *noun, medicine* restless tossing in illness; bodily agitation. ⓒ 17c: from Latin *jactitare, jactitatum* to throw.

Jacuzzi /dʒə'kuːzɪ/ ▻ *noun* (***Jacuzzis***) **1** *trademark* a large bath or pool with underwater jets that massage and invigorate the body. **2** (*usually* **jacuzzi**) a bath in such a pool. ⓒ 1960s.

jade¹ ▻ *noun* **1** *geol* a very hard, green, white, brown or yellow semi-precious stone consisting of either JADEITE or NEPHRITE, used to make vases and carved ornaments. **2** the intense green colour of jade. ⓒ 18c: French *le jade*, from Spanish *piedra de ijada* stone of the ribs, from the belief that it helped to cure colic.

jade² ▻ *noun old use* **1** a disreputable or ill-natured woman. **2** a worn-out old horse. ⓒ 16c in sense 1; 14c in sense 2.

jaded /'dʒeɪdɪd/ ▻ *adj* fatigued; dull and bored. ⓒ 17c.

jadeite /'dʒeɪdaɪt/ ▻ *noun, geol* a tough fibrous mineral with a slightly greasy lustre, a translucent green form of which is the most highly prized form of JADE¹. ⓒ 19c.

Jaffa /'dʒafə/ ▻ *noun* a large oval orange with a particularly thick skin. ⓒ 19c: named after Jaffa, the Israeli city where this type of orange was first grown.

jag¹ ▻ *noun* **1** a sharp projection. **2** *Scots* an injection; an inoculation. ▻ *verb* (***jagged*** /dʒagd/ , ***jagging***) **1** to prick, sting or pierce something or someone. **2** to cut unevenly. **3** to make indentations in something. ⓒ 14c.

jag² ▻ *noun, slang* **1** a bout of heavy drinking or drug-taking. **2** a bout of indulgence in anything. ⓒ 20c.

jagged /'dʒagɪd/ ▻ *adj* having a rough or sharp uneven edge. • **jaggedly** *adverb*. • **jaggedness** *noun*. ⓒ 16c: from JAG¹.

jaggery see under PALM SUGAR

jaggy /'dʒagɪ/ ▻ *adj* (***jaggier***, ***jaggiest***) **1** having rough, untidy or uneven edges. **2** *Scots* prickly or stinging □ ***jaggy nettles***.

jaguar /'dʒagjʊə(r)/ ▻ *noun* the largest of the American BIG CATS, with a deep yellow or tawny coat covered with black spots, and found mainly in tropical forests. ⓒ 17c: from S American Indian (Tupí) *jaguara*.

jai alai see PELOTA

jail or **gaol** /dʒeɪl/ ▻ *noun* prison. ▻ *verb* (***jailed***, ***jailing***) to imprison. • **jailer** or **jailor** *noun*. ⓒ 13c: from French *gaole*.

jailbait ▻ *noun, slang* a girl who has not jet reached the legal age of consent.

jailbird or **gaolbird** ▻ *noun, colloq* a person who is, or has been, frequently in prison. ⓒ 17c.

jailbreak or **gaolbreak** ▻ *noun* an escape, especially by several prisoners, from jail.

Jain /dʒaɪn, dʒeɪn/ ▻ *noun* an adherent of **Jainism**, an indigenous religion of India which regards Vardhamana Mahavir (599–527 BC) as its founder. See also AHIMSA. ⓒ 19c: from Hindi *jaina* saint.

jalapeño /hɑːlə'peɪnjoʊ/ and **jalapeño pepper** ▻ *noun* (***jalapeños***) *chiefly US* an especially hot type of capsicum pepper, used in Mexican cooking. ⓒ 20c: American Spanish.

jalopy or **jaloppy** /dʒə'lɒpɪ/ ▻ *noun* (***jalopies*** or ***jaloppies***) *colloq* a worn-out old car. ⓒ 20c.

jalousie /ʒalʊ'ziː, 'ʒaluziː/ ▻ *noun* (***jalousies***) an outside shutter with slats. • **jalousied** *adj*. ⓒ 16c: French, literally 'jealousy', so called as someone behind the shutter could see out without being seen.

jam¹ ▻ *noun* a thick sticky food made from fruit boiled with sugar, used as a spread on bread, etc. • **jam tomorrow** *colloq* something agreeable which is constantly promised but which never arrives ⓒ 1871, from Lewis Carroll's *Through the Looking Glass* 'The rule is jam to-morrow and jam yesterday — but never jam to-day' • **money for jam** *colloq* money easily made. • **want jam on it** *colloq* to expect more than is reasonable. ⓒ 18c.

jam² ▻ *verb* (***jammed***, ***jamming***) **1** *often in passive* to stick or wedge something so as to make it immovable. **2** *tr & intr* said of machinery, etc: to stick or make it stick and stop working. **3** to push or shove something; to cram, press or pack. **4** (*also* **jam something up**) to fill (eg a street) so full that movement comes to a stop. **5** to cause interference to (a radio signal, etc), especially deliberately. **6** *intr, colloq* to play jazz in a JAM SESSION. ⓒ 18c: probably an imitation of the actions or its sound.

jamahiriya or **jamahiriyah** /dʒamɑːhiː'riːja/ ▻ *noun* a people's state; a state of the proletariat. ⓒ 20c: Arabic, from *jumhur* people.

Jamaican /dʒə'meɪkən/ ▻ *adj* belonging or relating to Jamaica, an island nation in the Caribbean Sea, or its inhabitants. ▻ *noun* a citizen or inhabitant of, or person born in, Jamaica.

jamb /dʒam/ ▻ *noun* the vertical post at the side of a door, window or fireplace. ⓒ 14c: from French *jambe* leg.

jambalaya /dʒambə'laɪə/ ▻ *noun* (***jambalayas***) *US* **1** a Creole or Cajun dish made with rice mixed with seafood or chicken, seasonings, etc. **2** a mixture generally. ⓒ 19c: Louisiana French, from Provençal *jambalaia*.

jamboree /dʒambə'riː/ ▻ *noun* (***jamborees***) **1** a large rally of Scouts, Guides, etc. **2** *colloq* a large and lively gathering. ⓒ 19c: originally US slang.

jammy ▷ *adj* (***jammier***, ***jammiest***) **1** covered or filled with jam. **2** *colloq* said of a person: lucky. **3** *colloq* said of a job, etc: profitable, especially at little cost in effort. ⓒ 19c.

jam-packed ▷ *adj*, *colloq* packed tight. ⓒ 20c.

jampan /'dʒampan/ ▷ *noun* an Indian sedan chair. • **jampanee** or **jampani** *noun* (***jampanees*** or ***jampanis***) its bearer. ⓒ 19c: from Bengali *jhampan*, Hindi *jhappan*.

jam sandwich ▷ *noun*, *colloq* a police squad car. ⓒ 1980s: so called because they are white with a reddish stripe along the middle of each side.

jam session ▷ *noun*, *slang* a session of live, especially improvised, jazz or popular music. ⓒ 20c: see JAM².

Jan. ▷ *abbreviation* January.

Jandal /'dʒandəl/ ▷ *noun*, *NZ trademark* a type of sandal with a thong between the big toe and the other toes.

JANET /'dʒanɪt/ ▷ *abbreviation* Joint Academic Network, a computer network linking UK universities, research bodies, etc, part of THE INTERNET.

jangle /'dʒaŋgəl/ ▷ *verb* (***jangled***, ***jangling***) **1** *tr & intr* to make or cause something to make an irritating, discordant ringing noise. **2** to upset or irritate. ▷ *noun* an unpleasant dissonant ringing sound. • **jangling** *noun*. • **jangly** *adj* (***janglier***, ***jangliest***). ⓒ 13c: from French *jangler*.

janissary /'dʒanɪsərɪ/ ▷ *noun* (***janissaries***) *historical* a soldier of the Turkish sultan's personal guard. ⓒ 16c: from Turkish *yeniçeri* new troops.

janitor /'dʒanɪtə(r)/ ▷ *noun* **1** *N Amer*, *Scottish* a caretaker, especially of a school. **2** a doorkeeper. • **janitorial** /-'tɔːrɪəl/ *adj*. ⓒ 17c: Latin, from *janua* door.

jankers /'dʒaŋkəz/ ▷ *noun*, *military slang* punishment, detention, etc for defaulting. ⓒ 20c.

January /'dʒanjʊrɪ, 'dʒanjʊərɪ/ ▷ *noun* (abbreviation **Jan.**) the first month of the year, which has 31 days. ⓒ 14c: from Latin *Januarius mensis* month of the god Janus.

Jap *offensive colloq* ▷ *noun* a Japanese person. ▷ *adj* Japanese.

japan /dʒə'pan/ ▷ *noun* **1** a hard glossy black lacquer, originally from Japan, used to coat wood and metal. **2** Japanese ware or work. ▷ *verb* (***japanned***, ***japanning***) to lacquer something with japan. ⓒ 17c: named after the country.

Japanese /dʒapə'niːz/ ▷ *adj* belonging or relating to Japan, an island state off the E coast of Asia, its inhabitants or their language. ▷ *noun* **1** (*plural* ***Japanese***) a native or citizen of Japan. **2** the official language of Japan.

jape /dʒeɪp/ ▷ *noun*, *old use* a trick, prank or joke. ▷ *verb* (***japed***, ***japing***) **1** *intr* to jest or joke. **2** *tr & intr* to mock. • **japer** *noun*. • **japing** *noun*. ⓒ 14c.

japonica /dʒə'pɒnɪkə/ ▷ *noun* (***japonicas***) **1** an ornamental, scarlet- or pink-flowered deciduous shrub of the quince family, native to E Asia, which bears round green, white or yellow fruit. Also called **Japanese quince**. **2** the CAMELLIA. ⓒ 19c: Latin, meaning 'Japanese'.

jar¹ ▷ *noun* **1** a wide-mouthed cylindrical container, usually made of glass **2** a JARFUL. **3** *colloq* a glass of beer. ⓒ 16c: from French *jarre*, from Arabic *jarrah* earthenware vessel.

jar² ▷ *verb* (***jarred***, ***jarring***) **1** *intr* to have a harsh effect; to grate. **2** *tr & intr* to jolt or vibrate. **3** *tr & intr* to make or cause something to make a harsh sound. **4** *intr* (*especially* **jar with something**) to clash or conflict with it □ *buildings that jar with the environment*. ▷ *noun* a jarring sensation, shock or jolt. • **jarring** *noun*, *adj*. • **jarringly** *adverb*. ⓒ 16c: imitating the sound or effect.

jardinière /ʒɑːdɪ'njɛə(r)/ ▷ *noun* **1** an ornamental pot or stand for flowers. **2** *cookery* an accompaniment of mixed vegetables for a meat dish. ⓒ 19c: French, feminine of *jardinier* gardener.

jarful ▷ *noun* (***jarfuls***) the amount a JAR¹ can hold.

jargon¹ /'dʒɑːgən/ ▷ *noun* **1** the specialized vocabulary of a particular trade, profession, group or activity. **2** *derog* language which uses this type of vocabulary in a pretentious or meaningless way. **3** confusing or meaningless talk; gibberish. • **jargoneer** or **jargonist** *noun* someone who uses jargon. • **jargonization** or **jargonisation** *noun*. • **jargonize** or **jargonise** *verb* (***jargonized***, ***jargonizing***) **1** to express something in jargon. **2** *intr* to speak jargon. ⓒ 14c: French.

jargon² /'dʒɑːgən/ or **jargoon** /-guːn/ ▷ *noun*, *mineralogy* a brilliant, colourless or pale zircon.

jarred and **jarring** see under JAR²

Jas. ▷ *abbreviation* **1** James. **2** Book of the Bible: the Letter of James. See table at BIBLE.

jasmine /'dʒazmɪn, 'dʒas-/ or **jessamine** /'dʒɛsəmɪn/ ▷ *noun* a shrub or vine native to Asia, widely cultivated as an ornamental plant and whose fragrant flowers are used as a source of jasmine oil in perfumery and also to scent tea. ⓒ 16c: from Persian *yasmin*.

jasper /'dʒaspə(r)/ ▷ *noun* **1** *geol* a red, yellow, brown or green semi-precious gemstone, an impure form of CHALCEDONY, used to make jewellery and ornaments. **2** (*also* **jasper ware**) a fine hard porcelain. ⓒ 14c: from Greek *iaspis*.

jataka /'dʒɑːtəkə/ ▷ *noun* (***jatakas***) *Buddhism* a nativity; the birth-story of Buddha. ⓒ 19c: Sanskrit, meaning 'born under'.

jato /'dʒeɪtoʊ/ ▷ *noun* (***jatos***) *aeronautics*, *etc* a jet-assisted take-off, using a **jato unit** consisting of one or more rocket motors, which is usually jettisoned after use. ⓒ 20c: from *j*et-*a*ssisted *t*ake-*o*ff.

jaundice /'dʒɔːndɪs/ ▷ *noun*, *pathol* a condition which turns the skin and the whites of the eyes a yellowish colour, resulting from an excess of BILIRUBIN in the blood, and often a symptom of liver disease. ⓒ 14c: from French *jaunisse*, from *jaune* yellow.

jaundiced ▷ *adj* **1** suffering from jaundice. **2** said of a person or attitude: bitter or resentful; cynical.

jaunt /dʒɔːnt/ ▷ *noun* a short journey for pleasure. ▷ *verb* (***jaunted***, ***jaunting***) *intr* to go for a jaunt. ⓒ 16c.

jaunty /'dʒɔːntɪ/ ▷ *adj* (***jauntier***, ***jauntiest***) **1** said of someone's manner or personality: breezy and exuberant. **2** said of dress, etc: smart; stylish. • **jauntily** *adverb*. • **jauntiness** *noun*. ⓒ 17c: from French *gentil* noble or gentle.

Java Man ▷ *noun* the first known fossil of *homo erectus*, who lived during the PALAEOLITHIC era. ⓒ 20c: the fossil was found in Java in the late 19c.

javelin /'dʒavəlɪn, 'dʒavlɪn/ ▷ *noun* **1** a light spear for throwing, either as a weapon or in sport. **2** (**the javelin**) the athletic event of throwing the javelin. ⓒ 16c: from French *javeline*.

jaw /dʒɔː/ ▷ *noun* **1** *zool*, *biol* in most vertebrates: either of the two bony structures that form the framework of the mouth and in which the teeth are set. See also MANDIBLE, MAXILLA. **2** the lower part of the face round the mouth and chin. **3** (**jaws**) the mouth, especially of an animal. **4** (**jaws**) a threshold, especially of something terrifying □ *the jaws of death*. **5** (**jaws**) in a machine or tool: a pair of opposing parts used for gripping, crushing, etc. **6** *colloq* a long conversation; a talking-to; talk; chatter. ▷ *verb* (***jawed***, ***jawing***) *intr*, *colloq* to chatter, gossip or talk. ⓒ 14c: from French *joue* cheek.

jawbone ▷ *noun*, *zool*, *non-technical* the upper or lower bone of the jaw. *Technical equivalents* MANDIBLE and MAXILLA.

jay¹ ▷ *noun* a noisy bird of the crow family, especially the **common jay** which has pinkish-brown plumage and blue, black and white bands on its wings. ⓒ 14c: from French *jai*.

jay² ▻ *noun* **1** a phonetic spelling for the letter J. See also J¹. **2** an object or mark of the same shape as the letter.

jaywalk ▻ *verb, intr* to cross streets wherever one likes, regardless of traffic signals. • **jaywalker** *noun*. • **jaywalking** *noun*. ◷ 20c: originally US, from *jay*, meaning 'fool'.

jazz ▻ *noun* **1** a type of popular music of Black American origin, with strong catchy rhythms, performed with much improvisation. **2** *colloq* talk; nonsense; business, stuff, etc. ▻ *verb* (***jazzed***, ***jazzing***) (*usually* **jazz something up**) *colloq* **1** to enliven or brighten it. **2** to give it a jazzy rhythm. • **... and all that jazz** *colloq* ... and all that sort of thing □ *philosophy and all that jazz.* ◷ 20c.

jazz poetry ▻ *noun* poetry which is recited to the accompaniment of jazz music, popular in the 1960s in Britain (especially London) and the USA. ◷ 20c.

jazzy ▻ *adj* (***jazzier***, ***jazziest***) **1** in the style of, or like, jazz. **2** *colloq* showy; flashy; stylish. • **jazzily** *adverb*.

JC ▻ *abbreviation* Jesus Christ.

JCB ▻ *noun* a type of mobile excavator used in the building industry, with a hydraulic shovel at the front and a digging arm at the back. ◷ 20c: named after *J*oseph *C*yril *B*amford (born 1916) the British manufacturer.

JCR ▻ *abbreviation* junior common room.

J-curve ▻ *noun, econ* a J-shaped curve on graphs, showing balance-of-trade statistics over a period of time after a currency has been devalued, which reflects a small initial decrease, followed by a large sustained increase, as the effect of cheaper exports and more expensive imports is felt.

jealous /ˈdʒɛləs/ ▻ *adj* (*often* **jealous of someone** or **something**) **1** envious of someone else, their possessions, success, talents, etc. **2** suspicious and resentful of possible rivals; possessive; unable to tolerate unfaithfulness or the thought of it □ *a jealous husband.* **3** anxiously protective of something one has. **4** *Bible* said of God: intolerant of disloyalty. **5** caused by jealousy □ *a jealous fury.* • **jealously** *adverb*. Compare ENVIOUS. ◷ 13c: from French *gelos*, from Greek *zelos* rivalry or jealousy.

jealousy ▻ *noun* (***jealousies***) **1** the emotion of envy or suspicious possessiveness. **2** (*usually* **jealousies**) an occurrence of this.

jeans /dʒiːnz/ ▻ *plural noun* casual trousers made especially of denim, corduroy or other similar material. ◷ 19c: from *jean* a strong cotton from Genoa (French *Gênes*).

Jeep ▻ *noun* **1** *trademark* a light military vehicle capable of travelling over rough country. **2** (*often* **jeep**) any similar vehicle. ◷ 20c: from *g*eneral-*p*urpose vehicle.

jeepers /ˈdʒiːpəz/ and **jeepers creepers** ▻ *exclamation, US colloq* expressing surprise. ◷ 20c: euphemism for *Jesus Christ*.

jeer /dʒɪə(r)/ ▻ *verb* (***jeered***, ***jeering***) **1** to mock or deride (a speaker, performer, etc). **2** *intr* (*also* **jeer at someone** or **something**) to laugh unkindly at them or it □ *jeered at his accent.* ▻ *noun* a taunt, insult or hoot of derision. • **jeerer** *noun*. • **jeering** *noun, adj*. • **jeeringly** *adverb*. ◷ 16c.

Jeez or **Jeeze** /dʒiːz/ ▻ *exclamation, slang* expressing surprise, enthusiasm or emphasis. ◷ 20c: originally US, corruption of *Jesus*.

jehad see JIHAD

Jehovah's Witness ▻ *noun* a member of a fundamentalist sect of Christians with their own translation of the Bible, who avoid worldly involvement and refuse to obey any law which they see as contradicting the word of God. ◷ 1930s: the organization was founded in the late 19c, but adopted this name in 1931; previously, they were called Millennial Dawnists and International Bible Students.

Jehu /ˈdʒiːhjuː/ ▻ *noun, humorous, colloq* a fast or reckless driver. ◷ 17c: named after a Biblical King of Israel (2 Kings 9.20) renowned for his furious chariot-driving.

jejune /dʒɪˈdʒuːn/ ▻ *adj, derog* **1** said of writing, ideas, etc: dull, banal, unoriginal and empty of imagination. **2** childish; naïve. • **jejunely** *adverb*. • **jejuneness** or **jejunity** *noun*. ◷ 17c: from Latin *jejunus* hungry or empty.

jejunum /dʒɪˈdʒuːnəm/ ▻ *noun, anatomy* in mammals: the part of the SMALL INTESTINE between the duodenum and the ileum, the main function of which is to absorb digested food. ◷ 16c: from Latin *jejunum intestinum* empty intestine (because it was thought always to be empty after death).

Jekyll and Hyde /ˈdʒɛkɪl — haɪd; *US* ˈdʒiːkɪl —/ ▻ *noun* a person with two distinct personalities, one good, the other evil. ◷ 19c: from *The Strange Case of Dr Jekyll and Mr Hyde*, a novel by Robert Louis Stevenson (1850–94).

jell or **gel** ▻ *verb* (***jelled***, ***jelling***) *intr* **1** to become firm; to set. **2** *colloq* to take definite shape. ◷ 19c: from JELLY.

jellied ▻ *adj* set in jelly □ *jellied eels.*

jellify ▻ *verb* (***jellified***, ***jellifying***) **1** to make something into jelly. **2** *intr* to become gelatinous. ◷ 19c.

jelly /ˈdʒɛlɪ/ ▻ *noun* (***jellies***) **1** a wobbly, transparent, fruit-flavoured dessert set with gelatine. **2** a clear jam made by boiling and straining fruit. **3** meat stock or other savoury medium set with gelatine. **4** any jelly-like substance. **5** *Scottish drug-taking slang* a Temazepam capsule. ◷ 14c in sense 3: from French *gelée*, from Latin *gelare* to freeze.

jelly baby and **jelly bean** ▻ *noun* a soft fruit-flavoured sweet in the shape of a baby or a bean, made with gelatine.

jelly bag ▻ *noun, cookery* a bag through which fruit is strained to make jelly.

jellyfish ▻ *noun, zool* any of various marine COELENTERATES, usually having an umbrella-shaped body and tentacles containing stinging cells. ◷ 19c in this sense.

jemmy /ˈdʒɛmɪ/ ▻ *noun* (***jemmies***) a small crowbar used by burglars for forcing open windows, etc. ▻ *verb* (***jemmies, jemmied***, ***jemmying***) (*usually* **jemmy something open**) to force it open with a jemmy or similar tool. ◷ 19c: from the name *James*.

Jena glass /ˈjeɪnə —/ ▻ *noun* a special type of glass which contains BORATES and free SILICA, and is resistant to chemical attack. ◷ 19c: originally produced in the German town of *Jena*.

a je ne sais quoi /— ʒə nə seɪ kwɑː/ ▻ *noun* (***je ne sais quois***) an indefinable something; a special unknown ingredient or quality. ◷ 17c: French, literally 'I don't know what'.

jennet /ˈdʒɛnɪt/ ▻ *noun* a small Spanish donkey. Also called **genet**. ◷ 15c: from French *genet*, ultimately from Spanish Arabic *zanati* a tribe renowned for its horsemanship.

jenny /ˈdʒɛnɪ/ ▻ *noun* (***jennies***) **1** a name given to the female of certain animals, especially the donkey, ass, owl and wren. **2** a SPINNING-JENNY. ◷ 17c: from the name *Jenny*.

jeopardize or **jeopardise** /ˈdʒɛpədaɪz/ ▻ *verb* (***jeopardized***, ***jeopardizing***) to put something at risk of harm, loss or destruction □ *She jeopardized her chances of passing the exam by doing very little revision.* ◷ 17c.

jeopardy /ˈdʒɛpədɪ/ ▻ *noun* **1** danger of harm, loss or destruction □ *His job was in jeopardy due to the takeover.* **2** *US law* the danger of trial and punishment faced by a person accused on a criminal charge. ◷ 14c: from French *jeu parti* a divided or even (ie uncertain) game.

jerboa /dʒɜːˈboʊə/ ▻ *noun* (***jerboas***) a small nocturnal burrowing rodent of N Africa and Asia, with long hind legs adapted for jumping, an extremely long tail and large ears. Also called **desert rat**. ⓒ 17c: from Arabic *yarba*.

jeremiad /dʒɛrəˈmaɪəd, -ad/ ▻ *noun, colloq* a lengthy and mournful tale of woe. ⓒ 18c: from French *jérémiade*, from *The Lamentations of Jeremiah* in the Old Testament.

jerk /dʒɜːk/ ▻ *noun* **1** a quick tug or pull. **2** a sudden movement; a jolt. **3** *weightlifting* a movement lifting the barbell from shoulder height to a position on outstretched arms above the head. See also **clean and jerk**. **4** *derog slang* a useless or idiotic person. ▻ *verb* (*jerked, jerking*) **1** to pull or tug sharply. **2** *intr* to move with sharp suddenness. ⓒ 16c.

■ **jerk someone around** *colloq* to treat them badly or unfairly.

■ **jerk off** or **jerk someone off** *coarse slang* to masturbate or masturbate them.

jerkin /ˈdʒɜːkɪn/ ▻ *noun* a sleeveless jacket, short coat or close-fitting waistcoat. ⓒ 16c.

jerky *adj* (*jerkier, jerkiest*) making sudden movements or jerks. ● **jerkily** *adverb*. ● **jerkiness** *noun*.

jeroboam /dʒɛrəˈboʊəm/ ▻ *noun* a large wine bottle holding the equivalent of four standard bottles. Compare REHOBOAM. ⓒ 19c: named after the Old Testament king Jeroboam (1 Kings 11.28).

Jerry /ˈdʒɛrɪ/ ▻ *noun* (*Jerries*) *Brit war slang* **a** a German soldier; a German; **b** German soldiers collectively; the Germans. ⓒ 20c: alteration of GERMAN.

jerry[1] /ˈdʒɛrɪ/ ▻ *noun* (*jerries*) *colloq, old use* a CHAMBERPOT. ⓒ 19c: from JEROBOAM.

jerry[2] /ˈdʒɛrɪ/ ▻ *noun, colloq* (*jerries*) **1** a JERRY-BUILDER. **2** *as adj* hastily made using poor materials.

jerry-builder ▻ *noun* a person who puts up flimsy buildings cheaply and quickly. ● **jerry-building** *noun*. ● **jerry-built** *adj* said of buildings, etc: built cheaply, hastily and incompetently. ⓒ 19c: possibly referring to the town of Jericho and the Biblical story in which its walls came tumbling down.

jerry can ▻ *noun* a flat-sided can used for carrying water, petrol, etc. ⓒ 20c: from JERRY[1].

jersey /ˈdʒɜːzɪ/ ▻ *noun* (*jerseys*) **1** a knitted garment worn on the upper part of the body, pulled on over the head; a pullover. **2** a fine knitted fabric, usually machine-knitted and slightly stretchy, in cotton, nylon, etc. **3** (**Jersey**) a breed of dairy cattle, with a fawn to dark-grey coat. ⓒ 16c: named after Jersey in the Channel Islands.

Jerusalem artichoke /dʒəˈruːsələm —/ ▻ *noun* **1** a tall perennial N American plant, related to the sunflower, widely cultivated for its edible tubers. **2** the underground tuber of this plant, with white flesh and knobbly brownish or reddish skin, which can be eaten as a vegetable. ⓒ 17c: a corruption of Italian *girasole* sunflower.

jess ▻ *noun* (*jesses*) *falconry* a short leather strap attached to the leg of a hawk. ● **jessed** *adj*. ⓒ 14c: from French *ges*, from Latin *jactus* a throw, from *jacere* to throw.

jessamine see JASMINE

Jessie or **jessie** /ˈdʒɛsɪ/ ▻ *noun* (*Jessies*) *Scots colloq* an effeminate, feeble or namby-pamby man or boy. ⓒ 1920s.

jest ▻ *noun* a joke or prank. ▻ *verb* (*jested, jesting*) *intr* to make a jest; to joke. ● **in jest** as a joke; not seriously. ● **jestful** *adj*. ● **jesting** *noun, adj*. ● **jestingly** *adverb*. ⓒ 13c: from French *geste* deed, from Latin *gesta* things done.

jester /ˈdʒɛstə(r)/ ▻ *noun, historical* a colourfully-dressed professional clown, employed by a king or noble to amuse the court. ⓒ 14c.

Jesuit /ˈdʒɛzjʊɪt/ ▻ *noun* a member of the Society of Jesus (**the Jesuits**), a male religious order founded in 1540 by Ignatius de Loyola. ▻ *adj* belonging or relating to the Jesuits. ⓒ 16c: from Latin *Jesuita*, from *Jesus*.

jesuitical /dʒɛzjʊˈɪtɪkəl/ ▻ *adj* **1** said of an argument: over-subtle; cleverly misleading. **2** said of a plan: crafty; cunning. ● **jesuitically** *adverb*. ⓒ 17c.

Jesus /ˈdʒiːzəs/ ▻ *noun* Jesus Christ, the central figure of the Christian faith. ▻ *exclamation* an exclamation of surprise, anger, etc.

jet[1] ▻ *noun, geol* **a** a hard black variety of LIGNITE that can be cut and polished and was formerly a popular gemstone, used to make jewellery and ornaments; **b** *as adj* □ *jet necklace*. ⓒ 14c: from French *jaiet*.

jet[2] ▻ *noun* **1** a strong continuous stream of liquid gas, forced under pressure from a narrow opening. **2** an orifice, nozzle or pipe through which such a stream is forced. **3** any device powered by such a stream of liquid or gas, especially a jet engine. **4** (*also* **jet aircraft**) an aircraft powered by a jet engine. ▻ *verb* (*jetted, jetting*) **1** *tr & intr, colloq* to travel or be transported by jet aircraft. **2** *intr* to emit liquid or gas in a jet; to spurt. ⓒ 16c: from French *jeter* to throw.

jet-black ▻ *adj* deep glossy black.

jet engine ▻ *noun* any engine, especially that of an aircraft, which generates all or most of its forward thrust by ejecting a jet of gases that have been formed as a result of combustion of its fuel. See also TURBOFAN, TURBOJET, TURBOPROP.

jetfoil ▻ *noun* an advanced form of HYDROFOIL (sense 2) propelled by water jets.

jet lag ▻ *noun* the tiredness and lethargy that result from the body's inability to adjust to the rapid changes of TIME ZONE that go with high-speed, long-distance air travel. ● **jet-lagged** *adj*.

jeton see JETTON

jet plane ▻ *noun* an aircraft powered by a jet engine.

jet-propelled ▻ *adj* **1** driven by jet propulsion. **2** *colloq* fast.

jet propulsion ▻ *noun* the forward thrust of a body brought about by means of a force produced by ejection of a jet of gas or liquid (eg combustion gases produced by the burning of fuel) to the rear of the body.

jetsam /ˈdʒɛtsəm/ ▻ *noun* goods jettisoned from a ship and washed up on the shore. Compare FLOTSAM. ⓒ 16c: contracted from JETTISON.

the jet set ▻ *singular or plural noun, colloq* wealthy people who lead a life of fast travel and expensive enjoyment. ● **jet-setter** *noun*. ● **jet-setting** *noun, adj*.

jet ski ▻ *noun* a powered craft, similar to a motorbike, adapted for skimming across water on a ski-like keel. ● **jet-ski** ▻ *verb, intr* to travel over water on a jet ski. 20c.

jet stream ▻ *noun* **1** *meteorol* very high winds more than 20 000 feet above the Earth. **2** the exhaust of a rocket engine.

jettison /ˈdʒɛtɪsən/ ▻ *verb* (*jettisoned, jettisoning*) **1** to throw (cargo) overboard to lighten a ship, aircraft, etc in an emergency. **2** *colloq* to abandon, reject or get rid of something. ⓒ 15c: from French *getaison*, from Latin *jactatio* a tossing.

jetton or **jeton** /ˈdʒɛtən/ ▻ *noun* **1** a counter or chip used in card games or other gambling games. **2** a token for operating a machine. ⓒ 18c: French *jeton*, from *jeter* to throw.

jetty /ˈdʒɛtɪ/ ▻ *noun* (*jetties*) **1** a stone or wooden landing-stage. **2** a stone barrier built out into the sea to protect a harbour from currents and high waves. ⓒ 15c: from French *jetee*, from *jeter* to throw.

Jew /dʒuː/ ▻ *noun* **1** a member of the Hebrew race. **2** someone who practises Judaism. **3** *offensive, old use* a miser; an unrelenting bargainer. ⓒ 12c: from French *Juiu*, from Latin *Judaeus*.

jewel /dʒʊəl/ ▻ *noun* **1** a precious stone. **2** a personal ornament made with precious stones and metals. **3** a gem used in the machinery of a watch. **4** someone or something greatly prized. ▷ *verb* (***jewelled, jewelling***) to adorn someone or something with jewels; to fit something with a jewel. ● **jewelled** *adj.* ◎ 13c: from French *joel.*

jeweller ▷ *noun* a person who deals in, makes or repairs jewellery, watches and objects of gold and silver.

jeweller's rouge see ROUGE *noun* 2

jewellery or (*US*) **jewelry** /ˈdʒʊəlrɪ/ ▷ *noun* articles worn for personal adornment, eg bracelets, necklaces, brooches and rings.

Jewess ▷ *noun, sometimes considered offensive* a Jewish woman or girl.

Jewish ▷ *adj* relating to the Jews or to Judaism.

Jewry /ˈdʒʊərɪ/ ▷ *noun* (*plural* in sense 3 only, ***Jewries***) *old use* **1** Jews collectively. **2** their culture or religion. **3** the Jewish quarter in a town.

Jew's harp ▷ *noun* a tiny, lyre-shaped musical instrument held between the teeth, with a narrow metal tongue that is twanged with the finger. ◎ 16c.

Jew's mallow see KERRIA

Jezebel /ˈdʒɛzəbel, -bəl/ ▷ *noun, derog* a shamelessly immoral or scheming woman. ◎ 16c: named after Ahab's wife in the Old Testament, 1 Kings 21; 2 Kings 9.30.

jib[1] ▷ *noun, naut* a small three-cornered sail in front of the mainsail of a yacht. ▷ *verb* (***jibbed, jibbing***) (*especially* **jib at something**) **1** *intr* said of a horse: to refuse a jump, etc. **2** *intr* said of a person: to object to it. **3** *tr & intr, naut* to GYBE. ◎ 17c.

jib[2] ▷ *noun* the projecting arm of a crane from which the lifting gear hangs. ◎ 18c: from GIBBET.

jib boom ▷ *noun, naut* an extension to the bowsprit on which the jib is spread.

jibe see GYBE

jiffy /ˈdʒɪfɪ/ or **jiff** ▷ *noun* (***jiffies*** or ***jiffs***) *colloq* a moment □ *just a jiffy.* ◎ 18c.

Jiffy bag ▷ *noun, trademark* a padded envelope.

jig ▷ *noun* **1** a lively country dance or folk dance. **2** music for such a dance. **3** a jerky movement. **4** *mech* a device that holds a piece of work in position and guides the tools being used on it. **5** *angling* a lure which moves jerkily when drawn through the water. ▷ *verb* (***jigged, jigging***) **1** *intr* to dance a jig. **2** *intr* to jump up and down. **3** *tr & intr* to jerk rapidly up and down. **4** *mech* to work on (something under construction) using a jig. ◎ 16c.

jigger[1] ▷ *noun* **1 a** a small quantity of alcoholic spirits; **b** a glass for measuring this. **2** *billiards, colloq* a cue rest. **3** *golf* an iron-headed club. **4** *N Amer colloq* an all-purpose term for a gadget when its name is not known or not remembered. ◎ 19c; 17c in the sense 'someone who jigs'.

jigger[2] see CHIGGER

jiggered /ˈdʒɪgəd/ ▷ *adj, colloq* exhausted. ● **I'll be jiggered** *colloq* an expression of astonishment. ◎ 19c: possibly euphemistic for *buggered.*

jiggery-pokery /ˈdʒɪgərɪˈpoʊkərɪ/ ▷ *noun, colloq* trickery or deceit. ◎ 19c: from Scots *joukery-pawkery*, from *jouk* to dodge + *pawk* trick.

jiggle /ˈdʒɪgəl/ ▷ *verb* (***jiggled, jiggling***) *tr & intr* to jump or make something jump or jerk about. ▷ *noun* a jiggling movement. ◎ 19c: from JIG 1.

jigsaw /ˈdʒɪgsɔː/ ▷ *noun* **1** (*also* **jigsaw puzzle**) a picture, mounted on wood or cardboard and cut into interlocking irregularly shaped pieces, to be fitted together again. **2** a fine-bladed saw for cutting intricate patterns. ▷ *verb* (***jigsawed, jigsawing***) *tr & intr* to cut something with a jigsaw. ◎ 19c: JIG + SAW[2].

jihad or **jehad** /dʒɪˈhɑːd/ ▷ *noun* a holy war, against infidels, fought by Muslims on behalf of Islam. ◎ 19c: Arabic, meaning 'struggle'.

jillaroo /jɪləˈruː/ ▷ *noun* (***jillaroos***) a female JACKAROO. ▷ *verb* (***jillarooed, jillarooing***) *intr* to work as a jillaroo.

jilt ▷ *noun, old use* a person, originally and especially a woman, who encourages and then rejects a lover. ▷ *verb* (***jilted, jilting***) to leave and abruptly discard a previously encouraged lover. ◎ 17c: from dialect *jillet* a flirt.

Jim Crow ▷ *noun, N Amer slang* **1** *offensive* a black person. **2 a** the policy of segregating blacks from whites, eg in public vehicles, public places or employment; **b** *as adj* for blacks only □ *Jim-Crow schools.* **3** a tool for bending iron bars. **4** a plane or other tool that works in both directions. ● **Jim-Crowism** *noun.* ◎ 19c: from the name of a black minstrel song.

jimjams /ˈdʒɪmdʒams/ ▷ *plural noun* **1** *colloq* a state of nervous excitement. **2** *slang* delirium tremens. **3** *colloq* pyjamas. ◎ 19c.

jingle /ˈdʒɪŋgəl/ ▷ *noun* **1** a light ringing or clinking sound, eg of small bells, coins, keys, etc. **2** something which makes such a sound, especially a metal disc on a tambourine. **3** a simple rhyming verse, song or tune, especially one used to advertise a product, etc. ▷ *verb* (***jingled, jingling***) *tr & intr* to make or cause something to make a ringing or clinking sound. ● **jingler** *noun.* ● **jingly** *adj.* ◎ 16c: probably imitating the sound.

jingle-jangle ▷ *noun* a dissonant continued jingling.

jingo or **Jingo** /ˈdʒɪŋgoʊ/ ▷ *noun* (***jingoes***) a ranting patriot. ● **jingoism** /ˈdʒɪ *noun* over-enthusiastic or aggressive patriotism. ● **jingoist** *noun.* ● **jingoistic** *adj.* ● **jingoistically** *adverb.* ● **By jingo** a mild oath. ◎ 19c from a chauvinistic song; 17c as an exclamation used by a conjuror.

jink ▷ *verb* (***jinked, jinking***) **1** *intr* **a** to dodge; **b** *aeronautics* to make a sudden evasive turn. **2 a** to elude; **b** to cheat. ▷ *noun* **1** a dodge; a jinking movement. **2** *aeronautics & rugby* a quick deceptive turn. ◎ 18c: imitating the sudden dodging movement.

jinni, **jinnee** or **djinni** /dʒɪnɪ/ and **djinn** /dʒɪn/ ▷ *noun* (*plural* ***jinn*** or ***djinn***) in Muslim folklore: a supernatural being able to adopt human or animal form. ◎ 19c: Arabic.

jin shin do /dʒɪn ʃɪn ˈdoʊ/ ▷ *noun, alternative therapy* a form of ACUPRESSURE. ◎ 1970s: Japanese, meaning 'the way of the compassionate spirit'.

jinx /dʒɪŋks/ ▷ *noun* (***jinxes***) **1** (*usually* **a jinx on something** or **someone**) an evil spell or influence, held responsible for misfortune. **2** someone or something that brings bad luck. ▷ *verb* (***jinxed, jinxing***) to bring bad luck to, or put a jinx on, someone or something. ● **jinxed** *adj.* ◎ 20c: from Greek *iynx* the wryneck, a bird used in spells; hence a spell or charm.

jism or **gism** /ˈdʒɪzəm/ and **jissom** /ˈdʒɪsəm/ ▷ *noun* **1** *chiefly US colloq* energy; force. **2** *taboo* semen. ◎ 19c.

JIT ▷ *abbreviation, business* just-in-time.

jitter /ˈdʒɪtə(r)/ *colloq* ▷ *verb* (***jittered, jittering***) *intr* to shake with nerves; to behave in a flustered way. ▷ *noun* (*usually* **the jitters**) an attack of nervousness □ *He's got the jitters.* ● **jitteriness** *noun.* ● **jittery** *adj.* ◎ 20c: variant of dialect and Scots *chitter* to shiver.

jitterbug ▷ *noun* **1** *US* an energetic dance like the JIVE, popular in the 1940s. **2** someone who performs this dance. **3** *Brit* an alarmist or scaremonger. ▷ *verb* (***jitterbugged, jitterbugging***) *intr* to dance the jitterbug. ◎ 20c: from JITTER.

jiu-jitsu see JU-JITSU

jive /dʒaɪv/ ▷ *noun* **1** a lively style of jazz music or swing, popular in the 1950s. **2** the style of dancing done to this music. **3** *slang* the jargon of Harlem and of jazz musicians. ▷ *verb* (***jived, jiving***) *intr* **1** to dance in this style. **2** to talk jive. ● **jiver** *noun.* ◎ 20c.

jizz /dʒɪz/ ▷ *noun* (***jizzes***) the characteristic features of a bird, animal or plant which distinguish it from other species that resemble it. ◎ 20c.

JJ see under J²

Jl ▷ *symbol, chem* joliotium.

Jnr or **jnr** ▷ *abbreviation* Junior or junior.

job ▷ *noun* **1** a person's regular paid employment. **2** a piece of work. **3** a completed task □ *made a good job of the pruning.* **4** a function or responsibility. **5** *colloq* a problem; difficulty □ *had a job finding it.* **6** a crime, especially a burglary □ *an inside job.* **7** an underhand scheme □ *a put-up job.* **8** *colloq* a do, affair, business, etc □ *The wedding was a proper church job.* **9** *colloq* a surgical operation, usually involving plastic surgery □ *a nose job.* **10** *colloq* a manufactured product, or other object □ *smart little jobs, these calculators.* ▷ *verb* (**jobbed, jobbing**) **1** *intr* to do casual jobs. **2** *tr & intr* to buy and sell (stocks) as a stockjobber; to act as stockjobber. **3** *tr & intr* to bring something about by, or practise, jobbery. **4** to hire or let out something for a period or a job. ● **a good job** *colloq* fortunate; lucky □ *It's a good job I was early.* ● **do the job** to succeed in doing what is required □ *This new lock should do the job.* ● **give something up as a bad job** to abandon a task, etc as impossible or not worthwhile. ● **jobs for the boys** *derog* jobs given to or created for one's supporters and friends. ● **just the job** exactly what is required. ● **make the best of a bad job** to do one's best in difficult circumstances. ⓒ 16c.

jobber ▷ *noun, stock exchange* a STOCKJOBBER. ⓒ 18c: from JOB.

jobbery ▷ *noun* the abuse of public office for private gain.

job centre or **Jobcentre** ▷ *noun, Brit* a government office displaying information on available jobs.

job club or **Jobclub** ▷ *noun, Brit* an association aimed at helping the jobless find work through learning and using the necessary skills of presentation, etc.

job description ▷ *noun, commerce, etc* a systematic and detailed listing of all the duties, responsibilities, activities, etc necessary to a specific job.

job evaluation ▷ *noun, commerce, etc* a method of assessing the relative position, and appropriate salary, for the different jobs in an organization by allocating points for the various aspects of each job as listed in a JOB DESCRIPTION.

jobless ▷ *adj* **1** having no paid employment; unemployed. **2** (**the jobless**) unemployed people as a group (see THE 4b).

job lot ▷ *noun* a mixed collection of objects sold as one item at an auction, etc.

Job's comforter /dʒoʊbz —/ ▷ *noun* a person whose attempts at sympathy have the effect of adding to one's distress. ⓒ 18c: referring to Job in the Old Testament, whose friends responded to his troubles by reproving him.

Job Seekers Allowance ▷ *noun* (abbreviation **JSA**) *Brit* a means-tested state allowance paid to people on low incomes and to the unemployed, replacing both unemployment benefit and income support in October 1996.

job-sharing ▷ *noun* the practice of sharing one full-time job between two or more part-time workers.

jobsworth ▷ *noun, derog slang* a minor official, especially one who sticks rigidly and unco-operatively to petty rules. ⓒ 20c: from 'It's more than my job's worth to let you …'.

Jock ▷ *noun, colloq, often derog* a Scotsman, especially a soldier. ⓒ 18c: Scottish variant of the name *Jack*.

jock ▷ *noun, colloq* **1** *US* a male athlete. **2** a jockey. **3** a disc-jockey. **4** a jockstrap. ⓒ 19c in sense 2.

jockey /'dʒɒkɪ/ ▷ *noun* (**jockeys**) **1** a rider, especially a professional one, in horse races. **2** someone who takes undue advantage in business. ▷ *verb* (**jockeyed, jockeying**) **1** to ride (a horse) in a race. **2** *tr & intr* (*also* **jockey someone into** or **out of something**) to manipulate them deviously. ● **jockeyism** *noun.* ● **jockeyship** *noun.* ● **jockey for position** to seek an advantage over rivals, especially unscrupulously. ⓒ 16c: diminutive of the personal name *Jock*, meaning 'lad'.

jockstrap /'dʒɒkstrap/ ▷ *noun* a garment for supporting the genitals, worn by male athletes. ⓒ 20c: from dialect *jock* penis.

jocose /dʒə'koʊs/ ▷ *adj* playful; humorous. ● **jocosely** *adverb.* ● **jocoseness** *noun.* ● **jocosity** /dʒə'kɒsɪtɪ/ *noun.* ⓒ 17c: from Latin *jocosus*, from *jocus* a joke.

jocular /'dʒɒkjʊlə(r)/ ▷ *adj* **1** said of a person: given to joking; good-humoured. **2** said of a remark, etc: intended as a joke. ● **jocularity** /dʒɒkjʊ'larɪtɪ/ *noun.* ● **jocularly** *adverb.* ⓒ 17c: from Latin *joculus* a little joke.

jocund /'dʒoʊkənd, 'dʒɒ-/ ▷ *adj* cheerful; merry; good-humoured. ● **jocundity** /dʒə'kʌndɪtɪ/ *noun.* ● **jocundly** *adverb.* ⓒ 14c: from Latin *jocundus* agreeable.

jodhpur boots ▷ *plural noun* ankle-high boots worn with jodhpurs for riding.

jodhpurs /'dʒɒdpəz/ ▷ *plural noun* riding-breeches that are loose-fitting over the buttocks and thighs, and tight-fitting from knee to calf. ⓒ 19c: named after Jodhpur in India.

Joe ▷ *noun* (**Joes**) a man; an ordinary fellow. ⓒ 19c.

Joe Bloggs and (*US, Austral*) **Joe Blow** ▷ *noun* the average man in the street. Also called **Joe Public**. ⓒ 20c.

joey /'dʒoʊɪ/ ▷ *noun* (**joeys**) **1** *Austral* a young animal, especially a kangaroo. **2** *NZ* an opossum. ⓒ 19c: from an Aboriginal language.

jog ▷ *verb* (**jogged, jogging**) **1** to knock or nudge slightly. **2 a** to remind someone; **b** to prompt (their memory). **3** *intr* (*also* **jog along** or **on**) to progress slowly and steadily; to plod. **4** *intr* to run at a slowish steady pace, especially for exercise. ▷ *noun* **1** a period or spell of jogging □ *go for a jog.* **2** a nudge, knock or jolt. ⓒ 14c: probably a variant of dialect *shog* to shake.

jogger ▷ *noun* **1** someone who jogs, especially on a regular basis for exercise. **2** a machine which aligns sheets of paper ready for stapling, binding, etc. **3** (**joggers**) jog pants.

jogger's nipple ▷ *noun, colloq* painful inflammation of the nipples caused by friction against clothing while running or jogging.

jogging ▷ *noun* running at a slowish steady pace.

joggle /'dʒɒgəl/ ▷ *verb* (**joggled, joggling**) *tr & intr* to jolt, shake or wobble. ▷ *noun* a shake or jolt. ⓒ 16c: from JOG.

jog pants ▷ *plural noun* loose-fitting trousers made of jersey fabric, elasticated at the waist and ankles, and worn for jogging.

jog-trot ▷ *noun* an easy pace like that of a horse between walking and trotting. ▷ *verb, intr* to move at such a pace. ⓒ 18c.

john /dʒɒn/ ▷ *noun, N Amer colloq* (*usually* **the john**) a lavatory. ⓒ 20c: from the name *John*.

John Dory see DORY¹

johnny ▷ *noun* (**johnnies**) **1** *Brit colloq, old use* a chap; a fellow. **2** a condom. ⓒ 17c: from the familiar name *Johnny*.

johnny-come-lately ▷ *noun* (**johnny-come-latelys**) *colloq* a newcomer.

joie de vivre /ʒwɑː də 'viːvrə/ ▷ *noun* enthusiasm for living; exuberant spirits. ⓒ 19c: French, meaning 'joy of living'.

join /dʒɔɪn/ ▷ *verb* (**joined, joining**) **1** (*often* **join one thing to another** or **join things up**) to connect, attach, link or unite. **2** *tr & intr* to become a member of (a society, firm, etc). **3** *tr & intr* said of roads, rivers, etc: to meet. **4** to come together with someone or something; to enter the company of (a person or group of people) □ *joined them for supper.* **5** *tr & intr* (*also* **join on to something**) to add oneself to it □ *join the queue.* **6** to take part in something. **7** to do the same as someone, for the sake of companionship □ *Who'll join me in a drink?* ▷ *noun* a seam or joint. ◷ 13c: from French *joindre*, from Latin *jungere* to yoke.

■ **join in** to take part.

■ **join in something** to participate in it.

■ **join up** to enlist as a member of an armed service.

■ **join up with someone** to come together with them for joint action, etc.

joiner ▷ *noun* **1** a craftsman who makes and fits wooden doors, window frames, stairs, shelves, etc. **2** *colloq* a sociable person who likes joining clubs and being a member of a group. • **joinery** *noun* the trade or work of a joiner. ◷ 14c.

joint /dʒɔɪnt/ ▷ *noun* **1** the place where two or more pieces join. **2** *anatomy* in vertebrates: the point of contact or articulation between two or more bones, together with the ligaments that surround it. **3** a piece of meat, usually containing a bone, for cooking or roasting. **4** *slang* a cheap shabby café, bar or nightclub, etc. **5** *slang* a cannabis cigarette. **6** *geol* a crack in a mass of rock. ▷ *verb* (*jointed, jointing*) **1** to connect to something by joints. **2** to divide (a bird or animal) into, or at, the joints for cooking. ▷ *adj* **1** owned or done, etc in common; shared □ *joint responsibility.* **2** working together. • **jointed** *adj* **1** having joints. **2** composed of segments. • **jointly** *adverb.* • **jointness** *noun.* • **out of joint** **1** said of a bone: dislocated. **2** in disorder. ◷ 13c: French, from *joindre* to join.

joint account ▷ *noun* a bank account held in the name of two or more people.

joint heir ▷ *noun* someone who inherits jointly with another or others.

joint-stock company ▷ *noun* a business whose capital is owned jointly by the shareholders.

jointure /ˈdʒɔɪntʃə(r)/ ▷ *noun* property settled on a woman by her husband for her use after his death. ▷ *verb* (*jointured, jointuring*) to provide (a woman) with a jointure. ◷ 14c: French, from Latin *junctura* joining.

joint venture ▷ *noun, business* a business activity undertaken by two or more companies acting together, sharing the costs, risks and profits.

joist /dʒɔɪst/ ▷ *noun* any of the beams supporting a floor or ceiling. ▷ *verb* (*joisted, joisting*) to fit something with joists. ◷ 14c: from French *giste*, from *gesir* to lie.

jojoba /hoʊˈhoʊbə/ ▷ *noun* (*jojobas*) a N American shrub whose edible seeds contain a waxy oil chemically similar to SPERMACETI, used in the manufacture of cosmetics and lubricants. ◷ 20c: Mexican Spanish.

joke /dʒoʊk/ ▷ *noun* **1** a humorous story □ *crack a joke.* **2** anything said or done in jest. **3** an amusing situation. **4** *colloq* something or someone ludicrous. ▷ *verb* (*joked, joking*) *intr* **1** to make jokes. **2** to speak in jest, not in earnest. • **the joke's on him, her**, *etc colloq* he, she, etc has become the victim of their own joke. • **joking apart** or **aside** used when changing the tone of what one is saying: seriously; to be serious. • **no joke** *colloq* a serious matter. • **play a joke on someone** to trick them. • **see the joke** *colloq* to see the funny side of a situation. • **take a joke** to be able to laugh at a joke played on one. ◷ 17c: from Latin *jocus* joke.

joker ▷ *noun* **1** *cards* an extra card in a pack, usually bearing a picture of a jester, used in certain games. **2** a cheerful person, always full of jokes. **3** *colloq* an irresponsible or incompetent person. **4** *colloq* a person. • **joker in the pack** someone or something whose effect on a situation is unpredictable.

jokey ▷ *adj* (*jokier, jokiest*) **1** given to joking, good-humoured. **2** as or in a joke. • **jokiness** *noun.*

jokingly ▷ *adverb* as a joke.

joliotium /dʒɒlɪˈoʊtɪəm/ ▷ *noun, chem* (symbol **Jl**, atomic number 105) a name proposed for the radioactive element UNNILPENTIUM.

jollify /ˈdʒɒlɪfaɪ/ ▷ *verb* (*jollifies, jollified, jollifying*) to make something jolly. • **jollification** *noun* an occasion of merrymaking, or of being jolly.

jollity /ˈdʒɒlɪtɪ/ ▷ *noun* **1** merriment. **2** (**jollities**) festivities.

jolly /ˈdʒɒlɪ/ ▷ *adj* (*jollier, jolliest*) **1** good-humoured; cheerful. **2** happy; enjoyable; convivial. ▷ *adverb, Brit colloq* very □ *jolly good.* ▷ *verb* (*jollies, jollied, jollying*) only in phrases below. • **jolliness** *noun.* • **jolly well** *Brit colloq* used for emphasis: certainly □ *You jolly well deserved it.* ◷ 14c: from French *jolif* pretty or merry.

■ **jolly someone along** to keep them cheerful and co-operative.

■ **jolly someone into** or **out of something** to coax or cajole them into or out of it.

■ **jolly someone up** to make them more cheerful.

jollyboat ▷ *noun* a small boat carried on a larger ship. ◷ 18c.

Jolly Roger ▷ *noun, historical or literary* a pirate-ship flag, black with a white skull-and-crossbones. ◷ 18c.

jolt ▷ *verb* (*jolted, jolting*) **1** *intr* to move along jerkily. **2** to shake, jog or jar. ▷ *noun* **1** a jarring shake. **2** an emotional shock. ◷ 16c: probably a combination of dialect *jot* and *joll*, both meaning 'to bump'.

Jonah /ˈdʒoʊnə/ ▷ *noun* (*Jonahs*) a person who seems to bring bad luck. ◷ 17c: named after Jonah in the Old Testament, who almost brought disaster to the ship on which he was sailing.

jonquil /ˈdʒɒŋkwɪl/ ▷ *noun* a species of small daffodil native to Europe and Asia, widely cultivated for its fragrant white or yellow flowers. ◷ 16c: from French *jonquille*.

josh *colloq, originally N Amer* ▷ *verb* (*joshes, joshed, joshing*) *tr & intr* to tease. ▷ *noun* (*joshes*) a bit of teasing; a joke. • **josher** *noun.* ◷ 19c.

joss-stick ▷ *noun* a stick of dried scented paste, burnt as incense. ◷ 19c: from pidgin Chinese *joss* household god, from Portuguese *deos* god.

jostle /ˈdʒɒsəl/ ▷ *verb* (*jostled, jostling*) **1** *intr* to push and shove. **2** to push against someone roughly. ◷ 14c: from JOUST.

■ **jostle with someone** to compete aggressively against them.

jot ▷ *noun* (*usually with negatives*) the least bit □ *not a jot of sympathy.* ▷ *verb* (*jotted, jotting*) now only in phrases below. ◷ 16c: from *iota* the Greek letter *i*, the smallest letter in the Greek alphabet.

■ **jot something down** to write it down hastily.

jotter /ˈdʒɒtə(r)/ ▷ *noun, especially Scottish* a school notebook for rough work and notes.

jotting ▷ *noun* (*usually* **jottings**) something jotted down.

joule /dʒuːl/ ▷ *noun, physics* (abbreviation **J**) in the SI system: a unit of work and energy, equal to the work done when a force of one newton moves through a distance of one metre in the direction of the force. ◷ 19c: named after James Joule (1818–89), British natural philosopher.

journal /ˈdʒɜːnəl/ ▷ *noun* **1** a magazine or periodical, eg one dealing with a specialized subject. **2** a diary in which one recounts one's daily activities. **3** *engineering* that part of an axle or rotating shaft that is in contact with and supported by a bearing. ▷ *verb* (***journalled, journalling***) to provide something with, or fix something as, a journal. ◷ 14c: from Latin *diurnalis* daily.

journalese /dʒɜːnəˈliːz/ ▷ *noun, derog* the language, typically shallow and full of clichés and jargon, used by less able journalists. ◷ 1880s.

journalism ▷ *noun* the profession of writing for newspapers and magazines, or for radio and television. • **journalist** *noun.* • **journalistic** *adj.* • **journalistically** *adverb.* ◷ 1830s: from French *journalisme*; see -ISM.

journalize or **journalise** ▷ *verb* (***journalized, journalizing***) **1** *intr* to write in or for a journal. **2** to enter something in a journal. • **journalization** *noun.*

journey /ˈdʒɜːnɪ/ ▷ *noun* (***journeys***) **1** a process of travelling from one place to another. **2** the distance covered by, or time taken for, a journey. ▷ *verb* (***journeyed, journeying***) *intr* to make a journey. ◷ 13c: from French *journee* day, or a day's travelling.

journeyman ▷ *noun* **1** a craftsman qualified in a particular trade and working for an employer. **2** an experienced and competent worker, but not an outstanding one. ◷ 15c: from JOURNEY in the obsolete sense 'a day's work'.

journo /ˈdʒɜːnoʊ/ ▷ *noun* (***journos*** or ***journoes***) *colloq, originally Austral* a journalist.

joust /dʒaʊst, dʒuːst/ ▷ *noun, historical* a contest between two knights on horseback armed with lances. ▷ *verb* (***jousted, jousting***) *intr* to take part in a joust. • **jouster** *noun.* ◷ 13c: from French *jouster*, from Latin *juxta* near.

Jove /dʒoʊv/ ▷ *noun* JUPITER. • **by Jove!** *Brit colloq, old use* an exclamation expressing surprise or emphasis. ◷ 14c: from Latin *Jupiter, Jovis* Jupiter.

jovial /ˈdʒoʊvɪəl/ ▷ *adj* good-humoured; merry; cheerful. • **joviality** /dʒoʊvɪˈalɪtɪ/ *noun.* • **jovially** /ˈdʒoʊvɪəlɪ/ *adverb.* ◷ 16c: from Latin *jovialis* relating to the planet JUPITER, believed to be a lucky influence.

jowl[1] /dʒaʊl/ ▷ *noun* **1** the lower jaw. **2** the cheek. • **jowled** *adj, usually in compounds* □ *heavy-jowled.* • **jowly** *adj* with heavy or droopy jaws. ◷ 16c: from Anglo-Saxon *ceafl* jaw.

jowl[2] /dʒaʊl/ ▷ *noun* (*usually* **jowls**) **1** in humans: loose flesh under the chin; a pendulous double chin. **2** in animals: fatty flesh hanging from the lower jaw, eg the DEWLAP of a bull. ◷ 16c: from Anglo-Saxon *ceole* throat.

joy /dʒɔɪ/ ▷ *noun* **1** a feeling of happiness; intense gladness; delight. **2** someone or something that causes delight □ *She's a joy to live with.* **3** *Brit colloq* satisfaction; success □ *Any joy at the enquiry desk?* • **joyless** *adj.* • **joylessly** *adverb.* • **joylessness** *noun.* ◷ 13c: from French *joie*, from Latin *gaudium*, from *gaudere* to be glad.

joyful ▷ *adj* **1** happy; full of joy. **2** expressing or resulting in joy. • **joyfully** *adverb.* • **joyfulness** *noun.*

joyous ▷ *adj* filled with, causing or showing joy. • **joyously** *adverb.* • **joyousness** *noun.*

joypop ▷ *verb, slang* to take addictive drugs from time to time, but without becoming addicted to them.

joyride ▷ *noun* a jaunt, especially a reckless drive in a stolen vehicle. ▷ *verb, intr* to go for such a jaunt. • **joyrider** *noun.* • **joyriding** *noun.* ◷ 20c: originally colloquial US.

joystick ▷ *noun, colloq* **1** the controlling lever of an aircraft, machine etc. **2** *computing* a lever for controlling the movement of the cursor on a VDU screen. ◷ 20c.

JP ▷ *abbreviation* justice of the peace.

Jr or **jr** ▷ *abbreviation* Junior or junior □ *John Smith, Jr.*

JSA ▷ *abbreviation* Job Seekers Allowance.

jubate /ˈdʒuːbeɪt/ ▷ *adj, zool, etc* maned.

jube ▷ *noun Austral & NZ colloq* shortened form of JUJUBE.

jubilant /ˈdʒuːbɪlənt/ ▷ *adj* showing and expressing triumphant joy; rejoicing. • **jubilantly** *adverb.* ◷ 17c: from Latin *jubilare* to shout for joy.

jubilation /dʒuːbɪˈleɪʃən/ ▷ *noun* **1** triumphant rejoicing. **2** (**jubilations**) celebrations. ◷ 14c: from Latin *jubilatio*.

jubilee /ˈdʒuːbɪliː, dʒuːbɪˈliː/ ▷ *noun* (***jubilees***) a special anniversary of a significant event, eg the succession of a monarch, especially the 25th (**silver jubilee**), 50th (**golden jubilee**) or 60th (**diamond jubilee**). ◷ 14c: from French *jubile*, from Latin *jubilaeus annus* the Jewish celebration of emancipation and restoration held every 50 years; ultimately from Hebrew *yobhel* the ram's horn or trumpet used to announce this.

Jud. ▷ *abbreviation* Books of the Bible: **1** Judges. **2** Judith (in the Apocrypha). See table at BIBLE.

Judaeo- or **Judeo-** /dʒʊˈdiːoʊ, -ˈdeɪoʊ/ ▷ *combining form, forming adjectives, signifying* Jewish □ *Judaeo-Hispanic.*

Judaic /dʒʊˈdeɪɪk/ ▷ *adj* relating to the Jews or Judaism.

Judas /ˈdʒuːdəs/ ▷ *noun* (***Judases***) a traitor, especially someone who betrays their friends. ◷ 15c: named after Judas Iscariot, who betrayed Jesus.

judder /ˈdʒʌdə(r)/ ▷ *verb* (***juddered, juddering***) *intr* said of machinery: to jolt, shake, shudder or vibrate. ▷ *noun* **1** a shuddering vibration, especially of machinery. **2** an intense jerking motion. ◷ 20c: perhaps from SHUDDER + JAR[2].

judge /dʒʌdʒ/ ▷ *noun* **1** a public officer who hears (see HEAR *verb* 5) and decides cases in a law court. See also JUSTICE *noun* 4, 6. **2** a person appointed to decide the winner of a contest. **3** someone qualified to assess something; someone who shows discrimination □ *a good judge of character.* **4** someone who decides or assesses □ *Let me be the judge of that.* ▷ *verb* (***judged, judging***) **1** to try (a legal case) in a law court as a judge; to decide (questions of guiltiness, etc). **2** to decide the winner of (a contest). **3** *intr* to act as judge or adjudicator. **4** to assess; to form an opinion about something or someone. **5** to estimate. **6** to consider or state something to be the case, after consideration □ *judged her fit to travel.* **7** to criticize someone or something, especially severely; to condemn. • **judgeship** *noun* the office or function of a judge. ◷ 14c: from French *juge*, from Latin *judicare* to judge.

judgement or **judgment** ▷ *noun* **1** the decision of a judge in a court of law. **2** the act or process of judging. **3** the ability to make wise or sensible decisions; good sense □ *I value his judgement.* **4** an opinion □ *in my judgement.* **5** (*usually* **a judgement on someone**) *old use* punishment regarded as sent by divine providence □ *His sickness was a judgement on him.* • **against one's better judgement** contrary to what one believes to be the sensible course. • **pass judgement on someone** to condemn them. • **pass judgement on someone** or **something** to give an opinion or verdict about them. • **reserve judgement** to postpone one's verdict. • **sit in judgement on someone** to assume the responsibility of judging them. ◷ 13c: from French *jugement*.

judgemental or **judgmental** /dʒʌdʒˈmɛntəl/ ▷ *adj* **1** involving judgement. **2** apt to pass judgement, especially to make moral judgements.

judicature /ˈdʒuːdɪkətʃə(r), dʒʊˈdɪ-/ ▷ *noun* **1** the administration of justice by legal trial. **2** the office of judge. **3** a body of judges. **4** a court or system of courts. ◷ 16c: from Latin *judicatura*.

judicial /dʒʊˈdɪʃəl/ ▷ *adj* relating or referring to a court of law, judges or the decisions of judges. • **judicially** *adverb.* ◷ 14c: from Latin *judicialis*, from *judicium* judgement.

judiciary /dʒʊˈdɪʃərɪ/ ▻ *noun* (***judiciaries***) **1** the branch of government concerned with the legal system and the administration of justice. **2** a country's body of judges. • **judiciarily** *adverb*. Ⓒ 16c: from Latin *judiciarius* relating to the law courts.

judicious /dʒʊˈdɪʃəs/ ▻ *adj* shrewd, sensible, wise or tactful. • **judiciously** *adverb*. • **judiciousness** *noun*. Ⓒ 16c: from Latin *judicium* judgement.

judo /ˈdʒuːdoʊ/ ▻ *noun* a Japanese sport and physical discipline based on unarmed self-defence techniques, developed from JU-JITSU. Ⓒ 19c: Japanese, from *ju* gentleness + *do* art.

judogi /ˈdʒuːdoʊgɪ, dʒʊˈdoʊgɪ/ ▻ *noun* (***judogis***) the costume (jacket and trousers) worn by a JUDOIST.

judoist and **judoka** /ˈdʒuːdoʊkə/ ▻ *noun* (***judoists*** or ***judokas***) a person who practises, or is expert in, judo.

jug ▻ *noun* **1** a deep container for liquids, with a handle and a shaped lip for pouring. **2** a JUGFUL. **3** *slang* prison. ▻ *verb* (***jugged***, ***jugging***) to stew (meat, especially hare) in an earthenware container. Ⓒ 16c: perhaps from the pet name *Jug* for Joan.

jugate /ˈdʒuːgeɪt, ˈdʒuːgət/ ▻ *adj* **1** *bot* paired. **2** *bot* having the leaflets in pairs. **3** joined side by side or overlapping. Ⓒ 19c: from Latin *jugare*, *jugatum* to join together.

jugful *noun* (***jugfuls***) the amount a jug can hold.

jugged hare ▻ *noun* hare cut in pieces and stewed with wine and other seasonings.

juggernaut /ˈdʒʌgənɔːt/ ▻ *noun* **1** *Brit colloq* a very large articulated lorry. **2** a mighty force sweeping away and destroying everything in its path. Ⓒ 19c in sense 1: named after the gigantic chariot of the Hindu god, Jagannatha.

juggins /ˈdʒʌgɪnz/ ▻ *noun, rather dated slang* a simpleton. Ⓒ 19c.

juggle /ˈdʒʌgəl/ ▻ *verb* (***juggled***, ***juggling***) **1** to keep several objects simultaneously in the air by skilful throwing and catching. **2** (*usually* **juggle with something**) to adjust (facts or figures) to create a misleading impression. • **juggler** *noun*. • **juggling** *noun, adj*. Ⓒ 14c: from French *jogler* to act as jester.

jugular /ˈdʒʌgjʊlə(r)/ ▻ *adj* relating to the neck or throat. ▻ *noun, anatomy* (*also* **jugular vein**) any of several veins that carry deoxygenated blood from the head to the heart in vertebrates. • **go for the jugular** to attack someone where they are most vulnerable. Ⓒ 16c: from Latin *jugulum* throat.

jugulate /ˈdʒʌgjʊleɪt/ ▻ *verb* (***jugulated***, ***jugulating***) **1** to cut the throat of (a person or animal). **2** to strangle. **3** to check (a disease, etc) by drastic means. Ⓒ 17c: from Latin *jugulare*, *jugulatum*.

juice /dʒuːs/ ▻ *noun* **1** the liquid or sap from fruit or vegetables. **2** (*usually* **juices**) the body's natural fluids □ ***digestive juices***. **3** vitality; piquancy. **4** *slang* power or fuel, especially electricity or petrol □ ***step on the juice***. **5** *US slang* alcoholic drink. ▻ *verb* (***juiced***, ***juicing***) to squeeze juice from (a fruit, etc). • **juiceless** *adj*. Ⓒ 13c: from French *jus*.

juicer and **juice extractor** ▻ *noun* a device for extracting the juice from fruit and vegetables.

juicy ▻ *adj* (***juicier***, ***juiciest***) **1** full of juice; rich and succulent. **2** *colloq* said of a problem, etc: challenging; meaty. **3** *colloq* said of gossip: intriguing; spicy. **4** *colloq* profitable; lucrative. • **juiciness** *noun*.

ju-jitsu or **jiu-jitsu** /dʒuːˈdʒɪtsuː/ ▻ *noun* a martial art founded on the ancient Japanese system of combat and self-defence without weapons, and the basis for many modern forms of combat sports, such as JUDO, AIKIDO and KARATE. Ⓒ 19c: from Japanese *ju* gentleness + *jutsu* art.

juju /ˈdʒuːdʒuː/ ▻ *noun* (***jujus***) **1** a charm or fetish used by W African tribes. **2** the magic contained in such a charm. Ⓒ 19c: from Hausa (W African language) *djudju* fetish.

jujube /ˈdʒuːdʒuːb/ ▻ *noun* (***jujubes***) **1** a soft fruit-flavoured sweet made with gelatine. Also shortened to JUBE. **2 a** a spiny shrub of the buckthorn family; **b** *historical* the fruit of this shrub, dried and eaten as a sweet. Ⓒ 14c: from Latin *jujuba*, from Greek *zizyphon*.

jukebox /ˈdʒuːkbɒks/ ▻ *noun* a coin-operated machine that plays the record or CD one selects. Ⓒ 20c: from Gullah (W African language) *juke* disorderly + BOX[1] (*noun* 3a).

Jul. ▻ *abbreviation* July.

julep /ˈdʒuːlɪp/ ▻ *noun* **1** a sweet drink, often a medicated one. **2** especially in N America: an iced drink of spirits and sugar, flavoured especially with mint. Also called **mint julep**. Ⓒ 14c: from Persian *gulab* rosewater.

Julian calendar /ˈdʒuːlɪən —/ ▻ *noun* the calendar introduced by Julius Caesar in 46 BC, with a year of 365 days and 366 every leap year or centenary year. See also GREGORIAN CALENDAR.

julienne /dʒuːlɪˈɛn/ ▻ *noun, cookery* **1** a clear soup, with shredded vegetables. **2** any foodstuff which has been shredded. ▻ *adj* said of vegetables: in thin strips; shredded. Ⓒ 19c: from the French personal name.

Juliet /ˈdʒuːlɪət/ ▻ *noun, communications* in the NATO alphabet: the word used to denote the letter 'J' (see table at NATO ALPHABET).

juliet cap ▻ *noun* a round close-fitting skullcap worn by women. Ⓒ 20c: probably named after Juliet in Shakespeare's *Romeo and Juliet*.

July /dʒʊˈlaɪ, ˈdʒuːlaɪ/ ▻ *noun* (abbreviation **Jul.**) the seventh month of the year, which follows June and comes before August, and has 31 days. Ⓒ 13c: from Latin *Julius mensis* the month of Julius Caesar.

jumble /ˈdʒʌmbəl/ ▻ *verb* (***jumbled***, ***jumbling***) (*often* **jumble things up** or **together**) **1** to mix or confuse them, physically or mentally. **2** to throw them together untidily. ▻ *noun* **1** a confused mass. **2** unwanted possessions collected, or suitable, for a jumble sale. Ⓒ 16c: probably imitating the action of jumbling things up.

jumble sale ▻ *noun* a sale of unwanted possessions, eg used clothing, usually to raise money for charity.

jumbo /ˈdʒʌmboʊ/ *colloq* ▻ *adj* extra-large. ▻ *noun* (***jumbos***) a jumbo jet. Ⓒ 18c: probably from the name of an elephant exhibited in London in the 1880s, perhaps ultimately from MUMBO-JUMBO.

jumbo jet ▻ *noun, colloq* the popular name for a large wide-bodied jet airliner capable of carrying several hundred passengers.

jumbuck /ˈdʒʌmbʌk/ ▻ *noun, Austral colloq* a sheep. Ⓒ 19c: from an Aboriginal word.

jump ▻ *verb* (***jumped***, ***jumping***) **1** *intr* to spring off the ground, pushing off with the feet. **2** *intr* to leap or bound. **3** to get over or across something by jumping. **4** to make something (especially a horse) leap. **5** *intr* said of prices, levels, etc: to rise abruptly. **6** *intr* to make a startled movement. **7** *intr* to twitch, jerk or bounce. **8** *intr* to pass directly from one point to another, omitting intermediate matter or essential steps **9** to omit; to skip □ ***jump the next chapter***. **10** *colloq* to pounce on someone or something. **11** *N Amer colloq* to board and travel on (especially a train) without paying. **12** *intr* to make a descent by parachute from an aircraft. **13** to fall off or out of (rails, a groove, etc) □ ***The train jumped the rails***. **14** *colloq* said of a car: to pass through (a red traffic light). **15** *intr, colloq* to be lively □ ***The disco was jumping***. **16** *taboo* said of a male: to have sexual intercourse with someone. ▻ *noun* **1** an act of jumping. **2** an obstacle to be jumped, especially a fence to be jumped by a horse. **3** the height or distance jumped □ ***a jump of two metres***. **4** a jumping contest □ ***the high jump*** □ ***the long jump***. **5** a sudden rise in amount, cost or value □ ***a***

jump in prices. **6** an abrupt change or move. **7** a startled movement; a start □ *gave a jump of surprise.* **8** a parachute descent. **9** (**the jumps**) *slang* convulsive movements; chorea; delirium tremens. • **be** or **stay one jump ahead of someone** *colloq* to anticipate the moves of rivals, and so maintain an advantage over them. • **have the jump on someone** *colloq* to have an advantage over them. • **jump bail** to abscond, forfeiting bail. • **jump down someone's throat** *colloq* to snap at them impatiently. • **jump ship** *colloq* said of a sailor: to leave one's ship while still officially employed or in service, etc. • **jump the gun** to get off one's mark too soon; to act prematurely; to take an unfair advantage. • **jump the queue** to get ahead of one's turn. • **jump to conclusions** see under LEAP. • **jump to it** to hurry up. ◷ 16c: probably imitating the action of jumping.

■ **jump at something** to take or accept it eagerly.

■ **jump on someone** to attack them physically or verbally.

jump cut ▷ *noun* in filming: an abrupt change from one scene or subject to another, across an interval of time.

jumped-up ▷ *adj, derog colloq* having an inflated view of one's importance; cocky; arrogant.

jumper¹ ▷ *noun* **1** a knitted garment for the top half of the body. *N Amer equivalent* SWEATER. See also PULLOVER. **2** *N Amer* a pinafore dress. ◷ 19c: from old word *jump* a short coat.

jumper² ▷ *noun* **1** a person or animal that jumps. **2** *elec* a short length of conductor (eg wire) used to make a temporary connection between two points on a circuit, or to allow current to flow around an open circuit. **3** *engineering* a heavy drill with a jumping motion, that works by repeated impact.

jumpier, **jumpiest**, **jumpily** and **jumpiness** see under JUMPY

jumping-bean ▷ *noun* the seed of a Mexican plant, containing a moth larva which makes it move or jump.

jumping-jack ▷ *noun* a toy figure whose limbs jump up when a string is pulled.

jumping-off place ▷ *noun* **1** the terminus of a route; the destination. **2** a place from which one sets out into the wilds, the unknown, etc. **3** *US* somewhere very remote.

jump jet ▷ *noun* a jet aircraft capable of taking off and landing vertically.

jump-jockey ▷ *noun, horse-racing* a jockey who rides in steeplechases.

jump lead ▷ *noun* either of the two electrical cables used to supply power to start a motor vehicle with a flat battery, usually by connecting it to the charged battery of another vehicle.

jump-off ▷ *noun* **1** *showjumping* an extra round held in the event of a tie. **2** *US* the start; the starting-place.

jump seat ▷ *noun* **1** a movable seat in a car or aircraft. **2** a folding seat.

jump-start ▷ *verb* to start the engine of (a motor vehicle) that has a weak or flat battery by using JUMP LEADS or by pushing it and engaging the gears while it is moving. See also BUMP-START. ▷ *noun* the act of jump-starting a vehicle.

jumpsuit ▷ *noun* a one-piece garment combining trousers and top.

jump-up ▷ *noun, Caribb* a social dance.

jumpy ▷ *adj* (*jumpier, jumpiest*) **1** nervy; anxious. **2** moving jerkily. • **jumpily** *adverb.* • **jumpiness** *noun.* ◷ 19c.

Jun. ▷ *abbreviation* **1** June. **2** Junior.

jun. ▷ *abbreviation* junior.

junction /ˈdʒʌŋkʃən/ ▷ *noun* **1** a place where roads or railway lines meet or cross; an intersection. **2** a point of exit from, and access to, a motorway. **3** *electronics* the contact area between two or more semiconductor materials with different electrical properties. **4** *elec* the point at which wires or cables are connected. **5** the process, an instance or a point of joining. ◷ 18c: from Latin *junctio* joining.

junction box ▷ *noun* the casing for an electrical junction.

juncture /ˈdʒʌŋktʃə(r)/ ▷ *noun* **1** a joining; a union. **2** a point in time, especially a critical one. **3** *linguistics* a feature of pronunciation which marks the beginning or end of an utterance, or the transition between elements within it. ◷ 16c: from Latin *junctura* connection.

June /dʒuːn/ ▷ *noun* (abbreviation **Jun.**) the sixth month of the year, which follows May and comes before July, and has 30 days. ◷ Anglo-Saxon as *Junius*: from Latin *Junius mensis* the month of the goddess Juno.

Juneberry ▷ *noun* the fruit of the SHADBUSH.

June drop ▷ *noun* a falling of immature fruit through a variety of causes, at its height around June.

Jungian /ˈjʊŋɪən/ ▷ *adj* relating to or according to the theories of the Swiss psychologist, Carl Gustav Jung (1875–1961).

jungle /ˈdʒʌŋgəl/ ▷ *noun* **1 a** an area of dense vegetation in an open area of tropical rainforest, eg on the site of former tree clearings, along a river bank, or at the forest edge; **b** any area of dense vegetation. **2** a popular name for a tropical rainforest. **3** a mass of complexities difficult to penetrate □ *the jungle of building regulations.* **4** a complex or hostile environment where toughness is needed for survival □ *the concrete jungle.* **5** DRUM AND BASS. • **jungly** *adj* (*junglier, jungliest*). ◷ 18c: from Hindi *jangal* desert or waste or forest.

jungle fever ▷ *noun* a severe malarial fever.

junglefowl ▷ *noun* a pheasant native to E India and SE Asia, that inhabits forest and scrub.

jungle-green ▷ *adj* a very dark green.

jungle juice ▷ *noun, slang* alcoholic liquor, especially if it is very strong, of poor quality, or home-made.

junglier, **jungliest** and **jungly** see under JUNGLE

junior /ˈdʒuːnɪə(r)/ (abbreviation **Jr**, **Jnr**, **jnr**, **Jun.** or **jun.**) *adj* **1** (*often* **junior to someone**) **a** low or lower in rank; **b** younger. **2** relating or belonging to, or for, schoolchildren aged between 7 and 11 □ *junior schools.* **3** used after the name of a person with the same name as their parents: younger. ▷ *noun* **1** a person of low or lower rank in a profession, organization, etc. **2** a pupil in a junior school. **3** *N Amer, especially US* a third-year college or high-school student. **4** a person younger than the one in question □ *She's three years his junior.* **5** (*often* **Junior**) *N Amer, especially US* a name used to address or refer to the son of a family. ◷ 16c: Latin, meaning 'younger'.

junior common room ▷ *noun* (abbreviation **JCR**) in some universities: a common room for the use of students, as opposed to staff. Compare SENIOR COMMON ROOM.

juniper /ˈdʒuːnɪpə(r)/ ▷ *noun* an evergreen coniferous tree or shrub native to N temperate regions, with sharp greyish needles and purple berry-like cones, oils from which are used to flavour gin. ◷ 14c: from Latin *juniperus.*

junk¹ ▷ *noun, colloq* **1 a** worthless or rejected material; rubbish; **b** *as adj* cheap and worthless □ *junk jewellery.* **2** old or second-hand articles sold cheaply. **3** nonsense. **4** *slang* narcotic drugs, especially heroin. ▷ *verb* (*junked, junking*) *colloq* **1** to treat something as junk. **2** to discard or abandon something as useless. • **junky** *adj* (*junkier, junkiest*) rubbishy; worthless. ◷ 15c: from *jonke* pieces of old rope.

junk² ▷ *noun* a flat-bottomed square-sailed boat, with high forecastle and poop, from the Far East. ◷ 17c: from Portuguese *junco*, from Malay *jong.*

junk bond ▷ *noun, finance* a bond offering a high yield but with low security.

junk call ▷ *noun* an unsolicited telephone call from someone who is trying to sell a product or service.

junket /ˈdʒʌŋkɪt/ **1** *noun* a dessert made from sweetened and curdled milk. **2** a feast or celebration. **3** a trip made by a government official, businessman, academic, etc which they do not pay for themselves. ▷ *verb* (***junketed, junketing***) *intr* **1** to feast, celebrate or make merry. **2** to go on a junket. • **junketer** or **junketeer** *noun*. ◷ 14c: from French *jonquette* a rush basket for holding cheeses, etc; 15c in sense 1 (it was originally perhaps served in a rush basket).

junk fax ▷ *noun* unsolicited material sent by fax.

junk food ▷ *noun* food with little nutritional value.

junkie or **junky** ▷ *noun* (***junkies***) **1** *slang* a drug addict or drug-pusher. **2** *colloq* someone who is addicted to something ◻ ***a coffee junkie***. ◷ 1920s: from JUNK[1] 4.

junk mail ▷ *noun* unsolicited mail, such as advertising circulars, etc.

junky see under JUNK[1], JUNKIE

junta /ˈdʒʌntə, ˈhʊnta/ ▷ *noun* (***juntas***) **1** *derog* a group, clique or faction, usually of army officers, in control of a country after a coup d'état. **2** (*also* **junto** (***juntos***)) a body of men joined or united for some secret intrigue. ◷ 17c: Spanish, literally 'meeting' or 'council'.

Jupiter /ˈdʒuːpɪtə(r)/ ▷ *noun* **1** the chief god among the Romans, the parallel of the Greek Zeus. Also called **Jove**. **2** *astron* the fifth planet from the Sun, and the largest in the solar system, whose orbit lies between those of Mars and Saturn. ◷ 13c: Latin.

Jurassic /dʒʊˈrasɪk/ *geol* ▷ *noun* in the Mesozoic era, the period of geological time between the Triassic and Cretaceous periods, lasting from about 210 to 140 million years ago. ▷ *adj* belonging or relating to this period. See table at GEOLOGICAL TIME SCALE. ◷ 19c: named after the Jura, a limestone mountain range in E France.

jurat[1] /ˈdʒʊərat/ ▷ *noun* **1** especially in France and the Channel Islands: a magistrate. **2** *historical* a sworn officer. ◷ 16c: from Latin *juratus* sworn man.

jurat[2] /ˈdʒʊərat/ ▷ *noun, law* the official memorandum at the end of an affidavit, showing the time when and the person before whom it was sworn. ◷ 18c: from Latin *juratum* sworn, from *jurare* to swear.

juridical /dʒʊˈrɪdɪkəl/ or **juridic** ▷ *adj* relating or referring to the law or the administration of justice. • **juridically** *adverb*. ◷ 16c: from Latin *juridicus* relating to justice.

jurisconsult /dʒʊərɪsˈkɒnsʌlt/ ▷ *noun* **1** someone who is consulted on the law. **2** a lawyer who gives opinions on cases put to them. **3** a person knowledgeable in law. ◷ 17c: from Latin *jus, juris* law, and *consulere, consultum* to consult.

jurisdiction /dʒʊərɪsˈdɪkʃən/ ▷ *noun* **1** the right or authority to apply laws and administer justice. **2** the district or area over which this authority extends. **3** authority generally. • **jurisdictional** or **jurisdictive** *adj*. ◷ 13c: from Latin *jurisdictio* administration of justice.

jurisprudence /dʒʊərɪsˈpruːdəns/ ▷ *noun* **1** knowledge of or skill in law. **2** the science and philosophy of law. **3** a legal system. **4** a speciality within law ◻ ***medical jurisprudence***. ◷ 17c: from Latin *jurisprudentia*, from *jus* law + *prudentia* wisdom.

jurisprudent ▷ *adj* knowledgeable in jurisprudence. ▷ *noun* someone who is knowledgeable in jurisprudence. • **jurisprudential** /-prʊˈdɛnʃəl/ *adj* relating to or involving jurisprudence.

jurist /ˈdʒʊərɪst/ ▷ *noun* **1** an expert in the science of law, especially Roman or civil law. **2** a student of law. **3** a graduate in law. **4** *US* a lawyer. • **juristic** /ˈdʒʊəˈrɪstɪk/ or **juristical** *adj* **1** relating to jurists. **2** relating to law or its study. • **juristically** *adverb*. ◷ 15c: from French *juriste*.

juror /ˈdʒʊərə(r)/ ▷ *noun* **1** a member of a jury in a court of law. **2** someone who takes an oath. ◷ 14c.

jury /ˈdʒʊərɪ/ ▷ *noun* (***juries***) **1** a body of people sworn to give an honest verdict on the evidence presented to a court of law on a particular case. **2** a group of people selected to judge a contest. ◷ 14c: from French *juree* something sworn, from Latin *jurare* to swear.

jury box ▷ *noun* the enclosure in which the jury sit in a law court.

juryman and **jurywoman** ▷ *noun* a member of a jury; a juror.

jury service and **jury duty** ▷ *noun* the act of being a member of a jury.

just[1] ▷ *adj* (***juster, justest***) **1** fair; impartial. **2** reasonable; based on justice. **3** deserved. • **justly** *adverb*. • **justness** *noun*. ◷ 14c: from Latin *justus* just, upright or equitable.

just[2] ▷ *adverb* **1** exactly; precisely. **2** a short time before ◻ ***He had just gone.*** **3** at this or that very moment ◻ ***was just leaving.*** **4** and no earlier, more, etc ◻ ***only just enough.*** **5** barely; narrowly ◻ ***The bullet just missed his ear.*** **6** only; merely; simply ◻ ***just a brief note.*** **7** *colloq* used for emphasis ◻ ***That's just not true.*** **8** *colloq* absolutely ◻ ***just marvellous.*** • **just about** almost ◻ ***I'm just about ready.*** • **just about to do something** on the point of doing it. • **just a minute** or **second**, *etc* an instruction to wait a short while. • **just as well 1** fortunate; lucky ◻ ***It's just as well you came.*** **2** advisable ◻ ***It would be just as well to wait.*** • **just in case** as a precaution. • **just now** at this particular moment. • **just so 1** a formula of agreement. **2** neat and tidy ◻ ***They like everything just so.*** • **just then 1** at that particular moment. **2** in the next moment. • **just the same** nevertheless. • **not just yet** not immediately, but soon. ◷ 14c: from Latin *justus* right or proper.

justice /ˈdʒʌstɪs/ ▷ *noun* **1** the quality of being just; just treatment; fairness. **2** the quality of being reasonable. **3** the law, or administration of or conformity to the law ◻ ***a miscarriage of justice.*** **4** (**Justice**) the title of a judge. **5** a justice of the peace. **6** *N Amer, especially US* a judge. • **bring someone to justice** to arrest and try them. • **do justice to someone** or **something 1** to treat them fairly or properly. **2** to show their full merit, etc. **3** *colloq* to appreciate (a meal, etc) fully. • **do justice to oneself** or **do oneself justice** to fulfil one's potential. • **in justice to someone** or **something** to be fair to them. ◷ Anglo-Saxon as *justise*: from Latin *justitia*, from *justus* just.

justice of the peace ▷ *noun* (***justices of the peace***) (abbreviation **JP**) a person authorized to judge minor criminal cases .

justiceship ▷ *noun* the office or dignity of a justice or judge.

justiciary /dʒʌˈstɪʃərɪ/ ▷ *noun* (***justiciaries***) **1 a** an administrator of justice; **b** a judge. **2** the jurisdiction of a Scottish justiciary. ▷ *adj* belonging or relating to the administration of justice. ◷ 15c: from Latin *justiciarius*.

justificative /ˈdʒʌstɪfɪkətɪv/ and **justificatory** /-ˈkeɪtərɪ/ ▷ *adj* having power to justify.

justifiable /dʒʌstɪˈfaɪəbl, ˈdʒʌ-/ ▷ *adj* that can be justified. • **justifiability** *noun*. • **justifiableness** *noun*. • **justifiably** *adverb*.

justifiable homicide ▷ *noun* the killing of a person in self-defence, or to prevent an atrocious crime.

justification ▷ *noun* **1** the act or process of justifying. **2** something which justifies. **3** vindication. **4** absolution. **5** *law* a plea showing sufficient reason for an action.

justification by faith ▷ *noun, theol* the doctrine that mankind is absolved from sin by faith in Christ.

justificator and **justifier** ▷ *noun* **1** someone who defends or vindicates. **2** someone who pardons and absolves people from guilt and punishment.

justify /ˈdʒʌstɪfaɪ/ ▻ *verb* (***justifies, justified, justifying***) **1** to prove or show something to be right, just or reasonable. **2** *printing* to arrange (text) so that the margins are even-edged. • **justifier** *noun*. ⓘ 13c: from Latin *justus* just + *facere* to make.

just-in-time ▻ *noun, business* (abbreviation **JIT**) a method of stock control in which little or no warehoused stock is kept at the production site, supplies being delivered just in time for use .

justly and **justness** see under JUST[1]

jut ▻ *verb* (***jutted, jutting***) *intr* (*also* **jut out**) to stick out; to project. • **jutting** *adj*. ⓘ 16c: variant of JET[2].

Jute /dʒuːt/ ▻ *noun, historical* a member of a Germanic people whose original homeland was the northern part of the Danish peninsula (Jutland). ⓘ 14c: from Anglo-Saxon *Iotas* the Jutes.

jute /dʒuːt/ ▻ *noun* fibre from certain types of tropical bark, used for making sacking, ropes, etc. ⓘ 18c: from Bengali *jhuta*.

juv. ▻ *abbreviation* juvenile.

juvenescent /dʒuːvəˈnɛsənt/ ▻ *adj* becoming youthful. • **juvenescence** *noun*. ⓘ 19c: from Latin *juvenescere* to arrive at the age of youth.

juvenile /ˈdʒuːvənaɪl/ ▻ *adj* (abbreviation **juv.**) **1** young; youthful. **2** suitable for young people. **3** *derog* childish; immature. ▻ *noun* **1** a young person. **2** a young animal. **3** an actor playing youthful parts. ⓘ 17c: from Latin *juvenilis* youthful.

juvenile delinquency ▻ *noun* criminal or antisocial acts or behaviour of juvenile delinquents.

juvenile delinquent and **juvenile offender** ▻ *noun* a young person who is guilty of an offence, especially vandalism or antisocial behaviour.

juvenile hormone ▻ *noun, zool* a hormone necessary for growth and development during the immature stages in the life cycle of an insect, but which must eventually be absent for it to change into the adult form.

juvenilia /dʒuːvəˈnɪlɪə/ ▻ *plural noun* the works produced by a writer or artist during their youth. ⓘ 17c: from Latin *juvenilis* youthful.

juxtapose /dʒʌkstəˈpoʊz, ˈdʒʌkstəpoʊz/ ▻ *verb* (***juxtaposed, juxtaposing***) to place things side by side. ⓘ 19c.

juxtaposition /dʒʌkstəpəˈzɪʃən/ ▻ *noun* placing or being placed together. • **juxtapositional** *adj*. ⓘ 16c: from Latin *juxta* beside.

K

K[1] or **k** /keɪ/ ▷ *noun* (***Ks, K's*** or ***k's***) **1** the eleventh letter of the English alphabet.

K[2] /keɪ/ ▷ *noun* (*plural* ***K***) *colloq* **1** one thousand, especially £1 000 □ a *salary of 40K per annum plus company car.* **2** *computing* a unit of memory equal to 1024 bits, bytes or words. ◷ 20c: from KILO-.

K[3] ▷ *abbreviation* **1** *IVR* Kampuchea, now Cambodia. **2** *physics* kelvin, the kelvin scale or a degree on the kelvin scale. **3** kilo. **4** *computing* kilobyte. **5** *cards* king. **6** *chess* knight. **7** *knitting* knit a plain stitch. **8** *Köchel* (German), indicating the serial number in the catalogue of the works of Mozart. **9** krona, Swedish currency. **10** króna, Icelandic currency. **11** krone, Danish and Norwegian currency. **12** kwacha, Zambian currency.

K[4] ▷ *symbol* **1** *chem*: *kalium* (Latin), potassium. **2** *physics* kaon. **3** *chess* king. **4** one thousand.

k[1] ▷ *symbol* **1** *physics* Boltzmann constant. **2** *chem* velocity constant.

k[2] ▷ *abbreviation* **1** karat or CARAT. **2** KILO or KILO-.

Kabbala and **Kabala** see CABBALA

kabuki /kəˈbuːkɪ/ ▷ *noun* (***kabukis***) a popular traditional form of Japanese drama in which men play both male and female roles. ◷ 19c: Japanese, from *ka* song + *bu* dance + *ki* skill.

Kabyle /kəˈbaɪl/ ▷ *noun* **1** (*plural* ***Kabyle*** or ***Kabyles***) a member of the BERBER people of N Africa. **2** a dialect of BERBER. ◷ 19c: from Arabic *qaba'il*, plural of *qabila* a tribe.

kaccha /ˈkʌtʃə/ ▷ *noun* (***kacchas***) the short trousers traditionally worn by Sikhs; one of THE FIVE K'S.

Kaddish or **Qaddish** /ˈkadɪʃ/ ▷ *noun, Judaism* a form of prayer and thanksgiving used during a period of mourning. • **say kaddish** to be a mourner. ◷ 17c: from Aramaic *qaddish* holy or holy one.

Kadi see CADI

Kaffir or **Kafir** or **Kaffer** /ˈkafə(r)/ ▷ *noun* **1** *S Afr, offensive* a black African. **2** *old use* the XHOSA language, a Bantu language of South Africa. **3** KAFFIR CORN. **4** *stock exchange slang* S African mining shares. ◷ 16c: from Arabic *kafir* unbeliever.

kaffirboom /ˈkafərbuəm/ ▷ *noun* a S African deciduous flowering tree. ◷ 19c: from KAFFIR + Afrikaans *boom* tree.

kaffir corn ▷ *noun* a variety of SORGHUM grown in southern Africa.

kaffiyeh /kaːˈfiːjɛ/ or **keffiyeh** or **kufiyah** ▷ *noun* an Arab headdress of cloth folded and held by a cord around the head. ◷ 19c: from Arabic *kaffiyah*.

Kafir /ˈkafə(r), ˈkaː–/ ▷ *noun* **1** one of a people belonging to Kafiristan in E Afghanistan. **2** KAFFIR. ◷ 19c: Arabic, meaning 'unbeliever'.

Kafkaesque /kafkəˈɛsk/ ▷ *adj* in the style of, or reminiscent of the ideas or work, etc, of the Czech novelist Franz Kafka (1883–1924), especially in his vision of man's isolated existence in a dehumanized world. ◷ 1940s.

kaftan see CAFTAN

kagoule see CAGOULE

kagu /ˈkaːguː/ ▷ *noun* (***kagus***) *zool* a ground-dwelling bird with pale grey plumage and a loose crest, now an endangered species, confined to the Pacific island of New Caledonia. ◷ 19c: native name.

kai /kaɪ/ ▷ *noun* (***kais***) *NZ* **1** food. **2** a meal. ◷ 19c: Maori.

kail see KALE

kailyard see KALEYARD

kainite /ˈkaɪnaɪt, ˈkeɪnaɪt/ ▷ *noun* hydrated magnesium sulphate with potassium chloride, found in salt deposits, used as a fertilizer. ◷ 19c: from German *Kainit*, from Greek *kainos* new.

Kaiser /ˈkaɪzə(r)/ ▷ *noun, historical* any of the emperors of Germany, Austria or the Holy Roman Empire. • **kaiserdom** *noun.* ◷ 16c: German, from Latin *Caesar*, family name of the earliest Roman emperors.

kaka /ˈkaːkə/ ▷ *noun* (***kakas***) a green New Zealand parrot with a long bill. ◷ 18c: Maori, meaning 'parrot'.

kakapo /ˈkaːkəpoʊ/ (***kakapos***) ▷ *noun, zool* a nocturnal flightless parrot, resembling an owl, found only in the rainforests of New Zealand. ◷ 19c: from Maori *kaka* parrot + *po* night.

kakemono /kakɪˈmoʊnoʊ/ ▷ *noun* (***kakemonos***) a Japanese wall-picture or calligraphic inscription on a roller. ◷ 19c: Japanese, from *kake* to hang + *mono* thing.

kakiemon /kaːkɪˈeɪmɒn, ka-/ ▷ *noun* a type of Japanese porcelain first made in the 17c by Sakaida Kakiemon, recognizable from the characteristic use of iron-red. ◷ 1890s.

kala-azar /ˈkaːlə əˈzaː(r)/ ▷ *noun* a tropical fever, confined to the dry regions of NE Africa and S Asia which, if untreated, is often fatal. It is characterized by fever, acute anaemia and enlargement of the spleen and liver, caused by a parasite which is usually transmitted by sandfly bites. Compare LEISHMANIASIS. ◷ 19c: Assamese *kala* black + *azar* disease.

kalanchoe /kalənˈkoʊɪ/ ▷ *noun* (***kalanchoes***) *bot* a succulent herb or shrub which bears flower clusters on long stems, native to tropical Africa and Madagascar. In many species the leaf margins bear plantlets that develop into new plants. ◷ 19c: from the Mandarin name of one of the species.

kalashnikov /kəˈlaʃnɪkɒf/ ▷ *noun* a type of submachine-gun manufactured in the Soviet Union. ◷ 1970s: named after its Russian inventor, M T Kalashnikov (born 1919).

kale or **kail** ▷ *noun* **1** a variety of cabbage with loose wrinkled or curled leaves that do not form a head, widely cultivated in Europe as a vegetable and fodder crop. **2** *Scots* cabbage. ◷ Anglo-Saxon as *cawl*.

kaleidoscope /kəˈlaɪdəskoʊp/ ▷ *noun* **1** an optical toy, usually consisting of two or three long mirrors fixed at an angle to each other inside a tube containing small pieces of coloured plastic, glass or paper, so that multiple reflections produce random regular patterns when the tube is viewed through an eyepiece at one end and rotated or shaken. **2** any colourful and constantly changing scene or succession of events. • **kaleidoscopic** /-ˈskɒpɪk/ *adj.* • **kaleidoscopically** *adverb.* ◷ 19c: from Greek *kalos* beautiful + *eidos* form + -SCOPE.

kalends see CALENDS

kaleyard or **kailyard** ▷ *noun, Scots* a vegetable garden.

kaleyard school or **kailyard school** ▷ *noun* a late-

19c to early-20c group of Scottish writers of fiction which romanticized Scottish village life.

kali /ˈkɑːliː/ ▻ *noun* (***kalis***) the prickly SALTWORT or GLASSWORT. ⓘ 16c: from Arabic *qili*, as in the root of ALKALI.

kalif see CALIPH

kalmia /ˈkalmɪə/ ▻ *noun* (***kalmias***) a N American evergreen shrub belonging to the heath family, notable for its clusters of flowers. ⓘ 18c: named after Peter Kalm (1716–79), Swedish botanist.

kalong /ˈkɑːlɒŋ/ ▻ *noun* a large fruit bat. ⓘ 19c: Javanese.

Kamasutra or **Kama Sutra** /ˈkɑːmə ˈsuːtrə/ ▻ *noun* an ancient Sanskrit text on the art of lovemaking, which describes the pleasures to be attained form various sexual techniques. ⓘ 19c: Sanskrit, meaning 'book on love', from *kama* love + *sutra* a string or rule.

kame /keɪm/ ▻ *noun, geol* a long narrow steep-sided mound or ridge of gravel, sand, etc, deposited by water at the edge of a melting glacier. ⓘ 19c: Scots and N English variant of COMB, from its shape like a cock's comb.

kameez /kəˈmiːz/ ▻ *noun* (***kameezes***) a loose tunic with tight sleeves worn by women in or from S Asia. ⓘ 19c: from Urdu *kamis*, from Arabic *qamis*.

kamik /ˈkɑːmɪk/ ▻ *noun* a knee-length sealskin boot. ⓘ 19c: Inuit.

kamikaze /kamɪˈkɑːzɪ/ ▻ *noun* (***kamikazes***) **1** in World War II: a Japanese plane loaded with explosives that the pilot would deliberately crash into an enemy target. **2** the pilot of this kind of plane. ▻ *adj* **1** relating or referring to such an attack or the pilot concerned. **2** *colloq* said of exploits, missions, etc: suicidally dangerous. **3** *colloq* reckless; foolhardy. ⓘ 1940s: Japanese, literally 'divine wind'.

kampong /ˈkampɒŋ, kamˈpɒŋ/ ▻ *noun* a Malaysian village or settlement. ⓘ 19c: Malay, meaning settlement.

Kampuchean /kampʊˈtʃɪən/ ▻ *adj* belonging or relating to Kampuchea or its inhabitants. ● ▻ *noun* a citizen or inhabitant of, or person born in, Kampuchea. See also CAMBODIAN, KHMER. ⓘ 1970s: Kampuchea was the name given to Campodia by the Khmer Rouge government from 1976–1989.

Kan. see under KS

Kanak /kəˈnək/ ▻ *noun* **1** a Melanesian. **2** a citizen or inhabitant of New Caledonia, an island in the SW Pacific, east of Australia, who is seeking its independence from France. ⓘ 20c: from Hawaiian *kanaka* man.

Kanaka /kəˈnakə, ˈkanəkə/ ▻ *noun* (***Kanakas***) **1** a native Hawaiian. **2** (*also* **kanaka**) *derog* a native South Sea Islander, especially (*formerly*) one who was an indentured or forced labourer in Australia. **3** the Hawaiian language. ⓘ 19c: Hawaiian, meaning 'man'.

Kanarese or **Canarese** /kanəˈriːz/ ▻ *adj* belonging or relating to Kanara in western India. ▻ *noun* (*plural* ***Kanarese***) **1** one of the people of Kanara. **2** their DRAVIDIAN language, now usually called **Kannada**.

kanga or **khanga** /ˈkaŋgə/ ▻ *noun* (***kangas***) *originally E Afr* a piece of cotton cloth, usually brightly decorated, wound around the body as a woman's dress. ⓘ 20c: Swahili.

kangaroo /kaŋgəˈruː/ ▻ *noun* (***kangaroos***) **1** a herbivorous marsupial mammal with a thick muscular tail and large powerful hind legs adapted for leaping, native to Australia, Tasmania and New Guinea. **2** (**the Kangaroos**) the Australian Rugby league team. **3** (**kangaroos**) *stock exchange slang* Australian shares in land, mining, etc. ▻ *verb* (***kangarooed***, ***kangarooing***) *intr, colloq* said of a car: to move forward in jerks because of the driver's poor clutch control. ⓘ 18c: from *gangurru* in an Australian Aboriginal language.

kangaroo closure ▻ *noun, Brit* in parliamentary procedure: a type of closure where the chairperson selects which amendments will be discussed and which passed over.

kangaroo court ▻ *noun* a court composed eg of strikers to try strikebreakers, or of prisoners to try fellow prisoners, that has no legal status and which is usually perceived as delivering unfair or biased judgments.

kangaroo rat ▻ *noun, zool* a small nocturnal N and C American rodent which has very long hind legs and a long tail, so called because it hops in a manner similar to a kangaroo.

kangha /ˈkʌŋhə/ ▻ *noun* (***kanghas***) the comb traditionally worn by Sikhs in their hair; one of THE FIVE K'S. ⓘ 20c: Punjabi.

kanji /ˈkandʒɪ/ ▻ *noun* (***kanjis*** or ***kanji***) **1** a Japanese writing system using characters derived from Chinese ideographs. **2** one of these characters. ⓘ 1920s: Japanese, from Chinese *han* Chinese + *zi* character.

Kannada see under KANARESE

Kans. see under KS

Kantian /ˈkantɪən/ ▻ *adj* relating to the German philosopher Immanuel Kant (1724–1804) or to his philosophy. ● **Kantianism** or **Kantism** *noun* the doctrines or philosophy of Kant. ● **Kantist** *noun* a disciple or follower of Kant. ⓘ 18c.

KANU /ˈkɑːnuː/ ▻ *abbreviation* Kenya African National Union.

kaolin or **kaoline** /ˈkeɪəlɪn/ ▻ *noun* a soft white clay composed of KAOLINITE and other clay minerals, used for making fine porcelain, bricks and cement, as a filler in rubber, paper and paints, and medicinally to treat diarrhoea and vomiting. Also called **china clay**. ● **kaolinic** /-ˈlɪnɪk/ *adj*. ● **kaolinize** or **kaolinise** *verb*. ⓘ 18c: from Chinese *Gaoling*, literally 'high ridge', the name of a mountain in Northern China where it was mined.

kaolinite ▻ *noun, geol* a white, grey or yellowish clay mineral consisting of hydrated aluminium silicate formed as a result of the alteration of feldspars by steam from underground sources or weathering. ● **kaolinitic** *adj*. ⓘ 19c: KAOLIN + -ITE sense 4.

kaon /ˈkeɪɒn/ ▻ *noun, physics* (symbol **K**) an elementary particle, which with the pion and psi particles, comprises mesons involved in the forces holding together protons and neutrons in the atomic nucleus. Also called **K-meson**. ⓘ 20c: from *K*, modelled on MESON.

kapellmeister /kəˈpɛlmaɪstə(r)/ ▻ *noun* the director of an orchestra or choir, especially and originally in the 18c in the household of a German prince. ⓘ 19c: from German *Kapelle* chapel or orchestra + *Meister* master.

kapok /ˈkeɪpɒk/ ▻ *noun* the light waterproof silky fibres that surround the seeds of certain trees, especially the **kapok tree**, used for padding and stuffing eg pillows, cushions and mattresses. ⓘ 18c: from Malay *kapoq* the name of the tree.

Kaposi's sarcoma /kəˈpoʊsiːz —, ˈkapəsiːz —/ ▻ *noun* (abbreviation **KS**) a form of cancer characterized by multiple malignant tumours of the skin or lymph nodes, now a common feature of AIDS. ⓘ 19c: named after Hungarian-born dermatologist Moritz Kaposi (1837–1902) who first described the condition.

kappa /ˈkapə/ ▻ *noun* (***kappas***) the tenth letter of the Greek alphabet. See table at GREEK ALPHABET

kaput /kəˈpʊt/ ▻ *adj, colloq* **1** broken, from French *être capot* to hold no tricks in the card game piquet. **2** ruined; destroyed. ⓘ 19c: from German *kaputt* broken.

kara /ˈkʌrə/ ▻ *noun* (***karas***) the steel bangle signifying the unity of God, traditionally worn by Sikhs; one of THE FIVE K'S. ⓘ 20c: Punjabi.

karabiner /karəˈbiːnə(r)/ ▻ *noun, mountaineering, etc* a steel coupling link with a spring clip in one side. Also called **krab** or **snaplink**. ⓘ 1930s: shortened from German *Karabinerhaken* carbine hook.

karakul or **caracul** /ˈkɑːrəkuːl/ ▷ *noun* **1** (*often* **Karakul**) a breed of sheep, native to central Asia, which has coarse black, brown or grey wool. **2** the soft curly fleece of a lamb of this breed, used to make fur coats, etc. **3** any cloth that resembles such a fleece. Also called **Persian lamb**. ⓘ 19c: named after Kara Kul, a lake in central Asia, in the area where the sheep were originally bred.

karaoke /ˈkarɪoʊkɪ/ ▷ *noun* (*karaokes*) a form of entertainment originally developed in Japan, in which amateur performers sing pop songs to the accompaniment of pre-recorded music. It involves using a **karaoke machine** which, as well as providing the backing track also enables the singer to follow the words on a screen. ⓘ 1980s: Japanese, literally 'empty orchestra'.

karaoke bar ▷ *noun* a bar or pub that offers karaoke entertainment.

karat see CARAT

karate /kəˈrɑːtɪ/ ▷ *noun* a system of unarmed self-defence, using blows and kicks, originally Japanese, now a popular combative sport. ⓘ 1950s: Japanese, literally 'emptyhand'.

karate chop ▷ *noun* a sharp downward blow with the side of the hand.

karateka /kəˈrɑːtɪka/ ▷ *noun* (*karatekas*) a competitor or an expert in karate.

karma /ˈkɑːmə, ˈkɜːmə/ ▷ *noun* (*karmas*) *Buddhism, Hinduism* **1** the sum of someone's lifetime's actions, seen as governing their fate in the next life. **2** destiny; fate. **3** *popularly* an aura or quality that is perceived to be given off by someone or something, or by a place. • **karmic** *adj*. ⓘ 19c: from Sanskrit *karma* act or deed.

Karoo or **Karroo** /kəˈruː/ ▷ *noun* (*Karoos*) (*also* without capital) **1** any one of several high inland plateaus in S Africa. **2** *geol* a series of strata in S Africa of PERMIAN and TRIASSIC age. ⓘ 18c: from Afrikaans *karo*.

kaross /kəˈrɒs/ ▷ *noun* a S African sleeveless jacket made of animal skins with the hair left on. ⓘ 18c.

karri /ˈkarɪ/ ▷ *noun* (*karris*) **1** a W Australian eucalyptus tree. **2** the durable red wood of this tree. ⓘ 19c: Aboriginal.

Karroo see KAROO

karsey see KAZI

karst /kɑːst/ ▷ *noun, geol* any landscape characterized by gorges, caves, potholes, underground streams and other features produced by the action of water on limestone rock formations. ⓘ 19c: German, from *der* Karst, the name of a district east of the Adriatic.

karsy see KAZI

kart /kɑːt/ ▷ *noun, colloq* a GO-KART. • **karter** *noun*. • **karting** *noun* go-kart racing. ⓘ 1950s.

karyo- or **caryo-** /karɪoʊ, karɪˈɒ/ ▷ *prefix, denoting* nucleus. ⓘ From Greek *karyon* kernel.

karyokinesis ▷ *noun, biol* the complicated changes that occur during MITOSIS. ⓘ 19c.

karyology ▷ *noun, biol* a former name for the study of cell nuclei, especially of chromosomes, which is now covered under molecular biology. ⓘ 19c.

karyotype ▷ *noun genetics* **1** the number, size and structure of the chromosomes in the nucleus of a cell, characteristic of all the DIPLOID cells of a particular individual, strain or species. **2** the representation of this in a diagram or photograph. ▷ *verb* to investigate or determine the karyotype of (a cell). • **karyotypic** or **karyotypical** *adj*. ⓘ 1920s.

karzy see KAZI

kasbah or **casbah** /ˈkazbɑː/ (*sometimes* **Kasbah** or **Casbah**) ▷ *noun* **1** a castle or fortress in a N African town. **2** the area around it. ⓘ 18c: from Arabic dialect *kasba* fortress.

kasha /ˈkaʃə/ ▷ *noun* (*kashas*) a porridge or gruel-like dish, originating in E Europe, made from crushed cereal, usually buckwheat. ⓘ 19c: Russian.

Kashmiri /kaʃˈmɪərɪ/ ▷ *adj* belonging or relating to Kashmir, a region in the NW of the Indian subcontinent, its inhabitants, or their language • ▷ *noun* **1** a citizen or inhabitant of, or person born in, Kashmir. **2** the Indic language spoken in this region. See also CASHMERE. ⓘ 19c..

Kashrut or **Kashruth** /kaʃˈruːt/ and **Kashrus** /-ruːs/ (*also* **kashrut** or **kashrus**) ▷ *noun* **1** the Jewish system of dietary laws relating to the fitness and preparation of food. See also KOSHER. **2** the condition of being suitable for ritual use. ⓘ Early 20c: Hebrew, meaning 'fitness'.

kat or **khat** or **qat** /kɑːt/ ▷ *noun* **1** a shrub of E Africa, Arabia, etc. **2** the leaves of the plant chewed or used in an infusion for their stimulant effect. ⓘ 19c: from Arabic *qat*.

kata /ˈkatə/ ▷ *noun* (*katas*) *karate* a formal sequence of practice movements and exercises that are performed in martial arts such as judo and karate. ⓘ 20c: from Japanese, meaning 'shape' or 'pattern'.

katabatic /katəˈbatɪk/ ▷ *adj, meteorol* said of winds: blowing down a slope because of air density differences resulting from overnight cooling, etc. Compare ANABATIC. ⓘ Early 20c: from Greek *katabainein* to go down.

katakana /katəˈkɑːnə/ ▷ *noun* (*katakanas*) one of the two syllabic writing systems in Japanese. See also KIRAGANA. ⓘ 18c: Japanese.

katharometer /kaθəˈrɒmətə(r)/ ▷ *noun, chem* an instrument that compares the thermal conductivity of gases in a mixture, used to detect air pollution and in gas chromatography. ⓘ Early 20c: from Greek *katharos* pure.

katydid /ˈkeɪtɪdɪd/ ▷ *noun, N Amer* any of various species of grasshopper, with antennae often much longer than its body. ⓘ 18c: imitating the sound made nocturnally by the male with its modified front wings.

kauri /ˈkaʊərɪ/ ▷ *noun* (*kauris*) **1** (*in full* **kauri pine**) a tall broad-leaved coniferous tree, native to SE Asia and Australasia, the source of valuable timber and an important resin. **2** (*in full* **kauri gum**) the brownish resin of this tree, used mainly in varnishes and in the manufacture of linoleum. **3** the timber of this tree. ⓘ 19c: Maori.

kava /ˈkɑːvə/ ▷ *noun* (*kavas*) **1** an aromatic plant of the pepper family. **2** a narcotic drink prepared from the stem and root of this plant. ⓘ 18c: Polynesian, meaning 'bitter'.

kayak /ˈkaɪak/ ▷ *noun* **1** a sealskin-covered canoe for one person used by the Inuit. **2** a similar canvas-covered or fibreglass craft used in the sport of canoeing. ⓘ 18c: from Inuit *qayaq*.

kayo /keɪˈoʊ/ *boxing slang* ▷ *noun* (*kayos* or *kayoes*) a KNOCKOUT. ▷ *verb* (*kayoed, kayoing*) to KNOCK SOMEONE OUT (see under KNOCK). • **kayoing** *noun*. ⓘ 1920s: from the pronunciation of the abbreviation KO.

Kazak or **Kazakh** /kəˈzɑːk, ˈkazak/ ▷ *noun* (*Kazaks* or *Kazakhis*) **1** a member of a Turko-Tatar people of Central Asia, especially of Kazakhstan. **2** the Turkic dialect they speak. ⓘ 19c: from Russian.

kazi or **karzy** or **karsey** or **karsy** /ˈkɑːzɪ/ ▷ *noun* (*kazis, karzies, karseys* or *karsies*) *slang* a lavatory. ⓘ Early 1960s: from Italian *casa* house.

kazoo /kəˈzuː/ ▷ *noun* (*kazoos*) a crude wind instrument consisting of a short metal tube with a strip of parchment or plastic etc, stretched across a hole in its upper surface which vibrates with a buzz when someone blows or hums into it. ⓘ 19c: imitating the sound.

KB¹ ▷ *abbreviation* **1** *computing* kilobyte. **2** King's Bench. **3** knight bachelor.

KB² ▷ *symbol, chess* king's bishop.

KBE ▷ *abbreviation* Knight Commander of the Order of the British Empire.

KBS ▷ *abbreviation, computing* knowledge-based system.

kbyte ▷ *abbreviation, computing* kilobyte. Usually called KB or K.

KC ▷ *abbreviation* **1** Kennel Club. **2** King's Counsel.

kc ▷ *abbreviation* kilocycle.

kcal ▷ *abbreviation* kilocalorie.

KCB ▷ *abbreviation* Knight Commander of the Order of the Bath.

KCMG ▷ *abbreviation* Knight Commander of the Order of St Michael and St George.

KCVO ▷ *abbreviation* Knight Commander of the Royal Victorian Order.

Kčs ▷ *abbreviation* koruna.

KD ▷ *abbreviation* **1** *finance* knocked down (see KNOCK SOMETHING DOWN sense 2 at KNOCK). **2** Kuwaiti dinar, Kuwaiti unit of currency.

kea /kɪə, keɪə/ ▷ *noun* (***keas***) *zool* an olive-coloured parrot with blue and red markings on its wings, found only on South Island, New Zealand. ⓘ 19c: Maori, imitating the sound it makes.

kebab /kə'bab/ ▷ *noun* (*in full* **shish kebab**) a dish of small pieces of meat and vegetable grilled on a skewer. Compare DONER KEBAB. ▷ *verb* (***kebabbed, kebabbing***) to skewer something. ⓘ 17c: from Arabic *kabab* roast meat; SHISH from Turkish *şiş* skewer.

kecks see KEKS

kedge /kɛdʒ/ ▷ *verb* (***kedged, kedging***) *tr & intr* to manoeuvre by means of a hawser attached to a light anchor. ▷ *noun* a light anchor used for kedging. ⓘ 17c.

kedgeree /kɛdʒə'riː, 'kɛdʒəriː/ ▷ *noun* (***kedgerees***) *cookery* **1** a European, but especially British, dish, now usually a mixture of rice, fish and eggs. **2** a dish, originally from India, consisting of rice cooked with butter and dal, flavoured with spice and shredded onion, etc. ⓘ 17c: from Hindi *khichri* a dish of rice and sesame.

keek *Scots & N Eng* ▷ *noun* a peep. ▷ *verb* (***keeked, keeking***) *intr* to take a peep. ⓘ 14c: probably from Dutch *kiken* to look.

keel¹ ▷ *noun* **1** the timber or metal strut extending from stem to stern along the base of a ship, from which the hull is built up. **2** a structure resembling or corresponding to a ship's keel. **3** *biol* **a** the projection of bone from the sternum which the flight muscles of birds are attached to; **b** any similar structure functioning like a keel. ▷ *verb* (***keeled, keeling***) *tr & intr* to capsize. • **keeled** *adj* **1** *bot* keel-shaped. **2** having a ridge on the back. • **on an even keel** calm and steady. ⓘ 14c as *kele*: from Norse *kjölr*.

■ **keel over 1** said of a ship: to tip over sideways. **2** *colloq* to fall over, eg in a faint.

keel² ▷ *noun* a low flat-bottomed boat; a barge. Also called **keelboat**. ⓘ 14c: from Dutch *kiel* ship.

keelboat¹ ▷ *noun* a type of yacht with a heavy external keel providing weight to offset that of the sails.

keelboat² see under KEEL²

keelhaul ▷ *verb* **1** to drag someone under the keel of a ship from one side to the other, as a naval punishment. **2** to rebuke someone severely. ⓘ 17c.

keelman ▷ *noun* a man who works on a barge (see KEEL²).

keelson see KELSON

keen¹ ▷ *adj* **1** eager; willing. **2** said of competition or rivalry, etc: fierce. **3** said of the wind: bitter. **4** said of a blade, etc: sharp. **5** said of the mind or senses: quick; acute. **6** said of prices: low; competitive. • **keenly** *adverb*. • **keenness** *noun*. • **keen on someone** or **something** enthusiastic about them or it; fond of them or it. ⓘ Anglo-Saxon *cene* bold or fierce.

keen² ▷ *verb* (***keened, keening***) *tr & intr* especially in Ireland: to lament or mourn in a loud wailing voice. ▷ *noun* a lament for the dead. • **keening** *noun* wailing; lamentation. ⓘ 19c: from Irish *caoine* lament.

keep¹ ▷ *verb* (***kept, keeping***) **1** to have; to possess. **2** to continue to have something; not to part with it; to save. **3** to maintain or retain □ *keep one's temper*. **4** to store. **5** *tr & intr* to remain or cause something to remain in a certain state, position, place, etc. **6** *intr* to continue or be frequently doing something □ *keep smiling* □ *kept fainting*. **7** said of a shopkeeper, etc: to have something regularly in stock. **8** to own and look after (an animal, etc) □ *keep hens*. **9** to own or run (a shop, boarding-house, etc). **10** to look after something □ *keep house* □ *keep this for me*. **11** *intr* said of food: to remain fit to be eaten □ *This cake keeps well*. **12** to maintain (a record, diary, accounts, etc). **13** to obey (the law, etc). **14** to preserve (a secret). **15** to stick to (a promise or appointment). **16** to celebrate (a festival, etc) in the traditional way; to follow (a custom). **17** to support someone financially. **18** to employ □ *We keep a gardener*. **19** to protect □ *keep them from harm*. **20** *football* to guard (the goal). **21** *cricket* (*usually* **keep wicket**) to guard the wicket. **22** to remain firm on something □ *managed to keep his feet despite the strong wind*. ▷ *noun* **1** the cost of one's food and other daily expenses □ *earn one's keep*. **2** the central tower or stronghold in a Norman castle. • **for keeps** *colloq* permanently; for good. • **How are you keeping?** How are you? • **keep going** to persevere in spite of problems. • **keep someone going** to help them survive difficulties, etc. • **keep to oneself** to avoid the company of others. • **keep something to oneself** not to reveal it to others. • **keep up with the Joneses** *colloq* to compete with neighbours in a display of material prosperity. See also **keep up with someone** below. ⓘ Anglo-Saxon *cepan* to guard, observe or watch.

■ **keep at something** to persevere at or persist in it.

■ **keep something back 1** to conceal information, etc. **2** to suppress (laughter, tears, etc).

■ **keep down** to keep low; to hide.

■ **keep someone down** to oppress them; to prevent their development or progress, etc.

■ **keep something down 1** to control or limit (prices, development, etc). **2** to oppress or restrain it. **3** to manage not to vomit (food, etc).

■ **keep from something** to hold back from doing it or delay doing it □ *couldn't keep from laughing*.

■ **keep someone from something** to prevent them from doing it.

■ **keep something from someone** to prevent (information) from reaching them.

■ **keep someone in** to confine them; to prevent them from escaping □ *was kept in after school and given one hundred lines*.

■ **keep something in 1** to confine it; to hold it back. **2** to conceal it.

■ **keep in with someone** to remain on good terms with them, especially for selfish reasons.

■ **keep off something 1** to avoid (a harmful food, awkward topic, etc). **2** to stay away from it □ *Keep off my books!*

■ **keep someone off something** to prevent them from approaching or attacking it.

■ **keep on doing something** to persist in it.

■ **keep someone on** to continue to employ them.

■ **keep something on 1** to continue renting or using it □ *We had a flat in town but decided not to keep it on.* **2** to continue to wear (a piece of clothing) □ *Keep your gloves on.*

■ **keep on about something** or **someone** to talk continually and repetitively about it or them.

■ **keep on at someone** to nag or harass them.

■ **keep to something** not to leave it □ *Keep to the path.*

■ **keep someone to something** to make them adhere to (a promise, decision, etc). □ *I'll keep you to that.*

■ **keep someone under** to subdue, repress or crush them.

■ **keep something up 1** to prevent (eg spirits, morale, etc) from falling. **2** to maintain (a habit, friendship, pace, etc). **3** to go on making (payments, etc). **4** to maintain (a house, garden, etc) in good condition.

■ **keep up with someone 1** not to be left behind by them. **2** to maintain the pace or standard set by them.

keeper ▷ *noun* **1** a person who looks after something, eg a collection in a museum. **2** a person who looks after animals or birds in captivity. **3** a gamekeeper. **4** *colloq* a goalkeeper. **5** a wicketkeeper. **6** an iron or steel bar placed across the poles of a permanent magnet in order to preserve its magnetic properties when it is not in use. **7** the socket that receives the bolt of a lock. **8** a small band of leather, etc on a belt, strap, etc that stops the end from flopping about.

keeper ring ▷ *noun* a GUARD RING.

keep fit ▷ *noun* a series or system of exercises intended to improve the circulation and respiratory system, suppleness and stamina, etc. Also *as adj* □ *keep-fit classes.*

keeping ▷ *noun* care or charge. • **in keeping with something** in harmony with it. • **not in keeping with something** not appropriate for it.

keepnet ▷ *noun* a cone-shaped net suspended in a river, etc, in which fish caught by anglers can be kept alive.

keepsake ▷ *noun* something kept in memory of the giver, or of a particular event or place.

kef /kɛf, keɪf/ and **kif** /kɪf, kiːf/ ▷ *noun* **1** a state of dreamy euphoria. **2** any drug, especially marijuana, that produces this condition when smoked. **3** marijuana. Ⓒ 19c: from Arabic *kaif* pleasure.

keffiyeh see KAFFIYEH

kefuffle see CARFUFFLE

keg ▷ *noun* (abbreviation **kg**) **1** a small barrel, usually containing less than 10 gallons. **2** an aluminium cask for transporting and storing beer, in which the beer may be kept under gas pressure. Ⓒ 17c: from Norse *kaggi.*

keg beer ▷ *noun* any of various types of beer that have had carbon dioxide added to them and which are kept in and served from pressurized kegs.

keister /ˈkiːstə(r)/ ▷ *noun, chiefly N Amer* **1** *slang, especially US* the buttocks; arse. **2** a safe or strong box. **3** a case or box. Ⓒ 19c: possibly from German *Kiste* chest or case.

kelim see KILIM

keloid or **cheloid** /ˈkiːlɔɪd/ *medicine* ▷ *noun* excessive hard smooth growth of harmless scar tissue at the site of a skin injury, common in dark-skinned people but unusual in fair-skinned people. • **keloidal** *adj.* Ⓒ 19c: from Greek *chele* claw.

keks or **kecks** ▷ *singular noun, colloq* trousers.

kelp ▷ *noun* **1** a common name for any large brown seaweed that grows below the low-tide mark. **2** the ash obtained by burning kelp, used as an agricultural fertilizer and as a source of iodine. Ⓒ 14c as *culp.*

Kelper or **kelper** ▷ *noun* the local name for a citizen or inhabitant of, or person born in, the Falkland Islands. ▷ *adj* belonging or relating to the Falkland Islands. Ⓒ 1960s: from KELP.

kelpie or **kelpy** /ˈkɛlpɪ/ ▷ *noun* (*kelpies*) *Scottish folklore* **1** a malignant water spirit in the form of a horse, usually associated with fords. **2** an Australian breed of sheepdog. Ⓒ 17c.

kelson /ˈkɛlsən/ and **keelson** /ˈkɛlsən, ˈkiːlsən/ ▷ *noun* a timber fixed along a ship's keel for strength. Ⓒ 17c: from German *kielswin* keel swine, ie 'keel timber'.

Kelt see CELT

kelt ▷ *noun* a salmon that has just spawned. Ⓒ 14c.

kelter see KILTER

Keltic see CELTIC

kelvin /ˈkɛlvɪn/ ▷ *noun, physics* (abbreviation **K**) in the SI system: a unit of thermodynamic or ABSOLUTE TEMPERATURE, equal to 1/273.16 of the absolute temperature of the triple point of water, and equal in magnitude to one degree on the Celsius scale. ▷ *adj* relating to the Kelvin scale of temperature. Ⓒ 19c: named after the UK physicist Sir William Thomson, Lord Kelvin (1824–1907).

Kelvin scale ▷ *noun* a thermodynamic temperature scale starting at ABSOLUTE ZERO and increasing by the same unitary intervals as the CELSIUS SCALE, ie 0°C = 273K and 100°C = 373K, in which there are no negatives.

kempt ▷ *adj* said especially of hair: neatly combed or kept. Ⓒ Anglo-Saxon: related to COMB.

Ken. see under KY

ken ▷ *verb* (**kent** or **kenned**, **kenning**) *Scots & N Eng dialect* **1** to know. **2** to understand. ▷ *noun* range of knowledge; perception □ *beyond our ken.* Ⓒ Anglo-Saxon *cennan.*

kenaf /kəˈnaf/ ▷ *noun* a tropical Asian herbaceous plant, the fibres of which can be used as a substitute for wood pulp in making paper. Ⓒ 19c: Persian.

kendo /ˈkɛndoʊ/ ▷ *noun* a Japanese art of fencing using bamboo staves or sometimes real swords, while observing strict ritual. Ⓒ 1920s: Japanese, literally 'sword way'.

kennel /ˈkɛnəl/ ▷ *noun* (**kennels**) **1** a small shelter for a dog. **2** (**kennels**) an establishment where dogs are boarded or bred. **3** a pack of hounds. ▷ *verb* (**kennelled, kennelling**; *N Amer* **kenneled, kenneling**) **1** to put or keep (an animal) in a kennel. **2** *intr* to live in a kennel. Ⓒ 14c: from Latin *canis* dog.

Kennelly-Heaviside layer /kɛnəlɪ ˈhɛvɪsaɪd —/ and **Heaviside layer** ▷ *noun, dated physics* the E-LAYER. Ⓒ 1920s: named after Arthur Edwin Kennelly (1861–1939), and Oliver Heaviside (1850–1925), both of whom independently inferred its existence.

kennel maid and **kennel man** ▷ *noun* someone whose job is to look after dogs.

kenspeckle /ˈkɛnspɛkəl/ and **kenspeck** ▷ *adj, Scots & N Eng dialect* conspicuous; easily recognized. Ⓒ 18c.

kent *past tense, past participle of* KEN

Kentish /ˈkɛntɪʃ/ ▷ *adj* belonging or relating to the county of Kent in SE England. ▷ *noun* the dialect of Kent and Essex, etc. Ⓒ Anglo-Saxon *Centisc.*

Kenyan /ˈkɛnjən, ˈkiːnjən/ ▷ *adj, noun* ▷ *adj* belonging or relating to Kenya, a republic in E Africa, or to its inhabitants. • ▷ *noun* a citizen or inhabitant of, or a person born in, Kenya. Ⓒ 1930s.

kepi /ˈkeɪpiː/ ▷ *noun* (*kepis*) a French military cap with a flat circular crown and horizontal straight-edged peak. Ⓒ 19c: from French *képi*, from Swiss German *Käppi*, diminutive of German *Kappe* cap.

Kepler's laws /ˈkɛpləz —/ ▷ *noun* a set of three interrelated theorems of planetary motion that describe the properties of elliptical orbits. ⓒ 18c: named after the German astronomer Johann Kepler (1571–1630).

kept *past tense, past participle of* KEEP

kept man and **kept woman** ▷ *noun, derog* a man or woman supported financially by someone in return for being available to them as a sexual partner.

keratin /ˈkɛrətɪn/ ▷ *noun, biochem* a tough fibrous protein produced by the EPIDERMIS in vertebrates, and forming the main component of hair, nails, claws, horns, feathers and the dead outer layers of skin cells. • **keratinous** *adj.* ⓒ 19c.

keratinize or **keratinise** ▷ *verb* (***keratinized, keratinizing***) *tr & intr* to become or make something horny. • **keratinization** *noun* **1** formation of keratin. **2** becoming horny.

keratitis /kɛrəˈtaɪtɪs/ ▷ *noun, medicine* inflammation of the cornea. ⓒ 19c.

kerato- /kɛrətoʊ, kɛrəˈtɒ/ or (before a vowel) **kerat-** ▷ *combining form, denoting* **1** horn. **2** keratin. **3** the cornea. ⓒ From Greek *keras, keratos* horn.

keratogenous /kɛrəˈtɒdʒənəs/ ▷ *adj* producing horn or KERATIN.

keratoid ▷ *adj* resembling horn or KERATIN.

keratose /ˈkɛrətoʊs/ ▷ *adj* said especially of certain sponges: having a horny skeleton. ⓒ 19c.

keratosis /kɛrəˈtoʊsɪs/ ▷ *noun* (***keratoses*** /-siːz/) *medicine* **1** a horny growth on or over the skin, eg a wart. **2** a skin condition producing this. ⓒ 19c.

kerb or (*especially N Amer*) **curb** /kɜːb/ ▷ *noun* **1** the row of stones or concrete edging forming the edge of a pavement. **2** a kerbstone. **3** an edging or margin of various kinds. ▷ *adj* said of a market or dealing, etc: unofficial; outside official trading hours. ⓒ 17c variant of CURB.

kerb-crawler ▷ *noun* someone who indulges in **kerb-crawling**, the practice of driving slowly alongside the kerb in order to lure potential sexual partners into the car.

kerb drill ▷ *noun* the safe procedure for crossing a road recommended for pedestrians.

kerb-merchant, **kerb-trader** and **kerb-vendor** ▷ *noun* someone who sells goods on or beside the pavement.

kerbside ▷ *noun* the edge of the pavement.

kerbstone ▷ *noun* one of the stones used to form a kerb.

kerb weight ▷ *noun* the weight (of a vehicle) without passengers and luggage.

kerchief /ˈkɜːtʃɪf/ ▷ *noun* **1** a square of cloth or a scarf for wearing over the head or round the neck. **2** *old use* a handkerchief. ⓒ 13c: from French *cuevrechief*, from *covrir* to cover + *chef* head.

kerf /kɜːf/ ▷ *noun* **1** the cut, notch or groove, etc made by a saw. **2** the place where a cut is made. ⓒ Anglo-Saxon *cyrf* a cut.

kerfuffle see CARFUFFLE

kermes /ˈkɜːmiːz/ ▷ *noun* **1** the dried bodies of the female SCALE INSECT used as a red dyestuff. **2** (*also* **kermes oak**) a small evergreen oak tree on which the insects breed. ⓒ 16c: from Persian and Arabic *qirmiz*, from Sanskrit *krmija-* red dye, literally 'produced by a worm'.

kermesse /ˈkɜːmɪs/ ▷ *noun* (***kermesses***) a cycle race held in an urban area. ⓒ 1960s: French, from Flemish *kermis*; see KERMIS.

kermis or **kirmess** /ˈkɜːmɪs/ ▷ *noun* (***kermises*** or ***kirmesses***) *N Amer* a fair or festival held to raise money for charity. ⓒ 19c: Dutch name for an annual country festival, originally a festival to celebrate the dedication of a church, from *kerk* church + *mis* mass.

kernel /ˈkɜːnəl/ ▷ *noun* **1** the inner part of a seed, eg the edible part of a nut. **2** in cereal plants such as corn: the entire grain or seed. **3** the important, essential part of anything. ⓒ Anglo-Saxon *cyrnel*, diminutive of *corn* a grain.

kerosine or **kerosene** /ˈkɛrəsiːn/ ▷ *noun* **1** a combustible oily mixture of hydrocarbons obtained mainly by distillation of petroleum, used as a fuel for jet aircraft, domestic heating systems and lamps, and as a solvent. **2** *N Amer* PARAFFIN. ⓒ 19c: from Greek *keros* wax.

kerria /ˈkɛrɪə/ ▷ *noun* (***kerrias***) a deciduous yellow-flowered shrub. Also called **Jew's mallow.** ⓒ 19c: named after the English gardener, William Kerr (died 1814).

kersey /ˈkɜːzɪ/ ▷ *noun* (***kerseys***) a coarse woollen cloth. ⓒ 14c.

kesh /keɪʃ/ ▷ *noun* (***keshes***) the uncut beard and hair traditionally worn by Sikhs; one of THE FIVE K'S. ⓒ 20c: Punjabi.

kestrel /ˈkɛstrəl/ ▷ *noun* a small falcon with a long tail and broad pointed wings, often seen hovering a few metres above ground while searching for prey. ⓒ 16c as *castrell*.

keta /ˈkiːtə/ ▷ *noun* (***ketas***) a Pacific salmon. ⓒ 19c: Russian.

ketamine /ˈkiːtəmiːn/ ▷ *noun* a crystalline anaesthetic and analgesic substance often used in veterinary medicine and sometimes illicitly for its hallucinatory properties. ⓒ 1960s: from KETONE.

ketch /kɛtʃ/ ▷ *noun* a small two-masted sailing boat, the foremast being the taller. ⓒ 15c as *cache*; related to CATCH.

ketchup /ˈkɛtʃəp, ˈkɛtʃʌp/ ▷ *noun* **1** *popularly* a thick sauce made from tomatoes, vinegar, spices, etc. Also called **tomato ketchup**. **2** (*also* **catchup** or **catsup** /ˈkatsəp/) any of various sauces containing vinegar and the juices of vegetables, nuts, etc. ⓒ 18c: from Malay *kechap*.

keto- /kiːtoʊ/ or **ket-** ▷ *prefix, chem, denoting* a ketone compound or derivative.

ketone /ˈkiːtoʊn/ ▷ *noun chem* any of a class of organic chemical compounds that are formed by the oxidation of secondary alcohols, eg ACETONE. ⓒ 19c: from German *Keton*, from *Aketon* acetone.

ketone body ▷ *noun, biochem* any of three compounds that are produced in excessive amounts in the blood and urine of diabetics, and as a result of starvation.

ketonuria /kiːtəˈnʊərɪə/ ▷ *noun* the presence of abnormally large numbers of ketone bodies in urine, a characteristic sign of diabetes, prolonged starvation, etc. ⓒ Early 20c: from KETONE + URIA.

ketosis /kiːˈtoʊsɪs/ ▷ *noun, medicine* the excessive formation of acetone or ketone bodies in the body, due to incomplete oxidation of fats, which occurs in diabetes and is also an indicator of starvation. ⓒ Early 20c.

kettle /ˈkɛtəl/ ▷ *noun* **1** a container with a spout, lid and handle, for boiling water. **2** a metal container for heating liquids or cooking something in liquid □ *Simmer the salmon in the fish kettle.* • **a different kettle of fish** *colloq* an entirely different matter. • **a pretty kettle of fish** *colloq* an awkward situation. • **kettleful** *noun.* ⓒ Anglo-Saxon *cetel*.

kettledrum ▷ *noun* a percussion instrument, consisting of a large copper or brass cauldron-shaped drum mounted on a tripod, with a skin or other membrane stretched over the top, tuned by adjusting screws that alter the tension of the skin. • **kettledrummer** *noun.*

kettle hole ▷ *noun, geol* a circular hollow in rocks caused by the melting of a trapped block of ice or a basin in glacial drift (eg lake) derived from such melting.

Ketubah /kɛtuːˈvɑː/ ▷ *noun* a formal Jewish marriage contract which couples sign before their wedding. ◑ 19c: from Hebrew *kethubhah* document.

Kevlar /ˈkɛvlɑː(r)/ ▷ *noun, trademark* a lightweight synthetic fibre of exceptionally high strength and heat resistance, used in aerospace, fire-fighting equipment, etc. ◑ 1970s.

key[1] /kiː/ ▷ *noun* (***keys***) **1** a device for opening or closing a lock, or for winding up, turning, tuning, tightening or loosening. **2** one of a series of buttons or levers pressed to sound the notes on a musical instrument, or to print or display a character on a computer, typewriter, calculator, etc. **3** a system of musical notes related to one another in a scale. **4** pitch, tone or style □ ***spoke in a low key.*** **5** something that provides an answer or solution. **6** a means of achievement □ ***the key to success.*** **7** a set of answers, eg at the back of a book of puzzles, exercises, etc. **8** a table explaining signs and symbols used on a map, etc. **9** *elec* a lever-like switch that makes or breaks a circuit for as long as the handle is depressed. **10** the dry winged fruit of certain trees, eg ash, sycamore and maple, often hanging with others in a cluster like a bunch of keys. **11** the relative roughness of a surface, especially with regard to its ability to take paint, etc, more readily. **12** a fret pattern. **13** a pin or wedge for fixing something. **14** *biol* a taxonomic system for distinguishing similar species. ▷ *adj* centrally important □ ***key questions.*** ▷ *verb* (***keyed, keying***) **1** (*also* **key something in**) to enter (data) into a computer, calculator, etc by means of a keyboard; to KEYBOARD. **2** to lock or fasten something with a key. **3** to provide with a key or keys. **4** *tr & intr* to roughen (a surface) eg for decorating, plastering, etc. **5** *tr & intr* to give an advertisement a feature so that replies to it may be identified, eg a reference code added to the address. **6** *printing* to mark the position on the layout of something to be printed, using symbols. • **keyed** *adj* **1** equipped with a key or keys. **2** *music* set to a particular key. **3** in a state of tension or readiness. • **keyless** *adj.* • **keyed up** *colloq* excited; tense; anxious. • **under lock and key** **1** safely stored. **2** in prison. ◑ Anglo-Saxon *cæg*.

key[2] /kiː/ or **cay** /keɪ, kiː/ ▷ *noun* (***keys*** or ***cays***) a small low island or reef formed of sand, coral, rock or mud, especially one off the coast of Florida. ◑ 17c: from Spanish *cayo*.

keyboard ▷ *noun* **1** the set of keys on a piano, etc. **2** the bank of keys for operating a typewriter or computer. **3** *music* especially in jazz, rock, etc: an electronic musical instrument with a keyboard. ▷ *verb* **1** *intr* to operate the keyboard of a computer. **2** to set (text) using a computer keyboard. • **keyboarder** *noun*.

keyhole ▷ *noun* **1** the hole through which a key is inserted into a lock. **2** any small hole similar to this in shape or purpose.

keyhole saw ▷ *noun* a PADSAW.

keyhole surgery ▷ *noun* a technique that involves internal surgical operations being performed with minimal external excision through a small opening, and monitored via fibre optics on a screen.

key man ▷ *noun* an indispensable member of the staff or management of a business, essential to its continued success and survival.

key money ▷ *noun* a payment in addition to rent, demanded in return for the grant, renewal or continuance of a tenancy.

Keynesian /ˈkeɪnzɪən/ ▷ *adj* relating to the economic theories of J M Keynes (1883–1946), which advocated government funding of public works to maintain full employment. • ▷ *noun* someone who supports Keynesian financial policies.

keynote ▷ *noun* **1** the note on which a musical scale or key is based; the TONIC. **2** a central theme, principle or controlling thought. **3** *as adj* said of a speech, etc: **a** expounding central principles; **b** setting the tone for a meeting, etc. **4** *as adj* of fundamental importance. ▷ *verb tr & intr* **1** to deliver a keynote speech. **2** to give the keynote.

keypad ▷ *noun* **1** a small device with push-button controls, eg a TV remote control unit or a pocket calculator. **2** a small cluster of keys, usually numerical ones, positioned to one side of a keyboard or on a separate keyboard.

keypunch ▷ *noun* a device, operated by a keyboard, that transfers data on to cards by punching holes in them, formerly used when computer data was routinely stored on punched cards. ▷ *verb, tr & intr* to transfer (data) in this way.

key ring ▷ *noun* a ring for keeping keys on, usually with a FOB[2] attached.

key signature ▷ *noun, music* the sharps and flats shown on the stave at the start of a piece of music, or at the beginning of a line, indicating the key it is to be played in.

key stage ▷ *noun, Brit education* any of the four age-based levels of the NATIONAL CURRICULUM.

keystone ▷ *noun* **1** *archit* the central supporting stone at the high point of an arch. **2** the chief element that everything else depends on, eg the central point in a theory or argument.

keystroke ▷ *noun* a single press of a key on a keyboard, etc.

keyword ▷ *noun* **1** a word that sums up or gives an indication of the nature of the passage in which it occurs. **2** *computing* a group of letters or numbers that is used to identify a database record.

KG ▷ *abbreviation* Knight of the Order of the Garter.

kg ▷ *abbreviation* **1** keg or kegs. **2** kilogram or kilograms; kilogramme or kilogrammes.

KGB ▷ *abbreviation*: *Komitet gosudarstvennoi bezopasnosti* (Russian), Committee of State Security, the former Soviet and then Russian secret police, superseded in Russia by the FSK and then the FSB. ◑ 1950s.

kGy ▷ *abbreviation* kilogray or kilograys.

khaddar /ˈkʌdə(r)/ and **khadi** /ˈkʌdɪ/ ▷ *noun* (***khaddars*** or ***khadis***) hand-spun, hand-woven cotton cloth, produced in India. ◑ 1920s: from Hindi *khadar*.

khaki /ˈkɑːkɪ/ ▷ *noun* (***khakis***) **1** a dull brownish-yellow or brownish-green colour. **2** **a** cloth of this colour; **b** military uniform made of such cloth. ◑ 19c: Urdu and Persian, meaning 'dusty'.

khalif see CALIPH

Khalsa /ˈkalsə/ ▷ *noun* the order of baptized Sikhs who wear THE FIVE K'S.

khamsin /ˈkamsɪn, kamˈsiːn/ ▷ *noun* a hot south or south-east wind in Egypt, which blows for about 50 days from mid-March. ◑ 17c: Arabic, meaning 'fifty'.

khan[1] /kɑːn/ ▷ *noun* an Eastern inn, especially a CARAVANSERAI. ◑ 14c: Arabic, from Persian.

khan[2] /kɑːn/ ▷ *noun* **1** the title of a ruler or prince in central Asia. **2** in ancient Persia: a governor. ◑ 14c: related to Turkish *kagan* ruler.

khanga see KANGA

khat see KAT

khedive /kəˈdiːv/ ▷ *noun, historical* the title of the viceroy of Egypt during Turkish rule from1867-1914. • **khediva** *noun* (***khedivas***) the wife of the viceroy. • **khedival** or **khedivial** *adj.* • **khedivate** or **khediviate** *noun* (***khedivates*** or ***khediviates***) **1** the office of the khedive. **2** the territory of the khedive. ⌚ 19c: from Persian *khidiw* a prince.

Khmer /kmɛə(r)/ ▻ *adj* belonging or relating to the Khmer region of SE Asia, or to Cambodia, a republic in SE Asia, or to their inhabitants, or their language. • ▻ *noun* **1** a citizen or inhabitant of, or person born in, the Khmer region or Cambodia. **2** the language spoken there. See also KAMPUCHEAN, CAMBODIAN. ⌚ 19c: the local name for this area and country.

Khmer Rouge /— ruːʒ/ ▻ *noun* the communist guerilla movement in Cambodia.

khutbah /'kʊtbɑː/ ▻ *noun* a Muslim prayer and sermon delivered in the mosques on Fridays. ⌚ 19c: Arabic, from *khataba* to preach.

kHz ▻ *abbreviation* kilohertz.

kiang /kɪ'aŋ/ ▻ *noun* a variety of wild ass found in Tibet and neighbouring regions. ⌚ 19c: from Tibetan *rkyang*.

kia ora /kɪə'ɔːrə/ ▻ *exclamation, NZ* used eg as a greeting: good health! ⌚ 19c: Maori.

kibble[1] /'kɪbəl/ ▻ *noun* a bucket on a chain or rope used in a well, or one used in mining, etc. ⌚ 17c: from German *Kübel* tub.

kibble[2] /'kɪbəl/ ▻ *verb* (***kibbled***, ***kibbling***) to grind (cereal, etc) fairly coarsely. ⌚ 18c.

kibbutz /kɪ'bʊts/ ▻ *noun* (*plural* ***kibbutzim*** /-'siːm/) in Israel: a communal farm or other concern owned and run jointly as a co-operative by its workers. • **kibbutznik** *noun* someone who lives and works on a kibbutz. ⌚ 1930s: from Modern Hebrew *kibbus* a gathering.

kibe /kaɪb/ ▻ *noun* a chilblain, especially one on the heel. ⌚ 14c.

kibitz /'kɪbɪts/ *slang* ▻ *verb* (***kibitzed***, ***kibitzing***) *intr* **1** to give unwanted advice; to comment out of turn. **2** to meddle. ⌚ 1920s: from Yiddish, from German *kiebitzen* to look on at cards.

kibitzer /'kɪbɪtsə(r)/ *N Amer slang* ▻ *noun* **1** an onlooker, eg at cards, etc, who gives unwanted advice. **2** someone who interferes or meddles. **3** someone who jokes and chats, etc while others are trying to work. ⌚ 1920s: see KIBITZ.

kiblah or **qibla** /'kɪblɑː/ ▻ *noun, Islam* the direction of Mecca, the point which Muslims turn towards in prayer. ⌚ 18c: from Arabic *qiblah*, from *qabala* to be opposite.

kibosh or **kybosh** /'kaɪbɒʃ/ *colloq* ▻ *noun* rubbish; nonsense. • **put the kibosh on something** to put an end to it; to ruin it. ⌚ 19c.

kick ▻ *verb* (***kicked***, ***kicking***) **1** to hit with the foot ▫ *The pony kicked the groom.* **2** to propel something with the foot ▫ *kicks the ball.* **3** *intr* to strike out or thrust with one or both feet, eg when swimming, fighting, struggling, etc. **4** *tr & intr*, especially in dancing: to jerk (the leg) vigorously or swing it high. **5** *intr* said of a gun, etc: to recoil when fired. **6** *intr* (*sometimes* **kick against something**) to resist it; to show opposition ▫ *kick against discipline.* **7** to get rid of (a habit, etc). **8** *rugby* to score (a drop goal) or make (a conversion) by kicking the ball between the posts. **9** *intr, athletics* to put on an extra spurt ▫ *She kicked 200 metres from the finish.* ▻ *noun* **1** a blow or fling with the foot. **2** *dancing, gymnastics, etc*: a swing of the leg ▫ *high kicks.* **3** *swimming* any of various leg movements. **4** the recoil of a gun, etc after firing. **5** *colloq* a thrill of excitement ▫ *He gets a kick out of watching his son race.* **6** power; pungency. **7** *colloq* the powerful effect of certain drugs or strong drink, which is sometimes felt quite suddenly or unexpectedly ▫ *That fruit punch has quite a kick.* **8** *athletics* an extra spurt of speed; a sudden acceleration. **9** *colloq* a brief enthusiasm ▫ *We're on a culture kick.* • **kicker** *noun* **1** someone or something that kicks ▫ *Watch out, that horse is a kicker!* **2** *sport, especially Amer Football* a player whose function is to take kicks, especially set-piece shots. • **alive and kicking** see under ALIVE. • **for kicks** for thrills. • **kick ass** *slang* **1** to act in a forceful or domineering way. **2** to have power or influence. • **kick in the teeth** *colloq* a humiliating snub. • **kick oneself** to reproach oneself ▫ *I could have kicked myself for being so tactless.* • **kick over the traces** to throw off control. • **kick someone in the teeth** *colloq* to inflict a snub on them. • **kick someone upstairs** *colloq* to promote them to a position of higher rank but less influence. • **kick the bucket** *colloq* to die. • **kick up a fuss, row** or **stink** *colloq* to complain or disapprove strongly and vociferously. ⌚ 14c as *kiken*.

■ **kick about** or **around** *colloq* **1** to lie around unused and neglected ▫ *The old set's kicking around in the attic.* **2** to be idle; to go about aimlessly ▫ *kicking about with his mates.*

■ **kick someone about** or **around** *colloq* to treat them badly or roughly.

■ **kick something about** or **around** *colloq* to discuss (an idea, etc) informally among several people.

■ **kick in** to take effect ▫ *As the effects of the pay freeze kick in commitment decreases.*

■ **kick off 1** to start, or restart, a football game by kicking the ball away from the centre. **2** *colloq* (*also* **kick something off**) to begin a discussion or other activity involving several people.

■ **kick something off** *colloq* to begin (a discussion, etc).

■ **kick someone** or **something out** *colloq* to dismiss or get rid of them or it, especially using force.

kickback ▻ *noun* **1** part of a sum of money received that is paid to someone else for help or favours already received or to come, especially if this is illegally given. **2** money paid in return for protection. **3** *horse-racing* loose material thrown up from the track by a galloping horse. **4** a strong reaction.

kick boxing ▻ *noun* a martial art in which the combatants kick with bare feet and punch with gloved fists.

kickdown ▻ *noun* a method of changing gear in a car with automatic transmission, by pressing the accelerator pedal right down.

kick-off ▻ *noun* (***kick-offs***) **1** the start or restart of a football match ▫ *Gates open 1pm, kick-off 2.30pm.* **2** the first kick in a game of football that starts, or restarts, the match. **3** *colloq* the start of anything. • **for a kick-off** *colloq* for a start.

kick pleat ▻ *noun* a small pleat at the back of a skirt, which allows ease of movement.

kickshaw /'kɪkʃɔː/ ▻ *singular noun* a trinket; a cheap article of no value. ⌚ 16c as *kick-shawes*: from French *quelque chose* something.

kickstand ▻ *noun* a metal device attached to a bicycle or motorcycle, etc, which is kicked down into position to hold the vehicle upright when it is parked.

kick-start ▻ *noun* **1** (*also* **kick-starter**) a pedal on a motorcycle that is kicked vigorously downwards to start the engine. **2** the starting of an engine with this pedal. ▻ *verb* (***kick-started***, ***kick-starting***) **1** to start (a motorcycle) using this pedal. **2** to get something moving; to give an advantageous, and sometimes sudden, impulse to something.

kickturn ▻ *noun, skiing, skateboarding* a turn through 180 degrees.

kid[1] ▻ *noun* **1** *colloq* a child; a young person. **2** a young goat, antelope or other related animal. **3** the smooth soft leather made from the skin of such an animal. Also called **kid leather** and **kidskin**. ▻ *adj, colloq* younger ▫ *my kid sister.* ▻ *verb* (***kidded***, ***kidding***) *intr* said of a goat, etc: to give birth to young. • **handle someone with kid gloves**

see under KID GLOVE. ◉ 13c as *kide*: related to Norse *kith* young goat.

kid[2] ▷ *verb* (***kidded, kidding***) *colloq* (*sometimes* **kid someone on** or **along**) **1** to fool or deceive them, especially light-heartedly or in fun. **2** *intr* to bluff; to pretend. **3** *tr & intr* to tease. • **kidder** *noun*. • **kiddingly** *adverb*. • **kid oneself** to fool oneself about something □ *kidding himself all was well.* See also KID-ON. ◉ 19c: perhaps from KID[1].

Kidderminster /ˈkɪdəmɪnstə(r)/ ▷ *noun* a two-ply or ingrain reversible carpet. ◉ 17c: named after Kidderminster, the town in Worcestershire in England where this type of carpet was originally made.

kiddie or **kiddy** /ˈkɪdɪ/ ▷ *noun* (***kiddies***) *colloq* a small child. ◉ 19c in this sense; 16c meaning 'a young goat': from KID[1].

kiddiewink or **kiddywink** and **kiddiewinkie** ▷ *noun, sometimes facetious* a small child. ◉ 1950s: from KIDDIE.

kiddush /ˈkɪdəʃ/ ▷ *noun* (***kiddushes***) a Jewish blessing pronounced over wine and bread by the head of the household to usher in the Sabbath and other holy days. ◉ 18c: from Hebrew *qiddush* sanctification.

kid glove ▷ *noun* **1** a glove made of kidskin. **2** *as adj* overcareful; delicate; extremely tactful □ *kid-glove treatment of the star.* • **handle someone with kid gloves** to treat them with special care or caution.

kid leather see under KID[1]

kidnap /ˈkɪdnap/ ▷ *verb* (***kidnapped, kidnapping***; *N Amer* ***kidnaped, kidnaping***) to seize and hold someone prisoner illegally, usually demanding a ransom for their release. • **kidnapper** *noun*. ◉ 17c: from KID[1] + obsolete *nap* to steal, originally used in the context of the practice of stealing children as forced labour.

kidney /ˈkɪdnɪ/ ▷ *noun* (***kidneys***) **1** *anatomy* in vertebrates: either of a pair of organs at the back of the abdomen whose function is the removal of waste products from the blood, and the excretion of such compounds from the body, usually in the form of urine. See also RENAL. **2** animal kidneys as food. ◉ 14c as *kidenei*.

kidney bean ▷ *noun* **1** any one of various varieties of common bean plant that produce dark-red kidney-shaped edible seeds. **2** the seed of one of these plants eaten as a vegetable.

kidney machine ▷ *noun, medicine* a machine that removes toxic waste products, by dialysis, from the blood of someone whose kidneys have failed to function properly.

kidney-shaped ▷ *adj* basically oval, but curved so that the long sides are respectively convex and concave.

kidney stone ▷ *noun* **1** *medicine* a CALCULUS (sense 2). **2** *geol* NEPHRITE.

kidology /kɪˈdɒlədʒɪ/ ▷ *noun, colloq* the art of deceiving or bluffing, sometimes used to gain a psychological advantage. • **kidologist** *noun*. ◉ 1960s: KID[2] + -OLOGY.

kid-on ▷ *noun* (***kid-ons***) *colloq* a pretence; a bluff; a hoax.

kids' stuff ▷ *noun, colloq* **1** something so simple, easy, etc that it is considered fit only for young children. **2** *derog* something which is really easy or tame.

kidvid /ˈkɪdvɪd/ ▷ *noun, slang* television or video entertainment for children. ◉ Formed from KID[1] + VIDEO.

kie kie /ˈkiːkiː/ ▷ *noun* a New Zealand climbing plant with edible bracts. ◉ 19c: Maori.

kieselguhr /ˈkiːzəlgʊə(r)/ ▷ *noun, geol* a soft whitish powdery deposit containing silica and composed mainly of the remains of cell walls of DIATOMS, used as an abrasive, filler and insulator, and as an absorbent material in dynamite. Also called **diatomite**. ◉ 19c: German, from *Kiesel* flint + *Guhr* fermentation.

kif see KEF

kike /kaɪk/ ▷ *noun, N Amer offensive slang* a Jew. ◉ Early 20c.

kiley see KYLIE[1]

kilim or **kelim** /kɪˈliːm/ ▷ *noun* a woven rug without any pile, traditionally made in the Middle East. ◉ 19c: Turkish, from Persian *kilim*.

kill ▷ *verb* (***killed, killing***) **1** *tr & intr* to cause the death of (an animal or person); to put someone to death; to murder; to slaughter; to destroy someone or something. **2** *colloq* to cause severe pain to someone □ *My feet are killing me.* **3** *colloq* to cause something to fail; to put an end to it □ *how to kill a conversation.* **4** to defeat (a parliamentary bill); to veto (a proposal). **5** *colloq* to cause something to stop; to turn off or switch off (lights, machinery, etc) □ *Kill the engine.* **6** *colloq* to destroy the effect of something □ *The turquoise kills the green.* **7** *colloq* to deaden (pain, noise, etc). **8** to pass (time), especially aimlessly or wastefully, while waiting for some later event □ *killing an hour in the pub before his train left.* **9** *colloq, especially ironic* to exhaust or put a strain on someone □ *Don't kill yourself doing unpaid overtime.* **10** *colloq* to overwhelm someone with admiration, amazement, laughter, etc. **11** *football* to bring (a loose ball) under control. **12** *squash, tennis, etc* to play (a shot) so hard that an opponent is unable to return it. ▷ *noun* **1** an act of killing. **2** the prey killed by any creature. **3** game killed. **4** an act of destroying an enemy plane, ship or tank, etc. **5** such an enemy target destroyed. • **killer** *noun* **1 a** a person or creature that kills; **b** *as adj* □ *killer bees.* **2** a habitual murderer. **3** *colloq* a gruelling task or activity. **4** *Austral & NZ colloq* an animal intended for slaughter. • **be in at the kill** *colloq* to be present at someone's dramatic downfall, or some other kind of confrontation or culmination. • **kill oneself** *colloq* to be reduced to helpless laughter. □ *It was so funny we were absolutely killing ourselves.* • **kill the fatted calf** to prepare an elaborate feast, etc for a homecoming or welcome. • **kill two birds with one stone** to accomplish two things by one action. ◉ 13c as *cullen* or *killen*.

■ **kill someone** or **something off 1** to destroy completely; to exterminate □ *The frost killed off most of the greenfly.* **2** said of an author, scriptwriter, etc: to write in the death of (a character).

killdeer /ˈkɪldɪə(r)/ ▷ *noun* (*plural* ***killdeer*** or ***killdeers***) the largest N American ring-necked plover. ◉ 18c: imitating its call.

killer whale ▷ *noun* a toothed whale, having a black body with white underparts and white patches on its head, and a narrow triangular dorsal fin similar to that of a shark. It feeds on marine mammals, fish and squid.

killick or **killock** /ˈkɪlək/ ▷ *noun* a small anchor, especially an improvised one made from a heavy stone. ◉ 17c.

killifish /ˈkɪlɪfɪʃ/ ▷ *noun zool* any of various species of small fish, resembling a minnow, found in fresh and brackish waters. Because it eats mosquito larvae, it is used in mosquito control. ◉ 19c: from US dialect *kill* a river.

killing ▷ *noun* an act of slaying. ▷ *adj, colloq* **1** exhausting. **2** highly amusing. **3** deadly; fatal. • **killingly** *adverb*. • **make a killing** *colloq* to make a large amount of money, especially unexpectedly or in a quick transaction.

killjoy ▷ *noun* (***killjoys***) someone who spoils the pleasure of others.

kiln ▷ *noun* a heated oven or furnace used for drying timber, grain or hops, or for firing bricks, pottery, etc. ▷ *verb* (***kilned, kilning***) to dry or fire something in a kiln. ◉ Anglo-Saxon *cyln*: from Latin *culina* kitchen.

kiln-dry ▷ *verb* to dry in a kiln.

Kilner jar /ˈkɪlnə —/ ▷ *noun, trademark* a glass jar with an airtight lid, used for preserving fruit and vegetables.

kilo /ˈkiːloʊ/ ▷ *noun* (***kilos***) (symbol **k**) **1** a KILOGRAM. **2** a KILOMETRE. **3** (**Kilo**) *communications* in the NATO alphabet:

the word used to denote the letter 'K' (see table at NATO ALPHABET).

kilo- /kɪloʊ, kiː-kɪ'loʊ/ ▷ *combining form* (abbreviation **K** or **k**) **1** one thousand □ ***kilogram***. **2** *computing* when describing storage capacity: 1 024 (2^{10}). In other contexts in computing it is used in sense 1. ◷ From French, introduced in France at the institution of the metric system (1795), ultimately from Greek *chilioi* thousand.

kilobar ▷ *noun* 1 000 bars (see BAR^{2}).

kilobit ▷ *noun, computing* 1 024 bits.

kilobyte ▷ *noun* (abbreviation **KB** or **kbyte** or **K**) *computing* a unit of memory equal to 1024 BYTES.

kilocalorie and **kilogram calorie** ▷ *noun* (abbreviation **kcal**) a metric unit of heat or energy equal to 1 000 calories, now replaced by the SI unit KILOJOULE.

kilocycle ▷ *noun* (abbreviation **kc**) *old use* a KILOHERTZ.

kilogram or **kilogramme** ▷ *noun* (abbreviation **kg**) in the SI system: the basic unit of mass, equal to 1 000 grams (2.205 lb).

kilogray ▷ *noun* (abbreviation **kGy**) *physics* 1 000 grays, an SI unit used to measure the absorbed dose of radiation, eg in food irradiation. ◷ 20c: see GRAY^{1}.

kilohertz ▷ *noun* (abbreviation **kHz**) (*plural* ***kilohertz***) an SI unit of frequency equal to 1 000 HERTZ or 1 000 cycles per second, used to measure the frequency of sound and radio waves. Formerly called KILOCYCLE.

kilojoule ▷ *noun* (abbreviation **kJ**) 1 000 joules, an SI unit used to measure energy, work and heat, replacing the metric unit KILOCALORIE (1 kj = 0.2388 kcal).

kilolitre ▷ *noun* (abbreviation **kl**) a metric unit of liquid measure equal to 1 000 litres.

kilometre or (*N Amer*) **kilometer** /kɪ'lɒmɪtə(r), 'kɪləmiːtə(r)/ ▷ *noun* (abbreviation **km**) a metric unit of length equal to 1 000 metres (0.62 miles). • **kilometric** /kɪlə'mɛtrɪk/ *adj*.

kiloton or **kilotonne** ▷ *noun* (abbreviation **kT**) a metric unit of explosive power equivalent to that of 1 000 tonnes of TNT.

kilovolt ▷ *noun* (abbreviation **kV**) SI unit: 1 000 volts.

kilowatt ▷ *noun* (abbreviation **kW**) an SI unit of electrical power equal to 1000 watts or about 1.34 horsepower.

kilowatt hour ▷ *noun* (abbreviation **kWh**) a commercial metric unit of electrical energy, based on the SI unit, the WATT, equal to the energy consumed when an electrical appliance with a power of one kilowatt operates for one hour. This is the unit by which the electricity supply industry charges consumers.

kilt ▷ *noun* **1** a pleated tartan knee-length wraparound skirt, traditionally worn by men as part of Scottish Highland dress. **2** any similar garment. ▷ *verb* (***kilted, kilting***) **1** to pleat something vertically. **2** to tuck (skirts) up. • **kilted** *adj* **1** wearing a kilt. **2** vertically pleated. **3** said of skirts: tucked up. ◷ 14c as *verb*, 18c as *noun*: related to Danish *kilte* to tuck up.

kilter /'kɪltə(r)/ and **kelter** /'kɛltə(r)/ ▷ *noun* good condition. • **out of kilter** out of order; not working properly; out of condition. ◷ 17c.

kiltie or **kilty** ▷ *noun* (***kilties***) *colloq* a person wearing a KILT, especially a soldier in a Highland Regiment.

kimberlite /'kɪmbəlaɪt/ ▷ *noun, geol* a rare igneous rock, occurring chiefly in S Africa and Siberia, that often contains, and is mined for, diamonds. ◷ 19c: named after the S African city Kimberley.

kimchi /'kɪmtʃɪ/ ▷ *noun, cookery* a very spicy Korean dish made with a variety of raw vegetables. ◷ 19c: Korean.

kimono /kɪ'moʊnoʊ/ ▷ *noun* (***kimonos***) **1** a long, loose, wide-sleeved Japanese garment fastened by a sash at the waist. **2** a dressing-gown, etc, imitating this in style. ◷ 19c: Japanese, meaning 'clothing'.

kin ▷ *noun* **1** one's relatives. **2** people belonging to the same family. ▷ *adj* related □ ***kin to the duke***. ◷ Anglo-Saxon *cynn*.

-kin ▷ *suffix, indicating* a diminutive □ ***lambkin***. ◷ Used in proper names from 13c; in general use from 14c: from Dutch.

kinaesthesia or (*N Amer*) **kinesthesia** /kɪnɪs'θiːzɪə/ and **kinaesthesis** or (*N Amer*) **kinesthesis** ▷ *noun, medicine* the process whereby the relative positions and movements of the different parts of the body are perceived by sensory cells in muscles, tendons and joints. • **kinaesthetic** or (*N Amer*) **kinesthetic** *adj*. ◷ 19c: from Greek *kineein* to move + *aisthesis* sensation.

kind^{1} /kaɪnd/ ▷ *noun* **1** a group, class, sort, race or type. **2** a particular variety or a specimen belonging to a specific variety. **3** nature, character or distinguishing quality □ ***differ in kind***. • **a kind of ...** something like a ... □ ***a kind of magazine***. • **after its kind** according to its nature. • **in kind 1** said of payment: in goods instead of money. **2** said of repayment or retaliation: in the same form as the treatment received. • **kind of** or **kinda** *colloq* somewhat; slightly □ ***kind of old-fashioned***. • **nothing of the kind** not at all; completely the reverse. • **of a kind 1** of the same sort □ ***three of a kind***. **2** of doubtful worth □ ***an explanation of a kind***. ◷ Anglo-Saxon *gecynd* nature.

> ***kind***
>
> • Like **sort**, **kind** gives rise to a usage difficulty when it is followed by *of* with a plural noun and needs to be preceded by a demonstrative pronoun **this, that, these, those.** The grammatical sequences in use are as follows:
>
> **?** *I think these kind of comments are most unfair.*
>
> ✓ *This kind of component is much smaller and more reliable than a valve.*
>
> ✓ *Those are the kinds of assumptions (or assumption) being made.*
>
> • The first is sometimes rejected by language purists, but it is common especially in speech.
>
> ☆ RECOMMENDATION: to avoid difficulty, use **this kind of** + singular noun, or **these kinds of** + singular or plural noun.

kind^{2} /kaɪnd/ ▷ *adj* (***kinder, kindest***) **1** friendly, helpful, well-meaning, generous, benevolent or considerate. **2** warm; cordial □ ***kind regards***. • **kindness** *noun*. • **be so kind as to ...** or **be kind enough to ...** a polite formula of request for someone to do a specified thing. ◷ Anglo-Saxon *gecynde* in obsolete sense 'natural'.

kinda see under KIND^{1}

kindergarten /'kɪndəgɑːtən/ ▷ *noun* a school for young children, usually those aged between 4 and 6. ◷ 19c: German, literally 'children's garden'.

kind-hearted ▷ *adj* kind; generous; good-natured. • **kind-heartedly** *adverb*. • **kind-heartedness** *noun*.

kindle /'kɪndəl/ ▷ *verb* (***kindled, kindling***) *tr & intr* **1** to start or make something, etc start burning. **2** said of feelings: to stir or be stirred. • **kindler** *noun*. • **kindling** *noun* **1** materials for starting a fire, eg dry twigs or leaves, sticks, etc. **2** the act of causing something to burn. ◷ 13c: related to Norse *kyndill* torch.

kindly /'kaɪndlɪ/ ▷ *adverb* **1** in a kind manner □ ***She kindly offered me a lift***. **2** please □ ***Kindly remove your feet from the desk***. ▷ *adj* (***kindlier, kindliest***) kind, friendly, generous or good-natured. • **kindliness** *noun*. • **look kindly on someone** or **something** to approve of them or it. • **not take kindly to something** to be unwilling to put up with it. • **think kindly of someone** or **something** to have a good opinion of them or it.

kindness see under KIND²

kindred /ˈkɪndrəd/ ▷ *noun* **1** one's relatives; family. **2** relationship by blood or, less properly, by marriage. ▷ *adj* **1** related. **2** having qualities in common □ *kindred arts.* ⓒ Anglo-Saxon *cynred.*

kindred spirit ▷ *noun* someone who shares one's tastes, opinions, etc.

kindy /ˈkɪndɪ/ ▷ *noun* (***kindies***) *Austral & NZ* a kindergarten.

kine /kaɪn/ ▷ *plural noun, old use, especially Bible* cattle. ⓒ Anglo-Saxon *cyna* of cows.

kinematics /kɪnɪˈmatɪks, kaɪ-/ ▷ *singular noun, physics* the branch of mechanics concerned with the motion of objects, without consideration of the forces acting on them. • **kinematic** or **kinematical** *adj.* ⓒ 19c: from Greek *kinema* movement.

kinesics /kɪˈniːsɪks, kaɪ-/ ▷ *singular noun* **1** body movements which convey information in the absence of speech, eg frowning, winking. **2** the study of visual body language as communication. ⓒ 1950s: from Greek *kinesis* movement.

kinesiology /kɪniːsɪˈɒlədʒɪ/ ▷ *noun* the scientific study of the mechanics of human movement. • **kinesiologist** *noun.* ⓒ 19c: from Greek *kinesis* movement.

kinesis /kɪˈniːsɪs, kaɪ-/ ▷ *noun, zool* the movement of a living organism or cell in response to a simple stimulus (eg light or humidity), the rate of movement being dependent on the intensity as opposed to the direction of the stimulus. ⓒ Early 20c: Greek, meaning 'movement'.

kinesthesia, **kinesthesis** and **kinesthetic** see KINAESTHESIA

kinetic /kɪˈnɛtɪk, kaɪ-/ ▷ *adj* **1** *physics* relating to or producing motion. **2** *chem* relating to the speed of chemical reactions. • **kinetically** *adverb.* ⓒ 19c: from Greek *kinetikos*, from *kineein* to move.

kinetic art and **kinetic sculpture** ▷ *noun* art and sculpture which has movement (produced by air currents, electricity, etc) as an essential feature.

kinetic energy ▷ *noun* (abbreviation **KE**) the energy that an object possesses because of its motion.

kinetics /kɪˈnɛtɪks, kaɪ-/ ▷ *singular noun* **1** *physics* the branch of MECHANICS concerned with the relationship between moving objects, their masses and the forces acting on them. **2** *chem* the scientific study of the rates of chemical reactions. ⓒ 19c: from KINETIC.

kinetic theory ▷ *noun, physics* a theory which attempts to account for the physical properties of matter, especially gases, in terms of the movement of the atoms or molecules of which they are composed.

kinfolk and **kinfolks** see KINSFOLK

king ▷ *noun* **1** a male ruler of a nation, especially a hereditary monarch. **2** a ruler or chief. **3** a creature considered supreme in strength, ferocity, etc □ *the lion, king of beasts.* **4** *especially as adj* a large, or the largest, variety of something □ *king penguins* □ *king prawns.* **5** a leading or dominant figure in a specified field, eg a wealthy manufacturer or dealer □ *the diamond king.* **6** *cards* the court card bearing a picture of a king. **7** *chess* the most important piece, which must be protected from checkmate. **8** *draughts* a piece that, having crossed the board safely, has been crowned (see CROWN *verb* 6), and may move both forwards and backwards. • **kingless** *adj.* • **kingship** *noun* the state, office or dignity of a king. • **king it** to act as if superior to, or in authority over, others. • **live like a king** *colloq* to live in great luxury. ⓒ Anglo-Saxon *cyning.*

kingbird ▷ *noun* any one of several American FLYCATCHERS.

King Charles spaniel ▷ *noun* a small active dog with a black and tan coat, short legs and long silky ears. ⓒ 19c: so called because it was made popular by Charles II.

king cobra ▷ *noun, zool* the world's largest venomous snake, up to 5.5m in length, native to India and SE Asia, and found in forests, especially near water, where it feeds on snakes and monitor lizards. Also called **hamadryad**. ⓒ 19c.

king crab ▷ *noun, zool* a HORSESHOE CRAB.

kingcup ▷ *noun* the common name for any of various plants with yellow flowers, especially the MARSH MARIGOLD or the BUTTERCUP.

kingdom /ˈkɪŋdəm/ ▷ *noun* **1** a region, state or people ruled, or previously ruled, by a king or queen. **2** *biol* in taxonomy: any of the divisions (usually reckoned as five) corresponding to the highest rank in the classification of plants and animals, eg *Animalia* (animals) or *Fungi* (fungi). **3** the domain of, or area associated with, something □ *the kingdom of the imagination.* • **to** or **till kingdom come** *colloq* **1** into the next world □ *blow them all to kingdom come.* **2** until the coming of the next world; for ever □ *wait till kingdom come.* ⓒ Anglo-Saxon *cyningdom.*

kingfish ▷ *noun* **1** the OPAH. **2** *Austral, N Amer* any of various fish notable for their size or value.

kingfisher ▷ *noun* any one of a large family of brightly coloured birds with long pointed bills and short wings. They live by water and are adept at diving for fish, etc. See also HALCYON. ⓒ 15c, originally as *kyngys fyschare.*

King James Bible and **King James Version** see under AUTHORIZED VERSION

kingly ▷ *adj* (***kinglier***, ***kingliest***) belonging to, or suitable for, a king; royal; kinglike. Also *as adverb.* • **kingliness** *noun.*

kingmaker ▷ *noun* someone who has influence over the choice of people for high office.

king of arms and **king at arms** ▷ *noun* the most senior rank in heraldry; the chief herald.

king of the castle ▷ *noun* the most important and powerful person in a particular group. ⓒ 19c: from a children's game where the aim is to achieve and hold the highest position.

king penguin ▷ *noun* a large penguin, smaller than the EMPEROR PENGUIN.

kingpin ▷ *noun* **1** the most important person in an organization, team, etc. **2** *mech* a bolt serving as a pivot. **3** the tallest or most prominently placed pin, such as the front pin in the triangular arrangement in TENPIN BOWLING.

king post ▷ *noun, archit* a perpendicular beam in the frame of a roof, rising from the TIE BEAM to the RIDGE.

king prawn ▷ *noun* a large prawn, especially one of a variety found around Australia.

Kings ▷ *noun, Bible* the title of two historical books of the Old Testament. See table at BIBLE.

King's Bench see QUEEN'S BENCH

King's Counsel see QUEEN'S COUNSEL

King's English see QUEEN'S ENGLISH

King's evidence see QUEEN'S EVIDENCE

King's evil ▷ *noun, old use* SCROFULA, formerly believed to be curable by the touch of a monarch.

King's Guide see QUEEN'S GUIDE

King's highway see QUEEN'S HIGHWAY

kingship see under KING

king-size and **king-sized** ▷ *adj* of a large or larger-than-standard size.

King's Scout see QUEEN'S SCOUT

King's Speech see QUEEN'S SPEECH

kinin /ˈkaɪnɪn/ ▷ *noun* **1** *physiol* any of a group of PEPTIDES, found in blood, that are associated with inflammation (eg as a result of insect stings), and cause contraction of smooth muscles, dilation of blood vessels, and an increase in the permeability of capillaries. **2** *bot* any of a group of plant growth substances that stimulate cell division. Also called **cytokinin**. ◎ 1950s: from Greek *kinesis* movement.

kink ▷ *noun* **1** a bend or twist in hair or in a string, rope, wire, etc. **2** *colloq* an oddness of personality; an eccentricity, especially a strange sexual preference. **3** a crick in the neck or a similar spasm affecting a muscle. **4** an imperfection; a minor difficulty. ▷ *verb* (***kinked, kinking***) *tr & intr* to develop, or cause something to develop, a kink □ *Flow stopped due to the hose kinking.* ◎ 17c: probably Dutch, meaning 'a twist in a rope'.

kinkajou /'kɪŋkədʒuː/ ▷ *noun* (***kinkajous***) *zool* a nocturnal fruit-eating mammal of Central and S America, which has a rounded head, slender body, yellowish-brown fur and a long prehensile tail. Also called **honey bear**. ◎ 18c: from French *quincajou*, from Algonquian *kwingwaage* the wolverine.

kinky ▷ *adj* (***kinkier, kinkiest***) **1** *colloq* interested in or practising unusual or perverted sexual acts. **2** *colloq* said of clothing, etc: out of the ordinary in an attractive and often provocative way □ *kinky boots and a mini skirt.* **3** *colloq* eccentric; crazy. **4** said of cable, etc: twisted; in loops. **5** said of hair: curling. • **kinkiness** *noun*. ◎ 19c: from KINK.

kino /'kiːnoʊ/ ▷ *noun* (***kinos***) a resin exuded by various tropical trees, used as an astringent and in tanning. ◎ 18c: W African.

kinsfolk /'kɪnzfoʊk/ and (*N Amer*) **kinfolk** and **kinfolks** ▷ *plural noun* one's relations.

kinship ▷ *noun* **1** family relationship. **2** a state of having common properties or characteristics.

kinsman /'kɪnzmən/ and **kinswoman** ▷ *noun* a relative by blood or marriage.

kiosk /'kiːɒsk/ ▷ *noun* **1** a small, roofed and sometimes movable booth or stall for the sale of sweets, newspapers, etc. **2** a public telephone box. ◎ 17c: from French *kiosque* a stand in a public park, from Turkish *köşk* pavilion.

kip¹ ▷ *noun* **1** sleep or a sleep. **2** somewhere to sleep; a bed. ▷ *verb* (***kipped, kipping***) *intr* **1** to sleep. **2** (*also* **kip down**) to go to bed; to doss down. ◎ 18c: from Danish *kippe* a hovel.

kip² ▷ *noun* the skin of a young animal, especially a calf or lamb. ◎ 16c.

kip³ ▷ *noun, Austral* a small thin piece of wood used in the game of TWO-UP for spinning coins. ◎ 19c.

kipper /'kɪpə(r)/ ▷ *noun* **1** a fish, especially a herring, that has been split open, salted and smoked. **2** a male salmon during the spawning season. ▷ *verb* (***kippered, kippering***) to cure (herring, etc) by salting and smoking. ◎ Anglo-Saxon *cypera* spawning salmon.

kipskin ▷ *noun* **1** a kip (see KIP²). **2** leather made from the skin of young cattle.

kir /kɪə(r)/ ▷ *noun* a drink made from white wine and CASSIS. ◎ 1960s: named after the mayor of Dijon, Canon F Kir (1876–1968), who is credited with inventing it.

Kirbigrip (*trademark*) or **kirbigrip** or **kirby grip** /'kɜːbɪgrɪp/ ▷ *noun* a type of hairgrip with one straight side and the other bent into ridges to prevent slipping. Also (*colloq*) called **kirby** (***kirbies***). ◎ 1920s: named after Kirby, one of the original manufacturers, Kirby, Beard & Co. Ltd.

kirk /kɜːk; *Scottish* kɪrk/ *Scottish* ▷ *noun* **1** a church. **2** (**the Kirk**) the Church of Scotland. ▷ *verb* (***kirked, kirking***) to bring (a newly delivered mother, members of a newly appointed civic authority, etc) to church for special ceremonies. • **kirking** *noun*. ◎ Anglo-Saxon *kirke*, from Norse *kirkja*.

kirk session ▷ *noun* the lowest court of the Presbyterian Church, which is the governing body of a congregation, and consists of the minister and elders.

kirmess see KERMIS

kirpan /kɪə'pɑːn/ ▷ *noun* a small sword or dagger worn by Sikh men as a symbol of religious loyalty, one of THE FIVE K'S. ◎ 20c: Punjabi.

kirsch /kɪəʃ/ and **kirschwasser** /'kɪəʃvasə(r)/ ▷ *noun* a clear liqueur distilled from black cherries. ◎ 19c: German *Kirschwasser* cherry water.

kismet /'kɪzmet, 'kɪsmɛt/ ▷ *noun* **1** *Islam* the will of Allah. **2** fate or destiny. ◎ 19c: from Turkish *qismet* portion, lot or fate.

kiss ▷ *verb* (***kissed, kissing***) **1** to touch someone with the lips, or to press one's lips against them, as a greeting, sign of affection, etc. **2** *intr* to kiss one another on the lips. **3** to express something by kissing □ *kissed them goodbye.* **4** *intr* said of billiard or snooker balls: to touch each other gently while moving. ▷ *noun* (***kisses***) **1** an act of kissing. **2** a gentle touch. • **kissable** *adj*. • **kisser** *noun* **1** (*usually* with preceding *adj*) a person who kisses in a specified way □ *a good kisser* □ *a sloppy kisser.* **2** *slang* the mouth or face. • **kiss and tell** *colloq* to give an account of sexual exploits to a newspaper, etc, especially when these involve a celebrity. See also separate entry KISS-AND-TELL. • **kiss hands** to kiss the sovereign's hands on acceptance of high office. • **kiss my arse!** an exclamation used to express contempt or to reject or dismiss someone or something out of hand □ *You expect me to forgive you? Well, you can kiss my arse!* • **kiss someone's arse** *slang* to curry favour with them. • **kiss the dust** to be overthrown, humiliated, etc. • **kiss and make up** to be mutually forgiving and so become reconciled. • **kiss something better** to show loving sympathy towards someone's physical or emotional injury □ *Mummy, kiss my sore knee better.* • **kiss something goodbye** or **kiss goodbye to something** to lose the chance of having it, especially through folly, mismanagement, etc □ *guess we can kiss goodbye to a holiday this year.* ◎ Anglo-Saxon *cyssan*.

kissagram see KISSOGRAM

kiss-and-tell ▷ *adj* said of an interview or article, especially in a tabloid newspaper: publicizing the sexual experiences of a person. See also KISS AND TELL at KISS.

kiss curl ▷ *noun* a flat curl of hair pressed against the cheek or forehead.

kisser see under KISS

kissing gate ▷ *noun* a gate set in a U- or V-shaped frame, allowing only one person at a time to pass through.

kiss of death ▷ *noun, colloq* someone or something that brings failure or ruin on some enterprise; a fatal move.

kiss of life ▷ *noun* **1** MOUTH-TO-MOUTH. *Technical equivalent* ARTIFICIAL RESPIRATION. **2** a means of restoring vitality or vigour.

kissogram or **kissagram** ▷ *noun* **1** a fun greetings service that involves employing someone to deliver a kiss to someone else on a special occasion. **2** the kiss or greeting delivered in this way. **3** (*also* kissogram girl or man) someone whose job is to deliver such a greeting, usually wearing fancy dress. ◎ 20c: from KISS, modelled on TELEGRAM.

kit¹ ▷ *noun* **1** a set of instruments, equipment, etc needed for a purpose, especially one kept in a container. **2** a set of special clothing and personal equipment, eg for a soldier, footballer, etc. **3 a** a set of parts ready for assembling □ *building a car from a kit;* **b** *as adj* □ *kit car.* ▷ *verb* (***kitted, kitting***) (*also* **kit someone out**) to provide someone with the clothes and equipment necessary for a particular occupation, assignment, etc. • **get one's kit off** *slang* to remove one's clothes, especially prior to sexual intercourse. ◎ 18c; 14c in obsolete sense 'a circular wooden vessel': from Dutch *kitte* tankard.

kit² ▻ *noun* **1** a kitten. **2** the young of various smaller fur-bearing animals, eg the polecat, ferret and fox. ⓒ 16c: shortened form of KITTEN.

kitbag ▻ *noun* a soldier's or sailor's bag, usually cylinder-shaped and made of canvas, for holding kit.

kitchen /ˈkɪtʃən/ ▻ *noun* a room or an area in a building where food is prepared and cooked. Also *as adj* □ *kitchen knife*. • **everything but the kitchen sink** everything possible, especially including unnecessary or useless items. ⓒ Anglo-Saxon *cycene*, from Latin *coquina* from *coquere* to cook.

kitchen cabinet ▻ *noun* an apparently influential, but informal, unelected group of advisers to someone who holds high political office. ⓒ 19c: US; see CABINET (*noun* 3).

kitchenette ▻ *noun* a small kitchen, or a section of a room serving as a kitchen. ⓒ Early 20c.

kitchen garden ▻ *noun* a garden, or a section of one, where vegetables, and sometimes fruit, are grown.

kitchen-sink ▻ *adj* said of plays, etc: dealing with dull or sordid real-life situations. ⓒ 1950s.

kitchen tea ▻ *noun, Austral, NZ* a party held for a bride before her wedding, when the guests bring gifts of kitchen equipment.

kitchen unit ▻ *noun* one of a set of fitted kitchen cupboards.

kitchenware ▻ *noun* pots and pans, cutlery and utensils, etc, that are used in kitchens.

kite ▻ *noun* **1** a bird of prey of the hawk family, noted for its long pointed wings, deeply forked tail, and soaring graceful flight. **2** a light frame covered in paper or some other light material, with a long holding string attached to it, for flying in the air for fun, etc. **3** (*also* **box kite**) a more complicated structure built of boxes, sometimes used for carrying recording equipment or a person in the air. **4** *naut* a light additional sail, usually set high up. **5** *slang* an aircraft. ▻ *verb* (***kited, kiting***) **1** *colloq* to write (a cheque) before one has sufficient funds in one's account to cover it. 2 *intr* to fly like a kite; to soar. • **kiting** *noun*. • **fly a kite** **1** to send up and control a kite. **2** *finance* to deal in fictitious accommodation papers in order to raise money. **3** to spread a rumour or suggestion intended to provoke reaction and so test public opinion. ⓒ Anglo-Saxon *cyta*.

kite-balloon ▻ *noun* a weather observation balloon for measuring atmospheric pressure.

kite flying ▻ *noun* the act of flying a kite (see FLY A KITE at KITE).

Kite mark or **kite mark** ▻ *noun, Brit* a kite-shaped mark indicating that a manufactured item meets the specifications of the British Standards Institution.

kith ▻ *noun* friends. • **kith and kin** friends and relations. ⓒ Anglo-Saxon *cythth*, from *cunnan* to know.

kitsch /kɪtʃ/ ▻ *noun* sentimental, pretentious or vulgar tastelessness in art, design, writing, film-making, etc. Also *as adj*. • **kitschy** *adj* (***kitschier, kitschiest***). ⓒ 1920: German, from *kitschen* to throw (a work of art together).

kitten /ˈkɪtən/ ▻ *noun* **1** a young cat. **2** the young of various other small mammals, eg the rabbit. ▻ *verb* (***kittened, kittening***) *tr & intr* said of a cat: to give birth. • **kittenish** *adj* **1** like a kitten; playful. **2** said of a woman: affectedly playful; flirtatious. • **have kittens** *colloq* to become extremely agitated. ⓒ 14c: from Norman French *caton*, diminutive of *cat*.

kittiwake /ˈkɪtɪweɪk/ ▻ *noun* either of two species of gull found on open water far from shore, especially that found in Arctic and N Atlantic coastal regions, which has white plumage with dark-grey back and wings, a yellow bill and black legs. ⓒ 17c: imitating its cry.

kitty¹ /ˈkɪtɪ/ ▻ *noun* (***kitties***) **1** a fund contributed to jointly, for communal use by a group of people. **2** *cards* a pool of money used in certain games. **3** *bowls* the jack. ⓒ 19c.

kitty² /ˈkɪtɪ/ ▻ *noun* an affectionate name for a cat or kitten.

kiwi /ˈkiːwiː/ ▻ *noun* (***kiwis***) **1** a nocturnal flightless bird with hair-like brown or grey feathers, a long slender bill and no tail, found only in pine forests in New Zealand and used as its national emblem. **2** *colloq* a New Zealander. **3** *colloq* a kiwi fruit. ⓒ 19c: Maori.

kiwi fruit ▻ *noun* an oval edible fruit with pale-green juicy flesh studded with small hard black seeds and enclosed by a brown hairy skin, produced by a climbing plant native to China. Also called **Chinese gooseberry**. ⓒ 1960s: so called because the fruit was exported to Europe, etc from New Zealand.

kJ ▻ *abbreviation* kilojoule or kilojoules.

KKK ▻ *abbreviation* Ku Klux Klan.

kl ▻ *abbreviation* kilolitre or kilolitres.

the Klan and **Klansman** see under KU KLUX KLAN

klaxon /ˈklaksən/ ▻ *noun* a loud horn used as a warning signal on ambulances, fire engines, etc. ⓒ Early 20c: originally a tradename for a type of hooter on early cars.

Klebsiella /ˈklɛbzɪɛlə, klɛbzɪˈɛlə/ ▻ *noun, pathol* a genus of GRAM-NEGATIVE rodlike bacteria which cause various diseases, including pneumonia, in humans and animals. ⓒ 1920s: named after the German pathologist E Klebs (1834–1913).

Kleenex /ˈkliːnɛks/ ▻ *noun* (***Kleenex*** or ***Kleenexes***) *trademark* a kind of soft paper tissue used as a handkerchief. ⓒ 1920s.

Klein bottle ▻ *noun, math* a one-sided four-dimensional surface, which in three dimensions can be represented as a surface obtained by pulling the narrow end of a tapering tube over the wall of the tube and then stretching the narrow end and joining it to the larger end. ⓒ 1940s: named after Felix Klein (1849–1925), German mathematician.

kleptomania /klɛptoʊˈmeɪnɪə/ ▻ *noun* an irresistible urge to steal, especially objects that are not desired for themselves and are of little monetary value. • **kleptomaniac** *noun, adj*. ⓒ 19c: from Greek *kleptein* to steal + -MANIA.

klezmer /ˈklɛzmə(r)/ ▻ *noun, music* traditional E European Yiddish music, revived in the 1980s with a jazz influence.

Klieg light or **klieg light** /kliːg —/ ▻ *noun* an intense type of floodlight used in film studios, etc. ⓒ 1920s: named after the German-born American brothers J H (1869–1959) and A (1872–1927) Kliegl, the inventors.

klipspringer /ˈklɪpsprɪŋə(r)/ ▻ *noun, zool* a dwarf antelope native to African scrubland south of the Sahara. It has a thick yellowish-grey speckled coat, short vertical horns, rounded ears with dark radiating lines and black feet. ⓒ 18c: Afrikaans, from Dutch *klip* rock + *springer* jumper.

KLM ▻ *abbreviation: Koninklijke Luchtvaart Maatschappij* (Dutch), Royal Dutch Airlines.

Klondike or **Klondyke** /ˈklɒndaɪk/ ▻ *noun* a very rich source of wealth. ▻ *verb* (***klondiked, klondiking***) *tr & intr* **1** to export (fresh fish, especially herring) direct from Scotland to Europe, etc. **2** to tranship (fish) at sea. • **klondyker** or **klondiker** *noun* a factory ship. ⓒ 19c: so called because of the gold rush to the Klondike region in the Yukon, US beginning 1896.

kloof /kluːf/ ▻ *noun, S Afr* a mountain ravine or pass. ⓒ 18c: Afrikaans, from Dutch *clove* a cleft.

kludge /klʌdʒ, kluːdʒ/ ▻ *noun, computing, colloq* a botched or makeshift device or program which is unreliable or inadequate in function. ⓒ 1960s.

klutz /klʌts/ ▻ *noun* (*klutzes*) *US slang* an idiot; an awkward, stupid person. • **klutzy** *adj* (*klutzier, klutziest*). ⓒ 1960s: Yiddish, from German *Klotz* meaning 'a block of wood'.

klystron /ˈklaɪstrɒn/ ▻ *noun, electronics* an evacuated ELECTRON TUBE used to generate or amplify microwaves. ⓒ 1930s: from Greek *klyzein* to washover + -TRON.

KM ▻ *abbreviation* Knight of Malta.

km ▻ *abbreviation* kilometre, or kilometres.

K-meson see under KAON

km/h ▻ *abbreviation* kilometres per hour.

kn ▻ *abbreviation, naut* knot (see KNOT[1] *noun* 11).

knack /nak/ ▻ *noun* **1** the ability to do something effectively and skilfully. **2** a habit or tendency, especially an intuitive or unconscious one. ⓒ 14c: probably related to obsolete *knack* a sharp blow or sound.

knacker /ˈnakə(r)/ ▻ *noun* **1** a buyer of worn-out old horses for slaughter. **2** someone who buys and breaks up old houses, ships, etc. ▻ *verb* (*knackered, knackering*) *colloq* **1** to exhaust □ *I was knackered after the climb.* **2** to break or wear out □ *These batteries are knackered.* ⓒ 16c.

knacker's yard ▻ *noun* **1** a slaughterhouse dealing with horses. **2** colloq destruction; the end; the scrap heap.

knackwurst /ˈnakwɜːst/ and **knockwurst** /ˈnɒk-/ ▻ *noun* a variety of highly seasoned sausage. ⓒ 1930s: German, from *knacken* to crack + *Wurst* a sausage.

knag /nag/ ▻ *noun* **1** a knot in wood. **2** a peg. • **knaggy** *adj* (*knaggier, knaggiest*) **1** knotty. **2** rugged. ⓒ 15c as *knagge*.

knapsack /ˈnapsak/ ▻ *noun* a hiker's or traveller's bag for food, clothes, etc, traditionally made of canvas or leather, carried on the back or over the shoulder. ⓒ 17c: from German *knappen* eat + *sack* bag.

knapweed /ˈnapwiːd/ ▻ *noun* a perennial plant native to Europe, with tough stems, toothed basal leaves with shallow lobes,untoothed stem leaves, and hard knob-like reddish-purple flower heads. ⓒ 15c as *knopwed*.

knar /nɑː(r)/ ▻ *noun* a knot on a tree. • **knarred** gnarled; knotty. ⓒ 14c: from German *kuarren*, from Dutch *knar* a stump.

knave /neɪv/ ▻ *noun old use* **1** *cards* the JACK. **2** a mischievous young man; a scoundrel. • **knavery** *noun* mischief; trickery. • **knavish** *adj*. ⓒ Anglo-Saxon *cnafa* a boy or youth.

knead /niːd/ ▻ *verb* (*kneaded, kneading*) **1** to work (dough) with one's fingers and knuckles into a uniform mass. **2** to massage (flesh) with firm finger-movements. • **kneader** *noun*. ⓒ Anglo-Saxon *cnedan*.

knee /niː/ ▻ *noun* (*knees*) **1** in humans: the joint in the middle of the leg where the lower end of the FEMUR articulates with the upper end of the TIBIA. **2 a** the corresponding joint in the hindlimb of other vertebrates; **b** in a horse's foreleg: the joint corresponding to the wrist. **3** the area surrounding this joint. Also *as adj* and *in compounds* □ *knee-length*. **4** the lap □ *sat with the child on her knee*. **5** the part of a garment covering the knee □ *patches on the knee and elbow*. **6** something which resembles the knee in action or shape. **7** *bot* a root upgrowth that trees growing in swamps breathe through. ▻ *verb* (*kneed, kneeing*) **1** to hit, nudge or shove someone or something with the knee. **2** to make (clothing) baggy at the knee. • **kneed** or **knee'd** *adj* **1** said of trousers: baggy at the knees. **2** having knees or angular joints. • **at one's mother's knee** said of truths, lessons, etc: (first learnt, heard, etc) when one was very young. • **bend** or **bow the knee** *formal or literary* to kneel; to submit. • **bring someone their knees** to defeat, prostrate, humiliate or ruin them utterly. • **go weak at the knees** *colloq* to be overcome by emotion. • **on one's knees** **1** kneeling. **2** exhausted. **3** begging. ⓒ Anglo-Saxon *cneow*.

knee-breeches ▻ *plural noun* breeches extending to just below the knee.

kneecap ▻ *noun* (*also* **kneepan**) a small plate of bone situated in front of and protecting the knee joint in humans and most other mammals. Also called PATELLA. ▻ *verb* to shoot or otherwise damage someone's kneecaps as a form of revenge, torture or unofficial punishment. • **kneecapping** *noun*.

knee-deep ▻ *adj, adverb* **1** rising or reaching to someone's knees □ *The pond is only knee-deep.* **2** sunk to the knees □ *standing knee-deep in mud.* **3** deeply involved.

knee-high ▻ *adj* rising or reaching to the knees □ *knee-high grass.* • **knee-high to a grasshopper** **1** very young. **2** very small.

kneehole ▻ *noun* the space beneath a desk, etc for one's knees.

knee-jerk ▻ *noun* an involuntary kick of the lower leg, caused by a reflex response when the tendon just below the kneecap is tapped sharply. ▻ *adj* said of a response or reaction: automatic; unthinking; predictable.

knee joint ▻ *noun* **1** the joint of the knee. **2** *carpentry, etc* a joint with two pieces at an angle, so as to be very tight when pressed into a straight line.

kneel /niːl/ ▻ *verb* (*knelt* or *kneeled, kneeling*) *intr* (*often* **kneel down**) to support one's weight on, or lower oneself onto, one's knees. • **kneeler** *noun* **1** a cushion for kneeling on, especially in church. **2** someone who is kneeling. ⓒ Anglo-Saxon *cneowlian*.

knee-length ▻ *adj* coming down or up as far as the knees □ *knee-length skirt* □ *knee-length socks*.

kneepad ▻ *noun* a protective cover for the knee.

knees-up ▻ *noun* (*knees-ups*) *Brit colloq* a riotous party or dance; an uninhibited celebration.

knee-trembler ▻ *noun* **1** *slang* an act of sexual intercourse performed while standing up. **2** *loosely* any sexual adventure.

knell /nɛl/ ▻ *noun* **1** the tolling of a bell announcing a death or funeral. **2** something that signals the end of anything. ▻ *verb* (*knelled, knelling*) to announce something or summon someone by, or as if by, a tolling bell. ⓒ Anglo-Saxon *cnyll*.

knelt *past tense, past participle of* KNEEL

knew *past tense of* KNOW

knickerbocker glory ▻ *noun* a large and extravagant ice-cream sundae, usually served in a tall glass.

knickerbockers /ˈnɪkəbɒkəz/ and (*US*) **knickers** ▻ *plural noun* baggy trousers tied just below the knee or at the ankle. ⓒ 19c: named after Diedrich Knickerbocker, the pseudonym of the author of Washington Irving's *History of New York*, 1809.

knickers /ˈnɪkəz/ ▻ *plural noun* an undergarment with two separate legs or legholes. They are worn by women and girls, and cover part or all of the lower abdomen and buttocks and sometimes the thighs. ▻ *exclamation, colloq* a mild expression of exasperation, etc. • **get one's knickers in a twist** *colloq* to be anxious or agitated; to panic. ⓒ 19c: short form of KNICKERBOCKERS.

knick-knack or **nick-nack** /ˈnɪknak/ ▻ *noun* a little trinket or ornament. ⓒ 17c: from KNACK in the obsolete sense 'toy'.

knife /naɪf/ ▻ *noun* (*knives* /naɪvz/) **1** a cutting instrument, typically in the form of a blade fitted into a handle or into machinery, and sometimes also used for spreading. Also *in compounds* □ *steak-knife* □ *butter-knife*. **2** such an instrument used as a weapon. ▻ *verb* (*knifed, knifing*) **1** to cut. **2** to stab or kill with a knife. **3** to try to defeat by treachery. • **knifing** *noun* the act of attacking and injuring someone using a knife. • **have one's knife in** or **into someone** *colloq* **1** to bear a grudge against them. **2** to be persistently hostile or spiteful to them. • **the knives are out** *colloq* the argument has taken a savage turn. • **twist the knife (in the wound)** to deliberately to increase someone's distress or embarrassment by constant reminders of the circumstances that caused it. • **under the knife** *colloq* having a surgical operation. ⓔ Anglo-Saxon *cnif.*

■ **knife into something** to penetrate it.

■ **knife through something** to cut through it as if with a knife.

knife block ▷ *noun* a wooden block with slots of various sizes where kitchen knives are stored

knife edge ▷ *noun* **1** the cutting edge of a knife. **2** any sharp edge or sharp-edged ridge. **3 a** a sharp edge, eg of a piece of steel, that serves as the axis of a balance, etc; **b** *as adj* delicately poised on the edge of danger □ *a knife-edge decision.* • **on a knife edge** in a state of extreme uncertainty; at a critical point.

knife pleat ▷ *noun* a flat narrow pleat.

knifepoint ▷ *noun* the sharp tip of a knife. • **at knifepoint** under threat of injury from a knife.

knife switch ▷ *noun, elec* a switch in an electric circuit, in which the moving element consists of a flat blade which engages with fixed contacts.

knight /naɪt/ ▷ *noun* **1** a man who has been awarded the highest or second highest class of distinction in any of the four British orders of chivalry, ie honours for service or merit awarded by the Queen or the Government. See also DAME. **2** *historical* in medieval Europe: a man-at-arms of high social status, usually mounted, serving a feudal lord. **3** *historical* the armed champion of a lady, devoted to her service. **4** *chess* a piece shaped like a horse's head. ▷ *verb* (***knighted***, ***knighting***) to confer a knighthood on someone. • **knighthood** *noun* **1** the rank of a knight, just below that of a baronet, conferring the title 'Sir'. **2** the order or fraternity of knights. • **knightly** *adj* (***knightlier***, ***knightliest***) relating to, like or befitting a knight; chivalrous. ⓔ Anglo-Saxon *cniht* a boy, servant or warrior.

knight bachelor ▷ *noun* (***knights bachelor***) a knight belonging to no special order of knighthood, the lowest form in rank and earliest in origin.

knight commander see COMMANDER

knight errant ▷ *noun* (***knights errant***) *historical* a knight who travelled about in search of opportunities for daring and chivalrous deeds. • **knight errantry** *noun.*

knight of the road ▷ *noun, colloq, usually facetious* **1** a tramp. **2** a commercial traveller. **3** a truck driver. **4** a highwayman.

kniphofia /nɪˈfoʊfɪə/ ▷ *noun* (***kniphofias***) *bot* a RED-HOT POKER. ⓔ 19c: named after J H Kniphof (1704–63), a German botanist.

knish /knɪʃ/ ▷ *noun* (***knishes***) in Jewish cookery: dough with a filling of potato, meat, etc, baked or fried. ⓔ 1930s: Yiddish, from Russian *knysh* a type of cake.

knit /nɪt/ ▷ *verb* (***knitted*** or *old use* ***knit***, ***knitting***) **1** *tr & intr* to produce a fabric composed of interlocking loops of yarn, using a pair of KNITTING NEEDLES or a **knitting machine**. **2** to make (garments, etc) by this means. **3** to make (a stitch) in plain knitting. **4** to unite something □ *The tragedy served to knit them closer together.* **5** *tr & intr* said of broken bones: to grow or make them grow together again. **6** to draw (one's brows) together in a frown. **7** *poetic* to intertwine something. ▷ *adj, in compounds* united in a specified way □ *a close-knit family* □ *a loosely-knit alliance.* ▷ *noun* a fabric or a garment made by knitting □ *cotton knits for summer.* • **knitter** *noun.* • **knitting** *noun* **1** a garment, etc that is in the process of being knitted. **2** the art or process of producing something knitted. ⓔ Anglo-Saxon *cnyttan* in obsolete sense 'to tie'.

knitting needle ▷ *noun* an implement like a long stout pin used to knit with, made of metal, plastic or wood, and used for holding the stitches in knitting.

knitwear ▷ *noun* knitted clothing, especially sweaters and cardigans.

knives see under KNIFE

knob /nɒb/ ▷ *noun* **1** a hard rounded projection. **2** a handle, especially a rounded one, on a door or drawer. **3** a button on mechanical or electrical equipment that is pressed or rotated to operate it. **4** a small roundish lump □ *a knob of butter.* **5** *coarse slang* **a** the penis; **b** a stupid person. • **knobble** *noun* a little knob. • **knobbly** *adj* (***knobblier***, ***knobbliest***) covered with or full of knobs; knotty. • **knobby** *adj* (***knobbier***, ***knobbiest***) • **with knobs on** *Brit colloq* with interest; more so. ⓔ 14c: from German *knobbe* a knot in wood.

knobkerrie /ˈnɒbkɛrɪ/ ▷ *noun* (***knobkerries***) a stick with a knob on the end used as a club and missile by S African tribesmen. ⓔ 19c: from Afrikaans *knopkierie*, from *knop* knob + *kierie* a stick.

knock /nɒk/ ▷ *verb* (***knocked***, ***knocking***) **1** *intr* to tap or rap with the knuckles or some object, especially on a door for admittance. **2** to strike and so push someone or something, especially accidentally. **3** to put someone or something into a specified condition by hitting them or it □ *knocked him senseless.* **4** to make by striking □ *knocked a hole in the boat.* **5** *tr & intr* (*usually* **knock against** or **on** or **into something** or **someone**) to strike, bump or bang against it or them. **6** *colloq* to find fault with or criticize someone or something, especially unfairly. **7** *intr* said of an internal combustion engine: to make a metallic knocking sound caused by the explosion of an unburned mixture of fuel vapour and air before it is ignited by the spark. Also called **pink**. **8** *intr* said of machinery: to rattle or clank with a regular rhythm (sometimes a symptom of wear). **9** *coarse slang* to have sexual intercourse with someone. ▷ *noun* **1** an act of knocking. **2** a tap or rap. **3** a push or shove. **4** *colloq* a personal misfortune, blow, setback, calamity, etc. **5** in an internal combustion engine: a metallic knocking sound caused by the explosion of an unburned mixture of fuel vapour and air before it is ignited by the spark. **6** the sound of knocking in machinery. **7** *colloq* a criticism. • **knock someone into the middle of next week** *colloq* **1** to hit them extremely hard. **2** to surprise them. • **knock something on the head** *colloq* to put an end to it in a firm or definite manner. ⓔ Anglo-Saxon *cnucian.*

■ **knock about** or **around** *colloq* **1** to wander about (a place) in a casual and aimless way; to lie about unused; to be idle □ *knocking about the streets.* **2** to travel about, roughing it and having varied experiences □ *knocked about Europe for the summer.*

■ **knock someone about** or **around** *colloq* to treat them roughly; to hit or batter them.

■ **knock about with someone** *colloq* to associate or go about with them.

■ **knock someone back** **1** *colloq* to cost them (a specified amount) □ *knocked me back 500 quid.* 2 to surprise, dismay, or disappoint them. 3 to rebuff or reject them; to turn them down.

■ **knock something back** *colloq* to eat or drink it quickly and with relish.

■ **knock someone down** to strike them to the ground □ *knocked down by a car.*

■ **knock something down** **1** to demolish (a building). 2 *colloq* to reduce its price □ *knocked these down to a fiver each.*

■ **knock something down to someone** *colloq* to sell (goods) to them at auction.

■ **knock into someone** to meet them by chance or unexpectedly.

■ **knock into someone** or **something** to collide with them.

■ **knock something into someone** *colloq* to teach it to them forcefully □ *needs to have some sense knocked into him.*

■ **knock off** *colloq* to finish work □ *We knock off at 5pm.*

■ **knock someone off 1** *slang* to kill them. **2** *coarse slang* to have sexual intercourse with them.

■ **knock something off 1** *colloq* to produce it or them at speed or in quick succession, apparently quite easily □ *knocks off several books a year.* **2** *colloq* to deduct (a certain amount) □ *knocked off £15 for a quick sale.* **3** *slang* to rob or steal it □ *He knocked off 10 grand* □ *They knocked off a bank.* **4** *slang* to copy and distribute illegally □ *caught knocking off videos and computer games.* **5** *colloq* often in commands: to stop it □ *Knock it off!*

■ **knock on** *rugby* to commit the foul of pushing the ball forward with the hand. See also KNOCK-ON.

■ **knock someone out 1** to make them unconscious, especially by hitting them. **2** *boxing* to make them unconscious or render them incapable of rising in the required time. **3** to defeat them in a knockout competition. **4** *colloq* to amaze them; to impress them greatly. See also KNOCKOUT.

■ **knock someone** or **something over** to collide with them or it, usually accidentally, causing them or it to fall □ *I'm so sorry, but I've knocked over the vase of flowers.*

■ **knock something out 1** to dislodge it by a blow. **2** *colloq* to make it stop functioning; to damage or destroy it. **3** *colloq* to produce something, especially if done quickly or roughly.

■ **knock someone sideways** *colloq* to come as a severe shock to them; to devastate or disconcert them □ *Her death knocked him sideways.*

■ **knock something together** *colloq* to make it hurriedly.

■ **knock up** *tennis* to exchange practice shots with one's opponent before a match.

■ **knock someone up 1** to wake them by knocking. **2** *colloq* to exhaust them. **3** *coarse slang* to make them pregnant.

■ **knock something up 1** *colloq* to make it hurriedly. **2** *cricket* to score (a number of runs).

knockabout ▷ *adj* said of comedy: boisterous; slapstick. ▷ *noun* **1** a boisterous performance with horseplay. **2** someone who performs such turns. **3** *Austral* an odd-job man or station-hand.

knock-back ▷ *noun* **1** a setback, especially a financial one; a rejection or refusal. **2** *slang* a refusal of parole from prison.

knockdown ▷ *adj, colloq* **1** very low; cheap □ *knockdown prices.* **2** said of furniture: able to be taken to pieces easily. **3** said of an argument: overwhelmingly strong.

knocker *noun* **1** (*also* **doorknocker**) a heavy piece of metal, usually of a decorative shape, fixed to a door by a hinge and used for knocking. **2** someone who knocks. **3** someone who makes unsolicited door-to-door calls on householders, usually hoping either to sell to them or to purchase from them for a quick profit. **4** *colloq* a critic. **5** (**knockers**) *slang* a woman's breasts.

knocker-up ▷ *noun* someone whose job is to rouse workers in the morning.

knock-for-knock agreement or **policy** ▷ *noun* an arrangement between motor insurance companies by which, after an accident involving two cars, each company settles the damage to the car it insures regardless of which driver was to blame.

knocking ▷ *noun* **1** a rap or beating on a door, etc. **2** a noise that resembles knocking. **3** KNOCK (*noun* 5). **4** the practice of making unsolicited calls on householders, usually in the hope of selling something to them, or buying valuables from them. ● **knocking on** *colloq* getting to be a fair age. ● **knocking on for ...** approaching the age of ... □ *must be knocking on for 60 by now.*

knocking copy ▷ *noun* advertising material which denigrates rival products on the market.

knocking shop ▷ *noun, slang* a brothel.

knock knee or (*popularly*) **knock knees** ▷ *noun* a condition in which the lower legs curve inward, causing the knees to touch when the person is standing with their feet slightly apart. ● **knock-kneed** *adj.* Compare BANDY.

knock-on ▷ *adj* causing or caused by a series of consequences. ▷ *noun, rugby* the illegal move of knocking the ball forward with an arm or hand.

knock-on effect ▷ *noun* a secondary or indirect effect of some action, etc on one or more indirectly-related matters or circumstances □ *The stagnant housing market has a knock-on effect for the economy.*

knockout ▷ *noun* **1** *colloq* someone or something stunning □ *Brad Pitt is such a knockout!* **2** a competition in which the defeated teams or competitors are dropped after each round. **3** *boxing, etc* **a** the act of rendering someone unconscious; **b** a blow that renders the opponent or victim unconscious. ▷ *adj* **1** said of a competition: in which the losers in each round are eliminated. **2** said of a punch, etc: leaving the victim unconscious. **3** *colloq* stunningly attractive; excellent.

knockout drops ▷ *plural noun, colloq* a drug put in a drink, etc to make the drinker unconscious.

knock-up ▷ *noun, tennis, etc* practice play, especially just before a match.

knockwurst see KNACKWURST

knoll /nɒl, noʊl/ ▷ *noun* a small round, usually grassy hill. ⓒ Anglo-Saxon *cnoll.*

knot¹ /nɒt/ ▷ *noun* **1** a join or tie in string, etc made by looping the ends around each other and pulling tight. **2** a bond or uniting link. **3** a coil or bun in the hair. **4** a decoratively tied ribbon, etc. **5** a tangle in hair, string, etc. **6** a difficulty or complexity. **7** a hard mass of wood at the point where a branch has grown out from a tree trunk. **8** a scar on a piece of timber, representing a cross-section through such a mass. **9** a node or joint in a stem, especially of grass. **10** a small gathering or cluster of people, etc. **11** (abbreviation **kn**) used in meteorology and in navigation by aircraft and at sea: a unit of speed equal to one nautical mile (1.85km) per hour. **12** *loosely* a nautical mile. **13** a tight feeling, eg in the stomach, caused by nervousness. ▷ *verb* (**knotted**, **knotting**) **1** to tie something in a knot. **2** *tr & intr* to tangle; to form knots. **3** *intr* said eg of the stomach: to become tight with nervousness, etc. ● **knotless** *adj.* ● **knotted** *adj* **1** full of knots. **2** having a knot or knots. ● **knotty** *adj* (**knottier**, **knottiest**) **1** full of knots. **2** said of a problem, etc: difficult, complex or intricate. ● **at a rate of knots** *colloq* very fast. ● **get knotted!** *Brit colloq* an expression of disagreement, refusal or dismissiveness. ● **tie someone** or **oneself in knots** to bewilder, confuse or perplex them or oneself. ● **tie the knot** *colloq* to get married. ⓒ Anglo-Saxon *cnotta.*

knot² /nɒt/ ▷ *noun* a small wading bird of the sandpiper family with grey plumage and a short bill. ⓒ 15c.

knot garden ▷ *noun* a formal garden with intricate designs of flowerbeds, shrubs, etc.

knotgrass and **knotweed** ▷ *noun* an annual plant which is widespread throughout most of Europe. It has slender branched stems that bear small narrow leaves and tiny white or pink flowers.

knothole ▷ *noun* a hole left in a piece of wood where a knot has fallen out.

know /noʊ/ ▷ *verb* (***knew*** /njuː/, ***known***, ***knowing***) **1** *tr & intr* (*usually* **know something** or **know of** or **about something**) to be aware of it; to be certain about it. **2** to have learnt and remembered something. **3** to have an understanding or grasp of something. **4** to be familiar with someone or something □ *know her well.* **5** to be able to recognize or identify someone or something. **6** to be able to distinguish someone or something, or to tell them apart □ *wouldn't know him from Adam.* **7** *intr* to have enough experience or training □ *knew not to question him further.* **8** to experience or be subject to something □ *has never known poverty.* **9** *old use, eg Bible* to have sexual intercourse with someone. • **knowable** *adj* capable of being known, discovered, or understood. • **Heaven** or **God knows** *colloq* I have no idea. • **in the know** *colloq* **1** having information not known to most people. **2** initiated. • **I wouldn't know** I am not in a position to know. • **know all the answers** to be fully informed on everything, or to think one is. • **know a thing or two** *colloq* to be pretty shrewd. • **know better than to do something** to be wiser, or better instructed, than to do it. • **know how many beans make five** to be sensible or aware; to have one's wits about one. • **know the ropes** to understand the detail or procedure. • **know what's what** to be shrewd, wise or hard to deceive. • **know which side one's bread is buttered on** to be fully aware of one's own best interests. • **let it be known** to reveal, especially indirectly. • **make oneself known** to introduce oneself. • **there's no knowing** it's impossible to predict. • **what do you know?** *colloq* an expression of surprise. • **you never know** *colloq* it's not impossible; perhaps. ◷ Anglo-Saxon *cnawan.*

▪ **be known as something** to be called it; to have it as one's name.

▪ **know someone as** or **for something** to think of or have experience of them as (a specified thing) □ *knew him as a kindly man.*

▪ **know something backwards** *colloq* to know it thoroughly.

know-all ▷ *noun* (***know-alls***) *derog* someone who seems, or claims, to know more than others.

know-how ▷ *noun* **1** *colloq* ability; adroitness; skill. **2** specialized skill.

knowing /ˈnoʊɪŋ/ *adj* **1** shrewd; canny; clever. **2** said of a glance, etc: signifying secret awareness. **3** deliberate. • **knowingly** *adverb* **1** in a knowing manner. **2** on purpose; deliberately; consciously. • **knowingness** *noun.*

knowledge /ˈnɒlɪdʒ/ ▷ *noun* **1** the fact of knowing; awareness; understanding. **2** what one knows; the information one has acquired through learning or experience. **3** learning; the sciences □ *a branch of knowledge.* **4 a** specific information about a subject; **b** (**the knowledge**) the detailed information about streets, routes, etc that London taxi-drivers are tested on before they are licensed. • **to one's** or **to the best of one's knowledge** as far as one knows. ◷ 14c as *knouleche.*

knowledgeable or **knowledgable** /ˈnɒlɪdʒəbəl/ ▷ *adj* well-informed. • **knowledgeability** *noun.* • **knowledgeably** *adverb.*

knowledge base ▷ *noun, computing* a collection of specialist knowledge formulated for use from human experience (eg medical diagnostics), especially in EXPERT SYSTEMS.

knowledge-based system ▷ *noun* (abbreviation **KBS**) *computing* a program that stores and utilizes a large collection of encoded specialist knowledge to solve a problem, using the methods of ARTIFICIAL INTELLIGENCE.

knowledge engineering ▷ *noun, computing* the application of artificial intelligence techniques in constructing EXPERT SYSTEMS.

known ▷ *verb, past participle of* KNOW. ▷ *adj* **1** widely recognized. **2** identified by the police □ *a known thief.*

knuckle /ˈnʌkəl/ ▷ *noun* **1** a joint of a finger, especially one that links a finger to the hand. **2** cookery, *etc* the knee or ankle joint of an animal, especially with the surrounding flesh, as food. ▷ *verb* (***knuckled, knuckling***) to touch or press something with the knuckle or knuckles. • **near the knuckle** *colloq* bordering on the indecent or obscene. ◷ 14c as *knokel*: related to German *knochen* bone.

▪ **knuckle down to something** to begin to work hard at it.

▪ **knuckle under** *colloq* to submit, yield or give way.

knucklebone ▷ *noun* **1** *cookery* any bone with a rounded end. **2** (**knucklebones**) the game of JACKS.

knuckle-duster ▷ *noun* a set of metal links or other metal device worn over the knuckles as a weapon.

knucklehead ▷ *noun, colloq* a fool; an idiot. • **knuckleheaded** *adj.*

knuckle joint ▷ *noun* **1** any of the finger joints. **2** *mech* a hinged joint in which two pieces of machinery are joined by a pin through eyes at their ends, one piece being forked and enclosing the other.

knuckle sandwich ▷ *noun, colloq* a blow with the fist.

knur or **knurr** /nɜː(r)/ ▷ *noun* **1** a knot on a tree (see KNOT[1] *noun* 7). **2** a hard ball or knot of wood. ◷ 16c.

knurl or **nurl** /nɜːl/ ▷ *noun* a ridge, especially one of a series. ▷ *verb* (***knurled, knurling***) to make ridges in something. • **knurled** *adj* covered with ridges. • **knurling** *noun* mouldings or other woodwork decorated along the edge with a series of ridges or beadings. • **knurly** *adj.* ◷ 17c.

KO or **k.o.** ▷ /keɪˈoʊ/ ▷ *abbreviation* **1** kick-off. **2** knockout. **3** knock out. ▷ *noun* (***KO's*** or ***k.o.'s***) *colloq* a knockout. ▷ *verb colloq* (***KO'd*** or ***k.o.'d***, ***KO'ing*** or ***k.o.ing***) to knock someone out.

koa /koʊə/ ▷ *noun* (***koas***) *bot* an ACACIA native to Hawaii. ◷ 19c: the local Hawaiian name for this tree.

koala /koʊˈɑːlə/ ▷ *noun* (***koalas***) an Australian tree-climbing marsupial resembling a very small bear. It has thick grey fur and bushy ears and feeds on eucalyptus leaves. Also (*Austral*) called **native bear**. ◷ 19c: from an extinct Aboriginal language *gula.*

koan /ˈkoʊan/ ▷ *noun* in Zen Buddhism: a nonsensical question given to students as a subject for meditation in order to demonstrate the uselessness of logical thinking. ◷ 1940s: Japanese, meaning 'a public proposal or plan'.

kobold /ˈkoʊbɒld/ ▷ *noun, German folklore* **1** a spirit of the mines. **2** a domestic brownie. ◷ 19c: German.

Kodiak /ˈkoʊdɪak/ and **Kodiak bear** ▷ *noun* a large variety of brown bear, found in W Alaska and the Aleutian Islands. ◷ 19c: named after Kodiak Island, Alaska.

kofta /ˈkɒftə/ ▷ *noun* (***koftas***) in Indian cookery: minced and seasoned meat or vegetables, shaped into balls and fried. ◷ 19c: Hindi, meaning 'pounded meat'.

kohl /koʊl/ ▷ *noun* a cosmetic for darkening the eyelids. It was originally used in the East in the form of a black powder. ◷ 18c: from Arabic *koh'l* powdered antimony.

kohlrabi /koʊlˈrɑːbɪ/ ▷ *noun* (***kohlrabis*** or ***kohlrabi***) a variety of cabbage with a short swollen green or purple edible stem. It resembles a turnip, and is eaten as a vegetable and used as animal feed. ◷ 19c: German, from Italian *cavolrape* cabbage turnip, from Latin *caulis* cabbage + *rapa* turnip.

koi /kɔɪ/ ⊳ *noun* (*plural* ***koi***) any one of various ornamental varieties of common carp. ◷ 18c: Japanese.

koine or **Koine** /'kɔɪniː, -neɪ/ ⊳ *noun* (***koines***) any dialect which has come to be used as the common language of a larger area. Compare LINGUA FRANCA. ◷ 19c: from Greek *koine dialektos* common dialect, the name given to the written variety of Greek used throughout the Eastern Mediterranean and Middle East from the Hellenistic until the Byzantine periods.

KO'ing or **k.o.ing** *present participle of* KO

kola see COLA

kolinsky /kə'lɪnskɪ/ ⊳ *noun* (***kolinskies***) **1** any variety of the Siberian mink which has a brown coat even in winter. **2** the fur of this animal. ◷ 19c: from Russian *kolinski* of the Kola Peninsula, an area of Murmansk.

kolkhoz /kɒl'xɒz/ ⊳ *noun* (*plural* ***kolkhoz***, ***kolkhozes*** or ***kolkhozy***) a large-scale collective farm in the former Soviet Union. ◷ 1920s: Russian *abbreviation* of *kollektivnoe khozyaistvo*.

Kol Nidre /kɒl'niːdreɪ/ ⊳ *noun, Judaism* **1** the opening prayer said at the service on the eve of YOM KIPPUR. **2** this evening service. **3** the traditional musical setting for this prayer. ◷ 19c: the Aramaic opening words of the prayer, meaning 'all vows'.

komatik /'kɒmətɪk/ ⊳ *noun* an Inuit sled with wooden runners and drawn by dogs. ◷ 19c: Inuit.

kombu /'kɒmbuː/ ⊳ *noun* (***kombus***) an edible brown seaweed, used especially for making stock. ◷ 19c: Japanese.

Komodo dragon /kə'moʊdoʊ —/ and **Komodo lizard** ⊳ *noun, zool* the largest living lizard, now an endangered species, up to 3m in length, and confined to a few Indonesian islands. ◷ 1920s: the name of one of the islands.

koodoo see KUDU

kook /kuːk/ *N Amer colloq* ⊳ *noun* a crazy or eccentric person. • **kooky** or **kookie** *adj* (***kookier***, ***kookiest***). ◷ 1960s.

kookaburra /'kʊkəbʌrə/ ⊳ *noun* (***kookaburras***) either of two species of large bird of the kingfisher family, found in Australia and New Guinea and known for its chuckling cry. Also called **laughing jackass**. ◷ 19c: from Wiradhuri (Australian Aboriginal language) *gugubarra*.

koori /'kʊərɪ/ ⊳ *noun* (***kooris***) *Austral* **1** an Aborigine. **2** a young Aboriginal woman. ◷ 19c: Aboriginal.

kop ⊳ *noun* **1** *S Afr* a hill. **2 a** a bank of terracing at a football ground, especially and originally in Anfield, the ground of Liverpool FC; **b** (**the kop**) Liverpool FC's most dedicated and enthusiastic supporters as a group. ◷ 19c: from Afrikaans *kopje* a little head, from Dutch *kop* the head.

kopeck or **kopek** or **copek** /'koʊpɛk/ ⊳ *noun* a coin or unit of currency of Russia, and the former Soviet Union, worth one hundredth of a rouble. ◷ 17c: from Russian *kopeika*.

koppie or (*S Afr*) **kopje** /'kɒpɪ/ ⊳ *noun* (***koppies*** or ***kopjes***) a low hill. ◷ 19c: see KOP.

kora /'kɔːrə/ ⊳ *noun* (***koras***) *music* a W African stringed instrument, rather like a harp. ◷ 18c.

Koran or **Qoran** or **Quran** or **Qur'an** /kɔː'rɑːn, kə'rɑːn/ ⊳ *noun, Islam* the holy book of Islam, believed by Muslims to be composed of the true word of Allah as dictated to Muhammad. • **Koranic** /-'ranɪk/ *adj*. ◷ 17c: from Arabic *qur'an* book, from *qara'a* to read.

korfball /'kɔːfbɔːl/ ⊳ *noun* a game similar to basketball, played by two teams, consisting each of six men and six women. ◷ Early 20c: from Dutch *korfbal*, from *korf* basket + *bal* ball.

korma /'kɔːmə/ ⊳ *noun* (***kormas***) in Indian cookery: a mild-flavoured dish of meat or vegetables braised in stock, yoghurt or cream. ▫ *chicken korma*. ◷ 19c: Urdu.

koruna /kɒ'ruːnə/ ⊳ *noun* (***korunas***) (abbreviation **Kčs**) the standard unit of currency of the Czech Republic and Slovakia. ◷ 1920s: Czech, meaning 'crown'.

KO's or **k.o.'s** *plural of* KO

kosher /'koʊʃə(r)/ ⊳ *adj* **1** in accordance with Jewish law. **2** said of food: prepared as prescribed by Jewish dietary laws. Opposite of TREFA. **3** *colloq* genuine. **4** *colloq* legitimate. ⊳ *noun* **1** kosher food. **2** a shop selling it. ◷ 19c: Yiddish, from Hebrew *kasher* right or fit.

koto /'koʊtoʊ/ ⊳ *noun* (***kotos***) a Japanese musical instrument consisting of a long box strung with 13 silk strings. ◷ 18c: Japanese.

koumiss see KUMISS

kouprey /'kuːpreɪ/ ⊳ *noun* (***koupreys***) *zool* an endangered species of wild cattle, native to the forests of SE Asia, with a large blackish-brown body, white legs, and cylindrical horns. It is believed to be closely related to the ancestors of modern domestic cattle. ◷ 1940s: Cambodian native name, from Pali *go* cow + Khmer *brai* forest.

kowhai /'koʊhaɪ, 'koʊwaɪ/ ⊳ *noun* (***kowhais***) *bot* a small leguminous tree which bears clusters of golden flowers, found in New Zealand and Chile. ◷ 19c: Maori.

kowtow /kaʊ'taʊ/ ⊳ *verb* **1** *intr* (*usually* **kowtow to someone**) *colloq* to defer to them, especially in an over-submissive or obsequious way. **2** to touch the forehead to the ground in a gesture of submission, originally a Chinese ceremonial custom ⊳ *noun* an act of kowtowing. ◷ 19c: from Chinese *ke tou* to strike the head.

KP ⊳ *abbreviation* Knight of the Order of St Patrick.

kpg ⊳ *abbreviation* kilometres per gallon.

kph ⊳ *abbreviation* kilometres per hour.

Kr ⊳ *symbol, chem* krypton.

kr ⊳ *abbreviation* **1** krona, Swedish currency **2** króna, Icelandic currency **3** krone, Danish and Norwegian currency

kraal /krɑːl/ ⊳ *noun* **1** a S African village of huts surrounded by a fence. **2** *S Afr* an enclosure for cattle, sheep, etc. ◷ 18c: Afrikaans, from Portuguese *curral* pen.

krab see under KARABINER

kraft /krɑːft/ and **kraft paper** ⊳ *noun* a type of strong brown wrapping paper. ◷ Early 20c: German, meaning 'strength'.

krait /kraɪt/ ⊳ *noun* a venomous S Asian rock snake. ◷ 19c: from Hindi *karait*.

kraken /'krɑːkən, 'kreɪkən/ ⊳ *noun, mythol* a legendary gigantic sea monster. ◷ 18c: Norwegian.

krans /'krɑːns/ or **kranz** or **krantz** /krɑːnts/ ⊳ *noun* (***kranses***, ***kranzes*** or ***krantzes***) *S Afr* **1** a crown of rock on a mountain top. **2** a precipice. ◷ 18c: Afrikaans, from Dutch *krans* a coronet.

kraut /kraʊt/ ⊳ *noun, offensive or derog slang* a German. ◷ Early 20c: from SAUERKRAUT.

Krebs cycle ⊳ *noun, biochem* in the cells of living organisms: a sequence of biochemical reactions in which, subject to the availability of oxygen, the products of GLYCOLYSIS are broken down to form carbon dioxide and water, with the release of large amounts of energy. Also called **tricarboxylic acid cycle**. ◷ 1940s: named after the German-born UK biochemist Hans Krebs (1900–81).

kremlin /'krɛmlɪn/ ⊳ *noun* **1** the citadel of a Russian town, especially (**the Kremlin**) that of Moscow. **2** (**the Kremlin**) the government of the former Soviet Union. ◷ 17c: from Russian *kreml* a citadel.

krill ▷ *noun* (*plural* ***krill***) a shrimp-like crustacean that feeds on plankton and which lives in enormous swarms. They constitute the main food of baleen whales and large fishes. ⓘ Early 20c: from Norwegian *kril* small fry or young fish.

krimmer /ˈkrɪmə(r)/ ▷ *noun* a tightly curled grey or black fur from a Crimean type of lamb. ⓘ 19c: from German *Krim* Crimea.

kris /kriːs, krɪs/ ▷ *noun* (***krises***) a Malay or Indonesian dagger with a wavy blade. ⓘ 16c: Malay.

Krishnaism /ˈkrɪʃnəɪzəm/ ▷ *noun* the worship of Krishna, one of the most important gods in HINDUISM. See also VISHNU. ⓘ 19c.

kromesky /krəˈmɛskɪ/ ▷ *noun* (***kromeskys***) a croquette of minced beef or fish cooked with a binding sauce and allowed to cool. It is then sliced, coated in flour and fried. ⓘ 19c: from Polish *kroméczka* a little slice.

krona /ˈkroʊnə/ ▷ *noun* (*plural* ***kronor*** /-nə/) the standard unit of currency of Sweden. (abbreviation **K**). ⓘ 19c: Swedish and Icelandic, meaning 'crown'.

króna /ˈkroʊnə/ ▷ *noun* (*plural* ***krónur*** /-nə/) (abbreviation **Kr**) the standard unit of currency of Iceland. ⓘ 19c: Iclandic, meaning 'crown'.

krone /ˈkroʊnə/ ▷ *noun* (*plural* ***kroner*** /-nə/) (abbreviation **K**) the standard unit of currency of Denmark and Norway. ⓘ 19c: Danish & Norwegian, meaning 'crown'.

Krugerrand or **krugerrand** /ˈkruːgərand/ ▷ *noun* a S African one-ounce (or 28-gram) gold coin minted only for investment, which bears a portrait of Paul Kruger (1825–1904), Boer statesman. Also called **rand**. ⓘ 1960s: see RAND.

krummhorn or **crumhorn** /ˈkrʊmhɔːn, krʌm-/ ▷ *noun, music* an early double-reed wind instrument with a curved end. ⓘ 17c: German, meaning 'curved horn'.

krypton /ˈkrɪptɒn/ ▷ *noun* (symbol **Kr**, atomic number 36) a colourless odourless tasteless noble gas that is almost inert, used in lasers, fluorescent lamps and discharge tubes. ⓘ 19c: from Greek *kryptos* hidden or secret.

KS ▷ *abbreviation* **1** *US state* Kansas. Also written **Kan.**, **Kans. Ks.** **2** *medicine* Kaposi's sarcoma.

KT ▷ *abbreviation* Knight of the Thistle.

Kt¹ ▷ *abbreviation* kiloton or kilotons, kilotonne or kilotonnes.

Kt² ▷ *symbol, chess* Knight.

kt ▷ *abbreviation* **1** (*also* **kT**) kiloton or kilotonne. **2** karat or carat. **3** *naut* knot.

Ku ▷ *symbol, chem* kurchatovium.

kudos /ˈkjuːdɒs/ ▷ *noun* credit, honour or prestige. ⓘ 18c: Greek, meaning 'glory'.

kudu or **koodoo** /ˈkuːduː/ ▷ *noun* (***kudus*** or ***koodoos***) *zool* either of two species of lightly striped African antelope, the male of which has long spiral horns. ⓘ 18c: from Afrikaans *koedoe*.

kudzu /ˈkʊdzuː/ ▷ *noun* (***kudzus***) *bot* an ornamental climbing plant with edible root tubers and a stem from which fibre can be obtained. ⓘ 19c: from Japanese *kuzu*.

kufiyah see KAFFIYEH

Ku Klux Klan /kuː klʌks klan/ and **the Klan** ▷ *noun* (abbreviation **KKK**) a secret society of White Protestants of the southern US, originally formed after the civil war of 1861–65, and during the 20c using violence against Blacks, Jews and Catholics. • **Ku Klux Klanner** or **Ku Klux Klansman** or **Klansman** *noun* a member of this organization. ⓘ 19c: probably from Greek *kyklos* circle + *klan*, a variant of CLAN.

kukri /ˈkʊkrɪ/ ▷ *noun* (***kukris***) a heavy curved knife or short sword used by Gurkhas. ⓘ 19c: Hindi.

kulak /ˈkuːlak/ ▷ *noun, historical* a wealthy, property-owning Russian peasant. ⓘ 19c: Russian, literally 'fist' or 'tight-fisted person'.

kumara /ˈkuːmərə/ ▷ *noun* (***kumaras***) *NZ* the SWEET POTATO. ⓘ 18c: Maori.

kumiss or **koumiss** /ˈkuːmɪs/ ▷ *noun* (***kumisses*** or ***koumisses***) a drink made from fermented milk, especially mare's milk. ⓘ 17c: from Russian *kumis*, from Tatar *kumiz*.

kümmel /ˈkʊməl/ ▷ *noun* a German liqueur flavoured with cumin and caraway seeds. ⓘ 19c: German, from *Kumin* cumin.

kumquat or **cumquat** /ˈkʌmkwɒt/ ▷ *noun* **1** a small spiny evergreen citrus shrub or tree, native to China. **2** the small round orange citrus fruit produced by this plant, resembling a miniature orange and containing an acidic pulp surrounded by a sweet rind. ⓘ 17c: from Cantonese Chinese *kam kwat* golden orange.

kung fu /kʌŋ fuː/ ▷ *noun* a Chinese martial art with similarities to karate and judo. ⓘ 1960s: Chinese, meaning 'combat skill'.

Kuo-yü see under PUTONGHUA

kupfernickel see under NICCOLITE

kurchatovium /kɜːtʃəˈtoʊvɪəm/ ▷ *noun* (symbol **Ku**, atomic number 104) an alternative name proposed by Soviet scientists for the element UNNILQUADIUM. ⓘ 1960s: in honour of the Russian nuclear physicist, Igor Kurchatov (1903–1960).

Kurd /kɜːd/ ▷ *noun* a member of the Islamic people of Kurdistan, a mountainous region of Turkey, Iran and Iraq.

Kurdish ▷ *adj* belonging or relating to the Kurds or their language. ▷ *noun* the language of the Kurds. ⓘ 19c.

kuri /ˈkʊrɪ/ ▷ *noun* (***kuris***) *NZ* a mongrel dog. ⓘ 19c: Maori name for a native dog, now extinct.

kurrajong or **currajong** /ˈkʌrədʒɒŋ/ ▷ *noun* a name for various Australian trees and shrubs with tough fibrous bark. ⓘ 19c: Aboriginal, from *garrajung* a fibrous fishing line.

kurtosis /kɜːˈtoʊsɪs/ ▷ *noun* (*plural* ***kurtoses*** /-siːz/) *statistics* the relative sharpness of the peak on a frequency-distribution curve, which indicates the concentration of a distribution about its mean value. ⓘ Early 20c: Greek, meaning 'bulging or swelling'.

Kuwaiti /kʊˈweɪtɪ/ ▷ *adj* belonging or relating to Kuwait, a state in the Persian Gulf, or to its inhabitants. ▷ *noun* a citizen or inhabitant of, or person born in, Kuwait. ⓘ 1920s: from Arabic *Kuwayt*.

kuzu /ˈkuːzuː/ ▷ *noun, cookery* an arrowroot thickening agent, acceptable in a macrobiotic diet. ⓘ Japanese, meaning 'arrowroot'.

kV ▷ *abbreviation* kilovolt or kilovolts.

kvass /kvɑːs/ ▷ *noun* (***kvasses***) an E European rye beer. ⓘ 16c: from Russian *kvas* leaven.

kvetch /kvɛtʃ/ *chiefly US slang* ▷ *verb* (***kvetched***, ***kvetching***) *intr* to complain or whine, especially incessantly. ▷ *noun* (*also* **kvetcher**) a complainer; a fault-finder. ⓘ 1960s: Yiddish, from German *quetsche* crusher.

kW ▷ *symbol* kilowatt or kilowatts.

KWAC /kwak/ ▷ *abbreviation, chiefly computing* keyword and context.

kwacha /ˈkwatʃə/ ▷ *noun* (abbreviation **K**) (*plural* ***kwacha*** or ***kwachas***) the standard unit of currency of Zambia and Malawi. ⓘ 1960s: native name, literally 'dawn'.

kwanza /ˈkwanzə/ ▷ *noun* (*plural* ***kwanza*** or ***kwanzas***) the standard unit of currency in Angola. ⓘ 1970s.

kwashiorkor /kwɒʃɪˈɔːkɔː(r)/ ▷ *noun, medicine* a serious nutritional deficiency disease, caused by lack of protein in the diet, most common in infants and young children in tropical Africa. ⌚ 1930s: a Ghanaian name.

kWh ⊳ *abbreviation* kilowatt hour or kilowatt hours.

KWIC /kwɪk/ ⊳ *abbreviation, chiefly computing* keyword in context.

KWOC /kwɒk/ ⊳ *abbreviation, chiefly computing* keyword out of context.

KWT ⊳ *abbreviation, IVR* Kuwait.

KY ⊳ *abbreviation, US state* Kentucky. Also written **Ken.**, **Ky.**

kyanite /ˈkaɪənaɪt/ or **cyanite** /ˈsaɪənaɪt/ ⊳ *noun* a mineral, an aluminium silicate, generally sky-blue. ⌚ 18c: from Greek *kyanos* blue.

kyanize or **kyanise** /ˈkaɪənaɪz/ ⊳ *verb* (***kyanized, kyanizing***) to preserve (wood) from decay by injecting corrosive sublimate into its pores. ⌚ 19c: named after the Irishman, John H Kyan (1774–1850).

kybosh see KIBOSH

kyle /kaɪl/ ⊳ *noun* (***kyles***) *Scottish* a channel, strait or sound, a common element in placenames. ⌚ 16c: from Gaelic *caoil* a narrow strait.

kylie or **kiley** /ˈkaɪlɪ/ ⊳ *noun* (***kylies*** or ***kileys***) *Austral* a type of boomerang. ⌚ 19c: Aboriginal.

kyloe /ˈkaɪloʊ/ and **kylie** /-lɪ/ ⊳ *noun* (***kyloes, kylies***) one of the small long-haired cattle of the Scottish Highlands and Hebrides. ⌚ 18c: from Gaelic *gaidhealach* Gaelic or Highland.

kymograph /ˈkaɪməgrɑːf/ ⊳ *noun* originally an apparatus comprising a slowly rotating cylinder encircled with sooted paper such that physiological responses (especially muscle contraction) could be recorded continuously by a tracking stylus scraping the soot from the paper, but now exclusively an electronic apparatus based on the same principle. • **kymogram** *noun* a record made by this device. • **kymographic** *adj.* • **kymography** *noun*. ⌚ 19c: from Greek *kyma* a wave.

kyphosis /kaɪˈfoʊsɪs/ ⊳ *noun* (***kyphoses*** /-siːz/) *pathol* excessive curvature of the spine causing a convex backwards arching of the back. Compare LORDOSIS. ⌚ 19c: Greek, from *kyphos* a hump.

Kyrie eleison /ˈkɪərɪ ɛˈleɪɪsɒn/ ⊳ *noun, Christianity* **1** a form of prayer in all the ancient Greek liturgies, retained in the RC mass, following immediately after the INTROIT, including both words and music. **2** one of the responses to the commandments in the Anglican ante-communion service. **3** (*often* **Kyrie**) a musical setting of these. ⌚ 14c: from Greek *kyrie eleeson* Lord have mercy.

kyu /kjuː/ ⊳ *noun* (*plural* ***kyu***) *judo* **1** one of the six novice grades (the least experienced being sixth kyu). **2** a novice in one of these grades. ⌚ 1930s: Japanese.

L

L^1 or **l** /ɛl/ ▻ *noun* (*Ls, L's* or *l's*) **1** the twelfth letter of the English alphabet. **2 a** the shape of an L ▫ ***arranged the sofas in an L***; **b** a building that has had an extension added perpendicular to the original so that the whole thing then forms the shape of an L. **3** the speech sound represented by this letter.

L^2 ▻ *abbreviation* **1** lake. **2** learner driver. **3** Liberal. **4** licentiate. **5** lira or lire.

L^3 ▻ *symbol* the Roman numeral for 50.

L^4 see ELEVATED RAILROAD

l ▻ *abbreviation* **1** left. **2** length. **3** line. **4** lira or lire. **5** litre.

LA ▻ *abbreviation* **1** Los Angeles. **2** *US state* Louisiana. Also written **La**.

La ▻ *symbol, chem* lanthanum.

la see LAH

Lab ▻ *abbreviation* **1** Labour. **2** Labrador.

lab ▻ *contraction* short form of LABORATORY, which now seems to be preferred to the full form.

label /'leɪbəl/ ▻ *noun* **1 a** a note, tag or sticker that specifies details of something's contents, destination, ownership, etc; **b** a tag or sticker attached to something, which carries advice about how to use it, wash it, care for it, etc. **2** a word or short phrase which is used to describe a person, movement or school of thought ▫ ***The label 'Left-wing' is a relative one.*** **3** a small strip of material, etc which has the name of the maker or designer on it. **4 a** a recording company's trademark; **b** the sticker in the middle of a RECORD (*noun* 4) that has information about the music, performers, production, etc on it. **5** *computing* a character or set of characters used as a means of identifying the position of an INSTRUCTION by citing it in a particular place in a PROGRAM, and which, having been declared as a label, can then be referred to from elsewhere in the program. **6** *chem* an element, often a radioactive atom, that is used for the identification or monitoring of a chemical reaction, molecule, living organism, etc. ▻ *verb* (***labelled, labelling*** or *US* ***labeled, labeling***) **1 a** to mark something in a specified way with a special tag, sticker, etc; **b** to attach a tag, sticker, etc to something. **2** to call someone or some group by a specified name. **3** *chem* to use an element, often a radioactive atom, to identify or monitor (a chemical reaction, a molecule, organism, etc). ◷ 14c: French, meaning 'ribbon'.

labial /'leɪbɪəl/ ▻ *adj* **1 a** relating to or beside the lips; **b** relating to or beside the LABIA. **2** *phonetics* said of a sound: produced by the active use of one or both lips. ▻ *noun* a sound that involves some active use of one of the lips in its production. • **labially** *adverb*. ◷ 16c: from Latin *labium* lip.

labiate /'leɪbɪeɪt, -bɪət/ ▻ *noun, bot* any of a family of flowering plants, including mint and thyme, in which the stems are usually square, and the COROLLA of petals is divided into two lips. ▻ *adj, bot* **1** referring or relating to this family of plants. **2** *anatomy* having or resembling lips. ◷ 18c: from Latin *labium* lip.

labile /'leɪbaɪl or (*especially* US) 'leɪbəl/ ▻ *adj* **1** unstable. **2** *chem* said of a chemical compound: readily altered by heat, etc. Compare INERT. ◷ 15c: from Latin *labilis*, from *labi* to slip.

labium /'leɪbɪəm/ ▻ *noun* (*labia* /-bɪə/) **1** a lip or lip-like structure. **2** (*usually* **labia**) one section of the two pairs of fleshy folds which form part of the VULVA in the human female. ◷ 16c: Latin, meaning 'lip'.

laboratory /lə'bɒrətərɪ or (*especially N Amer*) 'labərətɔrɪ/ ▻ *noun* (***laboratories***) **1** a room or building specially equipped for scientific experiments, research, the preparation of drugs, etc. **2** a room in a school, college, etc where the practical side of the sciences is taught. Often shortened to LAB. ◷ 17c: from Latin *laborare, laboratum* to work.

Labor Day ▻ *noun, N Amer* a national holiday held on the first Monday in September, when all businesses close and people celebrate with group picnics, parades, sporting events, etc. Compare LABOUR DAY.

laborious /lə'bɔːrɪəs/ ▻ *adj* **1** said of a task, etc: requiring hard work or much effort, especially when the work involved is tedious and boring. **2** said of someone's written or spoken expression: not natural; not fluent ▫ ***waded through pages of laborious prose.*** • **laboriously** *adverb*. • **laboriousness** *noun*. ◷ 14c: from LABOUR .

labour or (*N Amer*) **labor** /'leɪbə(r)/ *noun* **1** strenuous and prolonged work, especially of the physical kind that is done for payment. **2** (*usually* **labours**) the amount of effort someone puts in to something ▫ ***Despite his labours, the garden was still a mess.*** **3** working people or their productive output regarded collectively as a resource or as a political force ▫ ***talks between management and labour.*** **4** the process of giving birth, especially from the point when the contractions of the uterus begin. **5** (**Labour**) *Brit* the Labour Party. **6** *as adj* **a** *in compounds* referring or relating to hard work; **b** referring or relating to working people or their productive output ▫ ***joined the labour force.*** ▻ *verb* (***laboured, labouring***) **1** *intr* to work hard or with difficulty. **2** *intr* to progress or move slowly and with difficulty ▫ ***The old man laboured up the hill.*** **3** *intr* to spend a lot of time and effort in the hope of achieving something ▫ ***laboured endlessly for Scottish devolution.*** • **labour a** or **the point 1** to spend an excessive length of time on one particular subject or issue. **2** to go into one particular subject or issue in too much detail. **3** to keep returning to one particular subject or issue, especially in a tedious or patronizing manner and when it has already been adequately covered. • **labour under a misapprehension** to mistakenly carry on doing or thinking something without being fully aware of all the pertinent facts. ◷ 14c: from Latin *labor*.

labour camp or **labor camp** ▻ *noun* **1** a prison camp where part of the punishment involves hard physical work. **2** a place where temporary accommodation is set up for migratory workers.

Labour Day ▻ *noun* a public holiday held in many industrialized countries on 1 May, when the importance of working people is often celebrated with marches, speeches, etc. Compare LABOR DAY.

laboured or (*especially N Amer*) **labored** ▻ *adj* **1** showing signs of effort or difficulty ▫ ***His breathing was laboured.*** **2** not natural or spontaneous ▫ ***a boring and laboured prose style.***

labourer or (*especially N Amer*) **laborer** ▻ *noun* someone who is employed to do heavy, usually unskilled, physical work.

labour exchange ▻ *noun, Brit* the former name for a JOB CENTRE, which is sometimes still used informally.

labour force ▷ *noun* the body of people available for work, especially in a particular company or area, or in a country as a whole.

labour-intensive ▷ *adj* said of an industry or enterprise: requiring a large resource of people as distinct from machinery. Compare CAPITAL-INTENSIVE.

labour of love ▷ *noun* (***labours of love***) an undertaking made mainly for personal satisfaction or pleasure rather than for profit or material advantage.

Labour Party ▷ *noun* **1** *Brit* a political party founded by members of trades unions and socialist organizations who felt that the rights of workers were not adequately represented by the LIBERAL PARTY or the CONSERVATIVE PARTY. The party was originally committed to policies of public ownership, establishing a welfare state and national health service, etc, although, in recent times, its stance on such issues would appear to have given way to one that is more middle-of-the-road. **2** (*often* **Labor Party**) any similarly orientated political party in several other countries. ◷ 1906: in Britain previously known as the Labour Representative Committee (1900–06), and before 1900, in less well-developed form, as the Independent Labour Party.

labour-saving ▷ *adj* having the effect of reducing the amount of work or effort needed ▫ *labour-saving devices.*

Labrador /ˈlabrədɔː(r)/ ▷ *noun* a medium-sized breed of retriever with a short black or golden coat often kept as a family pet or used as a shooting dog. Often shortened to LAB. ◷ 19c: named after Labrador, a peninsula in E Canada where the breed was developed.

laburnum /ləˈbɜːnəm/ ▷ *noun* a small tree of the pea family, all parts of which are poisonous, especially the seeds, and which has hanging clusters of bright yellow flowers. ◷ 16c: Latin.

labyrinth /ˈlabɪrɪnθ/ ▷ *noun* **1** a highly complex network of interconnected, sometimes underground, passages and chambers designed to be difficult to find one's way around. **2** anything that is complicated, intricate or difficult to negotiate ▫ *a labyrinth of tiny cobbled back streets.* **3** *anatomy* the complex arrangement of membranous and bony structures that form the organs of hearing and balance in the inner ear of vertebrates. **4** *electronics* a loudspeaker enclosure whose function is to absorb certain unwanted sound waves. **5** a MAZE. ◷ 14c: from Greek *labyrinthos*, originally applied to the legendary structure that Daedalus was said to have built for King Minos in Crete, which in 20c is usually believed to be a folk-memory of the intricate palace of Knossos itself.

labyrinthine /labɪˈrɪnθaɪn/ ▷ *adj* extremely complex or confusing.

lac /lak/ ▷ *noun* a resinous substance produced by certain tropical Asian insects and deposited on the twigs of various trees, used to make varnish, especially SHELLAC, as well as sealing wax, abrasives and a red dye. ◷ 16c: from Hindi *lakh* 100 000, because of the vast numbers of insects required for the production of small quantities of the substance.

Lacanian /ləˈkeɪnɪən/ ▷ *adj* referring or relating to the thoughts or writings of the French psychoanalyst Jacques Lacan (1901–81), an important figure in STRUCTURALISM. ◷ 1970s.

laccolith /ˈlakəlɪθ/ ▷ *noun, geol* a lens-shaped mass of IGNEOUS rock, usually with a domed upper surface and a flat base, formed when MAGMA bursts into the surrounding strata (see STRATUM) and then cools and solidifies. • **laccolithic** *adj.* ◷ 19c: from Greek *lakkos* a reservoir + -LITH.

lace /leɪs/ ▷ *noun* **1** a delicate material, usually used to decorate clothes or for table linen, etc, made by knotting, looping or twisting thread into open intricate symmetrical patterns. **2** a string or cord drawn through holes or round hooks and used for fastening shoes, etc. ▷ *verb* (***laced, lacing***) **1** *tr & intr* to fasten or be fastened with a lace or laces. **2** to put a lace or laces into (shoes, etc). **3** to flavour, strengthen or adulterate something with alcohol, drugs, poison, etc ▫ ***laced the trifle with sherry.*** **4** to trim with lace. **5** to weave in and out of something; to intertwine. **6** to mark or streak with colour ▫ ***a pink carnation laced with deep red.*** ◷ 13c: from Latin *laqueum* noose.

■ **lace into someone** *colloq* to attack them physically or with words.

■ **lace something up 1** to tighten or fasten (shoes, etc) with laces. See also LACE-UP. **2** to feed (film or tape) into the appropriate channels or guidelines on a projector, tape recorder, etc.

laced ▷ *adj* **1** said of food, drink, etc: having alcohol, drugs, poison, etc added to it. **2** said of a bicycle wheel: having spokes that radiate from the hub to the rim in such a way that they overlap near the hub.

lacerate /ˈlasəreɪt/ ▷ *verb* (***lacerated, lacerating***) **1** to tear or cut (especially flesh) roughly. **2** to wound or hurt (someone's feelings). ▷ *adj, bot* having serrated or ragged edges ▫ ***the lacerate leaves of the dandelion.*** • **lacerated** *adj.* • **laceration** *noun.* ◷ 16c: from Latin *lacerare, laceratum* to tear.

lace-up ▷ *noun* a shoe fastened with a lace. ▷ *adj* said of shoes: fastened with a lace or laces.

lacewing and **lacewing fly** ▷ *noun* an insect with long antennae, a slender body and two pairs of distinctly-veined gauzy wings.

laches /ˈlatʃɪz/ ▷ *noun, law* negligence or excessive delay in carrying out some legal duty or in asserting a right. ◷ 14c: from French *lasche* slack.

lachrymal /ˈlakrɪməl/ ▷ *adj* **1** (*also* **lacrimal**) *anatomy* referring or relating to tears or the glands that secrete them. **2** *literary* relating to or producing tears. ◷ 15c: from Latin *lacrima* tear.

lachrymal gland or **lacrimal gland** ▷ *noun, anatomy* a gland at the upper outer edge of the eye that produces tears.

lachrymose /ˈlakrɪmous/ ▷ *adj, literary* **1** prone to frequent bouts of crying; liable to cry without much provocation. **2** said of a novel, play, film, etc: very sad; likely to make someone cry. • **lachrymosely** *adverb.* ◷ 17c: from Latin *lacrima* tear.

lacing ▷ *noun* **1** (*also* **lacing course**) *Brit, building* a reinforcing COURSE (sense 11) of bricks, stones, etc incorporated in a wall, especially a wall that is constructed from flint, rubble, small stones, etc. **2** (*often* **lacings**) LACE 2. **3** a decoration or trimming made of lace or braiding. **4** the action of putting something into food, drink, etc, especially a small amount of alcohol, usually a spirit, into a drink, etc. ◷ 15c: from LACE + -ING[3].

laciniate /ləˈsɪnɪeɪt/ *biol* ▷ *adj* said of a leaf, petal, the mouthparts of some insects, etc: deeply jagged. • **laciniation** *noun.* ◷ 18c: from *lacinia* a lappet.

lack ▷ *noun* something missing or in short supply; a deficiency or want. ▷ *verb* (***lacked, lacking***) to be without or to have too little of something ▫ ***His argument lacked any real substance.*** • **lacking** *adj.* • **lack of something** absence of something expected or required ▫ ***showed a complete lack of understanding.*** • **no lack of something** a plentiful supply of it. ◷ 13c.

■ **lack for something** to be in need of it.

lackadaisical /lakəˈdeɪzɪkəl/ ▷ *adj* **1** showing little energy, interest, enthusiasm, etc. **2** lazy or idle, especially in a nonchalant way. • **lackadaisically** *adverb.* ◷ 18c: from *alack the day*, an obsolete exclamation of surprise, shock, regret, etc.

lackey /ˈlakɪ/ ▻ *noun* (***lackeys***) **1** someone who does menial work. **2** *derog* a grovelling or servile follower. **3** *old use* a male servant, especially a footman or valet. ▻ *verb* (***lackeyed, lackeying***) *usually intr* **1** to do menial work, especially under the direction of someone else. **2 a** to behave in a grovelling manner towards someone; **b** to follow in a slavish manner. **3** *old use* to work as a servant, especially a footman or valet. ⓒ 16c: from French *laquais* a foot-soldier.

lacklustre or (*US*) **lackluster** ▻ *adj* having or showing little energy, enthusiasm, brightness, etc.

laconic /ləˈkɒnɪk/ ▻ *adj* said of someone's speech or writing: using few words; neatly concise and to the point. • **laconically** *adverb*. ⓒ 16c: from Greek *lakonikos* belonging to Laconia, an area in ancient Greece whose capital was Sparta and whose inhabitants were noted for their terse style of speech.

lacquer /ˈlakə(r)/ ▻ *noun* **1** a substance made by dissolving natural or man-made resins in alcohol and used to form a hard shiny and usually transparent covering on wood and metal. **2** the sap from some trees, used as a varnish for wood. **3** HAIRSPRAY. ▻ *verb* (***lacquered, lacquering***) to cover with lacquer. • **lacquered** *adj*. ⓒ 17c.

lacquer-ware ▻ *noun, art* pieces of decorative art, especially of Asian origin, often inlaid with ivory, mother-of-pearl, precious metals, etc, and coated with hard shiny lacquer, usually depicting landscapes with flamboyantly blossomed trees, pagodas, etc. ⓒ 17c.

lacrimal see under LACHRYMAL

lacrosse /ləˈkrɒs/ ▻ *noun* a team game where each player has a long stick with a netted pocket which is used for catching, carrying and throwing a small ball, the object being to put the ball into the opponents' goal-net. ⓒ 18c: French *la* the + *crosse* hooked stick, a French-Canadian name for the N American Indian game *baggataway*.

lactate[1] /lakˈteɪt/ ▻ *verb* (***lactated, lactating***) *physiol, intr* said of the mammary glands of mammals: to secrete milk. ⓒ 19c: from Latin *lactare, lactatum* to suckle.

lactate[2] /ˈlakteɪt/ ▻ *noun, biochem* a salt or ester of lactic acid. ⓒ 18c.

lactation /lakˈteɪʃən/ ▻ *noun, physiol* in mammals: the hormonally controlled secretion of milk by the mammary glands in order to feed a baby or young animal until it is weaned (see WEAN). • **lactational** *adj*. ⓒ 19c.

lacteal /ˈlaktɪəl/ ▻ *adj* **1** referring or relating to, or consisting of, milk. **2** *anatomy* said of certain lymphatic vessels: carrying a milky fluid such as CHYLE. ▻ *noun, anatomy* any small lymphatic vessel that absorbs the products of digestion of fats in the small intestine. ⓒ 17c: from Latin *lacteus* milky + -AL[1].

lactic /ˈlaktɪk/ ▻ *adj* relating to, derived from or containing milk. ⓒ 18c: from Latin *lac, lactis* milk + -IC.

lactic acid ▻ *noun, biochem* (formula $CH_3CH(OH)COOH$) an organic acid produced during the souring of milk by a bacterial fermentation process that is used commercially in the manufacture of cheese, yoghurt and other dairy products. It is also produced in animal muscle when there is insufficient oxygen available to break down carbohydrate.

lacto- /ˈlaktoʊ/ or (before a vowel) **lact-** ▻ *combining form, signifying* milk. ⓒ From Latin *lac, lactis* milk.

lactose /ˈlaktoʊs/ ▻ *noun, biochem* (formula $C_{12}H_{22}O_{11}$) a white crystalline disaccharide sugar which consists of a GALACTOSE molecule linked to a GLUCOSE molecule, found only in milk and used in the manufacture of baby milk, and as a laxative and diuretic. *Non-technical equivalent* **milk sugar** or **sugar of milk**. ⓒ 19c.

lactovegetarian /laktoʊvɛdʒɪˈtɛərɪən/ and **lactarian** /lakˈtɛərɪən/ ▻ *noun* a vegetarian whose diet includes milk and other dairy products. ▻ *adj* relating to someone who practices this or to this kind of diet. Compare VEGAN.

lacuna /ləˈkjuːnə/ ▻ *noun* (***lacunae*** /-niː/ or ***lacunas***) **1** a gap or a space where something is missing, especially in printed text. **2** *anatomy* a tiny cavity in bone or cartilage tissue. **3** *bot* any air space in the centre of a plant stem or root. ⓒ 17c: Latin, meaning 'hole'.

lacustrine /ləˈkʌstraɪn/ ▻ *adj* **1** referring or relating to lakes. **2** said of plants and animals: living in lakes or on lake shores. ⓒ 19c: from Latin *lacus* a pool.

lacy /ˈleɪsɪ/ ▻ *adj* (***lacier, laciest***) **1** like lace, especially when used to suggest the fine delicate nature of something □ *The frost left a lacy pattern on the window.* **2** made of lace or trimmed with lace. • **lacily** *adverb*. • **laciness** *noun*.

lad ▻ *noun* **1** a boy or youth. **2** (*usually* **the lads**) *colloq* a group of male friends who drink together, go to football matches together, etc on a regular basis. **3** *Brit* someone who works in a stable, regardless of their age or sex. **4** *Scots* a boyfriend. • **laddish** see separate entry. • **a bit of a lad** *colloq* a man who indulges in occasional bouts of heavy drinking, chasing women, etc. • **my lad** *colloq* an endearing or familiar term of address, often used by mothers to their sons. • **one of the lads** a person, usually a man who is thought of as fairly ordinary, but who is also good company and willing to join in the fun. *N Amer equivalent* **regular guy**. ⓒ 14c.

ladder /ˈladə(r)/ ▻ *noun* **1** a piece of equipment which is used for climbing up or down, usually made of wood, metal or rope, and consisting of a set of parallel horizontal rungs or steps set at right angles between two long vertical supports. See also FISH-LADDER. **2** *chiefly Brit* a long narrow flaw, especially in a stocking, tights or other knitted garment, where a row of stitches has broken. Also called RUN. **3** a hierarchical or graded route of advancement or progress □ *determined to climb the social ladder.* **4** anything that is like a ladder in arrangement, eg a list of names of players in a competition on which names are moved up or down depending on whether the players win or lose. ▻ *verb* (***laddered, laddering***) *chiefly Brit* said of stockings, etc: **a** to cause a ladder to appear; **b** to develop a ladder. • **laddered** *adj* said of stockings, etc: having a ladder or ladders. ⓒ Anglo-Saxon *hlæder*.

laddie /ˈladɪ/ ▻ *noun, dialect* (***laddies***) *colloq* **1** a young boy or lad, often used as a familiar or endearing form of address. **2** a son. ⓒ 16c.

laddish ▻ *adj* said of some young males or their behaviour: characterized by loud swaggering arrogance, vulgarity and sometimes aggression, often brought on by excessive drinking. • **laddishness** *noun*. See also LAGER LOUT. ⓒ 1980s: derived from such concepts as being 'one of the lads' and 'a bit of a lad'.

lade ▻ *verb* (*past tense* ***laded***, *past participle* ***laden***, *present participle* ***lading***) In most senses the only surviving form is that of the past participle LADEN used adjectivally. **1 a** to load (cargo, etc) on to a ship; **b** said of a ship: to take cargo, etc on board. **2** to put a burden, especially one of guilt, on someone. **3** to scoop out (water) using a ladle, etc. ⓒ Anglo-Saxon *hladen* to load or to draw up.

laden /ˈleɪdən/ ▻ *adj* **1** said of a ship: loaded with cargo. **2** said of a person, an animal, the sky, a vehicle, etc: heavily loaded, weighed down, burdened □ *trees laden with fruit.* **3** said of a person: oppressed, especially with guilt, worry, etc. **4** *in compounds* □ *guilt-laden* □ *heavy-laden.* ⓒ Anglo-Saxon *hladen* to load or to draw up.

la-di-da or **lah-di-dah** /lɑːdɪˈdɑː/ ▻ *adj, adverb, colloq* in a pretentiously 'posh' way □ *talks so la-di-da you'd never guess he comes from Aberdeen.* ⓒ 19c: an imitation of this affected way of talking.

ladies /ˈleɪdɪz/ ▻ *singular and plural noun* a lavatory in a restaurant, pub, etc for women only; a women's public lavatory.

lading /ˈleɪdɪŋ/ ▷ *noun* **1** the cargo or load that a ship, etc carries. **2** the act of loading cargo or goods onto a ship, etc. See also BILL OF LADING. ⓒ Anglo-Saxon *hladen* to load or to draw up.

ladle /ˈleɪdəl/ ▷ *noun* a large spoon with a long handle and deep bowl, for serving or transferring liquid. ▷ *verb* (***ladled, ladling***) to serve or transfer with a ladle. ⓒ Anglo-Saxon *hlædel*.

■ **ladle something out** to serve or distribute (praise, blame, etc) generously or excessively.

ladleful ▷ *noun* (***ladlefuls***) the amount a ladle can hold.

lady /ˈleɪdɪ/ ▷ *noun* (***ladies***) **1** a woman who is regarded as having good manners and elegant or refined behaviour. **2** a polite word for a woman generally. **3** *historical* a woman of the upper classes. **4** (**Lady**) *Brit* **a** a title of honour used for peeresses (but not duchesses), the wives and daughters of peers and knights, and for certain women of importance, eg mayoresses; **b** (**my lady**) the formal way of addressing someone who holds such an honorary title. **5** *as adj, now rather dated* said of the female gender: **a** used especially for occupations, etc formerly considered to be the domain of men □ *a lady doctor*; **b** used especially when the attendant noun fails to signal gender □ *went on holiday with his lady friend*. • **lady of the house** *usually facetious* the woman who is head of a household. • **lady of the night** or **evening** *euphemistic* a prostitute. ⓒ Anglo-Saxon *hlæfdige*, meaning 'bread-kneader'.

ladybird and (*N Amer*) **ladybug** ▷ *noun* a kind of small beetle whose oval body is usually bright red or yellow with black spots, and which feeds mainly on aphids and scale insects, playing an important part in the control of garden pests.

Lady Chapel ▷ *noun, Christianity, chiefly RC Church* a chapel dedicated to the Virgin Mary, usually built behind and to the east of the main altar.

Lady Day ▷ *noun, Christianity* 25 March, the feast of the ANNUNCIATION.

lady-in-waiting ▷ *noun* (***ladies-in-waiting***) a woman who attends a queen, princess, etc.

lady-killer ▷ *noun, colloq* a man who is considered, or who considers himself to be, irresistibly attractive to women.

ladylike ▷ *adj* showing attributes, such as social poise, good manners, elegance, etc, that are like or appropriate to those of a lady.

lady luck ▷ *noun* a personification of the concept of good fortune □ *Lady luck was smiling on the winner of the lottery*.

Lady Mayoress ▷ *noun* the wife of a LORD MAYOR.

lady's finger ▷ *noun* **1** OKRA. **2** the popular name for the wild flower, kidney VETCH. **3** a SPONGE FINGER.

Ladyship ▷ *noun* (*usually* **Your** or **Her Ladyship**) **a** a title used to address peeresses (but not duchesses) and the wives and daughters of peers and knights; **b** *also ironic* used to address or refer to someone whose behaviour suggests that they think of themselves as being are more important than they are □ *Her ladyship expected everything to be done for her*.

lady's man or **ladies' man** ▷ *noun* a man who enjoys and cultivates the company of women.

lady's-slipper ▷ *noun* an orchid with a large yellow slipper-like lip.

laevorotation /liːvoʊroʊˈteɪʃən/ ▷ *noun* an action of turning to the left. • **laevorotationary** *adj*. ⓒ 19c: from Latin *lævus* turned to the left.

lag¹ ▷ *verb* (***lagged, lagging***) *intr* (*usually* **lag behind**) to move or progress so slowly as to become separated or left behind. ▷ *noun* **1** a lagging behind; a delay. **2** the amount by which one thing is delayed behind another. ⓒ 16c.

lag² ▷ *verb* (***lagged, lagging***) to cover (a boiler, water pipes, etc) with thick insulating material in order to minimize heat loss. ⓒ 19c.

lager /ˈlɑːɡə(r)/ ▷ *noun* a light beer available in bottles or on draught. ⓒ 19c: from German *lagern* to store.

lager lout ▷ *noun* **1** a youngish male who, after an extended drinking bout, starts behaving in an aggressive or unruly manner. **2** anyone whose antisocial behaviour can be attributed to excessive drinking. • **lager-loutery** *noun*. Compare LADDISH. ⓒ 1988: first coined by *Sun* journalist, Simon Walters, following the Conservative minister John Patten's use of lager culture.

laggard /ˈlaɡəd/ ▷ *noun* someone or something that lags behind.

lagging ▷ *noun* insulating cover for pipes, boilers, etc.

lagomorph /ˈlaɡoʊmɔːf/ ▷ *noun, zool* a mammal such as a rabbit or hare with upper front teeth specially adapted for gnawing. ⓒ 19c: from Greek *lagos* a hare + -MORPH.

lagoon /ləˈɡuːn/ ▷ *noun* a relatively shallow body of often brackish water that is separated from the open sea by a barrier such as a reef or a narrow bank of sand or shingle. ⓒ 17c: from Latin *lacuna* a pool.

lah or **la** /lɑː/ ▷ *noun, music* in SOL-FA notation: the sixth note of the major scale. ⓒ 14c: see SOL-FA.

laid *past tense, past participle of* LAY¹

laid-back ▷ *adj, colloq* relaxed; not inclined to get upset; easy-going.

laid paper ▷ *noun* a type of paper that has faint lines running across the surface.

laid-up ▷ *adj* **1** said of someone: confined to bed because of illness or injury. **2** said of a car, boat, etc: off the road, on shore or in dry dock for repairs, refitting, etc.

lain *past participle of* LIE²

lair /lɛə(r)/ ▷ *noun* **1** a wild animal's den. **2** *colloq* a place of refuge or hiding. ⓒ Anglo-Saxon *leger* a bed or lying place.

laird /lɛəd; *Scots* lerd/ ▷ *noun, Scots* someone who owns a large estate, especially one that is divided up amongst tenant farmers. ⓒ 15c: a variant of LORD.

laissez-faire or **laisser-faire** /lɛseɪˈfɛə(r)/ ▷ *noun* a policy of not interfering in what others are doing. ⓒ 19c: French.

laissez-passer or **laisser-passer** /lɛseɪˈpɑːseɪ/ ▷ *noun* a permit that allows someone to travel to or through a particular area. ⓒ Early 20c: French.

laity /ˈleɪɪtɪ/ ▷ *noun* (*usually* **the laity**) the people who are not members of a particular profession, especially those who are not part of the clergy. ⓒ 16c: from LAY³.

lake¹ ▷ *noun* **1** a large area of still fresh or salt water, surrounded by land and lying in a depression in the Earth's surface, which receives water from rivers, streams, springs, etc. **2** a surplus of a liquid commodity, usually one that has been created because of specific economic conditions □ *a wine lake*. ⓒ 14c: from Latin *lacus* a vat or pool.

lake² ▷ *noun* **1** a reddish dye, originally obtained from LAC, but now more usually obtained from COCHINEAL. **2** a dye, mainly used in the textile industry, that is made by combining animal, vegetable or coal-tar pigment with a metallic oxide or earth. ⓒ 17c: a variant spelling of LAC.

lake dwelling ▷ *noun* a house that is constructed on top of a platform which is supported by piles driven into a lake-bed or into the soft ground near the shore of a lake so that dampness and pests such as rodents can be avoided. ⓒ 19c.

lakeside ▷ *adj* situated beside a lake.

-lalia /leɪlɪə/ ▷ *combining form, denoting* speech of a specified kind, usually defective or idiosyncratic in some way. ⓒ Greek, meaning 'speech' or 'chatter'.

Lalique glass /la'liːk —/ ▻ *noun* a type of decorative glassware and jewellery. ⓒ Early 20c: named after René Lalique (1860–1945), French glassware and jewellery designer.

Lallans /'lalənz/ ▻ *singular noun* a name applied to any of the varieties of SCOTS created and used in 18c and 20c revivals of the language as a literary medium. ⓒ 18c: Scots variant of LOWLANDS.

lam *slang* ▻ *verb* (***lammed, lamming***) to thrash. ▻ *noun, chiefly N Amer* an escape, especially from the police. • **on the lam** trying to avoid being captured. ⓒ 16c: from Norse *lemja* to make someone lame.

■ **lam into someone** to beat them up.

Lam. ▻ *abbreviation* Book of the Bible: Lamentations (of Jeremiah). See table at BIBLE.

lama /'lɑːmə/ ▻ *noun* (***lamas***) the title of a Buddhist priest or monk in Tibet and Mongolia. See also DALAI LAMA. ⓒ 17c: from Tibetan *blama.*

Lamaism /'lɑːməɪzəm/ ▻ *noun* the branch of Buddhism that is prevalent in Tibet and Mongolia. • **Lamaist** *noun.* • **Lamaistic** *adj.* ⓒ 19c: from LAMA.

Lamarckism /lɑː'mɑːkɪzəm/ ▻ *noun* one of the earliest theories of evolution, now discredited, which proposed that characteristics acquired during the lifetime of an organism could be transmitted from parents to offspring. Compare DARWINISM. ⓒ 19c: named after the French naturalist Jean Baptiste Lamarck (1744–1829).

the Lamb and **the Lamb of God** ▻ *noun, Christianity* a title given to Christ (John 1.29 and Revelation 17.14, etc) because of the sacrificial nature of his death.

lamb /lam/ ▻ *noun* **1** a young sheep. **2** the flesh of a lamb or sheep. **3** *colloq* **a** a quiet and well-behaved child; **b** a kind, gentle, good, sweet, etc person. ▻ *verb* (***lambed, lambing***) *intr* **1** said of a ewe: to give birth to a lamb or lambs. **2** said of a shepherd or farmer: to look after ewes that are lambing. • **like a lamb to the slaughter** innocently and without resistance. ⓒ Anglo-Saxon.

lambada /lam'bɑːdə/ ▻ *noun* (***lambadas***) **1** a Brazilian dance in which couples make fast erotic hip movements. **2** the music for this style of dancing, influenced by SALSA, CALYPSO and REGGAE. ⓒ 1990s: Portuguese, meaning 'a crack of a whip'; the dance became popular outside Brazil only after the film *Dirty Dancing* (1987).

lambaste or **lambast** /lam'bast/ ▻ *verb* (***lambasted, lambasting***) **1** to thrash or beat severely. **2** to scold severely. ⓒ 17c: LAM + BASTE³.

lambda /'lamdə/ ▻ *noun* (***lambdas***) the eleventh letter of the Greek alphabet. See table at GREEK ALPHABET.

lambent /'lambənt/ ▻ *adj* **1** said of a flame or light: flickering over a surface. **2** said of eyes, the sky, etc: gently sparkling. **3** said of wit, writing style, etc: playfully light and clever. • **lambency** *noun.* • **lambently** *adverb.* ⓒ 17c: from Latin *lambere* to lick.

lambert /'lambət/ ▻ *noun* a former unit of brightness, equal to the luminance radiated into a hemisphere by one square centimetre of a uniformly diffusing surface. Compare LUMEN. ⓒ Early 20c: named after the German mathematician, Johann Heinrich Lambert (1728–77).

lambing ▻ *noun* **1** the time when ewes give birth to lambs. **2** the work involved in caring for ewes and their newborn lambs. ⓒ 16c.

Lambrusco /lam'brʊskoʊ/ ▻ *noun* (***Lambruscos***) **1** a variety of white or red grape frequently used in wine-making in Italy. **2** the light sparkling wine made from this kind of grape.

lamb's fry ▻ *noun* lamb's offal, especially lamb's testicles.

lambskin ▻ *noun* the skin of a lamb, usually with the wool left on it, used to make slippers, coats, etc. ⓒ 14c.

lamb's lettuce see CORN SALAD

lamb's tails ▻ *noun, colloq* the CATKINS which hang from the hazel tree. ⓒ 19c: from the notion that these particular catkins look very like the tails of lambs.

lambswool ▻ *noun* fine wool, especially that from a lamb's first shearing. Also *as adj.* ⓒ 16c.

LAMDA /'lamdə/ ▻ *abbreviation* London Academy of Music and Dramatic Art.

lame ▻ *adj* (***lamer, lamest***) **1** not able to walk properly, especially due to an injury or defect of the leg, hip, etc. **2** said of an excuse, argument, etc: not convincing; weak; ineffective. ▻ *verb* (***lamed, laming***) to make lame. • **lamely** *adverb.* • **lameness** *noun.* ⓒ Anglo-Saxon *lama.*

lamé /'lɑːmeɪ/ ▻ *noun* a fabric which has metallic threads, usually gold or silver, woven into it. ⓒ 1920s: French, meaning 'having metal plates or strips'.

lamebrain ▻ *noun, colloq* someone who is considered to be extremely stupid. • **lamebrained** *adj.* ⓒ 1920s.

lame duck ▻ *noun* **1** someone who depends on the help of others to an excessive extent. **2** *US* an elected official who is in the final months of office, after a successor has been appointed. **3** a company that has financial problems, especially one that is looking for government subsidy to survive. **4** *stock exchange* someone who is unable to meet the financial liabilities they have taken on. Compare BEAR² *noun* 4, BULL¹ *noun* 4. ⓒ 18c: originally a stock market term which extended to a more general meaning in 19c.

lamella /lə'mɛlə/ ▻ *noun* (***lamellae*** /-liː/) **1** *anatomy* a thin sheet or plate of tissue, especially one of the many thin layers of which compact bone is formed. **2** *bot* any of the thin sheet-like membranes that are present within the CHLOROPLASTS of plant cells. **3** *biol* any of the vertical SPORE-bearing structures or gills that radiate outwards from the stalk on the underside of the cap of a mushroom or toadstool. Also called **gill**. ⓒ 17c: Latin, meaning 'thin layer'.

lamellibranch /lə'mɛlɪbraŋk/ ▻ *noun* (***lamellibranchs***) *zool* any of various BIVALVE molluscs, including oysters and mussels, that have large gills which are used to filter microscopic food particles from the water. ⓒ 19c: from LAMELLA + Greek *branchia* gills.

lamellicorn ▻ *noun, zool* any of a group of beetles, such as the DUNG-BEETLE, characterized by antennae with platelike clubs at their ends. Also *as adj.* ⓒ 19c: from LAMELLA + Latin *cornu* a horn.

lament /lə'mɛnt/ ▻ *verb* (***lamented, lamenting***) *tr & intr* to feel or express regret or sadness. ▻ *noun* **1** an expression of sadness, grief, regret, etc. **2** a poem, song, etc which expresses great grief, especially following someone's death. ⓒ 16c: from Latin *lamentari* to wail or moan.

lamentable /'laməntəbəl, lə'mɛn-/ ▻ *adj* **1** regrettable, shameful or deplorable. **2** inadequate; useless. • **lamentably** *adverb.* ⓒ 15c.

lamentation /lamən'teɪʃən/ ▻ *noun* an act of lamenting; a lament.

Lamentations and **Lamentations of Jeremiah** ▻ *noun* Book of the Bible: the title of a book in the Old Testament. See table at BIBLE.

lamented ▻ *adj* said of a dead person: sadly missed; mourned for □ *her late lamented father.*

lamina /'lamɪnə/ ▻ *noun* (***laminae*** /-niː/) **1** a thin plate or layer of a material of uniform thickness, especially bone, rock or metal. **2** *bot* the flattened part of a leaf blade. ⓒ 17c: Latin, meaning 'thin plate'.

laminar flow ▻ *noun* **1** *physics* the streamlined flow of a viscous incompressible fluid in which all particles of the fluid travel along distinct and separate lines. **2** *meteorol* non-turbulent flow. ⓒ 1940s.

laminate ▻ *verb* /'lamɪneɪt/ (***laminated, laminating***) **1** to beat (a material, especially metal) into thin sheets. **2** to form (a composite material) by bonding or gluing together two or more thin sheets of that material. **3** to cover or overlay (a surface) with a thin sheet of protective material, eg transparent plastic film. **4** *tr & intr* to separate or be separated into thin layers. ▷ *noun* /ˈlamɪnət/ a sheet of composite material formed by bonding or gluing together two or more thin sheets of that material, usually with the application of pressure or heat, eg plywood, reinforced plastic, laminated glass. ▷ *adj* /ˈlamɪnət/ **1** laminated. **2** said of a material, especially metal: beaten into thin sheets. • **lamination** *noun*. ⓒ 17c: from Latin *lamina* thin plate.

laminated ▷ *adj* **1** composed of two or more thin sheets of a material, bonded or glued together. **2** covered with a thin layer of protective or strengthening material. **3** arranged in thin layers or plates. **4** said of a material, especially metal: beaten into thin sheets. ⓒ 17c.

Lammas /ˈlaməs/ ▷ *noun, Christianity* an old feast day in the early church calendar held on 1 August, one of the four QUARTER DAYS in Scotland. ⓒ Anglo-Saxon *hlafmæsse*, from *hlaf* loaf + *mæsse* mass, because the festival celebrated the harvesting of the first crops.

lammergeyer or **lammergeier** /ˈlaməgaɪə(r)/ ▷ *noun* a large rare vulture with a wingspan of nearly 3m, a feathered neck and dark tufts of feathers on either side of its beak, found in the remote mountain regions of Europe, Africa and Asia (especially the Himalayas). ⓒ 19c: from German *Lämmergeier*, literally 'lamb vulture'.

lamp ▷ *noun* **1** a piece of equipment designed to give out light, now especially one with an electricity supply, a means of holding a light-bulb and a shade. **2** an appliance used as a source of light, that has a glass case covering a flame produced by burning oil, etc. **3** any piece of equipment that produces ultraviolet or infrared radiation and which is used in the treatment of certain medical conditions. ⓒ 12c: from Greek *lampein* to shine.

lampblack ▷ *noun* soot obtained from burning carbon and used as a pigment. ⓒ 15c.

lamplight ▷ *noun* the light given off by a lamp or lamps. ⓒ 16c.

lamplighter ▷ *noun, formerly* a person whose job was to light and extinguish gas streetlights. ⓒ 18c.

lampoon /lamˈpuːn/ ▷ *noun* an attack, usually in the form of satirical prose or verse, on someone or on the style or content of their writing. ▷ *verb* (***lampooned, lampooning***) to use a lampoon to attack or laugh at someone or their writing. • **lampooner** *noun*. • **lampoonery** *noun*. • **lampoonist** *noun*. ⓒ 17c: from French *lampons* let's booze.

lamppost ▷ *noun* a tall post that supports a streetlamp.

lamprey /ˈlamprɪ/ ▷ *noun* (***lampreys***) *zool* any of about 30 species of primitive jawless fish resembling eels, which feed by clinging to other fishes with their sucker-like mouths and sucking the blood of their hosts. ⓒ 13c: from French *lampreie*.

lampshade ▷ *noun* a shade placed over a lamp or light bulb to soften or direct the light coming from it.

lampshell see BRACHIOPOD

LAN ▷ *abbreviation, computing* local area network, a computer network that operates over a small area, such as an office or group of offices, and which links word processors, disk drives, printers, etc together. Compare WAN.

Lancastrian /laŋˈkastrɪən/ ▷ *noun* **1** someone who comes from or lives in Lancaster or Lancashire. **2** *historical* a supporter of the House of Lancaster in the Wars of the Roses. Compare YORKIST. ▷ *adj* relating to Lancaster, the House of Lancaster or Lancashire. ⓒ 19c.

lance /lɑːns/ ▷ *noun* **1** a long spear with a hard pointed head at one end and sometimes a small flag at the other, used as a weapon by charging horsemen. **2** any similarly shaped implement used in hunting, whaling, etc. ▷ *verb* (***lanced, lancing***) **1** to cut open (a boil, abscess, etc) with a lancet. **2** to pierce with, or as if with, a lance. ⓒ 13c: from Latin *lancea* a light spear with a leather thong attached.

lance corporal ▷ *noun*, **1** in the British army: a rank between private and corporal, the lowest rank of non-commissioned officer. **2** a soldier who holds this rank.

lanceolate /ˈlɑːnsɪəleɪt/ ▷ *adj, chiefly scientific* said of an object: having the shape of the head of a spear, ie with its length much greater than its width and both ends tapered to a point. ⓒ 18c: from Latin *lanceola* small lance.

lancer /ˈlɑːnsə(r)/ ▷ *noun* **1** *formerly* a cavalry soldier belonging to a regiment armed with lances. **2** someone who belongs to a regiment that has retained the word *Lancers* in its title.

lancers /ˈlɑːnsəz/ ▷ *singular noun* a set of quadrilles (see QUADRILLE[1]), or the music for it.

lancet /ˈlɑːnsɪt/ ▷ *noun* a small pointed surgical knife which has both edges sharpened. ⓒ 15c: from French *lancette* a small lance.

lancet arch ▷ *noun, archit* a high narrow pointed arch.

lancet window ▷ *noun, archit* a high narrow pointed window.

Lancs. /laŋks/ ▷ *abbreviation, English county* Lancashire.

land ▷ *noun* **1** the solid part of the Earth's surface as opposed to the area covered by water. **2** ground or soil, especially with regard to its use or quality □ *farm land.* **3** ground that is used for agriculture. **4** a country, state or region □ *native land.* **5** (**lands**) estates. **6** *in compounds* any area of ground that is characterized in a specified way □ *gangland* □ *hinterland.* ▷ *verb* (***landed, landing***) **1** *tr & intr* to come or bring to rest on the ground or water, or in a particular place, after flight through the air □ *The plane landed on time.* **2** *intr* to end up in a specified place or position, especially after a fall, jump, throw, etc. **3** to bring on to the land from a ship □ *landed the cargo.* **4** to bring (a fish, especially one caught on a line) out of the water. **5** *colloq* to be successful in getting (a job, contract, prize, etc). **6** *colloq* to give someone (a punch or slap). • **by land** over the ground, as opposed to flying or sailing. • **in the land of the living** *colloq* alive. • **land lucky** to find oneself in an unexpectedly fortunate position. • **land on one's feet** to end up in a favourable situation, especially after some setback, misdemeanour, indiscretion, etc. • **see how the land lies** to make investigations into something, especially before taking some decision. ⓒ Anglo-Saxon.

■ **land someone** or **oneself in something** *colloq* to put them, or to find oneself, in a certain position or situation, usually one that is unwelcome or unfavourable □ *landed themselves in trouble.*

■ **land up** *colloq* to come to be in a certain position or situation, usually one that is worse than the previous one □ *landed up homeless after losing his job.*

■ **land someone with something** *colloq* to give or pass something unpleasant or unwanted to them □ *landed us with all the bills to pay.*

Land /land/ ▷ *noun* (*plural* ***Länder*** /ˈlɛndə(r)/) **1** any of the federal states which make up the Federal Republic of Germany and function as a unit of local government. **2** any of the provinces of Austria.

land agent ▷ *noun* **1** someone who manages a large estate for the owner. **2** someone who takes care of the sale of estates.

landau /ˈlandɔː, -daʊ/ ▷ *noun* (***landaus***) a four-wheeled horse-drawn carriage with a removable front cover and a back cover which folds down. ⓒ 18c: named after Landau in Germany, where they were first made.

land bank ▷ *noun, US* a bank that finances real-estate transactions using the land as security.

landed ▻ *adj* **1** owning land or estates □ *landed gentry.* **2** consisting of or derived from land □ *landed estates.*

landed interest ▻ *noun* the collective interests of people owning lands.

Länder *plural of* LAND

landfall ▻ *noun* **1** the first land visible towards the end of a journey by sea or air. **2** an approach to, or a sighting of, land towards the end of a journey by sea or air.

landfill ▻ *noun* **1** a site where rubbish is disposed of by burying it under layers of earth. **2** the rubbish that is disposed of in this way. ◷ 1940s.

land-girl ▻ *noun, Brit, formerly* a woman, a member of the Women's Land Army, who worked on a farm, especially during World War I and II.

landing ▻ *noun* **1** the act of coming or being put ashore or of returning to the ground. **2** a place for disembarking, especially from a ship. **3** a level part of a staircase either between two flights of steps, or at the very top. ◷ 15c.

landing-craft ▻ *noun* (*plural* ***landing-craft***) **1** *military* a low open vessel, capable of beaching itself, that is used for putting troops, tanks, equipment, etc ashore. **2** a part of a spacecraft that disengages from the main part and lands on a planet or moon.

landing-field ▻ *noun* a stretch of ground where aircraft can take off and land.

landing-gear ▻ *noun* the wheels and supporting structure which allow an aircraft to land and take off.

landing-net ▻ *noun* a large hand-held net used for taking fish that are already hooked out of the water.

landing-stage ▻ *noun* a platform, either fixed or floating, where passengers, cargo, etc from a ship can come ashore.

landing-strip ▻ *noun* a long narrow stretch of ground where aircraft can take off and land.

landlady ▻ *noun* **1** a woman who rents property out to a tenant or tenants. **2** a woman who owns or runs a public house or hotel.

landlocked ▻ *adj* said of a country or a piece of land: almost or completely enclosed by land.

landlord ▻ *noun* **1** a man who rents property out to a tenant or tenants. **2** a man who owns or runs a public house or hotel.

landlubber ▻ *noun, derog* a sailors' name for someone who lives and works on the land and has no experience of the sea.

landmark ▻ *noun* **1** a distinctive feature on the land that is conspicuous or well-known, especially when it can be used by sailors or travellers as an indication of where they are. **2** an occasion, event or development of importance, especially one that is significant in the history or progress of something □ *'Citizen Kane' is regarded as a landmark in cinema history.* **3** anything that functions as a means of indicating a land boundary.

landmass ▻ *noun* a large area of land unbroken by seas.

land mine ▻ *noun* an explosive device that is laid on or near the surface of the ground and which detonates if it is disturbed from above.

land of milk and honey ▻ *noun* **1** *originally Bible* the fertile land promised to the Israelites when they left Egypt (Ezekiel 20.6). **2** any place or region believed to be particularly rich and prosperous.

land of Nod ▻ *noun* **1** *originally Bible* the region to the east of Eden where Cain went after he had killed Able (Genesis 4.16). **2** used as a pun: sleep.

landowner ▻ *noun* someone who owns land.

Landrover ▻ *noun, trademark* a strong four-wheel-drive motor vehicle used for driving over rough ground.

landscape /ˈlandskeɪp/ ▻ *noun* **1** the area and features of land that can be seen in a broad view, especially when they form a particular type of scenery. **2 a** a painting, drawing, photograph, etc of the countryside, often depicting natural elements, such as trees, rivers, mountains, etc; **b** the genre of this. **3** *as adj* **a** consisting of landscape; having landscape as one's subject; **b** said of the orientation of a page, illustration, etc: wider than it is tall or deep. Compare PORTRAIT. ▻ *verb* (***landscaped, landscaping***) to improve the look of (a garden, park, the layout of a housing estate, etc) by enhancing the existing natural features or by artificially creating new ones. ◷ 17c: from Dutch *land* + *schap* creation, originally introduced as a technical term in painting.

landscape gardening ▻ *noun* the art of laying out a garden or grounds to produce the effect of a natural landscape, especially a picturesque one. • **landscape gardener** *noun.*

landside ▻ *noun* that part of an airport accessible to the general public. Compare AIRSIDE.

landslide ▻ *noun* **1** (*also* **landslip**) **a** the sudden downward movement of a mass of soil and rock material, especially in mountainous areas, under the influence of gravity, usually as a result of heavy rain or snow, earthquakes, or blasting operations; **b** the accumulation of soil and rock material from a landslide. **2** a victory in an election by an overwhelming majority.

landward /landwəd/ ▻ *adj* lying or facing toward the land. ▻ *adverb* (*also* **landwards**) towards land. See also INLAND.

land yacht ▻ *noun* a recreational vehicle with wheels and sails, powered by wind as a conventional yacht, and used on beaches.

lane ▻ *noun* **1** a narrow road or street. **2 a** a subdivision of a road for a single line of traffic; **b** the traffic occupying one such subdivision. **3** a regular course taken by ships across the sea, or by aircraft through the air □ *shipping lane.* **4** a marked subdivision of a running track or swimming pool for one competitor. **5** *ten-pin bowling* each subdivision of a bowling alley, down which the balls are bowled towards the pins. **6** a passage through a crowd. ◷ Anglo-Saxon *lanu.*

lang. ▻ *abbreviation* language.

Langerhans see under ISLETS OF LANGERHANS

langlauf /ˈlɑːŋlaʊf/ ▻ *noun* cross-country skiing. • **langlaufer** *noun.* ◷ 1920s: German, from *lang* long + *Lauf* run.

langouste /lɑ̃ŋˈguːst/ ▻ *noun* a salt-water crustacean similar to the lobster but rather smaller and with no claws. Also called **spiny lobster**. ◷ 19c: French, related to Latin *locusta* a lobster or locust.

langoustine /lɑ̃ŋgʊˈstiːn/ ▻ *noun* a saltwater crustacean similar to the crayfish and rather bigger than the king prawn. ◷ 1940s: French diminutive of *langouste.*

lang syne /laŋˈsaɪn/ *Scots* ▻ *adverb* long ago. ▻ *noun* days gone by, especially those that evoke nostalgic memories. ◷ 16c: from Scots *lang* long + *syne* before or since.

language /ˈlaŋgwɪdʒ/ ▻ *noun* **1** any formalized system of communication, especially one that uses sounds or written symbols which the majority of a particular community will readily understand. **2** the speech and writing of a particular nation or social group. **3** the faculty of speech. **4** a specified style of speech or verbal expression □ *elegant language.* **5** any other way of communicating or expressing meaning □ *sign language.* **6** professional or specialized vocabulary □ *legal language.* **7** a system of signs and symbols used to write computer programs. See also LOW-LEVEL LANGUAGE, HIGH-LEVEL LANGUAGE. • **bad language** words that some people might consider rude or offensive. • **body language** see separate entry. • **dead language** a language, eg Sanskrit,

Latin or classical Greek, that is no longer passed on from one generation to another as a mother tongue and which has therefore become fossilized. • **first language** or **native language 1** the language that someone learns as a child, usually from a parent or parents. **2** the language that someone in a multilingual community chooses to use in preference to other language options. See also MOTHER TONGUE. • **second** or **third**, *etc* **language** language that is learned subsequent to the mother tongue □ *Polish was his first language, French was his second language and English his third.* • **speak the same language** to think in similar ways or share the same kind of tastes. ⓒ 13c: from French *langage*.

language laboratory ▷ *noun* a room with separate cubicles equipped with tape recorders and pre-recorded tapes, used for language learning.

langue /lɑ̃g/ ▷ *noun, linguistics* the entire language system of a particular speech community, theoretically available to every member of that community. Compare PAROLE. ⓒ 1915: French; first coined in *Cours de linguistique générale*, a compilation of his students' notes from lectures by the Swiss linguist Ferdinand de Saussure (1857-1913).

langue de chat /lɑ̃ŋ də 'ʃɑː/ ▷ *noun* (***langues de chat***) a very thin finger-shaped biscuit or piece of chocolate. ⓒ Early 20c: French, meaning 'cat's tongue'.

languid /'laŋgwɪd/ ▷ *adj* **1** lacking in energy or vitality; listless. **2** slow-moving; sluggish. • **languidly** *adverb*. • **languidness** *noun*. ⓒ 16c: from Latin *languere* to grow faint.

languish /'laŋgwɪʃ/ ▷ *verb* (***languishes, languished, languishing***) *intr* **1** to spend time in hardship or discomfort. **2** to grow weak; to lose energy or vitality. **3** to look sorrowful. **4** to pine. • **languishing** *adj*. ⓒ 14c: see LANGUID.

languor /'laŋgə(r)/ ▷ *noun* **1** a feeling of dullness or lack of energy. **2** tender softness or sentiment. **3** a stuffy suffocating atmosphere or stillness. • **languorous** *adj*. ⓒ 14c: from Latin *languere* to grow faint.

langur /lʌŋ'gʊə(r)/ *noun* a long-tailed monkey, native to S and SE Asia. See also WANDEROO 1. ⓒ 19c: Hindi

lank ▷ *adj* (**lanker, lankest**) **1** long and thin. **2** said of hair: long, straight, limp, dull and unhealthy-looking. • **lankness** *noun*. ⓒ Anglo-Saxon *hlanc*.

lanky /'laŋkɪ/ ▷ *adj* (***lankier, lankiest***) said of a person or animal: thin and tall, especially in an awkward and ungainly way. • **lankiness** *noun*. ⓒ Anglo-Saxon *hlanc*.

lanneret /'lanərət/ ▷ *noun* the male LANNER FALCON.

lanner falcon /'lanər —/ ▷ *noun* **1** a species of large falcon that lives in the arid lands of the Mediterranean, Africa and SE Asia and which mainly eats other birds. **2** the female of this species. Compare LANNERET. ⓒ 15c: from French *lanier* cowardly.

lanolin /'lanəlɪn/ ▷ *noun* a yellowish viscous substance derived from the grease that occurs naturally in sheep's wool, used in cosmetics, ointments and soaps, and for treating leather. ⓒ 19c: from Latin *lana* wool + *oleum* oil.

lantern /'lantən/ ▷ *noun* **1** a lamp or light contained in a transparent case, usually of glass, so that it can be held or carried. **2** a fixed lamp or light in this style. **3** the top part of a lighthouse, where the light is kept. **4** a structure, especially on the top of a dome, that admits light and air. See also CHINESE LANTERN, MAGIC LANTERN. ⓒ 14c: from French *lanterne*.

lantern jaws ▷ *plural noun* long thin jaws that give the face a hollow drawn appearance. • **lantern-jawed** *adj*.

lanthanide /'lanθənaɪd/ ▷ *noun, chem* any of a group of 15 highly reactive metallic elements in the periodic table with atomic numbers ranging from 57 (lanthanum) to 71 (lutetium). Also called RARE-EARTH. ⓒ 1920s: see LANTHANUM.

lanthanum /'lanθənəm/ ▷ *noun, chem* (symbol **La**, atomic number 57) a silvery-white metallic (one of the lanthanide series) that ignites spontaneously in air, and is used in rocket propellants, electronic devices, alloys for lighter flints and as a catalyst for the cracking of petroleum. ⓒ 19c: from Greek *lanthanein* to escape notice, because it is hidden in rare minerals.

lanugo /lə'njuːgoʊ/ ▷ *noun* (***lanugos***) **1** the soft downy hairs that cover the body of the human fetus from about 20 weeks, which are shed in the ninth month of gestation and so are usually only seen on premature babies. **2** the fine hairs that sometimes appear as one of the symptoms of ANOREXIA NERVOSA. ⓒ 17c: Latin.

lanyard or **laniard** /'lanjəd/ ▷ *noun* **1** a cord for hanging a knife, whistle, etc round the neck, especially as worn by sailors. **2** *naut* a short rope for fastening rigging, etc. ⓒ 15c: from French *laniere*.

lap[1] ▷ *verb* (***lapped, lapping***) **1** usually said of an animal: to drink milk, water, etc using the tongue. **2** *tr & intr* said of water, etc: to wash or flow against a shore or other surface with a light splashing sound. ▷ *noun* **1** the sound of waves gently splashing or lapping. **2** the act of lapping or the amount lapped up. ⓒ Anglo-Saxon *lapian*.

▪ **lap something up 1** to drink it, especially eagerly or greedily, using the tongue. **2** to listen eagerly to (praise, gossip, information, etc). **3** to be avidly enthusiastic about it □ *She laps up anything written by Jim Thompson.*

lap[2] ▷ *noun* **1** the front part, from the waist to the knees, of someone's body when they are sitting down. **2** the part of someone's clothing, especially of a skirt or dress, which covers this part of the body. • **fall in, into** or **land in someone's lap** to come within their grasp, power, sphere of influence, etc, or to become a possibility, especially suddenly or unexpectedly □ *The chance of a trip to New York fell in her lap.* • **drop** or **dump something in someone's lap** to make it their responsibility, especially suddenly or unexpectedly □ *dumped the job of cleaning up the mess in his lap.* • **in the lap of the gods** said of a situation: beyond human control. • **in the lap of luxury** in very comfortable conditions. ⓒ Anglo-Saxon *læppa*.

lap[3] ▷ *noun* **1** one circuit of a racecourse or other track. **2** one section of a journey. **3** a part which overlaps or the amount it overlaps by. **4** the amount of thread or material wound once round a reel, etc. ▷ *verb* **1** to get ahead of (another competitor in a race) by one or more laps. **2** to make something overlap something else. **3** *intr* to lie with an overlap. ⓒ 14c as *lappen* to enfold.

▪ **lap someone in something** to wrap them in (clothing etc), especially as a protection.

▪ **lap something round someone** to fold (a piece of clothing, etc) round them.

laparoscope /'lapərəskoʊp/ ▷ *noun, surgery* an instrument consisting of a narrow flexible illuminated tube that can be inserted through a small incision in the abdominal wall so that the surgeon can examine the abdominal cavity for signs of disease or abnormality. If necessary, material can be taken for a biopsy, or relatively minor surgery carried out, without the need for fully invasive surgery. • **laparoscopy** /-'rɒskəpɪ/ *noun* (***laparoscopies***) examination or treatment using a laparoscope. • **laparoscopic** /-rə'skɒpɪk/ *adj*. ⓒ 19c: from Greek *lapara* flank.

laparotomy /lapə'rɪtəmɪ/ ▷ *noun* (***laparotomies***) *surgery* an incision into the abdominal wall. ⓒ 19c: from Greek *lapara* flank.

lap belt ▷ *noun* a type of SAFETY BELT that merely crosses from one hip to the other, and not also diagonally from one shoulder to the opposite hip.

lap dissolve ▷ *noun, cinematog* a technique of moving from one scene to the next where one scene fades out while the next scene simultaneously fades in, so that the two images momentarily overlap. The technique is usually employed to suggest the passing of time.

lapdog ▷ *noun* a small pet dog. ⓘ 17c: from LAP[2].

lapel /lə'pɛl/ ▷ *noun* the part of a collar on a coat or jacket that is folded out across the chest towards the shoulders. • **lapelled** *adj*. ⓘ 18c: a diminutive of LAP[2].

lapidary /'lapɪdərɪ/ ▷ *noun* (***lapidaries***) someone whose job is to cut and polish gemstones. ▷ *adj* **1** relating to stones. **2** engraved on stone. **3** said of a writing style: concise and to the point, in the way that an inscription on a monument has to be. ⓘ 14c: from Latin *lapidarius*, from *lapis* stone.

lapis lazuli /'lapɪs 'lazjʊliː/ ▷ *noun* **1** *geol* a gemstone, consisting of the deep-blue mineral lazurite embedded in a matrix of white calcite, together with dark specks of pyrite. **2** its bright-blue colour. ⓘ 14c: Latin, from *lapis* stone + *lazuli* azure.

lap joint ▷ *noun* a joint formed in rails, timbers, etc, by reducing their thickness at the ends and overlapping them.

lap of honour ▷ *noun* (***laps of honour***) a ceremonial circuit of a racecourse or sports ground by the winner or winners to acknowledge the support of the audience and to accept their applause.

Lapp ▷ *noun* **1** (*also* **Laplander**) a member of a mainly nomadic people who live in the far north of Scandinavia and the area around the White Sea in Russia. **2** (*also* **Lappish**) the language spoken by this people. ▷ *adj* referring or relating to this people, their language or their culture. ⓘ 19c: Swedish, meaning 'lip'; there is evidence linking the word to German *läppisch* silly, the implication being that these nomads were perceived as being more stupid and less sophisticated than their neighbours.

lappet /'lapɪt/ ▷ *noun* **1** a small flap or fold in material, a piece of clothing, etc. **2** a piece of loose hanging flesh. ⓘ 16c: a diminutive of LAP[2].

lapsang /'lapsaŋ/ and **lapsang souchong** /— suː'ʃɒŋ, — suː'tʃɒŋ/ ▷ *noun* (*also* **Lapsang**) a type of tea with a particularly smoky flavour. ⓘ 19c: *souchong* from Chinese *xiao-zhong* small sort; *lapsang* is an invented name.

lapse /laps/ ▷ *noun* **1** a slight mistake or failure. **2** a perceived decline in standards of behaviour, etc ▫ *His drunken lapses are getting more frequent.* **3** a passing of time. **4** *law* the loss of a right or privilege because of failure to renew a claim to it. ▷ *verb* (***lapsed, lapsing***) *intr* **1** to fail to behave in what is perceived as a proper or morally acceptable way. **2** to turn away from a faith or belief. **3** *law* said of a right, privilege, etc: to become invalid because the claim to it has not been renewed. **4** said of a membership of a club, society, etc: to become invalid, usually because the fees have not been paid or some other condition has not been met. ⓘ 16c: from Latin *lapsus* a slip.

▪ **lapse into something** to pass into or return to (a specified state) ▫ *lapsed into his old drinking habits.*

lapsed /lapst/ ▷ *adj* **1** having fallen into bad habits or having resumed former bad habits. **2** no longer practising a religion, or being a member of a club or society, etc ▫ *a lapsed Catholic.* **3** no longer used or valid.

lapse rate ▷ *noun, meteorol* the rate of change of temperature in relation to atmospheric height.

lapsus linguae /'lapsəs 'lɪŋgwaɪ, — 'lɪŋgwiː/ ▷ *noun* (*plural* ***lapsus linguae***) a slip of the tongue. ⓘ 17c: Latin.

laptop ▷ *noun, computing* a portable personal computer, small enough to be used on someone's lap. It can be either mains- or battery-operated and has a lid that folds back to reveal a flat display screen and a compact keyboard. Compare NOTEBOOK 2. ⓘ 1980s: originally *laptop computer*.

lapwing /'lapwɪŋ/ ▷ *noun* a subgroup of the plover family, the only nesting species in Europe having greenish-black and white feathers and a crest. Also called PEEWIT. ⓘ Anglo-Saxon *hleapewince*.

larceny /'lɑːsənɪ/ ▷ *noun* (***larcenies***) *law, old use* theft of personal property. • **larcenous** *adj*. ⓘ 15c: from French *larcin*.

larch /lɑːtʃ/ ▷ *noun* (***larches***) **1** any of various deciduous coniferous trees, native to cold northern regions, with short linear needles arranged spirally in rosettes on woody terminal shoots, and egg-shaped cones. **2** the wood of this tree, used to make telegraph poles, stakes, etc. ⓘ 16c: from German *Lärche*.

lard ▷ *noun, cookery, etc* a soft white preparation made from the purified fat of pigs, used in cooking and baking, ointments and perfumes. ▷ *verb* (***larded, larding***) **1** to coat (meat, etc) in lard. **2** to insert strips of bacon or pork into (lean meat) in order to make it more moist and tender once it is cooked. **3** to sprinkle (a piece of writing, etc) with technical details or over-elaborate words, etc. ⓘ 15c: from Latin *laridum* bacon fat.

larder /'lɑːdə(r)/ ▷ *noun* **1** a cool room or cupboard for storing food, originally bacon. **2** a wild animal's winter store of food. ⓘ 14c: from French *lardier*, from Latin *laridum* bacon fat.

larding ▷ *noun, cookery* the action of adding LARDONs to improve the cooking of some meats. ⓘ 15c.

lardon /'lɑːdən/ and **lardoon** /lɑː'duːn/ ▷ *noun, cookery* a strip or cube of fatty bacon or pork used in LARDING and sometimes in French salads. ⓘ 15c.

large /lɑːdʒ/ ▷ *adj* (***larger, largest***) **1** occupying a comparatively big space. **2** comparatively big in size, extent, amount, etc. **3** broad in scope; wide-ranging; comprehensive. **4** generous. **5** *euphemistic* said of a person: fat. ▷ *adverb* importantly; prominently. • **largeness** *noun*. • **largish** *adj*. • **as large as life** *colloq* in person. • **at large** **1** said of criminals, prisoners, etc: free and threatening. **2** in general; as a whole ▫ *people at large.* **3** at length and with full details. • **loom large** to figure prominently. ⓘ 12c: French, from Latin *largus* plentiful.

large intestine ▷ *noun, anatomy* in mammals: the part of the alimentary canal comprising the CAECUM, COLON and RECTUM, the principal function of which is the absorption of water and the forming of faeces. See also SMALL INTESTINE.

largely ▷ *adverb* **1** mainly or chiefly. **2** to a great extent. ⓘ 13c.

large-scale ▷ *adj* **1** said of maps, models, etc: made on a relatively large scale, though small in comparison with the original. **2** extensive; widespread.

largesse or **largess** /lɑː'dʒɛs, lɑː'ʒɛs/ ▷ *noun* **1** generosity. **2** gifts, money, etc given generously. ⓘ 13c: French, from Latin *largus* plentiful.

largo /'lɑːgoʊ/ *music* ▷ *adverb* slowly and with dignity. ▷ *adj* slow and dignified. ▷ *noun* (***largos***) a piece of music to be played in this way. ⓘ 17c: Italian, meaning 'broad'.

lariat /'larɪət/ ▷ *noun* **1** a lasso. **2** a rope used for tethering animals. ⓘ 19c: from Spanish *la reata* the lasso.

lark[1] ▷ *noun* any of various different kinds of bird, but especially the skylark, that are usually gregarious, brownish in colour, ground-nesting and characterized by their tuneful song which they often deliver while in flight. • **as happy as a lark** extremely carefree. • **get up** or **be up with the lark** to be up and about very early in the morning. ⓘ Anglo-Saxon *lawerce*.

lark[2] ▷ *noun, colloq* **1** a joke or piece of fun. **2** *Brit colloq* a job or activity ▫ *the navy lark.* ▷ *verb* (***larked, larking***) *intr* (*usually* **lark about** or **around**) *colloq* to play or fool about frivolously. ⓘ 19c.

larkspur ▷ *noun* a plant with spur-like calyces and blue, white or pink flowers, related to the delphinium. ⓒ 16c.

larrigan /'larɪgən/ ▷ *noun, N Amer* a knee-high boot made of oiled leather and worn by lumberjacks, trappers, etc. ⓒ 19c.

larrikin /'larɪkɪn/ ▷ *noun, Austral & NZ slang* a hooligan or lout.

larva /'lɑːvə/ ▷ *noun* (***larvae*** /-viː/) *zool* the immature stage in the life cycle of many insects, amphibians and fish, in which it hatches from the fertilized egg and is capable of independent existence, eg the caterpillar of butterflies, the tadpole of frogs, etc. • **larval** *adj*. ⓒ 18c in this sense; 17c, meaning 'ghost': Latin, meaning 'ghost', or 'mask'.

laryngeal /lə'rɪndʒəl/ ▷ *adj* relating to the LARYNX. ⓒ 18c.

laryngitis /larɪn'dʒaɪtɪs/ ▷ *noun* an inflammation of the larynx that causes pain and makes it difficult to speak.

larynx /'larɪŋks/ ▷ *noun* (***larynges*** /lə'rɪndʒiːz/ or ***larynxes***) in mammals and other higher vertebrates: the expanded upper part of the trachea, which contains the vocal cords and is responsible for the production of vocal sounds. ⓒ 16c: Greek.

lasagne or **lasagna** /lə'zanjə, lə'sanjə/ ▷ *noun* **1** pasta in the form of thin flat sheets which can be flavoured with spinach, tomato, etc. **2** a dish made up of layers of these sheets of pasta alternating with layers of, traditionally, minced beef (or alternatively vegetables) in a tomato sauce, topped with a cheese sauce and then browned in the oven. ⓒ 18c: Italian; *lasagne* is the plural form and *lasagna* is the singular.

lascivious /lə'sɪvɪəs/ ▷ *adj* **1** said of behaviour, thoughts, etc: lewd; lecherous. **2** said of poetry, prose, art, etc: causing or inciting lewd or lecherous behaviour, thoughts, etc. • **lasciviously** *adverb*. • **lasciviousness** *noun*. ⓒ 15c: from Latin *lascivus* playful or wanton.

laser /'leɪzə(r)/ ▷ *noun* a device that produces a very powerful narrow beam of coherent light of a single wavelength by stimulating the emission of photons from atoms, molecules or ions. ⓒ 1960s: from *l*ight *a*mplification by *s*timulated *e*mission of *r*adiation, modelled on MASER.

laser disc ▷ *noun* a play-only disc on which analogue video and digital audio material is recorded as a series of microscopic pits readable only by laser beam.

laser mass spectrometer ▷ *noun* a mass spectrometer which uses a laser to convert a sample for analysis into a form which can pass through the analysing system.

laser printer ▷ *noun, computing* a fast high-quality printer that projects a laser beam on to a rotating drum coated with a material that becomes electrically charged and attracts a metallic powder, the powder image then being transferred to paper and fixed to it by heat. Compare DOT MATRIX PRINTER, INKJET PRINTER.

lash¹ ▷ *noun* (***lashes***) **1 a** a stroke or blow, usually one made with a whip and delivered as a form of punishment; **b** a crack of a whip in the air; **c** a verbal attack. **2** the flexible part of a whip. **3** an eyelash. **4** (**the lash**) punishment by whipping. ▷ *verb* (***lashes, lashed, lashing***) **1** to hit or beat with a lash. **2** *tr & intr* to move suddenly, restlessly, uncontrollably, etc. **3** to attack with harsh scolding words or criticism. **4** *intr* to make a sudden whip-like movement. **5** *tr & intr* said of waves or rain: to beat or strike with great force. **6** to urge on as if with a whip. ⓒ 14c as *lashe*, generally thought to be onomatopoeic.

▪ **lash out 1 a** to hit out violently; **b** to speak in a very hostile or aggressive manner. **2** *colloq* to spend money extravagantly.

lash² ▷ *verb, chiefly naut* to fasten with a rope or cord. ⓒ 17c.

lashing¹ ▷ *noun* **1** a beating with a whip. **2** (**lashings**) a generous amount. ▷ *adj* said of rain: falling heavily and persistently. ⓒ 15c: from LASH¹.

lashing² ▷ *noun* a rope used for tying things fast. ⓒ 17c: from LASH².

lass ▷ *noun* (***lasses***) *Scots & N Eng dialect* **1** a girl or young woman. **2** an affectionate form of address used for females of any age. ⓒ 14c.

Lassa fever /'lasə —/ ▷ *noun* a viral disease of tropical Africa whose symptoms include high temperature, diarrhoea, headache, vomiting and chest pains and which, in its severest form, can prove fatal. ⓒ 1970s: named after Lassa, a village in NE Nigeria where it was first identified.

lassie /'lasɪ/ ▷ *noun* (***lassies***) *Scots & N Eng dialect, colloq* **1** often used as a familiar or endearing form of address: a young girl. **2** a daughter. ⓒ 18c.

lassitude /'lasɪtʃuːd/ ▷ *noun* a feeling of physical or mental tiredness; a lack of energy and enthusiasm. ⓒ 16c: from Latin *lassus* weary.

lasso /lə'suː/ ▷ *noun* (***lassos*** or ***lassoes***) a long rope used for catching cattle, horses, etc with a sliding loop at one end so that, when the rope is pulled, the noose tightens around the animal's neck. ▷ *verb* (***lassoes, lassoed, lassoing***) to catch with a lasso. ⓒ 18c: from Spanish *lazo*.

last¹ /lɑːst/ ▷ *adj* **1** being, coming or occurring at the end of a series or after all others. **2** usually applied to dates, time, etc: most recent; happening immediately before the present (week, month, year, etc). **3** only remaining after all the rest have gone or been used up ▫ *gave him her last sweet*. **4** least likely, desirable, suitable, etc ▫ *the last person to expect help from*. **5** final ▫ *administered the last rites*. ▷ *adverb* **1** most recently ▫ *When did you see her last?*. **2** lastly; at the end (of a series of events, etc) ▫ *and last she served the coffee*. • **at last** or **at long last** in the end, especially after a long delay. • **at the last minute** at the last possible moment. Compare LAST-MINUTE. • **last but not least** finally but not less importantly. • **last thing** *colloq* after doing everything else, especially before leaving or going to bed. • **on its last legs** *colloq* near to being no longer usable; worn. • **on one's last legs** *usually euphemistic* near to death or total collapse. • **the last 1** the person or thing that is at the end or behind the rest. **2** the end; last moment, part, etc ▫ *That's the last of the milk*. **3** the final appearance or mention ▫ *We haven't heard the last of him*. • **to the last** until the very end, especially until death. ⓒ Anglo-Saxon *latost* latest.

last² ▷ *verb* (***lasted, lasting***) *tr & intr* **1** to take a specified amount of time to complete, happen, come to an end, etc. **2** to be adequate, or to be adequate for someone ▫ *enough water to last us a week*. **3** to be or keep fresh or in good condition ▫ *The bread will only last one more day*. ⓒ Anglo-Saxon *læstan*.

▪ **last out** to survive for a given or implied length of time.

last³ ▷ *noun* a foot-shaped piece of wood or metal used in the making and repairing of shoes. ⓒ Anglo-Saxon *læste*.

last-ditch ▷ *adj* done as a last resort ▫ *a last-ditch attempt*.

lasting ▷ *adj* existing or continuing for a long time or permanently.

Last Judgement see DAY OF JUDGEMENT

lastly ▷ *adverb* used to introduce the last item or items in a series or list: finally.

last-minute ▷ *adj* made, done or given at the latest possible moment.

last name ▷ *noun* a less formal term for SURNAME.

the last post ▷ *noun, military* **1** the final bugle call of a series denotes that it is time to retire at night. **2** the farewell bugle call at military funerals.

the last rites ▻ *plural noun, Christianity* the formalized ceremonial acts performed for someone who is dying.

the last straw ▻ *noun, colloq* an inconvenience that in itself would be considered insignificant but which, if it occurs after a series of other misfortunes, difficulties, accidents, etc, finally serves to make the whole situation intolerable.

the Last Supper ▻ *noun, Christianity* the final meal Jesus had with his disciples before the Crucifixion, and which is commemorated in the EUCHARIST.

the last word ▻ *noun* **1** the final or definitive remark in an argument or debate. **2** the final decision. **3** the most up-to-date or fashionable thing ◻ *the last word in elegance*.

Lat. ▻ *abbreviation* Latin.

lat. ▻ *abbreviation* latitude.

latch ▻ *noun* (*latches*) **1** a door catch consisting of a bar which is lowered or raised from its notch by a lever or string. **2** a door lock by which a door may be opened from the inside using a handle, and from the outside by using a key. ▻ *verb* (*latches*, *latched*, *latching*) *tr & intr* to fasten or be fastened with a latch. • **on the latch** said of a door: shut but not locked; able to be opened by the latch. ⓒ Anglo-Saxon *læccan*.

■ **latch on** *colloq* to understand.

■ **latch on to someone** *colloq* to become closely attached to them, often without the person concerned wanting such closeness.

■ **latch on to something** *colloq* **1** to cling to it, often obsessively ◻ *He latched on to the idea of buying a sports car.* **2** to realize its significance.

latchkey ▻ *noun* a key for a door, gate, etc that has a latch.

latchkey child and **latchkey kid** ▻ *noun* a child who comes home from school while the parent or parents are still out at work.

latchstring ▻ *noun* a string that is attached to a latch so that it can be lifted from outside or from a distance.

late ▻ *adj* (*later*, *latest*) **1** coming, arriving, etc after the expected or usual time. **2 a** far on in the day or night ◻ *late afternoon*; **b** well into the evening or night; **c** *in compounds* occurring towards the end of a specified historical period, etc ◻ *late-Georgian architecture*; **d** written, painted, etc towards the end of someone's life or towards the end of their active career ◻ *a late Picasso*. **3** happening, growing, etc at a relatively advanced time ◻ *Let's go to the late showing*. **4** dead ◻ *his late father*. **5** former ◻ *the late prime minister*. **6** recent ◻ *quite a late model of car*. ▻ *adverb* **1** after the expected or usual time ◻ *He arrived late for the meeting.* **2** far on in the day or night ◻ *He arrived late on Thursday.* **3** at an advanced time ◻ *flower late in the season.* **4** recently ◻ *The letter was sent as late as this morning.* **5** formerly, but no longer ◻ *late of Glasgow*. • **lately** see separate entry. • **lateness** *noun*. • **later, latest** see separate entries. • **better late than never** said of an event, arrival, occurrence, etc: preferable that it should happen at some late point in time than not at all. • **late in the day** at a late stage, especially when it is too late to be of any use. • **late in life** happening later in someone's life than is usual or expected ◻ *married late in life*. • **of late** lately; recently ◻ *There has been some unpleasantness of late, but it has now been resolved.* ⓒ Anglo-Saxon *læt*.

latecomer ▻ *noun* someone who arrives late.

lateen /lə'tiːn/ ▻ *adj, naut* said of a ship: having a triangular sail on a long sloping yard. ⓒ 18c: from French *voile latine* Latin sail, because this type of sail is common on the Mediterranean.

lately ▻ *adverb* in the recent past; not long ago. ⓒ 15c.

La Tène /la 'tɛn/ ▻ *adj* relating to the ancient central and western European culture which flourished during the second Iron Age. ⓒ 19c: named after a district at the eastern end of Lake Neuchâtel in Switzerland where artefacts belonging to this culture were first discovered.

late-night shopping ▻ *noun, Brit* shopping that can be done outside the shops' usual opening hours, especially on a specific evening every week.

latent /'leɪtənt/ ▻ *adj* **1** said of a characteristic, tendency, etc: present or existing in an undeveloped or hidden form. **2** *pathol* said of a disease: failing to present or not yet presenting the usual or expected symptoms. Opposite of MANIFEST. • **latency** *noun*. • **latently** *adverb*. ⓒ 17c: from Latin *latere* to lie hidden.

latent heat ▻ *noun, physics* the amount of heat energy required to change a solid to a liquid, or a liquid to a gas, without a change in temperature, the same amount of energy being released when the liquid changes back to a solid, or the gas changes back to a liquid.

latent image ▻ *noun, photog* on a photosensitive emulsion: an invisible image that is made visible by the development process.

latent period ▻ *noun* **1** *physiol* the period between the arrival of a nerve impulse at a muscle fibre and the time when that fibre starts to contract. **2** *pathol* the INCUBATION PERIOD.

latent virus ▻ *noun* a virus in a plant or animal that is present but not causing any harm, although it can still be passed on to another individual in whom the expected symptoms might be manifested. ⓒ 1930s.

later /'leɪtə(r)/ ▻ *adj* more late. ▻ *adverb* at some time after, or in the near future. • **later on** at some unspecified time in the future ◻ *I'll tidy up later on.* • **see** or **catch you later** *colloq* goodbye. ⓒ 16c:.

lateral /'latərəl/ ▻ *adj* at, from or relating to a side or the side of something ◻ *lateral fins*. ▻ *noun* **1** something, eg a branch, shoot, side road, tributary, etc, that forks off from the main part. **2** *phonetics* a consonant, eg any of the various *l* sounds of English, that is articulated by making a partial closure between the tongue and the gums at the side of the mouth, creating just enough of a gap to allow the air stream to pass through. • **laterally** *adverb*. ⓒ 17c: from Latin *latus, lateris* side.

laterality /latə'ralɪtɪ/ and **lateralization** ▻ *noun* **1** the state of being lateral or to the side; physical one-sidedness, either right or left. **2** *physiol* the specialization of the left and right cerebral hemispheres of the human brain for different functions. In the majority of people this involves specialization of the left hemisphere for language functions, eg reading, writing, speaking and understanding, and specialization of the right hemisphere for the perception of complex patterns.

lateral line ▻ *noun, zool* in fish: a line of specialized receptor cells along the sides of the body that are sensitive to vibrations and water pressure.

lateral thinking ▻ *noun* a form of thinking which seeks new and unusual ways of approaching and solving problems, and does not merely proceed by logical steps from the starting point of what is known or believed.

laterite /'latəraɪt/ ▻ *noun, geol* a soft porous soil or hard dense rock, composed mainly of hydroxides of iron and aluminium, formed as a result of the weathering of igneous rocks in humid tropical climates, and often used as a building material. ⓒ 19c: from Latin *later* brick + -ITE 4.

latest /'leɪtɪst/ ▻ *adj* most recent ◻ *the latest update on the news*. **2** (**the latest**) the most recent news, occurrence, fashion, etc. ▻ **at the latest** not later than a specified time. ⓒ 16c.

late tackle ▻ *noun, rugby, football, hockey, etc* an attempt to get the ball when the player who has had possession of it has already released it, especially when the attempt fouls or injures the other player.

latex /ˈleɪtɛks/ ▷ *noun* (*latexes* or *latices* /ˈleɪtɪsiːz/) **1** a thick milky juice that is produced by some plants and used commercially, especially in the manufacture of rubber. **2** a synthetic product that has similar properties to those of rubber. ◷ 17c: Latin, meaning 'liquid'.

lath /lɑːθ/ (*laths* /lɑːθs, lɑːðz/) ▷ *noun* a thin narrow strip of wood, especially one of a series used to support plaster, tiles, slates, etc. ▷ *verb* (*lathed, lathing*) to prepare a ceiling, wall, roof, etc with laths before plastering, tiling, etc. ◷ Anglo-Saxon *lætt*.

lathe /leɪð/ ▷ *noun* (*lathes*) a machine tool used to cut, drill or polish a piece of metal, wood or plastic that is rotated against the cutting edge of the lathe. ◷ 17c.

lather /ˈlɑːðə(r)/ ▷ *noun* **1** a foam made by mixing water and soap or detergent. **2** foamy sweat, especially the kind that forms on a horse during strenuous exercise. ▷ *verb* (*lathered, lathering*) **1** *intr* to form a lather. **2** to cover something with lather. • **lathery** *adj*. • **in a lather** *colloq* extremely agitated or excited. ◷ Anglo-Saxon *leathor* washing soda.

lathi /ˈlɑːtiː/ ▷ *noun* (*lathis*) *Indian subcontinent* a long heavy wooden or bamboo stick used as a weapon. ◷ 19c: Hindi.

latices *plural of* LATEX

Latin /ˈlatɪn/ ▷ *noun* **1** the language of ancient Rome and its empire, which became a dead language (see under LANGUAGE) well over a thousand years ago, but was adopted as the language of education, government, the church, the law and cultured society in medieval Europe. As a result many English words are derived from it. **2** a person of Italian, Spanish or Portuguese extraction. **3** an inhabitant of ancient Latium in central Italy. ▷ *adj* **1** relating to, or in, the Latin language. **2** applied to languages derived from Latin, especially Italian, Spanish and Portuguese. **3** said of a person: Italian, Spanish or Portuguese in origin. **4** passionate or easily excitable ▫ *his Latin temperament.* **5** referring or relating to the Roman Catholic Church. ◷ Anglo-Saxon: from Latin *Latinus* of Latium.

Latin American ▷ *noun* an inhabitant of Latin America, the areas in America where languages such as Spanish and Portuguese are spoken. ▷ *adj* (**Latin-American**) belonging or relating to any of these areas, their inhabitants or culture ▫ *Latin-American dancing.*

Latinate ▷ *adj* said of someone's writing style or vocabulary: resembling or derived from Latin. ◷ Early 20c.

Latin cross ▷ *noun* an upright cross with the lowest limb longer than the other three.

Latinism ▷ *noun* a word or idiom borrowed from Latin.

Latinist ▷ *noun* someone who has specialist knowledge of the Latin language.

Latinize or **Latinise** ▷ *verb* (*Latinized, Latinizing*) **1** to translate something into Latin. **2** to change (a ceremony, custom, etc) so that it conforms more closely with the ways of the Roman Catholic Church. ◷ 16c.

Latino /laˈtiːnoʊ/ and **Latina** /-nə/ ▷ *noun* (*Latinos* or *Latinas*) a man or woman respectively, usually a N American, who is of Latin American descent. ◷ 1940s.

latish /ˈleɪtɪʃ/ ▷ *adj, adverb* slightly late.

latitude /ˈlatɪtʃuːd/ ▷ *noun* **1** *geog* any of a series of imaginary circles drawn around the Earth parallel to the EQUATOR, representing the angular distance north or south of the equator, measured from 0 degrees at the equator to 90 degrees at the north and south poles. See also LINE OF LATITUDE. Compare LONGITUDE. **2** (*usually* **latitudes**) *geog* a region or area thought of in terms of its distance from the equator or its climate ▫ *warm latitudes.* **3** scope for freedom of action or choice. • **latitudinal** *adj*. • **latitudinally** *adverb*. ◷ 14c: from Latin *latitudo* breadth.

Pronunciation of Latin in English

Most Latin words and phrases used in English are said with a strongly anglicized pronunciation, which is quite different from the way they were pronounced in ancient Rome. Other Latin expressions came into English from church Latin, or from medieval Latin, which were pronounced in yet another way.

It is therefore not always easy to predict the exact anglicized pronunciation of Latin words and phrases, but the following rules generally apply:

- Unstressed ***i***'s are pronounced /ɪ/.
- Stressed ***i***'s are usually pronounced /aɪ/, as in **ad infinitum** /ad ɪnfɪˈnaɪtəm/ and **bona fide** /ˈboʊnə ˈfaɪdɪ/, but if they are short they too are pronounced /ɪ/, as in **ab initio** /ab ɪˈnɪʃɪoʊ/.
- At the end of a word, Latin ***-i*** is pronounced /aɪ/, as in the plurals **cacti** and **stimuli**, and in technical scientific names such as **Musci** /ˈmʌsaɪ/, the mosses.
- The letters ***ae*** are normally pronounced /iː/, as commonly in technical scientific names such as **Compositae** /kɒmˈpɒzɪtiː/, the botanical name for the family of flowering plants that includes the daisy and dandelion.

Occasionally, and unpredictably, some Latin words and phrases are not normally anglicized in pronunciation. In **curriculum vitae**, for example, **vitae** is normally pronounced /ˈviːtaɪ/ as in Classical Latin or /ˈviːteɪ/ as in church Latin, rather than the expected /ˈvaɪtiː/ of anglicized Latin.

As examples of the pronunciation of other vowels, note the following: **inter alia** /ɪntəˈreɪlɪa/, **quod erat demonstrandum** /kwɒd ˈɛrat dɛmənˈstrandəm/, **pro bono publico** /proʊ ˈboʊnoʊ ˈpʊblɪkoʊ/, **modus operandi** /ˈmoʊdəs ɒpəˈrandaɪ/.

Pronunciation of ***c*** and ***g*** varies in different contexts:

- Before ***a*** and ***o***: ***c*** and ***g*** are pronounced /k/ and /g/ respectively.
- Before ***e*** and ***i***: ***c*** is usually pronounced /s/, as in **circa** /ˈsɜːkə/, and ***g*** is pronounced /dʒ/, as in **fungi** /ˈfʌndʒaɪ/.
- However, before ***i***: ***c*** (and also ***t***) may be pronounced /ʃ/, as in **prima facie** /ˈpraɪmə ˈfeɪʃɪ/ and **ab initio** /ab ɪˈnɪʃɪoʊ/.

latitudinarian /latɪtʃuːdɪˈnɛərɪən/ ▷ *noun* someone who believes in freedom of choice, thought, action, etc, especially in religious matters. ◷ 17c: modelled on TRINITARIAN.

latrine /ləˈtriːn/ ▷ *noun* a lavatory, especially in a barracks or camp, etc. ◷ 17c: from Latin *lavatrina* a privy.

latter /ˈlatə(r)/ ▷ *adj* **1** nearer the end than the beginning ▫ *the latter part of the holiday.* **2** used when referring to two people or things: mentioned, considered, etc second. • **the latter** said of two people or things: the second one mentioned, considered, etc ▫ *Andy and Liz were both up for the job, but the latter had more experience.* Compare FORMER. See Usage Note overleaf. ◷ Anglo-Saxon *lætra*.

latter-day ▷ *adj* recent or modern.

Latter-day Saints ▷ *noun* the name that the MORMONS prefer to call themselves.

latterly ▷ *adverb* **1** recently. **2** towards the end. ◷ 18c.

lattice /ˈlatɪs/ ▷ *plural noun* **1** (*also* **lattice-work**) an open frame made by crossing narrow strips of wood or metal over each other to form an ornamental pattern and used especially in gates and fences. **2** (*also* **lattice window**) a window with small diamond-shaped panels of glass held in place with strips of lead. **3** *chem* the regular three-dimensional arrangement of atoms, ions or molecules that forms the structure of a crystalline solid. • **latticed** *adj.* ⓒ 14c: from French *lattis*, from *latte* lath.

Latvian /ˈlatvɪən/ ▻ *adj* belonging or relating to Latvia, a European country bordering the Baltic Sea, its inhabitants, or their language. ▻ *noun* **1** a citizen or inhabitant of, or person born in, Latvia. **2** (*also* **Lettish**) the official language of Latvia.

latter

• In sense 2, **latter** strictly refers to the second of two choices (and **former** refers to the first) □ *Do I have to choose between goat's cheese and chocolate cake? Sometimes I prefer the latter, sometimes the former* □ *He and Mr Doran – the latter complaining mightily about his lumbago – pushed the cakes to the back of the table.*

• More loosely, especially in speech, it refers to the last of several choices □ *The story is reported in the Express, Guardian and Telegraph. The latter also has extensive photo coverage.*

• In sense 1, it does not contrast with **former**, and it means more or less the same as **later,** to which it is related in origin □ *An upturn in profits was recorded in the latter part of the decade* □ *It will not be long before her name appears in the latter stages of the world's leading tournaments.*

laud /lɔːd/ *formal* ▻ *verb* (***lauded, lauding***) **1** to praise. **2** to sing or speak the praises of someone or something, especially a god. ▻ *noun* praise. See also LAUDS. ⓒ 14c: from Latin *laus, laudis* praise.

laudable ▻ *adj* worthy of praise; commendable. • **laudability** *noun.* • **laudably** *adverb.* ⓒ 15c.

laudanum /ˈlɔːdənəm/ ▻ *noun* a solution of morphine in alcohol, prepared from raw opium, formerly often taken by mouth to relieve pain, aid sleep, etc. ⓒ 17c: a Latinized name first coined by the physician and alchemist, Paracelsus (c.1490–1541), for his expensive medicine containing opium.

laudatory /ˈlɔːdətərɪ/ ▻ *adj* containing or expressing praise. ⓒ 16c: from Latin *laudatorius.*

laudable, laudatory

• **Laudable** means deserving praise and **laudatory** means expressing it:

✓ *There is nothing that is not laudable and praiseworthy in this scheme.*

✓ *It was all very laudable bringing culture to the masses.*

✓ *The paper continued to write laudatory pieces about the embattled Mr Young.*

• **Laudatory** is the more often confused, as in the following incorrect example:

✗ *Mr Rossi seems to have led a laudatory existence for a man of his calling.*

lauds /lɔːdz/ ▻ *plural noun, now especially RC Church* the first of the CANONICAL HOURS of the day, now often taken together with MATINS and the time when the traditional morning prayers and psalms are said and sung. ⓒ 14c: plural of LAUD.

laugh /lɑːf/ ▻ *verb* (***laughed, laughing***) **1** *intr* to make spontaneous sounds associated with happiness, amusement, scorn, etc. **2** to express (a feeling, etc) by laughing □ *laughed his contempt.* ▻ *noun* **1** an act or sound of laughing. **2** *colloq* someone or something that is good fun, amusing, etc. • **be laughing** *colloq* to be in, or almost in, a very favourable situation □ *Once he gets that new job, he'll be laughing.* • **be laughing all the way to the bank** *colloq* to have successfully pulled off a financial ruse or swindle. • **don't make me laugh** *ironic* expressing contempt, scorn, etc for some idea, suggested possibility, etc □ *Harry go in to work five days in a row? Don't make me laugh!* • **have the last laugh** *colloq* to win or succeed in the end, especially after setbacks; to be finally proved right. • **laugh oneself silly**, *etc* to bring oneself into a specified state (often figuratively) through laughing. • **laugh one's head off** to laugh exuberantly, etc. • **laugh on the other side of one's face** to become annoyed or distressed after previously having been in good spirits. • **laugh someone out of court** to dismiss them, or their views or achievements, with ridicule. • **laugh up one's sleeve** to be secretly or gleefully amused or pleased. ⓒ Anglo-Saxon *hlæhhan.*

■ **laugh at someone** or **something 1** to make fun of or ridicule them or it. **2** to find it funny.

■ **laugh something off** to treat lightly or trivially (especially an injury, an insult, an embarrassment, etc) □ *He laughed off his broken leg as just one of those things.*

laughable ▻ *adj* **1** deserving to be laughed at. **2** absurd; ludicrous. • **laughably** *adverb.*

laughing ▻ *noun* laughter. • **laughingly** *adverb.* • **no laughing matter** or **not a laughing matter** a very serious business, state of affairs, etc.

laughing gas ▻ *noun* popular name for NITROUS OXIDE, especially when used as an anaesthetic, so called because it may induce spontaneous laughter or giggling when inhaled.

laughing hyena see HYENA

laughing jackass see KOOKABURRA

laughing-stock ▻ *noun* someone or something that is the object of ridicule, mockery, contempt, etc.

laughter ▻ *noun* the act or sound of laughing.

launch¹ /lɔːntʃ/ ▻ *verb* (***launches, launched, launching***) **1 a** to send (a ship or boat, etc) into the water at the beginning of a voyage; **b** to send (a newly-built ship or boat) into the water for the first time. **2** to send (a spacecraft, missile, etc) into space or into the air. **3** to start someone or something off in a specified direction. **4** to bring (a new product) on to the market, especially with promotions and publicity. **5** to begin (an attack of some kind) □ *launched an aerial attack.* ▻ *noun* (***launches***) **1** the action or an instance of a ship, spacecraft, missile, etc being sent off into the water or into the air. **2** the start of something □ *press coverage for the launch of the new product.* ⓒ 15c: from Latin *lanceare* to wield a lance.

■ **launch into something a** to begin (an undertaking, etc) with vigour and enthusiasm; **b** to begin (a story or speech, especially a long one).

launch² /lɔːntʃ/ ▻ *noun* **1** a large powerful motorboat. **2** *historical* the largest boat carried by a man-of-war. ⓒ 17c: from Spanish *lancha.*

launcher ▻ *noun* a device used for launching a spacecraft or missile, etc.

launching-pad and **launch pad** ▻ *noun* the area or platform for launching a spacecraft or missile, etc.

launch vehicle ▻ *noun, astron* a rocket-propelled vehicle that is used to carry a spacecraft, eg a satellite or space probe, from the Earth's surface into space.

launch window ▻ *noun, astron* the period of time during which the launch of a spacecraft must take place if it is to put a satellite, space probe, etc in the right orbit or on the right flight path.

launder /ˈlɔːndə(r)/ ▻ *verb* (***laundered, laundering***) **1** to wash and iron (clothes, linen, etc). **2** *colloq* to transfer

Latin Phrases Used in English

ab initio from the beginning
ab ovo from the egg; from the beginning
absit omen a superstitious formula; may there be no ill omen (as in a reference just made)
ad hoc towards this; for one particular purpose
ad hominem to the man; appealing not to logic or reason but to personal preference or feelings
ad infinitum to infinity; for ever; without limit
ad litem for the lawsuit; used of a guardian appointed to act in court (eg because of insanity or insufficient age of the litigant)
ad nauseam to the point of sickness; excessively
ad referendum for reference; to be further considered
ad valorem to value; according to what it is worth, often used of taxes, etc
a fortiori from the stronger (argument); for a stronger reason
anno Domini in the year of the Lord; used in giving dates since the birth of Christ
ante meridiem before midday; between midnight and noon; abbreviated to **am**
a posteriori from the later; based on observation or experience
a priori from the previous; working from cause to effect
bona fide in good faith; genuine or sincere
carpe diem seize the day; enjoy the pleasures of the present moment while they last
caveat emptor let the buyer beware; warns the buyer to examine carefully the article they are about to purchase
compos mentis having control of one's mind; of sound mind; rational
contra mundum against the world; denotes defiant perseverance despite universal criticism
cum grano salis with a grain (pinch) of salt
de facto from the fact; actually, though not necessarily legally, so
de gustibus non est disputandum (often in English shortened for convenience to *de gustibus*) there is no disputing about tastes; there is no sense in challenging people's preferences
de jure according to law; denotes the legal or theoretical position, which may not correspond with reality
deo volente God willing
eheu fugaces opening of a quotation (Horace *Odes* II, XIV, 1–2) alas! the fleeting years slip away; bemoans the brevity of human existence
et al. *et alia* and other things; *et alii* and other people; used to avoid giving a complete and possibly over-lengthy list of all items eg of authors
et tu, Brute you too, Brutus (Caesar's alleged exclamation when he saw Brutus among his assassins); denotes surprise and dismay that a supposed friend has joined in a conspiracy against one
ex cathedra from the chair; with authority
ex gratia as a favour; given as a favour
ex officio from office, by virtue of office; by virtue of one's official position
ex parte from (one) part; on behalf of one side only in legal proceedings; partial, prejudiced
fidus Achates the faithful Achates (Aeneas' friend); a loyal follower
fons et origo the source and origin
habeas corpus have the body; requiring a prisoner to be brought into court
hic jacet here lies; the first words of an epitaph; memorial inscription
honoris causa for the sake of honour; as a token of respect; used to designate honorary university degrees
in absentia in absence; in a person's absence
in camera in the chamber; in a private room; in secret
in extremis in the last; in desperate circumstances; at the point of death
in flagrante delicto in the blazing crime; in the very act of committing the crime
infra dig below dignity; beneath one's dignity
in loco parentis in the place of a parent
inter alia among other things
in vitro in glass; in a test tube
ipso facto by the fact itself; thereby
mea culpa through my fault; I am to blame
mens sana in corpore sano a sound mind in a sound body (Juvenal *Satires* X, 356); the guiding rule of the 19c English educational system
mirabile dictu wonderful to tell (Virgil *Georgics* II, 30); an expression of (sometimes ironic) amazement
multum in parvo much in little; a large amount in a small space
mutatis mutandis having changed what needs to be changed
ne plus ultra not more beyond; extreme perfection
non sequitur it does not follow; an illogical step in an argument
nota bene observe well, note well; often abbreviated to **NB**
O tempora! O mores! O the times! O the manners! (Cicero *In Catalinam*) a condemnation of present times, as contrasted with a past which is seen as golden
panem et circenses bread and circuses, or food and the big match (Juvenal *Satires* X, 80); amusements which divert the populace from unpleasant realities
per capita by heads; for each person
post meridiem after noon; between midday and the following midnight; abbreviated to **pm**
prima facie at first sight; on the evidence available
primus inter pares first among equals
pro bono publico for the public good; something done for no fee
quid pro quo something for something; something given or taken as equivalent to or in retaliation for something else
quod erat demonstrandum which was to be shown; often used in its abbreviated form **QED**
reductio ad absurdum reduction to absurdity; originally used in logic to mean the proof of a proposition by proving the falsity of its contradictory; the application of a principle so strictly that it is carried to absurd lengths
sic transit gloria mundi so passes away earthly glory
sine die without a day; with no future time fixed
sine qua non without which not; an essential condition or requirement
sub judice under a judge; under consideration by a court
sub rosa under the rose; in secret, privately
summa cum laude with the highest praise; with great distinction; the highest class of degreee that can be gained by a US college student
summum bonum the chief good
tempus fugit time flies; delay cannot be tolerated
ultra vires beyond strength, beyond powers; beyond one's power or authority
urbi et orbi to the city and the world; used of the Pope's pronouncements; to everyone

(money, etc) that has been obtained illegally through banks or legitimate businesses to cover up its origins. **3** *intr* to be capable of being washed without ill-effect □ *This shirt launders well.* 🕔 14c: from Latin *lavandarius* needing to be washed, from Latin *lavare* to wash.

launderette or **laundrette** /lɔːndəˈrɛt, -ˈdrɛt/ ▷ *noun* a place where coin-operated washing machines and tumble driers are used by customers for washing and drying clothes, etc. *N Amer equivalent* **laundromat**. 🕔 1940s: originally a trademark.

laundress ▷ *noun* (***laundresses***) a woman who washes and irons clothes, linen, etc, especially one who does this for a living.

laundry /ˈlɔːndrɪ/ ▷ *noun* (***laundries***) **1** a place where clothes, linen, etc are washed. **2** clothes, linen, etc for washing or newly washed.

Laurasia /lɔːˈreɪʒə/ ▷ *noun, geol* an ancient SUPERCONTINENT, thought to have existed in the northern hemisphere during the Mesozoic era, which subsequently split to form N America, Greenland, Europe and N Asia. ◷ 1930s: named after the *Laurentian* strata of the Canadian Shield + Eur*asia*.

laureate /ˈlɔːrɪət, ˈlɒrɪət, -eɪt/ ▷ *adj* **1** *often following a noun* honoured for artistic or intellectual distinction □ *poet laureate.* **2** crowned with laurel leaves as a sign of honour or distinction. ▷ *noun* (***laureates***) someone honoured for artistic or intellectual achievement, especially a POET LAUREATE. ◷ 14c: from Latin *laureatus*, from *laurus* laurel.

laurel /ˈlɒrəl/ ▷ *noun* **1** (*also* **bay tree**, **sweet bay tree** and **bay laurel**) a small evergreen tree with smooth dark shiny leaves that are used for flavouring in cooking and sometimes medicinally. **2** a crown of laurel leaves worn as a symbol of victory or mark of honour. **3** (**laurels**) honour; praise. ● **look to one's laurels** to beware of losing one's reputation by being outclassed. ● **rest on one's laurels** to be satisfied with one's past successes and so not bother to achieve anything more. ◷ 14c: from Latin *laurus*.

LAUTRO /ˈlaʊtroʊ/ ▷ *abbreviation* Life Assurance and Unit Trust Regulatory Organization.

lav ▷ *noun, colloq* short form of LAVATORY.

lava /ˈlɑːvə/ ▷ *noun* (***lavas***) **1** *geol* MAGMA that has erupted from a volcano or fissure and flowed on to the Earth's surface or the ocean floor. **2** the solid rock that forms as a result of cooling and solidification of this material. ◷ 18c: Italian, originally meaning 'a sudden stream of water, caused by rain'.

lavatorial /lavəˈtɔːrɪəl/ ▷ *adj* said especially of humour: relating to lavatories and excretion.

lavatory /ˈlavətərɪ/ ▷ *noun* (***lavatories***) **1** a piece of equipment, usually bowl-shaped with a seat, where urine and faeces are deposited and then flushed away by water into a sewer. **2** a room or building containing one or more of these. ◷ 14c: from Latin *lavare* to wash.

lavender /ˈlavəndə(r)/ ▷ *noun* **1** a plant or shrub with sweet-smelling pale bluish-purple flowers. **2** the dried flowers from this plant, used to perfume clothes or linen. **3** the pale bluish-purple colour of the flowers. **4** a kind of perfume made from the distilled flowers of this plant. Also called **lavender water**. ◷ 13c: from Latin *lavendula*.

laver /ˈleɪvə(r)/ ▷ *noun* any of various edible seaweeds, used to make laver bread. ◷ 17c: Latin, meaning 'water plant'.

laver bread ▷ *noun* a Welsh dish made from boiled laver dipped in oatmeal and fried.

lavish /ˈlavɪʃ/ ▷ *adj* **1** spending or giving generously. **2** gorgeous or luxurious □ *lavish decoration.* **3** too generous; extravagant or excessive. ▷ *verb* (***lavishes, lavished, lavishing***) to spend (money) or give (praise, etc) freely or generously. ● **lavishly** *adverb*. ● **lavishness** *noun*. ◷ 15c: from French *lavasse* deluge of rain.

law /lɔː/ ▷ *noun* **1** a customary rule recognized as allowing or prohibiting certain actions. **2** a collection of such rules according to which people live or a country or state is governed. **3** the control which such rules exercise □ *law and order.* **4** a controlling force □ *Their word is law.* **5** a collection of laws as a social system or a subject for study. **6** a group of laws relating to a particular activity □ *commercial law.* **7** (**laws**) jurisprudence. **8** one of a group of rules which set out how certain games, sports, etc should be played. **9** the legal system as a recourse; litigation □ *go to law.* **10** a rule in science, philosophy, etc, based on practice or observation, which says that under certain conditions certain things will always happen. ● **be a law unto oneself** to act as one wants and not according to laws or custom. ● **have** or **get the law on someone** *colloq* usually said as a threat: to ensure that legal action is taken against them. ● **lay down the law** see under LAY[1]. ● **take the law into one's own hands** to get justice in one's own way, without involving the law or the police. ● **the law 1** people who are knowledgeable about law, especially professionally. **2** *colloq* the police or a member of the police. ● **the long arm of the law** the law thought of in terms of its power and extent □ *They fled to Dublin but the long arm of the law soon caught up with them.* ◷ Anglo-Saxon *lagu*.

law-abiding /ˈlɔːəbaɪdɪŋ/ ▷ *adj* obeying the law.

lawbreaker ▷ *noun* someone who breaks the law.

law centre ▷ *noun, Brit* a publicly funded free legal advisory service.

lawcourt ▷ *noun* (*also* **court of law**) a place where people accused of crimes are tried and legal disagreements settled.

lawful ▷ *adj* **1** allowed by or according to law. **2** just or rightful. ● **lawfully** *adverb*. ● **lawfulness** *noun*.

lawless ▷ *adj* **1** ignoring or breaking the law, especially violently. **2** having no laws. ● **lawlessly** *adverb*. ● **lawlessness** *noun*.

Law Lord ▷ *noun* **1** a peer in the House of Lords who holds or has held high legal office, and who sits in the highest COURT OF APPEAL. **2** *Scottish* a judge in the COURT OF SESSION.

lawn[1] ▷ *noun* an area of smooth mown cultivated grass, especially as part of a garden or park. ◷ 18c in this sense; 16c as *laune*, meaning 'glade'.

lawn[2] *noun* fine linen or cotton. ◷ 15c.

lawnmower ▷ *noun* an electric, petrol-driven or manually powered machine for cutting grass. ◷ 19c.

lawn tennis ▷ *noun* TENNIS (sense 1). Compare REAL TENNIS.

law of averages ▷ *noun* the theory that if something happens, its opposite is likely to happen also, so that balance may be maintained.

law of diminishing returns see DIMINISHING RETURNS

Law of Moses ▷ *noun* Jewish law as it is laid down in the first five books of the Old Testament, or the PENTATEUCH.

law of nature ▷ *noun* **1** a LAW (sense 10) observed in the natural world. **2** *loosely, colloq* a recurring phenomenon in human experience, unjustifiably elevated to this status.

law of the jungle ▷ *noun* the principle that one should protect one's own interests ruthlessly and competitively.

lawrencium /ləˈrensɪəm, lɒ-, lɔː-/ ▷ *noun, chem* (symbol **Lr**, atomic number 103) a synthetic radioactive metallic element formed by bombarding CALIFORNIUM with BORON ions. ◷ 1960s: named after the US physicist, Ernest Orlando Lawrence (1901–58), the founder of the laboratory where it was discovered.

lawsuit ▷ *noun* an argument or disagreement taken to a court of law to be settled.

lawyer /lɔːjə(r)/ ▷ *noun* a person, especially a solicitor, whose job is to know about the law, and give legal advice and help. ◷ 14c.

lax[1] ▷ *adj* (***laxer, laxest***) **1** showing little care or concern over behaviour, morals, etc. **2** loose, slack or flabby. **3** negligent. ● **laxity** *noun*. ● **laxly** *adverb*. ◷ 14c: from Latin *laxus* loose.

lax² ▻ *noun* (***laxes*** or ***lax***) a salmon, especially one caught in Norwegian or Swedish waters. ◷ Anglo-Saxon *leax*.

laxative /'laksətɪv/ ▻ *adj* inducing movement of the bowels. ▻ *noun* a medicine or food that induces movement of the bowels. ◷ 14c: from Latin *laxare* to loosen.

lay¹ ▻ *verb* (***laid***, ***laying***) **1** to place something on a surface, especially in a lying or horizontal position □ *laid the letter on the table.* **2** to put or bring something to a stated position or condition □ *laid her hand on his arm.* **3** to design, arrange or prepare □ *lay plans.* **4** to put plates and cutlery, etc on (a table) ready for a meal. **5** to prepare (a fire) by putting coal, etc in the grate. **6** *tr & intr* said of a female bird: to produce (eggs). **7** to present □ *laid his case before the court.* **8** to set something down as a basis □ *laid the ground rules.* **9** to deal with or remove □ *lay a fear.* **10** *colloq* to place (a bet) □ *I'll lay 20 quid you can't eat the whole plateful.* **11** *slang* to have sexual intercourse with someone, especially a woman. ▻ *noun* **1** the way or position in which something is lying □ *the lay of the surrounding countryside.* **2** *slang* **a** a partner in sexual intercourse; **b** an act of sexual intercourse. ● **get laid** *colloq* to succeed in having sexual intercourse. ● **lay about one** to strike blows in all directions. ● **lay something bare** to reveal or explain (a plan or intention that has been kept secret). ● **lay down the law** to dictate in a forceful and domineering way. ● **lay down one's arms** to surrender or call a truce. ● **lay it on thick** *colloq* to exaggerate, especially in connection with flattery, praise, etc. ● **lay low** to overthrow, fell or kill. ● **lay one's hands on someone** or **something** *colloq* to succeed in getting hold of them or it. ● **lay oneself open to something** to expose oneself to criticism or attack. ● **lay something on someone 1** to assign or attribute it to them □ *laid the blame on his friends.* **2** *colloq* to give it to them, especially unexpectedly or without payment. ● **lay someone low** said of an illness: to affect them severely. ● **lay something open 1** to uncover or reveal it. **2** to cut it open. ● **lay someone to rest** to bury (a dead body). ● **lay waste** to destroy or devastate completely. ◷ Anglo-Saxon *lecgan*.

■ **lay something aside 1** to put it to one side, especially for later use or treatment. **2** to discard or abandon it.

■ **lay something by** to put it away for future use.

■ **lay something down 1** to put it on the ground or some other surface. **2** to give it as a deposit, pledge, etc. **3** to give up or sacrifice □ *lay down one's life.* **4** to formulate or devise □ *lay down a plan.* **5** to store (wine) in a cellar. **6** to begin to build (a ship or railway). **7** to put (music) onto tape, CD, etc □ *laid down ten tracks in only three days.*

■ **lay something in** to get and store a supply of it.

■ **lay into someone** *colloq* to attack or scold them severely.

■ **lay into something** to eat it quickly and with enthusiasm.

■ **lay someone off 1** to dismiss (an employee) when there is no work available. See also LAY-OFF.

■ **lay off something** *colloq* to stop it.

■ **lay off someone** *colloq* to leave them alone.

■ **lay something on** to provide a supply of it.

■ **lay someone out 1** *colloq* to knock them unconscious. **2** to prepare (a dead body) for burial.

■ **lay something out 1** to plan and arrange (especially land or natural features). **2** to spread it out or display it. **3** *colloq* to spend it. See also LAYOUT.

■ **lay someone up** *colloq* to force them to stay in bed or at home.

■ **lay something up 1** to keep or store it □ *laid up some of her delicious jam.* **2** to put (a ship) out of use, especially for repairs.

lay, lie

● These two verbs are commonly confused - even by native speakers - because their meanings are close and their forms overlap, since **lay** is also the past of **lie**:

✓ *When she reached her room Lucy lay on the bed to review the situation.*

✗ *I got so tired I used to lay down on the bunk.*

✓ *Many individual units had begun to lay down their arms.*

● Another cause of confusion is the closeness in form of **laid** and **lain**, and the fact that **laid** is the past and past participle of **lay**; but **lain** is only the past participle of **lie**:

✓ *He paused, then laid a hand on her shoulder.*

✗ *She had also lain aside her clothes and was dressed in nothing but an orange robe.*

✓ *After waking he had lain and thought of the day ahead.*

lay² *past tense of* LIE²

lay³ ▻ *adj* **1** relating to or involving people who are not members of the clergy. **2** not having specialized or professional knowledge of a particular subject. ◷ 14c: from Greek *laos* the people.

lay⁴ ▻ *noun* (***lays***) a short narrative or lyric poem, especially one that is meant to be sung. ◷ 13c.

layabout ▻ *noun, colloq* someone who is habitually lazy or idle.

lay-by ▻ *noun* (***lay-bys***) *Brit* an area off to the side of a road where cars can stop safely without disrupting the flow of traffic.

layer /leɪə(r), lɛə(r)/ ▻ *noun* **1** a thickness or covering, especially one of several on top of each other. **2** *in compounds* someone or something that lays something specified □ *bricklayer.* **3** a hen that regularly lays eggs. **4** a shoot from a plant fastened into the soil so that it can take root while still attached to the parent plant. ▻ *verb* (***layered***, ***layering***) **1** to arrange or cut in layers. **2** to produce (a new plant) by preparing a layer from the parent plant. ● **layered** *adj* composed of layers. ◷ 16c: from LAY¹.

layette /leɪ'ɛt/ ▻ *noun, old use* a complete set of clothes, blankets, etc for a new baby. ◷ 19c: French.

lay figure ▻ *noun* **1** a jointed adjustable model of the human body used by painters and sculptors, especially when they want to study the effects of drapery. **2 a** someone who lacks individuality; **b** a character in a novel who is unconvincing or unrealistic. ◷ 18c: from Dutch *leeman* jointed man + FIGURE (*noun* 5).

layman, **laywoman** and **layperson** ▻ *noun* **1** someone who is not a member of the clergy. **2** someone who does not have specialized or professional knowledge of a particular subject. See also LAITY. ◷ 15c: from LAY³.

lay-off ▻ *noun* a dismissal of employees when there is no work available. ◷ 19c.

layout ▻ *noun* **1** an arrangement or plan of how land, buildings, pages of a book, etc are to be set out. **2** the things displayed or arranged in this way. **3** the general appearance of a printed page.

lay reader ▻ *noun* an unordained person licensed to undertake some religious duties.

laze ▻ *verb* (***lazed***, ***lazing***) *intr* to be idle or lazy. ▻ *noun* a period of time spent lazing. ◷ 16c: a back-formation from LAZY.

■ **laze about** or **around** to spend time doing nothing.

lazy /'leɪzɪ/ ▻ *adj* (***lazier***, ***laziest***) **1** disinclined to work or do anything requiring effort. **2** idle. **3** appropriate to idleness. **4** said of a river: slow-moving; sluggish. ● **lazily** *adverb*. ● **laziness** *noun*. ⓒ 16c.

lazy-bones ▻ *noun* (*plural* ***lazy-bones***) *colloq* someone who is lazy.

lazy Susan ▻ *noun* a revolving tray, usually divided into sections each of which may be filled with a different kind of food and placed on a dining table.

lb ▻ *abbreviation* **1** *libra* (Latin), a pound weight. **2** *cricket* leg bye.

lbw or **l.b.w.** ▻ *abbreviation, cricket* leg before wicket.

lc ▻ *abbreviation* **1** *loco citato* (Latin), in the place cited. **2** *printing* lower case.

LCD ▻ *abbreviation* **1** liquid crystal display. **2** (*also* **lcd**) lowest common denominator.

LCM or **lcm** ▻ *abbreviation* lowest common multiple.

L/Cpl ▻ *abbreviation* Lance Corporal.

***L*-dopa** see under DOPA

L-driver ▻ *noun* a learner driver (see LEARNER 3).

LEA ▻ *abbreviation, Brit* Local Education Authority.

lea¹ ▻ *noun, poetic* a field, meadow or piece of arable or pasture land. ⓒ Anglo-Saxon *leah*.

lea² ▻ *adj* fallow. ▻ *noun* arable land that has been left uncultivated. ⓒ 14c: from Anglo-Saxon *lage*.

leach ▻ *verb* (***leaches***, ***leached***, ***leaching***) **1** *chem* to wash a soluble substance out of (a solid) by allowing a suitable liquid solvent to percolate through it. **2** to make liquid seep through (ash, soil, etc), in order to remove substances from that material. **3 a** to remove (soluble substances) by having liquid seep through; **b** *intr* said of soluble substances: to be removed in this way. ⓒ probably Anglo-Saxon *leccan* to water.

■ **leach something away** or **out** to remove (soluble substances) by having liquid seep through.

lead¹ /liːd/ ▻ *verb* (***led***, ***leading***) **1** *tr & intr* to guide by going in front. **2** to precede. **3** to guide or make someone or something go in a certain direction by holding or pulling with the hand, etc. **4** to guide. **5** to conduct. **6** to induce. **7** to cause to live or experience. **8** *tr & intr* to direct or be in control (of something). **9** to make someone act, feel or think in a certain way. **10** to live, pass or experience □ *lead a miserable existence.* **11** *tr & intr* to go or take someone in a certain direction □ *The road leads to the village.* **12** *tr & intr* to be foremost or first; to be the most important or influential in (a group) in a particular field □ *They lead the world in engineering.* **14** *intr* (*usually* **lead with** or **on**) said of a newspaper: to have (a particular story) as its most important article □ *The tabloids all lead with the latest atrocity.* **15** *Brit* to be the leader of (an orchestra). **16** to conduct liquid along a channel or course. **17** *tr & intr, cards* to begin a round of cards by playing (the first card, especially of a particular suit). **18** *Scots law* to adduce. **19** (*often* **lead in**) to cart crops to the farmyard. ▻ *noun* **1** an instance of guidance given by leading. **2** the first, leading, or most prominent place; leadership. **3** the amount by which someone or something, etc is in front of others in a race, contest, etc □ *had a lead of about a metre.* **4** a strap or chain for leading or holding a dog, etc. **5** an initial clue or piece of information which might help solve a problem, mystery, etc. **6** the principal part in a play, film, etc; the actor playing this role. **7** the most important story in a newspaper. **8** a precedent or example. **9** precedence. **10** an indication. **11** direction. **12** initiative. **13** a wire or conductor taking electricity from a source to an appliance. **14** *cards* the act or right of playing first, the first card played or the play of someone who plays first. **15** the first player in some team sports and games. **16** a watercourse leading to a mill. **17** a channel through ice. **18** a main conductor in electrical distribution. ● **lead someone astray** to entice them into a wrong or misguided course. ● **lead someone by the nose** to force them to follow. ● **lead someone a (merry) dance** see under DANCE. ● **lead someone up the garden path** see under GARDEN. ● **lead the life of Riley** to have an easy life. ● **lead the way** to go first, especially to guide others. ⓒ Anglo-Saxon *lædan*.

■ **lead off** to begin.

■ **lead someone on 1** to persuade them to go further than intended. **2** to deceive or mislead them.

■ **lead someone** or **something out** to bring them or it out by preceding □ *led the team out to tremendous applause.*

■ **lead to something** to result in it.

■ **lead up to something 1** to approach (a topic of conversation) reluctantly or by gradual steps or stages □ *leading up to the question of money.* **2** to be an underlying cause of it □ *Persistent lateness lead up to his dismissal.*

lead² /lɛd/ ▻ *noun* **1** (symbol **Pb**, atomic number 82) a soft, heavy, bluish-grey, highly toxic metallic element that is resistant to corrosion, used in the building and roofing trades, as a protective shielding against radiation and as a component of high-quality glass and numerous alloys. **2** graphite. **3** a thin stick of graphite, or some other coloured substance, used in pencils. **4** a lump of lead used for measuring the depth of the water, especially at sea. **5** (**leads**) a sheet of lead for covering roofs; a roof covered with lead sheets. **6** a lead frame for a small window-pane, eg in stained glass windows. **7** a lead weight or piece of lead shot used at the end of a fishing line and in cartridges. ▻ *adj* made of lead. ▻ *verb* (***leaded*** /'lɛdɪd/, ***leading*** /'lɛdɪŋ/) **1** to fit or surround with lead. **2** to cover or weight with lead. **3** to set (eg window panes) in lead. **4** *printing* to separate (type) with lead or leads. ● **leading** see separate entry. ● **go down like a lead balloon** *facetious* to be spectacularly unsuccessful. ⓒ Anglo-Saxon.

lead acetate see under SUGAR OF LEAD

leaden /'lɛdən/ ▻ *adj* **1** made of lead. **2** dull grey in colour. **3** heavy or slow. **4** depressing; dull. ● **leadenly** *adverb*. ● **leadenness** *noun*.

leader /'liːdə(r)/ ▻ *noun* **1** someone or something that leads or guides others. **2** someone who organizes or is in charge of a group. **3 a** *Brit* the principal violinist in an orchestra. *N American equivalent* **concert master**; **b** *US* an alternative name for a conductor of an orchestra, etc. **4** *Brit* (*also* **leading article**) an article in a newspaper, etc written to express the opinions of the editor. **5** (**Leader** or **Leader of the House of Commons** or **Lords**) *Brit* a member of the government officially responsible for introducing business in Parliament. **6** a short blank strip at the beginning and end of a film or tape, used for loading the film or tape on to a spool. **7** a horse or dog in front place in a team or pair. **8** a long shoot growing from the stem or branch of a plant. **9** a tendon. **10** a connection between a fishing-line and the hook. **11** *printing* a line of dots to guide the eye from something listed on one edge of the page over to the other edge. **12** the principal wheel in any machinery.

leadership ▻ *noun* **1** the state of being a leader. **2** the ability to lead others. **3** leaders as a group.

lead-free see UNLEADED

lead-in /'liːd-/ ▻ *noun* **1** an introduction to an article, discussion, piece of music, commercial, etc. **2** a cable connecting a television, radio, receiver or transmitter with the elevated part of an outside aerial.

leading¹ /'liːdɪŋ/ ▻ *adj* **1** acting as leader. **2** guiding. **3** directing. ▻ *noun* guidance; leadership.

leading² /'lɛdɪŋ/ ▻ *noun, printing* a thin strip of metal used formerly to produce a space between lines.

leading aircraftman and **leading aircraftwoman** ▻ *noun* a man or woman with the rank above aircraftman or aircraftwoman.

leading article see LEADER 4

leading business ▻ *noun* the acting of the principal parts or roles in films and plays.

leading edge ▻ *noun* **1** the foremost edge of an aerofoil or propeller blade. **2** said especially of technology, etc: the forefront. ▻ *adj* (**leading-edge**) said especially of technology, etc: most up-to-date.

leading lady and **leading man** ▻ *noun* someone who plays the principal female or male role in a film or play.

leading light ▻ *noun* someone who is very important and influential in a particular field or subject.

leading note ▻ *noun, music* the seventh note of the diatonic scale in any key.

leading question ▻ *noun* a question asked in such a way as to suggest the answer wanted.

lead monoxide ▻ *noun* a bright yellow solid compound used in pigments and paints, and in the manufacture of glass and ceramics.

lead-off ▻ *noun* a first move.

lead pencil ▻ *noun* a pencil with a thin stick of graphite in the middle.

lead poisoning ▻ *noun* **1** severe poisoning caused by the absorption of lead into the body, usually by inhalation of lead fumes. **2** *slang* injury or death by shooting.

leads and lags ▻ *noun, commerce* in international trade: the early payment of bills, etc to concerns abroad, and the delayed invoicing of foreign customers in order to take advantage of expected changes in the rate of exchange.

lead time /liːd —/ ▻ *noun* **1** the time between the conception or design of a product, etc and its actual production, completion, etc. **2** the time between the ordering and the delivery of goods.

lead-up ▻ *noun* **1** something that introduces or causes something else. **2** the period of time or the process involved immediately prior to something happening □ *the lead-up to the election.*

leadwort see PLUMBAGO

leaf ▻ *noun* (***leaves***) **1** an expanded outgrowth, usually green and flattened, from the stem of a plant, that contains the pigment CHLOROPHYLL and is the main site of PHOTOSYNTHESIS in green plants. **2** anything like a leaf, such as a scale or a petal. **3** leaves regarded collectively. **4** a single sheet of paper forming two pages in a book. **5** a very thin sheet of metal □ *gold leaf.* **6** a hinged or sliding extra part or flap on a table, door, etc. **7** *drug-taking slang* marijuana. ▻ *verb* (***leafed***, ***leafing***) said of plants: to produce leaves. • **in leaf** the condition of having leaves. • **take a leaf out of someone's book** see under BOOK. • **turn over a new leaf** to begin a new and better way of behaving or working. ◷ Anglo-Saxon *leaf.*

■ **leaf through something** to turn the pages of (a book, magazine, etc) quickly and cursorily.

leafage ▻ *noun* the leaves of plants.

leaf-base ▻ *noun* the bottom of the stalk of a leaf where it joins the stem.

leaf-bud ▻ *noun* a bud which will produce a leaf or leaves rather than a flower.

leaf-curl ▻ *noun* a plant disease that causes the leaves to curl up.

leaf-cutting ▻ *noun* a leaf taken from a plant and used in propagation.

leaf-fall ▻ *noun* **1** the shedding of leaves. **2** the time when leaves are shed, usually autumn.

leaf-hopper ▻ *noun* a name for various hopping insects which suck juices from plants.

leaf insect ▻ *noun* an insect with wing covers that look like leaves. Compare STICK INSECT.

leafless ▻ *adj* without leaves.

leaflet ▻ *noun* **1** a single sheet of paper, or several sheets of paper folded together, giving information, advertising products, etc, usually given away free. **2** a small or immature leaf. **3** a division of a compound leaf. ▻ *verb* (***leafleted***, ***leafleting***) *tr & intr* to distribute leaflets.

leaf mosaic ▻ *noun* a name for various viral diseases of potato, tobacco, etc, in which the leaves become mottled.

leaf mould ▻ *noun* earth formed from rotted leaves, used as a compost for plants.

leaf stalk ▻ *noun, bot* the part in a plant that attaches a leaf to the stem. *Technical equivalent* **petiole**.

leafy ▻ *adj* (***leafier***, ***leafiest***) **1** having or covered with leaves. **2** shaded by leaves □ *the leafy lane.* **3** like a leaf.

league[1] /liːg/ ▻ *noun* **1** a union of persons, nations, etc formed for the benefit of the members. **2** a group of sports clubs which compete over a period for a championship. **3** a class or group, considered in terms of ability, importance, etc. ▻ *verb* (***leagued***, ***leaguing***) *tr & intr* to form or be formed into a league. • **bottom** or **top of the league** the lowest or highest in a particular field of achievement, or in quality. • **in league with someone** acting or planning with them, usually for some unfavourable outcome or purpose. • **in the big league** *colloq* amongst the most important, powerful, etc people, organizations, etc. • **not in the same league as** not of the same calibre, ability, importance, etc, as. ◷ 15c: from Latin *ligare* to bind.

league[2] /liːg/ ▻ *noun, old use* **1** a unit for measuring distance travelled, usually taken to be about 4.8km (3ml). **2** *naut* a measure, 1/20th of a degree, 3 international nautical miles, 5.556km (3.456 statute miles). ◷ 14c: from Latin *leuga* a Gaulish unit of distance.

league match ▻ *noun* a game played between people, teams or clubs from the same league. Compare CUP MATCH.

league table ▻ *noun* **1** a table in which people or clubs are placed according to their performances. **2** any grouping where relative success or importance is compared or monitored.

leak ▻ *noun* **1 a** an unwanted crack or hole in a container, pipe, etc where liquid or gas can pass in or out; **b** the act or fact of liquid or gas escaping in this way; **c** liquid or gas which has escaped in this way. **2 a** a revelation of secret information, especially when unauthorized or apparently unauthorized; **b** information revealed in this way; **c** someone who reveals information in this way. **3** (*usually in* **take a leak**) *slang* an act of urinating. **4** a loss of electricity from a conductor, etc, usually because of faulty insulation. **5** *electronics* a high resistance, especially serving as a discharging path for a condenser. ▻ *verb* (***leaked***, ***leaking***) **1 a** said of liquid, gas, etc: to pass accidentally in or out of an unwanted crack or hole; **b** *intr* to allow (liquid, gas, etc) to pass accidentally in or out. **2 a** to reveal (secret information) without authorization, or apparently so; **b** *intr* said of secret information: to become known. **3** to urinate. • **leaking** *noun, adj.* • **spring a leak** to become leaky, especially suddenly or unexpectedly. ◷ 15c as *leken*: from Norse *leka.*

■ **leak out 1** to escape. **2** to be revealed.

leakage ▻ *noun* **1** an act or instance of leaking. **2** something that enters or escapes through a leak.

leaky ▻ *adj* (***leakier***, ***leakiest***) **1** having a leak or leaks. **2** habitually divulging secrets. • **leakiness** *noun.*

lean[1] ▻ *verb* (***leant*** /lɛnt/ or ***leaned*** /liːnd, lɛnt/, ***leaning***) **1** *tr & intr* to slope or be placed in a sloping position. **2** *tr & intr* to rest or be rested against something for support.

3 *intr* (*usually* **lean towards**) to have an inclination to, a preference for or tendency towards. ▻ *noun* **1** an act or condition of leaning. **2** a slope. ● **lean over backwards** or **bend over backwards** see under BACKWARDS.

lean² ▻ *adj* **1** said of a person or animal: thin. **2** said of meat: containing little or no fat. **3** producing very little food, money, etc; unfruitful □ *lean years.* ▻ *noun* meat with little or no fat. ● **leanness** *noun*. ⓒ Anglo-Saxon *hlæne*.

lean-burn ▻ *adj* using, referring or relating to a fuel-air mixture containing a large amount of air in proportion to its fuel content, so that both the amount of fuel consumed and the level of pollution caused is reduced.

leaning ▻ *noun* a liking or preference; tendency □ *What is your political leaning?*

leant *past tense, past participle of* LEAN¹

lean-to ▻ *noun* (*lean-tos*) a shed or other light construction built against another building or a wall.

leap ▻ *verb* (*leapt* /lɛpt/ or *leaped* /liːpt, lɛpt/, *leaping*) **1** *intr* to jump or spring suddenly or with force. **2** to jump over. **3** *intr* to move in bounds. **4** *intr* said of prices: to go up by a large amount suddenly and quickly. **5** *intr* said of fish: to jump up out of the water, usually to propel themselves up some fast-flowing stretch of river. **6** *intr* to rush suddenly and unexpectedly. **7** to make something jump □ *leapt the horse over the fence.* ▻ *noun* **1** an act of leaping or jumping. **2** the distance leaped. **3** a place where leaping takes place □ *a salmon leap.* ● **by leaps and bounds** extremely rapidly. ● **a leap in the dark** an action, decision, etc whose results cannot be guessed in advance. ● **leap** or **jump to conclusions** to decide on something without being aware of all the issues involved. ⓒ Anglo-Saxon *hleapan*.

■ **leap at something** *colloq* to accept it eagerly.

leap-frog ▻ *noun* a game, usually played by children, in which each player in turn jumps over the back of the stooping player in front. ▻ *verb* (*leap-frogged*, *leap-frogging*) *tr & intr* **1** to jump over (someone's back) in this way. **2** said of two or more people, vehicles, etc: to keep passing each other so that the leader is continually changing □ *The executives would leap-frog each other in the promotion stakes.* ● **leap-frogging** *noun, adj.* ⓒ Late 19c.

leap year ▻ *noun* a year of 366 days, with an INTERCALARY day on 29 February, which occurs once every four years when the year is divisible by 4 (eg 1996). For end-of-century years, the year must be divisible by 400, thus accommodating the extra approximately quarter-day per year that it takes the Earth to circle the Sun. ⓒ 14c: possibly from the fact that any day falling after 29 February will not fall on the day of the week after the day it fell on in the previous year as is usual, but will leap over to the next day.

learn /lɜːn/ ▻ *verb* (*learnt* or *learned*, *learning*) **1** *tr & intr* to be or become informed or to hear of something. **2** *tr & intr* to gain knowledge of or skill in something through study, teaching, instruction or experience. **3** to get to know by heart; to memorize. **4** *non-standard* to teach. ● **learn how to do something** to gradually become skilful at it. ● **learn the hard way** to become experienced in something only after having suffered some kind of setback or trouble. ● **learn the ropes** *colloq* to understand gradually how to do something. ⓒ Anglo-Saxon *leornian*.

■ **learn about** or **of something** to hear about or of it.

■ **learn by** or **from something** to gain experience through it.

learned /lɜːnɪd/ ▻ *adj* **1** having great knowledge or learning, especially through years of study. **2** referring or relating to learned people; scholarly. **3** (**the learned**) those who have great knowledge. ● **learnedly** *adverb*. ● **my learned friend** *law* a title of courtesy used by lawyers or barristers to address each other in court.

learner ▻ *noun* **1** someone who is learning or being taught something. **2** someone who is in the early stages of learning or being taught something. **3** someone who is learning to drive a motor vehicle, and has not passed a driving test.

learning ▻ *noun* **1** knowledge gained through study. **2** what is learned. **3** scholarship.

learning curve ▻ *noun* **1** a graph used in education and research to represent progress in learning. **2** the process of becoming familiar with a subject or activity, especially in relation to its speed.

learning disabilities ▻ *plural noun, sociol* the currently favoured term for MENTAL HANDICAP.

learning support ▻ *noun* teaching intended to help pupils with learning difficulties. See also REMEDIAL.

lease /liːs/ ▻ *noun* **1** a contract by which the owner of a house, land, etc agrees to let someone else use it for a stated period of time in return for payment. **2** the duration of such a contract □ *a six-month lease.* **3** the tenure or rights under such a contract. ▻ *verb* (*leased*, *leasing*) **1** said of an owner: to allow someone else to use (a house, land, etc) under the terms of a lease. **2** said of an occupier: to borrow (a house, land, etc) from the owner under the terms of a lease. ● **leasable** *adj.* ● **leaser** *noun* a LESSEE. ● **give someone** or **something a new lease of life** to cause them or it to have a longer or better life or period of usefulness than might have been expected. ⓒ 13c: from French *lais*.

leaseback ▻ *noun* an arrangement whereby the seller of a property, land, etc then leases it from the buyer. Also called **sale and leaseback**.

leasehold ▻ *noun* **1** the holding of land or buildings by lease. **2** the land or buildings held by lease. Compare FREEHOLD. ● **leaseholder** *noun*.

lease-lend see LEND-LEASE

leash ▻ *noun* (*leashes*) a strip of leather or chain used for leading or holding a dog or other animal. ▻ *verb* (*leashes*, *leashed*, *leashing*) **1** to put a leash on. **2** to control or restrain. **3** to bind. ● **straining at the leash** impatient or eager to begin. ⓒ 14c: from French *laisser* to let a dog run on a leash.

least (used as the superlative of LITTLE) ▻ *adj* smallest; slightest; *denoting* the smallest number or amount. ▻ *adverb* in the smallest or lowest degree. ▻ *pronoun* the smallest amount □ *I think he has least to offer.* ● **at least** **1** if nothing else; at any rate. **2** not less than □ *at least half an hour late.* ● **not in the least** or **not in the least bit** not at all. ● **the least** the minimum □ *The least you could do is visit from time to time.* ⓒ Anglo-Saxon *læst*.

leather /ˈlɛðə(r)/ ▻ *noun* **1** the skin of an animal made smooth by tanning. **2** a small piece of leather for polishing or cleaning. **3** the leather part of something. **4** (*usually* **leathers**) **a** riding breeches made of leather; **b** clothes made of leather, especially as worn by motorcyclists. **5** *as adj* **a** made of leather □ *a leather wallet*; **b** relating to or for sado-masochists □ *leather porn* □ *leather-bar.* ▻ *verb* (*leathered*, *leathering*) **1** to cover or polish with leather. **2** *colloq or dialect* to thrash. ● **leathern** *adj, archaic.* ● **leathering** *noun, colloq* a severe beating. ⓒ Anglo-Saxon *lether*.

leather-back ▻ *noun* the largest sea turtle, the adult of which has small bony plates embedded in its leathery skin, but no shell.

leatherette ▻ *adj, trademark* cloth, paper etc treated to resemble leather.

leather-jacket ▻ *noun* **1** a popular name for the larva of certain species of CRANEFLY, which has a greyish-brown leathery skin and often causes serious damage to plant roots. **2** any of several species of tropical fish which have a leathery skin.

leather-neck ▻ *noun, slang* **1** a sailor's name for a soldier or marine. **2** *US* a marine. ◷ 19c: from the leather stock or cravat once worn by marines.

leathery ▻ *adj* **1** tough. **2** looking or feeling like leather.

leave¹ ▻ *verb* (***left, leaving***) **1** *intr* to go away from someone or somewhere. **2** to allow something to remain behind, especially by mistake □ *left the keys at home.* **3** to move out of somewhere. **4** to abandon. **5** *intr* to resign or quit. **6** to allow someone or something to remain in a particular state or condition □ *leave the window open.* **7** to deliver to or deposit with someone □ *I'll leave the keys with a neighbour.* **8** to cause □ *It may leave a scar.* **9** to have as a remainder □ *Three minus one leaves two.* **10** to make a gift of something in a will □ *left all her money to charity.* **11** to be survived by □ *leaves a wife and daughter.* **12** to cause (especially food or drink) to remain unfinished □ *She left half her dinner.* **13** to hand or turn something over to someone else □ *left the driving to her.* • **be left with** to be burdened with □ *He was left with a huge bill.* • **leave someone** or **something be 1** to allow them or it to remain unchanged. **2** to leave them or it alone. • **leave for dead** to abandon someone who is assumed to be dead. • **leave go** *colloq* to let go. • **leave someone holding the baby** to abandon them to an unpleasant task or fate. • **leave someone in the lurch** see under LURCH². • **leave it at that** to take no further action, make no more comment on, etc. • **leave it out!** *slang* stop it! • **leave little** or **much to be desired** to be slightly or very inadequate or unsatisfactory. • **leave something unsaid** to hold back from saying it. • **leave well alone** to refrain from interfering with something, especially when it is functioning adequately. ◷ Anglo-Saxon *læfan* to remain.

■ **leave someone** or **something alone** to allow them or it to remain undisturbed.

■ **leave someone** or **something behind 1** to go without taking them or it, either intentionally or accidently. **2** to outdistance them.

■ **leave for somewhere** to set out for a place.

■ **leave off something** to stop doing it.

■ **leave something on** to leave it switched on, usually by mistake.

■ **leave someone** or **something out** to exclude or omit it or them .

leave² ▻ *noun* **1** permission to do something. **2** permission to be absent, especially from work or military duties. **3** permitted absence from work or military duties. **4** the length of time this lasts □ *took a week's leave.* **5** *old use* a formal parting or farewell. • **on leave** officially absent from work. • **take leave** to assume permission. • **take leave of one's senses** to become irrational, especially suddenly and without any apparent reason. • **take one's leave** *formal, old use* to depart. ◷ Anglo-Saxon *leafe* permission.

leaven /ˈlɛvən/ ▻ *noun* (*also* **leavening**) **1** a substance, especially yeast, added to dough to make it rise. **2** anything which is an influence and causes change. ▻ *verb* (***leavened, leavening***) **1** to cause (dough) to rise with leaven. **2** to influence or cause change in. ◷ 14c: from Latin *levamen* a means of raising.

leaver ▻ *noun* someone who leaves. See also SCHOOL-LEAVER.

leaves *plural of* LEAF

leavings ▻ *plural noun, colloq* things which are left over; rubbish.

Lebensraum /ˈleɪbənzraʊm/ ▻ *noun* (*sometimes* **lebensraum**) space in which to live and, if necessary, expand. **2** *historical* territory outside Germany that the Nazis claimed was necessary for continued economic growth. ◷ Early 20c: German *Lebens* of life + *Raum* space.

lech /lɛtʃ/ ▻ *noun* (***leches***) *slang* **1** someone who acts lustfully. **2** a lustful act. ▻ *verb* (***leches, leched, leching***) *slang* to behave lustfully. ◷ 18c: back-formation from LECHER.

lecher /ˈlɛtʃə(r)/ ▻ *noun* someone who acts lustfully. ▻ *verb* (***lechered, lechering***) to behave in a lustful way. Often shortened to LECH. ◷ 12c: from French *lechier* to lick.

lecherous ▻ *adj* having or showing great or excessive sexual desire, especially in ways which are offensive. • **lecherously** *adverb.* • **lecherousness** *noun.*

lechery ▻ *noun* excessive sexual desire, especially in ways which are offensive.

lechwe /ˈliːtʃwiː, ˈlɛtʃweɪ/ ▻ *noun* (***lechwes***) an African antelope, related to but smaller than the waterbuck, with a light brownish-yellow coat. ◷ 19c: Sechuana, related to Sesuto *letsa* an antelope.

lecithin /ˈlɛsɪθɪn/ ▻ *noun, biochem* an organic chemical compound that is a major component of cell membranes in higher animals and plants, and is also used in foods, pharmaceuticals, cosmetics and paints. ◷ 19c: from Greek *lekithos* egg-yolk.

lectern /ˈlɛktən/ ▻ *noun* a stand with a sloping surface for holding a book, notes, etc for someone to read from, especially in a church or lecture-hall. ◷ 14c: from Latin *legere, lectum* to read.

lectin /ˈlɛktɪn/ ▻ *noun* any of numerous proteins, found mainly in plant seeds, some of which cause agglutination of the red blood cells in certain blood groups. ◷ 1950s: from Latin *legere, lectum* to pick.

lection /ˈlɛkʃən/ ▻ *noun* **1** a reading. **2** a lesson read in church. ◷ 17c: from Latin *legere, lectum* to read.

lector /ˈlɛktɔː(r)/ ▻ *noun* **1** a reader, especially in a college or university. **2** someone who reads the Scripture lesson in a church service. **3** in some monasteries and convents: an ecclesiastic of a minor order whose original duty was to read lessons aloud, especially at mealtimes. ◷ 15c: Latin.

lecture /ˈlɛktʃə(r)/ ▻ *noun* **1** a formal talk on a particular subject given to an audience. **2** a lesson or period of instruction, especially as delivered at a college or university. **3** a long and tedious scolding or warning. ▻ *verb* (***lectured, lecturing***) **1** *tr & intr* to give or read a lecture or lectures to (a group of people). **2** to scold someone at length. **3** to instruct by lectures, especially in a college or university. **4** to instruct authoritatively. ◷ 14c: from Latin *lectura,* from *legere* to read.

lecturer ▻ *noun* someone who lectures, especially in a college or university. • **lectureship** *noun* a position or post held by a lecturer.

LED ▻ *abbreviation, electronics* light-emitting diode, a semiconductor diode which gives out light when an electric current is passed through it, used in the self-luminous displays of calculators, digital watch faces, etc.

led *past tense, past participle of* LEAD¹

lederhosen /ˈleɪdəhoʊzən/ ▻ *plural noun* men's short leather trousers with braces, worn in various regions around the Alps. ◷ 1930s: German *Leder* leather + *Hosen* trousers.

ledge ▻ *noun* **1** a narrow horizontal shelf or shelf-like part. **2** a ridge or shelf of rock, especially one on a mountain side or under the sea. **3** a lode or vein of ore or rock. ◷ 14c: from *legge,* perhaps from *leggen* to lay.

ledger /ˈlɛdʒə(r)/ ▻ *noun* **1** the chief book of accounts of an office or shop, in which details of all transactions are recorded. **2** a horizontal timber in scaffolding. **3** a flat grave slab. **4** *angling* a weighted line. ▻ *verb* (***ledgered, ledgering***) *intr, angling* to fish with a weighted line. ◷ 15c: from *leggen* to lay.

ledger-bait ▻ *noun, angling* fishing bait that is designed to stay in one place.

ledger line or **leger line** ▻ *noun, music* a short line added above or below a musical stave on which to mark a note higher or lower than the stave allows for.

ledger-line or **leger-line** ▻ *noun, angling* a fishing line that is fixed in one place.

ledger-tackle ▻ *noun, angling* nets or lines that have been weighted.

lee ▻ *noun* (***lees***) **1** shelter given by a neighbouring object. **2** the sheltered side, away from the wind. ▻ *adj* relating to the sheltered side. See also LEEWARD, LEEWAY. ◷ Anglo-Saxon *hleo* shelter.

lee-board ▻ *noun, naut* a board lowered on the lee side of a vessel, to lessen drift to leeward.

leech[1] ▻ *noun* (***leeches***) **1** any of various annelid worms with a cylindrical or flattened body bearing suckers at each end, especially a blood-sucking species which was formerly used for bloodletting as a treatment for many ailments. **2** a person who befriends another in the hope of personal gain. **3** *archaic* a doctor or physician. ▻ *verb* (***leeches, leeched, leeching***) *medicine, archaic* to treat (a patient) by applying leeches. ◷ Anglo-Saxon *læce*.

■ **leech off someone** or **something** to use them or it to one's advantage, usually without permission and often in an objectionable way.

■ **leech on to someone** or **something** to cling to them or it.

leech[2] ▻ *noun, naut* the side edge of a sail. ◷ 15c.

lee-gage or **lee-gauge** ▻ *noun, naut* position to the leeward. Opposite of WEATHER-GAGE.

leek ▻ *noun* a long thin vegetable with broad flat dark green leaves and a white base, closely related to the onion, and adopted as the national emblem of Wales. ◷ Anglo-Saxon *leac*.

leer ▻ *noun* **1** a lecherous look or grin. **2** a sideways look. ▻ *verb* (***leered, leering***) *intr* **1** to look or grin lecherously. **2** to look sideways. • **leering** *adj, noun*. • **leeringly** *adverb*. ◷ 16c: Anglo-Saxon *hleor* face or cheek.

leery ▻ *adj* (***leerier, leeriest***) *now chiefly dialect* sly; cunning. • **be leery of someone** or **something** *slang* to be wary or suspicious of them or it.

lees /liːz/ ▻ *plural noun* **1** the sediment that settles at the bottom of liquids and alcoholic drinks, especially wine. **2** the worst part or parts. ◷ 14c: from French *lie*.

leeside ▻ *noun, naut* the sheltered side.

leet ▻ *noun, Scots* (*usually* **short leet**) a list of candidates for some office or position; a shortlist.

leetide ▻ *noun, naut* a tide that flows in the same direction as the wind blows.

leeward /ˈliːwəd, ˈljuəd/ *naut* ▻ *adj, adverb* in or towards the direction in which the wind blows. ▻ *noun* the sheltered side.

leeway ▻ *noun* **1** scope for freedom of movement or action. **2** *naut* a ship's drift sideways, away from its true course. • **make up leeway** to make up for lost progress or time.

left[1] ▻ *adj* **1** referring, relating to, or indicating the side facing west from the point of view of someone or something facing north, which normally in human beings has the weaker and less skilful hand. **2** relatively liberal, democratic, progressive, innovative, either in general disposition or in political outlook. **3** inclined towards socialism or communism. ▻ *adverb* on or towards the left side. ▻ *noun* **1** the left side, part, direction, etc. **2** the region to the left side. **3** (**the Left**) **a** people, political parties, etc in favour of socialism; **b** the members of any political party that holds the most progressive, democratic, socialist, radical or actively innovating views ◷ from the practice in some legislatures of this group sitting to the president's left See also RIGHT (*noun* 5), CENTRE (*noun* 8). **4** the left hand □ ***a boxer who leads with his left***. **5** a blow with the left hand. **6** said of one of a pair: a glove, shoe, etc which fits the left hand or foot. **7** a turning to the left. • **have two left feet** to be very awkward or clumsy, especially when trying to dance. • **left, right and centre** in or from all directions; everywhere. ◷ Anglo-Saxon *left* weak.

left[2] *past tense, past participle of* LEAVE[1]

Left Bank ▻ *noun* **1** traditionally the artistic and student quarter of Paris on the south side of the River Seine. **2** *as adj* (*often* **left bank**) having artistic, unconventional or eccentric ways □ ***thinks of himself as very left bank.***

left-footed ▻ *adj* **1** done with the left foot. **2** having more strength or skill in the left foot.

left-footer ▻ *noun, Brit derog slang* a Roman Catholic. ◷ 1940s: originating in communal turf-cutting in Ulster, where, traditionally, the Roman Catholics would use spades with lugs to the left of the shaft, requiring them to use the left foot to push the spade into the turf, while Protestants used spades with lugs to the right.

left-hand ▻ *adj* **1** relating to, on or towards the left. **2** done with the left hand.

left-hand drive ▻ *adj* said of vehicles intended for use on the right-hand side of the road: having the driving mechanisms on the left.

left-handed ▻ *adj* **1** having the left hand stronger and more skilful than the right. **2** for use by left-handed people, or the left hand. **3** awkward; clumsy. **4** said of compliments, etc: dubious or ambiguous; only seeming to be sincere. **5** anti-clockwise. **6** said of a marriage: where one partner is of a considerably lower rank than the other and the marriage does not improve the lower-ranking person's status. Compare MORGANATIC. • **left-handedly** *adverb*. • **left-handedness** *noun*.

left-hander ▻ *noun* **1** a left-handed person. **2** a punch with the left hand.

leftism ▻ *noun* **1** the principles and policies of the political left. **2** support for and promotion of this. • **leftist** *noun* a supporter of the political left. ▻ *adj* relating to or characteristic of the political left.

left-luggage ▻ *noun* in an airport, railway or coach station: an area containing lockers where one can store luggage.

left-luggage office ▻ *noun* a room at an airport or a railway or coach station where travellers may leave luggage in return for a small payment.

left-of-centre ▻ *adj* in politics: inclining slightly towards a group's, a party's or a political system's more liberal policies. ▻ *noun* (**left of centre**) those in a group, party or political system that favour comparatively liberal policies or views. Compare RIGHT-OF-CENTRE.

left-over ▻ *adj* not used up, not eaten, etc □ ***Put the left-over soup in the fridge.*** ▻ *noun* (**leftovers**) food that remains uneaten at the end of a meal □ ***gave the left overs to the dog.***

left wing ▻ *noun* **1** the members of a political party or group who are most inclined towards a socialist viewpoint. **2** *sport* **a** the extreme left side of a pitch or team in a field game □ ***took the ball down the left wing***; **b** (*also* **left-winger**) a player playing on this side □ ***The left wing scored a hat-trick.*** **3** the left side of an army. • **left-wing** *adj* belonging or relating to the left wing. • **left-winger** *noun*.

lefty ▻ *noun* (***lefties***) *colloq, often derog* **1** *politics* a left-winger. **2** a left-handed person.

leg ▻ *noun* **1** one of the limbs on which animals, birds and people walk and stand. **2** an animal's or bird's leg used as food. **3** the part of a piece of clothing that covers one of these limbs. **4** a long narrow support of a table, chair, etc. **5** one stage in a journey. **6** a section of a competition or lap of a race. **7** *cricket* **a** (*also* **leg side**) the side of the field that is to the left of a right-handed batsman or to the right of a left-handed batsman; **b** a fielder positioned on this side of the field. See also FINE LEG, LONG LEG, SHORT LEG, SQUARE LEG. **8** a branch or limb of a forked or jointed object □ *the sharp leg of the compasses.* ▷ *verb* (***legged***, ***legging***) to propel (a barge) through a canal tunnel by pushing with the feet on the walls or roof. • **legged** /lɛgd, 'lɛgɪd/ *adj, in compounds* having a specified number or type of legs □ *a three-legged cat* □ *a bow-legged man.* • **get** or **have one's leg over** *slang* to have sexual intercourse. • **give someone a leg up** *colloq* to help them climb up or over something. • **leg it** *colloq* to walk briskly, to run or dash away. • **not have a leg to stand on** or **be without a leg to stand on** *colloq* to have no way of excusing one's behaviour or supporting one's arguments with facts. • **pull someone's leg** *colloq* to try to make them believe something which is not true, especially as a joke. ⓒ 13c: from Norse *leggr.*

leg. ▷ *abbreviation* **1** legal. **2** legate. **3** legislature.

legacy /'lɛgəsɪ/ ▷ *noun* (***legacies***) **1** an amount of property or money left in a will. **2** something handed on or left unfinished by a past owner or predecessor □ *a legacy of mismanagement.* ⓒ 15c: from Latin *legare* to leave by will.

legal /li:gəl/ ▷ *adj* **1** lawful; allowed by the law. **2** referring or relating to the law or lawyers. **3** created by law. ⓒ 16c: from Latin *legalis.*

legal aid ▷ *noun* financial assistance from public funds given to people who cannot afford to pay for legal advice or proceedings. ⓒ Late 19c.

legal eagle ▷ *noun* a successful lawyer, especially one who is young, bright and dynamic. ⓒ 1940s.

legalese /li:gə'li:z/ ▷ *noun* complicated legal jargon.

legalism ▷ *noun* **1** strict adherence to the law. **2** the tendency to observe the letter or form of the law rather than the spirit. **3** *theol* the doctrine that salvation depends on strict adherence to the law. ⓒ 19c: from Latin *legalis.*

legalist ▷ *noun* someone who adheres strictly to the law.

legalistic ▷ *adj* adhering strictly to the law. • **legalistically** *adverb.*

legality /lɪ'galɪtɪ/ ▷ *noun* (*plural* in sense 2 only ***legalities***) **1** the state of being legal; lawfulness. **2** a legal obligation.

legalization or **legalisation** /li:gəlaɪ'zeɪʃən/ ▷ *noun* the process of making something that was once against the law legal or lawful □ *pressed for the legalization of cannabis.*

legalize or **legalise** /'li:gəlaɪz/ ▷ *verb* (***legalized***, ***legalizing***) to make something that was once against the law legal or lawful. ⓒ 18c.

legally ▷ *adverb* in accordance with or as regards the law.

legal tender ▷ *noun* **1** currency which, by law, must be accepted in payment of a debt. **2** the banknotes and coins used by a particular country □ *The Scottish £1 note is legal tender in England.*

legal year ▷ *noun* the year by which dates are reckoned; in Scotland since 1600 and in England since 1752, it has been taken to begin on 1 January, but, for six centuries before 1752, 25 March was used.

legate /'lɛgət/ ▷ *noun* **1** an ambassador or representative, especially from the Pope. **2** a delegate, deputy. **3** *originally* a Roman general's lieutenant. **4** *historical* the governor of a Papal province. ⓒ 12c: from Latin *legare, legatum* to send as a deputy.

legatee ▷ *noun* (***legatees***) someone who is left a legacy by the terms of a will. ⓒ 17c: from Latin *legare, legatum* to leave by will.

legation /lɪ'geɪʃən/ ▷ *noun* **1** a diplomatic mission or group of delegates. **2** the official residence of such a mission or group. **3** the office or status of a legate. **4** *historical* a Papal province. ⓒ 15c: from Latin *legare, legatum* to send as a deputy.

legato /lɪ'gɑ:toʊ/ *music* ▷ *adverb* smoothly, with the notes running into each other. ▷ *adj* smooth and flowing. ▷ *noun* (***legatos***) **1** a piece of music to be played in this way. **2** a legato style of playing. • **legatissimo** *adverb, adj* extremely legato. ⓒ 19c: Italian *legato* bound.

leg before wicket and **leg before** ▷ *noun, cricket* (abbreviation **lbw**) a way of being given out for having prevented a ball from hitting the wicket with any part of the body other than the hand.

leg break ▷ *noun, cricket* **1** a ball that breaks from the eg side to towards the off side on pitching. Also called LEG SPIN. **2** a ball bowled to have this kind of effect. **3** spin imparted to a ball to achieve this effect.

leg bye ▷ *noun, cricket* a run made when the ball touches any part of the batsman's body apart from the hand.

legend /'lɛdʒənd/ ▷ *noun* **1** a traditional story which has popularly come to be regarded as true, but has not been confirmed as such. **2** such stories collectively. **3** someone famous about whom popularly-believed stories are told □ *a legend in her own lifetime.* **4** words accompanying a map or picture, etc which explain the symbols used. **5** an inscription on a coin, medal or coat of arms. **6** *originally* the story of a saint's life. ⓒ 14c: from Latin *legenda* things to be read.

legendary ▷ *adj* **1** relating to or in the nature of legend. **2** described or spoken about in legend. **3** *colloq* very famous □ *His temper tantrums were legendary.* **4** romantic. ▷ *noun* (***legendaries***) **1** a writer of legends. **2** a book of legends.

legerdemain /lɛdʒədə'meɪn/ ▷ *noun* **1** skill in deceiving or conjuring with the hands. **2** trickery. ⓒ 15c: French *léger* light + *de* of + *main* hand.

leger line see LEDGER LINE

leggings ▷ *plural noun* **1** close-fitting stretch coverings for the legs, worn by girls and women. **2** *formerly* outer and extra protective coverings for the lower legs.

leg guard ▷ *noun, cricket* padded protection for the lower part of the legs.

leggy ▷ *adj* (***leggier***, ***leggiest***) **1** said especially of a woman: having attractively long slim legs. **2** said of a plant: having a long stem.

leghorn /'lɛghɔ:n, 'lɛgɔ:n/ ▷ *noun* **1** fine straw plait made in Tuscany. **2** a hat or bonnet made from this. **3** a breed of small domestic fowl. ⓒ 18c: from the Italian town Legorno, now called Livorno.

legible /'lɛdʒɪbəl/ ▷ *adj* said especially of handwriting: clear enough to be read. • **legibility** *noun.* • **legibly** *adverb.* ⓒ 14c: from Latin *legibilis.*

legion /'li:dʒən/ ▷ *noun* **1** *historical* a unit in the ancient Roman army, containing between three thousand and six thousand soldiers. **2** a very great number. **3** the name of certain military forces □ *the French Foreign Legion.* ▷ *adj* great in number □ *Books on this subject are legion.* See also ROYAL BRITISH LEGION. ⓒ 13c: from Latin *legere* to choose.

legionary ▷ *noun* (***legionaries***) *historical* a soldier in an ancient Roman legion. ▷ *adj* relating to legions.

legionnaire /li:dʒə'nɛə(r)/ ▷ *noun* a member of a legion, especially of the French Foreign Legion.

Legionnaires' Disease or **Legionnaire's Disease** ▷ *noun, pathol* a severe and sometimes fatal disease caused by a bacterial infection of the lungs. ⓒ 1970s: so called because it was first identified after an outbreak at a convention of the American Legion in 1976 in Pennsylvania.

leg-iron ▷ *noun* a fetter for the leg.

legislate /ˈlɛdʒɪsleɪt/ ▷ *verb* (***legislated***, ***legislating***) *intr* to make laws. • **legislate for something** to make provision for it. ⓒ 18c: back-formation from LEGISLATOR.

legislation ▷ *noun* **1** the process of legislating. **2** a group of laws.

legislative /ˈlɛdʒɪslətɪv/ ▷ *adj* **1** relating to or concerned with law-making. **2** having the power to make laws □ *a legislative assembly.* ▷ *noun* **1** law-making power. **2** the law-making body.

legislator ▷ *noun* someone who makes laws, especially a member of a legislative body. • **legislatorial** /lɛdʒɪsləˈtɔːrɪəl/ *adj.* ⓒ 17c: Latin, from *lex, legis* law + *lator* from *ferre, latum* to bring.

legislature /ˈlɛdʒɪsleɪtʃə(r)/ ▷ *noun* the part of the government which has the power to make laws.

legit. or **legit** /ləˈdʒɪt/ ▷ *abbreviation, colloq* legitimate. • **on the legit.** legally □ *For once he was working on the legit.*

legitimacy /ləˈdʒɪtɪməsɪ/ ▷ *noun* the state or fact of being legitimate.

legitimate ▷ *adj* /ləˈdʒɪtɪmət/ **1** lawful. **2** born to parents who are married to each other, either at the time of the birth or subsequently. **3** said of an argument or conclusion, etc: reasonable or logical. **4** said of a sovereign: ruling according to strict hereditary right. **5** genuine. **6** conforming to an accepted standard. **7** according to strict rules of heredity and primogeniture. ▷ *verb* /-meɪt/ (***legitimated***, ***legitimating***) **1** to make lawful or legitimate. **2** to give someone the rights of a legitimate child. • **legitimateness** *noun.* ⓒ 15c: from Latin *legitimare* to declare as lawful.

legitimately ▷ *adverb* lawfully; with justification.

legitimate theatre or **legitimate drama** ▷ *noun* the body of plays by traditional dramatists as distinct from other kinds of dramatic productions such as films, TV drama, vaudeville, etc.

legitimization or **legitimisation** ▷ *noun* said especially about conferring the rights and privileges of legitimate birth: making legitimate.

legitimize or **legitimise** /lɛˈdʒɪtəmaɪz/ ▷ *verb* (***legitimized***, ***legitimizing***) **1** to make legitimate. **2** to make (an illegitimate child) the legal heir to its parents and so able to claim the same rights and privileges as a legitimate child.

legless ▷ *adj* **1** *colloq* very drunk. **2** having no legs. • **leglessness** *noun.*

leg-man and **leg-woman** ▷ *noun, chiefly N Amer* **1** someone who goes out of the office to gather information. **2** *informal* a reporter for a newspaper.

Lego /ˈlɛgoʊ/ ▷ *noun, trademark* a children's toy construction system consisting of small plastic bricks, windows, wheels etc which can be fastened together to form model houses, trains, spaceships, etc. ⓒ 20c: from Danish *lege godt* to play well.

leg-of-mutton or **leg-o'-mutton** ▷ *adj* **1** said of sleeves: narrow at the wrist and much wider at the shoulder. **2** said of sails: wide at the bottom and tapering towards the top.

leg-over ▷ *noun, slang* an act of sexual intercourse.

leg-pull ▷ *noun, colloq* a joking attempt to make someone believe something which is not true. • **leg-puller** *noun.* • **leg-pulling** *noun.*

leg-rest ▷ *noun* something that supports the legs.

legroom ▷ *noun* the amount of space available for someone's legs, especially in a confined area such as a car, aeroplane, cinema, theatre, etc.

leg side ▷ *noun* see LEG (*noun* 7)

leg slip ▷ *noun, cricket* a fielder or position slightly behind the batsman.

leg spin ▷ *noun, cricket* a LEG BREAK. • **leg spinner** *noun* someone who bowls leg breaks.

leg stump ▷ *noun, cricket* the stump nearest the batsman.

leg theory ▷ *noun, cricket* the policy of bowling on the striker's legs with a trap of leg-side fielders. See also BODYLINE.

legume /ˈlɛgjuːm, lɪˈgjuːm/ ▷ *noun, bot, technical* **1** any of a family of flowering plants that produce a dry DEHISCENT fruit in the form of a pod, eg pea, bean, lentil. **2** the fruit of such a plant, containing one to many edible seeds rich in protein. **3** the edible seeds of this plant. • **leguminous** /lɪˈgjuːmɪnəs/ **1** referring to the family of pulse vegetables. **2** bearing legumes. ⓒ 17c: from Latin *legere* to gather.

legwarmers ▷ *plural noun* long footless socks, often worn during exercise or dance practice.

leg-woman see LEG-MAN

legwork ▷ *noun* work that involves a lot of research or travelling around.

lei[1] /leɪ/ ▷ *noun* (***leis***) a Polynesian garland of flowers, shells or feathers worn round the neck, often given as a symbol of welcome or affection. ⓒ 19c: Hawaiian.

lei[2] *plural of* LEU

Leics ▷ *abbreviation, English county* Leicestershire.

leishmaniasis /liːʃməˈnaɪəsɪs/ ▷ *noun, pathol* an infection common in tropical and subtropical regions, caused by a parasitic PROTOZOAN which is transmitted by sandflies. ⓒ Early 20c: named after the Scots bacteriologist, Sir William Leishman (1865–1926), who discovered the cure for the fever form of the disease, KALA-AZAR.

leisure /ˈlɛʒə(r)/ or (*US*) /ˈliːʒə(r)/ ▷ *noun* **1** time when one is free to relax and do as one wishes. • **at leisure** **1** not occupied. **2** without hurrying. • **at one's leisure** at a time one finds convenient. • **of leisure** *jocular* out of work, either involuntarily or by choice. ⓒ 14c: from Latin *licere* to be permitted.

leisure centre ▷ *noun* a centre providing a wide variety of recreational facilities, especially sporting ones for families.

leisured ▷ *adj* having ample leisure time □ *leisured classes.*

leisurely ▷ *adj* not hurried; relaxed. ▷ *adverb* without hurrying; taking plenty of time.

leitmotif or **leitmotiv** /ˈlaɪtmoutiːf/ ▷ *noun* **1** a theme or image, etc which recurs throughout a piece of music, novel, etc. **2** *music* in musical dramas, especially Wagnerian ones: a short piece of music that is always associated with a particular person, idea, feeling, etc. ⓒ 19c: German *Leitmotiv*, from *leiten* to lead + *Motiv* motif.

lek[1] ▷ *noun* the Albanian unit of currency, equal to 100 qintars.

lek[2] ▷ *noun* **1 a** a piece of ground where certain male game birds such as the black grouse and the capercailzie perform sexual displays to attract females; **b** this kind of display. **2** the season during which this kind of display takes place. ▷ *verb* (***lekked***, ***lekking***) *intr* to perform this kind of display. ⓒ 19c.

lekythos /ˈlɛkɪθɒs/ ▷ *noun* (***lekythi*** /-iː/ or ***lekythoi*** /-ɔɪ/) a Greek flask or vase with a narrow neck. ⓒ 19c: Greek.

LEM or **lem** /lɛm/ ▷ *abbreviation* Lunar Excursion Module.

lemma /ˈlɛmə/ ▷ *noun* (***lemmas*** or ***lemmata*** /ˈlɛmətə/) **1** *math* a preliminary proposition, or a premise taken for granted. **2** a heading or outline of an argument in a piece of literary writing. **3** *linguistics* a headword, especially in a dictionary, thesaurus, etc. • **lemmatical** *adj.* ⓒ 16c: Greek, in sense 2, from *lambanein* to take.

lemmatize or **lemmatise** ▷ *verb* (**lemmatized**, **lemmatizing**) to organize (words in a text) so that all inflected and variant forms of the same word are grouped together under one lemma or headword. ⓒ 1960s.

lemming /'lɛmɪŋ/ ▷ *noun* **1** a small burrowing rodent, native to northern regions of Europe, Asia and N America, which occasionally participates in huge migrations once popularly but erroneously believed to result in mass drownings at sea. **2** someone who blindly follows other people on a course to predictable disaster. • **lemming-like** *adverb* foolishly and without thinking. ⓒ 16c: Norwegian *lemmen*.

lemon /'lɛmən/ ▷ *noun* **1** a small oval citrus fruit with pointed ends and a tough yellow rind enclosing sour-tasting juicy flesh rich in vitamin C. **2** the small evergreen tree that produces this fruit. **3** a pale yellow colour. **4** *colloq* someone or something thought of as worthless, disappointing, unattractive or defective. ▷ *adj* **1** pale yellow in colour. **2** tasting of or flavoured with lemon. • **lemony** *adj* **1** tasting of or flavoured with lemon. **2** having a vaguely lemon colour. ⓒ 15c: from Arabic *lima* citrus fruits, closely related to LIME.

lemonade ▷ *noun* a fizzy or still drink flavoured with or made from lemons.

lemon balm see BALM

lemon curd and **lemon cheese** ▷ *noun* a thick creamy paste made from lemons, sugar, butter and egg.

lemon drop ▷ *noun* a hard lemon-flavoured sweet.

lemon grass ▷ *noun* a lemon-scented perennial grass grown in India for its oil.

lemon meringue pie ▷ *noun* a dessert with a pastry base, lemon filling and meringue topping.

lemon peel ▷ *noun* the skin of lemons, often candied.

lemon sole ▷ *noun* a European FLATFISH used as food.

lemon squash ▷ *noun, Brit* a concentrated drink made from lemons.

lemon squeezer ▷ *noun* any of various devices used to extract the juice from lemons.

lempira /lɛm'pɪərə/ ▷ *noun* (**lempiras**) the unit of currency of Honduras, equal to 100 centavos. ⓒ 20c: named after a local chief.

lemur /'liːmə(r)/ ▷ *noun* a nocturnal tree-dwelling PRIMATE, now confined to Madagascar, with large eyes and a long bushy tail, many species of which are now endangered. ⓒ 18c: from Latin *lemures* ghosts.

lend ▷ *verb* (**lent**, **lending**) **1** to allow someone to use something on the understanding that it (or its equivalent) will be returned. **2** to give someone the use of something (usually money), especially in return for interest paid on it. **3** to give or add (interest, beauty, etc) to something or someone □ *The lighting lends a calming atmosphere.* • **lend a hand** to help, though not necessarily by using the hands □ *Can you lend a hand with working out this sum?* • **lend an ear** to listen. ⓒ Anglo-Saxon *lænan*.

■ **lend itself to something** to be suitable for (a purpose) □ *The hall lends itself to staging live bands.*

■ **lend oneself to something** to adapt oneself or set oneself up to be treated in a specified way □ *He lends himself to ridicule.*

lend, loan

Lend is always a verb; **loan** can be used as a noun or a verb, although some people prefer **lend** to **loan** as the verb form in general senses.

lender ▷ *noun* someone who lends something, especially money.

lending library ▷ *noun* a library where books may be taken away to be read, as opposed to a **reference library** where they must be consulted on the premises.

lend-lease and **lease-lend** ▷ *noun* **1** *originally* in World War II: an arrangement whereby the President of the US could supply vital equipment such as warships to Britain and other countries at war with Germany in exchange for access to British bases. **2** *now* any arrangement that involves the parties mutually agreeing to lend or lease something to each other.

lenes *plural of* LENIS

length /lɛŋθ/ ▷ *noun* **1** the distance from one end of an object to the other, normally the longest dimension. Compare BREADTH. **2** *often in compounds* the distance something extends □ *a knee-length skirt.* **3** the quality of being long. **4** a long piece of something or a stated amount of something long □ *a length of rope.* **5** the extent from end to end of a horse, boat, etc, as a way of measuring one participant's lead over another in a race □ *won by two lengths.* **6** (*often* **in length**) a stretch or extent □ *The film was 90 minutes in length.* **7** *swimming* **a** the longer measurement of a swimming pool; **b** this distance swum □ *did twenty lengths a day.* **8** in racket sports: the placing of a shot so as to land well into the opponent's court □ *used topspin to get the length.* **9 a** an extent of time; **b** *phonetics, music* the amount of time a vowel, syllable, note, etc sounds. **10** *cricket* a perfect distance for pitching a ball. • **at length 1** in full. **2** at last. **3** monotonously and tediously □ *went on at length about the golf.* • **go to great lengths** or **go to any length** or **lengths** or **go to all lengths** to try all the possible ways of achieving something, even if it means going beyond expected or accepted boundaries. • **the length and breadth of something** the entire extent of it. ⓒ Anglo-Saxon *lengthu*.

lengthen ▷ *verb* (**lengthened**, **lengthening**) *tr & intr* to make or become longer.

lengthman ▷ *noun* someone who is responsible for the upkeep of a particular stretch of road or railway.

length mark ▷ *noun, phonetics* a symbol used to indicate the relative length of a vowel.

lengthways and **lengthwise** ▷ *adverb, adj* in the direction of or according to something's length.

lengthy ▷ *adj* (**lengthier**, **lengthiest**) **1** being of great, often excessive, length. **2** said of speech, etc: long and tedious. • **lengthily** *adverb*. • **lengthiness** *noun*.

lenient /'liːnɪənt/ ▷ *adj* mild and tolerant, especially in punishing; not severe. • **lenience** or **leniency** *noun*. • **leniently** *adverb*. ⓒ 17c: from Latin *lenis* soft.

Leninism /'lɛnɪnɪzəm/ ▷ *noun* the political, economic and social principles and practices of the Russian revolutionary leader Lenin, especially his theory of government by the proletariat, based on his interpretation of MARXISM. See also MARXISM-LENINISM. Compare STALINISM. • **Leninist** or **Leninite** *noun*. ⓒ 1918: named after Vladimir Ilyich Ulyanov (1870–1924) who assumed the pseudonym Lenin in 1901.

lenis /'liːnɪs/ *phonetics* ▷ *adj* articulated with relatively little muscular effort and pressure of breath. ▷ *noun* (*plural* **lenes** /'liːniːz/) a consonant that is pronounced in this way. Compare FORTIS. ⓒ 1920s: Latin, meaning 'soft'.

lenity /'lɛnɪtɪ/ ▷ *noun, old use* mildness; mercifulness. ⓒ 16c: from Latin *lenis* soft.

lens /lɛnz/ ▷ *noun* (**lenses**) **1 a** an optical device consisting of a piece of glass, clear plastic, etc curved on one or both sides, used for converging or diverging a beam of light; **b** a contact lens. **2** (*technical*, also called **crystalline lens**) in the eye of many vertebrates, including humans: the transparent biconvex structure behind the iris which focuses light from an object on to the RETINA, forming an image. **3** in a camera: a mechanical equivalent of the lens of an eye which allows the image to fall on the photographer's eye or, when the shutter is open, on the film plane. See also FISH-EYE LENS, TELEPHOTO LENS, WIDE-ANGLE LENS. ⓒ 17c: Latin, meaning 'lentil' (because of the shape).

Lent ▷ *noun, Christianity* the time, lasting from Ash Wednesday to Easter Sunday, of fasting or, more commonly now, going without something, in remembrance of Christ's fast in the wilderness (Matthew 4.2). ◎ Anglo-Saxon *lencten* spring.

lent *past tense, past participle of* LEND

Lenten ▷ *adj* relating to or during LENT.

lentic /ˈlɛntɪk/ ▷ *adj* **1** *ecol* associated with standing water. **2** living in ponds, swamps, etc. ◎ 1930s: from Latin *lentus* slow or calm.

lenticle /ˈlɛntɪkəl/ ▷ *noun, geol* a mass that is lens-shaped. ◎ 19c: from Latin *lenticula*, diminutive of *lens* a lentil.

lenticular /lɛnˈtɪkjʊlə(r)/ ▷ *adj* shaped like a lens or lentil. • **lenticularly** *adverb*.

lentil /ˈlɛntɪl, ˈlɛntəl/ ▷ *noun* **1** a small orange, brown or green seed used as food. **2** the leguminous annual pulse common in the Mediterranean and W Asia which produces these seeds. ◎ 13c: from Latin *lens*.

lent-lily ▷ *noun* a DAFFODIL. ◎ 19c: so called because it flowers during LENT.

lento /ˈlɛntoʊ/ *music* ▷ *adverb* slowly. ▷ *adj* slow. ▷ *noun* (***lentos*** or ***lenti*** /-tiː/) a piece of music to be performed in this way. ◎ 18c: Italian.

Leo /ˈliːoʊ/ ▷ *noun* (*plural* ***Leos*** *in sense 2b*) **1** *astron* a large conspicuous northern constellation of the zodiac, containing numerous galaxies, so called because the outline of some of its brighter stars bears some resemblance to the profile of a lion. **2** *astrol* **a** the fifth sign of the zodiac; **b** a person born between 21 July and 22 August, under this sign. See table at ZODIAC. ◎ 11c: Latin, meaning 'lion'.

leone /lɪˈoʊn/ ▷ *noun* the standard currency of Sierra Leone, equal to 100 Sierra Leone cents.

leonine /ˈlɪənaɪn/ ▷ *adj* relating to or like a lion. ◎ 14c: from Latin *leoninus*, from *leo* lion.

leopard /ˈlɛpəd/ ▷ *noun* **1** a large member of the cat family, native to Africa and Asia, which has tawny yellow fur covered with small black spots, and whitish underparts. Sometimes called the PANTHER. **2** the male of this animal. **3** *N Amer* the jaguar or any similar kind of big cat. See SNOW LEOPARD. • **leopards don't** or **can't change their spots** people's personality traits, ways of doing things, etc do not change. ◎ 13c: Greek *leon* lion + *pardos* panther, because the animal was once thought to have been the result of these two interbreeding.

leopard-cat ▷ *noun* a spotted wild cat of India.

leopardess ▷ *noun* (***leopardesses***) a female leopard.

leopard-moth ▷ *noun* a white moth which has black spots on its wings and body and an unusually long larval stage.

leotard /ˈlɪətɑːd/ ▷ *noun* a stretchy one-piece tight-fitting garment worn for dancing and exercise, made in a variety of different styles from long-sleeved to sleeveless and with or without legs. Compare BODY (*noun* 13). ◎ 1920s: named after Jules Léotard (1830–70), a French trapeze artist.

leper /ˈlɛpə(r)/ ▷ *noun* **1** *medicine* someone who has leprosy. **2** *derog* someone who is avoided, especially on moral grounds. ◎ 14c: from Greek *lepros* scaly.

Lepidoptera /lɛpɪˈdɒptərə/ ▷ *plural noun, zool, technical* the order of insects that includes butterflies and moths, adult members of which typically have two pairs of wings, often brightly coloured, and a long narrow coiled PROBOSCIS for sucking up nectar. • **lepidopterous** *adj*. ◎ 18c: from Greek *lepis* scale + *pteron* wing.

lepidopterist /lɛpɪˈdɒptərɪst/ ▷ *noun* a person who studies butterflies and moths. ◎ 18c: from LEPIDOPTERA.

leporine /ˈlɛpəraɪn/ ▷ *adj* relating to or resembling the hare. ◎ 17c: from Latin *leporinus*.

leprechaun /ˈlɛprəkɔːn/ ▷ *noun, Irish folklore* a small elf who spends his time making shoes and who traditionally has a CROCK² of gold. He might be persuaded to part with this to a human if they were to threaten him with violence and if they could keep their eyes fixed on him for long enough. ◎ 17c: from Irish *lúchorpán* from *lú* small + *corp* body.

leprosy /ˈlɛprəsɪ/ ▷ *noun, pathol* an infectious disease of the skin, mucous membranes and nerves, mainly occurring in tropical regions, caused by a bacterium, formerly often leading to paralysis, disfigurement and deformity but now treatable with antibacterial drugs. ◎ 16c: from Greek *lepros* scaly.

leprous /ˈlɛprəs/ ▷ *adj, pathol* **1** suffering from leprosy. **2** related to leprosy.

-lepsy /lɛpsɪ/ ▷ *combining form, medicine, signifying* a seizing or seizure □ ***catalepsy***.

lepton¹ /ˈlɛptɒn/ ▷ *noun* (***leptons***) *physics* **1** any of various subatomic particles, including electrons, muons and tau particles, that only participate in weak interactions with other particles. **2** formerly used to refer to any light particle, eg an electron, as opposed to a heavy one. • **leptonic** *adj*. Opposite of BARYON. ◎ 1940s: from Greek *leptos* small or thin.

lepton² /ˈlɛptɒn/ ▷ *noun* (***lepta*** /-tə/) a modern Greek coin worth 1/100th of a drachma. ◎ 18c: from Greek *leptos* to make slender.

leptosome /ˈlɛptoʊsoʊm/ ▷ *noun* someone with a slender physical build. Compare ATHLETIC 3, ASTHENIC 2, PYKNIC. • **leptosomatic** or **leptosomic** *adj*. ◎ 1930s: from Greek *leptos* + -SOME¹.

les see LEZ

lesbian /ˈlɛzbɪən/ ▷ *noun* a woman who is sexually attracted to other women. ▷ *adj* for, relating to or referring to lesbians. See also LEZ. Compare DYKE. • **lesbianism** *noun*. ◎ 19c: from Lesbos, Aegean island and home in the 7c BC of the Greek poetess Sappho, whose work explores themes of love, jealousy and hate as they relate to women and not, as is widely supposed, homosexual relations between women.

lese-majesty /leɪzˈmadʒəstɪ/ ▷ *noun* an insult to a sovereign; treason. ◎ 15c: from French *lèse-majesté*, from Latin *laesa majestas* injured majesty.

lesion /ˈliːʒən/ ▷ *noun* **1** an injury or wound. **2** *pathol* an abnormal change in the structure of an organ or tissue as a result of disease or injury. ◎ 15c: from Latin *laesio*, from *laedere* to injure.

less (used as the comparative of LITTLE) ▷ *adj* **1** *denoting* a smaller size, quantity, duration, etc □ ***drank less wine than you***. **2** *colloq* fewer in number □ ***smoke less cigarettes***. See note. ▷ *adverb* not so much; to a smaller extent □ ***exercises less nowadays***. ▷ *pronoun* a smaller amount or number □ ***tried to eat less***. ▷ *prep* without; minus □ ***£100 less the discount***. • **less than no time** *jocular* a very short time indeed. • **much less** used to link alternatives so that the extent of one's disapproval, surprise, etc is emphasized: □ ***didn't even cut the grass, much less do the weeding***. • **no less 1** *usually ironic* tagged on, usually after a title, a well-known name, etc in order to hint that the person, thing or action concerned is not really as highly respected as might be supposed: □ ***a compliment from the director, no less***. **2** *usually contemptuous* tagged on, usually at the end of a sentence, in order to devalue what has just been said: □ ***actually worked a full week, no less***. • **nothing less than** as much as; tantamount to □ ***amounts to nothing less than a swindle***. ◎ Anglo-Saxon *læssa*.

-less /ləs/ ▷ *suffix, forming adjectives* **1** free from; lacking; without □ ***painless*** □ ***penniless***. Compare -FREE at FREE. **2** not subject to the action of the specified verb □ ***dauntless***. ◎ Anglo-Saxon *leas* free from.

lessee /lɛˈsiː/ ▷ *noun* (***lessees***) someone granted the use of property by lease.

less, fewer

• **Less** is a grammatically complex word with several part-of-speech functions, as the entry shows. Its use overlaps with **fewer** when it qualifies plural nouns, especially in conversation:

? *They admitted this measure will lead to less prosecutions.*

Strictly, **fewer** is more correct in this case. The reason **less** is used here instead of **fewer** is that the total amount predominates in the mind over the plurality implied by the strict grammar of the noun. This is especially true

• when measurements (including time and distance) and words like **dozen**, **hundred**, etc, are used,

• when **less** is to be identified with a singular or indivisible subject,

• and when the construction is **less than**:

✓ *There were less than twelve hours before the big day.*

✓ *A baby girl less than two years old.*

✓ *Less than twenty of them made it back to England.*

✓ *People who are 65 years of age or less.*

✓ *The murders were committed less than three weeks ago.*

✓ *They were sentenced to imprisonment with hard labour for not less than three years.*

• In all these cases, **fewer** would be unidiomatic or even ungrammatical, and not typical of current English.

☆ RECOMMENDATION: it is legitimate to use **less** instead of **fewer** when the sense requires it; use **fewer** with straightforward plurals.

lessen /'lɛsən/ ▻ *verb* (***lessened, lessening***) *tr & intr* to make or become less.

lesser ▻ *adj* used in names, especially plant, animal and place names: smaller in size, quantity or importance □ *lesser celandine.* See also GREATER at GREAT. • **lesser of two evils** the slightly better option or outcome of two unpleasant possibilities.

lesson /'lɛsən/ ▻ *noun* **1** an amount taught or learned at one time. **2** a period of teaching. **3 (lessons)** instruction in a particular subject given over a period of time. **4** an experience or example which one should take as a warning or encouragement □ *Let that be a lesson to you.* **5** a passage from the Bible read during a church service. ◷ 16c: from French *leçon*, from Latin *lectio* a reading.

lessor ▻ *noun* someone who rents out property by lease.

lest ▻ *conj, formal or literary* **1** in case □ *speak quietly lest they hear us.* **2** that □ *worried lest we are late.* ◷ 13c: from Anglo-Saxon *thy læs the* the less that.

let¹ ▻ *verb* (***let, letting***) **1 a** to allow, permit, or cause to do something □ *let her daughter borrow the car*; **b** used in commands, orders, warnings, etc: □ *let him go*; **c (let's)** *contraction* let us, used in suggestions: shall we □ *Let's go.* **2** *Brit* to give the use of (rooms, a building, or land) in return for payment. **3** *math, philos* to suggest a symbol or a hypothesis be understood as something □ *Let 'D' be the distance travelled.* ▻ *noun, Brit* **1** the leasing of a property, etc □ *got the let of the cottage for £100 a week.* **2** the period of time for which a property, etc is leased □ *a two-week let.* • **lettable** *adj* fit to be leased or capable of being leased. • **let alone** used to link alternatives so that the extent of one's disapproval, surprise, etc is emphasized: □ *didn't even clear the table let alone do the washing up.* • **let fall 1** to drop. **2** to mention or hint. • **let fly at someone** to attack them physically or verbally. • **let go of something** to release or stop holding it. • **let off steam** to show emotion, especially anger, in an unrestrained way. • **let oneself go 1** to act without restraint. **2** to allow one's appearance or lifestyle, etc to deteriorate. • **let someone alone** or **let someone be** to avoid disturbing or worrying them. • **let someone have it** *colloq* to attack them either physically or verbally. • **let someone know** *colloq* to tell them something at a later time □ *let you know tomorrow if I can go.* • **let someone off the hook** to free them from a responsibility, commitment or promise. • **let something drop** to make secret information, etc known, especially unintentionally. • **let something loose** to release it. • **let the cat out of the bag** to let a secret out. • **let well alone** to hold back from interfering in something for fear of making it worse. • **to let** said of property: available for rent. ◷ Anglo-Saxon *lætan* to permit.

■ **let someone** or **something down 1** to disappoint or fail to help them at a crucial time. **2** to lower them or it. **3** to allow the air to escape from something inflated □ *let down the tyres.* **4** to make longer □ *let the hem down.*

■ **let someone** or **something in, out**, *etc* to allow or cause them to pass in, out, etc □ *Will someone let the cat in?*

■ **let someone in for something** *colloq* to involve them in something difficult or unpleasant.

■ **let someone in on something** *colloq* to share a secret, etc with them.

■ **let off** *euphemistic, colloq* to fart.

■ **let someone off 1** to allow them to go without punishment, etc. **2** to release them from work, duties, etc.

■ **let something off 1** to fire (a gun) or explode (a bomb). **2** to release (liquid or gas).

■ **let someone** or **something out** to release them or it.

■ **let something out 1** to enlarge it □ *let out the waist of the jeans.* **2** to emit (a sound) □ *let out a horrible scream.*

■ **let up** to stop or to become less strong or violent □ *The rain let up at last.*

let² ▻ *noun* **1** *sport* especially racket games: an obstruction during service of the ball, shuttlecock etc, eg by the net in tennis and badminton or by an opponent in squash, requiring the ball to be served again. **2** a service affected in this way. • **without let or hindrance** without anything hindering or preventing action or progress. ◷ 19c: Anglo-Saxon *lettan* to hinder.

-let /-lət/ ▻ *suffix, signifying* a small or young example □ *leaflet* □ *piglet.*

let-down ▻ *noun* a disappointment.

lethal /'li:θəl/ ▻ *adj* causing or enough to cause death. • **lethally** *adverb.* ◷ 17c: from Latin *let(h)um* death.

lethargic /lə'θɑ:dʒɪk/ ▻ *adj* lacking in energy or vitality. • **lethargically** *adverb.*

lethargy /'lɛθədʒɪ/ ▻ *noun* **1** lack of energy and vitality. **2** *pathol* a state of abnormal drowsiness and inactivity caused by inadequate rest, anaemia, lack of food, recent illness, etc. ◷ 14c: from Greek *lethargos* drowsy.

let-off ▻ *noun, colloq* an escape or a lucky break.

let-out ▻ *noun* a chance to escape, avoid keeping an agreement, contract, etc.

LETS /lɛts/ ▻ *abbreviation* Local Exchange Trading System, a system of sharing skills and resources with a local nominal currency counted in units, named after a local feature such as bobbins in Manchester and reekies in Edinburgh. It can be used to purchase services of any type, ranging from baby-sitting and dog-walking to catering, computer training, business services, bricklaying, etc. ◷ 1980s: pioneered by Scottish-born

Canadian Michael Linton as a way to stimulate local economies and counter unemployment.

letter /'lɛtə(r)/ ▷ *noun* **1** a conventional written or printed mark, usually part of an alphabet, used to represent a speech sound or sounds. **2** a written or printed message normally sent by post in an envelope. **3** (**the letter**) the strict literal meaning of words, especially in legal documents, or how such words can be interpreted □ *according to the letter of the law*. **4** printing type. ▷ *verb* (***lettered***, ***lettering***) to write or mark letters on something. • **to the letter** exactly; in every detail □ *followed the instructions to the letter*. ◎ 13c: from Latin *littera* letter of the alphabet.

letter bomb ▷ *noun* an envelope containing a device that is designed to explode when someone opens it.

letter box ▷ *noun, Brit* **1** a slot in a door, sometimes with a box behind it, through which letters are delivered to homes and buildings. **2** a large box with a slot in the front, for people to post letters. Also **post box** and **pillar box**. **3** (**letter-box**) *as adj, cinematog* referring to a print of a film where the ASPECT RATIO of a WIDESCREEN image has been masked to accommodate it for TV or release on video. • **letter-boxing** *noun* the screening of films of this kind.

lettered ▷ *adj* **1** well educated; literary. **2** marked with letters.

letterhead ▷ *noun* **1** a printed heading on notepaper, giving a company's or an individual's name, address, etc. **2** a piece of notepaper with this kind of heading.

lettering ▷ *noun* **1** the act of forming letters; the way in which they are formed. **2** letters which have been written, painted or inscribed.

letter of credit ▷ *noun* (***letters of credit***) a letter authorizing a bank, etc to issue credit or money up to a set amount, to the person bearing it.

letterpress ▷ *noun* **1 a** a technique of printing where ink is applied to raised surfaces and then pressed onto paper; **b** anything printed using this technique. **2** in a book with pictures, diagrams, photographs, etc: the printed words as opposed to the illustrations.

letters ▷ *plural noun* **1** literature. **2** learning. • **letters after his** or **her name** *Brit colloq* **1** a qualification at degree level. **2** an official title of some kind. • **a man** or **woman of letters** someone with a wide knowledge of literature or, occasionally, an author.

letters of credence and **letters credential** ▷ *plural noun* the formal document a diplomat uses to establish their status with foreign governments.

letters-of-marque and **letter-of-marque** ▷ *noun* a licence granted to a privateer by a state or nation to seize merchandise from ships or vessels from other nations. Sometimes shortened to **marque**.

letters patent ▷ *plural noun* an official document giving a patent to an inventor, etc.

Lettish see under LATVIAN

lettuce /'lɛtɪs/ ▷ *noun* a green plant with large edible leaves used in salads. ◎ 13c: from Latin *lactuca*, from *lac* milk, because of its milky juice.

let-up ▷ *noun* end; respite; relief □ *no let-up in the bombardment*.

leu /'leɪuː/ ▷ *noun* (***lei*** /leɪ/) the standard Romanian unit of currency, equal to 100 bani. ◎ 19c: Romanian, meaning 'lion'.

leucine /'luːsiːn/ or **leucin** /-sɪn/ ▷ *noun, biochem* an essential amino acid, found in proteins. ◎ 19c: Greek *leukos* white + -INE².

leuco- or **leuko-** /luːkoʊ, lʊ'kɪ/, or (before a vowel) **leuc-** or **leuk-** ▷ *combining form, signifying* white or colourless. ◎ From Greek *leukos* white.

leucoblast or **leukoblast** /'luːkoʊblɑːst/ ▷ *noun* an immature white blood cell. ◎ 19c.

leucocyte or **leukocyte** /'luːkəsaɪt/ ▷ *noun, anatomy* a white blood cell or CORPUSCLE. ◎ 19c.

leucoma or (*US*) **leukoma** /lʊ'koʊmə/ ▷ *noun* (***leucomas***) *pathol* an opaque white spot on the cornea of the eye, usually caused by scarring. ◎ 18c: LEUCO- + -OMA.

leucorrhoea /luːkə'rɪə/ ▷ *noun* (*also* (*informal*) **the whites**) *medicine* a white or yellowish discharge from the vagina, which often occurs normally, but if excessive may be a symptom of infection. ◎ 18c: LEUCO- + *rhein* to flow.

leucotomy or **leukotomy** /lʊ'kɒtəmɪ/ ▷ *noun* (*often* **frontal** or **pre-frontal leucotomy**) *surgery* a LOBOTOMY (sense 2). ◎ 1930s.

leukaemia or (*especially US*) **leukemia** /lʊ'kiːmɪə/ ▷ *noun* any of various malignant diseases which affect the bone marrow and other blood-forming organs, resulting in the overproduction of abnormal white blood cells, and extreme susceptibility to infection. ◎ 19c.

lev /lɛf/ ▷ *noun* (***leva*** /'lɛvə/) the standard unit of Bulgarian currency, equal to 100 stotinki. ◎ 20c: Bulgarian, meaning 'lion'.

Levant /lə'vant/ ▷ *noun* **1** (**the Levant**) *formerly* the islands and countries of the eastern Mediterranean. **2** (**levant**) a strong easterly wind. Also called **levanter**. **3** (**levant**) a kind of morocco leather. ◎ 15c: from French *levaunt* the place where the sun rises.

Levantine /'lɛvəntaɪn/ ▷ *adj* **1** relating or referring to the Levant. **2** said of ships: trading to the Levant.

levator /lə'veɪtə(r)/ ▷ *noun, anatomy* any muscle contraction which raises a part of the body. Opposite of DEPRESSOR. ◎ 17c: from Latin *levare* to raise.

levee¹ /'lɛvɪ/ ▷ *noun* (***levees***) **1** *US* especially on the Lower Mississippi: the natural embankment of silt and sand that is deposited along the banks of a river or stream during flooding. **2** an artificial embankment constructed along a watercourse. **3** a quay. ◎ 18c: from French *levée* raised.

levee² /'lɛvɪ, 'lɛveɪ/ ▷ *noun* **1** *historical* the first official meeting of a sovereign or other high-ranking person after they have got up from bed. **2** *old use* an official reception of guests or visitors in the morning or relatively early in the day. ◎ 17c: from French *levée*, from *lever* to raise.

level /'lɛvəl/ ▷ *noun* **1** a horizontal plane or line. **2** a specified height, value or extent □ *village lay just above sea level* □ *put prices up to a ridiculous level*. **3** position, status, or importance in a scale of values □ *offer help on a practical level*. **4** a stage or degree of progress □ *took exams at an advanced level*. **5** any device for checking whether a surface is horizontal or not □ *spirit level*. **6** (**the level**) a flat area of land. **7** a storey of a building. ▷ *adj* (***leveller***, ***levellest***) **1** having a flat smooth even surface. **2** horizontal. **3** (**level with something**) the same height as it. **4** having the same standard (as something else); equal □ *came out level in the test*. **5** steady; constant; regular □ *keep one's body temperature level*. **6** *cookery* said of measurements (usually of spoons in Britain and cups in N America): filled so as to be even with the rim □ *3 level tablespoons*. Compare ROUNDED. ▷ *verb* (***levelled***, ***levelling***) **1** to make flat, smooth or horizontal. **2** to make equal. **3** to pull down or demolish □ *A mortar bomb completely levelled the church*. • **levelly** *adverb*. • **levelness** *noun*. • **do one's level best** *colloq* to make the greatest possible effort. • **find one's level** to find one's proper place, rank, etc among others, or a comfortable rate of work, etc. • **on the level** *slang* fair; honest; genuine. ◎ 14c: from Latin *libella* little scale.

■ **level off** or **level something off** to make or become flat, even, steady, regular, etc.

■ **level out** or **level something out** to make or become level □ *The fluctuations in interest rates eventually levelled out*.

■ **level something at someone** to point (a gun, etc) at them.

■ **level something at** or **against someone** to direct (an accusation, criticism, etc).

■ **level with someone** *colloq* to speak honestly to them.

level crossing ▷ *noun, Brit, Austral & NZ* a place where a road and a railway line cross at the same level and where there are usually gates or other barriers which close when a train is due and so prevent traffic from crossing.

level-headed ▷ *adj* **1** often said of someone during a crisis: sensible; well-balanced. **2** said of someone in business: shrewd.

leveller ▷ *noun* someone or something that flattens or makes equal □ *Death is the one great leveller.*

level pegging ▷ *noun* equality of scores or accomplishments among rivals.

level playing field and **flat playing field** ▷ *noun* equal terms on which to compete.

lever /ˈliːvə(r); *N Amer* ˈlɛvər/ ▷ *noun* **1** a simple device for lifting and moving heavy loads, consisting of a rigid bar supported by and pivoting about a FULCRUM at some point along its length, so that an effort applied at one point can be used to move an object (the load) at another point. **2** a strong bar for moving heavy objects, prising things open, etc. **3** a handle for operating a machine. **4** anything that can be used to gain an advantage. ▷ *verb* (***levered, levering***) to move or open using a lever. ◷ 13c: from Latin *levare* to raise.

leverage /ˈliːvərɪdʒ; *N Amer* ˈlɛ-/ ▷ *noun* **1** the mechanical power or advantage gained through using a lever. **2** the action of a lever. **3** power or advantage.

leveret /ˈlɛvərət/ ▷ *noun* a young hare, especially one less than a year old. ◷ 16c: from Latin *lepus* hare.

leviathan or **Leviathan** /ləˈvaɪəθən/ ▷ *noun* **1** *Bible* a sea-monster. **2** the personification of a conquering or enslaving power □ *Egypt was the Hebrews' leviathan.* **3** anything which is large or powerful. ◷ 14c: from Hebrew *liwyathan.*

levigate /ˈlɛvɪgeɪt/ ▷ *verb* (***levigated, levigating***) **1** to smooth. **2** to crush something into a powder or paste. ◷ 17c: from Latin *levigare, levigatum,* from *levis* smooth.

Levis /ˈliːvaɪz/ ▷ *plural noun, trademark* jeans with points of particular strain strengthened by copper rivets. ◷ 1920s: named after Levi Strauss who first manufactured them in the US in the 1860s as working trousers..

levitate /ˈlɛvɪteɪt/ ▷ *verb* (***levitated, levitating***) *tr & intr* to float or cause to float in the air, especially by invoking some supernatural power or through spiritualism. ● **levitation** *noun.* ◷ 17c: from Latin *levis* light, modelled on GRAVITATE.

levity /ˈlɛvɪtɪ/ ▷ *noun* **1** a lack of seriousness; silliness. **2** fickleness. **3** *old use* lightness. ◷ 16c: from French *levité,* from Latin *levis* light.

levy /ˈlɛvɪ/ ▷ *verb* (***levies, levied, levying***) **1** to calculate and then collect (a tax, etc). **2** to raise (an army or the money needed to fund a war). ▷ *noun* (***levies***) **1** the collection of a tax, etc. **2** the amount of money raised by collecting a tax, etc. **3** the act of raising an army or the money needed to fund a war. **4** soldiers or money collected in preparation for a war. ◷ 14c: from Latin *levare* to raise.

lewd /luːd, ljuːd/ ▷ *adj* (***lewder, lewdest***) **1** feeling, expressing or designed to stimulate crude sexual desire or lust. **2** obscene; indecent. ● **lewdly** *adverb.* ● **lewdness** *noun.* ◷ 14c: Anglo-Saxon *læwede* unlearned.

lewis /ˈluːɪs/ ▷ *noun* (***lewises***) a dovetail iron TENON for lifting large stone blocks, etc. ◷ 18c.

Lewis gun ▷ *noun* a light machine-gun used in World Wars I and II. ◷ Early 20c: named after Col. Isaac Newton Lewis (1858–1932) who perfected the original design by his fellow American, Samuel McLean.

lewisia /luːˈɪsɪə/ ▷ *noun* (***lewisias***) a perennial herb that has a rosette of leaves at ground level and pink or white flowers. ◷ 19c: named after the American explorer, Meriwether Lewis (1774–1809).

lewisite /ˈluːɪsaɪt/ ▷ *noun* **1** a dark brown mineral. **2** an oily liquid that forms a toxic gas, used in chemical warfare in World War I. ◷ Early 20c: named after the US chemist, Winford Lee Lewis (1858–1931).

lexeme /ˈlɛksiːm/ and **lexical item** ▷ *noun, linguistics* a unit of language consisting of one or more written words, or occasionally just a part of a written word, that maintains a constant semantic element in its various forms. For example, the words *buys, buying* and *bought* are variant forms of the lexeme *buy,* and *am* and *'m* (as in *I'm*) are forms of the lexeme *am.* Compare MORPHEME. ◷ 1940s: from LEX(ICON), modelled on PHONEME.

lexical /ˈlɛksɪkəl/ ▷ *adj* **1** *linguistics* referring or relating to the meanings of words in a language as opposed to their grammatical functions. **2** referring or relating to a lexicon. ● **lexically** *adverb.* ◷ 19c: from Greek *lexis* word.

lexical verb see AUXILIARY VERB

lexicographer /lɛksɪˈkɒgrəfə(r)/ ▷ *noun* a writer, compiler or editor of dictionaries.

lexicography /lɛksɪˈkɒgrəfɪ/ ▷ *noun* the writing, compiling and editing of dictionaries. ● **lexicographic** /-kəˈgrafɪk/ or **lexicographical** *adj.* ● **lexicographist** /-ˈkɒgrəfɪst/ *noun.* ◷ 17c: from Greek *lexis* word + -GRAPHY 2.

lexicology /lɛksɪˈkɒlədʒɪ/ ▷ *noun* **1** the study of the history and meaning of words. **2** the analytical study of lexicography.

lexicon /ˈlɛksɪkən/ ▷ *noun* **1** a dictionary, especially one for Arabic, Greek, Hebrew or Syriac. **2** the vocabulary of terms as used in a particular branch of knowledge □ *The word 'nigger' is now regarded as a positive one in the black lexicon.* **3** the vocabulary of a language or used by an individual person. ◷ 17c: Greek, from *lexis* word.

lexigram /ˈlɛksɪgram/ ▷ *noun* a sign which represents a whole word. ◷ Late 20c: from Greek *lexis* word.

lexigraphy /lɛkˈsɪgrəfɪ/ ▷ *noun* a system of writing, such as Chinese, where each word is represented by a single sign. ● **lexigraphic** /-sɪˈgrafɪk/ or **lexigraphical** *adj.* ◷ 19c: from Greek *lexis* word + -GRAPHY 1.

lexis /ˈlɛksɪs/ ▷ *noun* **1** the way a piece of writing is expressed in words. **2** diction. **3** the total stock of words in a language. **4** *linguistics* the meanings of components of language as opposed to their grammatical functions. ◷ 1960s: Greek, meaning 'word'.

ley /leɪ/ and **ley line** ▷ *noun* (***leys***) a straight line, thought to be the route of a prehistoric road, that joins prominent features of the landscape, most commonly hilltops, and that is supposed to have had some kind of scientific or magical significance in the past. ◷ 1920s: variant of LEA[1].

Leyden jar /ˈleɪdən —/ ▷ *noun, physics* a glass jar coated inside and out with layers of metal foil and used as an early form of electricity condenser. ◷ 18c: named after Leyden (now Leiden), a city in the Netherlands, where it was invented.

lez, les or **lezz** /lɛz/ and **lezzy** or **lezzie** /ˈlɛzɪ/ and **lesbo** /ˈlɛzboʊ/ ▷ *noun* (*plural* ***lezzes, lezzies*** or ***lesbos***) *derog slang* short forms of LESBIAN. ◷ 1920s (although *lesbo* did not become current until 1940s): previously used by heterosexuals as derisive insults to gay women, though it seems that gay women are now using the words to describe themselves in positive terms.

LF ▷ *abbreviation, radio* low frequency.

LGU ▻ *abbreviation* Ladies' Golf Union.

LH ▻ *abbreviation* luteinizing hormone.

lh ▻ *abbreviation* left-hand.

lhasa apso /ˈlɑːsə ˈapsoʊ/ ▻ *noun* (***lhasa apsos***) a breed of small terrier originally from Tibet. ◷ Early 20c: named after Lhasa, the capital of Tibet.

LHD ▻ *abbreviation*: *Litterarum Humaniorum Doctor*, (Latin), Doctor of the Humaner Letters or Doctor of Humanities.

lhd ▻ *abbreviation* left-hand drive.

Li ▻ *symbol, chem* lithium.

liability /laɪəˈbɪlɪtɪ/ ▻ *noun* (***liabilities***) **1** the state of being legally liable or responsible for something. **2** a debt or obligation. **3** someone or something one is responsible for. **4** someone or something that is a problem or that causes a problem. **5** a likelihood. **6** a tendency. ◷ 18c.

liable /ˈlaɪəbəl/ ▻ *adj* **1** legally bound or responsible. **2** given or inclined (to) ◻ ***She is very liable to outbursts of temper.*** **3** likely. **4** susceptible. ◷ 16c: perhaps from French *lier* to bind.

liaise /lɪˈeɪz/ ▻ *verb* (***liaised, liaising***) *tr & intr* (*usually* **liaise with someone**) to communicate with or be in contact with them, often in order to discuss something of mutual benefit. ◷ 1920s: back-formation from LIAISON.

liaison /lɪˈeɪzən/ ▻ *noun* **1** communication or co-operation between individuals or groups. **2** a sexual or romantic relationship which is kept secret, especially when it is illicit or adulterous. ◷ 17c: French, from Latin *ligare* to bind.

liaison officer ▻ *noun* someone who communicates with or is in contact with some other person or group to exchange information or to organize something.

liana /lɪˈɑːnə/ or **liane** /lɪˈɑːn/ ▻ *noun* (***lianas***) any of various woody climbing plants found mainly in tropical rain forests. ◷ 18c: from French *liane*.

liar /ˈlaɪə(r)/ ▻ *noun* someone who tells lies, especially habitually. ◷ Anglo-Saxon.

Lias /ˈlaɪəs/ ▻ *noun, geol* the series of rocks formed during the Lower Jurassic period. • **Liassic** *adj*. ◷ 19c: French *lias*.

lib ▻ *noun, colloq* used especially in the names of movements: short form of LIBERATION ◻ ***gay lib*** ◻ ***women's lib.***

Lib. ▻ *abbreviation* Liberal.

lib. ▻ *abbreviation* **1** *liber* (Latin), book. **2** librarian. **3** library.

libation /laɪˈbeɪʃən, lɪ-/ ▻ *noun* **1** the pouring out of wine, etc in honour of a god. **2** this drink once it has been poured. **3** *facetious* **a** an alcoholic drink; **b** the act of drinking, especially alcohol. ◷ 14c: from Latin *libare*, *libatum* to pour.

libber /ˈlɪbə(r)/ ▻ *noun, colloq* short form of LIBERATIONIST ◻ ***women's libber.***

libel /ˈlaɪbəl/ ▻ *noun* **1** *Brit, law* **a** the publication of a statement in some permanent form (including broadcasting) which has the potential to damage someone's reputation and which is claimed to be false; **b** the act of publishing this kind of statement. **2 a** any false or potentially damaging description of someone; **b** a depiction, such as a portrait or sculpture, that is unflattering. ▻ *verb* (***libelled, libelling*** or *US* ***libeled, libeling***) **1** *law* to publish a libellous statement about someone. **2** to accuse wrongly and spitefully. Compare SLANDER. ◷ 14c: from Latin *libellus* little book.

libel, slander

There is often confusion between **libel** and **slander**: in English and American law, **libel** refers to an untrue defamatory statement made in some permanent form, usually in writing, whereas **slander** refers to something spoken. In Scots law, however, both are **slander**.

libellant or (*US*) **libelant** /ˈlaɪbələnt/ ▻ *noun* a LIBELLER.

libellee ▻ *noun* (***libellees***) someone who has something libellous written, broadcast or published against them.

libeller or (*US*) **libeler** ▻ *noun* someone who writes, broadcasts or publishes something libellous.

libellous or (*US*) **libelous** /ˈlaɪbələs/ *law* ▻ *adj* containing or forming a libel; damaging to someone's reputation. • **libellously** or (*US*) **libelously** *adverb*.

liberal /ˈlɪbərəl/ ▻ *adj* **1** given or giving generously, freely or abundantly. **2** tolerant of different opinions; open-minded. **3** lavish; extensive ◻ ***poured liberal glasses of wine.*** **4** in favour of social and political reform, progressive. **5** (**Liberal**) belonging to the LIBERAL PARTY. **6** said of education: aiming to develop general cultural interests and to broaden the mind, as opposed to being technically or professionally orientated ◻ ***a liberal arts student.*** **7** free from restraint; not rigorous ◻ ***a liberal interpretation.*** ▻ *noun* **1** someone who has liberal views, either politically or in general. **2** (**Liberal**) a member or supporter of the LIBERAL PARTY. • **liberally** *adverb* freely; generously. ◷ 14c: from Latin *liberalis*, from *liber* free.

liberal democracy ▻ *noun, politics* a state or political system which combines the right to individual freedom with the right to representative government.

Liberal Democrat and **Lib-Dem** ▻ *noun, Brit politics* a member or supporter of a political party (the **Liberal Democrats**), slightly to the left of centre, which evolved from the LIBERAL PARTY. ◷ 1989.

liberalism ▻ *noun* liberal views on moral, religious, social or political issues. • **liberalist** *noun*. • **liberalistic** *adj*.

liberality /lɪbəˈralɪtɪ/ ▻ *noun* **1** the quality of being generous. **2** the quality of being open-minded and free from prejudice.

liberalize or **liberalise** /ˈlɪbərəlaɪz/ ▻ *verb* (***liberalized, liberalizing***) *tr & intr* to make or become more liberal or less strict. • **liberalization** *noun*. • **liberalized** *adj*. • **liberalizer** *noun*. • **liberalizing** *adj*. ◷ 18c.

Liberal Party ▻ *noun* **1** *Brit* a political party (derived from the declining WHIGS), which from the 1860s until the early 1920s was the main party in opposition to the TORY Party. Since then it has diminished considerably in importance while undergoing a number of changes to its constitution, most notably the absorption, in 1988, of the remnants of the SOCIAL DEMOCRATIC PARTY. In 1989, after two previous name changes, it became the LIBERAL DEMOCRATS. **2** *Austral* (*in full* **The Liberal Party of Australia**) the more conservative of the two major parties, the other being The **Australian Labor Party** or **ALP**. See also under LABOUR PARTY. **3** *more generally* any political party advocating democratic reform and individual liberalism. ◷ 19c for the British sense, but 1940s for the Australian one.

liberate /ˈlɪbəreɪt/ ▻ *verb* (***liberated, liberating***) *tr & intr* **1** to set free. **2** to free (a country) from enemy occupation. **3** to free from accepted moral or social conventions or from traditional gender-based roles. **4** *chem* to give off (a gas). ◷ 17c: from Latin *liberare* to free.

liberated ▻ *adj* **1** not bound by traditional ideas about sexuality, morality, the roles conventionally assigned to men and women, etc. **2** freed from enemy occupation.

liberation /lɪbəˈreɪʃən/ ▻ *noun* the act or process of liberating.

liberationist ▻ *noun* someone who supports the cause of social freedom and equality for sections of society perceived to be underprivileged or discriminated against. • **liberationism** *noun*.

liberation theology ▻ *noun* a development of Christian doctrine that began in the 1960s in Latin America, which emphasizes a commitment to liberation from social, political and economic oppression, based on the belief in Christ's own mission to help the underprivileged and disadvantaged.

liberator ▷ *noun* someone who liberates, especially from oppression.

Liberian /laɪˈbɪərɪən/ ▷ *adj* belonging or relating to Liberia, a republic in W Africa, its inhabitants or its commonly used FLAG OF CONVENIENCE. ▷ *noun* **1** a citizen or inhabitant of, or person born in, Liberia. **2** a Liberian-registered ship.

libero /ˈliːbəroʊ/ ▷ *noun* (***liberos***) *football* a SWEEPER (sense 3). ⓘ 1990s: Italian, literally 'free'.

libertarian /lɪbəˈtɛərɪən/ ▷ *noun* **1** someone who advocates that people should be free to express themselves, their ideas, etc as they like. **2** someone who believes in the doctrine of FREE WILL and the power of self-determination. • **libertarianism** *noun*. ⓘ 18c.

libertine /ˈlɪbətiːn/ ▷ *noun, old use* someone, especially a man, who is not bound by the generally accepted codes of morality. ▷ *adj* unrestrained; dissolute; promiscuous □ *his libertine ways*. • **libertinism**. ⓘ 14c: from Latin *libertus* made free.

liberty /ˈlɪbətɪ/ ▷ *noun* (***liberties***) **1** freedom from captivity, slavery, restrictions, etc. **2** freedom to act and think as one pleases. **3** (*usually* **liberties**) a natural right or privilege. See CIVIL LIBERTY. **4** an action or utterance thought of as over-familiar or presumptuous. • **at liberty 1** free from prison or control; **2** allowed or permitted (to) □ *at liberty to use the company car*. • **take liberties 1** to treat someone with too much familiarity; to be too presumptuous or impertinent. **2** to act in an unauthorized way; to be deliberately inaccurate. • **take the liberty to** or **of** to do or venture to do something, usually without permission. ⓘ 14c: from Latin *liber* free.

liberty hall ▷ *noun, colloq* (*sometimes* **Liberty Hall**) a place where one may do as one pleases.

libidinal /lɪˈbɪdɪnəl/ ▷ *adj* referring to or related to libido.

libidinous /lɪˈbɪdɪnəs/ ▷ *adj* lustful; lewd. • **libidinously** *adverb*. • **libidinousness** *noun*. ⓘ 15c: from Latin *libido, libidinis* desire + -OUS.

libido /lɪˈbiːdoʊ/ ▷ *noun* (***libidos***) **1** sexual urge or desire. **2** *psychoanal* in FREUDIAN terms: psychic energy or impulse, especially that associated with forms of creativity and derived from the ID. See CATHEXIS. ⓘ Early 20c: Latin, meaning 'desire'.

Libra /ˈliːbrə/ ▷ *noun* (*plural* ***Libras*** in sense 2b) **1** *astron* a constellation of the zodiac. **2** *astrol* **a** the seventh sign of the zodiac. **b** a person born between 23 September and 22 October, under this sign. • **Libran** *adj, noun*. See table at ZODIAC. ⓘ From Latin *libra* pound weight.

librarian /laɪˈbrɛərɪən/ ▷ *noun* someone who works in a library or is in charge of a library.

librarianship ▷ *noun* the work of a librarian.

library /ˈlaɪbrərɪ, ˈlaɪbrɪ/ ▷ *noun* (***libraries***) **1** a room, rooms or building where books, films, records, videos, etc are kept for study, reference, reading or for lending. **2** a collection of books, films, records, videos, etc for public or private use. **3** a group of books published as a series. **4** *computing* a collection of computer programs that can be accessed when required. **5** *computing* a collection of related computer files. **6** a collection of items kept for reference □ *a library of DNA material*. See also LENDING LIBRARY, PUBLIC LIBRARY, REFERENCE LIBRARY. ⓘ 14c: from Latin *librarium* bookcase.

library book ▷ *noun* a book that may be borrowed from a library and which must be returned within a certain period of time.

library edition ▷ *noun* a book that has been specially produced with a strong binding for use in libraries.

library pictures ▷ *noun* a title that appears under film footage on TV to indicate that the images are not live.

librettist /lɪˈbrɛtɪst/ ▷ *noun* someone who writes opera libretti.

libretto /lɪˈbrɛtoʊ/ ▷ *noun* (***libretti*** /-tiː/ or ***librettos***) the words or text of an opera, oratorio or musical. ⓘ 18c: Italian, meaning 'little book'.

Libyan /ˈlɪbɪən/ ▷ *adj* belonging or relating to Libya, a republic in N Africa, or its inhabitants. ▷ *noun* a citizen or inhabitant of, or person born in, Libya.

lice *plural of* LOUSE

licence or (*US*) **license** /ˈlaɪsəns/ ▷ *noun* **1 a** an official document that allows someone to drive; **b** an official document that allows someone to own a dog, gun, etc; **c** *Brit* an official document showing that a household has paid a fee and may therefore watch TV and listen to the radio; **d** official permission to sell alcohol; **e** official permission for two people to marry. **2** permission or leave in general. **3** excessive freedom of action or speech. **4** a departure from a rule or convention, especially by writers and artists, for effect □ *poetic licence*. • **on licence** said of a prisoner: released before serving all of a sentence. ⓘ 14c: from Latin *licentia*, from *licere* to be allowed.

license /ˈlaɪsəns/ ▷ *verb* (***licensed, licensing***) **1** to give a licence or permit for something such as the sale of alcohol. **2** to give a licence or permit to someone to do something such as drive, own a dog, get married, etc. ⓘ 14c.

licensed ▷ *adj* said of a shop, hotel, etc: legally allowed to sell alcohol.

licensee /laɪsənˈsiː/ ▷ *noun* (***licensees***) someone who has been given a licence, especially to sell alcohol.

licentiate /laɪˈsɛnʃɪət/ ▷ *noun* **1** someone who holds a certificate of competence to practise a profession. **2** someone licensed to preach in the Presbyterian church. **3** in certain European universities: someone who has graduated but who has not yet obtained their doctorate. ⓘ 15c: from Latin *licentia* licence.

licentious /laɪˈsɛnʃəs/ ▷ *adj* immoral or promiscuous. • **licentiously** *adverb*. • **licentiousness** *noun*. ⓘ 16c: from Latin *licentia* licence.

lichee see LYCHEE

lichen /ˈlaɪkən, ˈlɪtʃən/ ▷ *noun* any of numerous primitive plants formed by the symbiotic association between a FUNGUS and a green or blue-green alga (see ALGAE), usually found on rocks, walls or tree trunks. ⓘ 17c: from Greek *leichen*.

lichgate or **lychgate** ▷ *noun* a roofed gateway to a churchyard, originally used to shelter a coffin until a member of the clergy arrived to conduct the funeral. ⓘ 15c: Anglo-Saxon *lic* corpse + GATE.

licit /ˈlɪsɪt/ ▷ *adj* lawful; permitted. • **licitly** *adverb*. ⓘ 15c: from Latin *licitus*, from *licere* to be lawful.

lick ▷ *verb* (***licked, licking***) **1** to pass the tongue over in order to moisten, taste or clean. **2** often said of flames: to flicker over or around. **3** *colloq* to defeat. **4** *colloq* to beat or hit repeatedly. ▷ *noun* **1** an act of licking with the tongue. **2** *colloq* a small amount. **3** *colloq* a quick speed □ *drove away at some lick*. **4** *colloq* a sharp blow. • **a lick and a promise** *colloq* a short and not very thorough wash. • **lick into shape** *colloq* to make more efficient or satisfactory. • **lick one's lips** or **chops** *colloq* to look forward to something with relish. • **lick one's wounds** to recover after having been thoroughly defeated or humiliated. • **lick the dust** to die. ⓘ Anglo-Saxon *liccian*.

licking ▷ *noun, colloq* a thrashing, both physical and figurative. • **get** or **take a licking** to be thrashed □ *got a licking from his mum for being late* □ *took a licking in the chess championship*. • **give someone a licking** to thrash them.

licorice see LIQUORICE

lictor /ˈlɪktɔː(r), ˈlɪktə(r)/ ▷ *noun, Roman hist* an officer who attended a magistrate, usually carrying the FASCES, and who had various duties such as clearing a way for the magistrate through a crowd and seeing that sentences on offenders were carried out.

lid ▷ *noun* **1** a removable or hinged cover for a pot, box, etc. **2** an eyelid. • **lidded** *adj* having a lid. • **lidless** *adj*. • **blow, take** or **lift the lid off something** *colloq* to expose or reveal something that is scandalous, shocking, etc. • **flip one's lid** see under FLIP. • **put the lid on it 1** to put an end to something. **2** to be the last in a series of injustices or misfortunes □ *and the flat tyre just put the lid on it.* ◷ Anglo-Saxon *hlid* covering.

lido /ˈliːdoʊ/ ▷ *noun* (***lidos***) **1** a fashionable beach. **2** a public open-air swimming pool. ◷ 1930s: named after Lido, an island in the Venice lagoon which has a fashionable beach, from Latin *litus* a shore.

lie[1] ▷ *noun* **1** a false statement made with the intention of deceiving. **2** anything misleading; a fraud □ *live a lie.* ▷ *verb* (***lied, lying***) *intr* **1** to say things that are not true with the intention of deceiving. **2** to give a wrong or false impression □ *The camera never lies.* • **give the lie to someone** or **something 1** *originally* to accuse them of lying. **2** *now* to show (a statement, etc) to be false. • **lie through one's teeth** to tell blatant lies. See LIAR, WHITE LIE. ◷ Anglo-Saxon *lyge*.

lie[2] ▷ *verb* (*past tense* ***lay***, *past participle* ***lain***, *present participle* ***lying***) *intr* **1** to be in or take on a flat or more or less horizontal position on a supporting surface. **2** to be situated □ *The village lies to the west of here.* **3** to stretch or be spread out to view □ *The harbour lay before us.* **4** said of subjects for discussion: to remain undiscussed □ *let matters lie.* **5 a** to be or remain in a particular state □ *lie dormant*; **b** to be buried □ *Jim's remains lie in a cemetery in Paris.* ▷ *noun* **1 a** the way or direction in which something is lying; **b** *golf* the relative position of a ball that has been struck □ *Despite finding the rough, he had a good lie.* **2** an animal's or bird's hiding-place. • **lie in wait** or **lie in wait for someone** to hide before ambushing them. • **lie low** to stay quiet or hidden. • **take something lying down** *often with negatives* to accept a rebuke or disappointment, etc meekly and without protest. ◷ Anglo-Saxon *licgan*.

■ **lie back 1** to lean back on a support. **2** to rest, especially after a period of hard work.

■ **lie down** to take a flat or horizontal position, especially to sleep or have a short rest.

■ **lie in 1** to stay in bed later than usual in the morning **2** *old use* to be in bed giving birth to a child.

■ **lie in something** to consist of it or have it as an essential part □ *Success lies in hard work.*

■ **lie to** *naut* said of a ship: to be almost at a complete standstill.

■ **lie up** said of a ship: to go into or be in dock.

■ **lie with someone 1** said of a duty or responsibility: to rest with them. **2** *old use* to have sexual intercourse with them.

lie

See Usage Note at **lay**.

Liebfraumilch /ˈliːbfraʊmɪlk/ ▷ *noun* a white wine from the Rhine region of Germany. ◷ 19c: German, meaning 'milk of Our Lady'.

lied /liːd; *German* liːt/ ▷ *noun* (***lieder*** /ˈliːdə(r)/; *German* /lidɛə/) a German song for solo voice and piano accompaniment as developed by Schubert and his successors during the ROMANTIC period. ◷ 19c: German *Lied* song, plural *Lieder*.

lie detector ▷ *noun* **1** a machine that is connected to someone's body during interrogation in order to measure changes in blood pressure, perspiration and pulse, for interpretation as an indication as to whether or not the subject is lying. *Technical equivalent* **polygraph**. **2** any form of test, such as Carl Jung's word association test, that is thought to show whether or not someone is lying.

lie-down ▷ *noun* a short rest taken lying down.

liege /liːdʒ/ *feudalism* ▷ *adj* **1** entitled to receive feudal service or homage from a VASSAL. **2** bound to give feudal service or homage to a SUPERIOR (*noun* 3). ▷ *noun* **1** (*also* **liege lord**) a feudal superior, lord or sovereign. **2** (*also* **liege man**) a feudal subject or vassal. ◷ 13c: French.

lie-in ▷ *noun* a long stay in bed in the morning.

lien /lɪən, liːn/ ▷ *noun, law* a right to keep someone's property until a debt has been paid. ◷ 16c: French, from Latin *ligare* to bind.

lie of the land ▷ *noun* the current state of affairs.

lieu /ljuː, luː/ ▷ *noun* • **in lieu** instead □ *got time off in lieu of overtime pay.* ◷ 13c: French, meaning 'place'.

Lieut or **Lieut.** ▷ *abbreviation* Lieutenant.

lieutenancy ▷ *noun* (***lieutenancies***) the rank of lieutenant.

lieutenant /lɛfˈtɛnənt, lə-; *US* luː-/ ▷ *noun* **1** a deputy acting for a superior. **2** an officer in the British army and navy. See table at RANKS. **3** *US* a police officer or fireman with the rank immediately below captain. ◷ 14c: French, from *lieu* place + *tenant* holding.

lieutenant colonel ▷ *noun* an officer in the army. See table at RANK.

lieutenant commander ▷ *noun* an officer with the rank immediately below commander. See table at RANK.

lieutenant general ▷ *noun* an officer in the army. See table at RANK.

life /laɪf/ ▷ *noun* (***lives***) **1 a** the quality or state which distinguishes living animals and plants from dead ones; **b** collectively, the characteristics which distinguish living animals, plants, etc from inanimate objects, especially the ability to grow, develop and reproduce. **2 a** the period between one's birth and death (compare LIFETIME); **b** the period between one's birth and the present time □ *has led a very sheltered life*; **c** the period between the present time and one's death □ *had his life carefully mapped out.* **3** the length of time a thing exists or is able to function □ *a long shelf life.* Also *in compounds* □ *long-life milk.* **4** living things in general or as a group □ *marine life.* **5** a living thing, especially a human □ *many lives lost in war.* **6** a way or manner of living □ *leads a very busy life.* **7** *in compounds* a specified aspect of one's life □ *love-life.* **8** liveliness; energy; high spirits □ *full of life.* **9** a source of liveliness, energy or high spirits □ *the life and soul of the party.* **10** a written account of someone's life. **11** *colloq* a LIFE SENTENCE □ *got life for murdering a taxi-driver.* **12** any of a number of chances a player has of remaining in a game □ *got to level six without losing a life.* **13** *as adj* for the duration of one's life □ *a life member of the Labour Party.* • **as large as life** *colloq* in person; real and living. • **bring something to life** to make (eg a story) lively or interesting. • **come to life** to become lively or interesting. • **for life** until death □ *friends for life.* • **for the life of me** despite trying very hard □ *For the life of me, I just can't understand what she sees in him.* • **get a life!** *colloq* stop being so petty, boring, conventional, sad, etc. • **the high life** see separate entry. • **the life of Riley** /— ˈraɪlɪ/ *colloq* an easy, carefree (often irresponsible) life. • **not on your life!** *colloq* certainly not! • **take one's life in one's hands** to take a very important decision which will have serious consequences for oneself; to put one's life at risk. • **to the life** exactly like the original. ◷ Anglo-Saxon *lif*.

life-and-death ▷ *adj* extremely serious or critical.

life assurance and **life insurance** ▷ *noun* an insurance policy that guarantees that a sum of money will be paid to the policyholder when they reach a certain age, or to the policyholder's named dependant(s) if the policyholder dies before that age.

lifebelt ▷ *noun* a ring or belt that floats in water and can be used to support someone in danger of drowning.

lifeblood ▷ *noun* **1** the blood necessary for life. **2** anything that is an essential part or factor.

lifeboat ▷ *noun* **1** a boat for rescuing people who are in trouble at sea. **2** a small boat, often one of several, carried on a larger ship for use in emergencies.

lifebuoy ▷ *noun* a float for supporting someone in the water until they are rescued.

life-cycle ▷ *noun* the sequence of often markedly different stages through which a living organism passes from the time of fusion of male and female gametes until the same stage in the next generation.

life expectancy ▷ *noun* **1** the average length of time (currently in the UK around 75 years) for which a person from a particular location might be expected to live if not affected by disease, war, famine, etc. **2** the length of time for which any living organism might be expected to live.

lifeguard ▷ *noun* **1** an expert swimmer employed at a swimming-pool or beach to rescue people in danger of drowning. **2** a bodyguard.

Life Guards ▷ *plural noun* a British army regiment which guards the monarch, especially on ceremonial occasions.

life jacket ▷ *noun* an inflatable sleeveless jacket for supporting someone in the water until help is available.

lifeless ▷ *adj* **1** dead. **2** unconscious. **3** having no energy or vivacity; dull. **4** said of food and drink: insipid. **5** said of a habitat: not able to support living things. • **lifelessly** *adverb*. • **lifelessness** *noun*.

lifelike ▷ *adj* said of a portrait, etc: very like the person or thing represented.

lifeline ▷ *noun* **1** a rope for support in dangerous operations or for saving lives. **2** a vital means of communication or support. **3** a line used by a diver for signalling.

lifelong ▷ *adj* lasting the whole of someone's life.

life peer and **life peeress** ▷ *noun* a peer whose title is not hereditary. • **life peerage** *noun*.

lifer ▷ *noun, slang* someone sent to prison for life.

life raft ▷ *noun* a raft kept on a ship, for use in emergencies.

life-renter ▷ *noun, Scots law* someone who enjoys the right of use of something for life. Compare FIAR.

life-saver ▷ *noun* **1** someone or something that saves lives, or that saves someone from difficulty. **2** *colloq* someone or something that comes to one's aid at a critical moment.

life-saving ▷ *noun* the act or skill of rescuing people who are in danger of drowning. ▷ *adj* designed to save life, especially from drowning.

life sciences ▷ *plural noun* the branches of science concerned with the study of living organisms and their structure, functioning, behaviour, etc, eg biochemistry, genetics, etc.

life sentence ▷ *noun, Brit* a prison sentence that is for the rest of the offender's life, but which seldom means this as the Home Secretary, on the advice of a parole board, can recommend release on licence.

life-size and **life-sized** ▷ *adj* said of a copy, drawing, etc: the same size as the original.

life story ▷ *noun* a biography or autobiography, especially in the form of a book, film or play that aims to entertain rather than be factual.

lifestyle ▷ *noun* **1** the way of living of a group or individual. **2** a fashionable way of living.

lifestyle drug ▷ *noun, medicine* a prescription drug taken to improve the quality of a person's life or to counter a condition, such as obesity, caused by their lifestyle rather than to cure or counter a medical disorder. ⓒ 1990s.

life-support ▷ *adj* said of machines, etc: allowing someone to remain alive, eg in an unfavourable environment such as space, or when seriously ill □ *life-support machine* □ *life-support system*. ▷ *noun* (*also* **life support machine** or **life support**) a machine or system which allows someone to remain alive.

lifetime ▷ *noun* **1** the duration of someone's life. **2** *informal* a very long time or what seems like a very long time □ *had to wait a lifetime for the bus.*

LIFFE /laɪf/ ▷ *abbreviation* London International Financial Futures Exchange.

LIFO /'laɪfoʊ/ ▷ *abbreviation* last in, first out, a method of pricing goods, controlling stock, storing data in a computer, or determining the likely order of redundancies. Compare FIFO.

lift ▷ *verb* (*lifted, lifting*) **1** *tr & intr* to raise or rise to a higher position. **2** to move (especially one's eyes or face) upwards. **3** to take and carry away; to remove. **4** to raise to a better or more agreeable level □ *lift one's spirits.* **5** *intr* **a** said of cloud, fog, etc: to clear; **b** said of winds: to become less strong. **6** to remove or annul □ *They will lift the trading restrictions.* **7** to dig up (crops growing in the ground, eg potatoes). **8** *colloq* to plagiarize from someone else's work or from published material. **9** *slang* to arrest. **10** *colloq* to steal. ▷ *noun* **1** an act of lifting. **2** lifting power. **3** the upward force of the air on an aircraft, etc. **4** *Brit* a device for moving people and goods between floors of a building, consisting of a compartment which moves up and down in a vertical shaft. *N Amer equivalent* **elevator**. **5** *Brit* a ride in a person's car or other vehicle, often given without payment as a favour. *N Amer equivalent* **ride**. **6** a boost to the spirits or sudden feeling of happiness. **7** a step in advancement, promotion, etc. **8** a mechanism for raising or lowering a vessel to another level of a canal. **9** a layer in the heel of a shoe to give extra height. • **to have one's face lifted** to have a FACELIFT. • **lift a** or **one's hand** to threaten to hit someone. • **lift a finger** or **hand** *with negatives* to make the smallest effort (to help, etc) □ *He just sat there without lifting a finger to help.* ⓒ 13c: from Norse *lypta*.

■ **lift off** said of a spacecraft: to rise, especially vertically, from the ground.

lift-off ▷ *noun* the vertical launching of a spacecraft or rocket.

lig ▷ *verb* (*ligged, ligging*) **1** to lie about idly. **2** to FREELOAD, especially in the media or entertainment industries. • **ligger** *noun*. ⓒ 1960s: from dialect variant of LIE[2]

ligament /'lɪgəmənt/ ▷ *noun* **1** anything that binds. **2** *anatomy* a band of tough connective tissue that holds two bones together at a joint. **3** a bond or tie. ⓒ 14c: from Latin *ligare* to bind.

ligand /'lɪgənd, 'laɪ-/ ▷ *noun, chem* an atom, molecule, radicle or ion attached to the central atom of certain types of compound. ⓒ 1950s: from Latin *ligare* to bind.

ligase /'laɪgeɪz/ ▷ *noun, biochem* any of a class of enzymes that play an important part in the synthesis and repair of certain complex molecules, including DNA, in living cells. ⓒ 1960s: from Latin *ligare* to bind.

ligate /'laɪgeɪt/ ▷ *verb* (*ligated, ligating*) *chiefly surgery* to tie up (a blood vessel or duct). ⓒ 16c: from Latin *ligare* to bind.

ligation /laɪ'geɪʃən/ ▷ *noun* **1** the act of binding, especially with a ligature. **2** the state of being bound. **3** *biol* the joining together of two linear nucleic acid molecules. ⓒ 16c: from Latin *ligare* to bind.

ligature /ˈlɪɡətʃə(r)/ ▷ *noun* **1** anything that binds or ties. **2 a** a thread, etc for tying, especially for sealing blood vessels during surgery; **b** the act or process of tying with a ligature. **3** *music* a symbol on a sheet of music indicating that a SLUR (*noun* 3b) joining a sequence of notes should be played. **4** *printing* a character formed from two or more characters joined together, for example, the Old English DIGRAPH, ASH[3], as it is written in *mediæval* or in *aesthetic*. ▷ *verb* (***ligatured***, ***ligaturing***) to bind with a ligature. ◷ 14c: from Latin *ligare* to bind.

liger /ˈlaɪɡə(r)/ ▷ *noun* the offspring of a *li*on and a female ti*ger*. ◷ 1930s.

ligger¹ /ˈlɪɡə(r)/ ▷ *noun* a lower millstone. ◷ 15c: from *lig*, Northern form of LIE².

ligger² see under LIG

light¹ /laɪt/ ▷ *noun* **1** a form of electromagnetic radiation that travels freely through space, and can be absorbed and reflected, especially that part of the spectrum which can be seen with the human eye. **2** any source of light, such as the Sun, a lamp, a candle, etc. **3** an appearance of brightness; a shine or gleam □ *see a light away in the distance*. **4** (**the lights**) traffic lights □ *turn left at the lights*. **5** the time during the day when it is daylight. **6** dawn. **7** a particular quality or amount of light □ *a good light for taking photographs*. **8** a flame or spark for igniting. **9** a means of producing a flame for igniting, such as a match. **10** a way in which something is thought of or regarded □ *see the problem in a new light*. **11** a hint, clue or help towards understanding. **12** a glow in the eyes or on the face as a sign of energy, liveliness, happiness or excitement. **13** someone who is well regarded in a particular field □ *a leading light*. **14** an opening in a wall that lets in light, such as a window. **15** (**lights**) *formal* someone's mental ability, knowledge or understanding □ *act according to one's lights*. ▷ *adj* **1** having light; not dark. **2** said of a colour: pale; closer to white than black. ▷ *verb* (*past tense* and *past participle* ***lit*** or ***lighted***, *present participle* ***lighting***) **1** to provide light for something □ *light the stage*. **2** *tr & intr* to begin to burn, or to make something begin to burn □ *light the fire*. **3** to guide or show someone the way using a light or torch. **4** *tr & intr* to make or become bright, sparkling with liveliness, happiness or excitement. • **lightish** *adj*. • **lightness** *noun*. • **bring something to light** to make it known or cause it to be noticed. • **come to light** to be made known or discovered. • **go out like a light** to fall sound asleep soon after going to bed. • **hide one's light under a bushel** see under BUSHEL. • **in a good** or **bad light** putting a favourable or unfavourable construction on something. • **in the light of something** taking it into consideration. • **light at the end of the tunnel** an indication of success or completion. • **lights out 1** *military* a bugle or trumpet call for lights to be put out. **2** the time at night when lights in a dormitory or barracks have to be put out. • **see the light 1** to understand something. **2** to have a religious conversion. • **see the light of day 1** to be born, discovered or produced. **2** to come to public notice. • **shed** or **throw light on something** to make it clear or help to explain it. • **strike a light!** *chiefly Austral slang* expressing surprise. ◷ Anglo-Saxon *leoht*.

■ **light up** *colloq* to light (a cigarette, etc) and begin smoking.

light² or (in senses 21 and 22) **lite** /laɪt/ ▷ *adj* **1** being of little weight; easy to lift or carry. **2** low in weight, amount or density □ *light rain*. **3** not pressing heavily; gentle □ *a light touch*. **4** easy to bear, suffer or do □ *light work*. **5** being of less weight than is correct or proper. **6** equipped with only hand-held weapons □ *light infantry*. **7** without problems, sorrow, etc; cheerful □ *a light heart*. **8** graceful and quick; nimble □ *a light skip*. **9** not serious or profound, but for amusement only □ *light reading*. **10** *old use* not chaste. **11** thoughtless or trivial □ *a light remark*. **12** not thinking clearly or seriously; giddy □ *a light head*. **13** said of a syllable: not stressed. **14** said of food: easily digested. **15** *technical* said of wine: with an alcohol content of between 5.5% and 15% by volume. **16** *non-technical* said of wine: with a delicate fresh flavour. **17** said of cakes, etc: spongy and well risen. **18** said of soil: loose and sandy. **19** said of a vehicle or ship: designed to carry light loads only. **20** said of a ship: unloaded. **21** (*also* **lite**) said of alcoholic drinks: low in alcohol. **22** (*also* **lite**) said of food and non-alcholic drinks: containing little fat and/or sugar and so healthier. **23** said of industry: producing small consumer articles, usually without the use of heavy machinery. ▷ *adverb* **1** in a light manner. **2** with little luggage □ *travel light*. ▷ *noun* (**lights**) see separate entry. • **lightish** *adj*. • **lightly** see separate entry. • **lightness** *noun*. • **make light of something** to treat it as unimportant or trivial. ◷ Anglo-Saxon *leoht*.

light³ /laɪt/ ▷ *verb* (*past tense* and *past participle* ***lit*** or ***lighted***, *present participle* ***lighting***) said especially of birds: to come to rest after flight. ◷ Anglo-Saxon *lihtan* to alight.

■ **light on** or **upon something** to come upon or find it by chance □ *suddenly lit upon the idea*.

light bulb ▷ *noun* an airtight glass ENVELOPE surrounding an electric FILAMENT which emits visible light when a current is passed through it.

light-emitting diode see LED

lighten¹ /ˈlaɪtən/ ▷ *verb* (***lightened***, ***lightening***) **1** *tr & intr* to make or become brighter. **2** to cast light on. **3** *intr* to shine or glow. ◷ 14c.

lighten² /ˈlaɪtən/ ▷ *verb* (***lightened***, ***lightening***) **1** *tr & intr* to make or become less heavy. **2** *tr & intr* to make or become happier or more cheerful. **3** to make (a problem, unhappy mood, etc) less □ *tried to lighten her sadness*. • **lightening** *noun*. ◷ 14c.

■ **lighten up** *slang* **1** to relax. **2** to become less serious, angry, etc.

lighter¹ ▷ *noun* **1** a device for lighting cigarettes, etc. **2** someone who sets something alight. ◷ 16c.

lighter² ▷ *noun* a large open boat used for transferring goods between ships, or between a ship and a wharf. ◷ 15c: from Anglo-Saxon *lihtan* to relieve of a weight.

lighter-than-air ▷ *adj* said of an aircraft: weighing less than the air it displaces. ▷ *noun* an aircraft of this kind. ◷ 19c.

light-fingered ▷ *adj* having a habitual tendency to steal. ◷ 16c.

light-flyweight ▷ *noun* an amateur boxer whose maximum weight must be 48kg.

light-footed ▷ *adj* nimble; active.

light-headed ▷ *adj* **1** having a dizzy feeling in the head, especially one brought on by alcohol or drugs. **2** thoughtless and silly; frivolous. • **light-headedly** *adverb*. • **light-headedness** *noun*.

light-hearted ▷ *adj* **1** said of entertainment, etc: not serious; cheerful and amusing. **2** happy and carefree. • **light-heartedly** *adverb*. • **light-heartedness** *noun*.

light-heavyweight ▷ *noun* a class of boxers, wrestlers and weightlifters of not more than a specified weight (79kg or 175lb in professional boxing, similar weights in the other sports). **2** a boxer, etc weighing not more than the specified amount for their category.

lighthouse ▷ *noun* a building on the coast with a flashing light to guide ships or warn them of rocks, etc.

lighthousekeeper and **lighthouseman** ▷ *noun* a person in charge of a lighthouse.

light industry ▷ *noun* a factory or factories involving the production of smaller goods, eg knitwear, glass, electronics components, etc. Compare HEAVY INDUSTRY.

lighting ▷ *noun* **1** equipment for providing light. **2** light, usually of a specified kind □ *subdued lighting*.

lighting cameraman ▷ *noun*, *cinematog* someone who oversees the lighting of sets to be filmed.

lighting-up time ▻ *noun* the time of day when road vehicles must have their lights turned on.

lightly ▻ *adverb* **1** in a light manner. **2** slightly. ● **get off lightly** to escape without serious rebuke or punishment. ◷ Anglo-Saxon.

light meter ▻ *noun, photog* a meter for measuring the amount of light present. Also called EXPOSURE METER.

light-middleweight see under MIDDLEWEIGHT

lightning /ˈlaɪtnɪŋ/ ▻ *noun, meteorol* a bright flash of light produced by the discharge of static electricity between or within clouds, or between a cloud and the Earth's surface, accompanied by THUNDER. ▻ *adj* very quick and sudden □ *made a lightning dash to catch the bus.*

lightning-conductor and **lightning-rod** ▻ *noun* a metal rod, usually projecting above the roof of a tall building, designed to prevent structural damage by diverting lightning directly to earth.

lightning strike ▻ *noun* an industrial or military strike that happens without warning.

light opera ▻ *noun* operetta.

light pen ▻ *noun* **1** *computing* especially in computer-aided design and graphics: a light-sensitive pen-like device that can be used to generate or modify images and and move them about on a computer screen by touching the device to the screen. **2** a bar-code reader.

light pollution ▻ *noun* an excessive amount of artificial lighting, especially in large cities.

lightproof and **light-tight** ▻ *adj* having the capacity to stop light penetrating.

lights ▻ *plural noun* the lungs of an animal, used as food. ● **put** or **punch someone's lights out** to give them a severe beating. ◷ 13c: a specialized use of LIGHT[2].

light-sensitive ▻ *adj, physics* denoting materials that display certain photoelectric properties, eg an increase or decrease in electrical resistance, when exposed to light.

lightship ▻ *noun* a ship with a beacon, that acts as a lighthouse.

light show ▻ *noun* **1** *originally* the colourful spectacle of moving lights that often accompanies rock and pop bands at live performances, usually projected on to a large screen. **2** *now also* an entertainment where such lights are synthesized with recorded (usually instrumental) music.

lightweight ▻ *adj* **1** light in weight. **2** *derog* having little importance or authority. **3** belonging to or relating to the lightweight class of boxing, etc. ▻ *noun* **1** a person or thing of little physical weight. **2** *derog* a person or thing having little importance or authority. **3** a class for boxers, wrestlers and weight-lifters of not more than a specified weight (61.2kg (135lb) in professional boxing, different but similar weights in amateur boxing and the other sports). **4** a boxer, etc of this class.

light-year ▻ *noun* the distance travelled by a beam of light in a vacuum in one year, equal to about 9.46 trillion km or 5.88 trillion miles, used as a unit of measurement for the distances between stars and galaxies.

ligneous /ˈlɪgnɪəs/ ▻ *adj, technical* composed of or resembling wood; woody. ◷ 17c: from Latin *lignum* wood.

lignify /ˈlɪgnɪfaɪ/ ▻ *verb* (***lignifies, lignified, lignifying***) *intr* said of the walls of plant cells: to thicken and become woody as a result of the deposition of lignin. ◷ 19c.

lignin /ˈlɪgnɪn/ ▻ *noun, bot* the complex polymer that cements together the fibres within the cell walls of plants, making them woody and rigid. ◷ 19c: from Latin *lignum* wood + -IN.

lignite /ˈlɪgnaɪt/ ▻ *noun, geol* a soft brown low-grade form of coal, intermediate between peat and bituminous coal, that burns with a smoky flame and give out little heat. Also called **brown coal**. ◷ 19c.

ligno- /lɪgnoʊ, -nə/ or **ligni-** /lɪgnɪ/ or (before a vowel) **lign-** ▻ *combining form, signifying* wood. ◷ From Latin *lignum* wood.

lignocaine /ˈlɪgnəkeɪn/ ▻ *noun, pharmacol* a local anaesthetic widely used during minor surgery and dental operations. ◷ 1950s: from LIGNO- and *cocaine*.

lignum /ˈlɪgnəm/ ▻ *noun, bot* the woody outer surface of certain plants. ◷ 19c.

lignum vitae /lɪgnəm ˈvaɪtiː/ ▻ *noun* the wood of a tropical American genus of trees, Guaiacum. ◷ 16c: Latin, literally 'wood of life'.

likable see LIKEABLE

like[1] ▻ *adj* **1** similar; resembling □ *as like as two peas.* **2** typical of □ *It's just like them to forget.* **3** used in asking someone for a description of someone or something □ *What's he like?* ▻ *prep* **1** in the same manner as; to the same extent as □ *run like a deer.* **2** such as □ *animals like cats and dogs.* ▻ *adverb* **1** *colloq* approximately. **2** *colloq* as it were □ *It was magic, like.* ▻ *conj, colloq* **1** as if; as though □ *It's like I've been here before.* **2** in the same way as □ *not pretty like you are.* ▻ *noun* usually preceded by a possessive pronoun: the counterpart or equal of someone or something □ *people of their like.* ● **anything like** *often with negatives* nearly □ *not anything like as good as the other one.* ● **the like a** things of the same kind □ *TVs, radios and the like are on the third floor;* **b** *with negatives and in questions* anything similar □ *never see the like again.* ● **the likes of** *usually contemptuous* people or things such as □ *wouldn't have much to do with the likes of them.* ● **like as not** *dialect* probably □ *She'll be on time, like as not.* ● **nothing like** not nearly □ *His new film is nothing like as good as his last one.* ● **something like** approximately □ *paid something like £150 to get her car repaired.* ● **like a …** see under the following noun, eg for *like a bat out of hell* see under BAT. ● **like crazy** or **mad** *colloq* furiously; very much, fast, etc □ *drove like crazy.* ● **like one of the family** *colloq* as though someone or something was a member of one's family □ *She treats that cat like one of the family.* ● **like what** *non-standard* in the same way as □ *He's not mad like what you are.* ● **more like it a** nearer to what is wanted or required □ *A cup of tea? A large brandy would be more like it;* **b** nearer to the truth □ *calls her his research assistant but dogsbody is more like it.* ◷ Anglo-Saxon *gelic* alike.

like[2] ▻ *verb* (***liked, liking***) **1** to be pleased with something. **2** to find someone or something pleasant or agreeable. **3** to be fond of someone or something. **4** to prefer □ *She likes her tea without sugar.* **5** to wish, or wish for □ *if you like.* ▻ *noun* (**likes**) things that someone has a preference for □ *likes and dislikes.* ● **I like that!** *ironic* expressing surprise or shock. ● **(to do something) and like it** (to put up with doing something that is unpleasant) without complaining. ● **like it or lump it** see under LUMP. ◷ Anglo-Saxon *lician* to please.

-like ▻ *adj, forming adjectives, signifying* **a** resembling □ *catlike;* **b** typical of □ *childlike;* **c** *colloq* somewhat □ *weird-like.*

likeable or **likable** /ˈlaɪkəbəl/ ▻ *adj* **1** easy to like. **2** lovable. **3** pleasant.

likelihood /ˈlaɪklɪhʊd/ and **likeliness** ▻ *noun* probability. ● **in all likelihood** very probably.

likely ▻ *adj* **1** probable. **2** suitable or useful for a particular purpose □ *a likely spot for a picnic.* **3** *ironic* credible □ *a likely tale.* ▻ *adverb* probably. ● **as likely as not** probably. ● **not likely** *colloq* (often with a swear-word) absolutely not.

like-minded ▻ *adj* sharing a similar outlook or having similar opinions, tastes or purpose.

liken ▻ *verb* (***likened, likening***) **1** (*usually* **liken something to something else**) to see two things as being the same or similar. **2** to compare.

likeness ▻ *noun* (***likenesses***) **1** a similarity □ *a family likeness.* **2** *formerly* a portrait or formal photograph.

likewise ▷ *adverb* **1** in the same or a similar manner. **2** also; in addition.

liking ▷ *noun* **1** a fondness □ ***a liking for chocolates.*** **2** affection. **3** taste; preference □ ***to one's liking.***

lilac /ˈlaɪlək/ ▷ *noun* **1** a small European tree or shrub of the olive family, with white or pale pinkish-purple sweet-smelling flowers. **2** a lilac colour. ▷ *adj* pale pinkish-purple in colour. ⓒ 17c: from Persian *nilak* bluish, from *nil* blue.

Lilliputian /lɪlɪˈpjuːʃən/ ▷ *noun* someone or something very small. ▷ *adj* (*also* **lilliputian**) very small. ⓒ 18c: from Lilliput, an imaginary country inhabited by tiny people in Swift's *Gulliver's Travels.*

Lilo /ˈlaɪloʊ/ (*also* **Li-lo** or **lilo**) ▷ *noun* (***Lilos***) *trademark* a type of inflatable mattress used in camping or on the beach, etc. ⓒ 1930s: from LIE[2] + LOW.

lilt ▷ *noun* **1** a light graceful swinging rhythm. **2** a tune, song or voice with such a rhythm. **3** a springing, swinging quality in someone's walk. ▷ *verb* (***lilted, lilting***) *intr* to speak, sing or move with a lilt. ● **lilting** *adj.* ⓒ 16c.

lily /ˈlɪlɪ/ ▷ *noun* (***lilies***) **1** *strictly* any of various perennial plants that have underground bulbs, narrow leaves, and white or brightly coloured flowers, often spotted, with long protruding stamens. **2** *loosely* any of various plants with flowers superficially resembling those of a lily, eg water lily. **3** someone or something considered exceptionally pure. **4** a FLEUR-DE-LIS. ▷ *adj* pale; white. ● **liliaceous** *adj.* ● **gild the lily** see under GILD. ⓒ Anglo-Saxon, from Latin *lilium.*

lily-livered ▷ *adj* cowardly.

lily-of-the-valley ▷ *noun* (***lilies-of-the-valley***) a spring plant with small white bell-shaped flowers that have a sweet smell.

lily pad ▷ *noun* a large water lily leaf that sits on top of a pond, etc.

lily-white ▷ *adj* **1** pure white. **2** without blame.

Lima /ˈliːmə/ ▷ *noun, communications* in the NATO alphabet: the word used to denote the letter 'L'. See table at NATO ALPHABET.

lima bean and **lima** /ˈliːmə, ˈlaɪmə/ ▷ *noun* (***limas***) a flat white edible bean from tropical America. ⓒ 19c: named after Lima, the capital of Peru.

limb¹ /lɪm/ ▷ *noun* **1** an arm, leg or wing. **2** a projecting part. **3** a main branch on a tree. **4** a spur of a mountain. **5** a branch or section of a larger organization. ● **limbed** *adj in compounds* having limbs of a specified number or type □ ***long-limbed.*** ● **limbless** *adj* having no limbs. ● **out on a limb** exposed or isolated, especially as regards an opinion or attitude. ⓒ Anglo-Saxon *lim.*

limb² /lɪm/ ▷ *noun* **1** an edge of the disk of the Sun, Moon or a planet □ ***the northern limb.*** **2** the edge of a sextant. **3** *bot* the expanded blade-like part of a leaf or petal. ⓒ 15c: from Latin *limbus* border.

limber¹ /ˈlɪmbə(r)/ ▷ *adj* flexible and supple. ▷ *verb* (***limbered, limbering***) to make flexible and supple.

■ **limber up** to stretch and warm up before taking exercise. ⓒ 20c in this sense; 18c, meaning 'to make supple', perhaps from LIMB[1].

limber² ▷ *noun* the detachable front part of a gun carriage, consisting of an axle, pole and two wheels. ▷ *verb* (***limbered, limbering***) to attach (a gun) to a limber. ⓒ 15c: as *lymour.*

limbic system /ˈlɪmbɪk —/ ▷ *noun, anatomy* the part of the brain concerned with basic emotions. ⓒ 19c: from Latin *limbus* border.

limbo¹ or **Limbo** /ˈlɪmboʊ/ ▷ *noun* (***limbos***) **1** *Christianity* an area between heaven and hell that is believed to be reserved for the unbaptized dead, either children or the righteous who died before Christ. **2** a place of oblivion or neglect. **3** prison. ● **in limbo** in a state of uncertainty or waiting. ⓒ 14c: from Latin *in limbo* on the border.

limbo² /ˈlɪmboʊ/ ▷ *noun* a West Indian dance in which the object is to lean backwards and shuffle under a rope or bar which is gradually lowered towards the floor, a highly skilled performer being able to do this with only a few inches clearance. ⓒ 1950s: from Jamaican English *limba* to bend.

limb of Satan ▷ *noun* a mischievous child.

Limburger /ˈlɪmbɜːɡə(r)/ and **limburger cheese** ▷ *noun* a white strong-tasting and strong-smelling cheese. ⓒ 19c: named after Limburg in Belgium where the cheese is made.

lime¹ ▷ *noun* **1** *loosely* CALCIUM OXIDE. **2** *loosely* SLAKED LIME. **3** *loosely* LIMESTONE. **4** BIRD-LIME. **5** *dialect* any slimy or gluey substance. ▷ *verb* (***liming, limed***) **1** to cover with lime. **2** to apply ground limestone as a fertilizer to (soil). **3** to trap (usually birds, but sometimes animals) using bird-lime. ● **liminess** *noun.* ● **limy** see separate entry. ⓒ Anglo-Saxon *lim.*

lime² ▷ *noun* **1** a small, round or oval, green or yellowish-green citrus fruit with a sour taste, used as a garnish, flavouring for drinks, etc. **2** the yellowish-green colour of this fruit. **3** the small spiny evergreen tree, native to Asia, that bears this fruit. ▷ *adj* (*often* **lime green**) being of a yellowish-green colour. ● **limy** see separate entry. ⓒ 17c: from Spanish *lima* lemon.

lime³ ▷ *noun* **1** (*also* **lime-tree** and **linden** /ˈlɪndən/) any of various deciduous trees and shrubs which have heart-shaped leaves and pendulous clusters of fragrant yellow, green or white flowers. **2** the wood from this tree. ⓒ 17c: from Anglo-Saxon *lind* linden.

limekiln ▷ *noun* a kiln for heating limestone to produce lime.

limelight ▷ *noun* **1** formerly used in theatres: a bright white light produced by heating a block of lime in a flame. **2** the glare of publicity □ ***in the limelight.*** ▷ *verb* to subject someone or something to the glare of limelight. ⓒ 19c.

limerick /ˈlɪmərɪk/ ▷ *noun* (*sometimes* **Limerick**) a humorous poem with five lines that always have the same RHYME and METRE[2] patterns, lines one, two and five sharing the same rhyme and lines three and four rhyming with each other. The opening line usually begins something like: *There was a young lady from ...* ⓒ 19c: said to be from *Will you come up to Limerick?*, a refrain sung between the verses of extemporized versions of this kind of poem at parties in the Irish town of Limerick.

limestone ▷ *noun, geol* any of various sedimentary rocks composed mainly of CALCIUM CARBONATE, used as a building material and in iron smelting, cement manufacture, etc.

limewash see WHITEWASH

limewater ▷ *noun, chem* an alkaline solution of calcium hydroxide in water, sometimes used as an antacid.

limey /ˈlaɪmɪ/ ▷ *noun* (***limeys***) *N Amer, Austral & NZ slang* **1** a British person. **2** *formerly* a British sailor or ship. ⓒ 19c: from LIME[2], because British sailors used to take lime-juice to prevent scurvy.

liming /ˈlaɪmɪŋ/ ▷ *noun* **1** in the preparation of leather, etc: the soaking of skins in limewater to remove the hair. **2 a** the application of whitewash to walls; **b** the application of lime to the ground as a fertilizer.

limit /ˈlɪmɪt/ ▷ *noun* **1** a point, degree, amount or boundary, especially one which cannot or should not be passed. **2** a restriction. **3** *stock exchange* a predetermined price at which a broker is instructed to buy or sell. **4** *math* in calculus: a value that is approached increasingly closely, but never reached. **5** the boundary or edge of an area □ ***city limits.*** **6** the greatest or smallest extent, degree, etc allowed. **7** (**the limit**) *colloq, sometimes facetious* someone or something that is intolerable or extremely annoying. ▻ *verb* (**limited**, **limiting**) **1** to be a limit or boundary to someone or something. **2** to restrict. • **limitable** *adj.* • **limiter** *noun.* • **limitary** *adj.* • **off limits** out of bounds. • **over the limit** said of someone who has been driving: **a** registering more than the permitted level of alcohol in the blood; **b** exceeding the legal speed limit. • **within limits** with only a moderate degree of freedom. ◷ 14c: from Latin *limes* boundary.

limitation ▻ *noun* **1** an act of limiting or the condition of being limited. **2** *law* a specified period within which an action must be brought. **3** (*often* **limitations**) someone's weakness, lack of ability, etc which sets a limit on what they can achieve □ *know one's limitations.* **4** *law* a period of time within which an action must be brought.

limited ▻ *adj* **1** having a limit or limits. **2** *derog* narrow; restricted □ *a limited understanding.* • **limitedly** *adverb.* • **limitedness** *noun.*

limited company and **limited liability company** ▻ *noun* a company owned by its shareholders, who have liability for debts, etc only according to the extent of their stake in the company.

limited edition ▻ *noun* an edition of a book, art print, etc of which only a certain number of copies are printed or made.

limitless ▻ *adj* **1** having no limit. **2** endless. **3** immense. • **limitlessly** *adverb.* • **limitlessness** *noun.*

limnology /lɪm'nɒlədʒɪ/ ▻ *noun* the scientific study of freshwater habitats, including chemical, physical and biological factors. • **limnological** /-nə'lɒdʒɪkəl/ *adj.* • **limnologist** *noun.* ◷ 19c: from Greek *limne* lake.

limo /lɪmoʊ/ ▻ *noun* (**limos**) *colloq* short form of LIMOUSINE. See also STRETCH LIMO.

limousine /'lɪməziːn, lɪmə'ziːn/ ▻ *noun* a large, luxurious motor car, especially one with a screen separating the driver from the passengers. ◷ 20c: French, originally meaning 'a cloak worn by shepherds in Limousin, a province in France'.

limp¹ ▻ *verb* (**limped**, **limping**) *intr* **1** to walk with an awkward or uneven step, often because one leg is weak or injured. **2** said of a damaged ship or aircraft: to move with difficulty. ▻ *noun* the walk of someone who limps. Compare LAME. ◷ From Anglo-Saxon *lemphealt*, from *lemp* to happen + *healt* limp.

limp² ▻ *adj* **1** not stiff or firm; hanging loosely. **2** without energy or vitality; drooping. **3** said of a book: with a soft cover not stiffened by boards. • **limply** *adverb.* • **limpness** *noun.* ◷ 18c: probably Scandinavian.

limpet /'lɪmpɪt/ ▻ *noun* **1** any of various marine gastropod molluscs that have a ridged conical shell and cling firmly to rock surfaces by means of a muscular foot. **2** *derog* someone who is difficult to get rid of. ◷ Anglo-Saxon *lempedu*, from Latin *lampreda*, from *lambere* to lick + *petra* a stone.

limpet mine ▻ *noun* a mine which attaches itself to its target with a magnet.

limpid /'lɪmpɪd/ ▻ *adj* **1** said of water, the air, eyes, etc: clear; transparent. **2** said of speeches, writing, etc: easily understood. • **limpidity** /lɪm'pɪdɪtɪ/ *noun.* • **limpidly** *adverb.* • **limpidness** *noun.* ◷ 17c: from Latin *limpidus*, from *lympha* clear liquid.

limping ▻ *noun* the act of walking with a limp. ▻ *adj* involving a limp; halting. • **limpingly** *adverb.*

limpkin /'lɪmpkɪn/ ▻ *noun* an American wading bird similar to a rail. ◷ 19c: so called because of its limping way of walking.

limp-wristed ▻ *adj, derog slang* said of a man: effeminate. • **limp-wrist** *noun.*

limy¹ /'laɪmɪ/ *adj* (**limier**, **limiest**) **1** like or having the consistency of LIME¹. **2** coated with BIRD-LIME.

limy² /'laɪmɪ/ *adj* (**limier**, **limiest**) tasting of the citrus fruit, LIME².

lin see LINN

lin. *abbreviation* **1** lineal. **2** linear.

linage or **lineage** /'laɪnɪdʒ/ ▻ *noun* **1** the number of lines in a piece of printed matter. **2** *journalism* measurement or payment by the line. ◷ 14c: from LINE¹ + -AGE.

linchpin /'lɪntʃpɪn/ ▻ *noun* **1** a pin-shaped rod passed through an axle to keep a wheel in place. **2** someone or something essential to a business, plan, etc. ◷ 14c: from Anglo-Saxon *lynis* axle.

Lincoln green /'lɪŋkən —/ ▻ *noun* **1** a bright-green cloth once made in Lincoln and said to have been worn by Robin Hood and his men. **2** the bright green of this cloth. ▻ *adj* bright green in colour. ◷ 16c.

lincomycin /lɪŋkoʊ'maɪsɪn/ ▻ *noun, pharmacol* an antibiotic used to treat infections caused by certain bacteria, including staphylococci and streptococci. ◷ 1960s: *linco-* because it is made from the bacterium streptomyces *linco*lnensis, + *-mycin* meaning 'coming from a fungus', from Greek *mykes* mushroom.

Lincs /lɪŋks/ ▻ *abbreviation, English county* Lincolnshire.

linctus /'lɪŋktəs/ ▻ *noun* (**linctuses**) *Brit* a syrupy liquid medicine, taken by mouth to relieve coughs and sore throats. ◷ 17c: Latin, meaning 'a licking', from *lingere*, *linctum* to lick.

linden see under LIME³

line¹ ▻ *noun* **1** a long narrow mark, streak or stripe. **2** *often in compounds* a length of thread, rope, wire, etc used for specified purposes □ *a washing line* □ *mending the telephone lines.* **3** a wrinkle or furrow, especially on the skin. **4** *math* something that has length but no breadth or thickness. **5** the path which a moving object is considered to leave behind it, having length but no breadth. **6** a row. **7** a row of words or printed or written characters □ *a line from Shakespeare.* **8** (**lines**) the words of an actor's part. **9** (*often* **lines**) an outline or shape □ *a car of stylish lines.* **10** (**lines**) a punishment at school where a phrase or sentence has to be written out a set number of times. **11** *music* any one of the five horizontal marks forming a musical stave. **12** *music* a series of notes forming a melody. **13** *colloq* a short letter or note □ *drop him a line.* **14** a series or group of people coming one after the other, especially in the same family or profession □ *from a long line of doctors.* **15** a field of activity, interest, study or work □ *his line of business.* **16** a course or way of acting, behaving, thinking or reasoning □ *think along different lines.* **17** the rules or limits of acceptable behaviour □ *overstep the line.* **18** a group or class of goods for sale □ *a new line in tonic water.* **19** a production line. **20** *N Amer, especially US* a physical boundary □ *the county line.* Compare LIMIT. **21** a figurative boundary or point of change □ *a thin line between genius and madness.* **22** one of several white marks outlining a pitch, race-track, etc on a field □ *goal line.* **23** a single track for trains or trams. **24** a branch or route of a railway system. **25** a route, track or direction of movement □ *line of fire.* **26** a continuous system, eg of telephone cables, connecting one place with another. **27 a** a telephone connection □ *trying to get a line to Aberdeen;* **b** *in compounds* a telephone number that connects the caller to some kind of special service, such as CHILDLINE or HOT LINE. **28** a company running regular services of ships, buses or aircraft between two or more places. **29** an arrangement of troops or ships side by side and ready to fight. **30** (*always* **lines**) a connected series of military defences □ *behind enemy lines.* **31** the regular army. **32** one of several narrow horizontal bands forming a television picture. **33** (*often* **the Line**) the equator. **34** *N Amer* a queue. **35** *drug-taking slang* a small amount of powdered drugs, usually cocaine, arranged in a narrow channel, ready to be sniffed. **36** *slang* a remark, usually insincere, that someone uses in the hope of getting some kind of benefit □ *He spun her a line.* **37** *Scots* a short note written by someone in authority □ *The doctor's line covered her absence.* **38** (**lines**) *Scots* a licence or certificate, eg of marriage or of church membership. ▻ *verb* (***lined***, ***lining***) **1** to mark or cover something with lines. See also WHITE LINE. **2** to form a line along something □ *Crowds lined the streets.* • **all along the line** at every point. • **be in someone's line** to be the kind of thing someone is comfortable with □ *Dealing with children is not in her line.* • **bring someone** or **something into line** to make them or it conform. • **down the line 1** *sport* said of the action of a ball, shot or player: very close to the edge of the court or pitch. **2** *colloq* in the future. • **draw the line** see under DRAW. • **end of the line** *colloq* the point at which it is useless or impossible to carry on. • **get a line on someone** or **something** *colloq* to get information about them or it. • **hard lines!** *colloq* bad luck! • **in line for something** likely to get it □ *in line for promotion.* • **in line to someone** in a line of succession □ *second in line to the boss.* • **in line with someone** or **something** in agreement or harmony with them or it. • **lay it on the line** to speak frankly. • **lay** or **put something on the line** to risk one's reputation or career over something. • **on** or **along the lines of something** sticking loosely to a specified way of doing it. • **on** or **along the right line** or **lines** *colloq* approximately correct. • **out of line 1** not aligned. **2** impudent. **3** exhibiting unacceptable behaviour. • **read between the lines** to understand something which is not actually stated. • **step out of line** see under STEP. ◷ 13c: from French *ligne*, combined with Anglo-Saxon *line* rope.

■ **line people** or **things up 1** to form them into a line. **2** to align them.

■ **line something up** to organize it □ *lined herself up a new job.*

■ **line up 1** to form a line. **2** to make a stand, eg in support of or against something. See LINE-UP.

line² ▻ *verb* **1** to cover the inside of (clothes, boxes, curtains, etc) with some other material. **2** to cover as if with a lining □ *line the walls with books.* **3** *colloq* to fill, especially with large amounts. • **lining** *noun* **1** the action of inserting a lining into something. **2** the material used for lining something. • **line one's pocket** or **pockets** to make a profit, especially by dishonest means. ◷ 14c: Anglo-Saxon *lin* flax.

lineage¹ /ˈlɪnɪɪdʒ/ ▻ *noun* ancestry, especially when it can be traced from one particular ancestor. ◷ 14c: from Latin *linea* LINE¹.

lineage² see LINAGE

lineal /ˈlɪnɪəl/ ▻ *adj* **1** said of family descent: in a direct line. **2** referring to or transmitted by direct line of descent or legitimate descent. **3** being of or in lines. • **lineally** *adverb.* ◷ 14c: from Latin *linealis*, from *linea* LINE¹.

lineament /ˈlɪnɪəmənt/ ▻ *noun* (*usually* **lineaments**) **1** a feature. **2** a distinguishing feature, especially on the face. ◷ 15c: from Latin *linea* LINE¹.

linear /ˈlɪnɪə(r)/ ▻ *adj* **1** referring to, consisting of or like a line or lines. **2** in or of one dimension only. **3** in the direction of a line. **4** long and very narrow with parallel sides. **5** *math* denoting an equation or relationship that can be represented by a straight line on a graph. **6** referring to any scientific or technical system in which a charge in one aspect, eg input, has a directly proportional effect on another, eg output. **7** relating to length. **8** *art* referring mainly to paintings: of a style where perspective, light and shade, etc are achieved by lines rather than through the use of colour. • **linearity** *noun.* ◷ 17c: from Latin *linearis* of lines.

Linear A ▻ *noun* an ancient script as yet undeciphered, but related to the later LINEAR B, and which seems to inscribe a Semitic language of Crete, where the clay tablets engraved with the script were found. ◷ 1940s: called *linear script...Class A* by Sir Arthur Evans (1851–1941), the English archaeologist who first discovered the tablets in the 1890s.

linear accelerator ▻ *noun* a device where electrons are made to move more quickly down a metal tube or tubes, by means of such things as electromagnetic waves. ◷ 1962.

Linear B ▻ *noun* an ancient script dating from around 1400 BC and later, found in Crete and in mainland Greece, inscribing a very early form of Greek. ◷ 1950: called *linear script...Class B* by Sir Arthur Evans; compare LINEAR A.

linear equation ▻ *noun, math* an equation with two or more terms, of which none is raised above the power of one.

linear momentum ▻ *noun, physics* for a particle moving in a straight line: the product of its mass and its velocity.

linear motor ▻ *noun* an electric motor that produces direct thrust without using gears. ◷ 1950s.

linear programming ▻ *noun* programming which enables a computer to give an optimum result when fed with a number of unrelated variables, used in determining the most efficient arrangement of something such as an industrial process. ◷ 1940s.

lineation /lɪnɪˈeɪʃən/ ▻ *noun* **1** the act of marking something with lines. **2** an arrangement of lines.

lined¹ *adj* having lines □ *lined paper.*

lined² *adj* having a lining □ *a lined jacket.*

line-dancing ▻ *noun* a form of dancing to country music in which the dancers dance in lines without partners.

line drawing ▻ *noun* a drawing in pen or pencil using lines only.

line judge ▻ *noun, sport* someone who watches a line (LINE¹ *noun* 22), eg in tennis, and who declares whether a service, a ball or a player is inside or outside of it. Compare LINESMAN.

line management ▻ *noun* a hierarchical system of management structured like a pyramid, where authority and responsibility are passed downwards and accountability is passed upwards via **line managers**. ◷ 1960s.

linen /ˈlɪnɪn/ ▻ *noun* **1** cloth made from flax. **2** household articles such as sheets, tablecloths, tea-towels, etc originally made from linen, now more likely to be made from cotton or man-made fibres. **3** underwear, which was originally made of linen. ▻ *adj* made of or like linen. • **wash one's dirty linen in public** to let personal problems and quarrels, often of a sordid nature, become generally known. ◷ Anglo-Saxon, from *lin* flax.

line of country ▻ *noun, colloq* someone's field of expertise, study or interest.

line of fire ▻ *noun* the range or scope of a weapon, etc □ *Journalists found they were in the snipers' line of fire* □ *in the line of fire of her vicious tongue.*

line of latitude ▻ *noun, geog* any reference or locational circle lying parallel to the north or south of the EQUATOR, defined in terms of the number of degrees any given line is from the equator. The measurement increases slightly irregularly (because the Earth is not a perfect sphere) towards the two poles where it becomes 90°. See LATITUDE. Compare LINE OF LONGITUDE.

line of longitude ▻ *noun, geog* any reference or locational circle passing through both poles, defined in terms of the number of degrees a given line lies to the east or west of the PRIME MERIDIAN, the measurement regularly increasing the further a line is from the prime meridian until it reaches a maximum of 180°. The physical distance between lines of longitude 1° apart is greatest nearest the EQUATOR (111.32km or 69.172 ml), diminishing to zero at the two poles. See LONGITUDE. Compare LINE OF LATITUDE.

line of vision and **line of sight** ▷ *noun* the line along which the eye can look in any one direction.

line-out ▷ *noun, rugby union* the way play restarts after the ball goes into TOUCH, by the forwards of both teams forming two rows facing the touch-line and trying to catch or deflect the ball which is thrown in by someone from the team which did not cause the infringement.

line printer ▷ *noun* a printer attached to a computer which prints a line at a time rather than one character.

liner¹ /ˈlaɪnə(r)/ ▷ *noun* a large passenger-ship or aircraft.

liner² /ˈlaɪnə(r)/ ▷ *noun, often in compounds* something used for lining □ *bin-liner.*

liner³ /ˈlaɪnə(r)/ ▷ *noun* **1** someone who makes, marks, draws, paints or writes lines. **2** a brush for making lines. **3** *often in compounds* colouring used to outline the eyes or the lips □ *eye-liner.*

linesman ▷ *noun* an official at a boundary line in some sports, eg football, whose job is to indicate when the ball has gone out of play. Compare LINE JUDGE.

line-up ▷ *noun* **1** an arrangement of things or people in line. **2** a list of people selected for a sports team □ *Jess was included in the Scotland line-up.* **3** the artistes appearing in an entertainment or show. **4** an identity parade.

ling¹ ▷ *noun* (***ling*** or ***lings***) a fish which has a long slender body, and is a member of the cod family. ⓘ 13c: possibly related to 'long'.

ling² ▷ *noun* HEATHER. ⓘ 14c: from Norse *lyng.*

ling. ▷ *abbreviation* linguistics.

-ling ▷ *suffix* **1** *often* expressing affection: a young, small, or minor person or thing □ *duckling* □ *darling.* **2** *sometimes derog* someone who has the specified attribute or position □ *weakling* □ *underling.*

lingam /ˈlɪŋgəm/ and **linga** /ˈlɪŋgə/ ▷ *noun* the Hindu phallus, a symbol of the god Siva. Compare YONI. ⓘ 18c: Sanskrit.

linger /ˈlɪŋgə(r)/ ▷ *verb* (***lingering, lingered***) *intr* **1** *often* said of sensations: to remain for a long time □ *The smell of garlic lingered in the kitchen.* **2** to be slow or reluctant to leave. **3** said of someone who is dying: to die very slowly. **4** to tarry. **5** to loiter. • **lingerer** *noun.* • **lingering** *noun.* • **lingeringly** *adverb.* ⓘ From Anglo-Saxon *lengan* to lengthen.

■ **linger over something** to spend a long time with it or doing it.

lingerie /ˈlɛ̃ʒərɪ/ ▷ *noun* women's underwear and nightclothes. ⓘ 19c: French, from Latin *linum* flax.

lingering ▷ *adj* **1** said especially of a sensation, a memory or a thought: persisting. **2** drawn out. • **lingeringly** *adverb.*

lingo /ˈlɪŋgoʊ/ ▷ *noun* (***lingos***) *colloq, often derog* **1** a language, especially one that is not highly thought of ~ or that is not understood □ *doesn't speak the lingo.* **2** the specialized vocabulary used by a particular group of people or profession □ *medical lingo.* ⓘ 17c: from Latin *lingua* tongue or language.

lingua franca /lɪŋgwə ˈfraŋkə/ ▷ *noun* (***lingua francas***) **1** a language, or often a simplified form of it, that has been chosen as a means of communication amongst the speakers of different languages. **2** any hybrid language that has been chosen as a means of communication amongst the speakers of different languages. **3** *usually* with reference to music and the arts: any system or set of conventions that are readily and easily understood □ *the lingua franca of ballet.* **4** *historical* a form of Italian with a mixture of French, Spanish, Greek and Arabic words, used in the eastern part of the Mediterranean to make trading easier. ⓘ 17c: Italian *lingua franca* Frankish language.

lingual /ˈlɪŋgwəl/ ▷ *adj* **1** referring or relating to the tongue. **2** *phonetics* pronounced using the tongue. **3** *in compounds* **a** knowing or expressed in the specified number of languages □ *monolingual;* **b** relating to the acquisition of speech □ *prelingual.* • **lingually** *adverb.* ⓘ 17c: from Latin *lingua* tongue or language.

linguini /lɪŋˈgwiːnɪ/ *plural noun* flat ribbon-like strips of pasta. ⓘ 1940s: Italian plural of *linguina* a little tongue.

linguist /ˈlɪŋgwɪst/ ▷ *noun* **1** someone who has an excellent knowledge of languages. **2** someone who studies linguistics, especially professionally. **3** *W Afr* someone who acts as an intermediary between the chief or priest of a tribe and the people. ⓘ 16c: from Latin *lingua* tongue or language.

linguistic ▷ *adj* **1** relating to language. **2** relating to linguistics. • **linguistically** *adverb.*

linguistic atlas ▷ *noun* an atlas that charts the spread and distribution of features of a language or dialect, such as pronunciation and vocabulary.

linguistician ▷ *noun* someone who studies linguistics.

linguistics /lɪŋˈgwɪstɪks/ ▷ *singular noun* the scientific study of language.

liniment /ˈlɪnɪmənt/ ▷ *noun* a kind of thin oily cream for rubbing into the skin to ease muscle pain. ⓘ 15c: from Latin *linire* to smear.

lining see under LINE²

link ▷ *noun* **1** a ring of a chain, or in chain-mail. **2** someone or something that connects. **3** a means of communication or travel. **4** a piece, part or scene that serves to hold two more important elements together □ *A jingle formed the link between the two radio programmes.* **5** a unit of measurement, equal to one hundredth of a surveyor's chain, 7.92in (c.20cm). **6** a cuff-link. ▷ *verb* (***linked, linking***) **1** to connect or join. **2** to associate. **3** *intr* to be or become connected. ⓘ 14c: from Norse *link.*

■ **link up 1** to connect. **2** to be connected □ *They linked up to satellite TV.*

linkage /ˈlɪŋkɪdʒ/ ▷ *noun* **1** an act, method or fact of linking. **2** a chemical bond. **3** *genetics* the association between two or more genes that occur close together on the same chromosome and therefore tend to be inherited together.

link man ▷ *noun, broadcasting* someone who provides some kind of connection between two parts or items on TV, radio, etc.

links ▷ *plural noun* **1** a stretch of more or less flat ground along a shore near the sea. **2** a golf course by the sea. ⓘ From Anglo-Saxon *hlinc* ridge.

link-up ▷ *noun* especially said of spacecraft, military manoeuvres, and telecommunications: a connection or union, especially of two different systems.

linn or **lin** ▷ *noun, now chiefly Scottish* **1** a waterfall. **2** a pool at the foot of a waterfall. **3** a deep ravine. ⓘ 16c: from Anglo-Saxon *hlynn.*

Linnaean /lɪˈnɪən/ ▷ *noun* **1** relating to Carolus Linnaeus. **2** relating to his BINOMIAL system of naming and classifying living organisms. ⓘ 18c: named after the Swedish botanist, Carolus Linnaeus (also known as Carl von Linné), who invented the system in 1735.

linnet /ˈlɪnɪt/ ▷ *noun* a small brown songbird of the finch family. ⓘ 11c: from French *linette,* from Latin *linum* flax, so called because it feeds on flax seeds.

lino /ˈlaɪnoʊ/ ▷ *noun* (***linos***) *colloq* LINOLEUM.

linocut ▷ *noun* **1** a design cut in relief in linoleum. **2** a print made from this.

linoleum /lɪˈnoʊlɪəm/ ▻ *noun, dated* a smooth hard-wearing covering for floors, made by impregnating a fabric with a mixture of substances such as linseed oil and cork. ⓒ 19c: from Latin *linum* flax + *oleum* oil.

Linotype /ˈlaɪnoʊtaɪp/ ▻ *noun, trademark* **a** a machine for producing stereotyped lines of printer's type; **b** a slug or line of printing-type cast in one piece by this method.

linseed /ˈlɪnsiːd/ ▻ *noun* the seed of the FLAX which contains linseed oil. ⓒ Anglo-Saxon *linsæd*.

linseed oil ▻ *noun* a pale-yellow oil, extracted from flax seed, which hardens on exposure to air, used in paints, varnishes, enamels, etc. ⓒ 19c.

lint ▻ *noun* **1** linen or cotton with a raised nap on one side, for dressing wounds. **2** fine, very small pieces of wool, cotton, etc; fluff. ⓒ 14c as *lynt*.

lintel /ˈlɪntəl/ ▻ *noun* a horizontal wooden or stone beam placed over a doorway or window. ⓒ 14c: from French *lintel* threshold, from Latin *limes* boundary or border.

lion /ˈlaɪən/ ▻ *noun* **1** a large member of the cat family, found mainly in Africa, with a tawny coat, a tufted tail, and, in the male, a long thick tawny or black mane on the head, neck and shoulders. **2** the male of this species, as opposed to the female. **3** someone who is brave. **4** someone who is the centre of public attention. **5** (**the Lion**) **a** *astron* the constellation of LEO; **b** *astrol* the sign of the zodiac, LEO. • **the lion's share** the largest share. • **put one's head in the lion's mouth** to put oneself in a dangerous position. See LEONINE, LIONESS. ⓒ 13c: from French *luin*, direct from Latin *leo*.

lioness ▻ *noun* (***lionesses***) **1** a female lion. **2** a brave or celebrated woman.

lion-heart ▻ *noun* someone who is very brave. • **lion-hearted** *adj* very brave or tenacious.

lionize or **lionise** /ˈlaɪənaɪz/ ▻ *verb* (***lionized, lionizing***) to treat someone as a celebrity or hero.

lip ▻ *noun* **1** either of the two fleshy parts which form the edge of the mouth. **2** the edge or rim of something, especially a container for liquid. **3** part of the edge of such a rim that has been extended to form a small spout □ *the lip of the milk jug.* **4** *slang* cheek. • **lippy** *adj* cheeky. • **to give someone lip** to talk in a cheeky way. • **keep a stiff upper lip** to show no emotion or worry when faced with difficulties. ⓒ Anglo-Saxon as *lippa*.

lip- see LIPO-

lip gloss ▻ *noun* a substance applied to the lips to give them a glossy appearance.

lipid /ˈlɪpɪd/ ▻ *noun, biochem* any of a group of organic compounds, mainly oils and fats, that occur naturally in living organisms, and are generally insoluble in water. ⓒ 1920s: LIP- + -ID².

lipo- /lɪpoʊ, laɪpoʊ, -ˈpɒ/ or (before vowels) **lip-** ▻ *combining form, signifying* fat. ⓒ From Greek *lipos* fat.

lipogram /ˈlɪpoʊgram/ ▻ *noun* a piece of writing, usually in verse form, in which all the words containing a certain letter are omitted. ⓒ 18c: from Greek *lipogrammatos* lacking a letter.

lipography /lɪˈpɒgrəfɪ/ ▻ *noun* the accidental omission of a letter or letters in writing or typing. ⓒ 19c: from Greek *leipein* to leave and -GRAPHY.

lipoprotein ▻ *noun* a water-soluble protein that carries cholesterol in the blood. ⓒ Early 20c.

liposome /ˈlɪpoʊsoʊm, ˈlaɪpoʊ-/ ▻ *noun* **1** a naturally-occurring lipid globule in the cytoplasm of a cell. **2** an artificial droplet of an aqueous substance surrounded by a lipid, used in the treatment of various diseases. ⓒ Early 20c.

liposuction ▻ *noun* a surgical process, done for cosmetic reasons, where excess fat is removed from the body by sucking it out through an incision in the skin. ⓒ Late 20c.

lipped ▻ *adj* said especially of a container: having a lip.

lip-read /ˈlɪpriːd/ ▻ *verb* said eg of a deaf person: to make sense of what someone is saying by watching the movement of their lips. • **lip-reader** *noun*. • **lip-reading** *noun*.

lip-service ▻ *noun* **1** insincere praise or worship. **2** respect or loyalty that someone appears to show, but which is not really held. • **pay lip-service to someone** or **something** to pretend to agree with someone or approve of an idea, etc without really doing so.

lip-smacking ▻ *adj, colloq* delicious.

lipstick ▻ *noun* a stick of cosmetic colouring for the lips.

lip-synch or **lip-sync** /ˈlɪpsɪŋk/ ▻ *verb* (***lip-synched, lip-synching***) to move the lips to make it look as though some pre-recorded music or dialogue is actually happening live. ▻ *noun* **1** the act of lip-synching. **2** in dubbing: the synchronization of sound with already-filmed lip movements. ⓒ 1950s: from *lip* + *synch*ronize.

liq. ▻ *abbreviation* **1** liquid. **2** liquor.

liquefaction /lɪkwɪˈfakʃən/ ▻ *noun* the process of LIQUEFYING.

liquefied natural gas ▻ *noun* (abbreviation **LNG**) NATURAL GAS in the liquid state, consisting mainly of methane, used as a domestic fuel.

liquefied petroleum gas ▻ *noun* (abbreviation **LPG**) butane, propane or pentane in liquid form, used as a portable fuel, eg in cigarette lighters and camping stoves.

liquefy /ˈlɪkwɪfaɪ/ ▻ *verb* (***liquefies, liquefied, liquefying***) *tr & intr* to make or become liquid. • **liquefiable** *adj*. • **liquefier** *noun*. ⓒ 15c: from Latin *liquere* to be liquid + *facere* to make.

liqueur /lɪˈkjʊə(r)/ ▻ *noun* **1** a potent alcoholic drink, sweetened and highly flavoured, and usually drunk at the end of a meal. **2** a sweet, usually with a chocolate outer shell and a filling that has the flavour of a particular liqueur. ⓒ 18c: from Latin *liquor*, from *liquere* to be liquid.

liqueur glass ▻ *noun* a very small glass used for serving liqueurs.

liquid /ˈlɪkwɪd/ ▻ *noun* **1 a** a state of matter between SOLID and GAS, where the volume remains constant, but the shape depends on that of its container; **b** any substance in a water-like state. **2** *phonetics* the sound of *l* or *r*. ▻ *adj* **1** said of a substance: able to flow and change shape. **2** like water in appearance, especially in being clear. **3** flowing and smooth. **4** said of sounds: harmonious. **5** said of assets: able to be easily changed into cash. **6** said of eyes: tearful. ⓒ 14c: from Latin *liquidus* liquid or clear.

liquid ammonia see AMMONIA

liquidate /ˈlɪkwɪdeɪt/ ▻ *verb* (***liquidated, liquidating***) **1** to bring to an end the trading of (an individual or a company), and have debts and assets calculated. **2** to turn (assets) into cash. **3** to pay off (a debt). **4** to eliminate. **5** *euphemistic, slang* **a** to get rid of someone by killing, often violently and in mass numbers; **b** to suppress or put an end to something or get rid of something, usually by violent or illegal means. ⓒ 16c: from Latin *liquidare* to make clear.

liquidation /lɪkwɪˈdeɪʃən/ ▻ *noun* **1** the bringing to an end of a company's trading. **2** *euphemistic, slang* **a** killing, often violently and in mass numbers; **b** suppressing, ending or getting rid of something, usually in a violent or illegal way. • **go into liquidation** said of a company, etc: to stop trading and have debts and assets calculated.

liquidator ▻ *noun* **1** an accountant called in to wind up a company's trading. **2** *euphemistic, slang* a group or someone who carries out a violent killing or killings or puts an end to something violently or illegally.

liquid crystal ▻ *noun, chem* any of a number of organic compounds that flow like a liquid but resemble solid crystalline substances in their optical properties, eg having colour that is temperature-dependent. They are used in electronic devices, and in medicine, eg to indicate small temperature differences of the skin. Ⓒ Late 19c.

liquid crystal display ▻ *noun* (abbreviation **LCD**) in digital watches, calculators, etc: a display of numbers or letters produced by applying an electric field across a LIQUID CRYSTAL solution sandwiched between two transparent electrodes, so that individual segments of the display are selectively darkened. Ⓒ 1960s.

liquidize or **liquidise** ▻ *verb* (***liquidized, liquidizing***) **1** to make liquid. **2** to make food, etc into a liquid or purée, especially by using a liquidizer. Ⓒ 19c.

liquidizer or **liquidiser** ▻ *noun* a machine used to liquidize or purée food.

liquid lunch ▻ *noun, Brit jocular* a lunchtime refreshment consisting of alcohol rather than food.

liquid oxygen ▻ *noun* a pale blue transparent liquid formed by the cooling of oxygen gas, used in rocket propellants.

liquid paper see CORRECTING FLUID

liquid paraffin ▻ *noun* a colourless mineral oil derived from petroleum, used as a lubricant and laxative. *N Amer equivalent* MINERAL OIL

liquor /ˈlɪkə(r)/ ▻ *noun* **1** strong alcoholic drink, especially some that has been distilled. **2** any fluid substance, especially water or liquid produced in cooking. **3** *pharmacol* a solution of a drug or chemical in water. Ⓒ 13c: from Latin *liquor*, from *liquere* to be liquid.

liquorice or **licorice** /ˈlɪkərɪs, -ɪʃ/ ▻ *noun* **1** a Mediterranean plant with sweet roots used to make confectionery and also in medicine, mainly as a laxative. **2** a black sticky sweet made from the juice of the roots of this plant. Ⓒ 13c: from Greek *glykys* sweet + *rhiza* root.

liquorice allsorts ▻ *plural noun* an assortment of liquorice-flavoured sweets.

lira /ˈlɪərə/ ▻ *noun* (***lire*** or ***liras***) the standard unit of currency in Italy and Turkey. Ⓒ 17c: Italian, from Latin *libra* pound.

lisle /laɪl/ ▻ *noun* fine smooth cotton thread used for making gloves, stockings and underwear. Ⓒ 19c: named after Lisle (now Lille), a town in N France, where it was first made.

LISP /lɪsp/ ▻ *noun* a general purpose programming language in which the expressions are represented as lists. Ⓒ 1950s: from *list* + *processing*.

lisp ▻ *verb* (***lisped, lisping***) **1** *intr* to pronounce the sounds of *s* and *z* in the same way as the *th* sounds in *thin* and *this* respectively. **2** to say or pronounce in this way. **3** to speak in an affectedly childish way. ▻ *noun* **1** the act or habit of lisping. **2** a speech defect distinguished by lisping. • **lisper** *noun*. • **lisping** *noun, adj*. • **lispingly** *adverb*. Ⓒ Anglo-Saxon *wlisp* lisping.

lissom or **lissome** /ˈlɪsəm/ ▻ *adj* graceful and supple in shape or movement. Ⓒ 19c: from LITHE + -SOME[1].

list[1] ▻ *noun* **1** a series of names, numbers, prices, etc printed out, written down or said one after the other. **2** *computing* an arrangement of data in a file. ▻ *verb* (***listed, listing***) **1** to make a list of something. **2** to add to a list. **3** to include in a list. See LISTS, LISTING, LISTED BUILDING. Ⓒ From Anglo-Saxon *liste* border.

list[2] ▻ *verb* (***listed, listing***) *intr* said especially of ships: to lean over to one side. ▻ *noun* the act of listing or a listing position. Ⓒ 17c.

list[3] ▻ *noun* **1** the SELVAGE on woven textile fabrics. **2** a strip, especially one cut from a border. **3** a border. ▻ *verb* (***listed, listing***) to border. See LISTS. Ⓒ From Anglo-Saxon *liste* border.

list[4] ▻ *verb* (***listed, listing***) *archaic, poetic* **1** *intr* to listen. **2** to listen to something. Ⓒ Anglo-Saxon *hlystan*.

listed building ▻ *noun* a building of particular architectural or historical interest, which it is not permitted to destroy or change.

listed company ▻ *noun, stock exchange* a company that has securities listed on the Stock Exchange.

listen /ˈlɪsən/ ▻ *verb* (***listened, listening***) *intr* **1** (*also* listen to someone or **something**) to try to hear them or it. **2** (*also* **listen to someone** or **something**) to pay attention to them or it. **3** to follow advice □ *I warned him but he wouldn't listen*. • **listen to reason** see under REASON.

listener ▻ *noun* **1** someone who listens. **2** someone who listens to radio programmes.

listeria /lɪˈstɪərɪə/ ▻ *noun* a bacterium sometimes found in certain foods, eg chicken and soft cheese, which if not killed in cooking may cause the serious disease **listeriosis**, which can cause death or miscarriage. Ⓒ 1940: named after Joseph Lister (1827–1912), British surgeon and pioneer of antiseptics.

listing ▻ *noun* **1** a list. **2** a position in a list. **3** *computing* a printout of a file or a program. **4** *stock exchange* an official quotation for stock so that it can be traded on the Stock Exchange. **5** (**listings**) a guide to what is currently available in entertainment such as the cinema, live music or the theatre. Ⓒ 17c: from Anglo-Saxon *list*.

listless ▻ *adj* tired and lacking energy or interest. • **listlessly** *adverb*. • **listlessness** *noun*. Ⓒ 15c: from 13c *list* desire + -LESS.

list price ▻ *noun* **1** the recommended price for something as shown in a manufacturer's catalogue or advertisement. **2** the price of something before any deductions have been made.

lists ▻ *plural noun, historical* **1** the barriers enclosing an area used for jousting and tournaments. **2** any scene of combat or conflict. • **enter the lists 1** to give or accept a challenge. **2** to start or become involved in a fight or controversy. Ⓒ 14c: from Anglo-Saxon *liste* a border.

lit[1] *past tense, past participle of* LIGHT[1], LIGHT[3]

lit[2] or **lit.** ▻ *abbreviation* **1** literary or literature. **2** literal or literally.

litany /ˈlɪtənɪ/ ▻ *noun* (***litanies***) **1** *Christianity* a series of prayers or supplications with a response which is repeated several times by the congregation. **2** (**the Litany**) the 'general supplication' as it appears in the Book of Common Prayer. **3** a long tedious list □ *a litany of jobs to be done*. Ⓒ 13c: from Greek *litaneia* prayer.

litchi see LYCHEE

lit crit see under LITERARY CRITICISM

lite see LIGHT[2]

liter see LITRE

literacy /ˈlɪtərəsɪ/ ▻ *noun* **1** the ability to read and write. **2** the ability to use language in an accomplished and efficient way. Ⓒ 15c: from LITERATE.

literal /ˈlɪtərəl/ ▻ *adj* **1** said of words or a text: following the exact meaning, without allegorical or metaphorical interpretation. **2** said of a translation: following the words of the original exactly. **3** *derog* said of a person: unimaginative and matter-of-fact. **4** true; exact □ *the literal truth*. ▻ *noun, printing* a misprint of one letter. Ⓒ 15c: from Latin *literalis*, from *litera* letter.

literalism ▻ *noun* **1** strict adherence to the literal meaning of words. **2** *art, derog* the representation of a subject in an exact and unimaginative way.

literalist ▻ *noun* an advocate of literalism, especially in cinema, art, literature, theatre, etc.

literally ▻ *adverb* **1** word for word. **2 a** often used as an intensifier in figurative contexts: actually; really; absolutely □ *They literally flew down the road*; **b** said of an interpretation of words, etc that is without allusion or metaphor: really □ *Put that mirror away — I didn't mean that you literally had egg on your face!*

> ***literally***
>
> ● In sense 2a, **literally** is often regarded as incorrect or as poor style, but it is an appropriate intensifier within the context of the idiom it is intensifying; other intensifiers like **really** and **utterly** would not work within the image or metaphor on which the the idiom is based □ *The red carpet was literally out for them* □ *Nurses are literally worrying themselves sick trying to cope with the increased pressures of their jobs* □ *It was literally a dream come true.*
>
> ● Often, the use of **literally** signals the relevance and punning nature of the idiom, especially when it is a cliché, as in some of the examples above. Occasionally, the effect is comic: □ *People have been literally beside themselves with frustration.*
>
> ☆ RECOMMENDATION: **literally** is in common use to intensify an idiom, and this is not incorrect; but beware of unintentionally bizarre or humorous effects.

literary /ˈlɪtərərɪ/ ▷ *adj* **1** referring or relating to, or concerned with, literature or writing. **2** said of a person: knowing a great deal about canonical literature. **3** said of a word: formal; used in literature, especially older literature. ⓒ 17c: from Latin *literarius*, from *litera* letter.

literary agent ▷ *noun* someone who acts on behalf of a writer, especially in dealing with publishers.

literary critic ▷ *noun* someone who evaluates and writes about works of literature.

literary criticism ▷ *noun* (abbreviation **lit crit**) the business of forming evaluative opinions and writing about works of literature. ⓒ Late 19c.

literate /ˈlɪtərət/ ▷ *adj* **1** able to read and write. **2** educated. **3** *in compounds* competent and experienced in something specified □ *computer-literate.* ▷ *noun* **1** someone who is literate. **2** someone who is educated, but who does not hold a university degree, especially a candidate for the priesthood. ⓒ 15c: from Latin *literatus* from *litera* letter.

literati /lɪtəˈrɑːtiː/ ▷ *plural noun* **1** learned people. **2** people who consider themselves to be knowledgeable about literature. ⓒ 17c: Latin, from *literatus* literate.

literature /ˈlɪtərətʃə(r), ˈlɪtrə-/ ▷ *noun* **1** written material, such as novels, poems and plays, that is valued for its language and content. **2** the whole body of written works of a particular country or period in time □ *American literature.* **3** the whole body of information published on a particular subject □ *scientific literature.* **4** the art or works produced by a writer. **5** *colloq* any printed matter, especially advertising leaflets. ⓒ 14c: from Latin *literatura*, from *litera* letter.

-lith ▷ *combining form, denoting* stone or rock □ *monolith.* ⓒ From Greek *lithos* stone.

litharge /ˈlɪθɑːdʒ/ ▷ *noun* lead monoxide. ⓒ 14c: from Greek *lithos* stone + *argyros* silver.

lithe /laɪð/ ▷ *adj* (*lither, lithest*) supple and flexible. ● **lithely** *adverb.* ● **litheness** *noun.* ⓒ 15c in this sense; Anglo-Saxon *meaning* 'gentle' or 'soft'.

lithia /ˈlɪθɪə/ ▷ *noun* lithium oxide, a white or colourless powder used in ceramics and in the manufacture of lithium salts. ⓒ 19c: from Greek *lithos* stone.

lithium /ˈlɪθɪəm/ ▷ *noun, chem* (symbol **Li**, atomic number 3) a soft silvery reactive metal, the lightest solid element, used in batteries and certain alloys, compounds of which are used in lubricants, glass, ceramics and drugs for treating certain psychiatric disorders. ⓒ 19c: from Greek *lithos* stone.

litho /ˈlaɪθoʊ/ ▷ *noun* (*lithos*) **1** a LITHOGRAPH. **2** LITHOGRAPHY. ▷ *adj* lithographic. ▷ *verb* (*lithos* or *lithoes, lithoed, lithoeing*) to lithograph.

litho- /lɪθoʊ, laɪ-, -θə; lɪˈθɒ, laɪ-/ or (*before a vowel*) **lith-** ▷ *combining form, denoting* stone. ⓒ From Greek *lithos* stone.

lithograph /ˈlɪθəgrɑːf/ ▷ *noun* a picture or print made using lithography. ▷ *verb* (*lithographed, lithographing*) to print (images, etc) using lithography. ⓒ 18c.

lithographic /lɪθəˈgrafɪk/ ▷ *adj* relating to or using lithography. ● **lithographically** *adverb.*

lithography /lɪˈθɒgrəfɪ/ ▷ *noun* a method of printing using a stone or metal plate which has been treated so that the ink adheres only to the design or image to be printed. ● **lithographer** *noun.* ⓒ 18c: LITHO- + -GRAPHY 2.

lithology /lɪˈθɒlədʒɪ/ *mineralogy* ▷ *noun* the study and description of the gross physical characteristics that define a particular rock, including colour, texture, mineral composition, and grain size. ● **lithological** /lɪθəˈlɪdʒɪkəl/ *adj.* ● **lithologist** *noun.* ⓒ 18c.

lithophyte /ˈlɪθəfaɪt/ ▷ *noun* **1** *bot* any plant that grows on rocks or stones. **2** *zool* any polyp that is partly composed of hard or stony material, eg a coral. ● **lithophytic** /-ˈfɪtɪk/ *adj.* ⓒ 18c.

lithosphere /ˈlɪθoʊsfɪə(r)/ *geol* ▷ *noun* the rigid outer layer of the Earth, consisting of the crust and the solid, outermost layer of the upper MANTLE. ● **lithospheric** /-ˈsfɛrɪk/ *adj.* ⓒ 19c.

lithotomy /lɪˈθɪtəmɪ/ ▷ *noun* (*lithotomies*) a surgical operation to remove a calculus from an organ of the body, especially from the bladder. ⓒ 18c.

lithotripsy /ˈlɪθoʊtrɪpsɪ/ and **lithotrity** *surgery* ▷ *noun* the crushing of a stone in the bladder, kidney or gall bladder, so that its fragments can then be passed in the urine. ● **lithotripter** or **lithotriptor** *noun* a device, often using ULTRASOUND, that administers a high-energy shock wave to shatter stones in the bladder, etc, which can then be passed in the urine. ⓒ 19c: from LITHO- + Greek *thruptein* to crush.

Lithuanian /lɪθjʊˈeɪnɪən/ ▷ *adj* **1** belonging or relating to Lithuania, a republic in NE Europe that borders on the Baltic, or to its inhabitants, or their language. ▷ *noun* **1** a citizen or inhabitant of, or person born in, Lithuania. **2** the official language of Lithuania.

litigant /ˈlɪtɪgənt/ ▷ *noun* someone involved in a lawsuit.

litigate /ˈlɪtɪgeɪt/ ▷ *verb* (*litigated, litigating*) **1** *intr* to be involved in a lawsuit. **2** to contest (a point, claim, etc) in a lawsuit. ⓒ 17c: from Latin *litigare*, from *lis* lawsuit + *agere* to do.

litigation /lɪtɪˈgeɪʃən/ ▷ *noun* **1** action at law. **2** legal contest.

litigious /lɪˈtɪdʒəs/ ▷ *adj* **1** relating to litigation or lawsuits. **2** inclined to taking legal action over arguments, problems, etc. **3** disputable in a court of law. ● **litigiously** *adverb.* ● **litigiousness** *noun.* ⓒ 14c: from Latin *litigium* quarrel.

litmus /ˈlɪtməs/ ▷ *noun, chem* a dye obtained from certain lichens, widely used as an indicator to distinguish between acid solutions, in which it turns red, and alkaline ones, in which it turns blue. ⓒ 16c: from Norse *litmosi* dyeing-moss.

litmus paper ▷ *noun, chem* paper that has been treated with litmus, and which is used to test for acidity and alkalinity.

litmus test ▷ *noun* **1** *chem* a chemical test for relative acidity or alkalinity using litmus paper. **2** *non-technical* an event or action that serves as a definitive test or trial of something.

litotes /ˈlaɪtoutiːz/ ▻ *noun, rhetoric* understatement used for effect, especially by negating the opposite, as in *not a little angry* meaning *furious*. Also called **meiosis**. Compare HYPERBOLE. ⓒ 17c: Greek, meaning 'small'.

litre or (*N Amer, especially US*) **liter** /ˈliːtə(r)/ ▻ *noun* (*litres*) **1 a** in the metric system: the basic unit of volume, equal to one cubic decimetre (10 000 cubic centimetres) or about 1.76 pints; **b** from 1901 to 1964, this was defined as the volume of a kilogram of distilled water at 4°C at standard atmospheric pressure. **2** *in compounds, signifying* the capacity of the cylinders of a motor vehicle engine □ *a three-litre engine*. ⓒ 18c: suggested by *litron* an obsolete French measure of capacity, from Greek *litra* pound.

litter /ˈlɪtə(r)/ ▻ *noun* **1** discarded paper, rubbish, etc lying in a public place. **2** a number of animals born to the same mother at the same time □ *a litter of five grey kittens*. **3** any scattered or confused collection of objects. **4** straw, hay, etc used as bedding for animals. **5** *old use* a framework consisting of cloth stretched tight between two long poles, used to carry sick or wounded people. **6** *old use* a framework consisting of a couch covered by curtains, with poles on either side, for transporting a single passenger. ▻ *verb* (*littered, littering*) **1** to make something untidy by spreading litter or objects about. **2** said of objects: to lie untidily around (a room, etc). **3** said of animals: to give birth to (young). **4** to give bedding litter to (animals). ⓒ 14c: from French *litiere*.

litter bin and **litter basket** ▻ *noun* a container in which small items of rubbish can be put.

litter-lout ▻ *noun, Brit colloq* someone who deliberately drops litter outside.

litter tray ▻ *noun* a tray kept indoors, in which a cat can urinate and defecate.

little /ˈlɪtəl/ ▻ *adj* (*littler, littlest*) (often having connotations of affection or another emotion and used instead of the more formal *small*) **1** small in size, extent or amount. **2** young; younger □ *a little girl* □ *her little brother*. **3** small in importance □ *a little mishap*. **4** trivial □ *a little misunderstanding*. **5** petty □ *a little disagreement*. **6** used as a way of detracting from a potentially disparaging implication: not troublesome □ *funny little ways*. **7** small-minded or mean □ *He's a little liar*. ▻ *adverb* (*comparative* **less**, *superlative* **least**) not much or at all □ *They little understood the implications*. ▻ *pronoun* not much □ *little to be gained from that course of action*. • **a little** (with a noun such as *bit, while, way* understood but not expressed) **1** a small amount □ *do a little to help out*. **2** a short time □ *He'll be here in a little*. **3** a short distance □ *down the road a little*. **4** a small degree or extent □ *run around a little to keep warm*. • **little by little** gradually; by degrees. • **make little of something** **1** to treat it as unimportant or trivial. **2** to understand only a little of it. • **think little of something** or **someone** to have a low opinion of it or them; to disapprove of it or them. • **not a little** very □ *He was not a little upset*. See also LESS, LESSER, LEAST. ⓒ Anglo-Saxon *lytel*.

the Little Bear (*Brit*) and (*US*) **the Little Dipper** ▻ *noun* URSA MINOR.

little end ▻ *noun* the smaller end of the main connecting rod in a car engine. Compare BIG END.

little finger ▻ *noun* the fifth and smallest finger of the hand. See also PINKIE. • **wrap** or **twist someone round one's little finger** see under FINGER.

little grebe ▻ *noun* a small waterfowl belonging to the GREBE family. Also called **dabchick**.

little green men *plural* ▻ *noun* imagined alien life forms. ⓒ 1906.

little people ▻ *plural noun, folklore* fairies. ⓒ 18c.

little slam and **small slam** ▻ *noun, cards, especially bridge*: the winning of all but one trick, or the contract to do so. Compare GRAND SLAM.

littoral /ˈlɪtərəl/ ▻ *adj* **1** on or near the shore of a sea or lake. **2** said of plants or animals: inhabiting the area on or near the shore of a sea or lake. ▻ *noun* the shore or an area of land on a shore or coast. ⓒ 17c: from Latin *littoralis*, from *litus* shore.

liturgy /ˈlɪtədʒɪ/ ▻ *noun* (*liturgies*) **1** the standard form of service in a church. **2** the service of Holy Communion in the Eastern Orthodox Church. • **liturgical** /lɪˈtɜːdʒɪkəl/ *adj*. • **liturgically** *adverb*. ⓒ 16c: from Greek *leitourgia* public service.

live[1] /lɪv/ ▻ *verb* (*lived, living*) (*intr* in all senses except 7 and 9) **1** to have life. **2** to be alive. **3** to continue to be alive. **4** to survive or to escape death. **5** to have a home or dwelling □ *We live in a small flat*. **6** to lead one's life in a certain way □ *live well*. **7** to pass or spend □ *live a happy life in the country*. **8** to enjoy life passionately or to the full □ *They really know how to live*. **9** to express (one's beliefs, etc) in one's life; to live in accordance with (one's beliefs, etc) □ *live one's religion*. • **live and breathe something** *colloq* to be very enthusiastic about it □ *lives and breathes football*. • **live and learn** *colloq* to learn by experience. • **live beyond one's means** *colloq* to spend more than one can really afford. Compare *live within one's means* below. • **live and let live** *colloq* to be tolerant of others and expect toleration in return. • **live by one's wits** see under WIT. • **lived-in** see separate entry. • **live for the moment** *colloq* to live without thinking of the future. • **live from hand to mouth** see under HAND. • **live in an ivory tower** *colloq* often said of academics: to be shut off from reality. • **live it up** *colloq* to fill one's life with excitement and pleasure, often excessively. • **live on borrowed time** *colloq* to live longer than might have been expected. • **live out of a suitcase** *colloq* to live in different places for very short spells, never having time to unpack. • **live through something** to undergo (an unpleasant experience). • **live within one's means** *colloq* to spend no more than one can afford. • **live with oneself** *with negatives and in questions* to maintain one's self-respect. ⓒ Anglo-Saxon *lifian* and *libban*.

■ **live by something** **1** to get a living from it □ *live by farming*. **2** to order one's life according to (certain principles) □ *lived by the teachings of Christ*.

■ **live something down** said after someone has made a mistake or blunder: to carry on living until something has been forgotten or forgiven by other people □ *He lived down the shame of his arrest*.

■ **live for someone** or **something** **1** to make them or it one's main concern. **2** to look forward to it.

■ **live in** to live in accommodation supplied at one's workplace.

■ **live off someone** or **something** to be supported by them or it □ *live off the land*.

■ **live on** to continue or last □ *Memories live on*.

■ **live on something** to have a diet that mainly consists of (one kind of food) □ *live on rice*.

■ **live with someone** usually said where a sexual relationship is implied: to share accommodation with them □ *He lives with his girlfriend*.

■ **live with something** **1** to continue to suffer from or be haunted by the memory of it □ *will live with the mistake for the rest of his life*. **2** to put up with it □ *He has to live with psoriasis*.

■ **live together** said of a couple, especially one in a sexual relationship: to share the same home.

■ **live up to someone** or **something** **1** to become as respected as them □ *could never live up to his brother*. **2** to turn out in a manner worthy of them or it □ *tried to live up to her parents' expectations*.

live[2] /laɪv/ ▻ *adj* **1** having life; not dead. **2** said of a radio or TV broadcast: heard or seen as the event takes place and not from a recording. **3** said of a record, video, etc: recorded during a performance. **4** said of a wire:

connected to a source of electrical power. **5** said of coal, etc: still glowing or burning. **6** said of a bomb, etc: still capable of exploding. **7** up-to-date; relevant □ *tackles live issues.* **8** said of a volcano: still liable to erupt. **9** said of entertainments: playing to an audience □ *a good live band.* **10** *computing* fully operational. **11** said of yoghurt: containing live bacteria. **12** authentic □ *saw a real live astronaut.* **13** *acoustics* having a long reverberation time. ▻ *adverb* at, during, or as a live performance □ *They had to perform live on stage.* Ⓒ 16c: from ALIVE.

liveable /ˈlɪvəbəl/ ▻ *adj* **1** said of a house, etc: fit to live in. **2** said of life: worth living. • **liveable with** *colloq* said of a person: friendly and easy to live with.

live-cell therapy ▻ *noun, medicine* the injection of specially prepared animal tissue into the muscles of humans in order to stimulate the regeneration of damaged cells and tissues. Also called **cellular therapy.**

lived-in /ˈlɪvdɪn/ ▻ *adj* **1** said of a room, etc: having a comfortable, homely feeling. **2** said of a face: marked by life's experiences.

live-in /ˈlɪvɪn/ ▻ *adj* **1** said of a worker: living where one works □ *a live-in nanny.* **2** said of a sexual partner: sharing the same home □ *a live-in lover.*

livelihood /ˈlaɪvlɪhʊd/ ▻ *noun* a means of earning a living. Ⓒ Anglo-Saxon *liflad*, from *lif* life + *lad* course.

livelong /ˈlɪvlɒŋ/ ▻ *adj, poetic* said of the day or night: complete, in all its pleasant or tedious length. Ⓒ 14c: from *lief* dear + *longe* long.

lively /ˈlaɪvlɪ/ ▻ *adj* (*livelier, liveliest*) **1** active and full of life, energy and high spirits. **2** brisk. **3** vivid or bright. • **liveliness** *noun.* • **look lively!** *colloq* get going! Ⓒ Anglo-Saxon *liflic.*

liven /ˈlaɪvən/ ▻ *verb* (**livened, livening**) *tr & intr* (*usually* **liven up**) to make or become lively.

liver¹ /ˈlɪvə(r)/ ▻ *noun* **1** in vertebrates: a large dark red glandular organ situated just below the diaphragm, whose main function is to regulate the chemical composition of the blood. **2** this organ in certain animals, used as food. ▻ *adj* dark reddish-brown in colour. Ⓒ Anglo-Saxon *lifer.*

liver² ▻ *noun in compounds* someone who lives their life in the way specified □ *a riotous liver.*

liver fluke ▻ *noun* a leaf-like parasitic flatworm that invades the liver of vertebrates and can be a serious pest of domesticated animals.

liverish ▻ *adj* **1** *old use* suffering from a disordered liver. **2** easily annoyed or made angry. • **liverishness** *noun.*

Liverpudlian /lɪvəˈpʌdlɪən/ ▻ *noun* a native or citizen of Liverpool in NW England. ▻ *adj* referring or related to Liverpool or its inhabitants. Ⓒ 19c: from Liverpool, with *-puddle* facetiously substituted for *-pool* + -IAN.

liver salts ▻ *plural noun* mineral salts taken to relieve indigestion and upset stomachs.

liver sausage and *N Amer* **liverwurst** /ˈlɪvəwɜːst/ ▻ *noun* finely minced liver combined with either pork or veal and made into a sausage shape, served as a spread on bread, toast or canapes.

liver spot ▻ *noun* a brown mark on the skin, usually appearing in old age.

liveware /ˈlaɪvwɛə(r)/ ▻ *noun, colloq* the people who work with a computer system, as distinct from HARDWARE and SOFTWARE.

liverwort /ˈlɪvəwɜːt/ ▻ *noun* any of a class of small spore-bearing plants without a vascular system, closely related to mosses, typically growing in moist shady conditions. Ⓒ Anglo-Saxon *liferwyrt*, so called because the leaves resemble the lobes of a liver and because the plant was once used to treat complaints of the liver.

livery /ˈlɪvərɪ/ ▻ *noun* (**liveries**) **1** a distinctive uniform worn by male servants belonging to a particular household or by the members of a particular trade guild. **2** any distinctive uniform or style, especially as used by companies so that their employees, vehicles, etc can be easily identified. **3** the distinctive colours and decoration used to identify the buses, aircraft, etc operated by a particular company. **4** the feeding, care, stabling and hiring out of horses for money. **5** *literary* distinctive markings or outward appearance □ *the trees in their autumn livery.* • **liveried** *adj.* Ⓒ 14c: from French *livree*, from Latin *liberare* to free.

livery company ▻ *noun, Brit* any of several trade guilds in the City of London, whose members began to wear distinctive clothes in the 14c.

livery horse ▻ *noun* a horse kept in a livery stable.

liveryman ▻ *noun* **1** *Brit* a freeman of the City of London entitled to certain privileges and to wear the livery of his company. **2** someone who works in or keeps a livery stable.

livery stable ▻ *noun* a place where people may keep their horses or where horses may be hired.

lives /laɪvz/ *plural of* LIFE

livestock /ˈlaɪvstɒk/ ▻ *singular or plural noun* domesticated animals, especially sheep, cattle, pigs and poultry, kept for the production of meat, milk, wool, etc, or for breeding purposes. Ⓒ 18c:.

live wire /ˈlaɪv —/ ▻ *noun, colloq* someone who is full of energy and enthusiasm.

livid /ˈlɪvɪd/ ▻ *adj* **1** *colloq* extremely angry. **2** having the greyish colour of lead. **3** said of a bruise: black and blue. **4** white or very pale. • **lividity** *noun.* • **lividly** *adverb.* • **lividness** *noun.* Ⓒ 17c: from Latin *lividus* lead-coloured.

living /ˈlɪvɪŋ/ ▻ *adj* **1** having life; alive. **2** currently in existence, use or activity. **3** said of a likeness: exact. **4** (**the living**) people who are alive (see THE 4b). ▻ *noun* **1** livelihood or means of subsisting. **2** a manner of life □ *riotous living.* **3** *C of E* a position as a vicar or rector which has an income or property attached to it. • **beat** or **scare the living daylights out of someone** to give them a severe beating or fright. • **within living memory** within a period of time remembered by people who are still alive. Ⓒ 14c: from Anglo-Saxon *lifian, libban.*

living death ▻ *noun* a time of unrelenting misery.

living proof ▻ *noun* an excellent example □ *living proof that the treatment worked.*

living-room ▻ *noun* a room in a house, etc where people sit and relax.

Livingstone daisy /ˈlɪvɪŋstən —/ ▻ *noun* a succulent plant, native to arid regions of S Africa, with swollen fleshy leaves and large colourful daisy-like yellow, pink or mauve flowers. Ⓒ 1930s.

living wage ▻ *noun* a wage which can support a wage-earner and family.

lizard /ˈlɪzəd/ ▻ *noun* any of numerous small reptiles, closely related to snakes, but with movable eyelids, much less flexible jaws and in most species four well-developed limbs and a tapering tail. Ⓒ 14c: from Latin *lacerta* lizard.

LJ ▻ *abbreviation* Lord Justice.

L.L. ▻ *abbreviation* Late Latin or Low Latin.

'll /l, əl/ ▻ *verb* (usually with a pronoun) ▻ *contraction of* SHALL and WILL □ *I'll* □ *they'll.*

llama /ˈlɑːmə/ ▻ *noun* (**llamas**) **1** a domesticated hoofed S American mammal related to the camel, with a long shaggy white, brown or black coat, a long neck and large ears, kept for its meat, milk and wool, and used as a beast of burden. **2** the wool obtained from this animal. **3** cloth made of this wool. Ⓒ 17c: Spanish, from Quechua.

LLB ▻ *abbreviation*: *legum baccalaureus* (Latin), Bachelor of Laws.

LLD ▻ *abbreviation*: *legum doctor* (Latin), Doctor of Laws.

lm ▷ *abbreviation, physics* lumen, the SI unit of luminous flux.

LMS ▷ *abbreviation* local management of schools, the system where a school's board of governors is responsible for managing its allocated budget.

LNG ▷ *abbreviation* liquefied natural gas.

lo /loʊ/ ▷ *exclamation, old use* look! see! • **lo and behold** *usually facetious* an exclamation used to introduce some startling revelation. ◷ Anglo-Saxon *la*.

loach /loʊtʃ/ ▷ *noun* (***loaches***) a small freshwater fish of the carp family, found throughout Europe and Asia, usually under 10cm (4in) in length, with a slender body and spines around its mouth, often kept as an aquarium fish. ◷ 14c: from French *loche*.

load ▷ *noun* **1** something that is carried or transported. **2 a** an amount that is or can be carried or transported at one time; **b** *in compounds* □ *lorryload of bricks*. **3** a burden. **4** a cargo. **5** a specific quantity, varying according to the type of goods. **6** the weight carried by a structure, etc. **7** (**loads**) *colloq* a large amount □ *loads of time*. **8** duties, feelings, etc which are oppressive and heavy to bear. **9** an amount or number of things to be dealt with at one time. **10** the power carried by an electric circuit. **11** the power output of an engine. **12** the amount of work imposed on or expected of someone □ *a heavy teaching load*. **13** a single discharge from a gun. ▷ *verb* (***loaded, loading***) **1** to put (cargo, passengers, etc) on (a ship, vehicle, plane, etc). **2** to put something in or on something else as a load □ *load the dishwasher*. **3** *photog* to put (film) in (a camera). **4** to weigh down or overburden. **5** to be a weight on or burden to someone or something; to oppress. **6** *computing* **a** to put (a disk, computer tape, etc) into a drive, so that it may be used; **b** to transfer (a program or data) into main memory, so that it may be used. See DOWNLOAD. **7** to put (ammunition) into (a gun). **8** to give weight or bias to (dice, a roulette wheel, a question, etc). **9** to put a large amount of (paint) on (a paintbrush or canvas). **10** *insurance* to add charges to. **11** to add a substance to (wine, etc). • **a load of something** *colloq, derisive* a lot of it □ *What a load of rubbish!* • **a load off one's mind** a relief. • **get a load of something** *slang* to pay attention to, listen to, or look at it □ *Get a load of those orange leggings!* • **have** or **get a load on** *N Amer slang* to be under the influence of alcohol or drugs, especially cocaine or marijuana. • **load the dice against someone** to deprive them of a fair chance. ◷ Anglo-Saxon *lad* course or journey.

▪ **load up** to take or pick up a load.

▪ **load someone with something** to give it lavishly or in great amounts to them.

load-bearing ▷ *adj* said of a wall, etc: supporting a structure, carrying a weight.

loaded ▷ *adj* **1** carrying a load; with a load in place. **2** said of a gun: containing bullets. **3** said of a camera: containing film. **4** *colloq* very wealthy. **5** *N Amer slang* under the influence of alcohol or drugs, especially cocaine or marijuana.

loaded question ▷ *noun* a question that is designed to bring out a specific kind of response.

loader ▷ *noun, in compounds* **1** said of a gun or machine, etc: loaded in a specified way □ *breech-loader*.

loading bay ▷ *noun* a space for loading and unloading vehicles.

loading gauge ▷ *noun* **1** a suspended bar that marks how high a railway truck may be loaded. **2** the maximum horizontal and vertical space that rolling-stock may safely occupy above the track.

loadline ▷ *noun* a line on a ship's side to mark the depth to which her cargo may be allowed to sink her. Also called PLIMSOLL LINE.

loadmaster ▷ *noun* the member of an aircrew who is in charge of the cargo.

loadsa- ▷ *combining form, signifying* a large amount. ◷ 1980s: a colloquialism for *loads of*, especially in *Loadsamoney*, a grotesque character created by the comedian, Harry Enfield.

load-shedding ▷ *noun* temporarily reducing the amount of electricity sent out by a power station.

loadstar see LODESTAR

loadstone see LODESTONE

lodestone or **loadstone** ▷ *noun* **1** *geol* a black, naturally occurring variety of the mineral magnetite, which has strong magnetic properties. **2** an elongated piece of this used as a magnet. **3** someone or something that attracts. ◷ 16c.

loaf¹ ▷ *noun* (***loaves*** /ˈloʊvz/) **1** a shaped lump of dough, especially after it has risen and been baked. **2** *in compounds* a quantity of food formed into a regular shape □ *meatloaf*. **3** *slang* the head or brains □ *Use your loaf*. ◷ Anglo-Saxon *hlaf*.

loaf² ▷ *verb* (***loafed, loafing***) *intr* to loiter. ▷ *noun* an act of loitering or lazing around. ◷ 19c.

▪ **loaf about, around** or **away** to pass the time or stand about idly; to hang about.

loafer ▷ *noun* **1** someone who loafs about. **2** a light casual shoe like a moccasin.

loaf sugar see SUGAR LOAF

loam ▷ *noun* **1** a dark fertile easily worked soil composed of sand, silt, small amounts of clay and humus. **2** a mixture basically of moist clay and sand used in making bricks, casting-moulds, plastering walls, etc. ▷ *verb* (***loamed, loaming***) to treat, cover or dress something with loam. • **loaminess** *noun*. • **loamy** *adj*. ◷ Anglo-Saxon *lam*.

loan ▷ *noun* **1** anything lent, especially money lent at interest. **2** an act of lending. **3** a state of being lent. **4** an arrangement for lending. **5** permission to use something □ *He asked for a loan of the car*. **6** short form of LOAN WORD. ▷ *verb* (***loaned, loaning***) to lend (especially money). • **on loan** given as a loan. ◷ 13c: from Norse *lan*.

> ***loan***
>
> See Usage Note at **lend**.

loan shark ▷ *noun, colloq* someone who lends money at exorbitant rates of interest. • **loan sharking** *noun* the business of lending money at very high interest rates.

loan translation see CALQUE

loanword ▷ *noun* a word taken into one language from another, usually retaining the original spelling; for example *penchant* is a French loanword in English, and *weekend* is an English loanword in French.

> ***loanword***
>
> Examples of **loanwords** are, from French, *blasé*, *café* and *gauche*; from German, *echt* and *leitmotif*, and, from Russian, *glasnost* and *sputnik*.

loath or **loth** /loʊθ/ ▷ *adj* unwilling; reluctant □ *were loath to admit it*. • **nothing loath** willing or willingly. ◷ Anglo-Saxon *lath* hated.

> ***loath, lothe***
>
> These words are often confused with each other.

loathe /loʊð/ ▷ *verb* (***loathed, loathing***) **1** to dislike intensely. **2** to find someone or something disgusting. ◷ Anglo-Saxon *lathian* to hate.

loathing ▷ *noun* intense dislike or disgust.

loathsome ▷ *adj* causing intense dislike or disgust.

loaves *plural of* LOAF[1]

lob ▷ *noun* **1** *tennis* a ball hit in a high overhead path. **2** *cricket* a slow high underhand ball. **3** *sport* any high looping ball. ▷ *verb* (***lobbed, lobbing***) **1** to hit, kick or throw (a ball) in this way. **2** to send a high ball over (an opponent) □ ***tried to lob the goalkeeper.*** ⓒ 14c.

lobar /ˈloʊbə(r)/ ▷ *adj* relating to or affecting a lobe, especially in the lungs.

lobate /ˈloʊbeɪt/ ▷ *adj* having lobes.

lobby /ˈlɒbɪ/ ▷ *noun* (***lobbies***) **1** a small entrance-hall, passage or waiting-room from which several rooms open. **2** a common entrance giving access to several flats or apartments. **3** an antechamber of a legislative hall. **4** *Brit* (*also* **division lobby**) either of two corridors in the House of Commons that members pass into when they vote. **5** *Brit* a hall in the House of Commons where members of the public meet politicians. **6** a group of people who try to influence the Government, politicians, legislators, etc to favour their particular cause. **7** the particular cause that such a group tries to promote. ▷ *verb* (***lobbied, lobbying***) **1** to try to influence (the Government, politicians, legislators, etc) to favour a particular cause. **2** *intr* to frequent the lobby in order to influence members or to collect political information. **3** *intr* to conduct a campaign in order to influence public officials. • **lobbying** *noun*. • **lobbyist** *noun*. ⓒ 16c: from Latin *lobia* covered walk or cloister.

lobe ▷ *noun* **1** (*also* **earlobe**) the soft lower part of the outer ear. **2** a division of an organ or gland in the body, especially the lungs, brain or liver. **3** a broad, usually rounded division or projection of a larger object. **4** a division of a leaf. • **lobed** *adj*. ⓒ 16c: from Greek *lobos* ear lobe.

lobectomy /loʊˈbɛktəmɪ/ ▷ *noun* (***lobectomies***) the surgical removal of a lobe from an organ or gland of the body. ⓒ Early 20c: from Greek *lobos* earlobe.

lobelia /loʊˈbiːlɪə/ ▷ *noun* (***lobelias***) a garden plant with red, white, purple, blue or yellow flowers. ⓒ 18c: named after Matthias de Lobel (1538–1616), Flemish botanist.

lobo /ˈloʊboʊ/ ▷ *noun* (***lobos***) *US* a timber wolf. ⓒ 19c: Spanish, from Latin *lupus* a wolf.

lobotomy /loʊˈbɒtəmɪ/ ▷ *noun* (***lobotomies***) *surgery* **1** any operation that involves cutting into a lobe of an organ or gland. **2** (*especially* **prefrontal lobotomy**) an operation in which the nerve fibres connecting the frontal lobes with the rest of the brain are severed, in an attempt to treat certain severe mental disorders. • **lobotomize** or **lobotomise** *verb*. ⓒ 1930s: from Greek *lobos* earlobe + -TOMY.

lobster /ˈlɒbstə(r)/ ▷ *noun* **1** any of various large decapod crustaceans, typically having four pairs of walking legs, a pair of large pincers and a hard bluish-black outer shell which turns bright red when cooked. **2** the flesh of this animal used as food. ⓒ Anglo-Saxon *loppestre*, related to Latin *locusta* a locust.

lobster pot ▷ *noun* a basket for catching lobsters.

lobule /ˈlɒbjuːl/ ▷ *noun* a small lobe. ⓒ 17c: from Latin *lobulus*, from *lobus* a lobe.

lobworm /ˈlɒbwɜːm/ ▷ *noun* a LUGWORM.

local /ˈloʊkəl/ ▷ *adj* **1** referring or belonging to a particular place. **2** relating or belonging to one's home area or neighbourhood. **3** said of a train or bus: stopping at all the stations or stops in a neighbourhood or small area. **4** *medicine* affecting or confined to a small area or part of the body □ ***a local infection.*** ▷ *noun* **1** someone who lives in a particular area. **2** *Brit* someone's nearest and most regularly visited pub. **3** a local bus or train. **4** a local anaesthetic. ⓒ 14c: from Latin *localis*, from *locus* place.

local anaesthetic ▷ *noun, medicine* **a** an injection that anaesthetizes only a small part of the body; **b** the medication used for this. Compare GENERAL ANAESTHETIC.

local area network ▷ *noun, computing* (abbreviation **LAN**) a computer network operating over a small area such as an office or a group of offices, in which a high rate of data transfer is possible.

local authority ▷ *noun* the elected local government body in an area.

local call ▷ *noun* a telephone call within the same exchange or group of exchanges and so charged at a cheap rate.

local colour ▷ *noun* details in a story, etc which are characteristic of the time or place in which it is set.

local derby see DERBY[1]

locale /loʊˈkɑːl/ ▷ *noun* the scene of some event or occurrence. ⓒ 18c: from French *local* local.

local education authority ▷ *noun* (abbreviation **LEA**) the department of a local authority which administers state education.

Local Exchange Trading System see under LETS

local government ▷ *noun* government of town or county affairs by a locally elected authority, as distinct from national or central government.

locality /loʊˈkalɪtɪ/ ▷ *noun* (***localities***) **1** a district or neighbourhood. **2** the scene of an event. **3** the position of a thing. ⓒ 17c: from Latin *localitas*, from *locus* place.

localize or **localise** /ˈloʊkəlaɪz/ ▷ *verb* (***localized, localizing***) **1** to restrict something to a place or area. **2** to mark something with the characteristics of a particular place. • **localization** *noun*. • **localized** *adj*. ⓒ 18c: from Latin *localis*, from *locus* place.

lo-call /ˈloʊkɔːl/ ▷ *noun, Brit telecomm, trademark* a telephone service for businesses, whose numbers are preceded by 0345, which allows calls from anywhere in the country to be charged at the local rate. Compare FREEFONE.

locally ▷ *adverb* within or in terms of a particular area or the people living in it.

local radio ▷ *noun* a radio station, often an independent one, which broadcasts to a fairly limited area and whose programmes are frequently of local interest or on local themes.

local time ▷ *noun* the time in one specific place in contrast to the time in any area to the east or west of that place.

locate /loʊˈkeɪt/ ▷ *verb* (***located, locating***) **1** to set in a particular place or position. **2** to find the exact position of something or someone. **3** to establish something in its proper place or position. **4** to describe or state the position of something. **5** *intr, originally N Amer* to become settled in business or residence in an area. ⓒ 17c: from Latin *locare, locatum*.

location /loʊˈkeɪʃən/ ▷ *noun* **1** a position or situation. **2** the act of locating or process of being located. **3** an authentic place or natural setting for making a film or broadcast, as distinct from an artificial setting in a studio. **4** *S Afr* under apartheid: any of the townships or other areas where Black or Coloured people were forced to live. **5** *computing* a position in a memory which can hold a unit of information. **6** *Austral* a farm. • **on location** *cinema* said of filming: taking place at an authentic cite as opposed to in the studio □ ***The whole film was shot on location.*** ⓒ 16c.

locative /ˈlɒkətɪv/ *grammar* ▷ *adj* indicating the case that suggests 'the place where'. ▷ *noun* **a** the locative case; **b** a word that is in the locative case. ⓒ 19c: from Latin *locare, locatum* to locate + -IVE.

loc cit /lɒk ˈsɪt/ ▷ *abbreviation*: *loco citato* (Latin), in the passage just quoted.

loch /lɒk; *Scottish* lɒx/ ▷ *noun, Scottish* **1** a lake. **2** (*also* **sea loch**) a long narrow arm of the sea surrounded by land on three sides. • **lochan** *noun* a small loch. ◷ 14c: Gaelic and Irish.

lochia /ˈlɒkɪə, ˈloʊ-/ ▷ *plural noun medicine* discharge from the uterus through the vagina after childbirth. • **lochial** *adj.* ◷ 17c: from Greek *lokhos* childbirth.

loci *plural of* LOCUS

lock¹ ▷ *noun* **1** a mechanical device, usually consisting of a sliding bolt moved by turning a key, dial, etc, that provides security by fastening a door, lid, machine, item of movable property, etc. **2** an enclosed section of a canal or river in which the water level can be altered by means of gates, enabling boats to move from a higher section of the waterway to a lower one, or vice versa. **3** a state of being jammed or fixed together, and completely immovable. **4** the part of a gun that explodes the charge. **5** *wrestling* a tight hold which prevents an opponent from moving. **6** the full amount by which the front wheels of a vehicle will turn. **7** (*also* **lock forward**) *rugby* either of the two inside players in the second row of a scrum. **8** an airlock. ▷ *verb* (***locked***, ***locking***) **1** to fasten (a door, box, bag, etc) with a lock. **2** *intr* said of a door, window, etc: to become or have the means of becoming locked. **3** to shut up or secure a building, etc by locking all the doors and windows. **4** *tr & intr* to jam or make something jam. **5** *tr & intr* to fasten or make something be fastened so as to prevent movement. **6** to hold someone closely in an embrace or tussle. • **lock horns** to engage in battle, either physical or verbal. • **lock, stock and barrel** completely; including everything. • **lock the stable door after the horse has bolted** to take action to stop something happening after it has already happened. • **under lock and key 1** securely locked up. **2** in prison. ◷ Anglo-Saxon.

▪ **lock someone in** to prevent them from getting out of a building or room by locking the doors.

▪ **lock on** or **lock on to something** said of a radar beam, etc: to track it automatically.

▪ **lock someone out 1** to prevent them from getting into a building or room by locking the doors. **2** to exclude (employees) from a factory or other workplace.

▪ **lock something out** *computing* to prevent other users from accessing (a file) while one user is reading it or updating it.

▪ **lock someone up** to confine them or prevent them from leaving by locking them in.

▪ **lock something up** to lock (a building, etc) securely.

lock² ▷ *noun* **1** a section or curl of hair. **2** (**locks**) *literary* hair. ◷ Anglo-Saxon *locc*.

lockable ▷ *adj* said especially of a room or building: able to be locked.

lockage ▷ *noun* referring or relating throughout to locks on canals or rivers: **1** the system of locks. **2** the difference in levels between the locks. **3** materials used for locks. **4** water lost by the use of a lock. **5** tolls paid for passing through locks.

locker ▷ *noun* a small lockable cupboard for personal, temporary use, eg for luggage at a station, for clothes and sports equipment at a gym or sports hall.

locker room ▷ *noun* a room with lockers, which is often also used for dressing and undressing in.

locket /ˈlɒkɪt/ ▷ *noun* a small decorated case for holding a photograph or memento, worn on a chain round the neck. ◷ 17c: from French *loquet* latch.

lock gate ▷ *noun* a gate for opening or closing a lock on a canal, river or dock entrance.

lockjaw ▷ *noun* **1** difficulty in opening the mouth, caused by spasm of the jaw muscles, usually a symptom of tetanus, or associated with hysteria or dental disease. **2** *sometimes* TETANUS itself. *Technical equivalent* **trismus**.

lockout ▷ *noun* the shutting out of employees by the management from their place of work during an industrial dispute, as a means of imposing certain conditions.

locksmith ▷ *noun* someone who makes and mends locks.

lockup ▷ *noun* **1** *Brit* a building, etc that can be locked up. **2** a cell for holding prisoners. **3** *Brit* a small shop with no living quarters attached. **4** the action or time of locking up a building, etc.

loco¹ /ˈloʊkoʊ/ ▷ *noun* (***locos***) *colloq* a locomotive.

loco² /ˈloʊkoʊ/ ▷ *adj, slang* **1** crazy; mad. **2** *US* said of cattle: suffering from LOCO DISEASE. ◷ 19c: from Spanish *loco* insane.

loco disease ▷ *noun, US* a disease of farm animals that is caused by eating locoweed and whose symptoms are disordered vision and paralysis.

locomotion /loʊkəˈmoʊʃən/ ▷ *noun* the power, process or capacity of moving from one place to another. ◷ 17c: from Latin *locus* place + *motio* motion.

locomotive /loʊkəˈmoʊtɪv/ ▷ *noun* a railway engine driven by steam, electricity or diesel power, used for pulling trains. ▷ *adj* relating to, capable of or causing locomotion. ◷ 17c.

locomotor /loʊkəˈmoʊtə(r)/ and **locomotory** ▷ *adj* relating to locomotion.

locomotor ataxia ▷ *noun, pathol* failure of muscle co-ordination in the late stages of syphilis, caused by degeneration of the nerve fibres.

locoweed /ˈloʊkoʊwiːd/ ▷ *noun, N Amer* **1** any of the leguminous plants which are known to cause loco disease. **2** *slang* marijuana.

loculus /ˈlɒkjʊləs/ ▷ *noun* (***loculi*** /-laɪ/) *biol* a small compartment or chamber. • **locular** *adj.* ◷ 19c: Latin diminutive of *locus* place.

locum /ˈloʊkəm/ (*in full* **locum tenens**) /— ˈtɛnɛnz/ ▷ *noun* (***locums*** or ***locum tenentes*** /— tɛnɛntiːz/) **1** someone who temporarily stands in for someone else, especially in the medical and clerical professions. **2** the work of a locum □ *She did a locum for the chemist in July*. • **locum tenency** *noun.* ◷ 15c: from Latin *locus* place + *tenere* to hold.

locus /ˈloʊkəs, ˈlɒkəs/ ▷ *noun* (***loci*** /-saɪ, -kiː/) **1** *law* an exact place or location, especially one where some incident has taken place. **2** a passage in a book; a piece of writing. **3** *math* the set of points or values that satisfy an equation or a particular set of conditions. **4** *genetics* the position of a particular gene on a chromosome. ◷ 18c: Latin.

locus classicus /— ˈklasɪkəs/ ▷ *noun* the passage regarded as the principal authority on a subject, etc. ◷ 19c: Latin, meaning 'classical place'.

locus standi /— ˈstandaɪ/ ▷ *noun* **1** a recognized position. **2** *law* a right to appear in court. ◷ 19c: Latin, meaning 'a place for standing'.

locust¹ /ˈloʊkəst/ ▷ *noun* **1** any of various large grasshoppers noted for their tendency to form dense swarms and migrate, eating all the vegetation in their path, including crops. **2** someone or something that destroys or devours. ◷ 13c: from Latin *locusta* lobster or locust.

locust² /ˈloʊkəst/ ▷ *noun* **1** (*also* **locust tree**) the CAROB. **2** (*also* **locust bean**) the edible seed pod of this tree, often ground and used as a substitute for chocolate. ◷ 17c: because the seed pod resembles a LOCUST.

locust bird ▷ *noun* any of several species of bird which feed on locusts.

locution /lə'kjuːʃən, loʊ-/ ▷ *noun* **1** a style of speech. **2** an expression, a word or phrase. ◷ 15c: from Latin *locutio* an utterance.

lode ▷ *noun* **1** a thin band or strip of rock containing metallic ore. **2** a reach of water. **3** *dialect* when referring to channels in fenny areas: a waterway. ◷ Anglo-Saxon *lad* course or journey.

loden /'loʊdən/ ▷ *noun* **1** a thick waterproof, often dark-green, woollen cloth, with a short pile. **2** (*also* **loden coat**) a coat made of this cloth.

lodestar or **loadstar** ▷ *noun* **1** a star used as a guide by sailors and astronomers, especially the Pole Star. **2** any guide or guiding principle. ◷ 14c: from Anglo-Saxon *lad* + *steorra*.

lodestone or **loadstone** ▷ *noun* **1** a form of magnetite which exhibits polarity, behaving, when freely suspended, as a magnet. **2** a magnet. **3** something that attracts.

lodge /lɒdʒ/ ▷ *noun* **1** a cottage at the gateway to the grounds of a large house or mansion. **2** a small house in the country originally used by people taking part in field sports. Also *in compounds* □ *a hunting-lodge*. **3** a porter's room in a university or college, etc. **4 a** the meeting-place of a local branch of certain societies such as the FREEMASONS and the ORANGE ORDER; **b** the members of a branch of these societies. **5** a beaver's nest, made of sticks plastered together with mud, and having an underwater entrance. **6** the home of some Native Americans. ▷ *verb* (***lodging***, ***lodged***) **1** *intr* to live, usually temporarily, in rented accommodation, especially in someone else's home. **2** *tr & intr* **a** to become or cause something to become firmly fixed; **b** said of feelings, ideas, thoughts, etc: to become implanted □ *The idea was firmly lodged in his mind.* **3 a** to bring (a charge or accusation) against someone; **b** to make (a complaint) officially. **4** to provide with rented, usually temporary, accommodation, especially in one's home. ◷ 13c: from French *loge* hut.

▪ **lodge in** or **with someone** said of power, authority, etc: to be in or under their control □ *The power to hire and fire lodges with the board.*

▪ **lodge something with someone** to deposit (money or valuables) with them, especially for safe-keeping.

lodger ▷ *noun* someone who rents accommodation in someone else's home, often temporarily.

lodging ▷ *noun* **1** (*usually* **lodgings**) a room or rooms rented in someone else's home. **2** temporary accommodation.

lodging house ▷ *noun* **1** a house where rooms are rented out. **2** a building where the homeless can have temporary accommodation.

loess /'loʊɪs, lɜːs/ *geol* ▷ *noun* a fine-grained loose quartz-based wind-blown loam found mostly in river valleys in central US, N Europe, Russia, China and Argentina. • **loessial** *adj.* • **loessic** *adj.* ◷ 19c: from German *löss* loose.

loft ▷ *noun* **1** a room or space under a roof. **2** a gallery in a church or hall □ *an organ loft*. **3** a room used for storage, especially one over a stable for storing hay. **4 a** (*also* **pigeon loft**) a room or shed where pigeons are kept; **b** a group of pigeons. **5** *golf* the relative backward slant of the face of a golf club, the higher-numbered clubs slanting more than the lower-numbered ones. **6** *golf* **a** a stroke that causes a golf ball to rise up high; **b** the amount of height that a player gives a ball. ▷ *verb* (***lofted***, ***lofting***) to strike, kick or throw (a ball, etc) high up in the air. • **lofted** *adj* **a** said of a golf club: having a slanting face rather than a vertical one; **b** said of a ball that has been struck: lifted into the air. ◷ Anglo-Saxon *loft* sky or upper room.

lofty ▷ *adj* (***loftier***, ***loftiest***) **1** very tall; being of great or imposing height. **2** *often* of high or noble character □ *lofty thoughts*. **3** haughty or proud. • **loftily** *adverb* imposingly; proudly; haughtily. • **loftiness** *noun*. ◷ 16c: from LOFT.

log¹ ▷ *noun* **1 a** part of a tree trunk or branch that has been cut, especially for firewood; **b** a tree trunk or large branch that has fallen to the ground. **2** a detailed record of events occurring during the voyage of a ship or aircraft, etc. **3** a logbook. **4** a float, originally made of wood, attached by a line to a ship and used for measuring its speed. ▷ *verb* (***logged***, ***logging***) **1 a** to record (distances covered on a journey, events, etc) in a book or logbook; **b** to record (speed) over a set distance. **2** to cut (trees or branches) into logs. **3** *intr* to cut logs. • **sleep like a log** to sleep very soundly. ◷ 14c.

▪ **log in** or **on** *computing* **a** to start a session on a computer system, usually one shared by several USERS and requiring a PASSWORD to be entered; **b** to make a connection with another computer over a NETWORK.

▪ **log out** or **off** *computing* **a** to end a session on a computer system by keying in a closing COMMAND (*noun* 7); **b** to close a connection with another computer which has been accessed over a NETWORK.

log² see under LOGARITHM

loganberry /'loʊɡənbərɪ, -berɪ/ ▷ *noun* **1** a large dark red berry eaten as a fruit and sometimes used as a filling for pies or used to make wine. **2** the plant that produces it, believed to be a cross between a raspberry and a wild blackberry. ◷ 19c: named after Judge J H Logan (1841–1928), the American lawyer and horticulturist who first grew it in his garden in California in 1881.

logarithm /'lɒɡərɪðəm/ *math* ▷ *noun* (*often* abbreviation **log**) the power to which a real number, called the BASE (sense 9), must be raised in order to give another number or variable, eg the logarithm of 100 to the base 10 is 2 (*written* $\log_{10} 100 = 2$). • **logarithmic** *adj.* • **logarithmically** *adverb*. Also called **Napierian logarithm**. See also ANTILOGARITHM. ◷ 1614: first coined by John Napier (1550–1617), Scottish mathematician, from Greek *logos* word or ratio + *arithmos* number.

logarithmic function ▷ *noun, math* **a** any mathematical function of the form $a = \log b$; **b** any function that can be expressed in this form.

logarithmic scale ▷ *noun, math* a scale of measurement that varies logarithmically with the quantity being measured.

logbook ▷ *noun* **1** a book containing an official record of the voyage of a ship, aircraft, etc, including details of crew and any incidents which occur. **2** *Brit, formerly* the registration documents of a motor vehicle, now called VEHICLE REGISTRATION DOCUMENT.

logged *adj, in compounds* filled with, saturated in, etc a specified thing □ *water-logged* □ *smoke-logged*.

loggerhead ▷ *noun* **1** (*also* **loggerhead turtle**) a large sea turtle with a big head, whose shell can be up to 0.9m (3ft) long and which weighs around 136kg (300lb). **2** a device with a long handle and a metal sphere at the end, which is heated and plunged into liquids such as tar to melt them. • **at loggerheads** arguing or disagreeing fiercely ◷ apparently from the use of the tar-melter as a weapon. ◷ 16c as *logger* a dialect word meaning 'something heavy and clumsy' + HEAD.

loggia /'lɒdʒɪə/ ▷ *noun* (***loggias***) a roofed gallery or arcade on the side of a building that usually opens onto a garden. ◷ 18c: Italian, meaning 'lodge'.

logging ▷ *noun* **1** the work of cutting trees and preparing timber. **2** the action of recording something, especially in a logbook.

logic /'lɒdʒɪk/ ▷ *noun* **1 a** *philos* the exploration of the validity or otherwise of arguments and reasoning, where the aim is not to prove or disprove the legitimacy of statements or PREMISSes, but rather to show that the underlying thinking behind what is being proposed is well-founded. See also FALLACY, SYLLOGISM; **b** *math* the analysis of the principles of reasoning on which mathematical systems are based. **2** the rules or reasoning governing a particular subject or activity □ ***the logic of the absurd.*** **3 a** the extent to which someone's reasoning is sound □ ***I didn't understand his logic — it was obvious it wouldn't work***; **b** the convincing and compelling force of an argument □ ***The logic for having exams is dubious***; **c** rationalized thinking □ ***Logic dictated that she shouldn't go.*** **4** the way that a string of related events or facts is inter-connected. **5** *electronics, computing* the system underlying the design and operation of computers, comprising elements that perform specified elementary arithmetical functions, using BOOLEAN ALGEBRA. **6** an individual, personal or particular way of reasoning □ ***with child-like logic.*** ⓘ 14c: from Greek *logos* word or ratio.

logical /lɒdʒɪkəl/ ▻ *adj* **1** relating or according to logic □ ***a logical truth.*** **2** correctly reasoned or thought out □ ***a logical conclusion.*** **3** able to reason correctly □ ***a logical mind.*** **4** following reasonably or necessarily from facts or events □ ***the logical choice.*** **5** *computing, electronics* referring or relating to LOGIC (*noun* 5). • **logicality** *noun.* • **logically** *adverb.* ⓘ 16c.

-logical and **-logic** ▻ *combining form* forming adjectives corresponding to nouns in -LOGY □ ***archaeological*** □ ***pathological.***

logical positivism ▻ *noun, philos* the theories of a philosophical movement of the 1920s whose members believed that only those statements or ideas which could be proved to have an EMPIRICAL basis were worth consideration, and hence eg metaphysics, ethics and religion were not worth consideration. ⓘ 1931.

logic bomb ▻ *noun, computing* an unauthorized program designed to interfere with the operation of a computer system when inserted into it and activated.

logic circuit ▻ *noun, computing* an electronic circuit with one or more input signals that produces a single output signal, used as a basic component in the construction of integrated circuits in digital computers.

logician /lə'dʒɪʃən/ ▻ *noun* **1** someone who studies or writes about logic. **2** someone who is particularly good at thinking things through in a logical way.

logistics /lə'dʒɪstɪks/ ▻ *singular or plural noun* **1** the organizing of everything needed for any large-scale operation. **2** the control and regulation of the flow of goods, materials, staff, etc in a business. **3** the art of moving and supplying troops and military equipment. • **logistic** *adj.* • **logistical** *adj.* • **logistically** *adverb.* ⓘ 19c: from French *logistique*, from *loger* to LODGE.

log jam ▻ *noun* **1** a blockage of logs being floated down a river. **2** a place in a river where logs tend to wedge together. **3** any complete stopping of movement or progress; a deadlock.

loglog ▻ *noun* a LOGARITHM of a logarithm.

logo /'loʊgoʊ/ ▻ *noun* (**logos**) any easily recognizable or significant badge or emblem used by a company, organization, etc as a trademark or symbol. ⓘ 1930s: contraction of *logotype*.

logo- /lɒgoʊ, -gə, lɒgɒ/ ▻ *combining form, signifying* referring or relating to words or speech. ⓘ From Greek *logos* a word.

logocentrism /lɒgoʊ'sɛntrɪzəm/ ▻ *noun* **1** the belief that, by concentrating on the language of a text and ignoring such things as the spectrum of knowledge and experience readers can bring to the text, some kind of fixed MEANING will emerge. **2** *loosely* the prioritizing of the language of a text over its content, an activity that is usually perceived very negatively. ⓘ 1967: first coined by Jacques Derrida.

logodaedalus /lɒgoʊ'diːdələs/ ▻ *noun* (***logodaedali*** /-aɪ/) someone who is skilled in the manipulative use of words. ⓘ 17c: from LOGO- + Daedalus, the name of an artist and inventor in Greek mythology.

logograph /'lɒgəgrɑːf/ and **logogram** /'lɒgəgram/ ▻ *noun* **1** used especially in eg SHORTHAND or scientific notation and in the orthography of languages like Chinese and Japanese: a single symbol which consistently stands for a MORPHEME, word or phrase, such as & for *and*. **2** *loosely* any simple symbol which represents something, eg the digging man inside a red triangle as a warning of road works or the care symbols on clothes that suggest how they should be washed. Compare IDEOGRAM, PICTOGRAPH. ⓘ 1930s.

logorrhoea or (*US*) **logorrhea** /lɒgə'rɪə/ ▻ *noun* **1** *medical* a condition associated with certain mental illnesses characterized by incoherent and very rapid talking, often using nonsense words. **2** *loosely* the unnecessary use of lots of words (also called VERBAL DIARRHOEA). ⓘ Early 20c: from LOGO-, modelled on DIARRHOEA.

logotype /'lɒgoʊtaɪp/ ▻ *noun* **1** a LOGO. **2** *printing* a section of type with more than one letter or character on it. ⓘ 19c.

-logue or (*US*) **-log** /lɒg/ ▻ *combining form, signifying* **1** speech or discourse □ ***monologue*** □ ***dialogue.*** **2** a list or compilation □ ***catalogue*** □ ***travelogue.*** **3** an agent noun corresponding to a noun in -LOGY □ ***ideologue.*** ⓘ From Greek *logos* word.

-logy /lədʒɪ/ or **-ology** /'ɒlədʒɪ/ ▻ *combining form, forming nouns, denoting* **1** a science or study □ ***geology.*** **2** writing or speech □ ***trilogy.*** ⓘ From Greek *logos* word or reason.

loin /lɔɪn/ ▻ *noun* **1** (**loins**) the area of the back and side in humans and some animals, stretching from the bottom rib to the pelvis. **2** a cut of meat from the lower back area of an animal. **3** (**loins**) *euphemistic or poetic* the genital area in humans. • **fruit of one's loins** one's children. • **gird** or **gird up one's loins** see under GIRD. ⓘ 14c: from French dialect *loigne* a loin of veal.

loincloth ▻ *noun* a piece of material worn round the hips, covering the genitals, especially by people in non-industrial societies.

loiter /'lɔɪtə(r)/ ▻ *verb* (***loitered, loitering***) *intr* **1** to walk slowly; to dawdle. **2** to wait around, especially furtively; to skulk. **3** to stand around or pass one's time doing nothing. • **loiterer** *noun.* • **loiter with intent** to stand about waiting for an opportunity (to commit a crime). ⓘ 15c: from Dutch *loteren* to wag (like a loose tooth).

loll /lɒl/ ▻ *verb* (***lolled, lolling***) *intr* **1** (*often* **loll about**) to lie or sit about lazily; to lounge or sprawl. **2** said of the tongue: to hang down or out. • **loller** *noun.* • **lollingly** *adverb.* ⓘ 14c.

lollipop /'lɒlɪpɒp/ ▻ *noun* a sweet on a stick. ⓘ 18c: from dialect *lolly* tongue + POP[1] 2.

lollipop lady and **lollipop man** ▻ *noun* someone employed to see that children get across busy roads safely, especially when they are going to or coming from school. ⓘ 1971: from the pole they carry which has a round sign at the top telling drivers they must stop, which looks like a LOLLIPOP.

lollop /'lɒləp/ ▻ *verb* (***lolloped, lolloping***) *intr, colloq* to bound around, especially with big ungainly strides. ⓘ 18c: onomatopoeic extension of LOLL.

lolly /'lɒlɪ/ ▻ *noun* (**lollies**) **1** *colloq* **a** short form of LOLLIPOP; **b** an ICE LOLLY. **2** money. ⓘ 19c in sense 1a; 1930s in sense 1b; 1940s in sense 3.

London pride ▻ *noun* a plant with pink flowers, a member of the saxifrage family.

lone /loʊn/ ▻ *adj* **1 a** without a companion; **b** only □ ***the lone car in the carpark.*** **2** *poetic* said of a place: isolated and unfrequented. ⓘ 14c: from ALONE.

lonely /'loʊnlɪ/ ▻ *adj* (***lonelier, loneliest***) **1** said of a person: sad because they have no companions or friends.

2 solitary and without companionship □ *a lonely existence.* 3 said of a place: isolated and unfrequented □ *in a lonely street.* • **loneliness** *noun.*

lonely heart ▻ *noun* someone who is lonely and looking for a loving relationship.

lonelyhearts and **lonelyhearts column** ▻ *noun* 1 a regular newspaper column where people give a brief, often humorous, account of themselves in the hope that someone will contact them and they will find romance. 2 advice given in a regular newspaper column to people who do not have a partner. ◷ 1930s: given further prominence by Nathanael West's 1933 novel, *Miss Lonelyhearts.*

loner ▻ *noun, sometimes derog* someone who prefers to be alone and who avoids close relationships.

lonesome /'lounsəm/ ▻ *adj* 1 sad and lonely. 2 causing feelings of loneliness. • **on** or **by one's lonesome** *colloq, often jocular* **a** completely alone; **b** without any help □ *cooked the exotic dinner all on her lonesome.*

lone wolf ▻ *noun* someone who prefers to live or act alone. ◷ Early 20c.

long¹ ▻ *adj* (***longer*** /lɒŋgə(r)/, ***longest*** /lɒŋgəst/) 1 **a** measuring a great distance in space from one end to the other; **b** said of time: lasting for an extensive period. 2 *often in compounds* **a** measuring a specified amount □ *six centimetres long*; **b** lasting a specified time □ *a three-hour-long movie.* 3 having a large number of items □ *a long list.* 4 **a** measuring more than is usual, expected or wanted □ *She has really long hair*; **b** lasting a greater time than is usual, expected or wanted □ *The breakdown made it a really long journey.* 5 said of someone's memory: able to recall things that happened a considerable time ago. 6 having greater length than breadth. 7 **a** said of a dress or skirt: reaching down to the feet; **b** said of trousers: covering the whole of the legs □ *Older boys were allowed to wear long trousers.* 8 said of a cold drink: large and thirst-quenching. 9 said of stocks: bought in large amounts in expectation of a rise in prices. 10 **a** *phonetics* said of a vowel: having the greater of two recognized lengths; **b** said of a syllable in verse: stressed; **c** *popularly* said of a vowel or syllable: taking a long time to pronounce in comparison with another, eg *mate* as compared to *mat.* 11 *cricket* said of fielders: covering the area near the boundary. ▻ *adverb* 1 for, during or by a long period of time □ *They had long expected such news.* 2 throughout the whole time □ *all night long.* ▻ *noun* 1 a comparatively long time □ *won't be there for long.* 2 a syllable that takes a comparatively long time to pronounce. 3 **a** a signal in MORSE code that corresponds with the DASH¹ (*noun* 5); **b** a long blast from a ship's siren, etc that forms part of a signal □ *Three shorts and one long means head for the lifeboats.* • **as long as** or **so long as** 1 provided that. 2 while; during the time that. • **before long** in the near future; soon. • **long ago** in the very distant past. • **the long and the short of it** the most important facts in a few words. • **long on something** *colloq* having a lot of it □ *not too long on brains.* • **no longer** not now as it was in the past. • **not long for this world** *euphemistic* about to die. • **so long** *colloq* goodbye. ◷ Anglo-Saxon *lang.*

long² ▻ *verb* (***longed, longing***) *intr* 1 (*often* **long for something** or **someone**) to desire it or them very much □ *He longed for her to come back.* 2 (**long to**) to have a strong desire to (do something) □ *He longed to hear from her.* ◷ Anglo-Saxon *langian* to have a yearning desire.

long arm ▻ *noun* the extent of an organization's powers □ *long arm of the law.*

long barrow see under BARROW²

longboat ▻ *noun, formerly* the largest boat carried by a sailing ship, used for ferrying people and goods from ship to shore and vice versa, or in times of emergency.

longbow /'lɒŋbou/ ▻ *noun* a large bow, drawn by hand, used for hunting and as a weapon, especially in England in the Middle Ages.

longcase clock ▻ *noun* a grandfather clock.

long cripple ▻ *noun, dialect* the slow-worm.

long-dated ▻ *adj, finance* said of securities: not due to be redeemed for at least fifteen years. See also MEDIUM-DATED, SHORT-DATED.

long-distance ▻ *adj* covering, travelling, operating, etc between or over long distances □ *a long-distance runner* □ *long-distance telephone calls.* ▻ *adverb* over a long distance □ *called New York long-distance.*

long division ▻ *noun, math* a calculation that involves DIVISION, where the DIVISOR is usually greater than 12 and the working is shown in full.

long-drawn-out ▻ *adj* taking too long □ *a long-drawn-out argument.*

long-eared ▻ *adj* said of various birds and animals: having either very long ears, ears with tufts of feathers or fur on them, or ear-like tufts of feathers or fur.

longevity /lɒn'dʒɛvɪtɪ/ ▻ *noun* great length of life. ◷ 17c: from Latin *longaevitas.*

long face ▻ *noun* a dismal, miserable or disappointed expression. • **long-faced** *adj.*

long field ▻ *noun, cricket* 1 a fielder who covers an area near the boundary. 2 the part of the pitch near the boundary.

long-hair *noun, colloq* someone or something that is LONG-HAIRED in any sense □ *A long-hair takes a great deal of grooming.*

long-haired ▻ *adj* 1 having long hair. 2 having long fur □ *a long-haired cat.* 3 *colloq, all frequently derisive* **a** having aesthetic or intellectual pretensions; **b** referring or relating to HIPPIES or to their beliefs; **c** referring or relating to classical music.

longhand ▻ *noun* ordinary handwriting as opposed to SHORTHAND, typing or word-processing.

long haul ▻ *noun* 1 **a** the carrying of cargo or passengers over a long distance; **b** *as adj* □ *a long-haul flight to India.* 2 anything requiring great effort or considerable time.

long-headed ▻ *adj* 1 having a head that is much longer than it is broad. 2 perceptive; discriminating. • **long-headedness** *noun.*

longhorn ▻ *plural noun* a breed of beef cattle characterized by their long horns.

long-house ▻ *noun* a long communal house found in Malaysia, Indonesia and in some Native American villages.

longing ▻ *noun* 1 an intense desire or yearning. 2 *as adj* having or exhibiting this feeling □ *a longing look.* • **longingly** *adverb.*

longish /'lɒŋɪʃ/ ▻ *adj* quite long.

longitude /'lɒŋgɪtʃuːd, 'lɪndʒɪ-/ ▻ *noun* 1 any of a series of imaginary circles that pass around the Earth through both poles, representing the angular distance east or west of the PRIME MERIDIAN, measured from 0 degrees at this meridian to 180 degrees east or west of it. See LINE OF LONGITUDE. Compare LATITUDE. 2 length. ◷ 14c: from Latin *longus* long.

longitudinal /lɒŋgɪ'tjuːdɪnəl, lɒndʒɪ-/ ▻ *adj* 1 relating to longitude; measured by longitude. 2 relating to length. 3 lengthways. • **longitudinally** *adverb.*

longitudinal wave ▻ *noun, physics* a wave in which particles are displaced in the same direction as that in which the wave is being propagated, eg sound waves.

long johns ▻ *plural noun, colloq* underpants with long legs, worn for warmth.

long jump ▻ *noun* an athletics event in which competitors take a running start and try to jump as far as possible, usually into a sandy pit. • **long-jumper** *noun.* • **long-jumping** *noun.*

long-lasting ▻ *adj* effective, or continuing, or remaining, etc for a long period □ *long-lasting relief from pain.*

long leg ▻ *noun, cricket* **a** the part of the pitch that is out towards the boundary, behind and to the left of a right-handed batsman or behind and to the right of a left-handed batsman; **b** the fielder who covers this part of the pitch.

long-legged /-lɛgd, -lɛgɪd/ ▻ *adj* having long legs.

long-life ▻ *adj* said of food and drink: treated so that, even without refrigeration, it may be stored for a long time in an unopened container and will remain fit for consumption □ *long-life milk.*

long-line[1] or **long line** ▻ *noun, angling* a long line with lots of hooks on it, used in deep sea fishing.

long-line[2] ▻ *adj* said of certain items of clothing: extending longer than is usual □ *a long-line bra.*

long-lived /lɒŋ'lɪvd/ ▻ *adj* having a long life.

long odds ▻ *plural noun, betting* a very remote possibility.

long off ▻ *noun, cricket* **a** the part of the pitch that is out towards the boundary, in front and to the right of a right-handed batsman or in front and to the left of a left-handed batsman; **b** the fielder who covers this part of the pitch.

long on ▻ *noun, cricket* **a** the part of the pitch that is out towards the boundary, in front and to the left of a right-handed batsman or in front and to the right of a left-handed batsman; **b** the fielder who covers this part of the pitch.

long pig ▻ *noun* human flesh, used as food. ⌚ 19c: translating a Polynesian cannibal term.

long-playing ▻ *adj* (abbreviation **LP**) denoting a RECORD (*noun* 4) which replaced the SEVENTY-EIGHT, designed to be played at 33¹/₃ rpm, each side lasting approximately 25 minutes. Compare EXTENDED-PLAY, FORTY-FIVE, TWELVE-INCH.

long-range ▻ *adj* **1** said of predictions, etc: looking well into the future □ *a long-range weather forecast.* **2** said of a missile or weapon: able to reach remote or far-off targets. **3** said of vehicles or aircraft: able to travel long distances without having to refuel.

long run ▻ *noun, theat* a long continuous staging (of a play, etc). • **long-running** *adj, theat* said of a play, etc: staged continuously over a long period □ *a long-running success.* • **in the long run a** ultimately; **b** when things have run their various courses.

longship ▻ *noun, historical* a long narrow Viking warship with a large squarish sail, which could also be powered by banks of rowers.

longshore /'lɒŋʃɔː(r)/ ▻ *adj* **a** found on or employed along the shore; **b** living on or frequently visiting the shore. ⌚ 19c: from *alongshore.*

longshoreman ▻ *noun, N Amer* someone who loads and unloads cargo from ships. *Brit equivalent* **docker**.

long shot ▻ *noun* **1** *colloq* **a** a guess, attempt, etc which is unlikely to be successful; **b** a bet made in the knowledge that there is only a slim chance of winning; **c** a participant in a competition, etc generally thought to have little chance of winning □ *The horse was a real long shot.* **2** *cinematog* a camera shot that makes viewers feel they are at a considerable distance from the scene. Opposite of CLOSE-UP. • **not by a long shot** not by any means.

long-sighted ▻ *adj* **1** only able to see distant objects clearly. Compare SHORT-SIGHTED. **2 a** tending to consider what effect actions, etc might have on the future; **b** wise. • **long-sightedness** *noun.*

long slip ▻ *noun, cricket* a fielder who is positioned at some distance behind the batsman on the OFF SIDE.

long-standing ▻ *adj* having existed or continued for a long time □ *a long-standing feud with a neighbour.* ▻ *noun* (**long standing**) someone or something that is well-established and generally held in high esteem □ *a family of long standing.*

long-stay ▻ *adj* **1 a** said of a hospital: looking after patients who need to be cared for either permanently or over long periods; **b** said of patients: needing to be cared for either permanently or over long periods. **2** said of a carpark: catering for motorists who want to leave their cars for days or weeks rather than just a few hours.

long-suffering ▻ *adj* patiently tolerating difficulties, hardship, unreasonable behaviour, etc □ *his long-suffering wife.* ▻ *noun* (**long suffering**) patient toleration (of hardship or something that is annoying), especially over an extended period of time □ *her long suffering of his excessive drinking.*

long-term ▻ *adj* said of a plan, etc: occurring in or concerning the future □ *The long-term outlook was not good.* ▻ *adverb* in the future □ *didn't think about the effects long-term.* ▻ *noun* (**the long term**) the future.

longtime ▻ *adj* **1** having been so for a long time □ *a longtime friend.* **2** lasting for a long time.

longueur /lɒŋ'gɜːr/ ▻ *noun* **a** any period of extreme tedium or boredom; **b** *music* a spell where the listener's attention has a tendency to wander. ⌚ 18c: French, meaning 'length'.

long vacation and **long vac** ▻ *noun, originally N Amer* the time in the summer when traditionally universities, colleges, etc suspend their usual teaching routine.

long wave ▻ *noun* an electromagnetic wave, especially a radio wave, with a wavelength greater than 1000m. Compare MEDIUM WAVE, SHORT WAVE.

longways ▻ *adverb, adj* in the direction of a thing's length; lengthways.

long weekend ▻ *noun* an extended weekend that includes having either the Friday or the Monday, or both, away from work.

long-winded ▻ *adj* said of a speaker or speech: using or having far more words than are necessary and so tending to bore those listening. • **long-windedly** *adverb.* • **long-windedness** *noun.*

loo[1] ▻ *noun* (***loos***) *Brit colloq* a lavatory. ⌚ 1920s.

loo[2] ▻ *noun* a card game played by anything from five to nine players where the object is to win other people's STAKE[2] (*noun* 1) money by taking TRICKS. ⌚ 17c: shortened from the older form of *lanterloo.*

loofah, **loofa** or **luffa** /'luːfə/ ▻ *noun* (***loofahs***, ***loofas*** or ***luffas***) the roughly cylindrical dried inner part of a tropical gourd-like fruit, used as a kind of rough sponge. ⌚ 19c: from Egyptian Arabic *lufah* the name for the whole plant which produces these fruits.

look /lʊk/ ▻ *verb* (***looked***, ***looking***) **1** *intr* to direct one's sight □ *looked out of the window.* **2** to seem to be; to have the appearance of being □ *She looked much younger than she was* □ *She looked an absolute sight.* **3** *intr* to face or be turned in a specified direction □ *The window looks south.* **4** to express by a look □ *She was looking daggers at him.* **5** to consider or realize □ *Just look what you've done!* ▻ *noun* **1 a** an act or the action of looking; a glance or view □ *had a look through his photos*; **b** a glance or stare that conveys a particular feeling or emotion □ *gave her an impatient look.* **2** (*sometimes* **looks**) the outward appearance of something or someone □ *She always has that tired look* □ *She didn't like the looks of the restaurant.* **3** (**looks**) beauty; attractiveness. **4** a particular way of dressing, etc, especially one that is different or particularly up-to-date □ *went for a punk look.* **5 a** a search □ *I'll have another look for that missing CD*; **b** a browse. **6** (*sometimes* **Look here!**) used as an exclamation to call for attention or to express protest □ *Look, you just can't behave like that!* □ *Look here! What do you think you're doing?* • **be nothing** or **nothing much to look at** or **not be much to look at** *colloq* to be plain or unattractive. • **by the look** or **looks of someone** or **something** *colloq* going by appearances □ *By the look of him, he's in need of a rest.* • **by the look of things** *colloq* going by how things stand at the moment □ *By the look of things, we won't get this finished today.* • **Here's looking at you** *colloq* said when dedicating a toast: let's drink to your continued health. • **look down one's nose at someone** or **something** *colloq* to disapprove of them or it; to treat them or it with contempt. • **have** or **take a**

look at something to make an inspection of it. ● **look as if** or **look as though** to appear to be the case that; to give the impression that □ *looks as though she'd seen a ghost.* ● **look like** *colloq* **1** to seem probable □ *looks like it will rain.* **2** to appear to be similar to □ *looks like her sister.* **3** to seem to be □ *He looks like a nice guy.* ● **look oneself** to seem to be as healthy as usual □ *He doesn't quite look himself yet, does he?* ● **look the part** to appear to be very well suited (to do or be something) □ *In the yellow lizard costume, he really did look the part.* ● **look a picture** said usually of a female: to be extremely attractive □ *The bride looked an absolute picture.* ● **look right** or **straight through someone** *colloq* to ignore them on purpose. ● **look sharp** *colloq* to hurry up □ *We'd better look sharp if we're going to be there for seven.* ● **look someone up and down** to take in someone's entire appearance. ● **never look back** to continue to make progress or to prosper □ *After the operation he never looked back.* ● **not know where to look** to feel acutely embarrassed. ⓒ Anglo-Saxon *locian.*

■ **look after someone** or **something** to attend to or take care of them or it.

■ **look ahead** to consider what will happen in the future.

■ **look around** to hunt about for something.

■ **look at 1** to turn the eyes in a certain direction so as to see; to use one's sight. **2** to think about something □ *We have to look at all the implications.* **3** to consider someone as a possible sexual or romantic partner □ *never looked at another woman.* **4** *colloq* to be expecting, hoping, facing, etc something or to do something □ *His lawyer said he was looking at five years for the robbery.*

■ **look back** to think about the past; to reminisce.

■ **look down on** or **upon someone** or **something** to consider them or it inferior or contemptible.

■ **look for someone** or **something a** to search for them or it; **b** *colloq* to be hoping for it □ *He was looking for around £100 for the bike.*

■ **look forward to something** to anticipate it with pleasure.

■ **look in on someone** to visit them briefly.

■ **look into something** to investigate it.

■ **look on** to watch without taking part.

■ **look on** or **upon someone** or **something in a certain way** to think of or consider them or it in that way □ *Look on it as a bonus* □ *You should look upon me as a friend.*

■ **look out a** to keep watch and be careful; **b** used as an exclamation warning of imminent danger. See also LOOKOUT.

■ **look out something** to find it by searching □ *I'll look out that magazine for you.*

■ **look out for someone** or **something 1** to be alert about finding them or it. **2** *colloq* to protect □ *He has always looked out for his younger brother.*

■ **look over something** to check it cursorily or quickly □ *looked over her daughter's homework.*

■ **look through something** to read or examine it.

■ **look to someone** or **something** to rely on, turn to or refer to them or it □ *looked to her for support.*

■ **look up** to show signs of improving □ *The weather's looking up at last.*

■ **look someone up** *colloq* to visit or get in touch with them □ *I'll look you up when I'm next in town.*

■ **look something up** to search for (an item of information) in a reference book.

■ **look up to someone** to respect their behaviour, opinions, etc.

lookalike ▻ *noun* someone or something that looks very much like someone or something else; a double.

look and say ▻ *noun, education* **1** a method of teaching reading to young children that encourages them to recognize whole words instead of getting them to pronounce separate syllables. **2** *as adj* □ *the look-and-say method.*

looker ▻ *noun, colloq* someone, usually a woman, who is considered attractive.

looker-on ▻ *noun* (***lookers-on***) someone who chooses to watch an event rather than participate in it.

look-in ▻ *noun* a chance of joining in, being included, or doing something.

looking-glass ▻ *noun, old use* a mirror.

lookout ▻ *noun* **1** a careful watch. **2** a place from which such a watch can be kept. **3** someone who has to keep watch, eg on board ship. **4** *colloq* a personal concern or problem □ *That's your lookout.* ● **be on the lookout for someone** or **something** to be watching for them or it □ *She was always on the lookout for a bargain.*

look-see ▻ *noun* (***look-sees***) *colloq* a quick look around or inspection.

loom¹ ▻ *noun* a machine, either hand-powered or mechanical, that weaves thread into fabric. ⓒ Anglo-Saxon *geloma* a tool.

loom² /luːm/ ▻ *verb* (***loomed, looming***) *intr* **1** to appear indistinctly and usually in some enlarged or threatening form. **2** said of an event: to be imminent, especially in some menacing or threatening way. ● **loom large** to take over a major part of someone's thoughts, life, etc □ *The exams were looming large.* ⓒ 16c.

loon¹ ▻ *noun, N Amer* a DIVER (*noun* 3). ⓒ 17c.

loon² ▻ *noun, N Scots* a boy; a son.

loony /ˈluːnɪ/ *slang* ▻ *noun* (***loonies***) someone who is mad. ▻ *adj* (***loonier, looniest***) **1** crazy; mad. **2** overzealous; fanatical □ *some loony fringe group.* ⓒ 19c: shortened from LUNATIC.

loony-bin ▻ *noun, slang* a psychiatric home or hospital.

loop ▻ *noun* **1** a rounded or oval-shaped single coil in a piece of thread, string, rope, chain, etc, formed as it crosses over itself. **2** any similar oval-shaped or U-shaped bend, eg in a river, the path of a planet, etc. **3** a manoeuvre in which an aircraft describes a complete vertical circle in the sky. **4** a strip of magnetic tape or motion-picture film whose ends have been spliced (see SPLICE *verb* 3) together to form a loop so that the sound or images on it can be continually repeated. **5** *electronics* a CLOSED CIRCUIT which a signal can pass round, as, for example, in a FEEDBACK (sense 3) control system. **6** *computing* a series of instructions in a program that is repeated until a certain condition is met. **7** *math* a line on a graph which begins and ends at the same point. **8** *physics* a closed curve on a graph, such as a HYSTERESIS loop. **9** a branch of a railway, telegraph line, etc that leaves the main line and then rejoins it. **10** an intrauterine contraceptive coil. **11** in knitting and crochet: a STITCH. **12** one of four possible categories of FINGERPRINT. **13** *skating* a curved figure that is traced by the skater. ▻ *verb* (***looped, looping***) **1** to fasten with or enclose in a loop. **2** to form into a loop or loops. ● **loop the loop** said of an aircraft, etc: to make a loop in the sky. ⓒ 15c as *loupe*: the verb is not attested until 19c.

looper ▻ *noun* a caterpillar of the **geometrid** /dʒɪˈɪmətrɪd/ moth, which moves by forming its body into a loop and planting its hinder legs close behind its six true legs.

loophole ▻ *noun* **1** *now* an inherent flaw, gap or ambiguity in a law, rule, contract, agreement, etc, especially one that is advantageous to a particular person or party, or one that allows someone to evade a responsibility, duty, obligation, etc legitimately. **2** *originally* a vertical slit in a wall, functioning as a window but sometimes also used as a place where the occupants of a castle, etc could defend themselves by firing arrows, missiles, etc at their attackers without risking their own lives too much. ◷ 16c.

loopy ▷ *adj* (**loopier**, **loopiest**) *slang* mad; crazy.

loo roll ▷ *noun, colloq* a toilet roll.

loose /luːs/ ▷ *adj* (**looser**, **loosest**) **1** not or no longer tied up or attached to something else; free. **2** said of clothes, etc: not tight or close-fitting. **3 a** not held together; not fastened or firmly fixed in place ▫ *Jane kept wiggling her loose tooth*; **b** not packaged ▫ *Get the loose oranges rather than the pre-packed ones.* **4** not tightly-packed or compact ▫ *loose soil.* **5** vague or inexact ▫ *a loose translation.* **6** *usually* said of a woman: promiscuous; tending to indulge in disreputable behaviour. **7** indiscreet ▫ *loose talk.* **8** *sport* said of a ball, etc: in play but not under a player's control. **9** hanging; droopy; baggy. **10** said of the bowels: moving frequently and producing softer faeces than is usual. **11** said of a cough: producing phlegm easily. ▷ *adverb* in an unrestrained way ▫ *The dog can run loose in the park.* ▷ *noun* (**the loose**) *rugby* any time in a game when there is not a SCRUM or LINE-OUT. ▷ *verb* (**loosed**, **loosing**) **1** to release or set free. **2** to unfasten or untie. **3** to make less tight, compact or dense. **4** to relax ▫ *loose one's hold.* **5** to discharge (a gun, bullet, arrow, etc). • **loosely** see separate entry. • **looseness** *noun.* • **on the loose** free from confinement or control. ◷ 14c: from Norse *lauss*.

> *loose*
>
> A word often confused with this one is **lose**.

loose box ▷ *noun* a part of a stable or horse-box where horses are kept untied.

loose change ▷ *noun* coins that are kept in a pocket, purse or bag for small expenses ▫ *made sure he had plenty of loose change for the phone.*

loose end ▷ *noun* (*often* **loose ends**) something that has been left unfinished or that has not been explained or decided ▫ *signed the contract after the loose ends had been tied up.* • **at a loose end** lacking something to do.

loose-leaf ▷ *adj* said of a folder, binder, etc: having clips or rings which open to allow pages to be taken out or put in.

loosely ▷ *adverb* **1** not tightly; droopily; insecurely. **2** roughly; approximately; without precision ▫ *The film's loosely based on Jim Thompson's novel.*

loosen /ˈluːsən/ ▷ *verb* (**loosened**, **loosening**) **1** *tr & intr* to make or become loose or looser. **2** to untie. **3** to free; to cause to become free or freer ▫ *Drink always loosened his tongue.* • **loosening** *noun.* ◷ 14c.

> ■ **loosen up 1** to make or become less dense, stiff or compacted ▫ *loosened up the soil.* **2** *colloq* to relax or become more relaxed.

loot ▷ *verb* (**looted**, **looting**) **1** *intr* **a** said especially of a mob: to steal from shops, warehouses, etc, often with attendant vandalism or violence during or following rioting; **b** to steal from an enemy in wartime. **2** *colloq* to steal from someone or something ▫ *looted his son's piggy-bank.* ▷ *noun* **1 a** money, goods or supplies stolen from shops, warehouses, etc, especially when taken during or following rioting; **b** money or goods stolen from an enemy in wartime. **2** an act of looting. **3** *slang* money. • **looter** *noun.* ◷ 18c: from Hindi *lut*.

looting ▷ *noun* the theft of money, goods or supplies, especially when they have been taken from an enemy during a war or from shops, warehouses, etc during rioting ▫ *The looting went on all night.* Also *as adj* ▫ *a looting spree.*

lop[1] ▷ *verb* (**lopped**, **lopping**) (*often* **lop off**) to cut off (especially the branches of a tree). ◷ 15c.

> ■ **lop something off** or **away** to cut away the unnecessary or superfluous parts of something ▫ *lopped five pages off the article.*

lop[2] ▷ *verb, intr* to hang down loosely. ◷ 16c.

lope ▷ *verb* (**loped**, **loping**) *intr* to run with long bounding steps. ▷ *noun* a bounding leap. ◷ 14c: from Norse *hlaupa* to leap.

lop-eared ▷ *adj* said of animals: having ears that droop. ◷ 17c: from LOP[2].

lopsided ▷ *adj* **1** with one side smaller, lower or lighter than the other. **2** leaning over to one side; unbalanced. ◷ 18c: from LOP[2].

loquacious /ləˈkweɪʃəs/ ▷ *adj* very talkative. • **loquaciously** *adverb.* • **loquaciousness** *noun.* ◷ 17c: from Latin *loquax*, from *loqui* to speak.

loquacity /ləˈkwasɪtɪ/ ▷ *noun* talkativeness. ◷ 17c: from French *loquacité*.

loquat /ˈloʊkwɒt, -kwat/ ▷ *noun* **1** a small evergreen tree with very hairy branches, originally found in China but now widely grown in S Europe. **2** the small round yellowish-orange edible fruits of this tree. ◷ 19c: Chinese, from Cantonese Chinese *luh kwat* rush orange.

loran or **Loran** /ˈlɔːrən/ ▷ *noun* a widely used long-range radio navigation system that works by measuring the time of arrival of signals from two fixed synchronized transmitters. ◷ 1940s: from *lo*ng-*ra*nge *n*avigation.

lord /lɔːd/ ▷ *noun* **1** a master or ruler. **2** *feudalism* someone who is in a superior position, with charge over a number of VASSALS who have received FIEFS from him in exchange for their oaths of loyalty. Compare LIEGE LORD. **3** *chiefly Brit* **a** a man who is a member of the aristocracy; **b** (**Lord**) a title used to address certain members of the aristocracy. **4** (**My Lord** or **my lord**) **a** /məˈlʌd/ a conventional way for lawyers, barristers, etc to address a judge in court; **b** a formal way of addressing certain members of the clergy and aristocracy. **5** (**Lord** or **Our Lord** or **the Lord**) *Christianity* a way of addressing or referring to both God and Jesus Christ. **6** (**Lord**) *in compounds* forming part of the titles of some high-ranking officials ▫ *Lord Provost* ▫ *Lord Privy Seal.* **7** (**Lord!**) expressing shock, surprise, dismay, etc ▫ *Good Lord! You mean he slept with his brother's wife?* **8** *formerly* a husband ▫ *my lord and master.* • **lordless** *adj.* • **lordlike** *adj.* • **drunk as a lord** very drunk indeed. • **live like a lord** to lead a luxurious life. • **lord it over someone** to behave in a condescending or overbearing manner towards them. • **Lord knows who, what, why,** *etc colloq* used to express complete bewilderment at something ▫ *Lord knows what she wants to go out with him for.* ◷ Anglo-Saxon *hlaf* loaf + *ward* keeper.

Lord Advocate ▷ *noun, Scot* see ATTORNEY GENERAL.

Lord Chamberlain ▷ *noun, Brit* the head of the royal household, in charge of eg the Ecclesiastical and Medical Households, the Honourable Corps of Gentlemen-at-Arms and the Yeomen of the Guard and with oversight over a variety of royal officials such as the poet laureate and the keeper of the royal swans. ◷ 13c.

Lord Chancellor and **Lord High Chancellor** ▷ *noun, Brit government* a member of the CABINET who, as head of the judiciary in England and Wales, advises on the appointment of magistrates, circuit judges and other senior law officers and whose other duties include being Speaker of the HOUSE OF LORDS. For Scotland see LORD PRESIDENT. ◷ 15c.

Lord Chief Justice and **Lord Chief Justice of England** and **Lord Chief Justice of Northern Ireland** ▷ *noun, Brit* the head of the Queen's Bench division, ranked immediately below the LORD CHANCELLOR. For Scotland see LORD JUSTICE GENERAL.

Lord Justice General ▷ *noun, Scottish* the president of the Court of Justiciary, the supreme criminal court of Scotland. See also LORD PRESIDENT.

Lord Lieutenant ▷ *noun* a title, now mainly honorary, for the Crown's representative in the English counties and shires, the Welsh and Northern Irish counties and the former counties of Scotland.

lordly ▷ *adj* (***lordlier, lordliest***) **1** having attributes that are popularly associated with lords, especially in being grand or haughty. **2 a** referring or relating to a lord or lords; **b** suitable for a lord or lords. • **lordliness**.

Lord Lyon see under LYON KING OF ARMS

Lord Mayor and **Lady Mayoress** ▷ *noun* a title formerly held only by the mayors of the City of London, York and Dublin, but now also given to the mayors of some of England's larger boroughs and cities such as Birmingham, Liverpool and Sheffield.

lordosis /lɔːˈdoʊsɪs/ ▷ *noun, pathol* a medical condition characterized by excessive inward curvature of the lumbar region of the spine, which may be congenital, or caused by faulty posture, muscular weakness, or disorders of the spine or hip. • **lordotic** /-ˈdɒtɪk/ *adj.* ◷ 18c: Latin, from Greek *lordos* bent backward.

Lord President ▷ *noun, Scottish* the president of the Court of Session (the supreme civil court of Scotland), and head of the Scottish justiciary. The position of LORD JUSTICE GENERAL is now also held by the same person.

Lord Privy Seal ▷ *noun* the leader of the House of Lords and a senior British cabinet minister without official duties. ◷ 15c.

Lord Provost ▷ *noun* the title of the PROVOST of five of Scotland's cities, namely Aberdeen, Dundee, Edinburgh, Glasgow and Perth.

the Lords *singular noun* shortened form of HOUSE OF LORDS.

lords-and-ladies ▷ *noun* a perennial European plant with large leaves shaped like arrow-heads, and a pale-green SPATHE partially surrounding a club-shaped reddish-purple SPADIX, which emits a fetid odour that attracts pollinating insects. Also called **cuckoo-pint**.

the Lord's Day ▷ *noun, Christianity* another term for Sunday, especially when drawing attention to the perceived holiness of the day.

Lordship ▷ *noun* (**His** or **Your Lordship**) **a** a title used to address bishops, judges and all peers except dukes; **b** *facetious* a form of address used to mock someone behaving in a pretentious or overbearing way.

the Lord's Prayer ▷ *noun, Christianity* the prayer that commonly begins, 'Our Father who art in heaven' (Matthew 6.9-13 and Luke 11.2-4), that was used by Jesus to teach his disciples the way of praying that would be most acceptable to God. Also called **Our Father** and, especially in the Latin version, **Paternoster**.

Lords Spiritual ▷ *noun, Brit* the English and Welsh Anglican archbishops and bishops entitled to sit in the House of Lords. Compare LORDS TEMPORAL.

the Lord's Supper ▷ *noun, Christianity* a Protestant (especially Presbyterian) term for MASS, COMMUNION (sense 3) or the EUCHARIST.

Lords Temporal ▷ *noun, Brit* all the members of the House of Lords who are not archbishops or bishops. Compare LORDS SPIRITUAL.

lore /lɔː(r)/ ▷ *noun* the whole body of knowledge on a particular subject, especially the kind of knowledge that has been enhanced by legends, anecdotes, traditional beliefs, etc □ ***folklore***. ◷ Anglo-Saxon *lar*.

Lorelei /ˈlɒrəlaɪ/ ▷ *noun* (***Loreleis***) **1** a rock in the river Rhine famous for its echo. **2 a** in German legend: a beautiful woman who drowned herself in the river Rhine after discovering her lover had been unfaithful and who was afterwards believed to sit on the Lorelei rock, luring sailors to their death by her singing; **b** any woman who is considered to exert a powerful attraction over men, especially when it results in their downfall. See also SIREN, FEMME FATALE. ◷ 19c: sense 2 is from the novel *Godwi* (1800-1802) by Clemens Brentano (1778-1842).

lorgnette /lɔːnˈjɛt/ ▷ *noun* a pair of spectacles that are held up to the eyes using a long handle, as opposed to the kind that rest on the nose. ◷ 19c: French, from *lorgner* to squint.

loris /ˈlɔːrɪs/ ▷ *noun* (*plural* ***lorises*** or ***loris***) a small primitive S Asian primate with a pale face and large eyes with dark rings around them. ◷ 18c.

lorry /ˈlɒrɪ/ ▷ *noun* (***lorries***) *Brit* a large road vehicle for transporting heavy loads. *N Amer equivalent* **truck**. ◷ Early 20c.

lose /luːz/ ▷ *verb* (***lost, losing***) **1 a** to fail to keep or obtain something, especially because of a mistake, carelessness, etc □ ***lost his money through a hole in his pocket***; **b** to stop or begin to stop having (some distinguishing quality, characteristic or property) □ ***She was losing her nerve*** □ ***Despite everything, he hasn't lost his sense of humour***; **c** to become less marked, noticeable, intense, etc in a specified way □ ***These roses have lost their smell.*** **2 a** to misplace something, especially temporarily □ ***I've lost the car keys***; **b** to be unable to find something; **c** to leave accidentally □ ***I lost the umbrella at the cinema.*** **3 a** to suffer the loss of someone (usually a close friend or relative) through death; **b** to suffer the loss of (an unborn baby) through miscarriage or stillbirth; **c** to fail to save the life of (especially a patient); **d** to be deprived of someone or something (life, possessions, etc), especially in a war, fire, natural disaster, etc □ ***The village lost half its population in the earthquake***; **e** (**be lost**) to be killed or drowned, especially at sea. **4** to fail to use or get something; to miss (an opportunity). **5 a** *tr & intr* to fail to win (a game, vote, proposal, election, battle, bet, etc); **b** to give away; to forfeit □ ***lost £50 on the horses.*** **6 a** to be unable or no longer able to hear, see, understand, etc someone or something □ ***Sorry, I lost what you said when that noisy bus went by***; **b** to confuse or bewilder someone □ ***Sorry, you've lost me there.*** **7 a** to escape or get away from someone or something; **b** said of a competitor in a race, etc: to leave (the rest of the field, etc) behind. **8** said of a clock or watch: to become slow by (a specified amount). • **lose one's cool** *colloq* to become upset. • **lose face** to be humiliated or discredited. • **lose one's grip** or **lose one's grip on something** to be unable to control or understand things. • **lose ground** to slip back or behind □ ***Major steadily lost ground in the opinion polls.*** • **lose one's head** to become angry or irrational. • **lose heart** to become discouraged; to despair. • **lose one's heart** or **lose one's heart to someone** to fall in love (with them). • **lose one's licence** to be disqualified from driving, usually for exceeding the limit of alcohol in the blood or for driving dangerously. • **lose one's marbles** *slang* to go completely crazy. • **lose one's mind** or **reason** to behave irrationally, especially temporarily. • **lose one's rag** or **lose the rag** *Brit colloq* to become very angry. • **lose sight of someone** or **something** **1** to be unable or no longer able to see them or it. **2** to forget or ignore the importance of them or it □ ***They lost sight of their original aims.*** • **lose sleep over something** to worry about it or be preoccupied by it. • **lose one's temper** to become angry. • **lose one's touch** to forget how to do something; to be less proficient at doing something than one used to be. • **lose touch with someone** or **something** to no longer be in contact with them or it. • **lose track of someone** or **something** to fail to notice or monitor the passing or progress of them or it. • **lose one's voice** to be unable or hardly able to speak, especially due to having a sore throat, a cold or flu. • **lose one's way** or **lose the way** to be unable or no longer able to tell where one is or in which direction one should be going; to stray from one's intended route by mistake. ⓒ Anglo-Saxon *losian* to be lost.

■ **lose oneself in something** to have all of one's attention taken up by it.

■ **lose out** *colloq* **1** to suffer loss or be at a disadvantage. **2** to fail to get something one wants.

■ **lose out on something** *colloq* to fail to benefit from it.

■ **lose to someone** to be beaten by them □ *He lost to a more experienced player.*

lose

A word often confused with this one is **loose**.

loser /'luːzər/ ▻ *noun* **1** someone or something that is defeated □ *The horse always looked a loser.* **2** *colloq* someone who is habitually unsuccessful. ● **a bad, poor** or **good loser** someone who loses in bad, poor or good spirit. ● **a two-time, three-time, big-time**, *etc* **loser** someone who has been to prison two, three, many etc times.

losing /'luːzɪŋ/ ▻ *adj* failing; never likely to be successful □ *fighting a losing battle.*

loss ▻ *noun* (*losses*) **1** the act or fact of losing or being lost □ *paid for his stupidity with the loss of his driving licence.* **2** the thing, amount, etc lost □ *His loss of hearing was severe.* **3** the disadvantage that results when someone or something goes □ *a great loss to the company.* **4 a** the death of a close friend or relative □ *He couldn't come to terms with the loss of his mother*; **b** the sadness felt after such a death □ *He did his best to console her in her loss.* ● **at a loss 1** puzzled; uncertain; unable to understand □ *Her tantrums left me at a complete loss.* **2** said of a selling price, etc: lower than the buying price □ *had to sell the car at a loss.* **3** said of a company, etc: losing more money than it is making □ *trading at a loss.* ● **at a loss for words** speechless through shock, amazement, etc. ⓒ Anglo-Saxon.

loss adjuster ▻ *noun, insurance* someone who assesses claims for compensation on behalf of an insurance company.

loss leader ▻ *noun, commerce* an item on sale at a loss, as a means of attracting custom for a wider range of goods.

lost¹ ▻ *adj* **1 a** missing □ *the lost child*; **b** having gone astray □ *a lost cat*; **c** no longer found, done or practised □ *the lost art of conversation*; **d** unable to find one's way. **2** confused; puzzled. **3** said especially of soldiers or people at sea: missing and presumed dead or drowned. **4** wasted □ *made up for lost time.* **5** *old use* **a** lacking in morals □ *lost women*; **b** damned □ *lost souls.* ● **get lost** *slang* **1** to go away and stay away. **2** used to express mild derision □ *Oh, get lost! You don't really mean that.* ● **lost and found** a column in local newspapers where people who have either lost something or found something can advertise. ● **lost in something 1** absorbed in it □ *She was completely lost in thought.* **2** hidden, indistinguishable, camouflaged, etc in or by it. ● **lost on someone** not appreciated or understood by them □ *The joke about the lizard was lost on her.* ● **lost to someone** no longer open or available to them. ● **lost to something** no longer capable of feeling (an emotion), or of responding morally or rationally. ⓒ 16c: past participle of LOSE.

lost² *past tense, past participle of* LOSE

lost cause ▻ *noun* an aim, ideal, person, etc that has no chance of success.

lost generation ▻ *noun* **1** *originally* the men who died in the trenches between 1914 and 1918. **2** the group of US expatriate writers living in Paris in the 1920s that included Ernest Hemingway and F Scott Fitzgerald, whose work explores and reflects the disillusionment that was felt after World War I and the concomitant breakdown of order and values. **3** *now* any generational group which is perceived to have lost or rejected traditional value systems. ⓒ 1920s: quoted by Ernest Hemingway in *The Sun Also Rises* (1926) as coined in conversation by Gertrude Stein.

lost property ▻ *noun* things that have been lost by their owners and found and handed in by someone else. ● **lost property office** or **department** an official place where lost property is stored until it is claimed, or disposed of if it is not claimed.

lot ▻ *noun* **1** *colloq* (*usually* **a lot of** or **lots of**) a large number or amount of something □ *an awful lot of work to do* □ *lots of children.* **2 a** (**the lot**) everything; the total; the whole number or amount □ *He just sat down and ate the lot*; **b** (**one's lot**) *colloq* all one is getting □ *That's your lot!* **3** a group of people or things that have something, often a specified attribute or quality, in common □ *Get a move on, you lazy lot.* **4 a** a straw, slip of paper, etc that is drawn from a group of similar objects, in order to reach a fair and impartial decision □ *They drew lots to see who'd go first*; **b** the use of lots to arrive at a decision, choice, etc □ *made their selection by lot.* **5** someone's fortune, destiny, plight, etc □ *Something must be done to remedy the lot of the homeless.* **6** an item or set of items for sale by auction, usually identified by a number □ *Lot 49 looks intriguing.* **7** *N Amer* an area of land for a specified purpose □ *parking lot.* **8** the area around a film studio used for outside filming. ● **a bad lot** a group or person considered to be dishonest, immoral, etc or that is thought of as having a reputation for behaving improperly □ *Unfortunately he got in with a thoroughly bad lot.* ● **a lot** often □ *went to the cinema a lot.* ● **cast** or **throw in one's lot with someone** to decide to share their fortunes. ● **this** or **that little lot** used, usually disparagingly, to refer to a specific group, series of events, etc □ *What a mess! She won't be happy when she sees this little lot.* ⓒ Anglo-Saxon *hlot* portion or choice.

loth see LOATH

lotion /'loʊʃən/ ▻ *noun* any liquid, used either as a medicine or a cosmetic, for healing or cleaning the skin. ⓒ 15c: from Latin *lotio*, from *lavare*, *lotum* to wash.

lottery /'lɒtərɪ/ ▻ *noun* (*lotteries*) **1** a system for raising money which involves randomly drawing numbered tickets from a drum, etc and giving prizes to those who hold the tickets with the same numbers as the ones that have been picked out. Compare RAFFLE, TOMBOLA. **2** anything which is thought of as being a matter of chance. See also NATIONAL LOTTERY. ⓒ 16c: from French *loterie*, related to LOT.

lotto /'lɒtoʊ/ ▻ *noun* an earlier name for the game now usually called BINGO.

lotus /'loʊtəs/ ▻ *noun* (*lotuses*) a popular name for a variety of different plants many of which are cultivated for their ornamental value: **1 a** the jujube shrub, native to the Mediterranean region; **b** *Greek mythol* the fruit of this shrub, used by the ancient Greeks to make bread and wine, consumption of which was thought to produce a state of blissful and dreamy forgetfulness. **2** a species of water lily sacred to the ancient Egyptians and often depicted in Egyptian art. **3** either of two species of water lily belonging to a separate genus, widely cultivated as ornamental plants, one native to Asia, with pink flowers and traditionally associated with Buddhism and Hinduism, and the other native to southern USA, with yellow flowers. ⓒ 16c: from Greek *lotos*.

lotus-eater ▻ *noun* **1** *originally Greek mythol* one of the people who tried to detain Odysseus's men by getting them to consume food made from the LOTUS (see sense 1b). **2** *now* someone who lives a lazy and indulgent life. ⓒ 19c.

lotus position ▻ *noun, yoga* a seated position with the legs crossed and each foot resting on the opposite thigh.

loud /laʊd/ ▷ *adj* (***louder***, ***loudest***) **1** making a relatively great sound; noisy. **2** capable of making a relatively great sound □ *a loud horn.* **3** emphatic and insistent □ *loud complaints.* **4** said disparagingly of colours, clothes, designs, etc: tastelessly bright, garish or gaudy. **5** said of someone or their behaviour: aggressively noisy and coarse. ▷ *adverb* in a loud manner. • **loudish** *adj.* • **loudly** *adverb.* • **loudness** *noun.* • **loud and clear** usually said of the quality of transmitted messages: easily heard and understood. • **out loud** said of something someone says: having the capacity of being heard by others □ *expressed her contempt out loud.* ⓒ Anglo-Saxon *hlud.*

loudhailer ▷ *noun* a portable device for amplifying the voice.

loud-mouth ▷ *noun, colloq* someone who is very noisy and aggressively boastful. • **loud-mouthed** *adj.*

loudspeaker (*often just* **speaker**) ▷ *noun, electronics* an electronic device that converts electrical signals into audible sound waves, used in radio, television, telephone receivers, hi-fi systems, etc.

lough /lɒk; *Irish* lɒx/ ▷ *noun, Irish* a LOCH. ⓒ 14c: Irish Gaelic *loch.*

lounge /laʊndʒ/ ▷ *verb* (***lounged***, ***lounging***) *intr* **1** to lie, sit, stand, recline etc in a relaxed and comfortable way. **2** to pass the time without doing very much □ *He would lounge from morning to night.* ▷ *noun* **1** a sitting-room in a private house. **2** a large room in a public building, such as a hotel, where people can sit and relax. **3** (*also* **departure lounge**) an area or large room in an airport, ferry terminal, etc, where passengers can relax prior to being called to board the aeroplane, ferry, etc. **4** *Brit* (*also* **lounge bar**) the more up-market bar of a pub or hotel. Compare PUBLIC BAR. **5** an act or spell of lounging. ⓒ 16c.

■ **lounge about** or **around** to lie about idly or lazily.

■ **lounge away** to pass (one's time) idly.

lounge lizard ▷ *noun* a man who tries to inveigle himself into the fashionable parties, etc of the rich in the hope of finding a female benefactor.

lounger ▷ *noun* **1** someone who lounges. **2** an extending chair or lightweight couch for lounging on. **3** any loose garment that is worn when relaxing.

lounge suit ▷ *noun, Brit* matching jacket and trousers worn by men for ordinary everyday wear.

lounge suite ▷ *noun* a set of furniture usually consisting of a sofa and two armchairs.

loupe /luːp/ ▷ *noun* a small magnifying glass held in the eye socket and used by jewellers, watchmakers, etc for close, intricate work or for examining pieces to assess their value.

lour or **lower** /laʊə(r)/ ▷ *verb* (***loured***, ***louring***) *intr* **1** said of the sky or elements: to darken or threaten rain or storms. **2** to scowl or look angry or gloomy. ▷ *noun* a scowl. • **louring** *adj.* ⓒ 13c in sense 2; 15c in sense 1.

louse /laʊs/ ▷ *noun* **1** (*plural* ***lice***) a wingless parasitic insect with a flat body and short legs, which survives by sucking the blood of its HOST, causing itchiness, and which is transmitted by direct contact, the adults laying eggs (NITs) on hair, fur, feathers, clothing, etc. **2** (*plural* ***louses***) *slang* a scornful term of abuse for a person. ▷ *verb* (***loused***, ***lousing***) to get rid of lice from (clothing, hair, etc). • **lousing** *noun.* ⓒ Anglo-Saxon *lus.*

■ **louse something up** *slang* to spoil or ruin it.

lousy /ˈlaʊzɪ/ ▷ *adj* (***lousier***, ***lousiest***) **1** having lice. **2** *slang* very bad, unpleasant or disgusting. **3** poor or second-rate. • **lousily** *adverb.* • **lousiness** *noun.* • **lousy with something** *slang* swarming with or having a great deal of it □ *The place was lousy with cops.*

lout /laʊt/ ▷ *noun* **1** *formerly* someone, usually male, who has little or no education or who behaves in a rude or ill-mannered way. **2** *now* someone, usually a teenage male, whose behaviour, especially in public, is generally considered unacceptable. • **loutish** *adj.* • **loutishness** *noun.* See also LAGER LOUT, LITTER LOUT. ⓒ 16c.

louvre or (*N Amer*) **louver** /ˈluːvə(r)/ ▷ *noun* **1** any one of a set of horizontal sloping overlapping slats in a door, etc which let air in but keep rain and light out. **2** a dome-like structure on a roof for letting smoke out and light and air in. • **louvred** *adj.* ⓒ 16c; 14c in sense 2: from French *lovier.*

lovable or **loveable** /ˈlʌvəbəl/ ▷ *adj* worthy of or inspiring love or affection.

lovage /ˈlʌvɪdʒ/ ▷ *noun* a S European flowering plant used medicinally and for flavouring. ⓒ 14c: from French *luvesche.*

lovat /ˈlʌvət/ ▷ *noun* **1** a palish dusky green colour. **2** a tweed suit in this colour. ▷ *adj* palish dusky green in colour. • **lovat-green** *adj.* ⓒ Early 20c: named after Lovat, a town in the Scottish Highlands famous for producing tweed of this colour.

love /lʌv/ ▷ *verb* (***loved***, ***loving***) **1 a** to feel great affection for (especially a close relative, friend, etc); **b** to feel great affection and sexual attraction for (especially a sexual partner, a person one is romantically involved with, etc). **2 a** to enjoy very much □ *I love to boogie*; **b** to like very much □ *I love chocolate biscuits.* ▷ *noun* **1** a feeling of great affection □ *brotherly love.* **2** a strong liking □ *a love of the outdoors.* **3** sexual attraction. **4** *as adj* relating or referring to love, romance, sexual relations, etc □ *love letters.* **5** often used as a term of address: **a** to a person one loves □ *my love*; **b** *Brit colloq* to anyone regardless of affection. **5** *tennis, squash, whist, etc* no score. • **fall in love with someone** to develop feelings of love and sexual attraction for them. • **in love** or **in love with someone** having strong feelings of affection and sexual attraction (for them). • **love at first sight** instant sexual attraction. • **make love to** or **with someone 1** to be sexually intimate with them, especially when this culminates in sexual intercourse. **2** *old use* to woo. • **not for love or money** under no circumstances. • **no love lost between (two or more people)** mutual dislike □ *Since the divorce, there's no love lost between them.* ⓒ Anglo-Saxon *lufu.*

love affair ▷ *noun* a romantic relationship which may or may not be a sexual one, especially one that is fleeting or illicit.

lovebird ▷ *noun* **1** a small parrot found in Africa and Madagascar, sometimes kept as a cagebird. It shows strong attachment to its mate through frequent mutual preening sessions. **2** (**lovebirds**) lovers who openly display their affection for each other in public.

love bite ▷ *noun* a patch of bruised skin, usually found on a woman's breast or on the neck of either sex, caused by a sucking kiss. *N Amer equivalent* **hickey**, **hickie**.

love-child ▷ *noun, old use* an illegitimate child.

love handles ▷ *plural noun, facetious* an affectionate term for the deposit of fat sometimes found in both men and women on either side of the back just below the waist. ⓒ 1980s: so called because it is commonly the place where sexual partners grip each other.

love-hate ▷ *adj* said of feelings towards someone or something: ambivalent or oscillating □ *a love-hate relationship.*

love-in-a-mist ▷ *noun* a garden plant with pale blue or white flowers and feathery leaves.

love juice ▷ *noun, vulgar* secretions produced during sexual arousal. ⓒ 19c.

loveless ▷ *adj* devoid of love □ *trapped in a loveless marriage.*

love letter ▷ *noun* a letter addressed to one's lover expressing feelings of affection.

love-lies-bleeding ▷ *noun* a garden plant with drooping spikes of reddish-purple flowers.

love life ▷ *noun* the area of someone's life that includes their personal relationships.

lovelorn /ˈlʌvlɔːn/ ▷ *adj* sad because the love one feels for someone else is not returned. ◷ 17c.

lovely ▷ *adj* (***lovelier***, ***loveliest***) **1** strikingly attractive; beautiful. **2** *colloq* delightful or pleasing. ▷ *noun* (***lovelies***) *colloq* a pretty woman. ◷ Anglo-Saxon *luflic*.

love-making ▷ *noun* **a** *formerly* courting; **b** *now* any form of sexual activity. ◷ 15c.

love nest ▷ *noun* a place where lovers can be together undisturbed.

love potion ▷ *noun* an APHRODISIAC.

lover ▷ *noun* **1** someone who is in love with someone else, especially in a romantic or sexual way. **2** (**lovers**) two people who are in love with one another or who are sharing a sexual relationship. **3** *in compounds* someone who enjoys or is fond of a specified thing □ *a cat-lover*.

lovesick ▷ *adj* **a** infatuated with someone; **b** lovelorn. ◷ 16c.

lovey-dovey /ˈlʌvɪˈdʌvɪ/ ▷ *adj, colloq* said of a couple: ostentatiously displaying affection, especially in a silly or sentimental way. ◷ 19c.

loving ▷ *adj* **1** affectionate and caring. **2** *in compounds* enjoying, valuing, cherishing or appreciating a specified thing □ *fun-loving*. ● **lovingly** *adverb*. ◷ 15c.

loving-cup ▷ *noun* a large two-handled drinking cup passed round at the end of a banquet. ◷ 19c.

loving kindness ▷ *noun* tenderness; compassion. ◷ 16c.

low¹ /loʊ/ ▷ *adj* (***lower***, ***lowest***) **1** said of a building, hill, etc: measuring comparatively little from top to bottom. **2** close to the ground, sea-level, the horizon, etc □ *low cloud*. **3** said of a temperature, volume of water, score, etc: measuring comparatively less than is usual or average □ *The river is low*. **4** having little value; not costing very much. **5** said of numbers: small. **6** not near the top □ *Shopping was low on her list of priorities*. **7** coarse, rude, vulgar, etc. **8** being of humble rank or position. **9** not very advanced; unsophisticated □ *Worms are a low form of animal life*. **10** said of the neckline of a garment: leaving the neck and upper part of the chest bare. **11** said of a sound, note, voice, etc: **a** quiet; soft □ *The fridge gives out a low hum*; **b** produced by slow vibrations and having a deep pitch. **12 a** weak; lacking in energy or vitality □ *feeling low after the operation*; **b** depressed; dispirited □ *feeling low after losing his job*. **13** unfavourable □ *a low opinion*. **14** underhanded; unprincipled □ *How low can you get?* **15** giving a relatively slow engine speed □ *a low gear*. **16** subdued □ *low lighting*. **17** not prominent or conspicuous □ *keeping a low profile*. **18** said of latitudes: near the equator. **19** *phonetics* said of a vowel: produced with the tongue or part of the tongue comparatively depressed and away from the palate. Also called OPEN. ▷ *adverb* **1** in or to a low position, state or manner □ *aimed low and fired* □ *brought low by his gambling debts*. **2** in a small quantity or to a small degree. **3** said of a sound, etc: **a** quietly; **b** with or in a deep pitch. **4** *in compounds* **a** not measuring much in a specified respect □ *low-voltage*; **b** not far off the ground □ *low-slung*; **c** deeply □ *low-cut*; **d** lowly □ *low-born*. ▷ *noun* **1** a depth, position, level, etc which is low or lowest □ *The pound has reached an all-time low*. **2** *meteorol* a CYCLONE 1. ● **lowness** *noun*. ● **lay low** see under LAY. ● **lie low** see under LIE. ● **lowest of the low** the most contemptible. ● **low in something** containing less than the average amount, etc of it □ *low in fat*. ● **low on something 1** *sometimes euphemistic* not having much of it □ *We're low on coffee* □ *She's a bit low on the brains front*. **2** not having much of it left □ *running low on petrol*. ◷ 12c: from Norse *lagr*.

low² /loʊ/ ▷ *verb* (***lowed***, ***lowing***) *intr* said of cattle: to make a gentle mooing sound. ▷ *noun* the gentle mooing sound made by cattle. ● **lowing** *noun*. ◷ Anglo-Saxon *hlowan*.

low-alcohol ▷ *adj* containing less alcohol by volume than is standard.

low-born ▷ *adj* being of humble birth.

lowbrow ▷ *adj* thought of as having or involving relatively popular tastes. ▷ *noun* someone who is thought to be more inclined towards the popular than the classical. Compare MIDDLEBROW, HIGHBROW.

low-cal ▷ *adj* said of certain food or drinks: having fewer calories than the standard variety.

Low Church ▷ *noun* a group within the Church of England which puts little value on ceremony or the authority of the priesthood, but which stresses evangelical theology. ▷ *adj* (**Low-Church**) referring or relating to this group or its practices. ◷ 17c.

low comedy ▷ *noun* comedy which relies on farcical situations, slapstick, pratfalls, etc for its humour rather than anything more sophisticated. ◷ 18c.

the lowdown ▷ *noun, colloq* information about someone or something, especially if it is disreputable or acquired surreptitiously □ *I've got all the lowdown on their affair*. ◷ Early 20c.

low-down ▷ *adj, colloq* mean and dishonourable □ *a low-down dirty trick*. ◷ 16c.

lower¹ /loʊə(r)/ ▷ *adj* **1** not as high in position, status, height, value, etc □ *lower middle class*. **2** said of an animal or plant: less highly developed than other species. **3** said of part of a river or the area of land around it: relatively far from the source □ *lower Deeside*. **4** in place names: **a** relatively far south; **b** geographically not so high. ▷ *adverb* in or to a lower position. ▷ *verb* (***lowered***, ***lowering***) **1** to lessen or become less in amount, value, status, sound, etc. **2 a** to pull down □ *We'd better lower the window*; **b** to cause or allow something to come down □ *lowered the lifeboat*. **3** to reduce or cause something to be reduced □ *The rejection lowered his confidence*. ◷ 13c.

lower² see LOUR

lower-case *printing* (abbreviation **lc**) ▷ *adj* referring or relating to small letters as opposed to capitals or UPPER-CASE letters. ▷ *noun* (**lower case**) a letter or letters of this kind □ *A novel written entirely in lower case*. ◷ 17c: so called because of the way the tray or CASE containing a compositor's type was divided up, the capital or UPPER-CASE letters being held in the top half and the uncapitalized small ones in the bottom half.

lower class ▷ *noun* the social group that traditionally includes manual workers and their families. ▷ *adj* (**lower-class**) referring or relating to this social group. ◷ 18c.

lower house and **lower chamber** ▷ *noun* in a BICAMERAL parliament: usually the larger section, more representative of the population as a whole, such as the House of Commons in the United Kingdom. ◷ 16c.

lowest common denominator ▷ *noun, math* (abbreviation **LCD** or **lcd**) in a group of fractions, the lowest common multiple of all the denominators, eg the LCD of $^1/_3$ and $^1/_4$ is 12. See also COMMON DENOMINATOR.

lowest common multiple ▷ *noun, math* (abbreviation **LCM** or **lcm**) the smallest number into which every member of a group of numbers will divide exactly, eg the LCM of 2, 3 and 4 is 12.

low-fat ▷ *adj* said of some processed foods: containing less fat than the full-fat versions of the same food.

low frequency ▷ *noun* **1** a radio band where the number of cycles per second is between 30 and 300 kilohertz. **2** *as adj* referring or relating to electric currents, voltages, sound waves, etc which fall into this category □ *low-frequency vibrations.*

Low German ▷ *noun* a term that covers some of the dialects of German, especially those spoken in Saxony and Westphalia, but excluding those of HIGH GERMAN. Also called **Plattdeutsch** /'plɑːtdɔɪtʃ/.

low-key ▷ *adj* **1** said of a painting, photograph, etc: made up of mostly dark, subdued shades with little or no highlighting. **2** restrained and subdued. **3** unobtrusive; not sensationalist □ *kept the news coverage very low-key.*

lowland ▷ *noun* **1** (*also* **lowlands**) land which is comparatively low-lying and flat. **2** (**the Lowlands**) the less mountainous region of Scotland lying to the south and east of the Highlands, but usually thought of as excluding the BORDERS. **3** (*also* **lowland** or **Lowland**) *as adj* referring or relating to lowlands or the Scottish Lowlands. • **lowlander** or **Lowlander** *noun.* ⓒ 16c.

Lowland Scots ▷ *noun* Scots, the language spoken in the Lowlands of Scotland.

Low Latin ▷ *noun* any of the forms of Latin used after the classical period, eg that used in medieval Europe.

low-level language ▷ *noun, computing* a programming language in which each instruction represents a single MACHINE-CODE operation. See also HIGH-LEVEL LANGUAGE.

low-life ▷ *adj* **1** common, vulgar, disreputable, etc □ *low-life scum.* **2** *used as a noun* (*usually* **lowlife**, *plural usually* **lowlifes**) **a** the criminal fraternity itself; **b** someone who is a member of the criminal fraternity or who closely associates with criminals; **c** anyone who is considered dishonest or disreputable □ *associating with lowlifes like her.* ⓒ 18c.

lowly ▷ *adj* (**lowlier**, **lowliest**) **1** humble in rank, status or behaviour. **2** simple, modest and unpretentious. • **lowliness** *noun.*

Low Mass ▷ *noun, Christianity* a mass celebrated without music or incense.

low-pitched ▷ *adj* **1** said of a sound: low in pitch. **2** said of a roof: having a gentle slope.

low-pressure ▷ *adj* said of steam, steam-engines, atmosphere, etc: using or creating little pressure.

low profile ▷ *noun* a deliberate avoidance of publicity and attention. ▷ *adj* (**low-profile**) **1** unobtrusive; getting little publicity □ *low-profile talks on N Ireland.* **2** said of car tyres: wider than is usual.

low-spirited ▷ *adj* dejected or depressed.

low tech ▷ *noun, colloq* **1** simple unsophisticated technology used to make basic products. **2** *as adj* □ *preferred the low-tech approach.* ⓒ 1970s: from LOW TECHNOLOGY, modelled on HIGH TECH.

low tide ▷ *noun* the minimum level reached by a falling tide. Also called **low water**.

low-water mark ▷ *noun* **1 a** the level that a low tide reaches; **b** a naturally occurring or artificial line that marks this level. **2** the lowest point it is possible to reach.

lox[1] /lɒks/ ▷ *noun* (**lox** or **loxes**) a type of smoked salmon. ⓒ 1940s: from Yiddish *laks*.

lox[2] /lɒks/ ▷ *abbreviation* liquid oxygen especially as used to support the combustion of rocket fuel. ⓒ 1920s.

loyal /'lɔɪəl/ ▷ *adj* **1** faithful and true. **2** personally devoted to a sovereign, government, leader, friend, partner, etc. **3** expressing or showing loyalty □ *the loyal toast to the Queen.* • **loyally** *adverb.* ⓒ 16c: from French *loial*, from Latin *legalis* legal.

loyalist ▷ *noun* **1** a loyal supporter, especially of a sovereign or an established government. **2** (**Loyalist**) in N Ireland: a protestant who is in favour of continuing their country's parliamentary union with Great Britain, as opposed to someone who advocates the union of N Ireland and Eire. See also UNIONIST. **3** *US* during the American War of Independence: an American who was in favour of continuing the US's links with Great Britain. Compare REPUBLICAN. ⓒ 17c.

loyalty ▷ *noun* (**loyalties**) **1** the state or quality of being loyal. **2** (*often* **loyalties**) a feeling of loyalty or duty towards someone or to an institution □ *divided loyalties.* ⓒ 15c.

lozenge /'lɒzɪndʒ/ ▷ *noun* **1** a small sweet or tablet, especially one with some kind of medicinal property, which dissolves in the mouth. **2** *math, now* a less common term for a RHOMBUS. **3** *heraldry* a diamond-shaped DEVICE whose longer axis is placed vertically. ⓒ 14c: from French *losenge*.

LP ▷ *abbreviation* **1** long-playing. **2** long-playing record.

lp ▷ *abbreviation* line printer.

LPG and **LP gas** ▷ *abbreviation* liquefied petroleum gas.

L-plate ▷ *noun, Brit* a small square white sign with a red letter *L* on it which, by law, learner drivers must display on the back and front of their cars until they pass their driving test.

Lr ▷ *symbol, chem* lawrencium.

LRAM ▷ *abbreviation* Licentiate of the Royal Academy of Music.

LRCP ▷ *abbreviation* Licentiate of the Royal College of Physicians.

LRCS ▷ *abbreviation* Licentiate of the Royal College of Surgeons.

LSD ▷ *abbreviation* lysergic acid diethylamide, a hallucinatory drug which psychotherapists once experimented with in the hope of finding out more about the causes and effects of certain mental illnesses and which, since the 1960s, has been widely used illegally as a psychedelic recreational drug. Also (*colloq*) called **acid**.

L.S.D., **l.s.d.** or **£.s.d.** ▷ *abbreviation, Brit* pounds, shillings, pence, denominations of currency which were superseded in the early 1970s by DECIMAL CURRENCY. ⓒ 19c: from Latin *librae, solidi, denarii*.

LSE ▷ *abbreviation* London School of Economics.

LSO ▷ *abbreviation* London Symphony Orchestra.

Lt or **Lt.** ▷ *abbreviation* Lieutenant.

Ltd or **Ltd.** ▷ *abbreviation* Limited, as used at the end of the names of limited liability companies.

Lu ▷ *symbol, chem* lutetium.

lubber /'lʌbə(r)/ ▷ *noun* someone who is big, awkward and clumsy, especially if they are also thought of as tending to be lazy. • **lubberly** *adj, adverb.* ⓒ 14c as *lobre*.

lubricant /'luːbrɪkənt/ ▷ *noun* oil, grease, etc used to reduce friction. ▷ *adj* lubricating. ⓒ 19c: from Latin *lubricare* to make slippery or smooth.

lubricate /'luːbrɪkeɪt, 'ljuː-/ ▷ *verb* (**lubricated**, **lubricating**) **1** to coat (engine parts, etc) with oil, grease, etc in order to reduce friction. **2** to make smooth, slippery or greasy. **3** *intr* to act as a lubricant. • **lubricating** *adj.* • **lubrication** *noun.* ⓒ 17c: from Latin *lubricare*, *lubricatum* to make slippery or smooth.

lubricator ▷ *noun* **1** someone or something that lubricates. **2** any appliance that contains oil, etc for lubricating engines, etc.

lubricity /lʊ'brɪsɪtɪ, ljʊ-/ ▷ *noun, literary* lewdness. • **lubricious** /-'brɪʃəs/ *adj.* ⓒ 17c: from Latin *lubricus* slippery.

lucent /'luːsənt, 'ljuː-/ ▷ *adj* bright; shiny. ⓒ 16c: Latin *lucere* to shine.

lucerne /lʊ'sɜːn/ ▷ *noun, Brit* ALFALFA. ⓒ 17c: from French *luzerne*.

lucid /ˈluːsɪd, ˈljuː-/ ▷ *adj* **1** said of a speech, piece of writing, argument, etc: **a** clearly presented and easily understood; **b** perceptive. **2** said of someone's mind or their ability to reason: not confused, especially in contrast to bouts of insanity or delirium. **3** bright; shining. • **lucidity** *noun*. • **lucidly** *adverb*. • **lucidness** *noun*. ◎ 16c: from Latin *lucidus* full of light.

Lucifer /ˈluːsɪfə(r), ˈljuː-/ ▷ *noun* Satan. ◎ 11c: Latin, meaning 'light-bringer', from *lux, lucis* light + *ferre* to bear.

luck ▷ *noun* **1** chance, especially as it is perceived as influencing someone's life at specific points in time □ *felt luck was on his side so he kept on betting.* **2** good fortune. **3** events in life which cannot be controlled and seem to happen by chance □ *She's had nothing but bad luck.* • **luckless** *adj*. • **down on one's luck** experiencing problems or suffering hardship. • **Good luck!** an exclamation wishing someone success in some venture they are about to undertake. • **in luck** fortunate □ *You're in luck; there's just one left.* • **just my, our, his,** *etc* **luck** *colloq* expressing how typical an unwelcome situation, event, outcome, etc is □ *Red wine all down my white shirt! Just my luck!* • **luck of the draw** a chance someone takes. • **luck of the Irish** extreme good fortune. • **no such luck** – *colloq* unfortunately not. • **out of luck** unfortunate □ *You're out of luck we sold the last one yesterday.* • **push one's luck** *colloq* to keep on doing something even when one is aware that something might well go wrong. • **Tough luck!** *colloq* expressing either genuine or mock sympathy to someone who has suffered a misfortune. • **try** or **test one's luck** to attempt something without being sure of the outcome. • **worse luck** *colloq* unfortunately. ◎ 15c: from Dutch *luk*.

▪ **luck into** or **onto something** *slang* to get or meet it by chance □ *We lucked into some really good bargains.*

▪ **luck out** *slang* to be fortunate or to get something by good fortune □ *really lucked out when they won the lottery.*

▪ **luck upon something** *slang* to come across it by chance.

lucky /ˈlʌkɪ/ ▷ *adj* (**luckier, luckiest**) **1** having good fortune. **2** bringing good fortune. **3** happening by chance, especially when the outcome is advantageous □ *It was lucky the weather was good.* • **luckily** *adverb*. • **I, you, we,** *etc* **should be so lucky!** *ironic* emphasizing the improbability or undesirability of something happening □ *Him get a pay rise? He should be so lucky!* ◎ 16c.

lucky bag ▷ *noun, Brit* a bag sold to children without the contents being visible, usually containing an assortment of sweets, a small plastic toy, etc.

lucky charm ▷ *noun* an object someone carries with them in the belief that it will bring good fortune □ *My rabbit's foot is my lucky charm.*

lucky dip ▷ *noun* **1** a chance to rummage around in a tub or container full of shredded paper, sawdust, etc in which prizes have been hidden, and to draw out a prize at random. **2** the tub or container in which this goes on.

lucrative /ˈluːkrətɪv, ljuː-/ ▷ *adj* affording financial gain; profitable. • **lucratively** *adverb*. ◎ 15c: from Latin *lucrari, lucratus* to gain.

lucre /ˈluːkə(r), ˈljuː-/ ▷ *noun, derog* profit or financial gain, especially when it is obtained in a way that is considered dishonourable, greedy or exploitative. Compare FILTHY LUCRE. ◎ 14c: from Latin *lucrum* gain.

Luddite /ˈlʌdaɪt/ ▷ *noun* **1** (**the Luddites**) *historical* a group of artisans who, in the early 19c, systematically destroyed machinery, especially in the textile industry, because they feared that the increase in automation not only threatened their job security but also resulted in the production of much shoddier goods. **2** anyone who opposes new technology or industrial change. ◎ 1811: said to be named after Ned Lud or Ludd, who, far from being the leader of the group, as popularly believed, was someone who attacked hosiery manufacturing equipment in an insane frenzy some thirty years earlier.

ludicrous /ˈluːdɪkrəs, ˈljuː-/ ▷ *adj* **1** said of a situation, proposal, etc: completely ridiculous because of its incongruity, unsuitability, absurdity, etc. **2** (**the ludicrous**) things that are incongruous, inane, absurd, etc (see THE 4b). • **ludicrously** *adverb*. • **ludicrousness** *noun*. ◎ 17c: from Latin *ludere* to play.

ludism /ˈluːdɪzəm, ˈljuː-/ ▷ *noun, literary theory* the belief that a text and its language have no firm or absolute 'meaning' and the resultant playfulness on the part of both the author and the reader that can develop from this idea. • **ludic** *adj*. ◎ 1970s: from Latin *ludere* to play.

ludo /ˈluːdoʊ/ ▷ *noun, Brit* a children's board game where each player has four counters of the same colour which they move according to the number shown each time they throw the dice, the object being to get all one's counters 'home', after a complete circuit of the board, before anyone else. ◎ 19c: Latin, meaning 'I play'.

luff ▷ *verb* (**luffed, luffing**) **1** to steer a ship towards the wind, especially with accompanying flapping of the sails. **2** to sail a ship in a particular direction, whilst keeping close to the wind. **3** to move the jib of a crane or derrick up or down. ▷ *noun* the forward edge of a fore-and-aft sail. ◎ 13c.

lug[1] ▷ *verb* (**lugged, lugging**) to carry, pull or drag something with difficulty, especially something that is bulky or heavy. ◎ 14c.

lug[2] ▷ *noun* **1** *dialect or colloq* an ear. **2 a** a protruding part on something, especially one that acts as a kind of handle, allowing the object to be carried or turned; **b** a projecting part on a spade or other similar implement. **3** a flap on a bonnet or hat that could cover the ear. ◎ 15c in sense 3; 16c in sense 1 in Scots and Northern English dialects.

luge /luːʒ/ ▷ *noun* a toboggan for either one or two people who must lie back in an almost flat, optimally aerodynamic position, steering with the feet and a hand rope. ▷ *verb* (**luged, luging,** or **lugeing**) *intr* **1** to travel across snow or ice on this type of toboggan. **2** to race on a specially constructed course using this type of toboggan. ◎ Early 20c: Swiss dialect.

Luger /luːgə(r)/ ▷ *noun* a type of automatic pistol. ◎ Early 20c: named after the German firearms expert, Georg Luger.

luggage /ˈlʌgɪdʒ/ ▷ *noun, Brit* suitcases, bags, etc used when travelling. ◎ 16c: from LUG[1].

lugger ▷ *noun* a small vessel with square sails, attached to yards, which hang obliquely to the masts. ◎ 18c.

lughole ▷ *noun, colloq* the ear.

lugubrious /lʊˈguːbrɪəs, lʊˈgjuː-/ ▷ *adj* sad and gloomy; mournful. • **lugubriously** *adj*. • **lugubriousness** *noun*. ◎ 17c: Latin *lugere* to mourn.

lugworm ▷ *noun* a large marine worm which burrows in the sand and soft earth on sea-shores and river estuaries and which is often used as fishing bait. ◎ 17c: related to LUG[1].

lukewarm /ˈluːkwɔːm/ ▷ *adj* **1** said especially of liquids: moderately warm. **2** said of interest, support, response, etc: not enthusiastic; indifferent. • **lukewarmly** *adverb*. ◎ 14c: from Anglo-Saxon *hleuke* tepid + WARM.

lull ▷ *verb* (**lulled, lulling**) **1** to soothe or induce a feeling of well-being in someone, especially by caressing them, quietly singing, etc □ *lulled the baby to sleep.* **2** to allay (suspicions), especially falsely. ▷ *noun* a period of calm and quiet □ *a lull before the storm.* • **lull someone into a false sense of security** to create an atmosphere where any potential worries or anxieties they may have are allayed, especially when the intention is to cause the person harm at some future point in time. ⓔ 14c: imitating the sound of quiet singing.

lullaby /ˈlʌləbaɪ/ ▷ *noun* (***lullabies***) a soft soothing song, especially one meant to pacify babies and little children or to help send them to sleep. ⓔ 16c: from LULL + BYE² (as in GOODBYE).

lumbago /lʌmˈbeɪgoʊ/ ▷ *noun* chronic pain in the lower region of the back, usually caused by a strained muscle or ligament, arthritis, a slipped disc or a trapped nerve. ⓔ 17c: Latin *lumbago*, from *lumbus* loin.

lumbar /ˈlʌmbə(r)/ ▷ *adj, anatomy* relating to the back between the lowest ribs and the pelvis. ⓔ 19c: from Latin *lumbaris*, from *lumbus* loin.

lumbar puncture ▷ *noun, medicine* the insertion of a needle into the lower region of the spine, either to remove cerebrospinal fluid to aid diagnosis of a disease or disorder, or to inject a drug.

lumber¹ /ˈlʌmbə(r)/ ▷ *noun* **1** disused articles of furniture, odds and ends that are no longer used, etc which have been stored away. **2** *N Amer* timber, especially when partly cut up ready for use. **3** *dialect* someone one has a sexual encounter with. ▷ *verb* (***lumbered, lumbering***) **1** to fill something with lumber or other useless items. **2** *tr & intr, chiefly N Amer* to fell trees and saw the wood into timber for transportation. ⓔ 16c.

■ **lumber someone with something** *colloq* to burden them with an unwanted or difficult responsibility or task.

lumber² /ˈlʌmbə(r)/ ▷ *verb, intr* to move about heavily and clumsily. • **lumbering** *adj*. ⓔ 16c.

lumberjack ▷ *noun* someone who works at felling trees, sawing them up and moving them. ⓔ 19c: from LUMBER¹ + JACK *noun* 11.

lumberjacket ▷ *noun* a checked jacket made from warm fleecy or woolly material. ⓔ 1930s.

lumen /ˈluːmən, ˈljuː-/ ▷ *noun* (***lumina*** /-mɪnə/ or ***lumens***) **1** *physics* (symbol **lm**) in the SI system: a unit of LUMINOUS FLUX, defined as the amount of light emitted by a point source of intensity one CANDELA within a SOLID ANGLE of one STERADIAN. **2** *biol* in living organisms: the space enclosed by the walls of a vessel or tubular organ, eg within a blood vessel or intestine. ⓔ 19c: Latin, meaning 'light'.

luminance /ˈluːmɪnəns, ˈljuː-/ ▷ *noun* **1** *physics* (symbol **L**) a measure of the brightness of a surface that is radiating or reflecting light, expressed in CANDELAS per square metre. **2** the state or quality of radiating or reflecting light. **3** in TV and video signals: the component that controls the brightness of the screen, as opposed to its colour or CHROMINANCE. ⓔ 1950s: from Latin *lumen* light.

luminary /ˈluːmɪnərɪ, ˈljuː-/ ▷ *noun* (***luminaries***) **1** someone who is considered an expert or authority in a particular field. **2** a famous or prominent member of a group. **3** *literary* a natural source of light, such as the Sun or Moon. ⓔ 15c: from Latin *luminarium* a lamp.

luminescence /luːmɪˈnɛsəns, ljuː-/ ▷ *noun, physics* the emission of light by a substance, usually a solid, in the absence of a rise in temperature. • **luminescent** *adj* giving off light by LUMINESCENCE. ⓔ 19c: from Latin *lumen* a light.

luminosity /luːmɪˈnɒsɪtɪ, ˈljuː-/ ▷ *noun* (***luminosities***) **1** the property of emitting light. **2** *astron* the brightness of a celestial object, eg a star, equal to the total energy radiated per unit time. **3** *non-technical* brightness. ⓔ 17c: from LUMINOUS.

luminous /ˈluːmɪnəs, ˈljuː-/ ▷ *adj* **1** full of or giving out light. **2** *non-technical* glowing in the dark □ *a luminous clock face.* **3** *non-technical* said of certain colours: very bright and garish □ *luminous green socks.* • **luminously** *adverb*. ⓔ 15c: from Latin *lumen* a light + -OUS.

luminous flux ▷ *noun* a measure of the rate of flow of light energy, measured in LUMENs, and determined according to its ability to produce visual sensation.

luminous intensity ▷ *noun, physics* the amount of visible light capable of causing illumination that is emitted from a point source per unit SOLID ANGLE, usually measured in CANDELAS.

lummox /ˈlʌməks/ ▷ *noun* (***lummoxes***) *colloq* someone who is very clumsy or stupid. ⓔ 19c: originally US.

lump¹ ▷ *noun* **1** a small solid mass that has no definite shape □ *a lump of coal.* **2** a swelling or tumour. **3** a number of things taken as a single whole. **4** a heavy, dull or awkward person. **5** (**the lump**) *Brit* self-employed casual workers, especially in the building trade, paid in lump sums to evade tax. ▷ *verb* (***lumped, lumping***) to form or collect into a lump. • **a lump in one's throat** a sensation of tightness in one's throat, usually caused by a build-up of emotion. ⓔ 14c.

■ **lump together** to gather (especially dissimilar things) into a group or pile, often without any legitimate reason for doing so.

lump² ▷ *verb* (***lumped, lumping***) *colloq* to put up with something one finds unpleasant □ *like it or lump it.* ⓔ 19c: one of a group of words, such as *dump, grump, mump*, etc, the sounds of which are thought to be inherently characteristic of their meanings.

lumpectomy /lʌmˈpɛktəmɪ/ ▷ *noun* (**lumpectomies**) *surgery* the removal of a lump, especially a tumour that is, or is suspected of being, cancerous, from the breast. Compare MASTECTOMY. ⓔ 1970s: from LUMP¹ + -ECTOMY.

lumpen /ˈlʌmpən/ ▷ *adj* boorish and stupid; incapable of, or not interested in, self-improvement. ⓔ 1940s: from LUMPENPROLETARIAT.

lumpenproletariat ▷ *noun* **1** (**Lumpenprotelariat**) people in a society who, for whatever reason, do not work, eg the homeless, beggars, criminals, etc. **2** *now derog* people of the lower classes in a society who are perceived as having no interest in improving themselves intellectually, financially, etc. • **lumpenproletarian** *adj*. ⓔ 1920s: from German *Lumpen* rag + PROLETARIAT; first coined by Karl Marx in 1850.

lumpfish and **lumpsucker** ▷ *noun* (***lumpfish*** or ***lumpfishes***) a fish widespread in cold northern seas, which has a heavy rounded body with rows of spiny plates and a large sucker on its underside, and which is eaten salted or smoked. Its eggs are often dyed black and used as a substitute for caviar. ⓔ 17c.

lumpish ▷ *adj* heavy, dull or awkward. • **lumpishly** *adverb*. • **lumpishness** *noun*.

lump sugar ▷ *noun* sugar formed into small lumps or cubes.

lump sum ▷ *noun* a comparatively large single payment, as opposed to several smaller ones spread out over a period of time.

lumpy ▷ *adj* (***lumpier, lumpiest***) **1** full of lumps. **2** said of a person: having a heavy body or a body that is fat in parts. • **lumpily** *adverb*. • **lumpiness** *noun*. ⓔ 18c.

lunacy /ˈluːnəsɪ/ ▷ *noun* (***lunacies***) **1** insanity. **2** great foolishness or stupidity; a misguided or misjudged action □ *It would be sheer lunacy to do that.* ⓔ 16c.

lunar /ˈluːnə(r)/ ▷ *adj* **1** resembling the Moon. **2** relating to or caused by the Moon. **3** measured in terms of the Moon's waxing and waning (see WAX, WANE). **4** for use on the surface of the Moon or in connection with travel to the Moon □ *lunar vehicle.* ⓔ 17c: from Latin *luna* moon + -AR¹.

lunar eclipse see under ECLIPSE

lunar month ▷ *noun* the length of time taken (29.53 days) for the Moon to orbit the Earth once.

lunate /ˈluːneɪt/ ▷ *adj, biol* crescent-shaped. ⓔ 18c: from Latin *luna* moon + -ATE¹ sense 3.

lunatic /ˈluːnətɪk/ ▻ *adj* **1** **a** *formerly* insane; **b** *law* being of unsound mind and so not legally responsible for any actions taken. **2** foolish, stupid or wildly eccentric. ▻ *noun* **1** someone who is foolish or highly eccentric. **2** **a** *formerly* someone who is considered insane; **b** *law* someone who is lunatic. ◷ 13c: from Latin *lunaticus* moonstruck, from *luna* moon, from the belief that intermittent insanity was caused by the phases of the Moon.

lunatic asylum ▻ *noun* **1** *formerly* a place where people who were regarded as insane were forcibly kept. **2** *derog* a psychiatric hospital. ◷ 18c.

lunatic fringe ▻ *noun* the most extreme, fanatical or eccentric members of any group. ◷ 1930s.

lunch ▻ *noun* (***lunches***) a light meal eaten in the middle of the day. ▻ *verb* (***lunches, lunched, lunching***) *intr* to eat lunch. • **out to lunch** *slang* absolutely mad; completely out of touch with reality. ◷ 16c.

luncheon /ˈlʌntʃən/ ▻ *noun* **1** a formal meal served in the middle of the day. **2** *formal* lunch. ◷ 16c.

luncheon meat ▻ *noun* a type of pre-cooked meat, processed and mixed with cereal, originally tinned and served cold. ◷ 1940s.

luncheon voucher ▻ *noun, Brit* a voucher of a specified value given by employers to their workers so that they can use it in part-payment for food at certain restaurants and shops. ◷ 1950s.

lunchtime ▻ *noun* the time at which lunch is eaten. ◷ 19c.

lunette /luˈnɛt/ ▻ *noun* **1** anything that is crescent-shaped. **2** an arched opening in a domed ceiling that allows light in. **3** **a** a semi-circular space, eg in a wall or ceiling, that contains a window or mural; **b** a painting, sculpture, etc that decorates such a space. ◷ 17c: French, meaning 'little moon'.

lung ▻ *noun* **1** in the chest cavity of air-breathing vertebrates: one of a pair of large spongy respiratory organs which remove carbon dioxide from the blood and replace it with oxygen. **2** in some terrestrial molluscs, eg slugs and snails: a simple respiratory organ. ◷ Anglo-Saxon *lungen*.

lunge /lʌndʒ/ ▻ *noun* **1** a sudden plunge forwards. **2** *fencing* a sudden thrust with a sword. ▻ *verb* (***lunged, lunging***) *intr* **1** to make a sudden strong or thrusting movement forwards. **2** *fencing* to make a sudden forward movement with a sword. ◷ 18c: from French *allonger* to lengthen.

■ **lunge at someone** or **something** to make a sudden forward movement towards them or it.

lungfish ▻ *noun* any of various relatively large freshwater fish, so called because, in addition to having gills, it has either one or a pair of lungs with which it breathes air at the water surface.

lungwort ▻ *noun* a perennial shade-loving plant with pale spotted leaves and clusters of pink or blue bell-shaped flowers. ◷ Anglo-Saxon, from *lungen* lung + *wyrt* root; so called because various preparations made from it were believed to alleviate conditions affecting the lungs.

lunula /ˈluːnjʊlə/ ▻ *noun* (***lunulae*** /-liː/) *technical* the whitish crescent-shaped area at the bottom of the human fingernail. Also called HALF-MOON. ◷ 19c: Latin, from *luna* a moon.

lupin /ˈluːpɪn/ ▻ *noun* a garden plant with long spikes of brightly coloured flowers. ◷ 15c.

lupine /ˈluːpaɪn, ˈljuː-/ ▻ *adj* relating to or like a wolf. ◷ 17c: from Latin *lupus* wolf.

lupus /ˈluːpəs, ˈljuː-/ ▻ *noun* (***lupuses*** or ***lupi*** /-paɪ/) any of a variety of skin diseases characterized by the formation of ulcers and lesions. ◷ 15c: Latin, meaning 'wolf'; so called because of the way it eats away the skin.

lurch¹ ▻ *verb* (***lurches, lurched, lurching***) *intr* **1** said of a person: to stagger unsteadily ▫ ***He lurched towards the nearest bar.*** **2** said of ships, etc: to make a sudden roll to one side. ▻ *noun* (***lurches***) **1** an act of staggering ▫ ***made a lurch for the door.*** **2** a sudden roll to one side. ◷ 18c.

lurch² ▻ *noun, cards* a state of play in cribbage, whist, etc where one side or player is being roundly beaten by the other. • **leave someone in the lurch** *colloq* to abandon them in a difficult situation, especially when they might have expected help. ◷ 16c: from French *lourche* a game which is believed to have been like backgammon, popular in 16c.

lurcher /ˈlɜːtʃə(r)/ ▻ *noun, Brit* a cross-bred hunting-dog, usually a cross between a greyhound and a collie, formerly kept by poachers for catching rabbits and hares. ◷ 17c: from obsolete *lurch* to lurk.

lure /ljʊə(r)/ ▻ *verb* (***lured, luring***) to tempt or entice, often by the offer of some reward. ▻ *noun* **1** someone or something which tempts, attracts or entices. **2** *falconry* a piece of meat attached to a bunch of feathers that a hawk, etc is allowed to eat during its training, so encouraging the bird to return to its falconer. **3** *angling* anything that an angler may put on a line to get fish to bite. See BAIT. ◷ 14c: from French *luerre* bait.

Lurex /ˈlʊərɛks, ˈljʊə-/ ▻ *noun, trademark* a type of material or yarn which has a shiny metallic thread running through it.

lurgy or **lurgi** /ˈlɜːgɪ/ ▻ *noun* (***lurgies***) **1** *originally* a highly infectious non-specific disease ▫ ***caught the dreaded lurgy.*** **2** *now* **a** any illness that is not very serious ▫ ***There's a 'flu lurgy going about;*** **b** anything that can be perceived as a scourge or burden ▫ ***that dreaded lurgy, marijuana.*** ◷ 1950s: although it is generally believed that this was first coined in the radio show, *The Goons*, there is slight etymological evidence that dialectal variations of it already existed, eg *fever-lurgy* a euphemism for 'laziness'.

lurid /ˈlʊərɪd, ˈljʊə-/ ▻ *adj* **1** glaringly bright, especially when the surroundings are dark ▫ ***a lurid light in the sky.*** **2** horrifying or sensational ▫ ***lurid details.*** **3** said especially of someone's complexion: pale or wan; having a sickly colour. • **luridly** *adj.* • **luridness** *noun.* ◷ 17c: Latin *luridus* pale-yellow or wan.

lurk ▻ *verb* (***lurked, lurking***) **1** to lie in wait, especially in ambush, with some sinister purpose in mind. **2** to linger unseen or furtively; to be latent ▫ ***The idea lurked at the back of his mind.*** • **a lurking suspicion** a feeling, especially one which is difficult to justify, that something is wrong. ◷ 14c.

luscious /ˈlʌʃəs/ ▻ *adj* **1** said of a smell, taste, etc: richly sweet; delicious. **2** attractive. • **lusciously** *adverb.* • **lusciousness** *noun.* ◷ 15c as *lucius*.

lush¹ ▻ *adj* (***lusher, lushest***) **1** said of grass, foliage, etc: green and growing abundantly. **2** said of fruit, etc: ripe and succulent. **3** luxurious; opulent. • **lushly** *adverb.* • **lushness** *noun.* ◷ 15c as *lusch*, meaning 'slack'.

lush² ▻ *noun* (***lushes***) *slang* someone who frequently or regularly drinks a lot of alcohol or who drinks alcohol habitually; an alcoholic. ◷ 19c.

lust ▻ *noun* **1** strong sexual desire. **2** enthusiasm; relish ▫ ***a lust for life.*** ▻ *verb* (***lusted, lusting***) *intr* **a** (*usually* **lust after someone**) to have a strong desire for them, especially a sexual one; **b** (*usually* **lust after something**) to want, crave or covet it. ◷ Anglo-Saxon, meaning 'desire' or 'appetite'.

lustful ▻ *adj* having or showing strong sexual desire; characterized by lust. • **lustfully** *adverb.* • **lustfulness** *noun.*

lustre or (*US*) **luster** /ˈlʌstə(r)/ ▻ *noun* **1** the shiny appearance of something in reflected light. **2** shine, brightness or gloss. **3** splendour and glory, on account of beauty or accomplishments, etc. **4** a glaze for pottery that imparts a particularly shiny appearance. ◷ 16c: French.

lustre ware or **lustreware** ▷ *noun* a type of pottery that is decorated with a shiny metallic-looking glaze.

lustrous /ˈlʌstrəs/ ▷ *adj* having a lustre; bright and shining. • **lustrously** *adverb.*

lusty /ˈlʌstɪ/ ▷ *adj* (***lustier, lustiest***) **1** vigorous or loud □ *a baby's lusty cries.* **2** strong and healthy. • **lustily** *adverb.* ◷ 13c.

lute /luːt, ljuːt/ ▷ *noun, music* a stringed instrument with a long neck and a body shaped like a half pear, which is played by plucking and which was especially popular in Europe from 14c to 17c. ◷ 14c: from Arabic *al 'ud* the wood.

lutein /ˈluːtiːɪn/ ▷ *noun, biochem* any of various yellow CAROTENOID pigments found in the CORPUS LUTEUM and in the egg yolk of animals, and in the leaves, flowers and fruits of certain plants. ◷ 19c: Latin *luteum* yolk of an egg, from *luteus* yellow.

luteinizing hormone /ˈluːtiːɪnaɪzɪŋ —/ ▷ *noun, physiol* (abbreviation **LH**) a hormone secreted by the pituitary gland in vertebrates, which stimulates ovulation and the formation of the CORPUS LUTEUM in females, and the secretion of testosterone by the testes in males. ◷ 1930s: from Latin *luteum* egg yolk.

lutenist or **lutanist** /ˈluːtənɪst, ˈljuː-/ and *N Amer* **lutist** ▷ *noun* someone who plays the lute.

lutetium or **lutecium** /luːˈtiːʃɪəm, ˈljuː-/ ▷ *noun, chem* (symbol **Lu**, atomic number 71) a very rare soft silvery metallic element, belonging to the LANTHANIDE series, usually obtained by the processing of other metals, and used as a catalyst and in nuclear technology. ◷ 1907: from Latin *Lutetia*, the Roman name for an ancient city on the cite of present-day Paris, where it was discovered.

Lutheran /ˈluːθərən/ ▷ *noun* a follower of Luther, or a member of the Lutheran Church. ▷ *adj* relating to Luther or his teaching. • **Lutheranism** *noun.* ◷ 16c: named after Martin Luther (1483–1546), German protestant reformer.

lutz /lʊts/ ▷ *noun, skating* a jump, including one or more rotations, from the back outer edge of one skate to the back outer edge of the other. ◷ 20c.

luvvie or **luvvy** /ˈlʌvɪ/ ▷ *noun* (***luvvies***) *Brit, facetious* someone, originally in the theatre, but now also generally, who speaks and behaves in an overly pretentious or camp manner.

lux /lʌks/ ▷ *noun* (*plural **lux***) *physics* in the SI system: a unit of illuminance, equal to one LUMEN per square metre. ◷ 19c: Latin, meaning 'light'.

luxe see DE LUXE

Luxembourger or **Luxemburger** /lʌksəmbɜːgə(r)/ ▷ *noun* **1** a citizen or inhabitant of, or person born in, Luxembourg, a small land-locked grand duchy in W Europe between France and Germany. **2** a native, inhabitant or citizen of its capital city, also called Luxembourg.

luxuriant /lʌgˈʒʊərɪənt/ ▷ *adj* **1** said of plants, etc: growing abundantly; lush. **2** said of someone's writing, imagination, language, etc: full of metaphors and very elaborate; fanciful and inventive; flowery or bombastic. **3** said of material things: ornate; overwrought. • **luxuriance** *noun.* • **luxuriantly** *adverb.* ◷ 16c: from Latin *luxuriare* to grow rank.

luxuriate /lʌgˈʒʊərɪeɪt/ ▷ *verb* (***luxuriated, luxuriating***) *intr* **1** to live in great comfort or luxury. **2** to grow richly or abundantly. ◷ 17c: from Latin *luxuriare*, *luxuriatum* to grow rank.

■ **luxuriate in something** to enjoy it greatly or revel in it.

luxurious /lʌgˈʒʊərɪəs/ ▷ *adj* **1** expensive and opulent □ *a luxurious hotel.* **2** enjoying luxury. • **luxuriously** *adverb.* ◷ 14c: from Latin *luxuria*, from *luxus* excess.

luxury /ˈlʌkʃərɪ/ ▷ *noun* (***luxuries***) **1** expensive, rich and extremely comfortable surroundings and possessions. **2** habitual indulgence in or enjoyment of luxurious surroundings. **3** something that is pleasant and enjoyable but not essential. ◷ 14c: from Latin *luxuria*, from *luxus* excess.

LV ▷ *abbreviation* luncheon voucher.

-ly /lɪ/ ▷ *suffix* **1** *forming adverbs, signifying* in a particular way □ *cleverly.* **2** *forming adjectives and adverbs, signifying* at intervals of; for the duration of □ *daily.* **3** *forming adjectives, signifying* in the manner of; like □ *brotherly.* ◷ From Anglo-Saxon *lic* like.

lycanthropy /laɪˈkanθrəpɪ, lɪ-/ ▷ *noun* **1** the supposed power to change from a human shape into that of an animal, usually a wolf in Europe but in other parts of the world bears, hyenas, leopards, tigers, etc. **2** *psychiatry* a condition in which sufferers believe they have taken on the characteristics of a wolf. ◷ 16c: from Greek *lykos* wolf + *anthropos* man.

lyceum /laɪˈsɪəm/ ▷ *noun* **1** a place or building devoted to teaching, especially literature and philosophy. **2** (**Lyceum**) Aristotelian philosophy and those who follow it. **3** an educational institution which organizes concerts and lectures, mostly on literature and science, for the public. ◷ 16c: from Greek *Lykeion*, from *lykeios* an epithet of Apollo, whose temple stood next to the garden in Athens where Aristotle taught and gave it its name.

lychee, **lichee** or **litchi** /laɪˈtʃiː, ˈlɪtʃiː/ ▷ *noun* (***lychees, lichees*** or ***litchis***) a small fruit with sweet white juicy flesh enclosing a single seed, originally from China but now widely cultivated in many tropical regions. ◷ 16c: from Chinese *lizhi*.

lychgate see LICHGATE

Lycra /ˈlaɪkrə/ ▷ *noun, trademark* a stretchy fibre or fabric made from lightweight polyurethane and used in the manufacture of clothes such as swimsuits and other sportswear, underwear, etc. ◷ 1950s.

lye /laɪ/ ▷ *noun* (***lyes***) **1** an alkaline solution made by LEACHing water through wood ash, etc. **2** a strong solution of sodium or potassium hydroxide. ◷ From Anglo-Saxon *leag* to leach.

lying *present participle of* LIE[1], LIE[2]

Lyme disease /laɪm —/ ▷ *noun* a viral disease transmitted to humans from ticks, affecting the joints, heart and nervous system. ◷ 20c: first identified in Lyme, Connecticut, USA.

lymph /lɪmf/ ▷ *noun, anatomy* in animals: a colourless fluid that bathes all the tissues and drains into the vessels of the LYMPHATIC SYSTEM, and which contains LYMPHOCYTES and antibodies which prevent the spread of infection. ◷ 17c: from Latin *lympha* water.

lymphatic /lɪmˈfatɪk/ ▷ *adj* **1** *anatomy* relating to lymph; carrying or secreting lymph. **2** said of someone: slow and lethargic.

lymphatic system ▷ *noun, anatomy* the network of vessels that transports LYMPH around the body.

lymphatic tissue ▷ *noun* body tissue such as the LYMPH NODES, SPLEEN and the THYMUS GLAND which form part of the LYMPHATIC SYSTEM.

lymph node and **lymph gland** ▷ *noun, anatomy* in the LYMPHATIC SYSTEM: any of a number of small rounded structures, found in large clusters in the neck, armpit, and groin, that produce antibodies in immune responses and filter bacteria and foreign bodies from the lymph.

lympho- or (before vowels) **lymph-** ▷ *combining form, denoting* referring or relating to LYMPH or the LYMPHATIC SYSTEM □ *lymphocyte.* ◷ From Latin *lympha* water.

lymphocyte /ˈlɪmfousaɪt/ ▷ *noun* a type of white blood cell with a dense nucleus and clear cytoplasm, present in large numbers in lymphatic tissues, and involved in immune responses. ◷ 19c.

lymphoid /ˈlɪmfɔɪd/ ▷ *adj* LYMPHATIC.

lymphoma /lɪmˈfoʊmə/ ▷ *noun* (***lymphomas*** or ***lymphomata*** /-ətə/) *pathol* any tumour of the lymphatic tissues, especially a malignant tumour of the lymph nodes.

lynch /lɪntʃ/ ▷ *verb* (***lynches***, ***lynched***, ***lynching***) said of a group of people: to decide mutually without holding a legal trial that someone is guilty of some crime or misdemeanour, and subsequently to put them to death, usually by hanging. • **lynching** *noun.* ◷ Early 19c: named after Captain William Lynch (1742–1820), who first presided over a self-created judicial tribunal in Virginia, USA around 1776.

lynch mob ▷ *noun* a group of incensed or angry people who are intent on lynching someone.

lynx /lɪŋks/ ▷ *noun* (***lynxes*** or ***lynx***) any of various wild members of the cat family with yellowish-grey or reddish fur, a short, stubby tail with a black tip, tufted ears and a ruff of fur around its face, found mainly in northern pine forests. ◷ 14c: Greek.

lynx-eyed ▷ *adj* sharp-sighted.

Lyon King of Arms ▷ *noun* the chief herald of the Scottish COLLEGE OF ARMS. Also called **Lord Lyon**. ◷ 14c: from an obsolete spelling of LION, adopted from the figure on the royal shield.

Lyonnaise /lɪəˈneɪz/ ▷ *adj, cookery* made with sautéed sliced potatoes and onions or potatoes in an onion sauce. ◷ 19c: named after the town of Lyon(s) in France.

lyophilic /laɪoʊˈfɪlɪk/ ▷ *adj, chem* denoting a substance that has an affinity for liquid solvents. ◷ Early 20c: from Greek *lye* separation + *phileein* to love.

lyophobic /laɪoʊˈfoubɪk/ ▷ *adj, chem* denoting a substance that tends to repel liquid solvents. ◷ Early 20c: from Greek *lye* separation + -PHOBIC.

lyre /laɪə(r)/ ▷ *noun* a small U-shaped instrument made from wood or tortoiseshell, with three to twelve strings which are plucked with the fingers or with a plectrum, used, especially in ancient Greece, to accompany songs and poetry. • **lyrate** *adj.* ◷ 13c: from Greek *lyra* lyre.

lyre-bird ▷ *noun* either of two species of ground-dwelling Australian bird, so called because the tail feathers of the male can be raised to form a sweeping lyre-shaped fan during courtship displays. ◷ 19c.

lyric /ˈlɪrɪk/ ▷ *adj* **1** *poetry* expressing personal, private or individual emotions. **2** having the form of a song; intended for singing, originally to the lyre. **3** referring or relating to the words of songs rather than the music or tunes. ▷ *noun* **1** a short poem or song, usually written in the first person and expressing a particular emotion □ *a love lyric.* **2** (**lyrics**) the words of a song. ◷ 16c: from Greek *lyrikos*, from *lyra* lyre.

lyrical /ˈlɪrɪkəl/ ▷ *adj* **1** lyric; song-like. **2** full of enthusiastic praise □ *waxing lyrical.* • **lyrically** *adverb.*

lyricism /ˈlɪrɪsɪzəm/ ▷ *noun* **1** the state or quality of being lyrical. **2** an affected pouring out of emotions.

lyricist /ˈlɪrɪsɪst/ ▷ *noun* **1** someone who writes the words to songs. **2** a lyric poet.

lysergic acid diethylamide /laɪˈsɜːdʒɪk — daɪˈɛθɪləmaɪd/ see LSD.

lysine /ˈlaɪsiːn/ ▷ *noun, biochem* an essential amino acid found in proteins. ◷ 19c: from Greek *lysis* dissolution.

lysis /ˈlaɪsɪs/ ▷ *noun* (***lyses*** /ˈlaɪsiːz/) *biol* any process that causes the destruction of a living cell by the disruption of the cell membrane and release of the cell contents. ◷ 20c in this sense: Greek, meaning 'dissolution'.

-lysis /lɪsɪs/ ▷ *combining form, denoting* a disintegration; a breaking down □ *electrolysis.* ◷ From Greek *lysis* dissolution.

lysosome /ˈlaɪsəsoum/ ▷ *noun, biol* a specialized membrane-bound structure, found mainly in animal cells, containing digestive enzymes which play an important role in the destruction of foreign particles and the breakdown of damaged or worn-out cells.

lysozyme /ˈlaɪsəzaɪm/ ▷ *noun, biochem* an enzyme that breaks down bacterial cell walls and is present in many body fluids and secretions, eg saliva, tears, mucus, etc. ◷ 1920s: from Greek *lysis* dissolution.

-lytic /ˈlɪtɪk/ ▷ *combining form, denoting* a loosening; a disintegration □ *electrolytic.* ◷ From Greek *lytikos* able to loosen.

M

M¹ or **m** /ɛm/ ▷ *noun* (***Ms, M's*** or ***m's***) **1** the thirteenth letter of the English alphabet. **2** something shaped like the letter M. See also EM.

M² ▷ *abbreviation* **1** *IVR* Malta. **2** mark or marks, the German currency unit. See also DM. **3** Master. **4** as a clothes size, etc: medium. **5** mega-. **6** million. **7** Monday (*also* MON.). **8** *econ* money supply (used in the UK to designate its seven categories: *M0, M1, M2, M3, M3c, M4* and M5; *M0* being the most liquid or readily-available category). **9** Monsieur. **10** Brit Motorway, followed by a number, as in M1. See also M-WAY.

M³ ▷ *symbol* as a Roman numeral: 1000. ◷ From Latin *mille* 1000.

m or **m.** ▷ *abbreviation* **1** male. **2** married. **3** masculine. **4** metre or metres. **5** mile or miles. **6** million or millions. **7** minute or minutes. **8** month.

m' /mə/ ▷ *contraction, formal* or *old use* my □ *m'lord.*

'm ▷ *contraction* **1** am □ *I'm going.* **2** *dated* (used deferentially in speech) madam □ *Yes'm, certainly'm.*

MA ▷ *abbreviation* **1** *US state* Massachusetts. Also written **Mass. 2** Master of Arts. **3** *IVR* Morocco.

ma /mɑː/ ▷ *noun* (***mas***) *colloq* a mother □ *How's your ma?* ◷ 19c: shortened from MAMA.

ma'am /mam or (mainly in addressing female royalty) mɑːm/ or (*colloq*) **marm** or **mum** /məm/ *contraction* used as a polite or respectful form of address to a lady: madam.

mac or **mack** ▷ *noun, colloq* short form of MACKINTOSH. ◷ Early 20c.

macabre /mə'kɑːbrə/ ▷ *adj* **1** connected, or to do with, death in some way. **2** causing fear or anxiety; ghastly; gruesome. ◷ 15c: from French *danse macabre* dance of Death; the earlier form *macabré* may be a corruption of *Macabé*, probably referring to Judas Maccabeus or his family the *Maccabees*, whose massacre is said to have been re-enacted in medieval drama.

macadam /mə'kadəm/ ▷ *noun, especially US* **1** a road-making material consisting of layers of compacted broken stones, usually bound with tar. **2** a road surface made with this. Compare BLACKTOP, TARMAC, TARMACADAM. See also ASPHALT, BITUMEN. ◷ 19c: named after its inventor, the Scottish engineer John McAdam (1756–1836).

macadamize or **macadamise** ▷ *verb* (***macadamized, macadamizing***) to build or cover (eg a road) with macadam, so as to form a smooth hard surface.

macadamia /makə'deɪmɪə/ ▷ *noun* (***macadamias***) **1** an evergreen tree belonging to a native Australian genus. Sometimes called **macadamia tree**. **2** the round edible oily nut of two species of macadamia, with a very hard shell. Also called **macadamia nut**. ◷ Early 20c: named after the Scottish-born Australian chemist, John Macadam (1827–65).

macaque /mə'kɑːk/ ▷ *noun* (***macaques***) a type of short-tailed or tailless monkey of Asia and Africa, with large cheek-pouches. ◷ 17c: French, from Portuguese *macaco* monkey.

macaroni /makə'rounɪ/ ▷ *noun* (***macaronis*** or ***macaronies***) **1** pasta in the form of short narrow tubes. **2** *historical* in 18c Britain: a DANDY, especially one who travelled abroad or imitated foreign habits, etc. ◷ 16c: from Italian dialect *maccaroni*, plural of *maccarone* (see MACAROON); sense 2 is derived from the *Macaroni Club* in London, founded and frequented in the 18c by a group of such fashionable dandies.

macaroni cheese ▷ *noun, cookery* macaroni served with a cheese sauce.

macaroon /makə'ruːn/ ▷ *noun* a sweet cake or biscuit made with sugar, eggs and crushed almonds or sometimes coconut. ◷ 17c: from French *macaron*, from Italian *maccarone*, probably from *maccare* to crush.

macassar oil see under YLANG-YLANG

macaw /mə'kɔː/ ▷ *noun* any of numerous large brilliantly-coloured parrots with long tails and strong beaks, found mainly in the tropical forests of Central and S America. ◷ 17c: from Portuguese *macao*.

Mace /meɪs/ and **Chemical Mace** ▷ *noun, US trademark* a type of TEAR GAS, used eg in a spray against an attacker, rioter, etc. ▷ *verb* (*usually* **mace**) (***maced, macing***) to spray, attack or disable someone with Mace. ◷ 1960s.

mace¹ /meɪs/ ▷ *noun* **1 a** a ceremonial staff carried by some public officials (eg the SPEAKER of the House of Commons) as a symbol of authority; **b** someone who carries a mace in a ceremonial procession. Also called **macebearer**. **2** *historical* a heavy club, usually with a spiked metal head, used as a weapon in medieval times. ◷ 13c in sense 2: French meaning 'a large hammer'.

mace² /meɪs/ ▷ *noun* a spice made from the layer around the NUTMEG seed, dried and ground up. ◷ 14c: French, from Latin *maciv* a red spicy bark.

macerate /'masəreɪt/ ▷ *verb* (***macerated, macerating***) *technical* **1** *tr & intr* to break up or make something break up or become soft by soaking it. **2** *intr* to waste away, or become emaciated, as a result of fasting. • **maceration** *noun*. • **macerator** *noun* a machine or person that macerates. ◷ 16c: from Latin *macerare* to soak.

Mach see under MACH NUMBER

machete /mə'ʃɛtɪ/ ▷ *noun* (***machetes***) a long heavy broad-bladed knife used as a weapon or cutting tool, especially in S America and the W Indies. ◷ 16c as *macheto*: from Spanish *machete*.

Machiavellian /makɪə'vɛlɪən/ ▷ *adj* said of a person or their conduct, political principles or activities, etc: crafty, amoral and opportunist; seeking power or advantage at any price. ▷ *noun* a cunning, amoral or unprincipled politician, statesman, etc. • **Machiavellianism** *noun*. ◷ 16c: from the name of the Italian political philosopher and statesman Niccolo Machiavelli (1469–1527).

machinate /'maʃɪneɪt, 'makɪneɪt/ ▷ *verb* (***machinated, machinating***) *intr* to form a plot or scheme, especially one to do something wrong or wicked, or designed to cause harm. • **machination** *noun* **1** (*usually* **machinations**) a crafty scheme or plot, especially a sinister one. **2** the act of machinating. • **machinator** *noun* ◷ 17c: from Latin *machinari, machinatus* to invent or contrive.

machine /mə'ʃiːn/ ▷ *noun* **1** a device with moving parts, and usually powered, designed to perform a particular task □ *sewing machine.* **2** a group of people or institutions, or a network of equipment, under a central control □ *the party's political machine.* **3** *colloq* a motor vehicle, especially a motorcycle. **4** *colloq* **a** a person with no initiative, capable only of following orders; **b** a tireless or mechanically efficient worker. **5** a WASHING MACHINE. ▷ *verb* (***machined, machining***) **1** to make, shape or cut something with a machine. **2** to stitch something with a sewing machine. • **machinable** or **machineable** *adj.* ⓒ 16c: French, from Latin *machina*, from Greek *mechana* a pulley.

machine code and **machine language** ▷ *noun, computing* a numerical code (eg a BINARY code) used for writing instructions in a form which a computer can understand.

machine-gun ▷ *noun* any of various portable guns, often used mounted on a stand, that fire a continuous rapid stream of bullets when the trigger is pressed. Also *as adj* □ *machine gun fire.* See also SUBMACHINE-GUN. ▷ *verb* (***machine-gunned, machine-gunning***) to shoot at someone or something with a machine-gun. • **machine-gunner** *noun.* ⓒ 19c.

machine-readable ▷ *adj, computing* said of data, text, etc: in a form that can be directly processed by a computer.

machinery /mə'ʃiːnərɪ/ ▷ *noun* (***machineries***) **1** machines in general. **2** the working or moving parts of a machine. **3** the combination of processes, systems or people that keeps anything working, or that produces the desired result.

machine shop ▷ *noun* a workshop where items such as metal parts are machined to shape using machine tools.

machine tool ▷ *noun* any stationary power-driven machine used to shape or finish metal, wood or plastic parts by cutting, planing, drilling, polishing, etc.

machine-washable ▷ *adj* said of a material, an item of clothing, etc: able to be washed in a washing machine without being damaged.

machinist ▷ *noun* **1** someone who operates a machine. **2** someone who makes or repairs machines. **3** a MECHANICIAN.

machismo /ma'tʃɪzmoʊ, ma'kɪzmoʊ/ ▷ *noun* (***machismos***) *usually derog* exaggerated manliness; the expression of male virility or masculine pride. ⓒ 1940s: American Spanish, from *macho* male.

Mach number /mɑːk —, mak —/ ▷ *noun* (often shortened to **Mach**) *aeronautics* a ratio of the speed of an object (such as an aircraft) to the speed of sound in the same medium, eg *Mach 2* is twice the speed of sound. ⓒ 1930s: devised by the Austrian physicist Ernst Mach (1838–1916).

macho /'matʃoʊ/ ▷ *adj, often derog* exaggeratedly or aggressively manly; virile in a very conspicuous or forced way. ▷ *noun* (***machos***) **1** *colloq* a macho man. **2** MACHISMO. ⓒ 1920s: Spanish, meaning 'male'.

macintosh see MACKINTOSH

mack see MAC

mackerel /'makərəl/ ▷ *noun* (***mackerels*** or ***mackerel***) **1** an important food fish of the tuna family, with a streamlined body that is blue-green above and silvery below, found especially in the N Atlantic. **2** the oily edible flesh of this fish □ *smoked mackerel.* ⓒ 14c: from French *maquerel.*

mackerel shark ▷ *noun* a large powerful shark found in open waters of the N Atlantic and Mediterranean.

mackerel sky ▷ *noun* a sky patterned with thin white ripples of fleecy cloud, reminiscent of the markings on a mackerel.

mackintosh or **macintosh** /'makɪntɒʃ/ ▷ *noun* **1** *chiefly Brit* a waterproof raincoat. Often shortened to MAC or MACK. **2** a kind of rubberized waterproof material. ⓒ 19c: named after Charles Macintosh (1766–1843), the Scottish chemist who patented the waterproofing process.

macramé /mə'krɑːmeɪ/ ▷ *noun* **1** the art or practice of knotting string or coarse thread into patterns. **2** decorative articles produced in this way; knotted threadwork. ⓒ 19c: French, ultimately from Turkish *maqrama* towel.

macro /'makroʊ/ ▷ *noun* (***macros***) *computing* a single instruction that brings a set of instructions into operation. Also (and originally) called **macroinstruction**.

macro- /makroʊ, ma'krɒ/ or (before a vowel) **macr-** ▷ *combining form, denoting* **1** large, long or large-scale. **2** *pathol* abnormally large or overdeveloped. ⓒ From Greek *makros* long or great.

macrobiotic ▷ *adj* **1** referring, belonging or relating to MACROBIOTICS □ *macrobiotic cookbook.* **2** prolonging life. **3** relating to longevity. ⓒ 18c in sense 2.

macrobiotics ▷ *singular noun* **1** the science of devising diets using whole grains and organically-grown fruit and vegetables. **2** the practice of following such a diet, thought to prolong life. ⓒ 1930s.

macrocephaly ▷ *noun, pathol* the condition of having an abnormally large head. • **macrocephalic** or **macrocephalous** *adj.* ⓒ 19c: from MACRO- + -CEPHALIC.

macrocosm /'makroʊkɒzəm/ ▷ *noun* **1** (**the macrocosm**) the universe as a whole. **2** any large or complex system or structure made up of similar smaller systems or structures known as microcosms (see MICROCOSM). • **macrocosmic** *adj.* • **macrocosmically** *adverb.* ⓒ 17c: from French *macrocosme*, from Greek *kosmos* world.

macroeconomics ▷ *singular noun* the study of economics on a large scale or in terms of large economic units such as national income, international trade, etc. Compare MICROECONOMICS. • **macroeconomic** *adj.* ⓒ 1940s.

macromolecule ▷ *noun, chem* a very large molecule, usually consisting of a large number of relatively simple structural units, eg proteins, DNA. • **macromolecular** *adj.* ⓒ 1930s.

macron /'makrɒn/ ▷ *noun* a straight horizontal bar (¯) placed over a letter to show that it is a long or stressed vowel. Compare BREVE. ⓒ 19c: from Greek *makros* long.

macropod ▷ *noun, zool* an animal that belongs to the MARSUPIAL family which comprises the kangaroos and wallabies. ⓒ 19c.

macroscopic *technical* ▷ *adj* **1** large enough to be seen by the naked eye. Compare MICROSCOPIC. **2** considered in terms of large units or elements. • **macroscopically** *adverb.* ⓒ 19c.

macula /'makjʊlə/ ▷ *noun* (***maculae*** /-liː/) *technical* a spot, discoloured mark or blemish, eg a freckle on the skin or a sunspot on the sun. • **macular** *adj.* • **maculation** *noun* **1** a spot or pattern of spots. **2** the act of spotting or staining. ⓒ 15c: Latin.

macula lutea /'makjʊlə 'luːtɪə/ ▷ *noun* (***maculae luteae*** /-liː -tɪiː/) *anatomy, zool, etc* a small area at the centre of the RETINA in vertebrates where vision is most distinct. Sometimes called **fovea** or YELLOW SPOT. ⓒ 19c: Latin, meaning 'yellow spot'.

mad ▷ *adj* (***madder, maddest***) **1** mentally disturbed; insane. **2** foolish or senseless; extravagantly carefree. **3** *colloq, originally & especially US* (*often* **mad at** or **with someone**) very angry; furious. **4** *colloq* (*usually* **mad about** or **on something**) extremely enthusiastic; fanatical; infatuated □ *My boys are mad about cricket* □ *she's football-mad.* **5** marked by extreme confusion, haste or excitement □ *a mad dash for the door.* **6** frantic with grief, pain or another violent emotion or desire. **7** said of a dog, etc: infected with rabies. • **madly** *adverb* **1** in a mad way. **2** *colloq* passionately. • **madness** *noun.* • **go mad 1** to become insane or demented. **2** *colloq* to become very angry. • **like mad** *colloq* frantically; very energetically □ *waving like mad at the back of the crowd.*

• **mad as a hatter** completely insane; crazy possibly from the fact that, in the manufacture of felt hats, hatters used nitrate of mercury, exposure to which caused mental and physical symptoms which were interpreted as madness.. • **mad as a March hare** see under MARCH HARE. • **mad keen** *colloq* extremely enthusiastic. ◷ 13c: from Anglo-Saxon *gemæded*, past participle of *gemædan* to madden.

Madagascan /madə'gaskən/ ▻ *adj* belonging or relating to Madagascar, an island republic lying off the E Coast of Africa that is noted for its unique species of plants and animals, or to its inhabitants. ▻ *noun* a citizen or inhabitant of, or person born on, Madagascar. See also MALAGASY. ◷ 19c.

madam /'madəm/ ▻ *noun* (*plural* in sense 1 ***mesdames*** /meɪdam/ or in other senses ***madams***) **1** a polite form of address to any woman, especially a married or elderly woman or any female customer in a shop, etc, used instead of a name. Equivalent to SIR for a man. Compare MISS² 1. **2** a form of address to a woman in authority, often prefixed to an official title ◻ *Madam Chairman.* **3** a woman who manages a brothel. **4** *colloq, especially Brit* an arrogant or spoiled girl or young woman ◻ *Cheeky little madam!* ◷ 13c (see MADAME); 20c in sense 3.

Madame /mə'dɑːm, 'madəm/ (abbreviation **Mme**) *noun* (***Mesdames*** /meɪdam/) (abbreviation **Mmes**) a title equivalent to MRS, used especially of a French or French-speaking woman, usually a married one. Compare MADEMOISELLE. ◷ 17c in this sense; 13c in same sense as MADAM 1: French, originally two words *ma* my + *dame* lady.

madcap ▻ *adj* **1** foolishly impulsive, wild or reckless. **2** exuberant and zany. ▻ *noun* **1** a foolishly impulsive person. **2** an exuberantly playful or zany person. ◷ 16c, originally meaning 'a madman'.

mad cow disease ▻ *noun, colloq* BSE.

madden /'madən/ ▻ *verb* (***maddened, maddening***) to make (a person or animal) mad, especially to enrage them or it. • **maddening** *adj* referring to something that drives one to madness or rage; extremely annoying. • **maddeningly** *adverb*. ◷ 18c.

madder /'madə(r)/ ▻ *noun* **1 a** a Eurasian herbaceous plant with yellow flowers and a red root; **b** any of various related plants. **2** a dark red dye, originally made from the root of this plant. ◷ Anglo-Saxon *mædere*.

made ▻ *verb, past tense, past participle of* MAKE. ▻ *adj* **1** (*especially* **made from, in** or **of something**) artificially produced or formed. **2** *in compounds, denoting* produced, constructed or formed in a specified way or place ◻ *homemade* ◻ *handmade.* **3** said of a road, etc: constructed with a surface of asphalt, tarmac, etc, as opposed to a gravel surface. Also called MADE-UP. **4** composed of various ingredients put together ◻ *made dish.* **5** said of a person, etc: whose success or prosperity is certain ◻ *a made man.* • **have it made** *colloq* to enjoy, or be assured of, complete success, happiness, etc. • **made for someone** or **something** ideally suited to or for that person or thing. • **made to measure** or **made to order** said of clothing, etc: made especially to suit an individual customer's requirements. See also BESPOKE.

Madeira /mə'dɪərə/ ▻ *noun* (***Madeiras***) a fortified wine made on the N Atlantic island of Madeira.

Madeira cake ▻ *noun* a kind of rich sponge cake.

madeleine /mad'lɛn, 'madəlɪn/ ▻ *noun* a type of small rich sponge cake, shaped like a shell. ◷ 19c: French, probably named after Madeleine Paulmier, a 19c French pastry cook.

Mademoiselle /madəmwə'zɛl, madmə'zɛl/ (abbreviation **Mlle**) *noun* (***Mesdemoiselles*** /meɪ-/ (abbreviation **Mlles**)) **1** a title equivalent to MISS, used of an unmarried French or French-speaking woman. **2** (**mademoiselle**) a French governess or teacher. Also shortened to **Mamselle** /mam'zɛl/ (***Mamselles***). ◷ 15c: French, originally two words *ma* my + *demoiselle* DAMSEL.

made up ▻ *adj* **1** said of a person: wearing make-up. **2** said of a story, etc: not true; invented. **3** dressed for a part; disguised ◻ *made up to look like a tramp.* **4** *colloq* said of a person: extremely pleased; chuffed. **5** said of a road: same as MADE 3. **6** put together, completed or parcelled up ◻ *two batches made up and ready to go.*

madhouse ▻ *noun* **1** *colloq* a place of great confusion and noise. **2** *old use* a mental hospital.

madly see under MAD

madman and **madwoman** ▻ *noun* **1** an insane person. **2** a very foolish person.

madness see under MAD

Madonna /mə'dɒnə/ ▻ *noun* (***Madonnas***) **1** (**the Madonna**) *especially RC Church* the Virgin Mary, mother of Christ. **2** (*sometimes* **madonna**) a picture, statue, icon, etc of the Virgin Mary. ◷ 16c: Italian, originally two words *ma* my + *donna* lady, from Latin *mea domina*.

madras /mə'drɑːs, -'dras/ ▻ *noun* **1** a large, usually brightly-coloured scarf, of a type formerly exported from Madras in SE India. **2** a fine cotton or silk fabric, often with a woven stripe. **3** a kind of medium-hot curry ◻ *a chicken madras.* ◷ 19c.

madrepore /'madrəpɔː(r)/ ▻ *noun, zool* any coral of the common, reef-building type, occurring especially in tropical seas. • **madreporic** /-'pɒrɪk/ *adj.* ◷ 18c: from Italian *madrepora*, meaning 'mother stone'.

madrigal /'madrɪgəl/ ▻ *noun* **1** *music* an unaccompanied PART SONG, typically about love or nature, of a type that originated in 14c Italy and became popular in England in the 16c and 17c. **2** a lyrical poem suitable for such treatment. ◷ 16c: from Italian *madrigale*, probably from Latin *matricalis* simple or primitive.

maelstrom /'meɪlstroʊm/ ▻ *noun, especially literary* **1** a place or state of uncontrollable confusion or destructive forces, especially one to which someone or something is inevitably drawn. **2** a violent whirlpool. ◷ 17c: Dutch, meaning 'whirlpool', from *malen* to whirl + *stroom* stream.

maenad /'miːnad/ ▻ *noun* **1** *Greek & Roman mythol* a female participant in orgies and rites in honour of Bacchus or Dionysus, the god of wine. **2** *literary* a woman who behaves in a frenzied or uncontrolled way. • **maenadic** /-'nadɪk/ *adj.* ◷ 16c: from Latin *maenas, maenadis*, from Greek *mainomai* to rave.

maestro /'maɪstroʊ/ ▻ *noun* (***maestros*** or ***maestri*** /-rɪ/) someone who is regarded as being specially gifted in a specified art, especially a distinguished musical composer, conductor, performer or teacher. Often used as a title (**Maestro**). ◷ 18c: Italian, literally 'master'.

Mae West /meɪ —/ ▻ *noun* (***Mae Wests***) an inflatable life jacket, especially as worn by pilots in World War II. ◷ 1940s: so called because its inflated shape was thought to be reminiscent of Mae West (1892–1980), an American actress famous for her large bust.

MAFF /maf/ ▻ *abbreviation, Brit* Ministry of Agriculture, Fisheries and Food.

Mafia /'mafɪə/ ▻ *noun* (***Mafias***) **1** (**the Mafia**) a secret international criminal organization, originating in Sicily, that controls numerous illegal activities worldwide, especially in Italy and the US. 2 (*often* **mafia**) any group that exerts a secret and powerful influence, especially one that uses unscrupulous or ruthless criminal methods. ◷ 19c: Sicilian Italian, literally 'hostility to the law'.

Mafioso or (*sometimes*) **mafioso** /mafɪ'oʊsoʊ, -zoʊ/ *noun* (***Mafiosi*** /-siː, -ziː/ or ***Mafiosos***) a member of the Mafia or a mafia. ◷ 19c: Italian.

mag ▻ *noun, colloq* a MAGAZINE or periodical. ◷ 19c.

magazine /magə'ziːn, 'magəziːn/ ▻ *noun* **1** a paperback periodical publication, usually a heavily illustrated one, containing articles, stories, etc by various writers. Sometimes shortened to MAG. **2 a** *TV, radio* a regular broadcast in which reports are presented on a variety of subjects; **b** *as adj* □ *magazine programme.* **3** in some automatic firearms: a metal container for several cartridges. **4 a** a storeroom for ammunition, explosives, etc; **b** any place, building, etc in which military supplies are stored. **5** *photog* a removable container from which slides are automatically fed through a projector, or film is fed through a movie camera, printer or processor. ⓒ 16c: French *magasin*, from Arabic *makhzan* storehouse.

Magellanic clouds /magəˈlanɪk —, madʒə- —/ ▻ *plural noun, astron* two galaxies visible in the southern hemisphere, the nearest galaxies to the Earth, that appear to the naked eye as though they were detached portions of the MILKY WAY. ⓒ 17c: named after the Portuguese navigator Ferdinand Magellan (c.1480–1521), who first recorded them.

magenta /məˈdʒɛntə/ ▻ *adj* dark, purplish-red in colour. ▻ *noun* (***magentas***) **1** a purplish-red colour. **2** an aniline dye of this colour. **3** FUCHSINE. ⓒ 1860s: named after Magenta, an Italian town which in 1859 (shortly before the discovery of this blood-red dye) was the scene of a bloody battle.

maggot /ˈmagət/ ▻ *noun* the worm-like larva of various flies, especially that of the housefly. • **maggoty** *adj* **1** full of or infected with maggots, or like maggots. **2** *slang, chiefly Austral* bad-tempered; crotchety. ⓒ 14c.

magi or **Magi** see under MAGUS

magic /ˈmadʒɪk/ ▻ *noun* **1** the supposed art or practice of using the power of supernatural forces, spells, etc to affect people, objects and events. Also called SORCERY, WITCHCRAFT. **2** the art or practice of performing entertaining illusions and conjuring tricks. **3** the quality of being wonderful, charming or delightful. **4** a secret or mysterious power over the imagination or will. See also BLACK MAGIC, WHITE MAGIC. ▻ *adj* **1** belonging or relating to, used in, or done by, sorcery or conjuring. **2** causing wonderful, startling or mysterious results. **3** *colloq* excellent; marvellous; great. Also *as exclamation.* ▻ *verb* (***magicked, magicking***) **1** to produce something by using, or as if by using, sorcery or conjuring □ *magicked a rabbit out of his hat.* **2** (*often* **magic something away** or **up**, *etc*) to move, transform or otherwise affect something by using, or as if by using, sorcery or conjuring. • **like magic** **1** mysteriously. **2** suddenly and unexpectedly. **3** excellently. ⓒ 14c: from Greek *magike techne* magic art.

magic, magical

• The adjective **magic** generally means 'relating to magic', and **magical** can have this meaning too, as in □ *The stone was believed to have magical properties.*

• However, only **magical** can mean 'enchanting, as if caused by magic', as in □ *It was a magical experience.*

magical ▻ *adj* **1** relating to the art or practice of magic. **2** causing wonderful, startling or mysterious results. **3** wonderful; charming; fascinating. • **magically** *adverb.*

magic bullet ▻ *noun* a drug which is capable of destroying bacteria, cancer cells, etc without adversely affecting the patient who receives it. ⓒ 1970s.

magic carpet ▻ *noun* in fairy stories: a carpet that can carry people magically through the air to faraway places.

magic eye ▻ *noun* **1** a light-sensitive electric switch; a PHOTOELECTRIC CELL. **2** *telecomm* a miniature CATHODE-RAY TUBE in a radio receiver which helps in tuning it.

magician /məˈdʒɪʃən/ ▻ *noun* **1** an entertainer who performs conjuring tricks, illusions, etc. **2** someone who practises black or white magic, or who uses supernatural powers; a sorcerer. **3** someone who has wonderful, surprising or extraordinary skills, powers, etc.

magicked and **magicking** see under MAGIC

magic lantern ▻ *noun* an early form of SLIDE PROJECTOR. ⓒ 17c.

magic mushroom ▻ *noun, colloq* any of various types of mushroom which contain hallucinogenic substances.

magic square ▻ *noun* a square filled with rows of figures arranged in such a way that the sums of all the rows (vertical, horizontal, diagonal) will be the same. ⓒ 18c.

magic wand ▻ *noun* a thin rod used by a magician or by a fairy, etc in a story, when performing a spell or magic trick.

magilp see MEGILP

magisterial /madʒɪˈstɪərɪəl/ ▻ *adj* **1** belonging or relating to, or administered by, a magistrate. **2** authoritative; commanding; dictatorial. **3** belonging or relating to, or suitable to, a teacher, instructor or master. • **magisterially** *adverb.* ⓒ 17c: from Latin *magister* master.

magistracy /ˈmadʒɪstrəsɪ/ ▻ *noun* (***magistracies***) **1** the rank or position of a magistrate. **2** (*usually* **the magistracy**) magistrates as a whole. Also called **magistrature**. ⓒ 16c in obsolete sense 'the existence of magistrates'.

magistral /ˈmadʒɪstrəl, məˈdʒɪ-/ ▻ *adj* **1** *pharmacol* said of a treatment or medicine: specially prescribed for a particular case. Compare OFFICINAL. **2** belonging or relating to a master; authoritative. ⓒ 17c: from Latin *magistralis.*

magistrate /ˈmadʒɪstreɪt/ ▻ *noun* **1** in England and Wales: a judge who presides in a lower court of law (**Magistrates' Court**), dealing with minor criminal and civil cases; a JUSTICE OF THE PEACE. Compare JUDGE, PROVOST, SHERIFF. **2** any public official administering the law. ⓒ 14c: from Latin *magistratus*, from *magister* master.

maglev /ˈmaglɛv/ ▻ *noun* a high-speed transport system in which magnetism is used to keep an electrically-powered train gliding above a track. Also *as adj.* ⓒ 1970s: from *mag*netic *lev*itation.

magma /ˈmagmə/ ▻ *noun* (***magmas*** or ***magmata*** /-mətə/) *geol* **1** hot molten rock material generated deep within the earth's crust or mantle. **2** a pasty or doughy mass of mineral or organic material. • **magmatic** /-ˈmatɪk/ *adj.* ⓒ 17c: from Greek, meaning 'a thick ointment'.

magnanimous /magˈnanɪməs/ ▻ *adj* having or showing admirable generosity of spirit towards another person or people; not spoiled by any mean or petty feelings; big-hearted. • **magnanimity** *noun.* • **magnanimously** *adverb.* ⓒ 16c: from Latin *magnanimus*, from *magnus* great + *animus* spirit or mind.

magnate /ˈmagneɪt, -nət/ ▻ *noun* someone of high rank or great power, especially in industry. ⓒ 15c in earlier sense 'a nobleman': from Latin *magnus* great.

magnate

There is sometimes a spelling confusion between **magnate** and **magnet**.

magnesia /magˈniːzɪə/ ▻ *noun* (***magnesias***) *chem* **1** the common name for MAGNESIUM OXIDE. **2** *pharmacol* a suspension of MAGNESIUM HYDROXIDE in water, used as an antacid and laxative. Also called **milk of magnesia**. • **magnesian** *adj.* ⓒ 14c as a hypothetical mineral sought by alchemists: named after Magnesia, a mineral-rich region in ancient Greece.

magnesium /magˈniːzɪəm/ ▻ *noun, chem* (symbol **Mg**, atomic number 12) a reactive silvery-grey metallic element that burns with a dazzling white flame, used in fireworks and in strong light alloys for aircraft components, etc. It is also an essential TRACE ELEMENT in plants and animals. ⓒ 19c: Latin; see MAGNESIA.

magnesium hydroxide ▷ *noun, pharmacol* a white powder with medicinal uses as an antacid and laxative, forming a viscous suspension when diluted in water. See also MAGNESIA 2.

magnesium oxide ▷ *noun* a light, white powder, used to line furnaces, and as a component of semiconductors, insulators, cosmetics, antacids, laxatives, etc.

magnet /ˈmagnɪt/ ▷ *noun* **1** a piece of metal, especially a piece of iron, with the power to attract and repel iron, and the tendency to point in an approximate north-south direction when freely suspended. **2** (*especially* **a magnet for** or **to something**) someone or something that attracts □ *That rubbish bin is a magnet to flies.* ◷ 15c, meaning 'LODESTONE' 1: from Greek *Magnetis lithos* Magnesian stone; see MAGNESIA.

> ***magnet***
>
> There is sometimes a spelling confusion between **magnet** and **magnate**.

magnetic /magˈnɛtɪk/ ▷ *adj* **1** belonging to, having the powers of, or operated by a magnet or magnetism. **2** said of a metal, etc: able to be made into a magnet. **3** said of a person, personality, etc: extremely charming or attractive; captivating; hypnotic. • **magnetically** *adverb*.

magnetic bubble see BUBBLE MEMORY

magnetic disk ▷ *noun, computing* a flat circular sheet of material coated with a magnetic oxide, used to store programs and data. Often shortened to **disk**. See also DISK FILE.

magnetic drum ▷ *noun, computing* a storage device used on large computers to allow very fast access to data, consisting of a rapidly-rotating drum covered with magnetic material, on which data can be read or written by a set of READ-WRITE HEADs.

magnetic equator ▷ *noun* the imaginary line around the Earth where the MAGNETIC NEEDLE remains horizontal, or a line drawn on a map of the Earth representing this.

magnetic field ▷ *noun, physics* the region of physical space surrounding a permanent magnet, electromagnetic wave or current-carrying conductor, within which magnetic forces may be detected.

magnetic flux ▷ *noun, physics* (SI unit WEBER) a measure of the amount of magnetism, considering both the strength and extent of the MAGNETIC FIELD. See also FLUX 6.

magnetic induction ▷ *noun, physics* the production of magnetic properties in a previously unmagnetized material.

magnetic ink character recognition ▷ *noun, computing* (abbreviation **MICR**) used eg in banking procedures: the reading of characters printed in **magnetic ink**, ie ink which contains a magnetic powder that activates an electronic character-reading device, so enabling the characters to be identified.

magnetic levitation ▷ *noun, physics* suspension by means of a magnetic field, eg suspension of a train above a track. See also MAGLEV.

magnetic mine ▷ *noun* a mine that is detonated by a pivoted MAGNETIC NEEDLE when it detects a magnetic field created by the presence of a large metal object such as a ship.

magnetic moment ▷ *noun, physics* a measure of the magnetic strength of a permanent magnet, or of a current-carrying coil, moving charge or individual atom in a magnetic field.

magnetic needle ▷ *noun* the slim rod or bar in a nautical compass which, because it is magnetized, always points to the north, or in other instruments is used to indicate the direction of a magnetic field.

magnetic north ▷ *noun* the direction in which a compass's MAGNETIC NEEDLE always points, slightly east or west of TRUE NORTH.

magnetic pole ▷ *noun* **1** *physics* either of two regions, usually at opposite ends of a magnet and referred to as north and SOUTH, from which the lines of force of a magnetic field appear to radiate. **2** *geol* either of two points on the Earth's surface, ie the NORTH POLE and SOUTH POLE, where the magnetic field is vertical, and to or from which a MAGNETIC NEEDLE points.

magnetic resonance imaging ▷ *noun, radiol* (abbreviation **MRI**) the use of NUCLEAR MAGNETIC RESONANCE of PROTONs to produce images of the human body, etc.

magnetic storm ▷ *noun, meteorol* a sudden severe disturbance of the earth's magnetic field caused by streams of particles from the sun.

magnetic stripe ▷ *noun* on the back of a credit card, identity card, etc: a dark horizontal stripe which can be read electronically to identify the card, etc.

magnetic tape ▷ *noun, electronics* a narrow plastic ribbon, coated on one side with magnetizable material, used to record and store data in audio and video tape recorders and computers.

magnetism /ˈmagnətɪzəm/ ▷ *noun* **1** the properties of attraction possessed by magnets. **2** the phenomena connected with magnets. **3** the scientific study of the properties of magnets and magnetic phenomena. **4** (*also* **personal magnetism**) the power of a personality to make itself felt and to exercise influence; strong personal charm.

magnetite /ˈmagnətaɪt/ ▷ *noun, geol* a shiny, black, strongly magnetic mineral form of iron oxide (see FERRIC OXIDE), an important ore of iron. See also LODESTONE.

magnetize or **magnetise** /ˈmagnətaɪz/ ▷ *verb* (***magnetized, magnetizing***) **1** to make something magnetic. **2** to attract something or someone strongly; to hypnotize or captivate. • **magnetizable** *adj*. • **magnetization** *noun*. • **magnetizer** *noun*.

magneto /magˈniːtoʊ/ ▷ *noun* (***magnetos***) *elec* a simple electric generator consisting of a rotating magnet that induces an alternating current in a coil surrounding it, used to provide the spark in the ignition system of petrol engines without batteries, eg in lawnmowers, outboard motors, etc. ◷ Late 19c: short for *magneto-electric generator* or *machine*.

magneto- /magˈniːtoʊ/ ▷ *combining form, signifying* **1** magnetic. **2** relating to magnetism. **3** magneto-electric.

magneto-electricity or **magneto electricity** ▷ *noun* **1** electricity produced by the action of magnets. **2** the science of this. • **magneto-electric** or **magneto-electrical** *adj*.

magnetometer /magnəˈtɒmɪtə(r)/ ▷ *noun, surveying, etc* an instrument for measuring the strength or direction of a magnetic field, especially that of the Earth. • **magnetometry** *noun* the measurement of magnetic fields using a magnetometer. ◷ 19c.

magnetomotive /magniːtoʊˈmoʊtɪv/ ▷ *adj, physics* said of a force, etc: producing a magnetic flux.

magnetosphere /magˈniːtoʊsfɪə(r)/ ▷ *noun* **1** *astron* the region of space surrounding the Earth that contains charged particles held around the Earth by its magnetic field. **2** a similar region around any other planet that has a magnetic field. ◷ 1950s.

magnetron /ˈmagnətrɒn/ ▷ *noun, physics* a device for generating MICROWAVEs, developed for use in radar transmitters, and now widely used in microwave ovens. ◷ 1920s: from MAGNET, modelled on ELECTRON.

magnet school and **magnet high school** ▷ *noun* in the US: a school which, in addition to providing a general education, specializes in teaching a particular subject, such as science, languages or the performing arts, drawing students who are interested in the specialized subject from a wide geographical area. ⓘ 1960s.

magnificat /mag'nɪfɪkat/ ▷ *noun, Christianity* **1** (*usually* **the Magnificat**) the Virgin Mary's hymn of praise to God, sung in services in certain branches of the Christian church. **2** any song of praise. ⓘ 13c: Latin, meaning 'magnifies', the opening word of the hymn in the VULGATE (Luke 1.46–55) which begins *Magnificat anima mea Dominum* My soul doth magnify the Lord.

magnification /magnɪfɪ'keɪʃən/ ▷ *noun* **1** *optics* a measure of the extent to which an image of an object produced by a lens or optical instrument is enlarged or reduced □ *enlarged by a magnification of seven*. Also called POWER (*noun* 15). **2** an appearance enlarged, especially by a stated amount. **3** an enlarged copy of something □ *The police studied a magnification of the photo*. **4** the action or an instance of magnifying (in any sense). **5** the state of being magnified. ⓘ 17c: see MAGNIFY.

magnificent /mag'nɪfɪsənt/ ▷ *adj* **1** splendidly impressive in size, extent or appearance. **2** *colloq* excellent; admirable. **3** *chiefly historical* said of a ruler, etc: noble; grand; elevated. • **magnificence** *noun*. • **magnificently** *adverb*. ⓘ 16c: French, from Latin *magnificus* great in deeds.

magnifier *noun* **1** an instrument which magnifies. **2** a MAGNIFYING GLASS. **3** *formal, church or old use* a person who magnifies, or who praises highly. ⓘ 14c.

magnify /'magnɪfaɪ/ ▷ *verb* (***magnifies***, ***magnified***, ***magnifying***) **1** to make something appear larger, eg by using a microscope or telescope. **2** to exaggerate something. **3** *formal, church or old use* to praise highly; to extol. • **magnifiable** *adj*. ⓘ 14c: from Latin *magnificare*, from *magnus* great.

magnifying glass ▷ *noun* a convex lens, especially a hand-held one, through which objects appear larger. Also called MAGNIFIER.

magniloquent /mag'nɪləkwənt/ *formal* ▷ *adj* speaking or spoken in a grand or pompous style; bombastic. • **magniloquence** *noun*. • **magniloquently** *adverb*. ⓘ 17c: from Latin *magnus* great + *loquus* speaking.

magnitude /'magnɪtjuːd/ ▷ *noun* **1** importance or extent. **2** physical size; largeness. **3** *astron* the degree of brightness of a star. • **of the first magnitude 1** *astron* said of a star: of the first degree of brightness. **2** of a very important, significant or catastrophic kind □ *a disaster of the first magnitude*. ⓘ 14c: from Latin *magnitudo*, from *magnus* great.

magnolia /mag'noʊlɪə/ ▷ *noun* (***magnolias***) **1 a** a tree or shrub with large sweet-smelling usually white or pink flowers; **b** one of its flowers. **2** a very pale, pinkish-white or beige colour. ▷ *adj* having the colour magnolia. ⓘ 18c: Latin, named after the French botanist Pierre Magnol (1638–1715).

magnox /'magnɒks/ ▷ *noun* (*sometimes* **Magnox**) **a** a material consisting of an aluminium-based alloy containing a small amount of magnesium, from which certain nuclear reactor fuel containers are made; **b** such a container or reactor. ⓘ 20c: from *mag*nesium *no* o*x*idation.

magnum /'magnəm/ ▷ *noun* a champagne or wine bottle that holds approximately 1.5 litres, ie twice the normal amount. ⓘ 18c: Latin, meaning 'something big'.

magnum opus /'magnəm 'oʊpəs/ ▷ *noun* (***magnum opuses*** or ***magna opera*** /'magnə 'oʊpərə/) a great work of art or literature, especially the greatest one produced by a particular artist or writer. ⓘ 18c: Latin, meaning 'great work'.

magpie /'magpaɪ/ ▷ *noun* **1 a** a black-and-white bird of the crow family, known for its chattering call and its habit of collecting shiny objects; **b** any of various other black-and-white or pied birds. **2** a person who hoards, steals or collects small objects, especially useless trinkets. **3** a chattering person. **4 a** the outermost division but one on a target; **b** a shot, eg in darts, archery, rifle shooting, etc that hits this part of a target. ⓘ 17c: from *Mag* (diminutive of the name *Margaret*) + PIE[3].

magus /'meɪgəs/ ▷ *noun* (***magi*** /'meɪdʒaɪ/) **1** (*usually* **the Magi**) *Christianity* the three wise men or astrologers from the east who brought gifts to the infant Jesus, guided by a star. Also called **the Three Kings** and **the Three Wise Men**. **2** *historical* a sorcerer, magician or astrologer in ancient times. **3** *historical* a Persian priest in ancient times. ⓘ 14c: from Persian *magus* magician.

Magyar /'magjɑː(r)/ ▷ *noun* **1** an individual belonging to the predominant race of people in Hungary, also found in NW Siberia. **2** the HUNGARIAN language. ▷ *adj* **1** belonging or relating to the Magyars or their language. **2** (**magyar**) said of a garment: cut, made, knitted, etc with the sleeves in one piece with the rest of the garment. ⓘ 18c: the native name.

maharajah or **maharaja** /mɑːhə'rɑːdʒə/ ▷ *noun* (***maharajahs*** or ***maharajas***) *historical* an Indian prince, especially any of the former rulers of the states of India. Also (**Maharajah**) used as a title. See also RAJA. ⓘ 17c: Hindi, from Sanskrit *mahat* great + *rajan* king.

maharani or **maharanee** /mɑːhə'rɑːnɪ/ ▷ *noun* (***maharanis*** or ***maharanees***) **1** the wife or widow of a maharajah. **2** a woman of the same rank as a maharajah in her own right. Also (**Maharani**) used as a title. See also RANI. ⓘ 19c: Hindi, from Sanskrit *mahat* great + *rani* queen.

maharishi /mɑːhɑː'riːʃɪ/ ▷ *noun* (***maharishis***) a Hindu religious teacher or spiritual leader. Often (***Maharishi***) used as a title. See also GURU. ⓘ 18c: Hindi, from Sanskrit *mahat* great + *rishi* sage.

mahatma /mə'hatmə, -hɑːtmə/ ▷ *noun* (***mahatmas***) a wise and holy Hindu leader. Often (**Mahatma**) used as a title. ⓘ 19c, in original sense 'a Buddhist sage with extraordinary powers': Hindi, from Sanskrit *mahat* great + *atman* soul.

Mahayana /mɑːhə'jɑːnə/ ▷ *noun* the most widespread form of Buddhism, practised especially in China, Japan, Tibet and the Himalayas. It focuses on enlightenment for all humanity, recognizes many texts as scripture and places special emphasis on compassion and wisdom and the concept of the BODHISATTVA. Also *as adj* □ *Mahayana Buddhism* □ *Mahayana Sutra*. Compare HINAYANA, ZEN. • **Mahayanist** *noun*. ⓘ 19c: Sanskrit, meaning 'great vehicle'.

Mahdi /'mɑːdiː/ ▷ *noun* (***Mahdis***) *Islam* **1** the name given by Sunni Muslims to the messianic deliverer who will eventually establish a reign of justice on Earth. **2** the title used by various insurrectionary leaders, especially Muhammad Ahmed who established a theocratic state in 19c Sudan. • **Mahdist** *noun, adj*. ⓘ 19c: Arabic, meaning 'divinely guided one'.

mah-jong or **mah-jongg** /mɑː 'dʒɒŋ/ ▷ *noun* an old game of Chinese origin, usually played by four players using a set of 144 small patterned tiles made of wood, ivory or bone, divided into suits and 'honours' tiles. The rules are similar to RUMMY. ⓘ 1920s: Shanghai Chinese *ma chiang*, meaning 'sparrows', perhaps alluding to the chattering sound made by the tiles during play.

mahlstick see MAULSTICK

mahogany /mə'hɒgənɪ/ ▷ *noun* (***mahoganies***) **1** any of various tall evergreen trees of tropical Africa and America, especially a species grown commercially for timber. **2** the highly-prized hard attractively-marked wood of this tree, used for furniture-making, cabinetwork, boat-building, etc. **3** the colour of the wood, a dark reddish-brown. ▷ *adj* **1** made from this wood. **2** dark reddish-brown in colour. ⓘ 17c.

mahout /mə'haʊt, -huːt/ ▷ *noun* used especially in India: someone who drives, trains and looks after elephants. ⓘ 17c: from Hindi *mahaut*.

maid /meɪd/ ▷ *noun* **1** a female servant. **2** *literary & old use* an unmarried woman. See also OLD MAID. ⓒ 13c: a shortened form of MAIDEN.

maiden /ˈmeɪdən/ ▷ *noun* **1** *literary & old use* a young, unmarried woman. **2** *literary & old use* a virgin. **3** *horse-racing* a horse that has never won a race. **4** *cricket* a MAIDEN OVER. ▷ *adj* **1** first ever □ ***maiden voyage*** □ ***maiden speech.*** **2** unmarried □ ***maiden aunt.*** **3** relating to a virgin or a young woman. **4** *literary* unused; fresh; referring to something that has never been captured, climbed, trodden, penetrated, pruned, etc □ ***maiden castle*** □ ***maiden soil.*** **5** said of a horse race: open to maidens only. • **maidenish** *adj.* • **maidenlike** *adj.* • **maidenly** *adj* suiting, or suitable for, a maiden; gentle or modest. ⓒ Anglo-Saxon *mægden.*

maidenhair ▷ *noun* any of various tropical ferns with delicate, fan-shaped leaves. ⓒ 15c.

maidenhair tree ▷ *noun* the GINGKO.

maidenhead ▷ *noun, literary* or *old use* **1** virginity. **2** the HYMEN. ⓒ 14c, meaning MAIDENHOOD.

maidenhood ▷ *noun* the state or time of being a maiden or virgin. ⓒ Anglo-Saxon *mægdenhad.*

maiden name ▷ *noun* the surname that a married woman had at birth, ie before she was married for the first time. See also NÉE.

maiden over ▷ *noun, cricket* an OVER (*noun* 1) from which no runs are scored.

maid of honour ▷ *noun* (***maids of honour***) **1** an unmarried female servant of a queen or princess. **2** the principal bridesmaid at a wedding, if she is unmarried. Compare MATRON OF HONOUR. **3** *Brit* a type of small cake flavoured with almonds.

maidservant ▷ *noun, old use* a female servant. See also MANSERVANT.

mail¹ ▷ *noun* **1** the postal system □ ***sent it through the mail*** □ ***came by hand not by mail.*** **2** letters, parcels, etc sent by post □ ***Collect your mail from the office.*** **3** a single collection or delivery of letters, etc □ ***Has the mail arrived yet?.*** **4** (*also* **mail train, mail van** *etc*) a vehicle carrying letters, etc. **5** *as adj* used for, or relating to mail □ ***mail room*** □ ***mail delivery.*** See also ELECTRONIC MAIL. ▷ *verb* (***mailed, mailing***) *especially N Amer* to send (a letter, parcel, etc) by post. Also called in all senses (*chiefly Brit*) POST. ⓒ 13c in old sense 'bag or wallet': from French *male*, from German *malha* a sack.

mail² ▷ *noun* **1** flexible armour for the body, made of small linked metal rings. Also called **chainmail**. **2** the protective covering of an animal such as the turtle. • **mailed** *adj.* ⓒ 14c in obsolete sense 'a small metal ring or plate' from which such armour was made: from French *maille* a MESH, from Latin *macula* a spot or mesh.

mailbag ▷ *noun* a large strong bag in which letters, etc are carried.

mailbox ▷ *noun* **1** *especially N Amer* a public or private letter box or postbox. **2** *computing* in an electronic mail system: a facility that allows computer messages from one user to be stored in the file of another.

mail-carrier see under MAILMAN

mail drop ▷ *noun, N Amer* **1** a letter box; a receptacle for mail or a slot for posting it through. **2** an address from which someone collects mail or messages, etc sent to them. See also PO BOX, POSTE RESTANTE.

mailed¹ *past participle of* MAIL¹

mailed² see under MAIL²

mailing *present participle of* MAIL¹

mailing list ▷ *noun* a list of the names and addresses of people to whom an organization or business, etc regularly sends information, especially advertising material, etc.

mailman ▷ *noun especially N Amer* a POSTMAN. Also called **mail-carrier**.

mailmerge ▷ *noun, wordprocessing, computing* **1** the process of producing a series of letters addressed to individuals by merging a file of names and addresses with a file containing the text of the letter. **2** a computer program which carries out this process, used eg in office administration, marketing or sales promotion. • **mailmerging** *noun.*

mail order ▷ *noun* **1** a system of buying and selling goods by post, in which customers receive a catalogue, leaflet, etc from which they choose and order their purchases, and their order is delivered directly to them. **2** an order of goods to be sent by post. **3** *as adj* relating to, bought, sold, sent or operating by mail order □ ***mail-order catalogue*** □ ***mail-order firm.***

mailshot ▷ *noun* **1** an unrequested item sent by post, especially a piece of advertising material. **2** the action or an instance of sending out a batch of such advertising, etc to potential customers by post.

mail train and **mail van** see under MAIL¹ *noun* 4

maim ▷ *verb* (***maimed, maiming***) to wound (a person or animal) seriously, especially to disable, mutilate or cripple them. • **maimed** *adj.* • **maiming** *noun.* ⓒ 13c: from French *mahaignier* to wound.

main ▷ *adj* **1** most important; chief; leading □ ***main event.*** **2** *literary* extreme; utmost; sheer □ ***main force.*** ▷ *noun* **1** (*often* **the mains**) the chief pipe, conduit or cable in a branching system □ ***a burst water main*** □ ***not connected to the mains.*** **2** (*usually* **the mains**) or *chiefly Brit* the network by which power, water, etc is distributed □ ***The electricity board came to connect us up with the mains.*** **3** (*always* **mains**) *as adj* belonging or relating to the mains (senses 1 and 2) □ ***mains supply.*** **4** *old use* great strength, now only usually in the phrase **with might and main**. See under MIGHT². **5** *old use* the open sea □ ***the Spanish main.*** • **in the main** mostly; on the whole. ⓒ Anglo-Saxon *mægen* (as *noun*) in obsolete sense 'strength'; partly from Norse *meginn* strong.

mainbrace ▷ *noun, naut* the rope or BRACE controlling the movement of a ship's mainsail. See also SPLICE THE MAINBRACE at SPLICE.

the main chance ▷ *noun* the chief object or best opportunity. • **an eye to the main chance** see under CHANCE.

main clause ▷ *noun, grammar* a clause which can stand alone as a sentence, eg *she picked it up* in *she picked it up and ran off.* Also called **independent clause, principal clause**. Compare SUBORDINATE CLAUSE.

main course ▷ *noun* the principle, and usually most substantial, course in a meal.

mainframe ▷ *noun, computing* a large powerful computer to which several smaller computers can be linked, that is capable of handling very large amounts of data at high speed and can usually run several programs simultaneously. Also *as adj* □ ***mainframe computer.***

mainland ▷ *noun* (*especially* **the mainland**) a country's principal mass of land, as distinct from a nearby island or islands forming part of the same country. Also *as adj* □ ***mainland Britain.*** • **mainlander** *noun.*

mainline ▷ *verb, tr & intr, slang* to inject (a drug) into a principal vein, so that it has the quickest possible effect. • **mainliner** *noun.* • **mainlining** *noun.* ⓒ 1930s: from MAIN LINE.

main line ▷ *noun* **1 a** the principal railway line between two places; **b** *as adj* (**mainline** or **main-line**) □ ***main-line station.*** **2** *US* a principal route, road, etc. **3** *slang* a major vein. ▷ **1** *adj* (*usually* **mainline**) principal; chief. **2** mainstream.

mainly ▷ *adverb* chiefly; for the most part; largely.

mainmast /'meɪnməst, -mɑːst/ ▻ *noun, naut* the principal mast of a sailing ship, usually the second mast from the prow. Compare FOREMAST.

mains see under MAIN

mainsail /'meɪnsəl, 'meɪnseɪl/ ▻ *noun, naut* the largest and lowest sail on a sailing ship, generally attached to the MAINMAST.

mainsheet ▻ *noun, naut* the rope or SHEET[2] attached to the lower corner of the MAINSAIL, for adjusting its angle, etc.

mainspring ▻ *noun* **1** the chief spring in a watch or clock, or other piece of machinery, that gives it motion. **2** a chief motive, reason or cause.

mainstay ▻ *noun* (***mainstays***) **1** *naut* a rope stretching forward and down from the top of the MAINMAST of a sailing ship. **2** a chief support □ *He has been my mainstay during this crisis.*

main store ▻ *noun, computing* the part of a computer's STORE (*noun* 4) that holds data and programs immediately before, during and immediately after processing or execution.

mainstream ▻ *noun* **1** (*usually* **the mainstream**) the chief trend, or direction of development, in any activity, business, movement, etc □ *His work is not part of the mainstream of modern art.* **2** the principal current of a river which has tributaries. **3** mainstream jazz (see *adj* 3). ▻ *adj* **1** belonging or relating to the mainstream. **2** in accordance with what is normal or standard □ *takes a mainstream view on this subject.* **3** *jazz* said of swing, etc: belonging or relating to a style that developed between early (ie traditional) and modern jazz. ▻ *verb, especially US, education* to integrate (children with learning difficulties or who need SPECIAL EDUCATION) into ordinary schools. • **mainstreaming** *noun* the introduction of SPECIAL NEEDS children into ordinary schools. ◷ 20c as *verb*; 17c in sense 2.

maintain /meɪn'teɪn, mən-/ ▻ *verb* (***maintained***, ***maintaining***) **1** to continue; to keep something in existence □ *must maintain this level of commitment.* **2** to keep something in good condition; to preserve it □ *The property has been beautifully maintained.* **3** to pay the expenses of someone or something; to support them financially □ *a duty to maintain his children.* **4** to continue to argue something; to affirm or assert (eg an opinion, one's innocence, etc). • **maintainable** *adj.* • **maintained** *adj, especially in compounds* said of a school, etc: financially supported, eg from public funds □ *grant-maintained.* • **maintainer** *noun.* ◷ 13c: from French *maintenir*, from Latin *manu tenere* to hold in the hand.

maintenance /'meɪntənəns/ ▻ *noun* **1 a** the process of keeping something in good condition; **b** *as adj* □ *a maintenance man.* **2 a** money paid by one person to support another, as ordered by a court of law, eg money paid to an ex-wife and/or children, following a divorce; **b** *as adj* □ *a maintenance order.* See also ALIMONY. **3** the process of continuing something or keeping it in existence. ◷ 15c: French; see MAINTAIN.

maiolica see MAJOLICA

maisonette or **maisonnette** /meɪzə'nɛt/ ▻ *noun* a flat within a larger house or block, especially one on two floors, usually with its own separate entrance. *US equivalent* DUPLEX. ◷ 19c: French diminutive of *maison* house.

maître d'hôtel /meɪtrədoʊ'tɛl/ ▻ *noun* **1** the manager or head waiter of a hotel or restaurant. **2** a head steward or major-domo of a household. Often (*colloq*) shortened to **maître d'** /meɪtrə'diː/ (***maîtres d'*** or ***maître d's***). ◷ 16c in sense 2: French, meaning 'master of the hotel'.

maize /meɪz/ ▻ *noun* **1** a tall cereal plant belonging to the grass family, widely grown for its edible yellow grain which grows in large spikes called CORNCOBS. **2** the grain of this plant, eaten ripe and unripe as a vegetable (SWEETCORN) and used as a source of oil, flour, starch and syrup. Also called CORN (*sense* 2), **Indian corn**. See also MEALIE. ◷ 16c: from Spanish *maíz*, from Taino (an extinct S American native language) *mahiz*.

Maj. ▻ *abbreviation* Major.

majestic /mə'dʒɛstɪk/ ▻ *adj* having or showing majesty; stately, dignified or grand in manner, style, appearance, etc. • **majestically** *adverb.*

majesty /'madʒəstɪ/ ▻ *noun* (***majesties***) **1** great and impressive dignity, sovereign power or authority, eg the supreme greatness and power of God. **2** splendour; grandeur. **3 His, Her** or **Your Majesty** (***Their*** or ***Your Majesties***) the title used when speaking of or to a king or queen. ◷ 14c: from French *majesté*, from Latin *majestas*.

majolica /mə'dʒɒlɪkə, mə'jɒ-/ or **maiolica** /mə'jɒ-/ ▻ *noun* colourfully glazed or enamelled earthenware, as produced in Italy from the 14c, and especially that of the early 16c decorated with scenes in the Renaissance style. Sometimes called **majolicaware**. ◷ 16c: Italian *maiolica*, from Latin *Majorica* Majorca, from where it was first imported and is thought to have been made originally by Moorish craftsmen.

major /'meɪdʒə(r)/ ▻ *adj* **1** great, or greater, in number, size, extent, value, importance, etc. **2** *music* **a** said of a scale: having two full tones between the first and third notes; **b** said of a key, chord, etc: based on such a scale. **3** *Brit, especially formerly* used after the surname of the elder of two brothers attending the same school: senior □ *Ask Simcox major to see me.* In all senses compare MINOR. ▻ *noun* **1 a** an officer in the army. See table at RANK; **b** an officer who is in charge of a military band □ *pipe major.* **2** *music* a major key, chord or scale. **3** *especially N Amer* **a** a student's main or special subject of study □ *English is his major*; **b** a student studying such a subject □ *He's a psychology major.* **4** someone who has reached the age of full legal responsibility, which in Britain and the US means a person of 18 years or over. Compare MINOR *noun* 1. See also MAJORITY 3. **5** a film company that produces mainstream Hollywood movies. **6** anything that is major as opposed to minor. ▻ *verb* (***majored***, ***majoring***) *intr* **1** (*always* **major in something**) *especially US* to specialize in (a particular subject of study). **2** (*usually* **major in** or **on something**) to specialize in (a particular product, area of interest, etc). ◷ 15c: Latin, comparative of *magnus* great.

Majorcan /mə'jɔːkən, mə'dʒɔː-/ ▻ *adj* belonging or relating to Majorca, a Spanish island in the Mediterranean, or to its inhabitants. ▻ *noun* a citizen or inhabitant of, or person born on, Majorca. Also called **Mallorcan** /mə'lɔːkən/. ◷ 17c.

major-domo /meɪdʒə'doʊmoʊ/ ▻ *noun* (***major-domos***) a chief servant or steward in charge of the management of a household. ◷ 16c: from Spanish *mayordomo*, from Latin *major domo*, meaning 'chief of the house'.

majorette /meɪdʒə'rɛt/ ▻ *noun* a member of a group of girls who march in parades, wearing decorative military-style uniforms with short skirts and performing elaborate displays of baton-twirling, etc. Also called **drum majorette**. • **majoretting** *noun* the practice of performing as a majorette. ◷ 1940s, originally US.

major-general ▻ *noun* an officer in the army. See table at RANK.

majority /mə'dʒɒrɪtɪ/ ▻ *noun* (***majorities***) **1 a** the greater number; the largest group; the bulk □ *The majority of the population is in favour*; **b** *as adj* □ *a majority verdict.* **2** the difference between the greater and the lesser number. **3** the winning margin of votes in an election □ *a Labour majority of 2 549.* **4** the age at which someone legally becomes an adult. See MAJOR (*noun* 4). Compare MINORITY. • **go over to the majority** or **join the majority** *euphemistic* to die. • **in the majority** forming the larger group or greater part. ◷ 16c: from French *majorité*, from Latin *majoritas*; see MAJOR.

majority

● Strictly, in sense 1 **majority** should only be used with reference to several things that could be numbered or counted:

✓ *The majority of our customers leave a generous gratuity.*

✓ *The majority of perennials flower during this period.*

● It should not be used when referring to things that are not countable, such as substances and concepts:

✗ *He spent the majority of his working life as a schoolteacher.*

● Although it is a singular noun, **majority** usually takes a plural verb in this sense, as in the examples given above.

majority rule ▷ *noun, politics* government by members of the largest racial, ethnic or religious group or groups in a country.

major league ▷ *noun, N Amer* **1** *sport, especially baseball* a group of sports teams or clubs at the highest professional national level, as distinct from the lower **minor league**. **2** *colloq* the top level in any activity, profession, etc. Often *as adj* □ *major league player.*

major mode see under MODE

major orders ▷ *plural noun, Christianity* in the Orthodox, Anglican and RC Churches: the higher levels of HOLY ORDERS, eg bishops, priests and deacons. Compare MINOR ORDERS, TERTIARY *noun* 2.

major premise ▷ *noun, logic* in a syllogism: the premise in which the **major term**, ie the term which is the predicate of the conclusion, occurs.

majuscule /'mədʒəskjuːl/ *printing* ▷ *noun* an extra large letter. ▷ *adj* **1** said of a letter: extra large. **2** relating to, printed in, etc large letters. Compare MINUSCULE. ● majuscular *adj.* ⓒ 18c: see MAJOR.

make /meɪk/ ▷ *verb* (***made*** /meɪd/, ***making***) **1** to form, create, manufacture or produce something by mixing, combining or shaping materials □ *make the tea* □ *made me a cake.* **2** to cause, bring about or create something by one's actions, etc □ *He's always making trouble* □ *I don't make the rules* □ *It makes no difference.* **3** to force, induce or cause someone to do something □ *Please don't make me go* □ *He makes me laugh.* **4** (*often* **make something** or **someone into something**) to cause it or them to change into something else; to transform or convert it or them □ *made the barn into a cottage.* **5** to cause something or someone to be, do or become a specified thing □ *made me cross* □ *made my head ache.* **6** to be capable of turning or developing into or serving as (a specified thing); to have or to develop the appropriate qualities for something □ *I make a terrible patient* □ *He will make a wonderful father* □ *He'll never make a salesman* □ *This box makes a good table.* **7** (*always* **make someone something**) to appoint them as something □ *They made her deputy head.* **8** (*also* **make someone** or **something into something**) to cause them or it to appear to be, or to represent them or it as being (a specified thing) □ *Long hair makes her look younger* □ *The course made them into effective sales reps.* **9** to gain, earn or acquire something □ *makes £400 a week* □ *Did you make a profit?* □ *He made a fortune but no friends* □ *made his name.* **10** to add up to or amount to something; to constitute □ *4 and 4 makes 8* □ *The book makes interesting reading* □ *will make a nice change.* **11** to calculate, judge or estimate something to be (a specified thing) □ *I make it three o'clock* □ *He made the total £28.70.* **12** to arrive at or reach something; to succeed in achieving, reaching or gaining it □ *should make the summit by midday* □ *can't make the party.* **13** to score or win (points, runs, card tricks, etc). **14** to tidy (a bed) after use by smoothing out and tucking in the sheets, rearranging the duvet, etc. **15** to bring about or ensure the success of something; to cap or complete something □ *It made my day* □ *Those curtains really make this room.* **16** to propose something or propose something to someone □ *make an offer* □ *make me an offer.* **17** to engage in something; to perform, carry out or produce something □ *make war* □ *make a speech* □ *make a decision.* ▷ *noun* **1** a manufacturer's brand □ *What make of car is it?* **2** *technical* the act, practice or process of making or manufacturing. **3** applied to a physical object, a person's body, etc: structure, type or build; the way in which it is made. **4** applied to an immaterial thing: disposition or character; manner. ● **makable** *adj.* ● **maker** and **making** see separate entries. ● **make as if** or **as though**, or (*US*) **make like something** or **make like to do something 1** to act or behave in a specified way □ *She made as if to leave.* **2** to pretend to be or do something □ *He made as if he hadn't heard* □ *He was making like a gorilla.* ● **make do** *colloq* to manage or get by □ *always having to make do.* ● **make do without something** *colloq* to manage without it. ● **make do with something** *colloq* to manage with, or make the best use, of a second or inferior choice □ *I've run out of butter, so you'll have to make do with margarine.* See also MAKE-DO. ● **make head or tail** or **head nor tail of something** *with negatives and in questions* to make any sense of it; to understand it □ *I can't make head or tail of this rota.* ● **make it** *colloq* **1** to be successful □ *to make it in show business.* **2** to survive □ *is so badly injured he might not make it.* ● **make it up to someone** to compensate or repay them for difficulties, inconvenience, etc which they have experienced on one's account, or for kindness, generosity, etc which they have shown to one. Compare *make up to someone* below. ● **make it with someone** *coarse slang* to have sexual intercourse with them. ● **make like something** see *make as if* above. ● **make or break something** or **someone** to be the crucial test that brings it or them either success or failure □ *The takeover will either make or break the company.* See also MAKE-OR-BREAK. ● **make to do something** to show an intention of doing it; to make an attempt or start to do it □ *He made to stand up, but changed his mind.* ● **make up one's mind** see under MIND. ● **on the make** *colloq* said of a person:. **1** seeking a large or illegal personal profit. **2** *slang* looking for a sexual partner. ⓒ Anglo-Saxon *macian.*

■ **make after someone** or **something** to follow or pursue them or it.

■ **make away with someone** to kill them.

■ **make away with something** see *make off* or *away with something* below.

■ **make for something** to bring it about; to have it as a specific result □ *Fine weather makes for an enjoyable holiday.*

■ **make for something** or **someone** to go towards it or them, especially rapidly, purposefully or suddenly.

■ **make of something** or **someone** to understand by it or them □ *What do you make of their comments?* □ *They did not know what to make of us.*

■ **make something of something** to construct it from (a material, etc).

■ **make off** to leave, especially in a hurry or secretly.

■ **make off** or **away with something** or **someone** to run off with it or them; to steal or kidnap it or them □ *The thief made off with my bag.*

■ **make out 1** *colloq* to progress or get along □ *How did you make out in the exam?* **2** *colloq, chiefly N Amer* to manage, succeed or survive □ *It's been tough, but we'll make out.* **3** *colloq, especially N Amer* to caress and fondle, snog or make love □ *They were making out in the back seat.*

■ **make out something** or **that something** to pretend or claim that it is so □ *He made out that he was ill.*

■ **make out something** or **make something out 1** to begin to discern it, especially to see or hear it □ *I could just make out a vague figure in the distance.* **2** to write or fill in a document, etc □ *made out a cheque for £20.*

■ **make something** or **someone out to be something** to portray them, or cause them to seem to be, what they are not □ *They made us out to be liars.*

■ **make over something** or **make something over 1** to transfer ownership of it □ *made over my shares to her when I retired.* **2** *N Amer, especially US* to convert or alter it. See also MAKEOVER.

■ **make up something** to assemble (text, illustration, etc) into (columns or pages).

■ **make up for something** to compensate or serve as an apology for it.

■ **make up to someone** *colloq* to seek their friendship or favour; to flirt with them.

■ **make up with someone** to resolve a disagreement with someone.

■ **make someone up** to apply cosmetics to their face.

■ **make something up 1** to fabricate or invent it □ *made up the story.* **2** to prepare or assemble it. **3** to constitute it; to be the parts of it □ *The three villages together make up a district.* **4** to form the final element in something; to complete it □ *another player to make up the team.* **5** to settle (disagreements, etc) □ *We made up our quarrel.*

make-believe ▻ *noun* pretence, especially playful or innocent imaginings □ *She likes to play make-believe with her dolls.* ▻ *adj* pretended; imaginary □ *She lives in a make-believe world, dreaming of becoming a pop star.* See also MAKE BELIEVE at BELIEVE.

make-do see under MAKESHIFT

make-or-break ▻ *adj* determining success or failure □ *This is a make-or-break moment for his career.* See also MAKE OR BREAK under MAKE.

makeover ▻ *noun* **1** a complete change in a person's style of dress, appearance, make-up, hair, etc. **2** a remake or reconstruction. **3** a transfer of ownership, title, etc. See also MAKE OVER SOMETHING under MAKE. Ⓒ 1960s.

maker ▻ *noun* **1** *especially in compounds* a person who makes something □ *clockmaker.* **2** (**Maker**) God, the Creator □ *to meet my Maker.*

makeshift ▻ *adj* serving as a temporary and less adequate substitute for something □ *use it as a makeshift bed.* Sometimes called **make-do**.

make-up ▻ *noun* **1 a** cosmetics such as mascara, lipstick, etc applied to the face, especially by women; **b** cosmetics worn by actors to give the required appearance for a part; **c** the technique or skill of applying cosmetics; **d** *as adj* □ *make-up bag* □ *make-up artist.* See also MAKE SOMEONE UP at MAKE. **4** the combination of characteristics or ingredients that form something, eg a personality or temperament □ *Greed is not in his make-up.* **5** *printing, etc* the arrangement of composed types, illustrations, etc into columns or pages. See also MAKE UP SOMETHING under MAKE.

makeweight ▻ *noun* **1** a small quantity added to a scale to get the required weight. **2** a person or thing of little value or importance, included only to make up for a deficiency.

making ▻ *noun* **1** *especially in compounds* the act or process of producing or forming the specified thing □ *breadmaking* □ *music-making.* **2** (**makings**) **a** the materials or qualities from which something can be made; **b** *colloq* the things needed to roll a joint, eg tobacco, cigarette papers, hash, matches, etc; **c** *colloq* the things needed to prepare a FIX (sense 2b) of heroin, etc. ● **be the making of someone** to ensure their success □ *This marriage will be the making of him.* Opposite of BE THE UNDOING OF SOMEONE under UNDOING. ● **have the makings of something** to have the ability to become, or to show signs of becoming, a specified thing □ *has the makings of a fine doctor.* ● **in the making** in the process of being made, formed or developed □ *She is a star in the making.* ● **of one's own making** brought about by one's own actions.

mako[1] /ˈmɑːkoʊ/ ▻ *noun* (*makos*) any of several types of shark. Also called **mako shark**. Ⓒ 18c: Maori.

mako[2] /ˈmɑːkoʊ/ ▻ *noun* (*makos*) a small evergreen tree of New Zealand with red berries that turn purple as they ripen. Also called **mako-mako** (*mako-makos*). Ⓒ 19c: Maori.

MAL ▻ *abbreviation, IVR* Malaysia.

mal see GRAND MAL, PETIT MAL

Mal. ▻ *abbreviation* Book of the Bible: Malachi. See table at BIBLE.

mal- ▻ *prefix, denoting* **1** bad or badly □ *malformed.* **2** incorrect or incorrectly □ *malfunction* □ *malpractice.* Ⓒ French, from Latin *male* badly.

malabsorption ▻ *noun, medicine* the poor or inadequate absorption of one or more nutrients, vitamins and minerals, etc from digested food material in the small intestine, seen in the UK especially as a symptom of COELIAC DISEASE.

malachite /ˈmaləkaɪt/ ▻ *noun, geol* a bright green copper mineral that is used as a gemstone and as a minor ore of copper. Ⓒ 14c: ultimately from Greek *malakhe* the MALLOW plant, whose leaves are a similar shade of green.

maladapted ▻ *adj* poorly or incorrectly adapted. ● **maladaptation** *noun*. ● **maladaptive** *adj* said of a species, etc: marked by, or tending to show, an inability to adapt, eg to its environment. Ⓒ 19c.

maladjusted ▻ *adj* **1** said of a person: psychologically unable to deal with everyday situations and relationships, usually as a result of an emotionally disturbing experience. **2** poorly or inadaquately adjusted, especially to environment or circumstances. ● **maladjustment** *noun*. Ⓒ 19c.

maladminister ▻ *verb* to manage (eg public affairs) badly, dishonestly or incompetently. ● **maladministration** *noun*. Ⓒ 18c.

maladroit /maləˈdrɔɪt/ ▻ *adj, rather formal* clumsy; tactless; unskilful □ *his maladroit performance at the meeting.* ● **maladroitly** *adverb*. ● **maladroitness** *noun*. Ⓒ 17c: French; see MAL- + ADROIT.

malady /ˈmalədɪ/ ▻ *noun* (*maladies*) *rather formal or old use* **1** an illness or disease. **2** a faulty or unhealthy condition. Ⓒ 13c: French, from *malade* sick.

Malagasy /maləˈgasɪ/ ▻ *adj* belonging or relating to Madagascar, an island republic off the coast of Mozambique, its inhabitants or their language. ▻ *noun* (***Malagasy*** or ***Malagasies***) **1** a citizen or inhabitant of, or person born in, Madagascar. **2** the official language of Madagascar, an AUSTRONESIAN language. Ⓒ 19c.

malaise /maˈleɪz/ ▻ *noun* (*malaises*) **1** a feeling of uneasiness, discontent, general depression or despondency. **2** a general feeling of physical ill health, not attributable to any particular disease. Ⓒ 18c: French, from *mal* ill + *aise* ease.

malapropism /ˈmaləprɒpɪzəm/ ▻ *noun* **1** the unintentional misuse of a word, usually with comic effect, through confusion with another word that sounds similar but has a different meaning. **2** a word misused in this way. Compare FREUDIAN SLIP. ◷ 18c: named after Mrs Malaprop, a character in Sheridan's play *The Rivals* (1775), who misuses words in this way; her name refers to the term MALAPROPOS.

malapropos /malaprə'poʊ/ *formal* ▷ *adj* out of place; unsuitable; inapt. ▷ *adverb* inappropriately or unsuitably. Opposite of APROPOS. ◷ 17c: from French *mal à propos* not to the purpose.

malaria /mə'lɛərɪə/ ▷ *noun* an infectious disease that produces anaemia and recurring bouts of fever, caused by a parasitic PROTOZOAN which is transmitted to humans by the bite of the mosquito. • **malarial** or **malarious** *adj*. ◷ 18c: from Italian *mal' aria*, literally 'bad air', which was formerly thought to be the cause of the disease.

malarkey or **malarky** /mə'lɑːkɪ/ ▷ *noun*, *colloq* nonsense; rubbish; absurd behaviour or talk. ◷ 1920s: originally US.

Malawian /mə'lɑːwɪən/ ▷ *adj* belonging or relating to Malawi, a republic in SE Africa, or to its inhabitants. ▷ *noun* a citizen or inhabitant of, or person born in, Malawi. ◷ 1960s.

Malay /mə'leɪ/ ▷ *noun* (***Malays***) **1** a member of a race of people inhabiting Malaysia, Singapore and Indonesia, formerly known as the Malay Peninsula. **2** the AUSTRONESIAN language of this people, the official language of Malaysia. ▷ *adj* belonging or relating to the Malays or their language or countries. Sometimes called **Malayan**. ◷ 16c: from Malay *malayu*.

Malaysian /mə'leɪzɪən, -ʒən/ ▷ *adj* **1** belonging or relating to Malaysia, an independent SE Asian federation of states, or its inhabitants **2** belonging or relating to the MALAY Peninsula. ▷ *noun* a citizen or inhabitant of, or person born in, Malaysia. ◷ 19c.

malcontent /'malkəntɛnt/ ▷ *adj* (*also* **malcontented**) said of a person: dissatisfied and inclined to rebel, especially in political matters; discontented. ▷ *noun* a dissatisfied or rebellious person. ◷ 16c: French.

mal de mer /mal də 'mɛə(r)/ ▷ *noun* seasickness. ◷ 18c: French.

Maldivian /mɔːl'dɪvɪən/ and **Maldivan** /-daɪvən/ ▷ *adj* belonging or relating to the Maldives, a republic consisting of an island archipelago in the Indian Ocean, its inhabitants, or their language. ▷ *noun* **1** a citizen or inhabitant of, or person born in, the Maldives. **2** the official language of the Maldives. ◷ 19c.

male ▷ *adj* **1** denoting the sex that produces sperm and fertilizes the egg cell (OVUM) produced by the female. **2** denoting the reproductive structure of a plant that produces the male GAMETE. **3** belonging to or characteristic of men; masculine □ ***male hormones***. **4** for or made up of men or boys □ ***male college***. **5** *engineering* said of a piece of machinery, etc: having a projecting part that fits into another part (the FEMALE *adj* 4). ▷ *noun* a male person, animal or plant. • **maleness** *noun*. ◷ 14c: from French *masle* or *male*, from Latin *masculus*, from *mas* a male.

> ***male, masculine***
>
> There is often confusion between **male** and **masculine**: **male** classifies, and refers to the fact of being a man; **masculine** describes and refers to characteristics that are typical of men.

male chauvinist or (*colloq*) **male chauvinist pig** (abbreviation **MCP**) *noun*, *derog* a man who believes in the superiority of men over women, is primarily concerned to promote men's interests and acts in a prejudiced manner towards women. • **male chauvinism** *noun* self-interested prejudice shown by men towards women. ◷ 1970s: see CHAUVINISM.

malediction /malɪ'dɪkʃən/ ▷ *noun*, *literary or formal* **1** a curse or defamation. **2** an act or the process of cursing; the uttering of a curse. • **maledictory** *adj* using or full of curses. ◷ 15c: from Latin *maledictio*, from *male* badly + *dicere* to speak.

malefactor /'malɪfaktə(r)/ ▷ *noun*, *literary, formal or old use* a criminal; an evil-doer or wrongdoer. • **malefaction** *noun* evil-doing; a criminal act. ◷ 15c: Latin.

male fern ▷ *noun* a common woodland fern that has long fronds each divided into many tapering lobes, or pinnae (see PINNA), themselves divided into smaller lobes, or PINNULEs on the underside of which are the spore-bearing structures, or sori (see SORUS).

maleficent /mə'lɛfɪsənt/ ▷ *adj*, *literary, formal or old use* **1** (*also* **malefic**) said of magical or astrological agencies or practices, etc: harmful; producing evil. **2** said of a person or their behaviour, etc: criminal; doing wrong. • **malefically** *adverb*. • **maleficence** *noun*. ◷ 17c: from Latin *maleficus*.

maleic acid /mə'leɪɪk —/ ▷ *noun*, *chem* (formula **HOOCCHCHCOOH**) an acid obtained from MALIC ACID.

male menopause ▷ *noun*, *colloq*, *especially facetious* a crisis of confidence identified in middle-aged men, comparable with the MENOPAUSE in women, but thought to be caused by psychological factors such as fear of ageing. ◷ 1960s.

maleness see under MALE

malevolent /mə'lɛvələnt/ ▷ *adj* wishing to do evil to others; malicious. • **malevolence** *noun*. • **malevolently** *adverb*. ◷ 16c: from Latin *malevolens* from *male* badly + *velle* to wish.

malfeasance /mal'fiːzəns/ ▷ *noun law* **1** wrongdoing; the committing of an unlawful act, especially by a public official. **2** an unlawful act, especially by a public official. • **malfeasant** *adj*. ◷ 17c: from French *malfaisance*, from Latin *male* badly + *facere* to do.

malformation ▷ *noun* **1** the state or condition of being badly or wrongly formed or shaped. **2** a badly or wrongly formed part; a deformity.

malformed *adj* **1** badly or wrongly formed. **2** deformed. ◷ 19c.

malfunction ▷ *verb*, *intr* to work imperfectly; to fail to work. ▷ *noun* failure of, or a fault or failure in, the operation of a machine, etc. ◷ 1920s.

Malian /'mɑːlɪən/ ▷ *adj* belonging or relating to Mali, a republic in W Africa, or its inhabitants. ▷ *noun* a citizen or inhabitant of, or person born in, Mali. ◷ 1960s.

malic acid /'malɪk —, 'meɪ- —/ ▷ *noun*, *chem* (formula **$HOOCCH_2CH(OH)COOH$**) an acid found in unripe fruits, and occurring in wines. ◷ 18c: from French *acide malique*, from Latin *malum* apple.

malice /'malɪs/ ▷ *noun* **1** the desire or intention to harm or hurt another or others. **2** a deliberately vicious, spiteful or cruel attitude of mind. ◷ 13c: French, from Latin *malitia*, from *malus* bad.

malice aforethought ▷ *noun*, *law* a firm intention to commit a crime, especially one against a person, such as murder or serious injury □ ***The prosecution must show that he acted with malice aforethought***. See also MENS REA.

malicious /mə'lɪʃəs/ ▷ *adj* **1** feeling, or motivated by, hatred or by a desire to cause harm. **2** deliberately vicious, spiteful or cruel. • **maliciously** *adverb*. • **maliciousness** *noun*. ◷ 13c: French, from MALICE.

malign /mə'laɪn/ ▷ *verb* (***maligned***, ***maligning***) to say or write bad or unpleasant things about someone, especially falsely or spitefully. See also DEFAME, LIBEL, SLANDER. ▷ *adj* **1** said of a person: evil in nature or influence; threatening; displaying ill-will. **2** said of a disease: harmful; malignant.

• **maligner** *noun*. • **malignity** *noun* (***malignities***) **1** the quality or state of being malign, evil or deadly. **2** an act of malevolence. **3** hatred. • **malignly** *adverb*. Ⓒ 14c: from Latin *malignus*, from *maligenus* of evil disposition.

malignancy /məˈlɪgnənsɪ/ *noun* (***malignancies***) **1** the quality or state of being malignant. **2** *medicine* a cancerous growth.

malignant /məˈlɪgnənt/ ▷ *adj* **1** said of a person: feeling or showing hatred or the desire to do harm to another or others; malicious or malevolent. **2** *medicine* **a** denoting any disorder that, if left untreated, may cause death; **b** said especially of a cancerous tumour: of a type that, especially if left untreated, invades and destroys the surrounding tissue and may spread to more distant parts of the body via the bloodstream or lymphatic system. Compare BENIGN. • **malignantly** *adverb*. Ⓒ 16c: from Latin *malignare* to act maliciously.

malinger /məˈlɪŋgə(r)/ ▷ *verb* (***malingered, malingering***) *intr* to pretend to be ill, especially in order to avoid having to work. • **malingerer** *noun*. Ⓒ 19c: from French *malingre* sickly.

mall /mɔːl, mal/ ▷ *noun* **1** a SHOPPING CENTRE (sense 2), street or area, etc with shops, that is closed to vehicles. **2** a public promenade, especially one that is broad and tree-lined. Ⓒ 1960s, originally N Amer in sense 1; 17c in obsolete senses 'a MALLET' (as used to hit the ball in the old game of *pall-mall*), and also 'an alley' (as used to play pall-mall on), and then more specifically *The Mall*, a street in London which was used as such in the time of Charles II and became a fashionable promenade.

mallard /ˈmalɑːd, -ləd/ ▷ *noun* (***mallard*** or ***mallards***) a very common species of wild duck that breeds on lakes, ponds, etc throughout most of the N hemisphere. The drake has a green head and neck with a white collar and dark brown breast while the female is simply brown. Ⓒ 14c: from French *mallart* wild drake.

malleable /ˈmalɪəbəl/ ▷ *adj* **1** said of certain metals and alloys, etc: able to be beaten into a different shape, hammered into thin sheets and bent, etc without breaking. **2** said eg of a person or personality: easily influenced. • **malleability** or *sometimes* **malleableness** *noun*. Ⓒ 14c: French, from Latin *malleabilis*, from *malleus* hammer.

mallet /ˈmalɪt/ ▷ *noun* **1** a hammer with a large head, usually made of wood. **2** in croquet, polo, etc: a long-handled wooden hammer used to strike the ball. **3** *music* a soft-headed stick used to beat a gong, etc. Ⓒ 15c: from French *maillet*, diminutive of *mail* a club or heavy wooden hammer.

malleus /ˈmalɪəs/ ▷ *noun* (***mallei*** /-ɪaɪ/) *anatomy* a small hammer-shaped bone in the MIDDLE EAR, which, together with the INCUS and STAPES, transmits sound waves from the eardrum to the inner ear. Ⓒ 17c: Latin, meaning 'a hammer'.

mallow /ˈmaloʊ/ ▷ *noun* any of various European plants with pink, purple or white flowers, and fine hairs on the leaves and stem. Ⓒ Anglo-Saxon *mealwe*, from Latin *malva*.

Mallorcan see MAJORCAN

malm /mɑːm/ ▷ *noun* **1** an artificial mixture of clay and chalk used in the manufacture of bricks. **2** *geol* **a** calcareous loam; **b** chalky earth of this kind. Ⓒ Anglo-Saxon *mealm*, as in *mealmstan*, literally 'soft stone'.

malmsey /ˈmɑːmzɪ/ ▷ *noun* (***malmseys***) a strong sweet wine originally from Greece but now usually from Spain, Madeira, etc. Ⓒ 15c: an English corruption of Greek *Monembasia*, the Greek port from which it was originally shipped.

malnourished ▷ *adj* suffering from MALNUTRITION. • **malnourishment** *noun*. Ⓒ 1920s.

malnutrition ▷ *noun* **1** *medicine* any of various disorders resulting from inadequate food intake, an unbalanced diet or inability to absorb nutrients from food. **2** general lack of food or a very unbalanced diet. Ⓒ 19c.

malodorous /malˈoʊdərəs/ ▷ *adj, formal* **1** *literally* foul-smelling. **2** said eg of conduct, business affairs, etc: highly unsavoury or improper; offensive. Ⓒ 19c.

malpractice ▷ *noun* **1** *law* **a** improper, careless, illegal or unethical professional conduct, eg medical treatment which shows a lack of reasonable skill or care, the misuse of a position of trust, etc; **b** an example or instance of this. See also NEGLIGENCE. **2** any wrong or illegal act. • **malpractitioner** *noun*. Ⓒ 17c.

malt /mɔːlt, mɒlt/ ▷ *noun* **1** *brewing* a mixture, used in brewing, prepared from barley or wheat grains that have been soaked in water, allowed to sprout and then dried in a kiln. **2** MALT WHISKY, or another liquor made with malt. ▷ *verb* (***malted, malting***) **1** to treat or combine (eg a liquor) with malt. **2** to make (a grain) into malt. • **malted** *adj* containing, made or flavoured with malt. • **malty** *adj*. Ⓒ Anglo-Saxon *mealt*.

maltase /mɔːlˈteɪs, mɒl-/ ▷ *noun, biochem* an enzyme in animals and plants that breaks down MALTOSE into glucose. Ⓒ 19c.

malted milk ▷ *noun* **1** a powdered mixture of malted grains and dehydrated milk. **2 a** a drink made with this mixture; **b** (*also* **malted**) *US* such a drink with added ice cream and flavouring, etc □ ***a strawberry malted.***

Maltese /mɔːlˈtiːz, mɒ-/ ▷ *adj* belonging or relating to Malta, an archipelago republic in the central Mediterranean Sea, its inhabitants, or their language. ▷ *noun* (*plural* ***Maltese***) **1** a citizen or inhabitant of, or a person born in, Malta. **2** the official language of Malta, a SEMITIC language with a strong Italian influence. **3** a small, toy spaniel with short legs concealed by a long thick coat of straight hair that reaches the ground. Ⓒ 17c.

Maltese cross ▷ *noun* a cross with four arms of equal length that taper towards the centre, each with a V cut into the end. Ⓒ Late 19c: it is the heraldic badge of the knights of Malta.

malt extract ▷ *noun* a sweet, sticky, liquid extract obtained from malt and used as a flavouring in food.

Malthusian /malˈθjuːzɪən/ ▷ *adj* relating to or supporting the theory which proposes that increases in populations tend to exceed the capacity to sustain them and that there should therefore be restraint or control of sexual activity. ▷ *noun* a supporter of this theory. Ⓒ 19c: named after the British economist, Thomas Malthus (1776–1834), who first put this theory forward.

malting and **malthouse** ▷ *noun* a building where malt is made.

maltose /ˈmɔːltoʊz, -s, ˈmɒl-/ ▷ *noun, biochem* a hard white crystalline sugar that occurs in starch and glycogen, and is composed of two GLUCOSE molecules linked together. Ⓒ 19c.

maltreat ▷ *verb* to treat someone or something roughly or cruelly. • **maltreatment** *noun*. Ⓒ 18c: from French *maltraiter*.

malt whisky ▷ *noun* whisky made entirely from malted barley. Often shortened to MALT.

malversation /malvəˈseɪʃən/ ▷ *noun, formal & rare* corruption in public affairs, eg extortion, bribery or embezzlement; illegal use of public funds. Ⓒ 16c: French, from Latin *versari, versatus* to behave oneself.

mam /mam/ ▷ *noun, dialect or colloq* mother. Ⓒ 16c: from MAMA.

mama /məˈmɑː, ˈmɑːmə/ or (*chiefly US*) **mamma** (*usually* /ˈmɑːmə/) and **mammy** /ˈmamɪ/ ▷ *noun* (***mamas, mammas*** or ***mammies***) **1** *rather dated* now used chiefly by young children: mother. Often shortened to MA, MAM. **2** *slang, chiefly US* a woman. See also MOM. Ⓒ 16c: repetition of the sound *ma* often heard in babbling baby-talk.

mamba /'mambə/ ▷ *noun* (***mambas***) a large, poisonous, black or green African snake. ⓒ 19c: from Zulu *imamba*.

mambo /'mamboʊ/ ▷ *noun* (***mambos***) **1** a rhythmic Latin American dance resembling the RUMBA. **2** a piece of music for this dance. ▷ *verb* (***mamboed, mamboing***) *intr* to dance the mambo. ⓒ 1940s: American Spanish, probably from Haitian meaning 'voodoo priestess'.

mamilla or (*N Amer*) **mammilla** /ma'mɪlə/ ▷ *noun* (***mamillae*** /-liː/) **1** *zool, anatomy* the nipple of the mammary gland. **2** a nipple-shaped protuberance. • **mamillary** *adj* **1** relating to the breast. **2** nipple-shaped. ⓒ 17c: Latin, diminutive of *mamma* breast.

mamma¹ /'mamə/ ▷ *noun* (***mammae*** /-miː/) *biol, anatomy, etc* the milk gland or MAMMARY GLAND; the breast, udder, etc in female mammals. ⓒ 17c: Latin, meaning 'breast'.

mamma² see under MAMA

mammal /'maməl/ ▷ *noun, zool* any warm-blooded, vertebrate animal characterized by the possession in the female of MAMMARY GLANDS which secrete milk to feed its young, eg a human, monkey, whale, etc. • **mammalian** /məm'eɪlɪən/ *adj* relating to or typical of mammals. ⓒ 19c: from scientific Latin *mammalis* of the breast, from Latin *mamma* breast.

mammary /'mamərɪ/ ▷ *adj, biol, medicine* belonging to, of the nature of, or relating to the breasts or other milk-producing glands. ⓒ 17c: see MAMMA¹.

mammary gland ▷ *noun, biol, anatomy, etc* the milk-producing gland of a mammal, eg a woman's breast or a cow's udder.

mammies *plural of* MAMMY

mammilla, mammillae and **mammillary** the *N Amer* spelling of MAMILLA, etc

mammography /ma'mɒgrəfɪ/ ▷ *noun, medicine* the process that involves an X-ray photograph of the breast (called a **mammograph** /'maməgrɑːf/ or **mammogram**) being taken, usually in order to detect any abnormal or malignant growths at an early stage. ⓒ 1930s.

mammon /'mamən/ ▷ *noun, chiefly literary or Bible* **1** wealth when considered as the source of evil and immorality. **2** (**Mammon**) the personification of this in the New Testament as a false god, the god of riches. • **mammonish** *adj* devoted to gaining wealth. • **mammonism** *noun*. • **mammonist** or **mammonite** *noun*. ⓒ 14c: from Greek *mamonas* or *mammonas* (as in the New Testament), from Aramaic *mamon* wealth, riches.

mammoth /'maməθ/ ▷ *noun* any of various extinct shaggy-haired, prehistoric elephants, some of which had long curved tusks up to 4m long. ▷ *adj* huge; giant-sized □ *It was a mammoth undertaking.* ⓒ 19c in adjectival sense; 18c: from Russian *mammot* or *mamont*.

mammy see under MAMA

Mamselle see under MADEMOISELLE

man ▷ *noun* (***men***) **1** an adult male human being. Opposite of WOMAN. Also *as adj* □ *men friends* □ *man child.* **2** *in compounds* a male person associated with a specified activity □ *postman* □ *businessman.* **3** *in compounds* a male person who was born in, or lives in, a specified country or place □ *Yorkshireman.* **4** human beings as a whole or as a genus (see HOMO¹); the human race □ *when man first walked the Earth.* Also called MANKIND. **5** *in compounds* **a** any subspecies of, or type of creature belonging to, the human genus *Homo* □ *Neanderthal man* □ *modern man*; **b** an individual member of such a group; a hominid □ *Java man.* **6** a human being; a person □ *the right man for the job* □ *Time waits for no man.* Often *in compounds* □ *manhunt* □ *man-made* □ *a two-man job.* **7 a** an ordinary employee, worker or member of the armed forces, as distinguished from a manager or officer □ *The new boss gets on well with the men.* Compare STAFF *noun* 1b; b) *as adj* □ *man-hours.* **8** an adult male human being displaying typical or expected masculine qualities, such as strength and courage □ *Stand up and be a man* □ *He's a real man.* **9** *sport, etc* a male member of a team, group, etc. **10** in various board games, eg draughts and chess: one of the movable pieces. **11** *colloq* a husband or boyfriend □ *Her man left her.* **12** *colloq* used as a form of address to an adult male, in various contexts, eg indicating impatience □ *Damn it, man!* □ *Just get on with it, man.* **13** *old use* any male servant, especially a valet. 14 *colloq* the perfect thing or person, especially for a specified job or purpose □ *If you need a good mechanic, David's your man* □ *When you're feeling down, a pint of plain's your man.* ▷ t *verb* (***manned, manning***) **1** to provide (eg a ship, industrial plant, fortress, etc) with men, ie workers, operators, defenders, especially male ones. Also *in compounds* □ *overmanning* □ *undermanned* □ *We are fully-manned today.* **2** to operate (a piece of equipment, etc) or to make it ready for action □ *man the pumps.* ▷ *exclamation, colloq, especially US* used to intensify a statement that follows it □ *Man, is she gorgeous!* • **manful**, **manly** see separate entries. • **manned** *adj* said of a ship, machine, spacecraft, etc: provided with men, operators, crew, etc. • **mannish** see separate entry. • **as one man** simultaneously; all together. • **be one's own man** to be independent, not relying on or controlled by anyone else. • **be someone's man** to be exactly the person they are looking for to do a particular job □ *You're my man.* • **make a man of someone** to cause him to acquire some or all of the stereotypical adult male qualities, such as strength, toughness, courage, self-sufficiency. • **man alive!** *chiefly US* an expression of surprise. • **man and boy** from childhood to manhood; for all of someone's life. • **man to man** openly or frankly; as one man to another. • **sort out** or **separate the men from the boys** *colloq* to serve as a test that will prove someone's ability, calibre, quality, etc or otherwise □ *It's a climb that will surely separate the men from the boys.* • **to a man** *slightly formal* or *old use* without exception □ *The board accepted my decision to a man.* • **men in grey suits** unseen establishment figures holding the ultimate power in an organization, political party, etc. ⓒ Anglo-Saxon *mann*.

man-about-town ▷ *noun* (***men-about-town***) a fashionable, sophisticated, city-dwelling, socializing man.

manacle /'manəkəl/ ▷ *noun* a handcuff; a shackle for the hand or wrist. Compare FETTER. ▷ *verb* (***manacled, manacling***) to handcuff someone; to restrain someone with manacles. ⓒ 14c: French, from Latin *manicula*, from *manus* hand.

manage /'manɪdʒ/ ▷ *verb* (***managed, managing***) **1** to be in overall control or charge of, or the manager of, something or someone □ *She manages the financial side of the business.* **2** to deal with something or handle it successfully or competently □ *I can manage my own affairs* □ *I don't know how to manage his temper tantrums.* **3** *tr & intr* to succeed in doing or producing something; to cope with it □ *Can you manage the food if I organize the drink?* □ *It's very heavy; I hope you can manage to lift it* □ *Shall I help? No, I can manage.* **4** to have, or to be able to find, enough room, time, etc for something □ *Can you manage another sandwich?* □ *I won't manage the meeting tomorrow after all.* **5** to handle (eg a tool or weapon) □ *She manages a spoon quite well now.* **6** to control (an animal). • **managing** *adj* having executive control; administering □ *managing editor.* ⓒ 16c: from Italian *maneggiare* to handle or train (a horse), from Latin *manus* hand.

> ■ **manage on something** to succeed in living on (a specified amount of money, etc) □ *expected to manage on £50 a week.*

manageable ▷ *adj* able to be managed or controlled, especially without much difficulty; governable. • **manageability** or **manageableness** *noun*. • **manageably** *adverb*.

managed fund ▷ *noun, finance* a UNIT-LINKED insurance or savings plan, etc invested by professional managers.

management ▷ *noun* **1** the skill or practice of controlling, directing or planning something, especially a commercial enterprise or activity. **2** the managers of a company, etc, as a group. **3** manner of directing, controlling or using something. ◷ 16c.

management accountant ▷ *noun, business* a COST-ACCOUNTANT who produces information on which managerial decisions are based. • **management accounting** *noun*.

management buyout ▷ *noun, business* the purchase of the majority of shares in a company by its own management so that they retain control of it, especially when a TAKEOVER by another company is imminent. ◷ 1970s.

management consultant ▷ *noun* a specialist, usually one employed on a freelance basis, who advises firms on the most efficient management methods and procedures applicable to their particular business or industry. • **management consulting** or **management consultancy** *noun*.

manager /'manɪdʒə(r)/ ▷ *noun* (abbreviation **Mgr**) **1** someone who manages, especially someone in overall charge or control of a commercial enterprise, organization, project, etc. See also MANAGERESS. Compare DIRECTOR, MANAGING DIRECTOR. **2** in an industrial firm or business: someone who deals with administration and with the design and marketing, etc of the product, as opposed to its actual construction, production, etc. **3** someone who organizes other people's business affairs or activities, especially one who manages actors, musicians, sportsmen and sportswomen, or a particular team, etc. **4** someone legally appointed to manage a business or property, etc as RECEIVER. **5** in British parliamentary procedure: any of several members of both Houses who are appointed to deal with any business that involves the House of Lords and the House of Commons. • **managerial** /manɪ'dʒɪərɪəl/ *adj* belonging or relating to a manager or management. • **managerially** *adverb*. • **managership** *noun*.

manageress /manɪdʒə'rɛs/ ▷ *noun* (***manageresses***) *sometimes considered offensive* a female manager of a business, etc. Not usually used in official titles.

> ***manageress***
>
> Like some other words in *-ess*, this is now commonly regarded as affected and condescending.

managing see under MANAGE

managing director ▷ *noun* (abbreviation **MD**) a director in overall charge of an organization and its day-to-day running, often carrying out the decisions of a board of directors. *N Amer equivalent* CHIEF EXECUTIVE OFFICER.

mañana or **manana** /man'jɑːnə/ ▷ *noun, adverb, colloq* tomorrow; some unspecified time, or at some unspecified time, in the future; later. ◷ 19c: Spanish, meaning 'tomorrow'.

man-at-arms ▷ *noun* (***men-at-arms***) *historical* a soldier, especially a heavily-armed, mounted soldier.

manatee /manə'tiː/ ▷ *noun* (***manatees***) a large plant-eating marine mammal of the tropical waters of America, Africa and the W Indies. Compare DUGONG. ◷ 16c: from Spanish *manatí*, from Carib (a West Indian language).

Mancunian /maŋ'kjuːnɪən, man-/ ▷ *noun* a citizen or inhabitant of, or person born in, the city of Manchester in NW England. ▷ *adj* belonging or relating to Manchester. ◷ Early 20c: from Latin *Mancunium* Manchester.

-mancy /mansɪ/ ▷ *combining form, forming nouns, denoting* divination by a specified method □ ***necromancy***. • **-mantic** *combining form, forming adjectives, denoting* belonging or relating to a specified method of divination. ◷ From Greek *manteia* divination.

mandala /'mandələ, mʌn-/ ▷ *noun* (***mandalas***) **1** *Buddhism, Hinduism, relig art* a circular symbol representing the Universe, usually a circle enclosing images of deities or geometric designs, used as an aid to meditation. **2** *psychol* in Jungian theory: a magical circular symbol that occurs in dreams, etc representing the wholeness of the self. ◷ 19c: Sanskrit, meaning 'disc or circle'.

mandamus /man'deɪməs/ ▷ *noun* (***mandamuses***) *law* a writ or COURT ORDER issued by a high court to a lower court, or to a tribunal, public official, etc, instructing it or them to perform a duty, especially one which it should have performed. ◷ 16c: Latin, meaning 'we command'.

mandarin /'mandərɪn/ ▷ *noun* **1 a** (*also* **mandarin orange**) a small citrus fruit, similar to the tangerine, with deep orange skin that peels easily; **b** the tree that produces this fruit. **2** (**Mandarin** or **Mandarin Chinese**) **a**) the name given to the form of Chinese spoken in the north, centre and west of China; **b**) the official spoken language of China, based on the Beijing variety of this language. Compare PUTONGHUA. **3** a high-ranking official or bureaucrat, especially one who is thought to be outside political control □ ***at the mercy of the mandarins at Whitehall***. **4** a person of great influence, especially a reactionary or pedantic literary figure. **5** *historical* a senior official belonging to any of the nine ranks of officials under the Chinese Empire. ◷ 18c in sense 1, probably referring to the colour of the skin, similar to that of a Chinese mandarin's robes: 16c in sense 5: from Portuguese *mandarim*, from Malay *mantri* counsellor.

mandarin collar and **mandarin neck** ▷ *noun, dressmaking, fashion* a high narrow stand-up collar which does not quite meet at the front ends. ◷ 1950s.

mandarin duck ▷ *noun* a crested Asiatic duck, with brightly-coloured, patterned plumage.

mandate /'mandeɪt/ ▷ *noun* **1** a right or authorization given to a nation, person, etc to act on behalf of others. **2** *politics* **a** legal authorization given to an MP or other elected official to act on behalf of other people; **b** permission to govern according to declared policies, considered to be given to a political party or leader by the electorate on the decisive outcome of an election. **3** *finance* **a** in banking: a form indicating that one customer may act on behalf of more than one □ ***joint account mandate***; **b** in banking: a form to instruct an employer, company, etc to pay salary, dividends, etc into one's bank account; **c** in building societies: an instruction for the regular payment of a specified sum between accounts held by the society. **4** an order given by a superior official, judge, etc to an inferior one ordering them how to act □ ***papal mandate***. **5** (*also* **Mandate**) *historical* **a** a territory administered by a country on behalf of the League of Nations. Also called **mandated territory**; **b** the power conferred on a country by the League of Nations to administer such a territory. ▷ *verb* (***mandated, mandating***) **1** to give authority or power to someone or something. **2** to assign (territory) to a nation under a mandate. ◷ 16c: from Latin *mandatum* a thing that is commanded, from *mandare* to command or charge.

mandatory /'mandətərɪ/ ▷ *adj* **1** not allowing any choice; compulsory. **2** referring to the nature of, or containing, a MANDATE or command.

man-day ▷ *noun* a unit of work equal to the work done by one person in one day.

Mandelbrot set /'mandəlbrɒt —/ ▷ *noun* a particular set of complex numbers important in fractal geometry and computer graphics. ◷ 20c: after Benoît B Mandelbrot (born 1924) Polish-born mathematician.

mandible /'mandɪbəl/ ▷ *noun, zool* **1** the lower jaw of a vertebrate. **2** the upper or lower part of a bird's beak. **3** one of a pair of jawlike mouthparts in insects, crustaceans, etc used for cutting food. See also JAW 1, JAWBONE. • **mandibular** /man'dɪbjʊlə(r)/ *adj*. ◷ 16c: from Latin *mandibula*, from *mandere* to chew.

mandolin or **mandoline** /'mandəlɪn/ ▻ *noun* a musical instrument like a small guitar. The eight metal strings are tuned in pairs and usually played with a plectrum. • **mandolinist** *noun*. ◷ 18c: from Italian *mandolino*, diminutive of *mandora* a three-stringed musical instrument.

mandrake /'mandreɪk/ ▻ *noun* **1** a Eurasian plant with purple flowers and a forked root, formerly thought to have magical powers. **2** the root of this plant, formerly used to make sleep-inducing drugs. ◷ 14c: from Latin *mandragora*.

mandrel or **mandril** /'mandrəl/ ▻ *noun, technical* **1** the rotating shaft on a lathe that the object being worked on is fixed to. **2** the axle of a circular saw or grinding wheel. ◷ 16c as *manderelle* in original sense 'a miner's pick': related to French *mandrin* lathe.

mandrill /'mandrɪl/ ▻ *noun* a large W African baboon with distinctive red and blue striped markings on its muzzle and hindquarters. ◷ 18c: probably from MAN + DRILL[4].

mane ▻ *noun* **1** on a horse, lion or other animal: the long hair growing from and around the neck. **2** on a human: a long, thick head of hair. • **maned** *adj* (also *in compounds*) □ *shaggy-maned*. • **maneless** *adj*. ◷ Anglo-Saxon *manu*.

-mane see -MANIAC

man-eater ▻ *noun* (***man-eaters***) **1** a wild animal, such as a tiger or shark, that has acquired the habit of attacking, killing and eating people. **2** *colloq* a woman who pursues men energetically or voraciously. • **man-eating** *adj*. ◷ 17c in original sense 'a cannibal'.

manège or **manege** /ma'neɪʒ/ ▻ *noun, technical* **1 a** the skill or practice of training or handling horses; horsemanship; **b** the movements taught to a horse in this way. **2** a riding-school. ◷ 17c: French, from Italian *maneggiare* (see MANAGE).

maneuver, **maneuvered**, *etc* the *N Amer* spellings of MANOEUVRE, etc.

man Friday ▻ *noun* (***man Fridays***) **1** a faithful or devoted manservant or male assistant. **2** a junior male worker given various duties, especially in an office. See also GIRL FRIDAY. ◷ 19c: after Friday, the loyal native servant in the novel *Robinson Crusoe* (1719) by Daniel Defoe.

manful ▻ *adj* brave and determined; manly. • **manfully** *adverb*. • **manfulness** *noun*. ◷ 14c.

manganese /'maŋgəniːz/ ▻ *noun, chem* (symbol **Mn**, atomic number 25) a hard brittle pinkish-grey metallic element, an essential TRACE ELEMENT for plants and animals which is also widely used to make alloys that are very hard and resistant to wear, eg in railways lines, etc. ◷ 17c: from French *manganèse*, from Latin *magnesia* MAGNESIA.

mange /meɪndʒ/ ▻ *noun, vet medicine* a skin disease due to mites, that affects hairy animals such as cats and dogs, causing itching and loss of hair. See also MANGY. ◷ 15c: from French *mangeue* itch.

mangel-wurzel /'maŋgəlwɜːzəl/ or (*US*) **mangel** ▻ *noun* a variety of beet with a large yellow root, used as cattle food. ◷ 18c: from German *Mangoldwurzel*, from *Mangold* beet + *Wurzel* root.

manger /'meɪndʒə(r)/ ▻ *noun, old use* an open box or trough from which cattle or horses feed. ◷ 14c: from French *mangeoire*, from *mangier* to eat.

mangetout /mɒndʒ'tuː, mɑ̃ʒ-/ and **mangetout pea** ▻ *noun* a variety of garden pea of which the whole pod, containing the peas, is eaten. See also **sugar pea**. ◷ 1920s: from French *mange tout*, literally 'eat-all'.

mangey, **mangier**, *etc* see under MANGY

mangle[1] /'maŋgəl/ ▻ *verb* (***mangled***, ***mangling***) **1** to damage or destroy something or someone by cutting, crushing, tearing, etc. **2** to spoil, ruin or bungle something □ *He mangled his opening lines*. • **mangled** *adj*. • **mangler** *noun*. ◷ 15c: from French *mangler*, probably from *mahaigner* to maim.

mangle[2] /'maŋgəl/ ▻ *noun* **1** *dated* a device, usually hand-operated, that consists of two large heavy rotating rollers which have wet laundry fed between them in order to squeeze most of the water out. Also called WRINGER. **2** *especially US* a machine that presses laundry by passing it between two large heated rollers. ▻ *verb* (***mangled***, ***mangling***) to pass (laundry, etc) through a mangle. ◷ 18c: from Dutch *mangel*, ultimately from Greek *manganon* a type of war machine.

mango /'maŋgoʊ/ ▻ *noun* (***mangos*** or ***mangoes***) **1** a heavy oblong fruit with a central stone surrounded by sweet, soft juicy orange flesh and a thick, green, yellow or red skin. **2** the large evergreen tropical tree that produces this fruit. ◷ 16c: from Portuguese *manga*, from Malay *mangga*, from Tamil *man-kay* mango-fruit.

mangosteen /'maŋgəstiːn/ ▻ *noun* **1** a fruit, shaped like an orange, with thick dark brown rind and juicy rose-coloured flesh. **2** the East Indian tree that produces this fruit. ◷ 16c: from Malay *mangustan*.

mangrove /'maŋgroʊv/ ▻ *noun* any of several tropical and subtropical evergreen trees that grow in salt marshes and on mudflats, along tropical coasts and in tidal estuaries, producing aerial roots from their branches that form a dense tangled network. ◷ 17c.

mangy or **mangey** /'meɪndʒɪ/ ▻ *adj* (***mangier***, ***mangiest***) **1** *vet medicine* **a** said of an animal: suffering from MANGE; **b** caused by or relating to mange. **2** *derog* shabby; dirty and scruffy. • **mangily** *adverb*. • **manginess** *noun*.

manhandle ▻ *verb* **1** to treat someone or something roughly; to push, shove or use force to move them or it. **2** to move or transport something using manpower, not machinery. ◷ 19c; 15c in obsolete sense 'to handle a tool'.

Manhattan /man'hatən/ ▻ *noun* a cocktail consisting of vermouth, whisky, a dash of Angostura bitters and sometimes curaçao or maraschino. ◷ 19c: named after Manhattan, the island and borough of New York City.

manhole ▻ *noun* an opening large enough to allow a person through, especially one in a road that leads down into a sewer.

manhood ▻ *noun* **1** the state of being an adult male. **2** manly qualities. **3** men collectively.

man-hour ▻ *noun* (***man-hours***) a unit of work equal to the work done by one person in one hour.

manhunt ▻ *noun* an intensive and usually large-scale organized search for someone, especially a criminal or fugitive.

mania /'meɪnɪə/ ▻ *noun* (***manias***) **1** *psychol* **a** a mental disorder characterized by great excitement or euphoria, rapid and incoherent thought and speech, hyperactivity, grandiose delusions and domineering behaviour which may become violent; **b** the elated phase of MANIC-DEPRESSIVE disorders. **2** *loosely* (*especially* **a mania for something**) a great desire or enthusiasm for it; a craze or obsession. ◷ 14c: Latin, from Greek, from *mainomai* to be mad.

-mania ▻ *combining form, forming nouns, denoting* **1** *psychol* an abnormal, uncontrollable or obsessive desire for a specified thing or of a specified kind □ *kleptomania* □ *egomania*. **2** a great desire or enthusiasm for a specified thing; a craze □ *technomania* □ *bibliomania*.

maniac /'meɪnɪak/ ▻ *noun* **1** *colloq* a person who behaves wildly □ *He is a maniac on the road*. **2** an extremely keen enthusiast □ *a video maniac*. **3** *psychol, old use* someone suffering from MANIA (sense 1a); a lunatic or madman. ▻ *adj* (*also* **maniacal**) **1** affected by or relating to MANIA (sense 1 or 2). **2** behaving like or characteristic of a maniac. **3** *in compounds* someone affected by an uncontrollable desire for, or with great enthusiasm for, a specified thing □ *pyromaniac.* • **maniacally** *adverb.* ◷ 17c.

manic /ˈmanɪk/ ▻ *adj* **1** *psychol* characteristic of, relating to or suffering from MANIA (*noun* 1). **2** *colloq* very energetic or active. • **manically** *adverb.* ◷ Early 20c.

manic-depressive *psychiatry* ▻ *adj* affected by or suffering from **manic-depressive psychosis** or **manic depression**, an illness which produces alternating phases of extreme elation (MANIA 1b) and severe depression. ▻ *noun* someone who is suffering from this kind of depression.

manicure /ˈmanɪkjʊə(r)/ ▻ *noun* **1** the care and cosmetic treatment of the hands, especially the fingernails, usually carried out by a trained professional or **manicurist**. **2** an individual treatment of this kind. Compare PEDICURE. ▻ *verb* (***manicured, manicuring***) to carry out a manicure on (a person or their hands) □ *She manicures customers all day* □ *She manicured his fingernails.* ◷ 19c: from Latin *manus* hand + *cura* care.

manifest /ˈmanɪfɛst/ ▻ *verb* (***manifested, manifesting***) *formal* **1** to show or display something clearly □ *a patient manifesting all the classic symptoms.* **2** (*usually* **manifest itself**) to reveal or declare itself □ *His frustration manifested itself in an uncharacteristic, angry outburst.* **3** to be evidence or proof of something □ *an act which manifested his sincerity.* ▻ *adj* **1** easily seen or perceived; obvious □ *a manifest lie.* **2** *psychol* said of the content of a dream: that is remembered by the dreamer on waking. Opposite of LATENT. ▻ *noun* **1** a customs document that gives details of a ship or aircraft, its cargo and its destination. **2** a passenger list, for an aeroplane, etc. • **manifestable** *adj* • **manifestly** *adverb* obviously; undoubtedly. ◷ 14c: from Latin *manifestare*, from *manifestus* clearly visible or evident.

manifestation /manɪfɛˈsteɪʃən, manɪfəˈsteɪʃən/ ▻ *noun* **1** the showing of something publicly; display or demonstration. **2** the act or process of making something manifest, especially of revealing something that is secret, hidden or obscure. **3** an apparition or ghost, etc.

manifesto /manɪˈfɛstoʊ/ ▻ *noun* (***manifestos*** or ***manifestoes***) a written public declaration of policies, intentions, opinions or motives, especially one produced by a political party or candidate. ◷ 17c, originally meaning 'a piece of evidence': Italian, from Latin *manifestare* to MANIFEST.

manifold /ˈmanɪfoʊld/ ▻ *adj*, *formal or literary* **1** many and various; of many different kinds □ *manifold pleasures.* **2** having many different features or functions. ▻ *noun* **1** (*also* **manifold pipe**) *technical* a pipe with several inlets and outlets. **2** *formal* something with many different forms, features or functions. • **manifoldly** *adverb.* ◷ Anglo-Saxon *manigfeald*; see MANY + -FOLD.

manikin or **mannikin** /ˈmanɪkɪn/ ▻ *noun* **1** a model of the human body, used in teaching art and anatomy, etc. **2** *old use* an abnormally small person; a dwarf. Compare MANNEQUIN. ◷ 16c: Dutch, double diminutive of *man* MAN.

manila or **manilla** /məˈnɪlə/ ▻ *noun* (*plural* ***manilas*** or ***manillas*** used only in sense 2) **1** (*also* manila paper or **manilla paper**) a type of thick strong brown paper, originally made from MANILA HEMP, that is used especially for wrapping. Also *as adj* □ *manila envelope.* **2** a type small cigar or CHEROOT. ◷ 19c: originally made in the city of Manila in the Philippines.

Manila hemp ▻ *noun* the fibre of the ABACA.

the man in the moon ▻ *noun* the features of a man's face which can be seen on the surface of the Moon as it is viewed from Earth.

the man in the street ▻ *noun* the ordinary, typical or average man. Compare JOE BLOGGS.

manioc /ˈmanɪɒk/ ▻ *noun* CASSAVA. ◷ 16c: from Tupí *mandioca*, the name for the roots of the plant.

manipulate /məˈnɪpjʊleɪt/ ▻ *verb* (***manipulated, manipulating***) **1** to handle something, or move or work it with the hands, especially in a skilful way. **2** to control or influence someone or something cleverly and unscrupulously, especially to one's own advantage. **3** to give false appearance to something, change its character, etc □ *manipulating the statistics to suit his argument.* **4** to apply therapeutic treatment with the hands to (a part of the body). **5** *word processing* to move, edit or alter (data, files, blocks of text, etc). • **manipulable** or **manipulatable** *adj.* • **manipulation** *noun.* • **manipulative** or **manipulatory** *adj* said of a person: given to or skilled in manipulating or exploiting people or circumstances. • **manipulator** *noun* a person or device that manipulates. ◷ 19c: a back-formation from 18c *manipulation*, ultimately from Latin *manipulus* handful, from *manus* hand + *plere* to fill.

man jack ▻ *noun*, *colloq* (*usually* **every man jack**) an individual person.

mankind /manˈkaɪnd, maŋ-/ ▻ *noun* **1** the human race as a whole; human beings collectively. **2** (*usually* /ˈmankaɪnd/) human males collectively. Opposite of WOMANKIND.

manky /ˈmaŋkɪ/ ▻ *adj* (***mankier, mankiest***) *colloq* or *dialect* **1** dirty. **2** of poor quality; shoddy; rotten. ◷ 1950s: from obsolete Scots *mank* defective, from French *manc.*

manly ▻ *adj* (***manlier, manliest***) **1** displaying qualities considered admirable in a man, such as strength, determination, courage, etc. **2** considered suitable for or characteristic of a man. See also MANNISH, WOMANISH. • **manliness** *noun.*

man-made ▻ *adj* **1** said of fibre or fabric, etc: artificial or synthetic, not natural or naturally produced. **2** made by or originated by humans.

man-management ▻ *noun*, *business* the organization of the work of members of staff.

manna /ˈmanə/ ▻ *noun* **1** in the Old Testament: the food miraculously provided by God for the Israelites in the wilderness (Exodus 16.14–36). **2** any unexpected gift or windfall □ *manna from heaven.* ◷ Anglo-Saxon: from Latin, perhaps ultimately from Hebrew *man* a gift, or *man hu* 'What is it?'.

manned see under MAN

mannequin /ˈmanəkɪn/ ▻ *noun* **1** a fashion model, especially a woman, employed to model clothes, etc. **2** a life-size dummy of the human body, used in the making or displaying of clothes. Compare MANIKIN. ◷ 18c: French, from Dutch *manneken*; see MANIKIN.

manner /ˈmanə(r)/ ▻ *noun* **1** way; fashion □ *Don't speak to him in that manner* □ *an unusual manner of walking.* **2** (*often* **manners**) behaviour towards others □ *has a very pleasant manner.* **3** (**manners**) good or polite social behaviour □ *She has no manners* □ *table manners.* **4** *formal* or *dated* kind or kinds □ *all manner of things* □ *What manner of man is he?* **5** style; character □ *dressed in the Chinese manner.* • **mannerless** *adj.* • **by no manner of means** or **not by any manner of means** under no circumstances; certainly not. • **in a manner of speaking** or **in a manner** in a way; to some degree; so to speak. • **to the manner born** said of a person: accustomed since birth to a particular occupation, activity, lifestyle, etc. ◷ 12c: from French *maniere*, from Latin *manuarius* of the hand.

mannered ▻ *adj*, *formal* **1** *usually derog* unnatural and artificial; affected. **2** *in compounds* having or displaying a specified kind of social behaviour □ *bad-mannered* □ *sweet-mannered.*

mannerism ▷ *noun* **1** an individual characteristic, such as a gesture or facial expression. **2** *derog* especially in art or literature: noticeable or excessive use of an individual or mannered style. **3** (*often* **Mannerism**) in art and architecture: a style prevalent in France, Spain, and especially 16c Italy, characterized by the playful use of Classical elements and trompe l'oeil effects in bizarre or dramatic compositions, often with the human body represented in an idealized rather than a natural form. • **mannerist** *noun*. • **manneristic** *adj*. • **manneristically** *adverb*.

mannerly ▷ *adj, old use* polite; showing good manners. • **mannerliness** *noun*.

mannikin same as MANIKIN

manning see under MAN

mannish /ˈmanɪʃ/ ▷ *adj* **1** said of a woman or child: having an appearance or qualities regarded as more typical of a man. **2** masculine; like or belonging to a man. • **mannishness** *noun*.

manoeuvre or (*N Amer*) **maneuver** /məˈnuːvə(r)/ ▷ *noun* **1** a movement requiring, or performed with, skill or intelligence, eg one carried out by the driver of a vehicle or pilot of an aircraft. **2** a clever or skilful handling of affairs, often one involving deception or inventiveness. **3** *military, navy* **a** (*usually* **manoeuvres**) a large-scale battle-training exercise by armed forces; **b** a skilful or clever tactical movement of troops or ships, etc. ▷ *verb* (***manoeuvred, manoeuvring***) **1** *tr & intr* to move something accurately and with skill ▫ *manoeuvred the car into the space.* **2** *tr & intr* to use ingenuity, and perhaps deceit, in handling something or someone. **3** *intr* to carry out military exercises. **4** *tr & intr* to change the position of (troops or ships, etc). • **manoeuvrability** *noun*. • **manoeuvrable** *adj*. • **manoeuvrer** *noun*. ⓒ 15c in obsolete sense 'hand-work': French, from Latin *manu* by hand + *opera* work.

man of God ▷ *noun* **1** a saint or holy man. **2** (*also* **man of the cloth**) a clergyman.

man of letters ▷ *noun* **1** a scholar. **2** an author.

man of straw ▷ *noun* **1** someone who is weak or of no substance, especially in financial terms. **2** a bogus or imaginary opponent, claim, allegation, etc set up for the sake of argument.

man of the moment ▷ *noun* especially in politics, etc: **1** the man who is dealing with, or is best able to deal with, the present situation. **2** someone, especially a man, who is most favoured at a particular time.

man of the world and **woman of the world** ▷ *noun* someone who is mature and widely experienced.

man-of-war or **man-o'-war** ▷ *noun, historical* an armed sailing ship used as a warship.

manometer /məˈnɒmɪtə(r)/ ▷ *noun, physics* an instrument for measuring the difference in pressure between two fluids (liquids or gases). • **manometric** /manəˈmɛtrɪk/ *adj*. • **manometry** /məˈnɒmɪtrɪ/ *noun*. ⓒ 18c: from French *manomètre*, from Greek *manos* rare or thin.

manor /ˈmanə(r)/ ▷ *noun* **1** (*also* **manor-house**) the principal residence on a country estate, often the former home of a medieval lord. **2** *historical* in medieval Europe: an area of land under the control of a lord. **3** *Brit colloq* the area in which a particular person or group, especially a police unit or a criminal, operates. • **manorial** /məˈnɒrɪəl/ *adj*. ⓒ 13c: from French *manoir*, from Latin *manere* to stay.

manpower ▷ *noun* **1** the number of available employees or people fit and ready to work. **2** human effort or energy, as opposed to mechanical power.

manqué /ˈmɒŋkeɪ; *French* mɑ̃ke/ ▷ *adj, following its noun, literary* applied to a specified kind of person: having once had the ambition or potential to be that kind of person, without achieving it; unfulfilled ▫ *an artist manqué.* ⓒ 18c: French, meaning 'having missed'.

mansard /ˈmansɑːd/ ▷ *noun, archit* (*in full* **mansard roof**) a four-sided roof, each side of which is in two parts, the lower part sloping more steeply. ⓒ 18c: from French *mansarde*, named after François Mansart (1598–1666), French architect.

manse /mans/ ▷ *noun* especially in Scotland: the house of a religious minister. ⓒ 15c in obsolete sense 'mansion house': from Latin *mansus* dwelling.

manservant ▷ *noun* (***menservants***) *old use* a male servant, especially a valet. See also MAIDSERVANT.

mansion /ˈmanʃən/ ▷ *noun* **1** a large house, usually a grand or luxurious one. **2** (**mansions** or **Mansions**) *Brit* used eg as the name or address of a residential property: a large building divided into luxury apartments ▫ *Belgravia Mansions.* **3** *now rare* a manor-house. ⓒ 14c in obsolete sense 'a dwelling place': French, from Latin *mansio* remaining.

man-sized and **man-size** ▷ *adj* **1** said eg of a task: suitable for a man; requiring, or appropriate for, a man. **2** *colloq* big.

manslaughter ▷ *noun* **1** *law* the crime of HOMICIDE without MALICE AFORETHOUGHT, eg as a result of gross negligence, provocation or diminished responsibility. *Scots equivalent* CULPABLE HOMICIDE. Compare MURDER. **2** *old use* the killing of a person by another. ⓒ 14c.

manta /ˈmantə/ and **manta ray** ▷ *noun* (***mantas*** or ***manta rays***) a type of fish, a giant RAY², that may exceed 9m (30ft) in width and 2 tonnes in weight, with a broad mouth situated across the front of the head. ⓒ 18c: Spanish, meaning 'cloak' or 'blanket'.

mantel /ˈmantəl/ ▷ *noun, chiefly old use* a mantelpiece or mantelshelf. ⓒ 15c: related to MANTLE.

mantelpiece ▷ *noun* the ornamental frame around a fireplace, especially the top part which forms a shelf.

mantelshelf ▷ *noun* the shelf part of a mantelpiece, over a fireplace.

mantilla /manˈtɪlə; *Spanish* manˈtiːja/ ▷ *noun* (***mantillas***) **1** a lace or silk scarf worn by women as a covering for the hair and shoulders, especially in Spain and S America. **2** a short lightweight cape or cloak. ⓒ 18c: Spanish, diminutive of *manta* a cloak.

mantis /ˈmantɪs/ ▷ *noun* (***mantises*** or ***mantes*** /-tiːz/) any of numerous mainly tropical insect-eating insects that have long bodies, large eyes and a tendency to sit in wait for prey with their two spikey front legs raised. Also called **praying mantis**. ⓒ 17c: Latin, from Greek *mantis* a prophet (because it looks as though it is praying).

mantissa /manˈtɪsə/ ▷ *noun* (***mantissas***) *math* the part of a logarithm comprising the decimal point and the figures following it. See also CHARACTERISTIC (*noun* 2). ⓒ 17c: Latin, 'something added'.

mantle /ˈmantəl/ ▷ *noun* **1** a cloak or loose outer garment. **2** *literary* a covering ▫ *a mantle of snow.* **3** *geol* the part of the Earth between the crust and the core. **4** a fireproof mesh around a gas or oil lamp, that glows when the lamp is lit. **5** *literary* a position of responsibility ▫ *The leader's mantle passed to him.* **6** a fold of the external skin of a mollusc, etc that secretes the substance which forms the shell. ▷ *verb* (***mantled, mantling***) *literary* to cover, conceal or obscure something or someone ▫ *mantled in darkness.* ⓒ 13c: from Latin *mantellum*, diminutive of *mantum* a cloak.

man-to-man ▷ *adj* said especially of personal discussion: open and frank. ▷ *adverb* in an open and frank manner; honestly.

mantra /ˈmantrə/ ▷ *noun* (***mantras***) **1 a** *Hinduism, Buddhism* a sacred phrase, word or sound chanted repeatedly as part of meditation and prayer, as an aid to concentration and the development of spiritual power; **b**

a word, sound or group of sounds repeated, often inwardly, as an aid to concentration when meditating. **2** *Hinduism* any of the hymns of praise in the Vedas (see VEDA), the ancient sacred scriptures. ⌚ 19c: Sanskrit, meaning 'instrument of thought'.

mantrap ▷ *noun* **1** a trap or snare for catching trespassers, poachers, etc. **2** any source of potential danger.

manual /'manjʊəl/ ▷ *adj* **1** belonging or relating to the hand or hands □ *a job requiring manual skill.* **2** using the body, rather than the mind; physical. **3** worked, controlled or operated by hand; not automatic or computer-operated, etc. ▷ *noun* **1** a book of instructions, eg for repairing a car or operating a machine. Also called HANDBOOK. **2** an organ keyboard or a key played by hand not by foot. **3** *military* drill in the use of weapons, etc. ● **manually** *adverb*. ⌚ 15c: from Latin *manualis*, from *manus* hand.

manufacture /manjʊ'faktʃə(r)/ ▷ *verb* (***manufactured, manufacturing***) **1** to make something from raw materials, especially in large quantities using machinery. **2** to invent or fabricate something. **3** *derog* to produce something in a mechanical fashion. ▷ *noun* **1** the practice, act or process of manufacturing something. **2** anything manufactured. ● **manufacturer** *noun* **1** a person or business that manufactures a product, etc. **2** a director or manager of a firm that manufactures goods. **3** a person who makes, fabricates or invents something. ● **manufacturing** *adj, noun*. ⌚ 16c: French, from Latin *manu* by hand + *facere* to make.

manuka /'mɑːnʊkɑː/ ▷ *noun* (***manukas***) an Australian and New Zealand tree of the myrtle family with hard wood and aromatic leaves. ⌚ 19c: Maori.

manumit /manjʊ'mɪt/ ▷ *verb* (***manumitted, manumitting***) *formal* to release (a person) from slavery; to set someone free. ● **manumission** *noun*. ● **manumitter** *noun*. ⌚ 15c: from Latin *manumittere* to send from one's hand or control, from *manus* hand + *mittere* to send.

manure /mə'njʊə(r)/ ▷ *noun* any substance, especially animal dung, used on soil as a fertilizer. ▷ *verb* (***manured, manuring***) to apply manure to (land, soil, etc); to enrich (soil) with a fertilizing substance. ● **manurer** *noun*. ● **manuring** *noun*. ⌚ 15c in obsolete verb senses 'to manage or cultivate (land)': from French *maynoverer* to work with the hands.

manuscript /'manjʊskrɪpt/ ▷ *noun* (abbreviation **MS** or **ms.**) **1** an author's handwritten or typed version of a book, play, etc before it has been printed. **2** a book or document written by hand. ▷ *adj* written by hand or typed, not printed □ *some rare manuscript poems.* ⌚ 16c: from Latin *manuscriptus* written by hand, from *manu* by hand + *scribere* to write.

Manx /maŋks/ ▷ *adj* **1** belonging or relating to the Isle of Man, a British Crown Dependency in the Irish Sea, its inhabitants, or their language. **2** (**the Manx**) the people of the Isle of Man; Manxmen and Manxwomen collectively (see THE 4b). ▷ *noun* an almost extinct Celtic language that was formerly widely spoken on the Isle of Man. ⌚ 16c: from *Maniske* Man-ish.

Manx cat ▷ *noun* a short-haired, tailless domestic cat of a breed originally from the Isle of Man.

Manxman and **Manxwoman** ▷ *noun* a man or woman born on or living in the Isle of Man.

many /'mɛnɪ/ ▷ *adj* (*comparative* ***more***, *superlative* ***most***) **1** (*sometimes* **a great many** or **good many**) consisting of a large number; numerous □ *Many teenagers smoke* □ *had to stop a good many times to rest.* **2** (**the many**) the majority or the crowd; ordinary people, not nobility or royalty. ▷ *pronoun* a great number (of people or things) □ *The sweets were so rich that I couldn't eat many.* See also MORE, MOST. ● **as many** the same number (of something) □ *She hasn't as many friends as you* □ *I don't want as many.* ● **have one too many** *colloq* to drink to excess. ● **how many?** how great a number? □ *How many people are coming?* ● **many a, an** or **another** as or being one of a number of (a specified thing) □ *many a man* □ *spent many a happy hour there.* ● **many's the time** *colloq* on a great many occasions □ *Many's the time I found her crying.* ● **too many** too great a number (of something); more than required □ *There are too many people in here.* ⌚ Anglo-Saxon *manig*.

many-sided ▷ *adj* **1** said of an argument, viewpoint, etc: having many qualities or aspects. **2** said of a person: having many interests or varied abilities.

manzanilla /manzə'nɪlə, -'niːjə/ ▷ *noun* (***manzanillas***) a very dry, light, pale sherry with a comparatively low alcohol content. ⌚ 19c: Spanish, diminutive of *manzana* apple, also meaning CAMOMILE.

Maoism /'maʊɪzəm/ ▷ *noun, politics* the policies and theories of Mao Zedong (or Mao Tse-tung) (1893–1976), the first leader of Communist China. ● **Maoist** *noun* a follower of Chinese communism as expounded by Mao Zedong. ▷ *adj* relating to or characteristic of Maoism or a Maoist. ⌚ 1950s.

Mao jacket and **Mao suit** ▷ *noun* a jacket or suit, especially one made of grey or blue cotton, in the simple style of those worn by Mao Zedong and his followers.

Maori /'maʊərɪ/ ▷ *noun* (***Maori*** or ***Maoris***) **1** a member of the aboriginal Polynesian people of New Zealand. **2** the language of this people, belonging to the AUSTRONESIAN family of languages. ▷ *adj* belonging or relating to this people or their language. ⌚ 19c: a native name.

map ▷ *noun* **1** a diagram of any part of the earth's surface, showing geographical and other features, eg the position of towns and roads. See also CARTOGRAPHY. **2** a similar diagram of the surface of the Moon or a planet. **3** a diagram showing the position of the stars in the sky. **4** a diagram of the layout of anything, eg one that describes a particular sequence of genes in a chromosome. ▷ *verb* (***mapped, mapping***) **1** to make a map of something. **2** *math* to place (the elements of a SET² (*noun* 2)) in one-to-one correspondence with the elements of another set. ● **mapper** *noun* someone or something that maps or makes maps. ● **mappable** *adj*. ● **mapping** *noun, chiefly math.* ● **off the map 1** said of a location: away from all main routes or roads, etc. **2** *colloq* out of existence; no longer significant. ● **put something** or **someone on the map** *colloq* to cause (eg a town, an actor, a trend, etc) to become well-known or important. ⌚ 16c: from Latin *mappa* a napkin or painted cloth.

■ **map something out** to plan (a route, course of action, etc) in detail □ *She seems to have her whole life mapped out.*

maple /'meɪpəl/ ▷ *noun* **1** (*also* **maple tree**) any of various broad-leaved deciduous trees of northern regions whose seeds float by means of winglike growths. **2** the hard light-coloured wood of these trees, used to make furniture, etc. Also *as adj* □ *maple leaf.* ⌚ Anglo-Saxon *mapul*.

maple leaf ▷ *noun* the leaf of a maple tree, especially as the national emblem of Canada.

maple syrup ▷ *noun, especially N Amer* the distinctively flavoured syrup made from the sap of the sugar-maple tree.

map-reading ▷ *noun* the practice, act, process or skill of interpreting what is on a geographical map, especially in order to direct or plan a route, journey, etc. ● **map-reader** *noun*.

maquette /ma'kɛt/ ▷ *noun* a small model of something to be made on a larger scale, especially a clay, wax or plaster model made by a sculptor as a preliminary study for a full-size work.

maquillage /makɪ'jɑːʒ/ ▷ *noun* **1** cosmetics; make-up. **2** the art of applying cosmetics to one's face. ⌚ 19c: from French *maquiller* to put on make-up.

maquis /mɑːˈkiː, ˈmɑːkiː/ ▷ *noun* (*plural* ***maquis***) **1** a type of thick, shrubby vegetation found in coastal areas of the Mediterranean. **2** (**the maquis** or **the Maquis**) *historical* **a** the French resistance movement that fought against German occupying forces during World War II; **b** a member of this movement. ⓒ 1940s in sense 2, from the idea of the thick vegetation providing cover for resistance members hiding in the hills; 19c: French, from Italian *macchia* thicket.

Mar. ▷ *abbreviation* March.

mar /mɑː(r)/ ▷ *verb* (***marred***, ***marring***) **1** to spoil something ▫ *The flavour was marred by too much vinegar.* **2** to injure or damage something ▫ *The landscape was marred by ugly pylons.* ⓒ Anglo-Saxon *merran*.

marabou or **marabout** /ˈmarəbuː/ or ▷ *noun* (*plural* in sense 1 only ***marabous*** or ***marabouts***) **1** a large black-and-white African stork. **2** its feathers, used to decorate clothes, trim hats, etc. ⓒ 19c: French, from Arabic *murabit* a hermit or holy man; the stork is considered holy in Islam.

maraca /məˈrakə/ ▷ *noun* (***maracas***) **1** originally and especially in Latin America: a hand-held percussion instrument, usually one of a pair, consisting of a gourd or similar hollow shell filled with dried beans, pebbles, etc which make a rattling noise when shaken. **2** (**maracas**) *US colloq* female breasts. ⓒ 19c: from Portuguese *maracá*.

maraschino /marəˈʃiːnoʊ, -ˈskiːnoʊ/ ▷ *noun* a liqueur made from cherries, with a taste like bitter almonds. ⓒ 18c: Italian, from *amarasca* a sour cherry, from Latin *amarus* bitter.

maraschino cherry ▷ *noun* a cherry preserved in MARASCHINO or something similar, used for decorating cocktails, cakes, etc.

marathon /ˈmarəθən/ ▷ *noun* **1** (sometimes **marathon race**) a long-distance race on foot, usually 42.195km (26ml 385yd). **2** any lengthy and difficult task. ▷ *adj* **1** belonging or relating to a marathon race. **2** requiring or displaying great powers of endurance or stamina ▫ *a marathon effort.* ⓒ 19c: named after Marathon in Greece, from where a messenger is said to have run to Athens with news of victory over the Persians in 490 BC; the length of the race is based on this distance.

maraud /məˈrɔːd/ ▷ *verb* (***marauded***, ***marauding***) **1** *intr* to wander in search of people to attack and property to steal or destroy. **2** to plunder (a place). • **marauder** *noun*. • **marauding** *adj*, *noun*. ⓒ 18c: from French *marauder* to prowl, from *maraud* a rogue.

marble /ˈmɑːbəl/ ▷ *noun* **1 a** *geol* a hard, metamorphic rock formed of recrystallized limestone or dolomite, white when pure but usually mottled or streaked; **b** any such rock that can be highly polished, used in building and sculpture. **2** in children's games: a small hard ball, now usually made of glass, but originally made of marble. See also MARBLES. **3** a work of art, tombstone, tomb, slab or other object made of marble. ▷ *verb* (***marbled***, ***marbling***) to stain, vein or paint something (especially paper) to resemble marble. • **marbled** *adj* **1** mottled, or having irregular streaks of different colours, like marble. **2** made with or of marble ▫ *marbled halls.* • **marbling** *noun* **1** a marbled appearance or colouring, eg in meat with streaks of fat. **2** the practice or act of streaking, veining or painting (especially the endpapers or edges of a book) in imitation of marble.• **marbly** *adj*. ⓒ 13c as *marbre*: French, from Latin *marmor*, from Greek *marmaros*, from *marmairein* to sparkle.

marbles ▷ *singular noun* any of several children's games played with marbles. See MARBLE (*noun* 2). • **have all one's marbles** or **lose one's marbles** to be in full possession of, or to lack, one's mental faculties.

marbling see under MARBLE[2]

marc /mɑːk/ ▷ *noun* **1** *technical* the leftover skins and stems of grapes used in winemaking. **2** a kind of brandy made from these. ⓒ 17c: French, from *marchier* to trample.

marcasite /ˈmɑːkəsaɪt/ ▷ *noun* **1** *geol* a pale yellow mineral, a compound of iron, formerly used in jewellery and now mined for use in the manufacture of sulphuric acid. **2** a polished gemstone made from this or any similar mineral. ⓒ 15c: from Latin *marcasita*, from Arabic *marqashita*.

marcato /mɑːˈkɑːtoʊ/ *music* ▷ *adverb* in an emphatic or strongly-accented manner. ▷ *adj* emphatic; strongly accented. ⓒ 19c: Italian, meaning 'marked'.

March /mɑːtʃ/ ▷ *noun* the third month of the year, which follows February and comes before April, and has 31 days. ⓒ 13c: from French *Marche*, from Latin *Martius* belonging to Mars, the Roman god of war.

march[1] /mɑːtʃ/ ▷ *verb* (***marches***, ***marched***, ***marching***) **1** *intr* to walk in a stiff, upright, formal manner, usually at a brisk pace and in step with others. **2** to make or force someone, especially a soldier or troop of soldiers, to walk in this way. **3** *intr* to walk in a purposeful and determined way ▫ *suddenly marched out of the room.* **4** *intr* to advance or continue, steadily or irresistibly ▫ *events marched on.* ▷ *noun* (***marches***) **1** an act of marching. **2** a distance travelled by marching. **3** a brisk walking pace. **4** a procession of people moving steadily forward. **5** *music* a piece of music written in a marching rhythm. **6** steady and unstoppable progress or movement ▫ *the march of time.* • **marcher** *noun* **1** someone who marches. **2** someone who takes part in a march. • **steal a march on someone** see under STEAL. • **on the march** said of an army, etc: marching; advancing. ⓒ 16c: from French *marcher* to walk.

march[2] /mɑːtʃ/ ▷ *noun* **1** a boundary or border. **2** a border district, especially (**the Marches**) those around the English–Welsh and English–Scottish borders, which were fought over continuously from the 13c to the 16c. ⓒ 13c: from French *marche*; related to MARK[1].

March hare ▷ *noun* a hare during its breeding season in March 15c: used as a proverbial example of madness because of its excitable and erratic behaviour. ▫ *mad as a March hare.* **2** *literary* one of the mad characters encountered by Alice in the children's book *Alice's Adventures in Wonderland* (1865) by Lewis Carroll.

marching orders ▷ *plural noun* **1** orders to march in a certain way, given to soldiers, etc. **2** *colloq* dismissal from a job, house, relationship, etc ▫ *The boss gave him his marching orders on the spot.* *N Amer equivalent* WALKING PAPERS.

marchioness /ˈmɑːʃənəs, -nɛs/ ▷ *noun* **1** the wife or widow of a MARQUIS. **2** a woman who holds the rank of marquis in her own right. ⓒ 16c: from Latin *marchionissa*, from *marchio* marquis.

march past ▷ *noun*, *military* a march performed by a body of troops, etc in front of a person, eg the sovereign or a senior officer, who reviews it.

Mardi Gras /ˈmɑːdɪ grɑː; *French* mardigʀa/ ▷ *noun* **1** SHROVE TUESDAY, a day celebrated with a festival in some places, especially famously in Rio de Janeiro, Brazil. **2** the festival held on this day. ⓒ 17c: French, literally 'fat Tuesday'.

mare[1] /mɛə(r)/ ▷ *noun* an adult female horse, ass, zebra, etc. See also STALLION, FOAL. ⓒ Anglo-Saxon *mere*.

mare[2] /ˈmɑːreɪ, ˈmar-/ ▷ *noun* (***maria*** /-rə/) *astron* any of numerous large, flat areas on the surface of the Moon or Mars, seen from Earth as dark patches and originally thought to be seas. ⓒ 18c: Latin, meaning 'sea'.

mare's nest ▷ *noun* **1** a discovery that proves to be untrue or without value; a hoax. **2** *chiefly US* a disordered or confused place or situation.

marg or **marge** /mɑːdʒ/ ▷ *contraction*, *colloq* margarine.

margarine /mɑːdʒəˈriːn, ˈmɑːgəriːn/ ▷ *noun* a food product, usually made from vegetable oils with water, flavourings, colourings, vitamins, etc, that is used as a substitute for butter. Also (*US*) called OLEO, OLEOMARGARINE. Ⓒ 1870s: French, from Greek *margaron* pearl.

margarita /mɑːgəˈriːtə/ ▷ *noun* (***margaritas***) a cocktail made with tequila, lemon or lime juice, and an orange-flavoured liqueur, often served with salt around the top of the glass. Ⓒ 1960s: from the Spanish personal name Margarita.

margin /ˈmɑːdʒɪn/ ▷ *noun* **1** the blank space around a page of writing or print. **2** any edge, border or fringe. **3** an extra amount, eg of time or money, beyond what should strictly be needed □ ***allow a margin for error.*** **4** an amount by which one thing exceeds another □ ***win by a large margin.*** **5** *business* the difference between the selling and buying price of an item; profit. **6** *econ, etc* an upper or lower limit, especially one beyond which it is impossible for a business, etc to exist or operate. **7** *finance* a deposit to protect a broker against loss. • **margined** *adj* provided with a margin; having a border. Ⓒ 14c: from Latin *margo, marginis* a border.

marginal ▷ *adj* **1** small and unimportant or insignificant. **2** near to the lower limit; barely sufficient. **3** *chiefly Brit* said of a political constituency: whose current MP or other representative was elected by only a small majority of votes at the last election. **4** said of a note, mark, design, etc: appearing in the margin of a page of text. **5** in, on, belonging or relating to a margin. ▷ *noun, chiefly Brit* a marginal constituency or seat. Compare SAFE SEAT. • **marginality** *noun.* • **marginally** *adverb.*

marginal cost ▷ *noun, business, econ* the cost to a firm of producing one extra unit of output. See also FIXED COSTS.

marginalia /mɑːdʒɪˈneɪlɪə/ ▷ *plural noun* notes written in the margin or margins of a page, book, etc. Also called **marginal notes**. Ⓒ 19c: from Latin *marginalis* marginal.

marginalize or **marginalise** /mɑːdʒɪnəlaɪz/ ▷ *verb* (***marginalized, marginalizing***) to push something or someone to the edges of anything (especially of society or one's consciousness), in order to reduce its or their effect, relevance, significance, etc. • **marginalization** *noun.* Ⓒ 1970s.

marginate /mɑːdʒɪneɪt/ ▷ *verb* (***marginated, marginating***) to provide something with a margin or margins. ▷ *adj* (*also* **marginated**) *biol, etc* having a well-marked border or margin. • **margination** *noun.* Ⓒ 17c.

marguerite /mɑːgəˈriːt/ ▷ *noun* a garden plant, such as the **oxeye daisy**, whose large flowers have pale yellow or white petals round a yellow centre. Ⓒ 19c: French, meaning 'daisy', from Latin *margarita* a pearl..

maria *plural of* MARE[2]

marigold /ˈmarɪgoʊld/ ▷ *noun* a garden plant with bright orange or yellow flowers and strongly-scented leaves. See also MARSH MARIGOLD. Ⓒ 14c: from *Mary* (the Virgin Mary) + *gold*, an obsolete name for the plant.

marijuana or **marihuana** /marɪˈwɑːnə/ ▷ *noun* CANNABIS.

marimba /məˈrɪmbə/ ▷ *noun* (***marimbas***) *music* a type of XYLOPHONE, originally from Africa, consisting of a set of hardwood strips which, when struck with hammers, vibrate metal plates underneath to produce a musical sound. Ⓒ 18c: from Kongo, a W African language.

marina /məˈriːnə/ ▷ *noun* (***marinas***) a harbour for berthing private pleasure boats, usually with associated facilities provided. Ⓒ 19c: from Italian and Spanish, from Latin *marinus* MARINE.

marinade /marɪˈneɪd/ ▷ *noun, cookery* **1** any liquid mixture, especially a mixture of oil, herbs, spices, vinegar or wine, etc, in which food, especially meat or fish, is soaked before cooking to add flavour or to tenderize it. **2** meat, fish, etc that has been soaked in such a mixture. ▷ *verb* (***marinaded, marinading***) *tr & intr* to soak (meat or fish, etc) in a marinade. Also called MARINATE. Ⓒ 17c: French, from Spanish *marinar* to pickle something in brine.

marinara /marəˈnarə/ ▷ *noun* an Italian-style tomato and seafood sauce, often with herbs, spices, white wine, etc, served with pasta dishes. • ▷ *adj denoting* pasta, gnocchi, etc that is served with this kind of sauce □ ***spaghetti marinara.*** Ⓒ 1940s: Italian, meaning 'in sailor's style', from *marina* sea.

marinate /ˈmarɪneɪt/ ▷ *verb* (***marinated, marinating***) to MARINADE something. Ⓒ 17c: from Italian *marinare* or French *mariner.*

marine /məˈriːn/ ▷ *adj* **1** belonging to or concerned with the sea □ ***marine landscape.*** **2** inhabiting, found in or obtained from the sea □ ***marine mammal.*** **3** belonging or relating to ships, shipping trade or the navy □ ***marine insurance*** □ ***marine architect.*** **4** done or used at sea □ ***marine compass.*** See also MARITIME. ▷ *noun* **1** (*often* **Marine**) **a** a soldier trained to serve on land or at sea; **b** a member of the Royal Marines or the US Marine Corps. **2** the merchant or naval ships of a nation collectively. • **tell that** or **it to the marines** *colloq* an expression of disbelief and ridicule. Ⓒ 15c: from Latin *marinus*, from *mare* sea.

mariner /məˈriːnə(r)/ ▷ *noun* a seaman. Ⓒ 13c: French.

marinière / *French* maʀinjɛʀ/ ▷ *adj, following its noun, cookery* said especially of mussels: cooked in white wine with onions and herbs □ ***moules marinières.*** Ⓒ 20c: from French *à la marinière*, meaning 'in the manner of the bargeman's wife'.

marionette /marɪəˈnɛt/ ▷ *noun* a puppet with jointed limbs moved by strings. Ⓒ 17c: French, diminutive of Marion, the woman's name.

marital /ˈmarɪtəl/ ▷ *adj* **1** belonging or relating to marriage □ ***marital status*** □ ***the marital home.*** See also CONNUBIAL, MATRIMONIAL. **2** belonging or relating to a husband □ ***denied him his marital rights.*** • **maritally** *adverb.* Ⓒ 17c: from Latin *maritalis* married, from *maritus* a husband.

maritime /ˈmarɪtaɪm/ ▷ *adj* **1** belonging or relating to the sea or ships, sea-trade, etc □ ***maritime communications.*** See also MARINE *adj.* **2** said of plants, etc: living or growing near the sea. **3** said of a climate: having relatively small temperature differences between summer and winter. **4** said of a country, etc: having a sea-coast. **5** said of a country, etc: having a navy and sea-trade □ ***a maritime nation.*** Ⓒ 16c: from Latin *maritimus* of the sea, from *mare* sea.

marjoram /ˈmɑːdʒərəm/ ▷ *noun* **1** (*in full* **sweet marjoram**) a purple-flowered Mediterranean plant whose sweet-smelling leaves are used to season food. **2** (*in full* **wild marjoram**) a similar but more pungent plant, used especially in pasta dishes. Also called OREGANO. Ⓒ 14c as *marjorane*: French, from Latin *majorana.*

mark[1] /mɑːk/ ▷ *noun* **1** a visible blemish, such as a scratch or stain. **2** a patch, stripe, spot, etc forming part of a larger pattern. **3 a** a grade or score awarded according to the proficiency of a student or competitor, etc; **b** a letter, number, or percentage used to denote this □ ***What mark did you get? Only C+.*** **4** a sign or symbol □ ***a question mark.*** **5** an indication or representation □ ***a mark of respect.*** **6** the position from which a competitor starts in a race. See also *on your marks* below. **7** an object or thing to be aimed at or striven for; a target or goal □ ***It fell wide of the mark.*** **8** a required or normal standard □ ***up to the mark.*** **9** an impression, distinguishing characteristic or influence □ ***Your work bears his mark.*** **10** noteworthiness; distinction □ ***someone of no mark.*** **11** a cross or other sign used instead of a signature □ ***Make your mark below.*** **12** *rugby* **a** a mark made with the heel on the ground by a player on making a fair catch; **b** the act of making a fair catch within one's own 22-metre line and marking the spot where the catch was made, from where a free kick can be taken. **13** (*often* **Mark**) (abbreviation **Mk**) applied especially to vehicles: a type of design; a model or issue □ *driving a Jaguar Mark II.* See also MARQUE. **14** *slang* a suitable victim for trickery, theft, etc □ ***a soft mark.*** ▷ *verb* (***marked, marking***) **1** *tr & intr* to spoil something with, or become spoiled by, a MARK (*noun* 1). **2** a) to read, correct and award (a grade) to a piece of written work, etc; b) to allot a score to someone or something. **3** to show; to be a sign of something □ *events marking a new era* □ *X marks the spot.* **4** (*often* **mark something down**) to make a note of something; to record it. **5** to pay close attention to something □ *mark my words.* **6** *sport* to stay close to (an opposing player) in order to try and prevent them from getting or passing the ball. **7** to characterize or label someone or something □ *This incident marks him as a criminal.* • **marked** and **marking** see separate entries. • **make** or **leave one's mark** to make a strong or permanent impression. • **mark someone's card** to correct them, especially quickly and forcefully, when they are under a false impression; to put them right. • **mark time 1** to move the feet up and down as if marching, but without going forward. **2** merely to keep things going, without making progress or speeding up. • **off the mark 1** not on target; off the subject or target. **2** said of an athlete, etc: getting away from the mark (*noun* 6) in a race, etc □ *slow off the mark.* See also QUICK OFF THE MARK at QUICK. • **on your marks** or **mark** *athletics* said to the runners before a race begins: get into your position, ready for the starting command or signal. • **up to the mark 1** said of work, etc: satisfactory; of a good standard. **2** said of a person: fit and well. ⓒ Anglo-Saxon *merc* boundary or limit.

■ **mark someone down** to give them or their work a lower mark □ *had to mark him down for poor spelling.*

■ **mark something down 1** to reduce its price □ *a jacket marked down from £70 to £55.* **2** to note it.

■ **mark something off** or **out 1** to indicate on a list, etc that (an issue, point, etc) has been dealt with. **2** to fix its boundaries or limits with marks of some kind.

■ **mark something out** to lay out its plans or outlines.

■ **mark something up** to increase its price; to make a profit for the seller on it. See also MARK-UP.

mark² /mɑːk/ ▷ *noun* **1** (abbreviation **M** and **DM**) the standard currency unit in Germany. See also DEUTSCHMARK. **2** *formerly* a unit of weight for gold and silver. ⓒ Anglo-Saxon *marc.*

mark-down ▷ *noun* a reduction in price, especially in determining level of profit.

marked ▷ *adj* **1** obvious or noticeable □ *a marked change in her attitude.* **2** said of a person: watched with suspicion; selected as the target for an attack □ *a marked man.* • **markedly** /ˈmɑːkɪdlɪ/ *adverb* noticeably. • **markedness** /ˈmɑːkɪdnəs/ *noun.* • **marked for something** destined or doomed for it.

marker ▷ *noun* **1** a pen with a thick point, for writing signs, etc. Also called **marker pen**. **2** someone who takes notes, eg of the score in a game. **3** anything used to mark the position of something.

market /ˈmɑːkɪt/ ▷ *noun* **1** a gathering of people that takes place periodically, where stalls, etc are set up allowing them to buy and sell a variety of goods or a specified type of goods. **2** a public place, square, building, etc in which this regularly takes place. **3** a particular region, country or section of the population, considered as a potential customer □ *the French market* □ *the teenage market.* **4** buying and selling; a level of trading □ *The market is slow.* **5** opportunity for buying and selling; demand □ *no market for these goods.* **6** *as adj* □ *market day* □ *market share* □ *market trader.* **7** *especially N Amer* a shop or supermarket. ▷ *verb* (***marketed, marketing***) **1** to offer something for sale; to promote (goods, etc). **2** *intr* to trade or deal, especially at a market. **3** *intr, especially US* to shop; to buy provisions. • **marketable** *adj.* • **marketability** *noun.* • **be in the market for something** to wish to buy it. • **on the market** on sale; able to be bought. See also STOCK MARKET. ⓒ Anglo-Saxon: from Latin *mercatus* trade or market.

market economy ▷ *noun* an economic system in which prices, wages, products and services are determined by MARKET FORCES of SUPPLY and DEMAND, without any state interference. Compare COMMAND ECONOMY, MIXED ECONOMY.

marketeer ▷ *noun* **1** someone who trades at a market. **2** *econ* someone who is involved with, or who promotes, a particular kind of market □ *free marketeer* □ *black marketeer.* Compare MARKETER.

marketer *noun* **1** someone who goes to, or trades at, a market. **2** *business* someone whose job is to sell the product produced by their company. Compare MARKETEER.

market forces ▷ *plural noun* the willingness of customers to buy goods or services that suppliers are willing to offer at a particular price; supply and demand.

market garden ▷ *noun* an area of land, usually near a large town or city, that is used commercially to grow produce, especially vegetables, salad crops, soft fruit and flowers, for immediate sale at a market. • **market gardener** *noun* the owner of or a person who tends a market garden. • **market gardening** *noun. N Amer equivalent* TRUCK FARM.

marketing ▷ *noun* **1** *business* the techniques or processes by which a product or service is sold, including assessment of its sales potential and responsibility for its promotion, distribution and development. **2** *especially N Amer* an act or process of shopping.

market-led ▷ *adj* referring or relating to the selling or development of a product, of research, etc, which is allowed to be influenced solely by economic and commercial factors rather than attracting any kind of subsidy, etc.

market leader ▷ *noun, business* **1** a company that sells more goods of a specific type than any other company. **2** a brand of goods that sells more than any other of its kind.

market maker ▷ *noun, stock exchange* a BROKER-DEALER. See also STOCKJOBBER.

market-place ▷ *noun* **1** the open space in a town, etc in which a market is held. **2** (**the market-place**) the commercial world of buying and selling □ *Can this product find a slot in the wider market-place?*

market price ▷ *noun* the price for which a thing can be sold, and is being sold, at a particular time. Also called **market value**.

market research ▷ *noun* study and analysis of the habits, needs and preferences of customers, often in regard to a particular product or service. • **market researcher** *noun.*

market town ▷ *noun* a town, often at the centre of a farming area, where a market is held regularly, usually on the same day every week.

marking ▷ *noun* **1** (*often* **markings**) a distinctive pattern of colours on an animal or plant. **2** the act or process of giving marks (eg to school work) or making marks on something.

markka /mɑːˈkɑː/ ▷ *noun* (***markkaa*** or ***markkas***) (symbol **Mk**) the standard currency unit in Finland. ⓒ Early 20c: Finnish; see MARK².

marksman and **markswoman** ▷ *noun* someone who can shoot a gun or other weapon accurately, especially a trained soldier, police officer, etc. • **marksmanship** *noun.* ⓒ 17c.

mark-up ▷ *noun, commerce* **1** an increase in price, especially in determining level of profit. **2** the difference between the WHOLESALE and RETAIL price of an item. See also MARK SOMETHING UP at MARK[1].

marl /mɑːl/ ▻ *noun, geol* a mixture of clay and limestone. ▻ *verb* (***marled***, ***marling***) to apply marl to (sandy soil, etc). • **marling** *noun, especially formerly* the process of adding marl to light sandy soil to improve its texture and fertility and to increase its water-holding capacity. • **marly** *adj.* ⓘ 14c: from French *marle*, from Latin *marga*.

marlin /'mɑːlɪn/ ▻ *noun* (***marlin*** or ***marlins***) a large fish found in warm and tropical seas which has a long spear-like upper jaw. Also called SPEARFISH. ⓘ 20c: from MARLINSPIKE, because of its pointed snout.

marline /'mɑːlɪn/ ▻ *noun, naut* a small rope for winding around a larger one, to keep it from wearing. ⓘ 15c: from Dutch *marlijn*, from *marren* to tie + *lijn* rope.

marlinspike or **marlinespike** ▻ *noun* (***marlinspikes*** or ***marlinespikes***) *naut* a pointed metal tool for separating the strands of rope to be spliced. ⓘ 17c: MARLINE + SPIKE[1].

marm see MA'AM

marmalade /'mɑːməleɪd/ ▻ *noun* jam made from the pulp and rind of any citrus fruit, especially oranges. ▻ *adj* said of a cat: with a coat marked with orange and brown streaks. ⓘ 16c: from Portuguese *marmelada*, from *marmelo* QUINCE, from which it was originally made.

marmelize or **marmelise** /'mɑːməlaɪz/ ▻ *verb* (***marmelized***, ***marmelizing***) *Brit colloq* to thrash or defeat someone heavily; to destroy them. ⓘ 20c: from MARMALADE, as though turning them into marmalade.

Marmite /'mɑːmaɪt/ ▻ *noun, trademark* a dark brown savoury spread made from yeast and vegetable extracts, eaten on toast, etc. ⓘ Early 20c: from MARMITE.

marmite /'mɑːmaɪt/ ▻ *noun* a lidded cooking pot, typically one made of glazed earthenware, used especially for making stock or soup. ⓘ 19c: French, meaning 'pot' or 'kettle'.

marmoreal /mɑː'mɔːrɪəl/ ▻ *adj, formal or literary* **1** like marble; cold, smooth, white, etc. **2** made of marble. • **marmoreally** *adverb.* ⓘ 18c: from Latin *marmor* marble.

marmoset /'mɑːməzɛt/ ▻ *noun* a small S American monkey with a long bushy tail and tufts of hair around the head and ears. ⓘ 14c: from French *marmouset* grotesque figure.

marmot /'mɑːmət/ ▻ *noun* a stout, coarse-haired, burrowing rodent of Europe, Asia and N America. See also WOODCHUCK. ⓘ 17c: from French *marmotte*.

maroon[1] /mə'ruːn/ ▻ *adj* dark brownish-red or purplish-red in colour. ▻ *noun* this colour. ⓘ 18c: from French *marron* chestnut.

maroon[2] /mə'ruːn/ ▻ *verb* (***marooned***, ***marooning***) **1** to leave someone in isolation in a deserted place, especially on a desert island. **2** to leave someone helpless or without support. ⓘ 18c in sense 1; 17c as *noun*, meaning 'a fugitive slave': from American Spanish *cimarrón* wild.

marque[1] /mɑːk/ ▻ *noun* (***marques***) applied especially to cars: a brand or make. ⓘ Early 20c: French, meaning 'mark' or 'sign'.

marque[2] see LETTERS-OF-MARQUE

marquee /mɑː'kiː/ ▻ *noun* (***marquees***) a very large tent used for circuses, parties, etc. ⓘ 17c: coined from MARQUISE in its obsolete sense 'a large tent', which was wrongly thought to be a plural form and a supposed singular was therefore created from it.

marquess /'mɑːkwɪs/ ▻ *noun, Brit* a member of the nobility. See also MARQUIS, MARQUISE. ⓘ 16c: from French *marchis*, from Latin *marchensis* prefect of the marches; see MARCH[2].

marquetry /'mɑːkətrɪ/ ▻ *noun* (***marquetries***) **1** the art or practice of making decorative arrangements or patterns out of pieces of different-coloured woods, ivory, etc, especially set into the surface of wooden furniture. Compare INLAY. **2** work made in this way. ⓘ 16c: French, from *marqueter* to inlay.

marquis /'mɑːkwɪs; *French* maʀki/ ▻ *noun* (***marquis*** or ***marquises***) **1** in various European countries: a nobleman next in rank above a count. **2** *sometimes* a MARQUESS. See also MARCHIONESS. ⓘ 17c: variant of MARQUESS.

marquise /mɑː'kiːz/ ▻ *noun* (***marquises***) **1** in various European countries: a MARCHIONESS. **2** **a** a ring set with gems arranged to form a pointed oval; **b** a gem cut into such a shape. ⓘ 19c.

marram /'marəm/ and **marram grass** ▻ *noun* a coarse grass that grows on sandy shores, often planted to stop sand erosion. ⓘ 17c: from Norse *maralmr*, from *marr* sea + *halmr* stem.

marriage /'marɪdʒ/ ▻ *noun* **1** the state or relationship of being husband and wife. **2** the act, or legal contract, of becoming husband and wife. **3** the civil or religious ceremony during which this act is performed; a wedding. **4** a joining together; a union. **5** *as adj* □ *marriage contract* □ *marriage vows.* ⓘ 13c: French; see MARRY.

marriageable ▻ *adj* said of a woman, or sometimes a man: suitable for marriage, especially in terms of being at a legal age for marriage. • **marriageability** or **marriageableness** *noun.*

marriage bureau ▻ *noun* an introduction agency which arranges for single people wishing to find a husband or wife to meet potential partners.

marriage certificate ▻ *noun* an official piece of paper showing that two people are legally married.

marriage guidance ▻ *noun* professional counselling given to couples with marital or personal problems.

marriage licence ▻ *noun* a paper that gives official permission for a marriage to take place.

marriage of convenience ▻ *noun* **1** a marriage entered into for the advantages it will bring, such as citizenship of the country of one's partner, rather than for love. **2** a close business union, partnership, etc entered into for practical reasons or advantages only. ⓘ 18c.

married /'marɪd/ ▻ *adj* **1** having a husband or wife. **2** belonging or relating to the state of marriage □ *married life.* **3** (*especially* **married to something**) closely fixed together; joined, especially inseparably or intimately, to it □ *He's married to his work.* ▻ *noun* (***marrieds***) *colloq* a married couple.

marrons glacés /'marən 'glaseɪ/ ▻ *plural noun, cookery* chestnuts poached in a vanilla-flavoured syrup and coated with a sugar glaze. ⓘ 19c: French, meaning 'iced chestnuts'.

marrow /'maroʊ/ ▻ *noun* **1** (*also* **bone marrow**) the soft tissue that fills the internal cavities of bones. **2** (*also* **vegetable marrow**) **a** an annual plant with large prickly leaves, native to tropical America but cultivated worldwide for its large, oblong, edible fruit; **b** the fruit of this plant which has a thick, green or striped skin, and soft white flesh, and is cooked as a vegetable. **3** the innermost, essential or best part of anything. • **marrowy** *adj.* • **to the marrow** right through. ⓘ Anglo-Saxon *mærg*.

marrowbone ▻ *noun* a bone containing edible marrow. Also *as adj* □ *marrowbone jelly.*

marrowfat and **marrowfat pea** ▻ *noun* **1** a variety of large, edible pea. **2** the plant that bears it.

marry[1] /'marɪ/ ▻ *verb* (***marries***, ***married***, ***marrying***) **1** to take someone as one's husband or wife □ *Will you marry me?* **2** said of a priest, minister, official, etc: to perform the ceremony of marriage between two people □ *My uncle married us.* **3** *intr* to become joined in marriage □ *We married last June.* **4** (*usually* **marry someone to someone**) said of a parent, guardian, etc: to give (a son, daughter or ward) in marriage to someone. **5** intr (*also* **marry something up**) to fit together, join up, or match (usually two things) correctly □ *The two sides do not* *marry*. • **marrying** *adj* likely to marry or inclined towards marriage □ *not the marrying kind.* ⓒ 13c: from French *marier*, from Latin *maritare*, from *maritus* a husband.

■ **marry into something 1** to become involved in or associated with it by marriage □ *married into a large, close-knit family.* **2** *colloq* to acquire it by marriage □ *He married into money.*

■ **marry someone off** (*colloq*) to find a husband or wife for them.

marry² /'marɪ/ ▷ *exclamation, archaic* an expression of surprise or earnest declaration; indeed!. ⓒ 14c: for 'By (the Virgin) Mary!'.

Mars /mɑːz/ ▷ *noun* **1** *astron* the fourth planet from the Sun, and the nearest planet to the Earth. ⓒ 14c: named after Mars, the Roman god of war, because of its fiery red appearance.

Marsala /mɑː'sɑːlə/ ▷ *noun* a dark, sweet, fortified wine made in Marsala in Sicily.

marsh /mɑːʃ/ ▷ *noun* (*marshes*) **1** a poorly-drained, low-lying, frequently-flooded area of land, commonly found at the mouths of rivers and alongside ponds and lakes. See also FEN, SWAMP. **2** (*also* **salt marsh**) such an area of land lying in the INTERTIDAL zone that is periodically flooded by seawater. ▷ *adj* inhabiting or found in marshes □ *marsh marigold.* ⓒ Anglo-Saxon *mersc* or *merisc*.

marshal /'mɑːʃəl/ ▷ *noun* **1** (*often* **Marshal**) *in compounds* **a** any of various high-ranking officers in the armed forces (see table at RANK) □ *Air Vice-Marshal* □ *field marshal*; **b** *Brit* a high-ranking officer of State □ *Earl Marshal.* **2** an official who organizes parades etc, or controls crowds at large public events. **3** *US* in some states: a chief police or fire officer. **4** a law-court official with various duties and responsibilities □ *judge's marshal.* ▷ *verb* (*marshalled, marshalling*; *US marshaled, marshaling*) **1** to arrange (troops, competitors, facts, etc) in order. **2** to direct, lead or show the way to (a crowd, procession, etc), especially in a formal or precise way. • **marshaller** *noun*. ⓒ 13c: French from *mareschal*, from German *marahscalh*, from *marah* horse + *scalh* servant.

marshalling-yard ▷ *noun* a place where railway wagons are arranged into trains.

marshal of the Royal Air Force ▷ *noun, Brit* an officer in the air force. See table at RANK.

marsh fever ▷ *noun* MALARIA.

marsh gas ▷ *noun* METHANE.

marsh harrier ▷ *noun* a HARRIER² hawk, found in marshy regions of Europe. It has an owl-like head, long wings and long legs.

marsh hawk ▷ *noun* a common N American hawk with a white patch on its rump.

marshland ▷ *noun* marshy country.

marshmallow ▷ *noun* **1** a spongy, pink or white sweet originally made from the root of the MARSH MALLOW. **2** sometimes *as adj* said of someone or something: excessively soft, sweet or sentimental. ⓒ 19c.

marsh mallow ▷ *noun* a pink-flowered plant that grows wild in coastal marshes. ⓒ Anglo-Saxon: *merscmealwe*.

marsh marigold ▷ *noun* a marsh plant with yellow flowers like large buttercups.

marshy ▷ *adj* (*marshier, marshiest*) **1** like, or of the nature of, a marsh. **2** covered with marshes.

marsupial /mɑː'suːpɪəl, -sjuː-/ ▷ *noun, zool* any of a group of mammals including the kangaroo, koala and wombat in which the female lacks a placenta and the young, which are tiny and very immature when born, are carried and suckled in an external pouch on the mother's body until they are mature enough to survive independently. ▷ *adj* belonging to or like a marsupial. ⓒ 17c: from Latin *marsupium* pouch.

mart /mɑːt/ ▷ *noun* a trading place; a market or auction. ⓒ 15c: from Dutch *markt*.

martello /mɑː'tɛloʊ/ ▷ *noun* (*martellos*) a small circular fortified tower used for coastal defence. Also called **martello tower**. ⓒ 19c: from Cape Mortella in Corsica, where such a tower was captured with difficulty by a British fleet in 1794.

marten /'mɑːtɪn/ ▷ *noun* **1** any of various small, tree-dwelling, predatory mammals with a long thin body and a bushy tail. See also PINE MARTEN. **2** their highly-valued, soft, black or brown fur. ⓒ 15c: from French *martre*.

martial /'mɑːʃəl/ ▷ *adj* belonging or relating to, or suitable for, war or the military; warlike; militant. • **martialism** *noun*. • **martially** *adverb*. ⓒ 14c: French, from Latin *martialis* belonging to MARS.

martial art ▷ *noun* any of various fighting sports or self-defence techniques of Far Eastern origin, eg karate or judo.

martial law ▷ *noun* law and order strictly enforced by the army, eg when ordinary civil law has broken down during a war, revolution, etc.

Martian /'mɑːʃən/ ▷ *adj* belonging or relating to, or supposedly coming from, the planet MARS. ▷ *noun* someone who is supposed to come from or inhabit Mars. ⓒ 14c: from Latin *Martius*.

martin /'mɑːtɪn/ ▷ *noun* any of various small birds of the swallow family, with a square or slightly forked tail, eg the HOUSE MARTIN or the SAND MARTIN. ⓒ 15c.

martinet /mɑːtɪ'nɛt/ ▷ *noun, derog* someone who maintains strict discipline. 17c: French, named after Jean Martinet (died 1672), one of Louis XIV's generals and a very stringent drillmaster.

martingale /'mɑːtɪŋgeɪl/ ▷ *noun* a strap that is passed between a horse's forelegs and fastened to the girth and to the bit, noseband or reins, used to keep the horse's head down. ⓒ 16c: French.

martini /mɑː'tiːnɪ/ ▷ *noun* (*martinis*) **1** (**Martini**) *trademark* an Italian brand of vermouth. **2** a cocktail made of gin and vermouth. ⓒ 19c: from the name of the Italian wine makers Martini and Rossi.

Martinmas /'mɑːtɪnməs/ ▷ *noun* St Martin's day, 11 November. ⓒ 13c.

martyr /'mɑːtə(r)/ ▷ *noun* **1** someone who chooses to be put to death as an act of witness to their faith, rather than abandon his or her religious beliefs. **2** someone who suffers or dies for their beliefs, or for a particular cause, etc. **3** (*usually* **a martyr to something**) *colloq* someone who suffers greatly on account of something (eg an illness, ailment or misfortune) □ *She is a martyr to arthritis.* **4** *colloq, usually derog* someone who wishes or chooses to be or to be seen as a suffering victim, especially in circumstances which they could have chosen to avoid. ▷ *verb* (*martyred, martyring*) to put someone to death as a martyr. • **martyrdom** *noun* the death or suffering of a martyr. • **make a martyr of oneself** *colloq* to put oneself deliberately in the position of a victim or someone who deserves sympathy or admiration for sacrificing their own happiness, comfort, etc. ⓒ Anglo-Saxon: from Latin, from Greek *martus* a witness.

marvel /'mɑːvəl/ ▷ *verb* (*marvelled, marvelling*; *US marveled, marveling*) *intr* (*especially* **marvel at something**) to be filled with astonishment or wonder. ▷ *noun* an astonishing or wonderful person or thing; a wonder. ⓒ 14c: from French *merveille*, from Latin *mirari* to wonder at.

marvellous or (*US*) **marvelous** /'mɑːvələs/ ▷ *adj* **1** so wonderful or astonishing as to be almost beyond belief. **2**

colloq excellent; extremely pleasing. ● **marvellously** *adverb*. ● **marvellousness** *noun*.

Marxism /'mɑːksɪzəm/ ▻ *noun, politics* the theories of Karl Marx (1818–83), the German economist and political philosopher, stating that the struggle between different social classes is the main influence on political change and that communism will eventually replace capitalism.

Marxism-Leninism ▻ *noun, politics* a distinct variant of MARXISM formulated and put into practice by Vladimir Ilyich Lenin (1870–1924), which became the basis of Communist ideology (see COMMUNISM). Compare LENINISM. ● **Marxist-Leninist** *adj, noun*.

Marxist ▻ *noun* **1** a follower of MARXISM. **2** someone who advocates MARXIST LITERARY THEORY. ▻ *adj* (*sometimes* **Marxian**) relating to or characteristic of Karl Marx, Marxism or Marxists.

Marxist literary theory or **Marxist literary criticism** ▻ *noun, literary theory* a complex and highly theoretical approach that, in its simplest form, emphasizes how important the effect of the struggle to control the material side of life is to the production of all art, past and present, both at the fundamental economic and social levels and at the level of influence this struggle has on ideas, beliefs, philosophies, etc, and which tends to stress this over any notion of creativity. Also *in compounds* □ ***Marxist-Feminist***. See also STRUCTURALISM, POST-STRUCTURALISM, MODERNISM, POST-MODERNISM, FORMALISM.

marzipan /'mɑːzɪpan/ ▻ *noun* a sweet paste made of ground almonds, sugar and egg whites, used to decorate cakes, make sweets, etc. ⓘ 15c: from Italian *marzapane*.

-mas /məs/ ▻ *combining form, forming nouns, denoting* a church festival or feast day □ ***Candlemas*** □ ***Christmas***. See MASS[2].

Masai /'mɑːsaɪ/ ▻ *noun* **1** (*plural* ***Masai***) a member of a pastoral people who inhabit hilly regions of Kenya and Tanzania in E Africa. **2** their language. ▻ *adj* belonging or relating to this people or their language. ⓘ 19c: Bantu.

masala /mə'sɑːlə/ ▻ *noun, cookery* **1** a blend of spices ground into a powder or paste used in Indian cookery. **2** a dish using this □ ***chicken tikka masala***. ⓘ 18c: Hindi, meaning 'spices'.

masc. ▻ *abbreviation* masculine.

mascara /ma'skɑːrə/ ▻ *noun* (***mascaras***) a cosmetic for darkening, lengthening and thickening the eyelashes, applied with a brush. ⓘ 19c: Spanish, meaning 'mask'.

mascarpone /maskə'poʊnɪ/ ▻ *noun* a soft Italian cream cheese. ⓘ 20c: Italian.

mascot /'maskət, -kɒt/ ▻ *noun* a person, animal or thing thought to bring good luck and adopted for this purpose by a person, team, etc. ⓘ 19c: from French *mascotte*, from Provençal *mascotto* charm.

masculine /'maskjʊlɪn/ ▻ *adj* **1** belonging to, typical of, peculiar to or suitable for a man or the male sex; male. **2** said of a woman: mannish; unfeminine. **3** *grammar* (abbreviation **m.** or **masc.**) in many languages: belonging or referring to one of the GENDERS into which nouns and pronouns are divided, ie that which includes most words denoting human and animal males, plus, in many languages, many other words. Compare COMMON GENDER, FEMININE, NEUTER. ▻ *noun, grammar* **a** the masculine gender; **b** a word belonging to this gender. ● **masculinity** *noun*. ⓘ 14c: from Latin *masculinus* male, from *mas* a male.

> ***masculine***
>
> See Usage Note at **male**.

masculinize or **masculinise** /'maskjʊlɪnaɪz/ ▻ *verb* (***masculinized, masculinizing***) *tr & intr* to make or become masculine in character or appearance, especially when induced in women by the use of steroids. ● **masculinization** *noun*. ⓘ Early 20c.

maser /'meɪzə(r)/ ▻ *noun* in radar and radio astronomy: a device for increasing the strength of MICROWAVE. Compare LASER. ⓘ 1950s: acronym for *m*icrowave *a*mplification by *s*timulated *e*mission of *r*adiation.

mash /maʃ/ ▻ *verb* (***mashes, mashed, mashing***) **1** (*also* **mash something up**) to beat or crush it into a pulpy mass. **2** in the brewing process: to mix (malt) with hot water. ▻ *noun* (*plural* in senses 1 and 3 only ***mashes***) **1** a boiled mixture of grain and water used to feed farm animals. **2** a mixture of crushed malt and hot water, used in brewing. **3** any soft or pulpy mass. **4** *colloq* mashed potatoes. ● **mashed** *adj*. ● **masher** *noun*. ⓘ Anglo-Saxon *masc*-, used in compounds.

mask /mɑːsk/ ▻ *noun* **1 a** any covering for the face or for part of the face, worn for amusement, protection or as a disguise, which is often painted and decorated □ ***Hallowe'en mask***. **b** a covering for the mouth and nose, such as an OXYGEN MASK, or a **surgical mask** worn by surgeons, nurses, etc to reduce the spread of infection. **2** a pretence; anything that disguises the truth, eg false behaviour □ ***a mask of light-heartedness***. **3** a moulded or sculpted cast of someone's face □ ***death-mask***. **4** a cosmetic FACE PACK. **5** *photog* see under MASKING. ▻ *verb* (***masked, masking***) **1** to put a mask on someone or something. **2** to disguise, conceal or cover □ ***Find something to mask the smell***. **3** to protect something with a mask, or as if with a mask, from some effect or process. **4** (*usually* **mask as something** or **someone**) *intr* to masquerade, or be disguised as, it or them. ● **masked** *adj* **1** wearing, concealed or protected by a mask. **2** for or with people wearing masks □ ***masked ball***. ● **masker** *noun*. ⓘ 16c as *masque*: French, from Spanish *máscara* or Italian *maschera* a mask or disguise.

masking ▻ *noun, photog* the process of using a screen (or **mask**) to cover part of a light-sensitive surface, usually so that a second image may be superimposed subsequently.

masking tape ▻ *noun* sticky paper tape, used eg in painting to cover the edge of a surface, eg of a window pane to be left unpainted.

masochism /'masəkɪzəm/ ▻ *noun* **1** *psychol* the practice of deriving sexual pleasure from pain or humiliation inflicted by another person. Compare SADISM, SADO-MASOCHISM. **2** *colloq* a tendency to take pleasure in one's own suffering. ● **masochist** *noun* **1** someone who derives sexual pleasure from pain or humiliation. **2** *colloq* someone who takes pleasure in their own suffering. ● **masochistic** *adj*. ⓘ 19c: named after Leopold von Sacher Masoch (1836–95), the Austrian novelist who described cases of it.

mason /'meɪsən/ ▻ *noun* **1** a STONEMASON. **2** (**Mason**) a FREEMASON. **3** *US* a skilled builder who works with bricks or stone. ● **masonic** /mə'sɒnɪk/ *adj* (*often* **Masonic**) belonging or relating to freemasons. ⓘ 13c: from French *masson*.

Mason-Dixon Line ▻ *noun* the boundary between Pennsylvania and Maryland, later thought of as separating the free Northern states from the slave states of the South. ⓘ 18c: named after Charles Mason and Jeremiah Dixon who surveyed it.

masonry /'meɪsənrɪ/ ▻ *noun* **1** the part of a building built by a mason; stonework and brickwork. **2** the craft or skill of a mason. **3** (*often* **Masonry**) FREEMASONRY.

masque /mɑːsk/ ▻ *noun* **1** *historical* in English royal courts during the 16c and 17c: a kind of dramatic entertainment performed to music by masked actors. **2** *chiefly old use* a masquerade or masked ball. ⓘ 16c: French, meaning 'MASK' *noun* 1.

masquerade /maskə'reɪd, mɑː-/ ▻ *noun* **1** a pretence or false show. **2 a** a formal dance at which the guests wear masks and costumes; **b** *chiefly US* any party or gathering to which costumes or disguises are worn; a FANCY DRESS party or ball. **3** *chiefly US* the costume or disguise worn at a masquerade, etc; fancy dress. ▷ *verb* (***masqueraded, masquerading***) *intr* (*especially* **masquerade as someone** or **something**) **1** to disguise oneself. **2** to pretend to be someone or something else □ *was masquerading as a vicar* □ *a squalid town masquerading as a city.* • **masquerader** *noun.* ⓘ 16c: from Spanish *mascarada*, from *máscara* MASK.

mass¹ /mas/ ▷ *noun* **1** *physics* the amount of matter that an object contains, which is a measure of its INERTIA. **2** a large quantity, usually a shapeless quantity, gathered together; a lump. **3** (*often* **masses**) *colloq* a large quantity or number □ *masses of room* □ *He has masses of books.* **4** (*usually* **the mass of something**) the majority or bulk of it. **5** *technical* a measure of the quantity of matter in a body. **6** (**the masses**) ordinary people; the people as a whole. **7** *art* an area of uniform colour or shading. **8** *as adj* **a** involving a large number of people □ *a mass meeting* □ *mass murder*; **b** belonging or relating to a mass, or to large quantities or numbers □ *mass production.* ▷ *verb* (***masses, massed, massing***) *chiefly intr* (*sometimes* **mass together**) to gather or form in a large quantity or number □ *Clouds were massing in the distance.* See also AMASS. ⓘ 14c: from French *masser*, from Latin *massa* lump.

mass² or **Mass** /mas/ ▷ *noun* **1** *Christianity* in the Roman Catholic and Orthodox Churches: **a** the EUCHARIST, a celebration of THE LAST SUPPER; **b** the ceremony in which this occurs. See also HIGH MASS, LOW MASS. Compare (in Protestant churches) COMMUNION, HOLY COMMUNION, THE LORD'S SUPPER. **2** a part of the text of the Roman Catholic liturgy set to music and sung by a choir or congregation □ *a requiem mass.* ⓘ Anglo-Saxon *mæsse*.

Mass. see MA

massacre /ˈmasəkə(r)/ ▷ *noun* **1** a cruel and indiscriminate killing of large numbers of people or animals. **2** *colloq* in a game, sports match, etc: an overwhelming defeat. ▷ *verb* (***massacred, massacring***) **1** to kill (people or animals) cruelly, indiscriminately and in large numbers. **2** *colloq* to defeat (the opposition or enemy, etc) overwhelmingly. ⓘ 16c: French.

massage /ˈmasɑːʒ, -sɑːdʒ/ ▷ *noun* **1** a technique of easing pain or stiffness in the body, especially the muscles, by rubbing, kneading and tapping with the hands. **2** a body treatment using this technique. ▷ *verb* (***massaged, massaging***) **1** to perform massage on someone. **2** to alter something (especially statistics or other data) to produce a more favourable result; to manipulate or doctor something to make it look better, more suitable, etc. • **massage someone's ego** *facetious* to flatter them, or treat them in any way that makes them feel more important or special. ⓘ 19c: French, from *masser* to massage, from Greek *massein* to knead.

massage parlour ▷ *noun* **1** an establishment that offers customers massage treatment, often with steam baths available also. **2** an establishment that ostensibly offers customers massage treatment, but which is often known to offer any of various sexual services. ⓘ Early 20c.

massé /ˈmasɪ, -eɪ/ ▷ *noun* (***massés***) *billiards* a sharp stroke made with the cue held vertically, or nearly vertically. ⓘ 19c: French, from *masse* a sledgehammer.

masses see under MASS¹

masseur /maˈsɜː(r)/ and **masseuse** /-ˈsɜːz/ ▷ *noun* (***masseurs*** or ***masseuses***) someone who is trained to carry out massage, especially as their profession. ⓘ 19c: French.

mass extinction ▷ *noun, biol* at certain times in the Earth's history: the dying out of many animal species at more or less the same time, eg the disappearance of the dinosaurs about 65 million years ago.

massif /ˈmasiːf/ ▷ *noun, geol* a mountainous plateau that differs from the surrounding lowland, usually composed of rocks that are older and harder. ⓘ 19c: French; see MASSIVE.

massive /ˈmasɪv/ ▷ *adj* **1** said of physical objects: very big, bulky, solid and heavy. **2** *colloq* very large; of great size or power □ *a massive salary* □ *a massive explosion.* **3** said of a mineral: without crystalline form. **4** not separated into parts, elements, layers, etc. • **massively** *adverb* in a massive way; to a massive degree. • **massiveness** *noun.* ⓘ 15c: from French *massif*, from *masse* MASS¹.

mass market ▷ *noun, econ* the market for goods that have been mass-produced. • **mass-marketing** *noun.*

mass media see MEDIA

mass noun ▷ *noun, grammar* a noun which cannot be qualified in the singular by the indefinite article and cannot be used in the plural, eg *furniture*. Compare COUNT NOUN.

mass number ▷ *noun, chem* the total number of protons and neutrons in the nucleus of an atom. Also called **nucleon number**.

mass-produce ▷ *verb* to produce (goods, etc) in a standard form in great quantities, especially using mechanization. • **mass-produced** *adj* said of an article: produced in a standardized form in large numbers. • **mass production** *noun.* ⓘ 1920s.

mass spectrograph ▷ *noun, chem, physics* a device used to give precise measurements of the ATOMIC MASS UNITS of different isotopes of an element, by passing beams of ions through electric and magnetic fields so that they can be separated according to the ratio of their CHARGE (*noun* 7) to their MASS. See also SPECTROGRAPH.

mass spectrometer ▷ *noun, chem, physics* a MASS SPECTROGRAPH used to measure the relative atomic masses of isotopes of chemical elements, and that uses an electrical detector, as opposed to a photographic plate, to determine the distribution of ION. • **mass spectrometry** *noun.*

mast¹ /mɑːst/ ▷ *noun* any upright wooden or metal supporting pole, especially one carrying the sails of a ship, or a radio or television aerial. • **masted** *adj, usually in compounds* having the specified type or number of masts □ *three-masted.* • **before the mast** *naut* serving as an apprentice seaman or ordinary sailor. • **half mast** see separate entry. ⓘ Anglo-Saxon *mæst*.

mast² /mɑːst/ ▷ *noun* the nuts of various forest trees, especially beech, oak and chestnut, used as food for pigs. ⓘ Anglo-Saxon *mæst*.

mastaba /ˈmastəbə/ ▷ *noun* (***mastabas***) *archaeol* an ancient Egyptian tomb built of brick or stone with sloping sides and a flat roof, having an outer area in which offerings were made, connected to a secret inner room from which a shaft led to an underground burial chamber. ⓘ 17c in original sense 'a stone bench or seat': from Arabic *mastabah* bench.

mastectomy /məˈstɛktəmɪ/ ▷ *noun* (***mastectomies***) *surgery* the surgical removal of a woman's breast. Compare LUMPECTOMY. ⓘ 1920s: from Greek *mastos*.

master /ˈmɑːstə(r)/ ▷ *noun* **1** someone especially a man, who commands or controls. **2** the owner, especially a male owner, of a dog, slave, etc. **3** someone with outstanding skill in a particular activity, eg art. See also OLD MASTER. **4** a fully qualified craftsman or tradesman, allowed to train and direct others. Also *as adj* □ *master builder* □ *master butcher.* **5** *rather dated* a male teacher. Compare MISTRESS 2. **6** the commanding officer on a merchant ship. **7** (**Master**) **a** a degree of the level above BACHELOR (sense 2). Usually called **Masters** □ *has a Masters in geophysics*; **b** someone who holds this degree □ *Master of Arts* □ *Master of Science.* **8** (**Master**) a title for a boy too young to be called MR. **9** an original document, film, recording, etc from which copies are made. Also called **master copy**. **10** (**Master**) a title for the heads of certain university colleges. **11** in England and Wales: an official of the Supreme Court. ▷ *adj* **1** fully qualified; highly skilled; expert. **2** main; principal □ *master bedroom*. **3** controlling □ *master switch*. ▷ *verb* (***mastered***, ***mastering***) **1** to overcome or defeat (eg feelings or an opponent). **2** to become skilled in something. ⓘ Anglo-Saxon *mægester*: from Latin *magister*, from *magnus* great.

master-at-arms ▷ *noun* (***masters-at-arms***) *naut* a ship's officer responsible for maintaining discipline.

master copy see MASTER *noun* 9

masterful ▷ *adj* showing the authority, skill or power of a master. • **masterfully** *adverb*. • **masterfulness** *noun*.

master key ▷ *noun* a key which opens a number of locks, each of which has its own different individual key.

masterly ▷ *adj* showing the skill of a master. • **masterliness** *noun*.

mastermind ▷ *noun* **1** someone who has great intellectual ability. **2** the person responsible for devising a complex scheme or plan. ▷ *verb* (***masterminded***, ***masterminding***) to be the mastermind of (a scheme, etc); to originate, think out and direct something. ⓘ 18c.

master of ceremonies ▷ *noun* (***masters of ceremonies***) (abbreviation **MC**; *plural* **MCs**) an announcer, especially one who announces the speakers at a formal dinner or the performers in a stage entertainment.

masterpiece ▷ *noun* an extremely skilful piece of work, especially the greatest work of an artist or writer. Sometimes called **masterwork**.

masterstroke ▷ *noun* a very clever or well-timed action.

mastery /ˈmɑːstərɪ/ ▷ *noun* (***masteries***) **1** (*usually* **mastery of something**) great skill or knowledge in it. **2** (*especially* **mastery over someone** or **something**) control over them or it. ⓘ 13c: French, from *maistre* MASTER.

masthead ▷ *noun* **1** *naut* the top of a ship's mast. **2** *journalism* the title of a newspaper or periodical, and other information such as logo, price and place of publication, printed at the top of its front page.

mastic /ˈmastɪk/ ▷ *noun* **1** a gum obtained from a Mediterranean evergreen tree, used in making varnish. **2** *building* any of various waterproof, putty-like pastes used as joint-sealers or fillers. ⓘ 14c: French, from Greek *mastiche*.

masticate /ˈmastɪkeɪt/ ▷ *verb* (***masticated***, ***masticating***) *tr & intr*, *formal or technical* **1** to chew (food). **2** to knead (eg india-rubber) mechanically. • **mastication** *noun* chewing. • **masticator** *noun*. • **masticatory** *adj*. ⓘ 17c: from Latin *masticare* to chew.

mastiff /ˈmastɪf/ ▷ *noun* a large powerful short-haired breed of dog, formerly used in hunting. ⓘ 14c: from French *mastin*, from Latin *mansuetus* tame.

mastitis /maˈstaɪtɪs/ ▷ *noun* inflammation of a woman's breast or an animal's udder, usually caused by bacterial infection. ⓘ 19c: Latin, from MASTO- + -ITIS.

masto- /mastoʊ/ or (before a vowel) **mast-** ▷ *combining form*, *denoting* **1** the breast or mammary glands. **2** a teat or nipple. ⓘ From Greek *mastos* breast.

mastodon /ˈmastədɒn/ ▷ *noun* any of several, now extinct, mammals from which elephants are thought to have evolved, which had two pairs of tusks, a long flexible trunk and a hairy coat. ⓘ Early 19c: from MASTO- + Greek *odontos* tooth, because of the teat-like prominences of its molar teeth.

mastoid /ˈmastɔɪd/ *anatomy* ▷ *adj* like a nipple or breast. ▷ *noun* **1** the raised area of bone behind the ear. **2** *colloq* MASTOIDITIS. ⓘ 18c: from Greek *mastoeides* like a breast.

mastoiditis ▷ *noun* inflammation of the mastoid air cells.

masturbate /ˈmastəbeɪt/ ▷ *verb* (***masturbated***, ***masturbating***) *tr & intr* to rub or stroke the genitals of (oneself or someone else) so as to produce sexual arousal, usually to the point of orgasm or ejaculation. • **masturbation** *noun*. • **masturbator** *noun*. • **masturbatory** *adj*. ⓘ 18c: from Latin *masturbari*.

mat¹ /mat/ ▷ *noun* **1** a flat piece of any carpet-like material, used as a decorative or protective floor-covering, for wiping shoes on to remove dirt, or absorbing impact on landing or falling in gymnastics, etc. **2** a smaller piece of fabric, or a harder material, used under a plate, vase, etc to protect a surface from heat or scratches. **3** a carpet-like, interwoven or tangled covering, eg of vegetation or hair. ▷ *verb* (***matted***, ***matting***) *tr & intr* to become, or make something become, tangled or interwoven into a dense untidy mass. • **matted** *adj* often said of hair: tangled. • **on the mat** see ON THE CARPET under CARPET. ⓘ Anglo-Saxon *matt* or *matte*: from Latin *matta*.

mat² see MATT

mat. ▷ *abbreviation* matinée.

matador /ˈmatədɔː(r)/ ▷ *noun* the principal TOREADOR who kills the bull in bullfighting. ⓘ 17c: Spanish, from *matar* to kill.

match¹ /matʃ/ ▷ *noun* (***matches***) **1** a formal contest or game. **2** (*especially* **a match for someone** or **something**) a person or thing that is similar or identical to, or combines well with, another. **3** a person or thing able to equal, or surpass, another □ *met his match*. **4** a partnership or pairing; a suitable partner, eg in marriage. **5** a condition of exact agreement, compatibility or close resemblance, especially between two colours. ▷ *verb* (***matches***, ***matched***, ***matching***) **1** *tr & intr* (*also* **match up** or **match something up**) to combine well; to be well suited, compatible or exactly alike; to put (matching people, colours, things, etc) together. **2** to set (people or things) in competition; to hold them up in comparison. **3** to be equal to something; to make, produce, perform, etc an equivalent to something □ *cannot match, let alone beat, the offer*. **4** *electronics* to make the IMPEDANCES of (two circuits) equal, so as to produce maximum transfer of energy. • **matchable** *adj*. • **matching** *adj* similar; compatible; part of the same set □ *a matching pair*. • **be a match for someone** to be as good at something as them; to be as successful, strong, forceful, etc as them. • **meet one's match 1** to have to deal with someone who is able to resist one successfully. **2** to meet, or have to compete with, someone who is as good as or better at something than one is oneself. ⓘ Anglo-Saxon *gemæcca* a mate or companion.

match² /matʃ/ ▷ *noun* (***matches***) **1** a short thin piece of wood or strip of card coated on the tip with a substance that ignites when rubbed against a rough surface, used to light fires, etc. See also SAFETY MATCH. **2** a slow-burning fuse used in cannons, etc. ⓘ 14c in obsolete sense 'the wick of a candle or lamp': from French *mesche*.

matchboard ▷ *noun* a board with a tongue cut along one edge and a groove in the opposite edge enabling it to fit together with other similar boards to make wall facings, etc.

matchbox ▷ *noun* a small cardboard box for holding matches.

matchless ▷ *adj* having no equal; superior to all. • **matchlessly** *adverb*. • **matchlessness** *noun*.

matchmaker ▷ *noun* someone who tries to arrange romantic partnerships or marriages between people. • **matchmaking** *noun, adj*. ⓘ 17c.

match play ▷ *noun, golf* scoring according to holes won and lost rather than the number of strokes taken. Compare STROKE PLAY.

match point ▻ *noun, tennis, etc* the stage in a game at which only one more point is needed by a player to win; the winning point.

matchstick ▻ *noun* the stem of a wooden MATCH² (sense 1). ▻ *adj* **1** very thin, like a matchstick ▫ *matchstick legs.* **2** said of figures in a drawing, etc: with limbs represented by single lines ▫ *matchstick men.*

matchwood ▻ *noun* **1** wood suitable for making matches. **2** TOUCHWOOD. **3** splinters.

mate¹ /meɪt/ ▻ *noun* **1** an animal's breeding partner. **2** *colloq* a person's sexual partner, especially a husband or wife. **3 a** *colloq* a companion or friend, especially one of one's own sex; **b** used as a form of address, especially to a man ▫ *alright, mate.* **4** *in compounds* a colleague; a person someone shares something with ▫ *workmate* ▫ *flatmate.* **5** a tradesman's assistant ▫ *plumber's mate.* **6** one of a pair. **7** *naut* any officer below the rank of master on a merchant ship ▫ *first mate.* ▻ *verb* (***mated, mating***) **1** *intr* said of animals: to copulate. **2** to bring (male and female animals) together for breeding. **3** *tr & intr* to marry. **4** to join (two things) as a pair. • **mateship** *noun, especially Austral* the bond between close friends or mates. ⓒ 14c: related to Anglo-Saxon *gemetta* a guest at one's table.

mate² see under CHECKMATE

maté or **mate** /ˈmɑːteɪ, ˈmateɪ/ ▻ *noun* (***matés*** or ***mates***) **1** a S American species of holly tree. **2** a type of tea made from its dried leaves. ⓒ 18c: American Spanish, from Quechua *mati* the gourd in which the tea is made.

mater /ˈmeɪtə(r)/ ▻ *noun, humorous or dated colloq* **1** a mother. **2** a form of address for mother, used chiefly by boys at public school. See also PATER. ⓒ 19c: Latin.

material /məˈtɪərɪəl/ ▻ *noun* **1** any substance out of which something is, or may be, made. See also RAW MATERIAL. **2** cloth; fabric. **3** (**materials**) instruments or tools needed for a particular activity or task. **4** information that provides the substance from which a book, TV programme, etc is prepared. **5** someone who is suitable for a specified occupation, training, etc ▫ *He is management material.* ▻ *adj* **1** relating to or consisting of solid matter, physical objects, etc; not abstract or spiritual ▫ *suffered no material damage* ▫ *the material world.* **2** relating to physical, as opposed to emotional, well-being or concerns ▫ *material comforts.* **3** (*usually* **material to something**) *technical* important; significant; relevant ▫ *facts not material to the discussion.* Compare IMMATERIAL. • **materially** *adverb.* • **materialness** or **materiality** /mətɪərɪːˈalɪtɪ/ *noun* ⓒ 14c as *adjective*: from Latin *materialis*, from *materia* matter.

materialist *noun* a follower of or believer in materialism. ▻ *adj* materialistic. • **materialistic** *adj* relating to or characteristic of materialism. • **materialistically** *adverb* **1** *formal* to an important or significant extent. **2** with regard to physical well-being or material conditions.

materialism /məˈtɪərɪəlɪzəm/ ▻ *noun* **1** *often derog* excessive interest in or devotion to material possessions and financial success. **2** *philos* the theory stating that only material things exist, especially denying the existence of a soul or spirit. ⓒ 18c.

materialize or **materialise** /məˈtɪərɪəlaɪz/ ▻ *verb* (***materialized, materializing***) **1** *intr* to become real, visible or tangible; to appear or take shape. **2** *intr, loosely* to become fact; to happen. **3** to cause (eg a spirit) to assume bodily form. • **materialization** *noun.* ⓒ 18c.

matériel /mətɪərɪˈɛl/ ▻ *noun* materials and equipment, especially the munitions, supplies, etc of an army. ⓒ 19c: French, meaning 'MATERIAL'.

maternal /məˈtɜːnəl/ ▻ *adj* **1** belonging to, typical of or like a mother. **2** said of a relative: related on the mother's side of the family ▫ *my maternal grandfather.* Compare PATERNAL. • **maternally** *adverb.* ⓒ 15c: from French *maternel*, from Latin *maternus*, from *mater* mother.

maternity /məˈtɜːnɪtɪ/ ▻ *noun* **1** the state of being or becoming a mother; motherhood. **2** *as adj* relating to pregnancy or giving birth ▫ *maternity hospital* ▫ *maternity wear.* **3** the qualities typical of a mother; motherliness. ⓒ 17c: from French *maternité*; see MATERNAL + -ITY.

maternity leave ▻ *noun* the period of statutory paid leave that a pregnant woman is entitled to from her employer.

matey or **maty** /ˈmeɪtɪ/ ▻ *adj* (***matier, matiest***) *colloq* friendly or familiar. ▻ *noun* (***mateys*** or ***maties***) *colloq* usually used in addressing a man: friend; pal. • **matily** *adverb.* • **matiness** or **mateyness** *noun.* ⓒ 19c: from MATE¹.

math ▻ *noun, N Amer colloq* mathematics. *Brit equivalent* MATHS.

math. ▻ *abbreviation* mathematics.

mathematical /maθəˈmatɪkəl/ ▻ *adj* **1** belonging or relating to, or using, mathematics. **2** said of calculations, etc: very exact or accurate. • **mathematically** *adverb.* ⓒ 16c.

mathematician /maθəməˈtɪʃən/ ▻ *noun* someone who specializes in or studies mathematics.

mathematics /maθəˈmatɪks/ ▻ *singular noun* the science dealing with measurements, numbers, quantities, and shapes, usually expressed as symbols. ⓒ 16c: from Greek *mathematike* relating to learning, from *manthanein* to learn.

maths ▻ *singular noun, Brit colloq* mathematics. *N Amer equivalent* MATH.

maties see under MATEY

Matilda /məˈtɪldə/ ▻ *noun, Austral* a tramp's bundle or SWAG. • **waltz Matilda** to travel around carrying one's swag. ⓒ 19c: from the female personal name.

matily see under MATEY

matinal /ˈmatɪnəl/ ▻ *adj, relig* belonging or relating to MATINS.

matinée or **matinee** /ˈmatɪneɪ/ ▻ *noun* (***matinées*** or ***matinees***) an afternoon performance of a play or showing of a film. ⓒ 19c: French, meaning 'morning'.

matinée jacket or **matinée coat** ▻ *noun* a baby's short jacket or coat.

matiness see under MATEY

matins /ˈmatɪnz/ ▻ *singular or plural noun* **1** *now especially RC Church* the first of the CANONICAL HOURS, originally at midnight, but often now taken together with LAUDS. **2** *C of E* (*also* **morning prayer**) the daily morning service. Compare EVENSONG. ⓒ 13c: French, from Latin *matutinus* of the morning, from *Matuta* the goddess of morning.

matri- /ˈmatrɪ/ ▻ *combining form, denoting* **1** a mother or mothers ▫ *matricide.* **2** a woman or women ▫ *matriarchal.* Compare PATRI-. ⓒ From Latin *mater* mother.

matriarch /ˈmeɪtrɪɑːk, ˈmat-/ ▻ *noun* **1** the female head of a family, community or tribe. **2** an elderly woman who dominates her family or associates. **3** an elderly and much respected woman of special dignity. • **matriarchal** *adj.* ⓒ 17c: from MATRI-, modelled on PATRIARCH.

matriarchy /ˈmeɪtrɪɑːkɪ, mat-/ ▻ *noun* (***matriarchies***) **1** a social system in which women are the heads of families or tribes, and property and power passes from mother to daughter. **2** a society or community, etc controlled by women. Compare PATRIARCHY. ⓒ 19c.

matrices /ˈmeɪtrɪsiːz, ˈmatrɪsiːz/ *a plural of* MATRIX

matricide /ˈmeɪtrɪsaɪd, ˈmatrɪsaɪd/ ▻ *noun* **1** the killing of a mother by her own child. **2** someone who kills their own mother. • **matricidal** *adj.* ⓒ 16c: from Latin *matricidium*: see MATRI- + -CIDE.

matriculate /məˈtrɪkjʊleɪt/ ▻ *verb* (***matriculated, matriculating***) **1** to admit someone as a member of a university or college, etc. **2** *intr* to register as a student at a university, college, etc, eg after passing an examination. • **matriculation** /-leɪʃən/ *noun* **1** the process of matriculating. **2** *colloq* (often shortened to **matric** /mə'trɪk/) a university or college entrance examination taken at school. Also *as adj* □ ***matriculation card.*** ⓘ 16c: French, from Latin *matriculare* to register.

matrilineal /matrɪ'lɪnɪəl/ ▷ *adj, anthropol, denoting* descent or kinship through the mother or through females of the line only. Compare PATRILINEAL. • **matrilineally** *adverb*. ⓘ Early 20c.

matrimony /'matrɪmənɪ/ ▷ *noun* (***matrimonies***) *formal* **1** the state of being married. Also called MARRIAGE, WEDLOCK. **2** the wedding ceremony. • **matrimonial** /-'moʊnɪəl/ *adj*. ⓘ 14c: from French *matremoyne*, from Latin *matrimonium* wedlock, from *mater* mother.

matrix /'meɪtrɪks, 'ma-/ ▷ *noun* (***matrices*** /-trɪsiːz/ or ***matrixes***) **1** *math* a square or rectangular arrangement of symbols or numbers, in rows or columns, used to summarize relationships between different quantities, etc. **2** *biol* in tissues such as bone and cartilage: the substance in which cells are embedded. **3** *anatomy* the tissue lying beneath the body and root of a fingernail or toenail, and from which it develops. **4** *geol* the rock in which a mineral or fossil is embedded. **5** *printing* a mould, especially one from which printing type is produced. **6** *old use* the womb. ⓘ 16c: Latin, meaning 'womb'.

matron /'meɪtrən/ ▷ *noun* **1** the former title of the head of the nursing staff in a hospital. Now usually called SENIOR NURSING OFFICER. **2** a woman in charge of nursing and domestic arrangements in an institution such as a boarding school or old people's home. **3** any dignified, worthy or respectable middle-aged or elderly woman, especially a married one. **4** *US* a prison wardress. • **matronly** *adj* said of a woman: **1** dignified; authoritative. **2** *euphemistic* plump or portly in build, because of middle-age. ⓘ 14c: French *matrone*, from Latin *mater* mother.

matron of honour ▷ *noun* (***matrons of honour***) a married woman who is a bride's chief attendant at a wedding. Compare MAID OF HONOUR.

matt or (*sometimes*) **mat** ▷ *adj* said eg of paint: having a dull surface without gloss or shine. ▷ *verb* (***matted, matting***) **1** to produce a dull surface on something. **2** to frost (glass). ⓘ 17c: from French *mat* a dull colour or unpolished surface.

Matt. ▷ *abbreviation* Book of the Bible: Matthew, the Gospel according to St Matthew. See table at BIBLE.

matte see under MATTE SHOT

matted *past tense, past participle of* MAT[1], MATT

matter /'matə(r)/ ▷ *noun* **1** the substance from which all physical things are made; material. **2** material of a particular kind □ ***vegetable matter*** □ ***reading matter.*** **3** a subject or topic; a concern, affair or question □ ***if it's a matter of money*** □ ***matters of principle.*** **4** *with negatives* importance, significance or consequence □ ***something of no matter.*** **5** content, as distinct from style or form. **6** *printing, publishing* **a** material to be printed; **b** type that has been set. **7** (*usually* **a matter of something**) **a** an approximate quantity or amount of (time, etc) □ ***I'll be there in a matter of minutes;*** **b** used in saying what is involved or necessary □ ***It's just a matter of asking her to do it.*** **8** (**the matter** or **the matter with someone** or **something**) something that is wrong; the trouble or difficulty □ ***What is the matter?*** □ ***I don't know what is the matter with him.*** **9** *medicine* pus or discharge. ▷ *verb* (***mattered, mattering***) **1** *intr* to be important or significant □ ***Your health is what matters.*** **2** to secrete or discharge pus. • **a matter of form** an official procedure or conventional etiquette. • **a matter of opinion** something about which different people have different opinions. • **as a matter of course** as something that one expects automatically to happen or be done, etc. • **as a matter of fact** in fact; actually. • **for that matter** used when referring to some alternative or additional possibility, etc: as far as that is concerned □ ***I could leave it until tomorrow, or until next week, for that matter.*** • **no matter** it is not important; it makes no difference. • **no matter how, what** or **where**, *etc* regardless of how or what, etc □ ***I'm leaving, no matter what you say.*** ⓘ 13c: French, from Latin *materia* subject or substance.

matter-of-fact ▷ *adj* calm and straightforward; not excited or emotional. • **matter-of-factly** *adverb*. • **matter-of-factness** *noun*.

matter of life and death ▷ *noun* something that is of great importance.

matte shot /mat —/ ▷ *noun, cinematog* a motion picture scene in which a mask (known as a **matte**) restricts the image exposed so that a second image can be superimposed subsequently. ⓘ 1930s: from French *matte*.

matting ▷ *verb, present participle of* MAT[1], MATT. ▷ *noun* **1** material of rough woven fibres used for making mats. **2** mat-making. **3** the act of becoming matted, or condition of being matted.

mattock /'matək/ ▷ *noun* a kind of pickaxe with a blade flattened horizontally at one end, used for breaking up soil, etc. ⓘ Anglo-Saxon *mattuc*.

mattress /'matrəs/ ▷ *noun* **1** a large flat fabric-covered pad, now often made of foam rubber or springs, used for sleeping on, by itself or on a supporting frame. **2** a mass of brushwood, etc used to form a foundation for roads, etc. ⓘ 13c: from Arabic *almatrah* a place where anything is thrown.

maturate /'matʃʊreɪt, matjʊr-/ ▷ *verb* (***maturated, maturating***) *tr & intr* **1** *medicine* to discharge or cause something to discharge pus. **2** to make or become mature. • **maturation** *noun* **1** *medicine* the process of suppurating fully (see SUPPURATE). **2** bringing or coming to maturity. • **maturative** *adj*. ⓘ 16c: from Latin *maturare* to ripen.

mature /mə'tʃʊə(r), -'tjʊə(r)/ ▷ *adj* (***maturer, maturest***) **1** fully grown or developed. **2** having or showing adult good sense, emotional and social development, etc. **3** said of cheese, wine, etc: having a fully developed flavour. **4** said of bonds, insurance policies, etc: paying out, or beginning to pay out, money to the holder. **5** *formal* carefully or thoroughly thought out. ▷ *verb* (***matured, maturing***) **1** *tr & intr* to make or become fully developed or adult in outlook. **2** *intr* said of a life insurance policy, etc: to begin to produce a return. • **maturely** *adverb*. • **maturity** *noun*. ⓘ 16c: from Latin *maturus* ripe.

mature student ▷ *noun, Brit* someone over 25 who, unlike the majority of students who go to college or university immediately or shortly after leaving school, has become a student later in life after working or starting a family, etc.

MATV ▷ *abbreviation, Brit* Master Antenna Television, the use of a single antenna to serve a number of TV receivers, either directly or from a central station by cable distribution.

maty see MATEY

matzo /'matsə, -soʊ/ ▷ *noun* (***matzos***) **1** a) unleavened bread; **b** *as adj* □ ***matzo ball.*** **2** a wafer or cracker made of this, now usually a large, thin, square one, eaten especially during Passover, etc. ⓘ 19c: from Yiddish *matse*, from Hebrew *massah*.

maudlin /'mɔːdlɪn/ ▷ *adj* said especially of a drunk person: foolishly sad or sentimental. ⓘ 14c: from French *Madelaine*, from Latin *Magdalena*, in reference to Mary Magdalene, the penitent woman (in Luke 7.38) who was often portrayed weeping.

maul /mɔːl/ ▷ *verb* (***mauled, mauling***) **1** to attack someone or something fiercely, usually tearing the flesh □ ***was mauled by lions.*** **2** to handle someone or something roughly or clumsily. **3** to subject someone to fierce criticism. ▷ *noun* **1** *rugby* a quickly-formed gathering of players from both teams around a player who is holding the ball. **2** a heavy wooden hammer. ⓒ 13c as *male* in obsolete sense 'a MACE[1]': from French *mail*, from Latin *malleus* a hammer.

maulstick or **mahlstick** /'mɔːlstɪk/ ▷ *noun, art* a stick or rod with a pad on one end, used by painters to steady their painting hand while executing delicate brushwork, by resting the padded end on the canvas or its frame. ⓒ 17c: from Dutch *malen* to paint.

maunder /'mɔːndə(r)/ ▷ *verb* (***maundered, maundering***) *intr* **1** (*also* **maunder on**) to talk in a rambling way; to drivel. **2** to wander about, or behave, in an aimless way. • **maundering** *adj*. ⓒ 17c.

maundy /'mɔːndɪ/ ▷ *noun* (***maundies***) *Christianity, formerly* a religious ceremony in which the sovereign washed the feet of the poor, in commemoration of Christ's washing of the disciples' feet, and distributed food, clothing and money (a tradition that remains only in the form of the ceremonial distribution of MAUNDY MONEY). ⓒ 13c: from French *mandé*, from Latin *mandatum* command, taken from Christ's command in John 23.34.

Maundy money ▷ *noun, Brit* silver money that is specially minted for the sovereign to distribute on **Maundy Thursday**, the day before Good Friday.

Mauritanian /mɒrɪ'teɪnɪən, mɔː-/ ▷ *adj* belonging or relating to Mauritania, an Islamic republic in NW Africa, or its inhabitants. ▷ *noun* a citizen or inhabitant of, or person born in, Mauritania.

mausoleum /mɔːsə'lɪəm/ ▷ *noun* (***mausoleums*** or ***mausolea*** /-lɪə/) a grand or monumental tomb. ⓒ 16c as *Mausoleum*, meaning specifically the Tomb of *Mausolus*, King of Caria, at Halicarnassus: Latin.

mauve /moʊv/ ▷ *adj* having a pale purple colour. ▷ *noun* this colour. ⓒ 19c: French, from Latin *malva* MALLOW.

maven /'meɪvən/ or **mavin** /-ɪn/ ▷ *noun, US colloq* an expert or pundit. ⓒ 1960s: Yiddish, from Hebrew *mevin* understanding.

maverick /'mavərɪk/ ▷ *noun* **1** *N Amer, especially US* an unbranded stray animal, especially a calf. **2** a determinedly independent person; a nonconformist. Also *as adj*. ⓒ 19c: named after Samuel Maverick (1803–70), a Texas cattle-raiser who left his calves unbranded.

mavis /'meɪvɪs/ ▷ *noun* (***mavises***) *colloq* another name for the song thrush. ⓒ 14c: from French *mauvis*.

maw /mɔː/ ▷ *noun* **1** the jaws, throat or stomach of a voracious animal. **2** *facetious* a greedy person's stomach. **3** something that seems to swallow things up insatiably. ⓒ Anglo-Saxon *maga*.

mawkish /'mɔːkɪʃ/ ▷ *adj* **1** weakly sentimental, maudlin or insipid. **2** sickly or disgusting. • **mawkishly** *noun*. • **mawkishness** *noun*. ⓒ 17c: from obsolete *mawk* a maggot, from Norse *mathkr*.

the max see under MAXIMUM

max. ▷ *abbreviation* maximum.

maxi /'maksɪ/ ▷ *adj, often in compounds* said of a skirt, coat, etc: **1** extra long; full length. **2** extra large. ▷ *noun* (***maxis***) **1** a maxi garment. Compare MINI. **2** a large racing yacht. ⓒ 1960s: from MAXIMUM.

maxilla /mak'sɪlə/ ▷ *noun* (***maxillae*** /-liː/) *biol* **1** the upper jaw or jawbone in animals. **2** the chewing organ or organs of an insect, just behind the mouth. See also JAW 1, JAWBONE. • **maxillary** *adj*. ⓒ 17c: Latin, meaning 'jaw'.

maxim /'maksɪm/ ▷ *noun* **1** a saying that expresses a general truth. **2** a general rule or principle. ⓒ 15c: from Latin *maxima propositio* or *sententia* greatest axiom or opinion.

maximal ▷ *adj* belonging or relating to a MAXIMUM; having the greatest possible size, value, etc. • **maximally** *adverb*.

maximalist ▷ *noun* someone who makes the fullest (especially political) demands and is unwilling to accept compromise.

maximin /'maksɪmɪn/ ▷ *noun* **1** *math* the highest value in a set of minimum values. **2** in game theory: the strategy of making all decisions in such a way as to maximize the chances of incurring the minimum potential loss. Compare MINIMAX. ⓒ 1950s: from *maxi*mum + *min*imum.

maximize or **maximise** /'maksɪmaɪz/ ▷ *verb* (***maximized, maximizing***) to make something as high or great, etc as possible. • **maximization** *noun*. • **maximizer** *noun*. ⓒ 19c: from Latin *maximus* greatest.

maximum /'maksɪməm/ (abbreviation **max.**) *adj* greatest possible. ▷ *noun* (***maximums*** or ***maxima*** /-mə/) **1** the greatest or most; the greatest possible number, quantity, degree, etc. Also (*chiefly US colloq*) called **the max**. **2** *geom* in co-ordinate geometry: the point at which the slope of a curve changes from positive to negative. ⓒ 18c: from Latin *maximus* greatest.

maxi-single see under 12 INCH

maxwell /'makswəl/ ▷ *noun, physics* (abbreviation **mx**) the CGS UNIT of magnetic flux, equal to 10^{-8} weber. ⓒ Early 20c: named after James Clerk Maxwell (1831–79), a Scottish physicist.

May ▷ *noun* the fifth month of the year, which follows April and comes before June, and has 31 days. ⓒ 13c: from French *Mai*, from Latin *Maius* the month of *Maia* who in Roman mythology is the mother of Hermes.

may[1] ▷ *auxiliary verb* (*past tense* ***might***) **1** used to express permission □ *You may go now.* **2** (*sometimes* **may well**) used to express a possibility □ *I may come with you if I get this finished.* **3** used to express an offer □ *May I help you?* **4** *formal* used to express a wish □ *May you prosper!* **5** *formal & old use* used to express purpose or result □ *Listen, so that you may learn.* **6** *affected, old use* or *facetious* used to express a question □ *And who may you be?* **7** used to express the idea of 'although' □ *You may be rich, but you're not happy.* See also MIGHT[1]. • **be that as it may** in spite of that. • **come what may** whatever happens. • **may I add** used to introduce an additional point. • **may I ask** *often ironic* used before or after a question. • **That's as may be** That may be so. ⓒ Anglo-Saxon *mæg*, present tense of *magan* to be able.

may

See Usage Note at **can**.

may[2] ▷ *noun* (***mays***) **1** the blossom of the HAWTHORN tree. Also called **mayflower**. **2** any variety of hawthorn tree. Also called **may tree**. ⓒ 16c: from MAY, the month in which it usually blooms.

maybe /'meɪbiː, -bɪ/ ▷ *adverb* it may be; it is possible; perhaps. Also used as a sentence substitute. ▷ *noun* (***maybes***) **1** a possibility. **2** a thing or person that may possibly be selected, appointed, etc. ⓒ 15c: MAY[1] + BE.

May beetle and **Maybug** see COCKCHAFER

mayday or **Mayday** ▷ *noun* (***maydays*** or ***Maydays***) the international radio distress signal sent out by ships and aircraft. ⓒ 1920s: a phonetic representation of French *m'aider* help me.

May Day ▷ *noun* the first day of May, a national holiday in many countries, on which socialist and labour demonstrations are held, and traditionally a day of festivities.

mayflower ▷ *noun* **1** see under MAY[2]. **2** any of several other flowers that bloom in May.

mayfly ▷ *noun* (***mayflies***) a short-lived insect with transparent wings, which appears briefly in spring. ⓒ 17c.

mayhem /'meɪhem/ ▷ *noun* **1** a state of great confusion and disorder; chaos. **2** *US & formerly law* the crime of maiming someone. ⓒ 15c in sense 2 as *mahyme* or *mayme*: from French *mahaignier* to wound.

mayn't /'meɪənt/ ▷ *contraction, colloq* may not.

mayonnaise /meɪə'neɪz/ ▷ *noun, cookery* **1** a cold, creamy sauce made of egg yolk, oil, vinegar or lemon juice and seasoning. **2** *in compounds* a dish in which a specified ingredient is mixed or coated with mayonnaise □ *egg mayonnaise*. Sometimes (*colloq*) shortened to **mayo** /'meɪoʊ/. ⓒ 19c: French.

mayor /mɛə(r)/ ▷ *noun* **1** in England, Wales and N Ireland: the head of the local council in a city, town or borough. Compare PROVOST. See also LORD MAYOR, LADY MAYORESS, MAYORESS. **2** in other countries: the head of any of various communities. • **mayoral** *adj* **1** belonging or relating to a mayor. **2** belonging or relating to the office of a mayor. • **mayoralty** /'mɛərəltɪ/ *noun* (***mayoralties***) the position, or period of office, of a mayor. ⓒ 13c: from French *maire*, from Latin *major*, the comparative of *magnus* great.

mayoress /mɛər'ɛs/ ▷ *noun* **1** a mayor's wife. **2** *old use* a female mayor. ⓒ 15c.

maypole ▷ *noun* a tall, decorated pole traditionally set up for dancing round on MAY DAY.

May queen ▷ *noun* a young woman crowned with flowers, chosen to preside over May Day festivities.

may tree see under MAY²

mayweed ▷ *noun* **1** a type of camomile. Also called **stinking camomile**. **2** any of various similar composite plants. ⓒ 16c.

maze /meɪz/ ▷ *noun* **1** a confusing network of paths bordered by high walls or hedges, laid out in a garden as a puzzling diversion in which a person might become lost or disorientated. **2** any confusingly complicated system, procedure, etc. • **mazy** *adj*. ⓒ 14c; 13c as the *maze* in obsolete sense 'delirium': related to AMAZE.

mazurka /mə'zɜːkə, mə'zʊəkə/ ▷ *noun* (***mazurkas***) **1** a lively Polish dance in triple time, quite like the POLKA. **2** a piece of music for this dance. ⓒ 19c: Polish, meaning 'a woman from Mazovia' a province in Poland.

MB ▷ *abbreviation* **1** Medicinae Baccalaureus (Latin), Bachelor of Medicine. **2** *computing* megabyte.

MBA ▷ *abbreviation* Master of Business Administration.

mbar ▷ *abbreviation* millibar or millibars.

MBE ▷ *abbreviation* Member of the Order of the British Empire.

MBO ▷ *abbreviation* management buyout.

MBSc ▷ *abbreviation* Master of Business Science.

mbyte ▷ *abbreviation* megabyte.

MC /ɛm'siː/ ▷ *abbreviation* **1** master of ceremonies. **2** *US* Member of Congress. **3** *Brit* Military Cross. **4** *IVR* Monaco.

MCC ▷ *abbreviation, Brit* Marylebone Cricket Club.

McCarthyism /mə'kɑːθiːɪzəm/ ▷ *noun* the policy of hunting down and removing from public employment all people suspected of having links with Communism. • **McCarthyite** *adj* belonging or relating to this purge, or to any manic purge of dissident factions in a political party, etc. ▷ *noun* someone who supports or practises McCarthyism. ⓒ 1950s: named after the US Republican senator Joseph R McCarthy (1909–57), who headed a fierce campaign to hunt out and interrogate suspected Communists in the US in the early 1950s.

McCoy /mə'kɔɪ/ ▷ *noun* • **the real McCoy** *colloq* the genuine article, not an imitation.

MCP ▷ *abbreviation* male chauvinist pig. See MALE CHAUVINIST.

MD ▷ *abbreviation* **1** managing director. **2** *US state* Maryland. Also written **Md**. **3** *Medicinae Doctor* (Latin), Doctor of Medicine. **4** mentally deficient.

Md ▷ *symbol, chem* mendelevium.

MDMA ▷ *abbreviation* methylenedioxymethamphetamine, the chemical name for ECSTASY.

MDS ▷ *abbreviation* Master of Dental Surgery.

MDT ▷ *abbreviation, N Amer* Mountain Daylight Time, the system of time used in the mountain time zone during the summer months.

ME ▷ *abbreviation* **1** *US state* Maine. Also written **Me**. **2** Middle English. **3** *medicine* myalgic encephalomyelitis.

me¹ /miː/ ▷ *pronoun* **1** the object form of I², used by a speaker or writer to refer to himself or herself □ ***asked me a question.*** **2** used for *I* after the verb BE or when standing alone □ ***It's only me.*** • **be me** *colloq* to be suited to me □ ***This dress isn't really me.*** ⓒ Anglo-Saxon: dative case of I².

me

For **between you and me**, etc see Usage Note at **I**.

me² or **mi** /miː/ ▷ *noun, music* in sol-fa notation: the third note of the major scale. ⓒ 16c: see SOL-FA.

mea culpa /meɪə 'kʊlpə/ ▷ *noun* ▷ *interjection, literary or facetious* as an acknowledgement of one's own guilt or mistake: I am to blame. ⓒ 14c: Latin, literally 'by my fault'.

mead¹ /miːd/ ▷ *noun* an alcoholic drink made by fermenting honey and water, usually with spices added. Also called **hydromel**. ⓒ Anglo-Saxon *meodu*.

mead² /miːd/ ▷ *noun, poetic or old use* a meadow. ⓒ Anglo-Saxon *mæd*.

meadow /'mɛdoʊ/ ▷ *noun* **1** a low-lying field of grass, used for grazing animals or making hay. **2** any moist, grassy area near a river. • **meadowy** *adj*. ⓒ Anglo-Saxon *mædwe*.

meadow pipit ▷ *noun* a ground-dwelling songbird with brown streaky plumage and a slender bill.

meadow saffron see AUTUMN CROCUS

meadowsweet ▷ *noun* a European and Asian wild plant of the rose family, with fragrant cream-coloured flowers. ⓒ 16c.

meagre or (*US*) **meager** /'miːgə(r)/ ▷ *adj* (***meagrer***, ***meagrest***; *US* ***meagerer***, ***meagerest***) **1** lacking in quality or quantity; inadequate; scanty. **2** said of a person: thin, especially unhealthily so. • **meagrely** *adverb*. • **meagreness** *noun*. ⓒ 14c: from French *maigre* thin, from Latin *macer* lean.

meal¹ /miːl/ ▷ *noun* **1** an occasion on which food is eaten, eg lunch, supper, dinner, etc. **2** an amount of food eaten on one such occasion. • **make a meal of something** **1** *colloq* to exaggerate the importance of it, or make it seem more complicated than it really is, eg by taking an unnecessary amount of time or trouble over it. **2** to eat it as a meal. ⓒ Anglo-Saxon *mæl*, meaning 'a measure' or 'a portion of time'.

meal² /miːl/ ▷ *noun, often in compounds* **1** the edible parts of any grain, usually excluding wheat, ground to a coarse powder □ ***oatmeal***. **2** any other food substance in ground form □ ***bone meal***. ⓒ Anglo-Saxon *melo*.

mealie /'miːlɪ/ ▷ *noun* (***mealies***) *S Afr* **1** an ear of MAIZE. **2** (*especially* **mealies**) MAIZE. ⓒ 19c: from Afrikaans *mielie* maize, from Portuguese *milho* millet.

mealie meal ▷ *noun, S Afr* maize ground to a fine flour.

meals-on-wheels ▷ *singular noun, Brit* a welfare service by which cooked meals are delivered by car, etc to the homes of old or sick people.

meal ticket ▷ *noun* **1** *colloq* a person or situation that provides a source of income or other means of living □ ***saw marriage as her meal ticket out of poverty.*** **2** *N Amer, especially US* a LUNCHEON VOUCHER.

mealy /ˈmiːlɪ/ ▷ *adj* (***mealier***, ***mealiest***) **1** containing MEAL[2]. **2** dry and powdery, or granular, like meal. • **mealiness** *noun*.

mealy-mouthed ▷ *adj, derog* said of a person: afraid to speak plainly or openly; not frank or sincere. ◷ 16c.

mean[1] /miːn/ ▷ *verb* (***meant*** /mɛnt/, ***meaning***) **1** to express or intend to express, show or indicate something. **2** to intend something; to have it as a purpose □ *didn't mean any harm.* **3** to be serious or sincere about something □ *He means what he says.* **4** to be important to the degree specified; to represent something □ *Your approval means a lot to me* □ *He meant nothing to me.* **5** to entail something necessarily; to involve or result in it □ *War means hardship.* **6** to foretell or portend something □ *Cold cloudless evenings mean overnight frost.* • **be meant for something** to be destined to it □ *She was meant for stardom.* • **mean well** to have good intentions. ◷ Anglo-Saxon *mænan*.

mean[2] /miːn/ ▷ *adj* (***meaner***, ***meanest***) **1** not generous. **2** low; despicable. **3** poor; shabby; characterized by inferior quality. **4** *colloq, especially N Amer* vicious; malicious; bad-tempered. **5** *colloq* good; skilful □ *plays a mean guitar.* • **meanly** *adverb*. • **meanness** *noun*. • **no mean something** *colloq* **1** an excellent one □ *He's no mean singer.* **2** not an easy one; a very difficult one □ *That was no mean feat.* ◷ Anglo-Saxon *gemæne* low in rank or birth, common.

mean[3] /miːn/ ▷ *adj* **1** midway; intermediate. **2** average. ▷ *noun* **1** a midway position or course, etc between two extremes. **2** *math, statistics* a mathematical AVERAGE, in particular: **a** the average value of a set of *n* numbers, equal to the sum of the numbers divided by *n*. Also called **arithmetic mean**; **b** the average value of a set of *n* numbers, also taking into account their frequency, by multiplying each number by the number of times it occurs, summing the resulting values and dividing them by *n*. Also called **weighted mean**; **c** the *n*th root of the product of *n* quantities or numbers, eg the geometric mean of 2 and 3 is the second (square) root of 6, ie $\sqrt{6}$. Also called **geometric mean**. Compare MEDIAN, MODE. ◷ 14c: from French *meien*, from Latin *medius* middle.

meander /mɪˈandə(r)/ ▷ *verb* (***meandered***, ***meandering***) *intr* **1** said of a river: to bend and curve. **2** (*also* **meander about**) to wander randomly or aimlessly. ▷ *noun* (*often* **meanders**) **1** a bend; a winding course. **2** *art* an intricate, winding, fret pattern. ◷ 16c: from Latin *Maeander*, a winding river in Turkey, now called the Menderes.

meanie or **meany** /ˈmiːnɪ/ ▷ *noun* (***meanies***) *colloq* **1** a selfish or ungenerous person. **2** *especially N Amer* a malicious or bad-tempered person.

meaning ▷ *noun* **1** the sense in which a statement, action, word, etc is intended to be understood. **2** significance, importance or purpose, especially when hidden or special. ▷ *adj* intended to express special significance □ *a meaning look.*

meaningful ▷ *adj* **1** having meaning; significant. **2** full of significance; expressive. **3** *logic* capable of interpretation. • **meaningfully** *adverb*.

meaningless ▷ *adj* **1** without meaning or reason. **2** having no importance. **3** having no purpose; pointless. • **meaninglessly** *adverb*. • **meaninglessness** *noun*.

means ▷ *singular or plural noun* **1** the instrument or method used to achieve some object. **2** wealth; resources. • **a means to an end** something treated merely as a way of achieving a desired result, considered unimportant in every other respect. • **by all means** *rather formal* yes, of course. • **by any means** using any available method. • **by fair means** see under FAIR. • **by means of something** with the help or use of it. • **by no means** or **not by any means** not at all; definitely not. ◷ 17c: from MEAN[3].

means test ▷ *noun* an official inquiry into someone's wealth or income to determine their eligibility for financial benefit from the state. ▷ *verb* (**means-test**) to carry out a means test. ◷ 1930s: see MEANS 2.

meant *past tense, past participle of* MEAN[1]

meantime ▷ *noun* (*especially* **in the meantime**) the time or period in between; the intervening time. ▷ *adverb* MEANWHILE. ◷ 14c.

meanwhile ▷ *adverb* **1** during the time in between. **2** at the same time. ◷ 14c.

meany see MEANIE

measles /ˈmiːzəlz/ ▷ *singular noun* **1** a highly infectious viral disease characterized by fever, a sore throat and a blotchy red rash that starts on the face and neck, and spreads to the rest of the body. See also GERMAN MEASLES. **2** *vet medicine* in pigs and cattle: a disease caused by larval tape worms. ◷ 14c.

measly /miːzəlɪ/ ▷ *adj* (***measlier***, ***measliest***) **1** *derog, colloq* said of an amount, value, etc: very small; miserable; paltry. **2** relating to, or suffering from, measles. • **measliness** *noun*.

measurable /mɛʒrəbəl, mɛʒərəbəl/ ▷ *adj* **1** able to be measured; large enough, or of sufficient quantity, to be measured. **2** noticeable; significant. • **measurably** *adverb*.

measure /ˈmɛʒə(r)/ ▷ *noun* **1** size, volume, etc determined by comparison with something of known size, etc, usually an instrument graded in standard units. **2** *often in compounds* such an instrument for taking a measurement of something □ *a tape-measure.* **3** a standard unit of size, etc; a standard amount □ *a measure of whisky.* **4** a system of such units □ *imperial measure* □ *metric measure.* **5** (*usually* **measures**) an action; a step □ *We must take drastic measures.* **6** a limited, or appropriate, amount or extent □ *a measure of politeness* □ *in some measure* □ *had my measure of luck.* **7** an enactment or bill. **8** *music* time or rhythm; a bar. **9** *poetry* rhythm or metre. **10** (*usually* **measures**) a layer of rock containing a particular mineral, etc □ *coal measures.* **11** *printing* the width of a page or column of type, usually expressed in EMs. **12** *old use* a dance □ *tread a measure.* ▷ *verb* (***measured***, ***measuring***) **1** *tr & intr* to determine the size, volume, etc of, usually with a specially made instrument or by comparing it to something else. **2** *intr* to be a specified size. **3** (*also* **measure off something** or **measure something off** or **out**) to mark or divide something into units of a given size, etc. **4** to set something in competition with something else □ *measure his strength against mine.* • **measuring** *noun*. Also *as adj, especially in compounds* referring to an object used for measuring □ *measuring-jug.* • **above** or **beyond measure** exceptionally great; to an exceedingly great degree. • **be the measure of something** to be the standard by which to judge its quality. • **for good measure** as something extra, or above the minimum necessary. • **get** or **have the measure of someone** or **have** or **get someone's measure** *rather formal* to form or have an idea or judgement of their character or abilities. • **measure one's length** to fall down at full length on the ground. • **without measure** inordinately; without restraint. ◷ 13c: from Latin *mensura*, from *metiri* to measure.

▪ **measure someone up** to find out and take note of a person's measurements □ *was measured up for a new suit.*

▪ **measure up to something** to reach the required standard; to be adequate □ *He just doesn't measure up to the job.*

measured ▷ *adj* **1** slow and steady. **2** carefully chosen or considered □ *a measured response.* • **measuredly** *adverb*.

measurement ▷ *noun* **1** (*often* **measurements**) a size, amount, etc determined by measuring □ *measurements for the new bedroom carpet.* **2** (*often* **measurements**) the size of a part of the body □ *What is his chest measurement?* **3** the act of measuring. **4** a standard system of measuring.

measuring-worm see INCHWORM

meat /miːt/ ▷ *noun* **1** the flesh of any animal used as food. See also RED MEAT, WHITE MEAT, GAME[1] *noun* 10. **2** the basic or most important part; the essence. **3** in something said or written: substance or content. **4** *old use* food in general; a meal. • **meatless** *adj.* • **meat and drink to someone 1** a source of enjoyment to them. **2** their basic means of support. ⓔ Anglo-Saxon *mete*.

meatball ▷ *noun, cookery* a small ball of minced meat mixed with breadcrumbs and seasonings.

meat loaf ▷ *noun* a loaf-shaped food made from chopped or minced meat, seasoning, etc, cooked and usually eaten cold in slices.

meatus /mɪ'eɪtəs/ ▷ *noun* (***meatuses***) *anatomy* a passage between body parts or an opening, eg the passage that leads from the external surface of the ear to the eardrum. ⓔ 17c: Latin, meaning 'passage', from *meare* to flow or run.

meaty /miːtɪ/ ▷ *adj* (***meatier, meatiest***) **1** full of, or containing, animal flesh. **2** resembling or tasting like meat, especially cooked meat. **3** full of interesting information or ideas □ *a meaty article.* • **meatily** *adverb.* • **meatiness** *noun.*

mecca or **Mecca** /'mɛkə/ ▷ *noun* (***meccas*** or ***Meccas***) any place of outstanding importance or significance to a particular group of people, especially one which they feel they have to visit □ *St Andrews, the mecca of golf.* ⓔ 19c: named after the city of Mecca in Saudi Arabia, the birthplace of Muhammad, to which all Muslims try to make at least one pilgrimage.

mech. ▷ *abbreviation* **1** mechanical. **2** mechanics.

mechanic /mə'kanɪk/ ▷ *noun* a skilled worker who repairs, maintains or constructs machinery. See also MECHANICIAN, MACHINIST. ⓔ 16c: see MECHANICAL.

mechanical ▷ *adj* **1** belonging to or concerning machines or mechanics. **2** worked by, or performed with, machinery or a mechanism. **3** said of an action or movement, etc: done without or not requiring much thought. **4** acting or done by physical means, rather than chemical. • **mechanically** *adverb.* ⓔ 15c: from Latin *mechanicus*, from Greek *mechane* a contrivance or machine.

mechanical advantage ▷ *noun, engineering* the ratio of the output force (or LOAD *noun* 11) to the input force for a simple machine.

mechanical drawing ▷ *noun, technical* a drawing of a machine, architectural construction, etc done with the aid of instruments.

mechanical engineering ▷ *noun* the branch of engineering concerned with the design, construction and operation of machines of all types.

mechanician /mɛkə'nɪʃən/ ▷ *noun* someone skilled in constructing machines and tools. See also MACHINIST, MECHANIC.

mechanics ▷ *singular noun* **1** the branch of physics that deals with the motion of bodies and the forces that act on them. See also DYNAMICS, STATICS. **2** the art or science of machine construction. ▷ *plural noun* **1** the system on which something works. **2** *colloq* routine procedures.

mechanism /'mɛkənɪzəm/ ▷ *noun* **1** a working part of a machine or its system of working parts. **2** the arrangements and action by which something is produced or achieved; the process. **3** *psychol* an action that serves some purpose, often a subconscious purpose □ *Laughter is a common defence mechanism.* ⓔ 17c: from Latin *mechanismus*; see MACHINE.

mechanistic /mɛkə'nɪstɪk/ ▷ *adj* **1** relating to mechanics. **2** relating to a mechanism. • **mechanistically** *adverb.*

mechanize or **mechanise** /'mɛkənaɪz/ ▷ *verb* (***mechanized, mechanizing***) **1** to change (the production of something, a procedure, etc) from a manual to a mechanical process. **2** *military* to provide (troops etc) with armoured armed vehicles. • **mechanization** *noun.* • **mechanizer** *noun.* ⓔ 17c.

meconium /mɪ'koʊnɪəm/ ▷ *noun, medicine* the first faeces passed by a baby after birth, or occasionally just before birth, which are dark-greenish and sticky. ⓔ 18c; 17c in obsolete sense 'poppy juice': Latin, from Greek *mekon* poppy.

the Med ▷ *noun, colloq* **1** the Mediterranean Sea. **2** the region of the Mediterranean.

MEd. ▷ *abbreviation* Master of Education.

med. ▷ *abbreviation* **1** medical. **2** medicine. **3** medieval. **4** medium.

medal /'mɛdəl/ ▷ *noun* a flat piece of metal decorated with a design or inscription and awarded, eg to a soldier, sportsperson, etc, for merit or bravery, or produced in celebration of a special occasion. • **medallist** *noun* **1** someone who is awarded a medal, especially for excellence in sport. **2** a designer, maker or collector of, or an expert on, medals. ⓔ 16c: from French *médaille*, from Latin *metallum* metal.

medallion /mə'dalɪən/ ▷ *noun* **1** a large medal-like piece of jewellery, usually worn on a chain. **2** in architecture or on textiles: an oval or circular decorative feature. **3** *cookery* a thin circular cut of meat. ⓔ 17c: from French *médaillon*; related to MEDAL.

meddle /'mɛdəl/ ▷ *verb* (***meddled, meddling***) *intr* **1** (*usually* **meddle in something**) to interfere in it. **2** (*usually* **meddle with something**) to tamper with it. • **meddler** *noun.* • **meddlesome** *adj, derog* fond of meddling. • **meddling** *noun, adj.* ⓔ 14c: from French *medler*, from Latin *miscere* to mix.

media /'miːdɪə/ ▷ *plural noun*: *plural of* MEDIUM. ▷ *singular or plural noun* (*usually* **the media** or **the mass media**) the means by which news and information, etc is communicated to the public, usually considered to be TV, radio and the press collectively.

> ***media***
>
> • When referring to newspapers and broadcasting, **media** is still more commonly treated as a plural noun:
>
> ✓ *The media are highly selective in their focus on sexual violence.*
>
> • Occasionally, however, it is used as a singular noun, especially when a unified concept is intended:
>
> **?** *These people have fears which the media has shamelessly played on over the years.*
>
> **?** *This may lead the media to slant its coverage.*
>
> • **Media** is often used before a noun (as an adjective), eg *media attention, media coverage.*

mediaeval, mediaevalism and **mediaevalist** an alternative (now less common) spelling of MEDIEVAL, etc.

mediagenic /miːdɪədʒɛnɪk, -dʒiːnɪk/ ▷ *adj* said of a person: able to communicate well or present a good image in the media, especially on TV. ⓔ 1980s: from MEDIA, modelled on PHOTOGENIC.

medial /'miːdɪəl/ ▷ *adj, technical* **1** belonging to or situated in the middle; intermediate. **2** *math* relating to a mean or average. **3** see MEDIAN *adj* 1 and 2. • **medially** *adverb.* ⓔ 16c: from Latin *medialis*, from *medius* middle.

median /'miːdɪən/ ▷ *noun* **1** a middle point or part. **2** *geom* a straight line between any VERTEX of a triangle and the centre of the opposite side. **3** *statistics* **a** the middle value in a set of numbers or measurements arranged from smallest to largest, eg the median of 1, 5 and 11 is 5; **b** said of an even number of measurements: the AVERAGE of the middle two measurements. Compare MEAN³, MODE. ▷ *adj* (*also* **medial**) **1** situated in or passing through the middle. **2** *statistics* belonging or relating to the median. ◷ 16c: from Latin *medianus*, from *medius* middle.

mediant /ˈmiːdɪənt/ ▷ *noun, music* the third degree of a major or minor scale, lying midway between the TONIC and the DOMINANT. ◷ 18c: from Italian *mediante*, from Latin *medius* middle.

mediastinum /miːdɪəˈstaɪnəm/ ▷ *noun* (***mediastina*** /-nə/) *anatomy* **1** a membranous partition, especially the one that separates the lungs. **2** the region of the thoracic cavity between the lungs where the heart lies. ◷ 16c: from Latin *mediastimus* an inferior servant or drudge.

mediate ▷ *verb* /ˈmiːdɪeɪt/ (***mediated, mediating***) **1 a** *intr* to act as the agent seeking to reconcile the two sides in a disagreement; **b** to intervene in or settle (a dispute) in this way. **2 a** to convey or transmit (views, etc) as an agent, intermediary or medium; **b** *intr* to act as an intermediary or medium. **3** *intr* to hold an intermediary position. ▷ *adj* /ˈmiːdɪət/ **1** resulting from mediation. **2** indirectly related or connected, eg through some other person. • **mediation** *noun* the act or process of mediating. • **mediator** *noun*. Compare MODERATE, MODERATOR. ◷ 16c: from Latin *mediatus*, from *mediare* to be in the middle.

medic /ˈmɛdɪk/ ▷ *noun, colloq* a doctor or medical student. Also called MEDICO. ◷ 17c.

medicable /ˈmɛdɪkəbəl/ ▷ *adj* said of a condition, illness, etc: able to be healed or treated.

Medicaid /ˈmɛdɪkaɪd/ ▷ *noun* in the USA: a state- or federal-funded scheme which provides assistance with medical expenses for people with low incomes. Compare MEDICARE. ◷ 1960s.

medical /ˈmɛdɪkəl/ ▷ *adj* **1** belonging or relating to doctors or the science or practice of medicine. **2** concerned with medicine, or treatment by medicine, rather than surgery. ▷ *noun* a medical examination to discover a person's physical health. • **medically** *adverb*. ◷ 17c: from French *médical*, from Latin *medicus* physician, from *mederi* to heal.

medical certificate ▷ *noun* **1** a certificate outlining a person's state of health, provided by a doctor who has carried out a medical examination on them, especially for employment purposes. **2** a certificate from a doctor stating that a person is, or has been, unfit for work.

medical jurisprudence ▷ *noun* FORENSIC MEDICINE.

Medical Officer or **medical officer** ▷ *noun* (abbreviation **MO**) in the armed services, etc: a doctor in charge of medical treatment.

medicament /məˈdɪkəmənt, ˈmɛ-/ ▷ *noun, formal* a medicine. ◷ 16c: from Latin *medicamentum*, from *medicare* to cure.

Medicare ▷ *noun* **1** in the USA: a scheme which provides medical insurance for people aged 65 and over, and for certain categories of disabled people. Compare MEDICAID. **2** in Australia: a system providing universal medical insurance. ◷ 1960s.

medicate /ˈmɛdɪkeɪt/ ▷ *verb* (***medicated, medicating***) **1** to treat someone with medicine. **2** to add a healing or health-giving substance to something. • **medication** *noun* medicine or treatment by medicine. ◷ 17c: from Latin *medicare* to cure.

medicinal /məˈdɪsɪnəl/ ▷ *adj* **1** having healing qualities; used as a medicine. **2** belonging or relating to healing. • **medicinally** *adverb*.

medicine /ˈmɛdɪsən, ˈmɛdsɪn/ ▷ *noun* **1 a** any substance used to treat or prevent disease or illness, especially one taken internally; **b** *as adj* □ *medicine bottle* □ *medicine cabinet*. **2** the science or practice of treating or preventing illness, especially using prepared substances rather than surgery. **3** medical practice or the profession of a physician. **4** in primitive societies: something regarded as magical or curative. • **have** or **get a taste** or **dose of one's own medicine** to suffer the same unpleasant treatment that one has given to other people. • **take one's medicine** to accept an unpleasant but deserved punishment. ◷ 13c: from French *medecine*, from Latin *medicina*, from *medicus* a physician.

medicine ball ▷ *noun* a heavy ball thrown from person to person as a form of exercise.

medicine man ▷ *noun* among certain peoples: a person believed to have magic powers, used for healing or sorcery.

medico /ˈmɛdɪkoʊ/ ▷ *noun* (***medicos***) *colloq* a MEDIC.

medico- /mɛdɪkoʊ/ ▷ *combining form, denoting* medicine or medical matters □ *medico-legal*.

medieval or (less commonly) **mediaeval** /mɛdɪˈiːvəl, mɛˈdiːvəl/ ▷ *adj* **1** belonging or relating to, or characteristic of, THE MIDDLE AGES. **2** *derog, colloq* extremely old and primitive. • **medievalism** *noun* **1** the spirit or style of the Middle Ages, or devotion to medieval ideals. **2** a practice or style revived or surviving from the Middle Ages. • **medievalist** *noun* a student of, or expert in, any area or aspect of study of the medieval period. ◷ 19c: from Latin *medius* middle + *aevum* age.

mediocre /miːdɪˈoʊkə(r)/ ▷ *adj* only ordinary or average; rather inferior. • **mediocrity** /miːdɪˈɒkrɪtɪ/ *noun* (***mediocrities***) **1** the quality of being mediocre. **2** a mediocre person or thing. ◷ 16c: from French *médiocre*, from Latin *mediocris*, meaning 'midway up a mountain', from *medius* middle + *ocris* stony mountain.

meditation *noun* **1** the act or process of meditating. **2** deep thought; contemplation, especially on a spiritual or religious theme. **3** a meditative discourse or literary or musical piece. See also TRANSCENDENTAL MEDITATION.

meditate /ˈmɛdɪteɪt/ ▷ *verb* (***meditated, meditating***) **1** *intr* to spend time in deep religious or spiritual thought, often with the mind in a practised state of emptiness. **2** (*often* **meditate about** or **on something**) to think deeply and carefully about something; to reflect upon it. • **meditative** /-ˈtətɪv/ *adj* **1** inclined to meditate. **2** encouraging or giving rise to meditation. • **meditatively** *adverb* ◷ 16c: from Latin *meditari* to reflect upon.

Mediterranean /mɛdɪtəˈreɪnɪən/ ▷ *adj* **1** in, belonging or relating to the area of the Mediterranean Sea, a large inland sea lying between S Europe, N Africa and SW Asia. **2** characteristic of this area. **3** *meteorol* said of a climate: characterized by hot, dry summers and mild, rainy winters. **4** said of a human physical type: slight to medium stature and with a dark complexion. ▷ *noun* **1** (**the Mediterranean**) the Mediterranean Sea and the area surrounding it, or both. **2** a person born or living in one of the countries which borders on to the Mediterranean Sea. ◷ 16c: from Latin *mediterraneus*, from *medius* middle + *terra* earth.

medium /ˈmiːdɪəm/ ▷ *noun* (*plural* in all senses except 2 and 7 ***mediums*** or, in all senses except 3, ***media*** /ˈmiːdɪə/) **1** something by or through which an effect is produced. **2** see MEDIA. **3** someone through whom the spirits of dead people are said to communicate with the living. **4** *art* a particular category of materials seen as a means of expression, eg watercolours, photography or clay. **5** *art* a substance, eg water, oil, turpentine, in which paint is thinned or mixed. **6** *biol* a CULTURE MEDIUM. **7** *computing* (*usually* **media**) any material on which data is recorded, eg magnetic disk. **8** a middle position, condition or course □ *a happy medium*. ▷ *adj* **1** intermediate; midway; average. **2** moderate. **3** said of meat, especially steak: cooked through so that it is not bloody when cut open. Compare RARE², WELL DONE. ◷ 16c: Latin, from *medius* middle.

medium-dated ▷ *adj, finance* said of securities: redeemable in five to fifteen years' time. See also LONG-DATED, SHORT-DATED.

medium wave ▻ *noun* a radio wave with a wavelength between 200 and 1000 metres. Compare LONG WAVE, SHORT WAVE. Also *as adj* □ *a medium-wave broadcast.*

medlar /'mɛdlə(r)/ ▻ *noun* **1** a small brown apple-like fruit eaten only when already decaying. **2** the small Eurasian tree that bears it. ◷ 14c: from French *medler*, from Latin *mespilum*.

medley /'mɛdlɪ/ ▻ *noun* (***medleys***) **1** a piece of music made up of pieces from other songs, tunes, etc. **2** a mixture or miscellany. **3** a race in stages with each stage a different length or, in swimming, with each stage swum using a different stroke. Also called **medley relay**. ◷ 15c in sense 2; 14c in obsolete sense 'fighting': from French *medlee*, from *medler* to mix.

medulla /mɛ'dʌlə/ ▻ *noun* (***medullae*** /-liː/ or ***medullas***) **1** *biol* the central part of an organ or tissue, when this differs in structure or function from the outer layer, eg the pith of a plant stem. **2** *anatomy* the MEDULLA OBLONGATA. • **medullary** or **medullar** *adj*. ◷ 17c: Latin, meaning 'pith'.

medulla oblongata /mɛ'dʌlə ɒblɒŋ'gɑːtə/ ▻ *noun* (***medullae oblongatae*** /-liː -tiː/ or ***medulla oblongatas***) *anatomy* in vertebrates: the part of the brain that arises from the spinal cord and forms the lower part of the BRAINSTEM, containing centres that control breathing, heartbeat, etc. ◷ 17c: Latin, meaning 'oblong marrow'.

medusa /mə'djuːzə, -sə/ ▻ *noun* (***medusas*** or ***medusae*** /-siː/) *zool* a free-swimming, disc-shaped or bell-shaped organism with marginal tentacles and a mouth in the centre of its underside, representing the sexually-reproducing stage in the life cycle of a jellyfish or other coelenterate. • **medusoid** /mə'djuːzɔɪd/ *adj*. ◷ 18c: from Latin *Medusa*, from Greek *Medousa*, one of the Gorgons in Greek mythology who had snakes for hair.

meek ▻ *adj* (***meeker***, ***meekest***) **1** having a mild and gentle temperament. **2** submissive. • **meekly** *adverb*. • **meekness** *noun*. ◷ 13c: from Norse *mjukr* soft, gentle.

meerkat /'mɪəkat/ ▻ *noun* any of several species of mongoose-like carnivores native to S Africa, that live in large social groups and nest in burrows. ◷ 15c in obsolete sense 'monkey'.

meerschaum /'mɪəʃəm, -ʃaʊm/ ▻ *noun* **1** a fine, whitish, clay-like mineral. **2** a tobacco pipe with a bowl made of this. ◷ 18c: German, from *Meer* sea + *Schaum* foam.

meet¹ ▻ *verb* (***met***, ***meeting***) **1** *tr & intr* to be introduced to someone for the first time. **2** *tr & intr* **a** (*also* **meet up with someone** or *US* **meet with someone**) to come together with them by chance or by arrangement; **b** said of two people, groups, etc: to come together, either by chance or arrangement. **3** to be present at the arrival of (a vehicle, etc) □ *met the train.* **4** *tr & intr* (*often* **meet with something**) to come into opposition against it □ *My plan met with fierce resistance.* **5** *tr & intr* to join; to come into contact with something □ *where the path meets the road.* **6** to satisfy □ *meet your requirements.* **7** to pay □ *meet costs.* **8** to come into the view, experience or presence of something □ *the sight that met my eyes.* **9** (*also* **meet with something**) to encounter or experience it □ *met his death* □ *met with disaster.* **10** (*also* **meet with something**) to receive it □ *My suggestions met with approval.* ▻ *noun* **1** the assembly of hounds and huntsmen and huntswomen before a fox-hunt begins. **2** a sporting event, especially a series of athletics competitions. • **meet someone halfway** to come to a compromise with them; to be willing to make some concessions to them, so that an agreement can be reached when they do the same. • **more than meets the eye** or **ear** more complicated, interesting, etc than it first appears or sounds. ◷ Anglo-Saxon *metan*.

■ **meet with something** to answer or oppose something □ *meet force with greater force.*

meet² ▻ *adj, old use* proper, correct or suitable. • **meetly** *adverb* correctly; suitably. ◷ Anglo-Saxon *gemæte*.

meeting ▻ *noun* **1** an act of coming together. **2** an assembly or gathering at a prearranged time, usually to discuss specific topics. **3** a sporting event, especially an athletics or horse-racing event □ *race meeting.*

meeting-house ▻ *noun* a house or building in which people meet for public worship, especially one used by the RELIGIOUS SOCIETY OF FRIENDS.

mega /'mɛgə/ ▻ *adj, colloq* excellent. ◷ 1980s: from MEGA-.

mega- /'mɛgə/ ▻ *combining form, denoting* **1** (symbol **M**) a million □ *megabit* □ *megawatt.* **2** (*also* **megalo-** /'mɛgəloʊ/) large or great. **3** *colloq* great □ *megastar.* ◷ From Greek *megas*, *megal-* big.

megabuck ▻ *noun N Amer colloq* **1** a million dollars. **2** (*usually* ***megabucks***) a huge sum of money. ◷ 1940s.

megabyte ▻ *noun, computing* a unit of storage capacity equal to 2^{20} or 1 048 576 bytes (abbreviation **mbyte** or **MB**). ◷ 1970s.

megadeath ▻ *noun* death of a million people, used as a unit in estimating casualties in nuclear war.

megaflop ▻ *noun, colloq* a complete failure, especially one that involves huge commercial losses.

megahertz ▻ *noun* (*plural* ***megahertz***) (symbol **MHz**) a unit of frequency equal to of one million hertz. Formerly called **megacycle**.

megalith /'mɛgəlɪθ/ ▻ *noun, archaeol* a very large stone, especially one that forms part of a prehistoric monument. See also CROMLECH. • **megalithic** *adj* **1** said of a period of prehistory: characterized by the use of megaliths in monuments, etc. **2** said of a prehistoric monument: made of megaliths. ◷ 19c.

megalo- see under MEGA-

megalomania /mɛgəloʊ'meɪnɪə/ ▻ *noun* **1** *medicine* a mental condition characterized by an exaggerated sense of power and self-importance. **2** *colloq* greed for power. ◷ 19c.

megalomaniac *noun* someone who is affected by megalomania. ▻ *adj* relating to or affected by megalomania.

megalosaur /'mɛgəloʊsɔː(r)/ and **megalosaurus** /-'sɔːrəs/ ▻ *noun* (***megalosaurs*** or ***megalosauri*** /-iː/) any gigantic bipedal carnivorous dinosaur of the Jurassic or Cretaceous period. ◷ 19c: Latin *megalosaurus*, from Greek *sauros* lizard.

megaphone ▻ *noun* a funnel-shaped device which, when someone speaks into it, amplifies the voice. ◷ 19c.

megastore ▻ *noun* a very large shop, especially any of the large chain stores. ◷ 1980s.

megaton /'mɛgətʌn/ ▻ *noun* **1** a unit of weight equal to one million tons. **2** a unit of explosive power equal to one million tons of TNT. Also *as adj* □ *megaton bomb.*

megilp or **magilp** /mə'gɪlp/ ▻ *noun, art* in oil-painting: a medium consisting of linseed oil and mastic varnish. ◷ 18c.

meiosis /maɪ'oʊsɪs/ ▻ *noun* (***meioses*** /-siːz/) **1** *biol* a type of cell division in which four daughter nuclei are produced, each containing half the number of chromosomes of the parent nucleus and resulting in the formation of male and female GAMETEs. Also called REDUCTION. **2** *rhetoric* a less common term for LITOTES. • **meiotic** /maɪ'ɒtɪk/ *adj*. ◷ Early 20c in sense 1; 16c in sense 2: from Greek *meion* less.

meister /'maɪstə(r)/ ▻ *noun* **1** someone who's an expert. **2** *in compounds* someone who's an expert in the specified thing □ *style meister* □ *scam meister* □ *image meister* □ *noise meister.*

meitnerium /maɪt'nɛərɪəm/ ▷ *noun, chem* (symbol **Mt**, atomic number 109) a name proposed for the radioactive element UNNILENNIUM.

melamine /'mɛləmiːn/ ▷ *noun, chem* **1** a white crystalline organic compound used to form artificial resins (**melamine resins**) that are resistant to heat, water and many chemicals. **2** one of these resins. **3** material made from one of these resins, widely used as laminated coatings. ⓒ 19c: from German *Melamin*.

melan- see under MELANO-

melancholia /mɛlən'koulɪə/ ▷ *noun* (*melancholiae* /-lɪaɪ/) *old use* mental depression. ⓒ 17c: Latin; see MELANCHOLY.

melancholy /'mɛlənkɒlɪ, -kəlɪ/ ▷ *noun* (*melancholies*) **1** a tendency to be gloomy or depressed. **2** prolonged sadness. **3** a sad, pensive state of mind. ▷ *adj* sad; causing or expressing sadness. • **melancholic** /mɛlən'kɒlɪk/ *adj* relating to or suffering from melancholia or melancholy. See also HUMOUR noun 6. ⓒ 14c: from Greek *melancholia*, from *melan* black + *chole* bile, because the condition was once thought to be due to an excess of black bile in the body.

Melanesian /mɛlə'niːzɪən, -'niːʒən/ ▷ *adj* belonging or relating to Melanesia, a group of islands NE of Australia, its inhabitants or their languages. ▷ *noun* **1** a citizen or inhabitant of, or person born in, Melanesia. **2** a group of languages spoken in Melanesia, or one of these languages. ⓒ 19c: from MELAN- (because the dominant race in these islands is dark-skinned), modelled on POLYNESIAN.

melange or **mélange** /meɪ'lɑːnʒ; *French* melɑ̃ʒ/ ▷ *noun* (*melanges* or *mélanges*) a mixture, especially a varied or confused one □ *a melange of strange characters* □ *a melange of winter vegetables*. ⓒ 17c: French.

melanin /'mɛlənɪn/ ▷ *noun, physiol, chem* the black or dark brown pigment found to varying degrees in the skin, hair and eyes of humans and animals. ⓒ 19c.

melano- /mɪlɑːnou-/ or (before a vowel) **melan-** ▷ *combining form, denoting* **1** black or dark. **2** melanin. ⓒ From Greek *melas, melanos* black.

melanocyte /'mɛlənousaɪt, mɪ'lan-/ ▷ *noun* (*melanocytes*) *zool* a cell that produces melanin. ⓒ 19c.

melanoma /mɛlə'noumə/ ▷ *noun* (*melanomas, melanomata* /-mətə/) *medicine* a cancerous tumour, usually of the skin, that is composed of MELANOCYTEs and may spread to other parts of the body, such as the lymph nodes. ⓒ 19c: Latin.

melatonin /mɛlə'tounɪn/ ▷ *noun, physiol* in vertebrates: a hormone secreted by the PINEAL GLAND that is involved in the control of certain daily and seasonal changes, and changes in pigmentation. ⓒ 1950s: modelled on SEROTONIN, from Greek *melas* black.

Melba toast /'mɛlbə —/ ▷ *noun* very thin, crisp toast. See also PEACH MELBA. ⓒ 1930s: named after Dame Nellie Melba (1861–1931), the Australian operatic soprano.

meld[1] ▷ *verb* (*melded, melding*) *tr & intr* to merge, blend or combine. ⓒ 1930s.

meld[2] ▷ *verb* (*melded, melding*) *tr & intr, cards* to declare; to lay down (cards) in order to score points. ▷ *noun* a laying down of cards. ⓒ 19c: from German *melden*, related to Anglo-Saxon *meldian* to show forth or make known.

melee or **mêlée** /'mɛleɪ/ ▷ *noun* (*melees* or *mêlées*) **1** a riotous brawl involving large numbers of people. **2** any confused or muddled collection. ⓒ 17c: French *mêlée*, from *mêler* to mix.

meliorate /'miːlɪəreɪt/ ▷ *verb* (*meliorated, meliorating*) *tr & intr* to improve. See also AMELIORATE. • **melioration** *noun*. • **meliorative** *adj*. ⓒ 16c: from Latin *meliorare*, from *melior* better.

mellifluous /mɪ'lɪfluəs/ or **mellifluent** /-fluənt/ ▷ *adj* said of sounds, speech, etc: having a smooth sweet flowing quality. • **mellifluously** or **mellifluently** *adverb*. • **mellifluousness** *noun*. ⓒ 15c: from Latin *mel* honey + *fluere* to flow.

mellow /'mɛlou/ ▷ *adj* (*mellower, mellowest*) **1** said of a person or their character: calm and relaxed with age or experience. **2** said of sound, colour, light, etc: soft, rich and pure. **3** said of wine, cheese, etc: fully flavoured with age; well matured. **4** said of fruit: sweet and ripe. **5** said of a person: pleasantly relaxed or warm-hearted through being slightly drunk or affected by a recreational drug. ▷ *verb* (*mellowed, mellowing*) *tr & intr* to make or become mellow. • **mellowness** *noun*. ⓒ 15c: perhaps from Anglo-Saxon *mearu* soft or tender.

■ **mellow out** to relax and release one's tensions and inhibitions.

melodeon or **melodion** /mə'loudɪən/ ▷ *noun* **1** a small reed-organ; a harmonium. **2** a kind of accordion. ⓒ 19c: German *Melodion*, from *Melodie* melody.

melodic /mə'lɒdɪk/ ▷ *adj* **1** relating or belonging to melody. **2** pleasant-sounding; tuneful; melodious. • **melodically** *adverb*. ⓒ 19c.

melodious /mə'loudɪəs/ ▷ *adj* **1** pleasant to listen to; tuneful. **2** having a recognizable melody. • **melodiousness** *noun*. ⓒ 14c.

melodist /'mɛlədɪst/ ▷ *noun* **1** someone who composes melodies. **2** *rather dated* a singer. ⓒ 18c in sense 2.

melodrama /'mɛlədrɑːmə/ ▷ *noun* (*melodramas*) **1** as a theatrical genre especially popular during the 19c: drama often including musical items and featuring simplified characters, sensational events and traditional justice, usually in the form of a happy ending. **2** a play or film of this kind, sometimes lacking the musical element and with an emphasis on appealing to the emotions. **3** *derog* excessively dramatic behaviour. • **melodramatic** /mɛlədrə'matɪk/ *adj* excessively emotional, sensational, etc; overstrained, characteristic of melodramas □ *stop being so melodramatic*. • **melodramatically** *adverb*. • **melodramatics** *plural noun* melodramatic behaviour. • **melodramatize** or **melodramatise** *verb*. ⓒ 19c: from French *mélodrame*, from Greek *melos* song + *drama* action or DRAMA.

melody /'mɛlədɪ/ ▷ *noun* (*melodies*) **1** *music* the sequence of single notes forming the core of a tune, as opposed to the HARMONY. **2** pleasantness of sound; tuneful music. **3** especially in poetry: pleasant arrangement or combination of sounds. ⓒ 13c: from Greek *melodia*, from *melos* song + *aoidein* to sing.

melon /'mɛlən/ ▷ *noun* **1** any of several plants of the gourd family, cultivated for their fruits. **2** the large rounded edible fruit of any of these plants, which generally have a thick skin, sweet juicy flesh and many seeds □ *watermelon*. ⓒ 14c: French, from Greek *melon* apple.

melt ▷ *verb* (*melted, melting*) *tr & intr* **1** (*sometimes* **melt down** or **melt something down**) to make or become soft or liquid, especially through the action of heat; to dissolve (something solid). **2** (*often* **melt into something**) to combine or fuse, or make something combine or fuse with something else, causing a loss of distinctness. **3** (*also* **melt away** or **melt something away**) to disappear or make something disappear or disperse □ *support for the scheme melted away*. **4** *colloq* to make or become emotionally or romantically tender or submissive □ *Her smile melted my heart*. ▷ *noun* **5** the act of melting. **6** the quantity or material melted. • **melting** *noun, adj*. • **meltingly** *adverb*. • **melt in the mouth** said of food: to be especially delicious, eg in lightness of texture. ⓒ Anglo-Saxon *meltan* (as the intransitive verb) and *mæltan* (the transitive).

■ **melt down 1** *technical* said of the core of a nuclear reactor: to overheat, causing radioactivity to escape. **2** to turn (metal, or metal articles) to a liquid state so that the raw material can be reused.

meltdown ▷ *noun* **1** *technical* the overheating of the core of a nuclear reactor, causing radioactivity to escape into the environment. **2** *colloq* a major disaster or failure.

melting point ▷ *noun* (abbreviation **mp**) the temperature at which a particular substance (usually one that is solid at room temperature, eg a metal) changes from a solid to a liquid.

melting-pot ▷ *noun* **1** a place or situation in which varying beliefs, ideas, cultures, etc come together. **2** a vessel for melting something, eg metal, in. • **in the melting-pot** in the process of changing and forming something new.

mem. ▷ *abbreviation* **1** (*also* **Mem.**) member. **2** memorandum. **3** memorial.

member /'mɛmbə(r)/ ▷ *noun* **1** someone who belongs to a group or organization. **2** (*often* **Member**) an elected representative of a governing body, eg a Member of Parliament, or of a local council, etc. **3 a** a part of a whole, especially a limb of an animal or a petal of a plant; **b** the penis. **4** *building* a constituent part of a structural framework. **5** a plant or animal belonging to a specific class or group. • **membered** *adj.* • **memberless** *adj.* ⓘ 13c in sense 3: from French *membre*, from Latin *membrum* limb or part.

Member of Parliament ▷ *noun* (abbreviation **MP**) **1** in the UK: a person elected to represent the people of a CONSTITUENCY in the HOUSE OF COMMONS. Sometimes shortened to MEMBER (sense 2) □ ***the Member for Huntingdon.*** **2** (*also* **member of parliament**) a person elected to a legislative assembly in various countries. See also MEP, MHR.

membership ▷ *noun* **1** the state of being a member □ ***has been refused membership of the club.*** **2 a** the members of an organization collectively; **b** the number of members □ ***Membership has fallen dramatically.***

membrane /'mɛmbreɪn/ ▷ *noun* **1** a thin sheet of tissue that lines a body cavity or surrounds a body part, organ, etc. **2** *biol* a thin layer of lipid and protein molecules that forms the boundary between a cell and its surroundings. Also called **cell membrane, plasma membrane**. **3** any thin, flexible covering or lining, eg plastic film. • **membranous** /'mɛmbrənəs/ *adj.* ⓘ 17c; 16c in obsolete sense 'parchment': from Latin *membrana* the skin of the body; parchment.

memento /mə'mɛntoʊ/ ▷ *noun* (***mementos*** or ***mementoes***) a thing that serves as a reminder of the past; a souvenir. ⓘ 15c: Latin, imperative of *meminisse* to remember.

memento mori /— 'mɔriː/ ▷ *noun* an object intended as a reminder of the inevitability of death, eg a skull. ⓘ Latin, literally 'Remember that you must die'.

memo /'mɛmoʊ/ ▷ *contraction* (***memos***) a short note. ⓘ 19c: shortened from MEMORANDUM.

memoir /'mɛmwɑː(r)/ ▷ *noun* **1** a written record of events in the past, especially one based on personal experience. **2** (*usually* **memoirs**) a person's written account of his or her own life; an autobiography. **3** a learned essay on any subject. • **memoirist** *noun.* ⓘ 16c: from French *mémoire* memory.

memorabilia /mɛmərə'bɪlɪə/ ▷ *plural noun* souvenirs of people or events. ⓘ 19c: Latin, meaning 'memorable things'.

memorable /'mɛmərəbəl/ ▷ *adj* worth remembering; easily remembered; remarkable. • **memorability** /-'bɪlɪtɪ/ *noun.* • **memorably** *adverb.* ⓘ 15c: from Latin *memorabilis*, from *memorare* to remember.

memorandum /mɛmə'randəm/ ▷ *noun* (***memorandums*** or ***memoranda*** /-də/) **1** a written statement or record, especially one circulated for the attention of colleagues at work. **2** a note of something to be remembered. **3** *law* a brief note of some transaction, recording the terms, etc. ⓘ 15c: Latin, meaning 'a thing to be remembered', from *memorare* to remember.

memorial /mə'mɔːrɪəl/ ▷ *noun* **1** a thing that honours or commemorates a person or an event, eg a statue or monument. **2** (*especially* **memorials**) *historical* a written statement of facts; a record. ▷ *adj* **1** serving to preserve the memory of a person or an event □ ***a memorial fund.*** **2** relating to or involving memory. ⓘ 14c: from Latin *memoriale* reminder.

Memorial Day ▷ *noun* in the USA: a national holiday held on the last Monday in May in honour of American war dead.

memorialize or **memorialise** /mə'mɔːrɪəlaɪz/ ▷ *verb* (***memorialized***, ***memorializing***) **1** to commemorate someone or something. **2** to address or present a memorial to someone. ⓘ 18c.

memorize or **memorise** /'mɛməraɪz/ ▷ *verb* (***memorized***, ***memorizing***) to learn something thoroughly, so as to be able to reproduce it exactly from memory. • **memorization** *noun.* ⓘ 19c.

memory /'mɛmərɪ/ ▷ *noun* (***memories***) **1** the ability of the mind to remember □ ***have a poor memory.*** **2** the mind's store of remembered events, impressions, knowledge and ideas □ ***searching my memory for the name.*** **3** the mental processes of memorizing information, retaining it, and recalling it on demand. **4** any such impression reproduced in the mind □ ***have no memory of the event.*** **5** *computing* the part of a computer that is used to store data and programs. Also called **store**. **6** the limit in the past beyond which one's store of mental impressions does not extend □ ***not within my memory.*** **7** the act of remembering; commemoration □ ***in memory of old friends.*** **8** reputation after death □ ***Her memory is still treasured here.*** ⓘ 14c: from French *memorie*, from Latin *memor* mindful.

memory lane ▷ *noun*, *colloq* the past as it is personally remembered, often with a degree of nostalgia or sentimentality □ ***got together for a chat and a jaunt down memory lane.***

memory mapping ▷ *noun* the way in which storage is organized in a computer, eg sections of memory allocated to the screen display, program code, etc.

memsahib /'mɛmsɑːɪb/ ▷ *noun*, *formerly* in India: a married European woman. Also used as a polite form of address. ⓘ 19c: from MA'AM + SAHIB.

men *plural of* MAN

menace /'mɛnəs, 'mɛnɪs/ ▷ *noun* **1** a source of threatening danger. **2** a threat; a show of hostility. **3** *colloq* something or someone that is very annoying or troublesome. ▷ *verb* (***menaced***, ***menacing***) *tr & intr* to threaten; to show an intention to damage or harm someone. • **menacer** *noun.* • **menacing** *adj.* • **menacingly** *adverb.* ⓘ 14c: from French, from Latin *minari* to threaten.

ménage /meɪ'nɑːʒ; *French* menɑːʒ/ ▷ *noun* (***ménages***) *literary* a group of people living together; a household. ⓘ 13c: French, from *manaige*, from Latin *mansio* dwelling.

ménage à trois / *French* menɑːʒ a trwɑ/ ▷ *noun* (***ménages à trois***) an arrangement or a household consisting of three people, especially a husband, a wife and the lover of one of them. ⓘ 19c: literally 'household of three'.

menagerie /mə'nadʒərɪ/ ▷ *noun* (***menageries***) **1 a** a collection of wild animals caged for exhibition; **b** the place where they are kept. **2** a varied or confused mixture, especially of people. ⓘ 18c: from French *ménagerie*, originally the management of a household and/or domestic livestock; related to MÉNAGE.

menarche /mɛ'nɑːkɪ/ ▷ *noun* (***menarches***) *physiol* the first menstruation. ⓘ Early 20c: from Greek *men* month + *arche* beginning.

mend ▻ *verb* (***mended, mending***) **1** to repair something. **2** *intr* to improve, especially in health; to heal or recover. **3** to improve or correct something ▫ *mend one's ways*. ▻ *noun* **1** on a garment, etc: a repaired part or place. **2** an act of mending. • **mendable** *adj*. • **mending** *noun* **1** the act or process of repairing. **2** articles that need to be mended, especially clothes. • **on the mend** getting better, especially in health. ◷ 13c: shortened from AMEND.

mendacious /mɛn'deɪʃəs/ ▻ *adj* lying, or likely to lie. • **mendaciously** *adverb*. ◷ 17c: from Latin *menitiri* to lie.

mendacity /mɛn'dasɪtɪ/ *noun* (***mendacities***) *formal* **1** untruthfulness; the tendency to lie. **2** a lie or falsehood.

mendelevium /mɛndə'liːvɪəm, -leɪvɪəm/ ▻ *noun*, *chem* (symbol **Md**, atomic number 101) an artificially-produced, radioactive, metallic element. ◷ 1950s: named after Dmitri I Mendeleyev (1834–1907), the Russian chemist who developed the periodic table of elements.

Mendelian /mɛn'diːlɪən/ ▻ *adj*, *biol* belonging or relating to the principles of heredity put forward by Gregor J Mendel (1822–84), an Austrian monk and botanist. ◷ Early 20c.

mendicant /'mɛndɪkənt/ ▻ *noun* **1** a monk who is a member of an order that is not allowed to own property and is therefore entirely dependent on charity, eg a Dominican or Franciscan friar. **2** *formal* a beggar. ▻ *adj* **1** dependent on charity. **2** *formal* begging. • **mendicancy** /-kənsɪ/ or **mendicity** /mɛn'dɪsɪtɪ/ *noun*. ◷ 14c as *noun* 2: from Latin *mendicare* to beg.

meneer see MYNHEER

menfolk ▻ *plural noun* **1** men collectively, especially the male members of a particular group. **2** a woman's male relatives, etc.

menhir /'mɛnhɪə(r)/ ▻ *noun* a prehistoric monument in the form of a single upright standing stone. ◷ 19c: French, from Breton *men* stone + *hir* long.

menial /'miːnɪəl/ ▻ *adj* **1** said of work: unskilled, uninteresting and of low status. **2** relating, belonging or suited to a servant. ▻ *noun*, *derog* a domestic servant. ◷ 15c in sense 2; 14c in obsolete adjectival sense 'domestic': French, from French *meinie* household.

meninges /me'nɪndʒiːz/ ▻ *plural noun* (*singular* ***meninx*** /'mɛnɪŋks/) *anatomy* the three membranes that cover the brain and spinal cord. See also ARACHNOID, DURA MATER, PIA MATER. • **meningeal** /-dʒɪəl/ *adj*. ◷ 17c: Latin, from Greek *meninx*, *meningos* membrane.

meningitis /mɛnɪn'dʒaɪtɪs/ ▻ *noun*, *pathol* inflammation of the MENINGES, usually caused by bacterial or viral infection, the main symptoms being severe headache, fever, stiffness of the neck and aversion to light. ◷ 19c.

meningococcus /mənɪŋgoʊ'kɒkəs/ ▻ *noun* a bacterium which causes epidemic cerebrospinal MENINGITIS. • **meningococcal** or **meningococcic** /-'kɒksɪk/ *adj*.

men in grey suits ▻ *plural noun* unseen establishment figures holding the ultimate power in an organization, political party, etc.

meniscus /mə'nɪskəs/ ▻ *noun* (***meniscuses*** or ***menisci*** /-skaɪ, -saɪ/) **1** *physics* the curved upper surface of a liquid in a partly-filled narrow tube, caused by the effects of surface tension. **2** *anatomy* a crescent-shaped structure, such as the disc of cartilage in the knee joint. **3** *optics* a lens that is convex on one side and concave on the other. ◷ 17c: Latin, from Greek *meniskos*, diminutive of *mene* moon.

Mennonite see AMISH

menopause /'mɛnəpɔːz/ ▻ *noun* the period in a woman's life, typically between the ages of 45 and 55, when menstruation ceases and pregnancy is no longer possible. Also called **change of life, the change**. See also MALE MENOPAUSE. • **menopausal** /mɛnə'pɔːzəl/ *adj* **1** relating to or experiencing the menopause and associated hormonal changes. **2** *colloq* suffering from strange moods and behaviour in middle age. ◷ 19c: from French *ménopause*, from Greek *men* month + *pausis* cessation.

menorah /mə'nɔːrə/ ▻ *noun* a candelabrum with seven branches used in Jewish worship and regarded as a symbol of Judaism. ◷ 19c: Hebrew, meaning 'candlestick'.

menorrhagia /mɛnə'reɪdʒɪə/ ▻ *noun*, *medicine* excessive and prolonged bleeding during menstruation. ◷ 18c: Latin, from Greek *men* month + *-rhagia*, from *rhegnynai* to break.

menorrhoea or (*US*) **menorrhea** /mɛnə'rɪə/ ▻ *noun*, *medicine* normal flow of blood during menstruation. See also AMENORRHOEA, DYSMENORRHOEA, MENORRHAGIA. ◷ 19c: from Greek *men* month + *rhoia* flow.

menses /'mɛnsiːz/ ▻ *plural noun*, *biol*, *medicine* **1** the fluids discharged from the womb during menstruation. **2** the time of menstruation. ◷ 16c: Latin, plural of *mensis* month.

Menshevik /'mɛnʃəvɪk/ ▻ *noun*, *historical* in Russia: a moderate or minority socialist. Compare BOLSHEVIK. ◷ Early 20c: Russian, from *menshye* smaller + *-vik* the agent suffix.

mens rea /mɛnz'rɪə/ ▻ *noun*, *law* criminal intent; knowledge on the part of a law-breaker of the unlawfulness of their act. See also MALICE AFORETHOUGHT. ◷ 19c: Latin, literally 'guilty mind'.

menstrual /'mɛnstrʊəl/ ▻ *adj* relating to or involving menstruation. ◷ 14c.

menstrual cycle ▻ *noun*, *biol* in some primates including humans: a repeating cycle of reproductive changes regulated by sex hormones, and during which OVULATION occurs, happening about once in every 28 days in humans.

menstruate /'mɛnstrʊeɪt/ ▻ *verb* (***menstruated, menstruating***) *intr*, *biol* to discharge blood and other fluids from the womb through the vagina during menstruation. ◷ 17c: from Latin *menstruare*, from *mensis* month.

menstruation /mɛnstrʊ'eɪʃən/ ▻ *noun*, *biol* **1** in women of childbearing age: the discharge through the vagina of blood and fragments of mucous membrane, that takes place at approximately monthly intervals if fertilization of an OVUM has not occurred. Also called MENSES, PERIOD *noun* 8. **2** the time or occurrence of menstruating. See also THE CURSE, MONTHLY *noun* 2.

mensurable /'mɛnʃərəbəl, 'mɛnsjʊrəbəl/ ▻ *adj* **1** *technical or formal* measurable. **2** *music* having a fixed, relative time-value for each note. • **mensurability** *noun*. ◷ 17c: from Latin *mensurare* to measure.

mensuration /mɛnʃə'reɪʃən, mɛnsjʊ'reɪʃən/ ▻ *noun* **1** *technical* the application of geometric principles to the calculation of measurements such as length, volume and area. **2** *formal* the process of measuring. ◷ 16c in sense 2: from Latin *mensurare* to measure.

menswear ▻ *noun* clothing for men.

-ment ▻ *suffix*, *forming nouns*, *denoting* **1** a process, action, result or means ▫ *repayment* ▫ *treatment*. **2** a quality, state or condition ▫ *enjoyment* ▫ *merriment*. ◷ From Latin *-mentum*.

mental /'mɛntəl/ ▻ *adj* **1** belonging or relating to, or done by using, the mind or intelligence ▫ *a mental process* ▫ *mental arithmetic*. **2** *old use* belonging to, or suffering from, an illness or illnesses of the mind ▫ *a mental patient*. **3** *colloq* foolish; stupid. **4** *colloq* ridiculous; unimaginable. • **mentally** *adverb*. ◷ 15c: French, from Latin *mentalis*, from *mens* the mind.

mental age ▻ *noun*, *psychol* the age at which an average child would have reached the same stage of mental development as the individual in question ▫ *He is 33, with a mental age of 10*.

mental cruelty ▷ *noun* conduct, not involving physical cruelty or violence, that wounds a person's feelings and personal dignity.

mental disorder ▷ *noun, psychol* any of various disorders with psychological or behavioural symptoms (eg dementia, schizophrenia) but excluding mental handicap, disorders of development and normal reactions to distressing events.

mental handicap ▷ *noun* a condition in which a person has impaired intellectual abilities, typically with an IQ of less than 70, and suffers from some form of social malfunction due to a congenital condition, brain damage, etc. Also called **mental deficiency, mental retardation** or, the currently favoured term, **learning disabilities**.

mental image see IMAGE

mentality /mɛn'talɪtɪ/ ▷ *noun* (***mentalities***) **1** an outlook; a certain way of thinking. **2** intellectual ability.

menthol /'mɛnθɒl/ ▷ *noun* a sharp-smelling substance obtained from peppermint oil, used as a decongestant and a painkiller. • **mentholated** *adj.* ◎ 19c: German, from Latin *mentha* mint.

mention /'mɛnʃən/ ▷ *verb* (***mentioned, mentioning***) **1** to speak of or make reference to something or someone. **2** to remark on something or someone, usually briefly or indirectly. ▷ *noun* **1** a remark, usually a brief reference □ *made no mention of it.* **2** a reference made to an individual's merit in an official report, especially a military one □ *a mention in dispatches.* • **mentionable** *adj.* • **don't mention it** *colloq* no apologies or words of thanks are needed. • **not to mention something** used to introduce (a subject or facts that the speaker is about to mention), usually for emphasis. ◎ 14c as *noun*: from Latin *mentio* a calling to mind.

mentor /'mɛntɔː(r), -tə(r)/ ▷ *noun* **1** a trusted teacher or adviser. **2** *business* a more senior or experienced colleague appointed to help and advise a junior employee. • **mentoring** *noun* the practice of acting as a mentor or of appointing mentors. • **mentorship** *noun.* ◎ 18c: French, from Greek *Mentor*, the name of the character in the poems of Homer, who was adviser to Odysseus's son, Telemachus.

menu /'mɛnjuː/ ▷ *noun* (***menus***) **1 a** the range of dishes available in a restaurant, etc; **b** the dishes to be served at a particular meal □ *the wedding menu*; **c** a list of these dishes □ *choose from the menu.* **2** *computing* **a** a set of options displayed on a computer screen □ *a pull-down menu*; **b** *in compounds* □ *a menu-driven program.* **3** any list of subjects, options, etc to be selected from. ◎ 19c: French, originally (as an *adj*) meaning 'small' or (as a *noun*) 'a small and detailed list', from Latin *minutus* small.

menu-driven ▷ *adj, computing* applied to an interactive program in which the command choices are displayed as MENUS (sense 2).

meow, meowed and **meowing** see under MIAOW

MEP ▷ *abbreviation* Member of the European Parliament.

mepacrine ▷ *noun* the anti-malarial drug ATEBRIN.

meperidine /mɛ'pɛrɪdiːn, -dɪn/ ▷ *noun, US* PETHIDINE.

-mer ▷ *combining form, chem, forming nouns, denoting* a substance of a specified class □ *isomer* □ *polymer.* ◎ From Greek *meros* a part.

mercantile /'mɜːkəntaɪl/ ▷ *adj* **1** *formal* belonging or relating to trade or traders; commercial. **2** belonging to, like or relating to mercantilism. ◎ 17c: French, from Italian, from *mercante* merchant.

mercantile marine see under MERCHANT NAVY

mercantilism /'mɜːkəntɪlɪzəm/ ▷ *noun* **1** *econ* the business of merchants; trade and commerce. **2** *historical* advocacy of the **mercantile system**, an old economic strategy based on the theory that a nation's interests were best served by development of overseas trade and restriction of imports. • **mercantilist** *noun, adj.* ◎ 19c.

Mercator's projection or **Mercator's map projection** or **Mercator projection** /mɜː'keɪtəz —/ ▷ *noun, map-making, geog* a representation of the surface of the globe in which the meridians are parallel straight lines, and the parallels of latitude are straight lines at right angles to these. This gives a true representation of shape but not of area, and makes the regions towards the poles exaggerated in size. Compare PETERS' PROJECTION. ◎ 17c: from Gerhardus Mercator, the Latin version of the name of the Flemish-born German cartographer Gerhard Kremer (1512–94).

mercenary /'mɜːsənərɪ, -sənrɪ/ ▷ *adj* **1** *derog* excessively concerned with the desire for personal gain, especially money. **2** hired for money. ▷ *noun* (***mercenaries***) a soldier available for hire by a country or group. ◎ 14c meaning 'someone who works for hire': from Latin *mercenarius*, from *merces* reward or hire.

mercer /'mɜːsə(r)/ ▷ *noun, Brit* a dealer in textiles, especially expensive ones. ◎ 13c: from French *mercier.*

mercerize or **mercerise** /'mɜːsəraɪz/ ▷ *verb* (***mercerized, mercerizing***) to treat a material, especially cotton, with a substance which strengthens it and gives it a silky appearance. • **mercerized** *adj.* ◎ 19c: named after John Mercer (1791–1866), an English textile manufacturer who invented the process.

merchandise /'mɜːtʃəndaɪz, -daɪs/ ▷ *noun* commercial goods. ▷ *verb* (***merchandised, merchandising***) *tr & intr* **1** to trade; to buy and sell. **2** to plan the advertising or supplying of, or the selling campaign for (a product). • **merchandiser** *noun.* • **merchandising** *noun.* ◎ 13c: from French *marchandise*; related to MERCHANT.

merchant /'mɜːtʃənt/ ▷ *noun* **1** a trader, especially a wholesale trader. **2** *N Amer, especially US & Scottish* a shopkeeper. **3** *colloq, in compounds* someone who indulges in a specified activity, especially one that is generally not acceptable or appropriate □ *gossip merchant.* ▷ *adj* used for trade; commercial □ *merchant ship.* ▷ *verb* (***merchanted, merchanting***) *tr & intr* to trade; to deal in something. • **merchantable** *adj.* ◎ 13c: from French *marchand*, from Latin *mercari* to trade.

merchant bank ▷ *noun* a bank whose main activities are financing international trade, lending money to industry and assisting in company takeovers, etc. • **merchant banker** *noun.*

merchantman ▷ *noun* a ship that carries merchandise; a trading ship. Also called **merchant ship**.

merchant navy and **merchant service** ▷ *noun* the ships and crews that are employed in a country's commerce. Also called **mercantile marine**.

merciful /'mɜːsɪfəl/ ▷ *adj* showing or exercising mercy; forgiving. • **mercifully** *adverb* **1** luckily; thankfully. **2** in a merciful way. • **mercifulness** *noun.*

merciless /'mɜːsɪləs/ ▷ *adj* without mercy; cruel; pitiless. • **mercilessly** *adverb.* • **mercilessness** *noun.*

mercurial /mɜː'kjʊərɪəl/ ▷ *adj* **1** relating to or containing mercury. **2** said of someone or their personality, mood, etc: lively or active; tending to change suddenly and unpredictably. **3** belonging or relating to either the god or the planet Mercury. • **mercurially** *adverb.* ◎ 14c.

mercuric /mɜː'kjʊərɪk/ ▷ *adj, chem* containing or relating to divalent mercury.

mercurous /'mɜːkjʊrəs/ ▷ *adj, chem* containing or relating to monovalent mercury.

mercury /'mɜːkjʊrɪ/ ▷ *noun* **1** (symbol **Hg**, atomic number 80) a dense, silvery-white metallic element, and the only metal that is liquid at room temperature. Also called QUICKSILVER. **2** (**Mercury**) *astron* the closest planet to the Sun. ◎ 14c: from Latin *Mercurius*, the Roman god Mercury, god of merchandise, theft and eloquence, and messenger of the gods, probably from *merx* merchandise.

mercy /ˈmɜːsɪ/ ▷ *noun* (***mercies***) **1** kindness or forgiveness shown when punishment is possible or justified. **2** an act or circumstance in which these qualities are displayed, especially by God. **3** a tendency to be forgiving. **4** a piece of good luck; a welcome happening □ *grateful for small mercies.* **5** compassion for the unfortunate. ● **at the mercy of someone** or **something** wholly in their or its power; liable to be harmed by them or it. ◷ 12c: from French *merci*, from Latin *merces* reward.

mercy flight ▷ *noun* a flight by an aeroplane or helicopter taking eg a seriously ill or injured person to hospital, when other means of transport are impracticable or unavailable.

mercy killing see under EUTHANASIA

mere[1] /mɪə(r)/ ▷ *adj* nothing more than; no better, more important or useful than (a specified thing) □ *but he's a mere boy.* ● **merely** *adverb* simply; only. ◷ 16c: from Latin *merus* pure, undiluted.

mere[2] /ˈmɛrɪ/ ▷ *noun, old use, poetic* often in English place names: a lake or pool. ◷ Anglo-Saxon.

-mere /mɪə(r)/ ▷ *combining form, biol, forming nouns, denoting* part □ *centromere.* ● **-meric** /mɛrɪk/ *combining form, forming adjectives*. ◷ From Greek *meros* part.

meretricious /mɛrəˈtrɪʃəs/ ▷ *adj, formal* **1** bright or attractive on the surface, but of no real value. **2** false and insincere. **3** *old use* relating to, characteristic of, or worthy of a prostitute. ● **meretriciously** *adverb*. ● **meretriciousness** *noun* ◷ 17c: from Latin *meretricius*, from *meretrix* prostitute, from *mereri* to earn money.

merganser /mɜːˈgansə(r)/ ▷ *noun* (***mergansers*** or ***merganser***) a kind of large diving duck found in northern countries, with a long, hooked, serrated bill. ◷ 18c: Latin, from *mergus* diving bird + *anser* goose.

merge /mɜːdʒ/ ▷ *verb* (***merged***, ***merging***) *tr & intr* (*often* **merge with something**) to blend, combine or join with something else. ◷ 17c: from Latin *mergere* to plunge.

■ **merge into something** to become part of it and therefore impossible to distinguish from it.

merger ▷ *noun* a joining together, especially of business firms. Also called **amalgamation**.

meridian /məˈrɪdɪən/ ▷ *noun* **1** *geog* **a** an imaginary line on the Earth's surface passing through the poles at right angles to the equator; a line of longitude; **b** a representation of this, eg on a map. **2** *literary* the peak, eg of success. **3** in Chinese medicine: any of several lines or pathways through the body along which life energy flows. ● **meridional** *adj* **1** *technical* belonging or relating to, or along, a meridian. **2** *literary* belonging or relating to the south, especially to S Europe. ◷ 14c: from Latin *meridianus*, from *meridies* midday, from *medius* middle + *dies* day.

meringue /məˈraŋ/ ▷ *noun* (***meringues***) **1** a crisp, cooked mixture of sugar and egg-whites. **2** a cake or dessert made from this, often with a filling of cream. ◷ 18c: French.

merino /məˈriːnoʊ/ ▷ *noun* (***merinos***) **1** a type of sheep bred for its long, fine wool. Also called **merino sheep**. **2** this wool. **3** fine yarn or fabric made from its wool. Also *as adj* □ *merino shawl.* ◷ 18c: Spanish.

meristem /ˈmɛrɪstɛm/ ▷ *noun, bot* in a plant: a region of actively-dividing cells, mainly at the tips of shoots and roots. ◷ 19c: from Greek *meristos* divisible.

merit /ˈmɛrɪt/ ▷ *noun* **1** worth, excellence or praiseworthiness. **2** (*often* **merits**) a good point or quality □ *got the job on his own merits.* ▷ *verb* (***merited***, ***meriting***) to deserve; to be worthy of or entitled to something. ● **meritless** *adj*. ◷ 13c: from French *merite*, from Latin *meritum* reward.

meritocracy /mɛrɪˈtɒkrəsɪ/ ▷ *noun* (***meritocracies***) **1** a social system based on leadership by people of great talent or intelligence, rather than of wealth or noble birth. **2** government by this kind of group. **3** a group of people who have been selected because of their talents. ● **meritocrat** /ˈmɛrɪtəkrət/ *noun*. ● **meritocratic** *adj*. ◷ 1950s.

meritorious /mɛrɪˈtɔːrɪəs/ ▷ *adj, formal* deserving reward or praise; having merit. ● **meritoriously** *adverb*. ● **meritoriousness** *noun*. ◷ 15c.

merlin /ˈmɜːlɪn/ ▷ *noun* a small, dark-coloured falcon of the N hemisphere, with a black-striped tail. ◷ 14c: from French *esmerillon*.

merlon /ˈmɜːlən/ ▷ *noun, fortification* in a battlement: the projecting part of the parapet between two embrasures (see EMBRASURE sense 1). ◷ 18c: French, from Italian *merlo* battlement.

Merlot /ˈmɜːləʊ/ ▷ *noun* **1** an important variety of black grape use, often in blends with CABERNET SAUVIGNON, in winemaking. **2** a vine that this variety of grape grows on. **3** a red wine that is produced from, or mainly from, this variety of grape. ◷ 19c: French, meaning 'baby blackbird'.

mermaid /ˈmɜːmeɪd/ ▷ *noun, folklore* a mythical sea creature with a woman's head and upper body and a fish's tail. ◷ 14c: from Anglo-Saxon MERE[2] + MAID.

merman /ˈmɜːman/ ▷ *noun* the male equivalent of a MERMAID. ◷ 17c.

Merovingian /mɛroʊˈvɪndʒɪən/ ▷ *noun, historical* a member of a Frankish dynasty which ruled in Gaul and parts of present-day Germany, between about AD 500 and AD 751. ▷ *adj* relating to the Merovingians. ◷ 17c: from *Merovingi*, the Latin name for *Merovaeus* or *Merovech* king of the Salian Franks from AD 448–457, grandfather of Clovis I who reputedly founded the dynasty.

merry /ˈmɛrɪ/ ▷ *adj* (***merrier***, ***merriest***) **1** cheerful and lively. **2** *colloq* slightly drunk. **3** causing or full of laughter. ● **merrily** *adverb*. ● **merriment** *noun* gaiety with laughter and noise; hilarity. ● **merriness** *noun*. ● **make merry** *old use* to have fun; to celebrate. ● **play merry hell with someone** or **something** see under PLAY. ◷ Anglo-Saxon *myrige* in old sense 'pleasing or agreeable'.

merry-go-round ▷ *noun* **1** a fairground ride consisting of a revolving platform fitted with rising and falling seats in the form of horses or other figures. Sometimes called ROUNDABOUT. **2** a whirl of activity. **3** *colloq* a course of activity that tends to keep repeating itself. ◷ 18c.

merrymaking ▷ *noun* cheerful celebration; revelry. ● **merrymaker** *noun* someone who is having fun; a reveller.

mes- see MESO-

mesa /ˈmeɪsə/ ▷ *noun* (***mesas***) *geol* an isolated, flat-topped hill with at least one steep side or cliff. ◷ 18c: Spanish, meaning 'table', from Latin *mensa*.

mésalliance /mɛˈzalɪəns; *French* mezaljɑ̃s/ ▷ *noun* (***mésalliances***) *literary* a marriage to someone of lower social status. ◷ 18c: literally 'misalliance'.

mescal /mɛˈskal/ ▷ *noun* **1** a globe-shaped cactus of Mexico and the SW USA, with buttonlike tubercles (called **mescal buttons**) on its stems which have an intoxicating and hallucinogenic effect when chewed or made into an infusion and drunk. Also called **peyote**. **2** a colourless Mexican spirit made from the sap of this and certain other plants. ◷ 18c: from Aztec *mexcalli*.

mescaline or **mescalin** /ˈmɛskəliːn, -lɪn/ ▷ *noun* a hallucinogenic drug obtained from the MESCAL cactus. ◷ 19c.

mesclun /ˈmɛskluːn/ ▷ *noun, cookery* a mixed green salad of young leaves and shoots, eg of endive, rocket, chicory, fennel, etc, usually dressed in vinaigrette flavoured with herbs. ◷ 20c: French, from *mesclumo* mixture.

Mesdames see under MADAME

mesdames see under MADAM

Mesdemoiselles see under MADEMOISELLE

mesencephalon /mɛsɛn'sɛfəlɒn/ ▻ *noun, anatomy* the MIDBRAIN. ◷ 19c: Latin, from Greek *encephalon* brain.

mesentery /'mɛsəntərɪ, 'mɛz-/ ▻ *noun* (***mesenteries***) *anatomy* in humans and animals: the double layer of membrane on the inner surface of the body wall that serves to hold the stomach, small intestine, spleen, etc in place. ◷ 16c: from Latin *mesenterium*, from Greek *enteron* intestine.

mesh ▻ *noun* **1** netting, or a piece of netting made of wire or thread. **2** each of the openings between the threads of a net. **3** (*usually* **meshes**) a network. ▻ *verb* (***meshes, meshed, meshing***) **1** *intr, technical* said of the teeth on gear wheels: to engage. **2** *intr* (*often* **mesh with something**) to fit or work together. **3** *intr* to become entangled. **4** to catch something in a mesh. ● **be in mesh** *technical* said of the teeth on gear wheels: to be engaged; to be locked or fitted together. ◷ 16c: from Dutch *maesche*.

mesial /'miːzɪəl/ ▻ *adj, anatomy* said of a body part, etc: situated in or belonging to the middle of the body. ● **mesially** *adverb*. ◷ 19c: from Greek *mesos* middle.

mesmeric see under MESMERIZE

mesmerism /'mɛzmərɪzəm/ ▻ *noun* **1** a former term for HYPNOTISM. **2** a former method of HYPNOSIS, based on the ideas of Franz Anton Mesmer (1734–1815), an Austrian physician. ● **mesmerist** *noun* a hypnotist. ◷ 19c.

mesmerize or **mesmerise** /'mɛzməraɪz/ ▻ *verb* (***mesmerized, mesmerizing***) **1** to grip the attention of someone; to fascinate. **2** *old use* to hypnotize someone. ● **mesmeric** /mɛz'mɛrɪk/ *adj*. ● **mesmerizing** *adj*. ◷ 19c.

meso- /mɛsoʊ, mɛzoʊ, 'miːsoʊ, 'miːzoʊ/ or (before a vowel) **mes-** *combining form, denoting* middle. ◷ From Greek *mesos* middle.

Mesoamerican ▻ *adj* relating to or originating from Central America (or **Mesoamerica**), ie between N Mexico and Panama.

mesocephalic see CEPHALIC INDEX

mesoderm ▻ *noun, zool* in a multicellular animal with two or more layers of body tissue: the layer of cells in an embryo between the ECTODERM and the ENDODERM, which develops into the circulatory system, muscles and reproductive organs, etc. Also called **mesoblast**. ◷ 19c.

Mesolithic or **mesolithic** ▻ *adj* belonging or relating to the middle period of the Stone Age. See table at GEOLOGICAL TIME SCALE. ◷ 19c.

mesomorph /'mɛsoʊmɔːf/ ▻ *noun* a person of muscular body build, associated with an aggressive and extroverted personality type. Compare ECTOMORPH, ENDOMORPH. ● **mesomorphic** /-'mɔːfɪk/ or **mesomorphous** *adj* **1** relating to a mesomorph. **2** *chem* relating to an intermediate state of matter between solid and liquid. ◷ 1940s.

meson /'miːzɒn, 'mɛsɒn/ ▻ *noun, physics* any of a group of unstable, strongly-interacting, elementary particles, with a mass between that of an ELECTRON and a NUCLEON. ◷ 1930s: from earlier *mesotron*.

mesophyll ▻ *noun, bot* the internal tissue between the upper and lower epidermal surfaces of a plant leaf. ◷ 19c.

mesosphere ▻ *noun, meteorol* the layer of the Earth's atmosphere above the STRATOSPHERE and below the THERMOSPHERE, in which temperature rapidly decreases with height. ● **mesopheric** *adj*. ◷ 1950s: from MESO- + -SPHERE.

Mesozoic /mɛsoʊ'zoʊɪk/ ▻ *adj* **1** *geol* belonging or relating to an era of geological time. See table at GEOLOGICAL TIME SCALE. **2** relating to the rocks formed during this era. ◷ 19c: from Greek *zoion* animal + -IC.

mess ▻ *noun* **1** an untidy or dirty state ▫ ***The kitchen's in a mess.*** **2** a state of disorder or confusion ▫ ***The accounts are in a mess.*** **3** a badly damaged state. **4** something or someone in a damaged, disordered or confused state ▫ ***My hair is a mess.*** **5** *colloq* animal faeces ▫ ***dog mess.*** **6** a communal dining room, especially in the armed forces ▫ ***the sergeants' mess.*** **7** *old use* a portion of any pulpy food ▫ ***a mess of potage.*** ▻ *verb* (***messes, messed, messing***) **1** (*often* **mess something up**) to put or get it into an untidy, dirty, confused or damaged state; to spoil ▫ ***Don't mess your clean shirt*** ▫ ***That really messed up our plans.*** **2** *intr* said of soldiers, etc: to eat, or live, together. ● **no messing** *colloq* **1** without difficulty ▫ ***did the job in ten minutes and no messing.*** **2** honestly; truthfully ▫ ***It's the truth, no messing.*** ◷ 13c in *noun* sense 7: French *mes* dish.

■ **mess about** or **around** *colloq* to behave in an annoyingly foolish way; to potter or tinker.

■ **mess about** or **around with someone** *colloq* **1** to flirt or have sexual intercourse with someone. **2** to defy and provoke someone.

■ **mess about** or **around with something** to play or tinker with something.

■ **mess someone about** or **around** to treat them roughly, badly or unfairly.

■ **mess with something** to meddle, tinker or interfere in it.

■ **mess with someone** *colloq* to become involved in argument or conflict with them; to cause them trouble or aggravation.

message /'mɛsɪdʒ/ ▻ *noun* **1** a spoken or written communication sent from one person to another. **2** the instructive principle contained within a story, poem, religious teaching, work of art, etc. **3** (*usually* **messages**) *chiefly Scottish* an errand; household shopping ▫ ***Just nipping out for the messages.*** ▻ *verb* (***messaged, messaging***) to transmit something by signalling, etc; to send it as a message. ● **get the message** *colloq* to understand. ◷ 13c: French, from Latin *mittere* to send.

messenger /'mɛsɪndʒə(r)/ ▻ *noun* **1** someone who carries communications between people; a courier. **2** someone who performs errands. ◷ 13c: from French *messager*; see MESSAGE.

messenger RNA ▻ *noun, biochem* (abbreviation **mRNA**) a single-stranded molecule of RNA that transports coded genetic instructions for the manufacture of proteins from the DNA in the nucleus to the RIBOSOMES in the cytoplasm.

Messiah /mə'saɪə/ ▻ *noun* (*usually* **the Messiah**) **1** *Christianity* Jesus Christ. **2** *Judaism* the king of the Jews still to be sent by God to free his people and restore Israel. **3** someone who sets a country or a people free. ● **Messianic** /mɛsɪ'anɪk/ *adj* **1** belonging or relating to, or associated with, a Messiah. **2** relating to any popular or inspirational leader, especially a liberator. ● **Messianism** /mə'saɪənɪzəm/ *noun, relig* belief in a Messiah, specifically applied to an expression of Judaism which anticipates a new and perfected age. ◷ 14c from French *Messie*, from Hebrew *mashiah* anointed.

Messieurs *plural of* MONSIEUR

Messrs *plural of* MR

messy /'mɛsɪ/ ▻ *adj* (***messier, messiest***) **1** involving or making dirt or mess. **2** confused, untidy. ● **messily** *adverb*. ● **messiness** *noun*.

mestizo /mɛ'stiːzoʊ/ and **mestiza** /-zə/ ▻ *noun* (***mestizos*** or ***mestizas***) a male and female respectively of mixed Spanish-American and Native American parentage. ◷ 16c: Spanish, from Latin *mixtus* mixed.

the Met ▻ *noun, colloq* **1** the London Metropolitan Police Force. **2** the Metropolitan Opera, New York. **3** *Brit* (*also* **the Met Office**) the Meteorological Office, the government department that monitors national weather conditions and produces weather forecasts.

met *past tense, past participle of* MEET[1]

meta- /'mɛtə/ or (before a vowel) **met-** ▻ *combining form, denoting* **1** a change ▫ *metabolism*. **2** an area of study related to another subject of study, but going beyond it in some way ▫ *metalinguistics*. **3** a position behind or beyond something ▫ *metacarpal*. **4** *chem* **a** a derivative of, or an isomer or polymer of, a specified substance ▫ *metaldehyde*; **b** an acid or hydroxide derived from the ORTHO- (sense 4b) form of a specified substance by loss of water molecules; **c** a benzene substitution product in which the substituted atoms or groups are attached to two carbon atoms which are themselves separated by one carbon atom ▫ . ⓒ From Greek *meta* among, with, beside or after.

metabolic /mɛtə'bɒlɪk/ ▻ *adj* **1** relating to an organism's metabolism. **2** exhibiting metamorphosis. • **metabolically** *adverb*.

metabolism /mə'tabəlɪzəm/ ▻ *noun, biochem* the sum of all the chemical reactions that occur within the cells of a living organism, including both ANABOLISM and CATABOLISM of complex organic compounds. ⓒ Late 19c: from Greek *metabole* change, from *ballein* to throw.

metabolite /mə'tabəlaɪt/ ▻ *noun, biochem* a molecule that participates in the biochemical reactions that take place in the cells of living organisms. ⓒ 19c: from METABOLISM.

metabolize or **metabolise** /mə'tabəlaɪz/ ▻ *verb* (***metabolized***, ***metabolizing***) *tr & intr, biochem* to break down complex organic compounds into simpler molecules. ⓒ 19c: from METABOLISM.

metacarpus /mɛtə'kɑːpəs/ ▻ *noun* (***metacarpi*** /-paɪ/) *anatomy* **1** the set of five bones (**metacarpal bones**) in the human hand between the wrist and the knuckles, or in the forefoot in other vertebrates. **2** the part of the hand that contains these. See also CARPAL. Compare METATARSUS. • **metacarpal** *adj*. ⓒ 19c: Latin, from META- + Greek *karpos* wrist.

metal /'mɛtəl/ ▻ *noun* **1** any of a class of chemical elements with certain shared characteristic properties, most being shiny, malleable, ductile and good conductors of heat and electricity, and all (except MERCURY) being solid at room temperature. See also ALLOY, ORE. **2** ROAD METAL. **3** (**metals**) the rails of a railway. ▻ *adj* made of, or mainly of, metal. ▻ *verb* (***metalled***, ***metalling***; *US* ***metaled***, ***metaling***) **1** to fit or cover something with metal. **2** to make or mend (a road) with small, broken stones. • **metallic** /mɛ'talɪk, mə-/ *adj* **1** made of metal. **2** characteristic of metal, eg in sound or appearance. • **metallically** *adverb*. See also METTLE. ⓒ 13c: French, from Greek *metallon* mine.

metalanguage ▻ *noun* a language or system of symbols used to discuss another language or symbolic system. Compare OBJECT LANGUAGE sense 1.

metal detector ▻ *noun* an instrument used for detecting buried metal objects or, in industrial production, one for detecting stray metal parts embedded in food products.

metallize or **metallise** /mɛtə'laɪz/ ▻ *verb* (***metallized***, ***metallizing***; *US* ***metalized***, ***metalizing***) **1** to give a metallic appearance to something. **2** to apply a thin coating of metal to (eg glass or plastic). • **metallization** *noun*. ⓒ 16c.

metalloid /mɛtə'lɔɪd/ ▻ *noun, chem* a chemical element that has both metallic and non-metallic properties, eg silicon and arsenic. ⓒ 19c.

metallurgy /mɛ'talədʒɪ, 'mɛtəlɜːdʒɪ/ ▻ *noun* the scientific study of the nature and properties of metals and their extraction from the ground. • **metallurgic** /mɛtə'lɜːdʒɪk/ or **metallurgical** *adj*. • **metallurgist** /mɛ'talədʒɪst/ *noun*. ⓒ 18c: from Latin *metallurgia*, from Greek *metallourgos* mining.

metalwork ▻ *noun* **1** the craft, process or practice of shaping metal and making items of metal. **2** articles made of metal. • **metalworker** *noun*.

metamorphic /mɛtə'mɔːfɪk/ ▻ *adj* **1** relating to METAMORPHOSIS. **2** *geol* said of any of a group of rocks: formed by METAMORPHISM. Compare IGNEOUS, SEDIMENTARY.

metamorphism *noun, geol* any changes in the structure or composition of a pre-existing rock resulting from the effects of intense heat or pressure beneath the Earth's surface or both.

metamorphose /mɛtə'mɔːfoʊz/ ▻ *verb* (***metamorphosed***, ***metamorphosing***) *tr & intr* to undergo or cause something to undergo metamorphosis.

metamorphosis /mɛtə'mɔːfəsɪs, mɛtəmɔː'foʊsɪs/ ▻ *noun* (***metamorphoses*** /-siːz/) **1** a change of form, appearance, character, etc; a transformation. **2** *biol* the change of physical form that occurs during the development into adulthood of some creatures, eg butterflies. ⓒ 16c: from META- + Greek *morphe* form + -OSIS.

metaphase ▻ *noun, genetics* in mitosis and meiosis: the second phase during which the membrane surrounding the nucleus breaks down. ⓒ 19c.

metaphor /'mɛtəfɔː(r), -fə(r)/ ▻ *noun* **1** an expression in which the person, action or thing referred to is described as if it really were what it merely resembles, eg a rejection described as 'a slap in the face', or a ferocious person as 'a tiger'. See also FIGURE OF SPEECH, MIXED METAPHOR. **2** such expressions in general. • **metaphorical** /mɛtə'fɔːrɪkəl/ *adj*. • **metaphorically** *adverb*. ⓒ 16c: from Greek *metaphora*, from META- + *pherein* to carry.

metaphysical ▻ *adj* **1** belonging or relating to METAPHYSICS. **2** abstract. **3** supernatural. **4** (*also* **Metaphysical**) said of a poet: whose work is seen as belonging to a style termed METAPHYSICAL POETRY. ▻ *noun* a poet writing in this style ▫ *the Metaphysicals*. • **metaphysically** *adverb* **1** in a metaphysical way. **2** in a metaphysical sense.

metaphysical painting ▻ *noun* a modern art movement that flourished in Italy c.1911–18 and was an important precursor of SURREALISM, founded by De Chirico and typified by his mysterious empty landscapes inhabited by tailors' dummies and classical busts casting threatening shadows.

metaphysical poetry ▻ *noun* a term applied to 17c English poetry, eg work by Donne and Marvell, which makes use of elaborate images, intricate word-play, paradox, flexible metre and rhythm, etc to express intense feelings and complex ideas. ⓒ 17c: the term was first applied in a derogatory sense by Dryden and Dr Johnson.

metaphysics /mɛtə'fɪzɪks/ ▻ *singular noun* **1** the branch of philosophy dealing with the nature of existence and the basic principles of truth and knowledge. **2** *colloq* any type of abstract discussion, writing or thinking. ⓒ 16c: from Greek *ta meta ta physika*, literally 'the things coming after natural science', from the order in which subjects are dealt with in Aristotle's writings.

metapsychology ▻ *noun* theories and theorizing on psychological matters which cannot be proved or disproved by experiment or reasoning. • **metapsychological** *adj*. ⓒ Early 20c.

metastasis /mɛ'tastəsɪs/ ▻ *noun* (***metastases*** /-siːz/) *medicine* **1** the spread of a disease, especially of a malignant tumour, from one part of the body to another via the bloodstream or lymphatic system, or across a body cavity. **2** a secondary tumour resulting from the spread of a malignant disease in this way. ⓒ 17c; 16c in the sense 'transition' or 'rapid removal from one place to another': Greek, meaning 'change of place'.

metastasize or **metastasise** /mɛˈtastəsaɪz/ ▻ *verb* (***metastasized***, ***metastasizing***) *intr* said of a disease, especially a cancerous tumour: to spread to another part of the body. ◷ Early 20c.

metatarsus /mɛtəˈtɑːsəs/ ▻ *noun* (***metatarsi*** /-saɪ/) *anatomy* **1** the set of five long bones (**metatarsal bones**) in the human foot between the ankle and the toes, or in the hindfoot of other vertebrates. **2** the part of the foot that contains these. See also TARSUS. Compare METACARPUS. • **metatarsal** *adj*. ◷ 17c: from META- + Greek *tarsos* instep.

metatheory ▻ *noun* **1** *loosely* any theory concerning another theory. **2** *logic* the investigation of the various properties of a formal language, eg whether the language is consistent and complete. ◷ 20c.

metathesis /mɛˈtaθəsɪs/ ▻ *noun, linguistics* alteration of the normal order of sounds or letters in a word, eg the word 'girn' (see GIRNER) is an instance of **r-metathesis**, where the 'i' and the 'r' of 'grin' have swapped places. ◷ 17c: from Greek META- + THESIS.

metazoan /mɛtəˈzoʊən/ ▻ *noun, zool* any multicellular animal that has specialized differentiated body tissues. Compare PROTOZOAN. ▻ *adj* belonging or relating to the Metazoa. ◷ 19c: Latin, from META- + Greek *zoion* animal.

mete /miːt/ ▻ *verb* (***meted***, ***meting***) *rather formal* (*now always* **mete something out** or **mete out something**) to give out or dispense something, especially punishment. ◷ Anglo-Saxon *metan* in the sense 'to measure'.

meteor /ˈmiːtɪə(r)/ ▻ *noun, astron* the streak of light seen when a meteoroid enters into the Earth's atmosphere, where it burns up as a result of friction. Also called SHOOTING STAR. See also METEOROID, METEOR SHOWER, Compare METEORITE. ◷ 15c: from Latin *meteorum*, from Greek *meteoron* a thing in the air or up high.

meteoric /miːtɪˈɒrɪk/ ▻ *adj* **1** belonging or relating to meteors. **2 a** said of success, etc: very rapid; very short-lived; **b** like a meteor in terms of brilliance, speed, transience, etc. • **meteorically** *adverb*.

meteorite /ˈmiːtɪəraɪt/ ▻ *noun, astron* the remains of a METEOROID which has survived burn-up in its passage through the Earth's atmosphere as a METEOR. • **meteoritic** /-ˈrɪtɪk/ *adj*. ◷ 19c.

meteoroid /ˈmiːtɪərɔɪd/ ▻ *noun, astron* in interplanetary space: a small, moving, solid object or dust particle, which becomes visible as a METEORITE or a METEOR if enters the Earth's atmosphere. ◷ 19c.

meteorology /miːtɪəˈrɒlədʒɪ/ ▻ *noun* the scientific study of weather and climate over a relatively short period. Compare CLIMATOLOGY. • **meteorological** *adj*. • **meteorologically** *adverb*. • **meteorologist** *noun*. ◷ 17c.

meteor shower ▻ *noun, astron* a display which occurs when the Earth passes through a trail of dust left by a comet in interplanetary space and tens of meteors per hour can be seen emanating from the same part of the sky.

meter[1] /ˈmiːtə(r)/ ▻ *noun* **1** an instrument for measuring and recording, especially quantities of electricity, gas, water, etc used. **2** a parking-meter. ▻ *verb* (***metered***, ***metering***) to measure and record (eg electricity) using a meter. ◷ 19c: first used in the sense 'gas-meter'; see -METER and also METE.

meter[2] the *US* spelling of METRE[1], METRE[2]

-meter ▻ *combining form, forming nouns, denoting* **1** an instrument for measuring □ ***thermometer***. **2** a line of poetry with a specified number of units of stress, or feet (see FOOT sense 8) □ ***pentameter***. ◷ From Greek *metron* a measure.

methadone /ˈmɛθədoʊn/ ▻ *noun* a drug similar to MORPHINE, but less addictive, used as a painkiller and as a heroin substitute for drug-addicts. ◷ 1940s: from di*methy*lamino-*d*iphenyl-petan*one*.

methamphetamine /mɛθamˈfɛtəmiːn/ ▻ *noun* a methyl derivative of AMPHETAMINE with rapid and long-lasting action, used as a stimulant. Also (*colloq*) called ICE (*noun* 2).

methanal /ˈmɛθənal/ ▻ *noun, chem* FORMALDEHYDE.

methane /ˈmiːθeɪn/ ▻ *noun, chem* (formula CH_4) a colourless odourless flammable gas, used in the manufacture of organic chemicals and hydrogen, and as a cooking and heating fuel (in the form of NATURAL GAS of which it is the main component), and which occurs naturally as MARSH GAS and as FIREDAMP. ◷ 19c.

methanoic acid see under FORMIC ACID

methanol /ˈmɛθənɒl/ ▻ *noun, chem* (formula CH_3OH) a colourless flammable toxic liquid used as a solvent and antifreeze, and which can be catalytically converted to petrol. Also called **methyl** /ˈmiːθaɪl, ˈmɛθɪl/ **alcohol**, **wood alcohol**. ◷ Late 19c: from METHANE + -OL; see also etymology at METHYLENE BLUE.

methinks /mɪˈθɪŋks/ ▻ *verb* (***methought*** /mɪˈθɔːt/) *old use* or *humorous* it seems to me; it seems to me that … ◷ Anglo-Saxon *me thyncth*, from *thyncan* to seem.

methionine /mɛˈθaɪəniːn/ ▻ *noun, biochem* an essential amino acid found in proteins. ◷ 1920s.

method /ˈmɛθəd/ ▻ *noun* **1** a way of doing something, especially an ordered set of procedures or an orderly system. **2** good planning; efficient organization. **3** (*often* **methods**) a technique used in a particular activity □ ***farming methods***. **4** (**Method** or **the method**) see under METHOD ACTING. • **methodical** /məˈθɒdɪkəl/ or (*now rarely*) **methodic** *adj* efficient and orderly; done in an orderly or systematic way. • **methodically** *adverb*. • **methodicalness** *noun*. • **method in one's madness** reason or good sense underlying what seems an odd or chaotic situation or procedure. ◷ 19c: referring to Shakespeare's *Hamlet* (II ii) 'Though this be madness, yet there is method in it'. ◷ 16c: from French *methode* or Latin *methodus*, from Greek *methodos*.

method acting ▻ *noun, theat* a technique of acting that involves the actor 'living' a part, tapping into the character's inner motivations, rather than merely giving a technical performance. Also called **Method** or **the method**. Also *as adj* □ ***DeNiro is one of Hollywood's greatest Method actors***. ◷ 1920s: a theory and practice of acting introduced by Konstantin Stanislavsky (1863–1938), Russian actor and director.

Methodist /ˈmɛθədɪst/ *Christianity* ▻ *noun* **1** a member of the Methodist Church, a denomination founded by John Wesley in 1779 as an evangelical movement within the Church of England, but which became a separate nonconformist body in 1795. **2** a supporter of Methodism. ▻ *adj* belonging or relating to Methodism. See also WESLEYAN. • **Methodism** *noun*. ◷ 16c as *methodist* in noun sense 'someone who observes method'; 18c in current sense, originally applied in 1729 to John Wesley's religious society of Oxford students, because of the emphasis Wesley put on the methodical approach to prayer and Bible study, etc.

methodology /məθəˈdɒlədʒɪ/ ▻ *noun* (***methodologies***) **1** the system of methods and principles used in a particular activity, science, etc. **2** the study of method and procedure. • **methodological** *adj*. • **methodologically** *adverb*. ◷ 19c: from French *methodologie*; see METHOD + -LOGY.

methought *past tense of* METHINKS

meths ▻ *singular noun, colloq, especially Brit* methylated spirits.

methuselah /mɪˈθuːzələ/ ▻ *noun* **1** a size of wine bottle that contains eight times as much as a standard 75cl bottle. **2** a very old person or thing. ◎ 14c in sense 2; 1930s in sense 1: named after Methuselah, a biblical patriarch reputed (see Genesis 5.27) to have lived to the age of 969.

methyl alcohol see under METHANOL

methylate /ˈmɛθɪleɪt/ ▷ *verb* (***methylated, methylating***) to mix or impregnate something with methanol. ◎ 19c.

methylated spirits or **methylated spirit** ▷ *singular noun* ethanol with small quantities of methanol and pyridine and often blue or purple dye added, to make it virtually undrinkable so that it can be sold without excise duty for use as a fuel and solvent.

methylene blue ▷ *noun, chem* a blue dye used as a pH indicator, as a stain in the preparation of slides of tissue specimens and as a dye for textiles. ◎ 19c: from *methylene* the hypothetical compound CH_2, from French *méthylène* methyl alcohol or METHANOL, from Greek *methu* wine + *hyle* wood.

methyl group /ˈmiːθaɪl —, ˈmɛθɪl —/ ▷ *noun, chem* in organic chemical compounds: the CH_3 group, eg METHYL ALCOHOL.

meticulous /məˈtɪkjʊləs/ ▷ *adj* paying, or showing, very careful attention to detail; scrupulously careful. • **meticulously** *adverb*. • **meticulousness** *noun*. ◎ 19c: from Latin *meticulosus* frightened.

métier /ˈmɛtɪeɪ; *French* metje/ ▷ *noun* **1** a person's business or line of work. **2** the field or subject, etc in which one is especially skilled; one's forte. ◎ 18c: French, from Latin *ministerium* work or service.

the Met Office see under THE MET

metol or **Metol** /ˈmiːtɒl/ ▷ *noun* a water-soluble colourless substance, used especially as the basis of a photographic developer. ◎ 19c: German, coined by the inventor.

metonymy /mɪˈtɒnɪmɪ/ ▷ *noun* (***metonymies***) *linguistics* the use of a word referring to an element or attribute of something to mean the thing itself, eg *the bottle* for 'the drinking of alcohol' or *the Crown* for 'the sovereign'. • **metonymic** /mɛtəˈnɪmɪk/ or **metonymical** *adj*. ◎ 16c: from Greek *metonymia*, literally 'change of name'.

metope /ˈmɛtəpɪ, ˈmɛtoʊp/ ▷ *noun, archit* in the frieze of a Doric entablature: a slab or tablet of plain or sculptured marble between the TRIGLYPH. ◎ 16c: from Greek, from *meta* between + *ope* an opening for the end of a beam.

metre[1] or (*US*) **meter** /ˈmiːtə(r)/ ▷ *noun* (abbreviation **m**) in the SI system: the principal unit of length, equal to 39.37in or 1.094yd. ◎ 18c: from French *mètre*, from Greek *metron* a measure.

metre[2] or (*US*) **meter** /ˈmiːtə(r)/ ▷ *noun* **1** *poetry* the arrangement of words and syllables, or feet (see FOOT sense 8), in a rhythmic pattern according to their length and stress; a particular pattern or scheme. **2** *music* **a** the basic pattern or structure of beats; **b** tempo. ◎ Anglo-Saxon *meter*, from Latin *metrum*, from Greek *metron* a measure.

metre-kilogram-second system ▷ *noun* (abbreviation **mks system** or **MKS system**) a system of scientific measurement that uses the metre, kilogram and second as its units of length, mass and time respectively. See also SI SYSTEM.

metric[1] /ˈmɛtrɪk/ ▷ *adj* relating to or based on the METRE[1] or the metric system. • **metrically** *adverb*. ◎ 19c: from French *métrique*, from *mètre* METRE[1].

metric[2] see METRICAL

-metric /ˈmɛtrik/ and **-metrical** ▷ *combining form, forming adjectives, denoting* scientific measurement □ *thermometric* □ *tachometrical*. ◎ See -METER.

metrical or **metric** ▷ *adj, technical* **1** in or relating to verse as distinct from prose. **2** belonging or relating to measurement. • **metrically** *adverb*. ◎ 15c: from Latin *metricus*; see METRE[2].

metricate /ˈmɛtrɪkeɪt/ ▷ *verb* (***metricated, metricating***) *tr & intr* to convert (a non-metric measurement, system, etc) to a metric one using units of the metric system. • **metrication** *noun*. Compare DECIMALIZE. ◎ 1960s.

metric system ▷ *noun* a standard system of measurement, based on DECIMAL units, in which each successive multiple of a unit is 10 times larger than the one before it. Technical equivalent SI. See table at SI UNITS.

metro /ˈmɛtroʊ/ ▷ *noun* (***metros***) an urban railway system, usually one that is mostly underground, especially and originally the **Métro**, the system in Paris. Compare THE UNDERGROUND, TUBE. ◎ Early 20c: from French *métro*, abbreviation of *chemin de fer métropolitain* metropolitan railway.

metronome /ˈmɛtrənoʊm/ ▷ *noun* a device that indicates musical tempo by means of a ticking pendulum that can be set to move at different speeds. • **metronomic** /-ˈnɒmɪk/ *adj* ◎ 19c: from Greek *metron* measure + *nomos* rule or law.

metronymic /mɛtrəˈnɪmɪk/ ▷ *adj* said of a name: derived from the name of one's mother or of another female ancestor. ▷ *noun* a name derived in this way. Compare PATRONYMIC. ◎ 19c: from Greek *meter* mother + *onoma* name.

metropolis /məˈtrɒpəlɪs/ ▷ *noun* (***metropolises*** /-lɪsɪz/) a large city, especially the capital city of a nation or region. ◎ 16c: Latin, from Greek, from *meter* mother + *polis* city.

metropolitan /mɛtrəˈpɒlɪtən/ ▷ *adj* **1** belonging or relating to, typical of, or situated in, a large city. **2** belonging or referring to a country's mainland, as opposed to its overseas territories. **3** belonging or relating to the mother church, or chief see, of a province. ▷ *noun* **1** *Christianity* in the Catholic and Orthodox Churches: a bishop, usually an archbishop, with authority over all the bishops in a province. **2** an inhabitant of a metropolis. ◎ 16c.

metropolitan county ▷ *noun* in English local government: any of six counties that cover the major, heavily-populated, metropolitan regions excluding Greater London (eg Merseyside, West Midlands, etc. They were set up in 1974 under local government reorganization and their councils were abolished in 1986.

-metry /mɛtrɪ/ ▷ *combining form, forming nouns, denoting* **1** a science involving measurement □ *geometry*. **2** a process of measuring. ◎ From Greek *-metria*, from *metron* a measure.

metteur-en-scène /*French* mɛtœːʀ ɑ̃ sɛn/ ▷ *noun, cinematog* someone, usually the film's director, whose job is to create the MISE-EN-SCÈNE and to oversee the editing. The term is sometimes used disparagingly of a director who is considered to lack originality. Compare AUTEUR.

mettle /ˈmɛtəl/ ▷ *noun, literary* **1** courage, determination and endurance. **2** character; personal qualities □ *show one's mettle*. • **put someone on their mettle** *literary* to encourage or force them to make their best effort. ◎ 16c: originally a variant of METAL.

mettlesome ▷ *adj, literary* said especially of horses: lively; high-spirited. ◎ 17c: METTLE + -SOME[1].

meunière /mɜːniːɛə(r)/ ▷ *adj* said of a method of cooking fish: prepared by lightly flouring the fish and frying it gently in butter and serving it with a small portion of butter, lemon juice and parsley □ *sole meunière*. ◎ 19c: French, from *à la meunière* in the manner of the miller's wife, so called because of the dusting of flour over the fish.

MeV ▷ *abbreviation, physics* mega-electron-volt or -volts.

mew[1] /mjuː/ ▻ *verb* (***mewed, mewing***) *intr* to make the cry of a cat; to MIAOW. ▻ *noun* a cat's cry. ⓒ 16c: imitating the sound.

mew[2] /mjuː/ ▻ *noun* a seagull. ⓒ Anglo-Saxon *mæw*.

mewl /mjuːl/ ▻ *verb* (***mewled, mewling***) *intr* said especially of a child: to cry feebly; to make a whimpering noise. ⓒ 17c: imitating the sound.

mews /mjuːs, mjuːz/ ▻ *singular noun* (***mews*** or ***mewses***) **1** a set of stables around a yard or square, especially one converted into residential accommodation or garages. **2** (**Mews**) used in street names. ⓒ 14c: plural of *mew* a cage for moulting hawks (from French *muer* to moult), originally referring to the cages for royal hawks and later the royal stables, at Charing Cross, London.

MEX ▻ *abbreviation, IVR* Mexico.

Mex. ▻ *abbreviation* **1** Mexican. **2** Mexico.

Mexican /ˈmɛksɪkən/ ▻ *adj* belonging or relating to Mexico, a federal republic in southern N America, its inhabitants, or the Nahuatl language. ▻ *noun* **1** a citizen or inhabitant of, or person born in, Mexico. **2** the AZTEC language.

Mexican wave ▻ *noun* a rippling wave effect that passes right around a stadium full of spectators, achieved when all the spectators in turn stand up with their arms raised and then sit down again with their arms lowered. ⓒ 1980s: so called because it was first publicized at the World Cup football competition in Mexico in 1986.

MEZ ▻ *abbreviation*: *Mitteleuropäische Zeit* (German), Central European Time.

mezuzah /məˈzʊzə/ ▻ *noun* (*plural* ***mezuzot, mezuzoth*** /-soʊt/ or ***mezuzahs***) *Judaism* a cylindrical box containing a parchment inscribed with religious texts from Deuteronomy, that is attached to the doorposts of some Jewish houses as a declaration of faith. ⓒ 17c: Hebrew, meaning 'doorpost'.

mezzanine /ˈmɛzəniːn, ˈmɛtsəniːn, / ▻ *noun* (***mezzanines***) **1** *archit* in a building: a small storey between two main floors, usually the ground and first floors. **2** *theat* **a** a room or floor below the stage; **b** *N Amer* the first balcony; the circle. Also *as adj* □ *mezzanine floor.* ⓒ 18c: French, from Italian *mezzanino*, from *mezzano* middle.

mezzanine finance and **mezzanine funding** ▻ *noun, business* funding to cover an intermediate stage in a takeover, etc, consisting of one or more unsecured high-interest loans.

mezzo /ˈmɛtsoʊ/ ▻ *adverb, music* moderately, quite or rather, as in **mezzo-forte** rather loud, and **mezzo-piano** rather soft. ⓒ 19c: Italian, literally 'half'.

mezzo-soprano ▻ *noun, music* **1** a singing voice with a range between soprano and contralto. **2** a singer with this kind of voice. **3** a musical part for this kind of voice.

mezzotint /ˈmɛtsoʊtɪnt/ ▻ *noun, chiefly historical* **1** a method of engraving a metal plate, especially a copper plate, by polishing and scraping to produce areas of light and shade, rendered obsolete by photographic reproduction in the late 19c. **2** a print made from a plate engraved in this way. ▻ *verb tr* to engrave (a plate) using this method. ⓒ 17c as *mezzotinto*: Italian, from *mezzo* half + *tinto* shade.

MF ▻ *abbreviation* **1** said of paper: machine finished. **2** *radio* medium frequency. **3** multi-frequency.

mf ▻ *abbreviation, music* mezzo-forte.

mfrs ▻ *abbreviation* manufacturers.

MG ▻ *abbreviation* Morris Garages, the original makers of a popular type of British sports car.

Mg ▻ *symbol, chem* magnesium.

mg ▻ *abbreviation* milligram or milligrams.

MGlam ▻ *abbreviation, Welsh county* Mid Glamorgan.

MGM ▻ *abbreviation* Metro-Goldwyn-Mayer, an American film production company.

Mgr ▻ *abbreviation* **1** manager. **2** Monseigneur. **3** (*also* **Monsig.**) Monsignor.

MHR ▻ *abbreviation* in the USA, Australia and New Zealand: Member of the House of Representatives.

MHz ▻ *abbreviation* megahertz.

MI ▻ *abbreviation* **1** *US state* Michigan. Also written **Mich**. **2** Military Intelligence.

mi see ME[2]

MI5 /ɛmaɪ ˈfaɪv/ ▻ *abbreviation, Brit* Military Intelligence Section 5, the popular name for what is now officially called the **Security Services**, the government agency concerned with state security.

MI6 /ɛm aɪ ˈsɪks/ ▻ *abbreviation, Brit* Military Intelligence Section 6, the popular name for what is now officially called the **Secret Intelligence Services** (abbreviation **SIS**), the government agency concerned with espionage. Compare CIA.

miaow or **meow** /mɪˈaʊ/ ▻ *verb* (***miaowed, miaowing; meowed, meowing***) *intr* to make the cry of a cat. ▻ *noun* a cat's cry. Also called MEW[1]. Compare PURR. ⓒ 17c as *miau*: imitating the sound.

miasma /mɪˈazmə, maɪˈazmə/ ▻ *noun* (***miasmata*** /-mətə/ or ***miasmas***) *literary* **1** a thick foul-smelling vapour, especially one given off by swamps, marshes, etc. **2** an evil influence or atmosphere. • **miasmal** *adj* containing miasma. • **miasmatic** or **miasmic** *adj* relating to or typical of miasma. ⓒ 17c: Latin, from Greek, meaning 'pollution'.

Mic. ▻ *abbreviation* Book of the Bible: Micah. See table at BIBLE.

mic /maɪk/ a short form of MICROPHONE.

mica /ˈmaɪkə/ ▻ *noun* (***micas***) *geol* any of a group of silicate minerals that split easily into thin flexible sheets and are used as electrical insulators, DIELECTRICS, etc because they are poor conductors of heat and electricity. See also ISINGLASS. ⓒ 18c: from Latin *mica* crumb.

mice *plural of* MOUSE

Mich. ▻ *abbreviation* **1** Michaelmas. **2** Michaelmas term. **3** see MI 1.

Michaelmas /ˈmɪkəlməs/ ▻ *noun, Christianity* a festival in honour of St Michael the archangel, held on 29 September. ⓒ Anglo-Saxon *Sanct Michaeles mæsse*; see MASS[2].

Michaelmas daisy ▻ *noun* a garden plant of the aster family with purple, pink or white flowers that bloom in autumn.

Michaelmas term ▻ *noun* at Oxford, Cambridge and some other universities, etc: the autumn term.

Michelangelo virus ▻ *noun, computing* a virus set to destroy data on a computer's hard disk when the system date reads 6 March in any year. ⓒ 1980s: named after the Italian sculptor, painter and architect, Michelangelo Buonarroti (1475–1564) whose birthday was 6 March.

mick ▻ *noun, offensive slang* **1** an Irishman. **2** *especially Austral* a Roman Catholic. ⓒ 19c: pet form of the name *Michael*, common in Ireland.

mickey /ˈmɪkɪ/ ▻ *noun*. • **take the mickey** or **take the mickey out of someone** *colloq* to tease or make fun of them. ⓒ 1950s.

Mickey Finn ▻ *noun* (***Mickey Finns***) *slang* a drink, especially an alcoholic one, with a drug or laxative, etc added secretly to it in order to knock out or debilitate the person who drinks it. Also shortened to **Mickey**. ⓒ 1920s.

Mickey-Mouse ▻ *adj, derog, colloq* **1** second-rate; of the nature of a cheap imitation. **2** ridiculously simple or unprofessional □ *Here's the Mickey-Mouse version of the manual.* ⓘ 1930s: from the name of a cartoon character created in 1928 by US artist and film producer Walt Disney (1901–66); the use of this term derives from the Mickey Mouse wristwatches and other marketing gimmicks produced since the 1940s.

mickle /'mɪkəl/ or **muckle** /'mʌkəl/ *archaic or N Eng dialect & Scots* ▻ *adj* much or great. ▻ *adverb* much. ▻ *noun* a great quantity. • **many a mickle makes a muckle** every little helps. ⓘ Anglo-Saxon *micel.*

MICR ▻ *abbreviation, computing* magnetic ink character recognition.

micro /'maɪkroʊ/ ▻ *noun* (***micros***) *colloq* **1** a microcomputer or microprocessor. **2** a microwave oven.

micro- /'maɪkroʊ, 'maɪkrə, maɪ'krɒ/ or (sometimes before a vowel) **micr-** ▻ *combining form, denoting* **1** very small □ *microchip.* **2** one millionth part; 10^{-6} (symbol μ) □ *micrometre.* **3** using, used in, or prepared for, microscopy. **4** dealing with minute quantities, objects or values □ *microchemistry.* ⓘ From Greek *mikros* little.

microbe /'maɪkroʊb/ ▻ *noun, loosely* any micro-organism, especially a bacterium that is capable of causing disease. • **microbial** /maɪ'kroʊbɪəl/ or **microbic** *adj.* ⓘ 19c: French, from Greek *mikros* little + *bios* life.

microbiology ▻ *noun* the branch of biology dealing with the study of micro-organisms. • **microbiological** *adj* • **microbiologist** *noun.* ⓘ 19c.

microcassette ▻ *noun* a tiny cassette that uses very thin recording tape to give a similar recording time to that of a standard-size cassette.

microchip see under SILICON CHIP

microcircuit ▻ *noun* an electronic circuit with components formed in one microchip. • **microcircuitry** *noun.* ⓘ 1950s.

microclimate ▻ *noun, biol* the local and rather uniform climate immediately surrounding a living organism, as opposed to the climate of the entire region in which the organism occurs. • **microclimatic** *adj.* ⓘ 1920s.

microcode ▻ *noun, computing* **1** a MICROINSTRUCTION. **2** a sequence of microinstructions.

microcomputer ▻ *noun* a small, relatively inexpensive computer designed for use by one person at a time, and containing an entire CPU on a single microchip. Now usually called PERSONAL COMPUTER. ⓘ 1970s.

microcosm /'maɪkroʊkɒzəm/ ▻ *noun* **1** any structure or system which contains, in miniature, all the features of the larger structure or system that it is part of. **2** *philos* humankind regarded as a model or epitome of the universe. Compare MACROCOSM. • **microcosmic** *adj.* • **in microcosm** on a small scale; in miniature. ⓘ 15c as *microcosme*: French, from Greek *kosmos* world.

microdot ▻ *noun* **1** a photograph, eg one taken of secret documents, reduced to the size of a pinhead. **2** *colloq* a very small pill containing concentrated LSD. ⓘ 1940s.

microeconomics ▻ *singular noun* the branch of economics concerned with the financial circumstances of individual households, firms, etc, and the way individual elements in an economy (eg specific products) behave. • **microeconomic** *adj.* ⓘ 1940s.

microelectronics ▻ *singular noun* the branch of electronics dealing with the design and use of small-scale electrical circuits or other very small electronic devices. • **microelectronic** *adj.* ⓘ 1960s.

microfibre ▻ *noun* a synthetic, very closely woven fabric.

microfiche /'maɪkrəfiːʃ, -roʊ-/ ▻ *noun* (***microfiche*** or ***microfiches***) *photog* a flat sheet of film of a size suitable for filing, with printed text on it that has been photographically reduced, used for storing library catalogues, newspaper texts, etc, especially before the widespread introduction of electronic databases and CD-ROMs. Often shortened to **fiche**. ⓘ 1950s: from French *fiche* a sheet of paper.

microfilm ▻ *noun* a length of thin photographic film on which printed material is stored in miniaturized form. ▻ *verb* (***microfilmed, microfilming***) to record something on microfilm. ⓘ 1930s.

microfloppy ▻ *noun, computing* a small magnetic floppy disk, usually 3.5in in diameter.

microgravity ▻ *noun* the state or condition of being subjected to little or no gravity, eg the near-weightlessness experienced in space.

microhabitat ▻ *noun, biol, ecol* a small area that has different environmental conditions from those of the surrounding area.

microinstruction ▻ *noun, computing* a single, simple command that encodes any of the individual steps to be carried out by a computer. See also MICROCODE.

microlight ▻ *noun* a very lightweight, small-engined aircraft, like a powered hang-glider. Also *as adj* □ *microlight plane.* ⓘ 1980s.

micromanipulation ▻ *noun, technical* **1** the technique of using delicate instruments to work on cells, bacteria, etc under high magnifications. **2** the technique of working with extremely small quantities, eg in chemistry.

micromesh ▻ *noun* a very fine kind of mesh used to make hosiery, etc. Also *as adj* □ *micromesh stockings.*

micrometer /maɪ'krɒmɪtə(r)/ ▻ *noun* an instrument of various kinds used for accurately measuring very small distances, thicknesses or angles. Also *as adj* □ *micrometer gauge.* • **micrometric** /-'mɛtrɪk/ *adj.* • **micrometry** /-'krɒmɪtrɪ/ *noun.* ⓘ 17c.

micrometre or (*US*) **micrometer** /'maɪkroʊmiːtə(r)/ ▻ *noun* in the SI or metric system: a unit of length equal to 10^{-6}m; one millionth of a metre. See also MICRON. ⓘ 1880s.

microminiaturize or **microminiaturise** ▻ *verb* (***microminiaturized, microminiaturizing***) to reduce (scientific or technical equipment, etc, or any part of such equipment) to an extremely small size. • **microminiaturization** *noun.*

micron /'maɪkrɒn/ ▻ *noun* (symbol μ) the former name for the MICROMETRE. ⓘ 1880s: Greek, from *mikros* small.

Micronesian ▻ *adj* belonging or relating to Micronesia, a group of small islands in the West Pacific, north of New Guinea, or specifically, since 1979, to the Federated States of Micronesia, its inhabitants or their languages. ▻ *noun* **1** a citizen or inhabitant of, or person born in, Micronesia. **2** the group of AUSTRONESIAN languages spoken in Micronesia. ⓘ 19c: from MICRO- + Greek *nesos* an island; compare POLYNESIA.

micronutrient ▻ *noun, biol* any TRACE ELEMENT, vitamin or other essential nutrient required in minute quantities by a living organism, eg zinc.

micro-organism ▻ *noun* any living organism that can only be observed with the aid of a microscope, eg bacteria, viruses, protozoans and single-celled algae. ⓘ 19c.

microphone /'maɪkrəfoʊn/ ▻ *noun* an electro magnetic transducer that converts sound waves into electrical signals which can be amplified, recorded or transmitted over long distances. Often (*colloq*) shortened to MIKE or MIC. • **microphonic** /-fɒnɪk/ *adj.* ⓘ 17c meaning 'an instrument for intensifying very small sounds'.

microphotography ▻ *noun* photography, especially of documents, plans and graphic material, in the form of greatly-reduced images of small area (**microphotographs**) which have to be viewed by magnification or enlarged projection. ⓘ 1850s.

microprint ▷ *noun* a MICROPHOTOGRAPH of eg printed text, reproduced on paper or card, etc. • **microprinted** *adj.*

microprocessor ▷ *noun, computing* a single circuit performing most of the basic functions of a CPU. Also shortened to MICRO. ◷ 1970s.

micropyle /ˈmaɪkroʊpaɪl/ ▷ *noun, bot* **1** in flowering plants: a small opening or pore at the tip of the OVULE through which the pollen tube normally enters during pollination. **2** *zool* a tiny opening or pore in the protective layer surrounding an insect's egg, through which sperm enters during the process of fertilization. ◷ 19c: French, from Greek *pyle* gate.

microscope /ˈmaɪkrəskoʊp/ ▷ *noun* any of a range of instruments consisting of a system of lenses which produce a magnified image of objects that are too small to be seen with the naked eye. See also ELECTRON MICROSCOPE. • **microscopic** /-ˈkɒpɪk/ *adj* **1** too small to be seen without the aid of a microscope. **2** *colloq* extremely small. **3** belonging or relating to, or by means of, a microscope. • **microscopically** *adverb.* • **microscopy** /maɪˈkrɒskəpɪ/ *noun* the practice or skill of using a microscope in scientific work, etc. • **come, go** or **be put under the microscope** to be subjected to minute examination.

microsecond ▷ *noun* in the SI or metric system: a unit of time equal to one millionth part of a second.

microsurgery ▷ *noun, medicine* any intricate surgical procedure that is performed on very small body structures by means of a powerful microscope and small specialized instruments, eg in eye or brain surgery. • **microsurgeon** *noun.* • **microsurgical** *adj.*

microtome /ˈmaɪkrətoʊm/ ▷ *noun, biol* an instrument for cutting thin sections of objects for microscopic examination. ◷ 19c: from MICRO- + Greek *tome* a cut.

microtubule /maɪkrəˈtjuːbjuːl/ ▷ *noun, biol* any of the microscopic, hollow, tubular filaments that are found in the cytoplasm of eukaryotic (see EUKARYOTE) cells, and are constituents of the cilia and flagella and of the CYTOSKELETON.

microwave ▷ *noun* **1** a form of electromagnetic radiation with wavelengths in the range 1mm to 0.3m (ie between those of INFRARED and RADIO WAVES), used in radar, communications and cooking. Also called **microwave radiation**. **2** a microwave oven. ▷ *verb* (***microwaved, microwaving***) to cook something in a microwave oven. • **microwaveable** or **microwavable** *adj* said of food: suitable for cooking in a microwave oven.

microwave oven ▷ *noun* an electrically operated oven that uses microwaves to cook food more rapidly than is possible in a conventional oven, by causing water molecules within the food to vibrate and generate heat.

micturate /ˈmɪktjʊreɪt/ ▷ *verb* (***micturated, micturating***) *intr, formal* to urinate. • **micturition** *noun* the act of urinating. ◷ 19c: from Latin *micturire* to wish to urinate, from *mingere* to urinate.

mid¹ ▷ *adj, often in compounds* (sometimes with hyphen) referring to the middle point or in the middle of something □ ***mid-March*** □ ***mid-ocean*** □ ***in mid sentence.*** ◷ Anglo-Saxon *midd.*

mid² or **'mid** *prep, poetic* a short form of AMID. ◷ 19c.

mid-air ▷ *noun* any area or point above the ground □ ***caught it in mid-air.*** Also *as adj* □ ***a mid-air collision.***

the Midas touch /— ˈmaɪdəs —/ ▷ *noun* the ability to make money easily. ◷ 19c: from the Greek legend telling of *Midas,* a king of Phrygia who turned everything he touched into gold.

mid-Atlantic ▷ *adj* said of an accent, etc: peppered with a mixture of British and N American characteristics.

midbrain ▷ *noun, anatomy* the part of the brain which connects the FOREBRAIN to the HINDBRAIN. *Technical equivalent* MESENCEPHALON. ◷ 19c.

midday ▷ *noun* the middle of the day; twelve o'clock. Also *as adj* □ ***a midday meeting.***

midden /ˈmɪdən/ ▷ *noun* **1** *chiefly old use or dialect* a rubbish heap; a pile of dung. **2** *colloq* an untidy mess. ◷ 14c: from Danish *mykdyngja,* from *myk* manure + *dyngja* pile.

middle /ˈmɪdəl/ ▷ *adj* **1** at, or being, a point or position between two others, usually two ends or extremes, and especially the same distance from each □ ***It's the middle house in the row.*** **2** intermediate; neither at the top or at the bottom end of the scale □ ***middle management*** □ ***middle income.*** **3** moderate, not extreme; taken, used, etc as a compromise □ ***middle ground.*** **4** (**Middle**) said especially of languages: belonging to a period coming after the Old period and before the Modern □ ***Middle English.*** ▷ *noun* **1** the middle point, part or position of something □ ***the middle of the night.*** **2** *colloq* the waist. ▷ *verb* (***middled, middling***) **1** to place something in the middle. **2** *cricket* to hit (the ball) with the middle of the bat, therefore to hit it firmly and accurately. • **be in the middle of something** to be busy with it and likely to remain so for some time. ◷ Anglo-Saxon *middel.*

middle age ▷ *noun* the years between youth and old age, usually thought of as between the ages of 40 and 60. ▷ *adj* **middle-aged** said of a person: in their middle age.

the Middle Ages ▷ *plural noun* in European history: **1** the period (c.500–1500 AD) between the fall of the Roman Empire in the West and the Renaissance. **2** *sometimes strictly* the period between 1100 and 1500.

middle-age spread or **middle-aged spread** ▷ *noun* fat around the waist, often regarded as a consequence of reaching middle age.

Middle America ▷ *noun* **1** the geographical area usually thought of as comprising Mexico and Central America. **2** people in the US of above average income, education, etc and usually thought of as being politically conservative and having very traditional lifestyles and outlooks. ◷ 19c.

middlebrow *derog* ▷ *adj* intended for, or appealing to, people with conventional tastes and average intelligence. ▷ *noun* a middlebrow person. Compare HIGHBROW, LOWBROW.

middle C ▷ *noun, music* **1** the C in the middle of the piano keyboard. **2** in printed or written music: the first line below the treble or above the bass stave.

middle class ▷ *noun* (*especially* **the middle class**) a social class between the working class and the upper class, traditionally thought of as being made up of educated people with professional or business careers. See also BOURGEOISIE. ▷ *adj* (**middle-class**) belonging or relating to, or characteristic of, the middle class. ◷ 18c.

middle distance ▷ *noun* **1** in a painting, photograph, etc: the area between the foreground and the background. **2** *athletics* in a race: a length of 400, 800 or 1500m. ▷ *adj* (**middle-distance**) **1** said of a race: run over any of these distances. **2** said of an athlete: competing in races of middle distance.

middle ear ▷ *noun, anatomy* in vertebrates: an air-filled cavity that lies between the eardrum and the inner ear containing three small sound-transmitting bones (the MALLEUS, INCUS and STAPES). Compare INNER EAR.

Middle East ▷ *noun* a loosely-defined geographical region encompassing the largely Arab states to the E of the Mediterranean, as well as Cyprus, Turkey and sometimes the countries of N Africa.

Middle Eastern ▷ *adj* relating to or characteristic of the Middle East.

Middle England ▷ *noun* English people of above average income, education, etc who tend to have fairly traditional views, lifestyles, etc. As potential voters, they are considered to be an important group to win over. ◎ 1990s: modelled on MIDDLE AMERICA sense 2.

middle finger salute ▷ *noun, slang* a gesture, often a feature of ROAD RAGE, that involves making a fist with the middle finger extended upwards. It is used to express contempt, anger, frustration, etc and is generally taken to mean 'fuck off' or 'fuck you'. ◎ 1980s.

middle lamella ▷ *noun, bot* a thin layer, composed mainly of pectins, that cements together the walls of adjacent plant cells. See LAMELLA 2.

middleman ▷ *noun* **1** a dealer who buys goods from a producer or manufacturer and sells them to shopkeepers or to the public. **2** any intermediary. ◎ 17c in obsolete sense 'a soldier in one of the middle ranks of a file ten men deep'.

middle management ▷ *noun, business* in a firm or institution: the junior managerial executives and senior supervisory personnel.

middlemost see under MIDMOST

middle name ▷ *noun* **1** a name which comes between a FIRST NAME and a SURNAME. **2** a quality or feature for which a person is well-known □ ***Punctuality is his middle name.***

middle-of-the-road ▷ *adj, often derog* **1** said eg of politics or opinions: not extreme; moderate. **2** said eg of music: **a** of widespread appeal (abbreviation **MOR**); **b** boringly average or familiar.

middle school ▷ *noun, England & Wales* a school for children between the ages of 8 or 9 and 12 or 13. Compare SECONDARY SCHOOL. See also JUNIOR, SENIOR.

middle-sized ▷ *adj* characterized by being of average or medium size.

middleweight ▷ *noun* **1** a class for boxers, wrestlers and weightlifters of not more than a specified weight, eg 73kg (161 lb) in professional boxing, 70kg (154 lb) for **light middleweight**, 77kg (170 lb) for **super-middleweight**, and similar but different weights in the other sports. **2** a boxer or wrestler, etc of this weight.

middling /'mɪdlɪŋ/ *colloq* ▷ *adj* average; moderate; mediocre. ▷ *adverb* said especially of a person's health: fairly good; moderately □ ***middling good.*** • **fair to middling** *colloq* not bad; fairly good. ◎ 15c: Scots.

Middx ▷ *abbreviation, former English county* Middlesex, now largely contained in Greater London.

middy /'mɪdɪ/ ▷ *noun* (***middies***) *Austral colloq* a measure of beer, varying in amount from one place to another.

midfield ▷ *noun, football* **1** the middle area of the pitch, not close to the goal of either team. **2** (**the midfield**) the players who operate in this area, acting as the links between a team's defending and attacking players. Also *as adj* □ ***midfield player.*** • **midfielder** *noun.*

midge /mɪdʒ/ ▷ *noun* any of various small insects that gather near water, especially one of the kinds that bite people. • **midgy** *adj* (***midgier, midgiest***). ◎ Anglo-Saxon *mycge.*

midget /'mɪdʒɪt/ ▷ *noun* **1** an unusually small person whose limbs and features are of normal proportions. **2** any thing that is smaller than others of its kind. Compare DWARF. ◎ 19c: from MIDGE.

MIDI ▷ *noun* a system enabling computer control of electronic musical instruments. ◎ 20c: from *m*usical *i*nstrument *d*igital *i*nterface.

midi /'mɪdɪ/ ▷ *noun* (***midis***) *colloq, fashion* a skirt or coat of medium length or medium size. Compare MAXI, MINI. ◎ 1960s: from MID[1].

midi- /'mɪdɪ/ ▷ *prefix, rather dated* (sometimes without hyphen) *denoting* of medium size or length □ ***midi-skirt.***

midiron /'mɪdaɪən/ ▷ *noun, golf* a heavy club used for long approach shots. See also IRON (*noun* 4).

midi system ▷ *noun* a set of small pieces of hi-fi equipment that can be stacked to form a single compact unit.

midland /'mɪdlənd/ ▷ *adj* belonging or relating to the central, inland part of a country.

midlife crisis ▷ *noun* a period of panic, frustration and feelings of pointlessness, sometimes experienced by a person when they reach middle age and realize that their youth has passed.

midmost *literary* ▷ *adverb* in the very middle. ▷ *adj* (*also* **middlemost**) nearest the middle. ◎ Anglo-Saxon *midmest.*

midnight ▷ *noun* **1** twelve o'clock at night. **2** *as adj* at midnight, or belonging or relating to midnight □ ***midnight feast*** □ ***midnight blue.***

midnight sun ▷ *noun, astron* a phenomenon that occurs during the summer in the Arctic and Antarctic regions, where the Sun remains visible for 24 hours a day.

mid-on and **mid-off** ▷ *noun, cricket* a fielder in a roughly-horizontal line with, but at a certain distance from, the non-striking batsman, on the on or off side respectively (see ON *adj* 6, OFF *adj* 4).

midpoint ▷ *noun* a point at or near the middle in distance or time.

midrib ▷ *noun, bot* the rib that runs along the centre of a leaf and forms an extension of the PETIOLE.

midriff /'mɪdrɪf/ ▷ *noun* **1** the part of the body between the chest and the waist. Also *as adj* □ ***midriff bulge.*** **2** the DIAPHRAGM. ◎ Anglo-Saxon *midhrif*, from *midd* MID[1] + *hrif* belly.

midshipman ▷ *noun, naut* a trainee naval officer, stationed on land. See table at RANK. ◎ 17c: a midshipman was originally housed in quarters located AMIDSHIPS.

midships see AMIDSHIPS

midst ▷ *noun* **1** (*always* **in the midst of something**) **a** among it or in the centre of it; **b** at the same time as something; during it. **2** (*always* **in someone's midst**) among them or in the same place as them. ◎ 15c as *middest*: from Anglo-Saxon *in middes* amidst.

midstream ▷ *noun* **1** the area of water in the middle of a river or stream, away from its banks. **2 a** the part in the middle of a flow or course, eg of urine; **b** *as adj* □ ***a midstream sample.*** • **in midstream** before a sentence, action, etc is finished □ ***She cut him off in midstream.***

midsummer ▷ *noun* the period of time in the middle of summer, or near the SUMMER SOLSTICE, ie around 21 June in the N hemisphere or 22 December in the S hemisphere. Also *as adj* □ ***midsummer fair.*** Opposite of MIDWINTER.

Midsummer Day or **Midsummer's Day** ▷ *noun* 24 June.

midterm ▷ *noun* **1** the middle of an academic term or term of office, etc. **2** a holiday, examination, etc in the middle of term. **3** the middle of a particular period of time, especially of a pregnancy. Also *as adj* □ ***midterm elections.***

midway ▷ *adj* ▷ *adverb* halfway between two points in distance or time.

midweek ▷ *noun* the period of time in the middle of the week, especially Wednesday. Also *as adj* □ ***a midweek break.***

Midwestern ▷ *adj* relating to or typical of the US Midwest, the states between the Great Lakes and the upper Mississippi river valley.

mid-wicket ▷ *noun, cricket* **1** the area between the stumps on the on side (see ON *adj* 6), roughly midway between the wicket and the boundary. **2** a fielder placed in this area.

midwife /'mɪdwaɪf/ ▷ *noun* a nurse, especially a female one, trained to assist women in childbirth and to provide care and advice for women before and after childbirth. • **midwifery** /ˈmɪdwɪfərɪ/ *noun* the skills or practice of a midwife; obstetrics. ⓒ 14c: from Anglo-Saxon *mid* with + *wif* woman.

midwife toad ▷ *noun* a European frog that lives and mates out of water, the male of which wraps the eggs around its legs and carries them until they hatch, and then transports the tadpoles to water.

midwinter ▷ *noun* the period of time in the middle of winter, or near the WINTER SOLSTICE, ie around 22 December in the N hemisphere or 21 June in the S hemisphere. Also *as adj*. Opposite of MIDSUMMER.

midyear ▷ *noun* **1** the middle, or middle part, of the year. Also *as adj* ▫ *midyear results*. **2** (*usually* **midyears**) *chiefly US* an examination held in the middle of the academic year.

mien /miːn/ ▷ *noun, formal or literary* an appearance, expression or manner, especially one that reflects a mood ▫ *her thoughtful mien*. ⓒ 16c.

miff *colloq* ▷ *verb* (***miffed, miffing***) **1** to offend someone. **2** *intr* (*usually* **miffed at, about** or **with someone** or **something**) to be offended. ▷ *noun* **1** a quarrel. **2** a fit of sulking; a huff. • **miffed** *adj* offended, upset or annoyed. • **miffy** *adj* (***miffier, miffiest***) easily offended; touchy. ⓒ 17c.

might¹ /maɪt/ ▷ *auxiliary verb* **1** *past tense of* MAY¹ ▫ *He asked if he might be of assistance*. **2** (*sometimes* **might well**) used to express a possibility ▫ *He might win if he tries hard* ▫ *You might well be right*. **3** used to request permission ▫ *Might I speak to you a moment?* **4** used in suggesting that a person should be doing a specified thing ▫ *You might carry these bags for me!* **5** *affected, old use or facetious* used in asking a question ▫ *And who might you be?* **6** used to express the sense of 'although' ▫ *You might be the boss, but you're still an idiot!* ⓒ Anglo-Saxon *miht*.

might² /maɪt/ ▷ *noun* power or strength. • **with might and main** *literary* with great strength; with all one's strength ▫ *pulled with all our might and main*. ⓒ Anglo-Saxon *miht*.

might-have-been ▷ *noun* (***might-have-beens***) *colloq* someone who might have been or might have come to something (eg been famous) or a thing which might have happened, etc.

mightn't /ˈmaɪtnt/ ▷ *contraction* might not.

mighty /maɪtɪ/ ▷ *adj* (***mightier, mightiest***) **1** having great strength or power. **2** very large. **3** very great or important. Also **the mighty** (see THE 4b). ▷ *adverb, colloq N Amer, especially US* very ▫ *mighty pretty*. • **mightily** *adverb* **1** powerfully. **2** to a great extent. • **mightiness** *noun*.

migmatite /ˈmɪgmətaɪt/ ▷ *noun, geol* a complex rock with a banded or veined appearance, consisting of a mixture of igneous and metamorphic rocks. ⓒ Early 20c: from Swedish *migmatit*, from Greek *migma* mixture + -ITE 4.

mignon /mɪnjɒn/ ▷ *adj* (following its noun) (feminine ***mignonne***) small and dainty ▫ *filet mignon*.

migraine /ˈmiːgreɪn, ˈmaɪgreɪn/ ▷ *noun* a type of severe and recurring throbbing headache that usually affects one side of the head and is often accompanied by nausea or vomiting, and sometimes preceded by visual disturbances. • **migrainous** *adj* ⓒ 18c; 14c as *megrim*: French, from Greek *hemikrania* half skull.

migrant /ˈmaɪgrənt/ ▷ *noun* a person or animal that migrates. ▷ *adj* regularly moving from one place to another. ⓒ 17c: see MIGRATE.

migrate /maɪˈgreɪt/ ▷ *verb* (***migrated, migrating***) *intr* **1** said of animals, especially birds: to travel from one region to another at certain times of the year. **2** said of people: to leave one place and settle in another, especially another country, often regularly. • **migrator** *noun*. • **migratory** *adj* **1** said eg of birds: that migrate or are accustomed to migrating. **2** wandering; itinerant. ⓒ 17c: from Latin *migrare* to move from one place to another.

migration *noun* **1** *zool* the movement of animals from one location to another, generally involving travel over very long distances by well-defined routes, in response to seasonal changes. **2** an act or occurrence of migrating. **3** a number of animals or people migrating.

mihrab /miːˈrɑːb/ ▷ *noun, Islam* a niche or slab in a mosque indicating the direction of Mecca. ⓒ 19c: Arabic, meaning 'a praying place'.

mikado or (*often*) **Mikado** /mɪˈkɑːdoʊ/ ▷ *noun* (***mikados*** or ***Mikados***) a title formerly given by foreigners to an emperor of Japan. ⓒ 18c: Japanese, literally 'exalted gate'.

Mike /maɪk/ ▷ *noun, communications* in the NATO alphabet: the word used to denote the letter 'M' (see table at NATO ALPHABET).

mike /maɪk/ ▷ *contraction, colloq* short for MICROPHONE. ▷ *verb* (***miked, miking***) (*always* **mike someone up**) to attach a microphone to their clothing, eg for a TV interview.

mil ▷ *noun* **1** a unit of length equal to one thousandth of an inch. **2** *cinematog, colloq* a millimetre. **3** *photog, etc, colloq* a millimetre. **4** in artillery, etc: a unit of angular measurement, equal to 1/6400 of a circle, used for aiming, etc. ⓒ 18c: from Latin *mille* a thousand.

mil. or **milit.** ▷ *abbreviation* military.

milady /mɪˈleɪdɪ/ ▷ *noun* (***miladies***) *dated* a term formerly used to address, or to refer to, a rich English woman, especially an aristocratic one. ⓒ 19c: French, from English *my lady*.

milch /mɪltʃ/ ▷ *adj* said of cattle: producing milk. ⓒ Anglo-Saxon *milce*.

milch cow ▷ *noun* something or someone that is seen as a source of easy income or profit.

mild /maɪld/ ▷ *adj* (***milder, mildest***) **1** gentle in temperament or behaviour. **2** not sharp or strong in flavour or effect. **3** not great or severe. **4** said of climate, etc: not characterized by extremes; rather warm. ▷ *noun* (*also* **mild ale**) dark beer less flavoured with hops than BITTER beer. • **mildly** *adverb*. • **mildness** *noun*. • **to put it mildly** to understate the case. ⓒ Anglo-Saxon *milde*.

mildew /ˈmɪldjuː/ ▷ *noun* **1** any of various parasitic fungi that produce a fine white powdery coating on the surface of infected plants, or white or grey patches on the surface of paper, leather or other materials made from plant or animal material and subsequently kept in damp conditions. **2** the white powdery coating itself, or the white or grey patches produced by these fungi. ▷ *verb* (***mildewed, mildewing***) *tr & intr* to affect or become affected by mildew. • **mildewed** *adj*. • **mildewy** *adj*. ⓒ Anglo-Saxon *mildeaw*.

mild steel ▷ *noun* steel that contains little carbon and is easily worked.

mile /maɪl/ ▷ *noun* (abbreviation **m, m.** or **ml**) **1** in the imperial system: a unit of distance equal to 1760yd (1.61km). See also NAUTICAL MILE. **2** a race over this distance, especially a race on foot. **3** *colloq* a great distance; a large margin ▫ *missed by a mile*. • **miler** *noun* an athlete or horse that runs races of one mile. • **miles** *adverb* **1** at a great distance ▫ *lives miles away*. **2** *colloq* very much ▫ *feel miles better*. ⓒ Anglo-Saxon *mil*: originally a Roman unit of length consisting of 1000 double paces from Latin *mille passuum* a thousand paces.

mileage /ˈmaɪlɪdʒ/ ▷ *noun* **1** the number of miles travelled or to be travelled. **2 a** the number of miles a motor vehicle will travel on a fixed amount of fuel; **b** the total number of miles a car has dones since new, as shown on the mileometer. **3** travelling allowance calculated at a set amount per mile. **4** *colloq* use; benefit; advantage ▫ *We* *can get a lot of mileage out of that story.* ⓘ 18c in sense 3.

mileometer or **milometer** /maɪˈlɒmɪtə(r)/ ▻ *noun* in a motor vehicle: an instrument for recording the total number of miles travelled. Also (*colloq*) called **clock**.

milestone ▻ *noun* **1** a very important event; a significant point or stage. **2** a stone pillar at a roadside showing distances in miles to various places.

miliaria see PRICKLY HEAT

milieu /ˈmiːljɜː/ ▻ *noun* (*milieus* or *milieux*) *literary* a social environment or set of surroundings. ⓘ 19c: French, meaning 'middle place'.

milit. see MIL.

militant /ˈmɪlɪtənt/ ▻ *adj* **1** taking, or ready to take, strong or violent action; aggressively active. **2** *formal* engaged in warfare. ▻ *noun* a militant person. • **militancy** *noun*. • **militantly** *adverb*. ⓘ 15c: French, from Latin *militare* to serve as a soldier.

militaria /mɪlɪˈteərɪə/ ▻ *plural noun* weapons, uniforms, medals, badges and other items connected with the military, often in the form of a collection. ⓘ 1960s: from MILITARY + -IA[2].

militarism /ˈmɪlɪtərɪzəm/ ▻ *noun, often derog* **1** an aggressive readiness to engage in warfare. **2** the vigorous pursuit of military aims and ideals. • **militarist** *noun*. • **militaristic** *adj*. • **militaristically** *adverb*.

militarize or **militarise** /ˈmɪlɪtəraɪz/ ▻ *verb* (*militarized, militarizing*) **1** to provide (a country, body, etc) with a military force. **2** to make something military in nature or character. • **militarization** *noun*.

military /ˈmɪlɪtrɪ, -tərɪ/ ▻ *adj* **1** by, for, or belonging or relating to the armed forces or warfare ▫ *military band* ▫ *military encounter.* **2** characteristic of members of the armed forces ▫ *military bearing.* ▻ *noun* (*militaries*) (*usually* **the military**) the armed forces. • **militarily** *adverb*. ⓘ 16c: from French *militaire*, from Latin *militaris*, from *miles* soldier.

Military Cross ▻ *noun, Brit* (abbreviation **MC**) a medal awarded to army officers.

military honours ▻ *plural noun* a display of respect shown to a dead soldier, etc by fellow soldiers, royalty, etc ▫ *They were buried with full military honours.*

military police or **Military Police** ▻ *noun* (abbreviation **MP**) a police force within an army, enforcing army rules. • **military policeman, military policewoman** *noun* (abbreviation **MP**).

military science ▻ *noun* the theoretical study of warfare and of the strategic, tactical and logistic principles behind it.

militate /ˈmɪlɪteɪt/ ▻ *verb* (*militated, militating*) *intr* (*usually* **militate for** or **against something**) said of facts, etc: to have a strong influence or effect ▫ *The evidence militates against your sworn statement.* ⓘ 17c: from Latin *militare* to serve as a soldier; see -ATE 1.

> **militate**
>
> A word often confused with this one is **mitigate**.

militia /mɪˈlɪʃə/ ▻ *noun* (*militias*) a civilian fighting force used to supplement a regular army in emergencies, eg the TERRITORIAL ARMY. ⓘ 16c: Latin, meaning 'a military force'.

militiaman ▻ *noun* a member of a militia.

milk ▻ *noun* **1** a white or yellowish liquid consisting mainly of water, with protein, fats, carbohydrates, vitamins and minerals (especially calcium), that is secreted by the MAMMARY GLANDs of female mammals to provide their young with nourishment. Also *as adj* ▫ *milk jug.* See also CONDENSED MILK, EVAPORATED MILK, SKIMMED MILK. **2** the whiteish, milk-like juice or sap of certain plants ▫ *coconut milk.* **3** any preparation that resembles milk ▫ *milk of magnesia.* ▻ *verb* (*milked, milking*) **1** to take milk from (an animal). **2** to extract or draw off a substance (eg venom or sap) from something. **3** *colloq* to obtain money, information or any other benefit from someone or something, cleverly or relentlessly; to exploit ▫ *milked the scandal for all it was worth.* **4** *intr* said of cattle: to yield milk. • **milker** *noun* **1** a cow that is kept for milking. **2** a person or machine that milks cows. • **milking** *noun* the act, skill or process of milking. Also *as adj* ▫ *milking shed* ▫ *milking machine.* ⓘ Anglo-Saxon *milc*.

milk and honey ▻ *noun* comfort; luxury; plenty. ⓘ Anglo-Saxon *meolce and hunie*; referring to the phrase in the Bible (Exodus 3.8) which describes the *'land flowing with milk and honey'*, ie the PROMISED LAND.

milk and water *derog* ▻ *noun* weak, insipid or weakly sentimental speech or writing. Also *as adj* (**milk-and-water**). ⓘ 16c in obsolete sense 'the colour of milk and water'.

milk chocolate ▻ *noun* chocolate containing milk. Compare PLAIN CHOCOLATE.

milk float ▻ *noun, Brit* a vehicle, usually an electrically-powered one, used for delivering milk.

milkily and **milkiness** see under MILKY

milk leg see WHITE-LEG

milkmaid ▻ *noun* a woman who milks cows, goats, etc.

milkman ▻ *noun, Brit* a man who delivers milk to people's houses.

milk of magnesia see under MAGNESIA

milk pudding ▻ *noun* a dessert made by baking or boiling grain (eg rice or tapioca) in milk, usually with added sugar and flavouring.

milk round ▻ *noun* **1** a milkman's regular daily route from house to house. **2** a series of visits made periodically, eg a tour of universities made by representatives of a large company in order to attract or recruit undergraduates.

milk run ▻ *noun* **1** *airmen's slang* a routine flight. **2** a MILK ROUND 1.

milkshake ▻ *noun* a drink consisting of a mixture of milk, flavouring and sometimes ice cream, whipped together until creamy.

milksop ▻ *noun, derog, old use* a weak, effeminate or ineffectual man or youth. ⓘ 15c in obsolete sense 'a piece of bread soaked in milk'; see SOP.

milk sugar see under LACTOSE

milk tooth ▻ *noun* any of a baby's or young mammal's first set of teeth. Also called **baby tooth**.

milky /ˈmɪlkɪ/ ▻ *adj* (*milkier, milkiest*) **1** like milk, eg in colour, opacity, mildness of taste or effect, etc. **2** made of or containing milk. • **milkily** *adverb*. • **milkiness** *noun*.

the Milky Way ▻ *noun, astron* **1** *strictly* a band of diffuse light that circles the night sky as seen from Earth, and represents the combined light of billions of stars in the plane of our Galaxy which are too faint to be seen individually. **2** the Galaxy to which our Sun belongs.

mill ▻ *noun* **1 a** a large machine that grinds grain into flour; **b** a building containing such a machine ▫ *watermill* ▫ *windmill.* **2** any of various smaller machines or devices for grinding a particular thing ▫ *a pepper mill.* **3 a** in manufacturing industry, etc: a large machine that presses, rolls or otherwise shapes something; **b** a factory containing one or more of these machines. **4** any factory ▫ *a woollen mill.* **5** an institution or place which seems to process (eg students) in an impersonal, factory-like way to deliver a standardized end-product. ▻ *verb* (*milled, milling*) **1** to grind (grain, etc). **2** to shape (eg metal) in a mill. **3** to cut grooves into the edge of (a coin). **4** *intr, colloq* (*especially* **mill about** or **around**) to move in an aimless or confused manner ▫ *people milling around outside.* •

miller *noun* **1** someone who owns or operates a mill, especially a grain mill. **2** a machine for milling. • **milling** *noun* **1** the grinding of cereal grain to produce flour for use in making bread and other foodstuffs. **2** the act or process of passing anything through a mill. **3** the grooves, or the process of making grooves, in the edge of a coin, etc. • **go** or **put someone** or **something through the mill** to undergo or make them or it undergo an unpleasant experience or difficult test. ◷ Anglo-Saxon *myln*: from Latin *molere* to grind.

millefeuille /*French* milfœj/ ▷ *noun* (***millefeuilles***) a type of layered cake made with puff pastry and cream, jam, etc. ◷ 19c: literally 'a thousand leaves'.

millenarian /mɪlə'nɛərɪən/ ▷ *noun, Christianity* a person who believes that the coming of the millennium (see MILLENNIUM 2a) is a certainty. ▷ *adj* relating or belonging to the millennium. • **millenarianism** *noun* the beliefs of a millenarian.

millenary /mɪ'lɛnərɪ, -'liː-/ ▷ *noun* (***millenaries***) **1** a thousand, especially a period of a thousand years. **2** a thousandth anniversary. ▷ *adj* consisting of, or relating to, a millenary. ◷ 17c: from Latin *millenarius* consisting of a thousand.

millennium /mɪ'lɛnɪəm/ ▷ *noun* (***millenniums*** or ***millennia***) **1** a period of a thousand years. **2** (**the millennium**) **a** a future period of a thousand years during which some Christians believe Christ will rule the world; **b** a future golden age of worldwide peace and happiness. • **millennial** *adj*. See also MILLENARIAN. ◷ 17c: from Latin *mille* a thousand + *annus* year.

millepede see MILLIPEDE

miller see under MILL

millesimal /mɪ'lɛsɪməl/ ▷ *adj* **1** thousandth. **2** consisting of or relating to thousandths. ▷ *noun* a thousandth part. ◷ 18c: from Latin *millesimus*, from *mille* a thousand.

millet ▷ *noun* **1** the common name for several cereal grasses, especially certain fast-growing varieties tolerant of drought and poor soil which are grown as an important food crop in the drier regions of Africa and Asia, especially India and China, and are widely used as animal fodder. **2** (*also* **millet-seed**) the grain of this plant. ◷ 15c: French, from Latin *milium*.

milli- /mɪlɪ/ ▷ *combining form, forming nouns, denoting* in the names of SI or metric units: a thousandth part □ *millilitre* □ *millimetre*. ◷ From Latin *mille* a thousand.

milliard /'mɪlɪɑːd, 'mɪljɑːd/ ▷ *noun, old use* a thousand million. Now called BILLION. ◷ 18c: French, from *mille* a thousand.

millibar ▷ *noun, physics, meteorol, etc* (symbol **mbar**) a unit of atmospheric pressure equal to 10^{-3} (one thousandth) of a bar. See also BAR².

milligram or **milligramme** ▷ *noun* (abbreviation **mg**) a unit of weight equal to one thousandth of a gram.

millilitre or (*US*) **milliliter** ▷ *noun* (abbreviation **ml**) a unit of volume, equal to one thousandth of a litre.

millimetre or (*US*) **millimeter** ▷ *noun* (abbreviation **mm**) a unit of length equal to one thousandth of a metre.

milliner /'mɪlɪnə(r)/ ▷ *noun* someone who makes or sells women's hats. • **millinery** *noun* **1** the hats and trimmings made or sold by milliners. **2** the craft of making such articles. ◷ 16c: from Milaner, a trader in the fancy goods, for which the Italian city of Milan was once famous.

million /'mɪljən/ ▷ *noun* (***millions*** or after a number ***million***) **1** the number or quantity 10^6, a thousand thousands. **2** a numeral, figure or symbol representing this, eg 1 000 000. **3** *colloq* a million pounds or dollars. **4** (*often* **millions**) *colloq* a great number □ *He's got millions of friends.* ▷ *adj* 1 000 000 in number. • **one in a million** something or someone very rare of their kind, and therefore very valuable or special. ◷ 14c: French, from Latin *millionis*, from *mille* a thousand.

millionaire /mɪljə'nɛə(r)/ ▷ *noun* someone whose wealth amounts to a million pounds, dollars, etc or more. ◷ 19c: French.

millionairess ▷ *noun* (***millionairesses***) a female millionaire.

millionth /mɪljənθ/ ▷ *noun* ▷ *adj* a thousand thousandth.

millipede or **millepede** /'mɪlɪpiːd/ ▷ *noun* (***millipedes*** or ***millepede***) any of various small wormlike creatures with many-jointed bodies and numerous pairs of legs. ◷ 17c: from Latin *millepeda* a woodlouse, from *pedis* foot.

millisecond ▷ *noun* (abbreviation **ms**) a unit of time equal to one thousandth of a second.

millpond ▷ *noun* a pond containing water which is, or used to be, used for driving a mill. • **like** or **as calm as a millpond** said of a stretch of water: completely smooth and calm.

millstone ▷ *noun* **1** either of the large, heavy stones between which grain is ground in a mill. **2** (*especially* **a millstone around someone's neck**) any heavy burden, eg a duty or responsibility, which someone has to bear.

millstream ▷ *noun* a stream of water that turns a millwheel.

millwheel ▷ *noun* a wheel, especially a waterwheel, used to drive a mill.

milometer see MILEOMETER

milord /mɪ'lɔːd/ ▷ *noun, dated* a term formerly used on the continent to address or refer to a rich English gentleman, especially an aristocrat. ◷ 16c: French, from English *my lord*.

milt ▷ *noun* the testis or sperm of a fish. ◷ 15c in current sense; Anglo-Saxon *milte* in original sense 'the spleen of a mammal'.

Miltonic /mɪl'tɒnɪk/ ▷ *adj* relating to or characteristic of the literary works or style of the English poet John Milton (1608–74).

mime /maɪm/ ▷ *noun* **1** the theatrical art of conveying meaning without words through gesture, movement and facial expression. **2** a play or dramatic sequence performed in this way. **3** an actor who practises this art. Also called **mime artist**. **4** *historical* in ancient Greek and Roman theatre: a farcical play with dialogue making great use of gesture and facial expression. ▷ *verb* (***mimed***, ***miming***) *tr & intr* **1** to act or express (feelings, etc) without words through gesture, movement and facial expression. **2** to mouth the words to a song in time with a recording, giving the illusion of singing. • **mimer** *noun*. ◷ 17c: from Latin *mimus*, from Greek *mimos* imitator.

mimeograph /'mɪmɪəgrɑːf/ ▷ *noun* **1** a machine that produces copies of printed or handwritten material from a stencil. **2** a copy produced in this way. ▷ *verb* (***mimeographed***, ***mimeographing***) to make a copy of something in this way. ◷ 19c: originally a trademark.

mimesis /mɪ'miːsɪs, maɪ'-/ ▷ *noun* **1** in art or literature: imitative representation. **2** *biol* mimicry. **3** *rhetoric* use of a person's supposed or alleged words. • **mimetic** /mɪ'mɛtɪk/ *adj* **1** consisting of, showing, or relating to imitation; imitative. **2** *biol* displaying mimicry. ◷ 16c: Greek, meaning 'imitation'.

mimic /'mɪmɪk/ ▷ *verb* (***mimicked***, ***mimicking***) **1** to imitate someone or something, especially for comic effect. **2** to copy. **3** to simulate. **4** *biol* to resemble something closely, especially as a defense mechanism. ▷ *noun* **1** someone who is skilled at imitating other people, especially in a comic manner. **2** *biol* a plant or animal displaying mimicry. ▷ *adj* **1** imitative. **2** mock or sham. • **mimicker** *noun*. • **mimicry** /'mɪmɪkrɪ/ *noun* (***mimicries***) **1** the skill or practice of mimicking. **2** *biol* the close resemblance of one animal or plant species to another species, or to a non-living feature of its natural environment, which protects it from predators or enables it to deceive its prey. ⓒ 16c: from Latin *mimicus* imitative, from Greek *mimikos*, from *mimos* imitator.

mimosa /mɪ'moʊzə, -sə/ ▷ *noun* (***mimosas*** or ***mimosae*** /-siː/) any of various tropical shrubs or trees which have leaves that droop when touched, and clusters of flowers, typically yellow ones. ⓒ 18c: Latin, from Greek *mimos* imitator; the movement of the leaf when touched was seen as an imitation of a cowering animal.

min ▷ *noun, colloq* a minute.

Min. ▷ *abbreviation* **1** Minister. **2** Ministry.

min. ▷ *abbreviation* **1** minimum. **2** minute or minutes.

mina see MYNA

minaret /mɪnə'rɛt, 'mɪnərɛt/ ▷ *noun* a tower on or attached to a mosque, with a balcony from which the MUEZZIN calls Muslims to prayer. ⓒ 17c: from Arabic *manarat* lighthouse.

minatory /'mɪnətərɪ, 'maɪn-/ ▷ *adj, formal* threatening. ⓒ 16c: from Latin *minari* to threaten.

mince /mɪns/ ▷ *verb* (***minced, mincing***) **1** to cut or shred something (especially meat) into very small pieces. **2** (*especially* **mince words with someone** or **mince one's words**, (*chiefly with negatives*) to restrain or soften the impact of (one's words, opinion, remarks, etc) when addressing someone □ *not one to mince his words.* **3** *intr, usually derog* to walk or speak with affected delicateness. ▷ *noun* **1** minced meat, especially beef. **2** a dish of cooked minced beef, often with carrots, onions and gravy. ● **mincer** *noun*. ⓒ 19c as *noun*; 14c as *verb*: from French *mincier*.

mincemeat ▷ *noun* a spiced mixture of dried fruits, apples, candied peel, etc and often suet, used as a filling for pies. ● **make mincemeat of someone** or **something** *colloq* to destroy or defeat them or it thoroughly.

mince pie ▷ *noun* a pie filled with mincemeat or with minced meat.

mincing ▷ *adj, usually derog* said of a manner of walking or behaving: over-delicate and affected. ● **mincingly** *adverb*. ⓒ 16c: from MINCE.

MIND /maɪnd/ ▷ *abbreviation, Brit* National Association of Mental Health.

mind /maɪnd/ ▷ *noun* **1** the power of thinking and understanding; the intelligence. **2** the place where thoughts, feelings and creative reasoning exist; the intellect. **3** memory; recollection □ *call something to mind.* **4** opinion; judgement □ *It's unjust, to my mind.* **5** attention □ *keep your mind on the job.* **6** wish; inclination □ *I have a mind to go.* **7** a very intelligent person □ *great minds agree.* **8** right senses; sanity □ *has lost his mind.* ▷ *verb* (***minded, minding***) **1** to look after, care for or keep something or someone safe □ *Stay here and mind the luggage.* **2** *tr & intr* to be upset, concerned or offended by something or someone □ *I don't mind the noise, just the smoke.* **3** (*also* **mind out** or **mind out for something**) to be careful or wary of it □ *Mind where you step.* See also *exclamation* below. **4** to take notice of or pay attention to something or someone □ *Mind your own business.* **5** to take care to control something □ *Mind your language.* **6** *tr & intr* to take care to protect something or someone □ *Mind your jacket near this wet paint!* **7** *tr & intr, dialect* to remember □ *Mind and hurry back now.* ▷ *exclamation* (*often* **mind out!**) be careful; watch out! □ *Mind! There's a car reversing.* See also *verb* 3 above. ● **minded** and **minder** see separate entries. ● **bear something in mind** to remember it. ● **do you mind!** an exclamation expressing disagreement or objection. ● **in one's mind's eye** in one's imagination. ● **in** or **of two minds** undecided. ● **know one's own mind** or **have a mind of one's own** to have firm opinions or intentions; to be strong-willed and independent. ● **make up one's mind** to come to a decision. ● **mind you** an expression used when adding a qualification to something already said □ *I refuse to go. Mind you, I'd like to be there just to see his face.* ● **of one** or **the same mind** agreed. ● **on one's mind** referring to something that is being thought about, considered, worried about, etc. ● **out of mind** forgotten; out of one's thoughts. ● **put one in mind of something** to remind one of it. ● **take one's** or **someone's mind off something** to distract one's or someone's thoughts from it. ● **to my mind** in my opinion. ⓒ 14c as *verb mynd*; Anglo-Saxon as *noun gemynd*, from *munan* to think.

■ **mind out** to beware or look out.

mind-bending ▷ *adj, colloq* **1** mind-blowing. **2** mind-boggling.

mind-blowing ▷ *adj, colloq* **1** very surprising, shocking, or exciting. **2** said of a drug: producing a state of hallucination or altered consciousness. ● **mind-blowingly** *adverb*.

mind-boggling ▷ *adj, colloq* too difficult, large, strange, etc to imagine or understand; impossible to take in. ● **mind-bogglingly** *adverb* □ *mind-bogglingly large.*

minded ▷ *adj* **1** *rather formal* having an intention or desire □ *not minded to reply to her letter.* **2** *in compounds* having the specified kind of mind or attitude □ *open-minded* □ *like-minded.*

minder ▷ *noun* **1** *in compounds* someone who takes care of or supervises someone or something □ *childminder.* **2** *colloq* a bodyguard. **3** someone who MINDs in any other sense.

mindful ▷ *adj* (*usually* **mindful of something**) keeping it in mind; attentive to it. ● **mindfully** *adverb*. ● **mindfulness** *noun*.

mindless ▷ *adj* **1** *derog* senseless; done without a reason □ *mindless violence.* **2** *derog* needing no effort of mind □ *watching mindless rubbish on TV.* **3** (*usually* **mindless of something**) taking no account of it □ *mindless of his responsibilities.* ● **mindlessly** *adverb*.

mind-numbing ▷ *adj, colloq* so boring or dull that it seems to deaden the brain. ● **mind-numbingly** *adverb*.

mind-reader ▷ *noun* someone who claims to be able to know other people's thoughts. ● **mind-reading** *noun* the process of apparently discovering another person's thoughts.

mindset ▷ *noun* an attitude or habit of mind, especially a firmly fixed one.

mine[1] /maɪn/ ▷ *pronoun* **1** something or someone belonging to, or connected with, me; the thing or things, etc belonging to me □ *Your coat is nice, but I prefer mine.* **2** my family or people □ *as long as it doesn't affect me or mine.* ▷ *adj, old use, poetic* used in place of MY before a vowel sound or *h* □ *mine eye* □ *mine host.* ● **of mine** belonging to, or connected with, me □ *a cousin of mine.* ⓒ Anglo-Saxon *min*.

mine[2] /maɪn/ ▷ *noun* **1** *often in compounds* an opening or excavation in the ground, used to remove minerals, metal ores, coal, etc, from the Earth's crust □ *coalmine* □ *goldmine.* **2** *sometimes in compounds* an explosive device that is placed just beneath the ground surface or in water, designed to destroy tanks, ships, etc, when detonated □ *land-mine.* **3** a rich source □ *He's a mine of information.* **4** an excavation dug underneath a military position, fortification, etc to enter or undermine it, blow it up, etc. ▷ *verb* (***mined, mining***) **1** *tr & intr* to dig for (minerals, etc) □ *They mine gold in those hills.* **2** (*also* **mine somewhere for something**) to dig (a particular area) in order to extract minerals, etc □ *started mining the western bay in the 50s for gold.* **3** to lay exploding mines in (land or water) □ *The beach has been mined.* **4** to destroy something with exploding mines □ *Our ship was mined.* ● **miner** *noun, often in compounds* someone who mines or works in a mine, especially a coal mine □ *coalminer* □

goldminer. • **mining** *noun* **1** the act or process of extracting minerals, etc from the ground. **2** the act or process of laying mines. ◷ 14c: French, from *miner* to mine.

minefield ▷ *noun* **1** an area of land or water in which mines (see MINE^2 *noun* 2) have been laid. **2** a subject or situation that presents many problems or dangers, especially hidden ones.

minelayer ▷ *noun* a ship or aircraft designed for laying mines.

mineral /ˈmɪnərəl/ ▷ *noun* **1** *technical* a naturally occurring substance that is inorganic, usually crystalline, and has characteristic physical and chemical properties by which it may be identified. **2** *loosely* any substance obtained by mining, including fossil fuels (eg coal, natural gas or petroleum) although they are organic. **3** any inorganic substance, ie one that is neither animal nor vegetable. **4** (**minerals**) see MINERAL WATER. ▷ *adj* belonging or relating to the nature of a mineral; containing minerals. ◷ 14c in sense 2: from Latin *mineralis* relating to mines.

mineralize or **mineralise** /ˈmɪnərəlaɪz/ ▷ *verb* (***mineralized, mineralizing***) **1** to give something the properties of a mineral. **2** to make something into a mineral. • **mineralization** *noun.* • **mineralizer** *noun.*

mineralogy /mɪnəˈralədʒɪ/ ▷ *noun* the scientific study of minerals. • **mineralogical** *adj.* • **mineralogist** *noun.*

mineral oil ▷ *noun* any oil obtained from minerals, rather than from a plant or animal source.

mineral water ▷ *noun* water containing small quantities of dissolved minerals, especially water that occurs naturally in this state at a spring. Sometimes called **minerals**.

minestrone /mɪnəˈstrounɪ/ ▷ *noun, cookery* a clear stock-based soup containing a variety of chunky vegetables and pasta, often served with grated cheese on top. ◷ 19c: Italian, from *minestrare* to serve.

minesweeper ▷ *noun* a ship equipped to clear mines from an area. • **minesweeping** *noun.*

Ming ▷ *adj* belonging or relating to the Chinese Ming dynasty (1368–1643), or especially to its pottery and other art ◻ *a Ming vase.*

mingle /ˈmɪŋgəl/ ▷ *verb* (***mingled, mingling***) (*often* **mingle with something** or **someone**) **1** *tr & intr* to become or make something become blended or mixed. **2** *intr* to move from person to person at a social engagement, briefly talking to each. **3** *tr & intr* to associate or have dealings with others. • **mingler** *noun.* • **mingling** *noun.* ◷ 15c: from Anglo-Saxon *mengan* to mix.

mingy /ˈmɪndʒɪ/ *Brit derog, colloq* ▷ *adj* (***mingier, mingiest***) ungenerous; mean; meagre. • **minginess** *noun.* ◷ Early 20c.

mini /ˈmɪnɪ/ *colloq* ▷ *noun* (***minis***) something small or short of its kind, especially a MINISKIRT, or a type of small car. ▷ *adj* small or short of its kind; miniature. ◷ 1960s.

mini- ▷ *prefix, forming nouns, denoting* smaller or shorter than the standard size ◻ *minibus* ◻ *mini-submarine.* Compare MAXI, MIDI-. ◷ 1960s: a shortening of MINIATURE or MINIMUM.

miniature /ˈmɪnɪtʃə(r)/ ▷ *noun* **1** a small copy, model or breed of anything. **2 a** a very small painting, especially a portrait on a very small scale; **b** the genre of painting that includes such pictures. **3** manuscript illumination. ▷ *adj* minute or small-scale; referring to the nature of a miniature. • **miniaturist** *noun* an artist who paints miniatures. • **in miniature** on a small scale. ◷ 16c: from Italian *miniatura*, from Latin, from *miniare* to illuminate (a manuscript), or to use red paint for printing, illuminating, etc, from *minium* red lead.

miniaturize or **miniaturise** /ˈmɪnɪtʃəraɪz/ ▷ *verb* (***miniaturized, miniaturizing***) **1** to make (eg technical equipment) on a small scale. **2** to make something very small; to reduce it significantly in size. • **miniaturization** *noun.*

minibreak ▷ *noun* a short holiday, usually a weekend or long weekend break.

minibus ▷ *noun* a small bus, usually one with between 12 and 15 seats in it.

minicab ▷ *noun* a taxi that is ordered by telephone from a private company, not one that can be stopped in the street. • **minicabbing** *noun* running a minicab or minicabs, as a line of work or business.

minicam ▷ *noun* a miniature, portable, shoulder-held TV camera, as used in news reporting. ◷ 1930s.

minicomputer ▷ *noun* a medium-sized computer, larger than a MICROCOMPUTER but smaller than a MAINFRAME.

minidisk ▷ *noun, computing* a very compact magnetic disk storage medium for microcomputers.

mini-flyweight ▷ *noun* an amateur boxer who weighs under 48kg (105 lb).

minim /ˈmɪnɪm/ ▷ *noun* **1** *music* a note half the length of a SEMIBREVE. Also called **half-note**. **2** in the imperial system: a unit of liquid volume, equal to 1/60 of a fluid drachm (0.06ml). **3** in handwriting: a short down-stroke. ◷ 15c: from Latin *minimus* smallest.

minimal /ˈmɪnɪməl/ ▷ *adj* **1** very little indeed; negligible ◻ *caused minimal damage.* **2** referring to the nature of a minimum. **3** said of art, etc: minimalist. • **minimally** *adverb* in a minimal way; to a minimal extent. ◷ 17c: see MINIMUM.

minimal invasive therapy ▷ *noun, surgery* an operating procedure that does not necessitate stitching or scarring, eg gallstone removal by endoscopy and laser treatment.

minimalism ▷ *noun* **1** especially in art, music and design: the policy of using the minimum means, eg the fewest and simplest elements, to achieve the desired result. **2** (*also* **minimal art**) painting, sculpture, etc making minimal use of form, colour, shape, etc, composed eg of large geometric areas of primary or monochrome colours.

minimalist *noun* **1** a follower of minimalism. **2** an artist whose work is characteristic of minimalism. **3** someone who believes in or advocates a policy of the least possible action or intervention. ▷ *adj* belonging to or characteristic of minimalism. ◷ 1960s.

minimax /ˈmɪnɪmaks, -na-/ ▷ *noun* **1** *math* the lowest value in a set of maximum values. **2** in game theory: the strategy of making all decisions in such a way as to minimize the chances of incurring the maximum potential loss. Compare MAXIMIN. ◷ 1940s: from *MINIMUM* + *MAXIMUM*.

minimize or **minimise** /ˈmɪnɪmaɪz/ ▷ *verb* (***minimized, minimizing***) **1** to reduce something to a minimum. **2** to treat something as being of little importance or significance. ◷ 19c.

minimum /ˈmɪnɪməm/ ▷ *noun* (***minimums*** or ***minima*** /-mə/) **1** the lowest possible number, value, quantity or degree. **2** (*sometimes* **a minimum of something**) the lowest number, value, quantity or degree reached or allowed ◻ *There must be a minimum of three people present* ◻ *Three is the minimum.* ▷ *adj* **1** relating or referring to the nature of a minimum; lowest possible ◻ *minimum waste.* **2** lowest reached or allowed ◻ *minimum age.* Opposite of MAXIMUM. ◷ 17c: Latin, from *minimus* smallest.

minimum lending rate ▷ *noun, Brit econ,* (abbreviation **MLR**) *formerly* the minimum rate of interest at which the Bank of England would lend to discount houses, which was superseded in 1981 by the BANK BASE-RATE.

minimum wage ▷ *noun* the lowest wage an employer is allowed to pay, by law or union agreement.

mining see under MINE[2]

minion /ˈmɪnjən/ ▷ *noun, derog* **1** an employee or follower, especially one who is fawning or subservient. **2** a favourite subordinate of a sovereign, VIP, etc. ⓒ 16c, originally meaning 'a darling or favourite': from French MIGNON.

minipill ▷ *noun* a low-dose oral contraceptive containing progesterone but no oestrogen.

miniscule

See Usage Note at **minuscule**.

mini-series ▷ *singular noun, TV* a short series of related programmes, especially dramas, usually broadcast over consecutive days or weeks. ⓒ 1970s.

miniskirt ▷ *noun* a very short skirt, with a hemline well above the knee. Often shortened to MINI. ⓒ 1960s.

minister /ˈmɪnɪstə(r)/ ▷ *noun* **1** the political head of, or a senior politician with responsibilities in, a government department. See also SECRETARY OF STATE, MINISTER OF STATE. **2** a member of the clergy in certain branches of the Christian church. Compare PRIEST. **3** a high-ranking diplomat, especially the next in rank below an ambassador. **4** *formal* a person acting as agent for another, especially in business. ▷ *verb* (***ministered, ministering***) *intr* **1** *formal* (*especially* **minister to someone**) to provide someone with help or some kind of service; to take care of them. **2** to perform the duties of a religious minister. ● **ministerial** /-ˈstɪərɪəl/ *adj* **1** belonging or relating to, or typical of, a minister or a ministry ▫ *ministerial duties.* **2** relating to or having executive authority. ● **ministerially** *adverb.* ⓒ 13c: French, from Latin *minister* servant.

Minister of State ▷ *noun, Brit* a minister who assists a MINISTER OF THE CROWN in a large government department, usually having no place in the Cabinet.

Minister of the Crown ▷ *noun, Brit* the political head of a government department and a member of THE CABINET.

minister without portfolio ▷ *noun* (***ministers without portfolio***) *Brit* a government minister who does not have responsibility for a specific department.

ministration /mɪnɪˈstreɪʃən/ ▷ *noun, formal* **1** the act or process of ministering. **2** (*usually* **ministrations**) help or service given. ● **ministrant** /ˈmɪnɪstrənt/ *adj, noun.* ● **ministrative** *adj.*

ministry /ˈmɪnɪstrɪ, -nə-/ ▷ *noun* (***ministries***) **1 a** a government department; **b** the premises it occupies. **2** (**the ministry**) **a** the profession, duties or period of service of a religious minister; **b** religious ministers collectively. **3** the act of ministering.

Minitel /ˈmɪnɪtɛl/ ▷ *noun* in France: a public videotext system that provides banking and mail order services, electronic messaging, etc.

miniver /ˈmɪnɪvə(r)/ ▷ *noun* a type of fur used for lining ceremonial robes. ⓒ 14c: French.

mink /mɪŋk/ ▷ *noun* (*plural* ***mink***) **1** a semi-aquatic European or N American mammal with a slender body, webbed feet and thick fur, brown except for a white patch on the chin. **2** the highly valued fur of this animal. Also *as adj* ▫ *mink coat.* **3** a garment, especially a coat, made of this fur ▫ *wearing her mink.* ⓒ 15c: perhaps from Swedish *mänk.*

minke whale see under RORQUAL

Minn. see under MN

minneola /mɪnɪˈoʊlə/ ▷ *noun* (***minneolas***) an orange-like citrus fruit which is a cross between a grapefruit and a tangerine. ⓒ 20c: perhaps named after *Mineola* in Texas, USA.

minnow /ˈmɪnoʊ/ ▷ *noun* **1** any of several kinds of small freshwater fish of the carp family. **2** an insignificant person, group, thing, etc. ⓒ 15c.

Minoan /mɪˈnoʊən, maɪ-/ ▷ *adj* belonging or relating to the Bronze Age civilization that flourished in Crete and other Aegean islands from approximately 3 000–1 100 BC. ▷ *noun* an individual belonging to this civilization. ⓒ 19c: from *Minos*, a mythological king of Crete.

minor /ˈmaɪnə(r)/ ▷ *adj* **1** not as great in importance or size; fairly or relatively small or insignificant ▫ *only a minor problem.* **2** *music* **a** said of a scale: having a semitone between the second and third, fifth and sixth, and seventh and eighth notes; **b** said of a key, chord, etc: based on such a scale. **3** *Brit, especially formerly* used after the surname of the younger of two brothers attending the same school: junior ▫ *Simcox minor.* **4** said of a person: below the age of legal majority or adulthood. In all senses compare MAJOR. ▷ *noun* **1** someone who is below the age of legal majority (see MAJORITY 3). **2** *music* a minor key, chord or scale. **3** *especially US* **a** a student's minor or subsidiary subject of study; **b** a student studying such a subject ▫ *He's a history minor.* ▷ *verb* (***minored, minoring***) *especially US* (*always* **minor in something**) to study a specified minor or subsidary subject at college or university. Compare MAJOR. ⓒ 13c: Latin meaning 'less'.

minority /maɪˈnɒrɪtɪ, mɪ-/ ▷ *noun* (***minorities***) **1** a small number, or the smaller of two numbers, sections or groups. **2** a group of people who are different, especially in terms of race or religion, from most of the people (ie the MAJORITY) in a country, region, etc. **3** the state of being the smaller or lesser of two groups ▫ *in a minority.* **4** the state of being below the age of legal majority. Often *as adj* ▫ *minority party* ▫ *minority rights* ▫ *minority view.* ⓒ 16c: from Latin *minoritas*; related to MINOR.

minor league see under MAJOR LEAGUE

minor mode see under MODE

minor orders ▷ *plural noun, Christianity* the lower degrees of HOLY ORDERS, eg an ACOLYTE.

minor planet see ASTEROID

minster /ˈmɪnstə(r)/ ▷ *noun* a large church or cathedral, especially one that was originally attached to a monastery ▫ *York Minster.* ⓒ Anglo-Saxon *mynster*, from Latin *monasterium* monastery.

minstrel /ˈmɪnstrəl/ ▷ *noun, historical* **1** in the Middle Ages: a travelling singer, musician and reciter of poetry, etc. **2** *formerly* in the USA and Britain: any of a group of white-skinned entertainers made up to look black, who performed song and dance routines superficially of Negro origin. ● **minstrelsy** *noun* the art or occupation of a medieval minstrel. ⓒ 13c: French, meaning 'someone employed' eg an attendant or musician, from Latin; see MINISTER.

mint[1] ▷ *noun* **1** any of various aromatic plants, including PEPPERMINT and SPEARMINT, with paired leaves and small, white or purple flowers, widely grown as a garden herb. **2** *cookery* the pungent-smelling leaves of this plant, used fresh or dried as a flavouring. **3** a sweet flavoured with mint, or with a synthetic substitute for mint. Also called PEPPERMINT. ● **minty** *adj* (***mintier, mintiest***) tasting or smelling of mint. ⓒ Anglo-Saxon *minte*: from Latin *mentha.*

mint[2] ▷ *noun* **1** a place where coins are produced under government authority. **2** *colloq* a very large sum of money ▫ *must be worth a mint.* ● **in mint condition** or **state** in perfect condition, as if brand new; never or hardly used. ▷ *verb* (***minted, minting***) **1** to manufacture (coins). **2** to invent or coin (a new word, phrase, etc). ● **mintage** *noun.* ⓒ 15c in *noun* sense 1; Anglo-Saxon *mynet* in obsolete sense 'money'.

mint julep see JULEP 2

mint sauce ▷ *noun, cookery* the chopped leaves of spearmint or other mint mixed with vinegar and sugar, served especially with roast lamb.

minuend /ˈmɪnjʊɛnd/ ▷ *noun, math* the number that another number is to be subtracted from. Compare SUBTRAHEND. ⓘ 18c: from Latin *minuendus*, from *minuere* to diminish.

minuet /mɪnjʊˈɛt/ ▷ *noun* **1** a slow formal dance with short steps in triple time, popular in the 17c and 18c. **2** a piece of music for this dance. ⓘ 17c: from French *menuet*, from *menu* small.

minus /ˈmaɪnəs/ ▷ *prep* **1** with the subtraction of (a specified number) □ ***Eight minus six equals two is usually written as 8 − 6 = 2.*** **2** *colloq* without □ ***arrived minus his wife.*** ▷ *adj* **1** negative or less than zero. **2** said of a student's grade, and placed after the grade: indicating a level slightly below that indicated by the letter □ ***got a B minus for my essay.*** **3** *colloq* characterized by being a disadvantage □ ***a minus point.*** ▷ *noun* (***minuses***) **1** a sign (−) indicating a negative quantity or that the quantity which follows it is to be subtracted. Also called **minus sign**. **2** *colloq* a negative point; a disadvantage. **3** a negative quantity or term. In all senses opposite of PLUS. ⓘ 15c: Latin, from *minor* less.

minuscule /ˈmɪnəskjuːl/ ▷ *adj* **1** extremely small. **2** said of letters or script: lower-case, not upper-case or capital. ▷ *noun* **1** *printing* a lower-case letter. **2** a variety of small, cursive script originated by monks in the 7c. Compare MAJUSCULE. • **minuscular** *adj*. ⓘ 18c in sense 2: from Latin *littera minuscula* small letter.

minuscule, miniscule

• **Minuscule** is originally a technical word that has developed a more general meaning. The grammar has also changed, because the word was originally a noun and is now familiar as an adjective, meaning 'very small'. This makes it awkward in use:

✓ *She struggled with a minuscule portion of chicken.*

✓ *His wide chest tapers to a minuscule waist and spindly useless legs.*

• For this reason, and because the word is not often marked by a distinct pronunciation, it is sometimes written as **miniscule**, under the influence of the productive prefix **mini-**:

? *She showed him a photograph album, with herself by a fjord in a miniscule bikini.*

• However, this spelling is not yet widely accepted.

☆ RECOMMENDATION: use **minuscule** in more formal writing and print; be cautious about using **miniscule**, although this form is likely to win in the end.

minute¹ /ˈmɪnɪt/ ▷ *noun* (abbreviation **min**) **1** a unit of time equal to ($^1/_{60}$) of an hour; 60 seconds. **2** *colloq* a short while □ ***Wait a minute.*** **3** a particular point in time □ ***At that minute the phone rang.*** **4** the distance that can be travelled in a minute □ ***a house five minutes away.*** **5** (*usually* **the minutes**) the official written record of what is said at a formal meeting. **6** a written note or statement sent to a colleague; a memorandum. **7** *geom* (symbol ′) a unit of angular measurement equal to ($^1/_{60}$) of a degree; 60 seconds. ▷ *verb* (***minuted, minuting***) **1** to make an official written record of what is said in (eg a meeting); to take or record something in the minutes of (eg a meeting). **2** to send a memorandum to someone. • **up to the minute** or **up-to-the-minute** very modern, recent or up-to-date; the latest. ⓘ 14c: French; related to MINUTE².

minute² /maɪˈnjuːt/ ▷ *adj* (***minuter, minutest***) **1** very small; tiny. **2** precise; detailed. **3** petty; trivial. • **minutely** *adverb*. • **minuteness** *noun*. ⓘ 15c: from Latin *minutus* small, from *minuere* to make something small or smaller.

minute hand /ˈmɪnɪt —/ ▷ *noun* on a clock or watch, etc: the hand that indicates the minutes.

Minuteman /ˈmɪnɪtman/ ▷ *noun, US historical* **1** especially in the War of Independence: a member of a group of militiamen, particularly in New England, who were prepared to take up arms at very short notice. **2** an informal name for a type of three-stage intercontinental missile that was developed in the US in the 1960s.

minute steak /ˈmɪnɪt —/ ▷ *noun* a thin steak, usually beef, that can be cooked quickly.

minutiae /mɪˈnjuːʃɪaɪ/ ▷ *plural noun* small and often unimportant details. ⓘ 18c: plural of Latin *minutia* smallness, from *minutus*; see MINUTE².

minx /mɪŋks/ ▷ *noun* (***minxes***) *humorous or rather dated* a cheeky, playful, sly or flirtatious young woman. ⓘ 16c, originally in obsolete sense 'a pet dog'.

Miocene /ˈmaɪəsiːn/ *geol* ▷ *noun* the fourth epoch of the Tertiary period. See table at GEOLOGICAL TIME SCALE. ▷ *adj* **1** belonging or relating to this epoch. **2** relating to rocks formed during this epoch. ⓘ 19c: from Greek *meion* smaller.

MIPS or **mips** /mɪps/ ▷ *abbreviation, computing* millions of instructions per second.

MIR ▷ *abbreviation* mortgage interest relief.

miracle /ˈmɪrəkəl/ ▷ *noun* **1** an act or event that breaks the laws of nature, and is therefore thought to be caused by the intervention of God or another supernatural force. **2** *colloq* a fortunate happening; an amazing event □ ***It's a miracle you called round when you did.*** **3** *colloq* an amazing example or achievement of something □ ***a miracle of modern technology.*** Also *as adj* □ ***miracle drug.*** • **work miracles** to have an amazingly positive effect □ ***She's worked miracles on him — he hardly drinks at all now.*** ⓘ 12c: French, from Latin *miraculum*, from *mirari* to be amazed at.

miracle play ▷ *noun* **1** an early form of MYSTERY PLAY. **2** an enactment of one of the miracles performed by the saints.

miraculous /mɪˈrakjʊləs/ ▷ *adj* **1** brought about by, relating to, or like a miracle. **2** *colloq* wonderful; amazing; amazingly fortunate □ ***a miraculous escape.*** • **miraculously** *adverb*. • **miraculousness** *noun*.

mirage /ˈmɪrɑːʒ, mɪˈrɑːʒ/ ▷ *noun* **1** an optical illusion that usually resembles a pool of water on the horizon reflecting light from the sky, commonly experienced in deserts, and caused by the REFRACTION of light by very hot air near to the ground. **2** anything illusory or imaginary. ⓘ 19c: French, from *mirer* to reflect.

MIRAS /ˈmaɪras/ ▷ *abbreviation, Brit* mortgage interest relief at source.

mire /maɪə(r)/ ▷ *noun* **1** deep mud; a boggy area. **2** trouble; difficulty; anything unpleasant and messy. ▷ *verb* (***mired, miring***) **1** *tr & intr* to sink, or to make something or someone sink, in a mire. **2** to soil something or someone with mud. **3** to involve someone in trouble or difficulties. • **miry** *adj*. ⓘ 14c: from Norse *myrr* bog.

mirin /mɪˈrɪn/ ▷ *noun* a sweet rice wine used in Japanese cookery. ⓘ 20c: Japanese.

mirk and **mirky** see under MURKY

mirror /ˈmɪrə(r)/ ▷ *noun* **1** **a** a smooth highly-polished surface, such as glass, coated with a thin layer of metal, such as silver, that reflects an image of what is in front of it; **b** a reflective surface of this kind in a frame and hung on the wall or as part of a wardrobe or dressing table, etc. **2** any surface that reflects light. **3** a faithful representation or reflection □ ***when art is a mirror of life.*** ▷ *verb* (***mirrored, mirroring***) **1** to represent or depict something faithfully. **2** to fit (eg a wall) with a mirror or mirrors. **3** to reflect something or someone as in a mirror. ⓘ 14c: French, from Latin *mirare* to look at.

mirror image ▷ *noun* **1** a reflected image as produced by a mirror, ie one in which the right and left sides are reversed. **2** an object that matches another as if it were its reflection in a mirror, ie with features reversed.

mirror writing ▷ *noun* writing which is like ordinary writing as seen in a mirror, ie writing in reverse.

mirth /mɜːθ/ ▷ *noun* laughter; merriment. • **mirthful** *adj.* • **mirthfully** *adverb.* • **mirthfulness** *noun.* • **mirthless** *adj.* • **mirthlessly** *adverb.* • **mirthlessness** *noun* ⓒ Anglo-Saxon *myrgth*, from *myrige* merry.

MIRV /mɜːv/ ▷ *noun, military* a missile that contains many thermonuclear warheads, each able to attack a separate target. ⓒ 1960s: acronym for *M*ultiple *I*ndependently Targeted *R*e-entry *V*ehicle.

miry see under MIRE

mis- ▷ *prefix, denoting* **1** wrong or wrongly; bad or badly □ *mismanagement* □ *misconceived.* **2** a lack or absence of something □ *mistrust.* ⓒ Anglo-Saxon; related to MISS[1].

misadventure ▷ *noun, formal* **1** bad luck. **2** an unfortunate happening. **3** *law* an accident, with total absence of negligence or intent to commit crime □ *death by misadventure.* ⓒ 13c: from French *mésaventure*, from *mésavenir* to turn out badly.

misadvise ▷ *verb* to advise someone wrongly or badly. • **misadvisedly** *adverb.*

misalign ▷ *verb* to align something wrongly. • **misalignment** *noun.*

misalliance ▷ *noun, formal* a relationship or alliance, especially a marriage, in which the parties are not suited to each other. ⓒ 18c: modelled on French *mésalliance* a marriage between two people of differing social classes.

misally /mɪsə'laɪ/ ▷ *verb* to ally (people, parties, etc) in an unsuitable way.

misanthrope /'mɪzənθroup, 'mɪs-/ or **misanthropist** /mɪz'anθrəpɪst/ ▷ *noun* **1** someone who has an irrational hatred or distrust of people in general. **2** someone whose hatred or distrust of people is so strong that they avoid all human contact. • **misanthropic** /-'θrɒpɪk/ *adj* • **misanthropically** *adverb.* • **misanthropy** /mɪz'anθrəpɪ/ *noun.* ⓒ 16c: from Greek *misos* hatred + *anthropos* man.

misapply ▷ *verb* **1** to apply something wrongly. **2** to use something unwisely or for the wrong purpose. • **misapplication** *noun.*

misapprehend ▷ *verb, formal* to misunderstand something; to understand it in the wrong sense, etc. • **misapprehension** *noun* misunderstanding. • **misapprehensive** *adj.*

misappropriate ▷ *verb, formal, especially law* **1** to take something (especially money) dishonestly for oneself. **2** to put something (eg funds) to a wrong use. • **misappropriation** *noun* embezzlement or theft. ⓒ 19c.

misbegotten ▷ *adj* **1** *literary* illegally obtained. **2** *literary* foolishly planned or thought out; ill-conceived. **3** *old use* illegitimate; bastard. ⓒ 16c: from past participle of BEGET.

misbehave ▷ *verb, intr* to behave badly. • **misbehaviour** or (*US*) **misbehavior** *noun.* ⓒ 15c.

misc. ▷ *abbreviation* miscellaneous.

miscalculate ▷ *verb, tr & intr* to calculate or estimate something wrongly. • **miscalculation** *noun.*

miscall ▷ *verb* **1** to call someone or something by the wrong name; to misname. **2** *intr* in games: to make a bad or inaccurate call (see CALL *noun* 13). **3** *dialect or old use* to abuse or malign someone.

miscarriage ▷ *noun* **1** *medicine* the expulsion of a fetus from the uterus before it is capable of independent survival, ie at any time up to about the 24th week of pregnancy. Also called **spontaneous abortion**. **2 a** an act or instance of failure or error; **b** failure of a plan, etc to reach a desired objective; **c** failure of goods, etc to reach a desired destination. **3** see under MISCARRIAGE OF JUSTICE.

miscarriage of justice ▷ *noun* (***miscarriages of justice***) a failure of a judicial system to do justice in a particular case. Sometimes shortened to **miscarriage**.

miscarry ▷ *verb, intr* **1** said of a woman: to have a MISCARRIAGE (sense 1). **2** *formal* said of a plan, etc: to go wrong or fail; to be carried out wrongly or badly. ⓒ 14c in obsolete sense 'to come to harm'.

miscast ▷ *verb* **1** *theat* to give an unsuitable part to (an actor) or put an unsuitable actor in (a part). **2** to CAST something (in any other sense) wrongly or badly.

miscegenation /mɪsɪdʒə'neɪʃən/ ▷ *noun, formal* marriage or breeding between people of different races, especially that between people of different skin colours. ⓒ 19c: from Latin *miscere* to mix + *genus* race.

miscellaneous /mɪsə'leɪnɪəs/ ▷ *adj* **1** made up of various kinds; mixed. **2** said of a person: with a many-sided personality or with a variety of talents, etc. • **miscellaneously** *adverb.* • **miscellaneousness** *noun.* ⓒ 17c: from Latin *miscellaneus*, from *miscere* to mix.

miscellany /mɪ'sɛlənɪ/ ▷ *noun* (***miscellanies***) a mixture of various kinds, especially a collection of writings on different subjects or by different authors. • **miscellanist** *noun* someone who writes or compiles miscellanies. ⓒ 17c: from Latin *miscellanea*; see MISCELLANEOUS.

mischance ▷ *noun* **1** bad luck. **2** an instance of bad luck. ⓒ 13c.

mischief /'mɪstʃɪf/ ▷ *noun* **1** behaviour that annoys or irritates people but does not mean or cause any serious harm □ *The children are getting up to mischief.* **2** the desire to behave in this way □ *full of mischief.* **3** a person, usually a child, with a tendency to be mischievous □ *He is such a mischief.* **4** damage or harm; an injury □ *You'll do yourself a mischief.* ⓒ 14c: from French *meschief* a disaster or bad end.

mischievous /'mɪstʃɪvəs/ ▷ *adj* **1** said of a child, etc: tending to make mischief. **2** said of behaviour: playfully troublesome. **3** *rather dated* said of a thing: damaging or harmful. • **mischievously** *adverb.* • **mischievousness** *noun.*

miscible /'mɪsɪbəl/ ▷ *adj, formal, chem* said of a liquid or liquids: capable of dissolving in each other to form a single phase (see PHASE *noun* 4). • **miscibility** *noun.* ⓒ 16c: from Latin *miscibilis* capable of mixing, from *miscere* to mix.

misconceive ▷ *verb* **1** *tr & intr* (*also* **misconceive of something**) to have the wrong idea or impression about it; to misunderstand it. **2** to plan or think something out badly. • **misconceived** *adj.*

misconception *noun* a wrong or misguided attitude, opinion or view.

misconduct ▷ *noun* /mɪs'kɒndʌkt/ **1** improper or unethical behaviour □ *professional misconduct.* **2** bad management. ▷ *verb* /mɪskən'dʌkt/ **1** to conduct (eg oneself) badly. **2** to manage (eg a business) badly.

misconstruction *noun* an interpretation that is wrong or mistaken.

misconstrue ▷ *verb* to interpret something wrongly or mistakenly.

miscount ▷ *verb, tr & intr* to count something wrongly; to miscalculate. ▷ *noun* an act or instance of counting wrongly.

miscreant /'mɪskrɪənt/ ▷ *noun, literary or old use* a malicious person; a villain or scoundrel. ▷ *adj* villainous or wicked. ⓒ 14c, originally meaning 'unbelieving' or 'heretical': from French *mescreant.*

miscue ▷ *verb* **1** *tr & intr*, in billiards, snooker and pool: to hit the CUE BALL wrongly with the cue (see CUE[2] *noun* 1); to make a miscue. **2** *intr, theat* to miss one's cue or answer the wrong cue (see CUE[1] 1). ▷ *noun* (***miscues***) **1** in billiards, snooker and pool: a stroke in which the cue does not hit the cue ball properly, slips off it or misses it. **2** an error or failure.

misdate ▻ *verb* to date (eg a letter) wrongly. ▻ *noun* (***misdates***) a wrong date.

misdeal ▻ *noun* in cards, etc: an incorrect deal. ▻ *verb, tr & intr* to deal or divide something (especially playing cards) wrongly.

misdeed ▻ *noun, literary or formal* an example of bad or criminal behaviour; a wrongdoing □ *will be punished for his misdeeds.*

misdemeanour or (*US*) **misdemeanor** ▻ *noun* **1** *formal* a wrongdoing; a misdeed. **2** *old use, law* a crime less serious than a FELONY. ⓒ 15c: from obsolete *misdemean* to misbehave.

misdiagnose ▻ *verb* **1** to diagnose something (eg a disease) wrongly. **2** to wrongly diagnose the condition of (eg a patient). ● **misdiagnosis** *noun.*

misdial ▻ *verb, tr & intr* to dial (a telephone number) incorrectly.

misdirect ▻ *verb* **1** *formal* to give wrong directions to someone; to direct, address or instruct something or someone wrongly. **2** *formal* to use something (especially funds) for an unsuitable purpose. **3** *law* said of a judge: to provide incorrect legal information to (a jury). ● **misdirection** *noun* **1** the process of misdirecting or being misdirected. **2** the wrong directions or address.

mise-en-scène /miːzɒn'sɛn; *French* miːzɑ̃sɛn/ ▻ *noun* (***mise-en-scènes***) **1** *theat* **a** the process of arranging scenery and props; **b** the arrangement of the scenery and props; **c** the visual effect such an arrangement has. Also called **stage setting**. **2** *cinematog* the composition of each frame. **3** *literary* the setting in which an event takes place. ⓒ 19c: French, literally 'a putting-on-stage'.

miser /'maɪzə(r)/ ▻ *noun* **1** someone who lives in bleak, uncomfortable, etc conditions in order to store up their wealth. **2** any ungenerous person. ● **miserliness** *noun.* ● **miserly** *adj.* ⓒ 16c: Latin, meaning 'wretched'.

miserable /'mɪzərəbəl, 'mɪzrəbəl/ ▻ *adj* **1** said of a person: **a** very unhappy; **b** habitually bad-tempered or depressed. **2** marked by great unhappiness □ *a miserable life.* **3** causing unhappiness or discomfort □ *miserable weather.* **4** marked by poverty or squalor □ *miserable living conditions.* **5** contemptible □ *The show was a miserable failure.* **6** *dialect* ungenerous; mean. ● **miserably** *adverb.* ⓒ 16c: from French *misérable*, from Latin *miserabilis*, from *miser*, see MISER.

misère /mɪ'zɛə(r)/ ▻ *noun* (***misères***) *cards* a call made by a player meaning that they undertake not to take any tricks (see TRICK *noun* 8). ⓒ 19c: French, meaning 'poverty'.

misericord /mɪ'zerɪkɔːd/ ▻ *noun* **1** in a church: a ledge on the underside of a seat in the choir stalls, often a finely carved one, which a standing person can use as a support when the seat is folded up. **2** *historical* in a monastery: a room where some relaxation of the rules was allowed. ⓒ 14c: from Latin *misericordia* compassion.

misery /'mɪzərɪ/ ▻ *noun* (***miseries***) **1** great unhappiness or suffering. **2** a cause of unhappiness □ *His biggest misery is the cold.* **3** poverty or squalor □ *living in misery.* **4** *colloq* a habitually sad or bad-tempered person □ *Don't be such a misery.* ● **put someone** or **something out of their misery 1** to relieve them from their physical suffering or their mental anguish. **2** to kill (an animal that is in great pain). ⓒ 14c: from French *miserie*, from Latin *miseria*.

misfile ▻ *verb* to file (eg papers) wrongly.

misfire ▻ *verb, intr* **1** said of a gun, etc: to fail to fire, or to fail to fire properly. **2** said of an engine or vehicle: to fail to ignite the fuel at the right time. **3** said of a plan, practical joke, etc: to be unsuccessful; to produce the wrong effect. ▻ *noun* an instance of misfiring.

misfit ▻ *noun* **1** someone who is not suited to the situation, job, social environment, etc that they are in. **2** something that fits badly or not at all. ⓒ 19c.

misfortune ▻ *noun* **1** bad luck. **2** an unfortunate incident.

misgiving ▻ *noun* (*often* **misgivings**) a feeling of uneasiness, doubt or suspicion.

misguided ▻ *adj* acting from or showing mistaken ideas or bad judgement. ● **misguidedly** *adverb.*

mishandle /mɪs'handəl/ ▻ *verb* **1** to deal with something or someone carelessly or without skill. **2** to handle something or someone roughly; to mistreat someone or something.

mishap /'mɪshap/ ▻ *noun* an unfortunate accident, especially a minor one; a piece of bad luck. ⓒ 14c: from obsolete *hap* luck or happening.

mishear /mɪs'hɪə(r)/ ▻ *verb* to hear something or someone incorrectly.

mishit ▻ *verb* /mɪs'hɪt/ *sport, etc* to fail to hit (eg a ball) cleanly or accurately. ▻ *noun* /'mɪshɪt/ **1** an act of mishitting. **2** a wrongly-hit ball, shot, etc.

mishmash /'mɪʃmaʃ/ ▻ *noun, colloq* a jumbled assortment or mixture. ⓒ 15c: a reduplication of MASH.

Mishnah /'mɪʃnə/ ▻ *noun* (***Mishnayoth*** /mɪʃnə'joʊθ/) *Judaism* an important collection of codes and laws, forming the first section of the TALMUD. ● **Mishnaic** /mɪʃ'neɪɪk/ *adj.* ⓒ 17c: Hebrew, from *shanah* to repeat, teach or learn in the oral tradition.

misinform ▻ *verb* to give someone incorrect or misleading information. ▻ *noun* **misinformation**.

misinterpret ▻ *verb* to understand or explain something incorrectly or misleadingly. ● **misinterpretation** *noun.*

misjudge ▻ *verb* to judge something or someone wrongly, or to have an unfairly low opinion of them. ● **misjudgement** or **misjudgment** *noun.*

miskey /mɪs'kiː/ ▻ *verb, computing, etc* to key (especially data) incorrectly.

miskick ▻ *verb* to kick (eg a ball) in the wrong direction. ▻ *noun* an act or instance of miskicking.

mislay ▻ *verb* **1** to lose something, usually temporarily, especially by forgetting where it was put. **2** to lay something badly or wrongly.

mislead /mɪs'liːd/ ▻ *verb* **1** to make someone take a wrong or undesirable course of action. **2** to cause someone to have a false impression or belief. ● **misleading** *adj* likely to mislead; deceptive. ● **misleadingly** *adverb.*

mismanage ▻ *verb* to manage or handle something or someone badly or carelessly. ● **mismanagement** *noun.*

mismatch ▻ *verb* /mɪs'matʃ/ to match (things or people) unsuitably or incorrectly. ▻ *noun* /'mɪsmatʃ/ an unsuitable or incorrect match.

misname ▻ *verb* **1** to call something or someone by the wrong name. **2** to give something an unsuitable name.

misnomer /mɪs'noʊmə(r)/ ▻ *noun* **1** a wrong or unsuitable name. **2** the use of an incorrect name or term. ⓒ 15c: from French *mesnommer* to misname, from *mes-* MIS-[1] + *nommer* to name, from Latin *nominare*.

miso /'miːsoʊ/ ▻ *noun, cookery* a soy bean paste that has been fermented in brine, used for flavouring food. ⓒ 18c: Japanese.

misogamy /mɪ'sɒgəmɪ/ ▻ *noun* hatred of marriage. ● **misogamist**. ⓒ 17c: from Greek *misogamos*.

misogyny /mɪ'sɒdʒɪnɪ/ ▻ *noun* hatred of women. Compare MISANTHROPY. ● **misogynist** *noun* someone who hates women. ● **misogynous** *adj.* ⓒ 17c: from Greek *misogynes*, from *misos* hatred + *gyne* woman.

misplace ▻ *verb* **1** to lose something, usually temporarily, especially by forgetting where it was put. **2** to give (trust, affection, etc) unwisely or inappropriately.

3 to put something in the wrong place or an unsuitable place.

misplay ▷ *verb* /mɪs'pleɪ/ in sports or games: to play (eg a ball, card, etc) wrongly or badly. ▷ *noun* /'mɪspleɪ/ an instance of wrong or bad play.

misprint ▷ *noun* /'mɪsprɪnt/ a mistake in printing, eg an incorrect or damaged character. ▷ *verb* /mɪs'prɪnt/ to print something wrongly.

misprision /mɪs'prɪʒən/ ▷ *noun, law* **1** a failure to inform the authorities of a serious crime. **2** (*also* **misprision of felony** or **treason**, *etc*) the deliberate concealment of knowledge of a serious crime, treason, etc. ⓘ 15c: from French *mesprision* error, from *mesprendre* to make a mistake.

mispronounce ▷ *verb* to pronounce (a word, etc) incorrectly. • **mispronunciation** *noun* a wrong or careless pronunciation.

misquote ▷ *verb* to quote something or someone inaccurately, sometimes with the intention of deceiving. • **misquotation** *noun*.

misread /mɪsri:d/ ▷ *verb* **1** to read something incorrectly. **2** to misunderstand or misinterpret something.

misreport ▷ *verb* to report (eg a story) incorrectly, falsely or misleadingly.

misrepresent ▷ *verb* to represent something or someone falsely, especially to give a false or misleading account or impression of it or them, often intentionally. • **misrepresentation** *noun* **1** the act or process of misrepresenting. **2** an inaccurate or misleading representation. • **misrepresentative** *adj*.

misrule ▷ *noun, formal* **1** bad or unjust government. **2** civil disorder. ▷ *verb* to govern (eg a country) in a disorderly or unjust way.

miss[1] ▷ *verb* (***misses, missed, missing***) **1** *tr & intr* to fail to hit or catch something □ *missed the ball.* **2** to fail to get on something □ *missed my train.* **3** to fail to take advantage of something □ *missed your chance.* **4** to feel or regret the absence or loss of someone or something □ *I miss you when you're away.* **5** to notice the absence of someone or something. **6** to fail to hear or see something □ *missed his last remark.* **7** to refrain from going to (a place or an event) □ *I'll have to miss the next class.* **8** to avoid or escape (especially a specified danger) □ *just missed being run over.* **9** *intr* said of an engine: to fail to burn fuel at the right time. ▷ *noun* (***misses***) a failure to hit or catch something, etc. • **missable** *adj*. • **missing** see separate entry. • **give something a miss** *colloq* to avoid it or refrain from it □ *I'd better give pudding a miss.* • **miss the boat** or **bus** *colloq* to miss an opportunity, especially by being too slow to act. ⓘ Anglo-Saxon *missan*.

■ **miss out** to fail to benefit from something enjoyable or worthwhile, etc □ *Buy some now; don't miss out!*

■ **miss out on something** to fail to benefit from it or participate in it □ *You missed out on a great day.*

■ **miss something out** or **miss out something** to fail to include it; to leave it out.

miss[2] ▷ *noun* **1** a girl or unmarried woman. **2** (**Miss**) a term used when addressing an unmarried woman (especially in front of her surname). See also MS. **3** (**Miss**) used by children: a term used when addressing a female school teacher, whether married or not. **4** (**Miss**) a title formerly given to a beauty queen and used in front of the name of the country, region, etc that she represents □ *Miss World* □ *Miss France.* **5** *sometimes derog* a girl, especially one who behaves in a specified way □ *thinks she's little miss perfect.* ⓘ 17c: an abbreviation of MISTRESS.

Miss. see under MS

missal /'mɪsəl/ ▷ *noun, RC Church* a book containing all the texts used in the service of mass throughout the year. ⓘ 14c: from Latin *missale*, from *missa* MASS[2].

missel thrush see MISTLE THRUSH

misshapen /mɪs'ʃeɪpən/ ▷ *adj* badly shaped; deformed. • **misshapenly** *adverb*. ⓘ 14c: from *shapen* obsolete past participle of SHAPE.

missile /'mɪsaɪl/ ▷ *noun* **1** a self-propelled flying bomb, eg a GUIDED MISSILE or a BALLISTIC MISSILE. **2** any weapon or object that is thrown or fired. ⓘ 17c: from Latin *missilis*, from *mittere* to send.

missing ▷ *adj* **1** absent; lost; not able to be found. **2** said of a soldier, military vehicle, etc: not able to be located, but not known to be dead or destroyed. • **go missing** to disappear, especially unexpectedly and inexplicably. ⓘ 16c: from MISS[1].

missing link ▷ *noun* (*especially* **the missing link**) **1** any one thing that is needed to complete a series. **2** a hypothetical extinct creature representing a supposed stage of evolutionary development between apes and humans.

mission /'mɪʃən/ ▷ *noun* **1** a purpose for which a person or group of people is sent. **2 a** a journey made for a scientific, military or religious purpose; **b** a group of people sent on such a journey. **3** a flight with a specific purpose, such as a bombing raid or a task assigned to the crew of a spacecraft. **4** a group of people sent somewhere to have discussions, especially political ones. **5** (*usually* **mission in life**) someone's chosen, designated or assumed purpose in life or vocation. **6 a** a group of missionaries; **b** the building occupied by them. **7** a centre run by a charitable or religious organization, etc to provide a particular service in the community. Also *as adj* □ *mission control.* ⓘ 16c: from Latin *missionis*, from *mittere* to send.

missionary /'mɪʃənrɪ, -nərɪ/ ▷ *noun* (***missionaries***) a member of a religious organization seeking to carry out charitable works and religious teaching. Also *as adj* □ *missionary work.*

missionary position ▷ *noun* in heterosexual sexual intercourse: the face-to-face position with the male on top. ⓘ 1960s: so called because this was the position advocated by missionaries to the native people that they were trying to convert to Christianity.

missis see MISSUS

missive /'mɪsɪv/ ▷ *noun, literary or law, etc* a letter, especially a long or official one. ⓘ 15c: French, from Latin *missivus*, from *mittere* to send.

misspell ▷ *verb* to spell something incorrectly. • **misspelling** *noun* a wrong spelling.

misspend ▷ *verb* to spend (money, time, etc) foolishly or wastefully.

missus or (*sometimes*) **missis** /'mɪsɪz/ ▷ *noun, colloq* **1** *humorous* a wife □ *Bring the missus.* **2** *old use* a term used to address an adult female stranger. See also MRS. ⓘ 18c: originally as a spoken form of MISTRESS, used by servants.

missy /'mɪsɪ/ ▷ *noun* (***missies***) *colloq, old use, usually facetious or derog* a term used to address a girl or young woman.

mist ▷ *noun* **1** condensed water vapour in the air near the ground; thin fog or low cloud. **2** a mass of tiny droplets of liquid, eg one forced from a pressurized container. **3** condensed water vapour on a surface. **4** *literary* a watery film □ *a mist of tears.* **5** *literary* an obscuring influence □ *the mists of time.* ▷ *verb* (***misted, misting***) *tr & intr* (*also* **mist up** or **over**) to cover or become covered with mist, or as if with mist. ⓘ Anglo-Saxon.

mistake /mɪs'teɪk/ ▷ *noun* **1** an error. **2** a regrettable action. **3** an act of understanding or interpreting something wrongly. ▷ *verb* (***mistook*** /-'tʊk/, ***mistaken, mistaking***) **1** to misinterpret or misunderstand something □ *I mistook your meaning.* **2** to make the wrong choice of something □ *He mistook the turning in the fog.* • **mistakable** *adj*. • **by mistake** accidentally. ⓘ

14c as *verb*: from Norse *mistaka* to take something wrongly.

■ **mistake someone** or **something for someone** or **something else** to identify them or it incorrectly as someone or something else; to wrongly assume or understand them to be what they are not □ *might mistake us for intruders* □ *She mistook my silence for disapproval.*

mistaken /mɪs'teɪkən/ ▻ *adj* **1** understood, thought, named, etc wrongly; incorrect □ *mistaken identity.* **2** guilty of, or displaying, a failure to understand or interpret correctly □ *You are mistaken in saying that he's English.* ▻ *verb, past participle of* MISTAKE • **mistakenly** *adverb.* • **and no mistake** *colloq* definitely; truly □ *and no mistake about it.*

mister /'mɪstə(r)/ ▻ *noun* **1** (**Mister**) the full form of the abbreviation MR. **2** a man not belonging to the nobility; an untitled man □ *He's the only mister on the board.* **3** *colloq* a term used when addressing an adult male stranger □ *Can I have my ball back please, mister?* ◷ 16c: originally a spoken form of MASTER.

mistily see under MISTY

mistime ▻ *verb* **1** to do or say something at a wrong or unsuitable time. **2** *sport* to misjudge the timing of (a stroke, kick, etc) in relation to the speed of an approaching ball.

mistiness see under MISTY

mistle thrush or **missel thrush** /'mɪsəl —/ ▻ *noun* a large European thrush that likes to feed on mistletoe berries. Also called **storm cock**. ◷ 18c: from Anglo-Saxon *mistel* mistletoe.

mistletoe /'mɪsəltoʊ/ ▻ *noun* an evergreen shrub that grows as a parasite on trees and produces clusters of white berries in winter. ◷ Anglo-Saxon *misteltan.*

mistook *past tense of* MISTAKE

the mistral /— 'mɪstrəl, — mɪ'strɑːl/ ▻ *noun, meteorol* a cold, gusty, strong northerly wind that blows down the Rhône valley in S France. ◷ 17c: French, from Latin *magistralis* masterful.

mistranslate ▻ *verb* to translate something incorrectly. • **mistranslation** *noun.*

mistreat ▻ *verb* to treat someone or something cruelly or without care. • **mistreatment** *noun* bad or cruel treatment.

mistress /'mɪstrɪs/ ▻ *noun* (***mistresses***) **1** the female lover of a man married to another woman. **2** *rather dated* a female teacher □ *She is the French mistress.* Compare MASTER. **3** a woman in a commanding or controlling position; a female head or owner. **4** (*especially* **Mistress**) *formerly* a term used when addressing any woman, especially one in authority. Compare MRS. ◷ 14c in senses 2 and 3: French.

mistrial /'mɪstraɪl/ ▻ *noun, law* **1** a trial not conducted properly according to the law and declared invalid. **2** *US* an inconclusive trial.

mistrust /mɪs'trʌst/ ▻ *verb* to have no trust in, or to be suspicious of, someone or something. ▻ *noun* a lack of trust. See also DISTRUST. • **mistrustful** *adj.* • **mistrustfully** *adverb.*

misty /'mɪstɪ/ ▻ *adj* (***mistier, mistiest***) **1** covered with, or obscured by, mist. **2** *literary* not clear; vague or blurred. **3** said of the eyes: filled with tears. **4** like mist. • **mistily** *adverb.* • **mistiness** *noun.*

misunderstand ▻ *verb, tr & intr* to fail to understand something or someone properly. • **misunderstanding** *noun* **1** a failure to understand properly. **2** a slight disagreement.

misunderstood ▻ *verb, past tense, past participle of* MISUNDERSTAND ▻ *adj* usually said of a person: not properly understood or appreciated as regards character, feelings, intentions, etc.

misuse ▻ *noun* /mɪs'juːs/ improper or inappropriate use □ *the misuse of funds.* Sometimes called **misusage**. ▻ *verb* /mɪs'juːz/ **1** to put something to improper or inappropriate use. **2** to treat something or someone badly. • **misuser** *noun.*

MIT ▻ *abbreviation* Massachusetts Institute of Technology, a US university.

mite¹ /maɪt/ ▻ *noun* a small, often microscopic, animal with a simple rounded body and eight short legs, some species of which are pests, transmit diseases or cause human allergies. ◷ Anglo-Saxon.

mite² /maɪt/ ▻ *noun* **1** any small person or animal, especially a child that is pitied □ *poor little mite.* **2** a small amount of anything, especially of money. • **a mite ...** *colloq* rather or somewhat ... □ *I'm a mite worried* □ *You've a right to be a mite jealous.* ◷ 14c: Dutch a small copper coin.

miter the *US* spelling of MITRE¹, MITRE².

mitigate /'mɪtɪgeɪt/ ▻ *verb* (***mitigated, mitigating***) **1** *law* to partially excuse something or make it less serious. **2** to make (pain, anger, etc) less severe. • **mitigation** *noun.* • **mitigating** *adj* □ *mitigating circumstances.* • **mitigator** *noun.* ◷ 15c: from Latin *mitigare* to calm or soothe.

mitigate, militate

• **Mitigate** is a transitive verb, and is often confused with **militate**, which is intransitive and has another meaning (**to militate against something**).

Mitigate is correctly used as in the following example:

✓ *That was wrong of me, but it in no way mitigates your own actions.*

It is incorrectly used in the following example, in which **militates** is wanted:

✗ *This is certainly a problem which mitigates against the widest acceptance of the language*

mitochondrion /maɪtoʊ'kɒndrɪən/ ▻ *noun* (***mitochondria*** /-ɪə/) *biol* in the cytoplasm of EUKARYOTIC cells, especially in the cells of muscle tissue: a specialized oval structure, consisting of a central matrix surrounded by two membranes. • **mitochondrial** *adj.* ◷ Early 20c: from Greek *mitos* thread + *khondrion* granule.

mitosis /maɪ'toʊsɪs/ ▻ *noun* (***mitoses*** /-siːz/) *biol* a type of cell division that results in the production of two DAUGHTER CELLS with identical nuclei, each of which contains the same genes and the same number of chromosomes as the parent nucleus. Compare MEIOSIS. • **mitotic** /maɪ'tɒtɪk/ *adj.* ◷ 19c: Latin, from Greek *mitos* fibre.

mitral valve /maɪtrəl —/ ▻ *noun, anatomy* the valve in the heart that allows blood to flow from the left atrium to the left ventricle but not in the opposite direction. ◷ 17c: so called because it has two flaps which make it resemble a bishop's MITRE.

mitre¹ or (*US*) **miter** /'maɪtə(r)/ ▻ *noun* the ceremonial headdress of a bishop or abbot, a tall pointed hat with separate front and back sections. ◷ 14c: French, from Greek *mitra* a turban.

mitre² or (*US*) **miter** /'maɪtə(r)/ ▻ *noun* in joinery, etc: a corner joint between two lengths of wood, etc made by fitting together two 45 sloping surfaces cut into their ends. Also called **mitre joint**. ▻ *verb* (***mitred, mitring***; *US* ***mitered, mitering***) to join (two lengths of wood, etc) with a mitre. ◷ 17c: perhaps the same word as MITRE¹.

mitt ▻ *noun* **1** *colloq* a hand □ *Keep your mitts off!* **2** *baseball* a large padded leather glove worn by the catcher. **3** a thick loosely-shaped glove designed for a specific, eg protective, purpose □ *oven mitt* □ *bath mitt.* **4** a mitten or fingerless glove. ⓒ 18c: a shortening of MITTEN.

mitten /ˈmɪtən/ ▷ *noun* **1** a glove with one covering for the thumb and a large covering for all the other fingers together. **2** a glove covering the hand and wrist but not the whole length of the fingers. Also shortened to MITT. ⓒ 14c: from French *mitaine*.

mittimus see under COMMITMENT

mix /mɪks/ ▷ *verb* (*mixes, mixed, mixing*) **1** (*especially* **mix something with something else**, or **mix something and something else together** or **up together**) to put (things, substances, etc) together or to combine them to form one mass. **2** to prepare or make something by doing this □ *mix a cake.* **3** *intr* to blend together to form one mass □ *Water and oil do not mix.* **4** *intr* said of a person: **a** to meet with people socially; **b** to feel at ease in social situations. **5** to do something at the same time as something else; to combine □ *I'm mixing business with pleasure.* **6** to drink (different types of alcoholic drink) on one occasion □ *it doesn't pay to mix your drinks!* **7** *technical* to adjust (separate sound elements, eg the sounds produced by individual musicians) electronically to create an overall balance or particular effect. See also REMIX. **8** *tr & intr* said of a DJ, etc: to sequence two records (the one playing and the one to follow it) together by matching the beats □ *mixes at the club right through the night.* ▷ *noun* **1** a collection of people or things mixed together. **2** a collection of ingredients, especially dried ingredients, from which something is prepared □ *cake mix.* **3** *technical* in music, broadcasting, cinema, etc: the combined sound or soundtrack, etc produced by mixing various recorded elements. • **mixable** *adj.* • **be mixed up** *colloq* to be upset or emotionally confused. • **be mixed up in something** or **with something** or **someone** *colloq* to be involved in it or with them, especially when it is something illicit or suspect. • **mix it** *slang, especially Brit* to cause trouble, argument, a fight, etc. ⓒ 16c: from Latin *miscere* to mix.

▪ **mix something** or **someone up 1** to confuse it or them for something else □ *I always mix him up with his brother.* **2** *colloq* to upset or put into a state of confusion □ *The divorce really mixed me up.* See also MIXED-UP.

mixed ▷ *adj* **1** consisting of different and often opposite kinds of things, elements, characters, etc □ *mixed feelings* □ *a mixed reaction.* **2** done, used, etc by people of both sexes □ *mixed bathing.* **3** mingled or combined by mixing.

mixed-ability ▷ *adj, education* involving or relating to the teaching of children of a wide range of ability in a single class □ *mixed-ability group.* Compare STREAM (*noun* 6). ⓒ 1960s.

mixed bag ▷ *noun, colloq* a collection of people or things of different kinds, characteristics, standards, backgrounds, etc □ *We are a very mixed bag on this committee.*

mixed blessing ▷ *noun* something which has both advantages and disadvantages □ *The dishwasher is a mixed blessing; we're always fighting about who should empty it.*

mixed doubles ▷ *plural noun, sport* in tennis, table-tennis and badminton: a match played by two pairs, each consisting of a man and a woman.

mixed economy ▷ *noun* an economic system in which some elements are state-owned and others are privately owned. Compare MARKET ECONOMY, COMMAND ECONOMY.

mixed farming ▷ *noun* a combination of ARABLE and LIVESTOCK farming.

mixed grill ▷ *noun, cookery* a dish of different kinds of grilled meat, often with tomatoes and mushrooms.

mixed marriage ▷ *noun* a marriage between people of different races or religions.

mixed metaphor ▷ *noun* a combination of two or more metaphors which produces an inconsistent or incongruous mental image, and is often regarded as a stylistic flaw, eg *There are concrete steps in the pipeline.*

mixed number ▷ *noun* a number consisting of an integer and a fraction, eg $2^1/_2$.

mixed-up ▷ *adj* **1** mentally or emotionally confused. **2** badly-adjusted socially.

mixer ▷ *noun* **1** a machine used for mixing □ *a food mixer* □ *a cement mixer.* **2** a soft drink for mixing with alcoholic drinks. **3** *colloq* someone considered in terms of their ability to mix socially □ *a good mixer.* **4** someone who mixes in any other sense. **5** *electronics* a device which combines two or more input signals into a single output signal.

mixer tap ▷ *noun* a tap which can mix the hot and cold water supplies, with one outlet for both hot and cold, and separate controls for adjusting the mix.

mixture /ˈmɪkstʃə(r)/ ▷ *noun* **1** a blend of ingredients prepared for a particular purpose □ *cough mixture.* **2** a combination □ *a mixture of sadness and relief.* **3** the act of mixing. **4** the product of mixing.

mix-up ▷ *noun* a confusion or misunderstanding; an act or occasion of mistaking one person or thing for another.

mizzenmast /ˈmɪzənmɑːst/ ▷ *noun, naut* on a ship with three or more masts: the third mast from the front of the ship. Often shortened to **mizzen**. ⓒ 15c: from Italian *mezzano* middle + MAST[1].

Mk ▷ *abbreviation* **1** mark, a type of design or model, especially of vehicles. See MARK[1] *noun* 13. **2** markka.

MKS or **mks** ▷ *abbreviation* metre-kilogram-second □ *mks unit* □ *MKS system.*

ml ▷ *abbreviation* **1** mile or miles. **2** millilitre or millilitres.

MLA ▷ *abbreviation* in Australian and Indian states, and Canadian states except Quebec: Member of the Legislative Assembly.

MLC ▷ *abbreviation* in Australian and some Indian states: Member of the Legislative Council.

MLitt. ▷ *abbreviation: Magister Litterarum* (Latin), Master of Letters.

Mlle ▷ *abbreviation:* (***Mlles***) *Mademoiselle* (French), Miss.

MLR ▷ *abbreviation* minimum lending rate.

MM ▷ *abbreviation* **1** *Messieurs* (French), gentlemen; sirs. *Brit equivalent* MESSRS (see under MR). **2** Military Medal.

mm ▷ *abbreviation* millimetre or millimetres.

MMC ▷ *abbreviation, Brit* Monopolies and Mergers Commission, a body set up by the government to investigate monopolies (where a monopoly is defined as 25% of the market) and proposed mergers of large companies.

Mme ▷ *abbreviation* (***Mmes***) *Madame* (French), Mrs.

MMR ▷ *abbreviation, medicine* measles, mumps and rubella, a vaccine given to protect children against these diseases.

MN ▷ *abbreviation* **1** Merchant Navy. **2** *US state* Minnesota. Also written **Minn**.

Mn ▷ *symbol, chem* manganese.

MNA ▷ *abbreviation, Can* in Quebec: Member of the National Assembly.

mnemonic /nɪˈmɒnɪk/ ▷ *noun* **1** a device or form of words, often a short verse, used as a memory-aid, eg *Richard of York gained battle in vain* as an aid to remembering the colours of the rainbow where the initial letters of each word stand respectively, for *red, orange, yellow, green, blue, indigo* and *violet.* **2** (**mnemonics**) **a** the art of helping or improving the memory; **b** a system for this. ▷ *adj* **1** serving to help the memory. **2** relating to mnemonics. • **mnemonically** *adverb.* ⓒ 18c: from Greek *mnemonikos*, from *mnemon* mindful from *mnasthai* to remember.

MO ▷ *abbreviation* **1** Medical Officer, an army doctor. **2** *US state* Missouri. Also written **Mo.** **3** *modus operandi* (Latin). **4** money order.

Mo ▷ *symbol, chem* molybdenum.

mo /moʊ/ ▷ *noun* (***mos***) *chiefly Brit colloq* a short while; a moment. ⓒ 19c: a shortening of MOMENT.

-mo /moʊ/ *bookbinding, publishing* ▷ *suffix, forming nouns and adjectives, denoting* **1** a specified number of leaves to the sheet. **2** a book or size of book made up of such sheets □ ***twelvemo*** □ ***sixteenmo.*** ⓒ From the Latin ablative ending *-mo*, as in *in duodecimo* in twelfth.

moa /ˈmoʊə/ ▷ *noun* (***moas***) a flightless ostrich-like bird of New Zealand that has been extinct since the end of the 18c. ⓒ 19c: Maori.

moan /moʊn/ ▷ *noun* **1** a low prolonged sound expressing sadness, grief or pain. **2** any similar sound, eg made by the wind or an engine. **3** *colloq* a complaint or grumble. **4** *colloq* someone who complains a lot. ▷ *verb* (***moaned, moaning***) **1** *intr* to utter or produce a moan. **2** *intr, colloq* to complain, especially without good reason. **3** to utter something with a moan or moans. • **moaner** *noun*. • **moanful** *adj*. • **moaning** *adj, noun*. ⓒ 13c.

moaning minnie ▷ *noun* (***moaning minnies***) **1** *colloq* someone who whines and complains a lot. **2** *war slang* an air-raid siren. ⓒ 1940s.

moat /moʊt/ ▷ *noun* a deep trench, often filled with water, dug round a castle or other fortified position to provide extra defence. • **moated** *adj*. ⓒ 14c: French from *mote* mound.

the Mob see under MAFIA

mob ▷ *noun* **1 a** a large, disorderly crowd; **b** *as adj* □ ***mob rule.*** **2** *colloq* any group or gang. **3** (**the mob**) *colloq* ordinary people; the masses. **4** (**the mob**) an organized gang of criminals, especially the MAFIA. **5** *Austral, NZ* a large herd or flock. ▷ *verb* (***mobbed, mobbing***) **1** to attack something or someone as a mob. **2** to crowd round someone or something, especially curiously or admiringly. **3** *intr* to form into a mob. **4** *especially N Amer* to crowd into (a building, shop, etc). • **mobbed** *adj, colloq* densely crowded; packed with people. ⓒ 17c: shortening of Latin *mobile vulgus* fickle masses.

mob-cap ▷ *noun, historical fashion* a woman's indoor morning cap with a puffy crown, broad band and frills. ⓒ 18c: from obsolete *mob* a loose woman + CAP.

mobile /ˈmoʊbaɪl/ ▷ *adj* **1** able to be moved easily; not fixed. **2** set up inside a vehicle travelling from place to place □ ***mobile shop*** □ ***mobile library.*** **3** said of a face: that frequently changes expression. **4** moving, or able to move, from one social class to another □ ***upwardly mobile.*** **5** *colloq* provided with transport and able to travel. **6** able, or willing, to move house or change jobs. ▷ *noun* **1** a hanging decoration or sculpture, etc made up of parts that are moved around by air currents. **2** *colloq* a mobile phone, shop, etc. **3** *in compounds* /məˈbiːl/ a vehicle specially designed for transporting a specific object, VIP, etc in □ ***the Popemobile.*** • **mobility** *noun* **1** the ability to move. **2** a tendency to move. **3** freedom or ease of movement. ⓒ 15c: French, from Latin *mobilis*, from *movere* to move.

mobile home ▷ *noun* a type of house without foundations, like a large caravan, which can be towed but is usually kept in one place and connected to the local utilities. ⓒ 1960s.

mobile phone ▷ *noun* a portable telephone that operates by means of a cellular radio system, and nowadays fits easily in a pocket or handbag. Often shortened to **mobile**. ⓒ 1980s.

mobilize or **mobilise** /ˈmoʊbɪlaɪz/ ▷ *verb* (***mobilized, mobilizing***) **1** to organize or prepare something or someone for use, action, etc. **2 a** to assemble and make (forces, etc) ready for war; **b** *intr* said of forces, etc: to assemble and become ready for war. **3** to make something movable, mobile or readily available. • **mobilization** *noun*. • **mobilizer** *noun*. ⓒ 19c.

Möbius strip /ˈmɜːbɪəs —/ ▷ *noun, math* the one-sided surface made by joining the ends of a long rectangular strip after twisting one end through 180°. ⓒ 20c: named after A F Möbius (1790–1868) the German mathematician.

mobster /ˈmɒbstə(r)/ ▷ *noun, slang* a member of a gang or an organized group of criminals, especially the MAFIA.

moccasin /ˈmɒkəsɪn/ ▷ *noun* **1** a deerskin or other soft leather shoe with a continuous sole and heel, as worn by Native Americans. **2** any slipper or shoe in this style. **3** a large poisonous snake of the swamps of the southern US. Also called **water moccasin**. ⓒ 17c: from Native American languages.

mocha /ˈmɒkə/ ▷ *noun* (***mochas***) **1 a** a flavouring made from coffee and chocolate; **b** *as adj* □ ***mocha ice cream.*** **2 a** a deep brown colour; **b** *as adj* □ ***mocha shoes.*** **3 a** dark brown coffee of fine quality; **b** *as adj* □ ***mocha beans.*** ⓒ 18c in sense 3: from *Mocha*, an Arabian port, now in the Yemen Arab Republic, from where the coffee was originally shipped.

mock ▷ *verb* (***mocked, mocking***) **1** *tr & intr* (*also* **mock at someone** or **something**) to speak or behave disparagingly, derisively, or contemptuously towards someone or something. **2** to mimic someone, usually in a way that makes fun of them. **3** *chiefly literary* to make something seem to be impossible or useless; to defy, disappoint or frustrate it, as though showing contempt for it □ ***Violent winds mocked my attempt to pitch the tent.*** ▷ *adj* **1** false; sham □ ***mock sincerity.*** **2** serving as practice for the similar but real or true thing, event, etc which is to come later □ ***a mock examination.*** ▷ *noun* **1** *colloq* in England and Wales: a mock examination. *Scottish equivalent* PRELIM. **2** an imitation; a mockery. **3** an act of mocking. • **mocker** *noun*. • **mocking** *adj, noun*. • **mockingly** *adverb*. ⓒ 15c: from French *mocquer* to deride or jeer.

mockers /ˈmɒkəz/ ▷ *plural noun* • **put the mockers on something** or **someone** *colloq* to spoil or end its or their chances of success □ ***Well, that's put the mockers on my promotion.*** ⓒ 1920s.

mockery ▷ *noun* (***mockeries***) **1** an imitation, especially a contemptible or insulting one. **2 a** any ridiculously inadequate person, action or thing; **b** the subject of ridicule or contempt □ ***make a mockery of someone.*** **3** ridicule; contempt. ⓒ 15c: from French *moquerie*; see MOCK.

mock-heroic ▷ *adj* said especially of verse: imitating the style of HEROIC VERSE in an exaggerated way, usually for comic or satirical effect. ▷ *noun* (**mock heroic**) mock-heroic composition or style.

mockingbird ▷ *noun* any of several black, white or grey American or Mexican birds that copy the calls of other birds. ⓒ 17c: from MOCK *verb* 2.

mock moon see PARASELENE

mock orange see under PHILADELPHUS

mock turtle soup ▷ *noun, cookery* soup made in the style of turtle soup, but using a calf's head.

mock-up ▷ *noun* **1** a full-size model or replica of something, built for experimental purposes. **2** a rough layout of a printed text or item, showing the size, colours, etc.

MOD or **MoD** ▷ *abbreviation, Brit* Ministry of Defence.

mod¹ ▷ *adj, colloq, dated* short form of MODERN. ▷ *noun* (**Mod**) originally in the 1960s: a follower of a British teenage culture characterized by a liking for smart clothes and motor scooters. Compare ROCKER. ⓒ 1960s.

mod² or **Mod** ▻ *noun* a Scottish Gaelic literary and musical festival, held annually. ⓘ 19c: Gaelic, from Norse *mot* an assembly.

mod. ▻ *abbreviation* **1** moderate. **2** *music* moderato. **3** modern.

modal /'moudəl/ ▻ *adj* **1** *grammar* belonging or relating to, or concerning, MOOD² or a mood. **2** said of music: using or relating to a particular mode. ▻ *noun, grammar* a verb used as the auxiliary of another verb to express grammatical mood such as condition, possibility and obligation, eg *can, could, may, shall, will, must, ought to*. Also called **modal auxiliary** or **modal verb**. See also AUXILIARY VERB. • **modally** *adverb*. ⓘ 16c: from Latin *modalis*; see mode.

modality /mou'dalɪtɪ/ ▻ *noun* (***modalities***) **1** *music* the quality or characteristic of music as determined by its MODE (*noun* 4). **2** *grammar* the modal property of a verb or construction.

mod cons /mɒd'kɒnz/ ▻ *plural noun, colloq* modern household conveniences, eg central heating, hot water, washing machine, etc. ⓘ 1930s: abbreviation of *modern conveniences*.

mode /moud/ ▻ *noun* **1** *rather formal* a way of doing something, or of living, acting, happening, operating, etc □ *a new mode of transport*. **2** a fashion or style, eg in clothes or art □ *the latest mode*. **3** *computing* a method of operation as provided by the software □ *print mode*. **4** *music* **a** any of several systems according to which notes in an octave are or were arranged □ *Lydian mode*; **b** since the 16c specifically: either of the two main scale systems (**major mode** and **minor mode**) now in use; **c** *old use* a method of time-division of notes. **5** *statistics* the value of greatest frequency in a set of numbers. Compare MEAN, MEDIAN. ⓘ 14c: from Latin *modus* manner or measure.

model /'mɒdəl/ ▻ *noun* **1** a small-scale representation of something that serves as a guide in constructing the full-scale version. **2 a** a small-scale replica; **b** *as adj* □ *model railway*. See also WORKING MODEL. **3** one of several types or designs of manufactured article □ *the latest model of car*. **4** a person whose job is to display clothes to potential buyers by wearing them. See also SUPERMODEL. **5** a person who is the subject of an artist's or photographer's work, etc, usually one who is paid for this service. **6** a thing from which something else is to be derived; a basis. **7 a** an excellent example; an example to be copied □ *She's a model of loyalty*; **b** *as adj* □ *a model boss*. ▻ *verb* (***modelled, modelling***; *US* ***modeled, modeling***) **1** *tr & intr* to display (clothes) by wearing them. **2** *intr* to work as a model for an artist, photographer, etc. **3** *tr & intr* to make models of something. **4** to shape (something mouldable) into a particular form □ *models clay*. **5** (*especially* **model something on something else**) to plan, build or create it according to a model. • **modeller** *noun*. ⓘ 16c: from French *modelle*, from Latin *modulus* a little measure.

modelling or (*US*) **modeling** ▻ *noun* **1** the act or activity of making a model or models. **2** the activity or occupation of a person who models clothes. **3** *psychol* the process of observing another person or group of people who are considered worthy of imitation, and adopting their characteristics or forms of behaviour.

modello /*Italian* mo'dɛlo/ ▻ *noun* (***modelli*** /-liː/) *art, historical* a small but complete and detailed painting or drawing made to present the artist's ideas for a full-size work. ⓘ 1930s: Italian, literally 'model'.

modem /'moudɛm/ ▻ *noun, computing* an electronic device that transmits information from one computer to another along a telephone line, converting digital data into audio signals and back again. ⓘ 1950s: contraction from *mo*dulator + *dem*odulator.

moderate ▻ *adj* /'mɒdərət/ **1** not extreme; not strong or violent. **2** average; middle rate □ *moderate intelligence*. ▻ *noun* /'mɒdərət/ someone who holds moderate views, especially on politics. ▻ *verb* /'mɒdəreɪt/ (***moderated, moderating***) **1** *tr & intr* to make or become less extreme, violent or intense. **2** *intr* (*also* **moderate over something**) to act as a moderator in any sense, eg over an assembly. • **moderately** *adverb*. • **moderateness** *noun*. ⓘ 15c: from Latin *moderatus*, from *moderari* to moderate.

moderation /mɒdə'reɪʃən/ ▻ *noun* **1** the quality or state of being moderate. **2** an act of becoming or making something moderate or less extreme. **3** lack of excess; self-control. **4** (**Moderations**) the first public examinations for BA at Oxford University. Also (*colloq*) called **Mods** or **mods**. • **in moderation 1** to a moderate degree. **2** in moderate amounts.

moderato /mɒdə'rɑːtou/ *music* ▻ *adverb, adj* at a restrained and moderate tempo. ▻ *noun* (***moderatos***) a piece of music to be played in this way. ⓘ 18c: Italian.

moderator /'mɒdəreɪtə(r)/ ▻ *noun* **1** *Christianity* in a Presbyterian church: a minister who presides over a court or assembly. **2** someone who settles disputes. Also called MEDIATOR. **3** *nuclear physics* a substance used for slowing down neutrons in nuclear reactors. **4** at Oxford and Cambridge universities: an officer who superintends degree examinations. **5** a person or thing that moderates in any other sense. • **moderatorship** *noun*.

modern /'mɒdən/ ▻ *adj* **1** belonging to the present or to recent times; not old or ancient. **2** said of techniques, equipment, etc: involving, using or being the very latest available □ *modern transport*. **3** (*often* **Modern**) said of a language: in the most recent stage of development; as used at present □ *Modern English*. Compare MIDDLE *adj* 4, OLD *adj* 12. ▻ *noun* a person living in modern times, especially someone who follows the latest trends. • **modernity** /mə'dɜːrnɪtɪ/ *noun*. ⓘ 16c: from French *moderne*, from Latin *modernus*, from *modo* just now.

modern dance ▻ *noun* an expressive style of dance developed in the early 20c, which rejects the stylized conventional movements and structure of classical ballet.

Modern Greek see GREEK

modernism /'mɒdənɪzəm/ ▻ *noun* **1** modern spirit or character. **2** a modern usage, expression or trait. **3** (**Modernism**) in early 20c art, literature, architecture, etc: a movement characterized by the use of unconventional subject matter and style, experimental techniques, etc.

modernist *noun* **1** an admirer of modern ideas, ways, etc. **2** (**Modernist**) in the arts: someone who practises or advocates Modernism. ▻ *adj* (*also* **modernistic**) *adj* relating to or typical of modern ideas, modernism or Modernism.

modernity see under MODERN

modernize or **modernise** /'mɒdənaɪz/ ▻ *verb* (***modernized, modernizing***) **1** to bring something up to modern standards, or adapt it to modern style, conditions, etc. **2** *intr* to switch to more modern methods or techniques □ *spent five years modernizing*. • **modernization** *noun*. • **modernizer** *noun*.

modern jazz ▻ *noun* a rhythmically and harmonically complex style of jazz which evolved in the early 1940s. Compare TRAD.

modern pentathlon see under PENTATHLON

modest /'mɒdɪst/ ▻ *adj* **1** not having or showing pride; humble; not pretentious or showy. **2** not large; moderate □ *a modest income*. **3** unassuming; shy or diffident. **4** *old use* said especially of clothing: plain and restrained; not offending standards of decency □ *a modest dress*. • **modestly** *adverb*. ⓘ 16c: from Latin *modestus* moderate.

modesty *noun* (***modesties***) the quality or fact of being modest.

modicum /'mɒdɪkəm/ ▻ *noun, formal* or *facetious* a small amount □ *At least have a modicum of decency and close the curtain before you undress*. ⓘ 15c: Latin, from *modicus* moderate.

modi operandi see under MODUS OPERANDI

modifier ▷ *noun* **1** *grammar* **a** a word or phrase that modifies or identifies the meaning of another word, eg *in the green hat* in the phrase *the man in the green hat*, and *vaguely* in the phrase *He was vaguely embarrassed*; **b** a noun that functions as an adjective, eg *mohair* in *mohair jumper*. **2** a person or thing that modifies in any sense.

modify /ˈmɒdɪfaɪ/ ▷ *verb* (***modifies***, ***modified***, ***modifying***) **1** to change the form or quality of something, usually only slightly. **2** *grammar* to act as a modifier of (a word). **3** to moderate. • **modifiable** *adj*. • **modification** *noun* **1** the act of modifying or state of being modified. **2** a change of form or condition; something that has been modified □ ***a few modifications to the original plan.*** ◷ 14c: from French *modifier*, from Latin *modificare*.

modish /ˈmoʊdɪʃ/ ▷ *adj, rather formal* stylish; fashionable. • **modishly** *adverb*. • **modishness** *noun*. ◷ 17c: MODE + -ISH.

Mods or **mods** see under MODERATION 4

modular /ˈmɒdjʊlə(r)/ ▷ *adj* **1** consisting of MODULES. **2** constructed like a module. **3** belonging or relating to, or consisting of, MODULI (see under MODULUS). • **modularity** *noun*.

modular construction ▷ *noun, electronics* a method of constructing a hardware or software system using standard compatible units which are quickly interchangeable or which may be built up in a variety of combinations.

modularize or **modularise** ▷ *verb* (***modularized***, ***modularizing***) said of a university, college, etc: to adopt a teaching system based on self-contained MODULES (sense 3) as opposed to courses lasting a term or an academic year. • **modularization** *noun*. ◷ 1980s.

modulate /ˈmɒdjʊleɪt/ ▷ *verb* (***modulated***, ***modulating***) **1** *technical* to alter the tone or volume of (a sound, or one's voice). **2** *formal* to change or alter. **3** *intr* (*often* **modulate to** or **into something**) *music* to pass from one key to another with a linking progression of chords. **4** *radio* to cause modulation of a CARRIER WAVE. **5** *physics* to vary the velocity of electrons in an electron beam. • **modulator** *noun* a person or device that modulates. ◷ 17c: from Latin *modulari*, *modulatus* to regulate.

modulation ▷ *noun* **1** the act or process of, or an instance of, modulating something. **2** *technical* in radio transmission: the process whereby the frequency or amplitude, etc of a CARRIER WAVE is increased or decreased in response to variations in the signal being transmitted. See also AMPLITUDE MODULATION, FREQUENCY MODULATION.

module /ˈmɒdjʊl/ ▷ *noun* **1** a separate self-contained unit that combines with others to form a larger unit, structure or system. **2** in a space vehicle: a separate self-contained part used for a particular purpose □ ***lunar module.*** **3** *education* a set course forming a unit in a training scheme, degree programme, etc. **4** *archit* a measure, eg the semi-diameter of a column, used to fix the proportions of other parts. ◷ 16c: French, from Latin *modulus* a small measure.

modulus /ˈmɒdjʊləs/ ▷ *noun* (***moduli*** /-laɪ/) *math* the absolute value of a real number, whether positive or negative. ◷ 19c: Latin, meaning 'a small measure'.

modus operandi /ˈmoʊdəs ɒpəˈrandaɪ/ ▷ *noun* (***modi operandi*** /-daɪ —/) a method of working; the way something operates. ◷ 17c: Latin, literally 'way of working'.

modus vivendi /ˈmoʊdəs vɪˈvendaɪ/ ▷ *noun* (***modi vivendi*** /-daɪ -daɪ/) **1** an arrangement by which people or groups in conflict can work or exist together; a compromise. **2** *affected* a way of living. ◷ 19c: Latin, meaning 'way of living'.

mog see under MOGGY

Mogadon /ˈmɒgədɒn/ ▷ *noun, trademark* NITRAZEPAM, a drug used to treat insomnia. ◷ 1950s.

moggy or **moggie** /ˈmɒgɪ/ ▷ *noun* (***moggies***) *Brit colloq* a cat, especially an ordinary domestic cat of mixed breeding. Often shortened to MOG. ◷ 19c: originally as dialect pet name for a calf.

mogul[1] /ˈmoʊgəl/ ▷ *noun* **1** an important, powerful, or influential person, especially in business or the film industry □ ***a movie mogul.*** See also MAGNATE. **2** (**Mogul**) *historical* a Muslim ruler of India between the 16c and 19c. ▷ *adj* (**Mogul**) typical of or relating to the Moguls or the Mogul empire. ◷ 16c: from Persian *Mughul* MONGOL.

mogul[2] /ˈmoʊgəl/ ▷ *noun, skiing* **1** a mound of hard snow created as an obstacle on a ski-slope. **2** (**moguls** or **mogul skiing**) a discipline or event that involves skiing down a run which includes moguls. • **moguled** *adj*. ◷ 1960s.

MOH ▷ *abbreviation, Brit* Medical Officer of Health.

mohair /ˈmoʊhɛə(r)/ ▷ *noun* **1** the long soft hair of the Angora goat. **2** a yarn or fabric made of this, either pure or mixed with wool. Also *as adj* □ ***a mohair jumper.*** See also ANGORA. ◷ 16c: from Arabic *mukhayyar*, influenced by English *hair*.

Mohammedan see MUHAMMADAN

Mohammedan

See Usage Note at **Muslim**.

mohel /ˈmoʊɛl, ˈmoʊhel/ ▷ *noun, Judaism* an official who performs circumcisions. ◷ 17c: Hebrew.

mohican /moʊˈhiːkən/ ▷ *noun* a hairstyle popular amongst PUNKs, in which the head is partially shaved, leaving a central, front-to-back band of hair, usually coloured and formed into a spiky crest. ◷ 1960s: the style is based on that associated with the Mohicans, a Native American tribe.

moiety /ˈmɔɪətɪ/ ▷ *noun* (***moieties***) *literary or law* a half; one of two parts or divisions. ◷ 14c: from French *moité*, from Latin *medius* middle.

the Moirai /ˈmɔɪəraɪ/ ▷ *plural noun, Greek mythol* the three goddesses believed to control the destiny of human beings. See also PARCAE.

moire /ˈmwɑː(r)/ ▷ *noun* (***moires***) a fabric, especially silk, with a pattern of glossy irregular waves. ◷ 17c: French, from English MOHAIR.

moiré /mwɑːreɪ/ ▷ *adj* said of a fabric: having a pattern of glossy irregular waves; watered. ▷ *noun* (***moirés***) this pattern on the surface of a fabric or metal. ◷ 19c: French, past participle of *moirer*, from MOIRE.

moist /mɔɪst/ ▷ *adj* (***moister***, ***moistest***) **1** damp or humid; slightly wet or watery. **2** said of food, especially cake: pleasantly soft and fresh, not dry. **3** said of a climate: rainy. • **moistly** *adverb*. • **moistness** *noun*. ◷ 14c: from French *moiste*.

moisten /ˈmɔɪsən/ ▷ *verb* (***moistened***, ***moistening***) *tr & intr* to make something moist, or become moist. ◷ 16c.

moisture /ˈmɔɪstʃə(r)/ ▷ *noun* liquid in vapour or spray form, or condensed as droplets. ◷ 14c.

moisturize or **moisturise** /ˈmɔɪstʃəraɪz/ ▷ *verb* (***moisturized***, ***moisturizing***) **1** to make something less dry; to add moisture to it. **2** *tr & intr* to apply a cosmetic moisturizer to the skin. • **moisturizer** *noun* something which moisturizes, especially a cosmetic cream which restores moisture to the skin.

moke ▷ *noun* (***mokes***) *slang* **1** *Brit* a donkey. **2** *Austral, NZ* a worn-out or inferior horse. ◷ 19c.

mol ▷ *symbol, chem* MOLE[4]

molal see under MOLE[4]

molar[1] /ˈmoʊlə(r)/ ▷ *noun* any of the large back teeth in humans and other mammals, used for chewing and grinding. Compare CANINE TOOTH, INCISOR. ▷ *adj* **1**

belonging or relating to a molar. **2** said of a tooth: used for grinding. ⓔ 17c: from Latin *mola* millstone, from *molare* to grind.

molar² see under MOLE⁴

molarity /mɒ'larɪtɪ/ ▷ *noun* (***molarities***) the concentration of a solution, expressed as the number of moles (see MOLE⁴) of a dissolved substance present in a litre of solution.

molasses /mə'lasɪz/ ▷ *singular noun* **1** the thickest kind of treacle, left over at the very end of the process of refining raw sugar. **2** *N Amer* treacle. ⓔ 16c: from Portuguese *melaço*.

mold, **molder**, **molding**, **moldy**, etc the *N Amer* spelling of MOULD, MOULDER, MOULDING, MOULDY, etc.

mole¹ /moʊl/ ▷ *noun* **1** a small insectivorous burrowing mammal with velvety greyish-black fur, a naked muzzle, very small eyes and strong front legs with very broad feet adapted for digging. **2** *colloq* a spy who works inside an organization and passes secret information to people outside it. ⓔ 20c in sense 2; 14c in sense 1.

mole² /moʊl/ ▷ *noun* a raised or flat, dark, permanent spot on the skin, caused by a concentration of melanin. *Technical equivalent* NAEVUS. See also FRECKLE. ⓔ Anglo-Saxon *mal*.

mole³ /moʊl/ ▷ *noun, pathol, medicine* an abnormal fleshy mass formed in the uterus. ⓔ 17c: from French *môle*, from Latin *moles* mass.

mole⁴ /moʊl/ ▷ *noun, chem* (symbol **mol**) the SI unit of amount of substance, equal to the amount of a substance (in grams) that contains as many atoms, molecules, etc, as there are atoms of carbon in 12 grams of the isotope carbon-12. ● **molal** *adj* said of a solution: containing one mole of dissolved substance per kilogram of solvent. ● **molar** *adj* **1** belonging or relating to a mole. **2** per mole or per unit amount of substance. ⓔ Early 20c: from German *Mol*, from *Molekül* molecule.

mole⁵ /moʊl/ ▷ *noun* **1** a pier, causeway or breakwater made of stone. **2** a harbour protected by any of these. ⓔ 16c: from Latin *moles* mass.

mole⁶ /'moʊlɪ/ ▷ *noun* (***moles*** /-liːz/) in Mexican cooking: a sauce made mainly with chilli and chocolate, served with meat dishes. ⓔ 1930s: American Spanish, from Nahuatl *molli* sauce.

molecular see under MOLECULE

molecular biology ▷ *noun* the branch of biology that is concerned with the study of the structure, properties and functions of the large organic molecules, or MACROMOLECULES, found in the cells of living organisms.

molecular genetics ▷ *singular noun* the study and manipulation of the molecular basis of heredity.

molecular weight see under RELATIVE MOLECULAR MASS

molecule /'mɒlɪkjuːl/ ▷ *noun* **1** *chem, physics* the smallest particle of an element or compound that can exist independently and participate in a reaction, consisting of two or more atoms bonded together. **2** *loosely* a tiny particle. ● **molecular** /mə'lɛkjʊlə(r)/ *adj* belonging or relating to molecules. ● **molecularity** *noun*. ● **molecularly** *adverb*. ⓔ 18c: from French *molécule*, from Latin *molecula*, from *moles* mass.

molehill ▷ *noun* a little pile of earth thrown up by a burrowing mole (see MOLE¹). ● **make a mountain out of a molehill** see under MOUNTAIN.

mole salamander see under AXOLOTL

moleskin ▷ *noun* **1** mole's fur. **2 a** a heavy twilled cotton fabric with a short nap. Also *as adj* □ ***moleskin jacket***. **b** (**moleskins**) trousers made of this fabric.

molest /mə'lɛst/ ▷ *verb* (***molested***, ***molesting***) **1** to attack or interfere with someone sexually. **2** *formal* to attack someone, causing them physical harm. **3** *old use* to disturb or upset. ● **molestation** *noun*. ● **molester** *noun*. ⓔ 14c: from Latin *molestare*, from *molestus* troublesome.

moll ▷ *noun, slang, old use* **1** a gangster's girlfriend. **2** a prostitute. ⓔ 16c; from the female name *Moll*, a diminutive of *Mary*.

mollify /'mɒlɪfaɪ/ ▷ *verb* (***mollifies***, ***mollified***, ***mollifying***) **1** to make someone calmer or less angry. **2** to soothe, ease, or soften something (eg someone's anger, etc). ● **mollification** *noun*. ● **mollifier** *noun*. ⓔ 16c: from French *mollifier*, from Latin *mollificare*, from *mollis* soft + *facere* to make.

mollusc /'mɒləsk/ ▷ *noun, zool* any of a large group of invertebrate animals, typically one with a soft unsegmented body with a large, flattened, muscular foot on the underside and a MANTLE (*noun* 6) covering its upper surface protected by a hard, chalky shell, eg the snail, mussel, etc. ⓔ 18c: from Latin *Mollusca*, the name of the phylum to which they belong, from Latin *molluscus* softish, from *mollis* soft.

mollycoddle ▷ *verb* (***mollycoddled***, ***mollycoddling***) *colloq* to treat someone with fussy care and protection. ⓔ 19c: from Molly, a female name + CODDLE.

Molotov cocktail /'mɒlətɒf —/ ▷ *noun* a small crude bomb for throwing, consisting of a bottle filled with petrol, usually with a burning cloth as a fuse. ⓔ 1940s: named after the Russian politician and premier V M Molotov (1890–1986).

molt the *N Amer* spelling of MOULT

molten /'moʊltən/ ▷ *adj* in a melted state; liquefied □ ***molten metal***. ⓔ 14c; an old past participle of MELT.

molto /'mɒltoʊ/ ▷ *adverb, adj, music* very; much □ ***molto allegro***. ⓔ 19c: Italian.

molybdenum /mə'lɪbdənəm/ ▷ *noun, chem* (symbol **Mo**, atomic number 42) a hard silvery metallic element that occurs most commonly in the lustrous crystalline mineral **molybdenite** and is used as a hardening agent in various alloys, etc. ⓔ 19c: Latin, from Greek *molybdaina* a lead-like substance.

mom, **momma** and **mommy** ▷ *noun* (***moms***, ***mommas***, or ***mommies***) *N Amer colloq* mother. *Brit equivalents* MUM, MUMMY.

moment /'moʊmənt/ ▷ *noun* **1** a short while □ ***It will only take a moment.*** Sometimes shortened to MO. **2** a particular point in time □ ***at that moment***. **3** (**the moment**) the present point, or the right point, in time □ ***cannot be disturbed at the moment***. **4** *formal* importance or significance □ ***a literary work of great moment***. **5** *physics* a measure of the TORQUE produced by a force which causes an object to rotate about an axis, which is equal to the force multiplied by the perpendicular distance of the axis from the line of action of the force. Also called **moment of force**. **6** *physics* MOMENT OF INERTIA. ● **have one's** or **its**, *etc* **moments** *colloq* to experience or provide occasional but irregular times of happiness, success, etc □ ***I've had my moments.*** ● **of the moment** currently very popular, important, fashionable, etc. ⓔ 14c: from Latin *momentum* movement.

momentarily /'moʊməntrɪlɪ, -'tɛrəlɪ/ ▷ *adverb* **1** for a moment □ ***paused momentarily***. **2** every moment □ ***kept pausing momentarily***. **3** *N Amer* at any moment.

momentary /'moʊməntrɪ/ ▷ *adj* lasting for only a moment □ ***My confusion was only momentary.***

moment of force see MOMENT sense 5

moment of inertia ▷ *noun, physics* in mechanics: the notion that, for a rotating object, the turning force required to make it turn faster depends on the way in which the object's mass is distributed about the axis of rotation.

moment of truth ▷ *noun* a very important or significant point in time, especially one when a person or thing is faced with stark reality or is put to the test. ⓔ

1930s: translated from the Spanish phrase *el momento de la verdad*, referring to the climax of a bullfight, when the matador delivers the final sword-stroke to kill the bull.

momentous /moʊ'mɛntəs, mə-/ ▷ *adj* describing something of great importance or significance ◻ *the momentous events in Berlin in November 1989.* • **momentously** *adverb.* • **momentousness** *noun.* Ⓒ 17c.

momentum /moʊ'mɛntəm, mə-/ ▷ *noun* (***momentums*** or ***momenta*** /-tə/) **1 a** a continuous speed of progress; impetus ◻ *The campaign gained momentum;* **b** the force that an object gains in movement. **2** *physics* the product of the mass and the velocity of a moving object. See also ANGULAR MOMENTUM, LINEAR MOMENTUM. Ⓒ 17c: Latin, meaning 'movement'.

momma and **mommy** see under MOM

Mon. ▷ *abbreviation* Monday.

mon- see MONO-

monad /'mɒnad/ ▷ *noun* **1** *philos* any self-contained non-physical unit of being, eg God, or a soul. **2** *biol* a single-celled organism. **3** *chem* a univalent element, atom or radical. • **monadic** /mɒ'nadɪk/ *adj.* Ⓒ 17c: from Greek *monas, monados* a unit.

monandrous /mɒ'nandrəs/ ▷ *adj* **1** *bot* having only one stamen in each flower. See also POLYANDROUS. **2** *sociol* having or allowing only one husband or male sexual partner at a time. • **monandry** *noun* the state or condition of being monandrous. Ⓒ 19c: from Greek *andros* man.

monarch /'mɒnək/ ▷ *noun* **1** a king, queen or other non-elected sovereign with a hereditary right to rule. **2** a large butterfly with orange and black wings. • **monarchic** /mə'nɑːkɪk/ or **monarchical** *adj.* Ⓒ 15c, originally meaning 'a sole and absolute ruler': from Latin *monarcha*, from MON- + Greek *archein* to rule.

monarchism ▷ *noun* **1** the principles of monarchic government. **2** support for monarchy. • **monarchist** *noun* someone who approves of rule by a monarch; a supporter of the monarchy. • **monarchistic** *adj.*

monarchy /'mɒnəkɪ/ ▷ *noun* (***monarchies***) **1** a form of government in which the head of state is a MONARCH. **2** a country which has this form of government.

monastery /'mɒnəstərɪ, -strɪ/ ▷ *noun* (***monasteries***) the home of a community of monks, or sometimes nuns. See also NUNNERY. Ⓒ 15c: from Greek *monasterion*, from *monazein* to live alone.

monastic /mə'nastɪk/ ▷ *adj* **1** belonging or relating to monasteries, monks or nuns. **2** marked by simplicity and self-discipline, like life in a monastery. See also MONKISH at MONK. • **monastically** *adverb.* • **monasticism** *noun* the monastic system or way of life. Ⓒ 17c: from Latin *monasticus*, from Greek *monastes* monk.

monaural /mɒ'nɔːrəl/ ▷ *adj* **1** having, using, or relating to, one ear only. **2** MONOPHONIC. • **monaurally** *adverb.* Ⓒ 19c.

Monday /'mʌndeɪ/ ▷ *noun* the second day of the week counting from Sunday; the beginning of the working week. Also *as adj* ◻ *a Monday holiday.* • **that Monday morning feeling** the feeling of tiredness and reluctance to work that people often feel after the weekend, at the thought of another week's work ahead. Ⓒ Anglo-Saxon *monandæg* moon day, translated from the Latin term *lunae dies.*

monetarism /'mʌnɪtərɪzəm/ ▷ *noun, econ* the theory or practice of basing an economy on, and curbing inflation by, control of the MONEY SUPPLY rather than by fiscal policy. Also called **monetarist theory**. • **monetarist** *noun* someone who advocates policies based on monetarism. ▷ *adj* relating to or typical of monetarism. Ⓒ 1960s: from MONETARY.

monetary /'mʌnɪtərɪ/ ▷ *adj* belonging or relating to, or consisting of, money. • **monetarily** *adverb.* Ⓒ 19c: from Latin *monetarius*, from *moneta* money or a mint.

monetary unit ▷ *noun* the principal unit of currency of a state or country.

money /'mʌnɪ/ ▷ *noun* (*plural* in sense 1b and 4 ***monies*** or ***moneys***) **1 a** coins or banknotes used as a means of buying things; **b** any currency used as LEGAL TENDER. **2** wealth in general. **3** *colloq* a rich person; rich people ◻ *marry money.* **4** *commerce, law* (*always* **monies** or **moneys**) sums of money. • **moneyed** or **monied** *adj* having much money; wealthy. • **be in the money** *colloq* to be wealthy. • **for my, our,** *etc* **money** *colloq* in my, our, etc opinion. • **get one's money's worth** to get full value for the money or other resources one has put into something. • **have money to burn** to have enough money to be able to spend in ways which others may find foolish. • **made of money** *colloq* said of a person: extremely rich. • **make money** to make a profit or acquire wealth. • **money down** money paid on the spot for something. • **money for old rope** *colloq* money obtained without any effort. • **money talks** an expression used to convey the idea that people with money have power and influence over others. • **on the money** *US slang* spot-on; exactly right. • **put money into something** to invest in it. • **put money on something** *colloq* to bet on it. • **put one's money where one's mouth is** to support what one has said by risking or investing money, or giving other material or practical help. Ⓒ 13c: from French *moneie*, from Latin *moneta.*

moneybags ▷ *singular noun, colloq* a very rich person.

money belt ▷ *noun* a belt with a pocket in or on it for holding money.

moneybox ▷ *noun* a box for saving or collecting money in, with a slot to insert the money through. See also PIGGY BANK.

moneychanger ▷ *noun* someone whose job is to exchange one currency for another. Ⓒ 14c.

moneyed see under MONEY

money-grubber ▷ *noun, derog, colloq* someone who greedily acquires as much money as possible. • **money-grubbing** *adj, noun.*

moneylender ▷ *noun* a person or small business that lends money to people at interest, especially at rates higher than general commercial interest rates. • **moneylending** *noun.*

moneymaker ▷ *noun, colloq* **1** *often derog* someone whose main interest in life is acquiring money. **2** a project or company, etc that makes, or is expected to make, a large profit. • **moneymaking** *adj, noun* profitable.

money market ▷ *noun* the finance companies, banks, dealers, etc of a country that borrow and lend money for short periods.

money order ▷ *noun* a written order for the transfer of money from one person to another, through a post office or bank. See also POSTAL ORDER.

money spider ▷ *noun* a very small spider, thought superstitiously to bring luck in money to anyone it climbs on.

money-spinner ▷ *noun, colloq* an idea or project, etc that brings in large sums of money. • **money-spinning** *adj, noun.*

money supply ▷ *noun, econ* the amount of money in circulation in an economy at a given time.

-monger /'mʌŋgə(r)/ ▷ *combining form, forming nouns, denoting* **1** a trader or dealer ◻ *fishmonger.* **2** someone who spreads or promotes something undesirable or evil ◻ *scandalmonger* ◻ *warmonger.* • **-mongering** or **-mongery** *combining form, forming nouns.* Ⓒ Anglo-Saxon *mangere* as a full *noun* in sense 1: from Latin *mango* dealer.

Mongol /'mɒŋgɒl, -gəl/ ▷ *noun* **1** see MONGOLIAN *noun.* **2** *historical* any member of the tribes of central Asia and S Siberia that were united under Genghis Khan in 1206. **3**

(**mongol** or **mongoloid**) *old use, now offensive* a person affected by DOWN'S SYNDROME. • **mongolism** *noun, old use, now offensive* DOWN'S SYNDROME. ⓒ 18c.

Mongolian /mɒŋ'goulɪən/ ▷ *adj* belonging or relating to Mongolia, a republic in E central Asia, its inhabitants, or their language. ▷ *noun* (*also* **Mongol**) **1** a citizen or inhabitant of, or person born in, Mongolia. **2** the official language of Mongolia. **3** a Mongoloid.

Mongoloid /'mɒŋgəlɔɪd/ ▷ *adj* **1** belonging or relating to a large racial group, mainly N, E and SE Asian but including the Inuit of N America, characterized by a flattish face, high cheekbones, a fold of the upper eyelid, straight black hair and medium skin colour. **2** (**mongoloid**) *offensive* relating to or affected by DOWN'S SYNDROME. ▷ *noun* **1** a member of the Mongoloid race. **2** (**mongoloid**) see MONGOL *noun* 3.

mongoose /'mɒŋguːs, 'mʌŋ-/ ▷ *noun* (***mongooses***) a small mammal of SE Asia, Africa and Madagascar that preys on snakes, etc, and has a long, slender body, pointed muzzle and a bushy tail. See also ICHNEUMON. ⓒ 17c: from Marathi (a language of India) *mangus*.

mongrel /'mʌŋgrəl/ ▷ *noun* **1** an animal, especially a dog, of mixed breeding. **2** *derog* a person or thing of mixed origin or nature. ▷ *adj* **1** characterized by being of mixed breeding, origin or nature. **2** neither one thing nor another. • **mongrelly** *adj*. ⓒ 15c.

monied and **monies** see under MONEY

moniker /'mɒnɪkə(r)/ ▷ *noun, slang* a nickname. ⓒ 19c.

monism /'mɒnɪzəm, 'moun-/ ▷ *noun, philos* the theory that reality exists in one form only, especially that there is no difference in substance between body and soul. Compare DUALISM. • **monist** *noun*. • **monistic** *adj*. ⓒ 19c: from Greek *monos* single; see also -ISM.

monition /mɒ'nɪʃən/ ▷ *noun, formal or literary* a warning or telling-off; an act or instance of admonishing. • **monitive** *adj*. ⓒ 14c: French, from Latin *monere* to warn or remind.

monitor /'mɒnɪtə(r)/ ▷ *noun* **1** any instrument designed to check, record or control something on a regular basis. **2** a high-quality screen used in closed-circuit television systems, in TV studios, etc to view the picture being transmitted, etc. **3** the visual display unit of a computer, used to present information to the user. **4** in a school: a pupil who helps with specific tasks, or a senior pupil who helps to enforce discipline over other pupils. **5** someone whose job is to monitor eg a situation, process, etc. **6** (*also* **monitor lizard**) any of various large carnivorous lizards of Africa, Asia and Australia, so called because they are thought to give a warning of the presence of crocodiles. **7** *telecomm* an apparatus for testing transmission without interfering with the regular transmission. ▷ *verb* (***monitored, monitoring***) to check, record, track or control something on a regular basis; to observe or act as a monitor of something. • **monitorial** /mɒnɪ'tɔːrɪəl/ *adj*. • **monitorship** *noun*. • **monitory** /'mɒnɪtərɪ/ *adj, formal* serving as a warning or telling-off. ⓒ 16c: from Latin *monere* to warn or advise.

monitoring service ▷ *noun* eg as part of a country's intelligence operations: an agency responsible for systematically checking foreign broadcasts. See also GCHQ.

monk /mʌŋk/ ▷ *noun* a member of a religious community of men living disciplined austere lives devoted primarily to worship, under vows of poverty, chastity and obedience. • **monkish** *adj* **1** relating to or like a monk. **2** *often rather derog* monastic. ⓒ Anglo-Saxon *munuc*: from Greek *monachos*, from *monos* alone.

monkey /'mʌŋkɪ/ ▷ *noun* (***monkeys***) **1** any mammal belonging to the PRIMATES other than a human, ape, chimpanzee, gibbon, orang utan or lemur, with a hairy coat, nails instead of claws and usually tree-dwelling. **2** *colloq* a mischievous child. **3** *Brit slang* £500. **4** *US slang* an oppressive burden or habit, especially a drug addiction. **5** the falling weight of a pile-driver, etc (see also MONKEY ENGINE). ▷ *verb* (***monkeys, monkeyed, monkeying***) *intr, colloq* (*especially* **monkey about** or **around with something**) to play, fool, interfere, etc with it. • **have a monkey on one's back** *US slang* to be addicted to drugs. • **make a monkey out of someone** *colloq* to make them seem ridiculous; to make a fool of them. • **not give a monkey's** *slang* not to care at all. ⓒ 16c.

monkey business ▷ *noun, colloq* mischief; illegal or dubious activities.

monkey engine ▷ *noun* a pile-driver.

monkey nut ▷ *noun* a peanut in its shell.

monkey puzzle tree ▷ *noun* a S American conifer with close-set, hard, prickly leaves covering its long, drooping branches. Often shortened to **monkey puzzle**. Also called **Chile pine**.

monkey tricks ▷ *plural noun, colloq* mischief; pranks. *US equivalent* **monkey shines**.

monkey wrench ▷ *noun* a spanner-like tool with movable jaws; an adjustable spanner.

monkfish ▷ *noun* **1** a large cartilaginous fish with a flattened head, lateral gill openings, broad pectoral fins and a slender tail. Also called **angel shark**. **2** any of several types of ANGLER fish.

monkish see under MONK

monkshood see under ACONITE

mono /'mɒnou/ *colloq* ▷ *adj* short form of MONOPHONIC and MONOUNSATURATED. ▷ *noun* monophonic sound reproduction, ie on one channel only, not split into two, as with STEREOPHONIC systems.

mono- /'mɒnou-/ or (before a vowel) **mon-** *combining form, denoting* one; single □ *monosyllable* □ *monoxide*. ⓒ From Greek *monos* single.

monocarp /'mɒnoukɑːp/ ▷ *noun, bot* a plant that flowers and fruits only once in its life cycle. • **monocarpic** or **monocarpous** *adj*. ⓒ 19c: from Greek *karpos* fruit.

monochromatic ▷ *adj* **1** *physics* **a** said of light: having only one wavelength; **b** said of radiation or oscillation: having a unique or very narrow band of frequency. **2** monochrome.

monochrome /mɒnə'kroum/ ▷ *adj* **1** said of visual reproduction: using or having one colour, or in black and white only. **2** said especially of painting: using shades of one colour only. **3** lacking any variety or interest; dull or monotonous. ▷ *noun* **1** a monochrome picture, photograph, drawing, etc. **2** representation in monochrome. **3** the art or technique of working in monochrome. Also called **monochromy** /mə'nɒkrəmɪ/ . • **monochromic** *adj*. ⓒ 17c: from medieval Latin *monochroma*, from Greek *chroma* colour.

monocle /'mɒnəkəl/ ▷ *noun* a lens for correcting the sight in one eye only, held in place between the bones of the cheek and brow. • **monocled** *adj*. ⓒ 19c: French, from Latin *oculus* eye.

monocline /'mɒnouklaɪn/ ▷ *noun, geol* in rock strata: a fold with one side that dips steeply, after which the strata resume their original direction. • **monoclinal** *adj*. ⓒ 19c: from Greek *klinein* to cause something to slope.

monoclonal /mɒnou'klounəl/ ▷ *adj, biol* said of an antibody: of a highly specific type produced artificially by any of various clones (see CLONE *noun* 1) and used in the identification of blood groups and the production of vaccines.

monocoque /'mɒnoukɒk/ ▷ *noun* (***monocoques***) **1** *aeronautics* a fuselage or NACELLE in which all the structural loads are carried by the skin. **2** *naut* the hull of a boat made all in one piece. **3** a structural type of vehicle in which the body and chassis are in one piece. Also *as adj.* ◷ 19c: French, literally 'single shell', from *coque* egg-shell.

monocotyledon ▻ *noun, bot* a flowering plant with an embryo that has one COTYLEDON, parallel leaf veins, vascular bundles throughout the stem and flower parts in multiples of three, eg daffodil, cereals, grasses and palms. Compare DICOTYLEDON. • **monocotyledonous** *adj.*

monocracy /mɒˈnɒkrəsɪ/ ▻ *noun* (***monocracies***) **1** government by one person only. **2** the rule of such a person. **3** a country, state, society, etc that is governed by one person. See also AUTOCRACY. • **monocrat** /ˈmɒnəkrat/ *noun.* • **monocratic** /-ˈkratɪk/ *adj.* ◷ 17c: MONO- + -CRACY.

monocular /məˈnɒkjʊlə(r)/ ▻ *adj* **1** for the use of, or relating to, one eye only. **2** *now rare* having, or having the use of, one eye only. ◷ 17c.

monoculture ▻ *noun* **1** *agric* the practice of growing the same crop each year on a given area of land, rather than growing different crops in rotation. **2** an area where there is just one, shared culture, eg a single ethnic, social or religious culture. • **monocultural** *adj* belonging or relating to, or consisting of, a monoculture.

monocyte ▻ *noun, biol* the largest type of white blood cell, which has a single, oval or kidney-shaped nucleus and clear cytoplasm. ◷ Early 20c: from German *Monozyt*, see -CYTE.

monody /ˈmɒnədɪ/ ▻ *noun* (***monodies***) **1** *literary* **a** especially in Greek tragedy: a mournful song or speech performed by a single actor; **b** any poem lamenting a death. **2** *music* a song in which the melody is sung by one voice only, with other voices accompanying. • **monodic** /məˈnɒdɪk/ *adj.* • **monodist** *noun.* ◷ 17c: from Greek *monoidia*, from *oide* song.

monoecious /mɒˈniːʃəs/ ▻ *adj* **1** *bot* said of a plant: with separate male and female reproductive parts in the same plant. **2** *biol* said of an animal: with both male and female sexual organs; hermaphrodite. Compare DIOECIOUS. ◷ 18c: from MONO- + Greek *oikos* house.

monofilament ▻ *noun* a single strand of synthetic fibre.

monogamy /məˈnɒgəmɪ/ ▻ *noun* **1 a** the state or practice of having only one husband or wife at any one time; **b** *loosely* the state or practice of having only one sexual partner at any one time. Compare POLYGAMY. **2** *zool* the state or practice of having only one mate. • **monogamist** *noun.* • **monogamous** *adj.* ◷ 17c.

monoglot ▻ *noun* a person who only knows and speaks one language. ▻ *adj* referring or relating to such a person. ◷ 19c.

monogram ▻ *noun* a design composed from letters, usually a person's initials, interlaced or written into a single character, often used on personal belongings, clothing, etc. ▻ *verb* (***monogrammed, monogramming***) to mark something with a monogram. • **monogrammatic** *adj.* ◷ 17c.

monograph ▻ *noun* a book or essay dealing with one particular subject or a specific aspect of it. ▻ *verb* (***monographed, monographing***) to write a monograph on (a subject). • **monographer** or **monographist** *noun.* • **monographic** or **monographical** *adj.* ◷ 19c.

monohull ▻ *noun* a sailing craft with one hull, as distinct from a CATAMARAN or a TRIMARAN.

monohybrid ▻ *noun, biol* a living organism that carries one dominant and one recessive ALLELE for a particular gene.

monolingual ▻ *adj* **1** said of a person: able to speak one language only. **2** expressed in, or dealing with, a single language ▫ ***a monolingual dictionary.*** • **monolingualism** *noun.* • **monolinguist** *noun.*

monolith /ˈmɒnəlɪθ/ ▻ *noun* **1** a single, tall block of stone, especially one shaped like or into a column or pillar. **2** anything resembling one of these in its uniformity, immovability or massiveness. **3** *civil engineering, etc* a large uniform mass of concrete or similar material. • **monolithic** /-ˈlɪθɪk/ *adj* **1** relating to or like a monolith. **2** said of an organization, etc: large, unchanging and difficult to deal with. ◷ 19c: from French *monolithe*, from Greek *monolithos* made of one piece of stone, from MONO- + *lithos* stone.

monologue or (*US*) **monolog** /ˈmɒnəlɒg/ ▻ *noun* (***monologues*** or ***monologs***) **1** *theat, etc* **a** a long speech by one actor in a film or play. See also SOLILOQUY; **b** a drama for one actor. **2** *usually derog* any long, uninterrupted piece of speech by one person, especially a tedious or opinionated speech that prevents any conversation. ◷ 17c: French, meaning 'a person who likes to talk at length'.

monomania ▻ *noun* **1** *psychol* domination of the mind by a single subject or concern, to an excessive degree. **2** an obsession or craze. • **monomaniac** *noun.* • **monomaniac** or **monomaniacal** *adj.* ◷ 19c: from French *monomanie*, from MANIA.

monomark ▻ *noun, Brit* a particular combination of letters or figures used as an identification mark.

monomer /ˈmɒnəmə(r)/ ▻ *noun, chem* a simple molecule that can be joined to many others to form a much larger molecule known as a POLYMER. • **monomeric** /-ˈmɛrɪk/ *adj.* ◷ Early 20c.

monomial /mɒˈnoʊmɪəl/ *math* ▻ *noun* an algebraic expression that consists of one term only. ▻ *adj* consisting of one term. ◷ 18c: from MONO-, modelled on BINOMIAL.

monomorphic and **monomorphous** ▻ *adj, biol* said of an organism: that exists in one form only throughout its life cycle. • **monomorphism** *noun.* ◷ 19c: from Greek *morphe* form.

mononuclear ▻ *adj* said of a cell: having a single nucleus.

mononucleosis /mɒnoʊnjuːklɪˈoʊsɪs/ ▻ *noun, pathol* a condition, especially INFECTIOUS MONONUCLEOSIS, in which an abnormally large number of lymphocytes (MONONUCLEAR cells) are present in the blood. ◷ 1920s: from MONONUCLEAR.

monophonic ▻ *adj* said of a recording or broadcasting system, record, etc: reproducing sound or records on one channel only, rather than splitting it into two, as with STEREOPHONIC systems. Now usually shortened to MONO. Also called MONAURAL. ◷ 19c: see -PHONIC.

monophthong /ˈmɒnəfθɒŋ/ ▻ *noun* a single vowel sound. Compare DIPHTHONG. ◷ 17c: from Greek *monophthongos*, from *mono-* MONO- + *phthongos* sound.

monoplane ▻ *noun* an aeroplane with a single set of wings. Compare BIPLANE. ◷ Early 20c: see PLANE² *noun* 2.

monoplegia /mɒnoʊˈpliːdʒɪə/ ▻ *noun, medicine* paralysis that affects only one part of the body, or one limb or muscle. Compare PARAPLEGIA. • **monoplegic** *adj, noun.* ◷ 19c: Latin, from Greek *plege* stroke or blow.

monopolize or **monopolise** /məˈnɒpəlaɪz/ ▻ *verb* (***monopolized, monopolizing***) **1** to have a monopoly or exclusive control of trade in (a commodity or service). **2** to dominate (eg a conversation or a person's attention), while excluding all others. • **monopolization** *noun.* • **monopolizer** *noun.* ◷ 17c.

monopoly /məˈnɒpəlɪ/ ▻ *noun* (***monopolies***) **1** the right to be, or the fact of being, the only supplier of a specified commodity or service. **2** a business that has such a monopoly. **3** a commodity or service controlled in this way. **4** exclusive possession or control of anything ▫ ***You don't have a monopoly on the truth!*** See also DUOPOLY, OLIGOPOLY. • **monopolist** *noun* someone who monopolizes, has a monopoly or favours monopoly. • **monopolistic** /-ˈlɪstɪk/ *adj.* ◷ 16c: from Latin *monopolium*, from Greek *poleein* to sell.

Monopoly money ▷ *noun, colloq* large sums of money, when treated lightly as if it were of no real value or significance. ◷ 1970s: named after the board game *Monopoly* (*trademark*) invented in 1933, in which streets, property, etc are 'bought' and 'sold' using imitation banknotes.

monorail ▷ *noun* a railway system in which the trains run on, or are suspended from, a single rail. Also *as adj* □ *monorail system.*

monosaccharide ▷ *noun, biochem* a simple sugar, eg GLUCOSE or FRUCTOSE, that cannot be broken down into smaller units.

mono-ski ▷ *noun* a broad single ski on which the skier places both feet. • **mono-skier** *noun*. • **mono-skiing** *noun*.

monosodium glutamate /ˈmɒnəsoudɪəm ˈɡluːtəmeɪt/ ▷ *noun* (abbreviation **MSG**) a white crystalline chemical substance used to enhance the flavour of many processed savoury foods without giving a taste of its own. ◷ 1920s: MONO- + SODIUM + GLUTAMIC ACID + -ATE.

monosyllabic /mɒnousɪˈlabɪk/ ▷ *adj* **1** consisting of one syllable only. **2** using short words, especially 'yes' and 'no' □ *a monosyllabic reply.* • **monosyllabically** *adverb*.

monosyllable ▷ *noun* a word consisting of only one syllable. • **in monosyllables** using simple language. ◷ 16c.

monotheism ▷ *noun* the belief that there is only one God. • **monotheist** *noun*. • **monotheistic** *adj*. • **monotheistically** *adverb*. ◷ 17c: from Greek *theos* god.

monotint ▷ *noun, art* representation in, or a drawing, painting, etc using, shades of one colour only; monochrome.

monotone ▷ *noun* **1** in speech or sound: a single unvarying tone. **2** a sequence of sounds of the same tone. **3** especially in colour: sameness; lack of variety. ▷ *adj* **1** lacking in variety; unchanging. **2** in monotone. ◷ 17c: from Latin *monotonus*, from Greek *monotonos*, from *tonos* tone.

monotonous /məˈnɒtənəs/ ▷ *adj* **1** lacking in variety; tediously unchanging. **2** said of speech or sound, etc: in one unvaried tone. • **monotonously** *adverb*. ◷ 18c.

monotony *noun* (*monotonies*) **1** the quality of being monotonous. **2** routine or dullness or sameness.

monotreme /ˈmɒnətriːm/ ▷ *noun, zool* an animal, such as the ECHIDNA or the DUCK-BILLED PLATYPUS, that differ from other mammals in having a single opening, the CLOACA, that serves for the passing of both urine and faeces. In females, this same opening is used for egg-laying and the receiving of sperm. ◷ 19c: from Latin *Monotremata*, from Greek *trematus* holed.

monotype ▷ *noun* **1** *art* a one-off print made by applying oil paint or ink on to a sheet of glass or metal plate, and pressing paper against the wet surface to create on it a reverse image of the original. **2** (**Monotype**) *trademark, printing* **a** a make of typesetting equipment; **b** originally a machine that cast and set type, letter by letter; **c** a reproduction made by this process. Also *as adj* □ *monotype operator.* ◷ 19c.

monotypic /mɒnouˈtɪpɪk/ ▷ *adj* said eg of a plant or animal species: consisting of only one type or example.

monounsaturated ▷ *adj* said especially of an oil or fat: containing only one double or triple bond per molecule. Also shortened to MONO. Compare POLYUNSATURATED.

monovalent ▷ *adj, chem* said of an atom of an element: with a valency of one; capable of combining with one atom of hydrogen or its equivalent. Also called **univalent**. • **monovalence** or **monovalency** *noun*. ◷ 19c.

monoxide /məˈnɒksaɪd/ ▷ *noun, chem* a compound that contains one oxygen atom in each molecule. ◷ 19c.

monozygotic twins see under IDENTICAL

Monseigneur /mɒnˈsɛnjə(r)/ ▷ *noun* (***Messeigneurs*** /meɪˈsɛn-/) a title equivalent to *My Lord*, used to address a French or French-speaking man of high rank or birth, eg a bishop or prince (abbreviation **Mgr** or *plural* **Mgrs**). ◷ 17c: French, from *mon* my + *seigneur* lord.

Monsieur /məˈsjɜː(r)/ ▷ *noun* (***Messieurs*** /meɪˈjɜː(r)s-/) a title equivalent to MR, used especially in front of the surname of a French or French-speaking man (abbreviation **M** or *plural* **MM**). **2** (**monsieur**) a Frenchman, when not used with a surname. ◷ 16c: French, originally *mon* my + *sieur* lord.

Monsignor /mɒnˈsiːnjə(r)/ ▷ *noun* (***Monsignors*** or ***Monsignori*** /-ˈnjɔːrɪ/) a title given to various high-ranking male members of the Roman Catholic church (abbreviation **Monsig.** or **Mgr**). ◷ 17c: Italian, from French *Monseigneur*, a title given to high-ranking clergy and nobility.

monsoon /mɒnˈsuːn/ ▷ *noun* **1** especially in the area around the Indian Ocean and S Asia: a wind that blows from the NE in winter (the **dry monsoon**) and from the SW in summer (the **wet monsoon**). **2** in India: the heavy rains that accompany the summer monsoon. **3** *colloq* an extremely heavy fall of rain. **4** any strong, relatively constant wind that blows in opposite directions at different times of year. • **monsoonal** *adj*. ◷ 16c: from Dutch *monssoen*, ultimately from Arabic *mawsim* season.

monster /ˈmɒnstə(r)/ ▷ *noun* **1** especially in fables and folklore: any large and frightening imaginary creature. **2** a cruel or evil person. **3** any unusually large thing. **4** *old use* a deformed person, animal or plant. ▷ *adj* huge; gigantic □ *monster portions.* ◷ 14c: from French *monstre*, from Latin *monstrum* an evil omen.

monstera /mɒnˈstɪərə/ ▷ *noun* (***monsteras***) a tall tropical American climbing plant, popular as a house plant, with large shiny heart-shaped leaves and tough aerial roots growing from the stem. Also called **Swiss cheese plant**, **cheese plant**. ◷ 19c: from Latin *monstrum*.

monstrance /ˈmɒnstrəns/ ▷ *noun* (***monstrances***) *RC Church* a large, gold or silver cup in which the HOST[3] is displayed to the congregation during Mass. ◷ 16c: French, from Latin *monstrare* to show.

monstrosity /mɒnˈstrɒsɪtɪ/ ▷ *noun* (***monstrosities***) **1** any very ugly or outrageous thing; a monster or freak. **2** the quality or state of being monstrous. ◷ 16c.

monstrous /ˈmɒnstrəs/ ▷ *adj* **1** like a monster; huge and horrible. **2** outrageous; absurd. **3** extremely cruel; evil. **4** *old use* deformed; abnormal. • **monstrously** *adverb*. • **monstrousness** *noun*.

Mont. see under MT

montage /mɒnˈtɑːʒ/ ▷ *noun* **1 a** the process of creating a picture by assembling and piecing together elements from other pictures, photographs, etc, and mounting them on to canvas, etc; **b** a picture made in this way. **2** the process of editing film material. **3** *cinema, TV* a film sequence made up of short clips, or images superimposed, dissolved together, etc, especially one used to condense events that take place over a long period. **4** *cinema, TV* extensive use of changes in camera position to create an impression of movement or action in a filmed scene. See also MISE-EN-SCÈNE. ◷ 1920s: French, from *monter* to mount.

montbretia /mɒnˈbriːʃə/ ▷ *noun* (***montbretias***) a perennial hybrid plant with sword-shaped leaves and yellow or orange trumpet-shaped flowers that grow in spikes. ◷ 19c: Latin, named after the French botanist A F E Coquebert de Montbret (1780–1801).

Montezuma's revenge /mɒntəˈzuːməz —/ ▷ *noun* diarrhoea caused by travelling and exposure to unfamiliar food, especially in Mexico. ◎ 20c: from Montezuma II, the Mexican ruler at the time of the Spanish conquest.

month /mʌnθ/ ▻ *noun* **1** any of the 12 named divisions of the year, which vary in length between 28 and 31 days. Also called **calendar month**. **2** a period of roughly four weeks or 30 days. **3** the period between identical dates in consecutive months. Also called **calendar month**. See also LUNAR MONTH, SOLAR MONTH. • **a month of Sundays** *colloq* a very long time. ◎ Anglo-Saxon *monath*, from *mona* moon.

monthly ▻ *adj* **1** happening, published, performed, etc once a month. **2** lasting one month. ▻ *adverb* once a month. ▻ *noun* (***monthlies***) **1** a monthly periodical. **2** *colloq* a menstrual period.

montmorillonite /mɒntməˈrɪlənaɪt/ ▻ *noun* (***montmorillonites***) *geol* a soft opaque clay mineral composed of aluminium silicate that expands when it absorbs liquids, used in decolouring solutions, as a base for paper and cosmetics, etc. See also FULLER'S EARTH. ◎ 19c: named after Montmorillon in France, where it was found.

monument /ˈmɒnjʊmənt/ ▻ *noun* **1** something, eg a statue, built to preserve the memory of a person or event. **2** any ancient building or structure preserved for its historical value. **3** *formal* something that serves as clear evidence of something; an excellent example □ ***This work is a monument to her artistic skill.*** **4** *formal* a tombstone. ◎ 14c, originally meaning 'a sepulchre': from Latin *monumentum*, from *monere* to remind.

monumental /mɒnjʊˈmɛntəl/ ▻ *adj* **1** like a monument, especially huge and impressive. **2** *colloq* very great; extreme □ ***monumental arrogance.*** **3** belonging or relating to, or taking the form of, a monument. **4** *formal* relating to tombstones □ ***monumental sculptor.*** • **monumentally** *adverb*.

moo ▻ *noun* (***moos***) **1** the long low sound made by a cow, ox, etc. **2** *Brit rather dated derog slang* a simple-minded woman. ▻ *verb* (***moos, mooed, mooing***) *intr* to make this sound. • **mooing** *noun*. ◎ 16c: imitating the sound.

mooch /muːtʃ/ ▻ *verb* (***mooches, mooched, mooching***) *colloq* **1** *intr* (*usually* **mooch about** or **around**) to wander around aimlessly. **2** *tr & intr* to cadge; to get something for nothing by asking directly. **3** *intr* to skulk or lurk about. 19c in current senses; 15c meaning 'to act the miser'.

mood¹ /muːd/ ▻ *noun* **1** a state of mind at a particular time □ ***See what sort of mood he's in before you ask him.*** **2** (*especially* **the mood**) a suitable or necessary state of mind □ ***not in the mood for dancing.*** **3** a temporary grumpy state of mind □ ***Now he's gone off in a mood.*** **4** an atmosphere □ ***The mood in the factory is tense.*** ◎ Anglo-Saxon *mod* in obsolete sense 'mind' or 'feeling'.

mood² /muːd/ ▻ *noun* **1** *grammar* each of several forms of a verb, indicating whether the verb is expressing a fact (see INDICATIVE), a wish, possibility or doubt (see SUBJUNCTIVE) or a command (see IMPERATIVE). **2** *logic* the form of the SYLLOGISM as determined by the quantity and quality of its three constituent propositions. ◎ 16c: originally a variant of MODE.

moody /ˈmuːdɪ/ ▻ *adj* (***moodier, moodiest***) **1** tending to change mood often. **2** frequently bad-tempered or sulky. • **moodily** *adverb*. • **moodiness** *noun*.

Moog synthesizer /muːg —/ ▻ *noun, trademark* an electronic musical instrument with a keyboard that can produce a wide range of sounds. Often shortened to **Moog**. ◎ 1960s: developed by the American engineer Robert Moog (b.1934).

mooli /ˈmuːlɪ/ ▻ *noun* (***moolis***) a long white carrot-shaped root that tastes similar to a radish. ◎ 20c: native E African word.

moon¹ /muːn/ ▻ *noun* **1** (*often* **Moon**) the Earth's natural satellite, illuminated to varying degrees by the Sun depending on its position and often visible in the sky, especially at night. **2** the appearance of the Moon to an observer on Earth, especially in terms of its degree of illumination, eg FULL MOON, HALF MOON. See also CRESCENT, NEW MOON. **3** a natural satellite of any planet □ ***the moons of Jupiter.*** **4** something impossible to obtain □ ***promised me the moon.*** **5** *literary* or *old use* a month. • **moonless** *adj*. • **over the moon** *colloq* thrilled; delighted. ◎ Anglo-Saxon *mona*.

moon² /muːn/ ▻ *verb* (***mooned, mooning***) *intr* **1** (*usually* **moon about** or **around**) to wander around aimlessly; to spend time idly. **2** *slang* to make a show of one's bare buttocks in public. • **mooner** *noun*. 1960s in sense 2, from a resemblance to the MOON¹; 19c in sense 1, referring to the behaviour of someone who is MOONSTRUCK.

moonbeam ▻ *noun* a ray of sunlight reflected from the moon.

moonface ▻ *noun* a full, round face. • **moon-faced** *adj*.

moonfish see under OPAH

Moonies see UNIFICATION CHURCH

moonlight ▻ *noun* **1** sunlight reflected by the moon. **2** *as adj* at night □ ***a moonlight flit.*** **3** illuminated by moonlight. □ ***a moonlight swim.*** ▻ *verb, intr, colloq* to work at a second job outside the working hours of one's main job, often evading income tax on the extra earnings. • **moonlighter** *noun*. • **moonlighting** *noun* the practice of working as a moonlighter.

moonlit ▻ *adj* illuminated by moonlight □ ***a clear, moonlit night.*** See also MOONLIGHT.

moonscape ▻ *noun* the appearance of the surface of the moon, or a representation of it.

moonshine ▻ *noun, colloq* **1** foolish talk; nonsense. **2** *chiefly N Amer* smuggled or illegally-distilled alcoholic spirit. **3** MOONLIGHT *noun* 1.

moonshot ▻ *noun* a launching of an object, craft, etc to orbit or land on the moon.

moonstone ▻ *noun, geol* a transparent or opalescent, silvery or bluish FELDSPAR, used as a semi-precious gemstone. ◎ 17c: so called because it was once thought that its appearance changed with the waxing and waning of the moon.

moonstruck ▻ *adj, colloq* behaving in an unusually distracted, dazed, or wild way, as if affected by the moon. See also LUNATIC. ◎ 17c.

moony /ˈmuːnɪ/ ▻ *adj* (***moonier, mooniest***) *colloq* in a dreamy, distracted mood.

Moor /mɔː(r), mʊə(r)/ ▻ *noun* a Muslim belonging to a mixed Arab/Berber race of NW Africa, that conquered the Iberian peninsula in the 8c. • **Moorish** *adj*. ◎ 14c as *More* or *Maur*: from French *More* or *Maure*, from Latin *Maurus*.

moor¹ /mɔː(r), mʊə(r)/ ▻ *noun* a large area of open, uncultivated upland with an acid peaty soil. ◎ Anglo-Saxon *mor*.

moor² /mɔː(r), mʊə(r)/ ▻ *verb* (***moored, mooring***) **1** to fasten (a ship or boat) by a rope, cable or anchor. **2** *intr* said of a ship, etc: to be fastened in this way. • **moorage** *noun*. ◎ 15c as *more*.

moorcock ▻ *noun* a male MOORFOWL.

moorfowl ▻ *noun* a red or black grouse.

moorhen ▻ *noun* **1** a small black water bird of the rail family (see RAIL³), with a red beak. **2** a female MOORFOWL.

mooring ▻ *noun* **1** a place where a boat is moored. **2** (**moorings**) the ropes, anchors, etc used to moor a boat. **3** something that provides security or stability.

Moorish see under MOOR

moorland ▻ *noun* a stretch of MOOR¹.

moose /muːs/ ▻ *noun* (*plural* ***moose***) a large deer with flat, rounded antlers, found in N America, and also in

Europe and Asia where it is called the **elk**. ⓘ 17c: from Algonquian (a Native American language) *moos*.

moot /muːt/ ▷ *verb* (***mooted***, ***mooting***) **1** to suggest; to bring something up for discussion. **2** *intr* to dispute or plead, especially as a form of academic exercise. ▷ *adj* (***mooter***, ***mootest***) open to argument; debatable □ ***a moot point.*** ▷ *noun* **1** *historical* in Anglo-Saxon England: a court or administrative assembly. **2** a discussion of a hypothetical legal case, especially as a form of academic exercise. ⓘ Anglo-Saxon as *mot* assembly.

mop /mɒp/ ▷ *noun* **1** a tool for washing or wiping floors, consisting of a large sponge or a set of thick threads fixed on to the end of a long handle. **2** a similar smaller tool for washing dishes. **3** *colloq* a thick or tangled mass of hair. ▷ *verb* (***mopped***, ***mopping***) **1** to wash or wipe (eg a floor) with a mop. **2** to wipe, dab or clean (eg a sweaty brow). • **mopper** *noun*. ⓘ 15c.

■ **mop up** or **mop something up 1** to clean something up (eg a spillage) with a mop. **2** *colloq* to capture or kill (remaining enemy troops) after a victory. **3** *colloq* to deal with or get rid of (anything that remains).

mope /moʊp/ ▷ *verb* (***moped***, ***moping***) *intr* **1** (*especially* **mope about** or **around**) to behave in a depressed, sulky or aimless way. **2** (*often* **mope along**) to move in a listless, aimless or depressed way. ▷ *noun* **1** a habitually sulky or depressed person. **2** (**the mopes**) low spirits; depression. • **moper** *noun*. ⓘ 16c.

moped /ˈmoʊpɛd/ ▷ *noun* a small-engined motorcycle (under 50cc), especially one that is started by using pedals. ⓘ 1950s: a shortening of *mo*tor-assisted *ped*al-cycle.

moppet /ˈmɒpɪt/ ▷ *noun* a term of affection used to a small child. See also POPPET. ⓘ 17c: diminutive of obsolete *mop* rag doll.

mop-up ▷ *noun* an act of mopping up. See MOP UP under MOP.

mopy /ˈmoʊpɪ/ ▷ *adj* (***mopier***, ***mopiest***) inclined to mope; dull, listless or miserable. • **mopily** *adverb*. • **mopiness** *noun*.

moquette /mɒˈkɛt/ ▷ *noun* thick velvety material used to make carpets and upholstery. ⓘ 18c: French.

MOR ▷ *abbreviation* especially in music broadcasting: middle-of-the-road.

moraine /məˈreɪn/ ▷ *noun, geol* an area covered by a jumbled accumulation of different-sized rock fragments that have been carried from their place of origin and deposited by a glacier or ice sheet. • **morainal** or **morainic** *adj*. ⓘ 18c: French.

moral /ˈmɒrəl/ ▷ *adj* **1** belonging or relating to the principles of good and evil, or right and wrong. **2** conforming to what is considered by society to be good, right or proper; ethical. **3** adhering to or based on conscience or a knowledge of what is right □ ***a moral obligation.*** **4** having a psychological rather than a practical effect □ ***moral support.*** **5** considered in terms of psychological effect, rather than outward appearance □ ***a moral victory.*** **6** said of a person: capable of distinguishing between right and wrong. **7** supported by reason or probability, though not provable □ ***a moral certainty.*** ▷ *noun* **1** a principle or practical lesson that can be learned from a story or event. **2** (**morals**) a sense of right and wrong, or a standard of behaviour based on this, especially in relation to sexual conduct □ ***loose morals.*** • **morally** *adverb*. ⓘ 14c: from Latin *moralis*, from *mores*, plural of *mos* a custom.

moral certainty ▷ *noun* something about which there is hardly any doubt.

morale /məˈrɑːl/ ▷ *noun* the level of confidence or optimism in a person or group; spirits □ ***The news boosted morale in the camp.*** ⓘ 18c: French, feminine of adjective *moral* MORAL.

moralism /ˈmɒrəlɪzəm/ ▷ *noun* **1** a moral saying. **2** moralizing. **3** morality as distinct from religion.

moralist /ˈmɒrəlɪst/ ▷ *noun* **1** someone who lives according to strict moral principles. **2** someone who tends to lecture others on their low moral standards. • **moralistic** *adj* **1** relating to or typical of a moralist. **2** given to moralizing. **3** characterized by moralism. • **moralistically** *adverb*.

morality /məˈralɪtɪ/ ▷ *noun* (***moralities***) **1** the quality of being moral. **2** behaviour in relation to accepted moral standards. **3** a particular system of moral standards.

morality play ▷ *noun, historical* an allegorical drama, originating in the Middle Ages, in which the characters act out a conflict between good and evil. Compare MYSTERY PLAY.

moralize or **moralise** /ˈmɒrəlaɪz/ ▷ *verb* (***moralized***, ***moralizing***) **1** *intr* to write or speak, especially critically, about moral standards. **2** to explain something in terms of morals. **3** to make someone or something moral or more moral. • **moralization** *noun*. • **moralizer** *noun*.

morally see under MORAL

moral majority ▷ *noun* in a society: the majority, who are presumed to be in favour of a strict moral code. Compare SILENT MAJORITY. ⓘ 1970s.

moral philosophy see under ETHICS

moral theology ▷ *noun, relig* a theological discipline concerned with ethical questions considered from a specifically Christian perspective.

morass /məˈras/ ▷ *noun* (***morasses***) **1** an area of marshy or swampy ground. **2** *literary* a dangerous or confused situation, especially one that entraps someone or prevents them from progressing. ⓘ 17c: from Dutch *moeras*, from French *maresc* a marsh.

moratorium /mɒrəˈtɔːrɪəm/ ▷ *noun* (***moratoriums*** or ***moratoria*** /-rɪə/) **1** an agreed temporary break in an activity. **2 a** a legally-authorized postponement of payment of a debt for a given time; **b** the period of time authorized for this. ⓘ 19c: Latin, from *mora* delay.

Moravian /məˈreɪvɪən/ ▷ *adj* belonging or relating to Moravia, an early medieval kingdom, later part of Bohemia, and now a province situated in the Czech Republic, or to its inhabitants or their dialect. ▷ *noun* **1** an inhabitant of, or person born in, Moravia. **2** the Czech dialect spoken in Moravia. **3** *Christianity* a member of the **Moravian Brethren**, an evangelical Protestant body first formed in 15c Bohemia. • **Moravianism** *noun*. ⓘ 16c: from Latin *Morava* the river March.

moray /ˈmɒreɪ/ ▷ *noun* (***morays***) a sharp-toothed eel of warm coastal waters. ⓘ 17c: from Portuguese *moreia*, from Latin *muraena*.

morbid /ˈmɔːbɪd/ ▷ *adj* **1** displaying an unhealthy interest in unpleasant things, especially death. **2** *medicine* relating to, or indicating the presence of, disease. • **morbidity** *noun* **1** a morbid state. **2** *medicine* the proportion of diseased people in a community. • **morbidly** *adverb*. • **morbidness** *noun*. ⓘ 17c: from Latin *morbus* disease.

mordant /ˈmɔːdənt/ ▷ *adj* **1** sharply sarcastic or critical; biting. **2** *chem* said of a substance: serving as a mordant. ▷ *noun* **1** *chem* a chemical compound, usually a metallic oxide or salt, that is used to fix colour on textiles, etc that cannot be dyed directly. **2** a corrosive substance. • **mordancy** *noun*. • **mordantly** *adverb*. ⓘ 15c; 14c, meaning 'a device that bites': French, literally 'biting', from Latin *mordere* to bite.

mordent /ˈmɔːdənt/ ▷ *noun, music* a GRACE NOTE in which the principal note and the note above or below it are played before the note itself. ⓘ 19c: German, from Italian *mordente*, from *mordere* to bite.

more /ˈmɔː(r)/ (used as the comparative of MANY and MUCH) ▷ *adj* greater; additional □ ***He has more clothes***

than me □ *Don't use more than two bags.* ▷ *adverb* **1** used to form the comparative form of many adjectives and most adverbs, especially those of two or more syllables □ *a more difficult problem* □ *Drive more carefully.* **2** to a greater degree; with a greater frequency □ *I miss him more than ever.* **3** again □ *Do it once more.* ▷ *pronoun* a greater, or additional, number or quantity of people or things □ *If we run out, I'll have to order more.* See also MOST. • **more and more** increasingly; continuing to increase. • **more of a something** better described as or closer to being (a specified thing) □ *more of a painter than a writer.* • **more or less 1** almost □ *more or less finished.* **2** roughly □ *It'll take two hours, more or less.* ⓒ Anglo-Saxon *mara* greater.

moreish or **morish** /'mɔːrɪʃ/ ▷ *adj, Eng colloq* said especially of a food: so tasty, delicious, etc that one wants to keep eating more of it. ⓒ 18c.

morel /mə'rɛl/ ▷ *noun, bot* an edible fungus whose fruiting body has a pale stalk and a brownish egg-shaped head covered with a network of ridges. ⓒ 17c: from French *morel* dark brown.

morello /mə'rɛloʊ/ ▷ *noun* (***morellos***) a bitter-tasting, dark-red cherry. ⓒ 17c: from Italian, meaning 'blackish'.

morendo /mɒ'rɛndoʊ/ ▷ *adj* ▷ *adverb, music* dying away, in speed and tone. ⓒ 19c: Italian, meaning 'dying'.

moreover /mɔː'roʊvə(r)/ ▷ *adverb, slightly formal* or *old use* also; besides; and what is more important. ⓒ 13c.

mores /'mɔːreɪz, -riːz/ ▷ *plural noun, formal* social customs that reflect the basic moral and social values of a particular society. ⓒ Early 20c: Latin, plural of *mos* custom.

morganatic /mɔːgə'natɪk/ ▷ *adj, technical* said of marriage: between a person of high social rank and one of low rank, and allowing neither the lower-ranking person nor any child from the marriage to inherit the title or property of the higher-ranking person. Compare LEFT-HANDED. • **morganatically** *adverb*. ⓒ 18c: from Latin *matrimonium ad morganaticam*, literally 'marriage with a morning gift'; the offering of the gift, after consummation, is the husband's only duty in such a marriage.

morgue /mɔːg/ ▷ *noun* (***morgues***) **1** a MORTUARY. **2** any gloomy or depressing place. **3** in a newspaper office, etc: a place where miscellaneous information is stored for reference. ⓒ 19c: French, originally the name of a building in Paris, the *Morgue*, in which dead bodies were laid out for identification.

MORI /'mɔːrɪ/ ▷ *abbreviation, Brit* Market and Opinion Research Institute. Also *as adj* □ *a MORI poll.*

moribund /'mɒrɪbʌnd/ ▷ *adj* **1** dying; near the end of existence. **2** lacking strength or vitality. ⓒ 18c: from Latin *moribundus*, from *mori* to die.

morish see MOREISH

Mormon /'mɔːmən/ ▷ *noun, Christianity* a member of the Church of Jesus Christ of Latter-Day Saints, established in the US by Joseph Smith in 1830, which accepts as scripture both the Bible and the *Book of Mormon*, regarded as a record of certain ancient American prophets. • **Mormonism** *noun*. ⓒ 18c: named after Mormon, the supposed author of the Book of Mormon.

morn /mɔːn/ ▷ *noun, poetic* morning. ⓒ 13c: from Anglo-Saxon *morgen*.

mornay or (*sometimes*) **Mornay** /'mɔːneɪ/ ▷ *adj* **1** (following its noun) *cookery* served in a cheese sauce □ *cod mornay.* **2** said of a sauce: made with cheese. ⓒ Early 20c.

morning /'mɔːnɪŋ/ ▷ *noun* **1** the part of the day from sunrise to midday, or from midnight to midday. **2** *as adj* taken, or taking place, in the morning □ *morning coffee.* **3** sunrise; dawn. **4** *poetic or literary* the early part of something □ *the morning of my life.* • **in the morning** *colloq* tomorrow morning □ *Come back in the morning.* • **the morning after** *colloq* the morning after a celebration, especially when one is affected by a hangover or other unpleasant after-effects. ⓒ 13c: from *morn*, modelled on EVENING.

morning-after pill ▷ *noun, medicine* a contraceptive drug, consisting of a combination of oestrogen and progestogen, which can be taken within 72 hours of unprotected sexual intercourse by a woman wanting to prevent conception.

morning coat ▷ *noun* a man's black or grey TAILCOAT worn as part of morning dress.

morning dress ▷ *noun* men's formal dress for the daytime, consisting of morning coat, grey trousers and usually a top hat.

morning glory ▷ *noun* a tropical climbing plant with blue, pink or white trumpet-shaped flowers that close in the afternoon.

morning prayer see under MATINS 2

mornings ▷ *adverb, colloq, dialect or US* in the morning, especially on a regular basis □ *I don't work mornings.*

morning sickness ▷ *noun, colloq* nausea and vomiting or both, often experienced during the early stages of pregnancy, frequently in the morning.

morning star ▷ *noun* a planet, usually Venus, seen in the eastern sky just before sunrise. See also EVENING STAR.

Moroccan /mə'rɒkən/ ▷ *adj* belonging or relating to Morocco, a kingdom in N Africa, or to its inhabitants. ▷ *noun* a citizen or inhabitant of, or person born in, Morocco. ⓒ 18c.

morocco /mə'rɒkoʊ/ ▷ *noun* (***moroccos***) a type of soft fine goatskin leather. Also called **morocco leather**. ⓒ 17c: named after Morocco, the country that this leather was originally brought from.

moron /'mɔːrɒn/ ▷ *noun* **1** *derog, colloq* a very stupid person. **2** *old use, now very offensive* a person with a mild degree of mental handicap. • **moronic** /-'rɒnɪk/ *adj* **1** *colloq* stupid; foolish. **2** *old use* like or characteristic of a moron. • **moronically** *adverb*. ⓒ Early 20c: originally US, from Greek *moros* foolish.

morose /mə'roʊs/ ▷ *adj* silently gloomy or bad-tempered. • **morosely** *adverb*. • **moroseness** *noun*. ⓒ 16c: from Latin *morosus* peevish.

morph- /mɔːf/ or (before a consonant) **morpho-** *combining form, denoting* form, shape or structure. ⓒ From Greek *morphe* form.

-morph ▷ *combining form, forming nouns, denoting* something of a specified form, shape or structure □ *endomorph.* • **-morphic** *combining form, forming adjectives.* • **-morphism** *combining form, forming nouns.* • **-morphy** *combining form, forming nouns.* ⓒ From Greek *morphe* form.

morpheme /'mɔːfiːm/ ▷ *noun, linguistics* any of the grammatically or lexically meaningful units forming or underlying a word, not divisible themselves into smaller meaningful units, eg the morphemes *out, go* and *ing* forming the word, or 'lexeme', *outgoing*, or the 'plural' morpheme seen in the inflections in *cars, buses children,* etc. Compare LEXEME. See also MORPHOLOGY. • **morphemic** *adj.* • **morphemically** *adverb*. ⓒ 19c: from French *morphème*, modelled on PHONEME.

morphine /'mɔːfiːn/ ▷ *noun* a highly-addictive, narcotic drug obtained from opium, used medicinally as an analgesic to relieve severe and persistent pain, and as a sedative to induce sleep. Also called (*especially formerly*) **morphia**. See also CODEINE, HEROIN. ⓒ 19c: from German *Morphin*, from Greek *Morpheus*, the name of the god of sleep.

morphing /'mɔːfɪŋ/ ▷ *noun, cinematog* the use of computer graphics to blend one screen image into another, eg to transform or manipulate an actor's body. ⓒ 20c.

-morphism see under -MORPH

morpho- see MORPH-

morphogenesis /mɔːfoʊ'dʒɛnəsɪs/ ▻ *noun, biol* the development of form and structure in a living organism as a result of the growth and differentiation of its cells and tissues. • **morphogenetic** /-dʒə'nɛtɪk/ *adj.* Ⓒ 19c.

morphology /mɔː'fɒlədʒɪ/ ▻ *noun* **1** *linguistics* the study of MORPHEMES and the rules by which they combine to form words. **2** *biol* the scientific study of the structure of plants and animals. **3** *formal* the structure of anything. • **morphological** *adj.* • **morphologist** *noun.* Ⓒ 19c.

-morphy see under -MORPH

morris dance ▻ *noun* a type of traditional English country dance, performed by men carrying sticks and wearing costumes with bells and ribbons attached. Often shortened to **morris**. • **morris dancer** *noun.* • **morris dancing** *noun.* Ⓒ 15c: from *Morys* Moorish; see under MOOR.

the morrow /'mɒroʊ/ ▻ *noun, old use* or *poetic* **1** the following day ▫ ***would return on the morrow.*** **2** the time after an event ▫ ***bright hope for the morrow.*** **3** the morning. Ⓒ 13c: see MORN.

Morse and **Morse code** ▻ *noun* **1** a code used for sending messages, each letter of a word being represented as a series of short or long radio signals or flashes of light. **2** a method of sending messages using these signals. Ⓒ 19c: named after the American electrician, Samuel Morse (1791–1872), who invented it.

morsel /'mɔːsəl/ ▻ *noun* a small piece of something, especially of food. Ⓒ 13c: French, from *mors* a bite.

mortadella /mɔːtə'dɛlə/ ▻ *noun* (***mortadelle*** /-'dɛlɪ/) a large Italian pork sausage, sometimes studded with peppercorns, green olives or pistachios. Ⓒ 17c: Italian, from Latin *murtatum* seasoned with myrtle berries.

mortal /'mɔːtəl/ ▻ *adj* **1** said especially of human beings: certain to die at some future time. **2** causing or resulting in death ▫ ***mortal injury*** ▫ ***mortal combat.*** **3** extreme ▫ ***mortal fear.*** **4** characterized by intense hostility; implacable ▫ ***mortal enemies.*** **5** used for emphasis: conceivable; single ▫ ***every mortal thing.*** ▻ *noun* a mortal being, especially a human being. • **mortally** *adverb.* Ⓒ 14c: from Latin *mortalis*, from *mori* to die.

mortality /mɔː'talɪtɪ/ ▻ *noun* (***mortalities***) **1** the state of being mortal. . **2** the number of deaths, eg in a war or epidemic; the death-rate. Also called **mortality rate**. **3** loss of life; death, especially on a broad scale.

mortal sin ▻ *noun, RC Church* a serious sin, for which there can be no forgiveness from God. Compare VENIAL SIN.

mortar /'mɔːtə(r)/ ▻ *noun* **1** *building* a mixture of sand, water and cement or lime, used to bond bricks or stones. **2** the small heavy dish in which substances are ground with a PESTLE. **3** a type of short-barrelled artillery gun for firing shells over short distances. ▻ *verb* (***mortared, mortaring***) **1** to fix something (especially bricks) in place with mortar. **2** to plaster (eg a wall) with mortar. **3** to bombard (a place or target, etc) using a mortar. Ⓒ 13c: from French *mortier*, from Latin *mortarium*.

mortarboard ▻ *noun* **1** *building* a flat board used by bricklayers to carry mortar, held horizontally by a handle underneath. Also called **hawk**. **2** a black cap with a hard, square, flat top, worn by academics at formal occasions. Also called **trencher**.

mortgage /'mɔːgɪdʒ/ ▻ *noun* **1 a** a legal agreement by which a building society or bank, etc (the **mortagee**) grants a client (the **mortgagor** or **mortgager**) a loan for the purpose of buying property, ownership of the property being held by the mortagee until the loan is repaid; **b** the deed that brings such a contract into effect. **2 a** the money borrowed for this; **b** the regular amounts of money repaid. **3** any loan for which property is used as security. ▻ *verb* (***mortgaged, mortgaging***) **1** to give ownership of (property) as security for a loan. **2** *colloq* to pledge something. • **mortgageable** *adj.* Ⓒ 14c: French, from *mort* dead + *gage* pledge, apparently because the property that is pledged is 'dead' to the borrower if the loan is not repaid, or because the pledge to the lender becomes void or 'dead' when the loan is repaid.

mortician /mɔː'tɪʃən/ ▻ *noun, N Amer, especially US* an undertaker. Ⓒ 19c: from Latin *mortis* death.

mortify /'mɔːtɪfaɪ/ ▻ *verb* (***mortifies, mortified, mortifying***) **1** to make someone feel humiliated or ashamed. **2** *relig* to control (physical desire) through self-discipline or self-inflicted hardship ▫ ***mortify the flesh.*** **3** *intr, pathol, old use* said of a limb, etc: to be affected by gangrene. • **mortification** /-fɪ'keɪʃən/. • **mortifying** *adj, noun.* Ⓒ 14c: from French *mortifier*, from Latin *mortificare* to put someone to death.

mortise or (*sometimes*) **mortice** /'mɔːtɪs/ *carpentry, etc,* ▻ *noun* a hole cut in a piece of wood, into which a TENON on another piece of wood fits to form a mortise and tenon joint. ▻ *verb* (***mortised, mortising***) **1** to cut a mortise in (a piece of wood, etc). **2** to join (two parts) with a mortise and tenon joint. • **mortiser** *noun* Ⓒ 15c: from French *mortaise*.

mortise lock ▻ *noun* a lock fitted into a hole cut in the side edge of a door, rather than on to the door's surface.

mortuary /'mɔːtʃʊərɪ, 'mɔːtʃʊrɪ/ ▻ *noun* (***mortuaries***) a building or room in which dead bodies are laid out for identification or kept until they are buried or cremated. Also called MORGUE. ▻ *adj* relating to or connected with death, or the burial of the dead. Ⓒ 14c, meaning 'a customary payment made to a parish priest on the death of parishioner': from Latin adjective *mortuarius*, from *mortuus* dead.

Mosaic /moʊ'zeɪɪk/ ▻ *adj* relating to Moses, the biblical prophet and lawgiver, or to the laws attributed to him ▫ ***Mosaic law.*** See also PENTATEUCH.

mosaic /moʊ'zeɪɪk/ ▻ *noun* **1 a**▻) a design or piece of work formed by fitting together lots of small pieces of coloured stone, glass, etc; **b** *as adj* ▫ ***mosaic floor.*** **2** the process of making a mosaic. **3** anything that resembles a mosaic or is pieced together in a similar way. **4** *bot* (*also* **mosaic disease**) a viral disease affecting the potato or tobacco plant, etc in which the leaf becomes mottled. • **mosaicist** /-'zeɪsɪst/ *noun* someone who is skilled in mosaic work. Ⓒ 15c: from French *mosaïque*.

moschatel /mɒskə'tɛl/ ▻ *noun* a small plant with pale-green flowers and a musky smell. Ⓒ 18c: from French *moscatelle*, from Italian *moscato* musk.

moselle or **Moselle** /moʊ'zɛl, mə-/ or **Mosel** /*German* 'moːzəl/ ▻ *noun* a dry, German, white wine produced in

Morse code

A	B	C	D	E	F	G	H	I	J	K	L	M
•—	—•••	—•—•	—••	•	••—•	——•	••••	••	•———	—•—	•—••	——

N	O	P	Q	R	S	T	U	V	W	X	Y	Z
—•	———	•——•	——•—	•—•	•••	—	••—	•••—	•——	—••—	—•——	——••

the regions around Moselle river which runs through NE France, Luxembourg and Germany. ⓒ 17c.

Moses basket ▷ *noun* a portable cot for babies, in the form of a basket with handles. ⓒ 1940s: so called because of the biblical story of the infant Moses who was put in a papyrus basket and left among the bulrushes.

mosey /ˈmoʊzɪ/ ▷ *verb* (***moseys, moseyed, moseying***) *intr* (*usually* **mosey along**) *colloq, originally & especially US* to walk in a leisurely way; to saunter or amble. ⓒ 19c.

moshing /ˈmɒʃɪŋ/ ▷ *noun, Brit slang* a style of energetic sinuous dancing done in a crowded space especially to heavy metal or thrash music and usually done in a **moshpit**, the area in front of the stage at a gig. ⓒ 1980s: perhaps a mixture of SQUASH + MASH.

Moslem see MUSLIM

Moslem

See Usage Note at **Muslim**.

mosque /mɒsk/ ▷ *noun* (***mosques***) a Muslim place of worship. ⓒ 15c: from French *mosquée*, from Arabic *masjid* temple.

mosquito /mɒˈskiːtoʊ/ ▷ *noun* (***mosquitos*** or ***mosquitoes***) any of numerous species of small two-winged insects with thin, feathery antennae, long legs and slender bodies, the females of which have piercing mouthparts for sucking the blood of birds and mammals. They are responsible for transmitting several diseases including MALARIA. ⓒ 16c: Spanish, diminutive of *mosca* a fly, from Latin *musca*.

mosquito net ▷ *noun* a fine net designed to keep out mosquitos, especially one that is hung over a bed at night.

moss ▷ *noun* (***mosses***) **1** the common name for a type of small spore-bearing plant without a vascular system, typically found growing in dense, spreading clusters in moist shady habitats. See also BRYOPHYTE. **2** any of various unrelated plants which superficially resemble true moss. **3** *dialect, especially Scottish & N Eng* an area of boggy ground. • **mosslike** *adj*. ⓒ Anglo-Saxon *mos* in the sense 'bog'.

MOSSAD /ˈmɒsad/ ▷ *noun* the Israeli state intelligence service, formed in 1951. ⓒ 1950s: short for *Mossad le Alujeh Beth*, Committee for Illegal Immigration, the original Hebrew name of the organization founded in 1937 to oversee illegal Jewish immigration into Palestine.

moss agate ▷ *noun* a variegated chalcedony containing darker mosslike, or branching, marks of manganese oxide, etc.

moss green ▷ *noun* muted yellowy-green. Also *as adj* □ *a moss-green sweater.*

mossie or **mozzie** /ˈmɒsɪ, ˈmɒzɪ/ ▷ *noun, colloq* a mosquito. ⓒ 1940s.

mosso /ˈmɒsoʊ/ ▷ *adverb, music* in a quick or animated manner. ⓒ 19c: Italian, past participle of *muovere* to move.

moss stitch ▷ *noun, knitting* alternating plain and purl stitches along each row and in succeeding rows, giving a mosslike effect.

mossy /ˈmɒsɪ/ ▷ *adj* (***mossier, mossiest***) consisting of, covered with or like, moss. • **mossiness** *noun*.

most /moʊst/ (used as the superlative of MANY and MUCH) ▷ *adj denoting* the greatest number, amount, etc □ *Most children enjoy parties.* ▷ *adverb* **1** (*also* **the most**) used to form the superlative of many adjectives and most adverbs, especially those of more than two syllables □ *the most difficult problem of all* □ *I chose the most perfectly produced copy.* **2** (*also* **the most**) to the greatest degree; with the greatest frequency □ *I miss him most at Christmas.* **3** extremely □ *a most annoying thing.* ▷ *pronoun* the greatest number or quantity, or the majority of people or things □ *Most of them are here* □ *Who has most to lose?* ▷ See also MORE. • **at the most** or **at most** certainly not more than (a specified number) □ *three drinks at the most.* • **for the most part** mostly. • **make the most of something** to take the greatest possible advantage of it. ⓒ Anglo-Saxon *mast* or *mæst*.

-most ▷ *combining form, forming adjectives and adverbs, denoting* farthest in a specified direction □ *southernmost.*

mostly ▷ *adverb* **1** mainly; almost completely. **2** usually.

MOT or **MoT** ▷ *noun, Brit* **1** (*also* **MOT test**) an official, annual test of roadworthiness, required by the Department of Transport on all vehicles over three years old. **2** (*also* **MOT certificate**) the certificate supplied when a vehicle has passed this test. ⓒ 1960s: abbreviation for *M*inistry *o*f *T*ransport, the name of the department when the test was introduced.

mote /moʊt/ ▷ *noun* a speck, especially a speck of dust. ⓒ Anglo-Saxon *mot*.

motel /moʊˈtɛl/ ▷ *noun* a hotel with extensive parking facilities, situated near a main road and intended for overnight stops by motorists. Sometimes called **motor lodge**. ⓒ 1920s: a blend of *mo*tor ho*tel*.

motet /moʊˈtɛt/ ▷ *noun* a short piece of sacred music for several voices. ⓒ 14c: French diminutive of *mot* word.

moth ▷ *noun* the common name for one of many winged insects belonging to the same order as butterflies but generally duller in colour and night-flying, typically having a PROBOSCIS and four broad wings which fold down when resting. See also CATERPILLAR, CHRYSALIS. ⓒ Anglo-Saxon *moththe*.

mothball ▷ *noun* a small ball of camphor or naphthalene that is hung in wardrobes, etc to keep away the CLOTHES MOTH. ▷ *verb* **1** to postpone work on something (eg a project), or to lay it aside, especially for an indefinitely long time. **2** to put (clothes, linen, etc), with mothballs, into a place for long-term storage. • **put something in mothballs** to mothball it.

moth-eaten ▷ *adj* **1** said of cloth, etc: damaged by clothes moths. **2** *colloq* old and worn.

mother /ˈmʌðə(r)/ ▷ *noun* **1** a female parent. Also *as adj* □ *mother hen.* **2** (*usually* **the mother**) the protective, nurturing, or loving qualities associated with a mother □ *brings out the mother in her.* Also *as adj* □ *mother figure* □ *mother love.* **3** (*also* **Mother**) as a term of address or a title for: **a** one's own female parent or stepmother, foster-mother, etc. See also MUM, MUMMY; **b** (*also* **Mother Superior**) the head of a Christian female religious community; **c** *old use* an old woman; **d** an ancestress. **4** the cause or origin; the source from which other things have sprung or developed □ *Necessity is the mother of invention.* Also *as adj* □ *mother cell* □ *mother church* □ *mother earth.* ▷ *verb* (***mothered, mothering***) **1** to give birth to or give rise to someone or something. **2** to treat someone with care and protection, especially excessively so. • **motherhood** *noun* the state or condition of being a mother. • **motherless** *adj*. • **motherly** see separate entry. • **to be mother** *colloq, facetious* to pour the tea or dish out the food □ *Shall I be mother?* • **every mother's son** every man, without exception. • **the mother and father of a something** or **of all somethings** *colloq* one that is bigger than any other □ *the mother and father of a hangover.* ⓒ Anglo-Saxon *modor*.

motherboard ▷ *noun, computing* a PRINTED CIRCUIT BOARD that can be plugged into the back of a computer, and into which other boards can be slotted to allow the computer to operate various peripherals. See PERIPHERAL *noun*.

mother country ▷ *noun* **1** a person's native country. Also called **motherland**. **2** the country that emigrants leave to settle elsewhere.

motherese ▷ *noun, linguistics* the speech used by adults to young children while they are learning to speak, typically using shortened expressions, clear pronunciation, a high-pitched voice and often with exaggerated intonation patterns. Also called **caretaker speech**. ⓒ 20c.

motherfucker ▷ *noun, coarse slang* a contemptible, repulsive or hateful person; a general term of abuse. • **motherfucking** *adj*. ⓒ 1950s.

Mothering Sunday ▷ *noun* in the UK: the fourth Sunday in Lent, a day on which children traditionally honour their mothers with gifts. See also MOTHER'S DAY.

mother-in-law ▷ *noun* (***mothers-in-law***) the mother of one's husband or wife.

motherland see under MOTHER COUNTRY

motherly /ˈmʌðəlɪ/ ▷ *adj* like or characteristic of a mother. • **motherliness** *noun*.

mother-of-pearl ▷ *noun* a hard shiny iridescent substance made mainly of calcium carbonate, that forms the inner layer of the shell of some molluscs (eg oysters) and is used to make buttons, beads, etc. Also called NACRE.

Mother's Day ▷ *noun* **1** *Brit* another name for Mothering Sunday. **2** in the USA, Canada and Australia: the second Sunday in May, a day set apart in honour of mothers.

Mother Superior see under MOTHER

mother-to-be ▷ *noun* (***mothers-to-be***) a pregnant woman, especially one who is expecting her first child. ⓒ 1960s.

mother tongue ▷ *noun* **1** one's native language. **2** a language from which another originated.

mothproof ▷ *adj* said of cloth: treated with chemicals which resist attack by CLOTHES MOTH. ▷ *verb* to treat (fabric) in this way.

motif /moʊˈtiːf/ ▷ *noun* **1** on clothing, etc: a single design or symbol. **2** a shape repeated many times within a pattern. Also called MOTIVE. **3** in the arts: something that is often repeated throughout a work or works, eg a passage of music in a symphony, or a theme in a novel. ⓒ 19c: French; see MOTIVE.

motile /ˈmoʊtaɪl, -tɪl/ ▷ *adj, biol* said of a living organism, such as spermatozoa, or a structure: capable of independent spontaneous movement. • **motility** /-ˈtɪlɪtɪ/ *noun*. ⓒ 19c: from Latin *motus* movement.

motion /ˈmoʊʃən/ ▷ *noun* **1** the act, state, process or manner of moving. **2** a single movement, especially one made by the body; a gesture or action. **3** the ability to move a part of the body. **4** a proposal for formal discussion at a meeting. **5** *law* an application made to a judge during a court case for an order or ruling to be made. **6** *Brit* **a** an act of discharging faeces from the bowels; **b** (**motions**) faeces. ▷ *verb* (***motioned***, ***motioning***) *tr & intr* (*often* **motion to someone**) to give a signal or direction. • **motionless** *adj*. • **motionlessly** *adverb*. • **go through the motions 1** to pretend to do something; to act something out. **2** to perform a task mechanically or half-heartedly. • **in motion** moving; operating. ⓒ 14c: from Latin *motio*, from *movere* to move.

motion picture ▷ *noun, N Amer, especially US* a cinema film. Also *as adj* □ *the motion picture industry*.

motion sickness see under TRAVEL SICKNESS.

motivate /ˈmoʊtɪveɪt/ ▷ *verb* (***motivated***, ***motivating***) **1** to be the motive of something or someone. **2** to cause or stimulate (a person) to act; to be the underlying cause of (an action) □ *He is motivated by greed*. • **motivation** *noun*. • **motivational** *adj*. • **motivationally** *adverb*.

motive /ˈmoʊtɪv/ ▷ *noun* **1** a reason for, or underlying cause of, action of a certain kind. **2** see MOTIF 2. ▷ *adj* **1** causing motion □ *motive power*. **2** stimulating action □ *motive force*. ⓒ 14c: French, from Latin *movere* to move.

mot juste / *French* mo ʒyst/ ▷ *noun* (***mots justes*** /mo ʒyst/) the word or expression which fits the context most exactly. ⓒ Early 20c: from French *le mot juste* the exact word.

motley /ˈmɒtlɪ/ ▷ *adj* (***motleyer***, ***motleyest***) **1** made up of many different kinds □ *a motley crew*. **2** many-coloured. ▷ *noun* (***motleys***) a jester's multicoloured costume. ⓒ 14c.

motocross /ˈmoʊtəkrɒs/ ▷ *noun* a form of motorcycle racing in which specially-adapted motorcycles compete across rough terrain. ⓒ 1950s: from *moto*rcycle + *cross*-country.

motor /ˈmoʊtə(r)/ ▷ *noun* **1 a** an engine, especially the INTERNAL-COMBUSTION ENGINE of a vehicle or machine; **b** *as adj* driven by a motor □ *motor boat*. **2 a** *colloq* a car; **b** *as adj* □ *motor show*. **3** a device, eg in a domestic appliance, that converts electrical energy into mechanical energy, using the forces that act on a current-carrying conductor such as a COIL1 (noun 3) in the presence of a magnetic field. Also called ELECTRIC MOTOR. ▷ *adj* **1** *anatomy* **a** said of a nerve: transmitting impulses from the CENTRAL NERVOUS SYSTEM to a muscle or gland; **b** said of a nerve cell: forming part of such a nerve. **2** *physiol* relating to muscular movement, or the sense of muscular movement. **3** giving or transmitting motion. ▷ *verb* (***motored***, ***motoring***) **1** *intr* to travel by motor vehicle, especially by private car. **2** to convey someone or something by motor vehicle. **3** *intr, colloq* to move or work, etc fast and effectively. • **motoring** *noun* travelling by car, especially for pleasure. Also *as adj* □ *motoring holiday*. • **motorist** *noun* someone who drives a car. Also called DRIVER. ⓒ 16c: Latin, from *movere* to move.

motorbike ▷ *noun, colloq* a MOTORCYCLE.

motorcade /ˈmoʊtəkeɪd/ ▷ *noun* a procession of cars carrying VIPs, especially political figures. ⓒ Early 20c: from MOTOR, modelled on CAVALCADE.

motor car ▷ *noun, old use* a CAR.

motorcycle ▷ *noun* any two-wheeled road vehicle powered by a two-stroke or four-stroke internal combustion engine that runs on petrol. Also called MOTORBIKE or sometimes BIKE (*noun* 2). Compare MOPED. • **motorcycling** *noun*. • **motorcyclist** *noun*.

motorize or **motorise** /ˈmoʊtəraɪz/ ▷ *verb* (***motorized***, ***motorizing***) **1** to fit a motor or motors to something. **2** to supply (eg soldiers) with motor vehicles. • **motorization** *noun*.

motor lodge see under MOTEL

motormouth ▷ *noun, derog, slang* a person who talks non-stop or too much.

motor neurone ▷ *noun, anatomy* a nerve cell that carries impulses from the spinal cord or the brain to an EFFECTOR organ such as a muscle or gland.

motor neurone disease ▷ *noun, medicine* a disease in which progressive damage to motor neurones leads to muscle weakness and degeneration.

motor-scooter see under SCOOTER

motorway ▷ *noun, Brit, Austral & NZ* a major road for fast-moving traffic, especially one with three lanes per carriageway and limited access and exit points. See also EXPRESSWAY, FREEWAY, SUPERHIGHWAY.

Motown /ˈmoʊtaʊn/ ▷ *noun, pop music* a style that combines pop with rhythm and blues or gospel rhythms. ⓒ 1960s: from *Tamla Mowtown* the name of a record label that specializes in this kind of music, from *Motor Town*, a nickname for Detroit in the USA famed for its car production, where the label is based.

motte and bailey /mɒt — —/ ▷ *noun, historical* especially in England in the late 11c and 12c: a type of fortification, originally of earth and timber, commonly built by the Normans, consisting of an artificial mound (the **motte**) surrounded by a ditch, with a walled outer court (the BAILEY) adjoining it to one side. ⓒ 19c, from 13c *motte*: from French *mote* or *motte* mound.

mottle /'mɒtəl/ ▻ *verb* (***mottled, mottling***) to give something a blotched, streaked or variegated appearance, surface, etc. • **mottled** *adj* with a pattern of different coloured blotches or streaks. • **mottling** *noun*. ⓒ 17c.

motto /'mɒtoʊ/ ▻ *noun* (***mottos*** or ***mottoes***) **1 a** a phrase adopted by a person, family, etc as a principle of behaviour; **b** such a phrase appearing on a coat of arms, crest, etc. **2** a printed phrase or verse contained in a paper cracker. **3** a quotation at the beginning of a book or chapter, hinting at what is to follow. ⓒ 17c: Italian, from Latin *muttum* utterance.

moue / *French* mu/ ▻ *noun* (***moues***) a grimace or pout expressing discontentment. ⓒ 19c: French, literally 'pout'.

mould[1] or (*N Amer*) **mold** /moʊld/ ▻ *noun* **1** any of various fungi that produce an abundant woolly network of threadlike strands which may be white, grey-green or black in colour. **2** a woolly growth of this sort on foods, plants, etc. See also MILDEW. ⓒ 15c.

mould[2] or (*N Amer*) **mold** /moʊld/ ▻ *noun* **1** a hollow, shaped container into which a liquid substance is poured so that it takes on the container's shape when it cools and sets. **2** food, eg a jelly or other pudding that has been shaped in such a container. **3** nature, character or personality □ *We need a leader in the traditional mould.* **4** a framework on which certain manufactured objects are built up. **5** *now rare* or *technical* form, model or pattern. ▻ *verb* (***moulded, moulding***) **1** to shape something in or using a mould. **2 a** to shape (a substance) with the hands □ *moulded the clay in her hands*; **b** to form something by shaping a substance with the hands □ *moulded a pot out of the clay.* **3** *tr & intr* to fit, or make something fit, tightly □ *The dress was moulded to her body.* **4** (*especially* **mould something** or **someone into something**) to exercise a controlling influence over the development of something or someone □ *moulding his pupils into future leaders.* • **mouldable** *adverb*. • **moulder** *noun*. ⓒ 13c: from French *modle*, from Latin *modulus* a measure.

mould[3] or (*N Amer*) **mold** /moʊld/ ▻ *noun* loose soft soil that is rich in decayed organic matter □ *leaf mould.* ⓒ Anglo-Saxon *molde*.

moulder or (*N Amer*) **molder** /moʊldə(r)/ ▻ *verb* (***mouldered, mouldering***) *intr* (*also* **moulder away**) to become gradually rotten with age; to decay. ⓒ 16c.

moulding or (*N Amer*) **molding** /moʊldɪŋ/ ▻ *noun* **1** a shaped, decorative strip, especially one made of wood or plaster. **2** the conversion of molten plastics, clay, glass, etc into specific three-dimensional shapes by using hollow moulds and applying heat or pressure. See also CASTING.

mouldy or (*N Amer*) **moldy** /moʊldɪ/ ▻ *adj* (***mouldier, mouldiest***) **1** covered with mould. **2** old and stale. **3** *derog, colloq* rotten or bad; a general term of dislike □ *I don't want your mouldy advice.* • **mouldiness** *noun*. ⓒ 14c: from MOULD[1].

moult or (*N Amer*) **molt** /moʊlt/ ▻ *verb* (***moulted, moulting***) *intr, zool* said of an animal: to shed feathers, hair or skin to make way for a new growth. ▻ *noun* **1** the act or process of moulting. **2** the time taken for this. ⓒ 14c: from Anglo-Saxon, from Latin *mutare* to change.

mound /maʊnd/ ▻ *noun* **1** any small hill, or bank of earth or rock, either natural or man-made. **2** a heap or pile. ▻ *verb* (***mounded, mounding***) (*now usually* **mound something up**) to form or pile up into a mound. ⓒ 16c, meaning 'a hedge or other boundary'.

mount[1] /maʊnt/ ▻ *verb* (***mounted, mounting***) **1** *tr & intr* to go up □ *mounting the stairs.* **2** *tr & intr* to get up on to (a horse, bicycle, etc). **3** *intr* (*also* **mount up**) to increase in level or intensity □ *The tension is mounting* □ *when pressure mounts up.* **4** to put (a picture, slide, etc) in a frame or on a background for display; to hang or put something up on a stand or support. **5** to organize or hold (a campaign, etc). **6** to carry out (an attack, etc); to put something into operation. See also MOUNT GUARD at GUARD. **7** to get (a weapon, etc) into position and ready for use. **8** said of a stallion, bull, etc: to copulate with (a female). Also called COVER *verb* 17. ▻ *noun* **1** a support or backing on which something is placed for display or use, etc. **2** a horse that is ridden. **3** *technical* the slide, etc used in mounting an object for viewing under the microscope. • **mounted** *adj* **1** said of a person, etc: on horseback. **2** said of a picture, etc: hung on a wall, or placed in a frame or on a background. **3** *in compounds* set in or with a specified material □ *silver-mounted.* ⓒ 14c: from French *monter*, related to MOUNT[2].

mount[2] /maʊnt/ ▻ *noun, chiefly poetic* or *old use* a mountain. Also **Mount** in place names. ⓒ Anglo-Saxon *munt*: from Latin *mons, montis* mountain.

mountain /'maʊntɪn/ ▻ *noun* **1 a** a very high, steep hill, often one of bare rock; **b** *as adj* □ *mountain peak.* **2** (*also* **mountains of something**) *colloq* a great quantity; a heap or mass □ *a mountain of washing.* **3** a huge surplus of some commodity □ *a butter mountain.* • **mountainous** *adj* **1** said of a region, etc: containing many mountains. **2** *colloq* huge; as big as a mountain. • **make a mountain out of a molehill** to exaggerate the seriousness or importance of some trivial matter. ⓒ 13c: from French *montaigne*, from Latin *mons, montis* mountain.

mountain ash see under ROWAN

mountain beaver ▻ *noun* a squirrel-like burrowing primitive rodent (not a true beaver) with a stocky body and a minute, hairy tail, living in cool moist regions of N America.

mountain bike ▻ *noun* a sturdy bicycle with thick, deep-tread tyres and straight handlebars, originally designed as an ALL-TERRAIN bike for riding off road, in hilly terrain, but now popular as an all-purpose bike for town and road cycling. • **mountain biker** *noun*. • **mountain biking** *noun*. ⓒ 1980s..

mountain dew ▻ *noun* whisky, especially illicitly-made whisky.

mountaineer /maʊntɪ'nɪə/ ▻ *noun* someone who climbs mountains. ▻ *verb* (***mountaineered, mountaineering***) *intr* to climb mountains. • **mountaineering** *noun* the sport of climbing mountains, usually aided by ropes, etc, either on snow and ice, as practised mainly on the higher peaks of the world, or on bare rock faces (also called **rock climbing**). ⓒ 19c: from MOUNTAIN + -EER.

mountain lion see under PUMA

mountain sickness ▻ *noun* feelings of nausea, light-headedness, headache, etc caused by breathing low-oxygen mountain air, especially affecting climbers, etc who make too quick an ascent. Also called **altitude sickness**.

mountainside ▻ *noun* the slope of a mountain.

mountebank /'maʊntɪbaŋk/ ▻ *noun, literary, derog* **1** *formerly* a medically unqualified person who sold supposed medicines from a public platform; a quack. **2** any person who swindles or deceives. ⓒ 16c: from Italian *montimbanco* a person who stands up, ie who MOUNTs, a bench.

mounted see under MOUNT[1]

Mountie or **Mounty** /'maʊntɪ/ ▻ *noun* (***Mounties***) *colloq* a member of the Royal Canadian Mounted Police. ⓒ Early 20c.

mourn /mɔːn/ ▻ *verb* (***mourned, mourning***) **1** *tr & intr* (*especially* **mourn for** or **over someone** or **something**) to feel or show deep sorrow at the death or loss of them or it. **2** *intr* to be in mourning or wear mourning. • **mourner** *noun* **1** someone who mourns. **2** someone attending a funeral. ⓒ Anglo-Saxon *murnan*.

mournful ▷ *adj* **1** feeling or expressing grief. **2** suggesting sadness or gloom □ *mournful music.* • **mournfully** *adverb.* • **mournfulness** *noun.*

mourning /ˈmɔːnɪŋ/ ▷ *noun* **1** grief felt or shown over a death. **2** a symbol of grief, especially black clothing or a black armband (a **mourning band**). **3** a period of time during which someone is officially mourning a death, especially one in which they wear black clothing and/or observe certain restrictions of behaviour, etc □ *She is in mourning for her husband.* Also *as adj* □ *mourning clothes.*

mouse /maʊs/ ▷ *noun* (*mice* /maɪs/ or in sense 3 *mouses*) **1 a** any of various small rodents found worldwide, such as the FIELDMOUSE and HARVEST MOUSE, with a grey or brown coat, pointed muzzle, bright eyes, sharp teeth and a long naked tail. Compare RAT. **b** any of various similar animals, eg voles and shrews. **2** *colloq* a very shy, quiet or timid person. **3** *computing* an input device which can be moved around on a flat surface, causing a CURSOR (sense 1) to move around the computer screen in response. It has one or more buttons which are clicked (see CLICK verb 4) to choose one of a number of specified options displayed. ▷ *verb* (*moused, mousing*) *intr* **1** said of an animal, especially a cat: to hunt mice. **2** (*especially* **mouse about** or **around**) to prowl. • **mouser** *noun* a cat that catches mice, or is kept especially for catching mice. • **mousing** *noun.* ◷ 1960s in sense 3; Anglo-Saxon *mus*; plural *mys.*

mouse deer see under CHEVROTAIN

mouse potato ▷ *noun, slang, computing* someone who spends a great deal of time using a computer, especially for leisure. ◷ 1990s: by analogy with COUCH POTATO.

mousetrap ▷ *noun* **1** a mechanical trap for catching or killing mice. **2** *colloq* mediocre or poor quality cheese.

mousier, mousiest, mousily and **mousiness** see under MOUSY

moussaka /mʊˈsɑːkə/ ▷ *noun* (*moussakas*) *cookery* a dish made with minced meat, aubergines, onions, tomatoes, etc, covered with a cheese sauce and baked, traditionally eaten in Greece, Turkey and the Balkans. ◷ 1940s: modern Greek.

mousse /muːs/ ▷ *noun* (*mousses*) **1** *cookery* **a** a dessert made from a whipped mixture of cream, eggs and flavouring, eaten cold; **b** a similar but savoury dish, made with meat, fish, etc. **2** (*also* **styling mousse**) a foamy or frothy chemical preparation applied to hair to add body or to make styling easier. ◷ 19c: French, literally 'froth' or 'moss'.

mousseline /muːsliːn/ ▷ *noun* (*mousselines*) **1** a fine French muslin. **2** a type of very thin glassware. **3** *cookery* a dish made with MOUSSELINE SAUCE. ◷ 17c: French; see under MUSLIN.

mousseline sauce ▷ *noun, cookery* HOLLANDAISE SAUCE lightened with whipped cream or egg white.

moustache and (*N Amer*) **mustache** /məˈstɑːʃ, ˈmʌˈstɑːʃ/ ▷ *noun* unshaved hair growing across the top of the upper lip. Compare MUSTACHIO, BEARD. • **moustached** *adj.* See also MUSTACHIOED. ◷ 16c: French, from Italian *mostaccio.*

mousy or **mousey** /ˈmaʊsɪ/ ▷ *adj* (*mousier, mousiest*) **1** like a mouse, or belonging or relating to a mouse. **2** said of hair: light dullish brown in colour. **3** said of a person: shy, quiet or timid, especially tiresomely so. • **mousily** *adverb.* • **mousiness** *noun.*

mouth ▷ *noun* /maʊθ/ (*mouths* /maʊðz/) **1 a** in humans, animals, etc: an opening in the head through which food is taken in and speech or sounds emitted, and containing the teeth, gums, tongue, etc; **b** in other creatures: an opening with similar functions. **2** the lips; the outer visible parts of the mouth. **3** an opening, eg of a bottle. **4** the part of a river that widens to meet the sea. **5** a person considered as a consumer of food □ *five mouths to feed.* **6** *derog, colloq* boastful talk □ *He's all mouth.* **7** *colloq* backchat or cheek □ *don't want any of your mouth.* **8** *derog, colloq* **a** someone who talks too much, especially indiscreetly; **b** *in compounds* □ *bigmouth* □ *loudmouth.* **9** *colloq* use of language; way of speaking □ *a foul mouth.* **10** the responsiveness of a horse to the bit (see BIT[2] sense 1). ▷ *verb* /maʊð/ (*mouthed, mouthing*) **1** to form (words) without actually speaking □ *mouthed a hello to me across the crowded room.* **2** *tr & intr, derog* to speak (words) pompously or insincerely □ *is always mouthing platitudes.* **3** *intr* to grimace. • **mouthed** /maʊðd/ *adj, in compounds* **1** using a specified kind of language □ *foul-mouthed.* **2** having a specified kind of mouth □ *wide-mouthed.* • **be all mouth** *derog, colloq* to be someone who is full of boastful or confident talk but who never actually acts upon it. • **have a big mouth** *colloq* to be in the habit of talking indiscreetly, loudly or too much. • **down in the mouth** see under DOWN. • **keep one's mouth shut** *colloq* to keep quiet; not to say or disclose anything. ◷ Anglo-Saxon *muth.*

■ **mouth off** *slang, especially US* **1** to express opinions forcefully or loudly. Also called SOUND OFF. **2** to boast or brag.

mouthful ▷ *noun* (*mouthfuls*) **1** as much food or drink as fills the mouth or is in one's mouth. **2** a small quantity, especially of food □ *couldn't eat another mouthful.* **3** *colloq* a word or phrase that is difficult to pronounce □ *His name is quite a mouthful.* **4** *colloq* an outburst of forceful and often abusive language □ *gave me such a mouthful.* See also EARFUL.

mouth organ see under HARMONICA

mouthparts ▷ *plural noun, zool* any of the appendages specially adapted for feeding, located around the mouth of an ARTHROPOD.

mouthpiece ▷ *noun* **1** the part of a musical instrument, telephone receiver, tobacco pipe, etc that is held in or against the mouth. **2** a person or publication that is used to express the views of a group.

mouth-to-mouth ▷ *adj* said of a method of resuscitation: involving someone breathing air directly into the mouth of the person to be revived in order to inflate their lungs. ▷ *noun* mouth-to-mouth resuscitation. Also called **kiss of life**. See also ARTIFICIAL RESPIRATION.

mouthwash ▷ *noun* an antiseptic liquid used for gargling or for rinsing or freshening the mouth.

mouth-watering ▷ *adj* **1** said of food: having a delicious appearance or smell. **2** *colloq* highly desirable.

movable or **moveable** /ˈmuːvəbəl/ ▷ *adj* **1** not fixed in one place; portable. **2** *especially Scots law* said of property: able to be removed; personal. **3** said of a religious festival: taking place on a different date each year □ *Easter is a movable feast.* • **movability** or **moveability** *noun.* • **movableness** or **moveableness** *noun.*

move /muːv/ ▷ *verb* (*moved, moving*) **1** *tr & intr* to change position or make something change position or go from one place to another. **2** *intr* to make progress of any kind □ *move towards a political solution.* **3** *chiefly intr* (*often* **move on** or **out** or **away**, *etc*) to change one's place of living, working, operating, etc. See also *move house* below. **4** to affect someone's feelings or emotions. **5** (*usually* **move someone to do something**) to prompt them or affect them in such a way that they do it □ *What moved him to say that?* **6** *tr & intr* to change the position of (a piece in a board game). **7** *tr & intr, formal* (*usually* **move for** or **that something**) to propose or request it formally, at a meeting, etc. **8** *intr* to spend time; to associate with people □ *move in fashionable circles.* **9** *intr, colloq* to take action; to become active or busy □ *must move on this matter straight away.* **10** *intr, colloq* to travel or progress fast □ *That bike can really move.* **11** *colloq* (*also* **get a move on** or **get moving**) to hurry up. **12** *tr & intr, colloq* to sell or be sold. **13 a** *intr* said of the bowels: to be evacuated; **b** to cause (the bowels) to evacuate. ▻ *noun* **1** an act of moving the body; a movement. **2** an act of changing homes or premises □ *How did your move go?* **3** *games* **a** an act of moving a piece on the board; **b** a particular player's turn to move a piece; **c** any of a series of actions taken as part of an overall strategy; **d** the rules governing how the pieces are moved. • **movable, mover** and **moving** see separate entries. • **make a move 1** *colloq* to start on one's way; to leave. **2** to take a step; to begin to proceed. • **move heaven and earth** to make strenuous efforts to achieve something. • **move house** to move to a new place of residence; to move one's possessions to a new home. • **on the move 1** moving from place to place. **2** advancing or making progress. ◎ 13c: from French *movoir*, from Latin *movere*.

■ **move in** or **into something** or **somewhere** to begin to occupy new premises.

■ **move in on someone 1** to advance towards them, especially threateningly. **2** to take steps towards controlling them or usurping their position, etc.

■ **move out** to vacate premises; to leave.

■ **move over** to move so as to make room for someone else.

movement /muːvmənt/ ▻ *noun* **1** a process of changing position or going from one point to another. **2** an act or manner of moving □ *made a sudden, jerky movement.* **3** an organization, association or group, especially one that promotes a particular cause □ *the women's movement.* **4** a general tendency or current of opinion, taste, etc □ *a movement towards healthy eating.* **5** *music* a section of a large-scale piece, especially a symphony. **6** (**movements**) a person's actions during a particular time □ *Can you account for your movements that night?* **7 a** an act of evacuating the bowels; **b** the waste matter evacuated. **8** the moving parts of a watch or clock. **9** the theatrical art of moving the body gracefully or with expression. **10** the suggestion of motion conveyed in a work of art.

mover ▻ *noun* **1** someone or something that moves. **2** *formal* someone who brings a MOTION (*noun* 4) at a meeting, etc. **3** *chiefly N Amer* a person whose job is to help people to move house or premises. *Brit equivalent* REMOVAL MAN. **4** *especially US* someone who puts ideas or plans, etc in motion or who makes good progress □ *prime mover.*

movers and shakers ▻ *plural noun, especially US* the people with power and influence. ◎ 1970s: from a poem (1874) by Arthur O'Shaughnessy 'Yet we are the movers and shakers of the world for ever, it seems'.

movie /muːvɪ/ ▻ *noun* (***movies***) *especially US* **1** a cinema film. *British equivalent* FILM. Also called PICTURE (*noun* 9). **2** (*especially* **the movies**) **a** cinema films in general; **b** the industry that produces them □ *He didn't make it in the movies.* Also *as adj* □ *movie-maker* □ *movie star.* ◎ 1912: a shortening of MOVING PICTURE.

moviegoer see CINEMA-GOER

moving ▻ *adj* **1** having an effect on the emotions; touching; stirring □ *What a moving story!* **2** in motion; not static □ *a moving staircase.* **3** causing motion. • **movingly** *adverb.*

moving picture ▻ *noun, old use* a MOTION PICTURE.

moving staircase ▻ *noun, old use* an ESCALATOR.

moving walkway see under TRAVOLATOR

mow /moʊ/ ▻ *verb* (***mowes, mowed, mown, mowing***) to cut (grass, a lawn, crop, etc) by hand or with a machine. • **mower** *noun* something or someone that mows, especially a machine with revolving blades for mowing grass □ *lawnmower.* ◎ Anglo-Saxon *mawan.*

■ **mow someone** or **something down** *colloq* to cut or knock them or it down, or kill them or it, in large numbers □ *mowed them down with machine-gun fire.*

moxa /ˈmɒksə/ ▻ *noun, alternative medicine* a pithy material (eg sunflower pith or cotton wool), formed into a cone or stick and used for applying heat in oriental medicine, ACUPUNCTURE, etc. Also *as adj* □ *moxa cone.* ◎ 17c: from Japanese *mogusa*, from *moe kusa* burning herb.

moxibustion /mɒksɪˈbʌstʃən/ ▻ *noun, alternative medicine* the application of local heat over ACUPUNCTURE points by burning MOXA or by heating needles, as a technique to relieve pain in arthritis, etc. ◎ 19c: from MOXA, modelled on COMBUSTION.

Mozambican or **Mozambiquan** /moʊzəmˈbiːkn/ ▻ *adj* belonging or relating to Mozambique, a republic in SE Africa, or its inhabitants. ▻ *noun* a citizen or inhabitant of, or person born in, Mozambique. ◎ 19c.

Mozartian or **Mozartean** /moutˈsɑːtɪən/ ▻ *adj* belonging or relating to, or characteristic of, the musical style or work, etc of the Austrian composer Wolfgang Amadeus Mozart (1756–91). ◎ 19c.

mozzarella /mɒtsəˈrɛlə/ ▻ *noun* a soft, white, Italian curd cheese, especially used as a topping for pizza and in salads. ◎ Early 20c: Italian.

mozzie see MOSSIE

MP ▻ *abbreviation* **1** Member of Parliament. **2** *Eng* Metropolitan Police. **3 a** Military Police; **b** military police officer. **3** mounted police.

mp ▻ *abbreviation* **1** (*also* **m.p.**) melting point. **2** *music* mezzo piano, fairly loud.

m.p. ▻ *abbreviation* melting point.

mpg ▻ *abbreviation* miles per gallon.

mph ▻ *abbreviation* miles per hour.

MPhil /ɛmˈfɪl/ ▻ *abbreviation* Master of Philosophy.

Mr /mɪstə(r)/ ▻ *noun* (*plural* ***Messrs*** /ˈmɛsəz/) **1** the standard title given to a man, used as a prefix before his surname □ *Mr Brown. French equivalent* MONSIEUR. **2** a title given to a man who holds one of various official positions, used as a prefix before his designation □ *Mr Chairman* □ *Mr Speaker.* **3** *colloq* a title given to a man with a specified quality, job, skill, etc, used as a prefix before the appropriate epithet □ *Mr Fixit.* • **Mr Right** see separate entry. ◎ 15c: originally as an abbreviation of MASTER, later of MISTER.

MRC ▻ *abbreviation, Brit* Medical Research Council.

MRCP ▻ *abbreviation, Brit* Member of the Royal College of Physicians.

MRI ▻ *abbreviation* magnetic resonance imaging.

mRNA ▻ *abbreviation, biochem* messenger RNA.

MRP ▻ *abbreviation* manufacturer's recommended price.

Mr Right ▻ *noun, colloq* the man considered to be the ideal partner or husband for someone □ *She thought she'd found Mr Right.*

Mrs /mɪsɪz/ ▻ *noun* the standard title given to a married woman, used as a prefix before her surname, or before her full name with either her own or her husband's first name. See also MISSUS, MS. ◎ 17c, as an abbreviation of MISTRESS.

MS or **ms.** ▻ *abbreviation* **1** (*plural* ***MSS*** or ***mss.***) manuscript. **2** Master of Surgery. **3** *IVR* Mauritius. **4** *US state* Mississippi. Also written **Miss. 5** multiple sclerosis.

Ms /məz, mɪz/ ▻ *noun* the standard title given to a woman, married or not, used as a prefix before her surname in place of MRS or MISS □ *Ms Brown.*

ms ▻ *abbreviation* **1** See under MS. **2** millisecond or milliseconds.

MSc ▻ *abbreviation* Master of Science.

MSDOS or **MS-DOS** /ɛmɛsˈdɒs/ ▻ *abbreviation, trademark, computing* Microsoft disk-operating system, a widely-used DISK OPERATING SYSTEM used as the standard system for all IBM-compatible computers. ⓘ 1970s: the system was developed by the US *Microsoft* Corporation.

MSF ▷ *abbreviation* **1** *Brit* Manufacturing, Science and Finance Union. **2** *Médecins sans Frontières* (French), literally 'doctors without frontiers'; a medical aid organization.

MSG ▷ *abbreviation* monosodium glutamate.

Msgr ▷ *abbreviation* Monsignor.

MSS or **mss** see under MS

MST ▷ *abbreviation, N Amer* Mountain Standard Time.

MT ▷ *abbreviation, US state* Montana. Also written **Mont.**

Mt[1] ▷ *abbreviation* **1** Mount □ *Mt Etna.* **2** metical or meticals, the Mozambican currency unit.

Mt[2] ▷ *symbol, chem* meitnerium.

MTech. /ɛm'tɛk/ ▷ *abbreviation* Master of Technology.

mth ▷ *abbreviation* month.

Mts ▷ *abbreviation* Mountains.

MTV ▷ *abbreviation* Music Television, a satellite TV channel.

mu /mjuː/ ▷ *noun* **1** the twelfth letter of the Greek alphabet. See table at GREEK ALPHABET. **2** *physics, chem, etc* the symbol (μ) for MICRO- 2 and MICRON. See also MUON.

much /mʌtʃ/ ▷ *adj* ▷ *pronoun* (*comparative* ***more****, superlative* ***most***) especially with negatives and in questions: **1** a great amount or quantity of something □ *You don't have much luck* □ *How much time is there left?* **2** (as *pronoun*) a great deal; anything of significance or value □ *Can you see much?* □ *My belongings don't amount to much.* ▷ *adverb* **1** by a great deal □ *That looks much prettier.* **2** to a great degree □ *don't like her much* □ *We are much alike.* **3** (*often* **much the same**) nearly the same; almost □ *Things look much as I left them.* See also MORE, MOST. ● **a bit much** *colloq* rather more that can be tolerated or accepted □ *His constant teasing is a bit much.* ● **as much as ...** or **much as ...** although ... □ *I cannot come, much as I would like to.* ● **make much of something** or **someone 1** to cherish or take special interest in them or it, or to treat them or it as very important. **2** *with negatives* to find much sense in, or to succeed in understanding, them or it □ *couldn't make much of what he was saying.* ● **not much of a something** *colloq* not a very good example of it; a rather poor one □ *I'm not much of a singer.* ● **not up to much** *colloq* of a poor standard; not much good. ● **too much** *colloq* more than can be tolerated or accepted □ *I find the noise too much.* ● **too much for someone** more than a match for them. ⓘ 13c: from Anglo-Saxon *mycel*; see MICKLE.

muchness ▷ *noun, old use* greatness. ● **much of a muchness** *colloq* very similar; more or less the same.

mucilage /'mjuːsɪlɪdʒ/ ▷ *noun* (***mucilages***) **1** *bot* a type of gum-like substance that becomes viscous and slimy when added to water, present in or secreted by various plants. **2** a sticky substance used as an adhesive. ● **mucilaginous** /-'ladʒɪnəs/ *adj.* ⓘ 15c as *muscilage*: from Latin *mucilago*, literally 'mouldy juice', from *mucere* to be mouldy.

muck ▷ *noun* **1** *colloq* dirt, especially wet or clinging dirt. **2** animal dung; manure. **3** *derog, colloq* anything disgusting or of very poor quality □ *How can you read that muck?* ▷ *verb* (***mucked, mucking***) to treat (soil) with manure. ● **make a muck of something** *colloq* to do it badly; to ruin or spoil it. ⓘ 13c.

■ **muck about** or **around** *colloq* to behave foolishly.

■ **muck about** or **around with something** *colloq* to interfere, tinker or fiddle about with it.

■ **muck someone about** or **around** to treat them inconsiderately; to try their patience.

■ **muck in** or **muck in with someone** *colloq* to take a share of the work or responsibilities with others.

■ **muck out** or **muck something out** to clear dung from (a farm building, etc) or clear dung from the stall, etc of (animals) □ *have to muck out the pigs.*

■ **muck something up** *colloq* **1** to do it badly or wrongly; to ruin or spoil it. **2** to make it dirty.

mucker ▷ *noun, slang* **1** *Brit, rather dated* a best friend, mate or sidekick. **2** *especially US, old use* a coarse, unrefined person. ⓘ 19c.

muckheap ▷ *noun* a pile of muck; a dunghill.

muckle see MICKLE

muck-rake ▷ *verb, intr, colloq* said eg of a journalist: to seek out and expose scandal. ● **muck-raker** *noun.* ● **muck-raking** *noun* the practice of searching for and exposing scandal, especially about famous people. ⓘ Early 20c in this sense, as a back formation from *muck-raker*; in the 17c *muck-raker* was used to mean 'a miser' or sometimes, literally, someone who rakes muck.

muckspread ▷ *verb, agric* to spread manure. ● **muckspreader** *noun* an agricultural machine for spreading manure. ● **muckspreading** *noun.*

mucky ▷ *adj* (***muckier, muckiest***) *colloq* **1** very dirty □ *mucky hands.* **2** said eg of films or magazines: featuring explicit sex; pornographic. **3** like or consisting of dirt.

mucosa /mjuː'koʊsə/ ▷ *noun* (***mucosae*** /-siː/) the technical term for MUCOUS MEMBRANE.

mucous /'mjuːkəs/ ▷ *adj* consisting of, like or producing MUCUS. ● **mucosity** /-'kɒsɪtɪ/ *noun.*

> ***mucous, mucus***
>
> These words are sometimes confused with each other.

mucous membrane ▷ *noun, zool, anatomy* in vertebrates: the moist, mucus-secreting lining of various internal cavities of the body, eg the nasal passages and the gut.

mucus /'mjuːkəs/ ▷ *noun* the thick slimy substance that protects and lubricates the surface of MUCOUS MEMBRANES and traps bacteria and dust particles. ⓘ 17c: Latin, meaning 'nasal mucus', from *mungere* to wipe away.

mud ▷ *noun* **1 a** soft, wet earth; **b** *as adj* □ *mud pie.* **2** any semi-solid mixture that resembles this. **3** *colloq* insults; slanderous attacks □ *throw mud at someone.* ● **clear as mud** *colloq* not at all clear. ● **here's mud in your eye** *Brit facetious, colloq* an exclamation used as a drinking-toast. ● **my, his,** *etc* **name is mud** *colloq* I am, he is, etc disgraced or out of favour. ⓘ 14c.

mudbath ▷ *noun* **1** a medical treatment in which the body is covered in mud, especially hot mud, rich in minerals. **2** *colloq* any outdoor event taking place in muddy conditions.

muddied, muddier, muddiest, muddily and **muddiness** see under MUDDY

muddle /'mʌdəl/ ▷ *verb* (***muddled, muddling***) (*also* **muddle something** or **someone up**) **1** to put it or them into a disordered or confused state □ *Someone has muddled my notes up.* **2 a** to confuse the mind of someone □ *You'll muddle him with all those figures*; **b** to confuse (different things) in the mind □ *I always muddle their names.* **3** *US* to mix or stir (drinks, etc). ▷ *noun* a state of disorder or mental confusion. ● **muddled** *adj* confused; disordered. ● **muddler** *noun.* ⓘ 17c, meaning 'to wallow in mud'.

■ **muddle along** *colloq* to manage or make progress slowly and haphazardly.

■ **muddle through** *colloq* to succeed by persevering in spite of difficulties.

muddle-headed ▷ *adj* said of a person: not capable of clear thinking; confused. • **muddle-headedly** *adverb*. • **muddle-headedness** *noun*.

muddy ▷ *adj* (***muddier***, ***muddiest***) **1** covered with or containing mud. **2** said of a colour, a liquid, etc: dull, cloudy or dirty. **3** said of thoughts, etc: not clear; vague. ▷ *verb* (***muddies***, ***muddied***, ***muddying***) to make something muddy, especially to make it unclear or difficult to understand. • **muddily** *adverb*. • **muddiness** *noun*.

mudflap ▷ *noun* a flap of rubber, etc fixed behind the wheel of a vehicle to prevent mud, etc being thrown up behind. *N Amer equivalent* SPLASH GUARD. Compare MUDGUARD.

mudflat ▷ *noun* (*often* **mudflats**) a relatively flat area of land near an estuary, etc formed by accumulated silt or mud brought in by the tide, and which is covered by a shallow layer of water at high tide.

mudguard ▷ *noun* a curved, metal guard over the upper half of the wheel of a bicycle or motorcycle to keep rain or mud from splashing up. Compare MUDFLAP.

mudhopper or **mudskipper** ▷ *noun* a type of fish that has raised eyes on the top of its head and paired fins used for moving itself across mud. It spends much of its time out of water and is found commonly on mudflats, etc in the Indo-Pacific.

mudpack ▷ *noun* a thick paste that is applied to the face as a skin cleanser and toner.

mudpuppy ▷ *noun* a brownish-grey N American AMPHIBIAN with feathery gills, that spends its entire life in water. It has limbs with four toes and a deep narrow tail. See also SALAMANDER.

mud-slinging ▷ *noun*, *colloq* the act or process of making slanderous personal attacks or allegations to discredit someone else. • **mud-slinger** *noun*.

mudstone ▷ *noun*, *geol* a fine-grained brittle sedimentary rock that is a hardened consolidated form of mud, formed of roughly equal amounts of clay and silt.

muesli /ˈmjuːzlɪ, ˈmuːzlɪ/ ▷ *noun* (***mueslis***) a mixture of crushed grain, nuts and dried fruit, eaten with milk, especially for breakfast. ◷ 1920s: Swiss German.

muezzin /mʊˈɛzɪn/ ▷ *noun*, *Islam* the Muslim official who calls worshippers to prayer, usually from a MINARET. ◷ 16c: from Arabic *mu'adhdhin*, from *adhana* to proclaim.

muff¹ ▷ *noun* a wide fur tube which the wearer, usually a woman, places their hands inside for warmth, one through each end. ◷ 16c: probably from Dutch *mof*, from *moffel* a mitten.

muff² *colloq* ▷ *verb* (***muffed***, ***muffing***) **1** *sport* **a** to miss (a catch); **b** to perform (a stroke, etc) awkwardly or unsuccessfully; to bungle or fluff something. **2** to miss (an opportunity, etc). ▷ *noun* a failure or bungle, especially a failure to hold a catch. ◷ 19c: originally meaning 'someone who is awkward or bungling at sport'.

muffin /ˈmʌfɪn/ ▷ *noun* **1** ▷ *Brit* a small round flat breadlike cake, usually eaten toasted or hot with butter. **2** *N Amer* a cup-shaped sweet cake, usually of a specified flavour □ ***blueberry muffins***. ◷ 18c.

muffle /ˈmʌfəl/ ▷ *verb* (***muffled***, ***muffling***) **1** to make something quieter; to suppress (sound). **2** to prevent someone from saying something. • **muffled** *adj*. • **muffler** *noun* **1** a thick scarf. **2** *US* a SILENCER. ◷ 15c.

■ **muffle up** to wrap up in warm clothing, especially around the head, as a protection against the cold.

mufti /ˈmʌftɪ/ ▷ *noun*, *old use* civilian clothes when worn by people who usually wear a uniform. ◷ 19c.

mug¹ ▷ *noun* **1** a drinking-vessel with a handle, used without a saucer. **2** a MUGFUL. **3** *colloq* a face or mouth. **4** *noun*, *colloq* someone who is easily fooled; a dupe. ▷ *verb* (***mugged***, ***mugging***) to attack and rob someone violently or under threat of violence. • **mugger** *noun*. • **mugging** *noun* **1** assault and robbery. **2** an act or incident of beating up. • **a mug's game** a worthless or foolish activity. ◷ 17c.

mug² ▷ *verb* (***mugged***, ***mugging***) *tr & intr* (*especially* **mug something up** or **mug up on something**) *colloq* to study or revise (a subject, etc) thoroughly, especially for an examination. ◷ 19c.

mugful /ˈmʌgfʊl/ ▷ *noun* (***mugfuls***) the amount a mug (see MUG¹) will hold.

muggins /ˈmʌgɪnz/ ▷ *noun*, *Brit colloq* a foolish person, used especially to describe oneself when one has been taken advantage of by others. ◷ 19c.

muggy /ˈmʌgɪ/ ▷ *adj* (***muggier***, ***muggiest***) said of the weather: unpleasantly warm and damp; close. • **mugginess** *noun*. ◷ 18c, from dialect *mug* drizzle or mist.

mugshot ▷ *noun*, *colloq* **1** *originally US* a photograph of a criminal's face, taken for police records. **2** a similar style of photograph taken of any person's face.

mugwump /ˈmʌgwʌmp/ ▷ *noun*, *N Amer* **1** someone who is politically aloof. **2** a great man; a boss. ◷ 19c: from Algonquian *mugquomp* a great chief.

Muhammadan or **Mohammedan** /məˈhamɪdən, moʊ-/ ▷ *adj*, *old use* belonging or relating to the prophet Muhammad (died AD 632), or to the religion (ISLAM) he founded. Now usually called ISLAMIC (see ISLAM). ▷ *noun* a MUSLIM. • **Muhammadism** *noun* Islam. ◷ 17c as *Muhammedan*.

Muharram /muːˈhʌrʌm/ ▷ *noun*, *Islam* **1** the first month of the Muslim year. **2** among Shiite Muslims: a period of mourning for Hasan and Husain, grandsons of Muhammad, which is marked during the first ten days of the month, by processions in which the faithful beat their breasts or whip themselves and fast on the ninth day. ◷ 19c: from Arabic *muharram* sacred.

mujaheddin, **mujahedin** or **mujahadeen** /muːdʒəhəˈdiːn/ ▷ *plural noun* (*usually* **the Mujaheddin**) in Afghanistan, Iran and Pakistan: Muslim fundamentalist guerillas who united to wage a JIHAD to defeat the Soviet invaders of Afghanistan after the 1979 invasion. ◷ 1950s: from Arabic *mujahidin* fighters of a jihad.

mulatto /mʊˈlatoʊ, mjʊ-/ ▷ *noun* (***mulattos*** or ***mulattoes***) *old use, now usually offensive* a person of mixed race, especially someone with one black and one white parent. ▷ *adj* relating to a mulatto. ◷ 16c: from Spanish *mulato* young mule.

mulberry /ˈmʌlbərɪ/ ▷ *noun* **1** a deciduous tree of temperate regions that produces small edible purple berries. **2** such a berry. **3** a dark purple colour. ▷ *adj* **1** belonging or relating to the tree or its berries. **2** having a dark purple colour. ◷ 14c: from Latin *marum* the mulberry.

mulch /mʌltʃ/ ▷ *noun* straw, compost, shredded bark, etc laid on the soil around plants to retain moisture and prevent the growth of weeds. ▷ *verb* (***mulches***, ***mulched***, ***mulching***) to cover (soil, etc) with mulch. ◷ 17c: from obsolete *mulch* soft.

mulct /mʌlkt/ *formal or old use* ▷ *noun* a fine or penalty. ▷ *verb* (***mulcted***, ***mulcting***) **1** to fine someone. **2** (*usually* **mulct someone of something**) to deprive them of it, especially by swindling them. ◷ 16c: from Latin *mulcta* fine.

mule¹ /mjuːl/ ▷ *noun* **1** the offspring of a male donkey and a female horse, used as a working animal in many countries. **2** a stubborn person. See also MULISH. **3** *slang* someone who smuggles drugs into a country for a dealer. **4** a cotton-spinning machine that produces yarn on spindles. Also called **spinning mule**. **5** *especially as adj* a hybrid, such as a cross between a canary and another finch (a **mule canary**). ◷ Anglo-Saxon *mul*: from Latin *mulus* or *mula*.

mule² /mjuːl/ ▻ *noun* a shoe or slipper with no back part covering the heel. ⓒ 16c; 15c, meaning 'a chilblain on the heel': from French *mules* chilblains.

muleteer /mjuːləˈtɪə(r)/ ▻ *noun* someone whose job is to drive mules. See MULE¹.

mulish /ˈmjuːlɪʃ/ ▻ *adj* stubborn; obstinate. • **mulishly** *adverb*. • **mulishness** *noun*. ⓒ 18c: from MULE¹ 2.

mull¹ ▻ *verb* (***mulled***, ***mulling***) (*now always* **mull something over**) to consider it carefully; to ponder on it. ⓒ 19c.

mull² ▻ *verb* (***mulled***, ***mulling***) to spice, sweeten and warm (wine or beer). • **mulled** *adj* ▫ *mulled wine*. ⓒ 17c.

mull³ ▻ *noun, Scots* a headland or promontory ▫ *the Mull of Kintyre*. ⓒ 14c: from Gaelic *maol*.

mullah /ˈmʌlə, ˈmʊlə/ ▻ *noun* **1** a Muslim scholar and adviser in Islamic religion and sacred law. **2** a title of respect used for such a scholar or adviser. ⓒ 17c: from Arabic *maula*.

mullein /ˈmʌlɪn/ ▻ *noun* any of several tall stiff yellow-flowered, woolly plants of the Mediterranean area, especially AARON'S ROD. ⓒ 15c: from French *moleine*.

mullet /ˈmʌlɪt/ ▻ *noun* any of a family of thick-bodied edible marine fish, eg the **red mullet**. ⓒ 15c: from French *mulet*, from Latin *mullus*.

mulligatawny /mʌlɪgəˈtɔːnɪ/ ▻ *noun, cookery* (*in full* **mulligatawny soup**) a thick curry-flavoured meat soup, originally made in E India from chicken stock. ⓒ 18c: from Tamil *milagu-tannir* pepper-water.

mullion /ˈmʌljən/ ▻ *noun, archit* a vertical bar or post separating the panes or casements of a window. • **mullioned** *adj* said of a window: having mullions. ⓒ 14c: from French *moinel*.

mullock /ˈmʌlək/ ▻ *noun, Austral* rubbish, especially mining refuse. • **poke mullock at someone** *colloq* to mock or ridicule them. See also POKE BORAK AT SOMEONE at BORAK. ⓒ 14c, from obsolete or dialect *mull* dust.

multi- /ˈmʌltɪ/ or (before a vowel) **mult-** *prefix, denoting* many ▫ *multicoloured*. ⓒ From Latin *multus* much.

multi-access see under MULTI-USER

multicellular ▻ *adj, biol* said of an organism, etc: having or made up of many cells.

multicoloured ▻ *adj* having many colours.

multicultural ▻ *adj* said especially of a society, community, etc: made up of, involving or relating to several distinct racial or religious cultures, etc. Compare MONOCULTURAL. • **multiculturalism** *noun* the policy of accommodating any number of distinct cultures within one society without prejudice or discrimination. • **multiculturalist** *adj, noun*.

multidimensional ▻ *adj* **1** having several aspects or dimensions ▫ *a multidimensional argument*. **2** *geom* having or relating to more than three DIMENSIONS .

multidirectional ▻ *adj* extending in a number of directions.

multidisciplinary ▻ *adj, education* involving a combination of several academic disciplines, methods, etc.

multifarious /mʌltɪˈfɛərɪəs/ ▻ *adj, formal* consisting of many different kinds; very varied. • **multifariously** ▻ *adverb*. • **multifariousness** *noun*. ⓒ 16c: from Latin *multifarius* manifold.

multiform ▻ *adj, formal* having many different forms or shapes. • **multiformity** *noun*.

multigrade ▻ *adj* said of a motor oil: with a viscosity that matches the properties of several separate grades of motor oil.

multigravida /mʌltɪˈgravɪdə/ ▻ *noun* (***multigravidae*** /-diː/ or ***multigravidas***) *obstetrics* a pregnant woman who has had one or more previous pregnancies. Compare MULTIPARA, PRIMIGRAVIDA. ⓒ 19c: Latin, from *gravida* pregnant.

multigym ▻ *noun* an apparatus consisting of an arrangement of weights and levers, designed for exercising and toning up all the muscles of the body.

multilateral ▻ *adj* **1** involving or affecting several people, groups, parties or nations ▫ *a multilateral treaty*. **2** many-sided. • **multilateralism** *noun* **1** *econ* support for an economic trading system where many countries are encouraged to trade with each other. **2** the quality of being multilateral. • **multilateralist** *noun, adj*. • **multilaterally** *adverb*. ⓒ 17c.

multilingual ▻ *adj* **1** written or expressed in several different languages. **2** said of a person: able to speak several different languages. See also POLYGLOT. Compare BILINGUAL, MONOLINGUAL, TRILINGUAL. • **multilingualism** *noun*. • **multilinguist** *noun*.

multimedia ▻ *adj* **1** in entertainment, education, etc: involving the use of a combination of different media, eg TV, radio, slides, hi-fi, visual arts. **2** *computing* said of a computer system: able to present and manipulate data in a variety of forms, eg text, graphics and sound, often simultaneously. ▻ *singular noun* a number of different media taken collectively.

multimillionaire ▻ *noun* someone whose wealth is valued at several million pounds, dollars, etc.

multinational ▻ *adj* said especially of a large business company: operating in several different countries. ▻ *noun* a multinational corporation, business or organization.

multinational corporation ▻ *noun* a large business company which has production and/or distribution operations in several countries, via subsidiaries, holding companies, etc.

multipara /mʌlˈtɪpərə/ ▻ *noun* (***multiparae*** /-riː/ or ***multiparas***) *obstetrics* a woman who has given birth for the second or subsequent time, or is about to do so. Compare MULTIGRAVIDA, PRIMIPARA. ⓒ 19c: Latin, from *parere* to bring forth.

multiparous /mʌlˈtɪpərəs/ ▻ *adj, zool* said of a mammal: producing several young at one birth. ⓒ 17c: from Latin *multiparus*, from Latin *parus* bearing.

multipartite /mʌltɪˈpɑːtaɪt/ ▻ *adj* divided into many parts or segments. ⓒ 18c: from Latin *partitus* divided.

multiparty ▻ *adj, politics* **1** said of a state, etc: having a political system that contains more than one organized party. **2** made up of several parties or members of several parties.

multiple /ˈmʌltɪpəl/ ▻ *adj* **1** having, involving or affecting many parts. **2** many, especially more than several. **3** multiplied or repeated. ▻ *noun* **1** *math* a number or expression for which a given number or expression is a FACTOR (sense 2), eg 24 is a multiple of 12. See also LOWEST COMMON MULTIPLE. **2** *colloq* a MULTIPLE SHOP. ⓒ 17c: from French, from Latin *multiplus* manifold.

multiple-choice ▻ *adj* said of a test, exam or question: giving a list of possible answers from which the candidate has to try to select the correct one.

multiple personality ▻ *noun, psychol* a condition in which two or more distinct personalities or types of behaviour co-exist in or are displayed by a single person. Also called **split personality**. Compare SCHIZOPHRENIA.

multiple sclerosis ▻ *noun* (abbreviation **MS**) a progressive disease of the central nervous system caused by degeneration of the MYELIN SHEATH that encloses the NEURONES in the brain and spinal cord, producing symptoms such as inability to coordinate movements, weakness of the muscles, speech difficulties, blurring of vision and an abnormal tingling sensation. Formerly called **disseminated sclerosis**.

multiple shop and **multiple store** ▷ *noun, chiefly Brit* a CHAIN STORE. Usually shortened to MULTIPLE.

multiplex /ˈmʌltɪplɛks/ ▷ *noun* (***multiplexes***) **1 a** a large cinema building divided into several smaller cinemas; **b** *as adj* □ *multiplex cinema.* **2 a** *telecomm* a system in which two or more signals may be sent simultaneously on one communications channel; **b** *as adj* □ *multiplex transmission.* ▷ *verb* (***multiplexes***, ***multiplexed***, ***multiplexing***) *telecomm* to incorporate or transmit (two or more signals) in a multiplex. ▷ *adj, formal* having very many parts; manifold; complex. ● **multiplexer** *noun, telecomm.* ⓒ 16c in obsolete mathematical sense, meaning MULTIPLE: Latin, meaning 'of many kinds', from *-plex* -fold, from *plicare* to fold.

multipliable and **multiplicable** see under MULTIPLY

multiplicand /mʌltɪplɪˈkand/ ▷ *noun, math* a number to be multiplied by a second number (the MULTIPLIER). ⓒ 16c: from Latin *multiplicare* to MULTIPLY.

multiplication /mʌltɪplɪˈkeɪʃən/ ▷ *noun* **1** *math* **a** an operation in which one number is added to itself as many times as is indicated by a second number, written using the MULTIPLICATION SIGN; **b** the process of performing this operation. Compare DIVISION. **2** the act or process of increasing in number; breeding. ⓒ 14c: French, from Latin *multiplicare* to MULTIPLY.

multiplication sign ▷ *noun, math* the symbol × used between two numbers to indicate that they are to be multiplied, as in 2 × 2 = 4.

multiplication table ▷ *noun, math* a table that lists the products of multiplying pairs of numbers together, especially all pairs from 1 to 12.

multiplicity /mʌltɪˈplɪsɪtɪ/ ▷ *noun* (***multiplicities***) *formal* **1** a great number and variety. **2** the state of being many and various. ⓒ 16c: from Latin *multiplicitas*; see MULTIPLEX.

multiplier /ˈmʌltɪplaɪə(r)/ ▷ *noun* **1** *math* a number indicating by how many times another number (the MULTIPLICAND), to which it is attached by a multiplication sign, is to be multiplied. **2** a person or thing that multiplies. **3** *physics* a device or instrument that intensifies some effect.

multiply /ˈmʌltɪplaɪ/ ▷ *verb* (***multiplies***, ***multiplied***, ***multiplying***) **1** (*especially* **multiply something by something**) **a** to add (one number or amount) to itself a specified number of times □ *Two multiplied by two equals four*; **b** (*sometimes* **multiply something and something together**) to combine (two numbers) by the process of MULTIPLICATION. **2** *intr* to increase in number, especially by breeding. ● **multipliable** or **multiplicable** /-ˈplɪkəbəl/ *adj.* ⓒ 13c as *multiplien*: from French *multiplier*, from Latin *multiplicare*, from *plicare* to fold.

multiprogramming ▷ *noun, computing* the simultaneous execution of two or more programs by a single CPU, usually achieved by carrying out several instructions from one program, and then rapidly switching to the next one.

multipurpose ▷ *adj* having many uses.

multiracial ▷ *adj* for, including, or consisting of, people of many different races. ● **multiracialism** *noun* the policy of recognizing and responding to the rights of all members of a multiracial society.

multiskilling ▷ *noun* the training of employees in a variety of skills so that they can be used for several different tasks.

multi-stage ▷ *adj* **1** said of a process, etc: made up of a series of distinct parts. **2** *aerospace* said of a rocket, etc: consisting of a number of parts that fall off in a planned sequence during the course of the flight.

multistorey ▷ *adj* said of a building: having many floors or levels. ▷ *noun* (***multistoreys***) *colloq* a car park that has several levels.

multitasking ▷ *noun, computing* the action of running several processes or jobs simultaneously on one system.

multi-track ▷ *adj* said of a recording: made up of several or many different tracks blended together. ▷ *noun* a recording of this kind. ▷ *verb* to make a recording of this kind. ● **multitracked** *adj.* ● **multitracking** *noun.*

multitude /ˈmʌltɪtʃuːd/ ▷ *noun* **1** a great number. **2** a huge crowd of people. **3** (**the multitude**) ordinary people. ● **multitudinous** /-ˈtʃuːdɪnəs/ *adj* very numerous. ● **multitudinously** *adverb.* ● **multitudinousness** *noun.* ⓒ 14c: French, from Latin *multitudo, multitudinis*, from *multus* much.

multi-user ▷ *adj, computing* said of a system: consisting of several terminals linked to a central computer, allowing access by several users at the same time. Also called **multi-access**. See also TIME-SHARING 2.

multivalent ▷ *adj, chem* having a VALENCY greater than one. Also called **polyvalent**. ● **multivalence** or **multivalency** *noun.* ⓒ 19c.

multi-vision ▷ *noun, telecomm* a technique of audiovisual presentation in which groups of slide projectors are programmed to show a complex sequence of images on a wide screen with accompanying sound from tape recording.

multivitamin ▷ *noun* a pill containing a combination of different vitamins, taken as a dietary supplement. ⓒ 1940s.

mum¹ ▷ *noun* **1** *colloq* a mother. **2** a term used to address or refer to one's own mother. See also MA, MOTHER, MUMMY. *N Amer equivalent* MOM. ⓒ 19c: shortened from MUMMY¹.

mum² ▷ *adj, colloq* silent; not speaking □ *keep mum about it.* ● **mum's the word!** *colloq* an entreaty, warning or reminder to someone to keep quiet about something. ⓒ 14c: imitating a sound produced with closed lips.

mum³ see MA'AM

mumble /ˈmʌmbəl/ ▷ *verb* (***mumbled***, ***mumbling***) *tr & intr* to speak or say something unclearly, especially with the mouth partly closed. ▷ *noun* the sound of unclear, muffled or hushed speech. ● **mumbler** *noun.* ● **mumbling** *noun, adj.* ● **mumblingly** *adverb.* ⓒ 14c, from MUM².

mumbo-jumbo /mʌmboʊ ˈdʒʌmboʊ/ ▷ *noun* (***mumbo-jumbos***) *colloq* **1** foolish talk, especially of a religious or spiritual kind. **2** baffling jargon. **3** something, eg a tribal statue, treated as an object of worship. ⓒ 18c in sense 3.

mu meson see under MUON

mummer /ˈmʌmə(r)/ ▷ *noun* **1** *historical* **a** an actor in a traditional mimed folk play, usually performed at Christmas; **b** in medieval England: one of a group of masked actors who visited houses during winter festivals, distributing gifts and performing dances, etc. **2** a disguised child taking part in traditional merrymaking during religious festivals, especially at Hallowe'en; a guiser. ● **mumming** *noun.* ⓒ 15c: from French *momeur*, from *momer* to mime.

mummery *noun* (***mummeries***) **1** a performance by a group of mummers. **2** *derog* ridiculous or pretentious ceremony.

mummify /ˈmʌmɪfaɪ/ ▷ *verb* (***mummifies***, ***mummified***, ***mummifying***) to preserve (a corpse) as a MUMMY². ● **mummification** /-fɪˈkeɪʃn/ *noun.* ● **mummified** *adj* said of a body, tissue, etc: dried up; shrivelled ⓒ 17c.

mummy¹ /ˈmʌmɪ/ ▷ *noun* (***mummies***) *chiefly Brit* **1** a child's word for mother. **2** a term used to address or refer to one's own mother. Often shortened to MUM. *N Amer equivalent* MOMMY. ⓒ 18c: originally a dialect alteration of MAMA.

mummy² /ˈmʌmɪ/ ▷ *noun* (***mummies***) especially in ancient Egypt: a human or animal corpse (with the internal organs removed), preserved with embalming spices and bandaged, in preparation for burial. ◷ 15c: from French *mumie*, from Arabic and Persian *mumiya*, from Persian *mum* wax.

mumps /mʌmps/ ▷ *singular noun* (*also* **the mumps**) *medicine* an infectious viral disease, mainly affecting children, that causes fever, headache and painful swelling of the salivary glands on one or both sides of the cheeks and under the jaw, and in older males, swelling and inflammation of one or both testes. ◷ 16c: from obsolete *mump* a grimace, and archaic *mump* to grimace.

mumsy /'mʌmzɪ/ ▷ *adj* (***mumsier***, ***mumsiest***) *colloq* **1** homely; comfy. **2** maternal, in an old-fashioned cosy way. ◷ 19c as *noun*, an affectionate variant of MUM[1].

munch /mʌntʃ/ ▷ *verb* (***munches***, ***munched***, ***munching***) *tr & intr* to chew with a steady movement of the jaws, especially noisily. • **muncher** *noun*. ◷ 14c.

Munchausen syndrome /'mʌntʃaʊzən —/ or **Munchausen's syndrome** ▷ *noun*, *psychol* a disorder in which a person pretends to have a serious physical illness or injury, and simulates all the appropriate symptoms, in order to obtain hospital treatment. ◷ 1950s: named after Baron Karl von Münchausen, the hero of a series of wildly improbable adventure stories written in English by the German R E Raspe (1737–94).

Munchausen by proxy ▷ *noun* (*in full* **Munchausen's syndrome by proxy**) *psychol* a disorder in which a person, often someone in the medical profession, induces illness, or inflicts injury on, someone else, especially a child or someone who is already ill or injured.

munchies /'mʌntʃɪz/ ▷ *plural noun*, *colloq* **1** (**the munchies**) a strong craving for food, especially one that is alcohol- or drug-induced. **2** food to snack on; nibbles. ◷ 1970s: from MUNCH.

mundane /mʌn'deɪn/ ▷ *adj* **1** ordinary; dull; everyday. **2** belonging or relating to this world, not another, spiritual world. • **mundanely** *adverb*. • **mundaneness** or **mundanity** /mʌn'danɪtɪ/ *noun*. ◷ 15c: from French *mondain*, from Latin *mundus* world.

mung bean /mʌŋ —, mʊŋ —/ ▷ *noun* **1** an E Asian plant that produces beans and beansprouts. **2** the edible green or yellow bean of this plant. See also BEANSPROUT. ◷ 19c: Hindi *mung*.

municipal /mjʊ'nɪsɪpəl/ ▷ *adj* belonging or relating to, or controlled by, the local government of a town or region. • **municipally** *adverb*. ◷ 16c: from Latin *municipalis*, from *municeps* an inhabitant of a free town, from *municipium* a free town.

municipality /mjʊnɪsɪ'palɪtɪ/ ▷ *noun* (***municipalities***) **1** a town or region that has its own local government. **2** the local government itself. ◷ 18c.

municipalize or **municipalise** /mjʊ'nɪsɪpəlaɪz/ ▷ *verb* (***municipalized***, ***municipalizing***) **1** to make (a town or region) into a municipality. **2** to bring something under municipal control or ownership. • **municipalization** *noun*.

munificence /mjʊ'nɪfɪsəns/ ▷ *noun*, *formal*, magnificent generosity. • **munificent** *adj* extremely generous. • **munificently** *adverb*. ◷ 16c: French, from Latin *munificentia*, from *munificus* generous, from *munus* gift + *facere* to make.

muniments /'mjʊnɪmənts/ ▷ *plural noun*, *law* official papers that prove ownership, especially title deeds to property. ◷ 14c: French, from Latin *munimentum* title deed, from *munire* to fortify.

munitions /mjʊ'nɪʃənz/ ▷ *plural noun* **1** military equipment, especially ammunition and weapons. **2** *as adj* (*also* **munition**) □ ***munitions factory*** □ ***munition worker***. ◷ 16c: French, from Latin *munire* to defend or fortify.

Munro /mʌn'roʊ/ ▷ *noun* (***Munros***) *Brit* a Scottish mountain over 3000ft. ◷ Early 20c: named after Sir H T Munro who compiled the original list of these (published 1891).

muntin /'mʌntɪn/ or **munting** /'mʌntɪŋ/ ▷ *noun*, *archit*, *building* a vertical framing piece that separates the panels of a door. ◷ 14c: from French *montant*, from *monter* to rise.

muntjac or **muntjak** /'mʌntdʒak/ ▷ *noun* a small deer native to India and SE Asia whose face has a V-shaped ridge with the arms of the 'V' continuing as projecting, bony columns, the ends of which bear short antlers in the male. ◷ 18c: from Sunda (a language of Java) *minchek*.

muon /'mjuːɒn/ ▷ *noun*, *physics* an elementary particle that behaves like a heavy ELECTRON, but decays to form an electron and NEUTRINO. Formerly called **mu meson**. • **muonic** /mjuː'ɒnɪk/ *adj*. ◷ 1950s: MU (sense 2) + -ON.

mural /'mjʊərəl/ ▷ *noun* (*also* **mural painting**) a painting that is painted directly on to a wall. ▷ *adj*, *formal* belonging or relating to, on or attached to, a wall or walls. • **muralist** *noun* someone who paints or designs murals. 15c: from French *muraille*, from Latin *murus* wall.

murder /'mɜːdə(r)/ ▷ *noun* **1** the act of unlawfully and intentionally killing a person. **2** *law* **a** in England and Wales: the killing of a person where there has been MALICE AFORETHOUGHT; **b** in Scotland and many US states: homicide committed purposefully and knowingly. Compare HOMICIDE, MANSLAUGHTER. **3** *colloq* slaughter or death that is felt to be needless, brutal or blameworthy, as a result of recklessness, excessive or foolish behaviour, etc. **4** *colloq* something, or a situation, which causes hardship or difficulty □ ***The traffic in town was murder today.*** ▷ *verb* (***murdered***, ***murdering***) **1** *tr & intr* to kill someone unlawfully and intentionally. **2** *colloq* to punish someone severely or cruelly; to be furious with them □ ***I'll murder him when he gets home.*** **3** *colloq* to spoil or ruin something (eg a piece of music), by performing it very badly. **4** *colloq* to defeat someone easily and by a huge margin □ ***Aberdeen murdered Rangers six nil.*** • **murderer** *noun*. • **murderess** *noun*. • **get away with murder** *colloq* to behave very badly or dishonestly and not be caught or punished. • **murder will out 1** murder cannot remain hidden. **2** (*also* **truth will out**) the truth will always come to light. • **scream, shout** or **cry blue murder** *colloq* to protest loudly or angrily. ◷ Anglo-Saxon *morthor*, from *morth* death.

murderous /mɜːdrəs/ ▷ *adj* **1** said of a person, weapon, etc: intending, intended for, or capable of, causing or committing murder □ ***a murderous look in his eyes.*** **2** *colloq* very unpleasant; causing hardship or difficulty. • **murderously** *adverb*. • **murderousness** *noun*.

murine /'mjʊəraɪn, -rɪn/ ▷ *adj* **1** mouselike. **2** *zool* belonging to the mouse family or subfamily. ◷ 17c: from Latin *murinus*, from *mus, muris* a mouse.

murk or (*rarely*) **mirk** /mɜːk/ ▷ *noun* darkness; gloom. ◷ Anglo-Saxon *mirce*.

murky or (*rarely*) **mirky** /'mɜːkɪ/ ▷ *adj* (***murkier***, ***murkiest***) **1** dark; gloomy. **2** said of water: dark and dirty. **3** suspiciously vague or unknown; shady □ ***her murky past.*** • **murkily** *adverb*. • **murkiness** *noun*.

murmur /'mɜːmə(r)/ ▷ *noun* **1** a quiet, continuous sound, eg of running water or low voices. **2** anything said in a low, indistinct voice. **3** a complaint, especially a subdued, muttering one. **4** *medicine* in AUSCULTATION: an abnormal rustling sound made by the heart, often indicating the presence of disease. Also called **heart murmur**. ▷ *verb* (***murmured***, ***murmuring***) **1** *tr & intr* to speak (words) softly and indistinctly. **2** *intr* to complain or grumble, especially in a subdued, muttering way. • **murmuring** *noun*, *adj*. • **murmuringly** *adverb*. • **murmurous** *adj*. ◷ 14c: from French *murmurer* to murmur, from Latin *murmurare*, from *murmur* a rumbling noise.

Murphy's law /ˈmɜːfɪz —/ ▷ *noun, originally US* another name for SOD'S LAW. ⓒ 1950s: from the common Irish surname *Murphy*.

murrain /ˈmʌrɪn, ˈmʌrən/ ▷ *noun, vet medicine* any infectious cattle disease, especially FOOT-AND-MOUTH DISEASE. ⓒ 14c in obsolete sense 'plague': from French *morine* a plague, from Latin *mori* to die.

mus. ▷ *abbreviation* **1** music. **2** musical.

MusB or **MusBac.** ▷ *abbreviation*: *Musicae Baccalaureus* (Latin), Bachelor of Music.

muscadel see MUSCATEL

Muscadet /ˈmʌskədeɪ/ ▷ *noun* **1** a dry white wine from the Loire region of France. **2** the variety of white grape from which it is produced. ⓒ 1920s: French, from Latin *muscus* musk.

muscat /ˈmʌskat, ˈmʌskət/ ▷ *noun* **1** (*also* **muscat wine**) muscatel. **2** (*also* **muscat grape**) a variety of white grape with a musky smell, used in wine-making and dried for raisins. ⓒ 16c: Provençal, literally 'musky'.

muscatel /mʌskəˈtɛl, ˈmʌskətɛl/ and **muscadel** /-dɛl/ ▷ *noun* a rich sweet white wine made from MUSCAT grapes. ⓒ 14c: French, from Provençal *muscadel*, diminutive of *muscat*.

muscle /ˈmʌsəl/ ▷ *noun* **1** an animal tissue composed of bundles of fibres that are capable of contracting to produce movement of part of the body. See also INVOLUNTARY MUSCLE, VOLUNTARY MUSCLE, CARDIAC MUSCLE. **2** a body structure or organ composed of this tissue, eg the BICEPS. **3** bodily strength. **4** power or influence of any kind □ *financial muscle*. ▷ verb (***muscled***, ***muscling***) *colloq* (*always* **muscle in on something**) to force one's way into it; to try to grab a share of or part in it. ● **muscly** /ˈmʌsəlɪ/ *adj*. ⓒ 16c: from Latin *musculus*, diminutive of *mus* a mouse, from the shape of some muscles.

muscle-bound ▷ *adj* having over-enlarged muscles that are stiff and difficult to move.

muscleman ▷ *noun* a man with very big muscles, especially one employed to intimidate people.

muscovado /mʌskəˈvɑːdoʊ/ ▷ *noun* (***muscovados***) sugar in its unrefined state after evaporating sugar-cane juice and draining off the molasses. Also called **muscovado sugar**. ⓒ 17c: from Spanish *mascabado* of the lowest quality.

Muscovite /ˈmʌskəvaɪt/ ▷ *noun* a citizen or inhabitant of, or person born in, Moscow, capital of the Russian Federation. ▷ *adj* belonging or relating to Moscow, or its inhabitants. ⓒ 16c: from *Muscovy*, an old French name for Russia, from Latin *Moscovia*.

muscovite /ˈmʌskəvaɪt/ ▷ *noun, geol* a colourless silvery-grey, or pale brown, heat-resistant mineral of the MICA group, used as an electrical and heat insulator, as a filler in paint, in wallpaper manufacture and roofing materials, etc. ⓒ 19c: from *Muscovy* glass, from *Muscovy* an old French name for Russia.

muscular /ˈmʌskjʊlə(r)/ ▷ *adj* **1** belonging or relating to, or consisting of, muscle. **2** having well-developed muscles; strong; brawny. ● **muscularity** /-ˈlarɪtɪ/ *noun*. ● **muscularly** *adverb*.

muscular dystrophy ▷ *noun, medicine* any of various forms of a hereditary disease in which there is progressive wasting of certain muscles, which are eventually replaced by fatty tissue. ⓒ 19c.

musculature /ˈmʌskjʊlətʃə(r)/ ▷ *noun* (***musculatures***) the arrangement, or degree of development, of muscles in a body or organ.

MusD or **MusDoc.** ▷ *abbreviation*: *Musicae Doctor* (Latin), Doctor of Music.

Muse /mjuːz/ ▷ *noun* **1** *Greek mythol, also literary, art, etc* any of the nine goddesses of the arts, said to be a source of creative inspiration to all artists, especially poets. **2** *literary* (*especially* **the Muse**) **a** poetic genius or inspiration; **b** poetry or art. ⓒ 14c: French, from Latin *Musa*, from Greek *mousa*.

muse /mjuːz/ ▷ *verb* (***mused***, ***musing***) **1** *intr* (*often* **muse on something**) to reflect or ponder silently. **2** to say something in a reflective way. **3** *intr* to gaze contemplatively. ● **musing** *adj* thoughtful; reflective. ▷ *noun* **1** (**musings**) *literary* thoughts. **2** the act of musing. ● **musingly** *adverb*. ⓒ 14c: from French *muser* to loiter or waste time.

museum /mjʊˈzɪəm/ ▷ *noun* a place where objects of artistic, scientific or historical interest are displayed to the public, preserved and studied. ⓒ 17c: Latin, from Greek *mouseion* temple of the Muses, a place dedicated to study.

museum piece ▷ *noun* **1** an article or specimen displayed in a museum, or something fit for this because of its special quality, age or interest. **2** *humorous, colloq* any very old or old-fashioned person or thing.

mush¹ /mʌʃ/ ▷ *noun* **1** a soft half-liquid mass of anything. **2** *derog, colloq* sloppy sentimentality. **3** *N Amer* a kind of thick cornmeal porridge. ⓒ 17c.

mush² /mʌʃ/ ▷ *exclamation, N Amer* used especially to a team of dogs: go on! go faster! ▷ *verb* (***mushes***, ***mushed***, ***mushing***) *intr* to travel on a sledge pulled by dogs. ▷ *noun* a journey on a sledge pulled by dogs. ⓒ 19c.

mushroom /ˈmʌʃruːm, -rʊm/ ▷ *noun* **1 a** any of various FUNGI that produce a fast-growing fruiting body consisting of a short white stem supporting a pale fleshy umbrella-shaped cap with numerous brown or pinkish spore-bearing gills on the underside. See also TOADSTOOL. **b** the edible species of such fungi. Also *as adj* □ *mushroom omelette*. **2** anything resembling this in shape, eg a wooden article used for darning. Also *as adj* □ *mushroom cloud*. **3** anything resembling this in the speed of its growth or development. Also *as adj* □ *mushroom business*. **4** a pinkish-brown colour. ▷ *adj* having a pinkish-brown colour. ▷ *verb* (***mushroomed***, ***mushrooming***) *intr* to develop or increase with alarming speed. See also MAGIC MUSHROOM. ⓒ 15c: from French *mousseron*.

mushroom cloud ▷ *noun* a huge, mushroom-shaped cloud of radioactive dust produced by a nuclear explosion. ⓒ 1950s.

mushy /ˈmʌʃɪ/ ▷ *adj* (***mushier***, ***mushiest***) **1** in a soft half-liquid state; consisting of or like MUSH¹. **2** sentimental in a sickly way.

music /ˈmjuːzɪk/ ▷ *noun* **1** the art of making sound in a rhythmically organized, harmonious form, either sung or produced with instruments, and usually communicating some idea or emotion. **2** such sound, especially that produced by instruments. **3 a** any written form or composition in which such sound is expressed; **b** musical forms or compositions collectively. **4** the performance of musical compositions. **5** written or printed copies of such compositions; sheet music, musical scores, etc collectively. **6** pleasing, harmonious or melodic sound. Also *as adj* □ *music lesson*. ● **face the music** see under FACE. ● **music to one's ears** news, etc that is particularly welcome. ⓒ 13c: from French *musique*, from Greek *mousike* relating to the MUSES.

musical /ˈmjuːzɪkəl/ ▷ *adj* **1** consisting of, involving, relating to or producing music. **2** pleasant to hear; melodious. **3** said of a person: having a talent or aptitude for music. ▷ *noun* a play or film that features singing and dancing. ● **musicality** /-ˈkalɪtɪ/ *noun* musical quality. ● **musically** /ˈmjuːzɪklɪ/ *adverb*. ⓒ 15c.

musical box and **music box** ▷ *noun* a small box containing a mechanical device that plays music when the box is opened. The device consists of a drum with teeth which pluck at a comb-like metal plate. ⓒ 19c.

musical bumps ▷ *singular noun* a children's party game that involves the participants dancing or running round while the music plays. When the music stops, the object is to drop to the floor as quickly as possible, the last player to do so being eliminated. ⓘ 1930s.

musical chairs ▷ *singular noun* **1** a party game that involves the participants walking or running round a decreasing number of chairs while the music plays. When the music stops, the object is to grab a chair, the player left without a seat being eliminated. **2** a series of position-changes and shuffles involving a number of people, when seen as rather comical or amusing. ⓘ 1920s.

musical comedy ▷ *noun* a form of light entertainment, derived from BURLESQUE and light opera, consisting of humorous or sentimental songs, dance and dialogue, held together by a flimsy plot.

musical director ▷ *noun* the conductor of an orchestra in a theatre, production, etc.

musical instrument see INSTRUMENT

musical statues see STATUE

music box see MUSICAL BOX

music centre ▷ *noun, dated* a hi-fi that incorporates an amplifier, radio, record-player, cassette recorder in one unit. Compare MIDI SYSTEM, STACK (sense 6), STEREO. ⓘ 1970s.

music drama ▷ *noun* **1** a term used to describe opera in which the musical, dramatic and visual elements are given equal emphasis. **2** an opera of this genre. Compare MUSIC THEATRE. ⓘ 19c: from German *Musikdrama*, a term coined by Wagner (see WAGNERIAN) to describe his later operas.

music hall ▷ *noun* **1** VARIETY (sense 4) entertainment. Also *as adj* □ ***music-hall act.*** **2** a theatre in which variety entertainment can be seen.

musician /mjʊˈzɪʃən/ ▷ *noun* **1** someone who is skilled in music, especially in performing or composing it. **2** someone who performs or composes music as their profession. • **musicianly** *adj.* • **musicianship** *noun* skill in music.

musicology /mjuːzɪˈkɒlədʒɪ/ ▷ *noun* the academic study of music in all its aspects. • **musicological** *adj.* • **musicologist** *noun.* ⓘ Early 20c.

music stool see under PIANO STOOL

music theatre ▷ *noun* especially in avant-garde music: a form of staged dramatic performance with music and usually singing, presented on a smaller scale than traditional opera. Compare MUSIC DRAMA.

music therapy ▷ *noun, psychol* the use of music in the treatment, etc, of people with physical or mental disabilities, and sometimes used as an aid to recovery from mental disorders.

musing and **musingly** see under MUSE

musique concrète / *French* myzik kɔ̃krɛt/ ▷ *noun* a type of mid-20c music made up of recorded sounds, not always musical ones, from various sources, which are mixed, distorted and manipulated on tape by the composer. Also called **concrete music**. ⓘ 1950s: French, literally 'concrete music'.

musk ▷ *noun* **1** a strong-smelling substance much used in perfumes, secreted by the glands of various animals, especially the male MUSK DEER. **2** any similar synthetic substance. **3** the smell of such substances. **4** *as adj* having or producing musk, or a scent of or like musk □ ***musk gland*** □ ***musk orchid.*** ⓘ 14c: from French *musc*, from Latin *muscus*, perhaps from Sanskrit *muska* testicle or scrotum, because of the resemblance of the deer's musk gland in its sac to this.

musk deer ▷ *noun* a small, hornless, central Asian mountain deer. See also MUSK.

musket /ˈmʌskət/ ▷ *noun, historical* an early rifle-like gun that was loaded through the barrel and fired from the shoulder, used by soldiers between the 16c and 19c. • **musketeer** *noun* a soldier armed with a musket. • **musketry** *noun* **1** muskets. **2** the use of, or skill in using, muskets. **3** a body of troops armed with muskets. ⓘ 16c: from French *mousquet*, from Italian *moschetto* a kind of sparrowhawk.

musk melon ▷ *noun* **1** any of various common varieties of melon, including the honeydew. **2** the fruit of any of these melon plants. ⓘ 16c: so called because of the musky smell of the flesh of a particular variety.

musk ox ▷ *noun* a long-haired ox of Canada and Greenland that emits a musky smell during rutting.

muskrat /ˈmʌskrat/ and **musquash** /ˈmʌskwɒʃ/ ▷ *noun* **1** a large, N American water rodent, which produces a musky smell. **2** its highly-prized thick brown fur, used to make clothes. ⓘ 17c: from Abnaki (an Algonquian language) *muskwessu*.

musk rose ▷ *noun* a Mediterranean rambling rose whose flowers have a musky scent.

musky /ˈmʌskɪ/ ▷ *adj* (***muskier***, ***muskiest***) containing, or like the smell of, musk. • **muskily** *adverb.* • **muskiness** *noun.*

Muslim /ˈmʊzlɪm, ˈmʌz-/ and **Moslem** /mɒz-/ ▷ *noun* a follower of the religion of Islam. ▷ *adj* belonging or relating to Muslims or to Islam. See also ISLAM, MUHAMMADAN. ⓘ 17c: from Arabic *muslim*, literally 'one who submits', from *salma* to submit (to God).

> ***Moslem, Muslim, Mohammedan***
>
> Both **Moslem** and **Muslim** are correct, but the second is now more common than the first. The term **Mohammedan** is considered offensive by many Muslims and is best avoided.

muslin /ˈmʌzlɪn/ ▷ *noun* a fine cotton cloth with a gauze-like appearance. Also *as adj.* ⓘ 17c: from French *mousseline*, from Italian *musselino*, from *Mussolo* the town of Mosul in Iraq, where it was originally produced.

muso /mjuːzoʊ/ ▷ *noun* (***musos***) *slang* **1** *Brit derog* a pop or rock musician who concentrates too much on technique. **2** *especially Austral* a musician or music enthusiast. ⓘ 1960s: from MUSIC.

musquash see MUSKRAT

muss *N Amer, especially US, colloq* ▷ *verb* (***musses***, ***mussed***, ***mussing***) (*usually* **muss something up**) to make something (especially clothes or hair) untidy; to mess up or disarrange. ▷ *noun* (***musses***) disorder or confusion; mess. • **mussed-up** *adj.* • **mussy** *adj.* ⓘ 19c.

mussel /ˈmʌsəl/ ▷ *noun* **1** a marine BIVALVE mollusc, especially the common or edible mussel, that has a bluish-black shell and uses a mass of tough threads to anchor itself to rocks, etc. **2** a similar freshwater bivalve mollusc which forms MOTHER-OF-PEARL on the inside of its shell. ⓘ Anglo-Saxon *muscle* or *musle*: from Latin *musculus*, diminutive of *mus* mouse.

must[1] /ˈmʌst/ ▷ *auxiliary verb* **1** used to express necessity □ ***I must earn some extra money*** □ ***Must you leave so soon?*** **2** used to express duty or obligation □ ***You must help him.*** **3** used to express certainty □ ***You must be Charles.*** **4** used to express determination □ ***I must remember to go to the bank.*** **5** used to express probability □ ***She must be there by now.*** **6** used to express inevitability □ ***We must all die some time.*** **7** used to express an invitation or suggestion □ ***You must come and see us soon*** □ ***You must read her other books.*** Also used with the main verb merely implied □ ***I must away.*** See also MUSTN'T. ▷ *noun* (*always* **a must**) a necessity; something essential □ ***Fitness is a must in professional sport.*** • **must needs** see NEEDS MUST at NEED. ⓘ Anglo-Saxon *moste*, originally as past tense of *mot* MAY.

must² /ˈmʌst/ ▻ *noun* the juice of grapes or other fruit before it is completely fermented to become wine. ⓘ Anglo-Saxon: from Latin *mustum vinum* new wine.

must³ /ˈmʌst/ ▻ *noun* mustiness; mould. ⓘ 17c.

must⁴ see MUSTH

mustache and **mustached** the *N Amer* spelling of MOUSTACHE and MOUSTACHED.

mustachio /məˈstɑːʃɪoʊ/ ▻ *noun* (*often* ***mustachios***) an elaborately curled moustache. • **mustachioed** *adj.* ⓘ 16c: from Spanish *mostacho* and Italian *mostaccio*; see MOUSTACHE.

mustang /ˈmʌstaŋ/ ▻ *noun* a small wild or half-wild horse native to the plains of the western US. ⓘ 19c: from a combination of two Spanish words, *mestengo* belonging to the *mesta* (graziers' union) + *mostrenco* homeless or stray.

mustard /ˈmʌstəd/ ▻ *noun* **1** an annual plant native to Europe and W Asia, with bright yellow flowers. **2** a hot-tasting paste used as a condiment or seasoning, made from powdered or crushed whole seeds of black or white mustard or both, mixed with water or vinegar. Also *as adj* □ *mustard pot.* **3** a light yellow or brown colour. ▻ *adj* having a light yellow or brown colour. • **as keen as mustard** *colloq* extremely keen or enthusiastic. ⓘ 13c: from French *moustarde*, from Latin *mustum* MUST², which was originally an ingredient of the condiment.

mustard and cress ▻ *singular noun* a mixture of the seedlings of the mustard plant and cress, used as a salad vegetable.

mustard gas ▻ *noun* a highly poisonous gas, or the colourless oily liquid of which it is the vapour, that causes severe blistering of the skin, widely used as a CHEMICAL WARFARE agent in World War I.

muster /ˈmʌstə(r)/ ▻ *verb* (***mustered***, ***mustering***) **1** *tr & intr* said especially of soldiers: to gather together for duty or inspection, etc. **2** (*also* **muster something up** or **muster up something**) to summon or gather (eg courage or energy) □ *pulled with all the strength I could muster.* **3** *Austral, NZ* to round up (livestock). ▻ *noun* **1** any assembly or gathering, especially of troops for duty or inspection. **2** *Austral, NZ* a round-up of livestock. • **pass muster** to be accepted as satisfactory, eg at an inspection. ⓘ 14c: from French *mostre*, from Latin *monstrare* to show.

▪ **muster someone in** *US military* to enrol or enlist them as a new recruit.

▪ **muster someone out** *US military* to discharge them from service.

musth or **must** /mʌst/ ▻ *noun* (*especially in* **to be in musth**) a dangerous frenzied state in certain male animals, especially bull elephants in the breeding season. ⓘ 19c: from Persian and Hindi *mast* intoxicated.

must-have ▻ *adj* referring to something that is desired by someone, eg the latest model on the market, or something indispensable to a dedicated follower of fashion □ *the latest must-have hair accessory* □ *it's a must-have.*

mustn't /ˈmʌsənt/ ▻ *contraction* must not.

musty /ˈmʌstɪ/ ▻ *adj* (***mustier***, ***mustiest***) **1** mouldy or damp. **2** smelling or tasting stale or old. • **mustily** *adverb.* • **mustiness** *noun.* ⓘ 16c.

mutable /ˈmjuːtəbəl/ ▻ *adj* subject to or able to change; variable. • **mutability** *noun.* • **mutably** *adverb.* ⓘ 14c: from Latin *mutabilis*, from *mutare* to change.

mutagen /ˈmjuːtədʒən/ ▻ *noun, biol* a chemical or physical agent, such as X-ray or ultraviolet radiation, that induces or increases the frequency of mutations in living organisms, either by altering the DNA of the genes, or by damaging the chromosomes. • **mutagenic** *adj.* ⓘ 1940s: from MUTATION.

mutant /ˈmjuːtənt/ ▻ *noun* a living organism or cell that carries a specific mutation of a gene which usually causes it to differ from previous generations in one particular characteristic. ▻ *adj* said of an organism or cell: carrying or resulting from a mutation. ⓘ Early 20c: from Latin *mutantem* changing, from *mutare* to change.

mutate /mjuːˈteɪt/ ▻ *verb* (***mutated***, ***mutating***) *tr & intr* **1** *biol* to undergo or cause to undergo MUTATION (sense 1). **2** *formal* to change. ⓘ 19c; back-formation from MUTATION.

mutation /mjʊˈteɪʃən/ ▻ *noun* **1** *genetics* in a living organism: a change in the structure of a single gene, the arrangement of genes on a chromosome or the number of chromosomes, which may result in a change in the appearance or behaviour of the organism. **2** *formal* a change of any kind. **3** *linguistics* in Celtic languages: a change in a speech sound, especially a vowel, because of the nature of the sound next to it. **4** *phonetics* an UMLAUT. • **mutational** *adj.* • **mutationally** *adverb.* ⓘ 14c: from Latin *mutatio*, from *mutare* to change.

mutatis mutandis /mjʊˈteɪtɪs mjʊˈtandɪs/ ▻ *adverb* allowing for respective differences of detail; with necessary adjustments made. ⓘ 15c: Latin, meaning 'having changed what needs to be changed'.

mute /mjuːt/ ▻ *adj* (***muter***, ***mutest***) **1** said of a person: physically or psychologically unable to speak; dumb. **2** silent. **3** felt, but not expressed in words □ *mute anger.* **4** said of a letter in a word: not sounded, like the final *e* in many English words, eg *bite*, *mute.* **5** *law* said of a person: refusing to plead. ▻ *noun* **1** *medicine* someone who is physically unable to speak, eg as a result of deafness since birth or brain damage. **2** *psychol* someone who refuses to speak, eg as a result of psychological trauma or illness. **3** any of various devices that soften or deaden the sound of a musical instrument. **4** an unsounded letter in a word. ▻ *verb* (***muted***, ***muting***) to soften or deaden the sound of (a musical instrument). • **mutely** *adverb.* • **muteness** *noun.* • **mutism** *noun, medicine, psychol* inability or refusal to speak. ⓘ 14c: French, from Latin *mutus* silent.

muted ▻ *adj* **1** said of sound or colour: not loud or harsh; soft. **2** said of feelings, etc: mildly expressed; not outspoken □ *muted criticism.*

mute swan ▻ *noun* the commonest European swan, with pure white plumage and an orange bill with a black bump at the base, which despite its name has a variety of calls.

muti /ˈmʊtɪ/ ▻ *noun, S Afr* **1** traditional medicine, especially that associated with witchcraft or witch doctors. **2** *colloq* medicine. ⓘ 19c: from Zulu *umuthi* tree, plant or medicine.

mutilate /ˈmjuːtɪleɪt/ ▻ *verb* (***mutilated***, ***mutilating***) **1** to cause severe injury to (a person or animal), especially by removing a limb or organ. **2** to damage something severely, especially to alter (eg a text, song, etc) beyond recognition. • **mutilation** *noun* **1** severe physical injury, usually visible and permanent injury. **2** severe damage. • **mutilator** *noun.* ⓘ 16c: from Latin *mutilare* to cut off, from *mutilus* maimed.

mutinous /ˈmjuːtɪnəs/ ▻ *adj* **1** said of a person, soldier, crew, etc: having mutinied or likely to mutiny. **2** belonging or relating to mutiny. • **mutinously** *adverb.* • **mutinousness** *noun.*

mutiny /mjuːtɪnɪ/ ▻ *noun* (***mutinies***) rebellion, or an act of rebellion, against established authority, especially in the armed services. ▻ *verb* (***mutinies***, ***mutinied***, ***mutinying***) *intr* to engage in mutiny. • **mutineer** *noun.* ⓘ 16c: from French *mutin* rebellious, from Latin *movere*, *motum* to move.

mutism see under MUTE

mutt ▻ *noun, slang* **1** a dog, especially a mongrel. **2** a foolish, clumsy person. ⓘ Early 20c: shortened from MUTTONHEAD.

mutter /ˈmʌtə(r)/ ▻ *verb* (***muttered***, ***muttering***) **1** *tr & intr* to utter (words) in a quiet, barely audible or indistinct voice. 2 *intr* to grumble or complain, especially in a low voice. ▻ *noun* 1 a soft, barely audible or indistinct tone of voice. 2 a muttered complaint. • **mutterer** *noun*. • **muttering** *noun, adj*. Ⓒ 14c.

mutton /'mʌtən/ ▻ *noun* the flesh of an adult sheep, used as food. • **mutton dressed as lamb** *derog, colloq* an older person, especially a woman, dressed in clothes designed or suitable for a young person, especially if they look foolish or unsightly. Ⓒ 13c: from French *moton* sheep.

muttonchops and **mutton-chop whiskers** ▻ *plural noun* men's long side whiskers, narrow at the ears and broad and rounded at the lower jaw. Ⓒ 19c; so called because their shape is similar to that of a meat chop.

muttonhead ▻ *noun, derog, colloq* a stupid person. • **mutton-headed** *adj*. Ⓒ 19c.

mutual /'mjuːtʃʊəl, -tjʊəl/ ▻ *adj* 1 felt by each of two or more people about the other or others; reciprocal □ *mutual admiration*. 2 to, towards or of each other □ *mutual supporters*. 3 *colloq* shared by each of two or more; common □ *a mutual friend*. 4 *finance* said of a financial institution such as a building society: owned by its customers. • **mutuality** *noun*. • **mutually** *adverb*. Ⓒ 15c: from French *mutuel*, from Latin *mutuus* borrowed or reciprocal.

mutual fund see under UNIT TRUST

mutual inductance ▻ *noun, elec engineering* (SI unit HENRY) generation of ELECTROMOTIVE FORCE in one system of conductors by a variation of current in another system linked to the first by MAGNETIC FLUX.

mutual inductor ▻ *noun, elec engineering* a component consisting of two coils designed to have a definite MUTUAL INDUCTANCE between them.

mutual insurance ▻ *noun, business* a system in which the policy-holders are also the shareholders of the company, sharing its profits, etc.

mutualism ▻ *noun, biol* a relationship between two organisms of different species, that is beneficial to both of them. Compare SYMBIOSIS. Ⓒ 19c.

mutuality and **mutually** see under MUTUAL

muu-muu /'muːmuː/ ▻ *noun* (***muu-muus***) a simple, loose, usually colourful dress, worn by women chiefly in Hawaii. Ⓒ 1920s: from Hawaiian *mu'u mu'u*, literally 'cut off'.

muzak see under PIPED MUSIC

muzzle /'mʌzəl/ ▻ *noun* 1 the projecting jaws and nose of an animal, eg a dog. 2 an arrangement of straps fitted round an animal's jaws to prevent it biting. 3 the open end of a gun barrel. ▻ *verb* (***muzzled, muzzling***) 1 to put a muzzle on (eg a dog). 2 to prevent someone from speaking or being heard; to silence or gag them. Ⓒ 15c: from French *musel*, from Latin *musellum*, from *musum* a snout.

muzzle-loader ▻ *noun* a firearm that is loaded through the muzzle. Compare BREECH-LOADER. • **muzzle-loading** *adj*.

muzzy /'mʌzɪ/ ▻ *adj* (***muzzier, muzziest***) 1 not thinking clearly; confused. 2 blurred; hazy. • **muzzily** *adverb*. • **muzziness** *noun*. Ⓒ 18c.

MVO ▻ *abbreviation, Brit* Member of the Royal Victorian Order.

MW ▻ *abbreviation* 1 *IVR* Malawi. 2 medium wave. 3 megawatt, or megawatts.

M-way ▻ *abbreviation* motorway.

mx ▻ *abbreviation, physics* maxwell, or maxwells.

my /maɪ/ ▻ *adj* 1 belonging or relating to ME □ *my book*. 2 used with nouns in various exclamations □ *My gosh!* □ *My foot!* 3 *old use* used in respectful terms of address such as *my lord*. 4 used in rather old-fashioned, affectionate or patronizing terms of address such as *my dear*. ▻ *exclamation* (*also* **my word, my goodness** or, more strongly, **my God**) expressing surprise or amazement. Ⓒ 12c, from Anglo-Saxon *min* genitive of ME[1].

my- see under MYO-

myalgia /maɪ'aldʒɪə/ ▻ *noun, medicine* pain in the muscles or a muscle. • **myalgic** *adj*. Ⓒ 19c.

myalgic encephalomyelitis ▻ *noun* (abbreviation **ME**) a non-specific or generalized virus-associated debilitating disorder, the existence of which is debatable. It is characterized by extreme fatigue, muscular pain, lack of concentration, memory loss and depression and it may last many months. Also called **postviral syndrome** and **chronic fatigue syndrome**.

Myanmar /'mjanmaː(r)/ ▻ *adj* belonging or relating to Myanmar, a republic in SE Asia (called Burma until 1989), or its inhabitants. ▻ *noun* a citizen or inhabitant of, or person born in, Myanmar. See also BURMESE.

myasthenia /maɪəs'θiːnɪə/ ▻ *noun, medicine* muscular weakness or debility. Ⓒ 19c: Latin, from Greek *astheneia* weakness.

mycelium /maɪ'siːlɪəm/ ▻ *noun* (***mycelia*** /-lɪə/) *biol* in multicellular fungi: a mass or network of threadlike filaments or hyphae (see HYPHA) formed when the non-reproductive tissues are growing. • **mycelial** *adj*. Ⓒ 19c: Latin, from MYC-.

Mycenaean /maɪsə'niːən/ ▻ *adj* 1 relating to the ancient Bronze Age civilization in Greece (1500–1100 BC), known from the Homeric poems and from remains at Mycenae and other sites in S Greece. 2 belonging or relating to the ancient city of Mycenae itself or its inhabitants. ▻ *noun* an inhabitant of the Mycenaean world. Ⓒ 16c.

myco- /maɪkoʊ, maɪkɒ/ or (before a vowel) **myc-** *combining form, denoting* fungus or mushroom. Ⓒ From Greek *mykes* mushroom.

mycology /maɪ'kɒlədʒɪ/ ▻ *noun, biol* the study of fungi. • **mycologic** /-kə'lɒdʒɪk/ or **mycological** *adj*. • **mycologist** /-'kɒlədʒɪst/ *noun*. Ⓒ 19c: from Latin *mycologia*.

mycosis /maɪ'koʊsɪs/ ▻ *noun, pathol* any disease that is due to the growth of a fungus. • **mycotic** /-'ɒtɪk/ *adj*. Ⓒ 19c.

mycotoxin ▻ *noun, biol* any poisonous substance produced by a fungus. Ⓒ 1960s.

myelin /'maɪəlɪn/ ▻ *noun, zool, anatomy* a soft white substance that forms a thin insulating sheath (**myelin sheath**) around the AXONs of the nerve cells of vertebrates. Ⓒ 19c: German, from Greek *myelos* marrow.

myelitis /maɪə'laɪtɪs/ ▻ *noun, pathol* 1 inflammation of the spinal cord, which results in paralysis of the body below the affected region. 2 inflammation of the bone marrow, caused by infection, characterized by severe pain and swelling, which if untreated may result in bone deformity. See also OSTEOMYELITIS. Ⓒ 19c: from Greek *myelos* marrow.

myeloma /maɪə'loʊmə/ ▻ *noun* (***myelomas*** or ***myelomata*** /-'loʊmətə/) *medicine, pathol* a tumour of the bone marrow, caused by the proliferation of malignant plasma cells. Ⓒ 19c: from Greek *myelos* marrow + -OMA.

my God and **my goodness** see under MY

mylonite /'maɪlənaɪt/ ▻ *noun, geol* a dark fine-grained hard metamorphic rock, often banded or streaked and with a glassy appearance. Ⓒ 19c: from Greek *mylon* mill.

myna, **mynah** or **mina** /'maɪnə/ ▻ *noun* (***mynas, mynahs, minas***) any of various large, SE Asian birds of the starling family, some of which can be taught to imitate human speech. Ⓒ 18c: from Hindi *maina*.

mynheer or **meneer** /maɪn'hɛə(r), mə'nɛə(r)/ ▻ *noun, S Afr* a form of address for a man, used in place of SIR or, when preceding a name, MR. Ⓒ 19c Afrikaans as *meneer*, 17c: from Dutch *mijn* my + *heer* lord.

myo- /maɪoʊ/ or (before a vowel) **my-** *scientific combining form, denoting* muscle □ *myology*. Ⓒ From Greek *mys, myos* muscle.

MYOB ▻ *abbreviation, colloq* mind your own business. See under MIND.

myocardial infarction ▻ *noun, pathol* death of part

of the heart muscle, usually caused by thickening and hardening of the arteries. Non technical HEART ATTACK.

myocarditis ▻ *noun, pathol* inflammation of the MYOCARDIUM.

myocardium ▻ *noun* (***myocardia***) *anatomy* the muscular tissue of the heart. • **myocardiac** or **myocardial** *adj*. ⓒ 19c.

myofibril /maɪoʊˈfaɪbrɪl/ ▻ *noun, anatomy* any of the minute filaments which together make up a single muscle fibre. ⓒ 19c.

myoglobin /maɪoʊˈgloʊbɪn/ ▻ *noun, biochem* a protein that stores oxygen in the muscles of vertebrates. ⓒ 1920s: German.

myopia /maɪˈoʊpɪə/ ▻ *noun, ophthalmol* short-sightedness, in which parallel rays of light entering the eye are brought to a focus in front of the retina rather than on it, so that distant objects appear blurred. • **myopic** /maɪˈɒpɪk/ *adj* **1** short-sighted. **2 a** said of someone: unable to understand or appreciate the views, opinions, etc of others; **b** said of someone's outlook, attitude, etc: not admitting the views, opinions, etc of others. • **myopically** *adverb*. ⓒ 17c: Latin, from Greek *myops* short-sighted, from *myein* to shut + *ops* the eye.

myriad /ˈmɪrɪəd/ ▻ *noun* (*especially* **myriads** or **a myriad of something**) an exceedingly great number. ▻ *adj* numberless; innumerable □ ***her myriad admirers***. ⓒ 16c: from Greek *myrias* ten thousand.

myriapod /ˈmɪrɪəpɒd/ ▻ *noun, zool* a crawling, many-legged ARTHROPOD, eg the centipede or millipede. ⓒ 19c: from Latin *Myriapoda*, from Greek *myriopous, myriopodos* many-footed.

myrmidon /ˈmɜːmɪdən/ ▻ *noun* (*sometimes* **Myrmidon**) *literary* **1** a hired thug; a henchman. **2** a follower. ⓒ 17c: named after the *Myrmidons* of Greek mythology, a band of warriors who went to the Trojan Wars with Achilles.

myrrh /mɜː(r)/ ▻ *noun* **1** any of various African and Asian trees and shrubs that produce a bitter, brown, aromatic resin. **2** the resin produced by these, used in medicines, perfumes, etc. ⓒ Anglo-Saxon *myrra*: from Greek *myrra*.

myrtle /ˈmɜːtəl/ ▻ *noun* **1** a S European evergreen shrub with pink or white flowers and dark blue, aromatic berries. **2** any of various related shrubs. ⓒ 15c: from French *myrtille*, from Greek *myrtos*.

myself /maɪˈsɛlf, mɪ-/ ▻ *pronoun* **1** the reflexive form of I (used instead of *me* when the speaker or writer is the object of an action he or she performs) □ ***I did myself a favour*** □ ***I burnt myself***. **2** used with *I* or *me*, to add emphasis or to clarify something □ ***I prefer tea myself*** □ ***I myself took no part in these events***. **3** my normal self □ ***I am not myself today***. **4** (*also* **by myself**) alone; without any help. ⓒ 14c; Anglo-Saxon *me seolf*.

mysterious /mɪˈstɪərɪəs/ ▻ *adj* **1** difficult or impossible to understand or explain; deeply curious. **2** creating, containing or suggesting mystery. • **mysteriously** *adverb*. • **mysteriousness** *noun*.

mystery /ˈmɪstərɪ/ ▻ *noun* (***mysteries***) **1** an event or phenomenon that cannot be, or has not been, explained. **2** the quality of being difficult or impossible to explain or understand, or of being odd or obscure and arousing curiosity. **3** someone about whom very little is known or understood. **4** a story about a crime that is difficult to solve. Also *as adj* □ ***a mystery writer***. **5** (*especially* **mysteries**) *Christianity* **a** a truth known only because it is revealed by God; **b** a sacrament. **6** a religious rite, especially the Eucharist. ⓒ 14c: from Latin *mysterium*, from Greek *mysterion*, from *myein* to close the eyes.

mystery play ▻ *adj* a medieval play originally based on the life of Christ or of a saint, or, later, on any biblical event. Originally **miracle play**, compare MORALITY PLAY.

mystery religion ▻ *noun, historical* in the Graeco-Roman world: a religious cult, admission to which was restricted to those who had undertaken secret initiation rites or mysteries.

mystery tour ▻ *noun* a round trip to a destination that is not revealed to the travellers in advance.

mystic /ˈmɪstɪk/ ▻ *noun, relig* someone whose life is devoted to meditation or prayer in an attempt to achieve direct communication with and knowledge of God, regarded as the ultimate reality. ▻ *adj* mystical. ⓒ 14c: from Greek *mystikos*, from *mystes* an initiate.

mystical /ˈmɪstɪkəl/ ▻ *adj* (*also* MYSTIC) **1** *relig* **a** relating to or involving truths about the nature of God and reality revealed only to those people with a spiritually-enlightened mind; esoteric; **b** relating to the mysteries or to mysticism. **2** mysterious. **3** wonderful or awe-inspiring. • **mystically** *adverb*.

mysticism /ˈmɪstɪsɪzəm/ ▻ *noun* **1** *relig* the practice of gaining direct communication with God through prayer and meditation. **2** the belief in the existence of a state of reality hidden from ordinary human understanding, such as occult or other mysterious forces.

mystify /ˈmɪstɪfaɪ/ ▻ *verb* (***mystifies, mystified, mystifying***) **1** to puzzle or bewilder. **2** to make something mysterious or obscure. • **mystification** *noun*. • **mystifying** *adj*. ⓒ 19c: from French *mystifier*.

mystique /mɪˈstiːk/ ▻ *noun* (***mystiques***) a mysterious, distinctive or compelling quality possessed by a person or thing. ⓒ 19c: French, as *adjective*, meaning MYSTIC.

myth /mɪθ/ ▻ *noun* **1** an ancient story that deals with gods and heroes, especially one used to explain some natural phenomenon. **2** such stories in general; mythology. **3** a commonly-held, false notion. **4** a non-existent, fictitious person or thing. See also URBAN MYTH. ⓒ 19c: from Greek *mythos*.

mythical /ˈmɪθɪkəl/ ▻ *adj* **1** relating to myth. **2** imaginary; untrue. • **mythically** *adverb*.

mythicize or **mythicise** /ˈmɪθɪsaɪz/ ▻ *verb* (***mythicized, mythicizing***) to make something or someone into a myth, or to explain it or them as a myth. • **mythicizer** or **mythicist** *noun*. ⓒ 19c.

mythologize or **mythologise** /mɪˈθɒlədʒaɪz/ ▻ *verb* (***mythologized, mythologizing***) **1** *intr* to create myths. **2** *intr* to relate, interpret or explain myths or a myth. **3** to MYTHICIZE. ⓒ 17c.

mythology /mɪˈθɒlədʒɪ/ ▻ *noun* (***mythologies***) **1** myths in general. **2** a collection of myths, eg about a specific subject. **3** the study of myth or myths. • **mythological** *adj* relating or belonging to mythology. • **mythologist** *noun*. ⓒ 15c: from Greek *mythos* myth.

my word see under MY

myxo- /mɪksoʊ, mɪksə/ or (before a vowel) **myx-** *scientific combining form, denoting* mucus. ⓒ From Greek *myxa* mucus.

myxoedema or (*US*) **myxedema** /mɪksɪˈdiːmə/ ▻ *noun, pathol* a disease characterized by increased thickness and dryness of the skin, weight gain, hair loss, and reduction in mental and metabolic activity, often resulting from HYPOTHYROIDISM. ⓒ 19c.

myxoma /mɪkˈsoʊmə/ ▻ *noun* (***myxomata*** /-ˈmɑːtə/) *biol, pathol* a tumour composed of jellylike or mucous material that usually forms just beneath the skin. ⓒ 19c.

myxomatosis /mɪksəməˈtoʊsɪs/ ▻ *noun, vet medicine, biol* an infectious, usually fatal, viral disease of rabbits, transmitted by fleas and causing the growth of numerous MYXOMAta through the body. ⓒ 1920s.

myxomycete /mɪksoʊmaɪˈsiːt/ ▻ *noun* (***myxomycetes*** /-siːtiːz/) *biol* a SLIME MOULD. ⓒ 19c: from Greek *mykes* mushroom.

myxovirus /ˈmɪksoʊvaɪrəs/ ▻ *noun, pathol* any of a group of related viruses that cause influenza, mumps, etc. ⓒ 1950s.

N

N[1] or **n** /ɛn/ ▻ *noun* (***Ns, N's*** or ***n's***) **1** the fourteenth letter of the English alphabet. **2** the nasal consonant sound represented by this letter. See also EN.

N[2] ▻ *abbreviation* **1** National. **2** Nationalist. **3** New. **4** *physics* newton. **5** *chem* nitrogen. **6** North. **7** Northern. **8** *IVR* Norway.

N[3] ▻ *symbol, chess* knight.

N- ▻ *combining form, denoting* nuclear.

n[1] /ɛn/ ▻ *noun* **1** *math* an indefinite number. **2** *colloq* a large number. ▻ *adj* of an indefinite or large number.

n[2] ▻ *abbreviation* **1** nano-. **2** neuter. **3** neutron. **4** new. **5** *grammar* nominative. **6** noon. **7** note. **8** *grammar* noun.

'n' or **'n'** /ən/ ▻ *abbreviation, colloq, in compounds* and □ *chicken 'n' chips.*

NA ▻ *abbreviation* **1** *IVR* Netherlands Antilles. **2** North America.

Na ▻ *symbol, chem* sodium. ◷ From Latin *natrium.*

n/a ▻ *abbreviation* not applicable.

NAACP ▻ *abbreviation* in the US: National Association for the Advancement of Colored People, a pressure group which aims to extend awareness of their political rights among the black population.

NAAFI /'nafɪ/ ▻ *abbreviation, Brit* Navy, Army and Air Force Institutes. ▻ *noun* (***NAAFIs***) a canteen or shop run by the NAAFI.

naan see NAN

naartje see NARTJIE

nab ▻ *verb* (***nabbed, nabbing***) *colloq* **1** to catch someone in the act of doing wrong. **2** to arrest someone. **3** to grab or take something. • **nabber** *noun.* ◷ 17c.

nabla /'nablə/ ▻ *noun* (***nablas***) *math* in Cartesian coordinates: the symbol ∇, an inverted capital delta, representing the vector operator

$$i\frac{\partial}{\partial x}+j\frac{\partial}{\partial y}+k\frac{\partial}{\partial z}$$

Also called **del**. ◷ 19c: Greek, meaning 'a Hebrew stringed instrument', apparently because of the shape.

nabob /'neɪbɒb/ ▻ *noun* **1** *colloq* a wealthy influential person. **2** *old use* a European man who has made a vast fortune in the East. **3** *historical* **a** a Muslim governor under the Mogul empire in India; **b** a NAWAB. ◷ 17c in sense 3: from Urdu *nawwab* deputy governor.

nacelle /nə'sɛl/ ▻ *noun* **1** the basket or gondola of a balloon or airship, etc. **2** *aeronautics* a streamlined structure on an aircraft that houses an engine or accommodates crew and passengers, etc. ◷ Early 20c: French, meaning 'a small boat', from Latin *navicella,* from *navis* ship.

nachos /'nɑːtʃoʊz, 'natʃ-/ ▻ *plural noun, cookery* a Mexican dish of tortilla chips topped with chillis, melted cheese, etc. ◷ 1940s.

nacre /'neɪkə(r)/ ▻ *noun* (***nacres***) **1** a shellfish that produces mother-of-pearl. **2** MOTHER-OF-PEARL. • **nacreous** /'neɪkrɪəs/ *adj.* ◷ 17c: from Arabic *naqqarah* shell or drum.

NACRO or **Nacro** /'nakroʊ/ ▻ *abbreviation* National Association for the Care and Resettlement of Offenders.

nadir /'neɪdɪə(r), 'nadɪə(r)/ ▻ *noun* **1** *astron* the point on the celestial sphere directly beneath the observer and opposite to the zenith. **2** the lowest point of anything, especially the absolute depths, eg of despair or degradation. ◷ 15c: from Arabic *nazir-as-samt* opposite the zenith.

naevus or (*US*) **nevus** /'niːvəs/ ▻ *noun* (***naevi*** /-vaɪ/) a birthmark or mole on the skin. • **naevoid** *adj* like or typical of a naevus. ◷ 19c: Latin.

naff ▻ *adj* (***naffer, naffest***) *slang* **1** stupid; foolish. **2** tasteless; vulgar. **3** rubbishy; of poor quality; worthless. ▻ *noun* an incompetent. • **naff all** nothing at all. • **naff off!** *offensive* go away! get lost! ◷ 1960s.

NAFTA or **Nafta** /'naftə/ ▻ *abbreviation* North American Free Trade Agreement, a CUSTOMS UNION comprising the USA, Canada and Mexico, established in 1993.

nag[1] ▻ *noun* **1** *derog* a broken-down old horse; an inferior horse. **2** a small riding-horse. ◷ 15c, meaning 'a riding-horse'.

nag[2] ▻ *verb* (***nagged, nagging***) **1** (*also* **nag at someone**) *tr & intr* to scold them constantly; to keep finding fault with them. **2** (*also* **nag at someone**) *intr* to worry them or cause them anxiety. **3** *intr* said of pain: to persist. ▻ *noun* someone who nags. • **nagger** *noun* a person or problem that nags or annoys. • **nagging** *adj* said of a problem or anxiety: constantly worrying or causing concern □ *a nagging suspicion.* ◷ 19c: from Norse *nagga* to rub, grumble or quarrel.

■ **nag someone into something** to keep urging them until they do it.

nagana /nɑː'gɑːnə/ ▻ *noun, vet medicine* a disease of horses and domestic cattle of central and southern Africa, caused by a TRYPANOSOME transmitted by the TSETSE. ◷ Late 19c: from Zulu *nakane.*

nagari /'nɑːgəriː/ ▻ *noun* **1** DEVANAGARI. **2** the group of alphabets to which DEVANAGARI belongs. ◷ 18c: Sanskrit, meaning 'town-script', from *nagaran* town; the addition of *deva-*, meaning 'of the gods', was a later development.

NAHT ▻ *abbreviation* National Association of Head Teachers.

Nahuatl see AZTEC

naiad /'naɪad/ ▻ *noun* (***naiades*** /-ədiːz/ or ***naiads***) **1** *Greek mythol* a river- or spring-nymph. **2** the aquatic larva of the dragonfly, mayfly, stone-fly or damselfly. **3** an aquatic plant with narrow leaves and small flowers. ◷ 17c: from Greek *naias,* from *naein* to flow.

naïf or **naif** /naɪ'iːf/ ▻ *adj* NAIVE. ◷ 16c.

nail /neɪl/ ▻ *noun* **1** the outer structure, composed of KERATIN, that grows from a tuck in the skin and protects part of the fleshy tip of a finger or toe. **2** a metal spike hammered into something, eg to join two objects together or to serve as a hook. ▻ *verb* (***nailed, nailing***) **1** to fasten something with, or as if with, a nail or nails. **2** *colloq* to catch, trap or corner someone. **3** to detect, identify or expose (a lie or deception, etc). • **nailer** *noun* a maker of nails. • **nailery** *noun* (***naileries***) a place where nails are made. • **a nail in one's** or **the coffin 1** any event or experience, etc that has the effect of shortening one's life. **2** a contributory factor in the downfall of anyone or anything. • **hard as nails** callous; unsympathetic; unsentimental. • **hit the nail on the head 1** to pinpoint a problem or issue exactly. **2** to describe something in terms that sum it up precisely. • **nail one's colours to the mast** see under COLOURS. • **on the nail** *colloq* immediately. Ⓒ Anglo-Saxon *nægl*.

■ **nail someone down** *colloq* to extract a definite decision or promise from them.

■ **nail something down 1** to fix it down with nails. **2** to define or identify it clearly.

nail-bed ▷ *noun* the structure beneath a NAIL (*noun* 1), damage to which may result in the whole nail being lost.

nail-biting ▷ *noun* nibbling at or chewing off the ends of one's fingernails. ▷ *adj* said of an event or experience: extremely exciting or full of suspense. • **nail-biter** *noun* **1** someone who bites their nails. **2** *colloq* a nail-biting event or experience.

nail bomb ▷ *noun* an explosive terrorist device containing nails and capable of causing widespread serious injuries.

nailbrush ▷ *noun* a brush for cleaning the fingernails or toenails.

nail enamel see NAIL POLISH

nailfile ▷ *noun* a FILE² (sense 2).

nail gun ▷ *noun* a tool used to drive in metal nails.

nail-head ▷ *noun* **1** the head of a NAIL (*noun* 2). **2** an ornament shaped like the head of a nail.

nail polish, **nail varnish** and (*especially N Amer*) **nail enamel** ▷ *noun* lacquer which can be applied to the fingernails and toenails to give them colour and shine.

nail scissors ▷ *noun* small scissors designed for trimming the fingernails and toenails.

nainsook /ˈneɪnsʊk/ ▷ *noun* a type of muslin. Ⓒ Early 19c: from Hindi *nainsukh*, from *nain* eye + *sukh* pleasure.

naira /ˈnaɪərə/ ▷ *noun* (*plural* ***naira***) the standard unit of currency in Nigeria. Ⓒ 1970s: altered from *Nigeria*.

naive or **naïve** /naɪˈiːv/ ▷ *adj* (***naiver, naivest***) **1** simple, innocent or unsophisticated. **2** *derog* too trusting; credulous; not worldly enough. • **naively** *adverb*. • **naivety** /-vətɪ/ or **naïveté** /-vəteɪ, naɪˈiːvtɪ/ *noun* (***naiveties*** or ***naivetés***) **1** excessive trust or innocence. **2** an act, statement or behaviour that is naïve. Ⓒ 17c: French (*naïve*) feminine of *naïf*, from Latin *nativus* native.

naked /ˈneɪkɪd/ ▷ *adj* **1** wearing no clothes. **2** without fur, feathers or foliage. **3** barren; blank; empty. **4** simple; without decoration; artless. **5** undisguised; blatant or flagrant □ *naked greed.* **6** said of a light or flame: uncovered; exposed. **7** said of the eye: unaided by an optical instrument of any kind. **8** *literary* vulnerable; defenceless. **9** without confirmation or supporting evidence. **10** *commerce, finance* lacking some element, eg financial backing, to complete a contract or make it valid. • **nakedly** *adverb*. • **nakedness** *noun*. Ⓒ Anglo-Saxon *nacod*.

naked lady and **naked ladies** ▷ *singular noun* the AUTUMN CROCUS.

NALGO /ˈnalgoʊ/ ▷ *abbreviation, historical* National and Local Government Officers Association, now part of UNISON.

namby-pamby /nambɪˈpambɪ/ ▷ *adj, derog* **1** feebly sentimental; soppy. **2** prim; over-demure. ▷ *noun* (*plural in sense 2 only* ***namby-pambies***) **1** namby-pamby writing or talk. **2** a namby-pamby person. Ⓒ 18c: from the scornful nickname given to the poet Ambrose Philips (1674–1749).

name /neɪm/ ▷ *noun* **1** a word or words by which an individual person, place or thing is identified and referred to. **2** reputation □ *get a bad name.* **3** a famous or important person or firm, etc □ *the big names in fashion.* ▷ *verb* (***named, naming***) *tr & intr* **1** to give a name to someone or something. **2** to mention or identify someone or something by name □ *name three French poets.* **3** to specify or decide on someone or something. **4** to choose or appoint. • **namable** or **nameable** *adj*. • **named** *adj*. • **call someone names** to insult or abuse them verbally. • **in all but name** in practice, though not officially □ *leader in all but name.* • **in name only** officially, but not in practice. • **in the name of someone** or **something 1** by their or its authority. **2** on behalf of them or it. **3** for the sake of them or it; using them or it as justification □ *were tortured in the name of religion.* • **make a name for oneself** to become famous. • **name names** to identify eg culprits by name. • **name the day** to fix a date, especially the date of one's wedding. • **the name of the game** *colloq* the predominant or essential aspect or aim of some activity. • **to one's name** belonging to one □ *doesn't have a penny to his name.* • **you name it** whatever you mention or want, etc. Ⓒ Anglo-Saxon *nama*.

■ **name someone** or **something after** or (*N Amer*) **for someone** or **something else** to give (eg a child or a place) the same name as another person, in their honour or by way of commemoration.

name brand ▷ *noun* a product that bears a manufacturer's name. Compare OWN BRAND.

name calling ▷ *noun* verbal abuse.

name day ▷ *noun* **1** the feast day of the saint after whom one is named. **2** *stock exchange* the day when the buyer's name, etc, is given to the seller.

name-dropping ▷ *noun, derog* the practice of casually referring to well-known people as if they were friends, to impress one's hearers. • **name-dropper** *noun*. Ⓒ 1950s.

nameless ▷ *adj* **1** having no name. **2** unidentified. **3** anonymous; undistinguished. **4** too awful to specify; unmentionable. • **namelessly** *adverb*. • **namelessness** *noun*.

namely /ˈneɪmlɪ/ ▷ *adverb* used to introduce an expansion or explanation of what has just been mentioned □ *which helps me to achieve the goal, namely to improve standards.*

name part ▷ *noun* a TITLE ROLE.

nameplate ▷ *noun* a plate on or beside the door of a building or room, etc bearing the name, and sometimes also occupation, etc of the occupant.

namesake ▷ *noun* someone with the same name as another person; someone named after another. Ⓒ 17c.

nametape ▷ *noun* a piece of tape attached to a garment, etc marked with the owner's name.

nan or **naan** /nɑːn/ and **nan bread** ▷ *noun* a slightly leavened bread, traditionally cooked in India and Pakistan, baked in a large round or teardrop shape. Ⓒ 1960s: Hindi.

nana¹ /ˈnɑːnə/ ▷ *noun* (***nanas***) **1** *derog slang* an idiot, a fool. **2** *Austral slang* the head. • **off one's nana** *Austral slang* mad. Ⓒ 19c: probably from BANANA.

nana² see NANNY

nancy /ˈnansɪ/ and **nancy boy** ▷ *noun* (***nancies*** or ***nancy boys***) *derog, colloq* **1** an effeminate young man or boy. **2** a homosexual youth. Ⓒ Early 20c: from Nancy, the girl's name.

nankeen /naŋˈkiːn/ ▷ *noun* **1** a buff-coloured cotton cloth. **2** a yellowish buff or grey colour. Also *as adj*. **3** (**nankeens**) clothes, especially trousers, made of nankeen. Ⓒ 18c: named after Nanking in China, where the cloth was first made.

nannoplankton see NANOPLANKTON

nanny /ˈnanɪ/ ▷ *noun* (***nannies***) **1** a children's nurse. **2** (*also* **nana** and **nanna** /ˈnanə/) *colloq* a child's name for GRANDMOTHER. ▷ *adj, derog* said of institutions or the state, etc: protective to an intrusive extent. ▷ *verb* (***nannies, nannied, nannying***) to over-protect or over-supervise. • **nannyish** *adj* overprotective. Ⓒ 18c: from Nanny, a pet-form of the name Ann.

nanny goat ▷ *noun* an adult female goat. Compare BILLY GOAT.

nano- /nanoʊ/ ▷ *combining form, denoting* **1** (abbreviation **n**) a thousand millionth, 10^{-9} ◻ *nanogram.* **2** of microscopic size. ⓒ From Greek *nanos* dwarf.

nanometre /ˈnanoʊmiːtə(r)/ ▷ *noun* (abbreviation **nm**) one thousand millionth of a metre.

nanoplankton or **nannoplankton** ▷ *noun, biol* plankton of microscopic size. ⓒ Early 20c.

nanosecond ▷ *noun* (abbreviation **ns**) one thousand millionth of a second. ⓒ 1950s.

nap¹ ▷ *noun* a short sleep. ▷ *verb* (***napped, napping***) *intr* to have a nap. • **catch someone napping** *colloq* to find them unprepared or off-guard. ⓒ Anglo-Saxon *hnappian.*

nap² ▷ *noun* **1** a woolly surface on cloth, raised by a finishing process, not made in weaving. Compare PILE³. **2** the direction in which this surface lies smooth. **3** any similar downy covering or surface. • **napless** *adj.* • **napped** *adj* said of fabric: with a nap. ⓒ 15c as *noppe.*

nap³ ▷ *noun* **1** the card game NAPOLEON. **2** in that game: **a** a call of five; **b** the winning of five tricks. **3** *horse-racing* a tip that is claimed to be a certainty. ▷ *verb* (***napped, napping***) *horse-racing* to name (a particular horse) as certain to win. • **go nap 1** to undertake to win all five tricks. **2** to risk all. ⓒ Late 19c.

napa or **nappa** /ˈnapə/ ▷ *noun* a soft leather made by a special tawing process (see TAW¹), from sheepskin or goatskin. ⓒ 19c: named after Napa in California, where it was first made.

napalm /ˈneɪpɑːm, ˈna-/ ▷ *noun* an aluminium SOAP consisting of a mixture of various FATTY ACIDS, used as an incendiary agent in bombs and flame-throwers. ▷ *verb* (***napalmed, napalming***) to attack or destroy something with napalm. ⓒ 1940s: from *na*phthenate *palm*itate.

nape /neɪp/ ▷ *noun* the back of the neck. ⓒ 14c.

naphtha /ˈnafθə, ˈnapθə/ ▷ *noun, chem* any of several flammable liquids distilled from coal or petroleum, used as solvents. ⓒ 16c: Greek.

naphthalene ▷ *noun, chem* (formula $C_{10}H_8$) a white crystalline hydrocarbon distilled from coal tar, used eg in mothballs and dyes. • **naphthalic** *adj* pertaining to or derived from naphthalene. ⓒ 19c.

Napierian logarithm see LOGARITHM

napkin /ˈnapkɪn/ ▷ *noun* **1** (*also* **table napkin**) a piece of cloth or paper for wiping one's mouth and fingers at mealtimes, and used to protect one's clothing. **2** *formal or old use* a baby's nappy. ⓒ 15c: diminutive of French *nappe* tablecloth, from Latin *mappa* cloth.

napkin ring ▷ *noun* a ring that holds a rolled table napkin when it is not being used.

napless see under NAP²

napoleon /nəˈpoʊlɪən/ ▷ *noun* **1** *historical* a twenty-franc gold coin issued by Napoleon I of France. **2** a French modification of the game of EUCHRE, each player receiving five cards and playing as an individual. Often shortened to **nap**. ⓒ 19c: from French *napoléon.*

Napoleonic /nəpoʊlɪˈɒnɪk/ ▷ *adj* belonging to, characteristic of, or relating to Napoleon I of France (1769–1821).

nappa see NAPA

nappe /nap/ ▷ *noun* **1** *geol* a large arch-shaped geological fold structure. **2** *math* one of the two parts of a conical surface defined by the vertex. ⓒ Early 20c: French, meaning 'tablecloth', from Latin *mappa* cloth.

napped see under NAP¹, NAP², NAP³

napping see under NAP¹, NAP³

napless see under NAP²

nappy¹ /ˈnapɪ/ ▷ *noun* (***nappies***) a pad of disposable material, or a folded piece of towelling or other soft cloth, secured round a baby's bottom to absorb urine and faeces. *N Amer equivalent* DIAPER. ⓒ 1920s: diminutive of NAPKIN.

nappy² /ˈnapɪ/ ▷ *adj* (***nappier, nappiest***) **1** said of beer: **a** with a head; frothy; **b** strong. **2** tipsy. **3** said of a horse: nervous; excitable. ▷ *noun* strong ale. ⓒ 16c: perhaps from *nappy* shaggy, from NAP².

nappy rash ▷ *noun* irritation of a baby's skin on the buttocks or genital area, usually caused by prolonged contact with wet or soiled nappies.

narc and **narco** /ˈnɑːkoʊ/ ▷ *noun* (***narcs*** or ***narcos***) *US slang* a narcotics agent. ⓒ 20c: NARCOTIC.

narcissism /nɑːˈsɪsɪzəm/ ▷ *noun* **1** excessive admiration for oneself or one's appearance. **2** *psychol* sensual pleasure and satisfaction found in one's own body. • **narcissistic** *adj.* ⓒ 19c: from *Narkissos,* a youth in Greek mythology who fell in love with his own reflection.

narcissus /nɑːˈsɪsəs/ ▷ *noun* (***narcissuses*** or ***narcissi*** /-saɪ/) a plant similar to the daffodil, which grows from a bulb and has white or yellow flowers, often heavily scented. ⓒ 16c: from Greek *narkissos,* supposedly from *narke* numbness, because of its narcotic properties.

narco- /nɑːkoʊ, nɑːˈkɒ/ or (before vowels) **narc-** ▷ *combining form, signifying* **1** numbness or torpor. **2** using drugs ◻ *narcoanalysis.* **3** relating to or resulting from the illicit production of drugs. ⓒ From Greek *narke.*

narcoanalysis ▷ *noun* psychoanalysis of a patient under the influence of narcotic drugs.

narcolepsy /ˈnɑːkəlɛpsɪ/ ▷ *noun* a condition marked by sudden episodes of irresistible sleepiness. ⓒ 19c: French *narcolepsie.*

narcosis /nɑːˈkoʊsɪs/ ▷ *noun* (***narcoses***) *pathol* drowsiness, unconsciousness, or other effects to the central nervous system produced by a narcotic. ⓒ 17c: from Greek *narkosis* a numbing.

narcosynthesis ▷ *noun* treatment using narcotics so that repressed emotions become freely accepted into the self.

narcoterrorism ▷ *noun* terrorism by or on behalf of an organization involved in narcotics or drug dealing.

narcotic /nɑːˈkɒtɪk/ ▷ *noun* **1** a drug causing numbness and drowsiness, and eventually unconsciousnesss, which deadens pain and produces a temporary sense of well-being, but which can be addictive. **2** *loosely* **a** any addictive drug; **b** an illegal drug. **3** any substance that has a narcotic effect, eg alcohol or an inert gas. ▷ *adj* **1** belonging or relating to narcotics or the users of narcotics. **2** relating to NARCOSIS. • **narcotically** *adverb.* ⓒ 14c as *narcotyk:* from Greek *narkotikos* numbing.

narcotism /ˈnɑːkətɪzəm/ ▷ *noun* **1** the influence of narcotics. **2** a state of addiction or stupor induced by narcotics. ⓒ 19c.

narcotize or **narcotise** ▷ *verb* (***narcotized, narcotizing***) to subject to the influence of a narcotic drug. • **narcotization** *noun*

nard ▷ *noun* **1** SPIKENARD. **2** an Indian plant of the valerian family, from which this is obtained. **3** any of several aromatic plants formerly used in medicine. ⓒ 16c in this form; from 14c *narde:* from Greek *nardos.*

nardoo /nɑːˈduː/ ▷ *noun* (***nardoos***) **1** an Australian cloverlike fern. **2** the spores of this plant used as food. ⓒ 19c: Aboriginal.

nares /ˈnɛəriːz/ ▷ *plural noun, anatomy* the paired openings of the nasal cavity, the **external nares** which are the NOSTRILS, and the **internal nares**, present only in air-breathing vertebrates, which open into the PHARYNX. ⓒ 17c: Latin.

narghile, **nargile** or **nargileh** /ˈnɑːgɪlɪ, -leɪ/ ▷ *noun* (***narghiles, nargiles*** or ***nargilehs***) a hookah. ⓒ 19c:

Persian *nargileh*, from *nargil* coconut, from which it used to be made.

narial /ˈnɛərɪəl/ and **narine** /-raɪn/ ▷ *adj* relating to the nostrils. ⓘ 19c: from Latin *naris* nostril.

nark ▷ *noun, slang* **1** a spy or informer working for the police. **2** a habitual grumbler. **3** *especially Austral & NZ* a spoilsport. ▷ *verb* (***narked, narking***) *colloq* **1** *tr & intr* to annoy. **2** *intr* to grumble. **3** *intr* to inform or spy, especially for the police. • **narked** *adj* annoyed. ⓘ 19c: perhaps from Romany *nak* nose.

■ **nark at someone** to annoy them with persistent criticism.

narky /ˈnɑːkɪ/ ▷ *adj* (***narkier, narkiest***) *colloq* irritable.

Narragansett /narəˈgansət/ ▷ *noun* **1** a member of a Native American people formerly living on Rhode Island. **2** an Algonquian language spoken by this people, now virtually extinct. ⓘ 17c.

narrate /nəˈreɪt/ ▷ *verb* (***narrated, narrating***) *tr & intr* **1** to tell (a story); to relate. **2** to give a running commentary on (a film, etc). • **narratable** *adj*. • **narration** *noun* **1** the act or process of telling something. **2** a continuous story or account. • **narrator** *noun* someone who tells a story or narrative. • **narratory** *adj*. ⓘ 17c: from Latin *narrare, narratum* to relate.

narrative /ˈnarətɪv/ ▷ *noun* **1** an account of events. **2** those parts of a book, etc that recount events. ▷ *adj* **1** telling a story; recounting events □ *narrative poetry.* **2** relating to the telling of stories □ *narrative skills.* • **narratively** *adverb*. ⓘ 15c: from Latin *narrativus*, from *narrare* to relate.

narrow /ˈnaroʊ/ ▷ *adj* (***narrower, narrowest***) **1** having little breadth, especially in comparison with length. **2** said of interests or experience: restricted; limited. **3** said of attitudes or ideas: illiberal or unenlightened; intolerant or bigoted. **4** said of the use of a word: restricted to its precise or original meaning; strict □ *in its narrowest sense.* **5** close; only just achieved, etc □ *a narrow escape.* ▷ *noun* **1** a narrow part or place. **2** (**narrows**) a narrow part of a channel or river, etc. ▷ *verb* (***narrowed, narrowing***) *tr & intr* **1** to make or become narrow. **2 a** (*also* **narrow something down**) said eg of a range of possibilities: to be reduced or limited; **b** (*also* **narrow something down**) to reduce it. • **narrowness** *noun*. ⓘ Anglo Saxon *nearu*.

narrow boat ▷ *noun* a canal barge, especially one that is 7ft (2.1m) wide or less.

narrowcast ▷ *verb* **1** *tr & intr* to transmit (TV programmes, etc) on a cable system. **2** *intr* said eg of advertisers, radio or TV stations or programming: to target a particular audience. • **narrowcasting** *noun* **1** cable TV. **2** the production and distribution of material on video tapes and cassettes, etc. ⓘ 1970s in sense 1; 1930s: from NARROW, modelled on BROADCAST.

narrow-gauge ▷ *adj* said of a railway: less than the standard gauge. See GAUGE.

narrowly ▷ *adverb* **1** only just; barely. **2** with close attention □ *eyed him narrowly.* **3** in a narrow or restricted way.

narrow-minded ▷ *adj, derog* **1** intolerant. **2** bigoted; prejudiced. • **narrow-mindedly** *adverb*. • **narrow-mindedness** *noun*.

narrowness see under NARROW

narrow squeak see under SQUEAK

narthex /ˈnɑːθɛks/ ▷ *noun* (***narthexes***) *archit* **1** a western portico of an early church or a basilica to which women and CATACHUMENS were admitted. **2** a vestibule between the church porch and the nave. ⓘ 17c: Greek, also meaning 'giant fennel', a 'cane', 'stalk' or 'casket'.

nartjie or (*originally*) **naartje** /ˈnɑːtʃɪ/ ▷ *noun* (***nartjies*** or ***naartjes***) *S Afr* a small sweet orange like a mandarin. ⓘ 18c: Afrikaans, probably originally connected with ORANGE.

narwhal /ˈnɑːwəl/ ▷ *noun* an arctic whale, the male of which has a long spiral tusk. ⓘ 17c: from Danish *narhval*, perhaps from Norse *nar* corpse + *hvalr* whale.

nary /ˈnɛərɪ/ ▷ *adverb, dialect* or *colloq* never; not. • **nary a ...** not one; never a ... □ *nary a hint of apology.* ⓘ 19c variant of *ne'er a* never a.

NASA /ˈnasə/ ▷ *abbreviation* National Aeronautics and Space Administration, a US body for research in extraterrestrial space.

nasal /ˈneɪzəl/ ▷ *adj* **1** belonging or relating to the nose. **2** said of a sound or letter such as *m* or *n*: pronounced through, or partly through, the nose. **3** said of a voice, etc: abnormally or exceptionally full of nasal sounds. ▷ *noun* **1** a sound uttered through the nose. **2** a letter representing such a sound. • **nasally** *adverb*. • **nasality** *noun*. ⓘ 17c: from Latin *nasus* nose.

nasalize or **nasalise** /ˈneɪzəlaɪz/ ▷ *verb* (***nasalized, nasalizing***) *tr & intr* to pronounce or speak (a sound or words, etc) nasally. • **nasalization** *noun*. ⓘ Early 19c.

nascent /ˈneɪsənt/ ▷ *adj* in the process of coming into being; in the early stages of development. • **nascency** *noun* **1** being brought into being. **2** birth. **3** *chem, formerly* the abnormally active condition of an element, especially hydrogen. ⓘ 17c: from Latin *nascens, nascentis*, from *nasci* to be born.

NASDAQ /ˈnazdak/ ▷ *abbreviation, finance* National Association of Securities Dealers Automated Quotation, a quotation system and associated market for American shares. Compare EASDAQ.

naso- /neɪzoʊ/ ▷ *combining form, denoting* **1** nose. **2** concerning or referring to the nose, with or without something else. ⓘ From Latin *nasus* nose.

nasofrontal ▷ *adj, anatomy* relating to the nose and frontal bone.

nasogastric tube ▷ *adj, medicine* a tube that is passed into the stomach through the nose.

nasolacrymal ▷ *adj, medicine* relating to the nose and tears □ *nasolacrymal duct.*

nasopharynx ▷ *noun, anatomy* the part of the pharynx above the soft palate.

nastic movement /ˈnastɪk —/ ▷ *noun, bot* the non-directional movement of a plant organ in response to an external stimulus. ⓘ Early 20c: from Greek *nastos* close-pressed.

nasturtium /nəˈstɜːʃəm/ ▷ *noun* a climbing garden plant with flat round leaves and red, orange or yellow trumpet-like flowers. ⓘ 16c: Latin, meaning 'cress', said to be from *nasus* nose + *torquere* to twist, because of its pungent taste.

nasty /ˈnɑːstɪ/ ▷ *adj* (***nastier, nastiest***) **1** unpleasant; disgusting. **2** malicious; ill-natured □ *a nasty person.* **3** worrying; serious □ *a nasty wound.* **4** said of weather: wet or stormy □ *a nasty day.* ▷ *noun* (***nasties***) someone or something unpleasant, disgusting or offensive. Especially *in compounds* □ *a video nasty.* • **nastily** *adverb*. • **nastiness** *noun*. • **a nasty bit** or piece of work a very unpleasant or malicious person. ⓘ 14c.

NAS/UWT ▷ *abbreviation* National Association of Schoolmasters/Union of Women Teachers.

Nat. ▷ *abbreviation* **1** National. **2** Nationalist.

nat ▷ *noun, colloq* a NATIONALIST.

nat. ▷ *abbreviation* **1** national. **2** native. **3** natural.

natal[1] /ˈneɪtəl/ ▷ *adj* **1** connected with birth. **2** *rare* native. • **natality** *noun* (***natalities***) **1** birth. **2** birth-rate. ⓘ 15c; 14c in obsolete sense 'presiding over birthdays': from Latin *natalis*, from *nasci, natus* to be born.

natal[2] see under NATES

natal therapy ▷ *noun* in psychoanalysis: the treatment of REBIRTHING.

natation /nəˈteɪʃən, neɪˈteɪʃən/ ▷ *noun, formal* swimming. ⓒ 17c: from Latin *natatio*, from *natare* to swim.

natatorial /neɪtəˈtɔːrɪəl/ and **natatory** ▷ *adj, formal or technical* **1** relating to swimming. **2** having the habit of swimming. **3** adapted or used for swimming. ⓒ 19c; 18c natatory: from Latin *natatorius*.

natch /nɑːtʃ/ ▷ *adverb, slang* of course. ⓒ 1940s: short for NATURALLY.

nates /ˈneɪtiːz/ ▷ *plural noun, anatomy* the buttocks. • **natal** /ˈneɪtəl/ *adj*. ⓒ 18c: Latin, plural of *natis* buttock.

nation /ˈneɪʃən/ ▷ *noun* **1** the people living in, belonging to, and together forming, a single state. **2** a race of people of common descent, history, language or culture, etc, but not necessarily bound by defined territorial limits of a state. **3** a Native American tribe or federation of tribes. • **nationhood** *noun*. ⓒ 13c: French, from Latin *natio* tribe.

national /ˈnaʃənəl/ ▷ *adj* **1** belonging to a particular nation. **2** concerning or covering the whole nation. **3** public; general. ▷ *noun* **1** a citizen of a particular nation. **2** a national newspaper. **3** (**the National**) *Brit* the GRAND NATIONAL. • **nationally** *adverb*.

national anthem ▷ *noun* a nation's official song.

national bank ▷ *noun, US* a commercial bank chartered by the Federal government and required by law to be a member of the Federal Reserve System.

national call ▷ *noun* a long-distance telephone call made within Britain, but outside the local area.

national code see AUSTRALIAN RULES

National Curriculum ▷ *noun, education* (abbreviation **NC**) the curriculum prescribed by the government to be used in maintained schools in England and Wales since 1989 (the curriculum established in Scotland is called 5–14).

national debt ▷ *noun* the money borrowed by the government of a country and not yet repaid.

National Front ▷ *noun* an extreme right-wing British political party with racist and fascist policies, first formed in 1960.

national grid ▷ *noun* **1** the network of high-voltage electric power lines in Britain. **2** the system of vertical and horizontal lines, or co-ordinates, used in Ordnance Survey maps of Britain.

National Guard ▷ *noun* **1** *US* an organized military force in individual states. **2** *historical* an armed force that took part in the French Revolution, first formed in 1789.

National Health Service ▷ *noun, Brit* (abbreviation **NHS**) the system set up in 1948 to provide medical treatment for all UK residents free, or at a nominal charge, at the point of delivery, financed mainly by taxation.

national insurance ▷ *noun, Brit* (abbreviation **NI**) a system of state insurance to which employers and employees contribute, to provide for the sick, unemployed and retired, and those on maternity leave.

nationalism ▷ *noun* **1** extreme pride in the history, culture and successes, etc of one's nation; loyalty to one's nation; patriotism. **2** extreme or fanatical patriotism. **3** a policy of, or movement aiming at, national unity or independence. • **nationalist** *noun, adj*. • **nationalistic** *adj* characterized by nationalism or excessive patriotism. • **nationalistically** *adverb*.

nationality /naʃəˈnalɪtɪ/ ▷ *noun* (***nationalities***) **1** the status of citizenship of a particular nation. **2** a group or set that has the character of a nation. **3** the racial or national group to which one belongs. **4** national character.

nationalize or **nationalise** ▷ *verb* (***nationalized, nationalizing***) **1** to bring (eg an industry) under state ownership and control. **2** to make something national. **3** to NATURALIZE. • **nationalization** *noun*.

National Lottery ▷ *noun* in the UK: a nationwide lottery, established in 1994, in which players choose six numbers between 1 and 49 and pay £1 for each chosen set. The lottery is run by a private company and a small proportion of the profits are set aside in a fund for the arts, sports, charitable organizations, etc.

nationally see under NATIONAL

national park ▷ *noun* an area of countryside, usually important for its natural beauty, wildlife, etc, under the ownership and care of the nation.

National Savings Bank ▷ *noun* a savings bank run by the government.

national service ▷ *noun* a period of compulsory service for young men in the armed forces, abolished in Britain in 1962, but in force in many countries.

National Socialism ▷ *noun* the doctrines and policies of the **National Socialist Party**, an extreme nationalistic fascist party led by Adolf Hitler, which ruled Germany from 1933–45. Also called NAZISM (see under NAZI).

National Trust and **National Trust for Scotland** ▷ *noun* charitable organizations concerned with preserving historic buildings and monuments, and areas of natural beauty, in the United Kingdom.

nationwide ▷ *adj* extending over the whole of a nation □ *nationwide coverage*. ▷ *adverb* with a coverage extending over the whole of a nation □ *The scheme will go nationwide next week*.

native /ˈneɪtɪv/ ▷ *adj* **1** being or belonging to the place of one's upbringing. **2** born a citizen of a particular place □ *a native Italian*. **3** belonging naturally to one; inborn or innate □ *native wit*. **4** having a particular language as one's first, or mother, tongue □ *my native tongue*. **5** originating in a particular place □ *native to China*. **6** belonging to the original inhabitants of a country □ *native Balinese music*. **7** natural; in a natural state. **8** said of metals: **a** occurring naturally as a mineral, ie not manufactured; **b** found naturally uncombined as an element, not as eg an ore. ▷ *noun* **1** someone born in a certain place. **2** a plant or animal originating in a particular place. **3** *often derog* one of the original inhabitants of a place as distinct from later, especially European, settlers. • **natively** *adverb*. • **nativeness** *noun*. • **go native** see under GO. ⓒ 14c: from Latin *nativus* natural, from *nasci* to be born.

Native American see AMERICAN INDIAN

native bear ▷ *noun, Austral* the KOALA.

native-born ▷ *adj* born in the country or place specified.

native companion see under BROLGA

native land ▷ *noun* the land to which someone belongs by birth.

native language ▷ *noun* the first language that someone learns, usually that of their native land.

native rock ▷ *noun* unquarried rock.

native speaker ▷ *noun* someone who speaks the language in question as their native language.

nativism /ˈneɪtɪvɪzəm/ ▷ *noun* **1** the belief that the mind possesses some ideas or forms of thought that are inborn. **2** the policy of favouring the natives of a country over immigrants. **3** the policy of protecting and encouraging native culture under threat from external influences. • **nativist** *noun*. • **nativistic** *adj*.

nativity /nəˈtɪvɪtɪ/ ▷ *noun* (***nativities***) **1** birth, advent or origin. **2** (**Nativity**) **a** the birth of Christ; **b** a picture representing it; **c** Christmas. ⓒ 14c: from Latin *nativitas* birth.

NATO or **Nato** /ˈneɪtoʊ/ ▷ *abbreviation* North Atlantic Treaty Organization, an international organization established in 1949, made up of US, Canada and a group of European states, having the aim of maintaining international peace.

NATO phonetic alphabet

This is the set of names used by the military and the police force in radio communication to identify letters of the alphabet.

letter	codename	pronunciation
A	Alpha	/ˈalfə/
B	Bravo	/ˈbrɑːvoʊ/
C	Charlie	/ˈtʃɑːlɪ/
D	Delta	/ˈdɛltə/
E	Echo	/ˈɛkoʊ/
F	Foxtrot	/ˈfɒkstrɒt/
G	Golf	/gɒlf/
H	Hotel	/hoʊˈtɛl/
I	India	/ˈɪndɪə/
J	Juliet	/ˈdʒuːlɪət/
K	Kilo	/ˈkiːloʊ/
L	Lima	/ˈliːmə/
M	Mike	/maɪk/
N	November	/noʊˈvɛmbə(r)/
O	Oscar	/ˈɒskə(r)/
P	Papa	/pəˈpɑː/
Q	Quebec	/kəˈbɛk/
R	Romeo	/ˈroʊmɪoʊ/
S	Sierra	/sɪˈɛrə/
T	Tango	/ˈtaŋgoʊ/
U	Uniform	/ˈjuːnɪfɔːm/
V	Victor	/ˈvɪktə(r)/
W	Whisky	/ˈwɪskɪ/
X	Xray	/ˈɛksreɪ/
Y	Yankee	/ˈjaŋkiː/
Z	Zulu	/ˈzuːluː/

natter /ˈnatə(r)/ *colloq* ▷ *verb* (***nattered, nattering***) *intr* to chat busily. ▷ *noun* an intensive chat. ◷ 19c: imitating the sound of chattering.

natterjack /ˈnatədʒak/ ▷ *noun, zool* a European toad with a yellow stripe down its spine and a rough green skin. ◷ 18c.

natty /ˈnatɪ/ ▷ *adj* (***nattier, nattiest***) *colloq* **1** said of clothes: flashily smart. **2** clever; ingenious. ● **nattily** *adverb* in a neat and smart manner □ *He was nattily dressed.* ● **nattiness** *noun.* ◷ 18c: related to NEAT.

natural /ˈnatʃərəl/ ▷ *adj* **1** normal; unsurprising. **2** instinctive; not learnt. **3** born in one; innate □ *a natural talent.* **4** being such because of inborn qualities □ *Christian is a natural communicator.* **5** said of manner, etc: simple, easy and direct; not artificial. **6** said of looks: not, or apparently not, improved on artificially. **7** relating to nature, or to parts of the physical world not made or altered by man □ *natural sciences* □ *areas of natural beauty.* **8** following the normal course of nature □ *died a natural death.* **9** said of materials, products, etc: derived from plants and animals as opposed to man-made □ *natural fibres.* **10** wild; uncultivated or uncivilized. **11** related to one by blood □ *one's natural parents.* **12** *euphemistic* see illegitimate □ *his natural son.* **13** *music* not sharp or flat. ▷ *noun* **1** *colloq* someone with an inborn feel for something □ *She's a natural when it comes to acting.* **2** a person or thing that is the obvious choice for something. **3** someone or something that is assured of success; a certainty. **4** *music* **a** a sign (♮) indicating a note that is not to be played sharp or flat; **b** such a note. ● **naturalness** *noun* a natural state or quality; being natural. ◷ 14c: from Latin *naturalis* from *natura* nature.

natural-born ▷ *adj* native □ *natural-born Scot.*

natural childbirth ▷ *noun* childbirth with as little medical intervention as possible, especially in terms of analgesia.

natural frequency ▷ *noun* **1** *physics* the frequency at which an object or system will vibrate freely, in the absence of external forces. **2** *elec* the frequency at which resonance occurs in an electrical circuit.

natural gas ▷ *noun* a gas mixture, mainly methane, found under the ground or sea-bed in petroleum-bearing regions, used as a fuel.

natural history ▷ *noun* an increasingly antiquated broad scientific term for the popular study of plants, animals and minerals.

natural immunity ▷ *noun* the level of resistance to infection, with which a person is born. Compare ACQUIRED IMMUNITY.

naturalism ▷ *noun* **1** a realistic, as opposed to idealistic, treatment of subjects in art or sculpture, etc. **2** the view that rejects supernatural explanations of phenomena, maintaining that all must be attributable to natural causes.

naturalist /ˈnatʃərəlɪst/ ▷ *noun* **1** someone who studies animal and plant life (NATURAL HISTORY). **2** a follower of naturalism.

naturalistic ▷ *adj* characterized by naturalism, or the realistic treatment of subjects in art and literature. ● **naturalistically** *adverb.*

naturalize or **naturalise** /ˈnatʃərəlaɪz/ ▷ *verb* (***naturalized, naturalizing***) **1** to confer citizenship on (a foreigner). **2** *tr & intr* to gradually come to be considered as (a word) that is part of a language, as opposed to being used in that language as a foreign word. **3** to gradually admit (a custom) among established traditions. **4** to make (an introduced species of plant or animal) adapt to the local environment. **5** *intr* said of a plant or animal: to adapt to a new environment. **6** to make something natural or lifelike. ● **naturalization** *noun* the process of naturalizing, especially conferring citizenship. ◷ 16c.

natural language ▷ *noun* a language which has evolved naturally. Compare ARTIFICIAL LANGUAGE.

natural logarithm ▷ *noun, math* a logarithm to the base constant *e* (2.718…).

naturally ▷ *adverb* **1** of course; not surprisingly. **2** in accordance with the normal course of things. **3** by nature; as a natural characteristic □ *Sympathy came naturally to her.* **4** by means of a natural process, as opposed to being produced by a man-made process. **5** in a relaxed or normal manner.

naturalness see under NATURAL

natural number ▷ *noun, math* any whole positive number, sometimes including zero.

natural philosophy ▷ *noun* physics, or physics together with dynamics.

natural resources ▷ *plural noun* sources of energy and wealth that occur naturally in the earth.

natural science ▷ *noun* the science of nature (including biology, chemistry, geology and physics) as distinguished from mental and moral science, and from mathematics.

natural selection ▷ *noun* the process by which plant and animal species that adapt most successfully to their environment survive, while others die out; the basis for EVOLUTION. See also DARWINISM.

natural theology ▷ *noun* religion based on reasoned facts rather than revelation, etc.

natural wastage ▷ *noun, business* non-replacement of employees that leave or retire, as a means of reducing staffing levels.

nature /ˈneɪtʃə(r)/ ▷ *noun* **1** (*also* **Nature**) the physical world not made by man; the forces that have formed it and control it. **2** animal and plant life as distinct from human life. **3** what something is, or consists of. **4** a fundamental tendency; essential character; attitude or outlook □ *human nature* □ *quiet and retiring by nature.* **5** a kind, sort or type. ● **from nature** using natural models in drawing or sculpting, etc. • **in the nature of something** with the characteristics of it; like it. ◎ 13c: from Latin *natura*.

nature cure ▷ *noun* the practice of or treatment by NATUROPATHY.

nature reserve ▷ *noun* an area of land specially managed and protected to preserve the flora and fauna that live in it.

nature strip ▷ *noun, Austral* a strip of grass, etc bordering a road or footpath or dividing two carriageways.

nature study ▷ *noun* the study, usually amateur study, of plants and animals.

nature trail ▷ *noun* a signposted walk or path in the countryside that provides opportunities for studying nature.

naturism /ˈneɪtʃərɪzəm/ ▷ *noun* **1** nudism, regarded as a natural instinct. **2** the worship of natural objects. • **naturist** *noun* a nudist. ◎ 1930s in sense 1.

naturopathy /neɪtʃəˈrɒpəθɪ, natʃə-/ ▷ *noun* **1** the promotion of good health and natural healing by a system of diet, exercise, manipulation and hydrotherapy. **2** the philosophy of this system. • **naturopath** /-paθ/ *noun* someone who practises naturopathy. • **naturopathic** *adj*. ◎ Early 20c.

naught /nɔːt/ ▷ *noun* **1** *old use* nothing. **2** *N Amer, especially US* NOUGHT. • **come to naught** *old use* to fail. • **set something at naught** *old use* to despise it. ◎ 14c: Anglo-Saxon *nawiht*, from *na* no + *wiht* thing.

naughty /ˈnɔːtɪ/ ▷ *adj* (***naughtier***, ***naughtiest***) **1** mischievous; disobedient. **2** mildly shocking or indecent; titillating □ *a naughty photo*. ▷ *noun* (***naughties***) *Austral & NZ colloq* an act of sexual intercourse. • **naughtily** *adverb*. • **naughtiness** *noun*. ◎ 16c in these senses; from NAUGHT in its earlier sense 'wickedness'.

nauplius /ˈnɔːplɪəs/ ▷ *noun* (***nauplii*** /-plɪaɪ/) *zool* the larval form of many crustaceans, with one eye and three pairs of limbs. ◎ 19c: Latin, meaning 'a kind of shellfish', from Greek Nauplios a son of Poseidon, from *naus* a ship + *pleein* to sail.

nausea /ˈnɔːzɪə, ˈnɔːsɪə/ ▷ *noun* **1** a sensation that one is about to vomit, either by a reflex (eg irritation of stomach nerves) or conditioned (eg smell) stimulus. **2** disgust; revulsion. ◎ 16c: from Greek *nausia* seasickness, from *naus* ship.

nauseate /ˈnɔːzɪeɪt, ˈnɔːsɪ-/ ▷ *verb* (***nauseated***, ***nauseating***) **1** to make someone feel nausea. **2** to disgust someone. • **nauseating** *adj* **1** offensively unpleasant. **2** causing nausea. • **nauseatingly** *adverb* to a nauseating degree; repulsively. ◎ 17c: from Latin *nauseare* to be seasick.

nauseous /ˈnɔːzɪəs, ˈnɔːsɪəs/ ▷ *adj* **1** sickening; disgusting □ *a nauseous smell*. **2** affected by nausea □ *The drugs made him nauseous*. • **nauseously** *adverb*. • **nauseousness** *noun*. ◎ 17c: from Latin *nauseosus*.

naut. ▷ *abbreviation* nautical.

nautical /ˈnɔːtɪkəl/ ▷ *adj* (abbreviation **naut.**) relating to ships, sailors or navigation. • **nautically** *adverb*. ◎ 17c: from Greek *nautikos*, from *nautes* sailor.

nautical mile ▷ *noun* (abbreviation **n mile**) a measure of distance traditionally used at sea, equal to about 1.85km. See also KNOT (*noun* 11).

nautilus /ˈnɔːtɪləs/ ▷ *noun* (***nautiluses*** or ***nautili*** /-ɪlaɪ/) a sea creature related to the squid and octopus, especially the **pearly nautilus** which has a spiral chambered shell that is pearly on its interior, or the PAPER NAUTILUS. ◎ 17c: from Greek *nautilos* sailor or pearly nautilus.

NAV ▷ *abbreviation* net asset value.

nav. ▷ *abbreviation* **1** naval. **2** navigable. **3** navigation. **4** navigator.

Navajo or **Navaho** /ˈnavəhoʊ/ ▷ *noun* (***Navajos*** or ***Navahos***) **1** a Native American people of Utah, Arizona and New Mexico. **2** one of these people. **3** the language of these people. ◎ 18c: from Spanish *Navajó*, the name of a particular PUEBLO.

naval /ˈneɪvəl/ ▷ *adj* relating to a navy or to ships generally. ◎ 17c: from Latin *navalis*, from *navis* ship.

naval architecture ▷ *noun* the designing of ships.

naval officer ▷ *noun* an officer in the navy.

navarin /ˈnavərɪn/ ▷ *noun, cookery* a stew of lamb or mutton with root vegetables such as turnip. ◎ 19c: French.

nave¹ /neɪv/ ▷ *noun, archit* the main central part of a church, where the congregation sits. ◎ 17c: from Latin *navis* ship, from its similarity to an inverted hull.

nave² /neɪv/ ▷ *noun* the hub or central part of a wheel. ◎ Anglo-Saxon *nafu*.

navel /ˈneɪvəl/ ▷ *noun* **1** in mammals: the small hollow or scar at the point where the umbilical cord was attached to the fetus. **2** the central point of something. ◎ Anglo-Saxon *nafela*, diminutive of *nafu* hub.

navel-gazing ▷ *noun* unproductive self-analysis when direction action is called for.

navel orange ▷ *noun* a seedless orange with a navel-like pit on top enclosing a second smaller fruit.

navelwort ▷ *noun, bot* pennywort.

navicular /nəˈvɪkjʊlə(r)/ ▷ *adj* **1** boat-shaped. **2** *zool* relating to the **navicular bone**. ▷ *noun* (*in full* **navicular bone**) a small boat-shaped bone in the wrist or ankle, or in the equivalent position in animals, eg horses. Also called **scaphoid**. ◎ 16c: from Latin *navicula*, diminutive of *navis* a ship.

navigable /ˈnavɪgəbəl/ ▷ *adj* **1** said of a river or channel, etc: able to be sailed along or through, etc. **2** said of a ship: seaworthy. **3** said of a balloon or other craft: steerable. • **navigability** *noun*. • **navigably** *adverb*. ◎ 16c: from Latin *navigabilis*, from *navigare* to sail.

navigate /ˈnavɪgeɪt/ ▷ *verb* (***navigated***, ***navigating***) **1** *intr* to direct the course of a ship, aircraft or other vehicle. **2** *intr* to find one's way and hold one's course. **3** to steer (a ship or aircraft). **4 a** to manage to sail along or through (a river or channel, etc); **b** to find one's way through, along, over or across something, etc. **5** *intr* said of a vehicle passenger: to give the driver directions on the correct route. ◎ 16c: from Latin *navigare*, from *navis* ship.

navigation ▷ *noun* **1** the act, skill or science of navigating. **2** the movement of ships and aircraft. • **navigational** *adj*.

navigator ▷ *noun* **1** someone who navigates, especially a ship or aircraft. **2** *old use* an explorer by sea.

navvy /ˈnavɪ/ ▷ *noun* (***navvies***) a labourer, especially one employed in road-building or canal-building, etc. ▷ *verb* (***navvied***, ***navvying***) *intr* to work as or like a navvy. ◎ 19c: from NAVIGATION in its earlier sense 'canal'.

navy /ˈneɪvɪ/ ▷ *noun* (***navies***) **1** (*often* **the Navy**) **a** the warships of a state, usually considered together with the officers and other personnel manning them; **b** the organization to which they belong, ie one of the three armed services. Compare ARMY 2, AIR FORCE. **2** a body or fleet of ships with their crews. Often *in compounds* □ *the merchant navy*. **3** (*also* **navy blue**) a dark blue colour, typically used for naval uniforms. ▷ *adj* (*also* **navy-blue**) having a navy blue in colour. ◎ 14c *navie*: from French *navie*, from Latin *navis* ship.

Navy List ▷ *noun* the list of all the commissioned officers in the Royal Navy.

navy yard ▷ *noun, especially US* a government dockyard.

nawab /nə'wɑːb, nə'wɔːb/ ▷ *noun, historical* a Muslim ruler or landowner in India. See also NABOB. ⓘ 18c: from Urdu *nawwab*, from Arabic *nuwwab*, plural of *na'ib* viceroy.

nay /neɪ/ ▷ *exclamation, old use or dialect* **1** no. **2** rather; to put it more strongly □ *a misfortune, nay, a tragedy.* ▷ *noun* (***nays***) **1** the word 'no'. **2** *formal* especially in parliament: **a** someone who casts a negative vote □ *Nays to the left, ayes to the right*; **b** a vote against. Compare AYE. • **say someone nay** to contradict, or refuse something to, them. ⓘ 12c as *nei*: from Norse.

Nazarene /'nazəriːn, nazə'riːn/ ▷ *adj* belonging to Nazareth. ▷ *noun* **1** someone from Nazareth. **2** (**the Nazarene**) *historical* Jesus Christ. **3** *historical* a Christian. ⓘ 13c: from Greek *Nazarenos.*

Nazarite /'nazəraɪt/ ▷ *noun* **1** (*also* **Nazirite**) a Jewish ASCETIC under a vow in ancient Israel. **2** a NAZARENE. ⓘ 16c: from Hebrew *nazar* to consecrate.

naze /neɪz/ ▷ *noun* a headland or cape. ⓘ 18c: from earlier *næs* in placenames.

Nazi /'nɑːtsɪ/ ▷ *noun* (***Nazis***) **1** *historical* a member of the German NATIONAL SOCIALIST PARTY, which came to power in Germany in 1933 under Adolf Hitler. **2** *derog colloq* someone with extreme racist and dogmatic opinions. • **Nazification** *noun*. • **Nazified** *adj* referring to a person or nation, etc that has adopted Nazism. • **Nazism** *noun* the principles of the Nazis; the Nazi movement. ⓘ 1930s: German contraction of *Nationalsozialist.*

NB ▷ *abbreviation* **1** *US state* Nebraska. Also written **Neb.** or **Nebr. 2** *Canadian province* New Brunswick. **3** *historical* North Britain; Scotland. **4** (*also* **nb**) *nota bene* (Latin), note well; take note.

Nb ▷ *symbol, chem* niobium.

NBA ▷ *abbreviation* Net Book Agreement, an agreement within the book trade that books should not be sold at less than the price fixed by the publisher. It was made in 1900 and upheld until 1995.

NBC ▷ *abbreviation* **1** in the US: National Broadcasting Company. **2** nuclear, biological and chemical (warfare, weapons, etc).

NBC suit ▷ *noun* a suit that protects against the physical effects of **NBC weapons**, nuclear, biological and chemical weapons.

NC ▷ *abbreviation* **1** National Curriculum. **2** *US state* North Carolina. Also written **N.C. 3** numerical control.

nc ▷ *abbreviation* no charge.

NCC ▷ *abbreviation* **1** National Curriculum Council. **2** Nature Conservancy Council.

NCCL ▷ *abbreviation* National Council for Civil Liberties.

NCO ▷ *noun* (***NCOs*** or ***NCO's***) non-commissioned officer.

NCP ▷ *abbreviation, Austral* National Country Party.

NCT ▷ *abbreviation* National Childbirth Trust.

NCVQ ▷ *abbreviation* National Council for Vocational Qualifications.

ND ▷ *abbreviation, US State* North Dakota. Also written **N.D.** or **N.Dak.**

Nd ▷ *symbol, chem* neodymium.

nd ▷ *abbreviation* no date.

NE ▷ *abbreviation* **1** *US State* Nebraska. Also written **Neb** or **Nebr. 2** New England. Also written **N.E. 3** north-east. **4** north-eastern.

Ne ▷ *symbol, chem* neon.

né /neɪ/ ▷ *adj* used in giving the original name of a titled man: born. Compare NÉE. ⓘ Early 20c: French.

Neanderthal /nɪ'andətɑːl/ ▷ *adj* **1** denoting a primitive type of man living in Europe during the PALAEOLITHIC period of the Stone Age, who had a receding forehead and prominent brow ridges. **2** (*sometimes* **neanderthal**) *colloq* primitive. **3** (*sometimes* **neanderthal**) *colloq* extremely old-fashioned and reactionary. ⓘ 19c: from Neandertal, a valley in Germany where remains were first found.

Neapolitan /nɪə'pɒlɪtən/ ▷ *adj* relating to the city or the former kingdom of Naples. ▷ *noun* a citizen or inhabitant of, or person born in, Naples. ⓘ 17c: from Greek *Neapolis* new town.

Neapolitan ice and **Neapolitan ice cream** ▷ *noun* ice cream made in layers of different colours and flavours. ⓘ 19c.

Neapolitan violet ▷ *noun* a scented double variety of sweet violet.

neap tide and **neap** ▷ *noun* a tide occurring at the first and last quarters of the Moon, when there is the least variation between high and low water. Compare SPRING TIDE. ⓘ Anglo-Saxon *nepflod* neap flood.

near /nɪə(r)/ ▷ *prep* (***nearer, nearest***) **1** at a short distance from something □ *lives near the town centre.* **2** close to something (in amount, etc) □ *nearer 600 than 500* □ *near tears.* ▷ *adverb* (***nearer, nearest***) **1** (*also* **near to**) close □ *came near to hitting her.* **2** *old use* or *colloq in compounds* almost; nearly □ *She damn near died.* ▷ *adj* (***nearer, nearest***) **1** being a short distance away; close. **2** closer of two □ *the near bank of the river.* **3** similar; comparable □ *that knife is the nearest thing I've got to a screwdriver.* **4** closely related to one □ *a near relative.* **5** *often in compounds* almost amounting to, or almost turning into the specified thing □ *a near tragedy* □ *near-disastrous results.* **6** *old use* mean; miserly. ▷ *verb* (***neared, nearing***) *tr & intr* to approach. • **nearly** see separate entry. • **nearness** *noun*. • **near as dammit** or **as near as damn it** *colloq* very nearly. • **near at hand** conveniently close. • **not to go near someone** or **something** to avoid them. ⓘ Anglo-Saxon, from *neah* nigh, and from (*adverb*) Norse *nær* nigher, from *na* NIGH.

near beer ▷ *noun, US* any of several beers containing 1/2 per cent alcohol or less. Compare LOW-ALCOHOL.

nearby ▷ *adj, adverb* a short distance away; close at hand.

Nearctic /nɪ'ɑːktɪk/ ▷ *adj* in zoogeography: referring to the region that includes the part of N America to the north of the Tropic of Cancer, and Greenland. ⓘ 19c: from Greek *neos* new + *arktikos* northern.

near-death experience ▷ *noun* an instance, when apparently on the brink of death, of experiencing, from outside the body, the situation and circumstances of dying.

Near East ▷ *noun* **1** MIDDLE EAST. **2** *formerly* an area including the Balkans and Turkey, and sometimes the countries to the west of Iran.

nearly ▷ *adverb* almost. • **not nearly** very far from; nothing like □ *not nearly finished.* ⓘ 16c; see NEAR.

near miss ▷ *noun* **1** something not quite achieved, eg a shot that almost hits the target. **2** something (eg an air collision) only just avoided.

nearness see under NEAR

nearside ▷ *noun* the side of a vehicle, horse or team of horses nearer the kerb, ie in the UK the left side, and in most other countries the right side. Also *as adj* □ *the nearside front tyre.*

near-sighted ▷ *adj* short-sighted. • **near-sightedness** *noun*.

near thing ▷ *noun* a narrow escape; a success only just achieved.

neat[1] /niːt/ ▷ *adj* (***neater, neatest***) **1** tidy; clean; orderly. **2** pleasingly small or regular. **3** elegantly or cleverly simple □ *a neat explanation.* **4** skilful or efficient □ *Neat work!* **5** *N Amer* excellent □ *That's neat!* **6** said especially of an alcoholic drink: undiluted. • **neatly** *adverb.* • **neatness** *noun.* ⓒ 16c: from French *net* clean or tidy.

neat² /niːt/ ▻ *noun* (*plural* ***neat***) *archaic or dialect* an ox, bull or cow, etc. ⓒ Anglo-Saxon meaning 'a beast' or 'cattle', from *neotan* to use.

neaten ▻ *verb* (***neatened, neatening***) to make something neat and tidy. ⓒ 16c.

neath or **'neath** /niːθ/ ▻ *prep, dialect or poetry* beneath. ⓒ 18: shortened form of older *aneath* or BENEATH.

NEB ▻ *abbreviation* **1** National Enterprise Board. **2** New English Bible.

Neb. see under NB

neb *Scots & N Eng* ▻ *noun* **1** a beak or bill. **2** the nose. **3** the sharp point, or a projecting part, of something. ▻ *verb* (***nebbed, nebbing***) *intr* to look around in a nosey way with the hope of seeing something to gossip about. ⓒ Anglo-Saxon *nebb* beak or face.

nebbich /ˈnɛbɪx/, **nebbish** or **nebish** /ˈnɛbɪʃ/ ▻ *noun* (***nebbiches, nebbishes*** or ***nebishes***) an insignificant person; an incompetent person; a perpetual victim. ⓒ 19c: Yiddish.

Nebr. see under NB

nebula /ˈnɛbjʊlə/ ▻ *noun* (***nebulae*** /-liː/ or ***nebulas***) *astron* **1** a luminous or dark patch in space representing a mass of dust or particles. **2** *old use* the luminous mass of a remote star cluster. • **nebular** *adj.* ⓒ 17c: Latin, meaning 'mist'.

nebulizer /ˈnɛbjʊlaɪzə(r)/ ▻ *noun, medicine* a device, either hand-operated or electrical, with a mouthpiece or facemask through which a drug is administered in the form of a fine mist. See also INHALER. ⓒ 19c: from *nebulize* to make into mist, from Latin *nebula* mist.

nebulous /ˈnɛbjʊləs/ ▻ *adj* vague; hazy; lacking distinct shape, form or nature. • **nebulously** *adverb.* • **nebulousness** *noun.* ⓒ 19c in this sense: from Latin *nebulosus*, from *nebula* mist.

NEC ▻ *abbreviation* **1** National Executive Committee. **2** National Exhibition Centre, in Birmingham.

necessarily /nɛsəˈsɛrɪlɪ/ ▻ *adverb* as a necessary or inevitable result; for certain □ *It won't necessarily rain.*

necessary /ˈnɛsəsərɪ/ ▻ *adj* **1** needed; essential; indispensable; that must be done. **2** that must be; inevitable; inescapable □ *a necessary evil.* **3** logically required or unavoidable. **4** said eg of an agent: not free. ▻ *noun* (***necessaries***) **1** (*usually* **necessaries**) something that is necessary; an essential item. **2** (**the necessary**) *humorous, colloq* **a** money needed for a purpose; **b** action that must be taken. ⓒ 14c: from Latin *necessarius*, from *necesse*.

necessitarianism /nəsɛsɪˈtɛərɪənɪzəm/ and **necessarianism** ▻ *noun, philos* the theory that human actions are determined by precursory circumstances and cannot be willed. • **necessitarian** or **necessarian** *adj, noun.* ⓒ 19c.

necessitate /nəˈsɛsɪtaɪt/ ▻ *verb* (***necessitated, necessitating***) **1** to make something necessary or unavoidable. **2** to compel someone to do something. ⓒ 17c: from Latin *necessitare*, from *necessitas* necessity.

necessitate

☆ PLAIN ENGLISH alternatives: **need, require, demand, involve, entail, call for.**

necessity /nəˈsɛsɪtɪ/ ▻ *noun* (***necessities***) **1** something necessary or essential. **2** circumstances that make something necessary, obligatory or unavoidable □ *from necessity rather than choice.* **3** a pressing need □ *no necessity to rush.* **4** poverty; want; need. • **of necessity** necessarily; unavoidably. ⓒ 14c: from Latin *necessitas.*

neck ▻ *noun* **1** the part of the body between the head and the shoulders. **2** the part of a garment at or covering the neck. **3** a narrow part; a narrow connecting part □ *joined to the mainland by a neck of land.* **4** *horse-racing* a head-and-neck's length; a small margin □ *won by a neck.* **5** the meat from the neck of an animal. **6** *colloq* impudence; boldness. ▻ *verb* (***necked, necking***) *tr & intr, slang* to hug and kiss amorously. • **get it in the neck** *colloq* to be severely rebuked or punished. • **neck and neck** said of competitors in a race or election, etc: exactly level. • **neck or nothing** risking everything. • **risk one's neck** see under RISK. • **save one's** or **someone's neck** or **skin** see under SAVE. • **stick one's neck out** see under STICK. • **up to one's neck in something** *colloq* deeply involved in (*especially* a troublesome situation); busy; preoccupied. ⓒ Anglo-Saxon *hnecca.*

neckband ▻ *noun* **1** a band or strip of material sewn round the neck of a garment to finish it, or as the base for a collar. **2** a band worn around the neck.

neckcloth ▻ *noun* a piece of cloth, usually white, or sometimes a piece of lace, folded and worn around the neck by men.

neckerchief /ˈnɛkətʃɪf, -tʃiːf/ ▻ *noun* (***neckerchiefs*** or ***neckerchieves***) a cloth worn round the neck. ⓒ 14c as *necke couercheues*; 17c in modern form: NECK + KERCHIEF.

necking ▻ *noun* **1** *colloq* kissing and embracing. **2** *archit* the neck of a column. **3** *archit* a moulding between the capital and shaft of a column.

necklace /ˈnɛkləs/ ▻ *noun* **1** a string of beads or jewels, etc, or a chain, worn round the neck as jewellery. **2** (*also* **necklacing**) in S Africa: the punishment of having a tyre soaked in petrol placed around the neck or shoulders and set alight, traditionally used by Blacks to kill Blacks thought to be sympathizers or supporters of the government then enforcing APARTHEID. ▻ *verb* (***necklaced, necklacing***) in S Africa: to kill someone with a necklace. ⓒ 16c: NECK + LACE in the sense 'cord' or 'tie'.

necklet ▻ *noun* a simple necklace.

neckline ▻ *noun* the edge of a garment at the neck, or its shape.

neck of the woods ▻ *noun, humorous* a neighbourhood or locality.

necktie ▻ *noun, especially N Amer* a man's TIE.

neckwear ▻ *noun* ties, scarves or other articles of clothing worn around the neck.

necro- /nɛkroʊ, nɛkrə, nɛˈkrɒ/ or (before a vowel) **necr-** *combining form, denoting* **1** dead. **2** dead body. **3** dead tissue. ⓒ From Greek *nekros* a dead body.

necrobiosis ▻ *noun, pathol* the natural degeneration and death of a cell. • **necrobiotic** *adj.* ⓒ Late 19c: see -BIOSIS.

necromancer *noun* **1** someone who practises necromancy or divination. **2** a magician; a sorcerer.

necromancy /ˈnɛkroʊmansɪ/ ▻ *noun* **1** divination or prophecy through communication with the dead. **2** black magic; sorcery; enchantment. • **necromantic** *adj.* • **necromantically** *adverb.* ⓒ 14c as *nigramanci*: from Latin *nigromantia*, from Greek *nekros* corpse + *mantis* prophet.

necrophagous /nɛˈkrɒfəgəs/ ▻ *adj* said of an animal or bird, etc: feeding on carrion. ⓒ 19c.

necrophilia ▻ *noun* obsessive interest, especially of an erotic kind, in dead bodies. • **necrophilic** *adj.* ⓒ 19c; see -PHILIA.

necrophiliac /nɛkroʊˈfɪlɪak/ or **necrophile** /ˈnɛkroʊfaɪl/ *noun* someone with an obsessive, especially an erotic, interest in dead bodies.

necrophobia ▻ *noun* a morbid horror of corpses. ⓒ 19c.

necropolis /nɛˈkrɒpəlɪs/ ▷ *noun* (***necropolises*** or ***necropoleis*** /-leɪs/) *archaeol* a cemetery or a burial site. ◷ 19c: from Greek *nekros* corpse + *polis* city.

necropsy /ˈnɛkrɒpsɪ, nɛˈkrɒpsɪ/ or **necroscopy** /-skɒpɪ/ ▷ *noun* (***necropsies*** or ***necroscopies***) a post-mortem examination. • **necroscopic** /-skɒpɪk/ *adj.* ◷ 19c.

necrosis /nɛˈkroʊsɪs/ ▷ *noun* (***necroses*** /-siːz/) *pathol* the death of living tissue or bone, especially where the blood supply has been interrupted. • **necrotic** /nɛˈkrɒtɪk/ *adj.* ◷ 17c: Greek, from *nekros* corpse.

nectar /ˈnɛktə(r)/ ▷ *noun* **1** a sugary substance produced in the flowers of plants to attract pollinating insects and which is collected by bees to make honey. **2** *Greek mythol* the special drink of the gods giving life and beauty. Compare AMBROSIA 1. **3** any delicious drink. **4** anything delightfully welcome to the senses, especially taste or smell. • **nectarean** /nɛkˈtɛərɪən/, **nectareous** or **nectarous** /ˈnɛktərəs/ *adj.* ◷ 16c: from Greek *nektar*.

nectarine /ˈnɛktərɪn/ ▷ *noun* a variety of peach with a shiny downless skin. ◷ 17c, originally as *adj* meaning 'like nectar'.

nectary /ˈnɛktərɪ/ ▷ *noun* (***nectaries***) *bot* in flowering plants: a specialized gland, usually situated at the base of the flower, that secretes nectar. ◷ 18c.

ned ▷ *noun, Scots slang* a young hooligan; a disruptive male adolescent. ◷ 1950s: possibly a familiar shortening of Edward; see also TED.

NEDC ▷ *abbreviation* in the UK: National Economic Development Council, an advisory body on economic issues from 1962 to 1992. Also (*colloq*) called **Neddy.**

neddy /ˈnɛdɪ/ ▷ *noun* (***neddies***) **1** *colloq* a donkey. **2** *colloq* a fool. **3** *Austral slang* a racehorse. ◷ 18c: from the personal name Edward.

née or **nee** /neɪ/ ▷ *adj* used in giving a married woman's maiden name: born ▫ *Jane Day, née Osborn.* Compare NÉ. ◷ 18c: French *née*, feminine of *né* born.

need ▷ *verb* (***needed, needing***) **1** to lack; to require. **2** *intr* (also *as auxiliary verb* — see Usage Note) to be required or obliged to be or do something ▫ *We need to find a replacement* ▫ *They needn't stay.* ▷ *noun* **1** something one requires. **2** (**need of** or **for something**) a condition of lacking or requiring it; an urge or desire. **3** (**need for something**) necessity or justification for it. • **if need** or needs be if necessary. • **in need** needing help or financial support. See also NEEDS. ◷ Anglo-Saxon *nead* or *nied*.

need

Need may be used either as an ordinary intransitive verb or as an auxiliary verb.

• When **need** is used as an intransitive verb, the form of the verb accompanying 'he/she/it' ends in '-s', questions and negative statements are formed with the auxiliary verb 'do', and a following verb is preceded by 'to' ▫ *If he needs to go, I'll just have to let him* ▫ *You don't need to go* ▫ *I didn't need to see him at all* ▫ *Didn't you need to tell him something?*

• When **need** is used as an auxiliary verb, the verb accompanying 'he/she/it' has no '-s' ending, questions and negative statements are formed without 'do', and there is no 'to' before the following verb ▫ *She needn't go if she doesn't want to* ▫ *Need we tell her at all?* This auxiliary-verb construction is possible only in questions and negative statements in the present tense.

needful ▷ *adj* necessary. ▷ *noun* (**the needful**) *humorous, colloq* **1** whatever action is necessary. **2** money needed for a purpose. • **needfully** *adverb.* • **needfulness** *noun.*

needier, neediest and **neediness** see under NEEDY

needle /ˈniːdəl/ ▷ *noun* **1** a slender pointed steel sewing instrument with a hole for the thread. **2** a longer, thicker implement of metal, wood, bone or plastic, etc, without a hole, for knitting, crocheting, etc. **3 a** a hypodermic syringe; **b** its pointed end. **4** *medicine* a slender instrument for suturing and dissection, etc. **5** a gramophone STYLUS. **6** the moving pointer on a compass or other instrument. **7** anything slender, sharp and pointed. **8** a pinnacle of rock. **9** an obelisk. **10** a long slender crystal. **11** the needle-shaped leaf of a tree such as the pine or fir. **12** a strong beam passed through a wall as a temporary support. **13** (**the needle**) *colloq* **a** provocation; **b** irritation; anger; **c** dislike. ▷ *verb* (***needled, needling***) *tr & intr* **1** *colloq* to provoke or irritate someone, especially deliberately. **2** to sew. • **look for a needle in a haystack** to undertake a hopeless search. ◷ Anglo-Saxon *nædl*.

needle bank ▷ *noun* a place where dependent drug-users may exchange old hypodermic syringes for new ones, usually free of charge, to help prevent the spread of disease or infection.

needlecord ▷ *noun* a finely ribbed CORDUROY.

needlecraft ▷ *noun* the art of needlework.

needlepoint ▷ *noun* **1** embroidery on canvas. **2** lace made over a paper pattern, with needles rather than bobbins.

needless /ˈniːdləs/ ▷ *adj* unnecessary. • **needlessly** *adverb* without any need. • **needlessness** *noun.*

needle time ▷ *noun, broadcasting* the amount of time allowed to a radio channel for playing recorded music.

needlewoman ▷ *noun* a woman who sews; a seamstress.

needlework ▷ *noun* sewing and embroidery.

needn't /ˈniːdənt/ ▷ *contraction, colloq* need not.

needs /niːdz/ ▷ *adverb, old use* of necessity; inevitably ▫ *He needs must leave.* ▷ *plural noun* what is required; necessities ▫ *Her needs are modest.* • **needs must** or **needs must when the devil drives** if it is necessary one must do it, even if it is disagreeable. ◷ Anglo-Saxon from NEED.

needy /ˈniːdɪ/ ▷ *adj* (***needier, neediest***) in severe need; poverty-stricken; destitute. • **neediness** *noun.*

neep ▷ *noun, Scots* a turnip. ◷ 15c as Scots *neip*; Anglo-Saxon *næp*: from Latin *napus*.

ne'er /nɛə(r)/ ▷ *adverb, poetic* ▷ *contraction* never.

ne'er-do-well ▷ *adj* good-for-nothing. ▷ *noun* an idle irresponsible useless person. ◷ 18c.

NEF ▷ *abbreviation* National Energy Foundation.

nefarious /nɪˈfɛərɪəs/ ▷ *adj* wicked; evil. • **nefariously** *adverb.* • **nefariousness** *noun.* ◷ 17c: from Latin *nefarius*, from *nefas* a crime.

neg. ▷ *abbreviation* **1** negative. **2** negatively. **3** negotiable.

negate /nɪˈgeɪt/ ▷ *verb* (***negated, negating***) **1** to cancel or destroy the effect of something. **2** to deny the existence of something. ◷ 17c: from Latin *negare*, *negatum* to deny.

negation /nɪˈgeɪʃən/ ▷ *noun* **1** the act of negating. **2** the absence or opposite of something. **3** the denial of the existence of something. **4** *logic* a negative proposition.

negationist ▷ *noun* someone who merely denies something without offering any positive assertion.

negative /ˈnɛgətɪv/ ▷ *adj* **1** meaning or saying 'no'; expressing denial, refusal or prohibition. Opposite of AFFIRMATIVE. **2** said of people or attitudes, etc: unenthusiastic, defeatist or pessimistic. **3** *logic* denying the connection between a subject and a predicate. **4** *math* less than zero. **5** contrary to, or cancelling the effect of, whatever is regarded as positive. **6** *math* measured in the opposite direction to that chosen as positive. **7** *elec* having the kind of electric charge produced by an excess of electrons. **8** *photog* said of film: having the light and shade of the actual image reversed, or complementary colours in place of actual ones. **9** *biol* in a direction away from the source of stimulus. ▻ *noun* **1** a word, statement or grammatical form expressing denial □ *replied in the negative.* **2** a photographic film with a negative image, from which prints are made. ▻ *verb* (***negatived***, ***negativing***) **1** to reject something; to veto it. **2** to deny something. **3** to neutralize or cancel out something. **4** to disprove or prove the contrary of POSITIVE or AFFIRMATIVE. Compare POSITIVE. • **negatively** *adverb*. • **negativeness** or **negativity** *noun*. ⓒ 16c: from Latin *negativus*, from *negare* to deny.

negative equity ▻ *noun, econ* the situation, caused by a fall in house prices, when the market value of property becomes less than the value of the mortgage on it. ⓒ 1990s.

negative feedback ▻ *noun* **1** said of a response to an enquiry, survey or questionnaire, etc: expressing lack of enthusiasm or opposition. **2** the return of part of an output signal back to the input, as a way of increasing the quality of amplified sound.

negative heliotropism see under HELIOTROPISM

negative ion therapy ▻ *noun, alternative medicine* treatment whereby the body is exposed to harmless ions, claimed to effect various cures.

negative pole ▻ *noun* that pole of a magnet which turns to the south when the magnet swings freely.

negative reinforcement ▻ *noun, psychol* the process by which an activity is learned through use of an unpleasant stimulus, eg electrical shock. See also AVERSION THERAPY. Compare POSITIVE REINFORCEMENT.

negative sign ▻ *noun* the symbol of subtraction (–), read as *minus*.

negativism /'nɛgətɪvɪzəm/ ▻ *noun* **1** a tendency to deny and criticize without offering any positive assertions; the doctrine or attitude of a NEGATIONIST. **2** a tendency to do the opposite of what one is asked to do. • **negativist** *noun, adj*. • **negativistic** *adj*. ⓒ 19c.

negativity see under NEGATIVE

negator /nɪ'geɪtə(r)/ ▻ *noun* **1** someone who denies something. **2** *grammar* a word or particle expressing negation, eg *not, never*.

neglect /nɪ'glɛkt/ ▻ *verb* (***neglected***, ***neglecting***) **1** not to give proper care and attention to someone or something. **2** to leave (duties, etc) undone. **3** to fail or omit (to do something). ▻ *noun* **1** lack of proper care. **2** a state of disuse or decay. • **neglectful** *adj* inattentive or negligent; undutiful or unconscientious. • **neglectfully** *adverb*. • **neglectfulness** *noun*. ⓒ 16c: from Latin *negligere* to neglect.

négligée or **negligee** /'nɛglɪʒeɪ/ ▻ *noun* (***négligées*** or ***negligees***) a woman's thin light dressing-gown. ⓒ 1930s in this sense; 18c meaning, 'a loose gown': from French *négligé* carelessness or undress.

negligence /'nɛglɪdʒəns/ ▻ *noun* **1** being negligent. **2** lack of proper attention or care; carelessness; neglect. **3** *law* a breach of a legal duty of care for others. ⓒ 14c.

negligent /'nɛglɪdʒənt/ ▻ *adj* **1** not giving proper care and attention. **2** careless or offhand. • **negligently** *adverb*. ⓒ 14c.

negligible /'nɛglɪdʒəbəl/ ▻ *adj* small or unimportant enough to ignore. • **negligibility** *noun*. • **negligibly** *adverb* so as to be negligible or insignificant □ *a negligibly small amount.* ⓒ 19c: from Latin *negligere* to disregard.

negotiable /nɪ'goʊʃɪəbəl/ ▻ *adj* **1** open to discussion □ *Terms and conditions are negotiable.* **2** said of a hazard or obstacle: able to be got past □ *The pass is no longer negotiable.* **3** said of a cash order, cheque, etc: that can legally be negotiated, ie transferred to another person in exchange for its value in money. • **negotiability** *noun*.

negotiate /nɪ'goʊʃɪeɪt/ ▻ *verb* (***negotiated***, ***negotiating***) **1** *intr* to confer; to bargain. **2** to bring about (an agreement), or arrange (a treaty, price, etc), by conferring. **3** to pass safely (a hazard on one's way, etc). **4** *colloq* to cope with something successfully. • **negotiator** *noun*. ⓒ 16c: from Latin *negotiari*, *negotiatus* to trade.

■ **negotiate with someone** to confer with them to reach agreement on terms or arrangements affecting both parties.

negotiation ▻ *noun* **1** the process of negotiating. **2** a round of negotiating.

Negress /'niːgrɛs/ ▻ *noun* (***Negresses***) *often offensive* a female NEGRO. ⓒ 18c.

Negrillo /nɪ'grɪloʊ/ ▻ *noun* (***Negrillos***) an African NEGRITO. ⓒ 19c: Spanish, diminutive of *negro* black.

Negrito /nɪ'griːtoʊ/ ▻ *noun* (***Negritoes*** or ***Negritos***) a member of any of a number of pygmy negroid races of SE Asia, Melanesia and Africa. ⓒ 19c: Spanish diminutive of *negro* black.

Negro /'niːgroʊ/ ▻ *noun* (***Negroes***) *often offensive* a person belonging to or descended from one of the black-skinned races originally from Africa. ▻ *adj* belonging to, characteristic of, or relating to these races. ⓒ 16c: Spanish, from Latin *niger* black.

Negroid /'niːgrɔɪd/ ▻ *adj* (*also* **negroid**) having the physical characteristics of the Negro races, eg dark skin, a broad nose and tightly curling hair. ▻ *noun* a Negroid person. • **negroidal** *adj*. ⓒ 19c.

Negroism /'niːgroʊɪzəm/ ▻ *noun* **1** any peculiarity of speech among Negroes, especially in the southern US. **2** *old use, sometimes derog* devotion to the causes of the Black Civil Rights movement. ⓒ 19c.

Negro spiritual ▻ *noun* a type of religious song that originated among Negro slaves in the southern states of N America, often with a subtext referring to a planned escape.

Neh. ▻ *abbreviation* Book of the Bible: Nehemiah. See table at BIBLE.

neigh /neɪ/ ▻ *noun* the characteristic cry of a horse. ▻ *verb* (***neighed***, ***neighing***) *intr* to make this cry or a sound like it. ⓒ Anglo-Saxon *hnægan* to neigh: imitating the sound.

neighbour or (*N Amer*) **neighbor** /'neɪbə(r)/ ▻ *noun* **1** someone near or next door to one. **2** an adjacent territory or person, etc. **3** *old use* any of one's fellow humans □ *Love your neighbour.* • **neighbouring** *adj* **1** nearby. **2** adjoining. ⓒ Anglo-Saxon *neahgebur*, from *neah* near + *gebur* dweller.

neighbourhood or (*N Amer*) **neighborhood** ▻ *noun* **1** a district or locality. **2** the inhabitants of a district; the local community. **3** the area near something or someone. **4** *math* all the points that surround a given point or curve in a specified degree of closeness. • **in the neighbourhood of** roughly □ *It cost in the neighbourhood of £500.*

neighbourhood watch ▻ *noun* a crime-prevention scheme under which local householders agree to keep a general watch on each other's property and the local streets. ⓒ 1970s: originally US and introduced as a scheme in Britain in the 1980s.

neighbourly or (*N Amer*) **neighborly** ▻ *adj* friendly, especially to the people around one. • **neighbourliness** *noun*. ⓒ 16c.

neither /'naɪðə(r), 'niːðə(r)/ ▻ *adj, pronoun* not the one nor the other (thing or person) □ *Neither proposal is acceptable* □ *Neither of the proposals is acceptable.* ▻ *conj* (used to introduce the first of two or more alternatives; usually paired with NOR) not □ *I neither know nor care.* ▻ *adverb* nor; also not □ *If you won't, neither will I.* • **neither here nor there** irrelevant; unimportant. ⓒ Anglo-Saxon *nawther* or *nahwæther*.

neither

• **Neither** is followed by a singular or plural verb, although a singular verb is usually regarded as more correct:

✓ *Neither of us likes the idea very much.*

✓ *Neither of the old women in the house was in bed.*

✓ *Neither of them were drunk.*

• It is sometimes impossible to tell whether the verb is singular or plural because there is no difference in form:

✓ *Neither of us spoke for a few minutes.*

This increases the uncertainty.

☆ RECOMMENDATION: use a singular verb for preference. Note that **neither** should be paired with **nor**, not with **or**:

✓ *He possessed neither arms nor armour.*

nekton /ˈnɛktɒn/ ▻ *noun, zool, collective* the actively swimming organisms that inhabit seas and lakes, etc, eg fish. Compare PLANKTON. ◷ 19c: Greek, meaning 'swimming'.

nelly¹ /ˈnɛlɪ/ ▻ *noun old slang* now only used in the phrase • **not on your nelly** certainly not. ◷ 1940s: perhaps from the phrase 'not on your Nelly Duff', rhyming slang for 'puff', meaning 'life'.

nelly² /ˈnɛlɪ/ ▻ *noun* (***nellies***) a large PETREL. ◷ 19c: perhaps the woman's name Nelly.

nelson /ˈnɛlsən/ and **full nelson** ▻ *noun, wrestling* a hold in which one passes one's arms under and over one's opponent's from behind, with the palms against the back of their neck. Compare HALF NELSON. ◷ 19c: from the name of Horatio Nelson.

nematode /ˈnɛmətoʊd/ ▻ *noun, zool* any of several long thin unsegmented cylindrical worms, occurring as parasites in plants and animals as well as in soil or sediment. ◷ 19c: from Greek *nema* thread + *eidos* form.

Nembutal /ˈnɛmbjʊtal/ ▻ *noun, trademark* proprietary name for pentobarbitone sodium, used as a sedative, hypnotic and antispasmodic drug. ◷ 1930s.

nem. con. /nɛm ˈkɒn/ ▻ *abbreviation: nemine contradicente* (Latin), with no one disagreeing; unanimously.

nem. diss. /nɛm ˈdɪs/ ▻ *abbreviation: nemine dissentiente* (Latin), with no one dissenting.

nemesia /nɛˈmiːʒə/ ▻ *noun* (***nemesias***) a plant of the figwort family, originally found in S Africa, grown for its brightly coloured flowers. ◷ 19c: from Greek *nemesion* the name for a similar plant.

nemesis /ˈnɛməsɪs/ ▻ *noun* (***nemeses*** /-siːz/) **1** retribution or just punishment. **2** something that brings this. ◷ 16c: from Nemesis, Greek goddess of retribution.

neo- /niːoʊ, nɪˈɒ/ ▻ *prefix, denoting* new, or a new form; modern. ◷ From Greek *neos* new.

neoclassical ▻ *adj* said of artistic or architectural style, especially in the late 18c and early 19c: imitating or adapting the styles of the ancient classical world. • **neoclassicism** *noun*.

neocolonialism ▻ *noun* the domination by powerful states of weaker but politically independent states by means of economic pressure. • **neocolonialist** *adj, noun*.

neo-Darwinism ▻ *noun, biol* a later development of DARWINISM, laying greater stress on natural selection and denying the inheritance of acquired characteristics. • **neo-Darwinist** or **neo-Darwinian** *noun, adj*.

neodymium /niːoʊˈdɪmɪəm/ ▻ *noun, chem* (symbol **Nd**, atomic number 60) a silvery metallic element, one of the rare earth elements. ◷ 19c: from *didymium*, a substance once thought to be an element.

Neofascism ▻ *noun* a movement attempting to reinstate the policies of FASCISM. • **Neofascist** *noun, adj*.

Neo-Gothic or **neo-gothic** ▻ *noun, adj* revived GOTHIC of the 19c.

Neo-impressionism ▻ *noun, art* a movement lasting from c.1885 to c.1900, started by a group of French painters, including Georges Seurat, as a reaction against the romanticism of IMPRESSIONISM, and involved the use of greater luminosity of colour by applying pure unmixed colours in small dots.

neolithic or **Neolithic**/niːoʊˈlɪθɪk/ ▻ *adj* belonging or relating to the later Stone Age, in Europe lasting from about 40 000 to 2 400 BC, and characterized by the manufacture of polished stone tools. ◷ 19c: from NEO- + Greek *lithos* stone.

neologism /nɪˈɒlədʒɪzəm/ ▻ *noun* **1** a new word or expression. **2** a new meaning acquired by an existing word or expression. **3** the practice of coining or introducing neologisms. • **neologist** *noun*. • **neologistic** or **neologistical** *adj*. • **neologize** or **neologise** *verb* (***neologized, neologizing***) to introduce new words; to coin neologisms. ◷ Early 19c: from French *néologisme*, from NEO- + Greek *logos* word.

neomycin /niːoʊˈmaɪsɪn/ ▻ *noun, pharmacol* an antibiotic used to treat skin and eye infections. ◷ 1940s: from NEO- + Greek *mykes* fungus + -IN.

neon /ˈniːɒn/ ▻ *noun, chem* (symbol **Ne**, atomic number 10) an element, a colourless gas that glows red when electricity is passed through it, used eg in illuminated signs and advertisements. Often *as adj* ▫ *neon sign*. ◷ Late 19c: Greek neuter of *neos* new.

neonatal ▻ *adj* relating to newly born children. ◷ 19c: from Latin *neonatus*.

neonate /ˈniːoʊneɪt/ ▻ *noun, biol, medicine* a newly born child.

Neo-Nazi ▻ *noun* a member or supporter of any of a number of modern movements supporting the principles of NATIONAL SOCIALISM. • **Neo-Nazism** *noun*.

neon lamp and **neon light** ▻ *noun* **1** a neon-filled glass tube used for lighting. **2** *loosely* any similar tubular fluorescent light.

neophilia ▻ *noun* love of novelty; obsessive keeping up with the latest fashions and trends. • **neophile** *noun*. • **neophilic** *adj*. ◷ 1940s.

neophobia ▻ *noun* a dread or hatred of novelty. • **neophobe** *noun*. • **neophobic** *adj*. ◷ 19c.

neophyte /ˈniːoʊfaɪt/ ▻ *noun* **1** a beginner. **2** a new convert to a religious faith. **3** a novice in a religious order. ◷ 16c: from Latin *neophytus*, from Greek *neophytos* newly planted.

Neoplatonism ▻ *noun* a philosophy developed in the 3c AD combining PLATONISM with oriental elements. • **Neoplatonic** *adj*. • **Neoplatonist** *noun, adj*.

neoprene /ˈniːoʊpriːn/ ▻ *noun* an oil-resisting and heat-resisting synthetic rubber made by polymerizing chloroprene. ◷ 1930s: from *neo-* + chloro*prene*.

neorealism ▻ *noun* in the arts and literature: a modern form of realism, especially a movement that originated in post-war Italy in cinematography, concentrating in particular on social themes and the realistic depiction of lower-class life. • **neorealist** *noun, adj*. • **neorealistic** *adj*.

neoteny /nɪˈɒtənɪ/ ▻ *noun, zool* retention of juvenile features in the adult form, an important mechanism in EVOLUTION. ◷ Early 20c: from Latin *neotenia*, from Greek *teneín* to stretch.

neoteric /niːoʊˈtɛrɪk/ ▻ *adj* modern; recent. ▻ *noun* a modern writer or philosopher. • **neoterically** *adverb*. ◷ 16c: from Greek *neoterikos*, from *neoteros* newer.

neotropical ▻ *adj* relating to ecological aspects of the Americas south of the Tropic of Cancer.

Neozoic /niːoʊˈzoʊɪk/ ▻ *adj, geol* relating to the period between the MESOZOIC and the present age. ▻ *noun* this period. See table at GEOLOGICAL TIME SCALE. ◷ 19c.

Nepalese /nɛpəˈliːz/ ▻ *adj* ▻ *noun* (*plural* ***Nepalese***) NEPALI.

Nepali /nɪˈpɔːlɪ/ ▻ *noun* (***Nepali*** or ***Nepalis***) **1** a citizen or inhabitant, or person born in Nepal, a kingdom in S Asia. **2** the official language of Nepal. ▻ *adj* belonging or relating to Nepal, its inhabitants or their language. ⓒ Late 19c.

nepenthe /nɪˈpɛnθɪ/ ▻ *noun* (***nepenthes***) *poetic* **1** a drug or drink that allows one to forget one's sorrows. **2** the plant that it is made from. • **nepenthean** *adj*. ⓒ 16c: from Greek *nepenthes*, from *ne-* not + *penthos* grief.

nephelometer /nɛfəˈlɒmɪtə(r)/ ▻ *noun* an instrument for measuring cloudiness, especially in liquids. • **nephelometric** /-ˈmɛtrɪk/ *adj*. • **nephelometry** *noun*. ⓒ 19c: from Greek *nephele* cloud.

nephew /ˈnɛfjuː, ˈnɛvjuː/ ▻ *noun* the son of one's brother or sister, or of the brother or sister of one's wife or husband. *Feminine equivalent* NIECE. ⓒ 13c: from French *neveu*, from Latin *nepos* grandson or nephew.

nephology /nɛˈfɒlədʒɪ/ ▻ *noun, meteorol* the study of clouds. • **nephologic** /nɛfəˈlɒdʒɪk/ or **nephological** *adj*. • **nephologist** *noun*. ⓒ 19c: from Greek *nephos* cloud.

nephrectomy /nɪˈfrɛktəmɪ/ ▻ *noun* (***nephrectomies***) *medicine* the surgical removal of a kidney. ⓒ 19c.

nephrite /ˈnɛfraɪt/ ▻ *noun, geol* a hard glistening mineral that occurs in a wide range of colours including black, green and white. Also called JADE or JADEITE. • **nephritic** /nɪˈfrɪtɪk/ *adj*. ⓒ 18c: from Greek *nephros* kidney, because it was formerly believed to be useful in curing kidney disease.

nephritis /nɪˈfraɪtɪs/ ▻ *noun, pathol* inflammation of a kidney. • **nephritic** *adj*. ⓒ 16c.

nephro- /nɛfroʊ, nɛˈfrɒ/ or (before a vowel) **nephr-** *combining form, denoting* one or both kidneys. ⓒ From Greek *nephros* kidney.

nephrology /nɛˈfrɒlədʒɪ/ ▻ *noun* the branch of medicine concerned with the study of the structure, function and diseases of the kidney. ⓒ 19c.

nephron /ˈnɛfrɒn/ ▻ *noun, anatomy* one of over a million functional units in the vertebrate kidney, responsible for reabsorption of water and nutrients and for the filtration of waste products from the blood to form urine. ⓒ 1930s.

ne plus ultra /niː plʌs ˈʌltrə, neː —/ ▻ *noun* nothing further; the uttermost point or extreme perfection of anything. ⓒ 17c: Latin.

nepotism /ˈnɛpətɪzəm/ ▻ *noun* the practice of favouring one's relatives or friends, especially in making official appointments. • **nepotistic** /nɛpəˈtɪstɪk/ or **nepotic** /nɪˈpɒtɪk/ *adj*. • **nepotist** *noun*. ⓒ 17c: from Latin *nepos* grandson or nephew.

neptunium /nɛpˈtjuːnɪəm/ ▻ *noun, chem* (symbol **Np**, atomic number 93) a metallic element obtained artificially in nuclear reactors during the production of PLUTONIUM. ⓒ 1940s: named after the planet Neptune.

NERC /nɜːk/ ▻ *abbreviation* Natural Environment Research Council.

nerd or **nurd** /nɜːd/ ▻ *noun, derog, slang* someone who is foolish or annoying, often because they are so wrapped up in something that isn't thought worthy of such interest. Also *in compounds* □ *a computer nerd*. • **nerdish** *adj*. • **nerdy** *adj*. ⓒ 1950s.

nereid /ˈnɪərɪːɪd/ ▻ *noun* (*plural* ***nereids*** or in sense 1 ***nereides*** /-diːz/) **1** (*also* **Nereid**) *Greek mythol* a sea-nymph, daughter of the god Nereus. **2** a marine worm. ⓒ 17c: Greek *nereis*, from *Nereus*, an ancient sea-god.

nerka /ˈnɜːkə/ ▻ *noun* (***nerkas***) the sockeye. ⓒ 18c.

neroli /ˈnɛrəlɪ/ and **neroli oil** ▻ *noun* an oil distilled from orange flowers. ⓒ 17c: said to be named after a French-born Italian princess of Neroli credited with its discovery.

nerve /nɜːv/ ▻ *noun* **1** one of the cords, consisting of a bundle of fibres, that carry instructions for movement and information on sensation between the brain or spinal cord and other parts of the body. **2** courage; assurance. **3** *colloq* cheek; impudence. **4** (**nerves**) *colloq* nervousness; tension or stress □ *calm one's nerves*. **5** (*usually* **nerves**) *colloq* one's capacity to cope with stress or excitement. **6** *bot* a leaf-vein or rib. **7** *entomol* a NERVURE in an insect's wing. ▻ *verb* (***nerved, nerving***) (*often* **nerve oneself for something**) to prepare (oneself) for (a challenge or ordeal). • **nerved** *adj* supplied with nerves. • **get on someone's nerves** *colloq* to annoy them. ⓒ 16c: from Latin *nervus* sinew, tendon or nerve.

nerve agent ▻ *noun* a NERVE GAS or similar substance.

nerve cell see under NEURONE

nerve centre ▻ *noun* **1** a cluster of nerve cells responsible for a particular bodily function. **2** the centre of control within an organization, etc.

nerve fibre ▻ *noun, zool* an AXON.

nerve gas ▻ *noun* a poisonous gas that acts on the nerves, especially those controlling respiration, used as a weapon.

nerve impulse see IMPULSE

nerveless ▻ *adj* **1** lacking feeling or strength; inert. **2** fearless. • **nervelessness** *noun*. • **nervelessly** *adverb*.

nerve-racking or **nerve-wracking** ▻ *adj* denoting something that makes one feel tense and anxious; distressing.

nervier, **nerviest**, **nervily** and **nerviness** see under NERVY

nervous /ˈnɜːvəs/ ▻ *adj* **1** timid; easily agitated. **2** apprehensive; uneasy. **3** relating to the nerves □ *nervous illnesses*. **4** consisting of nerves. • **nervously** *adverb*. • **nervousness** *noun*. ⓒ 17c; 15c, meaning 'muscular' or 'vigorous': from Latin *nervosus* sinewy.

nervous breakdown ▻ *noun* a mental illness attributed loosely to stress, with intense anxiety, low self-esteem and loss of concentration.

nervous system ▻ *noun* the network of communication, represented by the brain, nerves and spinal cord, that controls all one's mental and physical functions.

nervure /ˈnɜːvjʊə(r)/ ▻ *noun* **1** *bot* a leaf-vein. **2** *entomol* a CHITINOUS strut or rib that supports or strengthens an insect's wing. ⓒ 19c.

nervy /ˈnɜːvɪ/ ▻ *adj* (***nervier, nerviest***) **1** excitable. **2** nervous. **3** *N Amer colloq* impudent; bold. • **nervily** *adverb*. • **nerviness** *noun*.

NES ▻ *abbreviation* National Eczema Society.

nescience /ˈnɛsɪəns/ ▻ *noun, formal* lack of knowledge; ignorance. • **nescient** *adj*. ⓒ 17c: from Latin *nescire* to be ignorant of something, from *ne* not + *scire* to know.

ness ▻ *noun* a headland. ⓒ Anglo-Saxon *næs*.

-ness /nɪs, nəs/ ▻ *suffix forming nouns, denoting* a state, condition or degree of something □ *slowness* □ *darkness*.

nest ▻ *noun* **1** a structure built by birds or other creatures, eg rats and wasps, etc in which to lay eggs, or give birth to and look after young. **2** a cosy habitation or retreat. **3** a den or haunt, eg of thieves, or secret centre, eg of vice, crime, etc. **4** a brood, swarm, gang, etc. **5** a set of things that fit together or one inside the other □ *a nest of tables*. ▻ *verb* (***nested, nesting***) **1** *intr* to build and occupy a nest. **2** *tr & intr* to fit things together compactly, especially one inside another. **3** *intr* to go in search of birds' nests. ⓒ Anglo-Saxon.

nest egg ▻ *noun* **1** a real or artificial egg left in a nest to encourage laying. **2** *colloq* a sum of money saved up for the future; one's savings.

nesting box ▻ *noun* a box set up for birds to nest in.

nestle /'nɛsəl/ ▻ *verb* (***nestled, nestling***) *intr* (*often* **nestle up**, **down** or **together**, *etc*) to lie or settle snugly. ⓒ Anglo-Saxon *nestlian* to make a nest.

nestling /'nɛslɪŋ, 'nɛstlɪŋ/ ▻ *noun* a young bird still unable to fly. ⓒ 14c: NEST +-LING.

net[1] ▻ *noun* **1** an openwork material made of thread or cord, etc knotted, twisted or woven so as to form regularly shaped meshes. **2** a piece of this in any of various shapes or qualities appropriate to such uses as catching fish or insects, protecting fruit bushes, confining hair, etc. **3** a strip of net dividing a tennis or badminton court, etc. **4** *sport* the net-backed goal in hockey and football, etc. **5** (**nets**) *cricket* **a** a practice pitch enclosed in nets, indoors or outdoors; **b** a practice session in nets. **6** a snare or trap. **7** (**the net**) short for THE INTERNET. ▻ *adj* made of or like net. ▻ *verb* (***netted, netting***) **1** to catch something in a net. **2** to cover something with a net. **3** *sport* to hit or kick, etc (the ball) into the net or goal. **4** *intr* to construct net from thread or cord, etc. **5** *historical* to make (a purse, etc) using a knotting and looping process. • **netted** *adj* **1** made into a net. **2** reticulated. **3** caught in a net. **4** covered with a net. • **netting** *noun* **1** any material with meshes, made by knotting or twisting thread, cord or wire, etc. **2** the act or process of netting. ⓒ Anglo-Saxon *net* or *nett*.

net[2] ▻ *adj* **1** said of profit: remaining after all expenses, etc have been paid. Opposite of GROSS. **2** said of weight: excluding the packaging or container. ▻ *verb* (***netted, netting***) to produce, or earn, (an amount) as clear profit. ⓒ 14c: French, meaning 'clean'.

net asset value ▻ *noun* (abbreviation **NAV**) the total value of the assets of a company minus the current liabilities.

netball ▻ *noun* a game played between teams of seven women or girls on a hard court, indoors or outdoors, the aim being to score points by throwing the ball through a net hanging from a ring at the top of a pole.

Net Book Agreement see NBA

net game and **net play** ▻ *noun, tennis, badminton, etc* play near the net.

Neth. ▻ *abbreviation* Netherlands.

nether /'nɛðə(r)/ ▻ *adj, literary or old use* lower or under. • **nethermost** *adj* lowest; farthest down. ⓒ Anglo-Saxon *nither* down.

Netherlander /'nɛðəlandə(r)/ ▻ *noun* **1** a citizen or inhabitant of, or person born in, the Netherlands, a country in NW Europe on the North Sea. **2** *historical* an inhabitant of the Netherlands and the Flemish-speaking areas of Belgium. • **Netherlandic** or **Netherlandish** *adj* Dutch.

nether world ▻ *singular noun* and **nether regions** ▻ *plural noun* the underworld; hell.

Netiquette or **netiquette** ▻ *noun, computing* the rules of polite on-line behaviour. ⓒ 1990s: from NET[1] + ETIQUETTE.

netsuke /'nɛtsʊkɪ/ ▻ *noun* (***netsukes*** or ***netsuke***) a small Japanese carved ornament, once used to fasten small objects (eg a purse, or a pouch for tobacco or medicines, etc) to a sash. ⓒ 19c: Japanese *ne* root or bottom + *tsuke*, from *tsukeru* to attach.

netted and **netting** see under NET[1], NET[2]

nettle /'nɛtəl/ ▻ *noun* **1** a plant covered with hairs that sting if touched. **2** a plant that resembles this, but does not sting. See also DEAD NETTLE. ▻ *verb* (***nettled, nettling***) **1** to offend or irritate someone. **2** to sting someone. • **grasp the nettle** to deal boldly with a difficult situation. ⓒ Anglo-Saxon *netele*.

nettle rash ▻ *noun, non-technical* URTICARIA.

network ▻ *noun* **1** any system that resembles a mass of criss-crossing lines ▫ *a network of streets*. **2** any co-ordinated system involving large numbers of people or branches, etc ▫ *a telecommunications network*. **3** a group of radio or TV stations that broadcast the same programmes at the same time. **4** *computing* a linked set of computers capable of sharing power or storage facilities, organized as a ring or star. **5** NETTING 1 (see under NET[1]). ▻ *verb* **1** to broadcast something on a network. **2** *intr* to build or maintain relationships with a network of people for mutual benefit. **3** to link (computer terminals, etc to operate interactively. • **networker** *noun*. • **become networked** to set up a connection to a computer network, especially THE INTERNET.

neume or **neum** /nju:m/ ▻ *noun* in medieval music: **1** a succession of notes sung to one syllable. **2** a sign giving a rough indication of rise or fall of pitch. ⓒ 15c: French, from Greek *pneuma* breath.

neur- see NEURO-

neural /'njʊərəl/ ▻ *adj* relating to the nerves or nervous system. • **neurally** *adverb*. ⓒ 19c: from Greek *neuron* nerve.

neuralgia /njʊə'raldʒɪə/ ▻ *noun, pathol* spasmodic pain originating along the course of a nerve. • **neuralgic** *adj*. ⓒ 19c.

neural network ▻ *noun, computing* an artificial network, consisting of many computer processing units connected in parallel, that attempts to imitate some of the structural and functional properties of the human nervous system. Also called NEURAL NET.

neuritis /njʊə'raɪtɪs/ ▻ *noun, pathol* inflammation of a nerve or nerves, in some cases with defective functioning of the affected part. ⓒ 19c.

neuro- /njʊəroʊ, njʊə'rɒ/ or (before a vowel) **neur-** ▻ *combining form, denoting* a nerve or the nervous system ▫ *neurosurgery*.

neuroglia see GLIA

neurolinguistics ▻ *singular noun* the study of the neurological basis of language development and use. • **neurolinguist** *noun*. • **neurolinguistic** *adj*.

neurology /njʊ'rɒlədʒɪ/ ▻ *noun, medicine* the study of the structure, functions, diseases and disorders of the CENTRAL NERVOUS SYSTEM, and the peripheral nerves. • **neurological** /-'lɒdʒɪkəl/ *adj*. • **neurologist** *noun*. ⓒ 17c.

neurone /'njʊəroʊn/ or **neuron** /-rɒn/ ▻ *noun, anatomy* any of a large number of specialized cells that transmit nerve impulses from one part of the body to another. Also called **nerve cell**. ⓒ 19c: Greek *neuron* nerve.

neurosis /njʊə'roʊsɪs/ ▻ *noun* (***neuroses*** /-si:z/) **1** a mental disorder that causes obsessive fears, depression and unreasonable behaviour. Compare PSYCHOSIS. **2** *colloq* an anxiety or obsession. ⓒ 18c.

neurotic /njʊə'rɒtɪk/ ▻ *adj* **1** relating to, or suffering from, a neurosis. **2** *colloq* over-anxious, over-sensitive or obsessive. ▻ *noun* someone suffering from a neurosis. • **neurotically** *adverb*. ⓒ 19c.

neurotransmitter ▻ *noun, physiol* a chemical released from a nerve fibre by means of which an impulse passes to a muscle or another nerve. ⓒ 20c.

neut. ▻ *abbreviation* **1** *grammar* neuter. **2** neutral.

neuter /'nju:tə(r)/ ▻ *adj* (abbreviation **n.** or **neut.**) **1** *grammar* in many languages: belonging or referring to one of the GENDERS into which nouns and pronouns are divided, ie that to which nouns and pronouns that are neither MASCULINE nor FEMININE belong. See also COMMON GENDER. **2** said of plants: lacking pistils or stamens. **3** said of animals: sexually undeveloped or castrated. **4** said of insects: sexually undeveloped. **5** sexless or apparently sexless. ▻ *noun* **1** *grammar* **a** the neuter gender; **b** a word belonging to this gender. **2** a neuter plant, animal or insect, eg a worker bee or ant. **3** a castrated cat. ▻ *verb* (***neutered, neutering***) to castrate (an animal). ⓒ 14c: Latin *neuter* neither, from *ne* not + *uter* either.

neutral /ˈnjuːtrəl/ ▷ *adj* **1** not taking sides in a quarrel or war. **2** not belonging or relating to either side □ *neutral ground.* **3** said of colours, especially grey and fawn: indefinite enough to blend easily with brighter ones. **4** with no strong or noticeable qualities; not distinctive. **5** *elec* with no positive or negative electrical charge. **6** *chem* neither acidic nor alkaline. ▷ *noun* **1** a person or nation taking no part in a war or quarrel and not allied to any side. **2** the disengaged position of an engine's gears, with no power being transmitted to the moving parts. • **neutrally** *adverb.* ◷ 16c: from Latin *neutralis*, from *neuter* neither.

neutralism /ˈnjuːtrəlɪzəm/ ▷ *noun* the policy of not entering into alliance with other nations and avoiding taking sides ideologically. • **neutralist** *noun, adj.*

neutrality /njʊˈtralɪtɪ/ ▷ *noun* being neutral, especially in a war or dispute.

neutralize or **neutralise** /ˈnjuːtrəlaɪz/ ▷ *verb* (***neutralized***, ***neutralizing***) **1** to cancel out the effect of something; to make it useless or harmless. **2** to declare (a country, etc) neutral. • **neutralization** *noun.* • **neutralizer** *noun.* ◷ 18c.

neutrino /njʊˈtriːnoʊ/ ▷ *noun* (***neutrinos***) *physics* a stable SUBATOMIC PARTICLE that has no electric charge, virtually no mass, and travels at or near the speed of light. ◷ 1930s: Italian, from *neutro* neutral.

neutron /ˈnjuːtrɒn/ ▷ *noun, physics* one of the electrically uncharged particles in the nucleus of an atom. Compare PROTON. ◷ 1920s: from Latin *neuter* neither + -ON.

neutron bomb ▷ *noun* a type of bomb that destroys life by intense radiation, without the blast and heat effects that destroy buildings. ◷ 1950s.

neutron star ▷ *noun, astron* a star of very small size and very great density which has almost reached the end of its evolutionary life.

Nev. see under NV

névé /ˈneveɪ/ ▷ *noun* (***névés***) **1** the granular snow, not yet compacted into ice, that lies on the surface at the upper end of a glacier. **2** a field of such snow. ◷ 19c: French, from Latin *nix, nivis* snow.

never /ˈnevə(r)/ ▷ *adverb* **1** not ever; at no time. **2** not □ *I never realized that.* **3** emphatically not □ *This will never do.* **4** surely not □ *Those two are never twins!* • **never ever** absolutely never. • **well I never!** an expression of astonishment. ◷ Anglo-Saxon *næfre*, from *ne* not + *æfre* ever.

nevermore ▷ *adverb, formal or literary* never again.

never-never ▷ *noun, colloq* the hire-purchase system □ *bought it on the never-never.*

never-never land ▷ *noun* (*sometimes* **Never-Never-Land**) an imaginary place or conditions too fortunate to exist in reality. ◷ Early 20c.

nevertheless ▷ *adverb* in spite of that.

nevus see NAEVUS

new /njuː/ ▷ *adj* (***newer***, ***newest***) **1** recently made, bought, built, opened, etc □ *a new bike.* **2** recently discovered □ *a new planet.* **3** never having existed before; just invented, etc □ *new techniques.* **4** fresh; additional; supplementary □ *a new consignment.* **5** recently arrived, installed, etc. **6** (*chiefly* **new to someone** or **something**) unfamiliar with it; experienced or experiencing for the first time □ *He's new to the work.* **7** said of a person: changed physically, mentally or morally for the better. **8** renewed □ *gave us new hope.* **9** modern □ *the new generation.* **10** used in naming a place just founded after an old-established one □ *New York.* ▷ *adverb, usually in compounds* **1** only just; freshly □ *a newborn babe* □ *new-baked bread.* **2** anew. ▷ *noun* **1** *colloq* something which is new. **2** newness. • **newly** *adverb* **1** only just; recently □ *newly arrived.* **2** again; anew □ *newly awakened desire.* • **newness** *noun.* ◷ Anglo-Saxon *niwe.*

New Age ▷ *noun* **1** a modern cultural trend concerned with the union of mind, body and spirit, and expressing itself in an interest in a variety of beliefs and disciplines such as mysticism, meditation, astrology and holistic medicine. **2** (*also* **New Age Music**) a style of music first popular in the late 1980s, that uses synthesizers together with acoustic instruments, and draws on jazz, folk and classical music. ▷ *adj* **1** relating to or typical of a way of life in which these beliefs and disciplines form a central part. **2** relating to or typical of New Age Music.

New Age traveller ▷ *noun* a member of a group of people who are usually ecologically conscious, and who move around the country in converted caravans and adopt an alternative lifestyle.

New Australian ▷ *noun, Austral* a recent immigrant to Australia. See also NEW CHUM.

new blood see BLOOD (*noun* 7b)

new-blown ▷ *adj* said of a flower: just come into bloom.

newborn ▷ *adj* **1** just or very recently born. **2** said of faith, etc: reborn.

new broom ▷ *noun* a new person in charge, bent on making sweeping improvements.

Newcastle Disease ▷ *noun, vet medicine* an acute, highly contagious viral disease of birds, especially poultry. Also called **fowl-pest**. ◷ Named after Newcastle-upon-Tyne where the disease was first recorded in 1926.

new chum ▷ *noun* **1** *Austral & NZ colloq* a newly arrived and inexperienced immigrant. **2** *Austral slang* a beginner.

new-come ▷ *adj* recently arrived.

newcomer ▷ *noun* **1** someone recently arrived. **2** a beginner.

newel /ˈnjuːəl/ ▷ *noun* **1** the central spindle round which a spiral stair winds. **2** (*also* **newel post**) a post at the top or bottom of a flight of stairs, supporting the handrail. • **newelled** *adj.* ◷ 14c: from French *nouel* nut kernel.

New Englander ▷ *noun* a citizen or inhabitant, or a person born in New England.

newfangled /njuːˈfaŋgəld/ ▷ *adj* modern, especially objectionably so. • **newfangledness** *noun.* ◷ 14c: from Anglo-Saxon *newefangel* eager for novelty.

new-fashioned ▷ *adj* **1** made in a new way or fashion. **2** modern.

new-found ▷ *adj* newly discovered or devised.

Newfoundland /ˈnjuːfəndlənd, njuːˈfaʊnd-/ ▷ *noun* a breed of very large intelligent dog, originally and especially black, that are strong swimmers. ◷ 18c: originally from Newfoundland, a Province in E Canada.

newish /ˈnjuːɪʃ/ ▷ *adj* rather new or nearly new. • **newishly** *adverb.* • **newishness** *noun.*

new lad ▷ *noun* an affluent young man who holds reactionary political and social views and adopts an arrogant, sexist, beer-drinking lifestyle in open defiance of political correctness.

new-laid ▷ *adj* said of eggs: fresh.

New Latin ▷ *noun* the form of Latin used since the Renaissance, especially in legal and scientific use.

New Left ▷ *noun, politics* an extreme left-wing movement among students, etc in the 1960s.

new look ▷ *noun* **1** a radical modification in the appearance of something. **2** (**New Look**) a style of women's fashion introduced in 1947, notable for longer and fuller skirts.

newly see under NEW

newly-weds ▷ *plural noun* a recently married couple.

new man ▷ *noun* **1** a reformed character. **2** a fitter healthier man. **3** (*sometimes* **New Man**) a man who is supposed to be prepared to show his feelings, and who has adopted modern ideas, especially with regard to health, the environment, and sharing family and household responsibilities.

newmarket ▷ *noun, cards* a game in which the stakes are won by those who succeed in playing out cards whose duplicates lie on the table. ⓒ 19c: named after Newmarket, the Suffolk racing town.

new maths ▷ *singular noun* an approach to teaching mathematics that is more concerned with creating an early understanding of basic concepts than with drilling in arithmetic.

new moon ▷ *noun* **1** the Moon when it is visible as a narrow waxing crescent. **2** the time when the Moon becomes visible in this form.

newness see under NEW

new potatoes ▷ *plural noun* the first-dug potatoes of the new crop.

news /nju:z/ ▷ *singular noun* **1** information about recent events, now especially as reported in newspapers, on radio or TV, or via the Internet. **2** (**the news**) a radio or TV broadcast report of news. **3** any fresh interesting information. **4** a currently celebrated person, thing or event □ *He's big news in America.* ● **that's news to me** *colloq* I have not heard that before. ⓒ 15c, meaning 'new things'.

news agency ▷ *noun* an agency that collects news stories and supplies them to newspapers, etc.

newsagent ▷ *noun* a shop, or the proprietor of a shop, that sells newspapers and sometimes confectionery, etc.

newsboy and **newsgirl** see under PAPERBOY

newscast ▷ *noun* a radio or TV broadcast of news items. ● **newscaster** *noun* someone who reads out these news items. Also called **newsreader**. ● **newscasting** *noun*. ⓒ 1930s.

news conference see PRESS CONFERENCE

newsdealer ▷ *noun* a newsagent.

news fiction see FACTION²

newsflash ▷ *noun* a brief announcement of important news that interrups a radio or TV broadcast.

newshound ▷ *noun, facetious* a newspaper reporter.

newsier, **newsiest** and **newsiness** see under NEWSY

newsletter ▷ *noun* a sheet containing news issued to members of a society or other organization, etc.

newsman ▷ *noun* a male reporter for a newspaper or for a broadcast news programme.

newsmonger ▷ *noun, old use* a gossip.

newspaper ▷ *noun* **1** a daily or weekly publication composed of folded sheets, containing news, advertisements, topical articles, correspondence, etc. **2** the printed paper which makes up such a publication. ⓒ 17c.

newspaperman ▷ *noun* **1** a journalist. **2** the proprietor or owner of a newspaper. **3** a man who sells newspapers on the street.

newspeak ▷ *noun, ironic* the ambiguous language, full of the latest distortions and euphemisms, used by politicians and other persuaders. ⓒ 1949: from *Newspeak* a deliberately impoverished form of English used as an official language, in G Orwell's novel *Nineteen Eighty-Four*.

newsprint ▷ *noun* **1** the paper on which newspapers are printed. **2** the ink used to print newspapers.

newsreader see under NEWSCAST

newsreel ▷ *noun* a film of news events, once a regular cinema feature.

newsroom ▷ *noun* an office in a newspaper office or broadcasting station where news stories are received and edited for publication or broadcasting.

news stand ▷ *noun* a stall or kiosk that sells newspapers and magazines, etc.

New Style ▷ *noun* the present method of dating, using the GREGORIAN CALENDAR. Compare OLD STYLE.

newsvendor ▷ *noun* someone who sells newspapers.

newsworthy ▷ *adj* interesting or important enough to be reported as news.

newsy /'nju:zɪ/ ▷ *adj* (***newsier***, ***newsiest***) full of news, especially gossip. ● **newsiness** *noun*.

newt /nju:t/ ▷ *noun* a small amphibious animal with a long body and tail and short legs. ⓒ Anglo-Saxon *efeta*; *an ewt* came to be understood as *a newt*.

New Testament ▷ *noun* the part of the Bible concerned with the teachings of Christ and his earliest followers. See table at BIBLE. Compare OLD TESTAMENT.

newton /'nju:tən/ ▷ *noun, physics* ▷ (abbreviation **N**) in the SI system: a unit of force equivalent to that which gives a one kilogram mass an acceleration of one second every second (formerly the imperial unit POUNDAL). ⓒ 19c: named after Sir Isaac Newton (1642–1727), English scientist.

new town ▷ *noun* a town planned and built by a government commission as a unit, to relieve congestion in nearby cities and encourage development, especially one of those built around London after World War II.

new wave ▷ *noun* **1** an artistic, musical or cultural movement or grouping that abandons traditional ideas and style. **2** (**New Wave** or **Nouvelle Vague** /'nu:vɛl vag/) a movement in French cinema of the 1960s notable for fluid camera work. **3** *jazz* a movement aiming at freedom from set patterns and styles.

New World ▷ *noun* the entire American continent. See also OLD WORLD.

New Year ▷ *noun* the first day of the year or the days, usually festive ones, immediately following or preceding it.

New Year's Day ▷ *noun* 1 January.

New Year's Eve ▷ *noun* 31 December.

New Zealand flax see FLAX-BUSH

next ▷ *adj* **1** following in time or order □ *the next on the list* □ *the next day.* **2** following this one □ *next week.* **3** adjoining; neighbouring □ *in the next compartment.* **4** first, counting from now □ *the very next person I meet.* ▷ *noun* someone or something that is next. ▷ *adverb* **1** immediately after that or this □ *What happened next?* **2** on the next occasion □ *when I next saw her.* **3** following, in order of degree □ *the next longest river.* ● **next best** next lowest in degree after the best □ *At rush-hour, walking is the next best thing to cycling.* ● **next biggest** next lowest (or highest, depending on context) in degree after the previous one mentioned. ● **next to something** or **someone 1** beside it or them. **2** after it or them, in order of degree □ *Next to swimming I like dancing.* **3** almost □ *wearing next to no clothes* □ *next to nothing.* ⓒ Anglo-Saxon *nehst* the nearest, from *neah* near.

next-door ▷ *adj* dwelling in, occupying or belonging to the next room, house or shop, etc; neighbouring. ▷ *adverb* (**next door**) to or in the next room, house or shop, etc. ● **next door to something** near, bordering upon or very near it.

next of kin ▷ *noun* one's closest relative or relatives.

nexus /'nɛksəs/ ▷ *noun* (***nexus*** or ***nexuses***) **1** a connected series or group. **2** a bond or link. ⓒ 17c: Latin, from *nectere*, *nexum* to bind.

NF ▷ *abbreviation* **1** in the UK: National Front. **2** *US state* Newfoundland. Also written **Nfd** or **Nfld**.

NFER ▷ *abbreviation* National Foundation for Educational Research.

NFL ▻ *abbreviation, N Amer* National Football League.

NFS ▻ *abbreviation* not for sale.

NFSC ▻ *abbreviation* National Federation of (Football) Supporters' Clubs.

NFSE ▻ *abbreviation* National Federation of Self-Employed.

NFT ▻ *abbreviation* National Film Theatre.

NFU ▻ *abbreviation* National Farmers' Union.

NFWI ▻ *abbreviation* National Federation of Women's Institutes.

NG ▻ *abbreviation, US* National Guard.

NGA ▻ *abbreviation* National Graphical Association.

ngaio /'naɪoʊ/ ▻ *noun* (***ngaios***) an evergreen New Zealand tree with white wood. Ⓞ 19c: Maori.

NGO ▻ *abbreviation* non-governmental organization, said of organizations other than commercial companies that operate in various countries and are not associated with a particular government, such as the UN, aid organizations, etc.

NH ▻ *abbreviation, US state* New Hampshire. Also written N.H.

NHBRC ▻ *abbreviation* National House-Builders' Registration Council or Certificate.

NHI ▻ *abbreviation* National Health Insurance.

NHS ▻ *abbreviation* National Health Service.

NI ▻ *abbreviation* **1** National Insurance. **2** Northern Ireland.

Ni ▻ *symbol, chem* nickel.

niacin /'naɪəsɪn/ and **nicotinic acid** ▻ *noun* VITAMIN B_7. Ⓞ 1940s.

nib ▻ *noun* **1** the writing-point of a pen, especially a metal one with a divided tip. **2** a point or spike. **3** a bird's bill. **4** (**nibs**) crushed coffee or cocoa beans. **5** (**nibs**) small particles or lumps in varnish or wool, etc. ▻ *verb* (***nibbed, nibbing***) **1** to provide with a pen-point or nib. **2** to reduce to nibs. • **nibbed 1** with a nib. **2** said of nuts, etc: roughly crushed. Ⓞ 16c, meaning 'a bird's beak'.

nibble /'nɪbəl/ ▻ *verb* (***nibbled, nibbling***) *tr & intr* **1** to take very small bites of something; to eat a little at a time. **2** to bite gently. • **nibbler** *noun*. • **nibbling** *noun*. • **nibblingly** *adverb*. Ⓞ 16c.

■ **nibble at something 1** to nibble it. **2** *colloq* to show cautious interest in (a proposal, etc).

niblick /'nɪblɪk/ ▻ *noun, golf* an old-fashioned golf club with a heavy head and wide face, used for lofting.

nibs ▻ *singular noun* (*usually* **his** or **her nibs**) *facetious* a derogatory mock title for an important or would-be important person. Ⓞ 19c.

NIC ▻ *abbreviation, IVR* Nicaragua.

nicad /'naɪkad/ ▻ *noun* **1** nickel-cadmium, used to make batteries. **2** a battery, often a rechargeable one, made using nickel-cadmium. Ⓞ 1950s.

Nicam /'naɪkam/ ▻ *noun* a system by which digital stereo sound signals are transmitted along with the standard TV signal, allowing the viewer to receive sound of CD quality. Ⓞ 1990s: *n*ear-*i*nstantaneous *c*ompanded (compressed and expanded) *a*udio *m*ultiplexing.

niccolite /'nɪkəlaɪt/ ▻ *noun* a hexagonal mineral, nickel arsenide. Also called **nickeline** and **kupfernickel**. Ⓞ 19c.

nice /naɪs/ ▻ *adj* (***nicer, nicest***) **1** pleasant; agreeable; respectable. **2** *often ironic* good; satisfactory. **3** *ironic* nasty □ *a nice mess.* **4** fine; subtle □ *nice distinctions.* **5** exacting; particular □ *nice in matters of etiquette.* • **niceness** *noun*. • **nice and ...** *colloq* satisfactorily ... ; commendably ... □ *nice and firm.* Ⓞ 13c, meaning 'foolish', 'coy' or 'exotic'.

nicely ▻ *adverb* **1** in a nice or satisfactory way. **2** precisely; carefully □ *judged it nicely.* **3** suitably; effectively □ *That will do nicely.*

Nicene Creed /'naɪsiːn —/ ▻ *noun, Christianity* the creed recited as part of the Eucharistic liturgies of the Orthodox and Roman Catholic Churches, and many Protestant Churches. Ⓞ Based on the work of the first Council of Nicaea, a town in Asia Minor, in AD 325.

nicety /'naɪsətɪ/ ▻ *noun* (***niceties***) **1** precision. **2** a subtle point of detail. • **to a nicety** exactly.

niche /niːʃ, nɪtʃ/ ▻ *noun* **1** a shallow recess in a wall, suitable for a lamp, ornament or statue, etc. **2** a position in life in which one feels fulfilled or at ease, or both. **3** a small specialized group identified as a market for a particular range of products or services. Also *as adj* □ *niche marketing* □ *niche advertising.* ▻ *verb* (***niched, niching***) **1** to place something in a niche. **2** to ensconce (oneself). • **niched** *adj* placed in a niche. Ⓞ 17c; 1980s as *noun* 3: French, from Latin *nidus* nest.

Nick and **Old Nick** ▻ *noun* the devil.

nick ▻ *noun* **1** a small cut; a notch. **2** *colloq* a prison or police station. ▻ *verb* (***nicked, nicking***) **1** to make a small cut in something; to cut something slightly; to snip it. **2** *slang* to arrest (a criminal). **3** *slang* to steal. **4** to make a cut in (a horse's tail muscle), so that the tail is carried higher. • **in good nick** *colloq* in good condition. • **in the nick of time** at the last possible moment; just in time. Ⓞ 16c.

nickel /'nɪkəl/ ▻ *noun* **1** *chem* (symbol **Ni**, atomic number 28) one of the elements, a greyish-white metal used especially in alloys and for plating. **2** *N Amer* an American or Canadian coin worth five cents. ▻ *adj* made of or with nickel. ▻ *verb* (***nickelled, nickelling***) to plate something with nickel. Ⓞ 18c: from German *Küpfernickel* copper devil, so called by miners mistaking it for copper.

nickel-and-dime ▻ *adj* **1** involving only a small amount of money. **2** worth only a small amount of effort, concern, etc.

nickeline see under NICCOLITE

nickelodeon /nɪkə'loʊdɪən/ ▻ *noun, US old use* **1** a cinema charging five cents for admission. **2** an early form of jukebox. **3** a type of pianola, especially one operated by the insertion of a five-cent piece. Ⓞ 1920s: NICKEL + MELODEON.

nickel-plating ▻ *noun* the plating of metals with nickel.

nickel silver ▻ *noun, chem* an alloy of copper, zinc and nickel, that looks like silver.

nicker /'nɪkə(r)/ ▻ *noun* (***nicker***) *old slang* a pound sterling. Ⓞ Early 20c.

nick-nack see KNICK-KNACK

nickname /'nɪkneɪm/ ▻ *noun* a name, usually additional to the real one, given to a person or place in fun, affection or contempt. ▻ *verb* to give a nickname to someone. Ⓞ 15c: from *eke* addition or extra; *an ekename* came to be understood as *a nickname.*

nicotiana /nɪkoʊʃɪ'ɑːnə/ ▻ *noun* a plant related to tobacco, originally found in America and Australia, cultivated for its colourful flowers and scent. Ⓞ 16c: French, named after J Nicot (1530–1600), French diplomat, said to have introduced tobacco into France.

nicotine /'nɪkətiːn/ ▻ *noun* a poisonous alkaline substance contained in tobacco. Ⓞ 19c: French; see NICOTIANA.

nicotinic acid see NIACIN

nictate /'nɪkteɪt/ and **nictitate** /'nɪktɪteɪt/ ▻ *verb* (***nictated, nictitated; nictating, nictitating***) *intr* to wink or blink. • **nictation** or **nictitation** *noun*. Ⓞ 17c: from Latin *nictare, nictatum* to wink.

nictitating membrane ▷ *noun, zool* in many reptiles, amphibians, birds, and some mammals: a transparent membrane that forms a third eyelid which can be drawn across the eye for protection.

nidicolous /nɪˈdɪkələs/ ▷ *adj* said of the young of certain birds: remaining for longer than average in the nest. Compare ALTRICIAL, PRECOCIAL.

nidify /ˈnɪdɪfaɪ/ ▷ *verb* (***nidifies***, ***nidified***, ***nidifying***) *intr* said of a bird: to make a nest or nests. • **nidification** *noun*. ⓘ 17c.

niece /niːs/ ▷ *noun* the daughter of one's sister or brother, or the sister or brother of one's husband or wife. *Masculine equivalent* NEPHEW. ⓘ 13c: from French, from Latin *neptis* granddaughter or niece.

niello /nɪˈɛloʊ/ ▷ *noun* (***nielli*** /-liː/ or ***niellos***) **1** a method of ornamenting metal by engraving, and then filling up the lines with a black compound. **2** a piece of work produced in this way. **3** the compound used in niello work, sulphur with silver, lead or copper. ▷ *verb* (***nielloed***, ***nielloing***) to decorate something with niello. ⓘ 19c: Italian, from Latin *nigellum* a black enamel, from *niger* black.

nielsbohrium /niːlsˈbɔːrɪəm/ ▷ *noun* an alternative name proposed by Soviet scientists for the chemical element UNNILPENTIUM.

Nietzschean /ˈniːtʃɪən/ ▷ *noun* a follower of Friedrich Nietzsche (1844–1900), a German philosopher, poet and critic. ▷ *adj* relating to Nietzsche or his philosophy. • **Nietzscheanism** *noun*. ⓘ Early 20c.

niff ▷ *noun, slang* a bad smell. ▷ *verb* (***niffed***, ***niffing***) *intr* to smell bad. ⓘ 19c.

niffy /ˈnɪfɪ/ (***niffier***, ***niffiest***) ▷ *adj* smelly.

nifty /ˈnɪftɪ/ ▷ *adj* (***niftier***, ***niftiest***) **1** clever; adroit; agile. **2** stylish. • **niftily** *adverb*. • **niftiness** *noun*. ⓘ 19c.

nigella /naɪˈdʒɛlə/ ▷ *noun* (***nigellas***) one of a group of plants with finely dissected leaves and whitish, blue or yellow flowers, one variety of which is also known as **love-in-a-mist**. ⓘ 14c: feminine of Latin *nigellus* blackish, referring to the colour of the seeds.

niggard /ˈnɪɡəd/ ▷ *noun* a stingy person. ⓘ 14c.

niggardly /ˈnɪɡədlɪ/ ▷ *adj* **1** stingy; miserly. **2** meagre □ *niggardly praise*. • **niggardliness** *noun*.

nigger /ˈnɪɡə(r)/ ▷ *noun, offensive* a person of Black African origin or race. • **nigger in the woodpile** a hidden evil influence. ⓘ 18c: from French *nègre*, from Spanish *negro* black.

niggle /ˈnɪɡəl/ ▷ *verb* (***niggled***, ***niggling***) *intr* **1** to complain about small or unimportant details. **2** to bother, especially slightly but continually; to fuss. ▷ *noun* **1** a slight nagging worry. **2** a small complaint or criticism. • **niggler** *noun*. • **niggling** *adj* **1** fussy. **2** trivially troublesome or worrying. **3** persistently annoying. ⓘ 19c; 17c, meaning 'to trifle'.

nigh /naɪ/ ▷ *adverb, old use, dialect or poetic* near. • **nigh on** or well nigh nearly; almost. ⓘ Anglo-Saxon *neah*.

night /naɪt/ ▷ *noun* **1** the time of darkness between sunset and sunrise. **2** the time between going to bed and getting up in the morning. **3** evening □ *stayed at home last night*. **4** nightfall. **5** *poetic* darkness. **6** an evening on which a particular activity or event takes place □ *my aerobics night*. **7** a state of ignorance, evil or sorrow, etc. ▷ *adj* **1** belonging to, occurring, or done in the night □ *the night hours*. **2** working or on duty at night □ *the night shift*. • **nightly** *adj* done or happening at night or every night. ▷ *adverb* at night; every night. • **nights** *adverb, colloq* at night; most nights or every night. • **make a night of it** *colloq* to celebrate late into the night. ⓘ Anglo-Saxon *niht*.

night-bell ▷ *noun* a doorbell for use at night, especially at a hotel.

night-bird ▷ *noun* **1** a bird that flies or sings at night. **2** someone who is active, awake, or goes about at night.

night-blindness ▷ *noun* a common name for NYCTALOPIA.

nightcap ▷ *noun* **1** a drink, especially an alcoholic one, taken before going to bed. **2** *old use* a cap worn in bed at night.

nightclass ▷ *noun* a class at NIGHT SCHOOL.

nightclothes ▷ *plural noun* clothes for sleeping in, such as pyjamas or a nightdress, etc. Compare BEDCLOTHES.

nightclub ▷ *noun* a club open in the evening and running late into the night for drinking, dancing, entertainment, etc. • **nightclubber** *noun* a patron of a nightclub. • **nightclubbing** *noun* dancing, drinking and sometimes dining at a nightclub.

nightdress ▷ *noun* a loose garment for sleeping in, worn by women and girls.

nightfall ▷ *noun* the end of the day and the beginning of night; dusk.

nightgown ▷ *noun* a loose garment for sleeping in.

nightie or **nighty** /ˈnaɪtɪ/ ▷ *noun* (***nighties***) *colloq* a nightdress. ⓘ 19c.

nightingale /ˈnaɪtɪŋɡeɪl/ ▷ *noun* any of several species of small brown thrush, especially the **common nightingale**, known for its melodious song, heard especially at night. ⓘ Anglo-Saxon *nehtegale*.

nightjar ▷ *noun* a nocturnal bird of the swift family that has a harsh discordant cry. ⓘ 17c: NIGHT + JAR[2].

night latch ▷ *noun* a door lock worked by a key from outside and a knob from inside.

nightlife ▷ *noun* entertainment available in a city or resort, etc, late into the night.

night light ▷ *noun* a dim-shining lamp or slow-burning candle that can be left alight all night.

nightlong ▷ *adj, adverb* throughout the night.

nightly see under NIGHT

nightmare /ˈnaɪtmɛə(r)/ ▷ *noun* **1** a frightening dream. **2** an intensely distressing or frightful experience or situation. • **nightmarish** *adj* like a nightmare; intensely distressing or frightful. ⓘ 16c; 13c, meaning 'an incubus': from Anglo-Saxon *mare* an incubus or nightmare-producing monster.

night owl ▷ *noun* **1** an exclusively nocturnal owl. **2** someone who likes to stay up late at night or who is habitually more alert and active, etc, at night than earlier in the day. See also NIGHT-BIRD.

nights see under NIGHT

night safe ▷ *noun* a safe built into the outer wall of a bank, in which to deposit money when the bank is closed.

night school ▷ *noun* **1** classes held in the evening, chiefly for people who have left school, especially for those who may be at work during the day. **2** an institution providing such educational evening classes.

nightshade ▷ *noun* any of several wild plants, some with poisonous berries, including BELLADONNA. Also called **deadly nightshade**. ⓘ Anglo-Saxon *nihtscada*.

night shift ▷ *noun* **1** a session of work or duty during the night. **2** the staff working during this period. See also BACK SHIFT, DAY SHIFT.

nightshirt ▷ *noun* a loose garment like a long shirt for sleeping in.

night-soil ▷ *noun, old use* human excrement collected at night from privies etc, for use as a soil fertilizer.

night spot ▷ *noun, colloq* a nightclub.

nightstick ▷ *noun, N Amer* a police truncheon.

night-time ▷ *noun* the time of darkness between sunset and sunrise.

night watch ▷ *noun* **1** a guard or watch kept at night. **2** someone who is on guard at night. **3 a** a period of keeping watch at night; **b** the time that such a period lasts.

nightwatchman ▷ *noun* **1** someone who looks after a public building or industrial premises, etc at night. **2** *cricket* a batsman, not usually a high scorer, put in to defend a wicket till close of play.

nighty see NIGHTIE

nigrescent /naɪˈgresənt, nɪˈgresənt/ ▷ *adj* **1** growing black or dark. **2** blackish. • **nigrescence** *noun* blackness; dark colouring or pigmentation; blackening. ◷ 18c: from Latin *nigrescere* to grow black, from *niger* black.

nihilism /ˈnaɪɪlɪzəm/ ▷ *noun* **1** the rejection of moral and religious principles. **2** the view that nothing has real existence; extreme scepticism. **3** a 19c Russian movement aimed at overturning all social institutions. • **nihilist** *noun*. • **nihilistic** *adj*. ◷ 19c: from Latin *nihil* nothing.

nihility /naɪˈhɪlɪtɪ/ ▷ *noun* being nothing; nothingness.

-nik ▷ *suffix, forming nouns, sometimes derog, denoting* someone concerned or associated with the specified cause or activity, etc □ ***peacenik*** □ ***refusenik***. ◷ 1940s: from Yiddish, from Slavic.

Nikkei index /nɪˈkeɪ —/ ▷ *noun* the indicator of the relative prices of the stocks and shares on the Tokyo stock exchange. Also called **Nikkei average**. Compare FOOTSIE, DOW JONES INDEX. ◷ 1970s: from the title of the financial newspaper which publishes it.

nil ▷ *noun, games, sport, etc* a score of nothing; zero. ◷ 19c: from Latin *nihil* nothing.

Nile blue /naɪəl —/ ▷ *noun* a very pale greenish blue colour. ◷ 19c: from the colour of the river Nile.

Nile green /naɪəl —/ ▷ *noun* a very pale green colour. ◷ 19c: from the colour of the river Nile.

nilgai /ˈniːlgaɪ, ˈnɪlgaɪ/ or **nilgau** /nɪlˈgɔː/ ▷ *noun* (***nilgai*** or ***nilgais***; ***nilgau*** or ***nilgaus***) a large Indian antelope, the male being a slaty-grey colour, and the female tawny. ◷ 19c: from Persian and Hindi *nil* blue + Hindi *gai* or Persian *gaw* cow.

Nilot /ˈnaɪlɒt/ or **Nilote** /ˈnaɪloʊt/ ▷ *noun* (***Nilot*** or ***Nilots***; ***Nilote*** or ***Nilotes*** /-tiːz/) **1** an inhabitant of the banks of the Upper Nile. **2** a member of any of several peoples from E Africa and the Sudan. **3** a Negro of the Upper Nile. • **Nilotic** /naɪˈlɒtɪk/ *adj* **1** belonging or relating to the river Nile. **2** belonging or relating to the Nilots or their languages. ◷ 17c as *Nilotic*: from Greek *Neilotes*, from Greek *Neilos* the river Nile.

nim ▷ *noun* an old and widespread game in which two players take an item alternately from heaps or rows of objects (now eg matches) with the aim of taking, or not taking, the last item. ◷ Early 20c; the game was possibly originally Chinese.

nimbi *a plural of* NIMBUS

nimble /ˈnɪmbəl/ ▷ *adj* (***nimbler, nimblest***) **1** quick and light in movement; agile. **2** said of wits: sharp; alert. • **nimbleness** *noun*. • **nimbly** *adverb*. ◷ Apparently Anglo-Saxon *næmel* receptive or *numol* quick to learn.

nimble-fingered ▷ *adj* skilful with the fingers.

nimble-footed ▷ *adj* agile; swift.

nimble-witted ▷ *adj* quick-witted.

nimbostratus /nɪmboʊˈstrɑːtəs/ ▷ *noun* (***nimbostrati*** /-taɪ/) *meteorol* a low dark-coloured layer of cloud bringing rain. ◷ Early 20c.

nimbus /ˈnɪmbəs/ ▷ *noun* (***nimbuses*** or ***nimbi*** /-baɪ/) **1** *meteorol* a heavy dark type of cloud bringing rain or snow. **2** a luminous mist or halo surrounding a god or goddess, or a representation of this. ◷ 17c: Latin.

NIMBY or **Nimby** /nɪmbɪ/ ▷ *noun, colloq* someone who is willing to let something happen, eg the building of a new road, so long as it does not adversely affect them, or disrupt their locality. • **nimbyism** *noun*. ◷ 1980s: from *not in my back yard*.

niminy-piminy /ˈnɪmɪnɪˈpɪmɪnɪ/ ▷ *adj, derog* affectedly fine or delicate. ◷ 18c: imitating the sound of affected talk.

nincompoop /ˈnɪŋkəmpuːp/ ▷ *noun* a fool; an idiot. ◷ 17c.

nine /naɪn/ ▷ *noun* **1 a** the cardinal number 9; **b** the quantity that this represents, being one more than eight. **2** any symbol for this, eg **9**, **IX**. **3** the age of nine. **4** something, especially a garment or a person, whose size is denoted by the number 9. **5** the ninth hour after midnight or midday □ ***opens at nine*** □ ***9am*** □ ***9 o'clock***. **6** a set or group of nine people or things. **7** a playing-card with nine pips □ ***She played her nine***. **8** a score of nine points. ▷ *adj* **1** totalling nine. **2** aged nine. • **dressed up to the nines** *colloq* wearing one's best clothes; elaborately dressed. ◷ Anglo-Saxon *nigon*.

nine days' wonder ▷ *noun* something that grips everyone's attention for a brief time. ◷ 16c.

ninefold ▷ *adj* **1** equal to nine times as much or many. **2** divided into, or consisting of, nine parts. ▷ *adverb* by nine times as much.

nine-hole ▷ *adj* said of a golf course: having nine holes.

ninepins ▷ *singular noun* a game similar to skittles, using a wooden ball and nine skittles arranged in a triangle.

nineteen /naɪnˈtiːn/ ▷ *noun* **1 a** the cardinal number 19; **b** the quantity that this represents, being one more than eighteen, or the sum of ten and nine. **2** any symbol for this, eg **19**, **XIX**. **3** the age of nineteen. **4** something, especially a garment or a person, whose size is denoted by the number 19. **5** a set or group of nineteen people or things. ▷ *adj* **1** totalling nineteen. **2** aged nineteen. • **talk nineteen to the dozen** *colloq* to chatter away animatedly. ◷ Anglo-Saxon *nigontiene*.

nineteenth (often written **19th**) ▷ *adj* **1** in counting: **a** next after eighteenth; **b** last of nineteen. **2** in nineteenth position. **3** (**the nineteenth**) the nineteenth day of the month. ▷ *noun* **1** one of nineteen equal parts. Also *as adj* □ ***a nineteenth share***. **2** a FRACTION equal to one divided by nineteen (usually written 1/19). **3** someone who comes nineteenth, eg in a race or exam. ◷ Anglo-Saxon; see NINETEEN + -TH[1].

the nineteenth hole ▷ *noun, humorous* a golf clubhouse, especially the bar. ◷ Early 20c; ie where one goes after finishing the 18th hole.

nineties /ˈnaɪntɪz/ (often written **90s** or **90's**) ▷ *plural noun* **1** the period of time between one's ninetieth and hundredth birthdays □ ***Leonard is in his nineties***. **2** the range of temperatures between ninety and a hundred degrees. **3** the period of time between the ninetieth and hundredth years of a century □ ***the 1990s***.

ninetieth /ˈnaɪntɪəθ/ (often written **90th**) ▷ *adj* **1** in counting: **a** next after eighty-nineth; **b** last of ninety. **2** in ninetieth position. ▷ *noun* **1** one of ninety equal parts. **2** a FRACTION equal to one divided by ninety (usually written 1/90). **3** someone who comes ninetieth, eg in a race or competition, etc. ◷ Anglo-Saxon; see NINETY + -TH[1].

ninety /ˈnaɪntɪ/ ▷ *noun* **1 a** the cardinal number 90; **b** the quantity that this represents, being one more than eighty-nine, or the product of ten and nine. **2** any symbol for this, eg **90**, **XC**. Also *in compounds, forming adjectives and nouns*, with cardinal numbers between *one* and *nine* □ ***ninety-six***. **3** the age of ninety. **4** a set or group of ninety people or things. **5** a score of ninety points. ▷ *adj* **1** totalling ninety. Also *in compounds, forming adjectives*, with ordinal numbers between *first* and *ninth* □ ***ninety-ninth***. **2** aged ninety. See also NINETIES, NINETIETH. ◷ Anglo-Saxon; see NINE + -TY[2].

ninja /ˈnɪndʒə/ ▻ *noun* (***ninja*** or ***ninjas***) especially in medieval Japan: one of a body of professional assassins trained in martial arts and stealth. ◷ 1960s: Japanese, from *nin-* stealth + *ja* person.

ninjutsu /nɪnˈdʒʊtsuː/ or **ninjitsu** ▻ *noun* an armed Japanese martial art with strong emphasis on stealth and camouflage. ◷ 1960s: Japanese, from *nin* stealth + *jutsu* art.

ninny /ˈnɪnɪ/ ▻ *noun* (***ninnies***) a foolish person. ◷ 16c.

ninon /ˈniːnɒn/ ▻ *noun* a silk voile or other thin fabric. ◷ Early 20c: from French *Ninon*, a woman's name.

Nintendo /nɪnˈtɛndoʊ/ ▻ *noun, trademark* a video games console machine used in conjunction with a TV screen or monitor. See also GAME BOY. ◷ 1980s: the name of the manufacturer.

ninth /naɪnθ/ (often written **9th**) ▻ *adj* **1** in counting: **a** next after eighth; **b** last of nine. **2** in ninth position. **3** (**the ninth**) the nineth day of the month. ▻ *noun* **1** one of nine equal parts. Also *as adj* ◻ *a ninth share.* **2** a FRACTION equal to one divided by nine (usually written 1/9). **3** a person coming ninth, eg in a race or exam. ▻ *adverb* ninthly. • **ninthly** *adverb* used to introduce the ninth point in a list. ◷ Anglo-Saxon; see NINE + -TH[1]..

niobium /naɪˈoʊbɪəm/ ▻ *noun, chem* (symbol **Nb**, atomic number 41) a relatively unreactive soft greyish-blue metallic element with a brilliant lustre, resistant to corrosion and formerly known as **columbium**. ◷ 19c: Latin, from Niobe, the daugher of Tantalus in Greek mythology; it is found in *tantalite*.

Nip ▻ *noun, offensive* a Japanese person. ◷ 1940s: short for NIPPONESE.

nip[1] ▻ *verb* (***nipped, nipping***) **1** to pinch or squeeze something or someone sharply. **2** to give a sharp little bite to something. **3** (*often* **nip off something**) to remove or sever it by pinching or biting. **4** *tr & intr* to sting; to cause smarting. **5** to halt the growth or development of something ◻ *nip it in the bud.* **6** *N Amer colloq* to snatch something. ▻ *noun* **1** a pinch or squeeze. **2** a sharp little bite. **3** a sharp biting coldness, or stinging quality. ◷ 14c: from Norse *hnippa* to poke.

■ **nip off, away** or **round**, *etc* to go off, away, or round, etc quickly ◻ *nip round to the shop.*

nip[2] ▻ *noun* a small quantity of alcoholic spirits ◻ *a nip of brandy.* ◷ 18c: from Dutch *nippen* to sip.

nip and tuck *colloq* ▻ *noun* a surgical operation carried out for cosmetic reasons. ▻ *adj, adverb, N Amer* neck and neck.

nipper /ˈnɪpə(r)/ ▻ *noun* **1** the large claw of a crab or lobster, etc. **2** (**nippers**) pincers, tweezers, forceps, or another gripping or severing tool. **3** a horse's INCISOR, especially one of the middle four. **4** *old colloq use* a small child.

nipple /ˈnɪpəl/ ▻ *noun* **1** the deep-coloured pointed projection on a breast, in the female the outlet of the ducts from which the young suck milk. **2** *N Amer* the teat on a baby's feeding-bottle. **3** *mech* any small projection with a hole through which a flow is regulated or machine parts lubricated. ◷ 16c in early form *neble*.

nipplewort ▻ *noun* a tall plant with small yellow flower heads, now regarded as a weed, formerly used as a cure for sore nipples.

Nippon /nɪˈpɒn, ˈnɪpɒn/ ▻ *noun* the Japanese name for Japan. • **Nipponese** *noun, adj.* ◷ 19c: Japanese *ni* sun + *pon*, from *hon* origin.

nippy /ˈnɪpɪ/ ▻ *adj* (***nippier, nippiest***) *colloq* **1** cold; chilly. **2** quick-moving; nimble. **3** said of flavour: pungent or biting.• **nippiness** *noun.* ◷ 16c.

NIRC ▻ *abbreviation* National Industrial Relations Court.

NIREX /ˈnaɪrɛks/ ▻ *abbreviation* Nuclear Industry Radioactive Waste Executive.

nirvana or **Nirvana** /nɪəˈvɑːnə, nɜː-/ ▻ *noun* **1** *Buddhism, Hinduism* the ultimate state of spiritual tranquillity attained through release from everyday concerns and extinction of individual passions. **2** *colloq* a place or state of perfect bliss. ◷ 19c: Sanskrit, meaning 'extinction'.

nisei /ˈniːseɪ/ ▻ *noun* (*plural* ***nisei***) an American or Canadian born of Japanese immigrant parents. ◷ 1940s: Japanese, meaning 'second generation'.

nisi /ˈnaɪsaɪ/ ▻ *adj* said of a court order: to take effect on the date stated, unless in the meantime a reason is given why it should not. See also DECREE NISI. ◷ 19c: Latin, literally 'unless'.

Nissen hut /ˈnɪsən —/ ▻ *noun* a corrugated-iron hut in the shape of a semi-cylinder lying lengthwise. Compare QUONSET HUT. ◷ Early 20c: named after P N Nissen (1871–1930), its designer.

nit[1] ▻ *noun* the egg or young of a LOUSE, found eg in hair. • **nitty** *adj* (***nittier, nittiest***). ◷ Anglo-Saxon *hnitu*.

nit[2] ▻ *noun, slang* an idiot. ◷ 16c: from NIT[1], influenced by NITWIT.

nit[3] ▻ *noun* in the CGS UNIT system: a unit of luminance equal to one candela per square metre. ◷ 1950s.

nit-picking ▻ *noun* petty criticism or fault-finding. ▻ *adj* fussy. • **nit-picker** *noun.* ◷ 1950s: from NIT[1].

nitrate /ˈnaɪtreɪt/ *chem* ▻ *noun* **1** a salt or ester of NITRIC ACID. **2** sodium nitrate or potassium nitrate used as a soil fertilizer. ▻ *verb* (***nitrated, nitrating***) **1** to treat something with nitric acid or a nitrate. **2** *tr & intr* to convert something into a nitrate. • **nitration** *noun.* ◷ 18c.

nitrazepam /naɪˈtrazəpam, naɪˈtreɪ-/ ▻ *noun* a hypnotic drug taken for the relief of insomnia. ◷ 1960s: from NITRO-, modelled on DIAZEPAM.

nitre /ˈnaɪtə(r)/ ▻ *noun, chem* potassium nitrate (formula KNO_3); saltpetre. ◷ 15c: French, from Greek *nitron* sodium carbonate.

nitric /ˈnaɪtrɪk/ ▻ *adj, chem* belonging to or containing nitrogen. ◷ 18c.

nitric acid ▻ *noun, chem* (formula HNO_3) a colourless pungent caustic corrosive acid, used as an oxidizing agent and for making explosives, fertilizers and dyes. *Formerly called* **aqua fortis**.

nitric oxide ▻ *noun, chem* (formula **NO**) a colourless gas which reacts spontaneously with oxygen at room temperature, forming NITROGEN DIOXIDE.

nitride /ˈnaɪtraɪd/ ▻ *noun, chem* a compound of nitrogen with another, metallic, element. ◷ 19c.

nitrify /ˈnaɪtrɪfaɪ/ ▻ *verb* (***nitrifies, nitrified, nitrifying***) *tr & intr, chem* usually said of ammonia: to convert or be converted into nitrates or nitrites, through the action of bacteria. • **nitrification** *noun.* ◷ 19c.

nitrite /ˈnaɪtraɪt/ ▻ *noun, chem* a salt or ester of NITROUS ACID. ◷ 19c.

nitro- /naɪtroʊ, naɪˈtrɒ/ ▻ *combining form, chem* **1** made with, or containing, NITROGEN, NITRIC ACID or NITRE. **2** containing the group $-NO_2$.

nitrogen /ˈnaɪtrədʒən/ ▻ *noun* (symbol **N**, atomic number 7) *chem* an element which is the colourless, odourless and tasteless gas making up four-fifths of the air we breathe. • **nitrogenous** /-ˈtrɒdʒənəs/ *adj.* ◷ 18c: from NITRE + -GEN.

nitrogen cycle ▻ *noun, biol* the continuous circulation of nitrogen and its compounds between the ATMOSPHERE and the BIOSPHERE as a result of the activity of living organisms.

nitrogen dioxide ▻ *noun, chem* (formula NO_2) a reddish-brown gas, used in the production of nitric acid.

nitrogen monoxide ▻ *noun, chem* NITRIC OXIDE.

nitroglycerine or **nitroglycerin** ▻ *noun, chem* (formula $C_3H_5(ONO_2)_3$) an explosive liquid compound, used in dynamites, produced by treating glycerine with nitric and sulphuric acids. ⓘ 19c.

nitrous /'naɪtrəs/ ▻ *adj, chem* relating to or containing nitrogen in a low valency. ⓘ 17c.

nitrous acid ▻ *noun, chem* (formula HNO_2) a weak acid occurring only in solution or in nitrite salts.

nitrous oxide ▻ *noun, chem* (formula N_2O) dinitrogen oxide used as an anaesthetic and popularly known as LAUGHING GAS.

nittier, **nittiest** and **nitty** see under NIT[1]

the nitty-gritty /'nɪtɪ'grɪtɪ/ ▻ *noun, colloq* the fundamental issue or essential part of any matter, situation or activity, etc. ⓘ 1960s: originally US; perhaps rhyming compound of *grit*.

nitwit /'nɪtwɪt/ ▻ *noun* a stupid person. ⓘ 1920s: from German dialect *nit* (variant of *nicht* not) + WIT[1].

nix ▻ *noun* (***nixes***) *slang* nothing. ▻ *exclamation, N Amer* no. ⓘ 19c; 18c as *nicks*: from colloquial German *nix*, a form of *nichts* nothing.

NJ ▻ *abbreviation, US state* New Jersey. Also written **N.J.**

NL ▻ *abbreviation, IVR* Netherlands.

NM ▻ *abbreviation, US state* New Mexico. Also written **N.Mex.**

nm ▻ *abbreviation* **1** nanometre. **2** nautical mile.

n mile ▻ *abbreviation* (international) nautical mile.

NMR ▻ *abbreviation* nuclear magnetic resonance.

NNE ▻ *abbreviation* north-north-east.

NNW ▻ *abbreviation* north-north-west.

NO ▻ *abbreviation* New Orleans.

No[1], **No** or **no** ▻ *abbreviation* number.

No[2] ▻ *symbol, chem* nobelium.

No[3] see NOH

no[1] /noʊ/ ▻ *exclamation* **1** used as a negative reply, expressing denial, refusal or disagreement. **2** *colloq* used as a question tag expecting agreement □ ***It's a deal, no?*** **3** used as an astonished rejoinder □ ***No! You don't say!*** ▻ *adverb* **1** (*with comparative*) not any □ ***no bigger than one's thumb.*** **2** used to indicate a negative alternative: not □ ***whether he's willing or no.*** ▻ *noun* (***noes***) a negative reply or vote □ ***The noes have it.*** • **no more 1** destroyed; dead. **2** never again; not any longer. • **not take no for an answer** to continue with an activity in spite of refusals; to insist. ⓘ Anglo-Saxon *na*, from *ne* not + *a* ever.

no[2] /noʊ/ ▻ *adj* **1** not any □ ***There's no milk left.*** **2** certainly not or far from something specified □ ***He's no fool*** □ ***no easy task.*** **3** hardly any □ ***do it in no time.*** **4** not allowed □ ***no smoking.*** • **no go** *colloq* impossible; no good. • **no one** no single □ ***No one candidate is the obvious choice.*** • **no way** *colloq* no; definitely not. ⓘ Anglo-Saxon *na*, variant of *nane* NONE.

no[3] or **no'** /noʊ/ ▻ *adverb, Scots* not □ ***no bad.***

no[4] see NO[1]

n.o. ▻ *abbreviation, cricket* not out.

no-account ▻ *adj* worthless; useless.

nob[1] ▻ *noun* in the game of cribbage: the jack of the turned-up suit. ⓘ 19c.

nob[2] ▻ *noun, slang* someone of wealth or high social rank. ⓘ 19c.

nob[3] ▻ *noun, slang* the head. ⓘ 17c: probably from KNOB.

no-ball ▻ *noun, cricket, baseball, rounders, etc* a ball bowled in a manner that is not allowed by the rules.

nobble /'nɒbəl/ ▻ *verb* (***nobbled***, ***nobbling***) *colloq* **1** *horse-racing* to drug or otherwise interfere with (a horse) to stop it winning. **2** to persuade someone by bribes or threats □ ***tried to nobble the jury.*** **3** to obtain something dishonestly. **4** to catch (a criminal). **5** to swindle someone. ⓘ 19c: possibly from *an hobbler*, later understood as *a nobbler*, meaning 'a person who lames horses'.

nobelium /noʊ'biːlɪəm/ ▻ *noun, chem* (symbol **No**, atomic number 102) a radioactive element produced artificially from the element CURIUM. ⓘ 1950s: named after the Nobel Institute, Stockholm, where it was first produced in 1957.

Nobel laureate ▻ *noun* a winner or past winner of a NOBEL PRIZE.

Nobel prize ▻ *noun* any of the annual prizes, awarded since 1901, for exceptional work in physics, chemistry, medicine or physiology, literature, economics, and the promotion of peace. 1900: instituted by Alfred Nobel (1833–96), Swedish discoverer of dynamite.

nobility /noʊ'bɪlɪtɪ/ ▻ *noun* (***nobilities***) **1** the quality of being noble, in character, conduct or rank. **2** (**the nobility**) the class of people of noble birth. ⓘ 15c: from Latin *nobilitas*, from *nobilis* noble.

noble /'noʊbəl/ ▻ *adj* (***nobler***, ***noblest***) **1** honourable. **2** generous. **3** of high birth or rank. **4** grand, splendid or imposing in appearance. ▻ *noun* a person of noble rank. Compare ARISTOCRAT, PEER[1]. • **nobleness** *noun*. • **nobly** *adverb* with a noble manner; honourably. ⓘ 13c: from Latin *nobilis*, originally *gnobilis* knowable, ie well-known.

noble gas ▻ *noun, chem* any of the colourless odourless tasteless gases in group 0 (see GROUP *noun* 5) of the periodic table of the elements, ie helium, neon, argon, krypton, xenon and radon, in order of increasing atomic number. Also called **inert gas**. ⓘ Early 20c.

nobleman and **noblewoman** ▻ *noun* a member of the nobility.

noble metal ▻ *noun* a metal such as gold, silver or platinum, that is highly unreactive, and so does not easily tarnish on exposure to the air. Opposite of BASE METAL.

noble rot ▻ *noun, bot* on white grapes: a rot caused by the fungus *Botrytis cinerea*, which aids the production of sweet white wine.

noble savage ▻ *noun* a romantic and idealized view of primitive human beings.

noblesse oblige /noʊ'bles oʊ'bliːʒ/ ▻ *noun, usually ironic* it is the duty of those who are privileged to use their privilege to the benefit of the less fortunate. ⓘ 19c: French, meaning 'nobility obliges'.

nobly see under NOBLE

nobody /'noʊbədɪ, -bɒdɪ/ ▻ *pronoun* no person; no one. ▻ *noun* (***nobodies***) someone of no significance. • **like nobody's business** *colloq* very energetically; intensively □ ***She yelled like nobody's business.***

NOC ▻ *abbreviation* National Olympic Committee.

nociceptive /noʊsɪ'septɪv/ ▻ *adj, physiol* **1** sensitive to pain. **2** causing pain. ⓘ Early 20c: from Latin *nocere* to hurt, modelled on RECEPTIVE.

nock ▻ *noun* a notch, or a part carrying a notch, especially on an arrow or a bow. ▻ *verb* (***nocked***, ***nocking***) **1** to notch. **2** to fit (an arrow) on the string of a bow. ⓘ 14c.

no-claims bonus or **no-claim bonus** ▻ *noun* a reduction in the fee one pays for insurance if one has made no claim for payment over a particular period. Also called **no-claims discount**.

noctambulation /nɒktambjʊ'leɪʃən/ ▻ *noun* sleep-walking. Also called **noctambulism**. • **noctambulist** *noun*. ⓘ 18c: from Latin *nox*, *noctis* night + *ambulare*, *ambulatum* to walk.

nocti- /nɒktɪ/ or (before a vowel) **noct-** ▻ *combining form, denoting* night. ⓘ From Latin *nox*, *noctis* night.

noctilucent /nɒktɪ'luːsənt, -'ljuːsənt/ ▷ *adj* **1** *zool* phosphorescent; glowing in the dark. **2** *meteorol* said of high-altitude dust-clouds or ice-clouds: visible at night. • **noctilucence** *noun.* ⓒ 19c: from Latin *lucens, lucentis* shining.

noctule /'nɒktjuːl/ ▷ *noun, zool* a large brown bat, the largest found in Britain. ⓒ 18c: French, from Italian *nottola* bat.

nocturnal /nɒk'tɜːnəl/ ▷ *adj* **1** said of animals, etc: active at night. **2** happening at night. **3** belonging or relating to the night. • **nocturnally** *adverb* at night. ⓒ 15c: from Latin *nocturnus,* from *nox* night.

nocturne /'nɒktɜːn, nɒk'tɜːn/ ▷ *noun* **1** *music* a dreamy piece of music, usually for the piano. **2** *art* a night or moonlight scene. ⓒ 19c: French, from Latin *nocturnus* nocturnal.

nod ▷ *verb* (***nodded, nodding***) **1** *tr & intr* to make a brief bowing gesture with the head, in agreement or greeting, etc; to bow (the head) briefly. **2** *intr* to let the head droop with sleepiness; to become drowsy. See *nod off* below. **3** *intr* to make a mistake through momentary loss of concentration. **4** to indicate or direct by nodding □ *nodded her approval* □ *He was nodded towards the Customs.* **5** *intr* said of flowers and plumes, etc: to sway or bob about. ▷ *noun* a quick bending forward of the head; a slight bow; a movement of the head as a gesture of assent, greeting or command. • **on the nod** *colloq* said of the passing of a proposal, etc: by general agreement, without the formality of a vote. • **the Land of Nod** the imaginary country to which sleepers go. ⓒ 14c.

■ **nod off** *intr* to fall asleep.

■ **nod someone** or **something through** **1** in parliament: to allow someone to vote by proxy. **2** to pass something without a discussion or vote, etc.

nodal see under NODE

nodding aquaintance ▷ *noun* **1** slight aquaintance. **2** someone with whom one is only slightly acquainted. **3** slight or superficial knowledge of something, eg a subject.

nodding donkey ▷ *noun, colloq, especially N Amer* a kind of pump for pumping oil from land-based oil-wells.

noddle /'nɒdəl/ ▷ *noun* (***noddles***) *colloq* the head or brain. ⓒ 15c.

noddy /'nɒdɪ/ ▷ *noun* (***noddies***) **1** any of several tropical birds of the tern family, so unafraid of humans as to seem stupid. **2** a simpleton. ⓒ 16c: perhaps from an obsolete *adj* sense, meaning 'silly'.

node /noʊd/ ▷ *noun* **1** a knob, lump, swelling or knotty mass. **2** *bot* a swelling where a leaf is attached to a stem. **3** *geom* the point where a curve crosses itself. **4** *astron* **a** a point where the orbit of a body intersects the apparent path of the sun; **b** a point where any two GREAT CIRCLES of the celestial sphere intersect. **5** *elec* in a vibrating body: the point of least movement. • **nodal** *adj.* ⓒ 17c: from Latin *nodus* knot.

nodose /noʊ'doʊs, 'noʊdoʊs/ ▷ *adj* having nodes, knots or swellings. • **nodosity** /noʊ'dɒsɪtɪ/ *noun* **1** knottiness. **2** (***nodosities***) a knotty swelling.

nodulated /'nɒdjʊleɪtɪd/ ▷ *adj* having nodules. • **nodulation** *noun.*

nodule /'nɒdjuːl/ ▷ *noun* **1** a small round lump. **2** *bot* a swelling in a root of a LEGUMINOUS plant, inhabited by bacteria that convert nitrogen to the plant's use. • **nodular** *adj* **1** relating to a nodule or nodules. **2** consisting of a nodule or nodules. **3** like a nodule. • **nodulose** or **nodulous** *adj.* ⓒ 17c: from Latin *nodulus,* diminutive of *nodus* knot.

Noel or **Noël** /noʊ'ɛl/ ▷ *noun* now only used in Christmas cards and carols, etc: Christmas. Also written NOWELL. ⓒ 19c: French, from Latin *natalis* birthday.

noes *plural of* NO[1]

noesis /noʊ'iːsɪs/ ▷ *noun* **1** the activity of the intellect. **2** *philos* purely intellectual apprehension or perception. • **noetic** /noʊ'ɛtɪk/ *adj.* ⓒ 17c: Greek, from *noeein* to perceive or to think.

no-fault ▷ *adj* said of insurance compensation payments, etc: made without attachment to, or admission of blame by, any one person or party in particular.

no-frills ▷ *adj* basic, not elaborate or fancy.

nog[1] ▷ *noun* an alcoholic drink made with whipped eggs; an EGG NOG. ⓒ 19c; 17c, meaning 'a variety of strong ale'.

nog[2] ▷ *noun* **1** a wooden peg. **2** a brick-sized piece of wood inserted into a wall to receive nails. • **nogging** *noun* a brick or rough timber filling between timbers in a partition or wall. ⓒ 17c.

noggin /'nɒgɪn/ ▷ *noun* **1** a small measure or quantity of alcoholic spirits. **2** a small mug or wooden cup. **3** *colloq* one's head. ⓒ 17c.

no-go area ▷ *noun* an area of a city, etc, to which normal access is prevented, eg because it is controlled by one of the groups involved in an armed conflict or civil war.

no-good ▷ *adj* bad; worthless. ▷ *noun* a bad worthless person.

Noh or **No** /noʊ/ (*also* **noh** or **no**) ▷ *noun* (*plural* ***Noh*** or ***No***) Japanese drama in the traditional style, developed from religious dance. ⓒ 19c: Japanese, meaning 'ability'.

nohow /'noʊhaʊ/ ▷ *adverb, colloq or dialect* in no way, not at all. ⓒ 18c.

noise /nɔɪz/ ▷ *noun* **1** a sound. **2** a harsh disagreeable sound, or such sound; a din. **3** *radio* interference in a signal. **4** *computing* irrelevant or meaningless material appearing in output. **5** *facetious* something one says as a conventional response, vague indication of inclinations, etc □ *make polite noises.* ▷ *verb* (***noised, noising***) (*usually* **noise abroad** or **about**) to make something generally known; to spread (a rumour, etc). • **make a noise** *colloq* to talk or complain a great deal. • **noiseless** *adj* lacking noise; silent. • **noiselessly** *adverb.* • **noiselessness** *noun.* ⓒ 13c: French, from Latin *nausea* sea-sickness.

noise pollution ▷ *noun* an excessive or annoying degree of noise in a particular area, eg from traffic or aeroplane engines.

noisette /nwa'zɛt/ ▷ *noun* **1** a small piece of meat (usually lamb) cut off the bone and rolled. **2** a nutlike or nut-flavoured, especially hazelnut, sweet. ▷ *adj* flavoured with or containing hazelnuts. ⓒ 19c: French, meaning 'hazelnut'.

noisome /'nɔɪsəm/ ▷ *adj* **1** disgusting; offensive; stinking. **2** harmful; poisonous □ *noisome fumes.* • **noisomely** *adverb.* • **noisomeness** *noun.* ⓒ 14c, meaning 'harmful' or 'noxious' from earlier *noy,* a variant of ANNOY.

noisy /'nɔɪzɪ/ ▷ *adj* (***noisier, noisiest***) **1** making a lot of noise. **2** full of noise; accompanied by noise □ *noisy streets.* • **noisily** *adverb.* • **noisiness** *noun.*

nolens volens /'noʊlɛnz 'voʊlɛnz/ ▷ *adverb* willy-nilly. ⓒ 16c: Latin, literally 'unwilling, willing'.

nolle prosequi /'nɒlɪ 'prɒsəkwaɪ, -kwiː/ ▷ *noun, law* an entry on a court record that the plaintiff or prosecutor will proceed no further with (a part of) the suit. ⓒ 17c: Latin, meaning 'do not want to pursue'.

nolo contendere /'noʊloʊ kən'tɛndərɪ/ ▷ *noun, law* a plea by which the accused does not admit guilt, but accepts conviction. ⓒ 18c: Latin, meaning 'I do not wish to contend'.

nom. ▷ *abbreviation, grammar* nominative.

nomad /'noʊmad/ ▷ *noun* **1** a member of a people without a permanent home, who travel from place to place seeking food and pasture. **2** a wanderer. • **nomadic**

adj said of a people: wandering from place to place; not settled. • **nomadically** *adverb*. ◷ 16c: from Greek *nomas, nomados,* from *nomos* pasture.

nomadize or **nomadise** /ˈnoʊmadaɪz/ ⊳ *verb* (***nomadized, nomadizing***) **1** *intr* to lead the life of a nomad or vagabond. **2** to make (a person, etc) nomadic; to force (a person, etc) into a nomadic way of life. • **nomadism** *noun*. • **nomadization** *noun*. ◷ 18c.

no-man's-land ⊳ *noun* **1** unclaimed land; waste land. **2** neutral territory between opposing armies or between two countries with a common border. **3** a state or situation that is neither one thing nor another. ◷ 14c as *nonesmanneslond.*

nom de guerre /nɒm də gɛə(r)/ ⊳ *noun* (*plural* ***noms de guerre***) an assumed name. ◷ 17c: French, literally 'war name'.

nom-de-plume or **nom de plume** /nɒm də ˈpluːm/ ⊳ *noun* (***noms-de-plume*** or ***noms de plume***) a pseudonym used by a writer; a pen-name. ◷ 19c: pseudo-French, from French *nom* name + *de* of + *plume* pen.

nomenclature /noʊˈmɛŋklətʃə(r)/ ⊳ *noun* **1** a classified system of names, especially in science; terminology. **2** a list or set of names. ◷ 17c: from Latin *nomenclatura,* from *nomen* name + *calare* to call.

-nomial /ˈnoʊmɪəl/ ⊳ *combining form, math, denoting* consisting of a specified number of terms or variables. ◷ From Latin *nomen, nominis* name.

-nomic see under -NOMY

nominal /ˈnɒmɪnəl/ ⊳ *adj* **1** in name only; so called, but actually not something specified □ *a nominal head of state.* **2** very small in comparison to actual cost or value □ *a nominal rent.* **3** *grammar* belonging to, being or relating to a noun. **4** belonging to, being or relating to a name. **5** *space flight* according to plan. ⊳ *noun, grammar* a noun, or a phrase, etc standing as a noun. • **nominally** *adverb* **1** in name only. **2** theoretically rather than actually. **3** *grammar* as a noun. ◷ 15c: from Latin *nominalis,* from *nomen, nominis* name.

nominal accounts ⊳ *plural noun* accounts which are concerned with revenue and expenses, eg sales, purchases, etc.

nominalism ⊳ *noun, philos* the view that a general term such as 'book' is no more than a name, and does not refer to an actual entity. • **nominalist** *noun, adj.* • **nominalistic** *adj.*

nominal value ⊳ *noun* the stated or face value on a bond or share certificate, etc.

nominate /ˈnɒmɪneɪt/ ⊳ *verb* (***nominated, nominating***) **1** (*usually* **nominate someone for something**) to propose them formally as a candidate for election or for a job, etc. **2** (*usually* **nominate someone to something**) to appoint them to (a post or position). **3** to specify formally (eg a date). • **nomination** *noun* **1** the act of nominating, especially a formal proposal of a candidate for election or appointment. **2** the state of being nominated. **3** in horse-breeding: the arranged mating of a mare and stallion. • **nominator** *noun*. ◷ 16c: from Latin *nominare, nominatum* to name.

nominative /ˈnɒmɪnətɪv/ ⊳ *noun, grammar* (abbreviation **nom.**) **1** in certain languages, eg Latin, Greek and German: the form or CASE[2] (sense 7) used to mark the subject of a verb. **2** a noun, etc in this case. ⊳ *adj* **1** *grammar* belonging to or in this case. **2** appointed by nomination rather than election. • **nominatival** /-ˈtaɪvəl/ *adj.* • **nominatively** *adverb*. ◷ 14c as *adj*: from Latin *nominativus,* from *nominare* to name.

nominee /nɒmɪˈniː/ ⊳ *noun* (***nominees***) **1 a** someone who is nominated as a candidate for a job or position, etc; **b** someone nominated to or for a job or position, etc. **2** a person or organization appointed to act on behalf of another, especially in order to keep the identity of the first secret. **3** someone on whose life an annuity or lease depends. ◷ 17c: from Latin *nominare* to name; see -EE.

nomogram /ˈnɒməgram/ and **nomograph** /-grɑːf/ ⊳ *noun* a chart or diagram of scaled lines or curves used to help in mathematical calculations, comprising three scales in which a line joining values on two determines a third. Also called **isopleth**. • **nomographic** or **nomographical** *adj.* • **nomography** /nəˈmɒgrafɪ/ *noun* the art of making nomograms. ◷ Early 20c: from Greek *nomos* law.

-nomy /nəmɪ/ ⊳ *combining form, forming nouns, signifying* a science or field of knowledge, or the discipline of the study of these. • **-nomic** *combining form* forming adjectives corresponding to nouns in *-nomy.* ◷ From Greek *-nomia* administration or regulation.

non- /nɒn/ ⊳ *prefix, signifying* **1** not; the opposite of something specified □ *non-essential* □ *non-existent.* **2** *ironic* not deserving the name of something specified □ *a non-event.* **3** not belonging to the category of something specified □ *non-fiction* □ *non-metals.* **4** not having the skill or desire to be, or not participating in, something specified □ *non-swimmers* □ *non-voting.* **5** rejection, avoidance, or omission of something specified □ *non-co-operation* □ *non-payment.* **6** not liable to do something specified □ *non-shrink* □ *non-drip.* **7** not requiring a certain treatment □ *non-iron.* ◷ From Latin *non* not.

nonage /ˈnɒnɪdʒ, ˈnoʊnɪdʒ/ ⊳ *noun, law* the condition of being under age; one's minority or period of immaturity. ◷ 14c: French, from *non* non- + *age* age.

nonagenarian /noʊnədʒəˈnɛərɪən, nɒnə-/ ⊳ *noun* someone in their nineties, ie between the ages of 90 and 99 years old. ◷ 19c: from Latin *nonagenarius* containing or consisting of ninety.

Some words with NON- prefixed. The prefix is extremely productive, and many other words besides those defined in this dictionary, and those listed below, may be formed.

non-abrasive *adj.*
non-absorbent *adj.*
non-academic *adj.*
non-acceptance *noun.*
non-accessible *adj.*
non-addictive *adj.*
non-alcoholic *adj.*
non-allergic *adj.*
non-arrival *noun.*
non-automatic *adj, noun.*
non-believer *noun.*
non-belligerent *adj, noun.*
non-biological *adj.*
non-breakable *adj.*
noncarbonated *adj.*
non-Catholic *adj, noun.*
non-Christian *adj, noun.*
non-clinical *adj.*
noncombining *adj.*
non-commercial *adj.*
non-compliance *noun.*
noncommunicative *adj.*
noncompetitive *adj.*
non-conclusive *adj.*
nonconsenting *adj.*
non-contagious *adj.*
non-controversial *adj.*
noncorroding *adj.*
non-delivery *noun.*
non-democratic *adj.*
nondisciplinary *adj.*
nondiscriminating *adj.*
nondivisible *adj.*
non-drinker *noun.*
non-driver *noun.*
nonearning *adj.*

non-aggression ▷ *noun* ▷ *adj* abstaining from aggression □ *non-aggression pact.*

nonagon /ˈnɒnəgɒn/ ▷ *noun, geom* a nine-sided figure. ⓘ 17c: from Latin *nonus* ninth + Greek *gonia* angle.

non-aligned ▷ *adj* said of a country: not allied to any of the major power blocs in world politics; neutral. • **non-alignment** *noun.*

non-appearance ▷ *noun* failing or neglecting to appear, especially in a court of law.

nonary /ˈnoʊnərɪ/ ▷ *adj, math* said of a mathematical system: based on nine. ⓘ 19c: from Latin *nonarius* ninth.

non-attendance ▷ *noun* failure to attend; absence.

non-attributable ▷ *adj* said of a press statement, etc: having a source that is not able or permitted to be disclosed. • **non-attributably** *adverb.*

non-belligerent ▷ *adj* taking no part in a war. ▷ *noun* a non-belligerent country.

nonce[1] /nɒns/ ▷ *noun* now only used in the phrase • **for the nonce** for the time being; for the present. ⓘ 14c: originally *for then ones* for the once, *then once* coming to be understood as *the nonce.*

nonce[2] /nɒns/ ▷ *noun, prison slang* a sexual offender, especially one who assaults children. ⓘ 1970s.

nonce-word ▷ *noun* a word coined for one particular occasion.

nonchalant /ˈnɒnʃələnt/ ▷ *adj* calmly or indifferently unconcerned. • **nonchalance** /-ləns/ *noun.* • **nonchalantly** *adverb.* ⓘ 18c: French, from *non* not + *chaloir* to matter or concern.

non-claim ▷ *noun, law* a failure to make a claim within a set limit.

non-classified ▷ *adj* said of information: not classified as secret.

non-cognizable ▷ *adj, law* said of an offence: that cannot be judicially investigated.

non-com ▷ *noun, colloq* a NON-COMMISSIONED OFFICER.

non-combatant ▷ *noun* **1** any member of the armed forces whose duties do not include fighting, eg a surgeon or chaplain. **2** in time of war: a civilian.

non-comedogenic ▷ *adj* said of cosmetics: not liable to block the pores of the skin, or cause blackheads or spots.

non-commissioned officer ▷ *noun* (abbreviation **NCO**) an officer such as a corporal or sergeant, appointed from the lower ranks of the armed forces, not by being given a COMMISSION.

non-committal ▷ *adj* avoiding expressing a definite opinion or decision. • **non-committally** *adverb.*

non-communicant ▷ *noun* **1** *Christianity* someone who does not take communion on any particular occasion or in general. **2** someone who has not yet communicated.

non compos mentis /nɒn ˈkɒmpəs ˈmɛntɪs/ ▷ *adj, often humorous* not of sound mind. ⓘ 17c: Latin, meaning 'not in command of one's mind'.

non-conductor ▷ *noun* a substance that does not conduct heat, electricity or sound. • **non-conducting** *adj.*

nonconformist ▷ *noun* **1** someone who refuses to conform to generally accepted practice. **2** (**Nonconformist**) in England: a member of a Protestant church separated from the Church of England. ▷ *adj* of or relating to nonconformists. • **non-conforming** *adj.* • **non-conformism** *noun.* • **non-conformity** *noun* **1** refusal to conform to established practice. **2** lack of correspondence or agreement between things. ⓘ 17c.

non-content ▷ *adj* in the House of Lords: someone who casts a negative vote.

non-contributory ▷ *adj* **1** said of a pension scheme: paid for by the employer, without contributions from the employee. **2** said of a state benefit: not dependent on the payment of National Insurance contributions.

non-co-operation ▷ *noun* failure or refusal to co-operate.

non-custodial ▷ *adj* said of a judicial sentence: not involving imprisonment.

non-dairy ▷ *adj* said of foods: containing no dairy produce.

non-denominational ▷ *adj* **1** not linked with any particular religious denomination. **2** for the use or participation of members of all denominations.

nondescript /ˈnɒndɪskrɪpt/ ▷ *adj* with no strongly noticeable characteristics or distinctive features. ▷ *noun* a nondescript person or thing. ⓘ 17c, meaning 'not previously described': from Latin *describere, descriptum* to describe.

non-destructive testing ▷ *noun* the testing of structures or metals, etc, for flaws without impairing their quality.

non-drip ▷ *adj* said of paint: not liable to drip when being applied. See also THIXOTROPY.

none[1] /nʌn/ ▷ *pronoun* (with *singular* or *plural* verb; see note) **1** not any □ *There were none in the box.* **2** no one; not any □ *None were as kind as she.* • **none but …** only … □ *none but the finest ingredients.* • **none of …** I won't put up with … □ *None of your cheek!* • **none other than someone** or **something** the very person or thing mentioned or thought of. • **none the …** (followed by a

Some words with NON- prefixed. The prefix is extremely productive, and many other words besides those defined in this dictionary, and those listed below, may be formed.

noneconomic *adj.*	**noninfectious** *adj.*	**non-playing** *adj.*
non-essential *adj, noun.*	**noninflammable** *adj.*	**non-poisonous** *adj.*
nonethical *adj.*	**non-involvement** *noun.*	**non-professional** *adj, noun.*
non-existence *noun.*	**non-iron** *adj.*	**non-resisting** *adj.*
non-existent *adj.*	**non-linear** *adj.*	**non-racial** *adj.*
non-factual *adj.*	**non-marrying** *adj.*	**non-reader** *noun.*
non-fatal *adj.*	**non-member** *noun.*	**non-scientific** *adj.*
non-flowering *adj.*	**non-natural** *adj.*	**non-smoking** *adj, noun.*
non-fulfilment *noun.*	**non-nuclear** *adj.*	**non-swimmer** *noun.*
non-functional *adj.*	**non-operational** *adj.*	**non-specialist** *noun.*
nongovernmental *adj.*	**non-partisan** or **nonpartizan** *adj.*	**non-technical** *adj.*
non-harmonic *adj.*	**nonpaying** *adj.*	**non-toxic** *adj.*
nonhuman *adj.*	**non-payment** *noun.*	**non-verbal** *adj.*

comparative) not any ... □ *none the worse for his adventure.* • **none too ...** by no means ... □ *none too clean.* • **none the less** or **nonetheless** nevertheless; in spite of that. ⓒ Anglo-Saxon *nan* not one or no.

none

• When **none** refers to a number of individual people or things, it can be followed by a singular or a plural verb, rather like a collective noun, depending on whether the individuals or the group as a whole are intended □ *The hotel is half a mile from the beach and none of the rooms overlook the sea* □ *None of us has time for much else but the work in hand.*

none² /noʊn/ and **nones** /noʊnz/ ▻ *noun, especially RC Church* the fifth of the CANONICAL HOURS. ⓒ 18c: from Latin *nona hora* the ninth hour.

non-effective *military* ▻ *adj* unfit or unavailable for service. ▻ *noun* a member of a force who is unfit or unavailable for active service.

non-ego ▻ *noun, philos* the not-I, the object as opposed to the subject, whatever is not the conscious self.

non-elective ▻ *adj* not chosen by election.

nonentity /nɒ'nɛntɪtɪ/ ▻ *noun* **1** *derog* someone of no significance, character or ability, etc. **2** *derog* a thing of no importance. **3** a thing which does not exist. **4** the state of not being. ⓒ 17c.

nones¹ /noʊnz/ ▻ *plural noun* in the Roman calendar: the seventh day of March, May, July and October, and the fifth day of other months. ⓒ 15c: from Latin *nonae*, from *nonus* ninth: the nones were the ninth day before the IDES, counting inclusively.

nones² see NONE²

nonesuch or **nonsuch** /'nʌnsʌtʃ, 'nʌn-/ ▻ *noun, literary* a unique, unparalleled or extraordinary thing. ⓒ 16c.

nonet /noʊ'nɛt/ ▻ *noun* (***nonettos*** or ***nonetti*** /-tiː/) *music* **1** a composition for nine instruments or voices. **2** a group of nine instrumentalists or singers. ⓒ 19c: from Italian *nonetto*.

nonetheless see under NONE

non-Euclidean geometry ▻ *noun, math* any system of geometry that is not based on the theories of the Greek mathematician Euclid. Compare EUCLIDEAN GEOMETRY.

non-event ▻ *noun* an event one has been greatly looking forward to, or which was promised as being of great importance, that turns out to be insignificant or a disappointment.

non-executive director ▻ *noun* a director of a company who is not employed full-time by the company, but brought in as an advisor.

non-fat ▻ *adj* said of food: having had the fat removed. Compare LOW-FAT.

non-feasance /nɒn'fiːzəns/ ▻ *noun, law* omission of something which ought to be, or ought to have been, done. ⓒ 16c: from French *faisance* doing, from *faire* to do.

non-ferrous ▻ *adj* said of metals: **1** not iron or steel. **2** not containing iron.

non-fiction ▻ *adj* said of a literary work: factual. Also *as noun* □ *He only reads non-fiction.* • **non-fictional** *adj.*

non-flammable ▻ *adj* not liable to catch fire or burn easily.

nong /nɒŋ/ ▻ *noun, Austral & NZ slang* a fool or an idiot. ⓒ 1950s.

nonillion /noʊ'nɪlɪən/ ▻ *noun* **1** in certain EC countries: the number shown as 10^{54}, a million raised to the ninth power. **2** *N Amer* the number shown as 10^{30}, a thousand raised to the tenth power. • **nonillionth** *adj.* ⓒ 17c: from Latin *nonus* ninth, modelled on MILLION and BILLION.

non-intervention ▻ *noun* not interfering, especially a government policy of systematically not interfering in the affairs of other nations.

non-invasive ▻ *adj* said of medical treatment: not involving surgery or the insertion of instruments, etc into the patient.

non-judgemental or **non-judgmental** ▻ *adj* relating to or having an open attitude without implicit moral judgement. • **non-judgementally** *adverb.*

non-juring /nɒn'dʒʊərɪŋ/ ▻ *adj, formal* not swearing allegiance.

non-juror ▻ *noun, formal* someone who refuses to take an oath, especially to swear allegiance.

non-metal ▻ *noun, chem* any chemical element that does not have the properties of a metal or a metalloid, and that does not form positive ions. Also *as adj.* • **non-metallic** *adj.*

non-moral ▻ *adj* **1** involving no moral or ethical considerations. **2** unconcerned with morality.

non-negotiable ▻ *adj* not open to negotiation; said of a cheque, etc: not NEGOTIABLE.

no-no /'noʊ noʊ/ ▻ *noun* (***no-nos*** or ***no-noes***) *colloq* **1** something which must not be done, said, etc. **2** something which is impossible; a NON-STARTER 1.

non-objective ▻ *adj, art* not aiming to be realistic.

non-observance ▻ *noun* failure to observe a rule, etc.

no-nonsense ▻ *adj* sensible and straightforward; tolerating no nonsense; practical □ *a no-nonsense approach.*

nonpareil /nɒnpə'reɪl, 'nɒnpərəl/ ▻ *adj* having no equal; matchless. ▻ *noun* a person or thing without equal. ⓒ 16c: French, from *non-* not + *pareil* equal.

non-participating ▻ *adj* **1** not taking part. **2** said of shares, etc: not giving the holder a right to a share in profits.

non-party ▻ *adj* independent of party politics.

non-persistent ▻ *adj* said of insecticides and pesticides, etc: that decompose rapidly after application and do not linger in the environment.

non-person ▻ *noun* a person, once prominent, who has slipped into obscurity.

nonplus /nɒn'plʌs/ ▻ *verb* (***nonplussed***, ***nonplussing***; *US* ***nonplused***, ***nonplusing***) to puzzle; to disconcert. ⓒ 16c: from Latin *non plus* no further.

non-profit ▻ *adj* not making or involving profit.

non-profit-making ▻ *adj* said of a business, organization, etc: not organized with the purpose of making a profit, but usually with the aim of covering costs, ie breaking even.

non-proliferation ▻ *noun* lack or limitation of the production or spread of something, especially the policy of limiting the production and ownership of nuclear or chemical weapons.

non-renewable resource ▻ *noun* any naturally occurring substance that is economically valuable, but which forms over such a long period of time that for all practical purposes it cannot be replaced. Compare RENEWABLE RESOURCE.

non-representational ▻ *adj, art* not aiming at the realistic depiction of objects.

non-residence ▻ *noun* the fact of not (either permanently or for the moment) residing at a place, especially where one's official or social duties require one to reside, or where one is entitled to reside. • **non-resident** *adj, noun.*

non-resistance ▻ *noun* **1** the principle of not resisting violence by force, or of not resisting authority. **2** passive submission.

non-resistant ▷ *adj* **1** unable to resist; likely to be affected by a disease. **2** passively submissive.

non-restrictive ▷ *adj* **1** not restrictive. **2** *grammar* said of a relative clause: that does not restrict the people or things to which its antecedent may refer.

non-returnable ▷ *adj* **1** said of a bottle or other container: on which a returnable deposit is not paid and which will not be accepted after use by the vendor for recycling. **2** said of a deposit, etc: that will not be returned in case of cancellation, etc.

non-return valve ▷ *noun* a valve incorporating a device to ensure flow in one direction only.

non-scheduled ▷ *adj* **1** not according to a schedule. **2** said of an airline: operating between specified points but not to a specific schedule of flights.

nonsense /ˈnɒnsəns/ ▷ *noun* **1** words or ideas that do not make sense. **2** foolishness; silly behaviour. ▷ *exclamation* you're quite wrong. • **make a nonsense of something** to destroy the effect of it; to make it pointless. ⌚ 17c.

nonsense verse ▷ *noun* verse deliberately written to convey an absurd meaning or no meaning at all.

nonsensical /nɒnˈsɛnsɪkəl/ ▷ *adj* making no sense; absurd. • **nonsensicality** *noun*. • **nonsensically** *adverb*. • **nonsensicalness** *noun*.

non sequitur /nɒnˈsɛkwɪtə(r)/ ▷ *noun* (abbreviation **non seq.**) **1** an illogical step in an argument. **2** *logic* a conclusion that does not follow from the premisses. ⌚ 16c: Latin, literally 'it does not follow'.

non-skid and **non-slip** ▷ *adj* said of a surface: designed to reduce the chance of sliding or slipping to a minimum.

non-smoker ▷ *noun* someone who does not smoke.

non-smoking ▷ *adj* said of a train carriage, aeroplane or bus, etc: in which smoking is not allowed.

non-specific ▷ *adj* **1** not specific. **2** said of a disease: not caused by any specific agent that can be identified □ ***non-specific urethritis.***

non-standard ▷ *adj* **1** not standard. **2** said of use of language: different to the usage of educated speakers and considered by some incorrect.

non-starter ▷ *noun* **1** a person, thing or idea, etc that has no chance of success. **2** a horse which, though entered for a race, does not run.

nonsteroidal anti-inflammatory drug see NSAID

non-stick ▷ *adj* said of a pan, etc: that has a coating to which food does not stick during cooking.

non-stop ▷ *adj, adverb* without a stop; which does not stop.

nonsuch see NONESUCH

nonsuit /ˈnɒnsuːt, -sjuːt/ *Eng law* ▷ *noun* the stopping of a suit either by the voluntary withdrawal of the plaintiff, or by the judge when the plaintiff has failed to make out cause of action, or to bring evidence. ▷ *verb* (***nonsuited, nonsuiting***) to order that a suit be dismissed. ⌚ 14c: Anglo-French *nonsute* or *nounsute* does not pursue.

non-U /nɒnˈjuː/ ▷ *adj, Brit colloq* said of behaviour, language, etc: not acceptable among the upper classes. Compare U[2]. ⌚ 1950s.

non-union ▷ *adj* **1** not attached, belonging or relating to a trade union. **2** not approved of by a trade union. **3** employing, or produced by, workers who do not belong to a trade union.

non-violence ▷ *noun* the ideal or practice of refraining from violence on grounds of principle. • **non-violent** *adj*.

non-voter ▷ *noun* **1** someone who does not vote, usually on principle. **2** someone who is not eligible to vote.

non-voting ▷ *adj* **1** said of shares: not giving the holder the right to vote on company decisions. **2** relating to a non-voter.

non-white ▷ *adj* said of a person: not belonging to one of the white-skinned races. ▷ *noun* (***non-whites***) a non-white person.

noodle[1] /ˈnuːdəl/ ▷ *noun* (*usually* **noodles**) *cookery* a thin strip of pasta, often made with egg. ⌚ 18c: from German *Nudel*.

noodle[2] /ˈnuːdəl/ ▷ *noun* **1** *colloq* a simpleton. **2** *colloq* a blockhead. **3** *N Amer* the head. ⌚ 18c.

nook /nʊk/ ▷ *noun* **1** a secluded retreat. **2** a corner or recess. • **every nook and cranny** absolutely everywhere. ⌚ 13c.

nooky or **nookie** /ˈnʊkɪ/ ▷ *noun, slang* sexual activity. ⌚ 1920s.

noon /nuːn/ ▷ *noun* midday; twelve o'clock. ⌚ 13c in this sense; Anglo-Saxon in obsolete sense referring to the ninth hour after sunrise, ie about 3pm: from Latin *nona* (*hora*) the ninth hour.

noonday ▷ *noun* midday. ▷ *adj* belonging to or relating to midday □ ***the noonday sun.***

no one or **no-one** ▷ *noun* nobody; no person. ⌚ 17c.

noontide ▷ *noun, literary* midday.

noose /nuːs/ ▷ *noun* **1** a loop made in the end of a rope, etc, with a sliding knot, used eg for killing someone by hanging. **2** any snare or bond. ▷ *verb* (***noosed, noosing***) to tie or snare someone or something in a noose. • **put one's head in a noose** to put oneself in a dangerous or vulnerable situation. ⌚ 15c: from French *nous*, from Latin *nodus* knot.

NOP ▷ *abbreviation* National Opinion Poll or Polls.

nope /noʊp/ ▷ *exclamation, slang* emphatic form of NO[1].

Nor. ▷ *abbreviation* **1** Norman. **2** North. **3** Norway. **4** Norwegian.

nor /nɔː(r)/ ▷ *conj* **1** (used to introduce alternatives after NEITHER) □ ***He neither knows nor cares*** □ ***They eat neither fish nor meat.*** **2** and not □ ***It didn't look appetizing, nor was it.*** ▷ *adverb* not either □ ***If you won't, nor shall I.*** ⌚ 13c: a contraction of Anglo-Saxon *nother*, from *ne* not + *other* either.

nor

See Usage Note at **neither**.

nor' /nɔː(r)/ ▷ *adj, in compounds, naut* north □ ***a nor'-wester*** □ ***nor'-nor'-east.***

noradrenalin or **noradrenaline** /nɔːrəˈdrɛnəlɪn/ ▷ *noun* a hormone produced by the ADRENAL GLANDS, controlling a wide range of physiological functions, and also secreted by the nerve endings in the sympathetic nervous system, acting as a chemical transmitter of nerve impulses. Also (*especially US*) called **norepinephrine** /nɔːrɛpɪˈnɛfrɪn/ . ⌚ 1930s.

Nordic /ˈnɔːdɪk/ ▷ *adj* **1** relating or belonging to Scandinavia or its inhabitants. **2** Germanic or Scandinavian in appearance, typically tall, blond and blue-eyed. **3** (**nordic**) denoting a type of competitive skiing with cross-country racing and ski-jumping. ⌚ 19c: from French *nordique*, from *nord* north.

Norf. ▷ *abbreviation, English county* Norfolk.

Norfolk jacket ▷ *noun* a man's loose pleated single-breasted belted jacket with pockets, originally worn when shooting duck. ⌚ 19c: from the name of the county.

nori /ˈnɒrɪ, ˈnɔːrɪ/ ▷ *noun* a seaweed used in Japanese cookery, either in dried sheets or as a paste. ⌚ 19c: Japanese.

noria /ˈnɔːrɪə/ ▷ *noun* (***norias***) an endless chain of buckets on a wheel, for raising water, eg from a stream into irrigation channels. ◷ 18c: Spanish, from Arabic *na'urah*, from *na'ara* to creak.

nork ▷ *noun, Austral slang* a woman's breast. ◷ 1920s: probably from Norco Co-operative Ltd, a NSW butter manufacturer.

norm ▷ *noun* **1** (**the norm**) a typical pattern or situation. **2** an accepted way of behaving, etc □ *social norms*. **3** a standard, eg for achievement in industry □ *production norms*. ◷ 19c: from Latin *norma* carpenter's square or a rule.

norm. ▷ *abbreviation* normal.

normal /ˈnɔːməl/ ▷ *adj* **1** usual; typical; not extraordinary. **2** mentally or physically sound □ *a normal baby*. **3** (**normal to something**) *geom* perpendicular. **4** *chem* said of a solution: (abbreviation **N**) a standard measurement of concentration, being a solution containing one equivalent weight of a dissolved substance per litre, eg *1N*, *2N*, etc. **5** *chem* (**n-**) said of hydrocarbon molecules: containing a single unbranched chain of carbon atoms □ *n-butane* □ *n-propane*. ▷ *noun* **1** what is average or usual. **2** *geom* a perpendicular line or plane. • **normally** *adverb* **1** in an ordinary or natural way. **2** usually. ◷ 15c: from Latin *normalis* regulated by a carpenter's square, from *norma* carpenter's square.

normal distribution ▷ *noun, statistics* a frequency distribution represented by a symmetrical, bell-shaped curve within which typical characteristics of a population (eg height) are enclosed.

normality /nɔːˈmalətɪ/ and (*N Amer*) **normalcy** /ˈnɔːrməlsɪ/ ▷ *noun* being normal; a normal state or quality.

normalize or **normalise** /ˈnɔːməlaɪz/ ▷ *verb* (***normalized, normalizing***) **1** *tr & intr* to make or become normal or regular. **2** to heat (steel) in order to refine the crystal structure and to relieve internal stress and improve strength. • **normalization** *noun*.

normal school ▷ *noun* in certain countries, especially France and N America: a training college for teachers. ◷ 19c: from French *école normal*, the first being intended to be a model for others.

Norman /ˈnɔːmən/ ▷ *noun* **1** a person from Normandy, especially one of the descendants of the Scandinavian settlers of N France, who then conquered England in 1066. **2** Norman French. ▷ *adj* **1** relating to or belonging to the Normans, their language, etc, or to Normandy. **2** *archit* signifying or relating to a building style typical in 10c and 11c Normandy, and 11c and 12c England, similar to ROMANESQUE, with round arches and heavy massive pillars. ◷ 13c: from French *Normant*, from Norse *Northmathr*.

normative /ˈnɔːmətɪv/ ▷ *adj* establishing a guiding standard or rules □ *normative grammar*. ◷ 19c: from NORM.

norm referencing ▷ *noun, education* comparing a pupil's abilities with those of his or her peers.

Norse /nɔːs/ ▷ *adj* **1** relating or belonging to ancient or medieval Scandinavia. **2** Norwegian. ▷ *noun* **1** the Germanic language group of Scandinavia. **2** (*also* OLD NORSE) the language of this group used in medieval Norway and its colonies. ▷ *plural noun, especially historical* the Scandinavians, especially the Norwegians. ◷ 16c: perhaps from Dutch *noorsch*.

Norseman ▷ *noun* a Scandinavian; a VIKING.

north /nɔːθ/ ▷ *noun* (*also* **North** or **the North**) **1** the direction to one's left when one faces the rising Sun. **2** MAGNETIC NORTH. **3** (*usually* **the North**) **a** any part of the Earth, a country or a town, etc lying in the direction of north; **b** in England: that part of England lying north of the Humber; **c** (**the North**) that part of the USA lying north of Maryland and the Ohio River, especially those states lying north of the MASON-DIXON LINE during the American Civil War. **4** (**the North**) the industrialized nations. **5** (*also* **North**) *bridge* the player or position occupying the place designated 'north' on the table. ▷ *adj* (*also* **North**) **1** in the north; on the side that is on or nearest the north. **2** coming from the direction of the north □ *a north wind*. ▷ *adverb* towards the north. ◷ Anglo-Saxon.

Northants ▷ *abbreviation, English county* Northamptonshire.

North Atlantic Drift see GULF STREAM

northbound ▷ *adj* going or leading towards the north.

the North Country ▷ *noun* (*also* **north country**) the northern part of a country, especially NORTH (*noun* 3a and 3b). ▷ *adj* (**north-country**) belonging to the northern part of the country, especially of England.

north-east ▷ *noun* (*sometimes* **North-East**) **1** the direction midway between north and east. **2** any part of the earth, or a country, etc lying in that direction. ▷ *adj* **1** in the north-east. **2** from the direction of the north-east □ *a north-east wind*. ▷ *adverb* in, to or towards the north-east.

north-easter or **nor'-easter** ▷ *noun* a strong wind or storm from the north-east.

north-easterly ▷ *adj* ▷ *adverb* **1** from the north-east. **2** (*also* **north-eastward**) towards the north-east. ▷ *noun* a wind or storm blowing from the north-east.

north-eastern ▷ *adj* **1** belonging to the north-east. **2** in, toward or facing the north-east or that direction.

north-eastward ▷ *adj, adverb* toward the north-east. ▷ *noun* the region to the north-east. • **north-eastwardly** *adj, adverb*. • **north-eastwards** *adverb*.

norther /ˈnɔːθə(r), ˈnɔːðə(r)/ ▷ *noun* a wind or storm from the north, especially a winter wind that blows from the north over Texas and the Gulf of Mexico. ◷ 19c.

northerly /ˈnɔːðəlɪ/ ▷ *adj* **1** said of a wind, etc: coming from the north. **2** being, looking or lying, etc towards the north. ▷ *adverb* **1** to or towards the north. **2** from the north. ▷ *noun* (***northerlies***) a northerly wind. • **northerliness** *noun*.

northern /ˈnɔːðən/ ▷ *adj* **1** belonging or relating to the NORTH. **2** in the north or in the direction toward it. **3** said of winds, etc: proceeding from the north. • **northerner** *noun* (*sometimes* **Northerner**) a person who lives in or comes from the north, especially the northern counties of England or the northern states of the USA. • **northernmost** *adj* situated furthest north.

the northern lights ▷ *plural noun* the AURORA BOREALIS.

North Germanic see GERMANIC

northing /ˈnɔːðɪŋ, ˈnɔːθɪŋ/ ▷ *noun, chiefly naut* **1** motion, distance or tendency northward. **2** distance of a heavenly body from the equator northward. **3** difference of LATITUDE made by a ship in sailing. **4** deviation towards the north.

north-north-east or **north-northeast** ▷ *noun* a direction midway between north and north-east. ▷ *adj, adverb* in this direction.

north-north-west or **north-northwest** ▷ *noun* a direction midway between north and north-west. ▷ *adj, adverb* in this direction.

North Pole or **north pole** ▷ *noun* **1** (*usually* **the North Pole**) the point on the Earth's surface that represents the northern end of its axis. **2** *astron* see POLE 1 sense 2. **3** (**north pole**) the north-seeking pole of a magnet.

North Sea oil and **North Sea gas** ▷ *noun, Brit* oil and natural gas, respectively, obtained from deposits below the North Sea, an arm of the Atlantic Ocean between the continent of Europe and the British Isles.

North Star ▷ *noun* the POLE STAR.

Northumb. ▷ *abbreviation, English county* Northumberland.

Northumbrian /nɔːˈθʌmbrɪən/ ▷ *noun* **1** a native of the modern Northumberland. **2** a native of the modern region of Northumbria, made up of Northumberland, Tyne and Wear, County Durham, Cleveland and parts of N Yorkshire. **3** *historical* a native of the old Kingdom of Northumbria (Anglo-Saxon *Northhymbre, Northhymbraland*) which stretched from the Humber to the Forth. ▷ *adj* belonging or relating to Northumbria or Northumberland.

northward ▷ *adj* towards the north. ▷ *adverb* (*also* **northwards**) towards the north. ▷ *noun* the northward direction or sector, etc. • **northwardly** *adj, adverb*.

north-west ▷ *noun* (*sometimes* **North-West**) the direction midway between north and west or any part of the earth or a country, etc lying in that direction. ▷ *adj* **1** in the north-west. **2** from the north-west ◻ *a north-west wind*. ▷ *adverb* in, to or towards the north-west.

north-wester ▷ *noun* a strong north-west wind.

north-westerly ▷ *adj, adverb* **1** from the north-west. **2** (*also* **north-westward**) toward the north-west. ▷ *noun* a wind or storm blowing from the north-west.

north-western ▷ *adj* **1** belonging to the north west. **2** in, towards or facing the north-west or that direction.

north-westward ▷ *adj, adverb* toward the north-west. ▷ *noun* the region to the north-west. • **north-westwardly** *adj, adverb*. • **north-westwards** *adverb*.

Norway rat ▷ *noun* the BROWN RAT.

Norway spruce ▷ *noun* a common European dark-green spruce tree.

Norwegian /nɔːˈwiːdʒən/ ▷ *adj* belonging or relating to Norway, a kingdom in N W Europe in the W part of the Scandinavian peninsula, its inhabitants or their language. ▷ *noun* **1** a citizen or inhabitant of, or person born in, Norway. **2** the language of Norway. ⓒ 17c: from Latin *Norvegia*, from Norse *northr* north + *vegr* way.

Nos, **Nos** or **nos** ▷ *abbreviation* numbers.

nose /noʊz/ ▷ *noun* **1** the projecting organ above the mouth, with which one smells and breathes. **2** an animal's snout or muzzle. **3** the sense of smell ◻ *He has a good nose.* **4** a scent or aroma, esp a wine's bouquet. **5** the front or projecting part of anything, eg a motor vehicle. **6** the nose as a symbol of inquisitiveness or interference ◻ *poke one's nose into something*. ▷ *verb* (**nosed**, **nosing**) **1** *tr & intr* to move carefully forward ◻ *nosed the car out of the yard*. **2** to detect something by smelling. **3** said of an animal: to sniff at something or nuzzle it. • **nosed** *adj, in compounds* having a nose of a specified type ◻ *red-nosed*. • **noseless** *adj*. • **nosing** *noun*. • **a nose for something** a faculty for detecting or recognizing something ◻ *He has a nose for a bargain*. • **by a nose** by a narrow margin. • **cut off one's nose to spite one's face** to act from resentment in a way that can only cause injury to oneself. • **get up someone's nose** *colloq* to annoy them. • **keep one's nose clean** *colloq* to avoid doing anything that might get one into trouble. • **look down** or **turn up one's nose at something** or **someone** *colloq* to show disdain for it or them. • **nose to tail** said of cars: in a slow-moving queue with the front of one almost touching the rear of the one in front. • **not see beyond** or **further than the end of one's nose** not to see the long-term consequences of one's actions. • **on the nose 1** said of bets made in horse-racing: to win only, ie not to come second, etc. **2** *N Amer* exactly. **3** *Austral colloq* unsavoury; offensive. • **pay through the nose** *colloq* to pay an exorbitant price. • **put someone's nose out of joint** *colloq* to affront them. • **under one's nose** or **one's very nose** in full view and very obviously in front of one; close at hand. ⓒ Anglo-Saxon *nosu*.

▪ **nose about** or **around** *colloq* to pry.

▪ **nose something out** to discover it by prying; to track it down.

nosebag ▷ *noun* a food bag for a horse, hung over its head.

noseband ▷ *noun* the part of a bridle that goes over the horse's nose.

nosebleed ▷ *noun* a flow of blood from the nose.

nose cone ▷ *noun* the cone-shaped cap on the front of a rocket, etc.

nosedive ▷ *noun* **1** a steep nose-downward plunge by an aircraft. **2** a sharp plunge or fall. **3** a sudden drop, eg in prices. ▷ *verb, intr* to plunge or fall suddenly. ⓒ Early 20c.

nosegay /ˈnoʊzgeɪ/ ▷ *noun* (**nosegays**) *old use* a posy, traditionally made up of fragrant flowers. ⓒ 15c: NOSE + GAY in the obsolete sense 'ornament'.

nose job ▷ *noun, colloq* plastic surgery performed on the nose in an attempt to improve its appearance. *Technical equivalent* RHINOPLASTY. ⓒ 1960s.

nosepiece ▷ *noun* **1** a NOSEBAND. **2** the part of a pair of spectacles that bridges the nose. **3** the end of a microscope tube that carries the OBJECT GLASS. **4** armour for the nose, eg part of a helmet.

nose rag ▷ *noun, slang* a handkerchief.

nose ring ▷ *noun* **1** an ornament worn in the nose, either in the SEPTUM or on either side. **2** a ring in the septum of an animal's nose by which it can be led.

nose wheel ▷ *noun* a single wheel at the front of a vehicle, especially an aircraft.

nosey see NOSY

nosh *slang* ▷ *noun* food. ▷ *verb* (**noshed**, **noshing**) *intr* to eat. ⓒ 1950s: Yiddish, from German *naschen* to nibble at something.

no-show ▷ *noun* someone who does not arrive for something they have booked, and who fails to cancel the booking. ⓒ 1940s: originally US.

nosh-up ▷ *noun, Brit slang* a large and satisfying meal.

no-side ▷ *noun, rugby* the end of a game.

nosier, **nosiest**, *etc* see under NOSY

nosocomial /nɒsoʊˈkoʊmɪəl/ ▷ *adj* relating or belonging to a hospital. ⓒ 19c: from Greek *nosos* disease + *komeion* to tend.

nosode /ˈnoʊsoʊd/ ▷ *noun, alternative medicine* a homeopathic remedy consisting of diseased tissue or a substance discharged during an illness. ⓒ From Greek *nosos* disease + *eidos* form.

nosography /nɒˈsɒgrəfɪ/ ▷ *noun* the description of diseases. • **nosographer** *noun*. • **nosographic** *adj*. ⓒ 17c: from Greek *nosos* disease.

nosology /nɒˈsɒlədʒɪ/ ▷ *noun* that branch of medicine which deals with the classification of diseases. • **nosological** *adj*. • **nosologist** *noun*. ⓒ 18c: from Greek *nosos* disease.

nostalgia /nɒˈstaldʒə/ ▷ *noun* **1** a yearning for the past. **2** homesickness. • **nostalgic** *adj*. • **nostalgically** *adverb*. ⓒ 18c in sense 2: from Greek *nostos* homecoming.

nostoc /ˈnɒstɒk/ ▷ *noun* a blue-green alga of the genus **Nostoc**, which is motile, forming a slime layer, and is found in soil, fresh water and the sea. ⓒ 17c: coined by Paracelsus.

nostril /ˈnɒstrɪl/ ▷ *noun* either of the two external openings in the nose, through which one breathes and smells, etc. ⓒ Anglo-Saxon *nosthyrl*, from *nosu* nose + *thyrel* hole or opening.

nostrum /ˈnɒstrəm/ ▷ *noun* **1** a patent medicine; a panacea or cure-all. **2** a pet solution or remedy, eg one for political ills. ⓒ 17c: Latin, meaning 'our own (make or brand, etc)'.

nosy or **nosey** /ˈnoʊzɪ/ ▷ *adj* (*nosier*, *nosiest*) *derog* inquisitive; prying. ▷ *noun* (*nosies* or *noseys*) a nickname for a prying person. • **nosily** *adverb*. • **nosiness** *noun*. ◷ Early 20c: from NOSE.

nosy parker ▷ *noun, derog, colloq* a nosy person; a busybody. ◷ Early 20c.

not ▷ *adverb* (with auxiliary and modal verbs often shortened to **n't** and joined to the verb) **1** used to make a negative statement, etc □ *That is not fair.* □ *Those aren't right.* □ *Why didn't they come?* **2** used with verbs of opinion or intention, etc to make the clause or infinitive following the verb negative, as in *I don't think he's right*, meaning *I think he is not right.* **3** used in place of a negative clause or predicate □ *might be late, but I hope not.* **4** (indicating surprise or an expectation of agreement, etc) surely it is the case that □ *Haven't you heard?* □ *Lovely, isn't it?* **5** used to contrast the untrue with the true □ *It's a cloud, not a mountain.* **6** barely □ *with his face not two inches from mine.* **7** by no means □ *not nearly enough* □ *Not everyone would agree.* **8** *colloq* used by a speaker to emphatically deny what they have just said □ *looks a lot like Brad Pitt…not.* • **not a …** absolutely no … □ *not a sound.* • **not at all** don't mention it; it's a pleasure. • **not just** or not only, *etc* used to introduce what is usually the lesser of two points, etc □ *not just his family, but his wider public.* • **not on** *colloq* **1** not possible. **2** not morally or socially, etc acceptable. • **not that …** though it is not the case that … □ *not that I care.* ◷ 14c: a variant of NOUGHT.

nota bene /noʊtə ˈbɛnɪ/ ▷ *verb* (abbreviation **NB** or **nb**) take note; mark well. ◷ 18c: Latin.

notable /ˈnoʊtəbəl/ ▷ *adj* **1** worth noting; significant. **2** distinguished. ▷ *noun* a notable person. • **notability** *noun*. • **notableness** *noun*. • **notably** *adverb* as something or someone notable, especially in a list or group □ *several people, notably my father.* • **notable for something** famous on account of it. ◷ 14c: from Latin *notabilis*, from *notare* to note or observe.

notaphily /noʊˈtafɪlɪ/ ▷ *noun* the collecting of banknotes and cheques, etc as a hobby. • **notaphilic** *adj*. • **notaphilism** *noun*. • **notaphilist** *noun*. ◷ 1970s: from NOTE 5.

notarize or **notarise** /ˈnoʊtəraɪz/ ▷ *verb* (*notarized, notarizing*) **1** to attest to something. **2** to authenticate (a document, etc) as a notary. ◷ 1926s.

notary /ˈnoʊtərɪ/ ▷ *noun* (*notaries*) (*in full* **notary public**) (*plural notaries public*) a public official with the legal power to draw up and witness official documents, and to administer oaths, etc. • **notarial** /noʊˈtɛərɪəl/ *adj* **1** relating to notaries or their work. **2** said of a document: drawn up by a notary. • **notarially** *adverb*. • **notaryship** *noun*. ◷ 14c: from Latin *notarius* secretary or clerk.

notate ▷ *verb* (*notated, notating*) to write (music, etc) in notation. ◷ Early 20c.

notation /noʊˈteɪʃən/ ▷ *noun* **1** the representation of quantities, numbers, musical sounds or movements, etc by symbols. **2** any set of such symbols. **3** the act or process of notating. • **notational** *adj*. ◷ 16c in obsolete sense 'etymological sense of a word': from Latin *notatio* marking.

notch ▷ *noun* (*notches*) **1** a small V-shaped cut or indentation. **2** a nick. **3** *colloq* a step or level. **4** *N Amer* a narrow pass. ▷ *verb* (*notches, notched, notching*) **1** to cut a notch in something. **2** to record something with, or as if with, a notch. **3** to fit (an arrow) to a bowstring. • **notched** *adj*. • **notchy** *adj* (*notchier, notchiest*) **1** having notches. **2** said of a manual gearbox: not operating smoothly and easily. ◷ 16c: from French *oche*, then *an oche* coming to be understood as *a notch*.

■ **notch something up 1** to record it as a score □ *notched it up on the scoreboard.* **2** to achieve it.

note /noʊt/ ▷ *noun* **1** (*often* **notes**) a brief written record made for later reference □ *took a note of the number.* **2** a short informal letter □ *a note of thanks.* **3** a brief comment explaining a textual point, etc. Often *in compounds* □ *a footnote* □ *endnote.* **4** a short account or essay. **5 a** a banknote; **b** a promissory note. **6** especially in diplomacy: a formal communication. **7** attention; notice □ *buildings worthy of note.* **8** distinction; eminence □ *women of note.* **9** *music* **a** a written symbol indicating the pitch and length of a musical sound; **b** the sound itself; **c** a key on a keyboard instrument. **10** *especially poetic* the call or cry of a bird or animal. **11** an impression conveyed; feeling; mood □ *with a note of panic in her voice.* ▷ *verb* (*noted, noting*) **1** (*also* **note something down**) to write it down. **2** to notice something; to be aware of it. **3** to pay close attention to something. **4** to mention or to remark upon something. **5** *music* to write down (music) in notes. **6** to annotate something. • **noted** *adj* **1** famous; eminent □ *a noted surgeon* □ *noted for his use of colour.* **2** notorious. • **notedly** *adverb*. • **noteless** *adj*. • **compare notes** to exchange ideas and opinions, especially about a particular person, event or thing. • **of note 1** well-known; distinguished. **2** significant; worthy of attention. • **strike a false note** to act or speak inappropriately. • **strike the right note** to act or speak appropriately. • **take note** (*often* **take note of something**) to observe it carefully, to pay attention to it. ◷ 14c: from Latin *nota* a mark or sign.

notebook ▷ *noun* **1** a small book in which to write notes, etc. **2** a small portable computer, smaller than a LAPTOP. ◷ 16c; 1980s in sense 2.

notecase ▷ *noun* a wallet.

notelet /ˈnoʊtlɪt/ ▷ *noun* a folded piece of notepaper, often a decorated one, for writing short letters or NOTES (*noun* 2) on.

notepad ▷ *noun* a block of writing-paper for making notes on.

notepaper ▷ *noun* paper for writing letters on.

noteworthy ▷ *adj* worthy of notice; remarkable. • **noteworthiness** *noun*.

nothing /ˈnʌθɪŋ/ ▷ *noun* **1** no thing; not anything. **2 a** zero number or quantity; **b** the figure 0 representing this. **3 a** very little; **b** something of no importance or not very impressive; **c** no difficulty or trouble. **4** an absence of anything. ▷ *adverb* not at all □ *nothing daunted.* • **nothingness** *noun* **1** the state of being nothing or of not existing. **2** emptiness. **3** worthlessness. **4** a thing of no value. • **be nothing to something** to be much less than it; to be trivial compared with it □ *That's nothing to what I saw.* • **be nothing to do with someone** or **something 1** to be unconnected with them. **2** to be of no concern to them. • **come to nothing** to fail or peter out. • **for nothing 1** free; without payment or personal effort □ *You can have it for nothing.* **2** for no good reason; in vain □ *all that work for nothing.* **3** *derog* because it is so obvious that you should know □ *I'll tell you that for nothing.* • **have nothing on 1** to be free; to have no engagement. **2** to be naked. • **have nothing on someone** or **something 1** *colloq* to have no information about them □ *Local police had nothing on him till now.* **2** *colloq* to be not nearly as good, beautiful, skilled, etc as them □ *She has nothing on her sister.* • **have nothing to do with someone** or **something 1** to avoid them. **2** to be unconnected with them. **3** to be of no concern to them. • **like nothing on earth** *colloq* **1** grotesque. **2** frightful. • **make nothing of someone** or **something** not to understand them or it. • **mean nothing to someone 1** to be incomprehensible to them. **2** to be of no importance to them. • **nothing but …** usually said of something unwelcome: only; merely □ *nothing but trouble.* • **nothing doing** *colloq* **1** an expression of refusal. **2** no hope of success. • **nothing for it but to …** no alternative except to … □ *nothing for it but to own up.* • **nothing if not …** primarily, above all, or very … □ *nothing if not keen.* • **nothing like …** by no means … □ *nothing like good enough.* • **nothing like someone** or **something** not at all like them or it. • **nothing much** very little. • **nothing short of** or **less**

than something **1** downright; absolute ◻ *They were nothing less than criminals.* **2** only ◻ *will accept nothing less than an apology.* • **nothing to it** or **in it** straightforward; easy. • **think nothing of something 1** to regard it as normal or straightforward. **2** to feel no hesitation, guilt or regret about it ◻ *thinks nothing of leaving the dog alone all day.* • **think nothing of it** it doesn't matter; there is no need for thanks. • **to say nothing of something** as well as it; not to mention it. ◷ Anglo-Saxon.

notice /ˈnoʊtɪs/ ▻ *noun* **1** an announcement displayed or delivered publicly. **2** one's attention ◻ *It escaped my notice.* **3** a warning or notification given, eg before leaving, or dismissing someone from, a job ◻ *give in one's notice* ◻ *will continue until further notice.* **4** a review of a performance or book, etc. ▻ *verb* (***noticed, noticing***) **1** to observe; to become aware of something. **2** to remark on something. **3** to show signs of recognition of someone, etc. **4** to treat someone with polite attention. • **at short notice** with little warning or time for preparation, etc. • **take notice** to take interest in one's surroundings, etc. • **take notice of someone** or something to pay attention to them. ◷ 15c: French, from Latin *notitia*, from *notus* known.

noticeable ▻ *adj* easily seen; clearly apparent. • **noticeably** *adverb*.

noticeboard ▻ *noun* a board on which notices are displayed.

notification /noʊtɪfɪˈkeɪʃən/ ▻ *noun* **1** an announcement or warning. **2** the act or means of notifying.

notify /ˈnoʊtɪfaɪ/ ▻ *verb* (***notifies, notified, notifying***) to tell or to inform. • **notifiable** *adj* said of infectious diseases: that must be reported to the public health authorities. ◷ 14c: from Latin *notus* known + *facere* to make.

▪ **notify someone of something** to inform or warn them about it.

notion /ˈnoʊʃən/ ▻ *noun* **1** an impression, conception or understanding. **2** a belief or principle. **3** an inclination, whim or fancy. **4** (**notions**) *originally N Amer, especially US* small items used in sewing such as pins, needles, threads and fastenings, etc. • **notional** *adj* **1** existing in imagination only. **2** theoretical. **3** hypothetical. **4** *grammar* having a full meaning of its own. • **notionalist** *noun* a theorist. • **notionally** *adverb*. ◷ 16c: from Latin *notio* an idea.

notochord /ˈnoʊtoʊkɔːd/ or **notochordal** /-dəl/ *noun*, *zool* a flexible rod-like structure, which strengthens and supports the body in the embryos and adults of more primitive animals. In vertebrates it is replaced by the spinal column before birth. ◷ 19c: from Greek *notos* back + *chorde* a string.

notoriety /noʊtəˈraɪətɪ/ ▻ *noun* **1** fame or reputation, usually for something disreputable. **2** publicity; public exposure.

notorious /noʊˈtɔːrɪəs/ ▻ *adj* famous, usually for something disreputable ◻ *a notorious criminal.* • **notoriously** *adverb*. • **notoriousness** *noun*. ◷ 16c: from Latin *notorius* well-known.

not-out ▻ *adj, adverb, cricket* **1** still in. **2** at the end of the innings without having been put out.

not proven / — ˈproʊvən/ ▻ *noun, Scots law* an alternative verdict resorted to when there is insufficient evidence to convict, resulting in the freedom of the accused. Also *as adj* ◻ *not proven verdict.* Compare GUILTY 1, INNOCENT 2.

no-trump *bridge* ▻ *noun* (*also* **no-trumps**) a call for the playing of a hand without any trump suit. ▻ *adj* said of a hand: possible to play without trumps.

Notts. ▻ *abbreviation, English county* Nottinghamshire.

notwithstanding /nɒtwɪðˈstandɪŋ/ ▻ *prep* in spite of. ▻ *adverb* in spite of that; however. ▻ *conj* although.

nougat /ˈnuːgɑː, ˈnʌgət/ ▻ *noun* a chewy sweet containing chopped nuts, cherries, etc. ◷ 19c: French, from Latin *nux* nut.

nought /nɔːt/ ▻ *noun* **1** the figure 0; zero. **2** *old use* nothing; naught. • **set something at nought 1** to despise it. **2** to disregard it. ◷ Anglo-Saxon *noht*, from *ne* not + *owiht* aught.

noughts and crosses ▻ *singular noun* a game for two players taking alternate turns, the aim being to complete a row of three noughts (for one player) or three crosses (for the other) within a square framework of nine squares.

noun /naʊn/ ▻ *noun, grammar* (abbreviation **n.**) a word used as the name of a person, animal, thing, place or quality. • **nounal** *adj* (see also NOMINAL). • **nouny** *adj* nounlike. See also COMMON NOUN, PROPER NOUN, COUNT NOUN, MASS NOUN, ABSTRACT (*adj* 4), CONCRETE (*adj* 4). ◷ 14c as *nown*: from Latin *nomen* name.

nourish /ˈnʌrɪʃ/ ▻ *verb* (***nourishes, nourished, nourishing***) **1** to supply someone or something with food needed for survival and growth. **2 a** to encourage the growth of something; **b** to foster (an idea, etc). • **nourisher** *noun*. • **nourishing** *adj*. • **nourishment** *noun* **1** something that nourishes; food. **2** the act of nourishing. **3** the state of being nourished. ◷ 13c as *noris*, meaning 'to suckle' or 'to nurse': from French *norir*, from Latin *nutrire* to feed, foster or care for.

nous /naʊs/ ▻ *noun colloq* common sense; gumption. ◷ 18c; 17c in original sense 'the intellect': Greek, meaning 'mind'.

nouveau riche /ˈnuːvoʊ riːʃ/ ▻ *noun, derog* (*usually in plural* ***nouveaux riches*** /ˈnuːvoʊ riːʃ/) people who have recently acquired wealth but lack the upper-class breeding to go with it. ◷ 19c: French, meaning 'new rich'.

nouvelle cuisine /ˈnuːvɛl kwɪˈziːn/ ▻ *noun* a simple style of cookery characterized by much use of fresh produce and elegant presentation. ◷ 1980s: French, meaning 'new cookery'.

Nouvelle Vague see under NEW WAVE

Nov. ▻ *abbreviation* November.

nova /ˈnoʊvə/ ▻ *noun* (***novae*** /-viː/ or ***novas***) *astron* a normally faint star that suddenly flares into brightness and then fades again. ◷ 19c: from Latin *nova stella* new star.

novel[1] /ˈnɒvəl/ ▻ *noun* **1** a book-length fictional story usually involving relationships between characters, their emotional crises and events concerning them. **2** (**the novel**) such writing as a literary genre. • **novelish** *adj*. • **novelist** *noun* a writer of a novel or novels. • **novelistic** *adj* relating to, or characteristic of, novels. ◷ 15c: from Italian *novella* short story, from Latin *novellus* new.

novel[2] /ˈnɒvəl/ ▻ *adj* new; original; previously unheard-of. ◷ 15c: from Latin *novellus* new.

novelese /nɒvəˈliːz/ ▻ *noun, derog* a hackneyed style of writing typical of poor novels. ◷ Early 20c.

novelette /nɒvəˈlɛt/ ▻ *noun, derog* a short novel, especially one that is trite or sentimental. • **novelettish** *adj*. • **novelettist** *noun*. ◷ Early 19c.

novella /nɒˈvɛlə/ ▻ *noun* (***novellas***) a short story or short novel. ◷ Early 20c: Italian.

novelty /ˈnɒvəltɪ/ ▻ *noun* (***novelties***) **1** the quality of being new and intriguing. **2** something new and strange. **3** a small, cheap and usually kitsch toy or souvenir. ◷ 14c: from French *novelté*.

November /noʊˈvɛmbə(r)/ ▻ *noun* **1** (abbreviation **Nov.**) the eleventh month of the year, which follows October and comes before December. **2** *communications* in the NATO alphabet: the word used to denote the letter 'N' (see table at NATO ALPHABET). ◷ 13c: Latin, meaning 'the ninth month', from *novem* nine; in the Roman calendar the year began in March.

novena /noʊ'viːnə/ ▻ *noun* (***novenas***) *RC Church* a series of special prayers and services held over a period of nine days. ⓒ 19c: from Latin *noveni* nine each.

novice /'nɒvɪs/ ▻ *noun* **1** someone new in anything; a beginner. **2** someone who has recently joined a religious community but not yet taken vows; a probationary member of such a community. **3** *horse-racing* a horse that has not won a race in a season prior to the current season. **4** a competitor that has not yet won a recognized prize. ⓒ 14c: from Latin *novicius*, from *novus* new.

noviciate or **novitiate** /nə'vɪʃɪət/ ▻ *noun* **1** the period of being a novice, especially one in a religious community. **2** the state of being a novice. **3** the novices' quarters in a religious community. ⓒ 17c: from French *noviciat*.

Novocaine /'noʊvəkeɪn/ ▻ *noun, trademark* a proprietary name for PROCAINE.

now /naʊ/ ▻ *adverb* **1** at the present time or moment. **2** immediately. **3** in narrative: then □ ***He now turned from journalism to fiction.*** **4** in these circumstances; as things are □ ***I planned to go, but now I can't.*** **5** up to the present □ ***has now been teaching 13 years.*** **6** used in conversation to accompany explanations, warnings, commands, rebukes, words of comfort, etc □ ***Now, this is what happened*** □ ***Careful now!*** ▻ *noun* the present time. ▻ *conj* (*also* **now that**) because at last; because at this time □ ***Now we're all here, we'll begin.*** • **any day** or **moment** or **time now** at any time soon. • **as of now** from this time onward. • **for now** until later; for the time being. • **just now 1** a moment ago. **2** at this very moment. • **now and again** or **now and then** sometimes; occasionally. • **now for** used in anticipation, or in turning from one thing to another □ ***Now for some fun!*** • **now, now! 1** used to comfort someone □ ***Now, now, don't cry!*** **2** (*also* **now then!**) a warning or rebuke □ ***Now, now! Less noise please!*** • **now…, now…** one moment…, and the next… □ ***now crying, now laughing.*** ⓒ Anglo-Saxon *nu*.

nowadays /'naʊədeɪz/ ▻ *adverb* in these present times. ⓒ 14c.

noway /noʊ'weɪ/, **noways** /-'weɪz/ and **nowise** /noʊ'waɪz/ ▻ *adverb* in no way, manner or degree. See also NO WAY at NO².

Nowell or **Nowel** /noʊ'ɛl/ ▻ *noun* NOEL. ⓒ 14c: French.

nowhere /'noʊwɛə(r)/ ▻ *adverb* in or to no place; not anywhere. ▻ *noun* a non-existent place. • **from** or **out of nowhere** suddenly and inexplicably □ ***They appeared from nowhere.*** • **get nowhere** *colloq* to make no progress. • **in the middle of nowhere** *colloq* isolated; remote from towns or cities, etc. • **nowhere near** *colloq* not nearly; by no means □ ***nowhere near fast enough.*** • **nowhere to be found** or **seen** lost.

no-win ▻ *adj* said of a situation: in which one is bound to fail or lose, whatever one does. ⓒ 1960s.

nowt /naʊt/ ▻ *noun, colloq or dialect* nothing. ⓒ 19c variant of NAUGHT.

noxious /'nɒkʃəs/ ▻ *adj* harmful; poisonous. • **noxiously** *adverb*. • **noxiousness** *noun*. ⓒ 17c: from Latin *noxius* harmful.

nozzle /'nɒzəl/ ▻ *noun* an outlet tube or spout, especially as a fitting attached to the end of a hose, etc. ⓒ 17c: a diminutive of NOSE.

NP or **np** ▻ *abbreviation* **1** new paragraph. **2** (*always* **NP**) *IVR* New Providence, Bahamas. **3** Notary Public. **4** *grammar* noun phrase.

Np ▻ *symbol, chem* neptunium.

NPA ▻ *abbreviation* Newspaper Publishers' Association.

NPFA ▻ *abbreviation* National Playing Fields Association.

nr ▻ *abbreviation* near.

NRV ▻ *abbreviation* net realizable value.

NS ▻ *abbreviation* **1** (*also* **ns**) new series. **2** said of dates: New Style. **3** *Canadian province* Nova Scotia. **4** Nuclear Ship.

ns ▻ *abbreviation* **1** nanosecond or nanoseconds. **2** new series. **3** not specified. **4** (*also* **n/s**) non-smoker.

NSAID ▻ *abbreviation* nonsteroidal anti-inflammatory drug, any one of a class of drugs used for treating rheumatic diseases, eg aspirin.

NSB ▻ *abbreviation* National Savings Bank.

NSC ▻ *abbreviation* **1** National Safety Council. **2** *US* National Security Council.

NSPCC ▻ *abbreviation* National Society for the Prevention of Cruelty to Children.

NSU ▻ *abbreviation* non-specific urethritis.

NSW ▻ *abbreviation, Austral state* New South Wales.

NT ▻ *abbreviation* **1** National Trust. **2** New Testament. **3** *Austral state* Northern Territory. **4** *cards* no-trumps.

-n't /ənt/ ▻ *contraction* not. See under NOT.

NTA ▻ *abbreviation* National Training Award.

Nth ▻ *abbreviation* North.

nth /ɛnθ/ ▻ *adj* (*sometimes* **n^th^**)**1** denoting an indefinite position in a sequence □ ***to the nth degree.*** **2** denoting an item or occurrence that is many times removed from the first in a sequence □ ***I'm telling you for the nth time.***

NTP or **ntp** ▻ *abbreviation* normal temperature and pressure. Former name for STP.

NTS ▻ *abbreviation* National Trust for Scotland.

nt wt ▻ *abbreviation* net weight.

NU ▻ *abbreviation* name unknown.

nu /njuː/ ▻ *noun* the thirteenth letter of the Greek alphabet. See table at GREEK ALPHABET.

NUAAW ▻ *abbreviation* National Union of Agricultural and Allied Workers.

nuance /'njuːɑːns, njʊəns/ ▻ *noun* a subtle variation in colour, meaning or expression, etc. ⓒ 18c: French, meaning 'shade' or 'hue'.

the nub ▻ *noun* the central and most important issue; the crux □ ***the nub of the matter.*** ⓒ 19c: from German *knubbe*.

nubile /'njuːbaɪl/ ▻ *adj* said of a young woman: **1** sexually mature. **2** marriageable. **3** sexually attractive. • **nubility** *noun*. ⓒ 17c: from Latin *nubilis*, from *nubere* to veil oneself, (hence) to marry.

nuc. ▻ *abbreviation* nuclear.

nucellus /njʊ'sɛləs/ ▻ *noun* (***nucelli*** /-laɪ/) *bot* in seed-bearing plants: the greater part of the OVULE, containing the embryo sac and nutritive tissue. ⓒ 19c: from Latin *nucella* a little nut, from *nux*, *nucis* a nut.

nucha /'njuːkə/ ▻ *noun* (***nuchae*** /-kiː/) *anatomy* the nape of the neck. • **nuchal** *adj*. ⓒ 15c: Latin, from Arabic *nukha* spinal marrow.

nuciferous /njʊ'sɪfərəs/ ▻ *adj, bot* nut-bearing. ⓒ 17c: from Latin *nux*, *nucis* nut.

nucivorous /njʊ'sɪvərəs/ ▻ *adj, zool* nut-eating. ⓒ 19c: from Latin *nux*, *nucis* nut.

nuclear /'njuːklɪə(r)/ ▻ *adj* **1** having the nature of, or like, a NUCLEUS. **2** belonging or relating to atoms or their nuclei □ ***nuclear physics.*** **3** relating to or produced by the fission or fusion of atomic nuclei □ ***nuclear energy.*** ⓒ 19c.

nuclear chemistry ▻ *noun* the branch of chemistry concerned with the atomic nucleus and its reactions, involving large energy changes.

nuclear disarmament ▻ *noun* a country's act of giving up its nuclear weapons.

nuclear energy ▷ *noun* energy produced through a nuclear reaction. Also called **atomic energy**.

nuclear envelope see under ENVELOPE

nuclear family ▷ *noun* the basic family unit, thought of as the mother, father and children only. Compare EXTENDED FAMILY, SINGLE PARENT. ⓘ 1940s.

nuclear fission ▷ *noun* a reaction in which an atomic nucleus of a radioactive element splits by bombardment from an external source, with simultaneous release of large amounts of energy, used for electric power generation. ⓘ 1930s in this sense.

nuclear-free ▷ *adj* said of a zone or state, etc: where the manufacture, storage, transport and deployment of nuclear weapons, the manufacture or use of nuclear energy, and the transport or disposal of nuclear waste are all banned.

nuclear fuel ▷ *noun* material such as URANIUM or PLUTONIUM used to produce nuclear energy.

nuclear fusion ▷ *noun* a THERMONUCLEAR reaction in which two atomic nuclei combine (usually DEUTERIUM and TRITIUM with formation of HELIUM), with a release of large amounts of energy, the uncontrolled form of which was the basis of the hydrogen bomb. ⓘ 1950s in this sense.

nuclearize or **nuclearise** /ˈnjuːklɪəraɪz/ ▷ *verb* (***nuclearized, nuclearizing***) **1** to make something nuclear. **2** to supply or fit something with nuclear weapons. • **nuclearization** *noun*. ⓘ 1960s.

nuclear magnetic resonance ▷ *noun* (abbreviation **NMR**) the absorption of electromagnetic radiation at a precise frequency by an atomic nucleus with a MAGNETIC MOMENT in an external magnetic field.

nuclear medicine ▷ *noun* the branch of medicine concerned with the use of radioactive isotopes to study, diagnose and treat diseases.

nuclear physics ▷ *noun* the study of atomic nuclei, especially relating to the generation of NUCLEAR ENERGY.

nuclear power ▷ *noun* power, especially electricity, obtained from reactions by NUCLEAR FISSION or NUCLEAR FUSION. • **nuclear-powered** *adj*.

nuclear reaction ▷ *noun* a process of fusion or fission as atomic nuclei interact with each other or with another particle.

nuclear reactor ▷ *noun* an apparatus for producing nuclear energy, eg to generate electricity, by means of a sustained and controlled chain reaction of NUCLEAR FISSION. *Formerly called* **atomic pile**.

nuclear waste ▷ *noun* the radioactive waste material that is produced during the operation of a nuclear reactor, the manufacture of nuclear weapons, or the mining and extraction of nuclear fuels.

nuclear weapon ▷ *noun* a weapon that derives its destructive force from the energy released during NUCLEAR FISSION or NUCLEAR FUSION. Also called **atomic weapon**.

nuclear winter ▷ *noun* a period without light, heat or growth, predicted as a likely after-effect of nuclear war.

nuclease /ˈnjuːklɪeɪz/ ▷ *noun, biochem* any enzyme that catalyses the splitting of the chain of nucleotides comprising NUCLEIC ACIDS.

nucleate /ˈnjuːklɪeɪt/ ▷ *verb* (***nucleated, nucleating***) **1** *tr & intr* to form, or form something into, a nucleus. **2** *chem* to act as a nucleus for (a crystal). ▷ *adj* having a nucleus. • **nucleation** *noun*. ⓘ 19c.

nuclei *plural of* NUCLEUS

nucleic acid /njuːˈkliːɪk —/ ▷ *noun* a chain of nucleotides, either DNA or RNA, found in all living cells. ⓘ Late 19c.

nucleo- /njuːklɪoʊ/ ▷ *combining form, denoting* **1** nuclear. **2** nucleic acid. **3** nucleus.

nucleolus /njʊˈklɪələs, njuːklɪˈoʊləs/ ▷ *noun* (***nucleoli*** /-laɪ/) *biol* a spherical body in the nucleus of most plant and animal cells, comprising protein and NUCLEOTIDES, and concerned with the production of protein. ⓘ 19c.

nucleon /ˈnjuːklɪɒn/ ▷ *noun, physics* a PROTON or NEUTRON. ⓘ 1920s: from NUCLEUS.

nucleonics /njuːklɪˈɒnɪks/ ▷ *singular noun* the study of the uses of radioactivity and nuclear energy. ⓘ 1940s.

nucleon number ▷ *noun, chem* MASS NUMBER.

nucleoside /ˈnjuːklɪəsaɪd/ ▷ *noun, biochem* an organic compound, similar to a NUCLEOTIDE, but lacking the phosphate group. Compare NUCLEOTIDE. ⓘ Early 20c.

nucleotide ▷ *noun, biochem* an organic compound consisting of a PURINE or PYRIMIDINE base, a sugar molecule, and a phosphate group bonded together, four of which in DNA are combined in numerous permutations to form the GENETIC CODE. Compare NUCLEOSIDE. ⓘ Early 20c.

nucleus /ˈnjuːklɪəs/ ▷ *noun* (***nuclei*** /-klɪaɪ/) **1** *physics* the positively charged tiny central part of an atom, consisting of neutrons and protons and surrounded by electrons. **2** *biol* the central part of a plant or animal cell, containing genetic material. **3** *chem* a stable group of atoms in a molecule acting as a base for the formation of compounds. **4** *chem* a small particle acting as the basis on which crystals can grow. **5** a core round which things accumulate. ⓘ 18c, meaning 'a central part': Latin, meaning 'kernel'.

nuclide /ˈnjuːklaɪd/ ▷ *noun, physics* one of two or more atoms that contain the same number of PROTONS and the same number of NEUTRONS in their nuclei, and so have the same ATOMIC NUMBER and MASS NUMBER. ⓘ 1940s.

NUCPS ▷ *abbreviation* National Union of Civil and Public Servants.

nude /njuːd/ ▷ *adj* **1** wearing no clothes; naked. **2** bare; uncovered. **3** *law* **a** lacking a necessary legal requirement; **b** said of contracts and agreements, etc: made without a consideration. **4** flesh-coloured. ▷ *noun* **1** a representation of one or more naked figures in painting or sculpture, etc. **2** someone naked. **3** the state of nakedness □ *in the nude*. • **nudely** *adverb*. • **nudeness** *noun*. See also NUDISM. ⓘ 16c: from Latin *nudus* naked.

nudge /nʌdʒ/ ▷ *verb* (***nudged, nudging***) **1** to poke or push someone gently, especially with the elbow, to get attention, etc. **2** *intr* to push slightly, or little by little □ *The driver nudged forward out of the side street.* ▷ *noun* a gentle prod. • **nudge nudge, wink wink** or **nudge-nudge** *colloq* said (with a show of confidentiality) to imply some disreputable practice, or a sexual innuendo ⓘ 1970s catch phrase from the British TV comedy show *Monty Python's Flying Circus.* ⓘ 17c: possibly from Norwegian dialect *nugga* to push or rub.

nudibranch /ˈnjuːdɪbraŋk/ ▷ *noun* (***nudibranchs***) a shell-less marine gastropod with gills exposed on the back and sides of the body. ⓘ 19c: from Latin *nudus* naked + *branchia* gills.

nudie /ˈnjuːdɪ/ *colloq* ▷ *adj* said of films, shows and magazines, etc: featuring nudity. ▷ *noun* (***nudies***) such a film, etc.

nudism /ˈnjuːdɪzəm/ *noun* **1** the practice of not wearing clothes, as a matter of principle. **2** *US* NATURISM. • **nudist** *noun* someone who wears no clothes, as a matter of principle. Also *as adj*. • **nudity** *noun*.

nuée ardente /njueɪ ɑːˈdɑ̃t/ *noun* (***nuées ardentes*** /njueɪ ɑːˈdɑ̃t/) a cloud of hot gas and ash, etc from a volcano, spreading horizontally. ⓘ Early 20c: French, meaning 'burning cloud'.

nugatory /ˈnjuːgətərɪ/ ▷ *adj, formal* **1** worthless; trifling; valueless. **2** ineffective; futile. **3** invalid. • **nugatoriness** *noun*. ⓘ 17c: from Latin *nugae* trifles.

nugget /ˈnʌgɪt/ ▷ *noun* **1** a lump, especially of gold. **2** a small piece of something precious □ *nuggets of wisdom.* • **nuggety** *adj* **1** full of nuggets, or like nuggets. **2** *Austral* stocky; thickset. ⓒ 19c.

NUGMW ▷ *abbreviation* National Union of General and Municipal Workers.

nuisance /ˈnjuːsəns/ ▷ *noun* **1** an annoying or troublesome person, thing or circumstance. **2** *law* something obnoxious to the community or an individual, that is disallowed by law. • **make a nuisance of oneself** to behave annoyingly. ⓒ 15c: French, from *nuire* to injure.

NUJ ▷ *abbreviation* National Union of Journalists.

nuke /njuːk/ ▷ *verb* (***nuked, nuking***) *slang* to attack with nuclear weapons. ▷ *noun* a nuclear weapon. ⓒ 1950s.

null /nʌl/ ▷ *adj* **1** legally invalid □ *declared null and void.* **2** with no significance or value. **3** *math* said of a set: with no members; empty. • **nullity** *noun* **1** the state of being null or void. **2** (***nullities***) something without legal force or validity. **3** lack of existence, force or efficacy. • **nullness** *noun.* ⓒ 16c: from Latin *nullus* none.

nullify /ˈnʌlɪfaɪ/ ▷ *verb* (***nullifies, nullified, nullifying***) **1** to cause or declare something to be legally invalid. **2** to make something ineffective; to cancel it out. • **nullification** *noun.* • **nullifier** *noun.* ⓒ 16c: from Latin *nullus* of no account + *facere* to make.

NUM ▷ *abbreviation* National Union of Mineworkers.

Num. and **Numb.** ▷ *abbreviation* Book of the Bible: Numbers, or the Book of Numbers. See table at BIBLE.

num. ▷ *abbreviation* **1** number. **2** numeral.

numb /nʌm/ ▷ *adj* (***number, numbest***) **1** deprived completely, or to some degree, of sensation. **2** too stunned to feel emotion; stupefied □ *numb with shock.* ▷ *verb* (***numbed, numbing***) **1** to make something numb. **2** to deaden something. • **numbly** *adverb.* • **numbness** *noun.* ⓒ 15c as *nomen*, meaning 'seized', ie with paralysis: from *nim* to take.

numbat /ˈnʌmbat/ ▷ *noun, Austral* a small marsupial which feeds on termites. ⓒ 1920s: Aboriginal.

number /ˈnʌmbə(r)/ ▷ *noun* **1** the means or system by which groups or sets, etc of individual things, etc are counted; a quantity calculated in units. **2** one or more arithmetical symbols representing such a quantity; a numeral or set of numerals, eg *5* or *V*, *15* or *XV*. **3** a numeral or set of numerals identifying something or someone within a series □ *telephone numbers.* **4** (with a numeral) the person, animal, vehicle, etc bearing the specified numeral □ *Number 21 is pulling ahead.* **5** a single one of a series, eg an issue of a magazine. **6** a quantity of individuals. **7** an act or turn in a programme. **8** a piece of popular music or jazz. **9** *colloq* an article or person considered appreciatively □ *driving a white sports number.* **10** a group or set □ *isn't one of our number.* **11** (**numbers**) numerical superiority □ *overwhelmed by sheer weight of numbers.* **12** *grammar* the property of expressing, or classification of word forms into, SINGULAR and PLURAL and, in some languages, 'dual' (for two people, things, etc). ▷ *verb* (***numbered, numbering***) **1** to give a number to something; to mark it with a number. **2** to amount to (a specified amount) □ *a crowd numbering about 500.* **3** *tr & intr* to list; to enumerate. • **numberless** *adj* **1** too many to count; innumerable. **2** without a number. • **any number of something** many of it. • **by numbers** said of a procedure, etc: performed in simple stages, each stage being identified by a number. • **one's days are numbered** one is soon to die, or come to the end of something (eg a job) unpleasantly. • **get** or **have someone's number** *colloq* to understand them; to have them sized up. • **one's number is up** *colloq* one is due for some unpleasant fate, eg death or ruin. • **there is safety in numbers** in situations where there is a risk of harm, rejection or failure, etc it is better to be one of a group or to involve oneself in a number of activities or approach a number of people, etc. • **without number** more than can be counted; countless. ⓒ 13c: from French *nombre*, from Latin *numerus*.

■ **number among, in** or **with something** to include □ *I number her among my enemies.*

number-cruncher ▷ *noun* **1** a computer designed to carry out large quantities of complex numerical calculations. **2** someone who operates such a computer. **3** someone who carries out such calculations in their head. • **number-crunching** *noun.*

number one ▷ *noun* **1** first in a numbered series. **2** *colloq, ironic* oneself □ *look after number one.* ▷ *adj* (**number-one**) first; of primary importance □ *give it number-one priority.*

number plate ▷ *noun* one of the two plates at the front and rear of a motor vehicle, bearing its registration number.

numbers game, numbers pool and **numbers racket** ▷ *noun, US* an illegal form of gambling in which players bet on the appearance of a chosen sequence of numbers in the financial pages of a newspaper, etc. • **play the numbers game** to use arithmetical calculations, or figures generally, to make or win a point.

Number Ten ▷ *noun, colloq* 10 Downing Street, London, the official home of the Prime Minister.

number theory ▷ *noun* the branch of mathematics concerned with the abstract study of the relationships between, and properties of, positive whole numbers.

number two ▷ *noun, colloq* second-in-command.

numbly and **numbness** see under NUMB

numbskull see NUMSKULL

numen /ˈnjuːmen/ ▷ *noun* (***numina*** /-minə/) a presiding deity. See also NUMINOUS. ⓒ 17c: Latin, meaning 'divinity'.

numerable /ˈnjuːmərəbəl/ ▷ *adj* that may be numbered or counted. • **numerability** *noun.* • **numerably** *adverb.* ⓒ 16c.

numeral /ˈnjuːmərəl/ ▷ *noun* **1** an arithmetical symbol or group of symbols used to express a number; a figure, eg *5* or *V*, *29* or *XXIX*. **2** *grammar* a word used to denote a number. ▷ *adj* relating to, consisting of, or expressing a number. ⓒ 16c: from Latin *numerus* number.

numerate /ˈnjuːmərət/ ▷ *adj* **1** able to perform arithmetical operations. **2** having some understanding of mathematics and science. • **numeracy** /-rəsɪ/ *noun.* ⓒ 15c as *adj* meaning 'counted': from Latin *numerus* number, modelled on LITERATE.

numeration ▷ *noun* **1** the process of counting or numbering. **2** a system of numbering. ⓒ 15c: from Latin *numerare, numeratum* to count.

numerator /ˈnjuːməreɪtə(r)/ ▷ *noun* **1** the number above the line in a fraction. See also DENOMINATOR. **2** a person or thing which numbers. ⓒ 16c.

numeric /njʊˈmerɪk/ and **numerical** /-kəl/ ▷ *adj* relating to, using, or consisting of, numbers □ *numerical superiority.* • **numerically** *adverb.* ⓒ 17c.

numerical analysis ▷ *noun* the study of methods of approximation and their accuracy, etc.

numerical control and **computer numeric control** ▷ *noun* (abbreviation **NC** or **CNC**) automatic control of operation of machine tools by means of numerical data stored in computers, either obeying a preset program of instructions or reacting to feedback from sensors.

numeric keypad ▷ *noun* a numbered pad forming a separate section on a computer keyboard, used for inputting data or occasionally commands.

numerology /njuːməˈrɒlədʒɪ/ ▷ *noun* the study of numbers as supposed to predict future events or influence

Number Systems

Arabic	Roman	Binary	Arabic	Roman	Binary
1	I	1	50	L	110010
2	II	10	60	LX	111100
3	III	11	64	LXIV	1000000
4	IV	100	90	XC	1011010
5	V	101	99	XCIX	1100011
6	VI	110	100	C	1100100
7	VII	111	128	CXXVIII	10000000
8	VIII	1000	200	CC	11001000
9	IX	1001	256	CCLVI	100000000
10	X	1010	300	CCC	100101100
11	XI	1011	400	CD	110010000
12	XII	1100	500	D	111110100
13	XIII	1101	512	DXII	1000000000
14	XIV	1110	600	DC	1001011000
15	XV	1111	900	CM	1110000100
16	XVI	10000	1 000	M	1111101000
17	XVII	10001	1 024	MXXIV	10000000000
18	XVIII	10010	1 500	MD	10111011100
19	XIX	10011	2 000	MM	11111010000
20	XX	10100	4 000	MV̄	111110100000
21	XXI	10101	5 000	V̄	1001110001000
30	XXX	11110	10 000	X̄	10011100010000
32	XXXII	100000	20 000	X̄X̄	100111000100000
40	XL	101000	100 000	C̄	11000011010100000

human affairs. • **numerological** /-rəˈlɒdʒɪkəl/ *adj.* • **numerologist** *noun.* ⓒ Early 20c.

numero uno /ˈnuːmeroʊ ˈuːnoʊ/ ▷ *noun, colloq* number one; the most important person or thing; oneself. ⓒ 1970s: Italian.

numerous /ˈnjuːmərəs/ ▷ *adj* **1** many. **2** said of an assembly or a body of people, etc: containing a large number of people. • **numerously** *adverb.* ⓒ 16c: from Latin *numerosus.*

numina *plural of* NUMEN

numinous /ˈnjuːmɪnəs/ ▷ *adj* **1** mysterious; awe-inspiring. **2** characterized by the sense of a deity's presence. • **numinousness** *noun.* ⓒ 17c: from Latin *numen* deity.

numismatic /njuːmɪzˈmatɪk/ ▷ *adj* relating to **numismatics** and **numismatology** /njuːmɪzməˈtɒlədʒɪ/, the study or collecting of coins and medals. • **numismatist** or **numismatologist** someone who collects or studies coins and medals. ⓒ 18c: from Greek *nomisma* coin.

numskull or **numbskull** ▷ *noun, colloq* a stupid person. ⓒ 18c: NUMB + SKULL.

nun ▷ *noun* a member of a female religious order living within a community, in obedience to certain vows. • **nunnish** *adj.* ⓒ Anglo-Saxon *nunne*: from Latin *nonna*, originally meaning 'mother'.

nunc dimittis /nʌŋk dɪˈmɪtɪs/ ▷ *noun* (*also* **Nunc Dimittis**) *Christianity* the song of Simeon (Luke 2 29–32) in the Roman Catholic Breviary and the Anglican evening service. ⓒ 16c: the opening words in Latin, meaning 'now lettest thou depart'.

nunchaku /nʊnˈtʃaku/ and **nunchaku sticks** ▷ *noun* (***nunchakus***) a weapon that consists of two short thick sticks joined by a length of chain, used in certain martial arts. ⓒ 1970s: Japanese.

nuncio /ˈnʌnsɪoʊ/ ▷ *noun* (***nuncios***) an ambassador from the pope. • **nunciature** /ˈnʌnsiətjʊə(r)/ *noun* a nuncio's office or term of office. ⓒ 16c: from Latin *nuntius* messenger.

nunnery /ˈnʌnərɪ/ *noun* (***nunneries***) a house in which a group of nuns live; a CONVENT.

NUPE /ˈnjuːpɪ/ ▷ *abbreviation, historical* National Union of Public Employees, now part of UNISON.

nuptial /ˈnʌpʃəl/ ▷ *adj* **1** relating to marriage. **2** *zool* relating to mating. ▷ *noun* (*usually* **nuptials**) a marriage ceremony. • **nuptially** *adverb.* ⓒ 15c: from Latin *nuptialis*, from *nuptiae* marriage.

NUR ▷ *abbreviation, historical* National Union of Railwaymen, now part of RMT.

nurd see NERD

nurl see KNURL

nurse /nɜːs/ ▷ *noun* (***nurses***) **1** someone trained to look after sick, injured or feeble people, especially in hospital. **2** someone, especially a woman, who looks after small children in a household, etc. See also NURSEMAID, NURSERY NURSE, WET NURSE. **3** a worker ant, bee, etc, that tends the young in the colony. ▷ *verb* (***nursed, nursing***) **1** to look after (sick or injured people) especially in a hospital. **2** *intr* to follow a career as a nurse. **3** *tr & intr* **a** to breastfeed a baby; **b** said of a baby: to feed at the breast. **4** to hold something with care □ ***gave him the bag of meringues to nurse.*** **5** to tend something with concern □ ***was at home nursing a cold.*** **6** to encourage or indulge (a feeling) in oneself □ ***nursing her jealousy.*** • **nursing** *adj, noun.* • **put out to** or **put to nurse 1** to put (a baby) into the care of a nurse, usually away from home. **2** to put (an estate) into the care of trustees. ⓒ 14c: from French *norrice*, from Latin *nutrire* to nourish or care for.

nursehound ▷ *noun* a European dogfish. ⓒ 19c: from 15c *nusse*, possibly originally *an huss* a dogfish.

nurseling see NURSLING

nursemaid and **nurserymaid** ▷ *noun* a children's nurse in a household.

nursery /ˈnɜːsərɪ/ ▷ *noun* (***nurseries***) **1 a** a place where children are looked after while their parents are at work, etc; **b** a NURSERY SCHOOL. **2** a room in a house, etc, set apart for young children and, where appropriate, their nurse or other carer. **3** a place where plants are grown for sale. **4** a place where young animals are reared or tended. **5** a place where the growth of anything is promoted. ▷ *adj* relating or belonging to the nursery or early training. 🕒 14c as *norcery*, meaning 'upbringing' or 'nursing'.

nursery canon ▷ *noun, billiards* a canon, especially one of a series, with the three balls close together and being moved as little as possible.

nurseryman ▷ *noun* someone who grows plants for sale.

nursery nurse ▷ *noun* someone trained in the care of babies and young children.

nursery rhyme ▷ *noun* a short simple traditional rhyme or song for young children.

nursery school ▷ *noun* a school for young children, usually those aged between three and five. Also shortened to NURSERY.

nursery slopes ▷ *noun, skiing* the lower, more gentle slopes, used for practice by beginners.

nursery stakes ▷ *noun, horse-racing* a race for two-year-old horses.

nurse shark ▷ *noun* any of various sharks that have an external groove on each side of their head between nostril and mouth. 🕒 19c as *nusse*, meaning 'dogfish'; see NURSE HOUND.

nursing see under NURSE

nursing chair ▷ *noun* a low chair without arms, suitable for sitting in to breastfeed a baby.

nursing home ▷ *noun* a small private hospital or home, especially one for old people.

nursing officer ▷ *noun* any of several grades of nurse that have administrative duties.

nursling or **nurseling** ▷ *noun* a young child or animal that is being nursed or fostered. 🕒 16c.

nurture /ˈnɜːtʃə(r)/ ▷ *noun* care, nourishment and encouragement given to a growing child, animal or plant. ▷ *verb* (***nurtured***, ***nurturing***) **1** to nourish and tend (a growing child, animal or plant). **2** to encourage the development of (a project, idea or feeling, etc). • **nurtural** *adj.* • **nurturer** *noun.* 🕒 14c: from French *norriture*, from Latin *nutrire* to nourish.

NUS ▷ *abbreviation* **1** National Union of Seamen. **2** National Union of Students.

NUT ▷ *abbreviation* National Union of Teachers.

nut ▷ *noun* **1** *popularly* **a** a fruit consisting of a kernel contained in a hard shell, eg a hazlenut or walnut; **b** the kernel itself. **2** *bot* a hard dry INDEHISCENT one-seeded fruit. **3** *popularly* a roasted peanut. **4** a small, usually hexagonal, piece of metal with a hole through it, for screwing on the end of a bolt. **5** *colloq* a person's head. **6** *colloq* (*also* **nutter**) a crazy person. **7** *colloq, usually in compounds* an enthusiast; a person with an obsessive interest □ *a football nut.* **8** a small lump □ *a nut of butter.* **9** (**nuts**) *colloq* testicles. **10** *music* **a** the ridge at the top of the fingerboard on a violin, etc; **b** the mechanism for tightening the bow. **11** *in compounds* a small biscuit or cake □ *ginger nut.* ▷ *verb* (***nutted***, ***nutting***) **1** *intr* to look for and gather nuts. **2** *colloq* to butt someone with the head. • **nutter** see *noun* 6 above. • **nuttiness** *noun.* • **nutty** see separate entry. • **do one's nut** *colloq* to be furious. • **for nuts** *colloq* at all □ *can't sing for nuts.* • **a hard** or **tough nut to crack** *colloq* **1** a difficult problem to solve. **2** an awkward person to deal with. • **off one's nut** *colloq* mad. See also NUTS. 🕒 Anglo-Saxon *hnutu*.

nutant /ˈnjuːtənt/ ▷ *adj, bot* nodding; pendulous. 🕒 18c: from Latin *nutans, nutantis* nodding.

nutation /njʊˈteɪʃən/ ▷ *noun* **1** the act of nodding. **2** *astron* the irregular nodding or 'side-to-side' movement of the Earth's axis of rotation. **3** *bot* the spiral growth pattern of the parts of some plants, eg the tips of the stems of climbing plants. **4** the periodic oscillation of a spinning top or gyroscope. • **nutational** *adj.* 🕒 17c: from Latin *nutare* to nod.

nut-brown ▷ *adj* brown; reddish-brown.

nutcase ▷ *noun, colloq* a crazy person. 🕒 1950s.

nutcracker ▷ *noun* **1** (*usually* **nutcrackers**) a utensil for cracking nuts. **2** a bird which feeds on nuts or seeds, etc.

nutgall ▷ *noun* a gall shaped like a nut, produced by the gall wasp, chiefly on oak trees.

nuthatch ▷ *noun* any of various birds that seek out and feed on insects in the bark of trees, and also eat nuts and seeds. 🕒 14c as *notehache*: from *note* hut + *hache* (related to HACK[1] + HATCH[2]).

nuthouse ▷ *noun, colloq, offensive* a mental hospital.

nutmeg /ˈnʌtmɛg/ ▷ *noun* the hard aromatic seed of the fruit of an E Indian tree, used ground or grated as a spice. Compare MACE[2]. • **nutmeggy** *adj.* 🕒 14c as *notemugge*.

nut oil ▷ *noun* an oil obtained from nuts, eg walnuts.

nutria /ˈnjuːtrɪə/ ▷ *noun* (***nutrias***) **1** the coypu. **2** its fur. 🕒 19c: Spanish, meaning 'otter'.

nutrient /ˈnjuːtrɪənt/ ▷ *noun* any nourishing substance. ▷ *adj* nourishing. 🕒 17c as *adj*, meaning 'serving as nourishment': from Latin *nutrire* to nourish.

nutriment /ˈnjuːtrɪmənt/ ▷ *noun* nourishment; food. • **nutrimental** *adj.* 🕒 16c: from Latin *nutrimentum*.

nutrition /njʊˈtrɪʃən/ ▷ *noun* **1** the act or process of nourishing. **2** the study of the body's dietary needs. **3** food. • **nutritional** *adj* relating to nutrition or nourishment. • **nutritionist** *noun* an expert in foods and their nutritional values. 🕒 16c.

nutritious /njʊˈtrɪʃəs/ ▷ *adj* nourishing; providing nutrition. • **nutritiously** *adverb.* • **nutritiousness** *noun.*

nutritive /ˈnjuːtrətɪv/ ▷ *adj* **1** nourishing. **2** relating to nutrition. • **nutritively** *adverb.*

nuts *colloq* ▷ *adj* insane; crazy. ▷ *exclamation* expressing defiance, contempt or disappointment, etc. • **nuts about** or **on someone** or something infatuated with, or extremely fond of them.

the nuts and bolts ▷ *noun, colloq* the essential or practical details.

nutshell ▷ *noun* the case containing the kernel of a nut. • **in a nutshell** concisely or very briefly expressed □ *to put it in a nutshell, …*

nutter and **nuttiness** see under NUT

nutting ▷ *verb, present participle of* NUT. ▷ *noun* the gathering of nuts.

nut-tree ▷ *noun* any tree that bears nuts, especially the hazel.

nutty /ˈnʌtɪ/ ▷ *adj* (***nuttier***, ***nuttiest***) **1** full of, or tasting of, nuts. **2** *colloq* crazy.

nux vomica /nʌks ˈvɒmɪkə/ ▷ *noun* **1** the seed of an East Indian tree, containing strychnine. **2** the drug made from it. 🕒 16c: Latin, meaning 'vomiting nut'.

nuzzle /ˈnʌzəl/ ▷ *verb* (***nuzzled***, ***nuzzling***) *tr & intr* **1** to push or rub someone or something with the nose. **2** (*usually* **nuzzle up to** or **against someone**) to snuggle up against them. 🕒 17c: from NOSE.

NV ▷ *abbreviation* **1** *US state* Nevada. Also written **Nev. 2** new version.

NVALA and **NVLA** ▷ *abbreviation* National Viewers' and Listeners' Association.

nvd ▷ *abbreviation* no value declared.

NVQ ▷ *abbreviation* National Vocational Qualification, a qualification awarded in the workplace by the NCVQ for competence in job skills at any of five different levels from basic to university standard.

NW ▷ *abbreviation* **1** north-west. **2** north-western.

NWT ▻ *abbreviation* Northwest Territories, a Canadian territory.

NY ▻ *abbreviation* **1** *US state* New York. Also written **N.Y.** **2** New York, the city.

nyala /nˈjɑːlə, ˈnjɑːlə/ ▻ *noun* (***nyala*** or ***nyalas***) a large southern African antelope with a spiral horn. ◷ 19c: from Bantu *inyala*.

NYC ▻ *abbreviation* New York City.

nyctalopia /nɪktəˈloʊpɪə/ ▻ *noun, pathol* abnormal difficulty in seeing in a faint light. Also called **night-blindness**. • **nyctalopic** *adj.* ◷ 17c: from Greek *nyx, nyktos* night + *alaos* blind + *ops* eye or face.

nyctitropism /nɪkˈtɪtrəpɪzəm/ ▻ *noun, bot* said of parts of plants: the taking up of certain positions at night different from those assumed by day. • **nyctitropic** /nɪktəˈtroʊpɪk, -ˈtrɒpɪk/ *adj.* ◷ 19c: from Greek *nyx, nyktos* night + *tropos* turning.

nyctophobia /nɪktəˈfoʊbɪə/ ▻ *noun* a morbid fear of the night or of darkness. ◷ 20c: from Greek *nyx, nyktos* night + -PHOBIA.

nylon /ˈnaɪlɒn/ ▻ *noun* **1** any of numerous polymeric amides that can be formed into fibres, bristles or sheets, from which a wide variety of products are manufactured, including clothing, hosiery, ropes and brushes. **2** a yarn or cloth made of nylon. **3** (**nylons**) nylon stockings. ◷ 1930s: originally a tradename invented by the first manufacturer.

nymph /nɪmf/ ▻ *noun* **1** *mythol* a goddess that inhabits mountains, water, trees, etc. **2** *poetic* a beautiful young woman. **3** *zool* the immature larval form of certain insects. • **nymphal** *adj.* • **nymphean** /ˈnɪmfɪən/ *adj.* ◷ 14c: from Greek *nymphe* nymph or bride.

nymphet /ˈnɪmfɪt, nɪmˈfɛt/ ▻ *noun* a sexually attractive and precocious girl in early adolescence. ◷ 17c, meaning 'a young nymph'.

nympho /ˈnɪmfoʊ/ ▻ *noun* (***nymphos***) *colloq* a nymphomaniac. ◷ Early 20c.

nymphomania /nɪmfəˈmeɪnɪə/ ▻ *noun* in women: overpowering sexual desire. Compare SATYRIASIS. • **nymphomaniac** *noun, adj.* ◷ 18c.

NYO ▻ *abbreviation* National Youth Orchestra.

NYOS /ˈnaɪds/ *abbreviation* National Youth Orchestra of Scotland.

nystagmus /nɪˈstagməs/ ▻ *noun* (***nystagmuses***) *pathol* a spasmodic involuntary movement of the eye. • **nystagmic** or **nystagmoid** *adj.* ◷ 19c: Latin, from Greek *nystazein* to nap.

nystatin /ˈnɪstətɪn/ ▻ *noun* an antifungal and antibiotic agent. ◷ 1950s: from *New York State* (where it originated) + -IN.

Nyungar /ˈnjʊŋə(r)/ ▻ *noun* an Aboriginal language formerly spoken in SW Australia.

NZ ▻ *abbreviation* New Zealand.

O

O¹ or **o** /oʊ/ ▻ *noun* (*Oes, Os,* or *o's*) **1** the fifteenth letter of the English alphabet. **2** the shape of this letter ▫ *formed his mouth into an O.* **3** in telephone, etc jargon: zero; nought.

O² see under OH

O³ ▻ *abbreviation* **1** Ocean. **2** (*also* **o**) octavo. **3** see under OH. **4** Old. **5** ordinary, in eg O level or O Grade.

O⁴ ▻ *symbol* **1** *chem* oxygen. **2** an ABO BLOOD GROUP SYSTEM.

O' /oʊ/ ▻ *prefix* in surnames of Irish Gaelic origin: descendant of (a specified person). ◷ 18c: from Irish Gaelic *ó* or *ua* grandson or descendant, from earlier *aue*.

o' /ə, ɒ, oʊ/ ▻ *prep, chiefly archaic & dialect* **1** short form of OF. See also O'CLOCK. **2** short form of ON.

-o /oʊ/ ▻ *suffix, slang or colloquial, forming nouns* (*plural -os*) *signifying* an abbreviation or diminutive ▫ *wino* ▫ *aggro*.

oaf /oʊf/ ▻ *noun* (*oafs* or *rare oaves*) a stupid, awkward or loutish, usually male, person. • **oafish** *adj*. • **oafishly** *adverb*. • **oafishness** *noun*. ◷ 17c: originally meaning 'an elf's or goblin's child' or 'a changeling': from Norse *alfr* elf.

oak /oʊk/ ▻ *noun* **1** any tree or shrub which produces a fruit called an acorn and usually has lobed leaves. **2** the hard durable wood of this tree, widely used in building construction, furniture and flooring, and formerly for shipbuilding. **3** any of various other trees resembling the oak. **4** a heavy wooden door, especially that of a set of university rooms. **5** the leaves of the oak tree, especially when worn as a wreath or garland. ◷ Anglo-Saxon *ac*.

oak-apple and **oak-gall** ▻ *noun* any of various round brownish woody galls found on oak trees, produced by the larvae of certain wasps.

oaken /'oʊkən/ ▻ *adj, old use* made of oak wood.

the Oaks /— oʊks/ ▻ *singular noun* an annual horse-race at Epsom for three-year-old fillies. ◷ 18c: named after an estate near Epsom.

oakum /'oʊkəm/ ▻ *noun* pieces of old, usually tarred, rope untwisted and pulled apart, used to fill small holes and cracks in wooden boats and ships. ◷ Anglo-Saxon *acumba* off-combings, from *a-* away from + *cemban* to comb.

O & M ▻ *abbreviation* in studies of working methods: organization and method(s).

OAP ▻ *abbreviation, Brit* old age pensioner.

oar /ɔː(r)/ ▻ *noun* **1** a long pole with a broad flat blade at one end, used for rowing a boat. **2** something that resembles an oar in form or function. **3** an oarsman or oarswoman. ▻ *verb* (*oared, oaring*) **1** to row or propel (a boat, etc) with or as if with oars. **2** *intr* to row; to move as if propelled by oars. • **oared** *adj, especially in compounds* with an oar or oars, usually of a specified number ▫ *six-oared*. • **oarless** *adj*. • **lie** or **rest on one's oars 1** to stop rowing and lean on the handles of one's oars, thus lifting the blades out of the water. **2** *colloq* to stop working; to rest or relax. • **put** or **stick one's oar in something** *colloq* to interfere or meddle in it, especially by offering one's opinion when it is not wanted. ◷ Anglo-Saxon *ar*.

oarfish ▻ *noun* a long ribbon-shaped fish, up to 7m (23ft) in length, widespread in tropical and warm temperate seas, with an extremely slender body, a dorsal fin that extends the full length of the body, and no tail fin. ◷ 19c.

oarsman and **oarswoman** ▻ *noun* a man or woman skilled in rowing; a rower. • **oarsmanship** *noun* skill in rowing.

OAS ▻ *abbreviation* Organization of American States.

oasis /oʊ'eɪsɪs/ ▻ *noun* (*oases* /-siːz/) **1** a fertile area in a desert, where water is found and plants grow. **2** any place or period of rest or calm, etc in the middle of hard work, problems or trouble. **3** (**Oasis**) *trademark* a block of light firm foam material, used in flower-arranging as a base to hold cut flowers, etc in place. ◷ 1960s in sense 3; 17c: Latin, from Greek.

oast /oʊst/ ▻ *noun* **1** a kiln for drying hops or, formerly, malt. **2** (*also* **oast-house**) a building, usually with a conical roof, containing such kilns. ◷ Anglo-Saxon *ast* kiln.

oat /oʊt/ ▻ *noun* **1** (*usually* **oats**) a cereal and type of grass, thought to be native to the Mediterranean region and now cultivated mainly in cool moist temperate regions as a food crop. **2** (**oats**) the grains of this plant, used to make porridge, oatcakes, etc, and also as a feedstuff for livestock. **3** any of various other grasses related to or resembling this plant. • **feel one's oats** *chiefly N Amer colloq* **1** to feel lively or exuberant. **2** to feel self-important. • **get** or **have one's oats** *slang* to have sexual intercourse. • **off one's oats** *colloq* with no appetite; off one's food. • **sow one's oats** or **wild oats** *colloq* to indulge in excessive drinking or promiscuity, etc during youth and before settling down. ◷ Anglo-Saxon *ate*.

oatcake ▻ *noun* a thin dry savoury biscuit made from oatmeal.

oaten /'oʊtən/ ▻ *adj* **1** made of oats or oatmeal. **2** made of an oat stem or straw.

oat grass ▻ *noun* any of several oatlike grasses, used more as fodder than for its seed.

oath /oʊθ/ ▻ *noun* (*oaths* /oʊðz, oʊθs/) **1** a solemn promise to tell the truth or to be loyal, etc, usually naming God as a witness. **2** the form of words used to make such a promise. **3** a swear-word, obscenity or blasphemy. • **my oath** *Austral & NZ slang* yes; certainly; of course. • **on** or **under oath 1** having sworn to tell the truth, eg in a court of law. **2** attested by oath. • **take an oath** to pledge formally. ◷ Anglo-Saxon *ath*.

oatmeal ▻ *noun* **1** meal ground from oats, used to make oatcakes, etc. **2** the pale brownish-yellow flecked colour of oatmeal.

OAU ▻ *abbreviation* Organization of African Unity.

oaves *plural of* OAF

OB ▻ *abbreviation* **1** old boy. **2** outside broadcast.

ob. ▻ *abbreviation* **1** on tombstones, etc: *obiit* (Latin), he or she died. **2** *obiter* (Latin), by the way; in passing.

Obad. ▻ *abbreviation* Book of the Bible: Obadiah. See table at BIBLE.

obbligato or **obligato** /ɒblɪ'gɑːtoʊ/ *music* ▻ *noun* (*obbligatos* or *obbligati* /-tiː/) an accompaniment that forms an essential part of a piece of music, especially one played by a single instrument accompanying a voice. ▻ *adj* played with an obbligato. ◷ 18c: Italian, meaning 'obligatory'.

obconic /ɒb'kɒnɪk/ and **obconical** /-kəl/ ▻ *adj, bot* said of a fruit: conical and attached by the apex. ◷ 19c:

from Latin *ob-* in the opposite direction or reversed + CONIC.

obcordate /ɒbˈkɔːdeɪt/ ▷ *adj*, *bot* said eg of a leaf: inversely heart-shaped and attached by the point. ◷ 18c: from Latin *ob-* in the opposite direction or reversed + CORDATE.

obdurate /ˈɒbdjʊrət/ ▷ *adj* **1** hard-hearted. **2** stubborn; difficult to influence or change, especially morally. • **obduracy** /ˈɒbdjʊrəsɪ/ *noun*. • **obdurately** *adverb*. ◷ 15c: from Latin *obdurare* to harden, from *ob-* against + *durare* to harden.

OBE ▷ *abbreviation*, *Brit* (Officer of the) Order of the British Empire, an award given to honour personal or professional excellence, or services to the country.

obeah see OBI[1]

obedience /əˈbiːdɪəns/ ▷ *noun* **1** the act or practice of OBEYing. **2** willingness to obey orders.

obedient /əˈbiːdɪənt/ ▷ *adj* obeying; willing to obey. • **obediently** *adverb*. ◷ 13c: from French *obédient*, from Latin *oboedire* to OBEY.

obeisance /oʊˈbeɪsəns/ ▷ *noun* a bow, act or other expression of obedience or respect. • **obeisant** *adj*. ◷ 14c: from French *obéissance*, from *obéir* to OBEY.

obelisk /ˈɒbəlɪsk/ ▷ *noun* **1** a tall tapering, usually four-sided, stone pillar with a pyramidal top, erected as a landmark or for religious or commemorative purposes, etc. **2** an OBELUS. ◷ 16c: from Greek *obeliskos* a small spit.

obelus /ˈɒbələs/ ▷ *noun* (*plural* ***obeli*** /-laɪ/) **1** *printing* a dagger-shaped mark (†) used especially for referring to footnotes. **2** in ancient manuscripts: a sign used to mark words or passages, etc as spurious. ◷ 14c: Latin, from Greek *obelos* a spit.

obese /oʊˈbiːs/ ▷ *adj* very or abnormally fat. • **obeseness** *noun*. • **obesity** *noun* the condition of someone who is overweight as a result of the accumulation of excess fat in the body. ◷ 17c: from Latin *obesus* plump or having eaten oneself fat, from *ob-* completely + *edere*, *esum* to eat.

obey /əˈbeɪ, oʊˈbeɪ/ ▷ *verb* (***obeyed***, ***obeying***) **1** to do what one is told to do by someone. **2** to carry out (a command). **3** *intr* to do what one is told. **4** to be controlled by (a force or impulse, etc). ◷ 13c: from French *obéir*, from Latin *oboedire*, from *ob-* towards + *audire* to hear.

obfuscate /ˈɒbfəskeɪt/ ▷ *verb* (***obfuscated***, ***obfuscating***) **1** to darken or obscure something. **2** to obscure something or make it difficult to understand. **3** to bewilder or confuse someone. • **obfuscation** *noun*. • **obfuscatory** *adj* tending to obscure or confuse. ◷ 16c: from Latin *ob-* completely + *fuscare* to darken.

obi[1] /ˈoʊbɪ/ or **obeah** /ˈoʊbɪə/ ▷ *noun* (***obis***; ***obeahs***) **1** a kind of witchcraft practised in the W Indies and Guyana, etc. **2** a fetish or charm used in this kind of witchcraft. • **obi-man** or **obi-woman** a male or female practitioner of obi. ◷ 18c: W African.

obi[2] /ˈoʊbɪ/ ▷ *noun* (***obis*** or ***obi***) a broad sash, tied in a large flat bow at the back, that is worn with a Japanese kimono. ◷ 19c: Japanese, from *obiru* to wear.

obiter dictum /ˈɒbɪtə ˈdɪktəm/ ▷ *noun* (***obiter dicta*** /— ˈdɪktə/) **1** *law* a remark made by a judge on a point of law, etc but that has no binding authority. **2** a remark that is in some way related to, but not essential to, the main argument. ◷ 19c: Latin, meaning 'something said by the way'.

obituary /əˈbɪtjʊərɪ/ ▷ *noun* (***obituaries***) a notice or announcement, especially in a newspaper, of a person's death, often with a short account of their life. ▷ *adj* **1** relating to or recording the death of a person or persons. **2** like an obituary. • **obituarial** /-tjʊˈɛərɪəl/ *adj*. • **obituarist** *noun*. ◷ 18c: from Latin *obitus* death.

object[1] /ˈɒbdʒɪkt, ˈɒbdʒɛkt/ ▷ *noun* **1** a material thing that can be seen or touched. **2** an aim or purpose. **3** a person or thing to which action, feelings or thought are directed ▫ ***the object of his affections.*** **4** *colloq* an oddity; a ridiculous or pitiable person or sight, etc. **5** *grammar* **a** a noun, noun phrase or pronoun affected by the action of the verb. See also DIRECT OBJECT, INDIRECT OBJECT, ACCUSATIVE. **b** a noun, noun phrase or pronoun affected by a preposition. See also SUBJECT. **6** *philos* a thing which is outside of, and can be perceived by, the mind. **7** *computing* an information package and a description of its use. • **objectless** *adj*. • **no object** not a difficulty or obstacle ▫ ***Money's no object.*** ◷ 14c: from Latin *objectus* a throwing before, from Latin *objicere*; see OBJECT[2].

object[2] /əbˈdʒɛkt/ ▷ *verb* (***objected***, ***objecting***) **1** *intr* (*usually* **object to** or **against something**) to feel or express dislike or disapproval for it. **2** to state something as a ground for disapproval or objection. • **objector** *noun*. ◷ 15c: from Latin *objicere*, *objectum*, from *ob-* in the way of + *jacere* to throw.

object ball ▷ *noun* in snooker, billiards, etc: the ball which a player is aiming to strike with the cue ball.

object finder ▷ *noun* a device in microscopes for locating an object on a mounted slide at low power before examining it by a higher power.

object glass ▷ *noun*, *optics* in a camera or telescope, etc: the lens or combination of lenses nearest to the object being viewed. Also called **objective**.

objectify /əbˈdjɛktɪfaɪ/ ▷ *verb* (***objectifies***, ***objectified***, ***objectifying***) **1 a** to make something into or present it as an object; **b** to represent something concretely. **2** to make something objective. • **objectification** *noun*.

objection /əbˈdʒɛkʃən/ ▷ *noun* **1** the act of objecting. **2** an expression or feeling of disapproval, opposition or dislike, etc. **3** (*often* **objection against** or **to something**) a reason or cause for disapproving, opposing or disliking it, etc. ◷ 14c.

objectionable ▷ *adj* **1** capable of being objected to. **2** unpleasant; offensive. • **objectionably** *adverb*. ◷ 18c.

objective /əbˈdʒɛktɪv/ ▷ *adj* **1 a** not depending on, or influenced by, personal opinions or prejudices; **b** relating to external facts, etc as opposed to internal thoughts or feelings. **2** *philos* **a** having existence outside the mind; **b** based on fact or reality. Compare SUBJECTIVE. **3** *grammar* said of a case or word: **a** indicating the object; **b** in the relation of object to a verb or proposition. **4** *medicine* said of symptoms: perceptible to a person other than the individual affected. **5** *optics* said of lenses: nearest the object. ▷ *noun* **1** a thing aimed at or wished for; a goal. **2** something independent of or external to the mind. **3** *grammar* **a** the objective case; **b** a word or form in that case. **4** an OBJECT GLASS. • **objectival** /-ˈtaɪvəl/ *adj* relating to or the nature of an objective. • **objectively** *adverb*. • **objectivity** or **objectiveness** *noun* the fact or quality of being objective, especially of considering things without being dependent on, or influenced by, personal opinions or prejudices. ◷ 17c.

objective test ▷ *noun* an examination or test in which each question is set in such a way as to have only one correct answer.

objectivism /əbˈdʒɛktɪvɪzəm/ ▷ *noun* **1** the tendency to emphasize what is objective. **2** *philos* the belief that certain things exist apart from human knowledge or perception of them. **3** *chiefly derog* in Communist theory: an objective attitude to the conditions that exist, as opposed to a desire for change in accordance with revolutionary principles. **4** the quality of being objective. • **objectivist** *noun*, *adj*. • **objectivistic** *adj*. ◷ 19c.

objectivize or **objectivise** /əbˈdʒɛktɪvaɪz/ ▷ *verb* (***objectivized***, ***objectivizing***) to objectify. • **objectivization** *noun*. ◷ 19c.

object language ▷ *noun* **1** a language described by means of another language. Compare METALANGUAGE. **2** *philos* a language made up only of words that have meaning in isolation. **3** *computing* a language into which a program is translated by a compiler.

objectless see under OBJECT[1]

object lesson ▷ *noun* **1** a lesson based on a material object that is presented to the class. **2** an instructive experience or event, etc that provides a practical example of some principle or ideal.

objector see under OBJECT[2]

objet /'ɒbʒeɪ/ ▷ *noun* (***objets*** /'ɒbʒeɪ/) an object, usually one displayed as an ornament. ⓒ 19c: French.

objet d'art /'ɒbʒeɪ dɑː(r)/ ▷ *noun* (***objets d'art*** /'ɒbʒeɪ dɑː(r)/) a small object of artistic value. ⓒ 19c: French, meaning 'object of art'.

objet trouvé /'ɒbʒeɪ 'truːveɪ/ ▷ *noun* (***objets trouvés*** /ɒb'ʒeɪ 'truːveɪ/) a FOUND OBJECT.

objurgate /'ɒbdʒəgeɪt/ ▷ *verb* (***objurgated, objurgating***) *tr & intr, literary* to rebuke someone; to scold or chide. • **objurgation** *noun*. ⓒ 17c: from Latin *objurgare*, from *jurgare* to scold.

obl. ▷ *abbreviation* **1** oblique. **2** oblong.

oblast /'ɒbləst/ ▷ *noun* (***oblasts*** or ***oblasti*** /-tɪ/) in some republics of the former Soviet Union and earlier in Russia: an administrative district; a region. ⓒ 19c: Russian, from Slavonic, meaning 'government'.

oblate¹ /'ɒbleɪt, ɒ'bleɪt/ ▷ *adj, geom* said of something approximately spherical: flattened at the poles, like the Earth. Compare PROLATE. ⓒ 18c: from Latin *oblatus* lengthened, from *ob-* towards + *latus*, past participle of *ferre* to bring or carry.

oblate² /'ɒbleɪt/ ▷ *noun* someone dedicated to monastic life (but without having taken vows) or to a religious life. ⓒ 19c: from French *oblat*, from Latin *offerre*, *oblatum* to offer.

oblation /ɒ'bleɪʃən/ ▷ *noun* **1** *Christianity* the offering of the bread and wine to God at a Eucharist. **2** a religious or charitable offering. • **oblational** or **oblatory** /'ɒblətərɪ/ *adj*. ⓒ 15c: French, or from Latin *oblatio*, from *offerre* to offer.

obligate /'ɒblɪgeɪt/ ▷ *verb* (***obligated, obligating***) **1** to bind or oblige someone by contract, duty or moral obligation. **2** to bind someone by gratitude. ▷ *adj, biol* said of an organism, especially a bacterium: limited to specific functions and by specific conditions. ⓒ 16c: from Latin *obligare*, *obligatum*.

obligation /ɒblɪ'geɪʃən/ ▷ *noun* **1** a moral or legal duty or tie. **2** the binding power of such a duty or tie. **3** a debt of gratitude for a service ▫ ***be under obligation to her.***

obligato see OBBLIGATO

obligatory /ə'blɪgət(ə)rɪ/ ▷ *adj* **1** legally or morally binding. **2** compulsory. **3** *biol* OBLIGATE. • **obligatorily** *adverb*. • **obligatoriness** *noun*. ⓒ 15c.

oblige /ə'blaɪdʒ/ ▷ *verb* (***obliged, obliging***) **1** to bind someone morally or legally; to compel. **2** to bind someone by a service or favour. **3** to please or do a favour for someone ▫ ***Please oblige me by leaving at once.*** **4** to do something as a favour or contribution for someone ▫ ***obliged us with a song.*** • **much obliged** an expression of gratitude. ⓒ 13c: from French *obliger*, from Latin *obligare*, from *ob-* down + *ligare* to bind.

obliging /ə'blaɪdʒɪŋ/ ▷ *adj* ready to help others; courteously helpful. • **obligingly** *adverb*. • **obligingness** *noun*.

oblique /ə'bliːk/ (abbreviation **obl.**) *adj* **1** sloping; not vertical or horizontal. **2** *geom* **a** said of lines and planes, etc: not at a right angle; **b** said of an angle: less than 180 degrees but more than 90 degrees, ie more than a right angle. **3** not straight or direct; roundabout; underhand. **4** *grammar* denoting any case other than the NOMINATIVE or VOCATIVE. **5** *bot* said of a leaf: with unequal sides. ▷ *noun* **1** an oblique line; a solidus (/). **2** anything that is oblique. ▷ *verb* (***obliqued, obliquing***) *intr* to advance obliquely, especially (*military*) to face half right or left and then advance. • **obliquely** *adverb*. • **obliqueness** or **obliquity** *noun*. ⓒ 15c: French, from Latin *obliquus*.

> ***oblique***
>
> An **oblique**
>
> • indicates alternatives ▫ *Bring your swimming costume and/or a tennis racquet* ▫ *Tea/coffee will be served* ▫ *Dear Sir/Madam* ▫ *Each candidate will be required to give a report on his/her research.*
>
> • indicates the limits of a period of time ▫ *I was at university in the years 1960/64* ▫ *You will shortly receive your 1996/7 tax return.*
>
> ALTERNATIVE STYLE: a short dash ▫ *in the years 1960–64.*
>
> • It also links items on a route or itinerary ▫ *The London/Oxford/Birmingham express was derailed at Reading* ▫ *The Edinburgh/Amsterdam/Frankfurt flight is subject to a delay of thirty minutes.*
>
> ALTERNATIVE STYLE: a short dash ▫ *the London–Oxford–Birmingham express.*
>
> • It also indicates an abbreviation ▫ *His mail should be re-addressed c/o Brown, 16 Caven Place* ('care of') ▫ *Please quote your a/c number in all correspondence* ('account') ▫ *Major Bateman is the officer i/c provisions* ('in charge of').
>
> • It expresses rates or ratios in measurements ▫ *100 km/h* ▫ *60 lb/in²*.

obliterate /ə'blɪtəreɪt/ ▷ *verb* (***obliterated, obliterating***) **1** to destroy something completely. **2** to cover and prevent (eg writing, etc) from being seen. • **obliteration** *noun*. • **obliterative** *adj*. ⓒ 16c: from Latin *oblitterare* to blot out or erase, from *ob* out + *littera* letter.

oblivion /ə'blɪvɪən/ ▷ *noun* **1** the state or fact of having forgotten or of being unconscious. **2** the state of being forgotten. **3** *law* amnesty; pardon. ⓒ 14c: from Latin *oblivio* forgetfulness, from *oblivisci* to forget.

oblivious /ə'blɪvɪəs/ ▷ *adj* (*usually* **oblivious of** or **to something**) unaware or forgetful of it. • **obliviously** *adverb*. • **obliviousness** *noun*.

oblong /'ɒblɒŋ/ ▷ *adj* (abbreviation **obl.**) rectangular with adjacent sides of unequal length; with a greater breadth than height. ▷ *noun, non-technical* something that has this shape; a rectangular figure. ⓒ 15c: from Latin *oblongus*, from *ob-* over + *longus* long.

obloquy /'ɒbləkwɪ/ ▷ *noun* (***obloquies***) **1** abuse, blame or censure. **2** disgrace; loss of honour, good name or reputation. ⓒ 15c: from Latin *obloquium* contradiction, from *ob-* against + *loqui* to speak.

obnoxious /əb'nɒkʃəs/ ▷ *adj* **1** offensive; objectionable. **2** *rare* subject or liable to harm or injury. • **obnoxiously** *adverb*. • **obnoxiousness** *noun*. ⓒ 16c in sense 2: from Latin *obnoxius*, from *ob-* exposed to + *noxa* harm or injury.

oboe /'oʊboʊ/ ▷ *noun* (***oboes***) **1** a double-reed treble woodwind instrument with a penetrating tone. **2** an organ stop with a similar tone. **3** an oboe player in an orchestra ▫ ***The oboes stood up.*** • **oboist** /'oʊboʊɪst/ *noun*. ⓒ 18c: Italian, from French *hautbois*, literally 'high wood', with reference to the instrument's pitch.

oboe d'amore / — da'mɔːreɪ/ ▷ *noun* (***oboes d'amore*** or ***oboi d'amore*** /'oʊbɔɪ —/) an old type of oboe that has a pear-shaped bell and is pitched a minor third lower than the ordinary oboe, used especially in baroque music. ⓒ 19c: Italian, meaning 'oboe of love'.

obol /'ɒbɒl/ ▷ *noun* in ancient Greece: the sixth part of a drachma in weight or in money. ⓒ 16c: from Greek *obolos*, a variant of *obelos* a spit.

obscene /əb'siːn, ɒb'siːn/ ▷ *adj* (***obscener, obscenest***) **1** offensive to accepted standards of behaviour or morality, especially sexual morality. **2** *colloq* indecent; disgusting. **3** *Brit law* said of a publication: tending to deprave or corrupt. • **obscenely** *adverb*. ⓒ 16c: from French *obscène* or Latin *obscenus* ill-omened, foul or indecent.

obscenity /əbˈsɛnɪtɪ/ *noun* (***obscenities***) **1** the state or quality of being obscene. **2** an obscene word or act.

obscurantism /ɒbskjʊˈrantɪzəm/ ▷ *noun* opposition to inquiry or the spreading or use of new knowledge, up-to-date scientific research or reform, etc. • **obscurantist** *noun* (*also* **obscurant**) someone who tries to prevent enlightenment or reform. ▷ *adj* (*also* **obscurant**) relating to or characteristic of obscurantism. ⓒ 19c.

obscure /əbˈskjʊə(r)/ ▷ *adj* **1** dark; dim. **2** not clear; hidden; difficult to see. **3** not well known. **4** difficult to understand. ▷ *verb* (***obscured***, ***obscuring***) **1** to make something dark or dim. **2** *phonetics* to pronounce (a vowel) in a more centralized and weaker position. **3** to overshadow something. **4** to make something difficult to see or understand. • **obscurely** *adverb*. • **obscurity** *noun* (***obscurities***) **1** the state of being obscure. **2** someone or something that is obscure. ⓒ 14c: from French *obscur*, from Latin *obscurus* dark.

obsequent /ˈɒbsɪkwent/ ▷ *adj* said of a stream or river: flowing in a contrary direction to the original slope of the land. Compare CONSEQUENT, SUBSEQUENT. ⓒ 19c: from Latin *ob* away from + *sequi* to follow.

obsequies /ˈɒbsəkwɪz/ ▷ *plural noun* funeral rites. ⓒ 14c: from Latin *obsequiae*, perhaps a confusion of Latin *exsequiae* funeral rites and *obsequium* compliance.

obsequious /əbˈsiːkwɪəs/ ▷ *adj* submissively obedient; fawning. • **obsequiously** *adverb*. • **obsequiousness** *noun*. ⓒ 15c in sense 'dutiful' or 'obedient': from Latin *obsequiosus* compliant.

observance /əbˈzɜːvəns/ ▷ *noun* **1** the fact or act of obeying rules or keeping customs, etc. **2** a custom or religious rite observed. **3** the rule of a religious order. ⓒ 13c.

observation, observance

• These two nouns correspond to different meanings of **observe**.

• **Observance** relates to sense 4 of **observe** and is used mainly about laws, rules, rights and principles, especially religious principles:

✓ *He advocated a more meticulous observance of the canons of Islam.*

✓ *He had seen his father reviled by his neighbours for his strict observance of the Lord's Day.*

• **Observation** relates to senses 1, 2 and 3 of **observe** and is used more generally:

✓ *From our observations it is clear that the guidelines for use were rarely followed closely.*

✓ *Accuracy depends to a large extent on vigilance and observation, as well as concentration.*

• **Observation** also has the special meaning 'remark' (in sense 3), eg:

✓ *The newspaper article made one telling observation about him.*

• You will occasionally see **observation** used to mean **observance**, but this is not a typical meaning and is best avoided:

? *She considered all religious observation as ridiculous frivolity.*

observant /əbˈzɜːvənt/ ▷ *adj* **1** quick to notice; perceptive. **2** carefully attentive. • **observantly** *adverb*.

observation /ɒbzəˈveɪʃən/ ▷ *noun* **1 a** the act of noticing or watching; **b** the state of being observed or watched. **2** the ability to observe; perception. **3** a remark or comment. **4** the noting of behaviour, symptoms or phenomena, etc as they occur, especially before analysis or diagnosis □ ***keep the patient under observation***. **5** the result of such observing. • **take an observation** to observe the position of the Sun or stars in order to calculate one's geographical position.

observational ▷ *adj* **1** relating to or consisting of observing or noticing. **2** based on observation of behaviour or phenomena, etc rather than on experiments. • **observationally** *adverb*.

observation car ▷ *noun* a railway carriage with large windows to allow passengers to view the scenery.

observatory /əbˈzɜːvətərɪ/ ▷ *noun* (***observatories***) **1** a room or building, etc specially equipped for making systematic observations of natural phenomena, especially the stars and other celestial objects visible in the night sky. **2** a building or site that affords an extensive view of its surroundings; a viewpoint. ⓒ 17c: from Latin *observare*, *observatum*.

observe /əbˈzɜːv/ ▷ *verb* (***observed***, ***observing***) **1** to notice or become conscious of something. **2** to watch something carefully; to pay close attention to it. **3** *tr & intr* to examine and note (behaviour, symptoms or phenomena, etc). **4** to obey, follow or keep (a law, custom or religious rite, etc). **5** *tr & intr* to make a remark or comment □ ***observed that he was late again***. • **observable** *adj*. • **observably** *adverb*. • **observer** *noun*. ⓒ 14c: from Latin *observare*, from *ob-* towards + *servare* to keep or watch.

obsess /əbˈsɛs, ɒbˈsɛs/ ▷ *verb* (***obsesses***, ***obsessed***, ***obsessing***) **1** to occupy someone's thoughts or mind completely, persistently or constantly; to preoccupy or haunt □ ***She is obsessed by football***. **2** *intr*, *chiefly N Amer* to think or worry constantly about something. ⓒ 16c in sense 1: from Latin *obsidere*, *obsessum* to besiege, from *ob-* in front of + *sedere* to sit.

obsession /əbˈsɛʃən/ ▷ *noun* **1** a persistent or dominating thought, idea, feeling, etc. **2** *psychol* a form of neurosis in which a recurring thought, feeling or impulse, generally of an unpleasant nature and with no rational basis, preoccupies a person against their will and is a source of constant anxiety. **3** the act of obsessing or state of being obsessed. • **obsessional** *adj*. • **obsessionally** *adverb*. • **obsessionist** *noun*. ⓒ Early 20c in sense 2; 16c.

obsessive /əbˈsɛsɪv/ ▷ *adj* **1** relating to or resulting from obsession, an obsession or obsessions. **2** said of a person: affected by an obsession. ▷ *noun* someone affected or characterized by obsessive behaviour. • **obsessively** *adverb*. • **obsessiveness** *noun*. ⓒ Early 20c.

obsessive-compulsive disorder ▷ *noun*, *psychol* a form of neurosis in which a person becomes preoccupied with a recurring thought, feeling or impulse, which is a source of constant anxiety. See also OBSESSION.

obsidian /ɒbˈsɪdɪən/ ▷ *noun*, *geol* the commonest type of volcanic glass, usually black, but sometimes red or brown in colour, formed by the rapid cooling and solidification of granite magma. ⓒ 17c: from Latin *obsidianus*, an erroneous form of *(lapis) obsianus*, a stone supposedly found by one Obsius in Ethiopia.

obsolesce /ɒbsəˈlɛs/ ▷ *verb* (***obsolesced***, ***obsolescing***) *intr* to become obsolete; to be going out of use. ⓒ 19c.

obsolescent /ɒbsəˈlɛsənt/ ▷ *adj* going out of use; becoming out of date. • **obsolescence** *noun*. ⓒ 18c.

obsolete /ˈɒbsəliːt, ɒbsəˈliːt/ ▷ *adj* **1** no longer in use or in practice. **2** out of date; outmoded. **3** *biol* said of organs, etc: vestigial; no longer functional or fully developed. • **obsoletely** *adverb*. • **obsoleteness** *noun*. ⓒ 16c: from Latin *obsoletus* worn out, from *obsolescere* to fall into disuse, perhaps from *ob-* in the opposite direction + *solere* to be accustomed to.

obstacle /ˈɒbstəkəl/ ▷ *noun* someone or something that obstructs, or hinders or prevents advance. ⓒ 14c: from Latin *obstaculum*, from *ob-* before + *stare* to stand.

obstacle race ▷ *noun* a race in which participants have to climb over and crawl through, etc various obstacles.

obstetric /ɒb'stɛtrɪk/ or **obstetrical** *adj* relating to obstetrics. • **obstetrically** *adverb*. ⓘ 18c: originally meaning 'relating to a midwife', from Latin *obstetrix* a midwife, from *ob* before + *stare* to stand.

obstetrician /ɒbstə'trɪʃən/ ▷ *noun* **1** a physician who specializes in obstetrics. **2** *formerly* someone skilled in midwifery. ⓘ 19c.

obstetrics /ɒb'stɛtrɪks/ ▷ *singular noun* the branch of medicine and surgery that deals with pregnancy, childbirth and the care of the mother. ⓘ 19c.

obstinacy /'ɒbstɪnəsɪ/ ▷ *noun* (***obstinacies***) **1** the quality or state of being obstinate; stubbornness. **2 a** obstinate behaviour; **b** an obstinate act.

obstinate /'ɒbstɪnət/ ▷ *adj* **1** refusing to change one's opinion or course of action; stubborn; inflexible. **2 a** difficult to defeat or remove; **b** said especially of a disease or medical condition, etc: difficult to treat; unyielding. • **obstinately** *adverb*. ⓘ 14c: from Latin *obstinare*, *obstinatum* to persist.

obstreperous /əb'strɛpərəs, ɒb-/ ▷ *adj* noisy and hard to control; unruly. • **obstreperously** *adverb*. • **obstreperousness** *noun*. ⓘ 16c: from Latin *strepere* to make a noise.

obstruct /əb'strʌkt/ ▷ *verb* (***obstructed***, ***obstructing***) **1** to block or close (a passage or opening, etc). **2** to prevent or hinder the movement or progress of someone or something. **3** to oppose or stand in the way of (a person, a proposition or intention, etc). **4** to block or impede (a view or line of vision, etc). **5** *intr* to be or constitute an obstruction. **6** *intr* to practise OBSTRUCTIONISM. • **obstructor** *noun*. ⓘ 16c: from Latin *obstruere*, from *ob-* in the way of + *struere* to pile or build up.

obstruction ▷ *noun* **1** a thing that obstructs or blocks. **2** the act of obstructing. **3** *sport* an act of hindering or unfairly getting in the way of another player or competitor.

obstructionism ▷ *noun* the practice of obstructing parliamentary or legal action. Compare FILIBUSTER. • **obstructionist** *noun* someone, especially a politician, who practises obstruction. Also *as adj*. ⓘ 19c.

obstruction lights ▷ *noun, aeronautics* lights fixed to any structures near airports that could constitute a danger to aircraft in flight.

obstructive ▷ *adj* causing or designed to cause an obstruction. • **obstructively** *adverb*. • **obstructiveness** *noun*. ⓘ 17c.

obtain /əb'teɪn/ ▷ *verb* (***obtained***, ***obtaining***) **1** to get something; to become the owner, or come into possession, of something, often by effort or planning; to gain something. **2** *intr* to be established, exist or hold good. • **obtainable** *adj*. • **obtainer** *noun*. • **obtainment** *noun*. ⓘ 15c from Latin *obtinere* to lay hold of, from *tenere* to hold.

obtrude /əb'truːd/ ▷ *verb* (***obtruded***, ***obtruding***) **1** *intr* to be or become unpleasantly noticeable or prominent. **2** (*usually* **obtrude something on** or **upon someone**) to push oneself or one's opinions, etc forward, especially when they are unwelcome. • **obtruder** *noun*. • **obtrusion** /əb'truːʒən/ *noun*. ⓘ 16c: from Latin *obtrudere*, *obstrusum*, from *trudere* to thrust.

obtrusive /əb'truːsɪv/ ▷ *adj* **1** unpleasantly noticeable or prominent. **2** sticking out; protruding. • **obtrusively** *adverb*. • **obtrusiveness** *noun*. ⓘ 17c.

obtuse /əb'tjuːs/ ▷ *adj* **1** *chiefly bot & zool* said eg of a leaf or other flat part: blunt; not pointed or sharp; rounded at the tip. **2 a** stupid and slow to understand; **b** not very perceptive or sensitive. **3** *geom* said of an angle: greater than 90° and less than 180°. Compare ACUTE (*adj* 7) **4** said of pain or a sound, etc: indistinctly felt or heard, etc; dull. • **obtusely** *adverb*. • **obtuseness** *noun*. • **obtusity** *noun*. ⓘ 16c: from Latin *obtundere*, *obtusum* to blunt, or beat against, from *tundere* to beat.

obverse /'ɒbvɜːs/ ▷ *adj* **1** turned towards or facing the observer. **2** complemental; referring to something that is the opposite aspect of the same fact. **3** *bot* said of leaves, etc: with the base narrower than the apex. ▷ *noun* **1** the side of a coin with the head or main design on it. Opposite of REVERSE (*noun* 4). **2** the face or side, etc of anything which is normally on view. **3** an opposite or counterpart, eg of a fact or truth. • **obversely** *adverb*. • **obversion** *noun*. ⓘ 17c: from Latin *obversus* turned against or towards, from *vertere* to turn.

obviate /'ɒbvɪeɪt/ ▷ *verb* (***obviated***, ***obviating***) to prevent or remove (a potential difficulty or problem, etc) in advance; to forestall. • **obviation** *noun*. ⓘ 16c: from Latin *obviare*, *obviatum* to go to meet.

obvious /'ɒbvɪəs/ ▷ *adj* **1** easily seen or understood; clearly evident. **2** not subtle. **3** *noun* (**the obvious**) something which is obvious (see THE 4b) ▫ *to state the obvious*. • **obviously** *adverb*. • **obviousness** *noun*. ⓘ 16c: from Latin *obvius*, from *ob* in the way of + *via* way.

OC ▷ *abbreviation* **1** Officer Commanding. **2** Officer in Charge. **3** (Officer of the) Order of Canada. **4** *philately* original cover.

oc ▷ *abbreviation* only child.

o/c ▷ *abbreviation* overcharge.

ocarina /ɒkə'riːnə/ ▷ *noun* (***ocarinas***) a small simple fluty-toned wind instrument that has an egg-shaped body with fingerholes and a projecting mouthpiece. ⓘ 19c: Italian, from *oca* goose, so-called because of its shape.

OCCAM or **occam** ▷ *noun, computing* a software language.

occasion /ə'keɪʒən/ ▷ *noun* **1** a particular event or happening, or the time at which it occurs ▫ *met on three occasions*. **2** a special event or celebration. **3** a suitable opportunity or chance. **4** a reason; grounds ▫ *have no occasion to be angry*. **5** an event which determines the time at which something happens, but which is not the actual cause of it. ▷ *verb* (***occasioned***, ***occasioning***) to cause something; to bring it about, especially incidentally. • **on occasion 1** as the need or opportunity arises. **2** from time to time; occasionally. • **rise to the occasion** see under RISE. • **take occasion** to take advantage of an opportunity (to do something). ⓘ 14c: French, or from Latin *occasio* opportunity or cause, from *occidere*, from *oc-* in the way of + *cadere*, *casum* to fall.

occasional ▷ *adj* **1** happening irregularly and infrequently. **2** produced on or for a special occasion. • **occasionally** *adverb*.

occasionalism ▷ *noun, philos* the Cartesian doctrine that explains the apparent interaction of mind and matter as the direct intervention of God on the occasion of certain changes occurring in one or the other. • **occasionalist** *noun*. ⓘ 19c.

occasional table ▷ *noun* a small portable side-table used irregularly and for various purposes.

Occident /'ɒksɪdənt/ ▷ *noun* **1** (**the Occident**) the countries in the west, especially those in Europe and America regarded as culturally distinct from eastern countries (the ORIENT). **2** (*also* **occident**) *poetic* the part of the sky where the Sun sets; the west. Compare ORIENT. • **occidental** /-'dɛntəl/ *adj* (*also* **Occidental**) from or relating to the Occident; western. ▷ *noun* (*usually* **Occidental**) someone born in the Occident; a westerner. • **occidentally** *adverb*. ⓘ 14c: French, from Latin *occidens* setting, west or sunset, from *occidere* to go down.

occidentalize or **occidentalise** ▷ *verb* (***occidentalized***, ***occidentalizing***) to make occidental; to westernize (a culture or customs, etc). ⓘ 19c.

occipital /ɒk'sɪpɪtəl/ *anatomy* ▷ *adj* relating to or in the region of the back of the head. ▷ *noun* (*also* **occipital bone**) the bone that forms the back of the skull and part of its base, and encircles the spinal column. ⓒ 16c: French, from Latin *occipitalis*.

occiput /'ɒksɪpʌt, -pət/ ▷ *noun, anatomy* **1** the back of the head or skull. **2** the occipital bone. ⓒ 14c: Latin, from *oc-* over + *caput* head.

occlude /ə'klu:d/ ▷ *verb* (***occluded, occluding***) *technical* **1 a** to block up or cover (eg a pore or some other opening or orifice); **b** to block or obstruct (a passage). **2** to shut something in or out. **3** to cover (an eye) to prevent its use. **4** *chem* said of a solid: to absorb (a gas) so that its atoms or molecules occupy the spaces within the lattice structure of the solid. **5** *medicine* to close (an opening), eg to obstruct a blood vessel. **6** *dentistry* to close (the surfaces of the upper teeth) on those of the lower teeth. **7** *tr & intr, meteorol* to form or cause to form an OCCLUDED FRONT. • **occludent** *noun, adj*. • **occluder** *noun, ophthalmol* a device used to occlude an eye. ⓒ 16c: from Latin *occludere* to shut or close up, from *oc-* in the way of + *claudere* to close.

occluded front ▷ *noun, meteorol* the final stage in an atmospheric depression, when a cold front catches up with and overtakes a warm front, lifting the warm air mass off the ground. Also called **occlusion**.

occlusion /ə'klu:ʒən/ ▷ *noun* **1** the closing of an orifice, etc. **2** the act of occluding or absorbing. **3** *dentistry* **a** the bite or way in which the upper and lower teeth meet; **b** the state of having the jaws closed and the upper and lower teeth in contact. **4** *meteorol* an OCCLUDED FRONT. **5** *phonetics* the brief closing of the breath passage during the articulation of a consonant released orally, or of the mouth passage during the articulation of a nasal consonant. • **occlusive** *adj*. ▷ *noun, phonetics* a sound produced by occlusion. ⓒ 17c.

occult ▷ *adj* /ɒ'kʌlt, 'ɒkʌlt/ **1** involving, using or dealing with that which is magical, mystical or supernatural. **2** beyond ordinary understanding. **3** secret, hidden or esoteric. **4** (**the occult**) the knowledge and study of that which is magical, mystical or supernatural (see THE 4b). ▷ *verb* /ɒ'kʌlt/ (***occulted, occulting***) **1** *tr & intr* to hide or conceal something, or to be hidden or concealed. **2** *tr & intr, astron* said of a celestial body: to obscure (another celestial body) or to be obscured by occultation. **3** *intr* said of lights, especially the light in a lighthouse, or beacons, etc: to become temporarily invisible at regular intervals. • **occultism** *noun, relig* the doctrine or study of the supernatural, and practices purporting to achieve communication with things hidden and mysterious. • **occultist** *noun*. • **occultly** *adverb*. • **occultness** *noun*. ⓒ 16c: from Latin *occulere*, *occultum* to hide.

occultation ▷ *noun, astron* a phenomenon that is observed when one celestial body, eg a planet or moon, passes directly in front of another, eg a star, so obscuring it, as with an ECLIPSE (*noun* 1).

occupancy /'ɒkjʊpənsɪ/ ▷ *noun* (***occupancies***) **1** the act or condition of occupying (a house or flat, etc), or the fact of its being occupied. **2** the period of time during which a house, etc is occupied. **3** *law* the action of taking possession of property, especially land, that has no owner with the intention of acquiring its ownership. **4** the proportion of, or extent to which, accommodation is used or occupied. ⓒ 16c.

occupant /'ɒkjʊpənt/ ▷ *noun* **1** someone who occupies, holds or resides in property, or in a particular position, etc. **2** *law* someone who acquires by occupancy the title to property that previously had no owner. ⓒ 16c.

occupation /ɒkjʊ'peɪʃən/ ▷ *noun* **1** a person's job or profession. **2** an activity that occupies a person's attention or free time, etc. **3** the act of occupying or state of being occupied ▫ *the terrorists' occupation of the embassy.* **4** the period of time during which a town, house, etc is occupied. **5** the act of taking and keeping control of a foreign country by military power. • **occupational** *adj* related to or caused by a person's job ▫ *occupational pension* ▫ *occupational disease.* • **occupationally** *adverb*. ⓒ 16c: from Latin *occupatio* seizing.

occupational disease see INDUSTRIAL DISEASE

occupational hazard ▷ *noun* a risk or danger accepted as a consequence of the nature or working conditions of a particular job.

occupational psychology ▷ *noun, psychol* the scientific study of human behaviour in the workplace, including the study of work skills and the working environment, vocational guidance, personnel selection, all forms of training, and principles of management. • **occupational psychologist** *noun*.

occupational therapy ▷ *noun* a form of rehabilitation in which patients with physical or mental illnesses are encouraged to participate in selected activities that will equip them to function independently in everyday life, such as household management, educational programmes, art and crafts, etc. • **occupational therapist** *noun*.

occupy /'ɒkjʊpaɪ/ ▷ *verb* (***occupies, occupied, occupying***) **1** to have possession of or live in (a house, etc). **2** to be in or fill (time or space, etc). **3** to take possession of (a town or foreign country, etc) by force. **4** to enter and take possession of (a building, etc) often by force and without authority. **5 a** to keep (someone, oneself or one's mind, etc) busy; **b** to fill in (time) ▫ *occupied the three-hour journey with knitting.* **6** to hold (a post or office). • **occupier** *noun* someone who lives in a building, either as a tenant or owner; an occupant. ⓒ 14c: from Latin *occupare* to seize.

occur /ə'kɜ:(r)/ ▷ *verb* (***occurred, occurring***) *intr* **1** to happen or take place. **2** *intr* to be found or exist. • **occurrence** *noun* **1** anything that occurs; an event, especially an unexpected one. **2** the act or fact of occurring. • **occurrent** *adj*. ⓒ 15c: from Latin *occurrere* to run towards, to befall.

■ **occur to someone** to come into their mind, especially unexpectedly or by chance ▫ *It occurred to her that the train might be late.*

ocean /'oʊʃən/ ▷ *noun* **1** the continuous expanse of salt water that covers about 70% of the Earth's surface and surrounds the continental land masses. **2** any one of its five main divisions: the Atlantic, Indian, Pacific, Arctic and Southern. **3** the sea. **4** (*often* **oceans**) a very large number, amount or expanse ▫ *oceans of wine.* ⓒ 13c: from Latin *oceanus*, from Greek *Okeanos* the stream supposed by the ancients to run round the Earth.

oceanarium /oʊʃə'nɛərɪəm/ ▷ *noun* (***oceanariums*** or ***oceanaria***) *originally US* a large saltwater aquarium, or an enclosed part of the sea, in which sea creatures such as dolphins and porpoises, etc are kept for research purposes or for display to the public. ⓒ 1940s.

ocean-going ▷ *adj* said of a ship, etc: suitable for sailing across oceans.

Oceanian /oʊʃɪ'eɪnɪən/ ▷ *adj* referring or relating to Oceania, which includes Polynesia, Micronesia and Melanesia, and sometimes also Australasia and the Malay Archipelago. ▷ *noun* a citizen or inhabitant of, or person born in, Oceania, especially a Polynesian. ⓒ 19c.

oceanic /oʊʃɪ'anɪk/ ▷ *adj* **1** relating to the ocean. **2** *biol, geol* found or formed in the ocean beyond the edge of a CONTINENTAL SHELF. **3** like an ocean; immense. **4** *meteorol* said of a climate: influenced by proximity to the sea, and therefore with a relatively small temperature range and relatively high precipitation. • **oceanicity** /oʊʃə'nɪsɪtɪ/ *noun, meteorol* the state of being, or extent to which a climate is, oceanic. ⓒ 17c.

oceanography /oʊʃə'nɒgrəfɪ/ ▷ *noun* the scientific study of the oceans, including the structure and origin of the ocean floor, the chemical properties of sea water, physical processes such as currents, waves and tides, and the ecology of marine organisms. • **oceanographer** *noun.* • **oceanographic** /-ˈgrafɪk/ or **oceanographical** *adj.* Ⓒ 19c.

oceanology /oʊʃəˈnɒlədʒɪ/ ▷ *noun* the scientific study of the sea, especially of its economic geography. • **oceanological** /-nəˈlɒdʒɪkəl/ *adj.* • **oceanologist** *noun.* Ⓒ 19c.

ocellus /oʊˈsɛləs/ ▷ *noun* (*plural* **ocelli** /-laɪ/) *zool* **1** in insects and other lower animals: a simple eye or eyespot, as distinct from a compound eye. **2** an eyelike or ringed spot of colour, eg on a butterfly's wing, etc. • **ocellar** *adj.* • **ocellate** /ˈɒsəleɪt/ *adj.* • **ocellated** *adj* **1** with an eyelike spot or spots. **2** eyelike and ringed. • **ocellation** *noun.* Ⓒ 19c: Latin, diminutive of *oculus* eye.

ocelot /ˈɒsəlɒt, ˈoʊ-/ ▷ *noun* **1** a medium-sized wild cat, found in the forests of Central and S America, that has dark-yellow fur marked with spots and stripes. **2** its fur. Ⓒ 18c: French, from Nahuatl *ocelotl* jaguar.

och /ɒx/ ▷ *exclamation, Scots & Irish* expressing surprise, impatience, disagreement, annoyance or regret, etc. Ⓒ 16c.

oche /ˈɒkɪ/ ▷ *noun* (*oches*) *darts* the line, groove or ridge on the floor behind which a player must stand to throw. Also called **hockey** or **hockey line**. Ⓒ 1930s: perhaps related to Anglo-Saxon *oche* to lop, or French *ocher* to nick or cut a groove in something.

ocher the *N Amer* spelling of OCHRE

ochlocracy /ɒˈklɒkrəsɪ/ ▷ *noun* (*ochlocracies*) **1** mob rule; government by the populace. **2** a state, etc that is dominated or governed by the populace. • **ochlocrat** *noun.* • **ochlocratic** or **ochlocratical** *adj.* Ⓒ 16c: from Greek *okhlokratia*, from *okhlos* crowd + *kratos* power.

ochlophobia /ɒkloʊˈfoʊbɪə/ ▷ *noun* fear of crowds. • **ochlophobiac** *noun.* • **ochlophobic** *adj.* Ⓒ Late 19c: from Greek *okhlos* crowd.

ochre /ˈoʊkə(r)/ or *N Amer* **ocher** /ˈoʊkər/ *noun* (*ochres* or *ochers*) **1** any of various fine earths or clays that contain ferric oxide, silica or alumina, used as a red, yellow or brown pigment. **2** a pale brownish-yellow colour. ▷ *adj* with the colour of ochre. ▷ *verb* (*ochred, ochring*) to mark or colour something with ochre. • **ochraceous** /oʊˈkreɪʃəs/ , **ochreous** /ˈoʊkrɪəs/ , **ochrous** or **ochry** *adj* **1** like, containing or full of ochre. **2** with the colour of ochre; yellowish. Ⓒ 14c: from French *ocre*, from Greek *okhros* pale yellow.

ochrea or **ocrea** /ˈɒkrɪə/ *noun* (*plural* **ochreae** /ˈɒkrɪaɪ/) *bot* a sheath formed by two or more stipulate leaves joined round a stem. • **ochreate** *adj.* Ⓒ 19c: Latin, meaning 'a legging'.

-ock /-ək/ ▷ *suffix, forming nouns, indicating* a diminutive ◻ *hillock.* Ⓒ Anglo-Saxon *-oc* or *-uc*.

ocker /ˈɒkə(r)/ *Austral slang* ▷ *noun* (*often* **Ocker**) an oafish uncultured Australian man. ▷ *adj* typical of an ocker; boorish; uncultured. Ⓒ 1970s: a form of the name Oscar, the name of a TV character.

o'clock /əˈklɒk/ ▷ *adverb* after a number from one to twelve: **1** used in specifying the time, indicating the number of hours after midday or midnight ◻ *three o'clock.* **2** used to indicate position or direction relative to the observer and with reference to an imaginary clock face, twelve o'clock being directly ahead or above ◻ *enemy aircraft at two o'clock.* Ⓒ Early 20c in sense 2; 18c: a contraction of *of the clock.*

OCR ▷ *abbreviation, computing* optical character recognition, reader or reading.

Oct. ▷ *abbreviation* October.

oct. ▷ *abbreviation* octavo.

oct- and **octa-** see OCTO-

octachord *music* ▷ *adj* **1** relating to an eight-note scale. **2** with eight strings. ▷ *noun* **1** a diatonic series of eight notes. **2** an instrument with eight strings. Ⓒ 18c: from Latin *octachordos*, from Greek, from *octa-* OCTA- + *khorde* string.

octad /ˈɒktad/ ▷ *noun* a group, series or set, etc of eight things. • **octadic** *adj.* Ⓒ 19c: from Greek *oktas, oktados* a group of eight, from *okto* eight.

octadecanoic acid see STEARIC ACID

octagon /ˈɒktəgən/ ▷ *noun* **1** a flat figure with eight straight sides and eight angles. **2** something that has an octagonal shape. ▷ *adj* octagonal. • **octagonal** /ɒkˈtagənəl/ *adj* **1** shaped like an octagon. **2** with eight sides and angles. • **octagonally** *adverb.* Ⓒ 16c: from Latin *octagonum*, from Greek *okto* eight + *gonia* angle.

octagynous see OCTOGYNOUS

octahedron or **octohedron** /ɒktəˈhiːdrən/ ▷ *noun* (*octahedra* /-drə/ or *octahedrons*) a solid figure with eight plane faces. • **octahedral** *adj* **1** shaped like an octahedron. **2** with eight plane surfaces. Ⓒ 16c: from Greek *oktaedron*, from *okto* eight + *hedra* seat or base.

octal /ˈɒktəl/ *math, computing* ▷ *adj* relating to or based on the number 8. ▷ *noun* **1** octal notation: a numbering system using the base 8 and the digits 0 to 7, eg 9 (decimal) is 11 (octal). **2** an octal number. Ⓒ 1930s.

octameter /ɒkˈtamɪtə(r)/ ▷ *noun, poetry* a line of eight metrical feet. See also PENTAMETER, HEXAMETER. Ⓒ 19c.

octane /ˈɒkteɪn/ ▷ *noun, chem* (formula C_8H_{18}) a colourless liquid belonging to the alkane series of hydrocarbons, present in petroleum, used in petrol, as a solvent and in the manufacture of organic chemicals. Ⓒ 19c.

octane number and **octane rating** ▷ *noun* a numerical system for classifying motor fuels according to their resistance to knocking, such that the higher the octane number on a scale 0 to 125, the better the quality of the petrol, and the lower the likelihood of knocking (see KNOCK *verb* 7).

octangular /ɒkˈtaŋgjʊlə(r)/ ▷ *adj* with eight angles; octagonal. Ⓒ 17c.

octant /ˈɒktənt/ ▷ *noun* **1** *math* **a** one eighth of the circumference of a circle; **b** a section, formed by drawing two straight lines from the centre to the circumference, of one eighth of a circle. **2** *math* a division of space or of a solid body divided into eight by three planes, usually at right angles to each other. **3** *math* an angle-measuring instrument in the form of a graduated eighth of a circle, used especially in astronomy and navigation. **4** *astron, astrol* a position of 45° from another position, especially of the Moon from CONJUNCTION (*noun* 4) or OPPOSITION (*noun* 7). • **octantal** /ɒkˈtantəl/ *adj.* Ⓒ 17c: from Latin *octans* half quadrant, from *octo* eight.

octaroon see OCTOROON

octave /ˈɒktɪv, ˈɒkteɪv/ ▷ *noun* **1** any group or series of eight. **2** *music* **a** the range of sound, or the series of notes, between the first and the eighth notes of a major or minor scale, eg from C to the C above; **b** a musical note that is an eighth above or below another. **3** an organ stop sounding an octave higher than the ordinary pitch. **4** (*also* **octet**) *poetry* **a** a verse or stanza with eight lines; **b** the first eight lines of a sonnet. **5 a** the eighth day (when counted inclusively) after a church festival; **b** the eight days from a festival to its octave. **6** *fencing* **a** the eighth of eight basic parrying positions; **b** a parry made in this position. Ⓒ 14c: from Latin *octavus* eighth.

octavo /ɒkˈteɪvoʊ/ ▷ *noun* (*octavos*) *printing, publishing* (abbreviation **oct.**) **1** a size of book or page produced by folding a standard-sized sheet of paper three times to give eight leaves. **2** a book or page of this size. Ⓒ 16c: from Latin *in octavo* in an eighth (said of a sheet).

octennial /ɒkˈtɛnɪəl/ ▷ *adj* **1** happening every eight years. **2** lasting for eight years. • **octennially** *adverb.* Ⓒ 17c: from Latin *octennium* eight years, from *octo* eight + *annus* year.

octet or **octette** /ɒk'tɛt/ ▻ *noun* **1** any group of eight people or things. **2** *music* **a** a group of eight musicians or singers who perform together; **b** a piece of music written for eight instruments or voices. **3** *poetry* an OCTAVE 4. **4** *chem* a stable group of eight electrons. **5** *nuclear physics* a group of eight subatomic particles. ⓘ 19c: from OCT- (see under OCTO-), modelled on DUET, *etc.*

octillion /ɒk'tɪlɪən/ ▻ *noun* **1** in Britain and Germany: a million raised to the eighth power; 10^{48}. **2** in N America and France: a thousand raised to the ninth power; 10^{27}. ● **octillionth** *noun, adj.* ⓘ 17c: from OCT-, modelled on *million, billion, etc.*

octo- /ɒktoʊ, ɒk'tɒ/ or **octa-** /ɒktə, ɒk'ta/ or (before a vowel) **oct-** ▻ *combining form, signifying* eight. ⓘ From Latin *octo*, Greek *okto* eight.

October /ɒk'toʊbə(r)/ ▻ *noun* (abbreviation **Oct.**) the tenth month of the year, which follows September and comes before November, and has 31 days. ⓘ Anglo-Saxon: Latin, from *octo* eight, so called because it was the eighth month in the Roman calendar.

octocentenary /ɒktoʊsən'tiːnərɪ, -sɛn'tɛnərɪ/ ▻ *noun* an eight-hundredth anniversary. ● **octocentennial** *adj.* ⓘ 19c.

octogenarian /ɒktoʊdʒə'nɛərɪən/ ▻ *noun* someone who is 80 years old, or between 80 and 89 years old. ▻ *adj* **1** between 80 and 89 years old. **2** relating to an octogenarian or octogenarians. ⓘ 19c: from Latin *octogenarius* relating to eighty, from *octoginta* eighty.

octogynous /ɒk'tɒdʒɪnəs/ or **octagynous** /-'tadʒ-/ ▻ *adj, bot* with eight pistils or styles. ⓘ 19c.

octohedron see OCTAHEDRON

octopus /'ɒktəpəs/ ▻ *noun* (***octopuses***) **1** any of about 150 species of marine mollusc, found mainly in tropical regions, with a soft rounded body, no external shell, and eight arms, each of which bears two rows of suckers. **2** a person or organization, etc with widespread, often harmful or destructive, influence. **3** a fairground ride that approximately resembles the form of an octopus, with a set of rotating spokes or 'arms' from which passenger cars are suspended. ⓘ Late 19c in sense 2; 18c: Latin, from Greek *oktopous*, from *okto* eight + *pous* foot.

octopush /'ɒktəpʊʃ/ ▻ *noun* an underwater game similar to hockey, played in a swimming pool by two teams of six players who attempt to score goals by pushing a lead puck, called a **squid**, along the bottom and hitting it against the opposing team's end of the pool. ● **octopusher** *noun.* ⓘ 1970s: from *octo*pus + PUSH (*noun* 1).

octoroon or **octaroon** /ɒktə'ruːn/ ▻ *noun* a person having one black African or Caribbean great-grandparent; the offspring of a quadroon and person of European descent. ⓘ 19c: OCTO-, modelled on QUADROON.

octosyllable ▻ *noun* **1** a word with eight syllables. **2** a line of verse containing eight syllables. ▻ *adj* octosyllabic. ● **octosyllabic** *adj* consisting of eight syllables or composed of lines of eight syllables. ▻ *noun* a line containing eight syllables. ⓘ 18c.

octroi /'ɒktrwaː, ɒk'trwaː/ ▻ *noun* (***octrois***) **1** especially in some European countries: a duty levied on certain articles brought into a town. **2 a** the place where such a duty is paid; **b** the officials to whom it is paid. ⓘ 18c; 16c in obsolete sense 'concession' or 'privilege', ultimately from Latin *auctorizare* to authorize.

octuple /ɒk'tjuːpəl/ ▻ *adj* **1** eight times as large; eightfold. **2** *music* with eight beats in a bar. ▻ *verb* (***octupled, octupling***) *tr & intr* to multiply by eight; to become or make something eight times as many or as much, etc. ⓘ 17c: from Latin *octuplus*.

octuplet /'ɒktjʊplət/ ▻ *noun* **1** *music* a group of eight notes to be played in the time of six. **2** one of eight children or animals born at one birth.

ocular /'ɒkjʊlə(r)/ ▻ *adj* **1 a** relating to or in the region of the eye; **b** eyelike. **2** *entomol* relating to a compound eye. **3** relating to or obtained by vision; visual. ▻ *noun* **1** *jocular* the eye. **2** the eyepiece of an optical instrument. ● **ocularly** *adverb.* ⓘ 16c: from Latin *ocularis*, from *oculus* eye.

ocularist /'ɒkjʊlərɪst/ ▻ *noun* a maker of artificial eyes. ⓘ 19c: from French *oculariste*.

oculate /'ɒkjʊlət/ and **oculated** ▻ *adj, zool, bot* with eyelike spots or markings. ⓘ 16c, meaning 'with eyes': from Latin *oculatus*, from *oculus* eye.

oculist /'ɒkjʊlɪst/ ▻ *noun* a specialist in diseases and defects of the eye; an optician or ophthalmologist. ⓘ 16c.

oculo- /ɒkjʊloʊ, ɒkjʊ'lɒ/ ▻ *combining form, signifying* the eye or vision. ⓘ From Latin *oculus* eye.

oculomotor ▻ *adj* relating to or causing movement of the eye □ ***oculomotor nerves.*** ⓘ 19c.

oculus /'ɒkjʊləs/ ▻ *noun* (*plural* ***oculi*** /-laɪ/) *archit* a round window. See also ROSE WINDOW. ⓘ 19c.

OD[1] /oʊ'diː/ *slang* ▻ *noun* (***ODs*** or ***OD's***) an overdose of drugs. ▻ *verb* (***OD's, OD'd, OD'ing***) *intr* to take a drug overdose. ⓘ 1960s: from *over*dose.

OD[2] ▻ *abbreviation* **1** officer of the day. **2** (*also* **O/D**) on demand. **3** (*also* **O/D**) overdrawn. **4** ordnance datum.

ODA ▻ *abbreviation* Overseas Development Administration.

odalisque or **odalisk** /'oʊdəlɪsk/ ▻ *noun, historical* a female slave or concubine in a harem, especially in the harem belonging to the Turkish Sultan. ⓘ 17c: French, from Turkish *odalik*, from *oda* room.

odd /ɒd/ ▻ *adj* **1** left over when others are put into groups or pairs; remaining. **2** not matching □ ***odd socks.*** **3** not one of a complete set. **4** *math* said of a whole number: not exactly divisible by two, eg three is an odd number. Compare EVEN. **5** said of pages, etc that are numbered consecutively: referring to one with an odd number □ ***put pictures on the odd pages.*** **6** (***odder, oddest***) unusual; strange □ ***an odd face.*** **7** occasional; not regular; casual. **8** *in compounds* a little more than the specified number □ ***twenty-odd replies.*** **9** said of a place: out of the way; standing apart. ▻ *noun, golf* a stroke that makes a player's total number of strokes for a particular hole one more than their opponent's. ● **oddish** *adj.* ● **oddly** *adverb* **1** in an odd way or manner. **2** strangely; surprisingly □ ***Oddly, he refused to stay.*** ● **oddness** *noun.* ● **odd man** or **odd one out 1** someone that is set apart or in some way different from, and sometimes unwilling to be like, others forming a particular group. **2** a person or thing left over when a team or a set, etc has been formed. See also ODDS. ⓘ 14c: from Norse *oddi* point, triangle or odd number.

oddball /'ɒdbɔːl/ *originally US, colloq* ▻ *noun* a strange or eccentric person. ▻ *adj* said of a thing, a plan or circumstances, etc: eccentric; peculiar. ⓘ 1940s.

oddity /'ɒdɪtɪ/ ▻ *noun* (***oddities***) **1** a strange or odd person or thing. **2** an odd quality or characteristic; a peculiarity. **3** the state of being odd or unusual; strangeness. ⓘ 16c.

odd job ▻ *noun* (*usually* **odd jobs**) casual or occasional pieces of work, often routine or domestic. ● **odd jobber** and **odd-job man** *noun.*

odd lot ▻ *noun, stock exchange* a block of less than one hundred shares. ● **odd-lotter** *noun* someone who deals in odd lots.

oddly and **oddness** see under ODD

oddment /'ɒdmənt/ ▻ *noun* **1** something left over or remaining from a greater quantity □ ***oddments of fabric.*** **2** a miscellaneous article, especially a piece from a broken set. **3** *printing* (**oddments**) the parts of a book other than the main text. ⓘ 18c.

odds ▻ *plural noun* (sometimes treated as *singular*) **1** the chance or probability, expressed as a ratio, that something will or will not happen □ *The odds are 10–1 against.* **2** the difference, expressed as a ratio, between the amount placed as a bet and the money which might be won □ *offer odds of 2 to 1.* **3** an advantage that is thought to exist, especially in favour of one competitor over another □ *The odds are in her favour.* **4** likelihood □ *The odds are he'll be late again.* **5** an equalizing allowance given to a weaker side or competitor. • **against all the odds** or **against all odds** in spite of great difficulty or disadvantage. • **at odds** in disagreement or dispute; on bad terms. • **give** or **lay odds** to offer a bet with favourable odds. • **make no odds** to make no significant difference. • **over the odds** more than is normal, required or expected, etc. • **shout the odds** *slang* **1** to talk too much or too loudly. **2** to boast. • **take odds 1** to accept a bet. **2** to offer a bet with unfavourable odds. • **What's the odds?** *colloq* What difference does it make?; What does it matter? ◷ 16c, originally meaning 'unequal things'.

odds and ends ▻ *plural noun, colloq* miscellaneous objects or pieces of things, etc, usually of little value or importance.

odds and sods ▻ *plural noun, colloq* miscellaneous people or things, etc.

odds-on ▻ *adj* **1** said of a chance, the likelihood of a horse winning a race, etc: rated at even or better. **2** very likely to succeed, win or happen, etc.

ode /oʊd/ ▻ *noun* **1** a lyric poem, usually a fairly long one, with lines of different lengths and complex rhythms, addressed to a particular person or thing. **2** *originally* a poem intended to be sung. ◷ 16c: from Latin *oda*, from Greek *oide* song or singing, from *aeidein* to sing.

odious /ˈoʊdɪəs/ ▻ *adj* hateful; repulsive; extremely unpleasant or offensive. • **odiously** *adverb.* • **odiousness** *noun.* ◷ 14c: from Latin *odiosus.*

odium /ˈoʊdɪəm/ ▻ *noun* hatred, strong dislike, or disapproval of a person or thing, especially when widespread. ◷ 17c: Latin.

odometer /ɒˈdɒmɪtə, oʊˈdɒmɪtə/ or **hodometer** /hoʊ-/ ▻ *noun, N Amer* a device for measuring and displaying the distance travelled by a wheeled vehicle or a person, eg the milometer incorporated in the speedometer of a car. • **odometry** *noun.* ◷ 18c: from French *odomètre*, from Greek *hodos* way.

-odon ▻ *suffix, forming nouns, indicating* (in the names of animals) some characteristic of the teeth □ *chaetodon* □ *mastodon.* ◷ From Greek *odon*, from *odous* tooth.

-odont ▻ *suffix, forming adjectives and nouns, indicating* some characteristic of the teeth; toothed □ *bunodont* □ *thecodont.* ◷ From Greek *odous, odontos* tooth.

odontalgia /ɒdɒnˈtaldʒɪə/ or **odontalgy** ▻ *noun* toothache. ◷ 17c: Greek.

odontalgic /ɒdɒnˈtaldʒɪk/ ▻ *noun* a medicine for toothache. ▻ *adj* referring or relating to toothache.

odonto- /ɒdɒntoʊ, ɒdɒnˈtɒ/ or (before a vowel) **odont-** /ɒdɒnt/ ▻ *combining form, denoting* a tooth or teeth. ◷ From Greek *odous, odontos* tooth.

odontoblast ▻ *noun* a dentine-forming cell in the pulp of a tooth. ◷ 19c.

odontogeny /ɒdɒnˈtɒdʒənɪ/ ▻ *noun* the origin and development of teeth. ◷ 19c.

odontoid /əˈdɒntɔɪd/ ▻ *adj, zool, anatomy* **1** like a tooth. **2** relating to or associated with the ODONTOID PROCESS. ▻ *noun* a tooth-like structure, especially the odontoid process. ◷ 19c.

odontoid process and **odontoid peg** ▻ *noun, anatomy* in mammals and some other vertebrates: a toothlike projection from the second vertebra of the neck.

odontology /ɒdɒnˈtɒlədʒɪ/ ▻ *noun, anatomy* the structure, development and diseases of the teeth. • **odontological** *adj.* • **odontologist** *noun.* ◷ 19c.

odor the *N Amer* spelling of ODOUR

odoriferous /oʊdəˈrɪfərəs/ ▻ *adj* with or giving off a smell, usually a sweet or pleasant smell. • **odoriferously** *adverb.* • **odoriferousness** *noun.* ◷ 15c: from Latin *odorifer*, from *odor* smell.

odorous /ˈoʊdərəs/ ▻ *adj* **1** with or giving off an odour. **2** sweet-smelling; fragrant. **3** *colloq* bad-smelling; malodorous. • **odorously** *adverb.* • **odorousness** *noun.* ◷ 16c: from Latin *odorus* fragrant.

odour or (*N Amer*) **odor** /ˈoʊdə(r)/ ▻ *noun* **1** a distinctive smell; scent. **2** reputation; standing; relationship □ *in bad odour with someone.* **3** a characteristic or quality. • **odourless** *adj.* ◷ 13c: from French *odor* and *odur*, from Latin *odor* smell or scent.

odour of sanctity ▻ *noun* **1** a fragrance said to be given off by the bodies of saints at or after death. **2** a sanctimonious manner.

odyssey /ˈɒdɪsɪ/ ▻ *noun* (*odysseys*) **1 a** a long and adventurous journey or series of wanderings; **b** a story that relates such a journey. **2** a long and drawn-out process of change or development. • **Odyssean** /ɒdɪˈsɪən/ *adj* **1** relating to the Greek epic poem the Odyssey. **2** like an odyssey. ◷ 19c: from Greek *Odysseia*, the Greek epic poem, the *Odyssey*, attributed to Homer, that describes the adventures and wanderings of Odysseus (Ulysses) on his ten years' journey home to Ithica after the fall of Troy, .

OE ▻ *abbreviation* Old English.

Oe ▻ *symbol* oersted.

OECD ▻ *abbreviation* Organization for Economic Cooperation and Development.

oecumenic and **oecumenical** see ECUMENIC

OED ▻ *abbreviation* Oxford English Dictionary.

oedema or **edema** /ɪˈdiːmə/ ▻ *noun* (***oedemata*** /-mətə/ or ***oedemas***) **1** *pathol* an abnormal and excessive accumulation of fluid within body tissues or body cavities, causing generalized or local swelling. **2** *bot* an abnormal swelling in a plant caused by an accumulation of water in the tissues. • **oedematous** /ɪˈdiːmətəs, ɪˈdɛ-/ or **oedematose** /-toʊs/ *adj.* ◷ 15c: Latin, from Greek *oidema*, from *oidein* to swell.

Oedipus complex /ˈiːdɪpəs —/ ▻ *noun, psychoanal* **1** the repressed sexual desire of a son for his mother, and the subsequent rivalry with his father, considered by Freud to represent a normal stage of child development. **2** the corresponding sexual desire of a daughter for her father, and the subsequent rivalry with her mother. • **Oedipal** or **oedipal** *adj.* • **Oedipean** /iːdɪˈpɪən/ *adj.* ◷ Early 20c: from Greek *Oidipous* (literally 'Swell-foot'), the name of a legendary king of Thebes, who unwittingly killed his father and married his mother.

OEEC ▻ *abbreviation, historical* Organization for European Economic Cooperation, superseded in 1961 by the OECD.

oeno- /iːnoʊ, iːˈnɒ/ or (*N Amer*) **eno-** or (before a vowel) **oen-** or (*N Amer*) **en-** ▻ *combining form, denoting* wine. Also written **oino-** /ɔɪnoʊ, ɔɪˈnɒ/ or **oin-**. ◷ From Greek *oinos* wine.

oenology /iːˈnɒlədʒɪ/ ▻ *noun* the study or knowledge of wine. • **oenological** *adj.* • **oenologist** *noun.* ◷ 19c.

oenophile ▻ *noun* a lover or connoisseur of wine; an oenologist. • **oenophilic** *adj.* ◷ 1930s.

o'er /oʊə(r), ɔː(r)/ ▻ *prep, adverb, poetic or old use* short form of OVER.

Oerlikon or **oerlikon** /ˈɜːlɪkɒn/ ▻ *noun* any of various guns and fittings, especially a type of anti-aircraft cannon. ◷ 1940s: the name of a suburb of Zürich where these are produced.

oersted /ˈɜːstɛd, ˈɜːstɪd/ ▻ *noun* (symbol **Oe**) in the CGS UNIT system: a unit of magnetic field strength. ◷ 1930s: named after H C Oersted (1777–1851), Danish physicist.

Oes *plural of* O[1]

oesophagus or (*especially N Amer*) **esophagus** /iːˈsɒfəgəs/ ▷ *noun* (*oesophagi* /-gaɪ, -dʒaɪ/) *anatomy* the part of the alimentary canal between the pharynx and the stomach, a narrow muscular tube (in humans about 23cm long) by means of which food passes to the stomach. Also called GULLET. • **oesophageal** /-fəˈdʒɪəl/ *adj.* ◷ 14c: Latin, from Greek *oisophagos*.

oestradiol /iːstrəˈdaɪɒl, ɛstrə-/ or (*N Amer*) **estradiol** ▷ *noun, biochem* **1** the most important female sex hormone, a steroid that is produced by the ovary and controls the development of the female secondary sexual characteristics and the functioning of the reproductive organs. **2** a synthesized form of this hormone, used to treat breast cancer and menstrual disorders. ◷ 1930s.

oestrogen /ˈiːstrədʒən, ˈɛstrədʒən/ or (*N Amer*) **estrogen** ▷ *noun, biochem* **1** any of a group of steroid hormones, produced mainly by the ovaries, that control the growth and functioning of the female sex organs and the appearance of female secondary sexual characteristics, eg breast development, and that regulate the menstrual cycle. **2** *medicine* any such compound produced synthetically. • **oestrogenic** *adj.* ◷ 1920s: from OESTRUS.

oestrous cycle ▷ *noun* the series of hormonally controlled physiological changes that occur from the beginning of one period of oestrus to the beginning of the next. Compare MENSTRUAL CYCLE.

oestrus /ˈiːstrəs, ˈɛstrəs/ or (*N Amer*) **estrus** ▷ *noun, zool, physiol* a regularly occurring but restricted period of sexual receptivity that occurs in most female mammals apart from humans. See also IN or ON HEAT at HEAT. • **oestrous** *adj.* • **oestral** *adj.* ◷ 19c; 17c meaning 'a biting insect of the genus *Oestrus*': from Greek *oistros* a gadfly noted for its frenzy.

OF ▷ *abbreviation* Old French.

of /ɒv, (when unstressed) əv/ ▷ *prep* **1** used to show origin, cause or authorship □ ***people of Glasgow*** □ ***die of hunger*** □ ***poems of Keats.*** **2** belonging to or connected with something or someone. **3** used to specify a component, ingredient or characteristic, etc □ ***built of bricks*** □ ***an area of marsh*** □ ***a heart of gold.*** **4** at a given distance or amount of time from something □ ***within a minute of arriving.*** **5** about; concerning □ ***tales of Rome*** □ ***think of the children.*** **6** belonging to or forming a part of something □ ***most of the story.*** **7** existing or happening, etc, at, on, in or during something □ ***battle of Hastings*** □ ***He works of a night.*** **8** used with words denoting loss, removal or separation, etc □ ***cheated of the money*** □ ***cured of cancer.*** **9** used to show the connection between a verbal noun and the person or thing that is performing, or that is the object of, the action stated □ ***the eating of healthy food.*** **10** *N Amer, especially US* in giving the time: to; before a stated hour □ ***a quarter of one.*** **11** aged □ ***a boy of twelve.*** ◷ Anglo-Saxon.

ofay /ˈoʊfeɪ, oʊˈfeɪ/ ▷ *noun* (*ofays*) *US derog, Black slang* a white person. Also *as adj.* ◷ 1920s.

off /ɒf/ ▷ *adverb* **1** away; at or to a distance. **2** in or into a position which is not attached; loose; separate □ ***The handle came off.*** **3** *colloq* ahead in time □ ***Easter is a week off.*** **4** in or into a state of no longer working or operating; not on □ ***Turn the radio off.*** **5** in or into a state of being stopped or cancelled □ ***The match was rained off.*** **6** in or into a state of sleep □ ***nodded off.*** **7** to the end, so as to be completely finished □ ***Finish the work off.*** **8** away from work or one's duties □ ***Take an hour off.*** **9** away from a course; aside □ ***Turn off into a side street.*** **10** situated as regards money □ ***well off*** □ ***badly off.*** ▷ *adj* **1** said of an electrical device: not functioning or operating; disconnected; not on □ ***The radio was off.*** **2** cancelled; not taking place □ ***The meeting's off.*** **3** *originally naut* most distant; furthest away. **4** said of the side of a vehicle, etc: nearest the centre of the road, ie on the right in the UK. **5** not good; not up to standard □ ***an off day.*** **6** *cricket* on the side of the field towards which the batsman's feet are pointing, usually the bowler's left. Opposite of ON (*adj* 6). **7** in a restaurant, on a menu, etc: no longer available as a choice □ ***Peas are off.*** **8** said especially of food or drink: in a state of decay; gone bad or sour □ ***The milk was off.*** ▷ *prep* **1** from or away from something □ ***Lift it off the shelf.*** **2** removed from or no longer attached to something. **3** opening out of, leading from, or not far from something □ ***a side street off the main road.*** **4** not wanting or no longer attracted by something □ ***off one's food*** □ ***go off him.*** **5** no longer using something, etc □ ***be off the tablets.*** **6** not up to the usual standard of something □ ***off one's game.*** **7** out to sea from (a specified country, area of land, etc) □ ***off the coast of Spain.*** ▷ *noun* **1** (*usually* **the off**) the start, eg of a race or journey □ ***ready for the off.*** **2** *cricket* the side of a field towards which the batsman's feet are pointing, usually the bowler's left. • **a bit off** *colloq* said of behaviour, etc: unacceptable or unfair. • **off and on** now and then; occasionally. • **off one's face** **1** slightly mad. **2** very drunk. ◷ Anglo-Saxon *of* away.

offal /ˈɒfəl/ ▷ *noun* **1** the heart, brains, liver and kidneys, etc of an animal, used as food. **2** rubbish, waste or refuse. ◷ 14c: from *of* off + *fal* fall.

offbeat *music* ▷ *noun* any of the usually unaccented beats in a bar, eg the second or fourth in four-four time. ▷ *adj* **1** relating to offbeats; with a rhythm on the offbeats. **2** *colloq* unusual; unconventional; eccentric. ◷ 1920s.

off-break and **off-spin** ▷ *noun, cricket* **1** deviation in the direction of a ball inwards from the offside spin with which it is bowled. **2** a ball bowled so as to have such a deviation.

off-Broadway ▷ *noun, adj* a collective term used since the 1950s to designate the generally more experimental, less commercial theatres located outside the Broadway area in New York and the productions they perform.

off-centre ▷ *adj* not quite central.

off chance see ON THE OFF CHANCE at CHANCE

off-colour ▷ *adj* **1** said especially of a diamond: not of a satisfactory colour and therefore of inferior quality. **2** *Brit* slightly unwell; not in good health. **3** *chiefly N Amer* (**off-color**) said of humour: rude; smutty. ◷ 19c.

offcut ▷ *noun* a small piece of eg wood or cloth, etc cut off or left over from a larger quantity, especially when making or shaping something. ◷ 17c.

offence or (*chiefly US*) **offense** /əˈfɛns/ ▷ *noun* **1 a** the breaking of a rule or law, etc; **b** a crime. **2** any cause of anger, annoyance or displeasure. **3** displeasure, annoyance or resentment □ ***I mean no offence.*** **4** an attack or assault. **5** *sport* **a** those players in a team who take on the attacking role; **b** attacking play. • **give offence** to cause displeasure or annoyance. • **take offence at something** to be offended by it.

offend /əˈfɛnd/ ▷ *verb* (*offended, offending*) **1** to make someone feel hurt or angry; to insult them. **2** to be unpleasant or annoying to someone. **3** *intr* (*usually* **offend against someone** or **something**) **a** to commit a sin or crime against them; **b** to act in a way that is not in accordance with (custom, etc). • **offender** *noun.* • **offending** *adj.* ◷ 14c: from Latin *offendere*, from *of-* against + *fendere* to strike.

offensive /əˈfɛnsɪv/ ▷ *adj* **1** giving or likely to give offence; insulting. **2** unpleasant, disgusting and repulsive, especially to the senses □ ***an offensive smell.*** **3** *sport, military, etc* used for attacking □ ***offensive weapons.*** ▷ *noun* **1** an aggressive action or attitude □ ***go on the offensive.*** **2** an attack. **3** *especially in compounds* a great or aggressive effort to achieve something □ ***a peace offensive.*** • **offensively** *adverb.* • **offensiveness** *noun.* ◷ 16c.

offer /ˈɒfə(r)/ ▷ *verb* (*offered, offering*) **1** to put forward (a gift, payment or suggestion, etc) for acceptance, refusal or consideration. **2** *formal* to provide □ *a site offering the best view.* **3** *intr* to state one's willingness to do something. **4** to present something for sale. **5** to provide an opportunity for something □ *a job offering rapid promotion.* **6** *intr* to present itself; to occur □ *if opportunity offers.* **7** *tr & intr* to propose (a sum of money) as payment to someone □ *offer him £250 for the car.* **8** (*also* **offer something up**) to present (a prayer or sacrifice) to God. **9** to show (resistance, etc). **10** (*usually* **offer up something**) *technical* in eg joinery, etc: to position or hold up (a part, etc) to test its size or suitability, etc before fixing it. ▻ *noun* **1** an act of offering. **2** something that is offered, especially an amount of money offered to buy something. **3** *old use* a proposal, especially of marriage. • **offerer** or **offeror** /ˈɒfərə(r)/ *noun* someone who offers something, especially shares for sale. • **on offer** for sale, especially at a reduced price. • **under offer** said of a house or flat, etc for sale: for which a possible buyer has made an offer, but with the contracts still to be signed. ⓘ Anglo-Saxon *offrian*, from Latin *offerre*, from *ob-* towards + *ferre* to bring.

offering ▻ *noun* **1** the act of making an offer. **2** anything offered, especially a gift. **3** a gift of money given to a church, usually during a religious service, used for charity, etc. **4** a sacrifice made to God, a saint or a deity, etc in the course of worship. **5** (**offerings**) in the Church of England: certain dues payable at Easter.

offertory /ˈɒfətərɪ/ ▻ *noun* (*offertories*) *Christianity* **1** the offering of bread and wine to God during a Eucharist. **2** an anthem or hymn sung while this is happening. **3** money collected during a church service. ⓘ 14c: from Latin *offertorium* place of offering.

offhand and **offhanded** ▻ *adj* **1** casual or careless, often with the result of being rude □ *an offhand manner.* **2** impromptu. • **offhandedly** *adverb.* • **offhandedness** *noun.* ⓘ 17c.

office /ˈɒfɪs/ ▻ *noun* **1** the room, set of rooms or building in which the business of a firm is done, or in which a particular kind of business, clerical work, etc is done. **2** a local centre or department of a large business. **3** a position of authority, especially in the government or in public service □ *run for office.* **4 a** the length of time for which an official position is held; **b** said of a political party: the length of time for which it forms the government □ *in office* □ *hold office.* **5** (**Office**) *in compounds* a government department □ *the Home Office.* **6** the group of people working in an office. **7** a function or duty. **8** (*usually* **offices**) an act of kindness or service □ *through her good offices.* **9** (*often* **Office**) an authorized form of Christian worship or service, especially one for the dead. See also DIVINE OFFICE. **10** (**offices**) the parts of a large house, estate or farm given over to household work or storage, etc. **11** (*especially* **usual offices**) *euphemistic, slang* a lavatory. • **give the office** *slang* to give a signal or hint. ⓘ 13c: from Latin *officium* favour, duty or service, from *opus* work or service + *facere* to do.

office-bearer and **office-holder** ▻ *noun* someone who holds office; someone with an official duty in a society or a church organization, etc.

office block ▻ *noun* a large multistorey building divided into offices.

office boy and **office girl** ▻ *noun* a young person employed to do minor jobs in an office.

office hours ▻ *noun* the time during which an office is open for business, usually between 9am and 5pm Monday to Friday.

officer /ˈɒfɪsə(r)/ ▻ *noun* **1** someone in a position of authority and responsibility in the armed forces. **2** someone with an official position in an organization, society or government department. **3** a policeman or policewoman. **4** a person in authority on a non-naval ship. ▻ *verb* (*officered, officering*) **1** to provide officers for (the army or navy). **2** to act as officer for (some organization, etc). ⓘ 14c.

officer of the day ▻ *noun* (abbreviation **OD**) *military* the officer in charge of camp or unit security on any particular day.

official /əˈfɪʃəl/ ▻ *adj* **1** relating or belonging to an office or position of authority. **2** given or authorized by a person in authority □ *an official report.* **3** formal; suitable for or characteristic of a person holding office □ *official dinners.* **4** *medicine* said of a drug: recognized in the pharmacopoeia. ▻ *noun* someone who holds office or who is in a position of authority. • **officially** *adverb.*

officialdom ▻ *noun* **1** officials and bureaucrats as a group. **2** officialism.

officialese /əfɪʃəˈliːz/ ▻ *noun* unclear, wordy and pompous language or jargon, thought to be typical of officials or official letters and documents, etc. ⓘ 19c.

officialism ▻ *noun* **1** excessive devotion to official routine and detail. **2** official position. ⓘ 19c.

official receiver see under RECEIVER

officiate /əˈfɪʃɪeɪt/ ▻ *verb* (*officiated, officiating*) *intr* **1 a** to act in an official capacity; **b** to perform official duties, especially at a particular function. **2** to conduct a religious service. • **officiation** *noun.* • **officiant** or **officiator** *noun* someone who officiates at a religious ceremony. ⓘ 17c: from Latin *officiare* to serve.

officinal /ɒˈfɪsɪnəl, ɒfɪˈsaɪnəl/ ▻ *adj* **1** said of a drug, etc: **a** sold as a medicine; **b** used in medicine. **2** said of a medicinal preparation, etc: sold by pharmacists. Compare MAGISTRAL. ⓘ 17c: from Latin *officinalis*, from *officina* a storeroom for medicines, etc in a monastery.

officious /əˈfɪʃəs/ ▻ *adj* **1** too ready to offer help or advice, etc, especially when it is not wanted; interfering. **2** in diplomacy: informal; unofficial. • **officiously** *adverb.* • **officiousness** *noun.* ⓘ 16c: from Latin *officiosus* obliging or dutiful.

offing /ˈɒfɪŋ/ ▻ *noun, naut* the more distant part of the sea that is visible from the shore. • **in the offing** not far off; likely to happen soon. ⓘ 17c.

offish /ˈɒfɪʃ/ ▻ *adj, colloq* said of a person's manner, etc: aloof; distant. • **offishly** *adverb.* • **offishness** *noun.* ⓘ 19c.

off-key ▻ *adj, adverb* **1** *music* **a** in the wrong key; **b** out of tune. **2** *colloq* not quite suitable. ⓘ 1920s.

off-licence ▻ *noun, Brit* **1** a shop, or a counter in a pub or hotel, that is licensed to sell alcohol to be drunk elsewhere. **2** a licence that permits such sales. Compare ON-LICENCE. ⓘ 19c.

off-limits ▻ *adj, especially military* not to be entered; out of bounds. ▻ *adverb* (**off limits**) in or into an area that is out of bounds. ⓘ 1940s.

off-line ▻ *adj, computing* said of a peripheral device, eg a printer: **1** not connected to the central processing unit, and therefore not controlled by it. **2** not connected; switched off. Also *as adverb* □ *went off line at 2 o'clock.* Compare ON-LINE.

offload ▻ *verb* **1** *tr & intr* to unload. **2** to get rid of something, especially something unpleasant or unwanted, etc by passing it on to someone else. ⓘ 19c in sense 1: originally S African, modelled on Dutch *afladen*.

off-peak ▻ *adj* said of services, eg electricity, etc: used at a time when there is little demand, and therefore usually cheaper □ *off-peak supply* □ *off-peak travel.* Also *as adverb.*

off-piste ▻ *adj* relating to skiing on new unused snow, away from or off the regular runs.

offprint ▻ *noun* a separately printed copy of an article that originally formed part of a larger magazine or periodical. ⓘ 19c.

off-putting ▻ *adj, colloq* **1** disconcerting; distracting. **2** unpleasant; repulsive. ⓘ 19c.

off-road ▻ *adj* **1** said of vehicle use: not on public roads; especially on rough ground or terrain. **2** said of a car, bike or other vehicle: suitable for such use. • **off-roader** *noun* an off-road vehicle. • **off-roading** *noun* the practice of driving over rough terrain and driving off-road vehicles, especially as a sport. ⓒ 1960s.

off-sales ▻ *noun* sales of alcoholic drink for consumption elsewhere.

off-season ▻ *noun* the less popular and less busy period in a particular business or for a particular activity. ▻ *adj* relating to such a period □ *off-season reductions.* ▻ *adverb* (**off season**) in or at such a period. ⓒ 19c.

offset ▻ *noun* /ˈɒfsɛt/ **1** a start; the outset. **2** a side-shoot on a plant, used for developing new plants. **3** *printing* a process in which an image is inked on to a rubber roller which then transfers it to paper, etc. **4** anything which compensates or is a counterbalance for something else. **5** a spur or ridge projecting from a mountain range. **6** *archit* a ridge or sloping break in the surface of a wall or pier, etc, formed when the structure reduces in thickness towards the top. **7** *surveying* a short distance measured at right angles to a main survey line. **8** *elec* a small deviation of voltage or current, etc. ▻ *verb* /ɒfˈsɛt/ **1** to counterbalance or compensate for something □ *price rises offset by tax cuts.* **2** to print something using an offset process. **3** *archit* to construct an offset in a wall, etc. **4** *intr* **a** to develop as an offset; **b** to project as an offset. ⓒ 16c.

offset lithography ▻ *noun* a method of printing, developed at the beginning of the 20c, by which an image created by photographic means on a printing plate is transferred to a rubber 'blanket' cylinder and then to the paper, or other material such as metal or plastic. Often shortened to **offset litho**.

offshoot ▻ *noun* **1** a shoot growing from a plant's main stem. **2** anything which is a branch of, or has developed or derived from, something else.

offshore ▻ *adverb* ▻ *adj* **1** situated in, at, or on the sea, not far from the coast □ *offshore industries.* **2** said of the wind: blowing away from the coast; out to sea. Compare INSHORE.

offside ▻ *adj, adverb, football, rugby, etc* in an illegal position between the ball and the opponents' goal. Compare ONSIDE. ▻ *noun* the side of a vehicle or horse nearest the centre of the road, in the UK the right side.

off-spin see OFF-BREAK

offspring /ˈɒfsprɪŋ/ ▻ *noun* (*plural* ***offspring***) **1** a person's child or children. **2** the young of an animal. **3** progeny; descendants. **4** a result or outcome. ⓒ Anglo-Saxon *ofspring*, from *of* of or off + *springan* to spring.

off-stage ▻ *adj, adverb, theat* not on the stage and so unable to be seen by the audience.

off-stream ▻ *adj* said of an industrial plant, etc: not in operation or production.

off-street ▻ *adj* said of parking: not on a road; in a car park.

off the cuff see under CUFF[1]

off-the-peg ▻ *adj* said of clothing: ready to wear; ready-made.

off the record see under RECORD

off-the-shoulder ▻ *adj* said of a woman's dress, etc: worn so as to reveal the shoulders.

off-the-wall ▻ *adj, slang* said eg of humour: unorthodox; outlandish.

off-white ▻ *adj* yellowish or greyish white; very nearly but not quite white. ▻ *noun* **1** this colour. **2** anything which is this colour, eg paint. ⓒ 1920s.

OFGAS or **Ofgas** /ˈɒfgas/ ▻ *abbreviation* in the UK: Office of Gas Supply, the regulatory body for the gas industry.

OFLOT or **Oflot** /ˈɒflɒt/ ▻ *abbreviation* in the UK: Office of the National Lottery, the regulatory body for the UK National Lottery.

OFS ▻ *abbreviation* Orange Free State, a province in S Africa.

OFSTED or **Ofsted** /ˈɒfstɛd/ ▻ *abbreviation* in England and Wales: Office for Standards in Education, an organization for monitoring education standards in state schools.

OFT ▻ *abbreviation* in the UK: Office of Fair Trading.

oft ▻ *adverb, archaic, poetic* often. Now *chiefly in compounds* □ *oft-repeated promises.* ⓒ Anglo-Saxon.

OFTEL or **Oftel** /ˈɒftɛl/ ▻ *abbreviation* in the UK: Office of Telecommunications, a regulatory body for the telecommunications industry.

often /ˈɒfən, ˈɒftən/ ▻ *adverb* **1** many times; frequently. **2** in many cases. ▻ *adj, archaic* done, made or happening, etc many times; frequent. • **as often as not** quite often; in about half the cases. • **every so often** sometimes; now and then. • **more often than not** usually; in most of the cases. ⓒ 14c: variant before vowels and *h* of *ofte* OFT.

oftentimes /ˈɒfəntaɪmz, ˈɒftən-/ ▻ *adverb, archaic, literary* often.

OFWAT or **Ofwat** /ˈɒfwɒt/ ▻ *abbreviation* in the UK: Office of Water Services, a regulatory body for the water industry.

ogam or **ogham** /ˈɒgəm/ ▻ *noun* (*also* **Ogam** or **Ogham**) **1 a** an ancient alphabet, consisting of 20 or 25 characters, used from the 4c BC in Celtic and Pictish inscriptions, especially on stone monuments found in Ireland and Wales; **b** (*usually* **ogams**) any of these characters, composed of sets of parallel lines (numbering one to five) meeting or crossing a base line, usually the corner of a stone monument. **2** an inscription in this alphabet. • **ogamic** or **oghamic** /ɒˈgamɪk, ˈɒgəmik/ or **ogmic** *adj.* ⓒ 18c: Irish Gaelic, perhaps related to Ogma, the mythical inventor of the alphabet.

ogee /ˈoʊdʒiː, oʊˈdʒiː/ ▻ *noun* (***ogees***) **1** an S-shaped curve or line. **2** *archit* an S-shaped moulding. ⓒ 14c: ultimately from French *ogive* OGIVE.

oggin /ˈɒgɪn/ ▻ *noun, naut slang* the sea. ⓒ 1940s: a corruption of earlier *hogwash*, meaning 'the sea'.

ogive /oʊˈdʒaɪv, ˈoʊ-/ ▻ *noun* **1** *archit* **a** a diagonal rib of a vault; **b** a pointed arch or window. **2** something, especially the nose of a rocket or missile, that has the form of an ogive. **3** *statistics* the cumulatively formed curve of a frequency distribution. **4** *geol* a band of some dark substance that is seen to stretch across a glacier's surface. • **ogived** or **ogival** *adj.* ⓒ 17c: French.

ogle /ˈoʊgəl/ ▻ *verb* (***ogled, ogling***) **1** *intr* to cast flirtatious or amorous glances. **2** to look at or eye someone in an amorous or lecherous way. **3** to stare or gape at something. ▻ *noun* a flirtatious or lecherous look. ⓒ 17c: perhaps from German *oegeln*, from *oegen* to look at.

ogmic see under OGAM

O-grade and **Ordinary grade** ▻ *noun, formerly* in Scotland: **1** an examination in a subject usually taken at the end of the fourth year in secondary schools, now replaced by STANDARD GRADE. **2** a pass in this examination.

-ography /ˈɒgrəfɪ/ ▻ *suffix* a form of -GRAPHY □ *oceanography* □ *bibliography.* The *-o-* comes either from the first element of the word, or functions as a connective between the first element and the suffix.

ogre /ˈoʊgə(r)/ and **ogress** /ˈoʊgrɪs/ ▻ *noun* (***ogres; ogresses***) **1** in fairy stories: a frightening, cruel, ugly, man-eating male or female giant. **2** a cruel, frightening or ugly person. • **ogreish** or **ogrish** *adj.* ⓒ 18c: French (first used in Perrault's *Contes*, 1697), perhaps from Latin *Orcus*, the name of the Roman god of the underworld.

OH ▷ *abbreviation, US state* Ohio. Also written **O**.

oh /oʊ/ ▷ *exclamation* **1** expressing surprise, admiration, pleasure, anger or fear, etc. **2** (*also* **O** *poetic or relig*) used in apostrophizing or addressing a person or thing, or in expressing a wish □ *O God!*

OHG ▷ *abbreviation* Old High German.

ohm /oʊm/ ▷ *noun* (symbol Ω) in the SI and MKSA systems: a unit of electrical resistance, equal to the resistance of a circuit in which a potential difference of one volt is required to maintain a current of one ampere. • **ohmage** *noun*. ⓘ 19c: named after Georg Simon Ohm (1787–1854), German physicist.

ohmmeter /ˈoʊmmiːtə(r)/ ▷ *noun* a device for measuring electrical resistance. ⓘ Late 19c.

OHMS ▷ *abbreviation, Brit* On Her (or His) Majesty's Service, often written on mail from government departments.

Ohm's law ▷ *noun, physics* a law which states that the direct current flowing in an electrical circuit is directly proportional to the potential difference (voltage) applied to the circuit, and inversely proportional to the resistance of the circuit, ie $V = IR$, where V is voltage, I is current and R is resistance. ⓘ 19c.

oho /oʊˈhoʊ/ ▷ *exclamation, rather old use* an expression of surprise, triumphant satisfaction or derision.

-oholic and **-oholism** see -AHOLIC

ohone see OCHONE

OHP ▷ *abbreviation* overhead projector.

-oid /ɔɪd/ ▷ *suffix, forming nouns and adjectives, signifying* something similar to or with the form of the specified thing □ *humanoid* □ *factoid* □ *rhomboid*. • **-oidal** *suffix, forming adjectives*. ⓘ From Greek *eidos* shape.

oik /ɔɪk/ ▷ *noun, Brit colloq* someone thought of as inferior, especially because of being rude, ignorant, badly educated or lower class. ⓘ 1920s.

oil /ɔɪl/ ▷ *noun* **1** any greasy, viscous and usually flammable substance, liquid at room temperature (20°C) and insoluble in water but soluble in organic compounds, that is derived from animals, plants or mineral deposits, or manufactured artificially, and used as a fuel, lubricant or food. **2** PETROLEUM. **3 a** (*often* **oils**) OIL PAINT; **b** an oil painting. **4** (**oils**) *colloq* oilskins; oilskin garments. **5** *Austral & NZ slang* news; information. Also *as adj* and *in compounds* □ *oil pipeline* □ *oil slick* □ *oilfield*. ▷ *verb* (**oiled**, **oiling**) **1** to apply oil to something; to lubricate or treat something with oil. **2** *intr* to take oil aboard as fuel. **3** *tr & intr* said of butter, etc: to make or become oily, especially by heating or melting. • **oiled** and **oily** see separate entries. • **burn the midnight oil** to work or study late into the night. • **oil someone's palm** *colloq* to bribe them. • **oil the wheels** to do something in order to make things go more smoothly or successfully, etc. • **pour oil on troubled waters** to soothe or calm a person or situation. • **strike oil 1** to discover or reach a source of petroleum while drilling for it. **2** *colloq* to discover some source of wealth, usually rapid wealth; to become rich or successful through exploiting such a source. ⓘ 12c: from French *oile*, from Latin *oleum* (olive) oil, from Greek *elaia* olive tree.

oil bath ▷ *noun, mech* a receptacle that contains lubricating oil through which part of a machine passes.

oilbird ▷ *noun* a gregarious fruit-eating nocturnal bird of northern S America and Trinidad, that roosts in caves during the day. ⓘ 19c; so called because the young, which grow extremely fat, used to be killed and boiled to extract oil from their bodies..

oil cake ▷ *noun* a feedstuff for livestock, especially cattle, made from the crushed residue that remains after most of the oil has been extracted from linseed, soybean or other oil-bearing seeds.

oil can ▷ *noun* a can for carrying oil or applying lubricating oil.

oilcloth ▷ *noun* **1 a** cloth, often cotton, treated with oil to make it waterproof; oilskin; **b** (**oilcloths**) oilskins; oilskin garments. **2 a** canvas coated with linseed or other oil to make it waterproof, used (*especially formerly*) as a covering for tables, etc; **b** LINOLEUM. ⓘ 17c.

oil colour ▷ *noun* OIL PAINT.

oil drum ▷ *noun* a cylindrical metal barrel for containing or transporting oil.

oiled ▷ *adj* **1** smeared, treated, lubricated or impregnated with oil. **2** preserved in oil. **3** *slang* drunk □ *He was well oiled last night.*

oiler ▷ *noun* **1** a person or thing that oils. **2** an OIL CAN. **3** (**oilers**) *originally US colloq* oilskins; oilskin garments. **4** *US colloq* an OIL WELL. **5 a** a vehicle or vessel driven by oil; **b** a vehicle or vessel that carries oil.

oilfield ▷ *noun* an area of land that contains reserves of petroleum, especially one that is already being exploited.

oil-fired ▷ *adj* said of central heating, etc: using oil as a fuel.

oil gland ▷ *noun* a gland that secretes oil, especially the uropygial or coccygeal gland in birds that produces a secretion used in preening.

oilier, **oiliest**, **oilily** and **oiliness** see under OILY

oilman ▷ *noun* **1** a man who deals in oil. **2** a man who owns an oil well. **3** (*also* **oil worker**) someone involved in the operation of an oil well or oil rig, etc.

oil paint ▷ *noun* paint made by mixing ground pigment with oil, often linseed oil.

oil painting ▷ *noun* **1** a picture painted with oil paints. **2** the activity or art of painting in oils. • **no oil painting** *colloq* said of a person: not very attractive.

oil palm ▷ *noun* a W African palm tree, the fruit-pulp of which is a source of palm-oil.

oil pan ▷ *noun, mech* the sump in an internal-combustion engine.

oil paper ▷ *noun* paper that has been oiled, eg to make it waterproof.

oil platform ▷ *noun* a steel and/or concrete structure, either fixed or mobile, used in offshore drilling to support the rig and to keep stores, etc.

oil rig ▷ *noun* **1** the complete installation, required for drilling oil wells, including the equipment and machinery, etc that it supports. **2** *loosely* a mobile oil platform. Also called **rig**.

oil sand ▷ *noun* sand or sandstone that occurs naturally impregnated with petroleum.

oilseed ▷ *noun* any of various seeds, eg sesame and castor bean, etc from which oil is extracted.

oilseed rape ▷ *noun* an annual plant with bluish-green leaves and vivid yellow flowers, the seed of which contains large amounts of oil and is used in margarine, cooking oils and some lubricating oils.

oil shale ▷ *noun, geol* a fine-grained sedimentary rock containing high levels of organic matter, from which an oily substance can be distilled by heating the shale in the absence of air.

oilskin ▷ *noun* **1** cloth treated with oil to make it waterproof. **2** (*often* **oilskins**) an outer garment made of oilskin. ⓘ 18c.

oil slick see SLICK *noun* 1

oilstone ▷ *noun* a whetstone used with oil.

oil tanker ▷ *noun* a large ship for carrying oil in bulk.

oil well ▷ *noun* a well, usually a vertical one, bored in the ground or sea-bed to extract petroleum (mineral oil) from underground deposits.

oil worker see under OILMAN

oily ▻ *adj* (*oilier*, *oiliest*) **1 a** like oil; greasy; **b** containing or consisting of oil. **2** soaked in or covered with oil. **3** *derog* said of a person or behaviour, etc: smooth; unctuous; servile and flattering. • **oilily** *adverb*. • **oiliness** *noun*.

oink /ɔɪŋk/ ▻ *noun* **1** a representation of the characteristic grunting noise made by a pig. **2** a sound similar to this. Also *as exclamation*. ▻ *verb* (*oinked*, *oinking*) *intr* to make this noise. ◷ 1940s: imitating the sound.

oino- and **oin-** see OENO-

ointment /ˈɔɪntmənt/ ▻ *noun* any greasy or oily semi-solid preparation, usually medicated, that can be applied externally to the skin in order to heal, soothe or protect it. • **a fly in the ointment** see under FLY[1]. ◷ 14c: from French *oignement*, from Latin *unguentum* unguent, from *unguere* to anoint.

Oireachtas /ˈɛrəxθəs/ ▻ *noun* **1** a cultural festival held each year by the Gaelic League of Ireland. **2** the legislature or parliament of the Republic of Ireland, consisting of the president, Seanad and Dáil. ◷ Early 20c: Irish Gaelic, meaning 'assembly'.

OK[1] ▻ *abbreviation*, *US state* Oklahoma. Also written **Okla**.

OK[2] or **okay** /oʊˈkeɪ/ *colloq*, *originally US*, ▻ *adj* all correct; all right; satisfactory ▫ *an okay song*. ▻ *adverb* well; satisfactorily. ▻ *exclamation* expressing agreement or approval; yes; certainly ▫ *OK! I'll do it!* ▻ *noun* (*OKs*, *OK's* or *okays*) approval, sanction or agreement. ▻ *verb* (*OK'd* or *OK'ed*, *Ok'ing*; *okayed*, *okaying*) (*often* **give something the OK**) to approve or pass something as satisfactory. ◷ 19c: probably from American English *oll korrect*, a facetious spelling of *all correct*.

okapi /oʊˈkɑːpɪ/ ▻ *noun* (*okapis* or *okapi*) a ruminant animal from central Africa, the only living relative of the giraffe but with a shorter neck, that has a reddish- or blackish-brown coat, with thick irregular horizontal black and white stripes on the hindquarters and upper parts of the legs. ◷ Early 20c: the native name.

okey-doke /ˈoʊkɪˈdoʊk/ or **okey-dokey** ▻ *adverb* ▻ *adj*, *exclamation*, *colloq* OK; fine. ◷ 1930s.

Okla see OK[1]

okra /ˈɒkrə, ˈoʊkrə/ ▻ *noun* (*okras*) **1** a tall annual plant native to tropical Africa that has red and yellow flowers. **2** the edible fruit of this plant, consisting of long green seed pods, used in soups and stews, etc. Also called **gumbo**, **lady's finger**. **3** a dish prepared using these seedpods. ◷ 18c: from a W African name.

-ol ▻ *suffix*, *forming nouns*, *denoting* **1 a** substances that are alcohols or compounds analogous to ALCOHOLS; **b** substances derived from or related to PHENOLS. **2** oils and oil-based substances.

old /oʊld/ ▻ *adj* (**older** or **elder**, **oldest** or **eldest**) **1** advanced in age; that has existed for a long time; not young. **2** having a stated age ▫ *five years old*. **3** belonging or relating to the end period of a long life or existence ▫ *old age*. **4** (**the old**) old people as a group (see THE 4b). **5** worn out or shabby through long use ▫ *old shoes*. **6** no longer in use; out of date; old-fashioned. **7** belonging to the past. **8** former or previous; earliest of two or more things ▫ *went back to see their old house*. **9** of long standing or long existence ▫ *an old member of the society*. **10** familiar, practised or skilled through long experience ▫ *the same old excuses*. **11** with the characteristics, eg experience, maturity or appearance, of age ▫ *be old beyond one's years*. **12** (**Old**) said of a language: that is the earliest form known or recorded ▫ *Old English*. **13** *colloq*, *jocular* used in expressions of familiar affection or contempt, etc ▫ *good old Bill* ▫ *silly old fool*. **14** *colloq* used for emphasis ▫ *any old how*. **15** *colloq* (*usually* **high old**, **rare old**, *etc*) used for emphasis: great; excessive ▫ *rare old time*. ▻ *noun* an earlier time ▫ *men of old*. • **oldish** *adj*. • **as old as the hills** *colloq* very old. • **little old** *colloq* a familiar affectionate or jocular way of referring to someone or something. • **of old** formerly; a long time ago. ◷ Anglo-Saxon *eald*.

older
See Usage Note at **elder**.

old age ▻ *noun* the later part of life.

old age pension see under RETIREMENT PENSION. • **old age pensioner** *noun* (abbreviation **OAP**).

Old Bailey ▻ *noun* the **Central Criminal Court** in London, where the most serious cases are usually tried.

old bean ▻ *noun Brit*, *colloq* an affectionate form of address, usually to a man.

the Old Bill see THE BILL

old boy ▻ *noun* **1** *Brit* a former male pupil of a school. **2** *colloq* an elderly man. **3** *colloq* an affectionate or familiar form of address to a man.

old boy network ▻ *noun*, *Brit* the system by which former members of the same public school secure advantages for each other in later life. See also OLD SCHOOL TIE.

old country ▻ *noun* an immigrant's country of origin.

old dear ▻ *noun*, *slang*, *often derog* **1** an old woman. **2** one's mother.

olden /ˈoʊldən/ ▻ *adj*, *archaic* former; past ▫ *in olden days*.

Old English see under ANGLO-SAXON

Old English sheepdog ▻ *noun* a breed of dog developed in Britain in the 18c to protect cattle, having a large body, with the hindquarters higher than the shoulders, and a long shaggy coat, usually white with large dark patches, often hiding the ears and eyes.

older and **oldest** see under OLD

olde-worlde /ˈoʊldɪˈwɜːldɪ/ ▻ *adj* said of appearance, decorative style, etc: self-consciously imitative of the past or supposed past ▫ *an olde-worlde inn*.

old-face see under OLD STYLE

old-fashioned ▻ *adj* **1** belonging to, or in a style common to, some time ago; out of date. **2** said of a person: in favour of, or living and acting according to, the habits and moral views of the past. **3** *chiefly Scots & dialect* said of a child: with grown-up manners; precocious. ▻ *noun*, *N Amer* a cocktail made from whisky, bitters, water and sugar. • **old-fashionedness** *noun*.

old flame ▻ *noun*, *colloq* a former boyfriend or girlfriend.

old girl ▻ *noun* **1** *Brit* a former female pupil of a school. **2** *colloq* an elderly woman. **3** *colloq* an affectionate or familiar form of address to a girl or woman.

Old Glory ▻ *noun*, *US colloq* a nickname for the US flag; the Stars and Stripes. ◷ 19c.

old gold ▻ *noun* a dull yellowish colour like that of tarnished gold. Also (**old-gold**) *as adj*.

old guard ▻ *noun* the original or most conservative members of a society, group or organization.

old hand ▻ *noun*, *colloq* **1** an experienced person; an expert. **2** an ex-convict.

old hat ▻ *adj*, *colloq* tediously familiar or well known.

Old High German ▻ *noun* (abbreviation **OHG**) **1** the oldest form of official and literary German with written records dating from the 8c AD. **2** High German up to c.1200. See also GERMANIC, HIGH GERMAN.

oldie /ˈoʊldɪ/ ▻ *noun* (*oldies*) *colloq* **1** an old person. **2** something, eg a song or film, etc that is old or familiar.

old lady ▻ *noun, slang* a person's wife or mother.

old lag ▻ *noun, Brit slang* a habitual criminal.

old maid ▻ *noun* **1** *derog colloq* a woman who is not married and is thought of as being unlikely ever to marry; a spinster. **2** *derog, colloq* a woman or man who is prim and fussy. **3 a** a simple card game in which players pass and match up pairs of cards; **b** the player left with the unpaired card at the end of the game. • **old-maidish** *adj.* • **old-maidishly** *adverb.*

old man ▻ *noun* **1** *slang* someone's husband or father. **2** *colloq* an affectionate form of address for a man or boy, usually only said by a man addressing another man. **3** *colloq* someone in command, eg the captain of a merchant ship; a boss. **4** *theol* unregenerate human nature. **5** SOUTHERNWOOD. **6** *Austral* a full-grown male kangaroo.

old man's beard ▻ *noun* any of various plants with long trailing parts, especially TRAVELLER'S JOY.

old master ▻ *noun, art* **1** any of the great European painters from the period stretching from the Renaissance to about 1800. **2** a painting by one of these painters.

old moon ▻ *noun* the moon in its last quarter, before the NEW MOON.

Old Nick ▻ *noun, colloq* the devil. ⓒ 18c.

Old Norse ▻ *noun* (abbreviation **ON**) the old N Germanic language from around 700 AD to 1350 AD from which the Scandinavian languages are derived.

Old Persian ▻ *noun* the old form of Persian spoken in the area of present-day Iran from around 1000 BC, and with surviving written records from c.6c BC. See also FARSI, IRANIAN LANGUAGES.

old rose ▻ *noun* **1** any of several varieties of rose existing before the development of hybrid tea roses. **2** a deep pink colour. Also (**old-rose**) *as adj.* ⓒ 19c.

old school ▻ *noun* **1** a person's former school. **2** a group of people or section of society with traditional or old-fashioned ways of thinking, ideas or beliefs, etc. Also (**old-school**) *as adj.*

old school tie ▻ *noun* **1** a tie with a characteristic pattern or colour worn by former members of a public school. **2** *Brit* **a** the values, attitudes and traditionalism, etc associated with public schools; **b** the system by which former members of the same public school do favours for each other in later life. See also OLD BOY NETWORK.

oldster /ˈoʊldstə(r)/ ▻ *noun, colloq* an old or elderly person. ⓒ 19c.

old story ▻ *noun* (*often* **the old story** or **the same old story**) something which one has often heard before, especially an excuse, or something negative which has often happened before.

Old Style ▻ *noun* a former method of calculating dates using the JULIAN CALENDAR. Compare NEW STYLE.

old style ▻ *noun, printing* a typeface modelled on, but with a more regular design than, **old-face** (a typeface with little contrast between thick and thin strokes).

old-style ▻ *adj* outmoded; outdated □ *old-style propaganda.*

Old Testament ▻ *noun* the first part of the Christian Bible, containing the Hebrew scriptures. See table at BIBLE. Compare NEW TESTAMENT.

old-time ▻ *adj* belonging to or typical of the past; old-fashioned.

old-timer ▻ *noun, colloq* **1** someone who has been in a job, position or profession, etc, for a long time; a veteran. **2** an old-fashioned person. **3** *US* especially as a form of address: an old man.

old wives' tale ▻ *noun* an old belief, superstition or theory considered foolish and unscientific. ⓒ 17c.

old woman ▻ *noun, slang* **1** someone's wife or mother. **2** *derog* a person, especially a man, who is timid or fussy. • **old-womanish** *adj* characteristic of or like an old woman, especially in being fussy.

Old World ▻ *noun* the Eastern hemisphere, comprising Europe, Asia and Africa, which forms that part of the world known before the discovery of the NEW WORLD. Also (**Old-World**) *as adj.*

old-world ▻ *adj* belonging to earlier times, especially in being considered quaint or charming; not modern □ *old-world charm.*

olé /oʊˈleɪ; *Spanish* oˈle/ ▻ *exclamation* **1** especially associated with Spanish dancing and bullfighting, etc: expressing approval, support or encouragement, etc. **2** an expression of triumph. ▻ *noun* (***olés***) a cry of 'olé'. ⓒ 1920s: Spanish, meaning 'bravo'.

oleaceous /oʊlɪˈeɪʃəs/ ▻ *adj, bot* relating or belonging to the **Oleaceae** /-ʃiː/, a family of trees and shrubs that includes the olive, ash, jasmine and privet. ⓒ 19c: from Latin *olea* olive tree.

oleaginous /oʊlɪˈadʒɪnəs/ ▻ *adj* **1** like or containing oil; oily. **2** producing oil. **3** unctuous; obsequious. • **oleaginousness** *noun.* ⓒ 17c: from Latin *oleaginus*, from *oleum* oil.

oleander /oʊlɪˈandə(r)/ ▻ *noun* a poisonous shrub with leathery evergreen leaves and clusters of fragrant white, pink or purple flowers. Also called **rosebay**. ⓒ 16c: Latin.

olearia /oʊlɪˈɛərɪə/ ▻ *noun* (***olearias***) **1** an Australasian evergreen shrub of the COMPOSITE family, with white, yellow or mauve daisy-like flowers. **2** *colloq* a daisy-tree or bush. ⓒ 19c: named after Johann Gottfried Olearius (1635–1711), a German theologian and horticulturalist.

oleaster /oʊlɪˈastə(r)/ ▻ *noun* **1** *strictly* the true wild olive. **2** any of several small European trees. ⓒ Anglo-Saxon: Latin, from *olea* olive tree.

oleate /ˈoʊlɪeɪt/ ▻ *noun, chem* a salt or ester of oleic acid. ⓒ 19c.

olefin /ˈoʊlɪfɪn/ ▻ *noun, chem* ALKENE. ⓒ 19c: from French *oléfiant* (in *gaz oléfiant*), from *oléfier* to make oil.

oleic acid /oʊˈliːɪk —/ ▻ *noun, chem* an unsaturated fatty acid, a colourless tasteless oily liquid that occurs in most natural fats and is used in making soap, cosmetics and oils, etc. ⓒ 19c: from Latin *oleum* oil + -IC.

oleiferous /oʊlɪˈɪfərəs/ ▻ *adj* producing or yielding oil, as eg seeds do. ⓒ 19c: from Latin *oleum* oil + -FEROUS.

olein /ˈoʊliːɪn/ ▻ *noun, chem* a glycerine ester of oleic acid. ⓒ 19c: from French *oléine*, from Latin *oleum* oil + -IN.

oleo /ˈoʊlɪoʊ/ ▻ *noun* (***oleos***) short form of OLEOGRAPH or OLEOMARGARINE.

oleo- /oʊlɪoʊ/ ▻ *combining form, denoting* oil. ⓒ From Latin *oleum* oil.

oleograph /ˈoʊlɪəgrɑːf/ ▻ *noun, historical* a lithograph printed in oil colours to imitate an oil painting. • **oleography** *noun.* ⓒ 19c.

oleomargarine ▻ *noun* **1** a yellow fatty substance obtained from beef tallow and used in making margarine and soap, etc. **2** *US* margarine. ⓒ 19c.

oleophilic /oʊlɪoʊˈfɪlɪk/ ▻ *adj* **1** with an affinity for oils or oily substances. **2** wetted by oil rather than water. ⓒ 1960s.

oleraceous /ɒləˈreɪʃəs/ ▻ *adj* **1** of the nature of a pot-herb or culinary vegetable. **2** obtained from a pot-herb. ⓒ 17c: from Latin *(h)oleraceus*, from *(h)olus* or *(h)oleris* a pot-herb or vegetable.

oleum /ˈoʊlɪəm/ ▻ *noun* (***oleums*** or ***olea*** /ˈoʊlɪə/) *chem* a solution of sulphur trioxide in sulphuric acid. Also called **fuming sulphuric acid**. ⓒ Early 20c: Latin, meaning 'oil'.

O-level and **Ordinary level** ▻ *noun, formerly* **1** an examination in a subject usually taken at the end of the fifth year of school, now replaced by GENERAL CERTIFICATE OF SECONDARY EDUCATION. **2** a pass in this examination.

olfactory /ɒl'faktərɪ/ ▻ *adj* relating to the sense of smell. ▻ *noun* (*usually* **olfactories**) an organ or nerve of smell. ◷ 17c: from Latin *olfacere* to smell, from *olere* to smell + *facere* to make.

olfactronics /ɒlfak'trɒnɪks/ ▻ *singular noun* the precise detection, analysis and measurement of odours by means of electronic devices. ◷ 1960s: from Latin *olfacere, olfactum* to smell, modelled on ELECTRONICS.

olibanum /ɒ'lɪbənəm/ ▻ *noun* an aromatic gum obtained from trees found especially in Somaliland and Arabia; a kind of FRANKINCENSE. ◷ 14c: Latin, perhaps from Greek *libanos* frankincense.

oligarchy /'ɒlɪgɑːkɪ/ ▻ *noun* (***oligarchies***) **1** government by a small group of people. **2** a state or organization governed by a small group of people. **3** a small group of people which forms a government. • **oligarch** /'ɒlɪgɑːk/ *noun*. • **oligarchic** or **oligarchical** *adj*. ◷ 15c: from Greek *oligarkhia*, from *oligos* little or few.

oligo- /ɒlɪgoʊ, ɒlɪ'gɒ/ or (before a vowel) **olig-** ▻ *combining form, denoting* little; few in number. ◷ From Greek *oligos* little or few.

Oligocene /'ɒlɪgoʊsiːn, ɒ'lɪgoʊsiːn/ *geol* ▻ *noun* the third epoch of the Tertiary period. See table at GEOLOGICAL TIME SCALE. ▻ *adj* **1** relating to this epoch. **2** relating to rocks formed during this epoch. ◷ 19c.

oligopoly /ɒlɪ'gɒpəlɪ/ ▻ *noun* (***oligopolies***) *econ* a situation in which there are few sellers of a particular product or service, and a small number of competitive firms control the market. • **oligopolistic** /-'lɪstɪk/ *adj*. See also DUOPOLY, MONOPOLY. ◷ 19c: from OLIGO-, modelled on MONOPOLY.

oligopsony /ɒlɪ'gɒpsənɪ/ ▻ *noun* (***oligopsonies***) *econ* a market situation in which only a small number of buyers exist for a particular product. • **oligopsonistic** *adj*. ◷ 1940s: from OLIGO- + Greek *opsonein* to buy provisions.

oligotrophic /ɒlɪgoʊ'trɒfɪk/ ▻ *adj, ecol* said especially of a lake or similar habitat: with steep rocky shores and little vegetation, poor in nutrients but rich in oxygen at all levels. • **oligotrophy** *noun*. ◷ 1930s.

olio /'oʊlɪoʊ/ ▻ *noun* (***olios***) **1** *cookery* **a** a highly spiced Spanish or Portuguese stew of different sorts of meat and vegetables; **b** any dish containing a mixture of many different ingredients. **2** a mixture or medley. **3** a variety show. ◷ 17c: from Spanish *olla* and Portuguese *olha*, from Latin *olla* a jar or pot.

olivaceous /ɒlɪ'veɪʃəs/ ▻ *adj* olive-coloured; olive-green. ◷ 18c.

olive /'ɒlɪv/ ▻ *noun* **1 a** a small evergreen tree cultivated mainly in the Mediterranean region for its fruit and the oil obtained from the fruit; **b** any of several more or less similar trees. **2** the small oval edible fruit of this tree, which has a hard stone and bitter oily flesh, and is harvested either when green and unripe or when purplish-black and ripe. **3** the wood of the tree, used to make furniture. **4** (*also* **olive green**) a dull yellowish-green colour like that of unripe olives. **5** a slice of meat rolled and stuffed with onions, etc □ *beef olive*. ▻ *adj* **1** (*also* **olive-green**) dull yellowish-green in colour. **2** said of a complexion: sallow. **3** relating to or containing olives. ◷ 13c: French, from Latin *oliva* olive.

olive branch ▻ *noun* **1** a branch of an olive tree as a symbol of peace. **2** a sign or gesture that indicates a wish for peace or reconciliation.

olive drab ▻ *noun* the dull grey-green colour of US army uniforms. Also (**olive-drab**) *as adj*.

olive oil ▻ *noun* the pale-yellow oil obtained by pressing ripe olives, used as a cooking and salad oil, and also in soaps, ointments and lubricants.

olivine /'ɒlɪviːn/ ▻ *noun, geol* any of a group of hard glassy rock-forming silicate minerals, typically olive-green, but sometimes yellowish or brown. ◷ 18c.

olla /'ɒlə/ ▻ *noun* (***ollas***) **1** a jar or cooking pot. **2** short form of OLLA PODRIDA. ◷ 17c: Spanish, from Latin *olla* a jar or pot.

olla podrida /ɒljɑːpɒ'driːdɑː/ ▻ *noun* (***olla podridas***) **1** *cookery* a Spanish mixed stew or hash of meat and vegetables. **2** an incongruous mixture or miscellaneous collection. ◷ 16c: Spanish, literally 'rotten pot', from OLLA + *podrida* putrid.

olm /ɒlm, oʊlm/ ▻ *noun* a blind eel-like salamander, found in caves in Austria. ◷ Early 20c: German.

ology /'ɒlədʒɪ/ ▻ *noun* (***ologies***) *colloq, jocular* any science or branch of knowledge. See also -LOGY. ◷ 19c: from words such as bi*ology*, phil*ology*, etc.

-ology see -LOGY

oloroso /ɒlə'roʊsoʊ/ ▻ *noun* (***olorosos***) a golden-coloured medium-sweet sherry. ◷ 19c: Spanish, meaning 'fragrant'.

Olympiad /ə'lɪmpɪad/ ▻ *noun* **1** in ancient Greece: **a** a period of four years, the interval from one celebration of the Olympic games to another, used as a way of reckoning time; **b** a celebration of the Olympic Games. **2** a celebration of the modern Olympic Games. **3** a regular international contest, especially in chess or bridge. ◷ 14c.

Olympian /ə'lɪmpɪən/ ▻ *noun* **1** *Greek mythol* any of the twelve ancient Greek gods thought to live on Mount Olympus in N Greece. **2** someone who competes in the Olympic Games. **3** a citizen or inhabitant of ancient Olympia, a plain in Greece. **4** a godlike person. ▻ *adj* **1** *Greek mythol* relating or belonging to Mount Olympus or to the ancient Greek gods thought to live there. **2** relating or belonging to ancient Olympia, or its inhabitants. **3** godlike, especially in being superior or condescending in behaviour or manners. ◷ 17c: from Greek *Olympios*, from Greek *Olympos* Olympus.

Olympic /ə'lɪmpɪk/ ▻ *adj* **1** relating to the Olympic Games. **2** relating to ancient Olympia. ◷ 17c: from Greek *Olympikos*.

Olympic Games ▻ *singular or plural noun* **1** *historical* games celebrated every four years at Olympia in Greece, that included athletic, musical and literary competitions. **2** (*also* **the Olympics**) a modern international sports competition held every four years.

OM ▻ *abbreviation, Brit* (Member of the) Order of Merit.

om /oʊm, ɒm/ ▻ *noun, Hinduism, Buddhism* a sacred syllable intoned in mantras and prayers, etc that symbolizes the Vedic scriptures, the three worlds (Earth, atmosphere and air), and the Absolute. ◷ 18c: Sanskrit.

-oma /'oʊmə/ ▻ *suffix* (***-omas*** or ***-omata*** /-mətə/) *forming nouns, denoting* a tumour or abnormal growth, etc □ *carcinoma*. ◷ Greek.

omasum /oʊ'meɪsəm/ ▻ *noun* (*plural* ***omasa*** /-sə/) *zool* the third stomach of a ruminant; the psalterium or manyplies. ◷ 18c: Latin, meaning 'bullock's tripe'.

ombre or (*US*) **omber** /'ɒmbə, 'ɒmbreɪ/ ▻ *noun* a card game popular in the 17th and 18th centuries. ◷ 17c: from Spanish *hombre* man, with reference to the player who tries to win the stakes.

ombré /'ɒmbreɪ/ ▻ *adj* said of fabric, etc: with colours gradually shading into each other. ▻ *noun* (***ombrés***) a fabric, etc that has such shading. ◷ 19c: French, from *ombrer* to shade.

ombudsman /'ɒmbʊdzmən/ ▻ *noun* an official appointed to investigate complaints against public authorities, government departments or the people who work for them, especially such a person in Britain, officially called a **Parliamentary Commissioner for Administration**. ◷ Early 20c: Swedish, meaning 'legal representative' or 'commissioner'.

-ome /oʊm/ ▻ *suffix, forming nouns, denoting* a mass □ *rhizome* □ *biome*. ◷ Variant of -OMA.

omega /'oʊmɪgə; *US* oʊ'miːgə/ ▻ *noun* **1** the 24th and last letter of the Greek alphabet, pronounced as a long

Ologies

This list contains some of the words ending in *-logy* (usually *-ology*) that denote areas of knowledge and study. Other words having the same form, eg *apology* and *eulogy*, are not included.

anthropology study of human societies and cultures
archaeology study of ancient civilizations
astrology study of planetary influences on human life
bacteriology study of bacteria
biology study of living things
campanology study of bells; bell-ringing
chronology study of historical dates; a list of dates
climatology study of climates
cosmology study of the universe
criminology study of crime and criminals
cytology study of plant and animal cells
deltiology study or collecting of picture postcards
demonology study of demons
dendrochronology study of dating from tree-rings
dermatology study of the skin and skin diseases
ecology study of living things in relation to their environment
embryology study of embryos
entomology study of insects
epistemology study and theory of human knowledge
escapology study of methods of escape
ethnology study of peoples and cultures
etymology study or description of word origins and development
gemmology study of gems
genealogy study of family history
geology study of the Earth's structure
gynaecology study of diseases relating to women
haematology study of blood and blood diseases
histology study of plant and animal tissues
horology study of clocks and time-keeping
ideology study of ideas; ideas or doctrines
immunology study of the immune system
lexicology study of word meanings
meteorology study of the Earth's atmosphere and weather
microbiology study of micro-organisms
mineralogy study of minerals
musicology study of music
mycology study of fungi
mythology study of myths; myths
neurology study of the nervous system
oenology study of wines
oncology study of tumours
ontology study of the nature of being
ophthalmology study of the eye
ornithology study of birds
palaeontology study of fossils
parapsychology study of psychic phenomena
pathology study of human diseases
petrology study of rocks
pharmacology study of medicines and drugs
phonology study of speech sounds
physiology study of life processes
psephology study of election results and trends
psychology study of the human mind and behaviour
radiology study of radioactivity and radiation
Sinology study of Chinese language and culture
seismology study of earthquakes
sexology study of human sexuality
sociology study of human society
theology study of religion
toxicology study of poisons
ufology study of UFOs
urology study of the urinary system
vinology study of (grape-)vines
virology study of viruses

open o. See table at GREEK ALPHABET. **2** the last of a series; a conclusion. ⓔ 16c: from Greek *o mega*, literally 'great O'; compare OMICRON.

omelette or (*N Amer, especially US*) **omelet** /'ɒmlət/ ▷ *noun, cookery* a dish made of beaten eggs fried in a pan, often folded round a savoury or sometimes sweet filling such as cheese or jam. ⓔ 17c: French, from *amelette* altered, from *alemelle* a thin plate, from Latin *lamella* or *lamina*.

omen /'oʊmən/ ▷ *noun* **1** a circumstance, phenomenon, etc that is regarded as a sign of a future event, either good or evil. **2** threatening or prophetic character □ ***bird of ill omen.*** ▷ *verb* (***omened, omening***) to portend. ● **omened** *adj, in compounds* with omens of a specified kind □ *ill-omened*. See also OMINOUS. ⓔ 16c: Latin.

omentum /oʊ'mɛntəm/ ▷ *noun* (*plural* ***omenta***) *zool* abdominal lining linking the intestinal tract to other organs. ⓔ 16c: Latin.

omertà /ɒ'mɛəta/ ▷ *noun* **1** the Mafia code of honour that requires silence about criminal activities and stresses the disgrace of informing. **2** a criminal conspiracy of silence. ⓔ 19c: Italian, a dialect form of *umiltà* humility.

omicron /'ɒmɪkrɒn, oʊ-, 'maɪkrɒn/ ▷ *noun* the 15th letter of the Greek alphabet, pronounced as a short o. See table at GREEK ALPHABET. ⓔ 17c: from Greek *o mikron*, literally 'little O'; compare OMEGA.

ominous /'ɒmɪnəs/ ▷ *adj* threatening; containing a warning of something evil or bad that will happen. ● **ominously** *adverb*. ● **ominousness** *noun*. ⓔ 16c: from Latin *ominosus*, from *omen* omen.

omission /ə'mɪʃən/ ▷ *noun* **1** something that has been left out or neglected. **2** the act of leaving something out or neglecting it. ● **omissive** *adj*. ⓔ 14c: from Latin *omissio*, from *omittere* to omit.

omit /ə'mɪt/ ▷ *verb* (***omitted, omitting***) **1** to leave something out, either by mistake or on purpose. **2** to fail to do something. ● **omissible** *adj* referring to something that may be omitted. ⓔ 15c: from Latin *omittere*, from *ob-* in front + *mittere* to send.

ommateum /ɒmə'tɪəm/ ▷ *noun* (*plural* ***ommatea*** /-tɪə/) *entomol* a COMPOUND EYE. ⓔ 19c: Latin, from Greek *omma*, *ommatos* an eye.

ommatidium /ɒmə'tɪdɪəm/ ▷ *noun* (*plural* ***ommatidia*** /-dɪə/) *entomol* a simple conical element of a COMPOUND EYE. ⓔ 19c.

omni- /ɒmnɪ/ ▷ *combining form, signifying* all, every or everywhere. ⓔ From Latin *omnis* all or every.

omnibus /'ɒmnɪbəs, 'ɒmnɪbʌs/ ▷ *noun* (***omnibuses*** /-sɪz/) **1** *old use or formal* a BUS. **2** (*also* **omnibus book** or **omnibus volume**) a book that contains reprints of a number of works by a single author, or several works on the same subject or of a similar type. **3** (*also* **omnibus edition** or **omnibus programme**) a TV or radio programme made up of or edited from the preceding week's editions of a particular serial. ▷ *adj* said especially of a legislative bill: relating to, dealing with or made up of several different items or parts. ⓔ 19c: Latin, meaning 'for all', from *omnis* all.

omnidirectional ▷ *adj* said of an antenna: equally sensitive or powerful in all directions, especially horizontally. ● **omnidirectionality** *noun*. ● **omnidirectionally** *adverb*. ⓔ 1920s.

omnifarious /ɒmnɪ'fɛərɪəs/ ▷ *adj* comprising or dealing with many different things. ● **omnifariously**

adverb. • **omnifariousness** *noun*. ⓒ 17c: from Latin *omnifarius*, from *-farius* doing.

omnific /ɒm'nɪfɪk/ and **omnificent** /ɒm'nɪfɪsənt/ ▷ *adj* all-creating. • **omnificence** *noun*. ⓒ 17c: from OMNI-, modelled on MAGNIFICENT, etc.

OMNIMAX or **Omnimax** /'ɒmnɪmaks/ ▷ *adj, trademark* said of a film: designed to be viewed on a special domed screen that provides the audience with a near-hemispherical image.

omnipotent /ɒm'nɪpətənt/ ▷ *adj* **1** said of God or a deity: all-powerful; with infinite power. **2** with very great power or influence. ▷ *noun* (**the Omnipotent**) God. • **omnipotence** *noun*. • **omnipotently** *adverb*. ⓒ 14c: French, from Latin *omnis* all + *potens, potentis* able or powerful.

omnipresent ▷ *adj* said especially of a god: present everywhere at the same time. • **omnipresence** *noun*. ⓒ 17c.

omniscient /ɒm'nɪsɪənt/ ▷ *adj* **1** said especially of God: with infinite knowledge or understanding. **2** with very great knowledge; knowing everything. • **omniscience** /-sɪəns/ *noun*. • **omnisciently** *adverb*. ⓒ 17c: from Latin *omnis* all + *sciens, scientis* knowing.

omnium /'ɒmnɪəm/ ▷ *noun, stock exchange* the aggregate value of the different stocks in which a loan is funded. ⓒ 18c: Latin, meaning 'of all'.

omnium-gatherum /'ɒmnɪəm 'gaðərəm/ ▷ *noun* (***omnium-gatherums*** or ***omnium-gathera*** /-rə/) *colloq, often facetious* a miscellaneous collection of people or things, etc. ⓒ 16c: mock Latin, from Latin *omnium* 'of all' + GATHER.

omnivorous /ɒm'nɪvərəs/ ▷ *adj* **1** eating any type of food, especially both meat and vegetable matter. **2** taking in, reading or using, etc everything. • **omnivore** *noun* a person or animal that eats any type of food. • **omnivorously** *adverb*. • **omnivorousness** *noun*. • **omnivory** *noun*. ⓒ 17c: from Latin *omnivorus*, from *vorare* to devour.

ON ▷ *abbreviation* Old Norse.

on ▷ *prep* **1** touching, supported by, attached to, covering, or enclosing □ *a chair on the floor* □ *a dog on a lead*. **2** in or into (a vehicle, etc) □ *got on the bus*. **3** *colloq* carried with (a person) □ *I've got no money on me*. **4** very near to or along the side of something □ *a house on the shore*. **5** at or during (a certain day or time, etc) □ *on Monday* □ *on the hour*. **6** immediately after, at or before □ *He found the letter on his return*. **7** within the (given) limits of something □ *a picture on page nine*. **8** about □ *a book on Jane Austen*. **9** towards □ *marched on the town*. **10** through contact with or as a result of something □ *cut oneself on the broken bottle*. **11** in the state or process of something □ *on fire* □ *on a journey*. **12** using as a means of transport □ *goes to work on the bus*. **13** using as a means or medium □ *talk on the telephone* □ *a tune on the piano*. **14** on the occasion of something □ *shoot on sight*. **15** having as a basis or source □ *on good authority* □ *arrested on suspicion*. **16** working for or being a member of something □ *on the committee* □ *work on the case*. **17** at the expense of or to the disadvantage of something or someone □ *treatment on the National Health* □ *drinks on me* □ *the joke's on him*. **18** supported by something □ *live on bread and cheese*. **19** regularly taking or using something □ *on tranquillizers*. **20** in a specified manner □ *on the cheap*. **21** staked as a bet □ *put money on a horse*. **22** following □ *disappointment on disappointment*. ▷ *adverb* **1** said especially of clothes: in or into contact or a state of enclosing, covering, or being worn, etc □ *have no clothes on*. **2** ahead, forwards or towards in space or time □ *go on home* □ *later on*. **3** continuously; without interruption □ *keep on about something*. **4** in or into operation or activity □ *put the radio on*. ▷ *adj* **1** working, broadcasting or performing □ *You're on in two minutes*. **2** taking place □ *Which films are on this week?* **3** *colloq* possible, practicable or acceptable □ *That just isn't on*. **4** *colloq* talking continuously, especially to complain or nag □ *always on at him to try harder*. **5** in favour of a win □ *odds of 3 to 4 on*. **6** *cricket* on the side of the field towards which the bat is facing, usually the batsman's left and the bowler's right. Opposite of OFF 6. • **be on to someone** or **something** *colloq* **1** to realize their importance or intentions. **2** to be in touch with them □ *We'll be on to you about the party on Saturday*. • **get on to someone** *colloq* to get in touch with them. • **just on** almost exactly □ *have collected just on £50*. • **on and off** now and then; occasionally. • **on and on** continually; at length. • **on time** promptly; at the right time. • **on to** (*also* ONTO) to a position on or in. ⓒ Anglo-Saxon.

-on ▷ *combining form denoting* **1** physics an elementary particle □ *neutron*. **2** chem a molecular unit □ *codon*.

onager /'ɒnədʒə(r), 'ɒnəgə(r)/ ▷ *noun* a variety of wild ass found in central Asia. ⓒ 14c: Latin, from Greek *onagros*, from *onos* an ass + *agrios* wild.

onanism /'oʊnənɪzəm/ ▷ *noun* **1** sexual intercourse in which the penis is withdrawn from the vagina before ejaculation; coitus interruptus. **2** masturbation. • **onanist** *noun*. • **onanistic** *adj*. ⓒ 18c: named after the Biblical character Onan, son of Judah, who practised coitus interruptus (Genesis 38.9).

ONC ▷ *abbreviation* Ordinary National Certificate, a qualification in a technical subject, more or less equivalent to an A-level.

once /wʌns/ ▷ *adverb* **1 a** a single time □ *I'll say this only once*; **b** on one occasion □ *They came once*. **2** multiplied by one. **3** at some time in the past; formerly □ *lived in London once*. **4** *chiefly with negatives or conditionals* ever; at any time □ *if once you are late*. **5** by one degree of relationship □ *hasn't once visited* □ *a cousin once removed*. ▷ *conj* as soon as; when once or if once □ *Once you have finished you can go out*. ▷ *noun* one time or occasion □ *just this once*. • **all at once 1** suddenly. **2** all at the same time; simultaneously. • **at once 1** immediately; without any delay. **2** all at the same time; simultaneously. • **for once** on this one occasion if on no other; as an exception. • **once again** or **once more** one more time, as before. • **once and for all** or **once for all** for the last time; now and never again. • **once in a way** or **while** occasionally; rarely. • **once or twice** a few times. • **once upon a time** the usual way to begin fairy tales: at a certain time in the past. ⓒ Anglo-Saxon *anes*, originally meaning 'of one', from *an* one.

once-over ▷ *noun, colloq* **1** a quick, often casual, examination or appraisal □ *give the car the once-over*. **2** a violent beating. • **give someone or something the once-over** to beat them violently. ⓒ Early 20c.

oncer /'wʌnsə(r)/ ▷ *noun, colloq* **1 a** someone or something that does a particular thing only once; **b** something that happens only once. **2** *old use* a £1 note. **3** *Austral* **a** an MP who is considered likely to serve only one term; **b** the election of such an MP. ⓒ 19c.

onchocerciasis /ɒŋkoʊsə'kaɪəsɪs/ ▷ *noun, pathol* a human disease, common in tropical regions of America and Asia, caused by infestation by a filarial worm that is transmited by various species of blackfly, and characterized by subcutaneous nodules and often blindness. Also called **river blindness**. ⓒ Early 20c: Latin, from Greek *onkos* a hook or barb + *kerkos* a tail.

onco- /'ɒŋkoʊ/ ▷ *combining form, signifying* swelling, especially tumours. ⓒ From Greek *onkos* bulk, mass or swelling.

oncogene /'ɒŋkoʊdʒiːn/ ▷ *noun, genetics* a gene that causes a normal cell to develop into a cancerous cell, or to multiply in an uncontrolled manner. ⓒ 1960s.

oncogenesis /ɒŋkoʊ'dʒɛnɪsɪs/ ▷ *noun* the formation of cancerous tumours. • **oncogenic** /ɒŋkoʊ'dʒɛnɪk/ *adj* **1** relating to oncogenesis. **2** causing tumours. ⓒ 1930s.

oncology /ɒŋˈkɒlədʒɪ/ ▷ *noun* the branch of medicine that deals with the study of tumours, especially cancerous ones. • **oncologist** *noun*. ⓒ 19c.

oncoming ▷ *adj* approaching; advancing □ *oncoming traffic*. ▷ *noun* an approach.

oncost ▷ *noun* (*often* **oncosts**) overhead expenses. Also *as adj*.

OND ▷ *abbreviation* Ordinary National Diploma, a qualification in a technical subject reached after a two-year full-time or sandwich course, recognized by many professional institutions.

on-drive *cricket* ▷ *noun* a drive to the on side (see ON adj 6). ▷ *verb, tr & intr* to drive to the on side. ⓒ 19c.

one /wʌn/ ▷ *noun* **1 a** the cardinal number 1; **b** the quantity that this represents, being a single unit. **2** a unity or unit. **3** any symbol for this, eg **1**, **I**. **4** the age of one. **5** something, especially a garment or a person, whose size is denoted by the number 1. **6** the first hour after midnight or midday □ *Come at one o'clock* □ *1pm*. **7** a score of one point. **8** *colloq* a story or joke □ *heard the one about the singing policeman?* **9** (**one for something**) *colloq* an enthusiast of the specified thing □ *She's quite a one for chess*. **10** *colloq* a drink, especially an alcoholic one □ *drop in for a quick one*. **11** *colloq* a daring, remarkable or cheeky person □ *You are a one!* ▷ *adj* **1** being a single unit, number or thing. **2** being a particular person or thing, especially as distinct from another or others of the same kind □ *lift one leg and then the other*. **3** being a particular but unspecified instance or example □ *visit him one day soon*. **4** being the only such □ *the one woman who can beat her*. **5** same; identical □ *of one mind*. **6** undivided; forming a single whole □ *They sang with one voice*. **7** first □ *page one*. **8** *colloq* an exceptional example or instance of something □ *That was one big fellow*. **9** totalling one. **10** aged one. ▷ *pronoun* **1** (often referring to a noun already mentioned or implied) an individual person, thing or instance □ *buy the blue one*. **2** anybody □ *One can't do better than that*. **3** *formal or facetious* I; me □ *One doesn't like to pry*. • **all one** just the same; of no consequence □ *It's all one to me*. • **at one with someone** or **something** **1** in complete agreement with them. **2** in harmony with them □ *at one with nature*. • **be one up on someone** *colloq* to have an advantage over them. • **for one** as one person □ *I for one don't agree*. • **all in one 1** together; combined; as one unit or object, etc. **2** in one go or attempt. • **just one of those things** an unfortunate event or situation that must be accepted. • **one and all** everyone without exception. • **one and only** used for emphasis: only. • **one another** used as the object of a verb or preposition when an action takes place between two (or more than two) people, etc □ *Chris and Pat love one another*. • **one by one** one after the other; individually. • **one or two** *colloq* a few. ⓒ Anglo-Saxon *an*.

> ***one another***
>
> See Usage Note at **each**.

-one /oʊn/ ▷ *combining form, chem signifying* certain compounds, especially Ketones □ *acetone*.

one-armed bandit ▷ *noun* a fruit machine with a long handle at the side which is pulled down hard to make the machine work. ⓒ 1930s.

one-horse ▷ *adj* **1** using a single horse. **2** *colloq* small, poor and of little importance □ *a one-horse town*.

one-horse race ▷ *noun* a race or competition, etc in which one particular competitor or participant is certain to win.

oneiric or **oniric** /oʊˈnaɪərɪk/ ▷ *adj* belonging or relating to dreams or dreaming. ⓒ 19c: from Greek *oneiros* a dream.

one-liner ▷ *noun, colloq* a short amusing remark or joke made in a single sentence. ⓒ Early 20c.

one-man, **one-woman** and **one-person** ▷ *adj* consisting of, for or done by one person □ *a one-person tent*.

one-man band ▷ *noun* a musician who carries and plays several instruments simultaneously.

oneness /ˈwʌnnɪs/ ▷ *noun* **1** the state or quality of being one; singleness. **2** agreement. **3** the state of being the same. **4** the state of being unique.

one-night stand ▷ *noun* **1** a performance given only once in any place, the next performance taking place elsewhere. **2** *colloq* a sexual encounter that lasts only one night.

one-off *colloq, chiefly Brit* ▷ *adj* made or happening, etc on one occasion only. ▷ *noun* something that is one-off. ⓒ 1930s.

one-on-one see ONE-TO-ONE

one-parent family ▷ *noun* a family that consists of a child or children and one parent, the other parent being dead or estranged.

one-person see ONE-MAN

one-piece ▷ *adj* said of a garment, especially a swimsuit: made as a single piece as opposed to separate parts. ▷ *noun* a garment, especially a swimsuit, made in such a way. Compare BIKINI.

onerous /ˈoʊnərəs, ˈɒnərəs/ ▷ *adj* **1** heavy; difficult to do or bear; oppressive. **2** *law* said of a contract, etc: with or involving a legal burden or obligation. • **onerously** *adverb*. • **onerousness** *noun*. ⓒ 14c: from Latin *onerosus*, from *onus* burden.

oneself /wʌnˈsɛlf/ and **one's self** ▷ *pronoun* **1** the reflexive form of ONE (*pronoun*) □ *not able to help oneself*. **2** the emphatic form of ONE (*pronoun*) □ *One hasn't been there oneself*. **3** one's normal self □ *not feeling oneself after an operation*. • **by oneself** on one's own; alone. ⓒ 16c.

one-sided ▷ *adj* **1** said of a competition, etc: with one person or side having a great advantage over the other. **2** seeing, accepting, representing or favouring only one side of a subject or argument, etc; unfair; partial. **3** greater or more developed on one side. **4** occurring on or limited to one side only. • **one-sidedly** *adverb*. • **one-sidedness** *noun*.

one-step ▷ *noun* **1** an early form of the foxtrot in quadruple time, originating in the US. **2** a piece of music for this dance. ▷ *verb, intr* to dance the one-step. ⓒ Early 20c.

one-stop ▷ *adj* **1** said of a shop, etc: able to provide the complete range of goods or services that a customer might require. **2** said of an advisory service, consultancy, retailer, etc: providing answers to most questions concerning a particular issue or all products in a particular field, without referring the customer to another department, company, etc □ *one-stop advisory service* □ *one-stop house-purchase service*.

one-time ▷ *adj* former; past □ *one-time lover*.

one-to-one ▷ *adj* **1** with one person or thing exactly corresponding to or matching another. **2** in which a person is involved with only one other person □ *one-to-one teaching*. *N Amer equivalent* ONE-ON-ONE.

one-track ▷ *adj* **1** with only a single track. **2** *colloq* said of a person's mind: **a** incapable of dealing with more than one subject or activity, etc at a time; **b** obsessed with one idea. ⓒ 1920s.

one-two ▷ *noun, colloq* **1** *boxing* the delivery of a blow with one fist quickly followed by a blow with the other. **2** *football, hockey, etc* a move in which one player passes the ball to another then runs forward to receive the ball as it is immediately passed back again. ⓒ Early 19c.

one-up ▷ *adj, colloq* with a particular advantage over someone else. ⓒ Early 20c.

one-upmanship ▻ *noun, humorous* the art of gaining psychological, social or professional advantages over other people. ⓒ 1952: a term coined by Stephen Potter.

one-way ▻ *adj* **1 a** said of a road or street, etc: on which traffic is allowed to move in one direction only; **b** relating to or indicating such a traffic system □ *one-way sign.* **2** said of a feeling or relationship: not returned or reciprocated. **3** said of an agreement, etc: not involving any reciprocal action or obligation. **4** *N Amer, especially US* said of a ticket: valid for travel in one direction only; SINGLE (*noun* 4). **5** said of a window, glass or mirror, etc: able to be seen through from one side only and which appears from the other side to be a mirror.

one-woman see ONE-MAN

onfall ▻ *noun* an attack; an onslaught.

onflow ▻ *verb, intr* to flow on. ▻ *noun* **1** a flowing on. **2** an onward flow. ⓒ 19c.

ongoing ▻ *adj* **1** in progress; going on. **2** continuing. **3** current. ▻ *noun* **1** the action of going on. **2** (**ongoings**) **a** proceedings; **b** behaviour, especially misbehaviour; goings-on. ⓒ 17c.

onion /ˈʌnjən/ ▻ *noun* **1** any of numerous varieties of a biennial plant belonging to the lily family, native to SW Asia. **2** the edible bulb of this plant, which consists of white fleshy scales and a pungent oil, surrounded by a brown papery outer layer, and is eaten raw, cooked or pickled. **3** the long tubular leaves of a young onion plant (called a SPRING ONION), eaten as a salad vegetable. • **onion-like** *adj.* • **oniony** *adj.* • **know one's onions** *colloq* to know one's subject or job well. ⓒ 14c: from Anglo-Norman *union*, from French *oignon*, from Latin *unio* unity, a large pearl, or an onion.

onion dome ▻ *noun, archit* a bulb-shaped dome topped with a sharply tapering point, characteristic of Orthodox, especially Russian and Byzantine, church architecture. ⓒ 1940s.

oniric see ONEIRIC

on-licence ▻ *noun* a licence to sell alcoholic drink for consumption on the premises. Compare OFF-LICENCE.

on-line ▻ *adj* **1** *computing* said of a peripheral device, eg a printer: connected to and controlled by the central processor of a computer. Also *as adverb* □ *The telephone banking service went on line last year.* Compare OFF-LINE. **2** said of a service, etc: run with a direct connection to and interaction with a computer □ *on-line shopping.* ⓒ 1950s.

onlooker ▻ *noun* someone who watches and does not take part; an observer. • **onlooking** *adj.* ⓒ 17c.

only /ˈoʊnlɪ/ ▻ *adj* **1** without any others of the same type. **2** said of someone: having no brothers or sisters. **3** *colloq* best □ *Flying is the only way to travel.* ▻ *adverb* **1** not more than; just. **2** alone; solely. **3** not longer ago than; not until □ *only a minute ago.* **4** merely; with no other result than □ *I arrived only to find he had already left.* ▻ *conj* **1** but; however □ *Come if you want to, only don't complain if you're bored.* **2** if it were not for the fact that □ *I'd come too, only I know I'd slow you down.* • **if only** I wish □ *If only you could be on time for once.* • **only too** very; extremely □ *only too ready to help.* ⓒ Anglo-Saxon *anlic*.

o.n.o. ▻ *abbreviation* or near offer; or nearest offer.

on-off ▻ *adj* said of a switch: able to be set to one of only two positions, either 'on' or 'off'.

onomasticon /ɒnəˈmastɪkɒn/ ▻ *noun, linguistics* a dictionary or collection of proper names, especially personal ones. ⓒ 18c: from Greek *onomastikos* relating to names, from *onoma* a name.

onomastics /ɒnəˈmastɪks/ ▻ *singular noun, linguistics* the study of the history, development and geographical distribution of proper names, including eg personal first names and surnames, place names, home names, and the names of boats, trains and pets. ⓒ 1930s.

onomatopoeia /ɒnəmatəˈpɪə/ ▻ *noun* **1** the formation of words whose sounds imitate the sound or action they represent, eg *boo, hiss, squelch.* **2** a word formed in this way. **3** *rhetoric* the use, for rhetorical effect, of words whose sounds help to suggest their meaning. • **onomatopoeic** *adj* IMITATIVE. • **onomatopoeically** *adverb.* ⓒ 16c: Latin, from Greek *onomatopoios*, from *onoma* name + *poiein* to make.

onrush ▻ *noun* a sudden and strong movement forward. ⓒ 19c.

onscreen ▻ *adj* ▻ *adverb* relating to information that is displayed on a TV screen or VDU. ⓒ 1950s.

onset /ˈɒnsɛt/ ▻ *noun* **1** an attack; an assault. **2** a beginning, especially of something unpleasant. **3** *phonetics* **a** the movement of the speech organs in preparation for or at the beginning of the articulation of a sound; **b** the consonant or group of consonants at the beginning of a syllable. ⓒ 1930s in sense 3; 16c.

onshore ▻ *adverb* /ɒnˈʃɔː(r)/ towards, on, or on to the shore. ▻ *adj* /ˈɒnʃɔː(r)/ **1** said of the wind: blowing or moving from the sea towards the shore. **2** found or occurring on the shore or land. ⓒ 19c.

onside ▻ *adj, adverb, football, rugby, etc* said of a player: in a position where the ball may legally be played; not offside. Also written **on-side**. Compare OFFSIDE. ⓒ 19c.

onslaught /ˈɒnslɔːt/ ▻ *noun* a fierce attack; an onset. ⓒ 17c: from Dutch *aenslag*, from *aen* on + *slag* a blow.

on-stage ▻ *adj, adverb* on the stage and visible to the audience.

on-stream or **onstream** ▻ *adj* /ˈɒnstriːm/ said of an industrial plant or process, etc: relating to normal production. ▻ *adverb* /ɒnˈstriːm/ in operation or ready to go into operation. ⓒ 1930s.

Ont. ▻ *abbreviation, Canadian province* Ontario.

onto ▻ *prep* on to (see under ON). • **be onto someone** to be suspicious or aware of their (usually underhand) actions.

onto- /ɒntə, ɒnˈtɒ/ ▻ *combining form, signifying* being; existence. ⓒ From Greek *ont-*, *on* being (present participle of *einai* to be).

ontogenesis /ɒntoʊˈdʒɛnəsɪs/ ▻ *noun, biol* the history of the development of an individual living organism, from fertilization of the ovum to sexual maturity. Compare PHYLOGENESIS. • **ontogenetic** *adj.* • **ontogenetically** *adverb.* ⓒ 19c.

ontogeny /ɒnˈtɒdʒənɪ/ ▻ *noun, biol* **1** ONTOGENESIS. **2** the branch of science that deals with ontogenesis. • **ontogenic** /-ˈdʒɛnɪk/ *adj.* • **ontogenically** *adverb.* ⓒ 19c.

ontology /ɒnˈtɒlədʒɪ/ ▻ *noun, philos* the branch of metaphysics that deals with the nature and essence of things or of existence. • **ontologic** /ɒntəˈlɒdʒɪk/ or **ontological** *adj.* • **ontologically** *adverb.* ⓒ 18c.

onus /ˈoʊnəs/ ▻ *noun* (*onuses*) a responsibility or burden □ *The onus is on you to prove it.* ⓒ 17c: Latin, meaning 'burden'.

onward /ˈɒnwəd/ ▻ *adj* moving forward in place or time; advancing. ▻ *adverb* (*also* **onwards**) **1** towards or at a place or time which is advanced or in front; ahead. **2** forward. **3** continuing to move forwards or progress.

onyx /ˈɒnɪks/ ▻ *noun, geol* a very hard variety of agate with straight alternating bands of one or more colours, eg a form with black and white bands widely used to make jewellery and ornaments. ⓒ 13c: Latin, from Greek, meaning 'nail'.

oo- or **oö-** /oʊə, oʊˈɒ/ ▻ *combining form, denoting* egg or ovum. ⓒ From Greek *oion* egg or ovum.

o/o ▻ *abbreviation* offers over.

oocyte /ˈoʊəsaɪt/ ▻ *noun, biol* a cell that gives rise to an ovum by two meiotic divisions. **Primary oocytes** are diploid and undergo meiosis to give **secondary oocytes** which are haploid, and meisois of a secondary oocyte produces an ovum. ⓒ 19c.

oodles /ˈuːdəlz/ ▻ *plural noun, colloq* lots; a great quantity □ *oodles of money*. ⓒ 19c.

oof ▻ *noun, slang* money. ⓒ 19c: possibly from Yiddish *ooftish*, from German *auf (dem) Tisch*.

oogamy /oʊˈɒgəmɪ/ ▻ *noun, biol* a form of sexual reproduction in which a large non-motile female gamete (the ovum or egg cell) is fertilized by a small motile male gamete. • **oogamous** *adj*. ⓒ 19c.

oogenesis /oʊəˈdʒɛnəsɪs/ ▻ *noun, biol* the production and development of an ovum in the ovary of an animal. ⓒ 19c.

ooh /uː/ ▻ *exclamation* expressing pleasure, surprise, excitement or pain. ▻ *verb* (***oohed, oohing***) (*often* **ooh and aah**) to make an ooh sound to show surprise or excitement, etc. ⓒ Early 20c.

oolite /ˈoʊəlaɪt/ ▻ *noun, geol* **1** a sedimentary rock, usually a form of limestone, consisting of masses of small round particles, known as **ooliths** or **ooids**, that resemble fish eggs. **2** (*also* **Oolite**) stratigraphically the upper part of the Jurassic in Britain, consisting largely of oolites. • **oolitic** /-ˈlɪtɪk/ *adj*. ⓒ 18c: from French *oölithe*, from Latin *oolites*, literally 'egg stone'.

oology /oʊˈɒlədʒɪ/ ▻ *noun* the science or study of birds' eggs. • **oological** *adj*. • **oologist** *noun*. ⓒ 19c: from Latin *oologia*; see OO- + -LOGY.

oolong or **oulong** /ˈuːlɒŋ/ ▻ *noun* a variety of black China tea that is partly fermented before it is dried and has the flavour of green tea. ⓒ 19c: from Chinese *wu* black + *long* dragon.

oomiak see UMIAK

oompah or **oom-pah** /ˈuːmpɑː, ˈʊmpɑː/ ▻ *noun, colloq* a common way of representing the deep sound made by a large brass musical instrument, such as a tuba. ⓒ 19c.

oomph /ʊmf, uːmf/ ▻ *noun, colloq* **1** energy; enthusiasm. **2** personal attractiveness, especially sex appeal. ⓒ 1930s.

oophorectomy /oʊəfəˈrɛktəmɪ/ ▻ *noun* (***oophorectomies***) *surgery* removal of one or both ovaries. ⓒ 19c: from Latin *oophoron* ovary.

oophoritis /oʊəfəˈraɪtɪs/ ▻ *noun, pathol* inflammation of the ovary. ⓒ 19c: from Latin *oophoron* ovary, from Greek *iophoros* egg-bearing.

oops /ʊps, uːps/ ▻ *exclamation, colloq* expressing surprise or apology, eg when one makes a mistake or drops something, etc. ⓒ 1930s.

oops-a-daisy see UPS-A-DAISY

oorial see URIAL

oospore /ˈoʊəspɔː(r)/ ▻ *noun* **1** *biol* a fertilized ovum. **2** *bot* in certain algae and fungi: the zygote that is produced as a result of OOGAMY, which has a thick protective outer wall and contains food reserves. ⓒ 19c.

ooze¹ /uːz/ ▻ *verb* (***oozed, oozing***) **1** *intr* to flow or leak out gently or slowly. **2** *intr* said of a substance: to give out moisture. **3** to give out (a liquid, etc) slowly. **4** to overflow with (a quality or feeling); to exude □ *oozed charm*. ▻ *noun* **1** anything which oozes. **2** a slow gentle leaking or oozing. **3** an infusion of bark and other vegetable matter used for tanning leather. • **oozy** *adj* (***oozier, ooziest***) damp; giving out moisture. ⓒ Anglo-Saxon *wos* sap or juice.

ooze² /uːz/ ▻ *noun* **1** soft boggy ground. **2** mud or slime, especially the kind found on the beds of rivers or lakes. **3** *geol* a layer of fine organic sediments and shells of diatoms, etc that accumulates very slowly on the ocean floor over millions of years. • **oozy** *adj* (***oozier, ooziest***) like or containing ooze; slimy. • **oozily** *adverb*. • **ooziness** *noun*. ⓒ Anglo-Saxon *wase* marsh or mire.

OP ▻ *abbreviation* **1** *military* observation post; observation point. **2** *theat* opposite prompt. **3** *Ordo Praedicatorum* (Latin), Order of Preachers, the DOMINICAN Order.

op ▻ *noun, colloq* **1** a surgical operation. **2** a military operation. ⓒ 1920s short form.

op. ▻ *abbreviation* opus.

opacity /oʊˈpasɪtɪ/ ▻ *noun* **1** opaqueness. **2** the state of having an obscure meaning and being difficult to understand. **3** dullness; obtuseness. See also OPAQUE. ⓒ 16c: from Latin *opacitas*, from *opacus* opaque.

opah /ˈoʊpə/ ▻ *noun* a large brilliantly coloured sea-fish with a laterally flattened body. Also called **kingfish** or **moonfish**. ⓒ 18c: W African.

opal /ˈoʊpəl/ ▻ *noun, geol* a milky-white, black or coloured form of SILICA, combined with variable amounts of water, usually with a characteristic internal 'play' of coloured flashes caused by light reflected from different layers within the stone. They are used as gemstones. ⓒ 16c: from French *opale* or Latin *opalus*, perhaps ultimately from Sanskrit *upala* precious stone.

opalescent /oʊpəˈlɛsənt/ ▻ *adj* reflecting different colours as the surrounding light changes, like an opal; with a milky iridescence. • **opalescence** *noun*. ⓒ 19c.

opaline /ˈoʊpəliːn, -laɪn/ ▻ *adj* OPALESCENT. ▻ *noun* **1** a whitish semi-translucent glass. **2** translucent glass of some other colour. ⓒ 18c.

opaque /oʊˈpeɪk/ ▻ *adj* (***opaquer, opaquest***) **1** not allowing light to pass through; not transparent or translucent. **2** not transmitting other forms of radiation, such as sound or heat, etc. **3** difficult to understand; obscure. **4** impervious to sense; dull or unintelligent. ▻ *noun* **1** something, eg a space or medium, that is opaque. **2** an eye-shade. **3** *photog* **a** a substance used to block out areas of a negative; **b** a print made on opaque paper. ▻ *verb* (***opaqued, opaquing***) **1** to make something opaque. **2** *photog* to block out (areas of a negative) by means of an opaque. • **opaquely** *adverb*. • **opaqueness** *noun*. See also OPACITY. ⓒ 15c: from Latin *opacus* dark or shaded.

Op Art ▻ *noun* (*in full* **Optical Art**) a modern art movement that exploits the illusions created by abstract compositions of spirals, grids, undulating lines, stripes, spots, etc to produce sensations of movement, space and volume. ⓒ 1960s.

op. cit. /ɒp ˈsɪt/ ▻ *abbreviation*: *opere citato* (Latin), in the work already quoted, used in footnotes, etc to refer to the last citation that is given.

ope /oʊp/ *archaic or poetic* ▻ *adj* OPEN. ▻ *verb* (***oped, oping***) *tr & intr* to OPEN. ⓒ 15c.

OPEC /ˈoʊpɛk/ ▻ *abbreviation* Organization of Petroleum Exporting Countries.

open /ˈoʊpən/ ▻ *adj* **1 a** said of a door or barrier, etc: not closed or locked; **b** said of a building or an enclosed space, etc: allowing people or things to go in or out; with its door or gate, etc not closed or locked. **2** said of a container, etc: **a** not sealed or covered; **b** with the insides visible □ *an open cupboard*. **3** said of a space or area of land, etc: **a** not enclosed, confined or restricted □ *the open sea*; **b** unobstructed □ *an open view*. **4** not covered, guarded or protected □ *an open wound*. **5** expanded, spread out or unfolded □ *an open newspaper*. **6** said of a shop, etc: receiving customers; ready for business. **7** said of a river or port, etc: **a** free from ice or frost; unfrozen; **b** not closed for any other reason. **8** said of the climate or a season: free from frost. **9** *sport* **a** said of a player: not marked by a member of the opposing team; **b** said of a goal, etc: unguarded or unprotected; **c** said of a game or style of play, etc: with the action or players spread out over the field of play. **10** *phonetics* **a** said of a vowel: produced with the tongue positioned low in the mouth; **b** see separate entry OPEN SYLLABLE. **11** said of cloth or a texture, etc: with a lot of small openings or gaps; loose. **12** *music* **a** said of a string: not stopped by a finger; **b** said of a note: played on an open string, or without holes on the instrument being covered. **13** *math* **a** see separate entry OPEN SET; **b** said of an interval in the real line: without either of its end points. **14** *astron* said of the universe: with a negative or zero radius of curvature; always expanding; infinite. **15** generally known; public. **16** (*usually* **open to something**) liable or susceptible to it; defenceless against it □ *leave oneself open to abuse.* **17** said of a competition: not restricted; allowing anyone to compete or take part, especially both amateurs and professionals. **18** free from restraint or restrictions of any kind □ *the open fishing season.* **19** said of a problem or discussion, etc: not finally decided; still to be settled. **20** unprejudiced □ *have an open mind.* **21** (*usually* **open to something**) amenable to or ready to receive (eg new ideas or impressions) □ *open to suggestion.* **22** said of a person: ready and willing to talk honestly; candid. ▻ *verb* (***opened***, ***opening***) **1 a** to unfasten or move (eg a door or barrier) to allow access; **b** *intr* said of a door or barrier, etc: to become unfastened to allow access. **2** *tr & intr* to become or make something become open or more open, eg by removing obstructions, etc. **3** (*also* **open out** or **open something out**) *tr & intr* to spread it out or become spread out or unfolded, especially so as to make or become visible. **4** *tr & intr* to start or begin working □ *The office opens at nine.* **5** to declare something open with an official ceremony □ *open the new hospital.* **6** *tr & intr* to begin or start speaking or writing, etc □ *opened his talk with a joke.* **7** to arrange (a bank account, etc), usually by making an initial deposit. **8** *tr & intr, cricket* to begin (the batting) for one's team. **9** *intr, law* said of legal counsel: to make a preliminary statement about a case before beginning to call witnesses. **10** *cards* to bet or bid on a hand first. ▻ *noun* **1** (**the open**) an area of open country; an area not obstructed by buildings, etc. **2** (**the open**) public notice or attention (*especially* **bring something into the open** or **out into the open**). **3** (**Open**) *often in compounds* a sports contest which both amateurs and professionals may enter □ *the British Open.* • **openable** *adj.* • **opener** and **opening** see separate entries. • **openly** *adverb* **1** in an open way. **2** without trying to hide anything; in a direct and honest manner. • **openness** *noun.* • **open and above board** thoroughly honest or legal. • **open fire** to start shooting. • **with open arms** warmly; cordially □ *welcomed him with open arms.* ⓒ Anglo-Saxon.

■ **open into** or **onto something** to provide access to it.

■ **open out** or **up** to begin to reveal one's feelings and thoughts or to behave with less restraint.

■ **open up 1** to open the door. **2** to open a shop for the day. **3** to start firing. **4** said of a game, etc: to become more interesting as it develops.

■ **open something up 1** to make it more accessible or available. **2** said especially of a vehicle or engine, etc: to increase its speed.

■ **open up something** to someone to reveal (one's thoughts or mind, etc) to them.

open access ▻ *noun* a system that allows members of the public direct access to the material on the shelves of a library. Also (**open-access**) *as adj.*

open air ▻ *noun* unenclosed space outdoors. ▻ *adj* (**open-air**) in the open air; outside □ *open-air theatre.*

open-and-shut ▻ *adj* easily proved, decided or solved □ *an open-and-shut case.*

open book ▻ *noun* **1** anything that can be easily read or interpreted. **2** someone who keeps no secrets and is easily understood.

opencast *mining* ▻ *adj* using or relating to a method in which the substance to be mined, eg coal or copper, is exposed by removing the overlying layers of material, without the need for shafts or tunnels. ▻ *noun* a mine where such a method is used.

open chain ▻ *noun, chem* a chain of atoms, the ends of which are not joined together to form a RING (*noun* 17).

open cheque ▻ *noun* **1** a cheque that is not made out for a stated amount. **2** *formerly* an uncrossed cheque.

open circuit ▻ *noun* an electrical circuit that has been disrupted such that no current flow exits. Compare SHORT CIRCUIT.

open cluster ▻ *noun, astron* a cluster of several hundred to several thousand relatively young stars that are usually loosely distributed. Compare GLOBULAR CLUSTER.

open court ▻ *noun, law* a court whose proceedings are carried out in public. Also *as adverb*. Compare IN CAMERA.

open day ▻ *noun* a day when members of the public can visit an institution (eg a school) that is usually closed to them.

open door ▻ *noun* **1** free unrestricted admission or access. **2** a policy or practice of allowing immigrants free access to a country. **3** a policy or practice of granting other nations equal trading opportunities with a country. ▻ *adj* (**open-door**) **1** said of policy or a system, etc: providing or allowing, etc freedom of access; unrestricted. **2** done openly or publicly.

open-ended ▻ *adj* **1** with an open end or ends. **2** said of a contract or arrangement, etc: with no limits or restrictions, eg of time, set in advance. **3** said of a question or debate, etc: not limited to strictly 'yes' or 'no' answers; allowing for free expression of opinion. • **open-endedness** *noun.*

opener ▻ *noun* **1** a device for opening something. Often *in compounds* □ *bottle-opener* □ *tin-opener.* **2** someone who opens something. **3** *cards* a player who opens the bidding or betting. **4** *cricket* either of the two batsmen who begins the batting for their team. **5** the first item on a programme. **6** an opening remark, etc. **7** (**openers**) *cards* cards that entitle the person holding them to open the betting. • **for openers** *colloq* to start with.

open-eyed ▻ *adj* **1** with the eyes wide open, eg in surprise or amazement. **2** fully aware; watchful.

open fire see FIRE

open fracture see COMPOUND FRACTURE

open-handed ▻ *adj* generous. • **open-handedly** *adverb.* • **open-handedness** *noun.*

open-hearted ▻ *adj* **1** honest, direct and hiding nothing; candid. **2** kind; generous. • **open-heartedly** *adverb.* • **open-heartedness** *noun.*

open-hearth process ▻ *noun, metallurgy* a traditional steelmaking process in which hot flames heat a shallow open hearth containing pig iron, malleable scrap iron and a flux, in a furnace with a low roof.

open-heart surgery ▻ *noun* surgery performed on a heart that has been stopped and opened up while the blood circulation is maintained by a heart-lung machine.

open house ▻ *noun* the state of being willing to welcome and entertain visitors at any time □ *keep open house.*

opening ▻ *noun* **1** the act of making or becoming open. **2** a hole or gap, especially one that can serve as a passageway. **3** a beginning or first stage of something. **4** *theat* the first performance of a play or opera, etc. **5** *chess* a recognized sequence of moves played at the beginning of a game. **6** an opportunity or chance. **7** a vacancy. **8** *law* a preliminary statement about a legal case made by counsel before witnesses are called. **9** the two pages that are exposed together when a book, etc is opened. **10** *chiefly US* an area of ground in a forest, etc in which there are very few or no trees. *Brit equivalent* CLEARING. ▻ *adj* relating to or forming an opening; first □ *opening night at the opera* □ *opening batsman*.

opening time ▻ *noun* the time at which a public house, bar or hotel, etc can legally begin to sell alcoholic drinks.

open learning ▻ *noun* a system of education based on independent or part-time study, etc rather than on formally taught classes.

open letter ▻ *noun* a letter, especially one of protest, addressed to a particular person or organization, etc but intended to be made public, eg through publication in a newspaper or magazine.

openly see under OPEN

open market ▻ *noun* a market in which buyers and sellers are allowed to compete without restriction.

open marriage and **open relationship** ▻ *noun* a marriage or relationship in which the partners agree that each of them may have sexual relationships with other people. ⌚ 1970s.

open-minded ▻ *adj* willing to consider or receive new ideas; unprejudiced. • **open-mindedly** *adverb*. • **open-mindedness** *noun*.

open-mouthed ▻ *adj* **1** with an open mouth, especially in surprise or amazement. **2** greedy. **3** clamorous.

openness see under OPEN

open-plan ▻ *adj* said of a building or office, etc: with few internal walls and with large undivided rooms.

open prison ▻ *noun* a prison which allows prisoners who are considered to be neither dangerous nor violent greater freedom of movement than in normal prisons.

open question ▻ *noun* a matter that is undecided; a question on which differences of opinion are allowable.

open relationship see OPEN MARRIAGE

open sandwich ▻ *noun* a sandwich without a slice of bread on top.

open season ▻ *noun* **1** a specified period of the year in which particular animals, birds or fish, etc may be legally killed for sport. **2** *colloq* a period during which there are no restrictions on a particular activity.

open secret ▻ *noun* something that is supposedly a secret but that is in fact widely known.

open sesame ▻ *noun* a means of gaining access to something which is otherwise out of one's reach. ⌚ 19c: the magical words by which, in the story of Ali Baba and the Forty Thieves (from the *Arabian Nights' Entertainments*), the door of the robbers' den was made to open.

open set ▻ *noun, math* a set which excludes the limits that define that set. Compare CLOSED SET.

open shop ▻ *noun* a firm or business, etc that does not oblige its employees to belong to a trade union. See also CLOSED SHOP.

open side *rugby* ▻ *noun* the part of the field between the scrum, etc and the farther touch-line. ▻ *adj* (**open-side**) during scrums, etc: positioned in that part of the field.

open-skies or **open-sky** ▻ *adj, military* said of system or policy: **1** that allows for reciprocal freedom for aerial inspection of military establishments, etc. **2** that allows aircraft of any nation to fly over a particular territory.

open stage ▻ *noun, theat* a stage that is in the same space as the auditorium, especially a raised platform built against one wall of the auditorium, surrounded on three sides by the audience.

open syllable ▻ *noun, phonetics* a syllable ending in a vowel. Compare CLOSED SYLLABLE.

open-toe and **open-toed** ▻ *adj* said of a shoe or sandal: without a covering (on the upper) for the toes.

open-top and **open-topped** ▻ *adj* said especially of a vehicle: without a top or a fixed top.

the Open University ▻ *noun* in the UK: a university founded in 1969 that broadcasts lectures by TV and radio, holds summer schools and awards degrees to mature students who study mainly by correspondence.

open verdict ▻ *noun, law* a verdict given by the coroner's jury at the end of an inquest that death has occurred, but without giving details of whether it was suicide, accidental or murder, etc.

openwork ▻ *noun* work in cloth, metal or wood, etc constructed so as to have gaps or holes in it, used especially for decoration.

opera¹ /ˈɒpərə/ ▻ *noun* (***operas***) **1** a dramatic work set to music, in which the singers are usually accompanied by an orchestra. **2** the score or libretto, etc of such a work. **3** operas as an art-form. **4** a theatre where opera is performed. **5** a company that performs opera. • **operatic** /ɒpəˈratɪk/ *adj* **1** relating to or like opera. **2** dramatic or overly theatrical; exaggerated. • **operatically** *adverb*. ⌚ 17c: Italian, from Latin, meaning 'work' or 'a work', from *opus* work.

opera² *plural of* OPUS

operable and **operability** see under OPERATE

opera buffa /ˈɒpərə ˈbuːfə/ ▻ *noun* (***operas buffa***) comic opera in the form that developed in Italy in the 18c, characterized by a less formal style, lighter subject matter, and characters and plot drawn from everyday life. ⌚ 19c: Italian, meaning 'comic opera'.

opéra comique /ˈɒpərə kɒˈmiːk/ ▻ *noun* (***opéras comiques*** /ˈɒpərə kɒˈmiːk/) a type of French opera, originally humorous and later also romantic or tragic, with some spoken dialogue. ⌚ 18c: French, meaning 'comic opera'.

opera glass and **opera glasses** ▻ *noun* small binoculars used at the theatre or opera, etc.

opera hat ▻ *noun* a man's collapsible top hat.

opera house ▻ *noun* a theatre specially built for the performance of opera.

operand /ˈɒpərand/ ▻ *noun, math, logic* a quantity on which an OPERATION (sense 7) is performed. ⌚ 19c: from Latin *operandum*, from *operari* to work.

operant /ˈɒpərənt/ *formal or technical* ▻ *adj* operative; producing effects. ▻ *noun* **1** someone or something that operates; an operator. **2** *psychol* behaviour that is spontaneous as opposed to being a response to stimulus. ⌚ 15c.

opera seria /— ˈsɪərɪə/ ▻ *noun* (***operas seria***) a type of opera common in the late 17c and throughout most of the 18c, characterized by its formality, elaborate arias, and use of noble, often classical or mythological, themes. ⌚ 19c: Italian, meaning 'serious opera'.

operate /ˈɒpəreɪt/ ▻ *verb* (***operated, operating***) **1** *intr* to function or work. **2** to make (a machine, etc) function or work; to control its functioning. **3** (*usually* **operate on something**) *intr* to produce an effect or have an influence on it. **4** to manage, control or direct (a business, etc). **5** (*usually* **operate on someone**) *intr* to perform a surgical operation on them. **6** *intr* to perform military, naval or police, etc operations. • **operable** *adj* **1** *medicine* said of a disease or injury, etc: that can be treated by surgery. **2** that can be operated. • **operability** *noun*. ⌚ 17c: from Latin *operari, operatus* to work.

operatic and **operatically** see under OPERA¹

operating system ▻ *noun, computing* (abbreviation **OS**) a software system that controls all the main activities of a computer.

operating table ▻ *noun* a special table on which surgery is performed.

operating theatre and **operating room** ▻ *noun* the specially equipped room in a hospital, etc where surgical operations are performed.

operation /ɒpəˈreɪʃən/ ▻ *noun* **1** an act, method or process of working or operating. **2** the state of working or being active □ *The factory is not yet in operation.* **3** an activity; something done. **4** an action or series of actions which have a particular effect. **5** *medicine* any surgical procedure that is performed in order to treat a damaged or diseased part of the body (often shortened to **op**). **6** (*often* **operations**) one of a series of military, naval or police, etc actions, usually involving a large number of people, performed as part of a much larger plan (often shortened to **op**). **7** *math* a specific procedure, such as addition or multiplication, whereby one numerical value is derived from another value or values. **8** *computing* a series of actions that are specified by a single computer instruction. **9** a financial transaction. ◷ 14c: French, meaning 'action' or 'deed'.

operational ▻ *adj* **1** relating to an operation or operations. **2** able or ready to work or perform an intended function. **3** *military* ready for use in, or already involved in, operations. **4** *math* relating to or using operators. **5** *philos* relating to or in accordance with operationalism. • **operationally** *adverb.* ◷ 1920s.

operationalism or **operationism** ▻ *noun, philos* the theory that defines scientific concepts by means of the operations used to prove or determine them. • **operationalist** or **operationist** *noun, adj.* ◷ 1930s.

operational research and **operations research** ▻ *noun* (abbreviation **OR**) the analysis of problems in business and industry in order to bring about more efficient work practices. ◷ 1940s.

operative /ˈɒpərətɪv/ ▻ *adj* **1** working; in action; having an effect. **2** said of a word: especially important or significant □ *'Must' is the operative word.* **3** relating to a surgical operation. ▻ *noun* **1** a worker, especially one with special skills. **2** *N Amer, especially US* a private detective. • **operatively** *adj.* • **operativeness** *noun.*

operator ▻ *noun* **1** someone who operates a machine or apparatus. **2** someone who operates a telephone switchboard, connecting calls, etc. **3** someone who runs a business. **4** *math* any symbol used to indicate that a particular mathematical operation is to be carried out, eg × which shows that two numbers are to be multiplied. **5** *colloq* a calculating, shrewd and manipulative person.

operculum /oʊˈpɜːkjʊləm/ ▻ *noun* (*plural* ***opercula***) **1** *zool* **a** in some gastropods: a horny plate that covers the opening of the shell; **b** in bony fishes: a flap that protects the gills. **2** *bot* a cover or lid. • **opercular** *adj.* • **operculate** *adj* having an operculum. ◷ 18c: Latin, meaning 'lid' or 'covering', from *operire* to cover.

operetta /ɒpəˈrɛtə/ ▻ *noun* (***operettas***) a short light opera, with spoken dialogue and often dancing. • **operettist** *noun* a composer of operettas. ◷ 18c: Italian, a diminutive of OPERA[1].

ophidian /ɒˈfɪdɪən/ *zool* ▻ *adj* **1** belonging or relating to the suborder of reptiles **Ophidia** that includes snakes. **2** relating to snakes; snakelike. ▻ *noun* a snake. ◷ 19c: from Greek *ophis* snake.

ophio- /ɒfɪoʊ, ɒfɪˈɒ/ or (before a vowel) **ophi-** ▻ *combining form, signifying* snake. ◷ From Greek *ophis* snake.

ophite /ˈɒfaɪt/ ▻ *noun, geol* igneous rock in which large silicate crystals completely enclose smaller FELDSPARS. • **ophitic** /ɒˈfɪtɪk/ *adj.* ◷ 17c: from Latin *ophites*, from Greek *ophis* a snake, because of its serpentine markings.

ophthalmia /ɒfˈθalmɪə/ ▻ *noun, pathol* inflammation of the eye, especially of the conjunctiva. • **ophthalmic** *adj* pertaining or relating to the eye. ◷ 16c: Latin, from Greek *ophthalmos* eye.

ophthalmic optician ▻ *noun* an optician qualified both to examine the eyes and test vision, and to prescribe, make and sell glasses or contact lenses. Also called OPTOMETRIST.

ophthalmo- /ɒfθalmoʊ, ɒfθalˈmɒ/ or (before a vowel usually) **ophthalm-** ▻ *combining form, signifying* eye. ◷ From Greek *ophthalmos* eye.

ophthalmology /ɒfθalˈmɒlədʒɪ/ ▻ *noun, medicine* the study, diagnosis and treatment of diseases and defects of the eye. • **ophthalmological** *adj.* • **ophthalmologist** *noun.* ◷ 19c.

ophthalmoscope ▻ *noun* a device that is used to examine the interior of the eye, by directing a reflected beam of light through the pupil. • **ophthalmoscopic** *adj.* ◷ 19c.

opiate ▻ *noun* /ˈoʊpɪət/ **1** any of a group of drugs containing or derived from opium, eg morphine, heroin or codeine, that depress the central nervous system, and can be used as steroid ANALGESICS. **2** anything that dulls physical or mental sensation. ▻ *adj* soporific; sleep-inducing. ▻ *verb* /ˈoʊpɪeɪt/ (***opiated***, ***opiating***) **1** to treat or put someone to sleep with opium. **2** to dull or deaden (sensation, etc). ◷ 16c: from Latin *opiatus*, from *opium* OPIUM.

opine /oʊˈpaɪn/ ▻ *verb* (***opined***, ***opining***) *formal* to suppose or express something as an opinion. ◷ 16c: from Latin *opinari* to think.

opinion /əˈpɪnjən/ ▻ *noun* **1** a belief or judgement which seems likely to be true, but which is not based on proof. **2** (*usually* **opinion on** or **about something**) what one thinks about it. **3** a professional judgement given by an expert □ *medical opinion.* **4** estimation or appreciation □ *has a high opinion of himself.* • **a matter of opinion** a matter about which people have different opinions. • **be of the opinion that ...** to think or believe that .... ◷ 13c: from Latin *opinio* belief, from *opinari* to believe.

opinionated ▻ *adj* with very strong opinions that one refuses or is very unwilling to change; stubborn. • **opinionatedly** *adverb.* • **opinionatedness** *noun.*

opinion poll see under POLL

opium /ˈoʊpɪəm/ ▻ *noun* **1** a highly addictive narcotic drug extracted from the dried milky juice of the unripe seed capsules of the **opium poppy**, used in medicine to bring sleep and relieve pain. **2** anything which has a soothing, calming or dulling effect on people's minds. ◷ 14c: Latin, from Greek *opion* poppy juice or opium, diminutive of *opos* vegetable juice.

opossum /əˈpɒsəm/ ▻ *noun* (***opossums*** or ***opossum***) **1** any of several small tree-dwelling American marsupials with thick fur, an OPPOSABLE thumb on each hindfoot and a hairless prehensile tail. **2** any of various similar marsupials, native to Australasia, such as the PHALANGER. Also called **possum**. ◷ 17c: from Algonquian *opassom*, from *op* white + *assom* dog or doglike animal.

opp. ▻ *abbreviation* **1** opposed. **2** opposite.

opponent /əˈpoʊnənt/ ▻ *noun* someone who belongs to the opposing side in an argument, contest or battle, etc. ▻ *adj* **1** opposed; contrary. **2** opposite in position; opposing. • **opponency** *noun.* ◷ 16c: from Latin *opponens*, *opponentis* setting before or against, from *op-* in the way of + *ponere* to place.

opportune /ˈɒpətjuːn/ ▻ *adj* **1** said of an action: happening at a time which is suitable, proper or correct. **2** said of a time: suitable; proper. • **opportunely** *adverb.* • **opportuneness** *noun.* ◷ 15c: from Latin *opportunus*, from *ob-* before + *portus* harbour, used originally of a wind blowing towards a harbour.

opportunist ▻ *noun* someone whose actions and opinions are governed by the particular events and circumstances, etc of the moment rather than being based on settled principles. ▻ *adj* referring to such actions or opinions. • **opportunism** *noun.* ◷ 19c.

opportunistic /ɒpətjʊˈnɪstɪk/ ▻ *adj* **1** relating to, characterized, or determined by opportunism. **2** *pathol* said of an infection: not affecting healthy people but attacking those whose immune system is weakened by drugs or disease.

opportunity /ɒpəˈtjuːnɪtɪ/ ▷ *noun* (***opportunities***) **1** an occasion offering a possibility; a chance. **2** favourable or advantageous conditions. ⓒ 16c: from Latin *opportunitas*, from *opportunus* OPPORTUNE.

opportunity cost ▷ *noun, econ* the real cost of acquiring any item, which amounts to the value of an alternative item which is foregone in order to acquire the chosen item.

opposable /əˈpoʊzəbəl/ ▷ *adj* said of a digit, especially the thumb: able to be placed in a position so that it faces and can touch the ends of the other digits of the same hand or foot. • **opposability** *noun*. ⓒ 19c.

oppose /əˈpoʊz/ ▷ *verb* (***opposed, opposing***) **1** to resist or fight against someone or something by force or argument. **2** *intr* to object. **3** *intr* to compete in a game or contest, etc against another person or team; to act in opposition. **4** to place opposite or in contrast to something, so as to counterbalance. • **opposer** *noun*. • **opposing** *adj*. • **as opposed to** in contrast to; as distinct from. ⓒ 14c: from French *opposer*, from Latin *opponere* to set before or against.

opposite /ˈɒpəzɪt/ (abbreviation **opp.**) ▷ *adj* **1** placed or being on the other side of, or at the other end of, a real or imaginary line or space. **2** facing in a directly different direction □ *opposite sides of the coin.* **3** completely or diametrically different. **4** referring to something that is the other of a matching or contrasting pair □ *the opposite sex.* **5** *bot* **a** said of leaves: arranged in pairs on a stem, so that the two members of a pair are exactly opposite each other; **b** said of flower parts: on the same radius. **6** *math* said of a side of a triangle: facing a specified angle. ▷ *noun* an opposite person or thing. ▷ *adverb* in or into an opposite position □ *live opposite.* ▷ *prep* **1** (*also* **opposite to someone** or **something**) in a position across from and facing them or it □ *a house opposite the station.* **2** said of an actor: in a role which complements that taken by another actor; co-starring with them □ *played opposite Olivier.* • **oppositely** *adverb*. • **oppositeness** *noun*. ⓒ 14c: French, from Latin *opponere*, *oppositum*; see OPPONENT.

opposite number ▷ *noun* someone with an equivalent position or job in another company or country, etc; a counterpart.

opposition /ɒpəˈzɪʃən/ ▷ *noun* **1** the act of resisting or fighting against someone or something by force or argument. **2** the state of being hostile or in conflict. **3** a person or group of people who are opposed to something. **4** (*usually* **the Opposition**) a political party which opposes the party in power. Also (**opposition**) *as adj*. **5** an act of opposing or being placed opposite. **6** *logic* a difference of quantity or quality between two propositions with the same subject and predicate. **7** *astron, astrol* the position of a planet or star when it is directly opposite another, especially the Sun, as seen from the Earth. • **oppositional** *adj*.

oppress /əˈprɛs/ ▷ *verb* (***oppresses, oppressed, oppressing***) **1** to govern with cruelty and injustice. **2** to worry, trouble or make someone anxious; to weigh heavily upon them. **3** to distress or afflict someone. • **oppression** *noun*. • **oppressor** *noun*. ⓒ 14c: from Latin *oppressare*, from *op-* against + *premere, pressum* to press.

oppressive ▷ *adj* **1** cruel, tyrannical and unjust □ *an oppressive regime.* **2** causing worry or mental distress; weighing heavily on the mind. **3** said of the weather: heavy, hot and sultry. • **oppressively** *adverb*. • **oppressiveness** *noun*. ⓒ 17c.

opprobrious /əˈproʊbrɪəs/ ▷ *adj* **1** insulting, abusive or severely critical. **2** shameful; infamous. • **opprobriously** *adverb*. ⓒ 14c.

opprobrium /əˈproʊbrɪəm/ ▷ *noun* (*plural* in sense 2 ***opprobria***) **1** public shame, disgrace or loss of favour; infamy. **2** anything that brings such shame or disgrace, etc. ⓒ 17c: Latin, from *op-* against + *probrum* reproach or disgrace.

oppugn /əˈpjuːn/ ▷ *verb* (***oppugned, oppugning***) to call into question; to dispute. • **oppugner** *noun*. ⓒ 15c: from Latin *oppugnare*, from *op-* against + *pugnare* to fight.

opt ▷ *verb* (***opted, opting***) *intr* (*usually* **opt for something** or **to do something**) to decide between several possibilities; to choose. ⓒ 19c: from French *opter*, from Latin *optare* to choose or wish.

■ **opt in** to choose to take part or participate in something.

■ **opt out 1** to choose not to take part in something. **2** said of a school or hospital: to leave local authority control and become, respectively, a grant maintained school or a hospital trust. See also OPT-OUT.

optative /ˈɒptətɪv/ ▷ *adj* **1 a** characterized by desire or choice; **b** expressing a desire or wish. **2** *grammar* denoting or relating to a mood expressing a desire or wish. ▷ *noun, grammar* **1** the optative mood. **2** a verb in this mood. • **optatively** *adverb*. ⓒ 16c.

Optic /ˈɒptɪk/ ▷ *noun* (*also* **optic**) *trademark* a device attached to the neck of an inverted bottle for measuring the amount poured out, especially for measuring amounts of alcohol. ⓒ 1920s.

optic /ˈɒptɪk/ ▷ *adj* **1** relating to the eye or vision. **2** OPTICAL. ▷ *noun, jocular* the eye. ⓒ 16c: from Greek *optikos*, from *optos* seen or visible.

optical /ˈɒptɪkəl/ ▷ *adj* **1** relating to sight or to what one sees. **2** relating to light or optics. **3** said of a lens: designed to improve vision. • **optically** *adverb*. ⓒ 16c: from OPTIC.

optical activity ▷ *noun, chem* the ability of certain chemical compounds, when placed in the path of a beam of polarized light, to rotate the plane of polarization of the light to the left or to the right.

Optical Art see OP ART

optical character reader ▷ *noun, computing* (abbreviation **OCR**) a light-sensitive device for inputting data directly on to a computer by means of optical character recognition. • **optical character reading** *noun*. ⓒ 1960s.

optical character recognition ▷ *noun, computing* (abbreviation **OCR**) the scanning, identification and recording of printed characters by a photoelectric device attached to a computer. ⓒ 1960s.

optical fibre ▷ *noun, telecomm* a thin flexible strand of glass that transmits energy in the form of light waves, used to convey information and nowadays used extensively in modern communications systems, ie in the cables for telephones, cable TV, etc. Compare FIBRE OPTICS. ⓒ 1960s.

optical illusion ▷ *noun* **1** something that has an appearance which deceives the eye. **2** a misunderstanding caused by such a deceptive appearance.

optically see under OPTICAL

optician /ɒpˈtɪʃən/ ▷ *noun* **1** (*also* **dispensing optician**) someone who fits and sells glasses and contact lenses but is not qualified to prescribe them. **2** *loosely* an OPHTHALMIC OPTICIAN. See also OPTOMETRIST. ⓒ 17c: from French *opticien*, from Latin *optica* optics.

optic nerve ▷ *noun, anatomy* in vertebrates: the second cranial nerve, responsible for the sense of vision, which transmits information from the retina of the eye to the visual cortex of the brain.

optical brightener ▷ *noun* any of a number of fluorescent substances that increase the whiteness or brightness of a textile.

optics /ˈɒptɪks/ ▻ *singular noun, physics* the study of light (especially visible light, but also ultraviolet and infra-red light), including the phenomena associated with its generation, propagation and detection, and its practical applications in a range of devices and systems.

optimal /ˈɒptɪməl/ ▻ *adj* most favourable; optimum. ● **optimally** *adverb*. ● **optimalization** *noun*. ◎ 19c: from Latin *optimus* best.

optimism /ˈɒptɪmɪzəm/ ▻ *noun* **1** the tendency to take a bright, hopeful view of things and expect the best possible outcome. **2** *philos* the belief that we live in the best of all possible worlds. **3** the theory that good will ultimately triumph over evil. Compare PESSIMISM. ● **optimistic** *adj*. ● **optimistically** *adverb*. ◎ 18c: from French *optimisme*, from Latin *optimus* best.

optimist ▻ *noun* **1** someone who has a bright and hopeful nature. **2** someone who follows the doctrine of optimism.

optimize or **optimise** /ˈɒptɪmaɪz/ ▻ *verb* (***optimized***, ***optimizing***) **1** to make the most or best of (a particular situation or opportunity, etc). **2** to make the most efficient use of something, especially by analysing and planning. **3** *intr* to be optimistic or act optimistically. **4** *intr* to become optimal. **5** *computing* to prepare or modify (a computer system or program) so as to achieve the greatest possible efficiency. ● **optimization** *noun*. ◎ 19c.

optimum /ˈɒptɪməm/ ▻ *noun* (***optimums*** or ***optima*** /-mə/) the condition, situation, amount or level, etc that is the most favourable or gives the best results. ▻ *adj* best or most favourable. ◎ 19c: Latin, neuter of *optimus* best.

option /ˈɒpʃən/ ▻ *noun* **1** an act of choosing. **2** that which is or which may be chosen. **3** the power or right to choose ▫ ***You have no option.*** **4** *commerce* the exclusive right to buy or sell something, eg stocks, at a fixed price and within a specified time-limit. ▻ *verb* (***optioned***, ***optioning***) *chiefly US* **1** to buy or sell something under option. **2** to have or grant an option on something. ● **keep** or **leave one's options open** to avoid making a choice or committing oneself to a particular course of action. ● **soft option** the easiest choice or course of action. ◎ 16c: French, or from Latin *optio*, from *optare* to choose.

optional ▻ *adj* left to choice; not compulsory. ● **optionally** *adverb*.

optional extra ▻ *noun* an available accessory, that is useful or desirable, but not essential.

optometer /ɒpˈtɒmɪtə(r)/ ▻ *noun, ophthalmol* a device for testing vision. ◎ 18c.

optometry /ɒpˈtɒmətrɪ/ ▻ *noun, ophthalmol* **1** the science of vision and eyecare. **2** the practice of examining the eyes and vision. **3** the prescription and provision of glasses and contact lenses, etc for the improvement of vision. ● **optometric** *adj*. ● **optometrist** *noun* an OPHTHALMIC OPTICIAN. ◎ 19c: from Greek *optos* seen.

optophone ▻ *noun* /ˈɒptəfoun/ a device that, by translating printed characters into arbitrary sounds, enables a blind person to interpret printed type. ◎ Early 20c.

opt-out ▻ *noun* **1 a** the action or an act of opting out of something; **b** said of a school or hospital: the act of leaving local authority control. **2** *TV, radio* a programme broadcast by a regional station in place of the main network transmission. See also OPT. ◎ 1990s in sense 1b; 1960s in sense 2.

opulent /ˈɒpjʊlənt/ ▻ *adj* **1** rich; wealthy. **2** luxurious. **3** abundant. ● **opulence** *noun*. ● **opulently** *adverb*. ◎ 16c: from Latin *opulentus*, from *opes* wealth or resources.

opuntia /ouˈpʌnʃɪə/ ▻ *noun* (***opuntias***) a cactus of genus **Opuntia**, especially the PRICKLY PEAR. ◎ 17c: Latin, meaning 'of Opus', from Greek *Opous*, the name of a town of Locris where Pliny said it grew.

opus /ˈoupəs/ ▻ *noun* (***opuses*** or ***opera*** /ˈɒpərə/) (abbreviation **op.**) an artistic work, especially a musical composition, often used with a number to show the order in which a composer's works were written or catalogued. ◎ 18c: Latin, meaning 'work'.

OR ▻ *abbreviation* **1** operational research; operations research. **2** *US state* Oregon. Also written **Ore.** or **Oreg.** **3** *military* other ranks.

or[1] /ɔː(r)/ ▻ *conj* used to introduce: **1** alternatives ▫ ***red or pink or blue.*** **2** a synonym or explanation ▫ ***a puppy or young dog.*** **3** an afterthought ▫ ***She's laughing — or is she crying?*** **4** the second part of an indirect question ▫ ***Ask her whether she thinks he'll come or not.*** **5** because if not; or else ▫ ***Run or you'll be late.*** **6** and not ▫ ***never joins in or helps.*** ● **or else 1** otherwise. **2** *colloq* expressing a threat or warning ▫ ***Give it to me or else!*** ● **or rather** or to be more accurate ▫ ***He went too, or rather I heard he did.*** ● **or so** about; roughly ▫ ***been there two hours or so.*** ◎ 13c: a contraction of OTHER.

or[2] /ɔː(r)/ ▻ *noun, heraldry* a gold colour. ◎ 16c: French, from Latin *aurum* gold.

-or ▻ *suffix, forming nouns, denoting* a person or thing that performs an action or function ▫ ***actor*** ▫ ***elevator.*** ◎ Latin.

ora *plural of* OS[2]

Oracle /ˈɒrəkəl/ ▻ *noun, trademark* a former TELETEXT service run by the Independent Broadcasting Authority. ◎ 1970s: from *o*ptional *r*eception of *a*nnouncements by *c*oded *l*ine *e*lectronics.

oracle /ˈɒrəkəl/ ▻ *noun* **1** in ancient Greece or Rome: a holy place where a god was believed to give advice and prophecy. **2** a priest or priestess at an oracle, through whom the god was believed to speak. **3** the usually mysterious or ambiguous advice or prophecy given at an oracle. **4 a** someone who is believed to have great wisdom or be capable of prophesying the future; **b** a statement made by such a person. ● **oracular** /ɒˈrakjʊlə(r)/ *adj* **1** relating to or like an oracle. **2** difficult to interpret; mysterious and ambiguous. **3** prophetic. ◎ 14c: from Latin *oraculum*, from *orare* to speak or pray.

oracy /ˈɔːrəsɪ/ ▻ *noun* the ability to express oneself coherently and to communicate freely with others by word of mouth. ◎ 1960s: from ORAL, modelled on *literacy*.

oral /ˈɔːrəl/ ▻ *adj* **1** spoken; not written. **2** relating to or used in the mouth. **3** said of a medicine or drug, etc: taken in through the mouth ▫ ***oral contraceptive.*** **4** *psychol* relating to a supposed stage of infant development, when satisfaction is obtained by sucking. ▻ *noun* a spoken test or examination. ● **orally** *adverb*. ◎ 17c: from Latin *oralis*, from *os*, *oris* mouth.

oral

A word often confused with this one is **aural**.

oral history ▻ *noun* the collection and study of information about events and social conditions, etc of the past, obtained by interviewing and tape-recording people who experienced them.

oral rehydration therapy ▻ *noun* (abbreviation **ORT**) the treatment of dehydration (caused by diarrhoea, etc) by drinks of a water, glucose and salt solution.

oral sex ▻ *noun* sexual relations involving the use of the mouth, tongue, etc to stimulate the genitals of one's partner.

Orange /ˈɒrɪndʒ/ ▻ *adj* **1** *historical* relating to the family of the princes of Orange, a former principality in S France from 11c, passing by an heiress to the house of Nassau in 1531, the territory ceded to France in 1713. **2** relating to or favouring the Orangemen (see ORANGEMAN).

orange /ˈɒrɪndʒ/ ▻ *noun* **1** a round citrus fruit with a tough reddish-yellow outer rind or peel enclosing membranous segments filled with sweet or sharp-tasting juicy flesh that is rich in vitamin C. The **sweet orange** is eaten raw or squeezed for its juice, and the bitter **Seville orange** or **bitter orange** is used to make marmalade. **2** the evergreen tree, cultivated in most subtropical regions, that bears this fruit and also ORANGE BLOSSOM. **3** any of various similar trees or plants, or their fruits. **4** a reddish-yellow colour like that of the skin of an orange. **5** a pigment or dye of this colour. **6** an orange-flavoured drink. ▻ *adj* **1** orange-coloured. **2** orange-flavoured. • **orangey** *adj*. • **orangish** *adj*. ⌚ 14c: ultimately from Sanskrit *naranga*.

orangeade /ɒrɪnˈdʒeɪd/ ▻ *noun* an orange-flavoured drink, usually fizzy.

orange blossom ▻ *noun* the fragrant white blossom of the orange tree, traditionally worn by brides, and used as a source of essential oils for perfumery.

Orangeman ▻ *noun* a member of a society founded in 1795 to support Protestantism in Ireland. ⌚ 18c: from William of Orange, later William III of Great Britain and Ireland.

Orange Order ▻ *noun* the society to which an ORANGEMAN belongs.

orange pekoe ▻ *noun* a type of high quality black tea made from very small leaves, grown in India and Sri Lanka. ⌚ 19c.

orangery /ˈɒrɪndʒərɪ/ ▻ *noun* (***orangeries***) a greenhouse or other building in which orange trees can be grown in cool climates. ⌚ 17c.

orange squash ▻ *noun* an orange drink made from oranges, water and sugar, etc, usually in a highly concentrated form and drunk diluted with water.

orange stick ▻ *noun* a small wooden stick, originally of orangewood, used for manicuring the fingernails.

orange-tip ▻ *noun* any of various butterflies with an orange patch near the tip of the forewing.

orangey and **orangish** see under ORANGE

orang-utan /əˈraŋətan, ɔːˈraŋʊtan/ or **orang-outang** /-taŋ/ ▻ *noun* the only tree-dwelling great ape, found in tropical forests in Borneo and Sumatra, with long reddish hair and characteristic long strong arms. ⌚ 17c: from Malay *oranghutan*, from *orang* man + *hutan* forest, but said not to be applied by the Malays to the ape.

orate /ɔːˈreɪt/ ▻ *verb* (***orated, orating***) *intr, jocular or derog* **1** to make an oration. **2** to make a pompous or lengthy speech. ⌚ 17c.

oration /ɔːˈreɪʃən/ ▻ *noun* a formal or ceremonial public speech delivered in dignified language. ⌚ 14c: from Latin *oratio*, from *orare* to speak or pray.

orator /ˈɒrətə(r)/ ▻ *noun* **1** someone who is skilled in persuading, moving or exciting people through public speech. **2** someone who gives an oration. ⌚ 15c.

oratorial ▻ *adj* **1** relating to or characteristic of an orator. **2** relating to an oratorio.

oratorical /ɒrəˈtɒrɪkəl/ ▻ *adj* **1** relating to or characteristic of an orator. **2 a** relating to or like ORATORY², especially in using rhetoric; **b** given to using oratory. • **oratorically** *adverb*. ⌚ 16c.

oratorio /ɒrəˈtɔːrɪoʊ/ ▻ *noun* (***oratorios***) **1** a musical composition, usually based on a Biblical or religious theme or story, sung by soloists and a chorus accompanied by an orchestra, but with no scenery, costumes or acting. **2** this type of musical composition or performance as a genre. ⌚ 17c: Italian, from Latin *oratorium* ORATORY¹, so called because the form developed from the musical services held in the church of the Oratory of St Philip Neri in Rome.

oratory¹ /ˈɒrətərɪ/ ▻ *noun* (***oratories***) a chapel or small place set aside for private prayer. ⌚ 14c: from Latin *oratorium*, from *orare* to pray or plead.

oratory² /ˈɒrətərɪ/ ▻ *noun* **1** the art public speaking; rhetoric. **2** rhetorical style or language. ⌚ 16c: from Latin *ars oratoria* the art of public speaking.

orb ▻ *noun* **1** a globe with a cross on top that is decorated with jewels and is carried as part of a monarch's regalia. **2** anything in the shape of a globe or sphere. **3** *poetic* a star, the Sun or a planet. **4** *poetic* the eye or eyeball. ▻ *verb* (***orbed, orbing***) *poetic* **1** to form something into a circle or sphere. **2** to encircle something. ⌚ 16c: from Latin *orbis* a circle.

orbicular /ɔːˈbɪkjʊlə(r)/ ▻ *adj* **1** approximately circular or spherical. **2** *geol* with the component minerals crystallized in layers of spheroidal aggregates (rhythmic crystallization). ⌚ 15c.

orbiculate /ɔːˈbɪkjʊlət/ ▻ *adj, bot, zool* rounded; orbicular. ⌚ 18c.

orbit /ˈɔːbɪt/ ▻ *noun* **1** *astron* in space: the elliptical path of one celestial body around another, eg the Earth's orbit around the Sun, or of an artificial satellite or spacecraft, etc around a celestial body. **2** *physics* the path of an electron around the nucleus of an atom. **3** a sphere of influence or action. **4** *anatomy* in the skull of vertebrates: one of the two bony hollows in which the eyeball is situated; an eye socket. **5** *zool* the area surrounding the eye of a bird or insect. ▻ *verb* (***orbited, orbiting***) **1** said of a celestial body, or a spacecraft, etc: to circle (the Earth or another planet, etc) in space. **2** said of an aircraft: to fly in a circle around a given point. **3** *intr* to move in or go into orbit. **4** to put (a spacecraft, etc) into orbit. • **orbiter** *noun* a spacecraft or satellite that orbits the Earth or another planet but does not land on it. ⌚ 1940s as *verb*; 16c as *noun*: from Latin *orbitus*, from *orbis* circle.

orbital ▻ *noun, chem* any region of space outside the nucleus of an atom or molecule where there is a high probability of finding an electron. ▻ *adj* **1** relating to or going round in an orbit. **2** said of a road: forming a complete circle or loop round a city.

orc ▻ *noun* **1** any of various whales or ferocious sea creatures, eg the killer whale. **2** an ogre. ⌚ 16c: in sense 1 from French *orque* or Latin *orca*; in sense 2 perhaps from Latin *orcus* hell and Italian *orco* demon.

Orcadian /ɔːˈkeɪdɪən/ ▻ *noun* someone who lives or was born in the Orkney Islands, a group of islands lying off NE Scotland. ▻ *adj* belonging or relating to the Orkney Islands. ⌚ 17c: from Latin *Orcades* the Orkney Islands.

orchard /ˈɔːtʃəd/ ▻ *noun* **1** a garden or piece of land where fruit trees are grown. **2** a collection of cultivated fruit trees. ⌚ Anglo-Saxon *ortgeard*, from *ort* (representing Latin *hortus* garden) + *geard* a yard or enclosure.

orchestra /ˈɔːkɪstrə/ ▻ *noun* (***orchestras***) **1** a large group of instrumentalists who play together as an ensemble, led by a conductor, usually comprising four main sections, ie STRINGS, WOODWIND, BRASS and PERCUSSION. **2** *loosely* a small instrumental group, eg a group of musicians playing in a restaurant. **3** (*also* **orchestra pit**) the part of a theatre or opera house where the musicians sit, usually immediately in front of, or under the front part of, the stage. **4** (*also* **orchestral stalls**) the front stalls in a theatre. **5** in the ancient Greek theatre: a semicircular area in front of the stage where the chorus danced. **6** in the ancient Roman theatre: the area in front of the stage where the senators and other important people sat. • **orchestral** /ɔːˈkɛstrəl/ *adj*. • **orchestralist** *noun*. • **orchestrally** *adverb*. ⌚ 16c: Greek, from *orcheisthai* to dance.

orchestrate /ˈɔːkɪstreɪt/ ▻ *verb* (***orchestrated, orchestrating***) **1** to arrange, compose or score (a piece of music) for an orchestra. **2** to organize or arrange (elements of a plan or a situation, etc) so as to get the desired or best result. • **orchestration** *noun* **1** the process or technique of orchestrating music. **2** music which has been orchestrated. **3** the way in which something is orchestrated. • **orchestrator** *noun.* ⓒ 19c.

orchid /ˈɔːkɪd/ ▷ *noun* a perennial plant belonging to the family **Orchidaceae**, one of the largest families of flowering plants, containing about 30 000 species. Orchids are best known for their complex and exotic flowers, and for their highly sophisticated pollination mechanisms. ⓒ 19c: from Greek *orchis* testicle, so called because of the shape of its root-tubers.

orchil /ˈɔːtʃɪl/ or **orchilla** /ˈɔːtʃɪlə/ ▷ *noun* **1** a red or violet dye made from various lichens. **2** the lichen that yields it. Also called **archil** /ˈɑːtʃɪl/. ⓒ 15c.

ordain /ɔːˈdeɪn/ ▷ *verb* (***ordained***, ***ordaining***) **1** *Christianity* to appoint or admit someone as priest or vicar, etc; to confer holy orders on them. **2** to order, command or decree something formally. **3** *math* to destine, which shows that two numbers are to be multiplied. • **ordainer** *noun.* • **ordainment** *noun.* See also ORDINATION. ⓒ 13c: from Latin *ordinare*, from *ordo* order.

ordeal /ɔːˈdiːl, ˈɔːdiːl/ ▷ *noun* **1** a difficult, painful or testing experience. **2** *historical* a method of trial in which the accused person was subjected to physical danger from fire or water, etc, survival of which was taken as a sign from God of the person's innocence. ⓒ Anglo-Saxon *ordal* judgement or verdict.

order /ˈɔːdə(r)/ ▷ *noun* **1** a state in which everything is in its proper place; tidiness. **2** an arrangement of objects according to importance, value or position, etc. **3** a command, instruction or direction. **4** a state of peace and harmony in society, characterized by the absence of crime and the general obeying of laws. **5** the condition of being able to function properly □ *in working order.* **6** a social class or rank making up a distinct social group □ *the lower orders.* **7** a kind or sort □ *of the highest order.* **8** an instruction to a manufacturer, supplier or waiter, etc to provide something. **9** the goods or food, etc supplied. **10** an established system of society □ *a new world order.* **11** *biol* in taxonomy: any of the groups, eg *Carnivora* (the carnivores), into which a CLASS (sense 9) is divided and which is in turn subdivided into one or more families (see FAMILY sense 7). **12** *commerce* a written instruction to pay money. **13** the usual procedure followed at especially official meetings and during debates □ *a point of order.* **14** (**Order**) a religious community living according to a particular rule and bound by vows. Also called **religious order**. **15** any of the different grades of the Christian ministry. **16** (**orders**) HOLY ORDERS. **17** the specified form of a religious service □ *order of marriage.* **18** (**Order**) a group of people to which new members are admitted as a mark of honour or reward for services to the sovereign or country □ *Order of the British Empire.* **19** any of the five classical styles of architecture (DORIC, IONIC, CORINTHIAN, TUSCAN and COMPOSITE) characterized by the way a column and entablature are moulded and decorated. ▷ *verb* (***ordered***, ***ordering***) **1** to give a command to someone. **2** to command someone to go to a specified place □ *order the regiment to Germany.* **3** to instruct a manufacturer, supplier or waiter, etc to supply or provide something □ *ordered the fish.* **4** to arrange or regulate □ *order one's affairs.* **5** *intr* to give a command, request or order, especially to a waiter for food □ *ready to order.* ▷ *exclamation* (**Order! Order!**) a call for quiet, calm or proper behaviour to be restored, especially during a debate. • **a tall order** *colloq* a difficult or demanding job or task. • **call to order 1** to request calm or attention. **2** to declare a formal meeting open. • **in order 1** in accordance with the rules; properly arranged. **2** suitable or appropriate □ *Her conduct just isn't in order.* **3** in the correct sequence. • **in the order of something** approximately (the number specified). • **in order that** so that. • **in order to do something** so as to be able to do it. • **on order** said of goods: having been ordered but not yet supplied. • **out of order** not correct, proper or suitable. • **to order** according to a customer's particular or personal requirements. • **under orders** having been commanded or instructed (to do something). ⓒ 13c: from French *ordre*, from Latin *ordo*.

■ **order someone about** or **around** to give them orders continually and officiously.

■ **order someone off** *sport* to order a player to leave the field because of bad or illegal behaviour.

ordered ▷ *adj* **1** placed in order. **2** well organized or arranged.

orderly /ˈɔːdəlɪ/ ▷ *adj* **1** in good order; well arranged. **2** well behaved; quiet. ▷ *noun* (***orderlies***) **1** an attendant, usually without medical training, who does various jobs in a hospital, such as moving patients. **2** *military* a soldier who carries an officer's orders and messages. • **orderliness** *noun.* ⓒ 16c.

order of battle ▷ *noun* the positions adopted by soldiers or ships before a battle.

order of the day ▷ *noun* **1** an agenda, eg for a meeting or for business in Parliament. **2** something which is necessary, normal or fashionable at a given time.

order paper ▷ *noun* a programme showing the order of business, especially in Parliament.

ordinal /ˈɔːdɪnəl/ ▷ *noun* **1** a book containing the services for the ordination of ministers. **2** *RC Church* a service book. **3** (*also* **ordinal number**) a number which shows a position in a sequence, eg *first, second, third*, etc. See also CARDINAL NUMBER. ▷ *adj* **1** denoting a position in a sequence of numbers. **2** *biol* in animal or plant classification: relating to or characteristic of an ORDER (*noun* 11). ⓒ 14c.

ordinance /ˈɔːdɪnəns/ ▷ *noun* **1** a law, order or ruling. **2** an authorized religious ceremony. ⓒ 14c: from French *ordenance*, from Latin *ordinare* to ordain.

ordinand /ˈɔːdɪnand/ ▷ *noun* someone who is training to become a minister of the church; a candidate for ordination. ⓒ 19c.

ordinary /ˈɔːdɪnərɪ, ˈɔːdənrɪ/ ▷ *adj* **1** of the usual everyday kind; unexceptional. **2** plain; uninteresting. **3** *law* **a** said of a judge or jurisdiction: by virtue of office, not by deputation; **b** said of a judge in Scotland: belonging to the Outer House of the Court of Session. **4** *commerce* said of shares or stock, etc: forming part of the common stock, entitling holders to receive a dividend from the net profits. ▷ *noun* (***ordinaries***) **1** *law* a judge of ecclesiastical or other causes who acts in his own right, such as a bishop or his deputy. **2** (**Ordinary**) *RC Church* **a** those parts of the Mass which do not vary from day to day; **b** a rule that prescribes or book that contains the form of divine service, especially the Mass. **3** *historical* a PENNY-FARTHING bicycle. **4** *heraldry* **a** one of a class of armorial charges of a simple, common or conventional kind; **b** a reference book of heraldic charges. • **ordinarily** *adverb* in the normal course of events; usually; normally. • **ordinariness** *noun.* • **in ordinary** especially in titles, etc: in regular and customary attendance. • **in the ordinary way** if things are as normal; usually. • **out of the ordinary** unusual; strange. ⓒ 16c as *adj*; 13c in some *noun* senses: from Latin *ordinarius* orderly, usual, from *ordo* order.

Ordinary grade see O-GRADE

Ordinary level see O-LEVEL

ordinary seaman ▷ *noun* (abbreviation **OS**) a sailor of the lowest rank (below an ABLE SEAMAN) in the Royal Navy. See table at RANK.

ordinate /ɔːdɪnət/ ▷ *noun*, *math* in coordinate geometry: the second of a pair of numbers (x and y), known as the y coordinate. It specifies the distance of a point from the horizontal or x-axis. See also ABSCISSA. ⓒ 18c: from Latin *ordinatus* ordained.

ordination /ɔːdɪˈneɪʃən/ ▷ *noun* the act or ceremony of ORDAINing a priest or minister of the church.

ordnance /ˈɔːdnəns/ ▷ *noun* **1** heavy guns and military supplies. **2** the government department responsible for military supplies. ⓒ 14c.

ordnance datum ▷ *noun* (abbreviation **OD**) the standard sea-level of the Ordnance Survey, now taken as mean sea-level at Newlyn, Cornwall.

Ordnance Survey ▷ *noun* the preparation of maps by the Great Britain and N Ireland Ordnance Survey Department.

Ordovician /ɔːdoʊˈvɪʃɪən/ ▷ *adj, geol* denoting the second period of the Palaeozoic era, during which the first vertebrates (jawless fishes) appeared, graptolites and trilobites were abundant, and echinoderms (eg starfish and sea urchins) became more widespread. See table at GEOLOGICAL TIME SCALE. ⓒ 19c: from Latin *Ordovices*, the name of an ancient British tribe in N Wales.

ordure /ˈɔːdjʊə(r)/ ▷ *noun* **1** waste matter from the bowels; excrement. **2** anything unclean, corrupt or obscene, etc. • **ordurous** *adj.* ⓒ 14c: French, from *ord* foul or filthy.

Ore. or **Oreg.** see under OR

ore /ɔː(r)/ ▷ *noun, geol* a solid naturally occurring mineral deposit from which one or more economically valuable substances, especially metals, can be extracted, and for which it is mined. ⓒ Anglo-Saxon *ora* unwrought metal, combined with *ar* brass.

oregano /ɒrɪˈgɑːnoʊ; *US* əˈrɛgənoʊ/ ▷ *noun* (***oreganos***) **1** a sweet-smelling Mediterranean herb, a variety of wild MARJORAM. **2** the dried, often powdered, aromatic leaves of this plant, used as a flavouring in cooking. ⓒ 18c: Spanish and American Spanish, a variant of ORIGANUM.

organ /ˈɔːgən/ ▷ *noun* **1** a part of a body or plant which has a special function, eg a kidney, a leaf. **2** a usually large musical instrument with a keyboard and pedals, in which sound is produced by air being forced through pipes of different lengths. **3** any similar instrument without pipes, such as one producing sound electronically or with reeds. **4** a means of spreading information, especially a newspaper or journal of a particular group or organization, etc. **5** any instrument or means by which a purpose is achieved or a function carried out. **6** *euphemistic or humorous* the penis. • **organist** *noun* a person who plays the organ. ⓒ 13c: from Latin *organum* instrument, from Greek *organon* tool.

organdie or **organdy** /ˈɔːgəndɪ/ ▷ *noun* a very fine thin cotton fabric which has been stiffened. ⓒ 19c: from French *organdi*.

organelle /ɔːgəˈnɛl/ ▷ *noun, biol* in the cell of a living organism: any of various different types of membrane-bound structure, each of which has a specialized function, eg MITOCHONDRIA (see MITOCHONDRION), RIBOSOMES and CHLOROPLASTS. • **organellar** *adj.* ⓒ Early 20c: from Latin *organella*, from *organum*; see ORGAN.

organ-grinder ▷ *noun* a musician who plays a barrel organ in the streets for money.

organic /ɔːˈganɪk/ ▷ *adj* **1** *biol, medicine, etc* **a** relating to an organ of the body; **b** said of a disease: resulting from a physical or metabolic disorder, accompanied by changes in the structures involved. **2** *biol* relating to, derived from, or with the characteristics of a living organism. **3** *agric* **a** relating to farming practices that avoid the use of synthetic fertilizers and pesticides, etc; **b** relating to crops, especially fruit and vegetables, produced in this way. **4** being or formed as an inherent or natural part; fundamental. **5** systematically organized. **6** *chem* relating to ORGANIC CHEMISTRY. ▷ *noun* (*usually* **organics**) an organic compound. • **organically** *adverb.* ⓒ 16c, meaning 'serving as an organ'.

organic architecture ▷ *noun* architecture which appears to grow out of, or be closely linked with, the surrounding landscape.

organic chemistry ▷ *noun* the study of ORAGANIC COMPOUNDS, eg alcohols and plastics. Compare INORGANIC CHEMISTRY.

organic compound ▷ *noun, chem* any of six million known chemical compounds that, with a few exceptions, contain carbon atoms arranged in chains or rings, together with smaller amounts of other elements, mainly hydrogen and oxygen.

organic farming ▷ *noun* a system of farming that avoids the use of industrially manufactured chemical fertilizers and pesticides.

organic fertilizer ▷ *noun* a fertilizer that consists of natural animal or plant products, such as manure, compost or bonemeal.

organism /ˈɔːgənɪzəm/ ▷ *noun* **1** any living structure, such as a plant, animal, fungus or bacterium, capable of growth and reproduction. **2** any establishment, system or whole made up of parts that depend on each other. • **organismal** or **organismic** *adj.* • **organismically** *adverb.* ⓒ 18c.

organist see under ORGAN

organization or **organisation** ▷ *noun* **1** a group of people formed into a society, union or especially a business. **2** the act of organizing. **3** the state of being organized. **4** the way in which something is organized. • **organizational** *adj.* • **organizationally** *adverb.*

organize or **organise** /ˈɔːgənaɪz/ ▷ *verb* (***organized***, ***organizing***) **1** to form something into an organic whole. **2** to give an orderly structure to something □ ***organized the books into a neat pile.*** **3** to arrange, provide or prepare □ ***will organize a meal*** □ ***organized the tickets.*** **4** to form or enrol (people or a person) into a society or organization. **5** *intr* to form a society or organization, especially a trade union. • **organizer** *noun* **1** someone or something that organizes. **2** a PERSONAL ORGANIZER. ⓒ 15c: from Latin *organizare*, from Latin *organum* ORGAN.

organ point see UNDER PEDAL POINT

organ screen ▷ *noun* a decorated stone or wooden screen in a church, etc on which an organ is placed.

organza /ɔːˈganzə/ ▷ *noun* a very fine stiff dress material made of silk or synthetic fibres. ⓒ 19c.

organzine /ˈɔːgənziːn/ ▷ *noun* **1** a silk yarn formed by twisting together two or more threads. **2** (*also* **organzine silk**) a fabric made of this yarn. ⓒ 17c: from French *organsin*, from Italian *organzino*.

orgasm /ˈɔːgazəm/ ▷ *noun* **1 a** the climax of sexual excitement, experienced as an intensely pleasurable sensation caused by a series of strong involuntary contractions of the muscles of the genital organs; **b** an instance of this. **2** *rare* violent excitement. ▷ *verb* (***orgasmed***, ***orgasming***) *intr* to experience an orgasm. • **orgasmic** or **orgastic** *adj.* • **orgasmically** or **orgastically** *adverb.* ⓒ 17c: from French *orgasme* or Latin *orgasmus*, from Greek *orgasmos* swelling.

orgy /ˈɔːdʒɪ/ ▷ *noun* (***orgies***) **1** a wild party or celebration involving indiscriminate sexual activity and excessive drinking. **2** any act of excessive or frenzied indulgence □ ***an orgy of shopping.*** **3** *Greek & Roman historical* (*usually* **orgies**) secret rites practised during the worship of various deities, such as Dionysus or Bacchus, often involving dancing and drinking, etc. • **orgiastic** *adj.* ⓒ 16c: from Latin *orgia*, from Greek (in sense 3).

oribi /ˈɒrɪbɪ/ ▷ *noun* (***oribi*** or ***oribis***) a small fawn-coloured antelope found in the plains of southern and eastern Africa. ⓒ 18c: Afrikaans, probably from a native African word.

oriel /ˈɔːrɪəl/ ▷ *noun* **1** a small room or recess with a polygonal bay window, especially one supported on brackets or corbels. **2** (*also* **oriel window**) the window of an oriel. ⓒ 14c: from French *oriol* gallery.

orient /ˈɔːrɪənt/ ▷ *noun* **1** (**the Orient**) the countries in the east, especially those of E Asia regarded as culturally distinct from western countries (the OCCIDENT). **2** *poetic* the part of the sky where the Sun rises. Compare OCCIDENT. ▷ *verb* (***oriented***, ***orienting***) **1** to place something in a definite position in relation to the points of the compass or some other fixed or known point. **2** to acquaint (oneself or someone) with one's position or their position relative to points known, or relative to the details of a situation. **3** to position something so that it faces east. **4** to build (a church) so that it runs from east to west. ◷ 14c: French, from Latin *oriens, orientis* rising.

oriental /ɔːrɪˈɛntəl/ ▷ *adj* (*also* **Oriental**) from or relating to the Orient; eastern. ▷ *noun* (*usually* **Oriental**) a person born in the Orient; an Asiatic. • **Orientalist** *noun* someone who studies, or is expert in, oriental culture or languages, etc.

orientate /ˈɔːrɪənteɪt/ ▷ *verb* (***orientated***, ***orientating***) **1** to orient. **2** *intr* to face the east; to be oriented. ◷ 19c.

orientation ▷ *noun* **1** the act or an instance of orienting or being oriented. **2** a position relative to a fixed point. **3** a person's position or attitude relative to their situation or circumstances. **4** a meeting giving information or training needed for a new situation; a briefing.

oriented ▷ *adj* **1** directed towards something. **2** *usually in compounds* interested in a specified thing □ *career-oriented.*

orienteer *noun* someone who takes part in orienteering. ▷ *verb* (***orienteered***, ***orienteering***) *intr* to take part in orienteering.

orienteering /ɔːrɪɛnˈtɪərɪŋ/ ▷ *noun* a sport in which contestants race on foot and on skis, etc over an unfamiliar cross-country course, finding their way to official check points using a map and compass. ◷ 1940s: from Swedish *orientering*, originally meaning 'orientating'.

orifice /ˈɒrɪfɪs/ ▷ *noun* a usually small opening or mouthlike hole, especially one in the body or body cavity. • **orificial** /-ˈfɪʃəl/ *adj.* ◷ 16c: from Latin *orificium*, from *os* mouth + *facere* to make.

oriflamme /ˈɒrɪflam/ ▷ *noun, historical* a small banner of red silk split into many points and carried on a gilt staff, used as the ancient royal standard of France. ◷ 15c: French, from Latin *auriflamma*, from *aurum* gold + *flamma* flame.

orig. ▷ *abbreviation* **1** origin. **2** original. **3** originally.

origami /ɒrɪˈgɑːmɪ/ ▷ *noun* the originally Japanese art of folding paper into decorative shapes and figures. ◷ 1950s: Japanese, from *ori* fold + *kami* paper.

origanum /ɒˈrɪgənəm/ ▷ *noun* any of various aromatic herbs of the marjoram genus of LABIATES or other genus, used in cookery. See also OREGANO. ◷ 13c: Latin, from Greek *origanon*, perhaps from *oros* mountain + *ganos* joy or brightness.

origin /ˈɒrɪdʒɪn/ ▷ *noun* **1** a beginning or starting-point; a source. **2** (*usually* **origins**) a person's family background or ancestry. **3** *anatomy* **a** the point of attachment of a muscle; **b** the root of a nerve in the brain or spinal column. **4** *math* in coordinate geometry: the point on a graph where the horizontal *x*-axis and the vertical *y*-axis cross each other, having a value of zero on both axes. **5** *commerce* the place or country from which a product or commodity, etc comes. ◷ 16c: from Latin *origo, originis*, from *oriri* to rise.

original /əˈrɪdʒɪnəl/ ▷ *adj* **1** relating to an origin or beginning. **2** existing from the beginning; earliest; first. **3** said of an idea or concept, etc: not thought of before; fresh or new. **4** said of a person: creative or inventive. **5** being the first form from which copies, reproductions or translations are made; not copied or derived, etc from something else. ▷ *noun* **1** the first example of something, such as a document, photograph or text, etc, which is copied, reproduced or translated to produce others, but which is not itself copied or derived, etc from something else. **2** a work of art or literature that is not a copy, reproduction or imitation. **3** a person or thing that serves as a model in art or literature. **4** an odd or eccentric person. • **originally** *adverb* **1** in the first place, at the beginning. **2** in an original way. ◷ 14c.

originality /ərɪdʒɪˈnalɪtɪ/ ▷ *noun* (***originalities***) **1** the quality or condition of being original. **2** the ability to create or be innovative. **3** an original act, idea or saying, etc. ◷ 18c.

original sin ▷ *noun, Christianity* the supposed innate sinfulness of the human race, inherited from Adam who was disobedient to God.

originate /əˈrɪdʒɪneɪt/ ▷ *verb* (***originated***, ***originating***) *tr & intr* to bring or come into being; to start. • **origination** *noun.* • **originative** *adj* with the power to originate or bring into existence; creative. • **originator** *noun* an author, inventor or creator. ◷ 17c.

oriole /ˈɔːrɪoʊl/ ▷ *noun* **1** any of a family of brightly coloured songbirds native to the forests of Europe, Asia and Africa, especially the **golden oriole**, native to Europe, so called because of the male's bright yellow and black plumage. **2** any of a separate family of songbirds, native to the New World, typically with mainly black plumage with brightly coloured patterns. ◷ 18c: from Latin *oriolus*, from *aureolus*, from *aurum* gold.

Orion ▷ *noun* /əˈraɪən/ *astron* a large brilliant constellation that is visible in both hemispheres.

orison /ˈɒrɪzən/ ▷ *noun, archaic or literary* a prayer. ◷ 12c: from French *oreison*, from Latin *oratio*.

orle /ɔːl/ ▷ *noun* **1** *heraldry* **a** a border within a shield that follows the outline at a short distance from the edge; **b** a number of small charges forming such a border. **2** *historical* the wreath or chaplet around a knight's helmet, showing the crest. ◷ 16c: French, from *ourler* to hem, from Latin *ora* hem or border.

Orlon /ˈɔːlɒn/ ▷ *noun, trademark* a type of acrylic fibre or the crease-resistant fabric made from it, used for making clothes, etc. ◷ 1940s.

orlop /ˈɔːlɒp/ and **orlop deck** ▷ *noun, naut* in a ship with four or more decks: the lowest deck, forming a covering for the hold. ◷ 15c: from Dutch *overloop* covering, from *overloopen* to run or spill over.

ormer /ˈɔːmə(r)/ ▷ *noun* **1** a marine gastropod mollusc with an ear-shaped shell, the inside of which is bright and iridescent; a type of ABALONE. **2** any other abalone. ◷ 17c: Channel Islands French, from French *ormier*, from Latin *auris maris* sea ear.

ormolu /ˈɔːməluː/ ▷ *noun* (***ormolus***) **1 a** *originally* gold or gold leaf prepared for gilding bronze or brass, etc; **b** a gold-coloured alloy, eg copper, zinc or sometimes tin, that is used to decorate furniture, make ornaments, etc. **2** articles made from or decorated with this. ◷ 18c: from French or *moulu*, literally 'ground gold'.

ornament ▷ *noun* /ˈɔːnəmənt/ **1** something that decorates or adds grace or beauty to a person or thing. **2** embellishment or decoration. **3** a small, usually decorative object. **4** someone whose talents add honour to the group or company, etc to which they belong. **5** *music* a note or notes that embellish or decorate the melody or harmony but do not belong to it, eg a trill. **6** (*usually* **ornaments**) articles, such as vestments and the altar, etc used in the services of the Church. ▷ *verb* /-mɛnt/ (***ornamented***, ***ornamenting***) to decorate something with ornaments or serve as an ornament to something; to adorn. • **ornamentation** *noun.* • **ornamenter** or **ornamentist** *noun.* ◷ 18c as *verb*; 13c in obsolete sense 'trappings' or 'equipment': from French *ournement*, from Latin *ornamentum*.

ornamental /ɔːnəˈmɛntəl/ ▷ *adj* serving as an ornament; decorative. ▷ *noun* a plant grown for ornament or decoration. • **ornamentally** *adverb.* ◷ 17c.

ornate /ɔːˈneɪt/ ▷ *adj* (*ornater*, *ornatest*) **1** highly or excessively decorated. **2** said of language: not plain and simple; flowery; using many elaborate literary words or expressions. • **ornately** *adverb*. • **ornateness** *noun*. ⓘ 15c: from Latin *ornare*, *ornatus* to adorn.

ornery /ˈɔːnərɪ/ ▷ *adj*, *N Amer dialect or colloq* **1** stubborn or cantankerous. **2** mean; contemptible. **3** commonplace. • **orneriness** *noun*. ⓘ 19c: variant of ORDINARY.

ornithischian /ɔːnɪˈθɪskɪən/ *palaeontol* ▷ *adj* relating to or indicating the order **Ornithiscia** of herbivorous dinosaurs with a bird-like pelvic structure. ▷ *noun* a dinosaur belonging to this order. ⓘ Early 20c: Latin *Ornithiscia*, from Greek *ischion* hip joint.

ornitho- /ɔːnɪθoʊ, ɔːnɪˈθɒ/ or (before a vowel) **ornith-** ▷ *combining form, signifying* bird or birds. ⓘ From Greek *ornis*, *ornithos* bird.

ornithology /ɔːnɪˈθɒlədʒɪ/ ▷ *noun* the scientific study of birds and their behaviour. • **ornithological** *adj*. • **ornithologically** *adverb*. • **ornithologist** *noun*. ⓘ 17c.

ornithorhynchus /ɔːnɪθoʊˈrɪŋkəs/ ▷ *noun* **1** the scientific generic name for the DUCK-BILLED PLATYPUS. **2** (**Ornithorhynchus**) the duckbill genus. ⓘ 19c: from Greek *rhynchos* snout.

ornithosis /ɔːnɪˈθoʊsɪs/ ▷ *noun* (*ornithoses* /-siːz/ , *pathol* PSITTACOSIS, especially as transmitted to humans. ⓘ 1930s.

orogen /ˈɒroʊdʒɛn/ ▷ *noun*, *geol* a usually elongated region of the Earth's crust which has undergone an orogeny.

orogeny /ɒˈrɒdʒənɪ, ɔːˈrɒ-/ and **orogenesis** ▷ *noun* (*orogenies*; *orogeneses*) *geol* the process of mountain-building, often lasting for hundreds of millions of years, involving deformation and the subsequent uplift of rocks within the mountains. • **orogenic** or **orogenetic** *adj*. ⓘ Late 19c: from Greek *oros* mountain.

orography /ɒˈrɒgrəfɪ/ ▷ *noun* **1** the branch of physical geography that deals with the description, formation, etc of mountains. **2** the orographic features of a region. • **orographic** or **orographical** **1** relating to orography. **2** denoting effects that are related to the presence of mountains or high ground, eg rainfall. • **orographically** *adverb*. ⓘ 19c: from Greek *oros* mountain + -GRAPHY.

oroide /ˈɔːroʊaɪd/ ▷ *noun* an alloy of copper, nickel or tin, etc that imitates gold. ⓘ 19c: from French or gold + -oide -OID.

orology /ɒˈrɒlədʒɪ/ ▷ *noun* the scientific study of mountains. Also called OROGRAPHY. • **orological** *adj*. • **orologist** *noun*. ⓘ 18c.

oropharynx /ɔːroʊˈfarɪŋks/ ▷ *noun* (*oropharynges* /-fəˈrɪndʒiːz/ or *oropharynxes*) *anatomy* in mammals: the part of the pharynx that lies between the SOFT PALATE and the EPIGLOTTIS. ⓘ 19c: from Latin *os*, *oris* mouth.

orotund /ˈɒroʊtʌnd/ ▷ *adj* **1** said of the voice: full, loud and grand. **2** said of speech or writing: boastful or self-important; pompous. • **orotundity** *noun*. ⓘ 18c: from Latin *ore rotundo*, meaning 'with rounded mouth'.

orphan /ˈɔːfən/ ▷ *noun* a child who has lost both parents, or, more rarely, one parent. ▷ *verb* (*orphaned*, *orphaning*) *usually in passive* to make (a child) an orphan. ⓘ 15c: from Greek *orphanos* bereft or without parents.

orphanage /ˈɔːfənɪdʒ/ ▷ *noun* **1** a home for orphans. **2** (*now usually* **orphanhood**) the state or condition of being an orphan. ⓘ 19c; 16c in sense 2.

Orphean /ɔːˈfɪən/ ▷ *adj* **1** relating to Orpheus, a mythical Greek musician and poet who could move inanimate objects by the music of his lyre, the founder and interpreter of the ancient mysteries. **2** melodious or entrancing. **3** ORPHIC (*adj* 1). ▷ *noun* an adherent of Orphic philosophy. ⓘ 19c as *noun*; 16c.

Orphic /ˈɔːfɪk/ ▷ *adj* **1** **a** relating to Orpheus, especially with respect to the philosophical mysteries associated with him; **b** mysterious; esoteric. **2** like the music or poems of Orpheus; melodious or entrancing. **3** relating to or characteristic of ORPHISM 2. ▷ *noun* **1** (*often* **Orphics**) an Orphic song or hymn. **2** an adherent of the Orphic school of philosophy. • **Orphically** *adverb*. ⓘ 17c: from the Greek name *Orpheus*.

Orphism /ˈɔːfɪzəm/ **1** the religion or system of mystic philosophy of the Orphic school. **2** *art* a modern art movement that developed out of Cubism between 1910 and 1914, concerned with achieving harmony of colour and form within the Cubist framework. • **Orphist** *noun* a follower of Orphism in art. ⓘ 19c; early 20c in sense 2.

orphrey /ˈɔːfrɪ/ ▷ *noun* (*orphreys*) gold or other rich embroidery, especially that bordering an ecclesiastical vestment. ⓘ 14c: from French *orfreis*, from Latin *auriphrygium* Phrygian gold.

orpiment /ˈɔːpɪmənt/ ▷ *noun* a yellow mineral, arsenic trisulphide, used as a pigment. ⓘ 14c: French, from Latin *auripigmentum*, from *aurum* gold + *pigmentum* paint.

orpine or **orpin** /ˈɔːpɪn/ ▷ *noun* a purple-flowered broad-leafed STONECROP. ⓘ 14c: French *orpin*.

Orpington /ˈɔːpɪŋtən/ ▷ *noun* a breed of white, black or buff-coloured poultry. ⓘ 19c: from the name of a town in Kent.

orrery /ˈɒrərɪ/ ▷ *noun* (*orreries*) a clockwork model of the Sun and the planets which revolve around it. ⓘ 18c: named after Charles Boyle, Earl of Orrery (1676–1731), for whom one was made.

orris /ˈɒrɪs/ ▷ *noun* (*orrises*) **1** an iris, especially the Florentine iris which has white flowers and fragrant fleshy rhizomes. **2** (*also* **orris-root**) the dried sweet-smelling rhizome of this plant, used in perfumes and formerly in medicines. ⓘ 16c: a variant of IRIS.

ORT ▷ *abbreviation* oral rehydration therapy.

ortanique /ɔːtəˈniːk/ ▷ *noun* a citrus fruit grown in the W Indies, produced by crossing an orange and a tangerine. ⓘ 1930s: from *or*ange + *tan*gerine + *unique*.

ortho- /ɔːθoʊ, ɔːθə, ɔːˈθɒ/ or (before a vowel) **orth-** ▷ *combining form, signifying* **1** straight; upright. **2** at right angles; perpendicular. **3** correct; right. **4** (*often in italic*) *chem* **a** the names of salts and acids that contain one molecule of water more than the corresponding *meta*-compound; **b** two adjacent carbon atoms of the benzene ring. Compare META- sense 4b. ⓘ From Greek *orthos* straight or correct.

orthocentre ▷ *noun*, *geom* the point of intersection of the three altitudes of a triangle (see ALTITUDE 3). ⓘ 19c.

orthochromatic /ɔːθoʊkrəˈmatɪk/ ▷ *adj*, *photog* correct in rendering the relation of colours, without the usual photographic modifications. ⓘ 19c.

orthoclase /ˈɔːθoʊkleɪs/ ▷ *noun*, *mineralogy* common or potash feldspar, consisting of a monoclinic silicate of aluminium and potassium, with cleavages at right angles. ⓘ 19c: from Greek *klasis* fracture or cleavage.

orthodontics /ɔːθəˈdɒntɪks/ ▷ *singular noun*, *dentistry* the branch of dentistry concerned with the prevention and correction of irregularities in the alignment of the teeth or jaws. • **orthodontist** *noun*. ⓘ Early 20c: from Greek *odous*, *odontos* tooth.

orthodox /ˈɔːθədɒks/ ▷ *adj* **1** believing in, living according to, or conforming with established or generally accepted opinions, especially in religion or morals; conventional. **2** (*usually* **Orthodox**) belonging or relating to the ORTHODOX CHURCH. **3** (*usually* **Orthodox**) belonging or relating to the branch of Judaism which keeps to strict traditional interpretations of doctrine and scripture. • **orthodoxy** *noun*. ⓘ 16c: from Latin, from Greek *orthos* straight or correct + *doxa* opinion.

Orthodox Church ▷ *noun* a communion of self-governing Christian churches that recognize the primacy of the Patriarch of Constantinople, originating in the Byzantine Empire and including the Churches of Russia,

Bulgaria, Georgia, Romania, Greece, Poland, etc. Also called **Eastern Orthodox Church, Eastern Church**.

orthoepy /ɔːˈθoʊəpɪ, ˈɔːθoʊɛpɪ/ ▻ *noun* (*plural* in sense 2 only ***orthoepies***) **1** the study of (correct) pronunciation, especially the connection between pronunciation and spelling, and especially in the 17c and 18c. **2** accepted or usual pronunciation. ⓘ 17c: from Greek *orthoepeia*, ultimately from *epos* a word.

orthogenesis ▻ *noun, biol* **1** the evolution of organisms systematically in a definite 'goal-directed' direction and not accidentally in many directions. **2** determinate variation. • **orthogenetic** *adj*. • **orthogenetically** *adverb*. ⓘ 19c.

orthogonal /ɔːˈθɒɡənəl/ ▻ *adj* right-angled; perpendicular. • **orthogonally** *adverb*. ⓘ 16c.

orthographic /ɔːθəˈɡrafɪk/ or **orthographical** ▻ *adj* **1** relating to spelling. **2** said of a projection used in elevations, etc: in perspective projection, with the point of sight at infinity. • **orthographically** *adverb*. ⓘ 19c.

orthography /ɔːˈθɒɡrəfɪ/ ▻ *noun* (***orthographies***) **1** correct or standard spelling. **2** a particular system of spelling. **3** the study of spelling. **4** ORTHOGRAPHIC projection. • **orthographer** or **orthographist** *noun*. ⓘ 15c: from Latin *ortographia*, from Greek.

orthopaedics or (*US*) **orthopedics** /ɔːθəˈpiːdɪks/ ▻ *singular noun, medicine* the correction (originally in childhood) by surgery or manipulation, etc of deformities arising from injury or disease of the bones and joints, such as broken bones or dislocated joints. • **orthopaedic** *adj*. • **orthopaedically** *adverb*. • **orthopaedist** *noun*. ⓘ 19c: from French *orthopédie*.

orthophosphoric acid see PHOSPHORIC ACID

orthopteran /ɔːˈθɒptərən/ ▻ *noun* an insect of the cockroach order **Orthoptera**, with firm forewings that act as covers for the folded membranous hindwings. • **orthopterous** *adj*. ⓘ 19c: Latin, from Greek *pteron* wing.

orthoptics /ɔːˈθɒptɪks/ ▻ *singular noun, medicine* the science or practice of correcting defective vision by non-surgical methods, especially the use of specific exercises to strengthen weak eye muscles. • **orthoptic** *adj*. • **orthoptist** *noun*. ⓘ 1930s.

orthorhombic /ɔːθoʊˈrɒmbɪk/ ▻ *adj, crystallog* denoting or relating to a crystal system with three unequal axes at right angles to each other. ⓘ 19c.

orthoscopic /ɔːθəˈskɒpɪk/ ▻ *adj* with or giving correct vision, true proportion or a flat field of view. ⓘ 19c.

orthosis /ɔːˈθoʊsɪs/ ▻ *noun* (***orthoses*** /-siːz/) *medicine* an external device used to support, correct deformities in, or improve the movement of, the limbs or spine. ⓘ 1950s: Greek, from *orthoun* to straighten.

orthotics /ɔːˈθɒtɪks/ ▻ *singular noun, medicine* the rehabilitation of injured or weakened joints or muscles by the use of orthoses. • **orthotic** *adj*. • **orthotist** *noun*. ⓘ 1950s.

ortolan /ˈɔːtələn/ ▻ *noun* **1** a small bunting, native to Europe, Asia and N Africa, eaten as a delicacy. **2** any of several other birds eaten as delicacies, eg the bobolink. ⓘ 16c: French, from Latin *hortolanus*, from *hortulus*, diminutive of *hortus* garden.

Orwellian /ɔːˈwɛlɪən/ ▻ *adj* **1** relating to or in the style of the English writer George Orwell (pseudonym of Eric Blair, 1903–50). **2** characteristic of the dehumanized authoritarian society depicted in his novel *Nineteen Eighty Four*. See also NEWSPEAK. ⓘ 1950s.

-ory[1] /ərɪ; *US* ˈɪ/ ▻ *suffix, forming nouns, denoting* a place or object, etc for a specified activity or purpose □ *dormitory* □ *repository*. ⓘ From Latin *-orium, -oria*.

-ory[2] /ərɪ; *US* ˈɪ/ ▻ *suffix, forming adjectives and nouns* relating to or involving the action of the verb □ *depository* □ *signatory*. ⓘ From Latin *-orius*.

oryx /ˈɒrɪks/ ▻ *noun* (***oryxes*** /-siːz/ or ***oryx***) any large grazing antelope of the African genus **Oryx**, typically with very long slender horns. ⓘ 14c: Latin, from Greek, meaning 'a stonemason's pick-axe', because of the shape of the animal's horns.

OS ▻ *abbreviation* **1** Old Style. **2** *computing* operating system. **3** ordinary seaman. **4** Ordnance Survey. **5** outsize.

Os ▻ *symbol, chem* osmium.

os[1] ▻ *noun* (*plural* ***ossa*** /ˈɒsə/) *anatomy* BONE, used only in Latin names of particular bones. ⓘ 16c.

os[2] /ɒs/ ▻ *noun* (*plural* ***ora*** /ˈɔːrə/) *anatomy, zool* a mouth or mouthlike opening, originally used only in Latin names of particular structures. ⓘ 18c.

Oscar[1] /ˈɒskə(r)/ ▻ *noun* **1** each of a number of gold-plated statuettes awarded annually since 1928 by the American Academy of Motion Picture Arts and Sciences for outstanding acting or directing, etc in films during the previous year. Also called **Academy Award**. **2** *communications* in the NATO alphabet: the word used to denote the letter 'O' (see table at NATO ALPHABET). ⓘ 1930s: an Academy employee is said to have remarked that the statuette reminded her of her uncle Oscar.

Oscar[2] or **oscar** /ˈɒskə(r)/ ▻ *noun, Austral & NZ slang* cash; money. ⓘ Early 20c: rhyming slang for Oscar Asche (1871–1936), Australian actor.

OSCE ▻ *abbreviation* Organization for Security and Co-operation in Europe, an organization including most W and E European countries that is a forum for discussion on military security across the whole of Europe.

oscillate /ˈɒsɪleɪt/ ▻ *verb* (***oscillated, oscillating***) **1** *tr & intr* to swing or make something swing backwards and forwards like a pendulum. **2** *tr & intr* to vibrate. **3** *intr* to waver between opinions, choices, courses of action, etc. **4** *intr, electronics* said of an electrical current: to vary regularly in strength or direction between certain limits. • **oscillating** *adj*. • **oscillation** *noun*. • **oscillator** *noun* **1** an electronic device that produces an alternating current of a particular frequency, used to produce high-frequency radio waves for TV and radio, and to make electronic musical instruments. **2** someone or something that oscillates. • **oscillatory** *adverb*. ⓘ 18c: from Latin *oscillare, oscillatum* to swing.

oscillogram /əˈsɪləɡram/ ▻ *noun* a record made by an oscillograph. ⓘ Early 20c.

oscillograph /əˈsɪləɡrɑːf/ ▻ *noun* a device that displays or records graphically the rapidly changing values of an oscillating quantity, such as an electric current, over time. • **oscillographic** *adj*. • **oscillographically** *adverb*. ⓘ 19c.

oscilloscope /əˈsɪləskoʊp/ ▻ *noun* a device, or component of a device, that measures the rapidly changing values of an oscillating quantity, such as an electrical current, over time, and that displays the varying electrical signals graphically on the fluorescent screen of a cathode-ray tube. Also called **cathode-ray oscilloscope** (abbreviation **CRO**). ⓘ Early 20c.

oscine /ˈɒsaɪn/ ▻ *adj, ornithol* belonging or relating to the **Oscines**, the songbirds, the group of birds that forms the main body of the PASSERINES. ⓘ 19c: from Latin *oscen* a singing-bird.

oscular /ˈɒskjʊlə(r)/ ▻ *adj* **1** relating to the mouth or to kissing. **2** *zool* relating to an OSCULUM. ⓘ 19c: from Latin *osculum* a little mouth or a kiss.

osculate /ˈɒskjʊleɪt/ ▻ *verb* (***osculated, osculating***) **1** *tr & intr, jocular* to kiss. **2** *geom* **a** said of a curve: to touch (another curve) without crossing it, thereby having a common tangent; **b** *intr* said of two curves: to have a common tangent. **3** *intr* to be in close contact. • **osculation** *noun*. • **osculatory** *adj*. ⓘ 17c: from Latin *osculari, osculatus* to kiss.

osculum /ˈɒskjʊləm/ ▷ *noun* (***oscula*** /-lə/) *zool* a mouthlike aperture, especially in a sponge. ⓒ 18c.

-ose¹ /oʊs, oʊz/ ▷ *combining form, forming adjectives, denoting* having or possessing a particular quality □ *verbose.*

-ose² /oʊs, oʊz/ ▷ *combining form, chem, denoting* a carbohydrate.

osier /ˈoʊzɪə(r), ˈoʊʒə(r)/ ▷ *noun* **1** any of various species of willow tree or shrub. **2** a flexible branch or twig from this tree, used to make baskets, etc. ⓒ 14c: from French, from Latin *auseria.*

-osis /oʊsɪs/ ▷ *suffix* (*plural* ***-oses*** /-siːz/) *forming nouns, denoting* **1** a condition or process □ ***hypnosis*** □ ***metamorphosis.*** **2** a diseased or disordered state □ ***neurosis.*** ⓒ Latin or Greek.

Osmanli /ɒzˈmanlɪ/ ▷ *adj* **1** relating to the dynasty of Osman, who founded the Ottoman empire in Asia, and reigned 1288–1326. **2** relating to the Ottoman empire. **3** relating or belonging to the western branch of the Turks or to their language. ▷ *noun* (***Osmanli*** or ***Osmanlis***) **1** a member of the dynasty. **2** a Turk of Turkey. See also OTTOMAN. ⓒ 18c: Turkish, meaning 'referring or relating to Osman'.

osmiridium /ɒzmɪˈrɪdɪəm/ ▷ *noun, chem* a hard white naturally occurring alloy of osmium and iridium, in which the iridium content is less than 35 per cent, used to make the tips of pen nibs. ⓒ 19c: from *osmium* + *iridium.*

osmium /ˈɒzmɪəm/ ▷ *noun, chem* (symbol **Os**, atomic number 76) a very hard dense bluish-white metal, the densest known element, used as a catalyst, and as a hardening agent in alloys with platinum and iridium, eg in pen nibs. ⓒ 19c: from Greek *osme* smell (because of the unpleasant pungent smell of one of its forms, osmium tetroxide) + -IUM.

osmoregulation /ɒzmoʊrɛgjʊˈleɪʃən/ ▷ *noun, biol* the process whereby the water content and concentration of salts within a living organism are maintained at a constant level, thus counteracting OSMOSIS 1. ⓒ 1920s: from Greek *osmos* a push.

osmose /ˈɒzmoʊs, -moʊz/ ▷ *verb* (***osmosed, osmosing***) *tr & intr* to undergo or cause something to undergo osmosis. ⓒ 19c, originally as *noun*: from endo*smose* and ex*osmose*, related to Greek *osmos* a push.

osmosis /ɒzˈmoʊsɪs/ ▷ *noun* **1** *chem* the spontaneous movement of a solvent, eg water, across a semi-permeable membrane from a more dilute solution to a more concentrated one, which stops when the concentrations of the two solutions are equal, or when an external pressure is applied to the more concentrated solution. **2** a gradual, usually unconscious, process of assimilation or absorption of ideas or knowledge, etc. • **osmotic** /-ˈmɒtɪk/ *adj.* • **osmotically** *adverb.* ⓒ 19c: a Latinized form of OSMOSE; see also -OSIS.

osmotic pressure ▷ *noun, chem* the pressure that must be applied to prevent the spontaneous movement by osmosis of a solvent across a semipermeable membrane from a more dilute solution to a more concentrated one.

osp ▷ *abbreviation*: *obiit sine prole* (Latin), died without issue, meaning 'died without any known children'.

osprey /ˈɒsprɪ, ˈɒspreɪ/ ▷ *noun* (***ospreys***) **1** a large fish-eating bird of prey found near water in most parts of the world, with a dark-brown body, white head and legs, and a characteristic dark line on the side of the head. **2** any feather from various other birds, used for trimming women's hats. ⓒ 15c: from French *ospres.*

ossa *plural of* OS¹

osseous /ˈɒsɪəs/ ▷ *adj* relating to, like, containing, or formed from bone; bony. ⓒ 17c: from Latin *osseus*, from *os* bone.

ossia /ˈɒsiːə/ ▷ *conj, music* used in directions to indicate an alternative, usually easier, way of playing a particular passage: or; alternatively. ⓒ 19c: Italian.

ossicle /ˈɒsɪkəl/ ▷ *noun* **1** *anatomy, zool* a small bone, especially each of the three small bones of the middle ear. **2** *zool* a bonelike plate or joint, etc. ⓒ 16c: from Latin *ossiculum*, diminutive of *os* bone.

Ossie see under AUSSIE

ossifrage /ˈɒsɪfreɪdʒ/ ▷ *noun* **1** the LAMMERGEYER, a rare type of vulture. **2** the OSPREY. ⓒ 17c: from Latin *ossifragus*, literally 'bone-breaking', perhaps used as a *noun* in sense 1, from *os* bone + *frangere* to break.

ossify /ˈɒsɪfaɪ/ ▷ *verb* (***ossifies, ossified, ossifying***) **1** *tr & intr* to turn into or make something turn into bone or a bonelike substance. **2** *intr* said of one's opinions or habits, etc: to become rigid, fixed or inflexible. • **ossification** *noun.* ⓒ 18c: from French *ossifier*, from Latin *os* bone + *facere* to make.

ossuary /ˈɒsjʊərɪ/ ▷ *noun* (***ossuaries***) any place, eg a vault or charnel-house, or an urn or other container, in which the bones of the dead are kept. ⓒ 17c: from Latin *ossuarium.*

oste- see OSTEO-

osteal /ˈɒstɪəl/ ▷ *adj, medicine, etc* **1** relating to, composed of, or resembling bone. **2** sounding like bone on percussion. ⓒ 19c.

osteitis /ɒstɪˈaɪtɪs/ ▷ *noun, pathol* inflammation of a bone. ⓒ 19c.

ostensible /ɒˈstɛnsɪbəl/ ▷ *adj* said of reasons, etc: stated or claimed, but not necessarily true; apparent. • **ostensibility** *noun.* • **ostensibly** *adverb.* ⓒ 18c: from Latin *ostensibilis.*

ostensive /ɒˈstɛnsɪv/ ▷ *adj* **1** *logic* directly or manifestly demonstrative. **2** said of a definition: giving examples of things to which the defined word properly applies. **3** OSTENSIBLE. • **ostensively** *adverb.* • **ostensiveness** *noun.* ⓒ 16c: from Latin *ostentivus* provable, from Latin *ostendere, ostensum* to show.

ostentation /ɒstɛnˈteɪʃən, ɒstən-/ ▷ *noun* pretentious display of wealth or knowledge, etc, especially to attract attention or admiration. • **ostentatious** *adj.* • **ostentatiously** *adverb.* • **ostentatiousness** *noun.* ⓒ 15c: from Latin *ostendere* to show.

osteo- /ɒstɪoʊ, ɒstɪˈɒ/ or (before a vowel) **oste-** ▷ *combining form, signifying* bone or bones. ⓒ From Greek *osteon* bone.

osteoarthritis ▷ *noun, pathol* an alternative, but misleading, name for OSTEOARTHROSIS, since it implies an inflammatory condition. • **osteoarthritic** *adj.* ⓒ 19c.

osteoarthrosis ▷ *noun, pathol* chronic non-inflammatory disease of bones, found mainly in the elderly, in which degeneration of the cartilage overlying the bones at a joint (especially the hip, knee or thumb joint) leads to deformity of the bone surface, causing pain and stiffness. ⓒ 1930s.

osteoblast /ˈɒstɪoʊblɑːst/ ▷ *noun, zool* a bone-forming cell. ⓒ 19c.

osteoclast /ˈɒstɪoʊklast/ ▷ *noun, zool* a bone-absorbing cell. ⓒ 19c.

osteoclastoma /ɒstɪoʊklaˈstoʊmə/ ▷ *noun* (***osteoclastomas*** or ***osteoclastomata*** /-mətə/) *pathol* a tumour arising from OSTEOCLAST cells. Compare OSTEOSARCOMA.

osteogenesis /ɒstɪəˈdʒɛnɪsɪs/ ▷ *noun* formation of bone. • **osteogenetic** or **osteogenic** *adj.* ⓒ 19c.

osteology /ɒstɪˈɒlədʒɪ/ ▷ *noun* (*plural* in sense 2 only ***osteologies***) **1** the branch of human anatomy that deals with the study of bones and the skeleton. **2** the structure and arrangement of an animal's bones. • **osteological** *adj.* • **osteologically** *adverb.* • **osteologist** *noun.* ⓒ 17c.

osteoma /ɒstɪˈoʊmə/ ▷ *noun* (***osteomata*** /-ˈmɑːtə/ or ***osteomas***) *pathol* a benign tumour of bone or bonelike tissue. Ⓒ 19c.

osteomalacia /ɒstɪoʊməˈleɪʃɪə/ ▷ *noun, pathol* a disorder characterized by softening of the bones due to a reduction in the availability of calcium salts, caused by a deficiency of vitamin D. • **osteomalacial** or **osteomalacic** /-ˈlasɪk/ *adj.* Ⓒ 19c: from Greek *malakia* softness.

osteomyelitis /ɒstɪoʊmaɪəˈlaɪtɪs/ ▷ *noun, pathol* inflammation of bone and bone marrow, caused by infection. Ⓒ 19c.

osteopathy /ɒstɪˈɒpəθɪ/ ▷ *noun, medicine* a system of healing or treatment, mainly involving manipulation of the bones and joints and massage of the muscles, that provides relief for many bone and joint disorders. • **osteopath** /ˈɒstɪəpaθ, -oʊpaθ/ *noun* a practitioner of osteopathy. • **osteopathic** *adj.* • **osteopathically** *adverb.* Ⓒ 19c.

osteoplasty /ˈɒstɪəplastɪ/ ▷ *noun, medicine* plastic surgery of the bones, bone grafting, etc. • **osteoplastic** *adj.* Ⓒ 19c.

osteoporosis /ɒstɪoʊpɔːˈroʊsɪs, -pəˈroʊsɪs/ ▷ *noun, pathol* a disease, most commonly of post-menopausal women, in which the bones become porous, brittle and liable to fracture, owing to the loss of calcium from the bone substance. • **osteoporotic** *adj.* Ⓒ 19c: from OSTEO- + PORE[1] + -OSIS.

osteosarcoma ▷ *noun* (***osteosarcomas*** or ***osteosarcomata*** /-mɑːtə/) *pathol* a malignant tumour derived from osteoblasts. Compare OSTEOCLASTOMA. Ⓒ 19c.

ostinato /ɒstɪˈnɑːtoʊ/ *music* ▷ *adj* frequently repeated. ▷ *noun* (***ostinati*** /-tɪ/ or ***ostinatos***) a melodic phrase that recurs throughout a piece. Ⓒ 19c: Italian, meaning 'obstinate' or 'persistent'.

ostler /ˈɒslə(r)/ ▷ *noun, historical* someone who attends to horses at an inn. Ⓒ 15c: from HOSTEL.

Ostmark /ˈɒstmɑːk/ ▷ *noun, historical* the standard unit of currency in the former German Democratic Republic (East Germany). Ⓒ 1940s: German *Ost* east + *Mark* mark.

Ostpolitik /ˈɒstpɒlitiːk/ ▷ *noun, historical* the policy of establishing normal trade and diplomatic relations with the Communist countries of Eastern Europe, especially that initiated in the 1960s by the former West Germany. Ⓒ 1960s: German *Ost* east + *Politik* policy.

ostracize or **ostracise** /ˈɒstrəsaɪz/ ▷ *verb* (***ostracized***, ***ostracizing***) **1** to exclude someone from a group or society, etc; to refuse to associate with them. **2** *historical* in Athens and other ancient Greek cities: to banish someone by popular vote. The banishment was for a fixed period of up to ten years and did not involve loss of property or citizenship. • **ostracism** *noun.* Ⓒ 17c: from Greek *ostrakizein*, from *ostrakon* POTSHERD, because in ancient Greece the voters wrote on potsherds the name of the person they wished to banish.

ostrich /ˈɒstrɪtʃ/ ▷ *noun* (***ostriches*** or ***ostrich***) **1** the largest living bird, found on dry plains in E Africa, having an extremely long neck and legs, and only two toes on each foot, up to 2.5m in height and although flightless capable of running at speeds of up to 60km per hour (about 40mph). **2** *colloq* someone who refuses to face or accept unpleasant facts 16c: from the popular but mistaken belief that the ostrich buries its head in the sand to 'hide' from danger. • **ostrich-like** *adj, adverb.* Ⓒ 13c: from French *ostruce*, from Latin *avis* bird + late Latin *struthio* ostrich.

Ostrogoth /ˈɒstrəgɒθ/ ▷ *noun, historical* a member of the Eastern Goths, who established their power in Italy in the 5c and 6c. Compare VISIGOTH. Ⓒ 17c: from Latin *Ostrogothi*, with the first element meaning 'east'.

OT ▷ *abbreviation* **1** occupational therapy. **2** Old Testament.

otalgia /oʊˈtaldʒɪə/ ▷ *noun, medicine* earache. Ⓒ 17c: Greek, from *ous, otos* ear.

OTC ▷ *abbreviation, Brit* **1** Officers' Training Corps. **2** *stock exchange* over the counter.

OTE ▷ *abbreviation* on target earnings, the earnings of a salesman who achieves targeted sales.

other /ˈʌðə(r)/ ▷ *adj* **1** remaining from a group of two or more when one or some have been specified already ▫ *Now close the other eye.* **2** different from the one or ones already mentioned, understood or implied ▫ *other people.* **3** additional; further ▫ *need to buy one other thing.* **4** far or opposite ▫ *the other side of the world.* ▷ *pronoun* **1 a** another person or thing; **b (others)** other people or things. **2 (others)** further or additional ones ▫ *I'd like to see some others.* **3** (*usually* **the others**) the remaining people or things of a group ▫ *Go with the others.* ▷ *adverb* (*usually* **other than**) otherwise; differently ▫ *couldn't do other than hurry home.* ▷ *noun* **1** someone or something considered separate, different, additional to, apart from, etc the rest ▫ *introduced him as his significant other.* **2** *literary theory* (*often* **Other**) in Lacanian terms: someone who does not belong to a specified social, cultural, racial, etc group and who is therefore excluded from participation in the predominant group's interpretation of eg literary texts. • **otherness** *noun* the fact or condition of being other or different. • **every other** each alternate; every second ▫ *see him every other week.* • **in other words** this means ▫ *'I've really no time.' 'In other words you can't do it?'.* • **other than ...** **1** except ...; apart from ... ▫ *Other than that, there's no news.* **2** different from ... ▫ *do something other than watch TV.* • **other things being equal** circumstances or conditions being unchanged. • **someone, something** or **somewhere** , *etc* **or other** some unspecified person, thing or place, etc ▫ *It's here somewhere or other.* • **the other day** or **week,** *etc* a few days or weeks, etc ago. • **the other man** or **woman** the lover of a woman or man who is already married or in a relationship. Ⓒ Anglo-Saxon.

other ranks ▷ *plural noun* (abbreviation **OR**) *chiefly Brit* members of the armed services who do not hold a commissioned rank.

the other side ▷ *noun* the spiritual world, to which one is believed by many to pass after death.

otherwise /ˈʌðəwaɪz/ ▷ *conj* or else; if not. ▷ *adverb* **1** in other respects ▫ *He is good at languages but otherwise not very bright.* **2** in a different way ▫ *couldn't act otherwise than as she did.* **3** under different circumstances ▫ *might otherwise have been late.* ▷ *adj* different ▫ *The truth is otherwise.* • **or otherwise** or the opposite; or not ▫ *Check all cars, fast or otherwise.* • **rather ... than otherwise** rather ... than not. Ⓒ Anglo-Saxon *othre wisan* in other wise or manner.

otherworldly ▷ *adj* **1** belonging or relating to, or resembling, a world supposedly inhabited after death. **2** concerned with spiritual or intellectual matters to the exclusion of practical matters. • **otherworldliness** *noun.* Ⓒ 19c.

otic /ˈoʊtɪk/ ▷ *adj, medicine, anatomy* relating to the ear. Ⓒ 17c: from Greek *otikos*, from *ous, otos* ear.

otiose /ˈoʊtɪoʊs/ ▷ *adj, formal* **1** futile. **2** said eg of a word or expression, etc in a particular context: serving no purpose; unnecessary; superfluous. **3** lazy; idle. • **otiosity** or **otioseness** *noun.* Ⓒ 18c: from Latin *otiosus*, from *otium* leisure.

otitis /oʊˈtaɪtɪs/ ▷ *noun, pathol* inflammation of the ear or of part of the ear. Ⓒ 18c: Latin, from Greek *ous, otos* ear.

oto- /oʊtoʊ, oʊtə, oʊˈtɒ/ or (before a vowel) **ot-** ▷ *combining form, signifying* the ear. Ⓒ From Greek *ous, otos* ear.

otolaryngology ▷ *noun* the branch of medicine that deals with the ear and larynx. Also called OTORHINOLARYNGOLOGY. • **otolaryngological** *adj.* • **otolaryngologist** *noun.* ⓒ 19c.

otolith /ˈoʊtəlɪθ/ ▷ *noun, zool* any of the calcareous granules found in the inner ear of vertebrates, the movement of which helps the animal to maintain equilibrium. • **otolithic** *adj.* ⓒ 19c.

otology /oʊˈtɒlədʒɪ/ ▷ *noun* the branch of medicine concerned with the ear. • **otological** *adj.* • **otologist** *noun.* ⓒ 19c.

otorhinolaryngology ▷ *noun* the branch of medicine that deals with the ear, nose and throat. Also called OTOLARYNGOLOGY. ⓒ Early 20c.

otoscope /ˈoʊtəskoʊp/ ▷ *noun, medicine* a device used for examining the external ear. • **otoscopic** *adj.* ⓒ 19c.

OTT ▷ *abbreviation, slang* over the top (see under OVER).

otter /ˈɒtə(r)/ ▷ *noun* (***otters*** or ***otter***) **1** a solitary and rather elusive carnivorous semi-aquatic mammal, found in all parts of the world except Australasia and Antarctica, with a long body covered with short smooth fur, a broad flat head, short legs, a stout tail tapering towards the tip, large webbed hind feet. **2** the fur of this animal. **3** (*also* **otter board**) a type of fishing tackle consisting of a board with several hooked and baited lines attached. **4** a PARAVANE. ⓒ Anglo-Saxon *otor* or *ottor.*

otter hound ▷ *noun* a large rough-haired dog, formerly bred for otter hunting. ⓒ 17c.

Ottoman /ˈɒtəmən/ ▷ *adj, historical* relating to the Ottomans or to the **Ottoman Empire**, which lasted from the 13c until the end of World War I, and was centred in what is now Turkey, and at different times reached into Europe and the Near East. ▷ *noun* (***Ottomans***) **1** an inhabitant of the Ottoman Empire; a Turk. **2** (**ottoman**) a long low seat, usually without a back or arms, and often in the form of a padded and upholstered box. See also OSMANLI. ⓒ 16c: ultimately from Arabic *Utman* Othman or Osman (1259–1326), the founder of the Ottoman Empire.

OU ▷ *abbreviation* **1** Open University. **2** Oxford University.

oubliette /uːblɪˈɛt/ ▷ *noun, historical* a secret dungeon with a single, often concealed, opening at the top. ⓒ 18c: French, from *oublier* to forget.

ouch /aʊtʃ/ ▷ *exclamation* expressing sudden sharp pain. ⓒ 19c.

ought /ɔːt/ ▷ *auxiliary verb* used to express: **1** duty or obligation □ ***You ought to help if you can.*** **2** advisability □ ***You ought to see a doctor.*** **3** probability or expectation □ ***She ought to be here soon.*** **4** shortcoming or failure □ ***He ought to have been here hours ago.*** **5** enthusiastic desire on the part of the speaker □ ***You really ought to read this book.*** **6** logical consequence □ ***The answer ought to be 'four'.*** • **ought not to ...** used to express moral disapproval □ ***You ought not to speak to him like that.*** ⓒ Anglo-Saxon *ahte*, past tense of *agen* to owe.

Ouija /ˈwiːdʒə/ and **Ouija board** ▷ *noun, trademark* (*also* **ouija**) a board with the letters of the alphabet printed round the edge, used at SÉANCES with a glass, pointer or other object to spell out messages supposed to be from the dead. ⓒ 19c: from French *oui* yes + German *ja* yes.

oulong see OOLONG

ounce[1] /aʊns/ ▷ *noun* **1** (abbreviation **oz**) in the imperial system: a unit of weight equal to one sixteenth of a pound (28.35g). **2** *historical* a unit of weight equal to one twelfth of the (legally obsolete) Troy or Apothecaries' pound, one ounce being equal to 480 grains (approximately 31.1g). **3** short form of FLUID OUNCE. **4** a small amount or quantity. ⓒ 14c: from French *unce*, from Latin *uncia* twelfth part.

ounce[2] /aʊns/ ▷ *noun* the SNOW LEOPARD. ⓒ 18c; 14c in obsolete sense 'the Eurasian lynx' or any of various other cats: from French *once*, mistakenly from *lonce* as if *l'once*, from Greek *lynx* lynx.

our /aʊə(r)/ ▷ *adj* **1** relating or belonging to, associated with, or done by us □ ***our children.*** **2** relating or belonging to people in general, or to humanity □ ***our planet.*** **3** *formal* used by a sovereign: my □ ***our royal will.*** **4** *colloq* **a** (before a personal name) belonging to the same family; that is the son, daughter, brother or sister, etc □ ***our Bill*** □ ***our Susan***; **b** (before a surname, etc) that belongs to the same organization, etc □ ***our Miss Jackson.*** ⓒ Anglo-Saxon *ure.*

Our Father see under THE LORD'S PRAYER

Our Lady ▷ *noun, RC Church* the Virgin Mary.

ours /aʊəz/ ▷ *pronoun* the one or ones belonging to us □ ***They're ours*** □ ***Ours are better.*** • **of ours** relating or belonging to us □ ***a friend of ours.***

ourself /aʊəˈsɛlf/ ▷ *pronoun, archaic* formerly used by monarchs: myself. ⓒ 15c.

ourselves /aʊəˈsɛlvz/ ▷ *pronoun* **1** reflexive form of *we*; us □ ***We helped ourselves to cakes.*** **2** used for emphasis: we personally; our particular group of people □ ***We ourselves know nothing about that.*** **3** our normal self □ ***We can relax and be ourselves.*** **4** (*also* **by ourselves**) **a** alone □ ***went by ourselves***; **b** without anyone else's help □ ***did it all by ourselves.***

-ous /əs/ ▷ *suffix, forming adjectives, signifying* **1** a particular character, quality or nature □ ***marvellous*** □ ***venomous.*** **2** *chem* an element in its lower valency. ⓒ From Latin *-osus.*

ousel see OUZEL

oust /aʊst/ ▷ *verb* (***ousted***, ***ousting***) **1** *law* **a** to eject someone from a possession; to deprive them of an inheritance; **b** to take away (a privilege or right, etc). **2** to force someone out of a position and take their place. • **ouster** *noun* **1** *law* ejection; dispossession. **2** *chiefly N Amer* the act of forcing someone out of a place, position, etc. ⓒ 16c: from French *oster* to remove, from Latin *obstare* to hinder or oppose.

out /aʊt/ ▷ *adverb* **1** away from the inside; not in or at a place □ ***Go out into the garden.*** **2** not in one's home or place of work □ ***I called but you were out.*** **3** to or at an end; to or into a state of being completely finished, exhausted or extinct, etc □ ***The milk has run out*** □ ***before the day is out*** □ ***Put the candle out.*** **4** aloud □ ***cry out.*** **5** with care or taking care □ ***Listen out for the baby*** □ ***watch out.*** **6** in all directions from a central point □ ***Share out the sweets.*** **7** to the fullest extent or amount □ ***Spread the blanket out.*** **8** to public attention or notice; revealed □ ***The secret is out.*** **9** *sport* said of a person batting: no longer able to bat, eg because of having the ball caught by an opponent □ ***bowled out.*** **10** in or into a state of being removed, omitted or forgotten □ ***miss him out*** □ ***Rub out the mistake.*** **11** not to be considered; rejected □ ***That idea's out.*** **12** removed; dislocated □ ***have a tooth out.*** **13** not in authority; not having political power □ ***voted them out of office.*** **14** into unconsciousness □ ***pass out in the heat.*** **15** in error □ ***Your total is out by three.*** **16** *colloq* existing □ ***the best car out.*** **17** said of a flower: in bloom. **18** said of a book: published □ ***will be out in the autumn.*** **19** visible □ ***the moon's out.*** **20** no longer in fashion □ ***Drainpipes are out, flares are in.*** **21** said of workers: on strike □ ***called the miners out.*** **22** said of a jury: considering its verdict. **23** *old use* said of a young woman: introduced into fashionable society. **24** said of a tide: at or towards the lowest level of water □ ***going out.*** ▷ *adj* **1** external. **2** directing or showing direction outwards. ▷ *prep, colloq, especially US* out of something □ ***Get out the car.*** ▷ *exclamation* expressing: **1** *sport* that the batsman is dismissed. **2** that a radio transmission has finished □ ***over and out.*** ▷ *noun* a way out, a way of escape; an excuse. ▷ *verb* (***outed***, ***outing***) **1** *intr* to become publicly known □ ***Murder will***

out. **2** to make public the homosexuality of (a famous person who has been attempting to keep their homosexuality secret). Compare COME OUT (sense 10) at COME. • **be out for something** *colloq* to be determined to achieve it □ ***He's just out for revenge.*** • **out and about** active outside the house, especially after an illness. • **out and away** by far; much. • **out of something 1** from inside it □ ***drive out of the garage.*** **2** not in or within it □ ***be out of the house.*** **3** having exhausted a supply of it □ ***be out of butter.*** **4** from among several □ ***two out of three cats.*** **5** from a material □ ***made out of wood.*** **6** because of it □ ***out of anger.*** **7** beyond the range, scope or bounds of it □ ***out of reach*** □ ***out of the ordinary.*** **8** excluded from it □ ***leave him out of the team.*** **9** no longer in a stated condition □ ***out of practice.*** **10** at a stated distance from a place □ ***a mile out of town.*** **11** without or so as to be without something □ ***cheat him out of his money.*** • **out of date** old-fashioned and no longer of use; obsolete. • **out of it 1** *colloq* not part of, or wanted in, a group or activity, etc. **2** *slang* unable to behave normally or control oneself, usually because of drink or drugs. • **out of pocket** having spent more money than one can afford. • **out of the way 1** difficult to reach or arrive at. **2** unusual; uncommon. • **ins and outs** see INS AND OUTS at IN. • **out to lunch** *slang* said of a person: slightly crazy; in a dream world. • **out with it!** an exhortation to speak openly. ◷ Anglo-Saxon *ut.*

out- ⊳ *prefix, denoting* **1** an excelling or surpassing of the specified action □ ***outrun*** □ ***outmanoeuvre.*** **2** external; separate; from outside □ ***outpatient*** □ ***outhouse.*** **3** away from the inside, especially as a result of the specified action □ ***output*** □ ***outpouring.*** **4** going away or out of; outward □ ***outdoor*** □ ***outboard.***

outage /ˈaʊtɪdʒ/ ⊳ *noun* **1** the amount of a commodity lost in transport or storage. **2** a period of time during which a power supply fails to operate. ◷ Early 20c.

out-and-out ⊳ *adj* complete; utter; thorough □ ***an out-and-out liar.***

outback ⊳ *noun* isolated remote areas of a country, especially in Australia.

outbalance ⊳ *verb* to OUTWEIGH.

outbid ⊳ *verb* to offer a higher price than someone else, especially at an auction.

outboard ⊳ *adj* **1** said of a motor or engine: portable and designed to be attached to the outside of a boat's stern. **2** said of a boat: equipped with such a motor or engine. **3** positioned towards or nearer the side of a ship or aircraft. ⊳ *adverb, adj* nearer or towards the outside of a ship or aircraft. ⊳ *noun* **1** an outboard motor or engine. **2** a boat equipped with an outboard motor or engine. Compare INBOARD. ◷ 19c.

outbound ⊳ *adj* said of a vehicle, flight, carriageway, etc: going away from home or a station, etc; departing. Opposite of INBOUND.

outbreak ⊳ *noun* a sudden, usually violent beginning or occurrence, usually of something unpleasant, eg of disease or rioting, etc.

outbreeding ⊳ *noun, genetics* mating between distantly related or unrelated members of a species, resulting in the production of greater genetic variation among the offspring than INBREEDING. ◷ Early 20c.

outbuilding ⊳ *noun* a building such as a barn, stable or garage, that is separate from the main building of a house but within the grounds surrounding it. ◷ 17c.

outburst ⊳ *noun* **1** a sudden violent expression of strong emotion, especially anger. **2** an eruption or explosion.

outcast ⊳ *noun* **1** someone who has been rejected by their friends or by society. **2** an exile or vagabond. ⊳ *adj* rejected or cast out.

outcaste ⊳ *noun* **1** a Hindu who has lost their caste. **2** someone who has no caste.

outclass ⊳ *verb* **1** to be or become of a much better quality or class than something else. **2** to defeat someone easily, eg in style or in a competition, etc. ◷ 19c.

outcome ⊳ *noun* the result of some action or situation, etc; consequence.

outcrop ⊳ *noun* /ˈaʊtkrɒp/ **1** a rock or group of rocks which sticks out above the surface of the ground. **2** an appearance or occurrence. ⊳ *verb* /aʊtˈkrɒp/ *intr* said of a rock or group of rocks: to stick out from the ground.

outcry ⊳ *noun* a widespread and public show of anger or disapproval. ◷ 14c.

outdated ⊳ *adj* no longer useful or in fashion; obsolete. • **outdatedness** *noun.*

outdistance ⊳ *verb* to leave (a competitor) far behind.

outdo ⊳ *verb* **1** to do much better than someone or something else; to surpass them. **2** to overcome or defeat someone or something.

outdoor ⊳ *adj* **1** done, taking place, situated or for use, etc in the open air □ ***outdoor pursuits.*** **2** preferring to be in the open air or fond of outdoor activities and sport, etc □ ***an outdoor person.*** ◷ 18c.

outdoors ⊳ *adverb* (*also* **out-of-doors**) in or into the open air; outside a building. ⊳ *singular noun* the open air; the world outside buildings □ ***the great outdoors.*** ◷ 19c.

outer /ˈaʊtə(r)/ ⊳ *adj* **1** external; belonging to or for the outside. **2** further from the centre or middle. ⊳ *noun* **1** *archery* **a** the outermost ring on a target; **b** a shot which hits this. **2** *Austral, NZ* the unsheltered part of the spectator enclosure at a sports ground. • **on the outer** *Austral, NZ* excluded; out in the cold. ◷ Anglo-Saxon *uterra.*

outer bar ⊳ *noun, law* in England: the junior barristers, collectively, who plead outside the bar in court.

outer ear ⊳ *noun, anatomy* in vertebrates: the part of the ear that transmits sound waves from outside the ear to the eardrum.

outermost or **outmost** ⊳ *adj* nearest the edge; furthest from the centre; most remote. ◷ 14c.

Some words with *out-* prefixed: see OUT- for numbered senses specified below.

outact *verb* sense 1.	**outjump** *verb* sense 1.	**outsell** *verb* sense 1.
outbargain *verb* sense 1.	**outlast** *verb* sense 1.	**outshine** *verb* sense 1.
outdance *verb* sense 1.	**outmatch** *verb* sense 1.	**outshoot** *verb* sense 1.
outdrink *verb* sense 1.	**outmanoeuvre** *verb* sense 1.	**outsit** *verb* sense 1.
outeat *verb* sense 1.	**outnumber** *verb* sense 1.	**outswim** *verb* sense 1.
outfight *verb* sense 1.	**outpace** *verb* sense 1.	**outswing** *noun* senses 2 and 3.
outflowing *noun, adj* senses 2 and 3.	**outperform** *verb* sense 1.	**outthink** *verb* sense 1.
outfly *verb* sense 1.	**outplay** *verb* sense 1.	**outwalk** *verb* sense 1.
outgush *noun* sense 2.	**outrival** *verb* sense 1.	
outhit *verb* sense 1.	**outrun** *verb* sense 1.	

outer space ▷ *noun* any region of space beyond the Earth's atmosphere. ⓘ Early 20c.

outerwear ▷ *noun* clothing to be worn on top of other garments or for outdoors.

outface ▷ *verb* **1** to stare at someone until they look away. **2** to fight or deal with someone bravely or confidently. ⓘ 16c.

outfall ▷ *noun* the mouth of a river or sewer, etc where it flows into the sea; an outlet.

outfield ▷ *noun* **1** the outlying land on a farm. **2** *cricket* the area of the pitch far from the part where the stumps, etc are laid out. **3** *baseball* the area of the field beyond the diamond-shaped pitch where the bases are laid out. **4** *cricket, baseball* the players who have positions in these areas. Compare INFIELD. • **outfielder** *noun, cricket, baseball.*

outfit ▷ *noun* **1** a set of clothes worn together, especially for a particular occasion. **2** a set of articles, tools or equipment, etc for a particular task. **3** *colloq* a group of people working as a single unit or team. ▷ *verb* to provide someone with an outfit, especially of clothes. • **outfitter** *noun* someone who provides outfits, especially one who sells men's clothes. ⓘ 19c in these senses.

outflank ▷ *verb* **1** *military* to go round the side or sides of an enemy's position and attack from behind. **2** to get the better of someone or something, especially by a surprise action. ⓘ 18c.

outflow ▷ *noun* **1** a flowing out. **2** anything that flows out. **3** the amount that flows out. • **outflowing** *noun.*

outfox ▷ *verb* to get the better of someone by being more cunning; to outwit someone. ⓘ 1920s.

outgo ▷ *noun* /'aʊtgoʊ/ **1** the fact of going out. **2** cost; expenditure. **3** outflow. ▷ *verb* /aʊt'goʊ/ *archaic* to surpass; to outstrip. ⓘ 16c as *verb.*

outgoing ▷ *adj* **1** said of a person: friendly and sociable; extrovert. **2** leaving; departing. **3** said of an official, politician, etc: about to leave office □ *the outgoing president.* Opposite of INCOMING. ▷ *noun* the act of going out. ⓘ 1950s as *adj* 1; 14c as *noun.*

outgoings ▷ *plural noun* money spent; expenditure.

outgrow ▷ *verb* **1** to grow too large for (one's clothes). **2** to become too old for (childish ailments or children's games, etc). **3** to grow larger or faster than someone or something else. ⓘ 16c.

outgrowth ▷ *noun* **1** the act or process of growing out. **2** anything which grows out of something else; a by-product.

outgun ▷ *verb* **1** to defeat by means of superior weapons or force, etc. **2** to shoot better than someone else. **3** *colloq* to surpass or do better than someone else.

outhouse ▷ *noun* a building, usually a small one such as a shed, etc built close to a house. ⓘ 14c.

outing ▷ *noun* **1** a short pleasure trip or excursion. **2** *sport* an appearance at or participation in an outdoor race or other sporting event. **3** *colloq* the act of making public the homosexuality of a prominent person, often against their will, and especially to further a homosexual cause. ⓘ 1990s in sense 3; 19c.

outjockey ▷ *verb* (***outjockeyed***, ***outjockeying***) to outwit someone by trickery. ⓘ 18c.

outlandish /aʊt'landɪʃ/ ▷ *adj* said of appearance, manner or habit, etc: very strange; odd; bizarre. • **outlandishly** *adverb.* • **outlandishness** *noun.* ⓘ Anglo-Saxon *utlendisc* foreign.

outlaw ▷ *noun* **1** *originally* someone excluded from, and deprived of the protection of, the law. **2** a criminal who is a fugitive from the law. **3** *loosely* a bandit; a lawless person. ▷ *verb* (***outlawed***, ***outlawing***) **1** to deprive someone of the benefit and protection of the law; to make them an outlaw. **2** to forbid something officially. • **outlawry** *noun.* ⓘ Anglo-Saxon *utlaga.*

outlay ▷ *noun* /'aʊtleɪ/ money, or occasionally time, spent on something; expenditure. ▷ *verb* /aʊt'leɪ/ to spend (money, etc). ⓘ 16c as *verb.*

outlet /'aʊtlɛt, -lət/ ▷ *noun* **1** a vent or way out, especially for water or steam. **2** a way of releasing or using energy, talents or strong feeling, etc. Opposite of INLET. **3** a market for, or a shop that sells, the goods produced by a particular manufacturer. **4** an electrical power point. ⓘ 13c.

outlier /'aʊtlaɪə(r)/ ▷ *noun* **1** a detached portion of anything lying some way off or out. **2** *geol* an isolated remnant of rock surrouded by older rock. **3** someone who lives away from their place of work. ⓘ 17c.

outline ▷ *noun* **1** a line that forms or marks the outer edge of an object. **2** a drawing with only the outer lines and no shading. **3** the main points, etc without the details □ *an outline of the plot.* **4** (*usually* **outlines**) the most important features of something. **5** a line representing a word in shorthand. ▷ *verb* **1** to draw the outline of something. **2** to give a brief description of the main features of something. ⓘ 17c.

outlive ▷ *verb* **1** to live or survive longer than someone or something else. **2** to survive the effects of (a disease, etc).

outlook ▷ *noun* **1** a view from a particular place. **2** someone's mental attitude or point of view. **3** a prospect for the future.

outmoded /aʊt'moʊdɪd/ ▷ *adj* no longer in fashion; out of date.

outmost see OUTERMOST

out-of-body experience ▷ *noun* a sensation of being separate from one's own body, usually involving seeing it clearly from this external viewpoint.

outpatient ▷ *noun* a patient who receives treatment at a hospital or clinic but does not stay there overnight. Compare INPATIENT. Also *as adj* □ *outpatient treatment.* ⓘ 18c.

outpost ▷ *noun* **1** *military* a group of soldiers stationed at a distance from the main body, especially to protect it from a surprise attack. **2** a distant or remote settlement or branch. ⓘ 18c.

outpouring ▷ *noun* **1** (*usually* **outpourings**) a powerful or violent show of emotion. **2** the amount that pours out.

output ▷ *noun* **1** the quantity or amount of something produced. **2** *computing* the data that are transferred from the main memory of a computer to a disk, tape or output device such as a VDU or printer. **3** the power or energy produced by an electrical component or apparatus. ▷ *verb* **1** to produce (information or power, etc) as output. **2** *computing* to transfer data from the main memory of a computer to a disk or tape, or to an output device. Compare INPUT. ⓘ 19c; 1940s in sense 2.

output device ▷ *noun, computing* **1** a unit that presents computer-processed data to the user in an intelligible form, eg VDU, printer or plotter. **2** a unit that translates such data into a form suitable for computer reprocessing later.

outrage ▷ *noun* **1** an act of great cruelty or violence. **2** an act which breaks accepted standards of morality, honour and decency. **3** great anger or resentment. ▷ *verb* **1** to insult, shock or anger someone greatly. **2** to do physical violence to someone, especially (*euphemistic*) to rape them. ⓘ 13c in the sense 'excess': from French *outrer* to exceed.

outrageous /aʊt'reɪdʒəs/ ▷ *adj* **1** not moderate in behaviour; extravagant. **2** greatly offensive to accepted standards of morality, honour and decency. **3** *colloq* terrible; shocking. • **outrageously** *adverb*. • **outrageousness** *noun*. ◎ 14c.

outrank ▷ *verb* to have a higher rank than someone; to be superior to them.

outré /ˈuːtreɪ/ ▷ *adj* not conventional; eccentric; shocking. • **outréness** *noun*. ◎ 18c: French, from *outrer* to exceed.

outride ▷ *verb* **1** to ride faster than (another vehicle, horse, etc or someone else). **2** said especially of a ship: to come safely through (a storm).

outrider ▷ *noun* an attendant or guard who rides a horse or motorcycle at the side or ahead of a carriage or car conveying an important person.

outrigger ▷ *noun, naut* **1** a beam or framework sticking out from the side of a boat to help balance the vessel and prevent it capsizing. **2** a boat that is fitted with this sort of structure. ◎ 18c.

outright ▷ *adverb* /aʊtˈraɪt/ **1** completely □ *be proved outright*. **2** immediately; at once □ *killed outright*. **3** openly; honestly □ *ask outright*. ▷ *adj* /ˈaʊtraɪt/ **1** complete □ *an outright fool*. **2** clear □ *the outright winner*. **3** open; honest □ *outright disapproval*. ◎ 14c.

outset ▷ *noun* a beginning or start.

outside ▷ *noun* /ˈaʊtsaɪd/ **1** the outer surface; the external parts. Opposite of INSIDE. **2** everything that is not inside or within the bounds or scope of something. **3** the farthest limit. **4** the side of a pavement next to the road. ▷ *adj* /ˈaʊtsaɪd/ **1** relating to, on or near the outside. **2** not forming part of a group, organization or one's regular job, etc □ *outside interests*. **3** unlikely; remote. **4** said of a guess, etc: stating the highest possible amount. ▷ *adverb* /aʊtˈsaɪd/ **1** on or to the outside; outdoors. **2** *slang* not in prison. ▷ *prep* /aʊtˈsaɪd/ **1** on or to the outside of something. **2** beyond the limits of something. **3** except; apart from. • **at the outside** at the most. • **get outside of something** *slang* to eat or drink it. • **outside in** see under INSIDE OUT.

outside broadcast ▷ *noun* (abbreviation **OB**) a radio or TV programme that is recorded or filmed somewhere other than in a studio.

outside left and **outside right** ▷ *noun, Brit football* **1** the position at the extreme left or right of the middle of the field. **2** a player in this position.

outside line ▷ *noun* a connection by telephone from a building to another place.

outsider ▷ *noun* **1** someone who is not part of a group, etc or who refuses to accept the general values of society. **2** in a race or contest, etc: a competitor who is not expected to win.

outsize (abbreviation **os**) ▷ *adj* (*also* **outsized**) over normal or standard size. ▷ *noun* **1** anything, especially a garment, that is larger than standard size. ◎ 19c.

outskirts ▷ *plural noun* the outer parts or area, especially of a town or city. ◎ 16c.

outsmart ▷ *verb* (*outsmarted*, *outsmarting*) *colloq* to get the better of someone or something by being cleverer or more cunning; to outwit. ◎ 1920s.

outsource ▷ *verb* (*outsourced, outsourcing*) *originally US* said of a business, company, etc: **1** to subcontract (work) to another company; to contract (work) out. **2** to buy in (parts for a product) from another company rather than manufacture them. • **outsourcing** *noun*.

outspoken ▷ *adj, originally Scots* **1** said of a person: saying exactly what they think; frank. **2** of a remark or opinion, etc: candid; frank. • **outspokenly** *adverb*. • **outspokenness** *noun*. ◎ 19c.

outspread ▷ *verb* /aʊtˈsprɛd/ *tr & intr* to spread or stretch out; to extend. ▷ *adj* said of the arms, etc: stretched or spread out widely or fully. ▷ *noun* /ˈaʊtsprɛd/ a spreading out; an expansion.

outstanding ▷ *adj* **1** excellent; superior; remarkable. **2** not yet paid or done, etc □ *outstanding debts*. • **outstandingly** *adverb* in an excellent or remarkable way. 17c, meaning 'projecting'.

outstare ▷ *verb* to outdo someone in staring.

outstation ▷ *noun* a position, post or station in a remote or lonely area far from towns.

outstay ▷ *verb* **1** to stay longer than the length of (one's invitation, etc); to overstay □ *outstay one's welcome*. **2** to stay longer than (other people).

outstretch ▷ *verb* **1** to stretch or spread out; to expand. **2** to reach or stretch out (especially one's hand); to extend. • **outstretched** *adj*.

outstrip ▷ *verb* **1** to go faster than someone or something else. **2** to leave behind; to surpass. ◎ 16c.

outswinger ▷ *noun* **1** *cricket* a ball bowled to swing from leg to off. **2** *football* a ball kicked to swerve away from the goal or from the centre of the pitch. ◎ 1920s.

outtake ▷ *noun, cinema, TV* a section of film or tape removed from the final edited version of a motion picture or video. ◎ 1960s.

out tray ▷ *noun* a shallow tray or container used in offices for letters, etc that are ready to be sent out. ◎ 1940s.

outturn ▷ *noun* OUTPUT (*noun* 1). ◎ Early 19c.

outvote ▷ *verb* to obtain more votes than someone or something else; to defeat them by a majority of votes.

outward /ˈaʊtwəd/ ▷ *adj* **1** on or towards the outside. **2** said of a journey: away from a place. **3** apparent or seeming □ *outward appearances*. **4** relating to the outer or visible aspect of something as opposed to its inner nature, especially to the body as opposed to the mind or soul. **5** relating to the external material world. ▷ *adverb* (*also* **outwards**) towards the outside; in an outward direction. • **outwardly** *adverb* in appearance; on the outside; superficially □ *Outwardly he's very pleasant*. • **outwardness** *noun*. ◎ Anglo-Saxon.

outwear ▷ *verb* /aʊtˈwɛə(r)/ **1** to destroy something by wearing; to wear it away. **2** to wear or last longer than something else. **3** to exhaust something in strength or endurance, etc. **4** to overcome or defeat something in the process of time. ▷ *noun* /ˈaʊtwɛə(r)/ OUTERWEAR.

outweigh ▷ *verb* **1** to be greater than something in weight. **2** to be greater than something in value, importance or influence.

outwit ▷ *verb* (*outwitted*, *outwitting*) to get the better of or defeat someone by being cleverer or more cunning than they are. ◎ 17c.

outwith /ˈaʊtwɪθ/ ▷ *prep, chiefly Scots* outside; beyond. ◎ 13c.

outwork ▷ *noun* /ˈaʊtwɜːk/ **1** (*usually* **outworks**) a defence work that is outside the main line of fortifications. **2** work done for a company, factory or shop, etc by employees who work at home. ▷ *verb* /aʊtˈwɜːk/ to work harder or faster, etc than someone or something else. • **outworker** *noun*.

outworn ▷ *adj* said especially of an idea, belief or institution: no longer useful or in fashion; out of date; obsolete.

ouzel or **ousel** /ˈuːzəl/ ▷ *noun* **1** (*also* **ring ouzel**) a thrush, native to Europe, N Africa and SW Asia, with dark plumage, pale silvery wings and a characteristic broad white band across its throat. **2** (*also* **water ouzel**) any of various small aquatic songbirds that inhabit fast-flowing streams; a dipper. **3** *formerly* a blackbird. ◎ Anglo-Saxon *osle*.

ouzo /ˈuːzoʊ/ ▷ *noun* (*ouzos*) a Greek alcoholic drink flavoured with aniseed and usually diluted with water. ◎ 19c: from modern Greek *ouzon*.

ova *plural of* OVUM

oval /'oʊvəl/ ▷ *adj* **1** with the outline of an egg or shaped like an egg. **2** *loosely* elliptical or ellipsoidal. ▷ *noun* **1** any egg-shaped figure or object. **2** *Austral* a ground for Australian Rules football. • **ovality** or **ovalness** *noun*. • **ovally** *adverb*. ◷ 16c: from Latin *ovalis*, from *ovum* egg.

oval window ▷ *noun, anatomy* in vertebrates: the upper of two membrane-covered openings between the middle ear and the inner ear. Also called **fenestra ovalis**.

ovarian follicle see GRAAFIAN FOLLICLE

ovariectomy /oʊvɛərɪ'ɛktəmɪ/ ▷ *noun* (*ovariectomies*) *surgery* surgical removal of an ovary. ◷ 19c.

ovaritis /oʊvə'raɪtɪs/ ▷ *noun, pathol* inflammation of the ovary. ◷ 19c.

ovary /'oʊvərɪ/ ▷ *noun* (*ovaries*) **1** in a female animal: the reproductive organ in which the ova are produced. In vertebrates there are two ovaries, and they also produce oestrogen. **2** *bot* the enlarged hollow base of the carpel of a flower, which contains one or more ovules, the outer layer of which develops into a fruit after fertilization. • **ovarian** *adj*. ◷ 17c: from Latin *ovarium*, from *ovum* egg.

ovate /'oʊveɪt/ ▷ *adj* **1** egg-shaped. **2** *bot* with an outline like that of an egg; broadest below the middle. ▷ *noun, archaeol* an implement with an oval shape, especially a type of hand-axe from the lower Palaeolithic period. ◷ 18c: from Latin *ovatus* egg-shaped.

ovation /oʊ'veɪʃən/ ▷ *noun* **1** sustained applause or cheering to express approval or welcome, etc. **2** *historical* a processional entry into Rome by a victorious general or commander, but less glorious than a triumph. • **ovational** *adj*. ◷ 16c: from Latin *ovatio*, from *ovare* to exult, or to celebrate a lesser victory.

oven /'ʌvən/ ▷ *noun* **1** a closed compartment or arched cavity in which substances may be heated, used especially for baking or roasting food, drying clay, etc. **2** a small furnace. ◷ Anglo-Saxon *ofen*.

oven glove ▷ *noun* a padded glove used to protect the hand when removing hot dishes from an oven.

ovenproof ▷ *adj* said of dishes and plates, etc: suitable for use in an oven; that will not crack at a high temperature.

oven-ready ▷ *adj* said of food: prepared beforehand so as to be ready for cooking in the oven immediately after purchase.

ovenware ▷ *noun* heat-resistant or ovenproof dishes, bowls, etc.

over /'oʊvə(r)/ ▷ *adverb* **1** above and across. **2** outwards and downwards □ ***knock him over*** □ ***The kettle boiled over.*** **3** across a space; to or on the other side □ ***fly over from Australia.*** **4** from one person, side or condition to another □ ***win them over*** □ ***turn the card over.*** **5** through, from beginning to end, usually with concentration □ ***read the letter over*** □ ***think it over thoroughly.*** **6** again; in repetition □ ***do it twice over.*** **7** at an end □ ***The game is over.*** **8** so as to cover completely □ ***paper the cracks over.*** **9** beyond a limit; in excess (of) □ ***go over budget*** □ ***spend over £10.*** **10** remaining □ ***left over.*** **11** until a later time □ ***hold payment over until February.*** ▷ *prep* **1** in or to a position which is above or higher in place, importance, authority, value or number, etc. **2** above and from one side to another □ ***fly over the sea.*** **3** so as to cover □ ***flopped over his eyes.*** **4** out and down from □ ***fall over the edge.*** **5** throughout the extent of something □ ***read over that page again.*** **6** during a specified time or period □ ***sometime over the weekend.*** **7** until after a specified time □ ***stay over Monday night.*** **8** more than □ ***over a year ago.*** **9** concerning; about □ ***argue over who would pay.*** **10** while occupied with something □ ***chat about it over coffee.*** **11** occupying time with something □ ***spend a day over the preparations.*** **12** recovered from the effects of something □ ***be over the accident.*** **13** by means of something □ ***hear about it over the radio.*** **14** divided by □ ***Six over three is two.*** ▷ *adj* **1** upper; higher. **2** outer. **3** excessive. See also OVER-. ▷ *exclamation* used during two-way radio conversations: showing that one has finished speaking and expects a reply. ▷ *noun, cricket* **1** a series of six (or *formerly* in Australia eight) balls bowled by the same bowler from the same end of the pitch. **2** play during such a series of balls. • **be all over someone** *colloq* to make a great fuss of them, often ingratiatingly. • **over again** once more. • **over against something** opposite it; in contrast with it. • **over and above something** in addition to it. • **over and over again** repeatedly. • **over head and ears** completely submerged. • **over the top** (abbreviation **OTT**) *colloq* excessive; exaggerated. ◷ Anglo-Saxon *ofer*.

over- /oʊvə(r)/ ▷ *prefix, denoting* **1** excessive or excessively; beyond the agreed or desired limit □ ***overconfident.*** **2** above; in a higher position or authority □ ***overlord*** □ ***oversee.*** **3** position or movement above □ ***overhang.*** **4** outer; extra □ ***overcoat.*** **5** movement downwards; away from an upright position □ ***overturn.*** **6** completely □ ***overwhelm.***

overachieve ▷ *verb, tr & intr* to do better than expected or than (an expected goal or aim, etc). • **overachiever** *noun*. ◷ 1950s.

overact ▷ *verb, tr & intr* to act (a part) with too much expression or emotion. ◷ 17c.

over-age ▷ *adj* **1** beyond a specified age limit. **2** too old.

overall ▷ *noun* /'oʊvərɔːl/ **1** *Brit* a loose-fitting coat-like garment worn over ordinary clothes to protect them. **2** (**overalls**) a one-piece garment with trousers to cover the legs and either a dungaree-type top, or top with sleeves, worn to protect clothes. Compare COVERALL. ▷ *adj* /'oʊvərɔːl/ **1** including everything □ ***the overall total.*** **2** from end to end □ ***the overall length.*** ▷ *adverb* /oʊvər'ɔːl/ as a whole; in general □ ***quite good, overall.*** ◷ 13c as *adverb*.

overarch ▷ *verb* to form an arch over something.

Some words with *over-* prefixed: see OVER- for numbered senses specified below.

overabundance *noun* sense 1.	**overcareful** *adj* sense 1.	**overeat** *verb* sense 1.
overambitious *adj* sense 1.	**overclad** *adj* sense 1.	**overemotional** *adj* sense 1.
overanxious *adj* sense 1.	**overcompensate** *verb* sense 1.	**over-exact** *adj* sense 1.
overanxiously *adverb* sense 1.	**overcomplicate** *verb* sense 1.	**overexcitable** *adj* sense 1.
overappreciative *adj* sense 1.	**overconfident** *adj* sense 1.	**overexcite** *verb* sense 1.
overassert *verb* sense 1.	**overcook** *verb* sense 1.	**overexert** *verb* sense 1.
overblanket *noun* sense 3.	**overcorrection** *noun* sense 1.	**overexertion** *noun* sense 1.
overboil *verb* sense 1.	**overcritical** *adj* sense 1.	**overfamiliar** *adj* sense 1.
overbold *adj* sense 1.	**overcrowd** *verb* sense 1.	**overfeed** *verb* sense 1.
overbook *verb* sense 1.	**overdevelop** *verb* sense 1.	**overfill** *verb* sense 1.
overbooked *adj* sense 1.	**overdramatize** *verb* sense 1.	**overfine** *adj* sense 1.

overarching ▷ *adj* **1** forming an arch over something. **2** referring or relating to something that covers various issues, the interests of various affected groups, etc □ *the overarching importance of the peace process* □ *one overarching body*.

overarm ▷ *adj, adverb* said of a ball, especially in cricket: bowled or thrown with the hand and arm raised over and moving round the shoulder.

overawe ▷ *verb* to subdue or restrain someone by filling them with awe, fear or astonishment. ⓒ 16c.

overbalance ▷ *verb, tr & intr* to make someone lose their balance (or to lose one's balance) and fall.

overbearing ▷ *adj* **1** domineering; too powerful and proud. **2** referring to someone or something of particularly great importance. ● **overbearingly** *adverb*.

overblown ▷ *adj* **1** overdone; excessive. **2** self-important and pretentious. **3** said of flowers: past their best; beginning to die.

overboard ▷ *adverb* over the side of a ship or boat into the water □ *fall overboard*. ● **go overboard** *colloq* to be very or too enthusiastic. ● **throw something** or **someone overboard** to abandon or get rid of it or them.

overburden ▷ *verb* to give someone too much to do, carry or think about.

overcast ▷ *adj* said of the sky or weather: cloudy.

overcharge ▷ *verb* **1** *tr & intr* to charge too much □ *overcharged him by £10*. **2** to overfill or overload something. ▷ *noun* /ˈoʊvə-/ **1** an excessive price or charge. **2** an excessive load.

overcloud ▷ *verb* **1** *tr & intr* to cover something, or become covered, with clouds. **2** to make someone sad or worried.

overcoat ▷ *noun* a warm heavy coat worn especially in winter. ⓒ Early 19c.

overcome ▷ *verb* **1** to defeat someone or something; to succeed in a struggle against them or it; to deal successfully with them or it. **2** to deal successfully with something □ *overcame his problems*. **3** *intr* to be victorious. **4** to affect someone strongly; to overwhelm them □ *was overcome by the fumes*. ⓒ Anglo-Saxon *ofercuman*.

overdo ▷ *verb* **1** to do something too much; to exaggerate. **2** to cook (food) for too long. **3** to use too much of something. ● **overdo it** or **things** to work too hard. ⓒ Anglo-Saxon *oferdon*.

overdose ▷ *noun* an excessive dose of a drug, etc. ▷ *verb, tr & intr* to take an overdose or give an excessive dose to someone. See also OD[1]. ⓒ 18c.

overdraft ▷ *noun* **1** a state in which one has taken more money out of one's bank account than was in it. **2** the excess of money taken from one's account over the sum that was in it. ⓒ 19c.

overdraw ▷ *verb* **1** *tr & intr* to draw more money from (one's bank account) than one has in it. **2** to exaggerate in describing something. ● **overdrawn** *adj* with an overdraft at a bank.

overdress ▷ *verb, tr & intr* to dress someone or oneself, or to be dressed, in clothes that are too formal, smart or expensive for the occasion. ▷ *noun* a dress that may be worn over a blouse or jumper, etc.

overdrive ▷ *noun* an additional very high gear in a motor vehicle's gearbox, which reduces wear on the engine and saves fuel when travelling at high speeds. ▷ *verb* to drive something too hard; to overwork it. ⓒ 1920s as *noun*.

overdue ▷ *adj* said of bills or work, etc: not yet paid, done or delivered, etc, although the date for doing this has passed.

overestimate ▷ *verb* to estimate or judge, etc something too highly. ▷ *noun* /-ˈɛstɪmɪt/ too high an estimate. ● **overestimation** *noun*.

overexpose ▷ *verb* **1** to expose someone to too much publicity. **2** to expose (photographic film) to too much light. ● **overexposure** *noun*.

overfish ▷ *verb* to remove too many fish from (a sea or river, etc) thereby depleting the population of certain species by reducing the number available to breed.

overflow ▷ *verb* **1** to flow over (a brim) or go beyond (the limits or edge of something). **2** *intr* said of a container, etc: to be filled so full that the contents spill over or out. **3** (*usually* **overflow with something**) *intr* to be full of it □ *was overflowing with gratitude*. ▷ *noun* /ˈoʊvə-/ **1** that which overflows. **2** the act of flowing over. **3** a pipe or outlet for surplus water. **4** an excess or abundance of something. ⓒ Anglo-Saxon *oferflowan*.

overgrown ▷ *adj* **1** said of a garden, etc: dense with plants that have grown too large and thick. **2** grown too large or beyond the normal size. ● **overgrowth** *noun*. ⓒ 14c in sense 2.

overhand ▷ *adj, adverb* thrown or performed, etc with the hand brought downwards from above the shoulder; overarm or with an overarm action.

overhang ▷ *verb* **1** *tr & intr* to project or hang out over something. **2** to threaten. ▷ *noun* /ˈoʊvə-/ **1** a piece of rock or part of a roof, etc that overhangs. **2** the amount by which something overhangs.

overhaul ▷ *verb* **1** to examine carefully and repair something. **2** to overtake. ▷ *noun* /ˈoʊvə-/ a thorough examination and repair.

overhead ▷ *adverb, adj* above; over one's head. ▷ *noun* (**overheads**) the regular costs of a business, such as rent, wages and electricity. ⓒ Early 20c as *noun*; 15c as *adverb*.

overhead projector ▷ *noun* (abbreviation **OHP**) a projector which sits on a speaker's desk and projects images on a screen behind it.

Some words with *over-* prefixed: see OVER- for numbered senses specified below.

overfond *adj* sense 1.
overfondly *adverb* sense 1.
overfull *adj* sense 1.
overgarment *noun* sense 3.
overgeneralization or **overgeneralisation** *noun* sense 1.
overgeneralize or **overgeneralise** *verb* sense 1.
overgenerous *adj* sense 1.
overhastily *adverb* sense 1.
overhasty *adj* sense 1.
overidealistic *adj* sense 1.
overindulge *verb* sense 1.
overindulgent *adj* sense 1.
overinsure *verb* sense 1.
overissue *verb* sense 1.
overkind *adj* sense 1.
overlong *adj, adverb* sense 1.
overman *verb* sense 1.
overoptimistic *adj* sense 1.
overpay *verb* sense 1.
overpopulate *verb* sense 1.
overpraise *verb* sense 1.
overprice *verb* sense 1.
overproduce *verb* sense 1.
overproduction *noun* sense 1.
overprotective *adj* sense 1.
over-refine *verb* sense 1.
over-refinement *noun* sense 1.
overripe *adj* sense 1.
overscrupulous *adj* sense 1.
oversensitive *adj*

overhear ▻ *verb, tr & intr* to hear (a person or remark, etc) without the speaker knowing, either by accident or on purpose.

overheat ▻ *verb* **1** to heat something excessively. **2** *intr* to become too hot. **3** *econ* to overstimulate (the economy) with the risk of increasing inflation. • **overheated** *adj* said of an argument, discussion, etc: angry and excited; passionate.

overjoyed /oʊvə'dʒɔɪd/ ▻ *adj* very glad; elated.

overkill ▻ *noun* /'oʊvəkɪl/ **1** the capability to destroy an enemy using a larger force than is actually needed to win a victory. **2** action, behaviour or treatment, etc that is far in excess of what is required. ▻ *verb, tr & intr* to practise overkill against, or subject someone or something to, overkill. ⓒ 1940s.

overladen ▻ *adj* overloaded.

overland ▻ *adverb, adj* said of a journey, etc: across land.

overlap ▻ *verb* /oʊvə'lap/ **1** said of part of an object: to partly cover (another object). **2** *intr* said of two parts: to have one part partly covering the other. **3** *intr* said of two things: to have something in common; to partly coincide. ▻ *noun* /'oʊvə-/ an overlapping part.

overlay ▻ *verb* **1** to lay one thing on or over another. **2** (*often* **overlay one thing with another**) **a** to cover or conceal it with something else; **b** to cover (a surface) with an applied decoration. **3** *printing* to obtain the correct printing pressure evenly over (a forme or plate) by adding to the appropriate areas of the packing. ▻ *noun* /'oʊvəleɪ/ **1** a covering; something that is laid over something else. **2** a layer, eg of gold leaf, applied to something for decoration. **3** a transparent sheet placed over a map or diagram, etc to give additional information or details. **4** *printing* material used to overlay a forme or plate. **5** *computing* **a** the process by which segments of a large program are brought from backing store for processing, with only those segments currently requiring processing being held in the main store; **b** a segment of a program transferred in this way.

overleaf ▻ *adverb* on the other side of the page.

overlie ▻ *verb* **1** to lie on. **2** to smother and kill (a baby or small animal) by lying on it.

overload ▻ *verb* **1** to load something too heavily. **2** to put too great an electric current through (a circuit). ▻ *noun* /'oʊvə-/ too great an electric current flowing through a circuit.

overlook ▻ *verb* **1** to give a view of something from a higher position □ *overlooks the garden.* **2** to fail to see or notice something. **3** to allow (a mistake or crime, etc) to go unpunished. **4** to supervise. **5** to look on someone with the evil eye; to bewitch them. ▻ *noun* /'oʊvə-/ **1** *chiefly US* a high place that gives a view of the area below. **2** a failure to see or notice something; an oversight.

overlord ▻ *noun* a lord or ruler with supreme power. • **overlordship** *noun*. ⓒ 13c.

overly /'oʊvəlɪ/ ▻ *adverb* too; excessively. ⓒ Anglo-Saxon *oferlice*.

overmaster ▻ *verb* to master someone or something completely; to overpower them.

overmatch *chiefly US* ▻ *verb* **1** to be more than a match for someone. **2** to match someone with a superior opponent. ▻ *noun* /'oʊvə-/ **1** a superior opponent. **2** a contest in which one of the opponents is superior.

overmuch ▻ *adverb, adj* too much; very much. ⓒ 13c.

overnice ▻ *adj* fussy; critical and hard to please.

overnight ▻ *adverb* **1** during the night. **2** for the duration of the night. **3** suddenly □ *Success came overnight.* ▻ *adj* /'oʊvə-/ **1** done or occurring in the night. **2** sudden □ *an overnight success.* **3** for use overnight.

overnight bag and **overnight case** ▻ *noun* a small grip or case for carrying the clothes and toilet articles, etc needed for an overnight stay.

overpass see under FLYOVER

overplay ▻ *verb* **1** to exaggerate or overemphasize (the importance of something). **2** *tr & intr* to exaggerate (an emotion, etc); to act in an exaggerated way. • **overplay one's hand** to overestimate or overtax one's talents or assets, etc.

overpower ▻ *verb* **1** to defeat or subdue by greater strength. **2** to weaken or reduce to helplessness. • **overpowering** **1** very great; overwhelming. **2** irresistible. *adj* • **overpoweringly** *adverb*.

overprint ▻ *verb* **1** to print over (something already printed, especially a postage stamp). **2** to print something in one colour on top of another. **3** *tr & intr* to print too many copies of (a book, etc). ▻ *noun* /'oʊvə-/ **1** the action of overprinting. **2** overprinted matter, especially on a postage stamp. **3** a postage stamp with overprinted matter.

overqualified ▻ *noun* with more qualifications or experience than are required for a particular job or post, etc.

overrate ▻ *verb* **1** to assess or think too highly of something or someone; to overestimate it or them. **2** *rowing* to row at a rate that is faster than (one's opponent). • **overrated** *adj*. ⓒ 17c in sense 1; 1960s in sense 2.

overreach ▻ *verb* **1** to defeat (oneself) by trying to do too much, or be too clever, etc. **2** to go beyond (a target, etc). **3** to strain (oneself) by trying to reach too far. **4** *tr & intr* to stretch out (an arm, etc) too far in attempting to reach for or grasp something. **5** *intr* said of a horse: to strike the hindfoot against the back of the forefoot, eg when jumping a fence.

overreact ▻ *verb, intr* to react excessively or too strongly. • **overreaction** *noun*. ⓒ 1960s.

Some words with *over-* prefixed: see OVER- for numbered senses specified below.

overshirt *noun* sense 3.
oversimplification *noun* sense 1.
oversimplify *verb* sense 1.
overskirt *noun* sense 3.
oversleeve *noun* sense 3.
overspecialize or **overspecialise** *verb* sense 1.
overspecialization or **overspecialisation** *noun* sense 1.
overspread *verb* sense 3.
overstaff *verb* sense 1.
overstain *verb* sense 3.
overstock *verb* sense 1.
overstock *noun* sense 1.
overstrain *verb* sense 1.
overstress *verb* sense 1.
overstretch *verb* sense 1.
overstrict *adj* sense 1.
overstuff *verb* sense 1.
oversubtle *adj* sense 1.
oversubtlety *noun* sense 1.
oversupply *verb* sense 1.
oversupply *noun* sense 1.
overtire *verb* sense 1.
overtrain *verb* sense 1.
overtrump *verb* sense 2.
overuse *verb* sense 1.
overuse *noun* sense 1.
overvalue *verb* sense 1.
overvaluation *noun* sense 1.
overviolent *adj* sense 1.
overwilling *adj* sense 1.
overweary *adj* sense 1.
overwise *adj* sense 1.

override ▷ *verb* **1** to ride over; to cross (an area) by riding. **2** to dominate or assume superiority over someone. **3** to annul something or set it aside. **4** to take manual control of (a normally automatically controlled operation). ▷ *noun* /ˈoʊvə-/ **1** the action or process of suspending an automatic control. **2** a device, especially a manual control, that does this. • **overriding** *adj* dominant; most important □ *overriding considerations*. ◷ Anglo-Saxon; 1940s as *noun*.

overrider /ˈoʊvəraɪdə(r)/ *noun* an attachment fitted to the bumper of a motor vehicle to prevent another bumper becoming interlocked with it.

overrule ▷ *verb* **1** to rule against or cancel (especially a previous decision or judgement) by higher authority. **2** to impose a decision on (a person) by higher authority.

overrun ▷ *verb* **1** to spread over or through something; to infest it □ *overrun with weeds*. **2** to invade and occupy (another country) quickly and by force. **3** *tr & intr* to go beyond (a fixed limit) □ *The talk overran by ten minutes*. **4** *intr* said of liquid or a container, etc: to spill over; to overflow. **5** *printing* to transfer or carry over (set type) to a new line or page. **6** *intr* said of a vehicle engine: to slow down in response to a reverse torque transmitted through the gears from the wheels. ▷ *noun* /ˈoʊvə-/ **1** the act or an instance of overrunning. **2** the extent to which something overruns. **3** an excess of production. ◷ Anglo-Saxon *oferyrnan*.

overrun brake ▷ *noun* a brake fitted to a trailer to prevent it from going faster than the towing vehicle when going downhill or when the towing vehicle is decelerating.

overseas ▷ *adverb* /oʊvəˈsiːz/ in or to a land beyond the sea; abroad □ *working overseas*. ▷ *adj* /ˈoʊvə-/ (*also* **oversea**) across or from beyond the sea; foreign □ *an overseas posting*. ▷ *noun* a foreign country or foreign countries in general □ *a visitor from overseas*. ◷ 16c.

oversee /oʊvəˈsiː/ ▷ *verb* to supervise. • **overseer** /ˈoʊvəsɪə(r)/ *noun* someone who oversees workers; a supervisor. ◷ Anglo-Saxon *oferseon* to overlook.

oversell ▷ *verb* **1** *tr & intr* to sell something at too high a price or in greater quantities than can be supplied. **2** to praise someone or something too highly. ▷ *noun* /ˈoʊvə-/ excessively aggressive or ambitious selling of commodities or goods, etc.

oversew ▷ *verb* to sew (two edges) together with close stitches that pass over both edges.

oversexed ▷ *adj* with unusually strong sexual urges.

overshadow ▷ *verb* **1** to seem much more important than someone or something else; to outshine them. **2** to cast a shadow over something; to make it seem more gloomy. ◷ Anglo-Saxon *ofersceadian*.

overshoe ▷ *noun* a shoe, usually made of rubber or plastic, worn over normal shoes to protect them in wet weather. ◷ 19c.

overshoot ▷ *verb* **1** to shoot or go farther than (a target aimed at). **2 a** said of an aircraft: to fly beyond or fail to come to a halt on (a runway); **b** said of a train: to fail to come to a halt at (a station). **3** (*especially* **overshoot the mark**) to make a mistake as a result of misjudging a situation. ▷ *noun* /ˈoʊvə-/ **1** the action or an act of overshooting. **2** the degree to which something overshoots. • **overshot** *adj* **1** with the upper jaw protruding beyond the lower one. **2** said of a waterwheel: fed from above.

oversight ▷ *noun* **1** a mistake or omission, especially one made through a failure to notice something. **2** supervision. ◷ 14c in sense 2.

oversize ▷ *adj* (*also* **oversized**) very large; larger then normal. ▷ *noun* /ˈoʊvə-/ **1** a size that is larger than normal. **2** something that is oversize.

oversleep ▷ *verb, intr* to sleep longer than one intended.

overspend ▷ *verb* **1** to exhaust something; to wear it out. **2** to spend in excess of (a specified amount or limit, etc). **3** *intr* to spend too much money; to spend beyond one's means. ▷ *noun* /ˈoʊvə-/ **1** the action or an act of overspending. **2** an amount that is overspent. ◷ 17c.

overspill ▷ *noun, Brit* the people leaving an overcrowded or derelict town area to live elsewhere. ◷ 19c.

overstate ▷ *verb* to state something too strongly or with undue emphasis; to exaggerate. • **overstatement** *noun*.

overstay ▷ *verb* to stay longer than the length of (one's invitation, etc) □ *overstay one's welcome*.

oversteer ▷ *verb, intr* said of a vehicle: to turn more sharply than the driver intends; to exaggerate the degree of turn applied by the steering wheel. ◷ 1930s.

overstep ▷ *verb* (*especially* **overstep the mark**) to go beyond or exceed (a certain limit, or what is prudent or reasonable). ◷ Anglo-Saxon *ofersteppan*.

overstrung ▷ *adj* **1** said of a person or temperament, etc: too sensitive and nervous; tense. **2** said of a piano: with two sets of strings crossing each other obliquely to save space. ◷ 19c.

oversubscribe ▷ *verb* to apply for or try to purchase (eg shares, etc) in larger quantities than are available. • **oversubscription** *noun*.

overt /oʊˈvɜːt, ˈoʊvɜːt/ ▷ *adj* not hidden or secret; open; public. • **overtly** *adverb*. ◷ 14c: from French *ouvert* open, from Latin *aperire, apertum*.

overt act ▷ *noun, law* something that is obviously done in execution of a criminal intent.

overtake ▷ *verb* **1** *tr & intr, chiefly Brit* to catch up with and go past (a car or a person, etc) moving in the same direction. **2** to draw level with and begin to do better than someone. **3** to come upon someone suddenly or without warning □ *overtaken by bad weather*.

overtax ▷ *verb* **1** to demand too much tax from someone. **2** to put too great a strain on someone or oneself.

over-the-counter ▷ *adj* **1** said of goods, eg drugs and medicines: legally sold directly to the customer. **2** (**over the counter**) involving trading in shares that are not on the official Stock Exchange list.

overthrow ▷ *verb* **1** to defeat completely (an established order or a government, etc). **2** to upset or overturn something. **3** to throw (a ball, etc) too far. ▷ *noun* /ˈoʊvə-/ **1** the act of overthrowing or state of being overthrown. **2** *cricket* an inaccurate return of the ball by a fielder which often allows the batsman to score extra runs.

overtime ▷ *noun* **1** time spent working at one's job beyond one's regular hours. **2** the money which is sometimes paid for this extra time. **3** *sport, N Amer* extra time. ▷ *adverb* during overtime; in addition to one's regular hours □ *work overtime*. ▷ *verb* /oʊvəˈtaɪm/ to go beyond the correct allowance of time for (a photographic exposure, etc).

overtly see under OVERT

overtone ▷ *noun* **1** (*often* **overtones**) a subtle hint, quality or meaning; a nuance □ *political overtones*. **2** *music* a tone that contributes towards a musical sound and adds to its quality. ◷ 19c: modelled on German *Oberton*, a contraction of *oberpartialton* upper partial tone.

overture /ˈoʊvətjʊə(r)/ ▷ *noun* **1** *music* **a** an orchestral introduction to an opera, oratorio or ballet; **b** a one-movement orchestral composition in a similar style. **2** (*usually* **overtures**) a proposal or offer intended to open a discussion, negotiations or a relationship, etc. ◷ 14c: French, meaning 'opening', ultimately from Latin *aperire, apertum* to open.

overturn ▷ *verb* **1** *tr & intr* to turn something or be turned over or upside down. **2** to bring down or destroy (a government). **3** to overrule or cancel (a previous legal decision).

overview ▻ *noun* a brief general account or description of a subject, etc; a summary.

overweening ▻ *adj* **1** said of a person: arrogant; conceited. **2** said of pride: inflated and excessive. • **overweeningly** *adverb*. • **overweeningness** *noun*. ⓘ 14c: from Anglo-Saxon *wenan* to WEEN.

overweight ▻ *adj* above the desired, required or usual weight. ▻ *noun* **1** extra weight; weight beyond what is required or allowed. **2** said of a person: the condition of being overweight. ▻ *verb* (***overweighted, overweighting***) **1** to give too much weight or importance to something. **2** to add too much weight to something; to overload it. ⓘ 16c.

overwhelm /oʊvə'wɛlm/ ▻ *verb* (***overwhelmed, overwhelming***) **1** to crush mentally; to overpower (a person's emotions or thoughts, etc). **2** to defeat completely by superior force or numbers. **3** to supply or offer something in great amounts □ *overwhelmed with offers of help*. ⓘ 14c: from *whelm* to turn or roll.

overwhelming ▻ *adj* physically or mentally crushing; intensely powerful. • **overwhelmingly** *adverb*. ⓘ 18c.

overwind ▻ *verb* to wind (a watch, etc) too far.

overwork ▻ *verb* **1** *intr* to work too hard. **2** to make someone work too hard. **3** to make too much use of something. **4** to decorate the surface of something. ▻ *noun* the act of working too hard; excessive work.

overwrite ▻ *verb* **1** to write too much about something. **2** to write in a laboured or excessively ornate style. **3** to write on top of something else. **4** *computing* to write new information over (existing data), thereby destroying (it). ⓘ 17c.

overwrought /oʊvə'rɔːt/ ▻ *adj* **1** very nervous or excited; over-emotional. **2** too elaborate; overdone. ⓘ 17c: from WROUGHT, old past participle of WORK.

ovi- /oʊvɪ/ or **ovo-** /oʊvoʊ/ ▻ *combining form, signifying* egg or ovum. ⓘ From Latin *ovum* egg.

oviduct /'oʊvɪdʌkt, 'ɒvɪ-/ ▻ *noun, anatomy, zool* the tube that conveys ova from the ovary to another organ, such as the uterus, or to the outside of the body. In mammals, this duct connects the ovary to the FALLOPIAN TUBE, which leads to the uterus. • **oviducal** or **oviductal** *adj*. ⓘ 18c.

oviform /'oʊvɪfɔːm/ ▻ *adj* egg-shaped. ⓘ 17c.

ovine /'oʊvaɪn/ ▻ *adj* relating to or characteristic of a sheep or sheep; sheeplike. ⓘ 19c: from Latin *ovinus*, from *ovis* sheep.

oviparous /oʊ'vɪpərəs/ ▻ *adj, zool* said of many birds, reptiles, amphibians, bony fishes, etc: laying eggs that develop and hatch outside the mother's body. Compare OVOVIVIPAROUS, VIVIPAROUS. • **oviparity** *noun*. • **oviparously** *adj*. ⓘ 17c.

ovipositor /oʊvɪ'pɒzɪtə(r)/ ▻ *noun, zool* **1** in female insects: the egg-laying organ, which is often long and tube-like, at the rear end of the abdomen and which may be used for stinging or boring. **2** in some female fishes: a similar organ, formed by the extension of the edges of the genital opening. ⓘ 19c: from OVI- + Latin *positor* placer.

ovo- see OVI-

ovoid /'oʊvɔɪd/ *chiefly zool & bot* ▻ *adj* egg-shaped; oval. ▻ *noun* an egg-shaped or oval form or object. ⓘ 19c: from French *ovoïde*, from Latin *ovum* egg.

ovolo /'oʊvəloʊ/ ▻ *noun* (*plural* ***ovoli***) *archit* a moulding with the rounded part composed of a quarter of a circle, or of an arc of an ellipse with the curve greatest at the top. ⓘ 17c: Italian, diminutive of *ouvo* or obsolete *ovo*, from Latin *ovum* egg.

ovoviviparous /oʊvoʊvɪ'vɪpərəs, -vaɪ'vɪpərəs/ ▻ *adj, zool* said of many insects and of certain fish and reptiles: producing eggs that hatch within the body of the mother. Compare OVIPAROUS and VIVIPAROUS. • **ovoviviparity** *noun*. ⓘ 19c.

ovulate /'ɒvjʊleɪt/ ▻ *verb* (***ovulated, ovulating***) *intr, physiol* **1** to release an ovum or egg cell from the ovary. **2** to form or produce ova. • **ovulation** *noun*. ⓘ 19c: from OVULE, or back formation from *ovulation*.

ovule /'ɒvjuːl/ ▻ *noun, bot* in flowering plants characteristic of SPERMATOPHYTES: the structure that develops into a seed after fertilization. • **ovular** *adj*. ⓘ 19c: French, from Latin *ovulum*, diminutive of *ovum* egg.

ovum /'oʊvəm/ ▻ *noun* (***ova*** /'oʊvə/) **1** *biol* an unfertilized egg or egg cell produced by the ovary of an animal; a female gamete. **2** *bot* the non-motile female gamete. ⓘ 18c in this sense: Latin, meaning 'egg'.

ow /aʊ/ ▻ *exclamation* expressing sudden, usually mild, pain. ⓘ Early 20c.

owe /oʊ/ ▻ *verb* (***owed, owing***) **1** *tr & intr* to be under an obligation to pay (money) to someone □ *owes him £5*. **2** to feel required by duty or gratitude to do or give someone something □ *owe you an explanation*. **3** (*often* **owe something to someone** or **something**) to have or enjoy it as a result of them or it □ *owes her promotion to her hard work*. **4** to hold or bear in the mind (a feeling, etc) against another person □ *owe a grudge*. ⓘ Anglo-Saxon *agan* to own.

owing ▻ *adj* still to be paid; due. • **owing to something** because of it; on account of it.

> ***owing***
>
> **Owing to** is often used as an alternative to **due to** when there is no noun or pronoun antecedent earlier in the sentence. See Usage Note at **due**.

owl /aʊl/ ▻ *noun* **1** a nocturnal bird of prey found in all parts of the world except Antarctica, with a large broad head, a flat face, large forward-facing eyes and a short hooked beak. It is noted for its distinctive hooting or howling call. **2** any of several varieties of fancy domestic pigeon with an owl-like head. **3** someone thought to look or behave like an owl, especially by looking solemn or wise, or sitting up late at night. • **owl-like** *adj*. ⓘ Anglo-Saxon *ule*.

owlet /'aʊlɪt/ ▻ *noun* a young or small owl. ⓘ 16c.

owlish ▻ *adj* **1** relating to or like an owl. **2** said of a person: **a** with an owl-like appearance, especially if wearing glasses; **b** solemn or wise. • **owlishly** *adverb*. • **owlishness** *noun*. ⓘ 17c.

own /oʊn/ ▻ *adj* often used for emphasis: belonging to or for oneself or itself □ *my own sister*. ▻ *pronoun* one belonging (or something belonging) to oneself or itself □ *lost his own, so I lent him mine*. ▻ *verb* (***owned, owning***) **1** to have something as a possession or property. **2** (*usually* **own to something**) *intr* to admit or confess to it □ *owned to many weaknesses*. **3** *rare* to concede or acknowledge. • **owner** *noun*. • **ownership** *noun*. • **come into one's own 1** to take possession of one's rights or what is due to one. **2** to have one's abilities or talents, etc duly recognized, or to realize one's potential. • **get one's own back on someone** *colloq* to get even with them; to have one's revenge. • **hold one's own** to maintain one's position, especially in spite of difficulty or opposition, etc; not to be defeated. • **on one's own 1** alone; by oneself. **2** without help. ⓘ Anglo-Saxon *agen*, past participle of *agan* to possess.

> ■ **own up** or **own up to something** to confess; to admit a wrongdoing, etc.

own brand and **own label** ▻ *noun* an article that carries the trademark or label, etc of the store that sells it rather than that of the producer. Compare NAME BRAND.

owner-occupier ▻ *noun* someone who owns the property they are living in. • **owner-occupied** *adj*.

own goal ▷ *noun* **1** *sport* a goal scored by mistake for the opposing side. **2** *colloq* an action that turns out to be to the disadvantage of the person who took it.

ox /ɒks/ ▷ *noun* (*plural* **oxen** /'ɒksən/) **1** the general name for any bovine mammal, especially the male or female of common domestic cattle. **2** an adult castrated male of any species of bovine mammal, especially domesticated species of cattle, used for pulling loads or as a source of meat. ⓒ Anglo-Saxon *oxa*.

oxalic acid /ɒk'salɪk —/ ▷ *noun, chem* (formula $(COOH)_2$) a highly poisonous white crystalline solid that occurs in the leaves of rhubarb, wood sorrel and certain other plants, used as a rust and stain remover, a cleaner for car radiators and in tanning and bleaching. Also called ETHANEDIOIC ACID. ⓒ 18c: from OXALIS.

oxalis /'ɒksəlɪs, ɒk'salɪs/ ▷ *noun* any of various plants with delicate white, pink, red or yellow flowers and clover-like leaves that contain oxalic acid. See also WOOD SORREL. ⓒ 17c: Greek, meaning 'sorrel', from *oxys* sour or acid, because of the sharp-tasting leaves.

oxblood ▷ *noun* a dark reddish-brown colour. Also *as adj.* ⓒ 18c.

oxbow /'ɒksboʊ/ ▷ *noun* **1** a collar for a yoked ox, formed from a piece of U-shaped wood the ends of which are attached to the yoke. **2** *geol* **a** a horseshoe-shaped bend or meander in a river; **b** (*also* **oxbow lake**) a shallow curved lake found on a flat floodplain alongside a meandering river, and formed when one of the meanders has been cut off by the formation of a stream across the neck of the bend. ⓒ 14c.

Oxbridge /'ɒksbrɪdʒ/ ▷ *noun, Brit* **1** the universities of Oxford and Cambridge considered together and usually in contrast to other universities. **2** *as adj* relating to or characteristic of these universities, especially when regarded as typical of traditional upper-class education, attitudes and privilege, etc. ⓒ 19c.

oxen *plural of* OX

ox-eyed ▷ *adj* with large round ox-like eyes.

oxeye daisy see MARGUERITE

OXFAM /'ɒksfam/ ▷ *abbreviation* Oxford Committee for Famine Relief, a major aid agency.

Oxford /'ɒksfəd/ ▷ *adj* relating to or characteristic of the city of Oxford or Oxford University. ▷ *noun* **1** (*also* **Oxford shoe**) a low-heeled shoe which laces up across the instep. **2** (*also* **Oxford cloth**) a cotton or synthetic woven fabric, used chiefly to make men's shirts.

Oxford bags ▷ *noun* trousers with very wide-cut baggy legs.

Oxford blue ▷ *noun* **1** a dark blue colour. Also (**Oxford-blue**) *as adj.* **2** someone awarded a BLUE (*noun* 4) from Oxford University.

Oxford movement see TRACTARIANISM

oxidant /'ɒksɪdənt/ ▷ *noun* **1** *chem* an oxidizing agent. **2** *engineering* a chemical compound, usually one containing oxygen, that is mixed with fuel and burned in the combustion chamber of a rocket. ⓒ 19c.

oxidase /'ɒksɪdeɪz/ ▷ *noun, biochem* any of a group of enzymes that catalyse oxidation in plant and animal cells. ⓒ 19c.

oxidation /ɒksɪ'deɪʃən/ ▷ *noun, chem* a chemical reaction that involves the addition of oxygen to or the removal of hydrogen from a substance which loses electrons, and which is always accompanied by REDUCTION (sense 4). ⓒ 18c.

oxidation-reduction see REDOX REACTION

oxide /'ɒksaɪd/ ▷ *noun, chem* any compound of oxygen and another element, often formed by burning that element or one of its compounds in oxygen or air. ⓒ 18c: French, from *ox(ygène)* oxygen + *(ac)ide* acid.

oxidize or **oxidise** /'ɒksɪdaɪz/ ▷ *verb* (**oxidized**, **oxidizing**) *tr & intr, chem* **1** to undergo, or cause (a substance) to undergo, a chemical reaction with oxygen. **2** to lose or cause (an atom or ion) to lose electrons. **3** to become, or make something become, rusty as a result of the formation of a layer of metal oxide. ● **oxidization** *noun*. ● **oxidizer** *noun* an oxidizing agent. ⓒ 19c.

oxidizing agent ▷ *noun, chem* any substance that oxidizes another substance in a chemical reaction, and is itself reduced in the process, by accepting electrons.

oxlip /'ɒkslɪp/ ▷ *noun* **1** a naturally occurring hybrid of the common primrose and the cowslip, with deep-yellow flowers. **2** the true oxlip, which is a separate species from the primrose and cowslip, and has pale-yellow flowers borne in a one-sided cluster. ⓒ Anglo-Saxon *oxanslyppe*, from *oxa* ox + *slyppe* slime.

Oxon. ▷ *abbreviation* **1** *English county* Oxfordshire ⓒ from Latin *Oxonia* Oxford. **2** used in degree titles and in bishop's signature: Oxford University ⓒ from Latin *Oxoniensis* of Oxford.

Oxonian /ɒk'soʊnɪən/ ▷ *noun* **1** an inhabitant of the city of Oxford. **2** a student or graduate of Oxford University. ▷ *adj* relating or belonging to Oxford or Oxford University. ⓒ 16c: from Latin *Oxonia* Oxford.

oxtail ▷ *noun* the tail of an ox, used especially in soups and stews.

oxter /'ɒkstə(r)/ ▷ *noun, Scots, Irish & N Eng dialect* the armpit. ⓒ Anglo-Saxon *oxta*.

ox-tongue ▷ *noun* **1** the tongue of an ox, used as food. **2** a plant of the daisy family with yellow flowers.

oxy- /ɒksɪ/ ▷ *combining form, signifying* **1** sharp; acute; acid. **2** oxygen. ⓒ From Greek *oxys* sour or acid.

oxyacetylene ▷ *noun* a mixture of oxygen and acetylene which burns with an extremely hot flame and is used in torches for cutting, welding or brazing metals. ⓒ Early 20c.

oxygen /'ɒksɪdʒən/ ▷ *noun* (symbol **O**, atomic number 8) a colourless odourless tasteless gas, the atmospheric form of which is produced by photosynthesis, and which is an essential requirement of most forms of plant and animal life. It is the most abundant element in the Earth's crust (50%), and constitutes about 21% (by volume) of the Earth's atmosphere. ● **oxygenous** /ɒk'sɪdʒɪnəs/ *adj* **1** containing or consisting of oxygen. **2** *originally* producing acids; acidifying. ⓒ 18c: from French *oxygène*, ultimately from Greek *oxys* sharp or acid + *gennaein* to generate, from the old belief that all acids contained oxygen.

oxygenate /'ɒksɪdʒəneɪt/ ▷ *verb* (**oxygenated**, **oxygenating**) to combine, treat, supply or enrich something (eg the blood) with oxygen. ● **oxygenation** *noun* **1** *physiol* the recharging of the blood with oxygen from air inhaled into the lungs. **2** *chem* treatment with or combination with oxygen. ● **oxygenator** *noun* any apparatus that supplies oxygen, especially one that is used to oxygenate the blood outside the body during open heart surgery. ⓒ 18c.

oxygen debt ▷ *noun, physiol* **1** a condition that occurs when the demand for oxygen, especially by muscle cells during a period of strenuous physical exercise, is greater than the amount of oxygen that can be supplied by the lungs. **2** the amount of oxygen that is required to restore normal levels in cells during the recovery period following muscular exercise.

oxygenize or **oxygenise** /'ɒksɪdʒənaɪz/ ▷ *verb* (**oxygenized**, **oxygenizing**) to OXYGENATE. ⓒ Early 19c.

oxygen mask ▷ *noun* a mask-like breathing apparatus that covers the nose and mouth, and is used to supply oxygen on demand, especially in rarefied atmospheres by mountaineers, aircraft passengers, etc.

oxygenous see under OXYGEN

oxygen tent ▷ *noun, medicine* a tent-like apparatus into which a controllable supply of oxygen can be pumped, erected around the bed of a patient to aid their breathing.

oxyhaemoglobin ▷ *noun, biochem* the red compound formed in blood by the combination of oxygen and the pigment HAEMOGLOBIN as a result of respiration. ◷ 19c.

oxymoron /ɒksɪ'mɔːrɒn/ ▷ *noun* a rhetorical figure of speech in which contradictory terms are used together, often for emphasis or effect, eg *horribly good*. • **oxymoronic** /ɒksɪmɔː'rɒnɪk/ *adj*. ◷ 17c: Greek, neuter of *oxymoros*, literally 'pointedly foolish', from *oxys* sharp + *moros* foolish.

oxytocic /ɒksɪ'toʊsɪk/ *medicine* ▷ *noun, adj* said of a drug: that stimulates uterine muscle contractions and therefore induces or accelerates labour. ▷ *noun* an oxytocic drug. ◷ 19c: from Greek *oxutokia* sudden delivery, from *oxys* sharp + *tokos* birth.

oxytocin /ɒksɪ'toʊsɪn/ ▷ *noun, medicine* a hormone, released by the pituitary gland, that induces contractions of the uterus during labour, and stimulates the flow of milk from the breasts during suckling. It is synthesized for use in accelerating labour. ◷ 1920s: from OXYTOCIC + -IN.

oxytone /'ɒksɪtoʊn/ *chiefly Greek grammar* ▷ *adj* with an acute accent on the last syllable. ▷ *noun* a word with such an accent. • **oxytonic** /-'tɒnɪk/ *adj*. ◷ 18c: from OXY-[1] + Greek *tonos* tone or pitch.

oyez or **oyes** /oʊ'jɛs, oʊ'jɛz/ ▷ *exclamation, historical* a cry for silence and attention, usually shouted three times by an official before a public announcement or in a court of law. ◷ 15c: from French *oyez* or *oiez*, meaning 'Hear!' or 'Hear ye!', imperative of *oir* to hear.

oyster /'ɔɪstə(r)/ ▷ *noun* **1** the common name for a family of marine bivalve mollusc with a soft fleshy body enclosed by a hinged shell, the fleshy part being a popular seafood. **2** any of several similar related molluscs such as the PEARL OYSTER. **3** the pale greyish beige or pink colour of an oyster. **4** an oyster-shaped piece of meat found in the hollow of the pelvic bone of a fowl, especially a chicken. **5** *colloq* a reserved or secretive person. ▷ *verb* (***oystered, oystering***) *intr* to fish for or gather oysters. • **the world is your** or **his**, *etc* **oyster** anything you, he, etc need or want is yours for the taking; you can go anywhere and do anything. ◷ 14c: from French *huistre*, from Greek *ostreon*.

oyster bed ▷ *noun* a place, especially on the sea-bed, where oysters breed, or where they are cultivated as a source of food or pearls.

oystercatcher ▷ *noun* a black-and-white wading bird with a long orange-red beak, found on shores and near the coast, that feeds on mussels, limpets and crabs, etc but, despite its name, not oysters. ◷ 18c.

oyster mushroom ▷ *noun* an edible fungus, found especially in clusters on dead wood.

oyster plant ▷ *noun* SALSIFY, or a blue-flowered plant growing on beaches, both supposed to taste like oysters.

Oz or **Ozzie** /'ɒzɪ/ *originally Austral slang* ▷ *adj* Australian. ▷ *noun* (***Ozzes*** or ***Ozzies***) **1** Australia. **2** an Australian. ◷ Early 20c as *Oss* or *Ossie*: imitating the pronunciation *Aus*tralia(n).

oz ▷ *abbreviation* OUNCE[1] (sense 1). ◷ 16c: from Italian *onza* ounce.

Ozalid /'ɒzəlɪd/ ▷ *noun, printing, trademark* **1** a method of duplicating printed matter onto chemically treated paper. **2** a reproduction made by this process. ◷ 1920s: from the reversal of *diazo*, a type of copying process, + *l*.

ozone /'oʊzoʊn/ ▷ *noun* **1** *chem* (formula O_3) a toxic pungent unstable bluish gas that is an ALLOTROPE of oxygen, and at ground level may be a pollutant (photochemical smog). Ozone is formed when ultraviolet light or an electric spark acts on oxygen, and is a strong oxidizing agent, used in controlled quantities for bleaching, sterilizing water and purifying air, etc. **2** *colloq* fresh bracing sea air. ◷ 19c: from Greek *ozein* to smell.

ozone-friendly ▷ *adj* said of products such as aerosols, etc: not harmful to the ozone layer; free from chemicals, eg chlorofluorocarbons, that deplete the ozone layer.

ozone layer and **ozonosphere** /oʊ'zoʊnəsfɪə(r)/ ▷ *noun* a layer of the upper atmosphere, between 15 and 30km above the Earth's surface, where ozone is formed, which filters harmful ultraviolet radiation from the Sun and prevents it from reaching the Earth.

ozonize or **ozonise** /'oʊzoʊnaɪz/ ▷ *verb* (***ozonized, ozonizing***) **1** to convert (oxygen) into ozone. **2** to treat or charge (a substance or environment) with ozone. • **ozonization** *noun*. • **ozonizer** *noun* an apparatus for turning oxygen into ozone. ◷ 19c.

Ozzie see OZ

P

P¹ or **p** /piː/ ▷ *noun* (***Ps, P's*** or ***p's***) the sixteenth letter of the English alphabet. • **mind one's p's and q's** *colloq* to behave well and carefully and with the etiquette suitable to a particular situation, particularly in what one says.

P² ▷ *abbreviation* **1** as a street sign: parking. **2** *IVR* Portugal. **3** *knitting* purl. **4** pula, the Botswanan currency unit.

P³ ▷ *symbol* **1** *chess* pawn. **2** *chem* phosphorus. **3** power.

p ▷ *abbreviation* **1** page. Also written **pg**. See also PP. **2** penny or pence.

PA ▷ *abbreviation* **1** *IVR* Panama. **2** *US state* Pennsylvania. Also written **Pa., Penn. 3** personal assistant. **4** Press Association. **5** public-address system. **6** Publishers Association.

Pa ▷ *abbreviation* **1** pascal. **2** *chem* protactinium.

pa /pɑː/ ▷ *noun* (***pas***) a familiar or childish word for FATHER. ◷ Early 19c.

p.a. ▷ *abbreviation* per annum.

PABX ▷ *abbreviation, telecomm* private automatic branch exchange. See also PBX.

paca /ˈpɑːkə, ˈpakə/ ▷ *noun* (***pacas***) a large rat-like nocturnal rodent, native to Central and S America, with a brown or black coat marked with four rows of white spots running along its flanks, a very short tail, and large cheek bones which form the outer walls of huge cheek pouches. ◷ 17c: Portuguese and Spanish, from Tupí.

pace¹ /peɪs/ ▷ *noun* **1** a single step. **2** the distance covered by one step when walking, about 80cm. **3** rate of walking or running, etc □ ***at a slow pace.*** **4** rate of movement or progress □ ***can't stand the pace*** □ ***at your own pace.*** **5** any of the gaits used by a horse. **6** a way of stepping, sometimes developed in horses, in which the legs on the same side are lifted together. ▷ *verb* (***paced, pacing***) **1** *tr & intr* (*often* **pace about** or **around**) to keep walking about, in a preoccupied or frustrated way □ ***was pacing about all morning*** □ ***began to pace the floor.*** **2** *intr* to walk steadily. **3** to set the pace for (others) in a race, etc. • **go through** or **show one's paces** to demonstrate one's skills at something. • **keep pace with someone** to go as fast as them. • **pace oneself** to work at a constant rate with the aim of achieving a particular goal, particularly when under pressure. • **put someone through their paces** to test them in some activity. • **set the pace** to be ahead of, and so set the rate for, others. ◷ 14c: from French *pas* step, from Latin *passus* step, literally 'stretch (of the leg)'.

■ **pace something out** to measure out (a distance) in paces.

pace² /ˈpeɪsiː, ˈpɑːkeɪ/ ▷ *prep* with the permission of or with due respect to (someone with whom one is disagreeing). ◷ 1860s: Latin ablative of *pax* peace or pardon.

pacebowler ▷ *noun, cricket* a bowler who characteristically delivers the ball fast.

pacemaker ▷ *noun* **1** *physiol* a small mass of specialized muscle-cells in the heart which control the rate and the rhythm of the heartbeat. **2** *medicine* an electronic device that stimulates the heart muscle to contract at a specific and regular rate, used to correct weak or irregular heart rhythms. **3** a pacesetter.

pacer /ˈpeɪsə(r)/ ▷ *noun* **1** someone who paces. **2 a** a horse whose usual gait is a PACE¹ (*noun* 6); **b** a horse trained to move in this way in harness racing.

pacesetter ▷ *noun* a person, horse, vehicle, etc that sets the pace in a race; a leader.

pacey and **pacy** /ˈpeɪsɪ/ ▷ *adj* (***pacier, paciest***) **1** fast. **2** lively; smart.

pachinko /pəˈtʃɪŋkoʊ/ ▷ *noun* a form of pinball popular in Japan. ◷ 1950s: from Japanese *pachin*, imitating a trigger sound.

pachisi /pɑːˈtʃiːsɪ, -zɪ/ ▷ *noun* an Indian board game resembling backgammon or ludo. ◷ Early 19c: from Hindi *pacisi*, meaning 'of 25', referring to the highest throw in the game.

pachyderm /ˈpakɪdɜːm/ ▷ *noun* **1** *zool, strictly* any animal belonging to a (now obsolete) category of large thick-skinned non-ruminant hoofed mammals, especially the elephant, rhinoceros or hippopotamus. **2** an elephant. **3** *colloq* an insensitive person. ◷ 1830s: from Greek *pachys* thick + *derma* skin.

Pacific /pəˈsɪfɪk/ ▷ *noun* (**the Pacific**) short for **Pacific Ocean**, the ocean between Asia and Australia, and North and South America. ▷ *adj* in or relating to the area of the Pacific Ocean, or the Pacific Islands. ◷ 1820s: from PACIFIC, so called by Ferdinand Magellan, the first European to sail it, because the ocean was notably calm when he crossed it in 1519.

pacific /pəˈsɪfɪk/ ▷ *adj* tending to make peace or keep the peace; peaceful; peaceable. ◷ 16c: from Latin *pacificus*, literally 'peacemaking', from *pax* peace.

pacification /pasɪfɪˈkeɪʃən/ ▷ *noun* the policy or process of pacifying; conciliation; appeasement.

Pacific Standard Time ▷ *noun* (abbreviation **PST**) the TIME ZONE for the US Pacific coastal region.

pacifier /ˈpasɪfaɪər/ ▷ *noun, N Amer* a baby's DUMMY.

pacifism /ˈpasɪfɪzəm/ ▷ *noun, politics* the beliefs and practices of pacifists. ◷ Early 20c.

pacifist /ˈpasɪfɪst/ ▷ *noun* someone who believes that violence is unjustified and who refuses to take part in making war, either from a secular moral standpoint, or on religious grounds, and usually actively advocates efforts to maintain peace by supporting disarmament. ◷ Early 20c: from French *pacifiste*; compare PACIFY.

pacify /ˈpasɪfaɪ/ ▷ *verb* (***pacifies, pacified, pacifying***) **1** to calm, soothe or appease someone. **2** to restore something to a peaceful condition. **3** *euphemistic* to subdue. ◷ 17c: from French *pacifier*, from Latin *pax* peace + *facere* to make.

pack¹ ▷ *noun* **1** a collection of things tied into a bundle for carrying. **2** a rucksack; a backpack. **3** a PACK OF CARDS; a complete set of PLAYING CARDS. **4** a troop of animals living and hunting together as a group, eg dogs or wolves. **5** a compact package, eg of equipment for a purpose □ ***a first-aid pack.*** **6** *in compounds* a collection of things of a specified number or for a specified purpose □ ***four-pack*** □ ***party-pack of balloons*** □ ***family-pack.*** **7** *derog* a collection or bunch □ ***a pack of idiots*** □ ***a pack of lies.*** **8** a group of Brownie Guides or Cub Scouts which meets regularly. **9** *rugby* the forwards in a team. **10** a medicinal or cosmetic skin preparation, eg a FACE PACK. **11** pack ice. ▷ *verb* (***packed, packing***) **1** to stow (goods, clothes, etc) compactly in cases, boxes, etc for transport or travel. **2** *intr* to put one's belongings into a suitcase, rucksack, travel bag, etc, ready for a journey □ *Have you packed yet?* **3** to put (goods, food, etc) into a container, or to wrap them, ready for sale. **4** *intr* to be capable of being formed into a compact shape. **5** to fill something tightly or compactly □ *packed the sandwich full of cheese* □ *The hall was packed.* **6** *tr & intr, N Amer colloq* to make a habit of carrying (a gun). **7** *intr* said of animals: to form a pack. • **pack a punch** *colloq* to be capable of giving a powerful punch or blow. • **packed like sardines** said eg of passengers on a bus or train during rush hour: crowded very closely together. • **pack it in!** *colloq* an exclamation expressing annoyance and irritation at what someone is doing, and telling them to stop doing it. • **send someone packing** *colloq* to send them away unceremoniously. ◷ 13c.

■ **pack something in 1 a** to push and cram it into something that is already quite full; **b** to cram (a great deal of activity) into a limited period □ *On holiday we packed in three excursions a day.* **2** to give something up or stop doing it □ *packed in her job.*

■ **pack into something** to crowd into (a bus, train, concert hall, etc which is already full) □ *The rush-hour passengers packed into the train.*

■ **pack someone off** to send them off hastily or abruptly □ *packed the children off to their friend's house.*

■ **pack something out** to fill (a container, concert hall, etc) very tightly, very full, etc.

■ **pack up 1** to stop work, etc at the end of the day or shift, etc. **2** *colloq* said of machinery, etc: to break down.

■ **pack something up** to put it in containers and store it.

pack² ▷ *verb* (***packed***, ***packing***) to fill (a jury, meeting, etc) illicitly with people one can rely on to support one. ◷ 16c, originally in obsolete sense 'to intrigue'.

package /ˈpakɪdʒ/ ▷ *noun* **1** something wrapped and secured with string, adhesive tape, etc; a parcel. **2** a case, box or other container for packing goods in. **3** a PACKAGE DEAL. **4** *computing* a group of related computer programs designed to perform a particular complex task.

package deal ▷ *noun* a deal covering a number of related proposals that must be accepted as a whole or not at all.

package holiday or **package tour** ▷ *noun* a holiday or tour for which one pays a fixed price that includes travel, accommodation, meals, etc.

packager ▷ *noun* an independent company specializing in the PACKAGING (sense 2) of something.

packaging ▷ *noun* **1 a** the wrappers or containers in which goods are packed and presented for sale; **b** the total presentation of a product for sale, ie both its wrappings and the design of these, intended to make the product as desirable as possible. **2** the design and complete production of eg illustrated books, programmes for television, etc for sale to a publisher, broadcasting company, etc.

pack animal ▷ *noun* an animal, eg a donkey, mule or horse, used to carry luggage or goods for sale.

packer ▷ *noun* **1** someone who packs, especially goods ready for distribution. **2** a machine for packing. **3** an employee or employer in the business of preparing and preserving food.

packet /ˈpakɪt/ ▷ *noun* **1** a wrapper or container made of paper, cardboard or plastic, with its contents □ *packet of biscuits.* **2** a small pack or package. **3** a mailboat that also carries cargo and passengers, and plies a fixed route. Also called **packet boat**. **4** *colloq* a large sum of money □ *cost a packet.* ◷ 16c: from French *pacquet*.

packet switching ▷ *noun, telecomm* a method of directing digitally-encoded data over a communications network by breaking it down into small units and reconstituting it as a whole at its destination.

packhorse ▷ *noun* a horse used to carry luggage or goods for sale.

pack ice ▷ *noun* a large area of free-floating sea ice, up to several kilometres in diameter, consisting of pieces that have been driven together by wind and currents to form a solid mass.

packing ▷ *noun* **1** materials used for padding or wrapping goods for transport, etc. **2** the act of putting anything into packs or tying it up for transporting or storing.

packing case and **packing box** ▷ *noun* a wooden crate in which to pack goods for transport or storage.

pack-load ▷ *noun* the load an animal can carry.

pack of cards ▷ *noun* a pack of playing cards used for card games, usually consisting of 52 cards divided into four SUITS, each of which contains 13 cards, ie the ACE, the numbers 2 to 10, and the three COURT CARDS.

pack of lies ▷ *noun* a completely false story, etc.

pack-rat ▷ *noun* a kind of long-tailed rat, native to the western part of N America.

pact ▷ *noun* an agreement reached between two or more parties, states, etc for mutual advantage. ◷ 15c: from Latin *pactum* agreement or covenant.

pacy see PACEY

pad¹ ▷ *noun* **1** a wad of material used to cushion, protect, shape or clean. **2** a leg-guard for a cricketer, etc. **3** a quantity of sheets of paper fixed together into a block. Also *in compounds* □ *notepad.* **4** a rocket-launching platform. **5** the soft fleshy underside of an animal's paw. **6** *N Amer* a large water lily leaf. **7** *slang* the place where someone lives. ▷ *verb* (***padded***, ***padding***) **1** to cover, fill, stuff, cushion or shape something with layers of soft material. **2** (*also* **pad something out**) *derog* to include unnecessary or irrelevant material in (a piece of writing, speech, etc) for the sake of length. ◷ 16c.

pad² ▷ *verb* (***padded***, ***padding***) **1** *intr* to walk softly or with a quiet or muffled tread. **2** *tr & intr* to tramp along (a road); to travel on foot. ◷ 16c: Dutch, meaning 'path'.

padded cell ▷ *noun* a room with walls softened by pads, used in psychiatric hospitals.

padding ▷ *noun* **1** material for cushioning, shaping or filling. **2** *derog* irrelevant or unnecessary matter in a speech or piece of writing, added to extend it to the desired length.

paddle¹ /ˈpadəl/ ▷ *verb* (***paddled***, ***paddling***) **1** *intr* to walk about barefoot in shallow water. **2** to trail or dabble (fingers, etc) in water. **3** *intr* to walk unsteadily or with short steps. ▷ *noun* a spell of paddling □ *went for a paddle in the sea.* ◷ 16c.

paddle² /ˈpadəl/ ▷ *noun* **1 a** a short light oar with a blade at one or both ends, used to propel and steer a canoe, kayak, etc; **b** the blade of such an oar. **2** one of the slats fitted round the edge of a paddle wheel or mill wheel. **3** a paddle-shaped instrument for stirring, beating, etc. **4** *US* a small bat, as used in table tennis. ▷ *verb* (***paddled***, ***paddling***) *tr & intr* **1** to propel (a canoe, kayak, etc) with paddles. **2** *intr* (*also* **paddle along**) to move through water using, or as if using, a paddle or paddles. **3** *US colloq* to spank someone. • **paddle one's own canoe** to be self-sufficient.

paddle steamer and **paddle boat** ▷ *noun* a boat driven by paddle wheels which are turned by a STEAM ENGINE.

paddle wheel ▷ *noun* a large engine-driven wheel at the side or back of a ship which propels the ship through the water as it turns.

paddock /ˈpadək/ ▷ *noun* **1** a small enclosed field for keeping a horse in. **2** *horse-racing* an enclosure beside a race track where horses are saddled and walked round before a race. ◎ 16c: from earlier *parrock*, from Anglo-Saxon *pearroc* fence or enclosure.

Paddy /ˈpadɪ/ ▷ *noun* (***Paddies***) **1** *sometimes derog* a familiar name for an Irishman. **2** (**paddy**) *colloq* a fit of rage. ◎ 18c: Irish, a familiar form of the name *Padraig* or Patrick.

paddy /ˈpadɪ/ ▷ *noun* (***paddies***) **1** (*also* **paddy field**) a field filled with water in which rice is grown. **2** rice as a growing crop; harvested rice grains that have not been processed in any way. ◎ 17c: from Malay *padi*.

padlock /ˈpadlɒk/ ▷ *noun* a detachable lock with a U-shaped bar that pivots at one side, so that it can be passed through a ring or chain and locked in position. ▷ *verb* (***padlocked, padlocking***) to fasten (a door, cupboard, etc) with a padlock. ◎ 15c.

padmasana /pʌdˈmɑːsənə/ ▷ *noun, yoga* the LOTUS. ◎ Late 19c: from Sanskrit *padma* LOTUS + ASANA.

padre /ˈpɑːdreɪ, ˈpɑːdrɪ/ ▷ *noun* a chaplain in any of the armed services. ◎ 16c: Portuguese, Spanish and Italian, meaning 'father', a form of address for a priest.

padsaw ▷ *noun* a small saw-blade with a detachable handle, used for cutting curves and awkward angles. ◎ 19c: PAD[1] (in the sense of a detachable handle which can be used with other tool heads) + SAW.

paean or (*US*) **pean** /pɪən/ ▷ *noun* a song of triumph, praise or thanksgiving. ◎ 16c: from Greek *Paian* the physician of the gods, used in hymns as a title for Apollo.

paed- see PAEDO-

paederasty and **paederast** see under PEDERASTY

paediatrician or (*N Amer*) **pediatrician** /piːdɪəˈtrɪʃən/ ▷ *noun* a doctor who specializes in the study, diagnosis and treatment of children's diseases.

paediatrics or (*N Amer*) **pediatrics** /piːdɪˈatrɪks/ ▷ *singular noun, medicine* the branch of medicine concerned with the care of children, and with the diagnosis and treatment of children's diseases. • **paediatric** or (*N Amer*) **pediatric** *adj* relating to or involving paediatrics. ◎ 19c.

paedo- or **pedo-** /piːdoʊ/ or (before a vowel) **paed-** or **ped-** ▷ *combining form, denoting* a child or children ▫ *paedophile* ▫ *paediatrics*. ◎ From Greek *paid-*, *pais* child.

paedology or (*N Amer*) **pedology** /piːˈdɒlədʒɪ/ *noun, medicine* the scientific study of physiological and psychological aspects of childhood. • **paedologist** *noun* a scientist who specializes in paedology. ◎ 19c.

paedomorphism ▷ *noun, biol* retention of juvenile physical characteristics in the mature stage of development. • **paedomorphic** *adj*. ◎ 1890s.

paedophile /ˈpiːdoufaɪl/ ▷ *noun* an adult who is sexually attracted to or engages in sexual activity with children.

paedophilia /piːdoʊˈfɪlɪə/ ▷ *noun* sexual attraction to children. ◎ Early 20c.

paella /paɪˈɛlə/ ▷ *noun* (***paellas***) *cookery* a Spanish rice dish of fish or chicken with vegetables and saffron. ◎ 19c: Catalan, from Latin *patella* pan.

paeony see PEONY

pagan /ˈpeɪgən/ ▷ *adj* **1 a** not a Christian, Jew, or Muslim; **b** belonging or relating to, or following, a religion in which a number of gods are worshipped. **2** without religious belief. ▷ *noun* a pagan person; a heathen. • **paganism** *noun*. ◎ 14c: from Latin *paganus* a rustic or villager (referring to the time when Christianity had been generally accepted in towns but not in rural areas), also a civilian (contrasting with Christians who called themselves 'soldiers of Christ').

paganize or **paganise** /ˈpeɪgənaiz/ ▷ *verb* (***paganized, paganizing***) **1** to convert someone to paganism. **2** *intr* to become pagan.

page[1] /peɪdʒ/ ▷ *noun* (abbreviation **p** or **pa**, *plural* ***pp***) **1** one side of a leaf in a book, etc. **2** a leaf of a book, etc. **3** *literary* an episode or incident in history, one's life, etc. ▷ *verb* (***paged, paging***) to paginate (a text). ◎ 16c: French, from Latin *pagina* a leaf of a book.

page[2] /peɪdʒ/ ▷ *noun* **1** *historical* a boy attendant serving a knight and training for knighthood. **2** a boy attending the bride at a wedding. See also BRIDESMAID. **3** a boy who carries messages or luggage, etc in hotels, clubs, etc. **4** in the US Congress: a messenger. ▷ *verb* (***paged, paging***) **1** to summon someone by calling their name out loud, or through a PUBLIC-ADDRESS SYSTEM or PAGER. **2** *rare* to attend someone as a page. ◎ 13c: French, from Italian *paggio*.

pageant /ˈpadʒənt/ ▷ *noun* **1** a series of tableaux or dramatic scenes, usually depicting local historical events or other topical matters. **2** any colourful and varied spectacle, especially one carried around in a procession. ◎ 14c: from Latin *pagina* page, scene or stage, the meaning possibly coming from the page of a manuscript being transferred into a scene.

pageantry /ˈpadʒəntrɪ/ ▷ *noun* splendid display; pomp.

pageboy ▷ *noun* **1** a PAGE[2] (*noun* 2). **2** a) a smooth jaw-length hairstyle with the ends curled under. **b** *as adj* ▫ *a pageboy cut*.

page description language ▷ *noun, computing* (abbreviation **PDL**) a programming language used to describe the composition of a printed page, which can be interpreted by a compatible printer.

pager /ˈpeɪdʒə(r)/ ▷ *noun, telecomm* a small individually-worn radio receiver and transmitter that enables its user, especially hospital personnel, to receive a signal (typically a 'beep' or a short message) to which they can respond with a phone call, etc to the sender. Also called **bleeper**, **bleep**.

page-three girl ▷ *noun* **1** a photograph of a nude or semi-nude female model, traditionally printed on the third page of certain popular tabloid newspapers. **2** a model who appears or has appeared in such a photograph.

page-turner ▷ *noun* a very absorbing book with a fast-moving story that is hard to put down.

paginate /ˈpadʒɪneɪt/ ▷ *verb* (***paginated, paginating***) to give consecutive numbers to the pages of (a text), carried out by a command within a word-processing package, or as part of the printing process, etc. Also called PAGE[1]. Compare FOLIATE. ◎ 19c: from Latin *pagina* page.

pagination /padʒɪˈneɪʃən/ ▷ *noun* **1** a system or process of paginating. **2** the figures and symbols used to mark pages.

paging *present participle of* PAGE[1], PAGE[2].

pagoda /pəˈgoʊdə/ ▷ *noun* (***pagodas***) **1** a Buddhist shrine or memorial-building in India, China and parts of SE Asia, especially in the form of a tall tower with many storeys, each one having its own projecting roof with upturned eaves. **2** an ornamental building imitating this. ◎ 17c: from Portuguese *pagode*, from Persian *butkada*, from *but* idol + *kada* temple.

pah! /pɑː/ ▷ *exclamation* expressing disgust, disbelief, etc. ◎ 16c.

pahoehoe /pəˈhoʊɪhoʊɪ/ ▷ *noun* (***pahoehoes***) a hardened lava with a smooth undulating shiny surface. ◎ Late 19c: Hawaiian.

paid ▷ *verb, past tense, past participle of* PAY[1]. • **put paid to something** to destroy any chances of success in it.

paid-up ▷ *adj* said of a society member, etc: having paid a membership fee ▫ *fully paid-up member*. See PAY UP at PAY[1].

pail /peɪl/ ▷ *noun* **1** a bucket. **2** the amount contained in a pail □ *a pail of milk.* ◎ Anglo-Saxon *pægel* gill (liquid measure), associated with French *paielle* pan.

pailful ▷ *noun* (***pailfuls***) the amount a pail can hold.

paillasse see PALLIASSE

pain /peɪn/ ▷ *noun* **1** an uncomfortable, distressing or agonizing sensation caused by the stimulation of specialized nerve endings by heat, cold, pressure or other strong stimuli. **2** emotional suffering. **3** *derog colloq* an irritating or troublesome person or thing. **4** (**pains**) trouble taken or efforts made in doing something. ▷ *verb* (***pained***, ***paining***) *rather formal* to cause distress to someone □ *It pained me to see the injured donkey.* • **be at pains to do something** to be anxious to do it with due care and thoroughness. • **for one's pains** *ironic* as a reward (usually a poor one) for the trouble one has taken. • **on pain of something** at the risk of incurring it as a punishment. • **take pains** to be careful to do something properly; to be thorough over a task, etc. ◎ 13c: from Latin *poena* punishment.

pained ▷ *adj* said of an expression, tone of voice, etc: expressing distress or disapproval.

painful ▷ *adj* **1** causing pain □ *a painful injury.* **2** said of part of the body: affected by some injury, etc which causes pain □ *a painful finger.* **3** causing distress □ *a painful duty.* **4** laborious and slow □ *painful progress.* • **painfully** *adverb.* • **painfulness** *noun.*

pain in the neck and **pain in the arse** ▷ *noun, slang* **1** an exasperating circumstance. **2** an annoying, irritating or tiresome person.

painkiller ▷ *noun* any drug or other agent that relieves pain; an ANALGESIC.

painless ▷ *adj* without pain. • **painlessly** *adverb.* • **painlessness** *noun.*

painstaking ▷ *adj* conscientious and thorough, ie taking pains or care □ *painstaking work* □ *painstaking about keeping records.* • **painstakingly** *adverb.*

paint /peɪnt/ ▷ *noun* **1** colouring matter in the form of a liquid which is applied to a surface and dries forming a hard surface. **2** a dried coating of this. **3** a tube or tablet of colouring matter for creating pictures. **4** *old use* face make-up; cosmetics. ▷ *verb* (***painted***, ***painting***) **1** to apply a coat of paint to (walls, woodwork, etc). **2** to turn something a certain colour by this means □ *paint the door yellow.* **3** *tr & intr* to make (pictures) using paint. **4** to depict (a person, place or thing) in paint. **5** to describe (a scene, place or person) as if in paint. **6** *tr & intr, old use* to put make-up on (one's face). • **paintable** *adj* suitable for painting. • **paint the town red** to go out and celebrate something lavishly. ◎ 13c: from French *peint*, past participle of *peindre* to paint.

paintball ▷ *noun* a type of WAR GAME in which participants stalk each other and fight battles with paint fired from compressed-air guns.

paintbox ▷ *noun* a case of dry watercolour paints in a variety of colours, for painting pictures.

paintbrush ▷ *noun* a brush of any kind used for applying paint, eg used by an artist or a decorator.

painted lady ▷ *noun* a type of butterfly, orange-red spotted with white and black.

painter[1] ▷ *noun* **1** someone who decorates houses internally or externally with paint. **2** an artist who paints pictures.

painter[2] /ˈpeɪntə(r)/ ▷ *noun, naut* a rope for fastening a boat. • **cut the painter** to sever ties. ◎ 15c: perhaps related to French *pentoir* rope.

painting ▷ *noun* **1** a painted picture. **2** the art or process of applying paint to walls, etc. **3** the art of creating pictures in paint. **4** a vivid description in words.

painty ▷ *adj* (***paintier***, ***paintiest***) **1** said of a smell, texture, etc: like paint. **2** smeared with paint. **3** overloaded with paint, and with colours considered too glaring.

pair /pɛə(r)/ ▷ *noun* **1** a set of two identical or corresponding things, eg shoes or gloves, intended for use together. **2** something consisting of two joined and corresponding parts □ *a pair of trousers* □ *a pair of scissors.* **3** one of a matching pair □ *Here's one earring—where's its pair?* **4** two people associated in a relationship; a couple. **5** two mating animals, birds, fishes, etc. **6** two horses harnessed together □ *a coach and pair.* **7** two playing cards of the same denomination. **8** in a parliament: **a** two voters on opposite sides in a parliament who have an agreement to abstain from voting on a specific motion or for a specific duration, usually because one or both will be absent from parliament at the time; **b** such an agreement. **9** *cricket* a duck (see DUCK[1] *noun* 5) in both innings. **10** *rowing* (symbol **2+** or **2-**) **a** a racing-boat manned by two oarsmen or oarswomen; **b** the crew of such a boat. Compare DOUBLE. ▷ *verb* (***paired***, ***pairing***) **1** *tr & intr* to divide into groups of two; to sort out in pairs. **2** *intr* said of two opposing voters in a parliament: to agree a PAIR (*noun* 8) above or to have such an agreement. • **paired** *adj.* • **in pairs** in twos. ◎ 13c: from French *paire* a couple, from Latin *par* equal.

■ **pair off** *colloq* to get together with someone romantically, sexually, etc, eg at a social gathering.

■ **pair something** or **someone off 1** to sort them into pairs. **2** to set (things or people) against each other, eg in a game. □ pair up with someone to join with them for some purpose.

pair bond ▷ *noun, zool* a continuing and exclusive relationship between a male and female, particularly during the courtship and mating of a pair of animals. • **pair bonding** *noun.*

pair of colours ▷ *noun, military* two flags carried by a regiment, one the national ensign, the other the flag of the regiment.

pair-royal and **prial** /ˈpraɪəl/ ▷ *noun* **1** *cards* a set of three cards of the same denomination, eg three queens, three sixes, etc. **2** a throw of three dice all falling with the same number face-up, eg three twos. ◎ 16c.

pairs ▷ *plural noun* another name for PELMANISM (sense 2).

pairwise ▷ *adverb* in pairs.

paisano /paɪˈzɑːnoʊ/ ▷ *noun* (***paisanos***) *US* **1** a person from the same area or town; a compatriot. **2** a pal; a friend. ◎ 19c: Spanish, from French *paysan* peasant.

paisley /ˈpeɪzlɪ/ ▷ *noun* (***paisleys***) **1** a fabric with a pattern resembling the PAISLEY PATTERN. **2** *as adj* decorated with this pattern □ *paisley pyjamas.* ◎ 19c: the pattern was used in the Paisley shawl, a shawl made in Paisley, Scotland.

paisley pattern ▷ *noun* a design whose characteristic feature is a highly ornate device which looks like a tree cone with a curving point. This device is arranged in a seemingly random fashion over the fabric.

pajamas see PYJAMAS

PAK ▷ *abbreviation, IVR* Pakistan.

pakapoo /pakəˈpuː/ ▷ *noun* (***pakapoos***) *Austral* a Chinese version of lotto, in which betting tickets are filled in with Chinese characters. ◎ Early 20c: Chinese *bai ge piao* white pigeon ticket.

Paki /ˈpakɪ/ ▷ *noun* (***Pakis***) *offensive Brit slang* **a** a Pakistani; **b** *loosely* someone from any part of the Indian subcontinent. Also *as adj.* ◎ 1960s.

Paki-bashing *Brit slang* ▷ *noun* the activity of making vicious and unprovoked physical or verbal attacks on Pakistani immigrants living in Britain. • **Paki-basher** *noun.*

Pakistani /pɑːkɪ'stɑːnɪ/ ▷ *adj* belonging or relating to Pakistan, a republic in S Asia, or to its inhabitants. ▷ *noun* (***Pakistanis***) **1** a citizen or inhabitant of, or person born in, Pakistan. **2** an immigrant from, or a person whose ancestors are immigrants from, Pakistan. ◎ 1940s.

pakora /pə'kɔːrə/ ▷ *noun* (***pakoras***) an Indian dish of chopped spiced vegetables formed into balls, coated in batter and deep-fried, served with a spicy sauce. ◎ 1950s: Hindi.

PAL ▷ *abbreviation* Phase Alternating Line, a coding system for colour TV used widely in Europe and many other parts of the world. See also SECAM.

pal *colloq* ▷ *noun* a friend; a mate. ▷ *verb* (***palled*** /pald/, ***palling***) *intr* (*usually* **pal up with someone**) to make friends with them. • **palliness** *noun*. • **pally** *adj* (compare PALSY[2]). ◎ 17c: Romany, meaning 'brother'.

palace /'paləs, 'palɪs/ ▷ *noun* **1** the official residence of a sovereign, bishop, archbishop or president. **2** a spacious and magnificent residence or other building; a palatial home. ◎ 13c: from French *paleis*, from Latin *Palatium* the Roman emperors' residence on the Palatine Hill.

palace revolution ▷ *noun* the overthrow of a sovereign or government by people within the high ranks of power, ie by those close to the monarch or leader.

paladin /'palədɪn/ ▷ *noun, historical* **1** any of the 12 peers of Charlemagne's court. **2** a KNIGHT ERRANT; a champion of a sovereign. ◎ 16c: from Italian *paladino*, from Latin *palatinus* belonging to the palace.

palae- see PALAEO-

palaeanthropology or **palaeoanthropology** ▷ *noun* the branch of ANTHROPOLOGY concerned with the study of fossil humanoids. • **palaeanthropic** *adj*. ◎ Early 20c.

palaeo- or **paleo-** /palɪoʊ, peɪ-, -lɪ'ɒ/ or (before a vowel) **palae-** or **pale-** ▷ *combining form, denoting* **1** old; ancient. **2** the very distant past. Most of the following forms can be spelt as either *palaeo-* or *paleo-*. ◎ From Greek *palaios* old.

palaeobiology ▷ *noun* the biological study of fossil plants and animals. ◎ 19c.

palaeobotany ▷ *noun, geol* the scientific study of fossil plants. ◎ 19c.

Palaeocene ▷ *adj, geol* the earliest epoch of the TERTIARY period, during which time many reptiles became extinct and mammals became the dominant vertebrates. See table at GEOLOGICAL TIME SCALE. ◎ 19c.

palaeoecology ▷ *noun, geol* the scientific study of the ecology of fossil animals and plants. ◎ 19c.

palaeography /palɪ'ɒgrəfɪ, peɪ-/ ▷ *noun* **1** the study of ancient writing and manuscripts. Compare CODICOLOGY. **2** an ancient handwriting. • **palaeographer** *noun*. ◎ 19c.

palaeolithic or **Palaeolithic** ▷ *adj* relating or belonging to an early period of the Stone Age, extending from about 2.5 million years ago to about 10 000 years ago, characterized by the use of tools made of unpolished chipped stone, during which CRO-MAGNON and NEANDERTHAL people lived. See table at GEOLOGICAL TIME SCALE. ◎ 19c.

Palaeolithic art ▷ *noun* the oldest known art, developed c.30 000 years ago, which includes cave paintings and small sculptures.

palaeontology ▷ *noun, geol* the scientific study of the structure, distribution, environment and evolution of extinct life forms by interpretation of their fossil remains. • **palaeontologist** *noun*. ◎ 19c: from PALAEO- + Greek *onta* being + -LOGY.

Palaeosiberian ▷ *adj* denoting four unrelated groups of languages spoken in NE Siberia, including the languages Chukchi, Yukaghir, Ket and Gilyak. ▷ *noun* the languages forming this group. ◎ 20c.

Palaeozoic /palɪoʊ'zoʊɪk/ ▷ *adj, geol* relating to the era of geological time extending from about 580 million to 250 million years ago, during which time the first vertebrates appeared. See table at GEOLOGICAL TIME SCALE. ◎ 19c: from Greek *zoion* animal.

palais de danse /'paleɪ də dɑːns/ ▷ *noun* (***palais de danse*** /'paleɪ or 'paleɪz — /) a dance-hall. ◎ Early 20c: French.

palamino see PALOMINO

palanquin or **palankeen** /palən'kiːn/ ▷ *noun, historical* a light covered litter used in the Orient, suspended from poles carried on the shoulders of four or six bearers. ◎ 16c: from Portuguese *palanquim*, originally from Sanskrit *paryanka* couch or litter.

palatable /'palətəbəl/ ▷ *adj* **1** having a pleasant taste; appetizing. **2** acceptable; agreeable. • **palatability** *noun*. • **palatably** *adverb*. ◎ 17c.

palatal /'palətəl/ ▷ *adj* **1** relating to the palate. **2** *phonetics* said of a speech sound: produced by bringing the tongue to or near the hard palate. ▷ *noun, phonetics* a sound produced in this way, eg /j/ as in *yellow* /jɛloʊ/. Compare PALATO-ALVEOLAR, VELAR.

palate /'palət/ ▷ *noun* **1** the roof of the mouth, consisting of the HARD PALATE in front and the SOFT PALATE behind. **2** the sense of taste. **3** an ability to discriminate between wines, different qualities of wine, etc. ◎ 14c: from Latin *palatum*.

palatial /pə'leɪʃəl/ ▷ *adj* like a palace in magnificence, spaciousness, etc. ◎ 18c: from Latin *palatium* PALACE.

palatine /'palətaɪn/ ▷ *adj* **1** referring to the Palatine Hill in Rome, or the palace of Roman emperors on that hill. **2** referring to a palace. **3** having royal privileges or jurisdiction. ◎ 15c.

palato-alveolar /'palətoʊ —/ *phonetics* ▷ *adj* said of a speech sound: produced by bringing the tip of the tongue to or near the roots of the upper teeth and raising the tongue towards the HARD PALATE. ▷ *noun* a sound produced in this way, eg the consonants in *church*. Compare ALVEOLAR. ◎ 20c: from *palato-*, scientific combining form denoting the PALATE + ALVEOLAR.

palaver /pə'lɑːvə(r)/ ▷ *noun* **1** a long, boring, complicated and seemingly pointless exercise; an unnecessary fuss ☐ *What a palaver!* **2** idle chatter. **3** *historical* an act of conferring between European traders, settlers, etc and native inhabitants. ▷ *verb* (***palavered***, ***palavering***) **1** *intr* to chatter idly. **2** to flatter; to cajole. ◎ 18c: from Portuguese *palavra*, from Latin *parabola* PARABLE, later meaning 'a word' or 'speech'.

palazzo /pa'latsoʊ/ ▷ *noun* (***palazzi*** /-tsiː/) **1** an Italian palace, often one converted into a museum. **2** a house built in this style. ◎ 17c: Italian.

palazzos /pa'latsoʊz/ ▷ *plural noun* loose trousers with wide straight legs, usually worn by women. ◎ 1970s: from PALAZZO.

pale[1] /peɪl/ ▷ *adj* (***paler***, ***palest***) **1** said of a person, face, etc: having less colour than normal, eg from illness, fear, shock, etc. **2** said of a colour: whitish; closer to white than black; light ☐ *pale-green*. **3** lacking brightness or vividness; subdued ☐ *pale sunlight*. ▷ *verb* (***paled***, ***paling***) *intr* **1** to become pale. **2** to fade or become weaker or less significant ☐ *My worries pale by comparison*. • **palely** *adverb*. • **paleness** *noun*. • **palish** *adj* somewhat pale; quite pale. • **pale into insignificance** to become relatively unimportant in comparison with something else. ◎ 13c: from French *palle*, from Latin *pallidus*, from *pallere* to be pale.

pale[2] /peɪl/ ▷ *noun* **1** a wooden or metal post or stake used for making fences. **2** a fence made of these; a boundary fence. **3** *heraldry* a broad stripe on a shield extending from top to bottom. • **paly** *adj, heraldry* divided by vertical lines. • **beyond the pale** outside the limits of acceptable behaviour; intolerable. See also PALING. ⓒ 14c: from Latin *palus* stake.

pale ale ▷ *noun* a light-coloured bitter ale.

palebuck ▷ *noun* the ORIBI.

paleface ▷ *noun, sometimes derog* the term supposed to have been used by Native Americans for the white settlers. ⓒ Early 19c.

palely and **paleness** see under PALE[1]

pale- and **paleo-** see PALAEO-

paler and **palest** see under PALE[1]

Palestinian /palə'stɪnɪən/ ▷ *noun* **1** an inhabitant of, or person born in, ancient or modern Palestine, a region bordering the E Mediterranean. **2** an Arab who was born in or is a descendant of someone born in the area of Palestine. ▷ *adj* belonging or relating to ancient or modern Palestine. ⓒ 19c as *adj*.

palette /'palət/ ▷ *noun* **1** a hand-held board with a thumb-hole, on which an artist mixes colours. **2** the assortment or range of colours used by a particular artist, in a particular picture, etc □ ***broadened his palette in later years.*** ⓒ 17c: French, literally 'small spade', from *pala* spade.

palette knife ▷ *noun* **1** an artist's knife for mixing and applying paint. **2** a flexible-bladed, round-ended knife used for spreading butter, mixing ingredients, etc.

Pali /'pɑːlɪ/ ▷ *noun* the sacred language of the Buddhists of India, closely related to Sanskrit. ⓒ 18c: from Sanskrit *pali-bhasa*, from *pali* canon + *bhasa* language, ie the canonical texts rather than commentaries on them.

palimony /'palɪmənɪ/ ▷ *noun, colloq* alimony or its equivalent demanded by one partner when the couple have been cohabiting without being married. ⓒ 1970s: from PAL, modelled on ALIMONY.

palimpsest /'palɪmpsɛst/ ▷ *noun* **1** a parchment or other ancient writing surface re-used after the original content has been erased. **2** a monumental brass that has been turned over and inscribed on the reverse. ⓒ 17c: from Greek *palin* again + *psaein* to rub smooth.

palindrome /'palɪndroum/ ▷ *noun* a word or phrase that reads the same backwards and forwards, eg *Hannah*, and *sums are not set as a test on Erasmus*, and (perhaps the first ever palindrome) *Madam, I'm Adam*. • **palindromic** /palɪn'drɒmɪk/ *adj* in the nature of a palindrome; having the same spelling backwards and forwards. • **palindromist** *noun* a writer who invents palindromes. ⓒ 17c: from Greek *palin* back + *dromein* run.

paling /'peɪlɪŋ/ ▷ *noun* **1** the act of constructing a fence with pales (see PALE[2] sense 1). **2** a fence of this kind. **3** an upright stake or board in a fence.

palisade /palɪ'seɪd/ ▷ *noun* a tall fence of pointed wooden stakes fixed edge to edge, for defence or protection. ⓒ 16c: from Provençal *palissada*, from Latin *palus* stake.

palish see under PALE[1]

pall[1] /pɔːl/ ▷ *noun* **1 a** the cloth that covers a coffin at a funeral; **b** the coffin itself. See also PALL-BEARER. **2** anything spreading or hanging over □ ***a pall of smoke.*** **3** a PALLIUM. ⓒ Anglo-Saxon *pæll* a robe or covering.

pall[2] /pɔːl/ ▷ *verb* (***palled, palling***) **1** *intr* to begin to bore or seem tedious. **2** to cloy; to bore. ⓒ 14c: a variant of APPAL.

palladium /pə'leɪdɪəm/ ▷ *noun, chem* (symbol **Pd**, atomic number 46) a soft silvery-white metallic element used as a catalyst, and in gold dental alloys, jewellery, electrical components, and catalytic converters for car exhausts. ⓒ Named after the asteroid Pallas, discovered at about the same time (1802).

pall-bearer ▷ *noun* one of the people carrying the coffin or walking beside it at a funeral.

palled see under PAL, PALL[2]

pallet[1] /'palɪt/ ▷ *noun* **1** a small wooden platform on which goods can be stacked for lifting and transporting, especially by forklift truck. **2** a flat-bladed wooden tool used for shaping pottery. ⓒ 16c in sense 2: from French *palette* (see PALETTE).

pallet[2] /'palɪt/ ▷ *noun* **1** a straw bed. **2** a small makeshift bed. ⓒ 14c: from French *paillet* a bundle or heap of straw, from *paille* straw.

palliasse or **paillasse** /palɪ'as, 'palɪas/ ▷ *noun* a straw-filled mattress. ⓒ 16c: from French *paillasse*, from *paille* straw.

palliate /'palɪeɪt/ ▷ *verb* (***palliated, palliating***) **1** to ease the symptoms of (a disease) without curing it. **2** to serve to lessen the gravity of (an offence, etc); to excuse something to some extent; to mitigate. **3** to reduce the effect of (anything disagreeable). ⓒ 16c: from Latin *palliare* to cloak.

palliative /'palɪətɪv/ ▷ *noun* anything used to reduce pain or anxiety. ▷ *adj* having the effect of alleviating or reducing pain. ⓒ 16c: French.

pallid /'palɪd/ ▷ *adj* (***pallider, pallidest***) **1** pale, especially unhealthily so. **2** lacking vigour or conviction. ⓒ 16c: from Latin *pallidus* pale.

palliness see under PAL

palling see under PAL, PALL[2]

pallium /'palɪəm/ ▷ *noun* (***pallia*** /-lɪə/ or ***palliums***) *relig* a white woollen vestment shaped like a double Y, embroidered with six purple crosses signifying episcopal power and union with the Holy See of Rome, worn by the pope and conferred by him on archbishops. Also called PALL[1]. ⓒ 16c: Latin, meaning 'a cloak'.

pallor /'palə(r)/ ▷ *noun* paleness, especially of complexion. ⓒ 17c: Latin.

pally see under PAL

palm[1] /pɑːm/ ▷ *noun* **1** the inner surface of the hand between the wrist and the fingers. **2** the part of a glove covering this. ▷ *verb* (***palmed, palming***) to conceal something in the palm of the hand. • **grease someone's palm** see under GREASE. • **in the palm of one's hand** in one's power; at one's command. ⓒ 14c as *paume*: French, originally from Latin *palma* palm of the hand; the spelling was gradually assimilated to the Latin form, resulting in the current spelling.

■ **palm something off on someone** or **palm someone off with something** *colloq* to give them something unwanted or unwelcome, especially by trickery.

palm[2] /pɑːm/ ▷ *noun* **1** any of various large tropical plants, most of which are trees with woody unbranched trunks bearing a crown of large fan-shaped or feather-shaped leaves, eg the date and the coconut. **2** a leaf of such a plant carried as a symbol of triumph or victory; the supreme prize. ⓒ Anglo-Saxon, from Latin *palma* palm of the hand.

palmaceous /pɑːl'meɪʃəs/ ▷ *adj, bot* belonging to the PALM[2] family. ⓒ 18c.

palmar /'palmə(r)/ ▷ *adj* relating to the palm of the hand. ⓒ 17c.

palmate /'palmeɪt, 'palmət/ or **palmated** ▷ *adj* **1** *bot* said of a leaf: divided into lobes that radiate from a central point, resembling an open hand. **2** *zool* said of an animal, especially an aquatic bird: having webbed toes. ⓒ 18c: from Latin *palmatus*, from *palma* palm of the hand.

palm cat and **palm civet** see under PARADOXURE

palm court ▷ *noun* a large room or conservatory in a hotel, etc, decorated with palm trees, where light music is traditionally played by a small orchestra and afternoon tea may be taken.

Palme d'Or /pɑːm'dɔ(r)/ ▻ *noun* (***Palmes d'or***) the highest award given at the annual Cannes International Film Festival. ⓒ 20c: French, meaning 'golden palm'.

palmetto /pal'mɛtoʊ/ ▻ *noun* (***palmettos*** or ***palmettoes***) any of various small palm trees, mainly native to tropical regions, which have fan-shaped leaves. ⓒ 16c: from Spanish *palmito* small palm.

palmhouse ▻ *noun* a glasshouse for palms and other tropical plants, usually found in botanical gardens in temperate climates where palms do not grow naturally.

palmist /'pɑːmɪst/ ▻ *noun* someone who practices palmistry.

palmistry /'pɑːmɪstrɪ/ ▻ *noun* the art and practice of telling someone's fortune by reading the lines on the palm of their hand. Also called **chiromancy**. ⓒ 15c.

palmitate /'pɑːlmiteɪt/ ▻ *noun, chem* a salt of palmitic acid. ⓒ 19c.

palmitic acid /pal'mɪtɪk —/ ▻ *noun, chem* (formula **$C_{15}H_{31}COOH$**) a fatty acid, obtained from many animal and plant oils and fats, used in the manufacture of soaps, lubricating oils and waterproofing agents.

palm oil ▻ *noun* the red oil obtained from the outer pulp of the fruit of the OIL PALM, used in cooking fats and margarines.

palm sugar ▻ *noun* sugar obtained from the sap of certain species of palm trees. Also called **jaggery**.

Palm Sunday ▻ *noun, Christianity* the Sunday before Easter, on which Christ's triumphal entry into Jerusalem, when the crowd spread palm branches before him, is commemorated.

palmtop ▻ *noun* a portable computer, smaller than a LAPTOP, and usually small enough to be held in the hand. See also NOTEBOOK.

palmy /'pɑːmɪ/ ▻ *adj* (***palmier***, ***palmiest***) effortlessly successful and prosperous □ ***one's palmy days***. ⓒ 17c: from PALM², as a symbol of triumph.

palmyra /pal'maɪərə/ ▻ *noun* (***palmyras***) an African and Asiatic palm yielding TODDY, JAGGERY and **palmyra nuts**. ⓒ 17c: from Portuguese *palmeira* palm tree, the spelling probably being influenced by the name of the ancient Syrian city *Palmyra*.

palolo /pə'loʊloʊ/ ▻ *noun* (***palolos***) an edible sea-worm that burrows in coral reefs, abundant in parts of the Pacific. ⓒ 19c: Samoan.

palomino or **palamino** /palə'miːnoʊ/ ▻ *noun* (***palominos*** or ***palaminos***) a golden or cream horse, largely of Arab blood, with a white or silver tail and mane. ⓒ Early 20c: American Spanish *palomino* dove-like.

palooka /pə'luːkə/ ▻ *noun* (***palookas***) *US slang* a stupid or clumsy person, especially in sports. ⓒ 1920s.

palp and **palpus** /'palpəs/ (***palps*** or ***palpi*** /-paɪ/) ▻ *noun, zool* a jointed sense-organ attached in pairs to the mouthparts of insects and crustaceans. • **palpal** *adj*. ⓒ 19c: from French *palpe*, from Latin *palpus* a feeler.

palpable /'palpəbəl/ ▻ *adj* **1** easily detected; obvious. **2** *medicine* said eg of an internal organ: able to be felt. • **palpability** *noun*. • **palpableness** *noun*. • **palpably** *adverb*. ⓒ 14c: from Latin *palpare* to touch.

palpate /'palpeɪt/ ▻ *verb* (***palpated***, ***palpating***) *medicine* to examine (the body or a part of it) by touching or pressing, especially in order to diagnose medical disorders or diseases. ⓒ 19c: from Latin *palpare* to touch.

palpitate /'palpɪteɪt/ ▻ *verb* (***palpitated***, ***palpitating***) *intr* **1** *medicine* said of the heart: to beat abnormally rapidly, eg as a result of physical exertion, fear, emotion or heart disease. **2** to tremble or throb. • **palpitation** *noun*. ⓒ 17c: from Latin *palpitare* to throb.

palpus see PALP

palsy¹ /'pɔːlzɪ, 'pɒlzɪ/ ▻ *noun* (***palsies***) paralysis, or loss of control or feeling in a part of the body. ▻ *verb* (***palsies***, ***palsied***, ***palsying***) to affect someone or something with palsy; to paralyse. ⓒ 13c: from French *paralisie*, from Latin and Greek *paralysis*.

palsy² /'palzɪ/ and **palsy-walsy** /-'walzɪ/ ▻ *adj, colloq* over-friendly; ingratiatingly intimate. ⓒ 1930s: from PAL.

paltry /'pɔːltrɪ, 'pɒltrɪ/ ▻ *adj* (***paltrier***, ***paltriest***) worthless; trivial; meagre; insignificant or insultingly inadequate □ ***a paltry sum***. • **paltriness** *noun*. • **paltrily** *adverb*. ⓒ 16c: from German dialect *paltrig* ragged.

paludal /pə'ljuːdəl, pə'luːdəl, 'paljʊdəl/ ▻ *adj* **1** relating to marshes; marshy. **2** arising from a marsh; malarial. ⓒ 19c: from Latin *paludis* a marsh.

paly see under PALE²

palynology /palɪ'nɒlədʒɪ/ ▻ *noun* the study and analysis of spores and pollen grains, especially those preserved in ancient sediments and soils, in order to reconstruct variations in vegetation over time. ⓒ 1940s: from Greek *palynein* to sprinkle + -LOGY.

pam. ▻ *abbreviation* pamphlet.

pampas grass ▻ *noun* /pampəs —/ a large perennial S American grass with dense tufts of arching bluish leaves and tall erect stems bearing silvery-white or pink plume-like panicles, used ornamentally in Europe. ⓒ 19c: from Spanish *Pampa* a vast prairie in S America south of the Amazon, from Peruvian *bamba* a steppe.

pamper /'pampə(r)/ ▻ *verb* (***pampered***, ***pampering***) to treat (a person or animal) over-indulgently and over-protectively; to cosset or spoil them. • **pamperer** *noun*. ⓒ 14c.

pamphlet /'pamflət/ ▻ *noun* (abbreviation **pam.**) a booklet or leaflet providing information or dealing with a current topic. ⓒ 14c: from French *pamphilet*, from the title of the Latin love poem *Pamphilus, seu de Amore*.

pan¹ ▻ *noun* **1** a pot, usually made of metal, used for cooking. **2** a PANFUL. **3** *often in compounds* any of various vessels, usually shallow ones, used for domestic, industrial and other purposes □ ***dustpan*** □ ***bedpan***. **4** the bowl of a lavatory. **5** either of the two dishes on a pair of scales. **6** a shallow hollow in the ground □ ***a salt pan***. **7** *historical* the hollow part of an old gunlock, that holds the priming. See also A FLASH IN THE PAN at FLASH. **8** *usually in compounds* any object similar to a pan in shape □ ***brainpan***. **9** a hard layer under or in the soil. **10** a hollow metal drum of the type played in a steel band. ▻ *verb* (***panned***, ***panning***) **1** (*often* **pan for something**) *tr & intr* to wash (river gravel) in a shallow metal vessel in search for (eg gold). **2** *colloq* to criticize something or review (a performance, book, etc) harshly. ⓒ Anglo-Saxon *panne*.

■ **pan out 1** to result or turn out. **2** to come to an end; to be exhausted.

pan² ▻ *verb* (***panned***, ***panning***) *tr & intr* said of a film camera, camcorder, etc: to swing round so as to follow a moving object or show a panoramic view. ▻ *noun* a panning movement or shot. ⓒ 1920s: a short form of PANORAMA.

pan- ▻ *combining form, denoting* **1** all; entire □ ***panorama*** □ ***panchromatic***. **2** referring to a movement or ideal to unite (a whole continent, group of people, religion, etc) politically, economically, etc □ ***pan-Africanism*** □ ***panhellenic***. Compare PANTO-. ⓒ From Greek *pas, pantos* all.

panacea /panə'sɪə/ ▻ *noun* (***panaceas***) a universal remedy; a cure-all for any ill, problem, etc. ⓒ 16c: from Greek *panakeia* universal remedy.

panache /pə'naʃ, pə'nɑːʃ/ ▻ *noun* flamboyant self-assurance; a grand manner. ⓒ 19c in this sense; 16c meaning 'plume' or 'decoration of feathers' (eg on a headdress or helmet): French, from Latin *pinnaculum*, diminutive of *pinna* feather.

panada /pə'nɑːdə/ ▷ *noun* (***panadas***) *cookery* **1** a dish made by boiling bread to a pulp in water or milk and flavouring it. **2** a thick binding sauce of flour or breadcrumbs, a liquid, and seasoning. ⓘ 17c: from Spanish *pan* bread.

pan-African ▷ *adj* **1** including or relating to the whole of the African continent. **2** referring or relating to pan-Africanism. ⓘ Early 20c.

pan-Africanism ▷ *noun* an ideal and a movement that draws its ideas from Black American and West Indian writers and activists, reflecting a pride in the African continent and culture, and a commitment to self-rule. • **pan-Africanist** *noun*.

PanAm ▷ *abbreviation* Pan-American World Airways Incorporated.

panama /'panəmɑː/ and **panama hat** ▷ *noun* (***panamas***) **1** a lightweight brimmed hat for men made from the plaited leaves of a palm-like Central American tree, made in Ecuador, not Panama. **2** a hat in this style. ⓘ 19c: named after Panama, a state in C America.

Panamanian /panə'meɪnɪən/ ▷ *adj* belonging or relating to Panama, a republic occupying the SE end of the isthmus of Central America, or to its inhabitants. ⓘ 19c.

pan-American ▷ *adj* including or relating to all the states of both N and S America, or all N and S Americans. • **pan-Americanism** *noun*. ⓘ 1890s.

pan-Arab or **pan-Arabic** ▷ *adj* relating to the ideal or policy of political unity between all Arab states. • **pan-Arabism** *noun*. ⓘ 1930s.

panatella /panə'tɛlə/ ▷ *noun* (***panatellas***) a long slim cigar. ⓘ Early 20c: American Spanish, meaning 'a long thin biscuit' and Italian, meaning 'small loaf'.

pancake ▷ *noun* a thin cake made from a batter of eggs, flour and milk, cooked on both sides in a frying-pan or on a griddle, and traditional in many parts of the world. Compare DROP SCONE, CREPE. ⓘ 15c: PAN[1] + CAKE.

Pancake Day ▷ *noun* SHROVE TUESDAY, when pancakes are traditionally eaten, originally in order to use up the fat and eggs in a house before fasting for Lent.

pancake ice ▷ *noun* polar sea ice in thin flat slabs, found as winter draws near.

pancake landing ▷ *noun* an aircraft landing made in an emergency, with the wheels up and landing flat on the belly of the aircraft.

pancake make-up ▷ *noun* cosmetic make-up in cake form which is moist or moistened before application.

panchax /'pantʃaks/ ▷ *noun* (***panchaxes***) any of several kinds of brightly coloured fish native to Africa and SE Asia. ⓘ 19c: Latin, former generic name.

panchromatic /paŋkroʊ'matɪk, pan-/ ▷ *adj, photog* said of a film: sensitive to all colours. ⓘ Early 20c.

pancreas /'paŋkrɪəs/ ▷ *noun, anatomy* in vertebrates: a large carrot-shaped gland lying between the duodenum and the spleen, that secretes PANCREATIC JUICE serving hormonal and digestive functions. See also SWEETBREAD. • **pancreatic** *adj*. ⓘ 16c: from Greek *pankreas*.

pancreatic juice ▷ *noun* a mixture of digestive enzymes secreted from the pancreas into the duodenum, which is strongly alkaline in order to counteract the acidity of food that has just passed from the stomach into the duodenum.

pancreatin /'paŋkrɪətɪn/ ▷ *noun* **1** *biochem* PANCREATIC JUICE. **2** a medicinal substance to aid the digestion, prepared from extracts of the pancreas of certain animals. ⓘ 19c.

panda /'pandə/ ▷ *noun* (***pandas***) **1** a GIANT PANDA. **2** a RED PANDA. ⓘ 1820s: Nepalese.

Pandean /pan'dɪən/ ▷ *adj* **1** relating to Pan, the Greek god of pastures, flocks and woods, represented as having a man's head, arms and torso, and goat's legs and feet. **2** relating to PANPIPES. ⓘ 19c.

pandemic /pan'dɛmɪk/ ▷ *adj, medicine* describing a widespread epidemic of a disease, one that affects a whole country, continent, etc. ⓘ 17c: from Greek *pan-* all + *demos* people.

pandemonium /pandə'moʊnɪəm/ ▷ *noun* **1** any very disorderly or noisy place or assembly. **2** noise, chaos and confusion. • **pandemonic** /-mɒnɪk/ *adj*. ⓘ 17c: John Milton's name for the capital of Hell in *Paradise Lost*, from Greek *pan-* all + *daimon* demon.

pander /'pandə(r)/ ▷ *noun* someone who obtains a sexual partner for someone else. ▷ *verb* (***pandered***, ***pandering***) *archaic* to play the pander for someone. ⓘ 16c: named after Pandarus in Chaucer and Shakespeare, the go-between who procures Cressida for Troilus.

> ■ **pander to someone** or **something** to indulge or gratify them or their wishes or tastes □ *John pandered to my every need.*

pandit see under PUNDIT

P & O ▷ *abbreviation* Peninsular and Oriental Steamship Navigation Company.

Pandora's box ▷ *noun* any source of great and unexpected troubles. ⓘ 16c: from Pandora (Greek, meaning 'all gifts'), the name of the first woman in Greek mythology, who, in one version of the myth, was given a box by Zeus which was opened against his advice, letting loose all the ills of the world, except for hope which was in the bottom of the box.

p & p ▷ *abbreviation* postage and packing.

pane /peɪn/ ▷ *noun* a sheet of glass, especially one fitted into a window or door. ⓘ 13c: from French *pan* a strip of cloth.

panegyric /panə'dʒɪrɪk/ ▷ *noun* a speech or piece of writing in praise of someone or something, especially an elaborate one; a eulogy. • **panegyric** or **panegyrical** *adj*. • **panegyrist** *noun*. ⓘ 17c: from Greek *panegyrikos* fit for a national festival, from *pan-* all + *agyris* an assembly.

panel /'panəl/ ▷ *noun* **1** a rectangular wooden board forming a section, especially an ornamentally sunken or raised one, of a wall or door. **2** one of several strips of fabric making up a garment. **3** any of the metal sections forming the bodywork of a vehicle. **4** a board bearing the instruments and dials for controlling an aircraft, etc □ *control panel*. **5** rectangular divisions on the page of a book, especially for illustrations. **6 a** a team of people selected to judge a contest, or to participate in a discussion, quiz or other game before an audience; **b** *as adj* □ *panel discussion* □ *panel game*. **7 a** a list of jurors; **b** the people serving on a jury. ▷ *verb* (***panelled***, ***panelling***; *especially N Amer* ***paneling***, ***paneled***) to fit (a wall or door) with wooden panels. ⓘ 13c: French diminutive of *pan* a strip of cloth, from Latin *pannus* a cloth.

panel-beating ▷ *noun* the removal of dents from metal, especially from the bodywork of a vehicle, using a soft-headed hammer. • **panel-beater** *noun*.

panel heating ▷ *noun* indoor heating diffused from panels in the floors, walls or ceilings.

panelling or (*N Amer*) **paneling** *noun* **1** panels covering a wall or part of a wall, usually as decoration. Also called **panel-work**. **2** material for making these.

panellist or (*N Amer*) **panelist** /'panəlɪst/ *noun* a member of a panel or team of people, especially in a panel game on TV or radio.

panel pin ▷ *noun* a small slender nail with a very small head, mainly used for fixing plywood or hardboard to supports.

panel saw ▷ *noun* a fine saw for cutting thin wood at right angles to the grain.

panettone /panə'toʊneɪ/ ▷ *noun* (***panettoni*** /niː/) a kind of spiced cake, usually containing sultanas, traditionally eaten at Christmas in Italy. ◷ 1920s: Italian, literally 'a small loaf'.

pan-European ▷ *adj* **1** referring or relating to the economics, politics, etc of all European countries, but usually exclusively referring to the countries of the EUROPEAN UNION. **2** referring or relating to the policy of or movement for political unity of all European states. ◷ Early 20c.

panful ▷ *noun* (***panfuls***) the amount a pan can hold.

pang /paŋ/ ▷ *noun* a brief but painfully acute feeling of hunger, guilt, remorse, etc □ ***a pang of guilt.*** ◷ 16c.

Pangaea or **Pangea** /pan'dʒɪə/ ▷ *noun, geol* the name given to the hypothetical supercontinent that is thought to have represented the entire landmass of the Earth about 200 million years ago, before it drifted apart to form LAURASIA and GONDWANALAND, which themselves drifted apart eventually forming the present continents of the Earth. ◷ 1920s: from PAN- + Greek *ge* earth.

pan-galactic ▷ *adj* relating or referring to all the galaxies in the Universe.

pan-Germanism ▷ *noun* especially in the 19c: an ideal of and movement for a Greater Germany or union of all German people. • **pan-German** *adj.*

pangolin /paŋ'goʊlɪn/ ▷ *noun* a toothless mammal that is covered with large overlapping horny plates, has a pointed head and a long broad tail, and can curl into an armoured ball when threatened by a predator. ◷ 18c: from Malay *peng-goling* roller.

pangram /'pangram/ ▷ *noun* a sentence or verse containing all the letters of the alphabet, such as *The quick brown fox jumps over the lazy dog.* • **pangrammatist** *noun* someone who contrives pangrams. ◷ 1930s.

panhandle ▷ *noun, especially US* a narrow strip of territory stretching out from the main body into another territory, eg part of a state which stretches into another.

panhellenic ▷ *adj* **1** said of either ancient or modern Greece: relating to, including or representing all Greeks, or the whole of Greece. **2** relating to Panhellenism. ◷ 19c.

Panhellenism ▷ *noun* especially in the late 19c: a movement or ideal for the union of all Greece or all Greeks. • **Panhellenist** *noun.*

panic /'panɪk/ ▷ *noun* a sudden overpowering fear that affects an individual, or especially one that grips a crowd or population. ▷ *verb* (***panicked, panicking***) *tr & intr* to feel panic, or make someone feel panic. ◷ 17c: from French *panique*, from Greek *panikon* baseless terror, referring to fear caused by harmless sounds heard in the mountains and valleys, thought to be made by Pan, the god of flocks and pastures.

panic attack ▷ *noun, psychol* an attack of intense terror and anxiety, lasting from several minutes to several hours.

panic button ▷ *noun* an alarm button operating any of various safety devices, eg one that stops an escalator, signals for assistance, etc.

panic-buy ▷ *verb* to buy (commodities or a commodity) in large quantities, in expectation of a shortage, often precipitating a greater shortage than might otherwise have occurred.

panicky /'panɪkɪ/ ▷ *adj* inclined to or affected by panic.

panicle /'panɪkəl/ ▷ *noun, bot* a branched flower-head, common in grasses, in which the youngest flowers are at the tip of the flower-stalk, and the oldest ones are near its base. • **panicled**, **paniculate** /pə'nɪkjʊlət/ or **paniculated** *adj* having, arranged in, or like, panicles. ◷ 16c: from Latin *panicula* tuft.

panic-stricken ▷ *adj* struck with sudden fear; terrified.

Panislamism /panɪz'lɑːmɪzəm/ ▷ *noun* especially in the 19c: the advocacy of a political union of the whole of the Muslim world. • **Panislam** *noun.* • **Panislamic** or **pan-Islamic** *adj.*

Panjabi see PUNJABI

panjandrum /pan'dʒandrəm/ ▷ *noun, humorous* a pompous official. ◷ 18c: from 'the Grand Panjandrum', used in a string of nonsense composed by Samuel Foote (1720–77), wit, actor and dramatist.

panne /pan/ ▷ *noun* a fabric resembling velvet, with a long nap. ◷ 18c: French.

panned *past tense, past participle of* PAN[1], PAN[2]

pannier /'panɪə(r)/ ▷ *noun* **1 a** one of a pair of baskets carried over the back of a donkey or other pack animal; **b** one of a pair of bags carried on either side of the wheel of a bicycle, etc. **2** *historical* **a** a system of hoops used for speading out a woman's dress at the hips; **b** a tucked-up arrangement of fabric on either side of a woman's skirt. ◷ 13c, originally referring to a large basket for carrying food: from French *panier*, from Latin *panarium* bread basket.

pannikin /'panɪkɪn/ ▷ *noun* **1** a small metal cup. **2** a small pan or saucer. ◷ 19c: from PAN[1] + -KIN.

panning *present participle of* PAN[1], PAN[2]

pannose /'panoʊs/ ▷ *adj, bot* like felt. ◷ 19c: from Latin *pannosus*, from *pannus* cloth.

pannus /'panəs/ ▷ *noun* (***pannuses***) *pathol* **1** a layer of new connective tissue that forms over the joints in rheumatoid arthritis. **2** an opaque membrane of inflammatory tissue that forms over the cornea in TRACHOMA. ◷ 18c: from Latin *pannus* cloth.

panocha /pə'noʊtʃə/ ▷ *noun* a coarse brown Mexican sugar. ◷ 19c: American Spanish.

panoply /'panəplɪ/ ▷ *noun* (***panoplies***) **1** the full splendid assemblage got together for a ceremony, etc □ ***the full panoply of a society wedding.*** **2** *historical* a full set of armour and weapons. ◷ 17c: from Greek *panoplia* full armour of heavy-armed Greek footsoldiers, from *pan-* all + *hopla* weapons.

panoptic /pan'ɒptɪk/ or **panoptical** ▷ *adj* all-embracing; viewing all aspects. ◷ 19c.

panorama /panə'rɑːmə/ ▷ *noun* (***panoramas***) **1** an open and extensive or all-round view, eg of a landscape. **2** a view of something in all its range and variety □ ***the panorama of history.*** ◷ 18c: from Greek *pan-* all + *horama* view.

panoramic /panə'ramɪk/ ▷ *adj* said of a view or prospect: like a panorama; open and extensive. • **panoramically** *adverb.*

panoramic camera ▷ *noun* a camera which takes very wide-angle views, generally by rotation about an axis and by exposing a roll of film through a vertical slit.

panoramic sight ▷ *noun* a gunsight that can be rotated, enabling the user to fire in any direction.

panpipes, **Pan pipes** or **Pan's pipes** ▷ *plural noun* a musical instrument, made of reeds of different lengths bound together and played by blowing across their open ends, of great antiquity and widely used in certain folk cultures such as those of S America and Romania. Also called **syrinx**. ◷ 19c: named after Pan, the Greek god of pastures, flocks and woods, who reputedly invented them.

pan-Slavic or **pan-Slav** ▷ *adj* **1** relating to, including or representing all Slavs. **2** relating to pan-Slavism.

pan-Slavism ▷ *noun* a movement for the union of all Slav peoples. • **pan-Slavist** *adj, noun.* ◷ 1850s: modelled on the German *Panslavismus.*

panspermatism /pan'spɜːmətɪzəm/ or **panspermism** ▷ *noun* the theory that life could be diffused through the Universe by means of germs carried by meterorites or that life was brought to Earth by this means. •

panspermatist or **panspermist** *noun*. ⓒ 19c: from Greek *sperma* seed.

pansy /ˈpanzɪ/ ▷ *noun* (***pansies***) **1** any of various species of violet, native to Europe, which have flat flowers with five rounded white, yellow or purple petals. **2** *offensive slang* an effeminate man or boy; a male homosexual. ⓒ 15c: from French *pensée* thought.

pant ▷ *verb* (***panted, panting***) **1** *intr* to breathe in and out with quick, shallow, short gasps as a result of physical exertion. **2** to say something breathlessly. ▷ *noun* a gasping breath. • **panting** *noun, adj*. • **pantingly** *adverb*. • **be panting for something** to be longing for it □ *panting for a drink.* ⓒ 15c: from French *pantaisier*, from Greek *phantasioun* to hallucinate.

pant- see PANTO-

pantaloons /pantəˈluːnz/ ▷ *plural noun* **1** baggy trousers gathered at the ankle. **2** various kinds of trousers, such as tight-fitting trousers for men with buttons or ribbons below the calf, worn at the turn of the 19c. ⓒ 16c: from *Pantalone*, a figure from Italian comedy, a skinny old man in tight hose.

pantechnicon /panˈtɛknɪkɒn/ ▷ *noun* a large furniture-removal van. ⓒ 19c: from Greek *pan-* all + *techne* art; originally the name of the premises of a London art dealer, which were later used as a furniture warehouse.

pantheism /ˈpanθiːɪzəm/ ▷ *noun* **1** the belief that equates all the matter and forces in the Universe with God. **2** readiness to believe in all or many gods. • **pantheist** *noun*. • **pantheistic** or **pantheistical** *adj*. ⓒ 18c: from Greek *pan-* all + *theos* god.

panthenol /ˈpanθənɒl/ ▷ *noun, US* PANTOTHENOL.

pantheon /ˈpanθɪən/ ▷ *noun* **1** all the gods of a particular people □ *the ancient Greek pantheon.* **2 a** a temple sacred to all the gods; **b** (**the Pantheon**) the temple built (c.119–125 AD) in Rome by the Emperor Hadrian, and regarded as one of the greatest surviving classical buildings. It was dedicated to the seven Roman planetary gods. **3** a building in which the glorious dead of a nation have memorials or are buried. ⓒ 14c: from Greek *pantheios* of all the gods.

panther /ˈpanθə(r)/ ▷ *noun* **1** a LEOPARD, especially a black one, formerly believed to be a different species. **2** *N Amer* a PUMA. • **pantherine** /-raɪn/ or **pantherish** *adj*. ⓒ 13c: from Latin *panthera*, from Greek *panther* leopard.

panties /ˈpantɪz/ ▷ *plural noun* thin light knickers, mainly for women and children. ⓒ Early 20c in this sense; 19c, meaning 'men's shorts or trousers': diminutive of PANTS.

pantihose see PANTY HOSE

pantile /ˈpantaɪl/ *building* ▷ *noun* a roofing tile with an S-shaped cross section, laid so that the upward curve of one tile fits under the downward curve of the next. • **pantiled** *adj*. • **pantiling** *noun*. ⓒ 17c: PAN[1] + TILE.

panto /ˈpantoʊ/ ▷ *noun* (***pantos***) *colloq* short form of PANTOMIME.

panto- /pantoʊ/ or (before a vowel) **pant-** ▷ *combining form, denoting* all or entire. Compare PAN-. ⓒ From Greek *pas, pantos* all.

pantograph /ˈpantəgrɑːf/ ▷ *noun* **1** a device consisting of jointed rods forming an adjustable parallelogram, for copying maps, plans, etc to any scale. **2** a similarly shaped metal framework on the roof of an electric train, transmitting current from an overhead wire. ⓒ 18c.

pantomime /ˈpantəmaɪm/ ▷ *noun* **1 a** a Christmas entertainment usually based on a popular fairy tale, with songs, dancing, comedy acts, etc; **b** *as adj* □ *pantomime season.* **2** communication by exaggerated gesture and facial expression, with no speech; mime. **3** a farcical or confused situation □ *What a pantomime!* • **pantomimic** /-ˈmɪmɪk/ or **pantomimical** *adj*. ⓒ 16c: from Greek *pantomimos* a mime actor, literally 'imitator of all'.

pantomimist /ˈpantəmaɪmɪst/ ▷ *noun* **1** an actor in pantomime. **2** a writer of pantomime.

pantothenic acid /pantəˈθɛnɪk —/ ▷ *noun, biochem* a member of the VITAMIN B COMPLEX that is found in many foods, especially cereal grains, egg yolk, liver, yeast and peas. See also PANTHENOL. ⓒ 1930s: from Greek *pantothen* from every side, because of its wide occurrence.

pantothenol ▷ *noun* a vitamin of the VITAMIN B COMPLEX. ⓒ 20c: see PANTOTHENIC ACID.

pantry /ˈpantrɪ/ ▷ *noun* (***pantries***) a small room or cupboard for storing food, cooking utensils, etc; a larder. ⓒ 13c: from French *paneterie* a place where bread was stored, from Latin *panis* bread.

pants ▷ *plural noun* **1** *Brit* an undergarment worn over the buttocks and genital area; underpants. **2** *N Amer* trousers. • **be caught with one's pants down** *colloq* to be caught at an embarrassing and unsuitable moment, completely unprepared. • **by the seat of one's pants** see under SEAT. • **scare, bore,** *etc* **the pants off someone** *slang* to scare, bore, etc them to a great extent. • **wear the pants** *N Amer colloq* wear the trousers (see under TROUSERS). ⓒ 19c: originally US, a shortening of PANTALOONS for trousers in general.

pant suit or **pants suit** ▷ *noun, N Amer* a TROUSER SUIT.

panty girdle ▷ *noun* a woman's undergarment consisting of tight elasticated pants which hold in the stomach and buttocks.

panty hose or **pantihose** ▷ *plural noun, N Amer* women's tights.

pap[1] ▷ *noun* **1** soft semi-liquid food for babies and sick people. **2** *derog* trivial or worthless reading matter or entertainment. • **pappy** *adj*. ⓒ 15c; 16c in sense 2; from German *pappe*, from Latin *papare* to feed with pap; probably imitating the sound of a baby eating.

pap[2] ▷ *noun* **1** *old use* a nipple or teat. **2** *Scots* in placenames: a round conical hill. ⓒ 13c: from Scandinavian; probably imitating a suckling sound.

papa ▷ *noun* **1** /pəˈpɑː/ (***papas***) *old use or jocular* a child's word for father. **2** /ˈpɑːpə/ (**Papa**) *communications* in the NATO alphabet: the word used to denote the letter 'P' (see table at NATO ALPHABET). ⓒ 17c: from French *papa* and Greek *pappas* father.

papacy /ˈpeɪpəsɪ/ ▷ *noun* (***papacies***) **1** the position, power or period of office of a POPE. **2** government by popes. ⓒ 14c: from Latin *papatia*, from *papa* pope.

papain /pəˈpeɪn/ ▷ *noun* a digestive enzyme in the juice of papaya fruits and leaves, used for tenderizing meat. ⓒ Late 19c.

papal /ˈpeɪpəl/ ▷ *adj* referring or relating to the POPE (*noun* 1) or the PAPACY. ⓒ 14c: from Latin *papalis*, from *papa* pope.

papal brief see BRIEF

papal bull ▷ *noun* a BULL[3]

papal cross ▷ *noun* a cross with three crossbars.

papalism ▷ *noun* the situation of the POPE (*noun* 1) as the head of the RC Church, his power and authority; the papal system. • **papalist** *noun* a supporter of the pope and of the papal system.

Papanicolaou smear and **Papanicolaou test** /papəˈniːkəlaʊ —/ ▷ *noun* a SMEAR TEST for detecting cancer or precancerous cells, especially cancer of the cervix. Often shortened to **pap test**. ⓒ 1940s: named after George Papanicolaou (1883–1962), US anatomist, who devised the test.

paparazzo /papəˈratsoʊ/ ▷ *noun* (***paparazzi*** /-tsiː/) a newspaper photographer who follows famous people about in the hope of photographing them in unguarded moments. ⓘ 1960s: from the name of the photographer in the film *La Dolce Vita* (1959).

papaverine /pəpeɪvəriːn, -rɪn/ ▻ *noun, medicine* a smooth-muscle relaxant drug found in opium. ⓘ 19c: from Latin *papaver* poppy.

papaw /pə'pɔː/ or **pawpaw** /'pɔːpɔː/ ▻ *noun* **1** a tree with purple flowers native to N America. **2** a small evergreen tree with a crown of large segmented leaves and yellow flowers, widely cultivated in the tropics for its edible fruit. **3** the large oblong yellow or orange fruit of this tree, which may be eaten raw, squeezed for its juice or canned, having sweet orange flesh and a central cavity filled with black seeds. Also called **custard apple**. Sometimes called **papaya** (***papayas***) ⓘ 15c: Spanish *papaya*, from a Caribbean dialect.

paper /'peɪpə(r)/ ▻ *noun* **1** a material manufactured in thin sheets from pulped wood, rags, or other forms of cellulose, used for writing and printing on, wrapping things, etc. **2** a loose piece of paper, eg a wrapper or printed sheet. **3** other material used for a similar purpose or with a similar appearance, eg PAPYRUS, RICE PAPER. **4** wallpaper. **5 a** a newspaper; **b (the papers)** newspapers collectively; the press. **6** a set of questions on a certain subject for a written examination □ *maths paper.* **7 a** a written article dealing with a certain subject, especially for reading to an audience at a meeting, conference, etc; **b** an essay written eg by a student. **8 (papers)** personal documents establishing one's identity, nationality, etc, required by customs, passport control, etc, and in some countries required by law to be carried at all times. **9 (papers)** a person's accumulated correspondence, diaries, etc. **10** *politics* see under GREEN PAPER, WHITE PAPER. **11** *stock exchange slang* stocks and shares. ▻ *adj* **1** consisting of or made of paper. **2** paper-like, especially thin like paper; papery. **3** on paper. ▻ *verb* (***papered, papering***) **1** to decorate (a wall, a room, etc) with wallpaper □ *paper the hall.* **2** to cover something with paper. • **paperer** *noun.* • **papering** *noun* **1** the activity of covering something with paper, especially wallpaper. **2** the paper used for this. • **on paper 1** in theory or in abstract as distinct from practice □ *The plans were good on paper, but not in practice.* **2** captured in written form □ *get one's ideas down on paper.* ⓘ 14c: from French *papier*, from Latin, from Greek *papyros* PAPYRUS.

■ **paper over something** or **paper over the cracks in something** to conceal or avoid (an awkward fact, mistake, etc).

paperback ▻ *noun* a book with a thin flexible paper binding, as opposed to a HARDBACK. Also *as adj.* ▻ *verb* to publish (a book) in paperback form.

paperboard ▻ *noun* a type of strong thick cardboard; PASTEBOARD.

paperboy and **papergirl** ▻ *noun* a boy or girl who delivers newspapers to people's homes, or sells them.

paper chase ▻ *noun* a cross-country race in which runners follow a trail of dropped shreds of paper. See also HARE AND HOUNDS.

paper chromatography ▻ *noun, chem* a form of CHROMATOGRAPHY used to separate and analyse complex mixtures of chemical compounds that are applied to one end of a sheet of a special grade of filter paper, which is then suspended vertically in a solvent.

paper clip ▻ *noun* **1** a metal clip formed from bent wire, for holding papers together. **2** a round-headed brass device with two flexible legs that can be pushed through papers, then separated and folded back to secure them. Also called **paper fastener**.

paper hanger ▻ *noun* someone who puts up wallpaper.

paper knife ▻ *noun* a knife for slitting open envelopes, cutting open the leaves of books, etc.

paperless ▻ *adj* using especially electronic means, rather than paper, for communicating, recording, etc □ *a paperless office.*

paper-mâché see PAPIER-MÂCHÉ

paper mill ▻ *noun* a place where paper is manufactured, traditionally a mill built beside a river, since a lot of water is required to produce paper pulp.

paper money ▻ *noun* bank notes, as opposed to coins.

paper nautilus ▻ *noun* any of various small octopuses, native to open seas, so called because the female secretes a thin-walled papery egg-case which is carried by her. ⓘ 19c: PAPER + NAUTILUS; apparently Aristotle believed that it used its arms as sails.

paper profits ▻ *plural noun* the appreciation in value of ASSETS (sense 3) without this being turned into money which can be spent, eg if someone owns a house which is worth more than what they paid for it, then they have paper profits. Compare NEGATIVE EQUITY.

paper tiger ▻ *noun* a person, organization or nation that appears to be powerful and is apparently threatening, but is in fact not. ⓘ 1950s: translation of a Chinese expression first used by Chairman Mao (1893-1976) about the US.

paperweight ▻ *noun* a heavy, usually ornamental, object kept on a desk for holding papers down.

paperwork ▻ *noun* routine written work, eg filling out forms, keeping files, writing letters and reports, etc, most of which is necessary to ensure the smooth running of a job, company, etc; clerical work.

papery /'peɪpərɪ/ ▻ *adj* like paper in texture.

Papiamento /papɪə'mentoʊ/ ▻ *noun* a creole language spoken in the Dutch Antilles, derived from Spanish and Portuguese, with vocabulary influence from Dutch. ⓘ 1940s: Spanish, from Spanish *papia* talk.

papier-mâché /papɪeɪ'maʃeɪ, papjeɪ-/ and **paper-mâché** ▻ *noun* a light hard material consisting of pulped paper mixed with glue and sometimes other substances such as paint. It is moulded into shape while wet and left to dry, and used to make boxes, jars, jewellery, masks, etc. Also *as adj.* ⓘ 18c: French, literally 'chewed paper'.

papilla /pə'pɪlə/ ▻ *noun* (***papillae*** /-liː/) *anatomy, biol* **1** a small nipple-like projection from the surface of a structure. **2** a minute elevation on the skin, especially that of the fingertips, the inner surface of the eyelids and upper surface of the tongue, in which a nerve ends. **3** a protuberance at the base of a hair, feather, tooth, etc. **4** a minute conical protuberance as on the surface of a petal. • **papillary** *adj* like or having papillae. • **papillate** or **papillated** or **papilliferous** /pap/ *adj* having papillae. • **papilliform** *adj* in the shape of a papilla. ⓘ 18c: Latin, diminutive of *papula* pimple.

papilloma /papɪ'loumə/ ▻ *noun* (***papillomas***) *medicine* a benign tumour formed by the abnormal enlargement of a papilla or papillae, such as a wart. • **papillomatous** /papɪ'loumətəs/ *adj.* ⓘ 19c.

papillon /'papɪjɔ̃/ ▻ *noun* a breed of toy dog (see TOY *noun* 3) related to the spaniel and developed in France, which has a small body and a long fine coat that is thickest on the neck, chest and upper legs. ⓘ Early 20c: French, meaning 'butterfly', because the fringes of hair on its ears resemble butterfly's wings.

papillote /'papɪlout/ ▻ *noun, cookery* **1** a small decorative paper frill used to garnish the bone end of a lamb or veal chop. **2** oiled or greased paper in which meat is cooked and served. • **en papillote** said of a dish: cooked and served inside oiled or greased paper. ⓘ 19c in these senses; 18c meaning 'a curl paper' for the hair: French, probably from *papillon* butterfly.

papist /'peɪpɪst/ ▻ *noun, offensive* a Roman Catholic. • **papism** or **papistry** *noun, often offensive* popery. ⓘ 16c: from Latin *papa* pope.

papoose /pə'puːs/ ▻ *noun* a Native American baby or young child. ⓘ 17c: from Algonquian *papoos*.

pappadom see POPPADOM

pappus /'papəs/ ▻ *noun* (***pappi*** /-pai/ or ***pappuses***) *bot* in composites and some other plants, eg dandelions and thistles: a ring or parachute of fine hair or down, which grows above the seed and helps in wind dispersal. ⓘ 18c: Latin, from Greek *pappos* a grandfather, because of its resemblance to an old man's beard.

pappy¹ /'papɪ/ ▻ *noun* (***pappies***) *US colloq* father; papa.

pappy² see under PAP¹

paprika /'paprɪkə, pə'priːkə/ ▻ *noun* a powdered hot spice made from red peppers. ⓘ 19c: Hungarian, from Serbo-Croat *papar* PEPPER.

pap test see under PAPANICOLAOU SMEAR

papula /'papjʊlə/ or **papule** /'papjuːl/ ▻ *noun* (***papulae*** /-liː/ or ***papules***) *biol* a pimple; a PAPILLA. • **papular** *adj*. ⓘ 18c: Latin.

papyrology /papɪ'rɒlədʒɪ/ ▻ *noun* the study of ancient papyruses. • **papyrologist** *noun* a scientist who specializes in papyrology. ⓘ 19c.

papyrus /pə'paɪərəs/ ▻ *noun* (***papyri*** /pə'paɪəraɪ/ or ***papyruses***) **1** a tall plant of the SEDGE family, common in ancient Egypt. **2** the writing material prepared from the pith of the flowering stems of this plant, used by the ancient Egyptians, Greeks and Romans. **3** an ancient manuscript written on this material. ⓘ 14c: from Greek *papyros*.

par /pɑː(r)/ ▻ *noun* **1** a normal level or standard. **2** *golf* the standard number of strokes that a good golfer would take for a certain course or hole. **3** *commerce* (*also* **par of exchange**) the established value of the unit of one national currency against that of another. • **above par** at a premium; at more than the nominal value. • **below** or **not up to par** *colloq* **1** not up to the usual or required standard. **2** slightly unwell. • **on a par with something** or **someone** equal to them; the equivalent of them. • **par for the course** *colloq* only to be expected; predictable; typical. ⓘ 17c: Latin, meaning 'equal'.

par. ▻ *abbreviation* **1** (*also* **para.**) /'parə/ paragraph. **2** parallel. **3** parish.

par- see PARA-¹, PARA-²

para /'parə/ ▻ *noun* (***paras***) *colloq* a paratrooper. ⓘ 1950s.

para-¹ /parə/ or (before a vowel) **par-** ▻ *combining form, denoting* **1** alongside; beside; side-by-side □ ***parathyroid***. **2** beyond □ ***parapsychology***. **3** resembling □ ***paramilitary***. **4** auxiliary □ ***paramedical***. **5** abnormal □ ***paraesthesia***. **6** *chem* having substituted atoms or groups attached to two opposite carbon atoms of the benzene ring, usually spelt ***p-*** and written in italics □ ***p*-xylene** □ ***para*-xylene**. **7** a polymer of, or compound related to, the specified compound. ⓘ From Greek *para* alongside.

para-² /'parə/ or (before a vowel) **par-** ▻ *combining form, denoting* protection or defence against the specified thing □ ***parachute*** □ ***parasol***. ⓘ French, from Italian, from Latin *parare* to defend.

para-³ /'parə/ ▻ *combining form, denoting* parachute □ ***paratrooper*** □ ***paradoctor***.

parable /'parəbəl/ ▻ *noun* **1** a story which is realistic but usually made-up, intended to convey a moral or religious lesson; an allegorical tale. **2** any of the stories of this kind recorded in the New Testament of the Bible, especially those told by Jesus. See also PARABOLIC. ⓘ 14c: from Latin *parabola* comparison, from Greek *parabole* analogy, from *paraballein* to set alongside or compare.

parabola /pə'rabələ/ ▻ *noun* (***parabolas***) *geom* **1** a CONIC SECTION produced when a plane intersects a cone, and the plane is parallel to the cone's sloping side. **2** the locus of a point equidistant from a fixed point (the FOCUS *noun* 8) and a fixed straight line (the DIRECTRIX). ⓘ 16c: from Greek *parabole* placing alongside.

parabolic /parə'bɒlɪk/ and **parabolical** ▻ *adj* **1** like or expressed in a parable. **2** like or in the form of a parabola. • **parabolically** *adverb*.

parabrake ▻ *noun* a parachute released behind an aircraft to help it slow down once it has landed. ⓘ 1950s.

paracentesis /parəsen'tiːsɪs/ ▻ *noun, surgery* the surgical piercing of a body cavity to remove gas, fluid, etc. ⓘ 16c: from Greek *parakenteein* to pierce at the side.

paracetamol /parə'siːtəmɒl, -'sɛtəmɒl/ ▻ *noun* **1** a mild analgesic drug, administered by mouth in order to relieve mild to moderate pain or to reduce fever. **2** a tablet of this drug. ⓘ 1950s: modelled on the medical name *para-acetylaminophenol*.

parachronism /pa'rakrənɪzəm/ ▻ *noun* an error in dating, especially when something is represented as later than it really was. ⓘ 17c: from PARA-¹, modelled on ANACHRONISM.

parachute /'parəʃuːt/ ▻ *noun* **1** an umbrella-shaped apparatus consisting of light fabric, with a harness for attaching to, and slowing the fall of, a person or package dropped from an aircraft. **2** any structure that serves a similar purpose. Also shortened to **chute**. ▻ *verb* (***parachuted***, ***parachuting***) *tr & intr* to drop from the air by parachute. • **parachutist** *noun*. ⓘ 18c: from PARA-² + French *chute* fall.

Paraclete /'parəkliːt/ ▻ *noun, Christianity* the Holy Ghost as an advocate. ⓘ 15c: from Latin *paracletus*, from Greek *parakaleein* to call in or comfort.

parade /pə'reɪd/ ▻ *noun* **1** a ceremonial procession of people, vehicles, etc. **2** said of soldiers, etc: **a** the state of being drawn up in rank for formal marching or inspection; **b** a group or body of soldiers, etc drawn up in this way. **3** a self-advertising display □ ***make a parade of one's generosity***. **4 a** a row of shops, a shopping street, etc; **b** (**the Parade**) used as the name or address of such a row. **5** *fencing* a PARRY. ▻ *verb* **1** (***paraded***, ***parading***) *tr & intr* to walk or make (a body of soldiers, etc) walk or march in procession, eg across a square, along a street, etc. **2** to display ostentatiously; to flaunt. ⓘ 17c: French, from Spanish *parada* a halt or stopping-place, from Latin *parare* to prepare.

parade ground ▻ *noun* the square or yard where soldiers assemble for inspection, marching practice, etc.

paradigm /'parədaɪm/ ▻ *noun* **1** an example, model or pattern. **2** a conceptual framework within which scientific theories are constructed, which is consistent within itself, but may need completely revising as evidence challenging the factual accuracy of some aspects of it accumulates. **3** *grammar* **a** a table of the inflected forms of a word serving as a pattern for words of the same declension or conjugation; **b** the words showing a particular pattern. • **paradigmatic** /-dɪg'matɪk/ or **paradigmatical** *adj*. • **paradigmatically** *adverb*. ⓘ 15c: from Greek *paradeigma* pattern.

paradisaic /parədɪ'seɪɪk/, **paradisaical** /-dɪ'zaɪəkəl/, **paradisal** /-'daɪsəl/ and **paradisiac** /-'dɪzɪak/ ▻ *adj* relating to or resembling paradise.

paradise /'parədaɪs/ ▻ *noun* **1** heaven. **2** a place of utter bliss or delight. **3** the Garden of Eden. ⓘ 12c as *paradis*: French, from Greek *paradeisos*, from Persian *pairidaeza* park.

paradise fish ▻ *noun* a Chinese freshwater fish with remarkable and beautiful colouring.

paradoctor ▻ *noun* a doctor who reaches patients in remote areas by parachuting down from an aeroplane. ⓘ 1940s.

paradox /'parədɒks/ ▻ *noun* (***paradoxes***) **1** a statement that seems to contradict itself, eg *More haste, less speed*, and *War is Peace, Freedom is Slavery, Ignorance is Strength* (from George Orwell's *Nineteen Eighty-Four*). **2** a situation involving apparently contradictory elements. **3** *logic* a proposition that is essentially absurd or leads to an absurd conclusion. • **paradoxical** *adj*. • **paradoxically** *adverb*. • **paradoxy** *noun* the quality of being paradoxical. ⓒ 16c: from Greek *paradoxos* incredible, from *para-* beyond + *doxos* opinion.

paradoxical sleep ▻ *noun, technical* REM SLEEP.

paradoxure /parə'dɒksjʊə(r)/ ▻ *noun* a civet-like carnivore of S Asia and Malaysia, with a very long curving tail. Also called **palm cat** or **palm civet**. ⓒ 19c: from PARADOX + Greek *oura* tail.

paraesthesia or (*US*) **paresthesia** /parɪs'θiːzɪə, parɛs-/ *noun, pathol* an abnormal tingling sensation in any part of the body, sometimes described as PINS AND NEEDLES, and often caused by pressure on a nerve. ⓒ 19c: from PARA-[1] sense 5 + Greek *aisthesis* sensation.

paraffin /'parəfɪn/ ▻ *noun* **1** a fuel oil obtained from petroleum or coal and used in aircraft, domestic heaters, etc. **2** any of a series of saturated aliphatic hydrocarbons derived from petroleum, including alkane gases such as methane and ethane, and liquids and waxy solids. Now more commonly called an **alkane**. **3** PARAFFIN WAX. **4** PETROLATUM. ⓒ 19c: from Latin *parum* little + *affinis* having an affinity, named by its discoverer, Reichenbach, because of its unreactiveness.

paraffin oil ▻ *noun* **1** *chem* a viscous yellow oil made from petroleum and used as a lubricant. **2** KEROSENE.

paraffin wax ▻ *noun, chem* a white tasteless odourless translucent solid, a type of PETROLEUM WAX, used to make candles, lubricants, polishes, wax crayons, cosmetics, etc.

paraffiny ▻ *adj* **1** relating to or suggestive of paraffin. **2** smelling of paraffin.

paragenesis /parə'dʒɛnɪsɪs/ and **paragenesia** /paradʒə'niːzɪə/ ▻ *noun, geol* **1** the order in which minerals have developed in a given mass of rock. **2** the development of minerals in such close contact that their formation is affected and they become a joined mass. • **paragenetic** *adj*. ⓒ 19c.

paragliding ▻ *noun* a sport in which the participant is towed through the air by a light aircraft while wearing a modified controllable and steerable type of parachute, then released to glide in the air and eventually drift to the ground, often to a predetermined location. • **paraglider** *noun*. ⓒ 1960s.

paragon /'parəgən/ ▻ *noun* someone who is a model of excellence or perfection. ⓒ 16c: French, from Italian *paragone* comparison.

paragraph /'parəgrɑːf/ ▻ *noun* **1** a section of a piece of writing of variable length, starting on a fresh, often indented, line, and dealing with a distinct point or idea. **2** a short report in a newspaper. **3** *music* a musical passage forming a unit. **4** (*also* **paragraph mark**) *printing* a sign (¶), indicating the start of a new paragraph. ▻ *verb* (***paragraphed***, ***paragraphing***) to divide (text) into paragraphs. ⓒ 16c: from Greek *paragraphe* marked passage, from *graphein* to write.

paragraphia /parə'grafɪə/ ▻ *noun, medicine* the writing of wrong words or letters in place of others, resulting from disease or injury of the brain. • **paragraphic** *adj*. ⓒ 19c: from Greek *-graphia* writing.

parainfluenza virus ▻ *noun* any of a group of viruses that cause influenza-like symptoms, especially in children.

parakeet or **parrakeet** /'parəkiːt/ ▻ *noun* any of various small brightly-coloured parrots with long pointed tails, native to tropical regions worldwide, which live in groups and usually roost in trees. ⓒ 16c: from French *paroquet* parrot.

paralalia /parə'leɪlɪə/ ▻ *noun, medicine* a form of speech disturbance, especially one in which a different sound or syllable is produced in place of the intended one. Compare APHASIA. ⓒ 19c.

paralanguage /'parə-/ ▻ *noun* those elements of communication other than words, ie tone of voice, whispering, gesture or body language, facial expression, etc. See also PARALINGUISTICS. ⓒ 1950s.

paraldehyde /pə'raldɪhaɪd/ ▻ *noun, chem* (formula $C_6H_{12}O_3$) a colourless flammable toxic liquid that is a polymer of ACETALDEHYDE, and is used as a solvent and sleep-inducing drug. ⓒ 19c.

paraleipsis /parə'laɪpsɪs/ or **paralipsis** /-'lɪpsɪs/ ▻ *noun* (***paraleipses*** or ***paralipses*** /-siːz/) *rhetoric* a rhetorical device by which the speaker draws attention to a subject by pretending to neglect it, as in *I will not speak of his generosity*. ⓒ 16c: from Greek *paraleipein* to leave aside.

paralinguistics ▻ *noun* the study of PARALANGUAGE. • **paralinguistic** *adj*.

parallax /'parəlaks/ ▻ *noun* (***parallaxes***) **1** *physics* the apparent change in the position of an object, relative to a distant background, when it is viewed from two different positions. **2** *astron* the angle between two straight lines joining two different observation points to a celestial body, used to measure the distance of stars from the Earth. • **parallactic** or **parallactical** *adj*. ⓒ 16c: from Greek *parallaxis* change or alteration.

parallel /'parəlɛl/ ▻ *adj* (*often* **parallel to something**) **1** said of lines, planes, etc: the same distance apart at every point; alongside and never meeting or intersecting ◻ *parallel lines* ◻ *a road parallel to the High Street*. **2** similar; exactly equivalent; corresponding; analogous ◻ *parallel careers*. ▻ *adverb* (*often* **parallel to something**) alongside and at an unvarying distance from it. ▻ *noun* **1** *geom* a line or plane parallel to another. **2** a corresponding or equivalent instance of something. **3** any of the lines of LATITUDE circling the Earth parallel to the equator and representing a particular angular degree of distance from it. Also called **parallel of latitude**. ▻ *verb* (***paralleled***, ***paralleling***) **1** to equal. **2** to correspond to or be equivalent to something. **3** to be or to run parallel to something. • **parallelwise** *adverb*. • **in parallel 1** said of electrical appliances: so co-ordinated that terminals of the same polarity are connected. **2** simultaneously. • **on a parallel with something** corresponding to it. • **without parallel** unequalled; unprecedented. ⓒ 16c: from Greek *parallelos* side by side.

parallel bars *gymnastics, plural noun* two parallel horizontal rails, fixed to upright posts, used by men for gymnastic exercises and display. ▻ *singular noun* an event in a gymnastics competition in which these bars are used.

parallel circuit ▻ *noun, physics* an electrical circuit arranged so that the current is split between two or more parallel paths.

parallelism /'parəlɛlɪzəm/ ▻ *noun* **1** the state or fact of being parallel. **2** resemblance in corresponding details. **3** a verse or sentence in which one part is a repetition of another, either in form or meaning.

parallel motion ▻ *noun, engineering* a name given to any linkage by which rotational motion may be changed into linear motion.

parallelogram /parə'lɛləgram/ ▻ *noun, geom* a two-dimensional four-sided figure in which opposite sides are parallel and equal in length, and opposite angles are equal. Compare QUADRILATERAL, RHOMBUS, TRAPEZIUM, RECTANGLE. ⓒ 16c: from Greek *parallelogrammon*.

parallelogram of vectors ▻ *noun, math* a figure that is constructed in order to add two vectors, by drawing them to scale so that they form two adjacent sides of the parallelogram.

parallel processing ▻ *noun, computing* the use of two or more processors simultaneously to carry out a single computing task, each processor being assigned a particular part of the task at any given time. This contrasts with single-processor computing in which the whole task is carried out sequentially by one processor.

parallel ruler ▷ *noun* two rulers joined by pivoted strips allowing the distance between them to be changed, used for drawing straight parallel lines.

parallel slalom ▷ *noun* a SLALOM race in which two competitors ski down parallel courses at the same time.

the Paralympics /parəˈlɪmpɪks/ ▷ *noun* an Olympic competition for people with physical disabilities, held at the same time as the traditional Olympic games. • **Paralympic** *adj.* ⌚ 1950s: from *paraplegic* + *Olympics*.

paralyse or (*N Amer*) **paralyze** /ˈparəlaɪz/ *verb* (***paralysed***, ***paralysing***) **1** to affect (a person or bodily part) with paralysis. **2** said of fear, etc: to have an immobilizing effect on someone. **3** to disrupt something or bring it to a standstill. • **paralyser** *noun.* ⌚ Early 19c.

paralysis /pəˈralɪsɪs/ ▷ *noun* (***paralyses*** /-siːz/) **1** a temporary or permanent loss of muscular function or sensation in any part of the body, usually caused by nerve damage, eg as a result of disease or injury. **2** a state of immobility; a standstill. ⌚ 16c: Greek, from *paralyein* to enfeeble.

paralytic /parəˈlɪtɪk/ ▷ *adj* **1** relating to, caused by or suffering from paralysis. **2** *colloq* helplessly drunk. ▷ *noun* a person affected by paralysis. • **paralytically** *adverb.*

paramatta or **parramatta** /parəˈmatə/ ▷ *noun* (***paramattas*** or ***parramattas***) a fabric like merino wool, made of worsted and cotton. ⌚ Early 19c: named after Parramatta, a town in New South Wales, Australia, where it was first produced.

Paramecium /parəˈmiːsɪəm/ ▷ *noun* a single-celled aquatic protozoan that is ovoid in shape and uniformly covered with hair-like processes known as CILIA. ⌚ 18c: from Greek *paramekes* long-shaped.

paramedic[1] /parəˈmɛdɪk/ ▷ *noun* a person, especially one trained in emergency medical procedures, whose work supplements and supports that of the medical profession. ⌚ 1970s.

paramedic[2] /parəˈmɛdɪk/ ▷ *noun, especially US* someone trained to give medical aid who reaches patients in remote areas by parachuting down from an aeroplane. ⌚ 1950s.

paramedical ▷ *adj, medicine* said of personnel or services, etc: supplementary to and supporting the work of the medical profession, eg physiotherapists, occupational therapists and ambulance crews.

parameter /pəˈramɪtə(r)/ ▷ *noun* **1** *math* a constant or variable that, when altered, affects the form of a mathematical expression in which it appears. **2** *physics* a quantity which under a particular set of conditions remains constant, but may be altered if the conditions change. **3** (*often* **parameters**) a limiting factor that serves to define the scope of a task, project, discussion, etc □ *What parameters are we working within?* • **parametric** /parəˈmɛtrɪk/ or **parametrical** *adj.* ⌚ 17c: from Latin *parametrum*, from Greek *para-* alongside + *metron* measure.

paramilitary ▷ *adj* organized on the same basis as a military force and usually reinforcing it, but not a professional military force. ▷ *noun* (***paramilitaries***) **1** a group organized in this way. **2** a member of such a group. ⌚ 1930s.

paramnesia /paramˈniːzɪə/ ▷ *noun* **1** a memory disorder in which words are remembered but not their proper meaning. **2** the condition of believing that one remembers events and circumstances which have not previously occurred. Compare DÉJÀ-VU, AMNESIA. ⌚ 19c: from Greek *para-* beyond + *mimneskein* to remind.

paramount /ˈparəmaʊnt/ ▷ *adj* foremost; supreme; of supreme importance. • **paramountcy** or **paramouncy** *noun.* ⌚ 16c: from French *par* by + *amont* above.

paramour /ˈparəmʊə(r)/ ▷ *noun* a male or female lover, usually the lover of someone who is married. ⌚ 14c: from French *par amour* by or through love.

paranoia /parəˈnɔɪə/ ▷ *noun* (***paranoias***) **1** *psychol* a rare mental disorder, characterized by delusions of persecution by others, especially if this is attributed to one's own importance or unique gifts. **2** a strong, usually irrational, feeling that one is being persecuted by others, resulting in a tendency to be suspicious and distrustful, and to become increasingly isolated. ⌚ 19c: Greek, from *para-* beyond + *nous* mind.

paranoid /parəˈnɔɪd/, **paranoiac** /-ˈnɔɪak/ and **paranoic** /-ɪk/ ▷ *adj* relating to or affected by paranoia. ▷ *noun* a person affected by paranoia.

paranormal ▷ *adj* said of phenomena, observations, occurrences, etc: beyond the normal scope of scientific explanation, and therefore not possible to explain in terms of current understanding of scientific laws. ▷ *noun* (**the paranormal**) paranormal occurrences. See also SUPERNATURAL. ⌚ 20c.

paranym /ˈparənɪm/ ▷ *noun* a word used to describe an event, etc which evades or conceals some important aspect of it, eg *liberation* used for *conquest*; a word which is nearly, but not exactly, a synonym. Compare EUPHEMISM. ⌚ 1960s: from PARA-[1] + Greek *onoma* name.

parapenting /ˈparəpɛntɪŋ, -pẽtɪŋ/ ▷ *noun* a cross between hang-gliding and parachuting, a sport in which the participant jumps from a high place wearing a modified type of parachute which is then used as a hang-glider. ⌚ 20c: from French *pente* slope.

parapet /ˈparəpɪt, -pət/ ▷ *noun* **1** a low wall along the edge of a bridge, balcony, roof, etc, sometimes with battlements and usually ornamental. **2** an embankment of earth or sandbags protecting the soldiers in a military trench. ⌚ 16c: from Italian *parapetto*, from *petto* chest or breast.

paraph /ˈparaf/ ▷ *noun* a mark or flourish under one's signature. ⌚ 16c in this sense; 14c in obsolete sense 'paragraph': from French *paraphe*, short for PARAGRAPH.

paraphernalia /parəfəˈneɪlɪə/ ▷ *plural noun, sometimes used as a singular noun* **1** the equipment and accessories associated with a particular activity, etc. **2** personal belongings. ⌚ 18c in sense 1; 17c as a legal term from Roman Law applied in various ways but generally referring to articles given to a married woman which were considered to belong to her: from Greek *parapherna* a bride's personal effects, ie not part of her dowry.

paraphrase /ˈparəfreɪz/ ▷ *noun* a restatement of something using different words, especially in order to clarify; a re-wording or re-phrasing. ▷ *verb* (***paraphrased***, ***paraphrasing***) to express something in other words. • **paraphrastic** /parəˈfrastɪk/ . ⌚ 16c: French, from Greek *paraphrasis*, from *para-* alongside + *phrasis* speaking.

paraplegia /parəˈpliːdʒɪə/ ▷ *noun, medicine* paralysis of the lower half of the body, usually caused by injury or disease of the spinal cord. Compare MONOPLEGIA, HEMIPLEGIA, QUADRIPLEGIA. ⌚ 17c: Greek, meaning 'a one-sided stroke', from *para-* alongside + *plege* blow.

paraplegic /parəˈpliːdʒɪk/ ▷ *adj* **1** affected with paraplegia. **2** marked by or typical of paraplegia. ▷ *noun* a person affected with paraplegia.

parapsychology ▷ *noun* the study of mental phenomena, such as telepathy and clairvoyance, that suggest the mind can gain knowledge by means other than the normal perceptual processes. • **parapsychological** *adj.* • **parapsychologically** *adverb.* • **parapsychologist** *noun.* ⌚ 1920s.

Paraquat /ˈparəkwɒt/ ▷ *noun, trademark* a highly toxic yellow solid, used as a herbicide and defoliant, that causes skin irritation and if ingested may cause liver or kidney failure. ◎ 1960s: from PARA-[1] 6 and *quaternary*, part of the technical description of the chemical.

parasailing ▷ *noun* a sport similar to PARAGLIDING in which the participant, wearing water-skis and a modified type of parachute, is towed into the air by a motorboat. ◎ 1970s.

parascending /ˈparəsɛndɪŋ/ ▷ *noun* a sport similar to PARAGLIDING in which the participant is towed into the wind behind a motor vehicle, becomes airborne and descends by means of a modified type of parachute. ◎ 1970s.

parascience ▷ *noun* the study of phenomena that are beyond the scope of traditional science since they cannot be explained by our current understanding of scientific laws. ◎ 1950s.

paraselene /parəsəˈliːniː/ ▷ *noun* (***paraselenae*** /-liːniː/) a bright spot in the Moon's halo, 22° to right or left of the Moon, due to refraction from ice crystals floating vertically. Also called **mock moon**. ◎ 17c: from Greek *selene* moon.

parasite /ˈparəsaɪt/ ▷ *noun* **1** a plant or animal that for all or part of its life obtains food and physical protection from a living organism of another species (the HOST[1] *noun* 5) which is usually damaged by and never benefits from its presence. **2** *derog* a person who lives at the expense of others, contributing nothing in return. ● **parasitic** /-ˈsɪtɪk/ or **parasitical** *adj*. ● **parasitically** *adverb*. ◎ 16c: from Greek *parasitos* someone who lives at another's expense.

parasitism /ˈparəsaɪtɪzəm/ ▷ *noun* **1** a close association between two living organisms in which one (the PARASITE) obtains food and physical protection from the other (the HOST[1] *noun* 5). Compare COMMENSALISM at COMMENSAL, SYMBIOSIS (sense 1). **2** the state of being a parasite. **3** the state of being infested with parasites.

parasitology /parəsaɪˈtɒlədʒɪ/ ▷ *noun, zool* the scientific study of parasites, especially protozoans, worms and arthropods that cause diseases or transmit them to humans and animals. ● **parasitologist** *noun*. ◎ 19c.

parasol /ˈparəsɒl/ ▷ *noun* a light umbrella used as a protection against the Sun; a sunshade. ◎ 17c: from French, from Italian *parasole*, from *sole* sun.

parasol mushroom ▷ *noun* a tall white edible mushroom that resembles a parasol.

parasuicide ▷ *noun* **1** a deliberate harmful act, such as taking an overdose of drugs, which appears to be an attempt at suicide but which was probably not intended to be successful. **2** someone who performs such an act. ◎ 20c.

parasympathetic nervous system ▷ *noun, zool* in vertebrates: a subdivision of the autonomic nervous system, which tends to slow down the heart rate, promote digestion, dilate blood vessels, and generally conserve energy. Compare SYMPATHETIC NERVOUS SYSTEM.

paratha /pəˈrɑːtə/ ▷ *noun* (***parathas***) a thin unleavened cake made of flour, water and clarified butter, originating in India. ◎ 1930s: Hindi.

parathormone /parəˈθɔːməʊn/ ▷ *noun, physiol* parathyroid hormone. ◎ 1920s.

parathyroid ▷ *adj, anatomy, medicine, etc* **1** situated beside the thyroid gland. **2** referring or relating to the parathyroid glands. ▷ *noun* a parathyroid gland. ◎ Late 19c.

parathyroid gland ▷ *noun, physiol* in mammals: any of four small glands near or within the thyroid, producing parathyroid hormone.

parathyroid hormone ▷ *noun, medicine* a hormone, released by the parathyroid glands, that raises blood calcium levels. Also called PARATHORMONE.

paratroops /ˈparətruːps/ ▷ *plural noun* a division of soldiers trained to parachute from aircraft into enemy territory or a battle zone. ● **paratrooper** *noun* a member of such a division. ◎ 1940s.

paratyphoid ▷ *noun, medicine* an infectious disease, similar to but milder than TYPHOID fever, caused by a bacterium and characterized by a pink rash, fever, abdominal pain and diarrhoea. ◎ Early 20c.

paravane /ˈparəvəɪn/ ▷ *noun* a torpedo-shaped device, with fins and vanes, towed from the bow of a vessel in order to deflect mines along a wire and to sever their moorings. Also called OTTER.

par avion /*French* par avjɔ̃/ ▷ *adverb* used as a label on mail which is to be sent by aeroplane: by air mail.

parawalker ▷ *noun* a metal structure like an external skeleton worn by a paraplegic to enable them to walk.

Parazoa /parəˈzoʊə/ *zool* ▷ *plural noun* a sub-kingdom of animal classification, the sponges, of the same rank as PROTOZOA and METAZOA. ● **parazoan** *singular noun* any member of this sub-kingdom. Also *as adj*. ◎ 19c: from Greek *zoion* animal.

parboil /ˈpɑːbɔɪl/ ▷ *verb* (***parboiled, parboiling***) to boil something until it is partially cooked. ◎ 15c: from French *parbo(u)illir*, from Latin *perbullire* to boil thoroughly; the meaning has been altered by confusion of *par-* with PART.

the Parcae /pɑːsaɪ/ ▷ *plural noun, mythol* the three Roman Fates, identified with the Greek MOIRAI.

parcel /ˈpɑːsəl/ ▷ *noun* **1** something wrapped in paper, etc and secured with string or sticky tape; a package. **2** a portion of something, eg of land. **3** a group of people, etc. **4** a lot or portion of goods for sale; a deal or transaction. ▷ *verb* (***parcelled, parcelling***) **1** (*also* **parcel something up**) to wrap it up in a parcel. **2** (*also* **parcel something out**) to divide it into portions and share it out. ◎ 14c: from French *parcelle*, from Latin *particula*, diminutive of *pars* part.

parcel bomb ▷ *noun* a parcel containing a bomb designed to detonate when someone opens it.

parch /pɑːtʃ/ ▷ *verb* (***parches, parched, parching***) **1** to dry something up; to deprive (soil, plants, etc) of water. **2** to make something or someone hot and very dry. **3** to roast (peas) slightly. ◎ 14c as *perchen*.

parched /pɑːʃt/ ▷ *adj* **1** *colloq* very thirsty. **2** very dry.

parchment /ˈpɑːtʃmənt/ ▷ *noun* **1 a** a material formerly used for bookbinding and for writing on, made from goatskin, calfskin or sheepskin; **b** a piece of this, or a manuscript written on it. **2** stiff off-white writing-paper resembling this. **3** *as adj* made of, or resembling, parchment □ ***parchment paper***. ◎ 13c: from French *parchemin*, from Latin *Pergamena charta* paper of Pergamum, influenced by French *parche* leather.

parchment bark see under PITTOSPORUM

parchment paper ▷ *noun* unsized paper made tough and transparent by dipping in sulphuric acid. Also called **vegetable parchment**.

pard /pɑːd/ and **pardner** /ˈpɑːdnə(r)/ ▷ *noun, US slang* friend or partner. ◎ 19c; late 18c as *pardner*.

pardon /ˈpɑːdən/ ▷ *verb* (***pardoned, pardoning***) **1** to forgive or excuse someone for a fault or offence □ ***pardon me*** □ ***pardon his rudeness*** □ ***pardon her for interrupting.*** **2** to allow someone who has been sentenced to go without the punishment. **3** *intr* to grant pardon. ▷ *noun* **1** forgiveness. **2** the cancellation of a punishment; remission. **3** a pardon from the pope; a papal indulgence. ● **pardonable** *adj*. ● **pardon me 1** a formula of apology. **2** (also shortened to **pardon**) a request to someone to repeat something said. ◎ 14c: from French *pardonner*, from Latin *perdonare* to overlook.

pardoner ▷ *noun* **1** someone who pardons. **2** *historical* in the Middle Ages: someone licensed to sell pardons from the pope, which freed people from being punished for their sins.

pare /pɛə(r)/ ▷ *verb* (***pared, paring***) **1** (*also* **pare something away**) to trim off (skin, etc) in layers. **2** to cut (fingernails or toenails). **3** to peel (fruit). **4** (*also* **pare something down**) to reduce (expenses, funding, etc) gradually, in order to economize. ⓒ 14c: from French *parer*, from Latin *parare* to prepare.

paregoric /parə'gɒrɪk/ ▷ *adj* soothing; lessening pain. ▷ *noun* a medicine that soothes pain, especially an alcoholic solution of opium, benzoic acid, camphor and oil of anise. ⓒ 17c: from Greek *paregoreein* to exhort or comfort.

parencephalon /parɛn'sɛfəlɒn/ ▷ *noun, anatomy* the CEREBELLUM. ⓒ 18c: from Greek *enkephalon* brain.

parenchyma /pə'rɛŋkɪmə/ ▷ *noun* (***parenchymata*** /-mətə/) **1** *bot* in plants: a tissue composed of thin-walled relatively unspecialized cells, that serves mainly as a packing tissue. **2** *zool* the loosely packed cells that form much of the body tissue of simple animals such as flatworms. ⓒ 17c: from Greek *enchyma* infusion.

parent /'pɛərənt/ ▷ *noun* **1** a father or mother. **2** the adopter or guardian of a child. **3** an animal or plant that has produced offspring. **4** something from which anything is derived; a source or origin. ▷ *verb* (***parented, parenting***) *tr & intr* to be or act as a parent; to care for someone or something as a parent. ▷ *adj* referring to an organization, etc that has established a branch or branches over which it retains some control. ⓒ 15c: from Latin *parens, parentis*, from *parere* to bring forth.

parentage /'pɛərəntɪdʒ/ ▷ *noun* **1** descent from parents. **2** rank or character derived from one's parents or ancestors. **3** the state or fact of being a parent.

parental /pə'rɛntəl/ ▷ *adj* **1** related to or concerning parents. **2** *biol, genetics* denoting the first generation that gives rise to all successive or filial generations. • **parentally** *adverb*.

parent company ▷ *noun* a business company that owns other, usually smaller, companies.

parenteral /pə'rɛntərəl/ ▷ *adj, medicine* **1** not intestinal. **2** said of the administration of a drug: not by way of the alimentary tract. • **parenterally** *adverb*. ⓒ Early 20c.

parenthesis /pə'rɛnθəsɪs/ ▷ *noun* (***parentheses*** /-siːz/) **1** a word or phrase inserted into a sentence as a comment, usually marked off by brackets or dashes. **2** (**parentheses**) a pair of round brackets ( ), used to enclose such a comment. **3** a digression. ⓒ 16c: Greek, from *tithenai* to place.

parenthesize or **parenthesise** /pə'rɛnθəsaɪz/ ▷ *verb* (***parenthesized, parenthesizing***) to place something within parentheses.

parenthetic /parən'θɛtɪk/ or **parenthetical** ▷ *adj* **1** referring to the nature of a parenthesis. **2** using parenthesis. • **parenthetically** *adverb*.

parenthood ▷ *noun* **1** being a parent. **2** the responsibilities of a parent.

parenting ▷ *noun* the activities and duties of a parent. ▷ *verb, present participle of* PARENT.

parentless ▷ *adj* without a parent.

paresis /'parəsɪs, pə'riːsɪs/ ▷ *noun, medicine* a partial form of paralysis affecting muscle movements but not diminishing sensation. • **paretic** /pə'rɛtɪk/ *adj*. ⓒ 17c: Latin, from Greek *parienai* to relax.

paresthesia the *US* spelling of PARAESTHESIA.

pareu /pa'reɪuː/ or **pareo** /pa'reɪoʊ/ ▷ *noun* (***pareus*** or ***pareos***) a wraparound skirt worn by women and men in Polynesia. ⓒ Late 19c: Tahitian.

par excellence /pɑː'rɛkselɑ̃s, -ləns/ ▷ *adverb* in the highest degree; in the truest sense of the word; beyond compare. ⓒ 17c: French, meaning 'as an example of excellence'.

parfait /pɑː'feɪ, 'pɑːfeɪ/ ▷ *noun* a kind of frozen dessert containing whipped cream, fruit and eggs. ⓒ Late 19c: French, meaning 'perfect'.

parget /'pɑːdʒɪt/ ▷ *noun* **1** plaster spread over a surface. **2** ornamental work in plaster. ▷ *verb* (***pargeted, pargeting***) **1** to plaster over something. **2** to cover something with ornamental plasterwork. ⓒ 14c: probably from French *parjeter* to throw all over.

parhelic circle /pɑː'hiːlɪk —/ ▷ *noun, meteorol* a band of luminosity parallel to the horizon, the result of diffraction caused by ice crystals in the atmosphere.

parhelion /pɑː'hiːlɪən/ ▷ *noun* (***parhelia*** /-lɪə/) *meteorol* a bright spot on the PARHELIC CIRCLE. • **parhelic** or **parheliacal** /pɑː'hɪlaɪəkəl/ *adj*. ⓒ 17c: Greek formed irregularly from *para* alongside + *helios* sun.

pariah /pə'raɪə, 'parɪə/ ▷ *noun* **1** someone scorned and avoided by others; a social outcast. **2** in S India and Burma: a member of a caste lower than the four Brahminical castes. ⓒ 17c: from Tamil *paraiyan* drummer.

pariah dog see PYE-DOG

parietal /pə'raɪətəl/ ▷ *adj, medicine, anatomy* relating to, or forming, the wall of a bodily cavity, eg the skull □ *the parietal bones*. ⓒ 16c: from Latin *paries* wall.

pari-mutuel /parɪ'mjuːtʃʊəl/ ▷ *noun* **1** a TOTALIZATOR. **2** the system of betting in which the winners receive a proportion of the total money staked, less the management charge. ⓒ Late 19c: French, literally 'mutual stake'.

paring *present participle of* PARE

pari passu /'pariː 'pasuː/ ▷ *adverb, usually law* with equal pace; together; proportionately. ⓒ 16c: Latin.

paripinnate /parɪ'pɪnət, -neɪt/ ▷ *adj, bot* pinnate without a terminal leaflet, ie with an even number of leaves. ⓒ 19c: from Latin *par* equal + PINNATE.

Paris green ▷ *noun* copper acetoarsenite, a pigment and insecticide. ⓒ 19c: named after the French capital city, Paris.

parish /'parɪʃ/ ▷ *noun* (***parishes***) (abbreviation **par.**) **1** a district or area served by its own church and priest or minister, usually the established church of that particular area. **2** especially in England: the smallest unit of local government. Also called **civil parish**. **3** the inhabitants of a parish □ *He has the full support of his parish*. ▷ *adj* **1** belonging or relating to a parish. **2** employed or supported by the parish. ⓒ 14c: from French *paroisse*, from Greek *paroikia*, from *paroikos* neighbour.

parish church ▷ *noun* the church of the establishment for a parish.

parish clerk ▷ *noun* an official who performs various duties connected with a parish church.

parish council ▷ *noun* in England: the elected administrative body of a PARISH (*noun* 2). • **parish councillor** *noun*. ⓒ 18c.

parishioner /pə'rɪʃənə(r)/ ▷ *noun* a member or inhabitant of a parish.

parish pump ▷ *noun* **a** petty local interests; parochialism; **b** *as adj* □ *parish-pump politics*. ⓒ Early 20c.

parish register ▷ *noun* a book in which the christenings, marriages, and deaths in a parish are recorded.

Parisian /pə'rɪzɪən/ ▷ *adj* relating or pertaining to Paris, capital of France. ▷ *noun* a man or woman who is a citizen or inhabitant of, or was born in, Paris. ⓒ 16c: from Latin *Parisii* the Gallic tribe of the Paris district.

Parisienne /parɪzɪ'ɛn/ ▷ *noun* a woman who is a native or resident of Paris.

parison /'parɪsən/ ▷ *noun* a lump of glass before it is moulded into its final shape. ⓒ 19c: from French *paraison*, from *parer* to pare, from Latin *parare* to prepare.

parity /ˈparɪtɪ/ ▷ *noun* (***parities***) **1** equality in status, eg in pay. **2** precise equivalence; exact correspondence. **3** *commerce* an established equivalence between a unit of national currency and an amount in another national currency. **4** *math* said of two or more numbers: the property of both or all being either odd or even. **5** said of the laws of physics: exact correspondence in a right- or left-handed system of co-ordinates. ⓘ 16c: from Latin *paritas*, from *par* equal.

parity check ▷ *noun, computing* a test applied to binary data to ensure that the parity is consistently either odd or even.

park /pɑːk/ ▷ *noun* **1** an area in a town with grass and trees, reserved for public recreation. **2** an area of land kept in its natural condition as a nature reserve, etc □ ***a wildlife park.*** **3** the woodland and pasture forming the estate of a large country house. **4** (**Park**) used in street names □ ***Waverley Park.*** **5** a place where vehicles can be left temporarily; a CAR PARK. **6** an area containing a group of buildings housing related enterprises □ ***a science park*** □ ***a business park.*** **7** *chiefly N Amer* a sports field or stadium. **8** (**the park**) *colloq* the pitch in use in a football game. ▷ *verb* (***parked, parking***) **1** *tr & intr* **a** to leave (a vehicle) temporarily at the side of the road or in a car park; **b** to manoeuvre (a vehicle) into such a position. **2** *colloq* to lay, place or leave something somewhere temporarily. **3** (**park oneself**) *colloq* to sit or install oneself. ⓘ 13c: from French *parc* enclosure.

parka /ˈpɑːkə/ ▷ *noun* (***parkas***) **1** a hooded jacket made of skins, worn by the Inuit and Aleut people of the Arctic. **2** a windproof jacket, especially a quilted one with a fur-trimmed hood; an anorak. ⓘ 18c: Aleut, meaning 'skin or coat', from Russian, meaning 'pelt' or 'skin jacket'.

park-and-ride ▷ *noun* **a** a system of travel to an urban centre by means of bus, tram or train, linked with large car parks on the outskirts, allowing car users to drive from outlying areas without having to congest and pollute the town centre; **b** *as adj* □ ***park-and-ride scheme.*** ⓘ Discussed and experimented with since the 1960s, but still not very widely used.

parkie /ˈpɑːkɪ/ ▷ *noun* (***parkies***) *colloq* a park keeper.

parkin /ˈpɑːkɪn/ or **perkin** /ˈpɜːkɪn/ ▷ *noun, Scots & N Eng* a moist ginger-flavoured oatmeal cake made with treacle. ⓘ 18c.

parking bay see under BAY[2]

parking lot ▷ *noun, N Amer* a CAR PARK.

parking meter ▷ *noun* a coin-operated meter in the street beside which a car may be parked for a limited period. Compare PAY-AND-DISPLAY.

parking ticket ▷ *noun* an official notice of a fine served on a motorist for parking illegally, eg on a yellow line, or with an expired pay-and-display ticket, etc.

Parkinson's disease /ˈpɑːkɪnsənz —/ ▷ *noun, medicine* the commonest form of PARKINSONISM, caused by degeneration of DOPAMINE-producing brain cells. Often shortened to **Parkinson's**. ⓘ 1920s.

parkinsonism /ˈpɑːkɪnsənɪzəm/ ▷ *noun, medicine* an incurable disorder, associated with DOPAMINE deficiency or the side effects of certain drugs, usually occurring later in life. The main symptoms are trembling of the hands and limbs, a mask-like facial expression, a flat voice, and a slow shuffling gait and stooping posture. ⓘ 19c: named after James Parkinson (1755–1824), English surgeon.

Parkinson's law /ˈpɑːkɪnsənz —/ ▷ *noun* the maxim that work expands to fill the time available for its completion. ⓘ 1950s: named after Cyril Northcote Parkinson (1909–93), historian and journalist, who proposed the concept.

park keeper ▷ *noun* a person employed to patrol a public park, keep order, etc. Also shortened to PARKIE.

parkland ▷ *noun* pasture and woodland forming part of a country estate.

parkway ▷ *noun, N Amer* a broad thoroughfare incorporating grassy areas and lined with trees, often connecting the parks of a town.

parky /ˈpɑːkɪ/ ▷ *adj* (***parkier, parkiest***) *Brit colloq* said of the weather: somewhat cold; chilly. ⓘ 19c.

parlance /ˈpɑːləns/ ▷ *noun* a particular style or way of using words □ ***in legal parlance*** □ ***in common parlance.*** ⓘ 16c: French, from *parler* to talk.

parlando /pɑːˈlandoʊ/ *music* ▷ *adj* said of a passage of vocal music: that the singer should actually speak, or give the impression of speaking. ▷ *adverb* in this manner. ▷ *noun* (***parlandos***) a passage to be performed in this way. ⓘ 19c: Italian, meaning 'speaking'.

parley /ˈpɑːlɪ/ ▷ *verb* (***parleyed, parleying***) *intr* to discuss peace terms, etc with an enemy, especially under truce. ▷ *noun* (***parleys***) a meeting with an enemy to discuss peace terms, etc. ⓘ 16c: from French *parler* to talk.

parliament /ˈpɑːləmənt/ ▷ *noun* **1** the highest law-making assembly of a nation. **2** (**Parliament**) in the UK: the House of Commons and House of Lords. ⓘ 13c: from French *parlement*, from *parler* to talk.

> ***Parliament***
>
> There is often uncertainty as to whether collective nouns such as **Parliament** should be followed by a singular or plural verb. Either is correct, depending on whether the group is being thought of as a single unit or as a number of individuals.

parliamentarian /pɑːləmenˈtɛərɪən/ ▷ *noun* **1** an expert in parliamentary procedure. **2** an experienced parliamentary debater. **3** *historical* a supporter of the Parliamentary party in the 17c English Civil War.

parliamentarianism or **parliamentarism** ▷ *noun* **1** the principles of parliamentary government. **2** the parliamentary system.

parliamentary /pɑːləˈmentərɪ/ ▷ *adj* **1** relating to, or issued by, a parliament. **2** said of conduct or procedure: in keeping with the rules of parliament. **3** said of language: admissible in parliament. • **parliamentarily** *adverb*.

Parliamentary Commissioner for Administration see under OMBUDSMAN

parlour /ˈpɑːlə(r)/ ▷ *noun* **1** *usually in compounds* a shop or commercial premises providing specified goods or services □ ***an ice-cream parlour*** □ ***piercing parlour*** □ ***funeral parlour.*** **2** *dated* a sitting-room for receiving visitors. ⓘ 13c: from French *parlur*, from *parler* to talk.

parlour game ▷ *noun* a game such as charades, suitable for playing in the sitting-room.

parlous /ˈpɑːləs/ ▷ *adj, archaic or facetious* precarious; perilous; dire. ⓘ 14c: a variant of PERILOUS.

Parmesan /ˈpɑːməzan, pɑːməˈzan/ and **Parmesan cheese** ▷ *noun* a hard dry Italian cheese made from skimmed milk mixed with rennet and saffron, often served grated with pasta dishes. ⓘ 16c: from Italian *Parmegiano*, meaning 'from Parma'.

paroccipital /parɒkˈsɪpɪtəl/ ▷ *adj, anatomy* situated beside or near the occiput. ⓘ 19c: from OCCIPUT.

parochial /pəˈroʊkɪəl/ ▷ *adj* **1** *derog* said of tastes, attitudes, etc: concerned only with local affairs; narrow, limited or provincial in outlook. **2** referring or relating to a parish. • **parochialism** or **parochiality** *noun*. • **parochially** *adverb*. ⓘ 14c in sense 2: from Latin *parochialis*, from *parochia* parish.

parochialism /pəˈroʊkɪəlɪzəm/ ▷ *noun* **1** narrowness of view; provincialism. **2** a system of local government based on the parish as a unit.

parody /ˈparədɪ/ ▷ *noun* (***parodies***) **1** a comic or satirical imitation of a work, or the style, of a particular writer, composer, etc. **2** a poor attempt at something; a mockery or travesty. ▷ *verb* (***parodies, parodied, parodying***) to ridicule something through parody; to mimic satirically. • **parodic** /pəˈrɒdɪk/ or **parodical** *adj.* • **parodist** *noun* the author of a parody. ◷ 16c: from Greek *paroidia*, from *para* beside + *oide* song.

parole /pəˈroʊl/ ▷ *noun* **1 a** the release of a prisoner before the end of their sentence, on promise of good behaviour □ ***released on parole***; **b** the duration of this conditional release. **2** the promise of a prisoner so released to behave well. **3** *as adj* □ ***the parole system.*** **4** /paˈrɔl/ *linguistics* language as manifested in the speech of individuals. Compare LANGUE. ◷ 1930s: French, meaning 'spoken word'. ▷ *verb* (***paroled, paroling***) to release or place (a prisoner) on parole. • **parolee** *noun* (***parolees***) a prisoner who has been conditionally released. ◷ 17c: from French *parole d'honneur* word of honour, from *parole* word, in the sense of 'formal promise'.

paronomasia /parənəˈmeɪzɪə/ ▷ *noun* (*plural* ***paronomasia***) a play on words, eg a pun. • **paronomastic** *adj.* ◷ 16c: Latin, from Greek *onoma* name.

paronym /ˈparənɪm/ ▷ *noun* a word from the same root, or having the same sound, as another; a COGNATE. ◷ 19c: see PARONOMASIA.

parotid /pəˈrɒtɪd, pəˈroʊtɪd/ ▷ *adj anatomy, medicine* situated beside or near the ear. ▷ *noun* the **parotid gland**, a salivary gland in front of the ear. ◷ 17c: from Greek *parotis*, from *para* beside + *os, otos* ear.

parousia /pəˈruːzɪə, pəˈraʊzɪə/ ▷ *noun, theol* the second coming of Christ which, in Christian thought, will be marked by a heavenly appearance, God's judgement of all humanity, and the resurrection of the dead. ◷ 19c: Greek, meaning 'presence' or 'arrival'.

paroxysm /ˈparəksɪzəm/ ▷ *noun* **1** a sudden emotional outburst, eg of rage or laughter. **2** a spasm, convulsion or seizure, eg of coughing or acute pain. **3** a sudden reappearance of or increase in the severity of the symptoms of a disease or disorder. • **paroxysmal** *adj.* ◷ 17c: from Greek *paroxysmos* a fit.

parpen /ˈpɑːpən/ or **perpend** /ˈpɜːpənd/ ▷ *noun* a stone forming part of a wall which can be seen from both sides. ◷ 15c: from French *parpain*.

parquet /ˈpɑːkeɪ, ˈpɑːkɪ/ ▷ *noun* **1** flooring composed of small inlaid blocks of wood arranged in a geometric pattern. **2** *as adj* made of parquet □ ***parquet floor.*** ◷ 19c: French, diminutive of *parc* enclosure.

parquetry /ˈpɑːkətrɪ/ ▷ *noun* inlaid work in wood arranged in a geometric pattern, used especially to cover floors or to decorate furniture, etc.

parr /pɑː(r)/ ▷ *noun* (***parr*** or ***parrs***) a young salmon aged up to two years, before it becomes a SMOLT. ◷ 18c.

parrakeet see PARAKEET

parramatta see PARAMATTA

parricide /ˈparɪsaɪd/ ▷ *noun* **1** the act of killing one's own parent or near relative. See also PATRICIDE, MATRICIDE. **2** someone who commits this act. • **parricidal** *adj.* ◷ 16c: French, from Latin *parricida*, possibly from *pater* father; see -CIDE.

parrot /ˈparət/ ▷ *noun* **1** any of numerous usually brightly-coloured birds, native to forests of warmer regions, with a large head, a strong hooked bill, and two of the four toes on each foot pointing backwards. **2** a person who merely imitates or mimics others. ▷ *verb* (***parroted, parroting***) to repeat or mimic (another's words, etc) unthinkingly. • **parroter** *noun.* ◷ 16c: from French *paroquet*, perhaps a diminutive of *Pierre*.

parrot-fashion ▷ *adverb* by mindless, unthinking repetition □ ***We learnt our tables parrot-fashion.***

parrot fish ▷ *noun* any of various brightly-coloured tropical marine fish, so called because its teeth are fused to form a parrot-like beak.

parry /ˈparɪ/ ▷ *verb* (***parries, parried, parrying***) **1** to fend off (a blow). **2** to sidestep (a question) adeptly. ▷ *noun* (***parries***) an act of parrying, especially in fencing. ◷ 17c: from French *parer* to ward off.

parse /pɑːz/ ▷ *verb* (***parsed, parsing***) *tr & intr* **1** *grammar* to analyse (a sentence) grammatically; to give the part of speech of and explain the grammatical role of (a word). **2** *computational linguistics* to analyse (a sentence, text, etc) into syntactic components and test its grammaticality against a given grammar. **3** *computing* to analyse (a string of input symbols) in terms of the computing language being used. • **parser** *noun, computing* a program which parses sentences. ◷ 16c: from Latin *pars orationis* part of speech.

parsec /ˈpɑːsɛk/ ▷ *noun, astron* a unit of astronomical measurement equal to 3.26 light years or 3.09×10^{13}km, being the distance at which a star would have a PARALLAX of 1 second of arc when viewed from two points which are the same distance apart as the Earth is from the Sun. ◷ Early 20c: from PARALLAX + SECOND².

Parsee or **Parsi** /ˈpɑːsiː, pɑːˈsiː/ ▷ *noun* (***Parsees*** or ***Parsis***) one of the descendants of the ancient ZOROASTRIANS, who fled from Persia in the 8c AD to escape Muslim persecution, and settled in the Bombay area of India. ◷ 14c: Persian *Parsee*, meaning 'Persian'.

parsimonious /pɑːsɪˈmoʊnɪəs/ ▷ *adj* too careful in spending money; stingy. • **parsimoniously** *adverb.* • **parsimoniousness** *noun.* ◷ 16c: from PARSIMONY + -OUS.

parsimony /ˈpɑːsɪmənɪ/ ▷ *noun* **1** reluctance or extreme care in spending money. **2** praiseworthy economy. **3** the avoiding of excess. **4** meanness. ◷ 15c: from Latin *parsimonia* thrift, from *parcere* to spare or save.

parsley /ˈpɑːslɪ/ ▷ *noun* (***parsleys***) **1** an annual or biennial plant with finely-divided bright green curly aromatic leaves, used fresh or dried as a culinary herb, and also used fresh as a garnish. **2** any of various similar or related plants □ ***cow parsley.*** ◷ Anglo-Saxon, from Greek *petroselinon* rock-parsley, from *petra* rock + *selinon* parsley.

parsnip /ˈpɑːsnɪp/ ▷ *noun* **1** a biennial plant widely grown for its thick fleshy edible tap root. **2** the long thick root of this plant, which has creamy-white flesh with a sweet flavour, eaten as a vegetable. ◷ 14c: from Latin *pastinacum*, from *pastinum* dibble; probably affected by NEEP.

parson /ˈpɑːsən/ ▷ *noun* **1** a parish priest in the Church of England. **2** any clergyman. ◷ 13c as *persone*: from Latin *persona* parish priest, person, personage or mask.

parsonage /ˈpɑːsnədʒ/ ▷ *noun* the residence of a parson.

parson bird ▷ *noun* the TUI.

parson's nose ▷ *noun, colloq* a piece of fatty flesh at the rump of a plucked fowl, especially a turkey or chicken. Also called **pope's nose**.

part /pɑːt/ ▷ *noun* **1** a portion, piece or bit; some but not all. **2** one of a set of equal divisions or amounts that compose a whole □ ***in the proportion of five parts cement to two of sand.*** **3** an essential piece; a component □ ***vehicle spare parts.*** **4** a section of a book; any of the episodes of a story, etc issued or broadcast as a serial. **5 a** a performer's role in a play, opera, etc; **b** the words, actions, etc belonging to the role. **6** the melody, etc given to a particular instrument or voice in a musical work. **7** one's share, responsibility or duty in something □ ***do one's part*** □ ***want no part in it.*** **8** (*usually* **parts**) a region □ ***foreign parts.*** **9** (**parts**) talents; abilities □ ***a man of many parts.*** ▷ *verb* (***parted, parting***) **1** to divide; to separate. **2** *intr* to become divided or separated. **3** to separate (eg curtains, combatants, etc). **4** *intr* said of more than one person: to leave one another; to go in different directions; to depart. **5** to put a parting in (hair). **6** *intr* to come or burst apart. ▷ *adj* in part; partial □ ***part payment.*** • **the better, best**

or **greater part of something** most of it; the majority of it. • **for the most part 1** usually. **2** mostly or mainly. • **for my part** as far as I am concerned. • **in great** or **large part** mostly. • **in part** partly; not wholly but to some extent. • **on the part of someone 1** as done by them. **2** so far as they are concerned. • **part and parcel of something** an essential part of it. • **part company with someone** to separate from them. • **part way** some of the way, without reaching; not all the way □ *go part way towards an objective*. • **play a part** to be involved. • **take something in good part** to take no offence at (a criticism, joke, etc). • **take part in something** to participate in it; to share in it. • **take someone's part** to support them; to take their side. ◐ 13c: from Latin *pars* part.

■ **part from** or **with someone** to leave them or separate from them.

■ **part with something** or **be parted from something** to give it up or hand it over □ *reluctant to part with their money* □ *reluctant to be parted from their money.*

on the part of, on behalf of

See Usage Note at **behalf**.

partake /pɑːˈteɪk/ ▻ *verb* (***partook*** /pɑːˈtʊk/, ***partaken, partaking***) *intr* (*usually* **partake in** or **of something**) **1** to participate in it. **2** to eat or drink. **3** *literary* to have a certain quality, etc to a degree. ◐ 16c: formed from *partaking*, from an earlier expression *part-taking*.

parted ▻ *adj* **1** divided; separated. **2** *bot* said of a leaf: divided deeply, almost to the base.

parterre /pɑːˈtɛə(r)/ ▻ *noun* **1** a formal ornamental flower-garden laid out with lawns and paths. **2** the pit of a theatre, especially the part under the galleries. ◐ 17c: from French *par terre* on the ground.

part exchange ▻ *noun* a purchase or sale of new goods made by exchanging used goods for part of the value of the new goods. Compare TRADE-IN.

parthenogenesis /pɑːθənoʊˈdʒɛnəsɪs/ ▻ *noun, biol* in some insects and plants: reproduction without fertilization by the male. • **parthenogenetic** *adj* /-dʒɛˈnetɪk/. ◐ 19c: from Greek *parthenos* maiden + -GENESIS.

Parthian /ˈpɑːθɪən/ ▻ *noun* a member of an ancient people who ruled an empire from the 3c BC from the Euphrates River to the Indus River, and were finally conquered in AD 224 by the Sassanids of Persia. ▻ *adj* relating to the Parthians. ◐ 16c.

Parthian shot see PARTING SHOT

partial /ˈpɑːʃəl/ ▻ *adj* **1** incomplete; in part only. **2** (*always* **partial to something**) having a liking for it. **3** favouring one side or person unfairly; biased. **4** *bot* forming one of the parts or divisions of a compound structure. ▻ *noun, acoustics* one of the single-frequency tones which go together to form a sound actually heard. Also called **partial tone**. ◐ 15c: from Latin *partialis*, from *pars* part.

partial derivative ▻ *noun, math* a derivative obtained by letting only one of several independent variables vary.

partial eclipse ▻ *noun, astron* an eclipse where only part of the Sun, etc is covered. Compare ANNULAR ECLIPSE, TOTAL ECLIPSE.

partial fraction ▻ *noun, math* one of a number of fractions into which another fraction can be separated, eg $^1/_2$ and $^1/_4$ are partial fractions of $^3/_4$.

partiality /pɑːʃɪˈalɪtɪ/ ▻ *noun* **1** being partial. **2** favourable bias or prejudice. **3** fondness.

partially /ˈpɑːʃəlɪ/ ▻ *adverb* not completely or wholly; not yet to the point of completion.

partially

See Usage Note at **partly**.

partial tone see under PARTIAL *noun*

partible /ˈpɑːtɪbəl/ ▻ *adj* said especially of inherited property: able to be divided up.

participant /pɑːˈtɪsɪpənt/ or **participator** ▻ *noun* a person or group that takes part in something. ▻ *adj* participating or sharing in something.

participate /pɑːˈtɪsɪpeɪt/ ▻ *verb* (***participated, participating***) *intr* (*often* **participate in something**) to take part or be involved in it. • **participation** *noun*. ◐ 16c: from Latin *pars, partis* part + *capere* to take.

participating insurance ▻ *noun* insurance that entitles policyholders to a share of the company's surplus profits.

participator /pɑːˈtɪsɪpeɪtə(r)/ ▻ *noun* **1** someone who participates in something. **2** someone who has a share in the capital or income of a company. • **participatory** /-ˈpeɪtərɪ/ *adj*.

participle /ˈpɑːtɪsɪpəl/ ▻ *noun, grammar* a word formed from a verb, which has adjectival qualities as well as verbal ones. There are two participles in English, the **present participle**, formed with the ending *-ing*, as in *going, swimming* or *shouting*, and the **past participle**, generally ending in *-d, -ed, -t* or *-n*, as in *chased, shouted, kept* and *shown*, but also with irregular forms such as *gone, swum*, etc. In English, present participles are used with the AUXILIARY verb *be* to form the PROGRESSIVE tenses (as in *I am going* and *she was singing*), and past participles are used with the auxiliary verb *have* to form the PERFECT tenses (as in *he has gone* and *they had left*), and with *be* to form PASSIVE constructions (as in *she was seen here yesterday*). A participle may also be used as an ADJECTIVE (as in *a screaming child* and *a grown woman*). • **participial** /pɑːtɪˈsɪpɪəl/ *adj* having the role of a participle □ *participial clause*. • **participially** *adverb*. ◐ 14c: from Latin *participium* a sharing, from *pars* part + *capere* to take, because participles share features of both a verb and an adjective.

particle /ˈpɑːtɪkəl/ ▻ *noun* **1** a tiny piece; a minute piece of matter. **2** the least bit □ *not a particle of sympathy*. **3** *physics* a tiny unit of matter such as a MOLECULE, ATOM or ELECTRON. **4** *grammar* a word which does not have any inflected forms, eg a PREPOSITION, CONJUNCTION or INTERJECTION. **5** *grammar* an AFFIX, such as *un-, de-, -fy* and *-ly*. **6** *RC Church* a crumb of consecrated bread, or a portion used in communion. ◐ 14c: from Latin *particula*, diminutive of *pars* part.

particle accelerator ▻ *noun, physics* a device that is used to accelerate charged subatomic particles, especially electrons or protons, to a high velocity. See also CYCLOTRON.

particle beam weapon ▻ *noun* a weapon in which high-energy subatomic particles, generated in nuclear accelerators, are directed into a narrow concentrated beam.

particle physics ▻ *singular noun* the branch of physics concerned with the study of the ELEMENTARY PARTICLES that are the fundamental components of matter, and the forces between them.

particoloured /ˈpɑːtɪkʌləd/ ▻ *adj* partly one colour, partly another; variegated. ◐ 16c: from French *parti* variegated.

particular /pəˈtɪkjʊlə(r)/ ▻ *adj* **1** specific; single; individually known or referred to □ *She liked that particular design*. **2** especial; exceptional □ *took particular care*. **3** difficult to satisfy; fastidious; exacting □ *He's very particular about the washing-up*. **4** exact; detailed. ▻ *noun* **1** a detail. **2** (**particulars**) personal details, eg name, date of birth, etc □ *took down her particulars*. •

particularness *noun*. • **in particular** particularly; especially; specifically; in detail. ◷ 14c: from Latin *particularis*, from *particula*, diminutive of *pars* part.

particular intention see INTENTION

particularism ▻ *noun* **1** attention to one's own group, class, sect, etc. **2** attention to the interests of a federal state before that of the confederation. **3** *theol* the doctrine that salvation is offered only to particular individuals, the elect, and not to everyone.

particularity /pətɪkjʊ'larɪtɪ/ ▻ *noun* **1** the quality of being particular. **2** minuteness of detail. **3** (*often* **particularities**) a single instance or case; a detail ▫ *the particularities of the case.*

particularize or **particularise** /pə'tɪkjʊləraɪz/ ▻ *verb* (***particularized***, ***particularizing***) **1** to specify individually. **2** to give specific examples of something. **3** *intr* to go into detail. • **particularization** *noun*. ◷ 16c: from French *particulariser*.

particularly ▻ *adverb* **1** more than usually ▫ *particularly good.* **2** specifically; especially ▫ *particularly hates board games.*

particulate /pɑː'tɪkjʊlət/ ▻ *adj* having the form of, or relating to, particles.

parting /'pɑːtɪŋ/ ▻ *noun* **1** the act of taking leave. **2** a divergence or separation ▫ *a parting of the ways.* **3** a line of exposed scalp that divides sections of hair brushed in opposite directions ▫ *a middle parting.* ▻ *adj* referring to, or at the time of, leaving; departing ▫ *a parting comment.*

parting shot ▻ *noun* a final hostile remark made on departing. Also called **Parthian shot**. ◷ 19c: referring to the practice of the horsemen of ancient Parthia of turning to shoot arrows at enemies following them as they rode off.

partisan /'pɑːtɪzan/ ▻ *noun* **1** an enthusiastic supporter of a party, person, cause, etc. **2** a member of an armed resistance group in a country occupied by an enemy. ▻ *adj* strongly loyal to one side, especially blindly so; biased. • **partisanship** *noun*. ◷ 16c: French, from *parte* PART.

partita /pɑː'tiːtə/ ▻ *noun, music* **1** (*plural* ***partite*** /-teɪ/) referring to the 17c: one of a set of instrumental variations. **2** (*plural* ***partitas***) referring especially to the 18c: a suite of instrumental dances, such as those by J S Bach. ◷ Late 19c: Italian, meaning 'a division', from Latin *partire* to divide.

partite /'pɑːtaɪt/ ▻ *adj* **1** *in compounds* divided into the specified number of parts ▫ *tripartite* ▫ *bipartite.* **2** *bot* said especially of leaves: cut nearly to the base, forming two or more parts. ◷ 16c: from Latin *partire* to divide.

partition /pɑː'tɪʃən/ ▻ *noun* **1** something which divides an object into a number of parts. **2** a screen or thin wall dividing a room. **3** the dividing of a country into two or more independent states. ▻ *verb* (***partitioned***, ***partitioning***) **1** to divide (a country) into independent states. **2** (*also* **partition something off**) to separate it off with a partition. ◷ 16c: from Latin *partitio* division.

partition wall ▻ *noun* a wall internal to a building, dividing the space into rooms.

partitive /'pɑːtɪtɪv/ *grammar* ▻ *adj* said of a word, form, etc: denoting a part of a whole of what is being described. ▻ *noun* a partitive word or form, eg *some*, *any*, *most*. ◷ 16c: from Latin *partire* to divide.

partly ▻ *adverb* in part, or in some parts; to a certain extent, not wholly.

partner /'pɑːtnə(r)/ ▻ *noun* **1** one of two or more people who jointly own or run a business or other enterprise on an equal footing. **2** a person with whom one has a sexual relationship, especially a long-term one, particularly in a committed unmarried or same-sex relationship. **3** a person one dances with ▫ *dance partner.* **4** a person who is on the same side as oneself in a game of eg bridge, tennis, etc. **5** *biol* an associate in COMMENSALISM or SYMBIOSIS. ▻ *verb* (***partnered***, ***partnering***) to join as a partner with someone; to be the partner of someone. ◷ 13c as *partener*: from *parcener* joint inheritor, influenced by PART.

> ***partly, partially***
>
> • These words are often used indiscriminately to mean 'in part' ▫ *A blow on the head left him partially deaf for the rest of his life* ▫ *About half the population is wholly or partially dependent on food aid* ▫ *Redpath was a good policeman partly because he was also a sensitive and humane man.*
>
> • Both words are found in conjunction with words like 'because, due to, explains, filled, obscured, open, responsible, successful, true'.
>
> • **Partly** is used more often when it is paired, either with itself or with **and also** or **but also** ▫ *Poor productivity is to be blamed partly on bad management of the workforce and partly on lack of investment* ▫ *It is partly a personal and partly a property tax* ▫ *The film was a big success, partly because of its openness about sex, but also because of the leading actors.*
>
> • **Partly** is also used more often when followed by an adjective or participle that is itself further qualified ▫ *The house is partly built of stone* (which refers to a completed house) ▫ *The house is partly / partially built* (which refers to an uncompleted house).
>
> ☆ RECOMMENDATION: generally prefer **partly**; use **partially** when there is a special sense of incompleteness.

partnership ▻ *noun* **1** a relationship in which two or more people or groups operate together as partners. **2** the status of a partner ▫ *offered her a partnership.* **3** a business or other enterprise jointly owned or run by two or more people, etc.

Partnership for Peace ▻ *noun* (abbreviation **PFP**) a scheme set up in 1993 as a link between NATO and some former Warsaw Pact countries, effectively giving the latter associate membership of NATO.

part-off ▻ *noun* (***part-offs***) *Caribb* a screen used to divide a room into two separate areas.

part of speech ▻ *noun* (***parts of speech***) *grammar* any of the grammatical classes of words, eg noun, adjective, verb or preposition. See note.

partook *past tense of* PARTAKE

part-owner ▻ *noun* a joint owner.

partridge /'pɑːtrɪdʒ/ ▻ *noun* (***partridge*** or ***partridges***) any of various plump ground-dwelling gamebirds, usually with brown or grey plumage, unfeathered legs and feet, and a very short tail. ◷ 13c as *pertrich*: from French *perdriz*, from Greek *perdix*.

part singing ▻ *noun* singing in which a number of harmonized parts are sung.

part song ▻ *noun* a song for singing in harmonized parts.

part-time ▻ *adj* done, attended, etc during only part of the full working day. ▻ *adverb* ▫ *studying part-time.* ▻ *verb* (***part-timed***, ***part-timing***) to work on a part-time basis. • **part-timer** *noun*. Compare FULL-TIME.

parturient /pɑː'tjʊərɪənt/ ▻ *adj, medicine* **1** referring or relating to childbirth. **2** giving birth or about to give birth. ◷ 16c: from Latin *parturire* to give birth, from *parere* to bring forth.

parturition /pɑːtjʊ'rɪʃən/ ▻ *noun, medicine* the process of giving birth; childbirth.

partwork ▻ *noun* one of a series of publications, especially magazines, issued at regular intervals, eventually forming a complete course or book.

party /ˈpɑːtɪ/ ▷ *noun* (*parties*) **1** a social gathering, especially of invited guests, for enjoyment or celebration. **2** a group of people involved in a certain activity together □ *search party*. **3** (*often* **Party**) an organization, especially a national organization, of people united by a common, especially political, aim. **4** *law* **a** each of the individuals or groups concerned in a contract, agreement, lawsuit, etc □ *no third party involved*; **b** *in compounds, as adj* □ *third-party insurance*. **5** *old facetious use* a person □ *an elderly party*. ▷ *verb* (*partied*, *partying*) *intr, colloq* to gather as a group to drink, chat, dance, etc for enjoyment; to have fun □ *We partied all night*. ● **be a party to something** to be involved in or partly responsible (for an agreement, decision, action, etc). ⓒ 13c: from French *partie* a part, share, etc, from *partir* to divide.

party line ▷ *noun* **1** a telephone line shared by two or more people. **2** the official opinion of a political party on any particular issue.

party man ▷ *noun* a man who is a faithful member of a political party.

party piece ▷ *noun* an act or turn, such as juggling, magic tricks, etc, that one can be called on to perform to entertain others, eg at a party.

party politics ▷ *singular or plural noun* political ideas and issues considered from the point of view of a particular party, or arranged to suit the views or interests of that party.

party pooper ▷ *noun* someone who spoils the enjoyment of others at a party or social occasion through lack of enthusiasm. ⓒ 1950s.

party-size ▷ *adj* said of a pack of food, etc: of a size suitable for a party.

party wall ▷ *noun* a wall that divides two houses, etc, being the joint responsibility of both owners.

par value ▷ *noun, finance, stock exchange* the value shown on a share certificate at time of issue; face value.

parvenu and **parvenue** /ˈpɑːvənjuː, -nuː/ ▷ *noun* (*parvenus* or *parvenues*) *derog* respectively a man or woman who has recently acquired substantial wealth but lacks the social refinement sometimes thought necessary to go with it. Also *as adj*. ⓒ Early 19c: French, literally 'arrived', from *parvenir* to arrive.

parvis /ˈpɑːvɪs/ or **parvise** /ˈpɑːviːs/ ▷ *noun* **1** an enclosed space, or sometimes a portico, at the front of a church. **2** *loosely* a room over a church porch. ⓒ 14c: from French *parevis*, from Latin *paradisum* PARADISE.

parvovirus /ˈpɑːvoʊvaɪərəs/ ▷ *noun* any of a group of very small viruses containing DNA, and which cause a number of animal, especially canine, diseases. ⓒ 1960s: from Latin *parvus* small + VIRUS.

pas /pɑː/ ▷ *noun* (*pas*) a step or dance, especially in ballet. ⓒ 18c: French.

PASCAL /pasˈkal/ ▷ *noun, computing* a high-level computer programming language, designed in the 1960s and still widely used for general programming purposes. ⓒ 1960s: named after Blaise Pascal (1623–62), French philosopher and scientist, because he devised and built a calculating machine.

pascal /ˈpaskəl/ ▷ *noun* (abbreviation **Pa**) in the SI system: a unit of pressure, equal to a force of one newton per square metre. ⓒ 1950s: named after Blaise Pascal (see PASCAL).

Pascal's triangle ▷ *noun* a triangular pattern of numbers with the number 1 at the apex, in which each digit, except for the number 1, is the sum of the two digits in the line immediately above it. ⓒ Late 19c: named after Blaise Pascal (see PASCAL), who described the triangle in his work.

Pasch /pask/ ▷ *noun* **1** the PASSOVER. **2** *archaic* Easter. ⓒ Anglo-Saxon as plural *pasches*: from Hebrew *pesach* the Passover.

paschal /ˈpaskəl/ ▷ *adj* **1** relating to the Jewish festival of PASSOVER. **2** relating to Easter. ⓒ 15c: from Latin *paschalis*; see PASCH.

pas de bourrée /pɑː də ˈbʊəreɪ/ ▷ *noun* (***pas de bourrée***) *ballet* a movement in which one foot is swiftly placed behind or in front of the other.

pas de chat /pɑː də ʃɑː/ ▷ *noun* (***pas de chat***) *ballet* a leap in which each foot is raised in turn to the opposite knee. ⓒ Early 20c: French.

pas de deux /pɑː də dɜː/ ▷ *noun* (*plural* ***pas de deux***) a dance sequence for two performers. ⓒ 18c: French, literally 'step for two'.

pash /paʃ/ ▷ *noun* (*pashes*) *slang* short form of PASSION.

pasha /ˈpaʃə, pɑːˈʃɑː/ ▷ *noun* (*pashas*) *historical* placed after the name in titles: a high-ranking Turkish official in the Ottoman Empire. ⓒ 17c: Turkish.

pashm /ˈpʌʃəm/ ▷ *noun* the fine underfleece of the goats of N India, used for making rugs, shawls, etc. ⓒ Late 19c: Persian, meaning 'wool'.

Pashto, **Pushto** /ˈpʌʃtoʊ/ or **Pushtu** /ˈpʌʃtuː/ ▷ *noun* (***Pashtos***, ***Pushtos*** or ***Pushtus***) **1** one of the official languages of Afghanistan, also spoken in NW Pakistan, an Iranian language of the Indo-European family. **2** a native speaker of this language; a PATHAN. ⓒ 18c: Persian and Afghan.

paso doble /ˈpasoʊ ˈdoʊbleɪ/ ▷ *noun* (***paso dobles*** or ***pasos dobles***) **1** a fast modern ballroom dance, based on a Latin American marching style. **2** the music for this dance usually in duple time. ⓒ 1920s: Spanish *paso* step + *doble* double.

pasqueflower /ˈpɑːskflaʊə(r)/ ▷ *noun* a low-growing hairy perennial plant with large dark- to pale-purple bell-shaped flowers, which are initially erect but droop as they begin to fade. ⓒ 16c: from French *passefleur*, from *passer* to surpass + *fleur* flower; influenced by PASCH.

pass /pɑːs/ ▷ *verb* (*passed* /pɑːst/, *passing*) **1** *tr & intr* to come alongside and progress beyond something or someone □ *passed her on the stairs*. **2** *intr* to run, flow, progress, etc □ *blood passing through our veins*. **3** *tr &*

---

parts of speech

Words that make up sentences can be grouped into different classes according to their function or role. For example, words such as *cat, car, Thomas* and *Liverpool* are nouns, ie words that name things, people and places, whereas words such as *big, black* and *angry* are adjectives, ie words that describe people and things.

Traditionally, English is said to have eight, or sometimes nine, wordclasses or parts of speech:

noun: *book, bread*;
verb: *sing, walk*;
adjective: *green, sad*;
adverb: *quickly, soon, very*;
pronoun: *I, us, you*;
preposition: *in, from, with*;
conjunction: *although, because, while*;
interjection: *ouch, alas, oh*;
and sometimes also
article: *the, a*.

In some modern grammars and dictionaries of English, several of these traditional parts of speech have been replaced or supplemented by others such as **determiner** and **intensifier**.

Note that many words belong to more than one part of speech. For example, *can* is a noun in *a can of worms*, an auxiliary verb in *I can come tomorrow*, and a lexical verb in *a factory where they can tomatoes*.

---

intr (*also* **pass through, into**, *etc* **something** or **pass something through, into**, *etc* **something**) to go or make it go, penetrate, etc □ *pass through a filter.* **4** *tr & intr* to move lightly across, over, etc something □ *pass a duster over the furniture.* **5** *intr* to move from one state or stage to another □ *pass from the larval to the pupal stage.* **6** to exceed or surpass □ *pass the target.* **7** *tr & intr* said of a vehicle: to overtake. **8 a** *tr & intr* to achieve the required standard in (a test, etc); **b** to award (a student, etc) the marks required for success in a test, etc. **9** *intr* to take place □ *what passed between them.* **10** *tr & intr* said of time: to go by; to use up (time) in some activity, etc. **11** *tr & intr* (*usually* **pass down** or **pass something down**) to be inherited; to hand it down. **12** *tr & intr, sport* to throw or kick (the ball, etc) to another player in one's team. **13** *tr & intr* to agree to (a proposal or resolution) or be agreed to; to vote (a law) into effect. **14** said of a judge or law court: to pronounce (judgement). **15** *intr* to go away after a while □ *her nausea passed.* **16** *intr* to be accepted, tolerated or ignored □ *let it pass.* **17** *intr* to choose not to answer in a quiz, etc or bid in a card game. **18** to make (a comment, etc). **19** to discharge (urine or faeces). ▷ *noun* (***passes***) **1** a route through a gap in a mountain range. **2** an official card or document permitting one to enter somewhere, be absent from duty, etc. **3** a successful result in an examination, but usually without distinction or honours. **4** *sport* a throw, kick, hit, etc to another player in one's team. **5** a state of affairs □ *came to a sorry pass.* **6** a decision not to answer in a quiz, etc, or not to bid in a card game. • **come** or **be brought to pass** to happen. • **make a pass at someone** to make a casual sexual advance towards them □ *made a pass at a gorgeous man at the party.* • **pass the buck** see under BUCK. • **pass the time of day** to exchange an ordinary greeting with someone. ⓘ 13c: from Latin *passus* step or pace.

■ **pass as** or **for someone** or **something** to be mistaken for or accepted as (a different person or thing).

■ **pass oneself off as someone** or **something** to represent oneself in that way □ *tried to pass themselves off as students.*

■ **pass away** or **on** *euphemistic* to die.

■ **pass by** to go past.

■ **pass by something** or **someone** to go past them.

■ **pass something** or **someone by** to overlook or ignore them.

■ **pass off 1** said of a sickness or feeling, etc: to go away; to diminish. **2** said of an arranged event: to take place with the result specified □ *The party passed off very well.*

■ **pass something off** to successfully present (something which is fraudulent).

■ **pass something on 1** to hand it on or transmit it to someone else. **2** see *pass something round* below.

■ **pass out 1** to faint. **2** to leave a military or police college having successfully completed one's training.

■ **pass over something** to overlook it; to ignore it.

■ **pass something round, on,** *etc* to circulate it; to hand or transfer it from one person to the next in succession □ *pass the memo round the office* □ *was passed on.*

■ **pass something up** *colloq* to neglect or sacrifice (an opportunity).

pass. ▷ *abbreviation, grammar* passive.

passable /ˈpɑːsəbəl/ ▷ *adj* **1** barely adequate. **2** *colloq* fairly good. **3** said of a road, etc: able to be travelled along, crossed, etc. • **passableness** *noun.* • **passably** *adverb.*

passacaglia /pasəˈkɑːljə/ ▷ *noun* (***passacaglias***) *music* **1** a slow stately old Spanish dance in triple time. **2** the music for this dance introduced into keyboard music in the 17c, and based on a set of uninterrupted variations on a continuously repeated bass line or harmonic progression. See also CHACONNE. ⓘ 17c: Italian, probably from Spanish *pasacalles* street song.

passade /paˈseɪd, pɑː-/ ▷ *noun, dressage* the motion of a horse to and fro over the same ground in dressage exercises. ⓘ 17c: French, from Spanish *pasada*, from Latin *passus* step.

passage[1] /ˈpasɪdʒ/ ▷ *noun* **1** a route through; a corridor, narrow street, or channel. **2** a tubular vessel in the body. **3** a piece of a text or musical composition of moderate length. **4** the process of passing □ *the passage of time.* **5 a** a journey, especially by ship or aeroplane; **b** the cost of such a journey. **6** permission or freedom to pass through a territory, etc. **7** the voting of a law, etc into effect □ *passage through parliament.* ⓘ 13c: French, from *passer* to pass, from Latin *passus* step.

passage[2] /paˈsɑːʒ, ˈpasɪdʒ/ *dressage* ▷ *noun* **1** a slow sideways walk. **2** a rhythmical trot with diagonal pairs of legs lifted high. ▷ *verb* (***passaged, passaging***) **1** *intr* to move at a passage. **2** to make (a horse) move at a passage. ⓘ 18c: from French *passager*, from Italian *passeggiare* to walk, from Latin *passus* step.

passage grave ▷ *noun, archaeol* an underground burial chamber connected to the surface by a passage.

passage of arms ▷ *noun* **1** any armed struggle. **2** an encounter, especially with words.

passageway ▷ *noun* a narrow passage or way, etc, usually with walls on each side; a corridor; an alley.

passata /pəˈsɑːtə/ ▷ *noun* (***passatas***) an Italian sauce of puréed and sieved tomatoes. ⓘ 1980s: Italian, meaning 'passed', ie passed through a sieve.

pass-back ▷ *noun, sport* an act of passing a ball, etc to a member of one's own team nearer one's own goal line.

passbook ▷ *noun* a book in which the amounts of money put into and taken out of a building society account, bank account, etc, are recorded.

passé /ˈpaseɪ, ˈpɑːseɪ/ ▷ *adj* outmoded; old-fashioned; having faded out of popularity. ⓘ 18c: French, meaning 'passed'.

passenger /ˈpasəndʒə(r)/ ▷ *noun* **1** a traveller in a vehicle, boat, aeroplane, etc driven, sailed or piloted by someone else. **2** *derog* someone not doing their share of the work in a joint project, etc. ▷ *adj* relating to, or for, passengers □ *passenger train.* ⓘ 14c: from French *passagier*, from *passage*, with inserted *n* as in messenger.

passe-partout /pɑːspɑːˈtuː, pas-/ ▷ *noun* **1** a means of passing anywhere, especially a master key. **2** a card or something similar cut as a mount for a picture. **3** a kind of simple picture-frame, usually of pasteboard, the picture being fixed by strips pasted over the edges. ⓘ 17c: French, meaning 'a master key', from *passer* to pass + *partout* everywhere.

passer-by ▷ *noun* (***passers-by***) someone who is walking past a house, shop, incident, etc.

passerine /ˈpasəraɪn/ *ornithol* ▷ *adj* belonging or relating to the largest order of birds, characterized by a perching habit and the possession of four toes, and which includes the songbirds. ▷ *noun* any bird belonging to this order. ⓘ 18c: from Latin *passer* sparrow.

pas seul /pɑːsɜːl/ ▷ *noun* (*plural* ***pas seul***) a dance for one person; a solo ballet dance. ⓘ 19c: French, literally 'step alone'.

passible /ˈpasɪbəl/ ▷ *adj* susceptible to or capable of suffering or feeling. ⓘ 14c: from Latin *passibilis*, from *pati*, *passus* to suffer.

passim /ˈpasɪm/ ▷ *adverb* said of a word, reference, etc: occurring frequently throughout the literary or academic work in question. ⓘ Early 19c: Latin, meaning 'here and there'.

passing /ˈpɑːsɪŋ/ ▻ *adj* **1** lasting only briefly. **2** casual; transitory ▫ ***a passing glance*** ▫ ***a passing reference to her absence.*** ▻ *noun* **1** a place where one may pass. **2** a coming to the end. **3** *euphemistic* death. • **in passing** while dealing with something else; casually; by allusion rather than directly ▫ ***mentioned the accident in passing.*** ◷ 14c: present participle of PASS.

passing note ▻ *noun, music* a note forming an unprepared discord in an unaccented place in the measure. Also (*N Amer*) called **passing tone**.

passing shot ▻ *noun, tennis* a shot hit past, and beyond the reach of, an opponent.

Passion ▻ *noun* **1** (*usually* **the Passion**) the suffering and death of Christ. **2** an account of this from one of the Gospels. **3** a musical setting of one of these accounts.

passion /ˈpaʃən/ ▻ *noun* **1** a violent emotion, eg hate, anger or envy. **2** a fit of anger. **3** sexual love or desire. **4 a** an enthusiasm ▫ ***has a passion for bikes***; **b** something for which one has great enthusiasm ▫ ***Bikes are his passion.*** **5** martyrdom. ◷ 12c: French, from Latin *passio*, from *pati* to suffer.

passional ▻ *adj* referring or relating to the sufferings of a Christian martyr. ▻ *noun* a book of the sufferings of saints and martyrs.

passionate /ˈpaʃənət/ ▻ *adj* **1** easily moved to passion; strongly emotional. **2** keen; enthusiastic; intense. • **passionately** *adverb*. • **passionateness** *noun*.

passion flower ▻ *noun* any of several tropical climbing plants with large distinctive flowers, the different parts of which were once thought to resemble the crown of thorns, nails, and other emblems of Christ's Passion. ◷ 17c.

passion fruit ▻ *noun* the round yellow or purple edible fruit of any of various species of passion flower.

passionless ▻ *adj* **1** free from or lacking passion, especially sexual desire. **2** not easily excited to anger.

passion play ▻ *noun* a religious drama representing the suffering and death of Christ.

Passion Sunday ▻ *noun, Christianity* the fifth Sunday in Lent.

Passiontide ▻ *noun, Christianity* the two weeks preceding Easter.

Passion week ▻ *noun, Christianity* **1** the week before Holy Week. **2** *sometimes* Holy Week.

passive /ˈpasɪv/ ▻ *adj* **1** lacking positive or assertive qualities; submissive. **2** lethargic; inert. **3** *grammar* (abbreviation **pass.**) **a** denoting or relating to a verbal construction which in English consists of *be* and the PAST PARTICIPLE (see under PARTICIPLE), which carries a meaning in which the subject undergoes, rather than performs, the action of the verb, such as *'the letter'* in *The letter was written by John.* Compare ACTIVE; **b** denoting or relating to the verb in such a construction. ▻ *noun, grammar* **1** (*also* **passive voice**) the form or forms that a passive verb takes. **2** a passive verb or construction. • **passively** *adverb*. • **passiveness** or **passivity** *noun*. ◷ 14c: from Latin *passivus*.

passive immunity ▻ *noun, medicine* the short-term immunity acquired either artificially, through the administration of antibodies, or naturally, as in the very young who receive antibodies through the placenta or in colostrum. Compare ACTIVE IMMUNITY.

passive resistance ▻ *noun* the use of non-violent means, eg fasting, peaceful demonstration, etc, as a protest against a government, law, regulation, etc. • **passive resister** *noun*.

passive smoking ▻ *noun* the involuntary breathing in of tobacco-smoke by non-smokers, especially within an enclosed area or for prolonged periods, which has injurious effects.

passkey ▻ *noun* a key designed to open a varied set of locks; a MASTER KEY.

pass law ▻ *noun* formerly in South Africa: a law restricting the movement of non-whites, requiring them to carry identification at all times.

Passover /ˈpɑːsouvə(r)/ ▻ *noun* an annual Jewish festival held 15–22 Nisan (in March or April), commemorating the deliverance of the Israelites from bondage in Egypt. See also PESACH. ◷ 16c: so called because the angel of death passed over the houses of the Israelites when he killed the firstborn of the Egyptians (Exodus 13).

passport /ˈpɑːspɔːt/ ▻ *noun* **1** an official document issued by the government, giving proof of the holder's identity and nationality, and permission to travel abroad with its protection. **2** an asset that guarantees one something, especially a privilege ▫ ***A degree is your passport to a good job.*** ◷ 15c: from French *passeport*, from *passer* to pass + *port* seaport.

password ▻ *noun* **1** *especially military* a secret word allowing entry to a high-security area or past a checkpoint, etc. **2** *computing* a set of characters personal to a user which they input to gain access to a computer or network.

past /pɑːst/ ▻ *adj* **1** referring to an earlier time; of long ago; bygone. **2** recently ended; just gone by ▫ ***the past year.*** **3** over; finished. **4** former; previous ▫ ***past presidents.*** **5** *grammar* said of the tense of a verb: indicating an action or condition which took place or began in the past, such as the simple past (as in *John wrote the letter*), past progressive (as in *John was writing the letter*), etc. Compare FUTURE (*noun* 2), PRESENT, PERFECT, PLUPERFECT, IMPERFECT. ▻ *prep* **1** up to and beyond ▫ ***went past me.*** **2** after in time or age ▫ ***past your bedtime.*** **3** beyond; farther away than ▫ ***the one past the library.*** **4** having advanced too far for something ▫ ***She's past playing with dolls.*** **5** beyond the reach of something ▫ ***past help*** ▫ ***What he did was past belief.*** ▻ *adverb* **1** so as to pass by ▫ ***watched me go past.*** **2** ago ▫ ***two months past.*** ▻ *noun* **1** (*usually* **the past**) **a** the time before the present; **b** events, etc belonging to this time. **2** one's earlier life or career ▫ ***My past is quite uninteresting.*** **3** a disreputable episode or period earlier in one's life ▫ ***a woman with a past.*** **4** *grammar* **a** the past tense; **b** a verb in the past tense. • **not put it past someone** *colloq* to believe them quite liable or disposed to do a certain thing. • **past it** or **past one's best** *colloq* having lost the vigour of one's youth or prime. ◷ 14c: an obsolete past participle of PASS.

pasta /ˈpastə/ ▻ *noun* (***pastas***) **1** a dough made with flour, water and eggs, shaped into a variety of forms such as spaghetti, macaroni, lasagne, etc. **2** a cooked dish of this, usually served with a sauce. ◷ 19c: Italian, from Latin, meaning 'paste' or 'dough', from Greek, meaning 'barley porridge'.

paste /peɪst/ ▻ *noun* **1** a stiff moist mixture made from a powder and water, and traditionally made from flour and water, used as an adhesive ▫ ***wallpaper paste.*** **2** a spread for sandwiches, etc made from ground meat or fish, etc ▫ ***salmon paste.*** **3** any fine, often sweet, dough-like mixture ▫ ***almond paste.*** **4** a hard brilliant glass used in making imitation gems. ▻ *verb* (***pasted, pasting***) **1** to stick something with paste. **2** (*also* **paste something up**) *printing* to mount (text, illustrations, etc) on a backing as a proof for printing from or photographing, etc. See also PASTE-UP. **3** *wordprocessing* to insert text, etc which has been copied or cut from another part of the document, etc. **4** *colloq* to thrash or beat soundly. ◷ 14c: French, from Latin *pasta* paste or dough.

pasteboard ▻ *noun* stiff board built up from thin sheets of paper glued or pasted together.

pastel /ˈpastəl, paˈstɛl/ ▻ *noun* **1** a chalk-like crayon made from ground pigment. **2** a picture drawn with pastels. ▻ *adj* **1** said of colours: delicately pale; soft, quiet.

2 drawn with pastels. ⓔ 17c: French, from Italian *pastello*, from Latin *pastillus* a ball or cake of something, from *pasta* PASTE.

pastern /ˈpastən/ ▷ *noun* the part of a horse's foot between the hoof and the fetlock. ⓔ 16c in this sense; 14c meaning 'a shackle or tether used when putting horses out to feed': from French *pasturon*, from *pasture* pasture or tether.

paste-up ▷ *noun* (***paste-ups***) a set of text, illustrations, etc mounted on a board, prepared for copying or photographing. See also PASTE SOMETHING UP at PASTE.

pasteurization or **pasteurisation** ▷ *noun* the partial sterilization of a food, especially milk, by heating it to a specific temperature for a short period before rapidly cooling it. ⓔ 1880s: named after Louis Pasteur (1822–95), French chemist and bacteriologist.

pasteurize or **pasteurise** /ˈpɑːstjʊraɪz, ˈpast-, -stəraɪz/ ▷ *verb* (***pasteurized, pasteurizing***) to subject (food, especially milk) to the process of pasteurization. • **pasteurizer** *noun* a machine for pasteurizing milk, etc.

pastiche /paˈstiːʃ/ ▷ *noun* a musical, artistic or literary work in someone else's style, or in a mixture of styles. ⓔ 19c: French, from Italian *pasticcio* a pasty or pie with a variety of ingredients.

pastier, pastiest see under PASTY[2]

pastille /ˈpastɪl, paˈstiːl/ ▷ *noun* **1** a small fruit-flavoured sweet, sometimes medicated ▫ *fruit pastille.* **2** a cone of fragrant paste, burned as incense, for scenting a room. ⓔ 17c: French, from Latin *pastillus* a ball or cake of something.

pastime /ˈpɑːstaɪm/ ▷ *noun* a spare-time pursuit; a hobby. ⓔ 15c: from PASS + TIME.

pastiness see under PASTY[2]

pasting /ˈpeɪstɪŋ/ ▷ *noun, colloq* a thrashing.

pastis /paˈstiːs/ ▷ *noun* (***pastises***) an alcoholic drink flavoured with anise. ⓔ 1920s: French.

past master ▷ *noun* **1** an expert; someone who is thoroughly proficient. **2** someone who has held the office of master, eg among the freemasons. ⓔ 18c.

pastor /ˈpɑːstə(r)/ ▷ *noun* a member of the clergy, especially in churches other than Anglican and Catholic, with responsibility for a congregation. ⓔ 14c: Latin, meaning 'shepherd', from *pascere* to feed.

pastoral /ˈpɑːstərəl/ ▷ *adj* **1 a** relating to the countryside or country life; **b** said of a poem, painting, musical work, etc: depicting the countryside or country life, especially expressing nostalgia for an idealized simple rural existence. **2** relating to a member of the clergy or their work. **3** relating to a shepherd or their work. **4** said of land: used for pasture. ▷ *noun* **1** a pastoral poem or painting. **2** *music* a PASTORALE. **3 a** a letter from a bishop to the clergy and people of the diocese; **b** a letter from a pastor to the people of their diocese. ⓔ 15c: from Latin *pastor, pastoris* shepherd.

pastoral care ▷ *noun* help, advice and moral guidance offered by a clergyman or other spiritual advisor to a group, such as the children in a school, members of the armed forces, a church congregation, etc.

pastorale /pastəˈrɑːl/ ▷ *noun, music* a musical work that evokes the countryside; a pastoral. ⓔ 18c: Italian, meaning 'pastoral'.

pastoralism /ˈpɑːstərəlɪzəm/ ▷ *noun, anthropol* a way of life characterized by keeping herds of animals, such as cattle, sheep, camels, reindeer, goats and llamas, which is common in dry, mountainous or severely cold climates not suitable for agriculture.

pastorate /ˈpɑːstərɪt/ ▷ *noun* **1** the office, authority or residence of a pastor. **2** a body of pastors.

past participle see under PARTICIPLE

past perfect see under PERFECT

pastrami /pəˈstrɑːmɪ/ ▷ *noun* (***pastramis***) a smoked highly-seasoned cut of beef, especially a shoulder. ⓔ 1930s: from Yiddish *pastrame*, from Rumanian *pastrama* pressed cured meat.

pastry /ˈpeɪstrɪ/ ▷ *noun* (***pastries***) **1** dough made with flour, fat and water, used for piecrusts. **2** a sweet baked article made with this; a pie, tart, etc. ⓔ 16c: from PASTE.

pasturage /ˈpɑːstʃərɪdʒ/ ▷ *noun* **1** an area of land where livestock is allowed to graze. **2** grass for feeding.

pasture /ˈpɑːstʃə(r), ˈpɑːstjʊə(r)/ ▷ *noun* an area of grassland suitable or used for the grazing of livestock. Also called **pastureland**. ▷ *verb* (***pastured, pasturing***) **1** to put (animals) in pasture to graze. **2** *intr* said of animals: to graze. • **pasturable** *adj* suitable for pasture. • **pastural** *adj*. • **pastureless** *adj*. ⓔ 14c: French, from Latin *pastura*, from *pascere* to feed.

pasty[1] /ˈpastɪ, ˈpɑːstɪ/ ▷ *noun* (***pasties***) a pie consisting of pastry folded round a savoury or sweet filling ▫ *Cornish pasty.* ⓔ 13c: from French *pastée*, from *pasta* PASTE.

pasty[2] /ˈpeɪstɪ/ ▷ *adj* (***pastier, pastiest***) **1** like a paste in texture. **2** said of the complexion: unhealthily pale. • **pastiness** *noun*. ⓔ 17c: from PASTE.

pasty-faced ▷ *adj* pale and dull of complexion.

pat ▷ *verb* (***patted, patting***) **1** to strike (a person or animal) lightly or affectionately with the palm of one's hand. **2** to shape something by striking it lightly with the palm or a flat instrument ▫ *pat it into shape.* ▷ *noun* **1** a light blow, especially an affectionate one, with the palm of the hand. **2** a round flat mass. ▷ *adverb* especially of things said: immediately and fluently, as if memorized ▫ *Their answers came too pat.* ▷ *adj* said of answers, etc: quickly and easily supplied. • **have** or **know something off pat** to have memorized it and know it perfectly. • **a pat on the back** an approving word or gesture. • **pat someone on the back** to congratulate them approvingly. • **stand pat** *N Amer* **1** to stand firmly by one's opinion, decision, etc. **2** *poker* to decide to play one's hand as it is. ⓔ 14c: probably imitating the sound it makes.

pat. ▷ *abbreviation* **1** patent. **2** patented.

patch ▷ *noun* **1** a piece of material sewn on or applied, eg to a garment or piece of fabric, etc, so as to cover a hole or reinforce a worn area. **2** a plot of earth ▫ *a vegetable patch.* **3** a pad or cover worn as protection over an injured eye. **4** a small expanse contrasting with its surroundings ▫ *patches of ice.* **5** *historical* a tiny piece of black silk worn on the face in imitation of a mole or beauty spot, to enhance the whiteness of the complexion. **6** a scrap or shred. **7** *colloq* a phase or period of time ▫ *go through a bad patch.* **8** *slang* the area patrolled by a policeman or covered by a particular police station. **9** *computing* a set of instructions added to a program to correct an error. ▷ *verb* (***patched, patching***) **1** to mend (a hole or garment) by sewing a patch or patches on or over it ▫ *patch the arm with an oval of leather.* **2** (*also* **patch something up**) to repair it hastily and temporarily ▫ *patch up the leaking pipe.* See also PATCH-UP. **3** *computing* to make a temporary correction in (a program). • **not a patch on someone** or **something** *colloq* not nearly as good as them. ⓔ 14c.

■ **patch something together** to assemble it hastily.

■ **patch something up** *colloq* to settle (a quarrel, etc), especially hurriedly or temporarily.

patchboard ▷ *noun* a panel with multiple electric terminals into which wires may be plugged to form a variety of temporary circuits, used in telephone exchanges, computer systems, etc.

patchily, patchiness see under PATCHY

patchouli /pəˈtʃuːlɪ, ˈpatʃʊlɪ/ ▷ *noun* (***patchoulis*** or ***patchoulies***) a shrubby perennial SE Asian plant that yields an aromatic ESSENTIAL OIL used in perfumery. ◐ 19c: from Tamil *pacculi*.

patch pocket ▷ *noun* a pocket made by sewing a piece of fabric on the outside of a garment.

patch test ▷ *noun* an allergy test in which substances are applied to areas of the skin which are later examined for signs of irritation.

patch-up ▷ *noun* (***patch-ups***) a provisional repair. See also PATCH SOMETHING UP at PATCH.

patchwork ▷ *noun* **1** needlework done by sewing together small pieces of contrastingly patterned fabric to make a larger piece of fabric. **2 a** a piece of work produced in this way, used to make eg cushions; **b** *as adj* □ ***patchwork quilt.*** **3** a variegated expanse □ ***a patchwork of fields.***

patchy /ˈpatʃɪ/ ▷ *adj* (***patchier, patchiest***) **1** forming, or occurring in, patches. **2** covered in patches. **3** uneven or variable in quality □ ***gave a patchy performance.*** • **patchily** *adverb.* • **patchiness** *noun.*

pate /peɪt/ ▷ *noun, old use or facetious* the head or skull, especially when alluding to baldness or intelligence. ◐ 14c.

pâté /ˈpateɪ/ ▷ *noun* a spread made from ground or chopped meat, fish or vegetables blended with herbs, spices, etc. ◐ Early 20c in this sense; 17c, French, meaning 'pie' or 'pasty'.

pâté de foie gras see under FOIE GRAS

patella /pəˈtɛlə/ ▷ *noun* (***patellae*** /-ˈtɛliː/ or ***patellas***) **1** *anatomy* the KNEECAP. **2** *archaeol* a little pan. ◐ 17c: Latin diminutive of *patina* a PATEN or small dish.

paten /ˈpatən/ ▷ *noun, relig* a circular metal plate, often of silver or gold, on which the bread is placed in the celebration of the Eucharist. ◐ 13c: French, from Latin *patina* a wide flat plate or dish.

patent /ˈpeɪtənt, ˈpatənt/ ▷ *noun* **1** an official licence from the government granting a person or business the sole right, for a certain period, to make and sell a particular article. **2** the right so granted. **3** the invention so protected. ▷ *verb* (***patented, patenting***) to obtain a patent for (an invention, design, etc). ▷ *adj* **1** very evident □ ***a patent violation of the law.*** **2** concerned with the granting of, or protection by, patents. **3** said of a product: made or protected under patent. **4** *colloq* ingenious; infallible; original. **5** open for inspection □ ***letters patent.*** • **patentable** *adj.* • **patently** /ˈpeɪtəntlɪ/ *adverb* openly; clearly □ ***patently obvious.*** ◐ 14c: from Latin *patens, patentis* lying open, from *patere* to lie open.

patent agent ▷ *noun* a person or organization that obtains patents on behalf of inventors, etc.

patentee /peɪtənˈtiː/ ▷ *noun* (***patentees***) the person obtaining or holding a patent.

patent leather ▷ *noun* leather made glossy by varnishing. ◐ 1920s.

patent medicine ▷ *noun* **1** *technical* a patented medicine which is available without prescription. **2** *colloq* any proprietary medicine, especially one claimed as an infallible cure.

Patent Office ▷ *noun* a government department that issues patents.

patentor /peɪtənˈtɔː/ ▷ *noun* a person, organization, authority, etc that grants patents.

patent right ▷ *noun* the exclusive right reserved by a patent.

patent rolls ▷ *plural noun* in Britain: the register of patents issued.

pater /ˈpeɪtə(r)/ ▷ *noun, old use or facetious* father. ◐ 14c: Latin.

paterfamilias /peɪtəfəˈmɪlɪas, pa-/ ▷ *noun* (***patresfamilias*** /peɪtreɪs-, patreɪz-/) the father as head of the household. ◐ 15c: Latin, from *pater* father + *familias* of a household; compare FAMILY.

paternal /pəˈtɜːnəl/ ▷ *adj* **1** referring, relating, or appropriate to a father □ ***paternal instincts.*** **2** said of a relation or ancestor: related on one's father's side □ ***paternal grandmother.*** Compare MATERNAL. • **paternally** *adverb.* ◐ 17c: from Latin *paternalis*, from *pater* father.

paternalism ▷ *noun* governmental or managerial benevolence towards its citizens, employees, etc taken to the extreme of overprotectiveness and authoritarianism. • **paternalistic** *adj.* • **paternalistically** *adverb.* ◐ 19c.

paternity /pəˈtɜːnɪtɪ/ ▷ *noun* **1** the quality or condition of being a father; fatherhood. **2** the relation of a father to his children. **3** the authorship, source or origin of something. ◐ 16c: from Latin *paternitas*, from *pater* father.

paternity leave ▷ *noun* leave of absence from an employer often granted to a father-to-be or father so that he can be with his wife or partner and assist her during and after the birth of a child. It is usually for around five to ten days where a formal agreement exists.

paternity suit ▷ *noun* a lawsuit brought by the mother of a child to establish that a certain man is the father of her child and therefore liable for its financial support.

paternoster /patəˈnɒstə(r)/ ▷ *noun, Christianity* **1** see THE LORD'S PRAYER. **2** every tenth bead in a rosary, which is larger than the rest and at which the Lord's Prayer is repeated. ◐ Anglo-Saxon: from Latin *Pater noster* Our Father, the first words of the Lord's Prayer.

Paterson's curse /ˈpatəsənz —/ ▷ *noun, Austral* any of various naturalized, originally European, herbs regarded as harmful to livestock. ◐ Early 20c: referring to an Australian family from whose garden in New South Wales a blue-flowered weed is said to have spread.

path /pɑːθ/ ▷ *noun* (***paths*** /pɑːðz/) **1** (*also* **pathway**) a track trodden by, or specially surfaced for, walking. **2** the line along which something is travelling □ ***the path of Jupiter.*** **3** a course of action □ ***the path to ruin.*** **4** *computing* the location of a file in terms of a computer's disk drives and directory structure. • **beat a path to someone's door** to visit them very often or in very large numbers. ◐ Anglo-Saxon *pæth*.

path. see PATHOL.

path- see PATHO-

-path /paθ/ ▷ *combining form, forming nouns, denoting* **1** a sufferer from a particular disorder □ ***psychopath.*** **2** a practitioner of a particular therapy □ ***homoeopath*** □ ***osteopath.*** ◐ From Greek *pathos* experience or suffering.

Pathan /pəˈtɑːn, pʌˈtɑːn/ ▷ *noun* **1** a member of the PASHTO-speaking people of SE Afghanistan and NW Pakistan. **2** one of the official languages of Afghanistan, also spoken in NW Pakistan, an Iranian language of the Indo-European family. **3** a native speaker of this language. ◐ 17c: Hindi, from Pashto *Pakhtun*.

pathetic /pəˈθɛtɪk/ ▷ *adj* **1** moving one to pity; touching, heart-rending, poignant or pitiful □ ***her pathetic sobs.*** **2** *derog, colloq* hopelessly inadequate □ ***a pathetic attempt.*** • **pathetically** *adverb.* ◐ 16c: from Greek *pathetikos* sensitive.

pathetic fallacy ▷ *noun* in literature: the transference of human feelings, etc to inanimate things, as in *a frowning landscape*.

pathfinder ▷ *noun* **1** an explorer who finds routes through unexplored territory; a pioneer. **2** someone who devises new methods of doing things. **3** a radar device used to aid the navigation of aircraft, or to guide missiles into a target area.

-pathic /paθɪk/ ▷ *combining form* forming adjectives corresponding to nouns in -PATHY.

patho- /paθoʊ, pə'θɒ/ or (before a vowel) **path-** *combining form, denoting* disease □ ***pathology***. ⓒ From Greek *pathos* experience or suffering.

pathogen /'paθədʒen/ ▷ *noun, pathol* any micro-organism, especially a bacterium or virus, that causes disease in a living organism. • **pathogenic** *adj*. • **pathogenicity** /-dʒə'nɪsɪtɪ/ *noun*. ⓒ Late 19c: PATHO- + -GEN.

pathogenesis and **pathogeny** /pə'θɒdʒənɪ/ ▷ *noun* the development of a disease or disorder, mainly as observed at the biochemical or cellular level. ⓒ 19c.

pathol. or **path.** ▷ *abbreviation* **1** pathology. **2** pathological.

pathological /paθə'lɒdʒɪkəl/ ▷ *adj* **1** relating to pathology. **2** caused by, or relating to, illness. **3** *colloq* compulsive; habitual □ ***a pathological liar***. • **pathologically** *adverb*.

pathologist /pə'θɒlədʒɪst/ ▷ *noun* a scientist who specializes in pathology, one of whose duties is usually to carry out postmortems.

pathology /pə'θɒlədʒɪ/ ▷ *noun* (***pathologies***) **1** the branch of medicine concerned with the study of the nature of diseases. **2** the manifestations, characteristic behaviour, etc of a disease. ⓒ 17c.

pathos /'peɪθɒs/ ▷ *noun* a quality in a situation, etc, especially in literature, that moves one to pity. ⓒ 17c: Greek, meaning 'feeling' or 'suffering'.

> ***pathos***
>
> A word sometimes confused with this one is **bathos**.

pathway ▷ *noun* **1** a PATH *sense* 1. **2** in neurology: a network of nerves linking specific organs. **3** in biochemistry: a network of components involved in physiological processes, especially those involving ENZYMES.

-pathy /pəθɪ/ ▷ *combining form, forming nouns, denoting* **1** feeling □ ***telepathy***. **2** disease or disorder □ ***psychopathy***. **3** a method of treating disease □ ***homoeopathy***. ⓒ From Greek *pathos* suffering.

patience /'peɪʃəns/ ▷ *noun* **1** the ability to endure delay, trouble, pain or hardship in a calm and contained way. **2** tolerance and forbearance. **3** perseverance. **4** *cards* a solo game in which the player, in turning each card over, has to fit it into a certain scheme. Also (*US*) called **solitaire**. ⓒ 13c: French, from Latin *patiens*, from *patientem* suffering.

patient /'peɪʃənt/ ▷ *adj* having or showing patience. ▷ *noun* a person who is being treated by, or is registered with, a doctor, dentist, etc. • **patiently** *adverb* in a patient way; with patience. ⓒ 14c.

patina /'patɪnə/ ▷ *noun* (***patinas***) **1** a coating formed on a metal surface by oxidation, especially the greenish coating of verdigris on bronze or copper. **2** a mature shine on wood resulting from continual polishing and handling. **3** any fine finish acquired with age. **4** *archaeol* a surface appearance that develops with prolonged exposure or burial. • **patinated** /-neɪtɪd/ *adj*. • **patination** *noun*. ⓒ 18c: Italian, meaning 'coating', from Latin meaning 'shallow dish'.

patio /'patɪoʊ/ ▷ *noun* (***patios***) **1** an open paved area beside a house. **2** an inner courtyard in a Spanish or Spanish-American house. ⓒ Early 19c: Spanish.

patisserie /pə'tiːsəriː/ ▷ *noun* (***patisseries***) **1** a shop or café selling fancy cakes, sweet pastries, etc in the continental style. **2** such cakes. ⓒ 18c: from French *pâtisserie*, from Latin *pasta* dough.

Patna rice /'patnə —/ ▷ *noun* a long-grained rice, originally grown at Patna in India, served with savoury dishes.

patois /'patwɑː/ ▷ *noun* (***patois***) **1** the local dialect of a region, used usually in informal everyday situations, as opposed to the language used in literature, education, etc. **2** jargon. ⓒ 17c: French.

pat. pend. ▷ *abbreviation* patent pending.

patresfamilias *plural of* PATERFAMILIAS

patri- /patrɪ/ ▷ *combining form, denoting* **1** a father or fathers □ ***patricide***. **2** a man or men □ ***patriarchal***. Compare MATRI-. ⓒ From Latin *pater, patris* father.

patrial /'peɪtrɪəl, 'pat-/ ▷ *noun, formerly* someone who, being a citizen of the UK, a British colony or the British Commonwealth, or the child or grandchild of someone born in the UK, has a legal right to live in the UK. • **patriality** *noun*. ⓒ 1970s in this sense, this right having been introduced by the Immigration Act 1971, but removed by the British Nationality Act 1981: from Latin *patria* fatherland.

patriarch /'peɪtrɪɑːk/ ▷ *noun* **1** the male head of a family or tribe. Compare MATRIARCH sense 1. **2** in the Eastern Orthodox Church: a high-ranking bishop. **3** in the RC Church: the pope. **4** in the Old Testament: any of the ancestors of the human race or of the tribes of Israel, eg Adam, Abraham or Jacob. **5** a venerable old man, especially the senior member of a community or group. ⓒ 13c: from Greek *patriarches* a senior bishop, or the father of a family.

patriarchal /peɪtrɪ'ɑːkəl/ ▷ *adj* **1** referring to the nature of a patriarch. **2** like a patriarch. **3** belonging to or subject to a patriarch. • **patriarchally** *adverb*.

patriarchal cross ▷ *noun* a cross with two horizontal bars, the upper one shorter than the lower one.

patriarchal society ▷ *noun* a society governed by a patriarch or patriarchs.

patriarchate /'peɪtrɪɑːkɪt/ ▷ *noun* the office, authority, or residence of a church patriarch.

patriarchy /'peɪtrɪɑːkɪ, 'patrɪ-/ ▷ *noun* (***patriarchies***) **1** a social system in which a male is head of the family and descent is traced through the male line. **2** a society based on this system. Compare MATRIARCHY.

patrician /pə'trɪʃən/ ▷ *noun* **1** *historical* a member of the aristocracy of ancient Rome. Compare PLEBEIAN (sense 1).**2** *historical* an aristocrat in certain medieval European provinces or cities. **3** an aristocrat. **4** someone who is thought of as refined and sophisticated. ▷ *adj* **1** belonging or relating to the aristocracy, especially that of ancient Rome. **2** refined and sophisticated. ⓒ 15c: from Latin *patricius* having a noble father, from *pater* father.

patricide /'patrɪsaɪd, 'peɪtrɪ-/ ▷ *noun* **1** the act of killing one's own father. **2** someone who commits this act. • **patricidal** *adj*. ⓒ 16c: a variant of earlier PARRICIDE, influenced by Latin *pater* father.

patrilineal /patrɪ'lɪnɪəl/ or **patrilinear** /-ɪə(r)/ ▷ *adj, anthropol* denoting descent or kinship reckoned through the father, or through males alone. Compare MATRILINEAL.

patrimony /'patrɪmənɪ/ ▷ *noun* (***patrimonies***) **1** property inherited from one's father or ancestors. **2** something inherited; a heritage. **3** a church estate or revenue. • **patrimonial** /-'moʊnɪəl/ *adj*. • **patrimonially** *adverb*. ⓒ 14c: from Latin *patrimonium*, from *pater* father.

patriot /'peɪtrɪət, 'pa-/ ▷ *noun* someone who loves and serves their fatherland or country devotedly. • **patriotic** /-'ɒtɪk/ *adj*. • **patriotically** *adverb*. ⓒ 16c: from Greek *patriotes* fellow-countryman.

patriotism ▷ *noun* loyalty and devotion to one's country.

patristic /pə'trɪstɪk/ ▷ *adj* referring or relating to the Fathers of the Christian Church. ⓒ 19c: from Greek *pater* father.

patrol /pə'troʊl/ ▷ *verb* (***patrolled, patrolling***) **1** *tr & intr* to make a regular systematic tour of (an area) to maintain security or surveillance. **2** *intr* said of a police officer: to be on duty on a beat. ▷ *noun* **1** the act of patrolling □ *on* *patrol.* **2** a person or group of people performing this duty. **3** a body of aircraft, ships, etc carrying out this duty. **4** any of the units of six or so into which a troop of Scouts or Guides is divided. • **patroller** *noun.* ⓒ 17c: from French *patrouiller.*

patrol car ▷ *noun* a police car equipped with a radio, etc, used to patrol streets and motorways.

patrolman and **patrolwoman** ▷ *noun* **1** *N Amer* the lowest-ranking police officer; a police officer on the beat. **2** someone employed by a motoring organization to patrol a certain area and help motorists in difficulty.

patron /'peɪtrən/ ▷ *noun* **1** someone who gives financial support and encouragement eg to an artist, the arts, a movement or charity □ ***a patron of the arts.*** **2** a regular customer of a shop, attender at a theatre, etc. **3** *C of E* someone who has the right to appoint to any office, especially to a living in the church. **4** a PATRON SAINT. • **patronal** /pə'troʊnəl/ *adj.* • **patronly** *adverb.* ⓒ 14c in the sense 'protector': from Latin *patronus* protector.

patronage /'patrənɪdʒ/ ▷ *noun* **1** the support given by a patron. **2** regular custom given to a shop, theatre, etc. **3** the power of bestowing, or recommending people for, offices.

patroness /'peɪtrənəs/ ▷ *noun, old use* a woman PATRON (senses 1 and 2). See note at AUTHORESS.

patronize or **patronise** /'patrənaɪz; *N Amer* 'peɪtrənaɪz/ ▷ *verb* (***patronized, patronizing***) **1** to treat someone condescendingly, or with benevolent superiority, especially inappropriately. **2** to act as a patron towards (an organization, individual, etc). **3** to give custom, especially regularly, to (a shop, theatre, restaurant, etc). • **patronizing** *adj.* • **patronizingly** *adverb.* ⓒ 16c in sense 2; late 18c in sense 1.

patron saint ▷ *noun* the guardian saint of a country, profession, craft, etc.

patronymic /patrə'nɪmɪk/ ▷ *noun* a name derived from one's father's or other male ancestor's name, usually with a suffix or prefix, as in *Donaldson* or *Macdonald*, or the Russian *Davidovich* or *Davidovna.* Compare MATRONYMIC. ⓒ 17c: from Greek *pater* father + *onyma* name.

patsy /'patsɪ/ ▷ *noun* (***patsies***) *slang, chiefly N Amer* an easy victim; a sucker; a scapegoat or fall guy. ⓒ Early 20c.

patten /'patən/ ▷ *noun, historical* an overshoe with a wooden or metal mount to raise the wearer above mud or water. ⓒ 14c: from French *patin* clog.

patter[1] /'patə(r)/ ▷ *verb* (***pattered, pattering***) *intr* **1** said of rain, footsteps, etc: to make a light rapid tapping noise. **2** to move with light rapid footsteps. ▷ *noun* the light rapid tapping of footsteps or rain □ ***heard the patter of tiny feet.*** ⓒ 17c: frequentative of PAT.

patter[2] /'patə(r)/ ▷ *noun* **1** the fast persuasive talk of a salesman, or the quick speech of a comedian. **2** the jargon or speech of a particular group or area □ ***Glasgow patter.*** ▷ *verb* (***pattered, pattering***) *tr & intr* to say or speak rapidly or glibly. ⓒ 14c: from PATERNOSTER, because of the fast mumbling style in which this prayer and others were recited.

pattern /'patən/ ▷ *noun* **1** a model, guide or set of instructions for making something □ ***a dress pattern.*** **2** a decorative design, often consisting of repeated motifs, eg on wallpaper or fabric. **3** a piece, eg of fabric, as a sample. **4** any excellent example suitable for imitation. **5** a coherent series of occurrences or set of features □ ***a pattern of events.*** ▷ *verb* (***patterned, patterning***) (*usually* **pattern something on another thing**) to model it on another type, design, etc. ⓒ 14c as *patron*; French, from Latin *patronus* example or defender.

patterned ▷ *adj* said of a fabric, etc: having a decorative design; not plain.

pattern race ▷ *noun* a horse race open to all comers in a particular category, eg of a certain age or weight, usually contested by top-class horses, with the purpose of finding the best.

patty /'patɪ/ ▷ *noun* (***patties***) **1** *N Amer* a flat round cake of minced meat, vegetables, etc. **2** a small meat pie. ⓒ 18c in sense 2: from French *pâté* PASTY 1.

pauciloquent /pɔː'sɪləkwənt/ ▷ *adj* speaking little, using few words, etc. ⓒ 17c: from Latin *paucus* a little + *loqui* to speak.

paucity /'pɔːsɪtɪ/ ▷ *noun* (***paucities***) smallness of quantity; fewness; a scarcity or lack; dearth. ⓒ 15c: from Latin *pauci* few.

Pauline /'pɔːlaɪn/ ▷ *adj* referring to the apostle St Paul. ▷ *noun* a member of any religious order named after him. ⓒ 14c as *noun*: from Latin adjective *Paulinus.*

paunch /pɔːntʃ/ ▷ *noun* (***paunches***) **1** a protruding belly, especially in a man. **2** the first and largest stomach of a ruminant. **3** *naut* a rope mat to prevent chafing. • **paunchiness** *noun.* • **paunchy** *adj* (***paunchier, paunchiest***). ⓒ 14c: from French *panche.*

pauper /'pɔːpə(r)/ ▷ *noun* **1** a poverty-stricken person. **2** *historical* someone living on charity or publicly provided money. • **pauperism** *noun* **1** the condition of paupers. **2** the existence of a pauper class. • **pauperize** or **pauperise** *verb* (***pauperized, pauperizing***) to make someone a pauper. • **pauperization** *noun.* ⓒ 16c: Latin, meaning 'poor'.

pause /pɔːz/ ▷ *noun* **1** a relatively short break in some activity, etc. **2** *music* **a** the prolonging of a note or rest beyond its normal duration; **b** a sign indicating this 𝄐, usually placed above the note, etc. Also called FERMATA. **3** said of a computer package, particularly a computer game: the command which causes the current operation to stop. ▷ *verb* (***paused, pausing***) *intr* **1** to have a break; to stop briefly □ ***paused for a few minutes before continuing his writing.*** **2** to hesitate □ ***paused before answering.*** • **give someone pause** to make them hesitate before acting. • **pauseless** *adj.* • **pauser** *noun.* • **pausing** *noun, adj.* ⓒ 15c: from Latin *pausa*, from Greek *pausis*, from *pauein* to make something cease.

pause button ▷ *noun* on a CD or tape machine, etc: the button which stops the running of the machine, ready to continue when it is pressed again.

pavan or **pavane** /'pavən, pə'vɑːn/ ▷ *noun* **1** a slow and sombre stately 16c and 17c dance. **2** a piece of music for this dance, in 4-4 time. ⓒ 16c: from Spanish or Italian *pavana*, from Spanish *pavo* peacock, or from Italian *Padovana* Paduan, or dance of Padua.

pave ▷ *verb* (***paved, paving***) to surface (especially a footpath, but also a street, etc) with stone slabs, cobbles, etc. • **paved** *adj.* • **pave the way for something** or **someone** to prepare for and make way for its introduction or development, or for their arrival. ⓒ 14c: from Latin *pavire* to ram or tread down.

pavement /'peɪvmənt/ ▷ *noun* **1** a raised footpath edging a road, etc, often but not always paved. *N Amer equivalent* SIDEWALK. **2** a paved road, area, expanse, etc □ ***a mosaic pavement.*** **3** a road surface; road-surfacing material. ⓒ 13c: French, from Latin *pavimentum* hard floor.

pavement artist ▷ *noun* **1** an artist who draws sketches and coloured pictures on a pavement, especially in order to receive money from passers-by. **2** an artist who sells pictures displayed on a pavement. ⓒ Late 19c.

pavement light ▷ *noun* a window of glass blocks in the pavement to light a cellar.

pavilion /pə'vɪlɪən/ ▷ *noun* **1** a building in a sports ground in which players change their clothes, store equipment, etc. **2** a light temporary building such as a marquee, in which to display exhibits at a trade fair, etc. **3** a summerhouse or ornamental shelter. **4** a large ornamental building for public pleasure and entertainment. **5** a large and elaborate tent. ◷ 13c: from French *pavillon*, from Latin *papilio* butterfly, later a tent.

paving /ˈpeɪvɪŋ/ ▷ *noun* **1** stones or slabs used to pave a surface. **2** a paved surface.

paving-stone ▷ *noun* a large flat regular-shaped stone used for paving.

pavlova /pavˈloʊvə/ ▷ *noun* (*pavlovas*) a dessert consisting of meringue topped with fruit and whipped cream. ◷ 1920s: named after Anna Pavlova (1885–1931), a Russian ballerina.

Pavlovian /pavˈloʊvɪən/ ▷ *adj, psychol, physiol* **1** relating to the work of the Russian physiologist, Ivan Pavlov (1849–1936), on conditioned reflexes. **2** said of reactions, responses, etc: automatic; unthinking. ◷ 1930s.

paw ▷ *noun* **1** the foot, usually clawed, of a four-legged mammal. **2** *colloq* a hand, especially when used clumsily. See also SOUTHPAW. ▷ *verb* (*pawed, pawing*) **1** to finger or handle something clumsily; to touch or caress someone with unwelcome familiarity. **2** (*also* **paw at something**) said of an animal: to scrape or strike it with a paw. ◷ 13c: from French *poue*.

pawky /pɔːkɪ/ ▷ *adj* (*pawkier, pawkiest*) *Scots or dialect* drily witty. ◷ 17c: from Scots *pawk* a trick.

pawl /pɔːl/ ▷ *noun, engineering* a catch that engages with the teeth of a ratchet wheel to limit its movement to one direction only. ◷ 17c.

pawn[1] ▷ *verb* (*pawned, pawning*) **1** to deposit (an article of value) with a pawnbroker as a pledge for a sum of money borrowed. **2** to pledge or stake something. ▷ *noun* **1** the condition of being deposited as a pledge □ *in pawn* □ *at pawn*. **2** an article pledged in this way. ◷ 15c: from French *pan* pledge or surety.

pawn[2] ▷ *noun* **1** *chess* (symbol **P**) a chess piece of lowest value. **2** a person used and manipulated by others. ◷ 14c: from French *poun*, from Latin *pedones* infantry.

pawnbroker /ˈpɔːnbroʊkə(r)/ and **pawnee** /pɔːˈniː/ ▷ *noun* someone who lends money in exchange for pawned articles. • **pawnbroking** *noun*. ◷ 17c.

pawner /ˈpɔːnə(r)/ ▷ *noun* someone who deposits something in pawn, especially with a pawnbroker, as a security for money borrowed.

pawnshop ▷ *noun* a pawnbroker's place of business.

pawpaw see under PAPAW, PAPAYA

pax ▷ *noun* (*paxes*) *formal church use* the kiss of peace, usually uttered as a greeting during the Eucharist. ▷ *exclamation, dated colloq* truce! let's call a truce! • **pax vobiscum** /paks vɒˈbɪskəm/ peace be with you. ◷ 15c: Latin, meaning 'peace'.

pay[1] ▷ *verb* (*pays, paid, paying*) **1** *tr & intr* to give (money) to someone in exchange for goods, services, etc □ *I paid him £10 for the books.* **2** *tr & intr* to settle (a bill, debt, etc). **3** *tr & intr* to give (wages or salary) to an employee. **4** *tr & intr* to make a profit, or make something as profit □ *businesses that don't pay* □ *an investment that pays £500 per annum.* **5** *tr & intr* to benefit; to be worthwhile □ *It pays one to be polite* □ *Dishonesty doesn't pay.* **6** *tr & intr* (*also* **pay for something**) to suffer a penalty on account of it; to be punished for it □ *pay dearly for one's crimes* □ *paid with his life.* **7 a** to do someone the honour of (a visit or call) □ *paid her a visit in hospital*; **b** to offer someone (a compliment, one's respects, etc) □ *paid him a compliment on his new haircut.* **8** to give (heed or attention). ▷ *noun* money given or received for work, etc; wages; salary. • **in the pay of someone** employed by them, especially for a secret or dishonest purpose. • **pay one's addresses to someone** *formal or old-fashioned* said of a man: to court (a woman). • **pay one's way** to pay all of one's own debts and living expenses. • **pay its way** to compensate adequately for initial outlay. • **put paid to something** or **someone** *colloq* to put an end to them; to deal effectively or finally with them. • **pay the piper** to bear the expense of something and therefore have control of it, ie CALL THE TUNE (see under CALL). • **pay through the nose** to pay a very high price □ *paid through the nose for the coach tour.* ◷ 13c: from French *paie*, from Latin *pacare* to pacify, settle (a debt).

■ **pay someone back** to revenge oneself on them.

■ **pay something back** to return (money owed).

■ **pay something down** to pay (eg a first instalment) in cash immediately.

■ **pay something in** to put (money, etc) into a bank account.

■ **pay off** to have profitable results.

■ **pay someone off** to make them redundant with a final payment.

■ **pay something off** to finish paying (a debt, etc). See also PAY-OFF.

■ **pay something out 1** to spend or give (money), eg to pay bills, debts, etc. **2** to release or slacken (a rope, etc) especially by passing it little by little through one's hands.

■ **pay up** *colloq* to pay the full amount that is due, especially reluctantly. See also PAID-UP.

pay[2] ▷ *verb* (*pays, payed, paying*) *naut* to smear (a wooden boat) with tar, etc as waterproofing. ◷ 17c: from French *peier*, from Latin *picare*, from *pic-*, *pix* pitch.

payable ▷ *adj* **1** that can or must be paid □ *Make cheques payable to me* □ *payable by 1 July.* **2** capable of being profitable.

pay-and-display ▷ *adj* referring to a system of paying for parking in a car park or on a street, in which a ticket is obtained from a nearby machine and displayed in the window of the car □ *pay-and-display ticket machine.* Compare PARKING METER.

pay-as-you-earn ▷ *noun* (abbreviation **PAYE**) in Britain and New Zealand: a method of collecting income tax from employees by deducting it from the wages or salary due to be paid to them.

pay-as-you-view see PAY-PER-VIEW

pay bed see PRIVATE PAY BED

pay day ▷ *noun* the day when wages or salaries are regularly paid.

pay dirt and **pay gravel** ▷ *noun* gravel or sand containing enough gold to be worth working. ◷ 19c.

payee /peɪˈiː/ ▷ *noun* (*payees*) someone to whom money is paid or a cheque is made out.

payer ▷ *noun* someone who pays for something.

paying guest ▷ *noun, euphemistic* a lodger.

payload ▷ *noun* **1** the part of a vehicle's load which earns revenue. **2** the operating equipment carried by a spaceship or satellite. **3** the quantity and strength of the explosive carried by a missile. **4** the quantity of goods, passengers, etc carried by an aircraft. ◷ 1930s.

paymaster ▷ *noun* an official in charge of the payment of wages and salaries.

payment ▷ *noun* **1** a sum of money paid. **2** the act of paying or process of being paid. **3** a reward or punishment. ◷ 14c.

pay-off ▷ *noun* (*pay-offs*) *colloq* **1** a fruitful result; a good return. **2** a bribe. **3** a final settling of accounts. **4** a climax, outcome or final resolution. See also PAY OFF, etc under PAY[1].

payola /peɪˈoʊlə/ ▷ *noun* (*payolas*) **1** a bribe for promoting a product, given to someone, eg a disc jockey, in a position to do this. **2** the practice of giving or receiving such bribes. ⓔ 1930s: from PAY[1], modelled on PIANOLA.

pay packet ▻ *noun* **1** an envelope or packet containing an employee's weekly wages. **2** the contents of this.

pay-per-view or **pay-as-you-view** ▻ *adj* said of satellite TV, cable TV, etc: **1** referring or relating to PAY TV. **2** referring or relating to a particular programme watched by such subscription.

payphone ▻ *noun* a telephone in a pub, restaurant, etc, or on the street, at a railway station, etc, that is operated by coins, a phonecard or credit card.

payroll ▻ *noun* **1** a register of employees that lists the wage or salary due to each. **2** the total amount of money required for employees' wages or salaries.

payroll giving ▻ *noun* contributions to charity which are deducted by the employer from an employee's wages and paid directly to the charity concerned.

paysage /'peɪzɑːʒ/ *art* ▻ *noun* a landscape or landscape painting. • **paysagist** /'peɪzɑːʒɪst/ *noun* a landscape painter. ⓔ 17c: French, from *pays* land.

pay slip ▻ *noun* a note of an employee's pay, showing deductions for tax or national insurance, supplied weekly or monthly.

pay TV or **pay television** ▻ *noun* TV programmes, video entertainment, etc distributed to an audience which pays for the programmes viewed by subscribing to a CABLE TV or SATELLITE TV network. Connection to a number of channels, or to an individual programme, is paid for by renting a decoder or using a smart card to unscramble signals received. Also called **subscription TV**.

pazzazz or **pazazz** see PIZZAZZ

Pb ▻ *symbol, chem* lead.

PBX ▻ *abbreviation, telecomm* private branch exchange, a telephone system that routes the internal and external calls of a company or organization. See also PABX.

PC ▻ *abbreviation* **1** personal computer. **2** Police Constable. **3 a** political correctness; **b** politically correct. **4** Privy Councillor.

pc ▻ *abbreviation* **1** per cent. **2** personal computer. **3** *colloq* postcard.

PCAS /'piːkas/ ▻ *abbreviation, formerly* Polytechnics Central Admissions System, an organization which formerly administered entry to polytechnics in the UK, now part of UCAS.

PCB ▻ *abbreviation, computing* printed circuit board.

pcm ▻ *abbreviation* per calendar month.

PCN ▻ *abbreviation* personal communications network, a network for mobile telephone users.

PCP ▻ *abbreviation, trademark* phencyclidine.

pct ▻ *abbreviation, N Amer* per cent.

Pd ▻ *symbol, chem* palladium.

pd ▻ *abbreviation* **1** paid. **2** (*also* **PD**) *physics* potential difference.

Pde ▻ *abbreviation* Parade, as a street name.

PDL ▻ *abbreviation, computing* page description language.

PDQ ▻ *abbreviation, colloq* pretty damn quick, ie as soon as possible.

PDSA ▻ *abbreviation* People's Dispensary for Sick Animals.

PE ▻ *abbreviation* **1** *IVR* Peru. **2** physical education. **3** *physics* potential energy.

pea /piː/ ▻ *noun* (***peas***) **1** an annual climbing plant of the pulse family, cultivated in cool temperate regions for its edible seeds, which are produced in long DEHISCENT pods. **2** the round protein-rich seed of this plant, which can be eaten fresh, or preserved by freezing, canning or drying. See also SPLIT PEAS. ⓔ 17c: a singular form of PEASE, which was spelt *peas* and mistaken for a plural.

peace /piːs/ ▻ *noun* **1** freedom from or absence of war. **2** a treaty or agreement ending a war. **3** freedom from or absence of noise, disturbance or disorder; quietness or calm. **4** freedom from mental agitation; serenity □ *peace of mind.* **5** *in compounds* usually referring to an organization, person, etc: promoting or advocating peace □ *peacemaker* □ *peace-camp* □ *peace activist* □ *peace talks.* • **at peace 1** not at war; not fighting. **2** in harmony or friendship. **3** in a calm or serene state. **4** freed from earthly worries; dead. • **hold one's peace** to remain silent. • **in peace** in a state of enjoying peace. • **keep the peace 1** *law* to preserve law and order. **2** to prevent, or refrain from, fighting or quarrelling. • **make peace** to end a war or quarrel, etc. • **make one's peace with someone** to reconcile or be reconciled with them. ⓔ 13c: from French *pais*, from Latin *pax* peace.

peaceable ▻ *adj* peace-loving; mild; placid. • **peaceably** *adverb*. • **peaceableness** *noun*.

Peace Corps ▻ *noun* a US government agency that sends volunteers to developing countries to help with agricultural, technological and educational projects. Compare VSO.

peace dividend ▻ *noun* money left over from a government's defence budget as a result of negotiated arms-reduction policies, available for non-military use. ⓔ 1980s.

peaceful ▻ *adj* **1** calm and quiet. **2** unworried; serene. **3** free from war, violence, disturbance, disorder, etc. • **peacefully** *adverb*. • **peacefulness** *noun*.

peacekeeper ▻ *noun* **1** an organization or country, etc which sends a peacekeeping force to a particular area. **2** (**peacekeepers**) the members of a peacekeeping force.

peacekeeping force ▻ *noun* a military force sent into a particular area with the task of preventing fighting between opposing factions □ *The UN sent a peacekeeping force to Bosnia in 1992.*

peacemaker ▻ *noun* **1** someone who makes or brings about peace with the enemy. **2** someone who reconciles enemies. • **peacemaking** *noun, adj*.

peace offering ▻ *noun* something offered to end a quarrel, or as an apology. ⓔ 16c: originally referring to an offering presented as a thanksgiving to God, a term of the Levitical law in the English Bible.

peace pipe ▻ *noun* a CALUMET.

peace sign ▻ *noun* a gesture or sign symbolizing victory, made with the index and middle fingers in the form of a V, with the palm turned outwards. See also V-SIGN.

peace studies ▻ *plural noun, education* educational courses designed to explore the role of the military in society, international strategic relationships, and those conditions that most promote peace and human welfare in society.

peace symbol ▻ *noun* the emblem ☮, used by the peace movement to symbolize the desire for world peace. ⓔ 1950s: devised in Britain from the N and the D of *N*uclear *D*isarmament in 1958 for the first ban-the-bomb march at Aldermaston, Berkshire.

peacetime ▻ *noun* periods that are free of war. ⓔ 16c.

peach[1] /piːtʃ/ ▻ *noun* (***peaches***) **1** any of numerous varieties of a small deciduous tree, widely cultivated in warm temperate regions for its edible fruit or for ornament. **2** the large round fruit of this tree, consisting of a hard stone surrounded by sweet juicy yellow flesh and a yellowish-pink velvety skin. **3** the yellowish-pink colour of this fruit. **4** *colloq* something delightful □ *a peach of a day.* **5** *colloq* a lovely young woman. ▻ *adj* peach-coloured □ *a peach blouse.* ⓔ 15c: from French *pesche*, from Latin *persicum malum* Persian apple.

peach² /piːtʃ/ ▻ *verb* (*peaches*, *peached*, *peaching*) (*always* **peach on someone**) *colloq* to betray or inform on them, especially on an accomplice. ⓒ 15c as *pesche* in obsolete sense 'to accuse or impeach', from obsolete *apeche* to hinder.

peach-blow ▻ *noun* **1 a** a purplish-pink colour, the colour of the blossom of the peach tree; **b** *as adj* □ *a peach-blow vase.* **2** a glaze of this colour on porcelain.

peach brandy ▻ *noun* a spirit distilled from the fermented juice of the peach.

peach melba /— 'mɛlbə/ ▻ *noun* (*peach melbas*) **1** a dessert consisting of peach halves, ice cream and raspberry sauce. **2** a flavour of ice cream that resembles this dessert. ⓒ 20c: named after Dame Nellie Melba (1861-1931), Australian operatic soprano.

peachy ▻ *adj* (*peachier*, *peachiest*) **1** coloured like or tasting like a peach. **2** *colloq* very good; excellent.

peacock /'piːkɒk/ ▻ *noun* (*peacock* or *peacocks*) **1** a large bird belonging to the pheasant family, the male of which has a train of green and gold eyespot feathers which it fans showily during courtship. Also called PEAFOWL. **2** the male peafowl (the female being known as the PEAHEN). **3** *derog* a vain person. • **peacockish** or **peacock-like** *adj.* ⓒ 14c: from Anglo-Saxon *pea* (from Latin *pavo* peacock) + COCK¹.

peacock-blue ▻ *adj* having the colour of the rich greenish blue in a peacock's plumage □ *a peacock-blue dress.* Also (**peacock blue**) *as noun.*

peacock butterfly ▻ *noun* a medium-sized butterfly with reddish-brown wings which have prominent eyespots.

peafowl ▻ *noun* a male or female peacock, although PEACOCK is usually used as the generic term. ⓒ 19c: from *peacock* + FOWL.

pea-green ▻ *adj* bright-green or yellowish-green in colour. Also (**pea green**) *as noun.*

peahen ▻ *noun* a female peacock. ⓒ 14c.

pea jacket ▻ *noun* a sailor's overcoat made of coarse woollen material. ⓒ 18c: probably from Dutch *pij-jakker*, from *pij* a type of coarse fabric + *jakker* jacket.

peak¹ ▻ *noun* **1 a** a sharp pointed summit; **b** a pointed mountain or hill. **2 a** a maximum, eg in consumer use □ *Consumption reaches its peak at around 7pm*; **b** *as adj* referring or relating to the period of highest use or demand □ *electricity consumed at peak periods* □ *peak viewing time.* **3** a time of maximum achievement, etc □ *His peak was in his early twenties.* **4** the front projecting part of a cap. **5** a pointed beard. **6** *naut* the upper outer corner of a sail extended by a gaff or yard. ▻ *verb* (*peaked*, *peaking*) *intr* **1** to reach a maximum. **2** to reach the height of one's powers or popularity. ⓒ 16c: probably related to PIKE².

peak² ▻ *verb* (*peaked*, *peaking*) *intr* to droop; to look thin or sickly. ⓒ 16c.

peaked ▻ *adj* **1** having a peak or peaks. **2** *in compounds* said of a mountain or hill: having a summit with the specified number of peaks □ *three-peaked* □ *twin-peaked.*

peak hour ▻ *noun* a period of the day when the volume of traffic is at its heaviest, or when the number of people watching TV is greatest.

peak load ▻ *noun* **1** the maximum demand of electricity in a particular area. **2** the maximum load on a power station.

peaky¹ ▻ *adj* **1** having a peak or peaks; sharp and pointed □ *a peaky summit.* **2** like a peak.

peaky² ▻ *adj* (*peakier*, *peakiest*) ill-looking; pallid. • **peakiness** *noun.* ⓒ 19c: related to PEAK².

peal ▻ *noun* **1** the ringing of a bell or set of bells. **2** *bell-ringing* a series of 5 040 changes (the maximum number of permutations possible with 7 bells) rung without a break and taking about 3 hours to complete. Compare CHANGE-RINGING. **3** *non-technical* a set of bells, each with a different note. Compare RING² *noun* 6. **4** a burst of noise □ *peals of laughter* □ *a peal of thunder.* ▻ *verb* (*pealed*, *pealing*) **1** *intr* to ring or resound. **2** to sound or signal (eg a welcome) by ringing. ⓒ 14c as *pele*, from obsolete *apele* APPEAL.

pean see PAEAN

peanut ▻ *noun* **1** a low-growing annual plant of the pulse family, native to tropical America, widely cultivated for its edible seeds which are produced under the ground in pods. **2** the protein-rich seed of this plant, which can be eaten raw or roasted, ground to make peanut butter, or used as a source of oil for cooking oil, margarine, soap, etc. Also called GROUNDNUT, MONKEY NUT. **3** (**peanuts**) *colloq* **a** something small, trivial or unimportant; **b** a small or paltry amount of money □ *He works for peanuts.* ⓒ 19c.

peanut butter ▻ *noun* a savoury spread made from ground roasted peanuts.

peapod ▻ *noun* the seedcase of a pea.

pear /pɛə(r)/ ▻ *noun* **1** a deciduous tree belonging to the rose family, widely cultivated in temperate regions for its edible fruit and ornamental flowers. **2** the edible cone-shaped fruit of this tree, consisting of a core of small seeds surrounded by sweet juicy white pulp and a yellowish-green skin. ⓒ Anglo-Saxon *peru*: from Latin *pirum* pear.

pear drop ▻ *noun* **1** a small boiled sweet shaped and flavoured like a pear. **2** a pear-shaped pendant.

pearl¹ /pɜːl/ ▻ *noun* **1** a bead of smooth hard lustrous material found inside the shell of certain molluscs, eg oysters, and used in jewellery as a gem. **2** an artificial imitation of this. **3** (**pearls**) a necklace of pearls □ *I was wearing my pearls.* **4** mother-of-pearl. **5** something resembling a pearl. **6** something valued or precious □ *pearls of wisdom.* ▻ *adj* **1** like a pearl in colour or shape. **2** made of or set with pearls or mother-of-pearl. See also CULTURED (sense 3). ▻ *verb* (*pearled*, *pearling*) **1** to set something with, or as if with, pearls. **2** to grind down (barley) into small pearl-like grains. **3** *intr* to form pearl-like beads or drops. **4** *intr* to fish for pearls. • **pearled** *adj.* • **pearler** *noun* **1** a pearl-fisher. **2** a pearl-fisher's boat. ⓒ 14c: from a diminutive of Latin *perna* sea mussel.

pearl² see PURL¹ *noun* 3

pearl barley ▻ *noun* seeds of barley ground into round polished grains, used in soups and stews.

pearl button ▻ *noun* a mother-of-pearl button.

pearl-grey or (*chiefly US*) **pearl-gray** ▻ *adj* pale bluish-grey in colour. Also (**pearl grey**) *as noun.*

pearlies /'pɜːlɪz/ ▻ *plural noun* **1** pearl buttons. **2** the traditional pearl-button-covered costume of costermongers.

pearlite see PERLITE.

pearlized or **pearlised** /'pɜːlaɪzd/ ▻ *adj* treated so as to give a pearly or lustrous surface.

pearl millet ▻ *noun* a grain grown widely in India.

pearl mussel ▻ *noun* a freshwater mussel that yields pearls.

pearl oyster ▻ *noun* any oyster that produces pearls.

pearl-shell ▻ *noun* **1** mother-of-pearl. **2** a pearl-bearing shell.

pearl spar ▻ *noun, geol* a crystalline carbonate mineral that has a pearly lustre.

pearly ▻ *adj* (*pearlier*, *pearliest*) **1** like a pearl or pearl; NACREOUS. **2** covered in pearl. • **pearliness** *noun.*

pearly gates ▻ *plural noun, colloq* the gates of Heaven. ⓒ 19c: referring to the biblical description in Revelation 21.21.

pearly king and **pearly queen** ▻ *noun* the London costermonger couple whose pearl-button-covered costumes are judged the most splendid.

pearly nautilus see under NAUTILUS

pearmain /ˈpɛəmeɪn/ ▷ *noun* a variety of apple. ⓘ 15c: originally referring to a type of pear, from French *parmain*.

pear-shaped ▷ *adj* **1** tapering towards one end and bulged at the other; in the shape of a pear. **2** said of a vocal quality: mellow, resonant and non-nasal.

peasant /ˈpɛzənt/ ▷ *noun* **1** in poor agricultural societies: a farm worker or small farmer. **2** *derog* a rough unmannerly or culturally ignorant person. • **peasantry** *noun* **1** the peasant class. **2** the condition of being a peasant. • **peasanty** *adj* in the style of a peasant. ⓘ 15c: from French *païsant*, from Latin *pagus* country district.

pease /piːz/ ▷ *noun* (***pease*** or *old* ***peason*** /ˈpiːzən/) *archaic* a pea or pea-plant. ⓘ Anglo-Saxon *pise* pea and *pisan* peas: from Latin *pisa*.

pease pudding ▷ *noun* a purée made from split peas soaked and then boiled.

pea-shooter ▷ *noun* a short tube through which to fire dried peas by blowing, used as a toy weapon.

pea soup ▷ *noun* thick soup made from dried peas.

pea-souper ▷ *noun, colloq* a very thick yellowish fog.

peat ▷ *noun* **1** a mass of dark-brown or black fibrous plant material, produced by the compression of partially decomposed vegetation, used in compost and manure, and in dried form as a fuel. **2** a cut block of this material. **3** *in compounds* **a** an area, bog, moor etc, covered with peat; **b** an area from which peat is dug □ ***peat bog*** □ ***peat land***. • **peaty** *adj* (***peatier***, ***peatiest***) **1** like or consisting of peat. **2** having a smoky taste or smell reminiscent of peat. ⓘ 13c in SE Scotland: from Anglo-Latin *peta* a peat, possibly from Celtic.

peat moss see SPHAGNUM

peau de soie /poʊ də swɑː/ ▷ *noun* a type of smooth silk or rayon fabric. ⓘ 19c: French, literally 'skin of silk'.

peavey or **peavy** /ˈpiːvɪ/ ▷ *noun* (***peaveys*** or ***peavies***) *N Amer* a lumberjack's spiked and hooked lever. ⓘ 19c: named after Joseph Peavey, its inventor.

pebble /ˈpɛbəl/ ▷ *noun* (***pebbles***) **1** a small fragment of rock, especially one worn round and smooth by the action of water. **2 a** transparent and colourless rock crystal; **b** a lens made from this. **3** a grained appearance on leather, as if pressed by pebbles. Also *as adj* □ ***a pebble beach***. ▷ *verb* (***pebbled***, ***pebbling***) **1** to cover with pebbles. **2** in leather manufacturing: to produce a rough and indented surface on (leather). • **pebbled** *adj* covered with pebbles. • **pebbly** *adj* (***pebblier***, ***pebbliest***) full of or covered with pebbles. ⓘ Anglo-Saxon *papol*.

pebbledash ▷ *noun, Brit* cement or plaster with small stones embedded in it, used as a coating for exterior walls. See also HARL[2], ROUGHCAST.

PEC or **pec** ▷ *abbreviation* photoelectric cell.

pec ▷ *noun* (*usually* **pecs**) *colloq* a PECTORAL MUSCLE. ⓘ 1960s.

pecan /pɪˈkan, ˈpiːkən/ ▷ *noun* **1** a deciduous N American tree, widely cultivated for its edible nut. Also called **pecan tree**. **2** the oblong reddish-brown edible nut, with a sweet oily kernel, produced by this tree. Also called **pecan nut**. ⓘ 18c: from the Native American name in various languages of the Algonquian language family, eg *pakan*, *pagann*.

peccable /ˈpɛkəbəl/ ▷ *adj, formal or literary* liable to sin. • **peccability** *noun*. Compare IMPECCABLE. ⓘ 17c: from Latin *peccare* to sin.

peccadillo /pɛkəˈdɪloʊ/ ▷ *noun* (***peccadillos*** or ***peccadilloes***) a minor misdeed. ⓘ 16c: from Spanish *pecadillo*, diminutive of *pecado* sin.

peccary /ˈpɛkərɪ/ ▷ *noun* (***peccaries***) a hoofed mammal, native to Central and S America, similar to but smaller than the Old World wild pig. ⓘ 17c: from Carib (a Native S American language) *pakira*.

peck[1] ▷ *verb* (***pecked***, ***pecking***) **1** (*also* **peck at something**) said of a bird: to strike, nip or pick at it with the beak □ ***pecked his finger*** □ ***pecked at the bark of the tree***. **2** to poke (a hole) with the beak. **3** to kiss someone or something in a quick or perfunctory way □ ***pecked her on the cheek***. ▷ *noun* **1** a tap or nip with the beak. **2** a perfunctory kiss. ⓘ 14c: probably related to PICK[1].

▪ **peck at something** **1** to eat (food) in a cursory, inattentive or dainty way, without enjoyment or application. **2** to nit-pick or quibble at it.

peck[2] ▷ *noun* **1** in the imperial system: a measure of capacity of dry goods, especially grain, equal to two gallons (9.1 litres) or a quarter of a BUSHEL. **2** a measuring container holding this quantity. **3** *old use* a large amount □ ***a peck of troubles***. ⓘ 13c: from French *pek*.

pecker ▷ *noun* **1** something that pecks; a beak. **2** a woodpecker. **3** *colloq* spirits; resolve □ ***keep one's pecker up***. **4** *N Amer coarse slang* the penis.

pecking order ▷ *noun* **1** a scale of ascendancy noticeably operating in a flock of poultry, such that any bird may peck one of lesser importance but must submit to being pecked by those of greater importance. **2** any social hierarchy in animals or humans, or system of ranks and associated privileges.

peckish /ˈpɛkɪʃ/ ▷ *adj* **1** *colloq* quite hungry □ ***feeling a bit peckish***. **2** *US colloq* irritable. • **peckishness** *noun*. ⓘ 18c: from PECK[1].

pecten /ˈpɛktɪn/ ▷ *noun* (***pectines*** /ˈpɛktɪniːz/ or ***pectens***) *anatomy, zool* **1** a comb-like structure, eg in a bird's or reptile's eye. **2** any comb-like organ. ⓘ 18c; 14c in obsolete senses 'metacarpus' and 'pubes': Latin, meaning 'a comb'.

pectic acid ▷ *noun, biochem* an acid that is obtained from the pectin found within ripening fruits.

pectin /ˈpɛktɪn/ ▷ *noun, biochem* a complex carbohydrate that functions as a cement-like material within and between plant cell-walls. It forms a gel at low temperatures and is widely used in jam-making. ⓘ 19c: from Greek *pektos* congealed.

pectinate /ˈpɛktɪneɪt/ or **pectinated** *biol* ▷ *adj* toothed like a comb; having narrow parallel segments or lobes. • **pectination** *noun*. ⓘ 18c: from Latin *pectinatus* combed, from *pecten* comb.

pectoral /ˈpɛktərəl/ ▷ *adj* **1** referring or relating to the breast or chest. **2** worn on the breast. ▷ *noun* **1** a pectoral muscle. **2** a pectoral fin. **3** a neck ornament worn covering the chest. **4** armour for the breast of a person or a horse. ⓘ 15c: from Latin *pectoralis*, from *pectus* chest.

pectoral cross ▷ *noun* a gold cross worn on the breast by bishops, etc.

pectoral fin ▷ *noun* in fishes: one of a pair of fins situated just behind the gills, used to control the angle of ascent or descent in the water, and for slowing down.

pectoral muscle ▷ *noun, anatomy* either of two muscles situated on either side of the top half of the chest, responsible for certain arm and shoulder movements. See also PEC.

pectose /ˈpɛktoʊs/ ▷ *noun, chem* a substance that yields PECTIN, contained in the fleshy pulp of unripe fruit.

peculate /ˈpɛkjʊleɪt/ *formal* ▷ *verb* (***peculated***, ***peculating***) *tr & intr* to appropriate something dishonestly for one's own use; to pilfer; to embezzle. • **peculation** *noun*. • **peculator** *noun*. ⓘ 18c: from Latin *peculari*, *peculatus*, from *peculium* private property; compare PECULIAR.

peculiar /pəˈkjuːlɪə(r)/ ▷ *adj* **1** strange; odd. **2** (**peculiar to someone** or **something**) exclusively or typically belonging to or associated with them □ ***habits peculiar to***

cats. **3** special; individual □ *their own peculiar methods.* **4** especial; particular □ *of peculiar interest.* ● **peculiarly** *adverb.* ⓘ 16c: from Latin *peculium* private property, originally cattle or money, from *pecus* cattle.

peculiarity /pəkjuːlɪ'arɪtɪ/ ▻ *noun* (***peculiarities***) **1** the quality of being strange or odd. **2** a distinctive feature, characteristic or trait. **3** an eccentricity or idiosyncrasy.

peculiarize or **peculiarise** ▻ *verb* (***peculiarized, peculiarizing***) to set something apart; to distinguish something (from another thing).

pecuniary /pɪ'kjuːnɪərɪ/ ▻ *adj* relating to, concerning or consisting of money. ⓘ 16c: from Latin *pecunia* money, from *pecus* flock or cattle.

ped- see PAEDO-

-ped /pɛd/ or **-pede** /piːd/ ▻ *combining form, forming nouns, denoting* foot □ *quadruped* □ *millipede.* ⓘ From Latin *pes, pedis* foot.

pedagogic /pɛdə'gɒdʒɪk, -'gɒgɪk/ or **pedagogical** ▻ *adj* relating to or characteristic of a pedagogue. ● **pedagogically** *adverb.*

pedagogue /'pɛdəgɒg/ ▻ *noun* (***pedagogues***) *old derog use* a teacher, especially a strict or pedantic one. ⓘ 14c: from Greek *paidagogos* a child's tutor.

pedagogy /'pɛdəgɒdʒɪ, -gɒgɪ/ ▻ *noun* the science, principles or work of teaching. ⓘ 17c: from French *pédagogie*, from Greek *paidagogia* tutorship, from *pais* child + *agein* to lead.

pedal /'pɛdəl/ ▻ *noun* **1** a lever operated by the foot, eg on a machine, vehicle or musical instrument. **2** *as adj* □ *pedal bike.* ▻ *verb* (***pedalled, pedalling***; or (*especially N Amer*) ***pedaled, pedaling***) *tr & intr* to move or operate by means of a pedal or pedals. ▻ *adj* /'piːdəl/ *zool* referring or relating to the foot or feet. ⓘ 17c: from Latin *pedalis* of the foot, from *pes* foot.

-pedal /piːdəl, pɛdəl/ ▻ *combining form, forming adjectives, indicating* foot □ *bipedal.* ⓘ From Latin *pes, pedis* foot.

pedalo /'pɛdəloʊ/ ▻ *noun* (***pedalos***) a small pedal-operated boat, used especially on lakes for pleasure. ⓘ 1960s.

pedal point ▻ *noun, music* a tone or tones sustained normally in the bass, while other parts move independently. Also called **organ point**.

pedalpushers ▻ *plural noun* women's knee-length breeches.

pedal steel guitar ▻ *noun* an electric steel guitar with foot pedals for adjusting pitch, creating glissando effects, etc.

pedant /'pɛdənt/ ▻ *noun, derog* someone who is over-concerned with correctness of detail, especially in academic matters. ⓘ 16c, originally meaning 'teacher' without derogatory connotation: from Italian *pedante* teacher.

pedantic /pə'dantɪk/ ▻ *adj* over-concerned with correctness. ● **pedantically** *adverb.*

pedantry /'pɛdəntrɪ/ ▻ *noun* **1** excessive concern with correctness. **2** a pedantic expression. **3** unnecessary formality.

pedate /'pɛdeɪt/ *biol* ▻ *adj* **1** footed or foot-like. **2** *bot* said of a leaf: with lobes radiating from one centre, the outer lobes deeply-cut, or branching into three leaflets with the outer branches forked. ● **pedately** *adverb.* ⓘ 18c: from Latin *pedatus* footed, from *pes* foot.

peddle /'pɛdəl/ ▻ *verb* (***peddled, peddling***) **1** *tr & intr* to go from place to place selling (a selection of small goods); to be a pedlar. **2** *colloq* to deal illegally in (narcotic drugs). **3** *colloq* to publicize and try to win acceptance for (ideas, theories, etc). ⓘ 16c: a back-formation from PEDLAR.

peddler ▻ *noun* **1** the usual *N Amer* spelling of PEDLAR. **2** someone who deals illegally in narcotics □ *a dope peddler.*

-pede see -PED

pederasty or **paederasty** /'pɛdərastɪ/ ▻ *noun* sexual relations between adults and children. ● **pederast** or **paederast** *noun* an adult who practises pederasty. ⓘ 16c: from Greek *pais, paidos* child + *erastes* lover.

pedestal /'pɛdəstəl/ ▻ *noun* the base on which a vase, statue, column, etc is placed or mounted. ● **put** or **place someone on a pedestal** to admire or revere them extremely; to idolize them. ⓘ 16c: from Italian *piedistallo* foot of stall.

pedestal desk ▻ *noun* a desk for which sets of drawers act as the side supports for the writing surface.

pedestrian /pə'dɛstrɪən/ ▻ *noun* someone travelling on foot, especially in a street; someone who is walking. ▻ *adj* **1** referring to, or for, pedestrians □ *a pedestrian walkway.* **2** dull; unimaginative; uninspired □ *a pedestrian rendering by the orchestra.* ⓘ 18c: from Latin *pedester* on foot.

pedestrian crossing ▻ *noun* a specially marked crossing-place for pedestrians, where they have priority over traffic. Compare ZEBRA CROSSING, PELICAN CROSSING. ⓘ 1930s.

pedestrianize or **pedestrianise** ▻ *verb* (***pedestrianized, pedestrianizing***) to convert (a shopping street, etc) into an area for pedestrians only by excluding through-traffic and usually paving over the street. ● **pedestrianization** *noun.* ⓘ 1960s in this sense; early 19c in the sense 'to walk'.

pedestrian precinct ▻ *noun* a shopping street or similar area from which traffic is excluded.

pediatrician, pediatric and **pediatrics** alternative *N Amer* spellings of PAEDIATRICIAN, PAEDIATRIC, PAEDIATRICS

pedicab /'pɛdɪkab/ ▻ *noun* a light vehicle consisting of a tricycle with a second seat attached, usually behind, covered by a half-hood for one or two passengers. ⓘ 1940s: from Latin *pes, pedis* foot + CAB.

pedicel /'pɛdɪsɛl/ ▻ *noun, biol* **1** the stalk of a single flower. Compare PEDUNCLE. **2** the stalk of a sedentary animal (see SEDENTARY 4b). **3** the stalk of an animal organ, eg a crab's eye. ⓘ 17c: from Latin *pedicelus*, diminutive of *pediculus* a little foot.

pedicle /'pɛdɪkəl/ ▻ *noun* **1** *bot* a short stalk; a pedicel. **2** *zool* in deer: a bony protrusion from the skull from which an antler grows. ⓘ 17c: from Latin *pediculus* a little foot, diminutive of *pes, pedis* foot.

pedicure /'pɛdɪkjʊə(r)/ ▻ *noun* a medical or cosmetic treatment of the feet and toenails. Compare MANICURE. ⓘ 19c: from Latin *pes, pedis* foot + *curare* to look after.

pedigree /'pɛdɪgriː/ ▻ *noun* (***pedigrees***) **1** a person's or animal's line of descent, especially if long and distinguished, or proof of pure breeding. **2** a genealogical table showing this; a family tree. ▻ *adj* said of an animal: pure-bred; descended from a long line of known ancestors of the same breed. ● **pedigreed** *adj* having a pedigree. ⓘ 15c: from French *pie de grue* foot of the crane, from its similarity to a branching family tree.

pediment /'pɛdɪmənt/ ▻ *noun* **1** *archit* a wide triangular gable set over a classical portico or the face of a building. **2** *geol* a gently sloping surface, usually consisting of bare rock covered by a thin layer of sediment, formed by the erosion of cliffs or steep slopes. ● **pedimented** *adj* **1** furnished with a pediment. **2** like a pediment. ⓘ 16c as *periment*, perhaps a corruption of PYRAMID.

pedlar /'pɛdlə(r)/ or (*chiefly N Amer*) **peddler** ▻ *noun* someone who peddles. ⓘ 14c.

pedo- see PAEDO-

pedology[1] /pɛ'dɒlədʒɪ/ ▻ *noun, geol* the scientific study of the origin, properties and uses of soil. ● **pedologist** *noun* a scientist who specializes in pedology. ⓘ 1920s: from Greek *pedon* ground.

pedology² the *N Amer* spelling of PAEDOLOGY

pedometer /pɪˈdɒmɪtə(r)/ ▷ *noun* a device that measures distance walked by recording the number of steps taken. ⓔ 18c: from Latin *pedi-* foot + Greek *metron* measure.

peduncle /pɪˈdʌŋkəl/ ▷ *noun* **1** *bot* a short stalk, eg one carrying an inflorescence or a single flower-head. Compare PEDICEL. **2** *anatomy, pathol* any stalk-like structure. • **peduncular**, **pedunculate** or **pedunculated** *adj*. ⓔ 18c: from Latin *pedunculus* small foot, from *pes*, *pedis* foot.

pee¹ *colloq* ▷ *verb* (***peed***, ***peeing***) *intr* to urinate. ▷ *noun* **1** an act of urinating. **2** urine. ⓔ 18c: a euphemism for PISS, based on the first letter.

pee² ▷ *singular or plural noun* a spelled-out form of the abbreviation P, penny or pence.

peek /piːk/ ▷ *verb* (***peeked***, ***peeking***) *intr* (*also* **peek at something**) to glance briefly and surreptitiously at it; to peep. ▷ *noun* a brief furtive glance. ⓔ 14c as *piken*.

peekaboo /ˈpiːkəbuː/ ▷ *noun* a child's game in which one person covers their face with their hands and suddenly uncovers it saying 'peekaboo', usually making a young child laugh. ⓔ 16c: from PEEK + BOO².

peel¹ ▷ *verb* (***peeled***, ***peeling***) **1** to strip the skin or rind off (a fruit or vegetable). **2** *intr* to be able to be peeled □ *Grapes don't peel easily.* **3** (*also* **peel something away** or **off**) to strip off (an outer layer). **4** *intr* said of a wall or other surface: to shed its outer coating in flaky strips. **5** *intr* said of skin, paint or other coverings: to flake off in patches. **6** *intr* said of a person or part of the body: to shed skin in flaky layers after sunburn. ▷ *noun* the skin or rind of vegetables or fruit, especially citrus fruit □ *candied peel.* • **peeler** *noun* a small knife or device for peeling fruit and vegetables. • **keep one's eyes peeled** or **skinned** see under EYE. ⓔ Anglo-Saxon: from Latin *pilare* to deprive of hair.

▪ **peel off 1** said of an aircraft or vehicle: to veer away from the main group. **2** *colloq* to undress.

peel² ▷ *noun* **1** a shovel, especially a baker's wooden shovel. **2** an instrument for hanging paper up to dry. ⓔ 14c: from French *pele*, from Latin *pala* a spade.

peelings ▷ *plural noun* strips of peel removed from a fruit or vegetable.

peen or **pein** /piːn/ ▷ *noun* the end of a hammer-head opposite the hammering face. ▷ *verb* (***peened***, ***peening***) to strike or work (metal) with a peen. ⓔ 17c.

peep¹ ▷ *verb* (***peeped***, ***peeping***) *intr* **1** (*often* **peep at something** or **someone** or **peep out**) to look quickly or covertly, eg through a narrow opening or from a place of concealment; to peek. **2** (*also* **peep out**) to emerge briefly or partially. ▷ *noun* **1** a quick covert look. **2** a first faint glimmering □ *at peep of day.* ⓔ 16c: a variant of PEEK.

peep² ▷ *noun* **1** the faint high-pitched cry of a baby bird, etc; a cheep. **2** the smallest utterance □ *not another peep out of you!* ▷ *verb* (***peeped***, ***peeping***) *intr* **1** said of a young bird, etc: to utter a high-pitched cry; to cheep. **2** *colloq* to sound or make something sound □ *peep the horn.* ⓔ 15c: imitating the sound.

peepers ▷ *plural noun, old colloq use* the eyes. ⓔ 18c: from PEEP¹.

peephole ▷ *noun* **1** a hole, crack, etc through which to peep. **2** a tiny aperture in a front door, fitted with a convex lens, through which one can check to see who is there before opening the door.

peeping Tom ▷ *noun* a man who furtively spies on other people, especially women undressing; a voyeur. ⓔ 19c: named after the tailor who, according to legend, peeped at Lady Godiva as she rode naked through the streets of Coventry in protest at her husband's high taxes.

peepshow ▷ *noun* a box with a peephole through which a series of moving pictures, especially erotic or pornographic ones, can be watched.

peepul see PIPAL

peer¹ /pɪə(r)/ ▷ *noun* **1** a member of the nobility, such as, in Britain, a DUKE, MARQUESS, EARL, VISCOUNT or BARON. Compare ARISTOCRAT, NOBLE. **2** a member of THE House of Lords, known as either a LIFE PEER or LIFE PEERESS, a **spiritual peer**, ie a bishop or archbishop, or a **temporal peer**, ie all other members of the House of Lords. See also PEER OF THE REALM. **3 a** someone who is one's equal in age, rank, etc; a contemporary, companion or fellow; **b** *as adj* □ *peer group.* ⓔ 14c: from French *per*, from Latin *par* equal.

peer² /pɪə(r)/ ▷ *verb* (***peered***, ***peering***) *intr* **1** (*also* **peer at something** or **someone**) to look hard at it or them, especially through narrowed eyes, as if having difficulty in seeing. **2** (*sometimes* **peer out**) *literary* to peep out or emerge briefly or partially. ⓔ 16c.

peerage /ˈpɪərɪdʒ/ ▷ *noun* **1** the title or rank of a peer □ *granted a peerage* □ *raised to the peerage.* **2** *singular or plural* the members of the nobility as a group. **3** a book containing a list of peers with details of their families and descent.

peeress /pɪəˈrɛs/ ▷ *noun* (***peeresses***) **1** the wife or widow of a peer. **2** a woman who holds the rank of peer in her own right.

peer group ▷ *noun* one's peers (PEER¹ *noun* 3) or companions as a group, especially as an influence on one's attitudes and aspirations.

peerless ▷ *adj* without equal; excelling all; matchless. • **peerlessly** *adverb*. ⓔ 14c: PEER1 + -LESS.

peer of the realm ▷ *noun* a member of the nobility with the right to sit in the House of Lords.

peer pressure ▷ *noun* compulsion to do or obtain the same things as others in one's PEER GROUP.

peeve ▷ *verb* (***peeved***, ***peeving***) *colloq* to irritate, annoy or offend. ▷ *noun, colloq* a cause of vexation or irritation. • **peeved** *adj*. ⓔ Early 20c: a back-formation from PEEVISH.

peevish /ˈpiːvɪʃ/ ▷ *adj* irritable; cantankerous; inclined to whine or complain. • **peevishly** *adverb*. • **peevishness** *noun*. ⓔ 14c.

peewit /ˈpiːwɪt/ and **pewit** /ˈpiːwɪt, ˈpjuːɪt/ ▷ *noun* a LAPWING. ⓔ 16c: imitating its cry.

peg ▷ *noun* **1** a little shaft of wood, metal or plastic shaped for any of various fixing, fastening or marking uses. **2** a coat hook fixed to a wall, etc. **3** a wooden or plastic clip for fastening washing to a line to dry; a clothes peg. **4** a small stake for securing tent ropes, marking a position, boundary, etc. **5** any of several wooden pins on a stringed instrument, which are turned to tune it. **6** a point of reference on which to base an argument, etc. **7** a pin for scoring, used eg in cribbage. **8** *colloq* a leg. **9** *colloq* a PEG LEG (sense 1). **10** *old colloq* a drink of spirits. ▷ *verb* (***pegged***, ***pegging***) **1** to insert a peg into something. **2** to fasten something with a peg or pegs. **3** to set or freeze (prices, incomes, etc) at a certain level. • **off the peg** said of clothes: ready to wear; ready-made. • **a square peg in a round hole** a person who does not fit in well in their environment, job, etc. • **take someone down a peg or two** *colloq* to humiliate them; to humble them. ⓔ 15c: from Dutch *pegge*.

▪ **peg away at something** *colloq* to work steadily at it.

▪ **peg back** or **peg something back** in sport, especially racing: to gain an advantage over an opponent.

▪ **peg someone down** to restrict them to an admission, following a certain course of action.

▪ **peg out 1** *colloq* to die. **2** to become exhausted. **3** *croquet* to finish by driving the ball against the peg. **4** *cribbage* to win by pegging the last hole before show of hands.

■ **peg something out** to mark out (ground) with pegs.

peg board ▻ *noun* a board with holes for receiving pegs that are used for scoring in games, or for attaching items for display.

peg leg ▻ *noun, colloq* **1** an artificial leg. **2** a person with an artificial leg.

pegmatite /ˈpɛgmətaɪt/ ▻ *noun, geol* any of various coarse-grained igneous rocks, many of which are sources of economically important minerals such as MICA, TOURMALINE and GARNET. ● **pegmatitic** /-məˈtɪtɪk/ *adj*. ⓒ 18c: from Greek *pegma* bond or framework.

PEI ▻ *abbreviation* Prince Edward Island.

peignoir /ˈpeɪnwɑː(r), ˈpɛnwɑː(r)/ ▻ *noun* a woman's light dressing-gown. ⓒ 19c: French, from *peigner* to comb.

pein see PEEN

pejorative /pəˈdʒɒrətɪv/ ▻ *adj* said of a word or expression: disapproving, derogatory, disparaging or uncomplimentary. ▻ *noun* a word or affix with derogatory force. ● **pejoratively** *adverb*. ⓒ 19c: from Latin *peiorare* to make worse.

pekan /ˈpɛkən/ ▻ *noun* a large N American marten with dark brown fur. ⓒ 18c: Canadian French, from Abnaki (an Algonquian language) *pékané*.

peke /piːk/ ▻ *noun* a Pekinese dog.

Pekinese or **Pekingese** /piːkɪˈniːz/ ▻ *noun* (***Pekinese***) **1** a small breed of pet dog with a long straight silky coat, short legs, a flat face, and a plumed tail curved over its back. Often shortened to PEKE. **2** someone who lives in or was born in Peking (Beijing), capital of the People's Republic of China. ▻ *adj* belonging or relating to Peking. ⓒ 19c: from *Peking* (Beijing).

pekoe /ˈpiːkoʊ, ˈpɛkoʊ/ ▻ *noun* (***pekoes***) a high-quality scented black China tea. ⓒ 18c: from Amoy Chinese *pek-ho* white down, because the leaves are picked young with the down still on them.

pelage /ˈpɛlɪdʒ/ ▻ *noun* an animal's coat of hair or wool. ⓒ 19c: French.

pelagic /pɪˈladʒɪk/ ▻ *adj* **1** *technical* relating to, or carried out on, the deep open sea. **2** denoting floating plankton and fish, and other organisms that swim freely in the surface waters. Compare BENTHOS, NEKTON. ⓒ 17c: from Greek *pelagos* sea.

pelargonium /pɛləˈgoʊnɪəm/ ▻ *noun* an annual or perennial plant with hairy stems, rounded or lobed aromatic leaves, and conspicuous scarlet, pink or white fragrant flowers borne in clusters, often cultivated under the name GERANIUM. ⓒ 19c: from Greek *pelargos* stork, modelled on GERANIUM.

pelf ▻ *noun, derog* riches; money; lucre. ⓒ 15c; 14c in obsolete sense 'stolen property': from French *pelfre* booty; compare PILFER.

pelham /ˈpɛləm/ ▻ *noun* a type of bit on a horse's bridle, a combination of the CURB (sense2) and SNAFFLE designs. ⓒ 19c: from the surname Pelham.

pelican /ˈpɛlɪkən/ ▻ *noun* (***pelican*** or ***pelicans***) a large aquatic bird that has an enormous beak with a pouch below it, and mainly white plumage. ⓒ Anglo-Saxon: from Latin *pelecanus*, from Greek *pelekan*.

pelican crossing ▻ *noun* a PEDESTRIAN CROSSING with a set of pedestrian-controlled traffic lights including an amber flashing light which indicates that the motorist may proceed only if the crossing is clear. ⓒ 1960s: adapted from *pe*destrian *li*ght-*con*trolled crossing.

pelisse /pɛˈliːs/ ▻ *noun, historical* **1** a long mantle of silk, velvet, etc, worn especially by women. **2** a fur or fur-lined garment, especially a military cloak. ⓒ 18c: French, from Latin *pellicea vestis* a garment of fur, from Latin *pellis* a skin.

pelite /ˈpiːlaɪt/ ▻ *noun, geol* any rock derived from clay or mud, such as shale. ● **pelitic** /pɪˈlɪtɪk/ *adj*. ⓒ 19c: from Greek *pelos* clay or mud.

pellagra /pəˈlagrə, pəˈleɪgrə/ ▻ *noun, medicine* a deficiency disease caused by lack of nicotinic acid or the amino acid tryptophan, characterized by scaly discoloration of the skin, diarrhoea, vomiting, and psychological disturbances. ● **pellagrin** *noun* someone afflicted with pellagra. ● **pellagrous** *adj* related to, like or afflicted with pellagra. ⓒ 19c: Italian, from Latin *pellis* skin + Greek *agra* seizure.

pellet /ˈpɛlɪt/ ▻ *noun* **1** a small rounded mass of compressed material, eg paper. **2** a piece of small shot for an airgun, etc. **3** a ball of undigested material regurgitated by an owl or hawk. ▻ *verb* (***pelleted, pelleting***) **1** to form (especially seeds) into pellets by coating it with a substance, eg to aid planting. **2** to bombard someone or something with pellets. ⓒ 14c: from French *pelote*, from Latin *pila* ball.

pellicle /ˈpɛlɪkəl/ ▻ *noun* **1** a thin skin or film. **2** *biol* a protein covering which preserves the shape of single-cell organisms. **3** *physics* a photographic emulsion used to monitor tracks of ionizing particles. ● **pellicular** /pɛˈlɪkjuːlə(r)/ *adj*. ⓒ 16c: from Latin *pellicula*, diminutive of *pellis* skin.

pellitory[1] /ˈpɛlɪtərɪ/ ▻ *noun* (***pellitories***) **1** a plant of the nettle family, growing especially on walls. Also called **pellitory of the wall**. **2** various similar plants. ⓒ 16c, also as *parietorie*, etc: from Latin *parietaria*, from *paries, parietis* a wall.

pellitory[2] /ˈpɛlɪtərɪ/ ▻ *noun* (***pellitories***) **1** a N African and S European plant related to camomile. Also called **pellitory of Spain**. **2** various similar plants, such as yarrow. ⓒ 16c: from Latin *pyrethrum*, from Greek *pyrethron* pellitory of Spain.

pell-mell /pɛlˈmɛl/ ▻ *adverb* headlong; in confused haste; helter-skelter. ▻ *adj* confusedly mingled; headlong. ▻ *noun* disorder; a confused mixture. ⓒ 16c: from French *pesle-mesle*, rhyming compound from *mesler* to mix.

pellucid /pɛˈluːsɪd/ ▻ *adj* **1** transparent. **2** absolutely clear in expression and meaning. ● **pellucidity** /pɛluːˈsɪdɪtɪ/ or **pellucidness** *noun*. ● **pellucidly** *adverb*. ⓒ 17c: from Latin *per* utterly + *lucidus* clear.

Pelmanism /ˈpɛlmənɪzəm/ ▻ *noun* **1** a system of mind-training to improve the memory. **2** (*usually* **pelmanism**) a card game in which the cards are spread out face down and must be turned up in matching pairs. Also called PAIRS. ⓒ Early 20c: named after The Pelman Institute, London, founded in 1899, which devised the system.

pelmet /ˈpɛlmɪt/ ▻ *noun* a strip of fabric or a narrow board fitted along the top of a window to conceal the curtain rail. ⓒ Early 20c.

pelorus /pɛˈlɔːrəs/ ▻ *noun* (***peloruses***) a kind of compass from which bearings can be taken. ⓒ 19c: named after Pelorus, Hannibal's pilot.

pelota /pɛˈloʊtə/ ▻ *noun* (***pelotas***) **1** a court game of Basque origin, played in Spain, SW France and Latin America, in which players use their hand or a basket-like device strapped to their wrists to catch and throw a ball against a specially marked wall. Also called JAI ALAI. **2** the ball used in this game. ⓒ 19c: Spanish, meaning 'ball'.

pelotherapy /piːloʊˈθɛrəpɪ/ ▻ *noun* therapeutic treatment using mud. ⓒ 1930s: from Greek *pelos* mud.

peloton /pɛləˈtɒn/ ▻ *noun, sport* the leading group of cyclists in a race, eg in the Tour de France. ⓒ 1990s: French, meaning 'the main body of runners or riders' or 'platoon'.

pelt¹ ▻ *verb* (***pelted, pelting***) **1** to bombard with missiles □ ***was pelted with stones.*** **2** *intr* to rush along at top speed □ ***pelting along the motorway.*** ▻ *noun* an act or spell of pelting. • **at full pelt** as fast as possible. ⓘ 15c.

■ **pelt down** *intr* said of rain, hail, etc: to fall fast and heavily □ ***The rain's pelting down.***

pelt² ▻ *noun* **1** the skin of a dead animal, especially with the fur still on it. Compare PELTRY. **2** the coat of a living animal. **3** a hide stripped of hair for tanning. ⓘ 15c: possibly back-formation from PELTRY.

peltry /'pɛltrɪ/ ▻ *noun* (***peltries***) the skins of animals with the fur on them; furs collectively. ⓘ 15c: probably from French *pelleterie* animal skins, from Latin *pellis* skin.

pelvic /'pɛlvɪk/ ▻ *adj* relating to or in the region of the pelvis.

pelvic fin ▻ *noun, zool* either of a pair of fins attached to the pelvic girdle of fishes, enabling control of steering.

pelvic girdle and **pelvic arch** ▻ *noun, zool, anatomy* the posterior limb-girdle of vertebrates, consisting of two hip bones, the SACRUM and the COCCYX, which articulates with the spine and the bones of the legs or hindlimbs.

pelvic inflammatory disease ▻ *noun* (abbreviation **PID**) *medicine* in women: any pelvic infection of the upper reproductive tract, usually affecting the uterus, Fallopian tubes and ovaries, often caused by the spread of infection from an infected organ nearby.

pelvis /'pɛlvɪs/ ▻ *noun* (***pelvises*** or ***pelves*** /-viːz/) *anatomy* **1** the basin-shaped cavity formed by the bones of the pelvic girdle. **2** the PELVIC GIRDLE. **3** in the mammalian kidney: the expanded upper end of the URETER, into which the urine drains. ⓘ 17c: Latin, meaning 'basin'.

pemmican or **pemican** /'pɛmɪkən/ ▻ *noun* **1** a Native American food of dried meat beaten to a paste and mixed with fat. **2** a similarly condensed and nutritious mixture of dried ingredients used as emergency rations. ⓘ 19c: from Cree (a Native American language) *pimekan*.

PEN /pɛn/ ▻ *abbreviation* International Association of Poets, Playwrights, Editors, Essayists, and Novelists.

pen¹ ▻ *noun* **1** a writing instrument that uses ink, formerly a quill, now any of various implements fitted with a nib (FOUNTAIN PEN), rotating ball (BALLPOINT), or felt or nylon point (FELT PEN). **2** this instrument as a symbol of the writing profession. ▻ *verb* (***penned, penning***) *formal* to compose and write (a letter, poem, etc) with a pen. • **penned** *adj* written; quilled. ⓘ 14c: from Latin *penna* feather.

pen² ▻ *noun* **1** a small enclosure, especially for animals. **2** *often in compounds* any small enclosure or area of confinement for the specified purpose □ ***a playpen.*** **3** a bomb-proof dock for submarines. **4** *Caribb* a cattle farm. **5** *Caribb* an estate or plantation. ▻ *verb* (***penned*** or ***pent, penning***) (*often* **pen someone** or **something in** or **up**) to enclose or confine them in a pen, or as if in a pen. ⓘ Anglo-Saxon *penn*.

pen³ ▻ *noun, N Amer colloq* a PENITENTIARY.

pen⁴ ▻ *noun* a female swan. See also COB¹ (sense 2), CYGNET. ⓘ 16c.

Pen. ▻ *abbreviation* Peninsula.

penal /'piːnəl/ ▻ *adj* relating to punishment, especially by law. • **penally** *adverb*. ⓘ 15c: from Latin *poenalis*, from *poena* penalty.

penal code ▻ *noun* a system of laws concerning the punishment of crime.

penalize or **penalise** /'piːnəlaɪz/ ▻ *verb* (***penalized, penalizing***) **1** to impose a penalty on someone, for wrongdoing, cheating, breaking a rule, committing a foul in sport, etc. **2** to disadvantage someone □ ***income groups that are penalized by the new tax laws.*** • **penalization** *noun*. ⓘ 19c.

penal servitude ▻ *noun, historical* imprisonment with HARD LABOUR, substituted in 1853 by TRANSPORTATION (*noun* 3), and abolished in 1948.

penalty /'pɛnəltɪ/ ▻ *noun* (***penalties***) **1** a punishment, such as imprisonment, a fine, etc, imposed for wrongdoing, breaking a contract or rule, etc. **2** a punishment that one brings on oneself through ill-advised action □ ***paid the penalty for my error.*** **3** *sport* a handicap imposed on a competitor or team for a foul or other infringement of the rules, in team games taking the form of an advantage awarded to the opposing side, such as a PENALTY KICK, penalty shot, etc, or time on the PENALTY BENCH, etc. **4** (**penalties**) *football* a series of penalty kicks by each side following EXTRA TIME to decide the outcome of a drawn game or winner of a cup, etc □ ***The 1994 World Cup was decided on penalties.*** Compare REPLAY. • **under** or **on penalty of something** with liability to the penalty of a particular punishment in case of violation of the law, etc □ ***swear on penalty of death.*** ⓘ 16c: from Latin *poenalitas*, from *poena* punishment.

penalty area ▻ *noun, football* an area in front of either goal within which a foul by any player in the defending team is punished by a penalty awarded to the attacking team.

penalty bench ▻ *noun, ice-hockey* an area or box beside the rink in which a player must stay for their allotted penalty period.

penalty box ▻ *noun* **1** *football* a PENALTY AREA. **2** *ice-hockey* a PENALTY BENCH.

penalty corner ▻ *noun, hockey* a free stroke taken on the goal line.

penalty goal ▻ *noun* a goal scored by a penalty kick or shot.

penalty kick ▻ *noun* **1** *rugby* a free kick. **2** *football* a free kick at goal from a distance of 12yd (11m), awarded to the attacking team for a foul committed in the PENALTY AREA by the defending team.

penalty spot ▻ *noun, football, hockey* a spot in front of the goal from which a penalty kick or shot is taken.

penance /'pɛnəns/ ▻ *noun* **1** repentance or atonement for an offence or wrongdoing, or an act of repentance □ ***do penance.*** **2** *RC Church* a sacrament involving confession, repentance, forgiveness, and the performance of a penance suggested by one's confessor. ⓘ 13c: from French *peneance*, from Latin *paenitentia* penitence.

pen-and-ink ▻ *noun* **1** writing materials. **2** a pen drawing. ▻ *adj* **1** engaged in writing. **2** said of a drawing: executed with pen and ink.

penannular /pɛ'nanjʊlə(r)/ ▻ *adj, technical* in the form of an almost complete ring. ⓘ 19c: from Latin *paene* almost + ANNULAR.

pence *a plural of* PENNY

-pence /pɛns, pəns/ ▻ *combining form* denoting a number of pennies (as a value) □ ***threepence.***

penchant /'pɑ̃ʃɑ̃/ ▻ *noun* a taste, liking, inclination or tendency □ ***a penchant for childish pranks.*** ⓘ 17c: French, present participle of *pencher* to lean.

pencil /'pɛnsɪl, -səl/ ▻ *noun* **1 a** a writing and drawing instrument consisting of a wooden shaft containing a stick of graphite or other material, which is sharpened for use, and makes more or less erasable marks; **b** *as adj* □ ***pencil drawing.*** **2** such material, especially with regard to the alterability of marks made with it □ ***written in pencil.*** **3** something with a similar function or shape, eg for medical or cosmetic purposes □ ***an eyebrow pencil.*** **4 a** something long, fine and narrow in shape; **b** *as adj* □ ***pencil pleat*** □ ***pencil torch.*** **5** a narrow beam of light □ ***a pencil of light.*** **6** *optics* a set of rays of light diverging from or converging to a point. ▻ *verb* (***pencilled, pencilling***; *N Amer* ***penciled, penciling***) to write, draw or mark something with a pencil. • **penciller** *noun*. ⓘ 15c: from

Latin *penicillus* painter's brush, diminutive of *peniculus* little tail, from *penis* tail.

■ **pencil something** or **someone in** to note down a provisional commitment, eg for a meeting, spending time with someone, etc, in one's diary, for later confirmation □ ***I'll pencil you in for 3 o'clock.***

pencil lead ▷ *noun* graphite for pencils.

pencilling or (*N Amer*) **penciling** *noun* **1** the art or act of painting, writing, sketching or marking with a pencil. **2** marks made with a pencil. **3** fine lines. **4** the marking of joints in brickwork with white paint.

pencil-sharpener ▷ *noun* an instrument for sharpening lead pencils into which the pencil is inserted and rotated against a blade or blades.

pendant or (*sometimes*) **pendent** /ˈpɛndənt/ ▷ *noun* **1 a** an ornament suspended from a neck chain, necklace, bracelet, etc; **b** a necklace with such an ornament hanging from it. **2** any of several hanging articles, eg an earring, ceiling light, etc. **3** a piece, eg a painting or poem, that is meant as a companion to another. **4** *naut* a PENNANT (*noun* 1). ◷ 14c: French, from *pendre* to hang, from Latin *pendere*.

pendent or (*sometimes*) **pendant** /ˈpɛndənt/ ▷ *adj* **1** hanging; suspended; dangling. **2** projecting; jutting; overhanging. **3** undetermined or undecided; pending. ● **pendently** *adverb*. ◷ 15c: from French *pendant*; see PENDANT.

pendente lite /pɛnˈdɛntɪ ˈlaɪtɪ, pɛnˈdɛnte ˈliːtɛ/ *law* while a law suit is pending; until trial. ◷ 18c: Latin.

pendentive /pɛnˈdɛntɪv/ ▷ *noun, archit* a spherical triangle shape formed by the space between a dome and a square base from which the dome rises, used in Byzantine and Romanesque architecture, etc. ◷ 18c: French, from Latin *pendens* hanging.

pending /ˈpɛndɪŋ/ ▷ *adj* **1** remaining undecided; waiting to be decided or dealt with. **2** said of a patent: about to come into effect. ▷ *prep* until; awaiting; during □ ***held in prison pending trial.*** ◷ 17c: from Latin *pendere* to hang.

pendulous /ˈpɛndjʊləs/ ▷ *adj* hanging down loosely; drooping; swinging freely. ● **pendulously** *adverb*. ● **pendulousness** *noun*. ◷ 17c: from Latin *pendulus* hanging.

pendulum /ˈpɛndjʊləm/ ▷ *noun* (***pendulums***) **1** *physics* a weight, suspended from a fixed point, that swings freely back and forth through a small angle with SIMPLE HARMONIC MOTION. **2** a swinging lever used to regulate the movement of a clock. **3** anything that undergoes obvious and regular shifts or reversals in direction, attitude, opinion, etc. ● **pendular** *adj* relating to or like a pendulum. ◷ 17c: Latin, neuter of *pendulus* hanging.

peneplain /ˈpiːnɪpleɪn/ ▷ *noun, geog* a land surface which is worn down to such an extent by DENUDATION as to be almost a plain. ◷ 19c: from Latin *pene* almost + PLAIN.

penes *a plural of* PENIS

penetrant /ˈpɛnətrənt/ ▷ *adj, literary or technical* penetrating. ▷ *noun, chem* a substance which increases the penetration of a liquid into a porous material or between contiguous surfaces, by lowering its surface tension.

penetrate /ˈpɛnətreɪt/ ▷ *verb* (***penetrated, penetrating***) **1** (*also* **penetrate into something**) to find a way into it; to enter it, especially with difficulty. **2** to gain access into and influence within (a country, organization, market, etc) for political, financial, etc purposes. **3** to find a way through something; to pierce or permeate □ ***penetrate enemy lines*** □ ***penetrated the silence.*** **4** *intr* to be understood □ ***The news didn't penetrate at first.*** **5** to see through (a disguise). **6** to fathom, solve, or understand (a mystery). **7** said of a man: to insert his penis into the vagina of (a woman) or anus of (a man or a woman). ● **penetrability** /pɛnətrəˈbɪlɪtɪ/ *noun*. ● **penetrable** *adj*. ● **penetrably** *adverb*. ● **penetrator** *noun*. ◷ 16c: from Latin *penetrare* to penetrate.

penetrating ▷ *adj* **1** said of a voice, etc: all too loud and clear; strident; carrying. **2** said of a person's mind: acute; discerning. **3** said of the eyes or of a look: piercing; probing. ● **penetratingly** *adverb*.

penetration /pɛnəˈtreɪʃən/ ▷ *noun* **1** the process of penetrating or being penetrated. **2** mental acuteness; perspicacity; insight.

penetrative /ˈpɛnətrətɪv/ ▷ *adj* **1** tending or able to penetrate. **2** piercing; having acute or deep insight. **3** said of sexual intercourse: in which the man penetrates his partner. **4** reaching and affecting the mind. ● **penetratively** *adverb*. ● **penetrativeness** *noun*.

penfold ▷ *noun* a small enclosure to keep cattle or sheep in.

pen friend and **pen pal** ▷ *noun* someone, usually living abroad, with whom one corresponds by letter, and whom one may not have met in person.

penguin /ˈpɛŋgwɪn/ ▷ *noun* any of various flightless sea birds with a stout body, small almost featherless wings, short legs, bluish-grey or black plumage, and a white belly. ◷ 16c: possibly from Welsh *pen* head + *gwyn* white.

penguinery /ˈpɛŋgwɪnərɪ/ (***penguineries***) ▷ *noun* **1** a group or colony of penguins. **2** a place where penguins breed.

penicillate /pɛnɪˈsɪlɪt, -eɪt/ ▷ *adj, biol* tufted; forming a tuft; brush-shaped.

penicillin /pɛnɪˈsɪlɪn/ ▷ *noun* any of various ANTIBIOTICs, derived from a mould or produced synthetically, that are widely used to treat bacterial infections. ◷ 1920s: from Latin *penicillus* painter's brush (referring to the hairy or tufty appearance of the mould).

penile /ˈpiːnaɪl/ ▷ *adj, anatomy, etc* relating to or resembling the penis.

penillion *plural of* PENNILL

peninsula /pəˈnɪnsjʊlə/ ▷ *noun* (***peninsulas***) a piece of land projecting into water from a larger landmass and almost completely surrounded by water. ● **peninsular** *adj*. ◷ 16c: from Latin *paene* almost + *insula* island.

penis /ˈpiːnɪs/ ▷ *noun* (***penises*** or ***penes*** /-niːz/) in higher vertebrates: the male organ of copulation which is used to transfer sperm to the female reproductive tract and also contains the URETHRA through which urine is passed. ◷ 17c: Latin, originally meaning 'tail'.

penis envy ▷ *noun, psychoanal* the Freudian concept of a woman's subconscious wish for male characteristics. ◷ 1920s.

penitent /ˈpɛnɪtənt/ ▷ *adj* regretful for wrong one has done, and feeling a desire to reform; repentant. ▷ *noun* **1** a repentant person, especially one doing penance on the instruction of a confessor. **2** *RC Church* a member of one of various orders devoted to penitential exercises, etc. ● **penitence** *noun*. ● **penitently** *adverb*. ◷ 14c: from Latin *paenitens* repentant.

penitential /pɛnɪˈtɛnʃəl/ ▷ *adj* referring to, showing or constituting penance □ ***penitential psalms.*** ▷ *noun, RC Church* **1** a book of rules relating to penance. **2** a penitent. ● **penitentially** *adverb*.

penitentiary /pɛnɪˈtɛnʃərɪ/ ▷ *noun* (***penitentiaries***) **1** *N Amer* a federal or state prison. Often shortened to **pen**. **2** a book for guidance in imposing penances. **3** *RC Church* an office at Rome dealing with cases of penance, dispensations, etc. ▷ *adj* **1** referring or relating to punishment or penance. **2** penal or reformatory. ◷ 16c.

penknife ▷ *noun* a pocket knife with blades that fold into the handle. ◷ 14c: from PEN[1] *noun* 1, because such a knife was originally used for cutting quills.

pen light ▻ *noun* a small electric torch shaped like a pen.

penmanship ▻ *noun* skill with the pen, whether calligraphic or literary.

Penn. see PA

penna /'pɛnə/ ▻ *noun* (***pennae*** /-niː/) *ornithol* a feather, especially one of the large feathers of the wings or tail. ◷ Latin, meaning 'feather' or 'wing'.

pen name ▻ *noun* a pseudonym used by a writer. ◷ 19c.

pennant /'pɛnənt/ ▻ *noun* **1** *naut* a dangling line from the masthead, etc, with a block for tackle, etc. Also called **pendant**. **2** *naut* a small narrow triangular flag, used on vessels for identification or signalling. Also called **pennon**. ◷ 17c: probably from PENNON + PENDANT.

pennate /'pɛneɪt/ ▻ *adj, biol* **1** winged; feathered; shaped like a wing. **2** PINNATE. ◷ 18c in sense 2: from Latin *pennatus* winged.

penned *past tense, past participle of* PEN[1], PEN[2]

penniless ▻ *adj* without money; poverty-stricken. • **pennilessness** *noun*. ◷ 14c.

pennill /'pɛnɪl; *Welsh* 'pɛnɪɬ/ ▻ *noun* (***penillion***) a form of Welsh improvised verse. ◷ 18c: Welsh, meaning 'verse' or 'stanza'.

penning *present participle of* PEN[1], PEN[2]

pennon /'pɛnən/ ▻ *noun* **1** *historical* a long narrow flag with a tapering divided tip, eg borne on his lance by a knight. **2** a PENNANT (*noun* 2). ◷ 14c: from Latin *penna* feather.

penny /'pɛnɪ/ ▻ *noun* (***pence*** /pɛns/ in senses 1 and 2, or ***pennies***) **1** (*singular* and *plural* ABBREVIATION **p** /piː/) in the UK: a hundredth part of £1, or a bronze coin having this value. **2** (*singular* and *plural* symbol **d**) in the UK before decimalization in 1971: 1/12 of a shilling or 1/240 of £1, or a bronze coin having this value. **3** *with negatives* the least quantity of money ▫ *won't cost a penny.* **4** *N Amer* one cent, or a coin having this value. **5** a coin of low value in certain other countries. **6** (**pennies**) money in general, usually a small amount ▫ *saving his pennies.* **7** /'pɛnɪ, pənɪ/ *in compounds* denoting a specified number of pennies (as a value) ▫ *a five-penny piece.* • **a pretty penny** *ironic* a huge sum ▫ *That must have cost a pretty penny.* • **in for a penny, in for a pound** (often shortened to **in for a penny**) once involved, one may as well be totally committed. • **in penny numbers** *colloq* in small quantities. • **pennies from heaven** money obtained without effort and unexpectedly. • **spend a penny** *euphemistic, colloq* to urinate. • **the penny dropped** *colloq* understanding about something finally came. • **turn an honest penny** *colloq* to earn one's living honestly. • **two a penny** or **ten a penny** very common; in abundant supply and of little value. ◷ Anglo-Saxon *pening*.

penny dreadful ▻ *noun, colloq* a cheap trivial novel or thriller. ◷ 19c.

penny farthing ▻ *noun, Brit* an early type of bicycle, dating from the 1860s, with a large front wheel and small back wheel. See also BONESHAKER. ◷ 1920s: a name applied retrospectively, comparing its wheels to the large PENNY and small FARTHING coins of the day; its contemporary name was the *ordinary*.

penny-halfpenny or **penny-ha'penny** ▻ *noun* formerly in the UK: one and a half pre-decimal pence.

penny-in-the-slot ▻ *adj* said of a machine: coin-operated.

penny-piece ▻ *noun, old use* a penny.

penny-pinching ▻ *adj, derog* too careful with one's money; miserly; stingy. • **penny-pincher** *noun*.

pennyroyal ▻ *noun* a species of mint with medicinal qualities. ◷ 16c as *puliol real*: from French *poliol* thyme.

penny share and **penny stock** ▻ *noun, stock exchange* a share or stock trading for less than £1 or $1, usually bought very speculatively.

pennyweight ▻ *noun* a unit equal to twenty-four grains of TROY WEIGHT, or 1/20 of an ounce troy.

penny whistle ▻ *noun* a tiny whistle or flageolet.

penny wise ▻ *adj* **1** (*usually* **penny wise and pound foolish**) thrifty about small things, but careless about large ones. **2** very concerned with saving small amounts of money.

pennywort ▻ *noun* a name given to various plants with round leaves. ◷ 13c: PENNY + WORT.

pennyworth /'pɛnəθ, 'pɛnɪwɜːθ/ ▻ *noun, old use* an amount that can be bought for one penny.

penology or **poenology** /piː'nɒlədʒɪ/ ▻ *noun* the study of crime and punishment. • **penological** /-'lɒdʒɪkəl/ *adj*. • **penologist** *noun*. ◷ 19c: from Greek *poine* punishment + -LOGY.

pen pal see PEN FRIEND

pen pusher ▻ *noun* a clerk or minor official whose job includes much tedious paperwork. • **pen-pushing** *noun, adj*. ◷ 19c: originally *pencil pusher*.

pensile /'pɛnsaɪl, 'pɛnsəl/ ▻ *adj* **1** hanging; suspended; overhanging. **2** *ornithol* said of birds: that build a hanging nest. • **pensileness** or **pensility** /pɛn'sɪlɪtɪ/ *noun*. ◷ 17c: from Latin *pensilis* hanging down, from *pendere* to hang.

pension /'pɛnʃən/ ▻ *noun* **1** a government allowance to a retired, disabled or widowed person. **2** a regular payment by an employer to a retired employee. **3** a regular payment from a private pension company to a person who contributed to a PENSION FUND for much of their working life. **4** an allowance paid as a bribe for future services. **5** /*French* pɑ̃sjɔ̃/ a boarding-house in continental Europe. See also EN PENSION. ▻ *verb* (***pensioned***, ***pensioning***) to grant a pension to (a person). • **pensioner** *noun* someone who is in receipt of a pension. • **pensionless** *adj*. ◷ 14c: French, from Latin *pensio* payment.

▪ **pension someone off** to put them into retirement, or make them redundant, on a pension.

pensionable ▻ *adj* entitling one to a pension; entitled to a pension ▫ *of pensionable age.*

pensionary /'pɛnʃənərɪ/ ▻ *adj* referring to the nature of a pension. ▻ *noun* (***pensionaries***) someone whose interest is bought by payment of a pension.

pension fund ▻ *noun* a fund into which a working person pays regular contributions which are invested on the stock market by the company running the fund, providing a return on retirement to individual members of the fund which varies according to the performance of the invested money.

pensive /'pɛnsɪv/ ▻ *adj* preoccupied with one's thoughts; thoughtful. • **pensively** *adverb*. • **pensiveness** *noun*. ◷ 14c: from French *pensif*, from *penser* to think.

penstemon /pɛn'stiːmən/ or **pentstemon** /pɛnt-/ ▻ *noun* a N American plant with showy flowers which have five stamens, one of which is sterile. ◷ 18c: from Greek *pente* five + *stemon* thread, here meaning 'stamen'.

penstock ▻ *noun* **1** a sluice. **2** in a hydroelectric power station: a valve-controlled water conduit. ◷ 17c.

pent *past tenses, past participle of* PEN[2]. See also PENT-UP.

penta- /pɛntə/ or (before a vowel) **pent-** *combining form, denoting* five ▫ *pentatonic.* ◷ From Greek *pente* five.

pentachord ▻ *noun* **1** a musical instrument with five strings. **2** a diatonic series of five notes. ◷ 18c: PENTA- + Greek *chorde* string.

pentacle /'pɛntəkəl/ ▻ *noun* a PENTAGRAM or similar figure or amulet used as a defence against demons. ◷ 16c:

from Latin *pentaculum*, or from French *pentacol*, from *pendre a col* to hang on the neck.

pentad /ˈpɛntad/ ▻ *noun* **1** a set of five things. **2** a period of five years or five days. ◷ 17c: from Greek *pentados* a group of five.

pentadactyl /pɛntəˈdaktɪl/ *zool* ▻ *noun* an animal with five digits on each limb, being the normal state in humans. ▻ *adj* said of the limbs of humans or animals: having five digits. ◷ 19c: from Greek *pente* five + *daktylos* finger or toe.

pentagon /ˈpɛntəgən, -gɒn/ ▻ *noun, geom* a plane figure (see PLANE² *adj* 3) with five sides and five angles. • **pentagonal** /pɛnˈtagənl/ *adj*. ◷ 16c: from Greek *pente* five + *gonia* angle.

pentagram /ˈpɛntəgram/ ▻ *noun* **1** a figure in the shape of a star with five points and consisting of five lines. **2** such a figure used as a magic symbol; a PENTACLE. ◷ Early 19c: from Greek *pentagrammos*, from *pente* five + *gramma* character or letter.

pentahedron /pɛntəˈhiːdrən/ ▻ *noun* (***pentahedrons*** or ***pentahedra*** /-drə/) *geom* a five-faced solid figure. • **pentahedral** *adj*. ◷ 18c: compare POLYHEDRON.

pentamerous /pɛnˈtamərəs/ ▻ *adj, biol* **1** consisting of five parts or members. **2** containing parts in groups of five. • **pentamerism** *noun*. ◷ 19c: compare TRIMEROUS.

pentameter /pɛnˈtamɪtə(r)/ ▻ *noun, poetry* a line of verse with five metrical feet. ◷ 16c: Latin, from Greek *pente* five + *metron* measure.

pentamidine /pɛnˈtamɪdiːn, -dɪn/ ▻ *noun, pharmacol* a drug first used to combat tropical diseases such as sleeping sickness, later found effective against a form of pneumonia common in AIDS patients. ◷ 1940s: from PENTANE + AMIDE + -INE².

pentane /ˈpɛnteɪn/ ▻ *noun, chem* (formula $\mathbf{C_5H_{12}}$) a hydrocarbon, fifth member of the methane series. ◷ 19c.

pentangle /ˈpɛntangəl/ ▻ *noun* **1** a PENTACLE. **2** *rare* a PENTAGON. • **pentangular** *adj*. ◷ 14c.

pentanoic acid ▻ *noun, chem* a colourless carboxylic acid used in the perfume industry. Also called **valeric acid**.

pentaprism ▻ *noun, photog* a five-sided prism that corrects lateral inversion by turning light through an angle of 90°, used in REFLEX CAMERAS to allow eye-level viewing. ◷ 1930s.

Pentateuch /ˈpɛntətjuːk/ ▻ *noun* the first five books of the Old Testament, ie Genesis, Exodus, Leviticus, Numbers and Deuteronomy. • **Pentateuchal** /-ˈtjuːkəl/ *adj*. ◷ 16c: from Greek *pentateuchos* five-volumed, from *penta-* five- + *teuchos* a tool, later a book.

pentathlon /pɛnˈtaθlən/ ▻ *noun* **1** any of several athletic competitions comprising five events all of which the contestants must compete in, based on a competition in the ancient Greek Olympics. **2** (*usually* **modern pentathlon**) such a competition at the Olympic games, consisting of swimming, cross-country riding and running, fencing and pistol-shooting. Compare HEPTATHLON, DECATHLON. ◷ 18c: from Greek *pente* five + *athlon* contest.

pentatonic /pɛntəˈtɒnɪk/ ▻ *adj, music* said of a musical scale: having five notes to the octave, most commonly equivalent to the first, second, third, fifth and sixth degrees of the major scale. ◷ 19c.

pentavalent /pɛntəˈveɪlənt/ and **quinquevalent** /kwɪnkwə-/ ▻ *adj, chem* said of an atom of a chemical element: having a valency of five. ◷ 19c.

Pentecost /ˈpɛntəkɒst/ ▻ *noun* **1** *Christianity* a festival on Whit Sunday, the seventh Sunday after Easter, commemorating the descent of the Holy Spirit on the Apostles. **2** *Judaism* the SHABUOTH. ◷ Anglo-Saxon: from Latin *pentecoste*, from Greek *pentecoste hemera* fiftieth day.

Pentecostal ▻ *adj* **1** denoting any of several fundamentalist Christian groups that put emphasis on God's gifts through the Holy Spirit, characterized by their literal interpretation of the Bible and informal worship with enthusiastic and spontaneous exclamations of praise and thanksgiving. **2** relating to Pentecost. ▻ *noun* a member of a Pentecostal church. • **Pentecostalism** *noun*. • **Pentecostalist** *noun, adj*.

penthouse /ˈpɛnthaʊs/ ▻ *noun* **1** an apartment, especially a luxuriously appointed one, built on to the roof of a tall building. Also *as adj* □ *penthouse suite*. **2** *real tennis* a roofed corridor running along three sides of the court. ◷ 1920s in sense 1; 14c, meaning 'annex' or 'outhouse', from earlier *pentice*: from French *appentis*, from Latin *appendicium* appendage.

pentimento /pɛntɪˈmɛntoʊ/ ▻ *noun* (*plural* ***pentimenti*** /-tiː/) *art* something painted out of a picture by an artist which later becomes visible again. ◷ Early 20c: Italian, literally 'repentance', from *pentirsi* to repent.

pentobarbitone /pɛntəˈbɑːbɪtoʊn/ or (*US*) **pentobarbital** /-ˈbɑːbɪtəl/ *noun, pharmacol* a barbiturate drug with hypnotic, sedative and anticonvulsant effects. ◷ 1930s.

pentose /ˈpɛntoʊs/ ▻ *noun, chem* any MONOSACCHARIDE with five carbon atoms. ◷ Late 19c: German, from Greek *pente* five + -OSE².

Pentothal /ˈpɛntoʊθəl/ ▻ *noun, trademark* THIOPENTONE SODIUM.

pentoxide /pɛnˈtɒksaɪd/ ▻ *noun, chem* a compound with five atoms of oxygen bonded to another element or radical. ◷ 19c.

pentstemon see PENSTEMON

pent-up (*also* **pent up**) ▻ *adj* said of feelings, energy, etc: repressed or stifled; bursting to be released □ *pent-up emotions*.

penult /pɛˈnʌlt/ or **penultima** /-ˈnʌltɪmə/ ▻ *noun* the last but one syllable in a word. ◷ 16c: from Latin *paenultimus* PENULTIMATE.

penultimate /pəˈnʌltɪmət, pɛ-/ ▻ *adj* last but one. ▻ *noun* **1** the penult. **2** the last but one. ◷ 17c: from Latin *paene* almost + *ultimus* last.

penumbra /pɛˈnʌmbrə/ ▻ *noun* (***penumbrae*** /-briː/ or ***penumbras***) **1** the lighter outer shadow that surrounds the dark central shadow produced by a large unfocused light-source shining on an opaque object. **2** *astron* the lighter area around the edge of a sunspot. • **penumbral** or **penumbrous** *adj*. ◷ 17c: Latin, from *paene* almost + *umbra* shadow.

penurious /pəˈnjʊərɪəs/ ▻ *adj* **1** mean with money; miserly. **2** poor; impoverished. • **penuriously** *adverb*. • **penuriousness** *noun*. ◷ 17c.

penury /ˈpɛnjərɪ/ ▻ *noun* (***penuries***) **1** extreme poverty. **2** lack; scarcity. ◷ 15c: from Latin *penuria* want.

peon /ˈpiːən/ ▻ *noun* **1** in India and Ceylon: an office messenger; an attendant. **2** in Latin America: **a** a farm labourer; **b** *especially formerly* someone required to work for a creditor until a debt is paid off. ◷ 17c: from Spanish *peón*, from Latin *pedo* foot soldier.

peonage /ˈpiːənɪdʒ/ and **peonism** /ˈpiːənɪzəm/ ▻ *noun* **1** the state of being a peon. **2** a system in which a debtor is required to work for a creditor until a debt is paid off.

peony or **paeony** /ˈpɪənɪ/ ▻ *noun* (***peonies*** or ***paeonies***) **1** a shrub or herbaceous plant with large, showy red, pink, yellow or white globular flowers with five to ten petals and numerous stamens. **2** the flower produced by this plant. ◷ Anglo-Saxon: from French *pione*, from Greek *paionia*, from *Paion* the healer of the gods, because of the plant's medicinal use.

people /ˈpiːpəl/ ▻ *noun, usually plural* **1** a set or group of persons. **2** men and women in general. **3** a body of persons held together by belief in common origin, speech, culture, political union, or by common leadership, etc. **4 a** (**the people**) ordinary citizens without special rank; the general populace; **b** *in compounds* denoting that the specified thing belongs or relates to the people, general populace, etc □ *people-power* □ *people-oriented.* **5** (**the people**) voters as a body. **6** subjects or supporters of a monarch, etc. **7** *singular* (*plural* ***peoples***) a nation or race □ *a warlike people.* **8** *colloq* one's parents, or the wider circle of one's relations. ▷ *verb* (***peopled***, ***peopling***) **1** to fill or supply (a region, etc) with people; to populate. **2** to inhabit. • **of all people 1** especially; more than anyone else □ *You, of all people, should know that.* **2** very strangely or unexpectedly □ *chose me, of all people, as spokesperson.* ⓒ 14c: from French *poeple*.

people's democracy ▷ *noun* a form of government in which the proletariat, represented by the Communist Party, holds power, and is seen ideologically as a transitional state on the way to full socialism.

people's front see POPULAR FRONT

PEP /pɛp/ ▷ *abbreviation* personal equity plan.

pep ▷ *noun, colloq* energy; vitality; go. ▷ *verb* (***pepped***, ***pepping***) (*always* **pep someone** or **something up**) to enliven or invigorate them or it. • **peppy** *adj* (***peppier***, ***peppiest***). Compare PEP TALK. ⓒ Early 20c: a shortening of PEPPER.

peperomia /pɛpə'roumɪə/ ▷ *noun* (***peperomias***) any one of a large genus of subtropical herbaceous plants, many of which are grown as house plants for their ornamental foliage. ⓒ 19c: Latin, from Greek *peperi* pepper + *homoios* like.

peperoni see PEPPERONI

pepino /pɛ'piːnou/ ▷ *noun* (***pepinos***) **1** a purple-striped pale yellow fruit with sweet flesh and an elongated oval shape. **2** the spiny-leaved S American plant that bears this fruit. ⓒ 19c: Spanish, meaning 'cucumber'.

peplum /'pɛpləm/ ▷ *noun* (***peplums*** or ***pepla*** /-lə/) a short skirt-like section attached to the waistline of a dress, blouse or jacket. ⓒ 17c: from Greek *peplos*, an outer robe or overskirt worn by women in ancient Greece.

pepo /'piːpou/ ▷ *noun* (***pepos***) *bot* **1** a large many-seeded berry, usually with a hard EPICARP. **2** the type of fruit found in the melon and cucumber family. ⓒ 19c: Latin, meaning 'pumpkin'.

pepper /'pɛpə(r)/ ▷ *noun* **1 a** a perennial climbing shrub, widely cultivated for its small red berries which are dried to form PEPPERCORNS; **b** a pungent seasoning prepared from the dried berries of this plant, usually by grinding them into a powder. See also BLACK PEPPER, WHITE PEPPER. **2 a** any of various tropical shrubs cultivated for their large red, green or yellow edible fruits, eg CHILLI pepper; **b** the fruit of these plants, eaten raw in salads or cooked as a vegetable. Also called **capsicum**, **sweet pepper**. **3** CAYENNE PEPPER. ▷ *verb* (***peppered***, ***peppering***) **1** to bombard something or someone (with missiles). **2** to sprinkle liberally □ *The text was peppered with errors.* **3** to season (a dish, etc) with pepper. • **peppery** *adj* see separate entry. ⓒ Anglo-Saxon *pipor*, from Latin *piper*.

pepper-and-salt ▷ *adj* **1** said of cloth: mingled with black and white. **2** said of hair: flecked with grey.

peppercorn ▷ *noun* **1** the dried berry of the PEPPER (*noun* 1) plant. **2** something of little value.

peppercorn rent ▷ *noun* rent that is very low or nominal.

peppermill ▷ *noun* a device for grinding peppercorns.

peppermint ▷ *noun* **1** a species of mint with dark-green leaves and spikes of small purple flowers, widely cultivated for its aromatic oil. **2** a food flavouring prepared from the aromatic oil produced by this plant. **3** a sweet flavoured with peppermint.

peppermint cream ▷ *noun* **1** a sweet creamy peppermint-flavoured substance. **2** a sweet made of this, often coated in chocolate.

pepperoni or **peperoni** /pɛpə'rounɪ/ ▷ *noun* (***pepperonies*** or ***peperonis***) a hard, spicy beef and pork sausage. ⓒ 1930s: Italian, plural of *peperone* chilli or pepper, from Latin *piper* pepper.

pepper pot ▷ *noun* **1** a small pot or container with small holes in the top from which ground pepper is sprinkled. **2** *cookery* a West Indian dish made from the juice of a bitter cassava, meat or dried fish, and vegetables, especially green okra and chillies.

peppery /'pɛpərɪ/ ▷ *adj* **1** well seasoned with pepper; tasting of pepper; hot-tasting or pungent. **2** short-tempered; irascible. • **pepperiness** *noun*.

pep pill ▷ *noun* a pill that contains a stimulant drug. ⓒ 1930s.

peppy see under PEP

pepsin /'pɛpsɪn/ ▷ *noun, biochem* in the stomach of vertebrates: a digestive enzyme produced by the gastric glands that catalyses the partial breakdown of dietary protein. ⓒ 19c: from Greek *pepsis* digestion; see -IN.

pep talk ▷ *noun* a brief talk intended to raise morale for a cause or course of action. Compare PEP. ⓒ 1920s.

peptic /'pɛptɪk/ ▷ *adj* **1** referring or relating to digestion. **2** referring or relating to the stomach. **3** referring or relating to pepsin. ⓒ 17c: from Greek *peptikos* able to digest, from *peptos* cooked or digested.

peptic ulcer ▷ *noun, pathol* an ulcer of the stomach, caused by destruction of part of the lining by excess gastric acid. See also DUODENAL ULCER.

peptide /'pɛptaɪd/ ▷ *noun, biochem* a molecule that consists of a relatively short chain of amino acids. ⓒ Early 20c: from Greek *pepsis* digestion.

per /pɜː(r), pə(r)/ ▷ *prep* **1** out of every □ *two per thousand.* **2** for every □ *£5 per head.* **3** in every □ *60 miles per hour* □ *100 accidents per week.* **4** through; by means of □ *per post.* • **as per ...** according to ... □ *proceed as per instructions.* • **as per usual** *colloq* as always. ⓒ 14c: Latin, meaning 'for', 'each' or 'by'.

per- /pɜː(r), pə(r)/ ▷ *prefix, denoting* **1** *chem* the highest state of oxidation of an element in a compound □ *peroxide.* **2** in words derived from Latin: through, beyond, thoroughly or utterly. ⓒ Latin, from *per* PER.

peradventure /pɜːrəd'vɛntʃə(r), pɛ-/ ▷ *adverb, archaic* perhaps; by chance. ⓒ 13c: from French *par aventure* by chance.

perambulate /pə'rambjʊleɪt/ ▷ *verb* (***perambulated***, ***perambulating***) *formal* **1** to walk about (a place). **2** *intr* to stroll around. • **perambulation** *noun*. • **perambulatory** *adj*. ⓒ 16c: from PER + Latin *ambulare* to walk.

perambulator /pə'rambjʊleɪtə(r)/ ▷ *noun* **1** *formal* a PRAM[1]. **2** a wheel-like instrument that surveyors use for measuring distances. ⓒ 17c; 19c in sense 1.

per annum /pər 'anəm/ ▷ *adverb* (abbreviation **p.a.** or **per an.**) for each year; yearly; by the year. ⓒ 17c: Latin.

per capita /pə 'kapɪtə/ ▷ *adverb, adj* for each person □ *income per capita* □ *GDP per capita.* ⓒ 20c in this sense; 17c in legal sense 'divided or shared equally by or among individuals': Latin, literally 'by heads'.

perceive /pə'siːv/ ▷ *verb* (***perceived***, ***perceiving***) **1** to observe, notice, or discern □ *perceived a change.* **2** to understand, interpret or view □ *how one perceives one's role.* • **perceivable** *adj*. ⓒ 14c: from French *percever*, from Latin *percipere*.

perceived noise decibel ▷ *noun* (abbreviation **PNdB**) a frequency-weighted noise unit used in measurement of aircraft noise.

per cent /pə 'sɛnt/ ▷ *adverb, adj* (symbol **%**) **1** in or for every 100 □ *Sales are 20 per cent down.* □ *a 15 per cent* *increase.* **2** on a scale of 1 to 100 □ ***90 per cent certain.*** ▻ *noun* (*usually* **percent**) **1** a percentage or proportion. **2** (*usually* **percents**) *in compounds* a security that yields a specified rate of interest □ ***invest in four-percents.*** **3** one part in or on every 100 □ ***half a percent.*** Ⓒ 16c: from Latin *per centum* for every 100.

percentage /pəˈsɛntɪdʒ/ ▻ *noun* **1** an amount, number or rate stated as a proportion of one hundred. **2** a proportion □ ***a large percentage of students fail.*** **3** *colloq* commission □ ***What percentage do you take?*** **4** profit; advantage. • **play the percentages** in sport, gambling, etc: to play, operate or proceed by means of unspectacular safe shots, moves, etc, as opposed to spectacular but risky ones which may not succeed, on the assumption that this is more likely to lead to success in the long run. Ⓒ 18c.

percentile /pəˈsɛntaɪl/ ▻ *noun, statistics* one of the points or values that divide a collection of statistical data, arranged in order, into 100 equal parts □ ***The 90th percentile is the value below which 90% of the scores lie.*** Ⓒ 19c.

percentile rank ▻ *noun* grading according to percentile group.

percept /ˈpɜːsɛpt/ ▻ *noun, psychol, etc* **1** an object perceived by the senses. **2** the mental result of perceiving. Ⓒ 19c.

perceptible /pəˈsɛptəbəl/ ▻ *adj* able to be perceived; noticeable; detectable. • **perceptibility** *noun.* • **perceptibly** *adverb.*

perception /pəˈsɛpʃən/ ▻ *noun* **1** *psychol* the process whereby information about one's environment, received by the senses, is organized and interpreted so that it becomes meaningful. **2** one's powers of observation; discernment; insight. **3** one's view or interpretation of something. **4** *bot* response to a stimulus, eg chemical or caused by light. • **perceptional** *adj.* Ⓒ 17c: from Latin *percipere* to perceive.

perceptive /pəˈsɛptɪv/ ▻ *adj* quick to notice or discern; astute. • **perceptively** *adverb.* • **perceptiveness** or **perceptivity** /-sɛpˈtɪvɪtɪ/ *noun.*

perch¹ /pɜːtʃ/ ▻ *noun* (***perches***) **1** a branch or other narrow support above ground for a bird to rest or roost on. **2** any place selected, especially temporarily, as a seat. **3** a high position or vantage point. **4** a POLE² (*noun* 2). ▻ *verb* (***perches, perched, perching***) **1** *intr* said of a bird: to alight and rest on a perch. **2** *intr* to sit, especially insecurely or temporarily. **3** *tr & intr* to sit or place high up. Ⓒ 13c as *perche*, meaning 'a pole or stick', from French, from Latin *pertica* rod.

perch² /pɜːtʃ/ ▻ *noun* (***perch*** or ***perches***) any of various freshwater fishes which have a streamlined body with a yellowish-green or olive-brown back patterned with dark vertical bars, and a silvery-white belly. See also PERCOID. Ⓒ 14c: from Greek *perke*.

perchance /pəˈtʃɑːns/ ▻ *adverb, old use* **1** by chance. **2** perhaps. Ⓒ 14c: from French *par chance* by chance.

percipient /pəˈsɪpɪənt/ ▻ *adj* perceptive; acutely observant; discerning. ▻ *noun* **1** someone or something that perceives or can perceive. **2** someone who receives impressions telepathically or by other extrasensory means. • **percipience** *noun.* • **percipiently** *adverb.* Ⓒ 17c: from Latin *percipere* to perceive.

percoid /ˈpɜːkɔɪd/ ▻ *adj* referring or relating to, or resembling, PERCH².

percolate /ˈpɜːkəleɪt/ ▻ *verb* (***percolated, percolating***) **1** *tr & intr* to undergo or subject (a liquid) to the process of percolation; to ooze, trickle or filter. **2** *intr* (*also* **percolate through**) *colloq* said of news or information: to trickle or spread slowly. **3** *tr & intr* said of coffee: to make or be made in a percolator. Sometimes shortened to **perk.** Ⓒ 17c: from Latin *percolare* to filter through, from *per* through + *colare* to strain.

percolation /pɜːkəˈleɪʃən/ ▻ *noun* **1** the gradual movement of a liquid through a porous material such as rock or soil. **2** the brewing of coffee in a percolator.

percolator /ˈpɜːkəleɪtə(r)/ ▻ *noun* a pot for making coffee, in which boiling water circulates up through a tube and down through ground coffee beans. Ⓒ 19c.

percuss /pəˈkʌs/ ▻ *verb* (***percusses, percussed, percussing***) *medicine* to tap (a part of the body) with the fingertips or a PLEXOR for purposes of diagnosis. Ⓒ Early 19c in this sense; 16c in obsolete sense 'to strike or tap sharply': from Latin *percutere*, from *per-* thoroughly + *quatere* to shake or strike.

percussion /pəˈkʌʃən/ ▻ *noun* **1** the striking of one hard object against another. **2 a** musical instruments played by striking, eg drums, cymbals, xylophone, etc; **b** these instruments collectively as a section of an orchestra. **3** *medicine* an AUSCULTATION technique whereby part of the body is examined by tapping it with the fingers. • **percussional** *adj.* • **percussive** *adj.* • **percussively** *adverb.* Ⓒ 16c: from Latin *percussio* striking, from *percutere*; see PERCUSS.

percussion cap ▻ *noun* a metal case containing a material that explodes when struck, formerly used for firing rifles.

percussion hammer see under PLEXOR

percussionist ▻ *noun* someone who plays percussion instruments, especially in an orchestra.

percussor see under PLEXOR

percutaneous /pɜːkjʊˈteɪnɪəs/ ▻ *adj* applied or effected through the skin. Ⓒ Late 19c: from Latin *per cutem* through the skin.

per diem /pər ˈdiːɛm/ ▻ *adverb, adj* for each day; daily; by the day. Ⓒ 16c: Latin.

perdition /pəˈdɪʃən/ ▻ *noun* everlasting punishment after death; damnation; hell. Ⓒ 14c: from Latin *perditio*, from *perdere* to lose utterly.

peregrinate /ˈpɛrəgrɪneɪt/ ▻ *verb* (***peregrinated, peregrinating***) *literary* **1** *intr* to travel, voyage or roam; to wander abroad. **2** to travel through (a place, region, etc). • **peregrination** *noun.* • **peregrinator** *noun.* Ⓒ 16c: from Latin *peregrinari, peregrinatus* to roam, from *per* through + *ager* field.

peregrine /ˈpɛrəgrɪn/ ▻ *noun* a large falcon with greyish-blue plumage on its back and wings, striped with darker bars, and paler underparts, also barred. Also called **peregrine falcon.** Ⓒ 14c: from Latin *peregrinus* wandering abroad, because the young birds were captured during their migration from the nesting-place, rather than being taken unfledged from the nest.

pereira /pəˈrɛərə/ ▻ *noun* (***pereiras***) **1** a Brazilian tree, the bark of which is used in herbal medicine. **2** the bark itself. Also called **pereira bark.** Ⓒ 19c: named after Jonathan Pereira, 19c English pharmacologist.

peremptory /pəˈrɛmptərɪ/ ▻ *adj* **1** said of an order: made in expectation of immediate compliance □ ***a peremptory summons.*** **2** said of a tone or manner: arrogantly impatient. **3** said of a statement, conclusion, etc: allowing no denial or discussion; dogmatic. • **peremptorily** *adverb.* • **peremptoriness** *noun.* Ⓒ 16c: from Latin *peremptorius* deadly.

perennial /pəˈrɛnɪəl/ ▻ *adj* **1** *bot* referring or relating to a plant that lives for several to many years, either growing continuously, as in the case of woody trees and shrubs, or having stems that die back each autumn. See also ANNUAL, BIENNIAL. **2** lasting throughout the year. **3** constant; continual. **4** said of insects: living for more than one year. ▻ *noun* a perennial plant. • **perenniality** *noun.* • **perennially** *adverb.* Ⓒ 17c: from Latin *perennis*, from *per* through + *annus* year.

perestroika /pɛrəˈstrɔɪkə/ ▻ *noun* a restructuring or reorganization, specifically that of the economic and political system of the former USSR instigated by Mikhail Gorbachev in the 1980s. ◷ 1980s: Russian, meaning 'reconstruction'.

perfect ▷ *adj* /'pɜːfɪkt/ **1** complete in all essential elements. **2** faultless; flawless. **3** excellent; absolutely satisfactory. **4** exact □ *a perfect circle.* **5** *colloq* absolute; utter □ *perfect nonsense.* **6** *bot* having ANDROECIUM and GYNAECEUM in the same flower. **7** *grammar* said of the tense or aspect of a verb: denoting an action completed at some time in the past or prior to the time spoken of. ▷ *noun* /'pɜːfɪkt/ *grammar* **1** the perfect tense, in English formed with the auxiliary verb *have* and the past PARTICIPLE, denoting an action completed in the past (**present perfect**, eg *I have written the letter*) or was or will be completed at the time being spoken of (**past perfect** or PLUPERFECT, eg *I had written the letter*; **future perfect**, eg *I will have written the letter*). **2** a verb in a perfect tense. Compare FUTURE, PAST, PRESENT, IMPERFECT, PLUPERFECT, PROGRESSIVE. ▷ *verb* /pə'fɛkt/ (***perfected, perfecting***) **1** to improve something to one's satisfaction □ *perfect one's Italian.* **2** to finalize or complete. **3** to develop (a technique, etc) to a reliable standard. • **perfectly** see separate entry. • **perfectness** *noun.* ◷ 13c: from Latin *perficere* to complete.

perfecta /pə'fɛktə/ ▷ *noun* (***perfectas***) a form of bet in which the punter has to select, and place in the correct order, the two horses, dogs, etc which will come first and second in a race. Compare QUINELLA, TRIFECTA, QUADRELLA. ◷ 1970s: originally US, from American Spanish *quiniela perfecta* perfect quinella.

perfect cadence ▷ *noun, music* a cadence that passes from the chord of the dominant to that of the tonic.

perfect fifth ▷ *noun, music* the interval between two sounds whose vibration frequencies are as 2 to 3.

perfect fourth ▷ *noun, music* the interval between two sounds whose vibration frequencies are as 3 to 4.

perfect gas see IDEAL GAS

perfectible ▷ *adj* capable of being made or becoming perfect. • **perfectibility** *noun.*

perfect insect ▷ *noun, entomol* an IMAGO or completely developed form of an insect.

perfect interval ▷ *noun, music* the fourth, fifth or octave.

perfection /pə'fɛkʃən/ ▷ *noun* **1** the state of being perfect. **2** the process of making or being made perfect, complete, etc. **3** flawlessness. **4** *colloq* an instance of absolute excellence □ *The meal was perfection.* • **to perfection** perfectly □ *did it to perfection.*

perfectionism ▷ *noun* **1** the doctrine that perfection is attainable. **2** an expectation of the very highest standard.

perfectionist ▷ *noun* someone who is inclined to be dissatisfied with standards of achievement, especially their own, if they are not absolutely perfect. • **perfectionistic** *adj.*

perfective /pə'fɛktɪv/ ▷ *adj* **1** tending to make perfect. **2** *grammar* said of a verbal aspect: denoting an action that is or was completed.

perfectly /'pɜːfɪktlɪ/ ▷ *adverb* **1** in a perfect way. **2** completely; quite □ *a perfectly reasonable reaction.*

perfect number ▷ *noun, math* a number that is equal to the sum of all its factors (except itself), eg the number 6, because the sum of its factors (1+2+3) is equal to 6. See FACTOR *noun* 2.

perfect pitch and **absolute pitch** ▷ *noun, music* the ability to recognize a note from its pitch, or spontaneously sing any note with correct pitch.

perfervid /pɜː'fɜːvɪd/ ▷ *adj, poetic* extremely fervid; ardent; eager. ◷ 19c: from Latin *perfervidus*, from *prae* before + *fervidus* fervid.

perfidious /pə'fɪdɪəs/ ▷ *adj* treacherous, double-dealing or disloyal. • **perfidiously** *adverb.* • **perfidiousness** or **perfidy** /'pɜːfɪdɪ/ *noun.* ◷ 16c: from Latin *perfidus* faithlessness, from *per* (implying destruction) + *fides* faith.

perfluorocarbon /pəfluəroʊ'kɑːbən/ ▷ *noun, chem* **1** a fluorocarbon in which the hydrogen directly attached to the carbon atoms has been completely replaced by fluorine. **2** any binary compound of carbon and fluorine, similar to a hydrocarbon.

perfoliate /pə'foulɪət, -lɪeɪt/ ▷ *adj, bot* said of a leaf: having the base joined around the stem, so as to appear pierced by the stem. • **perfoliation** *noun.* ◷ 17c: from Latin *perfoliatus*, from *per* through + *folium* leaf.

perforate /'pɜːfəreɪt/ ▷ *verb* (***perforated, perforating***) **1** to make a hole or holes in something; to pierce. **2** to make a row of holes in something, for ease of tearing. **3** *intr, medicine* said of an ulcer, diseased appendix, etc: to develop a hole; to burst. ◷ 16c: from Latin *perforare*, *perforatum* to pierce.

perforation /pɜːfə'reɪʃən/ ▷ *noun* **1** a hole made in something. **2** a row of small holes made in paper, a sheet of stamps, etc for ease of tearing. **3** the process of perforating or being perforated.

perforce /pə'fɔːs/ ▷ *adverb, chiefly old use* necessarily; inevitably or unavoidably. ◷ 14c: from French *par force* by force.

perform /pə'fɔːm/ ▷ *verb* (***performed, performing***) **1** to carry out (a task, job, action, etc); to do or accomplish. **2** to fulfil (a function) or provide (a service, etc). **3** *tr & intr* to act, sing, play, dance, etc (a play, song, piece of music, dance, etc) to entertain an audience. **4** *intr* said eg of an engine: to function. **5** *intr* to conduct oneself, especially when presenting oneself for assessment □ *performs well in interviews.* **6** *intr* said of commercial products, shares, currencies, etc: to fare in competition. • **performable** *adj.* • **performer** *noun.* ◷ 14c: from French *parfournir.*

performance /pə'fɔːməns/ ▷ *noun* **1 a** the performing of a play, part, dance, piece of music, etc before an audience; **b** a dramatic or artistic presentation or entertainment. **2** the act or process of performing a task, etc. **3** a level of achievement, success or, in commerce, profitability. **4** manner or efficiency of functioning. **5** *derog* an instance of outrageous behaviour, especially in public.

performance art ▷ *noun* a presentation in which several art forms are combined, such as acting, music, sculpture, photography, etc.

performing ▷ *adj* **1** referring to something or someone that performs. **2** trained to perform tricks □ *performing circus dogs.*

the performing arts ▷ *plural noun* the forms of art that require performance to be appreciated, especially music, drama and dance.

perfume ▷ *noun* /'pɜːfjuːm/ **1** a sweet smell; a scent or fragrance. **2** a fragrant liquid prepared from the extracts of flowers, etc, for applying to the skin or clothes; scent. ▷ *verb* /pə'fjuːm/ (***perfumed, perfuming***) to give a sweet smell to something; to apply perfume to something. • **perfumed** *adj.* • **perfumeless** *adj.* • **perfumer** /-'fjuːmə(r)/ *noun* a maker or seller of perfumes. • **perfumy** /'pɜːfjuːmɪ/ *adj.* ◷ 16c: from French *parfum*, from Latin *per* through + *fumare* to impregnate with smoke.

perfumery /pə'fjuːmərɪ/ ▷ *noun* (***perfumeries***) **1** perfumes in general. **2** the making or preparing of perfumes. **3** a place where perfumes are made or sold.

perfunctory /pə'fʌŋktərɪ/ ▷ *adj* done merely as a duty or routine, without genuine care or feeling. • **perfunctorily** *adverb.* • **perfunctoriness** *noun.* ◷ 16c: from Latin *perfunctorius* slapdash.

perfusion /pə'fjuːʒən/ ▷ *noun* **1** *biol* the movement of a fluid through a tissue or organ. **2** *medicine* the deliberate introduction of a fluid into a tissue or organ, usually by injection into a nearby blood vessel. ⓒ 16c: from Latin *perfusus* poured over.

pergola /ˈpɜːɡələ/ ▷ *noun* (***pergolas***) a framework constructed from slender branches, for plants to climb up; a trellis. ⓒ 17c: Italian, from Latin *pergula* shed.

perh. ▷ *abbreviation* perhaps.

perhaps /pəˈhaps or (*informal*) praps, pəˈraps/ ▷ *adverb* possibly; maybe. ⓒ 16c: from French *par* by + Norse *happ* fortune or chance.

peri- /pɛrɪ/ ▷ *prefix, denoting* **1** around □ *periscope* □ *pericardium.* **2** near □ *perinatal* □ *perigee.* ⓒ From Greek *peri* round or around.

perianth /ˈpɛrɪanθ/ ▷ *noun, bot* the outer part of a flower, usually consisting of a circle of petals within a circle of SEPALS. ⓒ 18c: from Latin *perianthium*, from Greek *anthos* flower.

periastron /pɛrɪˈastrɒn/ ▷ *noun, astron* the stage in the orbit of a comet, one component of a binary star, etc, when it is closest to the star around which it revolves. ⓒ 19c: from Greek *astron* star.

pericarditis /pɛrɪkɑːˈdaɪtɪs/ ▷ *noun, pathol* inflammation of the pericardium.

pericardium /pɛrɪˈkɑːdɪəm/ ▷ *noun* (***pericardia*** /-dɪə/) *anatomy* the sac, composed of fibrous tissue, that surrounds the heart. • **pericardiac** or **pericardial** *adj.* ⓒ 16c: Latin, from Greek *perikardion*, from *kardia* heart.

pericarp /ˈpɛrɪkɑːp/ ▷ *noun, bot* in plants: the wall of a fruit, which develops from the ovary wall after fertilization. • **pericarpial** /-ˈkɑːpɪəl/ *adj.* ⓒ 17c: from Latin *pericarpium*, from Greek *karpos* fruit.

perichondrium /pɛrɪˈkɒndrɪəm/ ▷ *noun* (***perichondria*** /-drɪə/) *anatomy* the fibrous membrane covering cartilage. ⓒ 18c: Latin, from Greek *chondros* cartilage.

periclase /ˈpɛrɪkleɪz, -kleɪs/ ▷ *noun, chem* a magnesium oxide occurring naturally in isometric crystals. ⓒ 19c: from Latin *periclasia*, formed in error from Greek *peri-* very + *klasis* fracture, because of its perfect chemical cleavage.

periclinal /pɛrɪˈklaɪnəl/ ▷ *adj* **1** *geol* sloping downwards in all directions from a point. **2** *bot* said of a cell wall, etc: parallel to the outer surface. ⓒ 19c: from Greek *periklines* sloping on all sides, from *klinein* to slope.

pericranium /pɛrɪˈkreɪnɪəm/ ▷ *noun* (***pericrania*** /-nɪə/) **1** *anatomy* the membrane surrounding the cranium. **2** *non-technical* the skull or brain. ⓒ 16c: Latin, from Greek *perikranion*, from *kranion* skull.

peridot /ˈpɛrɪdɒt/ ▷ *noun* **1** OLIVINE. **2** a green olivine used in jewellery. • **peridotic** /pɛrɪˈdɒtɪk/ *adj.* ⓒ 14c as *peritot*, etc: from French *péridot.*

peridotite /pɛrɪˈdoʊtaɪt/ ▷ *noun, geol* a coarse-grained igneous rock mainly composed of OLIVINE, thought to be a constituent of the Earth's upper mantle. ⓒ 19c: from French *péridot.*

perigee /ˈpɛrɪdʒiː/ ▷ *noun* (***perigees***) *astron* the point in the orbit of the Moon or an artificial satellite around the Earth when it is closest to the Earth. See also APOGEE. ⓒ 16c: from French *perigée*, from Greek *perigeion*, from *peri* near + *gaia, ge* earth.

periglacial /pɛrɪˈɡleɪsɪəl, pɛrɪˈɡleɪʃəl/ ▷ *adj* referring to or like a region bordering a glacier. ⓒ 1920s.

perihelion /pɛrɪˈhiːlɪən/ ▷ *noun* (***perihelia***) *astron* the point in the orbit of a planet or comet round the Sun when it is closest to the Sun. See also APHELION. ⓒ 17c: from Latin *perihelium*, from Greek *helios* sun.

perihepatic /pɛrɪhɛˈpatɪk/ ▷ *adj, anatomy, etc* surrounding the liver. ⓒ 19c.

perihepatitis /pɛrɪhɛpəˈtaɪtɪs/ ▷ *noun, pathol* inflammation of the PERITONEUM covering the liver. ⓒ 19c.

perikaryon /pɛrɪˈkarɪɒn/ ▷ *noun* (***perikarya*** /-rɪə/) *anatomy* the part of a nerve cell that contains the nucleus. ⓒ 19c: from Greek *karyon* kernel.

peril /ˈpɛrəl/ ▷ *noun* **1** grave danger. **2** a hazard. • **at one's peril** at the risk of one's life or safety, etc. ⓒ 13c: from French *péril*, from Latin *periculum* danger.

perilous /ˈpɛrələs/ ▷ *adj* very dangerous. • **perilously** *adverb.* • **perilousness** *noun.*

perilune /ˈpɛrɪluːn/ ▷ *noun, astron* the point in a spacecraft's orbit round the Moon when it is closest to the Moon. ⓒ 1960s: from Latin *luna* moon; compare PERIGEE, PERIHELION.

perimeter /pəˈrɪmɪtə(r)/ ▷ *noun* **1 a** the boundary of an enclosed area; **b** *as adj* □ *perimeter fence.* **2** *geom* **a** the boundary or circumference of any plane figure; **b** the length of this boundary. **3** *medicine* an instrument for measuring the field of vision. • **perimetric** /-ˈmɛtrɪk/ or **perimetrical** *adj.* ⓒ 16c: from Greek *perimetros*, from *metros* measure.

perimysium /pɛrɪˈmɪzɪəm/ ▷ *noun, anatomy* the connective tissue which surrounds and binds together muscle fibres. ⓒ 19c: based on Greek *mys* muscle.

perinatal /pɛrɪˈneɪtəl/ ▷ *adj, medicine* denoting or relating to the period extending from the 28th week of pregnancy to about one month after childbirth. ⓒ 1950s.

perinephrium /pɛrɪˈnɛfrɪəm/ ▷ *noun, anatomy* the fatty tissue surrounding the kidney. • **perinephric** *adj.* ⓒ 19c: from Greek *nephros* kidney.

perinephritis /pɛrɪnəˈfraɪtɪs/ *noun, pathol* inflammation of the perinephrium.

perineum /pɛrɪˈnɪəm/ ▷ *noun* (***perinea*** /-ˈnɪə/) *anatomy* the region of the body between the genital organs and the anus. • **perineal** *adj.* ⓒ 17c: from Latin *perinaeum*, from Greek *perinaion.*

period /ˈpɪərɪəd/ ▷ *noun* **1** a portion of time. **2** a phase or stage, eg in history, or in a person's life and development, etc. **3** an interval of time at the end of which events recur in the same order. **4** *geol* **a** a unit of geological time that is a subdivision of an ERA, and is itself divided into EPOCHS; **b** any long interval of geological time □ *glacial period.* **5** any of the sessions of equal length into which the school day is divided, and to which particular subjects or activities are assigned. **6** *especially N Amer* a FULL STOP. **7** *colloq* added to a statement to emphasize its finality □ *You may not go, period.* **8** the periodic discharge of blood during a woman's menstrual cycle □ *two weeks since her last period.* **9** *chem* in the periodic table: any of the seven horizontal rows of chemical elements. **10** *physics* the time interval after which a cyclical phenomenon, eg a wave motion, repeats itself; the reciprocal of the frequency. **11** *arith* the recurring part of a circulating decimal. ▷ *adj* dating from, or designed in the style of, the historical period in question □ *period costume* □ *period furniture.* • **period of grace** a specific time allowed to both parties to a contract to fulfil any obligations arising from it, or to withdraw from it completely. ⓒ 15c: from Greek *periodos* circuit or going round, from *peri* round + *hodos* way.

periodic /pɪərɪˈɒdɪk/ ▷ *adj* **1** happening at intervals, especially regular intervals. **2** occurring from time to time; occasional. **3** *chem* referring or relating to the periodic table.

periodical /pɪərɪˈɒdɪkəl/ ▷ *noun* a magazine published weekly, monthly, quarterly, etc. ▷ *adj* **1** referring or relating to such publications. **2** published at more or less regular intervals. **3** periodic. • **periodically** *adverb.*

periodic function ▷ *noun, math* a function that repeats itself at constant intervals.

periodicity /pɪərɪəˈdɪsɪtɪ/ ▷ *noun* the fact of recurring, or tendency to recur, at intervals; frequency.

periodic law ▷ *noun, chem* the law which states that the physical and chemical properties of the chemical elements tend to change in a periodic manner with increasing atomic number.

periodic sentence ▻ *noun, rhetoric* a sentence so constructed that it is not until the final clause that the requirements of sense and grammar are met, thus creating an element of suspense.

periodic table ▻ *noun, chem* a table of all the chemical elements arranged in order of increasing atomic number.

periodontal /pɛrɪoʊ'dɒntəl/ ▻ *adj, anatomy, etc* relating to tissues or regions around a tooth.

periodontics ▻ *singular noun* the branch of dentistry concerned with periodontal diseases. Also called **periodontology**. • **periodontical** *adj*. • **periodontist** *noun*. ⓒ Early 20c: from Greek *odous, odontos* tooth.

periodontitis /pɛrɪoʊdɒn'taɪtɪs/ ▻ *noun, pathol* inflammation of the tissues surrounding a tooth. ⓒ 19c.

period piece ▻ *noun* **1** a piece of furniture, etc dating from, and in the distinctive style of, a certain historical period. **2** *facetious* something quaintly old-fashioned.

periosteum /pɛrɪ'ɒstɪəm/ ▻ *noun* (***periostea*** /-tɪə/) *anatomy* a tough fibrous membrane covering the surface of bones, necessary for bone nutrition, and destruction of which prevents healing of fractures. • **periosteal** or **periostitic** *adj*. ⓒ 16c: Latin, from Greek *periosteon*, from *osteon* a bone.

peripatetic /pɛrɪpə'tɛtɪk/ ▻ *adj* **1** travelling about from place to place. **2** said of a teacher: employed by several schools and so obliged to travel between them. **3** (*also* **Peripatetic**) denoting the school of philosophers founded by Aristotle, given to promenading while lecturing. ▻ *noun* a peripatetic teacher or philosopher. • **peripatetically** *adverb*. ⓒ 16c: from Greek *peripatetikos*, from *peri* around + *pateein* to walk.

peripeteia or **peripetia** /pɛrɪpə'taɪə, pɛrɪpə'tiːə/ ▻ *noun* (***peripeteias***) especially in drama: a sudden change of fortune. ⓒ 16c: Greek, from *peri* around + *pet-*, the root of *piptein* to fall.

peripheral /pɛ'rɪfərəl/ ▻ *adj* **1** relating or belonging to the outer edge or outer surface □ *peripheral nerves*. **2** (**peripheral to something**) not central to the issue in hand; marginal. **3** *computing* supplementary; auxiliary. **4** relating to the outer edge of the field of vision. ▻ *noun, computing* a device concerned with the input, output or backup storage of data, eg a printer, mouse or disk drive. Also called **peripheral device**.

periphery /pə'rɪfərɪ/ ▻ *noun* (***peripheries***) **1** the edge or boundary of something. **2** the external surface of something. **3** a surrounding region. ⓒ 16c: from Greek *periphereia* circumference or surface.

periphrasis /pə'rɪfrəsɪs/ ▻ *noun* (***periphrases*** /-siːz/) a roundabout way of saying something; circumlocution. ⓒ 16c: Latin and Greek, from Greek *peri* around + *phrasis* speech.

periphrastic /pɛrɪ'frastɪk/ ▻ *adj* **1** using periphrasis. **2** *grammar* said especially of a verb tense involving an auxiliary: using at least two words instead of a single inflected form. • **periphrastically** *adverb*.

perique /pə'riːk/ ▻ *noun* a strongly-flavoured tobacco from Louisiana. ⓒ 19c: possibly from Périque, the nickname of a grower.

periscope /'pɛrɪskoʊp/ ▻ *noun, optics* a system of prisms or mirrors that enables the user to view objects that are above eye-level or obscured by a closer object, used in submarines, military tanks, etc. • **periscopic** /-skɒpɪk/ *adj*. ⓒ 19c: from Greek *periskopeein* to look around.

perish /'pɛrɪʃ/ ▻ *verb* (***perishes, perished, perishing***) **1** *intr* to die; to be destroyed or ruined. **2** **a** *intr* said of materials: to decay; **b** to cause (materials) to decay or rot. ⓒ 13c as *perissen*: from French *perir*, from Latin *perire*.

perishable ▻ *adj* said of commodities, especially food: liable to rot or go bad quickly. • **perishability** *noun*.

perished ▻ *adj* **1** *colloq* feeling the cold severely. **2** said of materials such as rubber: weakened and made liable to break or crack by age or exposure.

perisher ▻ *noun, old colloq use* a mischievous child or other troublesome person.

perishing ▻ *adj* **1** *colloq* said of weather, etc: very cold. **2** *old use, colloq* damned, infernal or confounded. • **perishingly** *adverb*.

perisperm /'pɛrɪspɜːm/ ▻ *noun, bot* nutritive tissue in a seed derived from the nucellus. ⓒ 19c: from Greek *sperma* seed.

perissodactyl /pərɪsoʊ'daktɪl/ ▻ *noun, zool* any UNGULATE with an odd number of toes, such as the horse, tapir or rhinoceros. ▻ *adj* referring, relating or belonging to the order **Perissodactyla**. ⓒ 19c: from Greek *perissos* odd + *daktylos* a finger or toe.

peristalith /pə'rɪstəlɪθ/ ▻ *noun* a stone circle. ⓒ 19c: from Greek *peristatos* standing around + *lithos* stone.

peristalsis /pɛrɪ'stalsɪs/ ▻ *noun* (***peristalses*** /-siːz/) *physiol* in hollow tubular organs, especially the intestines and oesophagus: the waves of involuntary muscle contractions that force the contents of the tube, eg food, further forward. • **peristaltic** *adj*. ⓒ 18c; *peristaltic*, first used in 17c: from Greek *peristellein* to contract round.

peristyle /'pɛrɪstaɪl/ ▻ *noun, archit* **1** a colonnade round a courtyard or building. **2** a court, square, etc surrounded by a colonnade. ⓒ 17c: from Greek *peri* round + *stylos* column.

peritoneum /pɛrɪtə'niːəm/ ▻ *noun* (***peritonea*** /-'niːə/ or ***peritoneums***) *anatomy* a SEROUS membrane that lines the abdominal cavity. • **peritoneal** *adj*. ⓒ 16c: Latin, from Greek *peritonaion*, from *periteinein* to stretch all round.

peritonitis /pɛrɪtə'naɪtɪs/ ▻ *noun, pathol* inflammation of the peritoneum. ⓒ 18c.

periwig /'pɛrɪwɪg/ ▻ *noun* a man's wig of the 17c and 18c. ⓒ 16c: a variant of PERUKE.

periwinkle¹ /'pɛrɪwɪŋkəl/ ▻ *noun* any of various climbing plants with slender trailing stems, oval shiny green leaves, and single bluish-purple flowers with five flat lobes. ⓒ Anglo-Saxon *perwince*: from Latin *pervinca*.

periwinkle² /'pɛrɪwɪŋkəl/ ▻ *noun* any of several species of herbivorous small marine mollusc with a spirally coiled shell, especially the **edible** or **common periwinkle**, sold by fishmongers as the **winkle**. ⓒ 16c: probably from Anglo-Saxon *pinewincle*.

perjure /'pɜːdʒə(r)/ ▻ *verb* (***perjured, perjuring***) (*now always* **perjure oneself**) to forswear oneself in a court of law, ie lie while under oath; to commit perjury. ⓒ 15c: from Latin *perjurare*, from *jurare* to swear.

perjury /'pɜːdʒərɪ/ ▻ *noun* (***perjuries***) the crime of lying while under oath in a court of law. • **perjurer** *noun*.

perk¹ ▻ *verb* (***perked, perking***) *tr & intr* **1** (*always* **perk up** or **perk someone up**) to become or make someone more lively and cheerful. **2** (*always* **perk up**) said of an animal's ears: to prick up. ⓒ 14c.

perk² ▻ *noun, colloq* a benefit, additional to income, derived from employment, such as membership of a health club, the use of a company car, etc. ⓒ 19c: a shortening of PERQUISITE.

perk³ ▻ *verb* (***perked, perking***) *tr & intr, colloq* to PERCOLATE (coffee). ⓒ 1930s.

perkin see PARKIN

perky /'pɜːkɪ/ ▻ *adj* (***perkier, perkiest***) lively and cheerful. • **perkily** *adverb*. • **perkiness** *noun*. ⓒ 19c, from PERK¹.

perlite or **pearlite** /'pɜːlaɪt/ ▻ *noun, geol* **1** any volcanic glass with small concentric spheroidal or spiral cracks between rectilineal ones. **2** a constituent of steel composed of alternate plates of ferrite and cementite. • **perlitic** or **pearlitic** /-'lɪtɪk/ *adj*. ⓒ 19c: French.

Periodic Table

The elements, listed with their symbols and atomic numbers, lie horizontally in order of their atomic numbers. Those with chemically similar

1 Hydrogen H								
3 Lithium Li	4 Beryllium Be							
11 Sodium Na	12 Magnesium Mg							
19 Potassium K	20 Calcium Ca	21 Scandium Sc	22 Titanium Ti	23 Vanadium V	24 Chromium Cr	25 Manganese Mn	26 Iron Fe	27 Cobalt Co
37 Rubidium Rb	38 Strontium Sr	39 Yttrium Y	40 Zirconium Zr	41 Niobium Nb	42 Molybdenum Mo	43 Technetium Tc	44 Ruthenium Ru	45 Rhodium Rh
55 Caesium Cs	56 Barium Ba	57–71 Lanthanide series	72 Hafnium Hf	73 Tantalum Ta	74 Wolfram W	75 Rhenium Re	76 Osmium Os	77 Iridium Ir
87 Francium Fr	88 Radium Ra	89–103 Actinide series	104 Rutherfordium Rf					
		57 Lanthanum La	58 Cerium Ce	59 Praseodymium Pr	60 Neodymium Nd	61 Prometheum Pm	62 Samarium Sm	63 Europium Eu
		89 Actinium Ac	90 Thorium Th	91 Protactinium Pa	92 Uranium U	93 Neptunium Np	94 Plutonium Pu	95 Americium Am

perlocution /pɜːləˈkjuːʃən/ ▻ *noun, philos* a speech act that involves persuading, convincing, etc and which may or may not prove successful. Compare ILLOCUTION. • **perlocutionary** *adj*. ◷ 1950s in this sense; 16c, meaning 'speaking': PER-^{2} + LOCUTION.

perm^{1} ▻ *noun* a hair treatment using chemicals that give a long-lasting wave or curl. ▻ *verb* (***permed, perming***) to curl or wave (hair) with a perm. ◷ 1920s: a shortening of PERMANENT WAVE.

perm^{2} *colloq* ▻ *noun* short form of PERMUTATION *noun* 2. ▻ *verb* (***permed***, ***perming***) short form of PERMUTE. ◷ 1950s.

permaculture /ˈpɜːməkʌltʃə(r)/ ▻ *noun, ecol* an ecologically friendly and self-sustaining system of agriculture. ◷ 20c: from *perma*nent + agri*culture*.

permafrost /ˈpɜːməfrɒst/ ▻ *noun, geol* an area of subsoil or rock that has remained frozen for at least a year, and usually much longer, found mainly in arctic, subarctic and alpine regions. ◷ 1940s, from *perma*nent *frost*.

permalloy /ˈpɜːmalɔɪ/ ▻ *noun* any of various alloys of iron and nickel, which often contain other elements, such as copper, molybdenum and chromium, and which have high magnetic permeability. ◷ 1920s: from *perm*eability + ALLOY.

permanence /ˈpɜːmənəns/ ▻ *noun* the fact or state of being permanent.

permanency /ˈpɜːmənənsɪ/ ▻ *noun* (***permanencies***) **1** someone or something that is permanent. **2** permanence.

permanent /ˈpɜːmənənt/ ▻ *adj* **1** lasting, or intended to last, indefinitely; not temporary. **2** said of a condition, etc: unlikely to alter. • **permanently** *adverb*. ◷ 15c: from Latin *permanere* to remain.

permanent magnet ▻ *noun, physics* a magnet that retains its magnetic properties after the force which magnetized it has been removed.

permanent tooth ▻ *noun, anatomy* in most mammals: any one of the set of teeth that develops after the MILK TEETH have been shed.

permanent wave ▻ *noun, old use* a PERM^{1}. ◷ Early 20c.

permanent way ▻ *noun* a railway track, including the rails, sleepers and stones.

permanganate /pəˈmaŋgəneɪt/ ▻ *noun, chem* any of the salts of **permanganic acid**, especially POTASSIUM PERMANGANATE, used as an oxidizing and bleaching agent and disinfectant. ◷ 19c.

permeability /pɜːmɪəˈbɪlɪtɪ/ ▻ *noun* **1** the ability of a porous material or membrane to allow a gas or liquid to pass through it. **2** *physics* a measure of the extent to which the presence of a material alters the magnetic field around it.

permeable /ˈpɜːmɪəbəl/ ▻ *adj* said of a porous material or membrane: allowing certain liquids or gases to pass through it. • **permeably** *adverb*. ◷ 15c: from Latin *permeabilis*; see PERMEATE.

permeance /ˈpɜːmɪəns/ ▻ *noun* **1** the act of permeating. **2** *elec engineering* the reciprocal of the reluctance of a magnetic circuit.

permeate /ˈpɜːmɪeɪt/ ▻ *verb* (***permeated, permeating***) (*also* **permeate through something**) **1** said of a liquid or gas: to pass, penetrate or diffuse through (a fine or porous material or a membrane). **2** *tr & intr* said of a smell, gas,

of Elements

properties fall under one another in the columns. Elements with atomic numbers of 93 and over are man-made.

								2 Helium He
			5 Boron B	6 Carbon C	7 Nitrogen N	8 Oxygen O	9 Fluorine F	10 Neon Ne
			13 Aluminium Al	14 Silicon Si	15 Phosphorus P	16 Sulphur S	17 Chlorine C	18 Argon Ar
28 Nickel Ni	29 Copper Cu	30 Zinc Zn	31 Gallium Ga	32 Germanium Ge	33 Arsenic As	34 Selenium Se	35 Bromine Br	36 Krypton Kr
46 Palladium Pd	47 Silver Ag	48 Cadmium Cd	49 Indium In	50 Tin Sn	51 Antimony Sb	52 Tellurium Te	53 Iodine I	54 Xenon Xe
78 Platinum Pt	79 Gold Au	80 Mercury Hg	81 Thallium Tl	82 Lead Pb	83 Bismuth Bi	84 Polonium Po	85 Astatine At	86 Radon Rn
64 Gadolinium Gd	65 Terbium Tb	66 Dysprosium Dy	67 Holmium Ho	68 Erbium Er	69 Thulium Tm	70 Ytterbium Yb	71 Lutecium Lu	
96 Curium Cm	97 Berkelium Bk	98 Californium Cf	99 Einsteinium Es	100 Fermium Fm	101 Mendelevium Md	102 Nobelium No	103 Lawrencium Lr	

etc: to spread through a room or other space; to fill or impregnate. ● **permeation** *noun*. ● **permeative** *adj*. ⓔ 17c: from Latin *permeare* to penetrate.

per mensum /pɛr 'mɛnsəm/ ▻ *adverb* for each month; monthly; by the month. ⓔ 17c: Latin.

Permian /'pɜːmɪən/ ▻ *adj* **1** *geol* relating to the last period of the Palaeozoic era, during which reptiles became more abundant and primitive conifers and GINKGOES appeared. **2** relating to the rocks formed during this period. See table at GEOLOGICAL TIME SCALE. ⓔ 19c: named after the Perm region in Russia where extensive areas of rock formed in this period are found.

permissible /pɜː'mɪsəbəl/ ▻ *adj* allowable; permitted. ● **permissibility** *noun*. ● **permissibly** *adverb*.

permission /pə'mɪʃən/ ▻ *noun* consent, agreement or authorization. ⓔ 15c: from Latin *permissio*, from *permittere*; see PERMIT.

permissive /pɜː'mɪsɪv/ ▻ *adj* **1** tolerant; liberal. **2** allowing usually excessive freedom, especially in sexual matters □ *the permissive society*. ● **permissively** *adverb*. ● **permissiveness** *noun*.

permit ▻ *verb* /pə'mɪt/ (***permitted***, ***permitting***) **1** to consent to or give permission for something. **2** to give (someone) leave or authorization. **3** to allow someone something □ *permitted him access to his children*. **4** (*also* **permit of something**) *formal* to enable it to happen or take effect; to give scope or opportunity for it □ *an outrage that permits of no excuses*. ▻ *noun* /'pɜːmɪt/ a document that authorizes something □ *a fishing permit*. ⓔ 15c: from Latin *permittere*, from *mittere* to let pass.

permittivity /pɜːmɪ'tɪvɪtɪ/ ▻ *noun*, *physics* (symbol ε) the ratio of the ELECTRIC DISPLACEMENT in a medium to the intensity of the electric field that is producing it, measured in FARADS per metre.

permutable /pə'mjuːtəbəl/ ▻ *adj* interchangeable. ● **permutability** *noun*. ⓔ 18c.

permutation /pɜːmjʊ'teɪʃən/ ▻ *noun* **1** *math* **a** any of several different ways in which a set of objects or numbers can be arranged; **b** any of the resulting combinations. **2** a fixed combination in football pools for selecting the results of matches. Often shortened to **perm**. ⓔ 14c: from Latin *permutatio*, from *permutare* (see PERMUTE).

permute /pə'mjuːt/ or **permutate** /'pɜːmjuteɪt/ ▻ *verb* (***permuted***, ***permuting***; ***permutated***, ***permutating***) to rearrange (a set of things) in different orders, especially in every possible order in succession; to go through the possible permutations of (a set of things). Also shortened to **perm**. ⓔ 14c: from Latin *permutare* to change completely or interchange, from *mutare* to change.

pernicious /pə'nɪʃəs/ ▻ *adj* harmful; destructive; deadly. ● **perniciously** *adverb*. ● **perniciousness** *noun*. ⓔ 16c: from Latin *perniciosus*, from *pernicies* ruin or bane.

pernicious anaemia ▻ *noun*, *medicine* a form of anaemia caused by a dietary deficiency of vitamin B_{12}, or by failure of the body to absorb the vitamin.

pernickety /pə'nɪkətɪ/ ▻ *adj* **1** said of a person: over-particular about small details; fussy. **2** said of a task: tricky; intricate. ● **pernicketiness** *noun*. ⓔ 19c: Scots.

Pernod /'pɛənoʊ, 'pɜːnoʊ/ ▻ *noun*, *trademark* an alcoholic drink made in France, flavoured with aniseed, and usually drunk with water as an aperitif. ⓔ Early 20c.

peroneal /pɛrə'nɪəl/ ▻ *adj, anatomy* referring or relating to the FIBULA. ⓒ Early 19c: from medical Latin *peronaeus*, from Greek *perone* fibula.

peroration /pɛrə'reɪʃən/ ▻ *noun* **1** the concluding section of a speech, in which the points made are summed up. **2** *colloq* a long formal speech. ● **perorate** /pɛrə'reɪt/ *verb* (***perorated***, ***perorating***) to make a peroration. ⓒ 15c: from Latin *peroratio*, from *per* through + *orare* to speak.

peroxide /pə'rɒksaɪd/ ▻ *noun* **1** *chem* any of various strong oxidizing agents that release hydrogen peroxide when treated with acid, used in rocket fuels, antiseptics, disinfectants and bleaches. **2 a** a solution of hydrogen peroxide used as a bleach for hair and textiles; **b** *as adj* □ *a peroxide blonde*. ▻ *verb* (***peroxided***, ***peroxiding***) to bleach (hair) with hydrogen peroxide. ⓒ 19c:.

perpend see PARPEN

perpendicular /pɜːpən'dɪkjʊlə(r)/ ▻ *adj* **1** vertical; upright; in the direction of gravity. **2** (*also* **perpendicular to something**) at right angles; forming a right angle with (a particular line or surface). **3** said of a cliff, etc: precipitous; steep. **4** (*usually* **Perpendicular**) *archit* referring or relating to the form of English Gothic architecture from late 14c to 16c, characterized by the use of slender vertical lines, vaulting and large areas of windows decorated with simple tracery and stained glass. ▻ *noun* **1** a perpendicular line, position or direction. **2** an instrument for determining the vertical line. ● **perpendicularity** *noun*. ● **perpendicularly** *adverb*. ⓒ 14c: from Latin *perpendicularis*, from *perpendiculum* a plumbline, from *pendere* to hang.

perpetrate /'pɜːpətreɪt/ ▻ *verb* (***perpetrated***, ***perpetrating***) to commit, or be guilty of (a crime, misdeed, error, etc). ● **perpetration** *noun*. ● **perpetrator** *noun*. ⓒ 16c: from Latin *perpetrare* to bring about or commit, from *patrare* to achieve.

perpetual /pə'pɛtʃʊəl/ ▻ *adj* **1** everlasting; eternal; continuous; permanent □ *in perpetual bliss*. **2** continual; continually recurring □ *perpetual quarrels*. **3** blooming continuously. ● **perpetually** *adverb*. ⓒ 14c: from Latin *perpetualis*, from *perpetuus* uninterrupted.

perpetual calendar ▻ *noun* **1** a calendar for ascertaining on which day of the week any date falls. **2** a calendar that is usable for any year or for several years.

perpetual check ▻ *noun, chess* a situation in which one player's king is continually placed in check by the other player who may thereby claim a draw.

perpetual motion ▻ *noun, physics* the motion of a hypothetical machine that continues to operate indefinitely without any external source of energy.

perpetuate /pə'pɛtʃueɪt/ ▻ *verb* (***perpetuated***, ***perpetuating***) **1** to make something last or continue □ *perpetuate a feud* □ *perpetuate a species*. **2** to preserve the memory of (a name, etc). **3** to repeat and pass on (an error, etc). ● **perpetuation** *noun*. ● **perpetuator** *noun*. ⓒ 16c: from Latin *perpetuare* to make perpetual.

perpetuity /pɜːpə'tjuːɪtɪ/ ▻ *noun* (***perpetuities***) **1** the state of being perpetual. **2** eternity. **3** duration for an indefinite period. **4** something perpetual, eg an allowance to be paid indefinitely. ● **in perpetuity** for ever. ⓒ 15c: from Latin *perpetuitas*, from *perpetuus* perpetual.

perplex /pə'plɛks/ ▻ *verb* (***perplexes***, ***perplexed*** /-'plɛkst/, ***perplexing***) **1** to puzzle, confuse or baffle someone with intricacies or difficulties. **2** to complicate. ● **perplexed** *adj*. ● **perplexedly** /pə'plɛksɪdlɪ, -'plɛkstlɪ/ *adverb*. ● **perplexing** *adj*. ● **perplexingly** *adverb*. ⓒ 16c: from Latin *per-* thoroughly + *plexus* entangled.

perplexity /pə'plɛksɪtɪ/ ▻ *noun* **1** the state of being perplexed. **2** (***perplexities***) something that perplexes.

per pro see under PP

perquisite /'pɜːkwɪzɪt/ ▻ *noun* **1** a PERK². **2** a customary tip expected on some occasions. **3** something regarded as due to one by right. ⓒ 18c in sense 2; 15c in obsolete legal sense of 'property acquired other than by inheritance': from Latin *perquisitum* something acquired.

Perrier /'pɛrɪeɪ/ ▻ *noun, trademark* a sparkling mineral water from a spring of that name in Southern France. ⓒ Early 20c.

perron /'pɛrən/ ▻ *noun* **1** a raised platform or terrace at an entrance door. **2** an external flight of steps leading up to this. ⓒ 14c: French, from Latin *petra* stone.

perry /'pɛrɪ/ ▻ *noun* (***perries***) an alcoholic drink made from fermented pear juice. ⓒ 14c: from French *peré*, from Latin *pirum* pear.

pers. ▻ *abbreviation* **1** person. **2** personal.

perse /pɜːs/ ▻ *adj* dark-blue; bluish-grey. ▻ *noun* **1** a dark blue colour. **2** a cloth of such colour. ⓒ 14c: from French *pers*.

per se /pɜː seɪ/ ▻ *adverb* in itself; intrinsically □ *not valuable per se*. ⓒ 16c: Latin, meaning 'through itself'.

persecute /'pɜːsɪkjuːt/ ▻ *verb* (***persecuted***, ***persecuting***) **1** to ill-treat, oppress, torment or put to death (a person or people), especially on the grounds of their religious or political beliefs. **2** to harass, pester or bother someone continually. ● **persecution** *noun*. ● **persecutor** *noun*. ⓒ 15c: from Latin *persequi*, *persecutus* to pursue or ill-treat.

persecution complex ▻ *noun, psychiatry* a morbid fear that one is being plotted against by other people.

perseverance /pɜːsə'vɪərəns/ ▻ *noun* the act or state of persevering; continued effort to achieve something one has begun, despite setbacks.

persevere /pɜːsə'vɪə(r)/ ▻ *verb* (***persevered***, ***persevering***) *intr* (*also* **persevere in** or **with something**) to keep on striving for it; to persist steadily with (an endeavour, which may be long and arduous to achieve). ● **persevering** *adj*. ● **perseveringly** *adverb*. ⓒ 14c: from French *perseverer*, from Latin *perseverare* to abide by something strictly.

Persian /'pɜːʃən, ʒən/ ▻ *adj* relating to ancient Persia or modern Iran, or to their people or language. ▻ *noun* **1** a citizen or inhabitant of, or person born in, ancient Persia or modern Iran. **2** the language of Persia or Iran. See also FARSI. **3** a Persian cat. **4** a Persian carpet. ⓒ 14c.

Persian blinds see under PERSIENNES

Persian carpet ▻ *noun* a distinctively-patterned hand-woven woollen or silk carpet made in Persia or elsewhere in the Near East.

Persian cat ▻ *noun* a domestic cat with a long silky coat and a bushy tail.

Persian lamb ▻ *noun* **1** the soft loosely-curled black fur of the lamb of a KARAKUL sheep, used to make coats, hats, etc. **2** the lamb from which this is obtained.

persienne /pɜːsɪ'ɛn/ ▻ *noun* an Eastern cambric or muslin fabric with a coloured printed pattern. ⓒ 19c: from French *persien* Persian.

persiennes /pɜːsɪ'ɛnz/ ▻ *plural noun* outside shutters made of thin movable slats in a frame. Also called **Persian blinds**. ⓒ 19c: from French *persien* Persian.

persiflage /'pɜːsɪflɑːʒ, pɜːsɪ'flɑːʒ/ ▻ *noun* banter; teasing; flippancy or frivolous talk. ⓒ 18c: French, from *persifler* to banter.

persimmon /pə'sɪmən, pɜː/ ▻ *noun* **1** any of various tall trees, native to warm temperate regions, widely cultivated for their hard wood and edible fruits. **2** the plum-like fruit of any of these trees. Also called DATE PLUM. ⓒ 17c: from an Algonquian language.

persist /pə'sɪst/ ▻ *verb* (***persisted***, ***persisting***) *intr* **1** (*also* **persist in** or **with something**) to continue with it in spite of resistance, difficulty, discouragement, etc. **2** said of rain, etc: to continue steadily. **3** said eg of a mistaken idea: to remain current. **4** to continue to exist. • **persistence** and **persistency** *noun*. ⓘ 16c: from Latin *persistere* to stand firm.

persistence of vision ▷ *noun, physiol* the persistence of a visual image on the retina for a short period after removal of the visual stimulus.

persistent /pəˈsɪstənt/ ▷ *adj* **1** continuing with determination in spite of discouragement; dogged; tenacious. **2** constant; unrelenting □ *persistent questions*. **3** *zool, bot* said of parts of animals and plants, such as horns, hair, leaves, etc: remaining after the time they usually fall off, wither or disappear. **4** *bot* continuing to grow beyond the usual time. **5** *ecol* said of a chemical: remaining relatively stable after release into the atmosphere. • **persistently** *adverb*.

persistent cruelty ▷ *noun, law* in matrimonial proceedings: behaviour likely to cause danger to the life or health of a spouse.

persistent vegetative state ▷ *noun, medicine* (abbreviation **PVS**) a deep comatose condition in which the patient shows no sign of higher brain activity and is only kept alive by means of various types of medical technology. ⓘ 1990s.

person /ˈpɜːsən/ ▷ *noun* (***persons*** or in sense 1 also ***people***) **1** an individual human being. **2** the body, often including clothes □ *A knife was found hidden on his person*. **3** *grammar* each of the three classes into which pronouns and verb forms fall, **first person** denoting the speaker (or the speaker and others, eg *I* and *we*), **second person** the person addressed (with or without others, eg *you*) and **third person** the person(s) or thing(s) spoken of (eg *she, he, it* or *they*). **4** (**Person**) *Christianity* any of the three forms or manifestations of God (Father, Son and Holy Spirit) that together form the TRINITY (sense 2). **5** *in compounds* used instead of *-man, -woman*, etc, to denote a specified activity or office, avoiding illegal or unnecessary discrimination on grounds of sex, eg in job advertisements □ *chairperson* □ *spokesperson*. Compare CHAIRMAN, CHAIRWOMAN, *etc*. • **be no respecter of persons** to make no allowances for rank or status. • **in person 1** actually present oneself □ *was there in person*. **2** doing something oneself, not asking or allowing others to do it for one. ⓘ 13c: from French *persone*, from Latin *persona* actor's mask.

persona /pəˈsoʊnə/ ▷ *noun* (***personae*** /-niː/ or ***personas***) **1** a character in fiction, especially in a play or novel. **2** in Jungian psychology: one's character as one presents it to the world, masking one's inner thoughts, feelings, etc. Compare ANIMA. See also PERSONA GRATA, PERSONA NON GRATA. ⓘ Early 20c: Latin, meaning 'an actor's mask'.

personable /ˈpɜːsənəbəl/ ▷ *adj* good-looking or likeable. • **personableness** *noun*. • **personably** *adverb*.

personage ▷ *noun* a well-known, important or distinguished person. ⓘ 15c: from Latin *personagium*, from *persona* person.

persona grata /— ˈgrɑːtə/ (***personae gratae*** /— -tiː/) ▷ *noun* a person who is acceptable, liked or favoured, especially one who is diplomatically acceptable to a foreign government. Compare PERSONA NON GRATA. ⓘ 19c: Latin, meaning 'a welcome person'.

personal /ˈpɜːsənəl/ ▷ *adj* **1** said of a comment, opinion, etc: coming from someone as an individual, not from a group or organization □ *my personal opinion*. **2** done, attended to, etc by the individual person in question, not by a substitute □ *give it my personal attention*. **3** relating to oneself in particular □ *a personal triumph*. **4** relating to one's private concerns □ *details of her personal life*. **5** said of remarks: referring, often disparagingly, to an individual's physical or other characteristics. **6** relating to the body □ *personal hygiene*. **7** *grammar* indicating PERSON (sense 3) □ *personal pronoun*. ⓘ 14c: from Latin *personalis*.

personal assistant ▷ *noun* (abbreviation **PA**) a secretary or administrator, especially one who helps a senior executive or manager, etc.

personal column ▷ *noun* a newspaper column or section in which members of the public may place advertisements, enquiries, etc.

personal computer ▷ *noun* (abbreviation **PC** or **pc**) a microcomputer designed for use by one person, which may be self-contained or networked to a larger system, used especially for wordprocessing, database or spreadsheet applications.

personal effects ▷ *plural noun* a person's belongings, especially those regularly carried about by them.

personal equation ▷ *noun* **1** a correction to be applied to the reading of an instrument on account of the observer's tendency to read too high or too low, etc. **2** any tendency to error or prejudice due to personal characteristics, for which allowance must be made.

personal equity plan ▷ *noun* (abbreviation **PEP**), *Brit finance* a type of investment scheme which allows relatively small investors to own shares in British companies, free from income tax and capital gains on any income and profits accrued.

personal identification number see PIN

personality /pɜːsəˈnalɪtɪ/ ▷ *noun* (***personalities***) **1** a person's nature or disposition; the qualities that give one's character individuality. **2** strength or distinctiveness of character □ *lots of personality*. **3** a well-known person; a celebrity. **4** (**personalities**) offensive personal remarks. **5** *psychol* all the physical, mental and emotional characteristics of an individual as an integrated whole, especially as they are presented to others. ⓘ 14c: from Latin *personalitas*, from *persona* person.

personality disorder ▷ *noun, psychiatry* any of various types of mental illness in which the sufferer tends to exhibit inappropriate behaviour.

personalize /ˈpɜːsənəlaɪz/ or **personalise** ▷ *verb* (***personalized, personalizing***) **1** to mark something distinctively, eg with name, initials, etc, as the property of a particular person. **2** to focus (a discussion, etc) on personalities instead of the matter in hand. **3** to personify. • **personalization** *noun*. ⓘ 18c.

personally /ˈpɜːsənəlɪ/ ▷ *adverb* **1** as far as one is concerned □ *Personally, I disapprove*. **2** in person. **3** as a person. **4** as directed against one □ *take a remark personally*.

personal pronoun ▷ *noun, grammar* any of the pronouns that represent a person or thing, eg *I, you, she, her, he, it, they, us*.

personal organizer ▷ *noun* **a** a small bag or wallet with sections in which personal notes and information may be kept; **b** a similar electronic device. Sometimes shortened to **organizer**. Compare FILOFAX.

personal property ▷ *noun* everything one owns other than land or buildings. Also called **personalty**. See also REAL PROPERTY.

personal stereo ▷ *noun* a small audio-cassette player with earphones, that can be worn attached to a belt or carried in a pocket. Also called WALKMAN.

persona non grata /— nɒn ˈgrɑːtə/ (***personae non gratae*** /— — -tiː/) ▷ *noun* someone who is not wanted or welcome within a particular group. Compare PERSONA GRATA. ⓘ 20c: Latin, meaning 'unwelcome person'.

personate /ˈpɜːsəneɪt/ ▷ *verb* (***personated, personating***) **1** to play the part of (a character in a play, etc). **2** to impersonate someone, especially with criminal intent. • **personation** *noun*. • **personator** *noun*. ⓘ 16c.

personification /pəsɒnɪfɪˈkeɪʃən/ ▷ *noun* **1** the attribution of human qualities to things or ideas. **2** in art or literature: the representation of an idea or quality as a person or human figure. **3** someone or something that personifies. **4** someone or something that is seen as embodying a particular quality □ *the personification of patience.*

personify /pə'sɒnɪfaɪ/ ▻ *verb* (***personifies, personified, personifying***) **1** in literature, etc: to represent (an abstract quality, etc) as a human being or as having human qualities. **2** said of a figure in art, etc: to represent or symbolize (a quality, etc). **3** to embody something in human form; to be the perfect example of it □ *She's patience personified.* • **personifier** *noun.* ⓒ 18c: probably from French *personnifier*; see also -FY.

personnel /pɜːsə'nɛl/ ▻ *plural noun* the people employed in a business company, an armed service or other organization. ▻ *singular noun* **a** a department within such an organization that deals with matters concerning employees; **b** *as adj* □ *a personnel officer* □ *the personnel department.* See also HUMAN RESOURCES. ⓒ 19c: French, meaning 'personal'.

personnel carrier ▻ *noun* a military vehicle, often an armoured one, for carrying troops.

perspective /pə'spɛktɪv/ ▻ *noun* **1** the observer's view of objects in relation to one another, especially with regard to the way they seem smaller the more distant they are. **2** the representation of this phenomenon in drawing and painting. **3** the balanced or objective view of a situation, in which all its elements assume their due importance □ *After a flustered few days, he finally got things into perspective.* **4** an individual way of regarding a situation, eg one influenced by personal experience or considerations. ⓒ 14c: from Latin *ars perspectiva* optical science.

perspectivism ▻ *noun* **1** *philos* the theory that things can only be known from an individual point of view at a particular time. **2** the use of subjective points of view in literature and art.

Perspex /'pɜːspɛks/ ▻ *noun, trademark* the trade name for POLYMETHYLMETHACRYLATE.

perspicacious /pɜːspɪ'keɪʃəs/ ▻ *adj* shrewd; astute; perceptive or discerning. • **perspicaciously** *adverb.* • **perspicacity** /-'kasɪtɪ/ *noun.* ⓒ 17c: from Latin *perspicax.*

perspicuous /pə'spɪkjʊəs/ ▻ *adj* said of speech or writing: clearly expressed and easily understood. • **perspicuously** *adverb.* • **perspicuity** /pɜːspɪ'kjuːətɪ/ *noun.* • **perspicuousness** *noun.* ⓒ 15c: from Latin *perspicuus* transparent or manifest.

perspiration /pɜːspɪ'reɪʃən/ ▻ *noun* **1** the secretion of fluid by the sweat glands of the skin, usually in response to heat or physical exertion. **2** the fluid secreted in this way.

perspire /pə'spaɪə(r)/ ▻ *verb* (***perspired, perspiring***) *intr* to secrete fluid from the sweat glands of the skin; to sweat. ⓒ 18c in this sense; 17c in obsolete sense referring to wind, meaning 'to blow gently through': from Latin *perspirare* to breathe through or sweat.

persuadable or **persuasible** ▻ *adj* capable of being persuaded. • **persuadability** or **persuasibility** *noun.*

persuade /pə'sweɪd/ ▻ *verb* (***persuaded, persuading***) **1** (*also* **persuade someone to do something**) to urge successfully; to prevail on or induce someone. **2** (*often* **persuade someone of something**) to convince them that it is true, valid, advisable, etc. • **persuader** *noun* **1** someone or something that persuades. **2** *slang* a gun. ⓒ 16c: from Latin *persuadere*, from *per* thoroughly + *suadere* to advise or recommend.

persuasion /pə'sweɪʒən/ ▻ *noun* **1** the act of urging, coaxing or persuading. **2** a creed, conviction, or set of beliefs, especially that of a political group or religious sect.

persuasive /pə'sweɪsɪv, -zɪv/ ▻ *adj* having the power to persuade; convincing or plausible. • **persuasively** *adverb.* • **persuasiveness** *noun.*

PERT ▻ *abbreviation* programme evaluation and review technique.

pert ▻ *adj* (***perter, pertest***) **1** impudent; cheeky. **2** said of clothing or style: jaunty; saucy. • **pertly** *adverb.* • **pertness** *noun.* ⓒ 14c: from French *apert* open.

pertain /pə'teɪn/ ▻ *verb* (***pertained, pertaining***) *intr* (*often* **pertain to someone** or **something**) **1** to concern or relate to them or it; to have to do with them or it. **2** to belong to them or it □ *skills pertaining to the job.* **3** to be appropriate; to apply. ⓒ 14c: from Latin *pertinere*, from *per-* utterly + *tenere* to hold.

pertinacious /pɜːtɪ'neɪʃəs/ ▻ *adj* determined in one's purpose; dogged; tenacious. • **pertinaciously** *adverb.* • **pertinaciousness** or **pertinacity** /-'nasɪtɪ/ *noun.* ⓒ 17c: from Latin *pertinax* holding fast.

pertinent /'pɜːtɪnənt/ ▻ *adj* (*also* **pertinent to someone** or **something**) relating to or concerned with them or it; relevant. • **pertinence** or **pertinency** *noun.* ⓒ 14c: from Latin *pertinens, pertinentem* pertaining, from *pertinere* to relate.

perturb /pə'tɜːb/ ▻ *verb* (***perturbed, perturbing***) to make someone anxious, agitated, worried, etc. • **perturbed** *adj.* • **perturbedly** *adverb.* ⓒ 14c: from Latin *perturbare* to throw into confusion, from *per* thoroughly + *turbare* to disturb.

perturbation /pɜːtə'beɪʃən/ ▻ *noun* **1** the act of perturbing or state of being perturbed. **2** *astron* a small deviation from the path of the orbit of a planet, etc because of the gravitational influence of neighbouring celestial bodies.

pertussis /pə'tʌsɪs/ ▻ *noun, medicine* whooping cough. • **pertussal** *adj.* ⓒ 18c: Latin from *tussis* cough.

peruke /pə'ruːk, 'pɛruːk/ ▻ *noun* a 17c and 18c style of wig, with side curls and a tail at the back. ⓒ 16c: from French *perruque* head of hair.

peruse /pə'ruːz/ ▻ *verb* (***perused, perusing***) **1** to read through (a book, magazine, etc) carefully. **2** to browse through something casually. **3** to examine or study (eg someone's face) attentively. • **perusal** *noun.* • **peruser** *noun.* ⓒ 16c in these senses; 15c meaning 'to use up': from PER- sense 2 + USE1.

Peruvian /pə'ruːvɪən/ ▻ *adj* belonging or relating to Peru, a republic on the W coast of S America, or its inhabitants. ▻ *noun* a citizen or inhabitant of, or person born in, Peru. ⓒ 18c.

perv ▻ *noun, slang* a pervert. ▻ *verb* (*also* **perve**) (***perved, perving***) *Austral* (*also* **perv at** or **on someone**) to look at them lustfully or for sexual pleasure. ⓒ 1940s: shortened from PERVERT.

pervade /pə'veɪd/ ▻ *verb* (***pervaded, pervading***) to spread or extend throughout something; to affect throughout something; to permeate. • **pervasion** /pə'veɪʒən/ *noun.* ⓒ 17c: from Latin *pervadere*, from *vadere* to go.

pervasive /pə'veɪsɪv/ ▻ *adj* tending to or having the power to spread everywhere. • **pervasively** *adverb.* • **pervasiveness** *noun.*

perverse /pə'vɜːs/ ▻ *adj* (***perverser, perversest***) **1** deliberately departing from what is normal and reasonable. **2** unreasonable; awkward; stubborn or wilful. • **perversely** *adverb.* • **perverseness** *noun.* • **perversity** *noun* the state or quality of being perverse. ⓒ 14c: from Latin *perversus*, from *pervertere*; see PERVERT.

perversion /pə'vɜːʃən, -ʒən/ ▻ *noun* **1** the process of perverting or condition of being perverted. **2** a distortion. **3** an abnormal sexual activity. ⓒ 14c: from Latin *pervertere*; see PERVERT.

pervert ▻ *verb* /pə'vɜːt/ (***perverted, perverting***) **1** to divert something or someone illicitly from what is normal or right □ *pervert the course of justice.* **2** to lead someone into evil or unnatural behaviour; to corrupt them. **3** to distort or misinterpret (words, etc). ▷ *noun* /ˈpɜːvɜːt/ someone who is morally or sexually perverted. ◷ 14c: from Latin *pervertere* to turn the wrong way, to overturn or to corrupt.

Pesach or **Pesah** /ˈpeɪsax/ ▷ *noun* the Hebrew name for PASSOVER. ◷ 17c: Hebrew.

peseta /pəˈseɪtə/ ▷ *noun* (***peseta*** or ***pesetas***) the standard unit of currency of Spain. ◷ 19c: Spanish, diminutive of *pesa* weight.

pesky /ˈpɛskɪ/ ▷ *adj* (***peskier***, ***peskiest***) *N Amer colloq* troublesome or infuriating. • **peskily** *adverb*. ◷ 18c: probably from PEST.

peso /ˈpeɪsoʊ/ ▷ *noun* (***pesos***) the standard unit of currency of many Central and S American countries and the Philippines. ◷ 16c: Spanish, literally 'weight'.

pessary /ˈpɛsərɪ/ ▷ *noun* (***pessaries***) **1** a vaginal SUPPOSITORY. **2** a cup-shaped device worn in the vagina as a contraceptive, or as a support for the womb. ◷ 14c: from Latin *pessarium*, from Greek *pessos* pebble or plug.

pessimism /ˈpɛsɪmɪzəm/ ▷ *noun* **1** the tendency to emphasize the gloomiest aspects of anything, and to expect the worst to happen. **2** the belief that this is the worst of all possible worlds, and that evil is triumphing over good. Compare OPTIMISM. • **pessimist** *noun* **1** someone who has a sombre gloomy nature. **2** someone who follows the doctrine of pessimism. • **pessimistic** *adj*. • **pessimistically** *adverb*. ◷ 18c: from Latin *pessimus* worst + -ISM.

pest ▷ *noun* **1** a living organism, such as an insect, fungus or weed, that has a damaging effect on animal livestock, crop plants or stored produce. **2** *colloq* a person or thing that is a constant nuisance. ◷ 16c: from Latin *pestis* plague.

pester /ˈpɛstə(r)/ ▷ *verb* (***pestered***, ***pestering***) **1** to annoy constantly. **2** to harass or hound someone with requests. • **pesterer** *noun*. • **pestering** *adj*. • **pesteringly** *adverb*. ◷ 16c: from French *empestrer* to entangle; influenced by PEST.

pesticide /ˈpɛstɪsaɪd/ ▷ *noun* any of various chemical compounds, including insecticides, herbicides and fungicides, that are used to kill pests. ◷ 1930s.

pestilence /ˈpɛstɪləns/ ▷ *noun* **1** a virulent epidemic or contagious disease, such as bubonic plague. **2** anything that is harmful to the morals. ◷ 14c: from Latin *pestilentia*, from *pestis* plague.

pestilent /ˈpɛstɪlənt/ ▷ *adj* **1** deadly, harmful or destructive. **2** *colloq, often facetious* infuriating; troublesome. • **pestilently** *adverb*. ◷ 15c: from Latin *pestilens*, from *pestis* plague.

pestilential /pɛstɪˈlɛnʃəl/ ▷ *adj* infuriating; troublesome. • **pestilentially** *adverb*.

pestle /ˈpɛsəl, ˈpɛstəl/ ▷ *noun* a club-shaped utensil for pounding, crushing and mixing substances in a MORTAR. ▷ *verb* (***pestled***, ***pestling***) to pound or crush, etc something with a pestle. ◷ 14c: from French *pestel*, from Latin *pistillum* a pounder, from *pinsere* to pound.

pesto /ˈpɛstoʊ/ ▷ *noun* (***pestos***) an Italian sauce for pasta, originating in Liguria and made by crushing and mixing together fresh basil leaves, pine kernels, olive oil, garlic and Parmesan cheese. ◷ 1930s: Italian, from *pestato* crushed, from *pestare* to crush or pound.

pestology /pɛsˈtɒlədʒɪ/ ▷ *noun* the study of agricultural pests and methods of combating them. • **pestologist** *noun*. ◷ 1920s.

PET /pɛt/ ▷ *abbreviation, medicine* positron emission tomography. Frequently as **PET scan**, **PET scanning**, a form of TOMOGRAPHY used especially for brain scans.

pet[1] ▷ *noun* **1** a tame animal or bird kept as a companion. **2** someone's favourite □ ***the teacher's pet***. **3** a darling or love. **4** a term of endearment. ▷ *adj* **1** kept as a pet □ ***a pet lamb***. **2** relating to pets or for pets □ ***pet food***. **3** favourite; own special □ ***her pet subject***. ▷ *verb* (***petted***, ***petting***) **1** to pat or stroke (an animal, etc). **2** to treat someone indulgently; to make a fuss of them. **3** *intr* said of two people: to fondle and caress each other for erotic pleasure. • **petting** *noun*. ◷ 16c.

pet[2] ▷ *noun* a fit of bad temper or sulks. See also PETTISH. ◷ 16c.

Pet. ▷ *abbreviation* Book of the Bible: Peter. See table at BIBLE.

peta- /ˈpɛtə/ ▷ *combining form* (symbol **P**) *denoting* one thousand million million; 10^{15} □ ***petajoule*** □ ***petametre***. ◷ 1970s: probably based on PENTA-.

petal /ˈpɛtəl/ ▷ *noun* **1** *bot* in a flower: one of the modified leaves, often scented and brightly coloured, which in insect-pollinated plants serve to attract passing insects. **2** a term of endearment. ◷ 18c: ultimately from Greek *petalon* leaf.

pétanque /peˈtɒŋk/ ▷ *noun* the name given in S France to a game that originated in Provence, in which steel bowls are rolled or hurled towards a wooden marker ball. Also called BOULES. ◷ 1950s: French.

petard /peˈtɑːd/ ▷ *noun, historical* a small bomb for blasting a hole in a wall, door, etc. • **hoist with one's own petard** blown up by one's own bomb, ie the victim of one's own trick or cunning; caught in one's own trap. ◷ 16c: from French *pétard* a banger or firecracker, from *péter* to break wind, from Latin *pedere*.

petechia /peˈtiːkɪə/ ▷ *noun* (***petechiae*** /-kiiː/) *medicine* a small red or purple spot on the skin. • **petechial** *adj*. ◷ 18c: Latinized from Italian *petecchia* freckle.

peter /ˈpiːtə(r)/ ▷ *verb* (***petered***, ***petering***) *intr* (*always* **peter out**) to dwindle away to nothing. ◷ 19c, originally US mining slang.

Peter Pan ▷ *noun* a youthful, boyish or immature man. ◷ Early 20c: the hero of J M Barrie's play *Peter Pan, the boy who wouldn't grow up* (1904).

Peter Pan collar ▷ *noun* a flat collar with rounded ends.

the Peter principle ▷ *noun, facetious* the theory that in a hierarchy people rise to the level at which they are incompetent. ◷ 1960s: the title of a book by Laurence Johnston Peter (born 1919), Canadian author.

petersham /ˈpiːtəʃəm/ ▷ *noun* **1** a stiff ribbed silk ribbon used for reinforcing waistbands, etc. **2 a** a heavy greatcoat; **b** rough-napped cloth, generally dark blue, from which these coats are made. ◷ 19c: named after Lord Petersham, a 19c English army officer.

Peter's pence ▷ *plural noun* **1** *historical* a tax, or tribute, of a silver penny paid to the Pope. **2** in modern times: a voluntary contribution to the Pope. ◷ 13c in sense 1: from St *Peter*, the first pope.

Peters' projection ▷ *noun, map-making* an equal area map projection, showing accurately the relative sizes of continents, oceans, etc, so giving a less Eurocentric view of the world. Compare MERCATOR'S PROJECTION. ◷ 1970s: named after Arno Peters (born 1916), German cartographer and mathematician.

pet hate ▷ *noun* something that one especially dislikes.

pethidine /ˈpɛθɪdiːn/ ▷ *noun* a mildly sedative pain-relieving drug, widely used in childbirth. Also called **meperidine**. ◷ 1940s.

petiole /ˈpɛtɪoʊl/ ▷ *noun* **1** *bot* the stalk that attaches a leaf to the stem of a plant. **2** *zool* a stalk-like structure, especially that of the abdomen in wasps, etc. ◷ 18c: from Latin *petiolus* little foot.

petit bourgeois /ˈpɛtɪ buəˈʒwɑː, — bɔːˈʒwɑː/ ▷ *noun* (***petits bourgeois*** /pɛtɪ —/) a member of the lower middle class. Also written **petty bourgeois**. ◷ 19c: French, literally 'little citizen'.

petite /pəˈtiːt/ ▻ *adj* said of a woman or girl: characterized by having a small and dainty build. ⓒ 18c: French, feminine of *petit* small.

petite bourgeoisie /pəˈtiːt bɔːʒwɑːˈziː/ ▻ *noun* (***petites bourgeoisies*** /pətiːt/) the lower middle class. ⓒ Early 20c: French.

petit four /ˈpɛtɪ fʊə(r), fɔː(r), ˈpətɪ —/ ▻ *noun* (***petits fours*** /— fʊəz, — fɔːz/) a small sweet biscuit, usually decorated with icing. ⓒ 19c: French, literally 'little oven'.

petition /pəˈtɪʃən/ ▻ *noun* **1** a formal written request to an authority to take some action, signed by a large number of people. **2** any appeal to a higher authority. **3** *law* an application to a court for some procedure to be set in motion. ▻ *verb* (***petitioned, petitioning***) *tr & intr* (*also* **petition someone for** or **against something**) to address a petition to them for or against some cause; to make an appeal or request. • **petitionary** *adj.* • **petitioner** *noun* **1** someone who petitions. **2** someone who applies for a divorce. ⓒ 15c: French, from Latin *petitio*, from *petere* to seek.

petit jury /ˈpɛtɪ —/ ▻ *noun, English law* a jury of twelve persons. Often written **petty jury**. Compare GRAND JURY.

petit mal /ˈpɛtɪ mal/ ▻ *noun, medicine* a mild form of EPILEPSY, without convulsions, characterized by short periods of loss of consciousness or 'absences'. Compare GRAND MAL. ⓒ Late 19c: French, literally 'little sickness or illness'.

petit point /ˈpɛtɪ pɔɪnt, — pwɛ̃/ ▻ *noun* **1** a small diagonal stitch used for fine work in needlepoint. **2** needlework using this stitch. ⓒ 19c: French, meaning 'small point'.

petits pois /ˈpɛtɪ pwɑː/ ▻ *plural noun* small young green peas. ⓒ 19c: French, meaning 'little peas'.

pet name ▻ *noun* a special name used as an endearment.

petrel /ˈpɛtrəl/ ▻ *noun* any of numerous small seabirds with a hooked bill and external tube-shaped nostrils, especially the STORM PETREL. ⓒ 17c: altered from earlier *pitteral*, perhaps from the name Peter by association with the story of St Peter walking on the water, as some species of storm petrel walk across the surface of the sea while feeding.

Petri dish /ˈpiːtrɪ —, ˈpɛtrɪ —/ ▻ *noun, biol* a shallow circular glass or plastic plate with a flat base and a loosely fitting lid, used for culturing bacteria, etc. ⓒ Late 19c: named after Julius R Petri (1852–1921), German bacteriologist.

petrifaction /pɛtrɪˈfakʃən/ or **petrification** /pɛtrɪfɪˈkeɪʃən/ ▻ *noun, geol* **1** a type of fossilization whereby organic remains are turned into stone as the original tissue is gradually replaced molecule-by-molecule by minerals. **2** the state of being petrified.

petrify /ˈpɛtrɪfaɪ/ ▻ *verb* (***petrifies, petrified, petrifying***) **1** to terrify; to paralyse someone with fright. **2** *tr & intr* said of organic remains: to turn into stone by the process of petrifaction. **3** *tr & intr* to fix or become fixed in an inflexible mould. ⓒ 16c: from French *pétrifier*, from Greek *petra* stone.

Petrine /ˈpiːtraɪn/ ▻ *adj* relating to the apostle Peter. ⓒ 19c: from Latin *Petrus* Peter.

petro-[1] /ˈpɛtroʊ/ ▻ *combining form, denoting* **1** petroleum and its products ▫ *petrochemical*. **2** referring or relating to the petroleum industry, eg production, export, sales, etc ▫ *petromoney*. ⓒ 1970s, from *petro*leum.

petro-[2] /ˈpɛtroʊ/ ▻ *combining form, denoting* stone or rocks ▫ *petrology*. ⓒ From Greek *petra* rock.

petrochemical ▻ *noun* any organic chemical derived from petroleum or natural gas. ▻ *adj* **1** referring or relating to such chemicals. **2** referring or relating to the petrochemical industry. • **petrochemically** *adverb.* ⓒ Early 20c.

petrochemistry ▻ *noun* **1** the scientific study of the chemistry of materials derived from petroleum or natural gas. **2** the scientific study of the chemical composition of rocks. ⓒ 1930s.

petrocurrency ▻ *noun* currency, usually in the form of US dollars (PETRODOLLARS), pounds sterling or Deutschmarks, available in oil-producing countries on their balance of payments and which is surplus to their own requirements. ⓒ 1970s.

petrodollar ▻ *noun* the US dollar as representative of the foreign currency earned by oil-exporting countries. ⓒ 1970s.

petroglyph /ˈpɛtroʊglɪf/ ▻ *noun* a rock-carving, especially a prehistoric one. ⓒ 19c: from French *pétroglyphe*, from Greek *petra* rock + *glyphein* to carve.

petrography /pɛˈtrɒgrəfɪ/ ▻ *noun* the systematic description and classification of rocks. ⓒ 17c: from Greek *petra* rock + -GRAPHY.

petrol /ˈpɛtrəl/ ▻ *noun* a volatile flammable liquid mixture of hydrocarbons, used as a fuel in most internal combustion engines. Also (*N Amer*) called GASOLINE. ⓒ Late 19c in this sense; 16c meaning PETROLEUM: from French *petrole*, from Latin *petroleum*.

petrolatum /pɛtrəˈleɪtəm/ ▻ *noun* a PARAFFIN-base PETROLEUM used as a lubricant or medicinally as an ointment. Also called **petroleum jelly**. ⓒ 19c: Latin, from PETROL.

petrol-blue ▻ *adj* a deep greenish blue. Also (**petrol blue**) *as noun.*

petrol bomb ▻ *noun* a crude bomb consisting of a petrol-filled bottle stopped with rags that are set alight just as the bottle is thrown. Compare MOLOTOV COCKTAIL.

petrol engine ▻ *noun* a type of INTERNAL COMBUSTION ENGINE, widely used in motor vehicles, in which a mixture of petrol and air is burned inside a cylinder fitted with a piston.

petroleum /pəˈtroʊlɪəm/ ▻ *noun* a naturally occurring oil consisting of a thick dark liquid mixture of hydrocarbons, distillation of which yields a wide range of petrochemicals, eg liquid and gas fuels, asphalt, and raw materials for the manufacture of plastics, solvents, drugs, etc. Compare PETROL. ⓒ 16c: Latin, from *petra* rock + *oleum* oil.

petroleum jelly ▻ *noun* PETROLATUM.

petroleum wax ▻ *noun* a solid hydrocarbon from PETROLEUM, being either a PARAFFIN WAX, microcrystalline wax or PETROLATUM wax.

petrology /pəˈtrɒlədʒɪ/ ▻ *noun, geol* the scientific study of the structure, origin, distribution and history of rocks. • **petrological** /pɛtrəˈlɒdʒɪkəl/ *adj.* • **petrologist** /-ˈtrɒl-/ *noun.* ⓒ 19c.

petrol station ▻ *noun* a FILLING STATION.

petrous /ˈpɛtrəs/ ▻ *adj* stony; characterized by having a consistency like rocks. ⓒ 16c: from Latin *petrosus*, from *petra* rock.

pe-tsai cabbage /peɪˈtsaɪ —/ ▻ *noun* CHINESE CABBAGE. ⓒ 18c: from Chinese *bai* white + *cai* vegetable.

petted *past tense, past participle of* PET[1]

petticoat /ˈpɛtɪkoʊt/ ▻ *noun* **1** a woman's underskirt. **2** (**petticoats**) *historical* skirts in general, or those worn by boys in early childhood in particular. **3** *as adj* said eg of organizations, tactics, etc: relating to or lead by women; feminine or female ▫ *petticoat government*. ⓒ 15c: from PETTY *adj* 1 + COAT.

pettifogger /ˈpɛtɪfɒgə(r)/ ▻ *noun* **1** a lawyer who deals with unimportant cases, especially somewhat deceitfully or quibblingly. **2** *derog* someone who argues over trivial details; a quibbler. • **pettifog** *verb* (***pettifogged, pettifogging***) *intr* to act as a pettifogger. • **pettifoggery** *noun.* • **pettifogging** *noun, adj.* ⓒ 16c: from PETTY + German dialect *voger* arranger.

petting see PET[1]

pettish /ˈpɛtɪʃ/ ▷ *adj* peevish; sulky. • **pettishly** *adverb*. • **pettishness** *noun*. ◷ 16c.

petty /ˈpɛtɪ/ ▷ *adj* (***pettier, pettiest***) **1** being of minor importance; trivial. **2** small-minded or childishly spiteful. **3** referring to a low or subordinate rank. • **pettily** *adverb*. • **pettiness** *noun*. ◷ 14c: from French *petit* small.

petty bourgeois see under PETIT BOURGEOIS

petty cash ▷ *noun* money kept for small everyday expenses in an office, etc.

petty jury see under PETIT JURY

petty officer ▷ *noun* a non-commissioned officer in the navy. See table at RANK.

petulant /ˈpɛtjʊlənt/ ▷ *adj* ill-tempered; peevish. • **petulance** or **petulancy** *noun*. • **petulantly** *adverb*. ◷ 16c: French, from Latin *petulans, petulantis*, from *petere* to seek.

petunia /pəˈtjuːnɪə/ ▷ *noun* (***petunias***) any of various annual plants with large funnel-shaped, often striped, flowers in a range of bright colours, including white, pink and purple. ◷ 19c: from French *petun* tobacco plant, because of its similarity to this, from Guaraní (S American Native language) *pety*.

pew /pjuː/ ▷ *noun* **1** one of the long benches with backs used as seating in a church. **2** *colloq* a seat □ ***take a pew***. ◷ 15c: from French *puie*, from Latin *podium* part of a choir stall.

pewit see PEEWIT

pewter /ˈpjuːtə(r)/ ▷ *noun* **1** a silvery alloy with a bluish tinge, composed of tin and lead, used to make tableware (eg tankards), jewellery and other decorative objects. **2** articles made of pewter. **3** *as adj* made of pewter. • **pewterer** *noun* someone who makes or works in pewter. ◷ 14c: from French *peutre*.

peyote /peɪˈoʊtɪ, peɪˈoʊteɪ/ ▷ *noun* (***peyotes***) **1** the MESCAL cactus, native to N Mexico and the south-west USA. **2** a hallucinogenic substance obtained from the button-like tops of this plant, taken sacramentally during certain Native American religious ceremonies. ◷ 19c: from Nahuatl (S American Native language) *peyotl*.

PF ▷ *abbreviation* **1** Patriotic Front. **2** Procurator Fiscal.

Pf ▷ *abbreviation* pfennig, or pfennigs.

pfennig /ˈfɛnɪg, ˈpfɛnɪg; *German* ˈpfɛnɪ/ ▷ *noun* (***pfennigs*** or ***pfennige*** /-nɪgə/) a German unit of currency worth a hundredth of a DEUTSCHMARK. ◷ 16c: German, related to PENNY.

PFP ▷ *abbreviation* Partnership for Peace.

PG ▷ *abbreviation* **1** as a film classification: parental guidance, ie containing scenes possibly unsuitable for children. **2** *colloq* paying guest.

pg. ▷ *abbreviation* page. See also P, PP.

PGA ▷ *abbreviation* Professional Golfers' Association.

pH /piːˈeɪtʃ/ and **pH value** ▷ *noun, chem* a measure of the relative acidity or alkalinity of a solution expressed as the logarithm of the reciprocal of the hydrogen-ion concentration of the solution. ◷ Early 20c: a shortening of German *Potenz* power or exponent + *H*, the symbol for hydrogen.

phacoid /ˈfakɔɪd, ˈfeɪ-/ ▷ *adj* **1** lentil-shaped. **2** lens-shaped. ◷ 19c: from Greek *phakos* a lentil + -OID.

Phaedra complex /ˈfiːdrə —/ ▷ *noun, psychol* the difficult relationship which can arise between a new step-parent and the son or daughter, usually teenage son or daughter, of the original marriage. ◷ 20c: named after Phaedra who, in Greek mythology, fell in love with her stepson and committed suicide after being rejected by him.

phaeton /ˈfeɪtən/ ▷ *noun* an open four-wheeled carriage for one or two horses. ◷ 16c: named after Phaeton who, in Greek mythology, was son of the god Helios and who drove his father's chariot so close to the Earth that he was destroyed by Zeus; from Greek *phaethon* shining.

phage /feɪdʒ/ ▷ *noun, biol* short for BACTERIOPHAGE.

-phage /feɪdʒ, fɑːʒ/ ▷ *combining form, forming nouns, denoting* something that eats or consumes the specified thing □ ***bacteriophage***. ◷ From Greek *phagein* to eat.

phago- /ˈfagoʊ/ or (before a vowel) **phag-** ▷ *combining form, denoting* feeding, eating or destroying □ ***phagocyte***. ◷ From Greek *phagein* to eat.

phagocyte /ˈfagoʊsaɪt/ ▷ *noun, biol* a cell, especially a white blood cell, that engulfs and usually destroys micro-organisms and other foreign particles. • **phagocytic** /-ˈsɪtɪk/ or **phagocytical** *adj*. ◷ 19c.

phagocytosis /fagoʊsaɪˈtoʊsɪs/ ▷ *noun, biol* the process whereby specialized cells, such as phagocytes and macrophages, engulf and digest bacteria, cell debris, or other solid material. ◷ 19c.

-phagous /fəgəs/ ▷ *combining form* forming adjectives corresponding to nouns in -PHAGE.

phalange /ˈfalandʒ/ ▷ *noun* **1** *anatomy* a PHALANX. **2** /*also* faˈlɑ̃ʒ/ the Christian right-wing group in Lebanon, modelled on the Spanish Falange. ◷ 16c: French.

phalanger /fəˈlandʒə(r)/ ▷ *noun* any of various nocturnal tree-dwelling marsupials, native to Australia and New Guinea, with thick fur, small fox-like ears and large forward-facing eyes. Also called **possum**. ◷ 18c: from Greek *phalangion* spider's web, because of its webbed toes.

phalangist /ˈfalandʒɪst/ ▷ *noun* a member of the PHALANGE (sense 2).

phalanx /ˈfalaŋks, ˈfeɪlaŋks/ ▷ *noun* (***phalanxes*** or in senses 3 and 4 ***phalanges*** /-dʒiːz/) **1** *historical* in ancient Greece: a body of infantry in close-packed formation. **2** a solid body of people, especially one representing united support or opposition. **3** *anatomy* in vertebrates: any of the bones of the digits. **4** *biol* a bundle of stamens. • **phalangeal** /fəˈlandʒɪəl/ or **phalangal** /fəˈlaŋgəl/ ◷ 16c: Greek, meaning 'a line of soldiers drawn up for battle'.

phalarope /ˈfaləroʊp/ ▷ *noun* any of various small aquatic birds of the sandpiper family, the female of which courts the male and the male incubates the eggs and cares for the young. ◷ 18c: from Latin *Phalaropus*, from Greek *phalaris* coot + *pous* foot.

phallic /ˈfalɪk/ ▷ *adj* **1** relating to or resembling a phallus. **2** *psychoanal* relating to a stage in psychosexual development when a child's interest is concentrated on the genital organs.

phallicism /ˈfalɪsɪzəm/ and **phallism** ▷ *noun* worship of the generative power of nature. • **phallicist** or **phallist** *noun*.

phallocentric /faloʊˈsɛntrɪk/ ▷ *adj* **1** centred on the phallus. **2** dominated by or expressive of male attitudes. • **phallocentricity** *noun*. ◷ 1920s.

phallocentrism ▷ *noun* in feminist theory: the concept that many artistic, cultural, social, etc systems assume and advance, either consciously or unconsciously, the idea that the masculine is the natural source of power, authority, etc and, as a consequence, the feminine becomes subjugated by this.

phallus /ˈfaləs/ ▷ *noun* (***phalluses*** or ***phalli*** /-laɪ/) **1** a penis. **2** a representation or image of an erect penis, especially as a symbol of male reproductive power. **3** (**Phallus**) the STINKHORN genus of fungi. ◷ 17c: Latin, from Greek *phallos*.

Phanerozoic /fanərəˈzoʊɪk/ ▷ *adj, geol* relating to the eon consisting of the Palaeozoic, Mesozoic and Cenozoic eras, extending from about 570 million years ago until the present time. See table at GEOLOGICAL TIME SCALE. Compare PROTEROZOIC. ◷ 19c: from Greek *phaneros* visible + *zoion* animal, because it is the eon that displays a broad range of animal life.

phantasm /'fantazəm/ ▻ *noun* **1** an illusion or fantasy. **2** a ghost or phantom. Also called **phantasma** (***phantasmata***). • **phantasmal** *adj.* • **phantasmally** *adverb.* ◷ 13c: from Greek *phantasma* apparition.

phantasmagoria /fantazmə'gɔːrɪə/ ▻ *noun* (***phantasmagorias***) a fantastic succession of real or illusory images seen as if in a dream. • **phantasmagoric** or **phantasmagorical** *adj.* ◷ 19c: perhaps from Greek *phantasma* apparition + *agora* assembly.

phantasy /'fantəsɪ/ ▻ *noun* (***phantasies***) an old spelling of FANTASY.

phantom /'fantəm/ ▻ *noun* **1** a ghost or spectre. **2** an illusory image or vision. ▻ *adj* **1** referring to the nature of a phantom; spectral. **2** imaginary; fancied; not real. ◷ 14c: from French *fantosme*, from Greek *phantasma* apparition.

phantom limb ▻ *noun, medicine* the perception of feeling in a limb that has been amputated.

phantom pregnancy see under PSEUDOCYESIS

phar. or **pharm.** ▻ *abbreviation* **1** pharmaceutical. **2** pharmacopoeia. **3** pharmacy.

Pharaoh /'fɛərou/ ▻ *noun* the title of the kings of ancient Eygpt, specifically the god-kings from the time of the New Kingdom (c.1500 BC) onwards. • **Pharaonic** /fɛəreɪ'ɒnɪk/ *adj.* ◷ Anglo-Saxon: from Greek *pharao*, from Egyptian *pr-'o* great house.

Pharisee /'farɪsiː/ ▻ *noun* (***Pharisees***) **1** a member of the Pharisees, an ancient Jewish sect whose strict interpretation of the Mosaic law led to an obsessive concern with the rules covering the details of everyday life. **2** *derog* anyone more careful of the outward forms than of the spirit of religion. **3** *derog* a self-righteous or hypocritical person. • **Pharisaic** or **pharisaic** /farɪ'seɪɪk/ *adj.* ◷ Anglo-Saxon: from Greek *pharisaios*, from Hebrew *parush* separated.

pharm. see PHAR.

pharmaceutical /fɑːmə'sjuːtɪkəl, -'suːtɪkəl, -'kjuːtɪkəl/ and **pharmaceutic** ▻ *adj* referring or relating to the preparation of drugs and medicines. • **pharmaceutically** *adverb.* ◷ 17c: from Latin *pharmaceutics*, from Greek *pharmakeutikos*, from *pharmakon* drug.

pharmaceutics /fɑːmə'sjuːtɪks, -'suːtɪks, -'kjuːtɪks/ ▻ *singular noun* the preparation and dispensing of drugs and medicine.

pharmacist /'fɑːməsɪst/ ▻ *noun* someone who is trained and licensed to prepare and dispense drugs and medicines. ◷ 19c: from PHARMACY + -IST.

pharmacology /fɑːmə'kɒlədʒɪ/ ▻ *noun* the scientific study of medicines and drugs and their effects and uses. • **pharmacological** /-kə'lɒdʒɪkəl/ *adj.* • **pharmacologically** *adverb.* • **pharmacologist** *noun.* ◷ 18c: from Greek *pharmakon* drug + -LOGY.

pharmacopoeia /fɑːməkə'piːə/ ▻ *noun* (***pharmacopoeias***) *medicine* an authoritative book that contains a list of drugs, together with details of their properties, uses, side-effects, methods of preparation and recommended dosages. ◷ 17c: Latin, from Greek *pharmakopoiia* preparation of drugs.

pharmacy /'fɑːməsɪ/ ▻ *noun* (***pharmacies***) **1** the mixing and dispensing of drugs and medicines. **2** a dispensary in a hospital, etc. **3** a pharmacist's or chemist's shop. ◷ 14c: from French *farmacie*, from Greek *pharmakeia* use of drugs.

pharyngeal /farən'dʒiːəl/ or **pharyngal** /fə'rɪŋgəl/ ▻ *adj, anatomy, medicine* relating to or in the region of the pharynx or throat.

pharyngitis /farɪn'dʒaɪtɪs/ ▻ *noun, medicine* inflammation of the mucous membrane of the pharynx, characterized by a sore throat, fever and difficulty in swallowing. ◷ 19c: medical Latin; see PHARNYX, -ITIS.

pharyngology /farɪn'dʒɒlədʒɪ/ ▻ *noun, medicine* the study of the pharynx and its diseases. ◷ 19c.

pharynx /'farɪŋks/ ▻ *noun* (***pharynxes*** or ***pharynges*** /-ɪndʒiːz/) **1** *anatomy* in mammals: the part of the alimentary canal that links the mouth and nasal passages with the oesophagus and trachea. **2** the throat. ◷ 17c: Greek, meaning 'throat'.

phase /feɪz/ ▻ *noun* **1** a stage or period in growth or development. **2** the appearance or aspect of anything at any stage. **3** *astron* any of the different shapes assumed by the illuminated surface of a celestial body, eg the Moon. **4** *physics* the stage that a periodically varying waveform has reached at a specific moment, usually in relation to another waveform of the same frequency. **5** *chem* a homogeneous part of a chemical system that is separated from other such parts of the system by distinct boundaries □ *Ice and water form a two-phase mixture.* ▻ *verb* (***phased***, ***phasing***) to organize or carry out (changes, etc) in stages. • **in** or **out of phase** coinciding, or failing to coincide, phase by phase throughout a series of changes. ◷ 19c: from Greek *phasis* appearance.

■ **phase something in** or **out** to introduce it, or get rid of it, gradually and in stages. See also PHASE-OUT.

phase difference ▻ *noun, physics* the amount by which one WAVE (*noun* 2) is behind or ahead of another wave of the same frequency.

phase-out ▻ *noun* an act or instance of phasing something out.

phatic communion /'fatɪk —/ ▻ *noun, linguistics* spoken language used for social reasons rather than to communicate ideas or facts, its main purpose being to maintain a rapport between people. It includes many conventional greetings such as *hello*, and statements or observations about the weather such as *Isn't it a nice day?* ◷ 1920s: from Greek *phatos* spoken.

PhD /piːeɪtʃ'diː/ ▻ *abbreviation*: *philosophiae doctor* (Latin), Doctor of Philosophy. See also DPH.

pheasant /'fɛzənt/ ▻ *noun* (***pheasant*** or ***pheasants***) **1** any of various species of ground-dwelling bird, the males of which are usually brightly coloured and have long pointed tails. **2** the common or ringed pheasant, a popular gamebird, the male of which has coppery plumage, with a dark-green head and neck, and red wattles around its eyes. ◷ 13c: from French *fesan*, from Greek *phasianos ornis* bird of the Phasis, ie the river in Asia Minor.

phellem /'fɛləm/ ▻ *noun, bot* the technical word for CORK (*noun* 1). ◷ 19c: German, from Greek *phellos* cork.

phencyclidine /fɛn'saɪklɪdiːn/ ▻ *noun, chem* (abbreviation **PCP**) an analgesic and anaesthetic drug, also used illegally as a hallucinogen. Also called **angel dust**. ◷ 1960s: from *phen-* + *cyclo-* + piper*idine*.

phenetics /fɛ'nɛtɪks/ ▻ *singular noun, biol* a system of classification of organisms based on observable similarities and differences irrespective of whether or not the organisms are related. • **phenetic** *adj.* ◷ 1960s: from PHENOTYPE, modelled on GENETICS.

pheno- /'fiːnou/ or (before a vowel) **phen-** *chem* ▻ *combining form, forming nouns, denoting* **1** something showing or visible □ *phenotype.* **2** a molecule that contains benzene rings. ◷ From Greek *phaino-* shining, from *phainein* to show.

phenobarbitone or (*chiefly N Amer*) **phenobarbital** *noun* a hypnotic and sedative drug used to treat insomnia, anxiety and epilepsy. ◷ 1930s.

phenocryst /'fiːnoukrɪst/ ▻ *noun, geol* in an igneous rock: a conspicuous crystal that is larger than the others. ◷ 19c: from French *phénocryste*; see PHENO-.

phenol /ˈfiːnɒl/ ▷ *noun, chem* **1** (formula C_6H_5OH) a colourless crystalline toxic solid used in the manufacture of phenolic and epoxy resins, nylon, solvents, explosives, drugs, dyes and perfumes. Also called **carbolic acid**. **2** any member of a group of weakly acidic organic chemical compounds, many of which are used as antiseptics, eg trichlorophenol (TCP). ◷ 19c: from *phene*, an old name for benzene + -OL.

phenolic resins /fɪˈnɒlɪk —/ ▷ *plural noun, chem* a group of plastics made from a PHENOL and an ALDEHYDE.

phenology /fɪˈnɒlədʒɪ/ ▷ *noun* the study of organisms as affected by climate, especially dates of seasonal phenomena, such as the opening of flowers, arrival of migrant animals, etc. • **phenological** /fiːnoʊˈlɒdʒɪkəl/ *adj*. • **phenologist** *noun*. ◷ 19c: from *pheno*menon + -LOGY.

phenolphthalein /fiːnɒlˈθeɪliːɪn/ ▷ *noun, chem* a dye which is colourless in acidic solutions and turns carmine red in alkaline solutions, used as a pH indicator and as a laxative. ◷ 19c.

phenomenal /fəˈnɒmənəl/ ▷ *adj* **1** remarkable; extraordinary; abnormal. **2** referring to the nature of a phenomenon. **3** relating to phenomena. • **phenomenally** *adverb*. ◷ 19c.

phenomenalism ▷ *noun, philos* a theory that human knowledge is confined to collections of sense-data (PHENOMENA), and that we know nothing that is not given to us by sense experience. • **phenomenalist** *noun, adj*. ◷ 19c.

phenomenology /fənɒmɪˈnɒlədʒɪ/ ▷ *noun* **1** the science of observing, or of describing, phenomena. **2** the philosophy of Edmund Husserl (1859-1938), concerned with the subjective experiences of the self, as opposed to ONTOLOGY. • **phenomenological** /-nəˈlɒdʒɪkəl/ *adj*. • **phenomenologist** *noun*. ◷ 18c: from PHENOMENON + -LOGY.

phenomenon /fəˈnɒmənən/ ▷ *noun* (***phenomena*** /-mənə/) **1** a happening perceived through the senses, especially something unusual or scientifically explainable. **2** an extraordinary or abnormal person or thing; a prodigy. **3** a feature of life, social existence, etc □ *stress as a work-related phenomenon.* ◷ 17c: from Greek *phainomenon* appearing, present participle of *phainesthai* to appear.

> ***phenomenon***
>
> Note that **phenomena** is plural. 'A phenomena' is often heard, but is not correct.

phenothiazine /fiːnoʊˈθaɪəziːn, fenoʊ-/ ▷ *noun* (formula $C_{12}H_9NS$) **1** a toxic heterocyclic compound used as a veterinary anthelminthic. **2** any of a number of derivatives of this, used as tranquillizers. ◷ 19c: from PHENO- + THIO- + AZINE.

phenotype ▷ *noun, genetics* **1** the observable characteristics of an organism, determined by the interaction between its GENOTYPE and environmental factors. **2** a group of individuals having the same characteristics of this kind. • **phenotypic** /-ˈtɪpɪk/ or **phenotypical** *adj*. ◷ Early 20c: from German *phaenotype*; see PHENO-.

phenyl /ˈfiːnɪl/ ▷ *noun, chem* (formula C_6H_5) an organic radical found in benzene, phenol, etc. ◷ 19c: from *phene*, an old name for benzene + -YL.

phenylalanine or **phenylalanin** /fiːnɪˈlaləniːn/ ▷ *noun, biochem* an essential amino acid, present in most proteins, that is readily converted to tyrosine. ◷ 19c: from German *phenylalanin*, PHENYL + ALANINE.

phenylketonuria /fiːnɪlkiːtoʊˈnjʊərɪə/ ▷ *noun, medicine, pathol* in infants: an inherited metabolic disorder in which phenylalanine accumulates in the body, damages the nervous system and may cause mental retardation. • **phenylketonuric** *noun* someone who suffers from phenylketonuria. ◷ 1930s.

pheromone /ˈfɛrəmoʊn/ ▷ *noun, zool* any chemical substance secreted in minute amounts by an animal, especially an insect or mammal, which has a specific effect on the behaviour of other members of the same species. ◷ 1950s: from Greek *pherein* to bear + HORMONE.

phew /fjuː/ ▷ *exclamation* used to express relief, astonishment or exhaustion. ◷ 17c: imitating the sound of a whistle.

phi /faɪ/ ▷ *noun* (***phis***) the twenty-first letter of the Greek alphabet. See table at GREEK ALPHABET.

phial /faɪəl/ ▷ *noun* a little medicine bottle. ◷ 14c: from Latin *phiala*, from Greek *phiale* shallow dish.

Phi Beta Kappa /faɪ ˈbiːtə ˈkapə, — ˈbeɪtə —/ ▷ *noun* in the US: **1** a national honorary society founded in 1776, whose members are chosen for their high academic distinction. **2** a member of this society. ◷ 18c: from the initial letters of its Greek motto, *Philosophia biou kybernetes* philosophy is the guide of life.

Phil. ▷ *abbreviation* **1** *US state* Philadelphia. **2** Book of the Bible: Philippians. See table at BIBLE. **3** philosophy. **4** *philosophiae* (Latin), of philosophy.

phil- see PHILO-

-phil see -PHILE

philadelphus /fɪləˈdɛlfəs/ ▷ *noun* (***philadelphuses***) any of various deciduous shrubs native to north temperate regions, especially the **mock orange**. ◷ 18c: from Greek *philadelphon* loving one's brother.

philander /fɪˈlandə(r)/ ▷ *verb* (***philandered***, ***philandering***) *intr* said of men: to flirt or have casual love affairs with women; to womanize. • **philanderer** *noun*. ◷ 16c: from Greek *philandros*, literally 'fond of men' but misapplied as 'a loving man', used in Greek literature as a proper name for a lover.

philanthropy /fɪˈlanθrəpɪ/ ▷ *noun* a charitable regard for one's fellow human beings, especially in the form of benevolence to those in need, usually characterized by contributing money, time, etc to various causes. • **philanthropic** /-lənˈθrɒpɪk/ *adj* benevolent. • **philanthropist** or **philanthrope** /ˈfɪlənθroʊp/ *noun*. ◷ 17c: from Greek *philanthropia*, from *phil-* loving + *anthropos* man.

philately /fɪˈlatəlɪ/ ▷ *noun* the study and collecting of postage stamps. • **philatelic** /fɪləˈtɛlɪk/ *adj*. • **philatelist** *noun*. ◷ 19c: from French *philatélie*, from Greek *phil-* PHILO- + *ateles* untaxed, indicating mail being delivered 'free' if prepaid by a stamp.

-phile /faɪl/ or **-phil** /fɪl/ ▷ *combining form, forming nouns, denoting* fondness, attraction or loving of the specified thing □ *bibliophile.* ◷ From Greek *philos* loving.

Philem. ▷ *abbreviation* Book of the Bible: Philemon. See table at BIBLE.

philharmonic /fɪləˈmɒnɪk, fɪlhɑːˈmɒnɪk/ ▷ *adj* used as part of the name of choirs and orchestras: dedicated to music, not indicating a particular type of music. ◷ 19c: from French *philharmonique*.

-philia /fɪlɪə, fiːlɪə/ ▷ *combining form, forming nouns, denoting* **1** a tendency towards an abnormal functioning of the specified thing □ *haemophilia.* **2** an abnormal and usually sexual liking or love of the specified thing □ *paedophilia.*

-philiac /fɪlɪak/ ▷ *combining form* forming nouns and adjectives corresponding to nouns in -PHILIA.

philibeg see FILIBEG

philippic /fɪˈlɪpɪk/ ▷ *noun* a speech making a bitter attack on someone or something. ◷ 16c: from the orations of the Athenian Demosthenes against Philip of Macedon.

philistine /ˈfɪlɪstaɪn/ ▷ *adj* having no interest in or appreciation of art, literature, music, etc, and tending rather towards materialism. ▷ *noun* a philistine person. • **philistinism** /-stɪnɪzəm/ *noun*. ⓒ 19c in this sense; 14c: from Greek Philistinos.

Phillips screw /ˈfɪlɪps —/ ▷ *noun, trademark* a screw with a recessed cross in the head, used with a corresponding **Phillips screwdriver** (*trademark*). ⓒ 1930s: named after the original US manufacturer, Philips Screws.

philo- /ˈfɪloʊ/ or (before a vowel) **phil-** /fɪl/ ▷ *combining form, denoting* fondness or liking of the specified thing. ⓒ From Greek *philos* loving.

philology /fɪˈlɒlədʒɪ/ ▷ *noun* **1** the study of language, its history and development; the comparative study of related languages; linguistics. **2** the study of literary and non-literary texts, especially older ones. • **philological** /fɪləˈlɒdʒɪkəl/ *adj*. • **philologically** *adverb*. • **philologist** *noun*. ⓒ 17c: from Greek *philologia* love of argument, literature or learning.

philosopher /fɪˈlɒsəfə(r)/ ▷ *noun* someone who studies philosophy, especially one who develops a particular set of doctrines or theories.

philosopher's stone ▷ *noun, historical* a hypothetical substance able to turn any metal into gold, long sought by alchemists. ⓒ 14c.

philosophical /fɪləˈsɒfɪkəl/ or **philosophic** ▷ *adj* **1** referring or relating to philosophy or philosophers. **2** calm and dispassionate in the face of adversity; resigned, stoical or patient □ *very philosophical about his problems*. • **philosophically** *adverb*.

philosophize or **philosophise** /fɪˈlɒsəfaɪz/ ▷ *verb* (***philosophized***, ***philosophizing***) *intr* **1** to form philosophical theories. **2** to reason or speculate in the manner of a philosopher. • **philosophizer** *noun*. ⓒ 16c.

philosophy /fɪˈlɒsəfɪ/ ▷ *noun* (***philosophies***) **1** the search for truth and knowledge concerning the universe, human existence, perception and behaviour, pursued by means of reflection, reasoning and argument. **2** any particular system or set of beliefs established as a result of this. **3** a set of principles that serves as a basis for making judgements and decisions □ *one's philosophy of life*. • **moral philosophy** and **natural philosophy** see separate entries. ⓒ 14c: from Greek *philosophia* love of wisdom, from *philo-* loving + *sophia* wisdom.

-philous /fɪləs/ ▷ *combining form* forming adjectives corresponding to nouns in -PHILIA.

philtre /ˈfɪltə(r)/ ▷ *noun* a magic potion for arousing sexual desire. ⓒ 17c: French, from Greek *philtron* love charm.

phimosis /faɪˈmoʊsɪs/ ▷ *noun, pathol* narrowness or constriction of the foreskin which prevents it being drawn back over the glans penis. ⓒ 17c: from Greek, meaning 'muzzling', from *phimos* a muzzle.

phiz and **phizog** /fɪˈzɒg/ ▷ *noun, slang, mainly Brit* the face. ⓒ 17c: shortening of PHYSIOGNOMY.

phlebitis /flɪˈbaɪtɪs/ ▷ *noun, pathol* inflammation of the wall of a vein, often resulting in the formation of a blood clot at the affected site. ⓒ 19c: Latin, from Greek *phleps, phlebos* vein + -ITIS.

phlebotomy /flɪˈbɒtəmɪ/ ▷ *noun* (***phlebotomies***) *surg* the removal of blood by puncturing or making a surgical incision in a vein. ⓒ 14c: from Latin *phlebotomia*, from Greek *phleps, phlebos* a vein + *-tomia* cutting.

phlegm /flɛm/ ▷ *noun* **1** a thick yellowish substance produced by the mucous membrane that lines the air passages, brought up by coughing. **2** calmness or impassiveness; stolidity or sluggishness of temperament. **3** *old physiol* one of the four humours (see HUMOUR *noun* 6) or bodily fluids, ie the humour characterized as cold and moist. • **phlegmy** /ˈflɛmɪ/ *adj*. ⓒ 14c as *fleume*: French, from Greek *phlegma* flame, heat, phlegm (thought to be the result of heat) or inflammation.

phlegmatic /flɛgˈmatɪk/ or **phlegmatical** ▷ *adj* **1** said of a person: calm; not easily excited. **2** producing or having phlegm. • **phlegmatically** *adverb*.

phloem /ˈfloʊəm/ ▷ *noun, bot* the plant tissue that is responsible for the transport of sugars and other nutrients from the leaves to all other parts of the plant. See also XYLEM. ⓒ 19c: German, from Greek *phloios* bark.

phlogiston /flɒˈdʒɪstən/ ▷ *noun, chem, historical* a substance believed in the 18c to be present in combustible materials and to separate from them during combustion, the observed actions of which were subsequently found to be due to oxygen. ⓒ 18c: Latin, from Greek *phlogistos, phlogiston* burnt up or inflammable.

phlomis /ˈfloʊmɪs/ ▷ *noun* (***phlomis*** or ***phlomises***) a plant belonging to a genus of labiate herbs and shrubs with whorls of white, yellow or purple flowers and wrinkled, often woolly, leaves. ⓒ 18c: Latin.

phlox /flɒks/ ▷ *noun* (***phlox*** or ***phloxes***) any of various mat-forming, trailing or erect plants with white, pink, red or purple tubular flowers borne in large dense terminal clusters. ⓒ 18c: Latin, from Greek, meaning 'flame' or 'wallflower'.

phlyctaena or **phlyctena** /flɪkˈtiːnə/ ▷ *noun* (***phlyctaenae*** or ***phlyctenae*** /-niː/) *medicine* a small blister or vesicle. ⓒ 17c: Latin, from Greek *phlyktaina* blister, from *phlyein* to swell.

-phobe /foʊb/ ▷ *combining form, forming nouns, denoting* someone affected by a phobia of the specified kind □ *Anglophobe* □ *xenophobe*. ⓒ French, from Greek *phobos* fear.

phobia /ˈfoʊbɪə/ ▷ *noun* (***phobias***) an obsessive and persistent fear of a specific object or situation, eg spiders, open spaces, etc, representing a form of neurosis. ⓒ 18c: from the combining form -PHOBIA.

-phobia /ˈfoʊbɪə/ ▷ *combining form, forming nouns, denoting* obsessive and persistent fear of the specified thing □ *claustrophobia* □ *hydrophobia*. ⓒ Greek, from *phobos* fear.

phobic /ˈfoʊbɪk/ ▷ *adj* **1** relating to or involving a phobia. **2** affected by a phobia. ⓒ 19c.

-phobic /ˈfoʊbɪk/ ▷ *combining form* forming adjectives corresponding to nouns in -PHOBIA.

phoebe /ˈfiːbɪ/ ▷ *noun* a N American flycatcher. ⓒ 19c: an imitation of its song.

Phoenician /fəˈnɪʃən, fəˈniːʃən/ ▷ *adj* belonging or relating to ancient Phoenicia, a narrow strip of land in the Eastern Mediterranean between the mountains of Lebanon and the sea, or to its people or culture. ▷ *noun* **1** a member of the Phoenician people. **2** their Semitic language. ⓒ 14c.

phoenix /ˈfiːnɪks/ ▷ *noun* (***phoenixes***) **1** in Arabian legend: a bird which every 500 years sets itself on fire and is reborn from its ashes to live a further 500 years. **2** someone or something of unique excellence or unsurpassable beauty. ⓒ Anglo-Saxon *fenix*: from Greek *phoinix*.

phoenixism ▷ *noun, stock exchange* the practice of forming a new company from a bankrupted one, usually with the same directors, workforce, premises, etc, which continues the same trading debt-free.

phon /fɒn/ ▷ *noun, acoustics* a unit of loudness, measured as the number of decibels above a pure tone with a

Some Common Phobias

Phobia	Meaning	Origin of name		
acrophobia	fear of heights and high places	Greek	*akron*	peak
aerophobia	fear of air or draughts	Greek	*aer*	air
agoraphobia	fear of open spaces	Greek	*agora*	market place
aichmophobia	fear of knives	Greek	*aichme*	point of a spear
ailurophobia	fear of cats	Greek	*ailouros*	cat
algophobia	fear of pain	Greek	*algos*	pain
androphobia	fear of men	Greek	*aner, andros*	man
anemophobia	fear of wind	Greek	*anemos*	wind
anthropophobia	fear of people	Greek	*anthropos*	person
arachnophobia	fear of spiders	Greek	*arachne*	spider
astrapophobia	fear of thunder and lightning	Greek	*astrape*	lightning
aviophobia	fear of flying	Latin	*avis*	bird
bathophobia	fear of depths and deep places	Greek	*bathos*	depth
belonephobia	fear of needles	Greek	*belone*	needle
bibliophobia	fear of books	Greek	*biblion*	book
claustrophobia	fear of confined spaces	Latin	*claustrum*	an enclosed space
cynophobia	fear of dogs or rabies	Greek	*kyon, kynos*	dog
dromophobia	fear of crossing a street	Greek	*dromos*	road
erotophobia	fear of sexual activity		*see*	EROTIC
erythrophobia	fear of the colour red, or of blushing	Greek	*erythros*	red
gephyrophobia	fear of crossing a bridge or river	Greek	*gephyra*	bridge
gerontophobia	fear of old people or old age	Greek	*geron, gerontos*	old man
graphophobia	fear of writing		*see*	GRAPH
gynophobia	fear of women	Greek	*gyne*	woman
haemophobia	fear of blood	Greek	*haima*	blood
hierophobia	fear of sacred objects or rituals	Greek	*hieros*	sacred
hodophobia	fear of travel	Greek	*hodos*	road, way
homophobia	fear of or hostility to homosexuals		*see*	HOMOSEXUAL
hydrophobia	fear of water	Greek	*hydor*	water
kenophobia	fear of empty spaces	Greek	*kenos*	empty
monophobia	fear of being alone	Greek	*monos*	alone
mysophobia	fear of contamination or dirt	Greek	*mysos*	contamination
necrophobia	fear of corpses or death	Greek	*nekros*	dead body
neophobia	fear of new situations, places, or objects	Greek	*neos*	new
nosophobia	fear of disease	Greek	*nosos*	disease
nyctophobia	fear of the night or darkness	Greek	*nyx, nyktos*	night
ochlophobia	fear of crowds	Greek	*ochlos*	crowd
oikophobia	fear of one's surroundings	Greek	*oikos*	house
ornithophobia	fear of birds	Greek	*ornis*	bird
ophidiophobia	fear of snakes	Greek	*ophidion*	snake
pantophobia	fear of everything	Greek	*pas, pantos*	everything
phagophobia	fear of food or eating	Greek	*phagein*	to eat
phengophobia	fear of daylight	Greek	*phengos*	light, brightness
phobophobia	fear of fearing	Greek	*phobos*	fear
phonophobia	fear of sounds or of speaking aloud	Greek	*phonos*	sound
photophobia	fear of light	Greek	*phos, photos*	light
ponophobia	fear of work	Greek	*ponos*	work, toil
pyrophobia	fear of fire	Greek	*pyr*	fire
scopophobia	fear of being looked at	Greek	*skopein*	to view
scotophobia	fear of the dark	Greek	*skotos*	dark
sitophobia	fear of food or eating	Greek	*sitos*	food
spectrophobia	fear of mirrors	Latin	*spectrum*	image
taphephobia	fear of being buried alive	Greek	*taphos*	tomb
theophobia	fear of God	Greek	*theos*	god
toxiphobia	fear of poisoning		*see*	TOXIC
triskaidekaphobia	fear of the number thirteen	Greek	*treiskaideka*	thirteen
xenophobia	fear of or hostility to foreigners	Greek	*xenos*	stranger
zoophobia	fear of animals	Greek	*zoion*	animal

frequency of 1000 hertz. ⓒ 1930s: German, from Greek *phone* sound.

phon- see PHONO-

phone¹ or **'phone** /foun/ ▻ *noun* a telephone. Also *as adj* □ *phone call* □ *phone box*. ▻ *verb* (***phoned***, ***phoning***) (*also* **phone someone up**) *tr & intr* to telephone someone. ⓒ 19c.

■ **phone in** to take part in a broadcast PHONE-IN.

phone² /foun/ ▻ *noun, phonetics* a single or elementary speech sound. ⓒ 19c: Greek, meaning 'sound'.

-phone /foun/ ▻ *combining form, forming nouns and adjectives, denoting* **1** an instrument that transmits or reproduces sound □ ***telephone*** □ ***microphone***. **2** a musical instrument □ *saxophone*. **3** a speech sound □ *homophone*. **4** speaking, or a speaker of, a language □ *Francophone*. See also -PHONIC. ⓒ From Greek *phone* 'sound' or 'voice'.

phone book see TELEPHONE DIRECTORY

phonecard ▷ *noun* a card that can be used to pay for phone calls from public telephones. ⓒ 1980s.

phone-in ▷ *noun* a radio or TV programme in which telephoned contributions from listeners or viewers are invited and discussed live by an expert or panel in the studio. ⓒ 1960s.

phoneme /'founi:m/ ▷ *noun, linguistics* the smallest unit of sound in a language that has significance in distinguishing one word from another. • **phonemic** /fə'ni:mɪk/ *adj.* • **phonemically** *adverb.* ⓒ Late 19c: French, from Greek *phonema* a sound uttered.

phonemics /fə'ni:mɪks/ ▷ *singular noun* **1** the study and analysis of phonemes. **2** the system or pattern of phonemes in a language. • **phonemicist** *noun.*

phone phreaking see PHREAKING

phonetic /fə'nɛtɪk/ ▷ *adj* **1** referring or relating to the sounds of a spoken language. **2** said eg of a spelling: intended to represent the pronunciation. **3** denoting a pronunciation scheme using symbols each of which represents one sound only. • **phonetically** *adverb.* ⓒ 19c: from Greek *phonetikos*, from *phoneein* to speak.

phonetic alphabet ▷ *noun* **1** a list of symbols used in phonetic transcriptions, such as the IPA. **2** used in voice communications: a system in which letters of the alphabet are identified by means of code words, eg *Delta* for *D*, *Echo* for *E*, *Foxtrot* for *F*, etc. Also called NATO ALPHABET (see table there).

phonetics /fə'nɛtɪks/ ▷ *singular noun* the branch of linguistics that deals with speech sounds, especially how they are produced and perceived. • **phonetician** /founɪ'tɪʃən/ *noun.* • **phonetist** /'founɪtɪst/ *noun.* ⓒ 19c.

phoney or (*US*) **phony** /'founɪ/ ▷ *adj* (***phonier, phoniest***) not genuine; fake, sham, bogus or insincere. ▷ *noun* (***phoneys*** or ***phonies***) someone or something bogus; a fake or humbug. • **phoneyness** or (*US*) **phoniness** *noun.* ⓒ Early 20c.

phonic /'founɪk, 'fɒnɪk/ ▷ *adj* **1** relating to sounds, especially vocal sounds. **2** *education* belonging or relating to the PHONIC METHOD (see PHONICS). • **phonically** *adverb.* ⓒ 19c: from Greek *phonikos*, from *phone* sound or voice.

-phonic ▷ *combining form* forming adjectives corresponding to nouns in -PHONE.

phonics or **phonic method** ▷ *singular noun* a method used in the teaching of reading, based on recognition of the relationships between individual letters, or groups of letters, and sounds. See also LOOK AND SAY.

phoniness an alternative *US* spelling of PHONEYNESS

phono- /founou, fə'nɒ/ or (before a vowel) **phon-** ▷ *combining form, denoting* sound or voice □ *phonology* □ *phonograph*. ⓒ From Greek *phone* sound or voice.

phonograph /'founəgrɑ:f/ ▷ *noun, N Amer, old use* a record-player. ⓒ 19c.

phonography /fou'nɒgrəfɪ/ ▷ *noun* a system in which each spoken sound is represented by a distinct character, eg in shorthand. ⓒ 19c.

phonolite /'founəlaɪt/ ▷ *noun* a fine-grained igneous rock that rings when struck by a hammer. Also called CLINKSTONE. ⓒ 19c.

phonology /fə'nɒlədʒɪ/ ▷ *noun* (***phonologies***) **1** the study of speech sounds in general, or of those in any particular language. **2** any particular system of speech sounds. • **phonological** /-'lɒdʒɪkəl/ *adj.* • **phonologically** *adverb.* • **phonologist** /fə'nɒlədʒɪst/ *noun.* ⓒ 18c, originally meaning PHONETICS.

phony an alternative *US* spelling of PHONEY

phooey /'fu:i:/ ▷ *exclamation, colloq* an exclamation of scorn, contempt, disbelief, etc. ⓒ 1920s: probably a variant of PHEW.

-phore or **-phor** /fɔ:(r)/ ▷ *combining form, forming nouns, denoting* carrier of a specified thing □ *semaphore* □ *chromatophore*. ⓒ French, from Latin *-phorus*, from Greek *-phoros*.

-phoresis /fə'ri:sɪs/ ▷ *combining form, forming nouns, denoting* transmission of a specified thing □ *electrophoresis*. ⓒ Greek, from *pherein* to bear or carry.

-phorous /fərəs/ ▷ *combining form* forming adjectives corresponding to nouns in -PHORE.

phosgene /'fɒsdʒi:n/ ▷ *noun, chem* ▷ (formula $\mathbf{COCl_2}$) a poisonous gas, carbonyl chloride, used in the manufacture of pesticides and dyes. ⓒ 19c: from Greek *phos* light + -GENE 1, because it was originally produced by exposing carbon monoxide and chlorine to sunlight.

phosphate /'fɒsfeɪt/ ▷ *noun, chem* any salt or ester of PHOSPHORIC ACID, found in living organisms and in many minerals, and used in fertilizers, detergents, water softeners, etc. ⓒ 18c.

phosphor /'fɒsfə(r)/ ▷ *noun, chem* any substance that is capable of phosphorescence, used to coat the inner surface of television screens and fluorescent light tubes, and as a brightener in detergents. ⓒ 17c: from Greek *phosphoros*; see PHOSPHORUS.

phosphoresce /fɒsfə'rɛs/ ▷ *verb* (***phosphoresced, phosphorescing***) *intr* to be phosphorescent; to shine in the dark.

phosphorescence /fɒsfə'rɛsəns/ ▷ *noun* **1** the emission of light from a substance after it has absorbed energy from a source such as ultraviolet radiation, and which continues for some time after the energy source has been removed. **2** a general term for the emission of light by a substance in the absence of a significant rise in temperature. • **phosphorescent** *adj.* ⓒ 18c.

phosphoric /fɒs'fɒrɪk/ ▷ *adj, chem* referring to or containing phosphorus in higher VALENCY.

phosphoric acid ▷ *noun, chem* (formula $\mathbf{H_3PO_4}$) a transparent crystalline water-soluble compound used in soft drinks, rust removers, and for forming a corrosion-resistant layer on iron and steel. Also called **orthophosphoric acid**.

phosphorous /'fɒsfərəs/ ▷ *adj, chem* referring to or containing phosphorus in lower VALENCY.

phosphorus /'fɒsfərəs/ ▷ *noun, chem* (symbol **P**, atomic number 15) a non-metallic element that exists as several different allotropes, including a whitish-yellow soft waxy solid that ignites spontaneously in air. ⓒ 17c: from Greek *phosphoros* bringer of light, from *phos* light + *pherein* to bring or carry.

phot /fɒt, fout/ ▷ *noun* in the cgs system: the unit of illumination equal to one LUMEN per square centimetre. ⓒ Early 20c in this sense: French from Greek *phos, photos* light.

phot. ▷ *abbreviation* **1** photographic. **2** photography.

photic /'foutɪk/ ▷ *adj* **1** referring to or concerned with light. **2** said of the turbidity of the uppermost layer of the sea or lakes: referring to the depth to which light can penetrate to allow photosynthesis. ⓒ 19c: from Greek *phos, photos* light.

photo /'foutou/ ▷ *noun* (***photos***) *colloq* a PHOTOGRAPH. ⓒ 1860s.

photo-[1] /foutou, fou'tɒ/ ▷ *combining form, denoting* photography □ *photocopier* □ *photomontage*. ⓒ An abbreviation of PHOTOGRAPH.

photo-[2] /foutou, fou'tɒ/ or **phot-** ▷ *combining form, denoting* light □ *photoelectric*. ⓒ From Greek *phos, photos* light.

photo call ▻ *noun* an arranged opportunity for press photographers to take publicity photographs of eg a celebrity.

photocell see PHOTOELECTRIC CELL

photochemistry ▻ *noun, chem* the branch of chemistry concerned with the study of chemical reactions that will only take place in the presence of visible light or ultraviolet radiation, as well as chemical reactions in which light is produced. • **photochemical** *adj*. • **photochemist** *noun*. ◷ 19c.

photocomposition see under FILMSETTING

photocopier ▻ *noun* a machine that makes copies of printed documents or illustrations by any of various photographic techniques, especially XEROGRAPHY.

photocopy ▻ *noun* (***photocopies***) a photographic copy of a document, drawing, etc. ▻ *verb* (***photocopies, photocopied, photocopying***) to make a photographic copy of (a document, etc). • **photocopiable** *adj*. • **photocopying** *noun*. ◷ 1920s.

photodegradable ▻ *adj* said of a substance or material: capable of being decomposed by the action of light or ultraviolet radiation. See also BIODEGRADABLE.

photoelectric ▻ *adj* referring or relating to the electrical effects of light, eg the emission of electrons or a change in resistance. ◷ 19c.

photoelectric cell ▻ *noun* (abbreviation **PEC** or **pec**) a light-sensitive device that converts light energy into electrical energy, used in light meters, burglar alarms, etc. Also called **photocell**.

photoelectric effect ▻ *noun, physics* the emission of electrons from the surface of some semi-metallic materials as a result of irradiation with light.

photoelectricity ▻ *noun* electricity produced when certain materials, such as selenium or silicon, are exposed to light or other forms of electromagnetic radiation.

photoengraving ▻ *noun* a technique for producing metal printing plates on cylinders carrying the image of continuous-tone and half-tone text and illustrations.

photo finish ▻ *noun* **1** a race finish in which the runners are so close that the result must be decided by looking at a photograph taken at the finishing line. **2** any race finish which is very close. ◷ 1930s.

Photofit or **photofit** ▻ *noun, trademark* **1** a system used by the police for building up a likeness of someone to fit a witness's description, similar to IDENTIKIT but using photographs rather than drawings of individual features. **2** a likeness produced in this way. Also *as adj* □ *photofit picture*. ◷ 1970s.

photogenic /foʊtə'dʒɛnɪk, -'dʒiːnɪk/ ▻ *adj* **1** said especially of a person: characterized by the quality of photographing well or looking attractive in photographs. **2** *biol* producing, or produced by, light. ◷ 1920s; mid 19c in sense 2.

photogram ▻ *noun* **1** a type of picture produced by placing an object on or near photographic paper which is then exposed to light. **2** *old use* a photograph. ◷ 19c in sense 2.

photogrammetry /foʊtoʊ'gramətrɪ/ ▻ *noun* the use of photographic records for precise measurements of distances or dimensions, eg aerial photographs used in surveying and map-making. ◷ 19c.

photograph ▻ *noun* a permanent record of an image that has been produced on photosensitive film or paper by the process of photography. ▻ *verb* (***photographed, photographing***) *tr & intr* to take a photograph of (a person, thing, etc). ◷ 19c.

photographer /fə'tɒgrəfə(r)/ ▻ *noun* someone who takes photographs, especially professionally.

photographic /foʊtə'grafɪk/ ▻ *adj* **1** relating to or similar to photographs or photography. **2** said of memory: retaining images in exact detail. • **photographically** *adverb*.

photography /fə'tɒgrəfɪ/ ▻ *noun* the process of making a permanent record of an image on light-sensitive film or some other sensitized material using visible light, X-rays, or some other form of radiant energy. ◷ 19c.

photogravure /foʊtoʊgrə'vjʊə(r)/ ▻ *noun* **1** a method of engraving in which the design is photographed on to a metal plate, and then etched in. **2** a picture produced in this way. ◷ 19c: PHOTO-[1] + GRAVURE.

photojournalism ▻ *noun* journalism consisting mainly of photographs to convey the meaning of the article, with written material playing a small role. • **photojournalist** *noun*. ◷ 1940s.

photolithography ▻ *noun* a process of lithographic printing from a photographically produced plate. ◷ 19c.

photoluminescence ▻ *noun, physics* luminescence produced by exposure of visible light, or infrared or ultraviolet radiation. • **photoluminescent** *adj*. ◷ 19c.

photolysis /foʊ'tɒlɪsɪs/ ▻ *noun, chem* a chemical reaction in which the breaking of a chemical bond within a molecule of a substance is brought about by exposure to light or ultraviolet radiation. • **photolytic** /foʊtoʊ'lɪtɪk/ *adj*. ◷ Early 20c.

photometry /foʊ'tɒmɪtrɪ/ ▻ *noun, physics* the measurement of visible light and its rate of flow, which has important applications in photography and lighting design. • **photometric** /foʊtə'mɛtrɪk/ *adj*. ◷ 18c.

photomicrograph ▻ *noun, physics* a photograph of an object observed through a microscope. • **photomicrography** *noun*. ◷ Mid 19c.

photomontage /foʊtoʊmɒn'tɑːʒ/ ▻ *noun* the assembling of selected photographic images, either by mounting cut-out portions of prints on a backing, or by combining several separate negatives in succession during printing. This technique is widely used in advertising display material and sometimes in artistic creations. See also MONTAGE. ◷ 1930s: from French *montage* mounting.

photomultiplier ▻ *noun, physics* a device for the electronic detection of very low intensities of light. ◷ 1940s.

photon /'foʊtɒn/ ▻ *noun, physics* a particle of electromagnetic radiation that travels at the speed of light, used to explain phenomena that require light to behave as particles rather than as waves. ◷ 1920s.

photo opportunity ▻ *noun* an event organized or attended by a public figure and intended to draw press photographers or television cameras to record it.

photoperiodism ▻ *noun, biol* the physiological and behavioural responses of living organisms to changes in day-length, eg flowering of plants or migration of animals. ◷ 1920s.

photophobia ▻ *noun, medicine* **1** a fear of or aversion to light. **2** an abnormal intolerance of and avoidance of light which may be a symptom of various disorders, eg migraine, measles or meningitis. ◷ 18c.

photoreceptor ▻ *noun, biol* a cell or group of cells that is sensitive to and responds to light stimuli. ◷ Early 20c.

photosensitive ▻ *adj* **1** readily stimulated by light or some other form of radiant energy. **2** said of skin: having an abnormal reaction to sunlight, characterized by burning and blistering. • **photosensitivity** *noun*. ◷ 19c.

photosphere ▻ *noun, astron* **1** the outermost visible layer of the Sun, representing the zone from which light is emitted. **2** the visible surface of any other star. ◷ 19c.

Photostat /'foʊtoʊstat/ ▻ *noun, trademark* **1** a photographic apparatus for copying documents, drawings, etc. **2** a copy made by this. ▻ *verb* (**photostat**) (*photostatted*, *photostatting*) to make a Photostat of (a document, etc). ◷ 1911.

photosynthesis ▷ *noun* **1** *bot* the process whereby green plants manufacture carbohydrates from carbon dioxide and water, using the light energy from sunlight trapped by the pigment CHLOROPHYLL in specialized structures known as CHLOROPLASTS. **2** a similar process that occurs in certain bacteria, whereby carbohydrates are manufactured using a hydrogen source other than water. • **photosynthetic** /-sɪn'θɛtɪk/ *adj*. ◷ 19c.

photosynthesize or **photosynthesise** ▷ *verb* (*photosynthesized*, *photosynthesizing*) *tr & intr* to carry out the process of photosynthesis.

phototaxis ▷ *noun*, *biol* the movement of a cell (eg a gamete) or a motile organism towards or away from a light source. • **phototactic** *adj*. ◷ 19c.

phototropism /foʊ'tɒtrəpɪzəm, foʊtoʊ'troʊpɪzəm/ ▷ *noun*, *bot* the growth of the roots or shoots of plants in response to light, eg shoots show 'positive phototropism' when they grow in the direction of light. ◷ Late 19c.

phototypesetter ▷ *noun*, *printing* **1** a machine for composing type (and certain illustrations) and creating an image of the composed type on film or on paper, ready for exposure to a plate for printing. **2** someone who operates such a machine. • **phototypesetting** *noun*. ◷ 1930s *phototypesetting*.

photovoltaic cell see SOLAR CELL

phrasal verb ▷ *noun*, *grammar* a phrase consisting of a verb plus an adverb or preposition, or both, frequently with a meaning or meanings that cannot be determined from the meanings of the individual words, eg *let on* or *come up with something*.

phrase /freɪz/ ▷ *noun* **1** a set of words expressing a single idea, forming part of a sentence though not constituting a CLAUSE (sense 1). **2** an idiomatic expression □ *What is the phrase she used?* See also COIN A PHRASE at COIN. **3** manner or style of speech or expression □ *ease of phrase*. See also TURN OF PHRASE. **4** *music* a run of notes making up an individually distinct part of a melody. ▷ *verb* (*phrased*, *phrasing*) **1** to express; to word something □ *He phrased his reply carefully.* **2** *music* to bring out the phrases in (music) as one plays. • **phrasal** *adj*. • **phrasally** *adverb*. ◷ 16c: from Greek *phrasis* expression, from *phrazein* to tell.

phrase book ▷ *noun* a book that lists words and phrases in a foreign language, especially for the use of visitors to a country where that language is spoken.

phraseogram /'freɪzɪəgram/ ▷ *noun* a single sign that represents a whole phrase, especially in shorthand. ◷ 19c.

phraseology /freɪzɪ'ɒlədʒɪ/ ▷ *noun* (*phraseologies*) **1** one's choice of words and way of combining them, in expressing oneself. **2** the language belonging to a particular subject, group, etc □ *legal phraseology*. • **phraseological** /-ɪə'lɒdʒɪkəl/ *adj*. ◷ 17c.

phrasing ▷ *noun* **1** the wording of a speech or passage. **2** *music* the grouping of the parts, sounds, etc into musical phrases.

phreaking and **phone phreaking** ▷ *noun*, *colloq* the practice of tampering electronically with a telephone to enable the user to make free calls. ◷ 1970s: a variant of FREAK, influenced by PHONE.

phreatic /frɪ'atɪk/ ▷ *adj*, *geol*, *etc* **1** relating to underground water-supplying wells or springs, or to the soil or rocks containing them. **2** said of underground gases, etc: present in or causing volcanic eruptions. ◷ 19c: from French *phréatique*, from Greek *phreatia* cistern.

phrenetic see FRENETIC

phrenic /'frɛnɪk/ ▷ *adj*, *anatomy* relating to the diaphragm, and especially the associated nerve. ◷ 18c: from French *phrénique*, from Greek *phren*, *phrenos* diaphragm.

phrenology /frə'nɒlədʒɪ/ ▷ *noun* the practice, popular in the 19c but now discredited, of assessing someone's character and aptitudes by examining the shape of their skull. • **phrenologic** /frɛnə'lɒdʒɪk/ or **phrenological** *adj*. • **phrenologist** /frə'nɒ-/ *noun*. ◷ 19c: from Greek *phren* mind + -LOGY.

Phrygian /'frɪdʒɪən/ ▷ *adj* belonging or relating to Phrygia, an ancient country in central Asia Minor, its inhabitants, or their language. ▷ *noun* **1** a citizen or inhabitant of, or person born in, Phrygia. **2** the Indo-European language of the ancient Phrygians. ◷ 15c as *noun* 1.

Phrygian cap ▷ *noun* an ancient type of conical cap with the top turned forward, which in the French Revolution came to symbolize liberty.

phthisis /'θaɪsɪs, 'fθaɪsɪs, 'taɪsɪs/ ▷ *noun* (*phthises* /-siːz/) *pathol* any wasting disease, especially tuberculosis. ◷ 16c: Greek, meaning 'emaciation' or 'consumption'.

phut /fʌt/ ▷ *noun*, *colloq* the noise of a small explosion. • **go phut 1** to break down or cease to function. **2** to go wrong. ◷ 19c: imitating the sound, or connected with Hindi and Urdu *phatna* to burst.

pH value see PH

phyco- /'faɪkoʊ/ ▷ *combining form*, *denoting* seaweed. ◷ From Greek *phykos* seaweed.

phycocyanin see under BLUE-GREEN ALGA

phycology /faɪ'kɒlədʒɪ/ ▷ *noun*, *bot* the scientific study of algae. ◷ 19c.

phycomycete /faɪ'koʊmaɪsiːt/ ▷ *noun*, *biol* primitive, mainly aquatic, fungus, often parasitic on fish. ◷ 19c.

phyla *plural of* PHYLUM

phylactery /fɪ'laktərɪ/ ▷ *noun* (*phylacteries*) **1** *Judaism* either of two small boxes containing religious texts worn on the left arm and forehead by Jewish men during prayers. **2** a reminder. **3** a charm or amulet. ◷ 14c: from Greek *phylakterion*, from *phylassein* to guard.

phyletic /faɪ'lɛtɪk/ ▷ *adj*, *biol* **1** relating to a PHYLUM. **2** referring to the evolutionary descent of organisms. ◷ 19c: from German *phyletisch*, from Greek *phyletikos*, from *phyle* a tribe.

phyllite /'fɪlaɪt/ ▷ *noun*, *geol* any of various fine-grained metamorphic rocks intermediate between slate and schist. ◷ 19c: from Greek *phyllon* a leaf.

phyllo see FILO

phylloclade /'fɪloʊkleɪd/ ▷ *noun*, *bot* a flattened branch with the shape and functions of a leaf. ◷ 19c: from Greek *phyllon* leaf + *klados* shoot.

phyllode /'fɪloʊd/ ▷ *noun*, *bot* a PETIOLE with the appearance and function of a leaf blade. ◷ 19c: from Greek *phyllon* leaf.

phyllomania /fɪloʊ'meɪnɪə/ ▷ *noun*, *bot* excessive production of leaves at the expense of flower or fruit production. ◷ 17c: from Greek *phyllon* leaf + *mania* MANIA.

phylloquinone /fɪloʊkwɪ'noʊn/ ▷ *noun*, *biochem* vitamin K_1, one of the fat-soluble vitamin K group essential for normal blood coagulation. ◷ 1930s: from Greek *phyllon* leaf + QUINONE.

phyllotaxis /fɪloʊ'taksɪs/ or **phyllotaxy** ▷ *noun* (*phyllotaxes* or *phyllotaxies*) *bot* the arrangement of leaves on a plant stem. • **phyllotactic** or **phyllotactical** *adj*. ◷ 19c: from Greek *phyllon* a leaf + *taxis* arrangement.

phylloxera /fɪlɒk'sɪərə, fɪ'lɒksərə/ ▷ *noun* (*phylloxerae* /-riː/ or *phylloxeras*) an aphid similar to GREENFLY that is very destructive to vines. ◷ 19c: from Greek *phyllon* leaf + *xeros* dry.

phylogenesis /faɪloʊ'dʒɛnɪsɪs/ and **phylogeny** /faɪ'lɒdʒənɪ/ ▷ *noun, biol* the sequence of changes that has occurred during the evolution of a particular species of living organism or a group of related organisms. • **phylogenetic** *adj.* ⓒ 19c: from German *phylogenie*, from Greek *phylon* race + *-geneia* origin.

phylum /'faɪləm/ ▷ *noun* (***phyla*** /-lə/) *biol, zool* in taxonomy: any of the major groups, eg *Chordata* (the vertebrates), into which the animal KINGDOM (sense 2) is divided and which in turn is subdivided into one or more CLASSes (sense 9). It corresponds to the DIVISION (sense 7) in the plant kingdom. See also PHYLETIC. ⓒ 19c: from Greek *phylon* race.

phys. ▷ *abbreviation* **1** physician. **2** physics. **3** physiology.

physic /'fɪzɪk/ *old use* ▷ *noun* **1** the skill or art of healing. **2** a medicine. **3** anything with a curative or reinvigorating effect. ▷ *verb* (***physicked***, ***physicking***) to dose someone with medicine. ⓒ 13c as *fisike*: from French *fisique*, from Greek *physike episteme* knowledge of nature.

physical /'fɪzɪkəl/ ▷ *adj* **1** relating to the body rather than the mind; bodily □ *physical strength.* **2** relating to objects that can be seen or felt; material □ *the physical world.* **3** relating to nature or to the laws of nature □ *physical features* □ *a physical impossibility.* **4** involving bodily contact. **5** relating to PHYSICS. • **physically** *adverb.* ⓒ 16c: from Latin *physicalis*, from *physica* PHYSIC.

physical anthropology ▷ *noun* the study of local biological adaptions in man and in man's evolutionary history.

physical chemistry ▷ *noun* the branch of chemistry concerned with the relationship between the chemical structure of compounds and their physical properties.

physical education ▷ *noun* (abbreviation **PE**) instruction in sport and gymnastics as part of a school or college curriculum.

physical geography ▷ *noun* the branch of geography concerned with the study of the earth's natural features, eg mountain ranges, ocean currents, etc.

physicalism ▷ *noun, philos* the theory that all phenomena are explicable in spatio-temporal terms and that all statements are either analytic or reducible to empirically verifiable assertions. ⓒ 1930s.

physicality /fɪzɪ'kalɪtɪ/ ▷ *noun* **1** a physical quality. **2** preoccupation with bodily matters.

physical jerks ▷ *noun, colloq* exercises, especially ones done regularly to keep fit.

physically see under PHYSICAL

physical science ▷ *noun* any of the sciences concerned with the study of non-living matter, eg astronomy, physics or geology.

physical training ▷ *noun* (abbreviation **PT**) instruction in sport and gymnastics, especially in the army.

physician /fɪ'zɪʃən/ ▷ *noun* **1** in the UK: a registered medical practitioner who specializes in medical as opposed to surgical treatment of diseases and disorders. **2** in other parts of the world: anyone who is legally qualified to practise medicine. ⓒ 13c as *fisicien*: French, from *fisique* (see PHYSIC).

physicism /'fɪzɪsɪzəm/ ▷ *noun* belief in the material and physical as opposed to the spiritual.

physicist /'fɪzɪsɪst/ ▷ *noun* a scientist who specializes in physics.

physics /'fɪzɪks/ ▷ *singular noun* the scientific study of the properties and inter-relationships of matter, energy, force and motion. ⓒ 16c: plural of PHYSIC in the old sense 'physical things', from Latin *physica* (see PHYSIC).

physio /'fɪzɪoʊ/ ▷ *noun* (***physios***) *colloq* **1** a PHYSIOTHERAPIST. **2** PHYSIOTHERAPY.

physio- /fɪzɪoʊ, fɪzɪ'ɒ/ or **physi-** ▷ *combining form, denoting* physical or physiological. ⓒ From Greek *physis* nature or make-up.

physiognomy /fɪzɪ'ɒnəmɪ/ ▷ *noun* (***physiognomies***) **1** the face or features, especially when used or seen as a key to someone's personality. **2** the art of judging character from appearance, especially from the face. **3** the general appearance of something, eg the countryside. • **physiognomic** /fɪzɪə'nɒmɪk/ or **physiognomical** *adj.* • **physiognomist** /-'ɒnəmɪst/ *noun.* ⓒ 14c as *phisonomie*, etc: from Latin *phisonomia*, from Greek *physis* nature + *gnomon* judge or interpreter.

physiography /fɪzɪ'ɒgrəfɪ/ ▷ *noun* physical geography. • **physiographer** *noun.* • **physiographic** /-'grafɪk/ or **physiographical** *adj.* ⓒ 19c.

physiology /fɪzɪ'ɒlədʒɪ/ ▷ *noun, biol* the branch of biology that is concerned with the internal processes and functions of living organisms, as opposed to their structure. • **physiologic** /-zɪə'lɒdʒɪk/ or **physiological** *adj* **1** referring or relating to physiology. **2** referring or relating to the normal functioning of a living organism. • **physiologically** *adverb.* • **physiologist** *noun* a scientist who specializes in physiology. ⓒ 16c: from Latin *physiologia*, from Greek *physis* nature.

physiotherapy ▷ *noun, medicine* the treatment of injury and disease by external physical methods, such as remedial exercises, manipulation or massage, rather than by drugs or surgery. • **physiotherapist** *noun.* See also PHYSIO. ⓒ Early 20c.

physique /fɪ'ziːk/ ▷ *noun* the structure of the body with regard to size, shape, proportions and muscular development; the build. ⓒ 19c: French, originally meaning 'physical', from Greek *physikos* of nature.

-phyte /faɪt/ ▷ *combining form, forming nouns, denoting* a plant belonging to a specified habitat or of a specified type □ *endophyte.* ⓒ From Greek *phyton* plant.

-phytic /fɪtɪk/ ▷ *combining form* forming adjectives corresponding to nouns in -PHYTE.

phyto- /faɪtoʊ, faɪ'tɒ/ ▷ *combining form, denoting* plant. ⓒ From Greek *phyton* plant.

phytochemical ▷ *noun* a chemical derived from a plant. ▷ *adj* referring to PHYTOCHEMISTRY. ⓒ 19c.

phytochemistry ▷ *noun* the chemistry of plant growth and metabolism, and of plant products. ⓒ 19c.

phytogenesis and **phytogeny** /faɪ'tɒdʒɪnɪ/ ▷ *noun* the branch of botany concerned with the evolution of plants. ⓒ 19c.

phytopathology ▷ *noun, bot* the scientific study of plant diseases. • **phytopathologist** *noun.* ⓒ 19c.

phytoplankton ▷ *noun, bot* that part of plankton which is composed of microscopic plants. ⓒ Late 19c.

PI ▷ *abbreviation* **1** *IVR* Philippines. **2** Private Investigator.

pi¹ /paɪ/ ▷ *noun* (***pis***) **1** the sixteenth letter of the Greek alphabet. See table at GREEK ALPHABET. **2** *math* this symbol (π), representing the ratio of the circumference of a circle to its diameter, in numerical terms 3.14159... • **pi-meson** see separate entry.

pi² /paɪ/ *Brit slang* ▷ *adj* a short form of PIOUS. ▷ *noun* (***pis***) a pious, religious or sanctimonious person or talk. ⓒ 19c.

pi³ see PIE²

piacevole /pɪə'tʃeɪvɒleɪ/ *music* ▷ *adverb* in a pleasant or playful manner. ▷ *adj* pleasant or playful. ⓒ Italian.

piaffe /pɪ'af/ ▷ *verb* (***piaffed***, ***piaffing***) *intr, dressage* to move at a piaffer. ⓒ 18c.

piaffer /pɪ'afə(r)/ ▷ *noun, dressage* a gait in which the horse's feet are lifted in the same succession as a trot, but more slowly. ⓒ 19c: from French *piaffer* to strut or make a show.

pia mater /ˈpaɪə ˈmeɪtə(r), ˈpɪə-/ ▷ *noun* (***piae matres*** /-iː -triːz/) ▷ *noun, anatomy* the delicate innermost membrane that encloses the brain and spinal cord. ⓒ 16c: Latin, literally 'tender mother', a translation of Arabic *umm raqiqah* thin mother.

pianissimo /pɪəˈnɪsɪmoʊ/ *music* ▷ *adverb* performed very softly. ▷ *adj* very soft. ▷ *noun* (***pianissimos***) a piece of music to be performed in this way. ⓒ 18c: Italian, superlative of *piano* quiet.

pianist /ˈpɪənɪst, ˈpjanɪst/ ▷ *noun* someone who plays the piano.

piano¹ /pɪˈanoʊ, ˈpjɑːnoʊ/ ▷ *noun* (***pianos***) a large musical instrument with a keyboard, the keys being pressed down to operate a set of hammers that strike tautened wires to produce the sound. ⓒ 19c: short form of PIANOFORTE.

piano² /ˈpjɑːnoʊ, pɪˈanoʊ/ *music* ▷ *adverb* softly. ▷ *adj* soft. ▷ *noun* (***pianos***) a passage of music to be played or performed softly. ⓒ 17c: Italian.

piano accordion see under ACCORDION

pianoforte /pɪanoʊˈfɔːtɪ, pjɑːnoʊˈfɔːteɪ/ ▷ *noun* the full formal term for a PIANO¹. ⓒ 18c: from Italian *piano e forte* soft and loud.

Pianola /pɪəˈnoʊlə/ ▷ *noun* (***Pianolas***) *trademark* a mechanical piano that is operated automatically by means of interchangeable paper rolls bearing coded music in the form of perforations; a kind of PLAYER PIANO. • **pianolist** *noun*. ⓒ Early 20c.

piano nobile /ˈpjɑːnoʊ ˈnoʊbɪleɪ/ ▷ *noun* (***piani nobili*** /-niː -liː/) *archit* the main floor of a large house or villa, usually on the first floor. ⓒ Early 20c: Italian, meaning 'noble storey'.

piano stool and **music stool** ▷ *noun* a stool for a pianist, usually adjustable in height and often hollow for the storage of music.

piassava /pɪəˈsɑːvə/ or **piassaba** /pɪəˈsɑːbə/ ▷ *noun* (***piassavas*** or ***piassabas***) **1** a coarse stiff fibre used for making brooms, etc, obtained from Brazilian palms. **2** the tree that yields it. ⓒ 19c: Portuguese, from Tupí.

piazza /pɪˈatsə/ ▷ *noun* (***piazzas***) **1** a public square in an Italian town. **2** *mainly Brit* a covered walkway. **3** *US* a veranda. ⓒ 16c: Italian, from Latin *platea* and Greek *plateia* street.

pibroch /ˈpiːbrɒx/ ▷ *noun* a series of variations on a martial theme or lament, played on the Scottish bagpipes. ⓒ 18c: from Gaelic *piobaireachd* pipe music, from *piobair* a piper, from *piob*, from English PIPE¹.

pic ▷ *noun* (***pics*** or ***pix***) *colloq* a photograph or picture. ⓒ 19c: short for PICTURE.

pica¹ /ˈpaɪkə/ ▷ *noun* (***picas***) *printing* an old type-size, giving about six lines to the inch, approximately 12-point and still used synonymously for that point size. ⓒ 15c: Latin, referring to a book of ecclesiastical rules for determining dates of religious festivals, from Latin *pica* magpie, because of the black and white appearance of the page in such a book; related to PIE².

pica² /ˈpaɪkə/ ▷ *noun* (***picas***) *medicine* an unnatural craving for unsuitable food, such as chalk, sand, clay, etc. ⓒ 16c: Latin, meaning 'magpie', referring to its indiscriminate diet.

picador /ˈpɪkədɔː(r)/ ▷ *noun, bullfighting* a TOREADOR who weakens the bull by wounding it with a lance. ⓒ 18c: Spanish, from *pica* lance.

picaresque /pɪkəˈrɛsk/ ▷ *adj* said of a novel, etc: telling of the adventures of a usually likeable rogue in separate, only loosely connected, episodes. ⓒ 19c: from Spanish *picaro* rogue.

picaroon /pɪkəˈruːn/ ▷ *noun, old use* a rogue, cheat or pirate. ⓒ 17c: from Spanish *picarón*, from *pícaro* rogue.

picayune /pɪkəˈjuːn/ *US colloq* ▷ *noun* **1** anything of little or no value. **2** any small coin of little value, especially a five-cent piece. ▷ *adj* petty; trifling. ⓒ 19c: from Provençal *picaioun*, an old Piedmontese copper coin.

piccalilli /pɪkəˈlɪlɪ, ˈpɪkəlɪlɪ/ ▷ *noun* (***piccalillis***) a pickle consisting of mixed vegetables in a mustard sauce. ⓒ 18c.

piccaninny or **pickaninny** /pɪkəˈnɪnɪ/ ▷ *noun* (***piccaninnies***) *offensive* **1** *N Amer, especially US* a Negro child. **2** *especially Austral* an Aboriginal child. ⓒ 17c: perhaps from Portuguese *pequenino*, diminutive of *pequeno* little.

piccolo /ˈpɪkəloʊ/ ▷ *noun* (***piccolos***) a small transverse FLUTE pitched one octave higher than the standard flute and with a range of about three octaves. ⓒ 19c: from Italian *flauto piccolo* little flute.

piccy /ˈpɪkɪ/ ▷ *noun* (***piccies***) *colloq* a photograph or picture. See also PIC. ⓒ 19c.

pichurim /ˈpɪtʃʊrɪm/ ▷ *noun* **1** a S American tree of the laurel family. **2** (*also* **pichurim bean**) its aromatic kernel. ⓒ 19c: Portuguese, from Tupí *puchury*.

pick¹ ▷ *verb* (***picked, picking***) **1** *tr & intr* to choose or select. **2** to detach and gather (flowers from a plant, fruit from a tree, etc). **3** to open (a lock) with a device other than a key, often to gain unauthorized entry. **4** to get, take or extract whatever is of use or value from something □ *pick a bone clean* □ *pick someone's brains*. **5** to steal money or valuables from (someone's pocket). See also PICKPOCKET. **6** to undo; to unpick □ *pick a dress to pieces*. **7** to make (a hole) by unpicking. **8** to remove pieces of matter from (one's nose, teeth, a scab, etc) with one's fingernails, etc. **9** to provoke (a fight, quarrel, etc) with someone. ▷ *noun* **1** the best of a group □ *the pick of the bunch*. **2** one's own preferred selection. • **have** or **take one's pick** to keep selecting and rejecting until one is satisfied. • **pick and choose** to be over-fussy in one's choice. • **pick holes in something** to find fault with it. • **pick one's way** to go carefully so as to avoid hazards □ *picked her way through the jungle*. • **pick someone's brains** to ask someone for information, ideas, etc, and then use it as your own. • **pick someone** or **something to pieces** to criticize them or it severely. • **pick someone up on something** to point out their error. • **pick up the pieces** to have to restore things to normality or make things better after some trouble or disaster. • **pick up speed** to increase speed or acelerate gradually. ⓒ 15c.

■ **pick at something 1** to eat only small quantities of (one's food). **2** to keep pulling at (a scab, etc) with one's fingernails.

■ **pick people** or **things off 1** to shoot them □ *picked the snipers off one by one*. **2** to deal with (opposition) bit by bit.

■ **pick on someone 1** to blame them unfairly. **2** to bully them. **3** to choose them for an unpleasant job.

■ **pick on something** to choose it; to light on it. □ pick oneself up to restore oneself to an upright position after a fall.

■ **pick someone out 1** to select them from a group. **2** to recognize or distinguish them among a group or crowd.

■ **pick something out 1** to play (a tune) uncertainly, especially by ear. **2** to mark it so as to distinguish it from its surroundings □ *beige walls with the picture rail picked out in brown*.

■ **pick something over** to examine (a collection of things) one by one and reject whatever is unwanted.

■ **pick up** said of a person, a person's health, or a situation: to recover or improve □ *She picked up after seeing you*. □ *Sales have picked up now*.

■ **pick up** or **pick something up** to resume □ *pick up where one left off* □ *pick up the threads of a relationship* □ *pick up the trail.*

■ **pick someone up 1** to arrest or seize them □ *was picked up by the police.* **2** to go and fetch them from where they are waiting □ *I'll pick you up at the station at 6pm.* **3** to stop one's vehicle for them and give them a lift □ *picked up a hitchhiker.* **4** *colloq* to approach them and successfully invite them, eg to go home with one, especially with a view to sexual relations. See also PICK-UP.

■ **pick something up 1** to lift or raise it from a surface, from the ground, etc. **2** to learn or acquire (a habit, skill, language, etc) over a time. **3** to notice or become aware of it □ *picked up a faint odour.* **4** to obtain or acquire it casually, by chance, etc □ *pick up a bargain* □ *pick up an infection.* **5** to go and fetch (something waiting to be collected). **6** *telecomm* to receive (a signal, programme, etc). **7** to refer back in conversation or discourse to (a point previously made), in order to deal with it further. **8** *colloq* to agree to pay (a bill, etc) □ *pick up the tab.*

■ **pick something up**, **off**, **out**, *etc* to lift, remove, detach or extract it □ *picked a crumb off the carpet.*

pick² ▷ *noun* **1** a tool with a long metal head pointed at one or both ends, for breaking ground, rock, ice, etc. **2** a poking or cleaning tool □ *a toothpick.* **3** a plectrum. ⓒ 14c, probably related to PIKE².

pickaback see PIGGYBACK

pickaninny see PICCANINNY

pickaxe /ˈpɪkaks/ ▷ *noun* a large pick, especially one with a point at one end of its head and a cutting edge at the other. ⓒ 14c as *pikoys*: from French *picois*.

picked /pɪkt/ ▷ *adj* selected or chosen. See also HAND-PICKED.

picker ▷ *noun* **1** a person who picks or gathers. **2** a tool or machine for picking.

pickerel /ˈpɪkərəl/ ▷ *noun* a young pike. ⓒ 14c: diminutive of PIKE¹.

picket /ˈpɪkɪt/ ▷ *noun* **1** a person or group of people stationed outside a place of work to persuade other employees not to go in during a strike. **2** a body of soldiers on patrol or sentry duty. **3** a stake fixed in the ground, eg as part of a fence. ▷ *verb* (*picketed*, *picketing*) **1** to station pickets or act as a PICKET (*noun* 1) at (a factory, etc). **2** to guard or patrol with, or as, a military picket. **3** to fence (an area, etc) with pickets (*noun* 3). ⓒ 18c: from French *piquet*, diminutive of *pic* PICK².

picket fence ▷ *noun* a fence made of pickets (see PICKET *noun* 3).

picket line ▷ *noun* a line of people acting as pickets (see PICKET *noun* 1) in an industrial dispute.

pickier, **pickiest**, **pickily** and **pickiness** see under PICKY

pickings ▷ *plural noun*, *colloq* profits made easily or casually from something □ *rich pickings.*

pickle /ˈpɪkəl/ ▷ *noun* **1** (*also* **pickles**) a preserve of vegetables, eg onions, cucumber or cauliflower, in vinegar, salt water or a tart sauce. **2** a vegetable preserved in this way. **3** the liquid used for this preserve. **4** *colloq* a mess; a quandary; a predicament □ *got herself in a terrible pickle.* **5** *colloq* a troublesome child. ▷ *verb* (*pickled*, *pickling*) to preserve something in vinegar, salt water, etc. ⓒ 14c: from German *pekel*.

pickled ▷ *adj* **1** preserved in pickle. **2** *colloq* drunk.

pickler ▷ *noun* **1** a container in which vegetables, etc are pickled. **2** a vegetable, etc suitable, or grown, for pickling. **3** someone who pickles.

picklock ▷ *noun* **1** an instrument for picking or opening locks. **2** someone who picks locks. ⓒ 16c.

pick-me-up ▷ *noun* **1** a stimulating drink, such as tea, a whisky, etc. **2** anything that revives and invigorates. ⓒ 19c.

pick-'n'-mix ▷ *noun* **1** an assortment, such as loose sweets, small pieces of individually wrapped cheese, etc, chosen by a customer from a range available at a self-service counter. **2** a discriminatory selection chosen to suit one's individual taste or needs. Also *as adj.*

pickpocket ▷ *noun* a thief who steals from people's pockets, usually in crowded areas. ⓒ 16c.

pick-up ▷ *noun* (*pick-ups*) **1** the STYLUS on a record-player. **2** a TRANSDUCER on electric musical instruments. **3** a small lorry, truck or van. **4** *colloq* **a** an acquaintance made casually, especially with a view to sexual relations; **b** the making of such an acquaintance. **5 a** a halt or place to load goods or passengers; **b** the goods or passengers loaded. See also PICK UP at PICK¹.

picky ▷ *adj* (*pickier*, *pickiest*) *colloq* choosy or fussy, especially excessively so; difficult to please. • **pickily** *adverb*. • **pickiness** *noun*. ⓒ 19c: from PICK¹.

pick-your-own ▷ *adj* **1** referring to a method of selling fruit or vegetables by which customers harvest the produce they wish to buy themselves. **2** said of produce: sold in this way. ⓒ 1960s.

picnic /ˈpɪknɪk/ ▷ *noun* **1** an outing on which one takes food for eating in the open air. **2** food taken or eaten in this way. ▷ *verb* (*picnicked*, *picnicking*) *intr* to have a picnic. • **no picnic** or **not a picnic** *colloq* a disagreeable or difficult job or situation □ *Minding young children is no picnic.* • **picnicker** *noun*. ⓒ 18c: from French *pique-nique*.

pico- /ˈpiːkoʊ, ˈpaɪkoʊ/ ▷ *prefix, forming nouns, denoting* a millionth of a millionth part, or 10^{-12}, of the specified unit □ *picocurie* □ *picosecond.* ⓒ Spanish, meaning 'a small quantity'.

picornavirus /pɪˈkɔːnəvaɪərəs/ ▷ *noun*, *biol* any of four viral genera including the ENTEROVIRUSes and RHINOVIRUSes. ⓒ 1960s: PICO- + RNA + VIRUS.

picot /ˈpiːkoʊ/ ▷ *noun* **1** a loop in an ornamental edging. **2** *embroidery* a raised knot. ⓒ 19c: French, meaning 'point' or 'prick'.

picotee /pɪkəˈtiː/ ▷ *noun* (*picotees*) a variety of carnation, originally speckled, now edged with a colour. ⓒ 18c: from French *picoté* marked with points.

picric acid /ˈpɪkrɪk —/ ▷ *noun*, *chem* (formula $C_6H_2(NO_2)_3OH$) a yellow compound used as a dyestuff and as the basis of high explosives. ⓒ 19c: from Greek *pikros* bitter.

Pict ▷ *noun* a member of an ancient N British people. ⓒ Anglo-Saxon *Peohtas*: from Latin *picti* painted men, coined by the Romans in the 3c.

Pictish /ˈpɪktɪʃ/ ▷ *adj* belonging or relating to the Picts. ▷ *noun* the language of the Picts. ⓒ 18c.

pictograph /ˈpɪktəgrɑːf/ and **pictogram** ▷ *noun* **1** a picture or symbol that represents a word, as in Chinese writing. **2** a pictorial or diagrammatic representation of values, statistics, etc. Compare IDEOGRAM, LOGOGRAPH. • **pictographic** /pɪktəˈgrafɪk/ *adj*. • **pictography** /-ˈtɒgrəfɪ/ *noun*. ⓒ 19c: from Latin *pictus* painted.

pictorial /pɪkˈtɔːrɪəl/ ▷ *adj* relating to, or consisting of, pictures. ▷ *noun* a periodical with a high proportion of pictures as opposed to text. • **pictorially** *adverb*. ⓒ 17c, meaning 'belonging or relating to a painter, or painting or drawing': from Latin *pictor* painter.

picture /ˈpɪktʃə(r)/ ▷ *noun* **1** a representation of someone or something on a flat surface; a drawing, painting or photograph. **2** someone's portrait. **3** a view; a mental image □ *a clear picture of the battle.* **4** a situation or outlook □ *a gloomy financial picture.* **5** a person or thing strikingly like another □ *She is the picture of her mother.* **6** a visible embodiment □ *was the picture of* *happiness.* **7** an image of beauty □ *looks a picture.* **8** the image received on a television screen □ *We get a good picture.* **9** a film; a motion picture. **10** (**the pictures**) *colloq* the cinema □ *went to the pictures last night.* ⊳ *verb* (*pictured, picturing*) **1** to imagine or visualize □ *Just picture that settee in our lounge.* **2** to describe something or someone vividly; to depict. **3** to represent or show someone or something in a picture or photograph. • **get the picture** *colloq* to understand something. • **in the picture** informed of all the relevant facts, etc. • **put me, her, him,** *etc* **in the picture** give me, them, etc all the relevant facts, information, etc. ◷ 15c: from Latin *pictura* painting.

picture card see under COURT CARD

picture gallery ⊳ *noun* **1** a gallery, hall or building where a selection of pictures are hung for exhibition and often for sale. **2** a hall or room of pictures hung for exhibition in a large private house, eg a manor house. **3** the collection itself.

picture postcard ⊳ *noun* a postcard with a picture on the front, usually a view of a village, town, landscape, holiday resort, etc. ⊳ *adj* (**picture-postcard**) very pretty or quaint, reflecting how many picture postcards look. ◷ 19c.

picture rail ⊳ *noun* a narrow moulding running round the walls of a room just below the ceiling, from which to hang pictures.

picture restorer ⊳ *noun* someone whose job is to preserve old pictures by cleaning and restoring them.

picturesque /pɪktʃə'rɛsk/ ⊳ *adj* **1** said of places or buildings: charming to look at, especially if rather quaint. **2** said of language: **a** colourful, expressive or graphic; **b** *facetious* vivid or strong to the point of being offensive. • **picturesquely** *adverb.* • **picturesqueness** *noun.* ◷ 18c: from French *pittoresque*, influenced by PICTURE.

picture window ⊳ *noun* an unusually large window with a plate-glass pane, usually affording an extensive view.

PID ⊳ *abbreviation* pelvic inflammatory disease.

piddle /'pɪdəl/ ⊳ *verb* (*piddled, piddling*) *intr, colloq* to urinate. ⊳ *noun* **1** ⊳ urine. **2** the act of urinating. • **piddler** *noun.* ◷ 18c in *verb* sense; 16c as phrasal *verb piddle about*, etc.

▪ **piddle about** or **around** to mess about or waste time.

piddling ⊳ *adj* trivial; trifling □ *piddling excuses.* ◷ 16c.

pidgin /'pɪdʒɪn/ ⊳ *noun* **1** a type of simplified language used especially for trading purposes between speakers of different languages, consisting of a combination and often simplification of the vocabulary, grammar and pronunciation systems of the languages concerned, commonly used in the East and West Indies, Africa and the Americas. See also CREOLE. **2** (*also* **pigeon**) *colloq* one's own affair, business or concern. ◷ 19c: said to be a Chinese pronunciation of *business*.

pidgin English ⊳ *noun* a PIDGIN (sense 1) in which one element is English, especially that formerly spoken between the Chinese and Europeans.

pi-dog see PYE-DOG

pie[1] /paɪ/ ⊳ *noun* a savoury or sweet dish, usually cooked in a container, consisting of a quantity of food with a covering of pastry, a base of pastry, or both. • **easy as pie** very easy. • **pie in the sky** some hoped-for but unguaranteed future prospect. ◷ 14c.

pie[2] or **pi** /paɪ/ ⊳ *noun* **1** *printing* confusedly mixed type. **2** a mixed state; confusion. ◷ 17c.

pie[3] /paɪ/ ⊳ *noun* an old name for MAGPIE (sense 1). ◷ 13c: French, from Latin *pica* magpie.

piebald /'paɪbɔːld/ ⊳ *adj* having contrasting patches of colour, especially black and white. Compare PIED. ⊳ *noun* a horse with black and white markings. ◷ 16c: PIE[3] + *bald* in the obsolete sense 'with white markings'.

piece /piːs/ ⊳ *noun* **1** a portion of some material; a bit. **2** any of the sections into which something (eg a cake) is divided; a portion taken from a whole. **3** a component part □ *a jigsaw piece.* **4 a** an item in a set; **b** *usually as adj* □ *an 18-piece teaset* □ *a 3-piece suite.* **5** an individual member of a class of things represented by a collective noun □ *a piece of fruit* □ *a piece of clothing.* **6** a specimen or example of something □ *a fine piece of Chippendale.* **7** an instance □ *a piece of nonsense.* **8** a musical, artistic, literary or dramatic work. **9** an article in a newspaper, etc. **10** a coin □ *a 50 pence piece* □ *pieces of eight.* **11** *chess* one of the tokens or men used in a board game. **12** a cannon or firearm. **13** *offensive, colloq* a woman. **14** *Scots* **a** a snack or meal, such as a sandwich, biscuit etc; **b** a piece of bread with butter, jam, etc. ⊳ *verb* (*pieced, piecing*). • **all in one piece** undamaged, unhurt, intact □ *returned from her travels, all in one piece.* • **all of a piece** forming an indivisible whole. • **go to pieces** *colloq* to lose emotional control; to panic. • **in pieces 1** separated into a number of component parts. **2** broken; shattered. • **of a piece with something** consistent or uniform with it. • **a piece of one's mind** a frank and outspoken reprimand. • **say one's piece** to make one's contribution to a discussion. • **to pieces 1** into its component parts □ *take to pieces.* **2** into fragments, shreds, tatters, etc □ *falling to pieces.* ◷ 13c as *pece*: from French *piece*.

▪ **piece something** or **things together** to join it or them together to form a whole.

▪ **piece something up** to patch or insert pieces into (a garment).

pièce de résistance /pɪ'ɛs də reɪ'zɪstɑ̃s/ (*pièces de résistance* /pɪ'ɛs də reɪ'zɪstɑ̃s/) ⊳ *noun* **1** the best or most impressive item. **2** the main dish of a meal. ◷ 19c: French.

piecemeal ⊳ *adverb* a bit at a time. ◷ 13c as *pecemele*: from PIECE + MEAL[1] in obsolete sense 'a measure'.

piece of cake ⊳ *noun* something that is easy, simple, etc. ◷ 1930s.

piece of eight ⊳ *noun* (*pieces of eight*) an old Spanish gold coin worth eight REAL[2]. ◷ 17c.

piece of piss ⊳ *noun, coarse slang* something that is easy, simple, etc.

piece of work ⊳ *noun* (*pieces of work*) **1** something that has been done or made □ *His essay was a magnificent piece of work.* **2** *colloq* a person □ *a nasty piece of work.*

piece rate ⊳ *noun* a fixed rate of pay for a particular amount of work done.

piecework ⊳ *noun* work paid for according to the amount done, not the time taken to do it.

pie chart, **pie diagram** and **pie graph** ⊳ *noun* a diagram used to display statistical data, consisting of a circle divided into sectors, each of which contains one category of information. The area of each sector indicates the category's relative importance in relation to the other categories. Compare BAR CHART.

piecrust ⊳ *noun* the dough or pastry covering or enclosing a pie.

piecrust table ⊳ *noun* an antique or reproduction table with a carved raised edge.

pied /paɪd/ ⊳ *adj* said of a bird: having variegated plumage, especially of black and white. ◷ 14c: from PIE[3].

pied-à-terre /pjeɪda'tɛə(r)/ ⊳ *noun* (*pieds-à-terre* /pjeɪda-/) a house or apartment, eg in a city, that one keeps as somewhere to stay on occasional visits there. ◷ 1920s: French, literally 'foot on the ground'.

pie-dog see PYE-DOG

pie-eyed ⊳ *adj, colloq* drunk. ◷ Early 20c.

pie graph see PIE CHART

pier /pɪə(r)/ ▷ *noun* **1 a** a structure built of stone, wood or iron, projecting into water for use as a landing-stage or breakwater; **b** such a structure used as a promenade with funfair-like sideshows, amusement arcades, etc. **2** a pillar supporting a bridge or arch. **3** the masonry between two openings in the wall of a building. ⓒ 12c as *per*: from Latin *pera*.

pierce /pɪəs/ ▷ *verb* (***pierced, piercing***) (*also* **pierce through something**) **1** said of a sharp object or a person using one: to make a hole in or through; to puncture; to make (a hole) with something sharp. **2** to penetrate or force a way through or into something □ *The wind pierced through her thin clothing.* **3** said of light or sound: to burst through (darkness or silence). **4** to affect or touch (someone's heart, soul, etc) keenly or painfully. ⓒ 13c: from French *percer*.

piercing ▷ *adj* **1** referring to something that pierces. **2** penetrating, acute, keen or sharp □ *a piercing cry*. ▷ *noun* BODY PIERCING. • **piercingly** *adverb*.

Pierrot or **pierrot** /ˈpɪəroʊ/ ▷ *noun* a clown dressed and made up like Pierrot, the traditional male character from French pantomime, with a whitened face, white frilled outfit and pointed hat. ⓒ 18c: a French name, diminutive of *Pierre* Peter, referring to the character originating from Pedrolino, a servant role in the commedia dell'arte and later developed by the 19c French pantomimist Deburau.

pietà /pɪeˈtɑː/ ▷ *noun* (***pietàs***) in painting and sculpture: a representation of the dead Christ mourned by angels, apostles or holy women. ⓒ 17c: Italian, from Latin *pieta* pity.

pietism /ˈpaɪətɪzəm/ ▷ *noun* pious feeling or an exaggerated show of piety. • **pietist** *noun*. • **pietistic** *adj*.

piety /ˈpaɪətɪ/ ▷ *noun* **1** dutifulness; devoutness. **2** the quality of being pious, dutiful or religiously devout. **3** sense of duty towards parents, benefactors, etc. ⓒ 17c in this sense: 14c in the obsolete sense 'pity', from Latin *pietas* dutifulness or piety.

piezoelectric crystal ▷ *noun* a non-conducting crystal exhibiting the piezoelectric effect.

piezoelectric effect /paiːzoʊɪˈlɛtrɪk —, piːzoʊ-—/ *physics*, *noun* **1** the generation of an electrical potential across non-conducting crystals, eg quartz, when they are stretched or compressed. **2** the reverse effect, in which an electrical potential can produce slight physical distortion in such crystals, used in quartz watches and clocks to keep almost perfect time.

piezoelectricity /paiːzoʊɪlɛkˈtrɪsɪtɪ, piːzoʊ —/ ▷ *noun* electricity produced by the piezoelectric effect in quartz crystals and other non-conducting crystals. • **piezoelectric** *adj*. ⓒ 19c: from Greek *piezein* to press + ELECTRICITY.

piffle /ˈpɪfəl/ ▷ *noun, colloq* nonsense; rubbish. ⓒ 19c, originally as a verb: from dialect.

piffling /ˈpɪflɪŋ/ ▷ *adj, colloq* trivial, trifling or petty.

pig ▷ *noun* **1** a hoofed omnivorous mammal with a stout heavy bristle-covered body, a protruding flattened snout and a corkscrew-like tail, kept worldwide for its meat. **2** an abusive term for a person, especially someone greedy, dirty, selfish or brutal, as these are traits erroneously attributed to pigs. **3** *slang* an unpleasant job or situation. **4** *offensive slang* a policeman. **5 a** a quantity of metal cast into an oblong mass; **b** the mould into which it is run. ▷ *verb* (***pigged, pigging***) **1** said of a pig: to produce young. **2** *tr & intr* said of a person: to eat greedily. See also *pig out* below. • **make a pig of oneself** *colloq* to eat greedily. • **make a pig's ear of something** *colloq* to make a mess of it; to botch it. • **a pig in a poke** *colloq* a purchase made without first inspecting it to see whether it is suitable. • **pig it** *colloq* **1** to eat greedily. **2** to live squalidly. • **pigs might fly** *colloq* an expression of scepticism: it's very unlikely. See also PORCINE. ⓒ 13c as *pigge*.

■ **pig out** to eat a large amount with relish and overindulgence; to overeat.

pigeon¹ /ˈpɪdʒən, -dʒɪn/ ▷ *noun* **1** a medium-sized bird with a plump body, a rounded tail and dense soft grey, brown or pink plumage. Compare DOVE. **2** *slang* a dupe or simpleton. See also STOOL-PIGEON. ⓒ 15c: from French *pijon*, from Latin *pipio*, from *pipare* to cheep.

pigeon² see PIDGIN (sense 2)

pigeon-breasted and **pigeon-chested** ▷ *adj* said of humans: having a narrow chest with the breastbone projecting, as a pigeon has.

pigeon-hearted ▷ *adj* timid; cowardly.

pigeonhole ▷ *noun* **1** any of a set of compartments, eg in a desk or on a wall, for filing letters or papers in. **2** a compartment of the mind or memory. ▷ *verb* (***pigeonholed, pigeonholing***) **1** to put something into a pigeonhole. **2** to put someone or something mentally into a category, especially too readily or rigidly. **3** to set something aside for future consideration. ⓒ 19c as *verb*; 17c in the original literal sense, ie an entrance hole in a dovecot.

pigeon loft see LOFT

pigeon-post ▷ *noun* conveyance of letters by pigeon.

pigeonry /ˈpɪdʒənrɪ/ ▷ *noun* (***pigeonries***) a place for keeping pigeons.

pigeon-toed ▷ *adj* said of a person: standing and walking with their toes turned in.

piggery /ˈpɪgərɪ/ ▷ *noun* (***piggeries***) **1** a place where pigs are bred. **2** *colloq* greediness or otherwise disgusting behaviour. ⓒ 18c.

piggish /ˈpɪgɪʃ/ ▷ *adj, derog* greedy, dirty, selfish, mean or ill-mannered. • **piggishly** *adverb*. • **piggishness** *noun*.

piggy or **piggie** /ˈpɪgɪ/ ▷ *noun* (***piggies***) a child's diminutive: **a** a pig; a little pig; **b** a toe, or, less commonly, a finger From the rhyme 'This little piggy went to market …' during the recital of which each of the toes or fingers is touched in turn.. ▷ *adj* (***piggier, piggiest***) **1** pig-like. **2** said of the eyes: small and mean-looking. ⓒ 18c.

piggyback or **pickaback** /ˈpɪkəbak/ ▷ *noun* a ride on someone's back, with the legs supported by the bearer's arms. ▷ *adj* **1** carried on the back of someone else. **2** said of a vehicle: conveyed on top of one another. **3** referring or relating to a type of heart transplant surgery in which the patient's own heart is not removed and continues to function in tandem with that of the donor. ▷ *adverb* on the back of someone else. ⓒ 16c.

piggy bank ▷ *noun* **1** a child's pig-shaped china container for saving money in. **2** a child's moneybox of any design. See also MONEYBOX. ⓒ 1940s.

pigheaded ▷ *adj* stupidly obstinate. • **pigheadedly** *adverb*. • **pigheadedness** *noun*. ⓒ 17c.

pig-in-the-middle or **piggy-in-the-middle** ▷ *noun* **1** a game in which one person stands between two others and tries to intercept the ball they are throwing to each other. **2** (***pigs-*** or ***piggies-in-the-middle***) any person helplessly caught between two contending parties.

pig iron ▷ *noun, metallurgy* an impure form of iron produced by smelting iron in a BLAST FURNACE, and usually processed subsequently to make steel. ⓒ 17c: from PIG *noun* 5.

piglet /ˈpɪglət/ ▷ *noun* a young pig.

pigment /ˈpɪgmənt/ ▷ *noun* **1** any insoluble colouring matter that is used in suspension in water, oil or other liquids to give colour to paint, paper, etc. Compare DYE. **2** a coloured substance that occurs naturally in living tissues, eg the red blood pigment HAEMOGLOBIN, or CHLOROPHYLL in the leaves of green plants. ▷ *verb* (***pigmented, pigmenting***) to colour something with pigment; to dye or stain. • **pigmentary** or **pigmented**

adj. ⓒ 14c: from Latin *pigmentum*, from *pigere* or *pingere* to paint.

pigmentation /pɪgmən'teɪʃən/ ▷ *noun* coloration or discoloration caused by deposits of pigments in plant or animal tissues which may occur normally or be a symptom of disease.

pigmy see PYGMY

pignut ▷ *noun* the EARTHNUT.

pigskin ▷ *noun* **1** leather made from the skin of a pig. **2** *N Amer colloq* a football.

pigsty /'pɪgstaɪ/ ▷ *noun* (***pigsties***) **1** a pen on a farm, etc for pigs; a STY. **2** *colloq* a filthy and disordered place.

pigswill /'pɪgswɪl/ ▷ *noun* kitchen or brewery waste for feeding to pigs.

pigtail ▷ *noun* a plaited length of hair, especially one of a pair, worn hanging at the sides or back of the head. Compare PONYTAIL. See also QUEUE *noun* 3. ⓒ 18c in this sense, but specifically as worn by sailors and soldiers; originally applied (in the 17c) to a thin twist of tobacco.

pika /'paɪkə/ ▷ *noun* (***pikas***) a mammal, native to Asia and N America, that resembles a small rabbit and has short legs, short rounded ears and a minute tail. Also called CONY. ⓒ 19c: from Tungus (an E Siberian language).

pike¹ ▷ *noun* (***pike*** or ***pikes***) any of various large predatory freshwater fish with a mottled yellowish-green body, a narrow pointed head and a small number of large teeth in the lower jaw. ⓒ 14c: from PIKE², referring to the shape of its head.

pike² /paɪk/ ▷ *noun* **1** *historical* a weapon like a spear, consisting of a metal point mounted on a long shaft. **2** a point or spike. **3** *N Eng dialect* a sharp-pointed hill or summit. ⓒ Anglo-Saxon *pic* point.

pike³ ▷ *noun* **1** a TURNPIKE. **2** *US* a main road. ⓒ 19c.

pike⁴ ▷ *adj, diving, gymnastics* (*also* **piked**) said of a body position: bent sharply at the hips with the legs kept straight at the knees and toes pointed. ▷ *verb* (***piked, piking***) *intr* to move into this position. ⓒ 1920s.

pikestaff ▷ *noun* the shaft of a PIKE². • **plain as a pikestaff** see under PLAIN.

pilaster /pɪ'lastə(r)/ ▷ *noun, archit* a rectangular column that stands out in relief from the façade of a building, as a decorative feature. • **pilastered** *adj*. ⓒ 16c: from French *pilastre*, from Latin *pila* pillar.

pilau /pɪ'laʊ/, **pilaf** or **pilaff** /pɪ'laf/ ▷ *noun* (***pilaus***) an oriental dish of spiced rice with, or to accompany, chicken, fish, etc. Also *as adj* □ ***pilau rice***. ⓒ 17c: from Persian *pilaw*, from Turkish.

pilchard /'pɪltʃəd/ ▷ *noun* a small edible marine fish of the herring family, bluish-green above and silvery below, covered with large scales. ⓒ 16c.

pile¹ ▷ *noun* **1** a number of things lying on top of each other; a quantity of something in a heap or mound. **2** (**a pile** or **piles**) *colloq* a large quantity. **3** *informal* a fortune □ ***made a pile on the horses***. **4** a massive or imposing building. **5** a PYRE. Also called **funeral pile**. **6** a NUCLEAR REACTOR, originally the graphite blocks forming the moderator for the reactor. Also called **atomic pile**. **7** *elec* a vertical series of plates of two different metals arranged alternately to produce an electric current. ▷ *verb* (***piled, piling***) *tr & intr* (*usually* **pile up** or **pile something up**) to accumulate into a pile. See also PILE-UP. • **pile it on** *colloq* to exaggerate. ⓒ 15c: from Latin *pila* a stone pier.

■ **pile in** or **into something** or **pile off, out**, *etc* to move in a crowd or confused bunch into or off it, etc □ ***piled into the bus***.

pile² ▷ *noun* a heavy wooden shaft, stone or concrete pillar, etc driven into the ground as a support for a building, bridge, etc. ⓒ Anglo-Saxon *pil*, from Latin *pilum* javelin.

pile³ /paɪl/ ▷ *noun* **1** the raised cropped threads that give a soft thick surface to carpeting, velvet, etc. Compare NAP². **2** soft fine hair, fur, wool, etc. ⓒ 15c: from Latin *pilus* hair.

pileate /'paɪlɪət/ or **pileated** /-eɪtəd/ ▷ *adj, biol* cap-shaped; capped; crested. ⓒ 18c: from Latin *pileatus* capped, from *pileus* (see PILEUS).

pile-cap¹ ▷ *noun* the top of a nuclear reactor. Compare PILE¹ *noun* 6.

pile-cap² ▷ *noun, civil engineering* a reinforced concrete block cast around a set of piles (see PILE²) to create a unified support.

pile-driver ▷ *noun* a machine for driving piles (see PILE²) into the ground.

piles /'paɪlz/ ▷ *plural noun* haemorrhoids. ⓒ 14c: from Latin *pila* ball.

pileum /'paɪlɪəm/ ▷ *noun* (***pilea*** /-lɪə/) *ornithol* the top of a bird's head. ⓒ 19c: Latin, from *pileus* cap.

pile-up ▷ *noun* (***pile-ups***) a vehicle collision in which following vehicles also crash, causing a number of collisions. ⓒ 1920s.

pileus /'paɪlɪəs/ ▷ *noun* (***pilei*** /-lɪaɪ/) *bot* the cap-shaped part of a mushroom, toadstool or other fungus. ⓒ 18c: Latin, from *pilleus* a felt cap.

pilfer /'pɪlfə(r)/ ▷ *verb* (***pilfered, pilfering***) *tr & intr* to steal in small quantities. • **pilferage** or **pilfering** *noun* petty theft. • **pilferer** *noun*. ⓒ 14c: from French *pelfre* booty.

pilgrim /'pɪlgrɪm/ ▷ *noun* **1** someone who makes a journey to a holy place as an act of reverence and religious faith. **2** a traveller. **3** *as adj* **a** belonging or relating to a pilgrim □ ***pilgrim staff***; **b** like a pilgrim □ ***pilgrim spirit***. ⓒ 12c as *pelegrim, pilegrim*: from Latin *peregrinus* foreigner or stranger.

pilgrimage /'pɪlgrɪmɪdʒ/ ▷ *noun* a journey to a shrine or other holy place, or to a place celebrated or made special by its associations, undertaken in order to gain a greater sense of closeness to the religion, etc or as a means of affirming one's faith. ▷ *verb* (***pilgrimaged, pilgrimaging***) to go on a pilgrimage. ⓒ 13c.

piliferous /paɪ'lɪfərəs/ ▷ *adj* said especially of plants: **1** bearing hairs. **2** ending in a hairlike point. • **piliform** *adj* hairlike. ⓒ 19c: from Latin *pilus* hair + -FEROUS.

Pilipino /pɪlɪ'piːnoʊ/ ▷ *noun* the national language of the Philippines, a standardized version of TAGÁLOG. ▷ *adj* relating to, or spoken or written in, Pilipino. ⓒ 1930s: from Spanish *Filipino* Philippine.

pill ▷ *noun* **1** a small ball or tablet of medicine, for swallowing. Compare CAPSULE, TABLET (sense 1). **2** something unpleasant that one must accept. **3** (**the pill**) any of various oral contraceptives, taken by some women (as opposed to men). See also MINIPILL, MORNING-AFTER PILL. • **be on the pill** to take oral contraceptives regularly. • **sugar** or **sweeten the pill** to make something that is unpleasant easier to accept or cope with. ⓒ 15c: from Latin *pila* ball.

pillage /'pɪlɪdʒ/ ▷ *verb* (***pillaged, pillaging***) *tr & intr* to plunder or loot. ▷ *noun* **1** the act of pillaging. **2** loot, plunder or booty. • **pillager** *noun*. ⓒ 14c: from French *piller*.

pillar /'pɪlə(r)/ ▷ *noun* **1** a vertical post of wood, stone, metal or concrete serving as a support to a main structure; a column. **2** any slender vertical mass of something, eg of smoke, rock, etc. **3** a strong and reliable supporter of a particular cause or organization □ ***He is a pillar of the village community***. • **from pillar to post** from one place to another, especially moving between these in desperation, frustration, etc □ ***rushing from pillar to post in search of a cash machine*** 15c as *from post to pillar*, derived from real tennis and referring to the way the ball is sent wildly about the court.. ◷ 13c: from French *piler*, from Latin *pila* pillar.

pillar box see under LETTER BOX

pillar-box red ⊳ *noun* a bright red colour, the colour of most British pillar boxes. Also **(pillar-box-red)** *as adj*.

pillbox ⊳ *noun* **1** a small round container for pills. **2** *military* a small, usually circular, concrete shelter for use as a lookout post and gun emplacement. **3** a small round flat-topped hat.

pillion /ˈpɪljən/ ⊳ *noun* a seat for a passenger on a motorcycle or horse, behind the driver or rider. Also *as adj* □ *pillion rider* □ *pillion seat*. ⊳ *adverb* on a pillion □ *to ride pillion*. ◷ 16c: from Scottish Gaelic *pillinn* or Irish Gaelic *pillín*, diminutive of *peall* skin or blanket.

pillock /ˈpɪlək/ ⊳ *noun, Brit slang* a stupid or foolish person. ◷ 1960s; 16c in N Eng dialect, meaning 'penis': from Norwegian dialect *pillicock* penis.

pillory /ˈpɪlərɪ/ ⊳ *noun* (*pillories*) *historical* a wooden frame with holes for the hands and head, into which wrongdoers were locked as a punishment and publicly ridiculed. ⊳ *verb* (*pillories, pilloried, pillorying*) **1** to hold someone up to public ridicule. **2** to put someone in a pillory. Also called **pillorize**. ◷ 13c: from French *pilori*.

pillow /ˈpɪloʊ/ ⊳ *noun* **1** a cushion for the head, especially a large rectangular one on a bed. **2** anything that resembles a pillow in shape, feel or function. ⊳ *verb* (*pillowed, pillowing*) **1** to rest (one's head) as though on a pillow □ *pillowed her head on her arms*. **2** to serve as a pillow for someone. ◷ Anglo-Saxon *pylwe*: from Latin *pulvinus* cushion.

pillowcase and **pillowslip** ⊳ *noun* a removable washable cover for a pillow.

pillow lace ⊳ *noun* lace worked over a cushion-like support, using bobbins.

pillow talk ⊳ *noun* confidential conversation with a sexual partner in bed.

pillpopper and **pillhead** ⊳ *noun, slang* a regular taker of sedative or stimulant pills or both, particularly an addict of these. ◷ 1960s.

pilose /ˈpaɪloʊs/ ⊳ *adj, biol* said especially of plants: having hairs. • **pilosity** /paɪˈlɒsɪtɪ/ *noun*. ◷ 18c: from Latin *pilosus*, from *pilus* hair.

pilot /ˈpaɪlət/ ⊳ *noun* **1** someone who flies an aircraft, hovercraft, spacecraft, etc. **2** someone employed to conduct or steer ships into and out of harbour. **3** someone who is qualified to act as pilot. **4** a guide. **5** *mech* a device that guides a tool or machine part. **6** *as adj* said of a scheme, programme, test, etc: serving as a preliminary test which may be modified before the final version is put into effect; experimental □ *a pilot project*. ⊳ *verb* (*piloted, piloting*) **1** to act as pilot to someone. **2** to direct, guide or steer (a project, etc). ◷ 16c: from French *pillote*, from Italian *pilota*, earlier *pedota*, from Greek *pedon* oar.

pilotage /ˈpaɪlətɪdʒ/ ⊳ *noun* **1** the act of piloting an aircraft, ship, etc. **2** a pilot's fee.

pilot fish ⊳ *noun* a fish that accompanies ships and is said to lead sharks to food.

pilot flag and **pilot jack** ⊳ *noun* the flag hoisted at the fore by a vessel needing a pilot.

pilot house ⊳ *noun* the WHEEL HOUSE.

pilot jacket ⊳ *noun* a PEA JACKET.

pilotless ⊳ *adj* **1** without a pilot. **2** said of an automatic aeroplane: not requiring a pilot.

pilot light ⊳ *noun* **1** a small permanent gas flame, eg on a gas cooker, that ignites the main burners when they are turned on. **2** an indicator light on an electrical apparatus showing when it is switched on.

pilot officer ⊳ *noun* an officer in the airforce. See table at RANK.

Pils /pɪls, pɪlz/ ⊳ *noun* any lager beer similar to PILSENER. ◷ 1960s: abbreviation.

Pilsener or **Pilsner** /ˈpɪlznə(r), ˈpɪlsnə(r)/ ⊳ *noun* a light, strongly-flavoured lager beer. ◷ 19c: from Pilsen, the German name of the Czech town of Plzeň; where it was originally brewed.

pilule /ˈpɪljuːl/ ⊳ *noun* a little pill. • **pilular** *adj*. ◷ 16c: French, from Latin *pilula* little ball, from *pila* ball.

pimento /pɪˈmɛntoʊ/ ⊳ *noun* (*pimentos*) **1** a small tropical evergreen tree, cultivated mainly in Jamaica. **2** any of the dried unripe berries of this tree which are a source of allspice. Also called **allspice**. **3** the PIMIENTO. ◷ 17c: altered from Spanish *pimiento*; see PIMIENTO.

pi-meson /paɪˈmiːzɒn/ ⊳ *noun, physics* the source of the nuclear force holding protons and neutrons together. Also called **pion**. See also MESON.

pimiento /pɪmɪˈɛntoʊ/ ⊳ *noun* (*pimientos*) **1** a variety of sweet pepper, native to tropical America, widely cultivated for its mild-flavoured red fruit. **2** the fruit of this plant, eaten raw in salads, cooked and eaten as a vegetable, or used as a relish, a stuffing for olives, etc. ◷ 19c: Spanish, meaning 'pepper', from Latin *pigmenta* spiced drink, spice or pepper.

pimp ⊳ *noun* a man who finds customers for a prostitute or a brothel and lives off the earnings. ⊳ *verb* (*pimped, pimping*) *intr* to act as a pimp. ◷ 17c: possibly related to French *pimpant* well-dressed or smart, from French *pimper* to dress smartly.

pimpernel /ˈpɪmpənɛl, -nəl/ ⊳ *noun* any of various small sprawling plants, especially the SCARLET PIMPERNEL. ◷ 15c: from French *pimprenelle*.

pimple /ˈpɪmpəl/ ⊳ *noun* a small raised often pus-containing swelling on the skin; a spot. *Technical equivalent* PAPULA, PAPULE and PUSTULE. • **pimpled** *adj* having pimples. ◷ 15c, related to Anglo-Saxon *pyplian* to break out in pimples: from Latin *papula* pimple.

pimply ⊳ *adj* (*pimplier, pimpliest*) having pimples.

PIN /pɪn/ ⊳ *abbreviation, noun* personal identification number, a multi-digit number used to authorize electronic transactions, such as cash withdrawal from a dispenser at a bank, access to an account via a telephone line, etc. Also called **PIN number**. ◷ 1980s.

pin ⊳ *noun* **1** a short slender implement with a sharp point and small round head, usually made of stainless steel, for fastening, attaching, etc, and used especially in dressmaking. **2** *in compounds* any of several fastening devices consisting of or incorporating a slender metal or wire shaft □ *hatpin* □ *safety pin*. **3** a narrow brooch. **4** *in compounds* any of several cylindrical wooden or metal objects with various functions □ *a rolling-pin*. **5** a peg of any of various kinds. **6** any or either of the cylindrical or square-sectioned legs on an electric plug. **7** a club-shaped object set upright for toppling with a ball □ *ten-pin bowling*. **8** the clip on a grenade, that is removed before it is thrown. **9** *golf* the metal shaft of the flag marking a hole. **10** (**pins**) *colloq* one's legs □ *shaky on my pins*. **11** *old use* the least bit □ *doesn't care a pin*. ⊳ *verb* (*pinned, pinning*) **1** (*also* **pin something together, back, up**, *etc*) to secure it with a pin. **2** to make a small hole in something. **3** *chess* to cause an opponent's piece to be unable to move without checking its own king. • **for two pins** *colloq* very readily; if given the smallest reason or encouragement, etc □ *For two pins, I'd come with you*. • **pin one's hopes** or **faith on something** or **someone** to rely on or trust in them entirely. ◷ Anglo-Saxon *pinn*: from Latin *pinna* point.

▪ **pin someone down** to force a commitment or definite expression of opinion from them.

▪ **pin something down** to identify or define it precisely.

▪ **pin something** or **someone down** to hold them fast or trap them □ *pinned the escaping prisoner down on the ground*.

▪ **pin something on someone** *colloq* to put the blame for (a crime or offence) on them.

pina colada or **piña colada** /ˈpiːnə kəˈlɑːdə, ˈpiːnjə —/ ▻ *noun* (***pina coladas***) a drink made from pineapple juice, rum and coconut. ◷ 1970s: Spanish, literally 'strained pineapple'.

pinafore /ˈpɪnəfɔː(r)/ ▻ *noun* **1** an apron, especially one with a bib. Sometimes shortened to **pinny**. **2** (*also* **pinafore dress**) a sleeveless dress for wearing over a blouse, sweater, etc. ◷ 17c: from pin + afore, because it was formerly 'pinned afore', ie pinned to the front of a dress.

pinball ▻ *noun* a game played on a slot machine, in which a small metal ball is propelled by flippers round a course, the score depending on what hazards it avoids and targets it hits; a form of BAGATELLE (sense 1). ◷ Early 20c.

pince-nez /ˈpansneɪ, ˈpɪnsneɪ/ ▻ *plural noun* spectacles that are held in position by a clip gripping the nose instead of being supported over the ears. ◷ 19c: French, literally 'pinch nose'.

pincer movement ▻ *noun, military* an advance that closes in on a target from both sides simultaneously. ◷ 1920s.

pincers /ˈpɪnsəz/ ▻ *plural noun* **1** a hinged tool with two claw-like jaws joined by a pivot, used for gripping objects, pulling nails, etc. **2** the modified claw-like appendage of a decapod crustacean, eg a crab or lobster, adapted for grasping. ◷ 14c: from French *pincier* to pinch.

pinch ▻ *verb* (***pinches***, ***pinched***, ***pinching***) **1** to squeeze or nip the flesh of someone or something, between thumb and finger. **2** to compress or squeeze something painfully. **3** said eg of cold or hunger: to affect someone or something painfully or injuriously. **4** *tr & intr* said of tight shoes: to hurt or chafe. **5** *tr & intr, colloq* to steal. **6** *intr* said of controls, restrictions, shortages, etc: to cause hardship. **7** *intr* to economize ▫ *had to pinch and scrape to get by.* **8** *colloq* to arrest someone. ▻ *noun* (***pinches***) **1** an act of pinching; a nip or squeeze. **2** the quantity of something (eg salt) that can be held between thumb and finger. **3** a very small amount. **4** a critical time of difficulty or hardship. • **at a pinch** *colloq* if absolutely necessary. • **feel the pinch** *colloq* to find life, work, etc difficult because of lack of money. • **know where the shoe pinches** to know by direct experience what the problem or difficulty is. ◷ 14c: from French *pincier* to pinch.

▪ **pinch something off**, **out**, **back**, *etc* to prune (a plant) by removing the tips of its shoots.

pinchbeck /ˈpɪntʃbɛk/ ▻ *noun* a copper-zinc alloy with the appearance of gold, used in cheap jewellery. ▻ *adj* cheap, artificial, sham, counterfeit or imitation. ◷ 18c: named after its inventor Christopher Pinchbeck (c.1670–1732), English watchmaker.

pinched ▻ *adj* said of a person's appearance: pale and haggard from tiredness, cold or other discomfort.

pinch-hit ▻ *verb* (***pinch-hit***, ***pinch-hitting***) **1** *baseball* to bat in place of someone else at short notice, especially at a critical point in the game. **2** to act as a substitute for someone in an emergency. ◷ Early 20c.

pincushion ▻ *noun* a pad into which to stick dressmaking pins for convenient storage.

pine[1] ▻ *noun* **1** (*also* **pine tree**) any of numerous evergreen coniferous trees with narrow needle-like leaves, native to cool northern temperate regions. **2** (*also* **pinewood**) the pale durable wood of this tree, used to make furniture, telegraph poles, paper pulp, etc, and widely used in construction work. Also *as adj* ▫ *pine table* ▫ *pine fragrance.* See also PINY. ◷ Anglo-Saxon *pin*: from Latin *pinus*.

pine[2] ▻ *verb* (***pined***, ***pining***) *intr* **1** (*also* **pine for someone** or **something**) to long or yearn for them or it. **2** (*also* **pine away**) to waste away from grief or longing. ◷ Anglo-Saxon *pinian* in obsolete sense 'to torment'.

pineal eye /ˈpɪnɪəl —/ ▻ *noun, zool* in certain cold-blooded vertebrates: a vestigial third eye in front of the PINEAL GLAND.

pineal gland and **pineal body** /ˈpɪnɪəl —/ ▻ *noun, anatomy* in vertebrates: a small outgrowth from the roof of the forebrain, which produces the hormone MELATONIN. Also called EPIPHYSIS. ◷ 17c: from French *pinéal*, from Latin from *pinea* pine cone.

pineapple /ˈpaɪnapəl/ ▻ *noun* **1** a tropical S American plant with spiky sword-shaped leaves, widely cultivated for its large edible fruit. **2** the fruit of this plant, which has sweet juicy yellow flesh covered by a yellowish-brown spiny skin and is crowned by a rosette of pointed leaves. ◷ 17c referring to the fruit; from 14c *pinappel* in now obsolete sense 'pine cone', ie 'the fruit of the pine'.

pine cone ▻ *noun* the egg-shaped woody fruit of the pine tree, which contains winged seeds.

pine marten ▻ *noun* either of two species of solitary nocturnal tree-dwelling mammal with a rich dark-brown coat and an irregularly shaped yellowish throat patch.

pine needle ▻ *noun* the slender sharp-pointed leaf of the pine tree.

pine nut and **pine kernel** ▻ *noun* the edible oily seed of various species of pine trees, especially the STONE PINE.

pine tar ▻ *noun* WOOD TAR.

pinewood ▻ *noun* **1** a wood of pine trees. **2** pine timber.

pin feather ▻ *noun, ornithol* a new and still unexpanded feather emerging from the skin of a bird.

ping ▻ *noun* a sharp ringing sound like that made by plucking a taut wire, lightly striking glass or metal, etc. ▻ *verb* (***pinged***, ***pinging***) *tr & intr* to make or cause something to make this sound. ◷ 19c: imitating the sound.

pinger /pɪŋə(r)/ ▻ *noun* a clockwork device used in the home, eg to time something that is being cooked, which can be set to give a warning signal such as a pinging sound, after a certain amount of time. ◷ 1950s.

pingo /ˈpɪŋgoʊ/ ▻ *noun* (***pingos*** or ***pingoes***) **1** a large cone-shaped mound with a core of ice formed by the upward expansion of freezing water surrounded by permafrost. **2** the lake formed when such a structure melts. ◷ 1920s: Eskimo, meaning 'conical hill'.

ping-pong /ˈpɪŋ pɒŋ/ ▻ *noun* TABLE TENNIS. Also written **Ping-Pong** (*trademark in US*). ◷ Early 20c: imitating the sound of the ball.

pinhead ▻ *noun* **1** the little rounded or flattened head of a pin. **2** something that is very small. **3** *slang* a stupid person. • **pinheaded** *adj*.

pinhole ▻ *noun* a tiny hole made by, or as if by, a pin.

pinhole camera ▻ *noun* a simple camera consisting of a box with a pin-size hole in it instead of a lens.

pinier and **piniest** see under PINY

pinion[1] /ˈpɪnjən/ ▻ *verb* (***pinioned***, ***pinioning***) **1** to immobilize someone by holding or binding their arms; to hold or bind (someone's arms). **2** to hold fast or bind ▫ *pinioned against a wall.* ▻ *noun* **1** the extreme tip of a bird's wing. **2** a bird's flight feather. ◷ 15c: from French *pignon* wing.

pinion[2] /ˈpɪnjən/ ▻ *noun* a small cogwheel that engages with a larger wheel or rack. ◷ 17c: from French *pignon* cogwheel.

pink[1] ▻ *noun* **1** a light or pale-red colour, between red and white. **2** an annual or perennial plant, eg a CARNATION or SWEET WILLIAM, which has stems with swollen nodes, grass-like bluish-green leaves and flowers with a tubular calyx and five spreading toothed or slightly frilled pink, red, white, purple, yellow, orange or variegated petals. **3 a**

a scarlet hunting-coat or its colour; **b** the person wearing it. **4** the highest point; the acme □ *in the pink of condition.* **5** a person of mildly left-wing views. Compare RED *noun* 7. ▷ *adj* **1** having, being or referring to the colour pink. **2** slightly left-wing. • **in the pink** *colloq* in the best of health. • **pinkish** *adj.* • **pinkness** *noun.* • **pinky** see separate entry. Ⓒ 16c as *noun* sense 2.

pink² ▷ *verb* (*pinked, pinking*) to cut (cloth) with a notched or serrated edge that frays less readily than a straight edge. See also PINKING SHEARS. Ⓒ Anglo-Saxon *pyngan* to prick.

pink³ ▷ *verb* (*pinked, pinking*) *intr* said of a vehicle engine: to KNOCK (*verb* 7). Ⓒ Early 20c: imitating the sound made.

pink elephant *noun* (*usually* **pink elephants**) a hallucination caused by over-indulgence in alcoholic drink.

pink eye see CONJUNCTIVITIS.

pink gin ▷ *noun* gin flavoured with and stained pink by ANGOSTURA BITTERS. Ⓒ 1930s.

pinkie or **pinky** /'pɪŋkɪ/ ▷ *noun* (*pinkies*) *Scots & N Amer* the little finger. Ⓒ 19c: from Dutch *pinkje*.

pinking shears ▷ *plural noun* scissors with a serrated blade for cutting a notched or zig-zag edge in cloth. See PINK².

pinko /'pɪnkoʊ/ ▷ *noun* (*pinkos*) *colloq* a mild or half-hearted socialist. Ⓒ 1950s.

pink pound ▷ *noun* the combined purchasing power of homosexuals considered as a consumer group. Ⓒ 1990s: *pink* refers to the PINK TRIANGLE.

pink triangle ▷ *noun* a symbol, in the form of a pink triangular cloth badge, worn by homosexuals as a sign of solidarity. Ⓒ Homosexual prisoners were forced to wear this symbol in the concentration camps of Nazi Germany, in the same way that Jews were marked by a yellow star.

pinky¹ /'pɪŋkɪ/ ▷ *adj* (*pinkier, pinkiest*) slightly pink. • **pinkiness** *noun.*

pinky² see PINKIE

pin money ▷ *noun* extra cash earned for spending on oneself, on luxury items, etc. Ⓒ 17c: originally referring to an allowance paid by a man to his wife for personal expenditure.

pinna /'pɪnə/ ▷ *noun* (*pinnae* /-niː/) **1** *anatomy* in mammals: the part of the outer ear that projects from the head and that in certain mammals can be moved independently in order to detect the direction of sounds. **2** in a compound leaf: one of the leaflets on either side of the midrib. **3** in birds: a feather or wing. **4** in fish: a fin. Ⓒ 18c: Latin, meaning 'feather' or 'wing'.

pinnace /'pɪnəs/ ▷ *noun* a small boat carried on a larger ship; a ship's boat. Ⓒ 16c: from French *pinace*, from Spanish *pinaza*, meaning 'something made of pine'.

pinnacle /'pɪnəkəl/ ▷ *noun* **1** a slender spire crowning a buttress, gable, roof or tower. **2** a rocky peak. **3** a high point of achievement □ *the pinnacle of her success.* ▷ *verb* (*pinnacled, pinnacling*) **1** to be the pinnacle of something. **2** to set something on a pinnacle. **3** to provide something with a pinnacle or pinnacles. Ⓒ 14c: from Latin *pinnaculum*, diminutive of *pinna* feather.

pinnate /'pɪneɪt, 'pɪnɪt/ ▷ *adj, bot* denoting a compound leaf that consists of pairs of leaflets arranged in two rows on either side of a central axis or midrib. • **pinnately** *adverb.* Ⓒ 18c: from Latin *pinnatus* feathered, from *pinna* feather or wing.

pinnatiped /pɪ'natɪpɛd/ ▷ *adj, zool* said of birds: having webbed feet. Ⓒ Early 19c: from Latin *pinnatus* winged + *pes, pedis* foot.

pinned, pinning see PIN

pinnule /'pɪnjuːl/ ▷ *noun* **1** *bot* a lobe of a leaflet of a pinnate leaf. **2** *zool* a branchlet of a crinoid arm. Ⓒ 16c: from Latin *pinnula*, diminutive of *pinna* wing.

PIN number see under PIN

pinny see PINAFORE

pinochle or **pinocle** /'pɪnəkəl, 'piː-/ ▷ *noun* **1** a card game derived from BÉZIQUE, in which two packs of 24 cards are shuffled together, with all cards of a lower value than nine discarded, the object of the game being to win tricks as in WHIST. **2** the combination of queen of spades and jack of diamonds together in this game. Ⓒ 1860s.

pinole /piː'noʊleɪ/ ▷ *noun* a fine flour made from parched Indian corn or other seeds, sweetened with sugar and eaten with milk, mainly in Mexico and SW states of the US. Ⓒ 19c: Spanish, from Nahuatl (S American Native language) *pinolli*.

pinpoint ▷ *verb* to place, define or identify something precisely. Ⓒ Early 20c.

pinprick ▷ *noun* **1** a tiny hole made by, or as if by, a pin. **2** a slight irritation or annoyance.

pins and needles ▷ *plural noun* an abnormal tingling or prickling sensation in a limb, etc, felt as the flow of blood returns to it after being temporarily obstructed. *Technical equivalent* PARAESTHESIA.

pinscher see DOBERMAN PINSCHER

pinstripe ▷ *noun* **1** a very narrow stripe in cloth. **2** cloth with such stripes. • **pinstriped** *adj* said of fabric or garments, especially suits: having pinstripes.

pint /paɪnt/ ▷ *noun* **1** in the UK, in the imperial system: a unit of liquid measure equivalent to 1/8 of a gallon or 20fl oz, equivalent to 0.568 litre (liquid or dry). **2** in the US: a unit of liquid measure equivalent to 1/8 of a gallon or 16 USfl oz, equivalent to 0.473 litre (liquid) and 0.551 litre (dry). **3** *colloq* a drink of beer of this quantity. Ⓒ 14c: from French *pinte*.

pinta¹ /'pɪntə/ ▷ *noun* a contagious bacterial skin infection occurring in the tropics, particularly Mexico, characterized by loss of skin pigmentation. Ⓒ 19c: Spanish, from Latin *pinctus*, from *pictus* painted.

pinta² /'paɪntə/ ▷ *noun* (*pintas*) *colloq* a pint of milk. Ⓒ 1950s: a contraction of *pint of*, originally used in an advertising slogan.

pintail ▷ *noun* a species of duck with a long slender neck, and a pointed tail which is greatly elongated in the male.

pintle /'pɪntəl/ ▷ *noun* **1** a bolt or pin, especially one which is turned by something. **2** the plunger or needle of the injection valve of an oil engine, opened by oil pressure on an annular face, and closed by a spring. Ⓒ Anglo-Saxon *pintel* in original and dialect sense 'penis'.

pinto /'pɪntoʊ/ *US* ▷ *adj* mottled; piebald. ▷ *noun* (*pintos*) a piebald horse. Ⓒ 19c: Spanish, meaning 'painted' or 'mottled', from Latin *pinctus*, from *pictus* painted.

pinto bean ▷ *noun* a kind of bean resembling a kidney bean, but mottled in colour. Ⓒ Early 20c.

pint-size or **pint-sized** ▷ *adj, humorous* said of a person: very small.

pin tuck ▷ *noun* a narrow decorative tuck in a garment.

pin-up ▷ *noun* **1** a picture of a pop star or a famous, glamorous or otherwise admirable person that one pins on one's wall. **2** someone whose picture is pinned up in this way. Ⓒ 1940s.

pinwheel ▷ *noun* **1** a whirling firework; a CATHERINE WHEEL. **2** *N Amer, especially US* a toy windmill.

piny /'paɪnɪ/ ▷ *adj* (*pinier, piniest*) referring to, resembling or covered in pine trees.

Pinyin /pɪn'jɪn/ ▷ *noun* a system for writing Chinese using letters of the Roman alphabet. Ⓒ 1960s: from Chinese *pinyin* phonetic spelling.

pion see under PI-MESON

pioneer /paɪəˈnɪə(r)/ ▷ *noun* **1** an explorer of, or settler in, hitherto unknown or wild country. **2** someone who breaks new ground in anything; an innovator or initiator. **3** *bot* a plant or species that is characteristically among the first to establish itself on bared ground. Also *as adj.* ▷ *verb* (***pioneered***, ***pioneering***) **1** *intr* to be a pioneer; to be innovative. **2** to explore and open up (a route, etc). **3** to try out, originate or develop (a new technique, etc). ◷ 16c: from French *peonier*, from Latin *pedo* foot soldier.

pious /ˈpaɪəs/ ▷ *adj* **1** religiously devout. **2** dutiful. **3** *derog* ostentatiously virtuous; sanctimonious. • **piously** *adverb*. • **piousness** *noun*. ◷ 16c: from Latin *pius* dutiful.

pip¹ ▷ *noun* the small seed of a fruit such as an apple, pear, orange or grape. • **pipless** *adj*. • **pippy** *adj*. ◷ 18c: shortening of PIPPIN sense 2.

pip² ▷ *noun* **1** one of a series of short high-pitched signals on the radio, telephone, etc. **2** (**the pips**) *colloq* the six pips broadcast as a time-signal by BBC radio, made up of five short ones and one long one which marks the start of the new minute and hour. ◷ Early 20c: imitating the sound.

pip³ ▷ *verb* (***pipped***, ***pipping***) to defeat someone narrowly. • **pipped at the post** *colloq* overtaken narrowly in the closing stages of a contest, etc. ◷ Late 19c: from PIP¹ or PIP⁴.

pip⁴ ▷ *noun* **1** one of the emblems or spots on playing-cards, dice or dominoes. **2** *military* in the British army: a star on a uniform indicating rank □ *got his second pip last month.* **3** on a radar screen: a mark, eg a spot of light, that indicates the presence of an object. **4** *bot* the single blossom or corolla in a cluster. ◷ 17c, originally as *peep*.

pip⁵ ▷ *noun, old use* a disease of poultry and other fowl. • **give someone the pip** *colloq* to irritate them. ◷ 15c as *pippe*: Dutch, perhaps ultimately from Latin *pituita* rheum or mucus.

pipa /ˈpiːpə/ ▷ *noun* (***pipas***) a S American toad, the female of which is noted for carrying her developing young on her back. Also called **Surinam toad**. ◷ 18c: Surinam dialect, probably of African origin.

pipal, **pipul** or **peepul** /ˈpiːpəl, ˈpiːpʌl/ ▷ *noun* the BO TREE. ◷ 18c: Hindu.

pipe¹ /paɪp/ ▷ *noun* **1** a tubular conveyance for water, gas, oil, etc. **2 a** a little bowl with a hollow stem for smoking tobacco, etc; **b** a quantity of tobacco smoked in one of these. **3** a wind instrument consisting of a simple wooden or metal tube. **4** (**the pipes**) the BAGPIPES. **5** any of the vertical metal tubes through which sound is produced on an organ. **6** a boatswain's whistle. **7** a pipe-like vent forming part of a volcano. **8** a cylindrical quantity of ore, etc. **9** *old use or in compounds* any of the air passages in an animal's body □ *the windpipe.* ▷ *verb* (***piped***, ***piping***) **1** to convey (gas, water, oil, etc) through pipes. **2** *tr & intr* to play on a pipe or the pipes □ *piped the same tune all evening.* **3** (*also* **pipe someone** or **something in**) to welcome or convey with music from a pipe or the bagpipes □ *piped in the haggis.* **4** *tr & intr* said of a child: to speak or say in a small shrill voice. **5** *intr* to sing shrilly as a bird does. **6 a** to use a bag with a nozzle in order to force (icing or cream, etc from the bag) into long strings for decorating a cake, dessert, etc; **b** to make (designs, etc) on a cake, etc by this means. **7** *computing* to direct (the output of one program) into another program as its input in order to increase the speed of execution. **8** *hortic* to propagate by using pipings (see PIPING *noun* 5). • **pipeless** *adj*. • **pipe-like** *adj*. • **piper** see separate entry. • **put that in your pipe and smoke it** *colloq* used dismissively in speech to emphasize and conclude some unwelcome statement, criticism, etc: think about that and see how you like it! ◷ Anglo-Saxon: from Latin *pipare* to chirp or play a pipe.

▪ **pipe down** *colloq* to stop talking; to be quiet □ *Will you please pipe down!*

▪ **pipe up** to speak unexpectedly, breaking a silence, etc.

pipe² /paɪp/ ▷ *noun* **1** a cask or butt of varying capacity, but usually about 105 gallons in Britain (equal to 126 US gallons), used for wine or oil. **2** a measure of this amount. ◷ 14c: French, meaning 'cask'.

pipeclay ▷ *noun* fine white clay for making tobacco pipes and delicate crockery.

pipe-cleaner ▷ *noun* a piece of wire with a woolly tufted covering for cleaning a tobacco pipe.

piped music ▷ *noun* light popular recorded music played continuously through loudspeakers, especially in public places, eg restaurants, shopping malls, supermarkets, etc. Also called **muzak** (*trademark*).

pipe dream ▷ *noun* a delightful fantasy of the kind indulged in while smoking a pipe, originally one filled with opium. • **pipe-dreamer** *noun*. ◷ Late 19c.

pipefish ▷ *noun* any of various fish of the seahorse family, a long thin fish covered with hard plates, its jaws forming a long tube.

pipeful ▷ *noun* (***pipefuls***) the amount a pipe can hold.

pipeline ▷ *noun* a series of connected pipes laid underground to carry oil, natural gas, water, etc, across large distances. • **pipelining** *noun*. • **in the pipeline** *colloq* under consideration; forthcoming or in preparation □ *Some reforms to the system are already in the pipeline.*

pipe of peace see under CALUMET

piper /ˈpaɪpə(r)/ ▷ *noun* a player of a pipe or the bagpipes.

pipe rack ▷ *noun* a rack for tobacco pipes.

piperidine /pɪˈpɛrɪdiːn/ ▷ *noun, chem* a liquid base with a peppery odour. ◷ 19c: French, from Latin *piper* pepper + -IDE + -INE².

piperine /ˈpɪpəraɪn/ ▷ *noun, chem* (formula $C_{17}H_{19}O_3N$) an alkaloid found in pepper. ◷ Early 19c: from Latin *piper* pepper + -INE².

pipestone ▷ *noun* a red clayey stone used by Native American people for making tobacco pipes.

pipette /pɪˈpɛt/ ▷ *noun* a small laboratory device usually consisting of a narrow tube into which liquid can be sucked and from which it can subsequently be dispensed in known amounts. ▷ *verb* (***pipetted***, ***pipetting***) to measure or transfer (a liquid) by means of such a device. ◷ 19c: French, diminutive of *pipe* pipe.

pipework ▷ *noun* **1** *mining* a vein of ore in the form of a pipe. **2** piping or pipes collectively.

piping /ˈpaɪpɪŋ/ ▷ *noun* **1 a** a length of pipe, or a system or series of pipes conveying water, oil, etc; **b** *as adj* □ *piping engineer.* **2** covered cord forming a decorative edging on upholstery or clothing. **3** strings and knots of icing or cream decorating a cake or dessert. **4** the art of playing a pipe or the bagpipes. **5** *hortic* a slip or cutting from a joint of a plant stem. ▷ *adj* said of a child's voice: small and shrill. • **piping hot** said of food: satisfyingly hot.

pipistrelle /pɪpɪˈstrɛl/ ▷ *noun* the smallest and most widespread European bat, which has a reddish-brown body and short triangular ears, and is frequently found roosting in barns and other large buildings. ◷ 18c: from French, from Italian *pipistrello*, from Latin *vespertilio* bat, from *vesper* evening.

pipit /ˈpɪpɪt/ ▷ *noun* any of various small ground-dwelling songbirds with a slender body, streaked brown plumage with paler underparts, a narrow beak and a long tail. ◷ 18c: imitating the sound of its call.

pipkin /ˈpɪpkɪn/ ▷ *noun* a small pot, now only an earthenware one. ◷ 16c: possibly a diminutive of PIPE².

pipless see under PIP¹

pippin ▷ *noun* **1** any of several varieties of eating apple with a green or rosy skin. **2** *obsolete or dialect* the seed or pip of a fruit. ◷ 13c in sense 2: from French *pepin*.

pippy see under PIP[1]

pipsqueak ▷ *noun, derog colloq* someone or something insignificant or contemptible. ⓒ Early 20c.

pipul see PIPAL

piquant /ˈpiːkənt, -kɑːnt/ ▷ *adj* **1** having a pleasantly spicy taste or tang. **2** amusing, intriguing, provocative or stimulating. ● **piquancy** *noun* the state of being piquant. ● **piquantly** *adverb*. ⓒ 16c: French, from *piquer* to prick.

pique /piːk/ ▷ *noun* resentment; hurt pride. ▷ *verb* (***piqued, piquing***) **1** to hurt someone's pride; to offend or nettle them. **2** to arouse (curiosity or interest). **3** to pride (oneself) on something □ *piqued himself on his good taste.* ⓒ 16c: French, from *piquer* to prick.

piqué /ˈpiːkeɪ/ ▷ *noun* a stiff corded fabric, especially of cotton. ⓒ 19c: French, meaning 'pricked', from *piquer* to prick.

piquet /pɪˈkɛt, pɪˈkeɪ/ ▷ *noun* a card game for two, played with 32 cards. ⓒ 17c: French, from *pic* the score of 30 points in this game, literally 'prick'.

Pir or **pir** /pɪə(r)/ ▷ *noun* a Muslim title of honour given to a holy man or religious leader. ⓒ 17c: Persian, meaning 'old man' or 'chief'.

piracy /ˈpaɪərəsɪ/ ▷ *noun* (***piracies***) **1** the activity of pirates, such as robbery on the high seas. **2** unauthorized publication or reproduction of copyright material. ⓒ 16c.

piranha /pɪˈrɑːnə/ or **piraña** /pəˈrɑːnjə/ ▷ *noun* any of various extremely aggressive S American freshwater fishes, usually dark in colour, with strong jaws, sharp interlocking saw-edged teeth and a slender muscular tail with a broad tail-fin. ⓒ 19c: Portuguese *piranha*, from Tupí (S American Native language) *piranya* scissors or piranha.

pirate /ˈpaɪərət/ ▷ *noun* **1** someone who attacks and robs ships at sea. **2** the ship used by pirates. **3** someone who publishes material without permission from the copyright-holder, or otherwise uses someone else's work illegally. **4** someone who runs a radio station without a licence. ▷ *verb* (***pirated, pirating***) to publish, reproduce or use (someone else's literary or artistic work, or ideas) without legal permission. ● **piratic** /paɪəˈratɪk/ or **piratical** *adj*. ● **piratically** *adverb*. ⓒ 15c: from Latin *pirata*, from Greek *peirates*, from *peiraein* to try one's fortune.

piri-piri[1] /ˈpɪriːpɪriː/ ▷ *noun* a spicy sauce made with red peppers. Also *as adj* □ *piri-piri chicken.* ⓒ 1960s: perhaps from Swahili *pilipili* pepper.

piri-piri[2] /ˈpɪəriːpɪərɪ/ ▷ *noun* a New Zealand weed with prickly burs, used medicinally and as a tea. ⓒ Late 19c: Maori.

pirouette /pɪrʊˈɛt/ ▷ *noun* a spin or twirl executed on tiptoe in dancing. ▷ *verb* (***pirouetted, pirouetting***) *intr* to execute a pirouette or a series of them. ⓒ 18c: French, originally meaning 'a spinning top'.

pirozhki /pɪˈrɒʒkɪ/ or **piroshki** /-ˈrɒʃkɪ/ ▷ *plural noun* small triangular pastries with meat, fish, cream cheese or vegetable fillings. ⓒ Early 20c: Russian, meaning 'small pastries'.

piscatorial /pɪskəˈtɔːrɪəl/ and **piscatory** /ˈpɪskətərɪ/ ▷ *adj, formal* relating to fish or fishing. ⓒ 17c as *piscatory*; early 19c as *piscatorial*: from Latin *piscatorius* fisherman.

Pisces /ˈpaɪsiːz/ ▷ *noun* **1** *astron* a constellation of the zodiac. **2** *astrol* **a** the twelfth sign of the zodiac; **b** someone born between 20 February and 20 March, under this sign. See table at ZODIAC. **3** *zool* in the animal kingdom: the superclass of fishes, consisting of the jawless fish (hagfish and lampreys), cartilaginous fish and bony fish. ● **Piscean** *adj*. ⓒ 14c: Latin, meaning 'fishes', from *piscis* fish.

pisci- /ˈpɪsɪ/ ▷ *combining form, denoting* fish or fishes. ⓒ From Latin *piscis* fish.

pisciculture /ˈpɪsɪkʌltʃʊə(r)/ ▷ *noun* the rearing of fish by artificial methods or under controlled conditions. ● **piscicultural** *adj*. ● **pisciculturist** *noun*. ⓒ 19c.

piscina /pɪˈsiːnə, pɪˈsaɪnə/ ▷ *noun* (***piscinae*** /-niː/ or ***piscinas***) a stone basin with a drain, found in older churches, in which to empty water used for rinsing the sacred vessels, generally situated in a niche on the south side of the altar. ⓒ 18c in this sense; 16c meaning 'fish pond', from Latin, meaning 'basin', 'tank' or 'fish pond'.

piscine /pɪˈsaɪn/ ▷ *adj* referring or relating to, or resembling, a fish or fishes. ⓒ 18c: from Latin *piscis* fish.

piscivorous /pɪˈsɪvərəs/ ▷ *adj* said of an animal: that feeds on fish. ⓒ 17c.

pish ▷ *exclamation* an expression of impatience, contempt or disgust. ⓒ 16c.

piss ▷ *verb* (***pissed, pissing***) **1** *intr, coarse slang, sometimes considered taboo* to urinate. **2** to discharge something (eg blood) in the urine. **3** to wet something with one's urine □ *piss the bed.* **4** *intr* (*also* **piss down**) to rain hard □ *It's pissing down outside.* ▷ *noun* (***pisses***) **1** urine. **2** an act of urinating. ● **take the piss out of someone** or **something** to ridicule them or it. See also PISS-TAKE. ⓒ 13c: from French *pisser*, from a colloquial Latin word; imitating the sound of urinating.

■ **piss about** or **around** to mess about; to waste time.

■ **piss someone about** or **around** to waste their time; to irritate them.

■ **piss off** to go away □ *Piss off, will you!*

■ **piss someone off** *Brit* to irritate or bore them □ *He really pisses me off.* □ *She's pissed off with him.*

piss-artist ▷ *noun, slang* **1** someone who presents themselves as being organized and productive but who is in fact incompetent. **2** a drunkard. ⓒ 1970s.

pissed /pɪst/ ▷ *adj* **1** *Brit coarse slang* drunk. **2** *N Amer* (*often* **pissed at someone** or **something**) irritated or annoyed with them or it. See also PISS SOMEONE OFF at PISS.

pisser ▷ *noun, coarse slang* **1** someone who pisses. **2** an annoying or irritating person or thing □ *What a pisser!* **3** a toilet. **4** the penis. ● **to pull someone's pisser** to joke with them; to pull their leg.

piss-head ▷ *noun* a drunkard. ⓒ 1970s.

pissoir / *French* piswaʀ/ ▷ *noun* a public urinal enclosed by a screen or wall. ⓒ Early 20c.

piss-poor ▷ *adj, slang* terrible; diabolical.

piss-take *slang* ▷ *noun* a parody. ● **piss-taker** *noun*. ● **piss-taking** *noun, adj*. ⓒ 1970s: derived from TAKE THE PISS OUT OF SOMEONE (see under PISS).

piss-up ▷ *noun, slang* **1** a party or gathering where most people drink a lot of alcohol. **2** a mess; a botched situation. ⓒ 1950s.

pistachio /pɪˈstɑːʃɪoʊ, -tʃɪoʊ/ ▷ *noun* (***pistachios***) **1** a small deciduous tree with greenish flowers borne in long loose heads, and reddish-brown nut-like fruits containing edible seeds. **2** the edible greenish seed of this tree which can be eaten salted or used as a food flavouring, in confectionery, etc. ⓒ 16c: from Italian *pistacchio*, ultimately from Persian *pistah*.

piste /piːst/ ▷ *noun* a ski slope or track of smooth compacted snow. ⓒ 18c: French, meaning 'race track', from Latin *pista* beaten track, from *pinsere* to pound or stamp.

pistil /ˈpɪstɪl/ ▷ *noun, bot* in a flowering plant: the female reproductive structure, which may be a single carpel consisting of a stigma, style and ovary, or a group of fused carpels. ⓒ 16c: from Latin *pistillum* pestle.

pistol /ˈpɪstəl/ ▷ *noun* a small gun held in one hand when fired. ● **hold a pistol to someone's head** to use threats to force them to do what one wants. ⓒ 16c: from French *pistole*, from German, from Czech *piötala* pistol, pipe or whistle.

pistole /pɪˈstoʊl/ ▷ *noun, historical* an old gold coin, especially a Spanish one. ⓒ 16c: from French, shortened from *pistolet* gold coin.

pistol grip ▷ *noun* a handle shaped like the butt of a pistol, eg for a camera. Also *as adj* □ ***pistol-grip camera.***

pistol-whip ▷ *verb* to hit someone with a pistol. ⓒ 1940s.

piston /ˈpɪstən/ ▷ *noun* **1** *engineering* a cylindrical device that moves up and down in the cylinder of a petrol, diesel or steam engine. **2** a sliding valve on a brass wind instrument. ⓒ 18c: French, from Italian *pistone*, from *pestare* to pound.

piston ring ▷ *noun, engineering* a split metal ring that forms an airtight seal between a piston and its containing cylinder.

piston rod ▷ *noun, engineering* in a vehicle engine: a rod attached to the piston, that transfers the piston's motion to the driving wheels by means of the crankshaft.

pit¹ ▷ *noun* **1** a big deep hole in the ground. **2** a mine, especially a coalmine. **3** a cavity sunk into the ground from which to inspect vehicle engines, etc. **4** (**the pits**) *motor sport* any of a set of areas beside a racetrack where vehicles can refuel, have wheel changes, etc. **5** an enclosure in which fighting animals or birds are put. **6 a** the floor of the auditorium in a theatre; **b** the people sitting there. **7** an ORCHESTRA PIT (see ORCHESTRA sense 3). **8** *anatomy* a hollow, indentation or depression, eg **pit of the stomach** the small hollow below the breastbone. **9** a scar left by a smallpox or acne pustule. **10** (**the pit**) *old use* hell. **11** (**the pits**) *slang* an awful or intolerable situation, person, etc. ▷ *verb* (***pitted, pitting***) **1** to mark something with scars and holes □ ***It's surface is pitted with craters.*** **2** to put something in a pit. ⓒ Anglo-Saxon *pytt*: from Latin *puteus* well.

■ **pit oneself against someone** to set or match oneself against them in competition or opposition □ ***pitted himself against the rest of the team.***

pit² ▷ *noun, N Amer* the stone in a peach, apricot, plum, etc. ▷ *verb* (***pitted, pitting***) to remove the stone from (a piece of fruit). ⓒ 19c: from Dutch, meaning 'kernel'.

pit-a-pat ▷ *noun* **1** a noise of pattering. **2** a succession of light taps. ▷ *adverb* with a pattering or tapping noise □ ***rain falling pit-a-pat.*** ▷ *verb* (***pit-a-patted, pit-a-patting***) to make a succession of quick light taps. ⓒ 16c: imitating the sound.

pit bull terrier ▷ *noun* a large breed of BULL TERRIER, originally developed for dogfighting. Often shortened to **pit bull**. ⓒ 1930s.

pitch¹ ▷ *verb* (***pitches, pitched, pitching***) **1** to set up (a tent or camp). **2** to throw or fling. **3** *tr & intr* to fall or make someone or something fall heavily forward. **4** *intr* said of a ship: to plunge and lift alternately at bow and stern. **5** *tr & intr* said of a roof: to slope □ ***is pitched at a steep angle.*** **6** to give a particular musical pitch to (one's voice or a note) in singing or playing, or to set (a song, etc) at a higher or lower level within a possible range □ ***The tune is pitched too high for me.*** **7** to choose a level, eg of difficulty, sophistication, etc at which to present (a talk, etc) □ ***was pitched too low for this audience.*** **8 a** *cricket* to bowl (the ball) so that it lands where the batsman can hit it; **b** *golf* to hit (the ball) high and gently, so that it stays where it is on landing; **c** *tr & intr, baseball* said of the PITCHER² (sense 1): to throw the ball overarm or underarm to the person batting. **9** to pave (a road) with stones set on end or on edge. ▷ *noun* (***pitches***) **1** the field or area of play in any of several sports. **2** an act or style of pitching or throwing. **3** a degree of intensity; a level □ ***reached such a pitch of excitement.*** **4 a** the angle of steepness of a slope; **b** such a slope. **5** *music* the degree of highness or lowness of a note that results from the frequency of the vibrations producing it. **6** a street trader's station. **7** a line in sales talk, especially one often made use of. **8** the distance between teeth on a saw, toothed wheel, etc, or between threads on a screw. **9** the plunging and rising motion of a ship. **10** the angle between the chord of the blade of a propeller and the plane of rotation. **11** *geol* the angle between a linear feature on the horizontal, measured in the inclined plane containing both. Compare PLUNGE. ● **pitcher** see separate entry. ● **pitch camp** to set up tents, etc upon arrival at a campsite, etc. ● **queer someone's pitch** see QUEER. ⓒ 13c as *picchen* to throw or put up.

■ **pitch in** *colloq* **1** to begin enthusiastically. **2** to join in; to make a contribution.

■ **pitch into someone** *colloq* to rebuke or blame them angrily.

pitch² ▷ *noun* (***pitches***) **1** a thick black sticky substance obtained from coal tar, used for filling ships' seams, etc. **2** any of various bituminous substances. Compare WOOD TAR. **3** in papermaking: a mixture of residues that interferes with paper quality. ▷ *verb* (***pitches, pitched, pitching***) to coat or treat something with pitch. ⓒ Anglo-Saxon *pic*.

pitch and putt ▷ *noun* **1** a small golf course in parks, etc, with short holes, needing only one pitch of the ball to reach the green from the tee. **2** the game played on such a course.

pitch-black or **pitch-dark** ▷ *adj* utterly, intensely or unrelievedly black or dark. ⓒ 16c.

pitchblende /ˈpɪtʃblɛnd/ ▷ *noun, geol* a radioactive glossy brown or black form of uraninite, the main ore of uranium and radium. ⓒ 18c: from German *Pechblende*, from *pech* PITCH² + BLENDE.

pitch circle ▷ *noun* in a toothed wheel: an imaginary circle along which the tooth pitch (see PITCH¹ *noun* 8) is measured and which would put the wheel in contact with another that meshed with it.

pitched battle ▷ *noun* **1** a prearranged battle between two sides on chosen ground. **2** a fierce dispute or violent confrontation, especially one that involves many people.

pitched roof ▷ *noun* a roof comprising two downward sloping surfaces meeting in a central ridge, contrasted with a flat one.

pitcher¹ /ˈpɪtʃə(r)/ ▷ *noun* a large earthenware jug with either one or two handles. ⓒ 13c: from French *pichier*, from Latin *bicarium* beaker.

pitcher² /ˈpɪtʃə(r)/ ▷ *noun* **1** *baseball* the player who throws the ball to the person batting to hit. **2** a paving-stone or sett. ⓒ 19c in these senses; see PITCH¹ *verb* 8c and 9.

pitcherful ▷ *noun* (***pitcherfuls***) the amount a PITCHER¹ can hold.

pitcher plant ▷ *noun* any of various insectivorous plants with modified leaves that collect rainwater, in which insects attracted to the plant are trapped and drowned. ⓒ 19c: so called because the leaves resemble pitchers (see PITCHER¹).

pitchfork ▷ *noun* a long-handled fork with two or three sharp prongs, for tossing hay. ⓒ 15c.

pitchpine ▷ *noun* a name for several N American pine trees that yield WOOD TAR and timber.

pitch pipe ▷ *noun* a small pipe used to pitch the voice or to tune an instrument with. ⓒ 18c.

pitchy /pɪtʃɪ/ ▷ *adj* (***pitchier, pitchiest***) **1** smeared with or full of PITCH². **2** black. **3** resembling PITCH². ● **pitchiness** *noun*.

piteous /ˈpɪtɪəs/ ▷ *adj* arousing one's pity; moving, poignant, heartrending or pathetic. ● **piteously** *adverb*. ● **piteousness** *noun*. Compare PITIABLE, PITIFUL. ⓒ 13c as *pitous*: from French *pitos*.

pitfall ▻ *noun* a hidden danger, unsuspected hazard or unforeseen difficulty. ⓘ 16c in this figurative sense.

pith ▻ *noun* **1** the soft white tissue that lies beneath the rind of many citrus fruits, eg orange. **2** *bot* in the stem of many plants: a central cylinder of generally soft tissue, composed of PARENCHYMA cells, used mainly for storage. **3** the most important part of an argument, etc. **4** substance, forcefulness or vigour as a quality in writing, etc. ▻ *verb* (*pithed, pithing*) **1** to remove the pith from (a plant). **2** to kill (animals) by severing, piercing or destroying the marrow or central nervous system. ⓘ Anglo-Saxon *pitha*.

pithead /'pɪthɛd/ ▻ *noun* the entrance to a mineshaft and the machinery round it. Also *as adj* □ *pithead ballot*. ⓘ 19c.

Pithecanthropus /pɪθɪ'kanθrəpəs, -'θroupəs/ ▻ *noun* a fossil hominid discovered in Java in 1891–2, a former genus of primitive man, now included in the genus HOMO. ⓘ 19c: from Greek *pithekos* ape + *anthropos* man.

pith helmet ▻ *noun* a large light rigid hat made from the pith of the sola plant, worn, especially formerly, in the tropics to protect the head from the Sun.

pithy /'pɪθɪ/ ▻ *adj* (*pithier, pithiest*) **1** said of a saying, comment, etc: brief, forceful and to the point. **2** referring to, resembling or full of pith. • **pithily** *adverb*. • **pithiness** *noun*. • **pithless** *adj*.

pitiable /'pɪtɪəbəl/ ▻ *adj* **1** arousing pity. **2** miserably inadequate; contemptible. ⓘ 15c.

pitiful /'pɪtɪfəl/ ▻ *adj* **1** arousing pity; wretched or pathetic □ *His clothes were in a pitiful state.* **2** sadly inadequate or ineffective □ *a pitiful attempt to be funny.* • **pitifully** *adverb*. • **pitifulness** *noun*. ⓘ 15c; 16c in sense 2.

pitiless ▻ *adj* showing no pity; merciless, cruel or relentless. • **pitilessly** *adverb*. • **pitilessness** *noun*.

piton /'piːtɒn/ ▻ *noun, mountaineering* a metal peg or spike with an eye for passing a rope through, hammered into a rockface as an aid to climbers. ⓘ 19c: French, meaning 'ringbolt'.

pit pony ▻ *noun, historical* a pony used for haulage in a coalmine.

pitstop ▻ *noun, motor sport* a pause made at a refuelling PIT[1] (*noun* 4) by a racing driver.

pitta /'pɪtə/ ▻ *noun* (*pittas*) **1** a Middle-Eastern slightly leavened bread, usually in a hollow oval shape that can be filled with other foods. **2** one such oval. Also called **pitta bread**. ⓘ 1950s: modern Greek, meaning 'cake' or 'pie'.

pittance /'pɪtəns/ ▻ *noun* a meagre allowance or wage □ *works for a pittance.* ⓘ 13c: from French *pietance* ration.

pitted *past tense, past participle of* PIT[1]

pitter-patter /'pɪtəpatə(r)/ ▻ *noun* the sound of pattering. ▻ *adverb* with this sound. ▻ *verb* (*pitter-pattered, pitter-pattering*) *intr* to make such a sound. ⓘ 15c: imitating the sound.

pitting *present participle of* PIT[1]

pittosporum /pɪ'tɒspərəm/ ▻ *noun* an evergreen shrub native to Australasia and parts of Africa and Asia, with leathery leaves and purple, white or greenish-yellow flowers. Also called PARCHMENT BARK. ⓘ 18c: Latin, from Greek *pitta* PITCH[2] + *sporos* seed.

pituitary /pɪ'tjuːɪtərɪ/ ▻ *noun* (*pituitaries*) short form of PITUITARY GLAND. ▻ *adj* relating to this gland. ⓘ 19c as *noun*; 17c in original adjectival sense 'relating to phlegm': from Latin *pituita* phlegm or rheum.

pituitary gland or **pituitary body** ▻ *noun, physiol* in vertebrates: an endocrine gland at the base of the brain that is responsible for the production of a number of important hormones, many of which control the activity of other glands, and therefore has a central role in the control of growth, sexual development, reproduction, water balance, adrenaline production and general metabolism.

pit viper ▻ *noun* any member of a N American group of snakes, including the RATTLESNAKE, with a small heat-sensitive pit on each side of the front of its head, used for sensing the prey's body heat while hunting in complete darkness.

pity /'pɪtɪ/ ▻ *noun* (*pities*) **1** a feeling of sorrow for the troubles and sufferings of others; compassion. **2** a cause of sorrow or regret. ▻ *verb* (*pities, pitied, pitying*) to feel or show pity for someone or something. • **for pity's sake** an expression of earnest entreaty or of exasperation. • **have** or **take pity on someone** to feel or show pity for them, especially in some practical way. • **more's the pity** *colloq* a phrase used to express regret: unfortunately; I'm sorry to say. ⓘ 13c: from French *pité*, from Latin *pietas* piety or dutifulness.

pitying ▻ *adj* **1** compassionate. **2** expressing pity, especially of a rather condescending or contemptuous sort □ *gave me a pitying look.* • **pityingly** *adverb*.

pityriasis /pɪtɪ'raɪəsɪs/ ▻ *noun, medicine, pathol* any of several skin diseases marked by the formation and flaking away of dry scales. ⓘ 17c: Latin, from Greek *pityron* bran.

più /pjuː/ ▻ *adverb, music, in compounds*, more, as in **più allegro** faster or **più lento** slower. ⓘ 18c: Italian.

piupiu /'piːuːpiːuː/ ▻ *noun* (*piupius*) a skirt, traditionally made from strips of flax, worn by Maori men and women for dances, celebrations and ceremonial occasions. ⓘ 19c: Maori.

pivot /'pɪvət/ ▻ *noun* **1** a central pin, spindle or pointed shaft round which something revolves, turns, balances or oscillates. **2** someone or something crucial, on which everyone or everything else depends. **3** a CENTRE-HALF in football or a similarly-placed player in other games. **4** the action of turning the body using one foot as a pivot. **5** the soldier or position from which a military formation takes its reference when altering its position, etc. ▻ *verb* (*pivoted, pivoting*) **1** *intr* (*often* **pivot on something**) **a** to turn, swivel or revolve □ *pivot on one's heel*; **b** to depend. **2** to mount something on a pivot. ⓘ 17c: French.

pivotal /'pɪvətəl/ ▻ *adj* **1** constructed as or acting like a pivot. **2** crucially important; critical □ *a pivotal moment in our history.* • **pivotally** *adverb*.

pivot bridge ▻ *noun, civil eng* a SWING BRIDGE moving on a vertical pivot in the middle.

pix[1] ▻ *noun* (*pixes*) PYX

pix[2] *a plural of* PIC

pixel /'pɪksəl/ ▻ *noun, electronics* the smallest element of the image displayed on a computer or TV screen, consisting of a single dot which may be illuminated (ie on) or dark (off). ⓘ 1960s: PIX[2] + *el*ement.

pixie or **pixy** /'pɪksɪ/ ▻ *noun* (*pixies*) *mythol* a kind of fairy, traditionally with mischievous tendencies. ⓘ 17c: originally dialect.

pixie hood ▻ *noun* a child's pointed hood, usually tied under the chin.

pixilated or **pixillated** /'pɪksɪleɪtɪd/ ▻ *adj, chiefly US* **1** bemused or bewildered. **2** mildly eccentric; slightly crazy. **3** *slang* drunk. ⓘ 19c: from PIXIE, modelled on *titillated, elated*, etc.

pixilation or **pixillation** /pɪksɪ'leɪʃən/ ▻ *noun* **1** bemusement, eccentricity, etc. **2** a technique for making human figures or animals appear to be animated artificially, eg by the use of stop-frame camera methods, usually used to create a whimsical effect. ⓘ 1940s in sense 2: from PIXILATED, modelled on ANIMATION.

pizza /'piːtsə/ ▻ *noun* (*pizzas*) a circle of dough spread with cheese, tomatoes, etc and baked, made originally in Italy. ⓘ 1930s: Italian.

pizzazz, **pazzazz**, **pizazz** or **pazazz** /pə'zaz/ ▻ *noun*, *colloq* a quality that is a combination of boldness, vigour, dash and flamboyance. ◷ 1930s: thought to have been coined by Diana Vreeland (c.1903–89), US fashion editor.

pizzeria /piːtsə'rɪə/ ▻ *noun* (***pizzerias***) a restaurant that specializes in pizzas. ◷ 1940s: Italian.

pizzicato /pɪtsɪ'kɑːtoʊ/ *music* ▻ *adj*, *adverb* said of music for stringed instruments: played using the fingers to pluck the strings. ▻ *noun* (***pizzicatos***) **1** a passage of music to be played in this way. **2** the playing or technique of playing a piece by plucking. ◷ 19c: Italian, literally 'twitched'.

Pk ▻ *abbreviation* used in street names: Park.

PL ▻ *abbreviation*, *IVR* Poland.

Pl. ▻ *abbreviation* used in street names: Place.

pl. ▻ *abbreviation* plural.

placable /'plakəbəl/ ▻ *adj* easily appeased. • **placability** or **placableness** *noun*. • **placably** *adverb*. ◷ 15c: from Latin *placabilis*, from *placare* to appease.

placard /'plakɑːd/ ▻ *noun* a board or stiff card bearing a notice, advertisement, slogan, message of protest, etc, carried or displayed in public. ▻ *verb* (***placarded***, ***placarding***) **1** to put placards on (a wall, etc). **2** to announce (a forthcoming event, etc) by placard. ◷ 15c: French, from *plaquier* to lay flat or plaster, from Flemish *placken* to plaster.

placate /plə'keɪt, pleɪ-/ ▻ *verb* (***placated***, ***placating***) to pacify or appease (someone who is angry, etc). • **placation** *noun*. • **placatory** *adj*. ◷ 17c: from Latin *placere* to appease.

place /pleɪs/ ▻ *noun* **1** a portion of the Earth's surface, particularly one considered as a unit, such as an area, region, district, locality, etc. **2** a geographic area or position, such as a country, city, town, village, etc. **3** a building, room, piece of ground, etc, particularly one assigned to some purpose ▫ *place of business* ▫ *place of worship*. **4** *colloq* one's home or lodging ▫ *Let's go to my place*. **5** *in compounds* somewhere with a specified association or function ▫ *one's birthplace* ▫ *a hiding-place*. **6** a seat or space, eg at table ▫ *lay three places*. **7** a seat in a theatre, on a train, bus, etc. **8** an area on the surface of something, eg on the body ▫ *point to the sore place*. **9** the customary position of something or someone ▫ *put it back in its place*. **10** a point reached, eg in a conversation, narrative, series of developments, etc ▫ *a good place to stop*. **11** a point in a book, etc, especially where one stopped reading ▫ *made me lose my place*. **12** a position within an order eg of competitors in a contest, a set of priorities, etc ▫ *finished in third place* ▫ *lost his place in the queue* ▫ *lets her family take second place*. **13** social or political rank ▫ *know one's place* ▫ *corruption in high places*. **14** a vacancy at an institution, on a committee, in a firm, etc ▫ *gain a university place*. **15** one's role, function, duty, etc ▫ *It's not my place to tell him*. **16** a useful role ▫ *There's a place for judicious lying*. **17 a** an open square or a row of houses ▫ *the market place*; **b** (**Place**) used in street names ▫ *Buccleuch Place*. **18** *math* the position of a number in a series, especially of decimals after the point. ▻ *verb* (***placed***, ***placing***) **1** to put, position, etc in a particular place. **2** to submit ▫ *place an order* ▫ *place an advertisement*. **3** to find a place, home, job, publisher, etc for someone ▫ *The agency were able to place her immediately with a company*. **4** to assign final positions to (contestants, etc) ▫ *was placed fourth*. **5** to identify or categorize ▫ *a familiar voice that I couldn't quite place*. **6** *commerce* to find a buyer for (stocks or shares, usually a large quantity of them). **7** to arrange (a bet, loan, etc). **8** *intr*, *especially N Amer* to finish a race or competition (in a specified position or, if unspecified, in second position) ▫ *The favourite placed third*. • **all over the place** in disorder or confusion. • **be placed 1** *horse-racing*, *athletics* to finish as one of the first three or, in some races, the first four. **2** to be in a position to do something ▫ *was well placed to influence the decision*. • **fall into place** to become clear; to make sense. • **give place to someone** or **something** to make way for or yield to them. • **go places** *colloq* **1** to travel. **2** to be successful. • **in place** in the correct position. • **in place of something** or **someone** instead of it or them. • **in the first place** in any event; anyway ▫ *I never liked it in the first place*. • **in the first, second**, *etc* **place** used to introduce successive points. • **in places** here and there. • **in your**, *etc* **place** if I were you, etc. • **know one's place** to show proper subservience (to someone, an organization, etc). • **lose one's place** to falter in following a text, etc; not to know what point has been reached. • **lose the place** *colloq* to become angry. • **out of place 1** not in the correct position. **2** inappropriate. • **put** or **keep someone in their place** to humble them as they deserve because of their arrogance, conceit, etc. • **take one's place** to assume one's usual or rightful position. • **take place** to happen, occur, be held, etc ▫ *the ceremony takes place next week in London*. • **take the place of someone** or **something** to replace or supersede them. ◷ 13c: from Anglo-Saxon *plæce* and French *place* an open place or street.

placebo /plə'siːboʊ/ ▻ *noun* (***placebos***) **1** *medicine* a substance that is administered as a drug but has no medicinal content, either given to a patient for its reassuring and therefore beneficial effect (the **placebo effect**), or used in a clinical trial of a real drug, in which participants who have been given a placebo (though believing that it is the real drug) serve as untreated CONTROL subjects for comparison with those actually given the drug. **2** *RC Church* the vespers for the dead. ◷ 18c in sense 1; 13c in sense 2: Latin, meaning 'I shall please', from the first word of the first antiphon of the vespers service, starting *Placebo Domino* I shall please the Lord.

place card ▻ *noun* a small card at someone's place at table, bearing their name.

place kick ▻ *noun*, *rugby* a kick made with the ball placed ready on the ground. Compare DROP KICK. • **place kicker** *noun*.

placeman ▻ *noun*, *colloq* someone appointed by a government, etc to a committee or organization and expected to represent the appointer's opinion. ◷ 18c.

place mat ▻ *noun* a table mat for use in a place setting.

placement ▻ *noun* **1** the act or process of placing or positioning. **2** the finding of a job or home for someone. **3** a temporary job providing work experience, especially for someone on a training course.

placename ▻ *noun* the name of a town, village, hill, lake, etc.

placenta /plə'sɛntə/ ▻ *noun* (***placentas*** or ***placentae*** /-tiː/) **1** in mammals: a disc-shaped organ attached to the lining of the uterus during pregnancy and through which the embryo obtains nutrients and oxygen. **2** *bot* in seed-bearing plants: that part of the ovary to which the ovules are attached. • **placental** *adj*. ◷ 17c: Latin, from Greek *plax*, *plakos* flat.

place of work see WORKPLACE

placer /'plasə(r), 'pleɪsə(r)/ ▻ *noun*, *mining* a superficial deposit containing gold or other valuable minerals, which can be washed from the deposit. ◷ 19c: American Spanish, meaning 'sandbank', from *plaza* place.

place setting see SETTING *noun* 2

placet /'pleɪsɛt, 'plakɛt/ ▻ *noun* **1** a vote of assent in a governing body. **2** *historical* permission given, especially by a sovereign, to publish and carry out an ecclesiastical order, such as a papal bull or edict. ◷ 16c: Latin, meaning 'it pleases', from *placere* to please.

placid /'plasɪd/ ▻ *adj* calm; tranquil. • **placidity** /plə'sɪdɪtɪ/ or **placidness** *noun*. • **placidly** *adverb*. ◷ 17c: from Latin *placidus*, from *placere* to please.

placket /'plakɪt/ ▷ *noun, dressmaking* **1** an opening in a skirt for a pocket or at the fastening. **2** a piece of material sewn behind this. ◷ 17c, originally meaning 'breastplate', a variant of *placard* (in the same sense).

placoderm /'plakoʊdɜːm/ *palaeontol* ▷ *adj* said of some fossil fishes: covered with bony plates. ▷ *noun* **1** a fish covered in this way. **2** a class of aquatic CHORDATES of the DEVONIAN period, which are vertebrates with armour formed of skin plates. ◷ 19c: from Greek *plax, plakos* anything flat + *derma* skin.

placoid /'plakɔɪd/ ▷ *adj, zool* **1** said of scales: plate-like. **2** said of fish, eg sharks: having irregular plates or scales of hard bone that do not overlap. ◷ 19c: from Greek *plax, plakos* anything flat.

plafond /plə'fɒn, pla'fɔ̃/ ▷ *noun* **1** a ceiling, especially a decorated one. **2** an earlier version of CONTRACT BRIDGE. ◷ 17c: French, meaning 'ceiling', from *plat* flat + *fond* bottom.

plagal /'pleɪgəl/ ▷ *adj, music* said of a Gregorian MODE (sense 4a): having the FINAL in the middle of the SCALE[1] (*noun* 7). Compare AUTHENTIC.

plagiarism /'pleɪdʒərɪzəm/ ▷ *noun* **1** an act of plagiarizing. **2** something plagiarized. • **plagiarist** *noun*. ◷ 17c: from early 17c *plagiary* a kidnapper, later a plagiarist, from Latin *plagiarius* kidnapper, from *plaga* a net.

plagiarize or **plagiarise** /'pleɪdʒəraɪz/ ▷ *verb* (***plagiarized, plagiarizing***) *tr & intr* to copy (ideas, passages of text, etc) from someone else's work and use them as if they were one's own. ◷ 18c; see PLAGIARISM.

plagioclase /'pleɪdʒɪoʊkleɪz/ ▷ *noun, mineralogy* a group of feldspars whose cleavages are not at right angles. ◷ Late 19c: from Greek *plagios* oblique + *klasis* fracture.

plagiostome /'pleɪdʒɪoʊstoʊm/ ▷ *noun, zool* a fish, such as the shark, whose mouth is a transverse slit on the underside of the head. ◷ 19c: from Greek *plagios* oblique + *stoma* mouth.

plague /pleɪg/ ▷ *noun* **1** *medicine* **a** any of several epidemic diseases with a high mortality rate; **b** specifically, an infectious epidemic disease of rats and other rodents, caused by a bacterium and transmitted to humans by flea bites, eg BUBONIC PLAGUE. **2** an overwhelming intrusion by something unwelcome □ *a plague of tourists.* **3** *colloq* a nuisance. **4** an affliction regarded as a sign of divine displeasure □ *a plague on both your houses.* ▷ *verb* (***plagued, plaguing***) **1** to afflict someone □ *plagued by headaches.* **2** to pester someone; to annoy them continually. • **avoid something like the plague** to keep well away from it; to shun it absolutely. ◷ 14c: from Latin *plaga* blow, disaster or pestilence.

plaguesome ▷ *adj, colloq* troublesome; annoying.

plaice /pleɪs/ ▷ *noun* (*plural* ***plaice***) **1** a flatfish that has a brown upper surface covered with bright orange spots,

Some Common Elements of Placenames

element	meaning	example
Aber-	mouth of a river…	Aberdeen, 'place at the mouth of the River Don'
Ard-	height, upland	Ardglass (Co Down), 'green height'
Auchen-/Auchin-	field	Auchencloich (Ayrshire), 'field with the boulder stone'
Auchter-	height, upland	Auchterarder (Perthshire), 'upland of the high stream'
Bally-	farm, village	Ballymena (Co Antrim,) 'middle village'
Blair-	plain, field	Blairgowrie (Perthshire), 'plain of the goat'
-b(o)rough/-burgh/ -bury	fortified place	Middlesbrough, 'middle fortified place' Roxburgh (Borders), 'Hroc's fortified place' Avebury (Wiltshire), 'Afa's fortified place'
Burn-/-burn/-bourne	stream, spring	Burnham (various), 'settlement by a stream' Broxburn (West Lothian), 'badger steam' Sittingbourne (Kent), 'stream of the slope-dwellers'
-by	farmstead, village	Ashby de la Zouch (Leicestershire), 'farm with ash trees, owned by feudal lord de la Zouch'
-caster/-cester/ -chester	city, Roman fortification	Lancaster, 'Roman station on the River Lune' Cirencester (Gloucestershire), 'Roman station at Corinium', Manchester, 'Roman fort at Mancunium'
-combe/-coombe	valley	Ilfracombe (Devon), 'valley of the people of Ielfred'
-dean/-den	valley, pasture	Figheldean (Wiltshire), 'Fygla's valley' Howden (Yorkshire), 'chief valley'
-ham	village, homestead	Caterham (Surrey), 'homestead by the throne-like hill'
-hampton	high farm, homestead	Wolverhampton, 'Wulfrun's high farm'
-holme/-hulme	small island	Levenshulme (Lancashire), 'Leofwine's island'
-hurst/-hirst	hillock, copse	Sissinghurst (Kent), 'wooden hill of Seaxa's people'
Inver-/-inver	mouth of a river	Inverness, 'place at the mouth of the River Ness'
Kin-	head of	Kinloch (various), 'place at the head of the loch'
Kil-	church	Kilmarnock (Ayrshire), 'church of St Ernan'
Kirk-/-kirk	church	Kirkby (various), 'village with a church' Falkirk (Stirlingshire), 'place of the speckled church'
Llan-	church	Llantrisant (Glamorgan), 'church of the three saints'
Pen-	top, hill, end	Penicuik (Lothian), 'hill of the cuckoo'
-rith/-reth	stream	Penrith (Cumbria), 'stream by a hill'
Shaw-/-shaw	small wood	Shawbury (Shropshire), 'place by a copse' Ushaw (Durham), 'wolves' wood'
Stoke-/-stoke	manor, religious place	Stokesay (Shropshire), 'manor held by Hugh de Sei'
Strath-	broad valley	Strathblane (Stirlingshire), 'place in the valley of the little flowers'
-thorpe	farm, secondary settlement	Swanthorpe (Hampshire), 'farm of the swineherds'
-thwaite	meadow, clearing	Southwaite (Cumbria), 'clay clearing'
Tor-	rock, rocky peak	Torbryan (Devon), 'rocky place held by Wydo de Brianne'
-wick/-wich	farm, dairy farm, saltworks	Fenwick (Ayrshire), 'dairy farm by a fen' Nantwich (Cheshire), 'renowned saltworks'

and is an important food fish. **2** *N Amer* any of several related fishes. ◷ 13c: from French *plais*, from Latin *platessa* flatfish.

plaid /plad, pleɪd/ ▻ *noun* **1** tartan cloth. **2** a long piece of woollen cloth worn over the shoulder, usually tartan and worn with a kilt as part of Scottish Highland dress, or checked as formerly worn by Lowland shepherds. **3** *as adj* with a tartan pattern or in tartan colours ▫ ***plaid trousers.*** ◷ 16c: from Gaelic *plaide* blanket.

Plaid Cymru /plaɪd 'kʌmrɪ/ ▻ *noun* the Welsh nationalist party. ◷ 1940s: Welsh, meaning 'party of Wales'.

plain /pleɪn/ ▻ *adj* **1** all of one colour; unpatterned; undecorated. **2** simple; unsophisticated; without improvement, embellishment or pretensions ▫ ***plain food*** ▫ ***not Dr or Professor, just plain Mr.*** **3** obvious; clear. **4** straightforward; direct ▫ ***plain language*** ▫ ***plain dealing.*** **5** frank; open. **6** said of a person: lacking beauty. **7** sheer; downright ▫ ***plain selfishness.*** ▻ *noun* **1** a large area of relatively smooth flat land without significant hills or valleys. **2** *knitting* the simpler of two basic stitches, with the wool passed round the front of the needle. See also PURL. ▻ *adverb* utterly; quite ▫ ***just plain stupid.*** • **plainly** *adverb.* • **plainness** *noun.* • **plain as a pikestaff** all too obvious. ◷ 13c: French, from Latin *planus* level.

plainchant see PLAINSONG

plain chocolate ▻ *noun* dark-coloured chocolate made without milk.

plain clothes ▻ *plural noun* ordinary clothes worn by police officers on duty, as distinct from a uniform. ▻ *adj* (**plain-clothes** or **plain-clothed**) said of police officers on duty: wearing ordinary clothes, not uniformed.

plain flour ▻ *noun* flour that contains no raising agent. Compare SELF-RAISING FLOUR.

plain Jane *derog colloq* ▻ *noun* (***plain Janes***) a plain and ordinary woman or girl. ▻ *adj* (**plain-Jane**) said especially of clothes: ordinary; plain. ◷ Early 20c.

plain language ▻ *noun* straighforward, uncomplicated, understandable language.

plainly and **plainness** see under PLAIN

plain sailing ▻ *noun* **1** easy unimpeded progress. **2** *naut* sailing in unobstructed waters. Compare PLANE SAILING.

plainsong or **plainchant** ▻ *noun* in the medieval Church, and still in the RC and some Anglican churches: music for unaccompanied voices, sung in unison. ◷ 16c.

plain-spoken ▻ *adj* frank to the point of bluntness.

plaint /pleɪnt/ ▻ *noun* **1** *poetic* an expression of woe; a lamentation. **2** *law* a written statement of grievance against someone, submitted to a court of law. ◷ 13c: from French *plainte*, from Latin *planctus* a blow.

plaintiff /'pleɪntɪf/ ▻ *noun, law* someone who brings a case against another person in a court of law. See also DEFENDANT. ◷ 14c: from French *plaintif* complaining, from Latin *planctus* PLAINT.

plaintive /'pleɪntɪv/ ▻ *adj* mournful-sounding; sad; wistful. • **plaintively** *adverb.* • **plaintiveness** *noun.* ◷ 16c in this sense; 14c meaning 'complaining': from French *plaintif.*

plait /plat/ ▻ *verb* (***plaited, plaiting***) to arrange something (especially hair) by interweaving three or more lengths of it. ▻ *noun* a length of hair or other material interwoven in this way. • **plaited** *adj.* • **plaiter** *noun.* ◷ 14c: from French *pleit*, from Latin *plicare* to fold.

plan ▻ *noun* **1** a thought-out arrangement or method for doing something. **2** (*usually* **plans**) intentions ▫ ***What are your plans for today?*** **3** a sketch, outline, scheme or set of guidelines. **4** a large-scale detailed drawing or diagram of a floor of a house, the streets of a town, etc done as though viewed from above. Often *in compounds* ▫ ***floor plan*** ▫ ***street plan.*** ▻ *verb* (***planned, planning***) **1** (*also* **plan for something**) to devise a scheme for it. **2** (*also* **plan for something**) to make preparations or arrangements for it. **3** *intr* to prepare; to make plans ▫ ***plan ahead.*** **4** (*also* **plan on something**) to intend or expect it. **5** to draw up plans for (eg a building); to design. • **not plan on** or **for something** not to reckon on or allow for it; to be surprised or embarrassed by it ▫ ***had not planned on all of them coming when I ordered the wine.*** ◷ 17c: French, meaning 'ground plan', from Latin *planus* flat.

planar see under PLANE²

planarian /plə'nɛərɪən/ ▻ *noun, zool* any of several kinds of aquatic flatworm. ◷ 19c: from the genus name *Planaria*, from Latin *planarius* flat.

planchet /'plɑːnʃɪt/ ▻ *noun* a blank disk to be stamped as a coin. ◷ 17c: diminutive of *planch* slab of metal.

Planck's constant /plaŋks —/ ▻ *noun, physics* (symbol ***h***) a fundamental constant, equal to 6.626×10^{-34} joule seconds, that relates the energy E of a quantum of light to its frequency v by the equation $E = hv$. ◷ Early 20c: named after Max Planck (1858–1957), German physicist.

plane¹ /pleɪn/ ▻ *noun* an AEROPLANE. ◷ Early 20c: short form.

plane² /pleɪn/ ▻ *noun* **1** *math* a flat surface, either real or imaginary, such that a straight line joining any two points lies entirely on it. **2** a level surface. **3** a level or standard ▫ ***on a higher intellectual plane.*** ▻ *adj* **1** flat; level. **2** having the character of a plane. **3** *math* lying in one plane ▫ ***a plane figure*** ▫ ***plane geometry.*** ▻ *verb* (***planed, planing***) *intr* **1** said of a boat: to skim over the surface of the water. **2** said of a bird: to wheel or soar with the wings motionless. • **planar** /'pleɪnə(r)/ *adj* **1** relating to a plane. **2** lying in a single plane. **3** flat. • **planeness** *noun.* ◷ 17c: from Latin *planum* level surface.

plane³ /pleɪn/ ▻ *noun* a carpenter's tool for smoothing wood by shaving away unevennesses. ▻ *verb* (***planed, planing***) (*also* **plane something down**) to smooth (a surface, especially wood) with a plane. • **planer** *noun* **1** someone who uses a plane. **2** a tool or machine for planing. ◷ 14c: French, from Latin *planare* to smooth.

■ **plane something off** or **away** to remove it from a surface with a plane.

plane⁴ /pleɪn/ ▻ *noun* **1** any of various large deciduous trees with pendulous bur-like fruits and thin bark which is shed in large flakes, revealing creamy or pink patches on the trunk. Also called **plane tree.** **2** *Scots* the sycamore. ◷ 14c: French, from Latin *platanus*, from Greek *platanos*, from *platys* broad.

plane angle ▻ *noun, geom* the two-dimensional angle formed by two lines in a plane figure (see PLANE² *adj* 3) such as a polygon. Compare SOLID ANGLE.

plane sailing ▻ *noun, naut* the calculation of a ship's place in its course as if the Earth were flat instead of spherical. Compare PLAIN SAILING. ◷ 17c.

planet /'planɪt/ ▻ *noun* **1** *astron* **a** a celestial body, in orbit around the Sun or another star, which has too small a mass to become a star itself, and shines by reflecting light from the star around which it revolves; **b** one of nine such bodies, Mercury, Venus, Earth, Mars, Jupiter, Saturn, Uranus, Neptune and Pluto, that revolve around the Sun in the solar system. Also called **major planet.** **c** a satellite of a planet. Also called **secondary planet.** **2** *astrol* the Sun, Moon, Mercury, Venus, Mars, Jupiter, Saturn, Uranus, Neptune or Pluto, thought to influence signs of the ZODIAC and used in the interpretation of horoscopes. ◷ 13c: from French *planète*, from Greek *planetes* wanderer.

planetarium /planə'tɛərɪəm/ ▻ *noun* (***planetaria*** /-rɪə/ or ***planetariums***) **1** a special projector by means of which the positions and movements of stars and planets can be projected on to a hemispherical domed ceiling in order to simulate the appearance of the night sky to an audience seated below. **2** the building that houses such a projector. ◐ 1920s in these senses; 18c referring to an ORRERY: from Latin *planetarius* planetary.

planetary /'planɪtərɪ/ ▷ *adj* **1** *astron* **a** relating to or resembling a planet; **b** consisting of or produced by planets; **c** revolving in an orbit. **2** *astrol* under the influence of a planet. **3** erratic.

planetoid /'planɪtɔɪd/ ▷ *noun, astron* a MINOR PLANET. ◐ 19c; see -OID.

planetology /planɪ'tɒlədʒɪ/ ▷ *noun, astron* the scientific study of the planets, their natural satellites and the interplanetary material of the solar system, including the asteroids and meteors. • **planetologist** *noun*. ◐ Early 20c.

plane tree see PLANE[4] (sense 1)

plangent /'plandʒənt/ ▷ *adj* said of a sound: deep, ringing and mournful. • **plangency** *noun*. • **plangently** *adverb*. ◐ 19c: from Latin *plangere* to beat or to lament aloud.

planimeter /plə'nɪmɪtə(r)/ ▷ *noun, engineering* an instrument that measures the area of an irregular plane surface (see PLANE[2]) by tracing its boundary. ◐ 19c: *plani-* (from Latin *planus* level) + -METER.

planing *present participle of* PLANE[2], PLANE[3]

planing-machine ▷ *noun* a machine used to PLANE[3] wood or metals.

planish /'planɪʃ/ ▷ *verb* (***planishes, planished, planishing***) **1** to polish (metal, etc). **2** to flatten (sheet metal, etc). • **planisher** *noun* a person or tool that planishes. ◐ 16c: from French *planissant*, from *planir* to smooth, from *plan* flat.

planisphere /'planɪsfɪə/ ▷ *noun* a sphere projected on a plane surface (see PLANE[2]). ◐ 14c: from Latin *planispharium*, from Latin *planus* flat + Greek *sphaira* SPHERE.

plank ▷ *noun* **1** a long flat piece of timber thicker than a board. **2** any of the policies forming the platform or programme of a political party. ▷ *verb* (***planked, planking***) to fit or cover something with planks. • **walk the plank** to be made by pirates to walk blindfold along a plank projecting over a ship's side until one falls into the sea and drowns. ◐ 14c: from French *planche* plank or small wooden bridge, from Latin *planca* board.

■ **plank something down** *colloq* to put it down roughly or noisily.

planking ▷ *noun* planks, or a surface, etc constructed of them.

plankton /'plaŋktən/ ▷ *noun, biol* microscopic animals and plants that passively float or drift with the current in the surface waters of seas and lakes. Compare NEKTON. • **planktonic** /-'tɒnɪk/ *adj*. ◐ 19c: from Greek *planktos* wandering.

planned economy see under COMMAND ECONOMY

planner ▷ *noun* **1** someone who draws up plans or designs ▫ ***a town planner***. **2** a wall calendar showing the whole year, on which holidays, etc can be marked, used for forward planning.

planning *present participle of* PLAN

planning permission ▷ *noun, Brit* permission required from a local authority to erect or convert a building or to change the use to which a building or piece of land is put.

plano- /pleɪnoʊ, planoʊ/ ▷ *combining form, signifying* flatness or planeness (see under PLANE[2]).

plano-concave ▷ *adj* said of a lens: characterized by being flat or PLANE[2] on one side and CONCAVE on the other. ◐ 17c.

plano-convex ▷ *adj* said of a lens: characterized by being flat or PLANE[2] on one side and CONVEX on the other. ◐ 17c.

planographic printing ▷ *noun* any method of printing from a flat surface, eg LITHOGRAPHY. ◐ 19c.

plant /plɑːnt/ ▷ *noun* **1** any living organism that is capable of manufacturing carbohydrates by the process of photosynthesis and that typically possesses cell walls containing cellulose. **2** a relatively small organism of this type, eg a herb or shrub as opposed to a tree. **3** the buildings, equipment and machinery used in the manufacturing or production industries, eg a factory, a power station, etc. **4** *colloq* something deliberately placed for others to find and be misled by. **5** *colloq* a spy placed in an organization in order to gain information, etc. **6** *snooker* a shot in which the player pockets (see POCKET *verb* 3), or tries to pocket, a red ball by causing it to be propelled by another red ball which has been struck by the cue ball or by some other red ball. ▷ *verb* (***planted, planting***) **1** to put (seeds or plants) into the ground to grow. **2** (*often* **plant something out**) to put plants or seeds into (ground, a garden, bed, etc). **3** to introduce (an idea, doubt, etc) into someone's mind. **4** to place something firmly. **5** to post someone as a spy in an office, factory, etc. **6** *colloq* to place something deliberately so as to mislead the finder, especially as a means of incriminating an innocent person. **7** to establish (a colony, etc). • **plantable** *adj*. ◐ Anglo-Saxon: from Latin *planta* a shoot or sprig.

■ **plant something on someone** to give them (a kiss or blow).

plantain[1] /'plantɪn/ ▷ *noun* **1** a plant belonging to the banana family, widely cultivated in humid tropical regions for its edible fruit. **2** the green-skinned banana-like edible fruit of this plant, which has a high starch content when ripe and can be cooked and eaten as a vegetable. ◐ 16c: from Spanish *plátano*.

plantain[2] /'plantɪn/ ▷ *noun* any of numerous northern temperate plants with a basal rosette of narrow lance-shaped to broadly oval leaves and an erect spike of small tightly-clustered flowers. ◐ 14c: from Latin *plantago*, from *planta* sole of the foot (referring to the shape of the leaf).

plantar /plantə(r)/ ▷ *adj, anatomy* belonging or relating to the sole of the foot. ◐ 18c: from Latin *plantaris*, from *planta* sole of the foot.

plantation /plɑːn'teɪʃən/ ▷ *noun* **1** an estate, especially in the tropics, that specializes in the large-scale production of a single cash crop, eg tea, coffee, cotton or rubber. **2** an area of land planted with a certain kind of tree for commercial purposes ▫ ***a conifer plantation***. **3** *historical* a colony. ◐ 15c: from Latin *plantatio* a planting.

planter ▷ *noun* **1** the owner or manager of a plantation. **2** a device for planting bulbs, etc. **3** a container for house plants.

plantigrade /'plantɪgreɪd/ *zool* ▷ *adj* said of an animal: that walks with the entire lower surface of the foot in contact with the ground, eg humans and bears. ▷ *noun* such an animal. Compare DIGITIGRADE. ◐ 19c: from Latin *plantigradus*, from *planta* sole of the foot + *gradi* to walk.

plant louse ▷ *noun* an aphis or greenfly.

plant pot ▷ *noun* a pot for growing a plant in.

plantsman and **plantswoman** ▷ *noun* someone who has extensive knowledge of and experience in gardening. ◐ 19c.

plaque /plɑːk, plak/ ▷ *noun* **1** a commemorative inscribed tablet fixed to or set into a wall. **2** a wall ornament made of pottery, etc. **3** *dentistry* a thin layer of food debris, bacteria and calcium salts that forms on the surface of teeth and may cause tooth decay. **4** *pathol* a raised area or patch on a body part or surface as a result of damage or disease. ◐ 19c: French, from *plaquer* to plate, from Dutch *placken* to patch.

plasm /'plazəm/ ▷ *noun* **1** *biol, in compounds and as combining form* a PROTOPLASM of the specified type ▫

cytoplasm □ *germ plasm*. **2** *physiol* PLASMA. ● **-plasmic** *combining form* forming adjectives corresponding to nouns in *-plasm*. ⓘ 19c in current senses.

plasma /'plazmə/ ▻ *noun* (***plasmas***) **1** *physiol* the colourless liquid component of blood or lymph, in which the blood cells are suspended. **2** *physics* a gas that has been heated to a very high temperature so that most of its atoms or molecules are broken down into free electrons and positive ions. **3** *geol* a bright green CHALCEDONY. ⓘ 18c: Latin, from Greek, meaning 'something moulded'.

plasma membrane see MEMBRANE sense 2

plasmapheresis /plazmə'fɛrəsɪs, plazməfə'riːsɪs/ ▻ *noun, medicine* the process of taking only the plasma from a blood donor, the blood cells being separated out by a centrifuge and returned to the donor. ⓘ Early 20c.

plasmatic /plaz'matɪk/ ▻ *adj* referring to, or occurring in, PLASMA.

plasmid /'plazmɪd/ ▻ *noun, biol* a small circular loop of DNA that moves from one bacterium to another, transferring genetic information and often endowing its host with useful characteristics, eg resistance to antibiotics. ⓘ 1950s.

plasmin /'plazmɪn/ ▻ *noun, physiol* FIBRINOLYSIN. ⓘ 1940s in this sense: from PLASMA.

plasminogen /plaz'mɪnədʒən/ ▻ *noun, physiol* the substance in blood plasma from which plasmin is formed. ⓘ 1940s.

plasmodesm /'plazmoudɛzəm/ ▻ *noun* (***plasmodesmata*** /-'dɛzmətə/) *bot* a thread of PROTOPLASM connecting cells. ⓘ Early 20c: from PLASMA + Greek *desmos* a chain.

plasmodium /plaz'moudɪəm/ ▻ *noun* (***plasmodia*** /-dɪə/) *biol* any of various species of parasitic protozoans that carry the micro-organisms which cause malaria in humans. ⓘ 19c.

-plast /plast/ *biol* ▻ *combining form, forming nouns, denoting* an ORGANELLE within a cell □ *chloroplast*. ⓘ From Greek *plastos* formed.

plaster /'plɑːstə(r)/ ▻ *noun* **1** a material consisting of lime, sand and water that is applied to walls when soft and dries to form a hard smooth surface. Also *as adj*. **2** a strip of material, usually with a lint pad and an adhesive backing, that is used for covering and protecting small wounds. Also called **sticking-plaster**. **3** PLASTER OF PARIS. ▻ *verb* (***plastered***, ***plastering***) **1** to apply plaster to (walls, etc). **2** (*usually* **plaster something with** or **on something**) *colloq* to coat or spread thickly □ *plaster gel on one's hair* □ *plaster one's hair with gel.* **3** to fix something with some wet or sticky substance □ *hair plastered to his skull.* **4** (*often* **plaster something with something**) to cover it liberally □ *walls plastered with pin-ups of Take That.* ● **plastering** *noun*. ● **plastery** *adj* like plaster. ⓘ Anglo-Saxon in an early sense of *noun* 2; 13c as *noun* 1: from French *plastre*, both from Latin *plastrum*, from Greek *emplastron* salve, from *en* on + *plassein* to mould or apply as a plaster.

plasterboard ▻ *noun* a material consisting of hardened plaster faced on both sides with paper or thin board, used to form or line interior walls.

plaster cast ▻ *noun* **1** a copy of an object, eg a sculpture, obtained by pouring a mixture of PLASTER OF PARIS and water into a mould formed from that object. **2** a covering of plaster of Paris for a broken limb, etc which immobilizes the limb while it heals, setting it in the desired position.

plastered ▻ *adj* **1** covered with PLASTER (*noun* 1). **2** *colloq* drunk; intoxicated.

plasterer ▻ *noun* **1** someone whose job is to apply plaster to walls, ceilings, etc. **2** an artist who works in plaster.

plaster of Paris ▻ *noun* a white powder consisting of a hydrated form of calcium sulphate (GYPSUM), mixed with water to make a paste that sets hard, used for sculpting and for making casts for broken limbs. ⓘ 15c: so called because originally prepared with gypsum taken from Montmartre in Paris.

plaster saint ▻ *noun* someone who pretends hypocritically to be virtuous. ⓘ 19c.

plasterwork ▻ *noun* **1** the finished work of a plasterer □ *The standard of his plasterwork is excellent.* **2** an ornate piece of plaster moulding, such as a cornice.

plastery see under PLASTER

plastic /'plastɪk, 'plɑː-/ ▻ *noun* **1** any of a large number of synthetic materials that can be moulded by heat and/or pressure into a rigid or semi-rigid shape, used to make bottles, bowls and other containers, fibres, film, packaging, toys, construction materials, etc. **2** *colloq* a credit card, or credit cards collectively □ *Can I pay with plastic?* ▻ *adj* **1** made of plastic. **2** easily moulded or shaped; pliant. **3** easily influenced. **4** *derog* artificial; lacking genuine substance. **5** said of money: in the form of, or funded by, a credit card. **6** relating to sculpture and modelling. ⓘ 17c: from Greek *plastikos* moulded, from *plassein* to mould.

plastic arts ▻ *plural noun* **a** the art of modelling or shaping in three dimensions, such as ceramics or sculpture; **b** art which is or appears to be three-dimensional.

plastic bomb ▻ *noun* a bomb made with plastic explosive.

plastic bullet ▻ *noun* a solid plastic cylinder fired by the police to disperse riots, etc.

plastic explosive ▻ *noun* an explosive substance resembling putty that can be moulded by hand, eg Semtex. ⓘ Early 20c.

Plasticine /'plastɪsiːn, 'plɑː-/ ▻ *noun, trademark* a non-hardening modelling material available in various colours, used especially by children. ⓘ Late 19c.

plasticity /pla'stɪsɪtɪ, plɑː-/ ▻ *noun* **1** the fact or property of being plastic. **2** the quality in a picture of appearing to be three-dimensional.

plasticize or **plasticise** /'plastɪsaɪz/ ▻ *verb* (***plasticized***, ***plasticizing***) *tr & intr* to make or become flexible, eg by adding a plasticizer.

plasticizer or **plasticiser** ▻ *noun, chem* an organic compound that is added to a rigid polymer in order to make it flexible and so more easily workable. ⓘ 1920s.

plastics ▻ *singular noun* the scientific study or industrial production of plastic materials.

plastic surgery ▻ *noun, medicine* the branch of surgery concerned with the repair or reconstruction of deformed or damaged tissue or body parts, the replacement of missing parts, and COSMETIC SURGERY. ● **plastic surgeon** *noun*.

plastid /'plastɪd/ ▻ *noun, bot* any of various highly specialized membrane-bound structures found within the CYTOPLASM of plant cells, eg chloroplasts. ⓘ 19c: German, from Greek *plastos* formed or moulded.

plastique /pla'stiːk/ ▻ *noun* graceful poses and movements in dancing. ⓘ 19c: French adjective, meaning 'plastic-like', used as a noun.

plastron /'plastrən/ ▻ *noun* **1** *zool* the ventral section of the shell of a turtle or tortoise. **2** *fencing* a fencer's wadded breast-shield. **3** the front of a DRESS SHIRT. **4** a separate ornamental front part of a woman's bodice. **5** *historical* a steel breastplate. ● **plastral** *adj*. ⓘ 16c: French, from Italian *piastrone*, from *piastra* breastplate.

platane or **platan** /'platən/ ▻ *noun* a PLANE TREE. ⓘ 14c: from Latin *platanus*, from Greek *platanos*, from *platys* broad.

plat du jour /plɑː duː 'ʒʊə(r)/ ▻ *noun* a dish on a restaurant menu specially recommended that day. Also called **dish of the day**. ⓘ Early 20c: French, meaning 'dish of the day'.

plate /pleɪt/ ▻ *noun* **1** a shallow dish, especially one made of earthenware or porcelain, for serving food on. Also *in compounds* □ *side plate* □ *dinner plate*. **2 a** the amount held by this; a PLATEFUL; **b** a portion served on a plate. **3** (*also* **collection plate**) a shallow vessel in which to take the collection in church. **4** a sheet of metal, glass or other rigid material. **5** a flat piece of metal, plastic, etc inscribed with a name, etc. Often *in compounds* □ *nameplate* □ *bookplate*. **6** gold and silver vessels or cutlery. **7 a** a gold or silver cup as the prize in a horse race, etc; **b** a race or contest for such a prize. See also SELLING PLATE. **8** a thin coating of gold, silver or tin applied to a base metal. Also called **plating** /pleɪtɪŋ/. **9** an illustration on glossy paper in a book. Compare BOOKPLATE. **10** *photog* a sheet of glass prepared with a light-sensitive coating for receiving an image. **11 a** a sheet of metal with an image engraved on it; **b** a print taken from one of these. **12** any of various surfaces set up with type ready for printing. **13 a** a rigid plastic fitting to which false teeth are attached; **b** a denture. **14** *geol* any of the rigid sections that make up the Earth's crust. See also PLATE TECTONICS. **15** *anatomy* a thin flat piece of bone or horn. **16** *baseball* a five-sided white slab at the home base. **17** (**plates**, *originally* **plates of meat**) *rhyming slang* the feet. **18** *building* a horizontal supporting timber. ▻ *verb* (***plated***, ***plating***) **1** to coat (a base metal) with a thin layer of a precious one. **2** to cover something with metal plates. • **plater** see separate entry. • **have a lot** or **much on one's plate** *colloq* to have a great deal of work, commitments, etc. • **hand** or **give someone something on a plate** *colloq* to present them with it without their having to make the least effort. ⓘ 13c: from French *plate* (feminine) something flat and *plat* (masculine) dish.

plateau /'platoʊ, pla'toʊ/ ▻ *noun* (***plateaux*** /-toʊ/ or ***plateaus*** /-toʊz/) **1** *geog* an extensive area of relatively flat high land, usually bounded by steep sides. **2** *econ* a stable unvarying condition of prices, etc after a rise □ *The production rate reached a plateau in August.* ▻ *verb* (***plateaued***, ***plateauing***) *intr* (*sometimes* **plateau out**) to reach a level; to even out. ⓘ 18c: from French *platel* something flat.

plated /'pleɪtɪd/ ▻ *adj* **1** covered with plates of metal. **2** *usually in compounds* covered with a coating of another metal, especially gold or silver. **3** *zool* said of an animal: armoured with hard scales or bone.

plateful ▻ *noun* (***platefuls***) **1** the amount a plate can hold. **2** (*usually* **platefuls**) *colloq* a great deal; a lot.

plate glass ▻ *noun* a high-quality form of glass that has been ground and polished to remove defects, used in shop windows, mirrors, etc. ▻ *adj* (**plate-glass**) **1** made with or consisting of plate glass. **2** said of a building: **a** having large plate-glass windows; **b** appearing to be built entirely of plate glass.

platelayer ▻ *noun* someone who lays and repairs railway lines. See PLATE RAIL.

platelet /'pleɪtlɪt/ ▻ *noun, physiol* in mammalian blood: any of the small disc-shaped cell fragments that are responsible for starting the formation of a blood clot when bleeding occurs. ⓘ 19c.

platen /'platən/ ▻ *noun* **1** in some printing-presses: a plate that pushes the paper against the type. **2** the roller of a typewriter. ⓘ 15c: from French *platine* metal plate.

plater ▻ *noun* **1** a metal, etc that is used to plate something. **2** someone who plates. **3** *horse-racing* a horse entered for a minor race, especially a SELLING RACE.

plate rack ▻ *noun* a rack for draining plates, dishes, etc on after washing them up.

plate rail ▻ *noun* a flat rail with a flange.

plate tectonics ▻ *singular noun, geol* a geological theory according to which the Earth's crust is composed of a small number of large plates of solid rock, whose movements in relation to each other are responsible for continental drift. See also TECTONICS. ⓘ 1960s.

platform /'platfɔːm/ ▻ *noun* **1** a raised floor for speakers, performers, etc. **2** the raised walkway alongside the track at a railway station, giving access to trains. **3** a floating installation moored to the sea bed, for oil-drilling, marine research, etc. Often *in compounds* □ *oil platform* □ *production platform*. **4** an open step at the back of some buses, especially older ones, for passengers getting on or off. **5 a** a very thick rigid sole for a shoe, fashionable particularly in the 1970s; **b** *as adj* □ *platform shoes*. **6** the publicly declared principles and intentions of a political party, forming the basis of its policies. **7** any situation that gives one access to an audience and that one can exploit to promote one's views. **8** see under PLATFORM GAME. ⓘ 16c: from French *platte forme* flat figure.

platform game ▻ *noun* a COMPUTER GAME in which the object is to progress to the next level, which is usually more difficult to complete than the one before.

plating see PLATE *noun 8*

platinic /plə'tɪnɪk/ ▻ *adj, chem* referring or relating to, or containing, platinum, especially in the tetravalent state.

platinize or **platinise** /'platɪnaɪz/ ▻ *verb* (***platinized***, ***platinizing***) to coat something with platinum. • **platinization** *noun*. ⓘ 19c.

platinous /'platɪnəs/ ▻ *adj, chem* referring or relating to, or containing bivalent platinum.

platinum /'platɪnəm/ ▻ *noun, chem* (symbol **Pt**, atomic number 78) a silvery-white precious metallic element that does not tarnish or corrode, used to make jewellery, coins, electrical contacts, thermocouples and surgical instruments. ⓘ 19c: Latin, from earlier *platina*, from Spanish *plata* silver.

platinum black ▻ *noun, chem* platinum in the form of a velvety black powder.

platinum-blonde or **platinum-blond** ▻ *adj* said of hair: having a silvery fairness. ▻ *noun* (**platinum blonde** or **platinum blond**) someone with hair of this colour. See usage note at BLONDE. ⓘ 1930s.

platinum disc ▻ *noun* **1** in Britain: **a** an album (ie an LP, CD, etc) that has sold 300 000 copies; **b** a single that has sold 600 000 copies. **2** in the US: an album or single that has sold one million copies. See also GOLD DISC, SILVER DISC. • **go platinum** *colloq* to sell the respective number of albums or singles, earning the artist a framed platinum disc from the recording company.

platitude /'platɪtjuːd/ ▻ *noun* an empty, unoriginal or redundant comment, especially one made as though it were important. ⓘ 19c: French, meaning 'flatness', from *plat* flat.

platitudinous /platɪ'tjuːdɪnəs/ ▻ *adj* **1** characterized by or of the nature of a platitude. **2** using platitudes. **3** full of platitudes.

Platonic /plə'tɒnɪk/ ▻ *adj* **1** belonging or relating to the Greek philosopher Plato. **2** (*usually* **platonic**) **a** said of human love: not involving sexual relations; **b** restricted to theorizing; not involving action. • **platonically** *adverb*. ⓘ 16c.

Platonic solid ▻ *noun, math* any of five solids whose faces are congruent regular polygons. These are the TETRAHEDRON, the CUBE, the OCTAHEDRON, the DODECAHEDRON and the ICOSAHEDRON.

Platonism /'pleɪtənɪzəm/ ▻ *noun* any philosophical position which includes many of the central features of Plato's philosophy. These include a belief in a transcendent realm of abstract entities, the power of reason to know these entities, bodily separability and the immortality of the soul. • **Platonist** *noun*.

platoon /plə'tuːn/ ▷ *noun* **1** *military* a subdivision of a COMPANY. **2** a squad of people acting in co-operation. ◷ 17c: from French *peloton*, diminutive of *pelote* ball.

Plattdeutsch see LOW GERMAN

platteland /'plɑːtəlɑːnt/ ▷ *noun, S Afr* rural districts. ◷ 1930s: Afrikaans, from Dutch *plat* flat + *land* country.

platter /'platə(r)/ ▷ *noun* **1** a large flat dish. **2** *N Amer colloq* a record (*noun* 4). ◷ 14c: from French *plater*, from *plat* plate.

platy- /'platɪ/ ▷ *combining form, signifying* flat or broad. ◷ From Greek *platys* broad.

platypus /'platɪpəs, 'platɪpus/ ▷ *noun* (***platypuses***) an egg-laying amphibious mammal with dense brown fur, a long flattened toothless snout, webbed feet and a broad flat tail, found in Tasmania and E Australia. Also called **duck-billed platypus**. ◷ 18c: Latin, from Greek *platys* broad + *pous* foot.

platyrrhine /'platɪraɪn/ *zool* ▷ *adj* **1** said of a human: broad-nosed. **2** said of a monkey: belonging to a S American division of monkeys with widely spaced nostrils. ▷ *noun* a New World monkey. ◷ 19c: from Greek *platys* broad + *rhis, rhinos* nose.

plaudit /'plɔːdɪt/ ▷ *noun* (*usually* **plaudits**) a commendation; an expression of praise. ◷ 17c: from Latin *plaudite*, imperative of *plaudere* to praise.

plausible /'plɔːzɪbəl/ ▷ *adj* **1** said of an explanation, etc: credible, reasonable or likely. **2** said of a person: characterized by having a pleasant and persuasive manner; smooth-tongued or glib. • **plausibility** or **plausibleness** *noun*. • **plausibly** *adverb*. ◷ 16c: from Latin *plausibilis* deserving applause.

play ▷ *verb* (***played, playing***) **1** *intr* said especially of children: to spend time in recreation, eg dancing about, kicking a ball around, doing things in make-believe, generally having fun, etc. **2** *intr* to pretend for fun; to behave without seriousness. **3** (*also* **play at something**) to take part in (a recreative pursuit, game, sport, match, round, etc) □ *We played rounders* □ *played at rounders.* **4** (*also* **play against someone**) to compete against them in a game or sport □ *St Johnstone played Aberdeen last week.* **5** *intr, colloq* to co-operate □ *He refuses to play.* **6** *sport* to include someone as a team member □ *playing McGuire in goal.* **7** *sport* to hit or kick (the ball), deliver (a shot), etc in a sport. **8** *cards* to use (a card) in the course of a game □ *played the three of clubs.* **9** to speculate or gamble on (the Stock Exchange, etc) □ *playing the market.* **10** *tr & intr* **a** to act or behave in a certain way □ *play it cool* □ *not playing fair*; **b** to pretend to be someone or something □ *play the dumb blonde.* **11** to act (a particular role) □ *play host to the delegates.* **12** (*usually* **play in something**) *tr & intr* to perform a role in (a play) □ *played Oliver in the school play.* **13** *tr & intr* said especially of a pop group: to perform in (a particular place or venue) □ *Oasis played London last year.* **14** *intr* said of a film, play, etc: to be shown or performed publicly □ *playing all next week.* **15** *music* **a** to perform (a specified type of music) on an instrument □ *plays jazz on the saxaphone* □ *plays the sax*; **b** to perform on (an instrument) **16** to turn on (a radio, a tape-recording, etc). **17** *intr* **a** said of recorded music, etc: to be heard from a radio, etc; **b** said of a radio, etc: to produce sound. **18** *intr* said of a fountain: to be in operation. **19** to direct (a hose, etc). **20** *angling* to allow (a fish) to tire itself by its struggles to get away. ▷ *noun* **1** recreation; playing games for fun and amusement □ *children at play.* **2** the playing of a game, performance in a sport, etc □ *rain stopped play.* **3** *colloq* behaviour; conduct □ *fair play* □ *foul play.* **4** (***plays***) a dramatic piece for the stage or a performance of it □ *The play is being put on at the Playhouse.* **5** fun; jest □ *said in play.* **6** range; scope □ *give full play to the imagination.* **7** freedom of movement; looseness □ *too much play in the steering.* **8** action or interaction □ *play of sunlight on water* □ *play of emotions.* **9** use □ *bring all one's cunning into play.* **10** the display that animals make in courtship. • **in** or **out of play** *sport* said of a ball: in, or not in, a position where it may be played. • **make a play for something** to try to get (eg someone's attention). • **make great play of something** to emphasize it or stress its importance. • **make play with something** to make effective or over-obvious use of it. • **play ball** *colloq* to co-operate. • **play fast and loose** to act in an irresponsible, inconsistent and reckless way. • **play for time** to delay action or decision in the hope or belief that conditions will become more favourable later. • **play the field** to spread one's interests, affections or efforts over a wide range of subjects, people, activities, etc, rather than concentrating on any single thing or person. • **play the game** see under GAME[1]. • **play hard to get** to make a show of unwillingness to co-operate or lack of interest, with a view to strengthening one's position. • **play hell** or **havoc with something** to damage it; to upset things. • **play hookey** see under HOOKEY. • **play into the hands of someone** to act so as to give, usually unintentionally, an advantage to them. • **play it** *colloq* to behave in, or manage, a situation in the stated way □ *play it cool* □ *play it slowly* □ *I'm not sure how to play it.* • **play it** or **one's cards close to one's chest** to be secretive about one's actions or intentions in a particular matter. • **play it by ear** to improvise a plan of action to meet the situation as it develops. • **play merry hell with someone or something** to harm or damage. • **play a part in something** to be instrumental in it; to take part in it. • **play possum** see under POSSUM. • **play safe** to take no risks. • **play with fire** to take foolish risks. ◷ Anglo-Saxon *plegan*.

■ **play about** or **around** to behave ineffectively or irresponsibly.

■ **play about** or **around with someone** to behave irresponsibly towards them, their affections, etc.

■ **play about** or **around with something** to fiddle or meddle with it.

■ **play someone along** to manipulate them, usually for one's own advantage.

■ **play along with someone** to co-operate with them for the time being; to humour them.

■ **play at something 1** to make a pretence of it, especially in play □ *play at being cowboys.* **2** to indulge in it trivially or flippantly □ *play at politics.* **3** *ironic* to try to achieve it □ *What are they playing at?*

■ **play something back** to play (a film or sound recording) through immediately after making it. See also PLAYBACK.

■ **play something down** to represent it as unimportant; to minimize, make light of or discount it.

■ **play off 1** to replay a match, etc after a draw. **2** *golf* to play from the tee. See also PLAY-OFF.

■ **play one person off against another** to set them in rivalry, especially for one's own advantage.

■ **play on something 1** to exploit (someone's fears, feelings, sympathies, etc) for one's own benefit. **2** to make a pun on it □ *played on the two meanings of 'batter'.*

■ **play something on someone** to perpetrate (a trick or joke) against them.

■ **play something out** to act out in real life a part, scene, etc that is so predictable that it could have come from a play. See also PLAYED OUT.

■ **play over** or **across something** said eg of light, facial expression, etc: to flicker over, across, etc (a surface, etc).

■ **play up 1** *colloq* to behave unco-operatively. **2** *colloq* to cause one pain or discomfort □ *His stomach is* *playing up again.* **3** *colloq* said of a machine, etc: to function faultily. **4** to try one's hardest in a game, match, etc.

■ **play something up** to highlight it or give prominence to it.

■ **play up to someone** to flatter them; to ingratiate oneself with them.

■ **play with oneself** *colloq* to masturbate oneself.

■ **play with someone 1** said especially of children: to spend time in recreation with them. **2** *colloq* to joke with them at their expense □ *I think you're just playing with me.* **3** *slang* to masturbate them.

■ **play with something** to contemplate (an idea, plan, etc) □ *played with the idea of becoming a writer.*

playa /'plɑːjə/ ▷ *noun* (***playas***) a basin which becomes a shallow lake after heavy rainfall and dries out again in hot weather. ⓘ 19c: Spanish, meaning 'shore' or 'beach'.

playable ▷ *adj* **1** said of a pitch, ground, etc: fit to be played on. **2** said of a ball: lying where it can be played. • **playability** *noun*.

play-act ▷ *verb, intr* to behave in an insincere fashion, disguising one's true feelings or intentions. ⓘ Late 19c.

playback ▷ *noun* a playing back of a sound recording or film. See also PLAY SOMETHING BACK at PLAY.

playbill ▷ *noun* a poster that advertises a play or show.

playboy ▷ *noun* a man of wealth, leisure and frivolous lifestyle.

played out ▷ *adj* exhausted; lacking energy. See also PLAY SOMETHING OUT at PLAY.

player ▷ *noun* **1** someone who plays. **2** someone who participates in a game or sport, particularly as their profession. **3** *colloq* a participant in a particular activity, especially a powerful one □ *a major player in the mafia scene.* **4** a performer on a musical instrument □ *guitar player.* **5** *old use* an actor.

player piano ▷ *noun* a piano fitted with a machinery enabling it to be played automatically, eg a PIANOLA.

playfellow see PLAYMATE

playful ▷ *adj* **1** full of fun; frisky. **2** said of a remark, etc: humorous. • **playfully** *adverb*. • **playfulness** *noun*.

playground ▷ *noun* **1** an area for children's recreation, especially one that is part of a school's grounds. Compare RECREATION GROUND. **2** a resort for people who take frivolous recreation seriously □ *The area became a yuppies' playground.*

playgroup ▷ *noun* an organized group of preschool children that meets for regular supervised play.

playhouse ▷ *noun, old use* a theatre.

playing-card ▷ *noun* a rectangular card belonging to a PACK OF CARDS used in card games. See also ACE, COURT CARD.

playing field ▷ *noun* a grassy outdoor area prepared and marked out for playing games on. See also LEVEL PLAYING FIELD.

playlist ▷ *noun* a list of records, CDs, etc, to be played on a particular radio programme, at a club, etc, usually consisting of a particular type of music.

playmate or **playfellow** ▷ *noun* a companion to play with.

play-off ▷ *noun* (***play-offs***) a match or game played to resolve a draw or other undecided contest. See also PLAY OFF at PLAY.

play on words ▷ *noun* **1** a pun. **2** punning.

playpen ▷ *noun* a collapsible frame that when erected forms an enclosure inside which a baby may safely play.

playschool ▷ *noun* a PLAYGROUP, or a school for children between the ages of two and five.

plaything ▷ *noun* a toy, or a person or thing treated as if they were a toy.

playtime ▷ *noun* a period for recreation, especially a set period for playing out of doors as part of a school timetable.

playwright ▷ *noun* an author of plays (see PLAY *noun* 4).

plaza /'plɑːzə/ ▷ *noun* (***plazas***) **1** a large public square or market place, especially one in a Spanish town. **2** *N Amer* a shopping centre or complex. ⓘ 17c: Spanish.

PLC or **plc** ▷ *abbreviation* public limited company.

plea /pliː/ ▷ *noun* (***pleas***) **1** an earnest appeal. **2** *law* a statement made in a court of law by or on behalf of the defendant. **3** an excuse □ *refused the invitation on the plea of a headache.* ⓘ 13c: from French *plaid* agreement or decision.

plea bargaining ▷ *noun, law, especially US* the practice of arranging more lenient treatment by the court in exchange for the accused's pleading guilty to the crime or turning State's evidence, etc.

plead /pliːd/ ▷ *verb* (***pleaded*** or *especially N Amer & Scots* ***pled***, ***pleading***) **1** (*usually* **plead with someone for something**) to appeal earnestly to them for it □ *pleading for mercy.* **2** *intr* said of an accused person: to state in a court of law that one is guilty or not guilty □ *decided to plead guilty* □ *He pleaded not guilty.* **3** (*also* **plead for something**) to argue in defence of it □ *plead someone's case.* **4** to give something as an excuse □ *plead ignorance.* • **pleadable** *adj*. • **pleader** *noun*. ⓘ 13c: from French *plaidier*, from Latin *placitum* that which pleases or is agreed upon.

pleading ▷ *adj* appealing earnestly; imploring. ▷ *noun, law* the act of putting forward or conducting a plea. See also SPECIAL PLEADING. • **pleadingly** *adverb*.

pleadings ▷ *plural noun, law* the formal statements submitted by defendant and plaintiff in a lawsuit.

pleasant /'plɛzənt/ ▷ *adj* (***pleasanter***, ***pleasantest***) **1** giving pleasure; enjoyable; agreeable. **2** said of a person: friendly; affable. • **pleasantly** *adverb*. • **pleasantness** *noun*. ⓘ 14c: from French *plaisant*, from *plaisir* to please.

pleasantry /'plɛzəntrɪ/ ▷ *noun* (***pleasantries***) **1** (*usually* **pleasantries**) a remark made for the sake of politeness or friendliness. **2** humour; teasing.

please /pliːz/ ▷ *verb* (***pleased***, ***pleasing***) **1** *tr & intr* to give satisfaction, pleasure or enjoyment; to be agreeable to someone. **2** (*with it as subject*) *formal* to be the inclination of someone or something □ *if it should please you to join us.* **3** *tr & intr* to choose; to like □ *Do what you please* □ *Do as you please.* ▷ *adverb, exclamation* used politely to accompany a request, order, acceptance of an offer, protest, a call for attention, etc. • **if you please 1** *old use, as adverb* please. **2** *ironic* of all things □ *is engaged to a baronet, if you please.* • **please oneself** to do as one likes □ *Please yourself, then.* ⓘ 14c: from French *plaisir* to please.

pleased ▷ *adj* **1** (*especially* **pleased about** or **with someone** or **something**) happy; satisfied; contented. **2** glad; delighted. • **pleased as Punch** delighted. • **pleased with oneself** *derog* self-satisfied; conceited.

pleasing ▷ *adj* causing pleasure or satisfaction □ *a very pleasing result.* • **pleasingly** *adverb*.

pleasurable /'plɛʒərəbəl/ ▷ *adj* enjoyable; pleasant. • **pleasurably** *adverb*.

pleasure /'plɛʒə(r)/ ▷ *noun* **1** a feeling of enjoyment or satisfaction □ *take pleasure in one's surroundings.* **2** a source of such a feeling □ *have the pleasure of your company.* **3** one's will, desire, wish, preference or inclination. **4** recreation; enjoyment □ *combine business with pleasure.* Also *as adj* □ *a pleasure boat* □ *a pleasure* *trip*. **5** gratification of a sensual kind □ ***pleasure and pain.*** ▻ *verb* (***pleasured, pleasuring***) *old use* **1** to give pleasure to someone, especially sexual pleasure. **2** (*usually* **pleasure in something**) to take pleasure in it. • **a pleasure** or **my pleasure** as a polite expression: not at all; it's no trouble. • **at pleasure** when or as one likes. • **with pleasure** as a polite expression: gladly; willingly; of course. ⓒ 14c: from French *plaisir*.

pleat /pliːt/ ▻ *noun* a fold sewn or pressed into cloth, etc. ▻ *verb* (***pleated, pleating***) to make pleats in (cloth, etc). ⓒ 14c: a variant of PLAIT.

pleb ▻ *noun, derog* someone who has coarse or vulgar tastes, manners or habits. • **plebby** *adj.* ⓒ 19c: a shortening of PLEBEIAN.

plebeian /plə'bɪən/ ▻ *noun* **1** a member of the common people, especially of ancient Rome. **2** *derog* someone who lacks refinement or culture. ▻ *adj* **1** referring or belonging to the common people. **2** *derog* coarse; vulgar; unrefined. ⓒ 16c: from Latin *plebeius*, from *plebs* the people.

plebiscite /'plɛbɪsɪt, 'plɛbɪsaɪt/ ▻ *noun* a vote of all the electors, taken to decide a matter of public importance; a referendum. • **plebiscitary** /-'bɪsɪtrɪ/ *adj.* ⓒ 16c: from Latin *plebiscitum* a decree of the plebs, from *plebis* of the people + *scitum* decree.

plectrum /'plɛktrəm/ ▻ *noun* (***plectrums*** or ***plectra*** /-rə/) a small flat implement of metal, plastic, horn, etc used for plucking the strings of a guitar. ⓒ 17c: Latin, from Greek *plectron*, from *plessein* to strike.

pled *a past tense, past participle of* PLEAD

pledge /plɛdʒ/ ▻ *noun* **1** a solemn promise. **2** something left as security with someone to whom one owes money, etc. **3** something put into pawn. **4** a token or symbol □ ***a ring as a pledge of love.*** **5** a toast drunk as proof of friendship, etc. ▻ *verb* (***pledged, pledging***) **1** to promise (money, loyalty, etc) to someone. **2** to bind or commit (oneself, etc). **3** to offer or give something as a pledge or guarantee. **4** *old use* to drink the health of someone. • **pledgeable** *adj.* • **pledgee** *noun* (***pledgees***) the person to whom a thing is pledged. • **pledger, pledgeor** or **pledgor** *noun* the person who pledges something. • **take** or **sign the pledge** *facetious, old use* to undertake to drink no alcohol. ⓒ 14c: from French *plege*.

pledget /'plɛdʒɪt/ ▻ *noun* a wad of lint, cotton, etc used to cover a wound or sore. ⓒ 16c.

-plegia /'pliːdʒɪə/ ▻ *combining form, forming nouns, denoting* paralysis of a specified kind □ ***paraplegia*** □ ***quadriplegia.*** ⓒ From Greek *plege* stroke, from *plessein* to strike.

-plegic /'pliːdʒɪk/ ▻ *combining form, forming adjectives and nouns* corresponding to nouns in -PLEGIA □ ***quadriplegic.***

pleiad /'plaɪad/ ▻ *noun* a brilliant and talented group of, usually seven, people or things. ⓒ 19c: from French *Pléiade*, a name applied by Ronsard (1524–85) to himself and a group of six other French poets, from Greek *Pleiades* the cluster of stars in Taurus which in mythology are the seven daughters of Atlas who were changed into stars after their deaths.

plein air /plɛ'nɛə(r)/ ▻ *adj, art history* said of pictures especially landscapes: **a** giving a vivid sense of the light and atmosphere of the open air; **b** painted out of doors, instead of in the studio. ⓒ 19c: French, meaning 'open air'.

Pleiocene see PLIOCENE

Pleistocene /'plaɪstoʊsiːn/ ▻ *adj, geol* denoting the first epoch of the Quaternary period, which contains the greatest proportion of fossil molluscs of living species and during which modern man evolved. See table at GEOLOGICAL TIME SCALE. ⓒ 19c: from Greek *pleistos* most + -CENE.

plenary /'pliːnərɪ, 'plɛnərɪ/ ▻ *adj* **1** full; complete □ ***plenary powers.*** **2** said of a meeting, assembly, council, etc: to be attended by all members, delegates, etc. Compare PLENUM. • **plenarily** *adverb.* ⓒ 16c: from Latin *plenarius*, from *plenus* full.

plenary indulgence ▻ *noun, RC Church* full or complete remission of temporal penalties to a repentant sinner.

plenary powers ▻ *plural noun* full powers to carry out some business or negotiations.

plenipotentiary /plɛnɪpə'tɛnʃərɪ/ ▻ *adj* entrusted with, or conveying, full authority to act on behalf of one's government or other organization. ▻ *noun* (***plenipotentiaries***) someone, eg an ambassador, invested with such authority. ⓒ 17c: from Latin *plenus* full + *potentia* power.

plenitude /'plɛnɪtjuːd/ ▻ *noun* **1** abundance; profusion. **2** completeness; fullness. ⓒ 15c: from Latin *plenitudo*, from *plenus* full.

plenteous /'plɛntɪəs/ ▻ *adj, literary* plentiful; abundant. • **plenteously** *adverb.* • **plenteousness** *noun.* ⓒ 14c as *plentivous*: from French *plentif*, from *plente* plenty.

plentiful /'plɛntɪfəl/ ▻ *adj* in good supply; copious; abundant. • **plentifully** *adverb.* • **plentifulness** *noun.* ⓒ 15c: from PLENTY.

plenty /'plɛntɪ/ ▻ *noun* **1** (*often* **plenty of something**) a lot □ ***plenty of folk would agree.*** **2** wealth or sufficiency; a sufficient amount □ ***in times of plenty.*** ▻ *pronoun* **1** enough, or more than enough □ ***That's plenty, thank you.*** **2** a lot; many □ ***I'm sure plenty would agree with me*** (ie plenty of folk; many people). ▻ *adverb, colloq* fully □ ***That should be plenty wide enough.*** • **in plenty** *rather formal or old use* in abundant quantities. ⓒ 13c: from French *plente*, from Latin *plenitas* abundance, from *plenus* full.

plenum /'pliːnəm/ ▻ *noun* (***plenums*** or ***plena*** /-nə/) **1** a meeting attended by all members. Compare PLENARY. **2** *physics* a space completely filled with matter. Opposite of VACUUM. ⓒ 17c: Latin, a shortening of *plenum spatium* full space.

plenum chamber ▻ *noun* a sealed chamber containing pressurized air.

plenum system and **plenum ventilation** ▻ *noun, building, archit* an air-conditioning system in which the air propelled into a building is maintained at a higher pressure than the atmosphere.

pleomorphism /pliːoʊ'mɔːfɪzəm/ ▻ *noun* POLYMORPHISM (senses 1 and 2)

pleonasm /'plɪənazəm/ ▻ *noun, grammar, rhetoric* **1** the use of more words than are needed to express something. **2** a superfluous word or words. • **pleonastic** *adj.* • **pleonastically** *adverb.* ⓒ 16c: from Greek *pleonasmos* superfluity.

plesiosaur /'pliːsɪoʊsɔː(r)/ ▻ *noun* any of various large reptiles of the Jurassic and Cretaceous eras with a long neck, short tail and four flippers. ⓒ 19c: from Greek *plesios* near + SAUR.

plethora /'plɛθərə/ ▻ *noun* (***plethoras***) a large or excessive amount. ⓒ 16c: Latin, from Greek, meaning 'fullness'.

pleura /'plʊərə/ ▻ *noun* (***pleurae*** /-riː/) *anatomy* in mammals: the double membrane that covers the lungs and lines the chest cavity. • **pleural** *adj.* ⓒ 17c: Latin, from Greek *pleuron, pleura* side or rib.

pleurisy /'plʊərɪsɪ/ ▻ *noun, pathol, medicine* inflammation of the pleura. • **pleuritic** /-'rɪtɪk/ *adj.* ⓒ 14c: from French *pleurisie*.

Plexiglas /'plɛksɪglɑːs/ ▻ *noun, US trademark* a tough transparent plastic; POLYMETHYLMETHACRYLATE. See also PERSPEX. ⓒ 20c.

plexor /'plɛksə(r)/ and **plessor** /'plɛsə(r)/ ▻ *noun, medicine* a small hammer used in percussing. Also called percussion hammer, percussor. ⓒ 19c: from Greek *plexis* a stroke, from *plessein* to strike.

plexus /ˈplɛksəs/ ▷ *noun* (***plexus*** or ***plexuses***) *anatomy* a network of nerves or blood vessels, eg the SOLAR PLEXUS behind the stomach. ⓒ 17c: Latin, literally 'weaving'.

pliable /ˈplaɪəbəl/ ▷ *adj* **1** easily bent; flexible. **2** adaptable or alterable. **3** easily persuaded or influenced. • **pliability** or **pliableness** *noun*. • **pliably** *adverb*. ⓒ 15c: French, from *plier* to fold or bend.

pliant /ˈplaɪənt/ ▷ *adj* **1** bending easily; pliable, flexible or supple. **2** easily influenced. • **pliancy** *noun*. • **pliantly** *adverb*. ⓒ 14c: French, from *plier* to fold or bend.

plié /ˈpliːeɪ/ ▷ *noun, ballet* a movement in which the knees are bent while the body remains upright. ⓒ 19c: French, meaning 'bent'.

plied and **plier** see under PLY[2]

pliers /ˈplaɪəz/ ▷ *plural noun* a hinged tool with jaws for gripping small objects, bending or cutting wire, etc. ⓒ 16c: from PLY[2].

plies see PLY[1], PLY[2]

plight[1] /plaɪt/ ▷ *noun* a danger, difficulty or situation of hardship that one finds oneself in; a predicament. ⓒ 14c as *plit* a fold or condition: from French *pleit*, from Latin *plicare* to fold, influenced by the spelling of PLIGHT[2].

plight[2] /plaɪt/ ▷ *verb* (***plighted***, ***plighting***) *old use* to promise something solemnly; to pledge. • **plight one's troth** to pledge oneself in marriage. ⓒ Anglo-Saxon *pliht* peril or risk.

plimsoll or **plimsole** /ˈplɪmsəl/ ▷ *noun, old use* a light rubber-soled canvas shoe worn for gymnastics, etc. Also called **gym shoe**. ⓒ Early 20c: from the resemblance of the line of the sole to the PLIMSOLL LINE.

Plimsoll line and **Plimsoll mark** ▷ *noun* any of several lines painted round a ship's hull showing, for different conditions, the depth to which it may be safely and legally immersed when loaded. ⓒ 19c: these lines were required by the Merchant Shipping Act of 1876, put forward by Samuel Plimsoll (1824–98).

plinth /plɪnθ/ ▷ *noun* **1** *archit* a square block serving as the base of a column, pillar, etc. **2** a base or pedestal for a statue or other sculpture, or for a vase. ⓒ 17c: from Latin *plinthus*, from Greek *plinthos* a brick or stone block.

Pliocene or **Pleiocene** /ˈplaɪoʊsiːn/ ▷ *adj, geol* the last epoch of the Tertiary period, during which the climate became cooler, many mammals became extinct and primates that walked upright appeared. See table at GEOLOGICAL TIME SCALE. ⓒ Early 19c: from Greek *pleion* more + -CENE.

plissé /ˈpliːseɪ, ˈplɪ-/ ▷ *adj* said of a fabric: chemically treated to produce a shirred or wrinkled effect. ⓒ 19c: French, meaning 'pleated'.

PLO ▷ *abbreviation* Palestine Liberation Organization.

plod ▷ *verb* (***plodded***, ***plodding***) *intr* **1** to walk slowly with a heavy tread. **2** to work slowly, methodically and thoroughly, if without inspiration. ▷ *noun* a heavy walk. • **plodding** *adj, noun*. • **ploddingly** *adverb*. ⓒ 16c: an imitation of the sound of a heavy tread.

plodder ▷ *noun* **1** someone who plods on. **2** a dull uninteresting person. **3** someone who progresses by toil rather than by inspiration.

ploidy /ˈplɔɪdɪ/ ▷ *noun* (***ploidies***) *biol* the number of complete chromosome sets present in a cell or living organism. ⓒ 1940s: from HAPLOIDY, POLYPLOIDY, etc.

-ploitation ▷ *combining form, forming nouns* referring to the commercial exploitation of the specified things in film and other media □ *sexploitation* □ *blaxploitation*. ⓒ 1980s.

plonk[1] /plɒŋk/ ▷ *colloq, noun* the resounding thud made by a heavy object falling. ▷ *verb* (***plonked***, ***plonking***) **1** to put or place something with a thud or with finality □ *plonked himself in the best chair*. **2** *intr* to place oneself or to fall with a plonk. ▷ *adverb* with a thud □ *landed plonk beside her*. ⓒ 19c: imitating the sound.

plonk[2] /plɒŋk/ ▷ *noun, colloq* cheap, undistinguished wine. ⓒ Early 20c: originally Australian slang, probably a corruption of *blanc* in French *vin blanc* white wine.

plonker ▷ *noun* **1** *colloq* anything large, especially a smacking kiss. **2** *slang* a stupid person; an idiot. **3** *slang* the penis. ⓒ 19c; 20c in slang senses.

plook see PLOUK

plop ▷ *noun* the sound of a small object dropping into water without a splash. ▷ *verb* (***plopped***, ***plopping***) *tr & intr* to fall or drop with this sound. ▷ *adverb* with a plop. ⓒ 19c: imitating the sound.

plosive /ˈploʊsɪv, ˈploʊzɪv/ *phonetics* ▷ *adj* said of a consonant: made by the sudden release of breath after stoppage. ▷ *noun* a plosive consonant or sound, such as /p/, /t/, /k/, etc. ⓒ 19c: a shortening of EXPLOSIVE.

plot[1] ▷ *noun* **1** a secret plan, especially one laid jointly with others, for contriving something illegal or evil; a conspiracy. **2** the story or scheme of a play, film, novel, etc. ▷ *verb* (***plotted***, ***plotting***) **1** *tr & intr* to plan something (especially something illegal or evil), usually with others. **2** to make a plan of something; to mark the course or progress of something. **3** *math* to mark (a series of individual points) on a graph, or to draw a curve through them. • **plotless** *adj*. ⓒ 16c: from PLOT[2], influenced by French *complot* conspiracy.

plot[2] ▷ *noun, often in compounds* a piece of ground for any of various uses □ *vegetable plot*. ⓒ Anglo-Saxon.

plotter ▷ *noun* **1** someone who plots. **2** an instrument, often the output device of a computer, which draws graphs, diagrams, contour maps, overhead slides, etc on paper or film using an automatically controlled pen.

the Plough ▷ *noun, astron* the seven brightest stars in the constellation URSA MAJOR whose configuration resembles the shape of a plough. Also (*N Amer*) called **the Big Dipper**.

plough or (*N Amer*) **plow** /plaʊ/ *noun* **1** a bladed farm implement used to turn over the surface of the soil and bury stubble, weeds, etc, in preparation for the cultivation of a crop. **2** any similar implement, especially a SNOWPLOUGH. **3** *hunting, etc* ploughed land. ▷ *verb* (***ploughed***, ***ploughing***; *N Amer* ***plowed***, ***plowing***) **1** (*also* **plough something up**) to till or turn over (soil, land, etc) with a plough. **2** *intr* to make a furrow or to turn over the surface of the soil with a plough. **3** *Brit colloq, old use* **a** to fail (a candidate in an examination); **b** *intr* said of a candidate: to fail an examination. • **plough a lonely furrow** to be separated from one's former friends and associates and go one's own way. • **put one's hand to the plough** to begin an undertaking. ⓒ Anglo-Saxon *plog* or *ploh*.

■ **plough something back** to re-invest (the profits of a business) in that business.

■ **plough something in** to mix (the remains of a crop) with the soil by means of a plough after harvesting □ *ploughed the stubble in*.

■ **plough into something** *colloq* said of a vehicle or its driver: to crash into it at speed □ *ploughed into the back of the lorry*.

■ **plough on** *colloq* to continue with something although progress is laborious.

■ **plough through something** **1** to move through it with a ploughing action □ *a boat ploughing through the waves*. **2** *colloq* to make steady but laborious progress with it.

ploughman or (*N Amer*) **plowman** *noun* someone who steers a plough.

ploughman's lunch ▻ *noun* a cold meal of bread, cheese, pickle and sometimes meat, often served in pubs as a bar meal.

ploughman's spikenard ▻ *noun* a European and N African SPIKENARD with yellow flowers and aromatic roots.

Plough Monday ▻ *noun, Brit* the Monday following Epiphany. ◷ 16c: so called because it was the day when traditionally ploughmen and others resumed their work after the Christmas holidays.

ploughshare or (*N Amer*) **plowshare** *noun* a blade of a plough. Also called **share**. ◷ 14c.

plouk or **plook** /pluːk/ ▻ *noun, Scots* a spot or pimple. ◷ 15c.

plover /ˈplʌvə(r)/ ▻ *noun* any of various wading birds with boldly patterned plumage, large pointed wings, long legs and a short straight bill. ◷ 14c: from French *plovier* rain bird, from Latin *pluvia* rain.

plow, *etc* the *N Amer* spelling of PLOUGH, *etc.*

ploy ▻ *noun* (***ploys***) **1** a stratagem, dodge or manoeuvre to gain an advantage. **2** any hobby or amusement with which one occupies oneself. ◷ 1950s; 18c in sense 2; 15c in obsolete sense 'to employ': possibly from Latin *plicare* to bend.

PLP ▻ *abbreviation, Brit* Parliamentary Labour Party.

PLR ▻ *abbreviation* public lending right.

pluck ▻ *verb* (***plucked, plucking***) **1** to pull the feathers off (a bird) before cooking it. **2** to pick (flowers or fruit) from a plant or tree. **3** (*often* **pluck something out**) to remove it by pulling □ ***Iain plucked out his grey hairs one by one.*** **4** to shape (the eyebrows) by removing hairs from them. **5** (*usually* **pluck** or **pluck at something**) to pull or tug it. **6** to sound (the strings of a violin, etc) using the fingers or a plectrum. **7** to grab or save someone or something at the last minute □ ***plucked from the jaws of death.*** **8** *slang* to rob or fleece someone; to swindle. ▻ *noun* **1** courage; guts. **2** a little tug. **3** the heart, liver and lungs of an animal. • **pluck up courage** to strengthen one's resolve for a difficult undertaking, etc. ◷ Anglo-Saxon *pluccian* to pluck or tear.

plucky ▻ *adj* (***pluckier, pluckiest***) *colloq* courageous; spirited. • **pluckily** *adverb*. • **pluckiness** *noun*.

plug ▻ *noun* **1** a piece of rubber, plastic, etc shaped to fit a hole as a stopper, eg in a bath or sink. **2** *often in compounds* any device or piece of material for a similar purpose □ ***earplugs.*** **3 a** the plastic or rubber device with metal pins, fitted to the end of the flex of an electrical apparatus, that is pushed into a socket to connect with the power supply; **b** *loosely* the socket or power point □ ***switch it off at the plug.*** **4** *colloq* a piece of favourable publicity given to a product, programme, etc, eg on television. **5** a SPARK PLUG. **6** an accumulation of solidified magma which fills the vent of a volcano. Also called **volcanic plug**. **7** a lump of tobacco for chewing. ▻ *verb* (***plugged, plugging***) **1** (*often* **plug something up**) to stop or block up (a hole, etc) with something. **2** *colloq* to give favourable publicity to (a product, programme, etc), especially repeatedly □ ***plugged her new book.*** **3** *slang* to shoot someone with a gun. • **plugger** *noun*. • **plug school** *slang* to play truant. • **pull the plug on something** or **someone 1** to stop being supportive of it or them. **2** to destroy them or it, eg by cutting off supplies, finance, etc. ◷ 17c: from Dutch *plugge* a bung or peg.

■ **plug away** or **along** *colloq* to work or progress steadily.

■ **plug something in** to connect (an electrical appliance) to the power supply by means of an electrical plug.

plug-and-play ▻ *adj* said of a computer, computer software, etc: having a facility allowing software to be used immediately without the user having to go through any complex processes to set it up.

plughole ▻ *noun* the hole in a bath or sink through which water flows into the wastepipe.

plug-ugly *colloq* ▻ *adj, derog* said of a person: very ugly. ▻ *noun* (***plug-uglies***) *US* a hoodlum; a ruffian. ◷ 19c.

plum ▻ *noun* **1** any of a number of varieties of shrub or small tree, cultivated in temperate regions for its edible fruit, or for its ornamental flowers or foliage. **2** the smooth-skinned red, purple, green or yellow fruit of this tree, which has a hard central stone surrounded by sweet juicy flesh, eg damson, greengage. **3** *in compounds* a raisin used in cakes, etc □ ***plum pudding.*** **4 a** *colloq* something especially valued or sought; **b** *as adj* □ ***a plum job.*** **5** a deep dark-red colour. ▻ *adj* plum-coloured. See also PLUMMY. ◷ Anglo-Saxon *plume*: from Greek *proumnon*, from *proumne* plum-tree.

plum, plumb

These words are sometimes confused with each other.

plumage /ˈpluːmɪdʒ/ ▻ *noun* a bird's feathers, especially with regard to colour. ◷ 15c: French, from *plume* feather.

plumb /plʌm/ ▻ *noun* a lead weight, usually suspended from a line, used for measuring water depth or for testing a wall, etc for perpendicularity. ▻ *adj* straight, vertical or perpendicular. ▻ *adverb* **1** in a straight, vertical or perpendicular way □ ***drops plumb to the sea bed.*** **2** *colloq* exactly □ ***plumb in the middle.*** **3** *N Amer, especially US colloq* utterly □ ***The guy is plumb crazy.*** ▻ *verb* (***plumbed, plumbing***) **1** to measure the depth of (water), test (a structure) for verticality, or adjust something to the vertical, using a plumb. **2** to penetrate, probe or understand (a mystery, etc). **3** (*usually* **plumb something in**) to connect (a water-using appliance) to the water supply or waste pipe. • **out of plumb** not vertical. • **plumb the depths of something** to experience the worst extreme of (a bad feeling, etc) □ ***plumbed the depths of misery.*** ◷ 13c: from French *plomb*, from Latin *plumbum* lead.

plumbago /plʌmˈbeɪgoʊ/ ▻ *noun* (***plumbagos***) **1** *chem* another name for GRAPHITE. **2** a Mediterranean and tropical plant with spikes of lead-coloured flowers. Also called LEADWORT. ◷ 18c; 17c in obsolete sense 'yellow oxide of lead': Latin, from Pliny's translation of Greek *molybdaina* lead or lead ore.

plumber /ˈplʌmə(r)/ ▻ *noun* someone who fits and repairs water pipes, and water- or gas-using appliances. ◷ 14c: from French *plummier*, from Latin *plumbarius*, from *plumbum* lead.

plumbing /ˈplʌmɪŋ/ ▻ *noun* **1** the system of water and gas pipes in a building, etc. **2** the work of a plumber. **3** *euphemistic* the lavatory. **4** *facetious* the human urinary excretory or reproductive systems.

plumbism /ˈplʌmbɪzəm/ ▻ *noun, pathol* lead poisoning. ◷ 19c: from Latin *plumbum* + -ISM.

plumbline ▻ *noun* a line with a PLUMB attached, used for measuring depth or testing for verticality.

plume /pluːm/ ▻ *noun* **1** a conspicuous feather of a bird. **2** such a feather, or bunch of feathers, worn as an ornament or crest, represented in a coat of arms, etc. **3** a curling column (of smoke etc). ▻ *verb* (***plumed, pluming***) **1** said of a bird: to clean or preen (itself or its feathers). **2** to decorate with plumes. **3** (*usually* **plume oneself on something**) to pride or congratulate oneself on it, usually on something trivial. ◷ 14c: French, from Latin *pluma* a soft feather.

plummet /ˈplʌmɪt/ ▻ *verb* (***plummeted, plummeting***) *intr* to fall or drop rapidly; to plunge or hurtle downwards. ▻ *noun* the weight on a plumbline or fishing-line. ◷ 14c:

from French *plommet* ball of lead, diminutive of *plomb* lead.

plummy ▷ *adj* (**plummier**, **plummiest**) **1** *colloq* said of a job, etc: desirable; worth having; choice. **2** *derog* said of a voice: affectedly or excessively rich and deep. **3** full of plums.

plump¹ ▷ *adj* (**plumper**, **plumpest**) full, rounded or chubby; not unattractively fat. ▷ *verb* (**plumped**, **plumping**) (*often* **plump something up**) to shake (cushions or pillows) to give them their full soft bulk. • **plumply** *adverb*. • **plumpness** *noun*. ◷ 16c in adjectival sense; 15c in obsolete sense 'dull' or 'blunt': from Dutch *plomp* blunt.

plump² *colloq* ▷ *verb* (**plumped**, **plumping**) *tr & intr* (*sometimes* **plump down** or **plump something down**) to put down, drop, fall or sit heavily. ▷ *noun* a sudden heavy fall or the sound this makes. ▷ *adverb* **1** suddenly; with a plump. **2** directly □ ***The fly landed plump in the middle of my soup.*** **3** in a blunt or direct way. Also *as adj*. ◷ 14c: imitating the sound made.

■ **plump for something** or **someone** to decide on or choose them; to make a decision in their favour.

plumule /'pluːmjuːl/ ▷ *noun* **1** *bot* the embryonic shoot of a germinating seedling. **2** *zool* one of the down feathers of a young bird. ◷ 18c: from Latin *plumula*, diminutive of *pluma* feather.

plumy /'pluːmɪ/ ▷ *adj* (**plumier**, **plumiest**) **1** covered or adorned with down or plumes. **2** like a plume.

plunder /'plʌndə(r)/ ▷ *verb* (**plundered**, **plundering**) *tr & intr* to steal (valuable goods) or loot (a place), especially with open force during a war; to rob or ransack. ▷ *noun* the goods plundered; loot; booty. • **plunderer** *noun*. ◷ 17c: from Dutch *plunderen* to rob of household goods.

plunge /plʌndʒ/ ▷ *verb* (**plunged**, **plunging**) **1** *intr* (*usually* **plunge in** or **into something**) to dive, throw oneself, fall or rush headlong in or into it. **2** *intr* (*usually* **plunge in** or **into something**) to involve oneself rapidly and enthusiastically. **3** to thrust or push something. **4** *tr & intr* to put something or someone into a particular state or condition □ ***The power failed and plunged the town into darkness.*** **5** to dip something briefly into water or other liquid. **6** *intr* to dip steeply □ ***The ship plunged and rose.*** **7** *intr* to gamble or squander recklessly. ▷ *noun* **1** an act of plunging; a dive. **2** *colloq* a dip or swim. **3** *geol* the inclination of a FOLD axis, measured in the vertical plane. Compare PITCH. • **take the plunge** *colloq* to commit oneself finally after hesitation; to take an irreversible decision. ◷ 14c: from French *plungier*, from an assumed Latin verb *plumbicare* to heave the lead, from *plumbum* lead.

plunger ▷ *noun* **1** a rubber suction cup at the end of a long handle, used to clear blocked drains, etc. **2** a part of a mechanism that moves up and down with a thrusting motion, like a piston.

plunk ▷ *verb* (**plunked**, **plunking**) **1** to pluck (the strings of a banjo, etc); to twang. **2** (*often* **plunk something down**) to drop it, especially suddenly. ▷ *noun* the act of plunking or the sound this makes. ◷ 19c: imitating the sound.

pluperfect /pluː'pɜːfɪkt/ *grammar* ▷ *adj* said of the tense of a verb: formed in English by the auxiliary verb *had* and a past PARTICIPLE, and referring to action already accomplished at the time of a past action being referred to, as in *They had often gone there before, but this time they lost their way*. ▷ *noun* **a** the pluperfect tense; **b** a verb in the pluperfect tense. Compare PAST, PRESENT, FUTURE, PERFECT, IMPERFECT. ◷ 16c: contracted from Latin *plus quam perfectum* more than perfect.

plural /'plʊərəl/ ▷ *adj* **1** *grammar* denoting or referring to two or more people, things, etc as opposed to only one. **2** consisting of more than one, or of different kinds. ▷ *noun, grammar* a word or form of a word expressing the idea or involvement of two or more people, things, etc. Compare SINGULAR. ◷ 14c: from French *plurel*, from Latin *pluralis*, from *plus* more.

pluralism ▷ *noun* **1** the existence within a society of a variety of ethnic, cultural and religious groups. **2** the holding of more than one post, especially in the Church. **3** *philos* the belief or theory that reality consists of more than two kinds of substance. Compare MONISM, DUALISM. • **pluralist** *noun, adj*. • **pluralistic** *adj*.

plurality /plʊə'ralɪtɪ/ ▷ *noun* (**pluralities**) **1** the state or condition of being plural. **2** PLURALISM (sense 2). **3** a large number or variety. **4** *US* a RELATIVE MAJORITY.

pluralize or **pluralise** /'plʊərəlaɪz/ ▷ *verb* (**pluralized**, **pluralizing**) to make or become plural. • **pluralization** *noun*. ◷ 19c.

plural society ▷ *noun* a society that consists of several interdependent groups which all have a say in the ruling of the society.

plus ▷ *prep* **1** *math* with the addition of (a specified number) □ ***2 plus 5 equals 7.*** **2** in combination with something; with the added factor of (a specified thing) □ ***Bad luck, plus his own obstinacy, cost him his job.*** ▷ *adverb* after a specified amount: with something more besides □ ***Helen earns £20 000 plus.*** ▷ *adj* **1** denoting the symbol '+' □ ***the plus sign.*** **2** mathematically positive; above zero □ ***plus 3.*** **3** advantageous □ ***a plus factor.*** **4** in grades: denoting a slightly higher mark than the letter alone □ ***B plus.*** **5** *physics, elec* electrically positive. ▷ *noun* (**pluses** /'plʌsɪz/) **1** (*also* **plus sign**) the symbol '+', denoting addition or positive value. **2** *colloq* something positive or good; a bonus, advantage, surplus, or extra □ ***The free crèche was a definite plus.*** ▷ *conj, colloq* in addition to the fact that □ ***That's a difficult question to answer, plus I'm late for an appointment.*** In all senses opposite of MINUS. ◷ 17c: Latin, meaning 'more'.

plus fours ▷ *plural noun* loose breeches gathered below the knee, still sometimes used as golfing wear. ◷ 1920s: from PLUS + FOUR, because four extra inches of fabric are required to make the breeches hang over the knee.

plush ▷ *noun* (**plushes**) a fabric with a long velvety pile. ▷ *adj* (**plusher**, **plushest**) **1** made of plush. **2** *colloq* plushy. ◷ 16c: from French *pluche*, from earlier *peluche* a hairy fabric, ultimately from Latin *pilus* hair.

plushy ▷ *adj* (**plushier**, **plushiest**) *colloq* luxurious, opulent, stylish or costly. ◷ 1920s in this sense.

plutocracy /pluː'tɒkrəsɪ/ ▷ *noun* (**plutocracies**) **1** government or domination by the wealthy. **2** a state governed by the wealthy. **3** an influential group whose power is backed by their wealth. ◷ 17c: from Greek *ploutos* wealth + -CRACY.

plutocrat /'pluːtoʊkrat/ ▷ *noun* **1** a member of a plutocracy. **2** *colloq* a wealthy person. • **plutocratic** /-'kratɪk/ *adj*.

plutonic /pluː'tɒnɪk/ ▷ *adj, geol* relating to coarse-grained igneous rocks that are formed by the slow crystallization of magma deep within the Earth's crust, eg GRANITES and GABBROS. ◷ 19c; 18c, meaning 'igneous': from Greek *Plouton* Pluto, the god of the underworld.

plutonium /pluː'toʊnɪəm/ ▷ *noun, chem* (abbreviation **Pu**, atomic number 94) a dense highly poisonous silvery-grey radioactive metallic element, whose isotope **plutonium-239** is used as an energy source for nuclear weapons and some nuclear reactors. ◷ 1940s in this sense: named after the planet Pluto.

pluvial /'pluːvɪəl/ ▷ *adj* relating to or characterized by rain; rainy. ▷ *noun, geol* a period of prolonged rainfall. ◷ 17c: from Latin *pluvia* rain.

ply¹ /plaɪ/ ▷ *noun* (**plies**) **1 a** thickness of yarn, rope or wood, measured by the number of strands or layers that compose it; **b** *in compounds, often as adj* specifying the number of strands or layers involved □ ***four-ply wool.*** **2** a strand or layer. ◷ 16c: from French *pli* fold, from *plier* to fold.

ply[2] /plaɪ/ ▻ *verb* (***plies, plied, plying***) **1** (*usually* **ply someone with something**) to keep supplying them with something or making a repeated, often annoying, onslaught on them □ ***plied them with drinks*** □ ***plying me with questions.*** **2** *tr & intr* (*often* **ply between one place and another**) to travel a route regularly; to go regularly to and fro between destinations. **3** *dated or literary* to work at (a trade). **4** *dated or literary* to use (a tool, etc) □ ***ply one's needle.*** • **plier** *noun*. ◷ 14c: from APPLY.

plywood ▻ *noun* wood which consists of thin layers glued together, widely used in the construction industry. ◷ Early 20c.

PM ▻ *abbreviation* **1** Past Master. **2** Postmaster. **3** Paymaster. **4** Prime Minister.

Pm ▻ *symbol, chem* promethium.

p.m., pm, P.M. or **PM** ▻ *abbreviation* **1** post meridiem. **2** post mortem.

PMG ▻ *abbreviation* Paymaster-General.

PMS ▻ *abbreviation* premenstrual syndrome.

PMT ▻ *abbreviation* premenstrual tension.

PNdB ▻ *abbreviation* perceived noise decibel.

pneumatic /njʊ'matɪk/ ▻ *adj* **1** relating to air or gases. **2** containing or inflated with compressed air □ ***pneumatic tyres.*** See TYRE. **3** said of a tool or piece of machinery: operated or driven by compressed air □ ***pneumatic drill.*** • **pneumatically** *adverb*. ◷ 17c: from Latin *pneumaticus*, from Greek *pneuma* wind or breath.

pneumoconiosis /njuːmoʊkoʊnɪ'oʊsɪs/ or **pneumonoconiosis** /njuːmənoʊkoʊnɪ'oʊsɪs/ ▻ *noun, pathol* any of various diseases of the lungs, caused by habitual inhalation of mineral or metallic dust. ◷ 19c: Latin, from Greek *pneumon* lung + *koniosis*, from *konis* dust.

pneumonia /njʊ'moʊnɪə/ ▻ *noun, pathol* inflammation of one or more lobes of the lungs, usually as a result of bacterial or viral infection, which was formerly a major cause of death but is now treatable with antibiotics. ◷ 17c: Latin, from Greek *pneumon* lung.

PNG ▻ *abbreviation, IVR* Papua New Guinea.

PO ▻ *abbreviation* **1** Personnel Officer. **2** Petty Officer. **3** Pilot Officer. **4** Post Office.

Po ▻ *symbol, chem* polonium.

po[1] /poʊ/ ▻ *noun* (***pos*** /poʊz/) *colloq* a chamberpot. ◷ 19c: contracted from French *pot de chambre*.

po[2] or **p.o.** ▻ *abbreviation* postal order.

poa /'poʊə/ ▻ *noun* (***poas***) *bot* any of various species of grass with green hairless leaves, often wrinkled or with a purplish tinge, abundant in meadows and pastures. ◷ 18c: from Greek *poa* grass.

poach[1] /poʊtʃ/ ▻ *verb* (***poaches, poached, poaching***) *cookery* **1** to cook (an egg without its shell) in or over boiling water. **2** to simmer (fish) in milk or other liquid. ◷ 15c: from French *pocher* to pocket (referring to the egg yolk inside the white), from *poche* pocket.

poach[2] /poʊtʃ/ ▻ *verb* (***poaches, poached, poaching***) **1** *tr & intr* to catch (game or fish) illegally on someone else's property. **2** to steal (ideas, etc). **3** to lure away (personnel at a rival business, etc) to work for one. **4** (*usually* **poach on something**) to intrude on (another's territory or area of responsibility). ◷ 17c: from French *pocher* to gouge.

poacher ▻ *noun* **1** a container in which to POACH[1] eggs. **2** someone who poaches (see POACH[2]) game, work, customers, etc.

poaching ▻ *noun* **1** cooking by gentle simmering. **2** the activity of a POACHER (sense 2); stealing.

PO box ▻ *abbreviation* Post Office box, a numbered box, pigeonhole, etc at a post office to which mail may be sent for collection by a recipient who does not have a permanent address, or who does not want to disclose their home or business address. Compare POSTE RESTANTE.

pochade /pɒ'ʃɑːd/ ▻ *noun, art* a quick sketch in colour, usually oils, made in the open air, often used by landscape painters as a preliminary stage in the planning of a full-size picture. ◷ 19c: French, from *pocher* to sketch in the rough.

pochard /'pɒtʃəd/ ▻ *noun* any of various diving ducks found in Europe and N America, the common variety of which has a short neck, a steep sloping forehead and a large bill. ◷ 16c.

pochoir /'pɒʃwɑː/ ▻ *noun, printing, publishing* a form of colour stencilling, by hand, on to a printed illustration. ◷ 1930s: French, meaning 'stencil'.

pock ▻ *noun* **1** a small inflamed area on the skin, containing pus, especially one caused by smallpox. **2** a POCKMARK. ◷ Anglo-Saxon *poc*.

pocket /'pɒkɪt/ ▻ *noun* **1** an extra piece sewn into or on to a garment to form a pouch for carrying things in. **2** any container similarly fitted or attached. **3** *as adj & in compounds* small enough to be carried in a pocket; smaller than standard □ ***pocketbook.*** Also **pocket-size**. **4** one's financial resources □ ***well beyond my pocket.*** **5** a rock cavity filled with ore. **6** in conditions of air turbulence: a place in the atmosphere where the air pressure drops or rises abruptly. **7** an isolated patch or area of something □ ***pockets of unemployment.*** **8** *billiards, etc* any of the holes, with nets or pouches beneath them, situated around the edges of the table and into which balls are potted. ▻ *verb* (***pocketed, pocketing***) **1** to put in one's pocket. **2** *colloq* to take something dishonestly; to steal it □ ***He pocketed the cash when he was alone in the office.*** **3** *billiards, etc* to drive (a ball) into a pocket. **4** to swallow or suppress (one's pride), eg to make a humble request. • **in one another's pocket** said of two people: in close intimacy with, or dependence on, one another. • **in** or **out of pocket** having gained, or lost, money on a transaction. • **in someone's pocket** influenced or controlled by them. • **out-of-pocket expenses** those incurred on behalf of an employer. • **line one's pockets** see under LINE[1]. • **put one's hand in one's pocket** to be willing to contribute money. ◷ 15c: from French *poquet*, diminutive of *poque*, from Dutch *poke* pocket.

pocketbook ▻ *noun* **1** *N Amer, especially US* a wallet for money and papers. **2** *N Amer, especially US* a woman's strapless handbag or purse. **3** a notebook.

pocket borough ▻ *noun, historical* in the UK before the 1832 Reform Act: an electoral constituency under the control of one person or family.

pocketful ▻ *noun* (***pocketfuls***) the amount a pocket can hold.

pocket knife ▻ *noun* a knife with folding blades. Also called PENKNIFE.

pocket money ▻ *noun* **1** *Brit* a weekly allowance given to children by their parents □ ***spent all his pocket money on sweets.*** **2** money carried for occasional expenses.

pockmark ▻ *noun* a small pit or hollow in the skin left by a pock, especially one caused by chickenpox or smallpox. • **pockmarked** *adj*.

poco /'poʊkoʊ/ *music* ▻ *adverb, adj in compounds* a little □ ***poco adagio.*** ◷ 18c: Italian.

poculiform /'pɒkjʊlɪfɔːm/ ▻ *adj, biol* cup-shaped. ◷ 19c: from Latin *poculum* cup.

pod /pɒd/ ▻ *noun* **1** *bot* **a** the long dry fruit produced by leguminous plants, eg peas and beans, consisting of a seedcase which splits down both sides to release its seeds; **b** the seedcase itself. **2** *aeronautics* in an aeroplane or space vehicle: a detachable container or housing, eg for an engine. ▻ *verb* (***podded, podding***) **1** to extract (peas, beans, etc) from their pods; to hull. **2** *intr* said of a plant: to produce pods. ◷ 17c.

-pod and **-pode** ▷ *combining form, forming nouns, denoting* something with a specified type, number, etc of feet □ *tripod.* ⊙ From Greek *pous, podos* foot.

podagra /pɒ'dagrə/ ▷ *noun, pathol* gout of the feet. • **podagral** *adj.* ⊙ 14c: from Greek *pous, podos* foot + *agra* a trap or seizure.

podgy /'pɒdʒɪ/ or **pudgy** /'pʌdʒɪ/ ▷ *adj* (***podgier***, ***podgiest***; ***pudgier***, ***pudgiest***) *derog* plump or chubby; short and squat. ⊙ 19c: from dialect *podge* a short fat person.

podiatry /pɒ'daɪətrɪ/ ▷ *noun, chiefly N Amer* chiropody. • **podiatrist** *noun.* ⊙ Early 20c: from Greek *pous, podos* foot + *iatros* doctor.

podium /'poʊdɪəm/ ▷ *noun* (***podiums*** or ***podia***) **1** a small platform for a public speaker, orchestra conductor, etc. **2** *archit* a projecting base for a colonnade, wall, etc. **3** a wall which encloses the arena of an amphitheatre. ⊙ 18c: Latin, meaning 'an elevated place', from Greek *podion*, from *pous, podos* foot.

podsol /'pɒdsɒl/ or **podzol** /-zɒl/ ▷ *noun, soil science* any of a group of soils, found under heathland and coniferous forests in cold temperate regions, characterized by a leached upper layer and a lower layer where leached compounds have accumulated. ⊙ Early 20c: Russian, from *pod* under + *zola* ash.

poem /'poʊɪm/ ▷ *noun* **1** a literary composition, typically, but not necessarily, in verse, often with elevated and/or imaginatively expressed content. **2** an object, scene or creation of inspiring beauty. See also POETRY. ⊙ 16c: from Greek *poiema* creation, poem, from *poieein* to make.

poenology see PENOLOGY

poesy /'poʊɪzɪ/ ▷ *noun* (***poesies***) *old use* poetry. ⊙ 14c: from Greek *poiesis*, from *poieein* to make.

poet /'poʊɪt/ and **poetess** /'poʊɪtəs, -'tɛs/ ▷ *noun* a male or female writer of poems. ⊙ 13c: from Latin *poeta*, from Greek *poietes*, from *poieein* to make.

poetic /poʊ'ɛtɪk/ or **poetical** ▷ *adj* **1** relating or suitable to poets or poetry. **2** possessing grace, beauty or inspiration suggestive of poetry. **3** written in verse □ *the complete poetical works.* • **poetically** *adverb.*

poetic justice ▷ *noun* a result or occurrence in which evil is punished or good is rewarded in a strikingly fitting way □ *It was poetic justice when the pickpocket had his wallet stolen.*

poetic licence ▷ *noun* a poet's or writer's departure from strict fact or standard grammar, for the sake of effect.

poet laureate ▷ *noun* (***poets laureate*** or ***poet laureates***) in the UK: an officially appointed court poet, commissioned to produce poems for state occasions. Sometimes shortened to **laureate**.

poetry /'poʊətrɪ/ ▷ *noun* (***poetries***) **1** the art of composing poems. **2** poems collectively. **3** poetic quality, feeling, beauty or grace. ⊙ 14c: from Latin *poetria*, from *poeta* poet.

po-faced ▷ *adj, derog colloq* **1** wearing a disapproving or solemn expression. **2** narrow-minded. ⊙ 1930s: perhaps from *po* (for POOH) or PO[1], influenced by POKER-FACED.

pogo /'poʊgoʊ/ ▷ *verb* (***pogoed***, ***pogoing***) *intr* **1** to jump on a pogo stick. **2** to jump up and down as if heading an imaginary football, especially as a form of dancing to punk music. ▷ *noun* (***pogos***) an instance of this. ⊙ 1970s in *verb* sense 2.

pogo stick /'poʊgoʊ —/ ▷ *noun* a spring-mounted pole with a handlebar and foot rests, on which to bounce, or progress by bounces. ⊙ 1920s.

pogrom /'pɒgrəm/ ▷ *noun* an organized persecution or massacre of a particular group of people, originally that of Jews in 19c Russia. ⊙ 20c: Russian, meaning 'destruction'.

poignant /'pɔɪnjənt, 'pɔɪnənt/ ▷ *adj* **1** painful to the feelings □ *a poignant reminder.* **2** deeply moving; full of pathos. **3** said of words or expressions: sharp; penetrating. **4** sharp or pungent in smell or taste. • **poignancy** *noun.* • **poignantly** *adverb.* ⊙ 14c: from French *puignant*, from *poindre* to sting, from Latin *pungere* to prick or pierce.

poikilothermic /pɔɪkɪloʊ'θɜːmɪk/ ▷ *adj, zool* COLD-BLOODED (sense 1). ⊙ 19c: from Greek *poikilos* variegated.

poinciana /pɔɪnsɪ'ɑːnə/ ▷ *noun* (***poincianas***) a tropical tree with large red or orange flowers. ⊙ 17c: Latin, named after De Poinci, a 17c Governor of the French West Indies.

poinsettia /pɔɪn'sɛtɪə/ ▷ *noun* (***poinsettias***) a deciduous Central American shrub with small greenish-yellow flowers surrounded by vermilion bracts that resemble petals, widely cultivated as houseplant. ⊙ 19c: Latin, named after J R Poinsett (1779–1851), US Minister to Mexico.

point /pɔɪnt/ ▷ *noun* **1** a sharp or tapering end or tip. **2** a dot, eg inserted (either on the line or above it) before a decimal fraction, as in *2.1* or *2·1* (*two point one*). **3** a punctuation mark, especially a full stop. **4** *geom* a position found by means of coordinates. **5** a position, place or location. Often *in compounds* □ *a look-out point.* **6** a moment □ *Sandy lost his temper at that point.* **7** a stage in a process, etc. **8** *in compounds* a stage, temperature, etc □ *boiling-point.* **9** the right moment for doing something □ *She lost courage when it came to the point.* **10** a feature or characteristic □ *She always hides her good points.* **11** in a statement, argument, etc: a detail, fact or particular used or mentioned. **12** aim or intention □ *What is the point of this procedure?* **13** use or value □ *There's no point in trying to change her mind.* **14** the significance (of a remark, story, joke, etc). **15** a unit or mark in scoring. **16** any of the 32 directions marked on, or indicated by, a compass. **17** (*often* **points**) an adjustable tapering rail by means of which a train changes lines. **18** *elec* a socket or POWER POINT. **19** (*usually* **points**) in an internal combustion engine: either of the two electrical contacts which complete the circuit in the distributor. **20** *printing* a unit of type measurement, equal to $^1/_{12}$ of a PICA[1]. Often *in compounds* □ *set in eight-point.* **21** *cricket* an off-side fielding position at right angles to the batsman. **22** (*usually* **points**) *ballet* **a** the tip of the toe; **b** a block inserted into the toe of a ballet shoe. **23** a headland or promontory. Often in place names □ *Lizard Point.* **24** (*usually* **points**) any of an animal's extremities, eg ears, tail and feet. **25** the tip of a deer's horn or antler. ▷ *verb* (***pointed***, ***pointing***) **1** to aim something □ *The hitman pointed a gun at her.* **2** *tr & intr* **a** to extend (one's finger or a pointed object) towards someone or something, so as to direct attention there; **b** said of a sign, etc: to indicate (a certain direction) □ *a weather vane pointing south.* **3** *intr* to extend or face in a certain direction □ *He lay on the floor with his toes pointing upward.* **4** *intr* said of a gun dog: to stand with the nose turned to where the dead game lies. **5** *often facetious* to direct someone □ *Just point me to the grub.* **6** (*usually* **point to something** or **someone**) to indicate or suggest it or them □ *It points to one solution.* **7** in dancing, etc: to extend (the toes) to form a point. **8** to fill gaps or cracks in (stonework or brickwork) with cement or mortar. • **beside the point** irrelevant. Compare *to the point* below. • **carry** or **gain one's point** to persuade others of the validity of one's opinion. • **come** or **get to the point** to cut out the irrelevancies and say what one wants to say □ *thought he would never get to the point.* • **in point of fact** actually; in truth. • **make a point of doing something** to be sure of doing it or take care to do it. • **make one's point** to state one's opinion forcefully. • **on the point of doing something** about to do it. • **score points off someone** to argue cleverly and successfully against them, usually on trivial or detailed grounds. • **to the point** relevant. Compare *beside the point* above. • **to the point of ...** to a degree that could be fairly described as ... □ *Ronald is brave to the point of recklessness.* • **up to a point** to a limited degree □ *I agree with you up to a point.* ⓒ 13c: French, from Latin *punctum* a dot, from *pungere* to pierce.

■ **point something out** to indicate or draw attention to it.

■ **point something up** to highlight or emphasize it.

point-blank ▷ *adj* **1** said of a shot: fired at very close range. **2** said of a question, refusal, etc: bluntly worded and direct. ▷ *adverb* **1** at close range. **2** in a blunt, direct manner □ *She refused point-blank.* ⓒ 16c.

point duty ▷ *noun* the task or station of a police officer or traffic warden who is directing traffic.

pointed ▷ *adj* **1** having or ending in a point. **2** said of a remark, etc: intended for, though not directly addressed to, a particular person; intended to convey a particular meaning or message although not directly expressing it. **3** keen or incisive. • **pointedly** *adverb.* • **pointedness** *noun.*

pointer ▷ *noun* **1** a rod used by a speaker for indicating positions on a wall map, chart, etc. **2** the indicating finger or needle on a measuring instrument. **3** *colloq* a suggestion or hint. **4** a gun dog trained to point its muzzle in the direction where the dead game lies.

pointillism /ˈpɔɪntɪlɪzəm, ˈpwan-/ ▷ *noun, art* a method of painting by which shapes and colour tones are suggested by means of small dabs of pure colour painted side by side. Also called **Divisionism.** • **pointillist** *noun, adj.* ⓒ Early 20c: from French *pointillisme*, from *pointillé* stippled.

pointing ▷ *noun* the cement or mortar filling the gaps between the bricks or stones of a wall. See POINT *verb* 8.

pointless ▷ *adj* **1** without a point. **2** lacking purpose or meaning. • **pointlessly** *adverb.*

point of honour ▷ *noun* (***points of honour***) **1** any scruple caused by a sense of duty, honour, self-respect, etc. **2** the obligation to demand and receive satisfaction for an insult, especially by duelling.

point of no return ▷ *noun* (***points of no return***) a stage reached in a process, etc after which there is no possibility of stopping or going back.

point of order ▷ *noun* (***points of order***) a question raised in an assembly, meeting, etc as to whether the business is being done according to the rules.

point of sale ▷ *noun* (abbreviation **POS**) (***points of sale***) **1** the place in a shop, etc where goods are paid for; a pay desk or checkout. **2** (**point-of-sale**) *as adj* made or installed at the point of sale □ *point-of-sale staff.* See also ELECTRONIC POINT OF SALE.

point of view ▷ *noun* (***points of view***) **1** one's own particular way of looking at or attitude towards something, influenced by personal considerations and experience. **2** the physical position from which one looks at something.

point-to-point ▷ *noun* (***point-to-points***) a horse race across open country, from landmark to landmark.

poise[1] /pɔɪz/ ▷ *noun* **1** self-confidence, calm or composure. **2** grace of posture or carriage. **3** a state of equilibrium, balance or stability, eg between extremes. ▷ *verb* (***poised, poising***) **1** *tr & intr, often in passive* to balance or suspend. **2** *in passive* to be in a state of readiness □ *She was poised to take over as leader.* ⓒ 16c in *noun* sense 3; 14c in obsolete sense 'to weigh': from French *pois*, from Latin *pensum*, from *pendere* to weigh.

poise[2] /pwɑːz, pɔɪz/ ▷ *noun* (***poises*** or ***poise***) *physics* in the cgs system of units: a unit of viscosity, equal to 10^{-1} newtons per second per square metre. ⓒ 20c: named after the French physiologist J L M Poiseuille (1799–1869).

poised ▷ *adj* **1** said of behaviour, etc: calm and dignified. **2** ready for action.

poison /ˈpɔɪzən/ ▷ *noun* **1** any substance that damages tissues or causes death when injected, absorbed or swallowed by living organisms, eg arsenic and cyanide. **2** any destructive or corrupting influence □ *a poison spreading through society.* **3** *chem* a substance that inhibits the action of a catalyst. **4** in a nuclear reactor: a substance which absorbs neutrons and so slows down the reaction. ▷ *verb* (***poisoned, poisoning***) **1** to harm or kill with poison. **2** to put poison into (food, etc). **3** to contaminate or pollute □ *rivers poisoned by effluents.* **4** to corrupt or pervert (someone's mind). **5** (*especially* **poison one person against another**) to influence them to be hostile. **6** to harm or spoil in an unpleasant or malicious way □ *Jealousy poisoned their relationship.* **7** *colloq* to infect. **8** to inhibit or stop (a chemical or nuclear reaction) by the addition of a poison. • **poisoner** *noun.* • **what's your poison?** *colloq* what would you like to drink? ⓒ 13c: from French *puisun*, from Latin *potio* a poisonous draft, from *potare* to drink.

poison gas ▷ *noun* any of several toxic gases, used in chemical warfare, that cause injury or death through contact or inhalation.

poison ivy ▷ *noun* any of various N American woody vines and shrubs, all parts of which produce a toxic chemical that causes an itching rash on contact with human skin.

poisonous /ˈpɔɪzənəs/ ▷ *adj* **1** liable to cause injury or death if swallowed, inhaled or absorbed by the skin. **2** containing or capable of injecting a poison □ *poisonous snakes.* **3** *colloq* said of a person, remark, etc: malicious. See also VENOMOUS. • **poisonously** *adverb.* • **poisonousness** *noun.*

poison-pen letter ▷ *noun* a malicious anonymous letter.

poison pill ▷ *noun, colloq, business* **1** any of various actions, such as merger, takeover or recapitalization, taken by a company to prevent or deter a threatened takeover bid. **2** a clause or clauses in a registered company's regulations which can be put into effect by an unwanted takeover, making such a takeover less attractive. ⓒ 1980s; 1930s in literal sense.

Poisson distribution /ˈpwɑːsɒn —, pwasɔ̃ —/ ▷ *noun, statistics* a distribution that, as a limiting form of BINOMIAL distribution, is characterized by a small probability of a specific event occurring during observations over a continuous interval (eg of time or distance). ⓒ 1920s: named after S D Poisson (1742–1840), French mathematician.

poke[1] ▷ *verb* (***poked, poking***) **1** (*often* **poke at something**) to thrust □ *Kevin poked at the hole with a stick.* **2** to prod or jab □ *Roy poked her in the ribs with his elbow.* **3** to make (a hole) by prodding. **4** *tr & intr* to project or make something project □ *Bob poked his head round the door* □ *Her big toe poked through a hole in her sock.* **5** to make (a fire) burn more brightly by stirring it with a poker. **6** *intr* (*especially* **poke about** or **around**) to search; to pry or snoop. **7** *slang* said of a man: to have sexual intercourse with (a woman). ▷ *noun* a jab or prod. **2** *slang* an act of sexual intercourse. • **poke fun at someone** to tease or laugh at them unkindly. • **poke one's nose into something** *colloq* to pry into or interfere in it. ⓒ 14c: Germanic origin.

poke[2] ▷ *noun, Scots* a paper bag. See also A PIG IN A POKE under PIG. ⓒ 13c: from French *poque*; see POCKET.

poker[1] /ˈpoʊkə(r)/ ▷ *noun* a metal rod for stirring a fire to make it burn better.

poker[2] /ˈpoʊkə(r)/ ▷ *noun* a card game in which players bet on the hands they hold, relying on bluff to outwit their opponents. The player who holds the highest ranking hand recognized in the game wins the pool (see POOL[2] *noun* 2). ⓒ 19c.

poker face ▻ *noun* a blank expressionless face that shows no emotion. • **poker-faced** *adj*. ⓘ 19c: from the practice of experienced poker players who tried to reveal nothing about the value of their cards by keeping their expression inscrutable.

pokeweed, **pokeberry** and **pokeroot** ▻ *noun, bot* a tall hardy American plant with pale yellow flowers and purple berries, used medicinally in a test for allergy. ⓘ 18c, orginally as *poke*: from Algonquian *puccoon*.

poky /ˈpoʊkɪ/ ▻ *adj* (***pokier, pokiest***) **1** *colloq* said of a room, house, etc: small and confined or cramped. **2** *US* slow; dull. • **pokiness** *noun*. ⓘ 19c: from POKE[1].

polar /ˈpoʊlə(r)/ ▻ *adj* **1** belonging or relating to the North or South Pole, or the regions round them. **2** relating to or having electric or magnetic poles. **3** having polarity. **4** as different as possible ◻ *polar opposites*. ⓘ 16c: from Latin *polaris*, from *polus* pole.

polar bear ▻ *noun* a large bear, found only in the Arctic region, which has thick creamy-white fur, a relatively small pointed head and long neck.

polar coordinates ▻ *plural noun, math* coordinates (see CO-ORDINATE) which define a point by means of a RADIUS VECTOR and the angle which it makes with a fixed line through the origin.

polarimetry /poʊləˈrɪmətrɪ/ ▻ *noun, physics* the measurement of the OPTICAL ACTIVITY of any of various chemical compounds, used to identify and measure concentrations of transparent solutions such as sugar solutions.

Polaris /poʊˈlɑːrɪs/ ▻ *noun* **1** the POLE STAR. **2** (*in full* **Polaris missile**) a first-generation US submarine-launched BALLISTIC MISSILE. See also TRIDENT. ⓘ 19c: from Latin *polaris* polar, from Greek *polos* pivot or axis or firmament.

polarity /poʊˈlarɪtɪ/ ▻ *noun* (***polarities***) **1** the state of having two opposite poles ◻ *magnetic polarity*. **2** the condition of having two properties that are opposite. **3** the tendency to develop differently in different directions along an axis. **4** *physics* the status, whether positive or negative, of the poles of a magnet, the terminals of an electrode, etc ◻ *negative polarity*. **5** the tendency to develop, or be drawn, in opposite directions; oppositeness or an opposite ◻ *the political polarities of left and right*.

polarization or **polarisation** /poʊləraɪˈzeɪʃən/ ▻ *noun* **1** *chem* the separation of the positive and negative charges of an atom or molecule, especially by an electric field. **2** *physics* the process whereby waves of electromagnetic radiation, eg light, are restricted to vibration in one direction only.

polarize or **polarise** /ˈpoʊləraɪz/ ▻ *verb* (***polarized, polarizing***) **1** to give magnetic or electrical polarity to something. **2** *physics* to restrict the vibrations of (electromagnetic waves, eg light) to one direction only by the process of polarization. **3** *tr & intr* said of people or opinions: to split according to opposing views.

polarizing filter ▻ *noun, photog* a filter which allows the passage of light polarized in one direction only, used for the control of surface reflections, eg from water, and to darken blue skies.

Polaroid /ˈpoʊlərɔɪd/ ▻ *noun, trademark* a plastic material that polarizes light, used in sunglasses, etc to reduce glare. ⓘ 1936.

Polaroid camera ▻ *noun* a camera with a special film containing a pod of developing agents which bursts when the film is ejected, producing a finished print within seconds of exposure to daylight.

polder /ˈpoʊldə(r)/ ▻ *noun* an area of low-lying land which has been reclaimed from the sea, a river or lake, especially in the Netherlands. ⓘ 17c: from Dutch *polre*.

Pole ▻ *noun* a citizen or inhabitant of, or person born in, Poland. See also POLISH.

pole¹ ▻ *noun* **1** either of two points representing the north and south ends of the axis about which the Earth rotates, known as the NORTH POLE and SOUTH POLE respectively. **2** *astron* either of two corresponding points on the celestial sphere, towards which the north and south ends of the Earth's axis point, and about which the stars appear to rotate daily. **3** a MAGNETIC POLE. **4** either of the two terminals of a battery. **5** either of two opposite positions in an argument, opinion, etc. • **poles apart** *colloq* widely different; as far apart as it is possible to be. ⓘ 14c: from Latin *polus*, from Greek *polos* axis or pivot.

pole² ▻ *noun* **1** a rod, especially one that is cylindrical in section and fixed in the ground as a support. **2** *historical* an old measure of length equal to 5½yd (5.03m). Also called **perch** or **rod**.

poleaxe ▻ *noun* **1** a short-handled axe with a spike or hammer opposite the blade, used, especially formerly, for slaughtering cattle. **2** *historical* a long-handled battleaxe. ▻ *verb* (***poleaxed, poleaxing***) to strike, fell or floor (an animal or person) with, or as if with, a poleaxe. ⓘ 14c as *pollax*, from POLL *noun* 4 + AXE.

polecat /ˈpoʊlkat/ ▻ *noun* **1** a mammal resembling a large weasel, with coarse dark-brown fur, creamy yellow underfur and white patches on its face, that produces a foul-smelling discharge when alarmed or when marking territory. **2** *N Amer, especially US* a skunk. ⓘ 14c.

polemic /pəˈlɛmɪk/ ▻ *noun* **1** a controversial speech or piece of writing that fiercely attacks or defends an idea, opinion, etc. **2** writing or oratory of this sort. **3** someone who argues in this way. ▻ *adj* (*also* **polemical**) relating to or involving polemics or controversy. • **polemically** *adverb*. • **polemicist** /pəˈlɛmɪsɪst/ *noun*. ⓘ 17c: from Greek *polemikos* relating to war, from *polemos* war.

polemics ▻ *singular noun* the art of verbal dispute and debate.

polenta /pɒˈlɛntə/ ▻ *noun* (***polentas***) an Italian dish of cooked ground maize. ⓘ 16c; 11c in obsolete sense 'pearl-barley': Latin, meaning 'hulled and crushed grain'.

pole position ▻ *noun* **1** *motor sport* the position at the inside of the front row of cars at the start of a race. **2** an advantageous position at the start of any contest.

Pole Star ▻ *noun* **1** *astron* the brightest star in the constellation URSA MINOR, formerly much used in navigation. Also called **Polaris**. **2** (**pole star**) *literary* a guide or director.

pole vault ▻ *noun, athletics* a field event in which athletes attempt to jump over a high horizontal bar with the help of a long flexible pole to haul themselves into the air. ▻ *verb* (**pole-vault**) *intr* to perform a pole vault or take part in a pole vault competition. • **pole vaulter** *noun*.

police /pəˈliːs/ ▻ *plural noun* **1** the body of men and women employed by the government of a country to keep order, enforce the law, prevent crime, etc. **2** members of this body ◻ *Over 200 police were on duty at the demonstration*. ▻ *verb* (***policed, policing***) **1** to keep law and order in (an area) using the police, army, etc. **2** to supervise (an operation, etc) to ensure that it is fairly or properly run. ⓘ 18c; 16c in obsolete sense 'civilization': French, from Latin *politia*, from Greek *politeia* political constitution.

police constable (abbreviation **PC**) ▻ *noun* a police officer of the lowest rank.

police dog ▻ *noun* a dog trained to work with police officers.

policeman and **policewoman** ▻ *noun* a male or female member of a police force.

police officer ▻ *noun* a member of a police force.

police state ▻ *noun* a state with a repressive government that operates through SECRET POLICE to eliminate opposition to it.

police station ▻ *noun* the office or headquarters of a local police force. See also NICK *noun* 2.

policy¹ /'pɒlɪsɪ/ ▻ *noun* (***policies***) **1** a plan of action, usually based on certain principles, decided on by a body or individual. **2** a principle or set of principles on which to base decisions □ *It is not our policy to charge for service.* **3** a course of conduct to be followed □ *Your best policy is to keep quiet and let us do the talking.* **4** prudence; acumen; wisdom. **5** (*usually* **policies**) *Scots* the surrounding grounds of a mansion □ *walk round the policies.* ◐ 15c in sense 4; 14c in obsolete sense 'governmental administration': from French *policie*, from Latin *politia*; see POLICE.

policy² /'pɒlɪsɪ/ ▻ *noun* (***policies***) **1** an insurance agreement. **2** the document confirming such an agreement. • **policy-holder** *noun*. ◐ 16c: from French *police*, from Latin *apodixis*, from Greek *apodeixis* proof.

policy unit ▻ *noun, politics* a group of officials in a government department or other public agency, whose role is to supply information, advice and analysis to policy-makers.

polio ▻ *noun* short form of POLIOMYELITIS.

poliomyelitis /poulɪoumaɪə'laɪtɪs/ ▻ *noun, pathol* a viral disease of the brain and spinal cord, which in some cases can result in permanent paralysis. ◐ 19c: from Greek *polios* grey + *myelos* marrow + -ITIS.

Polish /'poulɪʃ/ ▻ *adj* belonging or relating to Poland, a republic in Central Europe, its inhabitants, or their language. ▻ *noun* the official language of Poland. See also POLE. ◐ 17c.

polish /'pɒlɪʃ/ ▻ *verb* (***polishes***, ***polished***, ***polishing***) **1** *tr & intr* to make or become smooth and glossy by rubbing □ *polishing my shoes.* **2** to improve or perfect □ *She tried to polish her communication skills before the interview.* **3** *tr & intr* to make cultivated, refined or elegant □ *Henrietta polished her vowels before the speech day.* ▻ *noun* (***polishes***) **1** a substance used for polishing surfaces. Also *in compounds* □ *boot polish.* **2** a smooth shiny finish; a gloss □ *Look at the polish on the sideboard!* **3** an act of polishing. **4** refinement or elegance. • **polisher** a person, device or machine that polishes. ◐ 13c: from French *polir*, from Latin *polire*.

■ **polish off something** or **polish something off** to finish it quickly and completely, especially speedily □ *Iain polished off the sausage rolls without any trouble* □ *Matt polished his essay off, before playing frisbee.*

■ **polish up something** or **polish something up** **1** to work up a shine on it by polishing. **2** to improve a skill by practising it □ *Joe polished up his guitar-playing before the audition.*

politburo or **Politburo** /'pɒlɪtbjuərou/ ▻ *noun* (***politburos***) the supreme policy-making committee of a Communist state or party, especially that of the former Soviet Union. ◐ 1920s: from Russian *politbyuro*, from *politicheskoe* political + *byuro* bureau.

polite /pə'laɪt/ ▻ *adj* (***politer***, ***politest***) **1** said of a person or their actions, etc: well-mannered; considerate towards others; courteous. **2** well-bred, cultivated or refined □ *One does not pick one's nose in polite society.* • **politely** *adverb*. • **politeness** *noun*. ◐ 16c in sense 2; 15c in obsolete sense 'burnished': from Latin *politus*, from *polire* to polish.

politic /'pɒlɪtɪk/ ▻ *adj* **1** said of a course of action: prudent; wise; shrewd. **2** said of a person: cunning; crafty. **3** *old use* political. See also BODY POLITIC. ▻ *verb* (*also* **politick**) (***politicked***, ***politicking***) *intr, derog* to indulge in politics, especially to strike political bargains or to gain votes for oneself. ◐ 15c: from French *politique*, from Latin *politicus*, from Greek *politikos* civic, from *polites* citizen, from *polis* city.

political /pə'lɪtɪkəl/ ▻ *adj* **1** relating or belonging to government or public affairs. **2** relating to POLITICS. **3** interested or involved in POLITICS. **4** said of a course of action: made in the interests of gaining or keeping power. **5** said of a map: showing political and social structure rather than physical features. • **politically** *adverb*. ◐ 16c.

political asylum ▻ *noun* protection given by a country to refugees fleeing a foreign country for political reasons.

political correctness ▻ *noun* (abbreviation **PC**) the avoidance of expressions or actions that may be understood to exclude or denigrate certain people or groups of people on the grounds of race, gender, disability, sexual orientation, etc.

political correctness

Rightly or wrongly, many expressions that were generally considered inoffensive in the past are now deemed unacceptable by many people.

1. sexism

• Words ending in **-ess** should be used with caution. Many, such as *authoress* and *manageress*, are no longer used; a few, such as *Jewess* and *Negress*, are considered offensive.

• Avoid using **man** and **men** to refer to both men and women. Instead, use *people, humans* or *human beings*. Compounds which include 'man' should be replaced by sex-neutral terms: *synthetic* instead of *man-made, working hours* instead of *manhours, representative* instead of *spokesman*.

• It is rarely necessary to specify a person's sex when referring to the job they do. Avoid terms such as *lady doctor, woman judge* and *female reporter*. Equally, terms such as *male nurse* should be avoided.

2. physical and mental capability

• Avoid the terms **handicap** and **handicapped**; their association with the image of disabled people going 'cap in hand' onto the streets of Victorian Britain makes them nowadays unacceptable to people with disabilities.

• The term **disabled**, and terms such as **blind** and **deaf**, are all perfectly acceptable, but avoid referring to disabled people as **the disabled** or **the blind**. For disabled people, such terms connect too closely with the idea of charity. Instead use 'people with a disability', etc.

• Although the word **challenged** is common in North America, in compounds that refer to particular disabilities (such as *visually challenged* to mean *blind* or *partially sighted*), it tends to be avoided in the UK, where it has become the supreme satirical tool of those who lampoon the whole concept of political correctness.

political prisoner ▻ *noun* someone imprisoned for their political beliefs, activities, etc, usually because they differ from those of the government.

political science ▻ *noun* the study of politics and government, in terms of its principles, aims, methods, etc.

politician /pɒlɪ'tɪʃən/ ▻ *noun* **1** someone engaged in POLITICS, especially as a member of parliament. **2** *derog, chiefly US*, someone who enters politics for personal power and gain. ◐ 16c; see POLITIC.

politicize or **politicise** /pə'lɪtɪsaɪz/ ▻ *verb* (***politicized***, ***politicizing***) **1** *intr* to take part in political activities or discussion. **2** to give a political nature to something. **3** to make someone aware of or informed about politics. • **politicization** /pəlɪtɪsaɪ'zeɪʃən/ *noun*.

politico /pə'lɪtɪkou/ ▻ *noun* (***politicos*** or ***politicoes***) *colloq, usually derog* a politician or someone who is keen on politics. ◐ 17c: Italian or Spanish.

politico- ▻ *combining form, forming adjectives, denoting* political or politics □ *politico-philosophical writings.*

politics /ˈpɒlɪtɪks/ ▻ *singular noun* **1** the science or business of government. **2** POLITICAL SCIENCE. **3** a political life as a career □ *entered politics in 1961.* ▻ *singular or plural noun* political activities, wrangling, etc. ▻ *plural noun* **1** moves and manoeuvres concerned with the acquisition of power or getting one's way, eg in business. Also *in compounds* □ *office politics.* **2** one's political sympathies or principles □ *What are your politics?* ⓒ 16c in sense 1.

polity /ˈpɒlɪtɪ/ ▻ *noun* (***polities***) **1** a politically organized body such as a state, church or association. **2** any form of political institution or government. ⓒ 16c: from Latin *politia*; see POLICE.

polka /ˈpɒlkə, ˈpoʊlkə/ ▻ *noun* (***polkas***) **1** a lively Bohemian dance usually performed with a partner, which has a pattern of three steps followed by a hop. **2** a piece of music for this dance. ▻ *verb* (***polkaed, polkaing***) *intr* to dance a polka. ⓒ 19c: Czech, perhaps from *Polka*, feminine of *Polák* a Pole.

polka dot ▻ *noun* any one of numerous regularly-spaced dots forming a pattern on fabric, etc. Also *as adj* □ *a polka-dot bikini.* ⓒ 19c.

poll /poʊl/ ▻ *noun* **1** (**polls**) a political election □ *another Tory disaster at the polls.* **2** the voting or votes cast at an election □ *a heavy poll.* **3** (*also* **opinion poll**) a survey of public opinion carried out by directly questioning a representative sample of the populace. **4** *old use* the head. ▻ *verb* (***polled, polling***) **1** to win (a number of votes) in an election □ *He polled three votes at the by-election and lost his deposit.* **2** to register the votes of (a population). **3** *tr & intr* to cast (one's vote). **4** to conduct an opinion poll among (people, a specified group, etc) □ *We polled 300 voters to find out their favourite coffee.* **5** to cut off the horns of (cattle). **6** to cut the top off (a tree). ⓒ 13c as *polle*, meaning 'the hair of the head'.

pollack or **pollock** /ˈpɒlək/ ▻ *noun* (***pollack*** or ***pollacks***; ***pollock*** or ***pollocks***) **1** a marine fish belonging to the cod family, with a greenish-brown back, pale-yellow sides, a white belly and a projecting lower jaw. **2** *N Amer* COALFISH. ⓒ 17c.

pollan /ˈpɒlən/ ▻ *noun* (***pollan*** or ***pollans***) a type of whitefish found in the lakes of N Ireland. ⓒ 18c.

pollard /ˈpɒləd/ ▻ *noun* **1** a tree whose branches have been cut back, in order to produce a crown of shoots at the top of the trunk, so as to be out of reach of grazing animals, or for periodic harvesting for firewood or fencing, etc. **2** an animal whose horns have been removed. ▻ *verb* (***pollarded, pollarding***) to make a pollard of (a tree or animal). ⓒ 16c: from POLL *verb* 5, 6.

pollen /ˈpɒlən/ ▻ *noun* the fine, usually yellow, dust-like powder produced by the ANTHERS of flowering plants, and by the male cones of cone-bearing plants. See also POLLINATION. ⓒ 18c; 16c in obsolete sense 'fine dust': Latin, meaning 'fine dust'.

pollen count ▻ *noun* an estimate of the amount of pollen in the atmosphere at any particular time, published for the benefit of those who have a pollen allergy □ *Today's pollen count is low.*

pollen sac ▻ *noun, bot* in flowering plants: one of the four cavities in the ANTHER of a STAMEN, in which the pollen is produced and stored.

pollen tube ▻ *noun, bot* a slender tube that develops from the wall of a pollen grain after pollination, and which in flowering plants grows down through the STIGMA and STYLE and into the OVULE where fertilization takes place.

pollex /ˈpɒlɛks/ ▻ *noun* (***pollices*** /-lɪsiːz/) *zool, anatomy* the first digit on the forelimb of mammals, reptiles, amphibians and birds, eg the thumb in humans. ⓒ 19c: Latin, meaning 'big toe' or 'thumb'.

pollinate /ˈpɒlɪneɪt/ ▻ *verb* (***pollinated, pollinating***) *bot* in flowering and cone-bearing plants: to transfer pollen by the process of POLLINATION in order to achieve fertilization and subsequent development of seed. ⓒ 19c.

pollination /pɒlɪˈneɪʃən/ ▻ *noun, bot* **1** in flowering plants: the transfer of pollen from the ANTHER to the STIGMA. **2** in cone-bearing plants: the transfer of pollen from the male cone to the female cone.

polling-booth /ˈpoʊlɪŋ —/ ▻ *noun* an enclosed compartment at a polling-station in which a voter can mark their ballot paper in private.

polling-station /ˈpoʊlɪŋ —/ ▻ *noun* the building where voters go to cast their votes during an election.

pollock see POLLACK

pollster /ˈpoʊlstə(r)/ ▻ *noun* someone who organizes and carries out opinion polls.

poll tax ▻ *noun* **1** *historical* a fixed tax levied on each adult member of a population. **2** *formerly, informal* the COMMUNITY CHARGE. See also COUNCIL TAX.

pollutant ▻ *noun* any substance or agent that pollutes. ▻ *adj* polluting □ *pollutant emissions.*

pollute /pəˈluːt, pəˈljuːt/ ▻ *verb* (***polluted, polluting***) **1** to contaminate something with harmful substances or impurities; to cause pollution in something. **2** to corrupt (someone's mind, etc). **3** to defile. ⓒ 14c: from Latin *polluere* to soil or defile.

pollution ▻ *noun* the adverse effect on the natural environment, including human, animal or plant life, of a harmful substance that does not occur naturally, eg industrial and radioactive waste, or the concentration to harmful levels of a naturally occurring substance, eg nitrates. See also AIR POLLUTION, WATER POLLUTION.

pollyanna /pɒlɪˈanə/ ▻ *noun* someone who is unfailingly optimistic, often in a naive way. Also *as adj.* ⓒ 1920s: named after Pollyanna, a character in a novel of the same name by Eleanor Porter.

polo /ˈpoʊloʊ/ ▻ *noun* a game, similar to hockey, played on horseback by two teams of four players, using long-handled mallets to propel the ball along the ground. See also WATER POLO. ⓒ 19c: Balti (a Tibetan dialect), meaning 'ball'.

polonaise /pɒləˈneɪz/ ▻ *noun* **1** a stately Polish marching dance. **2** a piece of music for this dance. **3** an item of clothing consisting of a one-piece bodice and skirt, which reveals a decorative underskirt. ⓒ 18c: French, feminine of *polonais* Polish.

polo neck ▻ *noun* **1** a high close-fitting neckband on a sweater or shirt, which is doubled over. **2** a sweater or shirt with such a neck. **3** Also *as adj* □ *polo-neck jumper.*

polonium /pəˈloʊnɪəm/ ▻ *noun, chem* (abbreviation **Po**, atomic number 84) a rare radioactive metallic element that emits ALPHA PARTICLES and is used in portable radiation sources, as an energy source in satellites and for dissipating static electricity. ⓒ 19c: Latin, from *Polonia* Poland, the native country of Marie Curie who discovered it.

polony /pəˈloʊnɪ/ ▻ *noun* (***polonies***) a dry sausage made of partly cooked meat. ⓒ 18c: probably from Bologna a city in Italy.

polo shirt ▻ *noun* **1** a short-sleeved open-necked casual shirt with a collar, especially one made of a knitted cotton fabric. **2** *sometimes* a long-sleeved shirt of a similar style.

poltergeist /ˈpoʊltəgaɪst/ ▻ *noun* a type of mischievous ghost supposedly responsible for otherwise unaccountable noises and the movement of furniture and other objects. ⓒ 19c: German, from *poltern* to make a noise + *Geist* ghost.

poltroon /pɒlˈtruːn/ ▻ *noun, literary or old use* a despicable coward. ⓒ 16c: French, from Italian *poltrone* lazybones.

poly /'pɒlɪ/ ▻ *noun* (*polys*) ▻ *noun, informal* a polytechnic.

poly- /pɒlɪ 'pɒlɪ/ ▻ *combining form, denoting* **1** many or much; several □ *polytechnic.* **2** *chem* a POLYMER □ *polyvinyl.* ⓒ Greek, from *polys* many or much.

polyamide ▻ *noun, chem* a POLYMER formed by the linking of the AMINO GROUP of one molecule with the CARBOXYL GROUP of the next, eg nylon. ⓒ 1920s.

polyandrous /pɒlɪ'andrəs/ ▻ *adj* **1** *sociol* having more than one husband at the same time. **2** *bot* said of a flower: having many STAMENS. Compare MONANDROUS. ⓒ 19c: from Greek *aner, andros* man or husband.

polyandry /'pɒlɪandrɪ, pɒlɪ'andrɪ/ ▻ *noun* **1** *anthropol, etc* the custom or practice of having more than one husband at the same time. **2** *zool* the practice of a female animal having more than one mate in the same season. Compare POLYGYNY. ⓒ 18c: from Greek *aner, andros* man or husband.

polyanthus /pɒlɪ'anθəs/ ▻ *noun* (***polyanthuses*** or ***polyanthi*** /-θaɪ/) any of various hybrid varieties of primrose which have several large brightly-coloured flowers borne on a single stalk, widely cultivated as ornamental garden plants. ⓒ 18c: Latin, from Greek *anthos* flower.

polyarchy /'pɒlɪɑːkɪ/ ▻ *noun* (***polyarchies***) *politics* government of a state by many. Compare MONARCHY. ⓒ 17c: from Greek *polyarchia* rule by many.

polyatomic ▻ *adj, chem* said of a molecule: containing more than two atoms. ⓒ 19c.

polybasic ▻ *adj, chem* said of an acid: having several hydrogen atoms replaceable by a BASE (*noun* 6). ⓒ 19c.

polycarbonate ▻ *noun, chem* a strong rigid thermoplastic resin, used to make safety helmets, protective windows, soft-drink bottles, electrical terminals, etc. ⓒ 1930s in this sense.

polycarpic /pɒlɪ'kɑːpɪk/ or **polycarpous** /-pəs/ ▻ *adj, bot* said of a plant: able to produce fruit many times in succession. ⓒ 19c: from Greek *polykarpos*, from *karpos* fruit.

polycentrism ▻ *noun, politics* the condition of having, or the tendency to have, many ideological or political centres. ⓒ 1960s.

polychromatic ▻ *adj* **1** POLYCHROME. **2** said of electromagnetic radiation: composed of a number of different wavelengths. ⓒ 19c.

polychrome /'pɒlɪkroʊm/ ▻ *adj* (*also* **polychromatic**) multicoloured. Compare MONOCHROME. ▻ *noun* **1** varied colouring. **2** a work of art, especially a statue, in several colours. ⓒ 19c: from Greek *polychromos*, from CHROMA colour.

polychromy ▻ *noun* **1** *art* the practice of colouring sculpture, especially common in ancient Egypt and Greece and in medieval times. **2** *archit* the use of coloured marbles, bricks, flint, stone, etc on buildings for decorative effect. ⓒ 19c.

polyclinic ▻ *noun* a clinic or hospital which can treat many different diseases. ⓒ 19c.

polycotyledon ▻ *noun, bot* any plant which has more than two COTYLEDONS. • **polycotyledonous** *adj.* ⓒ 19c.

polydactyl ▻ *adj* (*also* **polydactylous**) said of man and other vertebrates: having more than the normal number of fingers and toes. ▻ *noun* a human or other animal of this sort. ⓒ 19c.

polyester /pɒlɪ'ɛstə(r)/ ▻ *noun* a synthetic resin used to form strong durable crease-resistant artificial fibres, such as Terylene, widely used in textiles for clothing, etc. ⓒ 20c.

polyethylene see under POLYTHENE

polygamy /pə'lɪgəmɪ/ ▻ *noun* the custom or practice of having more than one husband or wife at the same time. • **polygamist** *noun.* • **polygamous** *adj.* • **polygamously** *adverb.* Compare MONOGAMY. ⓒ 16c: from Greek *polygamia*, from *gamos* marriage.

polygene ▻ *noun, genetics* any of a group of GENEs that control quantitative characteristics, eg height, with their individual effects being too small to be noticed. ⓒ 1940s.

polyglot /'pɒlɪglɒt/ ▻ *adj* speaking, using or written in many languages. ▻ *noun* **1** someone who speaks many languages. **2** a collection of versions of the same work, especially a Bible, in different languages. • **polyglottal** *adj.* ⓒ 17c: from Greek *polyglottos*, from *glotta* tongue language.

polygon /'pɒlɪgɒn/ ▻ *noun, geom* a plane figure (see PLANE² *adj* 3) with a number of straight sides, usually more than three, eg a PENTAGON or a HEXAGON. • **polygonal** /pə'lɪgənəl/ *adj* **1** referring or relating to a polygon. **2** having the form of a polygon; many-sided. ⓒ 16c: from Greek *polygonon*, from *gonia* angle.

polygraph ▻ *noun* **1** *medicine* a device, sometimes used as a lie-detector, that monitors several body functions simultaneously, eg pulse, blood pressure and conductivity of the skin. **2** a device for producing identical copies of something. ⓒ 18c.

polygyny /pə'lɪdʒɪnɪ/ ▻ *noun* **1** *anthropol, etc* the condition or custom of having more than one wife at the same time. **2** *zool* the practice of a male animal having more than one mate in the same season. Compare POLYANDRY. ⓒ 18c: from Greek *gyne* woman or wife.

polyhedron /pɒlɪ'hiːdrən/ ▻ *noun* (***polyhedrons*** or ***polyhedra*** /-drə/) *geom* a solid figure with four or more faces, all of which are polygons, eg a TETRAHEDRON. • **polyhedral** *adj* **1** referring or relating to a polyhedron. **2** having the form of a polyhedron; many-sided. ⓒ 16c: Greek, from *hedra* seat, base or face.

polymath /'pɒlɪmaθ/ ▻ *noun* someone who is well educated in a wide variety of subjects. • **polymathic** *adj.* • **polymathy** /pə'lɪməθɪ/ *noun.* ⓒ 17c: from Greek *polymathes*, from *manthanein* to learn.

polymer /'pɒlɪmə(r)/ ▻ *noun, chem* a very large molecule consisting of a long chain of MONOMERS linked end to end to form a series of repeating units. • **polymeric** /-'mɛrɪk/ *adj.* ⓒ 19c: from Greek *polymeres* having many parts, from *meros* part.

polymerization or **polymerisation** ▻ *noun, chem* a chemical reaction in which two or more MONOMERS are joined together in a chain to form a POLYMER.

polymerize or **polymerise** /'pɒlɪməraɪz/ ▻ *verb* (***polymerized***, ***polymerizing***) *tr & intr, chem* to undergo or cause something to undergo polymerization. ⓒ 19c.

polymethylmethacrylate ▻ *noun* a tough transparent lightweight plastic used to make windshields, visors, domestic baths, advertising signs, etc. Also called PERSPEX and (*US*) PLEXIGLAS.

polymorphism /pɒlɪ'mɔːfɪzəm/ ▻ *noun* **1** *biol* the occurrence of a living organism in two or more different structural forms at different stages of its life cycle. **2** *genetics* the occurrence of several genetically determined and distinct forms within a single population, eg the different blood groups in humans. **3** *chem* the occurrence of a chemical substance in two or more different crystalline forms, eg diamond and graphite. Also called ALLOTROPY. • **polymorphic** or **polymorphous** *adj.* ⓒ 18c as *polymorphous*, in biological use meaning 'occurring in several different forms'.

Polynesian ▻ *adj* belonging or relating to Polynesia, a group of Pacific islands, its inhabitants, or their languages. ▻ *noun* **1** a citizen or inhabitant of, or person born in, Polynesia. **2** the group of languages including Maori, Hawaiian and Samoan. ⓒ 19c: from POLY- + Greek *nesos* an island; compare MICRONESIA.

polyneuritis ▻ *noun, pathol* simultaneous inflammation of several nerves. ⓒ 19c.

polynomial /pɒlɪ'noʊmɪəl/ *math* ▻ *adj* said of an expression: consisting of a sum of terms each containing a CONSTANT and one or more VARIABLEs raised to a power. ▻ *noun* an expression of this sort. ⓒ 17c as *noun*; modelled on BINOMIAL.

polynucleotide ▻ *noun, chem* a compound made up of a number of NUCLEOTIDEs. ⓒ Early 20c.

polyp /'pɒlɪp/ ▻ *noun* **1** *zool* a sessile COELENTERATE with a more or less cylindrical body and a mouth surrounded by tentacles. **2** *pathol* a small abnormal but usually benign growth projecting from a mucous membrane, especially inside the nose. • **polypous** *adj.* ⓒ 16c: from Latin *polypus*, from Greek *polypous*, from *pous* foot.

polypeptide ▻ *noun, chem* a PEPTIDE in which many amino acids are linked to form a chain. ⓒ Early 20c.

polyphagia /pɒlɪ'feɪdʒɪə/ ▻ *noun* **1** *pathol* an abnormal desire to eat to excess. **2** *zool* the habit of animals, especially insects, of eating many different kinds of food. ⓒ 17c: from Greek *polyphagos* eating much.

polyphone ▻ *noun* a letter which can be pronounced or sounded in more than one way, eg the letter *g* in English. ⓒ 19c in this sense.

polyphonic /pɒlɪ'fɒnɪk/ ▻ *adj* **1** having many voices. **2** relating to polyphony. **3** denoting a polyphone.

polyphony /pə'lɪfənɪ/ ▻ *noun* (***polyphonies***) **1** a style of musical composition in which each part or voice has an independent melodic value. **2** the use of polyphones. ⓒ 19c: from Greek *polyphonia* diversity of sounds, from *phone* a voice or sound.

polyploid /'pɒlɪplɔɪd/ *genetics* ▻ *adj* having more than twice the HAPLOID number of chromosomes. ▻ *noun* a polyploid organism. ⓒ 1920s.

polyploidy ▻ *noun, genetics* the condition in which three or more sets of chromosomes are present within a cell nucleus, common in many crop plants, including wheat. ⓒ 1920s.

polypous see under POLYP

polypropylene /pɒlɪ'proʊpəliːn/ and **polypropene** /-'proʊpiːn/ ▻ *noun, chem* a tough white translucent THERMOPLASTIC, formed by the POLYMERIZATION of propene, used to make fibres, film, rope and moulded articles, eg toys. ⓒ 1930s.

polyptych /'pɒlɪptɪk/ ▻ *noun* an altarpiece consisting of several panels with a separate picture in each, surrounded by an elaborate, usually gilded, frame. See also DIPTYCH, TRIPTYCH. ⓒ 19c: from Greek *ptychos* a fold.

polysaccharide ▻ *noun, biochem* a large carbohydrate molecule consisting of many MONOSACCHARIDEs linked together to form long chains, eg starch and cellulose. ⓒ 19c.

polysemy /pə'lɪsɪmɪ/ ▻ *noun, linguistics* the existence of more than one meaning for a single word, such as *table*. • **polysemous** *adj.* ⓒ Early 20c: from Greek (adj) *polysemos* of many senses, from *sema* sign.

polysome /'pɒlɪsoʊm/ ▻ *noun, biol* a form of RNA that is being processed simultaneously by several RIBOSOMEs in the synthesis of proteins. ⓒ 1960s: modelled on RIBOSOME.

polystyrene /pɒlɪ'staɪriːn/ ▻ *noun, chem* a tough transparent THERMOPLASTIC that is a good thermal and electrical insulator, used in packaging, insulation, ceiling tiles, etc. ⓒ 1920s.

polysyllable ▻ *noun* a word of three or more syllables. • **polysyllabic** *adj.* ⓒ 16c.

polysynthetic language ▻ *noun* a language type that uses long and complex words made up of many smaller words, parts of words, and inflected forms. ⓒ 19c.

polytechnic /pɒlɪ'tɛknɪk/ ▻ *noun, Brit education, formerly* a college of higher education providing courses in a large range of subjects, especially of a technical or vocational kind. In 1992 the polytechnics became universities. See also POLY, TECHNICAL COLLEGE, UNIVERSITY. ▻ *adj* relating to technical training. ⓒ Early 19c as *adjective*, from Greek *polytechnos* skilled in many arts, from *techne* art.

polytetrafluoroethylene /pɒlɪtɛtrəflʊəroʊ'ɛθɪliːn/ ▻ *noun* (abbreviation **PTFE**) a tough thermoplastic material, used especially to coat the surface of non-stick cooking utensils. ⓒ 20c.

polytheism /'pɒlɪθiːɪzəm/ ▻ *noun* belief in or worship of more than one god. • **polytheist** *noun.* • **polytheistic** *adj.* ⓒ 17c.

polythene /'pɒlɪθiːn/ ▻ *noun* a waxy translucent easily-moulded THERMOPLASTIC, used in the form of film or sheeting to package food products, clothing, etc, and to make pipes, moulded articles and electrical insulators. Also called **polyethylene** /-'ɛθəliːn/.

polyunsaturated ▻ *adj, chem* said of a compound, especially a fat or oil: containing two or more double bonds per molecule □ *polyunsaturated margarine*. Compare MONOUNSATURATED. ⓒ 1930s.

polyurethane ▻ *noun, chem* any of various polymers that contain the URETHANE group, and are used in protective coatings, adhesives, paints, varnishes, plastics, rubbers and foams. ⓒ 1940s.

polyvinyl chloride ▻ *noun, chem* (abbreviation **PVC**) a tough white THERMOPLASTIC, resistant to fire and chemicals and easily dyed and softened, used in pipes and other moulded products, records (see RECORD *noun* 4), food packaging, waterproof clothing and electrical insulation.

pom ▻ *noun, Austral & NZ derog colloq* a short form of POMMY.

pomace /'pʌmɪs/ ▻ *noun* **1 a** crushed apples for cider-making; **b** the residue of these or of any similar fruit after pressing. **2** anything crushed or ground to a pulp. ⓒ 16c: from Latin *pomum* fruit or apple.

pomade /pɒ'mɑːd, -'meɪd/ *historical* ▻ *noun* a perfumed ointment for the hair and scalp. ▻ *verb* (***pomaded***, ***pomading***) to put pomade on (a person's hair, etc). ⓒ 16c: from French *pommade*, from Latin *pomum* apple, a one-time ingredient of this.

pomander /pɒ'mandə(r), poʊ-/ ▻ *noun* **1** a perfumed ball composed of various aromatic substances, originally carried as scent or to ward off infection. **2** a perforated container for this. ⓒ 15c: from French *pomme d'ambre* apple of amber.

pome /poʊm/ ▻ *noun, bot* a type of fruit in which a fleshy outer layer surrounds a central core that contains a number of seeds, eg the apple and the pear. ⓒ 19c in this sense; 15c, meaning 'apple': from Latin *pomum* apple.

pomegranate /'pɒmɪgranət/ ▻ *noun* **1** a small deciduous tree or shrub widely cultivated in warm temperate regions for its edible fruit and its attractive white, orange or red flowers. **2** the round fruit of this plant, which has tough red or brown skin surrounding a mass of seeds, each of which is enclosed by red juicy edible flesh. ⓒ 14c: from French *pome grenate*, from Latin *pomum granatum* seedy apple.

pomelo /'pʌməloʊ, 'pɒməloʊ/ ▻ *noun* (***pomelos***) **1** a tropical tree, native to SE Asia, cultivated for its edible citrus fruit. **2** the round yellow edible fruit of this tree, resembling a grapefruit. **3** *Caribb* a GRAPEFRUIT. ⓒ 19c: from Dutch *pompelmoes* shaddock or grapefruit.

Pomeranian /pɒmə'reɪnɪən/ ▻ *noun* a breed of small dog with a sharp-pointed muzzle and thick double-layered white, creamy or black coat. ⓒ 19c in this sense; 18c as *adjective* 'belonging to Pomerania' (a region in N central Poland).

pomfret /ˈpɒmfrɪt, pʌm-/ and **pomfret cake** ▷ *noun* a disc-shaped liquorice sweet. ⓘ 19c: from French *Pontfret* Pontefract, where it was originally made.

pommel /ˈpɒməl, ˈpʌməl/ ▷ *noun* **1** the raised forepart of a saddle. **2** a rounded knob forming the end of a sword hilt. ▷ *verb* (***pommelled, pommelling***) to pummel. ⓘ 14c: from French *pomel* knob, from Latin *pommum* apple.

pommy /ˈpɒmɪ/ ▷ *noun* (***pommies***) *Austral & NZ derog colloq* a British, or especially English, person. Often shortened to **pom**. Also *as adj* □ *pommy scumbag.* ⓘ Early 20c.

pomp ▷ *noun* **1** ceremonial grandeur. **2** vain ostentation. ⓘ 14c: from Latin *pompa* procession.

pompadour /ˈpɒmpəˈdʊə(r)/ ▷ *noun, historical* a fashion of dressing women's hair by rolling it back from the forehead over a small cushion or pad, to give extra height. ⓘ 18c: named after the Marquise de Pompadour (1721–64), the mistress of Louis XV, who wore her hair in this way.

pompom /ˈpɒmpɒm/ or **pompon** ▷ *noun* **1** a ball made of cut wool or other yarn, used as a trimming on clothes, etc. **2 a** a variety of chrysanthemum with small globe-like flowers; **b** *as adj* □ *pompom dahlia.* ⓘ 18c: from French *pompon.*

pom-pom /ˈpɒmpɒm/ ▷ *noun* an automatic quick-firing gun, especially a multi-barrelled anti-aircraft gun. ⓘ Late 19c: imitating its sound.

pomposity /pɒmˈpɒsɪtɪ/ ▷ *noun* (***pomposities***) a pompous quality or manner.

pompous /ˈpɒmpəs/ ▷ *adj* **1** solemnly self-important. **2** said of language: inappropriately grand and flowery; pretentious. • **pompously** *adverb.* ⓘ 14c: from Latin *pomposus,* from *pompa* procession.

ponce /pɒns/ *offensive slang* ▷ *noun* **1** a pimp. **2** an effeminate man. ▷ *verb* (***ponced, poncing***) *intr* (*usually* **ponce about** or **around**) **1** to mince about in an effeminate manner. **2** to mess around. ⓘ 19c.

poncho /ˈpɒntʃoʊ/ ▷ *noun* (***ponchos***) an outer garment, originally S American, made of a large piece of cloth with a hole in the middle for the head to go through. ⓘ 18c: American Spanish.

pond ▷ *noun* **1** a small area of still fresh water surrounded by land, either lying in a natural depression in the Earth's surface, or artificially constructed, eg in a garden. **2** *N Amer slang* (*usually* **the Pond**) the sea, especially the Atlantic Ocean. ⓘ 13c, meaning 'enclosure'.

ponder /ˈpɒndə(r)/ ▷ *verb* (***pondered, pondering***) *tr & intr* (*often* **ponder on** or **over something**) to consider or contemplate it deeply. ⓘ 14c: from French *ponderer,* from Latin *ponderare* to weigh, from *pondus* weight.

ponderous /ˈpɒndərəs/ ▷ *adj* **1** said of speech, humour, etc: heavy-handed, laborious, over-solemn or pompous. **2** heavy or cumbersome; lumbering in movement. **3** weighty; important. • **ponderously** *adverb.* • **ponderousness** *noun.* ⓘ 14c: from Latin *ponderosus;* see PONDER.

pondok /ˈpɒndɒk/ or **pondokkie** /-ˈdɒkɪ/ ▷ *noun, S Afr derog* a crude dwelling hut; a shack. ⓘ 19c: Malay, meaning 'leaf house'.

pone¹ /poʊn/ ▷ *noun, US* a kind of maize bread. Also called **corn pone**. ⓘ 17c: Algonquian *apones.*

pone² /poʊn, poʊnɪ/ ▷ *noun, cards* the player to the right of the dealer. ⓘ 19c: Latin, meaning 'put', from *ponere* to place.

pong *colloq* ▷ *noun* a stink; a bad smell. ▷ *verb* (***ponged, ponging***) *intr* to smell badly. • **pongy** /ˈpɒŋɪ/ *adj* (***pongier, pongiest***) stinking; smelly. ⓘ Early 20c.

pongee /pɒnˈdʒiː/ ▷ *noun* **1** a soft unbleached silk made from the cocoons of a wild silkworm. **2** a fine cotton similar to this. ⓘ 19c: from Chinese *ben zhi* woven at home, from *ben* own or self + *zhi* to weave or knit.

pongo /ˈpɒŋgoʊ/ ▷ *noun* (***pongos***) an anthropoid ape, originally a gorilla but now used of an ORANG-UTAN. ⓘ 17c: from Congolese *mpongi.*

poniard /ˈpɒnjəd/ ▷ *noun* a slim-bladed dagger. ▷ *verb* (***poniarded, poniarding***) to stab someone or something with a poniard. ⓘ 16c: from French *poignard,* from *poing* fist.

pons /pɒnz/ ▷ *noun* (***pontes*** /ˈpɒntiːz/) *anatomy* in the brain of mammals: the mass of nerve fibres that connects the MEDULLA OBLONGATA to the THALAMUS, and relays nerve impulses between different parts of the brain. ⓘ 18c; 17c in full form *pons Varolii* bridge of Varoli, named after Constanzo Varoli (1543–75) Italian anatomist: Latin, literally 'bridge'.

pontiff /ˈpɒntɪf/ ▷ *noun* **1** a title for the Pope. **2** *formerly* any Roman Catholic bishop. ⓘ 17c: from French *pontife,* from Latin *pontifex* high priest.

pontifical /pɒnˈtɪfɪkəl/ ▷ *adj* **1** belonging or relating to a pontiff. **2** *derog* pompously opinionated; dogmatic. ▷ *noun, RC Church, C of E* an office-book containing the sacraments and other rites to be performed by a bishop. ⓘ 15c.

pontificals ▷ *plural noun* the ceremonial dress of a bishop or pope.

pontificate /pɒnˈtɪfɪkeɪt/ ▷ *verb* (***pontificated, pontificating***) *intr* **1** to pronounce one's opinion pompously and arrogantly. **2** to perform the duties of a pontiff. ▷ *noun* /pɒnˈtɪfɪkət/ the office of a pope. ⓘ 16c: from Latin *pontificatus* high-priesthood, from *pontifex* high priest.

pontoon¹ /pɒnˈtuːn/ ▷ *noun* any of a number of flat-bottomed craft, punts, barges, etc, anchored side by side across a river, to support a temporary bridge or platform, etc by providing buoyancy in the water. ⓘ 17c: from French *ponton,* from Latin *ponto* a punt, from *pons* a bridge.

pontoon² /pɒnˈtuːn/ ▷ *noun, cards* a game in which the object is to collect sets of cards that add up to or close to 21, without going over that total. Also called **twenty-one, vingt-et-un**. ⓘ Early 20c: a corruption of French *vingt-et-un* twenty-one.

pontoon bridge ▷ *noun* a bridge or platform, etc supported on pontoons.

pony /ˈpoʊnɪ/ ▷ *noun* (***ponies***) **1** any of several small hardy breeds of horse, usually less than 14.2 hands (1.5m) in height when fully grown, noted for their intelligence. **2** *Brit slang* a sum of £25. **3** *US slang* a crib or a translation prepared for use in an exam, etc. **4** *slang* a small glass. ⓘ 17c: from Scots *powney,* from French *poulenet,* diminutive of *poulain* colt, from Latin *pullus* a young animal or foal.

ponytail ▷ *noun* a hairstyle in which a person's hair is drawn back and gathered by a band at the back of the head, so that it hangs free like a pony's tail. Compare PIGTAIL. ⓘ 1950s.

pony trekking ▷ *noun* the recreational activity of riding ponies cross-country, especially in groups.

poo see POOP³

pooch /puːtʃ/ ▷ *noun* (***pooches***) *colloq* a dog, especially a mongrel. ⓘ 1920s.

poodle /ˈpuːdəl/ ▷ *noun* **1** a breed of lively pet dog of various sizes which has a narrow head with pendulous ears and a long curly black, white, grey or brown coat, often clipped into an elaborate style. **2** *derog* a lackey. ⓘ 19c: from German *Pudel,* short for *Pudelhund,* from *pudeln* to splash, as poodles were originally trained as water dogs.

poof /puːf/ and **poofter** /ˈpuːftə(r)/ ▷ *noun, offensive slang* a male homosexual. • **poofy** *adj* (***poofier, poofiest***) effeminate. ⓘ 19c: from French *pouffe* puff.

pooh /puː/ ▷ *exclamation, colloq* an exclamation of scorn or disgust, especially at an offensive smell. ◷ 17c: imitating the sound uttered.

pooh-pooh ▷ *verb* (***pooh-poohed, pooh-poohing***) *colloq* to express scorn for (a suggestion, etc); to dismiss (a suggestion, etc). ◷ 19c: from POOH.

pooka /ˈpuːkə/ ▷ *noun* (***pookas***) in Irish folklore: a malevolent goblin or spirit which sometimes assumes the form of an animal, and is said to haunt bogs and marshes. ◷ 19c: from Irish Gaelic *puca*.

pool¹ ▷ *noun* **1** a small area of still water. **2** a puddle; a patch of spilt liquid □ ***pools of blood.*** **3** a swimming pool. **4** a deep part of a stream or river. ◷ Anglo-Saxon *pol*.

pool² ▷ *noun* **1** a reserve of money, personnel, vehicles, etc used as a communal resource. Also *in compounds* □ ***typing pool.*** **2** the combined stakes of those betting on something; a jackpot. **3** *commerce* a group of businesses with a common arrangement to maintain high prices, so eliminating competition and preserving profits. **4** a game like BILLIARDS played with a white cue ball and usually 15 numbered coloured balls, the aim being to shoot specified balls into specified pockets using the cue ball. Compare SNOOKER. ▷ *verb* (***pooled, pooling***) to put (money or other resources) into a common supply for general use. ◷ 17c: from French *poule*, literally 'a hen', but associated in English with POOL¹ since the 18c.

the pools ▷ *plural noun, Brit* an organized syndicate which involves postal betting on the outcome of football matches. Also called **football pools**.

poop¹ *naut* ▷ *noun* **1** the raised enclosed part at the stern of old sailing ships. **2** the high deck at the stern of a ship. Also called **poop deck**. ▷ *verb* (***pooped, pooping***) **1** said of a wave: to break over the stern of (a ship). **2** said of a ship: to receive (a wave) over the stern. ◷ 15c: from French *pupe*, from Latin *puppis*.

poop² ▷ *verb* (***pooped, pooping***) *colloq* **1** *in passive* to become winded or exhausted □ ***Sheena was pooped after walking up the hill.*** **2** (*also* **poop someone out**) to tire them out; to make them exhausted or winded □ ***The swimming pooped me out.*** **3** *intr* (*usually* **poop out**) to give up from exhaustion. ◷ 1930s.

poop³ and **poo** *slang* ▷ *noun* faeces. ▷ *verb* (***pooped, pooping***) *intr* to defecate. ◷ 18c in this sense; 16c meaning 'a toot'.

poop-scoop and **pooper-scooper** ▷ *noun, colloq* a small scoop used to lift and remove dog faeces from pavements, etc. ◷ 1970s.

poor /pʊə(r), pɔː(r)/ ▷ *adj* **1** not having sufficient money or means to live comfortably. **2** (**the poor**) poor people in general (see THE 4). **3** (**poor in something**) not well supplied with it □ ***a country poor in minerals.*** **4** not good; weak; unsatisfactory □ ***poor eyesight.*** **5** unsatisfactorily small or sparse □ ***a poor attendance.*** **6** used in expressing pity or sympathy □ ***poor fellow!*** • **poorness** *noun*. See also POVERTY. • **poor man's ...** *derog* a substitute of lower quality or price than the specified thing □ ***This is only lumpfish, poor man's caviare.*** ◷ 13c: from French *povre*, from Latin *pauper* poor.

poor box ▷ *noun* a moneybox, especially one in a church, used to collect donations for the poor.

poorhouse ▷ *noun, historical* an institution maintained at public expense, for housing the poor; a WORKHOUSE.

poor law ▷ *noun, historical* a law or set of laws concerned with the public support of the poor.

poorly ▷ *adverb* not well; badly □ ***I speak French poorly.*** ▷ *adj, colloq or dialect* unwell □ ***Do you feel poorly?***

poor white ▷ *noun, derog* a member of an impoverished and deprived class of white people living among Blacks in the southern USA or South Africa. Often *as adj* □ ***poor white trash.***

pop¹ ▷ *noun* **1** a sharp explosive noise, like that of a cork coming out of a bottle. **2** *colloq, especially N Amer* any sweet non-alcoholic fizzy drink such as ginger beer. ▷ *verb* (***popped, popping***) **1** *tr & intr* to make or cause something to make a pop. **2** *tr & intr* to burst with a pop □ ***The balloon popped and landed at my feet.*** **3** (*especially* **pop out** or **up**) to spring out or up; to protrude. **4** *intr, colloq* to go quickly in a direction specified □ ***I'll just pop next door for a second.*** **5** *colloq* to put something somewhere quickly or briefly □ ***just pop it in the oven.*** **6** *slang* to pawn. **7** *drug-taking slang* to take or inject (a drug). ▷ *adverb* with a pop. • **pop the question** *humorous, colloq* to propose marriage. ◷ 16c as *verb* sense 1; 14c in obsolete sense 'to knock': imitating the sound.

■ **pop off** *colloq* **1** to leave quickly or suddenly. **2** to die.

■ **pop up** to appear or occur, especially unexpectedly. See also POP-UP.

pop² ▷ *noun* (*in full* **pop music**) a type of music which is primarily melody-driven and commercial, usually with a strong beat and characterized by its use of electronic equipment such as guitars and keyboards. ▷ *adj* popular □ ***pop culture.*** ◷ 19c, as a shortening of 'popular concert'.

pop³ ▷ *noun, informal, especially N Amer* father; dad. **2** often as a form of address: an elderly man. ◷ 19c; see PAPA.

pop. ▷ *abbreviation* **1** population. **2** popular. **3** popularly.

popcorn ▷ *noun* **1** (*also* **popping corn**) maize grains that puff up and burst open when heated. **2** the edible puffed-up kernels of this grain.

pope ▷ *noun* **1** (*often* **Pope**) the Bishop of Rome, the head of the Roman Catholic Church. **2** a priest in the Eastern Orthodox Church. • **popedom** *noun* the office, dignity or jurisdiction of the pope; a pope's tenure of office. ◷ Anglo-Saxon as *papa*: from Latin, from Greek *pappas* father, in the early Church a title used respectfully to bishops.

popery /ˈpoʊpərɪ/ ▷ *noun, offensive* Roman Catholicism.

pope's nose see under PARSON'S NOSE

pop-eyed ▷ *adj, colloq* with eyes protruding, especially in amazement.

popgun ▷ *noun* a toy gun that fires a cork or pellet with a pop.

popinjay /ˈpɒpɪndʒeɪ/ ▷ *noun, old use, derog* a vain or conceited person; a dandy or fop. ◷ 16c; 13c in archaic sense 'parrot': from French *papegai* parrot, from Spanish *papagayo*, from Arabic *babbaga*.

popish /ˈpoʊpɪʃ/ ▷ *adj, offensive* belonging or relating to Roman Catholicism.

poplar /ˈpɒplə(r)/ ▷ *noun* **1** a tall slender deciduous tree found in northern temperate regions, with broad simple leaves which tremble in a slight breeze, often planted for ornament or shelter. **2** the soft fine-grained yellowish wood of this tree, used to make plywood, matches, boxes and paper pulp. ◷ 14c: from French *poplier*, from Latin *populus*.

poplin /ˈpɒplɪn/ ▷ *noun* a strong cotton cloth with a finely ribbed finish. ◷ 18c: from French *popeline*, from Italian *papalina* papal cloth, because it was made in the papal city of Avignon.

popliteal /pɒpˈlɪtɪəl/ ▷ *adj, anatomy* belonging or relating to the part of the leg behind the knee. ◷ 18c: from Latin *poples* the ham of the knee.

pop music see POP²

poppadum, **poppadom** or **pappadom** /ˈpɒpədəm/ ▷ *noun* a paper-thin pancake, grilled or fried till crisp, served with Indian dishes. ◷ 19c: from Tamil *poppatam*, perhaps from *paruppa atam* lentil cake.

popper /ˈpɒpə(r)/ ▷ *noun* **1** someone or something that pops. **2** *informal* a PRESS STUD. **3** *especially N Amer* a container used to make popcorn. **4** (*often* **poppers**) *drug-taking slang* a small bottle of amyl nitrate or butyl nitrate which is inhaled.

poppet /ˈpɒpɪt/ ▷ *noun* **1** a term of endearment for someone lovable. **2** in vehicle engines: an unhinged valve that rises and falls in its housing. **3** a timber support used in launching a ship. ◎ 14c: an earlier form of PUPPET.

popping-crease ▷ *noun, cricket* the line at or behind which the batsman must stand, parallel to, and four feet in front of, the wicket. ◎ 18c: probably from POP[1] in the sense 'to hit or knock'.

popple /ˈpɒpəl/ ▷ *verb* (***poppled, poppling***) *intr* **1** said of boiling water or of sea water: to bubble or ripple. **2** (*often* **popple along**) to flow tumblingly. ▷ *noun* a poppling movement. ◎ 14c: imitating the sound made.

pop poetry ▷ *noun* a type of verse written primarily for public performance, which is often topical and satirical, and may be accompanied by music. ◎ 1970s.

poppy /ˈpɒpɪ/ ▷ *noun* (***poppies***) **1** any of numerous northern temperate plants with large brightly-coloured bowl-shaped flowers and a fruit in the form of a capsule, especially the **common poppy**. See also OPIUM POPPY. **2** an artificial red poppy, worn for Remembrance Day, symbolizing the poppies that grew on the battlefields of Flanders after World War I. ◎ Anglo-Saxon *popig*.

poppycock ▷ *noun, colloq* nonsense. ◎ 19c: from Dutch dialect *pappekak* soft dung.

Poppy Day see REMEMBRANCE DAY

pop socks ▷ *plural noun* knee-high nylon stockings.

popsy /ˈpɒpsɪ/ ▷ *noun* (***popsies***) *dated colloq* a term of endearment for a young girl or woman. ◎ 19c: diminutive of *pop*, shortened from POPPET (sense 1).

populace /ˈpɒpjʊləs/ ▷ *noun* the body of ordinary citizens; the common people. ◎ 16c: French, from Latin *populus* people.

popular /ˈpɒpjʊlə(r)/ ▷ *adj* **1** liked or enjoyed by most people □ *a pastime still popular with the young.* **2** said of beliefs, etc: accepted by many people □ *a popular misconception.* **3** catering for the tastes and abilities of ordinary people as distinct from specialists, etc □ *a popular history of science.* **4** said of a person: generally liked and admired. **5** involving the will or preferences of the public in general □ *by popular demand.* • **popularity** *noun.* • **popularly** *adverb.* ◎ 15c: from Latin *popularis*, from *populus* people.

popular front and **people's front** ▷ *noun* a left-wing group or faction, especially one set up from the 1930s onwards to oppose fascism.

popularize or **popularise** ▷ *verb* (***popularized, popularizing***) **1** to make something popular □ *popularized the mini skirt.* **2** to present something in a simple easily-understood way, so as to have general appeal. • **popularization** *noun.*

populate /ˈpɒpjʊleɪt/ ▷ *verb* (***populated, populating***) **1** said of people, animals or plants: to inhabit or live in (a certain area). **2** to supply (uninhabited places) with inhabitants; to people. ◎ 16c: from Latin *populare* to inhabit, from *populus* people.

population /pɒpjʊˈleɪʃən/ ▷ *noun* **1** all the people living in a particular country, area, etc. **2** the number of people living in a particular area, country, etc □ *The city has a population of two million.* **3** a group of animals or plants of the same species living in a certain area; the total number of these □ *the declining elephant population.* **4** the process of populating an area. **5** *statistics* a group that consists of all the possible quantities or values relevant to a statistical study, from which representative samples are taken in order to determine the characteristics of the whole.

population explosion ▷ *noun* a sudden or rapid increase in the size of a population, due to factors such as increased life expectancy.

populism ▷ *noun* political activity or notions that are thought to reflect the opinions and interests of ordinary people.

populist ▷ *noun* **1** a person who believes in the right and ability of the common people to play a major part in government. **2** a person who studies, supports or attracts the support of the common people. ▷ *adj* said of a political cause, programme, etc: appealing to the majority of the people.

populous ▷ *adj* densely inhabited. ◎ 15c: from Latin *populosus*, from *populus* people.

pop-up ▷ *adj* **1** said of a picture book, greetings card, etc: having cut-out parts designed to stand upright as the page is opened. **2** said of appliances, etc: having a mechanism which causes a component, or the item being prepared, to pop up □ *pop-up toaster.* See also POP UP at POP[1].

porbeagle /ˈpɔːbiːgəl/ ▷ *noun* a large heavily-built shark with a broad deep tail. ◎ 18c: a Cornish dialect word.

porcelain /ˈpɔːsəlɪn/ ▷ *noun* **1 a** a fine white translucent earthenware, originally made in China; **b** *as adj* □ *a porcelain dish.* **2** objects made of this. ◎ 16c: from French *porcelaine*, from Italian *porcellana* cowrie shell.

porch /pɔːtʃ/ ▷ *noun* (***porches***) **1** a structure that forms a covered entrance to the doorway of a building. **2** *N Amer* a verandah. ◎ 13c: from French *porche*, from Latin *porticus* colonnade.

porcine /ˈpɔːsaɪn/ ▷ *adj* relating to or resembling a pig. ◎ 17c: from Latin *porcinus*, from *porcus* pig.

porcupine /ˈpɔːkjʊpaɪn/ ▷ *noun* any of various large nocturnal rodents with long sharp black-and-white spikes or quills on the back and sides of the body. ◎ 14c: from French *porc d'espine* spiny pig.

pore[1] /pɔː(r)/ ▷ *noun* **1** a small, usually round opening in the surface of a living organism, eg in the skin, through which fluids, gases and other substances can pass. **2** any tiny cavity or gap, eg in soil or rock. ◎ 14c: French, from Latin *porus*, from Greek *poros* a passage or duct.

pore[2] /pɔː(r)/ ▷ *verb* (***pored, poring***) *intr* (*always* **pore over something**) to study (books, documents, etc) with intense concentration. ◎ 13c as *pouren*.

porge /pɔːʒ/ ▷ *verb* (***porged, porging***) *Judaism* to cleanse (a slaughtered animal) ceremonially by removing the forbidden fat, sinews, etc. ◎ 18c: from Jewish Spanish *porgar*, from Latin *purgare* to purge.

poriferan /pɒˈrɪfərən/ *zool* ▷ *adj* referring or relating to animals belonging to the phylum **Porifera**, the sponges. ▷ *noun* a member of this phylum. ◎ 19c: from Latin *porus* a pore + *ferre* to bear.

pork ▷ *noun* the flesh of a pig used as food. ◎ 13c: from French *porc*, from Latin *porcus* pig.

porker ▷ *noun* a pig that shows fast growth and reaches maturity at a relatively light weight, reared for fresh meat as opposed to processed meats such as bacon.

porky ▷ *adj* (***porkier, porkiest***) **1** resembling pork. **2** *colloq* plump.

porn and **porno** *colloq* ▷ *noun* pornography. ▷ *adj* pornographic.

pornography /pɔːˈnɒgrəfɪ/ ▷ *noun* books, pictures, films, etc designed to be sexually arousing, often offensive owing to their explicit nature. Often shortened to **porn** or **porno**. See also HARD PORN, SOFT PORN. • **pornographer** *noun.* • **pornographic** /pɔːnəˈgrafɪk/ *adj.* • **pornographically** *adverb.* ◎ 19c: from Greek *pornographos* writing about prostitutes, from *porne* prostitute + *graphein* to write.

porosity /pɔːˈrɒsɪtɪ/ ▻ *noun* (***porosities***) **1** said of a solid material: the property of being porous. **2** *geol* the ratio of the total volume occupied by pores and other spaces in a material, to the total volume occupied by that material.

porous /ˈpɔːrəs/ ▻ *adj* **1** referring or relating to a material that contains pores or cavities. **2** capable of being permeated by liquids or gases. ◷ 14c: from Latin *porosus*, from *porus* a pore.

porphyry /ˈpɔːfɪrɪ/ *geol* ▻ *noun* **1** *loosely* any igneous rock that contains large crystals surrounded by much smaller ones. **2** a very hard purple and white rock used in sculpture. • **porphyritic** /pɔːfɪˈrɪtɪk/ *adj.* ◷ 14c: from Latin *porphyrites*, ultimately from Greek *porphyrites lithos* purplish stone, from *porphyros* purple.

porpoise /ˈpɔːpəs/ ▻ *noun* **1** a beakless whale, smaller than a dolphin, with a blunt snout, found in northern coastal waters and around the coasts of S America and SE Asia. **2** *loosely* a DOLPHIN. ◷ 14c: from Latin *porcuspiscis*, from *porcus* pig + *piscis* fish.

porridge /ˈpɒrɪdʒ/ ▻ *noun* **1** a dish of oatmeal or some other cereal which is boiled in water or milk until it reaches a thick consistency. *N Amer equivalent* OATMEAL. **2** *Brit slang* a jail sentence. • **do porridge** *Brit slang* to serve a prison sentence □ *He's doing porridge now.* ◷ 17c in sense 1; 16c in obsolete sense 'thick soup'; a variant of POTTAGE.

porringer /ˈpɒrɪndʒə(r)/ ▻ *noun* a bowl, with a handle, for soup or porridge. ◷ 16c as *potinger*, variation of *potager* soup bowl; see POTTAGE.

port¹ ▻ *noun* **1** a harbour. **2** a town with a harbour. ◷ Anglo-Saxon: from Latin *portus*.

port² ▻ *noun* the left side of a ship or aircraft. Compare STARBOARD. ▻ *verb* (***ported***, ***porting***) *tr & intr* to turn or be turned to the left. ◷ 16c.

port³ ▻ *noun* **1** an opening in a ship's side for loading, etc. **2** a PORTHOLE. **3** *computing* a socket that connects the CPU of a computer to a peripheral device. **4** *now chiefly Scots* a town gate, or its former position. ◷ Anglo-Saxon: from Latin *porta* gate.

port⁴ ▻ *noun* a sweet dark-red or tawny fortified wine. ◷ 17c: from Oporto, the city in Portugal from where it was originally exported.

port⁵ ▻ *verb* (***ported***, ***porting***) *military* to hold (a rifle, etc) across the body with both hands, the barrel close to the left shoulder. ◷ 16c: from French *porter*, from Latin *portare* to carry.

portable /ˈpɔːtəbəl/ ▻ *adj* **1** easily carried or moved, and usually designed to be so. **2** *computing* said of a program: adaptable for use in a variety of systems. ▻ *noun* a portable radio, television, typewriter, etc. • **portability** *noun.* ◷ 14c: French, from Latin *portabilis*, from *portare* to carry.

portage /ˈpɔːtɪdʒ/ ▻ *noun* **1** an act of carrying. **2** the cost of carrying. **3** the transportation of ships, equipment, etc overland from one waterway to another. **4** the route used for this. ▻ *verb* (***portaged***, ***portaging***) to transport (ships, etc) overland. ◷ 15c: French, from *porter* to carry, from Latin *portare*.

Portakabin /ˈpɔːtəkabɪn/ ▻ *noun, trademark* a portable structure used as a temporary office, etc. ◷ 1960s.

portal /ˈpɔːtəl/ ▻ *noun, formal* an entrance, gateway or doorway, especially an imposing or awesome one. ◷ 14c: French, from Latin *portale*, from *porta* a gate.

portal vein ▻ *noun, anatomy* any vein that connects two networks of capillaries, eg the hepatic portal vein which connects the capillaries of the intestine to those of the liver. ◷ 19c: from Latin *porta* the transverse fissure of the liver, or a gate-like structure; see PORTAL.

portamento /pɔːtəˈmentoʊ/ ▻ *noun* (***portamenti*** /-tɪ/) *music* especially in stringed instruments: a continuous glide from one tone or note to another. ◷ 18c: Italian, literally 'a carrying', from Latin *portare* to carry.

portcullis /pɔːtˈkʌlɪs/ ▻ *noun, historical* a vertical iron or wooden grating fitted into a town gateway or castle entrance, which was lowered to keep intruders out. ◷ 14c: from French *porte coleice* sliding door or gate, from Latin porta *gate* + *colare* to filter.

portend /pɔːˈtend/ ▻ *verb* (***portended***, ***portending***) to warn of (usually something bad); to signify or foreshadow it. See also BODE. ◷ 15c: from Latin *portendere* to foreshadow or give a sign.

portent /ˈpɔːtent/ ▻ *noun* **1** a prophetic sign; an omen. **2** fateful significance □ *an event of grim portent.* **3** a marvel or prodigy. ◷ 16c: from Latin *portentum* a sign, from *portendere* (see PORTEND).

portentous /pɔːˈtentəs/ ▻ *adj* **1** ominous or fateful; relating to portents. **2** weighty, solemn or pompous. **3** amazing or marvellous. • **portentously** *adverb.* • **portentousness** *noun.*

porter¹ /ˈpɔːtə(r)/ ▻ *noun* a doorman, caretaker or janitor at a college, office or factory. ◷ 13c: from French *portier*, from Latin *portarius* gatekeeper.

porter² /ˈpɔːtə(r)/ ▻ *noun* **1** someone employed to carry luggage or parcels, eg at a railway station. **2** in a hospital: someone employed to move patients when required and to carry out other general duties. **3** a heavy dark-brown beer brewed from malt, formerly reputed to be popular with porters. **4** *N Amer* on a train: a sleeping-car attendant. ◷ 14c: from French *porteour*, from Latin *portator*, from *portare* to carry.

porterhouse ▻ *noun* **1** (*in full* **porterhouse steak**) a choice cut of beefsteak from the back of the sirloin. **2** *formerly* a public house where porter, beer, etc and steaks were served. ◷ 18c.

portfolio /pɔːtˈfoʊlɪoʊ/ ▻ *noun* (***portfolios***) **1** a flat case for carrying papers, drawings, photographs, etc. **2** the contents of such a case, as a demonstration of a person's work. **3** *politics* the post of a government minister with responsibility for a specific department. **4** a list of the investments or securities held by an individual, company, etc. ◷ 18c: from Italian *portafoglio*, from *portare* to carry + *foglio* a leaf.

porthole ▻ *noun* **1** an opening, usually a round one, in a ship's side to admit light and air. **2** an opening in a wall through which a gun can be fired. ◷ 16c.

portico /ˈpɔːtɪkoʊ/ ▻ *noun* (***porticos*** or ***porticoes***) *archit* a colonnade forming a porch or covered way alongside a building. ◷ 17c: Italian, from Latin *porticus* a porch, from *porta* a door.

portière / *French* pɔʀtjɛʀ/ ▻ *noun* a curtain hung over the door or doorway of a room. ◷ 19c: French, from Latin *porta* a door.

portion /ˈpɔːʃən/ ▻ *noun* **1** a piece or part of a whole □ *divided the cake into 12 equal portions.* **2** a share; a part allotted to one. **3** an individual helping of food. **4** *literary* one's destiny or fate. **5** *law* a woman's dowry. **6** *law* a share of money left to a child by their parents or guardians, intended as a permanent provision for them. ▻ *verb* (***portioned***, ***portioning***) (*now usually* **portion something out**) to divide it up; to share it out. ◷ 13c: from French *porcion*, from Latin *portio*, *portionis*.

portly /ˈpɔːtlɪ/ ▻ *adj* (***portlier***, ***portliest***) said especially of a man: somewhat stout. ◷ 16c: from *port* deportment or bearing (related to PORT⁵).

portmanteau /pɔːtˈmantoʊ/ ▻ *noun* (***portmanteaus*** or ***portmanteaux*** /-toʊz/) **1** a large travelling-bag that opens flat in two halves. See also GLADSTONE BAG. **2** *as adj* combining or covering two or more things of the same kind. ◷ 16c: French, meaning 'cloak carrier', from *porter* to carry + *manteau* coat or cloak.

portmanteau word ▻ *noun* a BLEND. ◷ 19c: originally used by Lewis Carroll (1832–98), English writer.

port of call ▷ *noun* (***ports of call***) **1** a place where a ship stops on a sea journey. **2** a place called at during a journey.

port of entry ▷ *noun* (***ports of entry***) a port by which people and merchandise may enter a country, supervised by immigration and customs officials.

portrait /ˈpɔːtrət/ ▷ *noun* **1** a drawing, painting or photograph of a person, especially of the face only. **2** a written description, film depiction, etc of someone or something □ ***a portrait of country life.*** ▷ *adj, printing* said of a page, illustration, etc: taller than it is wide. Compare LANDSCAPE. ⓒ 16c: French, from *portraire* to portray.

portraiture /ˈpɔːtrɪtʃə(r)/ ▷ *noun* **1** the art or act of making portraits. **2** a portrait, or portraits collectively.

portray /pɔːˈtreɪ/ ▷ *verb* (***portrayed, portraying***) **1** to make a portrait of someone or something. **2** to describe or depict something. **3** to act the part of (a character) in a play, film, etc. • **portrayal** *noun*. • **portrayer** *noun*. ⓒ 14c: from French *portraire* to represent, from Latin *protrahere* to draw forth.

Portuguese /pɔːtʃʊˈgiːz/ ▷ *adj* belonging or relating to Portugal, a country in SW Europe, its inhabitants or their language. ▷ *noun* (***Portuguese***) **1** a citizen or inhabitant of, or person born in, Portugal. **2** (**the Portuguese**) the people of Portugal in general (see THE sense 4). **3** the official language of Portugal. ⓒ 17c.

Portuguese man-of-war ▷ *noun* a genus of invertebrate animals resembling a large jellyfish that is native to tropical seas and consists of a colony of hundreds of small POLYPS with long stinging tentacles, clustered underneath a gas-filled bluish-purple bladder with a high crest. ⓒ 18c.

port-wine stain and **port-wine mark** ▷ *noun* a usually permanent purplish-red birthmark resulting from the formation of an extra-large network of blood vessels below the skin before birth. ⓒ 17c.

POS ▷ *abbreviation, commerce* point of sale.

pose ▷ *noun* **1** a position or attitude of the body □ ***a relaxed pose.*** **2** an artificial way of behaving, adopted for effect □ ***His punk style is just a pose.*** ▷ *verb* (***posed, posing***) **1** *tr & intr* to take up a position oneself, or position (someone else), for a photograph, portrait, etc. **2** *intr, derog* to behave in an exaggerated or artificial way so as to draw attention to oneself. **3** *intr* (*usually* **pose as someone** or **something**) to pretend to be someone or something that one is not □ ***The undercover detective posed as a drug addict to infiltrate the gang of dealers.*** **4** to ask or put forward (a question). **5** to cause (a problem, etc) or present (a threat, etc). • **strike a pose** to adopt a position or attitude, especially a commanding or impressive one. ⓒ 16c in verb sense 4; 15c in obsolete sense 'to suppose': from French *poser*, from Latin *pausare* to cease or pause, but influenced by Latin *ponere* to place.

poser[1] ▷ *noun* **1** someone who poses. **2** *derog* someone who tries to impress others by putting on an act and by dressing, behaving, etc so as to be noticed; a poseur. ⓒ 19c.

poser[2] ▷ *noun* **1** someone who sets difficult questions. **2** a puzzling or perplexing question. ⓒ 16c: from obsolete or rare *pose* to puzzle or perplex.

poseur /poʊˈzɜː(r)/ ▷ *noun, derog* someone who behaves in an affected or insincere way, especially to impress others. ⓒ 19c: French, from *poser* to POSE.

posh *colloq* ▷ *adj* **1** high-quality, expensive, smart or stylish. **2** upper-class. ▷ *adverb* in a way associated with the upper class □ ***Bert talks posh when he's on the telephone.*** ▷ *verb* (***poshed, poshing***) (*always* **posh something up**) to smarten it up. ⓒ 20c: popularly thought to be an acronym of *p*ort *o*utward *s*tarboard *h*ome, which was the most desirable position of cabins when sailing to and from the East, but more likely perhaps to be related to obsolete *posh* a dandy.

posit /ˈpɒzɪt/ ▷ *verb* (***posited, positing***) **1** to lay down or assume something as a basis for discussion; to postulate. **2** to place something in position. ▷ *noun, philos* a statement made on the assumption that it will be proved valid. ⓒ 17c: from Latin *ponere, positum* to place.

position /pəˈzɪʃən/ ▷ *noun* **1** a place where someone or something is □ ***The mansion was in a fine position overlooking the bay.*** **2** the right or proper place □ ***Volume 2 was out of position.*** **3** the relationship of things to one another in space; arrangement. **4** a way of sitting, standing, lying, facing, being held or placed, etc □ ***an upright position.*** **5** *military* a place occupied for strategic purposes. **6** one's opinion or viewpoint □ ***What's your position on euthanasia?*** **7** a job or post □ ***Bill holds a senior position at the bank.*** **8** rank; status; importance in society □ ***wealth and position.*** **9** the place of a competitor in the finishing order, or at an earlier stage in a contest □ ***lying in fourth position.*** **10** *sport* an allotted place in a team, especially on the pitch or playing-area □ ***the centre-forward position.*** **11** the set of circumstances in which one is placed □ ***not in a position to help*** □ ***found myself in an awkward position.*** ▷ *verb* (***positioned, positioning***) to place; to put something or someone in position. • **be in no position to do something** to have no right to (complain, criticize, etc). • **positional** *adj*. ⓒ 15c: French, from Latin *positio, positionis*, from *ponere* to place.

positive /ˈpɒzɪtɪv/ ▷ *adj* **1** sure; certain; convinced. **2** definite; allowing no doubt □ ***positive proof of her guilt.*** **3** expressing agreement or approval □ ***a positive response.*** **4** optimistic □ ***feeling more positive.*** **5** forceful or determined; not tentative. **6** constructive; contributing to progress or improvement; helpful. **7** clear and explicit □ ***positive directions.*** **8** *colloq* downright □ ***a positive scandal.*** **9** said of the result of a chemical test: confirming the existence of the suspected condition. **10** *math* said of a number or quantity: greater than zero. **11** *physics, elec* having a deficiency of electrons, and so being able to attract them, ie attracted by a negative charge. **12** *photog* said of a photographic image: in which light and dark tones and colours correspond to those in the original subject. **13** *grammar* expressing a quality in the simple form, as distinct from the COMPARATIVE or SUPERLATIVE forms. Compare NEGATIVE. ⓒ 14c: from French *positif, positive*, or Latin *positivus*, from *ponere* to place.

positive discrimination ▷ *noun* the creation of special employment opportunities, etc for those groups or members of society previously disadvantaged or discriminated against.

positive feedback ▷ *noun, engineering, biol* a form of feedback in which the output of a system is used to increase the input. Compare NEGATIVE FEEDBACK.

positive heliotropism see under HELIOTROPISM

positive hydrotropism see under HYDROTROPISM

positive reinforcement ▷ *noun, psychol* the process by which an activity is learned through use of a pleasant stimulus or reward, eg food. Compare NEGATIVE REINFORCEMENT.

positive vetting ▷ *noun* investigation of the connections and sympathies of a person being considered for a position of trust, eg in the senior civil service.

positivism /ˈpɒzɪtɪvɪzəm/ ▷ *noun* **1** a school of philosophy maintaining that knowledge can come only from observable phenomena and positive facts. **2** LOGICAL POSITIVISM. • **positivist** *noun, adj*.

positron /ˈpɒzɪtrɒn/ ▷ *noun, physics* an ANTIPARTICLE that has the same mass as an electron, and an equal but opposite charge. See also PET. ⓒ 1930s: a contraction of *positive electron*.

posology /pəˈsɒlədʒɪ/ ▷ *noun* the branch of medicine that deals with the quantities in which drugs or medicines should be administered. ⓒ 19c: from French *posologie*, from Greek *posos* how much.

poss. ▷ *abbreviation* **1** possible. Also (**poss**) *as colloq adj.* **2** possibly. **3** *grammar* possessive.

posse /'pɒsɪ/ ▷ *noun* **1** *N Amer, historical* a mounted troop of men at the service of a local sheriff. **2** *colloq* any group or band of people, especially friends. **3** *US* a Jamaican street gang. ◷ 17c in sense 1: from Latin *posse comitatus* force of the country.

possess /pə'zɛs/ ▷ *verb* (***possessed, possessing***) **1** to own. **2** to have something as a feature or quality □ *Frances possesses a quick mind.* **3** said of an emotion, evil spirit, etc: to occupy and dominate the mind of someone □ *What possessed you to behave like that?* **4** to be master of or have knowledge of someone or something. **5** to have sexual intercourse with someone. ● **possessor** *noun.* ◷ 15c: from French *possesser*, from Latin *possidere*.

possessed ▷ *adj* **1** (**possessed of something**) *formal* owning it; having it □ *possessed of great wealth.* **2** *following its noun* controlled or driven by demons, etc □ *screaming like a man possessed.*

possession /pə'zɛʃən/ ▷ *noun* **1** the condition of possessing something; ownership □ *took possession of the goods* □ *It came into my possession.* **2** the crime of possessing something illegally □ *The terrorist was charged with possession of firearms.* **3** occupancy of property □ *take possession of the house.* **4** *sport* control of the ball, puck, etc by one or other team in a match. **5** something owned. **6** (**possessions**) one's property or belongings. **7** (**possessions**) *formal* a country's dominions abroad □ *foreign possessions.* ● **be in possession of something** to hold or possess it.

possessive ▷ *adj* **1** relating to possession. **2** said of a person or of character: unwilling to share, or allow others to use, things they own □ *I'm very possessive about my car.* **3** said of a person or of character: inclined to dominate, monopolize and allow no independence to one's wife, husband, child, etc □ *a possessive husband.* **4** *grammar* denoting the form or CASE of a noun, pronoun or adjective which shows possession, eg *Kurt's, its, her.* ▷ *noun, grammar* **1** the possessive form or case of a word. **2** a word in the possessive case or in a possessive form. Compare GENITIVE. ● **possessively** *adverb.* ● **possessiveness** *noun.*

posset /'pɒsɪt/ ▷ *noun* a drink of hot milk, curdled with eg wine, ale or vinegar, and flavoured with spices, formerly used as a remedy for colds, etc. ▷ *verb* (***posseted, posseting***) *intr* **1** said of a baby: to bring up some curdled milk. **2** *old use* to make a posset. ◷ 15c; early 20c in verb sense 1.

possibility /pɒsɪ'bɪlətɪ/ ▷ *noun* (***possibilities***) **1** something that is possible. **2** the state of being possible. **3** a candidate for selection, etc. **4** (**possibilities**) promise or potential □ *This idea has definite possibilities.*

possible /'pɒsɪbəl/ ▷ *adj* **1** achievable; able to be done □ *a possible target of 50%.* **2** capable of happening □ *the possible outcome.* **3** imaginable; conceivable □ *It's possible that he's dead.* ▷ *noun* someone or something potentially selectable or attainable; a possibility. ◷ 14c: from Latin *possibilis* that can be done, from *posse* to be able.

possibly ▷ *adverb* **1** perhaps; maybe. **2** within the limits of possibility □ *We'll do all we possibly can.* **3** used for emphasis: at all □ *How could you possibly think that?*

possum /'pɒsəm/ ▷ *noun, colloq* **1** an OPOSSUM. **2** a PHALANGER. ● **play possum** to pretend to be unconscious, asleep or unaware of what is happening. ◷ 17c.

post¹ /poʊst/ ▷ *noun* **1** a shaft or rod fixed upright in the ground, as a support or marker, etc. **2** a vertical timber supporting a horizontal one. Often *in compounds* □ *a doorpost.* **3** an upright pole marking the beginning or end of a race track. **4** a GOALPOST. ▷ *verb* (***posted, posting***) **1** (*sometimes* **post something up**) to put up (a notice, etc) on a post or board, etc for public viewing. **2** to announce the name of someone among others in a published list □ *He was posted missing.* ◷ Anglo-Saxon: from Latin *postis* a doorpost.

post² /poʊst/ ▷ *noun* **1** a job □ ***a teaching post.*** **2** a position to which one is assigned for military duty □ ***never left his post.*** **3** a settlement or establishment, especially one in a remote area. Often *in compounds* □ ***trading-post*** □ ***military post.*** **4** *military* a bugle call summoning soldiers to their quarters at night. See also THE FIRST POST, THE LAST POST. ▷ *verb* (***posted, posting***) (*usually* **post someone to, at** or **in somewhere**) to station them there on duty; to transfer (personnel) to a new location □ ***I was posted abroad.*** ◷ 16c: from Italian *posto*, from Latin *postum*, from *ponere, positum* to place.

post³ /poʊst/ ▷ *noun* (*especially* **the post**) **1** the official system for the delivery of mail. See also POST OFFICE. **2** letters and parcels delivered by this system; mail. **3** a collection of mail, eg from a postbox □ *catch the next post.* **4** a delivery of mail □ *came by the second post.* **5** a place for mail collection; a postbox or post office □ *took it to the post.* **6** *historical* any of a series of riders stationed at various intervals along a route, who carried mail from one stage to another. **7** *historical* a stage or station on such a route. **8** used as a newspaper title □ *the Washington Post.* ▷ *verb* (***posted, posting***) **1** to put (mail) into a postbox; to send something by post. **2** *bookkeeping* **a** to enter (an item) in a ledger; **b** (*now usually* **post up something**) to update (a ledger). **3** to supply someone with the latest news □ *keep us posted.* See also POST¹ *verb.* ◷ 16c: from French *poste*, from Italian *posta*, from Latin *ponere, positum* to place.

post- /poʊst/ ▷ *prefix, denoting* **1** after □ *postwar* □ *postdate.* **2** behind □ *postnasal.* ◷ Latin.

postage ▷ *noun* the charge for sending a letter, etc through the POST³.

postage stamp ▷ *noun* a small printed gummed label stuck on a letter, etc indicating that the appropriate postage charge has been paid. Often shortened to **stamp**.

postal /'poʊstəl/ ▷ *adj* **1** relating or belonging to the POST OFFICE or to delivery of mail. **2** sent by post □ *a postal vote.*

postal code see under POSTCODE

postal order ▷ *noun* (abbreviation **po** or **p.o.**) a money order available from, and payable by, a post office.

postbag ▷ *noun* **1** a mailbag. **2** the letters received by eg a radio or TV programme, magazine or celebrated person, etc.

post box ▷ *noun* see under LETTER BOX

postbus ▷ *noun* a small bus, van or similar vehicle, used for delivering mail and carrying passengers, especially in rural areas.

postcard ▷ *noun* a card for writing messages on, often with a picture on one side, designed for sending through the post without an envelope.

post chaise ▷ *noun, historical* a fast, usually four-wheeled, coach carrying up to four passengers and mail, drawn by posthorses. ◷ 18c.

postcode ▷ *noun* a code used to identify a postal address, made up of a combination of letters and numerals. Also called **postal code**. *US equivalent* ZIP CODE. ◷ 1960s.

post-consumer waste ▷ *noun* newspapers and other household waste, as opposed to industrial waste; waste used for recycling.

postdate ▷ *verb* **1** to put a future date on (a cheque, etc). **2** to assign a later date than that previously accepted to (an event, etc). **3** to occur at a later date than (a specified date). ◷ 17c.

poster ▷ *noun* **1** a large notice or advertisement for public display. **2** a large printed picture. ◷ 19c: from POST¹.

poster art ▻ *noun* posters as an art form from the late 19c, as exemplified by Toulouse-Lautrec amongst others.

poste restante /poust 'rɛstɒnt/ ▻ *noun* **1** an address on mail indicating that it is to be held at a particular post office until it is collected by the recipient, used eg when a private address is not available. **2** the department of a post office which deals with such mail. Compare PO BOX. ◷ 18c: French, meaning 'post remaining'.

posterior /pɒ'stɪərɪə(r)/ ▻ *adj* **1** placed behind, after or at the back of something. **2** *formal or old use* coming after in time. Compare ANTERIOR. ▻ *noun, facetious* the buttocks. ◷ 16c: Latin, comparative of *posterus* coming after, from *post* after.

posterity /pɒ'stɛrɪtɪ/ ▻ *noun* **1** future generations. **2** one's descendants. ◷ 14c: from French *postérité*, from Latin *posteritas*, from *posterus* coming after.

postern /'pɒstən/ ▻ *noun, historical* a back door, back gate or private entrance. ◷ 13c: from French *posterne*, from Latin *posterula* a back way.

poster paint and **poster colour** ▻ *noun* a water-based paint in an opaque colour. 1920s.

post-free ▻ *adj* ▻ *adverb* **1** (*also* **post-paid**) with postage prepaid. **2** without charge for postage.

postgraduate ▻ *noun* **1** a person studying for an advanced degree or qualification after obtaining a first degree. **2** *as adj* relating to such a person or degree ◻ *postgraduate diploma*. Compare GRADUATE.

posthaste ▻ *adverb* with the utmost speed. ◷ 16c.

posthorse ▻ *noun, historical* a horse kept for conveying the mail. See also POST CHAISE.

posthouse ▻ *noun, historical* an inn where POSTHORSES were kept for the use of travellers wishing to change horses, etc.

posthumous /'pɒstjʊməs/ ▻ *adj* **1** said of a work: published after the death of the author, composer, etc. **2** said of a child: born after its father's death. **3** coming or occurring after death ◻ *posthumous fame*. • **posthumously** *adverb*. ◷ 17c: from Latin *postumus*, superlative of *posterus* coming after; *h* inserted by mistaken association with *humus* earth, ie burial.

postiche /pɒ'stiːʃ/ ▻ *adj* **1** said of a piece of architectural decoration: superfluous and inappropriately added to a finished work. **2** counterfeit; false. ▻ *noun* **1** anything that is falsely or superfluously added. **2** a hairpiece. ◷ 19c: French, meaning 'counterfeit', from Italian *apposticcio*; see APPOSITE.

postilion or **postillion** /pɒ'stɪlɪən/ ▻ *noun, historical* a rider on the nearside horse of one of the pairs of posthorses drawing a carriage, who, in the absence of a coachman, guides the team. ◷ 17c; 16c in obsolete sense 'a forerunner': from French *postillon*, from Italian *postiglione*, from *posta* POST[3].

postimpressionism or **Post-Impressionism** ▻ *noun, art* an imprecise term used to describe the more progressive forms of painting since c.1880, which developed as a reaction against IMPRESSIONISM and NEO-IMPRESSIONISM, with the aim of conveying the essence of their subjects through a simplification of form and developing the Impressionist style far beyond the merely representational. ◷ Early 20c: coined by the art critic Roger Fry (1866–1934).

post-industrial society ▻ *noun* an economically and technologically advanced society no longer dependent for its productivity on large-scale, labour-intensive industrial manufacture, and in which knowledge is the central preoccupation. ◷ 1973: coined by US sociologist Daniel Bell (born 1919).

Post-it ▻ *noun, trademark* (*in full* **Post-it note**) a small memo note with a strip of adhesive on the back so that it can be stuck wherever the reminder is needed, eg on a page in a diary, on a door, etc.

postman and **postwoman** ▻ *noun* a man or woman whose job is to deliver mail. *N Amer equivalent* MAILMAN. ◷ 16c, meaning POST[3] *noun* 6.

postman's knock ▻ *noun* a party game for children in which the 'postman' knocks on a door and exchanges a 'letter' for a kiss.

postmark ▻ *noun* a mark stamped on mail by the post office, cancelling the stamp and showing the date and place of posting. ▻ *verb* to mark (mail) in this way. Compare FRANK.

postmaster and **postmistress** ▻ *noun* the man or woman in charge of a local post office.

Postmaster General ▻ *noun* (***Postmasters General***) a government minister in charge of the country's postal services.

postmeridian ▻ *adj* **1** occurring after noon. **2** relating to the afternoon. ◷ 17c.

post meridiem /poust mə'rɪdɪəm/ ▻ *noun* (abbreviation **p.m.**, **pm**, **P.M.** or **PM**) after midday; in the afternoon. ◷ 17c: Latin.

postmillennialism /poustmɪ'lɛnɪəlɪzəm/ ▻ *noun* the doctrine that the Second Coming of Christ will follow the millennium. • **postmillennialist** *noun*. ◷ 19c.

post-modern ▻ *adj* exhibiting Post-modernism. ◷ 1960s.

Post-modernism ▻ *noun* a movement in the arts that takes many features of MODERNISM to new and more playful extremes, rejecting Modernism's tendency towards nihilistic pessimism and replacing it with a more comfortable acceptance of the solipsistic nature of life. There is also an inclination towards mishievous self-referentiality and witty intertextualizing. • **post-modernist** *noun, adj*. ◷ 1930s.

postmortem /poust'mɔːtəm/ (abbreviation **p.m.** or **pm**) ▻ *noun* **1** (*in full* **postmortem examination**) the dissection and examination of the internal organs of the body after death, in order to determine the cause of death. Also called **autopsy**. **2** *colloq* an after-the-event discussion. ▻ *adj* coming or happening after death. ◷ 18c as the phrase *post mortem*: Latin, meaning 'after death'.

postnasal ▻ *adj, chiefly medicine* situated or occurring at the back of the nose or nasal cavity.

postnatal ▻ *adj* relating to or occurring during the period immediately after childbirth. • **postnatally** *adverb*. ◷ 19c.

postnatal depression ▻ *noun, psychol* a relatively common form of usually mild depression that can affect a mother shortly after giving birth, and which mostly fades as her hormones settle down, although occasionally it becomes a severe and long-lasting condition. Also (*colloq*) called **baby blues**.

post office ▻ *noun* **1** a local office that handles postal business, the issuing of various types of licence, etc. **2** (**Post Office**; abbreviation **PO**) the government department in charge of postal services. See also PO BOX.

post-operative ▻ *adj* relating to or occurring during the period immediately following a surgical operation ◻ *post-operative discomfort*.

post-paid see under POST-FREE

postpartum /poust'pɑːtəm/ ▻ *adj, medicine* after childbirth. See also POSTNATAL. ◷ 19c: Latin *post partum* after birth.

postpone /pə'spoun, poust'poun/ ▻ *verb* (***postponed***, ***postponing***) to delay or put off something till later. Also DEFER. Compare CANCEL, ADJOURN. • **postponement** *noun*. ◷ 16c: from Latin *postponere*, from *ponere* to place.

postposition ▻ *noun, grammar* **1** the placing or position of a word after another word that it modifies and to which it is syntactically related. **2** a word used in this way. ◷ 17c: from Latin *postponere*, *postpositum* to place after.

postpositive *grammar* ▻ *adj* said of a modifier: following the word that it applies to, eg *elect* in *president elect*. ▻ *noun* a postpositive word. ◷ 19c: from *postposition*.

postprandial ▻ *adj, facetious* following a meal ▫ *a postprandial doze.* ⓒ 19c.

post-production ▻ *noun* the stages in the making of a film or video after shooting and before the first public showing, including recording and adding music and soundtrack, and final editing. ⓒ 1950s.

postscript ▻ *noun* **1** (abbreviation **PS** or **ps**) a message added to a letter as an afterthought, after one's signature. **2** anything that serves as an addition or follow-up to something. ⓒ 16c: from Latin *postscribere*, *postscriptum* to write something after.

Post-structuralism ▻ *noun* a revision of the STRUCTURALIST view of literature, holding that language has no objectively identifiable or absolute meaning, and that therefore texts allow any number of interpretations. • **Post-structuralist** *noun, adj.*

post-traumatic stress disorder and **post-traumatic stress syndrome** ▻ *noun, medicine, psychol* (abbreviation **PTSD**) a psychological disorder associated with an extremely traumatic event, such as military combat, rape or torture, and characterized by symptoms such as withdrawal, anxiety, nightmares, etc, which may not appear until many months after the event.

postulant /ˈpɒstjʊlənt/ ▻ *noun* someone who asks or petitions for something, especially a candidate for holy orders or for admission to a religious community. • **postulancy** *noun* (***postulancies***). ⓒ 18c: French, from Latin *postulare* to ask.

postulate /ˈpɒstjʊleɪt/ ▻ *verb* (***postulated, postulating***) **1** to assume or suggest something as the basis for discussion; to take it for granted. **2** to demand; to claim. **3** *church law* to nominate someone to an office or post, subject to the sanction of a higher authority. ▻ *noun* /ˈpɒstjʊlət/ **1** a stipulation or prerequisite. **2** a position assumed as self-evident. • **postulation** *noun*. ⓒ 16c: from Latin *postulare* to demand.

posture /ˈpɒstʃə(r)/ ▻ *noun* **1** the way one holds one's body while standing, sitting or walking. **2** a particular position or attitude of the body. **3** an attitude adopted towards a particular issue, etc. **4** a pose adopted for effect. ▻ *verb* (***postured, posturing***) **1** to take up a particular bodily attitude. **2** *intr, derog* to pose, strike attitudes, etc so as to draw attention to oneself. • **postural** *adj.* • **posturer** *noun*. ⓒ 17c: French, from Latin *positura*, from *ponere* to place.

postviral syndrome ▻ *noun* (abbreviation **PVS**) MYALGIC ENCEPHALOMYELITIS.

postwar ▻ *adj* relating or belonging to the period following a war.

posy /ˈpoʊzɪ/ ▻ *noun* (***posies***) a small bunch of flowers. ⓒ 16c: a variant of POESY.

pot[1] ▻ *noun* **1** any of various domestic containers, usually deep round ones, used as cooking or serving utensils, or for storage. **2** a POTFUL ▫ ***a pot of tea.*** **3** *pottery* any handmade container. **4** the pool of accumulated bets in any gambling game. **5** in snooker, billiards, pool, etc: a shot that pockets a ball. **6** a casual shot ▫ ***take a pot at something.*** **7** a CHAMBERPOT. **8** a FLOWERPOT or PLANT POT. **9** (**pots**) *colloq* a great deal, especially of money. **10** *colloq* a trophy, especially a cup. **11** a POT-BELLY. ▻ *verb* (***potted, potting***) **1** to plant something in a plant pot. **2** to preserve (a type of food) in a pot. **3** in snooker, billiards, pool, etc: to shoot (a ball) into a pocket ▫ ***couldn't pot the black.*** **4 a** *colloq* to shoot at (an animal, bird, etc), especially indiscriminately or wildly; **b** to win or secure, especially by shooting ▫ ***potted six grouse today.*** • **potted** *adj* see separate entry. • **go to pot** *colloq* to degenerate badly. • **keep the pot boiling** *colloq* to sustain public interest in something. ⓒ Anglo-Saxon *pott*.

pot[2] ▻ *noun, colloq* CANNABIS. ⓒ 1930s: probably from Mexican Spanish *potiguaya* marijuana leaves.

potable /ˈpoʊtəbəl/ ▻ *adj* fit or suitable for drinking. • **potability** *noun*. ⓒ 16c: French, from Latin *potare* to drink.

potage /pɒˈtɑːʒ/ ▻ *noun* a thick soup. ⓒ 16c: French; see POTTAGE.

potash /ˈpɒtaʃ/ ▻ *noun* (***potashes***) any of various compounds of potassium, especially potassium carbonate or potassium hydroxide. ⓒ 17c as *pot ashes*: from Dutch *potasschen*, because it was originally obtained by leading ashes and evaporating the product in a pot.

potassium /pəˈtasɪəm/ ▻ *noun, chem* (symbol **K**, atomic number 19) a soft silvery-white metallic element, compounds of which are used in fertilizers, explosives, laboratory reagents, soaps and some types of glass. ⓒ 19c: from POTASH.

potassium hydrogencarbonate ▻ *noun, chem* (formula $KHCO_3$) a white crystalline powder, soluble in water, used in baking powder, carbonated soft drinks, carbon-dioxide fire extinguishers and as an antacid. Also called **potassium bicarbonate**.

potassium hydrogentartrate ▻ *noun, chem* (formula $HOOC(CHOH)_2COOK$) a white crystalline powder, soluble in water, found in vegetables and fruit juices, and used in baking powders and carbonated drinks. Also called **cream of tartar**.

potassium hydroxide ▻ *noun, chem* (formula **KOH**) a highly corrosive white crystalline solid that dissolves in water to form a strong alkaline solution and is used in the manufacture of soft soap, and as an electrolyte in batteries. .

potassium nitrate ▻ *noun, chem* (formula KNO_3) a white or transparent highly explosive crystalline solid, used in the manufacture of fireworks, matches, gunpowder, fertilizers, etc and as a food preservative. Also called **nitre** or **saltpetre**.

potassium permanganate ▻ *noun, chem* (formula $KMnO_4$) a dark-purple water-soluble crystalline solid that is an extremely powerful oxidizing agent, used in disinfectants, fungicides, dyes and bleaches, and in chemical analysis. Also called **permanganate of potash** or **potassium manganate (VII)**.

potation /poʊˈteɪʃən/ *formal* or *humorous* **1** the act or an instance of drinking. **2** a drink, especially an alcoholic one. **3** a drinking binge. ⓒ 15c: from French *potacion*; see POTABLE.

potato /pəˈteɪtoʊ/ ▻ *noun* (***potatoes***) **1** a perennial plant that produces edible TUBERs and is a staple crop of temperate regions worldwide. **2** the starch-rich round or oval tuber of this plant, which can be cooked and eaten as a vegetable, or processed to form crisps or chips. Also *as adj* ▫ ***potato salad.*** ⓒ 16c: from Spanish *patata*, variant of *batata*, from Taino (a S American language).

potato blight ▻ *noun, bot* a widespread fungal disease of potato and related plants, in which the entire plant is affected and rapidly dies, especially in wet weather.

potato crisp ▻ *noun* see CRISP (noun)

pot-au-feu /pɒtoʊˈfɜː/ ▻ *noun* a traditional French dish made by slowly cooking various cuts of meat together with vegetables, eg carrots, leeks, onions, turnips, etc, and herbs in a large heavy pot. The meat is then usually removed and eaten separately and the vegetables and stock are served as soup. ⓒ 18c: French, literally 'pot on the fire'.

potbelly ▻ *noun* (***potbellies***) *colloq* **1** a large overhanging belly. **2** someone who has such a belly. • **pot-bellied** *adj.* ⓒ 18c.

potboiler ▻ *noun, derog* **1** an inferior work of literature or art produced by a writer or artist capable of better work, simply to make money and stay in the public view. **2** someone who produces such a work. ⓒ 19c: so called because it is something to KEEP THE POT BOILING (see under POT[1]).

potbound ▻ *adj* said of a pot plant: having its roots cramped by being in too small a pot, leaving no room for growth.

poteen /pɒˈtiːn, pɒˈtʃiːn/ ▻ *noun, Irish* illicitly distilled Irish whiskey. ⓒ 19c: from Irish *poitín*, diminutive of *pota* pot.

potent /ˈpoʊtənt/ ▻ *adj* **1** strong; effective; powerful. **2** said of an argument, etc: persuasive; convincing. **3** said of a drug or poison: powerful and swift in effect. **4** said of a male: capable of sexual intercourse. Opposite of IMPOTENT. • **potency** *noun* (***potencies***) **1** the state of being potent; power. **2** strength or effectiveness, eg of a drug. **3** the capacity for development. ⓒ 15c: from Latin *potens, potentis* present participle of *posse* to be able.

potentate /ˈpoʊtənteɪt/ ▻ *noun, especially historical or literary* a powerful ruler; a monarch. ⓒ 14c: from Latin *potentatus*, from *potens, potentis* powerful.

potential /pəˈtɛnʃəl/ ▻ *adj* possible or likely, though as yet not tested or actual ◻ ***a potential customer.*** ▻ *noun* **1** the range of capabilities that someone or something has; powers or resources not yet developed or made use of ◻ ***fulfil your potential.*** **2** *physics* the energy required to move a unit of mass, electric charge, etc from an infinite distance to the point in a gravitational or electric field where it is to be measured. • **potentiality** noun. • **potentialize** or **potentialise** (***potentialized, potentializing***). • **potentially** *adverb*. ⓒ 14c: from Latin *potentialis*, from *potentia* power.

potential difference ▻ *noun, physics* (abbreviation **pd** or **PD**) the WORK (sense 17) done in moving electric charge between two points in an electrical circuit.

potential energy ▻ *noun, physics* (abbreviation **PE**) the energy stored by an object by virtue of its position.

potentilla /poʊtənˈtɪlə/ ▻ *noun* (***potentillas***) *bot* any of various creeping plants or small shrubs which have leaves with three leaflets and flowers with four or five, often yellow, petals. ⓒ 16c: Latin, diminutive of *potens* powerful, because of the medicinal powers it was believed to have.

potentiometer /pətɛnʃɪˈɒmɪtə(r)/ ▻ *noun, physics* an instrument that measures electric POTENTIAL (noun 2), widely used as a volume control in transistor radios. ⓒ 19c.

potful ▻ *noun* (***potfuls***) the amount a pot can hold.

pothead /ˈpɒthɛd/ ▻ *noun* someone who smokes a lot of cannabis. ⓒ 1960s: from POT[2] + HEAD (*noun* sense 26).

pother /ˈpɒðə(r)/ ▻ *noun* **1** a fuss or commotion. **2** choking smoke or dust. ▻ *verb* (***pothered, pothering***) *tr & intr* to be, or make someone, flustered or upset. ⓒ 16c.

pot-herb ▻ *noun* any plant whose leaves or stems are used in cooking to season or garnish food.

pot-hole ▻ *noun* **1** a roughly circular hole worn in the bedrock of a river as pebbles are swirled around by water eddies. **2** a vertical cave system or deep hole eroded in limestone. **3** a hole worn in a road surface.

pot-holing ▻ *noun* the sport, pastime or activity of exploring deep caves and pot-holes. • **pot-holer** *noun*. ⓒ 19c.

pot-hook ▻ *noun* **1** a hook on which to hang a pot over a fire. **2** a hooked stroke in handwriting.

pot-hunter ▻ *noun* **1** someone whose motive in hunting game is merely profit and who ignores sporting rules and etiquette. **2** someone whose motive in taking part in a competition is merely to win a prize. ⓒ 18c.

potion /ˈpoʊʃən/ ▻ *noun* a draught of medicine, poison or some magic elixir. ⓒ 14c: French, from Latin *potare* to drink.

potlatch /ˈpɒtlatʃ/ ▻ *noun* a winter festival held by some Native American peoples, in which there is competitive and extravagant gift-giving, to demonstrate the status of the chief. ⓒ 19c: from Chinook *patlac* a gift.

pot luck ▻ *noun* whatever happens to be available. Also *as adj* ◻ ***pot-luck supper.*** • **take pot luck** to have whatever happens to be available.

potoroo /pɒtəˈruː/ ▻ *noun* (***potoroos***) a small marsupial related to the kangaroo, with a stocky body and long hindlegs. ⓒ 18c: Australian Aboriginal.

pot plant ▻ *noun* a plant grown in a pot and usually kept indoors for decoration.

potpourri /poʊˈpʊərɪ, poʊpʊˈriː/ ▻ *noun* (***potpourris***) **1** a fragrant mixture of dried flowers, leaves, etc placed in containers and used to scent rooms. **2** a medley or mixture. **3** a collection of old tunes. ⓒ 18c in sense 1; 17c in obsolete sense 'a dish of different kinds of meat': French, literally 'rotten pot'.

pot roast ▻ *noun, cookery* a cut of meat braised with a little water in a covered pot.

potsherd /ˈpɒtʃɜːd/ ▻ *noun, archaeol* a fragment of pottery. ⓒ 14c: POT[1] + SHERD.

pot shot ▻ *noun* **1** an easy shot at close range. **2** a shot made without taking careful aim. **3** a shot taken at game without regard for the rules of sport. ⓒ 19c, originally in sense 3, ie a shot made simply to fill the cooking pot.

pottage /ˈpɒtɪdʒ/ ▻ *noun* a thick soup. ⓒ 13c: from French *potage* that which is put in a pot.

potted ▻ *adj* **1** abridged, especially in order to give a simplified version ◻ ***a potted history.*** **2** said of food: preserved in a pot or jar ◻ ***potted meat.*** **3** said of a plant: growing or grown in a pot ◻ ***a potted begonia.***

potter[1] /ˈpɒtə(r)/ ▻ *noun* someone who makes pottery.

potter[2] /ˈpɒtə(r)/ ▻ *verb* (***pottered, pottering***) *intr* **1** (*usually* **potter about**) to busy oneself in a mild way with trifling tasks. **2** (*usually* **potter about** or **along**) to progress in an unhurried manner; to dawdle. • **potterer** *noun*. ⓒ 18c: from Anglo-Saxon *potian* to thrust.

potter's wheel ▻ *noun* an apparatus with a heavy rotating stone platter, on which clay pots can be shaped by hand before firing.

pottery ▻ *noun* (***potteries***) **1** containers, pots or other objects of baked clay. **2** the art or craft of making such objects. **3** a factory where such objects are produced commercially. ⓒ 15c.

potting-shed ▻ *noun* a shed where garden tools are kept, plants are put into pots, etc.

potto /ˈpɒtoʊ/ ▻ *noun* (***pottos***) a slow-moving lemur-like primate that lives in the equatorial forests of W Africa. ⓒ 18c.

Pott's disease ▻ *noun, pathol* a weakening disease of the spine, caused by tuberculous infection, often causing curvature of the back. ⓒ 19c: named after Sir Percivall Pott (1714–88) who first described it.

Pott's fracture ▻ *noun, medicine* a fracture and dislocation of the ankle joint in which the lower tibia and fibula are damaged, resulting in an outward displacement of the foot. ⓒ 19c: see POTT'S DISEASE.

potty[1] /ˈpɒtɪ/ ▻ *adj* (***pottier, pottiest***) *colloq* **1** mad; crazy. **2** (*usually* **potty about someone** or **something**) intensely interested in or keen on them or it. **3** trifling; insignificant. • **pottiness** *noun*. ⓒ 19c in sense 3: from POT[1].

potty[2] /ˈpɒtɪ/ ▻ *noun* (***potties***) *colloq* a child's chamberpot. ⓒ 1940s: diminutive of POT[1].

potty-train ▻ *verb* to teach (usually a toddler) to use a potty or the toilet. • **potty-trained** *adj* said especially of a toddler: no longer wearing nappies. • **potty-training** *noun*.

pouch /paʊtʃ/ ▷ *noun* (***pouches***) **1** *chiefly old use* a purse or small bag □ *a tobacco pouch.* **2** in marsupials such as the kangaroo: a pocket of skin on the belly, in which the young are carried until they are weaned. **3** a fleshy fold in the cheek of hamsters and other rodents, for storing undigested food. **4** a small lockable mailbag. ▷ *verb* (***pouched, pouching***) **1** to form, or form into, a pouch. **2** *colloq* to take possession of something. ● **pouched** *adj.* ● **pouchy** *adj.* 🕑 14c: from Old French *poche* pocket.

pouf and **poufter** ▷ *noun* a POOF.

pouffe or **pouf** /puːf/ ▷ *noun* **1** a firmly stuffed drum-shaped or cube-shaped cushion for use as a low seat. **2** *dressmaking* a part of a dress gathered up into a bunch. 🕑 19c: from French *pouf* something puffed out.

poulard /ˈpuːlɑːd/ ▷ *noun* a female hen that has been spayed and fattened for eating. Compare CAPON. 🕑 18c: from French *poularde*, from *poule* hen.

poult /poʊlt/ ▷ *noun* a young domestic fowl or game bird, eg a young chicken, turkey, pheasant, etc. 🕑 15c: a shortened form of French *poulet* a chicken.

poulterer /ˈpoʊltərə(r)/ ▷ *noun* a dealer in poultry and game. 🕑 17c: from French *pouletier*, from *poulet* PULLET.

poultice /ˈpoʊltɪs/ ▷ *noun, medicine* a hot, semi-liquid mixture spread on a bandage and applied to the skin to reduce inflammation or to help a boil, etc to come to a head. 🕑 16c: from Latin *pultes*, plural of *puls* thick porridge.

poultry /ˈpoʊltrɪ/ ▷ *noun* **1** *collective* domesticated birds kept for their eggs or meat, or both, eg chickens, ducks, turkeys, geese, etc. **2** the meat of such birds. 🕑 14c: from French *pouletrie*, from *pouletier* poultry seller.

pounce[1] /paʊns/ ▷ *verb* (***pounced, pouncing***) *intr* (*often* **pounce on something** or **someone**) **1** to leap or swoop on (a victim or prey), especially when trying to capture them or it. **2** to seize on it or them; to grab eagerly. ▷ *noun* **1** an act of pouncing. **2** the talon of a bird of prey. 🕑 15c in *noun* sense 2.

pounce[2] /paʊns/ ▷ *noun* **1** a fine powder for preparing a writing surface or absorbing ink. **2** coloured powder shaken through perforations to mark a pattern on the surface beneath. ▷ *verb* (***pounced, pouncing***) **1** to prepare with pounce. **2** to trace, transfer or mark (a surface, etc) with pounce. 🕑 18c: from French *ponce*, from Latin *pumex* pumice.

pound[1] /paʊnd/ ▷ *noun* **1** (symbol **£**) the standard unit of currency of the UK. Also called **pound sterling**. **2** the English name for the principal currency unit in several other countries, including Malta, Cyprus and Egypt. **3** (abbreviation **lb**) a measure of weight equal to 16 ounces (0.45kg) avoirdupois, or 12 ounces (0.37kg) troy. 🕑 Anglo-Saxon *pund*.

pound[2] /paʊnd/ ▷ *noun* **1** an enclosure where stray animals or illegally parked cars that have been taken into police charge are kept for collection. **2** a place where people are confined. See also COMPOUND[2]. ▷ *verb* (***pounded, pounding***) to enclose or confine something in a pound. See also IMPOUND. 🕑 Anglo-Saxon *pund-* used in compounds to mean 'enclosure'.

pound[3] /paʊnd/ ▷ *verb* (***pounded, pounding***) **1** *tr & intr* (*often* **pound on** or **at something**) to beat or bang it vigorously □ *pounding on the door.* **2** *intr* to walk or run with heavy thudding steps. **3** to crush or grind something to a powder. **4** to thump or beat especially with the fists □ *pounded him senseless.* **5** said of the heart: to beat with heavy thumping pulses, especially through fear, excitement, etc 🕑 Anglo-Saxon *punian*.

■ **pound something out** to produce it by, or as if by, pounding eg a typewriter, etc.

poundage ▷ *noun* a fee or commission charged per POUND[1] in weight or money.

poundal /ˈpɒndəl/ ▷ *noun, physics* a unit of force that is equivalent to the force required to make a mass weighing one pound accelerate by one foot per second per second. 🕑 19c.

pound cake ▷ *noun* a type of rich fruit cake that origianlly was made with a pound each of fruit, flour, butter, sugar, etc and which now applies to any cake with these ingredients in equal measure. 🕑 18c.

-pounder ▷ *noun, in compounds, denoting* **1** something weighing a specified number of pounds □ *My trout was a three-pounder.* **2** a field gun designed to fire shot weighing a specified number of pounds □ *a twenty-four-pounder.*

pound force ▷ *noun, physics* see POUNDAL

pound of flesh ▷ *noun* (*usually* **get** or **have one's pound of flesh**) what is strictly speaking due in the fulfilment of a bargain even if it means causing unreasonable suffering or difficulties to the other party. 🕑 16c: from Shakespeare's *The Merchant of Venice* IV. I, in which a pound of flesh is stipulated as a penalty in a bargain.

pound Scots ▷ *noun, historical* a former unit of currency varying in value from time to time and worth one shilling and eight pence at the time of THE UNION (sense 1) .

pound sign ▷ *noun* the symbol (**£**) used before a number to designate the POUND (sense 1).

pound sterling see under POUND[1]

pour /pɔː(r)/ ▷ *verb* (***poured, pouring***) **1** *tr & intr* to flow or cause something to flow in a downward stream. **2** *tr & intr* said of a jug, teapot, etc: to discharge (liquid) in a certain way □ *doesn't pour very well.* **3** (*also* **pour something out**) to serve (a drink, etc) by pouring □ *Pour me some tea.* **4** *intr* to rain heavily. **5** *intr* (*usually* **pour in** or **out**) to come or go in large numbers. **6** *intr* (*also* **pour in** or **out**, *etc*) to flow or issue plentifully □ *Donations poured in* □ *Words poured from her pen.* ● **pourer** *noun.* ● **it never rains but it pours** things, especially pieces of bad luck, etc, seldom come along unaccompanied by others □ *got the phone bill yesterday and now the gas bill — it never rains but it pours.* ● **pour cold water on something** to be discouraging or deprecatory about (an idea, scheme, etc). ● **pour scorn on something** to be contemptuous about it. 🕑 14c.

■ **pour something into something 1** to invest eg money, energy, etc liberally into it □ *poured all his savings into the company.* **2** to squeeze oneself or someone into (an item of clothing which fits very tightly).

■ **pour something out** to reveal without inhibition □ *poured out her feelings.*

pourboire / *French* puʀbwaʀ/ ▷ *noun* a tip or gratuity. 🕑 19c: French, literally 'for drinking'.

poussin /*French* pusɛ̃/ ▷ *noun* a young chicken reared for eating at the age of four to six weeks. 🕑 1930s: French, meaning 'a newly-born chicken'.

pout[1] /paʊt/ ▷ *verb* (***pouted, pouting***) **1** *tr & intr* to push the lower lip or both lips forward as an indication of sulkiness or seductiveness. **2** *intr* said of the lips: to stick out in this way. ▷ *noun* **1** an act of pouting. **2** a pouting expression. ● **poutingly** *adverb.* ● **pouty** *adj.* 🕑 14c.

pout[2] /paʊt/ ▷ *noun* (***pout*** or ***pouts***) a fish belonging to the cod family, which has barbels around its mouth. 🕑 Anglo-Saxon *puta*.

pouter ▷ *noun* **1** someone or something that pouts. **2** a breed of domestic pigeon, so called because it is capable of puffing out its large crop.

poverty /ˈpɒvətɪ/ ▷ *noun* **1** the condition of being poor; want. **2** poor quality. **3** inadequacy; deficiency □ *poverty of imagination.* 🕑 12c: from French *poverte*, from Latin *paupertas*, from *pauper* poor.

poverty line ▷ *noun* the minimum income needed to purchase the basic necessities of life □ *living below the poverty line.*

poverty-stricken ▷ *adj* suffering from poverty.

poverty trap ▷ *noun* the inescapable poverty of someone who, in achieving an improvement in income, has their state benefits cut.

POW ▷ *abbreviation* prisoner of war.

pow /paʊ/ ▷ *exclamation, colloq* an imitation of the noise of a blow or impact, etc. ⓒ 19c.

powder /ˈpaʊdə(r)/ ▷ *noun* **1** any substance in the form of fine dust-like particles □ *talcum powder.* **2** (*also* **face powder**) a cosmetic that is patted on to the skin to give it a soft smooth appearance. **3** GUNPOWDER. **4** a dose of medicine in powder form. ▷ *verb* (***powdered, powdering***) **1** to apply powder to (eg one's face); to sprinkle or cover something with powder. **2** to reduce something to a powder by crushing; to pulverize. • **powder one's nose** *euphemistic* **1** said of a woman: to go to the lavatory. **2** to snort cocaine. ⓒ 13c: from French *poudre*, from Latin *pulvis* dust.

powder blue ▷ *noun* a delicate pale blue colour. ▷ *adj* (**powder-blue**) having this colour.

powder keg ▷ *noun* **1** a barrel of gunpowder. **2** a potentially dangerous or explosive situation

powder metallurgy ▷ *noun, chem* a method of shaping heat-resistant metals or alloys by reducing them to powder, pressing them into moulds, and heating them to very high temperatures.

powder monkey ▷ *noun* **1** *historical* a boy who carried powder to the gunners on warships. **2** *US* someone who carries out blasting operations or is in charge of explosives.

powder puff ▷ *noun* a pad of velvety or fluffy material for patting POWDER (sense 2) on to the skin.

powder room ▷ *noun* a women's cloakroom or toilet in a restaurant, hotel, etc.

powder snow ▷ *noun* light dry snow that is good for skiing. ⓒ 1920s.

powdery ▷ *adj* (***powderier, powderiest***) **1** having the consistency or nature of powder; powderlike. **2** covered with or full of powder. **3** dusty. **4** friable.

power /ˈpaʊə(r)/ ▷ *noun* **1** control and influence exercised over others. **2** strength, vigour, force or effectiveness. **3** *usually in compounds* military strength □ *sea power* □ *air power.* **4** the physical ability, skill, opportunity or authority to do something. **5** an individual faculty or skill □ *the power of speech.* **6** a right, privilege or responsibility □ *the power of arrest.* **7** political control. **8** a state that has an influential role in international affairs. Also *in compounds* □ *superpower.* **9** a person or group exercising control or influence. **10** *colloq* a great deal □ *The rest did her a power of good.* **11** any form of energy, especially when used as the driving force for a machine. *Often in compounds* □ *nuclear power.* **12** *math* a less technical term for an EXPONENT (sense 3). **13** *physics* the rate of doing work or converting energy from one form into another. **14 a**) mechanical or electrical energy, as distinct from manual effort; **b** *as adj* □ *power tools.* **15** *optics* a measure of the extent to which a lens, optical instrument or curved mirror can deviate light rays and so magnify an image of an object. **16** in the traditional medieval hierarchy of nine ranks of angels: an angel of the sixth rank. Compare SERAPH, CHERUB, THRONE, DOMINION, VIRTUE, PRINCIPALITY, ARCHANGEL, ANGEL. ▷ *verb* (***powered, powering***) **1** to supply something with power. Also *in compounds* □ *wind-powered.* **2** *tr & intr, colloq* to move or cause something to move with great force, energy or speed. • **in power** elected; holding office □ *when Labour is in power.* • **the powers that be** the people who are in control or in authority. ⓒ 13c: from French *poer*, from Latin *posse* to be able.

■ **power something up** to recharge its power supply (especially that of a laptop computer) by attaching it to the mains electricity supply.

power base ▷ *noun* something or someone seen as the origin or foundation of authority, backing, support, etc, especially in politics, international relations, business, etc. ⓒ 1960s.

power block ▷ *noun* a politically important and powerful group or body, especially a group of allied states.

powerboat racing and **powerboating** ▷ *noun* the racing of boats fitted with high-powered and finely-tuned inboard or outboard engines, fuelled by petrol or diesel.

power breakfast see POWER LUNCH

power broker ▷ *noun* someone who has great influence, eg in politics, especially when they use this influence to sway policies, etc in their own or their party's favour. • **power-broking** *noun, adj.* ⓒ 1960s.

power cut ▷ *noun* a temporary break or reduction in an electricity supply.

power dive ▷ *noun* a steep dive made by an aeroplane, with its engines providing thrust. ▷ *verb* (**power-dive**) **1** *intr* said of an aircraft: to perform a power dive. **2** *tr& intr* to make (an aircraft) perform a power dive. ⓒ 1930s.

power dressing ▷ *noun* the wearing, by businesswomen, of severely tailored suits and dresses, intended to convey professionalism and assertiveness. ⓒ 1980s.

powerful ▷ *adj* **1** having great power, strength or vigour. **2** very effective or efficient □ *a powerful argument.* ▷ *adverb, dialect* extremely □ *June was powerful hot.* • **powerfully** *adverb.* • **powerfulness** *noun.*

powerhouse ▷ *noun* **1** a power station. **2** *colloq* a forceful or vigorous person.

powerless ▷ *adj* **1** deprived of power or authority. **2** completely unable (*usually* to do something) □ *I was powerless to help.* • **powerlessly** *adverb.* • **powerlessness** *noun.*

power line ▷ *noun* a conductor that carries electricity, especially one of several supported by pylons. ⓒ 19c.

power lunch and **power breakfast** ▷ *noun* a high-level business discussion held over lunch or breakfast.

power of attorney ▷ *noun* the right to act for another person in legal and business matters.

power pack ▷ *noun* a device for adjusting the voltage of a power source or battery to the voltage required by a particular electrical device.

power plant ▷ *noun* **1** an industrial plant for generating electrical energy from some other form of energy. **2** the engine and other equipment that supplies power to a motor vehicle, aeroplane, etc.

power play ▷ *noun* **1** *sport* strong attacking play designed to pressurize the defence by concentrating players and action in one small area. **2** in business, politics, etc: the concentration of resources, etc in a small area.

power point ▷ *noun, Brit* a wall socket where an electrical appliance may be connected to the mains.

power politics ▷ *singular or plural noun* political action based on influence, often involving a degree of coercion or force. ⓒ 1930s.

power-sharing ▷ *noun, politics* an agreement, especially between parties in a coalition, that policy-making, decision-taking, etc will be done jointly.

power station ▷ *noun* a building where electricity is generated on a large scale from another form of energy, such as coal, nuclear fuel, moving water, etc.

power steering and **power-assisted steering** ▷ *noun* in a motor vehicle: a system in which the rotating force exerted on the steering wheel is supplemented by engine power.

powwow /'paʊwaʊ/ ▷ *noun* **1** *colloq* a meeting for discussion. **2 a** a meeting of Native Americans; **b** a Native American ceremony or rite, often with feasting. Compare INDABA. **3** in certain Native American tribes: a medicine man. ▷ *verb* (***powwowed, powwowing***) *intr* to hold a powwow. ⓒ 17c: from Narragansett *powwaw* priest.

pox ▷ *noun* (***poxes***) **1** *medicine, often in compounds* any of various infectious viral diseases that cause a skin rash consisting of pimples containing pus □ ***chickenpox*** □ ***smallpox.*** **2** (*often* **the pox**) a former name for SYPHILIS. ⓒ 16c: a variant of *pocks*, the plural of POCK.

poxy /'pɒksɪ/ ▷ *adj* (***poxier, poxiest***) *Brit colloq* worthless, second-rate, trashy. ⓒ 1920s.

pozidriv /'pɒzɪdraɪv/ ▷ *noun, trademark* a type of screwdriver with a crossed end.

PP ▷ *abbreviation* **1** parish priest. **2** past president.

pp ▷ *abbreviation* **1** pages □ ***pp9–12.*** **2** usually written when signing a letter in the absence of the sender: *per procurationem* (Latin), for and on behalf of (the specified person). Also called **per pro**. **3** *music* pianissimo.

PPARC ▷ *abbreviation* Particle Physics and Astronomy Research Council.

PPE ▷ *abbreviation* Philosophy, Politics and Economics, a course at Oxford university.

ppm ▷ *abbreviation* parts per million.

PPS ▷ *abbreviation* **1** Parliamentary Private Secretary. **2** (*also* **pps**) *post postscriptum* (Latin), after the postscript, ie an additional postscript.

PR ▷ *abbreviation* **1** proportional representation. **2** public relations. **3** Puerto Rico.

Pr ▷ *symbol, chem* praseodymium.

practicable /'praktɪkəbəl/ ▷ *adj* **1** capable of being done, used or successfully carried out; feasible. **2** said eg of a road: fit for use. • **practicability** or **practicableness** *noun*. • **practicably** *adverb*. ⓒ 17c: from French *pratiquer* to practise; see PRACTICAL.

practicable, practical

• Both words mean 'able to be done, used, etc', and a plan (for example) can be said to be **practical** or **practicable**. But **practical** has the further connotation of 'efficient, sensible, useful' and is therefore more judgemental; it can also be applied to people, whereas **practicable** can not □ *It is perfectly practicable to make the journey by car* □ *They stood by to offer advice and practical assistance* □ *He was clever enough, but somehow he wasn't practical with it.*

practical /'praktɪkəl/ ▷ *adj* **1** concerned with or involving action rather than theory □ ***put her knowledge to practical use.*** **2** effective, or capable of being effective, in actual use. **3** said eg of clothes: designed for tough or everyday use; sensibly plain. **4** said of a person: **a** sensible and efficient in deciding and acting; **b** good at doing manual jobs. **5** in effect; virtual □ ***a practical walkover.*** ▷ *noun* a practical lesson or examination, eg in a scientific subject. • **practicality** *noun* (***practicalities***). ⓒ 17c: from Greek *praktikos*, from *prassein* to do.

practical joke ▷ *noun* a trick or prank which is played on someone, usually making them look silly. • **practical joker** *noun*.

practically ▷ *adverb* **1** almost; very nearly. **2** in a practical manner.

practice /'praktɪs/ ▷ *noun* **1** the process of carrying something out □ ***put ideas into practice.*** **2** a habit, activity, procedure or custom □ ***Don't make a practice of it!*** **3** repeated exercise to improve technique in an art or sport, etc. **4** the business or clientele of a doctor, dentist, lawyer, etc. • **be in** or **out of practice** to have maintained, or failed to maintain, one's skill in an art or sport, etc. ⓒ 16c: from PRACTISE.

practice, practise

• In British English, **practice** is the spelling of the noun, and **practise** the verb.

• American English uses **practice** for both.

practise or (*US*) **practice** /'praktɪs/ *verb* (***practised, practising***) **1** *tr & intr* to do exercises repeatedly in (an art or sport, etc) so as to improve one's performance. **2** to make a habit of something □ ***practise self-control.*** **3** to go in for something as a custom □ ***tribes that practise bigamy.*** **4** to work at or follow (an art or profession, especially medicine or law). **5** to perform (a wrongful act) against someone □ ***He practised a cruel deception on them.*** ⓒ 15c: from Latin *practicare*, from Greek *praktikos* practical work.

practised or (*US*) **practiced** *adj* (*often* **practised at something**) skilled; experienced; expert.

practising ▷ *adj* actively engaged in or currently pursuing or observing □ ***a practising lawyer*** □ ***a practising Christian.*** ▷ ▷ *noun* an act or the process of doing something for PRACTICE (sense 3) □ ***Practising the piano takes up a lot of her time.***

practitioner /prak'tɪʃənə(r)/ ▷ *noun* someone who practises an art or profession, especially medicine. See also GENERAL PRACTITIONER. ⓒ 16c: from French *praticien*, from Latin *practica* PRACTISE.

prädikat /preɪdɪ'kat/ ▷ *noun* **1** in Germany: a distinction awarded to a wine, based on the ripeness of the grapes used to produce it. **2** a wine that qualifies for this award. ⓒ 1980s: German meaning 'rating'.

prae- /priː/ ▷ *prefix* a form of PRE- used in words that are particularly Latinate or that relate to Roman antiquity.

praesidium see PRESIDIUM

praenomen /priː'noʊmən/ ▷ *noun, Roman history* someone's first or personal name, eg 'Gaius' in 'Gaius Julius Caesar'. ⓒ 17c: Latin, meaning 'first name'.

praetor /'priːtə(r)/ ▷ *noun, Roman history* one of the chief law officers of the state, elected annually, and second to the CONSUL in importance. ⓒ 15c: Latin, meaning 'one who goes before', from *prae* before + *ire* to go.

praetorian /priː'tɔːrɪən/ *Roman history* ▷ *adj* belonging or relating to, or having the authority of, a PRAETOR. ▷ *noun* a man of praetorian rank, especially one sent to a province to act as its governor. ⓒ 16c: see PRAETOR.

praetorian guard ▷ *noun, Roman history* the select group of soldiers whose duty was to act as bodyguard to the emperor.

pragmatic /prag'matɪk/ ▷ *adj* **1** concerned with what is practicable, expedient and convenient, rather than with theories and ideals; matter-of-fact; realistic. **2** relating to or concerning the affairs of a community or state. **3** *philos* relating to pragmatism. ⓒ 17c: from Latin *pragmaticus*, from Greek *pragma* a deed.

pragmatics ▷ *singular noun* the branch of lingustic study that deals with how language is used, especially the factors that influence people's choice of words.

pragmatism /'pragmətɪzəm/ ▷ *noun* **1** a practical matter-of-fact approach to dealing with problems, etc. **2** *philos* a school of thought that assesses the truth of concepts in terms of their practical implications. • **pragmatist** *noun*.

prahu see PROA

prairie /ˈprɛərɪ/ ▷ *noun* in N America: a large expanse of flat or rolling natural grassland, usually without trees. ◷ 18c: French, from Latin *pratum* meadow.

prairie dog ▷ *noun* a small burrowing GROUND SQUIRREL with a yellowish-brown or reddish-grey coat, small ears and a short tail. ◷ 18c: named 'dog' because of its barking alarm call.

prairie oyster ▷ *noun* an alcoholic drink, usually a large measure of spirits, with a seasoned raw egg in it. It is meant to be downed in one gulp and is supposed to cure a hangover. ◷ 19c.

praise /preɪz/ ▷ *verb* (***praised***, ***praising***) **1** to express admiration or approval of someone or something. **2** to worship or glorify (God) with hymns or thanksgiving, etc. ▷ *noun* **1** the expression of admiration or approval; commendation. **2** worship of God. • **sing someone's** or **something's praises** to commend them or it enthusiastically. ◷ 13c: from French *preisier*, from Latin *pretiare* to value.

praiseworthy ▷ *adj* deserving praise; commendable. • **praiseworthily** *adverb*. • **praiseworthiness** *noun*. ◷ 16c.

Prakrit /ˈprɑːkrɪt/ ▷ *noun* any of several Indic vernaculars spoken from ancient to medieval times and the medium of Buddhist and Jain literature. ◷ 18c: from Sanskrit *prakrta* natural, vulgar; compare SANSKRIT.

praline /ˈprɑːliːn/ ▷ *noun* a sweet consisting of nuts in caramelized sugar. ◷ 18c: from Marshal Duplessis-Praslin (1598–1675), a French soldier whose cook invented it.

pram ▷ *noun* a wheeled baby carriage pushed by someone on foot. ◷ 19c: a short form of PERAMBULATOR.

prana /ˈprɑːnə/ ▷ *noun, Hinduism* breath as the essential life force. ◷ 19c: Sanskrit.

prance /prɑːns/ ▷ *verb* (***pranced***, ***prancing***) **1** *intr* said especially of a horse: to walk with lively springing steps. **2** *intr* to frisk or skip about. **3** *intr* to parade about in a swaggering manner. **4** to make (a horse, etc) prance. ◷ 14c.

prandial /ˈprandɪəl/ ▷ *adj, often facetious* belonging or relating to dinner. See also POSTPRANDIAL. ◷ 19c: from Latin *prandium* a morning or midday meal.

prang *colloq* ▷ *verb* (***pranged***, ***pranging***) **1** to crash (a vehicle). **2** to bomb something from the air. ▷ *noun* **1** a vehicle crash. **2** a bombing raid. ◷ 1940s: originally RAF slang, imitating the sound made.

prank ▷ *noun* a playful trick; a practical joke. • **prankster** *noun*. ◷ 16c.

praseodymium /preɪzɪoʊˈdɪmɪəm/ ▷ *noun, chem* (symbol **Pr**, atomic number 59) a soft silvery metallic element, used in thermoelectric materials, glasses and glazes. ◷ 19c: Latin, from Greek *prasios* leek-green + DIDYMIUM.

prat ▷ *noun slang* **1** *offensive* a fool; an ineffectual person. **2** the buttocks. ◷ 16c.

prate ▷ *verb* (***prated***, ***prating***) *tr & intr* to talk or utter foolishly; to blab. ▷ *noun* idle chatter. ◷ 15c: from Dutch *praeten* to talk.

pratfall ▷ *noun* **1** a ridiculous tumble in which someone, especially a clown or comedian, lands on their bottom. **2** an embarrassing blunder. ◷ 1940s: PRAT + FALL.

pratincole /ˈpratɪŋkoʊl/ ▷ *noun* any of various species of bird related to the plover, with long pointed wings and a short beak. ◷ 18c: from Latin *pratincola*, from *pratum* a meadow + *incola* inhabitant.

prattle /ˈpratəl/ ▷ *verb* (***prattled***, ***prattling***) *tr & intr* to chatter or utter childishly or foolishly. ▷ *noun* childish or foolish chatter. • **prattler** *noun*. ◷ 16c: from German *pratelen* to chatter.

prau see PROA

prawn ▷ *noun* any of various small edible shrimp-like marine crustaceans with long tail fans, which are almost transparent when alive but pinkish-orange when cooked. ◷ 15c.

prawn cracker ▷ *noun* a light deep-fried prawn-flavoured type of crisp, traditionally eaten as an accompaniment to Chinese food.

praxis /ˈpraksɪs/ *noun* (*plural* ***praxes*** /-siːz/) **1** practice as opposed to theory. **2** an example or collection of examples for exercise. **3** accepted practice. ◷ 16c: Greek, from *prassein* to do.

pray ▷ *verb* (***prayed***, ***praying***) (*often* **pray for something** or **someone**) **1** *now usually intr* to address one's god, making earnest requests or giving thanks. **2** *old use, tr & intr* to entreat or implore □ *Stop, I pray you!* **3** *tr & intr* to hope desperately. ▷ *exclamation, old use* (*now* often uttered with quaint politeness or cold irony) please, or may I ask □ *Pray come in* □ *Who asked you, pray?* ◷ 13c: from French *preier*, from Latin *precari* to entreat.

> ***pray***
>
> A word often confused with this one is **prey**.

prayer¹ /prɛə(r)/ ▷ *noun* **1** an address to one's god, making a request or giving thanks. **2** the activity of praying. **3** an earnest hope, desire or entreaty. ◷ 13c: from French *preiere*, from Latin *precaria*, from *precari* to pray.

prayer² /preɪə(r)/ ▷ *noun* someone who prays.

prayer book ▷ *noun* a book of set prayers appropriate for various occasions and specific types of church service.

prayerful ▷ *adj* **1** said of someone: devout; tending to pray a lot or often. **2** said of a speech, etc: imploring. • **prayerfully** *adverb*. • **prayerfulness** *noun*.

prayer rug and **prayer mat** ▷ *noun* a small carpet on which a Muslim kneels when praying.

prayer shawl see TALLITH

prayer wheel ▷ *noun, Buddhism* a drum that turns on a spindle, inscribed with prayers, and containing a scroll of prayers, which are believed to be activated as the drum is rotated.

praying mantis see under MANTIS

PRB ▷ *abbreviation, historical* Pre-Raphaelite Brotherhood.

pre- /priː, prɪ/ ▷ *prefix, denoting* before **a** in time □ *pre-war*; **b** in position □ *premolar*; **c** in importance □ *pre-eminent*. ◷ From Latin *prae-* before.

preach ▷ *verb* (***preaches***, ***preached***, ***preaching***) **1** *tr & intr* to deliver (a sermon) as part of a religious service. **2** (*often* **preach at someone**) to give them advice in a tedious or obtrusive manner. **3** to advise or advocate something. • **preacher** *noun* someone who preaches, especially a minister of religion. ◷ 13c: from French *prechier*, from Latin *praedicare* to announce publicly.

preachy ▷ *adj* (***preachier***, ***preachiest***) *colloq* said of someone, their attitude, speech, etc: tending to be moralistic.

preadmonish ▷ *verb* to forewarn. ◷ 17c.

pre-adolescent ▷ *adj* **1** belonging or relating to the period immediately preceding adolescence. **2** said of a child: at this stage of development. ▷ *noun* a pre-adolescent child. • **pre-adolescence** *noun*.

preamble /prɪˈambəl/ ▷ *noun* an introduction or preface, eg to a speech or document; an opening statement. ◷ 14c: from Latin *praeambulare* to walk before.

preamplifier ▷ *noun* (*also colloq* **preamp**) an electronic device that boosts and clarifies the signal from a radio, microphone, etc before it reaches the main amplifier. ◷ 1930s.

prearrange ▷ *verb* to arrange something in advance. • **prearrangement** *noun*. ◷ 18c.

prebend /ˈprɛbənd/ ▷ *noun* **1** an allowance paid out of the revenues of a cathedral or collegiate church to its canons or chapter members. **2** the piece of land, etc which is the source of such revenue. **3** a prebendary. • **prebendal** /prɪˈbɛndəl/ *adj*. ◷ 15c: from Latin *praebenda* allowance, from *praebere* to offer.

prebendary /ˈprɛbəndərɪ/ ▷ *noun* (***prebendaries***) **1** a clergyman of a cathedral or collegiate church who is in receipt of a PREBEND. **2** *C of E* the honorary holder of a prebend.

Precambrian *geol* ▷ *adj* **1** relating to the earliest geological era, during which primitive forms of life appeared on Earth. See table at GEOLOGICAL TIME SCALE. **2** relating to the rocks formed during this period. ▷ *noun* (**the Precambrian**) the Precambrian era. ◷ 19c; see CAMBRIAN.

precancerous ▷ *adj* said especially of cells: showing early indications of possible malignancy. ◷ Late 19c.

precarious /prɪˈkɛərɪəs/ ▷ *adj* **1** unsafe; insecure; dangerous. **2** uncertain; chancy. • **precariously** *adverb*. • **precariousness** *noun*. ◷ 17c: from Latin *precarius* obtained by prayer, from *prex, precis* prayer.

precast ▷ *adj* said of concrete, etc: made into blocks, before being put into position. ◷ Early 20c.

precaution /prɪˈkɔːʃən/ ▷ *noun* **1** a measure taken to ensure a satisfactory outcome, or to avoid a risk or danger. **2** caution exercised beforehand. • **precautionary** *adj*. ◷ 17c: from Latin *praecautio*, from *cavere* to beware.

precede /prɪˈsiːd/ ▷ *verb* (***preceded, preceding***) *tr & intr* **1** to go or be before someone or something, in time, order, position, rank or importance. **2** to preface or introduce something. ◷ 15c: from Latin *praecedere* to go before.

precedence /ˈprɛsɪdəns, ˈpriːsɪdəns/ ▷ *noun* **1** priority □ *Safety takes precedence over all else.* **2** the fact of preceding, in order, rank, importance, etc. **3** the right to precede others. ◷ 16c.

precedent ▷ *noun* /ˈprɛsɪdənt, ˈpriː-/ **1** a previous incident or legal case, etc that has something in common with one under consideration, serving as a basis for a decision in the present one. **2** the judgement or decision given in such a case. ▷ *adj, now rare* /prɪˈsiːdənt, ˈprɛsɪdənt/ preceding. ◷ 14c as *adj*.

preceding ▷ *adj* going before in time, position, etc; previous.

precentor /prɪˈsɛntə(r)/ ▷ *noun, relig* someone who leads the singing of a church congregation, or the prayers in a synagogue. ◷ 17c: from Latin *praecentor*, from *prae-* before + *canere* to sing.

precept /ˈpriːsɛpt/ ▷ *noun* **1** a rule or principle, especially one of a moral kind, that is seen or used as a guide to behaviour. **2** *law* the written warrant of a magistrate. ◷ 14c: from Latin *praeceptum*, from *praecipere* to advise or, literally, to take before.

preceptor /prɪˈsɛptə(r)/ and **preceptress** /-trɪs/ ▷ *noun* a teacher or instructor. • **preceptorial** /priːsɛpˈtɔːrɪəl/ *adj*. • **preceptorship** *noun*. ◷ 15c: from Latin *praeceptor* an instructor.

precession /prɪˈsɛʃən/ ▷ *noun* **1** *physics* the gradual change in direction of the axis of rotation of a spinning body. **2** *astron* the progressively earlier occurrence of the equinoxes, resulting from the gradual change in direction of the Earth's axis of rotation. Also called **precession of the equinoxes**. **3** the act of preceding. • **precessional** *adj*. ◷ 16c: from Latin *praecessio, praecessionis*, from *praecedere* to PRECEDE.

precinct /ˈpriːsɪŋkt/ ▷ *noun* **1** (*also* **precincts**) the enclosed grounds of a large building, etc □ *the cathedral precinct.* **2** (*also* **precincts**) the neighbourhood or environs of a place. **3** a PEDESTRIAN PRECINCT. **4** *N Amer, especially US* **a)** any of the districts into which a city is divided for administrative or policing purposes; **b)** the police station of one of these districts. ◷ 15c: from Latin *praecingere, praecinctum* to surround.

preciosity /prɛʃɪˈɒsɪtɪ/ ▷ *noun* (***preciosities***) affectedness or exaggerated refinement in speech or manner. ◷ 19c see PRECIOUS.

precious /ˈprɛʃəs/ ▷ *adj* **1** valuable. **2** dear; beloved; treasured. **3** *derog* said of speech or manner: affected or over-precise. **4** *colloq, ironic* **a** confounded □ *Him and his precious goldfish!* **b** substantial □ *And a precious lot you'd care!* ▷ *noun* a rather sickly form of address □ *And how's my little precious today?* • **preciously** *adverb*. • **preciousness** *noun*. • **precious few** or **little** *colloq* almost none. ◷ 13c: from Latin *pretiosus* valuable, from *pretium* price.

precious metal ▷ *noun* gold, silver or platinum.

precious stone ▷ *noun* a gemstone, such as a diamond, ruby, etc, valued for its beauty and rarity, especially with regard to its use in jewellery or ornamentation.

precipice /ˈprɛsɪpɪs/ ▷ *noun* a steep, vertical or overhanging cliff or rock face. ◷ 17c: from Latin *praecipitare* to fall headlong.

precipitate ▷ *verb* /prɪˈsɪpɪteɪt/ (***precipitated, precipitating***) **1** to cause something or hasten its advent □ *precipitated a war.* **2** to throw or plunge □ *Jim precipitated himself into the controversy.* **3** *chem, tr & intr* to form or cause something to form a suspension of small solid particles in a solution, as a result of certain chemical reactions. **4** *meteorol* said of moisture, etc: to condense and fall as rain, snow, etc. ▷ *adj* /prɪˈsɪpɪtət/ said of actions or decisions: recklessly hasty or ill-considered. ▷ *noun* /prɪˈsɪpɪtət/ **1** *chem* a suspension of small solid particles formed in a solution as a result of certain chemical reactions. **2** *meteorol* moisture deposited as rain or snow, etc. • **precipitately** *adverb*. ◷ 16c: from Latin *praecipitare, praecipitatum* to fall or throw headlong.

precipitation /prɪsɪpɪˈteɪʃən/ ▷ *noun* **1** rash haste. **2** *meteorol* water that falls from clouds in the atmosphere to the Earth's surface in the form of rain, snow, etc. **3** the act of precipitating or process of being precipitated. **4** *chem* the formation of a precipitate.

precipitous /prɪˈsɪpɪtəs/ ▷ *adj* **1** dangerously steep. **2** said of actions or decisions: rash; precipitate. • **precipitously** *adverb*. • **precipitousness** *noun*.

précis /ˈpreɪsiː/ ▷ *noun* (*plural* ***précis***) a summary of a piece of writing. ▷ *verb* (***précised, précising***) to make a précis of something. ◷ 18c: French, meaning 'precise' or 'cut short'.

precise /prɪˈsaɪs/ ▷ *adj* (***preciser, precisest***) **1** exact; very □ *at this precise moment.* **2** clear; detailed □ *precise instructions.* **3** accurate □ *precise timing.* **4** said of someone: careful over details. • **preciseness** *noun*. ◷ 16c: from Latin *praecisus* shortened, from *praecidere* to cut short.

precisely ▷ *adverb* **1** exactly □ *began at eight o'clock precisely.* **2** in a precise manner. **3** said in response to a remark: you are quite right.

precision /prɪˈsɪʒən/ **1** *noun* accuracy. **2** *as adj* said of tools, etc: designed to operate with minute accuracy □ *precision timing.*

precision-approach radar ▷ *noun, aeronautics* (abbreviation **PAR**) a radar system that shows the exact position of an approaching aircraft, enabling an air traffic controller to give the pilot detailed landing instructions. ◷ 1950s.

preclinical ▷ *adj, medicine* **1** said of a disease, etc: at the stage before significant symptoms appear. **2** said of medical training or education: at the theoretical stage.

preclude /prɪˈkluːd/ ▷ *verb* (***precluded***, ***precluding***) **1** to rule out or eliminate something or make it impossible. **2** (*often* **preclude someone from something**) to prevent their involvement in it. • **preclusion** /prɪˈkluːʒən/ *noun*. • **preclusive** *adj*. ⓘ 17c: from Latin *praecludere*, *praeclusum* to impede, from *claudere* to shut.

precocial /prɪˈkoʊʃəl/ *ornith* ▷ *adj* said of the newly-hatched young of certain birds: covered with feathers and able to see, and so able to leave the nest relatively soon after hatching. ▷ *noun* a bird that produces such chicks. Compare ALTRICIAL, NIDICOLOUS. ⓘ 19c: see PRECOCIOUS.

precocious /prɪˈkoʊʃəs/ ▷ *adj* **1** said eg of a child: unusually advanced in mental development, speech, behaviour, etc. **2** said of behaviour, achievements, etc: indicating advanced development. • **precociously** *adverb*. • **precociousness** or **precocity** /prɪˈkɒsɪtɪ/ *noun*. ⓘ 17c: from Latin *praecox* ripening early, from *coquere* to cook or ripen.

precognition /priːkɒgˈnɪʃən/ ▷ *noun* the supposed ability to foresee events; foreknowledge. • **precognitive** /prɪˈkɒgnɪtɪv/ *adj*. ⓘ 17c: from Latin *praecognitio*, from *cognoscere* to know.

precolumbian or **preColumbian** ▷ *adj* denoting the period of American history before the discovery of America by Christopher Columbus. ⓘ 19c.

preconceive ▷ *verb* to form (an idea, etc) of something before having direct experience of it. • **preconceived** *adj*. ⓘ 16c.

preconception ▷ *noun* **1** an assumption about something not yet experienced. **2** (*often* **preconceptions**) a prejudice.

precondition ▷ *noun* a condition to be satisfied in advance. ▷ *verb* to accustom or train someone or something beforehand to behave or react in a particular way. ⓘ 19c.

preconize or **preconise** /ˈpriːkənaɪz/ ▷ *verb* (***preconized***, ***preconizing***) *formal* **1** to proclaim something publicly. **2** to summon someone publicly. **3** *RC Church* said of the pope: to proclaim and ratify the election of (a bishop). ⓘ 15c: from Latin *praeconizare*, from *praeco*, *praeconis* a herald.

precursor /prɪˈkɜːsə(r)/ ▷ *noun* **1** something that precedes, and is a sign of, an approaching event. **2** *chem* any chemical compound from which another compound is directly produced by some form of chemical modification. • **precursive** or **precursory** *adj*. ⓘ 16c: Latin, from *praecurrere*, *praecursum* to run before.

predacious /prɪˈdeɪʃəs/ ▷ *adj* said of animals: predatory. ⓘ 18c: from Latin *praeda* booty or prey.

predate[1] /priːˈdeɪt/ ▷ *verb* **1** to write a earlier date on (a document, cheque, etc). **2** to occur at an earlier date than (a specified date or event). ⓘ 19c.

predate[2] /prɪˈdeɪt/ ▷ *verb* said of an animal: **1** to eat or prey upon (another animal). **2** *intr* to hunt prey. ⓘ 1970s: back-formation from PREDATION.

predation /prɪˈdeɪʃən/ ▷ *noun* the killing and consuming of other animals for survival; the activity of preying. ⓘ 1930s in this sense; 15c in obsolete sense 'plundering': from Latin *praedari*, *praedatus* to plunder.

predator /ˈprɛdətə(r)/ ▷ *noun* **1** any animal that obtains food by catching, usually killing, and eating other animals. **2** *derog* a predatory person. ⓘ 1920s: from Latin *praedator* plunderer.

predatory /ˈprɛdətərɪ/ ▷ *adj* **1** said of an animal: obtaining food by catching and eating other animals. **2** said of someone: cruelly exploiting the weakness or goodwill of others for personal gain. • **predatorily** *adverb*. • **predatoriness** *noun*.

predecease ▷ *verb* to die before (another person). ⓘ 16c.

predecessor /ˈpriːdɪsɛsə(r)/ ▷ *noun* **1** the person who formerly held a job or position now held by someone else. **2** the previous version, model, etc of a particular thing or product. **3** an ancestor. ⓘ 14c: from Latin *praedecessor*, from *decedere* to go away.

predella /prɪˈdɛlə/ ▷ *noun* (***predellas***) **1** *art* a small painting or panel enclosed in a compartment attached to the lower edge of an altarpiece, especially one that illustrates scenes from the life of the saint represented in the main panel. **2** the platform or uppermost step on which an altar stands. **3** a RETABLE. ⓘ 19c: Italian, meaning 'stool' or 'footstool'.

predestination ▷ *noun* **1** the act of predestining or fact of being predestined. **2** *relig* the doctrine that whatever is to happen has been unalterably fixed by God from the beginning of time, especially with regard to which souls are to be saved and which damned.

predestine /priːˈdɛstɪn/ ▷ *verb* **1** to determine something beforehand. **2** to ordain or decree by fate. ⓘ 14c.

predetermine ▷ *verb* **1** to decide, settle or fix in advance. **2** to influence, shape or bias something in a certain way. • **predeterminable** *adj*. • **predeterminate** *adj*. • **predetermination** *noun*. ⓘ 17c.

predicable /ˈprɛdɪkəbəl/ ▷ *adj* able to be predicated or affirmed. ⓘ 16c: from Latin *praedicabilis*; see PREDICATE.

predicament /prɪˈdɪkəmənt/ ▷ *noun* **1** a difficulty plight or dilemma. **2** *logic* a category. ⓘ 14c: from Latin *praedicamentum* something asserted; see PREDICATE.

predicate ▷ *noun* /ˈprɛdɪkət/ **1** *grammar* the word or words in a sentence that make a statement about the subject, usually consisting of a verb and its complement, eg *ran* in *John ran* and *knew exactly what to do* in *The people in charge knew exactly what to do*. **2** *logic* what is stated as a property of the subject of a proposition. ▷ *verb* /ˈprɛdɪkeɪt/ (***predicated***, ***predicating***) **1** to assert. **2** to imply; to entail the existence of something. **3** *logic* to state something as a property of the subject of a proposition. **4** (*usually* **predicate on** or **upon something**) to make the viability of (an idea, etc) depend on something else being true □ ***Their success was predicated on the number of supporters they had***. • **predication** /prɛdɪˈkeɪʃən/ *noun*. ⓘ 16c: from Latin *praedicare* to assert, from *dicare* to declare.

predicate calculus ▷ *noun*, *math* a notation system by means of which the logical structure of simple propositions may be represented.

predicative /prɪˈdɪkətɪv/ ▷ *adj* **1** *grammar* said of an adjective: forming part of a PREDICATE, eg 'asleep' in *They were asleep*. Compare ATTRIBUTIVE. **2** relating to predicates. • **predicatively** *adverb*, *grammar* with a predicative function.

predict /prɪˈdɪkt/ ▷ *verb* (***predicted***, ***predicting***) to prophesy, foretell or forecast. ⓘ 17c: from Latin *praedicere* to foretell.

predictable ▷ *adj* **1** able to be predicted; easily foreseen. **2** *derog* boringly consistent in behaviour or reactions, etc; unoriginal. • **predictability** *noun*. • **predictably** *adverb*.

prediction /prɪˈdɪkʃən/ ▷ *noun* **1** the act or art of predicting. **2** something foretold.

predigest ▷ *verb* to digest (food) artificially before introducing it into the body. ⓘ 17c.

predikant /prɛdɪˈkant/ ▷ *noun* a minister in the Dutch Reformed Church, especially in S Africa. ⓘ 17c: Dutch, from Latin *predicare* to preach.

predilection /priːdɪˈlɛkʃən/ ▷ *noun* a special liking or preference for something. ⓘ 18c: from French prédilection, from Latin *praediligere*, *praedilectum* to prefer.

predispose ▷ *verb* **1** to incline someone to react in a particular way □ ***Clear handwriting will predispose the***

examiners in your favour. **2** to make someone susceptible to something (especially illness). • **predisposition** *noun.* ⓘ 17c.

prednisone /'prɛdnɪzoʊn/ ▻ *noun, pharmocology* a type of synthetic steroid used, like cortisone, to alleviate the symptoms of rheumatoid arthritis and as an anti-inflammatory agent in certain allergies. ⓘ 1950s.

predominant /prɪ'dɒmɪnənt/ ▻ *adj* **1** more numerous, prominent or powerful. **2** more frequent; prevailing. • **predominance** *noun.* • **predominantly** *adverb.*

predominate /prɪ'dɒmɪneɪt/ ▻ *verb, intr* **1** to be more numerous. **2** to be more noticeable or prominent. **3** to have more influence. ⓘ 16c.

pre-eclampsia /priːɪ'klampsɪə/ ▻ *noun, pathol* a toxic condition which can occur late in pregnancy and which may lead to ECLAMPSIA if left untreated. ⓘ 1920s.

pre-embryo ▻ *noun, biol, medicine* a human embryo in the first fourteen days after fertilization of an ovum, before DIFFERENTIATION (sense 3). ⓘ Early 20c.

pre-eminent /priː'ɛmɪnənt/ ▻ *adj* outstanding; better than all others. • **pre-eminence** *noun.* • **pre-eminently** *adverb.* ⓘ 15c: from Latin *praeeminere* to project forwards or stand out before.

pre-empt /priː'ɛmpt/ ▻ *verb* (***pre-empted, pre-empting***) **1** to do something ahead of someone else and so make pointless (an action they had planned). **2** to obtain something in advance. **3** *intr, bridge* to make a PRE-EMPTIVE (sense 3) bid. ⓘ 19c: a back-formation from PRE-EMPTION.

pre-emption ▻ *noun* **1** *law* the buying of, or right to buy, property, before others get the chance to do so. **2** the act of pre-empting. **3** a belligerent's right to seize neutral contraband at a fixed price. ⓘ 16c: from Latin *prae* before + *emptio, emptionis* buying.

pre-emptive ▻ *adj* **1** having the effect of pre-empting. **2** *military* said of an attack: effectively destroying the enemy's weapons before they can be used ◻ ***a pre-emptive strike.*** **3** *bridge* said of a bid: unusually high, with the intention of deterring other players from bidding.

preen ▻ *verb* (***preened, preening***) **1** *tr & intr* said of a bird: to clean and smooth (feathers, etc) with its beak. **2** said of a person: to groom (oneself, hair, clothes, etc), especially in a vain manner. ⓘ 15c.

▪ **preen oneself on something** to pride or congratulate oneself on account of it.

pre-exist ▻ *verb* to exist beforehand, especially in a previous life. ⓘ 16c.

pref. ▻ *abbreviation* **1** preface. **2** preference. **3** preferred.

prefab /'priːfab/ ▻ *noun* a prefabricated building, especially a domestic house. ⓘ 1940s: a shortened form of *prefabricated.*

prefabricate ▻ *verb* to manufacture standard sections of (a building) for later quick assembly. • **prefabrication** *noun.* ⓘ 1930s.

preface /'prɛfəs/ ▻ *noun* **1** an explanatory statement at the beginning of a book. **2** anything of an introductory or preliminary character. ▻ *verb* (***prefaced, prefacing***) **1** to provide (a book, etc) with a preface. **2** to introduce or precede something with some preliminary matter. ⓘ 14c: from French *préface,* from Latin *praefari* to say beforehand.

prefatory /'prɛfətərɪ/ ▻ *adj* **1** relating to a preface. **2** serving as a preface or introduction. **3** introductory. ⓘ 17c.

prefect /'priːfɛkt/ ▻ *noun* **1** in a school: a senior pupil with minor disciplinary powers. See also MONITOR (*noun* 4). **2** in some countries: the senior official of an administrative district. **3** *historical* in ancient Rome: any of various civil and military officers. • **prefectoral** /-'fɛktərəl/ and **prefectorial** /-'tɔːrɪəl/ *adj.* ⓘ 14c: from Latin *praefectus* an official in charge, from *praeficere* to place in authority over.

prefecture /'priːfɛktʃə(r)/ ▻ *noun* **1** the office or term of office of a prefect. **2** the district presided over by a prefect. **3** the official residence of a prefect. See PREFECT (sense 2). ⓘ 17c.

prefer /prɪ'fɜː(r)/ ▻ *verb* (***preferred, preferring***) **1** to like someone or something better than another ◻ ***Would you prefer tea?*** ◻ ***I prefer tea to coffee.*** **2** *law* to submit (a charge, accusation, etc) to a court of law for consideration. **3** *formal* to promote someone, especially over their colleagues. ⓘ 14c: from French *préférer,* from Latin *praeferre* to place before, especially in terms of esteem.

prefer

Prefer should be followed by **to**, not **than**, as in *He prefers tea to coffee.*

preferable /'prɛfərəbəl/ ▻ *adj* more desirable, suitable or advisable; better. • **preferably** *adverb.* ⓘ 17c.

preference /'prɛfərəns/ ▻ *noun* **1** the preferring of one person, thing, etc to another. **2** one's choice of, or liking for, someone or something particular. **3** favourable consideration. • **in preference to** rather than. ⓘ 17c.

preference shares ▻ *plural noun, stock exchange* shares on which the dividend must be paid before that on ORDINARY SHARES.

preferential /prɛfə'rɛnʃəl/ ▻ *adj* bestowing special favours or advantages ◻ ***preferential treatment.***

preferential voting ▻ *noun* an election system that requires voters to place candidates in order of their preference. It is often a feature of PROPORTIONAL REPRESENTATION. ⓘ 19c.

preferment /prɪ'fɜːmənt/ ▻ *noun* promotion to a more responsible position. ⓘ 15c: see PREFER 3.

prefigure /priː'fɪgə(r)/ ▻ *verb* **1** to be an advance sign or representation of something that is to come; to foreshadow. **2** to imagine beforehand. • **prefiguration** *noun.* ⓘ 15c: from Latin *praefigurare;* see PRE- + FIGURE *verb.*

prefix /'priːfɪks/ ▻ *noun* (***prefixes***) **1** *grammar* an element such as *un-, pre-, non-, de-,* etc which is added to the beginning of a word to create a new word. Compare AFFIX, INFIX, SUFFIX. **2** a title such as *Mr, Dr, Ms,* etc used before someone's name. ▻ *verb* **1** to add something as an introduction. **2** *grammar* to attach something as a prefix to a word. **3** to add (a prefix) to something. ⓘ 17c: PRE- (sense b) + FIX *verb.*

pre-flight ▻ *adj* prior to the take-off of an aeroplane or helicopter, etc ◻ ***pre-flight checks.*** ⓘ 1920s.

pre-frontal ▻ *adj, anatomy, etc* belonging or relating to the foremost area of the frontal lobe of the brain. ⓘ 19c.

pre-frontal leucotomy see under LEUCOTOMY

pre-frontal lobotomy see LOBOTOMY

preggers /'prɛgəz/ ▻ *adj, colloq* pregnant.

pregnable /'prɛgnəbəl/ ▻ *adj* capable of being taken by force; vulnerable. ⓘ 15c: from French *prenable,* from *prendre* to take, from Latin *prehendre* to seize.

pregnancy /'prɛgnənsɪ/ ▻ *noun* (***pregnancies***) *biol* in female mammals, including humans: the period between fertilization or conception and birth, during which a developing embryo is carried in the womb. Also called GESTATION. ⓘ 16c.

pregnant /'prɛgnənt/ ▻ *adj* **1** said of a female mammal, including humans: carrying a child or young in the womb. **2** said of a remark or pause, etc: loaded with significance. **3** fruitful in results. • **pregnantly** *adverb.* ⓘ 15c: from Latin *praegnans,* from *prae-* before + *(g)nasci* to be born.

preheat ▷ *verb* to heat (an oven, furnace, etc) before use. ◷ 19c.

prehensile /prɪˈhɛnsaɪl/ ▷ *adj, denoting* a part of an animal that is adapted for grasping, eg the tail of certain vertebrates. • **prehensility** /-hɛnˈsɪlɪtɪ/ *noun.* ◷ 18c: from French *préhensile*, from Latin *prehendere* to grasp.

prehension /prɪˈhɛnʃən/ ▷ *noun* **1** the act of grasping. **2** mental understanding. Compare APPREHENSION, COMPREHENSION. ◷ 19c: from Latin *prehendere* to seize.

prehistoric or **prehistorical** ▷ *adj* **1** belonging or relating to the period before written records. **2** *colloq* completely outdated or very old-fashioned. • **prehistorically** *adverb.* ◷ 19c.

prehistory ▷ *noun* the period before written records, classified as encompassing the STONE AGE, BRONZE AGE and IRON AGE. ◷ 19c.

pre-ignition ▷ *noun* in an internal-combustion engine: premature ignition of the explosive charge. ◷ 19c.

prejudge ▷ *verb* **1** to form an opinion on (an issue, etc) without having all the relevant facts. **2** to condemn someone unheard. • **prejudgement** *noun.* ◷ 16c.

prejudice /ˈprɛdʒʊdɪs/ ▷ *noun* **1** a biased opinion, based on insufficient knowledge. **2** hostility, eg towards a particular racial or religious group. **3** *law* harm; detriment; disadvantage □ *without prejudice to your parental rights.* ▷ *verb* (*prejudiced, prejudicing*) **1** to make someone feel prejudice; to bias. **2** to harm or endanger □ *A poor interview will prejudice your chances of success.* ◷ 13c: from French *préjudice*, from Latin *praejudicium* harm, from *prae-* PRE- + *judicium* judgement.

prejudicial /prɛdʒʊˈdɪʃəl/ ▷ *adj* **1** causing prejudice. **2** harmful. • **prejudicially** *adverb.*

prelacy /ˈprɛləsɪ/ ▷ *noun* (*prelacies*) *Christianity* **1** the office of a prelate. **2** the entire body of prelates. **3** administration of the church by prelates.

prelapsarian /priːlapˈsɛərɪən/ *adj* **1** belonging or relating to the time before THE FALL. **2** innocent; naive. ◷ 19c: from Latin *lapsus* a fall.

prelate /ˈprɛlət/ ▷ *noun, Christianity* a bishop, abbot or other high-ranking ecclesiastic. • **prelatic** /prɪˈlatɪk/ and **prelatical** *adj.* ◷ 13c: from French *prélat*, from Latin *praeferre, praelatum* to prefer.

preliminary /prɪˈlɪmɪnərɪ/ ▷ *adj* occurring at the beginning; introductory or preparatory. ▷ *noun* (*preliminaries*) **1** (*usually* **preliminaries**) something done or said by way of introduction or preparation □ *had no time for the usual preliminaries.* **2** a preliminary round in a competition. ◷ 17c: from Latin *praeliminaris*, from *prae–* before + *limen, liminis* threshold.

prelim /ˈpriːlɪm/ ▷ *noun, colloq* **1** in Scotland: any one of a set of school examinations taken before the public ones. **2** the first public examination in certain universities. **3** (**prelims**) *printing* the title page, contents page and other matter preceding the main text of a book. ◷ 19c: an abbreviation of *preliminaries.*

prelude /ˈprɛljuːd/ ▷ *noun* **1** *music* an introductory passage or first movement, eg of a fugue or suite. **2** a name sometimes given to a short musical piece or a poetical composition, etc. **3** (*especially* **a prelude to something**) some event that precedes, and prepares the ground for, something of greater significance. ▷ *verb* (*preluded, preluding*) **1** *tr & intr* to act as a prelude to something. **2** to introduce something with a prelude. • **prelusive** /prɪlˈjuːsɪv/ *adj.* ◷ 16c: from Latin *praeludium*, from *ludere* to play.

premarital ▷ *adj* belonging to or occurring in the period before marriage. • **premaritally** *adverb.* ◷ 19c.

premature /ˈprɛmətʃʊə(r), ˈpriː-/ ▷ *adj* **1** *medicine* said of human birth: occurring less than 37 weeks after conception. **2** occurring before the usual or expected time □ *premature senility.* **3** said of a decision, etc: over-hasty; impulsive. • **prematurely** *adverb.* ◷ 16c: from Latin *praematurus*, from *prae* before + *maturus* ripe.

premed /priːˈmɛd/ *colloq* ▷ *noun* **1** PREMEDICATION. **2** premedical studies. **3** a premedical student. ▷ *adj* PREMEDICAL. ◷ 1960s: abbreviation.

premedical ▷ *adj* belonging or relating to a course of study undertaken in preparation for professional medical training. ◷ Early 20c.

premedicate ▷ *verb* to give premedication to (a patient). ◷ 19c.

premedication ▷ *noun, medicine* drugs, usually including a sedative, given to a patient in preparation for a GENERAL ANAESTHETIC prior to surgery. Often shortened to PREMED. ◷ 1920s.

premeditate ▷ *verb* to plan; to think something out beforehand. • **premeditated** *adj* said especially of a crime: planned beforehand. • **premeditatedly** *adverb.* • **premeditation** *noun.* • **premeditative** *adj.* ◷ 16c.

premenstrual ▷ *adj* **1** relating to or occurring during the days immediately before a MENSTRUAL period. **2** said of a woman: in the days immediately before a menstrual period. ◷ 19c.

premenstrual tension and **premenstrual syndrome** ▷ *noun* (abbreviation **PMT** and **PMS**) *medicine* a group of symptoms associated with hormonal changes and experienced by some women before the onset of menstruation, characterized by fluid retention, headache, food cravings, depression and irritability. ◷ 1920s.

premier /ˈprɛmɪə(r), ˈpriː-/ ▷ *adj* **1** first in rank; most important; leading. **2** *Brit, denoting* the top two divisions in the football leagues in both England and Wales and Scotland. **3** first in time; earliest. ▷ *noun* **1** a prime minister. **2** in Australia and Canada: the head of government of a state or province. ◷ 15c: French, meaning 'first', from Latin *primarius* of first rank.

première or **premiere** /ˈprɛmɪɛə(r)/ ▷ *noun* **1** the first public performance of a play or showing of a film. Also called FIRST NIGHT. **2** the leading actress, female dancer, etc in a company. ▷ *verb* (*premièred, premièring*) **1** to present a première of (a film, etc). **2** *intr* said of a play, film, etc: to open. ◷ 19c: French feminine of *premier* first.

premiership ▷ *noun* **1** the office of prime minister. **2** (**the Premiership**) *football* in England and Wales: **a** the top division in the football league; **b** the competition in this division.

premillennialism /priːmɪˈlɛnɪəlɪzəm/ ▷ *noun* the doctrine that the Second Coming of Christ will be before the millennium (sense 2a). • **premillennialist** *noun.* ◷ 19c.

premise ▷ *noun* /ˈprɛmɪs/ **1** (*also* **premiss**) something assumed to be true as a basis for stating something further. **2** *logic* either of the propositions introducing a syllogism. ▷ *verb* /prɪˈmaɪz, ˈprɛmɪs/ to assume or state as a premise. ◷ 14c: from French *prémisse*, from Latin *praemissa* things preceding, from *praemittere* to put before.

premises /ˈprɛmɪsɪz/ ▷ *plural noun* **1** a building and its grounds, especially as a place of business. **2** *law* **a** the preliminary matter in a document, etc; **b** matters explained or property referred to earlier in the document. ◷ 18c in sense 1, 15c in sense 2b: from PREMISE.

premium /ˈpriːmɪəm/ ▷ *noun* **1** an amount paid, usually annually, on an insurance agreement. **2** an extra sum added to wages or to interest. **3** a prize. **4** *as adj* finest; exceptional □ *premium quality.* • **be at a premium** to be scarce and greatly in demand. • **put a premium on something** to attach special importance to it. ◷ 17c: from Latin *praemium* reward.

Premium Bond and **Premium Savings Bond** ▷ *noun* in the UK: a government bond that yields no interest, but is eligible for a monthly draw for cash prizes. See also ERNIE. ⓒ Early 20c.

premolar ▷ *noun* any of the teeth between the canine teeth and the molars. ▷ *adj* situated in front of a MOLAR tooth. ⓒ 19c.

premonition /prɛmə'nɪʃən, priː-/ ▷ *noun* a feeling that something is about to happen, before it actually does; an intuition or presentiment. ⓒ 16c: from Latin *praemonitio* a forewarning, from *prae* before + *monere* to warn.

prenatal ▷ *adj* relating to or occurring during the period before childbirth. ▷ *noun, colloq* any routine medical examination of a pregnant woman. • **prenatally** *adverb*. Compare ANTENATAL, POSTNATAL. ⓒ 19c.

preoccupation ▷ *noun* **1** the state or condition of being preoccupied. **2** something that preoccupies.

preoccupied ▷ *adj* **1** lost in thought. **2** (*often* **preoccupied by** or **with something**) having one's attention completely taken up; engrossed. **3** already occupied.

preoccupy ▷ *verb* **1** to occupy the attention of someone wholly; to engross or obsess. **2** to occupy or fill something before others. ⓒ 16c: from Latin *praeoccupare* to seize beforehand.

preordain /priːɔː'deɪn/ ▷ *verb* to decide or determine beforehand.

prep¹ ▷ *noun, colloq* **1** short for PREPARATION 3. **2** short for PREPARATORY □ *prep school.*

prep² ▷ *verb* (***prepped***, ***prepping***) to get (a patient) ready for an operation, etc, especially by giving a sedative.

prep. ▷ *abbreviation, grammar* preposition.

prepack ▷ *verb* to pack (food, etc) before offering it for sale. ⓒ 1920s.

prepaid see under PREPAY

preparation /prɛpə'reɪʃən/ ▷ *noun* **1** the process of preparing or being prepared. **2** (*usually* **preparations**) something done by way of preparing or getting ready. **3** *Brit, chiefly* in public schools: school work done out of school hours, done either in school or as HOMEWORK. Often shortened to **prep**. **4** a medicine, cosmetic or other such prepared substance.

preparatory /prə'parətərɪ/ ▷ *adj* **1** serving to prepare for something. **2** introductory; preliminary. • **preparatory to something** before it; in preparation for it. ⓒ 15c.

preparatory school ▷ *noun* **1** in the UK: a private school for children aged between seven and thirteen, usually preparing them for public school. **2** in the US: a private secondary school, preparing pupils for college. Often shortened to **prep school**. ⓒ 19c.

prepare /prɪ'pɛə(r)/ ▷ *verb* (***prepared***, ***preparing***) **1** *tr & intr* to make or get ready. **2** to make (a meal). **3** to clean or chop (vegetables or fruit). **4** to get someone or oneself into a fit state to receive a shock, surprise, etc □ *We prepared ourselves for bad news.* **5** *intr* to brace oneself (to do something) □ *prepare to jump.* ⓒ 15c: from Latin *praeparare*, from *prae* before + *parare* to make ready.

prepared ▷ *adj* **1** (*usually* **be prepared to do something**) said of a person: to be willing and able □ *I'm not prepared to lend any more.* **2** (*usually* **prepared for something**) expecting it or ready for it □ *We were prepared for the worst.* • **preparedness** /-rɪdnɪs/ *noun* a state of readiness.

prepay /priː'peɪ/ ▷ *verb* to pay for something, especially postage, in advance. • **prepaid** *adj* □ *a prepaid envelope.* • **prepayable** *adj*. • **prepayment** *noun*. ⓒ 19c.

prepense /prɪ'pɛns/ ▷ *adj, law* premeditated; intentional. Also called AFORETHOUGHT. ⓒ 18c: from French *purpensé*, from Latin *pensare* to consider.

preponderance /prɪ'pɒndərəns/ ▷ *noun* **1** the circumstance of predominating. **2** a superior number; a majority. • **preponderant** *adj*. ⓒ 17c.

preponderate /prɪ'pɒndəreɪt/ ▷ *verb* (***preponderated***, ***preponderating***) *intr* **1** (*often* **preponderate over something**) to be more numerous than it; to predominate. **2** to weigh more. ⓒ 17c: from Latin *ponderare* to weigh.

preposition /prɛpə'zɪʃən/ ▷ *noun, grammar* a word, or words, such as *to, from, into, out of*, etc, typically preceding nouns and pronouns, and describing their position, movement, etc in relation to other words in the sentence. • **prepositional** *adj*. • **prepositionally** *adverb*. ⓒ 14c: from Latin *praepositio*, from *praeponere, praepositum* to put before.

> ***preposition***
>
> In current English, a preposition can have various positions within a phrase, clause or sentence, and often comes at the end:
>
> ✓ *He was looking for a table to put his books on.*
>
> ✓ *He was looking for a table on which to put his books.*
>
> The notion still sometimes found, that a preposition should always come before the word or phrase it governs, is, like the split infinitive, an artificial rule that has no basis in usage or in principle. Often, especially in idiomatic uses, such a rule would produce absurd results:
>
> **?** *We don't have much on which to go.*
>
> ✓ *We don't have much to go on.*
>
> ☆ RECOMMENDATION: it is correct, and often more natural, to end a sentence with a preposition.

prepossess ▷ *verb, rather formal* **1** to charm. **2** to win over; to incline or bias. **3** to preoccupy someone in a specified way. ⓒ 17c: originally meaning 'to possess beforehand'.

prepossessing ▷ *adj* attractive; winning.

preposterous /prɪ'pɒstərəs/ ▷ *adj* ridiculous, absurd or outrageous. • **preposterously** *adverb*. ⓒ 16c: from Latin *praeposterus* back-to-front, from *prae* before + *posterus* coming after.

prepotent /priː'poutənt/ ▷ *adj* **1** powerfully more influential than others. **2** *biol* **a** said of one parent: more likely to pass on hereditary characteristics than the other; **b** having greater power of fertilization. • **prepotency** /prɪ'poutənsɪ/ *noun*. ⓒ 17c: from Latin *praepotens*, from *posse* to have power.

preppy /'prɛpɪ/ *informal, especially N Amer* ▷ *adj* (***preppier***, ***preppiest***) said of dress sense, etc: neat and conservative. ▷ *noun* (***preppies***) someone who dresses in such a way. ⓒ Early 20c: originally in the sense 'belonging to or characteristic of a PREPARATORY SCHOOL student'.

preprandial ▷ *adj, facetious* preceding a meal □ *a preprandial drink.* ⓒ 19c.

preproduction ▷ *noun* the groundwork that is done before a film, broadcast, etc starts being made. *Also as adj* □ *Brad Pitt was chosen for the role at the preproduction stage.*

prep school see PREPARATORY SCHOOL

prepuce /'priːpjuːs/ ▷ *noun, anatomy* **1** the fold of skin that covers the top of the penis. Also called FORESKIN. **2** the fold of skin that surrounds the clitoris. ⓒ 14c: from Latin *praeputium*.

prequel /'priːkwəl/ ▷ *noun* a book or film produced after one that has been a popular success, but with the story beginning prior to the start of the original story. ⓒ 1970s: from PRE-, modelled on SEQUEL.

Pre-Raphaelite /priː'rafəlaɪt/ ▷ *noun* a member of the Pre-Raphaelite Brotherhood (abbreviation **PRB**), a group of artists who advocated a truthful adherence to natural forms and effects. ▷ *adj* relating to or characteristic of the Pre-Raphaelites. ⓒ 19c: they adopted this name because of their aim to return to the style of painters before the Italian master Raphael (1483–1520).

prerecord ▷ *verb* to record (a programme for radio or TV) in advance of its scheduled broadcasting time. ⓒ 1930s.

prerequisite /priːˈrɛkwɪzɪt/ ▷ *noun* a preliminary requirement that must be satisfied. ▷ *adj* said of a condition, etc: required to be satisfied beforehand. ⓒ 17c.

prerogative /prɪˈrɒgətɪv/ ▷ *noun* **1** an exclusive right or privilege arising from one's rank or position. **2** any right or privilege. See also ROYAL PREROGATIVE. ▷ *adj* holding or exercising a prerogative. ⓒ 14c: from Latin *praerogativa* privilege, from *prae* before others + *rogare, rogatum* to ask.

Pres. ▷ *abbreviation* President.

pres. ▷ *abbreviation* present.

presage /ˈprɛsɪdʒ, prɪˈseɪdʒ/ ▷ *verb* (***presaged, presaging***) **1** to warn of or be a warning sign of something; to foreshadow, forebode or portend. **2** to have a premonition about something. ▷ *noun, formal or literary* **1** a portent, warning or omen. **2** a premonition. • **presageful** /prɪˈseɪdʒfəl/ *adj.* • **presager** *noun.* ⓒ 14c: from French *présage*, from Latin *praesagium*, from *praesagire* to forebode.

presbyopia /prɛzbɪˈoʊpɪə/ ▷ *noun, opthalmol* difficulty in focusing the eye on nearby objects, a defect that becomes more common in old age, caused by decreased elasticity of the lens of the eye. • **presbyopic** /-bɪˈopɪk/ *adj.* ⓒ 18c: Latin, from Greek *presbys* old man + *ops* eye.

presbyter /ˈprɛzbɪtə(r)/ ▷ *noun, Christianity* **1** in the early Christian church: an administrative official with some teaching and priestly duties. **2** in episcopal churches: a priest. **3** in presbyterian churches: an elder. ⓒ 16c: Latin, from Greek *presbyteros* an older man, from *presbys* old man.

presbyterian /prɛzbɪˈtɪərɪən/ ▷ *adj* **1** referring or relating to church administration by presbyters or elders. **2** (*often* **Presbyterian**) designating a church governed by elders. ▷ *noun* (**Presbyterian**) a member of a presbyterian church. ⓒ 17c.

presbytery /ˈprɛzbɪtərɪ/ ▷ *noun, Christianity* (***presbyteries***) **1** in a presbyterian church: an area of local administration. **2** a body of ministers and elders, especially one sitting as a local church court. **3** *archit* the eastern section of a church, beyond the choir. **4** the residence of a Roman Catholic priest. ⓒ 15c: from French *presbiterie* priest's house, from Latin *presbyterium*; see PRESBYTER.

preschool ▷ *adj* denoting or relating to children before they are old enough to attend school □ ***preschool playgroups.*** ⓒ 1920s.

preschool education ▷ *noun* the education of children who have not yet reached the statutory school age, which may be provided in a nursery, kindergarten, playgroup, etc.

prescience /ˈprɛsɪəns/ ▷ *noun* foreknowledge; foresight. • **prescient** *adj.* ⓒ 14c: from Latin *praescire* to know beforehand, from *scire* to know.

prescribe /prɪˈskraɪb/ ▷ *verb* (***prescribed, prescribing***) **1** said especially of a doctor: to advise (a medicine) as a remedy, especially by completing a prescription. **2** to recommend officially (eg a text for academic study). **3** to lay down or establish (a duty, penalty, etc) officially. • **prescriber** *noun.* ⓒ 16c: from Latin *praescribere* to write down beforehand, from *scribere* to write.

> ***prescribe***
>
> A word sometimes confused with this one is **proscribe**.

prescript /ˈpriːskrɪpt/ ▷ *noun, formal* a law, rule, principle, etc that has been laid down. ⓒ 16c: from Latin *praescriptum*, from *praescribere* to write down beforehand.

prescription /prɪˈskrɪpʃən/ ▷ *noun* **1 a** a set of written instructions from a doctor to a pharmacist regarding the preparation and dispensing of a drug, etc for a particular patient; **b** the drug, etc prescribed in this way by a doctor; **c** *as adj* □ ***prescription drugs.*** **2 a** a set of written instructions for an optician stating the type of lenses required to correct a patient's vision; **b** *as adj* □ ***prescription sunglasses.*** **3** the act of prescribing. **4** *law* uninterrupted use or possession of property over a period of time fixed by law, after which a title or right is acquired. • **on prescription** said of medicines: available only on the presentation to the pharmacist of a prescription from a doctor. ⓒ 14c: from Latin *praescriptio* an order; see PRESCRIBE.

prescriptive /prɪˈskrɪptɪv/ ▷ *adj* **1** authoritative; laying down rules. **2** said of a right, etc: established by custom. ⓒ 18c.

prescriptivism ▷ *noun* **1** *grammar* an authoritarian approach to language which advocates the strict application of certain rules governing how it should and should not be used, eg the avoidance of split infinitives or the use of '*I shall*' rather than '*I will*' to express future time. It is now generally frowned upon by linguists, teachers, etc because it fails to take into account how language is used and its potential for creativity. **2** *philos* the theory that moral judgements prescribe some course of action. Compare DESCRIPTIVISM. ⓒ 1950s.

preseason ▷ *noun* the period before a sporting, etc season starts.

presence /ˈprɛzəns/ ▷ *noun* **1** the state or circumstance of being present. **2** someone's company or nearness □ ***He said so in my presence*** □ ***Your presence is requested.*** **3** physical bearing, especially if it is commanding or authoritative □ ***people with presence.*** **4** a being felt to be close by, especially in a supernatural way. **5** a situation or activity demonstrating influence or power in a place □ ***maintain a military presence in the area.*** ⓒ 14c: French, from Latin *praesentia*, from *praeesse* to be before or at hand.

presence of mind ▷ *noun* the ability to act calmly and sensibly, especially in an emergency.

present¹ /ˈprɛzənt/ ▷ *adj* **1** being at the place or occasion in question. **2** existing, detectable or able to be found. **3** existing now □ ***the present situation.*** **4** now being considered □ ***the present subject.*** **5** *grammar* said of the tense of a verb: indicating action that is taking place now, or action that is continuing or habitual, as in *I walk the dog every morning* and *He's going to school.* ▷ *noun* **1** the present time. **2** *grammar* **a** the present tense; **b** a verb in the present tense. Compare PAST, PERFECT, IMPERFECT, PLUPERFECT, FUTURE. **3** (**presents**) *old use, law* the present document; this statement, these words, etc. • **at present** now. • **for the present** for the time being. ⓒ 13c: from Latin *praesens, praesentis.*

present² /prɪˈzɛnt/ ▷ *verb* (***presented, presenting***) **1** to give or award something, especially formally or ceremonially □ ***presented them with gold medals.*** **2** to introduce (a person), especially formally. **3** to introduce or compère (a TV or radio show). **4** to stage (a play), show (a film), etc. **5** to offer something for consideration; to submit. **6** to pose; to set □ ***shouldn't present any problem.*** **7** said of an idea: to suggest (itself). **8** to hand over (a cheque) for acceptance or (a bill) for payment. **9** to set out something □ ***presents her work neatly.*** **10** to depict or represent something or someone. **11** to put on (a specified appearance) in public. **12** to offer (one's compliments) formally. **13** to hold (a weapon) in aiming position. See also *present arms* below. **14** *intr, medicine* **a** to report to a doctor with certain symptoms or signs; **b** said of an illness, disease, etc: to manifest. **15** *intr, obstetrics* said of a baby's head or buttocks in childbirth: to be in a position to emerge first. • **present arms** to hold a rifle or other weapon vertically in front of one as a salute. • **present oneself** to appear in person. ⓘ 13c: from French *presenter*, from Latin *praesentare* to place before.

present[3] /ˈprɛzənt/ ▷ *noun* something given; a gift. ⓘ 13c: French, from the phrase *mettre une chose en présent à quelqu'un* to put something in the PRESENCE of someone, hence to offer as a gift to someone.

presentable /prɪˈzɛntəbəl/ ▷ *adj* **1** fit to be seen or to appear in company, etc. **2** passable; satisfactory. • **presentability** *noun*. • **presentably** *adverb*. ⓘ 19c: from PRESENT[2].

presentation /prɛzənˈteɪʃən/ ▷ *noun* **1** the act of presenting. **2** the manner in which something is presented, laid out, explained or advertised. **3** something performed for an audience, eg a play, show or other entertainment. **4** a formal report, usually delivered verbally. **5** *obstetrics* the position of a baby in the womb just before birth, ie whether with the head or buttocks downward.

present-day ▷ *adj* modern; contemporary.

presenter ▷ *noun* **1** *broadcasting* someone who introduces a programme and provides a linking commentary between items. **2** someone who presents (see PRESENT[2]).

presentiment /prɪˈzɛntɪmənt/ ▷ *noun* a feeling that something, especially something bad, is about to happen, just before it does. ⓘ 18c: French, from *pressentir* to sense beforehand.

presently /ˈprɛzəntlɪ/ ▷ *adverb* **1** soon; shortly. **2** *N Amer, especially US* at the present time; now.

presentment ▷ *noun* **1** an act of presenting or the state of being presented. **2** *law* the act of presenting information before a court, especially information known to a jury under oath.

present participle see under PARTICIPLE

present perfect see under PERFECT

preservation order ▷ *noun* a legally binding directive ordering the preservation of a building deemed to be historically important.

preservative /prɪˈzɜːvətɪv/ ▷ *noun* a chemical substance that, when added to food or other perishable material, slows down or prevents its decay by bacteria and fungi. ▷ *adj* having the effect of preserving.

preserve /prɪˈzɜːv/ ▷ *verb* (***preserved, preserving***) **1** to save something from loss, damage, decay or deterioration. **2** to treat (food), eg by freezing, smoking, drying, pickling or boiling in sugar, so that it will last. **3** to maintain (eg peace, the status quo, standards, etc). **4** to keep safe from danger or death. ▷ *noun* **1** an area of work or activity that is restricted to certain people □ *Politics was once a male preserve.* **2** an area of land or water where creatures are protected for private hunting, shooting or fishing. □ *game preserve.* **3** a jam, pickle or other form in which fruit or vegetables are preserved by cooking in sugar, salt, vinegar, etc. • **preservable** *adj*. • **preservation** *noun*. • **preserver** *noun*. ⓘ 14c: from Latin *praeservare* to guard beforehand, from *servare* to guard.

preset /priːˈsɛt/ ▷ *verb* to adjust (a piece of electronic equipment, etc) so that it will operate at the required time. ▷ *noun* /ˈpriːsɛt/ a device or facility for presetting. ⓘ 1940s.

preshrink ▷ *verb* to shrink (fabric) during manufacture, in order to prevent further shrinkage when it has been made into garments. ⓘ 1930s.

preside /prɪˈzaɪd/ ▷ *verb* (***presided, presiding***) *intr* (*often* **preside at** or **over something**) **1** to take the lead at (an event), the chair at (a meeting, etc); to be in charge. **2** to dominate; to be a dominating presence in (a place, etc) □ *His statue presides over the park.* ⓘ 17c: from Latin *praesidere* to command, from *prae* before + *sedere* to sit.

presidency /ˈprɛzɪdənsɪ/ ▷ *noun* (***presidencies***) the rank, office or term of a president.

president /ˈprɛzɪdənt/ ▷ *noun* **1** (*often* **President**) the elected head of state in a republic. **2** the chief office-bearer in a society or club. **3** *especially US* the head of a business organization, eg the chairman of a company, governor of a bank, etc. **4** the head of some colleges or other higher-education institutions. • **presidential** /-ˈdɛnʃəl/ *adj*. ⓘ 14c: from Latin *praesidens*; see PRESIDE.

presiding officer ▷ *noun* the person in charge of a POLLING STATION.

presidium or **praesidium** /prɪˈsɪdɪəm/ ▷ *noun* (***presidiums*** or ***presidia***) (*often with capital*) in a Communist state: a standing executive committee. ⓘ 1920s: from Russian *prezidium*, from Latin *presidium* a guard or garrison.

press[1] ▷ *verb* (***presses, pressed, pressing***) **1 a** *tr & intr* to push steadily, especially with the finger □ *press the bell*; **b** (*often* **press against** or **on** or **down on something**) to push it; to apply pressure to it □ *press down on the accelerator.* **2** to hold something firmly against something; to flatten □ *pressed her nose against the glass.* **3** to compress or squash. **4** to squeeze (eg someone's hand) affectionately. **5** to preserve (plants) by flattening and drying, eg between the pages of a book. **6 a** to squeeze (fruit) to extract juice; **b** to extract (juice) from fruit by squeezing. **7** to iron (clothes, etc). **8** to urge or compel someone; to ask them insistently. **9** to insist on something; to urge recognition or discussion of it □ *press your claim* □ *press the point.* **10** *law* to bring (charges) officially against someone. **11** to produce (eg a RECORD *noun* 4) from a mould by a compressing process. ▷ *noun* (***presses***) **1** an act of pressing. **2** any apparatus for pressing, flattening, squeezing, etc. **3** a PRINTING PRESS. **4** the process or art of printing. **5** a PRINTING HOUSE. **6 a** (**the press**) newspapers or journalists in general; **b** *as adj* belonging or relating to the newspaper industry □ *a press photographer.* **7** newspaper publicity or reviews received by a show, book, etc □ *got a poor press.* **8** a crowd □ *a press of onlookers.* **9** *Scottish* a cupboard. • **go to press** said of a book, etc: to be sent for printing. ⓘ 13c: from French *presser*, from Latin *premere*, *pressum* to press.

■ **press for something** to demand it □ *press for a payrise.*

■ **press on, ahead** or **forward** to hurry on; to continue, especially in spite of difficulties.

■ **press something on someone** to insist on giving it to them.

the press

There is often uncertainty as to whether collective nouns such as **press** should be followed by a singular or plural verb. Either is correct, depending on whether the group is being thought of as a single unit or as a number of individuals.

press[2] ▷ *verb* (***presses, pressed, pressing***) **1** to force (men) into the army or navy. **2** (*especially* **press something** or **someone into service**) to put it or them to use in a way that was not originally intended. ⓘ 16c: from older *prest* to recruit into military service, originally 'enlistment money'.

press agent ▷ *noun* someone who arranges newspaper advertising or publicity for a performer or other celebrity, etc.

press box ▷ *noun* an area at a stadium, arena, etc set aside for use by the press (see PRESS[1] *noun* 6).

press conference and **news conference** ▷ *noun* an interview granted to reporters by a politician or other person in the news, for the purpose of announcing something, answering questions, etc.

press cutting ▷ *noun* a paragraph or article cut from a newspaper, etc.

pressed ▷ *adj* said of a person: under pressure; in a hurry. • **be hard pressed** to be in difficulties ◻ *I'll be hard pressed to find a replacement.* • **be pressed for something** *colloq* to be short of it, especially time or money.

press gallery ▷ *noun* in the UK: the gallery reserved for journalists in parliament or the law courts.

pressgang ▷ *noun, historical* a gang employed to seize men and force them into the army or navy. ▷ *verb* (***pressganged, pressganging***) **1** to force (men) into the army or navy. **2** *facetious* to coerce someone into something.

pressie or **prezzie** /ˈprɛzɪ/ ▷ *noun, colloq* a present or gift. ⓔ 1930s: from PRESENT³.

pressing ▷ *adj* urgent ◻ *pressing engagements.* ▷ *noun* **1** in the music industry: a number of records produced from a single mould. **2** *sport* the tactic of pressurizing opponents when they have possession, in order to try and win possession from them, eg by marking very closely.

pressman and **presswoman** ▷ *noun* a journalist or reporter.

press officer ▷ *noun* someone employed by an organization to give information about it to journalists.

press proof ▷ *noun, printing* the final proof before the text is printed.

press release ▷ *noun* an official statement given to the press by an organization, etc.

press stud ▷ *noun* a type of button-like fastener, one part of which is pressed into the other. Also called POPPER.

press-up ▷ *noun* an exercise performed face down, raising and lowering the body on the arms while keeping the trunk and legs rigid. ⓔ 1940s.

pressure /ˈprɛʃə(r)/ ▷ *noun* **1** *physics* the force exerted on a surface divided by the area of the surface to which it is applied. **2** the act of pressing or process of being pressed. **3** force or coercion; forceful persuasion. **4** urgency; strong demand ◻ *work under pressure.* **5** tension or stress ◻ *the pressures of family life.* ▷ *verb* (***pressured, pressuring***) to try to persuade; to coerce, force or pressurize. ⓔ 14c: from Latin *pressura*, from *premere* to press.

pressure cooker ▷ *noun* a thick-walled pan with an airtight lid, in which food is cooked at speed by steam under high pressure.

pressure gauge ▷ *noun, physics* a gauge which measures the pressure of liquids or gases in enclosed vessels and containers, such as boilers and pipes.

pressure group ▷ *noun* a number of people who join together to influence public opinion and government policy on some issue.

pressure point ▷ *noun* any of various points on the body where pressure can be exerted to relieve pain, control the flow of arterial blood, etc.

pressure sore see BEDSORE

pressurize or **pressurise** /ˈprɛʃəraɪz/ ▷ *verb* (***pressurized, pressurizing***) **1** to adjust the pressure within (an enclosed compartment such as an aircraft cabin) so that nearly normal atmospheric pressure is constantly maintained. **2** to put pressure on someone or something; to force or coerce ◻ *I pressurized him into resigning.* ⓔ 1940s.

pressurized water reactor ▷ *noun* (abbreviation **PWR**) a type of nuclear reactor that uses normal water (as opposed to HEAVY WATER) under very high pressure as a coolant and moderator. ⓔ 1950s.

prestidigitation /prɛstɪdɪdʒɪˈteɪʃən/ ▷ *noun* SLEIGHT OF HAND. • **prestidigitator** *noun.* ⓔ 19c: from French *prestidigitateur*, from *preste* nimble + Latin *digitus* finger.

prestige /prɛˈstiːʒ/ ▷ *noun* **1** fame, distinction or reputation due to rank or success. **2 a** influence; glamour ◻ *a job with prestige*; **b** *as adj* ◻ *prestige cars.* • **prestigious** /prɛˈstɪdʒəs/ *adj.* ⓔ 19c in sense 1; 17c in obsolete sense 'illusion': from Latin *praestigiae* sleight of hand or magic tricks.

presto /ˈprɛstoʊ/ *music* ▷ *adverb* in a very fast manner. ▷ *adj* very fast. ▷ *noun* (***prestos***) a piece of music to be played in this way. • **hey presto** see separate entry. ⓔ 17c: Italian, meaning 'quick', from Latin *praestus*, from *praesto* ready.

pre-stressed ▷ *adj* said of concrete: embedded with stretched wires or rods in order to increase its tensile strength.

presumably /prɪˈzjuːməblɪ, -ˈzuːm-/ ▷ *adverb* I suppose; probably.

presume /prɪˈzjuːm, -ˈzuːm/ ▷ *verb* (***presumed, presuming***) **1** to suppose (something to be the case) without proof; to take something for granted ◻ *presumed he was dead.* **2** to be bold enough; especially without the proper right or knowledge; to venture ◻ *wouldn't presume to advise the experts.* ⓔ 14c: from Latin *praesumere* to take in advance.

■ **presume on** or **upon someone** or **something 1** to rely or count on them or it, especially unduly. **2** to take unfair advantage of (someone's good nature, etc).

presumption /prɪˈzʌmpʃən/ ▷ *noun* **1** ▷ something presumed ◻ *The presumption was that her first husband was dead.* **2** grounds or justification for presuming something. **3** inappropriate boldness in one's behaviour towards others; insolence or arrogance. **4** the act of presuming. ⓔ 13c: from Latin *praesumptio, praesumptionis.*

presumptive /prɪˈzʌmptɪv/ ▷ *adj* **1** presumed rather than absolutely certain. **2** giving grounds for presuming. See also HEIR PRESUMPTIVE.

presumptuous /prɪˈzʌmptʃʊəs/ ▷ *adj* over-bold in behaviour, especially towards others; insolent or arrogant. • **presumptuously** *adverb.* • **presumptuousness** *noun.*

presuppose /priːsəˈpoʊz/ ▷ *verb* **1** to take for granted; to assume as true. **2** to require as a necessary condition; to imply the existence of something. • **presupposition** *noun.* ⓔ 15c.

pre-tax ▷ *adj* before the deduction of tax ◻ *pre-tax profits.* Compare AFTER-TAX.

pretence or (*US*) **pretense** /prɪˈtɛns/ *noun* **1** the act of pretending. **2** make-believe. **3** an act someone puts on deliberately to mislead. **4** a claim, especially an unjustified one ◻ *make no pretence to expert knowledge.* **5** show, affectation or ostentation; pretentiousness. **6** (*usually* **pretences**) a misleading declaration of intention ◻ *won their support under false pretences.* **7** show or semblance ◻ *abandoned all pretence of fair play.* ⓔ 15c: from French *pretensse*, from Latin *praetendere* to PRETEND.

pretend /prɪˈtɛnd/ ▷ *verb* (***pretended, pretending***) **1** *tr & intr* to make believe; to act as if, or give the impression that, something is the case when it is not ◻ *Let's pretend we're dinosaurs* ◻ *pretend to be asleep.* **2** *tr & intr* to imply or claim falsely ◻ *pretended not to know.* **3** to claim to feel something; to profess something falsely ◻ *pretend friendship towards someone.* ▷ *adj, colloq* especially used by or to children: imaginary ◻ *a pretend cave.* ⓔ 15c: from Latin *praetendere* to stretch forth.

■ **pretend to something 1** to claim to have (a skill, etc), especially falsely. **2** *historical* to lay claim, especially doubtful claim, to (eg the throne).

pretender ▷ *noun* someone who pretends or pretended to something, especially the throne.

pretension /prɪ'tɛnʃən/ ▷ *noun* **1** foolish vanity, self-importance or affectation; pretentiousness. **2** a claim or aspiration ▫ ***had no pretensions to elegance.*** ⌚ 17c: see PRETEND.

pretentious /prɪ'tɛnʃəs/ ▷ *adj* **1** pompous, self-important or foolishly grandiose. **2** phoney or affected. **3** showy; ostentatious. • **pretentiously** *adverb.* • **pretentiousness** *noun.* ⌚ 19c.

preterite /'prɛtərɪt/ ▷ *noun, grammar* **1** a verb tense that expresses past action, eg *hit, moved, ran.* **2** a verb in this tense. ▷ *adj* denoting this tense. ⌚ 14c: from Latin *tempus praeteritum* past time.

preterm /priː'tɜːm/ ▷ *adj, adverb* born or occurring before the end of the normal length of a pregnancy.

preternatural /priːtə'natʃərəl/ ▷ *adj* **1** exceeding the normal; uncanny; extraordinary. **2** supernatural. • **preternaturally** *adverb.* ⌚ 16c: from Latin *praeter naturam* beyond nature.

pretext /'priːtɛkst/ ▷ *noun* a false reason given for doing something in order to disguise the real one; an excuse. ⌚ 16c: from Latin *praetextum*, from *praetexere* to weave before or to disguise.

prettify /'prɪtɪfaɪ/ ▷ *verb* (***prettifies, prettified, prettifying***) to attempt to make something or someone prettier by superficial ornamentation. • **prettification** *noun.* ⌚ 19c.

pretty /'prɪtɪ/ ▷ *adj* (***prettier, prettiest***) **1** usually said of a woman or girl: facially attractive, especially in a feminine way. **2** charming to look at; decorative. **3** said of music, sound, etc: delicately melodious. **4** neat, elegant or skilful ▫ ***a pretty solution.*** **5** *ironic* grand; fine ▫ ***a pretty mess.*** ▷ *adverb* fairly; satisfactorily; rather; decidedly. • **prettily** *adverb.* • **prettiness** *noun.* • **pretty much** *colloq* more or less. • **pretty nearly** almost. • **pretty well** *colloq* almost; more or less. • **sitting pretty** see under SIT. ⌚ Anglo-Saxon *prættig* astute.

a pretty pass ▷ *noun* (*especially* **come to** or **reach a pretty pass**) a deplorable state of affairs.

pretty-pretty ▷ *adj, derog colloq* pretty in an over-sweet way.

pretzel /'prɛtsəl/ ▷ *noun* a crisp salted biscuit in the shape of a knot. ⌚ 19c: German.

prevail /prɪ'veɪl/ ▷ *verb* (***prevailed, prevailing***) *intr* **1** (*often* **prevail over** or **against someone** or **something**) to be victorious; to win through ▫ ***Common sense prevailed.*** **2** to be the common, usual or generally accepted thing. **3** to be predominant. ⌚ 15c: from Latin *praevalere* to prove superior.

▪ **prevail on** or **upon someone** or **something** to persuade them or appeal to it.

prevailing ▷ *adj* most common or frequent.

prevailing wind ▷ *noun* the most frequently observed wind-direction in a particular region over a given period of time.

prevalent /'prɛvələnt/ ▷ *adj* common; widespread. • **prevalence** *noun.* • **prevalently** *adverb.* ⌚ 16c: see PREVAIL.

prevaricate /prɪ'varɪkeɪt/ ▷ *verb* (***prevaricated, prevaricating***) *intr* to avoid stating the truth or coming directly to the point; to behave or speak evasively. • **prevarication** *noun.* • **prevaricator** *noun.* ⌚ 17c: from Latin *praevaricari, praevaricatus* to walk with splayed legs, from *varus* bent.

prevaricate, procrastinate

• Both words are to do with failure to deal with a matter or to answer a question immediately or promptly, and they are sometimes confused.

• If you **prevaricate**, you respond to a question but avoid a direct or truthful answer, and you are therefore not being totally honest.

• If you **procrastinate**, you don't deal with the matter at all but put it off to some later time.

prevent /prɪ'vɛnt/ ▷ *verb* (***prevented, preventing***) **1** to stop someone from doing something, or something from happening; to hinder. **2** to stop the occurrence of something beforehand or to make it impossible; to avert. • **preventable** or **preventible** *adj.* ⌚ 16c: from Latin *praevenire* to anticipate or come before.

prevention ▷ *noun* **1** an act or process of preventing. **2** hindrance or obstruction.

preventive or **preventative** ▷ *adj* **1** tending or intended to prevent or hinder. **2** *medicine* tending or intended to prevent disease or illness. **3** in the UK: relating or belonging to the Coastguard or the department of Customs and Excise dealing with the prevention of smuggling. ▷ *noun* **1** a preventive drug. **2** a precautionary measure taken against something. ⌚ 17c.

preventive detention ▷ *noun* a term of imprisonment for a habitual or dangerous criminal.

preventive medicine ▷ *noun* the branch of medicine concerned with the prevention of disease, as opposed to its treatment and cure.

preview /'priːvjuː/ ▷ *noun* **1** an advance view. **2** an advance showing of a film, play, exhibition, etc before it is presented to the general public. ▷ *verb* to show or view (a film, etc) in advance to a select audience. ⌚ 19c.

previous /'priːvɪəs/ ▷ *adj* **1** earlier ▫ ***a previous occasion.*** **2** former ▫ ***the previous chairman.*** **3** prior ▫ ***a previous engagement.*** **4** *facetious* premature; over-prompt or over-hasty. **5** (*usually* **previous to something**) before (an event, etc). • **previously** *adverb.* ⌚ 17c: from Latin *praevius* leading the way, from *prae* before + *via* way.

pre-war ▷ *adj* belonging or relating to the period before a war, especially World War I or II. Also *as adverb* ▫ ***We met pre-war.*** ⌚ Early 20c.

pre-wash ▷ *noun* a preliminary wash before the main wash, especially in a washing machine. ▷ *verb* **1** to wash (jeans, etc) before sale. **2** to wash (very dirty clothes, etc) before a normal wash. ⌚ 1960s.

prey /preɪ/ ▷ *singular or plural noun* **1** an animal or animals hunted as food by another animal ▫ ***in search of prey.*** **2** a victim or victims ▫ ***easy prey for muggers.*** **3** (*usually* **a prey to something**) someone liable to suffer from (an illness, a bad feeling, etc). ▷ *verb* (***preyed, preying***) *intr* (*now especially* **prey on** or **upon something** or **someone**) **1** said of an animal: to hunt or catch (another animal) as food. **2 a** to bully, exploit or terrorize as victims; **b** to afflict them in an obsessive way ▫ ***preyed on by anxieties.*** ⌚ 13c: from French *preie*, from Latin *praeda* booty.

prey

A word often confused with this one is **pray**.

prezzie see PRESSIE

prial see under PAIR-ROYAL

priapism /'praɪəpɪzəm/ ▷ *noun, medicine* persistent abnormal erection of the penis, which may be a symptom of spinal injury, or of various diseases and disorders. ⌚ 17c: from Latin *priapismus*, from Greek *Priapos* the Greek and Roman god of procreation.

price ▷ *noun* **1** the amount, usually in money, for which a thing is sold or offered. **2** what must be given up or suffered in gaining something ▫ ***the price of celebrity.*** **3** the sum by which someone may be bribed. **4** *betting* odds. ▷ *verb* (***priced, pricing***) **1** to fix a price for or mark a price on something. **2** to find out the price of something. • **a price on someone's head** a reward offered for capturing or killing them. • **at a price** at great expense. • **at any price** no matter what it costs, eg in terms of money, sacrifice, etc. • **beyond** or **without price** invaluable. ⓒ 13c: from French *pris*, from Latin *pretium*.

price control ▷ *noun* a maximum or, rarely, minimum limit set on prices by the government.

price-fixing ▷ *noun, commerce* the fixing of a price by agreement between suppliers. ⓒ 1920s.

priceless ▷ *adj* **1** too valuable to have a price; inestimably precious. **2** *colloq* hilariously funny. • **pricelessly** *adverb*. • **pricelessness** *noun*.

price tag ▷ *noun* **1** a label showing a price. **2** the cost of something, eg a proposed building, etc.

price war ▷ *noun* a form of commercial competition in which retailers in the same market successively lower their prices to gain a larger share of that market.

pricey or **pricy** ▷ *adj* (***pricier***, ***priciest***) *colloq* expensive. ⓒ 1930s.

prick ▷ *verb* (***pricked***, ***pricking***) **1** to pierce slightly with a fine point. **2** to make (a hole) by this means. **3** *tr & intr* to hurt something or someone by this means. **4** *tr & intr* to smart or make something smart □ *feel one's eyes pricking.* **5** *tr & intr* (*also* **prick up**) **a** said of a dog, horse, etc: to stick (its ears) upright in response to sound; **b** said of a dog's, etc ears: to stand erect in this way. **6** to mark out (a pattern) in punctured holes. **7** to trouble □ *His conscience must be pricking him.* **8** to plant (seedlings, etc) in an area of soil that had had small holes marked out on it. ▷ *noun* **1** an act of pricking or feeling of being pricked. **2** the pain of this. **3** a puncture made by pricking. **4** *slang* the penis. **5** *derog slang* an abusive term for a man, especially a self-important fool. • **kick against the pricks** to react in vain against discipline or authority. • **prick up one's ears** *colloq* to start listening attentively. ⓒ Anglo-Saxon *prica* point.

prickle /ˈprɪkəl/ ▷ *noun* **1** a hard pointed structure growing from the surface of a plant or animal. **2** a pricking sensation. ▷ *verb* (***prickled***, ***prickling***) *tr & intr* to cause, affect something with or be affected with, a prickling sensation. ⓒ Anglo-Saxon *pricel*.

prickly ▷ *adj* (***pricklier***, ***prickliest***) **1** covered with or full of prickles. **2** causing prickling. **3** *colloq* said of a person: irritable; over-sensitive. **4** said of a topic: liable to cause controversy. • **prickliness** *noun*. ⓒ 16c.

prickly heat ▷ *noun* an itchy skin rash, most common in hot humid weather, caused by blockage of the sweat ducts. *Technical equivalent* **miliaria** /mɪlɪˈɛərɪə/.

prickly pear ▷ *noun* **1** any of various low-growing cacti with flattened or cylindrical spiny stem joints and bright yellow, orange or reddish flowers. See also OPUNTIA. **2** the large prickly reddish pear-shaped fruit of this plant, the juicy flesh and seeds of which are edible in some species. ⓒ 17c.

pride ▷ *noun* **1** a feeling of pleasure and satisfaction at one's own or another's accomplishments, possessions, etc. **2** the source of this feeling □ *That car is my pride and joy.* **3** self-respect; personal dignity. **4** an unjustified assumption of superiority; arrogance. **5** *poetic* the finest state; the prime. **6** the finest item □ *the pride of the collection.* **7** a number of lions keeping together as a group. ▷ *verb* (***prided***, ***priding***) (*always* **pride oneself on something**) to congratulate oneself on account of it □ *prided himself on his youthful figure.* • **swallow one's pride** see under SWALLOW[1]. • **take pride** or **take a pride in something** or **someone** **1** to be proud of it or them. **2** to be conscientious about maintaining high standards in (one's work, etc). ⓒ Anglo-Saxon *pryde*.

pride of place ▷ *noun* special prominence; the position of chief importance.

prie-dieu /priːˈdjɜː/ ▷ *noun* (***prie-dieux*** or ***prie-dieus***) a praying-desk which has a low surface on which to kneel and a support for a book or books. ⓒ 18c: French, meaning 'pray-God'.

pries and **pried** see under PRY[1], PRY[2]

priest /priːst/ ▷ *noun* **1** **a** in the Roman Catholic and Orthodox churches: an ordained minister authorized to administer the sacraments; **b** in the Anglican church: a minister ranking between deacon and bishop. **2** in non-Christian religions: an official who performs sacrifices and other religious rites. • **priestly** *adj*. ⓒ Anglo-Saxon *preost*: from Latin *presbyter* elder.

priestess ▷ *noun* in non-Christian religions: a female priest.

priesthood ▷ *noun* **1** the office of a priest. **2** the role or character of a priest. **3** priests collectively □ *members of the priesthood.*

priest's hole ▷ *noun, historical* a hiding place, especially a concealed room where a member of the clergy could hide during religious persecution.

prig ▷ *noun* someone who is self-righteously moralistic. • **priggery** *noun*. • **priggish** *adj*. • **priggishly** *adverb*. • **priggishness** *noun*. ⓒ 18c; 16c in obsolete sense 'a tinker'.

prim ▷ *adj* (***primmer***, ***primmest***) **1** stiffly formal, over-modest or over-proper. **2** prudishly disapproving. ▷ *verb* (***primmed***, ***primming***) **1** to purse (the mouth, lips, etc) into an expression of primness. **2** to make something prim. • **primly** *adverb*. • **primness** *noun*. ⓒ 17c.

prima ballerina /ˈpriːmə —/ ▷ *noun* the leading female dancer in a ballet company. ⓒ 19c: Italian, meaning 'first ballerina'.

primacy /ˈpraɪməsɪ/ ▷ *noun* (***primacies***) **1** the condition of being first in rank, importance or order. **2** the rank, office or area of jurisdiction of a PRIMATE of the church. ⓒ 14c: from Latin *primatia*, from *primus* first.

prima donna /ˈpriːmə ˈdɒnə/ ▷ *noun* (***prima donnas***) **1** a leading female opera singer. **2** someone difficult to please, especially someone given to melodramatic tantrums when displeased. ⓒ 18c: Italian, meaning 'first lady'.

primaeval see PRIMEVAL

prima facie /ˈpraɪmə ˈfeɪʃɪ/ *especially law* ▷ *adverb* at first sight; on the evidence available. ▷ *adj* apparent; based on first impressions □ *prima-facie evidence.* ⓒ 15c: Latin, meaning 'at first sight'.

primal /ˈpraɪməl/ ▷ *adj* **1** relating to the beginnings of life; original. **2** basic; fundamental. ⓒ 17c: from Latin *primalis*, from *primus* first.

primarily /ˈpraɪmərɪlɪ, praɪˈmɛrɪlɪ/ ▷ *adverb* **1** chiefly; mainly. **2** in the first place; initially. ⓒ 17c.

primary /ˈpraɪmərɪ/ ▷ *adj* **1** first or most important; principal. **2** earliest in order or development. **3** (**Primary**) *geol* PALAEOZOIC. See also SECONDARY, TERTIARY. **4** basic; fundamental. **5** at the elementary stage or level. **6** said of education, schools, classes etc: for children aged between 5 and 11 □ *Jane's in primary six.* See also SECONDARY, TERTIARY. **7** said of a bird's wing feather: outermost and longest. **8** firsthand; direct □ *primary sources of information.* **9** said of a product or industry: being or concerned with produce in its raw natural state. **10** *elec* **a** said of a battery or cell: producing electricity by an irreversible chemical reaction; **b** said of a circuit or current: inducing a current in a neighbouring circuit. ▷ *noun* (***primaries***) **1** something that is first or most important. **2** *US* a preliminary election, especially to select delegates for a presidential election. **3** *Brit colloq* a primary school □ *attends the local primary.* **4** a bird's primary feather. **5** (**the Primary**) the PALAEOZOIC era. See table at GEOLOGICAL TIME SCALE. ⓒ 15c: from Latin *primarius*, from *primus* first.

primary cell and **primary battery** ▷ *noun, physics* a non-rechargeable cell or battery that produces an electric current by chemical reactions that are not readily reversible. Also called **voltaic cell**.

primary colour ▷ *noun* **1** said of lights: any of the three colours (red, green and blue-violet) which together give white light, but can also be combined in various proportions to give all the other colours of the spectrum. **2** said of mixing pigments: any of the three colours (red, yellow and blue) which together give black, but can also be combined in various proportions to give all the other colours of the spectrum. ⓘ 17c.

primary school ▷ *noun* a school, especially a state one, for pupils aged between 5 and 11.

primary sexual characteristics ▷ *plural noun, zool* sexual features that are present from birth, ie the testes in males and the ovaries in females.

primary stress ▷ *noun, linguistics* the main STRESS (sense 5) in a word in which there is more than one stress, as in *fundamentalism*, in which the primary stress is on the syllable *-ment-*.

primate /ˈpraɪmeɪt, ˈpraɪmət/ ▷ *noun* **1** *zool* any member of an order of mammalian vertebrates which have a large brain, forward-facing eyes, nails instead of claws, and hands with grasping thumbs facing the other digits, eg a human, ape, etc. **2** *Christianity* an archbishop. ⓘ 13c: from Latin *primas, primatis*, from *primus* first.

prime ▷ *adj* **1** chief; fundamental. **2** the best quality. **3** excellent □ ***in prime condition.*** **4** supremely typical □ ***a prime example.*** **5** having the greatest potential for attracting interest or custom □ ***prime sites on the high street.*** ▷ *noun* the best, most productive or active stage in the life of a person or thing □ ***cut down in her prime.*** ▷ *verb* (***primed, priming***) **1** to prepare something (eg wood for painting) by applying a sealing coat of size, etc, (a gun or explosive device for firing or detonating) by inserting the igniting material, or (a pump for use) by filling it with water, etc. **2** to supply with the necessary facts in advance; to brief. **3** *facetious* to supply someone with drink or food by way of relaxing, emboldening or bribing them. ⓘ 14c: from Latin *primus* first.

prime cost ▷ *noun* the basic amount it costs in terms of labour, raw materials, etc to produce something.

prime lending rate see PRIME RATE

prime meridian ▷ *noun, geog* **1** a MERIDIAN chosen to represent 0, especially that passing through Greenwich, UK, from which other lines of longitude are calculated. **2** any representation of this, eg on a map.

prime minister ▷ *noun* (abbreviation **PM**) the chief minister of a government. ⓘ 17c.

prime mover ▷ *noun* the force that is most effective in setting something in motion.

prime number ▷ *noun, math* a whole number that can only be divided by itself and 1, eg 3, 5, 7, 11, etc.

primer[1] /ˈpraɪmə(r)/ ▷ *noun* a first or introductory book of instruction. ⓘ 14c: from Latin *primarium*, from *primarius* primary.

primer[2] /ˈpraɪmə(r)/ ▷ *noun* **1** any material that is used to provide an initial coating for a surface before it is painted. **2 a** a preparatory first coat of paint; **b** the particular type of paint used for this. **3** any device that ignites or detonates an explosive charge. ⓘ 19c in sense 3.

prime rate and **prime lending rate** ▷ *noun, econ* the lending rate, lower than other commerical lending rates, at which a bank will lend to its best customers, usually large companies or corporations.

prime time ▷ *noun, radio & TV* a period attracting the highest number of listeners or viewers. Also *as adj* □ ***prime-time viewing.***

primeval or **primaeval** /praɪˈmiːvəl/ ▷ *adj* **1** relating or belonging to the Earth's beginnings. **2** primitive. **3** instinctive. ⓘ 18c: from Latin *primaevus* young, from *primus* first + *aevum* age.

primigravida /praɪmɪˈgravɪdə/ ▷ *noun* (***primigravidae*** /-diː/ or ***primigravidas***) *obstetrics* a woman who is pregnant for the first time. Compare MULTIGRAVIDA. ⓘ 19c: from Latin *primus* first + *gravida* pregnant.

primipara /praɪˈmɪpərə/ ▷ *noun* (***primiparae*** /-riː/ or ***primiparas***) a woman who has given birth for the first time or is about to do so. Compare MULTIPARA. ⓘ 19c: from Latin *primus* first + *parere* to bring forth.

primitive /ˈprɪmɪtɪv/ ▷ *adj* **1** relating or belonging to earliest times or the earliest stages of development. **2** simple, rough, crude or rudimentary. **3** *art* simple, naïve or unsophisticated in style. **4** *biol* original; belonging to an early stage of development. ▷ *noun* **1** an unsophisticated person or thing. **2 a** a work by an artist in naïve style; **b** an artist who produces such a work. • **primitively** *adverb*. • **primitiveness** *noun*. ⓘ 15c: from Latin *primitivus*, meaning 'first of its kind', from *primus* first.

primitivism ▷ *noun, art* the deliberate rejection of Western techniques and skills in pursuit of stronger effects found, for example, in African tribal or Oceanic art. ⓘ 19c.

primly, **primmer**, **primmest** and **primness** see under PRIM

primo /ˈpriːmoʊ/ ▷ *noun* (***primos*** or ***primi*** /-miː/) *music* the upper or right-hand part in a piano duet. ⓘ 18c: Italian, meaning 'first'.

primogenitor /praɪmoʊˈdʒenɪtə(r)/ ▷ *noun* **1** a forefather or ancestor. **2** the earliest known ancestor of a race or people. ⓘ 17c: Latin, see PRIMOGENITURE.

primogeniture /praɪmoʊˈdʒenɪtʃə(r)/ ▷ *noun* **1** the fact or condition of being the firstborn child. **2** the right or principle of succession or inheritance of an eldest son. ⓘ 17c: from Latin *primogenitura*, from *primo* first + *genitura* birth.

primordial /praɪˈmɔːdɪəl/ ▷ *adj* **1** existing from the beginning; formed earliest □ ***primordial matter.*** **2** *biol* relating to an early stage in growth. • **primordiality** *noun*. • **primordially** *adverb*. ⓘ 14c: from Latin *primordialis*, from *primus* first + *ordiri* to begin.

primordial soup see under SOUP

primp ▷ *verb* (***primped, primping***) *tr & intr* to groom, preen or titivate. ⓘ 19c: related to PRIM.

primrose /ˈprɪmroʊz/ ▷ *noun* **1** a small perennial plant with a rosette of oval leaves, and long-stalked flowers with five pale yellow or (occasionally) pink petals. **2** (*in full* **primrose yellow**) **a** the pale-yellow colour of these flowers; **b** *as adj* □ ***a primrose dress.*** ⓘ 15c: from Latin *prima rosa* first rose (it flowers in early spring).

primrose path ▷ *noun* an untroubled pleasurable way of life.

primula /ˈprɪmjʊlə/ ▷ *noun* (***primulae*** /-liː/ or ***primulas***) any of various N temperate plants with white, pink, purple or yellow flowers with five spreading petals, including the primrose, cowslip and oxslip. ⓘ 18c: from Latin *primula veris* first little one of the spring.

primum mobile /ˈpraɪməm ˈmoʊbɪlɪ/ ▷ *noun* something that is considered as an important source or motivation of an action, etc. ⓘ 17c in this sense: Latin, literally 'first moving thing'.

Primus /ˈpraɪməs/ ▷ *noun* (***Primuses***) *trademark* a portable camping stove fuelled by vaporized oil. Also called **Primus stove**. ⓘ Early 20c.

prince ▷ *noun* **1** in the UK: the son of a sovereign. **2** a non-reigning male member of a royal or imperial family. **3** a sovereign of a small territory. **4** a ruler or sovereign generally. **5** a nobleman in certain countries. **6** someone or something celebrated or outstanding within a type or class □ ***the prince of highwaymen.*** See also PRINCIPALITY. ⓘ 13c: French, from Latin *princeps* leader.

Prince Albert ▻ *noun* **1** a man's double-breasted frock coat, worn especially in the early 20c. **2** a male genital piercing through the urethra and the head of the penis. ◷ 20c: named after Prince Albert, the consort of Queen Victoria.

Prince Charming ▻ *noun* a lover or hero, especially one who epitomizes the stereotypical female ideal of what a man should be in terms of looks, thoughtfulness, etc. ◷ 19c: from the prince in the tale of Cinderella, originally the name of the hero of Planché's *King Charming*.

prince consort ▻ *noun* (***princes consort***) the title given to a reigning queen's husband, who is himself a prince.

princedom ▻ *noun* a PRINCIPALITY; the estate, jurisdiction, sovereignty or rank of a prince.

princely ▻ *adj* **1** characteristic of or suitable for a prince. **2** *often ironic* lavish; generous ◻ *the princely sum of five pence.*

Prince of Darkness ▻ *noun* Satan.

Prince of Peace ▻ *noun* the Messiah, believed by Christians to be Jesus Christ.

Prince of Wales ▻ *noun* in the UK: a title usually conferred on the eldest son of the monarch.

prince regent ▻ *noun* (***princes regent***) a prince who rules on behalf of a sovereign who is too ill, young, etc to rule.

princess /'prɪnsɛs, prɪn'sɛs/ ▻ *noun* (***princesses***) **1** the wife or daughter of a prince. **2** the daughter of a sovereign. **3** a non-reigning female member of a royal or imperial family. **4** someone or something that is held in high esteem ◻ *Daddy's little princess* ◻ *the princess of boats.* ◷ 15c.

Princess Royal ▻ *noun* (***Princesses Royal***) in the UK: a title which can be conferred on the eldest daughter of a monarch.

principal /'prɪnsɪpəl/ ▻ *adj* first in rank or importance; chief; main. ▻ *noun* **1** the head of an educational institution. **2** a leading actor, singer or dancer in a theatrical production. **3** *law* the person on behalf of whom an agent is acting. **4** *law* someone ultimately responsible for fulfilling an obligation. **5** someone who commits or participates in a crime. **6** *commerce* the original sum of money on which interest is paid. **7** *music* the leading player of each section of an orchestra. • **principally** *adverb*. ◷ 13c: French, from Latin *principalis* chief, from *princeps* leader.

principal, principle

These words are often confused with each other.

principal boy ▻ *noun* the part of the young male hero in a pantomime, usually played by a woman.

principal clause see under MAIN CLAUSE

principality /prɪnsɪ'palɪtɪ/ ▻ *noun* (***principalities***) **1** a territory ruled by a prince, or one that he derives his title from. **2** (**the Principality**) in the UK: Wales. **3** in the traditional medieval hierarchy of nine ranks of angels: an angel of the seventh rank. Compare SERAPH, CHERUB, THRONE, DOMINION, VIRTUE, POWER, ARCHANGEL, ANGEL.

principal parts ▻ *plural noun, grammar* the main forms of a verb from which all other forms can be deduced, eg in English the infinitive, the past tense and the past participle.

principate /'prɪnsɪpeɪt/ ▻ *noun* **1** the area ruled by a prince; principality. **2** in the early Roman empire: a period of rule in which some republican forms survived.

principle /'prɪnsɪpəl/ ▻ *noun* **1** a general truth or assumption from which to argue. **2** a scientific law, especially one that explains a natural phenomenon or the way a machine works. **3** a general rule of morality that guides conduct; the having of or holding to such rules ◻ *a woman of principle.* **4** (**principles**) a set of such rules. **5** *technical* a norm of procedure ◻ *the principle of primogeniture.* **6** a fundamental element or source ◻ *the vital principle.* **7** *chem* a constituent of a substance that gives it its distinctive characteristics. • **in principle** said especially of agreement or disagreement to a plan, decision or action: in theory; in general, although not necessarily in a particular case ◻ *We approved the scheme in principle, subject to certain adjustments.* • **on principle** on the grounds of a particular principle of morality or wisdom. ◷ 14c: from Latin *principium* beginning or source.

principled ▻ *adj* holding, or proceeding from principles, especially high moral principles.

prink ▻ *verb* (***prinked, prinking***) *tr & intr* to dress (oneself) up; to smarten (oneself) up. ◷ 16c.

print ▻ *verb* (***printed, printing***) **1** to reproduce (text or pictures) on paper with ink, using a printing-press or other mechanical means. **2** to publish (a book, article, etc). **3** *tr & intr* to write in separate, as opposed to joined-up, letters, in the style of mechanically printed text. **4** to make (a positive photograph) from a negative. **5** to mark (a shape, pattern, etc) in or on a surface by pressure. **6** to mark designs on (fabric). **7** to fix (a scene) indelibly (on the memory, etc). ▻ *noun* **1** *often in compounds* a mark made on a surface by the pressure of something in contact with it ◻ *pawprint.* **2** a FINGERPRINT. **3** hand-done lettering with each letter written separately. **4 a** mechanically printed text, especially one produced on a printing press ◻ *small print*; **b** *as adj* ◻ *print media.* **5** a printed publication. **6** a design or picture printed from an engraved wood block or metal plate. **7** a positive photograph made from a negative. **8** a fabric with a printed or stamped design. • **be in** or **out of print** said of a publication: to be currently available, or no longer available, from a publisher. ◷ 13c: from French *priente*, from *priembre*, from Latin *premere* to press.

■ **print something out** to produce a printed version, eg of computer data. See also PRINTOUT.

printable ▻ *adj* **1** capable of being printed. **2** fit to be published.

printed circuit ▻ *noun, electronics* an electronic circuit in which circuit components are connected by thin strips of a conducting material that are printed or etched on to the surface of a thin board of insulating material. ◷ 1940s.

printed circuit board ▻ *noun* (abbreviation **PCB**) *electronics* a thin flat board on which strips of conducting material have been printed or etched, and which contains pre-drilled slots into which a variety of circuit components can be inserted.

printer ▻ *noun* **1** a person or business engaged in printing books, newspapers, etc. **2** a machine that prints, eg photographs. **3** *computing* any of various types of output device that produce printed copies of text or graphics on to paper.

printing ▻ *noun* **1** the art or business of producing books, etc in print. **2** the run of books, etc printed all at one time; an impression. **3** the form of handwriting in which the letters are separately written.

printing house ▻ *noun* a building or establishment where printing is carried out.

printing press ▻ *noun* any of various machines for printing books, newspapers, etc.

printout ▻ *noun, computing* output from a computer system in the form of a printed paper copy. See also PRINT SOMETHING OUT at PRINT.

print preview ▻ *noun, computing* a word-processing facility that allows the operator to see on screen how something will look when it is printed out.

print run ▷ *noun* the number of copies of a book, newspaper, etc printed at a time.

prior[1] /'praɪə(r)/ ▷ *adj* **1** said of an engagement: already arranged for the time in question; previous. **2** more urgent or pressing □ ***a prior claim.*** ● **prior to something** before an event □ ***prior to departure.*** ◷ 18c: Latin, meaning 'previous'.

prior[2] /'praɪə(r)/ ▷ *noun, Christianity* **1** the head of a community of certain orders of monks and friars. **2** in an abbey: the deputy of the abbot. ◷ 11c: Latin, meaning 'head' or 'chief'.

prioress /'praɪərəs/ ▷ *noun* a female PRIOR[2].

prioritize or **prioritise** /praɪ'ɒrɪtaɪz/ ▷ *verb* (***prioritized, prioritizing***) to schedule something for immediate or earliest attention. ◷ 1970s: from PRIORITY.

priority /praɪ'ɒrɪtɪ/ ▷ *noun* (***priorities***) **1** the right to be or go first; precedence or preference. **2** something that must be attended to before anything else. **3** the fact or condition of being earlier. ◷ 14c: from Latin *prioritas*, from *prior* previous.

priory /'praɪərɪ/ ▷ *noun* (***priories***) *Christianity* a religious house under the supervision of a prior or prioress. ◷ 13c.

prise or (*US*) **prize** /praɪz/ ▷ *verb* (***prised, prising***) **1** to lever something open, off, out, etc, usually with some difficulty □ ***prised open the lid*** □ ***prised the shell off the rock.*** **2** to get with difficulty □ ***prised the truth out of her.*** See also PRY[2]. ◷ 17c: French, meaning 'something captured', from Latin *prehendere* to seize.

prism /'prɪzəm/ ▷ *noun* **1** *geom* a solid figure in which the two ends are matching parallel polygons (eg triangles or squares) and all other surfaces are parallelograms. **2** *optics* a transparent block, usually of glass and with triangular ends and rectangular sides, that separates a beam of white light into the colours of the visible spectrum. ◷ 16c: from Greek *prisma* something sawn, from *prizein* to saw.

prismatic /prɪz'matɪk/ ▷ *adj* **1** produced by or relating to a prism □ ***a prismatic compass.*** **2** said of colour or light: produced or separated by, or as if by, a prism; bright and clear. ● **prismatically** *adverb*.

prison /'prɪzən/ ▷ *noun* **1** a building for the confinement of convicted criminals and certain accused persons awaiting trial. **2** any place of confinement or situation of intolerable restriction. **3** custody; imprisonment. ◷ 12c: from French *prisun*, from Latin *prehensio* a seizing.

prison camp ▷ *noun* an enclosed guarded camp where prisoners of war or political prisoners are kept.

prisoner ▷ *noun* **1** someone who is under arrest or confined in prison. **2** a captive, especially in war. ● **take no prisoners** to carry out some action right to its conclusions, without holding back for any reason. ● **take someone prisoner** to capture and hold them as a prisoner.

prisoner of conscience ▷ *noun* someone imprisoned for their political beliefs.

prisoner of war ▷ *noun* (abbreviation **POW**) someone taken prisoner during a war, especially a member of the armed forces.

prissy /'prɪsɪ/ ▷ *adj* (***prissier, prissiest***) insipidly prim and prudish. ● **prissily** *adverb*. ● **prissiness** *noun*. ◷ 19c: probably from PRIM + SISSY.

pristine /'prɪstiːn, 'prɪstaɪn/ ▷ *adj* **1** fresh, clean, unused or untouched. **2** original; unchanged or unspoilt □ ***still in its pristine state.*** **3** former. ◷ 16c: from Latin *pristinus* former or early.

prithie /'prɪðiː/ ▷ *contraction, archaic* please. ◷ 16c: from 'I pray thee'.

privacy /'prɪvəsɪ, 'praɪ-/ ▷ *noun* **1 a** freedom from intrusion by the public, especially as a right; **b** someone's right to this □ ***should respect her privacy.*** **2** seclusion; secrecy. ◷ 15c in sense 2.

private /'praɪvət/ ▷ *adj* **1** not open to, or available for the use of, the general public. **2** said of a person: not holding public office. **3** kept secret from others; confidential. **4** relating to someone's personal, as distinct from their professional, life □ ***a private engagement.*** **5** said of thoughts or opinions: personal and usually kept to oneself. **6** quiet and reserved by nature. **7** said of a place: secluded. **8 a** not coming under the state system of education, healthcare, social welfare, etc; **b** paid for or paying individually by fee, etc. **9** said of an industry, etc: owned and run by private individuals, not by the state. **10** said of a soldier: not an officer or NCO. **11** said of a member of parliament: not holding government office. ▷ *noun* **1** a private soldier. **2** (**privates**) *colloq* the PRIVATE PARTS. ● **privately** *adverb*. ● **in private** not in public; in secret; confidentially. ◷ 14c: from Latin *privatus* withdrawn from public life, from *privare* to deprive or separate.

private company ▷ *noun* a company with restrictions on the number of shareholders, whose shares may not be offered to the general public.

private detective and **private investigator** ▷ *noun* someone who is not a member of the police force, engaged to do detective work. Also called **private eye**.

private enterprise ▷ *noun* the management and financing of industry, etc by private individuals or companies, not by the state.

privateer /praɪvə'tɪə(r)/ ▷ *noun, historical* **1** a privately owned ship engaged by a government to seize and plunder an enemy's ships in wartime. **2** (*also* **privateersman**) the commander or a crew member of such a ship. ◷ 17c.

private eye ▷ *noun, colloq* a PRIVATE DETECTIVE.

private hotel ▷ *noun* a hotel, usually a small one run by the owner, who is not obliged to accept every prospective guest.

private international law see INTERNATIONAL LAW

private means and **private income** ▷ *noun* income from investments, etc, not from one's employment.

private member ▷ *noun* a member of a legislative body who does not have ministerial status or hold a government office.

private member's bill ▷ *noun, Brit politics* a parliamentary bill that is not a scheduled part of government legislature and is put forward by a private member.

private parts ▷ *plural noun, euphemistic* the external genitals and excretory organs.

private pay bed and **pay bed** ▷ *noun* a hospital bed, the occupant of which receives more privacy in exchange for a small payment.

private school ▷ *noun* a school run independently by an individual or group, especially for profit. Compare PUBLIC SCHOOL, STATE SCHOOL, GRANT-MAINTAINED.

private sector ▷ *noun* that part of a country's economy consisting of privately owned and operated businesses, etc.

privation /praɪ'veɪʃən/ ▷ *noun* the condition of not having, or being deprived of, life's comforts or necessities; a lack of something particular. ◷ 14c: from Latin *privatio, privationis* deprivation.

privative /'prɪvətɪv/ ▷ *adj* lacking some quality that is usually, or expected to be, present. ◷ 16c: from Latin *privativus*, from *privare* to deprive.

privatize or **privatise** /'praɪvətaɪz/ ▷ *verb* (***privatized, privatizing***) to transfer (a state-owned business) to private ownership. ● **privatization** *noun*. ◷ 1940s.

privet /ˈprɪvɪt/ ▻ *noun* any of various evergreen or deciduous shrubs with glossy lance-shaped dark-green leaves and strongly scented creamy-white flowers, used especially in garden hedges. ⓘ 16c.

privilege /ˈprɪvɪlɪdʒ/ ▻ *noun* **1** a right granted to an individual or a select few, bestowing an advantage not enjoyed by others. **2** advantages and power enjoyed by people of wealth and high social class. **3** an opportunity to do something that brings one delight; a pleasure or honour. ▻ *verb* **1** *tr & intr* to grant a right, privilege or special favour to someone or something. **2** (*usually* **privilege someone to do something**) to allow them a special right to do it. **3** (*usually* **privilege someone from something** to exempt them from a liability, etc. ⓘ 12c: from Latin *privilegium* prerogative, from *privus* private + *lex, legis* law.

privileged ▻ *adj* **1** enjoying the advantages of wealth and class. **2** favoured with the opportunity to do something.

privity /ˈprɪvɪtɪ/ ▻ *noun* (***privities***) **1** *law* a legally recognized relationship between two parties, eg in a contract, lease, etc. **2** (*usually* **privity to something**) the state of being privy (to a secret plans, etc). ⓘ 15c; 13c in obsolete sense 'something secret': from French *privité*, from Latin *privus* private or secret.

privy /ˈprɪvɪ/ ▻ *adj* **1** (*usually* **privy to something**) allowed to share in (secret discussions, etc) or be in the know about secret plans, happenings, etc. **2** *old use* secret; hidden. ▻ *noun* (***privies***) *old use* a lavatory. • **privily** *adverb*. ⓘ 13c: from French *privé* a private thing, from Latin *privatus* private.

Privy Council ▻ *noun* in the UK: a private advisory council appointed by the sovereign, consisting chiefly of current and former members of the Cabinet. Its functions are mainly formal. • **Privy Councillor** *noun*. ⓘ 14c.

Privy Purse ▻ *noun, Brit* **1** an allowance granted to the sovereign by Parliament for private expenses. **2** (*also* **Keeper of the Privy Purse**) the official in the royal household in charge of paying the royal expenses. ⓘ 17c.

privy seal ▻ *noun, Brit* a seal that is used on certain documents, especially those of lesser importance than the ones which require the GREAT SEAL. ⓘ 13c.

prize¹ ▻ *noun* **1** something won in a competition, lottery, etc. **2** a reward given in recognition of excellence. **3** something striven for, or worth striving for. **4** something captured or taken by force, especially a ship in war; a trophy. **5** *as adj* **a** deserving, or having won, a prize ▫ ***a prize bull***; **b** highly valued ▫ ***her prize possession***; **c** *ironic* perfect; great ▫ ***a prize fool***; **d** belonging or relating to, or given as, a prize. ▫ ***prize money.*** ▻ *verb* (***prized, prizing***) to value or regard highly. ⓘ 14c: related to PRICE and PRAISE, ultimately from Latin *prehendere* to seize.

prize² see PRISE

prizefight ▻ *noun* a boxing-match fought for a money prize. • **prizefighter** *noun*. • **prizefighting** *noun*. ⓘ 19c: from obsolete *prize* a contest + FIGHT.

PRO ▻ *abbreviation* **1** Public Records Office. **2** Public Relations Officer.

pro¹ /proʊ/ ▻ *prep* in favour of something. ▻ *noun* (***pros***) a reason, argument or choice in favour of something. See also PROS AND CONS. ▻ *adverb, colloq* in favour ▫ ***thought he would argue pro.*** Compare ANTI. ⓘ 15c: Latin, meaning 'for' or 'on behalf of'.

pro² /proʊ/ ▻ *noun* (***pros***) *colloq* **1** a professional. **2** a prostitute. ⓘ 19c abbreviation.

pro-¹ /proʊ/ ▻ *prefix, denoting* **1** in favour of (the specified thing); admiring or supporting ▫ ***pro-French.*** **2** serving in place of (the specified thing); acting for ▫ ***proconsul.*** ⓘ Latin.

pro-² /proʊ/ ▻ *prefix, denoting* before (the specified thing) in time or place; in front ▫ ***probosis.*** ⓘ Greek and Latin.

proa /ˈproʊə/, **prahu** or **prau** /ˈprɑːuː/ ▻ *noun* (***proas, prahus*** or ***praus***) a Malay boat, especially a fast one with a large triangular sail and an OUTRIGGER kept to the leeward side. ⓘ 16c: from Malay *prau*.

proactive /proʊˈaktɪv/ ▻ *adj* **1** actively initiating change in anticipation of future developments, rather than merely reacting to events as they occur. **2** *psychol* said of a prior mental experience: tending to affect, interfere with or inhibit a subsequent process, especially a learning process. ⓘ 1930s: from PRO- 2, modelled on REACTIVE.

pro-am /proʊˈam/ ▻ *adj, sport, especially golf* said of a tournament: involving both professionals and amateurs. ⓘ 1940s: from *pro*fessional-*am*ateur.

prob ▻ *noun, colloq* a problem ▫ ***OK, no probs. I'll post it off today.*** ⓘ 20c: abbreviation.

probability /prɒbəˈbɪlɪtɪ/ ▻ *noun* (***probabilities***) **1** the state of being probable; likelihood. **2** something that is probable. **3** *statistics* a mathematical expression of the likelihood or chance of a particular event occurring, usually expressed as a fraction or numeral ▫ ***a probability of one in four.*** • **in all probability** most probably.

probability theory ▻ *noun, math* the branch of mathematics concerned with the analysis of the likelihood of events occurring. It has important applications in statistics, the development of insurance company schemes, etc.

probable /ˈprɒbəbəl/ ▻ *adj* **1** likely to happen. **2** likely to be the case; likely to have happened. **3** said of an explanation, etc: likely to be correct; feasible. ▻ *noun* someone or something likely to be selected. ⓘ 14c: from Latin *probabilis*, from *probare* to prove.

probably ▻ *adverb* almost certainly. ⓘ 17c.

proband /ˈproʊband/ ▻ *noun, genetics* someone who is regarded as the starting point for an investigation of the inheritance of a particular disease or disorder within a family. ⓘ 1920s: from Latin *probandus* about to be or needing to be tested, from *probare* to test.

probang /ˈproʊbaŋ/ ▻ *noun, surgery* an instrument consisting of a flexible rod with a piece of sponge at the end, which is inserted into the oesophagus so as to apply medication or remove an obstruction. ⓘ 17c: named *provang* by its inventor, but probably influenced by PROBE.

probate /ˈproʊbeɪt/ ▻ *noun* **1** *law* the process of establishing that a will is valid. **2** an official copy of a will, with the document certifying its validity. ⓘ 15c: from Latin *probare, probatum* to prove.

probation /prəˈbeɪʃən/ ▻ *noun* **1** the system whereby offenders, especially young or first offenders, are allowed their freedom under supervision, on condition of good behaviour ▫ ***I was put on probation for six months.*** **2** in certain types of employment: a trial period during which a new employee is observed on the job, to confirm whether or not they can do it satisfactorily. • **probationary** *adj* **1** relating to or serving as probation. **2** on probation. **3** consisting of probationers. ⓘ 19c in sense 1; 15c, meaning 'trial': from Latin *probatio, probationis*, from *probare* to test or prove.

probationer ▻ *noun* someone on probation.

probation officer ▻ *noun* someone appointed to advise and supervise an offender on probation.

probe ▻ *noun* **1** a long, slender and usually metal instrument used by doctors to examine a wound, locate a bullet, etc. **2** a comprehensive investigation. **3** (*also* **space probe**) an unmanned spacecraft designed to study conditions in space, especially around one or more planets or their natural satellites. **4** an act of probing; a poke or prod. ▻ *verb* (***probed, probing***) (*often* **probe into something**) **1** to investigate it closely. **2** *tr & intr* to examine it with a probe. **3** *tr & intr* to poke or prod it. ⓘ 16c: from Latin *proba*, from *probare* to test or prove.

probiotics /proʊbaɪˈɒtɪks/ ▻ *singular noun, alternative medicine* treatment by taking into the body bacteria that support the useful and harmless bacteria that are already in the body against the harmful ones. 🕒 From PRO-¹ and BIOTIC.

probity /ˈproʊbɪtɪ/ ▷ *noun* integrity; honesty. 🕒 16c: from Latin *probitas*, from *probus* good.

problem /ˈprɒbləm/ ▷ *noun* **1** a situation or matter that is difficult to understand or deal with □ ***a problem with the software*** □ ***He's got a drink problem.*** **2** someone or something that is difficult to deal with. **3** a puzzle or mathematical question set for solving. **4** *as adj* **a** said of a child, etc: difficult to deal with, especially in being disruptive or anti-social; **b** said of a play, etc: dealing with a moral or social problem. • **have a problem with something 1** to be unable or unwilling to associate with it or to understand it □ ***Do you have a problem with her gayness?*** **2** to be troubled by it □ ***has a problem with gambling.*** • **no problem** *colloq* **1** said in response to a request, or to thanks: it's a pleasure, no trouble, etc. **2** easily □ ***found our way, no problem.*** 🕒 14c: from Greek *problema* a thing put forward, from *proballein* to put forth.

problematic /prɒbləˈmatɪk/ and **problematical** ▷ *adj* **1** causing problems. **2** uncertain. • **problematically** *adverb*.

problem page ▷ *noun* a page or section in a magazine that is devoted to dealing with readers' personal problems.

pro bono /proʊˈboʊnoʊ/ ▷ *adj, US law* **1** said of casework: undertaken free of charge, usually because the client is on a low income or not earning. **2** said of a lawyer: mainly doing this kind of work. 🕒 18c: Latin; see PRO BONO PUBLICO.

pro bono publico /— ˈpʊblɪkoʊ/ for the public good. 🕒 18c: Latin.

proboscis /proʊˈbɒsɪs, -ˈboʊsɪs/ ▷ *noun* (***proboscises*** or ***proboscides*** /-sɪdiːz/) **1** *zool* the flexible elongated snout of the elephant or tapir. **2** *entomol* the elongated tubular mouthparts of certain insects, eg the butterfly. **3** *facetious* the human nose. 🕒 17c: from Greek *proboskis*, from *pro* in front + *boskein* to nourish.

proboscis monkey ▷ *noun* an Old-World monkey, native to Borneo, with a long tail and a protruding nose, which in adult males becomes bulbous and pendulous.

procaine /ˈproʊkeɪn, proʊˈkeɪn/ ▷ *noun, chem* a colourless crystalline substance used as a local anaesthetic. See also **Novocaine**. 🕒 Early 20c: PRO-¹ (sense 2) + CO(CAINE).

procaryote see PROKARYOTE

procathedral ▷ *noun* a church serving as a temporary cathedral. 🕒 19c: from PRO-¹ (sense 2).

procedure /prəˈsiːdʒə(r)/ ▷ *noun* **1** the method and order followed in doing something. **2** an established routine for conducting business at a meeting or in a law case. **3** a course of action; a step or measure taken. • **procedural** *adj*. • **procedurally** *adverb*. 🕒 17c: from Latin *procedere* to advance or proceed.

proceed /prəˈsiːd/ ▷ *verb* (***proceeded, proceeding***) *intr* **1** *formal* to make one's way □ ***I proceeded along the road.*** **2** (*often* **proceed with something**) to go on with it; to continue after stopping. **3** to set about a task, etc. **4** *colloq* to begin □ ***proceeded to question her.*** 🕒 14c: from Latin *procedere* to advance or proceed.

▪ **proceed against someone** *law* to take legal action against them.

▪ **proceed from something** to arise from it □ ***Fear proceeds from ignorance.***

proceeding ▷ *noun* **1** an action; a piece of behaviour. **2** (**proceedings**) a published record of the business done or papers read at a meeting of a society, etc. **3** (**proceedings**) legal action □ ***begin divorce proceedings.***

proceeds /ˈproʊsiːdz/ ▷ *plural noun* money made by an event, sale, transaction, etc. 🕒 17c as proceed, originally meaning 'proceeding'.

process /ˈproʊsɛs/ ▷ *noun* (***processes***) **1** a series of operations performed during manufacture, etc. **2** a series of stages which a product, etc passes through, resulting in the development or transformation of it. **3** an operation or procedure □ ***a slow process.*** **4** *anatomy* a projection or outgrowth, especially one on a bone □ ***the mastoid process.*** **5** *law* a writ by which a person or matter is brought into court. **6** any series of changes, especially natural ones □ ***the aging process*** ▷ *verb* (***processes, processed, processing***) **1** to put something through the required process; to deal with (eg an application) appropriately. **2** to prepare (agricultural produce) for marketing, eg by canning, bottling or treating it chemically. **3** *computing* to perform operations on (data, etc). **4** *law* to instigate legal proceedings against someone. • **in the process of something** in the course of it. 🕒 14c: from Latin *processus* progression, from *procedere* to proceed.

procession /prəˈsɛʃən/ ▷ *noun* **1** a file of people or vehicles proceeding ceremonially in orderly formation. **2** this kind of succession or sequence. 🕒 12c: from Latin *processio, processionis* an advance.

processional ▷ *adj* relating or belonging to a procession. ▷ *noun, Christianity* **1** a book of litanies, hymns, etc for processions. **2** a hymn sung in procession. 🕒 15c.

processor ▷ *noun* **1** a machine or person that processes something. Often *in compounds* □ ***word processor*** □ ***food processor.*** **2** *computing* a CENTRAL PROCESSING UNIT.

pro-choice ▷ *adj* supporting the right of a woman to have an abortion. Compare PRO-LIFE. 🕒 1970s: PRO-1.

prochronism /ˈproʊkrɒnɪzəm/ ▷ *noun* the dating of an event which places it earlier than when it actually occurred. 🕒 17c: from PRO-² + Greek *chronos* time; modelled on ANACHRONISM.

proclaim /prəˈkleɪm/ ▷ *verb* (***proclaimed, proclaiming***) **1** to announce something publicly. **2** to declare someone to be something □ ***was proclaimed a traitor.*** **3** to attest or prove something all too clearly □ ***Cigar smoke proclaimed his presence.*** • **proclaimer** *noun*. 🕒 14c: from Latin *proclamare* to cry out.

proclamation /prɒkləˈmeɪʃən/ *noun* **1** an official public announcement of something nationally important. **2** the act of proclaiming. • **proclamatory** /prəˈklamətərɪ/ *adj*.

proclitic /proʊˈklɪtɪk/ *grammar* ▷ *adj* said of a word: closely attached to the following word and forming a single sound unit with it. ▷ *noun* a proclitic form. 🕒 19c: from Latin *procliticus*, from Greek *proklinein* to lean; modelled on ENCLITIC.

proclivity /prəˈklɪvɪtɪ, proʊ-/ ▷ *noun* (***proclivities***) *rather formal* a tendency, liking or preference □ ***sexual proclivity.*** 🕒 16c: from Latin *proclivitas*, from *proclivis* sloping.

proconsul ▷ *noun* **1** *Roman hist* a governor or military commander in a province. **2** a governor, eg of a colony, dependency, etc. • **proconsular** *adj*. 🕒 14c: Latin, from *proconsule* (someone acting) for the consul.

procrastinate /prəˈkrastɪneɪt/ ▷ *verb* (***procrastinated, procrastinating***) *intr* to put off doing something that should be done straight away, especially habitually or to an unspecified time. • **procrastination** *noun*. • **procrastinator** *noun*. 🕒 16c: from Latin *procrastinare*, from *pro-* onward + *cras* tomorrow.

procreate /ˈproʊkrɪeɪt/ ▷ *verb* (***procreated, procreating***) *tr & intr* to produce (offspring); to reproduce. • **procreant** /-krɪənt/ *noun*. • **procreation** *noun*. • **procreative** *adj*. • **procreator** *noun*. 🕒 16c: from Latin *procreare, procreatum* to beget.

Procrustean /proʊˈkrʌstɪən/ ▷ *adj* designed or intended to enforce rules or conformity by violent or forceful methods. 🕒 19c: from *Procrustes* the name of a robber in Greek mythology who stretched his victums or amputated their limbs to make them fit a bed; from Greek *procroustes* stretcher.

proctology /prɒk'tɒlədʒɪ/ ▻ *noun* the branch of medicine concerned with the anus and rectum. • **proctological** *adj*. • **proctologist** *noun*. ⓒ 19c: from Greek *proktos* the anus.

proctor /'prɒktə(r)/ ▻ *noun* in some English universities: an official whose functions include enforcement of discipline. • **proctorial** *adj*. • **proctorship** *noun*. ⓒ 14c: a contraction of PROCURATOR.

procumbent /proʊ'kʌmbənt/ ▻ *adj* **1** *bot* growing along the ground. **2** *technical* lying or leaning forward; prostrate. ⓒ 17c: from Latin *procumbere* to fall forwards.

procurator /'prɒkjʊreɪtə(r)/ ▻ *noun* **1** an agent with power of attorney in a law court. **2** in the Roman empire: a financial agent or administrator in a province. • **procuracy** or **procuratorship** *noun*. ⓒ 13c: from Latin, meaning 'agent' or 'manager', from *procurare* to attend to.

procurator fiscal ▻ *noun, Scots* a district official who combines the roles of coroner and public prosecutor. ⓒ 16c.

procure /prə'kjʊə(r)/ ▻ *verb* (***procured, procuring***) **1** to manage to obtain something or bring it about. **2** *tr & intr* to get (women or girls) to act as prostitutes. • **procurable** *adj*. • **procurement** *noun*. ⓒ 13c: from Latin *procurare* to take care of; see PRO-[1] + CURE.

procurer and **procuress** ▻ *noun* a man or woman who provides prostitutes for clients.

Prod, **Proddy** or **Proddie** ▻ *noun, offensive slang* a Protestant, especially in Ireland. ⓒ 1940s.

prod ▻ *verb* (***prodded, prodding***) **1** (*often* **prod at something**) to poke or jab it. **2** to nudge, prompt or spur (a person or animal) into action. ▻ *noun* **1** a poke, jab or nudge. **2** a reminder. **3** a goad or similar pointed instrument. ⓒ 16c.

prodigal /'prɒdɪgəl/ ▻ *adj* **1** heedlessly extravagant or wasteful. **2** (*often* **prodigal of something**) *formal or old use* lavish in bestowing it; generous. ▻ *noun* **1** a squanderer, wastrel or spendthrift. **2** (*also* **prodigal son**) a repentant ne'er-do-well or a returned wanderer. • **prodigality** *noun* **1** being prodigal or extravagant. **2** profusion. **3** great liberality. • **prodigally** *adverb*. ⓒ 16c: from Latin *prodigus* wasteful.

prodigious /prə'dɪdʒəs/ ▻ *adj* **1** extraordinary or marvellous. **2** enormous; vast. • **prodigiously** *adverb*. ⓒ 16c: from Latin *prodigiosus*; see PRODIGY.

prodigy /'prɒdɪdʒɪ/ ▻ *noun* (***prodigies***) **1** something that causes astonishment; a wonder; an extraordinary phenomenon. **2** someone, especially a child, of extraordinary brilliance or talent. ⓒ 17c: from Latin *prodigium* something portent.

produce ▻ *verb* /prə'dʒuːs/ (***produced, producing***) **1** to bring out or present something to view. **2** to bear (children, young, leaves, etc). **3** *tr & intr* to yield (crops, fruit, etc). **4** to secrete (a substance), give off (a smell), etc. **5** *tr & intr* to make or manufacture something. **6** to give rise to or prompt (a reaction) from people. **7** to direct (a play), arrange (a radio or television programme) for presentation, or finance and schedule the making of (a film). **8** *geom* to extend (a line). ▻ *noun* /'prɒdʒuːs/ foodstuffs derived from crops or animal livestock, eg fruit, vegetables, eggs and dairy products. • **producible** *adj*. ⓒ 15c: from Latin *producere* to bring forth.

producer ▻ *noun* **1** a person, organization or thing that produces. **2** *biol* in a food chain: any organism that manufactures carbohydrates by photosynthesis and serves as a source of energy for organisms higher up the chain.

product /'prɒdʌkt/ ▻ *noun* **1** something produced, eg through manufacture or agriculture. **2** a result □ *the product of much thought.* **3** *math* the value obtained by multiplying two or more numbers. **4** *chem* a substance formed during a chemical reaction. ⓒ 15c.

production /prə'dʌkʃən/ ▻ *noun* **1 a** the act of producing; **b** the process of producing or being produced □ *The new model goes into production next year.* **2** the quantity produced or rate of producing it. **3** something created; a literary or artistic work. **4** a particular presentation of a play, opera, ballet, etc. ⓒ 15c.

production line ▻ *noun* **1** a series of activities carried out in sequence as part of a manufacturing process. **2** the workers who carry out these activities.

productive /prə'dʌktɪv/ ▻ *adj* **1** yielding a lot; fertile; fruitful. **2** useful; profitable □ *a productive meeting.* **3** (*usually* **productive of something**) giving rise to it; resulting in it □ *productive of ideas.* • **productively** *adverb*. • **productiveness** *noun*.

productivity /prɒdʌk'tɪvɪtɪ/ ▻ *noun* the rate and efficiency of work, especially in industrial production, etc.

proem /'proʊɛm/ ▻ *noun* an introduction, prelude or preface, especially at the beginning of a book. ⓒ 14c: ultimately from Greek *pro* before + *oime* song.

prof ▻ *noun, colloq* a professor.

Prof. ▻ *abbreviation* Professor.

profane /prə'feɪn/ ▻ *adj* **1** showing disrespect for sacred things; irreverent. **2** not sacred or spiritual; temporal or worldly. **3** said especially of language: vulgar; blasphemous. ▻ *verb* (***profaned, profaning***) **1** to treat (something sacred) irreverently. **2** to violate or defile (what should be respected). • **profanation** /prɒfə'neɪʃən/ *noun*. • **profanely** *adverb*. ⓒ 14c: from Latin *profanus* outside the temple, hence not holy.

profanity /prə'fanɪtɪ/ ▻ *noun* (***profanities***) **1** lack of respect for sacred things. **2** blasphemous language; a blasphemy, swear word, oath, etc. ⓒ 17c.

profess /prə'fɛs/ ▻ *verb* (***professes, professed, professing***) **1** to make an open declaration of (beliefs, etc). **2** to declare adherence to something. **3** to claim or pretend □ *profess ignorance* □ *profess to be an expert.* Compare CONFESS. ⓒ 14c: from Latin *profiteri, professus* to declare.

professed ▻ *adj* **1** self-acknowledged; self-confessed. **2** claimed by oneself; pretended. **3** having taken the vows of a religious order. • **professedly** /prə'fɛsɪdlɪ/ *adverb*.

profession /prə'fɛʃən/ ▻ *noun* **1** an occupation, especially one that requires specialist academic and practical training, eg medicine, law, teaching, engineering, etc. **2** the body of people engaged in a particular one of these. **3** an act of professing; a declaration □ *a profession of loyalty.* **4** a declaration of religious belief made upon entering a religious order. • **the oldest profession** *colloq* prostitution. ⓒ 13c: from Latin *professio, professionis* a public declaration.

professional ▻ *adj* **1** earning a living in the performance, practice or teaching of something that is usually a pastime □ *a professional golfer.* **2** belonging to a trained profession. **3** like, appropriate to or having the competence, expertise or conscientiousness of someone with professional training □ *did a very professional job.* **4** *derog* habitually taking part in, or displaying a tendency towards, something that is despised or frowned upon □ *a professional misogynist.* ▻ *noun* **1** someone who belongs to one of the skilled professions. **2** someone who makes their living in an activity, etc that is also carried on at an amateur level. • **professionalism** *noun*. • **professionally** *adverb*.

professional foul ▻ *noun, football* a deliberate foul committed in order to prevent an opponent from scoring what looks like a certain goal.

professor /prə'fɛsə(r)/ ▻ *noun* **1** a teacher of the highest rank in a university; the head of a university department. **2** *N Amer, especially US* a university teacher. ● **professorial** /prɒfɛˈsɔːrɪəl/ *adj.* ● **professorship** *noun.* ⓒ 14c: Latin, meaning 'public teacher', from *profiteri* to PROFESS.

proffer /ˈprɒfə(r)/ ▷ *verb* (***proffered***, ***proffering***) to offer something for someone to accept; to tender. ▷ *noun* the act of proffering; an offer. ⓒ 13c: from French *proffrir*, from Latin *pro* forward + *offerre* to offer.

proficient /prəˈfɪʃənt/ ▷ *adj* fully trained and competent; expert. ▷ *noun* an expert. ● **proficiency** *noun.* ● **proficiently** *adverb.* ⓒ 16c: from Latin *proficere*, *profectum* to make progress.

profile /ˈproʊfaɪl/ ▷ *noun* **1 a** a side view of something, especially of a face or head; **b** a representation of this. **2** a brief outline, sketch or assessment. **3** *statistics* a list, table, graph, etc showing the extent to which a specified group, etc varies in certain characteristics □ *child development profiles.* ▷ *verb* **1** to represent in profile. **2** to give a brief outline (of a person, their career, a company, prospects, etc). ● **in profile** from the side view. ● **keep a low profile** to maintain a unobtrusive presence. ⓒ 17c: from Italian *profilo*, from *profilare* to outline.

profit /ˈprɒfɪt/ ▷ *noun* **1** the money gained from selling something for more than it originally cost. **2** an excess of income over expenses. **3** advantage or benefit. ▷ *verb* (***profited***, ***profiting***) *intr* (*often* **profit from** or **by something**) to benefit from it. ⓒ 14c: from Latin *profectus*, from *proficere* to advance.

profitable ▷ *adj* **1** said of a business, etc: making a profit. **2** useful; fruitful. ● **profitability** *noun.* ● **profitably** *adverb.* ⓒ 14c.

profit and loss ▷ *noun* (*in full* **profit and loss account**) *bookkeeping* an account that records income and other gains together with expenses, expenditures and losses and which is periodically, usually at the end of company's financial year, balanced to show the net profit or loss over the period.

profiteer /prɒfɪˈtɪə(r)/ ▷ *noun* someone who takes advantage of a shortage or other emergency to make exorbitant profits. ▷ *verb* (***profiteered***, ***profiteering***) *intr* to make excessive profits in such a way. ⓒ Early 20c.

profiterole /prəˈfɪtəroʊl/ ▷ *noun, cookery* a small puff of CHOUX PASTRY, with a sweet or savoury filling inside. ⓒ 16c: French, diminutive from *profit* profit.

profit margin ▷ *noun, commerce* the difference between the buying or production price of a product and the selling price. ⓒ 1920s.

profit-sharing ▷ *noun, business* an agreement whereby employees receive a proportion, fixed in advance, of a company's profits, usually in proportion to the employee's length of service. ⓒ 19c.

profligate /ˈprɒflɪgət/ ▷ *adj* **1** immoral and irresponsible; licentious or dissolute. **2** scandalously extravagant. ▷ *noun* a profligate person. ● **profligacy** /ˈprɒflɪgəsɪ/ *noun.* ● **profligately** *adverb.* ⓒ 17c: from Latin *profligare*, *profligatum* to strike down.

pro forma /proʊ ˈfɔːmə/ ▷ *adj, adverb* as a matter of form; following a certain procedure. ▷ *noun* **1** (*also* **pro-forma invoice**) an invoice sent in advance of the goods ordered. **2** *loosely* an official form for completion. ⓒ 16c: Latin, meaning 'for the sake of form'.

profound /prəˈfaʊnd/ ▷ *adj* (***profounder***, ***profoundest***) **1** radical, extensive, far-reaching □ *profound changes.* **2** deep; far below the surface. **3** said of a feeling: deeply felt or rooted. **4** said of comments, etc: showing understanding or penetration. **5** penetrating deeply into knowledge. **6** intense; impenetrable □ *profound deafness.* **7** said of sleep: deep; sound. ● **profoundly** *adverb.* ● **profundity** /prəˈfʌndɪtɪ/ *noun.* ⓒ 14c: from Latin *profundus* deep.

profuse /prəˈfjuːs/ ▷ *adj* **1** overflowing; exaggerated; excessive □ *profuse apologies.* **2** copious □ *profuse bleeding.* ● **profusely** *adverb.* ● **profusion** or **profuseness** *noun.* ⓒ 15c: from Latin *profusus* lavish, from *profundere* to pour forth.

progenitor /proʊˈdʒɛnɪtə(r)/ ▷ *noun* **1** an ancestor, forebear or forefather. **2** the founder or originator of a movement, etc. ⓒ 14c: Latin, from *progignere* to beget.

progeny /ˈprɒdʒənɪ/ ▷ *noun* (***progenies***) **1** children; offspring; descendants. **2** a result or conclusion. ⓒ 13c: from Latin *progenies* offspring.

progesterone /proʊˈdʒɛstəroʊn/ ▷ *noun, biochem* a steroid sex hormone that prepares the lining of the uterus for implantation of a fertilized egg and, if pregnancy occurs, is secreted in large amounts to maintain the pregnancy. ⓒ 1930s: from *progestin* + *sterol*.

progestogen /proʊˈdʒɛstədʒən/ and **progestin** /-ˈdʒɛstɪn/ ▷ *noun, biochem* any of a range of hormones of the PROGESTERONE type. Several synthetic progestogens are used in oral contraceptives. ⓒ 1930s.

prognosis /prɒgˈnoʊsɪs/ ▷ *noun* (***prognoses*** /-siːz/) **1** an informed forecast of developments in any situation. **2** a doctor's prediction regarding the probable course of a disease, disorder or injury. ⓒ 17c: Greek, meaning 'knowing before'.

prognostic /prɒgˈnɒstɪk/ ▷ *adj* **1** belonging or relating to a prognosis. **2** serving as a warning; foretelling. ▷ *noun* **1** something that acts, or can be taken, as an indication, eg of the possible presence of a disease, etc. **2** a warning or foretelling. ● **prognostically** *adverb.* ⓒ 15c: see PROGNOSIS.

prognosticate /prɒgˈnɒstɪkeɪt/ ▷ *verb* (***prognosticated***, ***prognosticating***) **1** to foretell. **2** to indicate in advance; to be a sign of something. ● **prognostication** *noun.* ● **prognosticator** *noun.* ⓒ 16c: from Latin *prognosticare*, *prognosticatum* to foretell.

programmable ▷ *adj* capable of being programmed to perform a task automatically.

programme or (*N Amer*) **program** /ˈproʊgram/ *noun* **1 a** the schedule of proceedings for, and list of participants in, a theatre performance, entertainment, ceremony, etc; **b** a leaflet or booklet describing these. **2** an agenda, plan or schedule. **3** a series of planned projects to be undertaken. **4** a scheduled radio or TV presentation. **5** (*usually* **program**) *computing* a set of coded instructions to a computer for the performance of a task or a series of operations, written in any of various PROGRAMMING LANGUAGES. ▷ *verb* (***programmed***, ***programming***; *N Amer also* ***programed***, ***programing***) **1** to include something in a programme; to schedule. **2** to draw up a programme for something. **3** to set (a computer) by program to perform a set of operations. **4** to prepare a program for a computer. **5** to set (a machine) so as to operate at the required time. **6** to train to respond in a specified way. ⓒ 18c: from Greek *programma* the order of the day or schedule.

programmed learning ▷ *noun, education* a form of learning in which the learner is given short chunks of information which they must follow with some active response, and in which correct answers are immediately reinforced. ⓒ 1950s: based on the behavourist learning theories of US psychologist B F Skinner (1904–).

programme evaluation and review technique ▷ *noun* (abbreviation **PERT**) *business* a method of planning, monitoring and reviewing the progress, costs, etc of a complex project.

programme music ▷ *noun* instrumental music which aims to depict a story or scene.

programmer ▷ *noun* someone who writes computer programs (see PROGRAMME *noun* 5).

programming language ▷ *noun, computing* any system of codes, symbols, rules, etc designed for writing computer programs (see PROGRAMME *noun* 5).

progress ▷ *noun* /ˈproʊgrɛs; *N Amer* ˈprɒ-/ **1** movement while travelling in any direction. **2** course □

followed the progress of the trial. **3** movement towards a destination, goal or state of completion □ ***make slow progress.*** **4** advances or development. **5** *old use* a journey made in state by a sovereign, etc. ▻ *verb* /prə'grɛs/ (***progresses***, ***progressed***, ***progressing***) **1** *intr* to move forwards or onwards; to proceed towards a goal. **2** *intr* to advance or develop. **3** *intr* to improve. **4** to put (something planned) into operation; to expedite. • **in progress** taking place; in the course of being done. ⓘ 15c: from Latin *progredi*, *progressus* to move forward.

progression /prə'grɛʃən/ ▻ *noun* **1** an act or the process of moving forwards or advancing in stages. **2** improvement. **3** *music* a succession of chords, the advance from one to the next being determined on a fixed pattern. **4** *math* a sequence of numbers, each of which bears a specific relationship to the preceding term. See ARITHMETIC PROGRESSION, GEOMETRIC PROGRESSION.

progressive /prə'grɛsɪv/ ▻ *adj* **1** advanced in outlook; using or favouring new methods. **2** moving forward or advancing continuously or by stages. **3** said of a disease: continuously increasing in severity or complication. **4** said of a dance or game: involving changes of partner at intervals. **5** said of taxation: increasing as the sum taxed increases. **6** *grammar* said of a verbal aspect or tense: expressing continuing action or a continuing state, formed in English with *be* and the present PARTICIPLE, as in *I am doing it* and *they will be going*. Also called CONTINUOUS. Compare PERFECT. ▻ *noun* **1** someone with progressive ideas. **2** *grammar* **a** the progressive aspect or tense; **b** a verb in a progressive aspect or tense. • **progressively** *adverb*. • **progressiveness** *noun*. • **progressivism** *noun*. • **progressivist** *noun, adj*.

progressive education ▻ *noun* an educational system which places greater emphasis on the needs and capacities of the individual child than traditional forms of teaching and which usually involves greater freedom of choice, activity and movement, stressing social as well as academic development. ⓘ 19c.

prohibit /prə'hɪbɪt/ ▻ *verb* (***prohibited***, ***prohibiting***) **1** to forbid something, especially by law; to ban. **2** to prevent or hinder. ⓘ 15c: from Latin *prohibere*, *prohibitum* to prevent.

prohibition /proʊɪ'bɪʃən, proʊhɪ-/ ▻ *noun* **1** the act of prohibiting or state of being prohibited. **2** a law or decree that prohibits something. **3** a ban by law, especially in the US from 1920–1933, on the manufacture and sale of alcoholic drinks. • **prohibitionary** *adj*. • **prohibitionist** *noun*.

prohibitive /prə'hɪbɪtɪv/ or **prohibitory** ▻ *adj* **1** banning; prohibiting. **2** tending to prevent or discourage. **3** said of prices, etc: unaffordably high. • **prohibitively** *adverb*. • **prohibitiveness** *noun*.

project ▻ *noun* /'prɒdʒɛkt/ **1** a plan, scheme or proposal. **2** a research or study assignment. ▻ *verb* /prə'dʒɛkt/ (***projected***, ***projecting***) **1** *intr* to jut out; to protrude. **2** to throw something forwards; to propel. **3** to throw (a shadow, image, etc) on to a surface, screen, etc. **4** to propose or plan. **5** to forecast something from present trends and other known data; to extrapolate. **6** to imagine (oneself) in another situation, especially a future one. **7** to ascribe (feelings of one's own) to other people. **8** to cause (a sound, especially the voice) to be heard clearly at some distance. **9** *intr, colloq* to make good contact with an audience through the strength of one's personality. ⓘ 17c: from Latin *projicere*, *projectum* to throw forward.

projectile /prə'dʒɛktaɪl/ ▻ *noun* an object designed to be projected by an external force, eg a guided missile, bullet, etc. ▻ *adj* **1** capable of being, or designed to be, hurled. **2** projecting. ⓘ 17c: from Latin *projectilis*; see PROJECT.

projection /prə'dʒɛkʃən/ ▻ *noun* **1** the act of projecting or process of being projected. **2** something that protrudes from a surface. **3** the process of showing of a film or transparencies on a screen. **4** a forecast based on present trends and other known data. **5** *math* especially on maps: the representation of a solid object, especially part of the Earth's sphere, on a flat surface. **6** *psychol* the reading of one's own emotions and experiences into a particular situation. **7** *psychol* the process whereby a person unconsciously attributes to others certain attitudes towards themselves, usually as a defence against their own guilt or inferiority, etc. ⓘ 16c.

projectionist ▻ *noun* someone who operates a projector, especially in a cinema. ⓘ 1920s.

projector ▻ *noun* an instrument containing a system of lenses that projects an enlarged version of an illuminated still or moving image on to a screen. ⓘ 19c.

prokaryote or **procaryote** /proʊ'karɪɒt/ ▻ *noun, biol* any organism, including all bacteria, in which each cell contains a single DNA molecule coiled in a loop, and not enclosed in a nucleus. • **prokaryotic** /-'ɒtɪk/ *adj*. • **prokaryotic** *adj*. See also EUKARYOTE. ⓘ 1960s: from PRO-[2] + Greek *karyon* kernel.

prolactin /proʊ'laktɪn/ ▻ *noun, physiol* a hormone, secreted by the PITUITARY GLAND, which initiates lactation in mammals, and stimulates the production of PROGESTERONE by the CORPUS LUTEUM. ⓘ 1930s: from PRO-[1] + *lact*ation + -IN.

prolapse /'proʊlaps/ or **prolapsus** /-səs/ ▻ *noun, pathol* the slipping out of place or falling down of an organ or other body part, especially the slipping of the uterus into the vagina. ▻ *verb* (***prolapsed***, ***prolapsing***) said of an organ: to slip out of place. ⓘ 18c: from Latin *prolabi*, *prolapsus* to slip forward.

prolate /'proʊleɪt/ ▻ *adj, geom* said of something approximately spherical: more pointed at the poles. Compare OBLATE. • **prolately** *adverb*. ⓘ 18c: from Latin *proferre*, *prolatum* to enlarge.

prole /proʊl/ ▻ *noun, adj, derog colloq* proletarian. ⓘ 19c.

prolegomenon /proʊlɪ'gɒmɪnən/ ▻ *noun* (***prolegomena*** /-nə/) a preface to a literary, critical or discursive work. • **prolegomenary** *adj*. • **prolegomenous** *adj*. ⓘ 17c: Latin, from Greek *prolegein*, from *legein* to say.

prolepsis /proʊ'lɛpsɪs/ ▻ *noun* (***prolepses*** /-siːz/) **1** a debating device that involves the speaker putting forward arguments or objections before they are raised by someone else in order to detract from their possible effects. **2** a rhetorical term for treating an event of the future as though it has already happened. • **proleptic** *adj*. ⓘ 16c: Latin, from Greek, from *prolambanein* to anticipate.

proletarian /proʊlə'tɛərɪən/ ▻ *adj* relating to the proletariat. ▻ *noun* a member of the proletariat. Compare PATRICIAN. ⓘ 17c: from Latin *proletarius* a citizen who has nothing to offer society but his offspring, from *proles* offspring.

proletariat /proʊlə'tɛərɪət, -rɪat/ ▻ *noun* **1** the working class, especially unskilled labourers and industrial workers. **2** in Marxist theory: the class of wage workers, especially industrial ones, whose chief source of income is the sale of their labour power. **3** *historical* in ancient Rome: the lowest class of people. ⓘ 19c.

pro-life ▻ *adj* said of a person or an organization: opposing abortion, euthanasia and experimentation on human embryos. • **pro-lifer** *noun*. Compare PRO-CHOICE. ⓘ 1970s.

proliferate /prə'lɪfəreɪt/ ▻ *verb* (***proliferated***, ***proliferating***) **1** *intr* said of a plant or animal species: to reproduce rapidly. **2** *intr* to increase in numbers; to multiply. **3** to reproduce (cells, etc) rapidly. ⓘ 19c: back-formation from PROLIFERATION.

proliferation /prəlɪfə'reɪʃən/ ▻ *noun* **1** a great and rapid increase in numbers. **2** *biol* in living organisms: the multiplication of cells, tissues or structures. **3** the spread of nuclear weapons to countries not already possessing them. ◷ 19c: from Latin *prolifer* bearing offspring, from *proles* offspring + *ferre* to bear.

prolific /prəˈlɪfɪk/ ▷ *adj* **1** abundant in growth; producing plentiful fruit or offspring. **2** said of a writer, artist, etc: constantly producing new work. **3** (*often* **prolific of** or **in something**) productive of it; abounding in it. • **prolificacy** *noun.* • **prolifically** *adverb.* • **prolificness** *noun.* ◷ 17c: from Latin *prolificus*, from *proles* offspring.

proline /ˈprouliːn/ ▷ *noun, biochem* an amino acid that is found in proteins. ◷ Early 20c: from German *Prolin*, a shortened form of PYRROLIDINE.

prolix /ˈproulɪks/ ▷ *adj* said of speech or writing: tediously long-winded; wordy; verbose. • **prolixity** *noun.* • **prolixly** *adverb.* ◷ 15c: from Latin *prolixus* stretched out.

prolocutor /prouˈlɒkjutə(r)/ ▷ *noun* a chairman, especially that of the Lower House of Convocation in the Anglican Church. ◷ 15c: Latin, from *loqui, locutus* to speak.

PROLOG /ˈproulɒg/ ▷ *noun, computing* a high-level programming language, often used in artificial intelligence research. ◷ 1970s: contraction of *programming in logic.*

prologue /ˈproulɒg/ ▷ *noun* **1** *theat* **a** a speech addressed to the audience at the beginning of a play; **b** the actor delivering it. **2** a preface to a literary work. **3** an event serving as an introduction or prelude. ▷ *verb* (***prologued, prologuing***) to introduce or preface something with a prologue. ◷ 13c: from Greek *prologos*, from *logos* discourse.

prolong /prəˈlɒŋ/ ▷ *verb* (***prolonged, prolonging***) to make something longer; to extend or protract. • **prolongation** /proulɒŋˈgeɪʃən/ *noun.* ◷ 15c: from Latin *prolongare* to lengthen or extend.

PROM ▷ *abbreviation, computing* programmable read-only memory, a type of read-only memory which can be programmed, usually only once, after manufacture and thereafter remains fixed.

prom ▷ *noun, colloq* **1** a walkway or promenade. **2** a PROMENADE CONCERT. **3** *N Amer* a formal school or college dance at the end of the academic year. ◷ 19c: abbreviation.

promenade /prɒməˈnɑːd/ ▷ *noun* **1** a broad paved walk, especially along a seafront. **2** *facetious* a stately stroll. ▷ *verb* (***promenaded, promenading***) **1** *intr* to stroll in a stately fashion. **2** to walk (the streets, etc). **3** to take someone out for some fresh air; to parade. • **promenader** *noun* **1** someone who promenades. **2** a member of the standing part of the audience at a promenade concert. ◷ 16c: French, from *promener* to lead forth.

promenade concert ▷ *noun* a concert, usually of classical music, at which part of the audience is accommodated in a standing area in which they can move about. ◷ 19c.

promenade deck ▷ *noun* an upper deck on board a passenger ship where people can walk about. ◷ 19c.

promethazine /prouˈmɛθəziːn/ ▷ *noun* an antihistamine drug used in the treatment of allergies and to prevent nausea, eg in seasickness. ◷ 1950s: from prophy + *meth*yl + phenothi*azine*.

Promethean /prəˈmiːθɪən/ ▷ *adj* daring and skilfully inventive. ◷ 16c: from Prometheus who, in Greek mythology, dared to steal fire from the gods and gave it to humans and taught them how to use it.

promethium /prəˈmiːθɪəm, prouˈ-/ ▷ *noun, chem* (abbreviation **Pm**, atomic number 61) a radioactive metallic element that occurs naturally in minute amounts and is manufactured artificially by bombarding neodymium with neutrons. It is used as an X-ray source and in phosphorescent paints. ◷ 1940s: Latin, named after Prometheus; see PROMETHEAN.

prominence ▷ *noun* **1** the state or quality of being prominent. **2** a prominent point or thing. **3** a projection. **4** *astron* a cloud of gas lying in the Sun's upper chromosphere, best seen during an eclipse.

prominent /ˈprɒmɪnənt/ ▷ *adj* **1** jutting out; projecting; protruding; bulging. **2** noticeable; conspicuous. **3** leading; notable. • **prominently** *adverb.* ◷ 16c: from Latin *prominere* to jut out.

promiscuous /prəˈmɪskjuəs/ ▷ *adj* **1** indulging in casual or indiscriminate sexual relations. **2** haphazardly mixed. • **promiscuity** /prɒmɪˈskjuːɪtɪ/ *noun.* • **promiscuously** *adverb.* • **promiscuousness** *noun.* ◷ 17c: from Latin *promiscuus* mixed up, from *miscere* to mix.

promise /ˈprɒmɪs/ ▷ *verb* (***promised, promising***) **1** *tr & intr* to give an undertaking (to do or not do something). **2** to undertake to give something to someone □ *promised him a treat.* **3** to show signs of bringing something □ *clouds that promise rain.* **4** to look likely (to do something) □ *promises to have a great future.* **5** to assure or warn □ *I promise nothing bad will happen.* ▷ *noun* **1** an assurance to give, do or not do something. **2** a sign □ *promise of spring in the air.* **3** signs of future excellence. • **promise well** or **badly** to give grounds for hope, or despondency. • **promisee** *noun.* • **promiser** or **promisor** *noun.* ◷ 14c: from Latin *promittere, promissum* to send forth.

promised land ▷ *noun* **1** *Bible* in the Old Testament: the fertile land promised by God to the Israelites. **2** *Christianity* heaven. **3** any longed-for place of contentment and prosperity. See also MILK AND HONEY.

promising ▷ *adj* **1** showing promise; talented; apt. **2** seeming to bode well for the future □ *a promising start.* • **promisingly** *adverb.*

promissory /ˈprɒmɪsərɪ/ ▷ *adj* containing, relating to or expressing a promise. ◷ 17c: from Latin *promissorius*, from *promittere* to promise or send forth.

promissory note ▷ *noun, finance* a note containing a written promise to pay a certain amount of money at a specified date or on demand.

promo /ˈproumou/ ▷ *noun* (***promos***) *colloq* something which is used to publicize a product, especially a video for a pop single. ◷ 1960s: short for PROMOTIONAL or PROMOTION.

promontory /ˈprɒməntərɪ/ ▷ *noun* (***promontories***) a usually hilly part of a coastline that projects into the sea. Also called HEADLAND. ◷ 16c: from Latin *promonturium* mountain ridge.

promote /prəˈmout/ ▷ *verb* (***promoted, promoting***) **1 a** to raise someone to a more senior position; **b**) *sport, especially football* to transfer (a team) to a higher division or league.Compare RELEGATE (sense 2). **2** to contribute to something □ *Exercise promotes health.* **3** to work for the cause of something □ *promote peace.* **4** to publicize; to try to boost the sales of (a product) by advertising. **5** to organize or finance (an undertaking). **6** *chess* to upgrade (a pawn that has reached the opponent's side of the board) to a higher rank. • **promotion** *noun.* • **promotional** *adj.* ◷ 14c: from Latin *promovere, promotum* to make something advance.

promoter ▷ *noun* the organizer or financer of a sporting event or other undertaking.

prompt ▷ *adj* (***prompter, promptest***) **1** immediate; quick; punctual. **2** instantly willing; ready; unhesitating. ▷ *adverb* punctually. ▷ *noun* **1** something serving as a reminder. **2** *theat* words supplied by a prompter to an actor. **3** *theat* a prompter. **4** *computing* a sign (usually >) on screen indicating that the computer is ready for input. ▷ *verb* (***prompted, prompting***) **1** to cause, lead or remind someone to do something. **2** to produce or elicit (a reaction or response). **3** *tr & intr* to help (an actor) to remember their next words by supplying the first few. • **promptitude** *noun*. • **promptly** *adverb*. • **promptness** *noun*. ⓒ 14c: from Latin *promptus* ready or quick.

prompter ▷ *noun* **1** *theat* someone positioned offstage to prompt actors if they forget their lines. **2** someone or something that prompts.

prompt side ▷ *noun, theat* the side of the stage where the prompter sits, usually to the actors' left, but often to their right in US.

promulgate /'prɒməlgeɪt/ ▷ *verb* (***promulgated, promulgating***) **1** to make (a decree, etc) effective by means of an official public announcement. **2** to publicize or promote (an idea, theory, etc) widely. • **promulgation** *noun*. • **promulgator** *noun*. ⓒ 16c: from Latin *promulgare, promulgatum* to make known.

pron. ▷ *abbreviation, grammar* pronoun.

pronator /proʊ'neɪtə(r)/ ▷ *noun, anatomy* a muscle in the forearm or forelimb that allows the hand or foot to face downwards. Compare SUPINATOR. ⓒ 17c: from Latin *pronane* to put (the hand or foot) downwards.

prone /proʊn/ ▷ *adj* **1** lying flat, especially face downwards. **2** (*often* **prone to something**) predisposed to it, or liable to suffer from it. Also *in compounds* □ *accident-prone*. **3** inclined or liable to do something. • **pronely** *adverb*. • **proneness** *noun*. ⓒ 14c: from Latin *pronus* bent forwards.

prong ▷ *noun* **1** a point or spike, especially one of those making up the head of a fork. **2** any pointed projection. ▷ *verb* (***pronged, pronging***) to stab or pierce something with or as with a prong. ⓒ 15c.

pronged ▷ *adj, in compounds* **1** said of a fork, etc: with a specified number of prongs or directions. **2** said of an attack, etc: made from a specified number of directions.

pronghorn and **prongbuck** ▷ *noun* a N American antelope-like mammal with a pale-brown coat, prominent eyes, short horns in the female and prong-like backward curving horns in the male. ⓒ 19c.

pronking /'prɒŋkɪŋ/ ▷ *noun, zool* behaviour exhibited by several hoofed mammals, eg the springbok, in which the back is arched and the legs are held stiffly downwards as the animal repeatedly leaps off the ground and lands on all four legs simultaneously. ⓒ 19c: from Afrikaans *pronk* to show off, strut or prance.

pronominal /proʊ'nɒmɪnəl/ *grammar* ▷ *adj* referring to or of the nature of a pronoun. • **pronominally** *adverb*. ⓒ 17c: from Latin *pronominalis*, from *pronomen* pronoun.

pronoun /'proʊnaʊn/ ▷ *noun, grammar* a word such as *she, him, they, it*, etc used in place of, and to refer to, a noun, phrase, clause, etc. ⓒ 16c: from Latin *pronomen*, from *pro* for + *nomen* noun.

pronounce /prə'naʊns/ ▷ *verb* (***pronounced, pronouncing***) **1** to say or utter (words, sounds, letters, etc); to articulate or enunciate. **2** to declare something officially, formally or authoritatively □ *pronounced her innocent*. **3** to pass or deliver (judgement). **4** *intr* (*usually* **pronounce on something**) to give an opinion or verdict on it. See also PRONUNCIATION. • **pronounceable** *adj*. ⓒ 14c: from Latin *pronuntiare* to declaim or pronounce.

pronounced ▷ *adj* **1** noticeable; distinct □ *a pronounced limp*. **2** spoken; articulated. • **pronouncedly** /prə'naʊnsɪdlɪ/ *adverb*.

pronouncement ▷ *noun* **1** a formal announcement. **2** a declaration of opinion; a verdict. **3** the act of pronouncing.

pronto /'prɒntoʊ/ ▷ *adverb, colloq* immediately. ⓒ Early 20c: Spanish, meaning 'quick', from Latin *promptus*.

pronunciation /prənʌnsɪ'eɪʃən/ ▷ *noun* **1** the act or a manner of pronouncing words, sounds, letters, etc. **2** the correct way of pronouncing a word, sound, etc in a given language. **3** a set of symbols indicating how a word, etc is to be pronounced.

proof ▷ *noun* **1** evidence, especially conclusive evidence, that something is true or a fact. **2** *law* the accumulated evidence on which a verdict is based. **3** *Scots law* a trial held before a judge without a jury. **4** the activity or process of testing or proving. **5** a test, trial or demonstration. **6** *math* a step-by-step verification of a proposed mathematical statement. **7** *printing* a trial copy of printed text used for examination or correction. **8** a trial print from a photographic negative. **9** a trial impression from an engraved plate. **10** a measure of the alcohol content of a distilled liquid, especially an alcoholic beverage, equal to 49.28% of alcohol by weight. ▷ *adj, especially in compounds* able or designed to withstand, deter or be free from or secure against a specified thing □ *proof against storms* □ *leakproof*. ▷ *verb* (***proofed, proofing***) **1** to make something resistant to or proof against a specified thing. Often *in compounds* □ *to damp-proof the walls*. **2** to take a proof of (printed material). **3** to proof-read. ⓒ 13c: from French *preuve*, from Latin *proba*, from *probare* to test.

proof-read ▷ *verb, tr & intr* to read and mark for correction the proofs of (a text, etc). • **proof-reader** *noun*. • **proof-reading** *noun*.

proof spirit ▷ *noun* a standard mixture of alcohol and water containing 49.28% alcohol by weight or 57.1% by volume. ⓒ 18c.

prop¹ ▷ *noun* **1** a rigid support, especially a vertical one, of any of various kinds □ *a clothes prop*. **2** a person or thing that one depends on for help or emotional support. **3** (*also* **prop forward**) *rugby* **a** the position at either end of the front row of the scrum; **b** a player in this position. ▷ *verb* (***propped, propping***) **1** (*often* **prop something up**) to support or hold it upright with, or as if with, a prop. **2** (*usually* **prop against something**) to lean against it; to put something against something else. **3** to serve as a prop to something. ⓒ 15c.

prop² ▷ *noun, colloq* (*in full* **property**) *theat* a portable object or piece of furniture used on stage during a performance.

prop³ ▷ *noun, colloq* a propeller. ⓒ Early 20c.

prop. ▷ *abbreviation* **1** proper. **2** properly. **3** property. **4** proposition. **5** proprietor.

propaganda /prɒpə'gandə/ ▷ *noun* **1 a** the organized circulation by a political group, etc of doctrine, information, misinformation, rumour or opinion, intended to influence public feeling, raise public awareness, bring about reform, etc; **b** the material circulated in this way. **2** (**Propaganda**) a Roman Catholic CONGREGATION (sense 4) responsible for foreign missions and the training of missionaries. • **propagandist** *noun*. ⓒ 18c: Italian, from the Latin *Congregatio de propaganda fide* congregation for propagating the faith.

propagandize or **propagandise** ▷ *verb* (***propagandized, propagandizing***) **1** to subject (a person, place, etc) to propaganda. **2** *intr* to circulate propaganda. ⓒ 19c.

propagate /'prɒpəgeɪt/ ▷ *verb* (***propagated, propagating***) **1** *tr & intr, bot* said of a plant: to multiply. **2** *bot* to grow (new plants), either by natural means or artificially. **3** to spread or popularize (ideas, etc). **4** *physics* to transmit energy, eg sound or electromagnetism, over a distance in wave form. ⓒ 16c: from Latin *propagare, propagatum* to grow plants by grafting, etc.

propagation /prɒpə'geɪʃən/ ▷ *noun* **1** *bot* the multiplication of plants, especially in horticulture, either by natural means, eg from seed, or by artificial methods, eg grafting and tissue culture. **2** *physics* the transmission of energy (eg sound or electromagnetism) from one point to another in the form of waves in a direction perpendicular to the wavefront.

propagator /'prɒpəgeɪtə(r)/ ▷ *noun* **1** someone or something that propagates. **2** a heated covered box in which plants may be grown from seed or cuttings.

propane /ˈproupeɪn/ ▷ *noun, chem* (formula C_3H_8) a colourless odourless flammable gas, obtained from petroleum. It readily liquefies under pressure and is used as a fuel supply for portable stoves, etc, and as a solvent and refrigerant. ⓒ 19c: from PROPIONIC ACID.

propanoic acid /proupəˈnouɪk —/ ▷ *noun, chem* (formula CH_3CH_2COOH) a fatty acid, a colourless liquid used to control the growth of certain moulds. Formerly called PROPIONIC ACID.

propanone /ˈproupənoun/ *noun* ACETONE.

propel /prəˈpɛl/ ▷ *verb* (***propelled, propelling***) **1** to drive or push something forward. **2** to steer or send someone or something in a certain direction. ⓒ 17c: from Latin *propellere* to drive.

propellant /prəˈpɛlənt/ ▷ *noun* **1** *chem* a compressed inert gas in an aerosol that is used to release the liquid contents as a fine spray when the pressure is released. **2** *engineering* the fuel and oxidizer that are burned in a rocket in order to provide thrust. **3** an explosive charge that is used to propel a projectile, eg a bullet or shell. **4** something that propels.

propellent /prəˈpɛlənt/ ▷ *adj* propelling; capable of driving or pushing forward.

propeller ▷ *noun* a device consisting of a revolving hub with radiating blades that produce thrust or power, used to propel aircraft, ships, etc. ⓒ 18c.

propelling pencil ▷ *noun* a type of pencil in which the lead is held in a casing and can be propelled forward as it is worn down. ⓒ 19c. ▷

propensity /prəˈpensətɪ/ ▷ *noun* (***propensities***) a tendency or inclination □ *a propensity for chocolate* □ *a propensity to drink too much.* ⓒ 16c: from Latin *propensus* hanging forward, from *propendere, propensum* to be inclined.

proper /ˈprɒpə(r)/ ▷ *adj* **1** real; genuine; able to be correctly described as (a specified thing). **2** right; correct. **3** appropriate □ *at the proper time.* **4** own; particular; correct □ *in its proper place.* **5** socially accepted; respectable. **6** *derog* morally strict; prim. **7** (*usually* **proper to something**) belonging or appropriate to it; suitable □ *the form of address proper to her rank.* **8** used immediately after a noun: strictly so called; itself, excluding others not immediately connected with it □ *We are now entering the city proper.* **9** *colloq* utter; complete; out-and-out □ *a proper idiot.* ▷ *adverb, non-standard* correctly □ *can't even speak proper.* ⓒ 13c: from French *propre*, from Latin *proprius* own or special.

proper fraction ▷ *noun, math* a fraction in which the NUMERATOR is less than the DENOMINATOR, eg $^1/_2$ or $^3/_7$. Compare IMPROPER FRACTION.

properly ▷ *adverb* **1** suitably; appropriately; correctly. **2** with strict accuracy. **3** fully; thoroughly; completely. **4** *colloq* utterly.

proper motion ▷ *noun, astron* the movement of a fixed star in space relative to the Sun.

proper noun and **proper name** ▷ *noun, grammar* the name of a particular person, place or thing, eg Kurt, Clapham, Internet. Compare COMMON NOUN.

propertied /ˈprɒpətɪd/ ▷ *adj* owning property, especially land.

property /ˈprɒpətɪ/ ▷ *noun* (***properties***) **1** something someone owns □ *That book is my property.* **2** possessions collectively. **3** the concept of ownership. **4 a** land or real estate; **b** an item of this. **5** a quality or attribute □ *has the property of dissolving easily.* **6** a PROP[2]. ⓒ 13c: from French *proprieté*, from Latin *proprietas* attribute, from *proprius* own.

property centre ▷ *noun* a place where local solicitors, estate agents and members of the public can advertize properties, businesses, etc that are for sale and prospective buyers can browse.

property man and **property mistress** ▷ *noun, theat* someone in charge of stage props (see PROP[2]).

propfan ▷ *noun* (*in full* **propeller fan**) an aircraft propeller consisting of a rotor carrying several blades working in a cylindrical casing, with swept-back blades allowing quieter operation for the rotational speeds involved.

prop forward see PROP[1] *noun* 3

prophase /ˈproufeɪz/ ▷ *noun, biol* in mitosis and meiosis: the first stage of cell division, during which the chromosomes coil, thicken and divide longitudinally to form CHROMATIDs, and the membrane surrounding the nucleus disintegrates. ⓒ 19c: PRO-[2] + PHASE.

prophecy /ˈprɒfəsɪ/ ▷ *noun* (***prophecies***) **1 a** the interpretation of divine will; **b** the act of revealing such interpretations. **2 a** the foretelling of the future; **b** something foretold; a prediction. **3** a gift or aptitude for predicting the future. ⓒ 13c: from French *prophecie*, from Greek *propheteia*; see PROPHET.

prophesy /ˈprɒfəsaɪ/ ▷ *verb* (***prophesies, prophesied, prophesying***) **1** *tr & intr* to foretell (future happenings); to predict. **2** *intr* to utter prophecies; to interpret divine will. ⓒ 14c: a variant of PROPHECY.

prophet /ˈprɒfɪt/ ▷ *noun* **1** someone who is able to express the will of God or a god. **2** *Bible* **a** any of the writers of prophecy in the Old Testament; **b** any of the books attributed to them. **3** *Islam* (**the Prophet**) Muhammad. **4** someone who claims to be able to tell what will happen in the future □ *a prophets of doom.* **5** a leading advocate of or spokesperson for a movement or cause. ⓒ 12c: from Greek *prophetes* someone who interprets or expresses the divine will, from *pro* for + *phanai* to speak.

prophetess ▷ *noun* (***prophetesses***) a female prophet (*especially* sense 1).

prophetic /prəˈfɛtɪk/ ▷ *adj* **1** foretelling the future. **2** relating or belonging to prophets or prophecy. • **prophetically** *adverb*.

prophylactic /prɒfɪˈlaktɪk/ ▷ *adj* guarding against or tending to prevent disease or other mishap. ▷ *noun* **1** a prophylactic drug or device; a precautionary measure. **2** a condom. ⓒ 16c: from Greek *prophylaktikos*, from *prophylassein* to take precautions against, from *phylax* a guard.

prophylaxis /prɒfɪˈlaksɪs/ ▷ *noun* (***prophylaxes*** /-siːz/) **1** action or treatment to prevent something unwanted; precautionary measures. **2** any treatment or other measures taken to prevent disease. ⓒ 19c: see PROPHYLACTIC.

propinquity /prəˈpɪŋkwɪtɪ/ ▷ *noun* **1** nearness in place or time; proximity. **2** closeness of kinship. ⓒ 14c: from Latin *propinquitas*, from *propinquus* near.

propionic acid /proupɪˈɒnɪk/ ▷ *noun* the former name for PROPANOIC ACID. ⓒ 19c: from PRO-[2] + Greek *pion* fat.

propitiate /prəˈpɪʃɪeɪt/ ▷ *verb* (***propitiated, propitiating***) to appease or placate (an angry or insulted person or god). • **propitiable** *adj*. • **propitiation** *noun*. • **propitiator** *noun*. • **propitiatory** *adj*. ⓒ 17c: from Latin *propitiare, propitiatum*, from *propitius* gracious.

propitious /prəˈpɪʃəs/ ▷ *adj* **1** favourable; auspicious; advantageous. **2** (*often* **propitious for** or **to something**) likely to favour or encourage it. • **propitiously** *adverb*. ⓒ 15c: from Latin *propitius* gracious.

proponent /prəˈpounənt/ ▷ *noun* a supporter or advocate of something; someone who argues in favour of their cause. ⓒ 16c: from Latin *proponere* to propose.

proportion /prəˈpɔːʃən/ ▷ *noun* **1** a comparative part of a total □ *a large proportion of the population.* **2** the size of one element or group in relation to the whole or total. **3** the size of one group or component in relation to another □ *in a proportion of two parts to one.* **4** the correct balance between parts or elements ◻ ***out of proportion*** ◻ ***get things into proportion.*** **5** (**proportions**) size; dimensions ◻ ***a garden of large proportions.*** **6** *math* correspondence between the ratios of two pairs of quantities, as expressed in *2 is to 8 as 3 is to 12.* ▷ *verb* (***proportioned, proportioning***) **1** to adjust the proportions, or balance the parts, of something. **2** (*usually* **proportion one thing to another**) to adjust their proportions relatively. • **in proportion to something 1** in relation to it; in comparison with it. **2** in parallel with it; in correspondence with it; at the same rate. ◷ 14c: from Latin *proportio*, from *pro portione* in respect of his share.

proportional ▷ *adj* **1** corresponding or matching in size, rate, etc. **2** in correct proportion; proportionate. ▷ *noun, math* a number or quantity in a proportion. • **proportionally** *adverb.*

proportional representation ▷ *noun* (abbreviation **PR**) any electoral system in which the number of representatives each political party has in parliament is in direct proportion to the number of votes it receives. Compare FIRST-PAST-THE-POST, ALTERNATIVE VOTE. ◷ 19c.

proportionate ▷ *adj* /prəˈpɔːʃənət/ (**proportionate to something**) due or in correct proportion. ▷ *verb* /-ʃəneɪt/ (***proportionated, proportionating***) to adjust in proportion. • **proportionately** *adverb.*

proposal ▷ *noun* **1** the act of proposing something. **2** something proposed or suggested; a plan. **3** an offer of marriage. ◷ 17c.

propose /prəˈpoʊz/ ▷ *verb* (***proposed, proposing***) **1** to offer (a plan, etc) for consideration; to suggest. **2** to suggest or nominate someone for a position, task, etc. **3** to be the proposer of (the motion in a debate). **4** to intend (to do something) ◻ ***don't propose to sell.*** **5** to suggest (a specified person, topic, etc) as the subject of a toast. **6** *intr* (*often* **propose to someone**) to make them an offer of marriage. ◷ 14c: from Latin *proponere, propositum* to propose.

proposer /prəˈpoʊzə(r)/ ▷ *noun* **1** someone who proposes or advocates something. **2** in a debate: the leading speaker in favour of the motion.

proposition /prɒpəˈzɪʃən/ ▷ *noun* **1** a proposal or suggestion. **2** something to be dealt with or undertaken ◻ ***an awkward proposition.*** **3** *euphemistic colloq* an invitation to have sexual intercourse. **4** *logic* a form of statement affirming or denying something, that can be true or false; a premise. **5** *math* a statement of a problem or theorem, especially one that incorporates its solution or proof. ▷ *verb* (***propositioned, propositioning***) *euphemistic colloq* to propose sexual intercourse to someone. ◷ 14c: from Latin *propositio* a setting forth, from *proponere* to propose.

propound /prəˈpaʊnd/ ▷ *verb* (***propounded, propounding***) **1** to put forward (an idea or theory, etc) for consideration or discussion. **2** *law* to produce (a will) for probate. ◷ 16c: from Latin *proponere* to propose.

propranolol /proʊˈpranəlɒl/ ▷ *noun, medicine* a BETA-BLOCKER used to treat abnormal heart rhythms, angina and high blood pressure, to prevent migraine attacks and relieve symptoms of anxiety. ◷ 1960s: from *pro*pyl + *propanol* (propyl alcohol).

proprietary /prəˈpraɪətərɪ/ (abbreviation **pty**) ▷ *adj* **1** said eg of rights: belonging to an owner or proprietor. **2** suggestive or indicative of ownership. **3** said of medicines, etc: marketed under a tradename. **4** *especially Austral, NZ & S Afr* (abbreviation **Pty**) said of a company etc: privately owned and managed. *UK equivalent* LTD. ▷ *noun* (***proprietaries***) **1** a body of proprietors. **2** proprietorship. ◷ 16c: from Latin *proprietas* ownership.

proprietary name ▷ *noun* a TRADENAME.

proprietor /prəˈpraɪətə(r)/ and **proprietress** ▷ *noun* an owner, especially of a shop, hotel, business, etc. ◷ 17c: from PROPRIETARY.

proprietorial /prəpraɪəˈtɔːrɪəl/ ▷ *adj* **1** said of a person: tending not to allow other people to have access to something, especially in regard to their work, study, etc ◻ ***Harry's very proprietorial and won't let you borrow his books.*** **2** belonging or relating to an owner or ownership.

propriety /prəˈpraɪətɪ/ ▷ *noun* (***proprieties***) **1** conformity to socially acceptable behaviour, especially between the sexes; modesty or decorum. **2** correctness; moral acceptability. **3** (**proprieties**) the details of correct behaviour; accepted standards of conduct. ◷ 17c: from French *propriété*, from Latin *proprietas*, from *proprius* own.

proprioceptor /proʊprɪəˈsɛptə(r)/ ▷ *noun, physiol* a cell or group of cells that is sensitive to movement, pressure or stretching within the body, and helps to maintain balance, posture and muscular coordination. ◷ Early 20c: from Latin *proprius* own + RECEPTOR.

props ▷ *singular noun, theat* a PROPERTY MAN or PROPERTY MISTRESS.

propulsion /prəˈpʌlʃən/ ▷ *noun* **1** the act of causing something to move forward. **2** a force exerted against a body which makes it move forward. Also *in compounds* ◻ ***jet propulsion.*** • **propulsive** *adj.* ◷ 18c: from Latin *propulsio*, from *propellere* to propel.

propyl /ˈproʊpɪl/ ▷ *noun* **1** the alcohol radical C_3H_7. **2** *as adj* ◻ ***propyl alcohol.*** ◷ 19c: from *prop*ionic acid + -YL.

propylaeum /prɒpɪˈlɪəm/ or **propylon** /ˈprɒpɪlɒn/ ▷ *noun* (***propylaea*** /–lɪə/, ***propyla*** /–lə/ or ***propylons***) *archit* in classical architecture: a monumental entrance gateway or vestibule, usually in front of a temple. ◷ 18c: Latin, from Greek *propylaion*, from *pro* before + *pyle* a gate.

pro rata /proʊ ˈrɑːtə/ ▷ *adverb* in proportion; in accordance with a certain rate. ◷ 16c: Latin, meaning 'for the rate'.

prorogue /prəˈroʊg, proʊˈroʊg/ ▷ *verb* (***prorogued, proroguing***) *formal* **1** to discontinue the meetings of (a legislative assembly) for a time, without dissolving it. **2** *intr* said of a legislative assembly: to suspend a session. • **prorogation** *noun.* ◷ 15c: from Latin *prorogare, prorogatum* to ask publicly.

prosaic /proʊˈzeɪɪk/ ▷ *adj* **1** unpoetic; unimaginative. **2** dull, ordinary and uninteresting. • **prosaically** *adverb.* ◷ 17c: from Latin *prosaicus*; see PROSE.

pros and cons ▷ *plural noun* the various advantages and disadvantages of a course of action, idea, etc. ◷ 16c: from PRO[1] + CON[4].

proscenium /proʊˈsiːnɪəm/ ▷ *noun* (***prosceniums*** or ***proscenia*** /-ə/) *theat* **1** the part of a stage in front of the curtain. **2** (*also* **proscenium arch**) the arch framing the stage and separating it from the auditorium. **3** in ancient theatres: the stage itself. ◷ 17c: from Greek *proskenion*, from *pro* before + *skene* stage.

prosciutto /proʊˈʃuːtoʊ, prɒˈʃuːtoʊ/ ▷ *noun* dry-cured uncooked ham. It is always thinly sliced and usually served as an hors d'oeuvre. ◷ 1940s: Italian, meaning 'pre-dried'.

proscribe /prəˈskraɪb/ ▷ *verb* (***proscribed, proscribing***) **1** to prohibit or condemn something (eg a practice). **2** *historical* to outlaw or exile someone. • **proscriber** *noun.* • **proscription** *noun.* • **proscriptive** *adj.* ◷ 16c: from Latin *proscribere, proscriptum* to write in front of, from *scribere* to write.

proscribe

A word sometimes confused with this one is **prescribe**.

prose /proʊz/ ▷ *noun* **1** the ordinary form of written or spoken language as distinct from verse or poetry. **2** a passage of prose set for translation into a foreign language. **3** dull and uninteresting discussion or speech, etc. Ⓒ 14c: from Latin *prosa oratio* straightforward speech, from *prorsus* straightforward.

prosecute /ˈprɒsɪkjuːt/ ▻ *verb* (***prosecuted, prosecuting***) **1** *tr & intr* to bring a criminal action against someone. **2** *formal* to carry on or carry out something (eg enquiries). • **prosecutable** *adj.* • **prosecutor** *noun.* Ⓒ 15c: from Latin *prosequi, prosecutus* to pursue.

prosecution /prɒsɪˈkjuːʃən/ ▻ *noun* **1** the act of prosecuting or process of being prosecuted. **2** the bringing of a criminal action against someone. **3 a** the prosecuting party in a criminal case; **b** the lawyers involved in this. **4** *formal* the process of carrying something out.

proselyte /ˈprɒsəlaɪt/ ▻ *noun* a convert, especially a Gentile turning to Judaism. • **proselytism** /ˈprɒsəlɪtɪzəm/ *noun.* Ⓒ 14c: from Greek *proselytos* new arrival or convert.

proselytize or **proselytise** /ˈprɒsəlɪtaɪz/ ▻ *verb* (***proselytized, proselytizing***) *tr & intr* to try to convert someone from one faith to another; to make converts. • **proselytizer** *noun.* Ⓒ 17c.

prose poem ▻ *noun* a work or passage printed continuously as prose but having many of the elements found in poetry, eg striking imagery, rhythm, internal rhyme, etc. • **prose poetry** *noun.* Ⓒ 19c: form established by Aloysius Bertrand's *Gaspard de la nuit* (1842).

prosimian /proʊˈsɪmɪən/ ▻ *noun, zool* any of several primitive primates, eg the lemur, loris, tarsier, etc. ▻ *adj* belonging or relating to these primates. Ⓒ 19c: from Latin *Prosimia*, from *simia* an ape.

prosier and **prosiest** see under PROSY

prosody /ˈprɒsədɪ, –zədɪ/ ▻ *noun* **1** the study of verse-composition, especially poetic metre. **2** (*also* **prosodics** /prəˈsɒdɪks/) the study of rhythm, stress and intonation in speech. • **prosodic** /-ˈsɒdɪk/ *adj.* • **prosodist** *noun.* Ⓒ 15c: from Latin *prosodia* the accent for a syllable, from Greek *pros* in addition to + *oide* song.

prospect ▻ *noun* /ˈprɒspɛkt/ **1** an expectation of something due or likely to happen. **2** an outlook for the future. **3** (**prospects**) chances of success, improvement, recovery, etc. **4** (**prospects**) opportunities for advancement, promotion, etc □ *a job with prospects.* **5** a potentially selectable candidate, team member, etc □ *He's a doubtful prospect for Saturday's match.* **6** a potential client or customer. **7** a broad view. **8** *gold-mining* **a** an area with potential as a mine; **b** the resulting yield of such a mine. ▻ *verb* /prəˈspɛkt/ (***prospected, prospecting***) **1** *tr & intr* to search or explore (an area, region, etc) for gold or other minerals. **2** *intr* to hunt for or look out for (eg a job). • **in prospect** expected soon. Ⓒ 15c: from Latin *prospectus* view, from *prospicere, prospectum* to look forward.

prospective /prəˈspɛktɪv/ ▻ *adj* likely or expected; future □ *a prospective buyer.* Ⓒ 18c.

prospector /prəˈspɛktə(r)/ ▻ *noun* someone prospecting for oil, gold, etc.

prospectus /prəˈspɛktəs/ ▻ *noun* (***prospectuses***) **1** a brochure giving information about a school or other institution, especially the courses on offer. **2** a document outlining a proposal for something, eg a literary work or an issue of shares. Ⓒ 18c: Latin, meaning a 'view'.

prosper /ˈprɒspə(r)/ ▻ *verb* (***prospered, prospering***) **1** said of someone: *intr* to do well, especially financially. **2** said of a business, etc: to thrive or flourish. Ⓒ 15c: from French *prospérer*, from Latin *prosperari* to succeed.

prosperity /prɒˈspɛrɪtɪ/ ▻ *noun* the state of being prosperous; success; wealth.

prosperous /ˈprɒspərəs/ ▻ *adj* wealthy and successful. • **prosperously** *adverb.* Ⓒ 15c.

prostaglandin /prɒstəˈglandɪn/ ▻ *noun, physiol* any of a group of hormones that have a wide range of specific effects and are sometimes used therapeutically to induce contractions of the uterus, either to accelerate labour or to induce abortion. Ⓒ 1930s: from *prosta*te *gland* (a major source of these).

prostate /ˈprɒsteɪt/ ▻ *noun* (*in full* **prostate gland**) *anatomy* in male mammals: a muscular gland around the base of the bladder, controlled by sex hormones, which produces an alkaline fluid that activates sperm during ejaculation. ▻ *adj* (*also* **prostatic**) relating or belonging to the prostate gland. Ⓒ 17c: from Greek *prostates* one that stands in front.

prostate, prostrate

These words are often confused with each other.

prosthesis /prɒsˈθiːsɪs/ ▻ *noun* (***prostheses*** /–siːz/) *medicine* **1** an artificial substitute for a part of the body that is missing (as a result of surgery or injury) or non-functional, eg dentures, an artificial limb or breast or a pacemaker. **2** the fitting of such a part to the body. **3** *linguistics* a less common term for PROTHESIS. • **prosthetic** /—ˈθɛtɪk/ *adj.* • **prosthetically** *adverb.* Ⓒ 18c in sense 2; 16c in the linguistic sense 'addition of a prefix to a word': Latin, from Greek, from *pros* in addition to + *tithenai* to put.

prosthetics /prɒsˈθɛtɪks/ ▻ *singular noun* the branch of surgery concerned with supplying, fitting and maintaining prostheses. Ⓒ 19c.

prostitute /ˈprɒstɪtjuːt/ ▻ *noun* **1** someone who performs sexual acts or intercourse in return for money. Also *in compounds* □ *male prostitute* □ *child prostitute.* **2** someone who offers their skills or talents, etc for unworthy ends. ▻ *verb* (***prostituted, prostituting***) **1** to offer (oneself or someone else) as a prostitute. • **prostitution** *noun.* **2** to put (eg one's talents) to an unworthy use. Ⓒ 16c: from Latin *prostituere, prostitutum* to offer for sale.

prostrate ▻ *adj* /ˈprɒstreɪt/ **1** lying face downwards in an attitude of abject submission, humility or adoration. **2** lying flat. **3** distraught with illness, grief, exhaustion, etc. ▻ *verb* /prɒˈstreɪt/ (***prostrated, prostrating***) **1** to throw (oneself) face down in submission or adoration. **2** said of exhaustion, illness, grief, etc: to overwhelm someone physically or emotionally. • **prostration** *noun.* Ⓒ 14c: from Latin *prosternere, prostratum* to throw forwards.

prosy /ˈproʊzɪ/ ▻ *adj* (***prosier, prosiest***) said of speech or writing: **1** prose-like. **2** dull and tedious.

prostyle /ˈproʊstaɪl/ ▻ *noun* in classical architecture: a type of portico in front of a Greek temple, where the columns, never exceeding four in number, are set in front of the building. ▻ *adj* said of a building: having this kind of portico. Ⓒ 17c: from Latin *prostylos*, from Greek *stylos* a column.

prot- see PROTO-

protactinium /proʊtakˈtɪnɪəm/ ▻ *noun* (symbol **Pa**, atomic number 91) *chem* a white highly-toxic radioactive metallic element that occurs naturally in minute quantities in uranium ores. Ⓒ Early 20c: PROT- + ACTINIUM.

protagonist /prəˈtagənɪst/ ▻ *noun* **1** the main character in a play, story, film, etc. **2** any person at the centre of a story or event. **3** *non-standard* a leader or champion of a movement or cause, etc. Ⓒ 17c: from Greek *protagonistes*, from *protos* first + *agonistes* combatant.

protasis /ˈprɒtəsɪs/ ▻ *noun* (***protases*** /-ˈsiːz/) *grammar, logic* the conditional clause of a conditional sentence, eg in *If Winter comes, can Spring be far behind?* the part before the comma is the protasis. Compare APODOSIS. Ⓒ 17c: Greek, meaning 'premise' or 'the first part of a drama'.

protea /ˈproʊtɪə/ ▻ *noun* (***proteas***) *bot* any of various evergreen shrubs and small trees, native to S Africa. They produce large heads of flowers surrounded by colourful bracts. 🕓 19c: named after Proteus, the Greek sea-god who assumed many shapes, and so called because of the varied character of these shrubs.

protean /ˈproʊtɪən/ ▻ *adj* **1** readily able to change shape or appearance; variable; changeable. **2** said especially of a writer, artist, actor, etc: versatile. 🕓 16c: from Proteus (see under PROTEA).

protease /ˈproʊtɪeɪs/ ▻ *noun, biochem* any enzyme that catalyses the breakdown of proteins. 🕓 Early 20c: from PROTEIN + -ASE.

protect /prəˈtɛkt/ ▻ *verb* (***protected, protecting***) **1** to shield someone or something from danger; to guard them or it against injury, destruction, etc; to keep safe. **2** to cover against loss, etc by insurance. **3** to shield (home industries) from foreign competition by taxing imports. 🕓 16c: from Latin *protegere, protectum* to cover in front.

protection ▻ *noun* **1** the action of protecting or condition of being protected; shelter, refuge, cover, safety or care. **2** something that protects. **3** (*also* **protectionism**) the system of protecting home industries against foreign competition by taxing imports. **4** *colloq* **a** the criminal practice of extorting money from shop-owners, etc in return for leaving their premises unharmed; **b** (*also* **protection money**) the money extorted in this way. **5** insurance cover. • **protectionist** *noun*.

protective ▻ *adj* **1** giving or designed to give protection ▫ *protective clothing*. **2** inclined or tending to protect. ▻ *noun* **1** something which protects. **2** a condom. • **protectively** *adverb*. • **protectiveness** *noun*.

protective custody ▻ *noun* the detention of someone in prison for their own safety, eg if they are the subject of a death threat.

protector and **protectress** ▻ *noun* **1** someone or something that protects. **2** a patron or benefactor. **3** someone who rules a country during the childhood of the sovereign or in the absence or incapacity of a sovereign; a regent. • **protectorship** *noun*.

protectorate /prəˈtɛktərət/ ▻ *noun* **1** the office or period of rule of a protector. **2 a** protectorship of a weak or backward country assumed by a more powerful one without actual annexation; **b** the status of a territory that is so protected. 🕓 17c.

protégé and **protégée** /ˈproʊtəʒeɪ/ ▻ *noun* (***protégés*** or ***protégées***) a person (male and female respectively) under the guidance, protection, tutelage, patronage, etc of someone wiser or more important. 🕓 18c: from French *protéger* to protect.

protein /ˈproʊtiːn/ ▻ *noun, biochem* any of thousands of different organic compounds, characteristic of all living organisms, that have large molecules consisting of long chains of amino acids. 🕓 19c: from French *protéine*, from Greek *proteios* primary.

pro tempore /proʊ tɛmˈpɔːreɪ/ ▻ *adverb, adj* for the time being. Often shortened to **pro tem**. 🕓 15c: Latin.

Proterozoic /proʊtəroʊˈzoʊɪk, prɒ-/ *geol* ▻ *adj* **1** relating to the geological era from which the oldest forms of life date. See table at GEOLOGICAL TIME SCALE. **2** *sometimes* denoting the entire PRECAMBRIAN period. ▻ *noun* (**the Proterozoic**) the Proterozoic era. 🕓 Early 20c: from Greek *proteros* earlier + *zoe* life + -IC.

protest ▻ *verb* /prəˈtɛst/ (***protested, protesting***) **1** *intr* to express an objection, disapproval, opposition or disagreement. **2** *N Amer, especially US* to challenge or object to (eg a decision or measure). **3** to declare something solemnly, eg in response to an accusation ▫ *protest one's innocence*. **4** *law* to obtain or write a protest with reference to (a bill). ▻ *noun* /ˈproʊtɛst/ **1** a declaration of disapproval or dissent; an objection. **2 a** an organized public demonstration of disapproval; **b** *as adj* ▫ *a protest march*. **3** *law* a written statement that a bill has been presented and payment refused. **4** the act of protesting. • **protester** or **protestor** *noun*. • **protestingly** *adverb*. • **under protest** reluctantly; unwillingly. 🕓 14c: from French *protester*, from Latin *protestari, protestatus* to declare formally.

Protestant or **protestant** /ˈprɒtɪstənt/ ▻ *noun* **1** a member of any of the Christian churches which embraced the principles of the Reformation and, rejecting the authority of the pope, separated from the Roman Catholic Church. **2** a member of any body descended from these. ▻ *adj* relating or belonging to Protestants. • **Protestantism** *noun*. 🕓 16c: originally applied to those princes and others who in 1529 protested against an edict denouncing the Reformation.

Protestant work ethic see under WORK ETHIC

protestation /prɒtəˈsteɪʃən/ ▻ *noun* **1** a protest or objection. **2** a solemn declaration or avowal.

prothallus /proʊˈθaləs/ ▻ *noun* (***prothalli*** /-liː/) *bot* in certain more primitive plants, eg the fern and some mosses: the small area of tissue where the reproductive organs develop.

prothesis /prɒˈθiːsɪs/ ▻ *noun* (***protheses*** /-siːz/) **1** *linguistics* the addition of a sound or syllable at the beginning of a word, eg the Spanish 'escuela' meaning 'school' developed in this way from Latin 'schola'. Also called **prosthesis**. **2** in Eastern Orthodox churches: **a** the preparation of the Eucharist and placing it on the table ready for use; **b** the table itself or the part of the church where the table stands. • **prothetic** /prəˈθɛtɪk/ *adj*. 🕓 17c: Greek, meaning 'a placing before'.

prothrombin /proʊˈθrɒmbɪn/ ▻ *noun, biochem* one of the clotting factors in blood, which is converted to the enzyme THROMBIN, which in turn causes the conversion of FIBRINOGEN to FIBRIN. 🕓 19c.

protist /ˈproʊtɪst/ ▻ *noun, biol* any member of the kingdom of organisms **Protista** /-ˈtɪstə/, including unicellular algae, bacteria, fungi, etc, which typically possess a true FLAGELLUM. 🕓 19c: from Greek *protistos* very first.

proto- /ˈproʊtoʊ/ or before a vowel **prot-** ▻ *combining form, denoting* **1** first; earliest in time ▫ *prototype*. **2** first of a series. 🕓 Latin and Greek, from Greek *protos* first.

protocol /ˈproʊtəkɒl/ ▻ *noun* **1** correct formal or diplomatic etiquette or procedure. **2** a first draft of a diplomatic document, eg one setting out the terms of a treaty. **3** *N Amer, especially US* a plan of a scientific experiment or other procedure. 🕓 16c: from Latin *protocollum*, from Greek *protokollon* a note of the contents of a document, glued to the front sheet, from *kolla* glue.

Proto-Indo-European see INDO-EUROPEAN

proton /ˈproʊtɒn/ ▻ *noun, physics* any of the positively charged subatomic particles that are found inside the nucleus at the centre of an atom. Compare NEUTRON. 🕓 1920s: Greek, from *protos* first.

protoplasm /ˈproʊtəplazəm, ˈproʊtoʊ-/ ▻ *noun, biol* the mass of protein material of which cells are composed, consisting of the cytoplasm and usually a nucleus. See also PLASM. • **protoplasmal** /-ˈplazməl/ *adj*. • **protoplasmatic** /-ˈmatɪk/ *adj*. • **protoplasmic** /-ˈplazmɪk/ *adj*. 🕓 19c.

prototype ▻ *noun* **1** an original model from which later forms are copied, developed or derived. **2** a first working version, eg of a vehicle or aircraft. **3** someone or something that exemplifies a type. **4** a primitive or ancestral form of something. • **prototypal** *adj*. • **prototypic** /-ˈtɪpɪk/ *adj*. • **prototypical** /-ˈtɪpɪkəl/ *adj*. • **prototypically** *adverb*. 🕓 17c: from Greek *prototypos* primitive or original.

protozoan /proʊtəˈzoʊən/ ▻ *noun* (***protozoa*** /–ˈzoʊə/) a member of a phylum of single-celled organisms, the

Protozoa, including both plant-like and animal-like forms, eg amoeba and disease-carrying parasites. ▷ *adj* relating to such organisms. • **protozoic** /-'zoʊɪk/ *adj*. • **protozoal** *adj*. ◷ 19c: from PROTO- + Greek *zoion* animal.

protract /prə'trakt/ ▷ *verb* (***protracted, protracting***) **1** to prolong; to cause something to last a long time. **2** to lengthen something out. **3** to draw something using a scale and protractor. • **protraction** *noun*. ◷ 16c: from Latin *protrahere, protractum* to drag forth.

protracted ▷ *adj* lasting longer than usual or longer than expected.

protractile /prə'traktaɪl/ ▷ *adj* said of a body part, eg a cat's claws: capable of being extended. ◷ 19c: see PROTRACT.

protractor ▷ *noun, geom* an instrument, usually a transparent plastic semicircle marked in degrees, used to draw and measure angles. ◷ 17c: see PROTRACT (sense 3).

protrude /prə'tru:d/ ▷ *verb* (***protruded, protruding***) **1** *intr* to project; to stick out. **2** to push something out or forward. • **protrusion** *noun*. • **protrusive** *adj*. ◷ 17c: from Latin *protrudere* to thrust forward.

protuberant /prə'tʃu:bərənt/ ▷ *adj* projecting; bulging; swelling out. • **protuberance** *noun*. ◷ 17c: from Latin *protuberare* to swell out.

protuberance, protuberant

These are often mispronounced and misspelt as if they were **protruberance** or **protruberant**, under the influence of **protrude**.

proud ▷ *adj* **1** (*often* **proud of someone** or **something**) feeling satisfaction, delight, etc with one's own or another's accomplishments, possessions, etc. **2** said of an event, occasion, etc: arousing justifiable pride □ *a proud day*. **3** arrogant; conceited. **4** concerned for one's dignity and self-respect. **5** honoured; gratified; delighted. **6** splendid; imposing; distinguished □ *a proud sight*. **7** *poetic* lofty; high. **8** *technical* projecting slightly from the surrounding surface □ *the top edge standing proud*. **9** said of flesh: forming a protuberant mass round a healing wound. • **proudly** *adverb*. • **proudness** *noun*. • **do oneself proud** to succeed gloriously. • **do someone proud** to entertain or treat them grandly. ◷ Anglo-Saxon *prud*.

Prov. ▷ *abbreviation* **1** Provence. **2** Book of the Bible: Proverbs. See table at BIBLE. **3** Provost.

prove /pru:v/ ▷ *verb* (*past tense* ***proved***, *past participle* ***proved*** or ***proven***, *present participle* ***proving***) **1** to show something to be true, correct or a fact. **2** to show something to be (a specified thing) □ *was proved innocent*. **3** *intr* to be found to be (a specified thing) when tried; to turn out to be the case □ *Her advice proved sound*. **4** to show (oneself) to be (of a specified type or quality, etc) □ *He proved himself reliable*. **5** to show (oneself) capable or daring. **6** *law* to establish the validity of (a will). **7** said of dough: to rise when baked. • **provable** or **proveable** *adj*. ◷ 12c: from French *prover*, from Latin *probare* to test or prove, from *probus* good.

proven /'proʊvən, 'pru:vən/ ▷ *verb, past participle of* PROVE. ▷ *adj* shown to be true, worthy, etc. □ *a proven statement* □ *an opportunity for a sales manager of proven ability*. See separate entry NOT PROVEN.

provenance /'prɒvənəns/ ▷ *noun* the place of origin (of a work of art, archaeological find, etc). ◷ 18c: French, from Latin *provenire* to come forth.

Provençal /prɒvɒn'sɑ:l/ ▷ *adj* **1** belonging or relating to Provence, an area in SE France, its inhabitants, their culture or language. **2** (*usually* **à la provençale**) denoting a style of French cookery that traditionally uses olive oil, tomatoes, onion, garlic and white wine and, in meat dishes, slow-cooking the beef, etc □ *eggs à la provençale*. ▷ *noun* **1** a citizen or inhabitant of, or person born in, Provence. **2** a language spoken in Provence, related to French, Italian and Catalan. ◷ 16c.

provender /'prɒvɪndə(r)/ ▷ *noun* **1** dry food for livestock, eg corn and hay. **2** *now usually facetious* food. ◷ 14c: from French *provendre*, from Latin *praebenda* payment.

proverb /'prɒvɜ:b/ ▷ *noun* any of a body of well-known neatly-expressed sayings that give advice or express a supposed truth. ◷ 14c: from French *proverbe*, from Latin *proverbium*, from *verbum* word.

proverbial /prə'vɜ:bɪəl/ ▷ *adj* **1** belonging or relating to a proverb. **2** referred to in a proverb; traditionally quoted; well known □ *turned up like the proverbial bad penny*. • **proverbially** *adverb*.

Proverbs ▷ *singular noun* the title of a book in the Old Testament. See table at BIBLE.

provide /prə'vaɪd/ ▷ *verb* (***provided, providing***) **1** to supply. **2** said of a circumstance or situation, etc: to offer (a specified thing) □ *provide enjoyment* □ *provide an opportunity*. **3** *chiefly law* to stipulate or require (that something should be done, etc). • **provider** *noun*. ◷ 15c: from Latin *providere* to see ahead.

■ **provide against** or **for something** to be prepared for (an unexpected contingency, an emergency, etc).

■ **provide for someone** or **something** to support or keep (a dependant, etc), or arrange for the means to do so □ *provided for his old age*.

■ **provide for something** *chiefly law* to specify it as a requirement, or enable it to be done.

provided and **providing** ▷ *conj* **1** on the condition or understanding (that a specified thing happens, etc) □ *You can come in provided you don't smoke*. **2** if and only if □ *Providing Joe gives me the money, I'll go out tonight*.

providence /'prɒvɪdəns/ ▷ *noun* **1 a** a mysterious power or force that operates to keep one from harm, etc; **b** the benevolent foresight of God. **2** (**Providence**) God or Nature regarded as an all-seeing protector of the world. **3** the quality of being provident; prudent foresight or thrifty planning. ◷ 14c: French, from Latin *providentia* foresight, from *providere* to provide.

provident /'prɒvɪdənt/ ▷ *adj* **1** having foresight and making provisions for the future. **2** careful and thrifty; frugal. • **providently** *adverb*.

providential /prɒvɪ'denʃəl/ ▷ *adj* due to providence; fortunate; lucky; opportune. • **providentially** *adverb*.

province /'prɒvɪns/ ▷ *noun* **1** an administrative division of a country. **2** *historical* in the Roman empire: a territory outside Italy, governed by Rome as part of its empire. **3** someone's allotted range of duties or field of knowledge or experience, etc. **4** (**the provinces**) the parts of a country away from the capital, typically thought of as culturally backward. **5** the district over which a bishop has jurisdiction. ◷ 14c: French, from Latin *provincia* official charge.

provincial /prə'vɪnʃəl/ ▷ *adj* **1** belonging or relating to a province. **2** relating to the parts of a country away from the capital □ *a provincial accent*. **3** *derog* supposedly typical of provinces in being culturally backward, unsophisticated or narrow in outlook □ *provincial attitudes*. • **provinciality** *noun*. • **provincialize** or **provincialise** *verb*. • **provincially** *adverb*. ◷ 14c: French, from Latin *provincialis*, from *provincia* province.

provincialism ▷ *noun* **1** being provincial. **2** the altitude, behaviour or speech peculiar to a province or country district. **3** a local expression. **4** ignorance and narrowness of interests. • **provincialist** *noun*.

proving-ground ▷ *noun* an area of scientific work where theories are tested; an area where something is tried out for the first time. ◷ 19c.

provirus ▻ *noun, biol* the form of a virus when it is integrated into the DNA of a host cell. • **proviral** *adj.* ⓒ 1950s.

provision /prəˈvɪʒən/ ▻ *noun* **1** the act or process of providing. **2** something provided or made available; facilities. **3** preparations; measures taken in advance ☐ *make provision for the future.* **4** (**provisions**) food and other necessities. **5** *law* a condition or requirement; a clause stipulating or enabling something. ▻ *verb* (***provisioned***, ***provisioning***) to supply (eg an army, country, boat) with food. ⓒ 14c: French, from Latin *provisio* forethought, from *providere* to provide.

Provisional ▻ *adj* belonging or relating to the breakaway wing of the Official IRA which advocates terrorism as the way to bring about Irish unity. ▻ *noun* a member of the Provisional IRA. See also PROVO.

provisional /prəˈvɪʒənəl/ ▻ *adj* temporary; for the time being or immediate purposes only; liable to be altered. • **provisionally** *adverb.*

proviso /prəˈvaɪzoʊ/ ▻ *noun* (***provisos***) **1** a condition or stipulation. **2** *law* a clause stating a condition. ⓒ 15c: from Latin *proviso quod* it being provided that.

provisory /prəˈvaɪzərɪ/ ▻ *adj* **1** containing a proviso or condition; conditional. **2** making provision for the time being; temporary. ⓒ 17c.

Provo /ˈproʊvoʊ/ *colloq* ▻ *noun* (***Provos***) a PROVISIONAL ▻ *adj* PROVISIONAL. ⓒ 1970s.

provocateur see AGENT PROVOCATEUR

provocation /prɒvəˈkeɪʃən/ ▻ *noun* **1** the act of provoking or state of being provoked; incitement. **2** a cause of anger, irritation or indignation. ⓒ 15c: from Latin *provocatio, provocationis* calling forth or challenge.

provocative /prəˈvɒkətɪv/ ▻ *adj* **1** tending or intended to cause anger; deliberately infuriating. **2** said of a debate, argument, etc: controversial, but often stimulating. **3** sexually arousing or stimulating, especially by design. • **provocatively** *adverb.* ⓒ 17c.

provoke /prəˈvoʊk/ ▻ *verb* (***provoked***, ***provoking***) **1** to annoy or infuriate someone, especially deliberately. **2** to incite or goad. **3** to rouse (someone's anger, etc). **4** to cause, stir up or bring about something ☐ *provoked a storm of protest.* • **provoking** *adj.* • **provokingly** *adverb.* ⓒ 15c: from Latin *provocare* to call forth.

provost /ˈprɒvəst/ ▻ *noun* **1** the head of some university colleges. **2** in Scotland: **a** the chief councillor of a district council; **b** *formerly* the chief magistrate of a burgh. **3** the senior cleric in a cathedral or collegiate church. ⓒ Anglo-Saxon *profost*: influenced by Latin *propositus* placed at the head.

provost marshal ▻ *noun* an officer in charge of military police. ⓒ 16c.

prow /praʊ/ ▻ *noun* the projecting front part of a ship; the BOW³. ⓒ 16c: from French *proue*, from Latin *prora*.

prowess /ˈpraʊɛs/ ▻ *noun* **1** skill; ability; expertise. **2** valour; dauntlessness. ⓒ 13c: from French *proesse*, from *prou* worthy.

prowl /praʊl/ ▻ *verb* (***prowled***, ***prowling***) *intr* **1** to go about stealthily, eg in search of prey ☐ *prowled the streets looking for likely victims.* **2** *intr* to pace restlessly. ▻ *noun* an act of prowling. • **prowler** *noun.* • **on the prowl 1** lurking about menacingly. **2** looking for a sexual partner. ⓒ 14c.

prox. ▻ *abbreviation* proximo.

proxemics /prɒkˈsiːmɪks/ ▻ *singular noun, sociol* the study of how people use physical space as an aspect of non-verbal communication, concerned with the intimate, personal, social and public distances that individuals, classes and cultures maintain when interacting. ⓒ 1960s: from PROXIMITY, modelled on PHONEMICS, etc.

Proxima Centauri ▻ *noun, astron* the closest star to the Sun, and a faint companion to the double star Alpha Centauri in the constellation Centaurus.

proximal /ˈprɒksɪməl/ ▻ *noun, biol* at the near, inner or attached end. • **proximally** *adverb.* Compare DISTAL. ⓒ 19c: from Latin *proximus* nearest.

proximate /ˈprɒksɪmət/ ▻ *adj* **1** nearest. **2** immediately before or after in time, place or chronology. • **proximately** *adverb.* ⓒ 16c: from Latin *proximare, proximatum* to approach, from *proximus* nearest.

proximity /prɒkˈsɪmɪtɪ/ ▻ *noun* (***proximities***) nearness; closeness in space or time. ⓒ 15c: from Latin *proximitas*, from *proximus* next.

proximo /ˈprɒksɪmoʊ/ ▻ *adverb* (abbreviation **prox.**) used mainly in formal correspondence: in or during the next month. Compare ULTIMO. ⓒ 19c: from Latin *proximo mense* during the next month.

proxy /ˈprɒksɪ/ ▻ *noun* (***proxies***) **1 a** a person authorized to act or vote on another's behalf; **b** the agency of such a person; **c** *as adj* ☐ *a proxy vote.* **2 a** the authority to act or vote for someone else; **b** a document granting this. ⓒ 15c: a contraction of PROCURACY.

Prozac /ˈproʊzak/ ▻ *noun, trademark* an anti-depressant drug that increases the levels of serotonin in the central nervous system.

PRS ▻ *abbreviation* **1** Performing Rights Society. **2** President of the Royal Society.

prude /pruːd/ ▻ *noun* someone who is, or affects to be, shocked by improper behaviour, mention of sexual matters, etc; a prim or priggish person. • **prudery** *noun.* • **prudish** *adj.* • **prudishness** *noun.* ⓒ 18c: French, from *prude femme* respectable woman.

prudent /ˈpruːdənt/ ▻ *adj* **1** wise or careful in conduct. **2** shrewd or thrifty in planning ahead. **3** wary; discreet. • **prudence** *noun.* • **prudently** *adverb.* ⓒ 14c: from Latin *prudens, prudentis*, from *providens* seeing ahead.

prudential /prʊˈdɛnʃəl/ ▻ *adj, old use* characterized by or exercising careful forethought. • **prudentially** *adverb.* ⓒ 17c.

prune¹ ▻ *verb* (***pruned***, ***pruning***) **1** to cut off (branches, etc) from (a tree or shrub) in order to stimulate its growth, improve the production of fruit or flowers, etc. **2** to cut out (superfluous matter) from (a piece of writing, etc); to trim or edit. **3** to cut back on (expenses, etc). ▻ *noun* an act of pruning. • **pruner** *noun.* ⓒ 15c: from French *proignier*, from *provigner* to prune vines.

prune² ▻ *noun* **1** a PLUM that has been preserved by drying, which gives it a black wrinkled appearance. **2** *colloq* a silly foolish person. ⓒ 14c: French, from Latin *prunum* plum.

prunella /pruːˈnɛlə/ ▻ *noun* a strong silk or woollen material, formerly used for academic and clerical gowns and women's shoes. ⓒ 17c.

pruning hook ▻ *noun* a garden tool with a curved blade, used for pruning, etc.

prurient /ˈprʊərɪənt/ ▻ *adj* **1** unhealthily or excessively interested in sexual matters. **2** tending to arouse such unhealthy interest. • **prurience** *noun.* • **pruriently** *adverb.* ⓒ 18c: from Latin *pruriens, prurientis* itching or lusting after.

prurigo /prʊəˈraɪgoʊ/ ▻ *noun* a skin disease characterized by red, slightly raised, intensely itchy patches. ⓒ 17c: Latin, meaning 'an itching'.

pruritus /prʊəˈraɪtəs/ ▻ *noun, medicine* itching. • **pruritic** /-ˈrɪtɪk/ *adj.* ⓒ 17c: Latin, from *prurire* to itch.

Prussian /ˈprʌʃən/ *historical* ▻ *adj* **1** belonging or relating to Prussia, a former N European state, or its inhabitants. **2** belonging or relating to this states militaristic tradition. ▻ *noun* a citizen or inhabitant of, or person born in, Prussia. ⓒ 16c.

Prussian blue ▻ *noun* **1** *chem* a dark blue crystalline compound, used as a pigment. **2** the colour of this. ▻ *adj* (**Prussian-blue**) Prussian-blue coloured.

prussic acid see under HYDROGEN CYANIDE

pry¹ ▻ *verb* (***pries, pried, prying***) *intr* **1** (*also* **pry into something**) to investigate, especially the personal affairs of others; to nose or snoop. **2** to peer or peep inquisitively. ▻ *noun* (***pries***) **1** the act of prying. **2** a nosey or inquisitive person. ⓔ 14c.

pry² ▻ *verb* (***pries, pried, prying***) *N Amer, especially US* to prise. ⓔ 19c.

PS ▻ *abbreviation* postscript.

PSA ▻ *abbreviation, Brit* Property Services Agency.

psalm /sɑːm/ ▻ *noun* a sacred song, especially one from the Book of Psalms in the Old Testament. ⓔ 10c: from Latin *psalmus*, from Greek *psalmos* a song sung to a harp, from *psallein* to play the harp.

psalmist /'sɑːmɪst/ ▻ *noun* a composer of psalms.

psalmody /'sɑːmədɪ, 'sal-/ ▻ *noun* (***psalmodies***) **1** the art of singing psalms. **2** a collected body of psalms. ⓔ 14c: from Greek *psalmos* psalm + *oide* song.

Psalms ▻ *noun* the title of a book in the Old Testament. See table at BIBLE.

psalter /'sɔːltə(r)/ ▻ *noun* **1** the PSALMS, often applied to a metrical version intended for singing. **2** a book containing the Biblical psalms. ⓔ 10c: from Latin *psalterium*, from Greek *psalterion* stringed instrument.

psaltery /'sɔːltərɪ/ ▻ *noun* (***psalteries***) *historical, music* a stringed instrument similar to a ZITHER, played by plucking. ⓔ 14c: see PSALTER.

p's and q's /piːzən'kjuːz/ ▻ *noun* • **watch** or **mind one's p's and q's** to be one one's best behaviour, especially by being careful not to use inappropriate language.

PSBR ▻ *abbreviation, econ* public sector borrowing requirement, the money needed by the public sector to finance services, etc not covered by revenue.

psephology /sɪ'fɒlədʒɪ/ ▻ *noun* the statistical study of elections and voting patterns. • **psephological** /siːfə'lɒdʒɪkəl, sɛfə-/ *adj*. • **psephologically** *adverb*. • **psephologist** *noun*. ⓔ 1950s: from Greek *psephos* a pebble or vote + -LOGY.

pseud /sjuːd, suːd/ *Brit colloq* ▻ *noun* a pretentious person; a bogus intellectual; a phoney. ▻ *adj* bogus, sham or phoney. ⓔ 1960s: from PSEUDO-.

pseudo ▻ *adj, colloq* false; sham; phoney.

pseudo- /'sjuːdoʊ, 'suːdoʊ/ or (before a vowel) **pseud-** ▻ *combining form, forming nouns and adjectives, denoting* **1** false; pretending to be something □ *pseudo-intellectuals*. **2** deceptively resembling □ *pseudo-scientific jargon*. ⓔ From Greek *pseudes* false.

pseudocarp /'sjuːdoʊkɑːp/ ▻ *noun, bot* a fruit that is formed from other parts of the flower in addition to the ovary, eg the strawberry, which includes the receptacle. *Non-technical equivalent* **false fruit**. ⓔ 19c: from Greek *karpos* fruit.

pseudocyesis /sjuːdoʊsaɪ'iːsɪs/ ▻ *noun, medicine* FALSE PREGNANCY. Also called **phantom pregnancy**. ⓔ 19c: from *pseudo-* + Greek *cyesis* pregnancy.

pseudomorph /'sjuːdoʊmɔːf/ ▻ *noun* **1** a crystal, etc that has undergone a chemical or other change so that it takes on a form that is more usual in another. **2** any false or deceptive form. • **pseudomorphic** /-'mɔːfɪk/ *adj*. • **pseudomorphism** /-'mɔːfɪzəm/ *noun*. ⓔ 19c: from Greek *morphe* form.

pseudonym /'sjuːdənɪm/ ▻ *noun* a false or assumed name, especially one used by an author; a pen name or nom de plume. • **pseudonymous** /-'dɒnɪməs/ *adj*. ⓔ 19c: from PSEUDO- 1 + Greek *onyma* name.

pseudopodium /sjuːdoʊ'poʊdɪəm/ ▻ *noun* (***pseudopodia*** /-ɪə/) *zool* any of a number of temporary lobe-like protrusions from the cell of a PROTOZOAN, produced by the streaming of cytoplasm and used to aid locomotion and to engulf food particles. ⓔ 19c: from PSEUDO-² + Greek *pous, podos* foot.

psi¹ /'psaɪ/ ▻ *noun* the twenty-third letter of the Greek alphabet. See table at GREEK ALPHABET.

psi² ▻ *abbreviation* pounds per square inch, a unit of pressure measurement.

psilocybin /saɪlə'saɪbɪn/ ▻ *noun* the substance found in certain mushrooms or toadstools which produces hallucinogenic effects similar to those of LSD. Formula $C_{12}H_{17}N_2O_4P$. ⓔ 1950s: German, from Latin *psilocybe*, form Greek *psilos* bare + *kybe* head.

psittacine /'sɪtəsaɪn/ ▻ *adj* belonging or relating to or resembling a parrot. ⓔ 19c: from Latin *psittacus* a parrot.

psittacosis /sɪtə'koʊsɪs/ ▻ *noun, pathol* a contagious disease of birds, especially parrots, that is caused by chlamydiae (see CHLAMYDIA) and which can be transmitted to human beings as a form of pneumonia. See also ORNITHOSIS. ⓔ 19c: Latin, from Greek *psittakos* parrot.

psoriasis /sə'raɪəsɪs/ ▻ *noun, pathol*, a common non-contagious skin disease of unknown cause, characterized by red patches covered with white scales, mainly on the elbows, knees, scalp and torso. ⓔ 17c: Latin, from Greek, from *psora* itch.

psst or **pst** /pst/ ▻ *exclamation* used to draw someone's attention quietly or surreptitiously. ⓔ 1920s.

PSV ▻ *abbreviation, Brit* public service vehicle, eg a bus.

psych or **psyche** /saɪk/ ▻ *verb* (***psyched, psyching***) *colloq* to psychoanalyse someone. ⓔ Early 20c: a shortening of PSYCHOANALYSE and other related words.

▪ **psych someone out** to undermine the confidence of (an opponent, etc); to intimidate or demoralize them.

▪ **psych oneself** or **someone up** to prepare or steel oneself, or them, for a challenge, etc.

psych- see PSYCHO-

psyche /'saɪkɪ/ ▻ *noun* (***psyches***) the mind or spirit, especially with regard to the deep feelings and attitudes that account for someone's opinions and behaviour. ⓔ 17c: Greek, meaning 'breath' or 'life'.

psychedelia /saɪkɪ'diːlɪə/ ▻ *plural noun* psychedelic items such as posters paintings, etc collectivley or generally. ⓔ 1960s.

psychedelic /saɪkə'dɛlɪk/ ▻ *adj* **1 a** said of a drug, especially LSD: inducing a state of altered consciousness characterized by an increase in perception, eg of colour, sound, etc, hallucinations, and an intensifying of emotions that will sometimes reveal significant underlying motivations; **b** said of an event or experience, etc: resembling such effects; bizarre □ *had a psychedelic vision*; **c** belonging or relating to this kind of drug, experience, etc □ *the psychedelic 60s*. **2** said of perceived phenomena, eg colour, music, etc: startlingly clear and vivid, often with a complex dazzling pattern. • **psychedelically** *adverb*. ⓔ 1950s: from PSYCHE + Greek *delos* clear.

psychedelic art ▻ *noun* an art style influenced by the prevalence of hallucinatory drugs, especially LSD, with typical designs featuring abstract swirls of intense colour with curvilinear calligraphy reminiscent of ART NOUVEAU. ⓔ 1960s.

psychiatry /saɪ'kaɪətrɪ/ ▻ *noun* the branch of medicine concerned with the study, diagnosis, treatment and prevention of mental and emotional disorders such as psychoses, neuroses, schizophrenia, depression, eating disorders, mental handicap, etc. • **psychiatric** /saɪkɪ'atrɪk/ *adj*. • **psychiatrist** *noun*. ⓔ 19c: from PSYCHE + Greek *iatros* doctor.

psychic /ˈsaɪkɪk/ ▻ *adj* **1** (*also* **psychical**) relating to mental processes or experiences that are not scientifically explainable, eg telepathy. **2** said of a person: sensitive to influences that produce such experiences; having mental powers that are not scientifically explainable. ▻ *noun* someone who possesses such powers. ⓒ 19c: from Greek *psychikos* relating to the PSYCHE.

psycho /ˈsaɪkoʊ/ *colloq* ▻ *noun* (***psychos*** /ˈsaɪkoʊz/) a psychopath. ▻ *adj* psychopathic. ⓒ 1940s; 1920s as shortening of PSYCHOANALYSIS.

psycho- /ˈsaɪkoʊ/ or (before a vowel) **psych-** /saɪk/ ▻ *combining form, denoting* the mind and its workings. ⓒ Greek: see PSYCHE.

psychoactive ▻ *adj* said of a drug: affecting the brain and influencing behaviour. Also called **psychotropic**. ⓒ 1960s.

psychoanalyse or (*US*) **psychoanalyze** ▻ *verb* to examine or treat someone by psychoanalysis. ⓒ Early 20c.

psychoanalysis ▻ *noun, psychol* a theory and method of treatment for mental and emotional disorders, which explores the effects of unconscious motivation and conflict on a person's behaviour. • **psychoanalyst** *noun*. • **psychoanalytic** or **psychoanalytical** *adj*. ⓒ 19c: from French *psychoanalyse*; pioneered by the Austrian neurologist Sigmund Freud (1856–1939).

psychoanalytic criticism ▻ *noun* an approach to literary criticism using the techniques and insights of psychoanalysis, making the assumption that the writer's unconscious desires may shape the text, etc.

psychobabble ▻ *noun, colloq* language that is impossible or very difficult to understand because it is too full of popular psychological jargon. ⓒ 1970s.

psychodrama ▻ *noun, psychol* a form of psychotherapy in which, by acting out real-life situations, a patient learns new ways of dealing with both emotional and interpersonal problems. ⓒ 1930s.

psychodynamics ▻ *singular noun, psychol* the study of mental and emotional forces, their source in past experience, and their effect. • **psychodynamic** *adj*. ⓒ 19c.

psychogenesis ▻ *noun* the study of the origin and development of the mind. • **psychogenetic** or **psychogenetically** *adj*. ⓒ 19c.

psychogenic ▻ *adj* said of symptoms, etc: originating in the mind. • **psychogenically** *adverb*. ⓒ 19c.

psychokinesis ▻ *noun* the apparent power to move objects, etc by non-physical means. ⓒ 19c.

psycholinguistics ▻ *singular noun* the psychological study of language development and the relationship between language and mental processes, eg memory, mental disorders, etc. ⓒ 1930s.

psychological /saɪkəˈlɒdʒɪkəl/ ▻ *adj* **1** relating or referring to PSYCHOLOGY. **2** relating or referring to the mind or mental processes. • **psychologically** *adverb*.

psychological moment ▻ *noun* the most suitable moment for achieving a particular purpose.

psychological warfare ▻ *noun* the use of propaganda and other methods in war-time to influence enemy opinion and sap enemy morale. ⓒ 1940s.

psychology /saɪˈkɒlədʒɪ/ ▻ *noun* **1** the scientific study of the mind and behaviour of humans and animals. **2** the mental attitudes and associated behaviour characteristic of a certain individual or group. **3** the ability to understand how people's minds work, useful when trying to influence them. • **psychologist** *noun*. ⓒ 17c; see PSYCHO-.

psychometrics ▻ *singular noun, psychol* the branch of psychology concerned with the measurement of psychological characteristics, especially intelligence, personality and mood states. ⓒ 1920s.

psychopath /ˈsaɪkəpaθ/ ▻ *noun* **1** *technical* someone with a personality disorder characterized by extreme callousness, who is liable to behave antisocially or violently in getting their own way, without any feelings of remorse. **2** *colloq* someone who is dangerously unstable mentally or emotionally. • **psychopathic** *adj*. • **psychopathically** *adverb*. ⓒ 19c.

psychopathology ▻ *noun, medicine* **1** the scientific study of mental disorders, as opposed to the treatment of such disorders. **2** the symptoms of a mental disorder.

psychopathy /saɪˈkɒpəθɪ/ ▻ *noun, psychol* a personality disorder characterized by an inability to form close relationships, the rejection of authority, and little or no guilt for antisocial behaviour. ⓒ 19c.

psychosexual ▻ *adj* belonging or relating to the psychological aspects of sex, eg sexual fantasies. ⓒ 19c.

psychosis /saɪˈkoʊsɪs/ ▻ *noun* (***psychoses*** /-siːz/) *psychol* one of the two divisions of psychiatric disorders, characterized by a loss of contact with reality, in the form of delusions or hallucinations and belief that only one's own actions are rational. Compare NEUROSIS. ⓒ 19c: from Greek, meaning 'animation', taken in modern use to mean 'condition of the psyche'.

psychosocial ▻ *adj* belonging or relating to matters which are both psychological and social. ⓒ 19c.

psychosomatic ▻ *adj, medicine* said of physical symptoms or disorders: strongly associated with psychological factors, especially mental stress, such as peptic ulcers and certain forms of eczema. • **psychosomatically** *adverb*. ⓒ 1930s.

psychosurgery ▻ *noun* brain surgery that is performed with the aim of treating a mental disorder. ⓒ 1930s.

psychotherapist ▻ *noun* an expert in psychotherapy.

psychotherapy ▻ *noun* the treatment of mental disorders and emotional and behavioural problems by psychological means, rather than by drugs or surgery. See also PSYCHOANALYSIS, GESTALT THERAPY. ⓒ 19c.

psychotic ▻ *adj* relating to or involving a PSYCHOSIS. ▻ *noun* someone suffering from a psychosis. • **psychotically** *adverb*.

psychotropic ▻ *adj* PSYCHOACTIVE. ⓒ 1950s.

PT ▻ *abbreviation* physical training.

Pt[1] ▻ *abbreviation* in placenames, etc: Port.

Pt[2] ▻ *symbol, chem* platinum.

pt ▻ *abbreviation* **1** part. **2** pint. **3** point.

PTA ▻ *abbreviation* Parent–Teacher Association.

ptarmigan /ˈtɑːmɪgən/ ▻ *noun* a mountain-dwelling game-bird with white winter plumage. ⓒ 16c: from Scottish Gaelic *tàrmachan*; the *p* was wrongly added under the influence of Greek words beginning with *pt-*.

Pte ▻ *abbreviation, military* Private, the title for an ordinary soldier.

-ptera /ptərə/ *zool* ▻ *combining form, forming plural nouns, denoting* organisms with a specified type or number of wings or wing-like parts. ⓒ From Greek *pteron* wing.

pteridophyte /ˈtɛrɪdəfaɪt/ ▻ *noun, bot* any member of the division of vascular plants **Pteridophyta** /–ˈdɒfɪtə/ which do not produce seeds, including ferns, clubmosses and horsetails. ⓒ 19c: from Greek *pteris, pteridos* fern + *phyton* plant.

pterodactyl /tɛrəˈdaktɪl/ ▻ *noun* a former name for PTEROSAUR. ⓒ 19c: from Greek *pteron* wing + *daktylos* finger.

pterosaur /ˈtɛrəsɔː(r)/ ▻ *noun* any of the order of extinct flying reptiles **Pterosauria** with narrow leathery wings, known from the late Triassic to the end of the Cretaceous period. Formerly called **pterodactyl**. ⓒ 19c: from Greek *pteron* wing + -SAUR.

PTFE ▷ *abbreviation* polytetrafluoroethylene.

PTO or **pto** ▷ *abbreviation* please turn over.

ptomaine /'toʊmeɪn/ ▷ *noun, biochem* any of a group of nitrogenous organic compounds, some of which are poisonous, produced during the bacterial decomposition of dead animal and plant matter. ⓒ 19c: from Italian *ptomaina*, from Greek *ptoma* corpse.

Pty ▷ *abbreviation* proprietary.

ptyalin /'taɪəlɪn/ ▷ *noun, biochem* in mammals: an enzyme present in the saliva that is responsible for the initial stages of the breakdown of starch. ⓒ 19c: from Greek *ptyalon* spittle.

Pu ▷ *symbol, chem* plutonium.

pub *colloq* ▷ *noun* a PUBLIC HOUSE. ▷ *verb* (***pubbed, pubbing***) *intr, colloq* to visit pubs. ⓒ 19c.

pub crawl ▷ *noun, colloq* an occasion of visiting, and drinking in, a number of pubs in succession.

puberty /'pjuːbətɪ/ ▷ *noun, biol* in humans and other primates: the onset of sexual maturity, when the secondary sexual characteristics appear and the reproductive organs become functional. ⓒ 14c: from Latin *pubertas* the age of maturity, from *puber* youth.

pubes /'pjuːbiːz/ ▷ *noun* (*plural* ***pubes***) **1** *anatomy* the pubic region of the lower abdomen; the groin. **2** (*also colloq treated as plural noun* /pjuːbz/) the hair that grows on this part from puberty onward. See also PUBIS. ⓒ 16c: Latin.

pubescence /pjuː'bɛsəns/ ▷ *noun* **1** the onset of puberty. **2** *biol* a soft downy covering on plants and animals. • **pubescent** *adj*. ⓒ 17c: French, from Latin *pubescere* to reach puberty.

pubic /'pjuːbɪk/ ▷ *adj* belonging or relating to the pubis or pubes.

pubis /'pjuːbɪs/ ▷ *noun* (*plural* ***pubes*** /-biːz/) *anatomy* in most vertebrates: one of the two bones forming the lower front part of each side of the pelvis. ⓒ 16c: shortened from Latin *os pubis* bone of the pubes.

public /'pʌblɪk/ ▷ *adj* **1** relating to or concerning all the people of a country or community □ *public health* □ *public opinion*. **2** relating to the organization and administration of a community. **3** provided for the use of the community □ *public library* □ *public toilet*. **4** well known through exposure in the media □ *a famous public figure*. **5** made, done or held, etc openly, for all to see, hear or participate in □ *a public inquiry*. **6** known to all □ *public knowledge* □ *make one's views public*. **7** watched or attended by an audience, spectators, etc. **8** open to view; not private or secluded □ *It's too public here*. **9** provided by or run by central or local government □ *under public ownership*. ▷ *singular or plural noun* **1** the people or community. **2** a particular class of people □ *the concert-going public*. **3** an author's or performer's, etc audience or group of devotees □ *mustn't disappoint my public*. • **go public 1** *business* to become a public company. **2** to make something previously private known to everyone. • **in public** in the presence of other people. • **in the public eye** said of a person, etc: well known through media exposure. ⓒ 15c: from Latin *publicus*, from *populus* people.

> ***public***
>
> • **Public** can be treated as a singular or plural noun; to reinforce the plural the phrase **members of the public** is often used □ *The public welcome the way we are treating teachers as a professional body* □ *You can hardly blame manufacturers for turning out what the public seems to want* □ *Most members of the public understand this fact.*

public-address system ▷ *noun* (abbreviation **PA system** or **PA**) a system of microphones, amplifiers and loudspeakers, used to communicate public announcements, etc over a large area. ⓒ 1920s.

publican /'pʌblɪkən/ ▷ *noun* **1** *Brit* the keeper of a PUBLIC HOUSE. **2** *Bible, etc* a tax-collector. ⓒ 18c in sense 1; 13c in sense 2: from Latin *publicanus* tax-farmer, from *publicum* the public revenue.

publication /pʌblɪ'keɪʃən/ ▷ *noun* **1** the act of publishing a printed work; the process of publishing or of being published. **2** a book, magazine, newspaper or other printed and published work. **3** the act of making something known to the public.

public bar ▷ *noun* in a public house: a bar which is less well furnished and serves drinks more cheaply than a lounge bar (see LOUNGE *noun* 4).

public company and **public limited company** (abbreviation **PLC** or **plc**) ▷ *noun, business* a company whose shares are available for purchase on the open market by the public. Compare LIMITED COMPANY.

public convenience ▷ *noun* a public toilet.

public enemy ▷ *noun* someone whose behaviour threatens the community, especially a criminal.

public health inspector ▷ *noun* a person whose job is to maintain the health of a community, eg by overseeing sanitation, drainage, hygienic food preparation, etc. See also SANITARY INSPECTOR.

public holiday ▷ *noun* a day kept as an official holiday, on which businesses, etc are usually closed.

public house ▷ *noun* **1** *Brit* an establishment licensed to sell alcoholic drinks for consumption on the premises. Often shortened to PUB. **2** an inn, tavern or small hotel. ⓒ 17c; 16c in obsolete sense 'a building open to the public'.

public image see IMAGE

public international law see INTERNATIONAL LAW

publicity /pʌ'blɪsɪtɪ/ ▷ *noun* **1** advertising or other activity designed to rouse public interest in something. **2** public interest attracted in this way. **3** the condition of being the object of public attention. ⓒ 18c.

publicize or **publicise** /'pʌblɪsaɪz/ ▷ *verb* (***publicized, publicizing***) **1** to make something generally or widely known. **2** to advertise. ⓒ 1920s.

public lending right ▷ *noun* (abbreviation **PLR**) an author's right to payment when their books are borrowed from public libraries.

public library ▷ *noun* a library which any member of the public can join and borrow books, records, etc from.

public limited company see PUBLIC COMPANY

public nuisance ▷ *noun* **1** an illegal act that causes trouble or danger to the general public. **2** *informal* an irritating or annoying person.

public prosecutor ▷ *noun, law* a public official whose job is to prosecute those charged with criminal offences.

public purse ▷ *noun* the nation's finances or wealth.

public relations (abbreviation **PR**) *singular or plural noun* the process of creating a good relationship between an organization, etc and the public, especially with regard to reputation, communication of information, etc. ▷ *singular noun* the department within an organization that is responsible for this. Also *as adj* □ *public relations department*. ⓒ 19c.

public school ▷ *noun* **1** in the UK: a secondary school, especially a boarding school run independently of the state, financed by endowments and by pupils' fees. **2** in the US: a school run by a public authority. *Brit equivalent* STATE SCHOOL. Compare PRIVATE SCHOOL, GRANT-MAINTAINED.

public sector ▻ *noun* the part of a country's economy which consists of nationalized industries and of institutions and services run by the state or local authorities.

public servant ▻ *noun* an elected or appointed holder of public office; a government employee.

public spending ▻ *noun* spending by a government or local authority, financed either by tax revenues or by borrowing.

public-spirited ▻ *adj* acting from or showing concern for the general good of the whole community.

public utility ▻ *noun* a company which provides a supply eg of gas, water or electricity, or other service, for a community.

public works ▻ *noun* buildings, roads, etc built by the state for public use.

publish /'pʌblɪʃ/ ▻ *verb* (***publishes***, ***published***, ***publishing***) *tr & intr* **1** to prepare, produce and distribute (printed material, computer software, etc) for sale to the public. **2** *tr & intr* said of an author: to have (their work) published. **3** to publish the work of (an author). **4** to announce something publicly. **5** *law* to circulate (a libel). ⓒ 14c: from French *publier*, from Latin *publicare* to make public.

publisher ▻ *noun* **1** a person or company engaged in the business of publishing books, newspapers, music, software, etc. **2** *N Amer* a newspaper proprietor.

publishing ▻ *noun* the activity or trade of a publisher or publishers, including the commissioning, production and marketing of material, eg books, magazines, newspapers, audio-visual material, computer-based information, etc.

pub quiz ▻ *noun* a quiz held in a pub, often on a regular basis, where teams of contestants try to answer questions on various subjects, eg general knowledge, sport, music, current affairs, etc. It is usually played in good spirits and the winners often receive a small prize.

puce /pjuːs/ ▻ *noun* a colour anywhere in the range between deep purplish-pink and purplish-brown. ▻ *adj* puce-coloured. ⓒ 18c: from French *couleur de puce* flea colour.

puck¹ ▻ *noun* a goblin or mischievous sprite. • **puckish** *adj*. ⓒ Anglo-Saxon *puca*.

puck² ▻ *noun, sport* **1** a thick disc of hard rubber used in ice hockey instead of a ball. **2** a hit of the ball in hurling. ▻ *verb* (***pucked***, ***pucking***) to hit (the ball) in hurling. ⓒ 19c.

pucker /'pʌkə(r)/ ▻ *verb* (***puckered***, ***puckering***) *tr & intr* to gather into creases, folds or wrinkles; to wrinkle. ▻ *noun* a wrinkle, fold or crease. ⓒ 16c.

pud /pʊd/ ▻ *noun, Brit colloq* pudding. ⓒ 18c.

pudding /'pʊdɪŋ/ ▻ *noun* **1** any of several sweet or savoury foods usually made with flour and eggs and cooked by steaming, boiling or baking. Often *in compounds* □ *rice pudding* □ *steak and kidney pudding*. **2** **a** any sweet food served as dessert; **b** the dessert course. **3** *in compounds* a type of sausage made with minced meat, spices, blood, oatmeal, etc □ *black pudding*. ⓒ 13c as *poding* a kind of sausage.

puddle /'pʌdəl/ ▻ *noun* **1** a small pool, especially one of rainwater on the road. **2** (*also* **puddle clay**) a non-porous watertight material consisting of thoroughly mixed clay, sand and water. ▻ *verb* (***puddled***, ***puddling***) **1** to make something watertight by means of puddle clay. **2** to knead (clay, sand and water) to make puddle clay. **3** *metallurgy* to produce (wrought iron) from molten pig by PUDDLING. **4** *intr* **a** to wallow in mud or shallow water; **b** to occupy oneself in something messy, or something not very productive. ⓒ 14c in sense 2 as *podel*: probably from Anglo-Saxon *pudd* ditch.

puddling ▻ *noun* the original process for converting pig iron into wrought iron by melting it in a furnace and stirring to remove carbon.

pudenda /pjuː'dɛndə/ ▻ *plural noun* (*rarely singular* ***pudendum*** /-dəm/) the external sexual organs, especially those of a woman. ⓒ 17c: Latin, literally 'things to be ashamed of', from *pudere* to be ashamed.

pudgy see PODGY

pueblo /'pwɛbloʊ/ ▻ *noun* (***pueblos***) in Spanish-speaking countries: a town or settlement. ⓒ 19c: Spanish, literally 'people', from Latin *populus* a people.

puerile /'pjʊəraɪl/ ▻ *adj* childish; silly; immature. • **puerility** /pjʊə'rɪlɪtɪ/ *noun*. ⓒ 17c: from Latin *puerilis*, from *puer* boy.

puerperal /pjʊ'ɜːpərəl/ ▻ *adj* **1** referring or relating to childbirth. **2** referring or relating to a woman who has just given birth. ⓒ 18c: from Latin *puerperium* childbirth, from *puerpera* a woman in labour.

puerperal fever ▻ *noun, pathol* fever accompanying blood-poisoning caused by infection of the uterus or vagina during or just after childbirth or miscarriage. ⓒ 18c.

puerperium /pjʊə'pɪərɪəm/ ▻ *noun, medicine* the period between childbirth and the return of the womb to its normal state, usually about six weeks. ⓒ 19c: Latin, from *puerpera* a woman in labour.

Puerto Rican /'pwɜːtə 'riːkən/ ▻ *adj* belonging or relating to Puerto Rico, the easternmost island of the Greater Antilles, or its inhabitants. ▻ *noun* a citizen or inhabitant of, or person born in, Puerto Rico. ⓒ 19c.

puff ▻ *noun* **1** **a** a small rush, gust or blast of air or wind, etc; **b** the sound made by it. **2** a small cloud of smoke, dust or steam emitted from something. **3** *colloq* breath □ *quite out of puff*. **4** an act of inhaling and exhaling smoke from a pipe or cigarette; a drag or draw. **5** *in compounds* a light pastry, often containing a sweet or savoury filling □ *jam puffs*. **6** a powder puff. **7** an item of publicity intended or serving as an advertisement. **8** *derog slang* a male homosexual. ▻ *verb* (***puffed***, ***puffing***) **1** *tr & intr* to blow or breathe in small blasts. **2** *intr* said of smoke or steam, etc: to emerge in small gusts or blasts. **3** *tr & intr* to inhale and exhale smoke from, or draw at (a cigarette, etc). **4** *intr* (*often* **puff along**) said of a train or boat, etc: to go along emitting puffs of steam. **5** *intr* to pant, or go along panting □ *puffing up the hill*. **6** (*often* **puff someone out**) *colloq* to leave them breathless after exertion. **7** *tr & intr* (*also* **puff out** or **up**) to swell or cause something to swell □ *puffed out its feathers*. **8** to praise something extravagantly by way of advertisement. ⓒ Anglo-Saxon *pyffan*.

puff adder ▻ *noun* any of various large thick-bodied vipers, native to Africa and the Middle East, which if alarmed emit a loud warning hiss and inflate their bodies with air. ⓒ 18c.

puffball ▻ *noun* **1** *bot* the spore-bearing structure of certain fungi, consisting of a hollow ball of white or beige fleshy tissue from which spores are released as puffs of fine dust through a hole in the top. **2** (*also* **puffball skirt**) *fashion* a tight-waisted full skirt gathered in at the hem so as to be shaped like a ball. ⓒ 17c; 1980s in sense 2.

puffed-out ▻ *noun, colloq* exhausted; out of breath.

puffed-up ▻ *adj, colloq* self-important; conceited.

puffer ▻ *noun* **1** *Scottish historical* a small steam-boat used to carry cargo around the west coast and Western Isles of Scotland. **2** someone or something which puffs.

puffer fish ▻ *noun, zool* any of several tropical fish capable of inflating their spine-covered bodies to become almost spherical, in response to attacks by predators.

puffin /'pʌfɪn/ ▻ *noun* a short stout black-and-white seabird of the AUK family, which has a large triangular bill with red, yellow and blue stripes. ⓒ 14c as *poffin*.

puff pastry ▷ *noun, cookery* light flaky pastry made with a high proportion of fat.

puffy ▷ *adj* (***puffier, puffiest***) swollen as a result of injury or ill health. • **puffily** *adverb*. • **puffiness** *noun*. ⓒ 17c.

pug¹ ▷ *noun* a small breed of dog with a compact body, a short coat, a flattened face with a wrinkled snout and a short curled tail. ⓒ 18c as *pug-dog*; 16c as a term of endearment: related to PUCK¹.

pug² ▷ *verb* (***pugged, pugging***) *building* **1** to mix (clay) with water so as to make it into a soft paste. **2** to pack with pugging. ⓒ 19c.

pugging ▷ *noun, building* clay, sawdust, plaster, etc put between floors to deaden sound.

pugilism /ˈpjuːdʒɪlɪzəm/ ▷ *noun, old use or facetious* the art or practice of boxing or prizefighting. • **pugilist** *noun*. ⓒ 18c: from Latin *pugil* boxer.

pugnacious /pʌgˈneɪʃəs/ ▷ *adj* given to fighting; quarrelsome, belligerent or combative. • **pugnaciously** *adverb*. • **pugnacity** /-ˈnasɪtɪ/ *noun*. ⓒ 17c: from Latin *pugnax, pugnacis*, from *pugnare* to fight.

pug nose ▷ *noun* a short upturned nose. • **pug-nosed** *adj*. ⓒ 18c: from PUG¹.

puisne /ˈpjuːnɪ/ ▷ *adj, law* said of a judge: junior; lesser in rank. ⓒ 17c: French *puisné* younger, from Latin *postea* after + *natus* born.

puissance /ˈpwiːsɑ̃ns/ ▷ *noun* **1** *showjumping* a competition that tests the horse's ability to jump high fences. **2** *chiefly poetic* power; strength. ⓒ 1950s in sense 1; 15c in sense 2: French.

puissant /ˈpwiːsɒnt; *US* ˈpjuːɪsənt/ ▷ *adj, old use, poetic* strong, mighty or powerful. ⓒ 15c: French, from Latin *posse* to be able or to have power.

puke /pjuːk/ *colloq* ▷ *verb* (***puked, puking***) *tr & intr* to vomit. ▷ *noun* **1** vomit. **2** an act of vomiting. **3** *chiefly US* a horrible person. ⓒ 16c: possibly imitating the sound.

pukeko /ˈpʊkəkoʊ/ ▷ *noun* (***pukekos***) a New Zealand wading bird with bright plumage. ⓒ 19c: Maori.

pukka /ˈpʌkə/ ▷ *adj, colloq* **1** superior; high-quality. **2** upper-class; well-bred. **3** genuine. ⓒ 17c: from Hindi *pakka* cooked, firm or ripe.

pulchritude /ˈpʌlkrɪtjuːd/ ▷ *noun, literary or formal* beauty of face and form. ⓒ 15c: from Latin *pulchritudo*, beauty, from *pulcher* beautiful.

pule /pjuːl/ ▷ *verb* (***puled, puling***) *tr & intr* to whimper or whine. • **puler** *noun*. • **puling** *noun, adj*. • **pulingly** *adverb*. • **puly** *adj*. ⓒ 16c: imitating the sound.

pull /pʊl/ ▷ *verb* (***pulled, pulling***) **1** *tr & intr* to grip something or someone strongly and draw or force it or them towards oneself; to tug or drag. **2** (*also* **pull something out** or **up**) to remove or extract (a cork, tooth, weeds, etc) with this action. **3** to operate (a trigger, lever or switch) with this action. **4** to draw (a trailer, etc). **5** to open or close (curtains or a blind). **6** (*often* **pull something on someone**) to produce (a weapon) as a threat to them. **7 a** *tr & intr* to row; **b** *intr* (*often* **pull away, off**, *etc*) said of a boat: to be rowed or made to move in a particular direction. **8** to draw (beer, etc) from a cask by operating a lever. **9** *intr* **a** said of a driver or vehicle: to steer or move (in a specified direction) ▫ *pulled right*; **b** said of a vehicle or its steering: (towards a specified direction), usually because of some defect. **10** *sport* in golf, cricket, snooker, etc: to hit (a ball) so that it veers off its intended course. **11** *intr* said of an engine or vehicle: to produce the required propelling power. **12** (*usually* **pull at** or **on something**) to inhale and exhale smoke from (a cigarette, etc); to draw or suck at it. **13** to attract (a crowd, votes, etc). **14** to strain (a muscle or tendon). **15** *printing* to print (a proof). **16** *tr & intr slang* to pick up (a sexual partner). ▷ *noun* **1** an act of pulling. **2** attraction; attracting force. **3** useful influence ▫ *has some pull with the education department*. **4** a drag at a pipe; a swallow of liquor, etc. **5** a tab, etc for pulling. **6** a stroke made with an oar. **7** *printing* a proof. **8** *slang* a sexual partner, especially a casual one. • **pull a fast one** to trick or cheat someone. • **pull one's punches** to be deliberately less hard-hitting than one might be. • **pull the other one** a dismissive expression used by the speaker to indicate that they are not being fooled by what has just been said ▫ *You've got a date with Brad Pitt? Pull the other one!* Other idioms containing 'pull' can be found under one of the other significant words, eg *pull someone's leg* is under LEG. • **pull someone up short 1** to check someone, often oneself. **2** to take them aback. ⓒ Anglo-Saxon *pullian* to pluck, draw or pull.

▪ **pull ahead of** or **away from someone** or **something 1** to get in front of them or it; to gain a lead over them or it. **2** to leave them or it behind.

▪ **pull something apart** or **to pieces 1** to rip or tear it; to reduce it to pieces. **2** to criticize it severely.

▪ **pull at something 1** to tug repeatedly down on it. **2** to execute strokes with (an oar). **3** see *verb* 12 above.

▪ **pull something back** to withdraw or or make it withdraw or retreat.

▪ **pull something down** to demolish (a building, etc).

▪ **pull in 1** said of a train: to arrive and halt at a station. **2** said of a driver or vehicle: to move to the side of the road.

▪ **pull someone in** *colloq* to arrest them.

▪ **pull something in** *slang* to make (money), especially a large amount.

▪ **pull something off** *colloq* to arrange or accomplish it successfully ▫ *pull off a deal*.

▪ **pull something on** to put on (an item of clothing) hastily.

▪ **pull out 1** to withdraw from combat, or from a competition, project, etc. See also PULL-OUT. **2** *intr* said of a driver or vehicle: to move away from the kerb or into the centre of the road to overtake.

▪ **pull something out** to extract or remove it.

▪ **pull over** said of a driver or vehicle: to move to the side of or off the road and stop.

▪ **pull round** or **through** to recover from an illness.

▪ **pull someone round** or **through** to help them to recover from an illness.

▪ **pull together** to work together towards a common aim; to co-operate.

▪ **pull up** said of a driver, vehicle or horse: to stop.

▪ **pull someone up** to criticize them or tell them off.

▪ **pull something up** to make (a vehicle or horse) stop.

▪ **pull up on** or **with someone** or **something** to catch up with or draw level with them or it.

pullet /ˈpʊlɪt/ ▷ *noun* a young female hen in its first laying year. ⓒ 14c: from French *poulet* chicken.

pulley /ˈpʊlɪ/ ▷ *noun* (***pulleys***) **1** a simple mechanism for lifting and lowering weights, consisting of a wheel with a grooved rim over which a rope or belt runs. **2** a clothes-drying frame suspended by ropes from the ceiling, lowered and raised by means of such a device. ⓒ 14c: from French *polie*, ultimately from Greek *polos* axis.

Pullman /ˈpʊlmən/ ▷ *noun* (***Pullmans***) a type of luxurious railway carriage. ⓒ 19c: named after its American originator George M Pullman (1831–1897).

pull-off ▷ *noun, N Amer* a LAY-BY.

pull-out ▻ *noun* **1** a self-contained detachable section of a magazine designed to be kept for reference. **2** a withdrawal from combat or competition, etc. See also PULL OUT at PULL.

pullover ▻ *noun* a knitted garment pulled on over the head; a sweater or jumper.

pullulate /ˈpʌljuleɪt/ ▻ *verb* (***pullulated, pullulating***) *intr* **1** *literary* to teem or abound. **2** *biol* to reproduce by pullulation. ◷ 17c: from Latin *pullulare, pullulatum* to sprout out, from *pullus* young animal.

pullulation ▻ *noun, biol* reproduction by vegetative budding, as in yeast cells.

pulmonary /ˈpʌlmənərɪ/ ▻ *adj* **1** belonging or relating to, or affecting, the lungs. **2** having the function of a lung. ◷ 18c: from Latin *pulmo, pulmonis* lung.

pulmonary emphysema ▻ *noun, pathol* a condition in which the ALVEOLI of the lungs are over-inflated and damaged, causing breathlessness and wheezing.

pulmonary tuberculosis see TUBERCULOSIS

pulmonary vein ▻ *noun, anatomy* a vein that carries oxygenated blood from the lungs to the heart.

pulp ▻ *noun* **1** the flesh of a fruit or vegetable. **2** a soft wet mass of mashed food or other material. **3** *derog* **a** worthless literature, novels, magazines, etc printed on poor paper; **b** *as adj* □ *pulp fiction.* **4** *anatomy* the tissue in the cavity of a tooth, containing nerves. ▻ *verb* (***pulped, pulping***) **1** *tr & intr* to reduce or be reduced to a pulp. **2** to remove the pulp from (fruit, etc). • **pulpy** *adj* (***pulpier, pulpiest***). ◷ 16c: from Latin *pulpa* flesh or fruit pulp.

pulpit /ˈpʊlpɪt/ ▻ *noun* **1** a small enclosed platform in a church, from which the preacher delivers the sermon. **2** (*usually* **the pulpit**) the clergy in general □ *the message from the pulpit.* **3** a place from where opinion is expressed, eg the press. ◷ 14c: from Latin *pulpitum* a stage.

pulque /ˈpʊlkeɪ/ ▻ *noun* an alcoholic drink made in Mexico from AGAVE sap. ◷ 17c: Mexican Spanish.

pulsar /ˈpʌlsɑː(r)/ ▻ *noun, astron* in space: a source of electromagnetic radiation emitted in brief regular pulses, mainly at radio frequency, believed to be a rapidly revolving NEUTRON STAR. ◷ 1960s: from *puls*ating st*ar*, modelled on QUASAR.

pulsate /pʌlˈseɪt/ ▻ *verb* (***pulsated, pulsating***) *intr* **1** to beat or throb. **2** to contract and expand rhythmically. **3** to vibrate. • **pulsation** *noun.* ◷ 18c: from Latin *pulsare, pulsatum* to beat.

pulsating star ▻ *noun, astron* a VARIABLE star whose brightness changes in a regular manner as it alternately expands and contracts.

pulse[1] /pʌls/ ▻ *noun* **1** *physiol* the rhythmic beat that can be detected in an artery, corresponding to the regular contraction of the left ventricle of the heart as it pumps blood around the body. **2** *medicine, etc* **a** the rate of this beat, often measured as an indicator of a person's state of health; **b** *as adj* □ *pulse rate.* **3** a regular throbbing beat in music. **4** *physics* a signal, eg one of light or electric current, of very short duration. **5** the hum or bustle of a busy place. **6** a thrill of excitement, etc. **7** the attitude or feelings of a group or community at any one time. ▻ *verb* (***pulsed, pulsing***) **1** *intr* to throb or pulsate. **2** to drive something by pulses. ◷ 14c: from French *pous*, from Latin *pulsus* a beating, from *pellere, pulsum* to beat.

pulse[2] /pʌls/ ▻ *noun* **1** the edible dried seed of a plant belonging to the pea family, eg pea, bean, lentil, etc. **2** any plant that bears this seed. ◷ 13c: from French *pols*, from Latin *puls* meal porridge or bean pottage.

pulse code ▻ *noun* the coding of data using pulses.

pulse code modulation ▻ *noun, telecomm* a technique that uses pulse modulation to represent a signal with a series of binary codes.

pulse modulation ▻ *noun* a type of modulation that involves varying pulses to represent a signal.

pulverize or **pulverise** /ˈpʌlvəraɪz/ ▻ *verb* (***pulverized, pulverizing***) **1** *tr & intr* to crush or crumble to dust or powder. **2** *colloq* to defeat utterly; to annihilate. • **pulverization** *noun.* ◷ 16c: from Latin *pulverizare*, from *pulvis* dust.

puma /ˈpjuːmə/ ▻ *noun* (***pumas***) one of the large cats of America, with short yellowish-brown or reddish fur, found in mountain regions, forests, plains and deserts. Also called **cougar, mountain lion** or **panther**. ◷ 18c: Spanish, from Quechua.

pumice /ˈpʌmɪs/ ▻ *noun* (*also* **pumice stone**) *geol* a very light porous white or grey form of solidified lava, used as an abrasive and polishing agent. ▻ *verb* (***pumiced, pumicing***) to polish or rub something with pumice. ◷ 15c: from French *pomis*, from Latin *pumex, pumicis*.

pummel /ˈpʌməl/ ▻ *verb* (***pummelled, pummelling***) to beat something repeatedly with the fists. ◷ 16c: a variant of POMMEL.

pump[1] ▻ *noun* **1** any of various piston-operated or other devices for forcing or driving liquids or gases into or out of something, etc. **2** a standing device with a handle that is worked up and down for raising water from beneath the ground, especially one serving as the water supply to a community. **3 a** a device for forcing air into a tyre; **b** *in compounds* □ *bicycle pump* □ *foot pump.* **4** (*also* **petrol pump**) a device for raising petrol from an underground storage tank to fill a vehicle's petrol tank. ▻ *verb* (***pumped, pumping***) **1** *tr & intr* to raise, force or drive (a liquid or gas) out of or into something with a pump. **2** (*usually* **pump something up**) to inflate (a tyre, etc) with a pump. **3** to force something in large gushes or flowing amounts. **4** to pour (money or other resources) into a project, etc. **5** to force out the contents of (someone's stomach) to rid it of a poison, etc. **6** to try to extract information from someone by persistent questioning. **7** to work something vigorously up and down, as though operating a pump handle. **8** to fire (bullets, etc), often into someone or something □ *pumped bullets into her.* • **pump iron** *colloq* to exercise with weights; to go in for weight-training. ◷ 15c: from Dutch *pumpe* pipe.

pump[2] ▻ *noun* **1** a light dancing shoe. **2** a plain, low-cut flat shoe for women. **3** a gymshoe or PLIMSOLL. ◷ 16c.

pumpernickel /ˈpʌmpənɪkəl, ˈpʊm-/ ▻ *noun* a dark heavy coarse ryebread, eaten especially in Germany. ◷ 18c: from German, meaning 'lout', perhaps literally 'stink-devil' or 'fart-devil', because of the after-effects of eating it.

pumpkin /ˈpʌmpkɪn/ ▻ *noun* **1** a perennial trailing or climbing plant which produces yellow flowers and large round fruits at ground level. **2** the fruit of this plant, which contains pulpy flesh and many seeds, enclosed by a hard leathery orange rind. ◷ 17c: from French *pompon*, from Greek *pepon* melon.

pun ▻ *noun* a form of joke consisting of the use of a word or phrase that can be understood in two different ways, especially one where an association is created between words of similar sound but different meaning. Also called **play on words**. ▻ *verb* (***punned, punning***) *intr* to make a pun. ◷ 17c.

Punch /pʌntʃ/ ▻ *noun* a humpbacked hook-nosed puppet character in the traditional show called *Punch and Judy*. • **pleased as Punch** extremely pleased. ◷ 18c: from Italian *Pulcinella* a commedia dell'arte character.

punch[1] /pʌntʃ/ ▻ *verb* (***punched, punching***) **1** *tr & intr* to hit someone or something with the fist. **2** *especially US & Austral* to poke or prod with a stick; to drive (cattle, etc). **3** to prod, poke or strike smartly, especially with a blunt object, the foot, etc □ *McCoist punched the ball into the back of the net.* ▻ *noun* (***punches***) **1** a blow with the fist. **2** vigour and effectiveness in speech or writing. • **pack a punch** see under PACK[1]. ◷ 14c: a variant of POUNCE[1].

punch[2] /pʌntʃ/ ▷ *noun* (***punches***) **1** a tool for cutting or piercing holes or notches, or stamping designs, in leather, paper, metal, etc. **2** a tool for driving nail-heads well down into a surface. ▷ *verb* (***punched***, ***punching***) **1** to pierce, notch or stamp something with a punch. **2** *computing, old use* to use a key punch to record (data) on (a card or tape). ◷ 15c: shortened from *puncheon* a piercing tool.

■ **punch in** or **out** *N Amer* to clock in or out.

punch[3] /pʌntʃ/ ▷ *noun* (***punches***) a drink, usually an alcoholic one, made up of a mixture of other drinks, which can be served either hot or cold. ◷ 17c: said to be from Hindi *panch* five, as the drink was originally made from five ingredients (spirits, water, lemon juice, sugar and spice).

punch[4] or **Punch** /pʌntʃ/ ▷ *noun* (***punches***) a short-legged draughthorse, usually chestnut in colour □ *a Suffolk Punch.* ◷ 19c.

punch-bag ▷ *noun* **1** a heavy stuffed leather bag hanging from the ceiling on a rope, used for boxing practice. **2** someone who is used and abused, either physically and emotionally.

punchball ▷ *noun* **1** a leather ball mounted on a flexible stand, used for boxing practice. **2** *US* a ball game similar to baseball. ◷ Early 20c; 1930s in sense 2.

punch bowl ▷ *noun* **1** a large bowl for mixing and serving PUNCH[3]. **2** *Brit* a bowl-shaped hollow in the mountains.

punch-drunk ▷ *adj* **1** said of a boxer: disorientated from repeated blows to the head, with resultant unsteadiness and confusion. **2** dazed from over-intensive work or some other shattering experience. ◷ Early 20c.

punched card or (*especially US*) **punch card** ▷ *noun, computing, old use* a card bearing coded data or instructions in the form of punched holes.

punchline ▷ *noun* the words that conclude a joke or funny story and contain its point, eg 'We're having another floor built on to our house — but that's another storey'. ◷ 1920s.

punch-up ▷ *noun, colloq* a fight. ◷ 1950s.

punchy ▷ *adj* (***punchier***, ***punchiest***) said of speech or writing: vigorous and effective; forcefully expressed. ● **punchily** *adverb*. ● **punchiness** *noun*.

punctilious /pʌŋk'tɪlɪəs/ ▷ *adj* carefully attentive to details of correct, polite or considerate behaviour; making a point of observing a rule or custom. ● **punctiliously** *adverb*. ● **punctiliousness** *noun*. ◷ 17c: from Italian *puntiglio*, from Spanish *puntillo* a little point.

punctual /'pʌŋktʃʊəl/ ▷ *adj* **1** arriving or happening at the arranged time; not late. **2** said of a person: making a habit of arriving on time. ● **punctuality** /-'alɪtɪ/ *noun*. ● **punctually** *adverb*. ◷ 17c in sense 1; 15c in obsolete sense 'sharp-pointed': from Latin *punctus* point.

punctuate /'pʌŋktʃʊeɪt/ ▷ *verb* (***punctuated***, ***punctuating***) **1** *tr & intr* to put punctuation marks into (a piece of writing). **2** to interrupt something repeatedly □ ***Bursts of applause punctuated his speech.*** ◷ 19c in sense 1; 17c in obsolete sense 'to point out': from Latin *punctuare*, *punctuatum* to prick or point.

punctuation ▷ *noun* **1** a system of conventional marks used in a text to clarify its meaning for the reader, indicating pauses, intonation, missing letters, etc. **2 a** the use of such marks; **b** the process of inserting them.

punctuation mark ▷ *noun* any of the set of marks such as the FULL STOP, COMMA, QUESTION MARK, COLON, etc that in written text conventionally indicate the pauses and intonations that would be used in speech, and which help to make the meaning clear to the reader.

puncture /'pʌŋktʃə(r)/ ▷ *noun* **1** a small hole pierced in something with a sharp point. **2 a** a perforation in an inflated object, especially one in a pneumatic tyre; **b** the resulting flat tyre. ▷ *verb* (***punctured***, ***puncturing***) **1** *tr & intr* to make a puncture in something, or to be punctured. **2** to deflate (someone's pride, self-importance, etc). ◷ 14c: from Latin *punctura*, from *pungere*, *punctum* to prick.

punctuation marks

See Usage Notes at **apostrophe**, **brackets**, **colon**, **comma**, **dash**, **exclamation mark**, **full stop**, **hyphen**, **oblique**, **question mark**, **quotation marks** and **semicolon**.

pundit /'pʌndɪt/ ▷ *noun* **1** an authority or supposed authority on a particular subject, especially one who is regularly consulted. **2** (*also* **pandit**) a Hindu learned in Hindu culture, philosophy and law. ◷ 17c: from Hindi *pandit*, from Sanskrit *pandita* skilled.

pungent /'pʌndʒənt/ ▷ *adj* **1** said of a taste or smell: sharp and strong. **2** said of remarks or wit, etc: cleverly caustic or biting. **3** said of grief or pain: keen or sharp. ● **pungency** *noun*. ● **pungently** *adverb*. ◷ 16c: from Latin *pungens*, *pungentis* pricking.

Punic /'pjuːnɪk/ ▷ *adj* **1** *historical* belonging or relating to ancient Carthage. **2** *literary* treacherous; deceitful. ◷ 15c: from Latin *Punicus* Carthaginian.

punier and **puniest** see under PUNY

punish /'pʌnɪʃ/ ▷ *verb* (***punishes***, ***punished***, ***punishing***) **1** to cause (an offender) to suffer for an offence. **2** to impose a penalty for (an offence). **3** *colloq* to treat something or someone roughly. **4** to beat or defeat (an opponent, etc) soundly. **5** *colloq* to consume large quantities of (eg drink). ● **punishable** *adj*. ● **punishing** *adj* harsh; severe. ◷ 14c: from French *punir*, from Latin *punire*, *punitum*, from *poena* a penalty.

punishment ▷ *noun* **1** the act of punishing or process of being punished. **2** a method of punishing; a type of penalty. See also CAPITAL PUNISHMENT, CORPORAL PUNISHMENT. **3** *colloq* rough treatment; suffering or hardship.

punitive /'pjuːnɪtɪv/ ▷ *adj* **1** relating to, inflicting or intended to inflict punishment. **2** severe; inflicting hardship. ● **punitively** *adverb*. ◷ 17c: see PUNISH.

Punjabi or **Panjabi** /pʌn'dʒɑːbɪ, pʊn'-/ ▷ *adj* belonging or relating to the Punjab, now divided as a state in NW India and a province in E Pakistan, their inhabitants or their language. ▷ *noun* (***Punjabis***) **1** a citizen or inhabitant of, or person born in, Punjab. **2** the INDO-ARYAN language of Punjab, also spoken in parts of India and Pakistan. ◷ 19c: Hindi *Panjabi*, from Persian *panj* five + *ab* water, referring to the five rivers which cross the region.

punk ▷ *noun* **1** a youth-orientated, anti-establishment movement, at its height in the mid- to late-70s, which was characterized by aggressive music and a dress style which included BONDAGE-wear, ripped clothes, vividly coloured hair and the wearing of cheap utility articles (eg safety pins) as ornament on or through various parts of the body. **2** a follower of punk styles or PUNK ROCK. **3** PUNK ROCK. **4** *N Amer* a worthless or stupid person. ▷ *adj* **1** relating to or characteristic of punk as a movement. **2** *N Amer* worthless; inferior. ◷ 19c in *adj* sense 2: perhaps a combination of 16c *punk* prostitute + 17c *punk* rotten wood.

punka or **punkah** /'pʌŋkə/ ▷ *noun* (***punkas*** or ***punkahs***) **1** a fan made from leaf-palm. **2** a large mechanical fan for cooling a room. ◷ 17c: from Hindi *pankha* fan.

punk rock ▷ *noun* a type of loud aggressive rock music, especially popular in the mid- to late-70s, with violent and often crude lyrics.

punned and **punning** see under PUN

punnet /'pʌnɪt/ ▷ *noun* a small basket or container, usually made of cardboard or plastic, for soft fruit. ◷ 19c.

punster ▷ *noun* someone who makes PUNS, especially habitually.

punt¹ ▷ *noun* a long, flat-bottomed open boat with square ends, propelled by a pole pushed against the bed of the river, etc. ▷ *verb* (***punted, punting***) **1** *intr* to travel by or operate a punt. **2** to propel (a punt, etc) with a pole. **3** to convey (passengers) in a punt. ◷ Anglo-Saxon: influenced by Latin *ponto* a punt or pontoon.

punt² ▷ *noun, rugby* a kick given with the toe of the boot to a ball dropped directly from the hands. ▷ *verb* (***punted, punting***) *tr & intr* to kick in this way. ◷ 19c.

punt³ ▷ *verb* (***punted, punting***) *intr* **1** *colloq* to bet on horses. **2** *cards* to bet against the bank. ▷ *noun* a gamble or bet. ◷ 18c: from French *ponter* to bet.

punt⁴ /pʊnt/ ▷ *noun* the standard unit of currency of the Republic of Ireland. ◷ 1970s: Irish Gaelic, meaning 'pound'.

punter ▷ *noun, colloq* **1** someone who bets on horses; a gambler. **2 a** the average consumer, customer or member of the public; **b** a prostitute's client.

puny /ˈpjuːnɪ/ ▷ *adj* (***punier, puniest***) **1** small, weak or undersized. **2** feeble or ineffective. ◷ 16c: originally PUISNE.

pup ▷ *noun* **1** a young dog. **2** the young of other animals, eg the seal, wolf and rat. Compare CUB. ▷ *verb* (***pupped, pupping***) *intr* to give birth to pups. • **be sold a pup** *colloq* to be swindled. • **in pup** said of a bitch: pregnant. ◷ 18c: from PUPPY.

pupa /ˈpjuːpə/ ▷ *noun* (***pupae*** /ˈpjuːpiː/ or ***pupas***) *zool* in the life cycle of certain insects, eg butterflies and moths: the inactive stage during which a larva is transformed into a sexually mature adult while enclosed in a protective case. • **pupal** *adj*. ◷ 18c: Latin, meaning 'doll'.

pupil¹ /ˈpjuːpəl/ ▷ *noun* **1** someone who is being taught; a schoolchild or student. **2** someone studying under a particular expert, etc. **3** *Scots law* a girl under the age of 12 or boy under the age of 14, who is in the care of a guardian. ◷ 14c: from Latin *pupillus* and *pupilla*, diminutives of *pupus* boy and *pupa* girl.

pupil² /ˈpjuːpəl/ ▷ *noun, anatomy* in the eye of vertebrates: the dark circular opening in the centre of the IRIS (sense 2), which varies in size allowing more or less light to pass to the retina. ◷ 16c: from Latin *pupilla*, diminutive of *pupa* girl or doll.

puppet /ˈpʌpɪt/ ▷ *noun* **1** a type of doll that can be moved in a number of ways, eg one operated by strings or sticks attached to its limbs, or one designed to fit over the hand and operated by the fingers and thumb. **2** a person, company, country, etc, who is being controlled or manipulated by someone or something else. ◷ 16c: ultimately from Latin *pupa* doll.

puppeteer /pʌpɪˈtɪə(r)/ ▷ *noun* someone skilled in manipulating puppets and giving puppet shows.

puppetry ▷ *noun* the art of making and manipulating puppets.

puppet show ▷ *noun* an entertainment with puppets as performers.

puppet state ▷ *noun* an apparently independent country actually under the control of another.

puppy /ˈpʌpɪ/ ▷ *noun* (***puppies***) **1** a young dog. **2** *informal, dated* a conceited young man. ◷ 15c: related to French *poupée* doll.

puppy fat ▷ *noun* a temporary plumpness in children, usually at the pre-adolescent stage, which disappears with maturity.

puppy love ▷ *noun* romantic love between adolescents, or of an adolescent for an older person. Also called **calf love**.

purblind /ˈpɜːblaɪnd/ ▷ *adj* **1** nearly blind; dim-sighted. **2** dull-witted; obtuse. ◷ 16c in sense 1; 13c in obsolete sense 'completely blind'; from PURE + BLIND.

purchase /ˈpɜːtʃəs/ ▷ *verb* (***purchased, purchasing***) **1** to obtain something in return for payment; to buy. **2** to get or achieve something through labour, effort, sacrifice or risk. ▷ *noun* **1** something that has been bought. **2** the act of buying. **3** firmness in holding or gripping; a sure grasp or foothold. **4** *mech* the advantage given by a device such as a pulley or lever. • **purchaser** *noun*. ◷ 14c: from French *pourchacier* to seek to obtain.

purchase tax ▷ *noun* a tax levied on those goods considered non-essential, at a higher rate than on other goods. It was replaced in the UK by VALUE-ADDED TAX.

purdah /ˈpɜːdə/ ▷ *noun* in some Muslim and Hindu societies: **1** the seclusion or veiling of women from public view. **2** a curtain or screen used to seclude women. ◷ 19c: from Hindi and Urdu *pardah* curtain.

pure /pjʊə(r)/ ▷ *adj* (***purer, purest***) **1** consisting of itself only; unmixed with anything else. **2** unpolluted; uncontaminated; wholesome. **3** virtuous; chaste; free from sin or guilt. **4** utter; sheer □ *pure lunacy*. **5** said of mathematics or science: dealing with theory and abstractions rather than practical applications. Compare APPLIED. **6** of unmixed blood or descent □ *pure Manx stock*. **7** said of sound, eg a sung note: clear, unwavering and exactly in tune. **8** absolutely true to type or style. **9** said of speech or language: free of imported, intrusive or debased elements. **10** *non-technical* said of a vowel: simple in sound quality, like the *o* in *box*, eg as distinct from a diphthong like the *oy* in *boy*. • **pureness** *noun*. See also PURITY. • **pure and simple** nothing but; without anything else □ *jealousy pure and simple*. ◷ 13c: from French *pur*, from Latin *purus* clean.

pure-bred ▷ *adj* said of an animal or plant: that is the offspring of parents of the same breed or variety.

purée /ˈpjʊəreɪ/ *cookery* ▷ *noun* (***purées***) a quantity of fruit, vegetables, meat, fish, game, etc reduced to a smooth pulp by liquidizing or rubbing through a sieve. ▷ *verb* (***purées, puréed, puréeing***) to reduce something to a purée. ◷ 18c: from French *purer* to strain.

purely ▷ *adverb* **1** in a pure way. **2** wholly; entirely. **3** merely.

purfle /ˈpɜːfəl/ ▷ *noun* a decorative border on clothing or furniture, etc. ▷ *verb* (***purfled, purfling***) to ornament (the edge of something) with such a border. ◷ 14c: from French *pourfiler* to border, from Latin *pro* forward + *filum* thread.

purgative /ˈpɜːgətɪv/ ▷ *noun* **1** a medicine that causes the bowels to empty. **2** something that cleanses or purifies. ▷ *adj* **1** said of a medicine, etc: having this effect. Also called LAXATIVE. **2** said of an action, etc: having a purifying, cleansing or cathartic effect. ◷ 15c: from Latin *purgare*, *purgatum* to clean out.

purgatory /ˈpɜːgətərɪ, -trɪ/ ▷ *noun* (***purgatories***) **1** (**Purgatory**) *chiefly RC Church* a place or state into which the soul passes after death, where it is cleansed of pardonable sins before going to heaven. **2** *humorous, colloq* any state of discomfort or suffering; an excruciating experience. • **purgatorial** /-ˈtɔːrɪəl/ *adj*. ◷ 13c: from Latin *purgatorium*, from *purgare* to cleanse.

purge /pɜːdʒ/ ▷ *verb* (***purged, purging***) **1 a** to rid (eg the soul or body) of unwholesome thoughts or substances; **b** to rid (anything) of impurities. **2** to rid (a political party, community, etc) of (undesirable members). **3** *old use* **a** to empty (the bowels), especially by taking a laxative; **b** to make someone empty their bowels, especially by giving them a laxative. **4** *law, relig, etc* to rid (oneself) of guilt by atoning for an offence. **5** *law* to clear (oneself or someone else) of an accusation. ▷ *noun* **1** an act of purging. **2** the process of purging a party or community of undesirable members. **3** *old use* the process of purging the bowels. **4** *old use* a LAXATIVE. ◷ 14c: from Latin *purgare* to cleanse, from *purus* pure.

puri /ˈpʊərɪ/ ▷ *noun* (***puris***) *cookery* a small cake of unleavened Indian bread, deep-fried and served hot. ◷ 1950s: Hindi.

purify /ˈpjʊərɪfaɪ/ ▻ *verb* (***purifies, purified, purifying***) **1** *tr & intr* to make or become pure. **2** to cleanse something of contaminating or harmful substances. **3** to rid something of intrusive elements. **4** *relig* to free someone from sin or guilt. • **purification** *noun*. • **purifier** *noun*. ⓒ 14c: from Latin *purificare*, from *purus* pure.

Purim /ˈpʊərɪm, -ˈriːm/ ▻ *noun, Judaism* the Feast of Lots, held about 1 March, in which the Jews celebrate their deliverance from a plot to have them massacred. ⓒ 14c: Hebrew, meaning 'lots'.

purine /ˈpjʊəriːn/ and **purin** /-rɪn/ ▻ *noun, biochem* a nitrogenous base with a double ring structure, the most important derivatives of which are major constituents of the nucleic acids DNA and RNA. ⓒ 19c: contracted from Latin *purum uricum acidum* pure uric acid.

purism /ˈpjʊərɪzəm/ ▻ *noun* insistence on the traditional elements of the content and style of a particular subject, especially of language. • **purist** *noun*. ⓒ 19c.

puritan /ˈpjʊərɪtən/ ▻ *noun* **1** (**Puritan**) *historical* in the 16c and 17c: a supporter of the Protestant movement in England and America that sought to rid church worship of ritual. **2** someone of strict, especially over-strict, moral principles; someone who disapproves generally of luxuries and amusements. ▻ *adj* **1** (**Puritan**) belonging or relating to the Puritans. **2** characteristic of a puritan. • **puritanical** /-ˈtanɪkəl/ *adj*. ⓒ 16c: from Latin *puritas* purity.

purity /ˈpjʊərɪtɪ/ ▻ *noun* **1** the state of being pure or unmixed. **2** freedom from contamination, pollution or unwholesome or intrusive elements. **3** chasteness or innocence. ⓒ 13c: from Latin *puritas*, from *purus* pure.

purl¹ /pɜːl/ ▻ *noun* **1** *knitting* a reverse PLAIN (*noun* 2) stitch. **2** cord made from gold or silver wire. **3** (*also* **pearl**) a decorative looped edging on lace or braid, etc. ▻ *verb* (***purled, purling***) to knit in purl. ⓒ 16c: from obsolete *pirl* to twist.

purl² /pɜːl/ ▻ *verb* (***purled, purling***) *intr* **1** to flow with a murmuring sound. **2** to eddy or swirl. ⓒ 16c: imitating the sound and related to Norwegian *purla* to bubble.

purlieu /ˈpɜːljuː/ ▻ *noun* (***purlieus***) **1** (*usually* **purlieus**) the surroundings or immediate neighbourhood of a place. **2** (*usually* **purlieus**) someone's usual haunts. **3** *Eng history* an area of land on the edge of a forest which was once considered part of the forest, and which still remained subject to some of its governing laws, even after separation. ⓒ 15c in sense 3: from French *puralé* a going through.

purlin or **purline** /ˈpɜːlɪn/ ▻ *noun, building* a roof timber stretching across the principal rafters or between the tops of walls, which supports the common or subsidiary rafters or the sheets of roof-covering material. ⓒ 15c.

purloin /pɜːˈlɔɪn/ ▻ *verb* (***purloined, purloining***) to steal, filch or pilfer. ⓒ 16c: from French *purloigner* to remove to a distance.

purple /ˈpɜːpəl/ ▻ *noun* **1** a colour that is a mixture of blue and red. **2** *historical* a crimson dye obtained from various shellfish. **3** crimson cloth, or a robe made from it, worn eg by emperors and cardinals, symbolic of their authority. **4** (**the purple**) high rank; power. ▻ *adj* **1** purple-coloured. **2** said of writing: especially fine in style; over-elaborate; flowery. • **born in the purple** born into a royal or noble family. ⓒ Anglo-Saxon: related to Greek *porphyra* a dye-yielding shellfish.

Purple Heart ▻ *noun military* (abbreviation **PH**) in the USA: a medal awarded for wounds received on active service. ⓒ 1932 in present form.

purple heart¹ ▻ *noun* **1** any of various trees native to tropical America, especially the Amazon region. **2** the purple-coloured wood of this tree. ⓒ 18c.

purple heart² ▻ *noun, colloq* a heart-shaped violet pill or tablet containing a stimulant drug, usually AMPHETAMINE. ⓒ 1960s.

purple patch ▻ *noun* **1** a passage in a piece of writing which is over-elaborate and ornate. **2** any period of time characterized by good luck.

purport ▻ *verb* /pɜːˈpɔːt/ (***purported, purporting***) **1** said of a picture, piece of writing, document, etc: to profess by its appearance, etc (to be something) □ ***a manuscript that purports to be written by Camus.*** **2** said of a piece of writing, or a speech, etc: to convey; to imply (that...). ▻ *noun* /ˈpɜːpɔːt/ meaning, significance, point or gist. ⓒ 15c: from French *purporter* to convey.

purpose /ˈpɜːpəs/ ▻ *noun* **1** the object or aim in doing something. **2** the function for which something is intended. **3** the intentions, aspirations, aim or goal □ ***no purpose in life.*** **4** determination; resolve □ ***a woman of purpose.*** ▻ *verb* (***purposed, purposing***) to intend (to do something). • **purposeless** *adj* without purpose; aimless. • **purposely** *adj* intentionally. • **on purpose** intentionally; deliberately. • **to little** or **no purpose** with few, or no, useful results. • **to the purpose** relevant; to the point. ⓒ 13c: from French *pourpos*, from Latin *proponere* to intend.

purpose-built ▻ *adj* designed or made to meet specific requirements.

purposeful ▻ *adj* determined; intent; resolute; showing a sense of purpose. • **purposefully** *adverb*.

purposefully, purposely

• **Purposefully** (= with purpose) refers to a person's manner or determination □ *He stood up and began to pace purposefully round the room.*
• **Purposely** (= on purpose) refers to intention □ *Earlier estimates had been purposely conservative.*

purposive /ˈpɜːpəsɪv/ ▻ *adj* **1** having a clear purpose. **2** purposeful. • **purposively** *adverb*. • **purposiveness** *noun*.

purr /pɜː(r)/ ▻ *verb* (***purred, purring***) **1** *intr* said of a cat: to make a soft low vibrating sound associated with contentment. **2** *intr* said of a vehicle or machine: to make a sound similar to this, suggestive of good running order. **3** *tr & intr* to express pleasure, or say something, in a tone vibrating with satisfaction. ▻ *noun* a purring sound. ⓒ 17c: imitating the sound.

purse /pɜːs/ ▻ *noun* **1** a small container carried in the pocket or handbag, for keeping cash, etc in. **2** *N Amer* a woman's handbag. **3** funds available for spending; resources. See also PUBLIC PURSE. **4** a sum of money offered as a present or prize. ▻ *verb* (***pursed, pursing***) to draw (the lips) together in disapproval or deep thought. ⓒ Anglo-Saxon *purs*.

purser ▻ *noun* the ship's officer responsible for keeping the accounts and, on a passenger ship, seeing to the welfare of passengers. ⓒ 15c.

purse-seine ▻ *noun* a type of fishing net with an open end which can be drawn up to form a bag shape. ⓒ 19c.

purse strings ▻ *plural noun, formerly* the two cords which, when pulled, draw the opening of a purse up in order to close it. • **hold** or **control the purse strings** to be in charge of the financial side of things, eg in a family, business, etc. • **loosen the purse strings** to allow for greater financial freedom. • **tighten the purse strings** to impose financial restraint. ⓒ 15c.

pursuance /pəˈsjuːəns/ ▻ *noun* the process of pursuing □ ***in pursuance of his duties.***

pursue /pəˈsjuː, ˈsuː/ ▻ *verb* (***pursued, pursuing***) **1** *tr & intr* to follow someone or something in order to overtake, capture or attack them or it, etc; to chase. **2** to proceed along (a course or route). **3** to put effort into achieving (a goal, aim, etc). **4** to occupy oneself with (one's career, etc). **5** to continue with or follow up (investigations or enquiries, etc). ⓒ 13c: from French *pursuer*, from Latin *prosequi*, from *sequi* to follow.

pursuer ▷ *noun* **1** someone who chases someone or something. **2** *Scots law* a plaintiff.

pursuit /pə'sjuːt/ ▷ *noun* **1** the act of pursuing or chasing. **2** an occupation or hobby. **3** in cycling: a race in which two riders start at opposite sides of the track and try to overtake each other. ◷ 15c in sense 1; 14c in obsolete sense 'persecution': from French *pursuete*, from *poursuivre* to pursue.

pursuivant /'pɜːsɪvənt, 'pɜːswɪ-/ ▷ *noun* **1** *heraldry* an officer of the College of Arms ranking below a herald. **2** *historical* a messenger or follower. ◷ 14c: from French *poursuivant*, from *poursuivre* to follow.

purulent /'pjʊərʊlənt, -jʊlənt/ *medicine, etc* ▷ *adj* belonging or relating to, or full of, pus. • **purulence** *noun*. • **purulently** *adverb*. ◷ 16c: from Latin *purulentus*, from *pus, puris* pus.

purvey /pə'veɪ/ ▷ *verb* (***purveyed, purveying***) *tr & intr* to supply (food or provisions, etc) as a business. • **purveyor** *noun*. ◷ 13c: from French *purveier*, from Latin *providere* to provide.

purveyance ▷ *noun* **1** the act of purveying. **2** *historical* the request for and collection of provisions for a monarch.

purview /'pɜːvjuː/ ▷ *noun, formal or technical* **1** scope of responsibility or concern, eg of a court of law. **2** the range of someone's knowledge, experience or activities. **3** *law* the body or enacting part of a statute, as distinct from the PREAMBLE. ◷ 15c: from French *purveu* provided, from *porveier* to PURVEY.

pus /pʌs/ ▷ *noun* the thick, usually yellowish liquid that forms in abscesses or infected wounds, composed of dead white blood cells, serum, bacteria and tissue debris. ◷ 16c: Latin.

push /pʊʃ/ ▷ *verb* (***pushes, pushed, pushing***) **1** (*often* **push against, at** or **on something**) to exert pressure to force it away from one; to press, thrust or shove it. **2** to hold (eg a wheelchair, trolley, pram, etc) and move it forward in front of one. **3** *tr & intr* (*often* **push through, in** or **past**, *etc*) to force one's way, thrusting aside people or obstacles. **4** *intr* to progress especially laboriously. **5** to force in a specified direction □ *push up prices.* **6** (*often* **push someone into something**) to coax, urge, persuade or goad them to do it □ *pushed me into agreeing.* **7** to pressurize someone (or oneself) into working harder, achieving more, etc. **8** (*usually* **push for something**) to recommend it strongly; to campaign or press for it. **9** to promote (products) or urge (acceptance of ideas). **10** to sell (drugs) illegally. ▷ *noun* (***pushes***) **1** an act of pushing; a thrust or shove. **2** a burst of effort towards achieving something. **3** determination, aggression or drive. • **at a push** *colloq* if forced; at a pinch. • **be pushing** *colloq* to be nearly (a specified age) □ *She is pushing 30.* • **get the push** *colloq* to be dismissed from a job, etc; to be rejected by someone. • **give someone the push** to dismiss or reject them. ◷ 13c: from French *pousser*, from Latin *pulsare*, from *pellere, pulsum*.

■ **push someone around** or **about** *colloq* **1** to bully them; to treat them roughly. **2** to dictate to them; to order them about.

■ **be pushed for something** *colloq* to be short of (eg time or money).

■ **push off** or **along** *colloq* to go away.

■ **push on** to continue on one's way or with a task, etc.

■ **push someone** or **something over** to knock them down.

■ **push something through** to force acceptance of (a proposal or bill, etc) by a legislative body, etc.

pushbike ▷ *noun, colloq* a bicycle propelled by pedals alone.

push button ▷ *noun* a button pressed to operate a machine, etc. Also *as adj* □ *a push-button phone.*

pushchair ▷ *noun* a small folding wheeled chair for a toddler. *N Amer equivalent* STROLLER. Also called **buggy** and **Baby Buggy**.

pusher ▷ *noun, colloq* **1** someone who sells illegal drugs. **2** someone who tries to get ahead, especially by being aggressive.

pushover ▷ *noun, colloq* **1** someone who is easily defeated or outwitted. **2** a task that is easily accomplished. ◷ Early 20c US slang.

push-start ▷ *verb* to roll (a vehicle) with its handbrake off and gear engaged until the engine begins to turn. ▷ *noun* an instance or the process of doing this. ◷ 1950s.

Pushto or **Pushtu** see PASHTO

pushy ▷ *adj* (***pushier, pushiest***) *colloq* aggressively self-assertive or ambitious. ◷ 1930s.

pusillanimous /pjuːsɪ'lanɪməs/ ▷ *adj* timid, cowardly, weak-spirited or faint-hearted. • **pusillanimity** /-lə'nɪmətɪ/ *noun*. • **pusillanimously** *adverb*. ◷ 16c: from Latin *pusillus* very small + *animus* spirit.

puss[1] /pʊs/ ▷ *noun* (***pusses***) *colloq* a cat. ◷ 16c.

puss[2] /pʊs/ ▷ *noun* (***pusses***) *slang* the face. ◷ 19c: Irish Gaelic, meaning 'mouth'.

pussy /'pʊsɪ/ ▷ *noun* (***pussies***) **1** (*also* **pussycat**) *colloq* a cat. **2** *coarse slang* **a** the female genitals; the vulva; **b** women collectively, especially when considered sexually. ◷ 16c; 19c in sense 2.

pussyfoot ▷ *verb* (***pussyfooted, pussyfooting***) *intr* **1** to behave indecisively; to avoid committing oneself. **2** to pad about stealthily. ◷ Early 20c.

pussy willow ▷ *noun* a willow tree with silky grey CATKINS.

pustule /'pʌstjuːl/ ▷ *noun* a small inflammation on the skin, containing pus; a pimple. • **pustular** *adj*. ◷ 14c: from Latin *pustula*.

put /pʊt/ ▷ *verb* (*past tense & past participle* ***put***, *present participle* ***putting***) **1** to place something or someone in or convey them or it to a specified position or situation. **2** to fit □ *Put a new lock on the door.* **3** to cause someone or something to be in a specified state □ *put him at ease.* **4** to apply. **5** to set or impose □ *put a tax on luxuries* □ *put an end to free lunches.* **6** to lay (blame, reliance, emphasis, etc) on something. **7** to set someone to work, etc or apply something to a good purpose, etc. **8** to translate □ *Put this into French.* **9** to invest or pour (energy, money or other resources) into something. **10** to classify or categorize something or put it in order □ *I put accuracy before speed.* **11** to submit (questions for answering or ideas for considering) to someone; to suggest □ *I put it to her that she was lying.* **12** to express something. **13** *colloq* to write or say □ *don't know what to put* □ *That's putting it mildly.* **14** *intr, naut* to sail in a certain direction □ *put to sea.* **15** *athletics* to throw (the shot). • **put it across someone** or **put one over on someone** *colloq* to trick, deceive or fool them. • **put it about** *colloq* **1** to spread a rumour, gossip, news, etc □ *put it about that he was leaving.* **2** to behave in a sexually promiscuous way. • **put it on** to feign or exaggerate □ *said she'd been really ill but she was putting it on.* • **put on an act** to pretend, especially in order to deceive, win sympath, etc. • **put something right** to mend it or make it better. • **put someone up to something** to urge them to do something they ought not to do. • **put up or shut up** to either give sensible or useful information, input, etc or make one's position on a matter clear; or else keep quiet. • **put up with someone** or **something** to tolerate them or it, especially grudgingly or reluctantly. Other idioms containing 'put' can be found under one of the other significant words, eg **put a sock in it** is under SOCK and **be hard put to do something** is under HARD. ◷ Anglo-Saxon *putian*.

■ **put about** *naut* to turn round; to change course.

■ **put something about** to spread (a report or rumour).

■ **put something across** to communicate (ideas, etc) to other people.

■ **put something aside 1** to save (money), especially regularly, for future use. **2** to discount or deliberately disregard (problems, differences of opinion, etc) for the sake of convenience or peace, etc.

■ **put something at something** *colloq* to estimate (costs, etc) as likely to be (a certain amount).

■ **put someone away** *colloq* **1** to imprison them. **2** to confine them in a mental institution.

■ **put something away 1** to replace it tidily where it belongs. **2** to save it for future use. **3** *colloq* to consume (food or drink), especially in large amounts. **4** *old use* to reject, discard or renounce it.

■ **put something back 1** to replace it. **2** to postpone (a match or meeting, etc). **3** to adjust (a clock, etc) to an earlier time.

■ **put something by** to save it for the future.

■ **put down** said of an aircraft: to land.

■ **put someone down** to humiliate or snub them. See also PUT-DOWN.

■ **put something down 1** to lay it on a surface after holding it, etc. **2** to crush (a revolt, etc). **3** to kill (an animal) painlessly, especially when it is suffering. **4** to write it down. **5** to pay (money) as a deposit on an intended purchase.

■ **put someone down for something 1** to sum them up or dismiss them as the specified thing □ *had put him down for a playboy.* **2** to include them in a list of participants or subscribers, etc for it.

■ **put something down to something** else to regard it as caused by something specified □ *The errors were put down to inexperience.*

■ **put someone forward** to propose their name for a post, etc; to nominate them.

■ **put something forward 1** to offer (a proposal or suggestion). **2** to advance (the time or date of an event or occasion). **3** to adjust (a clock, etc) to a later time.

■ **put in** *naut* to enter a port or harbour.

■ **put something in 1** to fit or install it. **2** to spend (time) working at something □ *puts in four hours' violin practice daily.* **3** to submit (a claim, etc). **4** to interrupt with (a comment, etc).

■ **put in for something** to apply for it.

■ **put someone off 1** to cancel or postpone an engagement with them. **2** to make them lose concentration; to distract them. **3** to cause them to lose enthusiasm or to feel disgust for something □ *Her accident put me off climbing* □ *was put off by its smell.*

■ **put something off 1** to switch off (a light, etc). **2** to postpone (an event or arrangement).

■ **put something on 1** to switch on (an electrical device, etc). **2** to dress in it. **3** to gain (weight or speed). **4** to present (a play or show, etc). **5** to provide (transport, etc). **6** to assume (an accent or manner, etc) for effect or to deceive. See also PUT-ON. **7** to bet (money) on a horse, etc.

■ **put someone on to someone** to give them an indication of their whereabouts or involvement □ *What put the police on to her?* **2** to connect them by telephone.

■ **put someone on to something** to recommend them to try it □ *A friend put me on to these biscuits.*

■ **put someone out 1** to inconvenience them. **2** to offend or annoy them. **3** *cricket* to dismiss (a player or team) from the batting.

■ **put something out 1** to extinguish (a light or fire). **2** to issue (a distress call, etc). **3** to publish (a leaflet, etc). **4** to strain or dislocate (a part of the body).

■ **put something over** to communicate (an idea, etc) to someone else.

■ **put something over on someone** to deceive them.

■ **put someone through 1** to connect them by telephone. **2** *colloq, football* said of a player: to pass the ball to another player so that they are in a good position to score □ *Irons put O'Boyle through only to see him fouled by the keeper.*

■ **put something through 1** to arrange (a deal or agreement, etc). **2** to make or connect (a telephone call).

■ **put something together** to join up the parts of it; to assemble it.

■ **put up** to stay for the night □ *We'd better put up at the local hotel.*

■ **put someone up** to give them a bed for the night.

■ **put something up 1** to build it; to erect it. **2** to raise (prices). **3** to present (a plan, etc). **4** to offer (a house, etc) for sale. **5** to provide (funds) for a project, etc. **6** to show (resistance); to offer (a fight).

■ **put someone** or **oneself up for something** to offer or nominate them, or oneself, as a candidate □ *We are putting you up for chairman.*

■ **put someone up to something** *colloq* to coerce or manipulate them into doing it, especially when it is devious or illicit.

■ **put up with someone** or **something** to bear or tolerate them or it.

■ **put upon someone** to presume on their good will; to take unfair advantage of them.

putative /ˈpjuːtətɪv/ ▷ *adj* supposed; assumed. ◷ 15c: from Latin *putativus*, from *putare, putatum* to think.

put-down ▷ *noun, colloq* a snub or humiliation. See also PUT DOWN, *etc* at PUT.

put-on ▷ *adj* said of an accent or manner, etc: assumed; pretended. ▷ *noun, colloq* a trick or deception. See also PUT SOMETHING ON at PUT.

Putonghua /puːtʊŋˈhwɑː/ ▷ *noun* the official spoken language of China, based on the Beijing variety of MANDARIN. Also called **Guo yu** or **Kuo-yü**. ◷ Early 20c: Chinese, meaning 'common language'.

put-put /pʌtˈpʌt/ ▷ *verb* (***put-putted, put-putting***) *intr* said of a vehicle, especially an old or broken one: to move along with a juddering motion or noise. ▷ *noun* **1** movement of this kind. **2** a car, etc that moves this way. ◷ Early 20c: imitating the sound.

putrefy /ˈpjuːtrɪfaɪ/ ▷ *verb* (***putrefies, putrefied, putrefying***) *intr* said of flesh or other organic matter: to go bad, rot or decay, especially with a foul smell. • **putrefaction** /-ˈfakʃən/ *noun*. ◷ 15c: from Latin *putrefacere*, from *puter* rotten.

putrescent /pjuːˈtrɛsənt/ ▷ *adj* decaying; rotting; putrefying. ◷ 18c: from Latin *putrescere* to become rotten.

putrid /ˈpjuːtrɪd/ ▷ *adj* **1** said of organic matter: decayed; rotten. **2** stinking; foul; disgusting. **3** *colloq* repellent; worthless. ◷ 16c: from Latin *putridus*, from *puter, putris* rotten.

putsch /pʊtʃ/ ▷ *noun* (***putsches***) a secretly-planned sudden attempt to remove a government from power. See also COUP D'ÉTAT. ◎ 1920s: Swiss German, meaning 'knock' or 'thrust'.

putt /pʌt/ ▷ *verb* (***putted, putting***) *tr & intr, golf, putting* to send (the ball) gently forward on the green and into or nearer the hole. ▷ *noun* a putting stroke. ◎ 17c: originally a form of PUT.

puttee /ˈpʌtiː/ ▷ *noun* (***puttees***) a long strip of cloth worn by wrapping it around the leg from the ankle to the knee and used as protection or support. ◎ 19c: from Hindi *patti* a band.

putter /ˈpʌtə(r)/ ▷ *noun, golf* **1** a club used for putting. **2** someone who putts. See also SHOTPUTTER.

putting /ˈpʌtɪŋ/ ▷ *noun* **1** the act of putting a ball towards a hole. **2** a game played on a PUTTING GREEN using only putting strokes. See also PITCH AND PUTT.

putting green ▷ *noun* **1** on a golf course: a smoothly mown patch of grass surrounding a hole. **2** an area of mown turf where PUTTING is played.

putto /ˈpʊtoʊ/ ▷ *noun* (*plural* ***putti*** /–tiː/) in Renaissance or Baroque art: an idealized representation of a naked young boy or cherub, often with wings. ◎ 17c: Italian, from Latin *putus* boy.

putty /ˈpʌtɪ/ ▷ *noun* (***putties***) **1** a paste of ground chalk and linseed oil, used for fixing glass in window frames, filling holes in wood, etc. Also called **glaziers' putty**. **2** a paste of slaked lime and water, used by plasterers. **3** a yellowish grey colour. ▷ *adj* putty-coloured. ▷ *verb* (***puttied, puttying***) to fix, coat or fill something with putty. • **be putty in someone's hands** to be easily manipulated or influenced by them. ◎ 17c: from French *potée* potful.

put-up job ▷ *noun* something dishonestly prearranged to give a false impression.

put-upon ▷ *adj* said of a person: taken advantage of, especially unfairly. See also PUT UPON SOMEONE at PUT.

puzzle /ˈpʌzəl/ ▷ *verb* (***puzzled, puzzling***) **1** to perplex, mystify, bewilder or baffle. ▷ *noun* **1** a baffling problem. **2** a game or toy that takes the form of something for solving, designed to test knowledge, memory, powers of reasoning or observation, manipulative skill, etc. • **puzzlement** *noun*. • **puzzling** *adj*. • **puzzlingly** *adverb*. • **puzzle one's brains** or **head** to think hard about a problem. ◎ 16c.

■ **puzzle about** or **over something** to brood, ponder, wonder or worry about it.

■ **puzzle something out** to solve it after prolonged thought.

puzzler ▷ *noun* **1** a challenging problem or question. Also called **poser**. **2** someone who enjoys solving puzzles.

PVC ▷ *abbreviation* polyvinyl chloride.

PVS ▷ *abbreviation* persistent vegetative state.

PW ▷ *abbreviation* policewoman.

PWA ▷ *abbreviation* **1** person with Aids. **2** (**PWAs**) people with Aids.

PY ▷ *abbreviation, IVR* Paraguay.

pyaemia or **pyemia** /paɪˈiːmɪə/ ▷ *noun, pathol* a form of BLOOD POISONING caused by the release of pus-forming micro-organisms, especially bacteria, into the bloodstream from an abscess or wound. ◎ 19c: Latin, from Greek *pyon* pus + *haima* blood.

pye-dog /ˈpaɪdɒɡ/ ▷ *noun* in Asia: an ownerless half-wild dog. Also called **pariah dog**. ◎ 19c: from Hindi *pahi* outsider.

pyelitis /paɪəˈlaɪtɪs/ *pathol, medicine* ▷ *noun* inflammation of the pelvis (sense 3) of the kidney. Also called **pyelonephritis** /-loʊnɪˈfraɪtɪs/. • **pyelitic** *adj*. ◎ 19c: from Greek *pyelos* trough; see also NEPHRITIS.

pygmy or **pigmy** /ˈpɪɡmɪ/ ▷ *noun* (***pygmies***) **1** (**Pygmy**) a member of one of the unusually short peoples of equatorial Africa. **2** an undersized person; a dwarf. **3** *derog* someone insignificant, especially in a specified field ▫ *an intellectual pygmy*. ▷ *adj* belonging or relating to a small-sized breed ▫ *pygmy hippopotamus*. • **pygmaean** or **pygmean** *adj*. ◎ 14c: from Greek *pygme* the distance from knuckle to elbow.

pygmy shrew ▷ *noun* a small shrew, the most widespread in Europe, with a brown coat and pale underparts.

pyjamas or (*N Amer*) **pajamas** /pəˈdʒɑːməz/ *plural noun* **1** a sleeping-suit consisting of a loose jacket or top, and trousers. Also (**pyjama**) *as adj* ▫ *pyjama bottoms* ▫ *pyjama case*. **2** loose-fitting trousers worn by either sex in the East. ◎ 19c: from Persian and Hindi *payjamah*, from *pay* leg + *jamah* clothing.

pyknic /ˈpɪknɪk/ ▷ *adj, anthropol* said of a human type: characterized by a short, stocky stature, with a domed abdomen and relatively short limbs and neck. Compare ATHLETIC 3, ASTHENIC 2, LEPTOSOME. ◎ 1920s: from Greek *pyknos* thick.

pylon /ˈpaɪlən/ ▷ *noun* **1** a tall steel structure for supporting electric power cables. **2** a post or tower to guide a pilot at an airfield. **3** an external structure on an aircraft for supporting an engine, etc. **4** *archaeol* a gate tower or ornamental gateway. ◎ Early 20c in senses 2 and 3; 19c in sense 4: Greek, from *pyle* gate.

pylorus /paɪˈlɔːrəs/ ▷ *noun* (***pylori*** /-raɪ/) *anatomy* the opening at the base of the stomach that allows partially digested food to pass into the duodenum. • **pyloric** *adj*. ◎ 17c: Latin.

pyorrhoea or (*especially US*) **pyorrhea** /paɪəˈrɪə/ *noun, dentistry* a discharge of pus, especially from the gums or tooth sockets. ◎ 19c: from Greek *pyon* pus + *rheein* to flow.

pyracantha /paɪərəˈkanθə/ ▷ *noun* (***pyracanthas***) a thorny evergreen shrub with bright red, yellow or orange berries. Also called FIRETHORN. ◎ 17c: from Greek *pyrakantha*, from *pyr* fire + *akanthos* thorn.

pyramid /ˈpɪrəmɪd/ ▷ *noun* **1** any of the huge ancient Egyptian royal tombs built on a square base, with four sloping triangular sides meeting in a common apex. **2** *geom* a solid of this shape, with a square or triangular base. **3** any structure or pile, etc of similar shape. • **pyramidal** /pɪˈramɪdəl/ *adj*. • **pyramidally** *adverb*. • **pyramidic**, **pyramidical** *adj*. • **pyramidically** *adverb*. ◎ 16c as *pyramis*: from Greek *pyramis, pyramidos*.

pyramid selling ▷ *noun, marketing* the sale of goods in bulk to a distributor who divides them and sells them on to sub-distributors at a profit, who do likewise to others, etc. ◎ 1970s.

pyre /paɪə(r)/ ▷ *noun* a pile of wood on which a dead body is ceremonially cremated. ◎ 17c: from Latin and Greek *pyra*, from Greek *pyr* fire.

Pyrenean mountain dog /pɪrəˈnɪən ——/ ▷ *noun* a dog with a large powerful body, a heavy head and a thick, usually pale coat. The breed was developed to protect sheep.

pyrethrum /paɪəˈriːθrəm/ ▷ *noun* **1** the name formerly used for any of various perennial plants of the CHRYSANTHEMUM genus, especially a species with finely divided silvery-grey leaves and solitary large white, pink, red or purple daisy-like flower-heads. **2** a natural insecticide prepared from extracts of the powdered dried flower-heads of a species of chrysanthemum. ◎ 16c: from Greek *pyrethron* feverfew.

pyretic /paɪəˈrɛtɪk/ ▷ *adj, medicine* relating to, accompanied by or producing fever. ◎ 19c: from Greek *pyretos* fever.

Pyrex /'paɪərɛks/ ▻ *noun, trademark* a type of heat-resistant glass widely used to make laboratory apparatus and cooking utensils, especially ovenware. ⊙ 1915.

pyrexia /paɪə'rɛksɪə/ ▻ *noun* (***pyrexias***) *medicine* fever. ⊙ 18c: from Greek *pyrexis*, from *pyressein* to be feverish.

pyridine /'pɪrɪdiːn/ ▻ *noun, chem* (formula C_5H_5N) a carcinogenic flammable colourless liquid with a strong unpleasant smell, used in the manufacture of other chemicals, in paints and textile dyes and as a solvent. ⊙ 19c: from Greek *pyr* fire.

pyridoxine /pɪrɪ'dɒksiːn/ ▻ *noun* VITAMIN B_6. ⊙ 1940s: from PYRIDINE with insertion of *-ox-* for OXYGEN.

pyrimidine /paɪə'rɪmɪdiːn/ ▻ *noun, biochem* a nitrogenous base with a single ring structure, the most important derivatives of which are major components of the nucleic acids DNA and RNA. ⊙ 19c: a variant of PYRIDINE.

pyrite /'paɪəraɪt/ ▻ *noun, geol* the commonest sulphide mineral, used as a source of sulphur, and in the production of sulphuric acid. Also called **iron pyrites** or **fool's gold**.

pyrites /paɪə'raɪtiːz/ ▻ *noun* **1** *geol* PYRITE. **2** *chem* any of a large class of mineral sulphides □ ***copper pyrites***. ⊙ 16c: Latin, meaning 'fire-stone'.

pyro- /paɪəroʊ, paɪə'rɒ/ or (before a vowel) **pyr-** ▻ *combining form, forming nouns and adjectives, denoting* **1** fire; heat; fever. **2** *chem* an acid or its corresponding salt. ⊙ Greek, from *pyr* fire.

pyroclast /'paɪərəklast/ *geol* ▻ *noun* an individual fragment of lava that has been ejected into the atmosphere during a volcanic eruption. • **pyroclastic** *adj.* ⊙ 19c: from Greek *klastos* broken.

pyrogallol /paɪərə'galɒl/ ▻ *noun, chem* (formula $C_6H_3(OH)_3$) a soluble crystalline phenol, used as a reducing agent in photographic developing. Also called **pyrogallic acid**. ⊙ 19c: from GALLIC ACID.

pyrogen /'paɪərədʒən/ *technical* ▻ *noun* a substance which causes heat or fever. • **pyrogenic** /-'dʒɛnɪk/ or **pyrogenous** /paɪ'rɒdʒənəs/ *adj.* ⊙ 19c.

pyrolusite /paɪəroʊ'luːsaɪt/ ▻ *noun, geol* (formula MnO_2) a soft black mineral that is the most important ore of manganese. ⊙ 19c: from Greek *lousis* washing.

pyrolysis /paɪə'rɒləsɪs/ ▻ *noun, chem* the chemical decomposition of a substance that occurs when it is heated to a high temperature in the absence of air. ⊙ 19c.

pyromania ▻ *noun, psychol* an obsessive urge to set fire to things. • **pyromaniac** *noun.* ⊙ 19c.

pyrometer /paɪə'rɒmɪtə(r)/ ▻ *noun, physics* a type of thermometer used to measure high temperatures. • **pyrometric** *adj.* • **pyrometrically** *adj.* • **pyrometry** *noun.* ⊙ 18c.

pyrope /'paɪəroʊp/ ▻ *noun* **1** a red magnesia-alumina GARNET, used as a gemstone. **2** any fiery red gemstone. ⊙ 14c: from French *pirope*, from Greek *pyropus* fiery-eyed.

pyrotechnics ▻ *singular noun* the art of making fireworks. ▻ *singular or plural noun* **1** ▻ a fireworks display. **2** a display of fiery brilliance in speech or music, etc. ⊙ 18c.

pyroxene /paɪə'rɒksiːn/ ▻ *noun, geol* any of a group of white, yellow, green, greenish-black or brown silicate minerals, including the most highly prized form of jade. ⊙ 19c: from PYRO- + Greek *xenos* stranger, because it was thought that pyroxene crystals in lava had been caught up accidentally.

Pyrrhic victory /'pɪrɪk —/ ▻ *noun* a victory won at so great a cost in lives, etc that it can hardly be regarded as a triumph at all. ⊙ 19c: named after Pyrrhus, king of Epirus in Greece, who won such victories against the Romans in 3c BC.

pyrrole /'pɪroʊl/ ▻ *noun, chem* a yellowish toxic oil used in the manufacture of drugs. Many naturally occurring compounds are derived from it, eg porphyrins and chlorophyll. ⊙ 19c: from Greek *pyrros* reddish + Latin *oleum* oil.

pyrrolidine /pɪ'rɒlədiːn/ ▻ *noun, chem* (formula C_4H_9N) a colourless strongly-alkaline base, both occurring naturally and produced from PYRROLE. ⊙ 19c: from PYRROLE + -INE^2.

pyruvic acid /paɪə'ruːvɪk —/ ▻ *noun, biochem* an organic acid that is the end-product of the breakdown of carbohydrates by GLYCOLYSIS. ⊙ 19c: from PYRO- + Latin *uva* grape.

Pythagoras's theorem /paɪ'θagərəsɪz —/ ▻ *noun, math* a theorem which states that, in a right-angled triangle, the square of the length of the hypotenuse is equal to the sum of the squares of the other two sides. ⊙ 19c: named after the Greek philosopher and mathematician Pythagoras (6c BC).

python /'paɪθən/ ▻ *noun* any non-venomous egg-laying snake of the BOA family that coils its body around its prey and squeezes it until it suffocates. • **pythonic** /–'θɒnɪk/ *adj.* ⊙ 19c: named after Python, a monster in Greek mythology killed by the god Apollo.

Pythonesque /paɪθə'nɛsk/ ▻ *adj* said of a style of humour: bizarre and surreal. ⊙ 1970s: named after *Monty Python's Flying Circus*, a British TV comedy show which ran from 1969–74; see -ESQUE.

pyx /pɪks/ ▻ *noun* (***pyxes***) **1** *Christianity* a container in which the consecrated Communion bread is kept. **2** a box at the Royal Mint in which sample coins for testing are kept. ⊙ 14c: from Latin and Greek *pyxis* a small box, from *pyxos* box tree.

pzazz see PIZZAZZ

Q

Q[1] or **q** /kjuː/ ▻ *noun* (***Qs, Q's*** or ***q's***) the seventeenth letter of the English alphabet.

Q[2] ▻ *abbreviation* **1** *IVR* Qatar. **2** quality. **3** quantity. **4** *printing* quarto. **5** Quebec. **6** Queen or Queen's. **7** *Austral state* Queensland. Also written **Qld**. **8** question.

Q[3] ▻ *symbol* **1** *physics* heat. **2** *cards, chess* queen.

q or **q.** ▻ *abbreviation* **1** quart. **2** quarter. **3** query. **4** quintal.

Qaddish see KADDISH

qadi see CADI

Qantas or **QANTAS** /ˈkwɒntəs/ ▻ *abbreviation* Queensland and Northern Territory Aerial Service the Australian international airline.

QARANC ▻ *abbreviation* Queen Alexandra's Royal Army Nursing Corps.

QARNNS ▻ *abbreviation* Queen Alexandra's Royal Naval Nursing Service.

qawwal /kəˈvɑːl/ ▻ *noun* a man who sings qawwali music.

qawwali /kəˈvɑːlɪ/ ▻ *noun* a type of Sufi music.

QB ▻ *abbreviation* Queen's Bench.

QC ▻ *abbreviation* **1** *law* Queen's Counsel. **2** quality control.

QED ▻ *abbreviation* used especially at the conclusion of a proof of a geometric theorem: *quod erat demonstrandum* /kwɒd ɛrat dɛmənˈstrandəm/ (Latin), which was the thing that had to be proved.

QE2 ▻ *abbreviation* Queen Elizabeth the Second, the Cunard liner.

Q-fever ▻ *noun, pathol* an acute disease with flu-like symptoms that is transmitted to humans by rickettsia, the same type of micro-organism that causes typhoid. ⊙ 1930s: from QUERY, because at first the cause of the diseases was unknown.

qi, **chi** or **ch'i** /tʃiː/ ▻ *noun, Chinese medicine* the life force that is believed to flow along a network of meridians in a person's body and which is vital to their physical and spiritual health. ⊙ 19c: Chinese, meaning 'breath' or 'energy'.

qibla see KIBLAH

qi gong or **chi kung** /tʃiː ˈguːŋ/ ▻ *noun* a system of meditational exercises for promoting physical and spiritual health by deep breathing. ⊙ 1990s: QI + Chinese *gong* skill or exercise.

Qld see under Q[2]

QM ▻ *abbreviation* quartermaster.

QMG ▻ *abbreviation* Quartermaster-General.

QMS ▻ *abbreviation* Quartermaster-Sergeant.

Qoran see KORAN

QPM ▻ *abbreviation, Brit* the Queen's Police Medal.

QPR ▻ *abbreviation, Brit* Queen's Park Rangers, the London football club.

qq ▻ *abbreviation, printing* quartos.

qqv ▻ *abbreviation* used in cross-referencing, when referring to more than one item: *quae vide* (Latin), which see. See also QV.

qr ▻ *abbreviation* quarter.

QSO ▻ *abbreviation* quasi-stellar object.

qt ▻ *abbreviation* **1** quantity. **2** quart.

q.t. see ON THE QUIET at QUIET

qto ▻ *abbreviation, printing* quarto.

qty ▻ *abbreviation* quantity.

Qu. ▻ *abbreviation* **1** Queen. **2** question.

qua /kweɪ, kwɑː/ ▻ *prep* in the capacity of something; considered as being something; in the role of something. ⊙ 17c: Latin, from *qui* who.

quack[1] /kwak/ ▻ *noun* the noise that a duck makes. ▻ *verb* (***quacked, quacking***) *intr* **1** said of a duck: to make this noise. **2** to talk in a loud silly voice. • **quacker** *noun*. ⊙ 17c: imitating the sound.

quack[2] /kwak/ ▻ *noun* **1** someone who practises medicine or who claims to have medical knowledge, but who has no formal training in the subject. **2** *colloq, often derog* a term for any doctor or medical practitioner, etc. **3** anyone who pretends to have a knowledge or skill that they do not possess. • **quackish** *adj*. ⊙ 17c: from Dutch *quacksalver*, from *kwakken* to quack + *salf* an ointment.

quackery ▻ *noun* (***quackeries***) the practices, methods and activities, etc that are typical of a quack or charlatan.

quad[1] /kwɒd/ ▻ *noun, colloq* a quadruplet. ⊙ Late 19c.

quad[2] /kwɒd/ ▻ *noun, colloq* a quadrangle. ⊙ 19c.

quad[3] /kwɒd/ *colloq* ▻ *adj* quadraphonic. ▻ *noun* **1** quadraphonics. **2** quadraphony. ⊙ 1970s.

quad[4] /kwɒd/ ▻ *noun* a small powerful four-wheel-drive vehicle that is used especially for towing a gun. ⊙ Early 20c: from QUADRUPLE.

quad[5] /kwɒd/ ▻ *noun, printing* (*in full* **quadrat**) a piece of blank type that is usually lower than the type face and which is used for spacing. ⊙ 19c.

quadragenarian /kwɒdrədʒɪənɛərɪən/ ▻ *noun* someone who is aged between 40 and 49. ▻ *adj* **1** aged between 40 and 49. **2** belonging, relating or referring to this age span. ⊙ 19c: from Latin *quadragenarius*, from *quadraginta* forty.

Quadragesima /kwɒdrəˈdʒɛsɪmə/ ▻ *noun* in the Christian calendar: the first Sunday in Lent. ⊙ 14c: from Latin *quadragesimus dies* fortieth day.

quadragesimal ▻ *adj* **1** belonging, relating or referring to Lent. **2** said of a fast: lasting for forty days.

quadrangle /ˈkwɒdraŋgəl/ ▻ *noun* **1** *geom* a square, rectangle or other four-sided two-dimensional figure. **2 a** an open rectangular courtyard, especially one that is in the grounds of a college or school, etc and which has buildings on all four sides of it; **b** a courtyard of this kind together with the buildings around it. Often shortened to **quad**. • **quadrangular** *adj*. • **quadrangularly** *adverb*. ⊙ 15c: from Latin *quadrangulum*, from *quattuor* four + *angulus* angle.

quadrant /ˈkwɒdrənt/ ▻ *noun* **1** *geom* **a** a quarter of the circumference of a circle; **b** a plane figure (see PLANE[2] *adj* 3) that is a quarter of a circle, ie an area bounded by two perpendicular radii and the arc between them; **c** a quarter of a sphere, ie a section cut by two planes that intersect at right angles at the centre. **2** any device or mechanical part in the shape of a 90° arc. **3** an instrument that was formerly used in astronomy and navigation and which consists of a graduated 90° arc allowing angular measurements, eg of the stars, to be taken and altitude calculated. • **quadrantal** *adj*. ⓒ 14c: from Latin *quadrans, quadrantis* a fourth part.

quadraphonic or **quadrophonic** ▷ *adj* said of a stereophonic sound recording or reproduction: using four loudspeakers that are fed by four separate channels so that there is the impression of front-to-back sound distribution as well as the side-to-side sound distribution. • **quadraphonically** *adverb*. • **quadraphony** /kwɒ'drɒfənɪ/ *noun*. ⓒ 1960s: from QUADRI-, modelled on STEREOPHONIC.

quadraphonics or **quadrophonics** ▷ *singular noun* a sound system that uses four loudspeakers which are fed by four separate amplified signals.

quadrat /'kwɒdrət/ ▷ *noun* **1** *ecol* a random sample area of ground enclosed within a frame, often one metre square, which is studied in order to determine what plant and animal species it supports. **2** *printing* QUAD[5]. ⓒ Early 20c: from Latin *quadratus* made square.

quadrate /'kwɒdreɪt, -drət/ ▷ *noun* **1** *anatomy* a body part, eg a muscle or bone, that has a square or rectangular shape. **2** *zool* in the upper jaw of bony fish, amphibians, birds and reptiles: one of a pair of bones that articulates with the lower jaw. ▷ *adj, bot* square or almost square in cross-section or face view. ▷ *verb* (***quadrated, quadrating***) **1** to make something square. **2** to conform or make something conform. ⓒ 14c: from Latin *quadrare* to make square.

quadratic /kwə'dratɪk/ *math* ▷ *noun* **1** (*in full* **quadratic equation**) an algebraic equation that involves the square, but no higher power, of an unknown quantity or variable. It has the general formula $ax^2 + bx + c = 0$, where x is the unknown variable. **2** (**quadratics**) the branch of algebra that deals with this type of equation. ▷ *adj* **1** involving the square of an unknown quantity or variable but no higher power. **2** square. ⓒ 17c.

quadrature /'kwɒdrətʃə(r)/ ▷ *noun* **1** *math* **a** the process that involves expressing a given area that is bounded by a curve, eg a circle, as an equivalent square area; **b** the process of making something square, or of dividing it into squares. **2** *astron* **a** either of the two points in space or time where the moon, when it is viewed from the Earth, is 90° distant from the sun; **b** any configuration where two celestial bodies are 90° away from each other. ⓒ 16c: from Latin *quadratura* a square or an act of squaring.

quadravalent see TETRAVALENT

quadrella /kwɒ'drelə/ ▷ *noun, Austral betting* **1** a type of bet where the punter selects the winner in four races. **2** the four specified races that are designated for this type of bet. Compare QUINELLA, PERFECTA, TRIFECTA. ⓒ 20c: diminutive, based on Latin *quattuor* four.

quadrennial /kwɒ'drenɪəl/ ▷ *adj* **1** lasting four years. **2** occurring every four years. • **quadrenially** *adverb*. ⓒ 17c: from Latin *quadriennium* a four-year period.

quadri- /kwɒdrɪ/ or (before a vowel) **quadr-** ▷ *combining form, denoting* four. ⓒ Latin, from *quattuor* four.

quadric /'kwɒdrɪk/ *math* ▷ *adj* said of function with more than two variables: being of the second degree. ▷ *noun* a quadric curve, surface or function. ⓒ 19c: from Latin *quadra* square.

quadriceps /'kwɒdrəseps/ ▷ *noun* (***quadricepses*** /-sepsɪz/ or ***quadriceps***) *anatomy* a large four-part muscle that extends the leg, which runs down the front of the thigh. • **quadricipital** /-'sɪpɪtəl/ *adj*. ⓒ 19c: Latin, from *caput, capitis* head.

quadrifid /'kwɒdrɪfɪd/ ▷ *adj, bot* said of a plant part: divided into four or having four lobes. ⓒ 17c: from Latin *quadrifidus*, from *findere* to cleave or cut.

quadrilateral ▷ *noun, geom* a two-dimensional figure that has four sides. ▷ *adj* four-sided. ⓒ 17c.

quadrille[1] /kwɒ'drɪl, kwə-/ ▷ *noun* **1** a square dance for four couples, in five or six movements. **2** music for this kind of dance. ⓒ 18c: French, from Spanish *cuadrilla* a troop.

quadrille[2] /kwə'drɪl/ ▷ *noun, cards* a game that is played by four players using only 40 cards, the eights, nines and tens being the ones left out. It was popular during the 18c and was superseded by whist. ⓒ 18c: French, from Spanish *cuartillo*, from *cuarto* fourth.

quadrillion /kwɒ'drɪljən/ ▷ *noun* (***quadrillion*** or ***quadrillions***) **1** in Britain, France and Germany: a number that is represented by a figure 1 followed by 24 zeros, ie 10^{24}. *N Amer equivalent* SEPTILLION. **2** in N America: a number that is represented by a figure 1 followed by 15 zeros, ie 10^{15}. • **quadrillionth** *adj*. ⓒ 17c: French, modelled on MILLION.

quadrinomial /kwɒdrɪ'noʊmɪəl/ *math* ▷ *adj* said of an algebraic expression: having four terms. ▷ *noun* an algebraic expression of this kind. ⓒ 18c.

quadripartite /kwɒdrɪ'pɑːtaɪt/ ▷ *adj* **1** *biol* said mainly of a plant or animal body part: divided into or composed of four parts. **2** *archit* said of a vault, etc: divided into four compartments. **3** said of talks or an agreement, etc: involving, concerning or ratified by, etc four parts, groups or nations, etc. ⓒ 15c: from Latin *partiri, partitum* to divide.

quadriplegia /kwɒdrɪ'pliːdʒɪə/ ▷ *noun, pathol* paralysis that affects both arms and both legs. Compare MONOPLEGIA, HEMIPLEGIA, PARAPLEGIA. ⓒ 1920s.

quadriplegic ▷ *adj* paralysed in all four limbs. ▷ *noun* someone who is paralysed in all four limbs.

quadrivalent ▷ *adj, chem* TETRAVALENT. ⓒ 1920s.

quadrivium /kwɒ'drɪvɪəm/ ▷ *noun, historical* a medieval university course consisting of arithmetic, geometry, astronomy and music. ⓒ 19c: Latin, meaning 'the place where four roads meet'.

quadroon /kwɒ'druːn/ ▷ *noun* **1** someone who is genetically one quarter Negro. **2** a person, plant or animal of mixed parental heritage. ⓒ 18c: from Spanish *cuarterón*, from *cuarto* a fourth or quarter.

quadrophonic, quadrophonics, *etc* see QUADRAPHONIC, QUADRAPHONICS

quadrumanous /kwɒ'druːmənəs/ ▷ *adj, zool* said of monkeys and apes: having feet that can function like hands. ⓒ 17c: from Latin *quadrumanus*, from *manus* a hand.

quadruped /'kwɒdrʊped/ ▷ *noun* an animal, especially a mammal, that has its four limbs specially adapted for walking. ▷ *adj* four-footed. • **quadrupedal** /kwɒdrʊ'piːdəl, kwɒ'druːpɪdəl/ *adj*. ⓒ 17c.

quadruple /'kwɒdrʊpəl, kwɒ'druːpəl/ ▷ *adj* **1** four times as great, much or many. **2** made up of four parts or things. **3** *music* said of time: having four beats to the bar. ▷ *verb* (***quadrupled, quadrupling***) *tr & intr* to make or become four times as great, much or many. ▷ *noun* **1** an amount that is four times greater than the original or usual, etc amount. **2** a group or series of four. • **quadruply** *adverb*. ⓒ 16c: French.

quadruplet /'kwɒdrʊplət, kwɒ'druːplət/ ▷ *noun* **1** one of four children or animals born to the same mother at the same time. Often shortened to **quad**. **2** a group of four similar things. **3** a group of four notes to be played in the time of three. ⓒ 18c: from QUADRUPLE, modelled on TRIPLET.

quadruple time ▷ *noun, music* a time with four beats in the bar.

quadruplicate ▷ *adj* /kwɒ'druːplɪkət/ **1** having four parts which are exactly alike. **2** being one of four identical copies. **3** quadrupled. ▷ *noun* any of four identical copies or four parts which are exactly alike. ▷ *verb* /-keɪt/ (***quadruplicated, quadruplicating***) to make something quadruple or fourfold. • **quadruplication** *noun.* • **in quadruplicate** copied four times. ⓘ 17c: from Latin *quadruplicare, quadruplicatum* to multiply by four.

quaff /kwɒf/ ▷ *verb* (***quaffed, quaffing***) *tr & intr, literary* to drink eagerly or deeply. • **quaffer** *noun.* ⓘ 16c.

■ **quaff something off** to drain (a cup or glass, etc) by taking long deep drinks.

quag /kwag/ ▷ *noun* a boggy or marshy place, especially one that has a layer of turf on it and which can be felt to shake or give way slightly underfoot. • **quagginess** *noun.* • **quaggy** *adj.* ⓘ 16c.

quagga /ˈkwagə/ ▷ *noun* (***quaggas***) an extinct member of the zebra family found in S Africa until the late 19c which had stripes only on the area around the head and shoulders, the rest of its body being a yellowish-brown colour. ⓘ 18c: a native name, believed to imitate the sound the animal made.

quagmire /ˈkwagmaɪə(r), ˈkwɒg-/ ▷ *noun* **1** an area of soft marshy ground; a bog. **2** a dangerous, difficult or awkward situation. ⓘ 16c.

quahog or **quahaug** /ˈkwɑːhɒg/ ▷ *noun* an edible round clam found off the Atlantic coast of N America. ⓘ 18c: from Narraganset (Native American language) *poquauhock*, from *pohkeni* dark + *hogki* shell.

quaich /kweɪx/ ▷ *noun, Scots* a two-handled drinking cup, the traditional ones being constructed from small wooden staves and hoops like barrels. ⓘ 17c: from Gaelic *cuach* a cup.

quail[1] /kweɪl/ ▷ *noun* (***quail*** or ***quails***) any of several small migratory game birds of the partridge family. ⓘ 14c: from French *quaille.*

quail[2] /kweɪl/ ▷ *verb* (***quailed, quailing***) *intr* to lose courage; to be apprehensive with fear; to flinch. ⓘ 15c.

quaint /kweɪnt/ ▷ *adj* (***quainter, quaintest***) old-fashioned, strange or unusual especially in a charming, pretty or dainty, etc way. • **quaintly** *adverb.* • **quaintness** *noun.* ⓘ 18c; 13c, meaning 'skilful', 'clever' or 'sly': from French *cointe*, from Latin *cognitum* known.

quake /kweɪk/ ▷ *verb* (***quaked, quaking***) *intr* **1** said of people: to shake or tremble with fear, etc. **2** said of a building, etc: to rock or shudder. ▷ *noun* **1** *colloq* an earthquake. **2** a shudder or tremor of fear, etc. • **quakiness** see under QUAKY. • **quaking** *adj, noun.* • **quakingly** *adverb.* • **quake in one's boots** to be very scared or act in a very frightened way. ⓘ Anglo-Saxon *cwacian.*

Quaker ▷ *noun* a member of THE RELIGIOUS SOCIETY OF FRIENDS, a Christian movement founded by George Fox in the 17c. • **Quakerish** *adj.* • **Quakerism** *noun.* • **Quakerly** *adj.* ⓘ 17c: so called either because of Fox's caution to his followers that they should 'tremble at the Word of the Lord' or because some of his adherents, especially the women, would become possessed by the holy spirit and go into trembling fits.

quaking ash ▷ *noun* another name for the ASPEN.

quaking grass ▷ *noun* any of various delicate grasses that tremble in the wind and which are chiefly found on moorland. ⓘ 16c.

quaky ▷ *adj* (***quakier, quakiest***) **1** tending to quake. **2** said of a sensation, etc: similar to quaking. • **quakiness** *noun.*

qualification ▷ *noun* **1 a** an official record that one has completed a training or performed satisfactorily in an examination, etc; **b** a document or certificate, etc that confirms this. **2** a skill or ability that fits one for some job, etc. **3** the act, process or fact of qualifying. **4** an addition to a statement, etc that modifies, narrows or restricts its implications; a condition, limitation or modification. ⓘ 16c: see QUALIFY.

qualified ▷ *adj* **1** having the necessary competency, ability or attributes, etc (to do something). **2** having completed a training or passed an examination, etc, especially in order to practise a specified profession or occupation, etc. **3** limited, modified or restricted; provisional. ⓘ 16c.

qualify /ˈkwɒlɪfaɪ/ ▷ *verb* (***qualifies, qualified, qualifying***) **1** *intr* to complete a training or pass an examination, etc, especially in order to practise a specified profession, occupation, etc. **2 a** (*often* **qualify someone for something**) to give or provide them with the necessary competency, ability or attributes, etc to do it; **b** to entitle ▫ *that qualifies you to get £10 discount.* **3** *intr* **a** to meet or fulfil the required conditions or guidelines, etc (in order to receive an award or privilege, etc); **b** (*usually* **qualify as something**) to have the right characteristics to be a specified thing. **4 a** to modify (a statement, document or agreement, etc) in such a way as to restrict, limit or moderate, etc it; **b** to add reservations to something; to tone down or restrict it. **5** *grammar* said of a word or phrase, especially an adjectival one: to modify, define or describe (another word or phrase, especially a nominal one). **6** *tr & intr, sport* to proceed or allow someone to proceed to the later stages or rounds, etc (of a competition, etc), usually by doing well in a preliminary round. • **qualifiable** *adj.* • **qualificatory** /-fɪˈkeɪtərɪ/ *adj.* • **qualifier** *noun.* • **qualifying** *adj, noun.* ⓘ 16c: from French *qualifier*, from Latin *qualis* of what kind + *facere* to make.

qualifying round ▷ *noun* a preliminary section of a competition, etc in which some of the entrants are eliminated.

qualitative /ˈkwɒlɪtətɪv, -teɪtɪv/ ▷ *adj* relating to, affecting or concerned with distinctions of the quality or standard of something. Compare QUANTITATIVE. • **qualitatively** *adverb.* ⓘ 17c.

qualitative analysis ▷ *noun, chem* the identification of the different constituents, eg the elements, ions and functioning groups, etc, that are present in a substance. Compare QUANTITATIVE ANALYSIS. ⓘ 19c.

quality /ˈkwɒlɪtɪ/ ▷ *noun* (***qualities***) **1** the degree or extent of excellence of something. **2 a** general excellence; high standard ▫ *articles of consistent quality*; **b** *as adj* being of or exhibiting a high quality or standard ▫ *the quality newspapers.* **3 a** a distinctive or distinguishing talent or attribute, etc; **b** the basic nature of something. **4 a** *music* the distinctive timbre that a voice or other sound has; **b** *phonetics* the distinctive character of a sound with regard to the various possible positions of the articulators. **5** *old use* high social status ▫ *families of quality.* ⓘ 13c: from French *qualité*, from Latin *qualis* of what kind.

quality control ▷ *noun* (abbreviation **QC**) a system or the process that involves regular sampling of the output of an industrial process in order to detect any variations in quality. • **quality controller** *noun.*

quality time ▷ *noun* a period of time when someone's attention is devoted entirely to someone else, eg a companion or child, without interruptions or distractions.

qualm /kwɑːm/ ▷ *noun* **1 a** a sudden feeling of nervousness or apprehension; **b** a feeling of uneasiness about whether a decision or course of action, etc is really for the best; **c** a scruple, misgiving or pang of conscience. **2** a feeling of faintness or nausea. • **qualmish** *adj.* ⓘ 16c.

quandary /ˈkwɒndərɪ/ ▷ *noun* (***quandaries***) **1** (*usually* **in a quandary about, over, as to,** *etc* **something**) a state of indecision, uncertainty, doubt or perplexity ▫ *in a quandary over whether to take the job.* **2** a situation that involves some kind of dilemma or predicament. ⓘ 16c.

quandong or **quandang** /ˈkwɒndɒŋ/ and **quantong** /ˈkwɒntɒŋ/ ▷ *noun, Austral* **1** a name for either of two native Australian trees. **2** the fruit or timber of one of these trees. ⓘ 19c: the Aboriginal Australian name.

quango /ˈkwaŋgou/ ▷ *noun* (***quangos***) a semi-public administrative body that functions outwith the civil service but which is government-funded and which has its senior appointments made by the government. ◎ 1960s: from *qua*si-autonomous *n*on-*g*overnmental *o*rganization.

quant /kwɒnt/ ▷ *noun* a type of punting pole that has a prong at the lower end so that it can be pushed into the bed of a river or canal, etc to propel a barge along. ▷ *verb* (***quanted, quanting***) to propel (a barge) along using a quant. ◎ 15c.

quanta see under QUANTUM

quantic /ˈkwɒntɪk/ ▷ *noun, math* a rational integral homogeneous function of two or more variables. • **quantical** *adj.* ◎ 19c: from Latin *quantus* how much.

quantify /ˈkwɒntɪfaɪ/ ▷ *verb* (***quantifies, quantified, quantifying***) **1** to determine the quantity of something or to measure or express it as a quantity. **2** *logic* to stipulate the extent of (a term or proposition) by using a word such as *all, some*, etc. • **quantifiable** *adj.* • **quantifiability** *noun.* • **quantification** *noun.* • **quantifier** *noun.* ◎ 19c: from Latin *quantus* how much + *facere* to make.

quantitative /ˈkwɒntɪtətɪv, -teɪtɪv/ ▷ *adj* **1** relating to or involving quantity. **2** estimated, or measurable, in terms of quantity. Compare QUALITATIVE. • **quantitatively** *adverb.* ◎ 16c.

quantitative analysis ▷ *noun, chem* the measurement of the amounts of the different constituents that are present in a substance. Compare QUALITATIVE ANALYSIS.

quantity /ˈkwɒntɪtɪ/ ▷ *noun* (***quantities***) (abbreviation **Q, qt** or **qty**) **1** the property that things have that allows them to be measured or counted; size or amount. **2** a specified amount or number, etc ▫ *a tiny quantity.* **3** largeness of amount; bulk ▫ *buy in quantity.* **4** (**quantities**) a large amount ▫ *quantities of food.* **5** *math* a value that may be expressed as a number, or the symbol or figure representing it. **6** *prosody* the length or duration of a vowel sound or syllable. • **an unknown quantity** someone or something whose importance or influence cannot be foreseen. ◎ 14c: from Latin *quantitas*, from *quantus* how much.

quantity surveyor ▷ *noun* a person whose job is to estimate the amount and cost of the various materials and labour, etc that a specified building project will require. ◎ Early 20c.

quantize or **quantise** /ˈkwɒntaɪz/ ▷ *verb* (***quantized, quantizing***) *physics* to form into QUANTA (see under QUANTUM). • **quantization** *noun.* ◎ 1920s.

quantum /ˈkwɒntəm/ ▷ *noun* (***quanta*** /-tə/) **1 a** an amount or quantity, especially a specified one; **b** a portion, part or share. **2** *physics* **a** the minimal indivisible amount of a specified physical property (eg momentum or electromagnetic radiation energy, etc) that can exist; **b** a unit of this, eg the PHOTON. Often *as adj* ▫ *quantum effect.* ▷ *adj* major, large or impressive but also sudden, unexpected or abrupt, etc. ◎ 17c: from Latin, neuter of *quantus* how much.

quantum electrodynamics ▷ *noun, physics* the branch of quantum theory that involves the study of the electromagnetic field in relation to the way it interacts with charged particles.

quantum leap or **quantum jump** ▷ *noun* **1** a sudden transition; a spectacular advance. **2** *physics* a sudden transition from one quantum state in an atom or molecule to another.

quantum mechanics ▷ *singular noun, physics* a mathematical theory that developed from the quantum theory and which is used in the interpretation the behaviour of particles, especially subatomic ones. ◎ 1920s.

quantum theory ▷ *noun, physics* a theory, developed by Max Planck (1858–1947) that is based on the principle that in physical systems, the energy associated with any QUANTUM is proportional to the frequency of the radiation.

quaquaversal /kweɪkwəˈvɜːsəl, kwɑː-/ ▷ *adj, geol* turned or pointing in every direction. • **quaquaversally** *adverb.* ◎ 18c: from Latin *quaqua* wheresoever + *versus* towards.

quarantine /ˈkwɒrəntiːn/ ▷ *noun* **1** the isolation of people or animals to prevent the spread of any infectious disease that they could be developing. **2** the duration or place of such isolation. ▷ *verb* (***quarantined, quarantining***) to impose such isolation on someone or something; to put (a person or animal) into quarantine. ◎ 17c: from Italian *quarantina* period of 40 days, from *quaranta* forty.

quark[1] /kwɔːk, kwɑːk/ ▷ *noun, physics* the smallest known bit of matter, being any of a group of subatomic particles which, in different combinations, are thought to make up all protons, neutrons and other hadrons and are believed to have a fractional electric charge though they have not yet been detected in the free state. ◎ 1960s in this sense, but first coined as 'Three Quarks for Muster Mark!' by the novelist James Joyce (1882–1941) in *Finnegans Wake* (1939) and adopted in this scientific sense by the American physicist Murray Gell-Mann (born 1929) before he knew that Joyce had already used it.

quark[2] /kwɑːk/ ▷ *noun* a type of low-fat soft cheese that is made from skimmed milk. ◎ 1930s: German.

quarrel /ˈkwɒrəl/ ▷ *noun* **1** an angry disagreement or argument. **2** a cause of such disagreement; a complaint. **3** a break in a friendship; a breach or rupture. ▷ *verb* (***quarrelled, quarrelling***; *US* ***quarreled, quarreling***) *intr* **1** to argue or dispute angrily. **2** to fall out; to disagree and remain on bad terms. **3** (*usually* **quarrel with someone** or **something**) to find fault with them or it. • **quarreller** *noun.* • **quarrelling** *adj, noun.* ◎ 13c: from Latin *querela*, from *queri* to complain.

quarrelsome ▷ *adj* inclined to quarrel or dispute; characterized by quarrelling. • **quarrelsomely** *adverb.* • **quarrelsomeness** *noun.* ◎ 16c.

quarry[1] /ˈkwɒrɪ/ ▷ *noun* (***quarries***) **1 a** an open excavation for the purpose of extracting stone or slate for building; **b** a place from which stone, etc can be excavated. **2** any source of information, data or knowledge, etc. ▷ *verb* (***quarries, quarried, quarrying***) **1** to extract (stone, etc) from a quarry. **2** to excavate a quarry in (land). **3 a** to get a supply of (material or information) from a source; **b** to search through and extract information or material, etc from (a source). • **quarrying** *noun.* ◎ 15c: from Latin *quadrare* to make (stones) square.

quarry[2] /ˈkwɒrɪ/ ▷ *noun* (***quarries***) **1** a animal or bird that is hunted, especially one that is the usual prey of some other animal or bird. **2** someone or something that is the object of pursuit. ◎ 17c; 14c meaning 'the entrails of a deer placed on the hide and given to hunting dogs as a reward': from French *cuiree*, from *cuir* hide.

quarry tile ▷ *noun* an unglazed floor tile.

quarryman ▷ *noun* a man who works in a quarry.

quart[1] /kwɔːt/ ▷ *noun* (abbreviation **q** or **qt**) **1** in the UK: **a** in the imperial system: a liquid measure equivalent to one quarter of a gallon, two pints (1.136 litres) or 40fl oz; **b** a container that holds this amount. **2** in the US: **a** a unit of liquid measure that is equivalent to one quarter of a gallon, two pints (0.946 litres) or 32fl oz; **b** a unit of dry measure that is equivalent to two pints (1.101 litres), an eighth of a peck or 67.2cu in. ◎ 14c: from French *quarte*, from Latin *quartus* fourth.

quart[2] or **quarte** /kɑːt/ ▷ *noun* **1** *fencing* the fourth of the eight parrying or attacking positions that fencers are taught. Also written **quarte** or **carte**. **2** *cards* a sequence of four cards in piquet. ⓒ 17c: from French *quarte*, from Latin *quartus* fourth.

quartan /ˈkwɔːtən/ ▷ *adj, pathol* said of a fever, etc: recurring every third day. ⓒ 18c: from Latin *febris quartana* a fever that occurs every fourth day (the day of the last flare-up being included).

quarter /ˈkwɔːtə(r)/ ▷ *noun* (abbreviation **q** or **qr**) **1 a** one of four equal parts that an object or quantity is or can be divided into; **b** (often written ¼) the number one when it is divided by four. **2** any of the three-month divisions of the year, especially one that begins or ends on a QUARTER DAY. **3** *N Amer* **a** 25 cents, ie quarter of a dollar; **b** a coin of this value. **4 a** a period of 15 minutes; **b** a point of time 15 minutes after or before any hour. **5** *astron* **a** a fourth part of the Moon's cycle; **b** either of the two phases of the Moon when half its surface is lit and visible at the point between the first and second and the third and fourth quarters of its cycle. **6** any of the four main compass directions; any direction. **7** a district of a city, etc □ *the Spanish quarter.* **8** (*also* **quarters**) a section of the public or society, etc; certain people or a certain person □ *no sympathy from that quarter.* **9** (**quarters**) lodgings or accommodation, eg for soldiers and their families □ *married quarters.* **10** in the imperial system: **a** a unit of weight equal to a quarter of a hundredweight, ie (*Brit*) 28 lbs or (*US*) 25 lbs; **b** *Brit colloq* 4 ozs or a quarter of a pound; **c** *Brit* a unit of measure for grain equal to eight bushels. **11 a** any of the four sections that an animal's or bird's carcass is divided into, each section having a leg or a wing; **b** (**quarters**) *historical* the four similar sections that a human body was divided into, especially after execution for treason. **12** mercy that is shown or offered, eg to a defeated enemy, etc □ *give no quarter.* **13** *heraldry* **a** any of the four sections of a shield which are formed by two perpendicular horizontal and vertical lines; **b** a device that occupies one of these sections in the upper third of a shield. **14** *sport, especially Amer football & Austral Rules football* any of the four equal periods that a game is divided into. **15** *naut* the side of a ship's hull that is between amidships and astern. ▷ *verb* (***quartered***, ***quartering***) **1** to divide something into quarters. **2 a** to accommodate or billet (troops, etc) in lodgings; **b** said especially of military personnel: to be accommodated or billeted in lodgings. **3** *historical* to divide (the body of a hanged traitor, etc) into four parts, each with a limb. **4** *heraldry* **a** to divide (a shield) into quarters using one horizontal and one vertical line; **b** to fill (each quarter of a shield) with bearings; **c** to add (someone else's coat of arms) to one's own hereditary arms. **5** said of a hunting dog or a bird of prey: to cross and recross (an area) searching for game. ⓒ 13c: from French *quartier*, from Latin *quartarius* a fourth part.

quarterage ▷ *noun* **1 a** a payment, tax or contribution, etc that is due quarterly; **b** a sum that is paid quarterly, eg wages, an allowance or a pension. **2** accommodation or lodgings. ⓒ 14c.

quarterback ▷ *noun, Amer football* a player who directs the attacking play. ⓒ 19c.

quarterbinding ▷ *noun* a form of bookbinding where the spine is bound in leather or some other material but the corners of the covers are not. • **quarterbound** *adj.* ⓒ 19c.

quarter day ▷ *noun, Brit* any of the four days when one of the QUARTERS (*noun* 2) of the year begins or ends. Traditionally they were the days that rent or interest fell due and when tenancies were agreed or renewed. ⓒ 15c.

quarterdeck ▷ *noun, naut* the stern part of a ship's upper deck which is usually reserved for officers and is traditionally the place where ceremonies are held. ⓒ 17c.

quarter final ▷ *noun* **1** a match or the round that involves the eight remaining participants or teams in a competition or cup, etc and which precedes the semi-final match or round. **2** (*often* **quarter finals**) the four matches that are played in one of these rounds. ⓒ 1920s.

quarter-finalist ▷ *noun* a team or a person that qualifies to take part in a quarter final.

quartering ▷ *noun* **1** *heraldry* (*usually* **quarterings**) the coats of arms displayed on a shield to indicate family alliances. **2** the provision of quarters for soldiers. **3** division into quarters.

quarterlight ▷ *noun* in older designs of cars: a small triangular window that pivots open for ventilation. ⓒ Late 19c.

quarterly ▷ *adj* produced, occurring, published, paid or due, etc once every quarter of a year. ▷ *adverb* once every quarter. ▷ *noun* (***quarterlies***) a quarterly publication. ⓒ 16c.

quartermaster ▷ *noun* **1** an army officer who is responsible for soldiers' accommodation, food and clothing. **2** *naut* (abbreviation **QM**) a petty officer who is responsible for navigation and signals. ⓒ 15c.

Quartermaster-General ▷ *noun* (***Quartermaster-Generals***) (abbreviation **QMG**) an army officer who is in charge of the department that is responsible for everything to do with the quartering of personnel. Also without hyphen.

Quartermaster-Sergeant ▷ *noun* (abbreviation **QMS**) a noncomissioned officer who is assigned to help the quartermaster. Also without hyphen.

quarter-miler ▷ *noun* an athlete who specializes in running races over a distance of quarter of a mile.

quarter note ▷ *noun, N Amer, music* a crotchet.

quarter pounder ▷ *noun, colloq* a name for a beefburger, cheeseburger, vegeburger, etc that has a main filling which weighs approximately quarter of a pound.

quartet or **quartette** /kwɔːˈtɛt/ ▷ *noun* **1** *music* **a** an ensemble of four singers or instrumentalists; **b** a piece of music for four performers. **2** any group or set of four. ⓒ 18c: from Italian *quartetto*.

quartic /ˈkwɔːtɪk/ ▷ *adj, math* involving the fourth degree. ▷ *noun* an equation, etc of this kind. ⓒ 19c: from Latin *quartus* fourth.

quartile /ˈkwɔːtaɪl/ ▷ *adj, astron* said of the aspect of two heavenly bodies: 90° apart. ▷ *noun* **1** *astrol* a quartile aspect between two heavenly bodies. **2** *statistics* in a frequency distribution: a value such that one quarter, one half or three quarters of the numbers considered are contained within it, these being called, respectively **first quartile**, **second quartile** and **third quartile**. ⓒ 16c: from Latin *quartilis*, from *quartus* fourth.

quarto /ˈkwɔːtoʊ/ ▷ *noun* (***quartos***) (abbreviation **Q**, **qto** *plural* **qq**; often written **4to**) *printing* **1** a size of paper produced by folding a sheet in half twice to give four leaves or eight pages. **2** a book that has its pages made up of sheets of paper that has been folded in this way and then had the outer folds cut. ⓒ 16c: from Latin *in quarto* in one fourth.

quartz /kwɔːts/ ▷ *noun* (***quartzes***) *geol* a common colourless mineral that is often tinged with impurities that give a wide variety of shades making it suitable as a gemstone, eg purple (amethyst), brown (cairngorm), pink (rose quartz), etc. In its pure form, it consists of silica or silicon dioxide. See also QUARTZITE. • **quartziferous** *adj.* • **quartzitic** *adj.* ⓒ 18c: German.

quartz clock and **quartz watch** ▷ *noun* a clock or watch that has a mechanism which is controlled by the vibrations of a QUARTZ CRYSTAL (sense 2).

quartz crystal ▷ *noun* **1** a transparent colourless form of quartz that occurs naturally or can be manufactured and which is used in optics and electronics. **2** a PIEZOELECTRIC CRYSTAL of quartz that is ground so that it vibrates at a specified frequency when a suitable electrical signal is applied to it.

quartzite ▷ *noun, geol* **1** any of various pale or white highly durable rocks that are composed largely or entirely of quartz and which are used as a construction material in the building industry. **2** a sandstone consisting of grains of quartz cemented together by silica. ⓒ 19c.

quasar /ˈkweɪzɑː(r), -sɑː(r)/ ▷ *noun, astron* a highly intense luminous star-like source of light and radio waves that exists thousands of millions of light years outside the Earth's galaxy and which has large redshifts. ⓒ 1960s: from *quasi*-stell*ar* object.

quash /kwɒʃ/ ▷ *verb* (***quashes, quashed, quashing***) **1** to subdue, crush or suppress, etc (eg a rebellion or protest). **2** to reject (a verdict, etc) as invalid. **3** to annul (a law, etc). ⓒ 14c: from Latin *quassare*, from *quatere* to shake.

quasi /ˈkweɪzaɪ/ ▷ *adverb* as it were; so to speak. ⓒ 15c: Latin, literally 'as if'.

quasi- /ˈkweɪzaɪ/ ▷ *combining form, denoting* **1** to some extent; virtually □ *a quasi-official role.* **2** seeming or seemingly, but not actually so □ *quasi-experts.* ⓒ From Latin *quasi* as if.

quasi-stellar object ▷ *noun* (abbreviation **QSO**) any astronomical body belonging to several classes of bodies, such as a QUASAR or a **quasi-stellar galaxy** both which have very large REDSHIFTS. ⓒ 1960s.

quassia /ˈkwɒʃə/ ▷ *noun* (***quassias***) **1** a S American tree whose bitter wood and bark are used as a tonic. **2** a W Indian tree of the same family. ⓒ 18c: named after an 18c Surinamese slave, Graman Quassi, who discovered its medicinal properties.

quaternary /kwɒˈtɜːnərɪ/ ▷ *adj* **1** having or consisting of four parts. **2** fourth in a series. **3** (**Quaternary**) *geol* belonging or relating to the most recent period of geological time when humans evolved. See table at GEOLOGICAL TIME SCALE. **4** *chem* **a** said of a compound, especially one containing nitrogen: having the central atom bound to four other atoms or groups; **b** said of an atom: bound to four other atoms or groups. ▷ *noun, geol* the Quartenary period or rock system. ⓒ 15c: from Latin *quaterni* four each.

quaternion /kwəˈtɜːnɪən/ ▷ *noun* **1** a set of four. **2** *math* the operation of changing one vector into another, or the quotient of two vectors, depending on four geometrical elements and expressible by an algebraical quadrinomial. ⓒ 14c: from Latin *quarternio*, from *quaterni* four.

quatorze /kəˈtɔːz/ ▷ *noun, cards* in piquet: a set of four aces, kings, queens, jacks or tens in a hand which scores 14. ⓒ 18c: French, meaning 'fourteen'.

quatrain /ˈkwɒtreɪn/ ▷ *noun, poetry* a verse or poem of four lines which usually rhyme alternately. ⓒ 16c: French, from *quatre* four.

quatrefoil /ˈkatrəfɔɪl/ ▷ *noun* **1** *bot* **a** a flower with four petals; **b** a leaf composed of four lobes or leaflets. **2** *archit* a four-lobed design, especially one that is used in open stonework. ⓒ 15c: French, from *quatre* four + *foil* leaf.

quattrocento /kwatroʊˈtʃɛntoʊ/ ▷ *noun* the 15c, especially with reference to Italian Renaissance art. • **quattrocentism** *noun*. • **quattrocentist** *adj, noun*. ⓒ 17c: Italian, meaning 'four hundred', but taken to mean 'fourteen hundred'.

quaver /ˈkweɪvə(r)/ ▷ *verb* (***quavered, quavering***) **1** *intr* said of a voice or a musical sound, etc: to be unsteady; to shake or tremble. **2** to say or sing something in a trembling voice. ▷ *noun* **1** *music* a note that lasts half as long as a crotchet and usually represented in notation by ♪. **2** a tremble in the voice. • **quaverer** *noun*. • **quavering** *adj*. • **quaveringly** *adverb*. • **quavery** *adj*. ⓒ 15c: a blending of QUAKE + WAVER.

quay /kiː/ ▷ *noun* an artificial structure that projects into the water for the loading and unloading of ships. ⓒ 17c: from French *kay*, partly assimilated to modern French *quai*.

quayage /ˈkiːɪdʒ/ ▷ *noun* **1** the amount that is levied for the use of a quay. **2** the amount of space that a quay affords.

quayside ▷ *noun* the area around a quay, especially the edge along the water.

Que. ▷ *abbreviation, Can province* Quebec.

queasy /ˈkwiːzɪ/ ▷ *adj* (***queasier, queasiest***) **1** said of a person: feeling slightly sick. **2** said of the stomach or digestion: easily upset. **3** said of the conscience: readily made uneasy. • **queasily** *adj*. • **queasiness** *noun*. ⓒ 15c.

Quebec /kəˈbɛk kwə-/ ▷ *noun, communications* in the NATO alphabet: the word used to denote the letter 'Q' (see table at NATO ALPHABET).

Quebecker or **Quebecer** /kwəˈbɛkə(r), kwɪˈ-, kə-/ and **Québecois** (*plural* **Québecois**) ▷ /*French* kebɛkwa/ ▷ *noun* **1** a citizen or inhabitant of, or a person born in, Quebec, a province in E Canada with a largely French-speaking population. **2** a citizen or inhabitant of, or a person born in, Quebec, a port in E Canada and the capital of the province of Quebec.

quebracho /keɪˈbrɑːtʃoʊ/ ▷ *noun* (***quebrachos***) **1** either of two types of S American trees with a hard wood which is rich in tannin. **2** the wood or bark of either of these trees, used in tanning and dyeing. ⓒ 19c: from American Spanish *quiebracha*, from *quebrar* to break + *hacha* an axe.

Quechua /ˈkɛtʃwə/ ▷ *noun* (***Quechua*** or ***Quechuas***) **1** a group of S American peoples that includes the INCAS, who inhabit Peru and parts of Bolivia, Chile, Colombia and Ecuador. **2** an individual belonging to this group of peoples. **3** their language, which is widely used in this area as a lingua franca. ▷ *adj* belonging or relating to this group or language. • **Quechuan** *noun, adj*. ⓒ 19c: Spanish, from Quechua *k'echua* plunderer.

queen /kwiːn/ ▷ *noun* **1 a** a woman who rules a country, having inherited her position by birth; **b** (*in full* **queen consort**) the wife of a king; **c** (*usually* **Queen**) the title applied to someone who holds either of these positions and which is usually followed by a designated first name or by the name of the country she rules □ *Queen Elizabeth I* □ *Mary Queen of Scots.* **2** a woman, place or thing considered supreme in some way □ *queen of people's hearts* □ *queen of European cities.* **3** a large fertile female ant, bee or wasp that lays eggs. **4** *chess* a piece that is able to move forwards, backwards, sideways or diagonally, making it the most powerful piece on the board. **5** *cards* any of the four high-ranking face cards that have a picture of a queen on them. **6 a** *derog* an effeminate male homosexual; **b** *gay* a male homosexual who likes to camp it up. **7** (*usually* **the Queen**) *Brit colloq* the national anthem when a woman is on the throne □ *Remember when the Queen was played in cinemas?* ▷ *verb* (***queened, queening***) **1** *chess* **a** to advance (a pawn) to the opponent's side of the board and convert it into a queen; **b** *intr* said of a pawn: to reach the opponent's side of the board and so be converted into a queen. **2** to make (a woman) queen. • **queendom** *noun*. • **queenlike** *adj*. • **queenship** *noun*. • **queen it** *colloq* said of a woman: to behave overbearingly. ⓒ Anglo-Saxon *cwene* a woman.

Queen Anne ▷ *adj, denoting* a style of English architecture and furniture, etc that was popular in the early 18c. ⓒ 18c: named after Queen Anne who reigned 1702–14.

Queen Anne's lace ▷ *noun* another name for COW PARSLEY.

queen bee ▷ *noun* (*also* **queen**) **1** the fertile female in a beehive. **2** the dominant, superior or controlling woman in an organization or group, etc.

queen cake ▷ *noun* a small sweet sponge cake, usually one with raisins in it.

queen consort ▷ *noun* the wife of a reigning king. Often shortened to **queen**.

queen dowager ▷ *noun* the widow of a king.

queenly ▷ *adj* (***queenlier***, ***queenliest***) **1** suitable for or appropriate to a queen. **2** majestic; like a queen. • **queenliness** *noun*.

queen mother ▷ *noun* the widow of a king who is also the mother of the reigning king or queen.

Queen Mum ▷ *noun, Brit colloq* an affectionate shortening of **queen mother** that is often applied to the mother of Queen Elizabeth II.

queen of puddings ▷ *noun* a dessert that is usually made from breadcrumbs, egg, milk and jam, often with a meringue topping.

Queen of the May see MAY QUEEN

queen post ▷ *noun, archit* in a trussed roof: one of two upright posts that connect the tie-beam to the principal rafters.

Queen's Bench (when the sovereign is a woman) or **King's Bench** (when the sovereign is a man) ▷ *noun* (abbreviation **QB**) in the UK: a division of the High Court of Justice.

Queensberry Rules /ˈkwiːnsbərɪ —/ ▷ *plural noun* **1** the code of rules that govern modern-day boxing. **2** *colloq* approved, mannerly, courteous or civilized, etc behaviour, especially in a dispute. ◷ Late 19c: named after Sir John Sholto Douglas (1844–1900), Marquis of Queensberry, who had a keen interest in the sport and who, in 1867, helped in drawing up the code.

Queen's Counsel (when the sovereign is a woman) or **King's Counsel** (when the sovereign is a man) ▷ *noun* (abbreviation **QC**) *law* **1** in England and Wales: a senior barrister who is recommended for appointment as Counsel to the Crown by the Lord Chancellor and who is allowed to sit within the bar and to wear silk gowns. **2** in Scotland: a senior advocate who is recommended for appointment as Counsel to the Crown by the Lord President and who has these same privileges. Also called **silk**.

Queen's English (when the sovereign is a woman) or **King's English** (when the sovereign is a man) ▷ *noun* a term that is used by some, but not by linguists, to designate the standard form of written or spoken Southern British English which they regard as the most correct or acceptable form. ◷ 16c.

Queen's evidence (when the sovereign is a woman) or **King's evidence** (when the sovereign is a man) ▷ *noun, Brit law* evidence that a participant or accomplice in a crime gives to support the case of the prosecution and which is usually not given as much weight as evidence from independent witnesses, because it is likely that the person giving it will try to minimize the extent of their own involvement. • **turn Queen's** or **King's evidence** said of a criminal: to decide to give such evidence, usually after a deal promising a more lenient sentence has been struck. *N Amer, especially US* equivalent STATE'S EVIDENCE.

Queen's Guide (when the sovereign is a woman) or **King's Guide** (when the sovereign is a man) *Brit,* ▷ *noun* **1** a GUIDE (*noun* 4) who has reached the highest level of proficiency. **2** this rank, its certificate or badge or the award of this rank.

Queen's highway (when the sovereign is a woman) or **King's highway** (when the sovereign is a man) ▷ *noun, Brit* a public road, regarded as being under royal control.

queen-size and **queen-sized** ▷ *adj* said especially of a bed or other piece of furniture: larger than the usual or normal size but not as large as king-size. ◷ 1950s.

Queenslander ▷ *noun* a citizen or inhabitant of, or a person born in, Queensland, a state in NE Australia.

Queensland nut ▷ *noun* another name for the MACADAMIA nut.

Queen's Scout (when the sovereign is a woman) and **King's Scout** (when the sovereign is a man) *Brit,* ▷ *noun* **1** a SCOUT (*noun* 2) who has reached the highest level of proficiency. **2** this rank, its certificate or badge or the award of this rank.

Queen's Speech (when the sovereign is a woman) and **King's Speech** (when the sovereign is a man) ▷ *noun, Brit* **1** the speech that the reigning monarch makes on the opening of a new session of parliament and which gives details of the government's proposed legislative agenda. **2** a traditional Christmas day broadcast on TV and radio in which the monarch addresses the nation and the Commonwealth.

queer /kwɪə(r)/ ▷ *adj* (***queerer***, ***queerest***) **1** *slang* said of a man: homosexual. Compare GAY *adj* 1. **2** odd, strange or unusual. **3** *colloq* slightly mad. **4** faint or ill. **5** *colloq* suspicious; shady. ▷ *noun, slang* a homosexual. ▷ *verb* (***queered***, ***queering***) to spoil something. • **queerish** *adj*. • **queerly** *adverb*. • **queerness** *noun*. • **in queer street** *Brit colloq* **1** in debt or financial difficulties. **2** in trouble. • **queer someone's pitch** *colloq* to spoil their plans; to thwart them. ◷ 1920s in sense 1; 16c in sense 2.

queer-bashing ▷ *noun* an act or instance, or the process of, maliciously attacking a homosexual, a group of homosexuals or homosexuals in general (or someone who is or people who are thought to be) homosexual, either physically or verbally and without any provocation. • **queer-basher** *noun*.

quell /kwɛl/ ▷ *verb* (***quelled***, ***quelling***) **1 a** to crush or subdue (riots, disturbances or opposition, etc); **b** to force (rebels or rioters, etc) to give in. **2** to suppress, overcome, alleviate or put an end to (sickness, unwanted feelings, etc). • **queller** *noun*. ◷ Anglo-Saxon *cwellan* to kill.

quench /kwɛnʃ, kwɛntʃ/ ▷ *verb* (***quenches***, ***quenched***, ***quenching***) **1 a** to satisfy (thirst) by drinking; **b** to satisfy (a desire, etc). **2** to extinguish (a fire or light, etc). **3** to damp or crush (ardour, enthusiasm or desire, etc). **4** *metallurgy* to cool (hot metal) rapidly by plunging in cold liquid in order to alter its properties. **5** *nuclear chem* to introduce an agent into a luminescent material to reduce the duration of phosphorescence. • **quenchable** *adj*. • **quencher** *noun*. • **quenchless** *adj*. • **quenching** *adj, noun*. ◷ Anglo-Saxon *acwencan*.

quenelle /kəˈnɛl/ ▷ *noun, cookery* an oval or sausage-shaped dumpling made from spiced meat-paste, eg fish, chicken or veal, etc, which is bound together with fat and eggs and poached in water. ◷ 19c: French, from German *Knodel* a dumpling.

querist /ˈkwɪərɪst/ ▷ *noun* someone who asks a question or makes an inquiry. ◷ 17c: from Latin *quaerere* to ask.

quern /kwɜːn/ ▷ *noun* **1** a mill, usually consisting of two circular stones (**quernstones**) one on top of the other, used for grinding grain by hand. **2** a small hand mill for grinding pepper or mustard, etc. ◷ Anglo-Saxon *cweorn*.

querulous /ˈkwɛrjʊləs, -rʊləs/ ▷ *adj* **1** said of someone or their disposition: inclined or ready to complain. **2** said of a voice, tone or comment, etc: complaining, grumbling or whining. • **querulously** *adverb*. • **querulousness** *noun*. ◷ 15c: from Latin *querulus*, from *queri* to complain.

query /ˈkwɪərɪ/ ▷ *noun* (***queries***) **1** a question, especially one that raises a doubt or objection, etc. **2** a request for information; an inquiry. **3** a less common name for a QUESTION MARK. ▷ *verb* (***queries***, ***queried***, ***querying***) **1** to raise a doubt about or an objection to something. **2** to ask ▫ *'How much?' she queried.* **3** *chiefly US* to interrogate or question someone. • **querying** *adj, noun*. • **queryingly** *adverb*. ◷ 17c: from Latin imperative *quaere* ask!, from *quaerere* to ask.

quest /kwɛst/ ▷ *noun* **1** a search or hunt. **2** a journey, especially one undertaken by a medieval knight, that involves searching for something (eg the Holy Grail) or achieving some goal and often resulting in various adventures which bring about some form self-improvement or self-discovery, etc. **3** the object of a search; an aim or goal. ▷ *verb* (***quested, questing***) *intr* **1** (*usually* **quest after** or **for something**) to search about; to roam around in search of it. **2** said of a dog: to search for game. ● **quester** or **questor** *noun*. ● **questing** *adj, noun*. ● **questingly** *adverb*. ● **in quest of something** in the process of looking for it. ⓒ 14c: from Latin *quaerere* to seek.

question /'kwɛstʃən/ ▷ *noun* **1 a** a written or spoken sentence that is worded in such a way as to request information or an answer; **b** the interrogative sentence or other form of words in which this is expressed. **2** a doubt or query □ *raises questions about their loyalty.* **3** a problem or difficulty □ *the Northern Ireland question.* **4** a problem set for discussion or solution in an examination paper, etc. **5** an investigation or search for information. **6** a matter, concern or issue □ *a question of safety.* ▷ *verb* (***questioned, questioning***) **1** to ask someone questions; to interrogate them. **2** to raise doubts about something; to query it. ● **questioner** *noun*. ● **questionless** *adj*. ● **be (only, simply** or **just**, *etc*) **a question of something** to be a situation, case or matter of a specified thing □ *It's just a question of time* □ *It's a question of whether or not he'll remember.* ● **beg the question** see under BEG. ● **beyond question** not in doubt; beyond doubt. ● **call something in** or **into question** to suggest reasons for doubting its validity or truth, etc. ● **in question 1** presently under discussion or being referred to □ *was away at the time in question.* **2** in doubt □ *Her ability is not in question.* ● **no question of something** no possibility or intention of it. ● **out of the question** impossible and so not worth considering. ● **pop the question** see under POP[1]. ● **without question** unhesitatingly. ⓒ 13c: from French *questiun*, from Latin *quaestio*, from *quaerere* to ask.

questionable ▷ *adj* **1** doubtful; debatable; ambiguous. **2** suspect; disreputable; obscure; shady. ● **questionability** *noun*. ● **questionably** *adverb*.

questioning ▷ *noun* an act or the process of asking a question or questions. ▷ *adj* **1** characterized by doubt or uncertainty; mildly confused □ *exchanged questioning looks.* **2** said especially of a person's mind: inquisitive; keen to learn. ● **questioningly** *adverb*.

question mark ▷ *noun* **1 a** the punctuation mark ? which is used to indicate that the sentence that comes before it is a question; **b** this mark when it is used to indicate that there is a possible error. **2** a doubt □ *still a question mark over funds.*

question mark

● A question mark is used to indicate a direct question □ *Is John coming?* □ *Which is your car?* Note that a question mark will sometimes be the only indication that a sentence is a question and not a statement □ *John's coming too?*

Sentences that are questions in form but requests or statements in meaning should not take a question mark □ *Can you pass me the butter, please.* □ *Would the parent of a little boy aged about four and answering to the name of Jeremy please come to the manager's office to collect him.*

● Informally, a question mark is used to indicate that an indirect question is really a polite request or a tentative direct question □ *I wonder if you could help me? I'm looking for Princes Street.* □ *I was wondering if you would like to come too?*

● It is used in parentheses to indicate that something in a statement is suspicious or uncertain □ *He gave his name as Ellis (?) and said he was looking for work.* □ *In this regard, we could consider the poetry of Geoffrey Chaucer (?1340–1400) and the paintings of Hieronymus Bosch (?1450–1516).*

question master ▷ *noun* someone who asks the questions and adjudicates the scores, etc in a quiz, etc.

questionnaire /kwɛstʃə'nɛə(r), kɛs-/ ▷ *noun* (***questionnaires***) **1** a set of questions that has been specially formulated as a means of collecting information and surveying opinions, etc on a specified subject or theme, etc. **2** a document that contains a set of questions of this kind. ⓒ Early 20c: French.

question time ▷ *noun, Brit* the period that is set aside each day that the House sits for MPs to put questions to government ministers.

quetzal /'kɛtsəl/ ▷ *noun* **1** the most flamboyant of the TROGON birds of Central and S America, the males of which have bright coppery-green feathers on their upper parts and crimson ones below, and enormously long wing and tail coverts which resemble graceful streamers. **2** (*plural* ***quetzales*** /-'sɑːlɛs/) the standard unit of currency of Guatemala. ⓒ 19c; early 20c in sense 2: American Spanish, from Nahuatl (the Aztec language) *quetzalli* a bird's tail-feather.

queue /kjuː/ ▷ *noun* **1** *Brit* a line or file of people or vehicles, etc, especially ones that are waiting for something. *N Amer equivalent* LINE. **2** *computing* a list of items, eg programs or data, held in a computer system in the order in which they are to be processed, the items that arrive earliest being processed first and subsequent ones placed at the end of the list. **3** a pigtail. ▷ *verb* (***queued, queuing***) *intr* **1** (*also* **queue up**) **a** to form a queue; **b** to stand or wait in a queue. **2** *computing* to line up tasks for a computer to process. ⓒ 19c as *noun* 3; 16c, meaning 'a tail': French.

queue-jump ▷ *verb, intr, Brit* to barge in front of other people in a queue in order to be served, dealt with, etc sooner. ● **queue-jumper** *noun*. ● **queue-jumping** *adj, noun*. ⓒ 1950s.

quibble /'kwɪbəl/ ▷ *verb* (***quibbled, quibbling***) *intr* to argue over trifles; to make petty objections □ *quibbled about his share of the bill.* ▷ *noun* **1** a trifling objection. **2** *old use* a pun. ● **quibbler** *noun*. ● **quibbling** *adj, noun*. ● **quibblingly** *adverb*. ⓒ 17c.

quiche /kiːʃ/ ▷ *noun* a type of open tart that is usually made with a filling of beaten eggs and cream with various savoury flavourings, and which can be served either hot or cold. ⓒ 1940s: French, from German *Kuchen* cake.

quiche lorraine /— lə'reɪn/ ▷ *noun* a traditional type of quiche that is flavoured with bacon.

quick /kwɪk/ ▷ *adj* (***quicker, quickest***) **1** taking little time. **2** brief. **3** fast; rapid; speedy. **4** not delayed; immediate. **5** intelligent; alert; sharp. **6** said of the temper: easily roused to anger. **7** nimble, deft or brisk. **8** not reluctant or slow (to do something); apt, eager or ready □ *quick to take offence.* ▷ *adverb, informal* rapidly. ▷ *noun* **1** an area of sensitive flesh, especially at the base of the fingernail or toenail. **2** the site where someone's emotions or feelings, etc are supposed to be located □ *Her words wounded him to the quick.* **3** (*usually* **the quick**) *old use* those who are alive □ *the quick and the dead.* ● **quickly** *adverb*. ● **quickness** *noun*. ● **be quick** to act immediately. ● **be quick off the mark** to act promptly. ● **be quick on the draw 1** to react or respond, etc promptly. **2** to pull a gun from its holster quickly. ⓒ Anglo-Saxon *cwic* alive.

quick assets ▷ *plural noun, accounting* assets that can easily and speedily be converted into cash.

quick-change artist ▷ *noun* a performer who makes several changes in costume or appearance during a single show.

quicken /'kwɪkən/ ▷ *verb* (***quickened, quickening***) **1** *tr & intr* to make or become quicker; to accelerate □ *Her heart quickened when she saw him.* **2** to stimulate, rouse or stir (interest or imagination, etc). **3** *intr* **a** said of a baby in the womb: to begin to move perceptibly; **b** said of a pregnant woman: to begin to feel her baby's movements. ● **quickener** *noun*. ● **quickening** *adj, noun*. ⓒ 16c in sense 3; 14c, meaning 'to give or receive life'.

quick-fire ▷ *adj* **1** said especially of repartee, etc: very rapid. **2** said of a gun, etc: designed or able to fire shots in rapid succession.

quick fix ▷ *noun* a remedy that has the benefit of being immediate but the drawback of not being very effective.

quick-freeze ▷ *verb* to freeze (especially soft fruit such as strawberries) rapidly by exposing it to moving air at a very low temperature, so that only small ice crystals form and the internal structure is not damaged. ● **quick-frozen** *adj.* ⓒ 1930s.

quickie ▷ *noun, colloq* **1** something that is dealt with or done rapidly or in a short time. **2** (*also* **a quick one**) a measure of alcohol that is drunk quickly. **3** a divorce that is settled quickly and without any complications. **4** a brief sexual encounter or act of sexual intercourse. ⓒ 1920s, specifically of a quickly-made film.

quicklime see CALCIUM OXIDE

quick march ▷ *noun, military* a march that proceeds in QUICK TIME. ▷ *exclamation* a command that instructs (soldiers, etc) to begin marching at this pace.

quicksand ▷ *noun* **1 a** loose, wet sand that can suck down anything that lands or falls on it, often swallowing it up completely; **b** an area of this. **2** a dangerous, testing, risky or threatening, etc situation or thing. ⓒ 15c.

quickset ▷ *noun* **1 a** a living slip or cutting from a plant, especially from a hawthorn or other shrub, that is put into the ground with others where they will grow to form a hedge; **b** a collection of such slips or cuttings. **2** a hedge that is formed from such slips or cuttings. ▷ *adj* said of a hedge: formed from such slips or cuttings. ⓒ 15c: from QUICK, meaning 'alive', 'living' or 'growing'.

quicksilver ▷ *noun* MERCURY 1. ▷ *adj* said of someone's mind or temper, etc: fast, especially unpredictably so; volatile. ▷ *verb* to coat (the back of a piece of glass) with an amalgam of tin in order to make it reflective. ● **quicksilvery** *adj.* ● **quicksilvering** *noun* the reflective backing in a mirror. ⓒ Anglo-Saxon *cwic seolfor*, modelled on Latin *argentum vivum* living silver.

quickstep ▷ *noun* **1 a** a fast modern ballroom dance in quadruple time; **b** a piece of music that is suitable for this kind of dance. **2** *military* the type of step that is used in QUICK TIME. ▷ *verb, intr* to dance the quickstep. ⓒ 19c.

quick-tempered ▷ *adj* easily angered; grouchy or irritable.

quickthorn ▷ *noun* the HAWTHORN.

quick time ▷ *noun, military* fast marching that is done at a rate of about 120 paces per minute. ⓒ Early 19c.

quick trick ▷ *noun, bridge* **1** a high-ranking card or combination of cards that is likely to win a trick. **2** a trick that is won by this kind of card or cards.

quick-witted ▷ *adj* **1** having fast reactions. **2** able to grasp or understand situations, etc quickly; clever. ● **quick-wittedness** *noun.*

quid[1] /kwɪd/ ▷ *noun* (*plural* ***quid***) *colloq* a pound sterling. ● **quids in** well-off; in a profitable or advantageous position. ⓒ 17c.

quid[2] /kwɪd/ ▷ *noun* a bit of tobacco that is kept in the mouth and chewed. ⓒ 18c: a dialectal variant of CUD.

quiddity /'kwɪdɪtɪ/ ▷ *noun* (***quiddities***) **1** the essence of something; the distinctive qualities, etc that make a thing what it is. **2** a quibble; a trifling detail or point. ⓒ 16c: from Latin *quidditas*, from *quid* what.

quid pro quo /kwɪd proʊ 'kwoʊ/ ▷ *noun* (***quid pro quos***) **1** something that is given or taken in exchange for something else of comparable value or status, etc. **2** an act or instance, or the process or result of, exchanging something for something else of comparable value or status, etc. ⓒ 16c: Latin, meaning 'something for something'.

quiescent /kwɪ'ɛːsənt/ ▷ *adj* **1** quiet, silent, at rest or in an inactive state, usually temporarily. **2** *phonetics* said of a consonant: not sounded. ● **quiescence** *noun.* ● **quiescency** *noun.* ● **quiescently** *adverb.* ⓒ 17c: from Latin *quiescere* to be quiet.

quiet /kwaɪət/ ▷ *adj* (***quieter***, ***quietest***) **1 a** making little or no noise; **b** said of a sound or voice, etc: soft; not loud. **2** said of a place, etc: peaceful; tranquil; without noise or bustle. **3** said of someone or their nature or disposition: reserved; unassertive; shy. **4** said of the weather or sea, etc: calm. **5** not disturbed by trouble or excitement. **6** without fuss or publicity; informal. **7** said of business or trade, etc: not flourishing or busy. **8** secret; private. **9** undisclosed or hidden □ *took a quiet satisfaction in his downfall.* **10** said of humour: subtle; not overdone. **11** enjoyed in peace □ *a quiet read.* **12** said of the mind or conscience: untroubled by anxiety or guilt, etc. **13** not showy or gaudy, etc □ *quiet tones of beige.* ▷ *noun* **1** absence of, or freedom from, noise or commotion, etc. **2** calm, tranquillity or repose. ▷ *verb* (***quieted***, ***quieting***) *tr & intr* (*usually* **quiet down**) to make something or become quiet or calm □ *told the class to quiet down.* ● **quietly** *adverb.* ● **quietness** *noun.* ● **keep quiet about something** or **keep something quiet** to remain silent or say nothing about it. ● **on the quiet** (*also* **on the q.t.**) secretly; discreetly. ⓒ 14c: from Latin *quietus*, from *quiescere* to come to rest.

quieten ▷ *verb* (***quietened***, ***quietening***) **1** (*often* **quieten down**) *tr & intr* to make or become quiet. **2** to calm (doubts or fears, etc). ⓒ 19c.

quietism /'kwaɪətɪzəm/ ▷ *noun* **1** a state of calmness and passivity. **2** (**Quietism**) a form of religious mysticism that involves the complete surrender of personal will to the will of God and the abandonment of anything connected to the senses in favour of dedication to devotion and contemplation. ● **quietistic** *adj.* ● **quietist** *noun, adj.* ⓒ 18c; 17c in sense 2; Quietism was founded by the Spanish priest Miguel de Molinos (1628–96).

quietude /'kwaɪətjuːd/ ▷ *noun* quietness; tranquillity. ⓒ 16c.

quietus /kwaɪ'iːtəs, kwiː'eɪtəs/ ▷ *noun* **1 a** release from life; death; **b** something that brings about death. **2** release or discharge from debts or duties. ⓒ 16c: from Latin *quietus est* he is quit, meaning 'he is considered to have discharged his debts'.

quiff /kwɪf/ ▷ *noun* a tuft of hair at the front of the head that is brushed up into a crest and which is sometimes made to hang over the forehead. ▷ *verb* (***quiffed***, ***quiffing***) (*also* **quiff up**) to style (hair) into a quiff. ⓒ 19c.

quill /kwɪl/ ▷ *noun* **1 a** a large stiff feather from a bird's wing or tail; **b** the hollow base part of this. **2** (*in full* **quill pen**) a pen that is made by sharpening and splitting the end of a feather, especially a goose feather. **3** a porcupine's long spine. **4** a hollow stem that is made into a musical pipe. **5** a curled tube of cinnamon bark. **6** a bobbin. **7** a plectrum, originally one made from a crow quill, that is used for plucking the strings of a musical instrument, especially a harpsicord. ▷ *verb* (***quilled***, ***quilling***) **1** to form (material in a ruff) into tubular folds. **2** to wind (thread, etc) on to a bobbin. ⓒ 15c.

quilt /kwɪlt/ ▷ *noun* **1** a type of bedcover that is made by sewing together two layers of fabric, usually with some kind of soft padding material, eg feathers or wadding, etc in between them. The padding is held in place by the stitching which is often made to form regular or decorative patterns. **2** a bedspread that is made in this way but which tends to be thinner. **3** *loosely* a duvet; a continental quilt. ▷ *verb* (***quilted***, ***quilting***) *tr & intr* **1** to sew (two layers of material, etc) together with a filling in between, usually by using stitching that produces regular or decorative patterns. **2** to cover or line something with padding. **3** to compile (a literary work) using extracts from various sources. ● **quilter** *noun.* ● **quilted** *adj.* ●

quilting *noun*. 🕓 13c: from French *cuilte*, from Latin *culcita* a mattress or cushion.

quilting bee and **quilting party** ▷ *noun, chiefly N Amer* an occasion when people gather, usually at someone's house, to work together on a quilt, catch up on gossip and have a good time.

quim /kwɪm/ ▷ *noun, slang* the external genital organs of a woman. 🕓 18c.

quin ▷ *noun, colloq* a shortened form of QUINTUPLET.

quinacrine /ˈkwɪnəkriːn/ ▷ *noun* MEPACRINE. 🕓 1930s: from *quinine* + *acridine*.

quinary /ˈkwaɪnərɪ/ ▷ *adj* **1** relating or referring to the number five. **2** said of a number system: based on the number five. **3** having or being composed of five parts. **4** fifth in a series. ▷ *noun* (***quinaries***) a set or group of five. 🕓 17c: from Latin *quinarius*, from *quinque* five.

quinate /ˈkwaɪnət/ ▷ *adj, bot* said of a leaf: having five leaflets. 🕓 Early 19c: from Latin *quinque* five.

quince /kwɪns/ ▷ *noun* **1** a small Asian tree of the rose family. **2** the acidic hard yellow fruit of this tree which is used in making jams and jellies, etc. **3** the fruit of certain other plants, eg the fruit of the JAPONICA. 🕓 14c: from the plural of English *quyne* quince, ultimately from Greek *melon Kydonion* apple of Cydonia, a town in Crete, now called *Canea*.

quincentenary ▷ *noun* **1** a 500th anniversary. **2** a celebration that is held to mark this. • **quincentennial** *adj*. 🕓 19c: from Latin *quinque* five + CENTENARY.

quincunx /ˈkwɪnkʌŋks/ ▷ *noun* (***quincunxes***) **1 a** an arrangement in which each of the four corners of a square or rectangle and the point at its the centre are all indicated by some object; **b** five objects that are arranged in this way. **2** a repeating pattern based on this arrangement, eg in tree-planting. • **quincunxial** /kwɪnˈkʌnʃɪəl/ *adj*. • **quincunxially** *adverb*. 🕓 17c: Latin, meaning 'five twelfths'.

quinella /kwɪˈnɛlə/ ▷ *noun* (***quinellas***) a type of bet where punters select two horses, dogs, etc, ie the one that comes second in a specified race as well as the race winner, although they do not have to specify which is which. Compare QUADRELLA, PERFECTA, TRIFECTA. 🕓 1940s: from American Spanish *quiniela*.

quinidine /ˈkwɪnədaɪn/ ▷ *noun, medicine* a drug that is obtained from the bark of the CINCHONA and which is used for treating irregularities in heartbeat rates. 🕓 19c; see QUININE.

quinine /kwɪˈniːn/ or (*especially US*) /ˈkwaɪnaɪn/ ▷ *noun* **1** an alkaloid that is found in the bark of the CINCHONA. **2** *medicine* a bitter-tasting toxic drug obtained from this alkaloid, and which was formerly taken as a tonic. It is effective in reducing fever and pain and was once widely used in treating malaria. 🕓 19c: from Spanish *quina* cinchona bark, from Quechua *kina* bark.

quinol /ˈkwɪnɒl/ ▷ *noun, chem* another name for HYDROQUINONE. 🕓 19c.

quinoline /ˈkwɪnəliːn, -lɪn/ ▷ *noun, chem* a water-soluble aromatic nitrogen compound in the form of an oily colourless liquid, used in the manufacture of dyes and antiseptics and as a food preservative. 🕓 19c.

quinone /ˈkwɪnoʊn/ ▷ *noun, chem* **1** a yellow crystalline compound that is made by oxidizing aniline, used in the manufacture of dyes. Also called **benzoquinone**. **2** any derivative of BENZENE where two hydrogen atoms are replaced by two oxygen ones. 🕓 19c; see QUININE, -ONE.

quinquagenerian /kwɪŋkwədʒɪˈnɛərɪən/ ▷ *noun* someone who is aged between 50 and 59. ▷ *adj* **1** aged between 50 and 59. **2** belonging, relating or referring to this age span. 🕓 19c; 16c, meaning 'a captain of 50 men': from Latin *quinquaginta* fifty.

Quinquagesima /kwɪŋkwəˈdʒɛsɪmə/ ▷ *noun* (*in full* **Quinquagesima Sunday**) in the Christian calendar: the Sunday before the beginning of Lent. 🕓 14c: from Latin *quinquagesima dies* fiftieth day, ie before Easter Day.

quinquennial /kwɪŋˈkwɛnɪəl/ ▷ *adj* **1** lasting for five years. **2** recurring once every five years. • **quinquennially** *adverb*. ▷ *noun* **1** a fifth anniversary. **2** a celebration of this. 🕓 15c: from Latin *quinque* five + *annus* year.

quinquennium /kwɪŋˈkwɛnɪəm/ ▷ *noun* (***quinquennia***) a period of five years. 🕓 17c.

quinquereme /ˈkwɪŋkwɪriːm/ ▷ *noun, historical* a type of ancient Roman or Greek galley ship that had five banks of oars or, possibly, five oarsmen to each oar. 🕓 17c: from Latin *quinque* five + *remus* oar.

quinquevalent /kwɪŋkwɪˈveɪlənt/ ▷ *adj, chem* PENTAVALENT.

quinsy /ˈkwɪnzɪ/ ▷ *noun, pathol* inflammation of the tonsils and the area of the throat round about them, accompanied by the formation of an abscess or abscesses on the tonsils. • **quinsied** *adj*. 🕓 14c: from Latin *quinancia*, from Greek *kyon* dog + *anchein* to strangle.

quint ▷ *noun* **1** /kɪnt/ *cards* in the game of piquet: a hand with a run of five cards of the same suit and which scores 15. **2** /kwɪnt/ (*in full* **quint stop**) an organ stop that gives a tone that is a fifth higher than normal. **3** /kwɪnt/ *US* a shortened form of QUINTUPLET. 🕓 17c: from French *quinte*, from Latin *quinque* five.

quinta /ˈkintə/ ▷ *noun* (***quintas***) a country house, villa or estate in Spain and Portugal. 🕓 18c: from Spanish and Portuguese *quinta parte* a fifth part, from the practice of letting a house or farm in exchange for a fifth of the annual produce.

quintal /ˈkwɪntəl/ ▷ *noun* **1** a unit of weight that is equal to a hundredweight, 112 lbs in Britain or 100 lbs in the US. **2** in the metric system: a unit of weight that is equal to 100 kg. 🕓 15c: French, from Arabic *qintar*, from Latin *centum* one hundred.

quintan /ˈkwɪntən/ ▷ *adj, pathol* said of a fever, etc: flaring up every fourth day. 🕓 18c: from Latin *febris quintana* a fever that occurs every fifth day (the day of the last flare-up being included).

quinte /kant, kɛ̃t/ ▷ *noun, fencing* the fifth of the eight parrying or attacking positions that fencers are taught. 🕓 18c: French, from Latin *quintus* fifth.

quintessence /kwɪnˈtɛsəns/ ▷ *noun* **1** (*usually* **quintessence of something**) a perfect example or embodiment of it. **2** the fundamental essential nature of something. **3** *old use* the purest, most concentrated extract of a substance. **4** in ancient and medieval philosophy: the fifth essence, after the four elements of fire, water, air and earth, which was believed to be present in all things and to be the major constituent of heavenly bodies. • **quintessential** /kwɪntɪˈsɛnʃəl/ *adj*. • **quintessentially** *adverb*. 🕓 15c: from Latin *quinta essentia* fifth essence.

quintet or **quintette** /kwɪnˈtɛt/ ▷ *noun* **1** a group of five singers or musicians. **2** a piece of music for five such performers. **3** any group or set of five. 🕓 19c: from French *quintette*, from Latin *quinto* fifth.

quintillion /kwɪnˈtɪljən/ ▷ *noun* (***quintillion*** or ***quintillions***) **1** in Britain: a number that is represented by a figure 1 followed by 30 zeros, ie 10^{30}. *N Amer equivalent* NONILLION. **2** in N America and France: a number that is represented by a figure 1 followed by 18 zeros, ie 10^{18}. • **quintillionth** *adj*. 🕓 17c: French, from Latin *quintus* fifth + *million*.

quintuple /ˈkwɪntjʊpəl/ ▷ *adj* **1** five times as great, much or many. **2** made up of five parts or things. **3** *music* said of time: having five beats to the bar. ▷ *verb* (***quintupled***, ***quintupling***) *tr & intr* to make or become five times as great, much or many. ▷ *noun* **1** an amount that is five times greater than the original or usual, etc amount. **2** a group or series of four. • **quintuply** *adverb*. 🕓 16c: French, from Latin *quintus* fifth, modelled on QUADRUPLE.

quintuplet /ˈkwɪntjʊplət/ ▷ *noun* **1** one of five children or animals born to the same mother at the same time. Often shortened to **quin** or (*US*) **quint**. **2** a group of five similar things. **3** a group of five notes to be played in the time of four. ⓒ 18c: from QUINTUPLE, modelled on TRIPLET.

quintuplicate ▷ *adj* /kwɪnˈtjuːplɪkət/ **1** having five parts which are exactly alike. **2** being one of five identical copies. **3** quintupled. ▷ *noun* any of five identical copies or five parts which are exactly alike. ▷ *verb* /-plɪkeɪt/ (***quintuplicated, quintuplicating***) to make something quintuple or fivefold. • **quintuplication** *noun*. • **in quintuplicate** copied five times. ⓒ 17c: from Latin *quintuplicare* to multiply by five.

quip /kwɪp/ ▷ *noun* **1** a witty saying. **2** a sarcastic or wounding remark. ▷ *verb* (***quipped, quipping***) **1** *intr* to make a quip or quips. **2** to answer someone with a quip. • **quippish** *adj*. • **quipster** *noun*. ⓒ 16c: from the earlier English *quippy* a quip, from Latin *quippe* indeed, which had sarcastic overtones.

quire /ˈkwaɪə(r)/ ▷ *noun* **1** a measure for paper that is equivalent to 25 (formerly 24) sheets and one-twentieth of a REAM. **2 a** a set of four sheets of parchment or paper folded in half together to form eight leaves; **b** *loosely* any set of folded sheets that is grouped together with other similar ones and bound into book form. • **in quires** not bound together; in sheets. ⓒ 15c: from French *quaier*, from Latin *quaterni* a set of four.

quirk /kwɜːk/ ▷ *noun* **1** an odd habit, mannerism or aspect of personality, etc. **2** an odd twist in affairs or turn of events; a strange coincidence. **3** *archit* a sharp-angled groove or hollow in a moulding. • **quirkish** *adj*. • **quirkiness** *noun*. ⓒ 16c.

quirky ▷ *adj* (***quirkier, quirkiest***) having quirks; odd; tricky.

quirt /kwɜːt/ ▷ *noun* a short-handled riding whip with a braided leather lash, about 61cm (2ft) long. ▷ *verb* (***quirted, quirting***) to strike (the flank of a horse) with a quirt. ⓒ 19c: from Spanish *cuerda* a cord.

quisling /ˈkwɪzlɪŋ/ ▷ *noun* **1** a traitor. **2** someone who collaborates with an enemy. ⓒ 1940s: named after the Norwegian officer and diplomatist, Major Vidkun Quisling (1887–1945), who was a known collaborator with the Germans during their occupation of his country.

quit /kwɪt/ ▷ *verb* (***quitted*** or ***quit, quitting***) **1** to leave or depart from (a place, etc). **2** *tr & intr* to leave, give up or resign (a job). **3** to exit (a computer program, application or game, etc). **4** *N Amer, especially US, colloq* to cease something or doing something. **5** *tr & intr* said of a tenant: to move out of rented premises. **6** *formal* to behave, especially in a specified manner □ *quit herself well.* ▷ *adj* (*usually* **quit of something**) free or rid of it. ⓒ 13c: from French *quiter*, from Latin *quietare* to make quiet.

quitch /kwɪtʃ/ ▷ *noun* (*in full* **quitch grass**; *plural* ***quitches***) another name for COUCH². ⓒ Anglo-Saxon *cwice*.

quite /kwaɪt/ ▷ *adverb* **1** completely; entirely □ *I quite understand* □ *It's not quite clear what happened.* **2** to a high degree □ *quite exceptional.* **3** rather; fairly; to some or a limited degree □ *quite a nice day* □ *quite enjoyed it.* **4** (*also* **quite so**) used in a reply: I agree, see your point, etc • **not quite** hardly; just short of or less than a specified thing. • **quite a** or **an** ... a striking, impressive, daunting, challenging, etc ... □ *That was quite a night.* • **quite a few** *colloq* a reasonably large number of (people or things, etc) □ *quite a few people brought their kids.* • **quite another matter** or **thing**, *etc* very different. • **quite some** ... a considerably large amount of ... □ *I might be quite some time.* • **quite something** very impressive □ *His flat is quite something.* ⓒ 14c: from (*adj*) QUIT.

quits ▷ *adj, colloq* **1** on an equal footing. **2** even, especially where money is concerned. • **call it quits 1** to agree to stop quarrelling or arguing, etc and accept that the outcome is even. **2** to agree that a situation, etc is even □ *Just give me a fiver and we'll call it quits.* • **double or quits** see under DOUBLE. ⓒ 15c.

quittance /ˈkwɪtəns/ ▷ *noun* **1** release from debt or other obligation. **2** a document that acknowledges this.

quitter ▷ *noun, colloq* **1** someone who gives up too easily. **2** a shirker.

quiver¹ /ˈkwɪvə(r)/ ▷ *verb* (***quivered, quivering***) **1** (*often* **quiver with something**) *intr* to shake or tremble slightly because of it; to shiver □ *Her voice quivered with fear.* **2** *intr* to shake or flutter □ *The snowdrops quivered in the wind.* **4** said of a bird: to make (its wings) vibrate rapidly. ▷ *noun* a tremble or shiver. • **quivering** *adj, noun*. • **quiveringly** *adverb*. • **quivery** *adj*. ⓒ 15c.

quiver² /ˈkwɪvə(r)/ ▷ *noun* a long narrow case that is used for carrying arrows. ⓒ 13c: from French *cuivre*.

qui vive /*French* ki viv/ ▷ *noun* (*usually* **be on the qui vive**) alert; ready for action. ⓒ 18c: French, meaning '(long) live who?', a challenge that a sentry, etc would issue to someone who wanted to pass in order to ascertain where their loyalties lay.

quixotic /kwɪkˈsɒtɪk/ ▷ *adj* **1** absurdly generous or chivalrous. **2** naively romantic, idealistic or impractical, etc. • **quixotically** *adverb*. • **quixotism** *noun*. • **quixotry** *noun*. ⓒ 19c: from Spanish *quijote* thigh armour, and named after the hero of *Don Quixote de la Mancha* (1605) a romantic novel by the Spanish writer Cervantes.

quiz /kwɪz/ ▷ *noun* (***quizzes***) **1** (*also* **quiz show**) an entertainment, eg on radio or TV, in which the knowledge of a panel of contestants is tested through a series of questions. **2** any series of questions as a test of general or specialized knowledge. **3** an interrogation. ▷ *verb* (***quizzes, quizzed, quizzing***) to question or interrogate someone. • **quizzer** *noun*. ⓒ 18c.

quizmaster ▷ *noun* someone who asks the questions and keeps the score, etc in a quiz show. ⓒ 1940s.

quizzical /ˈkwɪzɪkəl/ ▷ *adj* said of a look or expression, etc: mildly amused or perplexed; mocking; questioning. • **quizzicality** *noun*. • **quizzically** *adverb*. ⓒ 19c.

quod /kwɒd/ *Brit, slang* ▷ *noun* prison. ▷ *verb* (***quodded, quodding***) to imprison someone. ⓒ 18c.

quod erat demonstrandum see under QED

quodlibet /ˈkwɒdlɪbet/ ▷ *noun* **1** in philosophy or theology: a question or argument that is put forward for discussion or debate. **2** an informal or light-hearted musical medley of several well-known tunes. ⓒ 14c: from Latin *quod* what + *libet* it pleases.

quoin /kɔɪn, kwɔɪn/ ▷ *noun* **1** the external angle of a wall or building. **2** a cornerstone. **3 a** a wedge or wedge-shaped block used for various purposes, eg to stop barrels rolling on board ships or to raise or lower a gun; **b** *printing* a wedge used for locking type into a forme. ▷ *verb* (***quoined, quoining***) to secure or raise something with a wedge. ⓒ 16c: from French *coin*, from Latin *cuneus* a wedge.

quoit /kɔɪt, kwɔɪt/ ▷ *noun* **1** a ring made of metal, rubber or rope used in the game of quoits. **2** (**quoits**) a game that involves throwing these rings at pegs with the aim of encircling them or landing close to them. See also DECK QUOITS. ▷ *verb* (***quoited, quoiting***) **1** to throw something in a similar way to throwing a quoit. **2** *intr* to play quoits. • **quoiter** *noun*. ⓒ 15c.

quokka /ˈkwɒkə/ ▷ *noun* (***quokkas***) a small short-tailed wallaby that is found in SW Australia. ⓒ 19c: from Nyungar (an Aboriginal language) *kwaka*.

Quonset hut /ˈkwɒnsɪt —/ ▷ *noun, US trademark* a temporary semicircular prefabricated metal shelter for housing military personnel. Compare NISSEN HUT. ⓒ 1940s: named after Quonset Point, Rhode Island where the first huts were made.

quorate /ˈkwɔːrət/ ▷ *adj, Brit* said of a meeting, etc: attended by or consisting of enough people to form a quorum.

Quorn /ˈkwɔːrn/ ▻ *noun, trademark* a fibrous vegetable protein made from microscopic plant filaments and used as a low-calorie cholesterol-free meat substitute in cooking. ◷ 1980s: named after Quorn, a village in Leicestershire (now called Quorndon) which formed part of the original manufacturer's tradename.

quorum /ˈkwɔːrəm/ ▻ *noun* the fixed minimum number of members of an organization or society, etc who must be present at a meeting for its business to be valid. ◷ 17c: Latin, meaning 'of whom', part of the conventional formula used in certain Latin commissions.

quot. ▻ *abbreviation* quotation.

quota /ˈkwoʊtə/ ▻ *noun* (***quotas***) **1** the proportional or allocated share or part that is, or that should be, done, paid or contributed, etc out of a total amount, sum, etc. **2** the maximum or prescribed number or quantity that is permitted or required, eg of imported goods or students in an college intake, etc. ◷ 17c: Latin, from *quota pars* how big a share?.

quotable ▻ *adj* worthy of or suitable for quoting. • **quotability** *noun*.

quotation /kwoʊˈteɪʃən/ ▻ *noun* **1** a remark or a piece of writing, etc that is quoted. **2** the act or an instance of quoting. **3** *business* an estimated price for a job submitted by a contractor to a client. **4** *stock exchange* an amount that is stated as the current price of a commodity, stock or security, etc. **5** *music* a short extract from one piece that is put into another. ◷ 15c.

quotation mark ▻ *noun* each of a pair of punctuation marks which can be either single (' ') or double (" "). They are conventionally used to mark the beginning and end of a quoted passage or to indicate the title of an essay, article or song, etc, or put on either side of a word or phrase to draw the reader's attention to it, eg because it is colloquial, slang, jargon or a new coinage. Also called **inverted comma**.

quote /kwoʊt/ ▻ *verb* (***quoted, quoting***) *tr & intr* **1** to cite or offer (someone else or the words or ideas, etc of someone else) to substantiate an argument. **2** to repeat in writing or speech (the exact words, etc of someone else). **3** to cite or repeat (figures or data, etc). **4** *tr & intr* said of a contractor: to submit or suggest (a price) for doing a specified job or for buying something ◻ *quoted her £600 as a trade-in*. **5** *stock exchange* to state the price of (a security, commodity or stock, etc). **6** (*usually* **quote something at something**) to give (a racehorse) betting odds as specified ◻ *Desert Orchid is quoted at 2/1*. **7 a** to put quotation marks around (a written passage, word or title, etc); **b** (*also* **quote ... unquote**) to indicate (in speech) that a specified part has been said by someone else ◻ *The report says, quote, "The failure was deliberate but non-duplicitous." unquote*. **8** (*usually* **quote something as something**) to cite or offer it as (an example, model or standard, etc). **9** to refer to (a law, etc) as authority or support. ▻ *noun* **1** a quotation. **2** a price quoted. **3** (**quotes**) quotation marks. ◷ 14c: from Latin *quotare* to give passages reference numbers, from *quot* how many?

quoth /kwoʊθ/ ▻ *verb, old use* said ◻ *"Alas!" quoth he*. ◷ Anglo-Saxon *cwaeth*, the past tense of *cwethan* to say.

quotidian /kwoʊˈtɪdɪən/ ▻ *adj* **1** everyday; commonplace. **2** daily. **3** recurring daily. ▻ *noun* (*in full* **quotidian fever**) a fever that flares up every day. ◷ 14c: from Latin *quotidianus*, from *quotidie* daily.

quotation marks or inverted commas

• There are two types of **quotation marks**: **single'...'** and **double"..."**. Both are correct, but British English tends to favour single quotation marks, American English double.

• Quotation marks enclose direct speech ◻ *'Do come in,' he said.* ◻ *She asked him timidly, 'Will you be coming, too?'* ◻ *'Why not?' said Florence.* ◻ *'Help!' he shouted.* ◻ *He said to her firmly: 'You must help him.'*

Note, in the first two examples above, that the comma separating quoted material from the rest of the sentence goes inside the quotation marks when the quoted material comes first, and outside when what is quoted comes second. Note also, in the remaining examples, that all other punctuation goes inside the marks if it belongs to the quoted material, and outside if it belongs to the rest of the sentence.

Note that, where the end of a passage of quoted material coincides with the end of the whole sentence, usually only the punctuation inside the quotation is given ◻ *I think he said, 'I'll be there at five o'clock.'* ◻ *Why did you say 'Who's there?'*

• Quotation marks enclose a short quotation ◻ *Shakespeare once said that 'all the world's a stage'.*

Longer quotations are normally separated off more markedly from the rest of the text, for example by being given their own indented paragraph.

• Quotation marks enclose a word or phrase that the writer wishes to highlight ◻ *They spoke a very archaic kind of English, full of 'thee's and 'thou's.* ◻ *The table was what we in Scotland call 'shoogly'.* ◻ *What does 'an accessary after the fact' mean?*

Note that both single and double quotation marks are needed when a quoted passage itself contains quoted material ◻ *'Next week we shall examine the "stream of consciousness" technique in greater detail,' announced the tutor.*

quotient /ˈkwoʊʃənt/ ▻ *noun, math* **1** the result of a division sum, eg when 72 (the DIVIDEND) is divided by 12 (the DIVISOR), the quotient is 6, or when 80 is divided by 12, the quotient is still 6 with a REMAINDER (*noun* 2) of 8. **2** the number of times one number is contained within another. **3** a ratio of two numbers or quantities to be divided. See also INTELLIGENCE QUOTIENT. ◷ 15c: from Latin *quotiens* how often?

Qur'an or **Quran** see KORAN.

qv or **q.v.** ▻ *abbreviation* (*plural* ***qqv***) *quod vide* (Latin), which see.

qwerty or **QWERTY** /ˈkwɜːtɪ/ ▻ *adj* said of an English-language typewriter, word processor or other keyboard: having the standard arrangement of keys, ie with the letters *q w e r t y* appearing in that order at the top left of the letters section. ◷ 1920s.

qy ▻ *abbreviation* query.

R

R¹ or **r** /ɑː(r)/ ▻ *noun* (***Rs***, ***R's*** or ***r's***) the eighteenth letter of the English alphabet. See also THE THREE R'S.

> ***Linking r and intrusive r***
>
> In some accents of English, a written **r** is not pronounced before another consonant or at the end of a word, so that *cord* is pronounced /kɔːd/, and *bar* /bɑː/. In other accents, such as Scottish English, such **r**'s are pronounced. Accents of English can thus be divided between those that are *r-pronouncing* and those that are *non-r-pronouncing*.
>
> However, even in non-r-pronouncing accents, an **r** at the end of a word is pronounced when the word that follows begins with a vowel, so that *far away* is pronounced /fɑːrə'weɪ/. This is known as a **linking r**. It is signalled in the dictionary phonetics by (r), eg at RADAR.
>
> In some accents, however, speakers go further than this and pronounce an **r** in such cases even where there is no **r** in the written word, as in the infamous phrase *law and order*, which then becomes /lɔːrənd'ɔːdə/. This is known as an **intrusive r** and, although often condemned, is simply another characteristic of the speech habits of sections of the English-speaking community.

R² or **R.** ▻ *abbreviation* **1** rand. **2** Réaumur (scale). **3** *physics, electronics* resistance. **4 a** *Regina* (Latin), Queen; **b** *Rex* (Latin), King. **5** River. **6** Röntgen. **7** rupee.

r or **r.** ▻ *abbreviation* **1** radius. **2** right.

RA ▻ *abbreviation* **1** Rear Admiral. **2** *IVR* Republic of Argentina. **3 a** Royal Academician; **b** Royal Academy. **4** Royal Artillery.

Ra ▻ *symbol, chem* radium.

RAAF ▻ *abbreviation* Royal Australian Air Force.

rabbet /'rabɪt/ ▻ *noun* a groove cut along the edge of a piece of wood, etc, usually to join with a tongue or projection in a matching piece. ▻ *verb* (***rabbeted***, ***rabbeting***) **1** to cut a rabbet in something. **2** to join (eg two pieces of wood) with a rabbet. 🕒 15c: from French *rabattre* to beat down.

rabbi (with capital when prefixed or when used as a title, as in *Chief Rabbi*) /'rabaɪ/ ▻ *noun* (***rabbis***) **1** a Jewish religious leader. **2** a Jewish scholar or teacher of the law. • **rabbinical** /rə'bɪnɪkəl/ *adj* relating to the rabbis or to their opinions, learning or language. • **rabbinically** *adverb*. 🕒 13c: Hebrew, meaning 'my master'.

rabbinate /'rabɪnət/ ▻ *noun* **1** the post or tenure of office of a rabbi. **2** a body or gathering of rabbis. 🕒 18c.

rabbinic /rə'bɪnɪk/ ▻ *adj* rabbinical. ▻ *noun* (**Rabbinic**) the later Hebrew language.

rabbit /'rabɪt/ ▻ *noun* **1 a** a small burrowing herbivorous mammal belonging to the same family as the hare; **b** its flesh as food; **c** its fur, especially as used in clothing. **2** *Brit colloq* a poor performer in any sport or game. **3** a timid person. ▻ *verb* (***rabbited***, ***rabbiting***) *intr* **1** to hunt rabbits. **2** (*usually* **rabbit on** or **away**) *derog colloq* to talk at great length, often in a rambling way; to chatter inconsequentially 20c: originally rhyming slang *rabbit and pork* talk.. • **rabbiter** *noun* a person or animal that hunts rabbits. • **rabbity** *adj*. 🕒 14c: as *rabet*, perhaps from French.

rabbit punch ▻ *noun* a sharp blow on the back of the neck.

rabbitry ▻ *noun* (***rabbitries***) a place where rabbits are kept.

rabbit warren ▻ *noun* a system of burrows in which wild rabbits live.

rabble¹ /'rabəl/ ▻ *noun* **1** a noisy disorderly crowd or mob. **2** (**the rabble**) *contemptuous* the lowest class of people. 🕒 16c in this sense; 14c in obsolete sense 'a pack of animals'.

rabble² /'rabəl/ *metallurgy* ▻ *noun* a device for stirring molten iron, etc in a furnace. ▻ *verb* (***rabbled***, ***rabbling***) to stir with a rabble. • **rabbler** *noun*. 🕒 19c in this sense; 17c in obsolete sense 'a shovel used by charcoal-burners': from French *râble*, from Latin *rutabulum* a poker.

rabble-rouser ▻ *noun* someone who makes speeches, especially calling for social or political change, which are meant to arouse feelings of anger and violence in those listening. • **rabble-rousing** *adj, noun* the language and tactics of a rabble-rouser. 🕒 18c.

Rabelaisian /rabə'leɪzɪən/ ▻ *noun* a follower, admirer or student the French satirical writer of François Rabelais (c.1494–1553). ▻ *adj* **a** relating to, or characteristic of the works of Rabelais, especially in being satirical and coarsely humorous; **b** coarsely indecent; bawdy. • **Rabelaisianism** *noun*. 🕒 19c.

rabi /'rabiː/ ▻ *noun* in India, Pakistan, etc: the spring grain harvest. 🕒 19c: Arabic, meaning 'spring'.

rabid /'rabɪd, 'reɪ-/ ▻ *adj* **1** said of dogs, etc: suffering from rabies. **2 a** fanatical; unreasoning; **b** raging. • **rabidity** /rə'bɪdɪtɪ/ or **rabidness** *noun*. • **rabidly** *adverb*. 🕒 17c: from Latin *rabidus*, from *rabere* to be mad.

rabies /'reɪbiːz, 'reɪbɪz/ ▻ *noun* a viral disease of the central nervous system, usually fatal and transmitted in saliva from the bite of an infected animal, which causes convulsions, paralysis and fear of water. Also called HYDROPHOBIA. 🕒 16c: Latin, from *rabere* to be mad.

RAC ▻ *abbreviation* **1** Royal Armoured Corps. **2** Royal Automobile Club.

raccoon or **racoon** /rə'kuːn/ ▻ *noun* (***raccoons*** or ***raccoon***) **1** a smallish solitary nocturnal mammal, found in N and C America, which has dense greyish fur, characteristic black patches around the eyes and black rings on the tail. **2** its fur. 🕒 17c: from Algonquian *aroughcun*.

race¹ /reɪs/ ▻ *noun* **1** a contest of speed between runners, horses, cars, etc. **2** (*usually* **the races**) a series of such contests over a fixed course, especially for horses or dogs □ *a day at the races*. **3** any contest or rivalry, especially to be the first to do or get something □ *the arms race*. **4** a fixed course, track or path over which anything runs. **5** a strong or rapid current of water in the sea or a river. **6** a channel conveying water to and from a mill wheel. **7** a groove in which something, eg a ball-bearing, moves or slides. **8** a regular traverse of a fixed course, eg of the sun. ▻ *verb* (***raced***, ***racing***) **1** *intr* to take part in a race. **2** to have a race with someone. **3** to cause (a horse, car, etc) to race. **4** *intr* (*usually* **race about** or **along** or **around**) to run or move quickly and energetically. **5** *intr* said of eg an engine or a propeller: to run wildly fast when resistance is removed. **6** *tr & intr* to move or make something move more quickly than usual. **7** *intr* to own racehorses, or watch horse-racing as a hobby. • **racer** see separate entry. • **racing** *noun* the sport or practice of using animals (especially horses or dogs) or vehicles in contests of speed. Also *as adj* □ *racing car* □ *racing pigeon*. ◷ 13c: from Norse *ras*.

race² /reɪs/ ▻ *noun* **1** any of the major divisions of humankind distinguished by a particular set of physical characteristics, such as size, hair type or skin colour. **2** a tribe, nation or similar group of people thought of as distinct from others. **3** (**the human race**) human beings as a group. **4** a group of animals or plants within a species, which have characteristics distinguishing them from other members of that species. **5** said of wine: the special flavour by which its origin may be recognized. ◷ 16c: French, from Italian *razza*.

racecard ▻ *noun* a programme or list of all the competitors and races at a race meeting.

racecourse and **racetrack** ▻ *noun* a course or track used for racing horses, cars, bicycles, runners, etc.

racegoer ▻ *noun* someone who attends race meetings, especially regularly. • **racegoing** *noun*.

race hatred ▻ *noun* animosity arising from difference of race.

racehorse ▻ *noun* a horse bred and used for racing.

racemate /'rasɪmət/ ▻ *noun* a racemic mixture. • **racemation** /rasɪ'meɪʃən/ *noun* **1** a residue. **2** a cluster or bunch of grapes or of anything else.

raceme /rə'siːm, 'reɪ-, 'ra-/ ▻ *noun, bot* **1** a flower-head consisting of individual flowers attached to a main unbranched stem by means of short stalks, the youngest flowers being at the tip of the stem and the oldest ones near its base, eg bluebell, lupin. **2** a similar formation of spore cases. • **racemed** *adj* consisting of, or having, racemes. ◷ 18c: from Latin *racemus* bunch of grapes.

race meeting ▻ *noun* a series of races, especially horse races, taking place over the same course and on the same day or over a period of consecutive days.

racemic /rə'siːmɪk, rə'sɛmɪk, reɪ-/ ▻ *adj, chem* applied to an acid obtained from a certain kind of grape: an optically inactive form of tartaric acid.

racemize or **racemise** /'rasɪmaɪz/ ▻ *verb* (***racemized***, ***racemizing***) *chem* to change into a racemic form. • **racemism** *noun* the quality of being racemic. • **racemization** *noun*.

racemose /'rasɪmoʊs/ ▻ *adj* **1** like a raceme or racemes. **2** having racemes. **3** like a bunch of grapes.

racer ▻ *noun* **1** a person, animal or thing that races or is raced. **2** any of several non-venomous N American snakes.

race relations ▻ *plural noun* social relations between people of different races living in the same community or country.

race riot ▻ *noun* a riot caused either by hostility between people of different races, or by alleged discrimination against people of a particular race.

racetrack see RACECOURSE

raceway ▻ *noun, chiefly US* **1** a mill race. **2** a channel or groove for directing or controlling movement. **3** a racetrack.

rachi- /reɪkɪ, rə'kɪ/ ▻ *combining form, signifying* relating or referring to a rachis.

rachis or **rhachis** /'reɪkɪs/ ▻ *noun* (***rachises*** or ***rachides*** /-diːz/) **1** the spine. **2** *bot* the main axis of a compound leaf or a flower-head. **3** *zool* the main axis or shaft of a feather. ◷ 18c: Latin, from Greek *rhachis* spine, ridge, etc.

rachischisis /rə'kɪskɪsɪs/ ▻ *noun, medicine* a severe form of spina bifida. ◷ 19c: from RACHI- + Greek *schisis* cleavage, division.

rachitis /rə'kaɪtɪs/ ▻ *noun, medicine* RICKETS. • **rachitic** /rə'kɪtɪk/ *adj*. ◷ 18c: from Greek *rhachitis* inflammation of the spine, but adopted in 17c as the learned form of *rickets*.

Rachmanism /'rakmənɪzəm/ ▻ *noun* exploitation or extortion by a landlord of tenants living in slum conditions. • **Rachmanite** *adj*. ◷ 20c: named after a British property owner, exposed for such conduct in 1963.

racial /'reɪʃəl/ ▻ *adj* **1** relating to a particular race. **2** based on race. • **racialism** racism. • **racialist** *noun, adj*. • **racially** *adverb*.

racialism, racism

There is no difference in meaning between **racism** and **racialism**, although **racism** is now the more common form.

racier, **raciest**, **racily** and **raciness** see under RACY

racing see under RACE¹

racism /'reɪsɪzəm/ ▻ *noun* **1** hatred, rivalry or bad feeling between races. **2** belief in the inherent superiority of a particular race or races over others, usually with the implication of a right to be dominant. **3** discriminatory treatment based on such a belief. • **racist** *noun, adj*. ◷ 16c.

rack¹ ▻ *noun* **1** a framework with rails, shelves, hooks, etc for holding or storing things. **2** a framework for holding hay, etc from which livestock can feed. **3** a bar with teeth which connect with the teeth on a cogwheel or pinion to change the position of something, or to convert linear motion into rotary motion, or vice versa. **4 a** (**the rack**) *historical* a device for torturing people by stretching their bodies; **b** a device for stretching things. **5** something that causes extreme pain, anxiety or doubt. ▻ *verb* (***racked***, ***racking***) **1** to put something in a rack. **2** to move or adjust by rack and pinion. **3** *historical* to torture someone on a rack. **4** to stretch or move forcibly or excessively. **5** to cause pain or suffering to someone or something. • **racked** or (and usually regarded as an error) **wracked** *adj* tortured; tormented; distressed □ ***be racked with guilt***. Also *in compounds* □ ***disease-racked***. • **on the rack 1** extremely anxious or distressed. **2** said of skill, etc: stretched to its limits. • **rack one's brains** to think as hard as one can, especially in order to remember something. ◷ 14c: from Dutch *rec* shelf, framework.

rack² ▻ *noun* destruction. • **go to rack and ruin** to get into a state of neglect and decay □ ***The garden is going to rack and ruin***. ◷ 16c: variant of WRACK.

rack³ ▻ *verb* (***racked***, ***racking***) (*also* **rack something off**) to draw off (wine or beer) from its sediment. ◷ 15c: from Provençal *raca* dregs.

rack⁴ ▻ *noun* a joint of meat, especially of lamb, that includes the neck and front ribs. ◷ 16c.

rack⁵ ▻ *noun* a horse's gait in which the legs on either side in turn move nearly together. ▻ *verb* (***racked***, ***racking***) to move with such a gait. • **racker** *noun*. ◷ 16c.

rack and pinion ▻ *noun* a means of turning rotary motion into linear or linear motion into rotary by means of a toothed wheel engaging in a rack.

racket¹ or **racquet** /'rakɪt/ ▻ *noun* **1** a bat with a handle ending in a roughly oval head, made of a frame of wood, metal or other material, with a network of strings (originally catgut, now usually a synthetic material), used for playing tennis, badminton, squash, etc. **2** a snow-shoe of similar shape. ◷ 16c: from French *raquette*, from Arabic *rahat* palm of the hand.

racket² /'rakɪt/ ▻ *noun* **1** *colloq* a loud confused noise or disturbance; a din. **2** a fraudulent or illegal means of making money. **3** *slang* a job or occupation. • **racketeer** *noun*. • **rackety** *adj*. • **stand the racket 1** to endure the strain or noise. **2** to pay expenses, or the penalties of a deed. ◷ 16c: probably imitating a clattering noise.

racketeer /rakəˈtɪə(r)/ ▻ *noun* someone who makes money in some illegal way, often by threats of violence. ▻ *verb* (***racketeered***, ***racketeering***) *intr* to make money as a racketeer. • **racketeering** *noun*. ⓒ 1920s.

racket-press ▻ *noun* a device for keeping the strings of a racket taut when it is not being used.

rackets ▻ *singular noun* a simplified derivative of the old game of REAL TENNIS, similar to squash, played by two or four players in a court with four walls.

racket-tail ▻ *noun, ornithol* **1** a tail feather shaped like a racket. **2** a S American humming-bird with two long racket-shaped tail feathers. • **racket-tailed** *adj*.

rack rail ▻ *noun* a cogged rail, as on a RACK AND PINION railway.

rack railway ▻ *noun* a mountain railway with a toothed rack which engages with a cogged wheel on the locomotive.

rack-rent ▻ *noun* an excessive or unreasonably high rent. ▻ *verb* to charge (tenants) such rents. • **rack-renter** *noun*.

raclette /raˈklɛt/ ▻ *noun* a dish of melted cheese and jacket potatoes, originally from the Valais region of Switzerland. ⓒ 20c: French, meaning 'a small scraper', the dish being served by scraping the melted cheese onto a plate using such an implement.

racon /ˈreɪkɒn/ ▻ *noun, originally US* a RADAR BEACON. ⓒ 1940s: from *ra*dar + bea*con*.

raconteur /rakɒnˈtɜː(r)/ ▻ *noun* someone who tells anecdotes in an amusing or entertaining way. • **raconteuring** *noun*. • **raconteuse** /-ˈtɜːz/ *noun*. ⓒ 19c: French, from *raconter* to relate or tell.

racoon see RACCOON

racquet see RACKET[1]

racquetball ▻ *noun, originally & chiefly N Amer* a game played by two or four players in a walled court using a small rubber ball and short-handled rackets.

racy /ˈreɪsɪ/ ▻ *adj* (***racier***, ***raciest***) **1** said of writing, a way of life, etc: **a** lively or spirited; **b** slightly indecent; risqué. **2** said of wine: with a distinctive flavour imparted by the soil. • **racily** *adverb*. • **raciness** *noun*.

rad[1] (sometimes **Rad**) ▻ *noun, politics* short for RADICAL. ▻ *adj, originally & especially N Amer slang* a shortened form of RADICAL *adj* 9.

rad[2] ▻ *noun* (***rad*** or ***rads***) *physics* the unit formerly used to measure the amount of ionizing radiation absorbed, equal to 0.01 joule per kilogram of absorbing material, equivalent to 0.01 gray. ⓒ 1950s: from *r*adiation *a*bsorbed *d*ose.

rad[3] ▻ *abbreviation* radian.

rad. ▻ *abbreviation* radix.

RADA /ˈrɑːdə/ ▻ *abbreviation* Royal Academy of Dramatic Art.

radar /ˈreɪdɑː(r)/ ▻ *noun, originally US* **1** a system for detecting the presence of distant objects, or determining one's own position, by transmitting short pulses of high-frequency radio waves from a rotating aerial, and detecting the signals reflected back from the surface of any object in their path. **2** the equipment for sending out and receiving such radio waves. ⓒ 1940s: from *ra*dio *d*etecting *a*nd *r*anging.

radar astronomy ▻ *noun, astron* the use of pulsed radio signals to measure the distances and map the surfaces of objects in the solar system, and to determine their speed of rotation.

radar beacon ▻ *noun* a fixed radio transmitter whose signals enable an aircraft, by means of its radar equipment, to determine its position and direction.

radar gun ▻ *noun* a gun-like device used by the police which, when pointed at a moving vehicle and 'fired', records (by means of radar) the vehicle's speed.

radarscope ▻ *noun* a cathode-ray oscilloscope on which radar signals can be seen.

radar trap ▻ *noun* a device using radar which allows the police to detect vehicles travelling faster than the speed limit (see also SPEED TRAP).

RADC ▻ *abbreviation* Royal Army Dental Corps.

raddle /radəl/ ▻ *noun* red ochre; ruddle. ▻ *verb* (***raddled***, ***raddling***) **1** to colour or mark with red ochre. **2** to rouge coarsely. • **raddled** *adj* said of a person or a person's face: worn out and haggard-looking through debauchery. ⓒ 16c: a variant of RUDDLE.

radial /ˈreɪdɪəl/ ▻ *adj* **1** said of lines: spreading out from the centre of a circle, like rays. **2** relating to rays, a radius or radii. **3** along or in the direction of a radius or radii. **4** *anatomy* relating to the RADIUS. ▻ *noun* **1** a radiating part. **2** short for RADIAL-PLY TYRE. **3** *anatomy* a radial artery or nerve. • **radially** *adverb*. ⓒ 16c: from Latin *radialis*, from *radius*.

radial engine ▻ *noun* an engine which has its cylinders arranged radially, as opposed to in a line. Compare ROTARY ENGINE.

radial-ply tyre ▻ *noun* a tyre which has fabric cords laid at a right angle to the centre of the tread, allowing the walls to be flexible. See also CROSS-PLY.

radial symmetry ▻ *noun* the arrangement of parts in an object or living organism (eg in a jellyfish, or the stems and roots of a plant) such that a line drawn through its centre in any direction produces two halves that are mirror images of each other.

radial velocity ▻ *noun, astron* the velocity, along the observer's line of sight, of a star or other body.

radian /ˈreɪdɪən/ ▻ *noun, geom* (abbreviation **rad**) the SI unit of plane angular measurement, approximately 57°, defined as the angle that is made at the centre of a circle by an arc (a segment of the circumference) whose length is equal to the radius of the circle. ⓒ 19c: from RADIUS.

radiant /ˈreɪdɪənt/ ▻ *adj* **1** emitting electromagnetic radiation, eg rays of light or heat. **2** glowing or shining. **3** said of a person: beaming with joy, love, hope or health. **4** transmitted by or as radiation. ▻ *noun* **1** a point or object which emits electromagnetic radiation, eg light or heat. **2** *astron* the point in the sky from which meteors appear to radiate outward during a meteor shower. • **radiance** or **radiancy** *noun* **1** the state of being radiant. **2** a measure of the amount of electromagnetic radiation being transmitted from or to a point on a surface. • **radiantly** *adverb*. ⓒ 15c: Latin, from *radiare* to radiate, emit rays.

radiant energy ▻ *noun* energy given out as electromagnetic radiation.

radiant heat ▻ *noun* heat transmitted by electromagnetic radiation.

radiate /ˈreɪdɪeɪt/ ▻ *verb* (***radiated***, ***radiating***) **1** to send out rays (of light, heat, electromagnetic radiation, etc). **2** *intr* said of light, heat, radiation, etc: to be emitted in rays. **3** said of a person: to manifestly exhibit (happiness, good health, etc) □ *radiate vitality*. **4** *tr & intr* to spread or cause something to spread out from a central point as radii. ▻ *adj* having rays, radii or a radial structure. ⓒ 17c: from Latin *radiare*, radiation to shine, emit rays.

radiation /reɪdɪˈeɪʃən/ ▻ *noun* **1** energy (usually electromagnetic radiation, eg radio waves, microwaves, infrared, visible light, ultraviolet, X-rays) that is emitted from a source and travels in the form of waves or particles (photons) through a medium, eg air or a vacuum. **2** a stream of particles, eg alpha particles, beta particles, electrons, neutrons, etc, emitted by a radioactive substance. **3** the act or process of radiating.

radiation sickness ▻ *noun* illness caused by exposure to high levels of radiation, eg nuclear fallout, or to relatively low levels over a long period, and marked by symptoms such as diarrhoea, vomiting, loss of hair, internal bleeding, reduction in fertility, and a significantly increased risk of cancer, leukaemia, birth defects, etc. ◎ 1920s.

radiator /'reɪdɪeɪtə(r)/ ▷ *noun* **1** an apparatus for heating, consisting of a series of pipes through which hot water or hot oil is circulated. **2** an apparatus for heating in which wires are made hot by electricity. **3** an apparatus for cooling an internal combustion engine, eg in a car, consisting of a series of tubes which water passes through, and a fan.

radical /'radɪkəl/ ▷ *adj* **1** concerning or relating to the basic nature or root of something; fundamental; intrinsic. **2** far-reaching; thoroughgoing □ ***radical changes.*** **3** in favour of or tending to produce thoroughgoing or extreme political and social reforms. **4** relating to a political group or party in favour of extreme reforms. **5** *medicine* said of treatment: with the purpose of removing the source of a disease □ ***radical surgery.*** **6** *bot* from or relating to the root of a plant. **7** *math* relating to the root of a number. **8** *linguistics* relating to the roots of words. **9** *slang* fine, excellent; radically and admirably up to date. Often shortened to *rad* (see RAD1 *adj*). ▷ *noun* **1** a root or basis in any sense. **2** someone who is a member of a radical political group, or who holds radical political views. **3** *chem* within a molecule: a group of atoms which remains unchanged during a series of chemical reactions, but is normally incapable of independent existence □ ***free radical.*** **4** *math* the root of a number, usually denoted by the radical sign (√). **5** *linguistics* the root of a word. • **radicalism** *noun* **1** the beliefs and opinions of radicals, especially a set of ideas which advocates more substantial social and political change than is supported by the political mainstream. **2** extreme thoroughness. • **radically** *adverb.* • **radicalness** *noun.* ◎ 14c: from Latin *radicalis*, from *radix* root.

radicalize or **radicalise** ▷ *verb* (***radicalized, radicalizing***) to make or become radical. • **radicalization** or **radicalisation** *noun.*

radical sign ▷ *noun* the sign √, denoting a SQUARE ROOT.

radicchio /ra'diːkɪoʊ/ ▷ *noun* (***radicchios***) a purple-leaved variety of chicory from Italy, used raw in salads. ◎ 20c: Italian, meaning 'chicory'.

radices *plural of* RADIX

radicle /'radɪkəl/ ▷ *noun* **1** *bot* **a** the part of a plant embryo which develops into the root; **b** a little root. **2** *anatomy* the root-like origin of a vein or nerve. ◎ 18c: from Latin *radicula* small root, from *radix* root.

radii *plural of* RADIUS

radio /'reɪdɪoʊ/ ▷ *noun* (***radios***) **1** the use of RADIO WAVES to transmit and receive information such as television or radio programmes, telecommunications, and computer data, without connecting wires. **2** a wireless device that receives, and may also transmit, information in this manner. **3** a message or broadcast that is transmitted in this manner. **4** the business or profession of sound broadcasting □ ***to work in radio.*** ▷ *adj* **1** relating to radio. **2** for transmitting by, or transmitted by radio. **2** controlled by radio. ▷ *verb* (***radios, radioed, radioing***) **1** to send (a message) to someone by radio. **2** *intr* to broadcast or communicate by radio. ◎ Early 20c: from Latin *radius* spoke, ray.

radio- /reɪdɪoʊ, reɪdɪə/ ▷ *combining form, denoting* **1** radio or broadcasting. **2** radioactivity. **3** rays or radiation.

radioactive /reɪdɪoʊ'aktɪv/ ▷ *adj* relating to or affected by RADIOACTIVITY.

radioactive decay ▷ *noun, physics* the spontaneous decay of the nucleus of an atom, which results in the emission of alpha particles, beta particles or gamma rays.

radioactive tracer ▷ *noun, biochem* a radioactive isotope of a chemical element that is deliberately substituted for one of the atoms in a chemical compound in order to 'tag' it, thus enabling the path of a particular atom to be followed through a whole series of reactions.

radioactive waste see under NUCLEAR WASTE

radioactivity /reɪdɪoʊak'tɪvɪtɪ/ ▷ *noun* **1** the spontaneous disintegration (measured in units called BECQUERELS) of the nuclei of certain atoms, accompanied by the emission of alpha particles, beta particles or gamma rays. **2** the subatomic particles or radiation emitted during this process.

radio altimeter see ALTIMETER

radio astronomy ▷ *noun* **1** astronomical study by means of radar. **2** the study of the radio waves emitted or reflected in space.

radio beacon ▷ *noun* an apparatus that transmits signals for direction-finding.

radiobiology ▷ *noun, biol* the branch of biology concerned with the study of the effect of radiation and radioactive materials on living matter.

radiocarbon ▷ *noun* a radioactive isotope of carbon, especially carbon-14.

radiocarbon dating ▷ *noun* CARBON DATING.

radiochemistry ▷ *noun, chem* the branch of chemistry concerned with the study of radioactive elements and their compounds, including their preparation, properties and practical uses, increasingly used in medicine.

radio-compass ▷ *noun* a radio direction-finding instrument.

radioelement ▷ *noun* a RADIOISOTOPE.

radio frequency ▷ *noun* a frequency of electromagnetic waves used for radio and television broadcasting.

radio galaxy ▷ *noun, astron* a galaxy that is an intense source of cosmic radio waves.

radiogram ▷ *noun* **1** a RADIOGRAPH (see under RADIOGRAPHY). **2** a telegram sent by radio. **3** *old use* short for **radiogramophone**, an apparatus consisting of a radio and record-player.

radiography /reɪdɪ'ɒgrəfɪ/ ▷ *noun, medicine* the technique (widely used in medicine and dentistry, eg to detect tumours, broken bones, etc) of examining the interior of the body by means of recorded images, known as **radiographs**, which are produced by X-rays on photographic film. • **radiographer** *noun.* • **radiographic** *adj.*

radio immunoassay ▷ *noun* a method of detecting or quantifying antigens or antibodies using radiolabelled substances.

radioisotope ▷ *noun, physics* a naturally occurring or synthetic radioactive isotope of a chemical element (eg TRITIUM), used eg in RADIOTHERAPY, as RADIOACTIVE TRACERS, and as long-term power sources in spacecraft and satellites.

radiolabelled ▷ *adj* having had an atom replaced by a radioactive substance, for ease of identification in tests.

radiolocation ▷ *noun* position-finding by radio signals; RADAR.

radiology /reɪdɪ'ɒlədʒɪ/ ▷ *noun* the branch of medicine concerned with the use of RADIATION (eg X-rays) and radioactive isotopes to diagnose and treat diseases. • **radiological** *adj* **1** relating to or involving radiology. **2** involving radioactive materials. • **radiologist** *noun* a specialist in radiology.

radioluminescence ▷ *noun* light arising from RADIATION from a RADIOACTIVE material.

radio microphone ▷ *noun* a microphone with a miniature radio transmitter, and therefore not requiring any cable.

radionuclide /reɪdɪoʊ'njuːklaɪd/ ▷ *noun* any RADIOACTIVE atom of an element identified by the number of NEUTRONs and PROTONs in its NUCLEUS, and by its energy state.

radio-pager ▷ *noun* a very small radio receiver which emits a bleeping sound in response to a signal, used for PAGING people. • **radio-paging** *noun*.

radiophonic /reɪdɪə'fɒnɪk/ ▷ *adj* **1** said of sound, especially of music: produced electronically. **2** producing electronic music. • **radiophonics** *plural noun*. • **radiophonist** /reɪdɪ'ɒfənɪst/ *noun* ◷ 1950s in this sense; 19c meaning 'relating to sound produced by radiant energy'.

radioscopy /reɪdɪ'ɒskəpɪ/ ▷ *noun* the examination of the inside of the body, or of opaque objects, using X-rays. • **radioscopic** /reɪdɪə'skɒpɪk/ *adj*. • **radioscopically** *adverb*.

radiosensitive ▷ *adj* readily injured or changed by radiation.

radio telephone ▷ *noun* a telephone which works by radio waves, used especially in cars and other vehicles.

radio telescope ▷ *noun* a large, usually dish-shaped, aerial, together with amplifiers and recording equipment, that is used to study distant stars, galaxies, etc, by detecting the radio waves they emit.

radiotherapy and **radiotherapeutics** ▷ *noun* the treatment of disease, especially cancer, by X-rays and other forms of radiation. Compare CHEMOTHERAPY.

radio wave ▷ *noun, physics* an electromagnetic wave that has a low frequency and a long wavelength (in the range of about 1mm to 10^4m), widely used for communication.

radish /'radɪʃ/ ▷ *noun* a plant of the mustard family, with pungent-tasting red-skinned white roots, which are eaten raw in salads. ◷ Anglo-Saxon *rædic*: from Latin *radix* root.

radium /'reɪdɪəm/ ▷ *noun, chem* (symbol **Ra**, atomic number 88) a silvery-white highly toxic radioactive metallic element, discovered by Marie (1867—1934) and Pierre (1859—1906) Curie in 1898, obtained from uranium ores, especially pitchblende, and remarkable for its active spontaneous disintegration. ◷ 19c: from Latin *radius* ray.

radius /'reɪdɪəs/ ▷ *noun* (***radii*** /-aɪ/ or ***radiuses***) **1** *geom* **a** a straight line running from the centre to any point on the circumference of a circle or the surface of a sphere; **b** the length of such a line. **2** a radiating line. **3** anything placed like a radius, such as the spoke of a wheel. **4** a usually specified distance from a central point, thought of as limiting an area □ *all the houses within a radius of 10km*. **5** *anatomy* **a** the shorter of the two bones in the human forearm, on the thumb side; **b** the equivalent bone in other animals. Compare ULNA. • **radial** see separate entry. ◷ 16c: Latin, meaning a 'rod, spoke or ray'.

radius vector ▷ *noun* (***radii vectores*** /— vɛk'tɔːriːz/) a straight line joining a fixed point and a variable point.

radix /'reɪdɪks/ ▷ *noun* (***radices*** /'reɪdɪsiːz/) **1** a source, root or basis. **2** *math* the quantity on which a system of numeration or of logarithms, etc is based. ◷ 16c: Latin, meaning 'root'.

radome /'reɪdoum/ ▷ *noun* a protective covering for microwave radar antennae which is transparent to radio waves. ◷ 1940s: from *radar* + *dome*.

radon /'reɪdɒn/ ▷ *noun, chem* (symbol **Rn**, atomic number 86) a highly toxic, colourless, extremely dense, radioactive gas that emits alpha particles and is formed by the decay of radium. ◷ Early 20c: from *radium* + -ON.

radula /'radjʊlə/ ▷ *noun* (***radulae*** /-liː/) *zool* a tonguelike organ of molluscs, comprising a toothed, horny strip which is used for rasping, boring or scraping off particles of food. • **radular** *adj*. • **radulate** *adj*. ◷ 19c in this sense; 18c in sense 'scraper': from Latin *radere* to scrape.

radwaste /'radweɪst/ ▷ *noun, especially US* radioactive waste. ◷ 1970s: from *radioactive* + *waste*.

RAEC ▷ *abbreviation* Royal Army Educational Corps.

RAeS ▷ *abbreviation* Royal Aeronautic Society.

RAF /ɑːr eɪ 'ɛf, *informal* raf/ ▷ *abbreviation* Royal Air Force.

rafale /ra'fal/ ▷ *noun* **1** a burst of artillery in quick rounds. **2** a drum roll. ◷ Early 20c: French, literally 'a gust of wind'.

raffia or **raphia** /'rafɪə/ ▷ *noun* ribbon-like fibre obtained from the leaves of the RAPHIA palm, used for weaving mats, baskets, etc. ◷ 19c: a native word from Madagascar.

raffish /'rafɪʃ/ ▷ *adj* **1** said of appearance, dress, behaviour, etc: slightly shady or disreputable, often attractively so; rakish. **2** flashy; vulgar. • **raffishly** *adverb*. • **raffishness** *noun*. ◷ 19c: from RIFF-RAFF.

raffle /'rafəl/ ▷ *noun* a LOTTERY, often to raise money for charity, in which numbered tickets, which are drawn from a container holding all the numbers sold, win prizes for the holders of the tickets that match the numbers drawn. ▷ *verb* (***raffled***, ***raffling***) (*also* **raffle something off**) to offer something as a prize in a raffle. • **raffler** *noun*. ◷ 18c in this sense; 14c: meaning 'a French variety of the game of dice'.

raffle-ticket ▷ *noun* either of a pair of tickets each with the same number printed on it, one of which is bought by a participant in a raffle, the other one being placed with the rest of the tickets to be drawn to determine who has won.

raft ▷ *noun* **1** a flat structure of logs, timber, etc, fastened together so as to float on water, used for transport or as a platform. **2** a flat, floating mass of ice, vegetation, etc. **3** a wide layer of concrete to support a building on soft ground. ▷ *verb* (***rafted***, ***rafting***) **1 a** to transport something by raft; **b** to transport something in the form of a raft. **2** *intr* to travel by raft. **3** to cross or travel down (water, a river, etc) by raft. **4** *tr & intr* to form into a raft. **5** *intr* said of ice, etc: to pile up by overriding. ◷ 15c: from Norse *raptr*.

rafter¹ /'rɑːftə(r)/ ▷ *noun* a sloping beam supporting a roof. ▷ *verb* (***raftered***, ***raftering***) to equip with rafters. • **raftered** *adj* said of a building or structure: having (especially visible) rafters. • **raftering** *noun*. ◷ Anglo-Saxon *ræfter*.

rafter² ▷ *noun* a RAFTSMAN.

raftsman ▷ *noun* someone who works on a raft.

rag¹ ▷ *noun* **1** a worn, torn or waste scrap of cloth. **2** a shred, scrap or tiny portion of something. **3** (*usually* **rags**) old or tattered clothing □ *dressed in rags*. **4** *jocular* a flag, handkerchief or garment. **5** *derog, colloq* a newspaper □ *the local rag*. **6 a** RAGTIME; **b** a piece of ragtime music. ▷ *verb* (***ragged*** /ragd/ , ***ragging***) **1 a** to tear to rags; **b** to make RAGGED¹. **2** to perform (a piece of music or a dance) in RAGTIME. **3** *intr* said of clothing, a piece of cloth, etc: to become ragged; to fray. • **raggy** *adj*. • **from rags to riches** from poverty to wealth. • **lose one's rag** *slang* to lose one's temper. ◷ 14c: from Anglo-Saxon *raggig* shaggy.

rag² ▷ *verb* (***ragged*** /ragd/ , ***ragging***) **1** *especially Brit* to tease; to play rough tricks on someone. **2** to scold. ▷ *noun, Brit* a series of stunts and events put on by university or college students to raise money for charity. Also *as adj* □ *rag week*. • **ragging** *noun*. • **raggy** *adj, slang* irritated. ◷ 18c.

rag³ or **ragg** ▷ *noun* **1** a rough hard stone of various kinds, especially one which naturally breaks into slabs. **2** a large rough slate (3ft by 2ft, approximately 90cm by 30cm).

raga /'rɑːgə/ ▷ *noun* **1** in Hindu classical music: a traditional pattern of notes around which melodies can be improvised. **2** a piece of music composed around such a pattern. ⓒ 18c: Sanskrit *raga* colour or musical tone.

ragamuffin /ˈragəmʌfɪn/ ▷ *noun* **1** a ragged disreputable child. **2** RAGGA. ⓒ 14c: from *Ragamoffyn*, the name of a demon in the poem *Piers Plowman* by William Langland; probably from RAG[1].

rag-and-bone-man ▷ *noun* someone who collects and deals in goods of little value, eg old clothes, furniture, etc.

rag-bag ▷ *noun* **1** a bag for storing rags and scraps of material. **2** *colloq* a random or confused collection. **3** *colloq* a scruffy untidy person.

ragbolt ▷ *noun* a bolt with barb-like projections to prevent withdrawal once it is locked in position.

rag-book ▷ *noun* a child's book printed on cloth.

ragdoll ▷ *noun* a doll made from, and often stuffed with, scraps of cloth. ⓒ 19c.

rage /reɪdʒ/ ▷ *noun* **1** madness. **2 a** overpowering violent passion of any kind, such as desire or especially anger; **b** a fit of such passion. **3** said of the wind, the sea, a battle, etc: violent, stormy action. **4** an intense desire or passion for something. **5** *colloq* a widespread, usually temporary, fashion or craze. **6** *Austral & NZ colloq* a party or dance. ▷ *verb* (***raged***, ***raging***) *intr* **1** to be violently angry. **2** to speak wildly with anger or passion; to rave. **3** said of the wind, the sea, a battle, etc: to be stormy and unchecked. • **rager** *noun*. • **raging** *adj, noun*. • **ragingly** *adverb*. • **all the rage** *colloq* very much in fashion □ ***In the late 70s safety pins were all the rage.*** ⓒ 13c: from French, from Latin *rabies* madness.

ragg see RAG[3]

ragga /ˈragə/ ▷ *noun* a style of rap music influenced by dance rhythms. Also called **ragamuffin**. ⓒ 1980s: from RAGAMUFFIN because of the scruffy appearance of its exponents.

ragged[1] /ˈragɪd/ ▷ *adj* **1** said of clothes: old, worn and tattered. **2** said of a person: dressed in old, worn, tattered clothing. **3** with a rough and irregular edge; jagged. **4** untidy; straggly. **5** said of a performance or ability: uneven; not of consistent quality. • **raggedly** *adverb*. • **raggedness** *noun*. • **raggedy** *adj* uneven in quality. ⓒ 13c: probably from RAG[1].

ragged[2] *past tense, past participle of* RAG[1], RAG[2]

ragged robin ▷ *noun* a wild flower which is a type of campion, with pink ragged-edged petals.

ragged school ▷ *noun, historical* in the 19c: a voluntary school for destitute children.

raglan /ˈraglən/ ▷ *adj* **1** said of a sleeve: attached to a garment by two seams running diagonally from the neck to the armpit. **2** said of a garment: having such sleeves. ▷ *noun* an overcoat with the sleeve in one piece with the shoulder. ⓒ 19c: named after Lord Raglan (1788–1855), British commander in the Crimean war.

ragout /raˈguː/ ▷ *noun* a highly seasoned stew of meat and vegetables. ▷ *verb* (***ragouted*** /raˈguːd/ , ***ragouting*** /raˈguːɪŋ/) to make a ragout of meat, etc. ⓒ 17c: French, from *ragoûter* to revive the appetite.

rag-rolling ▷ *noun* a technique, used in house decoration, of rolling a folded cloth over a specially painted surface to produce a randomly shaded effect.

ragstone or **ragwork** *noun* undressed masonry in slabs. ⓒ 13c.

ragtag ▷ *noun* the rabble; the common herd. ▷ *adj* **1** relating to or like the rabble. **2** ragged, disorderly. ⓒ 19c.

ragtag and bobtail ▷ *noun* RIFF-RAFF.

ragtime ▷ *noun* a type of jazz piano music with a highly syncopated rhythm, originated by Black American musicians in the 1890s. ⓒ 19c: a contraction of RAGGED[1] + TIME.

rag trade ▷ *noun, colloq* the business of designing, making and selling clothes.

ragweed see RAGWORT

ragwork see under RAG[3]

ragworm ▷ *noun* a pearly white burrowing marine worm, used as bait by fishermen.

ragwort and **ragweed** ▷ *noun* a common plant which has yellow flowers with ragged petals.

rah or **'rah** /rɑː/ ▷ *exclamation, noun, verb* short form of HURRAH.

rai /raɪ/ ▷ *noun* a style of popular music from Algeria, blending traditional Arabic, Spanish flamenco and Western disco rhythms. ⓒ 20c: from Arabic *ra'y* opinion, view.

raid ▷ *noun* **1** a sudden unexpected attack. **2** an air attack. **3** an invasion unauthorized by government. **4** an incursion of police for the purpose of making arrests, or searching for suspected criminals or illicit goods. **5** an onset or onslaught for the purpose of obtaining or suppressing something. **6** *stock exchange slang* the selling of shares by a group of speculators in an attempt to lower share prices. ▷ *verb* (***raided***, ***raiding***) **1** to make a raid on (a person, place, etc). **2** *intr* to go on a raid. • **raider** *noun*. • **raid the market** *stock exchange* to upset prices of stocks artificially for future gain. ⓒ 15c Scots, from Anglo-Saxon *rad* incursion.

rail[1] ▷ *noun* **1** a bar, usually a horizontal one, supported by vertical posts, forming a fence or barrier. **2** a horizontal bar used to hang things on □ ***a picture rail***. **3** either of a pair of lengths of metal, usually steel, forming a track for the wheels of a train, tramcar or other vehicle. **4** the railway as a means of travel or transport □ ***go by rail***. **5** said of a door, wooden framework, etc: a horizontal section in panelling or framing. **6** (**the rails**) the fence which forms the inside barrier of a racecourse. **7** *naut* the capping part of bulwarks. ▷ *verb* (***railed***, ***railing***) **1** to provide with rails. **2** (*usually* **rail something in** or **off**) to enclose (eg a space) within a rail or rails. • **off the rails 1** mad; eccentric. **2** not functioning or behaving normally or properly. **3** disorganized. ⓒ 13c: from French *reille* iron rod, from Latin *regula* staff, rod.

rail[2] ▷ *verb* (***railed***, ***railing***) *intr* (*usually* **rail at** or **against something** or **someone**) to complain or criticize it or them abusively or bitterly. • **railer** *noun*. • **railing** *adj, noun*. • **railingly** *adverb*. ⓒ 15c: from French *railler* to deride.

rail[3] ▷ *noun* any of several birds which usually live near water and have short necks and wings and long legs, especially the water-rail, corncrake or coot. ⓒ 15c: from French *raale*.

railcar ▷ *noun* **1** *US* a railway carriage. **2** a self-propelled railway carriage.

railcard ▷ *noun* a special card, eg for students, the elderly, etc, giving the holder the right to reduced train fares.

railhead ▷ *noun* **1** a railway terminal. **2** the furthest point reached by a railway under construction.

railing ▷ *noun* **1 a** fencing; **b** material for building fences. **2** (*often* **railings**) a barrier or ornamental fence, usually of upright iron rods secured by horizontal connections.

raillery /ˈreɪlərɪ/ ▷ *noun* (***railleries***) **1** good-humoured teasing. **2** an instance of this. ⓒ 17c: related to RAIL[2].

railroad ▷ *noun, N Amer, especially US* a railway. ▷ *verb* (***railroaded***, ***railroading***) *colloq* **1** to rush or force someone unfairly into doing something. **2** to rush or force (a bill) through parliament. **3** to get rid of someone, especially by sending them to prison on a false charge.

railway ▷ *noun* (abbreviation **rly**) **1** a track or set of tracks for trains to run on, formed by two parallel steel rails fixed to sleepers (see SLEEPER sense 2). **2** a system of such tracks, plus all the trains, buildings and people required for it to function. **3** a company responsible for operating such a system. **4** a similar set of tracks for a different type of vehicle ◻ *funicular railway.* ◎ 18c.

railway carriage ▷ *noun* a railway vehicle for passengers.

railway crossing ▷ *noun* an intersection of railway lines, or of road and railway, especially without a bridge.

raiment /ˈreɪmənt/ ▷ *noun, archaic, poetic* clothing. ◎ 15c: from French *areer* to array.

rain ▷ *noun* **1 a** condensed moisture falling as separate water droplets from the atmosphere; **b** a shower; a fall of rain. **2** a fall, especially a heavy one, of anything in the manner of rain ◻ *a rain of bullets.* **3** (**rains**) the season of heavy rainfall in tropical countries. ▷ *verb* (***rained, raining***) **1** *intr* said of rain: to fall. **2** *tr & intr* to fall or cause something to fall like rain ◻ *rain down compliments on her head.* • **rainless** *adj.* • **come rain or shine** whatever the weather or circumstances. • **rain cats and dogs** *colloq* to rain very hard. • **rained off** *Brit* said of a sporting or other event: to be cancelled because of rain. • **right as rain** *colloq* perfectly all right or in order. See also RAINY. ◎ Anglo-Saxon *regn.*

rainbird ▷ *noun* a bird, such as the green woodpecker and various kinds of cuckoo, supposed to foretell rain when it calls.

rainbow /ˈreɪnboʊ/ ▷ *noun* **1** an arch of all the colours of the spectrum, ie red, orange, yellow, green, blue, indigo and violet, that can be seen in the sky when falling raindrops reflect and refract sunlight. **2** a collection or array of bright colours. ▷ *adj* **1** relating to, or coloured like, the rainbow. **2 rainbow-coloured.** • **rainbowy** or **rainbow-like** *adj.* • **chase rainbows** to pursue an impossible aim or hope. ◎ Anglo-Saxon *regnboga.*

rainbow coalition ▷ *noun* a political alliance between minority groups or parties of varying opinions.

rainbow trout ▷ *noun* a freshwater N American and European trout.

rain check ▷ *noun, chiefly N Amer* a ticket for future use, given to spectators when a game or sports meeting is cancelled or stopped due to bad weather. • **take a rain check** or **take a rain check on something** *colloq, originally N Amer* to promise to accept (an invitation) at a later date. ◎ 19c.

rain-cloud ▷ *noun* a dense dark sheet of cloud that may shed rain or snow. *Technical equivalent* NIMBUS.

raincoat ▷ *noun* a light waterproof coat worn to keep out the rain.

rain-doctor ▷ *noun* a RAIN-MAKER.

raindrop ▷ *noun* a drop of rain.

rainfall ▷ *noun* **1** the amount of rain that falls in a certain place over a certain period, measured by depth of water. **2** a shower of rain.

rainforest see TROPICAL RAINFOREST

rain-gauge ▷ *noun* an instrument for measuring rainfall.

rainier, **rainiest** and **raininess** see under RAINY

rain-maker ▷ *noun* **1** especially in tribal societies: someone who professes to bring rain. Also called **rain-doctor.** **2** *slang* a high-powered employee who generates a great deal of income for their employers.

rain-making ▷ *noun* attemping to cause rainfall by techniques such as seeding clouds.

rainproof ▷ *adj* more or less impervious to rain. ▷ *verb* to make something rainproof. ▷ *noun* a rainproof overcoat.

rain shadow ▷ *noun, meteorol* a region on the LEE side of mountains or hills that receives significantly less rainfall than land on the windward side, because prevailing winds are forced to rise, cool, and thereby lose most of their moisture by precipitation before reaching the lee, while moving across the high ground.

rain-tree ▷ *noun* a S American tree of the mimosa family, under which there is a constant rain of juice ejected by cicadas.

rainy ▷ *adj* (***rainier, rainiest***) said of a period of time: characterized by stretches of time when it is raining ◻ *a rainy afternoon.* • **raininess** *noun.* • **save** or **keep something for a rainy day** to keep it for a possible future time of need.

raise ▷ *verb* (***raised, raising***) **1** to move or lift to a higher position or level. **2** to put in an upright or standing position. **3** to build or erect. **4** to increase the value, amount or strength of something ◻ *raise prices* ◻ *raise one's voice.* **5** to put forward for consideration or discussion ◻ *raise an objection.* **6** to gather together or assemble ◻ *raise an army.* **7** to collect together or obtain (funds, money, etc) ◻ *raise money for charity.* **8** to stir up or incite ◻ *raise a protest.* **9** to bring into being; to provoke ◻ *raise a laugh* ◻ *raise the alarm.* **10** to promote to a higher rank. **11** to awaken or arouse from sleep or death. **12** to grow (vegetables, a crop, etc). **13** to bring up or rear (a child, children) ◻ *raise a family, or young.* **14** to bring to an end or remove ◻ *raise the siege.* **15** to cause (bread or dough) to rise with yeast. **16** to establish radio contact with. **17** *math* to increase (a quantity) to a given power (see POWER *noun* 12) ◻ *3 raised to the power of 4 is 81.* **18** *cards* to bet more than another player. **19** *naut* to cause (land) to come into sight by approaching. **20** to produce a nap on (cloth) by brushing. **21** to cause (a lump, blister, etc) to form or swell. ▷ *noun* **1** an act of raising or lifting. *Brit equivalent* RISE. **2** *colloq, especially N Amer* an increase in salary. • **raisable** or **raiseable** *adj.* • **raiser** *noun.* • **raising** *noun.* • **raise a hand to someone** or **something** to hit or generally treat them or it badly. • **raise an eyebrow** or **one's eyebrows** to look surprised (at). • **raise Cain** or **the roof** *colloq* **1** to make a lot of noise. **2** to be extremely angry. • **raise its ugly head** said of a difficult situation, problem, etc: to occur or appear. • **raise hell** or **the devil** *colloq* to make a lot of trouble. • **raise money on something** to get money for something by pawning or selling it, especially privately. • **raise one's glass** to drink a toast. • **raise one's hat** to take off one's hat in greeting. • **raise the wind** *slang* to get together the necessary money by any means. • **raise someone's hopes** to give them reason to be hopeful. • **raise someone's spirits** to make them more cheerful or optimistic. ◎ 12c: from Norse *reisa.*

raise

There is often a spelling confusion between **raise** and **raze**.

raised beach ▷ *noun, geol* an old sea margin above the present water-level.

raisin /ˈreɪzən/ ▷ *noun* a dried grape. • **raisiny** *adj.* ◎ 13c: French, meaning 'grape', from Latin *racemus* a cluster of grapes.

raison d'être /reɪzɑ̃ˈdɛːtrə/ ▷ *noun* (***raisons d'être*** /reɪzɑ̃ˈdɛːtrə/) a purpose or reason that justifies someone's or something's existence. ◎ 19c: French, meaning 'reason for being'.

raisonneur /reɪzɒˈnɜː(r)/ ▷ *noun* (***raisonneurs*** /reɪzɒˈnɜː(r)/) in a play, novel, etc: a character who embodies the author's point of view and expresses his or her opinions. ◎ Early 20c: French, meaning 'someone who argues or reasons'.

raita /rɑːˈiːtə/ ▷ *noun* (***raitas***) an Indian dish of chopped vegetables, especially cucumber, in yoghurt. ◎ 1960s: from Hindi *rayta.*

raj /rɑːdʒ/ ▷ *noun* **1** in India: **a** rule; sovereignty; **b** government. **2** *historical* (*usually* **the British Raj**) the

British government of India, 1858–1947. ◎ 19c: Hindi, from Sanskrit *rajan* king.

raja or **rajah** /ˈrɑːdʒə/ ▷ *noun* (***rajas*** or ***rajahs***) *historical* **1** an Indian king or prince. **2** a Malay or Javanese chief. See also RANI. See also MAHARAJAH. • **rajaship** or **rajahship** *noun*. ◎ 16c: Hindi, from Sanskrit *rajan* king.

Rajput or **Rajpoot** /ˈrɑːdʒpʊt/ ▷ *noun* a member of a race or class claiming descent from the original Hindu military and ruling caste. ◎ 16c: Hindi, from Sanskrit *rajan* king + *putra* son.

rake[1] /reɪk/ ▷ *noun* **1** a long-handled garden tool with a comb-like part at one end, used for smoothing or breaking up earth, gathering leaves together, etc. **2** any tool with a similar shape or use, eg a croupier's tool for gathering in money. **3** a wheeled farm implement with long teeth for gathering hay, scraping up weeds, etc. **4** a connected set of railway carriages or wagons. ▷ *verb* (***raked***, ***raking***) **1** (*usually* **rake things up** or **together**) to collect, gather or remove with, or as if with, a rake. **2** (*usually* **rake something over**) to make it smooth with a rake. **3** *intr* to work with, or as if with a rake. **4** *tr & intr* (*often* **rake through** or **among something**) to search carefully through or among it. **5** to sweep gradually along the length of something, especially with gunfire or one's eyes. **6** to scratch or scrape. ◎ Anglo-Saxon *raca*.

■ **rake something in** *colloq* said especially of money: to earn or acquire it in large amounts □ *The business is doing very well. They must be raking it in!*

■ **rake something up** *colloq* to revive or uncover (something forgotten or lost) □ *rake up old memories.*

rake[2] /reɪk/ ▷ *noun, old use* a fashionable man who lives a dissolute and immoral life. • **rakery** *noun* dissoluteness. • **rakish** *adj* dashing or jaunty, often with a suspicious or piratical appearance. • **rakishly** *adverb*. • **rakishness** *noun*. ◎ 17c: a short form of obsolete *rakehell* an utter scoundrel.

rake[3] /reɪk/ ▷ *noun* **1** a sloping position, especially of a ship's funnel or mast backwards towards the stern, or of a ship's bow or stern in relation to the keel. **2** *theat* the slope of a stage. **3** the amount by which something slopes. **4** the angle between the face of a cutting tool and the surface on which it is working. **5** the angle between the wings and body of an aircraft. ▷ *verb* (***raked***, ***raking***) **1** to set or construct at a sloping angle. **2** *intr* **a** said of a ship's mast or funnel: to slope backwards towards the stern; **b** said of a ship's bow or stern: to project out beyond the keel. **3** said of a theatre stage: to slope. • **rakish** *adj* **1** said of a ship: with raking masts. **2** swift-looking. • **rakishly** *adverb*. ◎ 17c: perhaps related to German *ragen* to project.

rake-off ▷ *noun, slang* a share of the profits, especially when dishonest or illegal.

rakery /ˈreɪkərɪ/ see under RAKE[2]

raki or **rakee** /ˈrɑːkɪ, ˈrakɪ/ ▷ *noun* an aromatic alcoholic liquor drunk in the Levant, Greece and Turkey. ◎ 17c: from Turkish *raqi*.

raku /ˈrɑːkuː/ ▷ *noun* a type of coarse-grained, lead-glazed pottery fired at low temperature, traditionally used in Japan to make tea bowls. ◎ 19c: Japanese, meaning 'pleasure or enjoyment'.

rale or **râle** /rɑːl/ ▷ *noun, pathol* an abnormal 'rattling' sound, caused by an accumulation of fluid, heard when listening to the lungs with a stethoscope. ◎ 19c: French.

rallentando /ralənˈtandoʊ/ *music* ▷ *adj, adverb* (abbreviation **rall**) as a musical direction: becoming gradually slower. ▷ *noun* (***rallentandos***, ***rallentandi*** /-diː/) in a piece of music: a passage to be played in this way. Also called **ritardando** /riːtɑːˈdandoʊ/ (abbreviation **rit.**). ◎ 19c: Italian, from *rallentare* to slow down.

rally /ˈralɪ/ ▷ *verb* (***rallies***, ***rallied***, ***rallying***) **1** to come or bring together again after being dispersed. **2** to come or bring together for some common cause or action. **3** *intr* to revive (one's spirits, strength, abilities, etc) by making an effort. **4** *intr* to recover one's lost health, fitness, strength, etc, especially after an illness. **5** *intr* said of share prices: to increase again after a fall. ▷ *noun* (***rallies***) **1** a reassembling of forces to make a new effort. **2** a mass meeting of people with a common cause or interest. **3** a recovering of lost health, fitness, strength, etc, especially after an illness. **4** *tennis* a series of strokes between players before one of them finally wins the point. **5** a competition to test skill in driving, usually held on public roads. • **rallier** *noun*. ◎ 16c: from French *rallier* to rejoin.

■ **rally round someone** to come together to support or help them at a time of crisis, etc.

rallycross ▷ *noun* motor racing over a course made up of both proper roads and rough ground.

rallying ▷ *noun* long distance motor racing over public roads. • **rallyist** *noun*.

rallying-cry ▷ *noun* a slogan to attract support for a cause, etc.

rallying-point ▷ *noun* a place of assembly, especially for a mass meeting.

RAM ▷ *abbreviation* **1** *computing* random access memory, a temporary memory which allows programs to be loaded and run, and data to be changed. Compare ROM. **2** Royal Academy of Music.

ram ▷ *noun* **1** an uncastrated male sheep; a tup. **2** *astrol, astron* (**Ram**) ARIES. **3** a BATTERING-RAM. **4** the falling weight of a pile-driver. **5** the striking head of a steam hammer. **6** **a** a piston or plunger operated by hydraulic or other power; **b** a machine with such a piston. **7** an act of ramming. **8** *naut, historical* **a** a pointed device on a warship's prow, for making holes in an enemy ship's hull; **b** a warship fitted with such a device. ▷ *verb* (***rammed***, ***ramming***) **1** to force something down or into position by pushing hard. **2** to strike or crash something violently (against, into, etc something or someone) □ *ram the car into the wall.* • **rammer** *noun*. • **ram something down someone's throat** *colloq* to force them to believe, accept or listen to (eg a statement, idea, etc) by talking about it or repeating it constantly. • **ram something home** to emphasize it forcefully. ◎ Anglo-Saxon *ramm*.

r.a.m. ▷ *abbreviation* relative atomic mass.

Ramadan or **Ramadhan** /raməˈdɑːn, ˈramədɑːn, -dan/ ▷ *noun* **1** the ninth month of the Muslim year, during which Muslims fast between sunrise and sunset. **2** the fast itself. ◎ 15c: Arabic, from *ramada* to be heated or hot.

ramakin see RAMEKIN

ramal see under RAMUS

Raman effect /ˈrɑːmən —/ ▷ *noun* in the study of molecules: a change in frequency of light passing through a transparent medium. ◎ 1920s: discovered by the Indian physicist, Sir Chandrasekhara Raman (1888–1970).

Ramapithecus /rɑːməˈpɪθəkəs/ ▷ *noun* an early PLIOCENE genus of primates, possibly an ancestor of modern man, known from fossil remains found in N India. • **ramapithecine** /-siːn/ *noun, adj*. ◎ 1930s: from *Rama*, the name of an Indian prince + Greek *pithekos* ape.

ramate see under RAMUS

ramble /ˈrambəl/ ▷ *verb* (***rambled***, ***rambling***) *intr* **1** to go where one pleases; to wander. **2** *now chiefly* to go for a long walk or walks, especially in the countryside, for pleasure. **3** (*often* **ramble on**) to speak or write, often at length, in an aimless or confused way. **4** said of the mind, thoughts or ideas: to wander or be confused. **5** said of eg a plant: to grow or extend in a straggling, trailing way. ▷ *noun* a walk, usually a longish one and especially in the countryside, for pleasure. • **rambler** *noun* **1** someone who goes walking in the countryside for pleasure. **2** a climbing plant, especially a rose. ◎ 17c: probably related to Dutch *rammelen* (said of animals) to roam about when on heat.

rambling *noun* walking for pleasure, especially in the countryside. ▷ *adj* **1** wandering; nomadic. **2** said of eg a building or structure: extending without any obvious plan or organization ▫ *a large rambling castle.* **3** said of speech, writing, thoughts, etc: confused, disorganized and often lengthy. **4** said of a plant: climbing, trailing or spreading freely ▫ *a rambling rose.* • **ramblingly** *adverb.*

rambunctious /ram'bʌŋkʃəs/ ▷ *adj, colloq* said of an animal or a person: **1** difficult to control. **2** boisterous; exuberant. • **rambunctiously** *adverb.* • **rambunctiousness** *noun.* ⓘ 19c.

rambutan /ram'bu:tən/ ▷ *noun* **1** a tree of the same family as the lychee, found throughout SE Asia. **2** the fruit of this tree, which has edible translucent flesh and a thick red shell covered with hooked hairs. ⓘ 18c: Malay, from *rambut* hair.

RAMC ▷ *abbreviation* Royal Army Medical Corps.

ramekin or **ramequin** or **ramakin** /'ramәkɪn/ ▷ *noun* **1** a small round straight-sided baking dish or mould for a single serving of food. **2** an individual serving of food, especially of a savoury dish containing cheese and eggs, served in such a dish. 17c: from French *ramequin.*

ramen /'rɑ:mɛn/ ▷ *noun* a Japanese dish of clear broth containing vegetables, noodles and often pieces of meat. ⓘ 20c: Japanese.

ramie /'ramɪ/ ▷ *noun* **1** a plant of the nettle family, long cultivated in China. **2** its fibre, used for weaving, paper-making, etc. ⓘ 19c: from Malay *rami.*

ramification /ramɪfɪ'keɪʃən/ ▷ *noun* **1** an arrangement of branches; a branched structure. **2** a single part or section of a complex subject, plot, situation, etc. **3** (*usually* **ramifications**) a consequence, especially a serious or complicated one. • **ramiform** *adj* having a branched shape. ⓘ 17c: from Latin *ramus* branch.

ramify *verb* (***ramifies, ramified, ramifying***) to separate or cause to separate into branches or sections.

ramin /ra'mi:n/ ▷ *noun* **1** a Malaysian tree that grows in swamps. **2** a light-coloured hardwood obtained from this tree, commonly used in making mouldings, frames, etc. ⓘ 1950s: Malay.

ramjet /'ramdʒɛt/ ▷ *noun, aeronautics* **1** (*in full* **ramjet engine**) a type of jet engine consisting of forward air intake, combustion chamber and rear expansion nozzle, in which thrust is generated by compression due solely to forward motion. **2** an aircraft or missile that is propelled by such an engine. ⓘ 1940s.

rammed, rammer and **ramming** see under RAM

ramose and **ramous** see under RAMUS

ramp[1] ▷ *noun* **1** a sloping surface between two different levels, especially one which can be used instead of steps. **2** a set of movable stairs for entering and leaving an aircraft. **3** a low hump lying across a road, designed to slow traffic down. **4** a place where the level of the road surface changes or is uneven due to roadworks. **5** the slope of a wall-top, or anything similar, between two levels. ▷ *verb* (***ramped, ramping***) **1** to provide with a ramp. **2** *intr* to slope from one level to another. **3** *intr* (*often* **ramp around** or **about**) to dash about in a wild, violent and threatening way. • **ramper** *noun.* ⓘ 18c: from French *ramper* (said of an animal) to creep or rear.

ramp[2] ▷ *noun, slang* a swindle, especially the exploitation of a special situation to increase the price of a commodity. ▷ *verb* (***ramped, ramping***) **1** *slang* to rob or swindle. **2** *commerce* (*usually* **ramp up**) to increase greatly (the price of eg shares, etc), usually dishonestly and for financial advantage. • **ramping** *noun* the practice of causing large false increases in the prices of shares, etc by dishonest means. ⓘ 19c in these senses; 16c, meaning 'snatch'.

rampage ▷ *verb* /ram'peɪdʒ/ (***rampaged, rampaging***) *intr* to rush about wildly, angrily, violently or excitedly. ▷ *noun* /'rampeɪdʒ, ram'peɪdʒ/ (*chiefly* **on the rampage**) storming about or behaving wildly and violently in anger, excitement, exuberance, etc. • **rampageous** *adj.* • **rampageousness** *noun.* • **rampaging** *noun.* ⓘ 18c: originally Scottish, probably related to RAMP[1].

rampant /'rampənt/ ▷ *adj* **1 a** uncontrolled; unrestrained; **b** unchecked in growth or prevalence ▫ *rampant growth.* **2** said of an animal: **a** rearing; **b** *heraldry, following its noun* in profile and standing erect on the left hind leg with the other legs raised ▫ *lion rampant.* **3** *archit* said of an arch: with abutments on different levels. • **rampancy** *noun.* • **rampantly** *adverb.* ⓘ 14c: related to RAMP[1].

rampart /'rampɑ:t, 'rampət/ ▷ *noun* **1** a broad mound or wall for defence, usually with a wall or parapet on top. **2** anything which performs such a defensive role. ▷ *verb* (***ramparted, ramparting***) to fortify or surround with ramparts. ⓘ 16c: from French *remparer* to defend, to fortify.

rampion /'rɑmpɪən/ ▷ *noun* a bell-flower whose root is eaten as a salad vegetable. ⓘ 16c.

ram-raid ▷ *noun* a raid carried out by smashing through the front window of a shop or store with a heavy vehicle and looting the goods inside. • **ram-raiding** *noun.* • **ram-raider** *noun.*

ramrod ▷ *noun* **1** a rod for ramming charge down into, or for cleaning, the barrel of a gun. **2** someone who is strict, stern and inflexible, both physically and morally.

ramshackle /'ramʃakəl/ ▷ *adj* said especially of buildings: tumbledown; rickety; badly made and likely to fall down; ⓘ 19c: from 17c *ramshackled,* from obsolete *ranshackle* to ransack.

ramsons /'ramzənz, -sənz/ ▷ *singular noun* **1** a wild garlic, native to woodland of Europe and Asia. **2** its bulbous root, eaten as a relish. ⓘ Anglo-Saxon *hramsa.*

ramus /'reɪməs/ ▷ *noun* (***rami*** /-mi:/) a branch of anything, especially a nerve. • **ramal** or **ramous** *adj* relating to a branch. • **ramate** or **ramose** *adj* branched. ⓘ 17c: Latin.

RAN ▷ *abbreviation* Royal Australian Navy.

ran *past tense of* RUN

ranch /rɑ:ntʃ/ ▷ *noun* **1** *especially N Amer & Austral* **a** an extensive grassland stock-farm where sheep, cattle or horses are raised; **b** such a farm including its buildings and the people employed on it. **2** any large farm that specializes in the production of a particular crop or animal ▫ *a mink ranch.* ▷ *verb* (***ranches, ranched, ranching***) **1** *intr* to own, manage or work on a ranch. **2** *tr* to rear (animals) on a ranch. **3** *tr* to use (land) as a ranch. • **rancher** *noun.* ⓘ 19c: from Mexican Spanish *rancho* mess-room.

rancid /'ransɪd/ ▷ *adj* said of butter, oil, etc that is going bad: tasting or smelling rank or sour. • **rancidity** /ran'sɪdɪtɪ/ or **rancidness** *noun.* ⓘ 17c: from Latin *rancidus,* from *rancere* to stink.

rancour /'raŋkə(r)/ ▷ *noun* a long-lasting feeling of bitterness, dislike or hatred. • **rancorous** *adj.* • **rancorously** *adverb.* ⓘ 14c: French, from Latin *rancor* rankness.

rand[1] /rand/ ▷ *noun* (***rand*** or ***rands***) (abbreviation **R**) the standard monetary unit used in South Africa and some neighbouring countries. See also KRUGERRAND. ⓘ 1960s, adopted at decimalization: named after Witwatersrand, a large gold-mining area near Johannesburg, and related to RAND[2].

rand[2] ▷ *noun* **1** a border or margin. **2** a ridge overlooking a valley. ⓘ Anglo-Saxon *rand.*

R & A ▷ *abbreviation* Royal and Ancient (Golf Club of St Andrews).

R & B ▷ *abbreviation* rhythm and blues.

R & D ▷ *abbreviation* research and development.

randem /ˈrandɛm/ ▷ *noun* a carriage or team of horses driven in tandem with three horses in a line, one in front of the other. ⓒ 19c: probably from *random* + *tandem*.

randier, **randiest**, **randily** and **randiness** see under RANDY

random /ˈrandəm/ ▷ *adj* lacking a definite plan, system or order; haphazard; irregular. • **at random** without any particular plan, system or purpose; haphazardly □ *chosen at random*. • **randomly** *adverb*. • **randomness** *noun*. • **randomwise** *adverb*. ⓒ 14c: from French *randon*, from *randir* to gallop.

random access ▷ *noun, computing* a method of accessing data stored on a disk or in the memory of a computer without having to read any other data stored on the same device, ie the data can be read out of sequence.

random access memory ▷ *noun, computing* see RAM.

randomize or **randomise** /ˈrandəmaɪz/ ▷ *verb* (***randomized***, ***randomizing***) to arrange or set up so as to occur in a random manner. • **randomization** *noun*. • **randomizer** *noun*. ⓒ 1920s.

random variable ▷ *noun, statistics* a VARIABLE which can take any one of a range of values which occur randomly.

R & R ▷ *abbreviation, originally US colloq* rest and recreation.

randy /ˈrandɪ/ ▷ *adj* (***randier***, ***randiest***) *colloq* sexually excited; lustful. • **randily** *adverb*. • **randiness** *noun*. ⓒ 17c.

ranee see RANI

rang see under RING²

range /reɪndʒ/ ▷ *noun* **1 a** an area between limits within which things may move, function, etc; **b** the limits forming this area. **2** a number of items, products, etc forming a distinct series. **3** *music* the distance between the lowest and highest notes which may be produced by a musical instrument or a singing voice. **4** the distance to which a gun may be fired or an object thrown. **5** the distance between a weapon and its target. **6** the distance that can be covered by a vehicle without it needing to refuel. **7** an area where shooting may be practised and rockets tested □ *firing range*. **8** a group of mountains forming a distinct series or row. **9** *N Amer* a large area of open land for grazing livestock. **10** the region over which a plant or animal is distributed. **11** *math* the set of values that a function or dependent variable may take. **12** an enclosed kitchen fireplace fitted with a large cooking stove with one or more ovens and a flat top surface for heating pans. ▷ *verb* (***ranged***, ***ranging***) **1** to put in a row or rows. **2** to put (someone, oneself, etc) into a specified category or group □ *She ranged herself among their enemies*. **3** *intr* to vary or change between specified limits. **4** (*usually* **range over** or **through something**) to roam freely in it. **5** *intr* to stretch or extend in a specified direction or over a specified area. ⓒ 13c: French, from *ranger* to place or position.

rangefinder ▷ *noun* an instrument which can estimate the distance of an object, especially a target to be shot or photographed.

ranger /ˈreɪndʒə(r)/ ▷ *noun* **1** someone who looks after a royal or national forest or park. **2** *N Amer* a soldier who has been specially trained for raiding and combat; a commando. **3** *N Amer* a member of a group of armed men who patrol and police a region. **4** (**Ranger** or **Ranger Guide**) *Brit* a member of the senior branch of the Guide Association.

rangy /ˈreɪndʒɪ/ ▷ *adj* (***rangier***, ***rangiest***) said of a person: with long thin limbs and a slender body.

rani or **ranee** /ˈrɑːnɪ/ ▷ *noun, historical* **1** an Indian queen or princess. **2** the wife or widow of a RAJA. See also MAHARANI. ⓒ 17c: Hindi, from Sanskrit *rajni* queen.

rank¹ ▷ *noun* **1** a line or row of people or things. **2** a line of soldiers standing side by side. **3** a position of seniority within an organization, society, the armed forces, etc. See table on next page. **4** a distinct class or group, eg according to ability. **5** high social position or status. **6** (**the ranks**) ordinary soldiers, eg privates and corporals, as opposed to officers. **7** *Brit* a place where taxis wait for passengers □ *taxi rank*. **8** *chess* a row of squares along the player's side of a chessboard. ▷ *verb* (***ranked***, ***ranking***) **1** to arrange (people or things) in a row or line. **2** *tr & intr* to give or have a particular grade, position or status in relation to others. **3** to have a higher position, status, etc than someone else; to outrank them. • **close ranks** said of a group of people: to keep their solidarity. • **pull rank** to use one's higher rank or status to get what one wants. • **the rank and file** **1** the ordinary members of an organization or society as opposed to the leaders or principal members. **2** the ordinary soldiers as opposed to the officers. ⓒ 16c: from French *renc* rank, row.

rank² ▷ *adj* **1** said of eg plants: coarsely overgrown and untidy. **2** offensively strong in smell or taste. **3** bold, open and shocking □ *rank disobedience*. **4** complete; utter □ *a rank beginner*. • **rankly** *adverb*. • **rankness** *noun*. ⓒ Anglo-Saxon *ranc* proud or overbearing.

ranker /ˈraŋkə(r)/ ▷ *noun* a soldier who serves or has served in the ranks, especially an officer who has been promoted up through the ranks.

rankle /ˈraŋkəl/ ▷ *verb* (***rankled***, ***rankling***) *intr* to continue to cause feelings of annoyance or bitterness □ *His refusal still rankles*. ⓒ 16c in this sense; 14c, meaning 'to fester, suppurate': from French *raoncle* or *rancle*, variant of *draoncle* festering sore, from Latin *dracunculus* a small dragon.

ransack /ˈransak/ ▷ *verb* (***ransacked***, ***ransacking***) **1** to search (eg a house) thoroughly and often roughly. **2** to rob or plunder. • **ransacker** *noun*. ⓒ 13c: from Norse *rannsaka*, from *rann* house + *sœkja* to seek.

ransom /ˈransəm/ ▷ *noun* **1** money demanded in return for the release of a kidnapped person, for the return of property, etc. **2** *relig* atonement; redemption. **3** (*usually* **a king's ransom**) an extortionate price; a vast amount of money. ▷ *verb* (***ransomed***, ***ransoming***) **1** to pay, demand or accept a ransom for someone or something. **2** *relig* to atone; to redeem. • **ransomable** *adj*. • **ransomless** *adj*. • **hold someone to ransom** **1** to keep them prisoner until a ransom is paid. **2** to blackmail them into agreeing to one's demands. ⓒ 14c: from French *ransoun*, from Latin *redemptio* redemption.

rant ▷ *verb* (***ranted***, ***ranting***) **1** *intr* to talk in a loud, angry, pompous way. **2** *tr & intr* to declaim in a loud, pompous, self-important way. ▷ *noun* **1** loud, pompous, empty speech. **2** an angry tirade. • **ranter** *noun* someone, especially a preacher, who rants. • **ranting** *noun, adj*. • **rantingly** *adverb*. ⓒ 16c: from Dutch *ranten* to rave.

RAOC ▷ *abbreviation, Brit* Royal Army Ordnance Corps.

rap¹ ▷ *noun* **1 a** a quick short tap or blow; **b** the sound made by this. **2** *slang* blame or punishment □ *take the rap*. **3** a fast rhythmic monologue recited over a musical backing with a pronounced beat. **4** RAP MUSIC. **5** *colloq* a conversation. ▷ *verb* (***rapped***, ***rapping***) **1** to strike sharply. **2** *intr* to make a sharp tapping sound. **3** (*usually* **rap something out**) to utter (eg a command) sharply and quickly. **4** to criticize sharply. **5** to communicate (a message) by raps or knocks. **6** *intr, colloq* to talk or have a discussion. **7** *intr, colloq* to perform a fast rhythmic monologue to music with a pronounced beat. • **rapper** *noun* **1** a person that raps something. **2** a performer of rap music. • **beat the rap** *N Amer slang* to escape punishment for a crime (whether guilty or not). ⓒ 14c: probably from Norse.

rap² ▷ *noun* the least bit □ *not care a rap*. ⓒ 19c: from the name of an 18c Irish counterfeit coin.

rapacious /rəˈpeɪʃəs/ ▷ *adj* **1** greedy and grasping, especially for money. **2** said of an animal or bird: living by catching prey. • **rapaciously** *adverb*. • **rapaciousness** or **rapacity** /rəˈpasɪtɪ/ *noun*. ⓒ 17c: from Latin *rapax* grasping, from *rapere* to seize.

rape[1] ▷ *noun* **1** the crime of forcing a person, especially a woman, to have sexual intercourse against their will. **2** violation, despoiling or abuse. ▷ *verb* (***raped, raping***) **1** to commit rape on someone. **2** to violate or despoil, especially a country or place in wartime. • **rapist** /ˈreɪpɪst/ *noun*. ⓒ 14c: from Latin *rapere* to seize and carry off.

rape[2] ▷ *noun* the refuse of grapes left after wine-making and used in making vinegar. ⓒ 17c: from French *râpe*.

rape[3] ▷ *noun* OILSEED RAPE. ⓒ 14c: from Latin *rapum* turnip.

raphia same as RAFFIA

rapid /ˈrapɪd/ ▷ *adj* **1** moving, acting or happening quickly; fast. **2** *photog* requiring short exposure. ▷ *noun* (*usually* **rapids**) a part of a river where the water flows quickly, usually over dangerous, sharply descending rocks. • **rapidity** /rəˈpɪdɪtɪ/ or **rapidness** *noun*. • **rapidly** *adverb*. ⓒ 17c: from Latin *rapidus*, from *rapere* to seize.

rapid eye movement ▷ *noun, physiol* (abbreviation **REM**) quick movements of the eyes from side to side behind the closed eyelids during REM SLEEP.

rapid fire ▷ *noun* the quickly repeated firing of guns, asking of questions, etc. ▷ *adj* (**rapid-fire**) fired, asked, etc in quick succession.

rapier /ˈreɪpɪə(r)/ ▷ *noun* a long thin sword for thrusting. ⓒ 16c: from French *rapière*.

rapine /ˈrapaɪn, ˈrapɪn/ ▷ *noun* **1** the seizing of property, etc by force. **2** plundering; robbery. ⓒ 15c: from Latin *rapere* to seize and carry off.

rapist see under RAPE[1]

rap music ▷ *noun* a style of music that has a strong background beat and rhythmic monologues. See also gangsta.

rapped, **rapper** and **rapping** see under RAP[1]

rapport /raˈpɔː(r)/ ▷ *noun* a feeling of sympathy and understanding; a close emotional bond. ⓒ 15c: French, from *rapprocher* to bring back.

rapprochement /raˈprɒʃmɑ̃/ ▷ *noun* the establishment or renewal of a close, friendly relationship, especially between states. ⓒ 19c: French, from *rapprocher* to bring together.

rapscallion /rapˈskalɪən/ ▷ *noun, old use* a rascal or scamp. ⓒ 17c: perhaps related to RASCAL.

rapt ▷ *adj* **1** enraptured; entranced. **2** completely absorbed. • **raptly** *adverb*. ⓒ 14c: from Latin *rapere*, *raptum* to seize and carry off.

raptor /ˈraptə(r)/ ▷ *noun, ornithol* any bird of prey, eg an owl or falcon. • **raptorial** /rapˈtɔːrɪəl/ *adj* **1** predatory. **2** adapted to predatory life. ⓒ 17c: Latin, meaning 'plunderer'.

rapture /ˈraptʃə(r)/ ▷ *noun* **1** great delight; ecstasy. **2** (**raptures**) great enthusiasm for or pleasure in something □ ***was in raptures about the concert.*** • **rapturous** *adj*. • **rapturously** *adverb*. ⓒ 17c: related to RAPT.

ra-ra skirt ▷ *noun* a very short gathered or pleated skirt, originally worn by cheerleaders. ⓒ Early 20c: probably from HURRAH.

rare[1] /rɛə(r)/ ▷ *adj* **1** not done, found or occurring very often; unusual. **2** same as RAREFIED. **3** excellent; unusually good □ ***rare talent.*** **4** *colloq* extreme; severe □ ***a rare old fright.*** **5** said of a gas or of high-altitude atmosphere, etc: rarefied; lacking the usual density. • **rarely** *adverb* **1** seldom; not often. **2** extremely well. • **rareness** *noun*. ⓒ 14c: from Latin *rarus* sparse.

rare[2] /rɛə(r)/ ▷ *adj* said of meat, especially a steak: only very lightly cooked, and often still bloody. Compare MEDIUM *adj* 3, WELL-DONE. ⓒ 18c: from Anglo-Saxon *hrere* lightly boiled.

rare bird ▷ *noun, colloq* an unusual or exceptional person or thing; a rarity.

rarebit see under WELSH RABBIT

rare earth ▷ *noun, chem* **1** an oxide of a **rare-earth element**, any of a group of metallic elements (the lanthanide series) which are similar in chemical properties and very difficult to separate. **2** *now usually* a rare-earth element itself.

rarefied /ˈrɛərɪfaɪd/ *adj* **1** said of the air, atmosphere, etc: thin; with a very low oxygen content. **2** refined; select;

Military Ranks

United Kingdom			USA		
Army	Air Force	Navy	Army	Air Force	Navy
Field Marshal	Marshal of the Royal Air Force	Admiral of the Fleet	General of the Army	General of the Air Force	Fleet Admiral
General	Air Chief Marshal	Admiral	General	General	Admiral
Lieutenant-General	Air Marshal	Vice-Admiral	Lieutenant-General	Lieutenant-General	Vice-Admiral
Major-General	Air Vice-Marshal	Rear-Admiral	Major-General	Major-General	Rear-Admiral
Brigadier	Air Commodore	Commodore Admiral	Brigadier-General	Brigadier-General	Commodore Admiral
Colonel	Group Captain	Captain RN	Colonel	Colonel	Captain
Lieutenant-Colonel	Wing Commander	Commander	Lieutenant-Colonel	Lieutenant-Colonel	Commander
Major	Squadron Leader	Lieutenant Commander	Major	Major	Lieutenant-Commander
Captain	Flight Lieutenant	Lieutenant	Captain	Captain	Lieutenant
Lieutenant	Flying Officer	Sub-Lieutenant	First-Lieutenant	First-Lieutenant	Lieutenant Junior Grade
Second-Lieutenant	Pilot Officer	Midshipman	Second-Lieutenant	Second-Lieutenant	Ensign

exclusive □ ***moves in rarefied circles.*** **3** esoteric; mysterious; spiritual.

rarefy /'rɛərɪfaɪ/ ▻ *verb* (***rarefies, rarefied, rarefying***) **1** to make or become rarer, or less dense or solid. **2** to refine or purify. • **rarefaction** /-'fakʃən/ *noun.* • **rarefactive** *adj.* • **rarefiable** *adj.* ⓒ 14c: from French *raréfier,* from Latin *rarefacere,* from *rarus* rare + *facere* to make.

rare gas ▻ *noun* a NOBLE GAS.

raring /'rɛərɪŋ/ ▻ *adj, colloq* (*chiefly* **raring to go**) keen and enthusiastic; willing and very ready to do something. ⓒ Early 20c: related to REAR[2].

rarity /'rɛərɪtɪ/ ▻ *noun* (***rarities***) **1** uncommonness. **2** something valued because it is rare.

RAS ▻ *abbreviation* Royal Astronomical Society.

rascal /'rɑːskəl/ ▻ *noun* **1** a dishonest person; a rogue. **2** *humorous* a fellow. **3** a cheeky or mischievous child. • **rascal-like** or **rascally** *adj.* ⓒ 14c: from French *rascaille* the rabble.

rase ▻ *verb* see RAZE

rash[1] ▻ *adj* **1** said of an action, etc: **a** over-hasty; reckless; **b** done without considering the consequences. **2** said of a person: lacking in caution; impetuous. • **rashly** *adverb.* • **rashness** *noun.* ⓒ 14c.

rash[2] ▻ *noun* **1** an outbreak of red spots or patches on the skin, usually either a symptom of an infectious disease such as measles or chickenpox, or of a skin allergy. **2** a large number of instances (of something happening) at the same time or in the same place □ ***a rash of burglaries.*** ⓒ 18c: from French *rasche,* from Latin *radere* to scratch or scrape.

rasher /'raʃə(r)/ ▻ *noun* a thin slice of bacon or ham. ⓒ 16c.

rasing see under RAZE

rasp[1] ▻ *noun* **1 a** a coarse, rough file; **b** any tool with a similar surface. **2** a harsh, rough, grating sound or feeling. ▻ *verb* (***rasped, rasping***) **1** to scrape roughly, especially with a rasp. **2** to grate upon or irritate (eg someone's nerves). **3** to speak or utter in a harsh, grating voice. • **rasping** *adj* • **raspingly** *adverb.* • **raspy** *adj.* ⓒ 16c: from French *rasper,* to scrape.

rasp[2] /rɑːsp/ ▻ *noun, colloq* a RASPBERRY.

raspberry /'rɑːzbərɪ, -brɪ/ ▻ *noun* (***raspberries***) **1** the cone-shaped berry made up of several usually reddish, but also black or pale yellow, DRUPELETs each of which contains a single seed. **2** the plant which produces this berry, a deciduous shrub which has upright thorny CANEs and is cultivated in Europe and N America. **3 a** a sound expressing disapproval or contempt, made by blowing through the lips. **b** *slang* a refusal or a rebuke. ▻ *adj* **1** like the red colour of a raspberry, ie varying from pale to deep bluish-pink. **2** made with or from raspberries. • **blow a raspberry** to make a *raspberry* (sense 3a) sound. ⓒ 17c.

Rastafarian /rastə'fɛərɪən/ and **Rastaman** ▻ *noun* a follower of an originally West Indian sect, which regards blacks as the chosen people, reveres Haile Selassie (1891–1975) the former Emperor of Ethiopia, as God. Often shortened to **Rasta**. ▻ *adj* (*also* **Rastafari**) relating to or characteristic of Rastafarians. • **Rastafarianism** *noun.* ⓒ 1950s: from *Ras Tafari,* the name and title of Haile Selassie.

raster /'rastə(r)/ ▻ *noun, TV* a complete set of scanning lines appearing at the receiver as a rectangular patch of light on which the image is reproduced. ⓒ 1930s: German, meaning 'screen or frame'.

rat ▻ *noun* **1** any of various small rodents, similar to mice but larger, which are found worldwide in huge numbers, and are notorious pests and transmitters of disease. **2** any of various unrelated rodents that resemble this animal, eg kangaroo rat. **3** *colloq* someone who is disloyal towards their friends, political party, etc. **4** *colloq* a strike-breaker; a blackleg. **5** *colloq* a despicable person. ▻ *verb* (***ratted, ratting***) *intr* **1** to hunt or chase rats. **2** (*usually* **rat on someone**) *colloq* to betray their trust or desert them. **3** *colloq* to work as a blackleg. • **ratter** *noun* a dog or other animal that catches and kills rats.• **smell a rat** *colloq* to sense that something is not as it should be. ⓒ Anglo-Saxon *ræt.*

ratability and **ratable** see under RATE

ratafia /ratə'fɪə/ ▻ *noun* **1** a flavouring essence made with the essential oil of almonds. **2** a cordial or liqueur flavoured with fruit kernels and almonds. **3** an almond-flavoured biscuit or small cake. ⓒ 17c: French.

ratan see RATTAN

ratarsed ▻ *adj, slang* extremely drunk.

rat-a-tat-tat ▻ *noun* a sound of knocking on a door. ⓒ 17c: imitating the sound of a series of knocks.

ratatouille /ratə'tuːɪ/ ▻ *noun* a southern French vegetable dish made with tomatoes, peppers, courgettes, aubergines, onions and garlic simmered in olive oil. 19c: French, from *touiller* to stir.

ratbag ▻ *noun, slang* a mean, despicable person.

rat-catcher ▻ *noun* someone who eradicates rats and other vermin.

ratchet /'ratʃɪt/ ▻ *noun* **1** a bar which fits into the notches of a toothed wheel so as to cause the wheel to turn in one direction only. **2** (*also* **ratchet-wheel**) a wheel with a toothed rim. **3** the mechanism of such a bar and toothed wheel together. ⓒ 17c: from French *rochet* a blunt head, eg of a lance.

rate[1] /reɪt/ ▻ *noun* **1** the number of times something happens, etc within a given period of time; the amount of something considered in relation to, or measured according to, another amount □ ***a high suicide rate*** □ ***at the rate of 40kph.*** **2a** a price or charge, often measured per unit □ ***the rate of pay for the job;*** **b** (**rates**) see separate entry. **3** a price or charge fixed according to a standard scale □ ***rate of exchange.*** **4** class or rank □ ***second-rate.*** **5** the speed of movement or change □ ***rate of progress.*** ▻ *verb* (***rated, rating***) **1** to give (a value) to something □ ***rate him number two in the world.*** **2** to be worthy of something; to deserve □ ***an answer that doesn't rate full marks.*** **3** *intr* (*usually* **rate as something**) to be placed in a certain class or rank □ ***rates as the best book on the subject.*** **4** in the UK until 1990: to determine the value of property for the purposes of assessing the RATES (sense 2) payable on it. • **rateable** or **ratable** see separate entries. • **at any rate** in any case; anyway. • **at this** or **that rate** if this or that is or continues to be the case. ⓒ 15c: from Latin *rata,* from *reri* to reckon.

rate[2] /reɪt/ ▻ *verb* (***rated, rating***) to scold or rebuke severely. ⓒ 14c.

rateable or **ratable** /'reɪtəbəl/ ▻ *adj* **1 a** said of property: able to have its value assessed for the purpose of payment of RATES; **b** liable to payment of rates. **2** able to be rated or evaluated. • **rateability** or **ratability** /-'bɪlɪtɪ/ *noun.*

rateable value ▻ *noun* the assessed value of a property, used to calculate the RATES to be paid on it.

rate-cap ▻ *verb* (***rate-capped, rate-capping***) said of central government: to set an upper limit on the level of RATES that could be levied by a local authority. • **rate-capping** *noun.* See also CAP *verb* 5.

ratel /'reɪtəl/ ▻ *noun* a HONEY BADGER.

rate of reaction ▻ *noun, chem* the speed of a chemical reaction, usually expressed in terms of the concentrations of REACTANT consumed in a given time, or the rate at which the products are formed.

ratepayer ▻ *noun, Brit* a person or institution that would have paid local RATES.

rates /reɪts/ ▻ *plural noun* **1** (*in full* **business rates**) in the UK: a tax paid by a business, based on the assessed value of property and land owned or leased and collected by a local authority to pay for public services. **2** in the UK until 1990: a tax payable by each household and collected by a local authority to pay for public services based on the assessed value of their property, replaced by the COMMUNITY CHARGE and subsequently by the COUNCIL TAX.

ratfink /'ratfɪŋk/ ▻ *noun, derog slang, especially N Amer* a mean, despicable or deceitful person.

rather /'rɑːðə(r)/ ▻ *adverb* **1 a** more readily; more willingly; **b** in preference ▫ ***I'd rather go to the cinema than watch TV.*** **2** more truly or correctly ▫ ***my parents, or rather my mother and stepfather.*** **3** to a limited degree; slightly. **4** ▫ ***It's rather good.*** **5** on the contrary ▫ ***She said she'd help me; rather, she just sat around watching TV.*** ▻ *exclamation* yes indeed; very much ▫ ***Would you like a chocolate? Rather!*** ⓘ Anglo-Saxon *hrathor*.

ratification /ratɪfɪ'keɪʃən/ ▻ *noun* **1** the act of ratifying or being ratified. **2** confirmation; sanction.

ratify /'ratɪfaɪ/ ▻ *verb* (***ratifies, ratified, ratifying***) to give formal consent to (eg a treaty, agreement, etc), especially by signature. ⓘ 14c: from Latin *ratificare*.

rating /'reɪtɪŋ/ ▻ *noun* **1** a classification according to order, rank or value. **2** *Brit* an ordinary seaman. **3** an estimated value of a person's position, especially as regards credit. **4** the proportion of viewers or listeners forming the estimated audience of a television or radio programme, used as a measure of that programme's popularity.

ratio /'reɪʃɪoʊ/ ▻ *noun* (**ratios**) **1** the number or degree of one class of things in relation to another, or between one thing and another, expressed as a proportion ▫ ***The ratio of dogs to cats is 5 to 3.*** **2** the number of times one mathematical quantity can be divided by another. ⓘ 17c: from Latin *ratio* reckoning, from *reri, ratus* to think.

ration /'raʃən/ ▻ *noun* **1** a fixed allowance of food, clothing, petrol, etc, during a time of war or shortage. **2** (**rations**) a daily allowance of food, especially in the army. ▻ *verb* (***rationed, rationing***) **1** (*often* **ration something out**) to distribute or share it out (especially when it is in short supply), usually in fixed amounts. **2** to restrict the supply of provisions to someone. • **rationing** *noun* **1** supplying rations. **2** dividing into rations. ⓘ 18c; 16c in obsolete sense 'ratio': French, from Latin *ratio* reason.

rational /'raʃənl/ ▻ *adj* **1** related to or based on reason or logic. **2** able to think, form opinions, make judgements, etc. **3** sensible; reasonable. **4** sane. **5** *math* said of a quantity, ratio, root: able to be expressed as a ratio of whole numbers. • **rationality** /raʃə'nalɪtɪ/ *noun* **1** being rational. **2** the possession or due exercise of reason. **3** reasonableness. • **rationally** *adverb*. ⓘ 14c: from Latin *rationalis*, from *ratio* reason.

rationale /raʃə'nɑːl/ ▻ *noun* the underlying principles or reasons on which a decision, belief, action, etc is based. ⓘ 17c: from Latin *rationalis* rational.

rational horizon see HORIZON sense 2

rationalism ▻ *noun* the theory that an individual's actions and beliefs should be based on reason rather than on intuition or the teachings of others. • **rationalist** *noun* someone who forms opinions by reasoning. • **rationalistic** *adj* • **rationalistically** *adverb*.

rationality see under RATIONAL

rationalize or **rationalise** ▻ *verb* (***rationalized, rationalizing***) **1** to attribute (one's behaviour or attitude) to sensible, well-thought-out reasons or motives, especially after the event. **2** *intr* to explain one's behaviour, etc in this way. **3** to make something logical or rational. **4** to make (an industry or organization) more efficient and profitable by reorganizing it to get rid of unnecessary costs and labour. • **rationalization** /-'zeɪʃən/ *noun*.

rational number ▻ *noun, math* any number able to be expressed as a fraction in the form $^m/_n$, where *m* and *n* are integers, and *n* is not equal to zero, eg $^2/_3$. Compare IRRATIONAL NUMBER.

ration book and **ration card** ▻ *noun* a book or card containing coupons which can be exchanged for rationed goods.

ratpack ▻ *noun, slang* **1** a rowdy gang of young people. **2** a group of photographers, especially from tabloid newspapers, who follow and photograph famous people.

rat race ▻ *noun, colloq* the fierce, unending competition for success, wealth, etc in business, society, etc.

rattan or **ratan** /rə'tan/ ▻ *noun* **1** a climbing palm with very long thin tough stems. **2** a cane made from the stem of this palm. **3** the stems collectively as WICKERWORK. ⓘ 17c: from Malay *rotan*.

ratted, ratter and **ratting** see under RAT

rattier and **rattiest** see under RATTY

rattle /'ratəl/ ▻ *verb* (***rattled, rattling***) **1** *intr* to make a series of short sharp hard sounds in quick succession. **2** to cause (eg crockery) to make such a noise. **3** *intr* to move along rapidly, often with a rattling noise. **4** *intr* (*usually* **rattle on**) to chatter thoughtlessly or idly. **5** *colloq* to make someone anxious or nervous; to upset them. ▻ *noun* **1** a series of short sharp sounds made in quick succession that gives the effect of a continuous sound. **2** a baby's toy made of a container filled with small pellets which rattle when it is shaken. **3** a device for making a whirring sound, used especially at football matches. **4** the loose horny structures at the end of a rattlesnake's tail, which produce a rattling sound when vibrated. **5** lively, empty chatter. **6** the rough harsh breathing sound caused by air passing through mucus in the back of the throat. ⓘ 14c.

■ **rattle something off** or **rattle through something** to say, recite or write it rapidly and unthinkingly.

rattler ▻ *noun, colloq* a rattlesnake.

rattlesnake ▻ *noun* any of several species of poisonous American snakes of the pit viper family, that gives birth to live young, and, if threatened, vibrates a series of dry horny structures at the end of its tail, producing a characteristic rattling sound.

rattletrap ▻ *noun, colloq* a broken-down rickety old vehicle, especially a car.

rattling *colloq old use* ▻ *adj, adverb* **1** smart or smartly. **2** brisk or briskly. **3** as a general intensifying word: good or well; very ▫ ***told us a rattling good yarn.***

rattly ▻ *adj* (***rattlier, rattliest***) making a rattling noise; often rattling.

ratty ▻ *adj* (***rattier, rattiest***) **1** relating to or like a rat. **2** *colloq* irritable.

raucous /'rɔːkəs/ ▻ *adj* said of a sound, especially a voice, shout, etc: hoarse; harsh. • **raucously** *adverb*. • **raucousness** *noun*. ⓘ 18c: from Latin *raucus* hoarse.

raunchy /'rɔːntʃɪ/ ▻ *adj* (***raunchier, raunchiest***) *colloq* coarsely or openly sexual; lewd or smutty. • **raunchily** *adverb*. • **raunchiness** *noun*. ⓘ 1960s.

rauwolfia /rɔː'wɒlfɪə/ ▻ *noun* any of various tropical trees and shrubs with clusters of white flowers and red or black berries, some of which were the natural basis for psychotropic drugs, including RESERPINE. ⓘ 18c: named after German physician and botanist Leonard Rauwolf (died 1596).

ravage /'ravɪdʒ/ ▻ *verb* (***ravaged, ravaging***) *tr & intr* to cause extensive damage to a place; to destroy it. ▻ *noun* (*usually* **ravages**) damage or destruction ▫ ***the ravages of time.*** ⓘ 17c: from French *ravir* to ravish.

rave /reɪv/ ▻ *verb* (***raved, raving***) **1** *intr* to talk wildly as if mad or delirious. **2** *intr* (*usually* **rave about** or **over**

something) to talk enthusiastically or passionately about it. ▻ *noun, colloq* **1** extravagant praise. **2** a RAVE-UP. **3** a gathering of lots of people in a large warehouse or open-air venue such as a field, etc for dancing to eg techno or acid-house music, etc where little alcohol is drunk but recreational drugs are usually available. ▻ *adj, colloq* extremely enthusiastic □ *rave reviews.* 14c.

ravel /'ravəl/ ▻ *verb* (**ravelled**, **ravelling**; *US* **raveled**, **raveling**) **1** *tr & intr* to tangle or become tangled up. **2** (*usually* **ravel something out**) **a** to untangle, unravel or untwist it; **b** to resolve it; to explain it or make it clear. **3** *intr* to fray. ▻ *noun* **1** a tangle or knot. **2** a complication. **3** a loose or broken thread. • **ravelling** *noun.* ⓒ 16c: perhaps from Dutch *ravelen* to tangle.

ravelin /'ravlɪn/ ▻ *noun, fortification* a detached work with two embankments raised before the counterscarp. ⓒ 16c: French.

raven /'reɪvən/ ▻ *noun* a large blue-black bird of the crow family. ▻ *adj* glossy blue-black in colour □ *raven-haired.* ⓒ Anglo-Saxon *hræfn.*

ravening /'ravənɪŋ/ ▻ *adj* said especially of meat-eating animals: hungrily seeking food. ⓒ 16c: from *raven* to devour or hunt for food.

ravenous /'ravənəs/ ▻ *adj* **1** extremely hungry or greedy. **2** said of hunger, a desire, etc: intensely strong. **3** said of an animal, etc: living on prey; predatory. • **ravenously** *adverb.* • **ravenousness** *noun.* ⓒ 15c: see RAVENING.

raver /'reɪvə(r)/ ▻ *noun, colloq* **1** someone who leads a full, very lively and often wild social life. **2** someone who attends a RAVE (sense 3).

rave-up ▻ *noun, colloq* a lively party or celebration.

ravine /rə'viːn/ ▻ *noun* a deep narrow steep-sided gorge. ⓒ 15c: from French *ravine* a violent rush (of water).

raving /'reɪvɪŋ/ ▻ *verb, present participle of* RAVE. ▻ *adj* ▻ *adverb* **1** frenzied; delirious. **2** *colloq* great; extreme □ *a raving beauty.* ▻ *noun* (*usually* **ravings**) wild, frenzied or delirious talk.

ravioli /ravɪ'oʊlɪ/ ▻ *singular or plural noun* small square pasta cases with a savoury filling of meat, cheese, etc. ⓒ 19c: Italian.

ravish /'ravɪʃ/ ▻ *verb* **1** to overwhelm someone with joy, delight, etc; to enrapture. **2** to rape someone. • **ravishing** *adj* delightful; lovely; very attractive. • **ravishingly** *adverb* delightfully.

raw /rɔː/ ▻ *adj* **1** said of meat, vegetables, etc: not cooked. **2** not processed, purified or refined • *raw silk.* **3** said of alcoholic spirit: undiluted. **4** said of statistics, data, etc: not analysed. **5** said of a person: not trained or experienced. **6** said of a wound, etc: with a sore, inflamed surface. **7** said of the weather: cold and damp. **8** said of an edge of material: not finished off and so liable to fray. **9** particularly sensitive • *touched a raw nerve.* ▻ *noun* a sore, inflamed or sensitive place. • **rawness** *noun.* • **in the raw 1** in a natural or crude state. **2** *colloq* naked. ⓒ Anglo-Saxon *hreaw.*

rawboned ▻ *adj* lean and gaunt.

raw deal ▻ *noun, colloq* harsh, unfair treatment.

rawhide ▻ *noun* **1** untanned leather. **2** a whip made from this.

raw material ▻ *noun* **1** any substance, in its natural unprocessed state, that serves as the starting point for a production or manufacturing process. **2** material out of which something is or can be made, or may develop.

raw sienna see SIENNA

raw umber ▻ *noun* untreated umber.

ray¹ /reɪ/ ▻ *noun* **1** a narrow beam of light or radioactive particles. **2** any of a set of lines fanning out from a central point. **3** a small amount of or the beginnings of something, especially hope or understanding. **4** any of the set of spines which support a fish's fin. ▻ *verb* (**rayed**, **raying**) **1** *tr & intr* to radiate. **2** to provide something with rays. ⓒ 14c: from French *rai*, from Latin *radius* rod.

ray² /reɪ/ ▻ *noun* any of numerous cartilaginous fish, related to the sharks, with a flattened body, large pectoral fins extending from the head to the base of the tail, and both eyes on the upper surface, eg stingray, manta ray, sawfish. ⓒ 14c: from French *raie*, from Latin *raia.*

ray³ or **re** /reɪ/ ▻ *noun, music* in sol-fa notation: the second note of the major scale. ⓒ 14c: see SOL-FA.

Ray-Bans ▻ *plural noun, trademark* a type of designer sunglasses with the manufacturer's name on the legs. Also (**Ray-Ban**) *as adj* □ *Ray-Ban shades.*

ray-gun ▻ *noun* especially in science fiction: a gun that fires destructive rays, used as a weapon.

Raynaud's disease /'reɪnoʊz —/ ▻ *noun, medicine* a disorder in which (usually in response to exposure to cold, or emotional stress) the fingers, toes, ears and nose turn white or develop a bluish tinge as a result of spasm of the arteries supplying the affected parts. ⓒ 19c: named after the French physician Maurice Raynaud (1834–81).

rayon /'reɪɒn/ ▻ *noun* a strong, durable, easily dyed artificial fibre consisting of regenerated cellulose that has been spun into filaments. It is used to make textiles for clothing, conveyer belts, hoses, etc. ⓒ 1920s: from RAY¹.

raze or **rase** /reɪz/ (**razed**, **razing**; **rased**, **rasing**) ▻ *verb* (*usually* **raze something to the ground**) **1** to destroy or demolish (buildings, a town, etc) completely. **2** to lay (a building) level with the ground. • **razed** *adj.* ⓒ 16c: from French *raser*, from Latin *radere* to scrape.

> ***raze***
>
> There is often a spelling confusion between **raze** and **raise**.

razoo /rɑː'zuː/ ▻ *noun* (**razoos**) *Austral & NZ colloq, with negatives* an imaginary coin of insignificant value □ *I don't have a brass razoo.* ⓒ 1930s.

razor /'reɪzə(r)/ ▻ *noun* a sharp-edged instrument used for shaving. ▻ *verb* **1** to use a razor on something or someone. **2** to shave or cut, especially closely. ⓒ 13c: from French *rasour*, from *raser* to shave.

razorbill ▻ *noun* a type of seabird with a sharp-edged bill.

razor edge ▻ *noun* **1** a very fine sharp edge. **2** *colloq* a critical delicately balanced situation.

razor shell ▻ *noun* a burrowing marine bivalve with two similar elongated shell valves, the two halves of the shell being closed by two muscles.

razor wire ▻ *noun* thick wire with sharp pieces of metal attached, used like barbed wire for fences, etc.

razzle /'razəl/ ▻ *noun, slang* (*often* **on the razzle**) a lively spree, outing or party, especially involving a lot of drinking □ *He's out on the razzle again tonight.* ⓒ Early 20c: from RAZZLE-DAZZLE.

razzle-dazzle /'razəldazəl/ ▻ *noun, slang* **1** excitement, confusion, dazzling show, etc. **2** a lively spree. ⓒ 19c: reduplication of DAZZLE.

razzmatazz /razmə'taz, 'razmətaz/ ▻ *noun* **1** razzle-dazzle. **2** humbug. ⓒ 19c.

Rb ▻ *symbol, chem* rubidium.

RC ▻ *abbreviation* **1** Red Cross. **2** *IVR* Republic of China, Taiwan. **3** Roman Catholic.

RCA ▻ *abbreviation* **1** Radio Corporation of America. **2** *IVR: Republique Centafricaine* (French), Central African Republic. **3** Royal Canadian Academy. **4** Royal College of Art.

RCAF ▻ *abbreviation* Royal Canadian Air Force.

RCB ▷ *abbreviation, IVR* Republic of the Congo (Brazzaville).

RCH ▷ *abbreviation, IVR* Republic of Chile.

RCM ▷ *abbreviation* Royal College of Music.

RCMP ▷ *abbreviation* Royal Canadian Mounted Police.

RCN ▷ *abbreviation* Royal Canadian Navy.

RCOG ▷ *abbreviation* Royal College of Obstetricians and Gynaecologists.

RCP ▷ *abbreviation* Royal College of Physicians.

RCR ▷ *abbreviation* Royal College of Radiologists.

RCS ▷ *abbreviation* **1** Royal College of Science. **2** Royal College of Surgeons. **3** Royal Corps of Signals.

RCT ▷ *abbreviation* Royal Corps of Transport.

RCVS ▷ *abbreviation* Royal College of Veterinary Surgeons.

RD ▷ *abbreviation* **1** written on a returned bank cheque: refer to drawer. **2** Rural Dean.

Rd ▷ *abbreviation* used in street names: Road.

rd ▷ *abbreviation* rutherford.

RDA ▷ *abbreviation* recommended daily (or dietary) allowance, the daily amount of essential nutrient, ie vitamins, protein, etc, needed to meet a normal healthy person's nutritional requirements.

RDF ▷ *abbreviation* refuse-derived fuel.

RE ▷ *abbreviation*, religious education.

Re ▷ *symbol, chem* rhenium.

re[1] /reɪ/ ▷ *prep* with regard to; concerning □ *re: your letter of 18th.* ◷ 18c: from Latin *res* thing.

re[2] see RAY[3]

re- ▷ *prefix* **1** *denoting* motion backwards or away, withdrawal, reversal, etc □ *recede* □ *recant.* **2** *denoting* again, or again and in a different way □ *reread* □ *rewrite.* ◷ Latin.

're /ə(r)/ ▷ *verb* short form of ARE[1]. □ *We're going to Paris.*

reach /riːtʃ/ ▷ *verb* (***reaches, reached, reaching***) **1** to arrive at or get as far as (a place, position, etc). **2** *tr & intr* to be able to touch or get hold of something. **3** *tr & intr* to project or extend to a point. **4** *intr* (*usually* **reach across, out, up,** *etc*) to stretch out one's arm to try to touch or get hold of something. **5** *colloq* to hand or pass something to someone □ *reach me that CD.* **6** to make contact or communicate with someone, especially by telephone □ *I couldn't reach her.* ▷ *noun* **1** the distance one can stretch one's arm, hand, etc □ *out of reach.* **2** a distance that can be travelled easily □ *within reach of London.* **3** an act of reaching out. **4** range of influence, power, understanding or abilities. **5** (*usually* **reaches**) a section within clear limits, eg part of a river or canal between two bends or locks. **6** (*usually* **reaches**) level or rank □ *the upper reaches of government.* ● **reachable** *adj.* ◷ Anglo-Saxon *rǣcan.*

reach-me-down ▷ *noun* a second-hand or ready-made item of clothing.

react /rɪ'akt/ ▷ *verb* (***reacted, reacting***) **1** *intr* **a** (*chiefly* **react to something** or **someone**) to act in response to something said or done, or to another person; **b** *loosely* to act or behave. **2** *intr* (*usually* **react against something**) **a** to respond to it in a way which shows dislike or disapproval; **b** to act in a contrary or opposing way. **3** *intr,*

Some words with *re-* prefixed, all of which refer to RE- sense 2.

reaccustom *verb.*
reacquaint *verb.*
reacquaintance *noun.*
reacquire *verb.*
readapt *verb.*
readaptation *noun.*
readdress *verb.*
readjust *verb.*
readjustment *noun.*
readmission *noun.*
readmit *verb.*
readmittance *noun.*
readopt *verb.*
readoption *noun.*
readvance *noun, verb.*
readvertise *verb.*
readvertisement *noun.*
readvise *verb.*
reaffirm *verb.*
reaffirmation *noun.*
realign *verb.*
realignment *noun.*
reallocate *verb.*
reallocation *noun.*
reallot *verb.*
reallotment *noun.*
reanimate *verb.*
reanimation *noun.*
reappear *verb, intr.*
reappearance *noun.*
reapplication *noun.*
reapply *verb.*
reappoint *verb.*
reappointment *noun.*
reapportion *verb.*
reapportionment *noun.*
reappraisal *noun.*
reappraise *verb.*
rearrange *verb.*
rearrangement *noun.*
rearrest *verb, noun.*
reassemble *verb.*
reassembly *noun.*
reassert *verb.*
reassertion *noun.*
reassess *verb.*
reassessment *noun.*
reassign *verb.*
reassignment *noun.*
reassume *verb.*
reassumption *noun.*
reattach *verb.*
reattachment *noun.*
reattain *verb.*
reattempt *verb, noun.*
reawake *verb.*
reawaken *verb.*
reawakening *noun*
rebaptism *noun.*
rebaptize or **rebaptise** *verb.*
rebid *verb, noun.*
rebroadcast *verb, noun.*
rebuild *verb.*
reburial *noun.*
rebury *verb.*
rebutton *verb.*
recalculate *verb.*
recapitalization or **recapitalisation** *noun.*
recapitalize or **recapitalise** *verb.*
recast *verb, noun.*
recentre *verb.*
recharge *verb.*
rechargeable *adj.*
recheck *verb, noun.*
rechristen *verb.*
recirculate *verb.*
reclassification *noun.*
reclassify *verb.*
reclimb *verb.*
reclothe *verb.*
recolonization or **recolonisation** *noun.*
recolonize or **recolonise** *verb.*
recombine *verb.*
recommence *verb.*
recommencement *noun.*
recommit *verb.*
recommitment *noun.*
recommital *noun.*
reconfirm *verb.*
reconfirmation *noun.*
reconnect *verb.*
reconnection *noun.*
reconquer *verb.*
reconquest *noun.*

physics to exert an equal force in the opposite direction. **4** *tr & intr, chem* to undergo or cause to undergo chemical change produced by a REAGENT. **5** *intr, stock exchange* said of share prices: to fall sharply after a rise. ⓘ 17c: from Latin *reagere, reactum*, from *agere* to do or act.

re-act ▻ *verb* to act (a scene, line, etc) again.

reactance /rɪˈaktəns/ ▻ *noun, elec* in an electric circuit carrying alternating current: the property of an INDUCTOR or CAPACITOR that causes it to oppose the flow of current. Compare IMPEDANCE. ⓘ 19c.

reactant /rɪˈaktənt/ ▻ *noun, chem* a substance which takes part in a chemical reaction. ⓘ 1920s.

reaction /rɪˈakʃən/ ▻ *noun* **1** a response to stimulus. **2** an action or change in the opposite direction. **3** a complete change of opinions, feelings, etc to the opposite of what they were ▫ *The idea was popular at first but then a reaction set in.* **4** a response which shows how someone feels or thinks about something ▫ *What was his reaction to the news?* **5** opposition to change, especially political change, reform, etc, and a tendency to revert to a former system, or state of affairs. **6** *physiol* a physical or mental effect caused by eg a drug, medicines, etc. **7** *chem* **a** a chemical process in which the electrons surrounding the nuclei in the atoms of one or more elements or compounds (REACTANTs) react to form one or more new compounds or products (see PRODUCT sense 4); **b** chemical change. **8** *physics* a nuclear reaction involving a change in an atomic nucleus, eg radioactive decay, nuclear fission, nuclear fusion. **9** *physics* the force offered by a body that is equal in magnitude but opposite in direction to the force applied to it. **10** *stock exchange* a sharp fall, in share prices, etc, after a rise. • **reactional** *adj*. ⓘ 17c: from REACT.

reactionary /rɪˈakʃənərɪ, -ʃənrɪ/ and **reactionist** /rɪˈakʃənɪst/ ▻ *adj* said of a person or policies: relating to or characterized by reaction, especially against radical social or political change, reform, etc, and in favour of reverting to a former system or state of affairs. ▻ *noun* (***reactionaries*** or ***reactionists***) someone who holds such political or social views. • **reactionism** *noun*. ⓘ Mid 19c.

reactivate /rɪˈaktɪveɪt/ ▻ *verb* (***reactivated, reactivating***) to make something active again. • **reactivation** /rɪaktɪˈveɪʃən/ *noun*. ⓘ Early 20c.

reactive /rɪˈaktɪv/ ▻ *adj* showing a reaction; liable to react; sensitive to stimuli.

reactor /rɪˈaktə(r)/ ▻ *noun* a NUCLEAR REACTOR.

read /riːd/ *verb* (***read*** /rɛd/, ***reading***) **1** to look at and understand (printed or written words). **2** to speak (words which are printed or written). **3** to learn or gain knowledge of something by reading ▫ *read the election results in the newspaper.* **4** *intr* to pass one's leisure time reading books, especially for pleasure ▫ *She doesn't read much.* **5** to look at or be able to see something and get information from it ▫ *cannot read the clock without my glasses.* **6** to interpret or understand the meaning of something other than writing, eg a map, a compass, the clouds, etc ▫ *read a map.* **7** to interpret or understand (signs, marks, etc) without using one's eyes ▫ *read Braille.* **8** to know (a language) well enough to be able to understand something written in it ▫ *speaks Chinese but cannot read it.* **9** *intr* to have a certain wording ▫ *The letter reads as follows.* **10** *tr & intr* to think that (a statement,

Some words with *re-* prefixed, all of which refer to RE- sense 2.

reconsecrate *verb*.
reconsecration *noun*.
reconsign *verb*.
reconsignment *noun*.
reconsolidate *verb*.
reconsolidation *noun*.
recontinue *verb*.
reconvene *verb*.
reconvey *verb*.
reconvict *verb*.
reconviction *noun*.
reconvert *verb*.
reconversion *noun*.
recross *verb* .
redeal *verb, noun*.
redecorate *verb*.
redefine *verb*.
redesign *verb*.
redial *verb*.
redirect *verb*.
rediscount *verb, noun*.
rediscover *verb*.
rediscovery *noun*.
redistribute *verb*.
redistribution *noun*.
redraw *verb*.
redrive *verb* .
re-elect *verb*.
re-election *noun*.
re-embark *verb*.
re-embarkation *noun*.
re-emerge *verb, intr*.
re-emergence *noun*.
re-emergent *adj*.
re-emphasize or **re-emphasise** *verb*.
re-enact *verb*.
re-enactment *noun*.
re-endorse *verb*.
re-endorsement *noun*.
re-engage *verb*.
re-engagement *noun*.
re-enlist *verb*.
re-enlistment *noun*.
re-equip *verb*.
re-erect *verb*.
re-erection *noun*.
re-establish *verb*.
re-establishment *noun*.
re-examination *noun*.
re-examine *verb*.
re-export *verb, noun*.
re-exportation *noun*.
refashion *verb*.
refloat *verb*.
reflower *verb, intr*.
reflowering *noun*.
refocus *verb*.
reformat *verb*.
reformulate *verb*.
reframe *verb*.
refreeze *verb*.
refurnish *verb*.
regrade *verb*.
regrind *verb*.
regroup *verb*.
regrow *verb*.
regrowth *noun*.
rehear *verb*.
rehearing *noun*.
reimport *verb*.
reinhabit *verb*.
reinsert *verb*.
reinsertion *noun*.
reinsure *verb*.
reintegrate *verb*.
reinterpret *verb*.
reinterpretation *noun*.
reinterpretative *adj*.
reintroduce *verb*.
reintroduction *noun*.
reissuable *adj*.
reissue *verb, noun*.
reinvent *verb*.
reinvest *verb*.
reinvigorate *verb*.
rekey *verb*.
rekindle *verb*.
relabel *verb*.
relearn *verb*.
relet *verb*.
relight *verb*.
reline *verb*.
reload *verb*.
rematch *noun*.
remarriage *noun*.

etc) has a particular meaning □ *read it as criticism.* **11** *intr* said of writing: to convey meaning in a specified way □ *an essay which reads well* □ *reads badly.* **12** said of a dial, instrument, etc: to show a particular measurement □ *The barometer reads 'fair'.* **13** to replace (a word, phrase, etc) by another □ *for 'three' read 'four'.* **14** to put into a specified condition by reading □ *She read the child to sleep.* **15** to study (a subject) at university. **16** to hear and understand, especially when using two-way radio □ *Do you read me?* ▷ *noun* **1** a period or act of reading. **2** a book, magazine, etc considered in terms of how readable it is □ *a good read.* • **read between the lines** to perceive a meaning which is implied but not stated. • **take something as read** /rɛd/ to accept or assume it. • **well** or **widely read** /rɛd/ educated, especially in literature, through reading. ◎ Anglo-Saxon *rædan.*

■ **read something into something** to find something in a person's writing, words, actions, etc (a meaning which is not stated clearly or made obvious and which may not have been intended).

■ **read something in** or **out** *computing* to transfer data from a disk or other storage device into the main memory of a computer.

■ **read something off from something** to take (figures, etc) as a reading from an instrument, database etc □ *read off the net profits from the speadsheet.*

■ **read something out** to read it aloud.

■ **read up on something** to learn a subject by reading books about it.

readable /'riːdəbəl/ ▷ *adj* **1** legible; able to be read. **2** pleasant or quite interesting to read. • **readability** /riːdə'bɪlɪtɪ/ or **readableness** *noun.*

reader /'riːdə(r)/ ▷ *noun* **1** someone who reads. **2** *Brit* a university lecturer of a rank between professor and senior lecturer. **3** someone who reads prayers in a church. See also LAY READER. **4** a book containing short texts, used for learning to read or for learning a foreign language □ *a German reader.* **5** someone who reads and reports on manuscripts for a publisher. **6** someone who reads and corrects proofs. **7** *computing* **a** a machine which produces a magnified image from a microfilm so that it can be read; a READING-MACHINE (sense 1); **b** a DOCUMENT READER.

readership ▷ *noun* **1** the total number of people who read a newspaper, the novels of a particular author, etc □ *has a readership of several thousand.* **2** *Brit* the post of reader in a university.

readier, **readiest**, **readily**, **readiness**, *etc* see under READY

reading /'riːdɪŋ/ ▷ *noun* **1** the action of someone who reads. **2** the ability to read □ *his reading is poor.* Also *as adj* □ *reading age* □ *reading glasses.* **3** any book, printed material, etc that can be read. **4** an event at which a play, poetry, etc is read to an audience. **5** *Brit politics* any one of the three stages (the **first reading**, **second reading** or **third reading**) in the passage of a bill through Parliament, when it is respectively introduced, discussed,

Some words with *re-* prefixed, all of which refer to RE- sense 2.

remarry *verb.*
remeasure *verb.*
remeasurement *noun.*
remilitarization or **remilitarisation** *noun.*
remilitarize or **remilitarise** *verb.*
remodel *verb.*
remodification *noun.*
remodify *verb.*
remoralize or **remoralise** *verb.*
remoralization or **remoralisation** *noun.*
remortgage *verb.*
rename *verb.*
renegotiable *adj.*
renegotiate *verb.*
renegotiation *noun.*
renominate *verb.*
renomination *noun.*
renotification *noun.*
renotify *verb.*
renumber *verb.*
reoccupation *noun.*
reoccupy *verb.*
reoccur *verb, intr.*
reoccurrence *noun.*
reoffend *verb, intr.*
reorder *verb.*
reorganization or **reorganisation** *noun.*
reorganize or **reorganise** *verb.*
reorient *verb.*
reorientate *verb.*
reorientation *noun.*
repack *verb.*
repaper *verb.*
repeople *verb.*
replan *verb.*
replant *verb.*
repopulate *verb.*
reposition *verb.*
repot *verb.*
repotting *noun.*
reprogramme *verb.*
republication *noun.*
republish *verb.*
repurchase *verb, noun.*
requote verb
reread *verb.*
reregulate *verb.*
reregulation *noun.*
re-revise *verb.*
re-roof *verb .*
resay *verb.*
reseal *verb.*
resealable *adj.*
reselect *verb.*
reselection *noun.*
resell *verb.*
resentence *verb.*
resettle *verb.*
resettlement *noun.*
reshape *verb.*
resite *verb.*
resole *verb.*
respell *verb.*
restaff *verb.*
restage *verb.*
restart *verb, noun.*
restate *verb.*
restatement *noun.*
restock *verb.*
restring *verb.*
restructure *verb.*
restyle *verb.*
resubmit *verb.*
resupply *verb.*
resurface *verb.*
resurvey *verb, noun.*
resynchronization or **resynchronisation** *noun.*
resynchronize or **resynchronise** *verb .*
retie *verb.*
retile *verb.*
retitle *verb.*
retune *verb.*
returf *verb.*
re-type *verb.*
reupholster *verb.*
reusable *adj.*
reuse *verb, noun.*
revarnish *verb.*
revictual *verb.*
revisit *verb, noun.*
rewash *verb.*
reweigh *verb.*
rewrap *verb.*

and reported on by a committee. **6** the actual word or words that can be read in a text, especially where more than one version is possible □ *one of many disputed readings in the Bible.* **7** information, figures, etc shown by an instrument or meter □ *thermometer reading.* **8** an understanding or interpretation of something written or said, or of circumstances, etc □ *her reading of the situation.* **9** knowledge gained from having read books. ▻ *adj* fond of or addicted to reading □ *the reading public.*

reading age ▻ *noun* the reading ability, especially of a child, calculated by comparison with the average ability at a certain age.

reading-book ▻ *noun* a book of exercises in reading, especially for a child who is learning to read.

reading-desk ▻ *noun* a desk for holding a book or paper while it is read; a lectern.

reading-lamp ▻ *noun* a lamp for reading by.

reading-machine ▻ *noun, computing* a DOCUMENT READER.

reading matter ▻ *noun* printed material, especially books, magazines, etc □ *get some reading-matter for the train.*

reading-room ▻ *noun* **1** a room, usually in a public building, where books, newspapers, etc may be consulted, read or studied. **2** a proof-reader's room.

read-only memory see ROM

read-out ▻ *noun, computing* **1** the act of copying data from the main memory of a computer into an external storage device, eg a disk or tape, or a display device, eg a VDU or plotter. **2** data that has been copied in this way. Compare PRINTOUT.

read-write head see under DISK DRIVE

read-write memory ▻ *noun, computing* a computer memory which allows data to be both read and changed.

ready /'rɛdɪ/ ▻ *adj* (***readier, readiest***) **1** prepared and available for use or action. **2** willing; eager □ *always ready to help.* **3** prompt; quick, usually too quick □ *He's always ready to find fault.* **4** likely or about to □ *a plant just ready to flower.* ▻ *noun* (**readies**) *colloq* short form of READY MONEY. ▻ *adverb* prepared or made beforehand □ *ready cooked meals.* ▻ *verb* (***readies, readied, readying***) to make ready; to prepare. • **readily** *adverb* willingly; quickly and without difficulty. • **readiness** *noun*. • **at the ready 1** said of a gun: aimed and ready to be fired. **2** ready for immediate action. • **ready, steady, go** or **ready, get set, go** a formulaic expression used to start a race. ◷ Anglo-Saxon *ræde*.

ready-made or **ready-to-wear** ▻ *adj* **1** said of clothes: made to a standard size, not made-to-measure. **2** convenient; useful □ *a ready-made excuse.* **3** hackneyed; unoriginal. ▻ *noun* an article, especially an article of clothing, that is ready-made.

ready money ▻ *noun, colloq* money at hand, especially bank notes, for immediate use; cash. Often shortened to **readies**.

ready reckoner ▻ *noun* a book of tables used as an aid in making calculations, especially working out interest, or the value of so many items at so much each, etc.

reafforest /riːə'fɒrəst, -rɪst/ ▻ *verb* (***reafforested, reafforesting***) to replant trees in a cleared area of land that was formerly forested. • **reafforestation** /riːəfɒrə'steɪʃən/ *noun*.

Reaganomics /reɪgə'nɒmɪks/ ▻ *singular noun* the economic practice of cutting taxes to stimulate production, as advocated by Ronald Reagan, US President 1981–9.

reagent /riː'eɪdʒənt/ ▻ *noun, chem* **1** any chemical compound that participates in a chemical reaction. **2** a common laboratory chemical with characteristic reactions, used in chemical analysis and experiments, eg hydrochloric acid, sodium hydroxide. • **reagency** *noun*. ◷ 19c: from Latin *reagere* to REACT.

real[1] /rɪəl/ ▻ *adj* **1** actually or physically existing; not imaginary. **2** actual; true □ *the real reason.* **3** not imitation; genuine; authentic □ *real leather.* **4 a** great, important or serious; **b** deserving to be so called □ *a real problem.* **5** *law* consisting of or relating to immoveable property, such as land and houses. See also REAL ESTATE. **6** said of income, etc: measured in terms of its buying power rather than its nominal value □ *in real terms.* **7** *math* involving or containing only REAL NUMBERS. ▻ *adverb, N Amer, Scots* really; very □ *real nice.* • **reality** and **really** see separate entries. • **realness** *noun*. • **for real** *slang* in reality; seriously. • **get real!** *originally N Amer slang, usually exclamation* be realistic! • **the real McCoy** see under McCOY. ◷ 15c: from French *réel*, from Latin *realis*, from *res* thing.

real[2] /reɪ'ɑːl/ ▻ *noun* (***reals*** or ***reales***) *historical* a small silver Spanish or Spanish-American coin. ◷ 17c: Spanish, from Latin *regalis* royal.

real ale ▻ *noun* ale or beer which is allowed to continue to ferment and mature in the cask after brewing and so is thought of as more traditional.

real estate see under REAL PROPERTY

realgar /rɪ'algə(r), -gɑː(r)/ ▻ *noun* a bright red MONOCLINIC mineral, arsenic monosulphide. ◷ 14c: Latin, from Arabic *rahj al-ghar* arsenic, literally 'powder of the mine'.

realise see REALIZE

realism /'rɪəlɪzəm/ ▻ *noun* **1** the tendency to consider, accept or deal with things as they really are. **2** a style in art, literature, etc that represents things in a realistic or lifelike way. **3** *philos* the theory that physical objects continue to exist even when they are not perceived by the mind. • **realist** *noun*. ◷ 19c: from REAL[1].

realistic /rɪə'lɪstɪk/ ▻ *adj* **1** showing awareness or acceptance of things as they really are. **2** representing things as they actually are; lifelike. **3** relating to realism or realists. • **realistically** *adverb*. ◷ 19c.

reality /rɪ'alɪtɪ/ ▻ *noun* (***realities***) **1** the state or fact of being real. **2** the real nature of something; the truth. **3** something which is real or actual and not imaginary. • **in reality** as a fact, often as distinct from a thought or idea; actually. ◷ 15c: from French *réalité*, from Latin *realitas*, from *realis* REAL[1].

realize or **realise** /'rɪəlaɪz/ ▻ *verb* (***realized, realizing***) **1** to become aware of something; to know or understand it □ *realize the danger.* **2** to make something real; to make something come true; to accomplish □ *realize my ambitions.* **3** to make something real or appear real. **4** to cause something to seem real; to act something out □ *realize the story on film.* **5** to convert (property or goods) into money. **6** to make (a sum of money) □ *realized £45 000 on the sale of the house.* • **realizable** *adj*. • **realizably** *adverb*. • **realization** *noun*. • **realizer** *noun*. ◷ 17c: from REAL.

real life ▻ *noun* everyday life as it is lived by ordinary people, as opposed to a more glamorous, fictional life □ *It wouldn't happen in real life.*

really /'rɪəlɪ/ ▻ *adverb* **1** actually; in fact. **2** very; genuinely □ *a really lovely day.* ▻ *exclamation* expressing surprise, doubt or mild protest.

realm /rɛlm/ ▻ *noun* **1** a kingdom. **2** a domain, province or region. **3** a field of interest, study or activity. • **realmless** *adj*. ◷ 13c: from French *realme*, ultimately from Latin *regalis* royal.

the real McCoy see McCOY.

real number ▻ *noun, math* any rational or irrational number.

realpolitik /reɪ'ɑːlpɒlɪtiːk/ ▻ *noun* practical politics based on the realities and necessities of life rather than on moral or ethical ideas. ⊙ Early 20c: German, meaning 'politics of realism'.

real property ▷ *noun* immoveable property, such as houses or land. Also (*N Amer*) called **real estate**, **realty** /ˈrɪəltɪ/. See also PERSONAL PROPERTY.

real tennis ▷ *noun* an early form of tennis played on a walled indoor court. Also called **royal tennis**. Compare LAWN TENNIS.

the real thing ▷ *noun* the genuine thing, not a cheap imitation.

real time ▷ *noun* the actual time during which an event takes place, especially a period which is analyzed by a computer as it happens, the data produced during it being processed as it is generated. Chiefly *as modifier* (**real-time**) □ *real-time processing.*

realtor or **Realtor** /ˈrɪəltə(r)/ ▷ *noun*, *N Amer* an estate agent, especially one who is a member of the National Association of Realtors. ⊙ Early 20c: from REALTY.

realty see under REAL ESTATE

ream[1] /riːm/ ▷ *noun* **1** (abbreviation **rm**) *printing* a number of sheets of paper equivalent to 20 QUIREs, formerly 480 (a **short ream**), now usually 500 (a **long ream**) or 516 (a **printer's ream**). **2** (**reams**) *colloq* a large quantity, especially of paper or writing □ *wrote reams.* ⊙ 14c: from French *reame*, from Arabic *rizmah* bale.

ream[2] /riːm/ ▷ *verb* (***reamed***, ***reaming***) to enlarge the bore of something. • **reamer** *noun* a rotating instrument for enlarging, shaping or finishing a bore. ⊙ 19c.

reap /riːp/ ▷ *verb* (***reaped***, ***reaping***) **1** to cut or gather (grain, etc); to harvest. **2** to clear (a field) by cutting a crop. **3** to receive something (especially an advantage or benefit) as a consequence of one's actions. ⊙ Anglo-Saxon *ripan*.

reaper ▷ *noun* **1** someone who reaps. **2** a reaping-machine. **3** (**the reaper** or **the grim reaper**) death.

reaping-hook ▷ *noun* a sickle.

rear[1] /rɪə(r)/ ▷ *noun* **1** the back part; the area at the back. **2** said of an army, fleet, etc: the part which is farthest away from the enemy. **3** a position behind or to the back. **4** *colloq* the buttocks. ▷ *adj* situated or positioned at the back □ *rear window.* • **bring up the rear** to come last (in a procession, etc). ⊙ 17c: see also ARREARS.

rear[2] /rɪə(r)/ ▷ *verb* (***reared***, ***rearing***) **1** to feed, care for and educate (children); to bring up (children). **2 a** to breed (animals); **b** to grow (crops). **3** to build or erect something. **4** *intr* (*often* **rear up**) said of an animal, especially a horse: to rise up on the hind legs. **5** *intr* said especially of tall buildings: to reach a great height, especially in relation to surroundings. ⊙ Anglo-Saxon *ræran*.

rear admiral ▷ *noun* a naval officer. See table at RANK[1].

rearguard /ˈrɪəgɑːd/ ▷ *noun* a group of soldiers who protect the rear of an army, especially in retreats. ⊙ 15c: from French *rereguarde*.

rearguard action ▷ *noun* **1** military action undertaken by the rearguard. **2** an effort to prevent or delay defeat, eg in an argument.

rear lamp and **rear light** ▷ *noun* a light attached to the back of a vehicle.

rearm /riːˈɑːm/ ▷ *verb* (***rearmed***, ***rearming***) to arm again; to arm with new or improved weapons. • **rearmament** *noun*. ⊙ 19c.

rearmost /ˈrɪəmoʊst/ ▷ *adj* last of all; nearest the back.

rear-view mirror ▷ *noun* a mirror attached to car or motorbike which allows the driver to see vehicles, etc behind without having to turn their head.

rearward ▷ *adj* positioned in or at the rear. ▷ *adverb* (*also* **rearwards**) **1** towards the back. **2** at the back.

rear-wheel drive ▷ *noun* a system in which the driving power is transmitted to the rear wheels of a vehicle, as opposed to the front wheels. Compare FRONT-WHEEL DRIVE, FOUR-BY-FOUR.

reason /ˈriːzən/ ▷ *noun* **1** a justification or motive for an action, belief, etc. **2** an underlying explanation or cause. **3** the power of the mind to think, form opinions and judgements, reach logical conclusions, etc. **4** sanity; sound mind □ *lose your reason.* ▷ *verb* (***reasoned***, ***reasoning***) *intr* to use one's mind to form opinions and judgements, reach logical conclusions, deduce, etc. • **by reason of something** because of it; as a consequence of it. • **for reasons best known to oneself** for reasons which do not seem obvious or sensible to others. • **it stands to reason** it is obvious or logical. • **listen to reason** to be persuaded to act in a reasonable or sensible way. • **within reason** in moderation; within the limits of what is sensible or possible. ⊙ 13c: from French *reisun*, from Latin *ratio* reckoning, from *reri*, *ratus* to think.

■ **reason someone into** or **out of something** to persuade or influence them with argument.

■ **reason something out** to think it through or set it out logically.

■ **reason with someone** to try to persuade them by means of reasonable or sensible argument.

reason

• Expressions like **the reason ..., the reason why ..., one reason (why) ...**, etc, are followed by *that* or *because*. Some more prescriptively minded people prefer *that*; but *because* is at least as common □ *The reason why the victim bought a stolen car was because he thought the accused was authorised to sell it* □ *The reason they do this is of course that they would like you to keep coming back.*

reasonable ▷ *adj* **1** sensible; rational; showing reason or good judgement. **2** willing to listen to reason or argument. **3** in accordance with reason. **4** fair or just; moderate; not extreme or excessive □ *a reasonable price.* **5** satisfactory or equal to what one might expect. • **reasonableness** *noun*. • **reasonably** *adverb*.

reasoned ▷ *adj* well thought out or argued.

reasoning ▷ *noun* **1** the forming of judgements or opinions using reason or careful argument. **2** the act or process of deducing logically from evidence. **3** the opinions or judgements formed, or deductions made, in this way.

reassure /rɪəˈʃʊə(r), rɪəˈʃɔː(r)/ ▷ *verb* (***reassured***, ***reassuring***) **1** to relieve someone of anxiety or worry. **2** to restore confidence to someone. **3** to confirm someone's opinion to them □ *reassured him he was correct.* **4** to assure again. **5** to reinsure. • **reassurance** *noun*. • **reassurer** *noun*. • **reassuring** *adj*. • **reassuringly** *adverb*. ⊙ 16c.

Réau. ▷ *abbreviation* Réaumur's thermometric scale.

Réaumur /ˈreɪoʊmjʊə(r)/ ▷ *adj* said of a thermometer or thermometer scale: marked with the freezing-point of water as 0° and the boiling-point as 80°. ⊙ 18c: named after R A F de Réaumur (1683–1757), the French physicist who introduced the scale.

re-bar /ˈriːbɑː(r)/ ▷ *noun* a steel bar in reinforced concrete. ⊙ 1960s: from *reinforcing* + *bar*.

rebarbative /rɪˈbɑːbətɪv/ ▷ *adj*, *literary* repellent; objectionable. ⊙ 19c: from French *rébarbatif*, from *barbe* beard.

rebate ▷ *noun* /ˈriːbeɪt/ **1** a refund of part of a sum of money paid. **2** a discount. ▷ *verb* /rɪˈbeɪt/ (***rebated***, ***rebating***) **1** to refund part of a sum of money paid. **2** to deduct part of an amount payable. • **rebatable** or **rebateable** *adj*. ⊙ 15c: from French *rabattre* to beat back.

rebel ▷ *verb* /rɪˈbɛl/ *intr* (***rebelled***, ***rebelling***) (*often* **rebel against something**) **1** to resist openly or fight against authority or oppressive conditions. **2** to refuse to conform to conventional rules of behaviour, dress, etc. **3** to feel aversion or dislike towards something. ▷ *noun* /'rɛbəl/ someone who rebels. Also *as adj* □ ***a rebel army.*** ◷ 13c: from French *rebelle*, from Latin *rebellis*, from *bellum* war.

rebellion /rɪ'bɛljən/ ▷ *noun* an act of rebelling; a revolt.

rebellious /rɪ'bɛljəs/ ▷ *adj* **1** rebelling or having a tendency to rebel. **2** characteristic of a rebel or a rebellion. **3** said of a difficulty, problem, etc: refractory; unmanageable. • **rebelliously** *adverb*. • **rebelliousness** *noun*.

rebind /riː'baɪnd/ ▷ *verb* to bind (especially a book) again. • **rebound** /riːbaʊnd/ *adj*. ◷ 19c.

rebirth /riː'bɜːθ/ ▷ *noun* **1** **a** a second or new birth; **b** reincarnation. **2** a revival, renaissance or renewal, especially a spiritual one. ▷ *verb* (***rebirthed, rebirthing***) to practise the techniques of REBIRTHING. ◷ 1970s as *verb*; 19c as *noun*.

rebirthing ▷ *noun* a type of psychotherapy that involves reliving the experience of being born in order to release anxieties believed to result from the original experience. • **rebirther** *noun*. ◷ 1970s.

reboot /riː'buːt/ ▷ *verb, computing* to restart (a computer), either by pressing a specified combination of keys or switching it off and on again at the power source when the computer has crashed or hung (see CRASH *verb* 6, HANG sense 13).

rebore ▷ *verb* /riː'bɔː(r)/ to renew or widen the bore of (a cylinder) in an internal combustion engine. ▷ *noun* /'riːbɔː(r)/ the process or result of this.

reborn /riː'bɔːn/ ▷ *adj* **1** **a** born again; **b** reincarnated. **2** revived or spiritually renewed. **3** converted to Christianity. See also BORN-AGAIN. ◷ 16c.

rebound¹ ▷ *verb* /rɪ'baʊnd/ *intr* **1** to bounce or spring back after an impact. **2** to recover after a setback. **3** (*also* **rebound on** or **upon someone**) said of an action: to have an unexpectedly bad effect on the person performing the action; to misfire. ▷ *noun* /'riːbaʊnd/ an instance of rebounding; a recoil. • **on the rebound** **1** *colloq* while still recovering from or reacting to an emotional shock, especially the ending of a love affair or attachment. **2** while bouncing. ◷ 14c: from French *rebondir*, from *bondir* to bound.

rebound² see under REBIND

rebuff /rɪ'bʌf/ ▷ *noun* **1** a sudden check, curb or setback. **2** an unexpected and blunt refusal or rejection, especially of help, advice, etc. **3** a slight or snub. ▷ *verb* **1** to check or curb. **2** to refuse or reject (an offer of help, advice, etc) bluntly. **3** to slight or snub someone. ◷ 16c: from French *rebuffer*, from Italian *ribuffo* a reproof, from *buffo* a gust or puff.

rebuke /rɪ'bjuːk/ ▷ *verb* (***rebuked, rebuking***) to speak severely to someone because they have done wrong; to reprimand. ▷ *noun* a stern reprimand or reproach. • **rebukable** *adj*. • **rebuker** *noun*. • **rebukingly** *adverb*. ◷ 14c: from French *rebuker*, from *bucher* to beat, strike.

rebus /'riːbəs/ ▷ *noun* (***rebuses***) **1** a sort of visual pun in which pictures, symbols or letters are used to represent words or syllables in order to form a message or phrase. **2** *heraldry* a device which shows the name of its bearer by means of such a pictorial or symbolic representation. ◷ 17c: from French *rébus*, from Latin *rebus* by things, from *res* thing.

rebut /rɪ'bʌt/ ▷ *verb* (***rebutted, rebutting***) **1** to disprove or refute (a charge or claim), especially by offering opposing evidence. **2** to drive back. • **rebuttable** *adj*. • **rebuttal** *noun*. ◷ 13c: from French *rebouter*, from *boter* to butt.

rebut

See Usage Note at **refute**.

rebutter /rɪ'bʌtə(r)/ ▷ *noun* **1** a person or an argument that rebuts. **2** *law* a defendant's reply to a plaintiff's surrejoinder.

rec ▷ *noun, colloq* **1** short form of RECREATION. **2** short form of RECREATION GROUND. ◷ 1920s.

recalcitrant /rɪ'kalsɪtrənt/ ▷ *adj* not willing to accept authority or discipline; refractory. • **recalcitrance** *noun*. ◷ 19c: from French *récalcitrant*, from Latin *recalcitrare* to kick back, from *calx* the heel.

recalesce /riːkə'lɛs/ ▷ *verb* to display a state of glowing heat again. • **recalescence** /riːkə'lɛsəns/ *noun, physics* the spontaneous renewed glowing of iron at a certain stage in cooling from white-heat. • **recalescent** *adj*. ◷ 19c: from Latin *calescere* to grow hot.

recall ▷ *verb* /rɪ'kɔːl/ **1** to call back. **2** to order to return. **3** to bring back by a summons. **4** *US* to remove someone from office by vote. **5** to remember. **6** to cancel or revoke. ▷ *noun* /'riːkɔːl/ **1** an act of recalling. **2** the ability to remember accurately and in detail □ ***total recall.*** • **recallable** *noun*. • **beyond recall** unable to be stopped or cancelled. ◷ 16c.

recant /rɪ'kant/ ▷ *verb* (***recanted, recanting***) **1** *intr* to revoke a former declaration. **2** *intr* to disclaim one's (usually religious or political) beliefs, especially publicly. **3** *tr & intr* to withdraw or retract (a statement, belief, etc). • **recantation** /riːkan'teɪʃən/ *noun* • **recanter** *noun*. ◷ 16c: from Latin *recantare* to revoke, from *cantare* to sing.

recap /'riːkap/ *colloq* ▷ *verb* (***recapped, recapping***) short form of RECAPITULATE sense 1. ▷ *noun* short form of RECAPITULATION (sense 1).

recapitulate /riːkə'pɪtʃʊleɪt/ ▷ *verb* **1** to go over the chief points of (an argument, statement, etc) again. **2** *biol* said of an embryo: to repeat (stages in the evolutionary development of its species) during embryonic development. **3** *music* to repeat (an earlier passage) in a piece of music. • **recapitulative** or **recapitulatory** *adj*. ◷ 16c.

recapitulation /riːkəpɪtʃʊ'leɪʃən/ ▷ *noun* **1** an act or instance of recapitulating or summing up. **2** *biol* **a** the repetition, in the developmental stages of an embryo, of the stages of evolutionary development of its species; **b** the debatable concept that ontogeny (individual development) recapitulates phylogeny (evolutionary history). **3** *music* the final repetition of themes, after DEVELOPMENT, in a movement written in sonata form. ◷ 14c.

recapture /riː'kaptʃə(r)/ ▷ *verb* **1** to capture again. **2** to convey, recreate or re-experience (eg images or sensations from the past) □ ***recapture the atmosphere of Victorian London.*** ▷ *noun* the act of recapturing or fact of being recaptured. ◷ 18c.

recce /'rɛkɪ/ *colloq* ▷ *noun* (*also* **recco**; *plural* ***recces*** or ***reccos***) RECONNAISSANCE. ▷ *verb* (***recced*** or ***recceed, recceing***) to RECONNOITRE. ◷ 1940s: originally military slang.

recede /rɪ'siːd/ ▷ *verb* (***receded, receding***) *intr* **1** to go or move back or backwards. **2** to become more distant. **3** to bend or slope backwards. **4** **a** said of a man's hair: to stop growing above the forehead and at the temples; **b** said of a man: to go bald gradually in this way. **5** (*usually* **recede from something**) to give up a claim; renounce a promise, etc. • **receding** *adj*. See also RE-CEDE. ◷ 15c: from Latin *recedere* to go back, from *cedere* to yield.

re-cede or **recede** ▷ *verb* to cede again, or give up something to a previous owner. ◷ 18c.

receipt /rɪ'siːt/ ▷ *noun* (abbreviation **recpt** or **rcpt**) **1** a printed or written note acknowledging that money, goods, etc have been received. **2** the act of receiving or being received □ ***We acknowledge receipt of the money.*** **3** (*usually* **receipts**) money received during a given period of time, especially by a shop or business □ ***Monthly receipts rose steadily this year*** ▷ *verb* (***receipted,***

receipting) **1** to mark (a bill) as paid. **2** *chiefly N Amer* to give a receipt for something . ◷ 14c: from French *receite*, from Latin *recipere* to receive.

receive /rɪ'siːv/ (***received, receiving***) ▷ *verb, chiefly tr* **1** to get, be given or accept (something offered, sent, etc). **2** to experience, undergo or suffer □ *receive injuries.* **3** to give attention to or consider something □ *receive a petition.* **4** to learn of or be informed of something □ *receive word of their arrival.* **5** to react to something in a specified way □ *The film was badly received.* **6** to admit or accept (an idea, principle, etc) as true. **7** to be awarded (an honour, etc) □ *receive the OBE.* **8** to support or bear the weight of something. **9** *tr & intr* to be at home to (guests or visitors). **10** to welcome or greet (guests), especially formally □ *They were received in the vestibule.* **11** to permit someone to become part of a particular body or group, or to take up a certain position □ *be received into the priesthood.* **12** *tr & intr, tennis, badminton* to be the player who returns (the opposing player's service). **13** *tr & intr, Christianity* to participate in communion. **14** *tr & intr, chiefly Brit* to buy or deal in (goods one knows are stolen). **15** to change (radio or television signals) into sounds or pictures. • **receivability** or **receivableness** *noun.* • **receivable** *adj.* • **received** *adj* generally accepted □ *received wisdom.* • **receiving** *noun, adj.* ◷ 13c: from French *receivre*, from Latin *recipere*, from + *capere* to take.

Received Pronunciation ▷ *noun* (abbreviation **RP**) the particular form of spoken British English (essentially an educated Southern English pronunciation) which is regarded by many as being the least regionally limited, the most socially acceptable and the most 'standard'. See also STANDARD ENGLISH.

Received Pronunciation

Of all the accents of English, **Received Pronunciation** or **RP** has come to be regarded as having most prestige, with its associations of respectable social standing and good education.

Although it can be found anywhere in the English-speaking community, RP is often associated with the south-east of England. This is where it developed in the late Middle Ages; it was (and perhaps still is) London that attracted most people seeking social advancement, and they adopted the accent they found there.

With the flourishing of Public Schools and the British Empire in the nineteenth century, RP rapidly became the accent of authority and power, and its pre-eminence was consolidated when it was adopted by by the BBC at the birth of radio broadcasting in the 1920s.

Still the most widely used accent today in the legal profession, in Parliament, and in other national institutions, as well as being the model for the teaching of English as a foreign language, RP is, in educated society generally, nevertheless losing some of its ground to regionally-modified speech, perhaps because of RP's traditional association with conservative values.

Although regional accents are still stigmatized in some quarters (a few BBC announcers with regionally modified accents still receive hate mail), increasing interest in and acceptance of all accents of the English-speaking community are surely to be welcomed.

Received Standard English and **Received English** ▷ *noun* the form of English generally spoken by educated British people and regarded as the standard of the language.

receiver /rɪ'siːvə(r)/ ▷ *noun* **1** someone or something that receives. **2** an officer who receives taxes. **3** (*in full* **official receiver**) a person appointed by a court to manage property under litigation, or to take control of the business of someone who has gone bankrupt or who is certified insane. **4** the part of a telephone which is held to the ear. **5** the equipment in a telephone, radio or television that changes signals into sounds and pictures, or both. **6** a RECEIVING-SET. **7** *chiefly Brit* a person who receives stolen goods. **8** *chem* a container for receiving the products of distillation or for someone holding gases. ◷ 14c.

receiver-general ▷ *noun* an officer who receives revenues.

receivership ▷ *noun* **1** (*usually* **in receivership**) the status of a business that is under the control of an official receiver. **2** the office of receiver.

receiving-house ▷ *noun* **1** a depot. **2** a house where letters, etc are left for transmission.

receiving-line ▷ *noun* a group of people standing in line formally to receive a VIP, guests, etc on arrival.

receiving-set ▷ *noun, telecomm* apparatus for receiving wireless communications.

recension /rɪ'sɛnʃən/ ▷ *noun* **1** a critical revision of a text. **2** a text revised in such a way. ◷ 17c: from Latin *censere* to value or assess.

recent /'riːsənt/ ▷ *adj* **1** happening, done, having appeared, etc not long ago. **2** fresh; new. **3** modern. **4** (**Recent**) *geol* HOLOCENE. • **recency** *noun.* • **recently** *adverb.* • **recentness** *noun.* ◷ 16c: from French *récent*, from Latin *recens* fresh.

receptacle /rɪ'sɛptəkəl/ ▷ *noun* **1** anything that receives, stores or holds something; a container. **2** *bot* **a** the top of a flower stalk, from which the different flower parts arise; **b** in flowerless plants, algae, etc: any of a number of swollen regions that contain the reproductive structures. ◷ 15c: from Latin *receptaculum* reservoir.

reception /rɪ'sɛpʃən/ ▷ *noun* **1** the act of receiving or fact of being received. **2** a response, reaction or welcome; the manner in which a person, information, an idea, etc is received □ *a hostile reception.* **3** a formal party or social function to welcome guests, especially after a wedding. **4** the quality of radio or television signals received □ *poor reception because of the weather.* **5** an area, office or desk where visitors or clients are welcomed on arrival, eg in a hotel or factory □ *ask at reception.* **6** short form of RECEPTION ROOM. ◷ 14c: from Latin *receptio*.

reception centre ▷ *noun* a place where people such as drug addicts, refugees, the victims of fire, disasters, etc and others in difficult circumstances, are received for immediate assistance.

reception class ▷ *noun* the class that receives the new intake of children at the beginning of the school year.

receptionist /rɪ'sɛpʃənɪst/ ▷ *noun* someone employed in a hotel, office, surgery, etc to deal with clients, visitors and guests, arrange appointments, etc.

reception order ▷ *noun* an order for the reception and detention of a person in a mental hospital.

reception room ▷ *noun* **1** a room, eg in a hotel, for formal receptions. **2** any public room in a house.

receptive /rɪ'sɛptɪv/ ▷ *adj* **1** capable of receiving. **2** able and quick to understand. **3** willing to accept new ideas, suggestions, etc. • **receptively** *adverb.* • **receptiveness** or **receptivity** /riːsɛp'tɪvɪtɪ/ *noun.* ◷ 16c: from French *réceptif*.

receptor /rɪ'sɛptə(r)/ ▷ *noun, biol* **1** an element of the nervous system adapted for reception of stimuli, eg a sense organ or sensory nerve-ending. **2** an area on the surface of a cell to which a specific antigen may bind. **3** a site in or on a cell to which a drug or hormone can bind, stimulating a reaction inside the cell. ◷ 15c: Latin.

recess ▷ *noun* /rɪ'sɛs, 'riːsɛs/ **1** a space, such as a niche or alcove, set in a wall. **2** part of a room formed by a receding of the wall □ *dining recess.* **3** (*often* **recesses**) a hidden, inner or secret place □ *the dark recesses of her mind.* **4** a temporary break from work, especially of a law-court or of Parliament during a vacation □ *summer recess.* **5** *N Amer* a short break between school classes. **6** *anatomy* a small indentation or cavity in an organ. ▷ *verb* /rɪˈsɛs/ (***recesses, recessed, recessing***) **1** to put something in a recess. **2** to make a recess in (a wall, etc). **3** *intr* said especially of law-courts or Parliament: to take a break or adjourn. • **recessed** *adj.* ◷ 16c: from Latin *recessus* a retreat, from *recedere* to RECEDE.

recession[1] /rɪˈsɛʃən/ ▷ *noun* **1** the act of receding or state of being set back. **2** *econ* a temporary decline in economic activity, trade and prosperity. **3** the departure of the clergy and choir after a church service. **4** part of a wall, etc that recedes. ◷ 17c.

recession[2] /rɪˈsɛʃən/ ▷ *noun* a ceding again or back; the act of restoring something to its former owner. ◷ 19c.

recessional /rɪˈsɛʃənəl/ ▷ *adj* relating to recession. ▷ *noun* a hymn sung during the departure of the clergy and choir after a church service. ◷ 19c: from RECESS.

recessive /rɪˈsɛsɪv/ ▷ *adj* **1** tending to recede. **2** *biol* **a** denoting an ALLELE (gene) appearing in an organism's visible characteristics only if its partner allele on a paired CHROMOSOME is also recessive, as opposed to DOMINANT; **b** denoting a characteristic determined by such a gene. See also DOMINANT. **3** *linguistics* said of stress: tending to move towards the beginning of the word. • **recessively** *adverb.* • **recessiveness** *noun.*

réchauffé /reɪˈʃoufeɪ/ ▷ *noun* **1** a warmed-up dish. **2** a reworking or revision of old material. ▷ *adj* **1** said of food: warmed-up; reheated. **2** reworked or revised. ◷ 19c: French, from *réchauffer* to warm up again.

recherché /rəˈʃɛəʃeɪ/ ▷ *adj* **1** rare, exotic or particularly exquisite. **2** obscure and affected. ◷ 17c: French, from *rechercher* to seek out.

rechipping /riːˈtʃɪpɪŋ/ ▷ *noun* the practice of changing the electronic identity of stolen mobile telephones in order to resell them. ◷ 1990s.

recidivism /rɪˈsɪdɪvɪzəm/ ▷ *noun* the habit of relapsing into crime. • **recidivist** *noun, adj.* ◷ 19c: from French *récidivisme*, from Latin *recidivus*, from *recidere* to fall back.

recipe /ˈrɛsɪpɪ/ ▷ *noun* (***recipes***) directions for making something, especially for preparing and cooking food, usually consisting of a list of ingredients and instructions point-by-point. *Also as adj* □ *recipe book.* • **a recipe for something** a method or means of achieving a desired end □ *a recipe for success.* ◷ 14c: Latin, originally meaning 'take' or 'take it' when written at the top of medical prescriptions, from *recipere* to take.

recipient /rɪˈsɪpɪənt/ ▷ *noun* a person or thing that receives something. ▷ *adj* receiving; receptive. • **recipience** or **recipiency** *noun.* ◷ 16c: from French *récipient*, from Latin *recipere* to receive.

reciprocal /rɪˈsɪprəkəl/ ▷ *adj* **1 a** giving and receiving, or given and received; mutual; **b** complementary. **2** *grammar* said of a pronoun: expressing a relationship between two people or things, or mutual action, eg *one another* in *John and Mary love one another.* ▷ *noun* **1** something that is reciprocal. **2** *math* the value obtained when 1 is divided by the number concerned, eg the reciprocal of 4 is $^1/_4$. • **reciprocality** /rɪsɪprəˈkalɪtɪ/ *noun.* • **reciprocally** *adverb.* ◷ 16c: from Latin *reciprocus* alternating.

reciprocate /rɪˈsɪprəkeɪt/ ▷ *verb* (***reciprocated, reciprocating***) **1 a** to give and receive mutually; to interchange; **b** to return (affection, love, etc). **2** *intr* said of part of a machine: to move backwards and forwards. • **reciprocation** *noun.* • **reciprocative** *adj.* • **reciprocator** *noun.* ◷ 17c: from Latin *reciprocare, reciprocatum.*

■ **reciprocate with something** to give it in return □ *reciprocate with an offer of money.*

reciprocating engine ▷ *noun* an engine in which the piston moves to and fro in a straight line.

reciprocity /rɛsɪˈprɒsɪtɪ/ ▷ *noun* **1** reciprocal action. **2** a mutual exchange of privileges or advantages between countries, trade organizations, businesses, etc. ◷ 18c.

recision /rɪˈsɪʒən/ ▷ *noun* the act of annulling or cancelling something; rescinding. ◷ 17c: from Latin *recidere, recisum* to cut back.

récit /reɪˈsiː/ ▷ *noun* (***récits*** /reɪˈsiː/) **1** *music* a solo part for the voice or an instrument. **2** *music* a principal part in a CONCERTED (sense 2) piece. **3** *music* a SWELL ORGAN. **4** a narrative, especially the narrative of a book as opposed to the dialogue. **5** a book consisting mainly of narrative. ◷ 20c in senses 4 and 5; 19c in other senses: French, from *reciter* to recite.

recital /rɪˈsaɪtəl/ ▷ *noun* **1** a public performance of music, usually by a soloist or a small group. **2** a detailed statement or list of something; an enumeration □ *a recital of his grievances.* **3** a narration. **4** an act of reciting or repeating something learned or prepared, especially in front of other people □ *a poetry recital.* **5** *law* the part of a deed which recites or states the circumstances and facts of a case. • **recitalist** *noun* someone who gives recitals. ◷ 16c.

recitative /rɛsɪtəˈtiːv/ ▷ *noun, music* **1** a style of singing resembling speech, used for narrative passages in opera or in oratorio. **2** a passage sung in this way. ▷ *adj* relating to or in the style of recitative. ◷ 17c: from Italian *recitativo.*

recite /rɪˈsaɪt/ ▷ *verb* (***recited, reciting***) **1** to repeat aloud (eg a poem, etc) from memory, especially before an audience. **2** to make a detailed statement; to list □ *recited his grievances.* • **recitable** *adj.* • **recitation** /rɛsɪˈteɪʃən/ *noun.* • **reciter** *noun.* ◷ 15c: from Latin.

reckless /ˈrɛklɪs/ ▷ *adj* **1** said of a person: **a** very careless; rash; **b** heedless of the consequences of their actions or behaviour. **2** said of an action or behaviour: **a** careless, especially wilfully so; rash; **b** done without consideration of the consequences. • **recklessly** *adverb.* • **recklessness** *noun.* ◷ Anglo-Saxon *recceleas.*

reckon /ˈrɛkən/ ▷ *verb* (***reckoned, reckoning***) **1** (*often* **reckon something up**) to calculate, compute or estimate it □ *reckon up the cost.* **2** to think of someone or something as belonging to a particular group; to class or place □ *reckon him among my friends.* **3** to consider or think of someone or something in a specified way; to judge □ *be reckoned a world authority.* **4** (*usually* **reckon that ...**) *colloq* to think or suppose ... □ *I reckon it's going to rain.* **5** *colloq* to esteem or admire someone or something highly. • **someone** or **something to be reckoned with** a person or thing of considerable importance or power that is not to be ignored. ◷ Anglo-Saxon *(ge)recenian* to recount or explain.

■ **reckon on someone** or **something** to rely on or expect them or it □ *We reckoned on their support.*

■ **reckon with** or **without someone** or **something** to expect, or not expect trouble or difficulties from them or it.

reckoner /ˈrɛkənə(r)/ ▷ *noun* **1** someone or something that reckons. **2** a table, device, etc used to help in making calculations, especially a READY RECKONER.

reckoning /ˈrɛkənɪŋ/ ▷ *noun* **1 a** calculation; counting; **b** estimation; conjecture □ *By my reckoning, we must be about eight miles from the town.* **2** an account or bill. **3** a settling of accounts, debts, grievances, etc. • **day of reckoning** a time when one has to account for one's actions; a time of judgement.

reclaim /rɪˈkleɪm/ ▷ *verb* **1** to seek to regain possession of something; to claim something back. **2** to make (especially marshland, also wasteland or previously developed land) available for agricultural or commercial use. **3** to recover useful materials from industrial or domestic waste. **4** *old use* to reform someone or convert them from evil, etc. ▷ *noun* the action of reclaiming something or someone, or the state of being reclaimed. ● **reclaimable** *adj.* ● **reclaimant** or **reclaimer** *noun.* ⓒ 13c: from French *réclamer*, from Latin *reclamare* to cry out or exclaim.

reclamation /rɛklə'meɪʃən/ ▷ *noun* **1** the action of reclaiming something or someone, or the state of being reclaimed. **2** the conversion of marshland, wasteland, etc to agricultural or commercial use. **3** the process of recovering useful materials from industrial or domestic waste.

reclinate /'rɛklɪneɪt/ ▷ *adj, bot* said especially of the leaf or stem of a plant: curved or bent down or backwards. ⓒ 18c: from Latin *reclinare, reclinatum* to recline.

recline /rɪ'klaɪn/ ▷ *verb* (***reclined, reclining***) **1** *intr* to lean or lie on one's back or side, especially when resting; to lie back. **2** to lean or lay something on its back, or in a resting position. **3** to incline or bend something backwards. ● **reclinable** *adj.* ● **reclining** *adj.* ⓒ 15c: from French *recliner*, from Latin *reclinare* to lean back.

recliner ▷ *noun* someone or something that reclines, especially a type of easy chair with a back which can be adjusted to slope at different angles.

recluse /rɪ'kluːs/ ▷ *noun* **1** someone who lives alone and has little contact with society. **2** a religious devotee who leads a life of seclusion. ▷ *adj* **1** said of a place: enclosed; secluded. **2** said of a person: retiring; solitary. ● **reclusion** /rɪ'kluːʒən/ *noun.* ● **reclusive** /rɪ'kluːsɪv/ *adj.* ⓒ 13c: from French *reclus*, from Latin *recludere*, from *claudere* to shut.

recognizance or **recognisance** /rɪ'kɒgnɪzəns, rɪ'kɒnɪ-/ ▷ *noun* **1** a legally binding promise made to a magistrate or court to do or not do something specified. **2** money pledged as a guarantee of such a promise being kept.

recognize or **recognise** /'rɛkəgnaɪz/ ▷ *verb* (***recognized, recognizing; recognised, recognising***) **1** to identify (a person or thing known or experienced before). **2** to admit or be aware of something ▫ *recognized his mistakes.* **3** to show approval of and gratitude for something; to reward something ▫ *recognized her courage by giving her a medal.* **4** to acknowledge the status or legality of (especially a government or state). **5** to acknowledge something. **6** to accept something as valid ▫ *recognize the authority of the court.* ● **recognizer** *noun.* ● **recognition** /rɛkəg'nɪʃən/ *noun* **1** the act or state of recognizing or being recognized. **2** acknowledgement. **3** a token or indication of recognizing. ● **recognizable** *adj.* ● **recognizably** *adverb.* ⓒ 15c: from Latin *recognoscere*, from *cognoscere* to know.

recoil ▷ *verb* /rɪ'kɔɪl/ (***recoiled, recoiling***) *intr* **1** to spring back or rebound. **2** said of a gun: to spring powerfully backwards under the force of being fired. ▷ *noun* /rɪ'kɔɪl, 'riːkɔɪl/ the act of recoiling, especially the backwards movement of a gun when fired. ● **recoiler** *noun.* ● **recoilless** *adj.* ⓒ 13c: from French *reculer* to move backwards, from Latin *culus* the rump.

■ **recoil at** or **from something** to move or jump back or away quickly or suddenly, usually in horror or fear.

recollect /rɛkə'lɛkt/ ▷ *verb* (***recollected, recollecting***) **1 a** to recall to memory; **b** to remember, especially with an effort. **2** (*usually* **recollect oneself**) to regain one's composure or resolution ▫ *She recollected herself and tried to smile.* **3** /riːkə'lɛkt/ to gather something together; to collect it again. ● **recollected** *adj.* ● **recollection** /rɛkə'lɛkʃən/ *noun.* **1** the act or power of recollecting. **2** a memory or reminiscence. **3** something remembered. ● **recollective** *adj.* ● **recollectively** *adverb.* ⓒ 16c: from Latin *recolligere, recolectum* to gather up or collect.

recombinant DNA /riː'kɒmbɪnənt —/ ▷ *noun, biol* genetic material produced by the joining of DNA components from different organisms.

recombination ▷ *noun, genetics* the process of rearranging or 'shuffling' genetic material during the formation of gametes, so that the offspring possess combinations of genetic characteristics that are different from those of either of the parents. ⓒ 20c in this sense.

recommend /rɛkə'mɛnd/ ▷ *verb* (***recommended, recommending***) **1** to suggest as being suitable to be accepted, chosen, etc; to commend ▫ *I can recommend a good restaurant.* **2** to make acceptable, desirable or pleasing ▫ *an applicant with very little to recommend him.* **3** *tr & intr* to advise, eg a particular course of action ▫ *recommended the first course of action.* ● **recommendable** *adj.* ● **recommendably** *adverb.* ● **recommendation** /rɛkəmɛn'deɪʃən/ *noun* **1** the act of recommending. **2 a** something that recommends; **b** a testimonial, especially a letter of recommendation. **3** something that is recommended. ● **recommendatory** *adj.* ● **recommender** *noun.* ⓒ 14c: from Latin *commendare* to commend.

recompense /'rɛkəmpɛns/ ▷ *verb* (***recompensed, recompensing***) **1** to repay or reward someone for service, work done, etc. **2** to compensate someone for loss, injury or hardship suffered. ▷ *noun* **1** repayment or reward. **2** compensation (usually financial) made for loss, injury, etc. ● **recompensable** *adj.* ● **recompenser** *noun.* ⓒ 15c: from French *recompenser*, from Latin *compensare* to compensate or to balance.

reconcile /'rɛkənsaɪl/ ▷ *verb* (***reconciled, reconciling***) **1 a** (*usually* **reconcile one person with another** or **one person and another**) to put them on friendly terms again, especially after a quarrel; **b** (**be reconciled**) said of two or more people: to be on friendly terms again. **2** (*usually* **reconcile one thing with another**) to bring two or more different aims, points of view, etc into agreement; to harmonize them. **3** (*usually* **be reconciled to something** or **reconcile oneself to something**) to agree to accept an unwelcome fact or situation patiently. ● **reconcilability** *noun.* ● **reconcilable** *adj.* ● **reconcilably** *adverb.* ● **reconcilement** *noun.* ● **reconciler** *noun.* ● **reconciliation** *noun.* ● **reconciliatory** /-'sɪlɪətərɪ/ *adj.* ⓒ 14c: from Latin *reconciliare*.

recondite /'rɛkəndaɪt, rɪ'kɒndaɪt/ ▷ *adj* **1** said of a subject or knowledge: difficult to understand; little known. **2** dealing with profound, abstruse or obscure knowledge. ● **reconditely** *adverb.* ● **reconditeness** *noun.* ⓒ 17c: from Latin *reconditus* hidden or put away, from *condere* hide or store.

recondition /riːkən'dɪʃən/ ▷ *verb* to repair or restore (an engine, piece of equipment, etc) to original or good working condition, eg by cleaning or replacing broken parts. ● **reconditioned** *adj* ▫ *bought a reconditioned washing machine.* ⓒ 1920s.

reconnaissance /rɪ'kɒnɪsəns/ ▷ *noun* **1** *military* a survey, eg of land or the position of troops, to obtain information about the enemy before advancing. **2** reconnoitring. **3** a preliminary survey. Often shortened to RECCE. ⓒ 19c: French.

reconnoitre or (*US*) **reconnoiter** /rɛkə'nɔɪtə(r)/ ▷ *verb* (***reconnoitred, reconnoitring; US reconnoitered, reconnoitering***) to examine or survey (land, enemy troops, etc), especially with a view to military operations etc. Often shortened to RECCE. ▷ *noun* the act of reconnoitring; a reconnaissance. ● **reconnoitrer** *noun.* ⓒ 18c: from French *reconnoître* to examine or recognize.

reconsider ▷ *verb* to consider (a decision, opinion, etc) again and possibly change or reverse it. ● **reconsideration** *noun.* ⓒ 16c.

reconstitute ▷ *verb* (***reconstituted, reconstituting***) **1** to restore (especially dried foods or concentrates; by adding water) to the original form or constitution. **2** to form or make up again; to reorganize. ● **reconstituent** /riːkən'stɪtjʊənt/ *adj, noun.* ● **reconstituted** *adj* ▫ *reconstituted eggs.* ● **reconstitution** *noun.* ⓒ Early 20c in sense 1; 19c in sense 2.

reconstruct /riːkən'strʌkt/ ▷ *verb* **1** to construct or form again; to rebuild. **2** to create a description or idea of (eg a crime or past event) from the evidence available. • **reconstructible** *adj.* • **reconstruction** *noun.* • **reconstructive** or **reconstructional** *adj.* • **reconstructor** *noun.* ⓒ 18c.

record ▷ *noun* /'rɛkɔːd/ **1** a formal written report or statement of facts, events or information. **2** (*often* **records**) information, facts, etc, collected usually over a fairly long period of time. ▫ *dental records.* **3** the state or fact of being recorded. **4** a thin plastic disc used as a recording medium for reproducing music or other sound. Also (*old use*) called **gramophone record**. **5a** especially in sports: a performance which is officially recognized as the best of a particular kind or in a particular class; **b** *as adj* ▫ *a record attempt*; **c** *as adj* unsurpassed ▫ *a record number of applications.* **6** a description of the history and achievements of a person, institution, company, etc. **7** a list of the crimes of which a person has been convicted. **8** *computing* in database systems: a subdivision of a file that can be treated as a single unit of stored information, consisting of a collection of related data or fields (see FIELD *noun* 16), each of which contains a particular item of information, eg a statistic, a piece of text, a name, address, etc. **9** anything that recalls or commemorates past events. ▷ *verb* /rɪ'kɔːd/ (**recorded**, **recording**) **1** to set something down in writing or some other permanent form, especially for use in the future. **2** *tr & intr* to register (sound, music, speech, etc) on a record or tape so that it can be listened to in the future. **3** said of a dial, instrument, person's face, etc: to show or register (a particular figure, feeling, etc). • **go on record** to make a public statement. • **off the record** said of information, statements, etc: not intended to be repeated or made public. • **on record** officially recorded; publicly known. • **set** or **put the record straight** to correct a mistake or false impression. ⓒ 13c: from French *recorder*, from Latin *recordari* to remember.

record-breaking ▷ *adj* said of a performance, and attempt, etc: beating the current RECORD (sense 5). • **record breaker** a person or performance that breaks the current record.

recorded delivery /rɪ'kɔːdɪd —/ *Brit*, ▷ *noun* **1** a Post Office service in which a record is kept of the sending and receiving of a letter, parcel, etc. **2** an item of mail sent via this service.

recorder /rɪ'kɔːdə(r)/ ▷ *noun* **1** a wooden or plastic wind instrument with a tapering mouthpiece and holes which are covered by the player's fingers in various configurations to make the notes. **2** a solicitor or barrister who sits as a part-time judge in a court. **3** someone or something that records. **4** short for TAPE-RECORDER.

recording /rɪ'kɔːdɪŋ/ ▷ *noun* **1** the process of registering sounds or images on a record, tape, video, etc. **2** sound or images which have been recorded.

record-player /'rɛkɔːd —/ ▷ *noun* an apparatus which reproduces the sounds recorded on records.

recount ▷ *verb* to narrate or tell (a story, etc) in detail. ⓒ 15c: from French *reconter*, from *conter* to tell.

re-count ▷ *verb* /riː'kaʊnt/ to count again. ▷ *noun* /'riːkaʊnt/ a second or new counting, especially of votes in an election to check the result because it is very close. ⓒ 18c.

recoup /rɪ'kuːp/ ▷ *verb* (**recouped**, **recouping**) **1** to recover or get back (something lost, eg money). **2** to compensate or reimburse someone (eg for something lost). **3** *law* to deduct or keep back (something due). • **recoupable** *adj.* • **recoupment** *noun.* ⓒ 15c: from French *recouper* to cut back.

recourse /rɪ'kɔːs/ ▷ *noun* **1 a** (*especially* **have recourse to someone** or **something**) the act of turning to someone, or resorting to a particular course of action, for help or protection, especially in an emergency or a case of extreme need; **b** a resort; a source of help or protection. **2** *law, commerce* the right to demand payment, especially by the drawer or endorser of a bill of exchange not met by the acceptor. • **without recourse** a qualified endorsement of a bill or promissory note indicating that the endorser takes no responsibility for non-payment. ⓒ 14c: from French *recours*, from Latin *recursus* a running back.

recover /rɪ'kʌvə(r)/ ▷ *verb* (**recovered**, **recovering**) **1** to get or find something again. **2** *intr* to regain one's good health, spirits or composure. **3** *intr* to regain a former and usually better condition ▫ *The economy recovered slightly last year.* **4** *intr* to get back into position (eg in a game of tennis). **5** to regain control of (one's emotions, actions, etc) ▫ *recover one's senses.* **6** *law* **a** to gain (compensation or damages) by legal action; **b** *intr* to be successful in a lawsuit. **7** to get money to make up for (expenses, loss, etc). **8** to obtain (a valuable or usable substance) from a waste product or by-product. • **recoverability** *noun.* • **recoverable** *adj.* • **recoverableness** *noun.* • **recoverer** *noun.* ⓒ 14c: from French *recoverer*, from Latin *recuperare* RECUPERATE.

re-cover or **recover** /riː'kʌvə(r)/ ▷ *verb* to cover something again.

recovery /rɪ'kʌvərɪ/ ▷ *noun* (**recoveries**) an act, instance or process of recovering, or state of having recovered, in any sense.

recpt ▷ *abbreviation* receipt.

recreant /'rɛkrɪənt/ *archaic* ▷ *noun* a cowardly or disloyal person. ▷ *adj* cowardly or disloyal. • **recreancy** ▷ *noun.* • **recreantly** *adverb.* ⓒ 14c: French.

recreate or **re-create** /riːkrɪ'eɪt/ ▷ *verb* to create something again; to reproduce. ⓒ 16c.

recreation[1] /rɛkrɪ'eɪʃən/ ▷ *noun* a pleasant, enjoyable and often refreshing activity done in one's spare time. • **recreational** *adj.* ⓒ 14c.

recreation[2] riːkrɪ'eɪʃən/ ▷ *noun* **1** the act of creating again. **2** a new creation.

recreation ground /rɛkrɪ'eɪʃən —/ ▷ *noun* an area of land on which sports, games, etc may be played. Often shortened to REC.

recriminate /rɪ'krɪmɪneɪt/ ▷ *verb* (**recriminated**, **recriminating**) *intr* to return an accusation against an accuser. • **recrimination** /rɪkrɪmɪ'neɪʃən/ *noun* the act of returning an accusation; a countercharge. • **recriminative** *adj.* • **recriminator** *noun.* • **recriminatory** *adj.* ⓒ 17c: from Latin *criminare* to accuse.

recrudesce /riːkruː'dɛs/ ▷ *verb* (**recrudesced**, **recrudescing**) said especially of a disease, troubles, etc: to become active again, especially after a dormant period; to break out again. • **recrudescenscе** *noun.* • **recrudescent** *adj.* ⓒ 19c: from Latin *recrudescere*, from *crudescere* to grow worse.

recruit /rɪ'kruːt/ ▷ *noun* **1** *military* a newly enlisted member of the army, air force, navy, etc. **2** a new member of a society, group, organization, company, etc. ▷ *verb* (**recruited**, **recruiting**) *tr & intr* **1** *military* **a** to enlist (people) as recruits; **b** to raise or reinforce (eg an army) by enlisting recruits. **2** to enrol or obtain new members, employees, etc. • **recruitable** *adj.* • **recruital** *noun.* • **recruiter** *noun.* • **recruiting** *adj.* • **recruitment** *noun.* ⓒ 17c: from French *recrute* new growth, from *recroître*, from Latin *crescere* to grow.

recrystallization or **recrystallisation** ▷ *noun* **1** *chem* the purification of a substance by repeated crystallization from fresh solvent. **2** a change in crystalline structure that is not accompanied by a chemical change.

Rect. ▷ *abbreviation* **1** Rector. **2** Rectory.

rect- or **recti-** /rɛktɪ/ ▷ *prefix, denoting* **1** right. **2** straight. ⓒ from Latin *rectus*, straight.

recta, **rectal** and **rectally** see under RECTUM

rectangle /ˈrɛktaŋgəl/ ▷ *noun* a four-sided figure with opposite sides of equal length and all its angles right angles. • **rectangled** *adj*. • **rectangular** /rɛkˈtaŋgjʊlə(r)/ *adj* **1** in the form of or like a rectangle. **2** placed at right angles. **3** right-angled. • **rectangularity** /-ˈlarɪtɪ/ *adj*. • **rectangularly** *adverb*. ⓒ 16c: from Latin *rectangulum*, from *rectus* straight + *angulus* angle.

rectangular hyperbola ▷ *noun* a HYPERBOLA with its ASYMPTOTES at right angles.

recti *plural of* RECTUS

rectifier /ˈrɛktɪfaɪə(r)/ ▷ *noun* **1** someone or something that rectifies. **2** *chem* a piece of equipment used for condensing hot vapour to liquid in distillation; a condenser. **3** *elec* an electrical device that is used to convert alternating current into direct current.

rectify /ˈrɛktɪfaɪ/ ▷ *verb* (***rectifies, rectified, rectifying***) **1 a** to put (a mistake, etc) right or correct; **b** to adjust something. **2** *chem* to purify (eg alcohol) by repeated distillation. **3** *elec* to change (alternating current) into direct current. **4** *math* to determine the length of (a curve or an arc). • **rectifiable** *adj*. • **rectification** *noun*. ⓒ 14c: from Latin *rectificare*, from *rectus* right + *facere* to make.

rectilineal and **rectilinear** ▷ *adj* **1** in or forming a straight line or straight lines; straight. **2** bounded by straight lines. • **rectilinearity** *noun*. • **rectilinearly** or **rectilineally** *adverb*. ⓒ 17c.

rectitude /ˈrɛktɪtjuːd/ ▷ *noun* **1** rightness; correctness of behaviour or judgement. **2** honesty; moral integrity. • **rectitudinous** /-ˈtjuːdɪnəs/ *adj* **1** showing moral correctness. **2** over-obviously righteous. ⓒ 15c: from Latin *rectitudo*.

recto /ˈrɛktoʊ/ ▷ *noun* (***rectos***) *printing* (abbreviation **ro**) **1** the right-hand page of an open book. **2** the front page of a sheet of paper. Compare VERSO. ⓒ 19c: from Latin *recto* on the right.

recto- /rɛktoʊ, rɛkˈto/ ▷ *combining form, denoting* the rectum.

rector /ˈrɛktə(r)/ ▷ *noun* **1** in the Church of England: a clergyman in charge of a parish who would, formerly, have been entitled to receive all the tithes of that parish. **2** in the Roman Catholic Church: a priest in charge of a congregation or a religious house, especially a Jesuit seminary. **3** *US, Scottish* in the Protestant Episcopal Church: a clergyman with charge of a congregation. **4** the headmaster of some schools and colleges, especially in Scotland. **5** *Scottish* a senior university official elected by and representing the students. • **rectorate** *noun*. • **rectorial** /rɛkˈtɔːrɪəl/ *adj*. • **rectorship** *noun*. ⓒ 14c: Latin, meaning 'ruler', from *regere* to rule.

rectory /ˈrɛktərɪ/ ▷ *noun* (***rectories***) the house or residence of a rector.

rectrix /ˈrɛktrɪks/ ▷ *noun* (***rectrices*** /ˈrɛktrɪsiːz/) a long stiff feather of a bird's tail, used to help control direction in flight. • **rectricial** /rɛkˈtrɪʃəl/ *adj*. ⓒ 17c: Latin feminine of *rector* rector.

rectum /ˈrɛktəm/ ▷ *noun* (***recta*** /-tə/ or ***rectums***) the lower part of the alimentary canal, ending at the anus. • **rectal** *adj*. • **rectally** *adverb*. ⓒ 16c: from Latin *rectum intestinum* straight intestine, from *rectus* straight.

rectus /ˈrɛktəs/ ▷ *noun* (***recti*** /-taɪ/) *anatomy* a straight muscle. ⓒ 18c: Latin, meaning 'straight'.

recumbent /rɪˈkʌmbənt/ ▷ *adj* **1** lying down; reclining. **2** said of an organ, etc: resting against the anatomical structure from which it extends. • **recumbence** or **recumbency** *noun*. • **recumbently** *adverb*. ⓒ 17c: from Latin *recumbere* to recline.

recuperate /rɪˈkuːpəreɪt/ ▷ *verb* (***recuperated, recuperating***) **1** *intr* to recover, especially from illness. **2** to recover (something lost). • **recuperable** *adj*. • **recuperation** *noun*. • **recuperative** *adj*. ⓒ 16c: from Latin *recuperare, recuperation* to recover, from *capere* to take.

recur /rɪˈkɜː(r)/ ▷ *verb* (***recurred, recurring***) *intr* **1 a** to happen or come round again; **b** to happen at intervals. **2** said of a thought, etc: to come back into one's mind. • **recurrence** /rɪˈkʌrəns/ *noun*. • **recurrent** /rɪˈkʌrənt/ *adj* **1** happening often or regularly. **2** said of a nerve, vein, etc: turning back to run in the opposite direction. • **recurrently** *adverb*. ⓒ 15c: from Latin *recurrere* to run back.

recurring decimal ▷ *noun, math* a decimal fraction in which a figure or group of figures would recur infinitely, eg 1 divided by 3 gives the recurring decimal 0.333333... Also called **repeating decimal**.

recursion /rɪˈkɜːʃən/ ▷ *noun* **1** a going back; a return. **2** *math* the repeated application of a function to its own values to produce an infinite series of values. • **recursive** *adj*.

recusant /ˈrɛkjʊzənt/ ▷ *noun* **1** *historical* said especially of Roman Catholics: someone who refused to attend Church of England services when these were obligatory (between c.1570 and c.1790). **2** someone who refuses to submit to authority. ▷ *adj* relating to or like a recusant. • **recusance** or **recusancy** *noun*. ⓒ 16c: from Latin *recusare* to refuse, from *causa* a cause.

recycle ▷ *verb* **1** to pass something through a series of changes or treatment in order to return it to its former state. **2** *now especially* to process or treat waste material (eg paper, glass, plastic, etc) so that it can be used again. **3** *loosely* to remake into something different; to re-use or find another use for something old. • **recyclable** *adj*. • **recycling** *noun*. ⓒ 1960s in sense 2; 1920s in sense 1.

red ▷ *adj* (***redder, reddest***) **1** referring to the colour of blood, or a colour similar to it. **2** said of hair, fur, etc: of a colour which varies between a golden brown and a deep reddish-brown. **3** said of the eyes: bloodshot or with red rims. **4** having a red or flushed face, especially from shame or anger, or from physical exertion. **5** said of wine: made with black grapes whose skins colour the wine a deep red. **6** *derog colloq* communist. **7** *chiefly colloq* (**Red**) relating to the former USSR; Soviet □ *the Red Army.* ⓒ 19c: originally referring to the colour of a socialist or communist party badge, and associated with the blood and fire of revolution. **8** indicating the most extreme urgency. See RED ALERT. ▷ *noun* **1** the colour of blood, or a similar shade. **2** red dye or paint. **3** red material or clothes. **4** the red traffic light, a sign that cars should stop. **5** anything red. **6** (*usually* **be in the red**) the debit side of an account; the state of being in debt, eg to a bank. Compare BLACK (*noun* 6). **7** *derog colloq* (*often* **Red**) a communist or socialist. • **reddish** and (*colloq*) **reddy** *adj* somewhat red. • **redly** *adverb*. • **redness** *noun*. • **paint the town red** *colloq* to go out to enjoy oneself in a lively, noisy and often drunken way. • **see red** *colloq* to become angry. See also REDDEN. ⓒ Anglo-Saxon *read*.

redact /rɪˈdakt/ ▷ *verb* (***redacted, redacting***) to edit; to put (a text) into the appropriate literary form. • **redaction** *noun*. • **redactional** *adj*. • **redactor** *noun*. • **redactorial** /-ˈtɔːrɪəl/ *adj*. ⓒ 15c: from Latin *redigere, redactum* to bring back.

red admiral ▷ *noun* a common butterfly of N America, Europe and Asia which has broad red bands on its wings.

red alert ▷ *noun* a state of readiness to deal with imminent crisis or emergency, eg war, natural disaster, etc. Compare YELLOW ALERT.

red alga ▷ *noun* (***red algae***) *bot* any of several ALGAE which typically have a pink or reddish colour due to the presence of the pigment phycoerythrin, which masks the green colour of chlorophyll.

redback and **redback spider** ▷ *noun* a poisonous Australian spider the female of which has a red stripe on its back.

red biddy ▻ *noun, Brit colloq* a cheap alcoholic drink made from red wine and methylated spirits. ⓒ 1930s.

red blood cell and **red corpuscle** ▻ *noun* a non-nucleated, disc-shaped blood cell, containing the pigment haemoglobin which gives the cell its red. Its function is to transport oxygen and carbon dioxide. Also called **erythrocyte**.

red-blooded ▻ *adj* **1** having red blood. **2** *colloq* full of vitality; very manly; virile ◻ ***a red-blooded male.*** • **red-bloodedness** *noun*.

redbreast ▻ *noun* any bird that has a red breast, especially a robin.

redbrick ▻ *adj* said of a British university: established in the late 19c or early 20c, eg Leeds, Manchester and Birmingham universities, as opposed to the more traditional ones such as Oxford, Cambridge, Edinburgh, etc.

red cabbage ▻ *noun* a purplish cabbage often used for pickling.

red-cap ▻ *noun* **1** a GOLDFINCH. **2** *Brit slang* a military policeman. **3** *N Amer* a railway porter.

red card ▻ *noun, football* a piece of red card or plastic shown by the referee to a player to indicate that they are being sent off. Compare YELLOW CARD. ▻ *verb* (**redcard**) said of a referee: to show (a player) a red card. See also CARD (*verb* 2).

red carpet ▻ *noun* a strip of carpet put out for an important person, especially a Royal or VIP, to walk on, eg on their arrival at a function. • **red-carpet treatment** special treatment, as for a very important person.

red cedar ▻ *noun* a name for various species of N American coniferous trees, especially the JUNIPER.

red cent ▻ *noun, chiefly US colloq* **1** a cent (formerly made of copper) considered as a very small amount. **2** a whit ◻ ***not have a red cent.***

redcoat ▻ *noun* **1** *historical* a British soldier. **2** *Can colloq* a MOUNTIE. **3** an attendant at a Butlin's holiday camp. ⓒ 1950s in sense 3; 16c in sense 1.

red corpuscle see RED BLOOD CELL

Red Crescent ▻ *noun* an organization equivalent to the Red Cross in Muslim countries that serves a similar function to the Red Cross.

Red Cross ▻ *noun* the copyrighted symbol of the international humanitarian organization **the Red Cross**, established to assist those wounded or captured in war and which now carries out extensive humanitarian relief and aid work worldwide.

redcurrant ▻ *noun* a small edible red berry which grows on a widely cultivated European shrub.

red deer ▻ *noun* a species of deer with a reddish-brown summer coat and brownish-grey winter coat, found in dense forest and on moorland in Europe, W Asia and NW Africa, and introduced to various other parts of the world.

redden /ˈrɛdən/ ▻ *verb* (***reddened, reddening***) **1** to make red or redder. **2** *intr* to become red; to blush.

redder, **reddest**, **reddish** and **reddy** see under RED

reddle see RUDDLE

red dwarf ▻ *noun, astron* a cool faint star of about one-tenth the mass and diameter of the Sun, eg Proxima Centauri or Barnard's Star.

redeem /rɪˈdiːm/ ▻ *verb* (***redeemed, redeeming***) **1** to buy someone or something back. **2** to recover (eg something that has been pawned or mortgaged) by payment or service. **3** to fulfil (a promise). **4** to set someone free or save them by paying a ransom. **5** to free (someone or oneself) from blame or debt. **6** *Christianity* said of Christ: to free (humanity) from sin by his death on the cross. **7** to make up or compensate for (something bad or wrong). **8** to exchange (tokens, vouchers, etc) for goods. **9** to exchange (bonds, shares, etc) for cash. • **redeemable** *adj*. • **redeemer** *noun* **1** someone who redeems. **2** (**the Redeemer**) a name for Jesus Christ. • **redeeming** *adj* making up for faults or shortcomings ◻ ***one of her redeeming features.*** ⓒ 15c: from French *redimer*, from Latin *redimere*, from *emere* to buy.

redemption /rɪˈdɛmpʃən/ ▻ *noun* **1** the act of redeeming or state of being redeemed. **2** anything which redeems. **3** *Christianity* the freeing of humanity from sin by Christ's death on the Cross. • **redemptive** or **redemptory** *adj*. • **redemptively** *adverb*. • **beyond** or **past redemption** too bad to be redeemed, improved or saved. ⓒ 14c: from Latin *redemptio* buying back.

Red Ensign see under ENSIGN

redeploy /riːdɪˈplɔɪ/ ▻ *verb* to transfer (soldiers, industrial workers, supplies, etc) to another place or job. • **redeployment** *noun*. ⓒ 1940s.

redevelop /riːdɪˈvɛləp/ ▻ *verb* **1** to develop again. **2** to develop again or renew (eg an area, such as a run-down urban area, a formerly active industrial site, etc) by renovating buildings, putting up new ones, encouraging investment, etc. • **redeveloper** *noun*. • **redevelopment** *noun*. ⓒ 1930s in sense 2; 19c in sense 1.

red-eye ▻ *noun* **1** the RUDD. **2** *US colloq* poor quality whisky. **3** *N Amer colloq* an overnight plane journey. **4** *colloq* a common fault in amateur flash photography, by which the pupils of the subject's eyes appear red.

red flag ▻ *noun* **1** a symbol of socialism or of revolution. **2** a flag used to warn of danger, defiance, no mercy, or as a signal to stop.

red fox ▻ *noun* a fox native to Europe, temperate Asia, N Africa and N America which has a reddish-brown coat with white underparts.

red giant ▻ *noun, astron* a large cool red star, 10 to 100 times the diameter of the Sun but of similar mass, that appears very bright because of its size, eg Betelgeuse.

Red Guard ▻ *noun* a member of a strict Maoist youth movement in China, especially active in the cultural revolution of the late 1960s.

red-handed ▻ *adj* (*chiefly* **catch someone red-handed**) in the very act of committing a crime or immediately after having committed it. See also IN FLAGRANTE DELICTO.

red hat ▻ *noun* **1** a cardinal's hat. **2** a symbol of a cardinal's office.

redhead ▻ *noun* a person, especially a woman, with red hair. • **redheaded** *adj* **1** said of a person: with red hair. **2** said of an animal, etc: with a red head.

red heat ▻ *noun* the temperature at which something is red-hot.

red herring ▻ *noun* **1** a herring which has been cured and smoked to a dark reddish colour. **2** a subject, idea, clue, etc introduced into a discussion, investigation, etc to divert attention from the real issue or to mislead. ⓒ 19c in sense 2, from the fact that a red herring drawn across a track would put a dog off the scent; 15c in sense 1.

red-hot ▻ *adj* **1** said of metal, etc: heated until it glows red. **2** feeling or showing passionate or intense emotion or excitement ◻ ***red-hot anger.*** **3** *colloq* feeling or showing great enthusiasm. **4** strongly tipped to win ◻ ***a red-hot favourite.*** **5** said of news, information, etc: completely new and up to date.

red-hot poker ▻ *noun* a tall straight garden plant with long spikes of (usually red or orange) flowers.

redid *past tense of* REDO

Red Indian ▻ *noun, now usually offensive* a Native American, especially of N America. ▻ *adj* relating to a Native American.

redingote /ˈrɛdɪŋgoʊt/ ▻ *noun* a long double-breasted overcoat, originally for a man, later for a woman. ⓒ 18c: French, from English *riding coat*.

red lead ▻ *noun* a bright red poisonous oxide of lead, used in making paints.

red-letter day ▻ *noun* a memorable or special day because something particularly pleasant or important happens on it. ◷ 18c: from the former custom of marking saints' days in red on calendars.

red light ▻ *noun* **1** a red warning light, especially the red traffic light at which vehicles have to stop. **2** a refusal or rejection. Compare GREEN LIGHT. **3** a red light displayed in a window to indicate that the building is a brothel. ▻ *adj* (**red-light**) *colloq* relating to brothels □ *red-light district.*

red-lining ▻ *noun* the practice of refusing credit to those living in an area with a bad record of repayment. ◷ 1970s: from the verb *red-line* to circle or mark in red ink.

redly see under RED

red meat ▻ *noun* dark-coloured meat, eg beef or lamb. See also WHITE MEAT.

red mud ▻ *noun* a type of industrial waste resulting from alumina processing, consisting of silicone dioxide, iron oxide, etc.

red mullet see MULLET

redneck ▻ *noun, US derog* in the south-western states: a poor white farm worker. ▻ *adj* ignorant, intolerant, narrow-minded and bigoted.

redness see under RED

redo /riː'duː/ ▻ *verb* (***redoes*** /riː'dʌz/ , ***redid, redone, redoing***) **1** to do something again or differently. **2** to redecorate (a room, etc). ◷ 19c in sense 2; 16c in sense 1.

redolent /'rɛdələnt/ ▻ *adj* **1** fragrant. **2** (*usually* **redolent of** or **with something**) **a** smelling strongly of it; **b** strongly suggestive or reminiscent of it □ *a street redolent of Victorian England.* • **redolence** or **redolency** *noun.* • **redolently** *adverb.* ◷ 14c: from Latin *redolere* to give off a smell.

redouble ▻ *verb* **1** to double; to repeat. **2** to make or become greater or more intense. **3** *bridge* to double (a bid that an opponent has already doubled). ▻ *noun, bridge* the act of redoubling. • **redoublement** *noun.*

redoubt /rɪ'daʊt/ ▻ *noun* **1** a fortification, especially a temporary one defending a pass or hilltop. **2** a stronghold. ◷ 17c: from French *redoute,* from Latin *reductus* refuge.

redoubtable /rɪ'daʊtəbəl/ ▻ *adj* **1** inspiring fear or respect; formidable. **2** brave; valiant. • **redoutably** *adverb.* ◷ 14c: from French *redouter* to fear greatly.

redound /rɪ'daʊnd/ ▻ *verb* (***redounded, redounding***) *intr* **1** (*always* **redound to someone**) to have a direct, usually beneficial, but also sometimes detrimental, effect on them. **2** (*chiefly* **redound on someone**) to come back to them as a consequence. ◷ 14c: from French *redonder,* from Latin *redundare* to surge, from *undara.*

redox reaction /'riːdɒks —/ ▻ *noun, chem* a chemical reaction in which one of the reacting substances (REACTANTS) is reduced, while the other is simultaneously oxidized. ◷ 1920s: from *red*uction + *ox*idation.

red panda ▻ *noun* a nocturnal tree-dwelling mammal with thick chestnut fur and white patches on its face, which is found in mountain forests of Asia.

red pepper ▻ *noun* **1** CAYENNE PEPPER. **2** a red CAPSICUM or SWEET PEPPER, eaten as a vegetable. Compare GREEN PEPPER.

red rag ▻ *noun* **1** *slang* the tongue. **2** *colloq* (*usually* **red rag to a bull**) something which is likely to provoke someone or make them very angry. ◷ 19c in sense 2, because the colour red is thought to infuriate bulls; 17c in sense 1.

redress /rɪ'drɛs/ ▻ *verb* (***redresses, redressed, redressing***) **1** to set right or compensate for (something wrong). **2** to make even or equal again □ *redress the balance.* ▻ *noun* **1** the act of redressing or being redressed. **2** money, etc paid as compensation for loss or wrong done. ◷ 14c: from French *redrecier* to straighten.

redshank /'rɛdʃank/ ▻ *noun* **1** a wading bird of the sandpiper family which has a scarlet bill and legs, a white rump and a broad white wing bar visible in flight. **2** *colloq, derog* a Highlander or an Irishman.

redshift ▻ *noun, astron* an increase in the wavelength of light or other electromagnetic radiation emitted by certain galaxies or quasars. ◷ 1920s: so called because an increase in wavelength moves light towards the red end of the visible SPECTRUM, which is generally interpreted as a DOPPLER EFFECT resulting from the movement of the source of radiation away from the Earth, and is regarded as evidence that the Universe is expanding..

red shirt ▻ *noun* **1** *historical* a follower of Garibaldi (1807–82), Italian revolutionary patriot. **2** a revolutionary or anarchist. ◷ 19c: so called because of Garibaldi's habit of wearing red.

redskin ▻ *noun, offensive colloq* a Native American.

red spider and **red spider mite** ▻ *noun* a pest that infests the underside of the leaves of plants causing severe damage in gardens, greenhouses, orchards, etc, and weaves sheet webs between the leaves and the main stem.

Red Spot ▻ *noun, astron* a gigantic storm system, larger than the Earth, in the atmosphere of the planet Jupiter, south of the planet's equator, formed as a result of interpolar differences in the rotation speeds of the planet's gaseous surface. Also called **Giant Red Spot**.

red squirrel ▻ *noun* a squirrel with reddish-brown fur, native to Europe and Asia.

redstart /'rɛdstɑːt/ ▻ *noun* **1** a European bird with a conspicuous chestnut-coloured tail. **2** an American warbler that is superficially similar. ◷ 18c in sense 2; 16c in sense 1.

red tape ▻ *noun, colloq* unnecessary rules and regulations which result in delay; bureaucracy in general. ◷ 18c: from the red tape used to bind official documents.

reduce /rɪ'dʒuːs/ ▻ *verb* (***reduced, reducing***) **1** *tr & intr* to make or become less, smaller, etc. **2** to change someone or something into a worse or less desirable state or form □ *reduced her to tears.* **3** *military* to lower the rank, status or grade of someone □ *reduce to the ranks.* **4** to bring someone into a state of obedience; to subdue. **5** to make weaker or poorer. **6** to lower (the price of something) □ *All prices were reduced by 20 per cent.* **7** *intr* to lose weight by dieting. **8** to convert (a substance) into a simpler form. **9** to simplify something or make it more easily understood by considering only its essential elements □ *reduce the plan to four main points.* **10** *tr & intr cookery* to thicken (a sauce) by slowly boiling off the excess liquid. **11** *chem* to cause (a substance) to undergo a chemical reaction whereby it gains hydrogen or loses oxygen. **12** *math* to convert (a fraction) to a form with the numerator and denominator as low in value as possible, eg $^3/_9$ to $^1/_3$. **13** *metallurgy* to convert (ore, etc) into metal. **14** *photog* to decrease the density of (a negative or print). **15** *surgery* to put back into a normal condition or position (eg an organ, dislocation or fracture). • **reducibility** *noun.* • **reducible** *adj.* ◷ 14c: from Latin *reducere* to lead back.

reduced circumstances ▻ *plural noun* a state of poverty, especially following a time of relative wealth.

reducer /rɪ'djuːsə(r)/ ▻ *noun* **1** someone or something that reduces. **2** *photog* a chemical substance used to decrease the density of a negative or print. **3** a joint-piece for connecting pipes of different diameters.

reducing agent ▻ *noun, chem* any substance that brings about the gain of electrons, loss of oxygen or gain of hydrogen by a different atom, molecule or ion and which is simultaneously oxidized.

reductase /rɪ'dʌkteɪz/ ▻ *noun, biochem* an enzyme which brings about the reduction of organic compounds. ◷ Early 20c.

reductio ad absurdum /rɪ'dʌkʃɪoʊ ad əb'sɜːdəm/ ▻ *noun* **1** proving a premise wrong by showing that its logical consequence is absurd. **2** indirectly proving a premise by showing the logical consequence of its contradictory to be absurd. **3** the application of a principle or rule so strictly that it is carried to absurd lengths. ◷ 18c: Latin, meaning 'reduction to the absurd'.

reduction /rɪ'dʌkʃən/ ▻ *noun* **1** an act, instance or process of reducing; the state of being reduced. **2** the amount by which something is reduced. **3 a** a copy of a picture, document, etc made on a smaller scale; **b** the action or process of making such a copy. **4** *chem* a chemical reaction that involves a REDUCING AGENT. See also OXIDATION. **5** *historical* a settlement of S American Indians converted to Christianity by the Jesuits and governed by them. • **reductive** *adj.* • **reductively** *adverb.* • **reductiveness** *noun.*

reductionism ▻ *noun* the belief that complex data, phenomena, etc can be explained in terms of something simpler. • **reductionist** *noun, adj.*

redundancy /rɪ'dʌndənsɪ/ ▻ *noun* (***redundancies***) **1** the state of being redundant, or an instance of this. **2a** the condition of being no longer needed in a company, organization, etc; **b** dismissal from work as a result of this; **c** someone who is dismissed in this way. **3** superfluity; the condition of being unnecessary to the meaning of the sentence, etc.

redundant /rɪ'dʌndənt/ ▻ *adj* **1** not needed; superfluous. **2** said of an employee: no longer needed and therefore dismissed. **3** said of a word or phrase: superfluous; expressing an idea or sense already conveyed by another word or phrase, and therefore able to be removed without affecting the overall meaning of the sentence, etc. • **redundantly** *adverb.* ◷ 17c: from Latin *redundare* to surge.

reduplicate ▻ *verb* /rɪ'djuːplɪkeɪt/ (***reduplicated, reduplicating***) **1** to repeat, copy or double something. **2** *grammar* to repeat (a word or syllable), often with some minor change, to form a new word, as in *hubble-bubble, riff-raff*, etc. ▻ *adj* /rɪ'djuːplɪkɪt/ **1** repeated, copied or doubled. **2** *grammar* reduplicated; referring to a word, sound, etc that is repeated. **3** *bot* said of petals or sepals: with edges turned outwards. • **reduplication** *noun.* • **reduplicative** *adj.* ◷ 16c: from Latin *reduplicare, reduplicatum.*

red-water ▻ *noun* a cattle disease, characterized by the passing of red-coloured urine, caused by a blood infection which destroys the red blood cells, releasing the pigment HAEMOGLOBIN.

redwing ▻ *noun* a type of thrush that has reddish sides below the wings.

redwood ▻ *noun* **1** an extremely tall and long-lived SEQUOIA, native to California, and reaches heights of 120m. **2** the reddish-brown wood of this tree.

reebok /'riːbɒk/ ▻ *noun* (***reeboks*** or ***reebok***) a S African antelope. ◷ 18c: Dutch, meaning 'roebuck'.

re-echo ▻ *verb* **1** to echo (a sound) back or again. **2** to repeat (a sound) like an echo. **3** *intr* to give back echoes; to resound. ▻ *noun* a re-echoing. ◷ 16c.

reed ▻ *noun* **1a** *bot* any of a group of grasses that grow in shallow water by the margins of streams, lakes and ponds; **b** a stalk of one of these plants used to make thatched roofs, furniture and fencing. **2** a thin piece of cane or metal in certain musical instruments which vibrates and makes a sound when air passes over it. **3** a wind instrument or organ pipe with reeds. **4** a comb-like device on a loom for spacing the threads of the warp evenly and putting the weft into position. ◷ Anglo-Saxon *hreod.*

reedier and **reediest** see under REEDY

reedmace ▻ *noun, bot* a reed-like plant that grows in marshy ground and which has a long tubular flowerhead made up of small, closely-packed brownish flowers. Also called **bulrush**.

reed pipe ▻ *noun* an organ pipe whose tone is produced by the vibration of a reed. Compare FLUE PIPE.

re-educate ▻ *verb* **1** to educate again. **2** to change someone's beliefs, especially their political ones. • **re-education** *noun.*

reed warbler ▻ *noun* a warbler that frequents marshy places and builds its nest on reeds.

reedy ▻ *adj* (***reedier, reediest***) **1** full of reeds. **2** having a tone like a reed instrument, especially in being thin and piping. **3** thin and weak. • **reedily** *adverb.* • **reediness** *noun.*

reef¹ ▻ *noun* **1** in shallow coastal water: a mass of rock, coral, sand, etc that either projects above the surface at low tide, or is permanently covered by shallow water. **2** *originally Austral* a gold-bearing lode or vein of rock. ◷ 16c: from Dutch *rif*, from Norse *rif* a rib.

reef² /riːf/ *naut* ▻ *noun* a part of a sail which may be folded in or let out so as to alter the area of sail exposed to the wind. ▻ *verb* (***reefed, reefing***) **1** to reduce the area of (a sail) exposed to the wind by folding in a reef. **2** to gather something up in a similar way. • **reefing** *noun.* ◷ 14c: from Norse *rif* a rib.

reef band ▻ *noun, naut* a reinforcing strip across a sail.

reefer /'riːfə(r)/ ▻ *noun* **1** (*in full* **reeferjacket**) a thick woollen double-breasted jacket. **2** *colloq* a cigarette containing marijuana.

reef knot ▻ *noun* a knot made by passing one end of a rope over and under the other end, then back over and under it again.

reef point ▻ *noun, naut* a short rope on a reef band for securing a reefed sail.

reek ▻ *noun* **1** a strong, unpleasant and often offensive smell. **2** *Scots & N Eng dialect* smoke. ▻ *verb* (***reeked, reeking***) *intr* **1** to give off a strong, usually unpleasant smell. **2** *Scots & N Eng dialect* to give off smoke. ◷ Anglo-Saxon *reocan.*

▪ **reek of something** to suggest or hint at (something unpleasant) □ *This scheme reeks of racism.*

reel ▻ *noun* **1** a round wheel-shaped or cylindrical object of plastic, metal, etc on which thread, film, fishing-lines, etc can be wound. **2** the quantity of film, thread, etc wound on one of these. **3** a device for winding and unwinding a fishing-line. **4** a lively Scottish or Irish dance, or the music for it. ▻ *verb* (***reeled, reeling***) **1** to wind something on a reel. **2** (*usually* **reel something in** or **up**) to pull it in or up using a reel □ *reel in a fish.* **3** *intr* to stagger or sway; to move unsteadily. **4** *intr* to whirl or appear to move □ *The room began to reel and then she fainted.* **5** *intr* (*also* **reel back**) to be shaken physically or mentally □ *reeled back in horror when he saw the body.* **6** *intr* to dance a reel. ◷ Anglo-Saxon *hreol.*

▪ **reel something off** to say, repeat or write it rapidly and often unthinkingly.

re-entry ▻ *noun* (***re-entries***) *astron* the return of a spacecraft to the Earth's atmosphere.

reeve¹ ▻ *noun, historical* **1** the chief magistrate of a town or district. **2** an official who supervises a lord's manor or estate. ◷ Anglo-Saxon *refa.*

reeve² ▻ *verb* (***rove, reeved, reeving***) to pass (a rope, etc) through a hole, opening or ring. ◷ 17c: from Dutch *reven* to reef.

reeve³ ▻ *noun* a female RUFF³.

ref ▻ *noun, colloq* short form of REFEREE (*noun* 2).

refectory /rɪ'fɛktərɪ/ ▻ *noun* (***refectories***) a dining-hall, especially one in a monastery or university. ⓘ 15c: from Latin *reficere*, *refectum* to refreshen.

refectory table ▷ *noun* a long narrow dining table.

refer /rɪ'fɜː(r)/ ▷ *verb* (***referred***, ***referring***) to direct a candidate to sit an examination again; to fail them. • **referable** or **referrable** /'rɛfərəbəl, rɪ'fɜːrəbəl/ *adj* capable of being referred or assigned. • **referral** /rɪ'fɜːrəl/ *noun* the act of referring to someone else or being referred to someone else, especially the sending of a patient by a GP to a specialist for treatment. ⓘ 14c: from French *référer*, from Latin *referre* to carry back.

> ▪ **refer to something** **1** *intr* to mention or make allusion to it. **2** *intr* to look to it for information, facts, etc □ *referred to the notes at the back of the book.* **3** *intr* to be relevant or relate to it.
>
> ▪ **refer someone to someone** or **something** to direct them to them or it.
>
> ▪ **refer something to someone** **1** to hand it over to them for consideration □ *referred the query to the manager.* **2** to hand it back to the person from whom it came because it is unacceptable.
>
> ▪ **refer something to something** to assign or attribute it to it.

referee /rɛfə'riː/ ▷ *noun* **1** a person to whom reference is made to settle a question, dispute, etc. **2** an umpire or judge, eg of a game or in a dispute. Sometimes shortened to **ref**. **3** someone who is willing to testify to a person's character, talents and abilities. **4** *law* someone appointed by a court to report on some matter. ▷ *verb* (***refereed***, ***refereeing***) *tr & intr* to act as a referee in a game, dispute, etc. ⓘ 16c.

reference /'rɛfərəns, 'rɛfrəns/ ▷ *noun* **1** (*usually* **reference to something**) a mention of it; an allusion to it. **2** a direction in a book to another passage or another book where information can be found. **3** a book or passage referred to. **4** the act of referring to a book or passage for information. **5 a** a written report on a person's character, talents and abilities, especially one describing their aptitude for a particular job or position; **b** a person referred to for such a report. **6 a** the providing of facts and information; **b** a source of facts or information; **c** *as adj* □ *a reference library.* **7** the directing of a person, question, etc to some authority for information, a decision, etc. **8** relation, correspondence or connection □ *with reference to your last letter.* **9** a standard for measuring or judging □ *a point of reference.* **10** *law* the act of submitting a dispute for investigaion or decision. ▷ *verb* (***referenced***, ***referencing***) **1** to make a reference to something. **2** to provide (a book, etc) with references to other sources. • **referential** /rɛfə'rɛnʃəl/ *adj* **1** containing a reference. **2** having reference to something. **3** used for reference. • **referentially** *adverb*. • **terms of reference** **1** a guiding statement that defines the scope and limits of an investigation, etc. **2** the scope itself. ⓘ 16c.

reference book ▷ *noun* any book, such as an encyclopedia or dictionary, that is consulted occasionally for information and which is not usually read through in the way that a novel, biography, etc is.

reference library see LENDING LIBRARY

referendum /rɛfə'rɛndəm/ ▷ *noun* (***referendums*** or ***referenda*** /-də/) the practice or principle of giving the people of a country the chance to state their opinion on a particular matter by voting for or against it. ⓘ 19c: from Latin *referre* to carry back.

referent /'rɛfərənt/ ▷ *noun* **1** what is being referred to. **2** the object or idea that a word, etc refers to. ⓘ 19c.

referred pain ▷ *noun, medicine* pain felt in a part of the body other than its actual source.

refill ▷ *noun* /'riːfɪl/ a new filling for something which becomes empty through use; a container for this plus contents. ▷ *verb* /riː'fɪl/ (***refilled***, ***refilling***) to fill again. • **refillable** *adj*. ⓘ 19c as *noun*; 17c as *verb*.

refine /rɪ'faɪn/ ▷ *verb* (***refined***, ***refining***) **1** to make something pure by removing dirt, waste substances, etc. **2** *tr & intr* to become or make something more elegant, polished or subtle. • **refining** *noun*. • **refined** *adj* **1** very polite; well-mannered; elegant. **2** with all the dirt, waste substances, etc removed. **3** improved; polished. • **refinedly** *adverb*. • **refinedness** *noun*. • **refinement** *noun* **1** the act or process of refining. **2** good manners or good taste; polite speech; elegance. **3** an improvement or perfection. **4** a subtle distinction. • **refiner** *noun*.

refinery /rɪ'faɪnərɪ/ ▷ *noun* (***refineries***) a factory where raw materials such as sugar and oil are purified. ⓘ 18c.

refit ▷ *verb* /riː'fɪt/ (***refitted***, ***refitting***) **1** to repair or fit new parts to (especially a ship). **2** *intr* said especially of a ship: to undergo repair or the fitting of new parts. ▷ *noun* /'riːfɪt/ the process of refitting or being refitted. • **refitment** or **refitting** *noun*. ⓘ 17c.

refl. ▷ *abbreviation* **1** reflection. **2** reflective. **3** reflex. **4** reflexive.

reflag /riː'flag/ ▷ *verb* (***reflagged***, ***reflagging***) to change the country of registration of (a merchant ship), usually for some commercial advantage.

reflate /riː'fleɪt/ ▷ *verb* (***reflated***, ***reflating***) to bring about reflation of (an economy). Compare INFLATE, DEFLATE. ⓘ 1930s: back-formation from REFLATION.

reflation /riː'fleɪʃən/ ▷ *noun* an increase in economic activity and in the amount of money and credit available, designed to increase industrial production after a period of deflation. Compare DEFLATION, INFLATION, STAGFLATION. • **reflationary** *adj*. ⓘ 1930s: from RE- + in*flation*.

reflect /rɪ'flɛkt/ ▷ *verb* (***reflected***, ***reflecting***) **1** *tr & intr* said of a surface: to send back (light, heat, sound, etc). **2** *tr & intr* said of a mirror, etc: to give an image of someone or something. **3** *intr* said of a sound, image, etc: to be sent back. **4** to have as a cause or be a consequence of □ *Price increases reflect greater demand for the goods.* **5** to show or give an idea of something □ *a poem which reflects the author's sadness.* **6** (*usually* **reflect on** or **upon something**) to consider it carefully; to contemplate it. ⓘ 15c: from Latin *reflectere* to bend back.

> ▪ **reflect on** or **upon someone** said of an action, etc: to bring about a specified result, attitude, etc □ *His behaviour during all the trouble reflects well on him.*

reflectance and **reflecting factor** ▷ *noun, physics* the ratio of the intensity of the radiation reflected by a surface to the intensity of radiation incident (ie falling) on that surface.

reflecting telescope ▷ *noun, astron* a telescope in which light rays are collected and focused by means of a concave mirror. Compare REFRACTING TELESCOPE.

reflection or **reflexion** /rɪ'flɛkʃən/ ▷ *noun* **1** the change in direction of a particle or wave, eg the turning back of a ray of light, either when it strikes a smooth surface that it does not penetrate, such as a mirror or polished metal, or when it reaches the boundary between two media. Compare REFRACTION. **2** the act of reflecting. **3** a reflected image □ *looked at his reflection in the mirror.* **4** careful and thoughtful consideration; contemplation. **5** blame, discredit or censure.

reflective /rɪ'flɛktɪv/ ▷ *adj* **1** said of a person: thoughtful; meditative. **2** said of a surface: able to reflect images, light, sound, etc. **3** reflected; resulting from reflection □ *reflective glare of the sun on the water.* • **reflectively** *adverb*. • **reflectiveness** *noun*. • **reflectivity** *noun* /riːflɛk'tɪvɪtɪ/ **1** ability to reflect rays. **2** reflectance.

reflector /rɪ'flɛktə(r)/ ▷ *noun* **1** a polished surface that reflects light, heat, etc. **2** a piece of red, white, etc plastic or glass attached to the back, front or spokes of a bicycle which glows when light shines on it. **3** a reflecting telescope.

reflet /rə'fleɪ/ ▷ *noun* (***reflets*** /rə'fleɪ/) an iridescent or metallic lustre, especially on ceramics. ⓘ 19c: French.

reflex /'riːflɛks/ ▻ *noun* (**reflexes**) **1** (*also* **reflex action**) *physiol* a response to a sensory, physical or chemical stimulus, either a **simple reflex** which is a rapid automatic response (usually noxious) acting through local sensory cells linked to the spinal cord, or a **conditioned reflex** involving a slower brain-mediated response to prior learning or experience. **2** the ability to respond rapidly to a stimulus. **3 a** reflected light, sound, heat, etc; **b** a reflected image. **4** a sign or expression of something. **5** *linguistics* a word or element of speech which has developed from a corresponding earlier form. ▻ *adj* **1** occurring as an automatic response without being thought about. **2** bent or turned backwards. **3** directed back on the source; reflected. **4** said of a thought: introspective. **5** *math* denoting an angle that is greater than 180° but less than 360°. Compare ACUTE (*adj* 7), OBTUSE (sense 3). ▻ *verb* /ri'flɛks/ (***reflexes***, ***reflexed***, ***reflexing***) to bend something back. ⓒ 16c: from Latin *reflexus* bent back.

reflex arc ▻ *noun, physiol* a nervous circuit involved in a SIMPLE REFLEX (see REFLEX) by which a rapid response is elicited via the spinal cord, the brain being aware of the response only after its occurrence.

reflex camera ▻ *noun* a camera in which the image transmitted through the lens is directed by a mirror to the viewfinder for more accurate composition and focusing.

reflexible /rɪ'flɛksɪbəl/ ▻ *adj* capable of being bent backwards. • **reflexibility** *noun*.

reflexion see REFLECTION

reflexive /rɪ'flɛksɪv/ ▻ *adj* **1** *grammar* said of a pronoun: showing that the object of a verb is the same as the subject, eg in *He cut himself, himself* is a reflexive pronoun. **2** *grammar* said of a verb: used with a reflexive pronoun as object, eg *shave* as in *He shaved himself*. **3** *physiol* relating to a reflex. ▻ *noun* a reflexive pronoun or verb. • **reflexively** *adverb*. • **reflexiveness** *noun*. • **reflexivity** *noun*.

reflexology /riːflɛk'sɒlədʒɪ/ ▻ *noun* therapy for particular health problems and illnesses in which the soles of the feet are massaged, based on the belief that different parts of the soles relate by way of meridians (see MERIDIAN 3) to different parts of the body and different organs. • **reflexologist** *noun* a therapist who specializes in reflexology. ⓒ 1970s.

reflux /'riːflʌks/ ▻ *noun, chem* **1** the boiling of a liquid for long periods in a container attached to a condenser (known as a **reflux condenser**), so that the vapour produced condenses and continuously flows back into the container. **2** the condensed vapour involved in this process. ▻ *verb tr & intr* to boil or be boiled under reflux. ⓒ 19c: Latin, from *fluxus* flow.

reform /rɪ'fɔːm/ ▻ *verb* (***reformed***, ***reforming***) **1** to improve or remove faults from (a person, behaviour, etc). **2** to improve (a law, institution, etc) by making changes or corrections to it. **3** *intr* (*also* **reform oneself**) to give up bad habits; to improve one's behaviour, etc. **4** to stop or abolish (misconduct, an abuse, etc). ▻ *noun* **1** a correction or improvement, especially in some social or political system. **2** improvement in one's behaviour or morals. • **reformability** *noun*. • **reformable** *adj*. • **reformative** *adj*. • **reformer** *noun* **1** someone who reforms. **2** (**Reformer**) *historical* one of those who took part in the Reformation of the 16c. ⓒ 14c: from Latin *reformare* to form again.

re-form /riː'fɔːm/ ▻ *verb tr & intr* to form again or in a different way. • **re-formation** *noun*. ⓒ 14c.

reformation /rɛfə'meɪʃən/ ▻ *noun* **1** the act or process of reforming or being reformed; improvement; amendment. **2** (**the Reformation**) the great religious and political revolution that took place in Europe in the 16c and resulted in the establishment of the Protestant Churches. • **reformationist** *noun*.

reformatory /rɪ'fɔːmətərɪ/ ▻ *noun* (***reformatories***) *old use* (*also* **reform school**) a school where young people who had broken the law or who exhibit disruptive behaviour were sent to be reformed. ▻ *adj* with the function or purpose of reforming. ⓒ 19c.

reformism /rɪ'fɔːmɪzəm/ ▻ *noun, politics* any doctrine or movement that advocates social and political change in a gradual manner within a democratic framework, rather than revolutionary change. • **reformist** *noun*.

Reform Judaism ▻ *noun* a form of Judaism, originating in the 19c, in which the Jewish Law is adapted so that it is more relevant to contemporary life.

refract /rɪ'frakt/ ▻ *verb* (***refracted***, ***refracting***) said of a medium, eg water, glass: to cause the direction of (a wave of light, sound, etc) to change when it crosses the boundary between this medium and another through which it travels at a different speed, eg between air and glass. • **refractable** REFRANGIBLE. • **refracted** *adj*. • **refractive** *adj* **1** relating to or involving refraction. **2** capable of causing refraction. • **refractivity** *noun*. • **refractor** *noun* **1** anything that refracts. **2** a REFRACTING TELESCOPE. ⓒ 17c: from Latin *refringere, refractum*, from *frangere* to break.

refracting telescope and **refractor** ▻ *noun, astron* a telescope in which light rays are collected by means of a lens of long focal length and magnified by a lens of short focal length. Compare REFLECTING TELESCOPE.

refraction /rɪ'frakʃən/ ▻ *noun* **1** *physics* **a** a change in the direction of a wave, eg of light or sound, when it passes from one medium to another in which its speed is different; **b** the amount by which the direction of a wave is changed. **2** the eye's ability to refract light. • **refractional** *adj*.

refraction correction ▻ *noun, astron* the correction made in the calculation of the position of a star, planet, etc to allow for the refraction of its light by the earth's atmosphere.

refractive index ▻ *noun, physics* (symbol ***n***) the ratio of the speed of electromagnetic radiation, especially light, in air or a vacuum to its speed in another medium.

refractometer /riːfrak'tɒmɪtə(r)/ ▻ *noun* an instrument for measuring refractive indices.

refractory /rɪ'fraktərɪ/ ▻ *adj* **1** difficult to control; stubborn; unmanageable. **2** *medicine* said of a disease: resistant to treatment. **3** *physiol* said of a nerve, etc: unresponsive to stimuli. **4** said of a material: resistant to heat; able to withstand high temperatures without fusing or melting. ▻ *noun* (***refractories***) *chem* a material that has a high melting point and is therefore able to withstand high temperatures without crumbling or softening, eg silica, fireclay and metal oxides, which are used to line furnaces, etc. • **refractorily** *adverb*. • **refractoriness** *noun*. ⓒ 17c: from Latin *refractarius* stubborn.

refrain[1] /rɪ'freɪn/ ▻ *noun* **1** a phrase or group of lines repeated at the end of each stanza or verse in a poem or song. **2** the music for such a phrase or group of lines. ⓒ 14c: French, from *refraindre*, from Latin *frangere* to break.

refrain[2] /rɪ'freɪn/ ▻ *verb* (***refrained***, ***refraining***) *intr* (*usually* **refrain from something**) to keep oneself from acting in some way or doing something; to avoid it. ⓒ 14c: from French *refréner*, from Latin *refrenare* to check with a bridle, from *frenum* a bridle.

refrangible /rɪ'frandʒɪbəl/ ▻ *adj* able to be refracted. • **refrangibility** *noun*. ⓒ 17c: from Latin *frangere* to break.

refresh /rɪ'frɛʃ/ ▻ *verb* (***refreshes***, ***refreshed***, ***refreshing***) **1** to make fresh again. **2** to make something brighter or livelier again. **3** said of drink, food, rest, etc: to give renewed strength, energy and enthusiasm to someone. **4** to revive (someone, oneself, etc) with drink, food, rest, etc. **5 a** to provide a new supply of something; **b** to replenish supplies of something. **6** to make cool. **7** to make (one's memory) clearer and stronger by reading or listening to the source of information again. **8** *computing* to update (especially a screen display) with data. •

refresher *noun* **1** anything that refreshes, eg a cold drink. **2** *law* an extra fee paid to counsel during a long case or an adjournment. ● **refreshing** *adj* **1** giving new strength, energy and enthusiasm. **2** cooling. **3** particularly pleasing because different, unexpected or new □ *His attitude was refreshing.* ● **refreshingly** *adverb.* ● **refreshment** *noun* **1** the act of refreshing or state of being refreshed. **2** anything that refreshes. **3** (**refreshments**) food and drink, especially a light meal. ⓒ 14c: from French *refreschir*, from *fresche* fresh.

refresher course ▷ *noun* a course of study or training intended to increase or update a person's previous knowledge or skill.

refrigerate /rɪ'frɪdʒəreɪt/ ▷ *verb* (***refrigerated, refrigerating***) **1 a** to freeze something or make it cold; **b** *intr* to become cold. **2** to make or keep (mainly food) cold or frozen to slow down the rate at which it goes bad. ● **refrigerant** *noun* a liquid used in the cooling mechanism of a refrigerator. ▷ *adj* cooling. ● **refrigeration** *noun* the process whereby a cabinet or room and its contents are kept at a temperature significantly lower than that of the surrounding environment, especially in order to slow down the rate of decay of food or other perishable materials. ● **refrigerative** *adj.* ⓒ 16c: from Latin *refrigerare, refrigeratum*, from *frigus* cold.

refrigerator *noun* an insulated cabinet or room maintained at a low temperature in order to slow down the rate of decay of food or other perishable materials stored within it. Usually shortened to FRIDGE. ● **refrigeratory** *adj* cooling.

refuel /riː'fjʊəl/ ▷ *verb* **1** to supply (an aircraft, car, etc) with more fuel. **2** *intr* said of an aircraft, car, etc: to take on more fuel.

refuge /'rɛfjuːdʒ/ ▷ *noun* **1** shelter or protection from danger or trouble. **2** any place, person or thing offering such shelter. **3** an establishment offering emergency accommodation, protection, support, etc, eg for battered women. **4** a street island for pedestrians. ● **seek, find** or **take refuge in something** to seek or get consolation, comfort, escape, etc in something. ⓒ 14c: French, from Latin *refugium*, from *fugere* to flee.

refugee /rɛfjʊ'dʒiː/ ▷ *noun* **1** someone who seeks refuge, especially from religious or political persecution, in another country. **2** a fugitive. Also *as adj* □ *a refugee camp.* ● **refugeeism** *noun.* ⓒ 17c: from French *réfugié*, from *réfugier* to take refuge.

refugium /rɪ'fjuːdʒɪəm/ ▷ *noun* (***refugia*** /-dʒɪə/) *biol* a region that has retained earlier geographical, climatic, etc conditions, and therefore becomes a haven for older varieties of flora and fauna. ⓒ 1950s: Latin, meaning 'a refuge'.

refulgent /rɪ'fʌldʒənt/ ▷ *adj, literary* shining brightly; radiant; beaming. ● **refulgence** or **refulgency** *noun.* ● **refulgently** *adverb.* ⓒ 16c: from Latin *refulgere* to shine brightly.

refund ▷ *verb* /rɪ'fʌnd/ (***refunded, refunding***) to pay (money, etc) back to someone because the goods or service that they had purchased was faulty, not up to standard, etc; to repay. ▷ *noun* /'riːfʌnd/ **1** the paying back of money, etc. **2** money, etc that is paid back. ● **refundable** /rɪ'fʌndəbəl/ *adj* said of a deposit, etc: able to be refunded. ● **refunder** /'riːfʌndə(r)/ *noun.* ⓒ 14c: from Latin *refundere* to pour back, from *fundere* to pour.

re-fund /riː'fʌnd/ ▷ *verb* (***refunded, refunding***) *finance* **1** to replace (an old issue of bonds) by a new one. **2** to borrow so as to pay off (an old loan). ⓒ 20c.

refurbish /riː'fɜːbɪʃ/ ▷ *verb* **1** to renovate. **2** to redecorate or brighten something up. ● **refurbishment** *noun.* ⓒ 17c.

refuse[1] /rɪ'fjuːz/ ▷ *verb* (***refused, refusing***) **1** *tr & intr* to declare oneself unwilling to do what one has been asked or told to do, etc; to say 'no'. **2** to decline to accept something □ *refuse the offer of help.* **3** not to allow (access, etc) or give (permission). **4** *tr & intr* to show or express unwillingness □ *The car refused to start.* **5** *tr & intr* said of a horse: to stop at a fence and not jump over it. **6** *cards* to fail to follow suit. ● **refusable** *adj.* ● **refusal** *noun* **1** an act of refusing. **2** (*usually* **first refusal**) the opportunity to buy, accept or refuse something before it is offered, given, sold, etc to anyone else □ *I'll give you first refusal if I decide to sell it.* ⓒ 14c: from French *refuser*.

refuse[2] /'rɛfjuːs/ ▷ *noun* **1** rubbish; waste. **2** anything that is thrown away. **3** *ecol* the combustible fraction of solid domestic waste. ⓒ 15c: from French *refus* rejection.

refuse-derived fuel ▷ *noun* (abbreviation **RDF**) **1** an energy source made by separating combustible material (refuse) from solid waste, and then mixing it with coal (1:1 ratio) or burning it in a specially-designed furnace. **2** the product of small-scale fermentation of domestic and animal waste to produce gas (methane) for domestic use. Also (in both senses) called **waste-derived fuel**.

refusenik or **refusnik** /rɪ'fjuːznɪk/ ▷ *noun* **1** in the former Sovet Union: someone, especially a Jew, who was refused permission to emigrate (usually to Israel). **2** someone who refuses to comply with laws or follow orders, especially as a protest. ⓒ 1970s: from REFUSE[1] + -NIK, modelled on Russian *otkaznik*, from *otkazat* to refuse.

refute /rɪ'fjuːt/ ▷ *verb* (***refuted, refuting***) **1** to prove that (a person, statement, theory, etc) is wrong. **2** *colloq* to deny. ● **refutable** *adj.* ● **refutably** *adverb.* ● **refutation** /rɛfjʊ'teɪʃən/ *noun* **1** refuting. **2** an argument, etc that refutes. ● **refuter** *noun.* ⓒ 16c: from Latin *refutare* to drive back or rebut.

refute, rebut, repudiate, reject

- If you simply deny an argument or allegation, you **reject** or **repudiate** it □ *The Prime Minister rejected the accusation the following day.* □ *He repudiated the suggestions as unwarranted.*
- If you **refute** or **rebut** the argument or allegation, you produce a reasoned counter-argument or proof □ *He had refuted criticisms of his work with patience and gentle good manners* □ *Wilson was hard put to rebut all these complaints.*
- You will sometimes see and hear **refute** used in the simpler sense of 'deny', which can give rise to ambiguity; in some sentences you won't know whether **refute** means reasoned proof or just emphatic denial □ *The fire official refuted past claims of a lack of fire cover, insisting it was now in many ways better.*

☆ RECOMMENDATION: use **refute** or **rebut** only when argument or proof is involved; otherwise use **reject** or **repudiate**.

reg /rɛdʒ/ ▷ *noun, Brit colloq often in compounds* a vehicle's REGISTRATION NUMBER, especially the letter that gives an indication of its age □ *What reg is your car?* □ *It's an A-reg.* ⓒ Late 20c.

regain /rɪ'geɪn/ ▷ *verb* **1** to get back again or recover □ *regained consciousness.* **2** to get back to (a place, position, etc) □ *regained her place as number one.* ● **regainer** *noun.*

regal /'riːgəl/ ▷ *adj* **1** relating to, like, or suitable for a king or queen. **2** royal. ● **regality** /rɪ'galɪtɪ/ *noun.* ● **regally** /'riːgəlɪ/ *adverb.* ⓒ 14c: from Latin *regalis* royal, from *rex* king.

regale /rɪ'geɪl/ ▷ *verb* (***regaled, regaling***) **1** (*usually* **regale someone with something**) to amuse them, eg with stories, etc. **2** to entertain someone lavishly. ● **regalement** *noun.* ⓒ 17c: from French *régaler*, from *gale* pleasure.

regalia /rɪ'geɪlɪə/ ▷ *plural noun* **1** the insignia of royalty, eg the crown and sceptre. **2** any ornaments, ceremonial clothes, etc, worn as a sign of importance or authority, eg by a mayor. ◉ 16c: Latin, meaning 'things worthy of a king', from *regalis* regal.

regard /rɪ'gɑːd/ ▷ *verb* (***regarded, regarding***) **1** to consider someone or something in a specified way □ *regarded him as a friend.* **2** to esteem or respect someone or something □ *regarded him highly.* **3 a** to pay attention to or take notice of something; **b** to heed. **4** to look attentively or steadily at someone or something. **5** to have a connection with or relate to something. ▷ *noun* **1 a** esteem; **b** respect and affection. **2** thought or attention. **3** care or consideration. **4** a gaze or look. **5** connection or relation. **6** (**regards**) **a** greetings; **b** respectful good wishes □ *Send him my regards.* • **regarder** *noun.* • **regardful** *adj* **1** (*often* **regardful of something**) paying attention to or taking notice of it. **2** showing regard or consideration. • **regardfully** *adverb.* • **regarding** *prep* about; concerning. • **as regards something** concerning it. • **with regard to something 1** about it; concerning it. **2** so far as this relates to it. ◉ 14c: from French *regarder* to look at or take notice of, from *garder* to guard or keep watch.

regardless ▷ *adverb* **1** not thinking or caring about problems, dangers, etc. **2** nevertheless; in spite of everything □ *carry on regardless.* ▷ *adj* (*usually* **regardless of something**) taking no notice of it □ *regardless of the consequences.* • **regardlessly** *adverb* **1** heedlessly. **2** inconsiderately. • **regardlessness** *noun.*

> ***regardless***
>
> Note that there is no word **irregardless**: it arises from a confusion between **regardless** and **irrespective**.

regatta /rɪ'gatə/ ▷ *noun* a yacht or boat race-meeting. ◉ 17c: from Italian (Venetian) *regata*, from obsolete *rigatta* a contest.

regelate /riːdʒɪ'leɪt/ ▷ *verb* (***regelated, regelating***) *tr & intr* to freeze together again. • **regelation** *noun* **1** the action of freezing together again. **2** the process of refreezing water to ice under pressure at a temperature below the freezing point of water, eg in skating-rinks. ◉ 19c from Latin *gelare, gelatum* to freeze.

regency /'riːdʒənsɪ/ ▷ *noun* (***regencies***) **1** (**Regency**) in Britain: the period from 1811–20 when the Prince of Wales was Prince Regent. **2** in France: the period from 1715–23 when Philip of Orleans was regent. **3** government by a regent; any period when a regent rules or ruled. **4** the office of a regent. ▷ *adj* (*also* **Regency**) said of art, furniture, etc: belonging to or in the style prevailing during the English or French Regency. ◉ 15c: from Latin *regentia*, from *regere* to rule..

regenerate ▷ *verb* /rɪ'dʒɛnəreɪt/ (***regenerated, regenerating***) **1** to produce again or anew. **2** *theol* to renew someone spiritually. **3** *tr & intr* to make or become morally or spiritually improved. **4** *tr & intr* **a** to develop or give new life or energy; **b** to be brought back or bring back to life or original strength again. **5** *physiol* to grow new tissue or organ to replace (a damaged part). **6** *physiol intr* said of a damaged part of the mammalian body: to be replaced by new tissue. **7** *elec* to magnify the amplitude of an electrical output by relaying part of the power back into the input circuit. ▷ *adj* /-rət/ **1** having been regenerated, especially in having improved morally, spiritually or physically. **2** changed from a natural to a spiritual state. • **regenerable** *adj.* • **regeneracy** *noun.* • **regeneration** /riːdʒɛnə'reɪʃən/ *noun.* • **regenerative** *adj.* • **regeneratively** *adverb.* • **regenerator** *noun.* • **regeneratory** *adj.* ◉ 16c: from Latin *regenerare, regeneratum* to bring forth again.

regent /'riːdʒənt/ ▷ *noun* someone who governs a country during a monarch's childhood or illness. ▷ *adj* **1** acting as regent □ *Prince regent.* **2** ruling. • **regentship** *noun.* ◉ 14c: see REGENCY.

reggae /'rɛgeɪ/ ▷ *noun* popular music of W Indian origin which has a strong syncopated beat, usually with four beats to the bar and a characteristic strongly-accented upbeat. ◉ 1960s: W Indian.

regicide /'rɛdʒɪsaɪd/ ▷ *noun* **1** the killing of a king. **2** someone who kills a king. Compare HOMICIDE, PARRICIDE. • **regicidal** /rɛdʒɪ'saɪdəl/ *adj.* ◉ 16c: from Latin *rex* king + -CIDE.

regime or **régime** /reɪ'ʒiːm/ ▷ *noun* **1** a system of government. **2** a particular government or administration. **3** a regimen. ◉ 15c: from French *régime*, from Latin *regimen*.

regimen /'rɛdʒɪmən/ ▷ *noun* **1** *medicine* a course of treatment, especially of diet and exercise, which is recommended for good health. **2 a** a system of government; **b** rule. ◉ 14c: Latin, from *regere* to rule.

regiment ▷ *noun* /'rɛdʒɪmənt/ (abbreviation **regt**) **1** *military* a body of soldiers, the largest permanent army unit, consisting of several companies, etc and commanded by a colonel. **2** a large number of people or things formed into an organized group. ▷ *verb* /'rɛdʒɪmɛnt/ (***regimented, regimenting***) **1** to organize or control (people, etc) strictly, usually too strictly. **2** *military* to form or group (soldiers, an army, etc) into a regiment or regiments. **3** to group (people or things) in an organized way. • **regimental** /rɛdʒɪ'mɛntəl/ *adj* belonging or relating to a regiment. • **regimentally** *adverb.* • **regimentation** /rɛdʒɪmɛn'teɪʃən/ *noun.* • **regimented** /'rɛdʒɪmɛntɪd/ *adj.* **1** formed into a regiment or regiments. **2** said of a routine, working practice, etc: overly strict or controlled. ◉ 14c: from French, from Latin *regimentum* rule, from *regere* to rule.

regimentals /rɛdʒɪ'mɛntəlz/ ▷ *plural noun* a military uniform, especially that of a particular regiment.

Regina /rɪ'dʒaɪnə/ ▷ *noun* **1** queen. **2** now used mainly on coins, official documents, etc: the title of a reigning queen. Also abbreviated to **R** in signature. □ *Elizabeth R.* Compare REX. ◉ 18c: Latin.

region /'riːdʒən/ ▷ *noun* **1** an area of the world or of a country, especially one with particular geographical, social, etc characteristics. **2** (**Region**) especially (1973–96) in Scotland: an administrative area. **3** *anatomy* an area of the body in the area of or near a specified part, organ, etc □ *the abdominal region.* **4** *geog* any of the different layers into which the atmosphere and sea are divided according to height or depth. **5** an area of activity or interest. • **regional** *adj* **1** relating to a region. **2** said of pain: affecting a particular area of the body. • **regionalization** or **regionalisation** *noun* the dividing of England (in 1972) and Scotland (in 1973) into regions for local government administration. • **regionally** *adverb.* • **in the region of** approximately; nearly □ *it cost in the region of a hundred pounds.* ◉ 14c: from Latin *regio*, from *regere* to rule.

régisseur /reɪʒɪ'sɜː; *French* ʀeʒisœʀ/ ▷ *noun, ballet* in a ballet company: a director. ◉ 19c: French, from *régir* to manage.

register /'rɛdʒɪstə(r)/ ▷ *noun* **1 a** a written list or record of names, events, etc; **b** a book containing such a list. **2** a machine or device which records and lists information, eg a CASH REGISTER. **3** *music* the range of tones produced by the human voice or a musical instrument. **4** *music* **a** an organ stop or stop-knob; **b** the set of pipes controlled by an organ stop. **5** a style of speech or language suitable for and used in a particular situation. **6** a device for regulating a draught. **7** *printing* exact adjustment of position, eg of colours in a picture. **8** *computing* a device for storing small amounts of data. ▷ *verb* (***registered, registering***) **1** to enter (an event, name, etc) in an official register. **2** *intr* to enter one's name and address in a hotel register on arrival. **3** *tr & intr* to enrol formally □ *Please register for the conference by Friday.* **4** to send (a letter, parcel, etc) by registered post. **5** said of a device: to record and usually show (speed, information, etc) automatically. **6** said of a person's face, expression, etc: to show (a particular feeling). **7** *intr, colloq* to make an impression on someone, eg by being understood, remembered, etc □ *The name didn't register.* • **registered** *adj* **1 a** recorded; **b** entered (in a list, etc). **2** enrolled. • **registrable** *adj.* • **registration** /rɛdʒɪ'streɪʃən/ *noun* **1** registering. **2** something registered. **3** *music* the art or act of combining stops in organ-playing. ⓒ 14c: from Latin *regesta* things recorded, from *regerere* to enter or record.

Registered General Nurse ▻ *noun* (abbreviation **RGN**) a nurse who has passed the examination of the General Nursing Council for Scotland. See also STATE REGISTERED NURSE.

registered post ▻ *noun, Brit* **1** a service offered by the Post Office whereby the sender is paid compensation for mail if it is lost or damaged. **2** mail sent using this service.

register office ▻ *noun, Brit* an office where records of births, deaths and marriages are kept and where marriages may be performed. Also called **registry office**.

registrar /'rɛdʒɪstrɑː(r), rɛdʒɪ'strɑː(r)/ ▻ *noun* **1** someone who keeps an official register, especially of births, deaths and marriages. **2** a senior administrator in a university, responsible for student records, enrolment, etc. **3** *Brit* a middle-ranking hospital doctor who is training to become a specialist, and who works under a consultant. • **registrarship** *noun.* ⓒ 17c: related to REGISTER.

registration number ▻ *noun* the sequence of letters and numbers displayed on a vehicle's number plate, by which its ownership is registered. See also VEHICLE REGISTRATION DOCUMENT.

registry /'rɛdʒɪstrɪ/ ▻ *noun* (***registries***) **1** an office or place where registers are kept. **2** registration.

Regius professor /'riːdʒɪəs —/ ▻ *noun, Brit* someone who holds a university CHAIR (sense 3) which was founded by a king or queen, or who was appointed to the position by the Crown. ⓒ 17c: from Latin *regius* royal, from *rex* king.

reglet /'rɛglɪt/ ▻ *noun* **1** *archit* a flat narrow moulding. **2** *printing* a narrow strip of wood or metal used for spacing between lines of type. ⓒ 16c: from French *réglet*, from *règle*, from Latin *regula* a rule.

regnal /'rɛgnəl/ ▻ *adj* **1** relating to a reign or to a monarch □ *in her 43rd regnal year.* **2** said of a number: indicating how many kings or queens have shared a specific name, eg the II in *Elizabeth II*. ⓒ 17c: from Latin *regnalis*, from *regnum* kingdom.

regnant /'rɛgnənt/ ▻ *adj* **1** *often following its noun* reigning □ *queen regnant.* **2** prevalent. ⓒ 17c: from Latin *regnare* to reign.

regorge /riː'gɔːdʒ/ ▻ *verb* **1 a** to disgorge; **b** to regurgitate. **2** *intr* said especially of water: to gush back. ⓒ 17c: probably from French *regorger* to overflow.

regress ▻ *verb* /rɪ'grɛs/ (***regresses, regressed, regressing***) **1** *intr* **a** to go back; **b** to return. **2** *intr* to revert to a former state or condition, usually a less desirable or less advanced one. **3** *tr & intr, psychol* to return to an earlier, less advanced stage of development or behaviour. **4** *statistics* to calculate the degree of association between one parameter (eg industrial output) and other parameters (eg time and costs). ▻ *noun* /'riːgrɛs/ **1 a** a going back; **b** a return. **2** a reversion to a former, less desirable or less advanced state or condition. • **regression** /rɪ'grɛʃən/ *noun* **1** an act of regressing. **2** *psychol* a return to an earlier level of functioning, eg an adult's reversion to infantile or adolescent behaviour. **3** *medicine* the stage of a disease in which symptoms subside. **4** *statistics* measurement of the relationship between the value of a particular variable and the values of one or more possibly related variables. **5** *ecol* the retreat of the sea from the land, which involves the boundary between marine and non-marine deposition moving towards the centre of a marine basin, or the conversion of deep-water to shallow-water conditions. • **regressive** *adj* **1 a** going back; **b** returning. **2** reverting. **3** said of taxation: with the rate decreasing as the taxable amount increases. • **regressively** *adverb.* • **regressiveness** or **regressivity** /riːgrɛ'sɪvɪtɪ/ *noun.* ⓒ 14c: from Latin from *regredi, regressus* to return or go back.

regret /rɪ'grɛt/ ▻ *verb* (***regretted, regretting***) **1 a** to feel sorry, repentant, distressed, disappointed, etc about (something one has done or that has happened); **b** to wish that things had been otherwise. **2** to remember someone or something with a sense of loss. ▻ *noun* **1 a** a feeling of sorrow, repentance, distress, disappointment, etc; **b** a wish that things had been otherwise. **2** a sense of loss. **3** (**regrets**) a polite expression of sorrow, disappointment, etc, used especially when declining an invitation. • **regretful** *adj.* • **regretfully** *adverb.* • **regrettable** *adj* **1** that should be regretted. **2** unwelcome; unfortunate. • **regrettably** *adverb* ⓒ 14c: from French *regreter*.

regt ▻ *abbreviation* regiment.

regular /'rɛgjʊlə(r)/ ▻ *adj* **1** usual; normal; customary. **2** arranged, occurring, acting, etc in a fixed pattern of predictable or equal intervals of space or time □ *visit my parents at regular intervals.* **3** agreeing with some rule, custom, established practice, etc, and commonly accepted as correct. **4** symmetrical or even. **5** said of a geometric figure: having all the faces, sides, angles, etc the same. **6** said of bowel movements or menstrual periods: occurring with normal frequency. **7** *originally US* medium-sized □ *a regular portion of fries.* **8** *colloq* complete; absolute □ *That child is a regular little monster.* **9** *grammar* said of a noun, verb, etc: following one of the usual patterns of formation, inflection, etc. **10** *military* said of troops, the army, etc: belonging to or forming a permanent professional body. **11 a**) officially qualified or recognized; **b** professional. **12** belonging to a religious order and subject to the rule of that order. **13** *N Amer colloq* behaving in a generally acceptable or likeable way □ *a regular guy.* **14** *astron* said of a satellite: keeping to or deviating only slightly from a circular orbit around its planet. ▻ *noun* **1** *military* a soldier in a professional permanent army. **2** *colloq* a frequent customer, especially of a pub, bar, shop, etc. **3** a member of a religious order who has taken the three vows of poverty, chastity and obedience. **4** *US politics* a loyal supporter of the party leader. • **regularity** /-'larɪtɪ/ *noun.* • **regularly** *adverb.* ⓒ 14c: from French *reguler*, from Latin *regula* rule.

regular guy see under LAD

regularize or **regularise** ▻ *verb* (***regularized, regularizing***) to make something regular. • **regularization** or **regularisation** *noun.*

regulate /'rɛgjʊleɪt/ ▻ *verb* (***regulated, regulating***) **1** to control or adjust (the amount of available heat, sound, etc). **2** to control or adjust (a machine) so that it functions correctly. **3** to control or direct (a person, thing, etc) according to a rule or rules. **4** *intr* to make regulations. • **regulation** *noun* **1** the act of regulating or state of being regulated. **2** a rule or instruction. **3** *law* a form of legislation used to bring the provisions of an act of Parliament into force. **4** in the EEC: a proposal from the commission which is approved by the council and immediately becomes law in all member states. **5** *as adj* **a** conforming to or governed by rules or by stated standards □ *the regulation model*; **b** normal; usual. • **regulative** /'rɛgjʊlətɪv/ or **regulatory** *adj.* • **regulatively** *adverb.* • **regulator** *noun* **1** someone or something that regulates. **2** a controllng device, especially one that controls the speed of a clock or watch. **3** *Brit* a change in the rate of taxation introduced by the Chancellor of the Exchequer between budgets to regulate the economy. ⓒ 17c: from Latin *regulare, regulatum*, from *regula* rule.

regulo /'rɛgjʊloʊ/ ▻ *noun* (***regulos***) any of several numbers in a series which indicate the temperature setting of a gas oven □ *bake at regulo five.* ⓒ 1930s, as *Regulo*, originally a trademark for a thermostatic control system for gas ovens.

regulus /ˈrɛgjʊləs/ ▷ *noun* (*reguluses* or *reguli* /-laiː/) **1** an impure metal formed as an intermediate product in the smelting of ores. **2** *obsolete* antimony. • **reguline** /-laɪn/ *adj*. ⓘ 16c: Latin, meaning 'a petty king', from *rex* king.

regurgitate /rɪˈgɜːdʒɪteɪt/ ▷ *verb* (*regurgitated*, *regurgitating*) **1 a** to pour back; **b** to cast out again. **2** to bring back (food) into the mouth after it has been swallowed. **3** *derog* to repeat exactly (something already said or expressed). **4** *intr* to gush back up again. • **regurgitant** *adj*. • **regurgitation** *noun*. ⓘ 17c: from Latin *regurgitare*, *regurgitatum*.

rehab /ˈriːhab/ *colloq* ▷ *noun* **1** REHABILITATION. **2** a REHABILITATION CENTRE. ▷ *verb* (*rehabbed*, *rehabbing*) REHABILITATE.

rehabilitate /riːəˈbɪlɪteɪt, riːhə-/ ▷ *verb* (*rehabilitated*, *rehabilitating*) **1** to help (usually someone who has been ill or is disabled, or a former prisoner) re-adapt to normal life, eg by providing therapy, vocational training, etc. **2** said of buildings, etc: to rebuild or restore to good condition. **3 a** to restore someone to a former state or rank; **b** to restore former rights or privileges. **4** to clear someone's character or restore their good reputation. **5** to bring something back into good condition. • **rehabilitation** *noun*. • **rehabilitative** *adj*. • **rehabilitator** *noun*. 16c: from Latin *rehabilitare*, *rehabilitatum* from *habilitas* skill or ability.

rehabilitation centre ▷ *noun* a place, usually residential, where people, eg those with problems related to drug or alcohol dependency, can get help.

rehash *colloq* ▷ *verb* /riːˈhaʃ/ to rework or reuse (material which has been used before), but with no significant changes or improvements. ▷ *noun* /ˈriːhaʃ/ a reworking or reuse of existing material with little or no change, especially a speech, book, etc which restates ideas which have already been expressed. ⓘ 19c.

rehearsal /rɪˈhɜːsəl/ ▷ *noun* **1** the act of rehearsing. **2** a practice session or performance of a play, etc before it is performed in front of an audience. • **in rehearsal** in the process of being rehearsed before public performance.

rehearse /rɪˈhɜːs/ ▷ *verb* (*rehearsed*, *rehearsing*) **1** *tr & intr* to practise (a play, piece of music, etc) before performing it in front of an audience. **2** to train (a person) for performing in front of an audience. **3** to give a list of something ▫ *rehearsed his grievances*. **4** to repeat or say something over again. • **rehearser** *noun*. • **rehearsing** *noun*. ⓘ 16c: from French *hercier* to harrow.

reheat ▷ *verb* /riːˈhiːt/ **1** to heat again. **2** *aeronautics* to add fuel (to the hot exhaust gases of a turbojet) in order to obtain increased thrust. ▷ *noun* /ˈriːhiːt/ *aeronautics* **1** a device for injecting fuel into the hot exhaust gases of a turbojet in order to obtain increased thrust. **2** the use of such a device. • **reheater** *noun*. ⓘ 18c as *verb* sense 1; 1950s in other senses.

rehoboam /riːəˈboʊəm/ ▷ *noun* a large liquor measure or vessel, especially for champagne, that holds six times the amount of a standard bottle. Compare JEROBOAM. ⓘ 19c: named after Rehoboam, a son of Solomon and king of Israel (1 Kings 11-14).

rehouse /riːˈhaʊz/ ▷ *verb* (*rehoused*, *rehousing*) to provide with new and usually better accommodation or premises. • **rehousing** *noun*. ⓘ 19c.

rehydrate /riːhaɪˈdreɪt/ ▷ *verb* **1** *intr* to absorb water again after dehydration. **2** to add water to (a dehydrated substance). **3** to enable (a dehydrated person) to absorb water. • **rehydration** *noun*. ⓘ 1920s.

Reich /raɪk, ʀaɪx/ ▷ *noun* (*in full* **the Third Reich**) the name given to the German state during the Nazi regime from 1933–1945. ⓘ 1920s: German, meaning 'kingdom'; the **First Reich** spanned the period of the Holy Roman Empire (962–1806) and the **Second Reich** the Hohenzollern empire (1871–1918), although they are not referred to as such in English.

Reichian /ˈraɪkɪən, ˈraɪxɪən/ ▷ *adj* relating or pertaining to the theories or practices of Austrian-born psychiatrist Wilhelm Reich (1897–1957), especially to his concept of a universal, sexually-generated life energy termed 'orgone'. ▷ *noun* a supporter of Reich and his theories. ⓘ 1950s.

Reichian therapy or **reichian therapy** ▷ *noun* therapy that aims to release inhibited or disturbed energies through the use of massage, controlled breathing, etc. Also called BIOENERGETICS.

Reichstag /ˈraɪkstɑːg, ˈraɪxs-/ ▷ *noun* **1** the lower house of the German parliament during the Second Reich and the Weimar Republic. **2** the building in Berlin in which it met, to become the site of the BUNDESTAG when the German parliament moves back to Berlin from Bonn.

reify /ˈreɪɪfaɪ, ˈriː-/ ▷ *verb* (*reifies*, *reified*, *reifying*) to think of (something abstract) as a material thing; to materialize. • **reification** *noun* **1** the turning of something abstract into an object; materialization. **2** especially in Marxist terminology: depersonalization. • **reificatory** *adj*. • **reifier** *noun*. ⓘ 19c: from Latin *res* thing.

reign /reɪn/ ▷ *noun* **1** the period of time for which a king or queen rules. **2** the period during which someone or something rules, is in control or dominates ▫ *reign of terror*. ▷ *verb* (*reigned*, *reigning*) *intr* **1** to be a ruling king or queen. **2** to prevail, exist or dominate ▫ *silence reigns*. • **reigning** *adj* **1 a** ruling; **b** prevailing. **2** said of a winner, champion, etc: currently holding the title of champion, etc. ⓘ 13c: from French *reigne*, from Latin *regnum* kingdom.

reiki /ˈreɪkiː/ ▷ *noun*, *alternative medicine* a form of therapy in which the practitioner places their hands on or just above certain points of the patient's body, allowing energy to transfer from the practitioner to the patient. ⓘ Japanese, meaning 'universal energy'.

reimburse /riːɪmˈbɜːs/ ▷ *verb* (*reimbursed*, *reimbursing*) **1** to repay (money spent) ▫ *will reimburse your costs*. **2** to pay (a person) money to compensate for or cover (expenses, losses, etc) ▫ *will reimburse you your costs*. • **reimbursable** *adj*. • **reimbursement** *noun*. • **reimburser** *noun*. ⓘ 17c: from Latin *imbursare* to put something into a purse, from *bursa* purse.

rein /reɪn/ ▷ *noun* **1** (*often* **reins**) the strap, or either of the two halves of the strap, attached to a bridle and used to guide and control a horse. **2** (*especially* **on a rein** or **the right** or **left rein**) the direction to right or left in which a rider turns their horse. **3** (*usually* **reins**) a device with straps for guiding a small child. Also called **walking reins**. **4** any means of controlling, governing or restraining. ▷ *verb* (*reined*, *reining*) **1** to provide with reins. **2** to guide or control (especially a horse) with reins. **3** (*usually* **rein someone** or **something in**) to stop or restrain them with or as if with reins. **4** (*usually* **rein in**) *intr* to stop or slow up. • **draw rein** said of a rider: to pull up; to stop. • **give rein** or **a free rein to someone** or **something** to allow them free play; to place no restraints on them. • **keep a tight rein on someone** or **something** to keep strict control of them or it. • **take** or **take up the reins** to take control. ⓘ 13c: from French *resne*, from Latin *retinere* to hold back.

■ **rein back** said of a horse: to step backwards.

■ **rein something back 1** to make (a horse) step backwards by applying pressure on the reins. **2** to take measures to stop (eg inflation, costs, etc) from continuing or increasing any further.

reincarnate ▷ *verb* (*reincarnated*, *reincarnating*) **1** to make (a person or soul) be born again after death in a different body. **2** to re-embody someone or something. ▷ *adj* reborn in a different body. • **reincarnation** *noun* **1** in some beliefs: the rebirth of the soul in a different body after death. **2** a being that has been reincarnated. **3** said of eg an idea or principle: representation or embodiment in a different form. • **reincarnationism** *noun* the doctrine of or belief in reincarnation. • **reincarnationist** *noun*. ⌚ 19c.

reindeer /ˈreɪndɪə(r)/ ▷ *noun* (***reindeer*** or ***reindeers***) a species of large deer, antlered in both sexes, that is found in arctic and subarctic regions of Europe and Asia and is closely related to the CARIBOU. ⌚ 14c: from Norse *hreindyri*.

reindeer moss ▷ *noun* a lichen that provides winter food for reindeer.

reinforce /riːɪnˈfɔːs/ ▷ *verb* **1** to strengthen or give additional support to something. **2** to stress or emphasize □ *reinforced his argument.* **3** to make (an army, force, etc) stronger by providing additional soldiers, weapons, etc. • **reinforcement** *noun* **1** the act of reinforcing. **2** anything which reinforces. **3** (*usually* **reinforcements**) soldiers, weapons, etc added to an army, force, etc to make it stronger. ⌚ 17c: from French *renforcer*.

reinforced concrete ▷ *noun, engineering* concrete in which steel bars or wires have been embedded in order to increase its tensile strength.

reinstate /riːɪnˈsteɪt/ ▷ *verb* **1** to instate someone again. **2** to restore someone or something to, or re-establish them in, a position, status or rank which they formerly held but resigned or were dismissed from for some misdemeanour. • **reinstatement** *noun*. ⌚ 16c.

reistafel see RIJSTAFEL

reiterate /riːˈɪtəreɪt/ ▷ *verb* **1** to repeat. **2** to repeat several times. • **reiteration** *noun*. • **reiterative** *adj*. ⌚ 16c: see ITERATE.

reject ▷ *verb* /rɪˈdʒɛkt/ (***rejected***, ***rejecting***) **1** to refuse to accept, agree to, admit, believe, etc. **2** to throw away or discard. **3** *medicine* said of the body: to fail to accept (new tissue or an organ from another body). ▷ *noun* /ˈriːdʒɛkt/ **1** someone or something that is rejected. **2** an imperfect article not accepted for import, normal sale, etc and offered for sale at a discount. • **rejectable** or **rejectible** *adj*. • **rejection** *noun*. • **rejective** *adj*. • **rejector** or **rejecter** *noun*. ⌚ 15c: from Latin *rejicere*, *rejectum* to throw back, from *jacere* to throw.

rejig ▷ *verb* /riːˈdʒɪɡ/ **1** to re-equip or refit (a factory, etc). **2** to rearrange or reorganize something. ▷ *noun* /ˈriːdʒɪɡ/ the act of rejigging. • **rejigger** *noun*. ⌚ 1940s.

rejoice /rɪˈdʒɔɪs/ ▷ *verb* (***rejoiced***, ***rejoicing***) **1** *intr* to feel, show or express great happiness or joy. **2** to give joy to someone; to make them glad. • **rejoicer** *noun*. • **rejoicing** *noun* **1** joyfulness. **2** an expression, subject or experience of joy. **3** festivities, celebrations, merrymaking, etc. • **rejoicingly** *adverb*. ⌚ 14c: from French *réjouir*, see JOY.

■ **rejoice in something** *often ironic* to revel or take delight in it □ *rejoices in the name Ben Pink Dandelion.*

rejoin[1] /rɪˈdʒɔɪn/ ▷ *verb* **1 a** to say something in reply, especially abruptly or wittily; **b** to retort. **2** *intr, law* to reply to a charge or pleading, especially to a plaintiff's replication. ⌚ 15c: from French *rejoindre*.

rejoin[2] /riːˈdʒɔɪn/ ▷ *verb, tr & intr* to join again.

rejoinder /rɪˈdʒɔɪndə(r)/ ▷ *noun* **1** an answer or remark, especially one made abruptly or wittily in reply to something; a retort. **2** *law* a defendant's answer to a plaintiff's replication. ⌚ 15c.

rejón /reˈxoʊn/ ▷ *noun* (***rejones*** /-neɪz/) *bullfighting* a lance with a wooden handle, usually thrust at a bull from horseback. ⌚ 19c: Spanish, meaning 'lance spear', from Latin *regula* a straight piece of wood.

rejuvenate /rɪˈdʒuːvəneɪt/ ▷ *verb* (***rejuvenated***, ***rejuvenating***) **1 a** to make young again; **b** to make someone feel, look, etc young again. **2** *intr* to rejuvenesce. **3** *geol* to restore to an earlier condition of active erosion. • **rejuvenation** *noun*. • **rejuvenator** *noun*. ⌚ 19c: from Latin *juvenis* young.

rejuvenesce /rɪdʒuːvəˈnɛs/ ▷ *verb* (***rejuvenesced***, ***rejuvenescing***) *tr & intr* **1 a** to make or become young again; **b** to recover youthful character, appearance, etc. **2** *biol* to bring about or undergo change in cell-contents to a different, usually more active, character. • **rejuvenescence** *noun*. • **rejuvenescent** *adj*. ⌚ 19c: from Latin *rejuvenescere*, from Latin *juvenis* young.

relapse ▷ *verb* /rɪˈlaps/ *intr* **1 a** to sink or fall back into a former state or condition, especially one involving evil or bad habits; **b** to backslide. **2** to become ill again after apparent or partial recovery. ▷ *noun* /rɪˈlaps, ˈriːlaps/ **1 a** the act or process of relapsing; **b** backsliding. **2** a return to ill health after apparent or partial recovery. • **relapsed** *adj*. • **relapser** *noun*. • **relapsing** *adj*. ⌚ 16c: from Latin *relabi*, *relapsus* to slide back.

relapsing fever ▷ *noun* a disease characterized by recurrent attacks of fever, notably MALARIA.

relate /rɪˈleɪt/ ▷ *verb* (***related***, ***relating***) **1** to tell or narrate (a story, anecdote, etc). **2** (*usually* **relate one thing to** or **with another**) to show or form a connection or relationship between facts, events, etc □ *related his unhappiness to a deprived childhood.* **3** *intr, law* said of a decision, etc: to date back in application; to be valid from a date earlier than that on which it was made. • **relatable** *adj*. ⌚ 16c: from Latin *referre*, *relatum* to bring back.

■ **relate to someone** *colloq* **1** to get on well with them. **2** to react favourably or sympathetically to them.

■ **relate to something** **1** to be about it or concerned with it □ *I have information that relates to their activities.* **2** to be able to understand it or show some empathy towards it. **3** (*also* **relate with something**) to have or form a connection or relationship with it □ *crime relates to poverty.*

related /rɪˈleɪtɪd/ ▷ *adj* **1 a** belonging to the same family; **b** connected by birth or marriage. **2** connected. **3** *music* referring to or indicating a key that shares notes with another key or keys. • **relatedness** *noun*.

relation /rɪˈleɪʃən/ ▷ *noun* **1** an act of relating. **2** a telling or narrating. **3** the state or way of being related. **4** a connection or relationship between one person or thing and another. **5** someone who belongs to the same family through birth or marriage; a relative. **6** kinship. **7 a** reference; **b** respect. **8** (**relations**) social, political or personal contact between people, countries, etc. **9** (**relations**) *euphemistic* sexual intercourse. **10** *philos* a quality that can be predicated, not of a single thing, but only of two or more things together. • **in** or **with relation to something** with respect to it.

relational ▷ *adj* **1** relating to or expressing relation. **2** *grammar* showing or expressing syntactic relation. **3** *computing* based on interconnected data □ *relational database.* • **relationally** *adverb*.

relationship ▷ *noun* **1** the state of being related. **2** the state of being related by birth or marriage. **3** friendship, contact, communications, etc between people, countries, etc. **4** an emotional or sexual affair.

relative /ˈrɛlətɪv/ ▷ *noun* a person who is related to someone else by birth or marriage. ▷ *adj* **1** compared with something else; comparative □ *the relative speeds of a car and train.* **2** existing only in relation to something else □ *'hot' and 'cold' are relative terms.* **3** (*chiefly* **relative to something**) in proportion to it; proportional □ *salary relative to experience.* **4** relevant □ *information relative to the problem.* **5** *grammar* **a** said of a pronoun or adjective: referring to someone or something that has already been named and attaching a subordinate clause to it, eg *who* in *the children who are playing*, although some clauses of this kind can have the relative word omitted, eg *playing in the park* is a relative clause in *the children playing in the park*; **b** said of a clause or phrase: attached to a preceding word, phrase, etc by a relative word such as *which* and *who* or *whose* in *the man whose cat was*. See also ANTECEDENT. Compare ABSOLUTE (*adj* 6a). **6** *music* said of major and minor keys: having the same key signature. • **relatively** *adverb*. • **relativeness** *noun*. • **relativity** see separate entry. ⓒ 16c: from Latin *relativus* referring.

relative aperture ▷ *noun, photog* in a camera: the ratio of the diameter of the lens to the FOCAL LENGTH, usually expressed as the F-NUMBER.

relative atomic mass ▷ *noun, chem* the average mass of one atom of all the naturally occurring isotopes of a particular chemical element, expressed in atomic mass units. Also (*formerly*) called **atomic weight**.

relative density ▷ *noun, physics* (abbreviation **rel.d.**) the ratio of the density of a particular substance to that of some standard, usually water at 20°C. Also called (*formerly*) **specific gravity**.

relative humidity ▷ *noun, physics* the ratio of the amount of water vapour present in the air to the amount that would be present if the air was saturated (at the same temperature and pressure), usually expressed as a percentage.

relative molecular mass ▷ *noun* the weight of one molecule of a substance relative to that of one-twelfth of the mass of a carbon-12 atom. Also called **molecular weight**.

relativism /'rɛlətɪvɪzəm/ ▷ *noun, philos* a philosophical position that maintains that there are truths and values, but denies that they are absolute, asserting that what may be true or rational in one situation may not be so in another. • **relativist** *noun*. • **relativistic** *adj*. ⓒ 19c.

relativity /rɛlə'tɪvɪtɪ/ ▷ *noun* **1** the condition of being relative to and therefore affected by something else. **2** two theories of motion, **special theory of relativity** (1905) and **general theory of relativity** (1915), developed by Albert Einstein, which recognize the dependence of space, time and other physical measurements on the position and motion of the observer who is making the measurements. • **relativitist** *noun* a person who studies or accepts relativity.

relativize or **relativise** ▷ *verb* (***relativized, relativizing***) to make or become relative.

relative majority ▷ *noun* in an election: an excess number of votes won by a candidate over a runner-up, when no candidate receives more than 50 per cent of all the votes cast. Also called **plurality**. Compare ABSOLUTE MAJORITY.

relax /rɪ'laks/ ▷ *verb* (***relaxes, relaxed, relaxing***) **1 a** to make (part of the body, muscles, one's grip, etc) less tense, stiff or rigid; **b** *intr* said of muscles, a grip, etc: to become less tense; to become looser or slacker. **2** *tr & intr* to make or become less tense, nervous or worried. **3** *intr* said of a person: to become less stiff or formal. **4** *tr & intr* to give or take rest from work or effort. **5** *tr & intr* said of discipline, rules, etc: to make or become less strict or severe. **6** to lessen the force, strength or intensity of something □ *relaxed his vigilance*. • **relaxed** *adj*. • **relaxedly** /rɪ'laksɪdlɪ/ *adverb*. • **relaxing** *adj*. ⓒ 15c: from Latin *relaxare* to loosen.

relaxant ▷ *adj* relating to or causing relaxation. ▷ *noun, medicine* a drug that makes a person feel less tense and helps them to relax, or one that relaxes the skeletal muscles. ⓒ 18c.

relaxation /riːlak'seɪʃən/ ▷ *noun* **1** the act of relaxing or state of being relaxed. **2 a** rest after work or effort; **b** recreation. **3** a relaxing activity. **4** *law* partial remission, eg of a punishment, etc. **5** *physics* the return of a system towards equilibrium.

relaxation therapy ▷ *noun, medicine* a form of therapy that involves learning to relax certain muscle groups, with the aim of eventually being able to relax the entire body, especially in stressful situations.

relaxin /rɪ'laksɪn/ ▷ *noun* **1** a hormone produced during pregnancy which has a relaxing effect on the pelvic muscles. **2** a preparation of this hormone which is used to facilitate childbirth. ⓒ 1930s.

relaxing see under RELAX

relay[1] ▷ *noun* /'riːleɪ/ **1** a set of workers, supply of materials, etc that replace others doing, or being used for, some task, etc. **2** *old use* a fresh supply of horses, posted at various points along a route, to replace others on a journey. **3** a RELAY RACE. **4** *electronics* an electrical switching device that, in response to a change in an electric circuit, eg a small change in current, opens or closes one or more contacts in the same or another circuit. **5** *telecomm* a device fitted at regular intervals along TV broadcasting networks, underwater telecommunications cables, etc to amplify weak signals and pass them on from one communication link to the next. **6 a** something which is relayed, especially a signal or broadcast; **b** the act of relaying it. **7** *as adj* □ ***a relay station***. ▷ *verb* /rɪ'leɪ, 'riːleɪ/ (***relays, relayed, relaying***) **1** to receive and pass on (news, a message, a TV programme, etc). **2** *radio* to rebroadcast (a programme received from another station or source). **3** *intr, old use* to get a fresh relay of horses. ⓒ 15c: from French *relaier* to leave behind, ultimately from Latin *laxare* to loosen.

relay[2] or **re-lay** /riː'leɪ/ ▷ *verb* (***relays, relaid, relaying***) to lay something again. ⓒ 16c.

relay race ▷ *noun* a race between teams of runners, swimmers, etc in which each member of the team covers part of the total distance to be covered.

rel.d. ▷ *abbreviation* relative density.

release[1] /rɪ'liːs/ ▷ *verb* (***released, releasing***) **1** to free (a prisoner, etc) from captivity. **2** to relieve someone who is suffering something considered unpleasant, such as a duty, burden, etc. **3** to loosen one's grip and stop holding something. **4** to make (news, information, etc) known publicly. **5** to offer (a film, record, book, etc) for sale, performance, etc. **6** to move (a catch, brake, etc) so that it no longer prevents something from moving, operating, etc. **7** to give off or emit (heat, gas, etc). ▷ *noun* **1** the act of releasing or state of being released, from captivity, duty, oppression, etc. **2** the act of making a film, record, book, etc available for sale, performance, publication, etc. **3** something made available for sale, performance, etc, especially a new record or film. **4** an item of news which is made public, or a document containing this □ *press release*. **5** an order or document allowing a prisoner, etc to be released. **6** a handle or catch which holds and releases part of a mechanism. • **releasable** *adj*. • **releaser** *noun*. ⓒ 13c: from French *relesser*, from Latin *relaxare* to relax.

release[2] /riː'liːs/ ▷ *verb* to grant a new lease for property, etc.

relegate /'rɛləgeɪt/ ▷ *verb* (***relegated, relegating***) **1** to move someone down to a lower grade, position, status, etc. **2** *sport, especially football* to move (a team) down to a lower league or division. Compare PROMOTE (sense 1b). **3** to refer (a decision, etc) to someone or something for action to be taken. • **relegable** /'rɛləgəbəl/ *adj*. • **relegation** *noun*. ⓒ 16c: from Latin *relegare, relegatum* to send away.

relent /rɪ'lɛnt/ ▷ *verb* (***relented, relenting***) *intr* **1** to become less severe or unkind; to soften. **2** to give way and agree to something one initially would not accept. • **relenting** *noun, adj*. ⓒ 14c: from Latin *lentus* flexible.

relentless ▷ *adj* **1 a** without pity; **b** harsh. **2** never stopping; unrelenting □ *a relentless fight against crime*. • **relentlessly** *adverb*. • **relentlessness** *noun*.

relevant /'rɛləvənt/ ▷ *adj* **1** directly connected with or related to the matter in hand; pertinent. **2** *Scots law* legally sufficient. • **relevance** or **relevancy** *noun*. • **relevantly** *adverb*. ⓒ 16c: from Latin *relevare* to raise up or relieve.

reliability, **reliable**, **reliably**, **reliance** and **reliant** see under RELY

relic /ˈrɛlɪk/ ▷ *noun* **1** (*usually* **relics**) a fragment or part of an object left after the rest has decayed □ ***unearthed relics from the stone-age village.*** **2** an object valued as a memorial or souvenir of the past. **3** something left from a past time, especially a custom, belief, practice, etc □ ***a relic of medieval Britain.*** **4** *RC Church, Orthodox Church* part of the body of a saint or martyr, or of some object connected with them, preserved as an object of veneration. **5** *colloq* **a** an old person; **b** something that is old or old-fashioned. **6** (**relics**) *archaic* the remains of a dead person; a corpse. **7** *biol* a relict species. ◷ 13c: from Latin *reliquiae* remains.

relict /ˈrɛlɪkt, rɪˈlɪkt/ ▷ *noun, biol* a species or organ occurring in circumstances different from those in which it originated. ◷ 16c: from Latin *relinquere, relictum* to leave.

relict organ ▷ *noun, biol* an organ that is no longer functional and is therefore seen as evidence of Darwinian evolution.

relied *past tense, past participle of* RELY

relief /rɪˈliːf/ ▷ *noun* **1** the lessening or removal of pain, worry, oppression or distress. **2** the feeling of calmness, relaxation, happiness, etc which follows the lessening or removal of pain, worry, etc. **3** anything which lessens pain, worry, boredom or monotony. **4** help, often in the form of money, food, clothing and medicine, given to people in need. **5** someone who takes over a job or task from another person, usually after a given period of time. **6** a bus, train, etc which supplements public transport at particularly busy times. **7** the freeing of a besieged or endangered town, fortress or military post. **8** *art* a method of sculpture in which figures project from a flat surface. See HIGH RELIEF, BAS-RELIEF. **9** a clear, sharp outline caused by contrast. **10** the variations in height above sea level of an area of land. ◷ 14c: French, from Latin *relevare* to reduce the load.

relief map ▷ *noun* a map which shows the variations in the height of the land, either by shading or by being a three-dimensional model.

relies see RELY

relieve /rɪˈliːv/ ▷ *verb* (***relieved, relieving***) **1** to lessen or stop (someone's pain, worry, boredom, etc). **2** (*usually* **relieve someone of something**) **a** to take a physical or mental burden from them □ ***relieved her of many responsibilities.***; **b** *euphemistic* to take or steal it from them □ ***The thief relieved him of his wallet.*** **3** to give help or assistance to someone in need. **4** to make something less monotonous or tedious, especially by providing a contrast. **5** to free or dismiss someone from a duty or restriction. **6** to take over a job or task from someone. **7** to come to the help of (a besieged town, fortress, military post, etc). • **relievable** *adj.* • **relieved** *adj* freed from anxiety or concern, usually about a particular matter. • **reliever** *noun.* • **relieve oneself** to urinate or defecate. ◷ 14c: from French *relever*, from Latin *relevare* to reduce the load, from *levare* to lighten.

relievo /rɪˈliːvoʊ/ or **rilievo** /rɪˈljeɪvoʊ/ ▷ *noun* (***relievos*** or ***riliev*** /-viː/) *art* **1** relief. **2** a work in relief. **3** appearance of relief. See RELIEF 8. ◷ 17c: Italian.

religieuse /*French* rəliʒjʊz/ ▷ *noun* (***religieuses*** / *French* rəliʒjʊz/) **1** a nun. **2** a cake made from two balls of choux pastry, the smaller placed on top of the larger one, filled with cream and covered with icing. ◷ 1920s in sense 2; 18c in sense 1: feminine form of RELIGIEUX.

religieux /*French* rəliʒjʊ/ ▷ *noun* (*plural* ***religieux*** /*French* rəliʒjʊ/) a monk or friar. ◷ 17c: French, from Latin *religiosus* religious.

religio- /rɪlɪdʒɪoʊ/ ▷ *combining form, denoting* religion or religious matters.

religion /rɪˈlɪdʒən/ ▷ *noun* **1** a belief in, or the worship of, a god or gods. **2** a particular system of belief or worship, such as Christianity or Judaism. **3** *colloq* anything to which one is totally devoted and which rules one's life □ ***mountaineering is his religion.*** **4** the monastic way of life. ◷ 12c: French, from Latin *religio* bond or obligation, etc, from *ligare* to bind.

religiose /rɪˈlɪdʒɪoʊs/ ▷ *adj* morbidly or sentimentally religious.

religious /rɪˈlɪdʒəs/ *adj* **1** relating to religion. **2 a** following the rules or forms of worship of a particular religion very closely; **b** pious; devout. **3 a** taking great care to do something properly; **b** conscientious. **4** belonging or relating to the monastic way of life. ▷ *noun* (*plural* ***religious***) a person bound by monastic vows, eg a monk or nun. • **religiosity** /-dʒɪˈɒsətɪ/ *noun.* • **religiously** *adverb* **1** in a religious way. **2** conscientiously. • **religiousness** *noun.*

religious order see ORDER (*noun* 14)

the Religious Society of Friends ▷ *noun* a pacifist Christian movement that was founded by George Fox in the 17c and whose members are often called QUAKERS. Fox stressed the importance of simplicity in all things and rejected the sacraments, formal doctrine and ordained ministry. Many 19c Quaker industrialists were noted for their philanthropic attitudes towards their workers. Often shortened to **Society of Friends**.

relinquish /rɪˈlɪŋkwɪʃ/ ▷ *verb* (***relinquished, relinquishing***) **1** to give up or abandon (a belief, task, etc). **2** to release one's hold of something; to let go of it. **3** to renounce possession or control of (a claim, right, etc). • **relinquishment** *noun.* ◷ 15c: from French *relinquir*, from Latin *linquere* to leave.

reliquary /ˈrɛlɪkwərɪ/ ▷ *noun* (***reliquaries***) a container for holy relics. ◷ 17c: from French *reliquaire*, from *relique* relic.

reliquiae /rəˈlɪkwiiː/ ▷ *plural noun* remains, especially fossil remains of plants or animals. ◷ 19c: Latin.

relish /ˈrɛlɪʃ/ ▷ *verb* (***relishes, relished, relishing***) **1** to enjoy something greatly or with discrimination. **2** to look forward to something with great pleasure. ▷ *noun* **1** pleasure; enjoyment. **2 a** a spicy appetizing flavour; **b** a sauce or pickle which adds such a flavour to food. **3** zest, charm, liveliness or gusto. • **relishable** *adj.* ◷ 16c: from French *relais* remainder, from *relaisser* to leave behind or release.

relive /riːˈlɪv/ ▷ *verb* **1** *intr* to live again. **2** to experience something again, especially in the imagination □ ***kept reliving the fight in his dreams.*** ◷ 16c.

relocate /riːloʊˈkeɪt/ ▷ *verb* **1** to locate again. **2** *tr & intr* to move (a business, one's home, etc) from one place, town, etc to another. • **relocation** *noun.*

reluctance /rɪˈlʌktəns/ ▷ *noun* **1 a** unwillingness; **b** lack of enthusiasm. **2** *physics* (symbol **R**) a measure of the opposition to magnetic flux in a magnetic circuit, analogous to resistance in an electric circuit. ◷ 16c: from Latin *reluctari* to resist.

reluctant *adj* unwilling or not wanting to do something. • **reluctantly** *adverb.*

rely /rɪˈlaɪ/ ▷ *verb* (***relied, relying, relies***) (*always* **rely on** or **upon someone** or **something**) **1** to depend on or need them or it. **2** to trust them to do something. **3** to be certain of it happening. • **reliability** /-əˈbɪlɪtɪ/ *noun.* • **reliable** *adj.* • **reliably** *adverb.* • **reliance** *noun.* • **reliant** *adj.* ◷ 14c: from French *relier* to bind together, from Latin *religare*, from *ligare* to bind.

REM /rɛm, ɑːr iːˈ ɛm/ ▷ *abbreviation* rapid eye movement.

rem /rɛm/ ▷ *noun* a former unit of radiation dosage, replaced by the SIEVERT (1 rem = 0.01 Sv). ◷ 1940s: from röntgen equivalent *man* or *mammal*.

remain /rɪˈmeɪn/ ▷ *verb* (***remained, remaining***) *intr* **1** to be left after others, or other parts of the whole, have been used up, taken away, lost, etc. **2 a** to stay behind; **b** to stay in the same place. **3** to stay the same or unchanged; to continue to exist in the same state, condition, etc. **4** to continue to need to be done, shown, dealt with, etc ▫ *That remains to be decided.* ⓘ 14c: from Latin *remanere* to stay behind.

remainder /rɪˈmeɪndə(r)/ ▻ *noun* **1** what is left after others, or other parts, have gone, been used up, taken away, etc; the rest. **2** *math* the amount left over when one number cannot be divided exactly by another number ▫ *7 divided by 2 gives 3 with a remainder of 1.* **3** *math* the amount left when one number is subtracted from another; the difference ▫ *8 minus 5 leaves 3 as a remainder.* **4** a copy or copies of a book sold at a reduced price when sales of that book have fallen off. **5** *law* an interest in an estate which comes into effect only if another interest established at the same time comes to an end. ▻ *verb* (***remaindered, remaindering***) to sell (a copy or copies of a book) at a reduced price because its sales have fallen off. • **remaindered** *adj* said of a book, especially a specified edition: offered for sale at a reduced price.

remains /rɪˈmeɪnz/ ▻ *plural noun* **1** what is left after part has been taken away, eaten, destroyed, etc. **2** a dead body. **3** relics. **4** literary works which are unpublished at the time of their author's death.

remake ▻ *verb* /riːˈmeɪk/ to make something again or in a new way. ▻ *noun* /ˈriːmeɪk/ **1 a** something that is made again; **b** *especially* a new version of an old film. **2** the act of making something again or in a new way. ⓘ 19c as *noun*; 17c as *verb*.

remand /rɪˈmɑːnd/ ▻ *verb* (***remanded, remanding***) **1** *law* to send (a person accused of a crime) back into custody to await trial, especially to allow more evidence to be collected. **2** *rare* to send back. ▻ *noun* **1** the act or process of sending an accused person back into custody to await trial. **2** the act of remanding or state of being remanded. • **on remand** in custody or on bail awaiting trial. ⓘ 15c: from Latin *remandare* to send back word or to repeat a command, from *mandare* to send word or to command.

remand centre ▻ *noun, Brit* a place of detention for those on remand.

remand home ▻ *noun, Brit* a place to which a judge may send a child or young person who has broken the law, either on remand or as punishment.

remanent /ˈrɛmənənt/ ▻ *adj* **1** remaining. **2** *physics* said of magnetism: remaining after removal of a magnetizing field. • **remanence** or **remanency** *noun*. ⓘ 19c in sense 2; 16c in sense 1: from Latin *remanere* to stay behind.

remark[1] /rɪˈmɑːk/ ▻ *verb* **1** *tr & intr* (*usually* **remark on something**) to notice and comment on it. **2** to make a casual comment. ▻ *noun* **1** a comment, often a casual one. **2** an observation. **3** noteworthiness. **4** notice; observation. **5** a REMARQUE. • **remarkable** *adj* **1** worth mentioning or commenting on. **2** unusual; extraordinary. • **remarkableness** *noun*. • **remarkably** *adverb*. • **remarked** *adj* conspicuous. • **remarker** *noun*. ⓘ 16c: from French *remarquer*.

remark[2] or **re-mark** ▻ *verb* /riːˈmɑːk/ to mark again. ▻ *noun* /ˈriːmɑːk/ the act of marking again. ⓘ 16c.

remarque or **remark** /rɪˈmɑːk/ ▻ *noun, engraving* an indication on the edge of a plate that usually takes the form of a small sketch denoting the stage that the engraving has reached. ⓘ 19c: French.

REME /ˈriːmɪ/ ▻ *abbreviation* Royal Electrical and Mechanical Engineers.

remedial /rɪˈmiːdɪəl/ *adj* **1** affording a remedy. **2** relating to or concerning the teaching of children with learning difficulties. • **remedially** *adverb*.

remedy /ˈrɛmədɪ/ ▻ *noun* (***remedies***) **1** any drug or treatment which cures or controls a disease. **2** (*old use*) anything which solves a problem or gets rid of something undesirable ▫ *a remedy for the country's economic problems.* **3** the range of tolerated variation from the standard weight or quality of a coin. ▻ *verb* (***remedies, remedied, remedying***) **1** to cure or control (a disease, etc). **2** to put right or correct (a problem, error, etc). • **remediable** /rɪˈmiːdɪəbəl/ *adj* • **remediably** *adverb*. • **remediless** *adj*. ⓘ 13c: from Latin *remedium* medicine or a cure, from *mederi* to heal.

remember /rɪˈmɛmbə(r)/ ▻ *verb* (***remembered, remembering***) **1** to bring someone or something from the past to mind. **2** to keep (a fact, idea, etc) in one's mind ▫ *remember to phone.* **3** to reward or make a present to someone, eg in a will or as a tip. **4** to commemorate. • **remembrance** /rɪˈmɛmbrəns/ *noun* **1** the act of remembering or being remembered. **2 a** something which reminds a person of something or someone; **b** a souvenir. **3** a memory or recollection ▫ *a dim remembrance of the night's events.* • **remember oneself** to regain one's good manners, usual composure, etc after a lapse. ⓘ 14c: from French *remembrer*, from Latin *rememorari*, from *memor* mindful.

▪ **remember someone to someone else** to pass on their good wishes and greetings to the other person ▫ *remember me to your parents.*

Remembrance Day and **Remembrance Sunday** ▻ *noun* in the UK: the Sunday nearest to 11 November, on which services are held to commemorate the servicemen and servicewomen who died in both World Wars and subsequent conflicts. Also called **Poppy Day**.

remembrancer /rɪˈmɛmbrənsə(r)/ ▻ *noun* **1** an officer of exchequer, especially one responsible for collecting debts due to the Crown (**Queen's Remembrancer** or **King's Remembrancer**). **2** an official representative of the City of London to Parliamentary committees, etc (**City Remembrancer**).

remex /ˈriːmɛks/ ▻ *noun* (***remiges*** /ˈrɛmɪdʒiːz/) *ornithol* any of the large primary or secondary flight feathers of a bird's wing. • **remigial** /rɪˈmɪdʒɪəl/ *adj*. ⓘ 17c in obsolete sense 'a rower': from Latin *remus* an oar.

remind /rɪˈmaɪnd/ ▻ *verb* (***reminded, reminding***) **1** to cause someone to remember (something or to do something) ▫ *remind me to speak to him.* **2** (*usually* **remind someone of something** or **someone**) to make them think about something or someone else, especially because of a similarity ▫ *She reminds me of her sister.* • **reminder** *noun* something that reminds. • **remindful** *adj*. ⓘ 17c.

remineralize or **remineralise** /riːˈmɪnərəlaɪz/ ▻ *verb, medicine* **1** to replace the depleted mineral content of bones, teeth, etc. **2** *intr* said of bones, teeth, etc: to regain or replace depleted minerals. • **remineralization** *noun* the naturally occurring replacement of depleted mineral content in bones, teeth, etc. ⓘ 20c.

reminisce /rɛmɪˈnɪs/ ▻ *verb* (***reminisced, reminiscing***) *intr* to think, talk or write about things remembered from the past. • **reminiscence** /rɛmɪˈnɪsəns/ *noun* **1** the act of thinking, talking or writing about the past. **2** (*often* **reminiscences**) an account of something remembered from the past. • **reminiscent** *adj* **1** (*usually* **reminiscent of something** or **someone**) similar, so as to remind one of them ▫ *a painting reminiscent of Turner.* **2** said of a person: **a** often thinking about the past. **3** relating to reminiscence. • **reminiscently** *adverb*. ⓘ 16c as *noun*: from Latin *reminisci* to remember.

remise /rɪˈmaɪz/ ▻ *verb* (***remised, remising***) **1** *law* to give up or surrender (a right, claim, etc). **2** *intr, fencing* to make a remise. ▻ *noun* **1** *law* the giving up or surrender of a right or claim. **2** *fencing* an effective second thrust made on the same lunge after the first has missed. ⓘ 15c: from French *remis*, from *remettre* to put back.

remiss /rɪˈmɪs/ ▻ *adj* **1** careless; failing to pay attention; negligent. **2** lacking vigour or energy. • **remissly** *adverb*. • **remissness** *noun*. ⓘ 15c: from Latin from *remittere*, *remissum* to loosen.

remission /rɪˈmɪʃən/ ▷ *noun* **1** a lessening in force or effect, especially in the symptoms of a disease such as cancer. **2** a reduction of a prison sentence. **3 a** pardon; **b** forgiveness from sin. **4** relinquishment of a claim. **5** the act of remitting or state of being remitted. • **remissibility** *noun*. • **remissible** /rɪˈmɪsəbəl/ *adj* able to be remitted. • **remissive** *adj* **1** remitting. **2** forgiving. • **remissively** *adverb*. ⓒ 13c: from Latin *remissio*.

remit ▷ *verb* /rɪˈmɪt/ (***remitted***, ***remitting***) **1** to cancel or refrain from demanding (a debt, punishment, etc). **2** *tr & intr* to make or become loose, slack or relaxed. **3** to send (money) in payment. **4** to refer (a matter for decision, etc) to some other authority. **5** *law* to refer (a case) to a lower court. **6** *intr* said of a disease, pain, rain, etc: to become less severe for a period of time. **7** to send or put something back into a previous state. **8** said of God: to forgive (sins). ▷ *noun* /ˈriːmɪt, rɪˈmɪt/ the authority or terms of reference given to an official, committee, etc in dealing with a matter. □ *not part of my remit to assess the cost*. • **remitment** or **remittal** *noun* **1** remission. **2** *law* reference to another court, etc. • **remittance** /rɪˈmɪtəns/ *noun* **1** the sending of money in payment. **2** the money sent. • **remittee** *noun* the person to whom a remittance is sent. • **remittent** *adj* said of a disease: becoming less severe at times. • **remittently** *adverb*. • **remitter** or **remittor** *noun* someone who makes a remittance. ⓒ 14c: from Latin *remittere* to loosen or send back.

remix ▷ *verb* /riːˈmɪks/ to mix again in a different way, especially to mix (a recording) again, changing the balance of the different parts, etc. ▷ *noun* /ˈriːmɪks/ a remixed recording. See also MIX (verb 7).

remnant /ˈrɛmnənt/ ▷ *noun* (*often* **remnants**) **1** a remaining small piece or amount of something larger, or a small number of things left from a larger quantity. **2** a remaining piece of fabric from the end of a roll. **3** a surviving trace or vestige. ⓒ 14c: from French *remenant* remaining, from *remanoir* to remain.

remonstrance /rɪˈmɒnstrəns/ *noun* **1** an act of remonstrating. **2** a strong, usually formal, protest. • **remonstrant** *noun*, *adj*.

remonstrate /ˈrɛmənstreɪt/ ▷ *verb* (***remonstrated***, ***remonstrating***) to protest forcefully; to say in remonstrance □ *remonstrated that they knew nothing about it*. • **remonstration** *noun*. • **remonstrative** /rɪˈmɒnstrətɪv/ *adj*. • **remonstrator** *noun*. ⓒ 16c: from Latin *remonstrare*, *remonstratum* to demonstrate.

■ **remonstrate with someone** to protest to them.

remontant /rɪˈmɒntənt/ *bot* ▷ *adj* **1** said especially of a rose: blooming more than once in the same season. **2** said of a strawberry plant: producing several crops in the same season. ▷ *noun* a remontant plant, especially a rose or a strawberry plant. ⓒ 19c: French, from *remonter* to come up again.

remora /ˈrɛmərə/ ▷ *noun* **1** any of several slender marine fish which attach themselves to rocks, other fish, etc by means of a large sucker on the top of the head. **2** a hindrance or obstacle. ⓒ 16c: Latin, from *mora* a delay, so called because formerly the fish was believed to stop ships by attaching itself to them.

remorse /rɪˈmɔːs/ ▷ *noun* **1 a** a deep feeling of guilt, regret and bitterness for something wrong or bad which one has done; **b** compunction. **2** compassion or pity. • **remorseful** *adj*. • **remorsefully** *adverb*. • **remorsefulness** *noun*. • **remorseless** *adj* **1** without remorse. **2** cruel. **3** without respite; relentless. • **remorselessly** *adverb*. • **remorselessness** *noun*. ⓒ 14c: from French *remors*, from Latin *remordere*, *remorsum* to vex, from *mordere* to bite or sting.

remote /rɪˈmoʊt/ ▷ *adj* **1** far away; distant in time or place. **2** out of the way; far from civilization. **3** operated or controlled from a distance; remote-controlled. **4** *computing* said of a computer terminal: located separately from the main processor but having a communication link with it. **5** distantly related or connected. **6** very small, slight or faint □ *a remote chance*. **7** said of someone's manner: not friendly or interested; aloof or distant. ▷ *noun* **1** *TV & radio, especially US* an outside broadcast. **2** a remote control device, eg for a TV. • **remotely** *adverb*. • **remoteness** *noun*. ⓒ 15c: from Latin *remotus* removed or distant.

remote access ▷ *noun, computing* access to a computer from a computer terminal at another site, usually in a different town or country.

remote control ▷ *noun* **1** the control of machinery or electrical devices from a distance, by the making or breaking of an electric circuit or by means of radio waves. **2** a battery-operated device for transmitting such waves. • **remote-controlled** *adj*.

remote handling equipment ▷ *noun, nuclear eng* equipment that enables dangerous (eg highly radioactive) materials to be manipulated from behind a shield or from a safe distance.

remote job entry ▷ *noun, computing* (abbreviation **RJE**) input of data or programs to a computer from a distant input device.

remote sensor ▷ *noun* a device which scans the earth and other planets from space in order to collect, and transmit to a central computer, data about them. • **remote sensing** *noun* TELEMETRY.

remoulade or **rémoulade** / *French* remulad/ ▷ *noun* (***remoulades*** / *French* remulad/) a sauce made by adding herbs, capers, mustard, etc to mayonnaise, and served with fish, salad, etc. ⓒ 19c: French, from dialect *ramolas* horseradish, from Latin *armoracea*.

remould ▷ *verb* /riːˈmoʊld/ **1** to mould again. **2** to bond new tread onto (an old or worn tyre). ▷ *noun* /ˈriːmoʊld/ a tyre that has had new tread bonded onto it. Also called **retread**. ⓒ 17c as *verb*, sense 1; 1950s in other senses.

remount ▷ *verb* /riːˈmaʊnt/ *tr & intr* **1** to get on or mount again (especially a horse, bicycle, etc). **2** to mount (a picture, etc) again. ▷ *noun* /ˈriːmaʊnt/ **1** a fresh horse. **2** a fresh supply of horses. ⓒ 14c.

remove /rɪˈmuːv/ ▷ *verb* **1** to move someone or something to a different place. **2** to take off (a piece of clothing). **3** to get rid of someone or something. **4** *euphemistic* to murder or assassinate. **5** to dismiss someone from a job, position, etc. **6** *intr, formal* **a** to change one's position, place, location, etc; **b** to move to a new house. ▷ *noun* **1** a removal. **2** the degree, usually specified, of difference separating two things □ *a form of government at only one remove from tyranny*. **3** *Brit* in some schools: an intermediate form or class. • **removability** *noun*. • **removable** *adj*. • **removal** *noun* **1** the act or process of removing or state of being removed. **2 a** the moving of possessions, furniture, etc to a new house; **b** *as adj* □ *removal van*. **3** *euphemistic* murder or assassination. • **removed** *adj* **1** separated, distant or remote. **2** usually said of cousins: separated by a specified number of generations or degrees of descent □ *first cousin once removed*. • **remover** *noun* **1** someone or something that removes. **2** someone whose job is to move possessions, furniture, etc from one house to another. ⓒ 14c: from French *remouvoir*.

REM sleep /rɛm—/ ▷ *noun* a phase of restless sleep characterized by brain patterns similar to those produced when awake, and including increased electrical activity of the brain, rapid eye movement, and dreaming. *Technical equivalent* **paradoxical sleep**.

remuage /rəmʊˈɑːʒ; *French* ʀəmˈaʒ/ ▷ *noun, wine-making* the process of turning or shaking wine bottles so that the sediment collects at the cork end for removal. • **remueur** /rəmʊˈɜː(r); *French* ʀəmˈœʀ/ *noun, wine-making* the person who turns the bottles. ⓒ 1920s: French, meaning 'moving about', from *remuer* to move or turn.

remunerate /rɪˈmjuːnəreɪt/ ▷ *verb* (***remunerated***, ***remunerating***) **1** to recompense. **2** to pay for services rendered. • **remunerable** *adj.* • **remuneration** *noun.* • **remunerative** *adj* profitable. • **remunerator** *noun.* • **remuneratory** *adj* giving a recompense. ⓘ 16c: from Latin *remunerari, remuneratus* from *munus* a gift.

renaissance /rɪˈneɪsəns, -sɑ̃s; *especially NAmer* ˈrɛnəsɑ̃s/ ▻ *noun* **1** a rebirth or revival, especially of learning, culture and the arts. **2** (**the Renaissance**) the revival of arts and letters which formed the transition from the Middle Ages to the modern world. ▻ *adj* relating to the Renaissance. ⓘ 19c: French, from Latin *renasci* to be born again.

renal /ˈriːnəl/ ▻ *adj* relating to, or in the area of, the kidneys. ⓘ 17c: from French *rénal*, from Latin *renalis*, from *renes* kidneys.

renascence /rɪˈnasəns/ ▻ *noun* **1** rebirth; the fact or process of being born again or into new life. **2** (**the Renascence**) Renaissance. • **renascent** /rɪˈnasənt, rɪˈneɪsənt/ *adj* **1** being reborn. **2** reviving; becoming active or lively again. ⓘ 18c: from Latin *renasci* to be born again.

rend ▻ *verb* (**rent**, **rending**) *old use* **1** to tear something apart, especially using force or violence; to split. **2** *intr* to tear or split, especially violently or with force. **3** to tear something forcibly or violently away from someone. **4** to tear (one's hair, clothes, etc) in grief, rage, etc. **5** said of a noise: to disturb (the silence, the air, etc) with a loud, piercing sound. ⓘ Anglo-Saxon.

render /ˈrɛndə(r)/ ▻ *verb* (**rendered**, **rendering**) **1** to cause something to be or become ◻ *render things more agreeable.* **2** to give or provide (a service, help, etc). **3** to show (obedience, honour, etc). **4** to pay (money) or perform (a duty), especially in return for something ◻ *render thanks to God.* **5** (*often* **render something back**) to give back or return something. **6** to give something in return or exchange. **7** (*also* **render something up**) to give up, release or yield something ◻ *The grave will never render up its dead.* **8** to translate something into another language ◻ *How do you render that in German?* **9** to perform (the role of a character in a play, a piece of music, etc). **10** to portray or reproduce someone or something, especially in painting or music. **11** to present or submit for payment, approval, consideration, etc. **12** to cover (brick or stone) with a coat of plaster. **13** (*often* **render something down**) **a** to melt down (fat), especially to clarify it; **b** to remove (fat) by melting it. **14** *law* said of a judge or jury: to deliver formally (a judgement or verdict). ▻ *noun* a first coat of plaster or rendering applied to brick or stonework. • **renderable** *adj.* • **renderer** *noun.* • **rendering** *noun* **1** a performance. **2** a coat of plaster. ⓘ 14c: from French *rendre*.

rendezvous /ˈrɑ̃deɪvuː, ˈrɒn-, -dɪvuː/ ▻ *noun* (***rendezvous*** /-vuːz/) **1 a** an appointment to meet at a specified time and place; **b** the meeting itself; **c** the place where such a meeting is to be. **2** a place where people generally meet. **3** *space flight* an arranged meeting, and usually docking, of two spacecraft in space. ▻ *verb* (***rendezvoused***, /-vuːd/ ***rendezvousing*** /-vuːɪŋ/) *intr* **1** to meet at an appointed place or time. **2** said of two spaccraft: to meet, and usually dock, in space. ⓘ 16c: French, meaning 'present yourselves', from *se rendre* to present oneself.

rendition /rɛnˈdɪʃən/ *noun* **1** an act of rendering. **2** a performance or interpretation of a piece of music, a dramatic role, etc. **3** a translation. **4** surrender.

rendzina /rɛndˈziːnə/ ▻ *noun, soil science* any of a group of dark fertile soils, typical of humid or semi-arid grassland and limestone regions, rich in humus and calcium carbonate, that have developed over limestone bedrock. ⓘ 1920s: Russian, from Polish *redzina*.

renegade /ˈrɛnəgeɪd/ ▻ *noun* **1 a** someone who deserts the religious, political, etc group which they belong to, and joins an enemy or rival group; **b** a turncoat. **2** a Christian turned Muslim. ⓘ 15c: from Spanish *renegado*, from Latin *negare* to deny.

renege or **renegue** /rɪˈniːg, rɪˈneɪg/ ▻ *verb* (***reneged***, ***reneging***) **1** *intr* (*often* **renege on something**) to go back on (a promise, agreement, deal, etc). **2** to renounce (a promise, etc) or desert (a person, faith, etc). **3** *cards* to revoke (sense 2). • **reneger** or **reneguer** *noun.* ⓘ 16c: from Latin *renegare* to renounce, from *negare* to deny.

renew /rɪˈnjuː/ ▻ *verb* (***renewed***, ***renewing***) **1 a** to make something fresh or like new again; **b** to restore something to its original condition. **2 a** to begin something or begin to do it again; **b** to repeat. **3** *tr & intr* to begin (some activity) again after a break. **4** *tr & intr* to make (a licence, lease, loan, etc) valid for a further period of time. **5** to replenish or replace ◻ *renew the water in the vases.* **6** to recover (youth, strength, etc). • **renewable** *adj.* • **renewal** *noun.* • **renewer** *noun.* • **renewing** *noun.*

renewable energy ▻ *noun* any energy source that is naturally occurring and that cannot in theory be exhausted, eg solar energy, tidal, wind or wave power, geothermal energy.

renewable resource ▻ *noun* a supply of living organisms that, after harvesting by regrowth or reproduction, can be replaced, unlike a NON-RENEWABLE RESOURCE.

reni- /ˈrɛnɪ, ˈriːnɪ/ ▻ *combining form, denoting* the kidneys or the area around the kidneys.

reniform ▻ *adj* kidney-shaped. ⓘ 18c.

renin /ˈriːnɪn/ ▻ *noun, physiol* an enzyme, produced by the kidneys, that is secreted into the bloodstream and is involved in the formation of a hormone which raises the blood pressure by constricting the arteries. ⓘ Early 20c: from Latin *renes* the kidneys.

renminbi yuan see under YUAN

rennet /ˈrɛnɪt/ ▻ *noun* a substance used for curdling milk, especially and originally an extract obtained from the stomachs of calves that contains the enzyme rennin. ⓘ 15c: related to Anglo-Saxon *gerinnan* to curdle.

rennin /ˈrɛnɪn/ ▻ *noun, biochem* an enzyme found in gastric juice that causes milk to curdle. ⓘ 19c: from RENNET.

renormalization or **renormalisation** ▻ *noun, physics* a method of obtaining finite answers to calculations (rather than infinites) by redefining the parameters, especially those of mass and charge. ⓘ 1940s.

renormalize or **renormalise** ▻ *verb* to subject to, or calculate using, renormalization.

renounce /rɪˈnaʊns/ ▻ *verb* (***renounced***, ***renouncing***) **1** to give up (a claim, title, right, etc), especially formally and publicly. **2** to refuse to recognize or associate with someone. **3** to give up (a bad habit). **4** *intr, cards* to fail to follow suit. ▻ *noun, cards* a failure to follow suit. • **renouncement** *noun.* • **renouncer** *noun.* ⓘ 14c: from French *renoncer*, from Latin *renuntiare* to announce.

renovate /ˈrɛnəveɪt/ ▻ *verb* (***renovated***, ***renovating***) **1 a** to renew or make new again; **b** to restore (especially a building) to a former and better condition. **2** to refresh or reinvigorate (one's spirits, etc). • **renovation** *noun.* • **renovator** *noun.* ⓘ 16c: from Latin *renovare, renovatum*.

renown /rɪˈnaʊn/ ▻ *noun* fame. • **renowned** *adj* famous; celebrated. ⓘ 14c: from French *renom*, from *renomer* to make famous.

rent[1] ▻ *noun* money paid periodically to the owner of a property by a tenant in return for the use or occupation of that property. ▻ *verb* (***rented***, ***renting***) **1** to pay rent for (a building, house, flat, etc). **2** (*usually* **rent something out**) to allow someone the use of (one's property) in return for payment of rent. **3** *intr* to be hired out for rent. • **rentability** *noun.* • **rentable** *adj.* • **rented** *adj* ◻ *rented accommodation.* • **renter** *noun.* ⓘ 12c: from French *rente* revenue, from Latin *rendere* to render.

rent[2] ▻ *noun, old use* **1** an opening or split made by tearing or rending. **2** a fissure. ▻ *verb, past tense, past participle of* REND. ⓘ 16c.

rent-a- or (before a vowel) **rent-an-** ▷ *prefix, derog or jocular denoting* as if rented, hired or organized for a specific occasion or purpose; quickly and artificially created, etc □ *rent-a-crowd* □ *rent-an-army*.

rental /ˈrɛntəl/ ▷ *noun* **1** the act of renting. **2** money paid as rent. **3** income derived from money paid as rent. **4** a list of rent owed to a property owner by tenants; a rent-roll. **5** property available for renting.

rent boy ▷ *noun* a young male prostitute who provides sexual services for men.

rent-free ▷ *adj, adverb* without payment of rent.

rent-restriction ▷ *noun* restriction of a landlord's right to raise rent controlled by legislation.

rent-roll ▷ *noun* **1** a list of property and rent. **2** the total income from rented property.

renunciation /rɪnʌnsɪˈeɪʃən/ ▷ *noun* **1** an act of renouncing. **2** a formal declaration of renouncing something. **3** self-denial. **4** *stock exchange* the surrendering to another of the rights to buy new shares in a rights issue. • **renunciative** /rɪˈnʌnsɪətɪv/ *adj*. • **renunciatory** /rɪˈnʌnsɪətərɪ/ *adj*. ◷ 14c: from Latin *renuntiare* to proclaim.

reopen /riːˈoʊpən/ ▷ *verb* **1** *tr & intr* to open again. **2** to begin to discuss again (a subject which has already been discussed). ◷ 18c.

rep[1] ▷ *noun, colloq* a representative, especially a travelling salesperson. Also *as adj*.

rep[2] or **repp** ▷ *noun* a corded cloth, made of wool, silk, cotton or rayon, used as a furnishing fabric. ◷ 19c: from French *reps*.

rep[3] see under REPERTORY.

repaint ▷ *verb* /riːˈpeɪnt/ to paint over or again. ▷ *noun* **1** the act or process of repainting or fact of being repainted. **2** a repainted golf ball. ◷ 17c.

repair[1] /rɪˈpɛə(r)/ ▷ *verb* (***repaired, repairing***) **1** to restore (something damaged or broken) to good working condition. **2** to put right, heal or make up for (some wrong that has been done). ▷ *noun* **1** an act or the process of repairing. **2** a condition or state □ *in good repair*. **3** a part or place that has been mended or repaired. • **repairable** *adj*. • **repairer** *noun*. ◷ 14c: from French *reparer*, from Latin *reparare*, from *parare* to put in order or make ready.

repair[2] /rɪˈpɛə(r)/ ▷ *verb* (***repaired, repairing***) *intr* (*usually* **repair to somewhere**) *old use* **1** to go there. **2** to take oneself off there. ◷ 14c: from French *repairer*, from Latin *repatriare* to return to one's homeland, from *patria* homeland.

repand /rɪˈpand/ ▷ *adj, bot, zool* with slightly wavy edge or margin. ◷ 18c: from Latin *repandus* bent backwards.

reparation /rɛpəˈreɪʃən/ ▷ *noun* **1** the act of making up for some wrong that has been done. **2** money paid or something done for this purpose. **3** (*usually* **reparations**) compensation paid after a war by a defeated nation for the damage caused. • **reparability** /rɛpərəˈbɪlɪtɪ/ *noun* • **reparable** /ˈrɛpərəbəl/ *adj* **1** able to be put right. **2** capable of being made good. • **reparably** *adverb*. • **reparatory** /rɪˈparətərɪ/ *adj*. ◷ 14c: from French *réparation*, from Latin *reparare* to repair.

repartee /rɛpɑːˈtiː/ ▷ *noun* (***repartees***) **1** the practice or skill of making spontaneous witty replies. **2** a quick witty reply or retort. **3** conversation with many such replies. ◷ 17c: from French *repartie*, from *repartir* to set out again or to retort.

repast /rɪˈpɑːst/ ▷ *noun, formal* or *old use* a meal. ◷ 14c: from French *repaistre* to eat a meal, from Latin *pascere* to feed.

repatriate /riːˈpatrɪeɪt, -ˈpeɪt-/ ▷ *verb* (***repatriated, repatriating***) to send (a refugee, prisoner of war, etc) back to their country of origin. ▷ *noun* a repatriated person. • **repatriation** *noun*. ◷ 17c as *verb*; 1920s as *noun*: from Latin *repatriare, repatriatum* to return home, from *patria* homeland.

repay /riːˈpeɪ, rɪ-/ ▷ *verb* **1** to pay back or refund (money). **2** to do or give something to someone in return for something they have done or given □ *repay his kindness*. • **repayable** *adj*. • **repayment** *noun*.

repeal /rɪˈpiːl/ ▷ *verb* (***repealed, repealing***) to make (a law, etc) no longer valid; to annul (a law, etc). ▷ *noun* the act of repealing (a law, etc); annulment. • **repealable** *adj*. • **repealer** *noun*. ◷ 14c: from French *repeler*, from *apeler* to appeal.

repeat /rɪˈpiːt/ ▷ *verb* (***repeated, repeating***) **1** to say, do, etc, again or several times. **2** to echo or say again exactly (the words already said by someone else). **3** to tell (something one has heard or been told in confidence) to someone else, especially when one ought not to. **4 a** to quote something from memory; **b** to recite (a poem, etc). **5** *intr* said of food: to be tasted again some time after being swallowed. **6** *intr* to occur again or several times; to recur. **7** (*usually* **repeat itself**) said of an event, occurrence, etc: to happen in exactly the same way more than once □ *history repeats itself*. **8** *intr* said of a gun: to fire several times without being reloaded. **9** *intr* said of a clock: to strike the hour or quarter hour. **10** *intr, US* to vote illegally more than once in the same election. **11** (**repeat oneself**) to say the same thing more than once, especially with the result of being repetitious or tedious. **12** said of a TV or radio company: to broadcast (a programme, series, etc) again □ *The BBC repeats 'Murder One' on Wednesdays* □ *'Murder One' is repeated on Wednesday*. ▷ *noun* **1 a** the act of repeating; **b** a repetition. **2** something that is repeated, especially a television or radio programme which has been broadcast before. **3** *music* **a** a passage in a piece of music that is to be repeated; **b** a sign which marks such a passage. **4** an order for goods, etc that is exactly the same as a previous one. ▷ *adj* repeated □ *a repeat showing*. • **repeatable** *adj* **1** able to be repeated. **2** suitable or fit to be told to others. • **repeated** *adj* **1** said, done, etc again or several times. **2** reiterated. • **repeatedly** *adverb* again and again; frequently. • **repeater** *noun* **1** someone or something that repeats. **2** a clock that strikes the hour or quarter hour. **3** a gun that can be fired several times without having to be reloaded. **4** *teleg* an instrument for automatically retransmitting a message. • **repeating** *noun, adj*. ◷ 14c: from French *répéter*.

repeating decimal see under RECURRING DECIMAL.

repechage /ˈrɛpəʃɑːʒ/ ▷ *noun, especially fencing & rowing* a supplementary heat in a competition that allows runners-up from earlier eliminating heats a second chance to go on to the final. ◷ 19c: from French *repêchage* a fishing out again, from *pêcher* to fish.

repel /rɪˈpɛl/ ▷ *verb* (***repelled, repelling***) **1 a** to force or drive something or someone back or away; **b** to repulse. **2** *tr & intr* to provoke a feeling of disgust or loathing. **3** to fail to mix with, absorb or be attracted by (something else) □ *oil repels water*. **4** to reject or rebuff, especially someone's advances. • **repeller** *noun*. • **repelling** *adj*. • **repellingly** *adverb*. ◷ 15c: from Latin *repellere* to drive back.

repellent or **repellant** *noun* **1** something that repels, especially that repels insects. **2** a substance used to treat fabric so as to make it resistant to water. ▷ *adj* **1** forcing or driving back or away; repelling. **2** provoking a feeling of disgust or loathing. • **repellence** or **repellency** *noun*. • **repellently** *adverb*.

repent[1] /rɪˈpɛnt/ ▷ *verb* (***repented, repenting***) **1** *tr & intr* (*often* **repent of something**) **a** to feel great sorrow or regret for something one has done; **b** to wish (an action, etc) undone. **2** *intr* to regret the evil or bad things one has done in the past and as a result change one's behaviour or conduct. • **repentance** *noun*. • **repentant** *adj* experiencing or expressing repentance. • **repentantly** *adverb*. • **repenter** *noun*. ◷ 13c: from French *repentir*.

repent² /ˈriːpənt/ ▷ *adj, bot* said of a plant: creeping, especially lying along the ground and rooting. ⓘ 17c: from Latin *repere* to creep.

repercussion /riːpəˈkʌʃən, rɛ-/ ▷ *noun* **1** (*usually* **repercussions**) the result or consequence of, or reaction to, some action, event, etc, and usually a bad, unforeseen or indirect one. **2** a reflection of a sound; an echo or reverberation. **3** a recoil or repulse after an impact. • **repercussive** *adj*. ⓘ 16c: from Latin *repercussio*.

repertoire /ˈrɛpətwɑː(r)/ ▷ *noun* **1** the list of songs, operas, plays, etc that a singer, performer, group of actors, etc is able or ready to perform. **2** the range or stock of skills, techniques, talents, etc that someone or something has. **3** *computing* the total list of codes and commands that a computer can accept and execute. ⓘ 19c: from French *répertoire*; see REPERTORY.

repertory /ˈrɛpətərɪ/ ▷ *noun* (**repertories**) **1** a repertoire, especially the complete list of plays that a theatre company is able and ready to perform. **2** the performance of a repertoire of plays at regular, short intervals. **3** a storehouse or repository. **4** short form of REPERTORY COMPANY. **5 a** short form of REPERTORY THEATRE; **b** repertory theatres collectively ▫ *worked in repertory for a few years.* Often shortened still further to **rep**. ⓘ 16c: from Latin *repertorium* inventory, from *reperire, repertum* to discover or find again.

repertory company ▷ *noun* a group of actors who perform a series of plays from their repertoire in the course of a season at one theatre.

repertory theatre ▷ *noun* a theatre where a repertory company performs its plays.

repetend /ˈrɛpɪtend, rɛpɪˈtend/ ▷ *noun* **1** *math* the figure or figures that repeat themselves in a RECURRING DECIMAL number. **2** a recurring note, word, refrain, etc. **3** anything that recurs or is repeated. ⓘ 18c: from Latin *repetendum*, something that should be repeated.

répétiteur /rɪpetɪˈtɜː(r)/ ▷ *noun* a coach or tutor, especially one who rehearses opera singers, ballet dancers, etc. ⓘ 1930s: French.

repetition /rɛpəˈtɪʃən/ ▷ *noun* **1** the act of repeating or being repeated. **2** something that is repeated. **3** a recital from memory, eg of a poem, piece of music, etc. **4** a copy or replica. **5** *music* the ability of a musical instrument to repeat a note quickly. • **repetitious** /rɛpəˈtɪʃəs/ or **repetitive** /rɪˈpɛtɪtɪv/ *adj* overinclined to repetition and so tedious and boring, etc. • **repetitiously** or **repetitively** *adverb*. • **repetitiousness** or **repetitiveness** *noun*. ⓘ 15c: from French *répétition*.

repetitive strain injury and **repetitive stress injury** ▷ *noun* (abbreviation **RSI**) inflammation of the tendons and joints of the hands and lower arms, caused by repeated performance of identical manual operations such as using a keyboard.

rephrase /riːˈfreɪz/ ▷ *verb* to put or express something in different words, especially to make it more understandable, acceptable, etc. ⓘ 19c.

repine /rɪˈpaɪn/ ▷ *verb* (**repined, repining**) *intr* (*usually* **repine at** or **against something**) **1** to fret. **2** to feel discontented. ⓘ 16c: from PINE².

replace /rɪˈpleɪs/ ▷ *verb* **1 a** to put something back in its previous position; **b** to return something to its proper position. **2** to take the place of or be a substitute for someone or something. **3** to supplant someone or something. **4** (*often* **replace someone** or **something by** or **with another**) to use or substitute another person or thing in place of an existing one ▫ *We want to replace the TV with a new one.* • **replaceable** *adj*. • **replacement** *noun* **1** the act of replacing something. **2** someone or something that replaces another. • **replacer** *noun*. ⓘ 16c.

> ***replace***
>
> See Usage Note at **substitute**.

> ***Could you rephrase that?***
>
> A glance at the following examples reveals the damage we can do when we construct our sentences loosely or clumsily:
>
> ✗ *If the baby does not thrive on raw milk, boil it.*
>
> ✗ *I have discussed the question of stocking the proposed poultry plant with my colleagues.*
>
> ✗ *County Council employees can sit on District Councils, and vice versa.*
>
> ✗ *Nothing is less likely to appeal to a young woman than the opinions of old men on the Pill.*
>
> ✗ *People in the South East keep their teeth longer than people in the North.*
>
> ✗ *Prices of different models vary and you should take the advice of an expert on the make.*
>
> A common error is to construct a sentence in such a way that there is no match between the subjects, or implied subjects, of the clauses:
>
> ✗ *Badly damaged by fire last year, I am in the process of rebuilding the house.*
>
> ✗ *Propped up against the wall like that, anyone could fall over those poles.*
>
> ✗ *As the biggest nation in the world, I want to learn as much about China as possible.*
>
> ✗ *Sitting in a hot stuffy office, it seemed as if five o'clock would never come.*

replay ▷ *noun* /ˈriːpleɪ/ **1** the playing of a game, football match, etc again, usually because there was no clear winner the first time. **2** ACTION REPLAY ▷ *verb* /riːˈpleɪ/ to play (a tape, recording, football match, etc) again. ⓘ 19c.

replenish /rɪˈplɛnɪʃ/ ▷ *verb* (**replenished, replenishing**) to fill up or make complete again, especially a supply of something which has been used up. • **replenisher** *noun*. • **replenishment** *noun*. ⓘ 14c: from French *replenir*, from Latin *plenus* full.

replete /rɪˈpliːt/ ▷ *adj* **1** (*often* **replete with something**) completely or well supplied with it. **2** *formal* **a** having eaten enough or more than enough; **b** satiated. • **repleteness** or **repletion** *noun*. ⓘ 14c: from Latin *replere, repletum* to fill.

replica /ˈrɛplɪkə/ ▷ *noun* (**replicas**) **1** an exact copy, especially of a work of art, sometimes by the original artist, and often on a smaller scale. **2** a facsimile or reproduction. **3** *music* a repeat. ⓘ 19c: Italian, from Latin *replicare* to repeat or fold back.

replicate ▷ *verb* /ˈrɛplɪkeɪt/ (**replicated, replicating**) **1 a** to make a replica of something; **b** to reproduce or copy something exactly. **2** to repeat (a scientific experiment). **3** *intr* said of a molecule, virus, etc: to make a replica of itself. **4** to fold back. ▷ *noun* /ˈrɛplɪkət/ **1** *music* a tone one or more octaves from a given tone. **2** a repetition of a scientific experiment. ▷ *adj* /ˈrɛplɪkət/ **1** *biol* said of a leaf, an insect's wing, etc: folded back. **2** said of a scientific experiment: being a replicate or repetition. • **replication** /rɛplɪˈkeɪʃən/ *noun* **1** the act of replicating. **2** *law* the plaintiff's answer to the defendant's plea. • **replicative** /ˈrɛplɪkətɪv/ *adj*. ⓘ 16c: from Latin *replicare, replicatum* to fold back.

reply /rɪˈplaɪ/ ▷ *verb* (**replies, replied, replying**) **1** *intr* to answer or respond to something in words, writing or action. **2** to say or do something in response. **3** *intr* to make a speech of thanks in answer to a speech of welcome. **4** *intr, law* to answer a defendant's plea. **5** *tr & intr* to echo; to return (a sound). ▷ *noun* (**replies**) **1** an answer; a response. **2** *law* the answer made to a defendant's plea on behalf of the plaintiff or prosecution. • **replier** *noun*. ⓘ 14c: from French *replier*, from Latin *replicare* to fold back reply.

repo /ˈriːpoʊ/ ▻ *noun* (***repos***) *chiefly US colloq* short form of REPOSSESSION. ⓒ 20c.

repoint /riːˈpɔɪnt/ ▻ *verb* to repair (stone or brickwork) by renewing the cement or mortar between the joins. ⓒ 19c.

report /rɪˈpɔːt/ ▻ *noun* (abbreviation **rept**) **1** a detailed statement, description or account, especially one made after some form of investigation. **2** a detailed and usually formal account of the discussions and decisions of a committee, inquiry or other group of people. **3** an account of some matter of news or a topical story □ *a newspaper report.* **4** a statement of a pupil's work and behaviour at school, usually made at the end of each school year or each term. **5 a** rumour; **b** general talk. **6** character or reputation. **7** a loud explosive noise, eg the sound of a gun firing. ▻ *verb* (***reported***, ***reporting***) **1** to bring back (information, etc) as an answer, news or account □ *reported that fighting had broken out.* **2** *intr* to state. **3** (*often* **to report on something**) to give a formal or official account or description of (findings, information, etc), especially after an investigation. **4** *US* said of a committee, etc: to make a formal report on (a bill, etc). **5 a** to give an account of (some matter of news, etc), especially for a newspaper, or TV or radio broadcast; **b** *intr* to act as a newspaper, TV or radio reporter. **6** to make a complaint about someone, especially to a person in authority. **7** to make something known to a person in authority. **8** *intr* (*usually* **report for something** or **to someone**) to present oneself at an appointed place or time for a particular purpose □ *Please report to reception on arrival.* **9** *intr* (*usually* **report to someone**) to be responsible to them or under their authority. **10** *intr* to account for oneself in a particular way □ *report sick.* **11** *law* to take down or record the details of a legal case, proceedings, etc. ● **reportable** *adj.* ● **reportedly** *adverb* according to report or general talk. ● **reporter** *noun* **1** someone who reports, especially for a newspaper, TV or radio. **2** *law* someone whose job is to prepare reports on legal proceedings. ⓒ 14c: from French *reporter*, from Latin *reportare* to carry back.

reportage /rɛpɔːˈtɑːʒ, rɪˈpɔːtɪdʒ/ ▻ *noun* **1** journalistic reporting. **2** the style and manner of this kind of reporting.

reported speech ▻ *noun, grammar* see INDIRECT SPEECH

report stage ▻ *noun* in the UK: the point when a parliamentary bill, which has been amended in committee, is reported to the House before the third reading.

repose¹ /rɪˈpoʊz/ ▻ *noun* **1** a state of rest, calm or peacefulness. **2** composure. ▻ *verb* (***reposed***, ***reposing***) **1** *intr* to rest. **2** to lay (oneself, one's head, etc) down to rest. **3** *intr, formal* to lie dead. **4** (*usually* **repose on something**) *formal* to be based on it. ● **reposed** *adj.* ● **reposedly** /rɪˈpoʊzɪdlɪ/ *adverb.* ● **reposedness** /rɪˈpoʊzɪdnəs/ *noun.* ● **reposeful** *adj.* ● **reposefully** *adverb.* ⓒ 15c: from French *reposer*, from Latin *repausare* to stop.

repose² /rɪˈpoʊz/ ▻ *verb* (***reposed***, ***reposing***) **1** to place (confidence, trust, etc) in a someone or something. **2** to place (an object) somewhere. ⓒ 15c: from Latin *reponere*, *repositum* to replace, restore, store up.

repository /rɪˈpɒzɪtərɪ/ ▻ *noun* (***repositories***) **1** a place or container where things may be stored. **2 a** a place where things are stored for exhibition; **b** a museum. **3** a warehouse. **4** someone or something thought of as a store of information, knowledge, etc. **5** a trusted person to whom one can confide secrets. **6** a tomb; a place of burial. ⓒ 15c: from Latin *repositorium*, from *reponere*, *repositum* to replace, to store up.

repossess ▻ *verb* said of a creditor: to regain possession of (property or goods), especially because the debtor has defaulted on payment. ● **repossession** *noun.* ● **repossessor** *noun.* ⓒ 15c.

repoussé /rəˈpuːseɪ/ ▻ *adj* said of metalwork: raised in relief by hammering from behind or within. ▻ *noun* a piece of metalwork made in this way. ● **repoussage** /-ˈsɑːʒ/ *noun.* ⓒ 19c: French.

repp see REP³

reprehend /rɛprɪˈhɛnd/ ▻ *verb* (***reprehended***, ***reprehending***) **1** to find fault with something. **2** to blame or reprove someone. ● **reprehensible** *adj* deserving blame or criticism. ● **reprehensibly** *adverb.* ● **reprehension** *noun.* ● **reprehensory** *adj.* ⓒ 14c: from Latin *reprehendere.*

represent /rɛprɪˈzɛnt/ ▻ *verb* (***represented***, ***representing***) **1 a** to serve as a symbol or sign for something □ *letters represent sounds*; **b** to stand for something or correspond to it □ *A thesis represents years of hard work.* **2** to speak or act on behalf of (someone else). **3 a** to be a good example of something; **b** to typify something □ *What he said represents the feelings of many people.* **4** to present an image of or portray someone or something, especially through painting or sculpture. **5** to bring someone or something clearly to mind □ *a film that represents all the horrors of war.* **6** to describe in a specified way; to attribute a specified character or quality to (someone, something, oneself, etc) □ *represented themselves as experts.* **7** to show, state or explain □ *represent the difficulties forcibly to the committee.* **8** to be an elected member of Parliament for (a constituency). **9** to act out or play the part of someone or something on stage. ● **representable** *adj.* ● **representability** *noun.* ⓒ 14c: from Latin *repraesentare* to exhibit, from *praesentare* to present.

re-present ▻ *verb* to present something again □ *Re-present the report on Monday when you've worked on it some more.* ⓒ 16c.

representation ▻ *noun* **1** the act or process of representing, or the state or fact of being represented. **2** a person or thing that represents someone or something else. **3 a** an image; **b** a picture or painting. **4** a dramatic performance. **5** a body of representatives. **6** (*often* **representations**) a strong statement made to present facts, opinions, complaints or demands. ● **representational** *adj* said especially of art: depicting objects in a realistic rather than an abstract form. ● **representationalism** or **representationism** *noun* **1** representational art. **2** *philos* the doctrine that, in the perception of the external world, the immediate object represents another object beyond the sphere of consciousness. ● **representationist** *noun.*

representative ▻ *adj* **1** representing. **2 a** standing as a good example of something; **b** typical. **3** standing or acting as a deputy for someone. **4** said of government: comprising elected people. ▻ *noun* **1** someone who represents someone or something else, especially someone who represents, or sells the goods of, a business or company; **b** someone who acts as someone's agent or who speaks on their behalf. **2** someone who represents a constituency in Parliament. **3** a typical example. ● **representatively** *adverb.* ● **representativeness** *noun.*

repress /rɪˈprɛs/ ▻ *verb* **1 a** to keep (an impulse, a desire to do something, etc) under control; **b** to restrain (an impulse, desire, etc). **2** to put down, especially using force □ *repress the insurrection.* **3** *psychol* to exclude (unacceptable thoughts, feelings, etc) from one's conscious mind. Compare SUPPRESS. ● **represser** or **repressor** *noun.* ● **repressible** *adj.* ● **repressibly** *adverb.* ● **repression** *noun* **1** the action or process of repressing. **2** *psychol* the defence mechanism whereby an unpleasant or unacceptable thought, memory or wish is deliberately excluded from the conscious mind. ● **repressive** *adj.* ● **repressively** *adverb.* ● **repressiveness** *noun.* ⓒ 14c: from Latin *reprimere*, *repressum* to press back.

re-press /ˈriːprɛs/ ▻ *verb* to press something again □ *re-pressed his trousers.*

repressed ▻ *adj* **1 a** controlled; **b** restrained. **2** *psychol* **a** tending to exclude unacceptable thoughts, feelings, etc from the conscious mind; **b** said of a thought, etc: excluded from the conscious mind.

reprieve /rɪ'priːv/ ▻ *verb* (***reprieved, reprieving***) **1** to delay or cancel (someone's punishment, especially the execution of a prisoner condemned to death). **2** to give temporary relief or respite from (trouble, difficulty, pain, etc). ▻ *noun* **1 a** the act of delaying or cancelling criminal sentence, especially a death sentence; **b** a warrant granting such a delay or cancellation. **2** temporary relief or respite from trouble, difficulty, pain, etc. ◷ 16c: from French *repris* taken back, from *reprendre* to take back; also from obsolete English *repreven* to reprove, in literal sense 'to test again'.

reprimand /'rɛprɪmɑːnd/ ▻ *verb* (***reprimanded, reprimanding***) to criticize or rebuke someone angrily or severely, especially publicly or formally. ▻ *noun* angry or severe and usually formal criticism or rebuke. ◷ 17c: from French *réprimande*, from Latin *reprimere* to press back, from *premere* to press.

reprint ▻ *verb* /riː'prɪnt/ **1** to print something again. **2** to print more copies of (a book, etc). **3** *intr* said of a book, etc: to have more copies printed. ▻ *noun* /'riːprɪnt/ **1** the act of reprinting. **2** a copy of a book or any already printed material made by reprinting the original without any changes. **3** the total number of copies made of a book which is reprinted □ ***a reprint of 3 000***. ● **reprinter** *noun*. ◷ 16c.

reprisal /rɪ'praɪzəl/ ▻ *noun* **1** revenge or retaliation. Also *as adj* □ ***a reprisal attack***. **2** (*often* **reprisals**) in war: revenge or retaliation against an enemy. **3** *historical* the usually forcible seizing of another country's property or people in retaliation. ◷ 15c: from French *reprisaille*, from Latin *reprehendere*, from *prehendere* to seize.

reprise /rɪ'priːz/ *music* ▻ *noun* the repeating of a passage or theme. ▻ *verb* (***reprised, reprising***) to repeat (an earlier passage or theme). ◷ 14c: from French *reprise* a taking back, from *reprendre* to take back.

reprivatize or **reprivatise** /riː'praɪvətaɪz/ ▻ *verb* (***reprivatized, reprivatizing***) to return (a company, etc) from public to private ownership. ● **reprivatization** *noun*. ◷ 1950s.

repro /'riːprəʊ/ *colloq* ▻ *noun* (***repros***) short form of REPRODUCTION 2. ▻ *adj* short form of REPRODUCTION.

reproach /rɪ'proutʃ/ ▻ *verb* (***reproaches, reproached, reproaching***) **a** to express disapproval of, or disappointment with, someone for a fault or some wrong done; **b** to blame someone. ▻ *noun* **1** an act of reproaching. **2** (*often* **reproaches**) a rebuke or expression of disappointment. **3** a cause of disgrace or shame. ● **reproachable** *adj*. ● **reproacher** *noun*. ● **reproachful** *adj*. ● **reproachfully** *adverb*. ● **reproachfulness** *noun*. ● **above** or **beyond reproach** too good to be criticized; perfect. ◷ 15c: from French *reprochier*, from Latin *prope* near.

reprobate /'rɛprəbeɪt/ ▻ *noun* **1** an immoral unprincipled person. **2** *Christianity* someone rejected by God. ▻ *adj* **1** immoral and unprincipled. **2** rejected or condemned. ▻ *verb* (***reprobated, reprobating***) **1 a** to disapprove of someone; **b** to censure something. **2** said of God: to reject or condemn (a person). ● **reprobacy** /'rɛprəbəsɪ/ *noun*. ● **reprobation** *noun*. ◷ 16c: from Latin *reprobatus* disapproved of, from *probare* to approve.

reprocess ▻ *verb* to process something again, especially to make (something already used, eg spent nuclear fuel) into a new reuseable form. ● **reprocessing** *noun, adj*. ◷ 1930s.

reproduce /riːprə'djuːs/ ▻ *verb* **1** to make or produce something again. **2 a** to make or produce a copy or imitation of something; **b** to duplicate it. **3** *tr & intr, biol* to produce (offspring) either sexually or asexually, so perpetuating a species. **4** *intr* **a** to be suitable for copying in some way; **b** to turn out (well, badly, etc) when copied. **5** to reconstruct something in imagination. ● **reproducer** *noun*. ● **reproducible** *adj*. ● **reproductive** /-'dʌktɪv/ *adj*. ● **reproductively** *adverb*. ● **reproductiveness** or **reproductivity** *noun*. ◷ 17c.

reproduction /riːprə'dʌkʃən/ *noun* **1** the act of reproducing. **2 a** a copy or imitation, especially of a work of art; **b** a facsimile. **3** *biol* **a** the act or process of reproducing offspring; **b** regeneration. ▻ *adj* said of furniture, etc: made in imitation of an earlier style. See also REPRO.

reproduction proof ▻ *noun, printing* a high-quality proof made from strips of typeset copy and photographed to produce a plate for printing from.

reprography /rɪ'prɒgrəfɪ/ ▻ *noun* the reproduction of graphic or typeset material, eg by photocopying, etc. ● **reprographer** *noun*. ● **reprographic** /rɛprə'grafɪk/ *adj*. ● **reprographically** *adverb*. ◷ 1960s: from German *Reprographie*, from *Reproduktion* reproduction + Photo*graphie* photography.

reproof¹ /rɪ'pruːf/ ▻ *noun* **1** an act of reproving. **2 a** a rebuke; **b** censure or blame. ◷ 14c: from French *reprove*, from *reprover* to reprove.

reproof² ▻ *verb* /riː'pruːf/ **1** to make (a coat, etc) waterproof again. **2** to make a new proof of (a book, printed material, etc). ▻ *noun* /'riːpruːf/ a second or new proof. ◷ 20c.

repro proof ▻ *noun* short form of REPRODUCTION PROOF.

reprove /rɪ'pruːv/ ▻ *verb* **1** to rebuke. **2** to blame or condemn someone for a fault, some wrong done, etc. ● **reprovable** *adj*. ● **reprover** *noun*. ● **reproving** *adj* **1** disapproving. **2** condemnatory. ● **reprovingly** *adverb*. ◷ 14c: from French *reprover*, from Latin *reprobare* to disapprove of.

rept ▻ *abbreviation* **1** receipt. **2** report.

reptant /'rɛptənt/ ▻ *adj, biol* creeping. ◷ 17c: from Latin *reptare* to creep.

reptile /'rɛptaɪl/ ▻ *noun* **1** *zool* any cold-blooded scaly vertebrate animal, eg lizards, snakes, tortoises, turtles, crocodiles, alligators, and many extinct species, including dinosaurs and pterodactyls. **2** a mean or despicable person. ▻ *adj* **1** creeping. **2** like a reptile. ● **reptilian** /rɛp'tɪlɪən/ *adj*. ● **reptiliferous** /rɛptɪ'lɪfərəs/ *adj, geol* said of rock: bearing fossil reptiles. ◷ 14c: from Latin *reptilis*, from *repere* to creep or crawl.

republic /rɪ'pʌblɪk/ ▻ *noun* **1** a form of government without a monarch and in which supreme power is held by the people or their elected representatives, especially one in which the head of state is an elected or nominated president. **2** a state or a governmental unit within a state that forms part of a nation or federation, eg in the individual republics making up the Russian Federation. ◷ 16c: from French *république*, from Latin *respublica*, from *res* concern or affair + *publicus* public.

republican /rɪ'pʌblɪkən/ ▻ *adj* **1** relating to or like a republic. **2** in favour of or supporting a republic as a form of government. **3** (**Republican**) *US* relating to the Republican Party. ▻ *noun* **1** someone who favours the republic as a form of government. **2** (**Republican**) *US* a member or supporter of the Republican Party. Compare DEMOCRAT. **3** (**Republican**) in N Ireland: someone who advocates the union of N Ireland and Eire. Compare LOYALIST. ● **republicanism** *noun* **1** the principles and theory of the republic as a form of government. **2 a** support for republican government; **b** a particular example of such support. ◷ 17c: from REPUBLIC.

repudiate /rɪ'pjuːdɪeɪt/ ▻ *verb* (***repudiated, repudiating***) **1** to deny or reject something as unfounded □ ***repudiate the suggestion***. **2** to refuse to recognize or have anything to do with (a person); to disown. **3** to refuse or cease to acknowledge (a debt, obligation, authority, etc). ● **repudiable** *adj*. ● **repudiation** *noun*. ● **repudiative** *adj*. ● **repudiator** *noun*. ◷ 16c: from Latin *repudiare, repudiatum* to put away, from *repudium* divorce.

> ***repudiate***
>
> See Usage Note at **refute**.

repugnant /rɪ'pʌgnənt/ ▷ *adj* **1** distasteful; disgusting. **2** (*usually* **repugnant with something**) said of things: inconsistent or incompatible with something else. • **repugnance** *noun*. • **repugnantly** *adverb*. ◷ 14c: from Latin *repugnare*, from *pugnare* to fight.

repulse /rɪ'pʌls/ ▷ *verb* (***repulsed***, ***repulsing***) **1** to drive or force back (an enemy, attacking force, etc). **2** to reject (someone's offer of help, kindness, etc) with coldness and discourtesy; to rebuff. **3** to bring on a feeling of disgust, horror or loathing in someone. ▷ *noun* **1** the act of repulsing or state of being repulsed. **2** a cold discourteous rejection; a rebuff. • **repulsion** *noun* **1** an act or the process of forcing back or of being forced back. **2** a feeling of disgust, horror or loathing. **3** *physics* a force that tends to push two objects further apart, such as that between like electric charges or like magnetic poles. Opposite of ATTRACTION. • **repulsive** *adj* **1** tending to repulse or drive off. **2** cold or reserved. **3** provoking a feeling of disgust, horror or loathing. **4** *physics* relating to, causing or being a repulsion. • **repulsively** *adverb*. • **repulsiveness** *noun*. ◷ 16c: from Latin *repellere, repulsum* to drive back.

repute /rɪ'pjuːt/ ▷ *verb* (***reputed***, ***reputing***) to consider someone or something to be as specified or to have some specified quality; to deem □ *She is reputed to be a fine tennis player*. ▷ *noun* **1** general opinion or impression. **2** reputation. • **reputable** /'rɛpjʊtəbəl/ *adj* **1 a** respectable; **b** well thought of. **2** trustworthy. • **reputably** *adverb*. • **reputation** /rɛpjʊ'teɪʃən/ *noun* **1** a generally held opinion about someone's abilities, moral character, etc. **2** fame or notoriety, especially as a result of a particular characteristic. **3 a** a high opinion generally held about someone or something; **b** good name. • **reputed** *adj* **1** supposed. **2** generally considered to be. • **reputedly** *adverb*. ◷ 15c: from French *réputer*.

request /rɪ'kwɛst/ ▷ *noun* **1** the act or an instance of asking for something. **2** something asked for. **3** (*usually* **in request**) the state of being asked for or sought after. **4 a** a letter, etc sent to a radio station, etc asking for a specified record to be played; **b** the record played in response to this. ▷ *verb* (***requested***, ***requesting***) to ask for something, especially politely or as a favour. • **requester** *noun*. • **on request** if or when requested. ◷ 14c: from French *requerre*, from Latin *requirere* to seek for.

request stop ▷ *noun* a bus stop that a bus will only stop at if asked to do so by a passenger on the bus, who rings the bell, or by someone waiting at the stop, who signals with their hand.

requiem /'rɛkwɪɛm, -əm/ ▷ *noun* **1** (*also* **Requiem**) *RC Church, music* **a** a mass for the souls of the dead; **b** a piece of music written to accompany this service. **2** *music* any piece of music composed or performed to commemorate the dead. ◷ 14c: from Latin *requiem* rest, the first word of the Latin version of the mass for the dead.

requiescat /rɛkwɪ'ɛskat/ ▷ *noun*, *Christianity* a prayer for the rest of the soul of the dead. ◷ 19c: Latin, from *requiescat in pace* may he or she rest in peace; see RIP.

require /rɪ'kwaɪə(r)/ ▷ *verb* (***required***, ***requiring***) **1 a** to need something; **b** to wish to have something. **2** to demand, exact or command by authority. **3** to have as a necessary or essential condition for success, fulfilment, etc. • **requirement** *noun* **1 a** a need; **b** something that is needed. **2** something that is asked for, essential, ordered, etc. **3** a necessary condition. • **requirer** *noun*. • **requiring** *noun*. ◷ 14c: from Latin *requirere* to seek for, from *quaerere* to seek or search for.

requisite /'rɛkwɪzɪt/ ▷ *adj* **1** required or necessary. **2** indispensable. ▷ *noun* something that is required, necessary or indispensable for some purpose □ *toilet requisites*. • **requisitely** *adverb*. • **requisiteness** *noun*. ◷ 15c: from Latin *requirere*, *requisitum* to search for something.

requisition /rɛkwɪ'zɪʃən/ ▷ *noun* **1 a** a formal and authoritative demand or request, usually written, especially for supplies or the use of something, and especially made by the army; **b** an official form on which such a demand or request is made. **2** the act of formally demanding, requesting or taking something. **3** the state of being in use or service. ▷ *verb* (***requisitioned***, ***requisitioning***) to demand, take or order (supplies, the use of something, etc) by official requisition. • **requisitionary** *adj*. • **requisitionist** *noun*. ◷ 14c: from Latin *requisitio* a searching for.

requite /rɪ'kwaɪt/ ▷ *verb* (***requited***, ***requiting***) *formal* **1** to make a suitable return in response to (someone's kindness or injury). **2** to repay someone for some act. **3** (*often* **requite one thing for** or **with another**) to repay (eg good with good or evil with evil). • **requitable** *adj*. • **requital** *noun* **1** the act of requiting. **2** recompense; reward. • **requiter** *noun*. ◷ 16c: from *quite* to pay.

reredos /'rɪədɒs/ ▷ *noun* a stone or wooden screen or partition wall, usually an ornamental one, behind an altar. ◷ 14c: from French *areredos*, from *arere* behind + *dos* back.

reroute /riː'ruːt/ ▷ *verb* to direct (traffic, aircraft, etc) along an alternative route, usually because the usual route cannot be used because of an accident, heavy traffic, bad weather, etc; to redirect. ◷ 1920s.

rerun ▷ *verb* /riː'rʌn/ **1** to run (a race, etc) again because a result could not be determined from the first run. **2** to broadcast (TV or radio programme or series) for a second or further time. ▷ *noun* /'riːrʌn/ **1** a race that is run again. **2** a TV or radio programme or series which is broadcast for a second or further time. **3** *computing* a repeat of part of a computer program. ◷ 19c.

res. ▷ *abbreviation* **1** research. **2** reserve. **3** residence. **4** resolution.

resale /'riːseɪl, riː'seɪl/ ▷ *noun* the selling of an article again. ◷ 17c.

resale price maintenance ▷ *noun*, *commerce* (abbreviation **RPM**) a system, now illegal in the UK, used by manufacturers acting together to prevent price-cutting by retailers, whereby they set a fixed or minimum price on their articles or products.

reschedule ▷ *verb* **1 a** to schedule again; **b** to arrange a new time or timetable for (a meeting, planned event, etc). **2** *econ* to rearrange (a country's debt repayment programme), usually to alleviate liquidity problems. ◷ 1960s.

rescind /rɪ'sɪnd/ ▷ *verb* (***rescinded***, ***rescinding***) to cancel, annul or revoke (an order, law, custom, etc). • **rescindment** or **rescission** *noun*. ◷ 16c: from Latin *rescindere*, *rescissum* to cut off.

rescore ▷ *verb music* to rewrite (a musical score) for different instruments, voices, etc.

rescript ▷ *noun* /'riːskrɪpt/ **1** the official answer from a pope to a question, petition, etc. **2** in ancient Rome: an emperor's written reply to a question, especially one on a point of law. **3** any official edict or decree. **4 a** the action of writing something again; **b** something that is written again; a copy. ◷ 16c: from Latin *rescribere*, *rescriptum*.

rescue /'rɛskjuː/ ▷ *verb* (***rescued***, ***rescuing***) **1** to free someone or something from danger, evil, trouble, captivity, etc; to save. **2** *law* **a** to free someone from legal custody by force; **b** to recover (goods) by force. ▷ *noun* **1** the act or an instance of rescuing or being rescued. **2** *law* **a** the freeing of someone from legal custody by force; **b** the recovery of goods by force. • **rescuer** *noun*. ◷ 14c: from French *rescourre*, to shake out or remove, ultimately from Latin *quatere* to shake.

research /rɪ'sɜːtʃ, 'riːsɜːtʃ/ ▷ *noun* (abbreviation **res.**) detailed and careful investigation into some subject or area of study with the aim of discovering and applying new facts or information. ▷ *verb tr & intr* (*often* **research into something**) to carry out such an investigation.

• **researcher** *noun*. ⌚ 16c: from French *recercher*, from *cercher* to seek.

research and development ▷ *noun* (abbreviation **R&D**) work in a company that concentrates on finding new or improved processes, products, etc and also on the optimum ways of introducing such innovations.

reseat /riː'siːt/ ▷ *verb* **1** to seat someone in a different chair or place. **2** to return someone to a former position or office. **3** to put a new seat on (a chair, etc). **4** to provide (a theatre, etc) with new seats. ⌚ 17c.

resect /rɪ'sɛkt/ ▷ *verb* (*resected*, *resecting*) **1** *surgery* to cut away or remove (part of a bone, organ, etc). **2** *surveying* to locate a (position or point) by resection. • **resection** *noun* **1** *surgery* the cutting away or removal of part of a bone, organ, etc. **2** *surveying* a method of fixing the position of a point by sighting it from three or more already known points. ⌚ 19c: from Latin *resecare*, *resectum* to cut off or away.

resemble /rɪ'zɛmbəl/ ▷ *verb* (*resembled*, *resembling*) to be like or similar to someone or something else, especially in appearance. • **resemblance** *noun* **1 a** likeness or similarity; **b** the degree of likeness or similarity between two people or things. **2** appearance. ⌚ 14c: from French *resembler*, ultimately from Latin *similis* like.

resent /rɪ'zɛnt/ ▷ *verb* (*resented*, *resenting*) **1** to take or consider something as an insult or an affront. **2** to feel anger, bitterness or ill-will towards someone or something. • **resentful** *adj*. • **resentfully** *adverb*. • **resentment** *noun*. ⌚ 16c: from French *ressentir* to be angry, from Latin *sentire* to feel.

reserpine /rɪ'zɜːpɪn, -piːn/ ▷ *noun* a drug obtained from various RAUWOLFIA plants, used to treat high blood pressure and as a tranquillizer. ⌚ 1950s.

reservation /rɛzə'veɪʃən/ ▷ *noun* **1** the act of reserving something for future use. **2 a** the act of booking or ordering in advance, eg a hotel room, a table in a restaurant, etc; **b** something, eg a hotel room, a table in a restaurant, etc, that has been reserved or booked in advance. **3** (*often* **reservations**) a doubt or objection which prevents one being able to accept or approve something, eg a plan, proposition, etc, wholeheartedly □ *She had reservations about the idea*. **4** a limiting condition, proviso or exception to an agreement, etc. **5** an area of land set aside for a particular purpose, especially one in the US and Canada for Native Americans. **6** *Brit* a CENTRAL RESERVATION. **7** in some Christian churches: the practice of keeping back part of the consecrated bread and wine for some particular purpose after the service, eg for taking to the sick. **8** *RC Church* **a** the right of the pope to nominate someone to a vacant benefice; **b** an act of exercising this right. **9** *law* **a** a clause of a deed by which someone reserves for themselves a right or interest in a property they are conveying, renting, etc to someone else; **b** the act of reserving this right or interest. ⌚ 14c: French.

reserve /rɪ'zɜːv/ (abbreviation **res**) *verb* (*reserved*, *reserving*) **1** to keep something back or set it aside for future use, for the use of a particular person, or for some particular purpose. **2** to keep or retain something for oneself. **3** to book or order (eg a hotel room, a table in a restaurant, etc) in advance. **4** (*especially* **reserve judgement**) to delay or postpone (a legal judgement, taking a decision, etc). ▷ *noun* **1** something kept back or set aside, epecially for future use or possible need. **2** the state or condition of being reserved or an act of reserving. **3 a** an area of land set aside for a particular purpose, especially for the protection of wildlife □ *a nature reserve*; **b** an area of land set aside for occupation by a particular people; a reservation. **4** *Austral, NZ* a public park. **5** coolness, distance or restraint of manner; diffidence or reticence. **6** *sport* **a** an extra player or participant who can take another's place if needed; a substitute; **b** (*usually* **the reserves**) the second or reserve team □ *playing for the reserves*. **7** (*also* **reserves**) *military* **a** part of an army or force kept out of immediate action to provide reinforcements when needed; **b** forces in addition to a nation's regular armed services, not usually in service but that may be called upon if necessary; **c** a member of such a force; a reservist. **8** (*often* **reserves**) *finance* a company's money or assets, or a country's gold and foreign currency, held at a bank to meet future liabilities. **9** (*usually* **reserves**) a supply of eg oil, gas, coal, etc, known to be present in a particular region and as yet unexploited. **10** (*usually* **reserves**) extra physical or mental power, energies, stamina, etc that can be drawn upon in a difficult or extreme situation □ *reserves of strength*. **11** a RESERVE PRICE. **12** in a competition, show, etc: **a** a distinction awarded to an exhibit, etc, which shows that it will be given a prize if another is disqualified; **b** the exhibit, etc that receives this distinction. Also *as adj* □ *a reserve supply*. • **without reserve** fully, or without reservations or restrictions; frankly. ⌚ 14c: from French *réserver*, from Latin *reservare* to keep something back.

re-serve /riː'sɜːv/ ▷ *verb* to serve again. ⌚ 19c.

reserve bank ▷ *noun* **1** one of the twelve US Federal Reserve banks. **2** *especially Austral & NZ* a central bank that holds currency reserves for other banks.

reserve currency ▷ *noun* a foreign currency acceptable in international transactions and held in reserve (see RESERVE *noun* 8) by central banks.

reserved /rɪ'zɜːvd/ ▷ *adj* **1** kept back, set aside or destined for a particular use or for a particular person. **2** said of a hotel room, a table in a restaurant, etc: booked or ordered in advance. **3** said of a person or their manner: cool, distant or restrained; diffident or reticent. • **reservedly** /rɪ'zɜːvɪdlɪ/ *adverb*. • **reservedness** *noun*. ⌚ 16c: from RESERVE.

reserved list ▷ *noun* a list of retired officers in the armed services who may be recalled for active service in the event of war.

reserved occupation ▷ *noun* a job of national importance that exempts one from being called up for service in time of war.

reserve price ▷ *noun* the lowest price that the owner of something which is being sold by auction is prepared to accept. Also called **floor price**.

reservist /rɪ'zɜːvɪst/ ▷ *noun, military* a member of a reserve force.

reservoir /'rɛzəvwɑː(r)/ ▷ *noun* **1** a large natural or man-made lake, or a tank, in which water is collected and stored for public use, irrigation, etc. **2** a part of a machine, device, etc where liquid is stored. **3** *biol* part of an animal or plant in which fluid is retained. **4** a large reserve or supply of something, eg of creativity, talent, etc. **5** a place where a large supply of something, now especially of fluid or vapour, is collected and stored. ⌚ 17c: from French *réservoir*, from *réserver* to RESERVE.

reservoir rock ▷ *noun, geol* porous rock that can hold a reservoir of oil or gas.

reset[1] ▷ *verb* /riː'sɛt/ **1** to set (eg a broken limb, the type of a book, a stone in a piece of jewellery, etc) again or differently. **2** to reposition (a counter, guage, etc) at zero. ▷ *noun* /'riːsɛt/ **1** the action of setting something again or differently. **2** something that is reset. ⌚ 17c.

reset[2] /riːsɛt/ *Scots law* ▷ *verb* to knowingly receive, handle or dispose of stolen goods. ▷ *noun* the act or an instance of doing this □ *was charged with reset*. • **resetter** *noun*. ⌚ 18c.

reshuffle ▷ *verb* /riː'ʃʌfəl/ **1** to shuffle (cards) again or differently. **2** to reorganize or redistribute (especially government posts). ▷ *noun* /'riːʃʌfəl/ an act of reshuffling □ *a cabinet reshuffle*. ⌚ 19c.

reside /rɪ'zaɪd/ ▷ *verb* (*resided*, *residing*) *intr* **1** (**reside in**, **at**, *etc usually* **somewhere**) *formal* to live or have one's home there, especially permanently. **2** (*usually* **reside in someone** or **something**) said of power, authority, particular quality, etc: to be present in or attributable to them or it. • **resider** *noun*. ⓘ 15c: from Latin *residere* to sit back, from *sedere* to sit.

residence /ˈrɛzɪdəns/ ▷ *noun* **1** *formal* a house or dwelling, especially a large, impressive and imposing one. **2 a** the act or an instance of living in a particular place; **b** the period of time someone lives there. • **in residence 1** living in a particular place, especially officially. **2** said especially of a creative writer, artist: working in a particular place for a certain period of time □ ***The university has an artist in residence.*** ⓘ 14c: French.

residency /ˈrɛzɪdənsɪ/ ▷ *noun* (***residencies***) **1** a residence. **2** a band's or singer's regular or permanent engagement at a particular venue. **3** *formerly* in India: a residence, especially the official dwelling of a governor in a colony, etc. **4** *N Amer* **a** the period, after internship, of advanced, specialized medical training for doctors in hospitals; **b** the post held during this period. ⓘ 16c.

resident /ˈrɛzɪdənt/ ▷ *noun* **1** someone who lives permanently in a particular place. **2** a registered guest staying, usually at least for a few days, in a hotel. **3** a bird or animal that is found permanently in a particular region or country and does not migrate. **4** *formerly* **a** a representative of a governor in a protected state; **b** a representative of the British governor general at the court of an Indian state. **5** *medicine* **a** a doctor who works at and usually lives in a hospital; **b** *N Amer* a doctor undergoing advanced or specialized training in a hospital. ▷ *adj* **1** living or dwelling in a particular place, especially permanently or for some length of time. **2** living or required to live in the place where one works. **3** said of birds and animals: not migrating. **4** said of qualities, etc: inherent. **5** *computing* said of files, programs, etc: placed permanently in the memory. • **residentship** *noun*. ⓘ 14c: from Latin *residere* to RESIDE.

residential /rɛzɪˈdɛnʃəl/ ▷ *adj* **1** said of a street, an area of a town, etc: containing private houses rather than factories, businesses, etc. **2** requiring residence in the same place as one works or studies □ ***a residential course.*** **3** used as a residence □ ***a residential home for the elderly.*** **4** relating to or connected with residence or residences. • **residentially** *adverb*. ⓘ 17c.

residentiary /rɛzɪˈdɛnʃərɪ/ ▷ *adj* **1** resident, especially officially, in a particular place. **2** relating to or involving official residence. ▷ *noun* (***residentiaries***) a person, especially a clergyman, who is obliged to reside in a particular place to carry out their duties. ⓘ 16c.

resider see under RESIDE

residual /rɪˈzɪdjʊəl/ ▷ *adj* **1** relating to a residue. **2** remaining; left over; unaccounted for. ▷ *noun* **1** something which remains or is left over as a residue. **2** *statistics* the difference between an observed or measured value of a quantity and its theoretical value. **3** (*often* **residuals**) a royalty paid to an actor or performer for a subsequent showing, playing, etc of a film, commercial, etc in which they have appeared. **4** *math* the remainder resulting from subtraction. • **residually** *adverb*. ⓘ 16c: from *residue*.

residue /ˈrɛzɪdjuː/ ▷ *noun* **1** what remains of something, or is left over, when a part has been taken away, used up, etc; the remainder. **2** *law* what is left of the estate of someone who has died, after all of the debts and legacies have been paid. **3** *chem* a substance which remains after evaporation, combustion or distillation. • **residuary** /rɪˈzɪdjʊərɪ/ *adj* **1** relating to or constituting a residue. **2** *law* relating or pertaining to the residue of an estate. ⓘ 14c: from French *résidu*, from Latin *residuus* remaining.

residuum /rɪˈzɪdjʊəm/ ▷ *noun* (***residua*** /-djʊə/) *formal* a residue. ⓘ 17c.

resign /rɪˈzaɪn/ ▷ *verb* (***resigned, resigning***) **1** *intr* (*often* **resign from a job, post**, *etc*) to give up employment or an official position, etc. **2** to give up or relinquish (a right, claim, etc). **3** (*usually* **resign oneself to something**) to come to accept it with patience, tolerance, etc, especially when it is unpleasant or unwelcome; to submit to it. • **resignation** /rɛzɪgˈneɪʃən/ *noun* **1** the act of resigning from a job, official position, etc. **2** a formal letter or notice of intention to resign from a job, post, etc. **3** the state or quality of having or showing patient and calm acceptance, especially of something unpleasant or something that is seen as inevitable. • **resigner** *noun*. ⓘ 14c: from French *résigner*, from Latin *resignare* to unseal or cancel.

re-sign /riːˈsaɪn/ ▷ *verb* (***re-signed, re-signing***) **1** to sign something again. **2** to sign (a contract) in order to engage or employ, eg someone for a further period of time. **3** *intr* said especially of footballers: to sign a contract with the same club for a further period of time. ⓘ 1930s in sense 3; 19c in senses 1 and 2.

resigned /rɪˈzaɪnd/ ▷ *adj* (*often* **resigned to something**) having or showing patient and calm acceptance of something, usually something unpleasant or unwelcome, that is considered inevitable. • **resignedly** /rɪˈzaɪnɪdlɪ/ *adverb*. • **resignedness** *noun*. ⓘ 17c.

resile /rɪˈzaɪl/ ▷ *verb* (***resiled, resiling***) *intr* **1** to draw back from a contract or agreement. **2** to draw back or withdraw from a particular course of action. **3** to recoil or draw back from something in aversion. **4** said of an object: to recover, or spring back to its original shape or position after being twisted, stretched, etc. ⓘ 16c: from Latin *resilere* to recoil or leap back.

resilient /rɪˈzɪlɪənt/ ▷ *adj* **1** said of a person: able to recover quickly from, or to deal readily with, illness, sudden, unexpected difficulties, hardship, etc. **2** said of an object, a material, etc: able to return quickly to its original shape or position after being bent, twisted, stretched, etc; elastic. • **resilience** or **resiliency** *noun*. • **resiliently** *adverb*. ⓘ 17c: from Latin *resilire* to recoil or leap back.

resin /ˈrɛzɪn/ ▷ *noun* **1** any of several substances (**natural resins**) obtained from the sap of various plants and trees, especially conifers, often aromatic and usually in the form of a brittle, translucent solid or a viscous liquid. Compare ROSIN. **2** *chem* a semisolid or solid complex amorphous mixture of organic compounds with no definite melting point and a tendency to crystallize. **3** *chem* any of several synthetic organic compounds (**synthetic resins**), mostly polymers, resembling natural resin and used in the production of plastics, paints, varnishes, textiles, etc. ▷ *verb* (***resined, resining***) **1** to treat something with resin. **2** to ROSIN. • **resinous** *adj*. • **resinously** *adverb*. ⓘ 14c: from French *resine*, from Latin *resina*, related to Greek *rhetine* resin from a pine.

resinate /ˈrɛzɪneɪt/ ▷ *verb* (***resinated, resinating***) to impregnate something with resin. ▷ *noun*, *chem* a salt of any of the acids occurring in natural resin. ⓘ 19c.

resinify /ˈrɛzɪnɪfaɪ/ ▷ *verb* (***resinifies, resinified, resinifying***) *tr & intr* to make into, or become, a resin or resinous. • **resinification** *noun*. ⓘ 19c.

resist /rɪˈzɪst/ ▷ *verb* (***resisted, resisting***) **1** *tr & intr* to oppose or fight against someone or something; to refuse to give in or comply to it. **2** to remain unchanged by, or withstand, something damaging □ ***a metal which resists corrosion.*** **3** to refuse to accept or comply with (an order, etc). **4** to refrain from something in spite of temptation or attraction □ ***He just can't resist chocolate.*** ▷ *noun* a protective coating of a resistant substance, especially one applied to parts of a fabric that are not to be dyed or printed, or a light-sensitive coating on a silicon wafer. Also *as adj*. • **resister** *noun*. • **resistibility** *noun*. • **resistible** *adj*. • **resistibly** *adverb*. ⓘ 14c: from Latin *resistere*, from *sistere* to stand firm.

resistance /rɪˈzɪstəns/ ▷ *noun* **1** the act or process of resisting. **2** the ability to, or degree to which, something damaging can be withstood, especially the body's natural ability to resist disease or infection □ *resistance is low during the winter months.* **3** *physics* in damped harmonic motion: the ratio of the frictional forces to the speed. **4** *elec* (symbol **R**) a measure of the extent to which a material or an electrical device opposes the flow of an electric current through it. See also OHM. **5** a measure of the extent to which a material opposes the flow of heat through it. Compare CONDUCTIVITY. **6** a RESISTOR. **7** (*usually* **the Resistance**) an underground organization fighting for the freedom of a country that has been occupied by an enemy force. • **resistant** *adj* able to resist, withstand or remain unaffected or undamaged by something. Often *in compounds* □ *water-resistant.* ▻ *noun* someone or something that resists. • **line of least resistance** the easiest, but not necessarily the best, course of action. ◷ 14c: from French *résistance.*

resistance thermometer ▻ *noun* a device for measuring high temperatures by means of the variation in the electrical resistance of a wire as the temperature changes.

resistivity /rɛzɪˈstɪvɪtɪ/ ▻ *noun, physics* (symbol ρ) the ability, measured in ohm metres, of a cubic metre of material to oppose the flow of an electric current. Formerly called **specific resistance.** ◷ 19c.

resistor /rɪˈzɪstə(r)/ ▻ *noun, elec* a device which introduces a known value of resistance to electrical flow into a circuit. ◷ Early 20c.

resit ▻ *verb* /riːˈsɪt/ *tr & intr* to take (an examination) again, usually having failed it before, or in order to improve one's grade. ▻ *noun* /ˈriːsɪt/ **1** the action of taking an examination again. **2** an examination that is taken again. ◷ 1950s.

resoluble /rɪˈzɒljʊbəl/ ▻ *adj* able to be resolved or analysed; resolvable. • **resolubility** *noun.* • **resolubleness** *noun.* ◷ 17c: from Latin *resolubilis,* from *resolvere* to resolve.

re-soluble /riːˈsɒljʊbəl/ ▻ *adj* able to be dissolved again. • **re-solubility** *noun.* • **re-solubleness** *noun.* ◷ 19c.

resolute /ˈrɛzəluːt, -ljuːt/ ▻ *adj* **1** said of a person or their attitude, etc: **a** with a fixed purpose or belief; **b** determined or steadfast in pursuing a particular purpose, course of action, etc. **2** said of an action, etc: characterized by determination or firmness □ *a resolute response.* • **resolutely** *adverb.* • **resoluteness** *noun.* ◷ 16c in these senses; 14c in earlier sense 'dissolved': from Latin *resolutus,* from *resolvere* to resolve.

resolution /rɛzəˈluːʃən, -ˈljuːʃən/ ▻ *noun* **1** the act or an instance of making a firm decision. **2** a firm decision. **3** determination or resoluteness. **4** the act or an instance of solving or finding the answer to (a problem, question, etc). **5** a formal decision, expression of opinion, etc by a group of people, eg at a public meeting. **6** the ability of a television screen, photographic film, etc to reproduce an image in very fine detail. **7** RESOLVING POWER. **8** *music* the passing of a chord from discord to concord. **9** the act of separating something (eg a chemical compound) into its constituent parts or elements. **10** *medicine* the disappearance or dispersal of a tumour or inflamation. **11** *prosody* substitution of two short syllables for a long one. • **resolutioner** *noun.* • **resolutionist** *noun.* ◷ 14c: from Latin *resolutus;* see RESOLUTE.

resolve /rɪˈzɒlv/ ▻ *verb* (***resolved, resolving***) **1** (*usually* **resolve on** or **to do something**) to decide firmly or to determine to do it. **2** to find an answer to (a problem, question, etc). **3** to take away or dispel (a doubt, difficulty, etc). **4** to bring (an argument, etc) to an end. **5** *tr & intr* to decide, or pass (a resolution), especially formally by vote. **6** said of a television screen, photographic film, etc: to produce an image of something in fine detail. **7** said of a microscope, telescope, etc: to distinguish clearly (eg objects which are very close together). **8** *tr & intr, music* said of a chord: to pass from discord into concord. **9** **a** to make something break up into separate or constituent parts or elements; **b** *intr* (*often* **resolve into**) to break up into constituent parts. **10** *medicine* to remove or disperse (a tumour or inflammation). ▻ *noun* **1** determination or firmness of purpose. **2** a firm decision; a resolution. • **resolvable** *adj.* • **resolvability** *noun.* • **resolver** *noun.* ◷ 14c: from Latin *solvere* to loosen, dissolve.

resolved /rɪˈzɒlvd/ ▻ *adj* said of a person: determined; firm in purpose. • **resolvedly** /rɪˈzɒlvɪdlɪ/ *adverb.* • **resolvedness** /rɪˈzɒlvɪdnɪs/ *noun.* ◷ 15c.

resolvent /rɪˈzɒlvənt/ ▻ *adj, chiefly medicine* able to bring about the resolution of a tumour or inflammation. ▻ *noun* a drug that resolves or reduces swelling or inflammation. ◷ 17c.

resolving power ▻ *noun* **1** *physics* the ability of a microscope, telescope, etc to distinguish between objects which are very close together. **2** *photog* the ability of an emulsion to produce fine detail in an image.

resonance /ˈrɛzənəns/ ▻ *noun* **1** the quality or state of being resonant. **2** sound produced by sympathetic vibration. **3** the ringing quality of the human voice when produced in such a way that the vibration of the vocal cords is accompanied by sympathetic vibration in the air spaces in the head, chest and throat. **4** *medicine* the sound heard in AUSCULTATION. **5** *physics* vibration that occurs when an object or system is made to oscillate at its natural frequency. **6** *chem* the movement of electrons from one atom of a molecule to another atom of the same molecule to form a stable structure called a **resonance hybrid.** **7** *physics* increased probability of a nuclear reaction when the energy of an incident particle or proton is around a certain value appropriate to the energy level of the compound nucleus. ◷ 15c: from Latin *resonantia* echo, from *resonare* to resound.

resonant /ˈrɛzənənt/ *adj* **1** said of sounds: echoing; continuing to sound; resounding. **2** producing echoing sounds □ *resonant walls.* **3** full of or intensified by a ringing quality □ *a resonant voice.* • **resonantly** *adverb.*

resonate /ˈrɛzəneɪt/ ▻ *verb* (***resonated, resonating***) *tr & intr* to resound or make something resound or echo. • **resonator** *noun* a resonating body or device, eg one for increasing sonority or analysing sound.

resorb /rɪˈsɔːb/ ▻ *verb* (***resorbed, resorbing***) **1** to absorb something again or absorb it back into itself. **2** *especially physiol* to absorb (material already absorbed into the tissue) back into the circulation; to reabsorb. • **resorbence** *noun.* • **resorbent** *adj.* ◷ 17c: from Latin *sorbere* to suck in.

resorcin /rɪˈzɔːsɪn/ or **resorcinol** /rɪˈzɔːsɪnɒl/ ▻ *noun, chem* (formula $\mathbf{C_6H_4(OH)_2}$) a white crystalline phenol used in dyeing, photography and pharmaceuticals, and also to make resins and adhesives. ◷ 19c: from *resin* + *orcin* a type of phenol.

resorption /rɪˈsɔːpʃən/ ▻ *noun* **1** the act of resorbing or state of being resorbed. **2** *geol* the remelting of a mineral by rock magma. **3** *medicine* the breaking down and assimilation of a substance into the body. • **resorptive** *adj.* ◷ 19c: from Latin *sorbere, sorptum* to suck in.

resort[1] /rɪˈzɔːt/ ▻ *verb* (***resorted, resorting***) *intr* (*usually* **resort to something or somewhere**) **1** to turn to it as a means of solving a problem, etc; to have recourse to it. **2** *formal* to go to (a place), especially habitually or in great numbers. ▻ *noun* **1** a place visited by many people, especially one, eg a seaside town, that provides accommodation and recreation for holidaymakers □ *a holiday resort* □ *the Spanish resorts.* **2** **a** the action of resorting or having recourse to someone or something for help; **b** the person or thing that is resorted to; someone or something looked to for help. • **resorter** *noun.* • **in the last resort** when all other means, methods, etc have failed. • **the last resort** the only remaining course of action or means of overcoming a difficulty, solving a problem, etc. ◷ 14c: from French *sortir* to go out.

resort² or **re-sort** /riːˈsɔːt/ ▻ *verb* to sort something again or differently. ⓒ 19c.

resound¹ /rɪˈzaʊnd/ ▻ *verb* **1** *intr* said of sounds: to ring or echo. **2** *intr* (**resound with** or **to something**) to be filled with (echoing or ringing sounds); to reverberate □ ***The hall resounded to their cheers.*** **3** *intr* to be widely known or celebrated □ ***Her fame resounded throughout the country.*** **4** said of a place: to make (a sound) echo or ring. **5** to repeat or spread (the praises of someone or something). • **resounding** *adj* **1** echoing and ringing; reverberating. **2** clear and decisive □ ***a resounding victory.*** • **resoundingly** *adverb*. ⓒ 14c: from Latin *resonare*.

resound² or **re-sound** /riːˈsaʊnd/ ▻ *verb, tr & intr* to sound or make something sound again. ⓒ 19c.

resource /rɪˈzɔːs, rɪˈsɔːs/ ▻ *noun* **1** someone or something that provides a source of help, support, etc when needed. **2** a means of solving difficulties, problems, etc. **3** skill at finding ways of solving difficulties, problems, etc; ingenuity. **4** anything that can be of use to people, either a NON-RENEWABLE RESOURCE or a RENEWABLE RESOURCE. **5** (*usually* **resources**) means of support, especially money or property. **6** (*usually* **resources**) the principal source of wealth or income of a country or institution □ ***natural resources.*** ▻ *verb* (***resourced, resourcing***) to provide support, usually financial, for someone or something. • **resourceful** *adj* skilled in finding ways of solving difficulties, problems, etc; ingenious. • **resourcefully** *adverb*. • **resourcefulness** *noun*. • **resourceless** *adj*. ⓒ 17c: from French *ressource*, ultimately from Latin *surgere* to rise.

respect /rɪˈspɛkt/ ▻ *noun* **1** admiration; good opinion □ ***be held in great respect.*** **2** the state of being honoured, admired or well thought of. **3** (**respect for something** or **someone**) consideration of or attention to them □ ***show no respect for his feelings.*** **4** (*often* **respects**) *formal* a polite greeting or expression of admiration, esteem and honour. **5** a particular detail, feature or characteristic □ ***In what respect are they different?*** **6** reference, relation or connection. ▻ *verb* (***respected, respecting***) **1** to show or feel admiration or high regard for someone or something □ ***He respected his grandfather.*** **2** to show consideration for, or thoughtfulness or attention to, something □ ***respect her wishes.*** **3** to heed or pay proper attention to (a rule, law, etc) □ ***respect the speed limit.*** • **respecter** *noun* **1** someone who respects. **2** someone or something that treats individuals unduly favourably □ ***The disease is no respecter of age or social class.*** • **in respect of** or **with respect to something** with reference to, or in connection with (a particular matter, point, etc). • **pay one's last respects to someone** to show respect for someone who has died by attending their funeral. • **pay one's respects to someone** *formal* to present oneself to them, or visit them as a mark of respect or out of politeness. • **with respect** or **with all due respect** a polite expression indicating disagreement and used before presenting one's own opinion. ⓒ 14c: from Latin *respicere, respectum* to look back at, pay attention to or consider.

respectable ▻ *adj* **1** worthy of or deserving respect. **2** having a reasonably good social standing; fairly well-to-do. **3** having a good reputation or character, especially as regards morals. **4** said of behaviour: correct; acceptable; conventional. **5** said of a person's appearance: presentable; decent. **6** fairly or relatively good or large □ ***a respectable turnout.*** • **respectability** *noun*. • **respectably** *adverb*. ⓒ 16c.

respectful ▻ *adj* having or showing respect. • **respectfully** *adverb*. • **respectfulness** *noun*.

respecting ▻ *prep* about; concerning; with regard to. ⓒ 18c.

respective ▻ *adj* belonging to or relating to each person or thing mentioned; particular; separate □ ***our respective homes.*** • **respectively** *adverb*. • **respectiveness** *noun*. ⓒ 16c.

respiration /rɛspɪˈreɪʃən/ ▻ *noun* **1** the act of respiring or breathing. **2** a single breath (inspiration and expiration). **3** (*also* **external respiration**) *physiol* a metabolic process in plants and animals whereby compounds are broken down to release energy, incorporated into ATP, commonly (but not exclusively) requiring oxygen, and with carbon dioxide as the end product. **4** (also **tissue respiration** or **internal respiration**) *biochem* a biochemical process that takes place in the cells of all living organisms, in all cases comprising firstly ANAEROBIC respiration and then, selectively, an energy-yielding stage requiring oxygen (AEROBIC respiration). ⓒ 15c: from Latin *respirare, respiratum* to breathe.

respirator /ˈrɛspɪreɪtə(r)/ ▻ *noun* **1** a mask worn over the mouth and nose to prevent poisonous gas, dust, etc being breathed in, or to warm cold air before it is breathed. **2** *medicine* apparatus used to help very ill or injured people breathe when they are unable to do so naturally.

respire /rɪˈspaɪə(r)/ ▻ *verb* (***respired, respiring***) **1** *tr & intr* to inhale and exhale (air, etc); to breathe. **2** *intr, biochem* to release energy as a result of the breakdown of organic compounds. • **respiratory** /ˈrɛspɪrətərɪ/ *adj*. ⓒ 14c: from Latin *respirare* to breathe.

respirometer /rɛspɪˈrɒmɪtə(r)/ ▻ *noun* a device for measuring breathing.

respite /ˈrɛspaɪt, ˈrɛspɪt/ ▻ *noun* **1** a period of rest or relief from, or a temporary stopping of, something unpleasant, difficult, etc. **2** a temporary delay. **3** *law* temporary suspension of the execution of a criminal; a reprieve. ▻ *verb* (***respited, respiting***) to grant a respite to someone; to reprieve. ⓒ 13c: from French *respit*, from Latin *respectare* to respect.

resplendent /rɪˈsplɛndənt/ ▻ *adj* brilliant or splendid in appearance. • **resplendence** or **resplendency** *noun*. • **resplendently** *adverb*. ⓒ 15c: from Latin *resplendere* to shine brightly.

respond /rɪˈspɒnd/ ▻ *verb* (***responded, responding***) **1** *tr & intr* to answer or reply; to say something in reply. **2** *intr* to react in reply to something □ ***I smiled at her, but she didn't respond.*** **3** *intr* (*usually* **respond to something**) to react favourably or well to it □ ***respond to treatment.*** **4** *intr, relig* to utter liturgical responses. ▻ *noun* **1** *relig* a response to a versicle in liturgy. **2** *archit* a half-pillar or half-pier attached to a wall to support an arch, especially one at the end of an arcade, etc. • **respondence** *noun*. • **respondency** *noun*. ⓒ 14c: from French *respondre*, from Latin *respondere* to return like for like.

respondent ▻ *noun* **1** someone who answers or makes replies. **2** *law* a defendant, especially in a divorce suit. **3** *psychol* a response to a specific stimulus. ▻ *adj* **1** answering; making a reply or response. **2** *psychol* responsive, especially to some specific stimulus.

response /rɪˈspɒns/ ▻ *noun* **1** an act of responding, replying or reacting to something. **2** a reply or answer. **3** a reaction □ ***met with little response.*** **4** (*usually* **responses**) *Christianity* an answer or reply, especially one in the form of a short verse which is either sung or spoken, made by the congregation or the choir to something said by the priest or minister during a service. **5** *electronics* the ratio of the output to the input level of a transmission system at any particular frequency. **6** *bridge* a bid made in reply to a partner's preceeding bid. • **responseless** *adj*. ⓒ 14c.

responsibility /rɪspɒnsɪˈbɪlɪtɪ/ *noun* (***responsibilities***) **1** the state of being responsible or of having important duties for which one is responsible. **2** something or someone for which one is responsible.

responsible /rɪˈspɒnsɪbəl/ ▻ *adj* **1** (*usually* **responsible for someone** or **something**) having charge or control over them or it and being accountable for them or it □ ***She was responsible for a class of 20 children*** □ ***He is responsible for ordering the stationery.*** **2**

(*usually* **responsible to someone**) accountable to them for one's actions □ ***responsible to her immediate superior.*** **3** said of a job, position, etc: with many important duties, such as taking important decisions; involving much responsibility. **4** (*often* **responsible for something**) being the cause of it □ ***Who was responsible for the accident?*** **5** said of a person: **a** able to be trusted; **b** able to answer for one's own conduct; capable of rational and socially acceptable behaviour □ ***She's an excellent babysitter and very responsible for her age.*** • **responsibleness** *noun*. • **responsibly** *adverb*. ⓒ 16c: French.

responsive /rɪ'spɒnsɪv/ ▻ *adj* **1** said of a person: ready and quick to react or respond. **2** reacting readily to stimulus. **3** reacting well or favourably to something □ ***a disease responsive to drugs.*** **4** made as or constituting a response □ ***a responsive smile.*** • **responsively** *adverb*. • **responsiveness** *noun*. ⓒ 14c: from Latin *responsivus*, from *respondere* to respond.

responsor /rɪ'spɒnsə(r)/ ▻ *noun, radar* a device that receives and processes the signals from a transponder. ⓒ 1940s.

responsory /rɪ'spɒnsərɪ/ ▻ *noun* (***responsories***) *relig* an anthem recited or sung after a lesson in a church service. ⓒ 15c: from Latin *responsorium*.

respray ▻ *verb* to spray (especially the bodywork of a vehicle) again, either with the same colour (especially part of the vehicle), or with a different colour of paint. ▻ *noun* /'riːspreɪ/ **1** the action of respraying. **2** the result of respraying. ⓒ 1930s.

rest¹ ▻ *noun* **1** a period of relaxation or freedom from work, activity, worry, etc. **2** sleep; repose. **3** calm; tranquillity. **4** a pause from some activity □ ***stopped half way up the hill for a rest.*** **5** death, when seen as repose. **6** a prop or support, eg for a billiard cue, etc. **7** often *in compounds* a place or thing which holds or supports something □ ***a headrest on a car seat.*** **8** a pause in reading, speaking, etc. **9** *music* **a** an interval of silence in a piece of music □ ***two bars' rest***; **b** a mark indicating the duration of this. **10** a place for resting, especially a lodging for sailors. ▻ *verb* (***rested, resting***) **1** *tr & intr* to stop or make something stop working or moving. **2** *intr* to relax, especially by sleeping or stopping some activity. **3** *tr & intr* to set, place or lie on or against something for support □ ***rested her arm on the chair.*** **4** *intr* to be calm and free from worry. **5** *tr & intr* to give or have as a basis or support □ ***will rest my argument on practicalities.*** **6** *tr & intr* to depend or make something depend or be based on or in. **7** *tr & intr* said of the eyes: to remain or make them remain looking in a certain direction, or at a certain person or thing. **8** *intr* to be left without further attention, discussion or action □ ***let the matter rest there.*** **9** *intr* to lie dead or buried. **10** *intr* said of farmland: to lie without a crop in order to regain its fertility. **11** *intr, colloq* said of an actor: to be unemployed. • **rester** *noun*. • **restful** *adj* **1** bringing or giving rest, or producing a sensation of calm, peace and rest. **2** relaxed; at rest. • **restfully** *adverb*. • **restfulness** *noun*. • **resting** *adj* **1** not moving, working, etc; at rest. **2** *colloq* said especially of an actor: not working; unemployed. • **restless** /'restlɪs/ *adj* **1** constantly moving about or fidgeting; unable to stay still or quiet. **2** constantly active or in motion; unceasing. **3** giving no rest; not restful □ ***a restless night.*** **4** worried, nervous and uneasy. • **restlessly** *adverb*. • **restlessness** *noun*. • **at rest 1** not moving or working; stationary. **2** free from trouble, worry, etc □ ***set his mind at rest.*** **3** asleep. **4** dead. • **lay someone to rest** to bury or inter them. • **rest one's case 1** *law* to conclude the calling of witnesses and presentation of arguments in a law case. **2** to bring one's argument to a close. ⓒ Anglo-Saxon *roest*.

rest² ▻ *noun* (*usually* **the rest**) **1** what is left when part of something is taken away, used, finished, etc; the remainder. **2** the others. ▻ *verb* (***rested, resting***) *intr* to continue to be; to remain □ ***rest assured.*** • **for the rest** concerning, or as regards, other matters. ⓒ 15c: from French *rester*, from Latin *restare* to remain, from *stare* to stand.

restaurant /'restərɒnt, -rənt, -rɒŋ, 'restrɒŋ/ ▻ *noun* an establishment where meals may be bought and eaten. • **restaurateur** /restərə'tɜː(r)/ *noun* the owner or manager of a restaurant. ⓒ 19c: French, from *restaurer* to restore.

restaurant car ▻ *noun* a carriage on a train in which meals are served to travellers. Also called **dining car**.

resting potential ▻ *noun, physiol* the difference in electrical potential across the membrane of a nerve cell that is not conducting an impulse. Compare ACTION POTENTIAL.

restitution /restɪ'tjuːʃən/ ▻ *noun* **1** the act of giving back to the rightful owner something lost or stolen. **2** the paying of compensation for loss or injury. **3** the return of an object or system to its original shape or position. • **restitutive** /rɪ'stɪtjʊtɪv, 'restɪtjuːtɪv/ *adj*. • **restitutor** /'restɪtjuːtə(r)/ *noun*. • **restitutory** /rɪ'stɪtjʊtərɪ/ *adj*. • **make restitution for something** to make amends for it, usually by paying some kind of compensation. ⓒ 13c: from Latin *restituere, restitutum* to restore or put up again, from *statuere* to set up.

restive /'restɪv/ ▻ *adj* **1** restless; nervous; uneasy. **2** unwilling to accept control or authority. **3** said of a horse: unwilling to move forwards. • **restively** *adverb*. • **restiveness** *noun*. ⓒ 17c: from French *restif* inert, from Latin *restare* to remain still or rest.

restoration /restə'reɪʃən/ ▻ *noun* **1** the act or process of restoring. **2** the act of giving back something lost or stolen. **3** something restored or given back. **4** a model or reconstruction (eg of a ruin, extinct animal, etc). **5** the act of returning to a former and higher status, rank, etc. **6** (*usually* **the Restoration**) *Brit historical* **a** the re-establishment of the monarchy in 1660; **b** the reign of Charles II (1660–85); **c** *as adj* relating to this period of history □ ***restoration comedy.*** • **restorationism** *noun, relig* **1** the receiving of a sinner to divine favour. **2** the final saving of all men. ⓒ 15c.

restorative /rɪ'stɒrətɪv, rɪ'stɔː-/ ▻ *adj* tending or helping to restore or improve health, strength, spirits, etc. ▻ *noun* a restorative food or medicine. • **restoratively** *adverb*.

restore /rɪ'stɔː(r)/ ▻ *verb* **1** to return (a building, painting, etc) to a former condition by repairing or cleaning it, etc. **2** to bring someone or something back to a normal or proper state or condition □ ***be restored to health.*** **3** to bring back (a normal or proper state); to reintroduce something □ ***restore discipline.*** **4** to return something lost or stolen to the rightful owner. **5** to bring or put back to a former and higher status, rank, etc. **6** to reconstruct or make a model or representation of (a ruin, extinct animal, etc). • **restorable** *adj*. • **restorer** *noun*. ⓒ 13c: from French *restorer*.

restrain /rɪ'streɪn/ ▻ *verb* (***restrained, restraining***) **1** to prevent (someone, oneself, etc) from doing something. **2** to keep (one's temper, ambition, etc) under control. **3** to take away someone's freedom, especially by arresting them. • **restrained** *adj* **1** controlled; able to control one's emotions. **2** showing restraint; without excess. • **restrainedly** *adverb*. • **restrainer** *noun*. • **restraint** *noun* **1** the act of restraining or state of being restrained. **2** a limit or restriction. **3** the avoidance of exaggeration or excess; the ability to remain calm and reasonable. ⓒ 14c: from French *restreindre*, from Latin *restringere*.

restrain

See Usage Note at **constrain**.

restrict /rɪ'strɪkt/ ▻ *verb* (***restricted, restricting***) **1** to keep someone or something within certain limits. **2** to limit or regulate something's use, especially to withhold it from general use. • **restricted** *adj* **1** limited in space; narrow; confined. **2** not for general use, circulation, etc. **3**

said of an area, place, etc: only for certain people, especially military personnel, may enter. • **restriction** *noun* **1** an act or instance of restricting. **2** something which restricts. **3** a regulation or rule which restricts or limits. • **restrictive** *adj* restricting or intended to restrict, especially excessively. • **restrictively** *adverb*. ◷ 16c: from Latin *restringere, restrictum* to restrain.

restricted area ▻ *noun* **1** an area in which a special speed limit is in force, eg in a built-up area. **2** an area to which access is limited.

restriction enzyme ▻ *noun, biochem* any of a large group of enzymes that can be used to break molecules of DNA at specific points, used extensively in genetic engineering to analyse the structure of chromosomes.

restrictive covenant ▻ *noun, law* a deed, most commonly found in title deeds for land or property, which in some way restricts the purchaser's use of the land or property.

restrictive practice ▻ *noun* (*often* **restrictive practices**) **1** an agreement between manufacturers, companies, etc to keep production of goods down or limit the supply of goods on the market to keep prices high. **2** a practice by a trade union which limits and restricts the activities of members of other trade unions.

rest room ▻ *noun, N Amer* a room with lavatories, wash basins and, sometimes, a seating area, eg in a shop, theatre, factory, etc, for the use of the staff or public.

restructuring ▻ *noun* the reorganization of a business, company, etc in order to improve efficiency, cut costs, etc, often involving redundancies.

result /rɪ'zʌlt/ ▻ *noun* **1** an outcome or consequence of something. **2** *colloq* (*often* **results**) a positive or favourable outcome or consequence □ ***His action got results.*** **3** a number or quantity obtained by calculation, etc. **4 a** *sport* a final score, eg in a football match, etc □ ***the result was six nil to Aberdeen***; **b** (**results**) a list of final scores eg published in a newspaper or broadcast on TV or radio □ ***listen to the results on the radio.*** **5** *colloq* a win in a game □ ***We got a result.*** **6** (**results**) a list of marks a student has obtained in an examination or series of examinations. ▻ *verb* (***resulted, resulting***) *intr* **1** (*usually* **result from something**) to be a consequence or outcome of some action, event, etc. **2** (*usually* **result in something**) to end in a specified way □ ***Carelessness results in mistakes.*** ◷ 15c: from Latin *resultare* to leap back, from *saltare* to leap.

resultant /rɪ'zʌltənt/ ▻ *adj* resulting. ▻ *noun, math, physics* a single force which is the equivalent of two or more forces acting on an object.

resume /rɪ'zjuːm/ ▻ *verb* (***resumed, resuming***) **1** *tr & intr* to return to something or begin it again after an interruption. **2** to take back or return to (a former position, etc) □ ***resume one's seat.*** • **resumable** *adj*. ◷ 15c: from Latin *resumere, resumptum* to take up again.

résumé /rɛ'zjʊmeɪ, 'reɪzʊmeɪ/ ▻ *noun* **1** a summary. **2** *N Amer* a curriculum vitae. ◷ 19c: French, from *résumer* to resume.

resumption /rɪ'zʌmpʃən/ ▻ *noun* the act of resuming. • **resumptive** *adj*. • **resumptively** *adverb*.

resupinate /rɪ'suːpɪneɪt, rɪ'sjuː-/ ▻ *adj, bot* said of parts of plants: inverted; appearing to be upside down because of a twist in the stem, etc. • **resupination** /-'neɪʃən/ *noun*. ◷ 18c: from Latin *resupinare, resupinatum* to bend back, *supinus* bent back.

resurface ▻ *verb* **1** to put a new surface on something, especially a road. **2** *intr* to reappear. • **resurfacing** *noun*.

resurgence /rɪ'sɜːdʒəns/ ▻ *noun* the act of returning to life, to a state of activity, importance, influence, etc after a period of decline. • **resurgent** *adj*. ◷ 19c: from Latin *resurgere* to rise again.

resurrect /rɛzə'rɛkt/ ▻ *verb* (***resurrected, resurrecting***) **1** to bring someone back to life from the dead. **2** to bring something back into general use, activity, etc.

resurrection /rɛzə'rɛkʃən/ ▻ *noun* **1** the act of resurrecting or bringing something back into use. **2** the act of coming back to life after death. **3** (**Resurrection**) *Christianity* **a** Christ's coming back to life three days after his death on the cross; **b** the coming back to life of all the dead at the Last Judgement. • **resurrectionary** *adj*. • **resurrectionist** *noun* **1** *old use* someone who robbed graves to get bodies for dissection. **2** a believer in the Resurrection. • **resurrector** *noun*. ◷ 13c: from French *résurrection*, from Latin *resurgere, resurrectum* to rise again.

resurrection plant ▻ *noun* any of several desert plants that curl into a ball and appear dead during a drought but revive when moistened.

resuscitate /rɪ'sʌsɪteɪt/ ▻ *verb* (***resuscitated, resuscitating***) **1** to bring someone or something back to life or consciousness; to revive them or it. **2** *intr* to revive or regain consciousness. • **resuscitable** *adj*. • **resuscitation** *noun*. • **resuscitative** *adj*. • **resuscitator** *noun*. ◷ 16c: from Latin *resuscitare, resuscitatum*, from *suscitare* to raise or revive.

ret ▻ *verb* (***retted, retting***) **1** to soften (flax, hemp, etc) by moistening or soaking. **2** *tr & intr* to spoil (hay, etc) by soaking or rotting.

retable /rɪ'teɪbəl/ ▻ *noun* a shelf or ornamental setting for panels, etc above and behind an altar. ◷ 19c: from French *rétable*, from Latin *retro-* behind + *tabula* table.

retail ▻ *noun* /'riːteɪl/ the sale of goods, either individually or in small quantities, to customers who will not resell them but who buy them for their own use. Compare WHOLESALE. ▻ *adj* relating to, concerned with, or engaged in such sale of goods. ▻ *adverb* **1** by retail. **2** at a retail price. ▻ *verb* (***retailed, retailing***) **1** /'riːteɪl/ **a** to sell (goods) in small quantities; **b** *intr* to be sold in small quantities to customers. **2** /riː'teɪl/ to tell or recount (a story, gossip, etc) in great detail. • **retailer** *noun*. ◷ 14c: from French *retailler* to cut off.

■ **retail at something** said of an article or goods: to be offered for sale at (a specified price) □ ***This wine retails at £3.50 a bottle or £36 a case.***

retail price index ▻ *noun, Brit* ▻ (abbreviation **RPI**) a monthly index of the retail prices of certain household goods, taken as indicative of the cost of living for that month, and as a way of monitoring changes in the cost of living over a period of time.

retain /rɪ'teɪn/ ▻ *verb* (***retained, retaining***) **1** to keep or continue to have something □ ***retain a sense of humour.*** **2** to be able, or continue, to hold or contain something □ ***retains moisture.*** **3** said of a person: to be able to remember (facts, information, etc) easily. **4** to hold something back or keep it in place. **5** to secure the services of (a person, especially a barrister) by paying a preliminary fee. **6** to keep something for future use by paying a small charge. • **retainable** *adj*. • **retainment** *noun*. ◷ 14c: from French *retenir*, from Latin *retinere* to hold back.

retainer /rɪ'teɪnə(r)/ ▻ *noun* **1** someone or something that retains. **2** *historical* a dependant or follower of a person of rank. **3** a domestic servant who has been with a family for a long time. **4** a fee paid to secure professional services, especially those of a lawyer or barrister. **5** a reduced rent paid for property while it is not occupied in order to reserve it for future use.

retaining wall ▻ *noun* a wall built to support and hold back a mass of earth, rock or water.

retake ▻ *verb* /riː'teɪk/ **1 a** to take again; **b** to take back. **2** to capture (eg a fortress) again. **3** to sit (an examination) again. **4** to film (eg a scene) again. ▻ *noun* /'riːteɪk/ **1** the action of retaking something. **2** an examination that someone sits again. **3 a** the act or process of filming a scene, recording a piece of music, etc again; **b** the scene, recording, etc resulting from this. • **retaker** *noun*. ◷ Early 20c as *noun*; 17c as *verb*.

retaliate /rɪ'talɪeɪt/ ▻ *verb* (***retaliated, retaliating***) **1** *intr* to repay an injury, wrong, etc in kind; to get revenge □ ***retaliated against the injustice*** □ ***retaliated with heavy gun fire.*** • **retaliation** *noun*. • **retaliative** /rɪ'talɪjətɪv/ *adj*. • **retaliator** *noun*. • **retaliatory** /rɪ'talɪətjərɪ, rɪtalɪ'eɪtərɪ/ *adj*. ⓒ 17c: from Latin *retaliare*, from *talis* such.

retard ▻ *verb* /rɪ'tɑːd/ (***retarded, retarding***) to slow down or delay something. ▻ *noun* /'riːtɑːd/ *especially US* a person of low intelligence or who acts in a particularly stupid way □ ***Tommy's such a retard - he's using smack again.*** • **retardation** /riːtɑː'deɪʃən/ or **retardment** /rɪ'tɑːdmənt/ *noun* **1** the act of retarding or state of being retarded. **2** something that retards. • **retardative** *adj*. • **retardatory** *adj*. ⓒ 15c: from French *retarder*, from Latin *tardus* slow.

retardant /rɪ'tɑːdənt/ ▻ *adj* having the effect of slowing down or delaying something. Often *in compounds* □ ***flame-retardant.*** ▻ *noun* a substance that retards, especially one that has the effect of slowing down or delaying some specified reaction, process, etc. Often *in compounds* □ ***fire retardant.***

retarded /rɪ'tɑːdɪd/ ▻ *adj* **1** slowed down or delayed. **2** *old use* said of a person: backward in physical or especially mental development.

retarder /rɪ'tɑːdə(r)/ ▻ *noun* a substance that is used to slow down the rate of some process, chemical change, etc, eg a substance used to delay or prevent the setting of cement.

retch ▻ *verb* (***retches, retched, retching***) *intr* to strain as if to vomit, but without actually doing so. ▻ *noun* an act of retching. ⓒ Anglo-Saxon *hræcan*.

retd ▻ *abbreviation* retired.

rete /'riːtiː/ ▻ *noun* (*plural* ***retia*** /'riːʃɪə, 'riːtɪə/) *anatomy* a network of blood vessels or nerves; a PLEXUS. • **retial** /'riːʃɪəl/ *adj*. ⓒ 16c in this sense; 14c in sense 'a metal network attached to an ASTROLABE, used to indicate the position of stars': Latin, meaning 'a net'.

retention /rɪ'tɛnʃən/ ▻ *noun* **1** the act of retaining something or the state of being retained. **2** the power of retaining or capacity to retain something. **3** the ability to remember experiences and things learnt. **4** *medicine* the failure to get rid of fluid from the body. • **retentionist** *noun* someone who advocates the retention of a policy, etc, especially the retention of capital punishment. • **retentive** *adj* **1** able to retain or keep, especially memories or information. **2** tending to retain (fluid, etc). • **retentively** *adverb*. • **retentiveness** *noun*. ⓒ 14c: from Latin *retentio*, from *retinere* to retain.

retexture /riː'tɛkstʃə(r)/ ▻ *verb* to treat (a blanket, garment, etc) with chemicals which restore the original texture of the material. ⓒ 19c.

rethink ▻ *verb* /riː'θɪŋk/ to think about or consider (a plan, etc) again, usually with a view to changing one's mind about it or reaching a different conclusion. ▻ *noun* /'riːθɪŋk/ an act of rethinking. ⓒ 1950s as *noun*; 18c as *verb*.

reticent /'rɛtɪsənt/ ▻ *adj* **1** not saying very much. **2** not willing to communicate; reserved. **3** not communicating everything that one knows. • **reticence** *noun*. • **reticently** *adverb*. ⓒ 19c: from Latin *reticere* to keep silent, from *tacere* to be silent.

reticle /'rɛtɪkəl/ ▻ *noun* an attachment to an optical instrument, consisting of a network of lines of reference. ⓒ 17c: from Latin *reticulum* a little net.

reticular /rɪ'tɪkjʊlə(r)/ ▻ *adj* **1** netted; netlike; reticulated. **2** *zool* related or pertaining to the reticulum.

reticulate ▻ *adj* /rɪ'tɪkjʊlɪt/ like a net or network, especially in having lines, veins, etc □ ***a reticulate leaf.*** ▻ *verb* /rɪ'tɪkjʊleɪt/ (***reticulated, reticulating***) *tr & intr* to form or be formed into a network; to mark or be marked with a network of lines, etc. • **reticulately** *adj*. • **reticulation** *noun*. ⓒ 17c: from Latin *reticulatus* like a net.

reticule /'rɛtɪkjuːl/ ▻ *noun* **1** *historical* a woman's small pouch-like bag, often netted or beaded, and fastening with a drawstring. **2** a RETICLE. ⓒ 18c: from Latin *reticulum* a little net.

reticulum /rɪ'tɪkjʊləm/ ▻ *noun* (***reticula*** /rɪ'tɪkjʊlə/) **1** *biol* a fine network, especially one of fibres, vessels, etc. **2** *zool* the second stomach of a ruminant. ⓒ 17c: Latin, meaning 'a little net'.

retiform /'riːtɪfɔːm/ ▻ *adj* having the form of a net; netlike. ⓒ 17c: from Latin *rete* a net.

retina /'rɛtɪnə/ ▻ *noun* (***retinas*** or ***retinae*** /'rɛtɪniː/) *anatomy* the light-sensitive tissue that lines much of the back of the eyeball, in which nerve impulses are generated. From here they are relayed to the brain, where they are interpreted as vision. • **retinal** *adj*. ⓒ 14c: Latin, probably from *rete* a net.

retinitis /rɛtɪ'naɪtɪs/ ▻ *noun, medicine* inflammation of the retina. ⓒ 19c.

retinol /'rɛtɪnɒl/ ▻ *noun* VITAMIN A. ⓒ 1960s.

retinoscope /'rɛtɪnəskoʊp/ ▻ *noun, medicine* an optical instrument used to examine the eye. • **retinoscopy** /rɛtɪ'nɒskəpɪ/ *noun* examination of the eye by observing the shadow on the retina. • **retinoscopically** *adverb*. • **retinoscopist** *noun*.

retinue /'rɛtɪnjuː/ ▻ *noun* the servants, officials, aides, etc who travel with and attend an important person. ⓒ 14c: from French *retenue*, from *retenir* to retain.

retire /rɪ'taɪə(r)/ ▻ *verb* (***retired, retiring***) **1** *tr & intr* to stop or make someone stop working permanently, usually on reaching an age at which a pension can be received □ ***retired at 60.*** **2** *intr, formal* to go away to rest, especially to go to bed. **3** *intr, formal* to go away (from or to a place); to leave □ ***retire to the drawing room.*** **4** *tr & intr* to withdraw or make someone withdraw from a sporting contest, especially because of injury. **5** *tr & intr* said of a military force, etc: to move or be moved back, away from a dangerous position. • **retiral** *noun* an act of retiring, eg from work, or of going away from a place. • **retired** *adj* **1** (abbreviation **retd**) having permanently stopped work because of one's age. **2** secluded. • **retirement** *noun* **1** the act of retiring or state of being retired from work. **2** seclusion and privacy. • **retiring** *adj* shy and reserved; not liking to be noticed. • **retiringly** *adverb*. ⓒ 16c: from French *retirer* to pull back.

retirement home ▻ *noun* **1** an easily-run flat or small house, usually part of a supervised complex, where a retired person or couple can live. **2** a residential institution for elderly people who need nursing care.

retirement pension ▻ *noun, Brit* a weekly payment from the state made to people who have retired from work.

retirement pregnancy ▻ *noun, medicine* artificially induced pregnancy in an elderly or postmenopausal woman.

retort /rɪ'tɔːt/ ▻ *verb* (***retorted, retorting***) **1** *intr* to make a quick and clever or angry reply. **2** to turn (an argument, criticism, blame, etc) back on the person who first used that argument, criticism, blame, etc. **3** *metallurgy* to heat and purify (metal) in a retort. ▻ *noun* **1** a quick and clever or angry reply. **2** an argument, criticism, blame, etc which is turned back upon the originator. **3** a glass vessel with a long neck which curves downwards, used in distilling. **4** *metallurgy* a vessel for heating metals such as iron and carbon to make steel, or for heating coal to produce gas. • **retortion** *noun*. ⓒ 16c: from Latin *retorquere* to twist back, from *torquere* to wrench or twist.

retouch ▻ *verb* /riː'tʌtʃ/ to improve or repair (a photograph, negative, painting, etc) by adding extra touches or making small alterations. ▻ *noun* /'riːtʌtʃ/ **1** an act of improving, especially of making small repairs or adjustments to a photograph by pencil-work on the negative. **2** a photograph, painting, etc that has been retouched. **3** the detail or area of a photograph, painting, etc that has been retouched. • **retoucher** *noun*. ⓘ 17c.

retrace ▷ *verb* **1** to go back over (a route, path, etc). **2** to trace something back to its origin □ *retrace her roots*. **3** to go over (recent events, etc) again in one's memory. **4** to trace something again with the eyes; to look at it again carefully. ⓘ 17c.

re-trace ▷ *verb* to trace or go over again (an outline, etc) with a pen, pencil, etc. ⓘ 18c.

retract /rɪ'trakt/ ▷ *verb* (***retracted***, ***retracting***) **1** to draw something in or back. **2 a** said of an animal: to draw or pull back (a part) into its body, shell, etc; **b** said of an aircraft: to draw up (landing equipment, etc) into the main body. **3** *tr & intr* to withdraw (a statement, claim, charge, etc) as wrong, offensive or unjustified. **4** *tr & intr* to go back on, or refuse to acknowledge (a promise, agreement, etc that one has made). • **retractable** or **retractible** *adj* **1** able to be drawn in, back or up; retractile. **2** said of a component part of an object: able to be drawn up or into the main body. **3** said of a statement, promise, etc: able to be retracted or withdrawn. • **retraction** *noun* **1** the act of drawing something in, back or up. **2** an act or instance of withdrawing, especially something one has said, agreed or promised. • **retractive** *adj*. ⓘ 16c: from Latin *retractere* to draw back, from *trahere* to drag or pull.

retractile /rɪ'traktaɪl/ ▷ *adj* said especially of parts of animals, eg of a cat's claws: able to be drawn in, back or up. • **retractility** *noun*.

retractor /rɪ'traktə(r)/ ▷ *noun* **1** *surgery* an instrument for holding back tissue, skin, an organ, etc from the area being operated on. **2** *anatomy* a muscle that retracts or pulls in a part of the body. **3** *chess* a problem involving the reversal of a previous move or moves.

retrain /riː'treɪn/ ▷ *verb* **1** to teach (a person or animal) new skills. **2** *intr* to learn new skills, especially with a view to finding alternative employment.

retread[1] /riː'trɛd/ ▷ *verb* to tread (a path, one's steps, etc) again. ⓘ 16c.

retread[2] ▷ *verb* /riː'trɛd/ (***retreaded***, ***retreading***) see REMOULD (verb 2). ▷ *noun* see REMOULD (noun)ⓘ Early 20c.

retreat[1] /rɪ'triːt/ ▷ *verb* (***retreated***, ***retreating***) **1** *intr* said of a military force, army, etc: to move back or away from the enemy or retire after defeat. **2** *intr* to retire or withdraw to a place of safety or seclusion. **3** *intr* to recede; to slope back. **4** *chess* to move (a piece) back. ▷ *noun* **1** the act of retreating, especially from battle, a military position, danger, etc. **2** *military* a signal to retreat, especially one given on a bugle. **3** a place of privacy, safety or seclusion. **4 a** a period of retirement or withdrawal from the world, especially for prayer, meditation, study, etc; **b** a place for such retirement or withdrawal. **5** an institution for the care and treatment of the elderly, the mentally ill, etc. ⓘ 14c: from French *retret*, from Latin *retrahere* to draw back.

retreat[2] or **re-treat** /riː'triːt/ ▷ *verb* to treat again. • **retreatment** *noun*. ⓘ 19c.

retrial see under RETRY

retrench /rɪ'trɛntʃ/ ▷ *verb* (***retrenched***, ***retrenching***) **1** *tr & intr* to reduce or cut down (expenses, money spent, etc); to economize. **2** to cut down, reduce, shorten or abridge something. • **retrenchment** *noun*. ⓘ 16c: from French *retrenchier* to cut off or back, from Latin *truncare* to maim.

retribution /rɛtrɪ'bjuːʃən/ ▷ *noun* **1** the act of punishing or taking vengeance for sin or wrongdoing. **2** deserved punishment, especially for sin or wrongdoing; vengeance. • **retributive** /rɪ'trɪbjʊtɪv/ *adj* being or forming a punishment which is deserved or suitable. • **retributively** *adverb*. ⓘ 14c: from Latin *retribuere*, *retributum* to give back.

retrieve /rɪ'triːv/ ▷ *verb* (***retrieved***, ***retrieving***) **1** to get or bring something back again; to recover. **2** to rescue or save something □ *retrieve the situation*. **3** to save (time). **4** to restore (honour or fortune). **5** to make good (a loss, error, etc). **6** *computing* to recover (information) from storage in a computer memory. **7** to remember or recall something to mind. **8** *tr & intr* said of a dog: to search for and bring back (game that has been shot, or a ball, stick, etc that has been thrown). **9** in tennis, etc: to return successfully (a shot that is difficult to reach). • **retrievable** *adj*. • **retrieval** *noun* **1** the act or possibility of retrieving something or getting it back. **2** *computing* the extraction of data from a file. ⓘ 15c: from French *retrover*.

retriever *noun* **1 a** a large dog with a golden or black water-resistant coat, that can be trained to retrieve game; **b** any dog that is trained to retrieve game. **2** someone or something that retrieves.

retro /'rɛtroʊ/ ▷ *adj* reminiscent of, reverting to, recreating or imitating a style, fashion, etc from the past. ▷ *noun* (***retros***) a RETRO-ROCKET. ⓘ 20c.

retro- /rɛtroʊ/ ▷ *prefix, denoting* **1** back or backwards in time or space. **2** behind. ⓘ Latin *retro* backwards.

retroact /'rɛtroʊakt/ ▷ *verb* (***retroacted***, ***retroacting***) *intr* **1** to react. **2** *law* to act retrospectively. • **retroactive** *adj* applying to or affecting things from a date in the past □ *retroactive legislation*. • **retroactively** *adverb*. • **retroactivity** *noun*. ⓘ 17c: from Latin *retroagere*, *retroactum* to drive back.

retrocede /rɛtroʊ'siːd/ ▷ *verb* (***retroceded***, ***retroceding***) **1** *intr* to move back; to recede. **2** to grant back (territory) to a government or country. • **retrocedent** *adj*. • **retrocession** *noun*. • **retrocessive** *adj*. ⓘ 17c: from Latin *retrocedere*, *cedere* to cede or yield.

retrochoir /'rɛtroʊkwaɪə(r)/ ▷ *noun*, *archit* an extension of a church behind the position of the high altar.

retrod and **retrodden** see under RETREAD[1]

retrofit /'rɛtroʊfɪt/ ▷ *verb* (***retrofitted***, ***retrofitting***) to modify (a house, car, aircraft, etc) some time after construction or manufacture by equipping with new or more up-to-date parts, etc.

retroflex /'rɛtroʊflɛks/ ▷ *adj* **1** *bot*, *anatomy* (*also* **retroflexed** or **retroflected**) turned or bent backwards. **2** *medicine*, *anatomy*, said especially of the uterus: arched backwards. Compare RETROVERSION. **3** *phonetics* (*also* **retroflexed**) said of sound, especially an 'r': pronounced with the tip of the tongue curled back. ▷ *verb*, *tr & intr* to turn or bend back. • **retroflexion** or **retroflection** *noun*. ⓘ 18c: from Latin *retroflectere*, *retroflexum*.

retrograde /'rɛtrəgreɪd/ ▷ *adj* **1** being, tending towards or causing a worse, less advanced or less desirable state. **2** moving or bending backwards. **3** in a reversed or opposite order. **4** *astron* said of a planet, etc: **a** seeming to move in the opposite or contrary direction to other planets, etc; **b** seeming to move from east to west. ▷ *verb* (***retrograded***, ***retrograding***) *intr* **1** to move backwards. **2** to deteriorate or decline. **3** *astron* said of a planet: to show retrograde movement. • **retrogradation** *noun*. • **retrogradely** *adverb*. ⓘ 14c: from Latin *retrogradus* going backwards, from *gradi* to go or walk.

retrogress /rɛtrə'grɛs/ ▷ *verb* (***retrogressed***, ***retrogresssing***) *intr* **1** to go back to an earlier, worse or less advanced condition or state; to deteriorate. **2** to recede or move backwards. • **retrogression** /rɛtrə'grɛʃən/ *noun* **1** a decline in quality or merit. **2** the act or process of going backward or reverting. **3** *astron* retrograde movement. • **retrogressive** *adj*. • **retrogressively** *adverb*. ⓘ 19c: from Latin *retrogressus* a movement backwards.

retro-rocket ▷ *noun*, *astron* a small rocket motor that is fired in the opposite direction from that in which a spacecraft, artificial satellite, etc is moving, in order to slow it down. Often shortened to RETRO. ⓒ 1960s.

retrorse /rɪ'trɔːs/ ▷ *adj* said especially of parts of plants: turned or pointing backwards. • **retrorsely** *adverb*. ⓒ 19c: from Latin *retrorsus*, from *retroversus*, from *vertere* to turn.

retrospect /'rɛtrəspɛkt/ (*especially* **in retrospect**) when considering or looking back on what has happened in the past □ *In retrospect, it wasn't a good idea.* • **retrospection** *noun* **1** the action of looking back at the past. **2** a survey of one's past life. • **retrospective** *adj* **1** said of a law, etc: applying to the past as well as to the present and to the future. **2** inclined to look back on past events. ▷ *noun* an exhibition which shows how an artist's work has developed over the years. • **retrospectively** *adverb*. ⓒ 17c: from Latin *retrospicere*, *retrospectum* to look back.

retroussé /rə'truːseɪ/ ▷ *adj* said especially of the nose: turned up at the end. ⓒ 19c: French, from *retrousser* to tuck or turn up.

retroversion /rɛtroʊ'vɜːʃən/ ▷ *noun* **1** the action of turning, or state of being turned, backwards. **2** *medicine, anatomy* said of an organ, etc, especially the uterus: the condition of being displaced backwards. Compare RETROFLEX. • **retroverted** *adj*.

Retrovir /'rɛtrəvɪə(r)/ ▷ *noun, trademark, pharmacol* the brand name for the drug AZT. ⓒ 1970s: from RETROVIRUS.

retrovirus /'rɛtroʊvaɪərəs/ ▷ *noun, biol* any of a group of viruses with genetic material consisting of RNA which is copied into DNA to allow integration into the host cell's DNA and including many carcinogenic viruses, as well as the HIV virus which causes AIDS. • **retroviral** *adj*. ⓒ 1970s: from *reverse transcriptase* (the active enzyme in these viruses) + -o- + *virus*.

retry ▷ *verb* **1** to submit to further judicial trial □ *were retried when new evidence came to light.* **2** to make a further attempt □ *retried the car but it still wouldn't start.* • **retrial** *noun* a further judicial trial.

retsina /rɛt'siːnə/ ▷ *noun* a Greek white or rosé wine flavoured with pine resin. ⓒ 1940s: Greek, from *retme* pine resin.

retted and **retting** see under RET

return /rɪ'tɜːn/ ▷ *verb* (***returned, returning***) **1** *intr* to come or go back again to a former place, state or owner □ *returned to Glasgow after two weeks.* **2** to give, send, put back, etc a particular thing in a former position. **3** *intr* to come back to in thought or speech □ *return to the topic later.* **4** to repay with something of the same value □ *return the compliment.* **5** *tr & intr* to answer or reply. **6** to report or state officially or formally. **7** to earn or produce (profit, interest, etc). **8** to elect as a Member of Parliament □ *was returned with an increased majority.* **9** *law* said of a jury: to deliver (a verdict). **10** *tennis, badminton, etc* to hit back (a ball, etc) served by one's opponent. ▷ *noun* **1** an act of coming back from a place, state, etc. **2** an act of returning something, especially to its former place, state, ownership, etc. **3** something returned, especially unsold newspapers and magazines returned to the publisher, or a theatre ticket returned to the theatre for resale. **4** profit from work, a business or investment. **5** (*often* **returns**) a statement of someone's income and allowances, used for calculating the tax which must be paid □ *tax returns.* **6** (*usually* **returns**) a statement of the votes polled in an election. **7** *Brit* a RETURN TICKET □ *a day return to Edinburgh.* **8** an answer or reply. **9 a** a ball, etc hit back after one's opponent's service in tennis, badminton, etc; **b** *as adj* forming, causing or relating to a return. **10** (*in full* **return key**) **a** a key on a computer or typewriter keyboard that takes the operator from the end of one line to the beginning of the line below; **b** a key on a computer keyboard used for various functions including the loading of software □ *Type 'install' and press 'Return'.* • **returnable** *adj*. • **by return of post** by the next post in the return direction, ie immediately or as soon as possible. • **in return** in exchange; in reply; as compensation. • **many happy returns (of the day)** an expression of good wishes on someone's birthday. ⓒ 14c: from French *retorner*, from Latin *tornare* to turn.

returning officer ▷ *noun* an official in charge of running an election in a constituency, counting the votes and declaring the result.

return match ▷ *noun, sport* a second match played between the same players or teams, usually at the home ground of the side previously playing away.

return ticket ▷ *noun* a ticket which allows someone to travel to a place and back again.

retuse /rɪ'tjuːs/ ▷ *adj, bot* with the tip blunt and broadly notched. ⓒ 18c: from Latin *retundere*, *retusum* to blunt.

reunify /riː'juːnɪfaɪ/ ▷ *verb* to unify (a country, republic, etc that has been divided) again or anew. • **reunification** *noun*. ⓒ 19c.

reunion /riː'juːnɪən, -njən/ ▷ *noun* **1** a meeting of people (eg relatives, friends, former colleagues, etc) who have not met for some time. **2** the act of reuniting or state of being reunited. ⓒ 17c.

reunite /riːjʊ'naɪt/ ▷ *verb, tr & intr* to bring or come together again after being separated. ⓒ 15c.

Rev or **Revd** ▷ *abbreviation* Reverend.

rev ▷ *noun, colloq* **1** (*often* **revs**) one cycle of events or one revolution in an internal combustion engine, the number of revolutions (usually RPM) often being used as an indication of engine speed. **2** an act of revving an engine, etc. ▷ *verb* (***revs, revved, revving***) *colloq* (*also* **rev up**) **1** to increase the speed of revolution of (a car engine, etc). **2** *intr* said of an engine or vehicle: to run faster. ⓒ 1920s: from REVOLUTION.

revalue or **revaluate** ▷ *verb* **1** to make a new valuation of something. **2** to adjust the exchange rate of (a currency), especially making it more valuable with respect to other currencies. Compare DEVALUE. ⓒ 20c as *revaluate*; 16c as *revalue*.

revamp /riː'vamp/ ▷ *verb* to revise, renovate or patch something up, usually with the aim of improving it. ▷ *noun* **1** the act of revamping. **2** something that has been revamped. ⓒ 19c.

revanchism /rɪ'vantʃɪzəm/ ▷ *noun* a policy directed towards recovery of territory lost to an enemy. • **revanchist** *noun, adj*. ⓒ 19c: from French *revanche* 'revenge'.

reveal[1] /rɪ'viːl/ ▷ *verb* (***revealed, revealing***) **1** to make (a secret, etc) known; to disclose it. **2** to show something; to allow it to be seen. **3** said of a deity: to make something known through divine inspiration or by supernatural means. • **revealable** *adj*. • **revealer** *noun*. • **revealing** *adj* **1** indicative; significant. **2** said of a dress, etc: allowing more than is usual of the body, especially a woman's breasts, to be seen. • **revealingly** *adverb*. ⓒ 14c: from French *reveler*, from Latin *velum* a veil.

reveal[2] /rɪ'viːl/ ▷ *noun, archit* the vertical side surface of a recess in a wall, especially the surface between the frame and the outer surface of the wall in the opening for a doorway or window. ⓒ 17c.

reveille /rɪ'valɪ/ ▷ *noun* **1** a signal given in the morning, usually by a drum or bugle call, to waken soldiers, etc. **2** the time at which this signal is given. ⓒ 17c: from French *réveillez!* wake up!

revel /'rɛvəl/ ▷ *verb* (***revelled, revelling***) *intr* to enjoy oneself in a noisy lively way; to make merry. ▷ *noun* (*usually* **revels**) an occasion of revelling; noisy lively enjoyment, festivities or merrymaking. • **reveller** *noun*. • **revelry** /'rɛvəlrɪ/ *noun* the action of revelling; noisy lively merrymaking. ⓒ 14c: from French *reveler* to riot, be merry, etc, from Latin *rebellare* to rebel.

▪ **revel in something** to take great delight or luxuriate in it.

Revelation /rɛvə'leɪʃən/ or (*popularly*) **Revelations** *singular noun* the last book of the New Testament, which contains prophecies of the end of the world. Also called **Apocalypse**.

revelation /rɛvə'leɪʃən/ ▷ *noun* **1** the act of revealing, showing or disclosing, especially in a dramatic or striking way, something previously unknown or unexpected. **2** something that is revealed or disclosed in this way. **3** the experience of discovering, especially in a striking way, something previously unknown or unexpected □ *It was a revelation to him when he discovered she was having an affair.* **4** *Christianity* something revealed, shown or made known to man by God through divine inspiration or by supernatural means. • **revelational** *adj*. • **revelationist** *noun* someone who believes in divine revelation. • **revelatory** /rɛvə'leɪtərɪ, 'rɛvələtərɪ/ *adj*. ⓘ 13c: from Latin *revelatio*, from *revelare* to unveil or reveal.

revenant /'rɛvənənt/ ▷ *noun* **1** someone who returns after a long absence, especially supposedly from the dead. **2** a ghost. ▷ *adj* returned, especially supposedly from the dead. ⓘ 19c: French, from *revenir* to return.

revenge /rɪ'vɛndʒ/ ▷ *noun* **1** malicious injury, harm or wrong done in return for injury, harm or wrong received; retaliation; vengeance. **2** something that is done as a means of returning like injury, harm, etc. **3** the desire to do such injury, harm, etc. **4** a return match or game, seen as an opportunity for the person, team, etc that was defeated the first time to even the score. *Also called as adj* □ *a revenge match.* ▷ *verb* (***revenged, revenging***) **1** to do similar injury, harm, etc in return for injury, harm, etc received. **2** to take revenge on someone on behalf of oneself or someone else; to avenge. • **revengeful** *adj*. • **revengefully** *adverb*. • **revengefulness** *noun*. • **revenger** *noun*. • **revenging** *adj*. ⓘ 14c: from French *revenger*, from Latin *vindicare* to vindicate.

revenue /'rɛvənju:/ ▷ *noun* **1** money which comes to a person, organization, etc from any source, eg property, shares, etc. **2** money raised by the government of a country or state from taxes, etc. **3** (*often* **Revenue**) a government department responsible for collecting this money. See also INLAND REVENUE. ⓘ 15c: from French *revenu*.

revenue cutter ▷ *noun, historical* a small armed vessel used to prevent smuggling.

reverb /'ri:vɜ:b, rɪ'vɜ:b/ ▷ *noun, colloq, music* **1** reverberation, especially that produced by an amplifier or an electronic musical instrument. **2** (*also* **reverb unit**) a device which produces an effect of reverberation. ⓘ 1960s.

reverberate /rɪ'vɜ:bəreɪt/ ▷ *verb* (***reverberated, reverberating***) **1** *intr* said of a sound, light, heat, etc: to be echoed, repeated or reflected repeatedly. **2** to echo, repeat or reflect (a sound, light, etc) repeatedly. **3** *intr* said of a story, scandal, etc: to circulate or be repeated many times. **4** *metallurgy* to heat (a metal, ore, etc) in a reverberatory furnace. • **reverberant** /rɪ'vɜ:bərənt/ *adj* resonant; reverberating. • **reverberantly** *adverb*. • **reverberation** /rɪvɜ:bə'reɪʃən/ *noun*. • **reverberative** *adj* **1** tending to reverberate. **2** like a reverberation. • **reverberator** *noun*. • **reverberatory** *adj*. ⓘ 16c: from Latin *reverberare, reverberatum* to beat back.

reverberatory furnace ▷ *noun, metallurgy* a furnace in which the material (eg steel, ceramics or glass) is not heated directly by the burning fuel, but by a flame directed at a low roof which radiates heat downwards on to it.

revere /rɪ'vɪə(r)/ ▷ *verb* (***revered, revering***) to feel or show great respect or reverence for someone or something; to venerate. • **reverer** *noun*. ⓘ 17c: from Latin *revereri*.

reverence /'rɛvərəns, 'rɛvrəns/ ▷ *noun* **1** great respect or veneration, especially that shown to something sacred or holy. **2** a feeling of, or the capacity to feel, such respect. **3** an act or gesture that shows such respect, such as an act of obeisance or a bow. **4** the state of being held in such respect. **5** (**His** or **Your Reverence**) a title used to address or refer to some members of the clergy, especially a priest in Ireland. ▷ *verb* (***reverenced, reverencing***) to regard someone or something with great reverence; to venerate. ⓘ 13c: from Latin *reverentia*.

reverend /'rɛvərənd, 'rɛvrənd/ ▷ *adj* **1** worthy of being revered or respected. **2** (**Reverend** abbreviation **Rev** or **Revd**) used before proper names as a title for members of the clergy, and in other titles such as **Most Reverend** for an archbishop or an Irish RC bishop, **Right Reverend** for a bishop or a Moderator of the Church of Scotland, **Very Reverend** for a dean or a former Moderator, and **Reverend Mother** for a Mother Superior of a convent. ▷ *noun, colloq* a member of the clergy. ⓘ 15c: from Latin *reverendus* worthy of reverence.

reverent /'rɛvərənt, 'rɛvrənt/ ▷ *adj* showing, feeling or characterized by great respect or reverence. • **reverently** *adverb*. ⓘ 14c.

reverential /rɛvə'rɛnʃəl/ ▷ *adj* reverent or very respectful. • **reverentially** *adverb*. ⓘ 16c.

reverie /'rɛvərɪ/ ▷ *noun* **1** a state of pleasantly dreamy and absented-minded thought. **2** a day-dream or absent-minded idea or thought. **3** *music* a piece of music suggestive of day-dreaming. ⓘ 14c: French.

revers /rɪ'vɪə(r)/ ▷ *noun* (*revers* /rɪ'vɪəz/) any part of a garment that is turned back, especially a lapel. ⓘ 19c: French, meaning 'reverse', from Latin *revertere, reversum* to turn back.

reversal /rɪ'vɜ:s(ə)l/ ▷ *noun* **1** an act of reversing something, or the state of being reversed. **2** a change in fortune, especially for the worse. Also called **reverse**. **3** *law* the action of setting aside or overthrowing a legal decision or judgement.

reverse /rɪ'vɜ:s/ ▷ *verb* (***reversed, reversing***) **1** *tr & intr* to move or make something move backwards or in an opposite direction □ *He reversed the car.* **2** to run (a mechanism, piece of machinery, etc) backwards or in the opposite direction from what is normal. **3** to put or arrange something in an opposite or contrary position, state, order, etc □ *reverse the names on the list.* **4** to turn something (eg an item of clothing) inside out. **5** to change (eg a policy, decision, etc) to its exact opposite or contrary. See also U-TURN. **6** *law* to set aside or overthrow (a legal decision, judgement, etc); to annul. ▷ *noun* **1** the opposite or contrary of something. **2** a change to an opposite or contrary position, direction, state, etc. **3** the back or rear side of something, eg the back cover of a book. **4** the side of a coin, medal, note, etc that has a secondary design on it. Opposite of OBVERSE. **5** a REVERSAL (sense 2). **6** a mechanism, especially a car gear, which makes a vehicle, piece of machinery, etc move or operate in a backwards direction. **7** *as adj* □ *reverse gear.* ▷ *adj* **1** opposite, contrary or turned round in order, position, direction, etc; inverted. **2** functioning or moving backwards, or in a direction opposite to the normal one. **3** *military* relating to or positioned at the rear. • **reversed** *adj* **1** turned the other way about, backwards or upside down; inverted. **2** said of a policy, legal decision, etc: overturned; annulled. • **reversedly** *adverb*. • **reversely** *adverb*. • **reverser** *noun*. • **reversing** *noun*. • **go into reverse** **1** to put a vehicle, mechanism, etc into reverse gear. **2** to move backwards or in an opposite direction to normal. • **in reverse** backwards or in an opposite direction to normal. • **reverse the charges** *Brit* to make a telephone call that is charged to the person being called instead of to the caller. *N Amer equivalent* CALL COLLECT (see under CALL). ⓘ 14c: from French, from Latin *revertere, reversum*.

reverse engineering ▷ *noun* the taking apart of a competitor's product to see how it is made, with a view to copying or improving it.

reverse takeover ▻ *noun, finance* **1** the taking over of a larger company by a smaller one, especially the purchase of a public company by a private one. **2** a takeover in which the company that has been taken over controls the new organization.

reverse transcriptase ▻ *noun* the enzyme in a retrovirus that makes a DNA copy of the virus's RNA genome and allows integration into host-cell DNA, in this way reversing the usual process of transferring gene information.

reversible /rɪˈvɜːsɪbəl/ ▻ *adj* **1** able to be reversed. **2** said of clothes or a fabric: able to be worn with either side out. ◻ *a reversible jacket.* ▻ *noun* a fabric or garment that can be worn either side out. • **reversibility** *noun.* • **reversibly** *adverb.* ◷ 17c.

reversible reaction ▻ *noun* **1** *chem* a chemical reaction that occurs in both directions simultaneously, so that products are being converted back to reactants at the same time that reactants are being converted to products. **2** a chemical reaction that can be made to proceed in one direction or the other by altering the conditions.

reversing light ▻ *noun* a light, usually a white one, on the rear of a vehicle which comes on when the vehicle is put into reverse gear to warn other drivers and pedestrians that it is going to move or that it is moving backwards and to allow the driver to see where they are going.

reversion /rɪˈvɜːʃən/ ▻ *noun* **1** a return to an earlier state, belief, etc. **2** *law* **a** the legal right (eg of an original owner or their heirs) to possess a property again at the end of a certain period, especially when the present owner dies; **b** property to which someone has such a right. **3** insurance which is paid on someone's death. **4** *biol* said of individuals, organs, etc: a return to an earlier ancestral, and usually less advanced, type. • **reversionary** *adj.* • **reversional** *adj.* • **reversionally** *adverb.* ◷ 14c: from Latin *reversio* a turning back.

revert /rɪˈvɜːt/ ▻ *verb* (***reverted, reverting***) (*usually intr* **revert to something**) **1** to return to as a topic in thought or conversation). **2** to return to a former and usually worse state, practice, way of behaving, etc ◻ *He reverted to his drinking.* **3** *biol* the change from a mutant physical characteristic of an individual to the characteristic most frequently found in natural populations (ie wild type). **4** *law* said especially of property: to return to an original owner or their heirs after belonging temporarily to someone else. **5** to turn something back. • **revertible** *adj.* ◷ 13c: from Latin *revertere* to turn back.

revetment /rɪˈvɛtmənt/ ▻ *noun, chiefly fortification* a facing of masonry or other material that protects or supports a wall, rampart, etc; a RETAINING WALL. ◷ 18c: from French *revêtement*, from *revêtir* to reclothe.

review /rɪˈvjuː/ ▻ *noun* **1** an act of examining, reviewing or revising, or the state of being examined, reviewed or revised. **2** a general survey of a particular subject, situation, etc. **3** a survey of the past and past events ◻ *the newspaper's annual review of the year.* **4** a critical report, especially one that is published in a newspaper or periodical, usually on a recent book, play, film, etc. **5** a magazine or newspaper, or a section of one, which contains mainly reviews of books, etc and other feature articles. **6** a second or additional study or consideration of certain facts, events, etc; a re-examination. **7** *military* a formal or official inspection of troops, ships, etc. **8** *law* a re-examination of a case, especially by a superior court. ▻ *verb* **1** to see or view something again. **2** to examine or go over something, especially critically or formally. **3** to look back on and examine (events in the past). **4** *intr* to write reviews, especially professionally. **5** to write, especially professionally, a critical report on (a book, play, film, etc). **6** *military* to inspect (troops, ships, etc), especially formally or officially. **7** *law* to re-examine (a case). • **reviewable** *adj.* • **reviewal** *noun.* • **in** or **under review** undergoing consideration, negotiation, etc. ◷ 16c: from French *revue.*

review body ▻ *noun* a committee set up to review eg salaries, etc.

review copy ▻ *noun* a copy of a newly published book that is sent out by the publisher eg to newspapers, periodicals, etc that may be interested in reviewing it.

reviewer *noun* someone who reviews, especially someone whose job is to write critical reviews of books, plays, etc.

revile /rɪˈvaɪl/ ▻ *verb* (***reviled, reviling***) **1** to abuse or criticize someone or something bitterly or scornfully. **2** *intr* to speak scornfully or use abusive language; to rail (see RAIL 2). • **revilement** *noun* **1** the act of reviling. **2** a reviling speech. • **reviler** *nouns.* ◷ 14c: from French *reviler*, from Latin *vilis* worthless.

revise /rɪˈvaɪz/ ▻ *verb* (***revised, revising***) **1** to examine something again in order to identify and correct faults, improve it or to take new circumstances into account, etc. **2** to correct faults and make improvements in, or bring up to date (a previously printed book), usually in preparing a new edition. **3** *tr & intr* to study or look at (a subject or one's notes on it) again, especially in preparation for an examination. **4** to reconsider or amend (eg an opinion, etc). ▻ *noun* **1** the action or result of revising; a revision. **2** *printing* a revised proof that includes corrections made to an earlier proof. • **revisable** *adj.* • **revisal** *noun* the action of revising; a revision. • **reviser** *noun.* • **revisory** *adj* **1** relating to revision. **2** capable of revising, or with the power to revise. ◷ 16c: from French *reviser*, from Latin *visere* to look at or examine.

Revised Standard Version ▻ *noun* (abbreviation **RSV**) a revision, made in 1946–52, of the Authorized Version of the Bible.

Revised Version ▻ *noun* (abbreviation **RV**) a revision, issued 1881–5, of the Authorized Version of the Bible.

revision /rɪˈvɪʒən/ ▻ *noun* **1** the action or result of revising, or process of being revised. **2** the action or process of studying or looking at a subject or notes on a subject again, especially in preparation for an examination. **3** a revised book, edition, article, etc. • **revisional** *adj.* • **revisionary** *adj.* ◷ 17c.

revisionism /rɪˈvɪʒənɪzəm/ ▻ *noun, politics* **1** the policy or practice of revising previously established political ideas, doctrines, etc. **2** a form of Communism that favours modification of stricter orthodox Communism and evolution rather than revolution as a way of achieving socialism. • **revisionist** *noun, adj.* ◷ Early 20c.

revitalize or **revitalise** /riːˈvaɪtəlaɪz/ ▻ *verb* to give new life or energy to someone or something. ◷ 19c.

revival /rɪˈvaɪvəl/ ▻ *noun* **1** the act or process of reviving or state of being revived. **2** a renewed interest, especially in old customs, fashions, styles, etc. **3** a new production or performance, especially of an old play or one that has not recently been staged. **4** a period of renewed religious faith and spirituality. **5** a series of evangelistic and often emotional meetings to encourage renewed religious faith. • **revivalism** *noun* the promotion of renewed religious faith and spirituality through evangelistic meetings. • **revivalist** *noun.* • **revivalistic** *adj.* ◷ 17c.

revive /rɪˈvaɪv/ ▻ *verb* (***revived, reviving***) *tr & intr* **1** to come or bring someone back to consciousness, strength, health, vitality, etc. **2** said of old customs, fashions, styles, etc: to come or bring back into use or fashion, to an active state, to notice, etc. **3** to perform again after a long time (a play that has not been recently staged). • **revivability** *noun.* • **revivable** *adj.* • **revivably** *adverb.* • **reviver** *noun* **1** someone or something that revives. **2** a substance that renovates or restores eg colour, lustre, etc. **3** *colloq* a stimulant, especially an alcoholic drink. • **reviving** *noun, adj.* • **revivingly** *adverb.* ◷ 15c: from French *revivre*, from Latin *revivere* to live again, from *vivere* to live.

revivify ▷ *verb* to put new life into someone or something; to revive. • **revivification** *noun*. ⓒ 17c.

revocable /ˈrɛvəkəbəl/ or **revokable** or **revokeable** /rɪˈvoʊkəbl/ ▷ *adj* capable of being revoked or recalled. • **revocability** *noun*. • **revocably** *adverb*. ⓒ 15c.

revoke /rɪˈvoʊk/ ▷ *verb* (***revoked, revoking***) **1** to cancel or make (a will, agreement, etc) no longer valid; to annul. **2** *intr, cards* to fail to follow suit in cards when one should and is able to do so. ▷ *noun, cards* an act of revoking. • **revoker** *noun, cards* someone who revokes. • **revocation** /rɛvəˈkeɪʃən/ *noun* the action of revoking or annulling something, or the state of being revoked or annulled; cancellation. • **revocatory** *adj*. ⓒ 14c: from Latin *revocare* to call back or withdraw, from *vocare* to call.

revolt /rɪˈvoʊlt/ ▷ *verb* (***revolted, revolting***) **1** *intr* to rebel or rise up against a government, authority, etc □ *revolted against the military junta.* **2 a** to provoke a feeling of disgust, loathing or revulsion □ *just the thought of it revolts me*; **b** *intr* to feel disgust, loathing or revulsion □ *I revolt at the very thought of it.* ▷ *noun* a rebellion or uprising against a government, authority, etc. • **revolted** *adj* disgusted; horrified. • **revolting** *adj* **1** causing a feeling of disgust, loathing, etc; nauseating. **2** rising in revolt; rebellious. • **revoltingly** *adverb*. ⓒ 16c: from French *révolter*.

revolute /ˈrɛvəluːt, rɛvəˈljuːt/ ▷ *adj, chiefly bot* said of the edges of a leaf: rolled backwards and usually downwards. ⓒ 18c: from Latin *revolvere, revolatum* to revolve.

revolution /rɛvəˈluːʃən/ ▷ *noun* **1** the overthrow or rejection of a government or political system by the governed, often, but not necessarily, involving violence. **2** in Marxism: **a** the class struggle ending with the working class taking control of the means of production and becoming the ruling class; **b** the transition from one system of production to another, the political changes brought about as a result of this, and ending with the establishment of Communism. **3** complete, drastic and usually far-reaching change in ideas, social habits, ways of doing things, etc □ *the Industrial Revolution.* **4 a** the action of turning or moving round an axis; **b** one complete circle or turn round an axis. **5** *astron* **a** the action of one planet or object moving in an orbit around another; **b** one such orbital movement; **c** the time taken to make one such orbital movement. **6 a** a cycle of events; **b** the time taken to go through such a cycle and return to the starting point. **7** *geol* a time of major change in the earth's features. • **revolutionism** *noun* the theory of or support for political, social, etc revolution. • **revolutionist** *noun* someone who supports or advocates revolution; a revolutionary. ▷ *adj* relating to revolution. ⓒ 14c: from French *révolution*.

revolutionary /rɛvəˈluːʃənərɪ/ ▷ *adj* **1** relating to or like a revolution. **2** in favour of and supporting political, social, etc revolution. **3** completely new or different; involving radical change. ▷ *noun* (***revolutionaries***) someone who takes part in or is in favour of political, social, etc revolution in general, or a particular revolution.

Revolutionary Calendar ▷ *noun* the calendar used in France from 1793 to 1805.

revolutionize or **revolutionise** ▷ *verb* (***revolutionized, revolutionizing***) **1** to bring about revolution, eg in a country's political system, government, etc. **2** to inspire (people) with revolutionary ideas. **3** to bring about great, radical or fundamental changes in (eg ideas, social habits, ways of doing things, etc) □ *computers have revolutionised many businesses.* ⓒ 18c.

revolve /rɪˈvɒlv/ ▷ *verb* (***revolved, revolving***) **1** *tr & intr* to move or turn, or make something move or turn, in a circle around a central point; to rotate. **2** *intr* (*usually* **revolve around** or **about something**) to have it as a centre, focus or main point. **3** *intr* to occur in cycles or at regular intervals. **4** *tr & intr* to consider or be considered in turn □ *revolve the ideas in her head.* ▷ *noun, theat* a section of a stage that can be rotated, providing a means of scene-changing. • **revolvable** *adj*. • **revolving** *adj* **1** able, designed, etc to revolve. **2** recurring at regular intervals. ⓒ 14c: from Latin *revolvere* to roll back.

revolver /rɪˈvɒlvə(r)/ ▷ *noun* a pistol with a revolving cylinder that holds several bullets, which allows the pistol to be fired several times without reloading. ⓒ 19c.

revolving credit ▷ *noun* credit that is automatically renewed as the sum borrowed is paid back, allowing the borrower to use the credit repeatedely provided the agreed maximum amount is not exceeded.

revolving door ▷ *noun* a door made up of several, usually four, sections rotating around a central axis.

revue /rɪˈvjuː/ ▷ *noun* a humorous theatrical show, that includes songs, sketches, etc which are often satirical. ⓒ 19c: French, meaning 'review'.

revulsion /rɪˈvʌlʃən/ ▷ *noun* **1** a feeling of complete disgust, distaste or repugnance. **2** a sudden and often violent change of feeling, especially from love to hate. **3** the action of drawing or state of being drawn back or away. • **revulsive** *adj*. ⓒ 16c: from Latin *revulsio*.

revved and **revving** see under REV

reward /rɪˈwɔːd/ ▷ *noun* **1** something given or received in return for work done, a service rendered, good behaviour, etc. **2** a sum of money offered, usually for finding or helping to find a criminal, stolen or lost property, etc. **3** something given or received in return, usually for usually for doing something good but sometimes for something evil. ▷ *verb* (***rewarded, rewarding***) to give something to someone to show gratitude or in recompense for work done, services rendered, help, good behaviour, etc. • **rewardable** *adj*. • **rewarder** *noun*. • **rewarding** *adj* giving personal pleasure or satisfaction; worthwhile □ *a rewarding job.* • **rewardless** *adj*. ⓒ 13c: from French *reguarder* to regard.

rewarewa /ˈreɪwəreɪwə/ ▷ *noun* **1** a tall New Zealand forest tree. **2** the light wood of this tree, used for making furniture. ⓒ 19c: Maori, from *rewa* to float.

rewind ▷ *verb* /riːˈwaɪnd/ (***rewound, rewinding***) **1** to wind (eg thread) again. **2** to wind (tape, film, etc) back to the beginning, to a specified place, or back onto its original reel. ▷ *noun* /ˈriːwaɪnd/ **1** the action of rewinding. **2** something that is rewound. **3** a mechanism for rewinding tape, film, etc. • **rewinder** *noun*. ⓒ 18c.

rewire ▷ *verb* to fit (a house, etc) with a new system of electrical wiring. • **rewirable** or **rewireable** *adj*. ⓒ Early 20c.

reword ▷ *verb* to express something in different words. • **rewording** *noun* **1** the action of expressing in different words. **2** something that is reworded. ⓒ 19c.

rework /riːˈwɜːk/ ▷ *verb* (***reworked, reworking***) **1** to work something again. **2** to alter or refashion something in order to use it again. **3** to revise or rewrite something. • **reworking** *noun* **1** the action of working something again, or of altering, revising it, etc. **2** something that is reworked, especially something that is revised or rewritten. ⓒ 19c.

rewrite ▷ *verb* /riːˈraɪt/ **1** to write something again or in different words. **2** *computing* to retain (data) in an area of store by recording it in the location from which it has been read. ▷ *noun* /ˈriːraɪt/ **1** the action of rewriting. **2** something that is rewritten.

Rex ▷ *noun* **1** king. **2** now used mainly on coins, official documents, etc: the title of the reigning king. Also abbreviated to **R** in signatures. Compare REGINA. ⓒ 17c: Latin.

Reye's syndrome /raɪz —/ ▷ *noun, medicine* a rare, acute, and often fatal metabolic disease of children that affects the brain and liver. ⓒ 1960s: named after the Australian paediatrician R D K Reye (1912–78).

Reynard or **reynard** /'reɪnɑːd, 'rɛ-/ ▷ *noun* a name for a fox, especially in stories, fables, etc.

Reynolds number /'rɛnəldz —/ ▷ *noun, mech* a number designating the type of flow of a fluid in a system. ⓒ Early 20c: named after the Irish engineer and physicist Osborne Reynolds (1842–1912).

RF ▷ *abbreviation* radio frequency.

Rf ▷ *symbol, chem* rutherfordium.

RFC ▷ *abbreviation* **1** Royal Flying Corps. **2** Rugby Football Club.

RFU ▷ *abbreviation* Rugby Football Union.

RGN ▷ *abbreviation* Registered General Nurse.

RGS ▷ *abbreviation* Royal Geographical Society.

RGV ▷ *abbreviation* Remote Guidance Vehicle.

RH ▷ *abbreviation* **1** *IVR* Republic of Haiti. **2** Royal Highness.

Rh ▷ *abbreviation* rhesus, especially in RH FACTOR. ▷ *symbol, chem* rhodium.

rh ▷ *abbreviation* right hand.

RHA ▷ *abbreviation* **1** Royal Hibernian Academy. **2** Royal Horse Artillery.

rhabdomancy /'rabdəmansɪ/ ▷ *noun* divination by rod or wand, especially divining for water or ore. • **rhabdomancer** *noun*. • **rhabdomantist** *noun*. ⓒ 17c: from Greek *rhabdos* a rod + -MANCY.

rhachis and **rhachides** see under RACHIS

Rhaetian /'riːʃən/ ▷ *noun* a generic name for the various Romance dialects spoken in Switzerland and N Italy, comprising **Romansch**, spoken in SE Switzerland and N Italy; **Ladin**, spoken in Italy (S Tyrol); and **Friulian**, spoken in N Italy. ▷ *adj* relating to these dialects. ⓒ 16c: named after Rhaetia, a province in the Roman Empire.

rhagades /'ragədiːz/ ▷ *plural noun, medicine* cracks or fissures in the skin. • **rhagadiform** *adj*. ⓒ 17c: Greek, plural of *rhagas* a tear or rent.

rhapsodize or **rhapsodise** /'rapsədaɪz/ ▷ *verb* (***rhapsodized***, ***rhapsodizing***) *tr & intr* to speak or write with great enthusiasm or emotion. • **rhapsodist** *noun*.

rhapsody /'rapsədɪ/ ▷ *noun* (***rhapsodies***) **1** *music* a piece of music, emotional in character and usually written to suggest a free form or improvisation. **2** an exaggeratedly enthusiastic and highly emotional speech, piece of writing, etc. **3** *historical* in ancient Greece: an epic poem, or part of one, of a length that makes it suitable to be recited all at one time. • **rhapsodic** /rap'sɒdɪk/ or **rhapsodical** *adj* **1** like, relating to or characteristic of a rhapsody. **2** exaggeratedly enthusiastic, highly emotional, etc. • **rhapsodically** *adverb*. ⓒ 16c: from Latin *rhapsodia*, from Greek *rhapsoidia* an epic, from *rhaptein* to sew or work together + *oide* song.

rhatany /'ratənɪ/ ▷ *noun* (***rhatanies***) **1** either of two S American leguminous plants. **2** the thick fleshy root of these plants used as an astringent. ⓒ 19c: from Spanish *ratania*, probably from Quechua *ratánya*.

rhea /rɪə/ ▷ *noun* (***rheas***) a S American flightless bird resembling the ostrich but smaller. ⓒ 19c: Latin, named after Rhea the mother of Zeus in Greek mythology.

Rhenish /'rɛnɪʃ/ ▷ *adj* relating to the River Rhine or the regions bordering it. ▷ *noun* RHINE WINE.

rhenium /'riːnɪəm/ ▷ *noun, chem* (symbol **Re**, atomic number 75) a rare silvery-white metallic element whose very high melting point (3180°C) makes it a useful ingredient in alloys. ⓒ 1920s: named by its discoverer after the River Rhine (*Rhenus* in Latin).

rheo- /riːoʊ/ ▷ *combining form, signifying* current or flow. ⓒ From Greek *rheos* a stream, or anything that flows, from *rhein* to flow.

rheology /rɪ'ɒlədʒɪ/ ▷ *noun, physics* the scientific study of the deformation and flow of matter subjected to force. • **rheological** *adj*. • **rheologist** *noun*. ⓒ 1920s.

rheostat /'rɪəstat/ ▷ *noun, elec* a variable resistor that enables the resistance to a current in an electric circuit to be increased or decreased, thereby varying the current without interrupting the current flow, eg as when dimming a light bulb. • **rheostatic** *adj*. ⓒ 19c.

rhesus /'riːsəs/ and **rhesus monkey** ▷ *noun* a macaque, a small N Indian monkey. ⓒ 19c: Latin, named after *Rhesos* a mythical king of Thrace in Greek mythology.

rhesus factor or **Rh factor** ▷ *noun, medicine* an ANTIGEN that is present on the surface of red blood cells of about 84% of the human population, who are said to be **rhesus positive**, and absent in the remaining 16%, who are said to be **rhesus negative**. It is necessary to discover whether someone is Rhesus positive or negative before a blood transfusion. ⓒ 1940s: named after the rhesus monkey, in which it was first discovered.

rhetoric ▷ *noun* /'rɛtərɪk/ **1** the art of speaking and writing well, elegantly and effectively, especially in order to persuade or influence others. **2** the theory and practice of using language effectively. **3** *derog* language which is full of unnecessarily long, formal or literary words and phrases, and which is also often insincere or meaningless ▫ *mere rhetoric*. • **rhetorical** /rɪ'tɒrɪkəl/ *adj* **1** relating to or using rhetoric. **2** over-elaborate or insincere in style. • **rhetorically** *adverb*. • **rhetorician** /rɛtə'rɪʃən/ *noun* **1** *historical* a teacher of the art of rhetoric. **2** an orator. **3** *derog* someone who uses rhetorical over-elaborate language. ⓒ 14c: from Greek *rhetorike techne* rhetorical art.

rhetorical question ▷ *noun* a question that is asked in order to produce an effect rather than to gain information, the answer usually being implied in the question. ⓒ 19c.

rheum /ruːm/ ▷ *noun* a watery mucous discharge from the nose or eyes. • **rheumed** *adj*. • **rheumy** *adj* **1** relating to or like rheum. **2** said especially of air: cold and damp. ⓒ 14c: from French *reume*, from Greek *rheuma* bodily HUMOUR, from *rhein* to flow.

rheumatic /rʊ'matɪk/ ▷ *adj* **1** relating to, like or caused by rheumatism. **2** affected with rheumatism. ▷ *noun* **1** someone who suffers from rheumatism. **2** (**rheumatics**) *colloq* rheumatism or pain caused by it. • **rheumatically** *adverb*. • **rheumaticky** *adj, colloq* like, or suffering from, rheumatism. ⓒ 14c: from French *reumatique*, from Greek *rheumatikos*, from *rheuma* rheum.

rheumatic fever ▷ *noun, medicine* a disease mainly affecting children and young adults, caused by a streptocccal bacterium that initially destroys blood cells. This can then lead to fever, arthritis that spreads from one joint to another, involuntary movements (Sydenham's chorea), skin disorders and inflammation of the heart valves which may cause permanent damage or lead to heart failure.

rheumatism /'ruːmətɪzəm/ ▷ *noun* a disease characterized by painful swelling of the joints (eg of the hips, knees, fingers, etc) and muscles, and which causes stiffness and pain when moving them. ⓒ 17c: from Latin *rheumatismus*, from Greek *rheumatismos*, from *rheuma* flow or rheum.

rheumatoid /'ruːmətɔɪd/ *adj* relating to or like rheumatism or rheumatoid arthritis.

rheumatoid arthritis ▷ *noun, medicine* a form of ARTHRITIS, particularly common in women, that causes pain, swelling, stiffness and deformity of the joints, especially of the fingers, wrists, ankles, feet or hips.

rheumatology /ruːmə'tɒlədʒɪ/ ▷ *noun, medicine* the branch of medicine that deals with the study of rheumatism and related disorders of the joints and muscles. • **rheumatological** *adj*. • **rheumatologist** *noun*. ⓒ 1940s.

rheumed and **rheumy** see under RHEUM

Rh factor see RHESUS FACTOR

RHG ▷ *abbreviation* Royal Horse Guards.

rhin- see RHINO-

rhinal /'raɪnəl/ ▷ *adj, anatomy* relating to the nose. ◷ 19c: from Greek *rhis, rhinos* nose.

rhinestone /'raɪnstoʊn/ ▷ *noun* **1** a rock crystal. **2** an imitation diamond usually made from glass or plastic. ◷ 19c: a translation of French *caillou du Rhin*, literally 'stone of the Rhine' referring to Strasbourg, a town on this river where such gems were made.

Rhine wine /raɪn waɪn/ ▷ *noun* an imprecise term for any wine made from grapes grown in the valley of the River Rhine.

rhinitis /raɪ'naɪtɪs/ ▷ *noun, medicine* inflammation of the mucous membrane of the nasal passages, accompanied by the discharge of mucus, eg as a symptom of the common cold or of certain allergies. ◷ 19c.

rhino¹ /raɪnoʊ/ ▷ *noun* (***rhinos*** or ***rhino***) short form of RHINOCEROS.

rhino² /'raɪnoʊ/ ▷ *noun, slang* money. ◷ 17c.

rhino- /'raɪnoʊ, raɪ'nɒ/ or (before a vowel) **rhin-** /raɪn/ ▷ *combining form*, denoting or relating to the nose. ◷ From Greek *rhis, rhinos* nose.

rhino bar see ROO BAR

rhinoceros /raɪ'nɒsərəs/ ▷ *noun* (***rhinoceroses*** or ***rhinoceros***) any of five species of a large herbivorous mammal, including three Asian species and two African species, with very thick skin that is usually almost hairless, and either one or two horns on its snout. • **rhinocerotic** /raɪnɒsə'rɒtɪk/ *adj.* ◷ 14c: from Greek *rhinokeros*, from *rhis, rhinos* nose + *keras* horn.

rhinology /raɪ'nɒlədʒɪ/ ▷ *noun* the branch of medicine that deals with the study of the nose. • **rhinological** *adj.* • **rhinologist** *noun.* ◷ 19c.

rhinoplasty /'raɪnoʊplastɪ/ ▷ *noun* plastic surgery of the nose. • **rhinoplastic** /-'plastɪk/ *adj.* ◷ 19c.

rhinoscopy /raɪ'nɒskəpɪ/ ▷ *noun, medicine* examination of the nasal passages, especially by means of an instrument called a **rhinoscope** /'raɪnoʊskoʊp/ . • **rhinoscopic** /raɪnoʊ'skɒpɪk/ *adj.* ◷ 19c.

rhinovirus /'raɪnoʊvaɪərəs/ ▷ *noun, biol* an RNA virus belonging to the PICORNAVIRUS family. The 90 different forms are responsible for 50% of cases of the common cold. ◷ 1960s.

rhizo- /raɪzoʊ, raɪ'zɒ/ or (before a vowel) **rhiz-** ▷ *combining form, denoting* root. ◷ From Greek *rhiza* root.

rhizocarp /'raɪzoʊkɑːp/ ▷ *noun, bot* **1** a perennial herb. **2** a plant that fruits underground. • **rhizocarpic** /-'kɑːpɪk/ or **rhizocarpous** /-'kɑːpəs/ *adj* said of plants: **1** with perennial roots but a stem that dies down each year. **2** producing fruit underground. ◷ 19c: from RHIZO- + Greek *karpos* flower.

rhizoid /'raɪzɔɪd/ ▷ *noun, bot* a small, often colourless, hairlike outgrowth that functions as a root in certain algae, and in mosses, liverworts and some ferns, absorbing water and mineral salts, and providing anchorage. • **rhizoidal** *adj.* ◷ 19c.

rhizome /'raɪzoʊm/ ▷ *noun, bot* a thick horizontal underground stem which produces roots and leafy shoots. • **rhizomatous** /raɪ'zoʊmətəs/ *adj.* ◷ 19c.

rhizopod ▷ *noun, zool* a protozoan with rootlike protrusions for movement and feeding. ◷ 19c.

rho /roʊ/ ▷ *noun* (***rhos***) the seventeenth letter of the Greek alphabet, corresponding to R. See table at GREEK ALPHABET. ◷ 14c.

rhod- see RHODO-

rhodamine /'roʊdəmiːn/ ▷ *noun* any of a group of synthetic dyestuffs, usually red or pink. ◷ 19c.

Rhode Island Red /roʊd — —/ ▷ *noun* an American breed of domestic fowl, usually with a browny-red plumage.

rhodie see RHODY

rhodium /'roʊdɪəm/ ▷ *noun, chem* (symbol **Rh**, atomic number 45) a hard, silvery-white metallic element, used to make temperature-resistant platinum alloys for thermocouples and electrical components, to plate jewellery, and to coat reflectors on optical instruments. It is also used as a catalyst to control car exhaust emissions. ◷ 19c: Latin, from Greek *rhodon* rose, from its rose-coloured salts.

rhodo- /roʊdoʊ, roʊ'dɒ/ or (before a vowel) **rhod-** ▷ *combining form, denoting* rose or rose-coloured. ◷ From Greek *rhodon* rose.

rhodochrosite /roʊdə'kroʊsaɪt/ ▷ *noun, mineralogy* manganese carbonate, occurring as a pink, brown or grey mineral in hexagonal crystalline form, principally used as a semiprecious stone. ◷ 19c: from Greek *rhodokhros*, from *khros* colour.

rhododendron /roʊdə'dɛndrən/ ▷ *noun* (***rhododendrons*** or ***rhododendra*** /-drə/) any of various trees and shrubs of the heath family, native to S Asia and widely cultivated in N temperate regions, usually with thick evergreen leaves and large showy colourful flowers. ◷ 17c: from Greek *rhodon* rose + *dendron* tree.

rhodolite /'roʊdəlaɪt/ ▷ *noun* a pink or purple garnet, used as a gemstone. ◷ 19c.

rhodonite /'roʊdənaɪt/ ▷ *noun, mineralogy* manganese silicate in crystalline form, often with some calcium, iron or magnesium, brownish in colour or rose-red when pure. ◷ 19c: from Greek *rhodon* rose + -ITE.

rhodopsin /roʊ'dɒpsɪn/ ▷ *noun, biochem* the light-sensitive pigment found in rod cells in the retina of the vertebrate eye which, on exposure to light, is chemically converted to its components, opsin and retinal, which stimulate the production of a nerve impulse to allow vision, particularly in dim light (night vision). Also called **visual purple**. ◷ 19c: from RHODO- + Greek *opsis* sight + -IN.

rhody or **rhodie** /'rɒdi/ ▷ *noun* (***rhodies***) *colloq* a short form of RHODODENDRON. ◷ 19c.

rhomb /rɒm, rɒmb/ ▷ *noun* **1** *geom* a RHOMBUS. **2** *crystallog* a RHOMBOHEDRON. ◷ 19c in sense 2; 16c in sense 1: from French *rhombe*; see RHOMBUS.

rhombohedron /rɒmboʊ'hiːdrən/ ▷ *noun* (***rhombohedra*** /-drə/ or ***rhombohedrons***) *chiefly crystallog* a solid object, especially a crystal, with six equal sides, each side being a rhombus. Also called RHOMB. • **rhombohedral** *adj.* ◷ 19c.

rhomboid /'rɒmbɔɪd/ ▷ *noun* a four-sided shape, usually one that is neither a rhombus nor a rectangle, that has opposite sides and angles equal, two angles being greater and two smaller than a right angle, and two sides being longer than the other two. ▷ *adj* (*also* **rhomboidal**) shaped like a rhomboid or a rhombus. ◷ 16c: from Greek *rhomboeides* shaped like a rhombus.

rhombus /'rɒmbəs/ ▷ *noun* (***rhombuses*** or ***rhombi*** /-baɪ/) **1** *geom* a four-sided shape with all four sides equal, two opposite angles being greater than a right angle and two smaller. Also called **rhomb**. **2** a lozenge or diamond shape, or an object with this shape. • **rhombic** /'rɒmbɪk/ *adj.* ◷ 16c: Latin, from Greek *rhombos* anything which may be spun round, from *rhembein* to spin aroun.

rhonchus /'rɒŋkəs/ ▷ *noun* (***rhonchi*** /-kaɪ/) a rasping or whistling, similar to the sound of snoring, produced when air passes through partly blocked or restricted bronchi. • **rhonchal** or **rhonchial** *adj* **1** relating to a rhonchus. **2** relating to snoring. ◷ 19c: Latin, from Greek *rhenchos* snoring.

RHS ▻ *abbreviation* **1** Royal Highland Show. **2** Royal Historical Society. **3** Royal Horticultural Society. **4** Royal Humane Society.

rhubarb /'ruːbɑːb/ ▻ *noun* **1** a perennial plant, cultivated in N temperate regions, that has very large poisonous leaves with long fleshy edible stalks. **2** the reddish fleshy leafstalks of this plant which can be sweetened with sugar, cooked and eaten. **3** the roots of a type of rhubarb found in China and Tibet, dried and used as a laxative. **4** *colloq* the continuous murmured sound made by actors to give the impression of indistinct background conversation, made especially by constantly repeating the word 'rhubarb'. **5** *colloq* nonsense; rubbish. • **rhubarbing** *noun, colloq* the use or practice of constantly repeating the word 'rhubarb' to give the impression of conversation. ⓘ 14c: from Greek *rheon barbaron* foreign rhubarb.

rhumb /rʌm/ ▻ *noun* **1** (*also* **rhumb-line**) an imaginary line on the surface of the earth that intersects all meridians at the same angle, used in navigation to plot direction on a chart. **2** (*also* **rhumb-line**) the course of a vessel or aircraft travelling in a fixed direction along such a line. **3** any point of the compass. ⓘ 16c: from Spanish *rumbo*, from Latin *rhombus* rhombus.

rhumba see RUMBA

rhyme /raɪm/ ▻ *noun* **1** a pattern of words which have the same final sounds at the ends of lines in a poem. **2** the use of such patterns in poetry, etc. **3** a word which has the same final sound as another □ ***'beef' is a rhyme for 'leaf'***. **4** a short poem, verse or jingle written in rhyme. ▻ *verb* (***rhymed, rhyming***) **1** *intr* said of words: to have the same final sounds and so form rhymes. **2** to use (a word) as a rhyme for another. **3** *intr* to write using rhymes. **4** to put (a story, etc) into rhyme. • **rhymed** *adj.* • **rhymeless** *adj.* • **rhymer** *noun.* • **rhymester** /'raɪmstə(r)/ *noun* a would-be poet, especially one who is not very talented. • **rhymist** *noun.* • **without rhyme or reason** lacking sense, reason or any discernible system. ⓘ 13c: from French *rimer* to rhyme, from German *rim* a series or row. Despite the current spelling of the word, it is probably not associated with Latin *rhythmus*, from Greek *rhythmos* rhythm.

rhyme-royal ▻ *noun* a seven line stanza with its lines rhyming in the pattern *a b a b b c c*, used by Chaucer, who encountered it in French.

rhyme-scheme ▻ *noun* the particular pattern of rhymes in a stanza, etc.

rhyming slang ▻ *noun* a type of slang, especially Cockney, in which the word meant is replaced by a phrase in which the last word rhymes with it, the phrase then often being shortened to only the first word, eg '*butcher's hook*' is rhyming slang for '*look*', and is normally shortened to '*butcher's*', as in '*have a butcher's*'.

rhyolite /'raɪəlaɪt/ ▻ *noun, geol* any of a group of fine-grained light-coloured igneous rocks, similar in chemical composition to granite, that often contain larger crystals of especially quartz or potassium feldspar. • **rhyolitic** /raɪə'lɪtɪk/ *adj.* ⓘ 19c: from Greek *rhyax* lava stream.

rhythm /'rɪðəm/ ▻ *noun* **1** a regularly repeated pattern, movement, beat or sequence of events. **2 a** the regular arrangement of stress, notes of different lengths, and pauses in a piece of music; **b** a particular pattern of stress, notes, etc in music □ ***tango rhythm***. **3** in poetry or other writing: a regular arrangement of sounds, and of stressed and unstressed syllables, giving a sense or feeling of movement; metre. **4** ability to sing, speak, move, etc rhythmically. **5** short form of RHYTHM SECTION. **6** in painting, sculpture, architecture, etc: a regular and harmonious pattern of shapes, colours, areas of shade and light, empty spaces, etc. • **rhythmic** /'rɪðmɪk/ or **rhythmical** *adj* **1** relating to rhythm. **2** said of music, language, etc: **a** characterized by rhythm; **b** with a pleasing rhythm. **3** said of movement, sound, some occurrence, etc: with a noticeable, regularly recurring pattern. • **rhythmically** *adverb.* • **rhythmicity** /rɪð'mɪsɪtɪ/ *noun* **1** the fact of being rhythmic. **2** ability to maintain a rhythm. • **rhythmist** /'rɪðmɪst/ *noun* someone who is knowledgeable about or skilled in rhythm. ⓘ 16c: from Latin *rhythmus*, from Greek *rhythmos*, from *rheein* to flow.

rhythm and blues ▻ *singular noun, music* (abbreviation **R & B**) a style of popular music, originating in the 1940s, when it was almost exclusively played by Black US artists. It combines certain features of the blues with lively rhythms more typical of rock music.

rhythm method ▻ *noun* a method of contraception that involves monitoring the woman's menstrual cycle and avoiding sexual intercourse on the days when conception is most likely to occur.

rhythm section ▻ *noun, music* **1** the instruments in a band or group, eg drums, double bass and piano, whose main function is to supply the rhthym. **2** the players of these instruments.

rhytidectomy /raɪtɪ'dɛktəmɪ/ ▻ *noun* (***rhytidectomies***) *surgery* **1** removal of wrinkles, especially from the face. **2** an operation to remove wrinkles, especially from the face. *Non-technical equivalent* FACELIFT. ⓘ 1930s: from Greek *rhytis* a wrinkle + -ECTOMY.

RI ▻ *abbreviation* **1 a** *Regina et Imperatrix* (Latin), Queen and Empress; **b** *Rex et Imperator* (Latin), King and Emperor. **2** religious instruction. **3** *IVR* Republic of Indonesia. **4** *US state* Rhode Island. **5** (Member of the) Royal Institute of Painters in Watercolours. **6** Royal Institution.

RIA ▻ *abbreviation* Royal Irish Academy.

ria /'rɪə/ ▻ *noun* (***rias***), *geog* a long narrow coastal inlet, differing from a fjord in that it gradually decreases in depth and width from its mouth inland, usually surrounded by hills, and formed by the flooding of river valleys. ⓘ 19c: from Spanish *ria* rivermouth.

rial /'raɪəl, 'riːɑːl/ ▻ *noun* **1** the standard unit of currency of Iran. **2** the standard unit of currency of Oman. **3** a RIYAL. ⓘ 1930s in these senses; historically a coin of various values.

RIAM ▻ *abbreviation* Royal Irish Academy of Music.

rib[1] ▻ *noun* **1** in vertebrates: any one of the slightly flexible bones which curve round and forward from the spine, forming the chest wall and protecting the heart and lungs. **2** a cut of meat containing one or more ribs. **3** any part or section of an object or structure that resembles a rib in form or fuction, eg part of a framework. **4** one of the pieces of wood which curve round and upward from a ship's keel to form the framework of the hull. **5** *archit* a curved raised band-like section or moulding of a structure that supports or defines a vault, dome or ceiling. **6** one of the parallel beams or girders that support a bridge. **7** *mining* a section of coal left in place to support the roof of the mine. **8** a rod-like bar which supports and strengthens a layer of fabric, membrane, etc, eg in an umbrella or in the wing of an insect or aircraft. **9** one of the larger veins in a leaf. **10** the shaft of a feather. **11** a vein of ore in rock. **12** a projecting ridge or strip of land. **13 a** a raised ridge in knitted or woven material; **b** *knitting* the series of such ridges, produced by alternating plain and purl stiches, eg around the waistband, wristbands, etc of a garment to provide elasticity. **14** *bookbinding* each of the raised lines on the spine of a book where the stitching runs across. ▻ *verb* (***ribbed, ribbing***) **1** to provide, support or enclose (an object, structure, etc) with ribs. **2** *knitting* to knit ribs on a garment. • **ribbed** *adj* with ribs or ridges, or riblike markings. • **ribbing** *noun* an arrangement of ribs or a rib-like structure. • **ribless** *adj.* ⓘ Anglo-Saxon *ribb*.

rib[2] ▻ *verb* (***ribbed, ribbing***) *colloq* to tease; to mock gently. • **ribbing** *noun.* ⓘ 1930s: perhaps from the verb *rib tickle* to make someone laugh.

RIBA ▻ *abbreviation* Royal Institute of British Architects.

ribald /'rɪbəld, 'raɪ-/ ▻ *adj* said of language, a speaker, humour, etc: humorous in an obscene, vulgar or indecently disrespectful way. ▷ *noun* someone who speaks, behaves, etc in such a way. • **ribaldry** *noun* ribald language or behaviour. ⓘ 13c: from French *ribauld*, from *riber* to lead a licentious life.

riband or **ribband** /ˈrɪbənd/ ▷ *noun* a ribbon, now especially one awarded as a prize in sport, etc. ⓘ 14c: from French *reubon*.

ribbon /ˈrɪbən/ ▷ *noun* **1 a** fine, usually coloured, material such as silk, etc, formed into a long narrow strip or band; **b** a strip of such material used for decorating clothes, tying hair, parcels, etc. **2** any ribbon-like long narrow strip, eg of some material, or the form of a road or path, etc. **3** a small strip of coloured cloth, worn to show membership of a team, as a sign of having won an award, medal, etc. **4** a long narrow strip of inked cloth used to produce print in a typewriter, printer, etc. **5** (*usually* **ribbons**) strips or tatters of torn material ▫ *hanging in ribbons.* ▷ *verb* (***ribboned, ribboning***) **1** to decorate or tie something with a ribbon or ribbons. **2** to mark something with ribbon-like stripes. **3** *tr & intr* to form or separate into narrow strips. **4** *intr* (*usually* **ribbon out**) said eg of a road or path, or of some viscous or flexible substance: to extend in the form of a ribbon or a long narrow band. ⓘ 16c: from French *reubon*.

ribbon-development ▷ *noun* the extensive building of houses, flats, etc along the side of a main road leading out of a town. ⓘ 1920s.

ribbonfish ▷ *noun* any of several fish with a long narrow flattened body, especially the oar fish.

ribbon microphone ▷ *noun* a microphone that picks up sound by means of a thin metallic strip. Also (*colloq*) called **ribbon mike**.

ribcage /ˈrɪbkeɪdʒ/ ▷ *noun* the chest wall, formed by the ribs, which protects the heart and lungs. ⓘ 20c.

ribless see under RIB[1]

ribo- /raɪboʊ/ ▷ *combining form, denoting* ribonucleic acid.

riboflavin /raɪboʊˈfleɪvɪn/ and **riboflavine** /-viːn/ ▷ *noun* VITAMIN B_2. ⓘ 1930s.

ribonuclease /raɪboʊˈnjuːklɪeɪs, -klɪeɪz/ ▷ *noun, biochem* (abbreviation **RNase**) an enzyme (the first to be synthesized) which splits selectively the nucleotide components of RNA. ⓘ 1940s: from *ribonucl*eic acid + -ASE.

ribonucleic acid /raɪboʊnjʊˈkleɪɪk, -kliːɪk —/ ▷ *noun, biochem* (abbreviation **RNA**) **1** the nucleic acid, containing the sugar ribose, that is present in all living cells and plays an important part in the synthesis of proteins. **2** the hereditary material of some viruses. Compare DNA. ⓘ 1930s.

ribose /ˈraɪboʊs/ ▷ *noun, biochem* (formula $C_5H_{10}O_5$) a monosaccharide sugar that is an important component of ribonucleic acid and whose derivative deoxyribose is a constituent of DNA. ⓘ 19c: German, from *arabinose* a sugar in gum arabic.

ribosome /ˈraɪboʊsoʊm/ ▷ *noun, biol* in the cytoplasm of a living cell: any of many small particles that are the site of protein manufacture, each consisting of two subunits of different sizes and composed of RNA and protein. • **ribosomal** *adj.* ⓘ 1950s.

rib-tickler ▷ *noun, colloq* a very funny joke or story. • **rib-tickling** *adj.*

ribwort ▷ *noun* a common plantain that has narrow pointed leaves with prominent ribs. Also called **ribwort plantain**.

RIC ▷ *abbreviation* Royal Irish Constabulary.

rice /raɪs/ ▷ *noun* **1** an important cereal plant of the grass family, native to SE Asia and having branched flower-heads bearing numerous starchy grain-like seeds. The commonest higher-yielding type, **Lowland rice**, is cultivated in flooded paddy fields, while **Upland rice** is cultivated on dry land, and can be grown in cooler drier regions. **2** the edible starchy seeds resembling grains (known either as **long-grain rice** or **short-grain rice** depending on their shape) that are produced by this plant and which form the staple food for over half the world's population. These grains are called **brown rice** when only the outer fibrous husk of the seed is removed by milling, and **white rice** when the bran is then removed by polishing. Also *as adj* ▫ *rice fields* ▫ *rice pudding.* ▷ *verb* (***riced, ricing***) *N Amer cookery* to press soft food, especially cooked potatoes, through a coarse sieve (a **ricer**), to form strands or to give it a roughly mashed consistency. • **ricey** or **ricy** *adj.* ⓘ 13c: from French *ris*, from Italian *riso*, from Greek *óryza*.

rice bowl ▷ *noun* **1** a small dish for eating rice. **2** a fertile area that produces large quantities of rice.

rice paper ▷ *noun* **1** a very thin, almost transparent, edible paper made from the flattened and dried pith of an Asiatic tree, used in baking biscuits and cakes, and also for painting, especially in the oriental style. **2** a similar sort of paper made from the straw of rice or from other plants.

rich /rɪtʃ/ ▷ *adj* **1 a** having a lot of money, property or possessions; wealthy; **b** (**the rich**) rich people as a group (see THE 4b). **2** said of decoration, furnishings, etc: luxurious, costly and elaborate ▫ *rich clothes.* **3** high in value or quality ▫ *a rich harvest.* **4** (*usually* **rich in** or **with something**) abundantly supplied with it ▫ *rich in minerals.* **5** *in compounds* abundantly supplied with something specified ▫ *oil-rich.* **6** said of soil, a region, etc: very productive; fertile. **7** said of colours: vivid and intense; deep ▫ *rich red.* **8** said of a drink, especially an alchoholic one: with a full mellow well-matured flavour. **9** said of food: **a** heavily seasoned, or strongly flavoured; **b** containing a lot of fat, oil or dried fruit. **10** said of an odour: pungent, spicy, or with a strong fragrance. **11** said of a voice or a sound: full, mellow and deep. **12** said of a remark, suggestion, etc: unacceptable or outrageous; ridiculous ▫ *That's a bit rich!* **13** said of the mixture in an internal combustion engine: with a high proportion of fuel to air. • **richly** *adverb* **1** in a rich or elaborate way. **2** fully and suitably ▫ *richly deserved.* • **richness** *noun* **1** the state of being rich; wealth. **2** abundance. ⓘ Anglo-Saxon *rice* strong or powerful.

riches /ˈrɪtʃɪz/ ▷ *plural noun* wealth in general, or a particular form of abundance or wealth ▫ *family riches* ▫ *architectural riches.* ⓘ 12c: from French *richesse*.

Richter scale /ˈrɪxtə —/ ▷ *noun, meteorol* a logarithmic scale, ranging from 0 to 10, that is used to measure the magnitude of an earthquake, 8.9 being the highest value ever recorded. ⓘ 1930s: named after its inventor, US seismologist Charles Francis Richter (1900–85).

rick[1] ▷ *noun* a stack or heap, eg of hay, corn, etc, especially one that is made in a regular shape and usually thatched on the top. ▷ *verb* (***ricked, ricking***) to stack or heap (especially hay, corn, etc). ⓘ Anglo-Saxon *hreac*.

rick[2] ▷ *verb* (***ricked, ricking***) to sprain or wrench (one's neck, back, etc). ▷ *noun* a sprain or wrench. ⓘ 18c.

ricker /ˈrɪkə(r)/ ▷ *noun, originally naut* a spar or pole made from a young tree trunk. ⓘ 19c.

rickets /ˈrɪkɪts/ ▷ *singular or plural noun* a disease, especially of children, caused by vitamin D deficiency (either due to a poor diet or lack of sunlight), characterized by softness and imperfect formation of the bones, and often resulting in bow legs. *Technical equivalent* RACHITIS. ⓘ 17c.

rickettsia /rɪˈketsɪə/ ▷ *noun* (***rickettsiae*** /-sɪiː/ or ***rickettsias***) *medicine* any of a group of parasitic micro-organisms found in lice, ticks, etc, which can cause serious diseases such as typhus when transferred to humans. • **rickettsial** *adj.* ⓘ Early 20c: named after US pathologist, Howard Taylor Ricketts (1871–1910).

Mercalli and Richter Scales

Mercalli		Richter
1	detected only by seismographs	<3
2	**feeble** just noticeable by some people	3–3.4
3	**slight** similar to passing of heavy lorries	3.5–4
4	**moderate** rocking of loose objects	4–4.4
5	**quite strong** felt by most people even when sleeping	4.5–4.8
6	**strong** trees rock and some structural damage is caused	4.9–5.4
7	**very strong** walls crack	5.5–6
8	**destructive** weak buildings collapse	6.1–6.5
9	**ruinous** houses collapse and ground pipes crack	6.6–7
10	**disastrous** landslides occur, ground cracks and buildings collapse	7.1–7.3
11	**very disastrous** few buildings remain standing	7.4–8.1
12	**catastrophic** ground rises and falls in waves	>8.1

rickety /ˈrɪkɪtɪ/ ▻ *adj* **1** said of a construction, piece of furniture, etc: unsteady and likely to collapse; shaky or unstable. **2** said of the mind, etc: feeble. **3 a** suffering from or affected by rickets; **b** relating to rickets; rachitic. • **ricketiness** *noun*. ◎ 17c.

rick-rack or **ric-rac** /ˈrɪkrak/ ▻ *noun* a zigzag braid for decorating or trimming clothes, soft furnishings, etc. ◎ 19c: related to RACK[1].

rickshaw /ˈrɪkʃɔː/ or **ricksha** /-ʃə/ ▻ *noun* a small two-wheeled hooded carriage, either drawn by a person on foot, or attached to a bicycle or motorcycle. ◎ 19c: shortened from Japanese *jinrikisha*, from *jin* a person + *-riki* power + *-sha* a vehicle.

ricochet /ˈrɪkəʃeɪ, -ʃɛt/ ▻ *noun* **1** the action, especially of a bullet or other missile, of hitting a surface and then rebounding. **2** the sound made by such an action. ▻ *verb, intr* (***ricocheted*** /-ʃeɪd/ or ***ricochetted*** /-ʃɛtɪd/ , ***ricocheting*** /-ʃeɪɪŋ/ or ***ricochetting*** /-ʃɛtɪŋ/) said of an object, especially a bullet, projectile, etc: to hit or glance off a surface and rebound. ◎ 18c: French.

ricotta /rɪˈkɒtə/ ▻ *noun* (*in full* **ricotta cheese**) a soft white unsalted Italian curd cheese made from sheep's or cow's milk and often used in sauces for ravioli, lasagne, etc. ◎ 19c: Italian, meaning 'recooked', from Latin *recocta*, from *recoquere*, from *coquere* to cook.

ric-rac see RICK-RACK

RICS ▻ *abbreviation* Royal Institute of Chartered Surveyors.

rictus /ˈrɪktəs/ ▻ *noun* (**rictus** or ***rictuses***) **1** the gape of an open mouth, especially of a bird's beak. **2** an unnatural fixed grin or grimace. • **rictal** *adj*. ◎ 18c: Latin, literally 'open mouth', from *ringi, rictus* to gape.

ricy see under RICE

rid ▻ *verb* (***rid*** or (*archaic*) ***ridded, ridding***) (*usually* **rid something, someone** or **oneself of something**) to disencumber or free it, them or oneself from something undesirable or unwanted. • **be rid of something** or **someone** to be freed or disencumbered of something or someone troublesome or unwanted. • **get rid of something** or **someone** to disencumber, free or relieve oneself of something or someone undesirable or unwanted. ◎ 13c: from Norse *rythja* to clear.

riddance /ˈrɪdəns/ ▻ *noun* the act of freeing oneself from something undesirable or unwanted. • **good riddance** a welcome relief from someone or something undesirable or unwanted.

riddle[1] /ˈrɪdəl/ ▻ *noun* **1** a short and usually humorous puzzle, often in the form of a question, which describes something or someone in an obscure or misleading way, and which can only be solved or understood using ingenuity. **2** a person, thing or fact that is puzzling or difficult to understand. ▻ *verb* (***riddled, riddling***) **1** *intr* to speak in riddles; to speak enigmatically or obscurely. **2** to solve, understand or explain (a riddle). • **riddler** *noun*. ◎ Anglo-Saxon *rædels*.

riddle[2] /ˈrɪdəl/ ▻ *noun* a large coarse sieve used eg for sifting gravel or grain. ▻ *verb* (***riddled, riddling***) **1** to pass (gravel, grain, etc) through a riddle. **2** (*usually* **riddle with something**) to pierce with many holes, especially with gunshot ▫ *The wall was riddled with bullets.* **3** (*usually* **riddle with something**) to spread through; to fill ▫ *a government department riddled with corruption.* ◎ Anglo-Saxon *hriddel*.

ride ▻ *verb* (***rode, ridden, riding***) **1** to sit, usually astride, on and control the movements of (especially a horse, bicycle, motorbike, etc). **2** *intr* (*usually* **ride on** or **in something**) to travel or be carried on (a horse, bicycle, etc) or in (a car, train or other vehicle) ▫ *He rode into town on the bus.* **3** *chiefly N Amer* to travel on (a vehicle). **4** *intr* to go on horseback, especially regularly ▫ *She rides every Sunday.* **5** to ride (a horse) in a race ▫ *rode Red Rum to victory.* **6** to move across or be carried over (eg the sea, sky, etc) ▫ *a ship riding the waves.* **7** said of a ship: **a** *intr* to float at anchor; **b** to be attached to (an anchor). **8** *intr* said especially of the moon: to appear to float or be carried on something ▫ *The moon was riding high.* **9** (*usually* **ride over** or **across** or **through**) to travel over, across, through, etc by horse, car, etc ▫ *rode across the desert on camels.* **10** *intr* (*after* **ride on something**) to rest on or be supported by it while moving ▫ *a kite riding on the wind.* **11** to bend before (a blow, punch, etc) to reduce its impact. **12** *coarse slang* to have sexual intercourse with someone. ▻ *noun* **1 a** a journey or certain distance covered on horseback, on a bicycle or in a vehicle; **b** the duration of this ▫ *a long ride home.* **2** the horse, vehicle, etc on which one rides. **3** an experience or series of events of a specified nature ▫ *a rough ride.* **4** *especially N Amer* a LIFT (*noun* 5). **5** the type of movement, usually specified, felt when driving or travelling in a vehicle ▫ *The car gives a very smooth ride.* **6** a path or track, especially one through a wood or across an area of countryside, reserved for horseback riding. **7** a fairground machine, such as a roller-coaster or big wheel, on which people ride for pleasure. **8** *coarse slang* **a** an act of sexual intercourse; **b** a sexual partner, especially a female one. • **rider 1** someone who rides. **2** an object that rests on or astride another. **3** an addition to what has already been said or written, especially an extra clause added to a document; a qualification or amendment. • **riderless** *adj*. • **riding** *noun* see separate entry. • **let something ride** to leave it undisturbed; to make no attempt to change or do anything about it. • **ride for a fall** to act or behave in a way that will inevitably lead to disaster, or a very bad reaction from others. • **ride to hounds** to take part in fox-hunting on horseback. • **riding high** going through a period of success, confidence, popularity, etc. • **take someone for a ride** *colloq* to trick, cheat or deceive them. ◎ Anglo-Saxon *ridan*.

■ **ride on something** to depend completely upon it ▫ *It all rides on his answer.*

■ **ride someone off** *polo* to bump against another player's horse that is moving in the same direction.

■ **ride something out** to come through (eg a difficult, period, situation, etc) successfully, or to endure it until it improves ▫ *ride out the storm.*

■ **ride up** *intr* said of an item of clothing: to move gradually up the body out of the correct position □ *Her skirt rode up as she sat down.*

ridge /rɪdʒ/ ▷ *noun* **1** a strip of ground raised either side of a ploughed furrow. **2** any long narrow raised area on an otherwise flat surface. **3** the top edge of something where two upward sloping surfaces meet, eg on a roof. **4** a long narrow strip of relatively high ground with steep slopes on either side, often found between valleys. **5** *meteorol* a long narrow area of high atmospheric pressure, often associated with fine weather and strong breezes. Compare TROUGH 4. ▷ *verb* (***ridged, ridging***) *tr & intr* to form or make something into ridges. ● **ridged** *adj.* ● **ridging** *noun.* ⓘ Anglo-Saxon *hrycg.*

ridgepole and **ridgepiece** ▷ *noun* **1** the beam along the ridge of a roof to which the upper ends of the rafters are attached. **2** the horizontal pole at the top of a tent.

ridge-tile ▷ *noun* a tile shaped to cover the ridge of a roof.

ridgeway ▷ *noun* a track along the crest or ridge of a hill, especially a long one.

ridicule /ˈrɪdɪkjuːl/ ▷ *noun* language, laughter, behaviour, etc intended to make someone or something appear foolish or humiliated; mockery or derision. ▷ *verb* (***ridiculed, ridiculing***) to laugh at someone or something; to make fun of them or mock them. ● **ridiculer** *noun.* ● **hold someone** or **something up to ridicule** to subject or expose them or it to mockery or derision. ⓘ 17c: French, from Latin *ridiculus* laughable, from *ridere* to laugh.

ridiculous /rɪˈdɪkjʊləs/ ▷ *adj* deserving or provoking ridicule; silly or absurd. ● **ridiculously** *adverb* **1** in a ridiculous way. **2** to a ridiculous degree or extent; absurdly □ *ridiculously expensive.* ● **ridiculousness** *noun.*

riding¹ /ˈraɪdɪŋ/ ▷ *noun* **1** the art and practice of riding horses. **2** a track or path for horseback riding. Also *as adj* □ *riding school* □ *riding-crop.*

riding² /ˈraɪdɪŋ/ ▷ *noun* (*often* **Riding** when part of a name) **1** any of the three former administrative divisions of Yorkshire, **East Riding**, **North Riding** and **West Riding**. **2** *Can* a political constituency. ⓘ Anglo-Saxon as *thriding*, from Norse *thrithjungr*: third part.

riding-light ▷ *noun, naut* a light hung from the rigging of a ship at night when it is riding at anchor.

riel /rɪəl/ ▷ *noun* the standard unit of currency of Cambodia (formerly Kampuchea). ⓘ 1950s: Khmer.

Riesling /ˈriːslɪŋ, riːz-/ ▷ *noun* **1** a dry white wine produced in Germany, Alsace, Austria and elsewhere. **2** the type of vine and grape from which it is made. ⓘ 19c: German.

rife ▷ *adj* usually said of something unfavourable: **1** very common or frequently occurring; extensive; current. **2** abundant; numerous. **3** (*usually* **rife with something**) having a large amount or number of something bad or undesirable □ *The garden was rife with weeds.* ● **rifeness** *noun.* ⓘ Anglo-Saxon *ryfe.*

riff ▷ *noun, jazz, rock music, pop music* a short passage of music played repeatedly, often over changing chords or harmonies, or as an accompaniment to a solo improvisation. ▷ *verb* (***riffed, riffing***) *intr* to play riffs. ⓘ 1930s.

riffle /ˈrɪfəl/ ▷ *verb* (***riffled, riffling***) **1** *tr & intr* (*often* **riffle through something**) to flick or leaf through (the pages of a book, a pile of papers, etc) rapidly, especially in a casual search for something. **2** to shuffle (playing-cards) by dividing the pack into two equal piles, bending the cards back slightly and controlling the fall of the corners of the cards with the thumbs, so that cards from each pile fall more or less alternately and overlap each other. **3** to make or form a ripple on the surface of water. ▷ *noun* **1 a** the action of riffling, eg cards; **b** the sound made by this. **2** *N Amer* a section of a stream or river where shallow water flows swiftly over a rough rocky surface. **3** *N Amer* a ripple or patch of ripples on the surface of water. **4** *mining* in eg gold-washing: a groove or slat in a sluice to catch free particles of ore. ⓘ 17c.

riff-raff /ˈrɪfraf/ ▷ *noun, derog* worthless, disreputable or undesirable people, especially those considered to be of a low social class; the rabble. ⓘ 15c: as *riff and raff* one and all, from French *rif et raf*, from *rifler* to spoil + *rafler* to snatch away.

rifle¹ /ˈraɪfəl/ ▷ *noun* **1** a large gun that is fired from the shoulder and has a long barrel with a spiral groove on the inside, giving the gun greater accuracy over a long distance. **2** a groove on the inside of the bore or barrel of a gun. **3** (*usually* **rifles**) a body of soldiers armed with rifles; riflemen. Also *as adj* □ *rifle shot* □ *rifle fire.* ▷ *verb* (***rifled, rifling***) **1** to cut spiral grooves in (a gun or its barrel). **2** *tr & intr* to fire at someone or something with a rifle. **3** to hit or kick (a ball, etc) very hard and direct at a target. ● **rifling** *noun* **1** the pattern of spiral grooves on the inside of the barrel of a gun. **2** the act of making these grooves. ⓘ 17c: from French *rifler* to scratch.

rifle² /ˈraɪfəl/ ▷ *verb* (***rifled, rifling***) **1** *tr & intr* to search through (eg a house, safe, etc) thoroughly, usually in order to steal something from it. **2** to steal something. ● **rifler** *noun.* ● **rifling** *noun.* ⓘ 14c: from French *rifler* to plunder.

rifle bird ▷ *noun* any of several Australian birds of paradise, with metallic-looking plumage and a long bill. ⓘ 19c.

rifle-green ▷ *noun* a dark green, the colour of a rifleman's uniform. ▷ *adj* having this colour.

rifleman ▷ *noun* **1 a** a soldier armed with a rifle; **b** a member of a rifle regiment. **2** someone skilled in using a rifle. **3** a small green and yellow wren of New Zealand.

rifle range ▷ *noun* **1** an area for practising rifle shooting. **2** the distance that a bullet fired from a rifle can reach.

rift ▷ *noun* **1** a split or crack, especially one in the earth or in rock; a fissure. **2** a gap in mist or clouds. **3** a break in previously friendly relations between people, nations, etc. ▷ *verb* (***rifted, rifting***) to tear or split something apart. ● **riftless** *adj.* ⓘ 13c: from Norse *ript* breaking of an agreement.

rift valley ▷ *noun, geol* a long steep-sided valley with a flat floor, formed when part of the Earth's crust subsides between two faults.

rig ▷ *verb* (***rigged, rigging***) **1** *naut* to fit (a ship, masts, etc) with ropes, sails and rigging. **2** *aeronautics* to position correctly the various parts and components of (an aircraft, etc). **3** *intr, naut, aeronautics* said of a ship, aircraft, etc: to be made ready for use; to be equipped. **4** to control or manipulate something for dishonest purposes, or for personal profit or advantage. ▷ *noun* **1** *naut* the particular arrangement of sails, ropes and masts on a ship. **2** an OIL RIG. **3** gear or equipment, especially that used for a specific task. **4** *N Amer* a lorry or truck. ● **rigging** *noun* **1** *naut* the system of ropes, wires, etc which support and control a ship's masts and sails. **2** *aeronautics* the ropes and wires, etc which support the structure of an airship or the wings of a biplane. ⓘ 15c.

■ **rig someone out 1** to dress them in clothes of a stated or special kind. **2** to provide them with special equipment.

■ **rig something up** to build or prepare it, especially hastily and with whatever material is available.

rigadoon /rɪɡəˈduːn/ ▷ *noun* **1** an old dance, of Provençal origin, in lively duple or quadruple time, for one couple. **2** the music for this dance. ⓘ 17c: from French *rigaudon*, perhaps named after Rigaud, a dancing master who is said to have invented it.

right /raɪt/ ▻ *adj* **1** indicating, relating or referring to, or on, the side facing east from the point of view of someone or something facing north. **2** said of a part of the body: on or towards the right side ▫ ***She broke her right leg.*** **3** said of an article of clothing, etc: worn on the right hand, foot, etc ▫ ***her right shoe.*** **4 a** on, towards or close to an observer's right; **b** on a stage: on or towards the performers' right ▫ ***stage right.*** **5** said of a river bank: on the right side of a person facing downstream. **6** correct; true ▫ ***the right answer.*** **7** said of a clock or watch: showing the correct time ▫ ***Is that clock right?*** **8** suitable; appropriate; proper ▫ ***It was the right job for him.*** **9** most appropriate or favourable ▫ ***It wasn't the right moment to ask.*** **10** in a correct, proper or satisfactory state or condition ▫ ***put things right.*** **11** mentally sound or stable; sane ▫ ***not in his right mind.*** **12** physically sound. **13** morally correct or good. **14** legally correct or good. **15** belonging to or on the side of a piece of fabric, a garment, etc which is intended to be seen or worn facing outwards ▫ ***turn the dress right side out.*** **16** *geom* **a** with an axis perpendicular to the base ▫ ***a right angle***; **b** straight. **17** (*sometimes* **Right**) **a** relating or belonging to, or indicating, the political right (see *noun* 5 below); **b** conservative; right-wing. **18** socially acceptable ▫ ***know all the right people.*** **19** *Brit colloq* complete; utter; real ▫ ***a right mess.*** ▻ *adverb* **1** on or towards the right side. **2** correctly; properly; satisfactorily. **3** exactly or precisely ▫ ***It happened right there.*** **4** immediately; without delay ▫ ***He'll be right over.*** **5** completely; absolutely ▫ ***It went right out of my mind.*** **6** all the way ▫ ***He drove right down to London.*** **7** said of movement, a direction, etc: straight; without deviating from a straight line ▫ ***right to the top.*** **8** towards or on the right side ▫ ***He looked right before crossing the road.*** **9** favourably or satisfactorily ▫ ***It turned out right in the end.*** **10** especially in religious titles: most; very ▫ ***right reverend.*** **11** *old use or dialect* very; to the full ▫ ***be right glad to see her.*** ▻ *noun* **1** (*often* **rights**) a power, privilege, title, etc that someone may claim legally or that is morally due to them. **2** (*often* **rights**) a just or legal claim to something. **3** fairness; truth; justice. **4** that which is correct, good or just ▫ ***the rights and wrongs of the case.*** **5** (*often* **the Right**) the political party, or a group of people within a party, etc which has the most conservative views ◷ from the practice of European parliaments in which members holding the most conservative views sit on the president's right. This originates from the first French National Assembly in 1789. **6** the right side, part or direction of something. **7** *boxing* **a** the right hand ▫ ***He was lethal with his right***; **b** a punch with the right hand ▫ ***He knocked him out with a right.*** **8** a glove, shoe, etc worn on the right hand or foot ▫ ***Can I try on the right?*** **9** (*often* **rights**) *commerce* the privilege given to a company's existing shareholders to buy new shares, usually for less than the market value. **10** (**rights**) the legal permission to print, publish, film, etc a book, usually sold to a company by the author or by another company. ▻ *verb* (***righted***, ***righting***) **1** *tr & intr* to put or come back to the correct or normal, especially upright, position ▫ ***They soon righted the boat.*** **2** (*especially* **to right a wrong**) to avenge or compensate for (some wrong done). **3** to correct something; to rectify it. **4** to put something in order or return it to order. ▻ *exclamation* expressing agreement, assent or readiness. • **rightable** *adj.* • **rightly** *adverb* **1** correctly. **2** justly. **3** fairly; properly. **4** with good reason; justifiably. **5** with certainty. • **rightness** *noun.* • **be a right one** *Brit colloq* to be or act in a silly or eccentric way. • **by right** or **rights** rightfully; properly. • **do right by someone** to treat them correctly or appropriately, in moral or legal terms. • **in one's own right** because of one's own qualifications, abilities, work, possessions, etc, rather than through a connection with someone else. • **in the right** right; with justice, reason, etc on one's side. • **keep on the right side of someone** to maintain their goodwill; not to do anything that will annoy or upset them. • **on the right side of** younger than (a specified age) ▫ ***on the right side of forty.*** • **put** or **set something** or **someone right** or **to rights** to put it or them in a proper order, place or state; to correct it or them. • **right away** or **right now** immediately; at once. • **right, left and centre** on all sides; all around. • **serve someone right** to be what they deserve, especially as a consequence of a foolish, ill-advised or malicious action. ◷ Anglo-Saxon *riht, reoht.*

right angle ▻ *noun* an angle of 90°, formed by two lines which are perpendicular to each other. • **at right angles** perpendicular. • **right-angled** *adj.*

right ascension ▻ *noun, astron* a coordinate on the celestial sphere that is analogous to longitude on Earth. It is measured in hours, minutes and seconds eastward along the celestial equator from the vernal equinox.

righteous /ˈraɪtʃəs/ ▻ *adj* **1** said of a person: virtuous, free from sin or guilt. **2** said of an action: morally good. **3** justifiable morally ▫ ***righteous indignation.*** • **righteously** *adverb.* • **righteousness** *noun.* ◷ Anglo-Saxon *rihtwis*, from *riht* right + *wise* manner.

rightful /ˈraɪtfʊl/ ▻ *adj* **1** having a legally just claim. **2** said of property, a privilege, etc: held by just RIGHT (*noun* 2). **3** fair; just; equitable. • **rightfully** *adverb.* • **rightfulness** *noun.*

right-hand ▻ *adj* **1** relating to, on or towards the right. **2** done with the right hand.

right-handed ▻ *adj* **1** said of a person: using the right hand more easily than the left. **2** said of a tool, etc: designed to be used in the right hand. **3** said of a blow, etc: done with the right hand. **4** said of a screw: needing to be turned clockwise to be screwed in. • **right-handedly** *adverb.* • **right-handedness** *noun.*

right-hander *noun* **1** a right-handed person. **2** a punch with the right hand.

right-hand man or **right-hand woman** ▻ *noun* a valuable, indispensable and trusted assistant.

Right Honourable ▻ *noun* a title given to British peers below the rank of marquis, to privy councillors, to present and past cabinet ministers, and to some Lord Mayors and Lord Provosts. Also *as adj* ▫ ***the Right Honourable Member.***

rightism ▻ *noun* **1** the political opinions of conservatives or the right. **2** support for and promotion of this. • **rightist** *noun* a supporter of the political right; a conservative. ▻ *adj* relating to or characteristic of the political right.

rightly see under RIGHT

right-minded ▻ *adj* thinking, judging and acting according to principles which are just, honest and sensible. • **right-mindedness** *noun.*

righto or **right-oh** /ˈraɪtoʊ/ ▻ *exclamation, colloq* expressing usually cheerful agreement or compliance.

right-of-centre ▻ *adj* in politics: inclining slightly towards a group's, a party's or a political system's more conservative policies. Compare LEFT-OF-CENTRE.

right of way ▻ *noun* (***rights of way***) **1 a** the right of the public to use a path that crosses private property; **b** a path used by this right. **2** the right of one vehicle to proceed before other vehicles coming from different directions eg at junctions, roundabouts, etc. **3** *US* the strip of land on which a railway track, road, etc lies.

right on ▻ *exclamation* expressing enthusiastic agreement or approval.

right-on ▻ *adj, colloq* **1** modern; up to date or trendy. **2** socially aware or relevant.

Right Reverend ▻ *noun* a title of a bishop. Also *as adj.*

rightward or **rightwards** ▻ *adj, adverb* on or towards the right.

right whale ▷ *noun* a baleen whale with a large head that represents up to 40 per cent of the total body length. ◷ 19c.

right wing ▷ *noun* **1** the more conservative members of a group or political party. **2** *sport* **a** the extreme right side of a pitch or team in a field game; **b** (*also* **right-winger**) the member of a team who plays in this position. **3** the right side of an army. • **right-wing** *adj* belonging or relating to the right wing. • **right-winger** *noun*.

rigid /ˈrɪdʒɪd/ ▷ *adj* **1** completely stiff and inflexible. **2** not able to be moved. **3** said of a person: strictly and inflexibly adhering to one's ideas, opinions, rules, etc. **4** said of rules, etc: strictly maintained and not relaxed. **5** said of an airship: having a rigid structure. • **rigidify** *verb* (*rigidifies, rigidified, rigidifying*) to become or make something rigid. • **rigidity** /rɪˈdʒɪdɪtɪ/ *noun*. • **rigidness** *noun*. • **rigidly** *adverb*. ◷ 16c: from Latin *rigidus*, from *rigere* to be stiff.

rigmarole /ˈrɪgmərοʊl/ ▷ *noun* **1** an unnecessarily or absurdly long, and often pointless or boring, complicated series of actions, instructions or procedures. **2** a long rambling or confused statement or speech. ◷ 18c: from the *Ragman Rolls*, a series of documents in which the Scottish nobles promised allegiance to Edward I of England in 1291–2 and 1296.

rigor /ˈrɪgə(r)/ ▷ *noun* **1** *medicine* a sense of chilliness accompanied by shivering, a preliminary symptom of many diseases. **2** a rigid irresponsive state caused by a sudden shock. ◷ 14c: Latin, meaning 'numbness' or 'stiffness'.

rigor mortis /rɪgə ˈmɔːtɪs/ ▷ *noun* the temporary stiffening of the body soon after death. ◷ 19c: Latin, meaning 'stiffness of death'.

rigorous /ˈrɪgərəs/ ▷ *adj* **1** showing or having rigour; strict; harsh; severe. **2** said especially of the weather or climate: cold, harsh and unpleasant. **3** strictly accurate. • **rigorously** *adverb*. • **rigorousness** *noun*.

rigour or (*US*) **rigor** /ˈrɪgə(r)/ ▷ *noun* **1** stiffness; hardness. **2** strictness or severity of temper, behaviour or judgement. **3** strict enforcement of rules or the law. **4** (*usually* **rigours**) said of a particular situation or circumstances, eg of weather or climate: harshness or severity. **5** harshness or severity of life; austerity. **6** strict precision or exactitude, eg of thought. ◷ 14c: from Latin *rigor* stiffness.

Rig-veda see VEDA

rijstafel or **reistafel** /ˈraɪstɑːfəl/ ▷ *noun* an Indonesian food consisting of a number of rice dishes served with a variety of foods. ◷ 19c: Dutch, from *rijst* rice + *tafel* table.

rile /raɪl/ ▷ *verb* (*riled, riling*) **1** to anger or annoy someone. **2** *N Amer* to agitate (water, etc). ◷ 19c: a variant of ROIL.

rilievo see RELIEVO

rill /raɪl/ ▷ *noun* **1** a small stream or brook. **2** a small trench or furrow. **3** *astron* see RILLE. **4** *phonetics* a fricative produced by forcing air out of a small gap formed between the tongue and the roof of the mouth. • **rilled** *adj*. ◷ 16c.

rille or **rill** /rɪl/ ▷ *noun, astron* a long narrow trench or valley on the moon, formed by volcanic activity. ◷ 19c: German, meaning 'a groove'.

rillettes /rɪˈjɛt/ ▷ *singular or plural noun* a French type of potted meat, made by cooking shreds of both lean and fat pork, etc in lard until crisp, then pounding them to form a paste. ◷ 19c: French.

RIM ▷ *abbreviation, IVR*: *République Islamique de Mauretanie*, Mauritania.

rim ▷ *noun* **1** a raised edge or border, especially of something curved or circular. **2** the outer circular edge of a wheel to which the tyre is attached. ▷ *verb* (*rimmed, rimming*) to form or provide an edge or rim to something; to edge. • **rimless** *adj*. • **rimmed** *adj*. ◷ Anglo-Saxon *rima*.

rim-brake ▷ *noun* a brake that acts on the rim of a wheel.

rime[1] /raɪm/ ▷ *noun* thick white frost formed especially from frozen water droplets from cloud or fog. ▷ *verb* (*rimed, riming*) to cover something with rime. • **rimy** /ˈraɪmɪ/ *adj* (*rimier, rimiest*) frosty; covered with rime. ◷ Anglo-Saxon *hrim*.

rime[2] see RHYME.

rim-lock ▷ *noun* a lock mechanism in a metal case that is screwed to the inner surface of a door.

rimu /ˈriːmuː/ ▷ *noun* **1** a tall evergreen coniferous tree of New Zealand. **2** the wood of this tree. ◷ 19c: Maori.

rind /raɪnd/ ▷ *noun* **1** a thick hard outer layer or covering on cheese or bacon. **2** the peel of a fruit. **3** the bark of a tree or plant. ▷ *verb* (*rinded, rinding*) to remove the rind from something, especially to strip the bark from a tree. • **rinded** *adj*. • **rindless** *adj*. ◷ Anglo-Saxon *rinde*.

rinderpest /ˈrɪndəpɛst/ ▷ *noun* a malignant and contagious disease of cattle causing fever, severe diarrhoea and discharges from the mucous membrane. ◷ 19c: German, from *Rinder* cattle + *Pest* plague.

ring[1] ▷ *noun* **1** a small circle or band of gold, silver or some other metal or material, worn on the finger. **2** a circle of metal, wood, plastic, etc, for holding, keeping in place, connecting, hanging, etc. **3** any object, mark or figure which is circular in shape. **4** a circular course or route. **5** a group of people or things arranged in a circle. **6** an enclosed and usually circular area in which circus acts are performed. **7** a square area on a platform, marked off by ropes, where boxers or wrestlers fight. **8** (**the ring**) boxing as a profession. **9** an enclosure for bookmakers at a race-course. **10** at agricultural shows, etc: an enclosure where cattle, horses, etc are paraded or exhibited for auction. **11** a group of people who act together to control eg an antiques or drugs market, betting, etc for their own advantage or profit. **12** a circular electric element or gas burner on top of a cooker. **13** a circular strip of bark cut from a tree. See RING-BARK. **14** a circular mark, seen when a tree trunk is examined in section, that represents the amount of growth made by that tree in one year. **15** a segment of a worm, caterpillar, etc. **16** a circle of fungus growth in turf; a FAIRY RING. **17** *chem* a closed chain of atoms in a molecule, eg six-membered ring system. **18** *geom* the area lying between two concentric circles. **19** *math* a system of elements in which addition is associative and commutative, and multiplication is associative and distributive with respect to addition. **20** a thin band of particles orbiting some planets, such as Saturn and Uranus. **21** *computing* a computer system suitable for a LAN, with several micro-computers or peripheral devices connected by cable in a ring. ▷ *verb* (*ringed, ringing*) **1** to make, form, draw, etc a ring round something, or to form it into a ring. **2** to cut something into rings. **3** to put a ring on (a bird's leg) as a means of identifying it. **4** to fit a ring in (a bull's nose) so that it can be lead easily. **5** to RING-BARK. • **ringed** *adj* **1** surrounded by, marked with, bearing or wearing a ring or rings. **2** ring-shaped. **3** made up of rings. • **make** or **run rings round someone** *colloq* to beat them or be much better than them. • **throw one's hat into the ring** *colloq* to offer oneself as a candidate or challenger. ◷ Anglo-Saxon *hring*.

ring[2] ▷ *verb* (*rang, rung, ringing*) **1 a** to sound (a bell) eg by striking it or by pulling a rope attached to it, often as a summons or to signal or announce something; **b** *intr* said of a bell: to sound in this way. **2 a** to make (a metal object, etc) give a resonant bell-like sound by striking it; **b** *intr* said of a metal object, etc: to sound in this way when struck. **3** *intr* said of a large building, etc: to resound; to be filled with a particular sound □ *The theatre rang with laughter and applause.* **4** *intr* said of a sound or noise: to resound; to re-echo □ *Applause rang through the theatre.*

5 *intr* (*usually* **ring out**) to make a sudden clear loud sound □ ***shots rang out.*** **6** *intr* to sound repeatedly; to resound □ ***Her criticisms rang in his ears.*** **7** *intr* said of the ears: to be filled with a buzzing, humming or ringing sensation or sound. **8** (*also* **ring someone up**) *chiefly Brit* to call by telephone. **9** (*usually* **ring for someone**) to ring a bell as a summons. **10** *intr* (*especially* **ring true** or **false**) said of words, etc: to give a specified impression, especially of being genuine or not □ ***His promises ring false.*** ▻ *noun* **1** the act of ringing a bell. **2** the act or sound of ringing. **3** the clear resonant sound of a bell, or a similarly resonant sound. **4** *Brit* a telephone call. **5** a suggestion or impression of a particular feeling or quality □ ***a story with a ring of truth about it.*** **6** a set of bells, each with a different note, especially in a church □ ***St Nicholas has a ring of six.*** • **ringing** *noun, adj.* • **ringingly** *adverb.* • **ring a bell** to bring to mind a vague memory of having been seen, heard, etc before □ ***His name rings a bell.*** • **ring the curtain down** or **up 1** *theat* to give the signal for lowering, or raising, the curtain. **2** (*usually* **ring the curtain down** or **up on something**) *colloq* to put an end to, or to begin, a project or undertaking. • **ring the changes 1** to vary the way something is done, used, said, etc. **2** *bell-ringing* to go through all the various orders possible when ringing a peal of church bells. See also CHANGE-RINGING. ⓒ Anglo-Saxon *hringan*.

■ **ring someone back 1** to telephone them again, usually to follow up an initial call. **2** to telephone a previous caller in response to their call.

■ **ring in** to make contact by telephone with someone.

■ **ring something in** to report (a piece of news, etc) by telephone.

■ **ring someone** or **something in** or **out** to announce their or its arrival or departure with, or as if with, bell-ringing □ ***ring out the old year and ring in the new.***

■ **ring off** to end a telephone call by replacing the receiver; to hang up.

■ **ring something up** to record the price of an item sold on a cash register.

ring-bark ▻ *verb* (***ring-barked, ring-barking***) to strip a ring of bark from a tree in order to stop it growing too fast.

ring binder ▻ *noun* a loose-leaf binder with metal rings which can be opened to add or take out pages.

ringbolt ▻ *noun* a bolt with a ring attached to the bolt head.

ringbone ▻ *noun* **1** a bony callus on a horse's pastern-bone. **2** the condition caused by this.

ring circuit ▻ *noun, elec* an electrical supply system in which a number of power points are connected to the main supply by a series of wires, forming a closed circuit.

ring-dove ▻ *noun* a woodpigeon.

ringed see under RING[1]

ringed plover ▻ *noun* a ring-necked plover of various kinds.

ringer /ˈrɪŋə(r)/ ▻ *noun* **1** someone or something that rings a bell, etc. **2** someone who rings the legs of birds. **3** (*also* **dead ringer**) *originally US, now colloq* someone or something that is almost identical to another. **4** *chiefly US* a horse or athlete entered into a race or competition under a false name or other false pretences. **5** *chiefly US colloq* an impostor or fake. **6** *curling* a stone lying within the circle round either tee. **7 a** a quoit thrown so as to encircle the pin it is aimed at; **b** such a throw. **8** *Austral* a station hand or stockman. **9** *Austral colloq* an expert, originally the fastest shearer in a shed. • **be a (dead) ringer for** or **of someone** or **something** to resemble them or it very closely.

ring-fence ▻ *noun* **1** a fence that completely encircles an estate. **2** a complete barrier. **3** the compulsory reservation of funds for use within a specific limited sector or department, eg of a government, company, etc. ▻ *verb* (***ring-fenced, ring-fencing***) **1** to enclose (an estate) with a ring-fence. **2** to apply a ring-fence to (a sector or department of government or a company).

ring finger ▻ *noun* the third finger, especially on the left hand, on which a wedding and/or engagement ring is worn.

ring fort ▻ *noun, archaeol* an Iron Age dwelling site with a strong circular wall.

ringhals /ˈrɪŋhals/ and **rinkhals** /ˈrɪŋkhals/ ▻ *noun* (***ringhals*** or ***ringhalses***; ***rinkhals*** or ***rinkhalses***) a venomous snake of southern Africa, that spits or sprays venom at its victims. ⓒ 18c: Afrikaans, from *ring* ring + *hals* neck.

ringleader ▻ *noun* the leader of a group of people who are doing something wrong or making trouble.

ringlet /ˈrɪŋlɪt/ ▻ *noun* **1** a long spiral curl of hair. **2** a small ring. **3** a circular pattern or formation, especially a fairy-ring. **4** any of several SATYRID butterflies. • **ringleted** *adj.* ⓒ 16c.

ring main ▻ *noun, elec* a domestic electrical supply system in which power points are connected to the mains in a closed circuit.

ringmaster ▻ *noun* the person who presents and is in charge of performances in a circus ring.

ring-necked ▻ *adj* said especially of certain birds or snakes: with a band of colour around the neck.

ring network ▻ *noun, computing* a network that forms a closed loop of connected terminals (eg a LAN).

ring ouzel see OUZEL

ring pull ▻ *noun* a tongue of metal with a ring attached to it, which when pulled breaks a seal and opens a can or similar container. ▻ *adj* (**ring-pull**) said of a can or tin: with a ring pull attached.

ring road ▻ *noun, Brit* a road, mainly for through traffic, that bypasses a town or goes through its suburbs, and which is designed to keep the town centre relatively free of traffic.

ringside ▻ *noun* **1** the seating area immediately next to a boxing-, circus- ring, etc. **2** any place that gives a good clear view.

ringtail[1] or **ringtailed** ▻ *adj* **1** said especially of certain lemurs: with a tail that is marked in bars or rings of colour. **2** said of certain opossums: with a prehensile tail that is curled at the end.

ringtail[2] ▻ *noun* **1** the female, or young male, of the hen-harrier, so called because of the rust-coloured ring on its tail-feathers. **2** a ringtailed cat.

ringworm ▻ *noun, pathol* any of various highly contagious fungal infections, characterized by the formation of small red itchy circular patches on soft areas of skin such as the scalp or groin, or between the toes (ATHLETE'S FOOT). Also called **tinea**. ⓒ 15c.

rink ▻ *noun* **1 a** an area of ice prepared for skating, curling or ice-hockey; **b** a building or enclosure containing this. **2 a** an area of smooth floor for roller-skating; **b** a building or enclosure containing this. **3** *bowls, curling* **a** a strip of grass or ice allotted to a team or set of players in bowling and curling; **b** a team or set of players using such a strip of grass or ice. ⓒ 14c: originally Scots, perhaps from French *renc* rank or row.

rinkhals see under RINGHALS

rinky-dink /ˈrɪŋkɪdɪŋk/ ▻ *noun, chiefly N Amer slang* **1** something worn out or old and run down. **2** something corny, trite or trivial. **3** a cheap place of entertainment. Also *as adj* □ ***rinky-dink sidestreets.*** ⓒ 19c.

rinse /rɪns/ ▻ *verb* (***rinsed, rinsing***) **1** to wash (soap, detergent, etc) out of (clothes, hair, dishes, etc) with clean water. **2** to remove (traces of dirt, etc) from something by washing it lightly in clean water, usually without soap □ *rinsed the wine out of the shirt.* **3** (*also* **rinse something out**) to clean (a cup, one's mouth, etc) by filling it with water, swirling the water round then throwing or spitting it out. **4** (*also* **rinse something away**) to remove (soap, detergent, dirt, etc) using clean water. **5** to give a temporary tint to (the hair) by using a rinse. ▷ *noun* **1** the action or an act of rinsing. **2** liquid used for rinsing. **3 a** a solution used in hairdressing to condition or give a temporary tint to the hair □ *a blue rinse*; **b** an application of such a solution. • **rinser** *noun* a board or rack for rinsing washed dishes. • **rinsing** *noun*. ⓒ 14c: from French *rincer* and *recincier*, perhaps ultimately from Latin *recens* fresh.

rioja /rɪ'ɒxə/ ▷ *noun* **1** a dry red, white or, occasionally, rosé wine produced in NE Spain. ⓒ Early 20c: named after the district of Rioja in NE Spain, from Spanish *río* river + *Oja*, a tributary of the river Ebro.

riot /'raɪət/ ▷ *noun* **1 a** *loosely* a noisy public disturbance or disorder, usually by a large group of people; **b** *law, technical* such a disturbance by three or more people; **c** *as adj* suitable for use in a riot □ *riot shields.* **2** uncontrolled or wild revelry and feasting. **3** *archaic* unrestrained squandering or indulgence. **4** said especially of colour: a striking display. **5** *colloq* someone or something that is very amusing or entertaining, especially in a wild or boisterous way. **6** a very, usually boisterously, successful show or performance. ▷ *verb* (***rioted, rioting***) *intr* **1** to take part in a riot. **2** to take part in boisterous revelry. • **rioter** *noun*. • **rioting** *noun*. • **run riot 1** to act, speak, etc in a wild or unrestrained way □ *The children ran riot.* **2** said of plants, vegetation, etc: to grow profusely or in an uncontrolled way □ *The weeds were running riot.* ⓒ 13c: from French *riote* a debate or quarrel.

Riot Act ▷ *noun, historical law* **1** an Act passed in 1715 and repealed in 1967, designed to prevent riotous assemblies by making it a felony, after the reading of a section of the act by a magistrate or other authority, for a gathering of more than 12 people to refuse to disperse within an hour. **2** the section of the act read as a warning to rioters to disperse. • **read the riot act** *jocular* to give an angry warning that bad behaviour must stop.

riot grrrls /— gɪrəlz/ ▷ *plural noun* a collective name for the members of certain, mainly US, female rock bands and their followers. Their music is aggressive and overtly sexual and their aim is to confront and challenge the male dominance of PUNK and, by implication, society in general. • **riot-grrrl** *adj* □ *Bikini Kill's riot-grrrl image.* ⓒ 1990s: from RIOT + an aggressive-looking and growling-sounding alteration of girl.

riotous /'raɪətəs/ ▷ *adj* **1** participating in, likely to start, or like, a riot. **2** very active, noisy, cheerful and wild □ *a riotous party.* **3** filled with wild revelry, parties, etc □ *riotous living.* • **riotously** *adverb*. • **riotousness** *noun*.

riot police ▷ *noun* police specially equipped with **riot gear**, ie riot shields, grenades, tear-gas, etc, for dealing with rioting crowds.

RIP ▷ *abbreviation*: *requiescat* (or *requiescant*) *in pace* (Latin), may he, she or they rest in peace, usually found on gravestones, death notices, etc.

rip[1] ▷ *verb* (***ripped, ripping***) **1** *tr & intr* to tear or come apart violently or roughly. **2** *intr, colloq* to rush along or move quickly without restraint □ *ripped through the store to find the best sale bargains.* **3** to saw (wood or timber) along the grain. ▷ *noun* **1** a violent or rough tear or split. **2** an unrestrained rush. **3** a RIPSAW. • **ripped** *adj* torn or rent. • **ripper** *noun* **1** someone who rips. **2** a murderer who rips or mutilates the bodies of their victims. **3** a tool for ripping, especially one attached to a tractor for breaking up hard soil, etc. **4** *chiefly Austral & NZ slang* an excellent or attractive person or thing. • **ripping** see separate entry. • **rippingly** *adverb*. • **let it rip** to let an action, process, etc continue in an unrestrained or reckless way. • **let rip 1** to speak, behave, etc violently or unrestrainedly. **2** to increase suddenly in speed, volume, etc. ⓒ 15c.

■ **rip someone off** to steal from, exploit, cheat or overcharge them. See also RIP-OFF.

■ **rip something off** or **out** or **up**, *etc* to remove it quickly and violently □ *ripped off the sticking plaster* □ *ripped out the page* □ *ripped up the roots of the tree.*

■ **rip something up** to shred or tear it into pieces □ *ripped up his letter.*

rip[2] ▷ *noun* **1** (*also* **riptide**) a disturbed state or stretch of the sea or in a river, caused by the meeting of currents. **2** (*also* **rip current** or **riptide**) a strong surface current coming out at intervals from the shore. **3** *chiefly US* any rough stretch of water in a river. ⓒ 18c: perhaps related to RIP[1].

RIPA ▷ *abbreviation* Royal Institute of Public Administration.

riparian /raɪ'pɛərɪən/ ▷ *adj, formal* relating to, occurring or living on a riverbank. ▷ *noun* an owner of land that borders a river. • **riparial** *adj*. ⓒ 19c: from Latin *riparius*, from *ripa* riverbank.

ripcord ▷ *noun* **1** a cord which, when pulled, releases a parachute from its pack. **2** a cord on the gas bag of a balloon which, when pulled, allows gas to escape and the balloon to descend.

ripe /raɪp/ ▷ *adj* **1** said of fruit, grain, etc: fully matured and ready to be picked or harvested and eaten. **2** said of cheese: **a** mature; having been allowed to age to develop its full flavour; **b** strong-smelling. **3** said of a flavour or taste, eg that of wine: rich or strong. **4** said eg of a person's complexion: resembling ripe fruit, especially in being plump and pink. **5** mature in mind and body; fully developed. **6** said of a person or their mind: mature in judgement or knowledge. **7** (*often* **ripe old age**) said of a person's age: very advanced, but still with good mental and physical health. **8** *slang* **a** complete; thorough; **b** excellent. **9** *slang* excessive. **10** *colloq* said of language, etc: slightly indecent; risqué. • **ripely** *adverb*. • **ripeness** *noun*. • **ripe for something 1** suitable or appropriate for a particular action or purpose □ *ripe for reform.* **2** eager or ready for a particular action or purpose. ⓒ Anglo-Saxon *ripe*.

ripen /'raɪpən/ ▷ *verb* (***ripened, ripening***) *tr & intr* to make or become ripe or riper. ⓒ 16c.

RIPHH ▷ *abbreviation* Royal Institute of Public Health and Hygiene.

ripieno /rɪ'pjeɪnoʊ/ *music* ▷ *adj* supplementary. ▷ *noun* (***ripieni*** /rɪ'pjeɪniː/ or ***ripienos***) **1** *originally* a supplementary instrument or player. **2** *now chiefly* in baroque music: the group of instruments accompanying the CONCERTINO. See also CONCERTO GROSSO. ⓒ 18c: Italian.

rip-off ▷ *noun* **1** an act or instance of stealing from someone, or cheating or defrauding them, etc. **2** an item which is outrageously overpriced. See also RIP OFF at RIP[1]. ⓒ 1970s.

riposte /rɪ'pɒst, rɪ'poʊst/ ▷ *noun* **1** a quick sharp reply; a retort. **2** *fencing* a quick return thrust after a parry. ▷ *verb* (***riposted, riposting***) *intr* to answer with a riposte. ⓒ 18c: French, from Italian *risposta*, from *rispondere* to respond.

ripped and **ripper** see under RIP[1]

ripping ▷ *verb present participle of* RIP[1]. ▷ *adj, old Brit slang* splendid; excellent.

ripple[1] /'rɪpəl/ ▷ *noun* **1** a slight wave or undulation, or a series of these, on the surface of water. **2** a similar wavy appearance or motion, eg in material, hair, etc. **3** said especially of laughter or applause: a sound that rises and falls quickly and gently like that of rippling water. **4** (**ripples**) repercussions; reverberations. **5** *electronics* small periodic variations in a steady current or voltage. **6** *geol* see RIPPLE-MARK. **7** a type of ice cream with coloured flavoured syrup mixed through it to give a marbled appearance □ ***raspberry ripple.*** **8** a way of firing missiles, etc in succession. ▻ *verb* (***rippled, rippling***) **1 a** to ruffle or agitate the surface of (water, etc); **b** to mark with ripples, or form ripples in (a surface, material, etc). **2** *intr* to form ripples or move with an undulating motion □ ***Her hair rippled over her shoulders.*** **3** *intr* said of a sound: to rise and fall quickly and gently. ● **rippling** *noun, adj.* ● **ripplingly** *adverb.* ● **ripply** *adj.* ⓘ 17c.

ripple² /ˈrɪpəl/ ▻ *noun* a toothed comb-like implement for removing seeds, etc from flax or hemp. ▻ *verb* (***rippled, rippling***) **1** to remove (seeds, etc) from flax or hemp by means of a ripple. **2** to clear (flax or hemp) of seeds, etc by drawing through a ripple. ● **rippler** *noun.* ⓘ 14c.

ripple effect ▻ *noun* the spreading outwards of the repercussions of a particular event or situation to areas beyond its initial location.

ripple-mark ▻ *noun, geol* an undulatory ridging formed in sediments by waves, currents or wind, often preserved in sedimentary rocks. ● **ripple-marked** *adj.*

ripple tank ▻ *noun, physics* a shallow tank of water, used to demonstrate the behaviour of waves, especially such properties as reflection, refraction, diffraction and interference.

rip-roaring ▻ *adj, colloq* wild, noisy and exciting. ● **rip-roaringly** *adverb* □ ***rip-roaringly good.***

ripsaw ▻ *noun* a saw for cutting along the grain of timber.

ripsnorter /ˈrɪpsnɔːtə(r)/ ▻ *noun, originally US slang* someone or something of exceptional appearance, quality, strength, etc. ● **ripsnorting** *adj.* ● **ripsnortingly** *adverb.* ⓘ 19c.

riptide see under RIP²

Rip Van Winkle /rɪp van ˈwɪŋkəl/ ▻ *noun* someone who is very much behind the times, especially in being unaware of social or political changes that have occurred over a considerable period of time. ● **Rip-Van-Winkleish** *adj.* ● **Rip-Van-Winkleism** *noun.* ⓘ 19c: the name of the hero of a story in Washington Irvine's *Sketch Book* (1819–20) who returned home, after having slept in the mountains for 20 years, to find the world greatly changed.

RISC /rɪsk/ ▻ *abbreviation, computing* reduced instruction set computer, a computer with a central processor which has a very small instruction set to enable faster processing. *Also as adj* □ ***RISC chips.*** ⓘ 1980s.

rise /raɪz/ ▻ *verb* (***rose, risen*** /ˈrɪzən/, ***rising*** /ˈraɪzɪŋ/) *intr* **1** to get or stand up, especially from a sitting, kneeling or lying position. **2** to get up from bed, especially after a night's sleep □ ***They always rise at seven.*** **3** to move upwards; to ascend. **4** to increase in size, amount, volume, strength, degree, intensity, etc □ ***sales have risen*** □ ***The wind rose at night.*** **5** said of the Sun, Moon, planets, etc: to appear above the horizon. **6** to stretch or slope upwards □ ***ground which rises gently.*** **7** (*usually* **rise up** or **rise against someone** or **something**) to rebel. **8** to move from a lower position, rank, level, etc to a higher one. **9** to begin or originate □ ***a river that rises in the mountains.*** **10** said especially of a person's spirits: to become more cheerful. **11** said of an animal's fur, a person's hair, etc: to become straight and stiff, especially from fear or anger. **12** said of a committee, court, parliament, etc: to finish a session; to adjourn. **13** to come back to life; to be resurrected □ ***rose from the dead.*** **14** said of fish: to come to the surface of the water. **15** said of birds: to fly up from the ground, etc □ ***The geese all rose from the lake.*** **16** said of dough, a cake, etc: to swell up; increase in volume. **17** to be built □ ***new office blocks rising all over town.*** **18** (*usually* **rise to something**) to respond to something, especially provocation or criticism. **19** said of the stomach or throat: to give a feeling of nausea □ ***His stomach rose at the sight.*** ▻ *noun* **1** an act of rising. **2** an increase in size, amount, volume, strength, status, rank, etc. **3** *Brit* an increase in salary □ ***asked for a rise.*** *US equivalent* RAISE. **4** a piece of rising ground; a slope or hill. **5** a beginning or origin. **6** the vertical height of a step or flight of stairs. ● **riser** /ˈraɪzə(r)/ *noun* **1** someone who gets out of bed, usually at a specified time □ ***an early riser*** □ ***a late riser.*** **2** any of the vertical parts between the horizontal steps of a set of stairs. **3** a vertical pipe, especially one within a building or on an oil rig. ● **rising** ▻ *noun* **1** the act or action of rising. **2** a rebellion. ▻ *adj* **1** moving or sloping upwards; getting higher. **2** approaching greater age, maturity, status, reputation or importance. **3** approaching a specified age □ ***the rising sevens.*** ● **get** or **take a rise out of someone** *colloq* to make them angry or upset, especially by teasing or provoking them. ● **give rise to something** to cause it or bring it about. ● **on the rise** to be rising or increasing □ ***Crime is on the rise in this area.*** ● **rise and shine** a facetiously cheerful invitation to someone to get out of bed briskly in the morning. ● **rise from the ranks 1** to work one's way up from being a private soldier to a commissioned officer. **2** to work one's way up within a particular field, profession, organization, etc. ● **rise to the bait** to do what someone else intends or suggests (usually by means of indirect suggestions, hints, etc) that one should do. ● **rise to the occasion** to prove oneself up to, or able to cope with, an unusual or special situation or circumstances. ⓘ Anglo-Saxon *risan.*

■ **rise above something** to remain unaffected by teasing, provocation, criticism, etc.

risible /ˈrɪzɪbəl/ ▻ *adj* **1** causing laughter; laughable; ludicrous. **2** *rare* inclined to laughter. ● **risibility** *noun.* ● **risibly** *adverb.* ⓘ 18c in sense 1; 16c in sense 2: from Latin *risibilis*, from *ridere* to laugh.

rising damp ▻ *noun, Brit* wetness which rises up through the bricks or stones of a wall.

risk ▻ *noun* **1** the chance or possibility of suffering loss, injury, damage, etc; danger. **2** someone or something likely to cause loss, injury, damage, etc. **3** *insurance* **a** the chance of some loss, damage, etc for which insurance could be claimed; **b** the type, usually specified, of such loss, damage, etc □ ***fire risk***; **c** someone or something thought of as likely (a **bad risk**) or unlikely (a **good risk**) to suffer loss, injury, damage, etc. ▻ *verb* (***risked, risking***) **1** to expose someone or something to loss, injury, danger, etc. **2** to act or do something in spite of the chances of loss, danger or some unfortunate consequences occurring. ● **at one's own risk** accepting personal responsibility for any loss, injury, etc which might occur. ● **at risk 1** in danger; in a situation or circumstances which might lead to loss, injury, etc. **2 a** said especially of a child: considered, eg by a social worker, etc, liable to be abused, neglected, etc; **b** referring or relating to such a child □ ***The parents are alcoholics and the children are on the 'at risk' register.*** ● **at the risk of something** with the possibility of loss, injury, losing face or some other unfortunate consequence □ ***at the risk of sounding pompous.*** ● **risk one's neck** to do something that puts one's life, job, etc in danger. ● **run the risk of something** to risk it; to be in danger of it □ ***run the risk of being late.*** ● **run** or **take a risk** to act in a certain way despite the risk involved. ⓘ 17c: from French *risque.*

risk analysis ▻ *noun* a methodical investigation undertaken to assess the financial and physical risks that may affect a business venture.

risk capital see VENTURE CAPITAL

risk factor ▻ *noun, medicine* a factor, such as one's age, living conditions or a habit such as smoking, that increases the likelihood of an individual developing a particular disease or medical problem.

risk money ▻ *noun* money allowed to a cashier to compensate for ordinary errors.

risky /ˈrɪskɪ/ ▻ *adj* (***riskier***, ***riskiest***) dangerous; likely to cause loss, damage, mishap, etc. ● **riskily** *adverb*. ● **riskiness** *noun*. ⓒ 19c.

risoluto /riːzəˈluːtoʊ/ ▻ *adverb*, *adj*, *music* with emphasis; boldly. ⓒ 18c: Italian.

risorgimento /rɪsɔːdʒɪˈmɛntoʊ/ ▻ *noun* (***risorgimenti*** /-tiː/ or ***risorgimentos***) **1** (**Risorgimento**) *historical* the liberation and unification of Italy in the 19c. **2** a revival; a rebirth. ⓒ 19c: Italian, meaning 'renewal, renaissance'.

risorius /rɪˈzɔːrɪəs, rɪˈsɔː-/ ▻ *noun*, *anatomy* a facial muscle situated at the corner of the mouth, that can be variable in form and is absent in some individuals. Also called **risorius muscle**. ⓒ 19c: Latin, from *risor* laugher.

risotto /rɪˈzɒtoʊ/ ▻ *noun* (***risottos***) an Italian dish of rice cooked in a meat or seafood stock with onions, tomatoes, cheese, etc. ⓒ 19c: Italian, from *riso* rice.

risqué /ˈrɪskeɪ, rɪsˈkeɪ/ ▻ *adj* said of a story, joke, etc: bordering on the rude or indecent. ⓒ 19c: French, from *risquer* to risk.

rissole /ˈrɪsoʊl/ ▻ *noun* a small fried cake or ball of chopped meat coated in breadcrumbs. ⓒ 18c: French.

Risso's dolphin see GRAMPUS

rit. *music* ▻ *abbreviation* **1** ritardando. **2** ritenuto.

ritardando see RALLENTANDO

rite /raɪt/ ▻ *noun* **1** a formal ceremony or observance, especially a religious one. **2** the required words or actions for such a ceremony. **3** a body of such acts or ceremonies which are characteristic of a particular church ▫ *the Latin rite of the Roman Catholic church.* ● **riteless** *adj*. ⓒ 14c: from Latin *ritus* religious ceremony.

ritenuto /rɪtəˈnjuːtoʊ/ ▻ *adj*, *adverb*, *music* (abbreviation **rit.**) with a sudden slowing down of tempo; restrained. ▻ *noun* (***ritenutos*** or ***ritenuti*** /-tiː/) a ritenuto passage or phrase. ⓒ 19c: Italian, from Latin *retinere* to restrain or hold back.

rite of passage ▻ *noun* (***rites of passage***) any ritual event or ceremony, such as those associated with birth, puberty, marriage or death, which marks a person's transition from one status to another within their society. ⓒ Early 20c: from French *rite de passage*.

ritornello /rɪtɔːˈnɛloʊ/ ▻ *noun* (***ritornellos*** or ***ritornelli*** /-liː/) *music* a short instrumental passage, eg a prelude or refrain, especially in a vocal work. Also called **ritornel** or **ritournelle**. ⓒ 17c: Italian, meaning 'a little return', from *ritorno* to return.

ritual /ˈrɪtʃʊəl, ˈrɪtjʊəl/ ▻ *noun* **1** the set order or words used in a religious ceremony. **2** a body of such rituals, especially of a particular church. **3** the use or performance of rituals in a religious ceremony. **4** an often repeated procedure or series of actions. **5 a** *psychol* a series of actions that are performed compulsively, their non-performance resulting in feelings of anxiety; **b** *colloq* anything that is performed regurlarly, habitually, etc; a routine. ▻ *adj* relating to, like or used for religious, social or other rites or ritual. ● **ritually** *adverb*. ⓒ 16c: from Latin *ritualis*, from *ritus* rite.

ritualism /ˈrɪtʃʊəlɪzm, ˈrɪtjʊə-/ ▻ *noun* excessive belief in the importance of, or excessive practice of, ritual, often without regard to its meaning or function. ⓒ 19c.

ritualist /ˈrɪtʃʊelɪst, ˈrɪtjʊə-/ ▻ *noun* **1** someone who is skilled in the rituals of a particular religious ceremony. **2** someone who believes in the practice and importance of religious ritual, often to an excessive degree. **3** *anthropol* someone who performs a tribal ritual. ⓒ 17c.

ritualistic ▻ *adj* **1** relating to or characteristic of ritualism. **2** fond of or devoted to ritual. **3** relating to ritual behaviour or actions. ● **ritualistically** *adverb*. ⓒ 19c.

ritualize or **ritualise** /ˈrɪtʃʊəlaɪz, ˈrɪtjʊə-/ ▻ *verb* (***ritualized***, ***ritualizing***) **1** *intr* to practise or convert to ritualism. **2** to turn (some action, procedure, behaviour, etc) into a ritual. ● **ritualization** *noun*. ⓒ 19c.

ritzy /ˈrɪtzɪ/ ▻ *adj* (***ritzier***, ***ritziest***) *colloq* **1** very smart and elegant. **2** ostentatiously rich; flashy. ● **ritzily** *adverb*. ● **ritziness** *noun*. ⓒ 1920s: named after the luxury hotels established by Swiss-born hotelier César Ritz (1850-1918).

rival /ˈraɪvəl/ ▻ *noun* **1** a person or group of people competing with another for the same objective or in the same field. **2** someone or something that is comparable with or equals another in quality, ability, etc. ▻ *adj* standing as a rival; in competition for the same objective or in the same field ▫ *rival companies.* ▻ *verb* (***rivalled***, ***rivalling***; *US* ***rivaled***, ***rivaling***) **1** to try to gain the same objective as someone or something else; to be in competition with them. **2** to try to equal or be better than someone or something else. **3** to equal or be comparable with someone or something else, in terms of quality, ability, etc. ● **rivalless** *adj*. ⓒ 16c: from Latin *rivalis*, originally meaning 'someone who uses the same stream as another', from *rivus* a stream.

rivalry /ˈraɪvəlrɪ/ *noun* (***rivalries***) **1** the state of being a rival or rivals. **2** the action of rivalling someone or something else.

rive /raɪv/ ▻ *verb* (*past tense* ***rived***, *past participle* ***rived*** or ***riven*** /ˈrɪvən/, *present participle* ***riving***) *poetic, archaic* **1** to tear something or tear it apart. **2** *intr* to split. ⓒ 13c: from Norse *rifa*.

river /ˈrɪvə(r)/ ▻ *noun* **1** *geol* a large permanent stream of water, originating at a source and flowing along a fixed course, usually into a lake or the sea at its mouth. *Also as adj* ▫ *rivermouth* ▫ *riverboat.* **2** an abundant or plentiful stream or flow of something ▫ *a river of wine* ▫ *rivers of tears.* ● **rivered** *adj* watered by rivers. ● **riverless** *adj*. ● **river-like** *adj*. ● **rivery** *adj*. ⓒ 13c: from French *riviere*, from Latin *riparius*, from *ripa* riverbank.

river basin ▻ *noun*, *geol* the area of land drained by a river and its tributaries. Also called **drainage basin**.

river blindness see ONCHOCERCIASIS

river dolphin ▻ *noun* any of various species of a small toothed whale with a long narrow beak, found in rivers and brackish water in S Asia and S America.

riverine /ˈrɪvəraɪn, -riːn/ ▻ *adj* **1** living or situated on or near a river; riparian. **2** belonging or relating to a river. ⓒ 19c.

riverside ▻ *noun* **1** the bank of a river. **2** the area of ground adjacent to or along a river. Also *as adj* situated beside a river ▫ *a riverside restaurant.*

river-terrace ▻ *noun*, *geol* a terrace formed when a river eats away the old alluvium deposited when its flood-level was higher.

rivet /ˈrɪvɪt/ ▻ *noun*, *engineering* a metal pin or bolt with a head at one end, used for joining pieces of metal, etc by passing it through a hole in each of the pieces, then hammering the protruding end flat. ▻ *verb* (***riveted***, ***riveting***) **1** to fasten (pieces of metal, etc) with a rivet. **2** to flatten or hammer out (the head of a nail, etc). **3** to fix something securely. **4** to attract (eg someone's attention) and hold it firmly; to engross someone. **5** to render someone motionless, especially with fascination, horror or fear, etc ▫ *I was riveted to the spot when I saw how he'd changed.* ● **riveter** *noun* **1** someone whose job is to rivet. **2** a machine for riveting. ⓒ 14c: from French *river* to fasten or clinch.

riveting ▻ *noun*, *engineering* the joining of pieces of metal, etc by means of a rivet or rivets. ▻ *adj* fascinating; enthralling. ● **rivetingly** *adverb*.

riviera /rɪvɪˈɛərə/ ▻ *noun* **1** a coastal area that has a warm climate and is popular as a holiday resort. **2** (**the Riviera**) the Mediterranean coast between Toulon in France and La Spezia in Italy, bordered by the Alps to the

N and including many popular holiday resorts. ◎ 18c: Italian, meaning 'coast or shore'.

rivière /rɪvɪ'ɛə(r)/ ▷ *noun* **1** in needlework: a row of openwork. **2** a necklace of diamonds or other precious stones, especially one made up of several strings. ◎ 19c: French, meaning 'river'.

rivulet /'rɪvjʊlət/ ▷ *noun* a small river or stream. ◎ 16c: perhaps from Italian *rivoletto*, from *rivo*, from Latin *rivulus*, from *rivus* a stream.

riyal /rɪ'jɑːl/ ▷ *noun* **1** the standard unit of currency of Qatar. **2** (*also* **rial**) the standard unit of currency of Saudi Arabia. **3** (*also* **rial**) the standard unit of currency of the Yemen Arab Republic. Compare RIAL.

riza /'riːzə/ ▷ *noun* an ornamental plate or plaque, usually of silver, that frames the face and other features of a Russian icon. ◎ 1920s: Russian, from Slavonic, meaning 'garment'.

RJE ▷ *abbreviation, computing* remote job entry.

RL ▷ *abbreviation* **1** reference library. **2** *IVR* Republic of Lebanon. **3** Rugby League.

RLC ▷ *abbreviation* Royal Logistic Corps.

rly ▷ *abbreviation* railway.

RM ▷ *abbreviation* **1** *IVR* Republic of Madagascar. **2** Resident Magistrate. **3** Royal Mail. **4** Royal Marines.

rm ▷ *abbreviation* **1** *printing* ream. **2** room.

RMA ▷ *abbreviation* Royal Military Academy, Sandhurst.

RMetS ▷ *abbreviation* Royal Meteorological Society.

RMM ▷ *abbreviation, IVR* Republic of Mali.

RMO ▷ *abbreviation* Resident Medical Officer.

RMP ▷ *abbreviation* (Corps of) Royal Military Police.

rms ▷ *abbreviation, math* root mean square.

RMT ▷ *abbreviation* (National Union of) Rail, Maritime and Transport Workers.

RN ▷ *abbreviation* **1** Royal Navy. **2** *N Amer* Registered Nurse. **3** *IVR* Republic of Niger.

Rn ▷ *symbol, chem* radon.

RNA ▷ *abbreviation, biochem* ribonucleic acid.

RNAS ▷ *abbreviation* **1** Royal Naval Air Service(s). **2** Royal Naval Air Station.

RNCM ▷ *abbreviation* Royal Northern College of Music.

RNIB ▷ *abbreviation* Royal National Institute for the Blind.

RNID ▷ *abbreviation* Royal National Institute for the Deaf.

RNLI ▷ *abbreviation* Royal National Lifeboat Institution.

RNR ▷ *abbreviation* Royal Naval Reserve.

RNT ▷ *abbreviation* Royal National Theatre.

RNVR ▷ *abbreviation* Royal Naval Volunteer Reserve.

RO ▷ *abbreviation, IVR* Romania.

ro ▷ *abbreviation* **1** *printing* recto. **2** *cricket* run out.

roach[1] /roʊtʃ/ ▷ *noun* (***roaches*** or ***roach***) **1** a silvery freshwater fish of the carp family. **2** *US* any of several small fish that resemble this. ◎ 14c: from French *roche*.

roach[2] /roʊtʃ/ ▷ *noun* **1** *chiefly N Amer* short form of COCKROACH. **2** *colloq* the butt of a cannabis cigarette. ◎ 19c in sense 1; 1930s in sense 2.

roach[3] /roʊtʃ/ ▷ *noun, naut* a concave curve in the foot of a square sail. ◎ 18c.

road ▷ *noun* **1** an open way, usually specially surfaced or paved, for people, vehicles or animals to travel on from one place to another. Also *as adj* □ *road traffic.* **2** a route or course □ *the road to ruin.* **3** (*usually* **roads** or *also* **roadstead** /'roʊdstɛd/) *naut* a relatively sheltered area of water near the shore where ships may be anchored. **4** *chiefly US* a railway. **5** a passage in a mine. • **roadless** *adj.* • **be** or **get in someone** or **something's road** *colloq* to obstruct or hinder them or it □ *His attitude towards women got in the road of his promotion.* • **hit the road** to leave; to depart. • **one for the road** a final, usually alcoholic, drink before leaving. • **on the road** travelling from place to place, especially as a commercial traveller, a musician on tour or a tramp. • **take the road** to depart; to set off. • **take to the road 1** to become a tramp. **2** to set off for or travel to somewhere. ◎ Anglo-Saxon *rad*, related to RIDE.

roadbed ▷ *noun* **1** the foundation of a railway track on which the sleepers are laid. **2** the material laid down to form a road and which forms a foundation for the road surface.

roadblock ▷ *noun* a barrier put across a road, usually by the police or army, to stop and check vehicles and drivers before letting them pass on their way.

road bridge ▷ *noun* a bridge that carries a road.

roadeo /'roʊdɪoʊ/ ▷ *noun* (***roadeos***) *N Amer* a show or contest of lorry driving skills. ◎ 1940s: modelled on RODEO.

road fund licence ▷ *noun, Brit* a certificate, usually stuck on a vehicle's windscreen, that shows that ROAD TAX has been paid. ◎ 1920s: from the former *road fund* established in 1920 for the building and maintenance of roads.

road-hog ▷ *noun, colloq* an aggressive, selfish or reckless driver, especially one who tries to intimidate other road-users. • **road-hoggish** *adj.* ◎ 1890s.

roadholding ▷ *noun* the extent to which a vehicle remains stable when turning corners at high speed, in wet conditions, etc.

roadhouse ▷ *noun* a public house or inn at the side of a major road.

road hump ▷ *noun* a SLEEPING POLICEMAN.

roadie /'roʊdɪ/ ▷ *noun, colloq* a person who helps move and organize the instruments and equipment for a rock or pop group, especially on tour. ◎ 1960s: shortened form of *road manager*.

roadman ▷ *noun* **1** someone whose job is to make roads or keep them in good repair. **2** a frequent road-user, eg a travelling representative for a company. **3** someone who competes in road races. ◎ 19c in sense 1; 20c in senses 2 and 3.

road metal ▷ *noun* broken stone or rock used for building or mending roads.

road movie ▷ *noun* a genre of film in which the main character or characters take to the road, often to escape from the law or in search of adventure. What unfolds usually symbolizes a path to self-discovery.

road pricing ▷ *noun* the system of charging drivers for the use of a road, eg with the aim of reducing traffic in a city centre.

road rage ▷ *noun* uncontrolled anger or aggression between road users, which usually takes the form of screaming obscenities, making rude gestures, etc, but which can erupt into violence. ◎ 1990s.

road roller ▷ *noun* a heavy roller used to flatten the surface of a road.

roadrunner ▷ *noun* either of two largish fast-running birds of the cuckoo family, the **greater roadrunner** of the southern US and Mexico and the **lesser roadrunner** found in Central America.

road sense ▷ *noun* ability to handle a vehicle well and with good consideration for other road users, especially in heavy traffic.

road show ▷ *noun* **1 a** a touring group of theatrical or musical performers; **b** a show given by such a group. **2 a** a touring disc jockey or radio or TV presenter and their team, equipment, etc; **b** a live broadcast, usually in front of an audience, presented by them from one of a series of venues on the tour. **3** **a** a promotional tour by a group or organization to publicize its policies, products, etc; **b** the performances given on such a tour. ◷ Early 20c.

roadside ▷ *noun* the ground or land beside or along a road.

road sign ▷ *noun* a sign beside or over a road, motorway, etc, that gives information on routes, speed limits, hazards, traffic systems, etc.

roadstead see ROAD 3

roadster /ˈroʊdstə(r)/ ▷ *noun* **1** *originally US old use* an open sports car for two people. **2** a strong bicycle. **3** a horse for riding, or pulling carriages, on roads.

road tax ▷ *noun* a tax, usually paid annually, that is levied on motor vehicles that use public roads.

road test ▷ *noun* **1** a test of a vehicle's performance and roadworthiness. **2** a practical test of a product, etc. ▷ *verb* (**road-test**) **1** to test (a vehicle's roadworthiness). **2** to test out the practicalities, suitability, etc of something (eg a new product, etc).

road train ▷ *noun, Austral* a number of linked trailers towed by a truck, for transporting cattle, etc.

roadway ▷ *noun* the part of a road or street used by cars. ◷ 19c; 16c in sense 'a way used as a road'.

roadwork ▷ *noun* athletic training, eg for marathons, boxing matches, etc, consisting of running on roads.

roadworks ▷ *plural noun* the building or repairing of a road, or other work that involves digging up a road.

roadworthy /ˈroʊdwɜːðɪ/ ▷ *adj* said of a vehicle: in a suitable condition and safe to be used on the road. • **roadworthiness** *noun*. ◷ 19c.

roam /roʊm/ ▷ *verb* (***roamed***, ***roaming***) **1** *intr* to ramble or wander, especially over a large area, with no fixed purpose or direction. **2** to ramble or wander about, over, through, etc (a particular area) in no fixed direction □ *roamed the streets*. ▷ *noun* **1** the act of roaming. **2** a ramble. ◷ 14c.

roan[1] /roʊn/ ▷ *adj* **1** said of a horse's coat: black (**blue roan**), bay (**red roan**) or chestnut (**strawberry roan**), thickly flecked with grey or white hairs. **2** said of the coats of other animals, eg cattle: reddish-brown or bay similarly flecked with grey or white hairs. ▷ *noun* **1** a roan colour. **2** an animal, especially a horse, with a coat of this type. ◷ 16c: French, from Spanish *roano*.

roan[2] /roʊn/ ▷ *noun* soft, grained sheepskin leather used in bookbinding. ◷ 19c.

roan[3] and **roanpipe** see RONE

roar /rɔː(r)/ ▷ *verb* (***roared***, ***roaring***) **1** *intr* said of a lion or other animal: to give a loud growling cry. **2** said of people: **a** *intr* to give a deep loud cry, especially in anger, pain or exhilaration; **b** to say something with a deep loud cry, especially in anger. **3** *intr* to laugh loudly and wildly. **4** *intr* said of cannons, busy traffic, wind or waves during a storm, a fiercely burning fire, etc: to make a deep loud reverberating sound. **5** (*often* **roar about**, **away**, **past**, *etc*) to move very fast and noisily, usually in a motor vehicle. **6** *intr* said of a diseased horse: to make a loud rasping sound when breathing. ▷ *noun* **1** a loud deep prolonged cry, such as that of a lion, a cheering crowd, a person in pain or anger, etc. **2** a loud deep prolonged sound, such as that made by cannons, busy traffic, an engine made to roar, wind or waves during a storm, a fiercely burning fire, etc. • **roarer** *noun*. ◷ Anglo-Saxon *rarian*.

■ **roar someone on** to shout encouragement to them.

roaring /ˈrɔːrɪŋ/ ▷ *noun* **1** any loud deep cry or sound. **2** a disease of horses marked by roaring. ▷ *adj* **1** uttering or emitting roars. **2** *colloq* riotous. **3** *colloq* proceeding with great activity or success. • **roaringly** *adverb*. • **roaring drunk** *colloq* rowdily or boisterously drunk. • **do a roaring trade** to do very brisk and profitable business.

roaring forties see under FORTIES

roaring twenties ▷ *plural noun* the 1920s, especially when thought of as a decade of post-war hedonism.

roast /roʊst/ ▷ *verb* (***roasted***, ***roasting***) **1** to cook (meat or other food) by exposure to dry heat, often with the addition of fat and especially in an oven. **2** to dry and brown (coffee beans, nuts, etc) by exposure to dry heat. **3** *intr* said of meat, coffee beans, nuts, etc: to be cooked or dried and made brown by exposure to dry heat. **4** *metallurgy* to heat (ores, etc) in a furnace to remove impurities and make them more workable. **5** *colloq* to warm or heat (oneself or something else) to an extreme or excessive degree □ *roast in the sun*. **6** *intr*, *colloq* to be uncomfortably hot. **7** *colloq* to criticize severely. ▷ *noun* **1** a piece of meat which has been roasted or is suitable for roasting. **2** *N Amer* a party in the open air at which food is roasted and eaten. ▷ *adj* roasted □ *roast potatoes*. • **roaster** *noun* **1** an oven or dish for roasting food. **2** a vegetable, fowl, etc, suitable for roasting. **3** *colloq* an extremely hot day. ◷ 13c: from French *rostir*.

roasting *colloq, adj* extremely or uncomfortably hot. ▷ *noun* a dose of severe criticism.

rob ▷ *verb* (***robbed***, ***robbing***) **1** to steal something from (a person or place), especially by force or threats. **2** *intr* to commit robbery. **3** to deprive someone of something expected as a right or due. • **robber** *noun* someone who robs; a thief. • **robbing** *noun*. • **rob Peter to pay Paul** **1** to deprive one person of something in order to satisfy another. **2** to raise a loan in order to pay off a debt. ◷ 12c: from French *rober*.

robber-crab ▷ *noun* a large, coconut-eating land crab found in the Indian Ocean.

robbery /ˈrɒbərɪ/ ▷ *noun* (***robberies***) the act or process, or an instance, of robbing, especially theft with threats, force or violence.

robe ▷ *noun* **1** (*often* **robes**) a long loose flowing garment, especially the official vestment worn on ceremonial occasions by peers, judges, mayors, academics, the clergy, etc. **2** a dressing-gown or bathrobe. ▷ *verb* (***robed***, ***robing***) to clothe (oneself or someone else) in a robe or robes. ◷ 13c: French, of Germanic origin, related to ROB, originally meaning 'booty' in the sense of clothes regarded as booty.

robin /ˈrɒbɪn/ ▷ *noun* **1** (*also* **robin redbreast**) a small brown European thrush with a red breast and white abdomen. **2** a N American thrush, larger than the European robin, with a brick-red breast, black and white speckled throat and white rings around its eyes. **3** any of various unrelated birds with a red, yellowish or white breast, native to Australia. ◷ 16c: a diminutive of the personal name *Robert*.

robing-room ▷ *noun* a room in which official or ceremonial robes are put on.

Robin Hood ▷ *noun* **1** a legendary medieval English outlaw who robbed the rich to give to the poor. **2** anyone who is considered to be philanthropic □ *He's our very own Robin Hood*. ◷ 15c.

robinia /rɒˈbɪnɪə/ ▷ *noun* (***robinias***) any of various leguminous plants, especially the locust or false acacia. ◷ 18c: named after Jean and Vespasien Robin, royal gardeners in Paris in the late 16c and early 17c who introduced them to Europe from America.

roborant /ˈrɒbərənt/ ▷ *noun* a strengthening drug or tonic. ▷ *adj* (*also* **roborating**) strengthening. ◷ 17c: from Latin *roborare*, from *robur* strength.

robot /ˈroʊbɒt/ ▷ *noun* **1** especially in science-fiction: a machine that vaguely resembles a human being and which can be programmed to carry out tasks. Compare ANDROID. **2** an automatic machine that can be programmed to perform specific tasks. **3** *colloq* someone who works efficiently but who lacks human warmth or sensitivity. **4** *chiefly S Afr* an automatic traffic signal. • **robotic** /roʊ'bɒtɪk/ *adj.* • **robotize** or **robotise** /'roʊbɒtaɪz/ *verb* (***robotized, robotizing***) to automate (a job, etc). • **robot-like** *adj.* ◷ 20c: Czech (in the title of Karl Capek's 1920 play *R.U.R.* (Rossum's Universal Robots), from *robota* forced labour.

robotics /roʊ'bɒtɪks/ ▻ *singular noun* **1** the branch of engineering concerned with the design, construction, operation and use of industrial robots, and which incorporates many of the concepts used in ARTIFICIAL INTELLIGENCE. **2** (*also* **robotic dancing** or **robot dancing**) a form of dancing in which dancers imitate the stiff jerky movements of robots.

robust /rə'bʌst/ ▻ *adj* **1** said of a person: strong and healthy; with a strong constitution. **2** strongly built or constructed. **3** said of exercise, etc: requiring strength and energy. **4** said of language, humour, etc: rough, earthy, slightly risqué. **5** said of wine, food, etc: with a full, rich quality. • **robustly** *adverb.* • **robustness** *noun.* ◷ 16c: from Latin *robustus*, from *robur* an oak or strength.

robusta /roʊ'bʌstə/ ▻ *noun* (***robustas***) a variety of coffee grown especially in E Africa, which is more disease-resistant than other arabicas but gives a coffee of an inferior quality. ◷ Early 20c.

ROC ▻ *abbreviation* Royal Observer Corps.

roc /rɒk/ ▻ *noun* in Arabian legends: an enormous bird that was strong enough to carry off an elephant. ◷ 16c: from Persian *rukh*.

rocaille /roʊ'kaɪ/ ▻ *noun* **1** ornate ornamental rockwork or shellwork. **2** a rococo style. ◷ 19c: French, from *roc* rock.

rocambole /'rɒkəmboʊl/ ▻ *noun* (***rocamboles***) a type of alliaceous plant with a garlic-like bulb used for seasoning. ◷ 17c: French, from German *Rockenbolle*, literally 'distaff bulb', so called because of its shape.

Roche limit /roʊʃ —/ ▻ *noun, astron* the lowest orbit that a satellite can maintain around its parent planet without being pulled apart by the tidal forces it creates. ◷ 19c: named after Edouard Roche (1820–83), the French astronomer who discovered it.

roche moutonnée /rɒʃ muːtɒ'neɪ/ ▻ *noun* (***roches moutonnées*** /— muːtɒ'neɪ/) *geog* a smooth, rounded, hummocky rock-surface formed by glaciation. • **roche moutonnéed** *adj.* ◷ 19c: French, literally 'fleecy rock'.

rochet /'rɒtʃɪt/ ▻ *noun, relig* a full-length white linen robe similar to a surplice, worn by bishops, especially of the Anglican Communion, on ceremonial occasions. ◷ 14c: French, from *roc* a coat.

rock[1] ▻ *noun* **1** *geol* a loose or consolidated mass of one or more minerals that forms part of the Earth's crust, eg granite, limestone, etc. **2** a large natural mass of this material forming a reef, tor, etc. **3** a large stone or boulder. **4** *N Amer, Austral* a stone or pebble. **5** someone or something that provides a firm foundation or support and can be depended upon. **6** *colloq* (*often* **rocks**) a cause or source of difficulty, danger or disaster. **7** *Brit* a hard sweet usually made in the form of long, cylindrical sticks, which is brightly coloured and flavoured with peppermint, etc, often sold at the seaside or in holiday resorts. **8** *slang* a precious stone, especially a diamond. **9** *Can* a curling-stone. **10** (**rocks**) *coarse slang* the testicles. **11** *slang* **a** the drug crack; **b** a small piece of crack. • **get one's rocks off** **1** *coarse slang* to achieve sexual gratification, especially to ejaculate. **2** *colloq* to derive pleasure or excitement ▫ ***gets his rocks off watching kung fu movies.*** • **on the rocks** *colloq* **1** said of a marriage: broken down; failed. **2** said of an alcoholic drink: served with ice cubes. **3** said of a business or firm: in a state of great financial difficulty. ◷ 14c: from French *rocque*.

rock[2] ▻ *verb* (***rocked, rocking***) **1** *tr & intr* to sway or make something sway gently backwards and forwards or from side to side ▫ ***rock the baby to sleep.*** **2** *tr & intr* to move or make something move or shake violently. **3** *colloq* to disturb, upset or shock ▫ ***The news rocked the sporting world.*** **4** *intr* to dance to or play rock music. ▻ *noun* **1** a rocking movement. **2** (*also* **rock music**) a form of popular music with a very strong beat, usually played on electronic instruments and derived from rock and roll. **3** rock and roll. • **rocker** and **rocky** see separate entries. • **rock the boat** to destabilize or disturb something especially unnecessarily or out of spite. ◷ Anglo-Saxon *roccian*.

rockabilly /'rɒkəbɪli/ ▻ *noun, originally US* **1** a style of music that combines elements from both rock and roll and hillbilly. **2** a devotee or performer of this style of music. ◷ 20c.

rock and roll or **rock 'n' roll** ▻ *noun* **1** a form of popular music originating in the 1950s, deriving from jazz, country and western and blues music, with a lively jive beat and simple melodies. **2** the type of dancing done to this music. ▻ *verb, intr* to dance to or play rock-and-roll music. • **rock and roller** or **rock 'n' roller** *noun.* ◷ 1950s: originally Black slang for 'sexual intercourse'.

rock bottom or **rock-bottom** ▻ *noun* **1** bedrock. **2** *colloq* the lowest possible level. ▻ *adj, colloq* said especially of prices: the lowest possible; unbeatable. • **reach** or **hit rock bottom** to arrive at the lowest possible level, eg of poverty or despair.

rock-bound ▻ *adj* said of a landscape, coast, etc: **a** hemmed in by rock or rocks; **b** rocky.

rock cake ▻ *noun* a small round bun with a rough surface, made with fruit and spices.

rock climbing see under MOUNTAINEER

rock crystal ▻ *noun, mineralogy* a transparent colourless quartz.

rock dove and **rock pigeon** ▻ *noun* a pigeon that nests on rocks, from which the domestic and feral varieties are descended.

rocker /'rɒkə(r)/ ▻ *noun* **1** one of usually two curved supports on which a chair, cradle, etc rocks. **2** something that rocks on such supports, especially a rocking chair. **3** someone or something that rocks. **4** a device which is operated with a movement from side to side, backwards and forwards, or up and down. Also *as adj* ▫ ***rocker switch.*** **5** (**Rocker**) *Brit* in the 1960s: a follower of a sometimes violent teenage movement, typically wearing a leather jacket and riding a motorcycle. Compare MOD[1] (*noun*). **6** an object with a part which is curved like a rocker, especially a skate with a curved blade. • **off one's rocker** *colloq* mad; crazy.

rocker switch ▻ *noun* a switch, eg for an electrical appliance, on a central pivot.

rockery /'rɒkərɪ/ ▻ *noun* (***rockeries***) a garden made with both rocks and earth, in which rock plants are grown.

rocket[1] /'rɒkɪt/ ▻ *noun* **1** a cylinder containing inflammable material, which when ignited is projected through the air, used eg for signalling purposes, carrying a line to a ship in distress, or as part of a firework display. **2** a projectile or vehicle, especially a space vehicle, that obtains its thrust from a backward jet of hot gases produced by the burning of a mixture of fuel (solid or liquid) and oxygen that is carried within the projectile or vehicle. **3** a missile propelled by a rocket system. **4** *Brit colloq* a severe reprimand. ▻ *verb* (***rocketed, rocketing***) **1** to propel (a spacecraft, etc) by means of a rocket. **2** *intr* to move, especially upwards, extremely quickly, as if with the speed of a rocket. **3** *intr* said of prices: to rise very quickly; to soar. **4** to attack with rockets. **5** *Brit colloq* to reprimand someone severely. • **rocketry** *noun* the scientific study and use of rockets. ◷ 17c: from French *roquette*, from Italian *rochetta*, a diminutive of *rocca* a distaff, with reference to its shape.

rocket[2] /ˈrɒkɪt/ ▷ *noun* **1** a salad plant of Mediterranean countries. **2** *in compounds* any of several other plants □ *garden rocket*. 16c: from Latin *eruca* a type of herb.

rocketeer /rɒkɪˈtɪə(r)/ ▷ *noun* **1** a rocket technician or pilot. **2** a specialist in rocketry, especially a rocket designer.

rocket engine and **rocket motor** ▷ *noun* a jet engine or motor that uses an internally stored oxidizer, instead of atmospheric oxygen, for combustion.

rocket range ▷ *noun* a place of experimentation for rocket projectiles.

rocket scientist ▷ *noun, stock exchange slang* someone who devises schemes to take advantage of price differentials on money markets.

rockfish ▷ *noun* **1** any of various types of fish that live among rocks. **2** ROCK SALMON.

rock garden ▷ *noun* a rockery, or a garden containing rockeries.

rock-hopper ▷ *noun* a small crested penguin.

rockily see under ROCKY[2]

rockiness see under ROCKY[1], ROCKY[2]

rocking chair ▷ *noun* a chair which rocks backwards and forwards on two curved supports.

rocking horse ▷ *noun* a toy horse mounted on two curved supports on which a child can sit and rock backwards and forwards.

rocking stone ▷ *noun* a boulder poised so finely, eg on another stone or some other surface, that it can be made to rock.

rockling ▷ *noun* (***rocklings*** or ***rockling***) any of several small fish of the cod family with barbels on both jaws, found in the N Atlantic Ocean. 17c.

rock melon ▷ *noun* the cantaloupe.

rock pigeon see ROCK DOVE

rock plant ▷ *noun* any small alpine plant which grows among rocks and needs very little soil.

rockrose ▷ *noun* a small evergreen shrub native to the Mediterranean region and parts of Asia, which has lance-shaped or oblong leaves, and white, yellow or red flowers with five petals.

rock salmon ▷ *noun* the dogfish or other fish, especially when sold as food.

rock salt ▷ *noun* common salt occurring as a mass of solid mineral.

rockshaft ▷ *noun* in engines: a shaft that oscillates rather than revolves.

rocksteady or **rock steady** ▷ *noun* **1** a type of dance music originally from Jamaica, with a slow tempo and heavily stressed off-beat. **2** the type of dancing done to this music. 1960s.

rock tripe ▷ *noun* any of various kinds of edible arctic lichen.

rock wool ▷ *noun* mineral wool, used as an insulating material.

rocky[1] ▷ *adj* (***rockier***, ***rockiest***) **1 a** full of rocks; **b** made of rock; **c** like rock. **2** *colloq* full of problems and obstacles. • **rockiness** *noun*. 15c.

rocky[2] ▷ *adj* (***rockier***, ***rockiest***) **1** said of an object: with a tendency to rock; shaky; unstable. **2** said of a person: dizzy; unsteady on their feet. • **rockily** *adverb*. • **rockiness** *noun*. 18c.

rococo /rəˈkoʊkoʊ/ ▷ *noun* (*also* **Rococo**) **1** a style of architecture, decoration and furniture-making originating in France in the early 18c, characterized by elaborate ornamentation and unsymmetrical and broken curves; a freer development of the baroque. **2** a style of music of the 18c characterized by similarly elaborate ornamentation. ▷ *adj* **1** relating to, or in, this style. **2** said of music, literature, etc: florid and elaborate. 19c: French from *rocaille* rock-work or shell-work.

rod ▷ *noun* **1** a long slender stick or bar of wood, metal, etc. **2** a stick or bundle of twigs used to beat people as a punishment. **3** a stick, wand or sceptre carried as a symbol of office or authority. **4** a fishing-rod. **5** in surveying: a unit of length equivalent to 5.5yd (5.03m). **6** *anatomy* in the retina of the vertebrate eye: one of over 100 million rod-shaped cells containing the light-sensitive pigment rhodopsin, concerned with the perception of light intensity and essential for vision in dim light. Compare CONE *noun* 3. **7** a rod-shaped bacterium. **8** a metal bar that forms part of the framework under a railway carriage. **9** *N Amer slang* a pistol. **10** *coarse slang* a penis. **11** a POLE[2] (*noun* 2). ▷ *verb* (***rodded***, ***rodding***) to push or force a rod through (a drain, etc) to clear it. • **rodless** *adj*. • **rodlike** *adj*. • **make a rod for one's own back** to create trouble for oneself. • **ride the rods** *US* to travel illegally on a railway, on the rods under railway carriages. Anglo-Saxon *rodd*.

rode *past tense of* RIDE

rodent /ˈroʊdənt/ ▷ *noun, zool* an animal belonging to the order of mostly nocturnal mammals that includes rats, mice, squirrels, beavers, etc. They have chisel-like incisor teeth that grow continuously and are adapted for gnawing. The order comprises half of all known species of mammal. ▷ *adj* **1** gnawing. **2** belonging to this order. 19c: from Latin *rodere* to gnaw.

rodenticide /roʊˈdɛntɪsaɪd/ ▷ *noun* a substance used to kill rodents. • **rodenticidal** *adj*. 1930s.

rodent officer ▷ *noun* an official employed to catch rats or other rodent pests.

rodent ulcer ▷ *noun, medicine* a slow-growing malignant tumour on the face, usually situated at the edges of the lips, nostrils or eyelids.

rodeo /ˈroʊdɪoʊ, roʊˈdeɪoʊ/ ▷ *noun* (***rodeos***) *originally N Amer* **1** a round-up of cattle, eg for purposes of counting or branding them. **2** a place where cattle are assembled for such purposes. **3** a show or contest of cowboy skills, including riding, lassoing and animal-handling. **4** a similar show or contest of other skills, such as motorcycle riding, etc. Compare ROADEO. 19c in senses 1 and 2: Spanish, from *rodear* to go round, from Latin *rotare* to rotate.

rodomontade /rɒdəmɒnˈteɪd, -ˈtɑːd/ *literary* ▷ *noun* **1** a boastful or bragging speech. **2** boastful or bragging words or behaviour. ▷ *verb* (***rodomontaded***, ***rodomontading***) to brag or boast. 17c: French, from Italian *rodomonte* a boaster, named after Rodomonte the boastful king of Algiers in Ariosto's *Orlando Furioso* (1516).

rod puppet ▷ *noun* a glove puppet that is held on one hand while its arms are manipulated by rods held in the other hand.

roe[1] /roʊ/ ▷ *noun* **1** (*also* **hard roe**) the mass of mature eggs contained in the ovaries of a female fish. **2** (*also* **soft roe**) the testis of a male fish containing mature sperm. **3** either of these used as food. See also CAVIAR. • **roed** *adj* containing roe. 15c.

roe[2] /roʊ/ and **roe deer** ▷ *noun* (***roes*** or ***roe***) a small deer, native to Europe and Asia, with a reddish-brown coat and white underparts in summer, turning greyish-fawn in winter, a white rump and virtually no tail. Anglo-Saxon *ra* and *rahdeor*.

roebuck /ˈroʊbʌk/ ▷ *noun* the male roe deer.

roentgen or **röntgen** /ˈrɜːntjən, ˈrɒnt-, ˈrʌnt-, -gən/ (*sometimes* **Roentgen** or **Röntgen**) ▷ *adj* relating to Wilhelm Konrad Roentgen (1845–1923), the German physicist who discovered ROENTGEN RAYS. ▷ *noun* (*in full* **roentgen unit**) a former unit for measurement of X-rays or gamma rays, defined in terms of the ionization produced in $1cm^3$ of air under specific conditions. • **roentgenography** *noun* radiography by means of X-rays. • **roentgenology** *noun* the study of these rays. ⓘ 19c.

roentgen rays ▷ *plural noun* X-rays.

roesti or ***rösti*** /ˈrʊsti/ ▷ *noun* a dish of potatoes that are grated, shaped into a pancake, then fried. ⓘ 1950s: Swiss German.

rogation /roʊˈgeɪʃən/ ▷ *noun, Christianity* (*usually* **rogations**) solemn supplication, especially in ceremonial form. ⓘ 14c: from Latin *rogatio*, from *rogare* to ask.

Rogation Day ▷ *noun, Christianity* (*usually* **Rogation Days**) the three days in **Rogation Week** before Ascension Day, when supplications are recited in procession.

Rogation Sunday ▷ *noun, Christianity* the Sunday before Ascension Day.

roger[1] /ˈrɒdʒə(r)/ ▷ *exclamation* **1** in radio communications and signalling, etc: message received and understood. **2** *colloq* I will; OK ▫ *Roger, will do — see you later.* ⓘ 1940s: from the name *Roger*, representing the letter *R* for *received*.

roger[2] /ˈrɒdʒə(r)/ ▷ *verb* (***rogered, rogering***) *coarse slang* said of a man: to have sexual intercourse with (a woman). • **rogering** *noun*. ⓘ 18c: from *Roger*, obsolete slang meaning 'penis'.

rogue /roʊg/ ▷ *noun* (***rogues***) **1** a dishonest or unscrupulous person. Also *as adj* ▫ *a rogue trader.* **2** someone, especially a child, who is playfully mischievous. **3** someone or something, especially a plant, which is not true to its type and is of inferior quality. **4** a horse, person or object that is troublesome and unruly. **5 a** a vicious wild animal that lives apart from, or has been driven from, its herd; **b** *as adj* ▫ *a rogue elephant.* **6** someone or something that has strayed or that is found in an unusual or unexpected place. ▷ *verb* (***rogued, roguing***) to eliminate rogues from (a crop, etc). • **roguer** *noun*. • **roguery** /ˈroʊgərɪ/ *noun* (***rogueries***) behaviour or an action that is typical of a rogue. • **roguing** *noun*. ⓘ 16c.

rogues' gallery ▷ *noun* **1** a collection of photographs of known criminals, kept by the police and used to identify suspects. **2** a group of disreputable or undesirable people.

roguish /ˈroʊgɪʃ/ ▷ *adj* **1** characteristic of a rogue. **2** dishonest; unprincipled. **3** playfully mischievous ▫ *a roguish grin.* • **roguishly** *adverb*. • **roguishness** *noun*. ⓘ 16c.

roil /ˈrɔɪl/ ▷ *verb* (***roiled, roiling***) **1** to make (water or other liquid) cloudy by mixing up dregs or sediment. **2** *US* to anger or upset. ⓘ 16c.

roister /ˈrɔɪstə(r)/ ▷ *verb* (***roistered, roistering***) *intr* **1** to enjoy oneself noisily and boisterously. **2** to bluster or swagger. • **roisterer** *noun*. • **roistering** *noun*. • **roisterous** *adj*. • **roisterously** *adverb*. ⓘ 16c: from French *rustre* a ruffian, an uncouth fellow, from Latin *rusticus* rustic, rural.

ROK ▷ *abbreviation, IVR* Republic of Korea.

Roland /ˈroʊlənd/ ▷ *noun, only in the phrase* **a Roland for an Oliver** /—ˈɒlɪvə(r)/ tit for tat; an effective retaliation or retort. ⓘ 16c: named after Roland, a legendary nephew of Charlemagne, celebrated in the medieval romance the *Chanson de Roland*, who fought a contest with his comrade Oliver.

role or **rôle** /roʊl/ ▷ *noun* **1** an actor's part or character in a play, film, etc. **2** a function, or a part played or taken on by someone or something in life, business, etc ▫ *in her role as head of the household* ▫ *the role of television as an educating medium.* **3** *psychol* someone's characteristic or expected function within a particular social setting. ⓘ 17c: French, originally meaning 'a roll of parchment on which an actor's part was written'.

role model ▷ *noun* someone whose character, life, behaviour, etc is taken as a good example to follow.

role-play or **role-playing** ▷ *noun* the assuming and performing of imaginary roles, usually as a method of instruction, training, therapy, etc.

Rolfing /ˈrɒlfɪŋ/ ▷ *noun* a therapeutic technique for correcting postural faults and improving physical wellbeing through manipulation of the muscles and joints, so that the body is realigned symmetrically and the best use made of gravity in maintaining balance. ⓘ 1950s: named after US physiotherapist Dr Ida Rolf (1897–1979), the originator of the technique.

roll /roʊl/ ▷ *noun* **1** a cylinder or tube formed by rolling up anything flat (such as paper, fabric, etc) ▫ *I used six rolls of wallpaper for this room.* **2** a rolled document; a scroll. **3 a** a small individually-baked portion of bread; **b** *in compounds* one of these with a specified filling ▫ *a cheese roll.* **4** a folded piece of pastry or cake with a filling ▫ *swiss roll* ▫ *sausage roll.* **5** a rolled mass of something ▫ *rolls of fat.* **6** an undulation, eg in a surface or of a landscape. **7 a** an official list of names, eg of school pupils, members of a club or people eligible to vote; **b** the total number registered on such a list. **8** an act of rolling. **9** a swaying or rolling movement, eg in walking or dancing, or of a ship. **10** a long low prolonged sound ▫ *a roll of thunder.* **11** a trill or trilling sound, especially an 'r' sound. **12** (*also* **a drum roll**) a series of quick beats on a drum. **13** a complete rotation around its longitudinal axis by an aircraft. **14** a roller or cylinder used to press, shape or apply something. **15 a** an act or bout of rolling ▫ *Sparky had a roll in the sand*; **b** a gymnastic exercise similar to, but less strenuous than, a somersault ▫ *a backward roll.* **16** *colloq* money, especially a wad of banknotes. ▷ *verb* (***rolled, rolling***) **1** *tr & intr* to move or make something move by turning over and over, as if on an axis, and often in a specified direction ▫ *rolled the dice.* **2** *tr & intr* to move or make something move on wheels, rollers, etc, or in a vehicle with wheels. **3** *intr* (*also* **roll over**) said of a person or animal, etc that is lying down: to turn with a rolling movement to face in another direction. **4** *tr & intr* to move or make something move or flow gently and steadily. **5** *intr* to seem to move like or in waves ▫ *a garden rolling down to the river.* **6** *intr* said eg of a ship: to sway or rock gently from side to side. **7** *intr* to walk with a swaying movement ▫ *rolled in drunk at six o'clock.* **8** *tr & intr* to begin to operate or work ▫ *the cameras rolled.* **9** *tr & intr* to move or make (one's eyes) move in a circle, especially in disbelief, despair or amazement. **10** *tr & intr* to form, or form something, into a tube or cylinder by winding or being wound round and round. **11** (*also* **roll up**) **a** to wrap something by rolling ▫ *rolled a spliff*; **b** to curl around ▫ *The hamster rolled up into a ball.* **12** (*also* **roll something out**) to spread it out or make it flat or flatter, especially by pressing and smoothing with something heavy ▫ *rolled out the pastry.* **13** *intr* to make a series of long low rumbling sounds. **14** to pronounce (especially an 'r' sound) with a trill. **15** *slang* to rob someone who is helpless, usually because they are drunk or asleep. **16 a** to make (the credits) appear on a screen; **b** to appear on a screen. **17 a** to make (a car) do a somersault; **b** *intr* said of a car: to overturn. • **rolled** *adj*. • **roller, rolling** see separate entries. • **a roll in the hay** *colloq* an act of sexual intercourse. • **heads will roll** severe punishment will be dealt out, especially involving loss of job or status. • **on a roll** *chiefly US colloq* going through a period of continuous good luck or success. • **rolled into one** combined in one person or in one thing. • **roll with the punches 1** said of a boxer: to move the body away from and in the same direction as an opponent's punches to reduce their impact. **2** to go along with something negative and to offer no resistance in order to lessen its impact. • **strike someone off the roll** to remove the right to practise from (a doctor, solicitor, etc), after professional misconduct. • **roll on ...** may a specified event, time, etc come soon ▫ *Roll on the holidays.* ⓘ 14c: from French *rolle*, from Latin *rotula*, diminutive of *rota* a wheel.

■ **roll by** or **on** or **past**, *etc* said especially of time: to pass or follow steadily and often quickly □ *The weeks rolled by.*

■ **roll in** to come or arrive in large quantities.

■ **be rolling in something** *colloq* to have large amounts of it (especially money).

■ **roll over 1** to overturn. **2** see *verb* 3 above. **3** said of a jackpot prize, eg in the UK National Lottery: to be carried across to the next week because it has not been won □ *the jackpot might roll over three times in one year.* See also ROLL-OVER.

■ **roll something over** *econ* to defer demand for repayment of (a debt, loan, etc) for a further term. See also ROLL-OVER.

■ **roll up 1** *colloq* to arrive. **2** to come in large numbers. See also ROLL-UP.

roll-bar ▷ *noun* a metal bar that strengthens the frame of a vehicle and reduces the danger to its occupants if the vehicle overturns, used especially in racing, rallying, etc.

roll-call ▷ *noun* an act or the process of calling out names from a list at an assembly, meeting, etc to check who is present.

rollcollar ▷ *noun* on a garment: a collar turned over in a curve.

rolled gold ▷ *noun* metal covered with a very thin coating of gold, usually used in inexpensive jewellery. The preferred term is now GOLD-PLATED.

roller /ˈroʊlə(r)/ ▷ *noun* **1** any cylindrical object or machine used for flattening, crushing, spreading, printing, applying paint, etc. **2** a rod for rolling cloth, etc round. **3** a small cylinder on which hair is rolled to make it curl. **4** a solid wheel or cylinder attached to heavy machinery, etc, which makes it easier to move. **5** a long heavy sea wave. **6** any of several birds of a family related to bee-eaters and kingfishers, found especially in Africa, which have a characteristic courtship display that involves spectacular tumbling and rolling flight. **7** *medicine* (*also* **roller-bandage**) a long bandage rolled into a cylinder before it is applied.

roller-bearing ▷ *noun* a bearing made up of two grooves between which a number of parallel or tapered rollers are located, usually in a cage, suitable for heavier loads than ball-bearings.

rollerblade ▷ *verb* (***rollerbladed, rollerblading***) *intr* to move about on Rollerblades, especially with gliding movements.

Rollerblades ▷ *plural noun, trademark* roller skates with wheels set in a single line from front to back along the sole of the shoe.

roller blind see BLIND *noun* 1

rollercoaster ▷ *noun* a raised railway with sharp curves and steep inclines and descents, ridden on for pleasure and excitement, usually found at funfairs.

roller hockey ▷ *noun* a form of hockey played by teams wearing roller skates.

roller skate ▷ *noun* a series of wheels attached to a framework which can be fitted onto a shoe, or a shoe with wheels attached to the sole. ▷ *verb* (**roller-skate**) *intr* to move, dance, etc on roller skates. • **roller-skater** *noun*. • **roller-skating** *noun*.

roller towel ▷ *noun* a towel, usually a long one, with the ends sewn together, that is hung on a roller.

rollick[1] /ˈrɒlɪk/ ▷ *verb* (***rollicked, rollicking***) *intr* to behave in a carefree, swaggering, boisterous or playful manner. ▷ *noun* a boisterous romp. • **rollicking** *adj* boisterous, noisy and carefree. ⓘ 19c.

rollick[2] /ˈrɒlɪk/ ▷ *verb* (***rollicked, rollicking***) *slang* to rebuke someone severely. • **rollicking** *noun* (*also* **rollocking**) a severe rebuke or scolding. ⓘ 20c: perhaps a variant of *bollock*.

rolling /ˈroʊlɪŋ/ ▷ *adj* **1** said of land, countryside, etc: with low, gentle hills and valleys, and without steep slopes and crags. **2** *colloq* extremely wealthy. **3** *colloq* staggering with drunkenness. **4** said of a contract: subject to review at regular intervals. **5** said of planned events, etc: organized so as to take place successively, on a relay or rota system, or with a steadily maintained or increasing effect.

rolling mill ▷ *noun* **1** a machine for rolling metal ingots into sheets, bars or other shapes between pairs of rollers revolving in opposite directions, often to improve the mechanical properties of a metal or to give it a bright finish. **2** a factory containing such machines.

rolling-pin ▷ *noun* a cylinder made of wood, pottery, marble, etc for flattening out pastry or dough.

rolling stock ▷ *noun* the engines, wagons, coaches, etc used on a railway.

rolling stone ▷ *noun* someone who leads a restless or unsettled life.

rollmop ▷ *noun* a fillet of raw herring rolled up usually round a slice of onion, and pickled in spiced vinegar. ⓘ Early 20c: from German *Rollmops*, from *rollen* to roll + *Mops* a pug-dog.

rollneck ▷ *adj* said of a garment: with a high neck which is folded over on itself.

rollocking see under ROLLICK[2]

roll-on ▷ *adj* contained in a bottle with a rotating ball at the top, by means of which the liquid is applied. ▷ *noun* **1** a roll-on deodorant, etc. **2** *Brit* a woman's light elastic corset.

roll-on roll-off ▷ *adj* (abbreviation **ro-ro**) said especially of a passenger ferry: with entrances at both the front and back of the ship, so that vehicles can be driven on through one entrance and off through the other. ▷ *noun* a ship of this kind.

roll-out ▷ *noun* **1** the first public showing of the prototype of an aircraft. **2** the part of an aircraft's landing during which it slows down after touching down.

roll-over ▷ *noun* **1 a** an instance of deferring demand for repayment of a debt, loan, etc for a further term; **b** *as adj* □ *roll-over loan.* **2** in the UK National Lottery: **a** an unwon jackpot prize which is carried forward from one week to the next and which is added to the next week's jackpot; **b** *as adj* □ *roll-over week.* See also ROLL OVER at ROLL.

roll-top desk ▷ *noun* a desk with a flexible cover of slats that may be rolled down when the desk is not being used.

roll-up ▷ *noun* **1** *Brit colloq* a cigarette which one makes oneself by rolling paper round loose tobacco. **2** *Austral* attendance; turn-out.

roly-poly /roʊlɪˈpoʊlɪ/ ▷ *adj* round and podgy. ▷ *noun* (***roly-polies***) **1** (*also* **roly-poly pudding**) a strip of suet pastry spread with jam and rolled up, then baked or steamed. **2** *colloq* a round podgy person. **3** the children's game of rolling over and over down a hill or grassy slope, etc. **4** *Austral* any of several bushy plants, found in arid regions, that break off and roll in the wind. ⓘ 19c.

ROM /rɒm/ ▷ *abbreviation, computing* read-only memory, a storage device which holds data permanently and allows it to be read and used but not changed. Compare RAM.

rom or **Rom** /rɒm/ ▷ *noun* (***roma*** /ˈrɒmə/ or ***romas***) a male Gypsy; a Romany. ⓘ 19c: Romany, meaning 'man', 'husband'.

Rom. ▷ *abbreviation* Book of the Bible: Romans. See table at BIBLE.

rom. ▷ *abbreviation, printing* roman (type).

Roman /'roʊmən/ ▻ *adj* **1** belonging or relating to modern or ancient Rome and the Roman Empire, its history, culture or inhabitants. **2** relating to the Roman Catholic Church. ▻ *noun* **1** an inhabitant of modern or ancient Rome. **2** a Roman Catholic.

roman /'roʊmən/ *printing* ▻ *adj* said of type: relating to or indicating the ordinary, upright kind most commonly used for printed material. Compare ITALIC. ▻ *noun* (abbreviation **rom.**) roman type. ⓒ 16c: so called because the form of the letters resembles that of ancient Roman inscriptions and manuscripts.

roman-à-clef /*French* rɔmɑ̃ a kle/ ▻ *noun* (***romans-à-clef***) a novel with characters based on real people under disguised names. ⓒ 19c: French, meaning 'novel with a key'.

roman alphabet ▻ *noun* the alphabet developed by the ancient Romans for writing Latin, and now used for most writing in W European languages, including English.

Roman candle ▻ *noun* a firework that discharges a succession of flaming white or coloured sparks, balls of fire, etc. ⓒ 19c.

Roman Catholic (abbreviation **RC**) ▻ *adj* belonging or relating to the **Roman Catholic Church**, the Christian church which recognizes the pope as its head. ▻ *noun* a member of this church. Often shortened to CATHOLIC. • **Roman Catholicism** *noun* the doctrines, worship and life of the Roman Catholic Church. ⓒ 17c.

romance /roʊ'mans/ ▻ *noun* **1** a love affair. **2** sentimentalized or idealized love, valued especially for its beauty, purity and the mutual devotion of the lovers. **3** the atmosphere, feelings or behaviour associated with romantic love. **4** a sentimental account, especially in writing or on film, of a love affair. **5** such writing, films, etc as a group or genre. **6** a fictitious story which deals with imaginary, adventurous and mysterious events, characters, places, etc. **7** a medieval verse narrative dealing with chivalry, highly idealized love and fantastic adventures. **8** an exaggeration or absurd account or lie. **9** (**Romance**) the group of languages, including French, Spanish, Italian and Romanian, which have developed from Latin. **10** *music* a short, informal, ballad-like piece. ▻ *adj* (**Romance**) belonging or relating to the languages which have developed from Latin, such as French, Spanish, Italian and Romanian. ▻ *verb* (***romanced***, ***romancing***) **1** to try to win someone's love. **2** *intr* to talk or write extravagantly, romantically or fantastically. **3** *intr* to lie. • **romancer** *noun*. • **romancing** *noun, adj*. ⓒ 13c: from French *romans*, from Latin *Romanicus* Roman.

Roman Empire ▻ *noun, historical* the ancient empire of Rome, established in 31 BC by Augustus, and divided in the 4c into the **Eastern Roman Empire** and **Western Roman Empire**. • **Roman Emperor** *noun*.

Romanes see ROMANY

Romanesque /roʊmə'nɛsk/ ▻ *noun* **1** the style of architecture found in W and S Europe from the 9c to the 12c, characterized by the use of a round arch, clear plans and elevations and, typically, a two-tower facade. **2** the style of sculpture, painting, etc of this period. ▻ *adj* in or relating to this style of architecture or art. ⓒ 18c: French.

roman-fleuve /*French* rɔmɑ̃ flœv/ ▻ *noun* (***romans-fleuves*** /*French* rɔmɑ̃ flœv/) a series of novels, each of which exists as a separate novel in its own right, but which are linked, usually because some or all of the characters appear in each successive work, eg the seven parts of Proust's *A la recherche du temps perdu* (1913–27) or John Galsworthy's *Forsyte Saga* (1906–28). ⓒ 20c: French, literally 'river novel'.

Romani see ROMANY

Romanian /roʊ'meɪnɪən/, **Rumanian** or **Roumanian** /rʊ-/ ▻ *adj* belonging or relating to Romania, a republic in SE Europe bordering on the Black Sea, its inhabitants or their language. ▻ *noun* **1** a citizen or inhabitant of, or a person born in Romania. **2** the official language of Romania.

Roman holiday ▻ *noun* an event or occasion when pleasure is taken from the suffering of others. ⓒ 19c: so called because days of gladiatorial combat in ancient Rome were public holidays.

Romanize or **Romanise** /'roʊmənaɪz/ ▻ *verb* (***Romanized***, ***Romanizing***) **1** to make (a ceremony, etc) Roman Catholic in character. **2** to convert someone to Roman Catholicism. **3** *intr* to become Roman Catholic in character or convert to Roman Catholicism. **4** to transcribe into the roman alphabet (a language, such as Arabic, Chinese, Greek or Hindi, that uses a different writing system). • **Romanization** *noun*. ⓒ 17c.

Roman nose ▻ *noun* a high-bridged or aquiline nose. • **Roman-nosed** *adj*.

Roman numeral ▻ *noun* (*often* **Roman numerals**) any of the figures in the NUMBER SYSTEM developed by the ancient Romans and used to represent cardinal numbers, eg I, V, X, etc. Compare ARABIC NUMERALS.

Romano- /roʊ'mɑːnoʊ/ ▻ *combining form, signifying* Roman ◻ *Romano-British*.

Romansch see under RHAETIAN

romantic /roʊ'mantɪk/ ▻ *adj* **1** characterized by or inclined towards sentimental and idealized love. **2** dealing with or suggesting adventure, mystery and sentimentalized love ◻ *romantic fiction*. **3** highly impractical or imaginative, and often also foolish. **4** (*often* **Romantic**) said of literature, art, music, etc: relating to or in the style of romanticism. ▻ *noun* **1** someone who has a romantic, idealized, impractical or sentimental view of love, etc. **2** (*often* **Romantic**) **a** a poet, writer, artist, composer, etc of the ROMANTIC PERIOD; **b** someone whose main influence or inspiration is the ROMANTIC PERIOD in the arts. • **romantically** *adverb*. ⓒ 17c: from French *romanz* romance.

romanticism or **Romanticism** /roʊ'mantɪsɪzəm/ ▻ *noun* a late 18c and early 19c movement in art, literature and music, characterized by an emphasis on feelings and emotions, often using imagery taken from nature, and creating forms which are relatively free from rules and set orders. • **romanticist** *noun* someone whose art or writing, etc is characterized by Romanticism. ⓒ 19c.

romanticize or **romanticise** /roʊ'mantɪsaɪz/ ▻ *verb* (***romanticized***, ***romanticizing***) **1** to make something seem romantic. **2** *tr & intr* to describe, think of or interpret something in a romantic, idealized, unrealistic and sometimes misleading way. **3** *intr* to hold romantic ideas or act in a romantic way. • **romanticization** *noun*.

romantic period ▻ *noun* the era from the late 18c to the early 19c when romanticism flourished.

Romany or **Romani** /'roʊmənɪ/ ▻ *noun* (***Romanies*** or ***Romanis***) **1** a GYPSY. **2** (*also* **Romanes** /'rɒmənɛs/) the language spoken by gypsies, belonging to the Indic branch of Indo-European, but now often showing regional variations from contact with other languages. ▻ *adj* relating or pertaining to the Romanies, their language or culture. ⓒ 19c: from Romany *rom* man.

Romeo /'roʊmɪoʊ/ ▻ *noun* (***Romeos***) **1** an ardent young male lover. **2** a womanizer. **3** *communications* in the NATO alphabet: the word used to denote the letter 'R' (see table at NATO ALPHABET). ⓒ 18c: the name of the love-struck hero in Shakespeare's *Romeo and Juliet*.

Romish /'roʊmɪʃ/ ▻ *adj, derog* Roman Catholic.

romneya /'rɒmnɪə/ ▻ *noun* (***romneyas***) *bot* either of two shrubby Californian plants with large white poppy-like flowers. ⓒ Late 20c: named after Thomas Romney Robinson (1792–1882), an Irish astronomer.

romp /rɒmp/ ▻ *verb* (***romped***, ***romping***) *intr* **1** to play or run about in a lively boisterous way. **2** (*usually* **romp in** or

home, *etc*) *colloq* to win a race, competition, etc quickly and easily. **3** (*usually* **romp through something**) *colloq* to complete (a task, etc) quickly and easily. ▻ *noun* **1** an act of romping; boisterous playing or running about. **2** a light-hearted outing or jaunt. **3** a swift pace. **4** *sport, colloq* an easily-won match, game, etc. • **romper** *noun*. • **rompingly** *adverb*. ◷ 18c.

rompers ▻ *plural noun* (*also* **romper suit**) *formerly* a baby's suit, usually one-piece, with short-legged trousers and either a short-sleeved top or a bib top. Compare BABYGRO.

rondavel /rɒn'dɑːvəl/ ▻ *noun, S Afr* a round hut or similar type of building, usually with a thatched roof. ◷ 19c: from Afrikaans *rondawel*.

rondeau /'rɒndoʊ/ ▻ *noun* (***rondeaux*** /-doʊ, -doʊz/) a poem of 13 or sometimes 10 lines with only two rhymes, and with the first line used as a refrain after the eighth and thirteenth lines. ◷ 16c: from French *rondel*, from *rond* round.

rondel /'rɒndəl/ ▻ *noun* a variation of the RONDEAU. ◷ 13c: French, meaning 'a little circle', from *rond* round.

rondo /'rɒndoʊ/ ▻ *noun* (***rondos***) *music* a piece of music, especially one forming the last movement of a sonata or a concerto, with a principal theme which recurs or is repeated as a refrain. ◷ 18c: Italian, from French rondeau; see RONDEAU.

rone or **roan** /roʊn/ and **ronepipe** or **roanpipe** ▻ *noun, Scottish* a roof-gutter. ◷ 19c.

ronggeng /'rɒŋgɛŋ/ ▻ *noun* **1** a Malaysian dancing-girl. **2** a popular kind of Malaysian dancing, often accompanied by singing. ◷ 19c: Malay.

röntgen, **röntgenography** and **röntgenology** see ROENTGEN

roo /ruː/ ▻ *noun, Austral colloq* a short form of KANGAROO. ◷ 20c.

roo-bar ▻ *noun, Austral colloq* a strong metal bar or grid fitted to the front of a vehicle as protection in case of collision with a kangaroo or other animal. Also called (*E Afr*) **rhino bar** or (*Brit*) **bull bar**.

rood /ruːd/ ▻ *noun* **1** a cross or crucifix, especially a large one set on a beam or screen at the entrance to a church chancel. **2** *literary* the Cross on which Christ was crucified. **3** a former unit of area, equal to a quarter of an acre, or 0.10117 hectare. **4** a former unit of area, equal to a square rod. ◷ Anglo-Saxon *rod* gallows or cross.

rood beam ▻ *noun* a beam for supporting a rood, often forming the top of a rood screen.

rood loft ▻ *noun* in a church: a gallery over the rood screen.

rood screen ▻ *noun* in a church: an ornamental wooden or stone screen separating the choir from the nave.

roof /ruːf/ ▻ *noun* (***roofs*** /ruːfs/ or common in spoken English, but *non-standard* in writing ***rooves*** /ruːvz/) **1 a** the top outside covering of a building; **b** the structure at the top of a building that supports this. **2** a similar top or covering for a vehicle, etc. **3** the interior overhead surface of a room, vault, cave, etc. **4** a dwelling or home ▫ *two families under the same roof.* **5** the top inner surface of an oven, refrigerator, etc. **6** (*usually* **roof of the mouth**) the upper inside surface of the mouth; the palate. **7** a high, or the highest, level; an upper limit ▫ *the roof of the world.* ▻ *verb* (***roofed***, ***roofing***) **1** to cover or provide something with a roof. **2** to serve as a roof or shelter for something. • **roofed** *adj* with a roof. • **roofer** *noun* someone who makes or repairs roofs. • **roofing** *noun* **1** materials for building a roof. **2** the roof itself. • **roofless** *adj*. • **rooflike** *adj*. • **have a roof over one's head** to have somewhere to live. • **go through** or **hit the roof** *colloq* to become very angry. • **raise the roof** *colloq* **1** to make a great deal of noise or fuss. **2** to become very angry. ◷ Anglo-Saxon *hrof*.

roof garden ▻ *noun* a garden on a flat roof of a building.

roof rack ▻ *noun* a frame attached to the roof of a car or other vehicle for carrying luggage, etc.

rooftop ▻ *noun* the outside of a roof of a building. Also *as adj* ▫ *a rooftop swimming pool.* • **shout it from the rooftops** to make public something that is better kept quiet.

roof tree ▻ *noun* **1** the ridge-pole of a roof. **2** the roof itself. ◷ 15c.

rooinek /'rɔɪnɛk/ ▻ *noun, S Afr jocular or derog slang* an English-speaking or British S African. ◷ 19c: Afrikaans, from *rooi* red + *nek* neck.

rook[1] /rʊk/ ▻ *noun* a large, crow-like bird with lustrous black plumage and a bare patch of grey skin at the base of its beak. It nests in colonies in the tops of trees and is found in Europe and Asia. ▻ *verb* (***rooked***, ***rooking***) *colloq* **1** to cheat or defraud, especially at cards. **2** to charge (a customer) an excessively high price. ◷ Anglo-Saxon *hroc*.

rook[2] /rʊk/ ▻ *noun, chess* a CASTLE. ◷ 14c: from Persian *rukh*.

rookery /'rʊkərɪ/ ▻ *noun* (***rookeries***) **1** a colony of rooks. **2** a colony of penguins or other sea birds, or of seals. ◷ 18c.

rookie or **rooky** /'rʊkɪ/ ▻ *noun* (***rookies***) *colloq* **1** a new or raw recruit, especially in the police or the army. **2** a beginner in a particular profession or field. **3** *sport, chiefly N Amer* a new member of a team, especially one who is playing in their first major league championship. ◷ 19c.

room /ruːm, rʊm/ ▻ *noun* **1 a** an area within a building enclosed by a ceiling, floor and walls; **b** *in compounds* ▫ *dining-room* ▫ *bedroom.* **2 a** sufficient or necessary space, especially free or unoccupied space, that is available to someone or for a particular purpose ▫ *no room for all her books.* ▫ *Have you room to get past?*; **b** *in compounds* ▫ *shelf room* **3** all the people present in a room ▫ *The room suddenly became silent.* **4** opportunity, scope or possibility ▫ *room for improvement.* **5** (**rooms**) rented lodgings, especially a set of rooms within a house, etc, that are rented out as an individual unit ▫ *returned to his rooms at Oxford.* ▻ *verb* (***roomed***, ***rooming***) *tr & intr, chiefly N Amer* to lodge; to occupy a room or rooms as a lodger. • **roomed** *adj, in compounds* having rooms of a specified kind or number. • **roomer** *noun, N Amer* a lodger, usually one who takes their meals elsewhere. • **leave the room** *euphemistic, old use* said especially by or about children in school: to go to the lavatory. ◷ Anglo-Saxon *rum*.

■ **room with someone** *N Amer* to share a room or rooms with them.

room-divider ▻ *noun* a low wall, partition or piece of furniture that divides a room or space into separate sections.

roomette ▻ *noun, N Amer* a sleeping compartment on a train.

roomful ▻ *noun* (***roomfuls***) as much or as many (people, objects, etc) as a room can hold ▫ *a roomful of books.*

rooming house ▻ *noun, N Amer* a house with furnished rooms to let.

roommate ▻ *noun* **1** someone who shares a room with another person, especially in a students' residence, hostel, etc. **2** *originally US* someone who lodges with or shares a flat, etc with another person or persons.

room service ▻ *noun* in a hotel: a facility that enables guests to order and be served food, drinks, etc in their rooms.

room temperature ▻ *noun* the average temperature of a living-room, usually about 20°C.

roomy ▷ *adj* (***roomier***, ***roomiest***) with plenty of room; spacious □ *The house is quite roomy.* ● **roomily** *adverb.* ● **roominess** *noun.* ⓒ 16c.

roost[1] /ruːst/ ▷ *noun* **1** a branch, perch, etc on which birds, especially domestic fowl, rest at night. **2** a group of birds, especially domestic fowl, resting together on the same branch or perch. **3** *colloq* a place that offers temporary sleeping accommodation. ▷ *verb* (***roosted***, ***roosting***) *intr* said especially of birds: to settle on a roost, especially for sleep. ● **the chickens have come home to roost** one's actions have had unpleasant consequences. ● **come home to roost** said of a scheme, etc: to have unpleasant consequences for, or a bad effect on, the originator. ⓒ Anglo-Saxon *hrost*.

roost[2] /ruːst/ ▷ *noun* around the islands of Orkney and Shetland: a strong tidal current. ⓒ 16c: from Norse *röst*.

rooster /ˈruːstə(r)/ ▷ *noun, chiefly N Amer* a farmyard cock. ⓒ 18c.

root[1] /ruːt/ ▷ *noun* **1 a** *bot* in vascular plants: the descending structure, lacking leaves and chlorophyll, that usually grows beneath the soil surface, and whose function is to anchor the plant in the soil and to absorb water and mineral nutrients; **b** *loosely* any of the branches of this structure; **c** a growing plant with its root; **d** *as adj* □ *root vegetable.* **2** the part by which anything is attached to or embedded in something larger. **3** *anatomy* the embedded part of eg a tooth, hair, nail or similar structure. **4 a** the basic cause, source or origin of something □ *the root of the problem*; **b** *as adj* □ *the root cause.* **5** (**roots**) **a** someone's ancestry or family origins; **b** someone's feeling of belonging, eg ethnically, culturally, etc, to a community or in a certain place □ *go back to one's roots.* **6** *linguistics* the basic element in a word which remains after all affixes have been removed, and which may form the basis of a number of related words, eg *love* is the root of *lovable*, *lovely*, *lover* and unloved. See also STEM. **7** *math* a factor of a quantity that, when multiplied by itself a specified number of times, produces that quantity, eg 2 is the square root of 4 and the cube root of 8. **8** *math* in an algebraic equation: the value or values of an unknown quantity or variable that represent the solution to that equation. Also called SOLUTION. **9** *music* in harmony: the fundamental note on which a chord is built. ▷ *verb* (***rooted***, ***rooting***) **1** *intr* to grow roots. **2** *intr* to become firmly established. **3** (*usually* **root something up** or **out**) to dig it up by the roots. **4** to fix something with or as if with roots. **5** to provide something with roots. **6** *tr & intr, Austral & NZ coarse slang* to have sexual intercourse with someone. ● **rootless** *adj* **1** with no roots. **2** with no fixed home; wandering. ● **rootlike** *adj.* ● **get to the root of something** to find its underlying cause. ● **root and branch** thoroughly; completely. ● **take** or **strike root** **1** to grow roots. **2** to become firmly established. ⓒ Anglo-Saxon *rot*.

■ **root something out** to remove or destroy it completely.

root[2] /ruːt/ ▷ *verb* **1** *intr* said especially of pigs: to dig up the earth with the snout in search of food. **2** *intr* (*usually* **root around** or **about**) *colloq* to look for something by poking about; to rummage. **3** (*usually* **root something out** or **up**) to find or extract it by rummaging. ● **rooter** *noun.* ⓒ Anglo-Saxon *wrotan*, from *wrot* snout.

root[3] /ruːt/ ▷ *verb* (***rooted***, ***rooting***) *intr* (*always* **root for someone**) *originally N Amer colloq* to support them with loud cheering and encouragement. ⓒ 19c.

root-ball ▷ *noun* the spherical mass formed by the roots of a plant and the surrounding soil.

root beer ▷ *noun, N Amer, especially US* a fizzy drink made from the roots of certain plants, such as dandelions, and flavoured with herbs.

root canal ▷ *noun* the passage through which the nerves and blood vessels of a tooth enter the pulp cavity. Also (*dentistry*) *as adj* □ *root-canal work.*

root climber ▷ *noun* any of various plants that climb by means of roots growing from the stem, eg ivy.

root crop ▷ *noun* any plant that is grown mainly for its edible root, tuber or corm, eg carrot, turnip, potato, sugar beet, etc.

rooted /ˈruːtɪd/ ▷ *adj* **1** fixed by or as if by roots. **2** firmly established. ● **rootedly** *adverb.* ● **rootedness** *noun.*

root hair ▷ *noun, bot* any of many fine tubular outgrowths from the surface cells of plant roots, serving to increase greatly the surface area of the root that is available to absorb water from the soil.

rootless see under ROOT[1]

rootlet /ˈruːtlɪt/ ▷ *noun* a small root.

root-mean-square ▷ *noun, math* (abbreviation **rms**) the square root of the sum of the squares of a set of quantities divided by the total number of quantities in the set.

roots ▷ *adj* **1** said especially of music: relating or referring to one's ethnic or cultural identity, especially insofar as it is authentic or unadulterated. **2** relating to roots music. ⓒ 20c.

roots music ▷ *noun* popular music of a style that shows the influence of folk music and has a certain ethnic identity, especially reggae of a kind that is considered authentic and unadulterated.

rootstock /ˈruːtstɒk/ ▷ *noun, bot* **1** an underground plant stem that bears buds; a rhizome. **2** a stock onto which another plant has been grafted.

rootsy ▷ *adj* said especially of music: influenced by, or incorporating, traditional ethnic or folk styles. ● **rootsiness** *noun.*

root vegetable ▷ *noun* **a** a vegetable with an edible root; **b** the root itself.

rope /roʊp/ ▷ *noun* **1 a** strong thick cord made by twisting fibres of hemp, wire or some other material together; **b** a length of this. **2** a number of objects, especially pearls or onions, strung together. **3** (**the rope**) **a** a hangman's noose; **b** execution by this means. **4** (**ropes**) the cords that mark off a boxing or wrestling ring, or the boundary of a cricket ground. **5** *Scottish* a clothes-line □ *hang the washing on the rope.* **6** *US* a lasso. **7** a long glutinous strand of a viscous substance found especially in contaminated beer. **8** *as adj* □ *a rope ladder* □ *rope-soles.* ▷ *verb* (***roped***, ***roping***) **1** to tie, fasten or bind with rope or as if with rope. **2** (*usually* **rope something in** or **off**) to enclose, separate or divide it with a rope. **3** *mountaineering* to tie (climbers) together with a rope for safety. **4** *chiefly N Amer* to catch (an animal) with a rope; to lasso. **5** *intr* said of a viscous substance: to form into a rope. ● **give someone (enough) rope (to hang themselves)** to allow them to bring about their own downfall as a result of their ill-considered or foolish actions, behaviour, etc. ● **know the ropes** to have a thorough knowledge and experience of what needs to be done in a particular circumstance or for a particular job. ● **on the ropes** **1** *boxing* driven back against the ropes of a boxing ring. **2** in a desperate position. ⓒ Anglo-Saxon *rap*.

■ **rope someone in** to persuade them to take part in some activity.

■ **rope up** said of a group of climbers: to tie themselves together with a rope for safety.

ropeable or **ropable** ▷ *adj* **1** able to be roped. **2** *Austral & NZ slang* said of cattle or horses: wild and unmanageable. **3** *Austral & NZ slang* said of a person: extremely or uncontrollably angry. ⓒ 19c.

rope-dance ▷ *noun* a tightrope performance. ● **rope-dancer** *noun.*

rope's end *historical* **1** *noun* a short piece of rope used for flogging, especially for flogging a sailor. **2** a hangman's noose. ▷ *verb* (***rope's-ended***, ***rope's-ending***) to flog someone with a rope's end. ⓒ 15c.

rope-trick ▷ *noun* a conjuring or other magic trick using a rope, especially an INDIAN ROPE-TRICK.

rope-walk ▷ *noun, historical* a long narrow shed or covered alley where ropes are made.

rope-walker ▷ *noun* a tightrope performer. • **rope-walking** *noun*.

ropeway ▷ *noun* **1** a cable railway. **2** a rope used as a means of transportation.

rope-yarn ▷ *noun* **1** yarn for making rope. **2** yarn obtained by unpicking rope.

roping-down ▷ *noun* abseiling.

ropy /'roʊpɪ/ or **ropey** ▷ *adj* (***ropier***, ***ropiest***) **1** said of a substance or its texture: **a** forming glutinous strands; **b** stringy. **2** rope-like. **3** *colloq* poor in quality. **4** *colloq* slightly unwell. • **ropily** *adverb*. • **ropiness** *noun*.

Roquefort /'rɒkfɔː(r)/ ▷ *noun, trademark* a strong soft blue-veined cheese made from ewes' milk. Also *as adj* □ *Roquefort dressing*. ⓒ 19c: named after the village in S France where it was originally made.

roquet /'roʊkeɪ, -kɪ/ ▷ *noun* in croquet: a stroke where a player strikes an opponent's ball with their own. ▷ *verb* (***roqueted*** /-keɪd, -kɪd/, ***roqueting*** /-keɪɪŋ, -kɪɪŋ/) *tr & intr* to strike another player's ball by a roquet; to play a roquet. ⓒ 19c: a variant of CROQUET.

ro-ro /'roʊroʊ/ ▷ *adj, noun* (***ro-ros***) acronym of ROLL-ON ROLL-OFF.

rorqual /'rɔːkwəl/ ▷ *noun* any of several baleen whales that have a longitudinally furrowed throat (allowing for expansion when feeding) and a small dorsal fin near the tail, especially the **common rorqual** or FIN WHALE, and the **lesser rorqual** or MINKE WHALE. ⓒ 19c: French, from Norwegian *ryrkval*, from Norse *reytharhvelr*, from *rauthr* red + *hvalr* whale.

Rorschach test /'rɔːʃak —, 'rɔːʃɑːk —/ ▷ *noun, psychol* a test designed to show intelligence, personality type, mental state, etc in which the subject is asked to interpret a number of inkblots of a standard type. ⓒ 20c: named after Hermann Rorschach (1884–1922), Swiss psychiatrist.

rort /rɔːt/ ▷ *noun, Austral slang* **1** a trick or fraud. **2** a lively or riotous party. ▷ *verb* (***rorted***, ***rorting***) *intr* **1** to shout or protest loudly. **2** at a race meeting: to call the odds. **3** *Austral slang* to commit fraud. • **rorter** *noun*. • **rorting** *noun* the action of commiting fraud. ⓒ 20c: back-formation from RORTY.

rorty *adj* **1** lively and enjoyable. **2** boisterous; rowdy. ⓒ 19c.

rosace /roʊ'zeɪs/ ▷ *noun, archit* **1** a ROSE WINDOW. **2** a rose-shaped ornament or decoration; a ROSETTE (*noun* 2). ⓒ 19c: French, from Latin *rosaceus* rosaceous.

rosaceous /roʊ'zeɪʃəs/ ▷ *adj* **1** *bot* denoting a plant that belongs to the family **Rosaceae**, including eg the rose, apple, strawberry, cherry and almond. **2** resembling a rose. ⓒ 18c: from Latin *rosaceus*, from *rosa* rose.

rosaniline ▷ *noun, chem* a base derived from aniline, used in dyeing and formerly as a medical fungicide. ⓒ 19c: ROSE[1] + ANILINE.

rosarian /roʊ'zeərɪən/ ▷ *noun* someone who is keen on cultivating varieties of roses, either professionally or as a pastime. ⓒ 19c.

rosarium /roʊ'zeərɪəm/ ▷ *noun* (***rosariums*** or ***rosaria*** /-rɪə/) a rose-garden. ⓒ 19c.

rosary /'roʊzərɪ/ ▷ *noun* (***rosaries***) **1 a** a rose-garden; **b** a rose-bed. Also called **rosery**. **2** *RC Church* a series of prayers with a set form and order in which five or fifteen decades of Aves are recited, each decade being preceded by a Paternoster and followed by a Gloria. **3** *RC Church* **a** a string of 165 beads divided into fifteen sets used to count such prayers as they are recited; **b** (*also* **lesser rosary**) *now especially* a similar string of 55 beads. **4** in other religions: a string of beads or length of knotted cord used in a similar way. ⓒ 14c: from Latin *rosarium* rose-garden, from *rosa* rose.

rose[1] /roʊz/ ▷ *noun* **1** an erect or climbing thorny shrub that produces large, often fragrant, flowers which may be red, pink, yellow, orange or white, or some combination of these colours, followed by bright-coloured fleshy fruits known as hips. **2** the flower of this plant. **3** a rose as the national emblem of England. **4** any flowering plant that superficially resembles a rose, eg the Christmas rose. **5** the colour of a rose, usually a darkish pink. **6** (**roses**) a light-pink, glowing complexion □ *put the roses back in one's cheeks*. **7** a perforated nozzle, usually attached to the end of a hose, watering can, shower-head, etc, that makes the water come out in a spray. **8** a circular fitting in a ceiling through which an electric light flex hangs. Also called **ceiling rose**. **9** a circular moulding from which a door handle projects. **10** a rose-like design, eg round the sound hole of a guitar or lute, etc. **11** a ROSE-DIAMOND. **12** a ROSE WINDOW. **13** a rosette. ▷ *adj* relating to or like a rose or roses, especially in colour, scent or form. • **roseless** *adj*. • **roselike** *adj*. • **all roses** or **roses all the way** pleasant or happy; free from problems or difficulties. • **bed of roses** an easy or comfortable situation. • **under the rose** in confidence; privately. Also called SUB ROSA. ⓒ Anglo-Saxon, from Latin *rosa*, probably from *rhodon* rose.

rose[2] *past tense of* RISE

rosé /'roʊzeɪ, roʊ'zeɪ/ ▷ *noun* (***rosés***) a light-pink wine properly made by removing the skins of red grapes after fermentation has begun. It is sometimes also made by mixing red and white wines. ⓒ 19c: French, literally 'pink'.

rose-apple ▷ *noun* **a** an E Indian tree of the clove genus; **b** its edible fruit.

roseate /'roʊzɪət, -eɪt/ ▷ *adj* **1** like a rose, especially in colour. **2** unrealistically hopeful or cheerful.

rosebay ▷ *noun* **1** the OLEANDER. **2** (*also* **rosebay willowherb**) a common wild plant that has spikes of pale purple flowers and produces many fluffy seeds. **3** any of several rhododendrons.

rose-beetle ▷ *noun* a ROSE-CHAFER.

rosebud ▷ *noun* **1** the bud of a rose. **2** something that is considered to be like a rosebud, especially in colour or beauty. **3** *literary* a pretty young woman. **4** *formerly* a member of the branch of the Guides for younger girls, now called BROWNIES. ⓒ 15c.

rose-campion ▷ *noun* a garden species of campion with pink flowers and woolly, down-covered leaves.

rose-chafer ▷ *noun* any of several beetles, with a greenish or yellowish metallic-looking body, that feed on roses.

rose-coloured and **rose-tinted** ▷ *adj* **1** pink; rosy. **2** seen or represented in too favourable a light. • **see** or **look through rose-coloured** or **rose-tinted spectacles** or **glasses** to view things in an unrealistically hopeful or cheerful way.

rose comb ▷ *noun* **1** a flat red or pinkish crest on the head of some fowls. **2** a fowl that has such a crest.

rose-cut ▷ *adj* said of a gem or diamond: cut in such a way as to be nearly hemispherical in form, with a flat base and many small facets rising to a low point above.

rose-diamond ▷ *noun* a rose-cut diamond.

rose-engine ▷ *noun* a lathe attachment for carving intricate patterns.

rose geranium ▷ *noun* any of several pelargoniums with small pink flowers and fragrant rose-scented leaves.

rosehip ▷ *noun* the red berry-like fruit of the rose.

rosella /roʊ'zɛlə/ ▷ *noun* any of various brightly coloured Australian parrots. ◷ 19c: probably from *Rosehiller*, from *Rose Hill*, Parramatta, near Sydney, where the birds were first observed.

rose madder ▷ *noun* the pinkish colour made from madder pigment or dye.

rose-mallow ▷ *noun* **1** hollyhock. **2** hibiscus.

rosemary /'roʊzmərɪ/ ▷ *noun* a fragrant evergreen shrub with stiff needle-like leaves, used in cookery and perfumery. ◷ 15c: from Latin *ros* dew + *marinus* of the sea.

rose of Jericho ▷ *noun* a plant of N Africa and Syria that curls up into a ball during drought. Also called RESURRECTION PLANT.

rose of Sharon ▷ *noun* **1** in the Bible, in *the Song of Solomon*: an unknown flowering plant, probably a type of narcissus. **2** *now* **a** a species of Hibiscus; **b** a species of Hypericum.

roseola /roʊ'zɪələ/ ▷ *noun* (***roseolas***) *medicine* **1** any rose-coloured rash. **2** *formerly* RUBELLA. • **roseolar** *adj.* ◷ 19c: Latin diminutive of *roseus* rosy.

rosery see ROSARY

rose-tinted see ROSE-COLOURED

rosette /roʊ'zɛt/ ▷ *noun* **1** a badge or decoration made in coloured ribbon to resemble the form of a rose, often awarded as a prize or worn to show membership of some group, etc. **2** *archit* a rose-shaped ornament on a wall or other surface. **3** *bot* **a** a naturally occurring cluster of leaves radiating from a central point, especially at the base of a stem; **b** an abnormal cluster of leaves on a stem that is a symptom of disease; **c** (*also* **rosette disease**) any of several plant diseases which result in such an abnormal cluster of leaves. **4** any rose-shaped structure, arrangement or figure. ▷ *verb* (***rosetted***, ***rosetting***) **1** to award a rosette to someone or something. **2** *intr*, *medicine* said of a cell or group of cells: to form into a rosette. • **rosetting** *noun*, *bot* the development of abnormal clusters of leaves as a symptom of plant disease. ◷ 18c: French, meaning 'little rose'.

rose-water ▷ *noun* water distilled from roses or scented with oil of roses, used as a perfume. ▷ *adj* **1** elegant and refined. **2** sentimental. **3** comfortable. ◷ 14c.

rose window ▷ *noun* a circular window with ornamental tracery radiating in a symmetrical pattern from the centre. Also called **rosace**.

rosewood ▷ *noun* **1** the valuable dark red or purplish wood of any of various tropical trees used in making high quality furniture. **2** a colour or shade similar to that of rosewood. ◷ 17c: so called because it is said to smell of roses when newly cut.

Rosh Hashanah or **Rosh Hashana** /rɒʃ hə'ʃɑːnə/ ▷ *noun* the Jewish festival of New Year, celebrated on the first and sometimes second of the month Tishri, which falls in September or October, at which, during the New Year's service, a ram's horn is blown as a call to repentance and spiritual renewal. ◷ 18c: Hebrew, literally 'head of the year', from *rosh* head + *hash-shanah* year.

Rosicrucian /roʊzɪ'kruːʃən, rɒ-/ ▷ *noun* **1** *historical* a member of a 17c-18c society that professed knowledge of the secrets of Nature, the transmutation of metals and other occult powers. **2** a member of any of various societies or organizations that derive from this. ▷ *adj* relating to or characteristic of this society or those derived from it. • **Rosicrucianism** *noun.* ◷ 17c: from Latin *rosa* rose + *crux* cross, probably translating the name of Christian Rosenkreutz, a German who supposedly founded the society in 1484.

rosier, **rosiest**, **rosily** and **rosiness** see under ROSY

rosin /'rɒzɪn/ ▷ *noun* a clear hard resin, produced by distilling turpentine prepared from dead pine wood, which is rubbed on the hair of the bows of stringed musical instruments. ▷ *verb* (***rosined***, ***rosining***) to rub rosin on (the bow of a violin, etc). • **rosiny** *adj.* ◷ 14c variant of RESIN.

rosolio or **rosoglio** /roʊ'zoʊljoʊ/ ▷ *noun* (***rosolios*** or ***rosoglios***) a sweet cordial, made especially in Italy, with raisins, alcohol, spices, etc. ◷ 19c: Italian, from Latin *ros* dew + *sol* sun.

RoSPA /'rɒspə/ ▷ *abbreviation* Royal Society for the Prevention of Accidents.

roster /'rɒstə(r)/ ▷ *noun* a list or roll of people's names, especially one that shows the order in which they are to do various duties, go on leave, etc. ▷ *verb* (***rostered***, ***rostering***) to put (someone's name) on a roster. • **rostering** *noun.* ◷ 18c: from Dutch *rooster* a gridiron, or a list or table (because of its ruled parallel lines), from *roosten* to roast.

rösti see ROESTI

rostrum /'rɒstrəm/ ▷ *noun* (***rostrums*** or ***rostra*** /-strə/) **1** a platform on which a public speaker stands. **2** a platform in front of an orchestra on which the conductor stands. **3** a raised platform for carrying a camera. **4** *zool* **a** a bird's beak; **b** a structure similar to a beak in other animals. • **rostral** *adj* relating to or like a rostrum. ◷ 16c: Latin, meaning 'beak' or 'beak-head', from *rodere* to gnaw. In the Forum of ancient Rome, the platform for public speaking (called the *Rostra*), was decorated with the beak-heads of captured ships.

rosy /'roʊzɪ/ ▷ *adj* (***rosier***, ***rosiest***) **1** rose-coloured; pink. **2** said of the complexion: with a healthy pink colour; glowing □ *rosy cheeks*. **3** filled or decorated with roses. **4** like a rose, especially in fragrance. **5** **a** hopeful or optimistic, often overly so □ *He tends to take a rosy view of things*; **b** promising □ *The situation looks quite rosy*. • **rosily** *adverb*. • **rosiness** *noun*. ◷ 14c.

rosy cross ▷ *noun* the emblem of the Rosicrucians.

rot /rɒt/ ▷ *verb* (***rotted***, ***rotting***) **1** *tr & intr* (*also* **rot down**) to decay or cause to decay or become putrefied as a result of the activity of bacteria and/or fungi. **2** *intr* to become corrupt. **3** *intr* to become physically weak, especially through being inert, confined, etc □ *Mike was left to rot in a Bangkok jail*. ▷ *noun* **1** **a** decay; **b** something which has decayed or decomposed. **2** *pathol* putrefaction of bodily tissues. **3** *colloq* nonsense; rubbish. **4** *in compounds* any of several plant or animal diseases caused by fungi or bacteria, eg FOOT ROT. ▷ *exclamation* expressing contemptuous disagreement. • **rotter** *noun*, *chiefly dated Brit slang* a thoroughly depraved, worthless or despicable person. See also ROTTEN. ◷ Anglo-Saxon *rotian*.

rota /'roʊtə/ ▷ *noun* **1** *Brit* a list of duties that are to be done with the names and order of the people who are to take turns doing them; a roster. **2** (**the Rota**) *RC Church* the supreme ecclesiastical tribunal. ◷ 17c: Latin, meaning 'wheel'.

Rotarian /roʊ'tɛərɪən/ ▷ *noun* a member of **Rotary International**, a society with branches throughout the world, that draws its membership from the business world and the professions and which aims to promote charity events and international goodwill. Also *as adj.* • **Rotarianism** *noun.*

rotary /'roʊtərɪ/ ▷ *adj* turning on an axis like a wheel. ▷ *noun* (***rotaries***) **1** a rotary machine. **2** *N Amer* a traffic roundabout. ◷ 18c: from Latin *rotarius*, from *rota* a wheel.

Rotary Club ▷ *noun* a local branch of Rotary International.

rotary engine ▷ *noun* a vehicle or aircraft engine with cylinders set in a circle, rotating around a fixed crankshaft. Compare RADIAL ENGINE.

rotate ▷ *verb* /roʊ'teɪt/ (***rotated***, ***rotating***) **1** *tr & intr* to turn or make something turn about an axis like a wheel; to revolve. **2** to arrange in an ordered sequence. **3** *intr* to change position, take turns in doing something, etc according to an ordered sequence. **4** to grow (different crops) in an ordered sequence on the same ground to avoid exhausting the soil and to resist the onset of plant-specific diseases. ▷ *adj* /ˈroʊteɪt/ *bot* said of the petals of a corolla: wheel-shaped; radiating like the spokes of a wheel. • **rotatable** *adj.* Ⓢ 17c: from Latin *rotare, rotatum*, from *rota* wheel.

rotation /roʊˈteɪʃən/ ▷ *noun* **1** the action of rotating or state of being rotated. **2** one complete turn around an axis. **3** a regular and recurring sequence or cycle. **4** CROP ROTATION.

rotator /roʊˈteɪtə(r)/ ▷ *noun* **1** a device that rotates or makes something else rotate. **2** *anatomy* a muscle that enables a limb, etc to rotate. Ⓢ 17c.

Rotavator or **Rotovator** /ˈroʊtəveɪtə(r)/ ▷ *noun, trademark* (*also* **rotavator** or **rotovator**) a machine with a rotating blade for breaking up the soil. Ⓢ 1930s: from *rota*ry culti*vator*.

rotavate or **rotovate** ▷ *verb* (***rotavated, rotavating***) **1** to break up (soil) with a Rotavator. **2** to work something into the soil by means of a Rotavator. Ⓢ 1950s: back-formation from ROTAVATOR.

rote ▷ *noun* mechanical use of the memory to repeat or perform something, without necessarily understanding what is memorized. • **by rote** mechanically; by heart, usually without understanding or regard to meaning □ *learn by rote.* Ⓢ 14c.

rotenone /ˈroʊtənoʊn/ ▷ *noun, chem* a toxic crystalline substance made from derris and other plants, commonly used in ecological studies to paralyse fish and medicinally to control head lice. Ⓢ 20c: from Japanese *roten* derris + -ONE.

rotgut ▷ *noun, slang* cheap alcoholic drink, especially spirits, of inferior quality. Also called **gutrot**.

roti /ˈroʊtɪ/ ▷ *noun* (***rotis***) **1** a cake of unleavened bread, traditionally made in parts of India and the Caribbean. **2** a kind of sandwich made from this bread wrapped around curried vegetables, seafood or chicken. Ⓢ 1920s: Hindi, meaning 'bread'.

rotifer /ˈroʊtɪfə(r)/ ▷ *noun, zool* any of various microscopic aquatic invertebrate animals that have an unsegmented body and swim by means of a ring of beating hair-like structures that resembles a spinning wheel. Also called **wheel animalcule**. Ⓢ 18c: from Latin *rota* wheel + *ferre* to carry.

rotisserie /roʊˈtɪsərɪ/ ▷ *noun* (***rotisseries***) **1** a cooking apparatus with a spit on which meat, poultry, etc is cooked by direct heat. **2** a shop or restaurant that sells or serves meat cooked in this way. Ⓢ 19c: from French *rôtisserie*, from *rôtir* to roast.

rotogravure /roʊtoʊgrəˈvjʊə(r)/ ▷ *noun, printing* **1** a photogravure process that uses a rotary press. **2** printed material, especially part of a magazine, produced by this method. Ⓢ Early 20c: from the name of a German company *Rotogravur*, from Latin *rota* wheel + GRAVURE.

rotometer /roʊˈtɒmɪtə(r), ˈroʊtəmiːtə(r)/ ▷ *noun* a small hand-held device for measuring distance travelled. Ⓢ Early 20c.

rotor /ˈroʊtə(r)/ ▷ *noun* **1** a rotating part of a machine, especially in an internal combustion engine. Compare STATOR. **2** a revolving cylinder attached to a ship to provide additional propulsion. **3** a system of blades, projecting from a cylinder, that rotate at high speed to provide the force to lift and propel a helicopter. **4** a rotating part of an encoding or decoding machine that changes codes by changing electrical circuits. Also *as adj* □ *rotor blade.* Ⓢ Early 20c: a variant of ROTATOR.

Rotovator see ROTAVATOR

rotted *past tense, past participle of* ROT

rotten /ˈrɒtən/ ▷ *adj* **1** gone bad, decayed, rotted. **2** falling or fallen to pieces from age, decay, etc. **3** morally corrupt. **4** *colloq* miserably unwell □ *She had a bad cold and felt rotten.* **5** *colloq* unsatisfactory □ *a rotten plan.* **6** *colloq* unpleasant; disagreeable □ *rotten weather.* ▷ *adverb, colloq* very much; extremely □ *She fancied him rotten.* • **rottenly** *adverb.* • **rottenness** *noun.* Ⓢ 13c: from Norse *rotinn*.

rotten apple ▷ *noun, colloq* a corrupt person.

rotten borough ▷ *noun, historical* before the Reform Act of 1832: a borough that could elect an MP even though it had few or no inhabitants.

rottenstone /ˈrɒtənstoʊn/ ▷ *noun* a decomposed silicious limestone, used as a powder for polishing metals.

rotter and **rotting** see under ROT

Rottweiler /ˈrɒtvaɪlə(r), -waɪlə(r)/ ▷ *noun* **1** a large, powerfully built black and tan dog with a smooth coat, originally from Germany. **2** (*often* **rottweiler**) *colloq* a rudely aggressive or brutish person. Also *as adj* □ *rottweiler politics.* Ⓢ Early 20c: named after Rottweil in SW Germany.

rotund /roʊˈtʌnd/ ▷ *adj* **1** *chiefly bot, zool* round or rounded in form; nearly spherical. **2** said of a person, part of the body, etc: plump. **3** said of speech, language, etc: impressive or grandiloquent. • **rotundity** *noun* **1** someone or something that is rotund. **2** roundness. • **rotundly** *adverb.* Ⓢ 15c: from Latin *rotundus*, from *rota* a wheel.

rotunda /roʊˈtʌndə/ ▷ *noun* (***rotundas***) a round, usually domed, building or hall. Ⓢ 17c: from Italian *rotonda* round.

ROU ▷ *abbreviation* Republic of Uruguay.

rouble or **ruble** /ˈruːbəl/ ▷ *noun* the standard unit of currency in Russia and some other states of the CIS. Ⓢ 16c: from Russian *rubl* a silver bar.

roucou /ruːˈkuː/ ▷ *noun* **a** ANNATTO; **b** the tropical American tree from which this comes. Ⓢ 17c: French, from Tupí *urucú*.

roué /ˈruːeɪ/ ▷ *noun* (***roués***) *old use* a debauched, disreputable man; a rake. Ⓢ 19c: French, meaning 'broken on the wheel', from *roue* a wheel. The name was first applied to the dissolute companions of Philippe, Duke of Orléans, Regent of France 1715–23, to suggest that they deserved such punishment.

rouge /ruːʒ/ ▷ *noun* **1** *old use* a pink or red cosmetic powder or cream used to colour the cheeks, originally a mixture of safflower and talc. Compare BLUSHER. **2** (*also* **jeweller's rouge**) a fine powder of hydrated ferric oxide used for polishing metal. **3** (*in full* **vin rouge**) French red wine. ▷ *verb* (***rouged, rouging***) **1** to apply rouge to (the cheeks, etc). **2** *intr* to use rouge. **3** *intr* to blush. Ⓢ 18c; 15c in obsolete sense 'red': French, meaning 'red'.

rouge-et-noir /ruːʒeɪˈnwɑː(r)/ ▷ *noun* a gambling card-game in which the stakes are laid on a table marked with two red and two black diamonds. Ⓢ 18c: French, meaning 'red and black'.

rough /rʌf/ ▷ *adj* **1** said of a surface or texture: not smooth, even or regular. **2** said of ground: covered with stones, tall grass, bushes and/or scrub. **3** said of an animal: covered with shaggy or coarse hair. **4** said of a sound: harsh or grating □ *a rough voice.* **5** said of a person's character, behaviour, etc: noisy, coarse or violent. **6** said of weather, the sea, etc: stormy. **7** requiring hard work or considerable physical effort, or involving great difficulty, tension, etc □ *a rough day at work.* **8** (*especially* **rough on someone**) unpleasant and hard for them to bear □ *a decision which is rough on the employees.* **9** said of a guess, calculation, etc: approximate. **10** not polished or refined □ *a rough draft.* **11** *colloq* slightly unwell and tired, especially because of heavy drinking or lack of sleep. **12** not well-kept □ *lives in a really rough area.* ▷ *noun* **1** (**the rough**) rough ground, especially the uncut grass at the side of a golf fairway. **2** the unpleasant or disagreeable side of something, *especially* **take the rough with the**

smooth. **3** a rough or crude state. **4** a crude preliminary sketch. **5** a thug or hooligan. ▻ *adverb* roughly. ▻ *verb* (***roughed***, ***roughing***) to make something rough; to roughen. • **roughish** *adj* somewhat rough. • **roughly** *adverb* **1** in a rough way. **2** approximately. • **roughness** *noun*. • **a bit of rough 1** someone, especially a man, whose lack of sophistication and coarse manner make them sexually attractive to some people. **2** sexual activity that involves a degree of violence. • **rough it** *colloq* to live in a very basic or primitive way, without the usual comforts of life one is accustomed to. • **sleep rough** to sleep in the open without proper shelter. ◷ Anglo-Saxon *ruh*.

▪ **rough something in** to outline or sketch it in roughly.

▪ **rough something out** to do a preliminary sketch of it or give a preliminary explanation of it.

▪ **rough someone up** *colloq* to beat them up.

roughage /ˈrʌfɪdʒ/ ▻ *noun* DIETARY FIBRE. ◷ 19c.

rough-and-ready ▻ *adj* **1** quickly prepared and not polished or perfect, but usually good enough for the purpose. **2** said of a person: friendly and pleasant but not polite or refined.

rough-and-tumble ▻ *noun* disorderly but usually friendly fighting or scuffling. ▻ *adj* haphazard; disorderly.

rough breathing ▻ *noun* in ancient Greek: the symbol (ʽ) denoting the sound *h* when inserted at the beginning of a word before a vowel or RHO.

roughcast /ˈrʌfkɑːst/ ▻ *noun* **1** a mixture of plaster and small stones used to cover the outside walls of buildings. **2** a rough or preliminary model, etc. ▻ *verb* (***roughcast***, ***roughcasting***) **1** to cover (a wall) with roughcast. **2** to prepare a rough or preliminary model, etc of something. ▻ *adj* said of a wall: covered or coated with roughcast.

rough diamond ▻ *noun* **1** an uncut and unpolished diamond. **2** *colloq* a good-natured person with rough unrefined manners.

rough-dry ▻ *adj* said of clothes: dried ready for ironing or pressing. ▻ *verb* (***rough-dried***, ***rough-drying***) to dry (clothes, etc) without ironing them.

roughen /ˈrʌfən/ ▻ *verb* (***roughened***, ***roughening***) *tr & intr* to make something rough or to become rough.

rough-hew ▻ *verb* to shape something crudely and without refining. • **rough-hewn** *adj* crude, unpolished, unrefined.

roughhouse /ˈrʌfhaʊs/ ▻ *noun, colloq* a disturbance or brawl. ▻ *verb* (***roughhoused***, ***roughhousing***) **1** *intr* to create a disturbance; to brawl. **2** to maltreat someone.

roughneck /ˈrʌfnɛk/ ▻ *noun, colloq* **1** a worker on an oil rig, especially an unskilled labourer. **2** a rough and rowdy person.

rough passage ▻ *noun* **1** a stormy sea voyage. **2** *colloq* a difficult trying time.

roughrider /ˈrʌfraɪdə(r)/ ▻ *noun* a rider of untrained horses; a horse-breaker.

roughshod /ˈrʌfʃɒd/ ▻ *adj* said of a horse: with horseshoes that have projecting nails which prevent the horse from slipping in wet weather. • **ride roughshod over someone** to treat them arrogantly and without regard for their feelings.

rough-stuff ▻ *noun* **1** coarse paint applied after priming and before finishing. **2** *colloq* violent behaviour.

rough trade ▻ *noun, slang* in homosexual use: **1** a casual sexual partner or partners. **2** a violent or sadistic male prostitute.

roulade /ruˈlɑːd/ ▻ *noun* **1** *music* **a** melodic embellishment; **b** a run, turn, etc sung to one syllable. **2** *cookery* something, usually meat, cooked in the shape of a roll, often with a filling. ◷ 18c: French, from *rouler* to roll.

roulette /ruˈlɛt/ ▻ *noun* **1** a gambling game in which a ball is dropped into a revolving wheel, the players betting on which of its many small, numbered compartments the ball will come to rest in. **2** a small tool with a toothed wheel, used for making a line of dots in etching or engraving, and perforating paper eg in making postage stamps. **3** *geom* a curve formed by a point on one curve when rolling along another curve. ◷ 18c: French, from *roue* a wheel.

Roumanian see ROMANIAN

round /raʊnd/ ▻ *adj* **1** shaped like, or approximately like, a circle or a ball. **2** not angular; with a curved outline. **3** said of a body or part of a body: curved and plump ▫ *a round face.* **4** moving in or forming a circle. **5** said of numbers: complete and exact ▫ *a round dozen.* **6** said of a number: without a fraction. **7** said of a number: approximate; without taking minor amounts into account. **8** said of a sum of money: considerable; substantial. **9** said of a character in a story or novel: fully and realistically developed. **10** plain-spoken; candid. **11** said of a vowel: pronounced with the lips forming a circle. **12** said of a sound: smooth; sonorous. **13** said of a pace: brisk; vigorous. ▻ *adverb* **1** in a circular direction or with a circular or revolving movement. **2** in or to the opposite direction, position or opinion ▫ *win someone round.* **3** in, by or along a circuitous or indirect route. **4** on all sides so as to surround ▫ *gather round.* **5** from one person to another successively ▫ *pass it round.* **6** in rotation, so as to return to the starting point ▫ *wait until spring comes round.* **7** from place to place ▫ *drive round for a while.* **8** in circumference ▫ *measures six feet round.* **9** to a particular place, especially someone's home ▫ *come round for supper.* ▻ *prep* **1** on all sides of so as to surround or enclose. **2** so as to move or revolve around a centre or axis and return to the starting point ▫ *run round the field.* **3** *colloq* having as a central point or basis ▫ *a story built round her experiences.* **4** from place to place in ▫ *We went round the town shopping.* **5** in all or various directions from somewhere; close to it. **6** so as to pass, or having passed, in a curved course ▫ *drive round the corner.* ▻ *noun* **1** something round, and often flat, in shape. **2 a** movement in a circle; **b** a complete revolution round a circuit or path. **3** a single slice of bread. **4** a sandwich, or two or more sandwiches, made from two slices of bread. **5** a cut of beef across the thigh-bone of an animal. **6** *golf* the playing of all 18 holes on a course in a single session. **7** one of a recurring series of events, actions, etc; a session ▫ *a round of talks.* **8** a series of regular activities; a daily routine ▫ *the daily round.* **9** a regular route followed, especially for the sale or delivery of goods ▫ *a milk round.* **10** (*usually* **rounds**) a sequence of visits, usually a regular one, made by a doctor to patients, either in a hospital or their homes. **11** a stage in a competition ▫ *through to the second round.* **12** a single turn by every member of a group of people playing a game, eg in a card game. **13** a single period of play, competition, etc in a group of such periods, eg in boxing, wrestling, etc. **14** a burst of applause or cheering. **15** a single bullet or charge of ammunition. **16** a number of drinks bought at the same time for all the members of a group. **17** *music* an unaccompanied song in which different people all sing the same part continuously but start, and therefore end, at different times. **18** a sequence in which each bell in a set or peal is rung once. ▻ *verb* (***rounded***, ***rounding***) **1 a** to make something round; **b** *intr* to become round. **2** to go round something ▫ *The car rounded the corner.* **3** to pronounce (a sound) with rounded lips. • **rounded** *adj* **1** curved; not angular. **2** complete; fully developed. **3** said of a sound or vowel: pronounced with the lips rounded. **4** *cookery* said of measurements (usually of spoons in Britain and cups in N America): filled so as to be slightly more than level with the rim. • **rounder** *noun* **1** someone or something that rounds. **2** in the game of ROUNDERS: a complete circuit. •

roundish *adj*. • **roundly** *adverb* **1 a** in a round way; **b** so as to be round. **2** frankly; bluntly. • **roundness** *noun*. • **go** or **make the rounds** said of news, information, etc: **1** to be passed round from person to person; to circulate. **2** to patrol. • **in the round 1** with all details shown or considered. **2** *theat* with the audience seated on at least three, and often four, sides of the stage. • **round about 1** on all sides; in a ring surrounding. **2** the other way about. **3** approximately □ *round about four o'clock*. • **round the clock** see ROUND-THE-CLOCK. ◷ 13c: from French *ront*, from Latin *rotundus*, from *rota* a wheel.

■ **round something down** to lower (a number) to the nearest convenient figure so that it can be expressed as a round number □ *round 15.47 down to 15.*

■ **round something off 1** to make its corners, angles, etc smooth. **2** to complete it successfully and pleasantly □ *round off the meal with a glass of brandy.*

■ **round on someone 1** to turn on or attack them. **2** to reply angrily to them, or attack them verbally.

■ **round something up 1** to raise (a number) to the nearest convenient figure so that it can be expressed as a round number □ *round 15.89 up to 16.* **2** to collect (wanted people, or things such as livestock or facts) together. See also ROUND-UP.

roundabout /ˈraʊndəbaʊt/ ▻ *noun* **1** *Brit* a circular road junction, usually with an island in the middle, where several roads meet, and around which traffic must travel in the same direction, giving way to vehicles coming from the right. **2** *Brit* a MERRY-GO-ROUND. ▻ *adj* not direct; circuitous □ *a roundabout way of explaining something.*

round-arm or **roundarm** ▻ *adj* **1** *cricket* **a** said of a bowling action: performed with a nearly horizontal outward swing of the arm; **b** said of a bowler: using such a bowling action. **2** said of a punch or blow, etc: given with an outward swing of the arm. ▻ *adverb* with a round-arm action. ◷ 19c.

round dance ▻ *noun* **1** a dance in which the dancers form a ring. **2** a dance, such as the waltz, in which the couples revolve about each other.

roundel /ˈraʊndəl/ ▻ *noun* **1** a small circular window or design. **2** a coloured, round identification disc on the wing of a military aircraft. ◷ 13c: from French *rondel* a little circle.

roundelay /ˈraʊndəleɪ/ ▻ *noun, music* **a** a simple song with a refrain; **b** a piece of music for such a song. ◷ 16c: from French *rondelet*, from *rondel* a little circle.

rounders ▻ *noun* a team game similar to baseball, in which each team sends players in to bat in turn while the other team bowls and fields. The batter scores a run if they successfully run round a square course in one go.

roundhand ▻ *noun* a style of hand-writing in which the letters are well rounded and free.

Roundhead ▻ *noun, historical* in the English Civil War (1642–9): a supporter of the parliamentary party against Charles I. ◷ 17c: so called because of their custom of wearing closely-cut hair.

roundhouse ▻ *noun* **1** *N Amer* an engine-house with a turntable. **2** *originally US, boxing slang* a wild swinging punch or style of punching. **3** *naut* a cabin on the after part of the quarterdeck, especially of a sailing ship. **4** *archaeol* a circular structure, eg a domestic buiding, especially one dating from the Bronze Age or Iron Age.

round robin ▻ *noun* **1 a** a petition or protest, especially one in which the names are written in a circle to conceal the ringleader; **b** any letter, petition, etc that is signed by many people. **2** *sport* a tournament in which every competitor plays each of the others in turn.

round-shouldered ▻ *adj* said of a person: with stooping shoulders and a back which bends forward slightly at the top.

round table ▻ *noun* **1** (**Round Table**) *historical* the table at which King Arthur and his knights sat. It was round in shape so that no individual knight should have precedence. **2 a** a meeting or conference at which the participants meet on equal terms; **b** *as adj* meeting on equal terms □ *round-table talks.*

round-the-clock ▻ *adj* lasting through the day and night □ *round-the-clock surveillance.* ▻ *adverb* (**round the clock**) all day and all night; for twenty-four hours.

round trip ▻ *noun* a trip to a place and back again, usually returning by a different route.

round-up ▻ *noun* **1** a gathering together of animals, especially all the cattle on a ranch. **2** a gathering together of people wanted by the police. **3** a summary or résumé of facts □ *a round-up of the news.* See also ROUND UP at ROUND.

round window ▻ *noun, anatomy* in vertebrates: the lower of the two membrane-covered openings between the middle ear and the inner ear. *Technical equivalent* **fenestra rotunda**.

roundworm ▻ *noun, zool* an invertebrate animal with a long slender unsegmented body. It is mostly parasitic within the bodies of humans and animals and can cause intestinal disorders.

roup /raʊp/ *Scots & N Eng dialect* ▻ *noun* a sale by auction. ▻ *verb* (***rouped, rouping***) to sell something by auction. ◷ 16c: Scandinavian, originally meaning 'to shout'.

rouse /raʊz/ ▻ *verb* (***roused, rousing***) **1** to arouse or awaken oneself or someone else from sleep, listlessness or lethargy. **2** *intr* to awaken or become more fully conscious or alert. **3** to excite or provoke □ *the injustice of it roused her anger.* **4** *intr* to become excited, provoked, etc. **5** to bring (game) out from cover or a lair. • **rouser** *noun*. • **rousing** *adj* stirring; exciting. • **rousingly** *adverb*. ◷ 15c, in the sense (said of a hawk) 'to ruffle or shake the feathers'.

rouseabout /ˈraʊszəbaʊt/ ▻ *noun, Austral, NZ* an odd-job man on a sheep station.

roustabout /ˈraʊstəbaʊt/ ▻ *noun* **1** an unskilled labourer, eg on an oil-rig or a farm. **2** *Austral, NZ* a variant of ROUSEABOUT.

rout[1] /raʊt/ ▻ *verb* (***routed, routing***) **1** to defeat (an army, troops, a sporting team, etc) completely. **2** to make (an army, troops, etc) retreat in disorderly confusion. ▻ *noun* **1** a complete and overwhelming defeat. **2** a confused and disorderly retreat. **3** *law* a group of three or more people gathered together to commit a crime or some unlawful act. **4** a disorderly and noisy group of people. ◷ 13c: from French *route*, from Latin *rupta* a detachment.

rout[2] /raʊt/ ▻ *verb* (***routed, routing***) **1** *tr & intr* to dig something up, especially (said of animals) with the snout. **2** (*usually* **rout someone out** or **up**) to find or fetch them by searching. ◷ 16c variant of ROOT[2].

route /ruːt; *Brit military & US general* raʊt/ ▻ *noun* **1** the way travelled on a regular journey. **2** a particular group of roads followed to get to a place. **3** *N Amer* a regular series of calls, eg for the collection or sale of goods; a round. ▻ *verb* (***routed, routeing*** or ***routing***) **1** to arrange a route for (a journey, etc). **2** to send someone or something by a particular route. ◷ 13c: from French *rute*, from Latin *rupta via* broken road, from *rumpere* to break.

route man or **routeman** ▻ *noun, N Amer* a shop-keeper's roundsman.

route march ▻ *noun* a long and tiring march, especially one for soldiers in training.

route-step ▻ *noun* a type of march in which soldiers are not required to keep step.

routine /ruːˈtiːn/ ▻ *noun* **1** a regular or unvarying series of actions or way of doing things □ *a daily routine.* **2** regular or unvarying procedure. **3** a set series of movements or steps in a dance, or in a skating performance, etc. **4** a comedian's or singer's act. **5** *computing* a program or part of one which performs a specific function. ▷ *adj* **1** unvarying. **2** standard; ordinary □ ***a routine examination***. **3** done as part of a routine. ● **routinely** *adverb*. ⓒ 17c: French, from *route* route, a regular or customary way.

routinize or **routinise** ▷ *verb* (***routinized, routinizing***) **1** to make something into a routine. **2** to subject something to routine or a routine. ● **routinization** *noun*.

roux /ruː/ ▷ *noun* (*plural* **roux** /ruː, ruːz/) *cookery* a cooked mixture of flour and fat, usually butter, used to thicken sauces. ⓒ 19c: French, from *beurre roux*, literally 'brown butter'.

rove[1] /roʊv/ ▷ *verb* (***roved, roving***) **1** *intr* to roam about aimlessly. **2** to wander over or through (a particular area, place, etc). **3** *intr* said of the eyes: to keep looking in different directions; to wander. ▷ *noun* the act of roving. ⓒ 16c: perhaps ultimately from Scandinavian.

rove[2] /roʊv/ ▷ *verb* (***roved, roving***) to twist (fibres of cotton or wool) slightly in preparation for spinning. ▷ *noun* a roved strand of fibre. ⓒ 18c.

rove[3] /roʊv/ ▷ *noun* a metal plate or ring through which a rivet is put and clinched. ⓒ 15c.

rove[4] *past tense, past participle of* REEVE

rover ▷ *noun* **1** someone who roves; a wanderer. **2** *archery* a random or distant mark selected as a target. **3** (*also* **Rover, rover scout** or **Rover Scout**) *formerly* a member of a senior branch of the (Boy) Scout organization. **4** in Australian Rules football: a player with no fixed position who forms part of the ruck. **5** *N Amer football*: a defensive linebacker. **6** in croquet: a ball or player ready to peg out. **7** a remote-controlled surface vehicle used in extra-terrestrial exploration.

roving /ˈroʊvɪŋ/ ▷ *adj* **1** wandering; likely to ramble or stray. **2** not confined to one particular place □ ***roving commission***. ● **rovingly** *adverb*. ● **have a roving eye** to have a tendency to show passing sexual interest in one person after another.

row[1] /roʊ/ ▷ *noun* **1** a number of people or things arranged in a line. **2** in a cinema or theatre: a line of seats. **3** a line of plants in a garden □ ***a row of cabbages***. **4** often in street-names: a street with a continuous line of houses on one or both sides. **5** *math* a horizontal arrangement of numbers, terms, etc. **6** in knitting: a complete line of stitches. ● **a hard row to hoe** a difficult job or destiny. ● **in a row 1** forming a row. **2** *colloq* in an unbroken sequence; in succession □ ***three telephone calls in a row***. ⓒ Anglo-Saxon *raw*.

row[2] /roʊ/ ▷ *verb* (***rowed, rowing***) **1** to move (a boat) through the water using oars. **2** to carry (people, goods, etc) in a rowing boat. **3** *intr* to race in rowing boats for sport. **4** *intr* to compete in a rowing race. ▷ *noun* **1** the action or an act of rowing a boat. **2 a** a period of rowing; **b** a distance of rowing. **3** a trip in a rowing boat. ● **rower** *noun*. See also OARSMAN. ● **rowing** *noun*. ⓒ Anglo-Saxon *rowan*.

■ **row over** to win a rowing race (usually a heat) by rowing the course unopposed.

row[3] /raʊ/ ▷ *noun* **1** a noisy quarrel. **2** a loud unpleasant noise or disturbance. **3** a severe reprimand. ▷ *verb* (***rowed, rowing***) *intr* to quarrel noisily. ⓒ 18c.

rowan /ˈroʊən, ˈraʊən/ ▷ *noun* **1** (*also* **rowan-tree**) a tree of the rose family, with small pinnate leaves. Also called **mountain ash**. **2** (*also* **rowan-berry**) the small red or pink berry-like fruit of this tree. ⓒ 15c: Scandinavian, related to Norse *reynir*, Norwegian *rogn, raun*.

rowboat ▷ *noun, N Amer* a ROWING BOAT.

rowdy /ˈraʊdɪ/ ▷ *adj* (***rowdier, rowdiest***) **a** noisy and rough; disorderly; creating disturbance □ ***a rowdy party***; **b** with a tendency to behave in a noisy disorderly way. ▷ *noun* (***rowdies***) *colloq* a noisy, rough, disorderly person. ● **rowdily** *adverb*. ● **rowdiness** *noun*. ● **rowdyism** *noun*. ⓒ 19c.

rowel /ˈraʊəl/ ▷ *noun* **1** a small spiked wheel attached to a spur. **2** *vet medicine, historical* a circular piece of material, often leather, inserted under the skin, especially of a horse, to produce a discharge. ▷ *verb* (***rowelled, rowelling***) **1** to spur (a horse) with a *rowel* (sense 1). **2** to treat (an animal, especially a horse) with a *rowel* (sense 2). ⓒ 14c: from French *roel* a small wheel, from Latin *rotella*, from *rota* a wheel.

rowel-spur ▷ *noun* a spur with a rowel attached.

rower see under ROW[2]

row house ▷ *noun, N Amer* a terraced house.

rowing boat ▷ *noun, Brit* a small boat which is moved by oars. *N Amer equivalent* **rowboat**.

rowing machine ▷ *noun* a static exercise machine with a sliding seat and handgrips that can be pulled to simulate rowing.

rowlock /ˈrɒlək/ ▷ *noun* a device that holds an oar in place and acts as a fulcrum for it. ⓒ 18c.

royal /ˈrɔɪəl/ ▷ *adj* **1** relating to or suitable for a king or queen. **2** (*sometimes* **Royal**) under the patronage or in the service of the monarch □ ***Royal Geographical Society***. **3** belonging to the monarch. **4** related to the monarch. **5** regal; magnificent. **6** larger or of better quality, etc than usual. **7** *naut* situated immediately above the top-gallant. ▷ *noun* **1** (*sometimes* **Royal**) *colloq* a member of a royal family. **2** any of various gold coins. **3** *naut* a sail immediately above the top-gallant sail on a royal mast. **4** (*also* **royal stag**) a stag with antlers of 12 or more points. **5** a size of paper, either 19 × 24in (483 × 610mm) of writing paper, or 20 × 25in (508 × 635mm) of printing paper. ● **royally** *adverb*. ● **the Royal We** or **the royal we 1** a monarch's use of 'we' instead of 'I' when speaking of himself or herself. **2** *jocular* the use by any individual of 'we' instead of 'I'. ⓒ 14c: from French *roial*, from Latin *regalis* regal, suitable for a king, from *rex* king.

royal assent ▷ *noun* in the UK: formal permission given by the sovereign for a parliamentary act to become law.

royal blue ▷ *noun* a rich bright deep-coloured blue.

Royal British Legion ▷ *noun* an association for former members of the armed forces, founded in 1921.

royal burgh ▷ *noun* in Scotland: a burgh established by a royal charter.

Royal Commission or **royal commission** ▷ *noun* in the UK: a group of people appointed by the crown, at the request of the government, to inquire into and report on some matter.

royal fern ▷ *noun* the most striking of British ferns, with very large fronds.

royal flush ▷ *noun*, in poker, etc: an unbeatable STRAIGHT FLUSH made up of the ten, jack, queen, king and ace.

royal icing ▷ *noun, cookery* a type of hard icing made with white of egg, used especially on rich fruit cakes.

royalist or **Royalist** /ˈrɔɪəlɪst/ (*also* **Royalist**) ▷ *noun* **1** a supporter of monarchy or of a specified monarchy. **2** *historical* during the English Civil War (1642–9): a supporter of Charles I. ▷ *adj* relating to royalists. ● **royalism** *noun*. ⓒ 17c.

royal jelly ▷ *noun* a rich protein substance secreted by worker bees and fed to all very young larvae and, throughout their development, to certain female larvae destined to become queen bees.

royal mast ▷ *noun, naut* the fourth and highest part of a mast, usually made in one piece with the top-gallant mast.

royal palm ▷ *noun* any of several palm trees found in tropical America.

royal prerogative ▻ *noun* the right of a monarch, in theory not restricted in any way but in practice established by custom.

royal standard ▻ *noun* a banner that bears the British royal arms, flown wherever the monarch is present.

royal tennis see REAL TENNIS

royalty /'rɔɪəltɪ/ ▻ *noun* (***royalties***) **1** the character, state, office or power of a king or queen. **2** members of royal families, either individually or collectively. **3** royal authority. **4** a percentage of the profits from each copy of a book, piece of music, invention, etc that is sold, publicly performed or used, which is paid to the author, composer, inventor, etc. **5** a payment made by companies who mine minerals, oil or gas to the person who owns the land the company is mining or the mineral rights to it. **6** a right, especially to minerals, granted by a king or queen to an individual or company. ◷ 14c.

royal warrant ▻ *noun* an official authorization to a tradesman to supply goods to a royal household.

rozzer /'rɒzə(r)/ ▻ *noun, Brit slang* a policeman. ◷ 19c.

RP ▻ *abbreviation* **1** Received Pronunciation. **2** Reformed Presbyterian. **3** Regius Professor. **4** *IVR* Republic of the Philippines. **5** Royal Society of Portrait Painters.

RPB ▻ *abbreviation* recognized professional body.

RPG ▻ *abbreviation, computing* report program generator, a programming language used in business.

RPI ▻ *abbreviation* retail price index.

RPM ▻ *abbreviation* retail price maintenance.

rpm ▻ *abbreviation* revolutions per minute.

RPO ▻ *abbreviation* Royal Philharmonic Orchestra.

RPS ▻ *abbreviation* Royal Photographic Society.

rps ▻ *abbreviation* revolutions per second.

RPV ▻ *abbreviation* remotely piloted vehicle.

RR ▻ *abbreviation* Right Reverend.

-rrhagia /reɪdʒɪə/ ▻ *combining form, pathol, denoting* abnormal or excessive discharge. ◷ Latin, from Greek *rhegnunai* to break or burst.

-rrhoea or (*especially US*) **-rrhea** /riːə/ ▻ *combining form, pathol, denoting* abnormal or excessive flow. ◷ Latin, from Greek *rhoia* a flow.

RRP ▻ *abbreviation* recommended retail price.

RS ▻ *abbreviation* Royal Society.

Rs ▻ *symbol* rupees.

RSA ▻ *abbreviation* **1** Republic of South Africa. **2** *NZ* Returned Services Association. **3 a** Royal Scottish Academy; **b** Royal Scottish Academician. **4** Royal Society of Arts.

RSC ▻ *abbreviation* **1** Royal Shakespeare Company. **2** Royal Society of Chemistry.

RSFSR ▻ *abbreviation, formerly* Russian Socialist Federative Socialist Republic, the largest administrative district of the Soviet Union.

RSI ▻ *abbreviation, medicine* repetitive strain injury.

RSL ▻ *abbreviation* **1** *Austral* Returned Services League. **2** Royal Society of Literature.

RSM ▻ *abbreviation* **1** regimental sergeant major. **2** *IVR* Republic of San Marino. **3** Royal School of Music. **4** Royal Society of Medicine.

RSNC ▻ *abbreviation* Royal Society for Nature Conservation.

RSNO ▻ *abbreviation* Royal Scottish National Orchestra (*formerly* SNO).

RSNZ ▻ *abbreviation* Royal Society of New Zealand.

RSPB ▻ *abbreviation* Royal Society for the Protection of Birds.

RSPCA ▻ *abbreviation* Royal Society for the Prevention of Cruelty to Animals.

RSSA ▻ *abbreviation* Royal Scottish Society of Arts.

RSSPCC ▻ *abbreviation* Royal Scottish Society for the Prevention of Cruelty to Children.

RSV ▻ *abbreviation* Revised Standard Version (of the Bible).

RSVP ▻ *abbreviation* often written on invitations: *répondez s'il vous plaît* (French), please reply.

RTE ▻ *abbreviation*: *Radio Telefís Éireann* (Irish Gaelic), Irish Radio and Television.

Rt Hon ▻ *abbreviation* Right Honourable.

Rt Rev ▻ *abbreviation* Right Reverend.

RU ▻ *abbreviation* **1** *IVR* Republic of Burundi. **2** Rugby Union.

Ru ▻ *symbol, chem* ruthenium.

rub ▻ *verb* (***rubbed, rubbing***) **1** to apply pressure and friction to something by moving one's hand or an object backwards and forwards over its surface. **2** *intr* (*usually* **rub against, on** or **along something**) to move backwards and forwards against, on or along it with pressure and friction. **3** (*usually* **rub something on** or **into something else**) to apply (ointment, polish, etc) to a surface with pressure so that it is evenly spread, absorbed, etc. **4** to clean something or polish, dry, smooth it, etc by applying pressure and friction. **5** *tr & intr* (*often* **rub something away, off, out,** *etc*) to remove it or be removed by pressure and friction. **6** *tr & intr* to be sore or make something sore by pressure and friction; to chafe. **7** *tr & intr* to fray by pressure and friction. **8** *intr, bowls* said of a bowl: to be slowed down or deflected by unevenness in the green, an obstacle, etc. ▻ *noun* **1** the process or an act of rubbing. **2** an obstacle or difficulty □ *It will cost a lot and there's the rub.* **3** *bowls* something that slows down or deflects a bowl. ● **rubber** see separate entries. ● **rubbing** *noun* **1** application of friction. **2** an impression or copy made by placing paper over a raised surface and rubbing the paper with crayon, wax, chalk, etc □ *a brass rubbing.* See also FROTTAGE (sense 1). ● **rub shoulders** to come into social contact. ● **rub someone's nose in it** to persist in reminding someone of a fault or mistake they have made. ● **rub someone up the wrong way** to annoy or irritate them, especially by dealing with them carelessly or tactlessly. ◷ 14c.

■ **rub along** *colloq* to manage to cope, make progress, etc without any particular difficulties.

■ **rub along with someone** *colloq* to be on more or less friendly terms with them.

■ **rub something down 1** to rub (one's body, a horse, etc) briskly from head to foot, eg to dry it. **2** to prepare (a surface) to receive new paint or varnish by rubbing the old paint or varnish off. **3** to become or make something smooth by rubbing.

■ **rub something in 1** to apply (ointment, etc) by rubbing. **2** *cookery* to mix (fat) into flour by rubbing one's fingertips together in the mixture. **3** *colloq* to insist on talking about or emphasizing (an embarrassing fact or circumstance).

■ **rub off on someone** to have an effect on or be passed to someone by close association □ *Some of his bad habits have rubbed off on you.*

■ **rub someone out** *N Amer slang* to murder them.

■ **rub something out** to remove it by rubbing, especially with an eraser.

■ **rub someone up** *slang* to rub against someone in an attempt to excite them or oneself sexually.

■ **rub something up 1** to polish it. **2** to refresh one's memory or knowledge of it.

rubaiyat /'ruːbaɪjat/ ▻ *noun* a Persian verse form consisting of four-line stanzas. ⓘ 19c: Arabic plural of *rubaiyah* a quatrain.

rubato /rʊ'bɑːtoʊ/ *music* ▻ *noun* (***rubatos*** or ***rubati*** /rʊ'bɑːtiː/) a modified or distorted tempo in which certain notes of a phrase, etc may be shortened (by a slight quickening of tempo) and others lengthened but the overall length of the phrase remains the same. ▻ *adverb, adj* with such freedom of tempo. ⓘ 18c: Italian, literally 'robbed', from *rubare* to steal.

rubber¹ /'rʌbə(r)/ ▻ *noun* **1** any of various natural or synthetic polymers characterized by their elasticity, strength and resilience, obtained from the latex of certain plants, especially the rubber tree, or manufactured artificially from petroleum and coal products. **2** *Brit* a small piece of rubber or plastic used for rubbing out pencil or ink marks on paper; an eraser. **3** *slang* a condom. **4** a cabinetmaker's cloth or pad used for polishing. **5** (**rubbers**) **a** *originally US* waterproof rubber overshoes; galoshes; **b** plimsolls. **6** any person, device or machine part that rubs. ⓘ 16c: from RUB.

rubber² /'rʌbə(r)/ ▻ *noun* **1** *bridge, whist, etc* **a** a match to play for the best of three or sometimes five games; **b** the winning of such a match. **2** *loosely* a session of card-playing. **3** a series of games in any of various sports, such as cricket, tennis, etc. ⓘ 16c.

rubber band ▻ *noun* an ELASTIC BAND.

rubber cement ▻ *noun* a type of adhesive made of rubber disolved in a solvent.

rubber cheque ▻ *noun, slang* a cheque that bounces.

rubber goods ▻ *plural noun, euphemistic* condoms.

rubberize or **rubberise** ▻ *verb* (***rubberized, rubberizing***) to coat or impregnate (a substance, especially a textile) with rubber.

rubberneck ▻ *noun, originally US slang* **1** someone who stares or gapes inquisitively or stupidly. **2** a tourist on a guided tour. ▻ *verb* (***rubbernecked, rubbernecking***) **1** *intr* to gape inquisitively or stupidly. **2** *intr* to go on a guided tour; to sightsee. **3** to stare at something. ⓘ 19c.

rubber plant ▻ *noun* **1** a plant with large glossy dark green leaves, native to S Asia, where it is cultivated as a source of rubber, and widely grown elsewhere as an ornamental pot plant. **2** a RUBBER TREE.

rubber stamp ▻ *noun* **1** a device made of rubber with figures, letters, names, etc marked on it, used to stamp a name, date, etc on books or papers. **2** an automatic, unthinking or routine agreement or authorization. **3** a person or group of people required to approve or authorize the decisions or actions of others, but who do not have the power, courage, etc to withold this approval or authorization. ▻ *verb* (**rubber-stamp**) **1** to mark something with a rubber stamp. **2** *colloq* to approve or authorize something automatically, unthinkingly or routinely.

rubber tree ▻ *noun* any of various trees which produce a milky white liquid that is used to make rubber, especially a large tree native to S America, and extensively cultivated in plantations in SE Asia, especially Malaya.

rubbery ▻ *adj* **1** like rubber. **2** flexible. • **rubberiness** *noun.*

rubbing see under RUB

rubbish /'rʌbɪʃ/ ▻ *noun* **1** waste material; refuse; litter. *Also as adj* □ ***rubbish bin.*** **2** worthless or useless material or objects. **3** *colloq* worthless or absurd talk, writing, etc; nonsense. ▻ *verb* (***rubbished, rubbishing***) *colloq* to criticize or dismiss something as worthless. • **rubbishy** *adj* worthless; trashy. ⓘ 14c as *noun;* 1950s as *verb.*

rubble /'rʌbəl/ ▻ *noun* **1** pieces of broken stones, bricks, plaster, etc, usually from ruined or demolished buildings. **2** small rough stones used in building, especially as a filling between walls. **3 a** (*also* **rubble-work**) coarse masonry made from such stones; **b** *as adj* □ ***rubble-stone.*** ⓘ 14c.

rub-down ▻ *noun* an act of rubbing something down, especially to clean or prepare a surface.

rube /ruːb/ ▻ *noun, N Amer slang* a country bumpkin; an uncouth or unsophisticated person. ⓘ 19c: from the personal name *Reuben.*

rubefacient /ruːbɪ'feɪʃənt/ *medicine* ▻ *adj* causing redness or mild inflammation. ▻ *noun* an external application that reddens the skin. ⓘ 19c.

rubefaction /ruːbɪ'fakʃən/ ▻ *noun* reddening or redness of the skin, especially one that is caused artificially. ⓘ 17c: from Latin *rubefacere, rubefactum* from *rubeus.*

rubella /rʊ'bɛlə/ ▻ *noun, medicine* a viral disease that is highly contagious, especially in childhood, characterized by a reddish-pink rash and swelling of the lymph glands. It is similar to measles but milder except for the possible harmful effects on the foetus of an expectant mother infected early in pregnancy. Also called **German measles.** ⓘ 19c: from Latin *rubellus* reddish, from *rubeus* red.

rubellite /'ruːbɪlaɪt/ ▻ *noun* a red variety of the mineral tourmaline, used as a gemstone. ⓘ 18c: from Latin *rubellus* reddish + -ITE.

rubeola /rʊ'bɪələ/ ▻ *noun, medicine* measles. ⓘ 19c in this sense; 17c in sense 'a rash of red spots or pimples': from Latin *rubeus* red.

Rubicon or **rubicon** /'ruːbɪkɒn/ ▻ *noun* **1** a boundary which, once crossed, commits someone crossing it to an irrevocable course of action. **2** *cards* in piquet: the winning of a game before one's opponent scores 100. • **cross** or **pass the Rubicon** to take a decisive and irrevocable step. ⓘ 17c: from the name of a stream in NE Italy that separated Julius Caesar's province of Cisalpine Gaul and Italy proper. By crossing the stream with his army in 49 BC Caesar effectively declared war on the Roman republic and began a civil war.

rubicund /'ruːbɪkənd/ ▻ *adj* said especially of the face or complexion: red or rosy; ruddy. ⓘ 16c: from Latin *rubicundus,* from *rubere* to be red, from *ruber* red.

rubidium /rʊ'bɪdɪəm/ ▻ *noun, chem* (symbol **Rb**, atomic number 37) a silvery-white, highly reactive metallic element, used in photoelectric cells. ⓘ 19c: from Latin *rubidus* red, so called because of the two red lines in its spectrum.

rubidium-strontium dating ▻ *noun* a method of determining the age of rocks that are more than 10 million years old by measuring the relative amounts of the naturally occurring radioactive isotope rubidium-87 and its beta decay product strontium-87.

rubies *plural of* RUBY

rubiginous /rʊ'bɪdʒɪnəs/ ▻ *adj* **1** rusty. **2** rust-coloured. ⓘ 17c: from Latin *rubiginosus,* from *rubigo* rust.

Rubik's cube /ruːbɪks —/ ▻ *noun* a cube-shaped puzzle consisting of 26 smaller cubes, the visible face of each being one of six colours, that are fixed to a central spindle, allowing them to be rotated on three axes. The object is to keep rotating the cubes until each face of the large cube is a uniform colour. ⓘ 1980s: named after the Hungarian designer Ernö Rubik (born 1940).

ruble see ROUBLE

rubric /'ruːbrɪk/ ▻ *noun* **1** a heading, especially one in a book or manuscript, originally one written or underlined in red. **2** *Christianity* a rule or direction for the conduct of divine service, added in red to the liturgy. **3** *law* the heading of a statute or section of a legal code. **4** an authoritative rule or set of rules. **5** something definitely settled. ⓘ 14c: from Latin *rubrica* red ochre.

rubricate /ˈruːbrɪkeɪt/ ▷ *verb* (***rubricated, rubricating***) **1** to write or mark something in red. **2** to put a rubric or rubrics into a text. • **rubrication** *noun* • **rubricator** *noun, historical* someone who rubricated parts of manuscripts or early printed books. • **rubrician** /ruˈbrɪʃən/ *noun* someone versed in liturgical rubrics. ◉ 16c.

ruby /ˈruːbɪ/ ▷ *noun* (***rubies***) **1** *geol* a valuable gemstone, a red impure variety of the mineral corundum, containing traces of chromium oxide which imparts its colour. It is used in lasers, and as bearings in watches and other precision intruments. **2** the rich deep-red colour characteristic of this stone. Also *as adj.* ◉ 14c: from Latin *rubinus lapis* red stone, from *ruber* red.

ruby wedding ▷ *noun* a fortieth wedding anniversary.

RUC ▷ *abbreviation* Royal Ulster Constabulary.

ruche /ruːʃ/ ▷ *noun* (***ruches*** /ˈruːʃɪz/) a pleated or gathered frill of lace, ribbon, etc, used as a trimming. ▷ *verb* (***ruched, ruching***) to trim (an item of clothing, etc) with a ruche or ruches. • **ruched** /ruːʃt/ *adj* trimmed with or gathered into a ruche or ruches. • **ruching** *noun.* ◉ 19c: French, literally 'beehive'.

ruck¹ ▷ *noun* **1** a heap or mass of indistinguishable people or things. **2** *rugby* a loose scrum that forms around a ball on the ground. **3** in Australian rules football: the three players who do not have fixed positions but follow the ball about the field. ▷ *verb* (***rucked, rucking***) **1** (*also* **ruck something up**) to heap or pile up (hay, etc). **2** *intr, rugby* to form a ruck. **3** *intr* in Australian rules football: to play as a member of the ruck. ◉ 13c.

ruck² ▷ *noun* a wrinkle or crease. ▷ *verb* (***rucked, rucking***) *tr & intr* (*also* **ruck up** or **ruck something up**) to wrinkle or crease. ◉ 18c: related to Norse *hrukka.*

rucksack /ˈrʌksak/ ▷ *noun* a bag carried on the back with straps over the shoulders, used especially by climbers and walkers. Also called BACKPACK. ◉ 19c: from German *Rucken* (a dialect variant of *Rücken* back) + *Sack* sack or bag.

ruckus /ˈrʌkəs/ ▷ *noun, originally chiefly N Amer* a disturbance; a commotion. ◉ 19c.

ruction /ˈrʌkʃən/ ▷ *noun, colloq* **1** a noisy disturbance; uproar. **2** (**ructions**) a noisy and usually unpleasant or violent argument or reaction. ◉ 19c.

rudaceous /ruˈdaɪʃəs/ *adj* said of rocks: composed mainly of fairly large fragments. Compare ARENACEOUS 1, ARGILLACEOUS.

rudbeckia /rʌdˈbɛkɪə, rʊd-/ ▷ *noun* any of various N American composite plants of the daisy family. ◉ 18c: named after Swedish botanist Olaf Rudbeck (1660–1740).

rudd ▷ *noun* a freshwater fish, widespread in European rivers and lakes, greenish-brown in colour on the back, with yellow sides and reddish fins. Also called **red-eye**. ◉ 17c.

rudder /ˈrʌdə(r)/ ▷ *noun* **1** *naut* a flat piece of wood, metal, etc fixed vertically to a ship's stern for steering. **2** *aeronautics* a movable aerofoil attached to the fin of an aircraft which helps control its movement along a horizontal plane. **3** anything that steers or guides. • **rudderless** *adj* **1** without a rudder. **2** aimless. ◉ Anglo-Saxon *rothor.*

ruddle /ˈrʌdəl/ or **raddle** /ˈra-/ or **reddle** /ˈrɛ-/ ▷ *noun* red ochre, used especially to mark sheep. ▷ *verb* (***ruddled, ruddling***) to mark (sheep) with ruddle. ◉ 16c: from Anglo-Saxon *rudu* redness.

ruddy /ˈrʌdɪ/ ▷ *adj* (***ruddier, ruddiest***) **1** said of the face, complexion, etc: glowing; with a healthy rosy or pink colour. **2** red; reddish. **3** *chiefly Brit colloq swear-word* bloody □ *ruddy fool.* Also *as adverb* □ *ruddy awful.* • **ruddily** *adverb.* • **ruddiness** *noun.* ◉ Anglo-Saxon *rudig.*

rude /ruːd/ ▷ *adj* **1** impolite; bad-mannered; discourteous. **2** roughly made; lacking refinement or polish □ *build a rude shelter.* **3** ignorant, uneducated or primitive. **4** sudden and unpleasant □ *a rude awakening.* **5** vigorous; robust □ *rude health.* **6** vulgar; indecent □ *a rude joke.* • **rudely** *adj.* • **rudeness** *noun* **1** being rude. **2** rude language or behaviour. • **rudery** *noun.* ◉ 14c: from French, from Latin *rudis* unwrought, rough.

ruderal /ˈruːdərəl/ ▷ *noun, bot* a plant that grows in waste places or among rubbish. Also *as adj.* ◉ 19c: from Latin *rudus, ruderis* rubble.

rudiment /ˈruːdɪmənt/ ▷ *noun* **1** (*usually* **rudiments**) the fundamental facts, rules or skills of a subject □ *the rudiments of cooking.* **2** (*usually* **rudiments**) the early and incomplete stages of something. **3** *biol* an organ or part which does not develop fully, usually because it has no function, such as the mammary glands in male mammals. • **rudimental** *adj* see RUDIMENTARY. ◉ 16c: from Latin *rudimentum,* from *rudis* unformed.

rudimentary /ruːdɪˈmɛnt(ə)rɪ/ ▷ *adj* **1** basic; fundamental. **2** crude; primitive. **3** *biol* said of an organ: **a** primitive or undeveloped; **b** only partially developed. • **rudimentarily** *adverb.* • **rudimentariness** *noun.* ◉ 19c.

rue¹ /ruː/ ▷ *verb* (***rued, ruing*** or ***rueing***) to regret; to wish that something had not been or had not happened. • **rueful** *adj* **1** feeling or showing sorrow or regret. **2** inspiring pity or sorrow. • **ruefully** *adverb.* • **ruefulness** *noun.* ◉ Anglo-Saxon *hreowan.*

rue² /ruː/ ▷ *noun* a strongly scented evergreen plant with bitter leaves which were formerly used in medicine. The plant is traditionally a symbol of repentance. ◉ 14c: from Greek *rhyte*; the symbol of repentance is in allusion to RUE¹

rufescent /ruˈfɛsənt/ ▷ *adj, bot, zool* tending to redness. ◉ 19c: from Latin *rufescere* to turn reddish, from *rufus* reddish.

ruff¹ ▷ *noun* **1** a circular pleated or frilled collar, worn in the late 16c and early 17c, or more recently by the members of some choirs. **2 a** a fringe or frill of feathers growing on a bird's neck; **b** a similar fringe of hair on an animal's neck. **3** a type of ruffed domestic pigeon. • **ruffed** /rʌft/ *adj.* ◉ 16c.

ruff² *cards* ▷ *verb* (***ruffed, ruffing***) *tr & intr* to trump. ▷ *noun* **1** an act of trumping. **2** an old card-game, similar to whist or trumps. ◉ 16c: from French *rouffle,* Italian *ronfa.*

ruff³ ▷ *noun* **a** a bird of the sandpiper family; **b** the male of this species, which grows a large ruff of feathers during the breeding season. See also REEVE. ◉ 17c.

ruff⁴ or **ruffe** /rʌf/ ▷ *noun* a small freshwater fish of the perch family, which has one dorsal fin.

ruffian /ˈrʌfɪən/ ▷ *noun* a coarse, violent, brutal or lawless person. ▷ *adj* **1** relating to a ruffian or ruffians. **2** brutal; violent. • **ruffianism** *noun.* • **ruffianly** *adj.* ◉ 16c: French, from Italian *ruffiano.*

ruffle /ˈrʌfəl/ ▷ *verb* (***ruffled, ruffling***) **1** to wrinkle or make something uneven; to spoil its smoothness. **2** *tr & intr* to make or become irritated, annoyed or discomposed. **3** said of a bird: to make (its feathers) erect, usually in anger or display. **4** to gather (lace, linen, etc) into a ruff or ruffle. **5** to flick or turn (pages of a book, etc) hastily. ▷ *noun* **1** a frill of lace, linen, etc worn either round the neck or wrists. **2** any ruffling or disturbance of the evenness and smoothness of a surface, or of the peace, someone's temper, etc. **3** the feathers round a bird's neck which are ruffled in anger or display; a ruff. • **ruffled** *adj.* • **ruffling** *noun.* ◉ 13c.

rufiyaa /ˈruːfiːjɑː/ ▷ *noun* (***rufiyaa***) the standard monetary unit of the Maldives. ◉ 20c: from Hindi *rupiya,* from Sanskrit *rupya* wrought silver.

rufous /ˈruːfəs/ ▷ *adj* said especially of a bird or animal: reddish or brownish-red in colour. ◉ 18c: from Latin *rufus* red or reddish.

rug ▷ *noun* **1** a thick heavy mat or small carpet for covering a floor. **2** a thick blanket or wrap, especially one used for travelling, or as a protective and often waterproof covering for horses. **3** *originally N Amer slang* a toupee or hairpiece. • **pull the rug (out) from under someone** to leave them without defence, support, etc, especially as a result of some sudden discovery, action or argument. ◷ 16c.

rugby /ˈrʌɡbɪ/ and **rugby football** ▷ *noun* a team game played with an oval ball which players may pick up and run with and may pass from hand to hand. Also as *adj* □ rugby club. ◷ 19c: named after Rugby, the public school in Warwickshire where the game was first played.

Rugby League ▷ *noun* **1** an association of rugby clubs formed in 1922 (previously called the Northern Union, from 1895). **2** (*usually* **rugby league**) a partly professional form of rugby, played with teams of 13 players according to Rugby League rules.

Rugby Union ▷ *noun* **1** an association of rugby clubs formed in 1871. **2** (*usually* **rugby union**) a formerly amateur now partly professional form of rugby, played with teams of 15 players according to Rugby Union rules (abbreviation **RU**).

rugged /ˈrʌɡɪd/ ▷ *adj* **1** said of landscape, hills, ground, etc: with a rough, uneven surface; steep and rocky. **2** said of someone's face: with features that are strongly marked, irregular and furrowed and that suggest physical strength. **3** said especially of someone's character: stern, austere and unbending. **4** said of manners, etc: unsophisticated; unrefined. **5** involving physical hardships □ *a rugged life.* **6** sturdy; robust □ *showed rugged individualism.* **7** said of machinery, equipment, etc: strongly or sturdily built to withstand vigorous use. • **ruggedly** *adverb*. • **ruggedness** *noun*. ◷ 14c.

rugger /ˈrʌɡə(r)/ ▷ *noun, colloq* RUGBY.

rugose /ˈruːɡoʊs, rʊˈɡoʊs/ ▷ *adj, bot, zool, anatomy* wrinkled; marked with folds or ridges. • **rugosely** *adverb*. • **rugosity** /rʊˈɡɒsɪtɪ/ *noun*. ◷ 18c: from Latin *rugosus*, from *ruga* a wrinkle or fold.

rug rat ▷ *noun, N Amer colloq* a child, especially one who has not yet learned to walk. ◷ 1960s.

ruin /ˈruːɪn/ ▷ *noun* **1** a broken, destroyed, decayed or collapsed state. **2** (*often* **ruins**) the remains of something which has been broken, destroyed or has decayed or collapsed, especially the remains of a building or group of buildings. **3** complete loss of wealth, social position, power, etc. **4** a person, company, etc that has lost all of their wealth, social position, power, etc. **5** something that brings about complete loss of wealth, social position, etc, or physical destruction, decay, etc. ▷ *verb* (***ruined***, ***ruining***) **1** to reduce or bring someone or something to ruin; to destroy them. **2** to spoil. • **ruination** /ruːɪˈneɪʃən/ *noun*. • **ruiner** *noun*. • **in ruins** said of a building, scheme, plan, etc: in a state of ruin; completely wrecked or destroyed. ◷ 14c: from French *ruine*, from Latin *ruina*, from *ruere* to tumble down.

ruing see under RUE[1]

ruinous /ˈruːɪnəs/ ▷ *adj* **1** likely to bring about ruin □ *ruinous prices.* **2** ruined; decayed; destroyed. • **ruinously** *adverb*. • **ruinousness** *noun*.

rule /ruːl/ ▷ *noun* **1** a principle, regulation, order or direction which governs or controls some action, function, form, use, etc. **2 a** government or control; **b** the period during which government or control is exercised. **3** a general principle, standard, guideline or custom □ *make it a rule always to be punctual.* **4** *Christianity* the laws and customs which form the basis of a monastic or religious order and are followed by all members of that order □ *the Benedictine rule.* **5** a RULER (sense 2). **6** *printing* a thin straight line or dash. **7** *law* an order made by a court and judge which applies to a particular case only. ▷ *verb* (***ruled***, ***ruling***) **1** *tr & intr* to govern; to exercise authority over someone. **2** to keep control of or restrain someone or something. **3** to make an authoritative and usually official or judicial decision. **4** *intr* to be common or prevalent □ *chaos ruled after the war.* **5** to draw a straight line. **6** to draw a straight line or a series of parallel lines eg on paper. • **rulable** *adj* **1** governable. **2** *US* allowable. • **ruleless** *adj*. • **as a rule** usually. • **be ruled** to take advice. • **rule the roost** to be dominant. ◷ 13c: from French, from Latin *regula* a straight stick, related to *regere* to rule, and *rex* king.

▪ **rule something off** to draw a line in order to separate it from something else.

▪ **rule something out 1** to leave it out or not consider it. **2** to make it no longer possible; to preclude it.

rule of three ▷ *noun, math* a method of finding the fourth term of a proportion when three are given.

rule of thumb ▷ *noun* a method of doing something, based on practical experience rather than theory or careful calculation. Also (**rule-of-thumb**) *as adj*.

ruler /ˈruːlə(r)/ ▷ *noun* **1** someone, eg a sovereign, who rules or governs. **2** a strip of wood, metal or plastic with straight edges that is marked off in units (usually inches or centimetres), and used for drawing straight lines and measuring.

ruling /ˈruːlɪŋ/ ▷ *noun* an official or authoritative decision. ▷ *adj* **1** governing; controlling. **2** most important or strongest; predominant.

rum[1] ▷ *noun* **1** an spirit distilled from fermented sugar-cane juice or from molasses. **2** *N Amer* alcoholic liquor in general. • **rummy** *adj*. ◷ 17c.

rum[2] ▷ *adj* (***rummer***, ***rummest***) *chiefly Brit colloq* strange; odd; bizarre. • **rumly** *adverb*. • **rumness** *noun*. ◷ 18c: perhaps from ROM.

Rumanian /rʊˈmeɪnɪən/ ▷ *noun* ▷ *adj, formerly* the preferred spelling of ROMANIAN.

rumba or **rhumba** /ˈrʌmbə, ˈrʊmbə/ ▷ *noun* (***rumbas***) **1 a** a lively Afro-Cuban dance; **b** a popular ballroom dance derived from this, with pronounced hip movements produced by transferring the weight from one foot to the other. **2** music for this dance, with a stressed second beat. ▷ *verb, intr* to dance the rumba. ◷ 1920s: American Spanish.

rum baba see BABA

rumble /ˈrʌmbəl/ ▷ *verb* (***rumbled***, ***rumbling***) **1** *intr* to make a deep low grumbling sound. **2** *intr* (*often* **rumble along** or **by** or **past**, *etc*) to move with a rumbling noise. **3** to say or utter something with a rumbling voice or sound. **4** *Brit slang* to find out the truth about or see through someone or something. **5** *intr, N Amer* to be involved in a street fight, especially one between gangs. ▷ *noun* **1** a deep low grumbling sound. **2** *N Amer slang* a street fight, especially one between gangs. **3** a part at the rear of a horse-drawn carriage used as a seat for servants or to carry luggage. Also called **dicky**. **4** (*also* **rumble seat**) *N Amer* a folding seat for extra passengers at the back of some early cars. • **rumbling** *adj* □ *a rumbling stomach.* ◷ 14c.

rumble strip and **rumble area** ▷ *noun* one of a series of rough-textured strips or areas set into a road surface to warn drivers (by the sound of their vehicle's tyres passing over them) of a hazard ahead.

rumbling ▷ *noun* **1** an act or instance of making a rumble. **2** (**rumblings**) early signs or indications □ *rumblings of discontent.*

rumbustious /rʌmˈbʌstʃəs/ ▷ *adj, Brit colloq* noisy and cheerful; boisterous. • **rumbustiously** *adverb*. • **rumbustiousness** *noun*. ◷ 18c.

rumen /ˈruːmɛn/ ▷ *noun* (***rumina*** /-mɪnə/ or ***rumens***) *zool* in a ruminant animal such as a cow or sheep: the first and largest chamber of the complex stomach, in which food is stored and partly digested before being regurgitated. ◷ 18c: Latin, meaning 'gullet'.

ruminant /ˈruːmɪnənt/ ▷ *noun* an even-toed hoofed mammal, eg a cow, sheep or goat, that chews the cud and has a complex stomach with four chambers. ▷ *adj* **1** relating or belonging to this group of mammals. **2** meditative or contemplative. • **ruminantly** *adverb*. ⓒ 17c: from Latin *ruminari* to chew the cud.

ruminate /ˈruːmɪneɪt/ ▷ *verb* (***ruminated, ruminating***) **1** *intr* said of a ruminant: to chew the cud. **2** to chew over something again. **3** *tr & intr* to think deeply about something; to contemplate. • **ruminatingly** *adj* thoughtfully. • **rumination** *noun*. • **ruminative** /-nətɪv/ *adj* meditative; contemplative. • **ruminatively** *adverb*. • **ruminator** *noun* someone who ruminates. ⓒ 16c: from Latin *ruminari*, ruminates to chew the cud.

rummage /ˈrʌmɪdʒ/ ▷ *verb* (***rummaged, rummaging***) **1** *tr & intr* (*usually* **rummage through something**) to search messily through (a collection of things, a cupboard, etc). **2** *intr* (*usually* **rummage about** or **around**) to search □ *rummage around for a pen.* ▷ *noun* **1** a search. **2** things found by rummaging, especially (*N Amer*) jumble. • **rummager** *noun*. ⓒ 16c: from French *arrumage* stowing of cargo on a ship.

rummage sale ▷ *noun* **1** *N Amer* a jumble sale. **2** a sale of unclaimed goods at a warehouse, etc.

rummer /ˈrʌmə(r)/ ▷ *noun* a large drinking-glass. ⓒ 17c: from Dutch *roemer* a drinking glass.

rummy¹ /ˈrʌmɪ/ ▷ *noun, originally US* a card game in which each player tries to collect sets or sequences of three or more cards. ⓒ Early 20c.

rummy² see under RUM¹

rumour or (*N Amer*) **rumor** /ˈruːmə(r)/ *noun* **1** a piece of news or information which is passed from person to person and which may or may not be true. **2** general talk or gossip; hearsay. ▷ *verb* (***rumoured, rumouring***) to report or spread (news, information, etc) by rumour □ *She is rumoured to be having an affair* □ *It is rumoured she is having an affair.* ⓒ 14c: French, from Latin *rumor* noise.

rump ▷ *noun* **1** the rear part of an animal's or bird's body; the area around the tail. **2** a person's buttocks. **3** (*also* **rump steak**) a cut of beef from the rump. **4** a small or inferior remnant. ⓒ 15c.

rumple /ˈrʌmpəl/ ▷ *verb* (***rumpled, rumpling***) *tr & intr* to become or to make (hair, clothes, etc) untidy, creased or wrinkled. ▷ *noun* a wrinkle or crease. • **rumpled** *adj* **1** crumpled. **2** dishevelled. • **rumply** *adj*. ⓒ 17c: from Dutch *rompel* wrinkle.

rumpus /ˈrʌmpəs/ ▷ *noun, colloq* a noisy disturbance, fuss, brawl or uproar. ⓒ 18c.

rumpus room ▷ *noun, originally N Amer* a room in which children can play freely and which does not need to be kept tidy.

rumpy-pumpy ▷ *noun, jocular* sexual intercourse. ⓒ 20c.

run ▷ *verb* (***ran, run, running***) **1** *intr* said of a person or an animal: to move at a pace quicker than walking and in such a way that both or all feet are off the ground together for an instant during part of each step. **2** to cover (a specified distance, etc) by running □ *run the marathon.* **3** to perform (an action) as if by running □ *run an errand.* **4** *intr* said especially of a vehicle: to move quickly and easily over a surface on, or as if on, wheels. **5** *intr* to flee; to run away. **6** *tr & intr* to move or make something move in a specified way or direction or with a specified result □ *run the car up the ramp* □ *let the dog run free* □ *run him out of town.* **7** *intr* to race or finish a race in a specified position. **8** to enter (a contestant) in a race or as a candidate for office. **9** *intr, chiefly N Amer* to stand as a candidate in an election □ *is running for governor.* **10** *intr* said of water, etc: to flow □ *rivers running to the sea.* **11** to make or allow (liquid) to flow □ *run cold water into the bath.* **12** *intr* said of the nose or eyes: to discharge liquid or mucous. **13** said of wax, etc: to melt and flow. **14** *tr & intr* said of a tap, container, etc: to give out or make it give out liquid □ *run the tap* □ *leave the tap running.* **15** to fill (a bath) with water □ *run a hot bath.* **16** *metallurgy* **a** *tr & intr* to melt or fuse; **b** to form (molten metal) into bars, etc; to cast. **17** *tr & intr* to come to a specified state or condition by, or as if by, flowing or running □ *run dry* □ *run short of time* □ *her blood ran cold.* **18** to be full of or flow with something. **19** **a** *tr & intr* said of machines, etc: to operate or function □ *The presses ran all night*; **b** *computing* to execute (a program). **20** to organize, manage or be in control of something □ *runs her own business.* **21** *intr* (*often* **run over, round** or **up**, *etc*) to make a brief trip or casual visit to a place, etc □ *run up to town for the afternoon.* **22** *tr & intr* said especially of public transport, etc: to travel or make (a vehicle) travel on a regular route □ *a train running between Paris and Nice* □ *run an extra train.* **23** *tr & intr* to continue or make something continue or extend in a specified direction, for a specified time or distance, or over a specified range □ *a road running south* □ *colours running from pink to deep red* □ *The play ran for ten years.* **24** *intr, law* to continue to have legal force □ *a lease with a year still to run.* **25** *colloq* to drive someone in a vehicle, usually to a specified place □ *run you to the station.* **26** *intr* to spread or diffuse □ *The colour in his shirt ran.* **27** *intr* said of news, information, etc: to spread or circulate quickly □ *The rumour ran through the office.* **28** *intr* said of a piece of writing or written material: to be worded □ *The report runs as follows.* **29** to be affected by or subjected to, or to be likely to be affected by, something □ *run a high temperature* □ *run risks.* **30** *intr* said of a physical feature, a quality, etc: to be inherent or recur frequently, especially within a family □ *blue eyes run in the family.* **31** to own, drive and maintain (a vehicle). **32** to publish □ *run the story in the magazine.* **33** *TV, radio* to show or broadcast (a programme, film, etc) □ *run a repeat of the series.* **34** *intr* said of a broadcast, play, exhibition, etc: to be shown, presented, etc. **35** *intr* **a** said of stitches: to come undone; **b** said of a garment, eg a pair of tights: to have some of its stitches come undone and form a ladder. **36** to set (cattle, etc) loose in a field or other area to graze □ *run cattle in the valley.* **37** to hunt or track down (an animal) □ *ran the fox to ground.* **38** to get past or through an obstacle, etc □ *run a blockade.* **39** to smuggle or deal illegally in something □ *run guns.* **40** *intr* said of fish: to migrate upstream, especially to spawn. **41** *cricket* to score a run by, or as if by, running. **42** *golf* to hit a ball in such a way that it rolls along the ground. **43** *bridge* **a** to take an uninterrupted succession of tricks in (a suit); **b** to take (several tricks) in this way. ▷ *noun* **1** an act of running. **2** the distance covered or time taken up by an act of running. **3** a rapid pace quicker than a walk □ *break into a run.* **4** a manner of running. **5** a mark, streak, etc made by the flowing of some liquid, eg paint. **6** a trip in a vehicle, especially one taken for pleasure □ *a run to the seaside.* **7** a continuous and unbroken period or series of something □ *a run of bad luck* □ *The play had a run of six weeks.* **8** freedom to move about or come and go as one pleases □ *have the run of the house.* **9** (*usually* **a run on something**) a high or urgent demand for (a currency, money, a commodity, etc) □ *a run on the pound.* **10** a route which is regularly travelled, eg by public transport, or as a delivery round, etc □ *a coach on the London to Glasgow run.* **11** a LADDER (*noun* 2). **12** the average type or class of something □ *the usual run of new students.* **13** (**the runs**) *colloq* diarrhoea. **14** the length of time for which a machine, etc functions or is operated. **15** the quantity produced in a single period of production □ *a print run.* **16** *music* a rapid scalelike passage of notes. **17** *military* (*also* **bombing run**) a flight, often a relatively short one and at a constant speed, made by an aircraft before and while dropping bombs at a target. **18** *cards* three or more playing cards in a series or sequence. **19** an inclined course, especially one covered with snow, used for skiing. **20** *chiefly US* a small stream. **21** *cricket* a point scored, usually by a batsman running from one wicket to the other. **22** a unit of scoring in baseball made by the batter successfully completing a circuit of four bases. **23** *golf* the distance a ball rolls after hitting the ground. **24** *Austral, NZ* a tract of land used for raising stock. **25** *often in compounds* an enclosure or pen for domestic fowls or animals □ *a chicken-run*. **26** a shoal of migrating fish. **27** a track used regularly by wild animals. **28** *computing* the complete execution of a program. See also TRIAL RUN. • **a (good) run for one's money** *colloq* **1** fierce competition. **2** enjoyment from an activity. • **on the run** fleeing, especially from the police. • **run for it** *colloq* to try to escape. • **run high** said of feelings, emotions, etc: to be very strong. • **run off one's feet** *Brit colloq* extremely busy. • **run someone ragged** to wear them out. • **run scared** *colloq* to be frightened. ◎ Anglo-Saxon *rinnan*.

■ **run across** or **into someone** to meet them unexpectedly.

■ **run after someone** or **something** to chase them or it.

■ **run along** *colloq* **1** *patronizing* (often as an imperative) to go away. **2** to leave □ *I'd better run along or I'll be late.*

■ **run** or **run something along, over, through,** *etc* to move or cause it to move or pass quickly, lightly or freely in the specified direction □ *run your eyes over the report* □ *Excitement ran through the audience.*

■ **run away** to escape or flee.

■ **run away with someone 1** to elope with them. **2** said of a horse: to gallop off uncontrollably with someone on its back.

■ **run away with something 1** to steal it. **2** said of someone: to be over-enthusiastic about or carried away by (an idea, etc). **3** to win a (competition, etc) comfortably.

■ **run down** said of a clock, battery, etc: to cease to work because of a gradual loss of power.

■ **run someone** or **something down 1** said of a vehicle or its driver: to knock them or it to the ground. **2** to speak badly of them or it usually without good reason. **3** to chase or search for them or it until they are found or captured. See also RUN-DOWN.

■ **run something down** to allow (eg an operation or business) to be gradually reduced or closed.

■ **run something in** *old use* to run (a new car or engine) gently to prevent damage to the engine.

■ **run someone in** *colloq* **1** to arrest them. **2** to give them a lift in a car, etc for a short distance, especially to a regular destination.

■ **run into someone** *colloq* to meet them unexpectedly.

■ **run into someone** or **something** to collide with them or it.

■ **run into something 1** to suffer from or be beset by (a problem, difficulty, etc) □ *Our plans quickly ran into problems.* **2** to reach as far as (an amount or quantity) □ *His debts run into hundreds.*

■ **run off 1** to leave quickly; to run away. **2** said of a liquid: to be drained.

■ **run something off 1** to produce, especially printed material, quickly or promptly. **2** to drain a liquid. **3** to decide a tied contest with a further round.

■ **run off with someone** to elope with them.

■ **run off with something 1** to steal it. **2** to win (a competition, etc) comfortably.

■ **run on 1** to talk at length or incessantly. **2** *printing* to continue in the same line without starting a new paragraph.

■ **run on something** said of a vehicle: to use (a specified fuel).

■ **run out** said of a supply: to come to an end; to be used up.

■ **run out of something** to use up a supply of it □ *run out of money.*

■ **run someone out 1** *cricket* to put out (a batsman running towards a wicket) by hitting that wicket with the ball. **2** *chiefly N Amer colloq* to force them to leave □ *run them out of town.*

■ **run out on someone** *colloq* to abandon or desert them.

■ **run over 1** to overflow. **2** to go beyond (a limit, etc).

■ **run over** or **through something** to read or perform a piece of music, a script, etc quickly, especially for practice or as a rehearsal.

■ **run someone** or **something over** said of a vehicle or driver: to knock them or it down and injure or kill them □ *reversed and ran the cat over.*

■ **run through something** to use up (money, resources, etc) quickly and recklessly.

■ **run someone through** to pierce them with a sword or similar weapon.

■ **run to something 1** to have enough money for it □ *We can't run to a holiday this year.* **2** said of money, resources, etc: to be sufficient for particular needs. **3** said of a text: to extend to (a specified extent). **4** to develop relatively quickly in (a specified direction); to tend towards it □ *run to fat.*

■ **run something up 1** to make (a piece of clothing, etc) quickly or promptly. **2** to amass or accumulate (bills, debts, etc). **3** to hoist (a flag).

■ **run up against someone** or **something** to be faced with (a challenging opponent or difficulty).

runabout /ˈrʌnəbɑʊt/ ▻ *noun* a small light car, boat or aircraft. Also *as adj.*

runaround ▻ *noun* a RUNABOUT car. • **give someone the runaround** *colloq* to behave repeatedly in a deceptive or evasive way towards them. • **get the runaround** *colloq* to be treated in this way.

runaway ▻ *noun* a person or animal that has run away or fled. ▻ *adj* **1** in the process of running away; out of control □ *a runaway train.* **2** said of a race, victory, etc: easily and convincingly won. **3** done or managed as a result of running away.

runcible spoon /ˈrʌnsɪbəl/ ▻ *noun* a pickle-fork with broad prongs and one sharp curved prong. ◎ 19c: a phrase coined by Edward Lear (1812-88), based on his nonsense word *runcible*.

run down ▻ *adj* **1** said of a person: tired or exhausted; in weakened health. **2** said of a building: shabby; dilapidated. ▻ *noun* (*usually* **rundown**) **1** a gradual reduction in numbers, size, etc. **2** a brief statement of the main points or items; a summary.

rune /ruːn/ ▻ *noun* **1** any of the letters of an early alphabet used by the Germanic peoples between about AD 200 and AD 600, used especially in inscriptions. **2** a mystical symbol or inscription. • **runic** *adj* **1** relating to, written in or inscribed with runes. **2** in the style of ancient interlaced ornamentation. ◎ 17c: from Norse *run*.

rung¹ ▻ *noun* **1** a step on a ladder. **2** a crosspiece on a chair. ◎ Anglo-Saxon *hrung*.

rung² *past participle of* RING²

run-in ▷ *noun* **1** an approach. **2** *colloq* a quarrel or argument.

runnable /ˈrʌnəbəl/ ▷ *adj* **1** said of a stag: fit for hunting. **2** said of a vehicle, machine, etc: *colloq* in a fit state to drive, be operated, etc.

runnel /ˈrʌnəl/ ▷ *noun* **1** a small stream. **2** a gutter. ◷ Anglo-Saxon *rynel*, diminutive of *ryne* a stream, related to *rinnan* to run.

runner /ˈrʌnə(r)/ ▷ *noun* **1** someone or something that runs. **2** a messenger. **3** a groove or strip along which a drawer, sliding door, curtain, etc slides. **4** either of the strips of metal or wood running the length of a sledge, on which it moves. **5** a blade on an ice skate. **6** *bot* in certain plants, eg strawberry, creeping buttercup, etc: a stem that grows horizontally along the surface of the ground, producing new plants either from axillary or terminal buds. *Technical equivalent* STOLON. **7** a long narrow strip of cloth or carpet used to decorate or cover a table, dresser, floor, etc. **8** a RUNNER BEAN. **9** a smuggler. • **do a runner** *slang* to leave a place hastily, especially to leave a shop, restaurant, etc without paying; to escape.

runner bean ▷ *noun* **1** a climbing plant which produces bright red flowers and long green edible beans. **2** the bean this plant produces.

runner-up ▷ *noun* (***runners-up***) **1** the team or the competitor that finishes in second place. **2** one of a number of teams or competitors that finish close behind the winner.

runnier and **runniest** see under RUNNY

running ▷ *noun* **1** the act of moving quickly. **2** the act of managing, organizing or operating. ▷ *adj* **1** relating to or for running □ *running shoes.* **2** done or performed while running, working, etc □ *running repairs* □ *a running jump.* **3** continuous □ *running battle.* **4** *following its noun* consecutive □ *two days running.* **5** flowing □ *running water.* **6** said of a wound or sore, etc: giving out pus. • **in** or **out of the running** having, or not having, a chance of success. • **make** or **take up the running** to take the lead or set the pace, eg in a competition, race, etc. • **take a running jump!** *slang* an expression of contempt, impatience, etc.

running battle ▷ *noun* **1** a military engagement with a constantly changing location. **2** a continuous fight or argument □ *a running battle with the Council.*

running-board ▷ *noun* a footboard along the side of a vehicle.

running commentary ▷ *noun* **1** a broadcast description of a game, event, etc as it is in progress. **2** any oral description especially a boring or over-elaborate one, of events as they happen or happened □ *gave a running commentary of his visit to the doctor.*

running head, **running headline** and **running title** ▷ *noun, printing* a title occurring at the top of several consecutive pages in a book.

running knot ▷ *noun* a knot that changes the size of a noose as one end of the string, etc is pulled.

running lights ▷ *noun* **1** *naut* the lights shown by vessels between sunset and sunrise. **2** small lights at the front and rear of a car that remain on while the engine is running.

running mate ▷ *noun* **1** a horse that is teamed with another, or that makes the pace for another in a race. **2** *politics* a candidate, standing for election to a post of secondary importance, when considered as the partner of the candidate for a more important post, especially the candidate for the post of vice-president of the US.

running repairs ▷ *plural noun* quick or temporary repairs to machinery, etc, carried out while it is operating or with a minimal break in its operation.

running water ▷ *noun* **1** an uninterrupted supply of water from a main or tap. **2** water in or taken from a flowing stream.

runny /ˈrʌnɪ/ ▷ *adj* (***runnier, runniest***) **1** tending to run or flow with liquid. **2** liquid; watery. **3** said of the nose: discharging mucous. ◷ 19c.

run-off ▷ *noun* **1 a** the action of running something off; **b** the quantity that is run off, especially by some mechanical process. **2 a** rainwater that moves over the ground and flows into surface streams and rivers under conditions of heavy rainfall, when the ground is saturated with water; **b** *N Amer* the period in which this occurs. **3** an extra race, contest, etc between two people or teams that have tied, to decide the winner.

run-of-the-mill ▷ *adj* ordinary; average; not special.

runt ▷ *noun* **1** the smallest animal in a litter. **2** *derog* an undersized and weak person. **3** a kind of large domestic pigeon. ◷ 16c.

run-through ▷ *noun* **1** a practice or rehearsal. **2** a summary.

run time ▷ *noun, computing* the time during which a computer program is executed.

run-up ▷ *noun* **1** *sport* a run made in preparation for a jump, throw, etc. **2** an approach to something or period of preparation, eg for some event □ *the run-up to Christmas.*

runway ▷ *noun* **1** a wide hard surface from which aircraft take off and on which they land. **2** in a theatre, etc: a narrow sloping or horizontal ramp projecting from a stage into the audience; a catwalk. **3 a** a groove in which something slides; **b** *N Amer* in forestry: an incline down which logs are slid.

rupee /ruːˈpiː/ ▷ *noun* (***rupees***) (symbol **Rs**) the standard unit of currency in India, Pakistan, Bhutan, Nepal, Sri Lanka, Mauritius and the Seychelles. ◷ 17c: from Hindi *rupiya*, from Sanskrit *rupya* wrought silver.

rupiah /ruːˈpɪə/ ▷ *noun* (***rupiah*** or ***rupiahs***) the standard unit of currency of Indonesia. ◷ 20c: from Hindi *rupiya*; see RUPEE.

rupture /ˈrʌptʃə(r)/ ▷ *noun* **1 a** a breach; a breaking or bursting; **b** the state of being broken or burst. **2** a breach of harmony or friendly relations. **3** *medicine* **a** a tearing or breaking of an organ, tissue, etc; **b** *non-technical* a hernia, especially an abdominal one. ▷ *verb* (***ruptured, rupturing***) **1** to break, tear or burst something. **2** to breach or break off (friendly relations). **3** *medicine* to cause a rupture in (an organ, tissue, etc). **4** *intr* to undergo or be affected by a rupture. ◷ 15c: from Latin *ruptura*, from *rumpere* to break, burst forth.

rural /ˈrʊərəl/ ▷ *adj* **a** relating to or suggestive of the country or countryside; **b** pastoral or agricultural. • **rurality** /rʊəˈralɪtɪ/ *noun*. Compare URBAN. ◷ 15c: French, from Latin *ruralis*, from *rus*, *ruris* the country.

rural dean ▷ *noun* in the Church of England: a clergyman with responsibility over a group of parishes.

ruralize or **ruralise** /ˈrʊərəlaɪz/ ▷ *verb* (***ruralized, ruralizing***) **1** to make something rural. **2** *intr* to adopt a rural way of life, rural habits, etc. • **ruralization** *noun*. ◷ 19c.

Ruritanian /rʊərɪˈteɪnɪən/ ▷ *adj* **1** belonging or relating to a fictitious land of historical romance, in SE Europe. **2** belonging or relating to any exciting or romantic setting. • **Ruritanian** *noun, adj*. ◷ 19c: from *Ruritania*, a country created by Anthony Hope (1863–1933) for several of his novels, including *The Prisoner of Zenda*.

rurp /rɜːp/ ▷ *noun, originally US mountaineering* a very small hook-like piton. ◷ 1960s: from *r*ealized *u*ltimate *r*eality *p*iton.

rusa /ˈruːsə/ ▷ *noun* (*plural* ***rusas*** or ***rusa***) (*also* **rusa deer**) a large E Indian deer, especially the sambar. ◷ 18c: Malay.

ruse /ruːz/ ▷ *noun* a clever strategem or plan intended to deceive or trick. ⓒ 16c in this sense; 14c, meaning 'to make a detour': from French *ruser* to retreat.

rush[1] ▷ *verb* (***rushed, rushing***) **1** *intr* to hurry; to move forward or go quickly. **2** to hurry someone or something forward; to make them go quickly. **3** to send, transport, etc someone or something quickly and urgently □ ***rushed her to hospital.*** **4** to perform or deal with something too quickly or hurriedly. **5** *intr* to come, flow, spread, etc quickly and suddenly □ ***colour rushed to her cheeks.*** **6** to attack someone or something suddenly. **7** (*usually* **rush into something**) to begin or enter into a course of action, an agreement, etc too hastily and often without giving it enough consideration. **8** to force someone to act or do something more quickly than they want to □ ***don't rush me.*** **9** *slang* to cheat someone by charging them an excessive amount for something. ▷ *noun* (***rushes***) **1** a sudden quick movement, especially forwards. **2** a sudden general movement or migration of people, usually towards a single goal □ ***a gold rush.*** **3** a sound or sensation of rushing. **4** haste; hurry □ ***be in a dreadful rush.*** **5** a period of great activity. **6** a sudden demand for a commodity. **7** *slang* a feeling of euphoria after taking a drug. **8** *rugby, Amer football* an attempt to force the ball through a line of defenders. **9** *Austral* a stampede. ▷ *adj* done, or needing to be done, quickly □ ***a rush job.*** • **be rushed off one's feet** to be frantically busy. • **rush one's fences** to act too hastily. ⓒ 14c: from French *ruser* to put to flight, from Latin *recusare* to push back.

rush[2] ▷ *noun* (***rushes***) **1** *bot* a densely tufted annual or evergreen perennial plant, typically found in cold wet regions of the northern hemisphere, usually on moors or marshy ground. **2** a stalk or stalklike leaf of this plant, often used as a material for making baskets, covering floors, etc. **3** *loosely* any of various plants more or less similar to RUSH (sense 1). **4** *colloq old use* something of very little value or importance (*especially* **not care** or **be worth a rush**). • **rushy** *adj.* ⓒ Anglo-Saxon *risc.*

rushes /'rʌʃɪz/ *usually* ▷ *plural noun, cinematog* **1** the first unedited prints of a scene or scenes. **2** a preliminary showing of these, often after a day's filming. ⓒ 1920s: from RUSH[1].

rush hour ▷ *noun* the period at the beginning or end of a weekday when traffic is at its busiest because people are travelling to or from work.

rush light ▷ *noun* **1** (*also* **rush candle**) a candle or night-light made from the pith of a rush dipped in tallow. **2** (**rushlight**) the light given by a rush candle.

rusk ▷ *noun* a piece of bread which has been rebaked, or a hard dry biscuit resembling this, given as food to babies. ⓒ 16c: from Spanish or Portuguese *rosca* a twist of bread.

russet /'rʌsɪt/ ▷ *noun* **1** a reddish-brown colour. **2** a variety of apple with a reddish-brown skin. **3** *archaic* a coarse homespun cloth, formerly used for clothing. ▷ *adj* **1** reddish-brown in colour. **2** *archaic* made of russet. • **russety** *adj.* ⓒ 13c: from French *rousset*, from Latin *russus* red.

russia leather or **Russia leather** /'rʌʃə —/ ▷ *noun* a fine brownish-red leather impregnated with birch tar oil, used especially in bookbinding. ⓒ 17c: so called because it originally came from Russia.

Russian /'rʌʃən/ ▷ *noun* **1** a person born in or living in Russia or (*loosely*) in any of the other former Soviet republics or in the former Soviet Union. **2** the Slavonic language spoken in Russia, the main official language of the former Soviet Union. ▷ *adj* relating to Russia or (*loosely*) to any of the other former Soviet republics or the former Soviet Union, their people, culture or language. ⓒ 16c: from Latin *Russianus.*

Russian doll ▷ *noun* a wooden painted figure which comes apart in the middle to reveal a smaller figure inside. There are usually about six dolls of this kind within the outer doll and they traditionally represent a Russian peasant woman. ⓒ 1930s.

Russianize or **Russianise** /'rʌʃənaɪz/ ▷ *verb* (***Russianized, Russianizing***) to make something Russian in style or character. • **Russianization** *noun.*

Russian roulette ▷ *noun* an act of daring or bravado, especially that of spinning the cylinder of a revolver which is loaded with one bullet only, pointing the revolver at one's own head, and pulling the trigger.

Russian salad ▷ *noun* a salad of diced mixed vegetables served with mayonnaise and pickles.

Russian tea ▷ *noun* tea with lemon and no milk, usually served in a glass.

Russify /'rʌsɪfaɪ/ ▷ *verb* (***Russified, Russifying***) to Russianize. • **Russification** *noun.*

Russky or **Russki** /'rʌskɪ/ *derog slang* ▷ *noun* (***Russkis*** or ***Russkies***) a Russian. ▷ *adj* Russian. ⓒ 19c.

Russo- /'rʌsoʊ/ ▷ *combining form, denoting* relating to Russia or (*loosely*) to any of the former Soviet republics or to the former Soviet Union □ ***a Russo-American treaty.***

rust ▷ *noun* **1** a reddish-brown coating that forms on the surface of iron or steel that has been exposed to air and moisture. **2** a similar coating which forms on other metals. **3** the colour of rust, usually a reddish-brown. **4 a** a parasitic fungus that causes a serious disease of cereals and other crops, characterized by the appearance of reddish-brown patches on the leaves and other surfaces of infected plants; **b** the disease caused by such a fungus, which may result in serious economic losses as it affects important cereal crops, such as wheat. ▷ *verb* (***rusted, rusting***) **1** *intr* to become rusty or coated with rust. **2** to make something rusty. **3** *intr* to become weaker, inefficient etc, usually through lack of use. • **rusted** *adj.* • **rusting** *noun, adj.* ⓒ Anglo-Saxon.

rust belt ▷ *noun* an area with a concentration of declining heavy industries, such as steel production, especially that in the Midwestern and NE USA.

rust-bucket ▷ *noun, colloq* a badly rusted car.

rustic /'rʌstɪk/ ▷ *adj* **1** relating to, characteristic of, or living in the country; rural. **2** with the characteristics of country life or country people, especially in being simple and unsophisticated. **3** awkward or uncouth. **4** made of rough untrimmed branches □ ***rustic furniture.*** **5** said of masonry: with a rusticated finish. ▷ *noun* **1** a person from, or who lives in, the country, especially one who is thought of as being simple and unsophisticated; a peasant. **2** a simple clownish person. **3 a** a rough-surfaced brick or stone; **b** rustic masonry. • **rustically** *adverb.* • **rusticism** /'rʌstɪsɪzəm/ *noun* a rustic saying or custom. • **rusticity** /rʌ'stɪsɪtɪ/ *noun* rustic manner; simplicity. ⓒ 15c: from Latin *rusticus*, from *rus* country.

rusticate /'rʌstɪkeɪt/ ▷ *verb* (***rusticated, rusticating***) **1 a** *intr* to live or go to live in the country; **b** to send someone to live in the country. **2** *Brit* to suspend (a student) temporarily from college or university because of some wrongdoing. **3 a** to give (masonry) a rough surface, and usually sunken or chamfered joints; **b** to build in rustic masonry. **4** to make something rustic or rural in style. • **rusticated** *adj.* • **rustication** *noun.* ⓒ 15c: from Latin *rusticari, rusticatus* to live in the country, from *rus* country.

rustic capitals ▷ *noun* a type of Roman script that uses simplified squared capital letters.

rustle /'rʌsəl/ ▷ *verb* (***rustled, rustling***) **1** *intr* to make a soft whispering sound like that of dry leaves. **2** *intr* to move with such a sound. **3** to make something move with or make such a sound □ ***rustled the papers on his desk.*** **4** *tr & intr, chiefly US* to round up and steal (cattle or horses). **5** *intr, chiefly US colloq* to work energetically; to hustle. ▷ *noun* a quick succession of small soft dry crisp sounds like that of dry leaves; a rustling. • **rustler** *noun* someone who steals cattle or horses. • **rustling** *noun, adj.* • **rustlingly** *adverb.* ⓒ 14c.

■ **rustle some people** or **things up** to gather them together, especially at short notice □ ***rustled up a few people to go to the meeting.***

■ **rustle something up** to arrange or prepare it, especially at short notice □ *I'll soon rustle up some lunch.*

rustproof /'rʌstpruːf, 'rʌspruːf/ ▷ *adj* **1** tending not to rust. **2** preventing. ▷ *verb* to make something rustproof. • **rustproofing** *noun.*

rusty /'rʌstɪ/ ▷ *adj* (***rustier, rustiest***) **1** said of iron, steel or other metals: covered with rust; rusted. **2** said of a plant: affected by rust (sense 4a). **3** said of a skill, knowledge of a subject, etc: not as good as it used to be through lack of practice □ *His French was rusty.* **4** said of a person: old or worn-out in appearance. **5** rust-coloured. **6** said especially of black or dark clothes: discoloured, often with a brownish sheen, through age. **7** said of a sound, the voice, etc: raucous; hoarse. • **rustily** *adverb.* • **rustiness** *noun.*

rusty nail ▷ *noun, colloq* an alcoholic cocktail containing whisky and Drambuie.

rut[1] ▷ *noun* **1** a deep track or furrow in soft ground, especially one made by wheels. **2** an established and usually boring or dreary routine. ▷ *verb* (***rutted, rutting***) to furrow (the ground) with ruts. • **rutty** *adj.* • **in a rut** stuck in a boring or dreary routine. ◷ 16c.

rut[2] ▷ *noun* **1** in many male ruminants, eg deer: a period of sexual excitement that occurs one or more times a year, during which they fight competitively for females and defend their territory prior to mating. **2** (*also* **rutting season**) the time of year when this occurs. ▷ *verb* (***rutted, rutting***) *intr* said of male animals: to be in a period of sexual excitement. • **rutting** *noun, adj.* • **ruttish** *adj.* ◷ 15c: French, from Latin *rugitus*, from *rugire* to roar.

rutabaga /ruːtə'beɪgə/ ▷ *noun, N Amer* a swede. ◷ 18c: from a Swedish dialect word *rotabagge*, literally 'root bag'.

ruthenium /rʊ'θiːnɪəm/ ▷ *noun, chem* (symbol **Ru**, atomic number 44) a brittle, silvery-white metallic element that occurs in small amounts in some platinum ores. It has a high melting point and is used to increase the hardness of platinum alloys. ◷ 19c: from Latin *Ruthenia* Russia, so called because it was discovered in ore from the Urals.

rutherford /'rʌðəfəd/ ▷ *noun, physics* (symbol **rd**) a former unit of radioactive disintegration, equal to 1 million disintegrations per second. Compare BECQUEREL, CURIE. ◷ 1940s: named after Ernest Rutherford (1871–1937), New Zealand-born British physicist.

rutherfordium /rʌðə'fɔːdɪəm/ ▷ *noun, chem* (symbol Rf) the name proposed in the USA for the radioactive elements of atomic number 104 (see UNNILQUADIUM) and 106 (see UNNILHEXIUM). ◷ 1960s: see RUTHERFORD.

ruthless /'ruːθlɪs/ ▷ *adj* without pity; merciless. • **ruthlessly** *adverb.* • **ruthlessness** *noun.* ◷ 14c: from obsolete *reuthe* pity.

rutile /'ruːtaɪl/ ▷ *noun, mineralogy* a reddish-brown or black lustrous mineral form of titanium oxide, commonly found in igneous and metamorphic rocks, and in beach sand. It is an important ore of titanium, and is used as a brilliant white pigment in paper, paint and plastics. ◷ 19c: from German *Rutil*, from Latin *rutilus* reddish.

rutted and **rutting** see under RUT[1], RUT[2]

ruttish see under RUT[2]

rutty see under RUT[1]

RV ▷ *abbreviation* Revised Version (of the Bible).

RWA ▷ *abbreviation, IVR* Rwanda.

-ry see -ERY

rya /rɪə/ and **rya rug** ▷ *noun* (***ryas***) **1** a type of Scandinavian knotted-pile rug with a distinctive colourful pattern. **2** the weave, pattern or style typical of such a rug. ◷ 1950s: Swedish.

rye /raɪ/ ▷ *noun* **1** **a** a cereal belonging to the grass family that resembles barley but has longer and narrower ears, cultivated mainly in central Europe and eastern Europe, eg Poland, Ukraine, Russia, etc; **b** its grain, used to make flour and in the distillation of whisky, gin, vodka and kvass. **2** *especially US* whiskey distilled from fermented rye. **3** *US* RYE BREAD. ◷ Anglo-Saxon *ryge*.

rye bread ▷ *noun* any of various breads made with rye flour.

ryokan /rɪ'oʊkan/ ▷ *noun* a traditional Japanese inn. ◷ 1960s: Japanese, from *ryo* travel + *kan* building.

ryot /'raɪət/ ▷ *noun* in the Indian subcontinent: a peasant or tenant farmer. ◷ 17c: from Arabic *ra'iyah* subjects, literally 'flock'.

RZS ▷ *abbreviation* Royal Zoological Society.

S

S¹ or **s** /ɛs/ ▷ *noun* (***Ss, S's*** or ***s's***) **1** the nineteenth letter of the English alphabet. **2** a consonant, usually pronounced as a voiceless sibilant (as in *sip*), but often voiced (as in *prise*). **3** anything shaped like an S.

S² ▷ *abbreviation* **1** Sabbath. **2** Saint. **3** schilling (Austrian currency). **4** Siemens. **5** Society. **6** South. **7** *IVR* Sweden.

S³ ▷ *symbol, chem* sulphur.

S⁴ or **s** ▷ *abbreviation, music* soprano.

s ▷ *abbreviation* **1** a second or seconds of time. **2** *formerly* in the UK: a shilling or shillings. Compare D. ⓘ From Latin *solidus*.

's¹ /z, s, ɪz/ ▷ *suffix* **1** a word-forming element used to form the possessive □ ***John's*** □ ***the children's***. **2** a word-forming element used to form the plural of numbers and symbols □ ***3's, X's***.

's² /z, s, ɪz/ ▷ *abbreviation* **1** the shortened form of IS, as in *he's not here*. **2** the shortened form of HAS, as in *she's taken it*. **3** the shortened form of US, as in *let's go*.

-s¹ /s, z/ and **-es** /ɪz/ ▷ *suffix* forming the plural of nouns □ ***dogs*** □ ***churches***.

-s² /s, z/ and **-es** /ɪz/ ▷ *suffix* forming the third person singular of the present tense of verbs □ ***walks*** □ ***misses***.

SA ▷ *abbreviation* **1** Salvation Army. **2** South Africa. **3** South America. **4** South Australia. **5** *historical*: *Sturmabteilung* (German), the Nazi assault troops.

sabadilla /sabə'dɪlə/ ▷ *noun* **1** a tropical plant of the lily genus. **2** the seeds of this plant, yielding the alkaloid VERATRINE. Also called **cebadilla, cevadilla**. ⓘ 19c: from Spanish *cebadilla*, a diminutive of *cebada* barley.

Sabahan /sə'bɑːhən/ ▷ *noun* a citizen or inhabitant of Sabah, a Malaysian state near the northern region of Borneo, which was formerly a British colony. ▷ *adj* from, belonging or relating to Sabah. ⓘ 1960s.

Sabbatarian /sabə'tɛərɪən/ ▷ *noun* **1** a person who recognizes Saturday as the Sabbath. **2** a person who believes in or practises strict observance of the Sabbath, ie Saturday or Sunday depending on the religion. • **Sabbatarianism** *noun*. ⓘ 17c: from Latin *sabbatarius* a Sabbath-keeper.

Sabbath /'sabəθ/ ▷ *noun* **1** a day of the week set aside for religious worship and rest from work, Saturday among Jews and Sunday among most Christians. **2** (**sabbath**) a time of rest. **3** a witches' midnight meeting. Also called **sabbat**. ▷ *adj* referring to or appropriate to the Sabbath. ⓘ Anglo-Saxon: from Greek *sabbaton*, from Hebrew *shabbath* rest.

sabbatical /sə'batɪkəl/ ▷ *adj* **1** relating to or being a period of leave usually given to lecturers or teachers in higher education, especially to study or to undertake a separate and related project. **2** (**Sabbatical**) relating to, resembling or typical of the Sabbath. ▷ *noun* a period of sabbatical leave. ⓘ 17c: from Greek *sabbatikos*, from *sabbaton*, from Hebrew *shabbath* rest.

saber *US* spelling of SABRE

sabin /'seɪbɪn/ ▷ *noun, physics* a unit of acoustic absorption. ⓘ 1930s: named after Wallace C Sabine (1868–1919), US physicist.

sable¹ /'seɪbəl/ ▷ *noun* (***sables*** or ***sable***) **1** a small carnivorous mammal, native to Europe and Asia, that is a species of the marten and inhabits coniferous forests, usually near streams. **2** the thick soft glossy dark brown or black coat of this animal, highly prized as valuable fur. **3** an artist's paintbrush made of this. **4** the sable antelope. ▷ *adj* made of sable fur. ⓘ 15c: French.

sable² /'seɪbəl/ ▷ *adj* **1** *poetic* dark. **2** *heraldry* black. ⓘ 14c.

sable antelope ▷ *noun* a large African antelope with long backward-curving horns, the male of which has a blackish coat with white underparts.

sabot /'sabou/ ▷ *noun* a wooden clog, or a shoe with a wooden sole, as formerly worn by the French peasantry. ⓘ 17c: French.

sabotage /'sabətɑːʒ/ ▷ *noun* **1** deliberate or underhand damage or destruction, especially carried out for military or political reasons. **2** action designed to disrupt any plan or scheme and prevent its achievement. ▷ *verb* (***sabotaged, sabotaging***) to deliberately destroy, damage or disrupt something. ⓘ 19c: from French *saboter* to ruin through carelessness.

saboteur /sabə'tɜː(r)/ ▷ *noun* someone who sabotages. ⓘ Early 20c.

sabra /'sɑːbrə/ ▷ *noun* (***sabras***) a native-born Israeli, not an immigrant. ⓘ 1940s: from Hebrew *sabrah* a type of cactus.

sabre or (*US*) **saber** /'seɪbə(r)/ *noun* (***sabres*** or ***sabers***) **1** a curved single-edged cavalry sword. **2** a lightweight sword with a tapering blade used for fencing. ▷ *verb* (***sabred, sabring***) to wound or kill using a sabre. ⓘ 17c: French.

sabre-rattling ▷ *noun* aggressive talk or action, especially from politicians or military leaders, intended to intimidate and display power.

sabretooth ▷ *noun, zool* an extinct member of the cat family, with extremely long upper canine teeth, that lived during the late Tertiary era. Also called **sabretoothed tiger**. ⓘ 19c.

sac ▷ *noun, biol* any bag-like part in a plant or animal. • **saccate** /'sakeɪt, 'sakɪt/ *adj* enclosed in a sac; pouchlike. ⓘ 18c: from Latin *saccus* bag.

saccade /sa'kɑːd, sə-, -'keɪd/ ▷ *noun* (***saccades***) **1** a short jerky movement of the eye as it switches from one point to another, and may be voluntary, as in reading, or involuntary. **2** any short jerky movement. **3** a short rapid tug on a horse's reins. • **saccadic** /sə'kadɪk/ *adj* jerky; consisting of or relating to saccades. • **saccadically** *adverb*. ⓘ 18c: French.

saccharide /'sakəraɪd/ ▷ *noun* (***saccharides***) *chem* any of a group of water-soluble carbohydrates composed of one or more simple sugars, and typically having a sweet taste, eg glucose, sucrose. ⓘ 19c: from Latin *saccharum* sugar.

saccharimeter /sakə'rɪmɪtə(r)/ ▷ *noun* a device for testing the concentration of sugar solutions. • **saccharimetry** *noun*. ⓘ 19c.

saccharin /'sakərɪn/ ▷ *noun* a white crystalline substance, about 550 times sweeter than sugar and with no energy value, used as an artificial sweetener, especially by diabetics and dieters. ⓘ 19c: from Greek *saccharon* sugar.

saccharine /'sakəriːn/ ▷ *adj* **1** relating to or containing sugar. **2** over-sentimental or sickly sweet; cloying. ⓘ 17c.

saccharose /'sakərous/ ▷ *noun, chem* **1** an alternative name for SUCROSE. **2** the basic unit of a CARBOHYDRATE. ⓒ 19c.

saccule /'sakju:l/ and **sacculus** /'sakjʊləs/ ▷ *noun* (***saccules*** /-ju:lz/ or *biol* ***sacculi*** /-laɪ/) **1** a small sac. **2** *biol* the smaller of two sacs in the vestibule of the ear. ⓒ 19c: from Latin *saccus* bag.

sacerdotal /sasə'doutəl/ ▷ *adj* **1** referring or relating to priests. **2** resembling a priest; priestly. • **sacerdotally** *adverb*. ⓒ 15c: from Latin *sacerdos* priest, from *sacer* sacred + *dare* to give.

sacerdotalism /sasə'doutəlɪzəm/ ▷ *noun* **1** the spirit and principles of priesthood. **2** the attribution of special and supernatural powers to the priesthood. **3** *derog* the excessive influence of priests over other people. ⓒ 19c.

sacerdotalize or **sacerdotalise** /sasə'doutəlaɪz/ ▷ *verb* (***sacerdotalized***, ***sacerdotalizing***) to render sacerdotal. • **sacerdotalist** *noun*. ⓒ 19c.

sachem /'seɪtʃəm/ ▷ *noun, US* **1** a political leader. **2** a SAGAMORE. ⓒ 17c: from Algonquian (a Native American language family) *sachim* leader.

sachet /'saʃeɪ/ ▷ *noun* **1** a small sealed packet, usually made of plastic, containing a liquid, cream or powder. **2** a small bag containing pot-pourri or a similar scented substance, used to perfume wardrobes, drawers, etc. ⓒ 15c: French, diminutive of *sac* bag.

sack[1] ▷ *noun* **1** a large bag, especially one made of coarse cloth or paper. **2** the amount a sack will hold; a sackful. **3** (**the sack**) *colloq* dismissal from employment □ ***gave the caretaker the sack*** □ ***She'll get the sack.*** **4** (**the sack**) *slang* bed. **5** (**the sack**) *Amer football* the instance of intervening or tackling the quarterback while still in possession of the ball. ▷ *verb* (***sacked***, ***sacking***) **1** to put into a sack or sacks. **2** *colloq* to dismiss from employment. **3** *Amer football* to tackle (the quarterback while still in possession of the ball). • **hit the sack** *slang* to go to bed. ⓒ Anglo-Saxon *sacc*, from Latin *saccus*, from Greek *sakkos* bag.

sack[2] ▷ *verb* (***sacked***, ***sacking***) to plunder, pillage and destroy a town. ▷ *noun* the act of sacking a town. ⓒ 16c: from French *mettre à sac* to put one's loot into a bag; to plunder.

sack[3] ▷ *noun, historical* a dry white wine from Spain, Portugal and the Canary Islands. ⓒ 16c: from French *sec*, from Latin *siccus* dry.

sackbut /'sakbʌt/ ▷ *noun* an early wind instrument with a slide like a trombone. ⓒ 16c: from French *saquebute*, from *saquer* to pull + *bouter* to push.

sackcloth ▷ *noun* **1** coarse cloth used to make sacks; sacking. **2** a garment made from this, formerly worn in mourning or as a penance. • **sackcloth and ashes** a display of mourning, sorrow or remorse. ⓒ 14c.

sackful ▷ *noun* (***sackfuls***) the amount a sack will hold.

sacking ▷ *noun* **1** coarse cloth used to make sacks. **2** *colloq* dismissal from, or the act of dismissing from, employment.

sackrace ▷ *noun* a race in which each contender's legs are encased in a sack.

sacra *plural of* SACRUM

sacral[1] /'seɪkrəl/ ▷ *adj* referring or relating to sacred rites. ⓒ 19c: from Latin *sacrum* a sacred object.

sacral[2] /'seɪkrəl/ ▷ *adj* relating to or in the region of the sacrum. ⓒ 18c: from Latin *sacralis* of the sacrum.

sacrament /'sakrəmənt/ ▷ *noun* **1** *Christianity* any of various religious rites or ceremonies, eg marriage or baptism, regarded as a channel to and from God or as a sign of grace. The Protestants recognize baptism and the Eucharist as sacraments, and the Roman Catholic and Orthodox Churches recognize baptism, confirmation, the Eucharist, penance, extreme unction, holy orders or ordination, and matrimony. **2** (**Sacrament**) *Christianity* **a** the service of the Eucharist or Holy Communion; **b** the consecrated bread and wine consumed at Holy Communion. **3** a spiritual or secret symbol. **4** a sign, token or pledge. ⓒ 12c: from Latin *sacramentum* an oath, from *sacrare* to consecrate, from *sacer* sacred.

sacramental /sakrə'mɛntəl/ ▷ *adj* relating to or having the nature of a sacrament. ▷ *noun, RC Church* an act or object that relates to the sacrament but is not actually named among them, eg the sign of the cross. • **sacramentalism** *noun*. • **sacramentalist** *noun*. • **sacramentally** *adverb*. ⓒ 15c: from Latin *sacramentalis*, from *sacrare* to consecrate, from *sacer* sacred.

sacrament of the sick ▷ *noun, RC Church* the act of anointing a person, who is very ill or badly injured, with consecrated oil.

sacrarium /seɪ'krɛərɪəm/ ▷ *noun* (***sacraria*** /-rɪə/) the area around the altar of a church; the sanctuary. ⓒ 18c: Latin, from *sacer* holy.

sacred /'seɪkrɪd/ ▷ *adj* **1** devoted to a deity, therefore regarded with deep and solemn respect; consecrated. **2** connected with religion or worship □ ***sacred music.*** **3** entitled to veneration, worship and respect. **4** said of rules, etc: not to be challenged, violated or breached in any circumstances. **5** dedicated or appropriate to a saint, deity, etc □ ***a church sacred to the Trinity.*** • **sacredly** *adverb*. • **sacredness** *noun*. ⓒ 14c: from Latin *sacrare* to worship, from *sacer* holy.

sacred cow ▷ *noun, colloq* a custom, institution, etc so revered that it is regarded as above criticism. ⓒ Early 20c: referring to the Hindu doctrine that cows are sacred.

sacred ibis ▷ *noun* an IBIS native to Africa and Arabia, with white plumage, a dark head and neck, and soft dark plumes on its tail.

sacrifice /'sakrɪfaɪs/ ▷ *noun* **1** the offering of a slaughtered person or animal on an altar to God or a god. **2** the person or animal slaughtered for such an offering. **3** any offering, symbolic or tangible, made to God or a god. **4** the destruction, surrender, or giving up of something valued for the sake of someone or something else, especially a higher consideration. **5** *theol* Christ's offering of himself for the sake of mankind. ▷ *verb* (***sacrificed***, ***sacrificing***) **1** to offer someone or something as a sacrifice to God or a god. **2** to surrender or give up something for the sake of some other person or thing. • **sacrificer** *noun*. ⓒ 13c: from Latin *sacrificium*, from *sacer* sacred + *facere* to make.

sacrificial /sakrɪ'fɪʃəl/ ▷ *adj* relating to, used in or having the nature of a sacrifice. • **sacrificially** *adverb*. ⓒ 17c.

sacrilege /'sakrɪlɪdʒ/ ▷ *noun* **1** a profanation or extreme disrespect for something holy or greatly respected. **2** the breaking into a holy or sacred place and stealing from it. • **sacrilegist** /-'li:dʒɪst/ *noun*. ⓒ 13c: from French *sacrilege*, from Latin *sacrilegus* stealer of sacred things.

sacrilegious /sakrɪ'lɪdʒəs/ ▷ *adj* **1** relating to or involving sacrilege. **2** guilty of committing sacrilege. ⓒ 16c.

sacristan /'sakrɪstən/ and **sacrist** /'sakrɪst, 'seɪkrɪst/ ▷ *noun* **1** someone responsible for the safety of the sacred vessels and other contents of a church. **2** a person responsible for the church buildings and churchyard; a sexton. ⓒ 14c: from Latin *sacristanus*, from *sacer* holy.

sacristy /'sakrɪstɪ/ ▷ *noun* (***sacristies***) a room in a church where sacred utensils and vestments are kept; a vestry. ⓒ 17c: from Latin *sacristia* vestry.

sacroiliac /sɑkrou'ɪlɪak/ ▷ *adj, anatomy* relating to the articulation of the sacrum and the ilium. ▷ *noun* this joint.

sacrosanct /'sakrousaŋkt/ ▷ *adj* supremely holy or sacred; inviolable. • **sacrosanctity** /-'saŋktɪtɪ/ *noun*. ⓒ 17c: from Latin *sacer* holy + *sanctus* hallowed.

sacrum /ˈseɪkrəm, ˈsak-/ ▻ *noun* (***sacra*** /-rə/) *anatomy* a large triangular bone composed of fused vertebrae, forming the keystone of the pelvic arch in humans. • **sacral** see separate entry. ⓒ 18c: from Latin *os sacrum* holy bone, from its use in sacrifices.

SAD ▻ *abbreviation, psychol* seasonal affective disorder.

sad ▻ *adj* (***sadder***, ***saddest***) **1** feeling unhappy or sorrowful. **2** causing unhappiness □ *sad news*. **3** expressing or suggesting unhappiness □ *sad music*. **4** very bad; deplorable □ *a sad state*. **5** *colloq* lacking in taste; inspiring ridicule □ *sad taste in music*. • **sadly** *adverb* **1** in a sad manner. **2** unfortunately; sad to relate. • **sadness** *noun*. ⓒ Anglo-Saxon *sæd* weary.

sadden /ˈsadən/ ▻ *verb* (***saddened***, ***saddening***) **1** to make someone sad. **2** *intr* to become sad. ⓒ 17c.

saddhu see SADHU

saddle /ˈsadəl/ ▻ *noun* **1** a leather seat for horse-riding, which fits on the horse's back and is secured under its belly. **2** a fixed seat on a bicycle or motorcycle. **3** a pad on the back of a draught animal, used for supporting the load. **4** the part of the back of an animal on which a saddle is placed. **5** a butcher's cut of meat including part of the backbone with the ribs. **6** the rear part of a male fowl's back extending towards the tail. **7** a mountain col or ridge between two peaks. **8** *civil engineering* in a structure, eg a bridge: a support with a groove shaped in a certain way to hold another part. ▻ *verb* (***saddled***, ***saddling***) **1** to put a saddle on (an animal). **2** *intr* to climb into a saddle. **3** to burden someone with a problem, duty, etc □ *He was saddled with the responsibility*. **4** said of a trainer: to be responsible for preparing and entering (a racehorse) for a race. **5** to ride (a horse, bicycle, etc). • **saddleless** *adj*. • **in the saddle 1** on horseback. **2** in a position of power or control. ⓒ Anglo-Saxon *sadol*.

saddleback ▻ *noun* **1** an animal or bird with a saddle-shaped marking on its back. **2** a saddle-shaped hill or mountain; one with a dip in the middle. **3** a saddle roof. • **saddlebacked** *adj*. ⓒ 16c.

saddlebag ▻ *noun* a small bag carried at or attached to the saddle of a horse or bicycle.

saddlebow /ˈsadəlboʊ/ ▻ *noun* the arched front of a saddle.

saddlecloth ▻ *noun* a cloth placed under a horse's saddle to prevent rubbing.

saddler /ˈsadlə(r)/ ▻ *noun* **1** a person who makes or sells saddles, harness, and related equipment for horses. **2** *military* a soldier who has charge of cavalry saddles. ⓒ 14c.

saddle roof ▻ *noun* a roof with two gables and a ridge.

saddlery /ˈsadlərɪ/ ▻ *noun* (***saddleries***) **1** the occupation or profession of a saddler. **2** a saddler's shop or stock-in-trade. **3** a room at a stables, etc for making or storing the saddles or related equipment. ⓒ 15c.

saddle soap ▻ *noun* a type of oily soap used for cleaning and preserving leather.

saddle sore ▻ *adj* said of a rider: chafed by rubbing against the saddle during riding.

saddle stitch ▻ *noun* **1** a form of needlework consisting of long stitches on the top surface and short stitches on the underside of the fabric. **2** one such stitch. **3** *bookbinding* a method of stitching or stapling a booklet, magazine, etc together through the back centre fold. ▻ *verb* (**saddle-stitch**) *tr & intr* to sew using saddle stitch. ⓒ 1930s.

saddle-tree ▻ *noun* the frame of a saddle.

saddling *present participle of* SADDLE

saddo ▻ *noun* (***saddos*** or ***saddoes***) *slang* someone who is to be pitied, despised or ridiculed. ⓒ From SAD.

Sadducee /ˈsadʒʊsiː/ ▻ *noun, historical* one of a Jewish priestly and aristocratic sect of traditionalists, who resisted the progressive views of the Pharisees, and who rejected, among other beliefs, that of life after death. • **Sadducaean** or **Sadducean** /sadʒʊˈsɪən/ *adj*. • **Sadduceeism** or **Sadducism** /ˈsadʒʊsɪzəm/ *noun* **1** the principles of the Sadducees. **2** scepticism. ⓒ Anglo-Saxon *sadduceas*, from Greek *Saddoukaios*, from Hebrew *Tsaduqim*, from *Zadok* the High Priest who founded the sect.

sadhu or **saddhu** /ˈsɑːduː/ ▻ *noun* a nomadic Hindu holy man, living an austere life and existing on charity. ⓒ 19c: Sanskrit.

sadism /ˈseɪdɪzəm/ ▻ *noun* **1** the pleasure, especially sexual, gained by inflicting pain on others. **2** any infliction of suffering on others for one's own satisfaction. Compare MASOCHISM. ⓒ 19c: named after Comte (called Marquis) de Sade (1740–1814), the French novelist who died insane, and who notoriously depicted this form of pleasure in his novels.

sadist /ˈseɪdɪst/ ▻ *noun* someone who indulges in sadism, or who gains pleasure, especially sexual, from inflicting pain on others. ⓒ Early 20c.

sadistic /səˈdɪstɪk/ ▻ *adj* relating to or involving sadism. • **sadistically** *adverb*. ⓒ 19c.

sado-masochism ▻ *noun* (abbreviation **SM**) **1** the existence of both sadism and masochism in a person. **2** the practice of deriving sexual pleasure from inflicting pain on another person, and having pain inflicted on oneself by another person. • **sado-masochist** *noun* a person who enjoys and indulges in sado-masochism. • **sado-masochistic** *adj* relating to or involving sado-masochism. ⓒ 1930s.

SAE or **sae** ▻ *abbreviation* stamped addressed envelope.

safari /səˈfɑːrɪ/ ▻ *noun* (***safaris***) **1** an expedition or tour to hunt or observe wild animals, especially in Africa □ *on safari*. **2** the people, vehicles, equipment, etc that go on safari. **3** a long expedition involving difficulty and requiring planning, usually in tropical regions. ⓒ 19c: Swahili, from Arabic *safar* journey.

safari park ▻ *noun* a large enclosed area in which wild animals, mostly non-native, roam freely and can be observed by the public from their vehicles. ⓒ 1970s.

safari suit ▻ *noun* a suit, typically made of khaki cotton, and consisting of a long square-cut **safari jacket** and long or short trousers.

safe ▻ *adj* **1** free from danger or harm. **2** unharmed. **3** giving protection from danger or harm; secure □ *a safe place*. **4** not dangerous or harmful □ *Is it safe to go out?* **5** involving no risk of loss; assured □ *a safe bet*. **6** said of a friend, companion, etc: reliable or trustworthy. **7** cautious □ *better safe than sorry*. ▻ *noun* a sturdily constructed cabinet, usually made of metal, in which money and valuables can be locked away. • **safely** *adverb*. • **safeness** *noun*. • **be** or **err on the safe side** to be doubly cautious; to choose the safer alternative. • **play safe** see under PLAY. • **safe and sound** secure and unharmed □ *They returned safe and sound from their trip*. • **safe as houses** *colloq* extremely safe and secure. ⓒ 15c: from French *sauf*, from Latin *salvus*.

safe-breaker and **safe-cracker** ▻ *noun* someone who illegally opens safes to steal the contents.

safe-conduct ▻ *noun* **1** an official permit to pass or travel, especially in wartime, with guarantee of freedom from interference or arrest. **2** a document authorizing this.

safe-deposit and **safety-deposit** ▻ *noun* a vault, eg in a bank, in which money and valuables can be locked away.

safeguard ▻ *noun* **1** a person, device or arrangement giving protection against danger or harm. **2** a safe-conduct. ▻ *verb* to protect from harm; to ensure the safety of someone or something.

safe haven ▷ *noun* **1 a** a demilitarized area in a region of conflict, a war zone, etc that is set aside by a government, an international organization, etc as a secure area for an ethnic minority or other oppressed group; **b** any refuge considered safe for a particular oppressed person or group. **2** *econ* a currency, financial institution, etc that is considered stable and secure for investment.

safe house ▷ *noun* a place of safety, especially one kept by the intelligence services or care agencies, whose location is unknown to possible pursuers.

safekeeping ▷ *noun* care and protection; safe custody □ *She put her jewellery away for safekeeping.*

safe light ▷ *noun* a light used in a photographic darkroom, etc, which emits light of an intensity and colour which will not damage the materials being processed.

safe period ▷ *noun, colloq* the part of the menstrual cycle during which conception is least likely.

safe seat ▷ *noun* a parliamentary seat which will almost certainly be won at an election by the same party that currently holds it.

safe sex ▷ *noun* sexual intercourse or activity in which the transmission of disease and viruses, especially HIV, is guarded against, eg by the use of a condom or the avoidance of penetration.

safety /'seɪftɪ/ ▷ *noun* **1** the quality or condition of being safe. **2** *Amer football* the most deeply-placed member of the defensive side. Also called **safetyman**. • **there is safety in numbers** it is easier and safer to do something risky when there is a larger group of people. ⓒ 13c: from French *sauveté*, from Latin *salvus* safe.

safety belt ▷ *noun* **1** in vehicles: a belt securing a driver or passenger to their seat as a precaution against injury in a crash. **2** a strap or belt attaching a workman, etc to a fixed object while carrying out a dangerous operation.

safety catch ▷ *noun* any catch to provide protection against something, eg the accidental firing of a gun.

safety curtain ▷ *noun* a fireproof curtain between the stage and audience, lowered to control the spread of fire.

safety-deposit see SAFE-DEPOSIT

safety factor ▷ *noun, mech & engineering* the ratio between the breaking stress in a material or structure, and the safe permissible stress in it.

safety glass ▷ *noun* **1** a laminate of plastic between sheets of glass used eg in windscreens. **2** glass that is strengthened to avoid shattering, eg by reinforcing it with wire.

safety-lamp ▷ *noun* a miner's oil lamp designed to prevent ignition of any flammable gases encountered in the mine by covering the flame with a wire gauze. Also called **Davy lamp**.

safety match ▷ *noun* a match that only ignites when struck on a specially prepared surface.

safety net ▷ *noun* **1** a large net stretched beneath acrobats, tightrope walkers, etc in case they accidentally fall. **2** any precautionary measure or means of protecting against loss or failure.

safety pin ▷ *noun* a U-shaped pin with an attached guard to cover the point.

safety razor ▷ *noun* a shaving razor with the blade protected by a guard to prevent deep cutting of the skin.

safety valve ▷ *noun* **1** a valve in a boiler or pipe system that opens when the pressure exceeds a certain level, and closes again when the pressure drops. **2** an outlet for harmlessly releasing emotion, eg anger or frustration.

saffian /'safɪən/ ▷ *noun* leather tanned with sumac and dyed in bright colours. ⓒ 16c: from Russian *saf'yan*, from Persian *sakhtiyan* goatskin, from *sakht* hard.

safflower /'saflaʊə(r)/ ▷ *noun* a plant with finely-toothed elliptical leaves and large thistle-like heads of orange-red flowers that yield yellow and red dyes, and seed that yield **safflower oil** which is used in cooking, margarine, medicines, paints and varnishes. ⓒ 16c: from Dutch *saffloer*, from French *saffleur*.

saffron /'safrən/ ▷ *noun* **1** an autumn-flowering species of crocus which has lilac flowers with large bright orange stigmas divided into three branches. **2** the dried stigmas of this species, used to dye and flavour food. **3** a bright orange-yellow colour. • **saffroned** *adj.* • **saffrony** *adj.* ⓒ 13c: from French *safran*, from Arabic *zafaran*.

safranine /'safrəniːn/ and **safranin** /'safrənɪn/ ▷ *noun* a coal-tar dye giving various different colours for fabrics. ⓒ 19c: SAFFRON + -INE².

sag ▷ *verb* (***sagged***, ***sagging***) *intr* **1** to bend, sink, or hang down, especially in the middle, under or as if under weight. **2** to yield or give way, under or as though under weight or pressure. **3** to hang loosely or bulge downwards; to droop. ▷ *noun* a sagging state or condition. • **saggy** see separate entry. ⓒ 15c: Norse.

saga /'sɑːgə/ ▷ *noun* (***sagas***) **1** a medieval prose tale of the deeds of legendary Icelandic or Norwegian heroes and events. **2** any long detailed story, especially a piece of modern serialized fiction depicting successive generations of the same family. **3** *colloq* a long series of events. ⓒ 18c: Norse.

sagacious /sə'geɪʃəs/ *formal* ▷ *adj* having or showing intelligence and good judgement; wise or discerning. • **sagaciously** *adverb.* • **sagacity** /sə'gasɪtɪ/ and **sagaciousness** *noun.* ⓒ 17c: from Latin *sagax*, from *sagire* to discern.

sagamore /'sagəmɔː(r)/ ▷ *noun* a Native North American chief. Also called SACHEM. ⓒ 17c: from Penobscot (a Native American language) *sagamo*.

sage¹ ▷ *noun* **1** a low-growing perennial shrub with wrinkled greyish-green aromatic leaves and bluish-lilac two-lipped flowers. **2** the leaves of this plant, used in cookery as a seasoning, especially in stuffing for poultry, and also as a medicinal herb. ⓒ 14c: from French *sauge*, from Latin *salvia* healing plant.

sage² ▷ *noun* someone of great wisdom and knowledge, especially an ancient philosopher. ▷ *adj* extremely wise and prudent. • **sagely** *adj.* • **sageness** *noun.* ⓒ 13c: French, from Latin *sapere* to be wise.

sagebrush ▷ *noun* any of various species of N American plant, especially an aromatic shrub with many branches, with wedge-shaped silvery leaves and small white flowers borne in large clusters. ⓒ 19c: SAGE¹ + BRUSH.

saggar or **sagger** /'sagə(r)/ ▷ *noun* a large clay box in which pottery is packed for firing in a kiln. ⓒ 17c: perhaps a variant of SAFEGUARD.

saggy ▷ *adj* (***saggier***, ***saggiest***) tending to sag.

Sagitta /sə'dʒɪtə/ ▷ *noun, astron* the Arrow, a small constellation in the Milky Way.

sagittal /'sadʒɪtəl/ ▷ *adj* **1** shaped like an arrow. **2** relating or parallel to the SAGITTAL SUTURE. • **sagitally** *adverb.* ⓒ 16c: from Latin *sagittalis*, from *sagitta* arrow.

sagittal suture ▷ *noun, anatomy* the serrated join between the two parietal bones forming the top and sides of the skull.

Sagittarian /sadʒɪ'tɛərɪən/ ▷ *noun* a person born under the sign of Sagittarius. Also *as adj.* ⓒ Early 20c.

Sagittarius /sadʒɪ'tɛərɪəs/ ▷ *noun* **1** *astron* the Archer, a large S constellation of the zodiac lying partly in the Milky Way. **2** *astrol* **a)** the ninth sign of the zodiac, the Archer; **b)** a person born between 22 November and 20 December, under this sign. See table at ZODIAC. ⓒ 14c: Latin, from *sagitta* arrow.

sago /ˈseɪɡoʊ/ ▻ *noun* **1** a starchy grain or powder obtained from the soft pith of the sago palm, a staple food in the tropics, and also widely used in desserts. **2** any of various species of palm that yield this substance. ◷ 16c: from Malay *sagu*.

sago palm ▻ *noun* a small tree with large feathery leaves, native to SE Asia and the Pacific region.

saguaro /səˈɡwɑːroʊ, səˈwɑːroʊ/ ▻ *noun* (***saguaros***) a giant cactus of up to 50ft (15m) in height, native to the south west US and Mexico, and with a tree-like trunk and edible red fruits. ◷ 19c: Mexican Spanish.

Saharan /səˈhɑːrən/ ▻ *adj* characteristic of, belonging or relating to the Sahara desert.

sahib /ˈsɑːɪb/ ▻ *noun* in India: a term of respect used after a man's name, equivalent to 'Mr' or 'Sir', and formerly used on its own to address or refer to a European man. Compare MEMSAHIB. ◷ 17c: Arabic, meaning 'lord or friend'.

said[1] /sɛd/ ▻ *verb, past tense, past participle of* SAY. ▻ *adj, often formal* previously or already mentioned ▫ ***the said occasion.***

said[2] see SAYYID

saiga /ˈsaɪɡə/ ▻ *noun* (***saiga*** or ***saigas***) a type of antelope from W Asia, with a characteristic swollen snout. ◷ 19c: Russian.

sail ▻ *noun* **1** a sheet of canvas, or similar structure, spread to catch the wind as a means of propelling a ship. **2** a framework of slats which drive a windmill by catching the wind. **3** sails collectively. **4** a trip in a boat or ship with or without sails. **5** a voyage of a specified distance travelled by boat or ship. **6** (usually ***sail***, especially after a number) *naut* a ship with sails ▫ ***thirty sail.*** ▻ *verb* (***sailed, sailing***) **1** *tr & intr* to travel by boat or ship ▫ ***sail the Pacific.*** **2** to control (a boat or ship) ▫ ***He sailed his ship around the world.*** **3** *intr* to depart by boat or ship ▫ ***We sail at two-thirty.*** **4** to cause (a toy boat, etc) to sail. • **sailable** *adj* navigable. • **sailed** *adj* having sails. • **sailless** *adj.* • **full sail** with all sails raised and filled with the wind. • **make sail 1** to raise more sail. **2** to set off on a voyage. • **put on sail** to set more sails in order to travel more quickly. • **sail close to** or **near the wind 1** *naut* to keep the boat's bow as close as possible to the direction from which the wind is blowing so that the sails catch as much wind as is safely possible. **2** to come dangerously close to overstepping a limit, eg of good taste or decency. • **set sail 1** to begin a journey by boat or ship. **2** to spread the sails. • **shorten sail** to reduce its open extent. • **strike sail** to lower a sail or sails. • **under sail 1** having the sails raised and spread. **2** propelled by sails. ◷ Anglo-Saxon *segel*.

■ **sail through something** *colloq* to succeed in it effortlessly ▫ ***She sailed through all her exams.***

sailboard ▻ *noun* a windsurfing board, like a surfboard with a sail attached, controlled by a hand-held boom. • **sailboarding** the sport of sailing such a craft; windsurfing.

sailboat ▻ *noun, especially N Amer* a usually small sailing boat.

sailcloth ▻ *noun* **1** strong cloth, such as canvas, used to make sails. **2** heavy cotton cloth used for garments.

sailer /ˈseɪlə(r)/ ▻ *noun* a boat or ship that can sail in a specific manner ▫ ***The new boat was viewed as a good sailer.***

sailfish ▻ *noun* a large agile fish, bluish-grey above and silvery beneath, named after its sail-like dorsal fin and highly prized as a sport fish.

sailing boat ▻ *noun* a boat propelled by sails, though often fitted with auxiliary motor power.

sailor /ˈseɪlə(r)/ ▻ *noun* **1** any member of a ship's crew, especially one who is not an officer. **2** someone regarded in terms of ability to tolerate travel on a ship without becoming seasick ▫ ***a good sailor.***

sailor-suit ▻ *noun* a suit, normally worn by children or women, that resembles a sailor's uniform.

sailplane ▻ *noun* a lightweight glider that can rise with upward currents.

sainfoin /ˈseɪnfɔɪn/ ▻ *noun* a leguminous perennial plant, widely cultivated as a fodder crop, with pinnate leaves, spiked flower-heads and bright pink to red flowers veined with purple. ◷ 17c: French, from Latin *sanum faenum* healthy hay.

saint /seɪnt/ or (when prefixed to a name) /sənt/ ▻ *noun* (abbreviation **St**) **1** (often written **Saint**) a person whose profound holiness is formally recognized after death by a Christian Church, and who is declared worthy of everlasting praise. **2** *colloq* a very good and kind person. **3** *Bible* any one of God's chosen people. **4** *Bible* an Israelite, a Christian or one of the blessed dead. **5** a member of various religious groups, especially Puritans, as used of themselves or as a nickname. ▻ *verb* (***sainted, sainting***) **1** to make a saint of someone. **2** to hail or recognize formally as a saint. • **sainthood** *noun* the position or status of a saint. • **saintlike** *adj.* ◷ 12c: from Latin *sanctus* holy.

St Agnes's Eve ▻ *noun* the night of 20 January when, according to tradition, a girl may dream the identity of her future husband. ◷ Named after Saint Agnes, the Christian martyr who was executed in AD 304 for her refusal to marry.

St Andrew's cross ▻ *noun* **1** a cross in the form of the letter X. **2** a similar white cross on a blue background, as used on the flag of Scotland.

St Anthony's fire see ERGOTISM and ERYSIPELAS

Saint Bernard and **Saint Bernard's dog** ▻ *noun* one of a breed of very heavy dogs, with an orange-brown and white coat, a broad head and large feet, originally used to track and rescue travellers trapped in mountain snow in the St Bernard passes in the Alps.

sainted /ˈseɪntɪd/ ▻ *adj* **1** formally declared a saint. **2** greatly respected or revered; hallowed. ◷ 16c.

St Elmo's fire ▻ *noun* an electrical discharge forming a glow around a church spire, ship's mast, etc, particularly common in bad weather.

St George's cross ▻ *noun* a red upright cross on a white background, used as the flag of England.

St John's wort ▻ *noun* any of several shrubs, most of which have five-petalled yellow flowers, believed to bloom on the 24 June, the feast of Saint John the Baptist.

St Leger /-ˈlɛdʒə(r)/ ▻ *noun* a horse race run annually at Doncaster. ◷ 1776: named after Colonel Barry St Leger who founded it.

saintly /ˈseɪntlɪ/ ▻ *adj* (***saintlier, saintliest***) **1** similar to, characteristic of, or befitting a saint. **2** very good or holy. • **saintliness** *noun.* ◷ 17c.

saintpaulia /səntˈpɔːlɪə/ ▻ *noun* a plant of the family to which the AFRICAN VIOLET belongs. ◷ 19c: named after Baron Walter von Saint Paul (1860–1910), who discovered it.

saint's day ▻ *noun* a day in the Church calendar on which a particular saint is honoured and commemorated.

St Swithin's Day ▻ *noun* 15 July, the feast day of Saint Swithin, a 9th-century bishop of Winchester, where according to a traditional rhyme, if it rains on this day, it will rain for 40 days, but if it is dry on this day, it will remain dry for 40 days.

St Valentine's Day ▻ *noun* 14 February, a day on which special greetings cards are sent to sweethearts or people to whom one is attracted. See also VALENTINE. ◷ 16c: originally this day was 15th February, on the feast of *Lupercalia*, the festival of fertility, but was moved forward to 14th February, the feast of Saint Valentine commemorating two Christian martyrs of this name, to be acceptable to the Church.

Saint Vitus's dance /— 'vaɪtəsɪz —/ ▻ *noun, pathol* chorea.

saith /seɪθ, sɛθ/ ▻ *verb, old use* says.

saithe /seɪθ/ ▻ *noun, Brit* the COLEY. Also called **coalfish**.

sake[1] ▻ *noun* **1** benefit or advantage; behalf; account □ *for my sake.* **2** purpose; object or aim. • **for God's** or **heaven's** , *etc* **sake** exclamations used in annoyance or when pleading, eg for forgiveness. • **for old time's sake** because of what happened or because it was done in the past □ *We should go to that bar for old time's sake.* • **for the sake of something** for the purpose of or in order to achieve or assure it □ *You should take these exams for the sake of your future.* ◷ Anglo-Saxon *sacu* lawsuit.

sake[2] or **saki** /'sɑːkɪ, 'sɑːkeɪ/ ▻ *noun* a Japanese fermented alcoholic drink made from rice. ◷ 17c: Japanese.

saker /'seɪkə(r)/ ▻ *noun* a species of falcon, especially the female, used in hawking. • **sakeret** *noun* a male saker. ◷ 14c: from French *sacre*, from Arabic *saqr*.

saki[1] /'sɑːkɪ/ ▻ *noun* a monkey native to South America, with a long bushy non-prehensile tail. ◷ 18c: French, from Tupí *sagui*.

saki[2] see SAKE[2]

sal /sal/ ▻ *noun, chem, pharmacol* a salt. ◷ 14c: Latin.

salaam /sə'lɑːm, sɑː'lɑːm/ ▻ *noun* **1** a word used as a greeting in Eastern countries, especially by Muslims. **2** a Muslim greeting or show of respect in the form of a low bow with the palm of the right hand on the forehead. **3** (**salaams**) greetings; compliments. ▻ *verb* (***salaamed, salaaming***) *tr & intr* to perform the salaam to someone. ◷ 17c: from Arabic *salam* peace.

salable see SALEABLE

salacious /sə'leɪʃəs/ ▻ *adj* **1** unnaturally preoccupied with sex; lecherous or lustful. **2** seeking to arouse sexual desire, especially crudely or obscenely. • **salaciously** *adverb*. • **salaciousness** or **salacity** /sə'lasɪtɪ/ *noun*. ◷ 17c: from Latin *salax* fond of leaping, from *salire* to leap.

salad /'saləd/ ▻ *noun* a cold dish of vegetables or herbs, either raw or pre-cooked, often served with a dressing, and eaten either on its own or as an accompaniment to a main meal. ◷ 15c: from French *salade*, from Latin *sal* salt.

salad cream ▻ *noun* a type of bottled mayonnaise for dressing a salad.

salad days ▻ *plural noun, literary* years of youthful inexperience and carefree innocence. ◷ 17c.

salad dressing ▻ *noun* any sauce served with a salad, eg mayonnaise or a mixture of oil and vinegar.

salamander /'saləmandə(r), salə'mandə(r)/ ▻ *noun* **1** any of numerous small amphibians found in damp regions or in water, superficially resembling a lizard, but with a rounded head, moist skin without scales, and toes without claws. **2** a mythical reptile or spirit believed to live in fire and be able to quench it with the chill of its body. **3** a hot metal plate for browning meat, etc. ◷ 14c: from French *salamandre*, from Greek *salamandra*.

salami /sə'lɑːmɪ/ ▻ *noun* (***salamis***) a highly seasoned type of sausage, usually served very thinly sliced. ◷ 19c: Italian, plural of *salame*, from Latin *salare* to salt.

salami tactics ▻ *plural noun* the business practice of cutting staff or undesirable parts of an organization one by one. ◷ 1960s.

sal ammoniac /— ə'moʊnɪak/ ▻ *noun, chem* another name for ammonium chloride, a white crystalline salt. See also AMMONIUM.

salaried /'salərɪd/ ▻ *adj* **1** having or receiving a salary. **2** said of employment: paid by a salary. ◷ 17c.

salary /'salərɪ/ ▻ *noun* (***salaries***) a fixed regular payment, usually made monthly, for especially non-manual work. ▻ *verb* (***salaries, salaried, salarying***) to pay a salary to someone. Compare WAGES. ◷ 14c: from French *salaire*, from Latin *salarium* soldier's allowance to buy salt, from *sal* salt.

salchow /'salkoʊ, 'salkɒv/ ▻ *noun, ice-skating* a jump where the skater takes off from the inside back edge of one skate, spins up to three times in the air, and lands on the outside back edge of the other skate. ◷ 1920s: named after Ulrich Salchow (1877–1949), the Swedish skater who devised it.

sale ▻ *noun* **1** the act or practice of selling. **2** the exchange of anything for a specified amount of money. **3** the power or opportunity of selling □ *There is no sale for fur coats in the Caribbean.* **4** an item sold. **5** a period during which goods in shops, etc are offered at reduced prices. **6** the sale of goods by auction. **7** any event at which certain goods can be bought □ *a book sale.* **8** (**sales**) the operations associated with, or the staff responsible for, selling □ *She has worked in sales for a year.* ▻ *adj* intended for selling, especially at reduced prices or by auction □ *sales items.* • **for** or **on sale** available for buying. ◷ Anglo-Saxon *sala*.

saleable or (*US*) **salable** /'seɪləbəl/ *adj* **1** suitable for selling. **2** in demand. • **saleability** *noun*. • **saleableness** *noun*. ◷ 16c.

sale and leaseback see LEASEBACK

sale of work ▻ *noun* a sale of items made by members of eg a church congregation or association in order to raise money for a charity or other organization.

sale or return and **sale and return** ▻ *noun* an arrangement by which a retailer may return any unsold goods to the wholesaler.

sale price ▻ *noun* the reduced price of a sale item.

saleroom and (*US*) **salesroom** ▻ *noun* a room where goods for sale, especially at a public auction, are displayed.

salesclerk ▻ *noun, N Amer* a sales assistant in a store or shop.

salesman, **salesgirl**, **saleswoman** and **salesperson** ▻ *noun* **1** a person who sells goods to customers, especially in a shop. **2** a person representing a company who often visits people's homes, offices, etc.

salesmanship ▻ *noun* **1** the art of selling. **2** the techniques used by a salesman to present goods in an appealing way so as to persuade people to buy them.

sales resistance ▻ *noun* unwillingness of potential customers to buy, despite persuasive and forceful selling techniques.

salesroom see SALEROOM

sales talk and **sales pitch** ▻ *noun* persuasive talk used by salespeople.

sales tax ▻ *noun, especially N Amer* a tax imposed on retail goods and services.

Salian /'seɪlɪən/ ▻ *adj, historical* referring or relating to a tribe of Franks, the **Salii**, which established itself on the lower Rhine in 4c. ▻ *noun* a member of this tribe. • **Salic** /'salɪk, 'seɪlɪk/ *adj*. ◷ 17c: from Latin *Salii*.

salicin or **salicine** /'salɪsɪn/ ▻ *noun, pharmacol* a bitter crystalline glucoside procured from willow-bark, used medicinally as an analgesic or painkiller. ◷ 19c: French, from Latin *salix, salicis* a willow.

salicylate /sə'lɪsɪleɪt/ ▻ *noun* a salt of salicylic acid. ◷ 19c.

salicylic acid /salɪ'sɪlɪk —/ ▻ *noun, chem* a white crystalline solid that occurs naturally in certain plants, used in the manufacture of aspirin, antiseptic ointments, dyes, food preservatives and perfumes. ◷ 19c: from Latin *salix* willow, from the bark of which it was originally prepared.

salient /'seɪlɪənt/ ▻ *adj* **1** striking; outstanding or prominent. **2** *archit* projecting outwards □ ***a salient angle.*** **3** *biol, heraldry* springing or leaping. ▻ *noun* a projecting angle, part or section, eg of a fortification or a defensive line of troops. • **salience** or **saliency** *noun.* • **saliently** *adverb.* Ⓔ 16c: from Latin *saliens*, present participle of *salire* to leap.

Salientia /seɪlɪ'ɛnʃə/ ▻ *noun* a genus of amphibians adapted for leaping, including frogs and toads. • **salientian** *adj* referring or belonging to this genus. Ⓔ 1940s: Latin, from *saliens* present participle of *salire* to leap.

Salii see under SALIAN

salina /sə'liːnə, sə'laɪnə/ ▻ *noun* (***salinas***) a salt lagoon, marsh, lake or spring. Also SALINE (*noun* 1). Ⓔ 17c: Spanish, from Latin, from *sal* salt.

saline /'seɪlaɪn, -liːn/ ▻ *adj* **1** said of a substance: containing sodium chloride (common salt); salty. **2** having the nature of a salt. **3** said of medicines: containing or having the nature of the salts of alkali metals and magnesium. ▻ *noun* **1** a salina. **2** (*also* **saline solution**) a solution of sodium chloride in water, having the same pH and concentration as body fluids, used in intravenous drips, etc. • **salinity** /sə'lɪnɪtɪ/ *noun.* Ⓔ 15c: from Latin *salinus*, from *sal* salt.

salinometer /salɪ'nɒmɪtə(r)/ ▻ *noun* a hydrometer for measuring the quantity of salt in water. Ⓔ 19c.

saliva /sə'laɪvə/ ▻ *noun* a clear alkaline liquid produced by the salivary glands of the mouth, that moistens and softens the food and begins the process of digestion. • **salivary** /sə'laɪvərɪ, 'salɪvərɪ/ *adj* relating to, secreting or conveying saliva. Ⓔ 17c: Latin.

salivary gland ▻ *noun* a gland that secretes saliva.

salivate /'salɪveɪt/ ▻ *verb* (***salivated, salivating***) *intr* **1** said of the salivary glands: to produce a flow of saliva into the mouth in response to the thought or sight of food. **2** to drool. **3** to produce excessive amounts of saliva. • **salivation** /salɪ'veɪʃən/ *noun* the flow of saliva, especially in excess as a result of the thought or expectation of food. Ⓔ 17c: from Latin *salivare, salivatum.*

Salk vaccine /sɔːk —, sɔːlk —/ ▻ *noun* a vaccine against poliomyelitis. Ⓔ 1954: named after Dr Jonas E Salk (1914–95), the US virologist who developed it.

sallow[1] /'saloʊ/ ▻ *adj* said of a person's complexion: being a pale yellowish colour, often through poor health. ▻ *verb* (***sallowed, sallowing***) *tr & intr* to make or become sallow. • **sallowish** *adj.* • **sallowness** *noun.* Ⓔ Anglo-Saxon *salo* or *salu.*

sallow[2] /'saloʊ/ ▻ *noun* a willow, especially the broader-leaved type with brittle twigs. • **sallowy** *adj* full of sallows. Ⓔ Anglo-Saxon *sealh*, from Latin *salix.*

sally[1] /'salɪ/ ▻ *noun* (***sallies***) **1** a sudden rushing forward or advance of troops to attack besiegers. **2** any sudden advance or outburst of action. **3** an excursion or outing. ▻ *verb* (***sallies, sallied, sallying***) *intr* **1** said of troops: to carry out a sally. **2** *humorous* (*also* **sally forth**) to rush out or surge forward. **3** to set off on an excursion. Ⓔ 16c: from French *saillie*, from *saillir* to surge forward, from Latin *salire* to leap.

sally[2] /'salɪ/ ▻ *noun* (***sallies***) *bell-ringing* the woolly grip for the hands on a bell rope. Ⓔ 17c: perhaps from SALLY[1].

Sally Lunn ▻ *noun* a sweet tea-cake, usually served hot with butter. Ⓔ 18c: named after a girl who sold them on the streets of Bath.

salmagundi or **salmagundy** /salmə'gʌndɪ/ ▻ *noun* (***salmagundies***) **1** a dish of minced meat with eggs, anchovies, vinegar and seasoning. **2** a medley or miscellany. Ⓔ 17c: from French *salmigondis.*

salmon /'samən/ ▻ *noun* (***salmon*** or ***salmons***) **1** any of various medium-sized to large silvery streamlined fish that migrate to freshwater rivers and streams in order to spawn, highly prized as a food and game fish. **2** any closely related fish, or one that resembles it superficially. **3** the edible reddish-orange flesh of this fish, highly prized as food. **4** (*also* **salmon pink**) an orange-pink colour. ▻ *adj* salmon-coloured □ ***a salmon jumper.*** Ⓔ 13c: from French *saumon*, from Latin *salmo*, from *salire* to leap.

salmonella /salmə'nɛlə/ ▻ *noun* (***salmonellae*** /-liː/ or ***salmonellas***) **1** (**Salmonella**) any of numerous rod-shaped bacteria found in the intestines of humans and animals, including many species associated with food poisoning, gastroenteritis, typhoid, etc. **2** food poisoning caused by such bacteria, characterized by violent diarrhoea and abdominal pain. Ⓔ Early 20c: named after Daniel E Salmon (1850–1914), US veterinary surgeon.

salmon ladder ▻ *noun* a series of steps built in a river to help salmon swim upstream, without obstruction, to lay eggs.

salmon trout ▻ *noun* a fish resembling a salmon, but smaller and thicker in proportion.

salon /'salɒn/ ▻ *noun* **1** a reception room, especially in a large house. **2** a social gathering of distinguished people in a fashionable household. **3** a shop or other business establishment where clients are beautified in some way □ ***a hairdressing salon.*** **4** a room or hall for exhibiting paintings, sculptures, etc. **5** (**Salon**) an annual exhibition of works by living artists in Paris. Ⓔ 18c: French, from Italian *salone.*

saloon /sə'luːn/ ▻ *noun* **1** a large public room for functions or some other specified purpose, such as billiards, dancing, hairdressing, etc. **2** a large public cabin or dining-room on a passenger ship, usually for passengers travelling first class. **3** (*also* **saloon bar**) a lounge bar; a quieter and more comfortable part of a public house, sometimes separated from it. **4** *N Amer, especially US* any bar where alcohol is sold. **5** *colloq* (*in full* **saloon car**) any motor car with two or four doors and an enclosed compartment, not an estate, coupé, convertible or sports model. Ⓔ 18c: from French *salon.*

salopettes /salə'pɛts/ ▻ *plural noun* a ski suit consisting of usually quilted trousers reaching to the chest, held up by shoulder-straps. Ⓔ 1970s: French.

Salopian /sə'loʊpɪən/ ▻ *adj* **1** referring to or coming from Shropshire, called Salop until 1980. **2** coming from or belonging to Shrewsbury School. ▻ *noun* **1** a native or inhabitant of Shropshire. **2** a pupil at or person educated at Shrewsbury School. Ⓔ 18c: from Anglo-Norman *Salopescira* Shropshire.

salpiglossis /salpɪ'glɒsɪs/ ▻ *noun* (***salpiglossises***) any plant of a family, some of which are grown specifically for their bright, trumpet-shaped flowers. Ⓔ 19c: from Greek *salpinx* trumpet + *glossa* tongue.

salpingectomy /salpɪn'dʒɛktəmɪ/ ▻ *noun* (***salpingectomies***) *medicine* the surgical removal of a Fallopian tube. Ⓔ 19c: from Greek *salpinx* trumpet, referring to the shape of the tube, + -ECTOMY.

salpingitis /salpɪn'dʒaɪtɪs/ ▻ *noun* inflammation of a Fallopian tube. Ⓔ 19c.

salpinx /'salpɪŋks/ ▻ *noun* (***salpinges*** /sal'pɪndʒiːz/) *anatomy* **1** the EUSTACHIAN TUBE. **2** either of the FALLOPIAN TUBES. Ⓔ 19c: Greek.

salsa /'salsə/ ▻ *noun* (***salsas***) **1** rhythmic music of Latin-American origin, containing elements of jazz and rock. **2** a dance performed to this music. **3** *cookery* a spicy Mexican sauce, made with tomatoes, onions, chillies and oil. Ⓔ 19c: Spanish, meaning 'sauce'.

salsify /'salsɪfɪ/ ▻ *noun* (***salsifies***) **1** a biennial plant with a long white cylindrical tap root, grass-like leaves and large solitary heads of violet-purple flowers surrounded by bracts. **2** the edible flesh root of this plant which can be boiled or baked and eaten as a vegetable, having a flavour resembling that of oysters. **3** the young leaves of this plant, which are sometimes used in salads.

See also OYSTER PLANT. ⓘ 17c: from French *salsifis*, from Italian *sassefrica*.

SALT ▷ *abbreviation* Strategic Arms Limitation Talks or Treaty.

salt /sɔːlt, sɒlt/ ▷ *noun* **1** SODIUM CHLORIDE, especially as used to season and preserve food. **2** a saltcellar. **3** *chem* a chemical compound that is formed when an acid reacts with a base. **4** liveliness; interest, wit or good sense □ ***Her opinion added salt to the debate.*** **5** (*also* **old salt**) an experienced and usually old sailor. **6** (**salts**) SMELLING-SALTS. **7** (**salts**) any substance resembling salt in appearance or taste, especially a medicine □ ***Epsom salts.*** **8** a SALTING or SALTMARSH. ▷ *adj* **1** containing salt □ ***salt water.*** **2** tasting of salt. **3** preserved or cured with salt □ ***salt pork.*** **4** covered over with or immersed in salt water. **5** said of a plant: growing in salt soil. ▷ *verb* (***salted***, ***salting***) **1** to season or preserve (food) with salt. **2** to cover (an icy road) with a scattering of salt to melt the ice. **3** to add piquancy, interest or wit to something. **4** *mining slang* to add gold, precious ore, etc to (a mine) to give a deceptive appearance of riches to the mine. • **saltish** *adj.* • **saltishness** *noun.* • **saltless** *adj.* • **saltly** *adverb.* • **lay, put** or **cast salt on someone's tail** to find or catch someone, from the humorously recommended method of catching a bird. • **go through something like a dose of salts** *colloq* to do or finish it very quickly. • **rub salt in someone's wounds** to add to their discomfort, sorrow, shame, etc. • **the salt of the earth** a consistently reliable or dependable person. • **take something with a pinch of salt** to treat a statement or proposition sceptically, or with suspicion and reservation. • **worth one's salt** competent or useful; worthy of respect. ⓘ Anglo-Saxon.

■ **salt something away** to store it up for future use; to hoard it, especially in a miserly way.

saltant /ˈsaltənt/ ▷ *adj, heraldry* said of animals: leaping. ⓘ 17c: from Latin *saltare* to jump.

saltation /salˈteɪʃən, sɔːl-, sɒl-/ ▷ *noun* **1** a leaping or jumping. **2** *genetics* a sudden mutation or variation in appearance in a species from one generation to another. **3** *geol* the movement of a particle being transported by wind or water, resembling a series of leaps. • **saltatorial** /saltəˈtɔːrɪəl/, **saltatorious** or **saltatory** /ˈsaltɪtərɪ/ *adj* **1** leaping or jumping. **2** *biol* displaying genetic saltation. ⓘ 17c: Latin, from *saltare* to jump around.

saltationism /salˈteɪʃənɪzəm, sɔːl-, sɒl-/ ▷ *noun* the process or concept of saltation, specifically the evolutionary theory that new species occur by way of saltation. • **saltationist** *noun* a person who believes in saltationism. ⓘ 1970s.

saltbush ▷ *noun* any shrubby plant of the goosefoot family, growing in arid regions.

saltcellar ▷ *noun* **1** a container holding salt when used as a condiment. **2** *anatomy* a depression behind the collar-bone. ⓘ 15c.

salted /ˈsɔːltɪd/ ▷ *adj* **1** cured or preserved in salt. **2** containing salt. ⓘ 14c.

salt flat ▷ *noun* a stretch of flat, salt-covered ground left after the evaporation of an area of salt water.

saltigrade /ˈsaltɪgreɪd/ ▷ *adj, biol* said of animals: adapted for or progressing by leaps. ▷ *noun* a type of jumping spider. ⓘ 19c: from Latin *saltus* a leap + *gradi* to go.

saltier and **saltiest** see under SALT

saltimbocca /saltɪmˈbɒkə/ ▷ *noun* (***saltimboccas***) *Italian cookery* a dish containing veal and ham rolled together and cooked with herbs and sometimes cheese. ⓘ 1930s: Italian, literally 'it jumps in the mouth'.

salting ▷ *noun* **1** the act of preserving, seasoning, etc (food) with salt. **2** (**saltings**) an area of land flooded by the tides. Compare SALT MARSH. ⓘ 14c.

saltire or **saltier** /ˈsɔːltaɪə(r), ˈsɒl-/ ▷ *noun* a heraldic design or ordinary in the form of a ST ANDREW'S CROSS. ⓘ 14c: from French *saultoir* or *sautoir*, from Latin *saltatorium* a stirrup.

salt lake ▷ *noun* an inland lake containing saline water.

salt lick ▷ *noun* **1** a place to which animals go in order to obtain salt. **2** an object coated in salt, given to pets with a salt deficiency.

salt marsh ▷ *noun* an area of land which is usually, or liable to be, flooded with salt water. See also SALTING.

salt pan ▷ *noun* **1** a natural land depression in which salt accumulates or is accumulated by evaporation of salt water. **2** a large basin for obtaining salt by evaporation of salt water.

saltpetre or (*US*) **saltpeter** /sɔːltˈpiːtə(r), sɒlt-/ *noun* potassium nitrate. ⓘ 16c: from Latin *salpetra* salt of rock.

saltus /ˈsaltəs/ ▷ *noun* (***saltuses***) a breach of continuity, especially a jump to a conclusion. ⓘ 17c: Latin, meaning 'a leap'.

saltworks ▷ *singular noun* a building or site, etc where salt is produced.

saltwort ▷ *noun* a fleshy prickly plant of the goosefoot family, with green flowers, which inhabits sandy seashores and salt marshes. ⓘ 16c: translation of Dutch *zoutkruid*.

salty /ˈsɔːltɪ/ ▷ *adj* (***saltier***, ***saltiest***) **1** containing salt. **2** tasting strongly or excessively of salt. **3** said of humour: sharp or witty; spirited. • **saltiness** *noun.* ⓘ 15c.

salubrious /səˈluːbrɪəs, səˈljuː-/ ▷ *adj* **1** *formal* promoting health or well-being; healthy □ ***a salubrious climate.*** **2** decent or respectable; pleasant □ ***not a very salubrious neighbourhood.*** • **salubriously** *adverb.* • **salubriousness** or **salubrity** *noun.* ⓘ 16c: from Latin *salubris*, from *salus* health.

saluki /səˈluːkɪ/ ▷ *noun* (***salukis***) a breed of dog of Arabian origin, with a tall slender body and a silky fawn, cream or white coat, with longer hair on the ears, tail and backs of the legs. ⓘ 19c: from Arabic *seluqi*.

salutary /ˈsaljʊtərɪ/ ▷ *adj* **1** beneficial; bringing or containing a timely warning. **2** promoting health and safety; wholesome. • **salutarily** *adverb.* • **salutariness** *noun.* ⓘ 17c: from Latin *salutaris*, from *salus* health.

salutation /saljʊˈteɪʃən/ ▷ *noun* **1** a word, act, or gesture of greeting. **2** a conventional form of greeting in a letter, such as 'Dear Sir or Madam'. • **salutational** *adj.* • **salutatory** /səˈluːtətərɪ/ *adj* relating to or having the nature of a salutation. • **salutatorily** *adverb.* ⓘ 14c: from Latin *salutare*, *salutatum* to greet.

salute /səˈluːt, səˈljuːt/ ▷ *verb* (***saluted***, ***saluting***) **1** to greet with friendly words or especially a gesture, such as a kiss. **2** to pay tribute to something or someone □ ***We salute your bravery.*** **3** *intr, military* to pay formal respect to someone or something with a set gesture, especially with the right arm or by firing a weapon, such as a cannon. ▷ *noun* **1** a greeting. **2** a military gesture of respect, for a person or an occasion. • **saluter** *noun.* ⓘ 14c: from Latin *salutare* to greet.

salvage /ˈsalvɪdʒ/ ▷ *noun* **1** the rescue of a ship or its cargo from the danger of destruction or loss. **2** the reward paid by a ship's owner to those involved in saving the ship from destruction or loss. **3** the rescue of any property from fire or other danger. **4** the saving and utilization of waste material. **5** the property salvaged in such situations. ▷ *verb* (***salvaged***, ***salvaging***) **1** to rescue (property or a ship) from potential destruction or loss, eg in a fire or shipwreck, or from disposal as waste. **2** to manage to retain (eg one's pride) in adverse circumstances. • **salvageable** *noun.* ⓘ 17c: from Latin *salvagium*, from *salvare* to save.

salvation /salˈveɪʃən/ ▷ *noun* **1** the act of saving someone or something from harm. **2** a person or thing that saves another from harm. **3** *relig* the liberation or saving of man from the influence of sin, and its consequences for his soul. ◷ 13c: from Latin *salvatus* saved, from *salvare* to save.

Salvation Army ▻ *noun* a Christian organization, with a military-like rank structure, aiming to help the poor and spread Christianity, founded by William Booth in 1865. • **Salvationist** *noun* a member of the Salvation Army.

salve /salv, sɑːv/ ▻ *noun* (*salves*) **1** ointment or remedy to heal or soothe □ *lip salve.* **2** anything that comforts, consoles or soothes. ▻ *verb* (*salved, salving*) **1** to smear with salve. **2** to ease or comfort □ *salve one's conscience.* ◷ Anglo-Saxon *sealf.*

salver /ˈsalvə(r)/ ▻ *noun* a small ornamented tray, usually of silver, on which something is presented. ◷ 17c: from French *salve* a tray for presenting the king's food for tasting.

salvia /ˈsalvɪə/ ▻ *noun* (*salvias*) *bot* any of numerous herbaceous plants or small shrubs of the mint family, including ornamental species and culinary herbs, eg sage. ◷ 19c: Latin, meaning 'sage'.

salvo /ˈsalvoʊ/ ▻ *noun* (*salvos* or *salvoes*) **1** a burst of gunfire from several guns firing simultaneously, as a salute or in battle. **2** a sudden round of applause. ◷ 17c: from Italian *salva* salute, from Latin *salve* hail.

sal volatile /sal vɒˈlatɪlɪ/ ▻ *noun* a former name for ammonium carbonate, especially in a solution used as SMELLING SALTS. See also AMMONIUM. ◷ 17c: Latin, meaning 'volatile salt'.

Salyut /salˈjuːt/ ▻ *noun, astron* any of a series of manned Earth-orbiting Soviet space stations, the first of which was launched in April 1971, the last in April 1982, which have demonstrated that astronauts can remain in orbit for periods of six months or more. ◷ 1970s: Russian, meaning 'salute'.

SAM ▻ *abbreviation* surface-to-air missile.

Sam. ▻ *abbreviation* Book of the Bible: Samuel. See table at BIBLE.

samara /səˈmɑːrə, ˈsamərə/ ▻ *noun* a dry, one-seeded fruit with a wing-like appendage allowing easier distribution on air currents. ◷ 16c: Latin, meaning 'seed'.

Samaritan /səˈmarɪtən/ ▻ *noun* **1** an inhabitant or citizen of Samaria. **2** the Aramaic dialect of Samaria. **3** (*in full* **Good Samaritan**) a kind, considerate or helpful person. **4** a voluntary worker with THE SAMARITANS. ▻ *adj* referring or relating to Samaria or the Samaritans. ◷ Anglo-Saxon, from Latin *Samaritanus.*

the Samaritans /səˈmarɪtənz/ ▻ *noun* a voluntary operation founded in 1953 by Chad Varah, an Anglican priest, offering help, support and counselling by telephone for those suffering from hardship, grief or distress.

samarium /səˈmeərɪəm/ ▻ *noun, chem* (symbol **Sm**, atomic number 62) a soft silvery metallic element, used in alloys with cobalt to make strong permanent magnets, and also used as a neutron absorber in nuclear reactor components. ◷ 19c: named after Col Samarski, a Russian engineer and mines inspector.

Sama-veda see VEDA

samba /ˈsambə/ ▻ *noun* (*sambas*) **1** a lively Brazilian dance in duple time. **2** a ballroom dance developed from this dance. **3** a piece of music written for either. ◷ 19c: Portuguese.

sambar or **sambur** /ˈsambə(r)/ ▻ *noun* (*sambars* or *sambar*; *samburs* or *sambur*) a large Indian or Asian deer with three-pronged antlers. ◷ 17c: from Hindi, from Sanskrit *sambara.*

Sambo /ˈsamboʊ/ (*sambos*) *offensive slang* **1** (*sometimes* **Sambo**) a black person. **2** a person of mixed race especially someone with one black and one Native American parent, or one black and one European parent. ◷ 18c: from American Spanish *zambo,* possibly from Greek *skambos* bow-legged.

Sam Browne and **Sam Browne belt** ▻ *noun* a military officer's belt with a strap over the right shoulder. ◷ Early 20c: named after General Sir Samuel J Browne (1824–1901) who invented it.

same ▻ *adj* **1** identical or very similar □ *This is the same film we saw last week.* **2** used as emphasis □ *He went home the very same day.* **3** unchanged or unvaried □ *This town is still the same as ever.* **4** previously mentioned; the actual one in question □ *this same man.* ▻ *pronoun* (**the same**) the same person or thing, or the one previously referred to □ *She drank whisky, and I drank the same.* ▻ *adverb* (**the same**) **1** similarly; likewise □ *I feel the same.* **2** *colloq* equally □ *We love each of you the same.* • **sameness** *noun* **1** being the same. **2** tedious monotony. • **all** or **just the same** nevertheless; anyhow. • **at the same time** still; however; on the other hand. • **be all the same to someone** to make no difference to them; to be of little or no importance. • **much the same** not very different; virtually unchanged □ *How are you? Much the same.* • **same here** *colloq* an expression of agreement or involvement. ◷ 12c: from Norse *samr.*

same-sex ▻ *adj* referring to a relationship or to sex between two men or two women; homosexual □ *same-sex partner* □ *same-sex marriage.*

samey /ˈseɪmɪ/ ▻ *adj, colloq* boringly similar or unchanging; monotonous □ *I quite like that band, but I think their songs are a bit samey.*

samfoo or **samfu** /ˈsamfuː/ ▻ *noun* a suit worn by Chinese women, comprising a jacket and trousers. ◷ 1950s: from Cantonese Chinese *sam* dress + *foo* trousers.

Samian /ˈseɪmɪən/ ▻ *adj* referring to or from the Greek island of Samos. ▻ *noun* a native or citizen of Samos. ◷ 16c.

Samian ware ▻ *noun* a brick-red or black earthenware pottery with a lustrous glaze, produced in Italy in the first century BC, later imitated in Roman Gaul and elsewhere in the Roman empire.

samisen /ˈsamɪsɛn/ ▻ *noun* a Japanese musical instrument, similar to a guitar, but with three strings, a long fingerboard and a rectangular soundbox. ◷ 17c: Japanese, from Chinese *san-xian,* from *san* three + *xian* string.

samizdat /ˈsamɪzdat/ ▻ *noun* **1** in the former Soviet Union: the secret printing and distribution of writings banned by the government. **2** the writings themselves. ◷ 1960s: Russian, meaning 'self-published'.

samosa /səˈmoʊsə, -zə/ ▻ *noun* (*samosas* or *samosa*) a small deep-fried triangular pastry turnover, of Indian origin, filled with spicy meat or vegetables. ◷ 1950s: Hindi.

samovar /ˈsaməvɑː(r), -ˈvɑː(r)/ ▻ *noun* a Russian water boiler, used for making tea, etc, often elaborately decorated, and traditionally heated by a central pipe filled with charcoal. ◷ 19c: Russian, literally 'self-boiler'.

Samoyed /samɔɪˈɛd, ˈsamɔɪɛd, (especially sense 1) səˈmɔɪɛd/ ▻ *noun* (*Samoyed* or *Samoyeds*) **1** (*also* **samoyed**) an active medium-sized dog of Siberian origin, with an extremely thick cream or white coat, and a tightly curled tail. **2 a** a member of a people from NW Siberia; **b** their URAL-ALTAIC language. • **Samoyedic** *adj.* ◷ 16c: from Russian *Samoed.*

sampan /ˈsampan/ or **sanpan** ▻ *noun* a small Oriental boat with no engine, which is propelled by oars. ◷ 17c: Chinese, from *san* three + *ban* plank.

samphire /ˈsamfaɪə(r)/ ▻ *noun* a fleshy perennial plant with strongly aromatic bluish-green leaves, formerly popular as a pickled delicacy, and flat-topped clusters of tiny yellowish-green flowers. ◷ 16c: from French *sampiere,* from *(herbe de) Saint Pierre* (herb of) St Peter.

sample /ˈsɑːmpəl/ ▷ *noun* **1** (***samples***) a specimen; a small portion or part used to represent the quality and nature of others or of a whole. **2** *pop music* an extract of music, sound, etc used in a song, recording, etc, often mixed using a SAMPLER (sense 2). ▷ *adj* used as or serving as a sample. ▷ *verb* (***sampled, sampling***) **1** to take or try as a sample. **2** to get experience of something □ ***He has sampled life abroad.*** **3** *pop music* to mix a short extract from one recording into a different backing track. **4** *pop music* to record a sound and program it into a synthesizer which can then reproduce it at the desired pitch. ◷ 13c: from French *essample*, from Latin *exemplum* example.

sampler /ˈsɑːmplə(r)/ ▷ *noun* **1** a collection of samples. **2** *pop music* the equipment used for sampling sound. **3** a piece of embroidery produced as a show or test of skill, often including the alphabet, figures, and sometimes the name of the person who embroidered it. ◷ 13c.

sampling /ˈsɑːmplɪŋ/ ▷ *noun* **1** the taking, testing, etc of a sample. **2** *pop music* the mixing of short extracts from previous sound recordings into a different backing track. ◷ 17c.

samurai /ˈsamʊraɪ, ˈsamjʊraɪ/ ▷ *noun* (***samurai***) **1** *Japanese historical* an aristocratic caste or class of Japanese warriors, between the 11c and 19c. **2** a member of this caste or class. **3** a samurai's sword; a two-handed sword with a curved blade. ◷ 18c: Japanese, from *samurau* to attend (one's lord).

sanative /ˈsanətɪv/ ▷ *noun* (***sanatives***) a remedy or cure. ▷ *adj* curing or healing. ◷ 15c: from Latin *sanativus*, from *sanare* to heal.

sanatorium /sanəˈtɔːrɪəm/ ▷ *noun* (***sanatoriums*** or ***sanatoria*** /-rɪə/) **1** a hospital for the chronically ill or convalescents, originally especially for consumptives. **2** a health farm. **3** *Brit* a sickroom in a boarding school, etc. ◷ 19c: Latin, from *sanare* to heal.

sanctify /ˈsaŋktɪfaɪ/ ▷ *verb* (***sanctifies, sanctified, sanctifying***) **1** to make, consider or show to be sacred or holy. **2** to set aside for sacred use. **3** to free from sin or evil. **4** to declare legitimate or binding in the eyes of the Church □ ***sanctify a marriage.*** • **sanctification** /saŋktɪfɪˈkeɪʃən/ *noun* the act of sanctifying or consecrating. • **sanctified** *adj* **1** made sacred or holy. **2** sanctimonious. • **sanctifier** *noun* **1** (*usually* **Sanctifier**) the Holy Spirit. **2** someone or something that sanctifies. ◷ 14c: from French *sanctifier*, from Latin *sanctificare*, from *sanctus* holy + *facere* to make.

sanctimonious /saŋktɪˈmoʊnɪəs/ ▷ *adj* affecting or simulating holiness or virtuousness, especially hypocritically. • **sanctimoniously** *adverb*. • **sanctimoniousness** or **sanctimony** /ˈsaŋktɪmənɪ/ *noun*. ◷ 17c: from Latin *sanctimonia* sanctity, from *sanctus* holy.

sanction /ˈsaŋkʃən/ ▷ *noun* **1** official permission or authority. **2** the act of giving permission or authority. **3** aid; support. **4** (*especially* **sanctions**) *politics* an economic or military measure taken by one nation against another as a means of coercion □ ***trade sanctions.*** **5** *law* a means of encouraging adherence to a social custom, eg a penalty for non-observance or reward for observance of a law or treaty. **6** any penalty attached to an offence. **7** *ethics* a motive or rationale for observance of and obedience to any moral or religious law. ▷ *verb* (***sanctioned, sanctioning***) **1** to authorize or confirm formally. **2** to countenance or permit. ◷ 16c: from Latin *sanctio*, *sanctionis*, from *sancire*, *sanctum* to decree.

sanction

• This does not mean 'impose sanctions on'; this meaning is expressed by **embargo** or **boycott**.

sanctitude /ˈsaŋktɪtʃuːd/ ▷ *noun* saintliness; sanctity. ◷ 15c: from Latin *sanctitudo*, *sanctitudinis*.

sanctity /ˈsaŋktɪtɪ/ ▷ *noun* (***sanctities***) **1** the quality of being holy or sacred. **2** purity or godliness; inviolability. **3** (***sanctities***) holy feelings, objects or obligations. ◷ 14c: from French *saintcete*, from Latin *sanctitas*, from *sanctus* holy.

sanctuary /ˈsaŋktʃʊərɪ/ ▷ *noun* (***sanctuaries***) **1** a holy or sacred place, eg a church or temple. **2** the most sacred part of a church or temple, eg around an altar. **3** a place, historically a church, providing immunity from arrest, persecution or other interference. **4** a place of private refuge or retreat, away from disturbance □ ***the sanctuary of the garden.*** **5** a nature reserve in which animals or plants are protected by law. ◷ 14c: from Latin *sanctuarium*, from *sanctus* holy.

sanctum /ˈsaŋktəm/ ▷ *noun* (***sanctums*** or ***sancta*** /-tə/) (*especially* **inner sanctum**) **1** a sacred place. **2** a place providing total privacy. ◷ 16c: from Latin *sanctum* holy.

sanctum sanctorum /saŋktəm saŋkˈtɔːrəm/ ▷ *noun* **1** the inner chamber of the Jewish tabernacle. Also called HOLY OF HOLIES. **2** any private retreat or room, free from disturbance. ◷ 15c: Latin, translated from Hebrew *qodhesh haqqodhashim* holy of holies.

Sanctus /ˈsaŋktəs/ ▷ *noun*, *Church* **1** the hymn beginning 'Holy, holy, holy', sung at the end of the Eucharistic preface. **2** the music for this hymn. ◷ 14c.

sanctus bell ▷ *noun*, *RC Church* **1** a bell rung at the singing of the Sanctus. **2** a bell rung in the more solemn parts of the Mass.

sand ▷ *noun* **1** *geol* tiny rounded particles or grains of rock, especially quartz. **2** (**sands**) an area of land covered with these particles or grains, such as a seashore or desert. ▷ *adj* **1** made of sand. **2** having the colour of sand, a light brownish-yellow colour. ▷ *verb* (***sanded, sanding***) **1** to smooth or polish a surface with sandpaper or a sander. **2** to sprinkle, cover or mix with sand. • **sanded** *adj* **1** sprinkled, covered or mixed with sand. **2** smoothed or polished with sandpaper or a sander. ◷ Anglo-Saxon.

sandal[1] /ˈsandəl/ ▷ *noun* a type of lightweight shoe consisting of a sole attached to the foot by straps. • **sandalled** *adj* wearing sandals. ◷ 14c: from Latin *sandalium*, from Greek *sandalon*.

sandal[2] see SANDALWOOD

sandalwood and **sandal tree** /ˈsandəl —/ ▷ *noun*, *bot* **1** an evergreen tree with OPPOSITE oval leaves and inconspicuous red bell-shaped flowers. **2** the hard pale fragrant timber obtained from this tree, which is used for ornamental carving and as an ingredient of incense, and also yields an aromatic oil used in perfumes. ◷ 16c: from Sanskrit *candana*.

sandarach or **sandarac** /ˈsandərak/ ▷ *noun* **1** (*in full* **sandarach tree**) a tree native to Australia, NW Africa, and N America, with sturdy fragrant wood. **2** (*in full* **gum sandarach** or **sandarac resin**) the resin from this tree which is powdered and used in making varnish. ◷ 14c: from Latin *sandaraca*, from Greek *sandarake*.

sandbag ▷ *noun* **1** a sack filled with sand or earth, used with others to form a protective barrier against bomb blasts, gunfire or floods, or used as ballast. **2** a similar small sack of sand used as a cosh. ▷ *verb* **1** to barricade or weigh down with sandbags. **2** to attack with a sandbag. • **sandbagger** *noun*.

sandbank ▷ *noun* a bank of sand in a river, river mouth or sea, formed by currents and often above the water level at low tide.

sandbar ▷ *noun* a long sandbank in a river, river mouth or sea.

sandblast ▷ *noun* a jet of sand forced from a tube by air or steam pressure, used for glass-engraving, cleaning and polishing metal and stone surfaces, etc. ▷ *verb* to clean or engrave with a sandblast.

sand-blind ▷ *adj* half-blind. Compare STONE-BLIND.

sandbox ▷ *noun* **1** a box of sand, especially one for sprinkling on railway lines or roads. **2** a sandpit.

sandboy ▷ *noun* a boy selling sand. • **as happy as a sandboy** see under HAPPY.

sandcastle ▷ *noun* a model of a castle made for fun out of wet sand by children on the beach or in a sandpit.

sand-dune ▷ *noun* a hill or ridge of sand on a beach or in a desert.

sand eel ▷ *noun* a long silvery fish, resembling an eel, living in wet sand at low tide. Also called LAUNCE.

sander /'sandə(r)/ ▷ *noun* a power-driven tool fitted with sandpaper or an abrasive disc, used for sanding wood, etc.

sand flea ▷ *noun* **1** the CHIGGER (sense 2). **2** the SANDHOPPER.

sandfly ▷ *noun* **1** a small bloodsucking midge. **2** a small mothlike bloodsucking midge that transmits **sandfly fever**, a fever due to a viral infection which can cause blindness.

sandgrouse ▷ *noun* a species of bird related to pigeons, living in sandy areas of the Old World, with long pointed wings and feathered legs.

sandhopper ▷ *noun* a semi-terrestrial burrowing crustacean with a flattened body, capable of vigorous jumping, often abundant on seashores.

sandier, **sandiest** and **sandiness** see under SAND

sand lizard ▷ *noun* a brown or green lizard with small dark rings and two pale lines along its back, found in heathland and sandy regions.

S and M ▷ *abbreviation* sadism and masochism; sado-masochism.

the sandman ▷ *noun, folklore* a man who supposedly sprinkles magical sand into children's eyes at bedtime to make them sleepy.

sand martin ▷ *noun* a small bird of the martin family that nests in colonies of burrows which are excavated in sand banks.

sandpaper ▷ *noun* abrasive paper with a coating originally of sand, now usually of crushed glass, glued to one side, used for smoothing and polishing surfaces. ▷ *verb* to smooth or polish with sandpaper.

sandpiper ▷ *noun* any of various ground-dwelling wading birds inhabiting shores in the N Hemisphere, with long legs and bills, camouflaged plumage, and a high-pitched piping call.

sandpit ▷ *noun* **1** a shallow pit filled with sand for children to play in. **2** a pit from which sand is dug.

sandshoe ▷ *noun* a shoe with a canvas upper and rubber sole; a plimsoll.

sandstone ▷ *noun, geol* a hard or soft sedimentary rock consisting of compacted sand cemented together with clay, silica, etc, widely used in the construction of buildings.

sandstorm ▷ *noun* a strong wind that sweeps clouds of sand through the air.

sandtrap ▷ *noun, golf* a bunker.

sandwich /'sandwɪdʒ, -wɪtʃ/ ▷ *noun* (***sandwiches***) **1** a snack consisting of two slices of bread or a roll with a filling of cheese, meat, etc. **2** anything with a similar arrangement or layout. ▷ *verb* (***sandwiches***, ***sandwiched***, ***sandwiching***) to place, especially with little or no gaps, between two layers. ⓒ 18c: named after John Montagu, the 4th Earl of Sandwich (1718–92), who ate such a snack so that he could remain at the gaming-table.

sandwich board ▷ *noun* either of two advertising boards carried by means of straps over the shoulders of their carrier, the **sandwich man**, so that one lies against the chest, the other against the back.

sandwich course ▷ *noun* an educational course involving alternate periods of academic study and work experience.

sandy /'sandɪ/ ▷ *adj* (***sandier***, ***sandiest***) **1** covered with or containing sand. **2** having the colour of sand, a light brownish-yellow colour □ *She has sandy hair.* • **sandiness** *noun*.

sand yacht and **land yacht** ▷ *noun* a boat fitted with wheels and a sail for running on land, usually on beaches. • **sand-yachting** *noun*.

sane ▷ *adj* **1** sound in mind; not mentally impaired. **2** sensible or rational; sound in judgement. • **sanely** *adverb*. • **saneness** *noun*. See also SANITY. ⓒ 17c: from Latin *sanus* healthy.

sang *past tense, past participle of* SING

sangfroid /sɒŋ'frwɑː/ ▷ *noun* calmness or composure; cool-headedness. ⓒ 18c: French, meaning 'cold blood'.

Sangraal, **Sangrail** or **Sangreal** /saŋ'greɪl, 'saŋ-/ ▷ *noun* the HOLY GRAIL. ⓒ 15c: from French *Saint Graal*.

sangria /saŋ'griːə/ ▷ *noun* a Spanish drink of red wine, fruit juice, sugar and spices. ⓒ 1960s: Spanish, meaning 'a bleeding'.

sanguinary /'saŋgwɪnərɪ/ ▷ *adj* **1** bloody; involving much bloodshed. **2** bloodthirsty; take pleasure in bloodshed. • **sanguinarily** *adverb*. • **sanguinariness** *noun*. ⓒ 17c: from Latin *sanguinarius*, from *sanguis* blood.

sanguine /'saŋgwɪn/ ▷ *adj* **1** cheerful, confident and full of hope. **2** said of a complexion: ruddy or flushed. ▷ *noun* **1** a blood-red colour. **2** a red chalk containing iron oxide, used for drawing. • **sanguinely** *adverb*. • **sanguineness** *noun*. ⓒ 14c: from Latin *sanguineus*, from *sanguis* blood.

sanguineous /saŋ'gwɪnɪəs/ ▷ *adj* **1** referring or relating to blood. **2** containing blood. **3** blood-red. ⓒ 17c: from Latin *sanguineus*, from *sanguis* blood.

Sanhedrim /san'hɛdrɪm, sanədrɪm, -'hiːdrɪm/ and **Sanhedrin** /-drɪn/ ▷ *noun, historical* a Jewish council or court, especially the supreme council and court in Jerusalem. ⓒ 16c: Hebrew, from Greek *synedrion*, from *syn* together + *hedra* a seat.

sanies /'seɪnɪiːz/ ▷ *noun, pathol* a watery discharge from wounds and sores, containing serum, blood, and pus. • **sanious** *adj*. ⓒ 16c: Latin.

sanitarian /sanɪ'tɛərɪən/ ▷ *noun* someone who favours or studies sanitary measures. ⓒ 19c.

sanitarium /sanɪ'tɛərɪəm/ ▷ *noun* (***sanitariums*** or ***sanitaria*** /-rɪə/) *especially US* a sanatorium.

sanitary /'sanɪtərɪ/ ▷ *adj* **1** concerned with and promoting hygiene, good health and the prevention of disease. **2** relating to health, especially drainage and sewage disposal. • **sanitarily** *adverb*. ⓒ 19c: from French *sanitaire*, from Latin *sanitarius*, from *sanitas* health.

sanitary engineering ▷ *noun* the branch of civil engineering concerned with the provision of a pure water supply, the disposal of waste, and conditions of public health.

sanitary inspector ▷ *noun, formerly* a person responsible for ensuring that standards of hygiene are adhered to, both in domestic and commercial environments. See also ENVIRONMENTAL HEALTH OFFICER, PUBLIC HEALTH INSPECTOR.

sanitary towel and (*US*) **sanitary napkin** ▷ *noun* an absorbent pad worn during menstruation.

sanitation /sanɪ'teɪʃən/ ▷ *noun* **1** standards of public hygiene. **2** measures taken to promote and preserve public health, especially through drainage and sewage disposal. • **sanitationist** *noun*. ⓒ 19c.

sanitize or **sanitise** /'sanɪtaɪz/ ▷ *verb* (***sanitized***, ***sanitizing***) **1** to make hygienic or sanitary. **2** to make less controversial or more acceptable by removing potentially offensive elements, aspects, connotations, etc. • **sanitization** *noun*. ⓒ 19c.

sanity /'sanɪtɪ/ ▻ *noun* **1** soundness of mind; rationality. **2** good sense and reason. ⓘ 15c: from Latin *sanitas* health, from *sanus* healthy.

sank *past tense, past participle of* SINK

sanpan see SAMPAN

sans /sanz; *French* sɑ̃/ ▻ *prep* without.

sansculotte /sanzkjʊ'lɒt, sanzkʊ'lɒt; *French* sɑ̃kylɔt/ ▻ *noun* **1** during the French Revolution: a nickname given to the democrats of the poorer classes. **2** a name used for any strong republican, democrat or revolutionary. • **sansculottism** *noun*. • **sansculottist** *noun*. ⓘ 18c: SANS + French *culotte* knee-breeches, so-called because the democrats in the French Revolution wore long trousers instead of knee-breeches.

sanserif or **sans serif** /san'sɛrɪf/ ▻ *noun, printing* a type in which the letters have no serifs. Also *as adj* □ ***sanserif type***. ⓘ 19c.

Sanskrit /'sanskrɪt/ ▻ *noun* the ancient Indo-European religious and literary language of India. ▻ *adj* relating to or expressed in this language. • **Sanskritic** *adj*. • **Sanskritist** *noun*. ⓘ 17c: from Sanskrit *samskrta* perfected.

Santa Claus /'santə klɔːz/ and **Santa** ▻ *noun* in folklore: a plump, white-bearded, jolly old man dressed in red who traditionally brings children presents on Christmas Eve or St Nicholas's Day, travelling on a sleigh which flies through the sky drawn by reindeers. Also called **Father Christmas**. ⓘ 18c: from Dutch dialect *Sante Klaas* St Nicholas; the original custom was for someone to dress as a bishop, ie as St Nicholas, and distribute presents to the good children on St Nicholas's Day (6 December).

santonica /san'tɒnɪkə/ ▻ *noun* the dried unopened flower-heads of a species of wormwood. ⓘ 17c: Latin.

santonin /'santənɪn/ ▻ *noun* a substance extracted from santonica, used as an anthelminthic. ⓘ 19c.

sap[1] ▻ *noun* **1** *bot* a vital liquid containing sugars and other nutrients that circulates in plants. **2** any liquid or fluid. **3** energy or vitality. **4** *slang* a weak or easily fooled person. ▻ *verb* (***sapped***, ***sapping***) **1** to drain or extract sap from something. **2** to weaken or exhaust; to drain energy from something. • **sappy** see separate entry. ⓘ Anglo-Saxon *sæp*.

sap[2] ▻ *noun* a hidden trench by which an attack is made on an enemy position. ▻ *verb* (***sapped***, ***sapping***) **1** *intr* to attack by means of a sap. **2** to undermine or weaken. ⓘ 16c: from French *sape*, from Italian *zappa* spadework.

sapele /sə'piːlɪ/ ▻ *noun* (***sapeles***) **1** a type of wood resembling mahogany, used to make furniture. **2** the tree that yields this wood. ⓘ Early 20c: W African.

sapid /'sapɪd/ ▻ *adj* **1** said of food: having a decided taste or flavour, usually pleasant. **2** pleasing or relishing; exhilarating. • **sapidity** *noun*. ⓘ 17c: from Latin *sapidus*, from *sapere* to taste.

sapience /'seɪpɪəns/ ▻ *noun* **1** discernment or judgement; sagacity. **2** *often ironic* wisdom. ⓘ 14c: from Latin *sapientia*, from *sapere* to be wise.

sapient /'seɪpɪənt/ ▻ *adj, formal, often ironic* having or showing good judgement; wise. • **sapiently** *adverb*. ⓘ 14c: from Latin *sapientia*, from *sapere* to be wise.

sapling /'saplɪŋ/ ▻ *noun* **1** a young tree. **2** a young, immature person. **3** a young greyhound.

sapodilla /sapə'dɪlə/ ▻ *noun* (***sapodillas***) **1** a large evergreen tree of tropical America. **2** its edible fruit. Also called **sapodilla plum**. **3** its durable wood. ⓘ 17c: from Spanish *zapotillo*, a diminutive of *zapote*, from Nahuatl *tzapotl*.

saponaceous /sapə'neɪʃəs/ ▻ *adj* soapy; similar to or containing soap. ⓘ 18c: from Latin *sapo* soap.

saponification ▻ *noun, chem* the hydrolysis of an ester by an alkali, a process which is used to convert fats into soap. ⓘ 19c: from Latin *sapo* soap.

saponify /sə'pɒnɪfaɪ/ ▻ *verb* (***saponifies***, ***saponified***, ***saponifying***) *chem* to carry out a process where the hydrolysis of an ester by an alkali converts fats into soap. • **saponification** *noun*. ⓘ 19c: from French *saponifier*, from Latin *saponificare*, from *sapo* soap.

saponin /'sapənɪn/ ▻ *noun* a glucoside extracted from plants, eg soapwort, which gives a soapy lather. ⓘ 19c: from French *saponine*, from Latin *sapo*, *saponis* soap.

sapor /'seɪpɔː(r)/ ▻ *noun, formal* taste; flavour. • **saporous** /'seɪpərəs/ *adj*. ⓘ 15c: Latin, from *sapere* to taste.

sapper /'sapə(r)/ ▻ *noun* **1** *Brit* a soldier, especially a private, in the Royal Engineers. **2** a soldier responsible for making saps (SAP[2]). ⓘ 17c.

Sapphic /'safɪk/ ▻ *adj* **1** *poetry* indicating the form of verses said to have been invented by Sappho, arranged in stanzas of four lines each, with a short fourth line. **2** referring or relating to Sappho. **3** lesbian. ▻ *noun* (*usually* **Sapphics** or **sapphics**) the form of verse invented by Sappho. • **Sapphism** *noun* (*also* **sapphism**) lesbianism. • **sapphist** *noun* a lesbian. ⓘ 16c: from Sappho (c.600 BC), the Greek poetess of the island of Lesbos, reputed to be a LESBIAN.

sapphire /'safaɪə(r)/ ▻ *noun* **1** any gem variety of the mineral corundum other than ruby, especially the hard transparent blue variety, prized as a gemstone, and also used in record player styluses, etc. **2** the deep blue colour of this stone. ▻ *adj* **1** made of sapphire. **2** having the colour of sapphire. ⓘ 13c: from Latin *sapphirus*, from Greek *sappheiros*, from Sanskrit *sanipriya* dear to the planet Saturn.

sappy /'sapɪ/ ▻ *adj* (***sappier***, ***sappiest***) **1** said of plants: full of sap. **2** full of energy. • **sappiness** *noun*.

sapro- /'saproʊ, sa'prɒ/ or (before a vowel) **sapr-** *combining form, signifying* rotten or decayed. ⓘ From Greek *sapros* rotten.

saprogenic /saproʊ'dʒɛnɪk/ and **saprogenous** /sa'prɒdʒənəs/ ▻ *adj, biol* **1** growing on decaying matter. **2** causing or caused by putrefaction or decay. ⓘ 19c: SAPRO- + -GENIC.

saprolite /'saproʊlaɪt/ ▻ *noun, geol* a soft earthy red or brown deposit formed by chemical weathering of igneous or metamorphic rock, especially in humid climates. ⓘ 19c: SAPRO- + Greek *lithos* stone.

saprophyte /'saproʊfaɪt, 'saprə-/ ▻ *noun, biol* a plant, especially a fungus, that feeds on dead and decaying organic matter. • **saprophytic** /-'fɪtɪk/ *adj*. ⓘ 19c: SAPRO- + Greek *phyton* plant.

saprozoic /saproʊ'zoʊɪk/ ▻ *adj, biol* said of organisms: feeding on dead or decaying organic matter. ⓘ Early 20c: SAPRO- + Greek *zoion* animal.

sapsucker ▻ *noun* a N American woodpecker which feeds on the sap of trees. ⓘ 18c.

sapwood ▻ *noun* the soft wood between the inner bark and the heartwood.

saraband or **sarabande** /'sarəband/ ▻ *noun* **1** a slow formal Spanish dance. **2** a piece of music written for this dance, where its rhythm is in 3-4 time with the second beat strongly accented. ⓘ 17c: from Spanish *zarabanda*.

Saracen /'sarəsən/ ▻ *noun* **1** in Roman times: a nomadic Syrian or Arab. **2** in later times: any Arab. **3** a Muslim defending the Holy Land from Christian crusaders. ▻ *adj* referring or relating to an Arab or Syrian from any of these times. • **Saracenic** /sarə'sɛnɪk/ *adj*. ⓘ Anglo-Saxon, from Latin *Saracenus*, from Greek *Sarakenos*.

sarcasm /'sɑːkazəm/ ▻ *noun* **1** an often ironical expression of scorn or contempt. **2** the use of such an expression. **3** its bitter, contemptuous quality. ◷ 16c: from Latin *sarcasmus*, from Greek *sarkasmos*, from *sarkazein* to tear the flesh.

sarcastic /sɑːˈkastɪk/ ▷ *adj* **1** containing sarcasm. **2** tending to use sarcasm. • **sarcastically** *adverb*. ◷ 17c.

sarcenet see SARSENET

sarco- /ˈsɑːkoʊ, sɑːˈkɒ/ ▷ *combining form, signifying* flesh. ◷ From Greek *sarx, sarkos* flesh.

sarcocarp /ˈsɑːkoʊkɑːp/ ▷ *noun, bot* the fleshy PERICARP of a stone fruit. ◷ 19c: SARCO- + Greek *karpos* fruit.

sarcoma /sɑːˈkoʊmə/ ▷ *noun* (***sarcomas*** or ***sarcomata*** /-mətə/) *pathol* a cancerous tumour arising in connective tissue. • **sarcomatous** *adj*. ◷ 17c: from Greek *sarkoma* fleshy growth, from *sarx* flesh.

sarcomatosis /sɑːkoʊməˈtoʊsɪs/ ▷ *noun, pathol* a condition characterized by the formation of sarcomas in several areas of the body. ◷ 19c.

sarcophagus /sɑːˈkɒfəgəs/ ▷ *noun* (***sarcophagi*** /-gaɪ, -dʒaɪ/ or ***sarcophaguses***) a stone coffin or tomb, especially one decorated with carvings. ◷ 17c: from Greek *sarkophagos* flesh-eating, from *sarx* flesh + *phagein* to eat, because the limestone which was used to make the coffins was believed to consume the flesh of the bodies.

sarcoplasm /ˈsɑːkoʊplazəm/ *anatomy* ▷ *noun* the cytoplasm separating the fibrils in muscle fibres. • **sarcoplasmic** /-ˈplazmɪk/ *adj*. ◷ 19c: SARCO- + Greek *plasma*, meaning 'a thing moulded', from *plassein* to mould.

sarcous /ˈsɑːkəs/ ▷ *adj* referring or relating to flesh or muscle. ◷ 19c: see SARCO-.

sard /sɑːd/ and **sardius** /ˈsɑːdɪəs/ ▷ *noun* a deep-red variety of CHALCEDONY. ◷ 14c: Latin, from Greek *sardion* a Sardian stone, from *Sardeis* Sardis, a city in Lydia.

sardine /sɑːˈdiːn/ ▷ *noun* (***sardines*** or ***sardine***) a young pilchard, an important food fish, commonly tinned in oil. • **packed like sardines** see under PACK. ◷ 15c: French, from Italian *sardina*, from Greek *sardinos*.

Sardinian /sɑːˈdɪnɪən/ ▷ *noun* **1** a native or inhabitant of Sardinia, a large island in the Mediterranean sea. **2** the Romance language spoken by the people of Sardinia. ▷ *adj* referring or relating to Sardinia or its people or language. ◷ 18c.

sardonic /sɑːˈdɒnɪk/ ▷ *adj* mocking or scornful; sneering. • **sardonically** *adverb*. ◷ 16c: from French *sardonique*, from Latin *sardonius*, from Greek *sardonion* a bitter-tasting plant from Sardinia which was said to screw up the face of the eater.

sardonyx /ˈsɑːdənɪks/ ▷ *noun, geol* a gem variety of CHALCEDONY with alternating straight parallel bands of colour, usually white and reddish-brown. ◷ 14c: Greek, from *Sardios* Sardian + *onyx* a nail.

sargasso /sɑːˈgasoʊ/ ▷ *noun* (***sargassos*** or ***sargassoes***) a brown seaweed with branching ribbon-like fronds that floats freely in huge masses, especially on the waters of the Sargasso Sea, a calm stretch of the N Atlantic ocean, near the West Indies. ◷ Early 20c: from Portuguese *sargaço*.

sarge /sɑːdʒ/ ▷ *noun, colloq* especially as a form of address: sergeant.

sari or **saree** /ˈsɑːrɪ/ ▷ *noun* (***saris*** or ***sarees***) a traditional garment of Hindu women, consisting of a single long piece of fabric wound round the waist and draped over one shoulder and sometimes the head. ◷ 16c: Hindi, from Sanskrit *sati*.

sarking /ˈsɑːkɪŋ/ ▷ *noun* a lining for a roof, usually made of wood or felt. ◷ Anglo-Saxon *serc*.

sarky /ˈsɑːkɪ/ ▷ *adj* (***sarkier, sarkiest***) *colloq* sarcastic.

Sarmatian /sɑːˈmeɪʃən/ ▷ *noun* **1** any of a nomadic tribe which used to inhabit Sarmatia. **2** the language that was spoken in Sarmatia. ▷ *adj* referring or relating to Sarmatia, historically a region which reached from the Vistula and Danube to the Volga and Caucasus rivers. • **Sarmatic** /sɑːˈmatɪk/ *adj*. ◷ 18c.

sarmentose /sɑːˈmɛntoʊs/ and **sarmentous** /sɑːˈmɛntəs/ ▷ *adj, bot* said of a plant: having runners. ◷ 18c: from Latin *sarmentum* a twig, from *sarpere* to prune.

sarnie /ˈsɑːnɪ/ ▷ *noun* (***sarnies***) *colloq* a sandwich. ◷ 1960s: shortened from 'sandwich'.

sarod /saˈroʊd/ ▷ *noun* an Indian stringed instrument similar to a cello, played with a bow or by plucking the strings. ◷ 19c: Hindi.

sarong /səˈrɒŋ/ ▷ *noun* **1** a Malay garment worn by both sexes, consisting of a long piece of fabric wrapped around the waist or chest. **2** the cloth, usually brightly coloured, used for making it. ◷ 19c: from Malay *sarung*, from Sanskrit *saranga* variegated.

saros /ˈsɛərɒs, ˈsɑːrɒs/ ▷ *noun* **1** *astron* a cycle of 6 585 days and 8 hours, or 18 years and 11 days, after which the relative positions of the Sun and Moon recur, so eclipses repeat their cycle. **2** a Babylonian cycle of 3 600 days. ◷ 17c: Greek, from Babylonian *sharu* 3 600.

sarrusophone /səˈrʌsəfoʊn/ ▷ *noun* a brass wind instrument, similar to an oboe. ◷ 19c: named after Sarrus, the French bandmaster who invented it.

sarsaparilla /sɑːspəˈrɪlə, sɑːsə-/ ▷ *noun* **1** any of various climbing or trailing tropical American plants with alternate leathery heart-shaped leaves, and greenish or yellowish flowers. **2** the long twisted aromatic root of this plant. **3** *US* a non-alcoholic drink flavoured with the dried root of this plant, used as a tonic. **4** a medicinal preparation derived from the dried root, used especially formerly to treat rheumatism and psoriasis. ◷ 16c: from Spanish *zarzaparrilla*, from *zarza* bramble + *parra* vine.

sarsenet or **sarcenet** /ˈsɑːsnɪt, ˈsɑːsnɛt/ ▷ *noun* a thin tissue of extremely fine silk. ▷ *adj* made of sarsenet. ◷ 15c: from Anglo-Norman *sarzinett*, from *Sarzin* Saracen.

sartorial /sɑːˈtɔːrɪəl/ ▷ *adj* **1** referring or relating to a tailor, tailoring or clothes in general □ *sartorial elegance*. **2** *anatomy* referring or relating to the sartorius. • **sartorially** *adverb*. ◷ 19c: from Latin *sartor* a patcher.

sartorius /sɑːˈtɔːrɪəs/ ▷ *noun* (***sartorii*** /-rɪaɪ/) *anatomy* a muscle in the thigh that crosses the leg, helping to flex the knee. ◷ 18c: from Latin *sartorius musculus* a tailor's muscle, so called because tailors customarily sat with crossed legs while working.

Sarum use /ˈsɛərəm —/ ▷ *noun* the medieval rites of Salisbury cathedral. ◷ 16c: from the ancient name of Salisbury.

SAS ▷ *abbreviation* Special Air Service.

sash¹ ▷ *noun* (***sashes***) a broad band of cloth, worn round the waist or over the shoulder, originally as part of a uniform. ▷ *verb* (***sashes, sashed, sashing***) to dress or adorn with a sash. ◷ 16c: from Arabic *shash* muslin.

sash² ▷ *noun* (***sashes***) a glazed frame, especially a sliding one, forming a SASH WINDOW. ▷ *verb* (***sashes, sashed, sashing***) to provide with sashes. ◷ 17c: from French *châssis* frame.

sashay /saˈʃeɪ/ ▷ *verb* (***sashays, sashayed, sashaying***) *intr* to walk or move in a gliding or ostentatious way. ▷ *noun* an excursion or trip. ◷ 19c: an alteration of French *chassé*.

sash cord ▷ *noun* a cord attaching a weight to the sash (SASH²) in order to balance it at any height.

sashimi /saˈʃiːmɪ/ ▷ *noun* a Japanese dish consisting of thinly sliced raw fish. ◷ 19c: from Japanese *sashi* pierce + *mi* flesh.

sash window ▷ *noun* a window consisting of two sashes (SASH²), one or either of which can slide vertically past the other.

Sask ▷ *abbreviation, Canadian province* Saskatchewan.

Saskatchewan /sas'katʃɪwən/ ▷ *noun* (abbreviation Sask) a W Canadian province.

sasquatch /'saskwatʃ, 'saskwɒtʃ/ ▷ *noun, folklore* a large hairy manlike creature believed by some to inhabit parts of N America and W Canada. ◷ 1920s: Salish (a Native American language).

sass *US colloq* ▷ *noun* impertinent talk or behaviour. ▷ *verb* (***sasses, sassed, sassing***) *intr* to speak or behave impertinently. • **sassy** *adj.* ◷ 19c.

sassaby /'sasəbɪ, sə'seɪbɪ/ ▷ *noun* (***sassabies***) a large S African antelope. ◷ 19c: from Tswana *tsessebe*.

sassafras /'sasəfras/ ▷ *noun* **1** any of various deciduous N American trees with oval aromatic leaves and long clusters of greenish-yellow flowers. **2** the aromatic dried bark obtained from the roots of this tree, which also yields a pungent oil (**sassafras oil**) that is used in tea, medicinal preparations, perfumes, and as a food flavouring. **3** an infusion of the bark. **4** a name extended to various plants with similar properties. ◷ 16c: from Spanish *sasafrás*.

Sassenach /'sasənax, -ak/ ▷ *noun, Scottish, usually derog* an English person; a Lowlander. ▷ *adj* English. ◷ 18c: from Gaelic *Sasunnach*, from Latin *Saxones* Saxons.

sat *past tense, past participle of* SIT

Sat. ▷ *abbreviation* Saturday.

Satan /'seɪtən/ ▷ *noun* the chief evil spirit, the adversary of God, and the tempter of human beings; the Devil; the chief fallen angel, Lucifer. ◷ Anglo-Saxon, from Hebrew, meaning 'enemy'.

satanic /sə'tanɪk/ and **satanical** ▷ *adj* **1** referring or relating to Satan. **2** evil; abominable. • **satanically** *adverb.* ◷ 17c.

Satanism /'seɪtənɪzəm/ ▷ *noun* (*also* **satanism**) **1** the worship of Satan. **2** a fiendish or devilish disposition. • **Satanist** *noun* a person who practises Satanism. Also *as adj.*

satay /'sateɪ/ ▷ *noun* **1** a Malaysian dish of marinated meat barbecued on skewers. **2** the spicy sauce served with this dish.

SATB ▷ *abbreviation* in choral music: soprano, alto, tenor, bass.

satchel /'satʃəl/ ▷ *noun* a small briefcase-like bag for schoolbooks, often leather, and usually with shoulder straps. • **satchelled** *adj.* ◷ 14c: from French *sachel* little bag, from Latin *saccellus*, a diminutive of *saccus* SACK[1].

sate /seɪt/ ▷ *verb* (***sated, sating***) to satisfy (a longing or appetite) to the full or to excess. • **sated** *adj.* • **satedness** *noun.* ◷ Anglo-Saxon *sadian*.

sateen /sa'tiːn/ ▷ *noun* a glossy cotton or woollen fabric, similar to satin. ◷ 19c: a variant of SATIN, modelled on VELVETEEN.

satellite /'satəlaɪt/ ▷ *noun* **1** (*in full* **natural satellite**) a celestial body that orbits a much larger celestial body, eg the Moon which orbits, and is a satellite of, the Earth. **2** (*in full* **artificial** or **earth satellite**) a man-made device that is launched into space by a rocket, etc, and is placed in orbit around a planet, especially the Earth, and used for communication, exploration and photography. **3** a smaller companion to anything. **4** a nation or state dependent, especially economically or politically, on a larger neighbour. **5** an obsequious follower; a hanger-on. • **satellitic** *adj.* ◷ 16c: from Latin *satelles* attendant.

satellite broadcasting, **satellite television** and **satellite TV** ▷ *noun, telecomm* the broadcasting of television by means of an artificial satellite.

satellite dish ▷ *noun* a saucer-shaped aerial for receiving television signals for programmes broadcast by means of an artificial satellite.

satellite town ▷ *noun* a small town built near a larger city to accommodate excess population.

sati /'sʌtiː/ see SUTTEE

satiable /'seɪʃəbəl, 'seɪʃɪəbəl/ ▷ *adj* able to be satisfied or satiated. • **satiability** *noun.*

satiate /'seɪʃɪeɪt/ ▷ *verb* (***satiated, satiating***) to gratify fully; to satisfy to excess. • **satiation** *noun* satisfaction. ◷ 15c: from Latin *satiare, satiatum*, from *satis* enough.

satiety /sə'taɪətɪ/ ▷ *noun* the state of being satiated; surfeit.

satin /'satɪn/ ▷ *noun* silk or rayon closely woven to produce a shiny finish, showing much of the warp. ▷ *adj* similar to or resembling satin. • **satiny** *adj.* ◷ 14c: from *Zaitun*, Arabic form of the former Chinese name of the town (probably Quanzhou) where it was originally produced or from which it was exported.

satinet or **satinette** /satɪ'nɛt/ ▷ *noun* **1** a thin satin. **2** a cloth with a cotton warp and a woollen weft. ◷ 18c: French, meaning 'small satin'.

satinwood ▷ *noun* **1** a shiny light-coloured ornamental hardwood from E India, used for fine furniture. **2** the tree that yields it.

satire /'sataɪə(r)/ ▷ *noun* **1** a literary composition, originally in verse, which holds up follies and vices for criticism, ridicule and scorn. **2** the use of instruments such as sarcasm, irony, wit and humour in such compositions. **3** satirical writing as a genre. ◷ 16c: from Latin *satira* mixture.

satirical /sə'tɪrɪkəl/ and **satiric** ▷ *adj* **1** relating to or containing satire. **2** characterized by satire. • **satirically** *adverb.*

satirist /'satɪrɪst/ ▷ *noun* **1** a writer or performer of satires. **2** a person who frequently uses satire.

satirize or **satirise** /'satɪraɪz/ ▷ *verb* (***satirized, satirizing***) **1** *intr* to write satire. **2** to mock, ridicule or criticize using satire. • **satirization** *noun* satirizing or being satirized. ◷ 17c.

satisfaction /satɪs'fakʃən/ ▷ *noun* **1** the act of satisfying, or the state or feeling of being satisfied. **2** something that satisfies. **3** gratification or comfort. **4** compensation for mistreatment. **5** the repayment of a debt; quittance. **6** the amendment of an honour, as by a duel. **7** *relig* atonement; the act of carrying out a penance. ◷ 14c.

satisfactory /satɪs'faktərɪ/ ▷ *adj* **1** adequate or acceptable. **2** giving satisfaction. **3** *relig* atoning; expiating one's sins. • **satisfactorily** *adverb.* • **satisfactoriness** *noun.* ◷ 16c.

satisfied /'satɪsfaɪd/ ▷ *adj* **1** pleased or contented. **2** said of a debt or bill: fully paid. **3** convinced or persuaded, eg in a debate or discussion.

satisfy /'satɪsfaɪ/ ▷ *verb* (***satisfies, satisfied, satisfying***) **1** *intr* to fulfil the needs, desires or expectations of someone. **2** to give enough to or be enough for someone or something. **3** to meet the requirements or fulfil the conditions of someone or something. **4** to pay in full. **5** to remove the doubts of someone; to convince them. **6** *intr* to please or gratify ▫ *Porridge is the only cereal that really satisfies.* **7** to amend. **8** to compensate or atone for something. **9** *intr* to make payment or atonement. • **satisfiable** *adj.* • **satisfying** *adj.* • **satisfyingly** *adverb.* ◷ 15c: from French *satisfier*, from Latin *satisfacere*, from *satis* enough + *facere* to make.

satori /sa'tɔːrɪ/ ▷ *noun* sudden enlightenment, sought in Zen Buddhism. ◷ 18c: Japanese, meaning 'awakening'.

satrap /'satrəp/ ▷ *noun* **1** a viceroy or governor of an ancient Persian province. **2** a provincial governor, especially if very powerful and ostentatiously rich. • **satrapal** *adj.* ◷ 14c: from Greek *satrapes*, from Persian *khshathrapavan* protector of the kingdom.

satrapy /'satrəpɪ/ ⊳ *noun* (***satrapies***) a satrap's province, office or period of office. ⓒ 17c.

Satsuma /sat'suːmə, 'satsʊmə/ ⊳ *noun* a former province in SW Japan, known for its **Satsuma ware**, a yellowish pottery with gilding and enamel, made from the end of the 16c.

satsuma /sat'suːmə/ ⊳ *noun* (***satsumas***) **1** a thin-skinned easily peeled seedless type of mandarin orange. **2** the tree that bears this fruit. ⓒ 19c: named after SATSUMA.

saturable /'satʃʊrəbəl/ ⊳ *adj, chem* able to be saturated. • **saturability** *noun*.

saturant /'satʃʊrənt/ ⊳ *adj* having a tendency to saturate. ⊳ *noun* a saturating substance; one that causes saturation.

saturate /'satʃʊreɪt/ ⊳ *verb* (***saturated***, ***saturating***) **1** to soak. **2** to fill or cover with a large amount of something. **3** to charge (air or vapour) with moisture to the fullest extent possible. **4** *chem* to add a solid, liquid or gas to (a solution) until no more of that substance can be dissolved at a given temperature. **5** *chem* to treat (an organic chemical compound) in such a way that it no longer contains any double or triple bonds. **6** *military* to cover (a target area) completely with bombs dropped simultaneously. ⊳ *adj* **1** saturated. **2** said of a colour: pure; deep. ⊳ *noun* a saturated compound. ⓒ 16c: from Latin *saturare*, *saturatum*, from *satur* full.

saturated ⊳ *adj* **1** *chem* said of a solution: containing as much of a solute as can be dissolved at a particular temperature and pressure. **2** *chem* said of a chemical, especially a fat: containing no carbon-carbon double bonds in the molecule and consequently not susceptible to addition reactions. **3** thoroughly wet or soaked.

saturated vapour pressure ⊳ *noun, physics* the pressure that is exerted by a vapour which is in equilibrium with the liquid form of the same substance.

saturation /satʃʊ'reɪʃən, satjʊ'reɪʃən/ ⊳ *noun* **1** the state of being saturated; saturating. **2** *chem* the point at which a solution contains the maximum possible amount of dissolved solid, liquid or gas at a given temperature. **3** *meteorol* the state of the atmosphere when fully saturated with water vapour at a given pressure. **4** *as adj* being of a great, or the greatest possible, intensity □ ***saturation bombing***. ⓒ 16c.

saturation point ⊳ *noun* **1** a limit beyond which no more can be added or accepted. **2** *chem* same as SATURATION 2.

Saturday /'satədɪ, 'satədeɪ/ ⊳ *noun* **1** the seventh day of the week, dedicated by the Romans to Saturn. **2** the Jewish SABBATH. ⓒ Anglo-Saxon *Sæterndæg* Saturn's day.

Saturn¹ /'satɜːn/ ⊳ *noun, Roman mythol* the ancient god of agriculture, commonly identified with the Greek Kronos. ⓒ Anglo-Saxon, from Latin *Saturnus*, from *satum*, past participle of *serere* to sow.

Saturn² /'satɜːn/ ⊳ *noun* **1** the planet: **a** *astron* the sixth planet from the Sun, with an orbit lying between those of Jupiter and Uranus, best known for its bright ring system called **Saturn's rings**; **b** *astrol* this planet, believed to induce a cold, melancholy and gloomy temperament, on account of its distance and slow orbit. **2** (*in full* **Saturn rocket**) any of a group of large US rockets used in the NASA Apollo programme. **3** *alchemy* the technical term for lead. ⓒ Anglo-Saxon.

Saturnalia /satə'neɪlɪə/ ⊳ *noun* (***Saturnalia*** or ***Saturnalias***) **1** *Roman history* the festival of the god Saturn in mid-December, a time of revelry and gift-giving when slaves were allowed temporary freedom. **2** (*often* **saturnalia**) a scene of rowdy celebration; a wild party or orgy. • **Saturnalian** *adj*. ⓒ 16c: Latin, from *Saturnalis* referring to SATURN¹.

Saturnian /sa'tɜːnɪən/ ⊳ *adj* **1** referring or relating to the god SATURN¹, especially in reference to his reign being called the golden age. **2** referring or relating to SATURN². ⊳ *noun* **1** someone born under the planet Saturn. **2** someone of saturnine temperament. ⓒ 17c.

saturnine /'satənaɪn/ ⊳ *noun* **1** having a grave and gloomy temperament; melancholy in character. **2** caused or poisoned by lead. • **saturnism** *noun* lead-poisoning. ⓒ 15c: especially with reference to SATURN² 1b.

satyagraha /'sʌtjəgrʌhə, sʌtjə'gruːhə/ ⊳ *noun* **1** Mahatma Gandhi's policy of non-violent and passive resistance to British rule in India. **2** any non-violent campaign for reform. • **satyagrahi** *noun* an exponent of this. ⓒ 1920s: Sanskrit, meaning 'reliance on truth', from *satya* truth + *agraha* persistence.

satyr /'satə(r)/ ⊳ *noun* **1** *Greek mythol* a lecherous woodland god, part man, part goat. **2** a lustful or lecherous man. • **satyric** or **satyrical** *adj*. ⓒ 14c: from Latin *satyrus*, from Greek *satyros*.

satyriasis /satɪ'raɪəsɪs/ ⊳ *noun* in men: overpowering sexual desire. Compare NYMPHOMANIA. ⓒ 17c: Greek, from SATYR + -IASIS.

satyrid /sə'tɪrɪd/ ⊳ *noun* any of several kinds of butterfly that have brownish wings marked with circles which resemble eyes. ⓒ Early 20c: from the genus name, *Satyridae*; see SATYR.

sauce /sɔːs/ ⊳ *noun* **1** any liquid, often thickened, cooked or served with food. **2** anything that adds relish, interest or excitement. **3** *colloq* impertinent language or behaviour; cheek. **4** *US* stewed fruit. ⊳ *verb* (***sauced***, ***saucing***) **1** to add sauce to (food). **2** to make interesting or pleasant. **3** *colloq* to be impertinent or cheeky to someone. ⓒ 14c: French, from Latin *salsa*, from *sal* salt.

sauce boat ⊳ *noun* **1** a long shallow jug for serving sauce. **2** *colloq* an attractive male.

saucepan ⊳ *noun* a deep cooking pot with a long handle and usually a lid. ⓒ 17c: so called as it was originally used only for making sauces.

saucer /'sɔːsə(r)/ ⊳ *noun* **1** a small shallow round dish, especially one for placing under a tea or coffee cup. **2** anything of a similar shape. ⓒ 14c: from French *saussiere*, from Latin *salsarium*, from *salsa* sauce.

saucerful ⊳ *noun* (***saucerfuls***) the amount a saucer will hold.

saucy /'sɔːsɪ/ ⊳ *adj* (***saucier***, ***sauciest***) *colloq* **1** similar to or tasting of sauce. **2** impertinent or cheeky; bold or forward. **3** referring to sex, especially in an amusing way □ ***saucy postcards***. **4** provocatively bold or audacious, especially arousing sexual desire. **5** said of clothes: smart. • **saucily** *adverb*. • **sauciness** *noun*. ⓒ 16c.

sauerkraut /'saʊəkraʊt/ ⊳ *noun* a popular German dish, consisting of shredded cabbage pickled in salt water. ⓒ 17c: German, literally 'sour cabbage'.

sauna /'sɔːnə, 'saʊnə/ ⊳ *noun* (***saunas***) **1** a Finnish-style bath where the person is exposed to dry heat, with occasional short blasts of steam created by pouring water on hot coals, usually followed by a cold plunge. **2** a building or room equipped for this. **3** a period spent in such a room. ⓒ 19c: Finnish.

saunter /'sɔːntə(r)/ ⊳ *verb* (***sauntered***, ***sauntering***) *intr* (*usually* **saunter along**, **past**, *etc*) to walk, often aimlessly, at a leisurely pace; to wander or stroll idly. ⊳ *noun* **1** a sauntering gait. **2** a leisurely walk or stroll; an amble. • **saunterer** *noun*. • **sauntering** *noun*. • **saunteringly** *adverb*. ⓒ 17c.

-saur /sɔː(r)/ and **-saurus** /'sɔːrəs/ ⊳ *combining form*, *denoting* an extinct reptile □ ***dinosaur*** □ ***brontosaurus***. ⓒ From Greek *sauros* lizard.

saurian /'sɔːrɪən/ *zool* ⊳ *noun* a lizard. ⊳ *adj* referring or relating to lizards; lizard-like. ⓒ 19c: from Greek *sauros* lizard.

saury /'sɔːrɪ/ ⊳ *noun* (***sauries***) a long sharp-nosed marine fish. Also called SKIPPER. ⓒ 18c: from Latin *saurus*, from Greek *sauros* lizard.

sausage /ˈsɒsɪdʒ/ ▷ *noun* **1** a mass of chopped or minced seasoned meat, especially pork or beef, sometimes mixed with fat, cereal, vegetables, etc, and stuffed into a tube of gut. **2** any object of a similar shape. • **not a sausage** *colloq* nothing at all. ◷ 15c: from French *saussiche*, from Latin *salsicia*, from *salsus* salted.

sausage dog ▷ *noun, colloq* a DACHSHUND.

sausage meat ▷ *noun* minced and seasoned meat of the kind used for making sausages.

sausage roll ▷ *noun, Brit* sausage meat baked in a roll (ROLL *noun* 3) of pastry.

sauté /ˈsoʊteɪ/ ▷ *verb* (***sautés, sautéed, sautéing*** or ***sautéeing***) to fry lightly for a short time. ▷ *noun* (***sautés***) a dish of sautéed food. ▷ *adj* fried in this way ▫ ***sauté potatoes***. ◷ 19c: French, meaning 'tossed', from *sauter* to jump.

savage /ˈsavɪdʒ/ ▷ *adj* **1** said of animals: untamed or undomesticated. **2** ferocious or furious ▫ ***He has a savage temper***. **3** said of eg behaviour: uncivilized; coarse. **4** cruel; barbaric. **5** said of land: uncultivated; wild and rugged. ▷ *noun* **1** *now offensive* a member of a primitive people. **2** an uncultured, fierce or cruel person. **3** a fierce or enraged animal. ▷ *verb* (***savaged, savaging***) to attack ferociously, especially with the teeth, causing severe injury. • **savagely** *adverb*. • **savageness** *noun*. ◷ 14c: from French *sauvage* wild, from Latin *silvaticus* of the woods, from *silva* a wood.

savagery /ˈsavɪdʒərɪ, -dʒrɪ/ ▷ *noun* (***savageries***) **1** cruelty, ferocity or barbarousness; an act of cruelty. **2** the state of being wild or uncivilized. ◷ 16c.

savanna or **savannah** /səˈvanə/ ▷ *noun* (***savannas*** or ***savannahs***) an expanse of level grassland, either treeless or dotted with trees and bushes, characteristic especially of tropical and subtropical Africa. ◷ 16c: from Spanish *zavana* (now *sabana*).

savant /ˈsavənt or *French* ˈsavɑ̃/ and **savante** /ˈsavənt or *French* savɑ̃t/ ▷ *noun* a wise and learned man or woman respectively. ◷ 18c: French, from *savoir* to know.

savate /sɑːˈvɑːt/ ▷ *noun* a form of boxing in which the feet as well as the fists are used. ◷ 19c: French, meaning 'old shoe'.

save ▷ *verb* (***saved, saving***) **1** to rescue, protect or preserve someone or something from danger, evil, loss or failure. **2** to use economically so as to prevent or avoid waste or loss. **3** *intr* to be economical, especially with money ▫ ***We're saving for the future.*** **4** to reserve or store for later use. **5** to spare from potential unpleasantness or inconvenience ▫ ***Doing a dissertation saves you having to do two exams*** ▫ ***That will save you having to make another trip.*** **6** to obviate or prevent. **7** *sport* to prevent (a ball or shot) from reaching the goal; to prevent (a goal) from being scored by the opposing team. **8** *tr & intr, relig* to deliver from the influence or consequences of sin; to act as a saviour ▫ ***Jesus saves.*** **9** *computing* to transfer (data, the contents of a computer file, etc) onto a disk or tape for storage. ▷ *noun* **1** an act of saving a ball or shot, or of preventing a goal ▫ ***He made a great save in that match.*** **2** *computing* the saving of data onto a disk or tape. ▷ *prep* (*sometimes* **save for**) except ▫ ***Save for one, John lost all the books*** ▫ ***We found all the tickets save one.*** ▷ *conj, old use* (*often* **save that**) were it not that; unless ▫ ***I would have gone with her, save that she had already left.*** • **savable** *adj*. • **saver** *noun*. • **saved by the bell** *often exclamation* rescued or saved from a difficult or unpleasant situation by a welcome interruption. ◷ from the bell which indicates the end of a round in a boxing match. • **save one's** or **someone's bacon** to enable oneself or them to escape or come off unscathed from a difficult situation. • **save one's** or **someone's face** to prevent oneself or them from appearing foolish or wrong; to avoid humiliation. • **save one's** or **someone's skin** or **neck** to save one's or their life ▫ ***You really saved my skin when you snared the tiger.*** • **save** or **keep something for a rainy day** see under RAINY. • **save the day** to prevent something from disaster, failure, etc ▫ ***Colin saved the day by remembering to bring the map of the maze with him.*** ◷ 13c: from French *sauver*, from Latin *salvare*, from *salvus* safe.

■ **save up** to set money aside for future use ▫ ***We're saving up for a holiday abroad next year.***

save as you earn ▷ *noun* (abbreviation **SAYE**) *Brit* a government-operated savings scheme in which regular deductions are made from one's earnings.

saveloy /ˈsavəlɔɪ/ ▷ *noun* (***saveloys***) a spicy smoked pork sausage, originally made from brains. ◷ 19c: from French *cervelat*, from Latin *cerebellum*, a diminutive of *cerebrum* the brain.

savin or **savine** /ˈsavɪn/ ▷ *noun* **1** a species of juniper with small leaves, native to Europe and Asia. **2** the irritant volatile oil extracted from the tops of this plant, originally used in drugs. ◷ Anglo-Saxon, from French *sabine*.

saving /ˈseɪvɪŋ/ ▷ *verb, present participle of* SAVE. ▷ *adj* **1** protecting or preserving. **2** economical or frugal. **3** *theol* protecting from sin; redeeming or securing salvation, as in SAVING GRACE. **4** *especially law* making an exception or reservation ▫ ***saving clause***. ▷ *noun* **1** something saved, especially an economy made ▫ ***We made a huge saving by buying in the January sales***. **2** anything saved. **3** (**savings**) money set aside for future use. • **savingly** *adverb*. ◷ 13c.

saving grace ▷ *noun* **1** a desirable virtue or feature that compensates for undesirable ones. **2** a divine grace that leads to salvation and redemption.

savings bank ▷ *noun* a bank established to encourage economy and thrift by taking small deposits and giving compound interest.

saviour /ˈseɪvjə(r)/ ▷ *noun* **1** a person who saves someone or something else from danger or destruction. **2** a person who saves others from sin or evil. **3** (**the Saviour**) *Christianity* a name for Christ. ◷ 14c: from French *sauveour*, from Latin *salvator*, from *salvare* to save.

savoir-faire /savwɑːˈfɛə(r)/ ▷ *noun* **1** instinctively knowing exactly what to do and how to do it; expertise. **2** tact or diplomacy. ◷ 19c: French, literally 'to know what to do'.

savory /ˈseɪvərɪ/ ▷ *noun* (***savories***) *bot* **1** any of various species of plant with square stems, OPPOSITE paired narrow leaves and loose spikes of two-lipped purplish or white flowers. **2** the leaves of certain species of this plant, used as a culinary herb. ◷ Anglo-Saxon *soetherie*, from Latin *satureia*.

savour or (*US*) **savor** /ˈseɪvə(r)/ *noun* **1** the characteristic taste or smell of something. **2** a faint but unmistakable quality. **3** a hint or trace. **4** relish or enjoyment. ▷ *verb* (***savoured, savouring***) **1** to taste or smell with relish. **2** to take pleasure in something. **3** to flavour or season. **4** to relish. **5** (*chiefly* **savour of something**) to show signs of it; to smack of it. • **savourless** *adj*. ◷ 13c: from French *savour*, from Latin *sapor*, from *sapere* to taste.

savoury or (*US*) **savory** /ˈseɪvərɪ/ *adj* **1** having a salty, sharp or piquant taste or smell; not sweet ▫ ***a savoury snack***. **2** having a good savour or relish; appetizing. **3** pleasant or attractive, especially morally pleasing or respectable ▫ ***He isn't a very savoury character***. ▷ *noun* (***savouries***) a savoury course or snack, especially served as an hors d'oeuvre. • **savoured** *adj*. • **savourily** *adverb*. • **savouriness** *noun*. ◷ 14c: from French *savure*, from *savourer*, from Latin *sapere* to taste.

savoy /səˈvɔɪ/ ▷ *noun* (***savoys***) (*in full* **savoy cabbage**) a winter variety of cabbage which has a large compact head and wrinkled leaves. ◷ 16c: from French *Savoie*, the region of SE France where it was originally grown.

Savoyard /ˈsavɔɪɑːd/ ▷ *noun* **1** a native or inhabitant of Savoy, the region in SE France. **2** a performer in or enthusiast of the Gilbert and Sullivan operas produced in the **Savoy Theatre**. ▷ *adj* referring or relating to Savoy or its inhabitants. ⓒ 18c: from French *Savoie*.

savvy /'savɪ/ *slang* ▷ *verb* (***savvies, savvied, savvying***) *tr & intr* to know or understand. ▷ *noun* **1** general ability or common sense; shrewdness. **2** skill; know-how. ▷ *adj* (***savvier, savviest***) knowledgeable or shrewd. ⓒ 18c: from Spanish *saber* to know, from Latin *sapere* to be wise.

saw[1] *past tense of* SEE[1]

saw[2] /sɔː/ ▷ *noun* any of various toothed cutting tools, either hand-operated or power-driven, used especially for cutting wood. ▷ *verb* (*past tense* ***sawed***, *past participle* ***sawn*** /sɔːn/ or ***sawed, sawing***) **1** to cut with, or as if with, a saw. **2** to shape by sawing. **3** *intr* to use a saw. **4** *intr* to make to-and-fro movements, as if using a hand-operated saw. ⓒ Anglo-Saxon *sagu*.

sawbones ▷ *noun* (***sawbones*** or ***sawboneses***) *slang* a surgeon.

sawdust ▷ *noun* dust or small particles of wood, made by sawing.

sawfish ▷ *noun* (***sawfish*** or ***sawfishes***) any of various large cartilaginous fishes, native to tropical and subtropical seas, with a long flattened sawlike snout bearing a row of sharp teeth on each side.

sawfly ▷ *noun* a wasplike insect characterized by its lack of a constricted waist, which uses its large egg-laying tube to deposit eggs deep within plant tissues.

sawhorse ▷ *noun* a trestle for supporting wood that is being sawn.

sawmill ▷ *noun* a factory in which timber is cut into planks.

sawn *past participle of* SAW

sawn-off and (*especially US*) **sawed off** ▷ *adj* **1** shortened by cutting with a saw □ *sawn-off shotgun.* **2** *colloq* short in height or stature.

sawn-off shotgun ▷ *noun* a shotgun with the end of the barrel cut off, making it easier to carry concealed.

saw set ▷ *noun* a device used for turning the saw teeth to the right and left.

sawyer /'sɔːjə(r)/ ▷ *noun* a person who saws timber, especially in a sawmill.

sax /saks/ ▷ *noun* (***saxes***) *colloq* short for SAXOPHONE.

Saxe blue, **Saxon blue** and **Saxony blue** ▷ *noun* a pale blue colour with a greyish tinge.

saxhorn /'saksho:n/ ▷ *noun* a valved brass instrument, similar to a small tuba, with a long winding tube and a bell opening, which is made in seven sizes. ⓒ 19c: named after Adolphe Sax (1814–94), the Belgian instrument maker who invented it.

saxicolous /sak'sɪkələs/ and **saxicoline** /-laɪn/ ▷ *adj, bot, zool* living or growing among rocks. ⓒ 19c: from Latin *saxicola*, from *saxum* rock + *colere* to inhabit.

saxifrage /'saksɪfreɪdʒ, -frɪdʒ/ ▷ *noun* any of numerous low-growing mainly alpine plants, often forming cushions or mats, with a basal rosette of fleshy leaves and small white, yellow, pink, red or purple flowers. • **saxifragaceous** /saksɪfrə'geɪʃəs/ *adj.* ⓒ 15c: from Latin *saxifraga* rock-breaker, from *saxum* rock + *frangere* to break.

Saxon /'saksən/ ▷ *noun* **1** a member of a Germanic people which invaded and conquered Britain in 5c and 6c. **2** any of various Germanic dialects spoken by this people. **3** a native, inhabitant or citizen of the region of **Saxony** in modern Germany. ▷ *adj* referring or relating to the Saxons, the ANGLO-SAXONS, their language, culture or architecture. ⓒ 13c: from Latin *Saxones*.

Saxon blue and **Saxony blue** see SAXE BLUE

saxophone /'saksəfoun/ ▷ *noun* a single-reeded wind instrument with a long S-shaped metal body, usually played in jazz and dance bands. Often shortened to SAX. • **saxophonist** /sak'sɒfənɪst/ *noun* someone who plays the saxophone. ⓒ 19c: named after Adolphe Sax (1814–94), the Belgian instrument maker who invented it.

say ▷ *verb* (***says*** /sɛz/, ***said*** /sɛd/ , ***saying***) **1** to speak, utter or articulate □ *He said he would come.* **2** to express in words □ *Say what you mean.* **3** to assert or declare; to state as an opinion □ *I say we should give it a try.* **4** to suppose □ *Say he doesn't come, what do we do then?* **5** to recite or repeat □ *say your prayers* □ *say a blessing.* **6** to judge or decide □ *It's difficult to say which is best.* **7** to convey information; to communicate □ *She talked for ages but didn't actually say much* □ *What is the artist trying to say here?* **8** to indicate □ *The clock says 10 o'clock* □ *The forecast says it'll be sunny today.* **9** to report or claim □ *Elvis Presley is said by some to be still alive.* **10** *tr & intr* to make a statement; to tell □ *I'd rather not say.* ▷ *noun* **1** a chance to express an opinion □ *You've had your say.* **2** the right to an opinion; the power to influence a decision □ *to have no say in the matter* □ *She will have a lot of say in the decision.* ▷ *exclamation, N Amer, especially US* **1** an expression of surprise, protest or sudden joy. **2** a way of attracting attention. • **sayer** *noun.* • **I say!** *especially Brit* an exclamation used for attracting attention, or expressing surprise, protest or sudden joy. • **I'll say!** *colloq* an expression of wholehearted agreement. • **it goes without saying** it is obvious. • **it is said** or **they say** it is commonly reputed or believed □ *They say that he killed his wife* □ *It is said to be a fake.* • **it**, *etc* **says** *colloq* the text runs □ *The paper says that it will rain tomorrow.* • **not to say** indeed; one might even go further and say □ *Train fares are expensive, not to say extortionate.* • **nothing to say for oneself 1** unable to defend oneself or to justify one's actions. **2** only engaging in small talk. • **say the word** give the signal or go-ahead □ *If you want me to go to the doctor with you, just say the word.* • **says you!** *colloq* expressing incredulity or disbelief. • **that is to say** in other words. • **there's no saying** it is impossible to guess or judge □ *There's no saying how long she'll take to recover.* • **to say nothing of something** not to mention it □ *He wastes all his money on alcohol, to say nothing of all those cigarettes.* • **to say the least** at least; without exaggeration □ *She is, to say the least, a rather irresponsible person.* • **what do you say to?** would you like? how about? □ *What do you say to a mug of hot chocolate?* • **You can say that again!** *colloq* You are absolutely right! I agree wholeheartedly! □ *'He is such a scandalmonger!' 'You can say that again!'* ⓒ Anglo-Saxon *secgan*.

■ **say for** or **against something** to argue in favour of or against it □ *There's a lot to be said for doing it yourself.*

SAYE ▷ *abbreviation* Save As You Earn.

saying /'seɪɪŋ/ ▷ *noun* **1** a proverb or maxim. **2** an expression □ *Family sayings can be meaningless to outsiders.* ⓒ 13c.

say-so ▷ *noun* **1** the right to make a final or authorized decision. **2** an authorized decision. **3** an unsupported claim or assertion.

sayyid or **sayid** or **said** /'saɪjɪd, 'seɪjɪd, 'sɑːɪd, 'seɪɪd/ ▷ *noun* **1** a descendant of Muhammad's daughter, Fatima. **2** an honorary title given to some Muslims. ⓒ 18c: Arabic, meaning 'lord'.

Sazerac /'sazərak/ ▷ *noun, trademark, US* a cocktail made from Pernod and whisky. ⓒ 1940s.

Sb ▷ *abbreviation, chem* antimony. ⓒ From Latin *stibium*.

SBN ▷ *abbreviation* Standard Book Number. Compare ISBN.

SC ▷ *abbreviation* **1** *Austral, NZ* School Certificate. **2** Signal Corps. **3** *US state* South Carolina.

Sc ▷ *abbreviation, chem* scandium.

sc ▷ *abbreviation, printing* small capitals.

sc. ▷ *abbreviation* **1** *scilicet* (Latin), namely. **2** *sculpsit* (Latin), he or she sculptured (this work).

scab ▷ *noun* **1** a crust of dried blood formed over a healing wound. **2** a contagious skin disease of sheep caused especially by mites, characterized by pustules or scales. **3** a plant disease caused by a fungus, producing crusty spots. **4** *derog, slang* a worker who defies a union's instruction to strike. Also called BLACKLEG. **5** *derog* a scoundrel; a contemptible person. ▷ *verb* (***scabbed, scabbing***) *intr* **1** (*also* **scab over**) to become covered by a scab. **2** *slang* to work or behave as a scab. ⓘ Anglo-Saxon *sceabb*.

scabbard /ˈskabəd/ ▷ *noun* a sheath, especially for a sword or dagger. ⓘ 13c: as *scauberc*, from French *escaubers*.

scabby /ˈskabɪ/ ▷ *adj* (***scabbier, scabbiest***) **1** covered with scabs. **2** *derog, colloq* contemptible; worthless. • **scabbiness** *noun*.

scabies /ˈskeɪbiːz/ ▷ *noun, pathol* a contagious skin disease characterized by severe itching, caused by a secretion of the itch mite, which bores under the skin to lay its eggs. ⓘ 15c: Latin, from *scabere* to scratch.

scabious /ˈskeɪbɪəs/ ▷ *noun* any of various annual or perennial plants with pinnately lobed leaves and flat heads of small bluish-lilac flowers. ⓘ 14c: from Latin *scabiosa herba* scabies plant, from *scabies* the itch, which the plant was used to treat.

scabrous /ˈskeɪbrəs/ ▷ *adj* **1** said of skin, etc: rough and flaky or scaly; scurfy. **2** bawdy; smutty or indecent. **3** beset with difficulties. • **scabrously** *adverb*. • **scabrousness** *noun*. ⓘ 17c: from Latin *scabrosus*, from *scaber* rough.

scad ▷ *noun* (***scad*** or ***scads***) a fish with an armoured and keeled lateral line, related to the mackerel. ⓘ 17c: Cornish dialect.

scaffie /ˈskafɪ/ ▷ *noun, Scots colloq* **1** a refuse collector. **2** a person who sweeps streets. ⓘ Late 19c: short for SCAVENGER.

scaffold /ˈskafould/ ▷ *noun* **1** a temporary framework of metal poles and planks used as a platform from which building repairs or construction can be carried out. **2** any temporary platform. **3** a raised platform for eg performers or spectators. **4** (**the scaffold**) **a** a temporary platform on which a person is executed; **b** hanging as a method of execution. ▷ *verb* (***scaffolded, scaffolding***) to supply with a scaffold. • **scaffolder** *noun*. ⓘ 14c: from French *escadafault*.

scaffolding /ˈskafəldɪŋ/ ▷ *noun* **1** a temporary scaffold or arrangement of scaffolds. **2** materials used for building scaffolds. ⓘ 14c.

scag or **skag** ▷ *noun, slang* heroin.

scalable /ˈskeɪləbəl/ ▷ *adj* able to be climbed or scaled. • **scalableness** *noun*. • **scalably** *adverb*. ⓘ 16c: from SCALE[1].

scalar /ˈskeɪlə(r)/ *math* ▷ *adj* denoting a quantity that has magnitude but not direction, such as distance, speed and mass. ▷ *noun* a scalar quantity. Compare VECTOR. ⓘ 17c: from Latin *scalaris*, from *scala* ladder.

scalawag see SCALLYWAG

scald /skɔːld/ ▷ *verb* (***scalded, scalding***) **1** to injure with hot liquid or steam. **2** to treat with hot water so as to sterilize. **3** to cook or heat to just short of boiling point. ▷ *noun* an injury caused by scalding. • **scalder** *noun*. • **scalding** *noun, adj*. ⓘ 13c: from French *escalder*, from Latin *excaldare* to bathe in warm water, from *ex* from + *calidus* hot.

scaldfish ▷ *noun* (***scaldfish*** or ***scaldfishes***) a small European flatfish with large scales. ⓘ 19c: from *scald*, meaning 'scabby', because the fish's scales are easily rubbed off, giving the fish a rather scabby appearance.

scale[1] ▷ *noun* **1** a series of markings or divisions at regular intervals, for use in measuring. **2** a system of such markings or divisions. **3** a measuring device with such markings. **4** the relationship between actual size and the size as represented on a model or drawing. **5** *music* **a** a sequence of definite notes; **b** (*usually* **scales**) a succession of these notes performed in ascending or descending order of pitch through one or more octaves. **6** *music* the range of a voice or instrument. **7** any graded system, eg of employees' salaries. **8** *math* a numeral system □ *logarithmic scale*. **9** extent or level relative to others □ *on a grand scale*. Also *as adj* □ *scale model*. ▷ *verb* (***scaled, scaling***) **1** to climb. **2** (*also* **scale up** and **scale down**) to change the size of something according to scale, making it either bigger or smaller than the original. • **on a large, small,** *etc* **scale** in a great, small, etc way. • **on the** or **a scale of 1** in the ratio of □ *on a scale of one to ten*. **2** (**on a scale of**) measuring between □ *How would you rate his performance on a scale of one to ten?* • **to scale** in proportion to the actual dimensions. ⓘ 15c: from Latin *scala* ladder, from *scandere* to mount.

scale[2] ▷ *noun* **1** any of the small thin plates that provide a protective covering on the skin of fish, reptiles and on the legs of birds. **2** *bot* a reduced leaf or leaf-base, often membranous or hard and woody. **3** any readily or easily detached flake. **4** a thin plate or lamina. **5** an overlapping plate making up **scale armour**. **6** *biol* a small flat detachable flake of cuticle. **7** *biol* one of many small flat structures covering and protecting the wings of moths, butterflies, etc. **8** tartar on the teeth. **9** a crusty white deposit formed when hard water is heated, especially in kettles. **10** a film formed eg as on iron being heated for forging. ▷ *verb* (***scaled, scaling***) **1** to clear something of scales. **2** to remove in thin layers. **3** *intr* to come off in thin layers or flakes. **4** *intr* to become encrusted with scale. • **scaled** *adj*. • **scaleless** *adj*. • **scalelike** *adj*. ⓘ 14c: from French *escale* husk.

scale[3] ▷ *noun* **1** (**scales**) a device for weighing. **2** the pan, or either of the two pans, of a balance. **3** (**the Scales**) *astron, astrol* same as LIBRA. ▷ *verb* (***scaled, scaling***) to weigh or weigh up. • **tip the scales** see under TIP[4]. ⓘ 13c: from Norse *skal* pan of a balance.

scale board ▷ *noun* a very thin strip of wood.

scale insect ▷ *noun, biol* any of various small bugs that feed on the sap of plants, including several serious pests of crops, the adult female of which is usually covered by a protective scale-like waxy or horny covering.

scalene /ˈskeɪliːn/ ▷ *adj* **1** *geom* said of a triangle: having each side a different length. **2** *geom* said of a cone or cylinder: having its axis oblique to the base. **3** *anatomy* denoting any of the **scalenus** muscles, connecting the upper ribs to the cervical vertebrae. ⓘ 18c: from Greek *skalenos* uneven.

scaler /ˈskeɪlə(r)/ ▷ *noun* **1** a person who scales fish, boilers, etc. **2** a device used to remove scale, eg for removing tartar from teeth.

scalier, **scaliest** and **scaliness** see under SCALY

scaling-ladder ▷ *noun* **1** a ladder used for climbing high walls, formerly for accessing fortresses, etc. **2** a fireman's ladder.

scallawag see SCALLYWAG

scallion /ˈskalɪən/ ▷ *noun* any of various onions with a small bulb and long edible leaves, eg the spring onion. ⓘ 14c: from French *escalogne*, from Latin *Ascalonia (cepa)* Ascalon (onion), from Ascalon, a port in Palestine.

scallop /ˈskɒləp, ˈskaləp/ and **escallop** /ɪˈskaləp/ ▷ *noun* **1** any of numerous species of marine bivalve molluscs with a strongly ribbed yellow, brown, pink or orange shell consisting of two valves with wavy edges that are almost circular in outline. **2** either of these shells, especially when served filled with food. **3** a shallow dish in which shellfish are cooked. **4** any of a series of curves forming a wavy edge, eg on fabric. **5** *cookery* an ESCALOPE.

6 *cookery* a potato slice fried in batter. **7** *historical* a scallop shell used as the badge of a pilgrim to the shrine of St James of Compostela. ▷ *verb* (***scalloped***, ***scalloping***) **1** to shape (an edge) into scallops or curves. **2** to bake in a scallop with a sauce and usually breadcrumbs. **3** *intr* to gather or search for scallops. • **scalloped** *adj* said eg of fabric: having the edge or border shaped into scallops or curves. ◷ 14c: from French *escalope*.

scallywag /ˈskalɪwag/ or **scalawag** /-əwag/ or **scallawag** /-əwag/ ▷ *noun, colloq* **1** a rascal or scamp; a good-for-nothing. **2** *old use* an undersized animal of little value. ◷ 19c.

scalp /skalp/ ▷ *noun* **1** the area of the head covered, or usually covered, by hair. **2** the skin itself on which the hair grows. **3** a piece of this skin with its hair, formerly taken from slain enemies as a trophy, especially by Native Americans. **4** *Scots dialect* a bare rock or mountain top. ▷ *verb* (***scalped***, ***scalping***) **1** to remove the scalp of someone or something. **2** *chiefly US colloq* to buy cheaply in order to resell quickly at a profit. **3** *colloq* to buy up eg theatre and travel tickets for resale at unofficial and inflated prices. • **scalper** *noun*. • **scalpless** *adj*. ◷ 14c: from Norse *skalpr* sheath.

scalpel /ˈskalpəl/ ▷ *noun* a small surgical knife with a thin blade. ◷ 18c: from Latin *scalpellum* small knife.

scaly /ˈskeɪlɪ/ ▷ *adj* (***scalier***, ***scaliest***) **1** covered with scales. **2** similar to or like scales. **3** peeling off in scales. • **scaliness** *noun*. ◷ 16c.

scam ▷ *noun, chiefly US slang* a trick or swindle.

scamp ▷ *noun* **1** a mischievous person, especially a child. **2** a rascal; an idler. • **scampish** *adj*. • **scampishly** *adverb*. • **scampishness** *noun*. ◷ 18c: from French *escamper* to decamp.

scamper /ˈskampə(r)/ ▷ *verb* (***scampered***, ***scampering***) *intr* to run or skip about briskly, especially in play. ▷ *noun* **1** an act of scampering. **2** a scampering movement or pace. ◷ 17c.

scampi /ˈskampɪ/ ▷ *plural noun* large prawns. ▷ *singular noun* a dish of these prawns, usually deep-fried in breadcrumbs. ◷ 1920s: from plural of Italian *scampo* shrimp.

scan ▷ *verb* (***scanned***, ***scanning***) **1** to read through or examine something carefully or critically. **2** to look or glance over something quickly. **3** to examine (all parts or components of something) in a systematic order. **4** to examine (the rhythm of a piece of verse); to analyse (verse) metrically. **5** to recite (verse) so as to bring out or emphasize the metrical structure. **6** *intr* said of verse: to conform to the rules of metre or rhythm. **7** *medicine* to examine (parts, especially internal organs, of the body) using techniques such as ultrasound. **8** in television: to pass a beam over (an area) so as to transmit its image. **9** to cast an eye negligently over something. **10** *engineering* to search or examine (an area) by means of radar or by sweeping a beam of light over it. **11** *computing* to examine (data) eg on a magnetic disk. ▷ *noun* **1** an act of scanning □ *brain scan.* **2** a scanning. **3** *medicine* an image obtained by scanning. ◷ 14c: from Latin *scandere* to climb.

scandal /ˈskandəl/ ▷ *noun* **1** widespread public outrage and loss of reputation. **2** any event or fact causing this. **3** any extremely objectionable fact, situation, person or thing. **4** malicious gossip or slander; a false imputation. • **scandalous** *adj* **1** giving or causing scandal or offence. **2** openly disgraceful, outrageous or defamatory. • **scandalously** *adverb*. ◷ 13c: from Latin *scandalum*, from Greek *skandalon* stumbling-block.

scandalize or **scandalise** /ˈskandəlaɪz/ ▷ *verb* (***scandalized***, ***scandalizing***) **1** to give or cause scandal or offence. **2** to shock or outrage. • **scandalization** *noun*. ◷ 15c.

scandalmonger ▷ *noun* someone who spreads or relishes malicious gossip.

Scandinavian /skandɪˈneɪvɪən/ ▷ *noun* **1** a citizen or inhabitant of, or a person born in, Scandinavia, the area of N Europe consisting of Norway, Sweden, Denmark, and often also including Finland and Iceland. **2** any of the group of N Germanic languages spoken in Scandinavia. ▷ *adj* belonging or relating to Scandinavia, its inhabitants or their languages. ◷ 18c.

scandium /ˈskandɪəm/ ▷ *noun, chem* (symbol **Sc**, atomic number 21) a soft silvery-white metallic element with a pinkish tinge, the oxide of which is used in ceramics and as a catalyst. ◷ 19c: named after Scandinavia, where it was discovered.

scanner /ˈskanə(r)/ ▷ *noun* **1** a person or device that scans or can scan. **2** *radar* the rotating aerial by which the beam is made to scan an area. **3** *computing* any device capable of recognizing characters, etc, in documents and generating signals corresponding to them, used especially to input text and graphics directly without the need for laborious keying. **4** *medicine* any device that produces an image of an internal organ or body part, eg in order to locate a tumour.

scanning electron microscope ▷ *noun, biol* (abbreviation **SEM**) an electron microscope that produces a three-dimensional image of an object, allowing the surface structure of a relatively thick specimen to be examined.

scansion /ˈskanʃən/ ▷ *noun* **1** the act or practice of scanning poetry. **2** the division of a verse into metrical feet. ◷ 17c: from Latin *scansio*.

scant ▷ *adj* **1** in short supply; deficient. **2** meagre or inadequate; scarcely sufficient. ▷ *adverb* barely; scantily. ▷ *verb* (***scanted***, ***scanting***) to limit, restrict or reduce something. • **scantly** *adverb*. • **scantness** *noun*. ◷ 14c: from Norse *skamt*.

scanty /ˈskantɪ/ ▷ *adj* (***scantier***, ***scantiest***) small or lacking in size or amount; barely enough □ *scanty clothing* □ *a scanty meal.* • **scantily** *adverb* in a scanty way; hardly or barely □ *scantily clad.* • **scantiness** *noun*. ◷ 17c.

-scape /skeɪp/ ▷ *suffix, indicating* a type of scene or view created by the specified thing □ *landscape* □ *soundscape* □ *officescape.*

scapegoat /ˈskeɪpgoʊt/ ▷ *noun* **1** someone made to take the blame or punishment for the errors and mistakes of others. **2** *Bible* a goat on which the Jewish high priest symbolically loaded the sins of the people, which was then released into the wilderness. ◷ 16c: from ESCAPE + GOAT, invented by William Tindale (1530), as a translation of the Hebrew *azazel*, incorrectly believed to mean 'the goat that escapes'.

scapegrace ▷ *noun* an incorrigible rogue or rascal. ◷ 19c: from ESCAPE + GRACE, meaning 'one who escapes God's grace'.

scaphoid /ˈskafɔɪd/ ▷ *adj* **1** shaped like a boat. **2** *anatomy* referring or relating to the SCAPHOID BONE. ◷ 18c: from Greek *skaphe* a boat + *eidos* form.

scaphoid bone /ˈskafɔɪd —/ ▷ *noun, anatomy* the NAVICULAR. ◷ 18c: from Greek *skaphe* a boat + *eidos* form.

scapula /ˈskapjʊlə/ ▷ *noun* (***scapulae*** /-liː/ or ***scapulas***) *anatomy* the broad flat triangular bone at the back of the shoulder. Also called **shoulder blade**. ◷ 16c: Latin.

scapular /ˈskapjʊlə(r)/ ▷ *adj, anatomy* relating to the scapula. ▷ *noun* **1** a monk's garment consisting of a broad strip of cloth with a hole for the head, hanging loosely over a habit in front and behind. **2** *RC Church* two small pieces of cloth joined by strings and worn over the shoulders by members of certain lay confraternities. **3** *ornithol* (*in full* **scapular feather**) a feather that grows from the shoulder. ◷ Anglo-Saxon, from Latin *scapulae* shoulder blades.

scapulary same as SCAPULAR (*noun*)

scar¹ ▷ *noun* **1** a mark left on the skin after a sore or wound has healed. **2** any permanent damaging emotional effect. **3** any mark or blemish. **4** a mark on a plant where a leaf was formerly attached. ▷ *verb* (***scarred, scarring***) *tr & intr* to mark or become marked with a scar. ◐ 14c: from French *escare*, from Greek *eschara* a burn or scab.

scar² or **scaur** /skɔː(r)/ ▷ *noun* a steep rocky outcrop or crag on the side of a hill or mountain; a cliff. ◐ 14c: from Norse *sker* low reef.

scarab /'skarəb/ ▷ *noun* **1** any of various dung beetles that are renowned for their habit of rolling and burying balls of dung, and which were regarded as sacred by the ancient Egyptians. **2** an image or carving of the sacred beetle, or a gemstone carved in its shape. ◐ 16c: from Latin *scarabaeus*.

scarabaeid /skarə'biːɪd/ ▷ *noun* any beetle of the large family which includes dung beetles. ▷ *adj* belonging or relating to this family. ◐ 19c: from Latin *scarabaeidae*.

scarce ▷ *adj* **1** not often found; rare. **2** in short supply. ▷ *adverb* scarcely; hardly ever □ ***We could scarce see it through the mist.*** • **scarceness** *noun*. • **make oneself scarce** *colloq* to leave quickly or stay away, often for reasons of prudence, tact, etc. ◐ 13c: from French *eschars* niggardly, from Latin *excerptus* past participle of *excerpere*, from *ex* out + *carpere* to pick.

scarcely /'skɛəslɪ/ ▷ *adverb* **1** only just. **2** hardly ever. **3** not really; not at all □ *That is scarcely a reason to hit him.* ◐ 14c.

scarcity /'skɛəsətɪ/ ▷ *noun* (***scarcities***) **1** a scarce state or fact. **2** a short supply or lack. ◐ 14c.

scare ▷ *verb* (***scared, scaring***) **1** *tr & intr* to make or become afraid □ *The cat scares her* □ *She scares easily.* **2** to startle. ▷ *noun* (***scares***) **1** a fright or panic. **2** a sudden, widespread and often unwarranted public alarm □ ***a bomb scare.*** • **scarer** *noun*. • **run scared** see under RUN. • **scare the daylights out of someone** or **scare the living daylights out of someone** or **scare the pants off someone** *colloq* to frighten them considerably or excessively. ◐ 12c: as *skerre*, from Norse *skirra* to avoid.

■ **scare someone** or **something away** or **off** to drive them away by frightening them.

scarecrow ▷ *noun* **1** a device, usually in the shape of a human figure, set up in fields to scare birds. **2** *colloq* a shabbily dressed person. **3** *colloq* a very thin person. ◐ 16c.

scaremonger ▷ *noun* an alarmist, or someone who causes panic or alarm by initiating or spreading rumours of disaster. • **scaremongering** *noun*. ◐ 19c.

scarf¹ ▷ *noun* (***scarves*** or ***scarfs***) **1** a strip or square of often patterned fabric, worn around the neck, shoulders or head for warmth or decoration. **2** a muffler. **3** a necktie or cravat. **4** a military or official sash. ◐ 16c: perhaps from French *escarpe* sash or sling.

scarf² ▷ *noun* **1** a joint made between two ends, especially of timber, cut so as to fit with overlapping, producing the effect of a continuous surface. **2** an end prepared for such a joint. **3** a longitudinal cut made in a whale's carcase. ▷ *verb* (***scarfed, scarfing***) **1** to join by means of a scarf-joint. **2** to make a scarf in something. ◐ 15c: from Norse *skarfr*.

scarier, **scariest**, *etc* see under SCARY

scarify /'skarɪfaɪ/ ▷ *verb* (***scarifies, scarified, scarifying***) **1** *chiefly surgery* to make a number of scratches, shallow cuts, or lacerations in (the skin, etc). **2** to break up the surface of soil with a wire rake, etc, without turning the soil over. **3** to hurt someone with severe criticism. • **scarification** *noun*. • **scarifier** *noun* an implement used for breaking up or loosening the surface of soil or of a road. ◐ 16c: from Latin *scarificare*, from Greek *skariphos* etching tool.

scarlatina /skɑːlə'tiːnə/ ▷ *noun, pathol* SCARLET FEVER. ◐ 19c: from Italian *scarlattina*, a diminutive of *scarlatto* scarlet.

scarlet /'skɑːlət/ ▷ *noun* **1** a brilliant red colour. **2** a brilliant red cloth or garment. ▷ *adj* **1** being scarlet in colour. **2** dressed in scarlet. ◐ 13c: from French *escarlate*, from Persian *saqalat* scarlet cloth.

scarlet fever ▷ *noun* an acute infectious childhood disease, caused by bacterial infection, and characterized by fever, sore throat, vomiting and a bright red skin rash.

scarlet letter ▷ *noun, historical* a scarlet-coloured letter 'A' worn by women convicted of adultery in the Puritan communities of New England.

scarlet pimpernel ▷ *noun* a plant of the primrose family, with small red, white or purple flowers that close when the weather is cloudy.

scarlet runner ▷ *noun* a scarlet-coloured climbing plant of the kidney bean genus, yielding edible beans.

scarlet woman ▷ *noun, derog* **1** a term applied to the Roman Catholic Church by some Protestant sects as an expression of their hostility (in allusion to Revelation 17). **2** a sexually promiscuous woman, especially a prostitute.

scarp ▷ *noun* **1** the steep side of a hill or rock; an escarpment. **2** *fortification* the inner side of a defensive ditch, situated nearest to the rampart. ▷ *verb* (***scarped, scarping***) to cut into a scarp or slope. ◐ 16c: from Italian *scarpa*.

scarp and dip ▷ *noun, geol* the two slopes, one steep and one relatively gentle, formed by the outcropping of a bed of sedimentary rock.

scarper /'skɑːpə(r)/ ▷ *verb* (***scarpered, scarpering***) *intr, colloq* to run away or escape; to go away unnoticed. ◐ 19c: from Italian *scappare* to escape.

scarves *plural of* SCARF¹

scary /'skɛərɪ/ ▷ *adverb* (***scarier, scariest***) *colloq* **1** causing fear or anxiety; frightening. **2** timorous; nervous. • **scarily** *adverb*. • **scariness** *noun*.

scat¹ ▷ *verb* (***scatted, scatting***) *intr, colloq* especially as a command: to go away; to run off. ◐ 19c: from the noise of a hiss + CAT, used to drive cats away.

scat² ▷ *noun* a form of jazz singing consisting of improvised sounds rather than words. ▷ *verb* (***scatted, scatting***) *intr* to sing jazz in this way. ◐ 1920s.

scathing /'skeɪðɪŋ/ ▷ *adj* scornfully critical; detrimental □ ***Margaret Thatcher launched a scathing attack on John Major.*** • **scathingly** *adverb*. ◐ 18c: from Norse *skathe* injury.

scatological /skatə'lɒdʒɪkəl/ ▷ *adj* **1** relating to or involving scatology. **2** characterized or preoccupied with obscenity. ◐ 1920s.

scatology /ska'tɒlədʒɪ/ ▷ *noun* **1** the scientific study of excrement, especially in medicine for the purpose of diagnosis. **2** the palaeontological study of fossilized excrement for the purpose of identifying and classifying fossils. **3** a morbid interest in or preoccupation with the obscene, especially with excrement, or with literature referring to it. **4** such literature containing these references. ◐ 19c: from Greek *skor, skatos* dung + -LOGY.

scatter /'skatə(r)/ ▷ *verb* (***scattered, scattering***) **1** to disperse. **2** to strew, sprinkle or throw around loosely. **3** *tr & intr* to depart or send off in different directions. **4** to reflect or disperse (especially waves or particles) irregularly. ▷ *noun* **1** an act of scattering. **2** a quantity of scattered items; a scattering. **3** *statistics* a measure of the extent to which the values of two random variables, plotted as paired values on a graph, are grouped close together or scattered apart. • **scatterer** *noun*. ◐ 12c: as *scateren*, a variant of *schateren* to SHATTER.

scatterbrain ▷ *noun, colloq* a person incapable of organized thought or attention. • **scatterbrained** *adj*. ◐ 18c.

scatter diagram ▷ *noun, math* a graph which shows the distribution of measurements of two random variables, indicating whether the mean value is representative of all the measurements.

scattering /ˈskatərɪŋ/ ▷ *noun* **1** dispersion. **2** something that is scattered. **3** a small amount. **4** *physics* the deflection of photons or particles as a result of collisions with other particles.

scatty /ˈskatɪ/ ▷ *adj* (***scattier***, ***scattiest***) *Brit colloq* **1** mentally disorganized. **2** crazy or daft; unpredictable in conduct. ◷ Early 20c: a shortening of SCATTERBRAINed.

scaur see SCAR[2]

scavenge /ˈskavɪndʒ/ ▷ *verb* (***scavenged***, ***scavenging***) **1** *intr* to behave or act as a scavenger. **2** *tr & intr* to search among waste for (usable items). **3** *chem* to cleanse, or remove impurities from, something. ◷ 17c: from SCAVENGER.

scavenger /ˈskavɪndʒə(r)/ ▷ *noun* **1** a person who searches among waste for usable items. **2** a person or apparatus that removes waste. **3** an animal that feeds on refuse or decaying flesh. ● **scavengery** *noun*. ◷ 16: from French *scawage* inspection.

ScB ▷ *abbreviation*: *Scientiae Baccalaureus* (Latin), Bachelor of Science.

SCCL ▷ *abbreviation* Scottish Council for Civil Liberties.

ScD ▷ *abbreviation*: *Scientiae Doctor* (Latin), Doctor of Science.

SCE ▷ *abbreviation* Scottish Certificate of Education.

scena /ˈʃeɪnə/ ▷ *noun* (*plural* ***scene*** /ˈʃeɪneɪ/) in opera: an elaborate and dramatic recitative followed by an aria. ◷ 19c: Italian, from Latin *scena* stage.

scenario /sɪˈnɑːrɪoʊ/ ▷ *noun* (***scenarios***) **1** a rough outline of a dramatic work, film, etc; a synopsis. **2** *cinematog* a detailed script. **3** any hypothetical situation or sequence of events. ◷ 19c: Italian, from Latin *scena* stage.

scene[1] /siːn/ ▷ *noun* **1** the setting in which a real or imaginary event takes place. **2** the representation of action on the stage. **3** a division of a play, indicated by the fall of the curtain, a change of place or the entry or exit of an important character. Compare ACT *noun* 5. **4** a unit of action in a book or film. **5** any of the pieces making up a stage or film set, or the set as a whole. **6** a landscape, situation or picture of a place or action as seen by someone ▫ *A delightful scene met their eyes.* **7** an embarrassing and unseemly display of emotion in public ▫ *make a scene.* **8** *colloq* the publicity, action, etc surrounding a particular activity or profession ▫ *the current music scene.* **9** *colloq* a liked or preferred area of interest or activity ▫ *Rock concerts are just not my scene.* **10** *colloq* a situation or state of affairs ▫ *That's the scene in Europe at the moment.* ● **behind the scenes 1** out of sight of the audience; backstage. **2** unknown to the public; in private. ● **come on the scene** to arrive; to become part of the current situation ▫ *Everything was fine until he came on the scene.* ● **set the scene** to describe the background to an event. ◷ 16c: from Latin *scena*, from Greek *skene* tent or stage.

scene[2] see SCENA

scenery /ˈsiːnərɪ/ ▷ *noun* (***sceneries***) **1** a picturesque landscape, especially one that is attractively rural. **2** the items making up a stage or film set. ◷ 18c.

scenic /ˈsiːnɪk/ ▷ *adj* **1** referring to, being or including attractive natural landscapes ▫ *We'll take the scenic route.* **2** referring or relating to scenery on stage or in film. ● **scenically** *adverb*. ◷ 17c: from Latin *scenicus*, from Greek *skenikos* theatrical.

scenic railway ▷ *noun* a small-scale railway, running through artificial representations of picturesque scenery, used as an amusement activity.

scent /sɛnt/ ▷ *noun* **1** the distinctive smell of a person, animal or plant. **2** a trail of this left behind ▫ *dogs on the scent.* **3** a series of clues or findings leading to a major discovery ▫ *The police are on the scent of the drug baron.* **4** perfume. ▷ *verb* (***scented***, ***scenting***) **1** to smell; to discover or discern by smell. **2** to sense; to be aware of something by instinct or intuition. **3** *intr* to give out a smell, especially a pleasant one. **4** to perfume. ● **scented** *adj* having a smell; fragrant or perfumed. ● **put** or **throw someone off the scent** to deliberately mislead them. ◷ 14c: from French *sentir*, from Latin *sentire* to perceive.

sceptic or (*N Amer*) **skeptic** /ˈskɛptɪk/ *noun* **1** someone with a tendency to disbelieve or doubt the validity or substance of other situations, people, etc. **2** someone who questions widely accepted, especially religious, doctrines and beliefs. ◷ 16c: from Latin *scepticus*, from Greek *skeptikos* thoughtful, from *skeptesthai* to consider.

sceptical or (*N Amer*) **skeptical** /ˈskɛptɪkəl/ *adj* doubtful; inclined to be incredulous. ● **sceptically** *adverb*.

> ***sceptical***
>
> See Usage Note at **cynical**.

scepticism or (*N Amer*) **skepticism** /ˈskɛptɪsɪzəm/ *noun* **1** doubt, or the general disposition to doubt. **2** the doctrine that no facts can be definitely known. **3** agnosticism.

sceptre /ˈsɛptə(r)/ ▷ *noun* a ceremonial staff or baton carried by a monarch as a symbol of sovereignty. ● **sceptred** *adj* regal; bearing a sceptre. ◷ 13c: from Latin *sceptrum*, from Greek *skeptron* staff.

SCF ▷ *abbreviation* Save the Children Fund.

Sch. ▷ *abbreviation* schilling.

schadenfreude /ˈʃɑːdənfrɔɪdə/ ▷ *noun* malicious pleasure in the misfortunes of others. ◷ 19c: German, from *Schade* hurt + *Freude* joy.

schedule /ˈʃɛdʒuːl, ˈskɛdʒuːl/ ▷ *noun* **1** a list of events or activities planned to take place at certain times. **2** the state of an event or activity occurring on time, according to plan ▫ *We are well behind schedule.* **3** any list or inventory. **4** a timetable or plan. **5** a supplement to a document. ▷ *verb* (***scheduled***, ***scheduling***) **1** to plan or arrange something to take place at a certain time. **2** to put something on a schedule. ◷ 14c: from Latin *schedula*, from *scheda* strip of papyrus.

scheduled castes ▷ *noun, especially formerly* in India: Hindus of a very low caste; the UNTOUCHABLES.

scheelite /ˈʃiːlaɪt/ ▷ *noun* the mineral calcium tungstate, a major source of tungsten. ◷ 19c: named after K W Scheele, (1742–86), the Swedish chemist who first discovered tungstic acid.

schema /ˈskiːmə/ ▷ *noun* (***schemata*** /-mətə/) **1** a scheme or plan. **2** a diagrammatic outline or synopsis. ◷ 18c: Greek.

schematic /skɪˈmatɪk/ ▷ *adj* **1** following or involving a particular plan or arrangement. **2** represented by a diagram or plan. ● **schematically** *adverb*. ◷ 18c.

schematize or **schematise** /ˈskiːmətaɪz/ ▷ *verb* (***schematized***, ***schematizing***) to reduce to or represent by a scheme. ● **schematization** /-ˈzeɪʃən/ *noun*. ● **schematism** *noun*. ◷ 17c.

scheme /skiːm/ ▷ *noun* **1** a plan of action. **2** a system or programme ▫ *a pension scheme.* **3** a careful arrangement of different components ▫ *a colour scheme.* **4** a secret plan intended to cause harm or damage. **5** a diagram or table. **6** a diagram of positions, especially (*astrol*) of planets. **7** *chiefly Scots* a HOUSING ESTATE. ▷ *verb* (***schemed***, ***scheming***) *intr* to plan or act secretly and often maliciously. ● **schemer** *noun*. ◷ 16c: Greek.

scheming ▷ *adj* tending to plot or scheme ▫ *She's a scheming so-and-so.* ▷ *noun* the act or process of making a plot or scheme. ◷ 19c.

scherzando /skɛət'sandoʊ, skɜːt-/ *music* ▻ *adverb* playfully. ▻ *adj* playful. ▻ *noun* (***scherzandos*** or ***scherzandi*** /-diː/) a playful movement, piece or passage. ⓒ Early 19c.

scherzo /'skɛətsoʊ, 'skɜːtsoʊ/ ▻ *noun* (***scherzos*** or ***scherzi*** /-siː/) a lively piece of music, usually with a trio (sense 3), generally the second or third part of a symphony, sonata, etc, replacing the minuet. ⓒ 19c: Italian, meaning 'joke'.

Schick test /'ʃɪk —/ or **Schick's test** ▻ *noun, medicine* a test carried out to determine susceptibility to diphtheria, done by injecting the skin with a measured amount of diphtheria toxin. ⓒ Early 20c: named after Bela Schick (1877–1967), the US paediatrician who devised it.

schilling /'ʃɪlɪŋ/ ▻ *noun* (abbreviation **Sch.**) the standard unit of currency of Austria. ⓒ 18c: German.

schism /'skɪzəm, 'sɪzəm/ ▻ *noun, relig* **1** a breach or separation from the main group, or into opposing groups. **2** the act of encouraging such a breach or separation. **3** the breakaway group formed. ⓒ 14c: from Greek *schisma* split.

schismatic /skɪz'matɪk, sɪz-/ and **schismatical** ▻ *adj* relating to or involving schism. • **schismatically** *adverb*. ⓒ 15c.

schist /ʃɪst/ ▻ *noun, geol* any of a group of common coarse-grained metamorphic rocks that characteristically contain broad wavy bands of minerals that readily split into layers. • **schistose** *adj*. ⓒ 18c: from French *schiste*, from Greek *schistos* split.

schistosomiasis /ʃɪstəsoʊ'maɪəsɪs/ ▻ *noun, pathol* a tropical disease, transmitted by contaminated water and caused by infestation with **schistosomes**, parasitic flukes which circulate in the blood and may affect other organs. Also called **bilharzia**. ⓒ Early 20c: from Greek *schistos* split.

schizo /'skɪtsoʊ/ *colloq* ▻ *noun* (***schizos***) a schizophrenic person. ▻ *adj* schizophrenic. ⓒ 1940s: a shortening of SCHIZOPHRENIC.

schizo- /'skɪtsoʊ, 'skaɪzoʊ, skɪtsə/ or (before a vowel) **schiz-** *combining form, signifying* a division or split. ⓒ from Greek *schizein* to split or cleave.

schizocarp /'skɪtsoʊkɑːp, 'skaɪzoʊ-/ ▻ *noun* a dry fruit that splits into two or more one-seeded portions. • **schizocarpous** or **schizocarpic** *adj*.

schizoid /'skɪtsɔɪd, -dzɔɪd/ ▻ *adj* displaying some symptoms of schizophrenia, such as introversion or tendency to fantasy, but without a diagnosed mental disorder. ▻ *noun* a schizoid person. • **schizoidal** *adj*. ⓒ 1920s.

schizomycete /skɪtsoʊmaɪ'siːt, skaɪzoʊ-/ ▻ *noun, biol* any micro-organism, including bacteria, belonging to the class **Schizomycetes**. • **schizomycetic** or **schizomycetous** *adj*. ⓒ 1870s.

schizophrenia /skɪtsə'friːnɪə/ ▻ *noun* any of various forms of a severe mental disorder characterized by loss of contact with reality, impairment of thought processes, a marked personality change, loss of emotional responsiveness and social withdrawal. ⓒ Early 20c: SCHIZO- + Greek *phren* mind.

schizophrenic /skɪtsə'frɛnɪk/ ▻ *noun* someone suffering from schizophrenia. ▻ *adj* relating to or suffering from schizophrenia. ⓒ Early 20c.

schizothymia /skɪtsoʊ'θaɪmɪə, skaɪzoʊ-/ ▻ *noun* a manifestation of schizoid traits and characteristics within normal limits. • **schizothymic** *adj*. ⓒ 1960s: SCHIZO- + Greek *thymos* spirit.

schlep or **schlepp** /ʃlɛp/ *slang* ▻ *verb* (***schlepped, schlepping***) to carry, pull or drag with difficulty. ▻ *noun* **1** a clumsy, stupid or incompetent person. **2** a journey or procedure requiring great effort or involving great difficulty. • **schleppy** *adj*. ⓒ 1920s: Yiddish.

schlock /ʃlɒk/ ▻ *noun* **1** inferior quality; shoddy production. **2** a shoddy or defective article. • **schlocky** *adj*. ⓒ Early 20c: Yiddish, from German *Schlag* a blow.

schmaltz /ʃmɔːlts, ʃmalts/ ▻ *noun* **1** *colloq* extreme or excessive sentimentality, especially in music or other art. **2** fat, especially chicken fat, used for cooking. • **schmaltzy** *adj*. ⓒ 1930s: Yiddish, from German *Schmalz* cooking fat.

schmooze /ʃmuːz/ ▻ *verb* (***schmoozed, schmoozing***) *intr* (*usually* **schmooze with someone**) to gossip or chat in a friendly or intimate manner. ▻ *noun* such a chat, especially at a social gathering. ⓒ 19c: from Yiddish *schmues* a chat.

schnapper same as SNAPPER 2

schnapps or **schnaps** /ʃnaps/ ▻ *noun* in N Europe: any strong dry alcoholic spirit, especially Dutch gin distilled from potatoes. ⓒ Early 19c: German meaning 'dram of liquor'.

Schnauzer /'ʃnaʊtsə(r)/ ▻ *noun* a type of German terrier with a thick wiry coat, marked eyebrows, moustache, beard and short pendulous ears. ⓒ 1920s: from German *Schnauze* snout.

schnitzel /'ʃnɪtsəl/ ▻ *noun* a veal cutlet. ⓒ 19c: German.

schnorkel see SNORKEL

schnozzle /'ʃnɒzəl/ ▻ *noun, chiefly US slang* a nose. ⓒ 1930s: probably from a combination of *nose* or *nozzle* and Yiddish *schnoitz* snout, *schnabe* beak, etc.

scholar /'skɒlə(r)/ ▻ *noun* **1** a learned person, especially an academic. **2** a person who studies; a pupil or student. **3** a person receiving a scholarship. **4** during times of less widespread education: a person who could read and write, or a learned person. **5** a person with extensive learning and knowledge, particularly in Greek and Latin, or with a scrupulous and critical approach to learning. • **scholarliness** *noun*. • **scholarly** *adj*. ⓒ Anglo-Saxon *scolere*, from French *escoler*, from Latin *scholaris*.

scholarship ▻ *noun* **1** the achievements or learning of a scholar. **2** a sum of money awarded, usually to an outstanding student, for the purposes of further study. **3** the status and emoluments of such a pupil or student. ⓒ 16c.

scholastic /skə'lastɪk, skɒ-/ ▻ *adj* **1** referring or relating to learning institutions, such as schools or universities, and to their teaching and education methods. **2** subtle; pedantic. **3** referring or relating to scholasticism. • **scholastically** *adverb*. ⓒ 16c: from Greek *scholastikos*.

scholasticism /skə'lastɪsɪzəm, skɒ-/ ▻ *noun* **1** the system of teaching, especially moral or religious, that dominated W Europe in the Middle Ages, based on the writings of Aristotle and the Church Fathers. **2** stubborn adherence to traditional teaching methods and values. ⓒ 18c.

scholiast /'skoʊlɪast/ ▻ *noun* someone who writes explanatory notes and comments on literary works, especially an ancient grammarian writing on manuscripts. • **scholiastic** *adj*. ⓒ 16c: from Greek *scholiastes*, from Latin *schole*.

school[1] /skuːl/ ▻ *noun* **1** a place or institution where education is received, especially primary or secondary education. **2** *in compounds* a place or institution offering instruction in a particular field or subject, often part of a university □ *music school* □ *art school*. **3** the building or room used for this purpose. **4** the work of such an institution. **5** the body of students and teachers that occupy any such a place. **6** the period of the day or year during which such a place is open to students □ *Stay behind after school*. **7** the disciples or adherents of a particular teacher. **8** a group of painters, writers or other artists sharing the same style, often as a result of having received instruction in the same place or from the same master. **9** any activity or set of surroundings as a provider of experience □ *Factories are the schools of life.* **10** *colloq* a group of people meeting regularly for some purpose, especially gambling □ *a card school.* **11** a method of instruction or tuition. **12** (**schools**) at Oxford University: the BA examinations. ▷ *verb* (***schooled***, ***schooling***) **1** to educate in a school. **2** to give training or instruction of a particular kind to. **3** to discipline. ⓒ Anglo-Saxon *scol*, from Latin *schola*, from Greek *schole* leisure or lecture-place.

school² /skuːl/ ▷ *noun* a group of fish, whales or other marine animals swimming together. ▷ *verb* (***schooled***, ***schooling***) *intr* to gather into or move about in a school. ⓒ 15c: Dutch.

schoolchild ▷ *noun* a child, a **schoolboy** or **schoolgirl**, who attends a school.

schoolhouse ▷ *noun* **1** a building used as a school. **2** a house provided for a teacher within the grounds of a school.

schooling ▷ *noun* education or instruction, especially received at school.

school-leaver ▷ *noun* a young person leaving school because they have completed the course of education.

schoolmarm /ˈskuːlmɑːm/ ▷ *noun, colloq* **1** *N Amer, especially US* a schoolmistress. **2** a prim woman with old-fashioned manners or attitudes. • **schoolmarmish** *adj* like or typical of a schoolmarm.

schoolmaster ▷ *noun* a male schoolteacher or head of a school.

schoolmate ▷ *noun* a friend from school; a classmate.

schoolmistress ▷ *noun* a female schoolteacher or head of a school.

schoolteacher ▷ *noun* a person who teaches in a school. • **schoolteaching** *noun*.

schoolyear ▷ *noun* the period of generally continual teaching through the year, usually starting in late summer, and usually divided into three terms, during which the pupil or student remains in the same class or classes.

schooner /ˈskuːnə(r)/ ▷ *noun* **1** a fast sailing-ship with two or more masts, and rigged fore-and-aft. **2** *Brit* a large sherry glass. **3** *N Amer, especially US* a large beer glass. ⓒ 18c: as *skooner* or *scooner*, possibly from dialect *scoon* to skim.

schottische /ʃɒˈtiːʃ, ˈʃɒtɪʃ/ ▷ *noun* (***schottisches***) **1** a German folk dance, similar to a slow polka. **2** the music for such a dance. ⓒ 19c: from German *der schottische Tanz* the Scottish dance.

schtook and **schtuk** see SHTOOK

schtoom see SHTOOM

schuss /ʃʊs/ *skiing* ▷ *noun* **1** a straight slope on which it is possible to make a fast run. **2** such a run. ▷ *verb* (***schussed***, ***schussing***) *intr* to make such a run. ⓒ 1930s: German.

schwa or **shwa** /ʃwɑː, ʃvɑː/ ▷ *noun* **1** the indistinct English vowel sound that occurs in unstressed syllables, as in the first and last syllables of *together* in normal speech, and in other words such as *to* and *the* in rapid speech. **2** the phonetic symbol (/ə/) used to represent this sound. ⓒ Late 19c: from Hebrew *schewa*.

sciatic /saɪˈatɪk/ ▷ *adj* **1** referring or relating to the hip region. **2** referring or relating to the sciatic nerve that runs from the pelvis to the thigh. **3** affected by sciatica. ⓒ 14c: from Latin *sciaticus*, from Greek *ischion* hip-joint.

sciatica /saɪˈatɪkə/ ▷ *noun, pathol* intense and intermittent pain in the lower back, buttocks and backs of the thighs caused by pressure on the sciatic nerve. ⓒ 15c: Latin, from Greek *ischion* hip-joint.

SCID ▷ *abbreviation, medicine* severe combined immunodeficiency.

science /ˈsaɪəns/ ▷ *noun* **1** the systematic observation and classification of natural phenomena in order to learn about them and bring them under general principles and laws. **2** a department or branch of such knowledge or study developed in this way, eg astronomy, genetics, chemistry. **3** any area of knowledge obtained using, or arranged according to, formal principles □ *political science.* **4** acquired skill or technique, as opposed to natural ability. • **sciential** /saɪˈɛnʃəl/ *adj* referring or relating to science; scientific. ⓒ 14c: from Latin *scientia* knowledge, from *scire* to know.

science fiction ▷ *noun* imaginative fiction presenting a view of life in the future, based on great scientific and technological advances, especially incorporating space or time travel, or the existence of life on other planets, or any other fantastic circumstances imagined by the writer. Often shortened to SCI-FI. ⓒ 1850s.

science park ▷ *noun* an industrial research centre, usually attached to a university, set up for the purpose of combining the academic and commercial world.

scientific /saɪənˈtɪfɪk/ ▷ *adj* **1** referring or relating to, or used in, science. **2** based on science. **3** displaying the kind of principled approach characteristic of science. • **scientifically** *adverb* in a scientific way; by scientific means. ⓒ 17c.

scientism /ˈsaɪəntɪzəm/ ▷ *noun* **1** the methods or attitudes of people of science. **2** the belief that methods used in natural sciences should also be applied to the study of human behaviour and condition, eg philosophy and social sciences. ⓒ 19c.

scientist /ˈsaɪəntɪst/ ▷ *noun* a person trained in or engaged in some field of science.

Scientology /saɪənˈtɒlədʒɪ/ ▷ *noun, trademark* a religious system which claims to improve the mental and physical wellbeing of its adherents by scientific means. ⓒ 1950s: founded by L Ron Hubbard.

sci-fi /ˈsaɪfaɪ/ ▷ *noun, colloq* science fiction. Also *as adj* □ *sci-fi novel.*

scilicet /ˈsaɪlɪset, ˈskiːlɪkɛt/ ▷ *adverb, formal,* (abbreviation **sc.**) only in writing: namely; that is to say. ⓒ 14c: from Latin *scire licet* it is permitted to know.

scilla /ˈsɪlə/ ▷ *noun, bot* the squill genus of the lily family, having bright blue spring flowers. ⓒ 19c: Latin, from Greek *skilla*.

Scillonian /sɪˈloʊnɪən/ ▷ *adj* referring, belonging to or concerning the Scilly Isles, situated off the SW coast of Britain. ▷ *noun* an inhabitant of these islands. ⓒ 18c.

scimitar /ˈsɪmɪtə(r)/ ▷ *noun* a sword with a short curved single-edged blade, broadest at the point end, used by Turks and Persians. ⓒ 16c: from Italian *scimitarra*, probably from Persian *shimshir*.

scintigraphy /sɪnˈtɪgrəfɪ/ ▷ *noun, medicine* a diagnostic technique in which a pictorial record of the pattern of gamma ray emission after injection of isotope into the body produces an image or **scintigram** of an internal organ by use of an external detector. ⓒ 1950s: from *scinti*llation + -GRAPHY.

scintilla /sɪnˈtɪlə/ ▷ *noun, literary* a hint or trace; an iota. ⓒ 17c: Latin, meaning 'spark'.

scintillate /ˈsɪntɪleɪt/ ▷ *verb* (***scintillated***, ***scintillating***) *intr* **1** to sparkle or emit sparks. **2** to capture attention or impress with one's vitality or wit. **3** *physics* said of an atom: to emit a unit of light after having been struck by a photon or a particle of ionizing radiation. • **scintillating** *adj* brilliant or sparkling; full of interest or wit. ⓒ 17c: from Latin *scintillare*, *scintillatum*, from *scintilla* spark.

scintillation /sɪntɪˈleɪʃən/ ▷ *noun* **1** *physics* the emission of a flash of light by an atom as it returns to its normal energy state after having been raised to a higher energy state by collision with a photon or a particle of ionizing radiation. **2** *astron* the twinkling of stars due to rapid changes in their brightness caused by variations in the density of the atmosphere through which the light rays pass.

scintillation counter ▷ *noun, physics* a device for detecting very low levels of radiation.

sciolism /'saɪəlɪzəm/ ▷ *noun* superficial pretensions to knowledge. • **sciolist** *noun*. • **sciolistic** or **sciolous** *adj*. ◷ Early 19c: from Latin *sciolus*, from *scire* to know.

scion /'saɪən/ ▷ *noun* **1** *bot* the detached shoot of a plant inserted into a cut in the outer stem of another plant when making a graft. **2** a descendant or offspring; a younger member of a family. ◷ 14c: from French *cion*.

scirocco see SIROCCO

scirrhus /'sɪrəs, 'skɪrəs/ ▷ *noun* (***scirrhi*** /'sɪraɪ/ or ***scirrhuses***) *pathol* a hard swelling, especially a hard cancer. • **scirrhoid** or **scirrhous** *adj*. ◷ 17c: from Latin *scirros*, from Greek *skiros* a hard substance or tumour.

scissor /'sɪzə(r)/ ▷ *verb* (***scissored, scissoring***) to cut with scissors.

scissors /'sɪzəz/ ▷ *plural noun* **1** a one-handed cutting device with two long blades pivoted in the middle so the cutting edges close and overlap. **2** any position or movement similar to that of scissors. **3** *gymnastics* a movement of the legs similar to the opening and closing of scissors. **4** *wrestling* a locking of the legs around the opponent's head or body. **5** a style of high jump where the jump is approached at an angle and the leg nearest the bar leads throughout. ◷ 14c: from French *cisoires*, from Latin *cisorium* cutting tool, from *caedere* to cut.

scissors kick ▷ *noun* a kick used in some swimming strokes in which the legs are moved in a scissor-like action.

sciurine /saɪ'jʊəraɪn, 'saɪjʊraɪn/ ▷ *adj* relating or belonging to a genus of rodents, including squirrels. ◷ 19c: from Latin *sciurus* squirrel, from Greek *skiouros*, from *skia* shadow + *oura* tail.

scler- see SCLERO-

sclera /'sklɪərə/ ▷ *noun* the outermost membrane of the eyeball. Also called SCLEROTIC. ◷ 19c: from Greek *skleros* hard.

sclerenchyma /sklɪə'rɛŋkɪmə/ ▷ *noun, bot* plant tissue consisting of cells with thick lignified walls, providing support for the inner tissue. • **sclerenchymatous** /-'kaɪmətəs/ *adj*. ◷ 19c: SCLER- + Greek *enchyma* in-filling.

sclero- /'sklɪəroʊ, sklɪərə/ or (before a vowel) **scler-** *combining form, signifying* hard. ◷ From Greek *skleros*.

scleroderma and **sclerodermia** ▷ *noun, pathol* a condition where the skin is hardened by fibrous tissue being replaced by subcutaneous fat. • **sclerodermic** *adj*. ◷ 1860s: SCLERO- + Greek *derma* skin.

scleroma /sklə'roʊmə, sklɪə'roʊmə/ ▷ *noun* (***scleromata*** /-mətə/) *pathol* a hardening of tissue, especially of mucous membrane or skin, eg forming nodules in the nose.

scleroprotein ▷ *noun* insoluble protein forming the skeletal parts of tissues. ◷ Early 20c.

sclerosis /sklə'roʊsɪs, sklɪə-/ ▷ *noun* **1** *pathol* abnormal hardening or thickening of an artery or other body part, especially as a result of inflammation or disease. **2** *bot* the hardening of plant tissue by thickening or lignification. ◷ 14c.

sclerotic /sklə'rɒtɪk, sklɪə-/ ▷ *noun, anatomy* in vertebrates: the white fibrous outer layer of the eyeball, which is modified at the front of the eye to form the transparent cornea. Also called SCLERA. ▷ *adj* **1** hard or firm. **2** relating to or affected with sclerosis. ◷ 16c: from Latin *scleroticus*, from Greek *skleros* hard.

sclerous /'sklɪərəs/ ▷ *adj* **1** *pathol* hardened or indurated. **2** *anatomy* ossified or bony. ◷ 1840s.

SCM ▷ *abbreviation* **1** State Certified Midwife. **2** Student Christian Movement.

scoff¹ ▷ *verb* (***scoffed, scoffing***) *intr* (*often* **scoff at someone** or **something**) to express scorn or contempt for them; to jeer. ▷ *noun* **1** an expression of scorn; a jeer. **2** an object of scorn or derision. • **scoffer** *noun*. • **scoffing** *noun, adj*. ◷ 14c: from Danish *scof* jest or mockery, from Frisian *schof*.

scoff² ▷ *colloq, verb* (***scoffed, scoffing***) *tr & intr* to eat (food) rapidly and greedily; to devour hungrily. ▷ *noun* food; a meal. ◷ 19c: from Scots *scaff* food.

scold /skoʊld/ ▷ *verb* (***scolded, scolding***) **1** to reprimand or rebuke. **2** *intr* to use strong or offensive language. ▷ *noun, old use* a nagging or quarrelsome person, especially a woman. • **scolder** *noun*. • **scolding** *noun* a telling-off. ◷ 13c: from Norse *skald*.

scoliosis /skɒlɪ'oʊsɪs/ ▷ *noun, pathol* lateral curvature of the spine. • **scoliotic** *adj*. ◷ 18c: from Greek *skoliosis* obliquity, from *skolios* bent.

scollop see SCALLOP

sconce¹ /skɒns/ ▷ *noun* a candlestick or lantern with a handle, or one fixed by bracket to a wall. ◷ 14c: from French *esconse*, from Latin *absconsa* dark lantern, from *abscondere* to hide.

sconce² /skɒns/ ▷ *noun* a small fort or earthwork, especially to defend a bridge, pass, etc. ◷ 16c: from Dutch *schans*, from German *Schanze* bundle of wood.

scone /skɒn, skoʊn/ ▷ *noun* a small flattish plain cake, baked with or without dried fruit, and usually eaten halved and spread with butter and jam, etc. ◷ 16c: perhaps from Dutch *schoon (brot)* fine (bread).

SCONUL /'skoʊnəl/ ▷ *abbreviation* Standing Conference of National and University Libraries.

scoop /skuːp/ ▷ *verb* (***scooped, scooping***) **1** (*also* **scoop something up**) to lift, dig or remove it with a sweeping circular movement. **2** (*also* **scoop something out**) to empty or hollow it with such movements. **3** to bail out (water). **4** to do better than (rival newspapers) in being the first to publish a story. ▷ *noun* **1** a spoonlike implement for handling or serving food. **2** a hollow shovel or lipped container for skimming or shovelling up loose material. **3** anything of a similar shape. **4** a scooping movement. **5** a quantity scooped. **6** a container for bailing out (water). **7** *surgery* a scooplike implement used for removing foreign material from the body. **8** a news story printed by one newspaper in advance of all others. **9** the forestalling of other papers in obtaining such a news story. • **scooper** *noun*. • **scoopful** *noun*. ◷ 14c: from Dutch *schoppe* shovel.

scoot /skuːt/ ▷ *verb* (***scooted, scooting***) *intr, colloq* to make off quickly or speedily. ▷ *noun* the act of scooting. ◷ 18c: from Norse *skjota* to SHOOT.

scooter /'skuːtə(r)/ ▷ *noun* **1** a child's toy vehicle consisting of a board on a two-wheeled frame, with tall handlebars connected to the front wheel, propelled by pushing against the ground with one foot. **2** (*in full* **motor-scooter**) a small-wheeled motorcycle with a protective front shield curving back to form a support for the feet. ◷ 19c: from SCOOT.

scope¹ ▷ *noun* **1** the size or range of a subject or topic covered. **2** the aim, intention or purpose of something. **3** the limits within which there is the opportunity to act. **4** range of understanding □ *beyond his scope*. **5** the length of mooring cable at which a vessel can ride freely. ◷ 16c: from Italian *scopo*, from Greek *skopos* watcher or point watched, from *skopeein* to view.

scope² ▷ *noun* a visual display unit, especially a radar screen □ *microscope, telescope, etc.* ▷ *verb* (***scoped, scoping***) *medicine* to examine internal organs of the body using a viewing device. ◷ 17c.

-scope /skoʊp/ ▷ *combining form, forming nouns signifying* a device for viewing, examining or detecting something □ ***telescope*** □ ***stethoscope***. ● **-scopic** /'skɒpɪk/ *combining form, forming adjectives*. ● **-scopy** /skəpɪ/ *combining form, forming nouns* denoting observation or examination, usually with the use of devices ending in *-scope* □ ***microscopy***. ⓒ From Greek *skopeein* to view.

scopolamine /'skəpɒləmiːn/ ▷ *noun* HYOSCINE. ⓒ 19c: named after G A Scopoli (1723–88), the Italian naturalist + AMINE.

scorbutic /skɔː'bjuːtɪk/ ▷ *adj, pathol* relating to or suffering from scurvy. ● **scorbutically** *adverb*. ⓒ 17c: from Latin *scorbuticus*, probably from German *schorbuk* scurvy.

scorch ▷ *verb* (***scorches***, ***scorched***, ***scorching***) **1** *tr & intr* to burn or be burned slightly or superficially. **2** to dry up, parch or wither. **3** to injure with severe criticism or scorn. ▷ *noun* **1** an act of scorching. **2** a scorched area or burn. **3** a mark made by scorching. ● **scorched** *adj*. ● **scorching** *adj, colloq* **1** said of the weather: very hot. **2** said of a criticism, etc: harsh. ● **scorchingly** *adverb*. ⓒ 15c: as *skorken*, from Norse *skorpna* to shrivel.

scorched-earth policy ▷ *noun* **1** in warfare: the practice of destroying everything in an area that may be of use to an advancing army. **2** any manoeuvre in which action is taken to reduce useful assets in order to minimize their value to any future opponents, owners, etc.

scorcher /'skɔːtʃə(r)/ ▷ *noun* **1** someone or something that scorches. **2** *colloq* an extremely hot day □ ***Tomorrow should be a scorcher***. **3** *Brit* someone or something that causes a sensation or excitement. ⓒ 19c.

score ▷ *noun* **1** a total number of points gained or achieved eg in a game. **2** an act of gaining or achieving a point, etc. **3** a scratch or shallow cut, especially one made as a tally. **4** a bold line marking a boundary or defined position. **5** a set of twenty □ ***three score***. **6** (**scores**) very many; lots □ ***I have scores of letters to write***. **7** *colloq* (**the score**) the current situation; the essential facts □ ***What's the score with your job?*** **8** a written or printed copy of music for several parts, set out vertically down the page. **9** the music from a film or play. **10** (**the score**) a reason; grounds □ ***He was accepted on the score of suitability***. **11** a grievance or grudge □ ***He has an old score to settle***. **12** a record of amounts owed. **13** *slang* a successful attempt to obtain drugs for illegal use. ▷ *verb* (***scored***, ***scoring***) **1** *tr & intr* to gain or achieve (a point) in a game. **2** *intr* to keep a record of points gained during a game. **3** to make cuts or scratches in the surface of something; to mark (a line) by a shallow cut. **4** to be equivalent to (a number of points) □ ***black king scores three***. **5** *music* **a** to break down music into parts for individual instruments or voices; **b** to adapt music for instruments or voices other than those originally intended. **6** to compose music for a film or play. **7** *intr* to achieve a rating; to be judged or regarded □ ***This film scores high for entertainment value***. **8** *intr, slang* to obtain drugs for illegal use. **9** (*often* **score with someone**) *slang* to succeed in having sexual intercourse with them. ● **scorer** *noun*. ● **know the score** to know or be aware of the facts of a situation. ● **on that score** as regards the matter or concern □ ***She has no worries on that score***. ● **over the score** *colloq* beyond reasonable limits; unfair. ● **pay off** or **settle a score** to repay an old grudge or debt. ● **score an own goal** *colloq* to do something unintentionally to one's own disadvantage. ⓒ Anglo-Saxon *scoru*, from Norse *skor*.

■ **score off someone** or **score points off someone** to humiliate them for personal advantage; to get the better of them.

■ **score something out** to cancel it by drawing a line through it.

scoreboard and **scoring board** ▷ *noun* a board on which the score in a game is displayed, altered according to the score changes.

scorecard and **scoring card** ▷ *noun* a card for recording the score in a game.

scoria /'skɔːrɪə/ ▷ *noun* (***scoriae*** /-rɪaɪ/) **1** dross or slag produced from the smelting of metal from its ore. **2** a quantity of cooled lava with steam-holes. ● **scorify** *verb* (***scorifies***, ***scorified***, ***scorifying***) to rid metals of impurities by forming scoria. ⓒ 14c: Latin, from Greek *skoria*, from *skor* dung.

scorn ▷ *noun* extreme or mocking contempt. ▷ *verb* (***scorned***, ***scorning***) **1** to treat someone or something with scorn; to express scorn for. **2** to refuse or reject with scorn. ● **scorner** *noun*. ● **scornful** *adj* contemptuous. ● **scornfully** *adverb*. ⓒ 12c: from French *escarn*, from German *skern* mockery.

Scorpio /'skɔːpɪoʊ/ ▷ *noun* (*plural* ***Scorpios*** in sense 2b) **1** *astron* the Scorpion, a large zodiacal constellation of the S hemisphere containing many star clusters that are visible through binoculars. Also called **Scorpius**. **2** *astrol* **a** the eighth sign of the zodiac, the Scorpion; **b** a person born between 23 October and 21 November, under this sign. See table at ZODIAC. ⓒ 14c: Latin for SCORPION.

scorpion /'skɔːpɪən/ ▷ *noun* **1** any of numerous species of invertebrate animal, found in hot regions, with eight legs, powerful claw-like pincers and a long thin segmented abdomen or 'tail', bearing a poisonous sting, that is carried arched over its back. **2** (**the Scorpion**) *astron, astrol* same as SCORPIO. **3** *Bible* a form of SCOURGE (*noun* 2). ⓒ 13c: from Latin *scorpio*, from Greek *skorpios*.

scorpion fish ▷ *noun* a marine fish with venomous spines on its fins.

Scot /skɒt/ ▷ *noun* **1** a native or inhabitant of Scotland. **2** *historical* one of a Gaelic-speaking people of Ireland who eventually settled in NW Britain in the 6c. ⓒ Anglo-Saxon *Scottas*, from Latin *Scottus*.

Scot. ▷ *abbreviation* **1** Scotland. **2** Scottish.

Scotch ▷ *adj* said of things, especially products, but not usually said of people: Scottish. ▷ *noun* Scotch whisky. ⓒ 17c: from SCOTTISH.

Scotch, Scots

See Usage Note at **Scottish**.

scotch¹ ▷ *verb* (***scotched***, ***scotching***) **1** to ruin or hinder eg plans. **2** to reveal (something, especially rumours) to be untrue. ▷ *noun* a line marked on the ground, especially for hopscotch.

scotch² ▷ *noun* a wedge or block to prevent turning or slipping eg of a wheel, gate or ladder. ▷ *verb* (***scotched***, ***scotching***) to stop or block. ⓒ 17c.

Scotch broth ▷ *noun* a thick soup made with mutton, barley and chopped vegetables.

Scotch egg ▷ *noun* a hard-boiled egg encased in sausage meat and fried in breadcrumbs.

Scotch mist ▷ *noun* very fine rain, common in the Scottish Highlands.

Scotch terrier see SCOTTISH TERRIER

scot-free ▷ *adj* unpunished or unharmed. ⓒ 13c: from obsolete *scot* payment or tax.

scotoma /skɒ'toʊmə/ ▷ *noun* (***scotomas*** or ***scotomata*** /skɒ'toʊmətə/) *pathol* a blind spot due to disease of the retina or optic nerve. ● **scotomatous** *adj*. ⓒ 16c: Latin, from Greek *skotoma* dizziness, from *skotos* darkness.

Scots ▷ *adj* **1** Scottish by birth. **2** said especially of law and language: Scottish. ▷ *noun* LOWLAND SCOTS. ⓒ 14c: from Scots *Scottis* Scottish.

Scotsman and **Scotswoman** ▷ *noun* a native of Scotland.

Scots pine ▷ *noun* a coniferous tree, native to Europe and Asia, with a bare reddish trunk, paired bluish-green needles and pointed female cones.

Scottie see SCOTTISH TERRIER

Scottish /ˈskɒtɪʃ/ ▻ *adj* belonging or relating to Scotland or its inhabitants. ⓒ Anglo-Saxon *Scottisc.*

Scottish, Scotch, Scots

- **Scottish** is the general term describing people and things from or in Scotland.
- **Scotch** is nowadays mainly reserved for produce, as in *Scotch beef* and *Scotch whisky*, being unacceptable to many Scottish people as a label of nationality.
- The word **Scots** as an adjective can be used to describe someone's nationality. Otherwise it is restricted to *Scots law*, the *Scots language*, *Scots pine*, and the names of certain army regiments, such as the *Scots Guards*.

Scottish Certificate of Education ▻ *noun* (abbreviation **SCE**) in Scottish secondary education: a certificate obtainable at Standard or Higher grades for proficiency in one or more subjects. Compare CSYS.

Scottish terrier ▻ *noun* a kind of dog with a sturdy body, thick wiry coat, and short erect ears and tail. Also called **Scotch terrier, Scottie**.

Scotvec or SCOTVEC /ˈskɒtvɛk/ ▻ *abbreviation* Scottish Vocational Education Council.

scoundrel /ˈskaʊndrəl/ ▻ *noun* an unprincipled or villainous rogue. ⓒ 16c.

scour[1] /ˈskaʊə(r)/ *verb* (*scoured, scouring*) **1** to clean, polish or remove by hard rubbing. **2** to free from dirt or grease. **3** to flush clean with a jet or current of water. **4** to wash (sheep wool) in order to remove grease and impurities. **5** *intr* in animals: to act as a purgative. ▻ *noun* **1** an act of scouring. **2** (*often* **scours**) in animal livestock: diarrhoea. • **scouring** *noun.* • **scourings** *plural noun* matter accumulated as a result of scouring. ⓒ 13c: from French *escurer*, from Latin *excurare* to cleanse.

scour[2] /ˈskaʊə(r)/ *verb* (*scoured, scouring*) **1** to make an exhaustive search of (an area). **2** to range over or move quickly over (an area). • **scourer** *noun* **1** someone who scours. **2** a device or container for scouring. ⓒ 14c: from Norse *skur* storm, shower.

scourge /skɜːdʒ/ ▻ *noun* **1** a cause of great suffering and affliction, especially to many people □ *Cancer is the scourge of Western society.* **2** a whip used for punishing. **3** someone or something that is an instrument of divine punishment. ▻ *verb* (*scourged, scourging*) **1** to cause suffering to; to afflict. **2** to whip. • **scourger** *noun.* ⓒ 13c: from French *escorge*, from Latin *excoriare* to flay.

Scouse /skaʊs/ *colloq* ▻ *noun* (*Scouses*) **1** the dialect of English spoken in and around Liverpool. **2** a native or inhabitant of Liverpool. Also called **Scouser**. **3** (**scouse**) *Liverpool dialect* a stew, often made with scraps of meat. ▻ *adj* referring or relating to Liverpool, its people or their dialect. ⓒ 19c: a shortening of *lobscouse* a sailor's stew.

scout[1] /skaʊt/ *noun* **1** *military* a person or group sent out to observe the enemy and bring back information. **2** (*often* **Scout**, *formerly* **Boy Scout**) a member of the Scout Association. See also VENTURE SCOUT, CUB SCOUT, BEAVER. **3** in the US: a member of the **Girl Scouts**, an organization similar to the Guides. **4** a TALENT SCOUT. **5** *colloq* a search □ *They had a scout around for it in the potting shed.* ▻ *verb* (*scouted, scouting*) *intr* **1** to act as a scout. **2** (*often* **scout about** or **around**) *colloq* to make a search □ *scouting about for new premises.* ⓒ 14c: from French *escouter*, from Latin *auscultare* to listen.

scout[2] /skaʊt/ *verb* (*scouted, scouting*) to dismiss or reject something or someone with disdain. ⓒ 17c: from Norse *skuta* a taunt.

Scout Association ▻ *noun* a worldwide youth organization, promoting outdoor skills, character development and community spirit. ⓒ 1908: founded by Lord Baden-Powell.

Scouter /ˈskaʊtə(r)/ ▻ *noun* an adult leader in the Scout Association.

scow /skaʊ/ ▻ *noun* a large flat-bottomed barge for freight. ⓒ 18c: from Dutch *schouw.*

scowl /skaʊl/ ▻ *verb* (*scowled, scowling*) *intr* **1** to wrinkle the brow in a malevolent or angry look. **2** to look disapprovingly, angrily or menacingly. ▻ *noun* a scowling expression. • **scowling** *adj.* • **scowlingly** *adverb.* ⓒ 14c: from Danish *skule* to cast down the eyes.

SCPS ▻ *abbreviation* Society of Civil and Public Servants.

SCR ▻ *abbreviation* Senior Common Room.

Scrabble /ˈskrabəl/ ▻ *noun, trademark* a game in which individual letter pieces are used by players to form words. ⓒ 1950s.

scrabble /ˈskrabəl/ ▻ *verb* (*scrabbled, scrabbling*) *intr* **1** to scratch, grope or struggle frantically. **2** to scrawl. ▻ *noun* an act of scrabbling. ⓒ 16c: from Dutch *schrabben* to scratch.

scrag ▻ *noun* **1** the thin part of a neck of mutton or veal, providing poor quality meat. Also **scrag-end**. **2** an unhealthily thin person or animal. **3** *slang* the human neck. ▻ *verb* (*scragged, scragging*) *colloq* **1** to wring the neck of (an animal); to throttle. **2** to attack or beat up. ⓒ 16c: perhaps from CRAG.

scraggy /ˈskragɪ/ ▻ *adj* (*scraggier, scraggiest*) unhealthily thin; scrawny. • **scragginess** *noun.*

scram /skram/ ▻ *verb* (*scrammed, scramming*) *intr, colloq* often as a command: to go away at once; to be off. ⓒ 1920s: perhaps from SCRAMBLE.

scramble /ˈskrambəl/ ▻ *verb* (*scrambled, scrambling*) **1** *intr* to crawl or climb using hands and feet, especially hurriedly or frantically. **2** *intr* to struggle violently against others □ *There are starving people scrambling to find food.* **3** to get along or cope somehow □ *We'll just have to scramble through.* **4** to cook (eggs) whisked up with milk, butter, etc. **5** to throw or jumble together haphazardly. **6** to rewrite (a message) in code form, for secret transmission. **7** to transmit (a message) in a distorted form intelligible only by means of an electronic scrambler. **8** *intr* said of military aircraft or air crew: to take off immediately in response to an emergency. ▻ *noun* **1** an act of scrambling. **2** a dash or struggle to beat others in getting something. **3** a disorderly or chaotic performance. **4** a walk or hike over rough ground. **5** an immediate take-off in an emergency. **6** a cross-country motorcar or motorcycle race. • **scrambling** *adj, noun.* ⓒ 16c: from dialect *scramb* to rake together with the hands.

scrambler /ˈskramblə(r)/ ▻ *noun, electronics* an electronic device, used to transmit secret communications, etc that modifies radio or telephone signals so that they can only be made intelligible by means of a special decoding device.

scrambling circuit ▻ *noun, electronics* in communication systems: a circuit used to prevent unauthorized personnel gaining access to sound, data or video signals, by using a scrambler to code the original signal before transmission.

scramjet /ˈskramdʒɛt/ ▻ *noun* a RAMJET engine that operates at supersonic speeds, the air required for combustion being compressed by the forward motion of the engine. ⓒ 1960s: from supersonic combustion *ramjet.*

scrap[1] ▻ *noun* **1** a small piece; a fragment. **2** waste material, especially metal, for recycling or re-using. **3** (**scraps**) leftover pieces of food. ▻ *verb* (*scrapped, scrapping*) to discard or cease to use; to abandon as unworkable. • **not a scrap** not even the smallest amount □ *He wasn't a scrap of use to us.* • **throw something on the scrap heap** to reject or discard it as useless. ⓒ 14c: from Norse *skrap.*

scrap² *colloq* ▻ *noun* a fight or quarrel, usually physical. ▻ *verb* (***scrapped***, ***scrapping***) *intr* to fight or quarrel. ◷ 17c: from SCRAPE.

scrapbook ▻ *noun* a book with blank pages for pasting in cuttings, pictures, etc.

scrape ▻ *verb* (***scraped***, ***scraping***) **1** (*also* **scrape something along, over,** *etc* **something**) to push or drag (especially a sharp object) along or over (a hard or rough surface). **2** *intr* to move along a surface with a grazing action. **3** to graze (the skin) by a scraping action. **4** to move along (a surface) with a grating sound. **5** *intr* to make a grating sound. **6** (*also* **scrape something off**) to remove it from or smooth a surface with such an action. **7** to make savings through hardship □ *We managed to scrape enough for a holiday.* **8** *intr*, *colloq* to play the fiddle. ▻ *noun* **1** an instance, process or act of dragging or grazing. **2** a part damaged or cleaned by scraping. **3** a scraped area in the ground. **4** a graze (of the skin). **5** a backward sliding movement of one foot accompanying a bow. **6** *colloq* a difficult or embarrassing situation or predicament. **7** *colloq* a fight or quarrel. ● **scraper** *noun* **1** a person who scrapes. **2** a scraping tool, device or machine. ● **bow and scrape** to be over-obsequious. ● **scrape acquaintance with someone** to contrive to get to know them. ● **scrape the bottom of the barrel** to utilize the very last and worst of one's resources, opinions, etc. ◷ Anglo-Saxon *scrapian*.

■ **scrape through** or **by** to manage or succeed in doing something narrowly or with difficulty □ *He just scraped through the interview.*

■ **scrape something together** or **up** to collect it little by little, usually with difficulty.

scraperboard and **scratchboard** ▻ *noun* a board covered with a thin layer of clay and ink which is scraped or scratched away using special blades, leaving a fine line. See also SGRAFFITO.

scrap heap ▻ *noun* **1** a place where unwanted and useless objects, eg old furniture, are collected. **2** the state of being discarded or abandoned □ *They consigned the idea to the scrap heap.*

scrapie /ˈskreɪpɪ/ ▻ *noun*, *agric* an often fatal disease of sheep, often characterized by severe itching and a tendency to rub against trees and other objects for relief, resulting in wool loss. ◷ Early 20c: from *scrape*.

scrappy /ˈskrapɪ/ ▻ *adj* (***scrappier***, ***scrappiest***) fragmentary or disjointed; not uniform or flowing. ● **scrappily** *adverb*. ● **scrappiness** *noun*.

scratch ▻ *verb* (***scratches***, ***scratched***, ***scratching***) **1** to draw a sharp or pointed object across (a surface), causing damage or making marks. **2** to make (a mark) by such action. **3** *tr & intr* to rub the skin with the fingernails, especially to relieve itching. **4** to dig or scrape with the claws. **5** (*usually* **scratch something out** or **off**) to erase or cancel it. **6** *intr* to make a grating noise. **7** *intr* to withdraw from a contest, competition, etc. ▻ *noun* (***scratches***) **1** an act of scratching. **2** a mark made by scratching. **3** a scratching sound. **4** a superficial wound or minor injury. ▻ *adj* **1** casually or hastily got together; improvised □ *a scratch meal.* **2** said of a competitor: not given a handicap. ● **scratcher** *noun*. ● **scratchily** *adverb*. ● **scratchiness** *noun*. ● **come up to scratch** *colloq* to meet the required or expected standard from the former meaning of the line in the ring up to which boxers were led before fighting.. ● **from scratch** from the beginning; without the benefit of any preparation or previous experience. ● **scratch the surface** to deal only superficially with an issue or problem. ● **you scratch my back and I'll scratch yours** *colloq* if you do me a favour I'll do you one in return. ◷ 15c: as *cracche* to scratch.

scratchboard see SCRAPERBOARD

scratchcard ▻ *noun* a form of lottery card covered with a thin opaque film, which is scratched off to reveal symbols or numbers which may correspond to prizes of various kinds, especially cash.

scratch pad ▻ *noun*, *chiefly US* a notepad or jotter.

scratch video ▻ *noun* a video film produced by piecing together images from other films.

scratchy /ˈskratʃɪ/ ▻ *adj* (***scratchier***, ***scratchiest***) **1** making the marks or noises of scratching. **2** causing or likely to cause itching.

scrawl ▻ *verb* (***scrawled***, ***scrawling***) *tr & intr* to write or draw illegibly, untidily or hurriedly □ *scrawled a note on the back of an envelope.* ▻ *noun* untidy or illegible handwriting. ● **scrawler** *noun*. ● **scrawly** *adj*. ◷ 17c: perhaps connected with CRAWL and SPRAWL.

scrawny /ˈskrɔːnɪ/ ▻ *adj* (***scrawnier***, ***scrawniest***) unhealthily thin and bony. ● **scrawnily** *adverb*. ● **scrawniness** *adj*.

scream ▻ *verb* (***screamed***, ***screaming***) **1** *tr & intr* to cry out in a loud high-pitched voice, as in fear, pain or anger. **2** *intr* to laugh shrilly or uproariously. **3** (*often* **scream at someone**) usually said of something unpleasant or garish: to be all too obvious or apparent □ *Those turquoise trousers really scream at you.* ▻ *noun* **1** a sudden loud piercing cry or noise. **2** *colloq* an extremely amusing person, thing or event. ● **screaming** *adj*. ● **screamingly** *adverb*. ◷ Anglo-Saxon *scræmen*.

■ **scream past, through,** *etc* to go at great speed, especially making a shrill noise □ *The train screamed through the tunnel.*

screamer ▻ *noun* **1** someone or something that screams. **2** any of three species of large spur-winged S American birds found near water or in marshland, the commonest of which is the **crested screamer**. **3** *printing, slang* an exclamation mark. ◷ 18c.

the screaming habdabs see HABDABS

scree ▻ *noun* (***screes***) *geol* a sloping mass of rock debris that piles up at the base of cliffs or on the side of a mountain. ◷ 18c: from Norse *skritha* landslip.

screech ▻ *noun* a harsh, shrill and sudden cry, voice or noise. ▻ *verb* (***screeches***, ***screeched***, ***screeching***) **1** *tr & intr* to utter a screech or make a sound like a screech. **2** to speak in such a way. ● **screecher** *noun*. ● **screechy** *adj*. ◷ 16c as *scrichen*.

screech owl ▻ *noun* **1** any of various small N American owls with grey or reddish-brown plumage, which are characterized by a long quavery cry. **2** a BARN OWL.

screed ▻ *noun* **1** a long and often tedious spoken or written passage. **2** *building* a strip of plaster laid on the surface of a wall as a guide to the thickness of the full coat of plaster to be applied. **3** *building* a layer of mortar applied to smooth off the surface of a floor. Also called **screeding**. ● **screeder** *noun*. ◷ Anglo-Saxon *screade* shred.

screen ▻ *noun* **1** a movable set of foldable hinged panels, used to partition off part of a room for privacy. **2** a single panel used for protection against strong heat or light, or any other outside influence. **3** a WINDSCREEN. **4** a sheltering row of trees, shrubs, etc. **5** a wire netting placed over windows for keeping out insects. **6** a coarse sifting apparatus or utensil. **7** a partition used to separate off a church choir or side chapel, usually from the nave. **8** the wide end of a TV set on which the images are formed. **9** a white surface onto which films or slides are projected. **10** (**the screen**) the medium of cinema or television □ *She is a star of the stage and the screen.* **11** *photog* a glass plate with a coarse surface on which the image of a photographed object is focused. **12** *printing* a glass plate with dots or closely-scored lines of a given coarseness or frequency for printing half-tone photographs. **13** *cricket* a SIGHT-SCREEN. **14** *electronics* a SCREEN GRID. **15** *military* a body of troops or formation of ships surrounding the bulk of the army or fleet as a cover or protection for its activity.

▷ *verb* (***screened, screening***) **1** to shelter or conceal. **2** to sift coarsely. **3** to subject someone to tests in order to discern their ability, reliability, worthiness, etc. **4** to test someone in order to check for the presence of disease. **5** to show or project (a film, programme, etc) at the cinema or on TV. **6** to make a motion picture or film of something. • **screener** *noun*. • **screening** *noun*. ⓘ 14c: from French *escran*.

■ **screen something off** to separate or partition it with a screen.

screen grid ▷ *noun, electronics* an electrode placed between the control grid and anode in a valve, having an invariable potential in order to eliminate positive feedback and instability.

screenings /ˈskriːnɪŋz/ ▷ *plural noun* material eliminated by sifting.

screenplay ▷ *noun* the script of a film, comprising dialogue, stage directions, and details for characters and sets.

screen printing, **screen process** and **silk-screen printing** ▷ *noun* a stencil technique in which coloured ink is forced through a fine silk or nylon mesh.

screen-saver ▷ *noun, computing* a program which temporarily blanks out a screen display, or displays a pre-set pattern, when a computer is switched on but is not in active use.

screen test ▷ *noun* a filmed audition to test whether or not an actor or actress is suitable for cinema work.

screen writer ▷ *noun* a writer of screenplays for film, television, etc.

screw ▷ *noun* **1** a small metal cylinder with a spiral ridge or THREAD down the shaft and a slot in its head, driven into position in wood, etc by rotation using a screwdriver, usually used as a fastening device. **2** any object similar in shape or function. **3** the turn or twist of a screw. **4** *snooker, billiards* a shot in which the cue ball is subjected to sidespin or backspin. **5** *slang* a prison officer. **6** *coarse slang* an act of sexual intercourse. **7** a SCREW PROPELLER or a ship driven by one. **8** a THUMBSCREW. **9** *colloq* wages or salary. ▷ *verb* (***screwed, screwing***) **1** to twist (a screw) into place. **2** to push or pull with a twisting action. **3** *colloq* to swindle or cheat. **4** *snooker, billiards* to put sidespin or backspin on (the cue ball). **5** *tr & intr, coarse slang* to have sexual intercourse with someone. • **screwer** *noun*. • **have one's head screwed on** or **screwed on the right way** *colloq* to be a sensible person. • **have a screw loose** *colloq* to be slightly mad or crazy. • **put the screws on someone** *colloq* to use force or pressure on them ⓘ a reference to thumbscrews, an old instrument of torture. • **screw** or **pluck up one's courage** to prepare oneself or become confident enough for an ordeal or difficulty. • **screw it, them, you,** *etc: coarse slang* an exclamation of disgust, frustration, scorn, etc. ⓘ 15c: from French *escroue*, ultimately from Latin *scrofa* SOW², because of the resemblance between a pig's curly tail and the thread of the screw.

■ **screw something from** or **out of someone** *colloq* to obtain it by intense persuasion or threats □ *They tried to screw more money out of them.*

■ **screw something up** or **together** to attach or assemble it by means of screws.

■ **screw someone up** *slang* to cause them to become extremely anxious, nervous or psychologically disturbed.

■ **screw something up** *slang* to ruin or bungle it.

screwball ▷ *noun, slang, N Amer, especially US* a crazy person; an eccentric. ▷ *adj* crazy; eccentric.

screwdriver ▷ *noun* a hand-held tool with a metal shaft with a shaped end that fits into the slot, etc on a screw's head, turned repeatedly to twist a screw into position.

screwed-up ▷ *adj, slang* said of a person: extremely anxious, nervous or psychologically disturbed.

screw eye ▷ *noun* a screw formed into a loop for attaching string, rope, wire, etc.

screw propeller ▷ *noun* a propeller with helical blades for powering a ship.

screw top ▷ *noun* **1** a round lid that is screwed off and on to open and re-seal a bottle or other container. **2** a container with such a top. ▷ *adj* (**screw-top**) referring or relating to such a lid or container □ *screw-top bottle.*

screw-up ▷ *noun, slang* **1** a disastrous occurrence or failure. **2** a person who has messed up (their life, etc).

screwy /ˈskruːɪ/ ▷ *adj* (***screwier, screwiest***) *colloq* crazy; eccentric.

scribble /ˈskrɪbəl/ ▷ *verb* (***scribbled, scribbling***) **1** *tr & intr* to write quickly or untidily; to scrawl. **2** *intr* to draw meaningless lines or shapes absent-mindedly. ▷ *noun* **1** untidy or illegible handwriting; scrawl. **2** meaningless written lines or shapes. • **scribbler** *derog* a worthless writer. • **scribbly** *adj*. ⓘ 15c: from Latin *scribillare*, from *scribere* to write.

scribe ▷ *noun* **1** a person employed to make handwritten copies of documents before printing was invented. **2** in biblical times: a Jewish lawyer or teacher of law. **3** a tool with a pointed blade for scoring lines on wood or metal. ▷ *verb* (***scribed, scribing***) to mark or score lines with a scribe or anything similar. • **scribal** *adj*. • **scriber** *noun* a scribing tool. ⓘ 14c: from Latin *scriba*, from *scribere* to write.

scrim ▷ *noun* a thin open cotton fabric used as lining in upholstery, in bookbinding, for curtains, etc. ⓘ 18c.

scrimmage /ˈskrɪmɪdʒ/ and **scrummage** /ˈskrʌ-/ ▷ *noun* **1** a noisy brawl or struggle. **2** *Amer football* play between the opposing teams beginning with the SNAP and ending when the ball is dead. **3** *rugby* a SCRUM (*noun* 9). ▷ *verb* (***scrimmaged, scrimmaging***) *intr* to take part in a scrimmage. ⓘ 15c: a variant of SKIRMISH.

scrimp ▷ *verb* (***scrimped, scrimping***) *intr* to live economically; to be frugal or sparing. • **scrimpiness** *noun*. • **scrimpy** *adj*. • **scrimp and save** to be sparing and niggardly, often out of necessity. ⓘ 18c: related to Swedish and Danish *skrumpen* shrivelled.

scrimshank or **skrimshank** /ˈskrɪmʃaŋk/ ▷ *verb* (***scrimshanked, scrimshanking***) *intr, military slang* to evade work or duties. • **scrimshanker** *noun*. ⓘ Late 19c.

scrimshaw /ˈskrɪmʃɔː/ ▷ *noun* handicrafts done by sailors in their spare time, such as engraving or carving designs on shells, ivory, bone, etc. ▷ *verb* (***scrimshawed, scrimshawing***) to work or decorate something in this way. ⓘ 19c.

scrip ▷ *noun* **1** a scrap of paper, especially one with writing on it. **2** *colloq* a doctor's prescription. **3** *commerce* a provisional certificate issued before a formal share certificate is drawn up. ⓘ 18c: a shortened form of PRESCRIPTION and SUBSCRIPTION.

script ▷ *noun* **1** a piece of handwriting. **2** type which imitates handwriting, or vice versa. **3** the printed text of a play, film or broadcast. **4** a set of characters used for writing; an alphabet □ *Cyrillic script.* **5** a candidate's examination answer paper. **6** *law* an original document. ▷ *verb* (***scripted, scripting***) to write the script of (a play, film or broadcast). ⓘ 14c: from Latin *scriptum*, from *scribere* to write.

scripture or **Scripture** /ˈskrɪptʃə(r)/ ▷ *noun* (***scriptures***) **1** the sacred writings of a religion. **2** (*also* **the Scriptures**) the Christian Bible. • **scriptural** *adj* relating to or derived from scripture. ⓘ 13c: from Latin *scriptura*, from *scribere* to write.

scriptwriter ▷ *noun* a person who writes scripts. • **scriptwriting** *noun*.

scrivener /ˈskrɪvənə(r)/ ▻ *noun, historical* a person who drafts or writes out copies of legal or other official documents. • **scrivening** *noun* writing. ◷ 14c: from French *escrivain*, from SCRIBE.

scrofula /ˈskrɒfjʊlə/ ▻ *noun, pathol* the former name for tuberculosis of the lymph nodes, especially of the neck. Also called **king's evil**. • **scrofulous** *adj*. ◷ 14c: from Latin *scrofulae*, from *scrofa* a SOW², apparently prone to it.

scroll /skroʊl/ ▻ *noun* **1** a roll of paper or parchment usually containing an inscription, now only a ceremonial format, eg for academic degrees. **2** an ancient text in this format □ *the Dead Sea Scrolls.* **3** a decorative spiral shape, eg carved in stonework or in handwriting. ▻ *verb* (*scrolled, scrolling*) **1** to roll into a scroll or scrolls. **2** to cut a length of material into scrolls. **3** *tr & intr, computing* (*often* **scroll up** or **down**) to move the text displayed on a VDU up or down to bring into view data that cannot all be seen at the same time. • **scrolled** *adj*. ◷ 15c as *scrowle*.

Scrooge /skruːdʒ/ ▻ *noun* a miserly person. ◷ 19c: named after Ebenezer Scrooge in *A Christmas Carol* (1843) by Charles Dickens (1812–70).

scrotum /ˈskroʊtəm/ ▻ *noun* (*scrota* /-tə/ or *scrotums*) *biol* the sac of skin that encloses the testicles. • **scrotal** *adj* relating to or in the region of the scrotum. ◷ 16c: Latin.

scrounge /skraʊndʒ/ ▻ *verb* (*scrounged, scrounging*) **1** *tr & intr, colloq* to get something by shamelessly asking or begging; to cadge or sponge □ *He scrounged a fiver off his old granny.* **2** *intr* (*often* **scrounge for something**) to hunt or search around for it. • **scrounger** *noun*. • **scrounging** *noun*. ◷ Early 20c: from dialect *scrunge* to steal.

scrub¹ ▻ *verb* (*scrubbed, scrubbing*) **1** *tr & intr* to rub hard, especially with a stiff brush, in order to remove dirt. **2** to wash or clean by hard rubbing. **3** *colloq* to cancel or abandon (plans, etc) □ *Scrub your plans for a day out, you're needed here.* **4** to purify (a gas). **5** *intr* to use a scrubbing brush. **6** *intr* to make a rapid to-and-fro movement as if scrubbing. ▻ *noun* an act of scrubbing. ◷ 14c: from German *schrubben*.

▪ **scrub up** said of a surgeon, etc: to wash the hands and arms thoroughly before performing, or assisting at, an operation.

scrub² ▻ *noun* **1** vegetation consisting of stunted trees and evergreen shrubs collectively. **2** (*also* **scrubland**) an area, usually with poor soil or low rainfall, containing such vegetation. **3** an inferior domestic animal of mixed or unknown parentage. **4** *N Amer* a player in a second or inferior team. **5** a small or insignificant person. **6** anything small or insignificant. **7** (**the scrub**) *Austral colloq* a remote place far from civilization. ▻ *adj* **1** small or insignificant. **2** *N Amer* said of a player: in a second or inferior team. ◷ 14c: a variant of SHRUB.

scrubber /ˈskrʌbə(r)/ ▻ *noun* **1** someone who scrubs. **2** apparatus used for filtering out impurities from gas. **3** *offensive slang* an unattractive woman. **4** *offensive slang* a woman who regularly indulges in casual sex. ◷ 19c.

scrubby /ˈskrʌbɪ/ ▻ *adj* (*scrubbier, scrubbiest*) **1** covered with scrub. **2** said of trees, shrubs, etc: stunted. **3** small or insignificant. ◷ 16c: from SCRUB².

scruff¹ ▻ *noun* the back or nape of the neck. ◷ 18c: a variant of dialect *scuft*, from Norse *skoft* the hair.

scruff² ▻ *noun, colloq* a dirty untidy person. ◷ 19c: see SCURF.

scruffy /ˈskrʌfɪ/ ▻ *adj* (*scruffier, scruffiest*) shabby and untidy. • **scruffily** *adverb*. • **scruffiness** *noun*. ◷ 17c.

scrum ▻ *noun* **1** *rugby* the restarting of play when the players from both teams hunch together and tightly interlock their arms and heads in readiness for the ball being thrown in by the SCRUM HALF. **2** *colloq* a riotous struggle. ◷ 19c: a shortening of SCRUMMAGE.

▪ **scrum down** to form a scrum.

scrum half ▻ *noun, rugby* the player from each side whose duty is to put the ball into scrums, then regain possession of it as soon as it re-emerges.

scrummage see SCRIMMAGE

scrummy /ˈskrʌmɪ/ ▻ *adj* (*scrummier, scrummiest*) *chiefly Brit colloq* delicious; scrumptious. ◷ Early 20c: from SCRUMPTIOUS.

scrumptious /ˈskrʌmpʃəs/ ▻ *adj, colloq* **1** delicious. **2** delightful. • **scrumptiously** *adverb*. ◷ 19c: probably from SUMPTUOUS.

scrumpy /ˈskrʌmpɪ/ ▻ *noun* (*scrumpies*) strong dry cider with a harsh taste made from small sweet apples, especially as brewed in the West Country. ◷ Early 20c: from dialect *scrump* withered apples.

scrunch ▻ *verb* (*scrunches, scrunched, scrunching*) **1** *tr & intr* to crunch or crush, especially with relation to the noise produced. **2** *intr* to make a crunching sound. ▻ *noun* an act or the sound of scrunching. ◷ 19c: a variant of CRUNCH.

scrunch-dry ▻ *verb* to scrunch (hair) into handfuls during blow-drying to give it more shape and body.

scrunchy /ˈskrʌntʃɪ/ ▻ *adj* (*scrunchier, scrunchiest*) referring or relating to a scrunching sound. ▻ *noun* (*also* **scrunchie**) (*plural* **scrunchies**) a tight ring of elastic covered in coloured fabric used to hold the hair in a ponytail.

scruple /ˈskruːpəl/ ▻ *noun* **1** (*usually* **scruples**) a sense of moral responsibility making one reluctant or unwilling to do wrong □ *He has no scruples.* **2** a unit of weight equal to 20 grains (GRAIN *noun* 9). ▻ *verb* (*scrupled, scrupling*) *intr* to be reluctant or unwilling because of scruples □ *I would scruple to steal even if we were starving.* • **make scruple** or **scruples about something** to offer moral objections to it. ◷ 14c: from Latin *scrupulus* pebble or anxiety, from *scrupus*.

scrupulous /ˈskruːpjʊləs/ ▻ *adj* **1** having scruples; being careful to do nothing morally wrong. **2** extremely conscientious and meticulous. • **scrupulosity** *noun*. • **scrupulously** *adverb*. • **scrupulousness** *noun*.

scrutineer /skruːtɪˈnɪə(r)/ ▻ *noun* a person who scrutinizes something, especially the collecting and counting of votes. ◷ 16c.

scrutinize or **scrutinise** /ˈskruːtɪnaɪz/ ▻ *verb* (*scrutinized, scrutinizing*) to subject to scrutiny; to examine closely. • **scrutinizer** *noun*. ◷ 17c.

scrutiny /ˈskruːtɪnɪ/ ▻ *noun* (*scrutinies*) **1** a close, careful and thorough examination or inspection. **2** a penetrating or searching look. **3** the official examination of election votes. ◷ 15c: from Latin *scrutinium*, from *scrutari* to search even to the rags, from *scruta* rags.

scuba /ˈskuːbə, ˈskjuːbə/ ▻ *noun* (*scubas*) a device used by skin-divers in **scuba diving**, consisting of one or two cylinders of compressed air connected by a tube to a mouthpiece allowing underwater breathing. ▻ *verb* (*scubaed, scubaing*) *intr* to swim using scuba gear. ◷ 1950s: from self-contained underwater breathing apparatus.

Scud ▻ *noun* a kind of surface-to-surface missile made in the former Soviet Union, originally designed to carry nuclear warheads but later modified for use with conventional weapons.

scud ▻ *verb* (*scudded, scudding*) *intr* **1** said especially of clouds: to sweep quickly and easily across the sky. **2** said especially of sailing vessels: to sail swiftly driven by the force of a strong wind. ▻ *noun* **1** the act of scudding. **2** cloud, rain or spray driven by the wind. • **scudder** *noun*. ◷ 16c: from German *schudden* to shake.

scuff ▻ *verb* (*scuffed, scuffing*) *tr & intr* **1** to brush, graze or scrape (especially shoes or heels) while walking. **2** to become grazed or shabby through wear. **3** to drag (the feet) when walking. ▷ *noun* **1** the act of scuffing. **2** an area worn away by scuffing. ◷ 19c: see SCUFFLE.

scuffle /ˈskʌfəl/ ▷ *noun* a confused fight or struggle. ▷ *verb* (***scuffled***, ***scuffling***) *intr* to take part in a scuffle. ◷ 16c: from Swedish *skuffa* to shove.

sculduggery see SKULDUGGERY

scull ▷ *noun* **1** either of a pair of short light oars used by one rower. **2 a** a small light racing boat propelled by one rower using a pair of such oars; **b (sculls)** a race between such boats. **3** a large single oar over the stern of a boat, moved from side to side to propel it forward. **4** an act or spell of sculling. ▷ *verb* (***sculled***, ***sculling***) to propel with a scull or sculls. • **sculler** *noun* **1** a person who sculls. **2** a small boat propelled by sculling. • **sculling** *noun*. ◷ 14c: as *sculle*.

scullery /ˈskʌlərɪ/ ▷ *noun* (***sculleries***) a room attached to the kitchen where basic chores, such as the cleaning of kitchen utensils, are carried out. ◷ 14c: from French *escuelerie*.

sculpt ▷ *verb* (***sculpted***, ***sculpting***) **1** *tr & intr* to carve or model. **2** to sculpture. ◷ 19c: from French *sculpter*, from Latin *sculpere* to carve.

sculptor /ˈskʌlptə(r)/ and **sculptress** /ˈskʌlptrəs/ ▷ *noun* a person who practises the art of sculpture. ◷ 17c: Latin.

sculpture /ˈskʌlptʃə(r)/ ▷ *noun* **1** the art or act of carving or modelling with clay, wood, stone, plaster, etc. **2** a work, or works, of art produced in this way. **3** *bot, zool* the natural ridges, spines, etc found on the surface of animals and plants. ▷ *verb* (***sculptured***, ***sculpturing***) **1** to carve, mould or sculpt. **2** to represent in sculpture. • **sculptural** *adj* **1** relating to sculpture. **2** having the qualities of sculpture. • **sculptured** *adj* **1** carved or engraved. **2** said of physical features: fine and regular, like those of figures in classical sculpture. **3** *bot, zool* having ridges, spines, etc. ◷ 14c: from Latin *sculptura*, from *sculpere* to carve.

sculpturesque /skʌlptʃəˈrɛsk/ ▷ *adj* similar to or characteristic of sculptures.

scum ▷ *noun* **1** dirt or waste matter floating on the surface of a liquid, especially in the form of foam or froth. **2** *colloq, derog* a worthless or contemptible person or such people. ▷ *verb* (***scummed***, ***scumming***) **1** to remove the scum from (a liquid). **2** *intr* to form or throw up a scum. • **scummer** *noun*. • **scummy** *adj*. ◷ 13c: from Dutch *schum* foam.

scumbag ▷ *noun* **1** *coarse slang* a contemptible person. **2** *chiefly US* a condom. ◷ 1960s.

scumble /ˈskʌmbəl/ ▷ *verb* (***scumbled***, ***scumbling***) to soften the effect of a drawing or painting by a very thin coat of opaque or semi-opaque colour, by light rubbing or by applying paint with a dry brush. ▷ *noun* **1** colour applied in this way. **2** the effect produced by this. • **scumbling** *noun*. ◷ 18c: perhaps related to SCUM.

scupper¹ /ˈskʌpə(r)/ ▷ *verb* (***scuppered***, ***scuppering***) **1** *colloq* to ruin or put an end to (a plan, an idea, etc). **2** to deliberately sink (a ship). ◷ 19c.

scupper² /ˈskʌpə(r)/ ▷ *noun* (*usually* **scuppers**) *naut* a hole or pipe in a ship's side through which water is drained off the deck. ◷ 15c: from *skopper*, perhaps related to SCOOP.

scurf ▷ *noun* **1** small flakes of dead skin, especially DANDRUFF. **2** any flaking or peeling substance. • **scurfiness** *noun*. • **scurfy** *adj*. ◷ Anglo-Saxon.

scurrilous /ˈskʌrɪləs/ ▷ *adj* indecently insulting or abusive, and unjustly damaging to the reputation □ *scurrilous remarks*. • **scurrilously** *adverb*. • **scurrility** /skəˈrɪlɪtɪ/ or **scurrilousness** *noun*. ◷ 16c: from Latin *scurrilis*, from *scurra* buffoon.

scurry /ˈskʌrɪ/ ▷ *noun* (***scurries***) **1** an act of or the sound of scurrying. **2** a sudden brief gust or fall, eg of wind or snow; a flurry. ◷ 16c: from *hurry-scurry* a reduplication of HURRY.

■ **scurry along, away, off,** *etc* to move hurriedly or briskly; to scuttle.

scurvy /ˈskɜːvɪ/ ▷ *noun, pathol* a disease caused by dietary deficiency of vitamin C and characterized by swollen bleeding gums, amnesia, bruising and pain in the joints. ▷ *adj* (***scurvier***, ***scurviest***) vile; contemptible. • **scurvily** *adverb*. • **scurviness** *noun*. ◷ Anglo-Saxon *scurf*.

scut ▷ *noun* a short tail, especially of a rabbit, hare or deer. ◷ 15c: from Norse *skutr* stern.

scutate /ˈskjuːteɪt/ ▷ *adj* **1** said of animals: protected by hard bony plates or scutes. **2** *bot* shield-shaped. ◷ 19c: from Latin *scutatus*, from *scutum* shield.

scute /skjuːt/ ▷ *noun* a hard bony plate forming part of the skin of animals such as armadillos, tortoises, etc. • **scutal** *adj*. ◷ 15c: from Latin *scutum* shield.

scutellum /skjʊˈtɛləm/ ▷ *noun* (***scutella*** /-tɛlə/) **1** *bot* in the seeds of certain flowering plants, eg maize: the tissue that surrounds, and serves as a food store for, the developing embryo. **2** the third dorsal plate of a segment of an insect's thorax. **3** a scale of a bird's foot. ◷ 18c: Latin, meaning 'tray', from *scutum* shield.

scutter /ˈskʌtə(r)/ *Brit dialect* ▷ *verb* (***scuttered***, ***scuttering***) *intr* to scurry or run hastily. ▷ *noun* a hasty run. ◷ 18c: a variant of SCUTTLE².

scuttle¹ /ˈskʌtəl/ ▷ *noun* **1** (*in full* **coal scuttle**) a container for holding coal, usually kept near a fire. **2** a shallow basket, especially one for holding vegetables, etc. • **scuttleful** *noun*. ◷ Anglo-Saxon *scutel*, from Latin *scutella* tray.

scuttle² /ˈskʌtəl/ ▷ *verb* (***scuttled***, ***scuttling***) *intr* to move quickly with haste; to scurry. ▷ *noun* a scuttling pace or movement. ◷ 15c: related to SCUD.

scuttle³ /ˈskʌtəl/ ▷ *noun* a lidded opening in a ship's side or deck. ▷ *verb* (***scuttled***, ***scuttling***) **1** *naut* to deliberately sink (a ship) by making holes in it or by opening the lids of the scuttles. **2** to ruin or destroy (eg plans). ◷ 15c: from French *escoutille* hatchway.

scutum /ˈskjuːtəm/ ▷ *noun* (***scuta*** /-tə/) **1** a SCUTE. **2** the second dorsal plate of an insect's thorax. ◷ 19c: Latin, meaning 'shield'.

scuzzy /ˈskʌzɪ/ ▷ *adj* (***scuzzier***, ***scuzziest***) *N Amer slang* filthy or scummy; sleazy. ◷ 1960s: perhaps a combination of SCUM and FUZZY.

Scylla /ˈsɪlə/ ▷ *noun, Greek mythol* a six-headed sea monster situated on a dangerous rock on the Italian side of the Straits of Messina, opposite **Charybdis** /kəˈrɪbdɪs/ a whirlpool. • **between Scylla and Charybdis** faced with danger on both sides, so that avoidance of one means exposure to the other. ◷ 16c: from Greek *Skylla*.

scythe /saɪð/ ▷ *noun* a tool with a wooden handle and a large curved blade, for cutting tall crops or grass by hand with a sweeping action. ▷ *verb* (***scythed***, ***scything***) to cut with a scythe. ◷ Anglo-Saxon *sithe*.

SD ▷ *abbreviation* **1** South Dakota. Also written **S Dak**. **2** *math* standard deviation.

SDA ▷ *abbreviation* Scottish Development Agency.

SDLP ▷ *abbreviation* Social and Democratic Labour Party.

SDP ▷ *abbreviation* Social Democratic Party.

SDR or **SDRs** ▷ *abbreviation* Special Drawing Rights.

SE ▷ *abbreviation* **1** Society of Engineers. **2** south-east or south-eastern. **3** *math* standard error.

Se ▷ *symbol, chem* selenium.

sea ▷ *noun* (***seas***) **1** (*usually* **the sea**) the large expanse of salt water covering the greater part of the Earth's surface. **2** any great expanse of water. **3** any geographical division of this, eg the Mediterranean Sea. **4** an area of this with reference to its calmness or turbulence □ *choppy seas*. **5** *as adj* □ *sea breeze*. **6** a large inland saltwater lake, eg the Dead Sea. **7** anything similar to the sea in its seemingly limitless mass or expanse □ *a sea of paperwork*. **8** a vast expanse or crowd □ *a sea of worshippers*. ● **all at sea** completely disorganized or at a loss. ● **at sea 1** away from land; in a ship on the sea or ocean. **2** completely disorganized or bewildered. ● **go to sea** to become a sailor. ● **put** or **put out to sea** to start a journey by sea. ◷ Anglo-Saxon *sæ*.

sea anchor ▷ *noun* a floating device dragged by a moving ship to slow it down or prevent it drifting off course.

sea anemone ▷ *noun* any of various marine invertebrates with a cylindrical and usually brightly-coloured body, numerous stinging tentacles, and attached by their bases to submerged weeds and rocks.

sea bed ▷ *noun* the bottom or floor of the sea.

seaboard ▷ *noun* a coast; the boundary between land and sea.

seaborgium /siː'bɔːgɪəm/ ▷ *noun, chem* (symbol **Sg**, atomic number 106) a name proposed for the radioactive element UNNILHEXIUM. ◷ Discovered 1974, but in March 1994 named after the US atomic scientist Glen Theodore Seaborg.

seaborne ▷ *adj* carried on or transported by the sea.

sea breeze ▷ *noun* a breeze blowing inland from the sea.

sea change ▷ *noun* a complete change or transformation.

sea cow ▷ *noun* **1** any of various large herbivorous mammals, especially the DUGONG or MANATEE. **2** formerly used to refer to the hippopotamus.

sea cucumber ▷ *noun* a sausage-shaped soft-bodied marine invertebrate, with a leathery skin and a mouth at one end surrounded by numerous tentacles.

sea dog ▷ *noun* an old or experienced sailor.

sea eagle ▷ *noun* any of several fish-eating eagles living near the sea.

seafaring ▷ *adj* travelling by or working at sea. ● **seafarer** *noun* a person who travels by sea; a sailor.

sea-floor spreading ▷ *noun, geol* the hypothesis that the oceanic crust is slowly expanding outwards sideways away from the oceanic ridges, as a result of the welling up of magma.

seafood ▷ *noun* shellfish and other edible marine fish.

seafront ▷ *noun* the side of the land, a town or a building facing the sea.

sea-girt ▷ *adj, poetry* surrounded by the sea.

seagoing ▷ *adj* said of a ship: designed or suitable for sea travel.

seagull see GULL[1]

sea holly ▷ *noun* a seashore plant similar to the thistle.

sea horse ▷ *noun* **1** any of various species of a small fish, native to warm coastal waters, that swims in an upright position, with its elongated head bent at right angles to its body. **2** *mythol* a sea monster with the body of a horse and the tail of a fish.

sea kale ▷ *noun* **1** a perennial maritime plant with broad fleshy bluish-green edible leaves and white flowers. **2** the young leaves and stems of this plant, which can be boiled and eaten as a vegetable.

seal[1] ▷ *noun* **1** a piece of wax, lead or other material, attached to a document and stamped with an official mark to show authenticity. **2** such a mark □ *the royal seal*. **3** an engraved metal stamp or ring for making such a mark eg on wax. **4** the mark itself. **5** a similar piece of material, with or without an official stamp, for keeping something closed. **6** a piece of rubber or other material serving to keep a joint airtight or watertight. **7** a token or object given, or a gesture made, as a pledge or guarantee. **8** a decorative adhesive label or stamp, usually sold for charity. **9** *RC Church* an obligation to keep discreet all that is said in confession. ▷ *verb* (***sealed, sealing***) **1** to fix a seal to something. **2** to fasten or stamp something with a seal. **3** to decide, settle or confirm □ *seal someone's fate* □ *seal a business agreement*. **4** to paint (eg wood) with a substance that protects against damage, especially the weather. **5** to close, especially permanently or for a long time. **6** *Austral, NZ* to tarmac. ● **set one's seal to something** to authorize, approve or formally endorse it. ◷ 13c: from French *seel*, from Latin *sigillum*, from *signum* mark.

■ **seal something off** to isolate an area, preventing entry by unauthorized persons.

■ **seal something up** to make it securely closed, airtight or watertight with a seal.

seal[2] ▷ *noun* **1** any of various marine mammals with a smooth-skinned or furry streamlined body and limbs modified to form webbed flippers, found mainly in cool coastal waters. Compare SEA LION. **2** sealskin. ▷ *verb* (***sealed, sealing***) *intr* to hunt seals. ● **sealer** *noun* a seal hunter. ◷ Anglo-Saxon *seolh*.

sealant /'siːlənt/ ▷ *noun* **1** any material used for sealing a gap to prevent the leaking of water, etc. **2** any material painted on to protect against weathering and wear. ◷ 1940s.

sealed-beam ▷ *noun* said of car headlights: consisting of a lens and reflector as a complete unit within a vacuum.

sea legs ▷ *plural noun* **1** the ability to resist seasickness. **2** the ability to walk steadily on the deck of a pitching ship.

sea level ▷ *noun* the mean level of the surface of the sea between high and low tides, therefore the point from which land height is measured.

sealing-wax ▷ *noun* a waxy mixture consisting of shellac, turpentine and colour, used for seals on documents.

sea lion ▷ *noun* any of numerous species of marine mammal with small ears (unlike seals, which have no external ears), long whiskers, paddle-like forelimbs and large hind flippers.

sea loch see LOCH 2

seal of approval ▷ *noun, often facetious* official approval.

seal ring ▷ *noun* a SIGNET RING.

sealskin ▷ *noun* **1** the prepared skin of a furry seal, or an imitation of it. **2** a garment made from this. **3** *as adj* □ *a sealskin jacket*.

Sealyham terrier /'siːlɪəm —/ ▷ *noun* a type of dog with a long body, a thick wiry pale coat, short legs and tail, a long head with eyebrows, moustache, beard and short pendulous ears. ◷ 19c: named after Sealyham estate near Haverfordwest, Wales, where it was first bred.

seam ▷ *noun* **1** a join between edges, especially one that has been welded. **2** a similar join where pieces of fabric have been stitched together. **3** *geol* a layer of coal or ore in the earth. **4** a wrinkle or scar, especially as a result of surgical incisions. **5** *cricket* SEAM BOWLING, as delivered by a SEAMER. ▷ *verb* (***seamed, seaming***) **1** to join edge to edge. **2** to scar or wrinkle. ◷ Anglo-Saxon, from *siwian* to sew.

seaman ▷ *noun* (***seamen***) a sailor below the rank of officer. ● **seamanlike** *adj*. ● **seamanly** *adj*. ● **seamanship** *noun* sailing skills, including navigation.

seam bowling ▷ *noun, cricket* bowling in which the seam of the ball is used by the bowler to make the ball swerve in flight, or first to swerve and then to break in the opposite direction in pitching. ◷ 19c.

seamer ▻ *noun, cricket* a ball delivered by seam bowling.

seamless ▻ *adj* having no seams; made from a single piece of fabric, etc.

seamstress /'siːmstrɪs/ ▻ *noun* a woman who sews, especially as a profession. ⓒ 17c.

seamy /'siːmɪ/ ▻ *adj* (***seamier***, ***seamiest***) sordid; disreputable. • **seaminess** *noun*. ⓒ 17c: from SEAM.

séance or **seance** /'seɪɑns, 'seɪɑ̃s/ ▻ *noun* a meeting at which a person, especially a spiritualist, attempts to contact the spirits of dead people on behalf of other people present. ⓒ 18c: French, meaning 'sitting', from Latin *sedere* to sit.

sea otter ▻ *noun* a marine mammal native to N Pacific coasts, with a broader body than freshwater otters.

sea pink ▻ *noun* THRIFT.

seaplane ▻ *noun* an aeroplane designed to take off from and land on water.

seaport ▻ *noun* a coastal town with a port for seagoing ships.

SEAQ /'siːak/ ▻ *abbreviation* Stock Exchange Automated Quotation.

sear /sɪə(r)/ ▻ *verb* (***seared***, ***searing***) **1** to scorch. **2** to dry out or wither. **3** to make someone callous or unfeeling. ▻ *noun* a mark made by scorching. • **searing** *adj* burning or intense □ *We sat outside in the searing heat.* ⓒ Anglo-Saxon *searian* to dry up.

search /sɜːtʃ/ ▻ *verb* (***searches***, ***searched***, ***searching***) **1** *tr & intr* to explore something thoroughly in order to try to find someone or something □ *searched the wardrobe for his pink shirt.* **2** to check the clothing or body of someone for concealed objects □ *Everyone is searched before entering the building.* **3** to examine closely or scrutinize □ *search one's conscience.* **4** to probe eg by thorough questioning. **5** to ransack. ▻ *noun* an act of searching. • **in search of someone** or **something** searching for it. • **search me** *colloq* I've no idea; I don't know. ⓒ 15c: from French *cerchier*, from Latin *circare* to go around.

■ **search something out** to uncover it after a thorough check or exploration.

search engine ▻ *noun, computing* software for retrieving information from the Internet. ⓒ 1990s.

searching /'sɜːtʃɪŋ/ ▻ *adj* seeking to discover the truth by intensive examination or observation □ *a searching inquiry.* • **searchingly** *adverb*.

searchlight ▻ *noun* **1** a lamp and reflector throwing a powerful beam of light for illuminating an area in darkness. **2** the beam of light projected in this way.

search party ▻ *noun* a group of people participating in an organized search for a missing person or thing.

search warrant ▻ *noun* a legal document authorizing a police officer to search premises.

seascape ▻ *noun* a picture or photograph of a scene at sea.

Sea Scout ▻ *noun* a member of a division of the Scout Association providing training in seamanship.

seashell ▻ *noun* the empty shell of a marine invertebrate, especially a mollusc.

seashore ▻ *noun* the land immediately adjacent to the sea.

seasick *adj* suffering from seasickness.

seasickness ▻ *noun* nausea caused by the rolling or dipping motion of a ship.

seaside ▻ *noun* **1** (*usually* **the seaside**) a coastal area or town, especially a holiday resort. **2** *as adj* □ *seaside town.*

season /'siːzən/ ▻ *noun* **1** any of the four major periods (SPRING, SUMMER, AUTUMN and WINTER) into which the year is divided according to changes in weather patterns and other natural phenomena. **2** any period having particular characteristics □ *rainy season* □ *our busy season.* **3** a period of the year during which a particular sport, activity, etc is played or carried out □ *fishing season* □ *holiday season.* **4** a period during which a particular fruit or vegetable is in plentiful supply. **5** any particular period of time. ▻ *verb* (***seasoned***, ***seasoning***) **1** to flavour (food) by adding salt, pepper and/or other herbs and spices. **2** to prepare something, especially timber, for use by drying it out. **3** to tone down or temper. **4** to add interest or liveliness to something. • **seasoner** *noun*. • **in season 1** said of food, especially fruit and vegetables: readily available, as determined by its growing season. **2** said of game animals: legally allowed to be hunted and killed, according to the time of year. **3** said of a female animal: ready to mate; on heat. • **out of season 1** said of food, especially fruit and vegetables: not yet available. **2** said of game animals: legally not yet to be hunted. ⓒ 14c: from French *seson*, from Latin *satio* a sowing.

seasonable /'siːzənəbəl/ ▻ *adj* **1** said of weather: appropriate to the particular season. **2** coming or occurring at the right time; opportune. • **seasonableness** *noun*. • **seasonably** *adverb*. ⓒ 14c.

seasonal /'siːzənəl/ ▻ *adj* available, taking place or occurring only at certain times of the year. • **seasonality** *noun*. • **seasonally** *adverb*. ⓒ 19c.

seasonable, seasonal

• **Seasonable** means appropriate to the season, ie opportune; **seasonal** is a more neutral word relating to the seasons of the year.

seasonal affective disorder ▻ *noun, psychol* (abbreviation **SAD**) a recurrent change in mood occurring at a particular time of year, especially a pattern of repeated depression during the winter months.

seasoned /'siːzənd/ ▻ *adj* **1** said of food: flavoured □ *a well seasoned dish.* **2** matured or conditioned □ *seasoned wood.* **3** experienced □ *seasoned travellers.*

seasoning /'siːzənɪŋ/ ▻ *noun* **1** the process by which anything is seasoned. **2** any substance such as salt, pepper, herbs, spices, etc used to season food. ⓒ 16c.

season ticket ▻ *noun* a ticket, usually bought at a reduced price, allowing a specified or unlimited number of visits or journeys during a fixed period.

sea surgeon ▻ *noun* a SURGEON FISH.

sea swallow ▻ *noun* a TERN.

seat ▻ *noun* **1** anything designed or intended for sitting on. **2** a chair, bench, saddle, etc. **3** the part of it on which a person sits. **4** a place for sitting, eg in a cinema or theatre, especially a reservation for such a place □ *We booked four seats for the theatre tomorrow night.* **5** the buttocks. **6** the part of a garment covering the buttocks. **7** the base of an object, or any part on which it rests or fits. **8** a parliamentary or local government constituency. **9** a position on a committee or other administrative body. **10** an established centre □ *seats of learning.* **11** a place where anything is located, settled or established. **12** a large country mansion. ▻ *verb* (***seated***, ***seating***) **1** to place on a seat. **2** to cause to sit down. **3** to assign a seat to someone, eg at a dinner table. **4** to provide seats for (a specified number of people) □ *My car seats five.* **5** to place in any site, situation or location. **6** to fit firmly and accurately. **7** *tr & intr* to make (a skirt, trousers, etc) or become baggy by sitting □ *an unlined skirt will seat.* • **by the seat of one's pants** instinctively; by intuition. • **take a seat** to sit down. • **take one's seat** to take up one's allocated place or position, especially in parliament. ⓒ 13c: from Norse *sæti*.

seat belt ▻ *noun* a safety belt that prevents a passenger in a car, aeroplane, etc from being thrown violently forward in the event of an emergency stop, a crash, etc.

-seater /ˈsiːtə(r)/ ▻ *combining form, indicating* that something has seats for the specified number of people □ *a three-seater sofa.*

seating /ˈsiːtɪŋ/ ▻ *noun* **1** the provision of seats. **2** the number, allocation or arrangement of seats, eg in a dining-room. **3** the fabric covering on seats. **4** *mech* a supporting surface for a part or fitting. ⓒ 16c.

SEATO /ˈsiːtoʊ/ ▻ *abbreviation* South-East Asia Treaty Organization.

sea trout ▻ *noun* the SALMON TROUT.

sea urchin ▻ *noun* a common name for any of numerous species of ECHINODERM that have a spherical or heart-shaped shell covered by sharp protective spines.

seaward /ˈsiːwəd/ ▻ *adj* facing or moving toward the sea. ▻ *adverb* (*also* **seawards**) towards the sea.

seaweed ▻ *noun* **1** *bot* the common name for any of numerous species of marine algae. **2** such plants collectively.

seaworthy /ˈsiːwɜːðɪ/ ▻ *adj* said of a ship: fit for a voyage at sea. • **seaworthiness** *noun.*

sebaceous /sɪˈbeɪʃəs/ ▻ *adj* similar to, characteristic of or secreting sebum. ⓒ 18c: Latin.

sebaceous gland ▻ *noun, anatomy* in mammals: any of the tiny glands in the DERMIS of the skin, that protect the skin by secretion of SEBUM.

seborrhoea or (*US*) **seborrhea** /sɛbəˈrɪə/ *noun, pathol* a disorder causing an excessive discharge of sebum from the sebaceous glands. • **seborrhoeic** *adj.* ⓒ 19c: from Latin *sebum* + Greek *rhoia* flow.

sebum /ˈsiːbəm/ ▻ *noun, biol* the oily substance secreted by the sebaceous glands that lubricates and waterproofs the hair and skin. ⓒ 18c: Latin, meaning 'grease'.

SEC ▻ *abbreviation* Securities and Exchange Commission.

Sec ▻ *abbreviation* Secretary.

sec¹ /sɛk/ ▻ *noun, colloq* short for SECOND² sense 3 □ *wait a sec.* ▻ *abbreviation* SECOND² sense 1.

sec² /sɛk/ ▻ *adj* **1** said of wine: dry. **2** said of champagne: medium sweet. ⓒ 19c: French, meaning 'dry'.

sec³ /sɛk/ ▻ *abbreviation* secant.

SECAM /ˈsiːkam/ ▻ *abbreviation*: *Séquentiel Couleur à Mémoire* (French), a broadcasting system for colour television. See also PAL. ⓒ 1960s: developed in France, and later adopted in the former USSR, E Europe and certain Middle East countries.

secant /ˈsiːkənt/ ▻ *noun* (abbreviation **sec**) **1** *geom* a straight line that cuts a curve at one or more places. **2** *math* for a given angle in a right-angled triangle: the ratio of the length of the hypotenuse to the length of the side adjacent to the angle under consideration; the reciprocal of the cosine of an angle. ⓒ 16c: from Latin *secans*, from *secare* to cut.

secateurs /ˈsɛkətɜːz, sɛkəˈtɜːz/ ▻ *plural noun* small sharp shears for pruning bushes, etc. ⓒ 19c: French.

secede /sɪˈsiːd/ ▻ *verb* (***seceded, seceding***) *intr* to withdraw formally, eg from a political or religious body or alliance. • **seceder** *noun* a country, etc that secedes. ⓒ 18c: from Latin *secedere* to go apart, from *se* apart + *cedere* to go.

secession /sɪˈsɛʃən/ ▻ *noun* **1** the act of seceding. **2** a group of seceders. ⓒ 17c: from Latin *secessio*, from *secedere* to SECEDE.

sech /sɛʃ, sɛtʃ, ʃɛk, sɛkˈeɪtʃ/ ▻ *noun* a hyperbolic secant.

seclude /sɪˈkluːd/ ▻ *verb* (***secluded, secluding***) **1** to keep away or isolate from other contacts, associations or influences. **2** to keep out of view. ⓒ 15c: from Latin *secludere*, from *se* apart + *claudere* to shut.

secluded /sɪˈkluːdɪd/ ▻ *adj* **1** protected or away from people and noise; private and quiet. **2** hidden from view. • **secludedly** *adverb.* ⓒ 17c.

seclusion /sɪˈkluːʒən/ ▻ *noun* **1** the state of being secluded or the act of secluding. **2** peacefulness and privacy. **3** a private place. ⓒ 17c.

second¹ /ˈsɛkənd/ ▻ *adj* **1** in counting: next after or below the first, in order of sequence or importance. **2** alternate; other □ ***every second week.*** **3** additional; supplementary □ ***have a second go.*** **4** subordinate; inferior □ *second to none.* **5** (**the second**) **a** the second day of the month; **b** *golf* the second hole. **6** closely resembling or similar to someone of a previous period □ *He has been heralded as the second Shakespeare.* **7** in a vehicle engine: referring to the next to bottom forward gear □ *go into second.* **8** *music* singing or playing a part in harmony which is subordinate or slightly lower in pitch to another part □ *second soprano* □ *second violin.* ▻ *noun* **1** someone or something next in sequence after the first; someone or something of second class. **2** a place in the second class or rank. **3** in a vehicle engine: the second gear. **4** *higher education* a second-class honours degree, usually graded into first and second divisions. **5** an assistant to a boxer or duellist. **6** *music* the interval between successive tones of the diatonic scale. **7** (**seconds**) flawed or imperfect goods sold at reduced prices. **8** (**seconds**) *colloq* a second helping of food. **9** (**seconds**) *colloq* the second course of a meal. **10** a Cub Scout or Brownie Guide next in rank to a sixer. ▻ *verb* (***seconded, seconding***) **1** to declare formal support for (a proposal, or the person making it). **2** to give support or encouragement of any kind to someone or something. **3** to act as second to (a boxer or duellist). ▻ *adverb* secondly. • **second-to-none** best or supreme; unsurpassed or exceptional. ⓒ 13c: from Latin *secundus.*

second² /ˈsɛkənd/ *noun* **1 a** (abbreviation **sec** or **s**) a unit of time equal to $^1/_{60}$ of a minute; **b** (symbol **s**) the SI unit of time defined in terms of the resonance vibration of the caesium-133 atom. **2** *geom* (symbol ″) a unit of angular measurement equal to $^1/_{3600}$ of a degree or $^1/_{60}$ of a minute. **3** a moment □ *wait a second.* ⓒ 14c: from Latin *secunda minuta* secondary minute.

second³ /səˈkɒnd/ ▻ *verb* (***seconded, seconding***) to transfer someone temporarily to a different post, place or duty. See also SECONDMENT. ⓒ Early 19c: from French *en second* in the second rank.

Second Advent see SECOND COMING

secondary /ˈsɛkəndərɪ/ ▻ *adj* **1** being of lesser importance than the principal or primary concern; subordinate. **2** developed from something earlier or original □ *a secondary infection.* **3** said of education: between primary and higher or further, for pupils aged between 11 and 18. **4** *electronics* said of an electric circuit: having a device that induces current, eg a transformer. Compare PRIMARY, TERTIARY. **5** *geol* (**Secondary**) relating to the MESOZOIC era. ▻ *noun* (***secondaries***) **1** a subordinate person or thing. **2** a delegate or deputy. **3** *pathol* a further malignant tumour in the body at some distance from an original cancer site. **4** a feather growing on the ulna of a bird's wing. **5** *electronics* the coil or windings of the second stage of a transformer. **6** (**the Secondary**) the MESOZOIC era. See table at GEOLOGICAL TIME SCALE. • **secondarily** /ˈsɛkəndərɪlɪ, -ˈdɛrəlɪ/ *adverb.* • **secondariness** *noun.* ⓒ 14c: from Latin *secundarius.*

secondary cell ▻ *noun, physics* an electrolytic cell that can be charged before use by passing an electric current through it, and which can then be recharged. ⓒ 19c.

secondary colour ▻ *noun* a colour obtained by mixing or superimposing two primary colours.

secondary emission ▻ *noun, physics* emission of **secondary electrons** from a surface or particle caused by bombardment with electrons, etc from another source.

secondary picketing ▻ *noun* the picketing of firms that have business or trading connections with the employer against whom industrial action is being taken.

secondary planet see under PLANET

secondary school ▻ *noun* a school, especially a state school, for pupils aged between 11 and 18.

secondary sexual characteristics ▻ *noun, zool* features other than reproductive organs that distinguish males from females after the onset of puberty, eg beard growth or breast development in humans.

secondary stress ▻ *noun, linguistics* the second-strongest stress in a word, etc. Compare PRIMARY STRESS.

second ballot ▻ *noun* an electoral system where a second vote is taken, after the elimination of the candidate or candidates who received the fewest votes in the first ballot.

second best ▻ *noun* the next after the best. • **come off second best** *colloq* to lose; to be beaten by someone.

second-best ▻ *adj* **1** next after the best. **2** somewhat inferior.

second childhood ▻ *noun* senility or dotage; mental weakness in extreme old age.

second class ▻ *noun* the next class or category after the first in quality or worth. ▻ *adj* (**second-class**) 1 referring or relating to the class below the first. **2** being of a poor standard; inferior. **3** said of mail: sent at a cheaper rate than first class, therefore taking longer for delivery. ▻ *adverb* by second-class mail or transport ◻ *sent it second class.*

second-class citizen ▻ *noun* a member of a community who does not have the full rights and privileges enjoyed by the community as a whole.

Second Coming ▻ *noun* the second coming of Christ to Earth on Judgement Day. Also called **Second Advent**.

second cousin ▻ *noun* a child of the first cousin of either parent.

second-degree ▻ *adj* **1** *medicine, denoting* the most serious of the three degrees of burning with blistering but not permanent damage to the skin. **2** *N Amer law, denoting* unlawful killing with intent, but no premeditation.

seconder /ˈsɛkəndə(r)/ ▻ *noun* a person who seconds (see SECOND¹ *verb* 1) a proposal or the person making it.

second estate see under ESTATE 5

second growth ▻ *noun* the new growth of a forest after cutting, fire, etc.

second hand ▻ *noun* the pointer on a watch or clock that measures and indicates the time in seconds.

second-hand ▻ *adj* **1** previously owned or used by someone else. **2** dealing or trading in second-hand goods. **3** not directly received or obtained, but known through an intermediary ◻ *second-hand information.* ▻ *adverb* **1** in a second-hand state ◻ *It's cheaper to buy furniture second-hand.* **2** not directly, but from someone else ◻ *They heard it second-hand.*

second home ▻ *noun* **1** a holiday home, owned in addition to one's main residence. **2** a place or location where one feels as much at home as in one's own house.

second lieutenant ▻ *noun* an army or navy officer of the lowest commissioned rank.

secondly /ˈsɛkəndlɪ/ ▻ *adverb* in the second place; as a second consideration.

secondment /sɪˈkɒndmənt/ ▻ *noun* a temporary transfer to another position or organization. See also SECOND³.

second nature ▻ *noun* a habit or tendency so deeply ingrained as to seem an innate part of a person's nature.

second person see under PERSON

second-rate ▻ *adj* inferior or mediocre; having a substandard quality, as opposed to FIRST-RATE, etc.

second sight ▻ *noun* the power believed to enable someone to see into the future or to see things happening elsewhere.

second slip see SLIP¹ *noun* 10

second strike ▻ *noun, military* in nuclear warfare: a counterattack following a first strike by the enemy.

second string ▻ *noun* an alternative course of action, choice, etc.

second thoughts ▻ *noun* **1** doubts ◻ *They're having second thoughts about getting married.* **2** a process of reconsideration leading to a different decision being made ◻ *On second thoughts I think I'll stay.*

second wind ▻ *noun* **1** the recovery of normal breathing after exertion. **2** a burst of renewed energy or enthusiasm.

secrecy /ˈsiːkrəsɪ/ ▻ *noun* **1** the state or fact of being secret. **2** confidentiality ◻ *I'm sworn to secrecy.* **3** the ability or tendency to keep information secret. ⌚ 15c: as *secretie*, from *secre* secret.

secret /ˈsiːkrət/ ▻ *adj* **1** kept hidden or away from the knowledge of others. **2** unknown or unobserved by others ◻ *a secret army.* **3** tending to conceal things from others; private or secretive. **4** guarded against discovery or observation ◻ *a secret location.* ▻ *noun* **1** something not disclosed, or not to be disclosed, to others. **2** an unknown or unrevealed method of achievement ◻ *the secret of eternal youth.* **3** a central but sometimes elusive principle, explanation, etc ◻ *the secret of a good marriage.* **4** a fact or purpose that remains unexplained or unidentified; a mystery. **5** *relig* a quietly spoken or silent prayer by the celebrant after the offertory and immediately before the preface. • **secretly** *adverb.* • **in secret** secretly; unknown to others. • **in on** or **in the secret** having knowledge of or participating in it. • **keep a secret** not to disclose or reveal it. ⌚ 14c: from Latin *secretus* set apart, from *se* apart + *cernere* to separate.

secret agent ▻ *noun* a member of the secret service; a spy.

secretaire /sɛkrəˈtɛə(r)/ ▻ *noun* (***secretaires***) a cabinet which folds out to form a writing desk. Also called ESCRITOIRE. ⌚ 18c: French, meaning 'SECRETARY'.

secretariat /sɛkrəˈtɛərɪət, -rɪat/ ▻ *noun* **1** the administrative department of any council, organization or legislative body. **2** its staff or premises. **3** a secretary's office. ⌚ 19c: French, from SECRETARY.

secretary /ˈsɛkrətərɪ/ ▻ *noun* (***secretaries***) **1** a person employed to perform administrative or clerical tasks for a company or individual. **2** the member of a club or society committee responsible for its correspondence and business records. **3** a senior civil servant assisting a government minister or ambassador. • **secretarial** /-ˈtɛərɪəl/ *adj* referring or relating to secretaries or their work. ⌚ 14c: from Latin *secretarius* person spoken to in confidence, from *secretum* SECRET.

secretary-bird ▻ *noun* a large ground-dwelling African bird with grey and black plumage, long stilt-like legs and an erectile crest of black-tipped feathers hanging down behind its head. ⌚ 19c: so called because the feathers on its head resemble pens held behind the ear of a secretary.

secretary-general ▻ *noun* (***secretaries-general***) the principal administrative official in a large, especially political organization, eg the United Nations.

Secretary of State ▻ *noun* **1** in the UK: a minister at the head of any of the major government departments. **2** in the US: the FOREIGN MINISTER.

secrete¹ /sɪˈkriːt/ ▻ *verb* (***secreted, secreting***) *biol, zool* said of a gland or similar organ: to form and release (a substance). ⌚ 18c: a shortening of SECRETION.

secrete[2] /sɪ'kriːt/ ▻ *verb* (***secreted***, ***secreting***) to hide away or conceal. ⓒ 18c: related to SECRET.

Secret Intelligence Services see under MI6.

secretion /sɪ'kriːʃən/ ▻ *noun* **1** the process whereby glands of the body discharge or release particular substances. **2** any of the substances produced by such glands, eg sweat, saliva, mucus, bile. ⓒ 17c: from Latin *secernere*, from *se* apart + *cernere* to separate.

secretive /'siːkrətɪv, sɪ'kriːtɪv/ ▻ *adj* inclined to or fond of secrecy; reticent. • **secretively** *adverb*. • **secretiveness** *noun*. ⓒ 15c.

secretory /sɪ'kriːtərɪ/ ▻ *adj* said of a gland, etc: referring or relating to or involved in the process of secretion. ⓒ 17c: related to SECRETE[1].

secret police ▻ *noun* a police force operating in secret to suppress opposition to the government.

secret service ▻ *noun* a government department responsible for espionage and national security matters.

sect ▻ *noun* **1** a religious or other group whose views and practices differ from those of an established body or from those of a body from which it has separated, used sometimes as an expression of disapproval by non-members. **2** a subdivision of one of the main religious divisions of mankind. **3** a body of followers of any doctrine, especially of an extreme political movement. ⓒ 14c: from Latin *secta* a following, from *sequi* to follow.

sectarian /sɛk'tɛərɪən/ ▻ *adj* **1** referring, relating or belonging to a sect. **2** having, showing or caused by hostility towards those outside one's own group or belonging to a particular group or sect □ ***sectarian violence***. ▻ *noun* a member of a sect, especially a bigoted person. • **sectarianism** *noun* loyalty or excessive attachment to a particular sect or party. ⓒ 17c: from SECTARY.

sectary /'sɛktərɪ/ ▻ *noun* (***sectaries***) **1** a member of a sect. **2** a dissenter from an established faith. ⓒ 16c.

section /'sɛkʃən/ ▻ *noun* **1** the act or process of cutting. **2** any of the parts into which something is or can be divided or of which it may be composed. **3** *geom* the surface formed when a plane cuts through a solid figure. **4** the act of cutting through a solid figure. **5** a plan or diagram showing a view of an object as if it had been cut through. **6** a smaller part of a document, newspaper, book, etc □ ***Where's the TV section of the newspaper?*** **7** *music* a subdivision of an orchestra or chorus consisting of players of similar instruments or voices □ ***the violin section*** □ ***the alto section***. **8** *printing* (*in full* **section mark**) a mark (§) used to indicate the beginning of a section of a book or used as a reference mark. **9** *geol* an exposure of rock in which the strata are cut across. **10** *biol* a thin slice of a specimen of tissue prepared for microscopic examination. **11** a subdivision of an army platoon. **12** a subdivision of a company or organization □ ***the marketing section***. **13** *surgery* the act or process of cutting, or the cut or division made. **14** *US* a land area of one square mile. **15** *NZ* a building plot. ▻ *verb* (***sectioned***, ***sectioning***) **1** to divide something into sections. **2** to draw a sectional plan of something. **3** *surgery* to cut a section through something. **4** *medicine* to issue an order for the compulsory admission of (a mentally ill person) to a psychiatric hospital under the relevant section of mental health legislation, eg the Mental Health Act in the UK. ⓒ 16c: from Latin *secare* to cut.

sectional /'sɛkʃənəl/ ▻ *adj* **1** made in sections. **2** referring or relating to a particular section. **3** restricted to a particular group or area. • **sectionalize** or **sectionalise** *verb*. • **sectionalization** *noun*. • **sectionally** *adverb*.

sectionalism /'sɛkʃənəlɪzəm/ ▻ *noun* a narrow-minded outlook or concern for the interests of a particular group, area, etc.

sector /'sɛktə(r)/ ▻ *noun* **1** *geom* a portion of a circle bounded by two radii and an arc. **2** *astron* an object of similar shape, especially one for measuring angular distance. **3** a division or section of a nation's economic operations. Compare PRIVATE SECTOR, PUBLIC SECTOR. **4** a part of an area divided up for military purposes. **5** a mathematical measuring instrument consisting of two graduated rules hinged together at one end. • **sectoral** *adj*. ⓒ 16c: Latin, from *secare* to cut.

sectorial /sɛk'tɔːrɪəl/ ▻ *adj* **1** sectoral; relating to a sector. **2** *zool* said of a tooth: designed for cutting and eating flesh. ⓒ 19c.

secular /'sɛkjʊlə(r)/ ▻ *adj* **1** relating to the present world rather than to heavenly or spiritual things. **2** not religious or ecclesiastical; civil or lay. **3** said of members of the clergy: not bound by vows to a particular monastic or religious order. **4** referring to the secular clergy. **5** lasting for a long duration of time. **6** occurring only once in a lifetime, century or age. ▻ *noun* a clergyman (eg parish priest) not bound by monastic rules; a layman. • **secularity** /sɛkjʊ'larɪtɪ/ *noun*. • **secularly** *adverb*. ⓒ 13c: from Latin *saecularis*, from *saeculum* generation or century.

secularism /'sɛkjʊlərɪzəm/ ▻ *noun* the view or belief that society's values and standards should not be influenced or controlled by religion or the Church. • **secularist** *noun* someone who favours secularism.

secularize /'sɛkjʊləraɪz/ or **secularise** ▻ *verb* (***secularized***, ***secularizing***) to make something secular. • **secularization** *noun*.

secund /'siːkʌnd, 'sɛkʌnd, sɪ'kʌnd/ ▻ *adj*, *bot* said eg of leaves: turned to or positioned on the same side. ⓒ 18c: from Latin *secundus* second or following.

secure /sɪ'kjʊə(r)/ ▻ *adj* **1** free from danger; providing safety. **2** free from trouble or worry. **3** free from uncertainty or mistrust; assured. **4** firmly fixed or attached. **5** not likely to be lost or taken away; safe or assured □ ***a secure job***. **6** in custody, usually of the police. ▻ *verb* (***secured***, ***securing***) **1** to fasten or attach firmly. **2** to get or assure possession of something □ ***She's secured a place on the course for next year***. **3** to make free from danger or risk; to make safe. **4** to contrive to get something. **5** to guarantee. • **securable** *adj*. • **securely** *adverb*. • **securer** *noun*. ⓒ 16c: from Latin *securus*, from *se-* without + *cura* care.

security /sɪ'kjʊərɪtɪ/ ▻ *noun* (***securities***) **1** the state of being secure. **2** protection from the possibility of future financial difficulty. **3** protection from physical harm, especially assassination. **4** protection from theft □ ***Our house has good security***. **5** the staff providing such protection against attack or theft. **6** freedom from vulnerability to political or military takeover □ ***national security***. **7** something given as a guarantee, especially to a creditor giving them the right to recover a debt. **8** (*usually* **securities**) a certificate stating ownership of stocks or shares, or the monetary value represented by such certificates. ▻ *adj* providing security □ ***security guard***. ⓒ 15c.

security blanket ▻ *noun* **1** a blanket or other familiar piece of cloth carried around by a toddler as a source of comfort and security. **2** any familiar object whose presence provides a sense of comfort or security.

Security Council ▻ *noun* a body of the United Nations whose responsibility is to maintain international peace and security.

security risk ▻ *noun* someone considered to be a threat to a nation's security, especially because of a likelihood of giving away military secrets as a result of their political affiliations.

Security Services see under MI5

SED ▻ *abbreviation* Scottish Education Department.

sedan /sɪ'dan/ ▻ *noun* **1** (*in full* **sedan chair**) *historical* a large enclosed chair for one person, carried on two horizontal poles by two bearers. **2** *N Amer* a saloon car. ◎ 17c.

sedate /sɪ'deɪt/ ▻ *adj* **1** calm and dignified in manner. **2** slow and unexciting. ▻ *verb* (***sedated, sedating***) to calm or quieten someone by means of a sedative. • **sedately** *adverb*. • **sedateness** *noun*. ◎ 17c: from Latin *sedatus*, from *sedare* to still.

sedation /sɪ'deɪʃən/ ▻ *noun, medicine* the act of calming or the state of having been calmed, especially by means of sedatives. ◎ 16c.

sedative /'sɛdətɪv/ ▻ *noun, medicine* any agent, especially a drug, that has a calming effect and is used to treat insomnia, pain, delirium, etc. ▻ *adj* said of a drug, etc: having a calming effect. ◎ 15c.

sedentary /'sɛdəntərɪ/ ▻ *adj* **1** said of work: involving much sitting. **2** said of a person: spending much time sitting; taking little exercise. **3** said of an animal: inactive; lethargic. **4** *zool* **a** said of a bird: not migratory; **b** said eg of a mollusc: attached to a substratum; not mobile. ◎ 16c: from Latin *sedentarius*, from *sedere* to sit.

Seder /'seɪdə(r)/ ▻ *noun, Judaism* the ceremonial meal and its rituals on the first night or first two nights of the Passover. ◎ 19c: from Hebrew *sedher* order.

sedge /sɛdʒ/ ▻ *noun* any member of a family of plants resembling grasses or rushes, found in bogs, fens, marshes and other poorly drained areas, and characterized by solid stems which are triangular in cross-section. • **sedgy** *adj*. ◎ Anglo-Saxon *secg*.

sedge warbler ▻ *noun* a common British warbler, found in marshy areas.

sediment /'sɛdɪmənt/ ▻ *noun* **1** insoluble solid particles that have settled at the bottom of a liquid in which they were previously suspended. **2** *geol* solid material, eg rock fragments or organic debris, that has been deposited by the action of gravity, wind, water or ice, especially at the bottom of a sea, lake or river. ◎ 16c: from Latin *sedimentum*, from *sedere* to sit.

sedimentary /sɛdɪ'mɛntərɪ/ ▻ *adj* **1** relating to or of the nature of sediment. **2** *geol* denoting any of a group of rocks, eg clay, limestone or sandstone, that have formed as a result of the accumulation and compaction of layers of sediment. ◎ 19c.

sedimentation /sɛdɪmɛn'teɪʃən/ ▻ *noun* **1** *chem* the settling of solid particles from a suspension, either naturally by gravity, or as a result of centrifugation. **2** *geol* the process of accumulating or depositing sediment in layers, especially during the formation of sedimentary rock. ◎ 19c.

sedition /sɪ'dɪʃən/ ▻ *noun* public speech, writing or action encouraging public disorder, especially rebellion against the government. ◎ 14c: from Latin *seditio* a going apart, from *sed* away + *ire* to go.

seditious /sɪ'dɪʃəs/ ▻ *adj* **1** relating to or involving sedition. **2** encouraging or participating in sedition. • **seditiously** *adverb*. • **seditiousness** *noun*.

seduce /sɪ'dʒuːs/ ▻ *verb* (***seduced, seducing***) **1** to lure or entice someone into having sexual intercourse. **2** to lead astray; to tempt, especially into wrongdoing. • **seducer** or **seductress** *noun*. ◎ 15c: from Latin *seducere* to lead aside.

seduction /sɪ'dʌkʃən/ ▻ *noun* the act or practice of seducing or the condition of being seduced. ◎ 16c: French, from SEDUCE.

seductive /sɪ'dʌktɪv/ ▻ *adj* **1** tending or intended to seduce. **2** sexually attractive and charming. **3** creating or designed to create the mood for sex □ *seductive lighting*. **4** tempting; enticing. • **seductively** *adverb*. • **seductiveness** *noun*. ◎ 18c: from Latin *seductivus*, from SEDUCE.

sedulous /'sɛdʒʊləs/ ▻ *adj, formal* **1** assiduous and diligent; steadily hardworking. **2** painstakingly carried out. • **sedulity** or **sedulousness** *noun*. • **sedulously** *adverb*. ◎ 16c: from Latin *sedulus*, from *se dolo* without deception.

sedum /'siːdəm/ ▻ *noun, bot* any of various rock plants with thick fleshy leaves and clusters of white, yellow or pink flowers. ◎ 15c: Latin, meaning 'houseleek'.

see[1] ▻ *verb* (*past tense* ***saw****, past participle* ***seen, seeing***) **1** to perceive by the sense operated in the eyes. **2** *intr* to have the power of vision. **3** *tr & intr* to perceive mentally; to understand or realize □ *Don't you see what she's trying to do?* **4** to watch □ *We're going to see a play.* **5** to be aware of or know, especially by looking or reading □ *I see from your letter that you're married.* **6** *tr & intr* to find out; to learn □ *We'll have to see what happens.* **7** to predict; to expect □ *We could see what was going to happen.* **8** to meet up with someone; to spend time with someone □ *I haven't seen her for ages.* **9** to spend time with someone regularly, especially romantically □ *He's been seeing her for quite a while now.* **10** to speak to someone; to consult □ *He's asking to see the manager.* **11** to receive as a visitor or client □ *The doctor will see you now.* **12** to make sure of something □ *See that you lock the door.* **13** to imagine, and often also to regard as likely □ *I can still see her as a little girl* □ *I can't see him agreeing.* **14** to consider □ *I see her more as an acquaintance than a friend.* **15** to encounter or experience □ *She's seen too much pain in her life.* **16** to be witness to something as a sight or event □ *We're now seeing huge increases in unemployment.* **17** to escort □ *I'll see you home.* **18** to refer to (the specified page, chapter, etc) for information □ *see page five.* **19** *cards* to match the bet of someone by staking the same sum □ *I'll see you and raise you five.* • **see fit to do something** to think it appropriate or proper to do it. • **see red** see under RED. • **see the light 1** to discover religious feelings within oneself. **2** to recognize and adopt the merits of a widely held point of view. **3** *humorous* to eventually come to understand and agree with someone else. • **see things** to have hallucinations. • **see you later** *colloq* an expression of temporary farewell. ◎ Anglo-Saxon *seon*.

■ **see about something** to attend to a matter or concern.

■ **see into something** to investigate it; to look into it.

■ **see something in someone** to find an attractive feature in them □ *I don't know what he sees in her.*

■ **see someone off 1** to accompany them to their place of departure □ *saw her off at the airport.* **2** *colloq* to get rid of them by force □ *saw the burgler off* □ *saw the cat off.*

■ **see someone out 1** to escort them out of the room, etc. **2** to outlive them.

■ **see something out** to stay until the end of it.

■ **see over something** to inspect it; to look over it.

■ **see through something 1** to discern what is implied by an idea or scheme, etc. **2** to detect or determine the truth underlying a lie □ *I saw through your plan straight away.*

■ **see something through** to participate in it to the end.

■ **see to something** to attend to it; to take care of it □ *Will you see to it?*

see[2] ▻ *noun* **1** the office of bishop of a particular diocese. **2** the area under the religious authority of a bishop or archbishop. **3** the HOLY SEE. ◎ 13c: from French *sied*, from Latin *sedes* seat, from *sedere* to sit.

seed ▻ *noun* (***seeds*** or ***seed***) **1** *bot* in flowering and cone-bearing plants: the highly resistant structure that develops from the ovule after fertilization, and is capable of developing into a new plant. **2** a small hard fruit or part in a fruit; a pip. **3** a source or origin □ *the seeds of the plan.* **4** *literary* offspring; descendants. **5** *literary* semen. **6** *sport* a seeded player □ *He is number one seed.* **7** *chem* a single crystal introduced to a concentrated solution to induce crystallization. ▷ *verb* (***seeded***, ***seeding***) **1** *intr* said of a plant: to produce seeds. **2** to sow or plant (seeds). **3** to remove seeds from (eg a fruit). **4** *chem* to use a single crystal to induce the formation of more crystals from (a concentrated solution). **5** to scatter particles of some substance into (a cloud) in order to induce rainfall, disperse a storm or freezing fog, etc. **6** *sport* to rank (a player in a tournament) according to their likelihood of winning □ *has been seeded number three for Wimbledon.* **7** *sport* to arrange (a tournament) so that high-ranking players only meet each other in the later stages of the contest. • **seeded** *adj* **1** having the seeds removed. **2** bearing or having seeds. **3** sown. **4** *sport* said of a tournament player: who has been seeded. • **seedless** *adj.* • **go** or **run to seed 1** *bot* said of a plant: to stop flowering prior to the development of seed. **2** *colloq* to allow oneself to become unkempt or unhealthy through lack of care. • **sow the seeds of something** to initiate it. ⓒ Anglo-Saxon *sæd.*

seedbed ▷ *noun* **1** a piece of ground prepared for the planting of seeds. **2** an environment in which something, especially something undesirable, develops.

seedcake ▷ *noun* a cake flavoured with caraway seeds.

seed coral ▷ *noun* coral that has formed into small irregular pieces.

seed corn ▷ *noun* **1** corn grains used for sowing. **2** assets likely to be profitable in the future.

seed drill ▷ *noun, agric* a farm implement that is used to sow seeds in rows and cover them with soil.

seed leaf ▷ *noun* a COTYLEDON.

seedling ▷ *noun* **1** a young plant grown from seed. **2** a young plant ready for transplanting from a seedbed. ⓒ 17c.

seed money ▷ *noun* the money with which a project or enterprise is set up.

seed-pearl ▷ *noun* a tiny pearl.

seed-potato ▷ *noun* a potato tuber kept for planting, from which a new potato plant grows.

seed vessel ▷ *noun, bot* the ovary of a flower; the PERICARP.

seedy /ˈsiːdɪ/ ▷ *adj* (***seedier***, ***seediest***) **1** said of a fruit, etc: full of seeds. **2** said of a plant: at the phase of producing seeds. **3** *colloq* mildly ill or unwell. **4** *colloq* shabby; dirty or disreputable □ *seedy areas of town* □ *a seedy club.* • **seediness** *noun.* ⓒ 16c.

seeing ▷ *noun* **1** the ability to see; the power of vision. **2** *astron* atmospheric conditions for good observation. ▷ *conj* (*usually* **seeing that**) given (that); since □ *Seeing you are opposed to the plan, I shall not pursue it.* ⓒ 14c.

seek ▷ *verb* (***sought*** /sɔːt/ , ***seeking***) **1** to look for someone or something. **2** to try to find, get or achieve something. **3** *intr* to try or endeavour □ *He's just seeking to please.* **4** to take oneself off to (a place, etc); to go to get □ *I'm seeking a place of refuge.* **5** to ask for something □ *We sought his advice.* • **seeker** *noun.* ⓒ Anglo-Saxon *secan.*

▪ **seek someone** or **something out** to search intensively for and find them.

seem ▷ *verb* (***seemed***, ***seeming***) *intr* **1** to appear to the eye; to give the impression of (being) □ *She seems happy today.* **2** to be apparent; to appear to the mind □ *There seems to be no good reason for refusing.* **3** to think or believe oneself (to be, do, etc) □ *I seem to know you from somewhere.* ⓒ 12c: from Norse *soemr* fitting.

seeming ▷ *adj* apparent; ostensible. ▷ *noun* appearance; a false appearance. • **seemingly** *adverb.* ⓒ 14c.

seemly /ˈsiːmlɪ/ ▷ *adj* (***seemlier***, ***seemliest***) fitting or suitable; becoming. ⓒ 13c.

seen *past participle of* SEE[1]

seep ▷ *verb* (***seeped***, ***seeping***) *intr* said of a liquid: to escape slowly or ooze through, or as if through, a narrow opening. • **seepage** *noun.* • **seepy** *adj.* ⓒ Perhaps from Anglo-Saxon *sipian* to soak.

seer /ˈsiːə(r), ˈsɪə(r)/ ▷ *noun* **1** a person who predicts future events; a clairvoyant. **2** a person of great wisdom and spiritual insight; a prophet. ⓒ 14c: SEE[1] + -ER[2], literally 'a person who sees'.

seersucker /ˈsɪəsʌkə(r)/ ▷ *noun* lightweight Indian cotton or linen fabric with a crinkly appearance, often with stripes. ⓒ 18c: from Persian *shir o shakkar* milk and sugar.

seesaw /ˈsiːsɔː/ ▷ *noun* **1** a plaything consisting of a plank balanced in the middle allowing people, especially children, when seated on the ends to propel each other up and down by pushing off the ground with the feet. **2** the activity of using a seesaw. **3** an alternate up-and-down or back-and-forth movement. ▷ *verb* (***seesawed***, ***seesawing***) *intr* to move alternately up-and-down or back-and-forth. ⓒ 17c: a reduplication of SAW[2], from the sawing action.

seethe /siːð/ ▷ *verb* (***seethed***, ***seething***) *intr* **1** said of a liquid: to churn and foam as if boiling. **2** to be extremely agitated, especially with anger. • **seething** *adj* **1** referring to something that seethes; boiling. **2** furious □ *He was seething with anger.* • **seethingly** *adverb.* ⓒ Anglo-Saxon *seothan.*

see-through ▷ *adj* said especially of a fabric or clothing: able to be seen through; transparent or translucent.

segment ▷ *noun* /ˈsɛgmənt/ **1** a part, section or portion. **2** *geom* in a circle or ellipse: the region enclosed by an arc and its chord. **3** *zool* in certain animals, eg some worms: each of a number of repeating units of which the body is composed. **4** *phonetics* the smallest sound unit of speech. ▷ *verb* /sɛgˈmɛnt/ (***segmented***, ***segmenting***) to divide into segments. • **segmental** *adj.* • **segmentary** *adj.* ⓒ 16c: from Latin *segmentum*, from *secare* to cut.

segmentation /sɛgmɛnˈteɪʃən/ ▷ *noun* **1** the act or process of dividing into segments; an instance of this. **2** *biol* the series of cell divisions which take place in an ovum immediately after fertilization. ⓒ 19c.

segregate /ˈsɛgrəgeɪt/ ▷ *verb* (***segregated***, ***segregating***) **1** to set apart or isolate. **2** *intr* to separate out into a group or groups. **3** *genetics* to separate into dominants and recessives. ⓒ 16c: from Latin *segregare*, *segregatum*, from *se-* apart + *grex* flock.

segregation /sɛgrəˈgeɪʃən/ ▷ *noun* **1** the process of segregating or the state of being segregated. **2** systematic isolation of one group, especially a racial or ethnic minority, from the rest of society. **3** *genetics* during meiosis: the separation of a pair of homologous chromosomes so that only one member of the pair is present in each gamete. • **segregational** *adj* involving or characterized by segregation. • **segregationist** *noun.* ⓒ 17c: from SEGREGATE.

segue /ˈsɛgweɪ, ˈseɪg-/ *music* ▷ *verb* (***segued***, ***segueing***) *intr* to proceed or follow on to the next song, movement, etc without a pause. ▷ *noun* **1** the term or direction to segue. **2** the act or result of segueing. ⓒ 18c: Italian, from *seguire* to follow.

seguidilla /sɛgɪˈdiːljə/ ▷ *noun* **1** a lively Spanish dance in triple time. **2** the music of this dance. ⓒ 18c: Spanish.

seigneur /sɛnˈjɜː(r)/ and **seignior** /ˈseɪnjə(r), ˈsiːnjə(r)/ ▷ *noun* a feudal lord, especially in France or French Canada. • **seigneurial** *adj.* ⓒ 16c: French, from Latin *senior.*

seigneury /ˈsɛnjərɪ/ ▷ *noun* (***seigneuries***) the domain of a seigneur. ⓒ 17c.

seine /seɪn, siːn/ ▷ *noun* a large vertical fishing net held underwater by floats and weights, and whose ends are brought together and hauled. ▷ *verb* (***seined, seining***) *tr & intr* to catch or fish with a seine. ◷ Anglo-Saxon *segne*.

seismic /ˈsaɪzmɪk/ ▷ *adj* **1** relating to or characteristic of earthquakes. **2** *colloq* gigantic □ *There was an increase of seismic proportions.* ◷ 19c: from Greek *seismos* a shaking.

seismo- /saɪzmoʊ, saɪzˈmɒ, saɪzmə/ or (before a vowel) **seism-** *combining form, denoting* earthquake. ◷ From Greek *seismos* a shaking, from *seiein* to shake.

seismogram /ˈsaɪzməgram/ ▷ *noun* a seismograph record. ◷ 19c.

seismograph /ˈsaɪzməgrɑːf/ ▷ *noun* an instrument that measures and records the force of earthquakes. • **seismographer** /saɪzˈmɒgrəfə(r)/ *noun*. • **seismographic** /saɪzməˈgrafɪk/ *adj*. ◷ 19c.

seismography /saɪzˈmɒgrəfɪ/ ▷ *noun* the scientific study of earthquakes. ◷ 19c.

seismology /saɪzˈmɒlədʒɪ/ ▷ *noun, geol* the scientific study of earthquakes, including possible methods by which they may be predicted. • **seismological** or **seismologic** *adj* relating to or involving seismology. • **seismologist** *noun* a scientist who specializes in seismology. ◷ 19c.

seize /siːz/ ▷ *verb* (***seized, seizing***) **1** to take or grab suddenly, eagerly or forcibly. **2** to take by force; to capture. **3** to affect suddenly and deeply; to overcome □ *He was seized by panic.* **4** to take legal possession of someone or something. **5** *naut* to lash or make fast. **6** (*often* **seize on** or **upon something**) to use or exploit it eagerly □ *She seized on the idea as soon as it was suggested* □ *They seized every chance to embarrass us.* • **seizable** *adj*. ◷ 13c: from French *saisir*.

▪ **seize up 1 a** said of a machine or engine: to become stiff or jammed, especially through overuse or lack of lubrication; **b** said of part of the body: to become stiff through over-exertion. **2** said of a person: to become overwhelmed eg with nerves, fear, etc □ *As soon as I saw him I just seized up.*

seizure /ˈsiːʒə(r)/ ▷ *noun* **1** the act of seizing. **2** a capture. **3** *pathol* a sudden attack of illness, especially producing spasms as in an epileptic fit.

selachian /sɪˈleɪkɪən/ ▷ *noun* any fish of the subclass **Selachii**, including sharks, rays, skates and dogfish. Also *as adj*.

seldom /ˈsɛldəm/ ▷ *adverb* rarely. ◷ Anglo-Saxon *seldum*.

select /səˈlɛkt/ ▷ *verb* (***selected, selecting***) to choose from several by preference. ▷ *adj* **1** picked out or chosen in preference to others. **2** restricted entrance or membership; exclusive □ *She mixes with a very select group.* • **selectness** *noun*. • **selector** *noun*. ◷ 16c: from Latin *seligere*, from *se* apart + *legere* to choose.

select committee ▷ *noun, politics* in Britain: a committee consisting of members of parliament chosen to report and advise on a particular matter, eg education or defence.

selection /səˈlɛkʃən/ ▷ *noun* **1** the act or process of selecting or being selected. **2** a thing or set of things selected. **3** a range from which to select. **4** a horse selected as the one most likely to win. **5** *biol* the process by which some individuals contribute more offspring than others to the next generation. See also NATURAL SELECTION. ◷ 17c: Latin, from SELECT.

selective /səˈlɛktɪv/ ▷ *adj* **1** exercising the right to select. **2** tending to select or choose; discriminating □ *a selective school.* **3** involving only certain people or things; exclusive. **4** *electronics* said especially of radio receivers: able to respond to a particular frequency without interference from other frequencies. • **selectively** *adj*. ◷ 17c.

selectivity /səlɛkˈtɪvɪtɪ/ ▷ *noun* **1** the ability to select or the state of being selective. **2** *electronics* the ability to respond to a particular frequency with no interference from other frequencies. ◷ Early 20c.

selenite /ˈsɛlənaɪt/ ▷ *noun, geol* a variety of gypsum occurring as clear colourless crystals. ◷ 16c: from Greek *selene* moon, as the crystals were originally believed to wax and wane with the Moon.

selenium /səˈliːnɪəm/ ▷ *noun, chem* (symbol **Se**, atomic number 34) a metalloid element that is a semiconductor, used in electronic devices, photoelectric cells and photographic exposure meters. ◷ Early 19c: from Greek *selene* moon.

seleno- /sɪˈliːnoʊ, sɛləˈnɒ/ or (before a vowel) **selen-** *combining form, signifying* moon. ◷ From Greek *selene*.

selenography /sɛləˈnɒgrəfɪ/ ▷ *noun* the study and mapping of the Moon and its physical features. • **selenographer** *noun*. • **selenographic** or **selenographical** *adj*. ◷ 17c.

selenology /sɛləˈnɒlədʒɪ/ ▷ *noun* the scientific study of the Moon. • **selenological** /səliːnəˈlɒdʒɪkəl/ *adj*. • **selenologist** *noun*. ◷ 19c.

self ▷ *noun* (***selves***) **1** personality, or a particular aspect of it. **2** a person's awareness of their own identity; ego. **3** a person as a whole, comprising a combination of characteristics of appearance and behaviour □ *He was his usual happy self.* **4** personal interest or advantage. ▷ *pronoun, colloq* myself, yourself, himself or herself. ▷ *adj* being of the same material or colour. ◷ Anglo-Saxon *seolf*.

self- ▷ *combining form, indicating* **1** by or for oneself; in relation to oneself □ *self-doubt* □ *self-inflicted.* **2** acting automatically □ *self-closing.*

self-abnegation ▷ *noun* denial and renunciation of one's own interest.

self-absorbed ▷ *adj* wrapped up in one's own thoughts, affairs or circumstances. • **self-absorption** *noun*.

self-abuse ▷ *noun* **1** revilement and criticism of oneself. **2** a condemnatory term for MASTURBATION. • **self-abuser** *noun*.

self-acting ▷ *adj* able to function without any external control; automatic.

self-addressed ▷ *adj* addressed by the sender for return to themselves.

self-appointed ▷ *adj* acting on one's own authority, without the choice or approval of others.

self-assertive and **self-asserting** ▷ *adj* always inclined to make others aware of one's presence and opinion, especially arrogantly or aggressively. • **self-assertion** *noun*.

self-assurance ▷ *noun* self-confidence. • **self-assured** *adj* secure in one's own abilities, opinions, position, etc.

self-catering ▷ *adj* said of a holiday, accommodation, etc: providing facilities allowing guests and residents to prepare their own meals.

self-centred ▷ *adj* interested only in oneself and one's own affairs; selfish.

self-coloured ▷ *adj* **1** having the same colour all over. **2** having its natural colour; undyed.

self-command ▷ *noun* SELF-CONTROL.

self-confessed ▷ *adj* as openly acknowledged and admitted by oneself □ *a self-confessed cheat.*

self-confidence ▷ *noun* confidence in or reliance on one's own abilities, sometimes with arrogance; total absence of shyness. • **self-confident** *adj*. • **self-confidently** *adverb*.

self-conscious ▷ *adj* **1** ill at ease in company as a result of irrationally believing oneself to be the subject of observation by others. **2** conscious of one's own identity, mind and its acts and states.

self-contained ▷ *adj* **1** said of accommodation: having no part that is shared with others. **2** said of a person: content to be on one's own; independent or reserved. **3** needing nothing added; complete in itself.

self-contradiction ▷ *noun* **1** the act or fact of contradicting oneself. **2** a statement whose elements are mutually contradictory. • **self-contradictory** *adj*.

self-control ▷ *noun* the ability to control one's emotions and impulses. • **self-controlled** *adj* characterized by or showing self-control.

self-deception and **self-deceit** ▷ *noun* the act or practice of deceiving oneself. • **self-deceiver** *noun*.

self-defence ▷ *noun* **1** the act or techniques of protecting or defending oneself from physical attack. **2** (*often* **the art of self-defence**) boxing as an act of defending oneself; now more loosely applied to any of a number of martial arts. **3** the act of defending one's own rights or principles.

self-denial ▷ *noun* the act or practice of denying one's own needs or desires. • **self-denying** *adj*.

self-destruction ▷ *noun* **1** the destruction of anything by itself. **2** the ending of one's life; suicide. • **self-destruct** *verb*. • **self-destructive** *adj*.

self-determination ▷ *noun* **1** the freedom to make one's own decisions without intervention from others. **2** a nation's freedom to decide its own government and political relations.

self-drive ▷ *adj* said of a hired motor vehicle: to be driven by the hirer. • **self-driven** *adj*.

self-effacing ▷ *adj* tending to avoid making others aware of one's presence or achievements out of shyness or modesty. • **self-effacement** *noun*.

self-employed ▷ *adj* working for oneself and under one's own control, rather than as an employee. • **self-employment** *noun*.

self-esteem ▷ *noun* **1** one's good opinion of oneself; self-respect □ *His low self-esteem increased as soon as the job offer came through.* **2** an excessively high opinion of oneself.

self-evident ▷ *adj* clear or evident enough without need for proof or explanation. • **self-evidence** *noun*.

self-explanatory and **self-explaining** ▷ *adj* easily understood or obvious; needing no further explanation.

self-expression ▷ *noun* the giving of expression of one's personality, especially in art, poetry, etc.

self-fulfilling ▷ *adj* referring or relating to a forecast which, by virtue of its being made, has the effect of bringing about the results it predicts especially in **a self-fulfilling prophecy**. • **self-fulfilment** *noun*.

self-government ▷ *noun* a government run by the people of a nation without any outside control or interference. • **self-governing** *adj*.

self-harming ▷ *noun* the habitual practice of inflicting physical damage on oneself.

self-heal ▷ *noun* a creeping perennial plant with oval leaves and dense heads of violet-blue two-lipped flowers. ⌚ 14c: so called because of its former use as a medicinal herb.

self-help ▷ *noun* the practice of solving one's own problems using abilities developed in oneself rather than relying on assistance from others. Also *as adj* □ *self-help groups.*

self-image ▷ *noun* one's own idea or perception of oneself.

self-important ▷ *adj* having an exaggerated sense of one's own importance or worth; arrogant or pompous. • **self-importantly** *adverb*. • **self-importance** *noun*.

self-imposed ▷ *adj* taken voluntarily on oneself; not imposed by others.

self-induced ▷ *adj* **1** brought on or induced by oneself. **2** *electronics* produced by self-induction.

self-induction ▷ *noun, electronics* the property of an electric circuit by which it resists any change in the current flowing in it.

self-indulgent ▷ *adj* giving in or indulging in one's own whims or desires. • **self-indulgence** *noun*.

self-inflicted ▷ *adj* inflicted by oneself on oneself.

self-interest ▷ *noun* **1** regard for oneself and one's own interests. **2** one's own personal welfare or advantage. • **self-interested** *adj*.

selfish /ˈsɛlfɪʃ/ ▷ *adj* **1** concerned only with one's personal welfare, with total disregard to that of others. **2** said of an act: revealing such a tendency. • **selfishly** *adverb*. • **selfishness** *noun*. ⌚ 17c.

self-justifying ▷ *adj* **1** justifying or making excuses for oneself and one's behaviour. **2** *printing* automatically arranging the length of the lines of type. • **self-justification** *noun*.

selfless ▷ *adj* **1** tending to consider the welfare of others before one's own; altruistic. **2** said of an act: revealing such a tendency. • **selflessly** *adverb*. • **selflessness** *noun*. ⌚ 19c.

self-love ▷ *noun* **1** the love of oneself. **2** the tendency to seek one's own welfare, happiness or advantage.

self-made ▷ *adj* having achieved wealth or success by working one's way up from poverty and obscurity, rather than by advantages acquired by birth.

self-opinionated ▷ *adj* tending to insist, obstinately and forcefully, that one's own opinions are superior to all others.

self-pity ▷ *noun* pity for oneself, especially involving excessive moaning about one's misfortunes.

self-pollination ▷ *noun, bot* in flowering plants: the transfer of pollen from the anther of the stamen to the stigma of the same flower. • **self-pollinated** *adj*.

self-possessed ▷ *adj* calm, controlled and collected, especially in an emergency. • **self-possession** *noun*.

self-preservation ▷ *noun* **1** the protection and care of one's own life. **2** the instinct underlying this.

self-propelled ▷ *adj* said of a vehicle or craft: having its own means of propulsion. • **self-propelling** *adj*.

self-raising ▷ *adj* said of flour: containing an ingredient to make dough or pastry rise.

self-realization ▷ *noun* the fulfilment of one's mental and moral potential.

self-referential ▷ *adj* **1** relating or belonging to the self. **2** said of a text, film, painting, etc: making reference to itself or to its own themes, etc. • **self-referentiality** *noun*.

self-regard ▷ *noun* respect for and interest in oneself.

self-reliant ▷ *adj* never needing or seeking help from others; independent. • **self-reliance** *noun* reliance on one's own abilities.

self-respect ▷ *noun* respect for oneself and one's character, and concern for one's dignity and reputation. • **self-respecting** *adj*.

self-restraint ▷ *noun* the act or ability to control one's own desires, feelings or impulses.

self-righteous ▷ *adj* having too high an opinion of one's own merits, and being intolerant of other people's faults. • **self-righteousness** *noun*.

self-sacrifice ▻ *noun* the forgoing of one's own needs, interests or happiness for the sake of others. • **self-sacrificing** *adj.*

selfsame ▻ *adj* the very same; identical □ *He left that selfsame day.*

self-satisfied ▻ *adj* feeling or showing complacent or arrogant satisfaction with oneself or one's achievements. • **self-satisfaction** *noun.*

self-sealing ▻ *adj* **1** said of an envelope: having two flaps coated with an adhesive so they can be stuck together without being moistened. **2** said of a tyre: capable of automatically sealing small punctures.

self-seeker ▻ *noun* **1** someone who looks mainly to their own interests or advantage. **2** a device which automatically tunes a radio to required wavelengths by means of a push-button control.

self-seeking ▻ *adj* preoccupied with one's own interests and opportunities for personal advantage. ▻ *noun* the act of self-seeking.

self-service ▻ *noun* a system, especially in a restaurant or petrol station, in which customers serve themselves and pay at a checkout. ▻ *adj* said of a restaurant, petrol station, etc: operating such a system.

self-serving ▻ *adj* benefiting or seeking to benefit oneself, often to the disadvantage of others.

self-sown and **self-seeded** ▻ *adj* said of plants: dispersed and sown naturally without man's agency.

self-starter ▻ *noun* **1** in a vehicle's engine: an automatic electric starting device. **2** *colloq* a person with initiative and motivation, therefore requiring little supervision in a job.

self-styled ▻ *adj* called or considered so only by oneself □ *a self-styled superstar.*

self-sufficient ▻ *adj* **1** said of a person or thing: able to provide for oneself or itself without outside help. **2** said of a person: being extremely and often overly confident in him- or herself. • **self-sufficiency** *noun.* • **self-sufficing** *adj.*

self-supporting ▻ *adj* **1** earning enough money to meet all one's own expenses; self-sufficient. **2** said of a structure, plant, etc: needing no additional supports or attachments to stay firmly fixed or upright. • **self-support** *noun.*

self-willed ▻ *adj* stubbornly or obstinately determined to do or have what one wants, especially to the disadvantage of others. • **self-will** *noun.*

self-winding ▻ *adj* said of a watch: containing a device that automatically rewinds it so there is no need for hand-winding.

sell ▻ *verb* (***sold, selling***) **1** to give something to someone in exchange for money □ *She sold it to her brother* □ *Can I sell you a crate of Southern Comfort?* **2** to have available for buying □ *Do you sell batteries?* **3** *intr* to be in demand among customers; to be sold □ *This particular style sells well.* **4** to promote the sale of something; to cause to be bought □ *The author's name sells the book.* **5** to convince or persuade someone to acquire or agree to something, especially by emphasizing its merits or advantages □ *It was difficult to sell them the idea.* **6** *colloq* to deceive or trick. **7** to lose or betray (eg one's principles) in the process of getting something, especially something dishonourable. ▻ *noun* **1** the act or process of selling. **2** the style of persuasion used in selling □ *the hard sell.* **3** *colloq* a trick or deception. • **sellable** *adj.* • **seller** *noun.* • **sell someone down the river** *colloq* to betray them. • **sell someone, something** or **oneself short 1** *colloq* to understate their good qualities; to belittle them. **2** *finance* to sell (eg stocks, etc) before one actually owns them, so one can buy them at a lower price just before selling them. • **sold on something** *colloq* convinced or enthusiastic about it. ⓘ Anglo-Saxon *sellan* to hand over, from Norse *selja*, from Gothic *saljan*.

■ **sell at** or **for something** to be available for buying at a specified price □ *These T-shirts sell at just under a tenner.*

■ **sell something off** to dispose of remaining goods by selling them quickly and cheaply.

■ **sell out of something** to sell one's entire stock of it.

■ **sell out to someone** to betray one's principles or associates to another party □ *He sold out to the opposition.*

■ **sell up** to sell one's house or business, usually because of debts.

sell-by date ▻ *noun* a date stamped on a manufacturer's or distributor's label indicating when goods, especially foods, are considered no longer fit to be sold. Compare BEST-BEFORE DATE.

seller's market or **sellers' market** ▻ *noun, commerce* a situation where demand exceeds supply and sellers may control the price of a commodity, product, etc. Compare BUYER'S MARKET.

selling race and **selling plate** ▻ *noun* a race of which the winning horse must be put up for auction.

Sellotape or **sellotape** /ˈsɛləteɪp/ ▻ *noun, trademark* a form of usually transparent adhesive tape, especially for use on paper. ▻ *verb* (***sellotaped, sellotaping***) to stick using Sellotape. ⓘ 1940s: from a variant of CELLULOSE + -O- + TAPE.

sell-out ▻ *noun* an event for which all the tickets have been sold.

sell-through ▻ *noun* retail sale, as opposed to rental, especially of video cassettes.

selva /ˈsɛlvə/ ▻ *noun* (*usually* **selvas**) a dense wet forest in the Amazonian basin. ⓘ 19c: Spanish and Portuguese, from Latin *silva* wood.

selvage or **selvedge** /ˈsɛlvɪdʒ/ ▻ *noun* **1** an edge of a length of fabric sewn or woven so as to prevent fraying. **2** an edge of a piece of cloth finished differently to the rest of the cloth. • **selvaged** *adj.* ⓘ 15c: from SELF + EDGE.

selves *plural of* SELF

SEM ▻ *abbreviation* **1** scanning electron microscope. **2** *math* standard error of the mean.

Sem. ▻ *abbreviation* **1** Seminary. **2** Semitic.

semantic /səˈmantɪk/ ▻ *adj* **1** referring or relating to meaning, especially of words. **2** referring or relating to semantics. • **semantically** *adverb.* ⓘ 17c: from Greek *semantikos* significant.

semantics /səˈmantɪks/ ▻ *singular noun* **1** the branch of linguistics that deals with the meaning of words. **2** the study of the differences and correlations between meanings of words. • **semanticist** *noun.* ⓘ 19c.

semaphore /ˈsɛməfɔː(r)/ ▻ *noun* **1** a signalling device, consisting primarily of a pole with arms that can be set in different positions. **2** a system of signalling in which flags, or simply the arms, are held in positions that represent individual letters and numbers. ▻ *verb* (***semaphored, semaphoring***) *tr & intr* to signal using semaphore or a semaphore. • **semaphoric** /sɛməˈfɒrɪk/ *adj.* ⓘ Early 19c: French, from Greek *sema* sign + -PHORE.

sematic /səˈmatɪk/ ▻ *adj, biol* said of an animal's colouring: serving for recognition, attraction or warning. ⓘ 19c: from Greek *sema* sign.

semblance /ˈsɛmbləns/ ▻ *noun* **1** outer appearance, especially when superficial or deceptive. **2** a hint or trace. ⓘ 13c: from French *sembler* to seem.

sememe /ˈsiːmiːm, ˈsɛmiːm/ ▻ *noun* a unit of meaning, specifically of the smallest linguistically analysable unit. ⓘ Early 20c: from Greek *sema* sign.

semen /'siːmən/ ▷ *noun* a thick whitish liquid carrying spermatozoa, ejaculated by the penis. See also SEMINAL. ⓘ 14c: Latin, meaning 'seed'.

semester /sə'mɛstə(r)/ ▷ *noun* in German and US, and now some UK, universities: an academic term lasting for half an academic year. ⓘ 19c: from Latin *semestris* six-monthly, from *sex* six + *mensis* month.

semi /'sɛmɪ; *US* 'sɛmaɪ/ ▷ *noun* (***semis***) **1** *colloq* a semi-detached house. **2** a semi-final.

semi- /'sɛmɪ/ ▷ *prefix, denoting* **1** half □ ***semiquaver***. **2** partly □ ***semiconscious***. **3** occurring twice in the stated period □ ***semiannual***. Compare DEMI-. ⓘ Latin, meaning 'half'.

semiannual ▷ *adj, chiefly N Amer* **1** happening every half-year. **2** being half a year in duration. • **semiannually** *adverb*.

semi-automatic ▷ *adj* **1** partially automatic. **2** said of a firearm: continuously reloading itself, but only firing one bullet at a time. • **semi-automatically** *adverb*.

semibreve /'sɛmɪbriːv/ ▷ *noun, music* the longest note in common use, equal to half a breve, two minims or four crotchets.

semicircle ▷ *noun* **1** one half of a circle. **2** an arrangement of anything in this form □ ***a semicircle of grass***. • **semicircular** *adj*.

semicircular canal ▷ *noun, anatomy* in the inner ear of vertebrates: one of the three fluid-filled semicircular tubes that are involved in the maintenance of balance.

semicolon /'sɛmɪkoʊlən, -'koʊlən/ ▷ *noun* a punctuation mark (;) indicating a pause stronger than that marked by a comma but weaker than that marked by a full stop □ ***We'll bring the drink; you can provide the food.***

semicolon

A **semicolon**

• is used to mark a break within a sentence, a more definite break than that marked by a comma, but less of a break than that between two separate sentences □ *He may have seemed a competent prime minister; yet, he totally failed to appreciate the changing circumstances of the country.*

• It is used when there is a balance or contrast between what is said in a pair of clauses □ *As a neighbour, he deserved our courtesy and consideration; as a politician, he provoked our silent scorn* □ *You may be sorry; I am delighted.*

ALTERNATIVE STYLE: a comma and a conjunction □ *You may be sorry, but I am delighted.*

• It is used to group parts of a long sentence that contains many commas:

✓ *Copies of the report have been faxed to our offices in Lagos, Nigeria; Nairobi, Kenya; and Harare, Zimbabwe.*

✓ *There was an alpine garden with sea-pinks, saxifrages, thyme and candytuft; a herbaceous border full of hosta, geum and delphinium; and at the far end there was a splendid wall of fuchsia, broom and other flowering shrubs.*

semiconductor ▷ *noun, electronics* a crystalline material that behaves either as an electrical conductor or as an insulator, eg silicon, used to make diodes, photoelectric devices, etc, and used in the form of silicon chips in the integrated circuits of computers, etc. • **semiconducting** *adj*. • **semiconductivity** *noun*.

semi-detached ▷ *adj* said of a house: forming part of the same building, with another house on the other side of the shared wall. ▷ *noun* a semi-detached house. Often shortened to SEMI.

semifinal ▷ *noun* in competitions, sports tournaments, etc: either of two matches, the winners of which play each other in the final. • **semifinalist** *noun*.

semi-fluid ▷ *adj* possessing properties of both a fluid and a solid; nearly solid but able to flow to some extent. ▷ *noun* a semi-fluid substance.

semi-lunar ▷ *adj* in the form of a half-moon or crescent. • **semi-lune** *noun* any object, body or structure that is semi-lunar in shape.

seminal /'sɛmɪnəl/ ▷ *adj* **1** referring or relating to seed, semen or reproduction in general. **2** referring or relating to the beginnings or early developments of an idea, study, etc. **3** highly original and at the root of a trend or movement □ ***seminal writings***. **4** generative; capable of creative and influential future development. • **seminally** *adverb*. ⓘ 14c: from Latin *seminalis*, from *semen* seed.

seminar /'sɛmɪnɑː(r)/ ▷ *noun* **1** a class in which a small group of students and a tutor discuss a particular topic. **2** a group of advanced students working in a specific subject of study under the supervision of a teacher. **3** any meeting set up for the discussion of any topic. ⓘ 19c: from Latin *seminarium* SEMINARY.

seminarian /sɛmɪ'nɛərɪən/ and **seminarist** /'sɛmɪnərɪst/ ▷ *noun* **1** a student in a seminary or in a seminar. **2** a Roman Catholic priest educated in a foreign seminary. **3** a teacher in a seminary. ⓘ 16c: from SEMINARY.

seminary /'sɛmɪnərɪ/ ▷ *noun* (***seminaries***) **1** a college for the training of priests, ministers and rabbis. **2** *old use* a secondary school, especially for girls. ⓘ 15c: from Latin *seminarium* seed-plot, from *semen* seed.

seminiferous /sɛmɪ'nɪfərəs/ ▷ *adj* **1** producing or conveying semen. **2** said of plants: bearing seeds. ⓘ 17c: from SEMEN.

seminiferous tubule ▷ *noun, anatomy* in mammals: any of many long tightly coiled tubules that form the bulk of the testes, and in which the sperm are produced. ⓘ 19c.

semiotics /sɛmɪ'ɒtɪks/ and **semiology** /sɛmɪ'ɒlədʒɪ/ ▷ *singular noun* **1** *linguistics* the study of human communication, especially the relationship between words and the objects or concepts they represent. **2** *pathol* the scientific study of disease symptoms. • **semiotic** *adj*. ⓘ 17c: from Greek *semeiotikos*, from *semeion* sign + -LOGY.

semi-permeable ▷ *adj* **1** only partly permeable. **2** *biol* denoting a membrane through which only certain molecules can pass. • **semi-permeability** *noun*.

semi-precious ▷ *adj* said of a gem: considered less valuable than a precious stone.

semi-professional ▷ *adj* **1** said of a person: engaging only part-time in a professional activity. **2** said of an activity: engaged in only by semi-professionals. ▷ *noun* a semi-professional person.

semiquaver ▷ *noun* a musical note equal to half a quaver or one-sixteenth of a semibreve.

semi-rigid ▷ *adj* said of an airship: having a flexible gas-bag supported by a stiffened keel.

semi-skilled ▷ *adj* **1** said of a job: having or requiring a degree of training less advanced than that needed for specialized work. **2** said of a person: possessing such skills.

Semitic /sə'mɪtɪk/ ▷ *noun* any of a group of Afro-Asiatic languages including Hebrew, Arabic and Aramaic, spoken by **Semites**, a group of people said to be descended from Shem, the eldest son of Noah (Genesis 10). ▷ *adj* **1** referring to or speaking any such language. **2** referring or relating to Semites. **3** referring or relating to the Jews; Jewish. ⓘ 19c: from Greek *Sem* Shem + -ITE.

semitone ▷ *noun, music* **1** half a tone. **2** the interval between adjacent notes on a keyboard instrument, and the smallest interval in a normal musical scale. • **semitonic** *adj*.

semi-tropical ▷ *adj* subtropical.

semivowel ▷ *noun* **1** a speech sound having the qualities of both a vowel and a consonant. **2** a letter representing such a sound, such as *y* and *w* in English.

semi-weekly see BI-WEEKLY

semolina /sɛmə'liːnə/ ▷ *noun* the hard particles of wheat not ground into flour during milling, used for thickening soups, making puddings, etc. ◷ 18c: from Italian *semolino*, diminutive of *semola* bran, from Latin *simila* fine flour.

Semtex /'sɛmtɛks/ ▷ *noun, trademark* a very powerful type of plastic explosive, favoured by terrorist groups because it has no detectable smell and can only be ignited by a detonator.

SEN ▷ *abbreviation* **1** State Enrolled Nurse. **2** Special Educational Needs.

Sen. ▷ *abbreviation* **1** senate. **2** senator. **3** senior.

senate /'sɛnət/ ▷ *noun* (*often* **Senate**) **1** in ancient Rome: the chief legislative and administrative body. **2** in the USA, Australia and other countries: a legislative body, especially the upper chamber of the national assembly. **3** a body of distinguished and venerable people. **4** the governing council in some British universities. ◷ 13c: from Latin *senatus* council, from *senex* old man.

senator /'sɛnətə(r)/ ▷ *noun* (*often* **Senator**) a member of a senate. • **senatorial** /sɛnə'tɔːrɪəl/ *adj* **1** relating to or characteristic of a senator. **2** made up of senators.

send ▷ *verb* (***sent, sending***) **1** to cause, direct or order to go or be conveyed. **2** to dispatch ▫ *I sent the letter yesterday.* **3** to force or propel ▫ *He sent me flying.* **4** to cause to pass into a specified state ▫ *She sent him into fits of laughter* ▫ *The din sent me mad.* **5** *radio* to cause a message, etc to be transmitted. **6** to bring about, especially by divine providence ▫ *a plague sent by God.* **7** *slang* originally said of jazz music: to rouse someone into a state of ecstasy; to thrill. • **sender** *noun* **1** a person who sends something, especially by post. **2** a transmitting device. • **send word** to send an intimation or announcement. ◷ Anglo-Saxon *sendan*.

▪ **send away for something** to order goods by post.

▪ **send someone down** **1** *colloq* to send them to prison. **2** to expel them from university.

▪ **send for someone** to ask or order them to come; to summon them.

▪ **send for something** to order it to be brought or delivered.

▪ **send something in** to submit it by post, especially an entry for a competition.

▪ **send someone off** in football, rugby, etc: to order a player to leave the field with no further participation in the game, usually after infringement of the rules.

▪ **send something off** to dispatch it, especially by post.

▪ **send off for something** to order (goods) by post.

▪ **send something on** **1** to post or send it, so as to arrive in advance of oneself. **2** to re-address and re-post a letter or parcel; to forward it.

▪ **send something out** **1** to distribute it by post. **2** to dispatch it.

▪ **send someone out for something** to send them to buy or fetch it.

▪ **send someone** or **something up** *Brit colloq* **1** to make fun of or parody them. **2** to send them to prison.

send-off ▷ *noun* a display of good wishes from a gathering of people to a departing person or group.

send-up ▷ *noun, Brit colloq* a parody or satire.

senescence /sɪ'nɛsəns/ ▷ *noun, biol* the changes that take place in a living organism during the process of ageing, eg the production of flowers and fruit in plants.

senescent /sɪ'nɛsənt/ ▷ *adj, formal* **1** growing old; ageing. **2** characteristic of old age. ◷ 17c: from Latin *senescere* to grow old, from *senex* old.

seneschal /'sɛnɪʃəl/ ▷ *noun* **1** *historical* a steward in charge of the household or estate of a medieval lord or prince. **2** *Brit* an administrative and judicial title still retained for certain cathedral officials. ◷ 14c: French, literally 'old servant'.

senile /'siːnaɪl/ ▷ *adj* **1** displaying the feebleness and decay of mind or body brought on by old age. **2** characterized or caused by old age. • **senility** /sə'nɪlɪtɪ/ *noun* **1** old age. **2** mental deterioration in old age. ◷ 17c: from Latin *senilis*, from *senex* old.

senile dementia ▷ *noun* a psychological disorder caused by irreversible degeneration of the brain, usually commencing after late middle age, and characterized by loss of memory, impaired intellectual ability and judgement.

senior /'siːnɪə(r)/ ▷ *adj* **1** older than someone. **2** higher in rank or authority than someone. **3** for or pertaining to schoolchildren over the age of 11. **4** *N Amer* referring to final-year college or university students. **5** (**Senior**) older than another person of the same name, especially distinguishing parent from child ▫ *James Smith, Senior.* ▷ *noun* **1** a person who is older or of a higher rank. **2** a pupil in a senior school, or in the senior part of a school. **3** *N Amer* a final-year student. ◷ 15c: Latin, meaning 'older', comparative of *senex* old.

senior citizen ▷ *noun* an elderly person, especially one retired; an old age pensioner.

senior common room ▷ *noun* in some universities: a common room used by staff. Compare JUNIOR COMMON ROOM.

seniority /siːnɪ'ɒrɪtɪ/ ▷ *noun* **1** the state or fact of being senior. **2** a privileged position earned through long service in a profession or with a company. ◷ 15c.

senior nursing officer ▷ *noun* a MATRON (sense 1).

senior service ▷ *noun* (*usually* **the senior service**) the Royal Navy.

senna /'sɛnə/ ▷ *noun* **1** any of various trees and shrubs, native to Africa and Arabia, with leaves divided into oval leaflets, and long clusters of yellow flowers. **2** the dried leaflets of certain species of these plants, used as a laxative. **3** the dried pods of certain species of these plants, used as a laxative. ◷ 16c: from Arabic *sana*.

Señor /sɛn'jɔː(r)/ ▷ *noun* **1** a Spanish gentleman. **2** in address: sir. **3** prefixed to a name: Mr. ◷ 17c: Spanish, from Latin *senior* older.

Señora /sɛn'jɔːrə/ ▷ *noun* (***Señoras***) **1** a Spanish lady. **2** in address: madam. **3** prefixed to a name: Mrs. ◷ 16c: a feminine form of SEÑOR.

Señorita /sɛnjɔː'riːtə/ ▷ *noun* (***Señoritas***) **1** a young Spanish lady. **2** a term of address. **3** prefixed to a name: Miss. ◷ 19c: a diminutive of SEÑORA.

sensation /sɛn'seɪʃən/ ▷ *noun* **1** an awareness of an external or internal stimulus, eg heat, pain or emotions, as a result of its perception by the senses. **2** a physical feeling ▫ *I've a burning sensation in my mouth.* **3** an emotion or general feeling; a thrill ▫ *a sensation of doubt* ▫ *We felt a sensation of terror as we faced the lion.* **4** a sudden widespread feeling of excitement or shock ▫ *His presence caused quite a sensation.* **5** the cause of such excitement or shock. ◷ 17c: from Latin *sensatio*, from *sentire* to feel.

sensational ▷ *adj* **1** causing or intended to cause strong feelings such as widespread excitement, intense interest or shock. **2** *colloq* excellent; marvellous ▫ *He's a sensational singer.* **3** referring or relating to the senses. • **sensationally** *adverb.* ◷ 1840s.

sensationalism ▷ *noun* **1** the practice of or methods used in deliberately setting out to cause widespread excitement, intense interest or shock. **2** *philos* the doctrine or belief that our ideas originate solely in sensation. • **sensationalist** *noun* **1** someone who aims to cause a sensation. **2** someone who believes that the senses are the ultimate source of all knowledge. • **sensationalistic** *adj.* ⓒ 19c.

sensationalize or **sensationalise** /sɛn'seɪʃənəlaɪz/ ▻ *verb* (***sensationalized***, ***sensationalizing***) to make (an event, situation, etc) appear more exciting, shocking, etc than it really is. ⓒ 19c.

sense /sɛns/ ▻ *noun* **1** any of the five main faculties used by an animal to obtain information about its external or internal environment, namely sight, hearing, smell, taste and touch. **2** an awareness or appreciation of, or an ability to make judgements regarding, some specified thing □ *She has a good sense of direction* □ *He has bad business sense.* **3** (**senses**) soundness of mind; one's wits or reason □ *He's lost his senses.* **4** wisdom; practical worth □ *There's no sense in doing it now.* **5** a general feeling or emotion, not perceived by any of the five natural powers □ *a sense of guilt.* **6** general, overall meaning □ *They understood the sense of the passage, if not all the words.* **7** specific meaning □ *In what sense do you mean?* **8** general opinion; consensus □ *the sense of the meeting.* ▻ *verb* (***sensed***, ***sensing***) **1** to detect a stimulus by means of any of the five main senses. **2** to be aware of something by means other than the five main senses □ *I sensed that someone was following me.* **3** to realize or comprehend. • **bring someone to their senses** to make them recognize the facts; to make them understand that they must rectify their behaviour. • **come to one's senses 1** to act sensibly and rationally after a period of foolishness. **2** to regain consciousness. • **in a sense** in one respect; in a way. • **make sense 1** to be understandable. **2** to be wise, rational or reasonable. • **make sense of something** to understand it; to see the purpose or explanation in it. • **take leave of one's senses** to begin behaving unreasonably or irrationally; to go mad. ⓒ 14c: from Latin *sensus*, from *sentire* to feel.

sense-datum ▻ *noun* (***sense-data***) something which is received immediately through the stimulation of a sense organ. ⓒ 19c.

senseless ▻ *adj* **1** unconscious. **2** unwise; without good sense or foolish. Also *as adverb* □ *He was beaten senseless.* • **senselessly** *adverb.* • **senselessness** *noun.* ⓒ 16c.

sense organ ▻ *noun, physiol* in animals: any organ consisting of specialized receptor cells that are capable of responding to a particular stimulus, eg the eye, ear, nose, skin and taste buds of the tongue.

sensibility /sɛnsɪ'bɪlɪtɪ/ ▻ *noun* (***sensibilities***) **1** the ability or capacity to feel or have sensations or emotions. **2** a delicacy of emotional response; sensitivity □ *There was a general sensibility to his grief.* **3** (**sensibilities**) feelings that can easily be offended or hurt. ⓒ 14c: see SENSIBLE.

sensible /'sɛnsɪbəl/ ▻ *adj* **1** having or showing reasonableness or good judgement; wise. **2** perceptible by the senses. **3** having the power of sensation; sensitive □ *sensible to pain.* • **sensibleness** *noun.* • **sensibly** *adverb.* ⓒ 14c: from Latin *sensibilis*, from *sentire* to feel.

sensible horizon see HORIZON

sensitive /'sɛnsɪtɪv/ ▻ *adj* **1** feeling or responding readily, strongly or painfully □ *sensitive to our feelings.* **2** *biol* responding to a stimulus. **3** easily upset or offended. **4** stimulating much strong feeling or difference of opinion □ *sensitive issues.* **5** said of documents, etc: not for public discussion or scrutiny as they contain secret or confidential information, eg concerning national security. **6** said of scientific instruments: reacting to or recording extremely small changes. **7** *photog* responding to the action of light. **8** *physics* responding to the action of some external force or stimulus □ *pressure-sensitive.* • **sensitively** *adverb.* ⓒ 14c: from Latin *sensitivus*, from *sentire* to feel.

sensitive plant ▻ *noun, bot* a perennial S American plant with a prickly stem and down-curved leaves divided into narrow leaflets which fold up at night or when touched.

sensitivity /sɛnsɪ'tɪvɪtɪ/ ▻ *noun* (***sensitivities***) **1** an abnormal response to an allergen, drug or other external stimulus of the senses. **2** heightened awareness of oneself and others within the context of social and personal relationships. **3** the readiness and delicacy of an instrument in recording changes. ⓒ Early 19c.

sensitize or **sensitise** /'sɛnsɪtaɪz/ ▻ *verb* (***sensitized***, ***sensitizing***) **1** to make sensitive. **2** *photog* to make a plate, film, etc more sensitive to light. • **sensitization** *noun.* ⓒ 19c.

sensitometer /sɛnsɪ'tɒmɪtə(r)/ ▻ *noun* a device for measuring sensitivity of photographic film, plates, etc. ⓒ 19c.

sensor /'sɛnsə(r)/ ▻ *noun, elec* any of various devices that detect or measure a change in a physical quantity, usually by converting it into an electrical signal, eg burglar alarms, smoke detectors, etc. ⓒ 1950s: from SENSE + -OR.

sensory /'sɛnsərɪ/ ▻ *adj* referring or relating to the senses or sensation. ⓒ 17c: from Latin *sensorium* brain, seat of the senses.

sensory nerve ▻ *noun, anatomy* a nerve that relays nerve impulses from sensory receptor cells and sense organs to the brain and spinal cord.

sensual /'sɛnʃʊəl/ ▻ *adj* **1** relating to the senses and the body rather than the mind or the spirit. **2** said of pleasures: connected with often undue gratification of the bodily senses. **3** pursuing physical pleasures, especially those derived from sex or food and drink. **4** stimulating carnal desires, especially sexual desires; voluptuous. • **sensually** *adverb.* ⓒ 15c: from Latin *sensualis*, from *sensus* sense.

sensual, sensuous

• Those who are precise about language assert a distinction between **sensual** and **sensuous**, by which **sensuous** relates to the senses in aesthetic contexts (principally seeing and hearing things of beauty), and **sensual** relates to carnal or sexual meanings □ *The shadowy interior is a sensuous mix of gilt and candle wax* □ *Select a sophisticated, sensual scent to match your little black dress.*

• In current use, the meanings overlap too much for the distinction to be maintained, and you will often find **sensuous** used in the same way as **sensual** □ *He felt her lips against his, soft, warm, sensuous.*

sensualism ▻ *noun* **1** sensual indulgence; the condition of being sensual. **2** the doctrine or belief that all our knowledge was originally derived from sensation; sensationalism. • **sensualist** *noun.* ⓒ Early 19c.

sensuality /sɛnʃʊ'alɪtɪ/ ▻ *noun* **1** the quality of being sensual. **2** indulgence in physical, especially sexual, pleasures. ⓒ 14c: from Latin *sensualitas*, from SENSUAL.

sensuous /'sɛnʃʊəs/ ▻ *adj* **1** appealing to the senses aesthetically, with no suggestion of sexual pleasure. **2** affected by or pleasing to the senses. **3** aware of what is perceived by the senses. • **sensuously** *adverb.* • **sensuousness** *noun.* ⓒ 17c: sense 1 apparently coined by Milton to distinguish it from the meanings of SENSUAL; from Latin *sensus* sense.

sent *past tense, past participle of* SEND

sentence /'sɛntəns/ ▻ *noun* **1** a sequence of words forming a meaningful grammatical structure that can stand alone as a complete utterance, and which in written English usually begins with a capital letter and ends with a full stop, question mark or exclamation mark. See note. **2** a punishment pronounced by a court or judge; its announcement in court. **3** a judgement, opinion or decision. ▻ *verb* (***sentenced***, ***sentencing***) **1** to announce the judgement or sentence to be given to someone. **2** to condemn someone to a punishment □ *They've sentenced him to five years' imprisonment.* • **sentential** *adj.* • **sententially** *adverb.* • **pass sentence on someone** to announce the punishment to be given to someone. ⓒ 13c: French, from Latin *sententia* opinion, from *sentire* to feel.

sentence

A **sentence** is sometimes defined as a grammatical structure that contains at least one CLAUSE with an expressed SUBJECT and a FINITE verb, as in *I'm going home* or *It'll be cooler outside* or *If you were as fit as that, would you waste your time doing press-ups?* However, in many sentences, sometimes known as **sentence fragments**, the subject and/or the verb may be implied rather than expressed □ *Where are you going?' 'To have a bath.'* (= 'I'm going to have a bath') □ *'What's he doing now?' 'Thinking.'* (= 'He's thinking'). The same is true for exclamations, such as *How awful!* and *What a pity!*

sententious /sɛn'tɛnʃəs/ ▻ *adj* **1** fond of using or full of sayings or proverbs; aphoristic. **2** tending to lecture others on morals. • **sententiously** *adverb.* • **sententiousness** *noun.* ⓒ 15c: from Latin *sententiosus* full of meaning, from SENTENCE.

sentient /'sɛnʃənt, 'sɛntɪənt/ ▻ *adj* capable of sensation or feeling; conscious or aware of something □ *sentient beings.* • **sentience** *noun.* ⓒ 17c: from Latin *sentiens*, from *sentire* to feel.

sentiment /'sɛntɪmənt/ ▻ *noun* **1** a thought or emotion, especially when expressed. **2** refined feelings, especially as expressed in art or literature. **3** emotion or emotional behaviour in general, especially when considered excessive, self-indulgent or insincere. **4** (*often* **sentiments**) an opinion or view □ *What are your sentiments on the matter?* ⓒ 14c: from Latin *sentimentum*, from *sentire* to feel.

sentimental /sɛntɪ'mentəl/ ▻ *adj* **1** readily feeling, indulging in or expressing tender emotions or sentiments, especially love, friendship and pity. **2** provoking or designed to provoke such emotions, especially in large measure and without subtlety. **3** closely associated with or moved by fond memories of the past; nostalgic □ *objects of sentimental value.* • **sentimentally** *adverb.* ⓒ 18c.

sentimentality /sɛntɪmen'talɪtɪ/ and **sentimentalism** ▻ *noun* **1** a sentimental quality or inclination. **2** a tendency to indulge in sentiment or to affect fine feelings. • **sentimentalist** *noun.* ⓒ 18c.

sentimentalize or **sentimentalise** /sɛntɪ'mentəlaɪz/ ▻ *verb* (***sentimentalized***, ***sentimentalizing***) **1** *intr* to behave sentimentally or indulge in sentimentality. **2** to make sentimental. **3** to regard something as sentimental □ *She's sentimentalizing the whole incident.* ⓒ 18c.

sentinel /'sɛntɪnəl/ ▻ *noun* someone posted on guard; a sentry. ▻ *verb* (***sentinelled***, ***sentinelling***; (*US*) ***sentineled***, ***sentineling***) **1** to watch over as a sentinel. **2** to post as or supply with a sentinel. ⓒ 16c: from French *sentinelle*, from Italian *sentinella*.

sentry /'sɛntrɪ/ ▻ *noun* (***sentries***) a person, usually a soldier, posted on guard to control entry or passage. ⓒ 17c: a shortening of *centronel*, variant of SENTINEL.

sentry-box ▻ *noun* a small open-fronted shelter for a sentry to use in bad weather.

Sep. and **Sept.** ▻ *abbreviation* September.

sepal /'sɛpəl, 'siːpəl/ ▻ *noun, bot* in a flower: one of the modified leaves, usually green but sometimes brightly coloured, that together form the CALYX which surrounds the petals. ⓒ 19c: from French *sépale*, coined by N J de Necker (d.1790) from Greek *skepe* cover.

separable /'sɛpərəbəl/ ▻ *adj* able to be separated or disjoined. • **separability** or **separableness** *noun.* • **separably** *adverb.* ⓒ 14c: from Latin *separabilis*, from SEPARATE.

separate ▻ *verb* /'sɛpəreɪt/ (***separated***, ***separating***) **1** to take, force or keep apart (from others or each other) □ *A hedge separates the two fields.* **2** *intr* said of a couple: to cease to be together or live together. **3** to disconnect or disunite; to sever. **4** to isolate or seclude □ *He should be separated from the others.* **5** to set apart for a purpose. **6** (*also* **separate up**) to divide or become divided into parts □ *The building is separated up into smaller apartments.* **7** *intr* to depart or withdraw; to secede. **8** *intr* to become disconnected or disunited. ▻ *adj* /'sɛpərət/ **1** separated; divided. **2** distinctly different or individual; unrelated □ *That is a separate issue.* **3** physically unattached; isolated. ▻ *noun* /'sɛpərət/ (*usually* **separates**) individual items which form a unit and which are often purchased separately to mix and match, eg items of women's clothing eg blouse, skirt, etc forming separate parts of an outfit, rather than a suit, or separate units of a hi-fi system such as a CD-player, amplifier, speakers, etc. • **separately** *adverb.* • **separateness** *noun.* • **separator** *noun.* ⓒ 15c: from Latin *separare*, from *se* aside + *parare* to put.

separation /sɛpə'reɪʃən/ ▻ *noun* **1** the act of separating or disjoining. **2** the state or process of being separated. **3** a place or line where there is a division. **4** a gap or interval that separates. **5** an arrangement, either approved mutually or by court, where a husband and wife live apart while still married, usually prior to divorce. ⓒ 15c.

separatist /'sɛpərətɪst/ ▻ *noun* **1** a person who encourages, or takes action to achieve, independence from an established church, federation, organization, etc. **2** *as adj* □ *a separatist tendency.* • **separatism** *noun* **1** a tendency to separate or to be separate. **2** support for separation. **3** the practices and principles of separatists. ⓒ 17c.

sepia /'siːpɪə/ ▻ *noun* **1** a rich reddish-brown pigment, obtained from a fluid secreted by the cuttlefish. **2** the colour of this pigment. **3** a brownish tint used in photography, especially in early photography. **4** a sepia drawing or photograph. ▻ *adj* **1** sepia-coloured. **2** done in sepia. ⓒ 16c: Greek, meaning 'cuttlefish'.

sepoy /'siːpɔɪ/ ▻ *noun* (***sepoys***) *historical* an Indian soldier in service with a European (especially British) army. ⓒ 17c: from Urdu and Persian *sipahi* horseman.

seppuku /sɛ'puːkuː/ ▻ *noun* HARA-KIRI. ⓒ 19c: Japanese.

sepsis /'sɛpsɪs/ ▻ *noun* (***sepses*** /-siːz/) *medicine* the presence of disease-causing micro-organisms, especially viruses or bacteria, and their toxins in the body tissues. ⓒ 19c: Greek, meaning 'putrefaction'.

sept ▻ *noun* especially in Scotland or Ireland: a clan; a division of a tribe. ⓒ 16c: an alteration of SECT.

Sept. see SEP.

septa *plural of* SEPTUM

September /sɛp'tɛmbə(r)/ ▻ *noun* the ninth month of the year, which follows August and comes before October and has 30 days. ⓒ Anglo-Saxon: Latin, meaning 'seventh', as it was the seventh month in the original Roman calendar.

septennial /sɛp'tɛnɪəl/ ▻ *adj* **1** occurring once every seven years. **2** lasting seven years. ⓒ 17c: from Latin *septem* seven + *annus* year.

septet or **septette** /sɛp'tɛt/ ▻ *noun* **1** a group of seven musicians. **2** a piece of music for seven performers. **3** any group or set of seven. ⓒ 19c: from Latin *septem* seven.

septic /'sɛptɪk/ ▷ *adj* **1** *medicine* said of a wound: contaminated with pathogenic bacteria. **2** putrefying. ⓘ 17c: from Greek *septikos*, related to SEPSIS.

septicaemia /sɛptɪ'siːmɪə/ ▷ *noun, pathol* the presence of pathogenic bacteria; blood-poisoning. ⓘ 19c: from Greek *septikos* putrefied + *haima* blood.

septic tank ▷ *noun* a tank, usually underground, in which sewage is decomposed by the action of bacteria.

septillion /sɛp'tɪlɪən/ ▷ *noun* (***septillion*** or ***septillions***) **1** in Britain, France and Germany: a number that is represented by a figure 1 followed by 42 zeros, ie 10^{42}. **2** in N Amer: a QUADRILLION (sense 1). ⓘ 17c: French, modelled on MILLION.

septuagenarian /sɛptʃʊədʒə'nɛərɪən/ ▷ *adj* aged between 70 and 79 years old. ▷ *noun* a septuagenarian person. ⓘ 18c: from Latin *septuaginta* seventy.

Septuagesima /sɛptʃʊə'dʒɛsɪmə/ ▷ *noun* the third Sunday before Lent (**Septuagesima Sunday**), apparently in continuation of the sequence Quadragesima, Quinquagesima, etc. ⓘ 14c: from Latin *septuagesimus* seventieth.

septum /'sɛptəm/ ▷ *noun* (***septa*** /'sɛptə/) *biol, anatomy* any partition between cavities, eg nostrils, areas of soft tissue, etc. ⓘ 18c: from Latin *saeptum* fence or enclosure, from *saepire* to fence.

septuple /'sɛptʃʊpəl, sɛp'tʃuːpəl/ ▷ *adj* being seven times as much or as many; sevenfold. ▷ *verb* (***septupled, septupling***) *tr & intr* to multiply or increase sevenfold. ⓘ 17c: from Latin *septuplus*, from *septem* seven.

septuplet /'sɛptʃʊplət, -'tʃuː-/ ▷ *noun* **1** any of seven children or animals born at one birth to the same mother. **2** *music* a group of seven notes played in four or six time. ⓘ 19c: from Latin *septuplus*, from *septem* seven.

sepulchral /sɪ'pʌlkrəl/ ▷ *adj* **1** referring or relating to a tomb or burial. **2** suggestive of death or burial; gloomy or funereal. ⓘ 17c.

sepulchre or (*US*) **sepulcher** /'sɛpəlkə(r)/ *noun* (***sepulchres*** or ***sepulchers***) **1** a tomb or burial vault. **2** *church architecture* a recess or structure, usually in the north chancel wall, to receive the reserved sacrament and the crucifix from Maundy Thursday or Good Friday till Easter. Also called **Easter sepulchre**. ▷ *verb* (***sepulchred, sepulchring***) to bury in a sepulchre; to entomb. ⓘ 12c: from Latin *sepulcrum*, from *sepelire* to bury.

sepulture /'sɛpəltʃʊə(r)/ ▷ *noun* the act of burial, especially in a sepulchre. • **sepultural** *adj*. ⓘ 13c: from Latin *sepultura* buried, from *sepelire* to bury.

sequel /'siːkwəl/ ▷ *noun* **1** a book, film or play that continues an earlier story. **2** anything that follows on from a previous event, etc. **3** a result or consequence. ⓘ 15c: from Latin *sequela*, from *sequi* to follow.

sequela /sɪ'kwiːlə/ ▷ *noun* (***sequelae*** /-laɪ/) (*usually* **sequelae**) *pathol* any abnormal condition following or related to a previous disease. ⓘ 18c: from SEQUEL.

sequence /'siːkwəns/ ▷ *noun* **1** the state or fact of being sequent or consequent. **2** a series or succession of things in a specific order; the order they follow. **3** a succession of short pieces of action making up a scene in a film. **4** *math* a set of values or quantities where each one is a fixed amount greater or smaller than its predecessor, as determined by a given rule. **5** *music* successive repetition of the same melody in higher or lower parts of the scale or in higher or lower keys. **6** *cards* a set of three or more cards, consecutive in value and generally of the same suit. **7** a hymn in rhythmical prose, sung after the GRADUAL (sense 1) and before the GOSPEL (sense 3). ⓘ 14c: from Latin *sequi* to follow.

sequencing ▷ *noun, biochem* **1** (*in full* **protein sequencing**) the process of determining the order of AMINO ACIDs in a protein. 2 (*in full* **gene sequencing**) the process of determining the order of NUCLEOTIDEs in DNA or RNA.

sequent /'siːkwənt/ ▷ *adj* successive or consequent; consecutive. ▷ *noun* a thing or quantity that follows. ⓘ 16c.

sequential /sɪ'kwɛnʃəl/ ▷ *adj* **1** in, having or following a particular order or sequence. **2** consequent; sequent. • **sequentiality** *noun*. • **sequentially** *adverb*. ⓘ 19c.

sequester /sɪ'kwɛstə(r)/ ▷ *verb* (***sequestered, sequestering***) **1** to set aside or isolate. **2** to set apart. **3** *law* to sequestrate. **4** *church law* to hold the income of (a vacant benefice) for the benefit of the next incumbent. **5** *law* to sequestrate the estate or benefice of (a person). **6** *chem* to remove or render ineffective (a metal ion) by adding a reagent that forms a complex with it (eg as a means of preventing or getting rid of precipitation in water). • **sequestered** *adj* secluded □ ***a sequestered garden***. ⓘ 14c: Latin, meaning 'depository'.

sequestrate /'siːkwəstreɪt/ ▷ *verb* (***sequestrated, sequestrating***) *law* to remove or confiscate (something, especially property) from someone's possession until a dispute or debt has been settled. • **sequestration** /siːkwə'streɪʃən/ *noun*. • **sequestrator** /'siːkwəstreɪtə(r), 'sɛk-/ *noun*. ⓘ 16c: from Latin *sequestrare*, from *sequester* depository.

sequin /'siːkwɪn/ ▷ *noun* **1** a small round shiny disc of foil or plastic, sewn on a garment for decoration. **2** an old Italian gold coin. • **sequined** *adj* covered or decorated with sequins. ⓘ 17c: from Italian *zecchino*, from *zecca* the mint, from Arabic *sikkah* coin.

sequoia /sɪ'kwɔɪə/ ▷ *noun* (***sequoias***) either of two species of massive evergreen trees, native to N America, the Californian REDWOOD (the tallest known tree) and the **giant sequoia** (the largest known tree). Also called **Wellingtonia**. ⓘ 19c: named after Sequoiah (d.1843) the Cherokee scholar.

seraglio /sə'rɑːlɪoʊ/ ▷ *noun* (***seraglios***) **1** women's quarters in a Muslim house or palace; a harem. **2** *historical* a Turkish palace, especially that of the sultans at Constantinople. ⓘ 16c: from Italian *serraglio*, from Persian *saray* palace.

serape /sə'rɑːpɪ/ ▷ *noun* (***serapes***) a Spanish-American woollen blanket or cape, usually brightly coloured, worn by men while riding. ⓘ 19c: Mexican-Spanish.

seraph /'sɛrəf/ ▷ *noun* (***seraphs*** or ***seraphim***) in the traditional medieval hierarchy of nine ranks of angels: an angel of the highest rank. Compare CHERUB, THRONE, DOMINION, VIRTUE, POWER, PRINCIPALITY, ARCHANGEL, ANGEL. • **seraphic** /sə'rafɪk/ or **seraphical** *adj*. • **seraphically** *adverb*. ⓘ 17c: Hebrew.

Serbian /'sɜːbɪən/ and **Serb** ▷ *adj* belonging or relating to Serbs, an ethnic group living in Yugoslavia and surrounding republics (see YUGOSLAV), or their language. ▷ *noun* **1** someone belonging to this ethnic group. **2** the Slavonic language spoken by Serbs; SERBO-CROAT.

Serbo-Croat /sɜːboʊ'kroʊat/ and **Serbo-Croatian** ▷ *noun* the official language of the former Yugoslavia, a Slavonic language spoken in Serbia, Croatia, etc. ▷ *adj* referring or relating to this language.

SERC ▷ *abbreviation, historical* Science and Engineering Research Council, now replaced by EPSRC and PPARC.

serenade /sɛrə'neɪd/ ▷ *noun* **1** a song or piece of music performed at night under a woman's window by her suitor. **2** any musical piece with a gentle tempo suggestive of romance and suitable for such a performance. **3** a piece of classical music similar to a symphony in length, but lighter in tone, having more movements and for a smaller orchestra. ▷ *verb* (***serenaded, serenading***) **1** to entertain (a person) with a serenade. **2** *intr* to perform a serenade. • **serenader** *noun*. ⓘ 17c: from Italian *serenata*, from Latin *serenus* bright clear sky, the meaning being influenced by Latin *serus* late.

serendipity /sɛrən'dɪpɪtɪ/ ▻ *noun* the state of frequently making lucky or beneficial finds. • **serendipitous** *adj* discovered by luck or chance. ⓒ 1754: from Serendip, a former name for Sri Lanka, a word coined by Horace Walpole from the folk tale *The Three Princes of Serendip*.

serene /sə'riːn/ ▻ *adj* **1** said of a person: calm and composed; at peace. **2** said of a sky: cloudless. **3** (**Serene**) a word incorporated in the titles of members of some European royal families □ ***Her Serene Highness.*** • **serenely** *adverb*. • **sereneness** *noun*. • **serenity** /sɪ'rɛnətɪ/ *noun*. ⓒ 16c: from Latin *serenus* clear.

serf /sɜːf/ ▻ *noun* in medieval Europe: a worker in modified slavery, bought and sold with the land on which they worked. • **serfdom** /'sɜːfdəm/ and **serfhood** *noun* the condition of a serf. ⓒ 15c: from Latin *servus* slave.

serge /sɜːdʒ/ ▻ *noun* a strong twilled fabric, especially of wool or worsted. ▻ *adj* made of serge. ⓒ 14c: French, from Latin *serica* silk.

sergeant or **serjeant** /'sɑːdʒənt/ ▻ *noun* **1** in the armed forces: a non-commissioned officer of the rank next above corporal. **2** in Britain: a police officer of the rank between constable and inspector. • **sergeancy** *noun* the office or rank of a sergeant. ⓒ 12c: from French *sergent*, from Latin *serviens* servant.

sergeant-at-arms or **serjeant-at-arms** ▻ *noun* an officer of a court or parliament who is responsible for keeping order.

sergeant-major ▻ *noun* a non-commissioned officer of the highest rank in the armed forces.

serial /'sɪərɪəl/ ▻ *noun* **1** a story, television programme, etc published or broadcast in regular instalments. **2** a periodical. ▻ *adj* **1** appearing in instalments. **2** forming a series or part of a series. **3** in series; in a row. **4** *music* using series as the basis of a composition. **5** *music* using serialism. ⓒ 19c: from Latin *serialis*, from SERIES.

serial, series

There is often confusion between **serial** and **series**: a **serial** is a single story presented in separate instalments, whereas a **series** is a set of separate stories featuring the same characters.

serialism ▻ *noun*, *music* the technique of using a series or succession of related notes as the basis for a musical composition, the most common type being 12-note serialism. ⓒ 1920s: first devised by Arnold Schoenberg (1874–1951), the Austrian composer.

serialize /'sɪərɪəlaɪz/ or **serialise** ▻ *verb* (***serialized***, ***serializing***) to publish or broadcast (a story, television programme, etc) in instalments. • **serialization** *noun* a production or publication in instalments. ⓒ 19c.

serial killer ▻ *noun* someone who commits a succession of murders, often choosing the same method of killing or the same type of victim.

serial number ▻ *noun* the individual identification number marked on each one of a series of identical products.

sericeous /sə'rɪʃəs/ ▻ *adj* **1** silky. **2** *bot* covered with soft silky hairs. **3** shiny like silk. ⓒ 18c: from Latin *sericeus*, from *sericus* silken.

sericulture /'sɛrɪkʌltʃə(r)/ ▻ *noun* the breeding of silkworms for producing raw silk. • **sericulturist** *noun*. ⓒ 19c.

series /'sɪərɪz, -riːz/ ▻ *noun* (*plural* ***series*** /'sɪərɪz, -riːz/) **1** a number of similar, related or identical things arranged or produced in line or in succession, such as a set of similar books issued by the same publishing house. **2** a TV or radio programme in which the same characters appear, or a similar subject is addressed, in regularly broadcast shows. **3** a set of things that differ progressively. **4** *math* in a sequence of numbers: the sum obtained when each term is added to the previous ones. **5** a taxonomic group. **6** *music* a set of notes in a particular order taken as the basis of a composition rather than a traditional scale. See SERIALISM. **7** *physics* an electric circuit whose components are arranged so that the same current passes through each of them in turn. **8** *geol* a group of rocks, fossils or minerals that can be arranged in a natural sequence on the basis of certain properties, eg composition. ⓒ 17c: Latin, meaning 'chain or row'.

series

See Usage Note at **serial**.

serif /'sɛrɪf/ ▻ *noun*, *printing* a short decorative line or stroke on the end of a printed letter, as opposed to SANSERIF. ⓒ 19c: perhaps from Dutch *schreef* stroke.

serigraph /'sɛrɪgrɑːf/ ▻ *noun* a print made by silk-screen process. • **serigrapher** *noun*. • **serigraphy** *noun*. ⓒ 19c: from Latin *sericum* silk.

serin /'sɛrɪn/ ▻ *noun* any of a genus of small European finches, including the canary. ⓒ 16c: French, meaning 'canary'.

serine /'seriːn/ ▻ *noun*, *biochem* an amino acid that is found in proteins. ⓒ 19c: from Greek *serikos* silken.

seriocomic /sɪərɪoʊ'kɒmɪk/ ▻ *adj* containing both serious and comic elements or qualities.

serious /'sɪərɪəs/ ▻ *adj* **1** grave or solemn; not inclined to flippancy or lightness of mood. **2** dealing with important issues □ ***a serious newspaper.*** **3** severe □ ***a serious accident.*** **4** important; significant □ ***There were serious differences of opinion.*** **5** showing firmness of intention; sincere or earnest □ ***I am serious about doing it.*** **6** *colloq* notable, renowned or in significant quantities □ ***That is a serious set of wheels*** □ ***serious money.*** • **seriously** *adverb*. • **seriousness** *noun*. ⓒ 15c: from Latin *seriosus*, from *serius*.

serjeant see SERGEANT

sermon /'sɜːmən/ ▻ *noun* **1** a public speech or discourse, especially one forming part of a church service, about morals, religious duties or some aspect of religious doctrine. **2** a lengthy moral or advisory speech, especially a reproving one. ⓒ 12c: from Latin *sermo* discourse.

sermonize or **sermonise** /'sɜːmənaɪz/ ▻ *verb* (***sermonized***, ***sermonizing***) **1** *intr* to compose and conduct sermons. **2** to preach or moralize. • **sermonizer** *noun*. ⓒ 17c.

sero- /sɪəroʊ, sɪə'rɒ/ ▻ *combining form*, *denoting* serum.

serology /sɪə'rɒlədʒɪ/ ▻ *noun*, *biol* the study of blood serum and its constituents, especially antibodies and antigens. • **serological** *adj*. • **serologically** *adverb*. • **serologist** *noun*. ⓒ Early 20c.

seropositive ▻ *adj* said of a person: having blood that is shown by tests to be infected by the specific disease tested for, usually Aids.

serotonin /sɪərə'toʊnɪn, sɛrə-/ ▻ *noun*, *physiol* a hormone that acts as a NEUROTRANSMITTER in the central nervous system, and also causes narrowing of blood vessels by stimulating their contraction. ⓒ 1940s: from SERUM + TONIC.

serous /'sɪərəs/ ▻ *adj* **1** characteristic of, relating to or containing serum. **2** said of a liquid: resembling serum; watery. ⓒ 16c.

serpent /'sɜːpənt/ ▻ *noun* **1** a snake. **2** a sneaky, treacherous or malicious person. **3** *music* an obsolete wooden bass wind instrument in the form of a writhing snake. ⓒ 14c: from Latin *serpens* creeping thing, from *serpere* to creep.

serpentine /'sɜːpəntaɪn/ ▻ *adj* **1** snake-like. **2** winding; full of twists and bends. ▻ *noun*, *geol* a soft green or white rock-forming mineral derived from magnesium silicates, so called because it is often mottled like a snake's skin. ◷ 14c: from Latin *serpentinum*, from SERPENT.

serpigo /sə'paɪgoʊ/ ▷ *noun, pathol* any spreading skin disease, especially ringworm. ◷ 14c: Latin, from *serpere* to creep.

SERPS or **Serps** /sɜːps/ ▷ *abbreviation* state earnings-related pension scheme.

serrate ▷ *adj* /'sɛreɪt/ **1** notched like the blade of a saw. **2** *bot, zool* possessing sharp forward-pointing teeth. ▷ *verb* /sə'reɪt/ (***serrated***, ***serrating***) to notch. • **serration** /sə'reɪʃən/ *noun* **1** the condition of being saw-like or serrated. **2** a sawlike tooth. ◷ 18c: from Latin *serra* saw.

serried /'sɛrɪd/ ▷ *adj* closely packed or grouped together □ ***soldiers in serried ranks.*** ◷ 17c: from French *serrer* to put close together.

serum /'sɪərəm/ ▷ *noun* (***serums*** or ***sera*** /'sɪərə/) **1** (in full **blood serum**) *anatomy* the yellowish fluid component of blood, which contains specific antibodies and can therefore be used in a vaccine. **2** *bot* the watery part of a plant fluid. ◷ 17c: Latin, meaning 'whey'.

serum hepatitis ▷ *noun, pathol* a virus infection of the liver, usually transmitted by transfusion of infected blood or use of contaminated instruments, especially needles, consequently occurring often in drug addicts. Also called HEPATITIS B.

servant /'sɜːvənt/ ▷ *noun* **1** *old use* a person employed by another to do household or menial work for them. **2** a person who acts for the good of others in any capacity. **3** a PUBLIC SERVANT. ◷ 13c: French, meaning 'serving', from Latin *servire* to serve.

serve /sɜːv/ ▷ *verb* (***served***, ***serving***) **1** to work for someone as a domestic servant; to be in the service of someone. **2** *intr* to be a servant. **3** to work for the benefit of someone; to aid □ ***He serves the community well.*** **4** *tr & intr* to attend to customers in a shop, etc; to provide to customers. **5** *tr & intr* to attend to the needs or requirements of someone □ ***These shoes have served me well.*** **6** *tr & intr* to bring, distribute or present (food or drink) to someone. **7** *intr* to wait at table. **8** to provide with or supply materials. **9** to render service and obedience to someone □ ***to serve God*** □ ***to serve the country.*** **10** *intr* to carry out duties as a member of some body or organization □ ***They serve on a committee.*** **11** *intr* to act as a member of the armed forces □ ***We served in the marines*** □ ***We served in France.*** **12** to provide specified facilities □ ***There are trams serving the entire city.*** **13** *tr & intr* to be of use; to suffice or fulfil a need □ ***There's no chair, but this box will serve*** □ ***This will serve our purpose.*** **14** *intr* to have a specific effect or result □ ***His speech just served to make matters worse.*** **15** to undergo as a requirement □ ***You have to serve an apprenticeship.*** **16** *tr & intr* in racket sports: to put (the ball) into play. **17** *law* to deliver or present (a legal document) □ ***serve with a writ*** □ ***He served a summons on her.*** **18** said of a male animal: to copulate with (a female). **19** *naut* to bind (rope, etc) with cord to guard and strengthen it. ▷ *noun* in racket sports: an act of serving. • **serve one's time** to undergo an apprenticeship or term in office. • **serve someone right** *colloq* to be the misfortune or punishment that they deserve. • **serve time** to undergo a term of imprisonment. ◷ 13c: from Latin *servire* to serve.

■ **serve as something** to act as or take the place of it □ ***This box will serve as a chair.***

■ **serve up** to bring food, etc to the table □ ***I'll serve up in about half an hour.***

server /'sɜːvə(r)/ ▷ *noun* **1** a person who serves. **2** in racket sports: the person who serves the ball. **3** *RC Church* a person who assists a priest during mass by organizing the altar, making the responses, etc. **4** a fork, spoon or other instrument for distributing food at the table. **5** a SALVER. ◷ 14c.

service /'sɜːvɪs/ ▷ *noun* **1** the condition or occupation of being a servant or someone who serves. **2** work carried out for or on behalf of others □ ***do someone a service.*** **3** the act or manner of serving. **4** use or usefulness □ ***Your services are no longer required*** □ ***This car has given me good service.*** **5** a favour or any beneficial act □ ***Can I be of service?*** **6** employment as a member of an organization working to serve or benefit others in some way; such an organization □ ***a public service*** □ ***the civil service.*** **7** the personnel employed in such an organization. **8** the requirements of members of such an organization. **9** assistance given to customers in a shop, restaurant, etc. **10** a facility provided □ ***British Rail ran an excellent service.*** **11** an occasion of worship or other religious ceremony; the words, etc used on such an occasion □ ***the marriage service.*** **12** a liturgical form or the musical setting of it. **13** a complete set of cutlery and crockery □ ***a dinner service.*** **14** (*usually* **services**) the supply eg of water, public transport, etc. **15** a periodic check and sometimes repair of the workings of a vehicle or other machine. **16** in racket sports: the act of putting the ball into play, or the game in which it is a particular player's turn to do so □ ***He lost his service game*** □ ***That was a poor service.*** **17** a SERVICE CHARGE, eg in a restaurant □ ***service not included.*** **18** (*often* **services**) any of the armed forces. **19** the participation of their members in warfare. **20** (**services**) a SERVICE AREA. **21** employment as a domestic servant. **22** the duty required of a feudal tenant. **23** cord or other material for serving a rope. **24** *as adj* for use by domestic servants □ ***service entrance.*** **25** *as adj* referring to the army, navy or air force. ▷ *verb* (***serviced***, ***servicing***) **1** to subject (a vehicle, etc) to a periodic check. **2** said of a male animal: to mate with (a female). • **at someone's service** ready to serve or give assistance to them. • **be of service to someone** to help or be useful to them. • **in service 1** in use or operation. **2** working as a domestic servant. • **out of service** broken; not in operation. ◷ 12c: from Latin *servitium*, from *servire* to serve.

serviceable ▷ *adj* **1** capable of being used. **2** able to give long-term use; durable. • **serviceability** *noun.* ◷ 14c.

service area ▷ *noun* an establishment near a motorway or major road providing facilities such as filling stations, garages, restaurants, toilets, etc.

service-berry ▷ *noun* one of the fruits of the SERVICE TREE.

service charge ▷ *noun* a percentage of a restaurant or hotel bill added on to cover the cost of service.

service flat ▷ *noun* a flat where the cost of certain services, eg domestic cleaning, is included in the rent.

service industry ▷ *noun* an industry whose business is providing services rather than manufacturing products, eg dry-cleaning, entertainment, transport, etc.

serviceman ▷ *noun* a male member of any of the armed forces.

service station ▷ *noun* a petrol station providing facilities for motorists, especially refuelling, car-washing, small shop, etc.

service tree ▷ *noun* a European flowering tree with toothed leaves, bearing edible fruit. Also called SORB.

servicewoman ▷ *noun* a female member of any of the armed forces.

serviette /sɜːvɪ'ɛt/ ▷ *noun* a table napkin. ◷ 15c: French, from *servir* to SERVE.

servile /'sɜːvaɪl/ ▷ *adj* **1** slavishly respectful or obedient; fawning or submissive. **2** referring or relating to, or suitable for, slaves or servants □ ***servile tasks.*** • **servilely** *adverb.* • **servility** /sɜː'vɪlɪtɪ/ *noun.* ◷ 14c: from Latin *servilis*, from *servus* slave.

serving /'sɜːvɪŋ/ ▷ *noun* a portion of food or drink served at one time; a helping.

serving hatch see HATCH[1]

servitude /ˈsɜːvɪtʃuːd/ ▻ *noun* **1** slavery; the state of being a slave. **2** subjection to irksome or taxing conditions. **3** *law* a burden on property obliging the owner to allow another person or thing an EASEMENT. ◷ 15c: from Latin *servitudo*, from *servus* slave.

servo /ˈsɜːvoʊ/ ▻ *adj* denoting a system in which the main mechanism is set in operation by a subsidiary mechanism and is able to develop a force greater than the force communicated to it □ *servo brakes*. ▻ *noun* (***servos***) an automatic device used to correct errors in the operation of machinery, used in satellite-tracking systems, power-steering systems on some cars, and to control robots and keep ships on course. ◷ Early 20c: from Latin *servus* slave.

sesame /ˈsɛsəmɪ/ ▻ *noun* (***sesames***) **1** an annual plant with opposite leaves below and alternate leaves above, and solitary white flowers, usually marked with purple or yellow. **2** the small edible husked seeds of this plant, used to garnish and flavour bread, rolls, cakes, confectionery, etc, and as a source of SESAME OIL. ◷ 15c: from Greek *sesamon*.

sesame oil ▻ *noun* a yellow oil obtained from sesame seeds, used as a cooking oil, and as an ingredient of margarine, soap, cosmetics and certain medicines.

sesamoid /ˈsɛsəmɔɪd/ ▻ *adj* shaped like a sesame seed. ▻ *noun, anatomy* (*in full* **sesamoid bone**) a small rounded bone or cartilage structure formed in the substance of a tendon, eg in the tendon of the big toe. ◷ 17c: from Latin *sesamoides* like sesame seed.

sesqui- /sɛskwɪ/ ▻ *combining form, denoting* the ratio of one and a half to one. ◷ Latin, from *semisque*, from *semis* half a unit + *que* and.

sesquicentennial and **sesquicentenary** ▻ *noun* a hundred and fiftieth anniversary. ◷ 1870s.

sesquipedalian /sɛskwɪpəˈdeɪlɪən/ and **sesquipedal** /səsˈkwɪpɪdəl/ ▻ *adj* **1** said of a words: polysyllabic. **2** inclined to use long or cumbersome words. • **sesquipedalianism** or **sesquipedality** /sɛskwɪ↓pəˈdalɪtɪ/ *noun*. ◷ 17c: SESQUI- + Latin *pes, pedis* foot.

sessile /ˈsɛsaɪl/ ▻ *adj* **1** said of a flower or leaf: attached directly to the plant, rather than by a stalk. **2** said of a part of the body: attached directly to the body. **3** said of an animal: stationary or immobile; sedentary. ◷ 18c: from Latin *sessilis* low or squat, from *sedere* to sit.

session /ˈsɛʃən/ ▻ *noun* **1** a meeting of a court, council or parliament, or the period during which such meetings are regularly held. **2** *colloq* a period of time spent engaged in any particular activity □ *a session of tennis* □ *a drinking session*. **3** an academic term or year. **4** the period during which classes are taught. • **sessional** *adj*. • **sessionally** *adverb*. • **in session** said of a court, committee, etc: conducting or engaged in a meeting □ *The court is now in session*. ◷ 14c: from Latin *sessio* a sitting, from *sedere* to sit.

sesterce /ˈsɛstɜːs/ and **sestertius** /sɛˈstɜːʃəs/ ▻ *noun* (***sesterces*** /ˈsɛstəsiːz/, ***sestertii*** /sɛˈstɜːʃɪaɪ/) *historical* a Roman coin, originally worth 2½ asses (see AS[2]), later worth 4 asses. ◷ 16c: from Latin *sestertius* two and a half, from *semis* half + *tertius* third.

sestet /sɛˈstɛt/ ▻ *noun* **1** a group of six people or things. **2** the last six lines of a sonnet. **3** *music* a composition for six performers; a SEXTET. ◷ Early 19c: from Italian *sestetto*, from Latin *sextus* sixth.

sestina /sɛˈstiːnə/ ▻ *noun* (***sestinas***) an old form of poetry consisting of six verses of six lines, where the end-words of the first verse are repeated in different orders in the last five verses. ◷ 1830s: Italian, from *sesto*, from Latin *sextus* sixth.

set[1] ▻ *verb* (***set, setting***) **1** to put, place or fix into a specified position or condition □ *set free* □ *set them straight*. **2** to array or arrange □ *Everything was set out beautifully*. **3** *tr & intr* to make or become solid, rigid, firm or motionless □ *The jelly has set* □ *set someone's jaw*. **4** to fix, establish or settle □ *Let's set a date*. **5** to embed □ *The lamp posts are set firmly in the cement*. **6** to stud, sprinkle or variegate. **7** to regulate. **8** to put into a state of readiness or preparation □ *set the table*. **9** to appoint, especially to a particular task or duty. **10** to appoint or call (a meeting, etc). **11** to ordain or fix (a procedure, etc). **12** to adjust (a measuring device, eg a clock) to the correct reading. **13** to adjust (a device) so that its controls are activated at a fixed time □ *Set the oven timer to 11 o'clock*. **14** in Scotland and Ireland: to lease or let to a tenant. **15** to propound. **16** to put something upon a course or start it off □ *set it going*. **17** to incite or direct. **18** to put in a position of opposition. **19** to fix (a broken bone) in its normal position for healing. **20** to impose or assign as an exercise or duty □ *set a test* □ *Which text has been set for the exam?* **21** to present or fix as a lead to be followed □ *We must set an example*. **22** to place on or against a certain background or surroundings □ *diamonds set in a gold bracelet*. **23** to decorate □ *She wore a bracelet set with diamonds*. **24** to stir, provoke or force into activity □ *That set me thinking* □ *We've set her to work*. **25** to treat (hair) when wet so that it stays in the required style when dry. **26** to hold or place as a value or consideration of worth □ *set a high price on honesty*. **27** *intr* said of the Sun or Moon: to disappear below the horizon. **28** to put down or advance (a pledge or deposit). **29** *printing* to arrange. **30** *intr* to have, take on or start along a particular course or direction. **31** said of a plant: to produce (seed). **32** *intr* said of a plant: to begin to form fruit or seed. **33** to compose or fit music to (words). **34** to position (a sail) so that it catches the wind. **35** to place (a novel, film, etc) in a specified period, location, etc □ *The Great Gatsby is set in the 1920s*. **36** *intr* to dance in a facing position □ *set to your partner*. **37** to put (a hen) on eggs to hatch them. **38** to put (eggs) under a hen for incubation. **39** to wager a bet. **40** said of a gun dog: **a** to point out (game); **b** *intr* to indicate the location of game by crouching. **41** to sharpen. **42** *bridge* to defeat (one's opponent's contract) usually by a stated number of tricks. **43** *tr & intr* said of a colour in dyeing: to become, or to make it become, permanent or to prevent it running. ▻ *noun* **1** the act or process of setting or the condition of being set. **2** a setting. **3** form; shape □ *the set of his jaw*. **4** habitual or temporary posture, carriage or bearing. **5** *theat, cinematog* the area within which the action takes place. **6** *theat, cinematog* the scenery and props used to create a particular location. **7 a** the process of setting hair; **b** a hairstyle produced by setting □ *a shampoo and set*. **8** the hang of a garment, especially when worn. **9** a plant-slip, bulb or tuber ready for planting. **10** a gun dog's indication of game. ▻ *adj* **1** fixed or rigid; allowing no alterations or variations □ *a set menu*. **2** established; never-changing □ *He's too set in his ways*. **3** predetermined or conventional □ *set phrases*. **4** ready or prepared □ *We're all set to go*. **5** about to receive or experience something; due □ *We're set for a pay rise*. **6** assigned; prescribed □ *These are the set texts for this year*. • **be set on something** to be determined to do it. • **set one's teeth** to clamp or clench them tightly together. • **set the pace** to start off at a pace to be followed by others, eg in a race. ◷ Anglo-Saxon *settan*.

■ **set about someone** to attack them.

■ **set about something** to start or begin it □ *They set about digging the garden*.

■ **set someone against someone else** to make them mutually hostile □ *They set him against his own family*.

■ **set something against something else 1** to compare or contrast them. **2** to deduct one from the other □ *set expenses against tax*.

■ **set something** or **someone apart** to separate or put them aside as different, especially superior.

■ **set something aside 1** to disregard or reject it. **2** to reserve it or put it away for later use.

■ **set something back 1** to delay or hinder its progress. **2** to cause it to return to a previous and less advanced stage □ *They've introduced changes that will set the health service back decades.* **3** *slang* to cost (in money) □ *How much did that set you back?*

■ **set someone down 1** to make them sit down □ *She set him down for a talk.* **2** to allow them to leave or alight from a vehicle at their destination. **3** to slight or snub them.

■ **set something down 1** to record it in writing. **2** to judge or view it (in a specified way) □ *The scheme was set down as a failure.*

■ **set something down to something else** to attribute it to it □ *His behaviour was set down to the stress he was under.*

■ **set forth** to begin a journey.

■ **set something forth** to declare, propose or explain it □ *She set forth her views.*

■ **set in 1** to become firmly established □ *We must leave before darkness sets in.* **2** said of a current or wind: to move or blow in the direction of the shore.

■ **set off** to start out on a journey □ *We'll set off in the morning.*

■ **set someone off** to provoke them into action or behaviour of a specified kind □ *He can always set us off laughing.*

■ **set something off 1** to start it or make it happen □ *You set off a terrible argument that day.* **2** to detonate (an explosive). **3** to show it off to good advantage or enhance its appearance □ *The colour of the dress sets off your eyes.* **4** to deduct it from another source; to offset it.

■ **set on someone** to attack them.

■ **set someone** or **something on someone** to order them to attack □ *I'll set the dogs on you if you don't leave!*

■ **set out 1** to begin or embark on a journey. **2** to resolve or intend (to do something) □ *She set out to cause trouble.*

■ **set something out 1** to present or explain it □ *She set out her proposals plainly.* **2** to lay it out for display.

■ **set to 1** to start working; to apply oneself to a task. **2** to start fighting or arguing. See also SET-TO.

■ **set someone up 1** to put them into a position of guaranteed security □ *The inheritance has set him up for life.* **2** to enable them to begin a new career. **3** to improve or restore their health. **4** *slang* to trick them into becoming a target for blame or accusations, or into feeling embarrassed or foolish. See also SET-UP.

■ **set something up 1** to bring it into being or operation; to establish it □ *He set the company up by himself.* **2** to arrange it. **3** to put up or erect something □ *Let's set the tents up over here.* See also SET-UP.

set² ▷ *noun* **1** a group of related people or things, especially of a kind that usually associate, occur or are used together □ *The class has two sets of twins* □ *These chairs only come in sets of six.* **2** *math* a group of objects, or elements, that have at least one characteristic in common, so that it is possible to decide exactly whether a given element does or does not belong to that group, eg the set of even numbers. When such a group is expressed diagrammatically it is called a VENN DIAGRAM. **3** a complete collection or series of pieces needed for a particular activity □ *a chess set* □ *a train set.* **4** the songs or tunes performed by a singer or a band at a concert □ *They played quite a varied set.* **5** *tennis, darts, etc* a group of games in which the winning player or players have to win a specified number, with a match lasting a certain number of sets. **6** a company performing a dance production. **7** a series of dance movements or figures. **8** a device for receiving or transmitting television or radio broadcasts. ◷ 14c: from French *sette*.

set³ or **sett** ▷ *noun* **1** a badger's burrow. **2** a block of stone or wood used in paving. **3** the number of a weaver's reed, determining the number of threads to the inch. **4** a square or pattern of tartan. ◷ 19c: from SET¹.

seta /ˈsiːtə/ ▷ *noun* (*setae* /-tiː/) *bot, zool* a bristle; a bristle-like structure. • **setaceous** /sɪˈteɪʃəs/ or **setose** /ˈsiːtous/ *adj.* ◷ 18c: Latin.

set-aside ▷ *noun* in the EC: the policy of taking agricultural land out of production, used to reduce surpluses of specific commodities, and compensated by specific payments.

setback ▷ *noun* **1** a delay, check or reversal to progress. **2** a disappointment or misfortune.

Seti ▷ *abbreviation* search for extraterrestrial intelligence.

setline ▷ *noun* any of various kinds of fishing lines suspended between buoys, etc and having shorter baited lines attached to it.

set-off ▷ *noun* **1** *law* a claim set against another. **2** *law* a cross-claim which partly offsets the original claim. **3** anything that counterbalances something else, eg a claim. **4** anything that sets off another object, eg an ornament, by way of contrast. **5** *printing, archit* an OFFSET.

set piece ▷ *noun* **1** a carefully prepared musical or literary performance. **2** *sport* a practised sequence of passes, movements, etc taken at free-kick, etc. **3** an elaborately arranged display of fireworks on a scaffold, etc.

set point ▷ *noun, tennis* **a** the moment in a match when a player needs one point to win a set (see SET² 5); **b** the point itself.

setscrew ▷ *noun* a screw that prevents relative motion by exerting pressure with its point.

set square ▷ *noun* a right-angled triangular plate, usually plastic, used as an aid for drawing or marking lines and angles.

Setswana see TSWANA

sett see SET³

settee /səˈtiː, sɛˈtiː/ ▷ *noun* (*settees*) a long indoor seat with a back and arms, usually able to hold two or more people; a sofa. ◷ 18c: a variant of SETTLE².

setter /ˈsɛtə(r)/ ▷ *noun* any of various large breeds of sporting dog with a long smooth coat (rich red in colour in the Irish setter and white with black, liver or tan markings in the English setter) and a feathered tail.

setting /ˈsɛtɪŋ/ ▷ *noun* **1 a** a situation or background within or against which action takes place; **b** *theat, cinematog* the scenery and props used in a single scene. **2** a set of cutlery, crockery and glassware laid out for use by one person. Also called **place setting**. **3** a position in which a machine's controls are set. **4** a mounting for a jewel. **5** the music composed specifically for a song, etc. ◷ 14c.

settle¹ /ˈsɛtəl/ ▷ *verb* (*settled, settling*) **1** *tr & intr* to make or become securely, comfortably or satisfactorily positioned or established. **2** *tr & intr* (*also* **settle on something**) to come to an agreement about it □ *settle an argument* □ *settle on a date.* **3** *intr* to come to rest. **4** to subside □ *Wait till the dust has settled.* **5** to establish a practice or routine □ *You'll soon settle into the job.* **6** *tr & intr* (*also* **settle down** or **settle someone down**) to make or become calm, quiet or disciplined after a period of noisy excitement or chaos. **7** to conclude or decide □ ***Let's settle this matter once and for all.*** **8** *tr & intr* to establish or take up a permanent home or residence □ ***They eventually settled in Australia.*** **9** *tr & intr* (*also* **settle up**) to pay off or clear (a bill or debt); to settle accounts □ ***I will settle the bill.*** **10** *intr* said of particles in a liquid: to sink to the bottom or form a scum. **11** to secure by gift or legal act. ◷ Anglo-Saxon *setlan* to place.

■ **settle for something** to accept it as a compromise or instead of something more suitable □ ***Would you settle for half the amount?***

■ **settle in** to adapt to a new living environment.

■ **settle something on someone** to transfer ownership of it legally to them □ ***She settled her estate on her son.***

■ **settle with someone** to come to an agreement or deal with them.

settle[2] /ˈsɛtəl/ ▷ *noun* a wooden bench with arms and a solid high back, often with a storage chest fitted below the seat. ◷ Anglo-Saxon *setl*.

settlement ▷ *noun* **1** the act of settling or the state of being settled. **2** a recently settled community or colony. **3** an agreement, especially one ending an official dispute. **4** subsidence or sinking. **5 a** an act of legally transferring ownership of property; **b** the document enforcing this. ◷ 17c.

settler /ˈsɛtlə(r)/ ▷ *noun* someone who settles in a country that is being newly populated. ◷ 16c.

settling day *noun, stock exchange* a date fixed for completion of transactions. See also TICKET DAY.

set-to ▷ *noun* **1** *colloq* a fight or argument. **2** a fierce contest. See also SET TO at SET[1].

set-up ▷ *noun* **1** *colloq* an arrangement or set of arrangements. **2** *slang* a trick to make a person unjustly blamed, accused or embarrassed. See also SET SOMEONE UP, SET SOMETHING UP at SET[1].

seven /ˈsɛvən/ ▷ *noun* **1 a** the cardinal number 7; **b** the quantity that this represents, being one more than six. **2** any symbol for this, eg **7** or **VII**. **3** the age of seven. **4** something, eg a shoe, or a person whose size is denoted by the number 7. **5** the seventh hour after midnight or midday □ ***Come at seven*** □ ***7 o'clock*** □ ***7pm.*** **6** a set or group of seven people or things. **7** a playing-card with 7 pips □ ***He played his seven.*** **8** a score of seven points. ▷ *adj* **1** totalling seven. **2** aged seven. ◷ Anglo-Saxon *seofon*.

the seven deadly sins ▷ *noun* pride, covetousness, lust, anger, gluttony, envy and sloth.

sevenfold /ˈsɛvənfoʊld/ ▷ *adj* **1** equal to seven times as much or as many. **2** divided into or consisting of seven parts. ▷ *adverb* by seven times as much or many. ◷ Anglo-Saxon *seofon feald*.

seven-inch and **7 inch** ▷ *noun* a RECORD (*noun* 4), usually with one track on each side, which is played at 45 rpm, now almost entirely replaced by the CD single.

seven seas ▷ *noun* (*usually* **the Seven Seas**) all the oceans of the world: the Arctic, Antarctic, N Atlantic, S Atlantic, Indian, N Pacific and S Pacific Oceans.

seventeen /sɛvənˈtiːn/ ▷ *noun* **1 a** the cardinal number 17; **b** the quantity that this represents, being one more than sixteen, or the sum of ten and seven. **2** any symbol for this, eg **17** or **XVII**. **3** the age of seventeen. **4** something, especially a garment, or a person, whose size is denoted by the number 17. **5** a set or group of seventeen people or things. **6** a score of seventeen points. ▷ *adj* **1** totalling seventeen. **2** aged seventeen. ◷ Anglo-Saxon *seofontiene*; see SEVEN + -TEEN.

seventeenth /sɛvənˈtiːnθ/ (often written **17th**) ▷ *adj* **1** in counting: **a** next after sixteenth; **b** last of seventeen. **2** in seventeenth position. **3** (**the seventeenth**) **a** the seventeenth day of the month; **b** *golf* the seventeenth hole. ▷ *noun* one of seventeen equal parts. Also *as adj* □ ***a seventeenth share.*** **2** a FRACTION equal to one divided by seventeen (usually written $^1/_{17}$). **3** a person coming seventeenth, eg in a race or exam □ ***He finished a bedraggled seventeenth.*** ▷ *adverb* seventeenthly. ● **seventeenthly** *adverb* used to introduce the seventeenth point in a list. ◷ Anglo-Saxon; see SEVENTEEN + -TH.

seventh /ˈsɛvənθ/ (often written **7th**) ▷ *adj* **1** in counting: **a** next after sixth; **b** last of seven. **2** in seventh position. **3** (**the seventh**) **a** the seventh day of the month; **b** *golf* the seventh hole. ▷ *noun* **1** one of seven equal parts. Also *as adj* □ ***a seventh share.*** **2** a FRACTION equal to one divided by seven (usually written $^1/_7$). **3** a person coming seventh, eg in a race or exam □ ***He finished a bedraggled seventh.*** **4** *music* (*also* **major seventh**) **a** an interval of a semitone less than an octave; **b** a note at that interval from another. ▷ *adverb* seventhly. ● **seventhly** *adverb* used to introduce the seventh point in a list. ◷ Anglo-Saxon; see SEVEN + -TH.

seventh heaven ▷ *noun* a state of extreme or intense happiness or joy.

seventies /ˈsɛvəntɪz/ (often written **70s** or **70's**) ▷ *plural noun* **1** (**one's seventies**) the period of time between one's seventieth and eightieth birthdays □ ***John is in his seventies.*** **3** the range of temperatures between seventy and eighty degrees □ ***It must be in the seventies today.*** **4** the period of time between the seventieth and eightieth years of a century □ ***born in the seventies.*** Also *as adj* □ ***I love seventies music.***

seventieth /ˈsɛvəntɪəθ/ (often written **70th**) ▷ *adj* **1** in counting: **a** next after sixty-ninth; **b** last of seventy. **2** in seventieth position. ▷ *noun* **1** one of seventy equal parts. Also *as adj* □ ***a seventieth share.*** **2** a FRACTION equal to one divided by seventy (usually written $^1/_{70}$). **3** a person coming seventieth, eg in a race or exam. ◷ 13c.

seventy /ˈsɛvəntɪ/ ▷ *noun* (***seventies***) **1** a) the cardinal number 70; **b** the quantity that this represents, being one more than sixty-nine, or the product of ten and seven. **2** any symbol for this, eg **70** or **LXX**. Also *in compounds, forming adjectives and nouns*, with cardinal numbers between *one* and *nine* □ ***seventy-two.*** **3** the age of seventy. **4** a set or group of seventy people or things. **5** a score of seventy points. ▷ *adj* **1** totalling seventy. Also *in compounds, forming adjectives and nouns*, with ordinal numbers between *first* and *ninth* □ ***seventy-second.*** **2** aged seventy. See also SEVENTIES, SEVENTIETH. ◷ Anglo-Saxon *seofontig*.

seventy-eight ▷ *noun, dated* a gramophone record which is played at 78 revolutions per minute. Compare FORTY-FIVE.

sever /ˈsɛvə(r)/ ▷ *verb* (***severed, severing***) **1** to cut off physically. **2** to separate or isolate. **3** to break off or end □ ***He's completely severed any relations with them.*** ● **severable** *adj*. ◷ 14c: from French *sevrer*, from Latin *separare* to SEPARATE.

several /ˈsɛvrəl, ˈsɛvərəl/ ▷ *adj* **1** more than a few, but not a great number □ ***I had several drinks that night.*** **2** various or assorted □ ***They were all there with their several backgrounds.*** **3** different and distinct; respective □ ***They went their several ways.*** **4** *law* separate; not jointly. ▷ *pronoun* quite a few people or things. ● **severally** *adj, formal* separately or singly □ ***travelling severally.*** ◷ 15c: French, from Latin *separalis*, from *separare* to SEPARATE.

severance /ˈsɛvərəns/ ▷ *noun* **1** the act or process of severing or being severed. **2** separation.

severance pay ▷ *noun* compensation paid by an employer to an employee dismissed through no fault of their own.

severe /səˈvɪə(r)/ ▷ *adj* **1** extreme and difficult to endure; marked by extreme conditions. **2** very strict towards others. **3** suggesting seriousness; austerely restrained □ *a severe appearance.* **4** having serious consequences; grave □ *a severe injury.* **5** demanding; conforming to a rigorous standard. • **severely** *adverb.* • **severity** /sə'vɛrɪtɪ/ *noun.* ⓒ 16c: from Latin *severus.*

severe combined immunodeficiency ▻ *noun, medicine* (abbreviation **SCID**) a severe form of congenital immunological deficiency.

sew /soʊ/ ▻ *verb* (*past tense* ***sewed****, past participle* ***sewed*** *or* ***sewn****, present participle* ***sewing***) **1** to stitch, attach or repair (especially fabric) with thread, either by hand with a needle or by machine. **2** to make (garments) by stitching pieces of fabric together. **3** *intr* to work using a needle and thread, or sewing-machine. • **sewer** *noun.* ⓒ Anglo-Saxon *siwian.*

■ **sew something up 1** to mend or join it by sewing. **2** *slang* to arrange or complete it successfully and satisfactorily.

sewage /'suːɪdʒ/ ▻ *noun* any liquid-borne waste matter, especially human excrement, carried away in drains. ⓒ 19c: from SEWER.

sewage farm ▻ *noun* a place where sewage is treated so that it can be used as fertilizer.

sewer /sʊə(r), sjʊə(r)/ ▻ *noun* a large underground pipe or channel for carrying away sewage from drains and water from road surfaces. ▻ *verb* (***sewered, sewering***) to provide with sewers. ⓒ 14c: from French *essever* to drain off.

sewerage /'sʊərɪdʒ, 'sjʊərɪdʒ/ ▻ *noun* **1** a system or network of sewers. **2** drainage of sewage and surface water using sewers. ⓒ 19c.

sewing /'soʊɪŋ/ ▻ *noun* **1** the act of sewing. **2** something that is being sewn □ *I keep my sewing in the basket.* ⓒ 13c.

sewing-machine ▻ *noun* a machine for sewing, especially an electric one for sewing clothes, etc.

sewn *past participle of* SEW

sex ▻ *noun* (***sexes***) **1** either of the two classes, male and female, into which animals and plants are divided according to their role in reproduction. **2** membership of one of these classes, or the characteristics that determine this. **3** sexual intercourse, or the activities, feelings, desires, etc associated with it. ▻ *adj* **1** referring or relating to sexual matters in general □ *sex education.* **2** due to or based on the fact of being male or female □ *sex discrimination.* ▻ *verb* (***sexed, sexing***) to identify or determine the sex of (an animal). ⓒ 14c: from Latin *sexus.*

sex- and **sexi-** ▻ *combining form, denoting* six. ⓒ Latin.

sexagenarian /sɛksədʒə'nɛərɪən/ ▻ *adj* said of a person: aged between 60 and 69. ▻ *noun* a person of this age. ⓒ 18c: from Latin *sexagenarius,* from *sexaginta* sixty.

Sexagesima /sɛksə'dʒɛsɪmə/ ▻ *noun* (*in full* **Sexagesima Sunday**) the second Sunday before Lent, apparently so called by analogy with Quadragesima and Quinquagesima. ⓒ 14c: from Latin *sexagesimus* sixtieth.

sexagesimal /sɛksə'dʒɛsɪməl/ ▻ *adj* referring to or based on 60. ▻ *noun* a sexagesimal fraction. ⓒ 17c: from Latin *sexagesimus* sixtieth.

sex aid ▻ *noun* any of, or the use of, various articles and devices to artificially aid or heighten sexual arousal.

sex appeal ▻ *noun* the power of exciting sexual desire in other people; sexual attractiveness.

sex bomb ▻ *noun, colloq* a person, especially a female, with a lot of sex appeal.

sex change ▻ *noun* the changing of sex in humans by the surgical alteration or re-forming of the sex organs, and by the use of hormone treatment.

sex chromosome ▻ *noun, genetics* any chromosome that carries the genes which determine the sex of an organism.

sex drive ▻ *noun* the natural urge and appetite for sexual activity or gratification.

sexed /sɛkst/ ▻ *adj, in compounds* having sexual desires or urges as specified to engage in sexual activity □ *highly sexed* □ *undersexed.*

sexism /'sɛksɪzəm/ ▻ *noun* contempt shown for or discrimination against a particular sex, usually by men of women, based on prejudice or stereotype. ⓒ 1960s.

sexist /'sɛksɪst/ ▻ *noun* someone whose beliefs and actions are characterized by sexism. ▻ *adj* relating to or characteristic of sexism □ *a sexist attitude.* ⓒ 1960s.

sex kitten ▻ *noun* a young woman who deliberately and mischievously plays up her sex appeal.

sexless /'sɛksləs/ ▻ *adj* **1** neither male nor female. **2** having no desire to engage in sexual activity. **3** *derog* lacking in sexual attractiveness. • **sexlessness** *noun.* ⓒ 16c.

sex linkage ▻ *noun, genetics* the tendency for certain inherited characteristics to occur predominantly or exclusively in one of the sexes because the genes for those characteristics are carried on the sex chromosomes.

sexology /sɛk'sɒlədʒɪ/ ▻ *noun* the study of human sexual behaviour, sexuality and relationships. • **sexologist** *noun* someone who studies human sexual behaviour. ⓒ Early 20c.

sexpert /'sɛkspɜːt/ ▻ *noun* especially in the US: an expert in human sexual behaviour. ⓒ 1920s: a combination of SEX and EXPERT.

sexploitation /sɛksplɔɪ'teɪʃən/ ▻ *noun* the commercial exploitation of sex in literature, films and other media. ⓒ 1940s: a blend of SEX and EXPLOITATION.

sexpot ▻ *noun, slang* a person of obvious and very great physical attraction.

sex shop ▻ *noun* a shop selling articles connected with sexual arousal and behaviour, such as pornographic photographs, sex aids, etc.

sext /'sɛkst/ ▻ *noun, now especially RC Church* the fourth of the CANONICAL HOURS. ⓒ 14c: from Latin *sextus* sixth.

sextant /'sɛkstənt/ ▻ *noun* **1** a device consisting of a small telescope mounted on a graded metal arc, used in navigation and surveying for measuring angular distances. **2** the sixth part of a circle or circumference. ⓒ 16c: from Latin *sextans* sixth, the arc being one sixth of a full circle.

sextet /sɛk'stɛt/ ▻ *noun* **1 a** a group of six singers or musicians; **b** a piece of music for this group. **2** any set of six. ⓒ 1840s: a variant of SESTET.

sex therapy ▻ *noun, medicine* a form of therapy that deals with physical and psychological problems relating to sexual relations, sexual intercourse, etc. • **sex therapist** *noun.*

sextillion /sɛk'stɪlɪən/ ▻ *noun* (***sextillions*** *or* ***sextillion***) **1** the sixth power of a million. **2** in the US: the seventh power of 1000. ⓒ 17c.

sexton /'sɛkstən/ ▻ *noun* someone responsible for the church buildings and churchyard, often also having bell-ringing, grave-digging and other duties. ⓒ 14c: from SACRISTAN.

sextuple /'sɛkstjʊpəl, sɛk'stjuːpəl/ ▻ *noun* a value or quantity six times as much. ▻ *adj* **1** sixfold. **2** made up of six parts. ▻ *verb* (***sextupled, sextupling***) *tr & intr* to multiply or increase sixfold. ⓒ 17c: from Latin *sextuplus.*

sextuplet /'sɛkstjʊplət, sɛk'stjuːplət/ ▻ *noun* **1** any of six children or animals born at the same time to the same mother. **2** *music* a group of six notes performed in the time of four. ⓒ 19c.

sexual /'sɛkʃʊəl, 'sɛksjʊəl/ ▻ *adj* **1** concerned with or suggestive of sex. **2** referring or relating to sexual reproduction involving the fusion of two gametes. **3**

concerned with, relating to or according to membership of the male or female sex. • **sexually** *adverb*. ◎ 17c.

sexual abuse ▻ *noun* subjection to sexual activity, such as rape, likely to cause physical or psychological harm.

sexual athlete ▻ *noun* someone who performs sexual intercourse skilfully and frequently.

sexual harassment ▻ *noun* harassment consisting of misplaced, unwelcome and often offensive sexual advances or remarks, especially from a senior colleague, male or female, in the workplace.

sexual intercourse ▻ *noun* the insertion of a man's penis into a woman's vagina, usually with the release of semen into the vagina.

sexuality /sɛkʃʊ'alɪtɪ, sɛksjʊ'alɪtɪ/ ▻ *noun* a sexual state or condition. ◎ Early 19c.

sexually transmitted disease ▻ *noun* (abbreviation **STD**) any disease that is characteristically transmitted by sexual intercourse, formerly known as **venereal disease**, eg AIDS, gonorrhoea, syphilis, chlamydia.

sexual reproduction ▻ *noun* a form of reproduction in which new individuals are produced by the fusion of two unlike GAMETEs, especially a sperm and an egg in higher animals, resulting in the offspring that differ genetically both from either of the parents and from each other. Compare ASEXUAL REPRODUCTION.

sexy /'sɛksɪ/ ▻ *adj* (***sexier, sexiest***) *colloq* **1** said of a person: sexually attractive; stimulating or arousing sexual desire. **2** said of an object, idea, etc: currently popular or interesting; attractive or tempting □ ***sexy products.*** • **sexily** *adverb*. • **sexiness** *noun*. ◎ 1920s.

SF ▻ *abbreviation* science fiction.

sf. and **sfz.** ▻ *abbreviation* sforzando.

SFA ▻ *abbreviation* **1** Scottish Football Association. **2** *slang* Sweet Fanny Adams, nothing at all.

sforzando /sfɔːt'sandoʊ/ and **sforzato** /sfɔːt'sɑːtoʊ/ ▻ *adverb, adj, music* played with sudden emphasis. Also *as noun*. ◎ Early 19c: Italian, from *sforzare* to force, from Latin *ex* out + *fortia* force.

sfumato /sfʊ'mɑːtoʊ/ ▻ *noun* (***sfumatos***) in painting and drawing: a misty indistinct effect obtained by gradually blending together areas of different colour or tone. ◎ 19c: Italian, from *sfumare* to shade off, from Latin *ex* out + *fumare* to smoke.

sfx /ɛsɛf'ɛks/ ▻ *noun* short for SPECIAL EFFECTS.

SG ▻ *abbreviation* Solicitor-General.

Sg ▻ *symbol, chem* seaborgium.

sgraffito /zgrə'fiːtoʊ/ and **graffito** ▻ *noun* (***sgraffiti*** /-tiː/) **1** a decorative technique in art in which one colour is laid over another and the top layer scratched away to form a design, by revealing the colour beneath. **2** pottery with such a decoration. ◎ 18c: from Italian *sgraffito*, from Latin *ex* + Greek *graphein* to write.

Sgt ▻ *abbreviation* Sergeant.

sh /ʃ/ ▻ *exclamation* hush; be quiet.

shabby /'ʃabɪ/ ▻ *adj* (***shabbier, shabbiest***) **1** said especially of clothes or furnishings: old and worn; threadbare or dingy. **2** said of a person: wearing such clothes; scruffy. **3** said of behaviour, conduct, etc: unworthy, discreditable or contemptible; nasty or mean. • **shabbily** *adverb*. • **shabbiness** *noun*. ◎ Anglo-Saxon *sceabb*.

Shabuoth /sha'vjuːnθ/ , **Shavuoth** and **Shavuot** ▻ *noun* the Jewish 'Feast of Weeks', celebrated seven weeks after the first day of Passover to commemorate the giving of the Law to Moses. ◎ 19c: Hebrew, meaning 'weeks'.

shack ▻ *noun* a crudely built hut or shanty. ◎ 19c.

■ **shack up** *slang* to live with someone, usually without being married □ ***They shacked up together.***

shackle /'ʃakəl/ ▻ *noun* **1** (*usually* **shackles**) a metal ring locked round the ankle or wrist of a prisoner or slave to limit movement, usually one of a pair joined by a chain. **2** (*usually* **shackles**) anything that restricts freedom; a hindrance or constraint. **3** a U-shaped metal loop or staple closed over by a **shackle-bolt**, used for fastening ropes or chains together. **4** the curved movable part of a padlock. ▻ *verb* (***shackled, shackling***) **1** to restrain with or as if with shackles. **2** to connect or couple. ◎ Anglo-Saxon *sceacul*.

shad ▻ *noun* (***shad, shads***) any of various marine fish resembling a large herring but with a deeper body. ◎ Anglo-Saxon *sceadd*.

shadbush ▻ *noun* a N American rosaceous shrub, flowering at shad spawning-time.

shade ▻ *noun* **1** the blocking or partial blocking out of sunlight, or the relative darkness caused by this. **2** an area from which sunlight has been completely or partially blocked. **3** any device used to modify direct light, eg a lampshade. **4** a device, eg a screen, used as a shield from direct heat, light, etc. **5** *US* a window-blind. **6** an obscure area or location. **7** a dark or shaded area in a drawing or painting. **8** the state of appearing less impressive than something or someone else □ ***He always lived in the shade of his brother's achievements*** □ ***Her singing puts mine in the shade.*** **9** a colour, especially one similar to but slightly different from a principal colour □ ***a lighter shade of blue.*** **10** a small amount; a touch □ ***My house is a shade smaller than that.*** **11** (**shades**) *colloq* sunglasses. **12** *literary* a ghost. ▻ *verb* (***shaded, shading***) **1** to block or partially block out sunlight from someone or something. **2** to draw or paint so as to give the impression of shade. **3** (*usually* **shade off** or **away**) to change gradually or unnoticeably. • **shadeless** *adj*. • **in the shade 1** sheltered from strong light or heat. **2** overlooked or forgotten; in relative obscurity. ◎ Anglo-Saxon *sceadu*.

shading /'ʃeɪdɪŋ/ ▻ *noun* in drawing and painting: the representation of areas of shade or shadows, eg by close parallel lines.

shadoof or **shaduf** /ʃɑː'duːf/ ▻ *noun* an irrigation device for lifting water from a river or watercourse and transferring it to the land, consisting of a bucket suspended from a counterpoised pivoted rod, used mainly for irrigation in the Nile flood plain. ◎ 19c: from Egyptian Arabic *shaduf*.

shadow /'ʃadoʊ/ ▻ *noun* **1** a dark shape cast on a surface when an object stands between the surface and the source of light. **2** an area darkened by the blocking out of light. **3** the darker areas of a picture. **4** a slight amount; a hint or trace □ ***without a shadow of a doubt.*** **5** a sense of gloom, trouble or foreboding □ ***The incident cast a shadow over the proceedings.*** **6** a weakened person or thing which has wasted away to almost nothing □ ***She's a shadow of her former self.*** **7** a constant companion. **8** a person following another closely and secretively, especially a spy or detective. **9** a ghost or spirit. ▻ *verb* (***shadowed, shadowing***) **1** to put into darkness by blocking out light. **2** to cloud or darken. **3** to follow closely and secretively. ▻ *adj, politics* in the main opposition party: denoting a political counterpart to a member or section of the government □ ***shadow Foreign Secretary.*** • **afraid of one's own shadow** extremely or excessively timid. ◎ Anglo-Saxon *sceadwe*, accusative case of *sceadu* SHADE.

shadow-boxing ▻ *noun* boxing against an imaginary opponent as training. • **shadow-box** *verb, intr* to practise shadow-boxing.

shadow cabinet ▻ *noun, politics* a body made up of leading members of an opposition party, holding shadow ministerial positions and ready to take office should their party assume power.

shadowgraph ▷ *noun* **1** a picture or image produced by throwing a shadow on a screen for entertainment. **2** a RADIOGRAPH (see under RADIOGRAPHY).

shadow-mask tube ▷ *noun* a type of cathode-ray tube for colour television, in which electron beams from three separate guns are deflected so that they fall on minute phosphor dots of the appropriate colour, which glow according to the intensity of the beam reaching them.

shadow puppet ▷ *noun* a puppet which is manipulated so as to cast a shadow on a screen.

shadowy /ˈʃadoʊɪ/ ▷ *adj* **1** dark and shady; not clearly visible □ *a shadowy figure.* **2** secluded; darkened by shadows. ● **shadowiness** *noun.* ◷ 14c.

shady /ˈʃeɪdɪ/ ▷ *adj* (***shadier***, ***shadiest***) **1** sheltered or giving shelter from heat or sunlight. **2** *colloq* underhand or disreputable, often dishonest or illegal □ *a shady character.* **3** shadowy or mysterious; sinister. ● **shadily** *adverb.* ● **shadiness** *noun.* ◷ 16c.

Shaef /ʃeɪf/ ▷ *abbreviation* Supreme Headquarters, Allied Expeditionary Force, World War II.

shaft /ʃɑːft/ ▷ *noun* **1** the long straight handle of a tool or weapon. **2** the long straight part or handle of anything. **3** a ray or beam of light. **4** a thing directed (usually at someone) with the violent force of an arrow or missile □ *shafts of sarcasm.* **5** in vehicle engines: a rotating rod that transmits motion. **6** a vertical passageway in a building, especially one through which a lift moves. **7** a well-like excavation or passage, eg into a mine. **8** either of the projecting parts of a cart, etc to which a horse is attached. **9** *anatomy* the middle section of any long bone. **10** *archit* the long middle part of a column, between the base and the capital. **11** the RACHIS of a feather. **12** *slang* the penis. ▷ *verb* (***shafted***, ***shafting***) **1** *US slang* to dupe, cheat or swindle. **2** *slang* to have sexual intercourse with (a woman). ◷ Anglo-Saxon *sceaft.*

shag¹ ▷ *noun* **1** a ragged mass of hair. **2** a long coarse pile or nap on fabric. **3** a type of tobacco cut into coarse shreds. ◷ Anglo-Saxon *sceacga.*

shag² ▷ *noun* a species of cormorant with glossy dark-green plumage, a long neck, webbed feet and an upright stance. ◷ Anglo-Saxon SHAG¹.

shag³ ▷ *coarse slang, verb* (***shagged***, ***shagging***) **1** to have sexual intercourse with someone. **2** (*usually* **shag out**) to tire. ▷ *noun* an act of sexual intercourse. ◷ 20c: probably from SHAG¹.

shaggy /ˈʃagɪ/ ▷ *adj* (***shaggier***, ***shaggiest***) **1** said of hair, fur, wool, etc: long and coarse; rough and untidy in appearance. **2** said of a person or animal: having shaggy hair or fur. ● **shaggily** *adverb.* ● **shagginess** *noun.* ◷ 16c.

shaggy dog story ▷ *noun* a story or joke, humorous because of its ridiculous length and the inconsequence of its ending.

shagreen /ʃəˈgriːn/ ▷ *noun* **1** a coarse granular leather, often dyed green, made from the skin of animals, especially a horse or donkey. **2** the skin of a shark, ray, etc covered with small nodules, used as an abrasive. ◷ 17c: from French *chagrin*, from Turkish *sagri* horse's rump.

shah /ʃɑː/ ▷ *noun, historical* a title of the former rulers of Iran and other Eastern countries. ◷ 16c: Persian.

shake ▷ *verb* (***shook***, ***shaken***, ***shaking***) **1** to move with quick, often forceful to-and-fro or up-and-down movements. **2** (*also* **shake something up**) to mix it in this way. **3** to wave violently and threateningly; to brandish □ *He shook his fist at them.* **4** *tr & intr* to tremble or make something or someone tremble, totter or shiver. **5** to cause intense shock to; to agitate profoundly □ *the accident that shook the nation.* **6** (*also* **shake someone up**) to disturb, unnerve or upset them greatly □ *He was very shaken after the accident.* **7** to make something or someone waver; to weaken □ *The experience shook my confidence.* **8** *intr* to shake hands. **9** *intr, music* to trill. ▷ *noun* **1** an act or the action of shaking. **2** *colloq* a very short while; a moment. **3** (**the shakes**) *colloq* a fit of uncontrollable trembling. **4** a milk shake. **5** *music* a trill. **6** a natural fissure formed in rock or growing timber. ● **shakeable** or **shakable** *adj.* ● **no great shakes** *colloq* not of great importance, ability or worth. ● **shake a leg** *colloq* to hurry up or get moving. ● **shake hands** or **shake hands with someone** **1** to greet them by clasping each others hands. **2** to seal a bargain, acknowledge an agreement, settle differences, etc. ● **shake one's head** to turn one's head from side to side as a sign of rejection, disagreement, disapproval, denial, etc. ● **two shakes (of a lamb's tail)** *colloq* a very short time. ◷ Anglo-Saxon *sceacan.*

■ **shake down** **1** to settle by shaking. **2** to go to bed, especially in a makeshift or temporary bed. See also SHAKEDOWN.

■ **shake someone down** **1** *slang* to extort money from them by threats or blackmail. **2** to frisk them (for weapons, drugs, etc). See also SHAKEDOWN.

■ **shake something down** **1** to make it settle by shaking. **2** *slang* to search it thoroughly.

■ **shake something** or **someone off** **1** to get rid of them; to free oneself from them. **2** to escape from them.

■ **shake out** to empty, or cause to spread or unfold, by shaking.

■ **shake someone up** *colloq* to stimulate them into action, especially from a state of lethargy or apathy. See also SHAKE-UP.

■ **shake something up** **1** to mix it. **2** *colloq* to reorganize it thoroughly. See also SHAKE-UP.

shakedown ▷ *noun, colloq* **1** a makeshift or temporary bed, originally made by shaking down straw. **2** an act of extortion. **3** *chiefly N Amer* a trial run or operation to familiarize personnel with equipment and procedures. See also SHAKEDOWN, SHAKE SOMEONE DOWN at SHAKE. ◷ 18c.

shaker /ˈʃeɪkə(r)/ ▷ *noun* **1** someone or something that shakes. **2** a container from which something, eg salt, is dispensed by shaking. **3** a container in which something, eg a cocktail, is mixed by shaking. ◷ 15c.

Shakespearean or **Shakespearian** /ʃeɪkˈspɪərɪən/ ▷ *adj* relating to or characteristic of the style of William Shakespeare (1564–1616), or his literary works. ◷ 18c.

shake-up and **shake-out** ▷ *noun, colloq* a fundamental change, disturbance or reorganization. See also SHAKE SOMEONE UP, SHAKE SOMETHING UP at SHAKE.

shako /ˈʃakoʊ/ ▷ *noun* (***shakos*** or ***shakoes***) a tall, and usually cylindrical, military cap with a plume. ◷ Early 19c: from Hungarian *csákó.*

shaky /ˈʃeɪkɪ/ ▷ *adj* (***shakier***, ***shakiest***) **1** trembling or inclined to tremble with, or as if with, weakness, fear or illness. **2** *colloq* wavering; not solid, sound or secure. **3** disputable or uncertain □ *shaky knowledge.* ● **shakily** *adverb.* ● **shakiness** *noun.* ◷ 18c.

shale ▷ *noun, geol* a fine-grained black, grey, brown or red sedimentary rock, easily split into thin layers, formed as a result of the compression of clay, silt or sand by overlying rocks. ● **shaly** *adj.* ◷ Anglo-Saxon *scealu.*

shall /ʃal, ʃəl/ ▷ *auxiliary verb* expressing: **1** the future tense of other verbs, especially when the subject is *I* or *we*. **2** determination, intention, certainty, and obligation, especially when the subject is *you, he, she, it* or *they* □ *They shall succeed* □ *You shall have what you want* □ *He shall become king* □ *You shall not kill.* **3** a question implying future action, often with the sense of an offer or suggestion, especially when the subject is *I* or *we* □ *What shall we do?* □ *Shall I give you a hand?* See note on next page. See also SHOULD, WILL. ◷ Anglo-Saxon *sceal.*

shall

- The rule about **shall** and **will** used to be as follows: to express the simple future, use **shall** with **I** and **we**, and **will** with **you, he, she, it** and **they**; to express permission, obligation or determination, use **will** with **I** and **we**, and **shall** with **you, he, she, it** and **they**.
- Nowadays, **I will** and **we will** are commonly used to express the simple future.
- Note that **shall** is often used in questions in the second person to show that the question is really a neutral request for information rather than a request that something be done □ *Shall you tell him about it?*

shallop /ˈʃaləp/ ▻ *noun* a dinghy; a small or light boat for use in shallow water. © 18c: from French *chaloupe*.

shallot or **shalot** /ʃəˈlɒt/ ▻ *noun* **1** a species of small onion, widely cultivated as a vegetable, that produces clusters of oval bulbs which are smaller and milder in flavour than the onion. **2** any of these small bulbs, widely used in cooking and for making pickles. © 17c: from French *eschalote*.

shallow /ˈʃaloʊ/ ▻ *adj* **1** having no great depth. **2** not profound or sincere; superficial □ *a shallow personality.* ▻ *noun* (*often* **shallows**) a shallow place or part, especially in water. ▻ *verb* (***shallowed***, ***shallowing***) to make something shallow. • **shallowly** *adverb.* • **shallowness** *noun.* © 15c.

shalom aleichem /ʃaˈlɒm əˈleɪxəm/ ▻ *noun* ▻ *exclamation* a Jewish greeting or farewell. Often shortened to **shalom**. © 19c: Hebrew, meaning 'peace be with you'.

shalt /ʃalt/ ▻ *verb, archaic* the second person singular of the verb SHALL, used with *thou*.

shaly see under SHALE

sham ▻ *adj* false, counterfeit or pretended; insincere. ▻ *verb* (***shammed***, ***shamming***) *tr & intr* **1** to pretend or feign. **2** to make false pretences or to pretend to be □ *to sham sick.* ▻ *noun* **1** anything not genuine. **2** a person who shams, especially an impostor. © 17c: derived from SHAME.

shaman /ˈʃeɪmən, ˈʃamən, ˈʃɑːmən/ ▻ *noun* (***shamans***) especially among certain N Asian and Native American peoples: a doctor-priest or medicine man or medicine woman using magic to cure illness, make contact with gods and spirits, predict the future, etc. © 17c: Russian, from Tungus *saman*, probably ultimately from Sanskrit *srama* religious practice.

shamanism /ˈʃeɪmənɪzəm, ˈʃa-, ˈʃɑː-/ ▻ *noun* especially among certain N Asian and Native American peoples: a religion dominated by shamans, based essentially on magic, spiritualism and sorcery. • **shamanist** *noun.* • **shamanistic** *adj.* © 18c.

shamateur /ˈʃamətɜː(r), ˈʃamətə(r), ˈʃamətjʊə(r)/ ▻ *noun* in sport: someone rated as an amateur, but still making money from playing or competing. © Late 19c: a blend of SHAM and AMATEUR.

shamble /ˈʃambəl/ ▻ *verb* (***shambled***, ***shambling***) *intr* (*usually* **shamble along, past**, *etc*) to walk with slow awkward tottering steps. ▻ *noun* a shambling walk or pace. • **shambling** *noun, adj.* © 17c: from SHAMBLES, in allusion to trestle-like legs.

shambles /ˈʃambəlz/ ▻ *singular noun* **1** *colloq* a confused mess or muddle; a state of total disorder □ *The whole event was a shambles.* **2** a meat market. **3** a slaughterhouse. **4** a scene or place of slaughter or carnage. • **shambolic** /-ˈbɒlɪk/ *adj, colloq* totally disorganized; chaotic. © Anglo-Saxon *scamel* stool, from Latin *scamellum*, diminutive of *scamnum* a bench.

shame ▻ *noun* **1** the humiliating feeling of having appeared unfavourably in one's own eyes, or those of others, as a result of one's own offensive or disrespectful actions, or those of an associate. **2** susceptibility to such a feeling or emotion. **3** fear or scorn of incurring or bringing disgrace or dishonour. **4** disgrace or loss of reputation □ *He's brought shame on the whole family.* **5** someone or something bringing this. **6** modesty or bashfulness. **7** a regrettable or disappointing event or situation □ *It's such a shame that he failed his exam.* ▻ *verb* (***shamed***, ***shaming***) **1** to make someone feel shame. **2** to bring disgrace on someone or something. • **put someone to shame 1** to disgrace them. **2** to make them seem inadequate by comparison. • **shame on you, them,** *etc* you, they, etc should be ashamed. © Anglo-Saxon *sceamu*.

■ **shame someone into something** to provoke them into taking action by inspiring feelings of shame □ *He shamed him into telling the truth.*

shamefaced /ˈʃeɪmfeɪst/ ▻ *adj* **1** showing shame or embarrassment; abashed. **2** modest or bashful. • **shamefacedly** /-ˈfeɪstlɪ, -ˈfeɪsɪdlɪ/ *adverb* in a shamefaced manner. © 16c: originally *shamefast* held by shame.

shameful ▻ *adj* bringing or deserving shame; disgraceful □ *shameful behaviour.* • **shamefully** *adverb.* • **shamefulness** *noun.* © Anglo-Saxon.

shameless ▻ *adj* **1** incapable of feeling shame; showing no shame. **2** carried out or done without shame; brazen or immodest. • **shamelessly** *adverb.* • **shamelessness** *noun.* © Anglo-Saxon.

shammy /ˈʃamɪ/ ▻ *noun* (***shammies***) *colloq* (*in full* **shammy leather**) a chamois leather. © 18c: from CHAMOIS.

shampoo /ʃamˈpuː/ ▻ *noun* (***shampoos***) **1** a soapy liquid for washing the hair and scalp. **2** a similar liquid for cleaning carpets or upholstery. **3** the act or an instance of treating with either liquid. ▻ *verb* (***shampooed***, ***shampooing***) to wash or clean with shampoo. © 18c: from Hindi *champo* squeeze, from *champna* to press.

shamrock /ˈʃamrɒk/ ▻ *noun* any of various plants with leaves divided into three rounded leaflets, especially various species of clover, adopted as the national emblem of Ireland. © 16c: from Irish Gaelic *seamrog*.

shandy /ˈʃandɪ/ ▻ *noun* (***shandies***) a mixture of beer or lager with lemonade or ginger beer. © 1880s.

shanghai /ʃaŋˈhaɪ/ ▻ *noun* (***shanghais***) *Austral, NZ* a catapult. ▻ *verb* (***shanghais***, ***shanghaied***, ***shanghaiing***) *colloq* **1** to kidnap and drug or make drunk and send to sea as a sailor. **2** to trick into any unpleasant situation. **3** *Austral, NZ* to shoot using a shanghai. © 19c: named after Shanghai in China, from the former use of this method in recruiting sailors for trips to the East.

shank ▻ *noun* **1** the lower leg between the knee and the foot. **2** the same part of the leg in an animal, especially a horse. **3** a cut of meat from the upper leg of an animal. **4** a shaft, stem or other long straight part. **5** the main section of the handle of a tool. **6** the part of a shoe connecting the sole to the heel. **7** the leg of a stocking. ▻ *verb* (***shanked***, ***shanking***) **1** *bot* to become affected with disease of the footstalk. **2** *golf* to strike the ball by mistake with the section of the club where the clubhead meets the shaft. © Anglo-Saxon *sceanca* leg.

shanks's pony and (*US*) **shank's mare** ▻ *noun, colloq* the use of one's own legs as a means of travelling.

shanny /ˈʃanɪ/ ▻ *noun* (***shannies***) the smooth blenny, a small marine fish found in rock pools and coastal areas. © 1830s.

shan't /ʃɑːnt/ ▻ *contraction, colloq* shall not.

shantung /ʃanˈtʌŋ/ ▻ *noun* **1** a plain and usually undyed fabric of wild silk with a rough finish. **2** a similar cotton or rayon fabric. © 19c: named after Shantung (Shandong) province in China where it was originally made.

shanty[1] /'ʃantɪ/ ▻ *noun* (***shanties***) **1** a roughly built hut or cabin; a shack. **2** *Austral, NZ* a rough public house, especially one selling alcohol illicitly. ◷ Early 19c: from Canadian French *chantier* woodcutter's cabin.

shanty[2] /'ʃantɪ/ ▻ *noun* (***shanties***) a rhythmical song with chorus and solo verses, formerly sung by sailors while working together. ◷ 19c: from French *chanter* to sing.

shanty town ▻ *noun* a town, or an area of one, in which poor people live in makeshift or ramshackle housing.

Shape ▻ *abbreviation* Supreme Headquarters, Allied Powers Europe, NATO.

shape ▻ *noun* **1** the outline or form of anything. **2** a person's body or figure. **3** a form, person, etc ▫ *I had an assistant in the shape of my brother.* **4** a desired form or condition ▫ *We'll have to get the contract into shape* ▫ *We like to keep in shape.* **5** a general condition ▫ *in bad shape.* **6** an unidentifiable figure; an apparition ▫ *There were shapes lurking in the dark.* **7** a mould or pattern. **8** a jelly, pudding, etc turned out of a mould. **9** a geometric figure. ▻ *verb* (***shaped***, ***shaping***) **1** to form or fashion; to give a particular form to something. **2** to influence to an important extent ▫ *the event that shaped history.* **3** to devise, determine or develop to suit a particular purpose. • **shapeable** or **shapable** *adj.* • **in any shape or form** at all ▫ *I'm not having it in any shape or form.* • **out of shape 1** unfit; in poor physical condition. **2** deformed or disfigured. • **take shape 1** to take on a definite form. **2** to finally become recognizable as the desired result of plans or theories. ◷ Anglo-Saxon *sceippan.*

▪ **shape up** *colloq* **1** to appear to be developing in a particular way ▫ *This project is shaping up well.* **2** to be promising; to progress or develop well. **3** to lose weight; to tone up ▫ *I'm trying to shape up for summer.*

shapeless ▻ *adj* **1** having an ill-defined or irregular shape. **2** unattractively shaped. • **shapelessness** *noun.* ◷ 13c.

shapely /'ʃeɪplɪ/ ▻ *adj* said especially of the human body: having an attractive, well-proportioned shape or figure. • **shapeliness.** ◷ 14c.

shard and **sherd** /ʃɜːd/ ▻ *noun* a fragment of something brittle, usually pottery, especially when found on an archaeological site. ◷ Anglo-Saxon *sceard.*

share[1] ▻ *noun* **1** a part allotted, contributed, or owned by each of several people or groups. **2** a portion, section or division. **3** (*usually* **shares**) the fixed units into which the total wealth of a business company is divided, ownership of which gives the right to receive a portion of the company's profits. ▻ *verb* (***shared***, ***sharing***) **1** to have in common ▫ *We share several interests.* **2** to use something with someone else ▫ *We had to share a book in class.* **3** (*also* **share in something**) to have joint possession or use of it, or joint responsibility for it, with another or others. **4** to divide into shares. • **sharer** *noun.* • **go shares** *colloq* to divide something. • **lion's share** see under LION. • **share and share alike 1** to give everyone their due share. **2** with or in equal shares. ◷ Anglo-Saxon *scearu.*

▪ **share something out** to divide it into portions and distribute it among several people or groups. See also SHARE-OUT.

share[2] ▻ *noun* a PLOUGHSHARE. ◷ Anglo-Saxon *scear.*

sharecropper ▻ *noun, especially US* a tenant farmer who supplies a share of their crops as rent payment. • **sharecrop** *verb, intr* to rent and work a farm in this way.

sharefarmer ▻ *noun, especially Austral* a tenant farmer who pays a share of the proceeds from the farm as rent.

shareholder ▻ *noun* someone who owns shares in a company. • **shareholding** *noun.*

share index ▻ *noun* an index showing the movement of shares in companies trading on a stock exchange.

share option ▻ *noun* the right of a person, on payment of a fee, to buy or sell shares for an agreed amount at or within a specified period of time.

share-out ▻ *noun* a distribution in or by shares. See also SHARE SOMETHING OUT at SHARE.

shareware ▻ *noun, computing* software readily available for a nominal fee.

sharia /ʃə'riːə/ and **shariat** /ʃə'riːət/ ▻ *noun* the body of Islamic religious law. ◷ 19c: from Arabic.

shark ▻ *noun* **1** any of 400 species of large cartilaginous fishes which have remained virtually unchanged for millions of years, with a spindle-shaped body covered with tooth-like scales, and a tail fin with a long upper lobe and shorter lower lobe. **2** *colloq* a ruthless or dishonest person, especially one who swindles, exploits or extorts. ◷ 16c in sense 2: perhaps from German *Schurke* scoundrel.

sharkskin ▻ *noun* **1** leather made from a shark's skin; shagreen. **2** smooth rayon fabric with a dull sheen. ◷ 1850s.

sharon fruit ▻ *noun* a PERSIMMON.

sharp ▻ *adj* **1** having a thin edge or point that cuts or pierces. **2** having a bitter pungent taste. **3** severely or harshly felt; penetrating ▫ *sharp pain.* **4** sudden and acute ▫ *sharp increases* ▫ *a sharp bend.* **5** abrupt or harsh in speech; sarcastic. **6** easily perceived; clear-cut or well-defined ▫ *a sharp contrast.* **7** keen or perceptive. **8** eager; alert to one's own interests. **9** barely honest; cunning. **10** fit; adept or able. **11** having abrupt or acute corners. **12** *colloq* stylish ▫ *a sharp dresser.* **13** *music* higher in pitch by a semitone ▫ *C sharp.* Compare FLAT[1] (*adj* 11b). **14** *music* slightly too high in pitch. ▻ *noun* **1** *music* a note raised by a semitone, or the sign indicating this (♯). **2** *music* the key producing this note. **3** *colloq* a practised cheat; a SHARPER ▫ *a card sharp.* **4** a long slender needle. **5** (**sharps**) the hard parts of wheat. ▻ *adverb* **1** punctually; on the dot ▫ *at 9 o'clock sharp.* **2** suddenly ▫ *pulled up sharp.* **3** *music* high or too high in pitch. • **sharply** *adverb.* • **sharpness** *noun.* • **at the sharp end** in the position of greatest difficulty, pressure, danger, stress, etc in any activity or situation. • **look sharp** *colloq* to hurry up; to be quick. ◷ Anglo-Saxon *scearp.*

sharpen /'ʃɑːpən/ ▻ *verb* (***sharpened***, ***sharpening***) *tr & intr* to make or become sharp. • **sharpener** *noun.*

sharper /'ʃɑːpə(r)/ ▻ *noun, colloq* a practised cheat; a sharp. ◷ 17c.

sharpish ▻ *adj* quite sharp. ▻ *adverb* quickly; promptly ▫ *I'd get there sharpish if I were you!*

sharp practice ▻ *noun* dishonesty or cheating; unscrupulous dealing.

sharp-set ▻ *adj* eager or keen in appetite for anything, especially food or sexual indulgence.

sharpshooter ▻ *noun* a good marksman. • **sharpshooting** *adj.*

sharp-tongued ▻ *adj* critical or harsh in speech; sarcastic.

sharp-witted ▻ *adj* quick to perceive, act or react; keenly intelligent or alert. • **sharp-wittedly** *adverb.*

shat *past tense, past participle of* SHIT

shatter /'ʃatə(r)/ ▻ *verb* (***shattered***, ***shattering***) **1** *tr & intr* to break into tiny fragments, usually suddenly or with force. **2** to destroy completely; to wreck. **3** to upset greatly. **4** *colloq* to tire out or exhaust. • **shattered** *adj, colloq* **1** exhausted. **2** extremely upset. • **shattering** *adj.* ◷ 14c: see SCATTER.

shatterproof /'ʃatəpruːf/ ▻ *adj* made to be specially resistant to shattering.

shave ▻ *verb* (*shaved*, *shaving*) **1** to cut off (hair) from (especially the face) with a razor or shaver. **2** *intr* to remove one's facial hair in this way. **3** to remove thin slivers from the surface of (especially wood) with a sharp bladed tool. **4** to graze the surface of something in passing. ▻ *noun* **1** an act or the process of shaving one's facial hair. **2** a tool for shaving or slicing wood. ⓘ Anglo-Saxon *sceafan*.

shaven /ˈʃeɪvən/ ▻ *adj* **1** shaved; close-cut or smooth. **2** tonsured. ⓘ 14c.

shaver /ˈʃeɪvə(r)/ ▻ *noun* **1** an electrical device with a moving blade or set of blades for shaving hair. **2** *old use*, *colloq* a young boy. ⓘ 15c.

shaving /ˈʃeɪvɪŋ/ ▻ *noun* **1** the removal of hair with a razor. **2** a thin sliver (especially of wood) taken off with a sharp bladed tool. ⓘ 14c.

Shavuot or **Shavuoth** see SHABUOTH

shawl ▻ *noun* a large single piece of fabric used to cover the head or shoulders or to wrap a baby. ⓘ 17c: from Persian *shal*.

shawm ▻ *noun, music* an instrument, a predecessor of the oboe, with a double reed and a flat circular mouthpiece. ⓘ 14c: from French *chalemie*, from Latin *calamus* reed.

she /ʃiː, ʃɪ/ ▻ *pronoun* a female person or animal, or thing thought of as female (eg a ship), named before or understood from the context. ▻ *noun* a female person or animal. ▻ *adj, especially in compounds* female □ *she-devil*. ⓘ Anglo-Saxon *seo*, feminine form of the definite article which replaced the pronoun *heo* in the 12c.

shea /ʃiː, ʃɪə/ ▻ *noun* (*sheas*) an African tree whose seeds, called **shea-nuts**, yield **shea-butter**. Also called **shea-tree**. ⓘ 18c: from W African *si*.

sheading /ˈʃiːdɪŋ/ ▻ *noun* any of the six divisions of the Isle of Man. ⓘ 16c: a variant of SHEDDING (from SHED²).

sheaf ▻ *noun* (*sheaves*) **1** a bundle of things tied together, especially of reaped corn. **2** a bundle of papers. **3** a bundle of usually 24 arrows in a quiver. ▻ *verb* (*also* **sheave**) (*sheafed*, *sheafing*; *sheaved*, *sheaving*) **1** to tie up in a bundle. **2** *intr* to make sheaves. • **sheaved** *adj*. ⓘ Anglo-Saxon *sceaf*.

shear ▻ *verb* (*past tense* ***sheared***, *past participle* ***sheared*** or ***shorn***, *present participle* ***shearing***) **1** to clip or cut off something, especially with a large pair of clippers. **2** to cut the fleece off (a sheep). **3** to cut excess nap from (fabric). **4** (*usually* **shear someone of something**) to strip or deprive them of it □ *We'll have to shear him of his privileges* □ *He was shorn of all authority*. **5** *tr & intr*, *engineering, physics* (*also* **shear off**) to subject to a shear. ▻ *noun* **1** the act of shearing. **2** (**shears**) a large pair of clippers, or a scissor-like cutting tool with a pivot or spring. **3** *engineering, physics* a force acting parallel to a plane rather than at right angles to it. • **shearer** *noun* someone who shears sheep. ⓘ Anglo-Saxon *sceran*.

shearling /ˈʃɪəlɪŋ/ ▻ *noun* **1** a young sheep that has been shorn for the first time. **2** the fleece of such a sheep. ⓘ 14c.

shear pin ▻ *noun* in a machine: a pin which, as a safety mechanism, will break and halt the machine or power-transmission when the correct load or stress is exceeded.

shearwater ▻ *noun* **1** a petrel with a long slender bill, dark plumage on the upper part of its body, and pale plumage beneath. **2** a SKIMMER (*noun* 3). ⓘ 17c.

sheath /ʃiːθ/ ▻ *noun* **1** a case or covering for the blade of a sword or knife. **2** a long close-fitting covering. **3** a condom. **4** (*also* **sheathdress**) a straight tight-fitting dress. **5** *biol* in plants and animals: any protective or encasing structure. ⓘ Anglo-Saxon *sceath*.

sheathe /ʃiːð/ ▻ *verb* (*sheathed*, *sheathing*) to put into or cover with a sheath or case. ⓘ 14c.

sheathing /ˈʃiːðɪŋ/ ▻ *noun* **1** something which sheathes; casing. **2** the protective covering, usually metal, of a ship's hull. ⓘ 14c.

sheave¹ /ʃiːv/ ▻ *noun* a grooved wheel, especially a pulley-wheel. ⓘ 14c.

sheave² see under SHEAF

shebang /ʃɪˈbaŋ/ ▻ *noun, originally US slang* an affair or matter; a situation □ *the whole shebang*. ⓘ 1860s: perhaps connected with SHEBEEN.

shebeen /ʃəˈbiːn/ ▻ *noun* **1** an illicit liquor-shop. **2** in Ireland: illicit and usually home-made alcohol. ⓘ 18c.

shed¹ ▻ *noun* a wooden or metal outbuilding, usually small, sometimes open-fronted, for working in, for storage or for shelter. ⓘ Anglo-Saxon *sced*, a variant of SHADE.

shed² ▻ *verb* (*shed*, *shedding*) **1** to release or make something flow □ *shed tears*. **2** to get rid of or cast off something □ *shed a skin* □ *shed jobs*. **3** to cast □ *It shed light on the whole problem*. **4** to allow to flow off □ *This fabric sheds water*. • **shedder** *noun*. ⓘ Anglo-Saxon *sceadan*.

she'd /ʃiːd, ʃɪd/ ▻ *contraction* **1** she had. **2** she would.

sheen ▻ *noun* shine, lustre or radiance; glossiness. • **sheeny** *adj*. ⓘ Anglo-Saxon *sciene* beautiful.

sheep ▻ *noun* (*plural* ***sheep***) **1** any of various wild or domesticated species of a herbivorous mammal with a stocky body covered with a thick woolly fleece, kept worldwide as a farm animal for its meat and wool. **2** a meek person, especially one who follows or obeys unquestioningly, like a sheep in a flock. **3** a member of a congregation, thought of as being looked after by the pastor. • **separate the sheep from the goats** to identify, especially by way of a test, the superior members of any group. ⓘ Anglo-Saxon *sceap*.

sheepcote /ˈʃiːpkout/ ▻ *noun* an enclosure for sheep. Also called **sheepfold**.

sheep-dip ▻ *noun* **1** a disinfectant insecticidal preparation in a dipping bath, used for washing sheep in order to control parasitic diseases such as sheep scab. **2** the trough or dipping bath for this preparation.

sheepdog ▻ *noun* **1** any working dog that is used to guard sheep from wild animals or to assist in herding. **2** any of several breeds of dog originally developed to herd sheep, eg Old English sheepdog, Shetland sheepdog, etc.

sheepish /ˈʃiːpɪʃ/ ▻ *adj* **1** embarrassed through having done something wrong or foolish. **2** sheep-like. • **sheepishly** *adverb*. • **sheepishness** *noun*.

sheepshank /ˈʃiːpʃaŋk/ ▻ *noun* a nautical knot used for shortening a rope.

sheepskin ▻ *noun* **1** the skin of a sheep, either with or without the fleece attached to it. **2** a rug or piece of clothing made from this. **3** leather made from sheep's skin.

sheepwalk ▻ *noun* a range of pasture for sheep.

sheer¹ ▻ *adj* **1** complete; absolute or downright □ *sheer madness*. **2** said of a cliff, etc: vertical or nearly vertical □ *a sheer drop*. **3** said eg of a fabric: so thin or fine as to be almost transparent □ *sheer tights*. ▻ *adverb* **1** completely. **2** vertically or nearly vertically □ *a rock face rising sheer*. • **sheerly** *adverb*. ⓘ 12c as *schere*: possibly from a lost Anglo-Saxon equivalent of Norse *skaerr* bright.

sheer² ▻ *noun* **1** a deviation. **2** the fore-and-aft upward curve of a ship's deck or sides. ▻ *verb* (***sheered***, ***sheering***) to make something change course or deviate. ⓘ 17c: partly another spelling of SHEAR; perhaps partly from German or Dutch equivalent *scheren* to cut or withdraw.

■ **sheer off** or **away 1** to change course suddenly; to swerve or deviate. **2** to move away, especially to evade someone or something disliked or feared.

sheet¹ ▻ *noun* **1** a large broad rectangular piece of fabric, especially for covering the mattress of a bed. **2** any large wide piece or expanse. **3** a piece of paper, especially if large and rectangular. **4** a pamphlet, broadsheet or newspaper. **5** *printing* a section of a book printed on one piece of paper. **6** *as adj* □ *sheet-metal.* ▷ *verb* (***sheeted, sheeting***) **1** to wrap or cover with or as if with a sheet. **2** to provide with sheets. **3** *intr* said of rain, ice, etc: to form in or fall in a sheet. ⓒ Anglo-Saxon *scete*.

sheet² ▷ *noun, naut* a controlling rope attached to the lower corner of a sail. ⓒ Anglo-Saxon *sceata* corner.

sheet-anchor ▷ *noun* **1** *naut* an extra anchor for use in an emergency. **2** a person or thing relied on for support, especially in a crisis; a last hope or refuge. ⓒ 15c: originally *shoot-anchor*.

sheeting ▷ *noun* **1** fabric used for making sheets. **2** protective boarding or metal covering. **3** the formation or process of making sheets. ⓒ 18c.

sheet lightning ▷ *noun* lightning that appears as a broad curtain of light.

sheet music ▷ *noun* music written or printed on unbound sheets of paper.

sheikh or **sheik** /ʃeɪk/ ▷ *noun* **1** the chief of an Arab tribe, village or family. **2** a Muslim leader. • **sheikhdom** *noun* the territory of a sheikh. ⓒ 16c: from Arabic *shaikh* old man, from *shakha* to be old.

sheila /'ʃiːlə/ ▷ *noun, Austral, NZ colloq* a woman or girl. ⓒ 19c: from the proper name.

shekel /'ʃɛkəl/ ▷ *noun* **1** the standard unit of currency in Israel, divided into 100 agorot. **2** an ancient Jewish weight (14 grams) and a coin of this weight. **3** (**shekels**) *slang* money. ⓒ 16c: from Hebrew *sheqel*, from *shaqal* to weigh.

sheldrake /'ʃɛldreɪk/ ▷ *noun* a male shelduck. ⓒ 14c: from dialect *sheld* variegated + DRAKE.

shelduck /'ʃɛldʌk/ ▷ *noun* a large goose-like duck which has white plumage with bold patterns of chestnut and black, a dark green head, a red bill and pink legs. ⓒ 18c: from dialect *sheld* variegated + DUCK.

shelf ▷ *noun* (***shelves***) **1** a usually narrow, flat board fixed to a wall or part of a cupboard, bookcase, etc, for storing or laying things on. **2** said especially of books: a shelf-ful. **3** a ledge of land, rock, etc; a sandbank. • **on the shelf 1** said of a person or thing: too old or worn out to be of any use. **2** said of a person, especially a woman: no longer likely to have the opportunity to marry, especially because of being too old. ⓒ Anglo-Saxon *scylf*.

shelf-life ▷ *noun* the length of time that a stored product remains usable, edible, etc.

shell ▷ *noun* **1** *bot* the hard protective structure covering the seed or fruit of some plants. **2** *zool* the hard protective structure covering the body of certain animals, especially shellfish, snails and tortoises. **3** the hard protective structure covering an egg. **4** the empty covering of eg a shellfish, found on the seashore. **5** any hard protective cover. **6** a round of ammunition for a large-bore gun, eg a mortar. **7** a shotgun cartridge. **8** an empty framework or outer case, especially the early stages of construction or the undestroyed remains of something, eg a building. **9** *computing* a program that acts as a user-friendly interface between an operating system and the user. **10** *chem* one of a series of concentric spheres representing the possible orbits of electrons as they revolve around the nucleus of an atom. **11** a type of light racing boat. ▷ *verb* (***shelled, shelling***) **1** to remove the shell from something. **2** to bombard with (eg mortar) shells □ *They shelled the city all night.* • **come out of one's shell** to cease to be shy and become more friendly or sociable. ⓒ Anglo-Saxon *scell*.

■ **shell out** or **shell out for something** *colloq* to pay out (money) or spend (money) on it □ *I had to shell out a fortune for it.*

she'll /ʃiːəl, ʃɪl/ ▷ *contraction* **1** she will. **2** she shall.

shellac /ʃə'lak/ ▷ *noun* **1** a yellow or orange resin produced by the lac insect. **2** a solution of this in alcohol, used as a varnish. Also called **shellac varnish**. **3** lac melted into thin plates, formerly used for making gramophone records. ▷ *verb* (***shellacked, shellacking***) **1** to coat with shellac. **2** *US colloq* to defeat convincingly; to trounce or thrash. ⓒ 18c: from SHELL + LAC, a translation of French *laque en ecailles* lac in thin plates.

shell company ▷ *noun, commerce* a company that exists on paper only, eg one set up as a potential takeover subject, to hold assets, or for corrupt financial purposes.

shellfire ▷ *noun* bombardment with artillery shells or ammunition.

shellfish ▷ *noun* (*plural* ***shellfish***) a shelled edible aquatic invertebrate, especially a mollusc or crustacean, eg prawn, crab, shrimp, lobster.

shelling /'ʃɛlɪŋ/ ▷ *noun* **1** removal of the shell or shells. **2** bombardment with ammunition; bombing. ⓒ 18c.

shellproof ▷ *adj* resistant to artillery shells or ammunition.

shell-shock ▷ *noun* a psychological disorder caused by prolonged exposure to military combat conditions, especially during World War I. • **shell-shocked** *adj*.

shell suit ▷ *noun* a type of lightweight multi-coloured tracksuit with a crinkly nylon outer layer and a cotton lining, commonly used as everyday casual wear.

Shelta /'ʃɛltə/ ▷ *noun* in Britain and Ireland: a secret jargon used by TRAVELLING PEOPLE. ⓒ 1870s: from *Shelru*, possibly a version of Irish *beulra* language.

shelter /'ʃɛltə(r)/ ▷ *noun* **1** protection against weather or danger. **2** a place or structure providing this. **3** a place of refuge, retreat or temporary lodging in distress. ▷ *verb* (***sheltered, sheltering***) **1** to protect someone or something from the effects of weather or danger. **2** to give asylum or lodging. **3** *intr* to take cover. • **shelterer** *noun*. ⓒ 16c: possibly from *sheltron* phalanx, from Anglo-Saxon *scieldtruma*, from *scield* shield + *truma* soldier.

sheltered ▷ *adj* **1** protected from the effects of weather. **2** protected from the harsh realities and unpleasantnesses of the world □ *a sheltered life.* ⓒ 16c.

sheltered housing ▷ *noun* flats or bungalows designed specially for elderly or disabled people, especially in a safe enclosed complex, allowing them to live as independently as possible, but with a resident warden.

sheltie or **shelty** /'ʃɛltɪ/ ▷ *noun* (***shelties***) a Shetland pony or Shetland sheepdog. ⓒ 17c: probably from Norse *Hjalti* Shetlander.

shelve /ʃɛlv/ ▷ *verb* (***shelved, shelving***) **1** to place or store on a shelf. **2** to fit with shelves. **3** to postpone or put aside; to abandon. **4** to remove from active service. **5** *intr* said of ground: to slope or incline. ⓒ 16c: from SHELF.

shelves see under SHELF

shelving /'ʃɛlvɪŋ/ ▷ *noun* **1** material used for making shelves. **2** shelves collectively. ⓒ 17c.

shemozzle /ʃɪ'mɒzəl/ ▷ *noun, slang* **1** a rumpus or commotion. **2** a mess or scrape. ⓒ Late 19c: Yiddish, from German *schlimm* bad + Hebrew *mazzal* luck.

SHEN /ʃɛn/ ▷ *noun, alternative therapy* a hands-on therapy that brings release from emotional and psychosomatic disorders. ⓒ From *S*pecific *H*uman *E*motional *N*exus.

shenanigans /ʃɪ'nanɪgənz/ ▷ *plural noun, colloq* **1** boisterous misbehaviour. **2** foolish behaviour; nonsense. **3** underhand dealings; trickery. ⓒ 1850s.

shepherd /'ʃɛpəd/ ▷ *noun* **1** someone who looks after, or herds, sheep. **2** *literary* a religious minister or pastor. ▷ *verb* (***shepherded, shepherding***) **1** to watch over or herd sheep. **2** to guide or herd (a group or crowd). ⓒ Anglo-Saxon *sceaphirde* sheep herd.

shepherdess /'ʃɛpədɛs/ ▷ *noun, old use* a female shepherd. ⓒ 14c.

shepherd's pie ▷ *noun* a dish consisting of minced meat baked with mashed potatoes on the top.

shepherd's purse ▷ *noun* a small annual weed with a rosette of oblong lobed leaves, white cross-shaped flowers, and heart-shaped seed capsules reminiscent of an old-style peasant's purse.

sherbet /ˈʃɜːbət/ ▷ *noun* **1** a fruit-flavoured powder eaten as confectionery, or made into an effervescent drink. **2** in Middle Eastern countries: a drink made of water and sweetened fruit juices. **3** *N Amer* a kind of water-ice. **4** *Austral colloq* beer. ⓘ 17c: Turkish and Persian, from Arabic *sharbah*, from *shariba* to drink.

sherd see SHARD

sherif or **shereef** /ʃəˈriːf/ ▷ *noun* **1** a descendant of Muhammad through his daughter Fatima. **2** a prince, especially the Sultan of Morocco. **3** the chief magistrate of Mecca. ⓘ 16c: from Arabic *sharif* noble or lofty.

sheriff /ˈʃɛrɪf/ ▷ *noun* **1** in a US county: the chief elected police officer mainly responsible for maintaining peace and order, attending courts, serving processes and executing judgements. **2** in England: the chief officer of the monarch in the shire or county, whose duties are now mainly ceremonial rather than judicial. **3** in Scotland: the chief judge of a sheriff court of a town or region. **4** *historical* the king's representative in a shire, with wide judicial and executive powers. • **sheriffdom** *noun* **1** the office, term of office or territory under the jurisdiction and authority of a sheriff. **2** in Scotland: one of six divisions of the judicature, made up of sheriff court districts. ⓘ Anglo-Saxon *scirgerefa*, from *scir* shire + *gerefa* reeve.

sheriff court ▷ *noun* in a Scottish town or region: a court dealing with civil actions and trying all but the most serious crimes.

sheriff officer ▷ *noun* in Scotland: an officer of the sheriff court who deals mainly with action against debtors and serving PROCESS.

Sherpa /ˈʃɜːpə/ ▷ *noun* (***Sherpa*** or ***Sherpas***) a member of an E Tibetan people living high on the south side of the Himalayas. ⓘ 19c: from Tibetan *shar* east + *pa* inhabitant.

sherry /ˈʃɛrɪ/ ▷ *noun* (***sherries***) **1** a fortified wine ranging in colour from pale gold to dark brown. **2** *loosely* a similar type of wine produced elsewhere. ⓘ 17c: from *Xeres*, an earlier form of *Jerez*, from Jerez de la Frontera, the S Spanish town where it is produced.

she's /ʃiːz; unstressed ʃɪz/ ▷ *contraction* **1** she is. **2** she has.

Shetland pony ▷ *noun* a kind of small sturdy pony with a long thick coat, originally bred in the Shetland Isles.

shewbread /ˈʃoʊbrɛd/ ▷ *noun* in ancient Israel: the twelve loaves offered every Sabbath on the table beside the altar of incense in the sanctuary by Jewish priests. Also called **showbread**. ⓘ 16c: from German *Schaubrot*, a translation of Hebrew *lechem panim* bread of the presence.

SHF or **shf** ▷ *abbreviation, radio* super high frequency.

Shia or **Shiah** /ʃɪə/ ▷ *noun* (*plural* in sense 2 only ***Shias*** or ***Shiahs***) **1** one of the two main branches of Islam, which regards Ali, Muhammad's cousin and son-in-law, as his true successor as leader of Islam. Compare SUNNI. **2** a member of this branch of Islam; a SHIITE. ⓘ 17c: Arabic, meaning 'sect'.

shiatsu or **shiatzu** /ʃɪˈatsuː/ ▷ *noun, medicine* a Japanese healing massage technique involving the application of pressure, mainly with the fingers and palms of hands, to parts of the body that are distant from the affected region. Also called ACUPRESSURE. ⓘ 1960s: Japanese, meaning 'finger pressure'.

shibboleth /ˈʃɪbəlɛθ/ ▷ *noun* **1** a common saying. **2** a slogan, catchphrase, custom or belief, especially if considered outdated. **3** a peculiarity of speech. **4** a use of a word, phrase or pronunciation that characterizes members of a particular group. ⓘ 14c: Hebrew, literally meaning 'ear of corn', used in the Old Testament as a test-word by Jephthah and his Gileadites to detect Ephraimites, who could not pronounce *sh*.

shied *past tense, past participle of* SHY[1] and SHY[2]

shield /ʃiːld/ ▷ *noun* **1** a piece of armour consisting of a broad plate, especially one with a straight top and tapering curved sides, carried to deflect weapons. **2** a protective plate, screen, pad or other guard. **3** any shield-shaped design or object, especially one used as an emblem or coat of arms. **4** a shield-shaped plate or medal presented as a prize. **5** someone or something that protects from danger or harm. **6** *geol* a large stable area of Pre-Cambrian rock in the earth's crust. Also called CRATON. ▷ *verb* (***shielded, shielding***) **1** to protect from danger or harm. **2** to ward off something. ⓘ Anglo-Saxon *sceld*.

shies see SHY[1], SHY[2]

shift ▷ *verb* (***shifted, shifting***) **1** *tr & intr* to change the position or direction of something; to change position or direction. **2** to transfer, switch or redirect □ *shift the blame on to someone else.* **3** in a vehicle: to change (gear). **4** to remove or dislodge someone or something □ *Nothing will shift that mark.* **5** *slang* to swallow or consume. **6** *intr, colloq* to move quickly. **7** *intr* (*also* **shift about**) **a** to fluctuate; to move from side to side; **b** to turn right round to the opposite point. **8** to take appropriate or urgent action. **9** to quit one thing for another □ *shift ideas.* **10** *intr* to manage or get along; to do as one can. **11** *linguistics* said of sounds: to undergo phonetic change. ▷ *noun* **1** a change, or change of position. **2** one of a set of consecutive periods into which a 24-hour working day is divided. **3** the group of workers on duty during any one of these periods. **4** a useful way of proceeding or dealing with something; an expedient. **5** a trick or other underhand scheme. **6** *computing* displacement of an ordered set of data to the left or right. **7** a general displacement of a series (as of lines in a spectrum, consonant or vowel sounds, faulted strata). **8** *music* in string instruments: a change in position of the left hand on the fingerboard. **9** a smock or loose dress, roughly oblong or triangular in shape. • **shift for oneself** *formal* to do without help from others; to depend on one's own resources. • **shift one's ground** to change the position or opinion one has taken, eg in a discussion. ⓘ Anglo-Saxon *sciftan* to divide, from Norse *skipta*.

shiftless /ˈʃɪftləs/ ▷ *adj* **1** having no motivation or initiative. **2** inefficient. • **shiftlessly** *adverb*. • **shiftlessness** *noun*. ⓘ 16c.

shifty /ˈʃɪftɪ/ ▷ *adj* (***shiftier, shiftiest***) **1** said of a person or behaviour: sly, shady or dubious; untrustworthy or dishonest. **2** said of a person or behaviour: evasive or tricky. **3** ready with shifts or expedients. • **shiftily** *adverb*. • **shiftiness** *noun*. ⓘ 16c.

shigella /ʃɪˈgɛlə/ ▷ *noun* a rod-shaped bacterium, especially one of a species that causes dysentery. ⓘ Early 20c: named after K Shiga (1870–1957), the Japanese bacteriologist who discovered it.

Shiite /ˈʃiːaɪt/ ▷ *noun* a Muslim who is an adherent of SHIA. ▷ *adj* referring or relating to Shia. • **Shiism** *noun*. • **Shiitic** *adj*. ⓘ 18c.

shilling /ˈʃɪlɪŋ/ ▷ *noun* **1** in the UK: a monetary unit and coin, before the introduction of decimal currency in 1971, worth one twentieth of a pound or 12 old pence (12d). **2** the standard unit of currency in Kenya, Tanzania, Uganda and Somalia, one shilling being worth 100 cents. ⓘ Anglo-Saxon *scilling*.

shilly-shally /ˈʃɪlɪʃalɪ/ ▷ *verb* (***shilly-shallies, shilly-shallied, shilly-shallying***) *intr* to be indecisive; to vacillate. ▷ *adverb* indecisively. ▷ *noun* (***shilly-shallies***) indecision; vacillation. • **shilly-shallier** *noun*. • **shilly-shallying** *noun*. ⓘ 17c: reduplication of *shall I?*.

shim ▷ *noun* a thin washer or slip of metal, wood, plastic, etc used to adjust or fill a gap between machine parts, especially gears. ▷ *verb* (***shimmed, shimming***) to fill or adjust with a shim or shims. ⓒ 18c.

shimmer ▷ *verb* (***shimmered, shimmering***) *intr* to shine tremulously and quiveringly with reflected light; to glisten. ▷ *noun* a tremulous or quivering gleam of reflected light. • **shimmery** *adj.* ⓒ Anglo-Saxon *scimerian*, from *scimian* to shine.

shimmy /ˈʃɪmɪ/ ▷ *noun* (***shimmies***) **1** a vivacious body-shaking dance, particularly popular during the 1920s. Also called **shimmy-shake**. **2** vibration in a motor vehicle, especially of the wheels, or an aeroplane. ▷ *verb* (***shimmies, shimmied, shimmying***) *intr* **1** to dance the shimmy, or to make similar movements. **2** to vibrate. ⓒ Early 20c: from CHEMISE.

shin ▷ *noun* **1** the bony front part of the leg below the knee. **2** the lower part of a leg of beef. ▷ *verb* (***shinned, shinning***) **1** *tr & intr* (*usually* **shin up**) to climb by gripping with the hands and legs. **2** to kick on the shins. ⓒ Anglo-Saxon *scinu*.

shinbone ▷ *noun* the TIBIA.

shindig /ˈʃɪndɪg/ ▷ *noun, colloq* **1** a lively party or celebration. **2** a noisy disturbance or row; a commotion. ⓒ 19c: see SHINDY.

shindy /ˈʃɪndɪ/ ▷ *noun* (***shindies***) a row or rumpus; a commotion. • **kick up a shindy** to make or cause a disturbance. ⓒ 19c: perhaps from SHINTY.

shine ▷ *verb* (***shone*** or in sense 4 ***shined, shining***) **1** *intr* to give out or reflect light; to beam with a steady radiance. **2** to direct the light from something □ *They shone the torch around the room.* **3** to be bright; to glow □ *Her face shone with joy.* **4** to make bright and gleaming by polishing. **5** *intr* to be outstandingly impressive in ability; to excel □ *She shines at maths.* **6** *intr* to be clear or conspicuous □ *Praise shone from his commentary.* ▷ *noun* **1** shining quality; brightness or lustre. **2** an act or process of polishing. • **come rain or shine** see under RAIN. • **take a shine to someone** *colloq* to like or fancy them on first acquaintance. ⓒ Anglo-Saxon *scinan*.

shiner /ˈʃaɪnə(r)/ ▷ *noun* **1** someone or something that shines. **2** any of various small glittering fish. **3** *colloq* a black eye. ⓒ 14c.

shingle¹ /ˈʃɪŋgəl/ ▷ *noun* **1** a thin rectangular tile, especially made of wood, laid with others in overlapping rows on a roof or wall. **2** these tiles collectively. **3** a board. **4** *US* a small signboard or plate, eg hung outside a doctor's office. **5** a woman's short hairstyle, cropped at the back into overlapping layers. ▷ *verb* (***shingled, shingling***) **1** to tile with shingles. **2** to cut in a shingle. ⓒ 12c: from Latin *scindula* wooden tile, from *scindere* to split.

shingle² /ˈʃɪŋgəl/ ▷ *noun, geol* **1** small pebbles that have been worn smooth by water, found especially in a series of parallel ridges on beaches. **2** a beach, bank or bed covered in gravel or stones. • **shingly** *adj.* ⓒ 16c.

shingles /ˈʃɪŋgəlz/ ▷ *singular noun, medicine* the disease herpes zoster, caused by the chickenpox virus, in which acute inflammation of spinal nerve ganglia produces pain and then a series of blisters along the path of the nerve, especially in the area of the waist and ribs, but sometimes around the head and face. ⓒ 14c: from Latin *cingulum* belt, from *cingere* to gird.

Shinto /ˈʃɪntoʊ/ ▷ *noun* the Japanese nature and hero cult, the indigenous religion of the country. ⓒ 18c: Japanese, from Chinese *shen dao*, from *shen* god + *dao* way or doctrine.

Shintoist /ˈʃɪntoʊɪst/ ▷ *noun* an adherent of Shinto. ▷ *adj* referring or relating to Shinto. • **Shintoism** *noun* the beliefs and practices of Shinto.

shinty /ˈʃɪntɪ/ ▷ *noun* (***shinties***) **1** a game, originally Scottish, similar to hockey, played by two teams of 12. **2** **a** (*also* **shinty-stick**) the stick used for this game; **b** the ball used. ⓒ 18c.

shiny /ˈʃaɪnɪ/ ▷ *adj* (***shinier, shiniest***) **1** reflecting light; polished to brightness. **2** said of part of a piece of clothing: having a glossy surface where the fabric has been badly worn.

ship ▷ *noun* **1** a large engine-propelled vessel, intended for sea travel. **2** a large sailing vessel, especially a three-masted, square-rigged sailing vessel. **3** a racing-boat. **4** any craft that floats on water. **5** a ship's crew. **6** *colloq* a spaceship or airship. ▷ *verb* (***shipped, shipping***) **1** to send or transport by ship. **2** to send or transport by land or air. **3** *naut* said of a boat: to take in (water, eg waves) over the side. **4** *intr* to embark. **5** *naut* to bring on board a boat or ship □ *ship oars.* **6** to fix an object in position. **7** to engage for service on board ship. • **when one's ship comes in** or **comes home** when one becomes rich. ⓒ Anglo-Saxon *scip*.

■ **ship someone off** *colloq* to send them away; to dispatch □ *They shipped the kids off to their grandparents.*

-ship ▷ *suffix, forming nouns, denoting* **1** position, rank or status □ *lordship.* **2** a period of office or rule □ *chairmanship.* **3** a state or condition □ *friendship.* **4** a specified type of skill □ *craftsmanship* □ *scholarship.* **5** a group of individuals having something in common □ *membership.* ⓒ Anglo-Saxon *-scipe*.

shipboard ▷ *noun* the side of a ship. ▷ *adj* occurring or situated on board a ship.

shipbuilder ▷ *noun* a person or company that constructs ships. • **shipbuilding** *noun.*

shipload ▷ *noun* the actual or possible load or capacity of a ship.

shipmate ▷ *noun* a fellow sailor.

shipment ▷ *noun* **1** the act or practice of shipping cargo. **2** a cargo or consignment transported, not necessarily by ship.

shipping ▷ *noun* **1** the commercial transportation of freight, especially by ship. **2** ships as traffic. **3** *as adj* □ *shipping forecast.*

ship's biscuit ▷ *noun* HARDTACK.

shipshape ▷ *adj* in good order; neat and tidy.

shipwreck ▷ *noun* **1** the accidental sinking or destruction of a ship. **2** the remains of a sunken or destroyed ship. **3** wreck or ruin; disaster. ▷ *verb* **1** *tr & intr* to be or make someone the victim of a ship's accidental sinking or destruction. **2** to wreck, ruin or destruct (eg plans).

shipwright ▷ *noun* a skilled wright or carpenter who builds or repairs (especially wooden) ships.

shipyard ▷ *noun* a place where ships are built and repaired.

shire /ʃaɪə(r)/ ▷ *noun* (***shires***) **1** a county. **2** /ʃə(r), ʃɪə(r)/ *in compounds* □ *Staffordshire.* **3** *Austral* a rural district having its own elected council. **4** a SHIRE HORSE. ⓒ Anglo-Saxon *scir* authority.

shire horse ▷ *noun* the largest kind of draught horse, once bred chiefly in the Midland shires, with a convex face, brown or bay coat with white markings, and long hair on its fetlocks.

the Shires ▷ *plural noun* the rural areas of England as opposed to the towns, specifically the Midland counties or the fox-hunting counties of Leicestershire, Northamptonshire and part of Lincolnshire.

shirk /ʃɜːk/ ▷ *verb* (***shirked, shirking***) **1** to evade (work, a duty, etc) □ *He's always trying to shirk responsibility.* **2** *intr* to avoid work, duty or responsibility. **3** *intr* to go or act evasively. ▷ *noun* someone who shirks. • **shirker** *noun.* ⓒ 17c: perhaps from German *Schurke* scoundrel.

shirt /ʃɜːt/ ▷ *noun* **1** a man's loose-sleeved garment for the upper body, typically with buttons down the front, and fitted collar and cuffs. **2** a woman's blouse of a similar form. **3** an undershirt. **4** a nightshirt. • **keep one's shirt on** *colloq* to control one's temper; to remain calm. • **put one's shirt on something** *colloq* to bet all one has on it. ⓘ Anglo-Saxon *scyrte*.

shirtsleeve ▷ *noun* a sleeve of a shirt. • **in one's shirtsleeves** not wearing a jersey, jacket or coat.

shirt-tail ▷ *noun* the longer flap hanging down at the back of a shirt.

shirtwaister ▷ *noun* a woman's tailored dress with a shirt-like bodice. Also called **shirt dress**. • **shirtwaist** *noun, US* a woman's blouse.

shirty /ˈʃɜːtɪ/ ▷ *adj* (***shirtier***, ***shirtiest***) *colloq* ill-tempered or irritable; annoyed. ⓘ 19c.

shish kebab see KEBAB

shit and **shite** *coarse slang* ▷ *noun* **1** excrement or faeces. **2** an act of defecating. **3** *derog* rubbish; nonsense. **4** *derog* a despicable person. **5** *drug-taking slang* marijuana or heroin. ▷ *verb* (***shit***, ***shitted*** or ***shat***, ***shitting***; ***shited***, ***shiting***) *intr* to defecate. ▷ *exclamation* expressing annoyance, disappointment or disgust. • **beat** or **kick the shit out of someone** to hit or attack them severely. • **get one's shit together** to get oneself and one's matters organized. • **No shit** *US slang* No fooling; You amaze me (*often ironic*). • **scared shitless** to be extremely scared or upset □ *I was scared shitless of him.* • **shit a brick** or **bricks** to be very anxious or scared. • **shit oneself** *slang* to be extremely frightened or scared. • **when the shit hits the fan** *slang* when the real trouble or conflict begins. • **up shit creek** in an extremely difficult or troublesome situation. ⓘ Anglo-Saxon *scitan* to defecate.

shitface ▷ *noun, slang* a contemptible person.

shithead ▷ *noun, slang* **1** a contemptible or detestable person. **2** a drug-user, especially a user of marijuana.

shithole ▷ *noun, slang* a filthy, disgusting or delapidated place or establishment.

shit-hot ▷ *adj, slang* often said of a person: excellent or first-rate; extraordinarily good.

shithouse ▷ *noun, slang* a lavatory.

the shits ▷ *singular noun, slang* diarrhoea.

shit-scared ▷ *adj, slang* very frightened □ *I'm shit-scared of spiders.*

shit-stirrer ▷ *noun, slang* someone who causes unnecessary trouble, especially for other people.

shitty /ˈʃɪtɪ/ ▷ *adj* (***shittier***, ***shittiest***) *coarse slang* **1** soiled with, or as if with, shit; filthy. **2** *derog* very bad or unpleasant; mean or despicable. • **shittiness** *noun*.

shiva /ˈʃiːvə/ or **Siva** /ˈsiːvə/ ▷ *noun, Hinduism* the third god of the Hindu trimurti, seen as the destroyer and reproducer. ⓘ Anglo-Saxon *sceadd*.

shiver[1] /ˈʃɪvə(r)/ ▷ *verb* (***shivered***, ***shivering***) *intr* **1** to quiver or tremble, eg with fear. **2** to make an involuntary muscular movement in response to the cold. ▷ *noun* **1** an act of shivering; a shivering movement or sensation. **2** (**the shivers**) *colloq* a fit of shivering. • **shivery** *adj* inclined to shiver. ⓘ 12c: as *chivere*.

shiver[2] /ˈʃɪvə(r)/ ▷ *noun* a splinter or other small fragment. ▷ *verb* (***shivered***, ***shivering***) *tr & intr* to shatter. • **shivery** *adj* brittle. • **shiver my timbers** a stage sailor's oath. ⓘ 12c: as *scifre*.

shm ▷ *abbreviation* simple harmonic motion.

shoal[1] *noun* **1** a multitude of fish swimming together. **2** a huge crowd or assemblage; a multitude, flock or swarm. ▷ *verb* (***shoaled***, ***shoaling***) *intr* to gather or move in a shoal; to swarm. ⓘ Anglo-Saxon *scolu* a troop.

shoal[2] ▷ *noun* **1** an area of shallow water in a river, lake or sea where sediment has accumulated. **2** such an accumulation of sediment, especially one exposed at high tide. ▷ *verb* (***shoaled***, ***shoaling***) **1** *tr & intr* to make or become shallow. **2** *intr, naut* to sail into shallow water. ▷ *adj* shallow. ⓘ Anglo-Saxon *sceald* shallow.

shock[1] ▷ *noun* **1** a strong emotional disturbance, especially a feeling of extreme surprise, outrage or disgust. **2** a cause of such a disturbance. **3** a heavy and violent impact, originally of charging warriors. **4** a clashing together. **5** outrage at something regarded as improper or wrong. **6** (*in full* **electric shock**) a convulsion caused by the passage of an electric current through the body. **7** a heavy jarring blow or impact. **8** *medicine* **a** a state of extreme physical collapse, characterized by lowered blood pressure and body temperature and a sweaty pallid skin, occurring as a result of haemorrhage, coronary thrombosis, severe burns, dehydration, drug overdose, extreme emotional disturbance, etc; **b** *Scots* a stroke. ▷ *verb* (***shocked***, ***shocking***) **1** to assail or attack with a shock. **2** to give a shock to someone. **3** to make someone feel extreme surprise, outrage or disgust. **4** to shake or jar suddenly and forcefully. **5** *intr* to outrage feelings. • **shock horror** *exclamation, colloq* an ironic expression used in response to something purporting or claiming to shock. • **shock-horror** *adj* used eg of banner headlines and other sensationalistic devices of the tabloid press. ⓘ 16c: from French *choc*, from *choquer*.

shock[2] ▷ *noun* a bushy mass of hair. ⓘ 19c.

shock[3] ▷ *noun* a number of sheaves of corn propped up against each other to dry. ▷ *verb* (***shocked***, ***shocking***) to set up in shocks. ⓘ 14c: as *schokke*.

shock absorber ▷ *noun* in a vehicle: a device, such as a coiled spring, that damps vibrations caused by the wheels passing over bumps in the road.

shocker ▷ *noun, colloq* **1** a very sensational tale. **2** any unpleasant or offensive person or thing.

shocking ▷ *adj* **1** giving a shock. **2** extremely surprising, outrageous or disgusting, especially to oversensitive feelings. **3** *colloq* deplorably bad □ *He has a shocking sense of humour.* • **shockingly** *adverb*. ⓘ 17c.

shockproof ▷ *adj* protected against or resistant to the effects of shock or impact. • **shockproofing** *noun*.

shock tactics ▷ *noun* any course of action that seeks to achieve its object by means of suddenness and force.

shock therapy and **shock treatment** ▷ *noun* see ELECTROCONVULSIVE THERAPY

shock wave ▷ *noun* **1** ▷ *physics* an exceptionally intense sound wave, caused by a violent explosion or the movement of an object at a speed greater than that of sound. **2** a feeling of shock which spreads through a community, etc, after some disturbing event □ *The mayor's arrest sent a shock wave through the town.*

shoddy /ˈʃɒdɪ/ ▷ *adj* (***shoddier***, ***shoddiest***) **1** of poor quality; carelessly done or made. **2** cheap and nasty. **3** made of shoddy. ▷ *noun* (***shoddies***) **1** wool made from shredded rags. **2** a cloth made from it, either on its own or mixed. **3** anything inferior intending to pass for better than it is. • **shoddily** *adverb*. • **shoddiness** *noun*.

shoe /ʃuː/ ▷ *noun* **1** either of a pair of shaped outer coverings for the feet, especially ones made of leather or other stiff material, usually finishing below the ankle. **2** anything like this in shape or function. **3** a horseshoe. **4** a metal tip or ferrule for protecting the end of a pole, stick, etc. **5** a strip of metal attached to the runners of a sledge to reduce friction. **6** a drag for the wheel of a vehicle. **7** a BRAKESHOE. **8** the contact on an electric train that slides along the third rail in order to pick up the current to power it. ▷ *verb* (***shod***, ***shoeing***) **1** to provide with shoes. **2** to fit (a horse) with shoes. • **in someone's shoes** in the same situation as them; in their position □ *I wouldn't like to be in his shoes now.* ⓘ Anglo-Saxon *scoh*.

shoehorn ▻ *noun* a curved piece of metal, plastic or (originally) horn, used for levering the heel into a shoe. ▻ *verb* (***shoehorned***, ***shoehorning***) to fit, squeeze or compress into a tight or insufficient space.

shoelace ▻ *noun* a string or cord passed through eyelet holes to fasten a shoe.

shoe leather ▻ *noun* leather used for making shoes.

shoemaker ▻ *noun* someone who makes, though now more often only sells or repairs, shoes and boots.

shoeshine ▻ *noun* **1** the act of polishing shoes. **2** the shiny appearance of polished shoes.

shoestring ▻ *noun, N Amer* a shoelace. Also *as adj* ◻ ***shoestring tie.*** • **on a shoestring** *colloq* with or using a very small or limited amount of money.

shoe tree ▻ *noun* a support, usually made of wood or metal, put inside a shoe to preserve its shape when it is not being worn.

shogi /'ʃoʊgɪ/ ▻ *noun* a Japanese form of chess, played on a squared board, each player having 20 pieces. Ⓒ 19c: Japanese.

shogun /'ʃoʊgʌn, 'ʃoʊgʊn/ ▻ *noun, Japanese history* any of the hereditary military governors who were the effective rulers of Japan from the 12c until 1867 when the emperor regained power. • **shogunal** *adj.* • **shogunate** *noun* the office, jurisdiction or state of a shogun. Ⓒ 17c: Japanese, from Chinese *jiangjun* general.

shone *past tense, past participle of* SHINE

shoo ▻ *exclamation* an expression used to scare or chase away a person or animal. ▻ *verb* (***shooed***, ***shooing***) **1** *intr* to cry 'Shoo!'. **2** (*usually* **shoo someone** or **something away** or **off**) to chase them away by, or as if by, shouting 'Shoo!'. Ⓒ 15c.

shoo-in ▻ *noun, US slang* **1** a horse that is allowed to win. **2** any certain or easy winner of something, especially a race, competition, etc; a sure thing. Ⓒ 1920s.

shook *past tense of* SHAKE

shoot ▻ *verb* (***shot***, ***shooting***) **1** *tr & intr* to fire a gun or other weapon. **2** to fire bullets, arrows or other missiles. **3** to hit, wound or kill with a weapon or missile. **4** to let fly with force ◻ ***The geyser shot water high into the air.*** **5** to launch or direct forcefully and rapidly ◻ ***He shot questions at them.*** **6** *tr & intr* to move or make someone or something move or progress quickly ◻ ***That last victory shot them to the top of the table.*** **7** *colloq* (*also* **shoot off**) to depart quickly ◻ ***I have to shoot or I'll miss my train.*** **8** *colloq* to tip out or dump (eg rubbish). **9** *tr & intr, sport* to strike (the ball, etc) at goal. **10** *golf* to score, for a hole or the round. **11** *tr & intr* to film (motion pictures), or take photographs of someone or something. **12** to variegate by adding different coloured specks of colour ◻ ***Her dress was black shot with burgundy.*** **13** *intr* said of pain: to dart with a stabbing sensation. **14** to pull (one's shirt sleeves) forward so that they protrude from the sleeves of one's jacket. **15** to slide (a bolt) along. **16** to slide a bolt into or out of its lock. **17** to elongate rapidly. **18** to protrude or jut out far or suddenly. **19** *colloq* to begin to speak one's mind or tell what one knows ◻ ***Go on, shoot!*** **20** to tower. **21** to throw or cast a die or dice. **22** to detonate. **23** *intr* to dart forth or forwards. **24** said of a cricket ball: to start forward rapidly near the ground. **25** *intr* to use a bow or gun in practice, competition, hunting, etc ◻ ***He likes to shoot regularly.*** **26** *intr* said of a plant: to produce new growth; to sprout. **27** *intr* said of a plant, especially a vegetable: to produce unwanted flowers and seeds. **28** *colloq* to pass through (red traffic lights) without stopping. **29** *colloq* to pass quickly through something ◻ ***shoot rapids.*** **30** *slang* to play a game of eg pool or golf; to have as a score at golf ◻ ***We could shoot pool at the club later.*** **31** *slang* to inject (especially oneself) with (drugs) illegally. ▻ *noun* **1** an act of shooting. **2** a shooting match or party. **3** an outing or expedition to hunt animals with firearms. **4** an area of land within which animals are hunted in this way. **5** the shooting of a film or a photographic modelling session. **6** a new or young plant growth. **7** the sprouting of a plant. **8** a dump or rubbish chute. • **shoot a line** *slang* to brag or exaggerate. • **shoot ahead** to advance quickly in front of others, eg in a race. • **shoot someone down in flames** *slang* **1** to scold or reprimand severely. **2** to destroy or humiliate, especially by the strength of one's argument ◻ ***His speech was shot down in flames by the opposition.*** • **shoot from the hip** *colloq* to speak hastily, bluntly or directly, without preparation or concern for the consequences. • **shoot home 1** to hit the target. **2** to put across an opinion, etc ◻ ***I think you've shot the point home.*** • **shoot it out** to settle (a dispute, competition, etc) by military action. • **shoot oneself in the foot** *colloq* to injure or harm one's own interests by ineptitude. • **shoot one's mouth off** *colloq* to speak freely, indiscreetly or boastfully. • **shoot through** *slang* to escape or leave quickly. • **the whole shoot** or **shooting-match** *colloq* the whole lot. Ⓒ Anglo-Saxon *sceotan.*

■ **shoot someone** or **something down 1** to fire guns at an aircraft so as to make it crash. **2** to kill with gunfire. **3** to dismiss mercilessly with criticism or ridicule.

■ **shoot up** to grow or increase extremely quickly ◻ ***He has really shot up since I last saw him.***

■ **shoot someone up** to kill or injure by shooting.

■ **shoot something up** *slang* to inject (heroin, etc).

shoot-'em-up *originally US, informal* ▻ *adj* signifying a computer game in which the object is to defeat the enemy by means of violence or attack. ▻ *noun* **1** such a computer game. **2** a film or television programme in which guns and shooting feature prominently. Ⓒ 1940s.

shooter ▻ *noun* **1** someone or something that shoots. **2** *colloq* a gun. Ⓒ 13c.

shooting-box and **shooting-lodge** ▻ *noun* a small country house for use during the hunting or shooting season.

shooting brake ▻ *noun, old use* an estate car.

shooting gallery ▻ *noun* a long room fitted out with targets used for practice or amusement with firearms.

shooting iron ▻ *noun, slang* a firearm, especially a revolver.

shooting range ▻ *noun* a place specifically used for shooting at targets.

shooting star ▻ *noun* a METEOR.

shooting stick ▻ *noun* a sturdy pointed walking-stick whose handle folds out to form a small seat.

shooting war ▻ *noun* actual war as opposed to cold war.

shootist /'ʃuːtɪst/ ▻ *noun, especially US slang* **1** someone who shoots. **2** a skilled or accomplished marksman.

shop ▻ *noun* **1** a room or building where goods are sold or services are provided. **2** a place providing specific goods or services ◻ ***a barber's shop*** ◻ ***a betting shop.*** **3** a spell of shopping, especially for food or household items. **4** a place where mechanics work, or where any kind of industry is pursued; a workshop ◻ ***machine shop.*** **5** a place of employment or activity. **6** *slang* prison. **7** talk about one's own business. ▻ *verb* (***shopped***, ***shopping***) **1** *intr* to visit a shop or shops, especially in order to buy goods. **2** *slang* to imprison, or cause to be imprisoned. **3** *slang* to betray or inform on someone to the police, etc. • **all over the shop** *colloq* scattered everywhere; in numerous places. • **set up shop** to establish or open a trading establishment. • **shut up shop** *colloq* to stop trading, either at the end of the working day or permanently. • **talk shop** *colloq* to talk about one's work or business, especially in a tedious way. Ⓒ Anglo-Saxon *sceoppa* treasury.

■ **shop around 1** to compare the price and quality of goods in various shops before making a purchase. **2** *colloq* to explore the full range of options available before committing oneself to any.

shop assistant ▷ *noun* someone serving customers in a shop.

shop floor ▷ *noun* **1** the part of a factory or workshop where the manual work is carried out. **2** the workers in a factory, as opposed to the management.

shopkeeper ▷ *noun* someone who owns and manages a shop.

shoplift ▷ *verb, tr & intr* to steal (goods) from shops. • **shoplifter** *noun*. • **shoplifting** *noun*.

shopper ▷ *noun* **1** someone who shops. **2** a shopping bag or basket. ◷ 1860s.

shopping ▷ *noun* **1** the act of visiting shops to look at or buy goods. **2** goods bought in shops. **3** *as adj* □ *a shopping basket.* ◷ 18c.

shopping centre ▷ *noun* **1** an area of a town or city containing a large number of shops of different kinds. **2** a collection of different shops within one building, usually providing other facilities, especially restaurants and toilets.

shopping list ▷ *noun* **1** a list of items to be bought when out shopping. **2** a list of items to be obtained, carried out, acted upon, considered, etc.

shop-soiled ▷ *adj* slightly dirty, faded or spoiled from being used as a display in a shop.

shop steward ▷ *noun* a worker elected by others to be an official trade union representative in negotiations with the management.

shopwalker ▷ *noun* someone who walks around a shop, especially a large department store, to supervise shop assistants and see that customers are attended to.

shop window ▷ *noun* **1** a window of a shop in which goods are arranged in a display. **2** any arrangement which displays something to advantage.

shoran /ˈʃɔːran/ ▷ *noun* a system of aircraft navigation using the measurement of the time taken for two dispatched radar signals to return from known locations. ◷ 1940s: from *short range navigation*.

shore[1] /ʃɔː(r)/ ▷ *noun* **1** a narrow strip of land bordering on the sea, a lake or any other large body of water. **2** land as opposed to the sea. **3** *law* the FORESHORE. **4** (**shores**) lands; countries □ *foreign shores.* ▷ *verb* (***shored, shoring***) to set on shore □ *shore a boat.* • **on shore** on the land; ashore. ◷ 14c: as *schore*.

shore[2] /ʃɔː(r)/ ▷ *noun* a prop. ▷ *verb* (*usually* **shore something up**) **1** to support it with props. **2** to give support to it; to sustain or strengthen it. • **shoring** *noun* **1** supporting by using props. **2** a set of props. ◷ 15c: from Dutch *schore*, from Norse *skortha*.

shoreline ▷ *noun* the line formed where land meets water.

shorn *past participle of* SHEAR

short ▷ *adj* **1** having little physical length; not long. **2** having little height. **3** having little extent or duration; brief; concise □ *short day.* **4** in the early future □ *short date.* **5** indicating a seemingly short length of time □ *For a few short weeks we could enjoy our time together.* **6** said of a temper: quickly and easily lost. **7** rudely abrupt; curt □ *She was very short with him.* **8** said of the memory: tending not to retain things for long. **9** said of a substance, especially food: brittle. **10** said of pastry: crisp and crumbling easily. **11** failing to reach the standard; not going far enough. **12** in short supply; in demand □ *We are two tickets short.* **13** in default. **14** referring to the sale of what one cannot supply. **15** *phonetics* said of a vowel sound: being the briefer of two possible lengths of vowel. **16** *poetry* said of a syllable: unaccented. **17** *colloq* said of an alcoholic drink, especially a spirit: not diluted with water; neat. **18** lacking in money □ *I'm a bit short at the moment.* **19** *cricket* said of fielding positions: relatively close to the batsman. **20** said of betting odds: providing the winner with only a small profit; near even. ▷ *adverb* **1** abruptly; briefly □ *stopped short.* **2** on this or the near side □ *The dart fell short of the board.* ▷ *noun* **1** something that is short. **2** shortness; abbreviation or summary. **3** *colloq* a drink of an alcoholic spirit. **4** a short cinema film shown before the main FEATURE FILM. **5** a SHORT CIRCUIT. ▷ *verb* (***shorted, shorting***) *tr & intr* to SHORT-CIRCUIT. • **shortness** *noun*. • **be caught** or **taken short** *colloq* to have an urgent need to urinate or defecate. • **cut someone** or **something short** see under CUT. • **fall short** to be insufficient; to be less than a required, expected or stated amount. • **for short** as an abbreviated form □ *She gets called Jenny for short.* • **go** or **run short of something** not to have enough of it; to have an insufficient supply of it □ *We're running short of milk.* • **in short** concisely stated; in a few words. • **in short order** very quickly. • **in short supply** not available in the required or desired quantity; scarce □ *Food is in short supply in Bosnia.* • **in the short run** within a short space of time; over a brief period. • **make short work of someone** or **something** to settle or dispose of quickly and thoroughly □ *I made short work of the essay.* • **short and sweet** *colloq* agreeably brief. • **short for something** an abbreviated form of it □ *Jenny is short for Jennifer.* • **short of** or **on something** deficient; lacking in it □ *We're always short of money* □ *She's a bit short on tact.* • **short of something** without going as far as it; except it □ *We tried every kind of persuasion short of threats.* • **stop short** to come to an abrupt halt or standstill. ◷ Anglo-Saxon *sceort*.

shortage /ˈʃɔːtɪdʒ/ ▷ *noun* a lack or deficiency.

shortbread ▷ *noun* a rich crumbly biscuit made with flour, butter and sugar.

shortcake ▷ *noun* **1** shortbread or other crumbly cake. **2** *US* a light cake, prepared in layers with fruit between, served with cream.

short-change ▷ *verb* **1** to give (a customer) less than the correct amount of change, either by accident or intentionally. **2** *colloq* to treat dishonestly; to cheat. • **short-changer** *noun*.

short circuit ▷ *noun* **1** *electronics* a connection across an electric circuit with a very low resistance, usually caused accidentally, eg by an insulation failure, which may damage electrical equipment or be a fire hazard. Compare OPEN CIRCUIT. **2** *surgery* an artificial connection between two normally separate tubular organs or parts.

short-circuit ▷ *verb* **1** to cause a short circuit in something. **2** to provide with a short cut or bypass. **3** *surgery* to interconnect where there was an obstruction.

shortcoming ▷ *noun* a fault or defect.

short cut ▷ *noun* **1** a quicker route than normal between two places. **2** a method that saves time or effort. ▷ *verb* (**short-cut**) **1** to take a short cut. **2** to use a shorter method.

short-dated ▷ *adj, finance* **1** said of a bill: having little time to run from its date. **2** said of securities: redeemable in under five years. See also LONG-DATED, MEDIUM-DATED.

shorten /ˈʃɔːtən/ ▷ *verb* (***shortened, shortening***) **1** *tr & intr* to make or become shorter. **2** to make something seem short or to fall short □ *Those trousers shorten your legs.* **3** to make (pastry) crumbly, by adding butter, lard, etc. **4** *naut* to draw in (the sails). **5** *cards* said of odds, etc: to make them shorten; to lower. ◷ 16c.

shortening ▷ *noun* butter, lard or other fat used for making pastry more crumbly. ◷ 16c.

shortfall ▷ *noun* **1** a failure to reach a desired or expected level or specification. **2** the amount or margin by which something is deficient □ *There is a shortfall of £100.*

short fuse ▷ *noun, colloq* a quick temper.

shorthand ▷ *noun* **1** any of various systems of combined strokes and dots representing speech sounds and groups of sounds, used as a fast way of recording speech in writing. **2** such a system of abbreviated handwriting. Also *as adj* □ *shorthand notebook.*

short-handed ▷ *adj* understaffed; short of workers.

shorthorn ▷ *noun* any of various breeds of beef and dairy cattle with very short horns and usually with a red and white, roan or white coat.

shortie see SHORTY

short leg ▷ *noun, cricket* **1** a fielding position near, and in line with, the batsman on the leg side. **2** a fielder who takes up this position.

shortlist ▷ *noun* (*also* **short leet**) a selection of the best candidates from the total number submitted or nominated, from which the successful candidate will be chosen. ▷ *verb* (**short-list**) to place on a shortlist.

short-lived ▷ *adj* living or lasting only for a short time.

shortly ▷ *adverb* **1** soon; within a short period of time □ *He'll arrive shortly.* **2** in a curt or abrupt manner.

short-range ▷ *adj* referring or relating to a short distance or length of time □ *short-range telescope.*

shorts ▷ *plural noun* trousers, worn by males or females, extending from the waist to anywhere between the upper thigh and the knee.

short shrift ▷ *noun* **1** *archaic* a brief period of time given to a prisoner for confession before execution. **2** discourteously brief or disdainful consideration □ *Their suggestions were given short shrift.* • **make short shrift of something** to discard it without due consideration.

short-sighted ▷ *adj* **1** said of a person: capable of seeing only near objects clearly; affected by MYOPIA. Compare LONG-SIGHTED. **2** said of a person, plan, etc: lacking or showing a lack of foresight. • **short-sightedly** *adverb.* • **short-sightedness** *noun.*

short-spoken ▷ *adj* curt in speech.

short-staffed ▷ *adj* having a reduced or insufficient staff.

short story ▷ *noun* a work of prose narrative shorter than a novel, usually concentrating on a specific episode or experience and its effect.

short-tempered ▷ *adj* easily made angry.

short-term ▷ *adj* **1** concerned only with the near or immediate future. **2** lasting only a short time. **3** *finance* maturing or effective within a brief period of time. • **short-termism** *noun* the tendency or inclination towards the adopting of short-term views, solutions to problems, etc.

short wave ▷ *noun* **1** a radio wave with a wavelength between 10 and 100 metres. **2** *physics* an electromagnetic wave with a wavelength no longer than that of visible light. **3** *as adj* □ *a short-wave radio station.*

short-winded ▷ *adj* easily and quickly running out of breath.

shorty or **shortie** /ˈʃɔːtɪ/ ▷ *noun* (***shorties***) *colloq* a person or thing (eg a garment) that is shorter than average.

shot¹ ▷ *noun* **1** an act of shooting or firing a gun. **2** the sound of a gun being fired. **3** *mining* an explosive charge or blast. **4** small metal pellets collectively, fired in clusters from a SHOTGUN. **5** a cannonball. **6** a single piece of filmed action recorded without a break by one camera. **7** a photographic exposure. **8** the range or extent of a camera □ *out of shot.* **9** a person considered in terms of their ability to fire a gun accurately □ *a good shot.* **10** *sport* an act or instance of shooting or playing a stroke eg in tennis, snooker, etc. **11** *athletics* a heavy metal ball thrown in the SHOT PUT. **12** *colloq* an attempt □ *I'll have a shot at it.* **13** *colloq* a spell or stint. **14** *colloq* a turn or go □ *I'll have a shot at it now.* **15** *colloq* a guess □ *Have a shot at the answer.* **16** an aggressive remark. **17** *colloq* an injection. **18 a** the flight of a missile; **b** the distance it travels. **19** a reach or range. **20** *N Amer, especially US colloq* a small drink of alcoholic spirit; a dram. **21** the launch of a spacecraft, especially a rocket □ *moon shot.* • **call the shots** see under CALL. • **like a shot** extremely quickly or without hesitation; eagerly or willingly. • **a long shot** a bet with little chance of success □ *It's a long shot, but I'll have a try.* ⓔ Anglo-Saxon *sceot.*

shot² ▷ *adj* **1** said of a fabric: woven with different-coloured threads in the warp and weft so that movement produces the effect of changing colours □ *shot silk.* **2** streaked with a different colour. **3** ruined; exhausted. ▷ *verb, past tense, past participle of* SHOOT. • **be** or **get shot of someone** or **something** *colloq* be rid of them.

shotgun ▷ *noun* a gun with a long, wide, smooth barrel for firing small shot.

shotgun wedding and **shotgun marriage** ▷ *noun* a marriage into which the couple has been forced, usually because of the woman's pregnancy.

a shot in the arm ▷ *noun, colloq* an uplifting or reviving influence; a boost.

a shot in the dark ▷ *noun* a wild guess.

shot put /— pʊt/ ▷ *noun, athletics* a field event in which a heavy metal ball is thrown from the shoulder as far as possible. • **shot-putter** *noun.*

should /ʃʊd/ ▷ *auxiliary verb* expressing: **1** obligation, duty or recommendation; ought to □ *You should brush your teeth regularly.* **2** likelihood or probability □ *He should have left by now.* **3 a condition** □ *If she should die before you, what would happen?*; **b** *with first person pronouns* the consequence of a condition □ *I should never be able to live with myself if that happened.* **4** *with first person pronouns* a past tense of *shall* in reported speech □ *I told them I should be back soon.* See note at SHALL. **5** statements in clauses with *that*, following expressions of feeling or mood □ *It seems odd that we should both have had the same idea.* **6** *with first person pronouns* doubt or polite indirectness in statements □ *I should imagine he's left* □ *I should think I'll get the job* □ *I should like to thank you all for coming.* **7** *literary* purpose □ *in order that we should not have to leave.* ⓔ Anglo-Saxon *sceolde.*

shoulder /ˈʃoʊldə(r)/ ▷ *noun* **1** in humans and animals: the part on either side of the body, just below the neck, where the arm or forelimb joins the trunk. **2** the part of a garment that covers this. **3** a cut of meat consisting of the animal's upper foreleg. **4** (**shoulders**) the bearer of burdens; the capacity to bear burdens □ *He has a lot of responsibility on his shoulders* □ *have broad shoulders.* **5** any object or part resembling a human shoulder. **6** any curve resembling that between the shoulder and the neck. **7** either edge of a road. ▷ *verb* (***shouldered, shouldering***) **1** to bear (eg a responsibility). **2** to carry on one's shoulders. **3** to thrust with the shoulder. • **give someone the cold shoulder** see under COLD. • **put one's shoulder to the wheel** *colloq* to get down to some hard work; to make a great effort. • **rub shoulders with someone** *colloq* to meet or associate with them. • **shoulder arms** *military* said of soldiers on a parade, etc: to bring the rifle to an upright position close to the right side of the body with the barrel against the shoulder. • **a shoulder to cry on** a person to tell one's troubles to. • **shoulder to shoulder** together in friendship or agreement; side by side. • **(straight) from the shoulder** *colloq* frankly and forcefully. ⓔ Anglo-Saxon *sculdor.*

shoulder bag ▷ *noun* a bag carried by a long strap over the shoulder.

shoulder blade ▷ *noun* the SCAPULA.

shoulder pad ▷ *noun* a pad inserted into the shoulder of a garment to raise and shape it.

shoulder strap ▷ *noun* a strap worn over the shoulder to support a garment or bag.

shouldn't /ˈʃʊdənt/ ▷ *contraction, colloq* should not.

shout ▷ *noun* **1** a loud cry or call. **2** *colloq* a round of drinks. **3** *colloq* a turn to buy a round of drinks. ▷ *verb* (***shouted, shouting***) **1** *tr & intr* (*also* **shout out**) to utter a loud cry or call. **2** *intr* to speak in raised or angry tones. **3** *Austral colloq* to stand drinks all round. • **shouter** *noun*. • **all over bar the shouting** said of a contest, event, etc: as good as over; virtually finished or decided. ◎ 14c as *schoute*, from Norse *skuta* a taunt.

■ **shout at someone** to speak loudly and angrily at them.

■ **shout someone down** to force them to give up speaking, or prevent them from being heard, by means of persistent shouting.

shove /ʃʌv/ ▷ *verb* (***shoved, shoving***) **1** *tr & intr* to push or thrust with force. **2** *colloq* to place or put, especially roughly □ *Just shove it in the bag.* ▷ *noun* a forceful push. • **shover** *noun*. ◎ Anglo-Saxon *scufan*.

■ **shove off** *colloq* to go away

■ **shove something off** to start a boat moving by pushing against the shore or jetty.

shove-halfpenny ▷ *noun* a game, similar to shovelboard, where coins or discs are driven along by the hand towards scoring lines.

shovel /ˈʃʌvəl/ ▷ *noun* **1** a tool with a deep-sided spade-like blade and a handle, for lifting and carrying loose material. **2** a machine, machine part or device with a scooping action. **3** a scoop; a shovelful. ▷ *verb* (***shovelled, shovelling***) **1** to lift or carry with, or as if with, a shovel. **2** to rapidly and crudely gather in large quantities □ *She shovelled food into her mouth.* ◎ Anglo-Saxon *scofl*, from *scufan* to SHOVE.

shovelboard and **shuffleboard** ▷ *noun* **1** an old game in which a coin or other disc was driven along a smooth table by the hand. **2** a modern development of this game played in N America. **3** a game, formerly played on board a ship, with wooden discs and cues. ◎ 16c.

shovelful ▷ *noun* (***shovelfuls***) the amount a shovel can hold.

shoveller or **shoveler** /ˈʃʌvələ(r)/ ▷ *noun* **1** someone or something that shovels. **2** *zool* a duck with a long rounded spade-like bill that inhabits marshes and muddy shallows. ◎ 14c.

show /ʃoʊ/ ▷ *verb* (*past tense* ***showed***, *past participle* ***shown*** or ***showed***, *present participle* ***showing***) **1** *tr & intr* to make or become visible, known or noticeable □ *Does my embarrassment show?* **2** to present to view. **3** to display or exhibit. **4** to prove, indicate or reveal □ *This shows us that man evolved from the ape.* **5** to prove oneself or itself to be □ *He always shows himself to be such a gentleman.* **6** to teach by demonstrating □ *She showed me how to draw.* **7** to lead, guide or escort □ *I'll show you to the door.* **8** to give □ *Show him some respect.* **9** to represent or manifest □ *The exam results show a marked improvement.* **10** *intr* said of a cinema film, theatre production, etc: to be part of a current programme □ *Rob Roy is now showing at the local Odeon.* **11** *intr, slang* to appear or arrive □ *What time did he show?* ▷ *noun* **1** an act of showing. **2** any form of entertainment or spectacle. **3** an exhibition. **4** a pretence □ *a show of friendship.* **5** a sign or indication □ *The slightest show of emotion made him uncomfortable.* **6** a display of true feeling. **7** *colloq* proceedings; affair. **8** *old use, colloq* effort; attempt □ *jolly good show.* **9** *medicine* in childbirth: a small discharge of blood and mucus at the start of labour. • **for show** for the sake of outward appearances; for effect. • **give the show away** to let out or reveal a secret. • **have something** or **nothing to show** have, or not have, a reward or benefit for one's efforts. • **on show** on display; available to be seen. • **run the show** *colloq* to be in charge; to take over or dominate. • **a show of hands** a vote carried out by raising hands. • **steal the show** see under STEAL. ◎ Anglo-Saxon *sceawian* to look.

■ **show someone in**, **out**, **over**, **round**, **up**, *etc* to usher or conduct them.

■ **show off 1** to display oneself or one's talents precociously, aimed at inviting attention or admiration. **2** to behave in an ostentatious manner. See also SHOW-OFF.

■ **show something off 1** to display it proudly, inviting admiration. **2** to display it to good effect □ *The cream rug shows off the red carpet nicely.*

■ **show up 1** *colloq* to arrive; to turn up. **2** to be clearly visible.

■ **show someone up** to embarrass or humiliate them in public.

■ **show something up** to make it appear inadequate or inferior by comparison.

show-and-tell ▷ *noun, US* an education exercise in which a pupil brings in an article to school and then talks about it to the rest of the class.

showbiz /ˈʃoʊbɪz/ ▷ *noun* ▷ *adj, colloq* show business.

showboat ▷ *noun* a river boat, usually a paddle-steamer, serving as a travelling theatre.

showbread see SHEWBREAD

show business ▷ *noun* the entertainment industry, especially light entertainment in film, theatre and television. Also *as adj* □ *his show-business friends.*

showcase ▷ *noun* **1** a glass case for displaying objects, especially in a museum or shop. **2** any setting in which someone or something is displayed to good advantage.

showdown ▷ *noun, colloq* a confrontation or fight by which a long-term dispute may be finally settled.

showed *past tense, past participle of* SHOW

shower /ˈʃaʊə(r)/ ▷ *noun* **1** a sudden but short and usually light fall of rain, snow or hail. **2** a fall of drops of any liquid. **3** a sudden (especially heavy) burst or fall □ *a shower of bullets* □ *a shower of abuse.* **4** *N Amer* **a** an abundance or accession of wedding gifts, gifts for a baby, etc; **b** *N Amer* a party at which such gifts are presented. **5** a device that produces a spray of water for bathing under, usually while standing. **6** a room or cubicle fitted with such a device or devices. **7** an act or an instance of bathing under such a device. **8** *physics* a large number of fast particles that arise from a high-energy particle. **9** *slang* a detestable or worthless person or group of people. ▷ *verb* (***showered, showering***) **1** *tr & intr* to cover, bestow, fall or come abundantly □ *He showers her with gifts* □ *Arrows showered down from the battlements.* **2** *intr* to bathe under a shower. **3** *intr* to rain in showers. • **showery** *adj*. ◎ Anglo-Saxon *scur*.

showgirl ▷ *noun* a girl who performs in variety entertainments, usually as a dancer or singer.

showhouse ▷ *noun* a house, usually on a new housing estate, opens to the public as an example of the builders' work and to stimulate sales.

showier, **showiest**, **showily** and **showiness** see SHOWY

showing ▷ *noun* **1** an act of exhibiting or displaying. **2** a screening of a cinema film. **3** a performance. **4** a display of behaviour as evidence of a fact □ *On this showing, he certainly won't get the job.*

showjumping ▷ *noun* a competitive sport in which riders on horseback take turns to jump a variety of obstacles, usually against the clock. Also *as adj* □ *showjumping event.* • **showjumper** *noun* a horse or rider that takes part in showjumping.

showman ▷ *noun* **1** someone who owns, exhibits or manages a circus, a stall at a fairground, or other entertainment. **2** someone skilled in displaying things, especially personal abilities. • **showmanship** *noun*.

shown *past participle of* SHOW

show-off ▷ *noun, colloq* someone who shows off to attract attention; an exhibitionist. See also SHOW OFF at SHOW.

show of hands ▷ *noun* a vote carried out by raising hands.

showpiece ▷ *noun* **1** an item on display; an exhibit. **2** an item presented as an excellent example of its type, to be copied or admired.

showplace ▷ *noun* **1** a place visited or shown as a sight. **2** a venue for shows and exhibitions.

showroom ▷ *noun* a room where examples of goods for sale, especially large and expensive items, are displayed.

show-stopper ▷ *noun* an act or performance that is very well received by the audience. • **show-stopping** *adj* ▫ *a totally show-stopping performance.*

showy /ˈʃoʊɪ/ ▷ *adj* (*showier*, *showiest*) **1** making an impressive or exciting display. **2** attractively and impressively bright. **3** ostentatious; gaudy; flashy. • **showily** *adverb*. • **showiness** *noun*.

shoyu /ˈʃoʊjuː/ ▷ *noun* a rich soy sauce made from soya beans naturally fermented with wheat or barley, and used as a flavouring in Japanese cookery. ⓒ 18c: Japanese.

shrank *past tense of* SHRINK

shrapnel /ˈʃrapnəl/ ▷ *noun* **1** a shell, filled with pellets or metal fragments, which explodes shortly before impact. **2** flying fragments of the casing of this or any exploding shell. ⓒ Early 19c: named after H Shrapnel (1761–1842), British inventor of the pellet-filled shell.

shred ▷ *noun* **1** a thin scrap or strip cut or ripped off. **2** the smallest piece or amount ▫ *There's not a shred of evidence.* ▷ *verb* (*shredded*, *shredding*) **1** to cut, tear or scrape into shreds. **2** *intr* to reduce to shreds by cutting or ripping. ⓒ Anglo-Saxon *screade*.

shredder /ˈʃrɛdə(r)/ ▷ *noun* a device for shredding eg documents.

shrew /ʃruː/ and **shrewmouse** ▷ *noun* **1** a small nocturnal mammal with velvety fur, small eyes and a pointed snout, that is extremely active and must feed almost continuously on worms, insects, etc in order to survive. **2** a quarrelsome or scolding woman. ⓒ Anglo-Saxon *screawa*.

shrewd /ʃruːd/ ▷ *adj* **1** possessing or showing keen judgement gained from practical experience; astute. **2** wily or crafty; calculating. • **shrewdly** *adverb*. • **shrewdness** *noun*. ⓒ 14c: as *shrewed* malicious, from SHREW.

shrewish /ˈʃruːɪʃ/ ▷ *adj* **1** like a shrew. **2** said of a woman: quarrelsome or scolding; ill-natured.

Shri see SRI

shriek /ʃriːk/ ▷ *verb* (*shrieked*, *shrieking*) *tr & intr* to cry out with a piercing scream. ▷ *noun* such a piercing cry. • **shrieker** *noun*. ⓒ 16c: from Norse *skoekja* to SCREECH.

shrieval /ˈʃriːvəl/ ▷ *adj* referring or relating to a sheriff. ⓒ 17c.

shrievalty /ˈʃriːvəltɪ/ ▷ *noun* (*shrievalties*) the office, term of office or jurisdiction area of a sheriff. ⓒ 16c: from *shrieve* an obsolete variant of SHERIFF.

shrift ▷ *noun* absolution; confession. See also SHORT SHRIFT.

shrike ▷ *noun* any of various small perching birds with a powerful slightly hooked beak, which feed on insects, small birds and rodents, often impaling their prey on thorns, twigs or barbed wire. ⓒ Anglo-Saxon *scric*.

shrill ▷ *adj* said of a voice, sound, etc: high-pitched and piercing. ▷ *verb* (*shrilled*, *shrilling*) to utter in such a high-pitched manner. • **shrilly** *adverb*. • **shrillness** *noun*. ⓒ 14c: from German *schrell*.

shrimp ▷ *noun* **1** any of numerous small aquatic crustaceans with a cylindrical semi-transparent body and five pairs of jointed legs, including several economically important edible species. **2** *colloq* a very small slight person. ▷ *verb* (*shrimped*, *shrimping*) *intr* to fish for shrimps. ⓒ 14c: from German *schrimpen* to shrink.

shrimping ▷ *noun, slang* the practice of sucking a partner's toes for sexual stimulation.

shrimp plant ▷ *noun* a perennial Mexican plant with arching stems, oval leaves and white hooded flowers, almost hidden by overlapping pinkish bracts, so called because its flower spikes superficially resemble a shrimp.

shrine ▷ *noun* **1** a sacred place of worship. **2** the tomb or monument of a saint or other holy person. **3** any place or thing greatly respected because of its associations. **4** a chest or casket containing relics. **5** *RC Church* a ledge or recess in a church for holy icons. ▷ *verb* (*shrined*, *shrining*) to enshrine. ⓒ Anglo-Saxon *scrin*.

shrink ▷ *verb* (*shrank*, *shrunk*, *shrinking*) **1** *tr & intr* to make or become smaller in size or extent, especially through exposure to heat, cold or moisture. **2** *tr & intr* to contract or make something contract. **3** *intr* to shrivel or wither. **4** (*often* **shrink from something**) to move away in horror or disgust; to recoil. **5** (*often* **shrink from something**) to be reluctant do it. **6** *colloq* to SHRINK-WRAP. ▷ *noun* **1** an act of shrinking. **2** *colloq* a psychiatrist. • **shrinkable** *adj*. ⓒ Anglo-Saxon *scrincan*.

shrinkage /ˈʃrɪnkɪdʒ/ ▷ *noun* **1** the act of shrinking. **2** the amount by which something shrinks. **3** in meat marketing: the loss of carcass weight during shipping, preparation for sale, etc. **4** in manufacturing, retail, etc: the loss of goods as a result of pilfering, breakages, etc. ⓒ 18c.

shrinking violet ▷ *noun, colloq* a shy hesitant person.

shrink-wrap ▷ *verb* to wrap (goods) in clear plastic film that is then shrunk, eg by heating, so that it fits tightly.

shrive ▷ *verb* (*past tense* **shrived** or **shrove**, *past participle* **shriven** or **shrived**, *present participle* **shriving**) *RC Church* **1** to hear a confession from and give absolution to someone. **2** to unburden by confession or otherwise. **3** to impose a penance on someone. **4** *intr* to receive or make confession. Compare SHRIFT. ⓒ Anglo-Saxon *scrifan* to write or prescribe penance, from Latin *scribere*.

shrivel /ˈʃrɪvəl/ ▷ *verb* (*shrivelled*, *shrivelling*) *tr & intr* (*also* **shrivel up**) to make or become shrunken and wrinkled, especially as a result of drying out. ⓒ 16c: from Swedish dialect *skryvla* to wrinkle.

shroud ▷ *noun* **1** a garment or cloth in which a corpse is wrapped. **2** anything that obscures, masks or hides ▫ *shrouds of fog.* **3** any protective covering, screen, shelter or shade. **4** (**shrouds**) *naut* a set of taut ropes running from the masthead to a ship's sides to support the mast. ▷ *verb* (*shrouded*, *shrouding*) **1** to wrap in a shroud. **2** to obscure, mask or hide ▫ *proceedings shrouded in secrecy.* **3** to cover or protect. ⓒ Anglo-Saxon *scrud* garment.

Shrovetide ▷ *noun* the three days preceeding Ash Wednesday.

Shrove Tuesday ▷ *noun* in the Christian calendar: the day before Ash Wednesday, on which it was customary to confess one's sins. See also PANCAKE DAY. ⓒ Anglo-Saxon *scrifan* to confess sins.

shrub[1] ▷ *noun, bot* a woody plant or bush, without any main trunk, which branches into several main stems at or just below ground level. ⓒ Anglo-Saxon *scrybb* scrub.

shrub[2] ▷ *noun* **1** a drink of lemon or other sweetened juice with spirits, especially rum. **2** *US* a drink made from raspberry juice with sugar and vinegar. ⓒ 18c: from Arabic *sharab*, from *shurb* drink.

shrubbery /ˈʃrʌbərɪ/ ▻ *noun* (***shrubberies***) **1** a place, especially a part of a garden, where shrubs are grown. **2** a collective name for shrubs. ⓘ 18c.

shrubby /ˈʃrʌbɪ/ ▻ *adj* (***shrubbier***, ***shrubbiest***) **1** having the character of or similar to a shrub. **2** covered with or full of shrubs. • **shrubbiness** *noun*. ⓘ 16c.

shrug ▻ *verb* (***shrugged***, ***shrugging***) *tr & intr* to raise up and drop the shoulders briefly as an indication of doubt, indifference, etc. ▻ *noun* an act of shrugging. ⓘ 14c as *schruggen* to shudder.

▪ **shrug something off 1** to shake off or get rid of it easily. **2** to dismiss (especially criticism) lightly; to be indifferent.

shrunk see under SHRINK

shrunken ▻ *adj* having shrunk or having been shrunk.

shtook or **schtook** or **schtuk** or **shtuk** /ʃtʊk/ ▻ *noun*, *slang* trouble; bother. • **in (dead) shtook**, *etc* in trouble or strife. ⓘ 1930s.

shtoom or **schtoom** or **shtum** or **shtumm** or **stumm** /ʃtʊm/ ▻ *adj*, *slang* silent; quiet. • **keep shtoom**, *etc* to remain silent. ⓘ 1950s: Yiddish, from German *stumm*.

shuck *N Amer* ▻ *noun* a husk, pod or shell. ▻ *verb* (***shucked***, ***shucking***) to remove the shuck from something. ▻ *exclamation*, *colloq* (**shucks**) an expression of disappointment, irritation or embarrassment. ⓘ 17c.

▪ **shuck something off** to remove or shed (clothing).

shudder /ˈʃʌdə(r)/ ▻ *verb* (***shuddered***, ***shuddering***) *intr* to shiver or tremble, especially with fear, cold or disgust. ▻ *noun* **1** such a trembling movement or feeling. **2** a heavy vibration or shaking. • **shuddering** *adj*. • **shudderingly** *adverb*. • **shuddery** *adj*. • **shudder to think something** to be inwardly embarrassed or appalled when imagining or considering (some consequence), etc □ *I shudder to think what he will do next.* ⓘ 14c: from German *schoderen*.

shuffle /ˈʃʌfəl/ ▻ *verb* (***shuffled***, ***shuffling***) **1** *tr & intr* to move or drag (one's feet) with short quick sliding steps; to walk in this fashion. **2** *intr* to shamble or walk awkwardly. **3** to rearrange or mix up roughly or carelessly □ *shuffle papers.* **4** *tr & intr* to jumble up (playing cards) randomly. **5** (*usually* **shuffle out, in, off**, *etc*) to put surreptitiously, evasively, scramblingly or in confusion. **6** to manipulate unfairly and deceptively. ▻ *noun* **1** an act or sound of shuffling. **2** a short quick sliding of the feet in dancing. • **shuffler** *noun*. ⓘ 16c: from German *schuffeln*.

▪ **shuffle something off** to throw or thrust it aside; to wriggle out of it □ *shuffle off problems.*

shuffleboard see SHOVELBOARD

shufti or **shufty** /ˈʃʊftɪ, ˈʃʌftɪ/ ▻ *noun*, *colloq* a look or glance. ⓘ 1940s: Arabic, literally meaning 'have you seen?', from *shaffa* to see.

shun ▻ *verb* (***shunned***, ***shunning***) to intentionally avoid or keep away from someone or something. ⓘ Anglo-Saxon *scunian*.

shunt ▻ *verb* (***shunted***, ***shunting***) **1** to move (a train or carriage) from one track to another. **2** *tr & intr* to turn or move aside. **3** to bypass or sidetrack. **4** to get rid of or transfer (eg a task) on to someone else, as an evasion. **5** *colloq* to crash (a car), especially one in the back of another. **6** *electronics* to divert or be diverted by means of a shunt. ▻ *noun* **1** an act of shunting or being shunted. **2** *electronics* a conductor diverting part of an electric current. **3** a railway siding. **4** *colloq* a minor collision between vehicles. • **shunter** *noun*. ⓘ 13c.

shush /ʃʊʃ, ʃʌʃ/ ▻ *exclamation* be quiet! ▻ *verb* (***shushes***, ***shushed***, ***shushing***) to make someone or something quiet by, or as if by, saying 'Shush!'.

shut ▻ *verb* (***shut***, ***shutting***) **1** *tr & intr* to place or move so as to close an opening □ *shut the door.* **2** *tr & intr* to close or make something close over, denying access to the contents or inside □ *shut the cupboard* □ *shut the book.* **3** *tr & intr* (*often* **shut up**) not to allow access to something; to forbid entrance into it □ *shut up the building* □ *The office shuts at weekends.* **4** to fasten or bar; to lock. **5** to bring together the parts or outer parts of something □ *Shut your eyes* □ *I can't shut the clasp.* **6** to confine □ *He shuts himself in his room for hours.* **7** to catch or pinch in a fastening □ *I shut my finger in the window.* **8** to end or terminate the operations of (a business, etc). **9** *intr* said of a business, etc: to cease to operate; to terminate. ▻ *adj* **1** not open; closed. **2** made fast; secure. • **shut it** *slang* to be quiet. ⓘ Anglo-Saxon *scyttan* to bar.

▪ **shut someone away** to isolate or confine them □ *He shuts himself away in his study day and night.*

▪ **shut something away** to keep it hidden or concealed □ *All the valuables are shut away in the attic.*

▪ **shut down** or **shut something down** to stop or make it stop working or operating, either for a time or permanently. See also SHUTDOWN.

▪ **shut someone** or **something in** to enclose or confine them or it □ *Remember to shut the cat in tonight.*

▪ **shut something off** to switch it off; to stop the flow of it. See also SHUT-OFF.

▪ **shut someone** or **something out 1** to prevent them or it entering a room, building, etc. **2** to exclude them or it. **3** to block out (eg light).

▪ **shut up** *colloq* to stop speaking.

▪ **shut someone up 1** *colloq* to make them stop speaking; to reduce them to silence. **2** to confine them.

▪ **shut something up** to close and lock (premises), either for a time or permanently □ *shut up shop.*

shutdown ▻ *noun* **1** a temporary closing of a factory or business. **2** a reduction of power to its minimum in a nuclear reactor, especially as a safety or emergency measure. See also SHUT DOWN at SHUT.

shuteye ▻ *noun*, *colloq* sleep.

shut-in ▻ *noun*, *US* an invalid or disabled person confined to his or her house.

shut-off ▻ *noun* a device that switches off the flow or operation of something; a stoppage. See also SHUT SOMETHING OFF at SHUT.

shut-out ▻ *adj* **1** excluded; remote. **2** *bridge* said of a bid: intended to deter the opposition from bidding.

shutter /ˈʃʌtə(r)/ ▻ *noun* **1** someone or something that shuts. **2** a movable internal or external cover for a window, especially one of a pair of hinged wooden or metal panels. **3** a device in a camera that regulates the opening and closing of the aperture, exposing the film to light. ▻ *verb* (***shuttered***, ***shuttering***) to fit or cover (a window) with a shutter or shutters. • **put up the shutters** *colloq* to stop trading, either for the day or permanently. ⓘ 16c: from SHUT.

shuttle /ˈʃʌtəl/ ▻ *noun* **1** *weaving* the device that carries the horizontal thread (the WEFT) backwards and forwards between the vertical threads (the WARP). **2** the device that carries the lower thread through the loop formed by the upper in a sewing-machine. **3** anything that makes a similar movement. **4** a rapid backwards-and-forwards movement between two points. **5** an aircraft, train or bus that runs a frequent service between two places, usually at a relatively short distance from one another. **6** a shuttlecock. ▻ *verb* (***shuttled***, ***shuttling***) *tr & intr* **1** to move or make someone or something move backwards and forwards. **2** to move regularly between two points. ⓘ Anglo-Saxon *scytel* dart.

shuttlecock /ˈʃʌtəlkɒk/ ▻ *noun* **1** a cone of feathers or of feathered plastic attached to a rounded cork, hit backwards and forwards with battledores or badminton racquets. **2** anything that is tossed backwards and forwards. ⓘ 16c.

shwa see SCHWA

shy¹ ▻ *adj* (***shyer, shyest***) **1** said of a person: embarrassed or unnerved by the company or attention of others. **2** easily scared; bashful or timid. **3** (**shy of something**) wary or distrustful of it. **4** warily reluctant. **5** especially in poker: short of or lacking funds. **6** *colloq* short in payment by a specified amount □ *10p shy.* ▻ *verb* (***shies, shied, shying***) *intr* said eg of a horse: to jump suddenly aside or back in fear; to be startled. ▻ *noun* (***shies***) an act of shying. • **shyly** *adverb.* • **shyness** *noun.* ⓘ Anglo-Saxon *sceoh* timid.

■ **shy away** or **off** to shrink from something or recoil, showing reluctance □ *He shied away from arguing with them* □ *I shy away from any sign of trouble.*

shy² ▻ *verb* (***shies, shied, shying***) to fling or throw. ▻ *noun* (***shies***) **1** a fling or throw. **2** *colloq* a gibe or taunt. **3** *colloq* an attempt or shot. **4** a COCONUT SHY. **5** *football* a THROW-IN.

Shylock /ˈʃaɪlɒk/ ▻ *noun* a ruthless creditor; a greedy grasping person. ⓘ 18c: named after Shylock, such a character from Shakespeare's play *The Merchant of Venice.*

shyster /ˈʃaɪstə(r)/ ▻ *noun, N Amer, especially US slang* **1** an unscrupulous or disreputable lawyer. **2** an unscrupulous or disreputable person in any business. ⓘ 19c: probably named after Scheuster, a disreputable US lawyer.

SI and **SI unit** ▻ *abbreviation* Système International d'Unités, the modern scientific system of units, used in the measurement of all physical quantities.

Si ▻ *symbol, chem* silicon.

si see TI

sial /ˈsaɪal, ˈsaɪəl/ ▻ *noun, geol* the granite rocks, rich in silica and aluminium, that form the upper layer of the Earth's crust. See also SIMA. ⓘ 1920s: from *si*lica and *al*umina).

siamang /ˈsɪəmaŋ, ˈsjɑːmaŋ/ ▻ *noun* a large black gibbon, native to Sumatra and the Malay Peninsula. ⓘ 19c: Malay.

Siamese /saɪəˈmiːz/ ▻ *adj* belonging or relating to Siam, a country in SE Asia, now called Thailand, its inhabitants, or their language. ▻ *noun* **1** (*plural* ***Siamese***) a citizen or inhabitant of, or person born in, Siam. **2** the official language of Siam. **3** (*plural* ***Siameses***) a Siamese cat.

Siamese cat ▻ *noun* any of numerous kinds of a short-haired variety of domestic cat with a triangular face, blue eyes, and a pale coat with darker patches on the ears, face, legs and tail.

Siamese twins ▻ *noun* **1** twins who are physically joined to each other from birth. **2** any two people always together.

SIB ▻ *abbreviation* Security and Investments Board.

sibilant /ˈsɪbɪlənt/ ▻ *adj* similar to, having or pronounced with a hissing sound. ▻ *noun, phonetics* a consonant with such a sound, eg *s* and *z*. • **sibilance** or **sibilancy** *noun.* ⓘ 17c: from Latin *sibilare* to hiss.

sibilate /ˈsɪbɪleɪt/ ▻ *verb* (***sibilated, sibilating***) *tr & intr* to produce or pronounce (words) with a hissing sound. • **sibilation** *noun.* ⓘ 17c.

sibling /ˈsɪblɪŋ/ ▻ *noun* a blood relation; a brother or sister. Also *as adj* □ *sibling rivalry.* ⓘ Anglo-Saxon *sibb* relationship + -LING.

Sibyl /ˈsɪbɪl/ ▻ *noun, mythol* any of several prophetesses of ancient Rome, Greece, Babylonia, Egypt, etc. ⓘ 13c: from Greek *Sybilla.*

Sibylline Books ▻ *noun, Roman hist* prophetic books supposedly produced by the Sibyl of the Greek colony of Cumae in Italy.

sic /sɪk, siːk/ ▻ *adverb* a term used in brackets after a word or phrase in a quotation to indicate that it is quoted accurately, even if it appears to be a mistake. ⓘ 19c: Latin, meaning 'thus' or 'so'.

siccative /ˈsɪkətɪv/ ▻ *adj* drying. ▻ *noun* a drying agent. ⓘ 16c: from Latin *siccativus,* from *siccare* to dry.

sick ▻ *adj* **1** vomiting; feeling the need to vomit. **2** ill; unwell. **3** referring or relating to ill health □ *sick pay.* **4** (*often* **sick for someone** or **something**) pining or longing for them or it. **5** (*often* **sick at** or **of someone** or **something**) extremely annoyed; disgusted □ *I'm sick of your attitude.* **6** (*often* **sick of someone** or **something**) thoroughly weary or fed up with them or it. **7** mentally deranged. **8** said of humour, comedy, jokes, etc: exploiting gruesome and morbid subjects in an unpleasant way. **9** *colloq* inadequate in comparison □ *makes my effort look a bit sick.* **10** out of working order. ▻ *noun, colloq* vomit. ▻ *verb* (***sicked, sicking***) *tr & intr* (*usually* **sick up**) to vomit. • **make someone sick** *colloq* to disgust or upset them □ *It makes me sick to think that no one offered to help.* • **sick and tired, sick of the sight** or **sick to death of someone** or **something** to be extremely weary of them. • **sick as a dog** *colloq* vomiting excessively and unrestrainedly. • **sick as a parrot** *colloq* extremely disappointed. • **sick to one's stomach 1** nauseated; about to vomit. **2** upset; disgusted. ⓘ Anglo-Saxon *seoc.*

sick bay ▻ *noun* **1** a compartment on board a ship for sick and wounded people. **2** any room where ill or injured people are treated, especially in a place of work.

sickbed ▻ *noun* a bed on which someone lies when sick.

sick benefit and **sickness benefit** ▻ *noun* a benefit paid to someone who is unable to work due to illness.

sick building syndrome ▻ *noun, medicine* a disorder first diagnosed among office workers in the 1980s, typical symptoms including headache, fatigue and sore throat, and thought to be caused by inadequate ventilation.

SI Units

Name of unit	Abbreviation of unit name	Physical quantity	Symbol
metre	m	length	*l*
kilogram	kg	mass	*m*
second	s	time	*t*
ampere	A	electric current	*I*
kelvin	K	thermodynamic temperature	*T*
candela	cd	luminous intensity	*I*
mole	mol	amount of substance	
radian	rad	plane angle	*α, β, θ*, etc
steradian	sr	solid angle	*Ω, ω*

sicken /ˈsɪkən/ ▷ *verb* (***sickened***, ***sickening***) **1** to make someone or something feel like vomiting. **2** to annoy greatly or disgust. ⓒ 12c: from SICK.

■ **sicken for something** to show symptoms of an illness □ *I'm sickening for the flu.*

sickening /ˈsɪkənɪŋ/ ▷ *adj* **1** causing nausea. **2** causing extreme annoyance or disgust. ● **sickeningly** *adverb*. ⓒ 18c.

sick headache ▷ *noun* a MIGRAINE.

sickie /ˈsɪkɪ/ ▷ *noun* (***sickies***) **1** *originally Austral & NZ colloq* a day's sick leave, often without the person actually being ill. **2** *N Amer* a sick person, either mentally or physically. ⓒ 1950s.

sickle /ˈsɪkəl/ ▷ *noun* a tool with a short handle and a curved blade for cutting grain crops with a horizontal sweeping action. ⓒ Anglo-Saxon *sicol*.

sick leave ▷ *noun* time taken off work as a result of sickness.

sicklebill ▷ *noun* a bird with a sickle-shaped bill, such as a species of bird of paradise, a species of hummingbird, etc.

sickle-cell anaemia ▷ *noun, pathol* a hereditary blood disorder, common in African peoples, in which the red blood cells contain an abnormal type of haemoglobin, become sickle-shaped and fragile, and are rapidly removed from the circulation, resulting in anaemia.

sick list ▷ *noun* a list of sick employees, pupils, soldiers, etc. ● **sick-listed** *adj* included on a sick list.

sickly ▷ *adj* (***sicklier***, ***sickliest***) **1** susceptible or prone to illness; ailing or feeble. **2** suggestive of illness. **3** inducing the desire to vomit □ *a sickly smell.* **4** unhealthy-looking; pallid □ *a sickly plant* □ *a sickly child.* **5** weakly sentimental; mawkish. ▷ *adverb* to an extent that suggests illness □ *sickly pale.* ● **sickliness** *noun*. ⓒ 14c.

sickness ▷ *noun* **1** the condition of being ill; an illness. **2** vomiting. **3** nausea.

sick pay ▷ *noun* the payments made to a worker while off sick.

sidalcea /sɪˈdalsɪə/ ▷ *noun* a herbaceous perennial plant of the mallow family with tall spikes of white, pink or purple flowers. ⓒ 19c: from Greek *side* a type of plant + *alkea* mallow.

side ▷ *noun* **1** any of the usually flat or flattish surfaces that form the outer extent of something; any of these surfaces other than the front, back, top or bottom. **2** an edge or border, or the area adjoining this □ *My car's at the side of the road.* **3** either of the parts or areas produced when the whole is divided up the middle □ *I'll take the left side of the room.* **4** the part of the body between the armpit and hip □ *He's paralysed down his left side.* **5** the area of space next to someone or something □ *He's round the side of the house* □ *He stayed by my side the whole evening.* **6** half of a carcass divided along the medial plane □ *a side of beef.* **7** either of the broad surfaces of a flat or flattish object □ *two sides of a coin.* **8** any of the lines forming a geometric figure. **9** any of the groups or teams, or opposing positions, in a conflict or competition. **10** an aspect □ *We've seen a different side to him.* **11** the slope of a hill. **12** the wall of a vessel, container or cavity. **13** a part of an area of land; district □ *I live in the north side of the town.* **14** the father's or mother's family or ancestors □ *She's related to him on her mother's side.* **15** a page □ *My essay covered 5 sides.* **16** *Brit colloq* television channel. **17** either of the two playing surfaces of a record or cassette. **18** in billiards, snooker, etc: spin given to a ball causing it to swerve and regulating its angle of rebound. Also called **sidespin**. **19** *slang* a pretentious or superior air. ▷ *adj* **1** located at the side □ *side entrance.* **2** subsidiary or subordinate □ *side road.* ▷ *verb* (***sided***, ***siding***) (*usually* **side with someone**) to take on their position or point of view; to join forces with them. ● **sided** /ˈsaɪdɪd/ *adj, in compounds* having a specified number of sides □ *one-sided argument* □ *a three-sided shape.* ● **bit on the side** see separate entry. ● **choose sides** to select teams. ● **let the side down** to fail one's colleagues or associates, or frustrate their efforts, by falling below their standards. ● **on** or **to one side** removed to a position away from the main concern; put aside. ● **on the side** in addition to or apart from ordinary occupation or income, often dishonest or illegal. ● **on the … side** *colloq* rather …; of a … nature □ *I found his comments a bit on the offensive side* □ *I thought his speech was a bit on the long side.* ● **put on side** to assume or take on pretentious airs. ● **side by side 1** close together. **2** with sides touching. ● **take sides** to support one particular side in a conflict, argument or dispute. ● **this side of …** between here or now and …; short of … □ *I doubt I'll see him this side of Tuesday.* ⓒ Anglo-Saxon.

sidearm ▷ *noun* (*usually* **sidearms**) a weapon worn at the side or in a belt.

sideband ▷ *noun, radio* a band of frequencies slightly above or below the carrier frequency, containing additional frequencies constituting the information to be conveyed, introduced by modulation.

sideboard ▷ *noun* **1** a large piece of furniture, often consisting of shelves or cabinets mounted above drawers or cupboards, for holding plates, ornaments, etc. **2** (**sideboards**) SIDEBURNS.

sideburn ▷ *noun* (*usually* **sideburns**) the lines of short hair growing down in front of each of a man's ears. Also called **side whiskers**. ⓒ 19c: a modification of the more extensive growth pioneered by General Burnside (1824–81) of America.

sidecar ▷ *noun* a small carriage for one or two passengers, attached to the side of a motorcycle.

side chain ▷ *noun, chem* a group of atoms attached to one or more of the locations in a CYCLIC OR HETEROCYCLIC compound.

sided see under SIDE

side dish ▷ *noun* a supplementary dish.

side drum ▷ *noun* a small double-headed drum with snares, usually slung from the drummer's side.

side effect ▷ *noun* **1** an additional and usually undesirable effect, especially of a drug, eg nausea, drowsiness. **2** any undesired additional effect.

sidekick ▷ *noun, colloq* a close or special friend; a partner or deputy.

sidelight ▷ *noun* **1** a small light fitted on the front and rear of a motor vehicle, used in fading daylight. **2** a light on each side of a moving boat or ship, one red light on the left side and a green one on the right. **3** light coming from the side. **4** a window above or at the side of a door. **5** any incidental illustration.

sideline ▷ *noun* **1** a line marking either side boundary of a sports pitch. **2** (**sidelines**) the areas just outside these boundaries. **3** (**sidelines**) the area to which spectators and non-participants in any activity are confined. **4** a business, occupation or trade in addition to regular work. ▷ *verb* **1** *sport* to remove or suspend (a player) from a team. **2** to demote or suspend from normal activity.

sidelong ▷ *adj* ▷ *adverb* from or to one side; not direct or directly □ *a sidelong glance.*

sidereal /saɪˈdɪərɪəl/ ▷ *adj* referring or relating to, or determined by the stars. ⓒ 17c: from Latin *sidus, sideris* star.

sidereal day ▷ *noun, astron* the time the Earth takes to make a revolution on its axis, relative to a particular star.

sidereal month ▷ *noun, astron* the time in which the Moon passes round the ECLIPTIC to the same point among the stars.

sidereal time ▷ *noun, astron* time measured with reference to the fixed stars.

sidereal year ▻ *noun, astron* the period required by the Sun to move from a given star to the same star again, having a mean value of 365 days, 6 hours, 9 minutes and 9.6 seconds.

siderite /ˈsɪdəraɪt/ ▻ *noun* **1** a meteorite consisting mainly of metallic iron. **2** *geol* a brown, grey, greenish or yellowish mineral form of ferrous carbonate (formula **$FeCO_3$**) that is an important ore of iron. ⓘ 16c: from Greek *sideros* iron.

side-road ▻ *noun* a BYROAD, especially one joining onto a main road.

siderosis /sɪdəˈroʊsɪs/ ▻ *noun, pathol* a lung disease caused by breathing in iron or other metal fragments. ⓘ 19c: from Greek *sideros* iron + -OSIS.

siderostat /ˈsɪdəroʊstat/ ▻ *noun* an astronomical device consisting of a mirror, or a telescope with a mirror, for reflecting the rays from a star in a constant direction. ⓘ 1870s.

side-saddle ▻ *noun* a horse's saddle designed to enable a woman in a skirt to sit with both legs on the same side. ▻ *adverb* sitting in this way.

sideshow ▻ *noun* **1** an exhibition or show subordinate to a larger one. **2** any subordinate or incidental activity or event.

sideslip ▻ *noun* **1** a skid, especially by a road vehicle. **2** a deliberate lateral movement of an aircraft. **3** *skiing* a side-on downward slide.

sidesman ▻ *noun* a deputy churchwarden.

side-splitting ▻ *adj* extremely funny; provoking uproarious and hysterical laughter.

sidestep ▻ *verb* **1** to avoid by, or as if by, stepping aside □ *You're sidestepping the issue.* **2** *intr* to step aside. ▻ *noun* a step taken to one side.

side street ▻ *noun* a minor street, especially one leading from a main street.

sideswipe ▻ *noun* **1** a blow coming from the side, as opposed to head-on. **2** a criticism or rebuke made in passing, incidentally to the main discussion.

sidetrack ▻ *verb* to divert the attention of away from the matter in hand.

sidewalk ▻ *noun, N Amer, especially US* a pavement.

sidewall ▻ *noun* the side section of a pneumatic tyre, between the tread and wheel rim.

sideways ▻ *adverb, adj* **1** from, to or towards one side. **2** with one side foremost □ *We skidded sideways into the hedge.*

side whiskers ▻ *noun* SIDEBURNS.

sidewinder /ˈsaɪdwaɪndə(r)/ ▻ *noun* **1** any snake which moves rapidly over soft sand by repeatedly winding its body forwards and sideways. **2** the N American horned rattlesnake, which usually moves by this method. **3** *US* a hard blow from the side.

siding /ˈsaɪdɪŋ/ ▻ *noun* a short dead-end railway line onto which trains, wagons, etc can be shunted temporarily from the main line.

sidle /ˈsaɪdəl/ ▻ *verb* (***sidled, sidling***) *intr* to go or edge along sideways, especially in a cautious, furtive and ingratiating manner. ⓘ 17c: a back-formation from obsolete *sideling* sideways.

SIDS ▻ *abbreviation* sudden infant death syndrome.

siege /siːdʒ/ ▻ *noun* **1** the act or process of surrounding a fort or town with troops, cutting off its supplies and subjecting it to persistent attack with the intention of forcing its surrender. **2** a police operation using similar tactics, eg to force a criminal out of a building. • **lay siege to a place** to subject it to a siege. ⓘ 13c: from French *sege*, from Latin *sedes* seat.

siemens /ˈsiːmənz/ ▻ *noun* (abbreviation **S**) the SI unit of conductance, equal to the conductance at which a potential of one volt produces a current of one ampere. ⓘ 1930s: named after Werner von Siemens (1816–92), German electrical engineer.

sienna /sɪˈɛnə/ ▻ *noun* **1** a pigment obtained from a type of earth with a high clay and iron content. **2** the yellowish-brown colour of this pigment in its original state (also called **raw sienna**). **3** the reddish-brown colour of this pigment when roasted (also called **burnt sienna**). ⓘ 18c: named after Siena in Italy.

sierra /sɪˈɛrə/ ▻ *noun* (***sierras***) especially in Spanish-speaking countries and the US: a mountain range, especially when jagged. ⓘ 17c: Spanish, meaning 'a saw'.

siesta /sɪˈɛstə/ ▻ *noun* (***siestas***) in hot countries: a sleep or rest after the midday meal. ⓘ 17c: Spanish, from Latin *sexta (hora)* sixth (hour).

sieve /sɪv/ ▻ *noun* a utensil with a meshed or perforated bottom, used for straining solids from liquids or for sifting large particles from smaller ones. ▻ *verb* (***sieved, sieving***) to strain or sift with a sieve. • **have a head** or **memory like a sieve** to be habitually forgetful. ⓘ Anglo-Saxon *sife*.

sievert /ˈsiːvət/ ▻ *noun, physics* (abbreviation **Sv**) the SI unit of radioaction DOSE equivalent, equal to the absorbed dose multiplied by its relative biological effectiveness, used in radiation safety measurements. ⓘ Early 20c: named after R M Sievert (1896–1966), the Swedish physicist.

sieve tube ▻ *noun, bot* in the phloem tissue of a flowering plant: any of the tubular columns, composed of long cells joined end to end, through which organic compounds manufactured in the leaves by photosynthesis are transported to the rest of the plant.

sift ▻ *verb* (***sifted, sifting***) **1** to pass through a sieve in order to separate out lumps or larger particles. **2** to separate out by, or as if by, passing through a sieve. **3** *intr* to use a sieve. **4** to examine closely and discriminatingly. • **sifter** *noun*. ⓘ Anglo-Saxon *siftan*, from *sife* sieve.

■ **sift through something** **1** to examine it closely by sifting. **2** to search among it.

sigh /saɪ/ ▻ *verb* (***sighed, sighing***) **1** *intr* to release a long deep audible breath, expressive of sadness, longing, tiredness or relief. **2** *intr* to make a similar sound, especially suggesting breakdown or failure □ *We heard the engine sigh.* **3** to express with such a sound. **4** (*often* **sigh for someone** or **something**) *literary* to regret, grieve over or yearn for them. ▻ *noun* an act or the sound of sighing. ⓘ Anglo-Saxon *sican*.

sight /saɪt/ ▻ *noun* **1** the power or faculty of seeing; vision. **2** a thing or object seen; view or spectacle □ *It's a lovely sight.* **3** someone's field of view or vision, or the opportunity to see things that this provides □ *within sight* □ *out of sight.* **4** (*usually* **sights**) places, buildings, etc that are particularly interesting or worth seeing □ *see the sights of the city.* **5** a device on a firearm through or along which one looks to take aim. **6** a similar device used as a guide to the eye on an optical or other instrument. **7** opinion or judgement; estimation □ *In his sight he was just a failure.* **8** *colloq* a person or thing unpleasant to look at □ *He looked a sight without his teeth in.* ▻ *verb* (***sighted, sighting***) **1** to get a look at or glimpse of someone or something □ *She was sighted there at around midnight.* **2** to adjust the sight of (a firearm). **3** to aim (a firearm) using the sight. • **a sight** *colloq* very many; a great deal □ *She may not be good, but she's a sight better than you!* • **a sight for sore eyes** a very welcome sight. • **a sight more** *colloq* a great deal or great many more □ *A sight more people than expected turned up.* • **at** or **on sight** **1** as soon as seen. **2** without previous view or study. • **catch sight of someone** or **something** to catch or get a glimpse of them or it. • **know someone** or **something by sight** to recognize them only by their appearance; to know who they are. • **lose sight of something** or **someone** **1** to no longer be able to see them or it. **2** to fail to keep them in mind; to lose touch with them. ● **set one's sights on something** to decide on it as an ambition or aim. ● **sight unseen** without seeing or having seen the object in question beforehand □ *I'd never buy a house sight unseen.* ⓒ Anglo-Saxon *sihth.*

sighted /ˈsaɪtɪd/ ▷ *adj* **1** having the power of sight; not blind. **2** *often in compounds* having a specified level of sight □ *partially sighted* □ *long-sighted.*

sightless /ˈsaɪtləs/ ▷ *adj* blind. ● **sightlessly** *adverb.* ● **sightlessness** *noun.*

sightly /ˈsaɪtlɪ/ ▷ *adj* pleasing to the eye; attractive or appealing. ● **sightliness** *noun.*

sight-reading ▷ *noun* playing or singing from printed music that one has not previously seen. ● **sight-read** *verb.*

sight-screen ▷ *noun, cricket* any of a set of large white movable screens at either end of a cricket ground that provide a background against which the batsman can see the ball clearly.

sightsee ▷ *verb, intr* to visit places of interest, especially as a tourist. ● **sightseer** *noun.* ● **sightseeing** *noun.*

sigillography /sɪdʒɪˈlɒgrəfɪ/ ▷ *noun* the study of seals used on documents, etc as a sign of authenticity, particularly useful in historical studies as a means of identifying, dating and validating documents. ⓒ 19c: from Latin *sigillum,* diminutive of *signum* sign + -GRAPHY.

sigla /ˈsɪglə/ ▷ *plural noun* abbreviations, symbols and signs, as used in manuscripts, seals, documents, etc. ⓒ 18c: Latin.

sigma /ˈsɪgmə/ ▷ *noun* (***sigmas***) the eighteenth letter of the Greek alphabet. See table at GREEK ALPHABET.

sign /saɪn/ ▷ *noun* **1** a printed mark with a meaning; a symbol □ *a multiplication sign.* **2** *math* an indication of positive or negative value □ *the minus sign.* **3** a gesture expressing a meaning; a signal. **4** an indication □ *signs of improvement.* **5** a portent or omen; a miraculous token. **6** a board or panel displaying information for public view. **7** a board or panel displaying a shopkeeper's name, trade, etc. **8** a device or symbol indicating an inn, shop, etc, instead of a street number. **9** *medicine* any external evidence or indication of disease, perceptible to an examining doctor, etc. **10** a trail or track of a wild animal, perceptible to a tracker. **11** *astrol* any of the twelve parts of the zodiac, bearing the name of, but not coincident with, a constellation. See table at ZODIAC. ▷ *verb* (***signed, signing***) **1** *tr & intr* to give a signal or indication. **2** to write a signature on something; to confirm one's assent to something with a signature. **3** to write (one's name) as a signature □ *sign a cheque.* **4** *tr & intr* to employ or become employed with the signing of a contract □ *Stoke City have signed a new player* □ *Rush has signed for another team.* **5** *tr & intr* to communicate using sign language. **6** to cross or make the sign of the cross over (oneself or someone else). See also SIGN OF THE CROSS. ● **signer** *noun.* ⓒ 13c: from French *signe,* from Latin *signum.*

■ **sign something away** to give it away or transfer it by signing a legally binding document.

■ **sign in** or **out** to record one's arrival or departure, eg at work, by signing one's name.

■ **sign someone in** to allow someone, usually a non-member, official entry to enter a club, society, etc by signing one's name.

■ **sign off 1** to bring a broadcast to an end. **2** to remove oneself from the register of unemployed people. **3** to stop work, etc. **4** *bridge* to indicate that one does not intend to bid further.

■ **sign someone off** to dismiss them from employment.

■ **sign on** *colloq* **1** to register as unemployed. **2** to return fortnightly to an unemployment office to sign one's name as a formal declaration that one is still unemployed.

■ **sign someone on** to engage them, eg for work.

■ **sign up 1** to enrol with an organization, especially the army. **2** to enrol for a task, outing, etc by signing a list. **3** to engage oneself for work by signing a contract.

■ **sign someone up** to engage them for work by signing a contract.

signal /ˈsɪgnəl/ ▷ *noun* **1** a message in the form of a gesture, light, sound, etc, conveying information or indicating the time for action, often over a distance. **2** (**signals**) the apparatus used to send such a message, eg coloured lights or movable arms or poles on a railway network. **3** an event marking the moment for action to be taken □ *Their arrival was a signal for the party to begin.* **4** any set of transmitted electrical impulses received as a sound or image, eg in television; the message conveyed by them. **5** *cards* a piece of play intended to convey information to one's partner. ▷ *verb* (***signalled, signalling***) **1** *tr & intr* to transmit or convey (a message) using signals. **2** to indicate. ▷ *adj* notable □ *a signal triumph.* ⓒ 14c: French, from Latin *signum.*

signal-box ▷ *noun* the cabin from which signals on a railway line are controlled.

signalize or **signalise** /ˈsɪgnəlaɪz/ ▷ *verb* (***signalized, signalizing***) to mark or distinguish; to make notable. ⓒ 17c.

signally /ˈsɪgnəlɪ/ ▷ *adverb* notably.

signalman ▷ *noun* a controller who works railway signals.

signal-to-noise ratio ▷ *noun, electronics* the ratio of the power of a desired electrical signal to the power of the unwanted background signal or noise, usually expressed in decibels.

signatory /ˈsɪgnətrɪ/ ▷ *noun* (***signatories***) a person, organization or state that is a party to a contract, treaty or other document. Also *as adj* □ *signatory nations.* ⓒ 17c: from Latin *signatorius,* from *signare* to sign.

signature /ˈsɪgnətʃə(r)/ ▷ *noun* **1** one's name written by oneself, or a representative symbol, as a formal mark of authorization, etc. **2** an indication of key (KEY SIGNATURE) or time (TIME SIGNATURE) at the beginning of a line of music, or where a change occurs. **3** a large sheet of paper with printed pages on it, each with a numeral or letter at the bottom, which when folded forms a section of a book. **4** a letter or number at the foot of such a sheet, indicating the sequence in which such sheets are to be put together. ⓒ 16c: from Latin *signatura,* from *signare* to sign.

signature tune ▷ *noun* a tune used to identify or introduce a specified radio or television programme or performer.

signet /ˈsɪgnɪt/ ▷ *noun* **1** a small seal used for stamping documents, etc. **2** the impression made by such a seal. **3** a signet-ring. ⓒ 14c: from Latin *signum* sign.

signet-ring ▷ *noun* a finger ring carrying a signet. Also called SEAL RING.

significance /sɪgˈnɪfɪkəns/ and **significancy** ▷ *noun* (***significances*** or ***significancies***) **1** meaning or importance. **2** the condition or quality of being significant. **3** a value of probability at which a particular hypothesis is held to be contradicted by the results of a statistical test. ⓒ 15c.

significance test ▷ *noun, math* a test which is used to demonstrate the probability that observed patterns cannot be explained by chance.

significant /sɪgˈnɪfɪkənt/ ▷ *adj* **1** important; worth noting or considering. **2** having some meaning; indicating or implying something. **3** said of data, etc: having statistical significance. ● **significantly** *adverb.* ⓒ 16c.

significant figures and **significant digits** ▷ *noun, math* digits that contribute to a number and are nor merely zeros filling vacant spaces at the beginning or end. They are used when specifying the degree of accuracy required, eg 2.157 to three significant figures is 2.16.

significant other ▷ *noun* a sexual partner.

signify /'sɪgnɪfaɪ/ ▷ *verb* (***signifies, signified, signifying***) **1** to be a sign for something or someone; to suggest or mean. **2** to be a symbol of something or someone; to denote. **3** to indicate or declare. **4** *intr* to be important or significant. Ⓒ 13c: from Latin *significare*, from *signum* sign + Latin *facere* to make.

sign language ▷ *noun* any form of communication using gestures to represent words and ideas, especially an official system of hand gestures used by deaf people.

sign of the cross ▷ *noun* a Christian sign made in representation of the cross, by moving the right hand from the forehead to the chest and then left to right across to each shoulder, or by making a similar movement in front of oneself.

sign of the zodiac see under ZODIAC

Signor /siːn'jɔː(r)/ and **Signore** /-reɪ/ ▷ *noun* (**Signori** /-riː/ or **Signors**) **1** an Italian form of address equivalent to Mr or sir. **2** (**signor**) a gentleman. Ⓒ 16c: Italian.

Signora /siːn'jɔːrə/ ▷ *noun* (**Signore** /-reɪ/ or **Signoras**) **1** an Italian form of address equivalent to Mrs or madam. **2** (**signora**) a lady. Ⓒ 17c: Italian

Signorina /siːnjɔː'riːnə/ ▷ *noun* (**Signorine** /-neɪ/ or **Signorinas**) **1** an Italian form of address equjivalent to Miss or miss. **2** (**signorina**) an unmarried lady. Ⓒ 19c: Italian diminutive of SIGNORA.

signpost ▷ *noun* **1** a post supporting a sign that gives information or directions to motorists or pedestrians. **2** an indication or clue. ▷ *verb* **1** to mark (a route) with signposts. **2** to give directions to someone.

sika /'siːkə/ ▷ *noun* (***sika*** or ***sikas***) a small deer that inhabits Japan and Eastern Asia, and develops a white spotted coat in the summer. Ⓒ 19c: from Japanese *shika*.

Sikh /siːk/ ▷ *noun* an adherent of the monotheistic religion established in the 16c by Guru Nanak who, together with former Hindus, rejected the authority of the Vedas, taking the **Granth** as their scripture. ▷ *adj* relating to the Sikhs, their beliefs or customs. • **Sikhism** *noun*. Ⓒ 18c: Hindi, meaning 'disciple'.

silage /'saɪlɪdʒ/ ▷ *noun* animal fodder made from forage crops such as grass, maize, etc which are compressed and then preserved by controlled fermentation, eg in a silo. Ⓒ 19c: an alteration of ENSILAGE, from SILO.

sild ▷ *noun* a young herring. Ⓒ 1920s: Norwegian.

silence /'saɪləns/ ▷ *noun* **1** absence of sound or speech. **2** a time of such absence of sound or speech. **3** failure or abstention from communication, disclosing information or secrets, etc. ▷ *verb* (***silenced, silencing***) to make someone or something stop speaking, making a noise, or giving away information. ▷ *exclamation* Be quiet! • **in silence** without speaking. Ⓒ 13c: from Latin *silere* to be quiet.

silencer /'saɪlənsə(r)/ ▷ *noun* **1** someone or something that silences. **2** a device fitted to a gun barrel or engine exhaust to reduce or eliminate the noise made. Ⓒ 17c.

silent /'saɪlənt/ ▷ *adj* **1** free from noise; unaccompanied by sound. **2** refraining from speech; not mentioning or divulging something. **3** unspoken but expressed □ *silent joy*. **4** not pronounced □ *the silent p in pneumonia*. **5** said of a cinema film: having no soundtrack. ▷ *noun* a silent film. • **silently** *adverb*. • **silentness** *noun*. Ⓒ 16c.

silent majority ▷ *noun* those, in any country the bulk of the population, who are assumed to have sensible, moderate opinions though they do not trouble to express them publicly.

silent partner see SLEEPING PARTNER

silenus /saɪ'liːnəs/ ▷ *noun* (***sileni*** /-naɪ/) in Greek mythology: **1** (**Silenus**) the foster-father of Bacchus, and the chief of the satyrs, depicted as a bearded, bald, pot-bellied old man. **2** a woodland god or elderly satyr. Ⓒ 18c: Latin, from Greek *Seilenos*.

silex /'saɪlɛks/ ▷ *noun* **1** a silica of quartz. **2** a heat-resistant and shock-resistant glass formed from fused quartz. Ⓒ 16c: Latin, meaning 'flint'.

silhouette /sɪlʊ'ɛt/ ▷ *noun* **1** a dark shape or shadow seen against a light background. **2** an outline drawing of an object or especially a person, in profile, usually filled in with black. ▷ *verb* (***silhouetted, silhouetting***) to represent, or make appear, as a silhouette. Ⓒ 18c: named after Etienne de Silhouette (1709–67), French finance minister in 1759.

silica /'sɪlɪkə/ ▷ *noun* (***silicas***) *geol* a hard white or colourless glassy solid that occurs naturally as quartz, sand and flint, and also as silicate compounds, and is used in the manufacture of glasses, glazes and enamels. Also called **silicon dioxide**.

silica gel ▷ *noun, chem* an absorbent form of silica used as a drying agent, and as a catalyst in many chemical processes.

silicate /'sɪlɪkeɪt/ ▷ *noun, chem* **1** any of various chemical compounds containing silicon, oxygen and one or more metals, including the main components of most rocks and many minerals, eg clay, mica, feldspar. **2** any salt of silicic acid. Ⓒ 19c.

siliceous or **silicious** /sɪ'lɪʃəs/ ▷ *adj* belonging or relating to, or containing, silica.

silicic /sɪ'lɪsɪk/ ▷ *adj* belonging or relating to, or containing, silicon or an acid containing silicon.

silicify /sɪ'lɪsɪfaɪ/ ▷ *verb* (***silicifies, silicified, silicifying***) to transform or make something transform into silica. • **silicification** *noun*.

silicon /'sɪlɪkən, -kɒn/ ▷ *noun* (symbol **Si**, atomic number 14) a non-metallic element that occurs naturally as silicate minerals in clays and rocks, and as silica in sand and quartz, used as a semiconductor to make transistors and silicon chips for the integrated circuits of computers, etc. Ⓒ Early 19c: from Latin *silex* flint.

> ***silicon, silicone***
>
> These words are often confused with each other.

silicon carbide ▷ *noun, chem* (formula **SiC**) a hard, iridescent, bluish-black, crystalline compound, widely used as an abrasive, in cutting, grinding and polishing instruments, and in light-emitting diodes. Also called CARBORUNDUM.

silicon chip ▷ *noun, electronics, computing* a very thin piece of silicon or other semiconductor material, only a few millimetres square, on which all the components of an integrated circuit are arranged. Also called **chip**, **microchip**.

silicon dioxide see SILICA

silicone /'sɪlɪkoun/ ▷ *noun, chem* any of numerous synthetic polymers, usually occurring in the form of oily liquids, waxes, plastics or rubbers, used in lubricants, electrical insulators, paints, water repellents, adhesives and surgical breast implants.

silicosis /sɪlɪ'kousɪs/ ▷ *noun, pathol* a lung disease caused by prolonged inhalation of dust containing silica. Compare ASBESTOSIS, ANTHRACOSIS.

silk ▷ *noun* **1** a fine soft fibre produced by the larva of the silkworm. **2** a similar fibre produced by another insect or spider. **3** an imitation (also called **artificial silk**) made by forcing a viscous solution of modified cellulose through small holes. **4** thread or fabric made from such fibres. **5** a garment made from such fabric. **6** **a** the silk gown worn by a Queen's or King's Counsel; **b** the rank conferred by this. Also *as adj* □ ***a silk blouse.*** • **take silk** said of a barrister: to be appointed a Queen's or King's Counsel. ◷ Anglo-Saxon *seolc*, from Latin *sericum*.

silken /ˈsɪlkən/ ▻ *adj, literary* **1** made of silk. **2** as soft or smooth as silk. **3** dressed in silk.

silk-screen printing see SCREEN PRINTING

silkworm ▻ *noun* the caterpillar of the silk moth, which spins a cocoon of unbroken silk thread, farmed in India, China and Japan to provide silk on a commercial basis.

silky /ˈsɪlkɪ/ ▻ *adj* (***silkier, silkiest***) **1** soft and shiny like silk. **2** made from silk. **3** said of a person's manner or voice: suave.

sill ▻ *noun* **1** the bottom part of the framework around the inside of a window or door. **2** the ledge of wood, stone or metal forming this. **3** *mining* a bed of rock. **4** *geol* a layer of intrusive igneous rock, more or less parallel to the bedding. ◷ Anglo-Saxon *syll*.

sillabub see SYLLABUB

silly /ˈsɪlɪ/ ▻ *adj* (***sillier, silliest***) **1** not sensible; foolish; trivial or frivolous. **2** dazed; senseless □ ***She laughed herself silly*** □ ***The blow knocked him silly.*** **3** *cricket* in a fielding position very near the batsman □ ***silly mid-on.*** ▻ *noun* (***sillies***) *colloq* (*also* **silly-billy**) a foolish person. • **silliness** *noun*. ◷ Anglo-Saxon *sælig* happy.

silo /ˈsaɪloʊ/ ▻ *noun* (***silos***) **1** a tall round airtight tower for storing green crops and converting them into silage. **2** an underground chamber housing a missile ready for firing. ◷ 19c: Spanish, from Latin *sirus*, from Greek *siros* pit.

silt ▻ *noun* sedimentary material, finer than sand and coarser than clay, consisting of very small rock fragments or mineral particles, deposited by or suspended in running or still water. ▻ *verb* (***silted, silting***) *intr* to become blocked up with silt. ◷ 15c: as *sylt*.

■ **silt up** to become or make something become blocked by silt.

Silurian /sɪˈlʊərɪən, sɪˈljʊərɪən/ ▻ *adj, geol* denoting the period of geological time between the Ordovician and Devonian periods, during which marine life predominated and the first jawed fish and primitive land plants appeared. See table at GEOLOGICAL TIME SCALE. ◷ 18c: from Latin *Silures* an ancient people of S Wales.

silvan see SYLVAN

silver /ˈsɪlvə(r)/ ▻ *noun* **1** (symbol **Ag**, atomic number 47) an element, a soft white lustrous precious metal that is an excellent conductor of heat and electricity, and is used in jewellery, ornaments, mirrors, coins, electrical contacts and for electroplating tableware. **2** coins made of this metal. **3** articles made of or coated with this metal, especially cutlery and other tableware. **4** a silver medal. ▻ *adj* **1** having a whitish-grey colour. **2** denoting a 25th wedding or other anniversary. **3** clear and ringing in tone eg of voice. ▻ *verb* (***silvered, silvering***) **1** to apply a thin coating of silver; to plate with silver. **2** to give a silvery sheen to something. **3** *intr* to become silvery. • **born with a silver spoon in one's mouth** born to affluence or wealthy surroundings. ◷ Anglo-Saxon *seolfor*.

silver birch ▻ *noun* a species of birch tree with silvery-white peeling bark.

silver disc ▻ *noun* in Britain: **a** an album (ie an LP, CD, etc) that has sold 60 000 copies; **b** a single that has sold 200 000 copies. See also GOLD DISC, PLATINUM DISC. • **go silver** *colloq* to sell the respective number of albums or singles, earning the artist a framed silver disc from the recording company.

silverfish ▻ *noun* a primitive wingless insect with a tapering body covered with silvery scales, commonly found in houses, especially in damp places such as cracks around sinks.

silver fox ▻ *noun* **1** an American fox with white-tipped black fur. **2** the fur from this animal.

silver-gilt ▻ *adj* gilded or overlaid with silver.

silver jubilee ▻ *noun* a 25th anniversary.

silver lining ▻ *noun* a positive aspect of an otherwise unpleasant or unfortunate situation.

silver medal ▻ *noun* especially in sporting competitions: a medal of silver awarded to the person or team in second place.

silver nitrate ▻ *noun, chem* (formula $\mathbf{AgNO_3}$) a colourless crystalline compound, soluble in water and sensitive to light, used in photographic film, silver plating, ink manufacture, mirror silvering, hair dyes, etc.

silver plate ▻ *noun* **1** a thin coating of silver or a silver alloy on a metallic object, eg cutlery. **2** such objects coated with silver. • **silver-plated** *adj*.

silver screen ▻ *noun* **1** (**the silver screen**) *colloq* the film industry or films in general. **2** the cinema screen.

silver service ▻ *noun* a method of serving food in a restaurant, etc, in which the waiter or waitress uses a spoon and fork held in one hand to transfer the food from the serving dish to the diners' plates.

silverside ▻ *noun* a fine cut of beef from the rump, just below the aitchbone.

silversmith ▻ *noun* someone who makes or repairs articles made of silver.

silverweed ▻ *noun* a creeping plant with silvery leaves and yellow flowers, whose starchy roots were used as food in prehistoric times.

silvery /ˈsɪlvərɪ/ ▻ *adj* **1** having the colour or shiny quality of silver. **2** having a pleasantly light ringing sound □ ***silvery bells.***

silviculture /ˈsɪlvɪkʌltʃə(r)/ ▻ *noun, bot* the cultivation of forest trees, or the management of woodland to produce timber, etc. ◷ 19c: from Latin *silva* wood + CULTURE.

sima /ˈsaɪmə/ ▻ *noun, geol* the basaltic rocks rich in silica and magnesium that form the lower layer of the Earth's crust. See also SIAL. ◷ Early 20c: from SILICON and MAGNESIUM.

simian /ˈsɪmɪən/ ▻ *noun* a monkey or ape. ▻ *adj* belonging or relating to, or resembling, a monkey or ape. ◷ 17c: from Latin *simia* ape.

similar /ˈsɪmɪlə(r)/ ▻ *adj* **1** having a close resemblance to something; being of the same kind, but not identical; alike. **2** *geom* exactly corresponding in shape, regardless of size. • **similarity** /sɪmɪˈlarɪtɪ/ *noun*. • **similarly** /ˈsɪmɪləlɪ/ *adverb*. ◷ 17c: from French *similaire*, from Latin *similis* like.

simile /ˈsɪmɪlɪ/ ▻ *noun* (***similes***) a figure of speech in which a thing is described by being likened to something, usually using *as* or *like*, as in *eyes sparkling like diamonds*, and in set phrases such as *bold as brass*. ◷ 14c: Latin.

similitude /sɪˈmɪlɪtʃuːd/ ▻ *noun, formal* similarity; resemblance. ◷ 14c: see SIMILAR.

simmer /ˈsɪmə(r)/ ▻ *verb* (***simmered, simmering***) **1** *tr & intr* to cook or make something cook gently at just below boiling point. **2** *intr* to be close to an outburst of emotion, usually anger. ▻ *noun* a simmering state. ◷ 17c: as *simperen*.

■ **simmer down** to calm down, especially after a commotion, eg an angry outburst.

simnel /ˈsɪmnəl/ ▻ *noun* a sweet fruit cake covered with marzipan, traditionally baked at Easter or Mid-Lent. ◷ 13c: from Latin *simila* fine flour.

simony /ˈsaɪmənɪ, ˈsɪmənɪ/ ▻ *noun* the practice of buying or selling a religious post, benefice or other privilege. ⓘ 13c: from Simon Magus, the Biblical sorcerer who offered money for the power to convey the gift of the Holy Spirit.

simoom /sɪ'muːm/ and **simoon** ▷ *noun* a hot suffocating desert wind in Arabia and N Africa. ⓘ 18c: from Arabic *samum*, from *samm* to poison.

simpatico /sɪm'patɪkoʊ/ ▷ *adj* sympathetic in the congenial sense. ⓘ 19c: Italian and Spanish.

simper /'sɪmpə(r)/ ▷ *verb* (***simpered, simpering***) **1** *intr* to smile in a weak affected manner. **2** to express by or while smiling in this way. ▷ *noun* a simpering smile. ⓘ 16c: from Norwegian *semper* smart.

simple /'sɪmpəl/ ▷ *adj* **1** easy; not difficult. **2** straightforward; not complex or complicated. **3** plain or basic; not elaborate or luxurious □ *a simple outfit.* **4** down-to-earth; unpretentious; honest. **5** *often ironic* foolish; gullible; lacking intelligence □ *He's a bit of a simple lad.* **6** plain; straightforward; not altered or adulterated □ *the simple facts.* **7** consisting of one thing or element. **8** *bot* not divided into leaflets. ▷ *noun* a medicine of one constituent. ⓘ 13c: French, from Latin *simplus*.

simple fraction ▷ *noun, math* a fraction with whole numbers as numerator and denominator.

simple fracture ▷ *noun* a fracture of the bone that does not involve an open skin wound. Compare COMPOUND FRACTURE.

simple harmonic motion ▷ *noun, physics* (abbreviation **shm**) continuous and repetitive motion whereby a body oscillates in such a way that it ranges an equal distance on either side of a central point, and its acceleration towards the point is proportional to its distance from it, as with a pendulum.

simple interest ▷ *noun* interest calculated only on the basic sum initially borrowed (see PRINCIPAL *noun* 6). Compare COMPOUND INTEREST.

simple-minded ▷ *adj* **1** lacking intelligence; foolish. **2** guileless; unsophisticated. • **simple-mindedness** *noun*.

simple sentence ▷ *noun* a sentence consisting of one MAIN CLAUSE. Compare COMPLEX SENTENCE, COMPOUND SENTENCE, COMPOUND-COMPLEX SENTENCE.

simpleton ▷ *noun* a foolish or unintelligent person. ⓘ 17c.

simplicity /sɪm'plɪsɪtɪ/ ▷ *noun* a simple state or quality. ⓘ 14c: from French *simplicite*, from *simple*.

simplify /'sɪmplɪfaɪ/ ▷ *verb* (***simplifies, simplified, simplifying***) to make something less difficult or complicated; to make it easier to understand. • **simplification** /sɪmplɪfɪ'keɪʃən/ *noun*. • **simplifier** *noun*. ⓘ 17c: from Latin *simplus* simple + *facere* to make.

simplistic /sɪm'plɪstɪk/ ▷ *adj* unrealistically straightforward or uncomplicated; oversimplified. • **simplistically** *adverb*. ⓘ 19c.

simply /'sɪmplɪ/ ▷ *adverb* **1** in a straightforward, uncomplicated manner. **2** just □ *It's simply not true.* **3** absolutely □ *simply marvellous.* **4** merely □ *We simply wanted to help.* ⓘ 13c.

simulate /'sɪmjʊleɪt/ ▷ *verb* (***simulated, simulating***) **1** to convincingly re-create (a set of conditions or a real-life event), especially for the purposes of training. **2** to assume a false appearance of someone or something. **3** to pretend to have, do or feel □ *She simulated anger.* • **simulated** *adj* not genuine; imitation □ *simulated leather.* • **simulation** *noun* **1** simulating; something that is simulated. **2** any model of a system or process □ *computer traffic simulation program.* ⓘ 17c: from Latin *simulare*.

simulator /'sɪmjʊleɪtə(r)/ ▷ *noun* a device that simulates a system, process or set of conditions, especially in order to test it, or for training purposes □ *flight simulator.*

simulcast /'sɪməlkɑːst/ ▷ *noun* **1** a programme broadcast simultaneously on radio and television. **2** the transmission of a programme in this way. ⓘ 1940s: from *simul*taneous broad*cast*.

simultaneous /sɪməl'teɪnɪəs/ ▷ *adj* happening, or carried out, at exactly the same time. • **simultaneously** *adverb*. • **simultaneousness** *noun*. ⓘ 17c: from Latin *simul* at the same time.

simultaneous equations ▷ *noun, math* two or more equations whose variables have the same values in both or all the equations.

sin¹ ▷ *noun* **1** an act that breaches a moral and especially a religious law or teaching. **2** the condition of offending a deity by committing a moral offence. **3** an act that offends common standards of morality or decency; an outrage. **4** a great shame. ▷ *verb* (***sinned, sinning***) *intr* (*often* **sin against**) to commit a sin. • **live in sin** *colloq* to live together as a couple without being married. ⓘ Anglo-Saxon *synn*.

sin² ▷ *abbreviation* sine (see SINE¹).

since /sɪns/ ▷ *conj* **1** from the time that; seeing that. **2** as; because □ *I'm not surprised you failed the exam since you did no work for it.* ▷ *prep* during or throughout the period between now and some earlier stated time □ *I've been there several times since it opened.* ▷ *adverb* **1** from that time onwards □ *I haven't been back since.* **2** ago □ *five years since.* ⓘ 15c: as *sithens*.

> ***since***
>
> See Usage Note at **ago**.

sincere /sɪn'sɪə(r)/ ▷ *adj* genuine; not pretended or affected. • **sincerely** *adverb*. • **sincerity** /sɪn'serɪtɪ/ *noun*. ⓘ 16c: from Latin *sincerus* clean.

sinciput /'sɪnsɪpʌt/ ▷ *noun* (***sinciputs*** or ***sincipita*** /-'sɪpɪtə/) *anatomy* the forepart of the head or skull. ⓘ 16c: Latin, from *semi-* half + *caput* head.

sine¹ /saɪn/ ▷ *noun, trig* (abbreviation **sin**) in a right-angled triangle: a FUNCTION (*noun* 4) of an angle, defined as the length of the side opposite the angle divided by the length of the hypotenuse. ⓘ 16c: from Latin *sinus* curve or bay.

sine² /'saɪnɪ, 'sɪnɛ/ ▷ *prep* without. ⓘ Latin.

sinecure /'sɪnɪkjʊə(r), 'saɪ-/ ▷ *noun* **1** *church* a BENEFICE without CURE (*noun* 4) of souls. **2** a paid job involving little or no work. ⓘ 17c: from Latin *sine* without + *cura* care.

sine die /'saɪnɪ 'daɪiː, 'sɪnɛ 'deɪ/ ▷ *adverb, adj* with no future time fixed; indefinitely. ⓘ 17c: Latin, meaning 'without a day'.

sine qua non /'saɪnɪ kweɪ nɒn, 'sɪnɛ kwɑː noːn/ ▷ *noun* an essential condition or requirement. ⓘ 16c: Latin, meaning 'without which not'.

sinew /'sɪnjuː/ ▷ *noun* **1** a strong piece of fibrous tissue joining a muscle to a bone; a tendon. **2** (**sinews**) physical strength; muscle. **3** (*often* **sinews**) strength or power of any kind, or a source of this. • **sinewy** *adj*. ⓘ Anglo-Saxon *sinu*.

sine wave ▷ *noun, math* a waveform whose shape resembles that obtained by plotting a graph of the size of an angle against the value of its sine.

sinfonia /sɪnfə'nɪə, sɪn'foʊnɪə/ ▷ *noun* (***sinfonie*** /sɪnfə'niːeɪ, sɪn'foʊnɪeɪ/ or ***sinfonias***) **1** an orchestral piece; a symphony. **2** a symphony or chamber orchestra. ⓘ 18c: Italian, meaning 'symphony'.

sinfonietta /sɪnfoʊnɪ'ɛtə/ ▷ *noun* (***sinfoniettas***) **1** an orchestral piece, usually in several movements but shorter and on a smaller scale than a symphony. **2** a small symphony or chamber orchestra. ⓘ Early 20c: Italian, a diminutive of SINFONIA.

sinful /'sɪnfəl/ ▷ *adj* wicked; involving sin; morally wrong. • **sinfully** *adverb*. • **sinfulness** *noun*.

sing ▻ *verb* (*past tense* ***sang***, *past participle* ***sung***, *present participle* ***singing***) **1** *tr & intr* to utter (words, sounds, etc) in a melodic rhythmic fashion, especially to the accompaniment of music. **2** *intr* to utter such sounds as a profession □ *Her mother was a dancer, but she sings.* **3** to make someone or something pass into a particular state with such sound □ *The mother sang her baby to sleep.* **4** *intr* to make a sound like a musical voice; to hum, ring or whistle □ *The kettle was singing on the stove* □ *Bullets were singing past his ears* □ *The wind was singing in the trees.* **5** *intr* to suffer a ringing sound □ *My ears were singing for days after the rock concert.* **6** *intr, especially US slang* to inform or confess; to squeal. **7** *intr* said of birds, specific insects, etc: to produce calls or sounds. **8** (*also* **sing of**) to write in poetry. **9** to proclaim or relate (an event, etc) in song or verse. • **sing someone's praises** to praise them enthusiastically. ⓒ Anglo-Saxon *singan*.

■ **sing along** said of an audience: to join in the familiar songs with the performer.

■ **sing out 1** to shout or call out. **2** to inform; to preach.

sing. ▻ *abbreviation* singular.

singalong ▻ *noun* a song in which an audience, etc can join in with the words.

singe /sɪndʒ/ ▻ *verb* (***singed***, ***singeing***) *tr & intr* to burn lightly on the surface; to scorch or become scorched. ▻ *noun* a light surface burn. ⓒ Anglo-Saxon *sengan*.

singer /ˈsɪŋə(r)/ ▻ *noun* **1** a person or bird that sings. **2** someone who sings professionally. **3** *especially US slang* an informer. ⓒ 14c.

Singhalese see SINHALESE

single /ˈsɪŋgəl/ ▻ *adj* **1** comprising only one part; solitary. **2** having no partner; unmarried, especially never having been married. **3** for use by one person only □ *a single room.* **4** said of a travel ticket: valid for an outward journey only; not return. **5** unique; individual. **6** one-fold; uncombined □ *single stitch.* **7** said of a combat: person-to-person. **8** even one □ *Not a single person turned up.* **9** said of a flower: having only one set of petals. ▻ *noun* (***singles***) **1** (*often* **singles**) a person without a partner, either marital or otherwise. **2** a single room, eg in a guest house. **3** a ticket for an outward journey only. **4** a RECORD (*noun* 4) usually with only one track on each side, now also referring to a CASSETTE SINGLE and those on compact disc. Compare ALBUM. **5** *Brit* a pound coin or note. **6** *US* a one-dollar note. **7** *cricket* a hit for one run. ▻ *verb* (***singled***, ***singling***) (*always* **single out**) to pick someone or something from among others □ *He was singled out for the team* □ *They singled him out as the culprit.* ⓒ 14c: French, from Latin *singuli* one by one.

single-breasted ▻ *adj* said of a coat or jacket: having only one row of buttons and a slight overlap at the front.

single combat ▻ *noun* fighting between two individuals.

single cream ▻ *noun* cream with a low fat-content, which does not thicken when beaten.

single-decker ▻ *noun* a vehicle, especially a bus, with only one deck. Compare DOUBLE-DECKER.

single figures ▻ *noun* the numbers from 1 to 9. • **single-figure** *adj* □ *a single-figure score.*

single file and **Indian file** ▻ *noun* a line of people, animals, etc standing or moving one behind the other. Also *as adverb* □ *They shuffled single-file into the hall.*

single-handed ▻ *adj, adverb* done, carried out etc by oneself, without any help from others. • **single-handedly** *adverb*.

single-minded ▻ *adj* determinedly pursuing one specific aim or object. • **single-mindedly** *adverb*. • **single-mindedness** *noun*.

single parent ▻ *noun* a mother or father bringing up a child alone.

singles /ˈsɪŋgəlz/ ▻ *noun* in tennis, etc: a match where one player competes against another.

singles bar and **singles club** ▻ *noun* a bar intended as a meeting place for unmarried or unattached people.

singlet /ˈsɪŋglət, -lɪt/ ▻ *noun* a sleeveless vest or undershirt. ⓒ 18c.

singleton /ˈsɪŋgəltən/ ▻ *noun* **1** the only playing-card of a particular suit in a hand. **2** a solitary person or thing. ⓒ 19c.

singly /ˈsɪŋglɪ/ ▻ *adverb* **1** one at a time; individually. **2** alone; by oneself.

singsong ▻ *noun* an informal gathering at which friends, etc sing together for pleasure. ▻ *adj* said of a speaking voice, etc: having a fluctuating intonation and rhythm.

singular /ˈsɪŋgjʊlə(r)/ ▻ *adj* **1** single; unique. **2** extraordinary; exceptional. **3** strange; odd. **4** *grammar* denoting or referring to one person, thing, etc as opposed to two or more. Compare PLURAL. ▻ *noun, grammar* a word or form of a word expressing the idea or involvement of one person, thing, etc as opposed to two or more. • **singularity** /sɪŋgjʊˈlarɪtɪ/ *noun* **1** being singular. **2** peculiarity; individuality. ⓒ 14c: from Latin *singularis*.

singularize or **singularise** /ˈsɪŋgjʊləraɪz/ ▻ *verb* (***singularized***, ***singularizing***) **1** to make (a word) singular. **2** to signalize. • **singularization** *noun*. ⓒ 16c.

singularly /ˈsɪŋgjʊləlɪ/ ▻ *adverb* **1** extraordinarily. **2** strangely. **3** singly. **4** very.

Sinhalese /sɪnhəˈliːz/ and **Singhalese** ▻ *noun* (*plural* ***Sinhalese***) **1** a member of a people living in Sri Lanka. **2** their language. ▻ *adj* belonging or relating to this people or their language. ⓒ Early 19c: from Sanskrit *Simhala* Sri Lanka.

sinister /ˈsɪnɪstə(r)/ ▻ *adj* **1** suggesting or threatening evil or danger; malign. **2** inauspicious; ominous. **3** *heraldry* on the left side of the shield from the bearer's point of view, as opposed to that of the observer. Compare DEXTER. • **sinisterly** *adverb*. ⓒ 14c: Latin, meaning 'left', believed by the Romans to be the unlucky side.

sinistral /ˈsɪnɪstrəl/ ▻ *adj* **1** positioned on or relating to the left side. **2** turning to the left side. **3** said of shells: coiled from right to left, contrary to normal. ⓒ 15c.

sinistrorse /sɪnɪˈstrɔːs, ˈsɪnɪstrɔːs/ ▻ *adj, bot* said of certain climbing plants: spiralling upwards from right to left. • **sinistrorsal** *adj*. ⓒ 19c: from Latin *sinistrorsus*, towards the left side, from *sinister* left + *vertere* to turn.

Sinitic /sɪˈnɪtɪk/ ▻ *adj* denoting a group of languages belonging to the Sino-Tibetan family, used mainly in China and Taiwan. ▻ *noun* the languages forming this group. ⓒ 19c: from Latin *Sinae* Chinese.

sink ▻ *verb* (*past tense* ***sank*** or ***sunk***, *past participle* ***sunk***, *present participle* ***sinking***) **1** *tr & intr* to fall or cause to fall and remain below the surface of water, either partially or completely. **2** *intr* to collapse downwardly or inwardly; to fall because of a collapsing base or foundation; to subside. **3** *intr* to be or become inwardly withdrawn or dejected □ *My heart sank at the news.* **4** to embed □ *They sank the pole into the ground.* **5** to pass steadily (and often dangerously) into a worse level or state □ *He sank into depression after her death.* **6** to slope away or dip. **7** to diminish or decline □ *My opinion of him sank after that incident.* **8** to invest (money) heavily □ *We sank a lot of money into this project.* **9** to pay (a debt). **10** *colloq* to ruin the plans of someone; to ruin (plans) □ *We are sunk.* **11** *colloq* to drink (especially alcohol) usually quickly □ *We sank four beers within the hour.* **12** *intr* said of the Sun or Moon: to disappear slowly below the horizon. **13** *colloq* to send (a ball) into a pocket in snooker, billiards, etc and into the hole in golf. **14** to excavate (a well, shaft, etc). **15** to let in or insert □ *screws sunk into the wall.* **16** to abandon or abolish □ *I'll sink the whole organization if I* *have to.* **17** to damn or ruin (especially in imprecation). ▻ *noun* **1** a basin, wall-mounted or in a SINK UNIT, with built-in water supply and drainage, for washing dishes, etc. **2** a place of immorality, vice and corruption. **3** a cesspool. **4** a depression in a surface. **5** an area without any surface drainage. **6** a depression in the ground where water, etc collects. **7** *physics* a method, natural or artificial, by which heat, fluid, etc is absorbed or discharged. ⓒ Anglo-Saxon *sincan.*

■ **sink in 1** *colloq* to be fully understood or realized □ *The bad news took a few days to sink in.* **2** to penetrate or be absorbed □ *Wait for the ink to sink in first.*

sinker /'sɪŋkə(r)/ ▻ *noun* **1** someone who sinks. **2** a weight used to sink something, eg a fishing-line. ⓒ 16c.

sinking fund ▻ *noun* a fund formed by setting aside income to accumulate at interest to pay off a debt.

sink unit ▻ *noun* a piece of kitchen furniture consisting of a sink and draining-board, usually also with cupboards underneath.

sinner /'sɪnə(r)/ ▻ *noun* someone who sins or has sinned. ⓒ 14c.

Sino- /'saɪnoʊ, sɪnoʊ, saɪ'nɒ, sɪ'nɒ/ ▻ *combining form, denoting* Chinese □ *Sino-Soviet.* ⓒ From Greek *Sinai* Chinese.

Sinology /saɪ'nɒlədʒɪ, sɪ-/ ▻ *noun* the study of China in all its aspects, especially cultural and political. • **Sinologist** *noun* an expert in Sinology. ⓒ 19c.

Sino-Tibetan ▻ *adj* denoting the family of languages spoken in China, Tibet and Burma (Myanma), consisting of around 300 languages, including the eight Chinese (or SINITIC) languages, Tibetan and Burmese. ▻ *noun* the languages forming this group.

sinter /'sɪntə(r)/ ▻ *noun* a siliceous deposit from hot springs. ▻ *verb* (***sintered***, ***sintering***) to heat a mixture of powdered metals, sometimes under pressure, to the melting-point of the metal in the mixture which has the lowest melting-point, which then binds together the harder particles. ⓒ 18c as *sinder* CINDER.

sinuate /'sɪnjʊeɪt/ ▻ *adj* **1** having many curves or bends; meandering. **2** having a twisting and turning motion. • **sinuation** *noun.* ⓒ 17c: from Latin *sinuatus*, from *sinuare* to bend or curve.

sinuous /'sɪnjʊəs/ ▻ *adj* wavy; winding; sinuate. • **sinuosity** /sɪnjʊ'ɒsɪtɪ/ or **sinuousness** *noun.* • **sinuously** *adverb.* ⓒ 16c: Latin, from *sinus* curve.

sinus /'saɪnəs/ ▻ *noun* (***sinuses***) **1** *anatomy* a cavity or depression filled with air, especially in the bones of mammals. **2** *anatomy* a cavity filled with blood, especially in the brain and certain blood vessels. **3** *bot* a notch or depression between two lobes in a leaf. ⓒ 16c: Latin, meaning 'curve'.

sinusitis /saɪnə'saɪtɪs/ ▻ *noun* inflammation of the lining of the sinuses, especially the nasal ones. ⓒ Early 20c.

sinusoid /'saɪnəsɔɪd/ ▻ *noun* **1** *math* the curve of sines. **2** *anatomy* a small blood vessel in certain organs, such as the liver, heart, etc. ▻ *adj* similar to or referring to a sinus. • **sinusoidal** *adj.* • **sinusoidally** *adverb.* ⓒ 19c.

Siouan /'suːən/ ▻ *adj* **1** referring or relating to the Sioux, or to a larger group to which the Sioux belong. **2** referring or relating to the languages of this group. ▻ *noun* the group of languages spoken by the Sioux. ⓒ 19c.

Sioux /suː/ ▻ *noun* (*plural* ***Sioux*** /suː, suːz/) **1** a Native American of a tribe now living in the Dakotas, Minnesota and Montana. **2** any of a group of languages spoken by them. ⓒ 18c: French, a shortening of Ottawan *Nadoussioux.*

sip ▻ *verb* (***sipped***, ***sipping***) *tr & intr* to drink in very small mouthfuls. ▻ *noun* **1** an act of sipping. **2** an amount sipped at one time. • **sipper** *noun.* ⓒ Anglo-Saxon *sypian*, perhaps a variation of SUP.

siphon or **syphon** /'saɪfən/ ▻ *noun* **1** a tube held in an inverted U-shape that can be used to transfer liquid from one container at a higher level into another at a lower level, used to empty car petrol tanks, etc. **2** (*in full* **soda siphon**) a bottle from which a liquid, especially soda water, is forced by pressure of gas. **3** *zool* in certain animals, eg bivalve molluscs: an organ resembling a tube through which water flows in and out. ▻ *verb* (***siphoned***, ***siphoning***) (*usually* **siphon something off**) **1** to transfer (liquid) from one container to another using such a device. **2** to take (money, funds, etc) slowly and continuously from a store or fund. ⓒ 17c: Greek, meaning 'pipe'.

sippet /'sɪpɪt/ ▻ *noun* a morsel of bread or toast, especially with soup. ⓒ 16c: from SIP.

sir /sɜː(r)/ ▻ *noun* **1** a polite and respectful address for a man. **2** (**Sir**) a title used before the Christian name of a knight or baronet. **3** (**Sir**) a word of address to a man in a formal letter □ *Sir!* □ *Dear Sir or Madam.* ⓒ 13c: see SIRE.

sire /saɪə(r)/ ▻ *noun* **1** the father of a horse or other animal. **2** *historical* a term of respect used in addressing a king. ▻ *verb* (***sired***, ***siring***) said of an animal: to father (young). ⓒ 12c: French, from Latin *senior* elder.

siren /'saɪərən/ ▻ *noun* **1** a device that gives out a loud wailing noise, usually as a warning signal. **2** an irresistible woman thought capable of ruining men's lives; a FEMME FATALE. **3** a bewitching and fascinating singer. **4** (**Siren**) *Greek mythol* a certain sea-nymph, part-woman, part-bird, whose seductive songs lured sailors to their deaths on the rocks. See also LORELEI. **5** any eel-like amphibian with no hind legs or external gills. ⓒ 14c: from Greek *Seiren.*

Sirius /'sɪrɪəs/ ▻ *noun, astron* the brightest star in the night sky (the **Dog Star**) in the constellation Canis Major. ⓒ 14c: Latin, from Greek *Seiros.*

sirloin /'sɜːlɔɪn/ ▻ *noun* a fine cut of beef from the loin or the upper part of the loin. ⓒ 16c: from French *surlonge*, from *sur* above + *longe* loin.

sirocco or **scirocco** /sɪ'rɒkoʊ/ ▻ *noun* (***siroccos*** or ***scirocos***) in S Europe: a dry hot dusty wind blowing from N Africa, and becoming more moist as it moves further north. ⓒ 17c: Italian, from Arabic *sharq* east wind.

sis ▻ *noun, colloq* short for SISTER.

sisal /'saɪsəl, 'saɪzəl/ ▻ *noun* (*in full* **sisal hemp** or **sisal grass**) **1** any of various perennial plants, native to Central America, which have a rosette of swollen stout sword-like leaves tipped with sharp spines. **2** the strong coarse durable yellowish fibre obtained from the leaves of this plant, used to make ropes, twine, brush bristles, sacking, matting, etc. ⓒ 19c: named after Sisal, the port in Yucatan in Mexico from where it was first exported.

siskin /'sɪskɪn/ ▻ *noun* any of various small finches, the male of which usually has yellowish-green plumage with a black crown and chin, a bold yellow rump and a deeply forked black tail. ⓒ 16c: from Dutch *siseken.*

sissy or **cissy** /'sɪsɪ/ ▻ *noun* (***sissies*** or ***cissies***) *derog* a feeble, cowardly or effeminate male. ▻ *adj* having the characteristics of a sissy. ⓒ 19c: from SISTER.

sister /'sɪstə(r)/ ▻ *noun* **1** a female child of the same parents as another. **2** a HALF-SISTER. **3** a nun. **4** a senior female nurse, especially one in charge of a ward. **5** a close female associate; a fellow female member of a profession, class or racial group. **6** often shortened from SOUL SISTER. ▻ *adj* being of the same origin, model or design □ *a sister ship.* ⓒ Anglo-Saxon *sweostor*, related to Norse *systir.*

sisterhood ▻ *noun* **1** the state of being a sister or sisters. **2** the relationship of sister. **3** a religious community of women; a body of nuns. **4** a group of women with common interests or beliefs.

sister-in-law ▷ *noun* (***sisters-in-law***) **1** the sister of one's husband or wife. **2** the wife of one's brother.

sisterly /'sɪstəlɪ/ ▷ *adj* said of a woman or her behaviour: like a sister, especially in being kind and affectionate. • **sisterliness** *noun*. ⓒ 16c.

sit ▷ *verb* (***sat, sitting***) **1** *intr* to rest the body on the buttocks, with the upper body more or less vertical. **2** said of an animal: to position itself on its hindquarters in a similar manner. **3** *intr* said of a bird: to perch or lie. **4** *intr* said of a bird: to brood. **5** *intr* said of an object: to lie, rest or hang □ ***There are a few cups sitting on the shelf*** □ ***The jacket sits nicely round your shoulders.*** **6** *intr* to lie unused □ ***I've got all my tools sitting in the shed.*** **7** *intr* to hold a meeting or other session □ ***The court sits tomorrow.*** **8** *intr* to be a member, taking regular part in meetings □ ***sit on a committee.*** **9** to have a seat, as in parliament. **10** to reside or inhabit. **11** to be a tenant. **12** to have a specific position □ ***The TV sits on this stand.*** **13** to be located or situated □ ***The TV sits in the corner.*** **14** said of the wind: to have a direction □ ***The wind sits south.*** **15** to take (an examination); to be a candidate for (a degree or other award) □ ***I'm sitting my first exam tomorrow.*** **16** to conduct to a seat; to assign a seat to someone □ ***They sat me next to him.*** **17** *intr* to be or exist in a specified comparison or relation □ ***His smoking sits awkwardly with his being a doctor.*** **18** *intr* to pose as an artist's or photographer's model. • **be sitting pretty** *colloq* to be in a very advantageous position. • **sit on the fence** see under FENCE. • **sit tight 1** to maintain one's position and opinion determinedly. **2** to wait patiently. ⓒ Anglo-Saxon *sittan*.

■ **sit back 1** to sit comfortably, especially with the head and back rested. **2** to observe rather than take an active part, especially when action is needed □ ***He's just happy to sit back and let everyone else make the effort.***

■ **sit down** or **sit someone down** to take, or make them take, a sitting position.

■ **sit down under something** to submit meekly to (an insult, etc).

■ **sit in on something** to be present at it as a visitor or observer, especially without participating.

■ **sit in for someone** to act as a substitute for them.

■ **sit on someone** *colloq* to force them to say or do nothing; to repress them.

■ **sit on something 1** to be a member of it □ ***I sit on the committee for the sports centre.*** **2** *colloq* to delay taking action over it. **3** *colloq* to keep it secret; to suppress it.

■ **sit something out 1** to stay until the end of it. **2** to take no part, especially in a dance or game.

■ **sit up 1** to move oneself from a slouching or lying position into an upright sitting position. **2** to remain out of bed longer than usual □ ***I sat up late writing my essay.*** **3** to take notice suddenly or show a sudden interest.

sitar /sɪ'tɑː(r), 'sɪ-/ ▷ *noun* a guitar-like instrument of Indian origin, with a long neck, rounded body and two sets of strings. ⓒ 19c: Hindi.

sitcom /'sɪtkɒm/ ▷ *noun*, *colloq* short for SITUATION COMEDY.

sit-down ▷ *noun*, *colloq* a short rest in a seated position. ▷ *adj* **1** said of a meal: for which the diners are seated. **2** said of a strike: in which the workers occupy the workplace until an agreement is reached.

site ▷ *noun* **1** the place where something was, is, or is to be situated □ ***the site of the museum*** □ ***the site of the rebellion.*** **2** an area set aside for a specific activity □ ***a camping site.*** ▷ *verb* (***sited, siting***) to position or situate. ⓒ 14c: from Latin *situs* position.

Site of Special Scientific Interest see SSSI

sit-in ▷ *noun* the occupation of a public building, factory, etc as a form of protest or as a means of applying pressure, especially towards the settling of a dispute. Also *as adj* □ ***a sit-in protest.***

Sitka spruce /'sɪtkə —/ ▷ *noun*, *bot* an evergreen coniferous tree, native to N temperate regions, widely cultivated for its timber and as an ornamental tree.

sitter /'sɪtə(r)/ ▷ *noun* **1** a person or animal that sits. **2** a person who poses for an artist or photographer. **3** a babysitter. **4** *in compounds* a person who looks after a house, pet, etc in the absence of its owner □ ***a flat sitter*** □ ***cat sitter.*** **5** an easy shot or catch □ ***He missed a sitter.*** **6** any easy task or activity. **7** a certain winner □ ***I backed a sitter in the 3.30 at Sandown Park.*** **8** *colloq* an easy target for crime or deception. **9** a person taking part in a seance, other than the medium. **10** a bird which sits on eggs to hatch them. ⓒ 14c.

sitting /'sɪtɪŋ/ ▷ *verb*, *present participle of* SIT. ▷ *noun* **1** the act or state of being seated. **2** a period of continuous activity, usually while sitting or in a similar position □ ***He wrote it at one sitting.*** **3** a turn to eat for any of two or more sections of a group too large to eat all at the same time in the same place, or the period set aside for each turn. **4** a period of posing for an artist or photographer. **5** a session or meeting of an official body. **6** brooding on eggs. **7** a clutch of eggs. ▷ *adj* **1** currently holding office □ ***He's the sitting MP for this constituency.*** **2** seated □ ***in a sitting position.*** **3** for people to sit in □ ***There's not enough sitting space.*** **4** brooding. ⓒ 12c.

sitting duck and **sitting target** ▷ *noun* someone or something in a defenceless or exposed position, easily attacked, criticized, etc.

sitting-room ▷ *noun* a room, especially in a private house, for relaxing in, entertaining visitors, etc.

sitting tenant ▷ *noun*, *Brit* a tenant occupying a property when it changes ownership.

situate ▷ *verb* /'sɪtʃʊeɪt/ (***situated, situating***) to place in a certain position, context or set of circumstances. ▷ *adj* /'sɪtʃʊət/ *especially law* situated. • **situated** in a particular position, setting or set of circumstances. ⓒ 16c: from Latin *situatus*, from *situare* to position, from *situs* SITE.

situation /sɪtʃʊ'eɪʃən/ ▷ *noun* **1** a set of circumstances or state of affairs. **2** a place, position or location. **3** a job; employment □ ***situations vacant.*** **4** a critical point in the action of a play or in the development of the plot of a novel. • **situational** *adj*. ⓒ 15c.

situation comedy ▷ *noun* a radio or TV comedy, often broadcast as a series of episodes in which the same characters appear in more or less the same surroundings, and which depends for its humour on the behaviour of the characters in particular, sometimes contrived, situations. Often shortened to SITCOM.

situation ethics ▷ *noun*, *philos* ethics based on the principle that what is good or right and what is bad or wrong may vary depending on the circumstances.

situationism ▷ *noun* the theory that behaviour is determined by surrounding situations rather than personal qualities. • **situationist** *noun*.

sit-up ▷ *noun* a physical exercise in which the body is raised up and over the thighs from a lying position, often with the hands behind the head.

Siva see SHIVA

six ▷ *noun* **1 a** the cardinal number 6; **b** the quantity that this represents, being one more than five. **2** any symbol for this, eg **6** or **vi**. **3** the age of six. **4** something, especially a garment or a person, whose size is denoted by the number 6. **5** the sixth hour after midnight or midday □ ***Come at six*** □ ***6 o'clock*** □ ***6pm.*** **6** a set or group of six people or things. **7** a playing-card with six pips □ ***He played his six.*** **8** a score of 6 points. **9** *cricket* a hit scoring 6 runs. **10** a team of (more or less) six Cub Scouts or Brownie Guides. ▷ *adj* **1** totalling six. **2** aged six. • **at**

sixes and sevens in a state of total disorder or confusion. • **hit** or **knock someone for six** *colloq* **1** to defeat or ruin them completely. **2** to shock or surprise them completely. • **six of one and half a dozen of the other** equal; equally acceptable or unacceptable; the same on both sides. Sometimes shortened to **six and half a dozen.** ⓔ Anglo-Saxon *siex*.

sixer /'sɪksə(r)/ ▻ *noun* the Cub Scout or Brownie Guide leader of a SIX (*noun* 10).

sixfold ▻ *adj* **1** equal to six times as much. **2** divided into or consisting of six parts. ▻ *adverb* by six times as much. ⓔ Anglo-Saxon; see SIX + -FOLD.

six-pack ▻ *noun* a pack containing six items sold as one unit, especially a pack of six cans of beer.

sixpence ▻ *noun* in Britain: a former small silver coin worth six old pennies (6d), equivalent in value to 2 $^1/_2$p.

sixpenny ▻ *adj* **1** worth or costing six old pennies. **2** cheap; worthless.

sixteen /sɪks'tiːn, 'sɪkstiːn/ ▻ *noun* **1 a** the cardinal number 16; **b** the quantity that this represents, being one more than fifteen, or the sum of ten and six. **2** any symbol for this, eg **16** or **XVI**. **3** the age of sixteen. **4** something, especially a garment or a person, whose size is denoted by the number 16. **5** a set or group of sixteen people or things. **6** a score of sixteen points. ▻ *adj* **1** totalling sixteen. **2** aged sixteen. ⓔ Anglo-Saxon; see SIX + -TEEN.

sixteenth /sɪk'stiːnθ/ (often written **16th**) ▻ *adj* **1** in counting: **a** next after fifteenth; **b** last of sixteen. **2** in sixteenth position. **3** (**the sixteenth**) **a** the sixteenth day of the month; **b** *golf* the sixteenth hole. ▻ *noun* **1** one of sixteen equal parts. Also *as adj* □ ***a sixteenth share.*** **2** a FRACTION equal to one divided by sixteen (usually written $^1/_{16}$). **3** a person coming ninth, eg in a race or exam □ ***In spite of all her training, she came in a poor sixteenth.*** ▻ *adverb* sixteenthly. ⓔ Anglo-Saxon; see SIXTEEN + -TH.

sixth /sɪksθ/ (often written **6th**) ▻ *adj* **1** in counting: **a** next after fifth; **b** last of six. **2** in sixth position. **3** (**the sixth**) **a** the sixth day of the month; **b** *golf* the sixth hole. ▻ *noun* **1** one of six equal parts. Also *as adj* □ ***a sixth share.*** **2** a FRACTION equal to one divided by six (usually written $^1/_6$). **3** a person coming sixth, eg in a race or exam □ ***She came in a weary but contented sixth.*** **4** *music* **a** the interval between two notes that are six notes apart (counting both the first and the last) on the diatonic scale; **b** a note at that interval from another, or a combination of two notes separated by that interval. ▻ *adverb* sixthly. • **sixthly** *adverb* used to introduce the sixth point in a list. ⓔ Anglo-Saxon; see SIX + -TH.

sixth form ▻ *noun* in secondary education: the stage in which school subjects are taught to a level that prepares for higher education. • **sixth-former** *noun* a member of a sixth form.

sixth sense ▻ *noun* an unexplained power of intuition by which one is aware of things that are not seen, heard, touched, smelled or tasted.

sixties /'sɪkstiːz/ (often written **60s** or **60's**) ▻ *plural noun* **1** (**one's sixties**) the period of time between one's sixtieth and seventieth birthdays □ ***Jean must be in her sixties by now.*** **2** (**the sixties**) **a** the range of temperatures between sixty and seventy degrees □ ***Temperatures reached the low sixties today***; **b** the period of time between the sixtieth and seventieth years of a century □ ***born in the 60s.*** Also *as adj* □ ***sixties flares.***

sixtieth /'sɪkstɪəθ/ (often written **60th**) ▻ *adj* **1** in counting: **a** next after fifty-ninth; **b** last of sixty. **2** in sixtieth position. ▻ *noun* **1** one of sixty equal parts. Also *as adj* □ ***a sixtieth share.*** **2** a FRACTION equal to one divided by sixty (usually written $^1/_{60}$). **3** a person coming sixtieth, eg in a race or exam □ ***He came in a triumphant sixtieth out of a field of sixty-three.*** ⓔ Anglo-Saxon; see SIXTY + -TH.

sixty /'sɪkstɪ/ ▻ *noun* **1 a** the cardinal number 60; **b** the quantity that this represents, being one more than fifty-nine, or the product of ten and six. **2** any symbol for this, eg **60** or **LX**. Also *in compounds, forming adjectives and nouns*, with cardinal numbers between *one* and *nine* □ ***sixty-four.*** **3** the age of sixty. **4** something, especially a garment, or a person, whose size is denoted by the number 60. **5** a set or group of sixty people or things. **6** a score of sixty points. ▻ *adj* **1** totalling sixty. Also *in compounds, forming adjectives and nouns*, with ordinal numbers between *first* and *ninth* □ ***sixty-fourth.*** **2** aged sixty. See also SIXTIES, SIXTIETH. ⓔ Anglo-Saxon; see SIX + -TY.

sixty-four dollar question and **sixty-four thousand dollar question** ▻ *noun* **1** in US quiz shows: the final and most difficult question a contestant must answer in order to win the top prize money. **2** any hard or crucial question.

sixtyish /'sɪkstɪɪʃ/ ▻ *adj* **1** about sixty years old. **2** about sixty in number □ ***How many turned up? Oh, sixtyish.***

sixty-nine see SOIXANTE-NEUF

sizar /'saɪzə(r)/ ▻ *noun* at Cambridge University and Trinity College in Dublin: a student receiving an allowance from their college towards expenses. • **sizarship** *noun*. ⓔ 16c.

size¹ /saɪz/ ▻ *noun* **1** length, breadth, height or volume, or a combination of these; the dimensions of something. **2** largeness; magnitude □ ***We were amazed at its size.*** **3** any of a range of graded measurements into which especially garments and shoes are divided □ ***She takes a size 12*** □ ***What is your shoe size?*** ▻ *verb* (***sized***, ***sizing***) **1** to measure something in order to determine size. **2** to sort or arrange something according to size. • **sized** *adj, usually in compounds* having a particular size □ ***medium-sized.*** • **sizer** *noun* **1** a measurer or gauge. **2** *slang* something of great or considerable size. • **of a size** being of the same size. • **the size of it** *colloq* an assessment of the present situation or state of affairs. ⓔ 13c: from French *sise*, a variant of *assise* ASSIZE.

■ **size someone** or **something up 1** to take a mental measurement of them or it. **2** *colloq* to mentally judge their or its nature, quality or worth.

size² /saɪz/ ▻ *noun* a weak kind of glue used to stiffen paper and fabric, and to prepare walls for plastering and wallpapering. ▻ *verb* (***sized***, ***sizing***) to cover or treat with size. ⓔ 15c.

sizeable or **sizable** /'saɪzəbəl/ ▻ *adj* fairly large; being of a considerable size.

sizeism or **sizism** /'saɪzɪzəm/ ▻ *noun* discrimination against overweight people. • **sizeist** *noun, adj*.

sizzle /'sɪzəl/ ▻ *verb* (***sizzled***, ***sizzling***) *intr* **1** to make a hissing sound when, or as if when, frying in hot fat. **2** to be extremely hot □ ***sizzling weather.*** **3** *colloq* to be in a state of intense emotion, especially anger or excitement. ▻ *noun* **1** a sizzling sound. **2** extreme heat. • **sizzler** *noun*. ⓔ 17c: imitating the sound.

SJ ▻ *abbreviation* Society of Jesus.

sjambok /'ʃambɒk/ ▻ *noun* in S Africa: a whip made from dried rhinoceros or hippopotamus hide. ⓔ 19c: Afrikaans, from Malay *samboq*, from Urdu *chabuk*.

ska /skɑː/ ▻ *noun* a style of Jamaican popular music similar to reggae, played on trumpet, saxophone, etc, in an unpolished style with fast blaring rhythms. ⓔ 1960s: perhaps imitating the characteristic sound of the music.

skag see under SCAG

skat /skat/ ▻ *noun* a three-handed card game using 32 cards. ⓔ 19c: from French *escart* laying aside.

skate¹ ▻ *noun* **1** a boot with a device fitted to the sole for gliding smoothly over surfaces, either a steel blade for use on ice (ICE SKATE) or a set of small wheels for use on wooden and other surfaces (ROLLER SKATE). **2** the blade of an ice-skate. **3** a spell of skating. ▻ *verb* (***skated***, ***skating***) *intr* to move around on skates. • **skater** *noun*. • **skating**

noun moving on skates. • **get one's skates on** *colloq* to hurry up □ *Come on, get your skates on or we'll be late!* • **skate on thin ice** to risk danger, harm or embarrassment, especially through lack of care or good judgement. ⓘ 17c: from Dutch *schaats*, from French *eschasse* stilt, from German *schake* shank.

■ **skate over something** to hurry or rush over it □ *We'll skate over this next chapter.*

■ **skate round something** to avoid dealing with something or considering (a difficulty, etc).

skate² ▷ *noun* (*skate* or *skates*) a large cartilaginous edible flatfish with a greyish-brown upper surface with black flecks, a long pointed snout, large wing-like pectoral fins and a long slim tail. ⓘ 14c: from Norse *skata*.

skateboard ▷ *noun* a narrow shaped board mounted on sets of small wheels, usually ridden in a standing or crouching position. ⓘ 1960s.

skating rink ▷ *noun* **1** a large surface covered in ice for the use of ice-skates. **2** the building that houses this structure.

skedaddle /skɪˈdadəl/ ▷ *verb* (*skedaddled*, *skedaddling*) *intr*, *colloq* to run away or leave quickly. ▷ *noun* a hurried departure. ⓘ 19c.

skeet ▷ *noun* a form of clay-pigeon shooting in which the targets are launched at various angles. ⓘ 1920s: from Norse *skota* to shoot.

skein /skeɪn/ ▷ *noun* **1** a loosely tied coil of wool or thread. **2** a tangle; a confused bundle of things. **3** a flock of wild geese in flight. ⓘ 15c: from French *escaigne*.

skeletal /ˈskɛlɪtəl/ ▷ *adj* **1** similar to or like a skeleton. **2** painfully or extremely thin. **3** existing in outline only.

skeleton /ˈskɛlɪtən/ ▷ *noun* **1** the framework of bones that supports and often protects the body of an animal, and to which the muscles are usually attached. **2** the supporting veins of a leaf. **3** an initial basic structure or idea upon or around which anything is built. **4** an outline or framework □ *the skeleton of the plot*. **5** a scheme reduced to its essential or indispensible elements. **6** SKELETON STAFF. **7** *colloq* an unhealthily thin person or animal. ⓘ 16c: Greek, from *skeleton soma* dried body, from *skellein* to dry.

skeleton in the cupboard and (*US*) **skeleton in the closet** ▷ *noun* a shameful or slanderous fact concerning oneself or one's family that one tries to keep secret.

skeletonize or **skeletonise** /ˈskɛlɪtənaɪz/ ▷ *verb* (*skeletonized*, *skeletonizing*) to reduce to a skeleton.

skeleton key ▷ *noun* a key whose serrated or shaped edge is filed in such a way that it can open many different locks.

skeleton staff ▷ *noun* a set of staff or workforce reduced to a bare minimum.

skep ▷ *noun* **1** a large round wickerwork basket. **2** a beehive, especially one made from straw. • **skepful** *noun* (*skepfuls*) the amount that a skep will hold. ⓘ Anglo-Saxon *sceppe*, from Norse *skeppa*.

skeptic, **skeptical** and **skepticism** an alternative *N Amer* spelling of SCEPTIC, *etc*.

skerrick /ˈskɛrɪk/ ▷ *noun*, *especially US, Austral & NZ dialect, usually with negatives* a minute quantity; a scrap. ⓘ 1930s.

skerry /ˈskɛrɪ/ ▷ *noun* (*skerries*) a reef of rock or a small rocky island. ⓘ 17c: from Norse *sker*.

sketch ▷ *noun* (*sketches*) **1** a rough drawing quickly done, especially one without much detail used as a study towards a more finished work. **2** a rough plan. **3** a short account or outline □ *She gave us a quick sketch of the story*. **4** any of several short pieces of comedy presented as a programme. **5** a short musical composition. **6** a short descriptive essay. ▷ *verb* (*sketches*, *sketched*, *sketching*) **1** *tr & intr* to do a rough drawing or drawings of something. **2** to give a rough outline of something. • **sketchable** *adj*. • **sketcher** *noun*. ⓘ 17c: from Dutch *schets*, from Italian *schizzo*, from Latin *schedium*, from Greek *schedios* offhand.

sketchy /ˈskɛtʃɪ/ ▷ *adj* (*sketchier*, *sketchiest*) **1** like a sketch. **2** lacking detail; not complete or substantial. • **sketchily** *adverb*. • **sketchiness** *noun*.

skew /skjuː/ ▷ *adj* **1** slanted; oblique; askew. **2** *math* **a** said of lines: not lying in the same plane; **b** said of statistics or a curve representing them: not symmetrical about the MEAN³. ▷ *verb* (*skewed*, *skewing*) **1** *tr & intr* to slant or cause to slant. **2** to distort. ▷ *noun* a slanting position; obliquity □ *on the skew*. • **skewed** *adj*. ⓘ 14c: from French *eschuer*.

skewbald /ˈskjuːbɔːld/ ▷ *adj* said of an animal, especially a horse: marked with patches of white and another colour (other than black). ▷ *noun* a skewbald horse. ⓘ 17c: from SKEW + (PIE)BALD.

skewer /ˈskjuːə(r)/ ▷ *noun* a long wooden or metal pin pushed through chunks of meat or vegetables which are to be roasted. ▷ *verb* (*skewered*, *skewering*) to fasten or pierce with, or as if with, a skewer. ⓘ 17c: from dialect *skiver*.

skewness /ˈskjuːnəs/ ▷ *noun*, *math* a measure of the degree of asymmetry about the central value of a distribution.

skew-whiff /skjuːˈwɪf/ ▷ *adj*, *adverb*, *colloq* lying in a slanted position; crooked; awry. ⓘ 18c.

ski /skiː/ ▷ *noun* (*skis*) **1** one of a pair of long narrow runners of wood, metal or plastic, upturned at the front and attached to each of a pair of boots or to a vehicle for gliding over snow. **2** a WATER-SKI. ▷ *verb* (*skis*, *skied* or *ski'd*, *skiing*) *intr* to move on skis, especially as a sport or leisure activity. • **skiable** *adj* said of a surface: having conditions suitable for skiing. ⓘ 18c: from Norse *skith* piece of split wood.

skid ▷ *verb* (*skidded*, *skidding*) **1** *intr* said of a wheel, etc: to slide along without revolving. **2** *intr* said of a vehicle: to slip or slide at an angle, especially out of control. **3** to cause a vehicle to slide out of control. ▷ *noun* **1** an instance of skidding. **2** a support on which something rests or is brought to the required level. **3** a support on which heavy objects are slid along short stretches. **4** a runner on an aeroplane used when landing. **5** a ship's wooden fender. **6** a shoe or other device for controlling a wheel on a down-slope. • **put the skids under someone** *colloq* **1** to cause them to hurry. **2** to bring about their downfall; to cause them to stop. ⓘ 17c: see SKI.

skid lid ▷ *noun*, *slang* a crash helmet.

skidoo /skɪˈduː/ ▷ *noun* (*skidoos*) a motorized sledge, fitted with tracks at the rear and steerable skis at the front. ▷ *verb* (*skidooed*, *skiddoing*) **1** to use a skidoo. **2** to leave or depart hastily. ⓘ 1960s as *noun*, although *verb* sense 2 dates from early 20c.

skid pan ▷ *noun* a special slippery track on which drivers learn to control skidding vehicles.

skid row and **skid road** ▷ *noun*, *especially US colloq* the poorest or most squalid part of a town where vagrants, drunks, etc live.

skier¹ /ˈskiːə(r)/ ▷ *noun* someone who skis.

skier² see SKYER

skies *plural of* SKY

skiff ▷ *noun* a small light boat. ⓘ 16c: from French *esquif*, from Italian *schifo*, related to SHIP.

skiffle /ˈskɪfəl/ ▷ *noun*, *Brit* a strongly accented type of folk music influenced by jazz and blues, played with guitars, drums, washboard and often other unconventional instruments. ⓘ 1950s.

skiing /ˈskiːɪŋ/ ▻ *noun* the art of propelling oneself along snow using skis, with the aid of poles.

ski-joring /ˈskiːjɔːrɪŋ, -ˈjɔːrɪŋ/ ▻ *noun* the activity of being towed along on skis by a horse or motor vehicle. ◷ 1920s: from Norwegian *ski-kjøring* ski-diving.

skilful or (*US*) **skillful** /ˈskɪlfəl/ *adj* having or showing skill. • **skilfully** *adverb*. • **skilfulness** *noun*.

ski lift ▻ *noun* a device for carrying skiers, either by towing or on chairs, to the top of a slope so that they can ski down.

skill ▻ *noun* **1** expertness; dexterity. **2** a talent, craft or accomplishment, naturally acquired or developed through training. **3** (**skills**) aptitudes and abilities appropriate for a specific job. ◷ 12c: from Norse *skil* distinction.

skilled /skɪld/ ▻ *adj* **1** said of people: possessing skills; trained or experienced. **2** said of a job: requiring skill or showing the use of skill.

skillet /ˈskɪlɪt/ ▻ *noun* **1** a small long-handled saucepan. **2** *especially N Amer* a frying-pan. ◷ 15c: from French *escuelete*, from Latin *scutella* tray.

skilly /ˈskɪlɪ/ ▻ *noun* (*skillies*) a thin gruel or soup, usually made from oatmeal. ◷ 19c: a shortening of *skilligalee*.

skim ▻ *verb* (*skimmed*, *skimming*) **1** to remove floating matter from the surface of (a liquid). **2** (*often* **skim off**) to take something off by skimming. **3** *tr & intr* to brush or cause something to brush against or glide lightly over (a surface) ▫ ***He skimmed the table as he went past*** ▫ ***The bird's wings skimmed over the water.*** **4** to throw an object over a surface so as to make it bounce ▫ ***We skimmed stones on the river.*** ▻ *noun* **1** the act or process of skimming. **2** SKIMMED MILK. • **skimming** *noun*. ◷ 15c: from French *escume* SCUM.

▪ **skim over something 1** to read (a page, passage, etc) superficially. **2** to evade or sidestep it ▫ ***I thought he skimmed over that issue.***

▪ **skim through something 1** to glance through (eg a book). **2** to deal with or discuss it superficially.

skimmed milk and **skim-milk** ▻ *noun* milk from which all or virtually all the fat has been removed.

skimmer /ˈskɪmə(r)/ ▻ *noun* **1** someone or something that skims. **2** a device for skimming milk. **3** a tropical bird, related to the terns, that catches fish by flying low with its long narrow lower bill cutting the water surface. Also called **shearwater**. ◷ 14c.

skimmia /ˈskɪmɪə/ ▻ *noun* (*skimmias*) any of various Asiatic evergreen shrubs, cultivated for their holly-like leaves and red berries. ◷ 19c: from Japanese *shikimi*.

skimp ▻ *verb* (*skimped*, *skimping*) **1** *intr* (*often* **skimp on something**) to spend, use or give too little or only just enough of it. **2** *intr* to stint or restrict. **3** to carry out hurriedly or recklessly. ▻ *adj* scanty. ◷ 19c: perhaps a combination of SCANT + SCRIMP.

skimpy /ˈskɪmpɪ/ ▻ *adj* (*skimpier*, *skimpiest*) **1** inadequate; barely enough. **2** said of clothes: leaving much of the body uncovered; scanty. • **skimpily** *adverb*. • **skimpiness** *noun*. ◷ 19c.

skin ▻ *noun* **1** the tough flexible waterproof covering of the human or animal body. **2** an animal hide, with or without the fur or hair attached. **3** the outer covering of certain fruits and vegetables. **4** any outer covering or integument ▫ ***sausage skin.*** **5** complexion ▫ ***greasy skin.*** **6** a membrane, especially covering internal organs in animals. **7** a semi-solid coating or film on the surface of a liquid. **8** a container for liquids made from an animal hide. **9** the outer covering of a craft, eg aircraft. **10** (*usually* **skins**) *colloq, jazz* drums. **11** *slang* a SKINHEAD. **12** *slang* a cigarette paper for making a JOINT (*noun* 5). ▻ *verb* (*skinned*, *skinning*) **1** to remove or strip the skin from something ▫ ***skin 2 lb tomatoes.*** **2** to injure by scraping the skin ▫ ***He skinned his elbow when he fell.*** **3** *slang* to cheat or swindle. **4** *intr* (*often* **skin over**) said of a wound, etc: to become covered with skin. • **by the skin of one's teeth** very narrowly; only just. • **get under someone's skin** *colloq* **1** to greatly annoy and irritate them. **2** to become their consuming passion or obsession. • **no skin off one's nose** *colloq* not a cause of even slight concern or nuisance to one ▫ ***It's no skin off my nose if he decides to resign.*** • **save one's** or **someone's skin** or **neck** see under SAVE. • **skin someone alive** to severely reprimand them ▫ ***I'll be skinned alive if I don't get back in time.*** ◷ 12c: from Norse *skinn*.

▪ **skin up** to prepare and roll a cigarette that contains an illegal substance, especially cannabis or cocaine.

skincare ▻ *noun* care and protection of the skin by using specific cosmetic products.

skin-deep ▻ *adj* superficial; shallow or not deeply fixed. ▻ *adverb* superficially.

skin-diving ▻ *noun* underwater swimming with breathing equipment carried on the back, but with no wet suit and no connection to a boat. • **skin-diver** *noun*.

skin flick ▻ *noun, slang* a pornographic film.

skinflint ▻ *noun, colloq* a very ungenerous or stingy person.

skinful /ˈskɪnfʊl/ ▻ *noun* (*skinfuls*) *slang* a large amount of alcohol, enough to make one thoroughly drunk.

skin graft ▻ *noun, surgery* the transplantation of a piece of skin from one part of the body to another where there has been an injury, especially a burn.

skinhead ▻ *noun* a person, especially a white youth and generally one of a gang, with closely cropped hair, tight jeans, heavy boots and anti-establishment attitudes.

skink ▻ *noun* a lizard found in tropical and temperate regions worldwide, usually with a long thin body, a broad rounded tongue, and short legs or none at all. ◷ 16c: from Latin *scincus*, from Greek *skinkos*.

skinned /skɪnd/ ▻ *verb, past tense, past participle of* SKIN. ▻ *adj* **1** having had the skin removed ▫ ***a skinned tomato.*** **2** *in compounds* having a specific type of skin ▫ ***brown-skinned.***

skinny /ˈskɪnɪ/ ▻ *adj* (*skinnier*, *skinniest*) **1** similar to or like skin. **2** said of a person or animal: very thin; emaciated. **3** *colloq* said of a pullover, T-shirt, etc: tight-fitting. ◷ 16c.

skinny-dip ▻ *verb, intr, colloq* to go swimming naked. • **skinny-dipper** *noun* a person who skinny-dips. • **skinny-dipping** *noun*.

skin search see under STRIP SEARCH

skint ▻ *adj, slang* without money; hard up; broke. ◷ 1930s: from SKINNED.

skin test ▻ *noun* a test made by applying a small amount of a substance to, or introducing a substance beneath, a person's skin in order to test for an allergy, immunity to disease, etc.

skin-tight ▻ *adj* said of a piece of clothing: very tight-fitting.

skip¹ ▻ *verb* (*skipped*, *skipping*) **1** *intr* to move along with light springing or hopping steps on alternate feet. **2** *intr* to make jumps over a skipping-rope. **3** to omit, leave out or pass over ▫ ***We'll skip the next chapter.*** **4** *colloq* not to attend eg a class in school. **5** to make (a stone) skim over a surface. **6** said of a stone: to skim over a surface. ▻ *noun* **1** a skipping movement. **2** the act of omitting or leaving something out. • **skipper** *noun* someone or something that skips. • **skip it!** *colloq* forget it; ignore it; it is not important. ◷ 13c: as *skippen*, from Norse *skopa* to run.

skip² ▻ *noun* **1** *Brit* a large metal container for rubbish from eg building work. **2** a large (especially wicker) chest for storing eg theatrical costumes, sports equipment, etc. **3** a lift in a coal mine for raising minerals. ⓒ 19c: a variant of SKEP.

ski pants ▷ *noun* trousers made from a stretch fabric and kept taut by a band under the foot, originally designed for skiing but often worn as casual wear.

skipjack ▷ *noun* (***skipjack*** or ***skipjacks***) **1** any of a number of different species of fish which are able to jump out of the water. **2** (*in full* **skipjack tuna**) a tropical fish with a striped body.

skipper[1] /'skɪpə(r)/ ▷ *noun* **1** a ship's captain. **2** the captain of an aeroplane. **3** the captain of a team. ▷ *verb* (***skippered, skippering***) to act as skipper of something. ⓒ 14c: from Dutch *schipper* shipper.

skipper[2] see SAURY

skippet /'skɪpɪt/ ▷ *noun* a flat wooden box for protecting a seal on a document. ⓒ 14c as *skipet*.

skipping /'skɪpɪŋ/ ▷ *noun* the art or activity of skipping using a skipping-rope.

skipping-rope ▷ *noun* a rope swung backwards and forwards or twirled in a circular motion, either by the person skipping or by two other people each holding an end, for jumping over as exercise or as a children's game.

skirl *Scots* ▷ *noun* the high-pitched sound of bagpipes. ▷ *verb* (***skirled, skirling***) **1** *intr* to make this sound. **2** *tr & intr* to shriek or sing in a high-pitched manner. ⓒ 14c: from Norwegian *skrella* crash.

skirmish /'skɜːmɪʃ/ ▷ *noun* (***skirmishes***) **1** a brief battle during a war, especially away from the main fighting. **2** any minor fight or dispute. ▷ *verb* (***skirmishes, skirmished, skirmishing***) *intr* to engage in a skirmish. ● **skirmisher** *noun*. ⓒ 14c: from French *escarmouche*.

skirt ▷ *noun* **1** a garment that hangs from the waist, worn chiefly by women and girls. **2** the part of a woman's dress, coat, gown, etc from the waist down. **3** any part or attachment resembling a skirt. **4** the flap around the base of a hovercraft containing the air-cushion. Also called APRON. **5** a saddle-flap. **6** a cut of beef from the rear part of the belly; the midriff. **7 a** *slang* a woman or women collectively; **b** (*also* **a bit of skirt**) *slang* a woman regarded as an object of sexual desire. ▷ *verb* (***skirted, skirting***) **1** to border something. **2** to pass along or around the edge of something. **3** to avoid confronting (eg a problem) □ *He's just skirting the issue.* **4** *intr* (*usually* **skirt along, around,** *etc* **something**) to be on or pass along the border of something. ● **skirted** *adj*. ⓒ 13c: from Norse *skyrta* shirt.

skirting /'skɜːtɪŋ/ ▷ *noun* **1** fabric used for skirts. **2** SKIRTING-BOARD.

skirting-board ▷ *noun* the narrow wooden board next to the floor round the walls of a room.

skit ▷ *noun* a short satirical piece of writing or drama. ⓒ 16c: perhaps related to Norse *skjota* to SHOOT.

skite ▷ *verb* (***skited, skiting***) *intr, Austral slang* to boast. ▷ *noun* **1** boastful chatter. **2** a boastful person. ⓒ 19c.

skitter /'skɪtə(r)/ ▷ *verb* (***skittered, skittering***) *intr* **1** to skim over the surface of water. **2** to fish by drawing the bait jerkily over the surface of the water. **3** to scamper or scuttle off. ⓒ 19c: perhaps from SKIT.

skittish /'skɪtɪʃ/ ▷ *adj* **1** lively and playful; spirited. **2** frequently changing mood or opinion; fickle or capricious. **3** said of a horse: easily frightened. ● **skittishly** *adverb*. ● **skittishness** *noun*. ⓒ 15c.

skittle /'skɪtəl/ ▷ *noun* **1** each of the upright bottle-shaped wooden or plastic targets used in a game of skittles. **2** (**skittles**) a game in which balls are rolled down an alley towards a set of nine of the above targets, the object being to knock over as many of these as possible. ⓒ 17c: perhaps from Norse *skutill*, and related to Danish *skyttel* shuttle.

skive ▷ *verb* (***skived, skiving***) **1** *intr* to pare or split leather. **2** *tr & intr, Brit colloq* (*also* **skive off**) to evade work or a duty, especially through laziness □ *I'm going to skive French today* □ *We're skiving off class today.* ▷ *noun* the act or an instance of skiving □ *I chose drama instead of PE 'cos it's such a skive.* ● **skiving** *noun*. ● **skivy** *adj*. ⓒ 19c: from Norse *skifa*.

skiver *noun* **1** split sheepskin leather. **2** a person or machine that skives (see SKIVE *verb* 1). **3** a person who avoids work or a duty.

skivvy /'skɪvɪ/ *colloq* ▷ *noun* (***skivvies***) **1** *derog* a servant, especially a woman, who does unpleasant household jobs. **2** *especially US slang* a man's undervest. **3** *Austral, NZ* a knitted cotton polo-necked sweater. ▷ *verb* (***skivvies, skivvied, skivvying***) *intr* to work as, or as if as, a skivvy. ⓒ Early 20c.

skoal /skoul/ or **skol** /skɒl/ ▷ *exclamation* hail!; a loud friendly toast before drinking. ⓒ 16c: from Norwegian *skaal* a bowl.

skrimshank see SCRIMSHANK

skua /'skjuːə/ ▷ *noun* (***skuas***) any of various large predatory gull-like seabirds, native to Arctic and Antarctic waters, usually with dark brown plumage and pale underparts. ⓒ 17c: from Norse *skufr*.

skulduggery or (*N Amer*) **skullduggery** /skʌl'dʌgərɪ/ *noun* (***skulduggeries***) unscrupulous, underhand or dishonest behaviour; trickery. Also written **sculduggery**. ⓒ 18c: from Scots *sculduddery* unchastity.

skulk ▷ *verb* (***skulked, skulking***) *intr* **1** to sneak off out of the way. **2** to hide or lurk, planning mischief. ● **skulker** *noun*. ● **skulking** *noun*. ⓒ 13c: Norse; related to Danish *skulke*.

skull ▷ *noun* **1** in vertebrates: the hard cartilaginous or bony framework of the head, including the cranium (which encloses the brain), face and jaws. **2** *colloq, often derog* the head or brain; intelligence □ *Can't you get it through your thick skull?* **3** a skullcap, especially one made of metal. ● **out of one's skull 1** mad or crazy. **2** extremely drunk. ⓒ 13c as *scolle*: from Norse *skalli*.

skull and crossbones ▷ *noun* a representation of a human skull with two femurs arranged like an X underneath, used formerly as a pirate's symbol, now as a symbol of death or danger.

skullcap ▷ *noun* **1** a small brimless cap fitting closely on the head. **2** the top of the skull. **3** *bot* any of various labiate plants with helmet-shaped flowers. ⓒ 17c.

skunk ▷ *noun* (***skunk*** or ***skunks***) **1** a small American mammal related to the weasel, best known for the foul-smelling liquid which it squirts from musk glands at the base of its tail in order to deter predators. **2** the fur from this animal. **3** *derog* a despised person. ⓒ 17c: from Algonquian *segonku*.

sky ▷ *noun* (***skies***) **1** the apparent dome of space in which the Sun, Moon and stars can be seen. **2** (**skies**) the heavens. **3** (*often* **skies**) the appearance of this area as a reflection of weather □ *dismal skies.* **4** the maximum limit or aim □ *Aim for the sky.* **5** the upper rows of pictures in a gallery. **6** sky-blue. ▷ *verb* (***skies, skied, skying***) **1** *cricket* to mishit (a ball) high into the air. **2** *rowing* to raise (the oar) too high. ● **the sky's the limit** there is no upper limit, eg to the amount of money that may be spent, or achievements to be made. ● **to the skies** in a lavish or extremely enthusiastic manner □ *He praised him to the skies.* ⓒ 13c: Norse, meaning 'cloud'.

sky-blue ▷ *noun* the colour of a cloudless sky; light blue. ▷ *adj* referring or relating to this colour.

sky-diving ▷ *noun* free-falling from an aircraft, often involving performing manoeuvres in mid-air, with a long delay before the parachute is opened. ● **sky-diver** *noun*.

skyer or **skier** /'skaɪə(r)/ ▷ *noun, cricket* a hit high into the air.

Skye terrier ▷ *noun* a small terrier with a long body, very short legs, a long wiry coat, and long hair on its head, ears and tail.

sky-high ▷ *adj, adverb* said especially of prices: very high.

skyjack ▷ *verb, slang* to hijack (an aircraft). • **skyjacker** *noun*. • **skyjacking** *noun*. ◷ 1960s: modelled on HIJACK.

Skylab ▷ *noun, astron* **1** the first US space station, launched from the Kennedy Space Center in May 1973, and manned over a period of nine months by three crews of three men each. **2** (**skylab**) any orbiting experimental space station. ◷ 1970s.

skylark ▷ *noun* a small lark, native to Europe and Asia, which inhabits open country and is known for its loud clear warbling song, performed in flight. ▷ *verb* (***skylarked, skylarking***) *intr, old use* to lark about; to frolic. • **skylarking** *noun*. ◷ 17c.

skylight ▷ *noun* a (usually small) window in a roof or ceiling.

skyline ▷ *noun* the outline of buildings, hills and trees seen against the sky; the horizon.

sky pilot ▷ *noun, slang* a clergyman, especially a military chaplain.

skyrocket ▷ *noun* a firework that explodes very high in the sky. ▷ *verb, intr* to rise high and fast.

skyscraper ▷ *noun* an extremely tall building.

skyward /'skaɪwəd/ ▷ *adj* directed towards the sky. ▷ *adverb* (*also* **skywards**) towards the sky.

skyway ▷ *noun* a route used by aircraft.

skywriting ▷ *noun* **1** the tracing of words in the sky by the release of smoke from an aircraft. **2** the words formed in this way.

slab ▷ *noun* **1** a thick flat rectangular piece of stone, etc. **2** a thick slice, especially of cake. **3** an outer plank sawn from a log. ▷ *verb* (***slabbed, slabbing***) **1** to cut or make into slabs. **2** to pave with concrete slabs. • **slabbed** *adj*. ◷ 13c as *sclabbe*.

slack¹ ▷ *adj* **1** limp or loose; not pulled or stretched tight. **2** not careful or diligent; lax or remiss. **3** not busy ◻ *Business is a bit slack these days.* **4** said of the tide, etc: still; neither ebbing nor flowing. **5** *phonetics* pronounced with the tongue relaxed; LAX. ▷ *adverb* in a slack manner; partially. ▷ *noun* **1** a loosely hanging part, especially of a rope. **2** a period of little trade or other activity. ▷ *verb* (*also* **slacken**) (***slacked, slacking; slackened, slackening***) (*often* **slack off**) **1** *intr* (*also* **slack off** or **up**) to become slower; to slow one's working pace through tiredness or laziness ◻ *Stop slacking!* **2** *tr & intr* to make or become looser. **3** *intr* to become less busy ◻ *work is slackening off for the winter.* **4** to fail or flag. **5** *tr & intr* to make or become less rigid and more easy or relaxed. ◷ Anglo-Saxon *slæc*.

slack² ▷ *noun* coal dust or tiny fragments of coal. ◷ 15c: from German *slecke*.

slacken see under SLACK

slacker /'slakə(r)/ ▷ *noun* an idle person; a shirker.

slacks ▷ *plural noun, dated* a type of loose casual trousers, worn by both males and females.

slag¹ ▷ *noun* **1** the layer of waste material that forms on the surface of molten metal ore during smelting and refining. **2** waste left over from coal mining. **3** scoriaceous lava. **4** vitrified cylinders. ▷ *verb* (***slagged, slagging***) *intr* said of molten metal ore: to throw up or form into a surface layer of slag. ◷ 16c: from German *slagge*.

slag² ▷ *verb* (***slagged, slagging***) *slang* (*usually* **slag someone off**) to criticize or deride them harshly or speak disparagingly about them ◻ *She's always slagging somebody* ◻ *Who are you slagging off now?* ◷ 1970s: from SLAG¹.

slag³ ▷ *noun, derog slang* someone, especially a woman, who regularly has casual sex with many different people. ◷ 18c: from SLAG¹.

slag heap ▷ *noun* **1** a hill or mound formed from coalmining waste. **2** an imaginary dumping ground ◻ *That's two more redundancies for the slag heap.*

slain *past participle of* SLAY

slake ▷ *verb* (***slaked, slaking***) **1** *literary* to satisfy or quench (thirst, desire or anger). **2** to cause (lime) to crumble by adding water. **3** to refresh with moisture. **4** *poetic* to abate or mitigate; to allay. ◷ Anglo-Saxon *slacian*.

slaked lime ▷ *noun* calcium hydroxide, **$Ca(OH)_2$**, manufactured from LIME, used in the production of cements. Also called **caustic lime**.

slalom /'slɑːləm/ ▷ *noun* a race, on skis or in canoes, in and out of obstacles on a winding course designed to test tactical skill. ◷ 1920s: Norwegian.

slam¹ ▷ *verb* (***slammed, slamming***) **1** *tr & intr* to shut loudly and with violence ◻ *The door slammed* ◻ *She slammed the window shut.* **2** *tr & intr* (*usually* **slam against, down, into**, *etc*) *colloq* to make or cause something to make loud heavy contact ◻ *He slammed his books down on the table.* **3** *slang* to criticize severely. ▷ *noun* **1** the act or sound of slamming. **2** a severe criticism. ◷ 17c: from Norwegian *slemma*.

slam² see GRAND SLAM, LITTLE SLAM

slammer /'slamə(r)/ ▷ *noun, slang* (**the slammer**) prison.

slander /'slɑːndə(r)/ ▷ *noun* **1** *law* damaging defamation by spoken words, or by looks or gestures. **2** a false, malicious and damaging spoken statement about a person. **3** the making of such statements; calumny. ▷ *verb* (***slandered, slandering***) to speak about someone in such a way. Compare LIBEL. • **slanderer** *noun*. • **slanderous** *adj* **1** said of words, reports, etc: characterized by or amounting to slander. **2** said of a person: given to using slander. ◷ 13c: from French *esclandre*, from Latin *scandalum*, from Greek *skandalon* snare or scandal.

> ***slander***
>
> See Usage Note at **libel**.

slang ▷ *noun* **1** originally the coarse language used by thieves and disreputable characters. **2** very informal words and phrases used by any class, profession or set of people. **3** language not accepted for dignified use. Also *as adj* ◻ *a slang dictionary.* ▷ *verb* (***slanged, slanging***) to speak abusively to someone using coarse language. • **slanginess** *noun*. • **slanging** *noun*. • **slangy** *adj*. ◷ 18c.

slanging match ▷ *noun, colloq* an angry exchange of insults or abuse.

slant /slɑːnt/ ▷ *verb* (***slanted, slanting***) **1** *intr* to be at an angle as opposed to horizontal or vertical; to slope. **2** to turn, strike or fall obliquely or at an angle. **3** to present (information, etc) in a biased way, or for a particular audience or readership. ▷ *noun* **1** a sloping position, surface or line. **2** a point of view, opinion or way of looking at a particular thing ◻ *Well, taking a slightly different slant, we can see him as a swindler.* ▷ *adj* sloping; lying at an angle. • **slanted** *adj*. • **slanting** *adj*. • **slantingly** *adverb*. ◷ 15c as *slent*.

slantwise and **slantways** ▷ *adverb, adj* at an angle; slanting.

slap ▷ *noun* **1** a blow with the palm of the hand or anything flat. **2** the sound made by such a blow, or by the impact of one flat surface with another. **3** a snub or rebuke. ▷ *verb* (***slapped, slapping***) **1** to strike with the open hand or anything flat. **2** to bring or send with a slapping sound ◻ *He slapped the newspaper down on the* *table.* **3** (*often* **slap something on**) *colloq* to apply thickly and carelessly □ *She quickly slapped make-up on her face.* **4** (*often* **slap someone down**) *colloq* to reject or contradict them abruptly; to rebuke them. ▻ *adverb, colloq* **1** exactly or precisely □ *slap in the middle.* **2** heavily or suddenly; with a slap □ *He fell slap on his face.* • **a slap in the face** *colloq* an insult or rebuff. • **a slap on the back** *colloq* congratulations. • **a slap on the wrist** *colloq, often facetious* a mild reprimand. ⓒ 17c: from German dialect *slapp.*

slap and tickle ▻ *noun, humorous colloq* kissing and cuddling; sexual activity of any kind.

slap-bang ▻ *adverb, colloq* **1** exactly or precisely □ *slap-bang in the middle.* **2** violently; directly and with force □ *He drove slap-bang into the wall.*

slapdash ▻ *adverb* in a careless and hurried manner. ▻ *adj* careless and hurried □ *a slapdash piece of work.*

slap-happy ▻ *adj, colloq* **1** cheerfully carefree or careless; happy-go-lucky. **2** punch-drunk.

slapstick ▻ *noun* (*in full* **slapstick comedy**) comedy in which the humour is derived from boisterous antics of all kinds. ⓒ 19c: from a mechanical sound effects device, used to punctuate (comic) stage fights with loud reports.

slap-up ▻ *adj, colloq* said of a meal: lavish; extravagant.

slash¹ ▻ *verb* (*slashes, slashed, slashing*) **1** *tr & intr* to make sweeping cuts or cutting strokes, especially repeatedly. **2** to cut by striking violently and often randomly. **3** to make long cuts or gashes in something. **4** to slit (a garment) so as to reveal the lining or material underneath. **5** *colloq* to reduce (prices, etc) suddenly and drastically. ▻ *noun* (*slashes*) **1** a sweeping cutting stroke. **2** a long and sometimes deep cut. **3** (*also* **slash mark**) an oblique line (/) in writing or printing; a solidus. **4** a cut in cloth intended to reveal the colours or material underneath. • **slashed** *adj.* • **slasher** *noun.* • **slashing** *noun, adj.* ⓒ 14c: probably from French *esclachier* to break.

slash² *coarse slang* ▻ *verb* (*slashes, slashed, slashing*) *intr* to urinate. ▻ *noun* (*slashes*) an act of urinating. ⓒ 1970s: perhaps from Scots dialect, meaning 'large splash'.

slash and burn ▻ *noun, agric* a system of agriculture, common in tropical regions, in which trees and natural undergrowth are cut down and burned, and crops are then grown on the bare soil for a few years until it loses its fertility.

slat ▻ *noun* a thin strip, especially of wood or metal. • **slatted** *adj* having, or made up of, slats. ⓒ 14c: from French *esclat.*

slate¹ ▻ *noun* **1** *geol* a shiny dark grey metamorphic rock that is easily split into thin flat layers, formed by the compression of clays and shales, and used for roofing and flooring. **2** a roofing tile made of this. **3** *formerly* a piece of this for writing on. **4** a record of credit given to a customer □ *put it on my slate.* **5** a dull grey colour. ▻ *verb* (*slated, slating*) to cover (a roof) with slates. ▻ *adj* **1** made of slate. **2** slate-coloured. • **slated** *adj.* • **slating** *noun.* • **slaty** *adj.* • **have a slate loose** to be mentally deranged or mad. • **on the slate** on credit. • **wipe the slate clean** to enable a person to make a fresh start in a job, relationship, etc by ignoring past mistakes, acts of crime, etc. See also CLEAN SLATE. ⓒ 14c: from French *esclate.*

slate² ▻ *verb* (*slated, slating*) *colloq* to criticize extremely harshly; to abuse or reprimand. ⓒ 19c: Norse.

slattern /ˈslatən/ ▻ *noun, old use* a woman of dirty or untidy appearance or habits; a slut. • **slatternly** *adj.* • **slatternliness** *noun.* ⓒ 17c: from dialect *slatter* to slop.

slaughter /ˈslɔːtə(r)/ ▻ *noun* **1** the killing of animals, especially for food. **2** cruel and violent murder. **3** the large-scale indiscriminate killing of people or animals. ▻ *verb* (*slaughtered, slaughtering*) **1** to subject to slaughter. **2** *colloq* to defeat resoundingly; to trounce □ *I was slaughtered at tennis yesterday.* • **slaughterer** *noun.* • **slaughterous** *adj* inclined to slaughter; murderous. ⓒ 13c: from Norse *slatr* butchers' meat.

slaughterhouse ▻ *noun* a place where animals are killed for food; an abattoir.

Slav /slɑːv/ ▻ *noun* a member of any of various Central and E European peoples speaking SLAVONIC languages including Russian, Czech, Slovak, Bulgarian, Polish, Serb and Slovenian. • **Slav** *adj* **1** referring or relating to the Slavs. **2** SLAVONIC. ⓒ 14c: from Latin *Sclavus.*

slave ▻ *noun* **1** *historical* someone owned by and acting as servant to another, with no personal freedom. **2** a person who is submissive under domination. **3** a person who works extremely hard for another; a drudge. **4** a person submissively devoted to another. **5** (*also* **a slave to something**) a person whose life is dominated by a specific activity or thing □ *She's a slave to her work.* **6** a mechanism controlled by another mechanism, eg in computing, by a central processor, or by remote control. ▻ *verb* (*slaved, slaving*) *intr* to work like or as a slave; to work hard and ceaselessly. ⓒ 13c: from French *esclave*, originally meaning a 'Slav'.

slave-driver ▻ *noun* **1** *historical* someone employed to supervise slaves to ensure they work hard. **2** *colloq* someone who demands very hard work from others.

slaver¹ /ˈsleɪvə(r)/ *noun, historical* **1** someone involved in the buying and selling of slaves. **2** a ship for transporting slaves. ⓒ Early 19c.

slaver² /ˈslavə(r), ˈsleɪvə(r)/ *noun* spittle running from the mouth. ▻ *verb* (*slavered, slavering*) *intr* **1** to let spittle run from the mouth; to dribble. **2** (*also* **slaver over someone**) to fawn over them, especially lustfully. **3** *colloq* to talk nonsense. • **slaverer** *noun.* • **slavering** *adj.* • **slaveringly** *adverb.* ⓒ 14c.

slavery /ˈsleɪvərɪ/ ▻ *noun* **1** the state of being a slave. **2** the practice of owning slaves. **3** extremely hard work; toil or drudgery. ⓒ 16c.

Slavic see under SLAVONIC

slavish /ˈsleɪvɪʃ/ ▻ *adj* **1** characteristic of, belonging to or befitting a slave. **2** rigid or unwavering in following rules or instructions. **3** very closely copied or imitated; unoriginal. • **slavishly** *adverb.* • **slavishness** *noun.*

Slavonic /sləˈvɒnɪk/ or **Slavic** /ˈslɑːvɪk/ ▻ *noun* a group of Central and E European languages that includes Russian, Polish, Bulgarian, Czech, Slovak, Croatian, Serbian and Slovenian. ▻ *adj* referring or relating to these languages, the peoples speaking them, or their cultures. ⓒ 17c: see SLAV.

slaw ▻ *noun, N Amer* cabbage salad; coleslaw. ⓒ 19c: from Dutch *sla*, short for *salade* SALAD.

slay /sleɪ/ ▻ *verb* (*slays, past tense* **slew** /sluː/, *past participle* **slain** /sleɪn/, *slaying*) **1** *tr & intr, archaic or literary* to kill. **2** to amuse or impress someone greatly. • **slayer** *noun.* ⓒ Anglo-Saxon *slean.*

sleaze / sliːz/ ▻ *noun, colloq* **1** sleaziness. **2** someone of low, especially moral, standards.

sleazy /ˈsliːzɪ/ ▻ *adj* (*sleazier, sleaziest*) *colloq* **1** dirty and neglected-looking. **2** cheaply suggestive of sex or crime; disreputable and considered to be of low standards, especially with regard to morals □ *a sleazy bar.* • **sleazily** *adverb.* • **sleaziness** *noun* the condition or state of being sleazy. ⓒ 17c.

sled ▻ *noun* **1** a SLEDGE. **2** a structure without wheels used for conveying goods, especially on snow. ▻ *verb* (*sledded, sledding*) **1** *intr* to SLEDGE. **2** to convey someone or something by sled. • **sledding** *noun.* ⓒ 14c: from German *sledde.*

sledge¹ ▻ *noun* **1** a vehicle with ski-like runners for travelling over snow, drawn by horses or dogs. **2** a smaller vehicle of a similar design for children, for sliding on the snow; a toboggan. **3** a framework without wheels used for dragging goods along. ▷ *verb* (***sledged***, ***sledging***) *intr* **1** to travel by sledge. **2** to play on a sledge. **3** to convey by sledge. • **sledger** *noun*. • **sledging** *noun*. ◷ 17c: from Dutch *sleedse*.

sledge² ▷ *noun* a SLEDGEHAMMER.

sledgehammer ▷ *noun* a large heavy hammer swung with both arms. ◷ Anglo-Saxon *slecg*, from *slean* to strike.

sleek ▷ *adj* (***sleeker***, ***sleekest***) **1** said of hair, fur, etc: smooth, soft and glossy. **2** having a well-fed and prosperous appearance. **3** insincerely polite or flattering; slick in manner. ▷ *verb* (***sleeked***, ***sleeking***) to smooth (especially hair). • **sleekly** *adverb*. • **sleekness** *noun*. ◷ 16c: a variant of SLICK.

sleep ▷ *noun* **1** in humans and many animals: a readily reversible state of natural unconsciousness during which the body's functional powers are restored, and physical movements are minimal. **2** a period of such rest. **3** *colloq* mucus that collects in the corners of the eyes during such rest. **4** *poetic* death. ▷ *verb* (***slept***, ***sleeping***) *intr* **1** to rest in a state of sleep. **2** to be motionless, inactive or dormant. **3** *tr* to provide or contain sleeping accommodation for (the specified number) □ *The caravan sleeps four.* **4** *colloq* to be in a dreamy state, not paying attention, etc. **5** *poetic* to be dead. • **go to sleep 1** to pass into a state of sleep. **2** *colloq* said of a limb: to be temporarily numb through lack of blood circulation. • **lose sleep over something** *colloq, usually with negatives* to be worried or preoccupied by it. • **put someone** or **something to sleep 1** to anaesthetize them. **2** *euphemistic* to kill (an animal) painlessly with an injected drug. ◷ Anglo-Saxon *slæp*.

■ **sleep around** to engage in casual sexual relations.

■ **sleep in 1** to sleep later than usual in the morning. **2** to sleep overnight at one's place of work; to live in.

■ **sleep something off** to recover from it by sleeping.

■ **sleep on something** to delay taking a decision about it until the following morning in the hope that one might have a better intuitive feel for the best course of action.

■ **sleep out 1** to sleep out of doors. **2** to sleep away from one's place of work; to live out.

■ **sleep with someone** to have sexual relations with them.

sleeper ▷ *noun* **1** someone who sleeps, especially in a specified way □ *a light sleeper* □ *a heavy sleeper.* **2** any of the horizontal wooden or concrete beams supporting the rails on a railway track. **3 a** a railway carriage providing sleeping accommodation for passengers; **b** a train with such carriages □ *took the sleeper to London.* **4** *colloq* a record, film, book, etc, which suddenly becomes popular after an initial period of uninterest. **5** a spy who spends a long time establishing him- or herself as an inoffensive citizen, usually in a foreign country, preparing for the time he or she will be required to pass on information. ◷ 13c.

sleepier, **sleepiest**, *etc* see under SLEEPY

sleeping-bag ▷ *noun* a large quilted sack for sleeping in when camping, etc.

sleeping car, **sleeping carriage** and **sleeping coach** ▷ *noun* a railway carriage fitted with sleeping compartments. See also SLEEPER sense 3.

sleeping partner ▷ *noun* a business partner who invests money in a business without taking part in its management. Also called **silent partner**.

sleeping pill ▷ *noun* a pill which contains a sedative drug that induces sleep.

sleeping policeman ▷ *noun, colloq* each of a series of low humps built into the surface of a road, intended to slow down motor traffic in residential areas, parks, etc.

sleeping sickness ▷ *noun* an infectious disease, caused by a parasitic protozoan and transmitted by the tsetse fly of E Africa, so called because, if left untreated, the later stages of the disease are characterized by extreme drowsiness, and eventually death.

sleepless ▷ *adj* **1** characterized by an inability to sleep □ *a sleepless night.* **2** unable to sleep. • **sleeplessly** *adverb*. • **sleeplessness** *noun*.

sleepwalking ▷ *noun* a condition in which the affected person walks about while asleep, but on waking has no memory of the event, sometimes a symptom of stress. Also called SOMNAMBULISM. • **sleepwalker** *noun*. • **sleepwalking** *noun*.

sleepy /ˈsliːpɪ/ ▷ *adj* (***sleepier***, ***sleepiest***) **1** feeling the desire or need to sleep; drowsy. **2** suggesting sleep or drowsiness □ *sleepy music.* **3** characterized by quietness and a lack of activity □ *a sleepy village.* • **sleepily** *adverb*. • **sleepiness** *noun*. ◷ 13c.

sleepyhead ▷ *noun, colloq* **1** a sleepy person. **2** someone who often feels sleepy, or who needs a lot of sleep. **3** someone who tends to daydream a lot.

sleet ▷ *noun* rain mixed with snow and/or hail. ▷ *verb* (***sleeted***, ***sleeting***) *intr* to rain and snow simultaneously. • **sleetiness** *noun*. • **sleety** *adj*. ◷ 13c as *slete*.

sleeve ▷ *noun* **1** the part of a garment that covers the arm. **2** any tube-like cover. **3** *engineering* a tube, especially of a different metal, fitted inside a metal cylinder or tube, either as protection or to decrease the diameter. **4** the cardboard or paper envelope in which a RECORD (*noun* 4) is stored. **5** a WINDSOCK. • **sleeveless** *adj* having no sleeves □ *a sleeveless dress.* • **laugh up one's sleeve** to laugh privately or secretly. • **roll up one's sleeves** to prepare oneself for a task, especially an unpleasant manual one. • **up one's sleeve** in secret reserve, possibly for later use. ◷ Anglo-Saxon *slefe*.

sleeve board ▷ *noun* a small board for ironing sleeves.

sleeved /sliːvd/ ▷ *adj* **1** having sleeves. **2** *in compounds* having sleeves of a specified kind □ *a short-sleeved blouse.*

sleeving /ˈsliːvɪŋ/ ▷ *noun, electronics* a tubular flexible insulation for bare conductor wires.

sleigh /sleɪ/ ▷ *noun, especially N Amer* a large horse-drawn sledge. ▷ *verb* (***sleighed***, ***sleighing***) *intr* to travel by sleigh. • **sleighing** *noun*. ◷ 17c: from Dutch *slee*.

sleigh bell ▷ *noun* a small bell attached to a sleigh-horse or its harness.

sleight /slaɪt/ ▷ *noun* **1** dexterity. **2** cunning or trickery. ◷ 13c: from Norse *slægth* cunning, from *slægr* sly.

sleight of hand ▷ *noun* the quick and deceptive movement of the hands in the performing of magic tricks.

slender /ˈslɛndə(r)/ ▷ *adj* **1** attractively slim. **2** thin or narrow; slight □ *by a slender margin.* **3** meagre □ *slender means.* • **slenderly** *adverb*. • **slenderness** *noun*. ◷ 14c as *slendre*.

slenderize or **slenderise** /ˈslɛndəraɪz/ ▷ *verb* (***slenderized***, ***slenderizing***) to make or become slender.

slept *past tense, past participle of* SLEEP

sleuth /sluːθ/ *colloq* ▷ *noun* a detective. ▷ *verb* (***sleuthed***, ***sleuthing***) *intr* to work as a detective. ◷ 19c: from Norse *sloth* trail.

S level /ɛs —/ (*in full* **Special level**) ▷ *noun* in England, Wales and N Ireland: **1** an examination in a single subject taken together with an A LEVEL in the same subject but that has a more advanced syllabus. **2** a pass in such an examination.

slew¹ *past tense of* SLAY

slew² or **slue** /sluː/ ▷ *verb* (***slewed***, ***slewing***) *tr & intr* **1** to turn about the axis. **2** to twist or cause to twist or swing round, especially suddenly and uncontrollably. ▷ *noun* an instance of slewing. • **slewed** *colloq* extremely drunk. ◷ 18c.

slice ▻ *noun* **1** a thin broad piece, wedge or segment that is cut off. **2** *colloq* a share or portion □ ***a slice of the business.*** **3** a kitchen utensil with a broad flat blade for sliding under and lifting solid food, especially fish. **4** a slash or swipe. **5** in golf and tennis: a stroke causing a ball to spin sideways and curve away in a particular direction; the spin itself. ▻ *verb* (***sliced***, ***slicing***) **1** to cut up into slices. **2** (*also* **slice something off**) to cut it off as or like a slice □ ***slice a piece off the end.*** **3** *intr* to cut deeply and easily; to move easily and forcefully □ ***a boat slicing through the water.*** **4** *intr* to slash. **5** to strike (a ball) with a slice. • **slicing** *noun, adj.* ⓒ 14c: from French *esclice*, from German *slizan* to split.

sliced loaf ▻ *noun* a loaf of bread sold sliced and wrapped.

slicer /ˈslaɪsə(r)/ ▻ *noun* a person or machine that slices.

slick ▻ *adj* **1** dishonestly or slyly clever. **2** glib; smooth-tongued or suave □ ***a slick operator.*** **3** impressively and superficially smart or efficient □ ***a slick organization.*** **4** said especially of hair: smooth and glossy; sleek. ▻ *verb* (***slicked***, ***slicking***) (*usually* **slick something back** or **down**) to smooth (especially hair). ▻ *noun* **1** (*in full* **oil slick**) a wide layer of spilled oil floating on the surface of water, often as a result of damage to or discharge from an oil tanker or pipelines, etc. **2** a smooth racing-car tyre. • **slickly** *adverb.* • **slickness** *noun.* ⓒ Anglo-Saxon *slician* to smooth.

slickenside ▻ *noun, geol* a smooth rock surface that has become polished and striated as a result of grinding or sliding against an adjacent rock mass during slippage along a fault plane. ⓒ 18c: from SLICK.

slicker /ˈslɪkə(r)/ ▻ *noun* **1** a sophisticated city-dweller. **2** a shifty or swindling person.

slide ▻ *verb* (***slid***, ***sliding***) **1** *tr & intr* to move or cause to move or run smoothly along a surface. **2** *intr* to lose one's footing, especially on a slippery surface; to slip or glide. **3** *tr & intr* to move or place softly and unobtrusively □ ***slid the letter into his pocket.*** **4** *intr* to pass gradually, especially through neglect or laziness; to lapse □ ***slid back into his old habits.*** ▻ *noun* **1** an act or instance of sliding. **2** a polished slippery track, eg on ice. **3** any part of something that glides smoothly, eg the moving part of a trombone. **4** an apparatus for children to play on, usually with a ladder to climb up and a narrow sloping part to slide down; a chute. **5** a small glass plate on which specimens are mounted to be viewed through a microscope. **6** a small transparent photograph viewed in magnified size by means of a projector. **7** a hair-clip, sometimes decorative. **8** a sliding seat, especially in a rowing boat. **9** *geol* a LANDSLIDE (sense 1). **10** *music* a PORTAMENTO. **11** a fall, especially in value, popularity, etc. • **slidable** *adj.* • **slider** *noun.* • **sliding** *noun, adj.* • **let something slide** to allow a situation to deteriorate. ⓒ Anglo-Saxon *slidan*.

slide projector ▻ *noun* an optical device which projects an enlarged image of a SLIDE onto a wall or screen. Formerly called **magic lantern**. See also PROJECTOR.

slide-rule ▻ *noun* a hand-held mechanical device used to perform quick numerical calculations, now largely superseded by the pocket calculator.

sliding scale ▻ *noun* a scale, eg of fees charged, that varies according to changes in conditions, eg unforeseen difficulties in performing the service requested, according to the client's income, etc.

slight /slaɪt/ ▻ *adj* **1** small in extent, significance or seriousness; negligible □ ***a slight problem.*** **2** slim or slender. **3** lacking solidity, weight or significance; flimsy. **4** lacking substance or value □ ***slight works of literature.*** ▻ *verb* (***slighted***, ***slighting***) to insult someone by ignoring or dismissing them abruptly; to snub them. ▻ *noun* an insult by snubbing or showing neglect. • **slightly** *adverb* to a small extent; in a small way. • **slightness** *noun.* • **not in the slightest** not at all; not even to the smallest degree. ⓒ Anglo-Saxon *eorthslihtes* close to the ground.

slighting /ˈslaɪtɪŋ/ ▻ *adj* scornful or disrespectful. • **slightingly** *adverb.*

slily see under SLY

slim ▻ *adj* (***slimmer***, ***slimmest***) **1** said of people: attractively thin; slender. **2** characterized by little thickness or width. **3** not great; slight or remote □ ***a slim chance.*** ▻ *verb* (***slimmed***, ***slimming***) *intr* **1** (*sometimes* **slim down**) to make oneself slimmer, especially by diet and/or exercise. **2** to try to lose weight. • **slimly** *adverb.* • **slimmer** *noun* someone who is trying to lose weight. • **slimming** *noun.* • **slimness** *noun.* ⓒ 17c: Dutch, meaning 'crafty', from German *sclimm* bad.

slime ▻ *noun* **1** any thin, unpleasantly slippery or gluey, mud-like substance. **2** any mucus-like substance secreted, eg by snails, slugs and certain fishes. ▻ *verb* (***slimed***, ***sliming***) to smear or cover with slime. ⓒ Anglo-Saxon *slim*.

slime mould ▻ *noun, biol* a small simple organism, resembling a fungus and usually consisting of a naked mass of PROTOPLASM. It lives in damp habitats and feeds on dead or decaying plant material.

slimy /ˈslaɪmɪ/ ▻ *adj* (***slimier***, ***slimiest***) **1** similar to, covered with or consisting of slime. **2** *colloq* exaggeratedly obedient or attentive; obsequious. • **slimily** *adverb.* • **sliminess** *noun.*

sling[1] ▻ *noun* **1** a cloth hoop that hangs from the neck to support an injured arm. **2 a** a weapon for hurling stones, consisting of a strap or pouch in which the stone is placed and swung round fast; **b** a catapult. **3** a strap or loop for hoisting, lowering or carrying a weight. **4** an act of throwing. ▻ *verb* (***slung***, ***slinging***) **1** *colloq* to throw, especially with force; to fling. **2** to hang something loosely □ ***a jacket slung over his shoulder.*** **3** *slang* to pass, give, etc □ ***sling her a cardigan.*** **4** to hurl, fling or toss. • **sling one's hook** *slang* to go away or remove oneself. ⓒ 13c: from Norse *slyngva* to fling.

■ **sling off at someone** *Austral & NZ colloq* to jeer at them.

sling[2] ▻ *noun* a drink of alcoholic spirit and water, usually sweetened and flavoured.

slingback and **slingback shoe** ▻ *noun* a shoe with no cover for the heel, just a strap fastening round it to hold the shoe on.

slingshot ▻ *noun, N Amer, especially US* a catapult.

slink ▻ *verb* (***slunk***, ***slinking***) *intr* **1** to go or move sneakingly or ashamedly. **2** to move in a lithe and seductive manner. ▻ *noun* a slinking gait. ⓒ Anglo-Saxon *slincan*.

slinky /ˈslɪŋkɪ/ ▻ *adj* (***slinkier***, ***slinkiest***) *colloq* **1** said of clothing: attractively close-fitting □ ***a slinky dress.*** **2** slender. **3** said of a person: walking in a slow and seductive manner. • **slinkily** *adverb.* • **slinkiness** *noun*

slip[1] ▻ *verb* (***slipped***, ***slipping***) **1** *intr* to lose one's footing and slide accidentally. **2** *intr* to make a slight mistake inadvertently rather than due to ignorance. **3** *intr* to lapse morally. **4** *tr & intr* said of a clutch in a vehicle: to fail to engage correctly. **5** *intr* to slide, move or drop accidentally □ ***The dish slipped from his hands.*** **6** to place smoothly, quietly or secretively □ ***She slipped the envelope into her pocket.*** **7** *tr & intr* to move or cause to move quietly, smoothly or unobtrusively with a sliding motion □ ***He slipped into the church in the middle of the service.*** **8** to pull free from someone or something smoothly and swiftly; to suddenly escape from them or it □ ***The dog slipped its lead*** □ ***The name has slipped my mind.*** **9** *colloq* to give or pass secretly □ ***She slipped him a fiver.*** **10** *intr, colloq* to lose one's former skill or expertise, or control of a situation. **11** to dislocate (a spinal disc). ▻ *noun* **1** an instance of losing one's footing and sliding accidentally. **2** a minor and usually inadvertent mistake. **3** a slight error or transgression. **4** an escape. **5** a slight dislocation. **6** a LANDSLIDE (sense 1). **7** a woman's undergarment, worn under a dress or skirt. **8** a loose covering for a pillow. **9** a SLIPWAY. **10** *cricket* **a** one of three fielders (**first slip**, **second slip** and **third slip**) standing near to and roughly in line with the wicket-keeper on the on side; **b** (*often* **slips**) this fielding position. • **give someone the slip** *colloq* to escape from them skilfully or adroitly. • **let something slip 1** to reveal it accidentally. **2** to fail to take advantage of something, especially an opportunity. • **slip of the tongue** or **pen** a word, phrase, etc said or written in error when something else was intended. ⓘ 13c: from German dialect *slippen*.

■ **slip in**, **out**, *etc* to move quietly and unnoticed.

■ **slip into something** *colloq* to put it on quickly and easily.

■ **slip off 1** to fall off. **2** to withdraw or go away quietly.

■ **slip something off** to take it off quickly and easily □ *She slipped off her coat.*

■ **slip something on** to put it on loosely or hastily.

■ **slip up** to make a slight mistake inadvertently. See also SLIP-UP.

slip² ▻ *noun* **1** a small strip or piece of paper. **2** anything slender or narrow. **3** a small pre-printed form. **4** a young or exceptionally slender person □ *She's just a slip of a girl.* ⓘ 15c as *slippe*.

slip³ ▻ *noun* a creamy mixture of clay and water used for decorating pottery. ⓘ Anglo-Saxon *slipa* paste.

slipcase ▻ *noun* a boxlike case for a book or set of books, open on one side and leaving the spine or spines visible.

slip-knot ▻ *noun* **1** a knot untied simply by pulling one end of the cord. **2** a knot finishing off a noose, and slipping along the cord to adjust the noose's tightness.

slip-on ▻ *noun* a shoe or other item of clothing that is easily put on due to having no laces, buttons or other fastenings. Also *as adj* □ *The slip-on style will fall off narrow feet.*

slippage ▻ *noun* **1** an act or instance of slipping. **2** *mech, commerce, etc* **a** a failure to reach a set target; **b** the amount by which the target is missed.

slipped disc ▻ *noun* a dislocation of one of the flat circular plates of cartilage situated between any of the vertebrae, resulting in painful pressure on a spinal nerve.

slipper /'slɪpə(r)/ ▻ *noun* **1** a soft loose laceless indoor shoe. **2** a lightweight dancing shoe. ▻ *verb* (***slippered***, ***slippering***) to beat with a slipper. • **slippered** *adj* wearing a slipper or slippers. ⓘ 15c: from SLIP¹.

slipperwort ▻ *noun* CALCEOLARIA.

slippery ▻ *adj* **1** so smooth, wet, etc as to cause or allow slipping. **2** difficult to catch or keep hold of; elusive or evasive. **3** unpredictable or untrustworthy □ *a slippery character.* • **slipperiness** *noun*.

slippy ▻ *adj* (***slippier***, ***slippiest***) *colloq* said of a thing: liable to slip; slippery. • **slippiness** *noun*.

slip road ▻ *noun* a road by which vehicles join or leave a motorway.

slipshod /'slɪpʃɒd/ ▻ *adj* untidy and careless; carelessly done.

slipstream ▻ *noun* **1** an area of decreased wind resistance immediately behind a quickly moving vehicle or other object. **2** a stream of air driven back by an aircraft propeller. ▻ *verb* to follow close behind (a vehicle) in order to benefit from the decreased air resistance created by its slipstream.

slip-up ▻ *noun, colloq* a minor and usually inadvertent mistake. See also SLIP UP at SLIP¹.

slipware ▻ *noun* pottery that has been decorated with slip.

slipway ▻ *noun* a ramp in a dock or shipyard that slopes into water, for launching boats.

slit ▻ *noun* a long narrow cut or opening. ▻ *verb* (***slit***, ***slitting***) **1** to cut a slit in something, especially lengthwise. **2** to cut something into strips. • **slitter** *noun*. ⓘ Anglo-Saxon *slitan* to split.

slither /'slɪðə(r)/ ▻ *verb* (***slithered***, ***slithering***) *intr* **1** to slide or slip unsteadily while walking, especially on ice. **2** to move slidingly, like a snake. ▻ *noun* a slithering movement. • **slithery** *adj* slippery. ⓘ Anglo-Saxon *slidrian*.

sliver /'slɪvə(r)/ ▻ *noun* **1** a long thin piece cut or broken off. **2** a slice. **3** a splinter. **4** a continuous strand of loose untwisted wool, cotton or other fibre. ▻ *verb* (***slivered***, ***slivering***) *tr & intr* to break or cut into slivers. ⓘ Anglo-Saxon *slifan* to cleave.

slivovitz /'slɪvəvɪts/ ▻ *noun* a dry colourless plum brandy from E Europe. ⓘ 19c: from Serbo-Croat *öljivovica*, from *öljiva* plum.

slob *colloq* ▻ *noun* a lazy, untidy and slovenly person. ▻ *verb* (***slobbed***, ***slobbing***) *intr* (*usually* **slob about** or **around**) to move or behave in a lazy, untidy or slovenly way. • **slobbish** or **slobby** *adj*. ⓘ 18c: from Irish Gaelic *slab* mud.

slobber /'slɒbə(r)/ ▻ *verb* (***slobbered***, ***slobbering***) **1** *intr* to let saliva run from the mouth; to dribble or slaver. **2** to wet with saliva □ *He slobbered his napkin.* ▻ *noun* dribbled saliva; slaver. • **slobbery** *adj*. ⓘ 14c: from Dutch *slobberen* to eat or work in a slovenly manner.

■ **slobber over something** *colloq* to express extreme or excessive enthusiasm or admiration for it.

sloe /sloʊ/ ▻ *noun* (***sloes***) **1** the fruit of the blackthorn bush. **2** the bush itself. ⓘ Anglo-Saxon *sla*.

sloe gin ▻ *noun* gin flavoured by having sloes soaked in it.

slog *colloq* ▻ *verb* (***slogged***, ***slogging***) **1** to hit hard and wildly. **2** *intr* to labour or toil. ▻ *noun* **1** a hard wild blow or stroke. **2** extremely tiring work. • **slogger** *noun*. ⓘ 19c: a variant of SLUG¹.

slogan /'sloʊgən/ ▻ *noun* **1** a phrase used to identify a group or organization, or to advertise a product. **2** *Scots hist* a clan warcry. ⓘ 16c: from Gaelic *sluagh* army + *gairm* cry.

sloop /sluːp/ ▻ *noun* **1** a single-masted sailing boat with fore-and-aft sails. **2** (*in full* **sloop-of-war**) *Brit historical* a war vessel of any rig, carrying between ten and eighteen guns on one deck only. ⓘ 17c: from Dutch *sloep*.

slop¹ ▻ *verb* (***slopped***, ***slopping***) **1** (*often* **slop about** or **around**) *tr & intr* to splash or cause to splash or spill violently. **2** *intr* to walk carelessly in slush or water. ▻ *noun* **1** spilled liquid; a puddle. **2** (**slops**) unappetizing watery food. **3** (**slops**) waste food. **4** (**slops**) semi-liquid food fed to pigs. **5** (**slops**) urine and excrement. **6** gushy sentiment. ⓘ Anglo-Saxon *cusloppe* cow dung.

■ **slop about** or **around** *colloq* to move or behave in an untidy or slovenly manner.

■ **slop out** said of prisoners: to empty SLOPS (*noun* 5).

slop² ▻ *noun* **1** (**slops**) poor quality ready-made clothing. **2** (**slops**) clothes and bedding issued to sailors. **3** a loose-fitting garment, eg a smock. ⓘ Anglo-Saxon *oferslop* a loose outer garment.

slope ▻ *noun* **1** a slanting surface; an incline. **2** a position or direction that is neither level nor upright; an upward or downward slant. **3** a specially prepared track for skiing, on the side of a snow-covered hill or mountain. ▻ *verb* (***sloped***, ***sloping***) *intr* **1** to rise or fall at an angle. **2** to be slanted or inclined. • **sloping** or **slopy** *adj*. • **slope arms** to place or hold a rifle on the shoulder with the barrel sloping back and up. ⓘ Anglo-Saxon *aslupan* to slip away.

■ **slope off** *colloq* to leave stealthily or furtively.

sloppy /ˈslɒpɪ/ ▻ *adj* (***sloppier***, ***sloppiest***) **1** wet or muddy. **2** watery. **3** over-sentimental. **4** said of language, work, etc: inaccurate or careless; shoddy. **5** said of clothes: baggy; loose-fitting. • **sloppily** *adverb*. • **sloppiness** *noun*.

sloppy Joe ▻ *noun* (***sloppy Joes***) a long loose sweater.

slosh ▻ *verb* (***sloshes***, ***sloshed***, ***sloshing***) **1** *tr & intr* (*often* **slosh about** or **around**) to splash or cause to splash or spill noisily. **2** *slang* to hit or strike with a heavy blow. ▻ *noun* (***sloshes***) **1** the sound of splashing or spilling. **2** slush; a watery mess. **3** *slang* a heavy blow. Ⓒ Early 19c: a variant of SLUSH.

sloshed /slɒʃt/ ▻ *adj*, *colloq* drunk; intoxicated.

slot ▻ *noun* **1** a long narrow rectangular opening into which something is fitted or inserted. **2** a slit. **3** a (usually regular) time, place or position within a schedule, eg of radio or TV broadcasts, or airport take-offs and landings. **4** a niche in an organization. ▻ *verb* (***slotted***, ***slotting***) to make a slot in. Ⓒ 14c: from French *esclot*.

■ **slot something in** to fit or insert it, or place it in a slot.

sloth /slouθ/ ▻ *noun* **1** a herbivorous tree-dwelling mammal with long slender limbs and hook-like claws, noted for its very slow movements. **2** the desire to avoid all activity or exertion; laziness; indolence. • **slothful** *adj* lazy; inactive. Ⓒ Anglo-Saxon *slæwth*, from *slaw* slow.

slot machine ▻ *noun* a machine operated by inserting a coin in a slot, eg a vending machine or fruit machine. Ⓒ 19c.

slouch /slaʊtʃ/ ▻ *verb* (***slouches***, ***slouched***, ***slouching***) **1** *intr* to sit, stand or walk with a tired, lazy or drooping posture. **2** to allow oneself to droop (the shoulders). ▻ *noun* such a posture. • **sloucher** *noun*. • **slouching** *adj*. • **no slouch at something** *colloq* said of a person: able or competent in some respect □ *She's no slouch at dancing.* Ⓒ 16c: from Norse *slokr* a slouching person.

slough[1] ▻ *noun* **1** /slaʊ/ a mud-filled hollow. **2** /sluː/ *N Amer* an area of boggy land; a marsh or mire. **3** /slaʊ/ *literary* a state of deep and gloomy emotion □ *a slough of depression.* Ⓒ Anglo-Saxon *sloh*.

slough[2] /slʌf/ ▻ *noun* **1** any outer part of an animal cast off or moulted, especially a snake's dead skin. **2** dead tissue in a sore or wound. ▻ *verb* (***sloughed***, ***sloughing***) **1** to shed (eg a dead skin). **2** to cast off or dismiss (eg worries). Ⓒ 13c as *sloh*.

Slovak /ˈslouvak/ ▻ *adj* belonging or relating to Slovakia, a republic in E Europe, its inhabitants, or their language. ▻ *noun* **1** a citizen or inhabitant of, or person born in, Slovakia. **2** the official language of Slovakia. • **Slovakian** *adj*. Ⓒ 19c.

sloven /ˈslʌvən/ ▻ *noun* **1** someone who is carelessly or untidily dressed; a person of shoddy appearance. **2** someone who is lazy and slipshod in work. Ⓒ 15c: from Dutch *slof*, from German *sluf* slow or indolent.

Slovenian /slouˈviːnɪən/ and **Slovene** /ˈslouviːn/ ▻ *adj* belonging or relating to Slovenia, a republic in SE Europe, its inhabitants or their language. ▻ *noun* **1** a citizen or inhabitant of, or a person born in, Slovenia. **2** the official language of Slovenia. Ⓒ 19c.

slovenly ▻ *adj* **1** careless, untidy or dirty in appearance. **2** careless or shoddy in habits or methods of working. ▻ *adverb* in a slovenly manner. • **slovenliness** *noun*.

slow /slou/ ▻ *adj* **1** having little speed or pace; not moving fast or swiftly. **2** taking a long time, or longer than usual or expected. **3** said of a watch or clock: showing a time earlier than the correct time. **4** said of a mind: unable to quickly and easily understand or appreciate. **5** said of wit or intellect: dull; unexciting or uninteresting. **6** progressing at a tediously gentle pace □ *a slow afternoon.* **7** boring or dull; tedious □ *a slow film.* **8** not allowing fast progress or movement □ *Traffic was slow.* **9** needing much provocation in order to do something □ *He's slow to get angry.* **10** said of a road lane, especially on a motorway: for the use of slower traffic. **11** said of business: slack. **12** said of photographic film: needing a relatively long exposure time. **13** said of a cooker, etc: heating gently; cooking slowly. ▻ *adverb* in a slow manner. ▻ *verb* (***slowed***, ***slowing***) *tr & intr* (*also* **slow down** or **up**) to reduce or make something reduce speed, pace or rate of progress. • **slowly** *adverb*. • **slowness** *noun*. Ⓒ Anglo-Saxon *slaw*.

slowcoach ▻ *noun*, *colloq* someone who moves or works at a slow pace.

slow match ▻ *noun* a slow-burning rope used when firing explosives.

slow motion ▻ *noun* **1** in film or television: a speed of movement that is much slower than real-life movement, created by increasing the speed at which the camera records the action. **2** an imitation of this in real-life movement. Also *as adj* □ *a slow-motion clip.*

slow neutron ▻ *noun*, *physics* a neutron with a relatively low energy content, used to initiate various nuclear reactions, especially nuclear fission.

slow virus ▻ *noun*, *pathol* a virus that produces disease only many years after infection, eg HIV.

slowworm ▻ *noun* a harmless species of legless lizard with a small mouth and a smooth shiny brownish-grey to coppery body. Ⓒ Anglo-Saxon *slawyrm*; the first part is not related to SLOW but has been assimilated to it.

SLR ▻ *abbreviation*, *photog* single-lens reflex.

slub ▻ *verb* (***slubbed***, ***slubbing***) to twist (fibre) after carding, so as to prepare for spinning. ▻ *noun* **1** a piece of fibre twisted in this way. **2** a lump in yarn. ▻ *adj* lumpy or knobbly in texture. • **slubbed** or **slubby** *adj*. • **slubber** *noun*. • **slubbing** *noun*. Ⓒ 19c.

sludge ▻ *noun* **1** soft slimy mud or mire. **2** muddy sediment. **3** sewage. **4** half-melted snow; slush. **5** a dark yellowish or brownish green colour □ *a sludge green coat.* • **sludgy** *adj*. Ⓒ 17c: probably from SLUSH.

slue see SLEW[2]

slug[1] ▻ *noun* **1** any of various terrestrial molluscs, including many garden pests, belonging to the same class as SNAILS, but having a long fleshy body and little or no shell. **2** the similar larvae of other insects, especially sawflies. **3** a sea slug. **4** a heavy or lazy person; a sluggard. **5** anything slow-moving. Ⓒ 15c: from Norwegian dialect *slugg* a heavy body, from *sluggje* a slow heavy person, from Swedish dialect *slogga* to be sluggish.

slug[2] ▻ *noun* **1** *colloq* **a** an irregularly formed bullet; **b** a bullet. **2** *printing* a solid line or section of metal type produced by a composing machine. Ⓒ 17c.

slug[3] ▻ *colloq*, *noun* a heavy blow. ▻ *verb* (***slugged***, ***slugging***) to strike with a heavy blow. • **slugger** *noun*. Ⓒ Early 19c: from SLOG.

slug[4] ▻ *noun*, *especially US colloq* a large gulp or mouthful of alcohol, especially spirit. Ⓒ 18c.

sluggard /ˈslʌgəd/ ▻ *noun* a habitually lazy or inactive person. Ⓒ 14c: as *slogarde*.

sluggish /ˈslʌgɪʃ/ ▻ *adj* **1** unenergetic; habitually lazy or inactive. **2** less lively, active or responsive than usual □ *This engine is a bit sluggish.* • **sluggishly** *adverb*. • **sluggishness** *noun*.

sluice /sluːs/ ▻ *noun* **1** a channel or drain for water. **2** (*in full* **sluicegate**) a valve or sliding gate for regulating the flow of water in such a channel. **3** a trough for washing gold or other minerals out of sand, etc. **4** an act of washing down or rinsing. ▻ *verb* (***sluiced***, ***sluicing***) **1** to let out or drain by means of a sluice. **2** to wash down or rinse by throwing water on. Ⓒ 14c: from French *escluse*, from Latin *exclusa (aqua)* (water) shut out.

slum ▻ *noun* **1** a run-down, dirty and usually overcrowded house. **2** (*often* **slums**) an area or neighbourhood containing such housing. ▻ *verb* (***slummed, slumming***) *intr* to visit an area of slums, especially out of curiosity or for amusement. • **slumming** *noun*. • **slummy** *adj* like a slum; run-down or squalid. • **slum it** *colloq, often facetious* to experience circumstances that are less affluent or more squalid than one is used to. ◷ Early 19c.

slumber /ˈslʌmbə(r)/ *chiefly poetic* ▻ *noun* sleep. ▻ *verb* (***slumbered, slumbering***) *intr* **1** to sleep, especially lightly. **2** to be inattentive or inactive. • **slumberer** *noun*. • **slumbering** *noun, adj*. ◷ Anglo-Saxon *sluma* chamber.

■ **slumber away** to spend time in slumber.

slumberous /ˈslʌmbərəs/ and **slumbrous** ▻ *adj* **1** inviting or causing sleep. **2** sleepy. • **slumberously** *adverb*.

slump ▻ *verb* (***slumped, slumping***) *intr* **1** to drop or sink suddenly and heavily, eg with tiredness □ *He slumped into an armchair.* **2** said of prices, trade, etc: to decline suddenly and sharply. **3** to fall or sink suddenly into water or mud. ▻ *noun* **1** an act or instance of slumping. **2** a serious and usually long-term decline, especially in a nation's economy. • **slumped** *adj*. ◷ 17c.

slung *past tense, past participle of* SLING[1]

slunk *past tense, past participle of* SLINK

slur /slɜː(r)/ ▻ *verb* (***slurred, slurring***) **1** to pronounce (words) indistinctly, eg through drunkenness. **2** to speak or write about something very disparagingly; to cast aspersions on it. **3** (*often* **slur over something**) to mention it only briefly or deal with only superficially. **4** *music* to sing or play (notes) as a flowing sequence without pauses. ▻ *noun* **1** a disparaging remark intended to damage a reputation. **2** a slurred word or slurring way of speaking. **3** *music* **a** a flowing pauseless style of singing or playing; **b** the curved line under the notes indicating this style. • **slurred** *adj*. • **slurring** *noun*. ◷ 17c.

slurp /slɜːp/ ▻ *verb* (***slurped, slurping***) to eat or drink noisily with a sucking action. ▻ *noun* a slurping sound. ◷ 17c: from Dutch *slurpen* to sip audibly.

slurry /ˈslʌrɪ/ ▻ *noun* (***slurries***) **1** a thin paste or semi-fluid mixture, especially watery concrete. **2** liquid manure that is treated so that it can be distributed on to fields. ◷ 15c: from SLUR.

slush ▻ *noun* **1** half-melted snow. **2** any watery half-liquid substance, eg liquid mud. **3** sickly sentimentality. ◷ 17c.

slush fund ▻ *noun* a fund of money used for dishonest purposes, eg bribery, especially by a political party.

slushy /ˈslʌʃɪ/ ▻ *adj* (***slushier, slushiest***) **1** like or consisting of slush. **2** sickeningly sentimental □ *a slushy film.*

slut ▻ *noun, derog* **1** a woman who regularly engages in casual sex. **2** a prostitute. **3** an untidy, dirty or slovenly woman. • **sluttish** *adj*. • **sluttishly** *adverb*. • **sluttishness** *noun*. ◷ 15c: from German dialect *schlutte*.

sly ▻ *adj* (***slyer, slyest***) **1** said of people: clever; cunning or wily. **2** surreptitious; secretively deceitful or dishonest. **3** playfully mischievous □ *a sly smile.* • **slyly** or **slily** *adverb*. • **slyness** *noun*. • **on the sly** *colloq* secretly or furtively; surreptitiously. ◷ 12c: from Norse *slægr*.

SM ▻ *abbreviation* **1** (*also* **s-m** or **s/m**) sado-masochism. **2** Sergeant-Major.

Sm ▻ *symbol, chem* samarium.

smack[1] ▻ *verb* (***smacked, smacking***) **1** to slap loudly and smartly, especially with the hand. **2** *tr & intr, colloq* to hit loudly and heavily □ *Her head smacked against the wall.* **3** to kiss loudly and noisily. **4** to part (the lips) loudly, with relish or in pleasant anticipation □ *She smacked her lips at the thought of the meal.* ▻ *noun* **1** an act, or the sound, of smacking. **2** a loud enthusiastic kiss. ▻ *adverb, colloq* **1** directly and with force □ *He drove smack into the tree.* **2** precisely □ *smack in the middle.* • **smacking** *noun, adj*. ◷ 16c: from Dutch *smacken*.

smack[2] ▻ *verb, intr* (*always* **smack of something**) **1** to have the flavour of it. **2** to have a trace or suggestion of it. ▻ *noun* **1** taste; distinctive flavour. **2** a hint or trace. ◷ Anglo-Saxon *smæc*.

smack[3] ▻ *noun* **1** a small single-masted fishing boat. **2** *US* a sailing vessel equipped with a tank in which fish can be kept alive. ◷ 17c: from Dutch *smak*.

smack[4] ▻ *noun, slang* heroin. ◷ 1960s: from Yiddish *schmeck* sniff.

smacker ▻ *noun* **1** *colloq* a loud enthusiastic kiss. **2** *slang* a pound sterling or a dollar bill.

small /smɔːl/ ▻ *adj* (***smaller, smallest***) **1** little in size or quantity. **2** little in extent, importance or worth; not great. **3** slender □ *of small build.* **4** humble □ *small beginnings.* **5** said of thought or action: petty; ungenerous or ignoble. **6** young □ *a small child.* **7** minor; insignificant □ *a small problem.* **8** said of a printed or written letter: lower-case; not capital. **9** humiliated □ *feel small.* **10** said eg of a business: not operating on a large scale. **11** fine in grain, texture, gauge, etc □ *small gravel.* ▻ *noun* **1** the narrow part, especially of the back. **2** (**smalls**) *colloq* underclothes. ▻ *adverb* **1** in a low or gentle tone. **2** on a small scale. **3** into small pieces. • **smallish** *adj*. • **smallness** *noun*. • **feel small** to feel silly, insignificant, ashamed, humiliated, etc. • **in a small way** unostentatiously. • **look small** to appear silly or insignificant. ◷ Anglo-Saxon *smæl*.

small ad ▻ *noun, colloq* a CLASSIFIED ADVERTISEMENT.

small arms ▻ *plural noun* hand-held firearms.

small beer ▻ *noun, colloq* something unimportant or trivial.

small calorie see CALORIE

small capitals ▻ *noun, printing* capital letters that are the same height as LOWER-CASE letters.

small change ▻ *noun* **1** coins of little value. **2** someone or something of little significance or importance.

small fry ▻ *singular or plural noun, colloq* **1** a person or thing, or people or things, of little importance or influence. **2** young children.

smallholding ▻ *noun* an area of cultivated land smaller than an ordinary farm. • **smallholder** *noun*.

small hours ▻ *noun* (**the small hours**) the hours immediately after midnight, very early in the morning.

small intestine ▻ *noun, anatomy* in mammals: the part of the intestine comprising the DUODENUM, JEJUNUM and ILEUM, the main function of which is to digest and absorb food. Compare LARGE INTESTINE.

small-minded ▻ *adj* narrow-minded; petty-minded. • **small-mindedly** *adverb*. • **small-mindedness** *noun*.

smallpox /ˈsmɔːlpɒks/ ▻ *noun, pathol* a highly contagious viral disease, characterized by fever, vomiting, backache and a rash that usually leaves permanent pitted scars (pocks) on the skin.

small print ▻ *noun* the details of a contract or other undertaking, often printed very small, especially when considered likely to contain unattractive conditions that the writer of the contract does not want to be noticed.

small-scale ▻ *adj* **1** said of maps, models, etc: made in accordance with a series of smaller measurements. **2** said of enterprises, etc: small in size, scope, etc.

the small screen ▻ *noun* television, as opposed to cinema.

small slam see LITTLE SLAM

small talk ▻ *noun* polite conversation about trivial matters.

small-time ▻ *adj* operating on a small scale; unimportant or insignificant.

smarm ▷ *verb* (***smarmed, smarming***) **1** *intr, colloq* to be exaggeratedly and insincerely flattering; to fawn ingratiatingly. **2** (*often* **smarm something down**) to smooth or flatten (the hair) with an oily substance. ▷ *noun, colloq* exaggerated or insincere flattery. ◷ Early 20c in sense 1; 19c in sense 2.

smarmy /'smɑːmɪ/ ▷ *adj* (***smarmier, smarmiest***) *colloq* **1** ingratiatingly flattering or respectful. **2** nauseously suave or charming. • **smarmily** *adverb*. • **smarminess** *noun*.

smart ▷ *adj* (***smarter, smartest***) **1** neat, trim and well-dressed. **2** clever; witty; astute or shrewd. **3** expensive, sophisticated and fashionable □ ***a smart hotel.*** **4** quick, adept and efficient in business. **5** said of pain, etc: sharp and stinging. **6** brisk □ ***He walked at a smart pace.*** **7** *computing* technologically advanced. **8** computer-guided or electronically controlled □ ***a smart bomb.*** **9** *colloq* impressive; excellent. ▷ *verb* (***smarted, smarting***) *intr* **1** to feel or be the cause of a sharp stinging pain □ ***My eyes smart if I use eyeshadow.*** **2** to feel or be the cause of acute irritation or distress □ ***He's still smarting after his relationship break-up.*** **3** (*often* **smart for something**) to suffer harsh consequences or punishment for it. ▷ *noun* a sharp stinging pain. ▷ *adverb* in a smart manner. • **smartly** *adverb*. • **smartness** *noun*. • **look smart** to hurry up. ◷ Anglo-Saxon *smeortan*.

smart alec and **smart aleck** *colloq* ▷ *noun* a person who thinks that they are cleverer than others; an irritating know-all. • **smart-alecky** *adj* characteristic of a smart alec.

smartarse and **smartass** ▷ *noun, derog slang* a SMART ALEC.

smart card ▷ *noun* a plastic card like a bank card, fitted with a microprocessor (including a memory) instead of a magnetic strip, used in commercial transactions, telecommunications, etc.

smart drug ▷ *noun* a drug designed to enhance mental powers or perception.

smarten /'smɑːtən/ ▷ *verb* (***smartened, smartening***) *tr & intr* (*usually* **smarten up**) to make or become smarter; to brighten up □ ***You need to smarten your appearance*** □ ***He should smarten up a bit.***

the smart money ▷ *noun* money invested by the experts.

smarty or **smartie** /'smɑːtɪ/ ▷ *noun* (***smarties***) *colloq* a know-all.

smartypants and **smartyboots** ▷ *singular noun, colloq* a SMARTY.

smash ▷ *verb* (***smashes, smashed, smashing***) **1** *tr & intr* to break or shatter violently into pieces; to destroy or be destroyed in this way. **2** *tr & intr* to strike with violence, often causing damage; to burst with great force □ ***He smashed his fist down on the table in anger*** □ ***They smashed through the door.*** **3** *colloq* to break up or ruin completely □ ***Police have smashed an international drugs ring.*** **4** *tr & intr* to become or cause to become bankrupt. **5** in racket sports: to hit (a ball) with a powerful overhead stroke. **6** to crash (a car). ▷ *noun* (***smashes***) **1** an act, or the sound, of smashing. **2** in racket sports: a powerful overhead stroke. **3** *colloq* a road traffic accident. **4** ruin or bankruptcy. **5** *colloq* a SMASH HIT. ▷ *adverb* with a smashing sound. ◷ 17c: probably from SMACK and MASH.

smash-and-grab ▷ *adj, colloq* said of a robbery: carried out by smashing a shop window and snatching the items on display. ▷ *noun* a robbery carried out in this way.

smashed ▷ *adj, slang* **1** extremely drunk. **2** high on drugs.

smasher ▷ *noun, colloq* **1** someone or something very much liked or admired. **2** anything great, charming or extraordinary.

smash hit ▷ *noun, colloq* a song, film, play, etc that is an overwhelming success.

smashing ▷ *adj, colloq* excellent; splendid □ ***It was a smashing trip.***

smash-up ▷ *noun, colloq* a serious road traffic accident.

smatter /'smatə(r)/ ▷ *noun* a smattering. ◷ 15c.

smattering /'smatərɪŋ/ ▷ *noun* **1** a few scraps of superficial knowledge. **2** a small amount scattered around. ◷ 16c as *smateren* to rattle.

smear ▷ *verb* (***smeared, smearing***) **1** to spread (something sticky or oily) thickly over (a surface). **2** *tr & intr* to make or become blurred; to smudge. **3** to say or write abusive and damaging things about someone. ▷ *noun* **1** a greasy mark or patch. **2** a damaging criticism or accusation; a slur. **3** an amount of a substance, especially of cervical tissue, placed on a slide for examination under a microscope. **4** *colloq* a CERVICAL SMEAR. ◷ Anglo-Saxon *smeru* fat, grease.

smear campaign ▷ *noun* a series of verbal or written attacks intended to defame and discredit an individual, group or organization.

smear tactics ▷ *plural noun* tactics employed in a smear campaign.

smear test ▷ *noun* a CERVICAL SMEAR.

smeary /'smɪərɪ/ ▷ *adj* sticky or greasy; showing smears. • **smearily** *adverb*. • **smeariness** *noun*.

smectic /'smɛktɪk/ ▷ *adj, chem* said of liquid crystals: having molecular layers oriented in parallel planes. ◷ 17c: from Latin *smecticus* cleansing, from Greek *smektikos* detergent (from the soapy consistency of a smectic substance).

smegma /'smɛgmə/ ▷ *noun* a thick white secretion that accumulates underneath the foreskin of the penis. ◷ Early 19c: from Greek *smegma* soap.

smell ▷ *noun* **1** the sense that allows different odours to be recognized by specialized receptors in the mucous membranes of the nose. **2** the characteristic odour of a particular substance □ ***It has a strong smell.*** **3** an unpleasant odour □ ***What a smell!*** **4** an act of using this sense □ ***Have a smell of this.*** **5** a sense, savour or suggestion of something □ ***The smell of money always brings him back.*** ▷ *verb* (***smelled*** or ***smelt, smelling***) **1** to recognize (a substance) by its odour. **2** *intr* to give off an unpleasant odour □ ***This rubbish tip really smells.*** **3** to give off a specified odour □ ***the perfume smells flowery.*** **4** to be aware of something by intuition; to recognize signs or traces of □ ***I smell a government cover-up.*** • **smeller** *noun*. • **smell a rat** see under RAT. ◷ 12c as *smel*.

▪ **smell of something** **1** to give off an odour of it. **2** to show signs or traces of it □ ***It is an organization smelling of corruption.***

▪ **smell someone** or **something out** to track them down by smell, or as if by smell.

smelling-salts ▷ *plural noun* a preparation of ammonium carbonate with a strong sharp odour, used to stimulate a return to consciousness after fainting.

smelly /'smɛlɪ/ ▷ *adj* (***smellier, smelliest***) *colloq* having a strong or unpleasant smell. • **smelliness** *noun*.

smelt¹ ▷ *verb* (***smelted, smelting***) to process (an ore), especially by melting it, in order to separate out the crude metal. • **smelting** *noun*. ◷ 16c: from German *smelten*.

smelt² ▷ *noun* (***smelts*** or ***smelt***) any of various small marine and freshwater fish of the salmon family, including several edible species, with a slender silvery body and a jutting lower jaw. ◷ Anglo-Saxon *smylt*.

smelt³ *past tense, past participle of* SMELL

smelter /'smɛltə(r)/ ▷ *noun* **1** a person whose work is smelting metal. **2** an industrial plant where smelting is done. ◷ 15c: from SMELT¹.

smidgen or **smidgeon** or **smidgin** /ˈsmɪdʒən, -dʒɪn/ ▷ *noun, colloq* a very small amount ▫ *You only need a smidgen of paprika.* ⓒ 19c.

smilax /ˈsmaɪlaks/ ▷ *noun, bot* **1** a climbing plant of the lily family, with net-veined leaves, some yielding SARSAPARILLA. **2** a southern African twining plant of the asparagus family with bright green foliage. ⓒ 17c: Greek.

smile ▷ *verb* (***smiled, smiling***) **1** *intr* to turn up the corners of the mouth, often showing the teeth, usually as an expression of pleasure, favour or amusement, but sometimes as an expression of slight contempt or displeasure. **2** to show or communicate with such an expression ▫ *He smiled his agreement.* ▷ *noun* an act or way of smiling. • **smiler** *noun*. • **smiling** *noun, adj*. • **smilingly** *adverb*. ⓒ 13c: as *smilen*.

■ **smile at someone** or **something** to react to them or it with a smile.

■ **smile on someone** or **something** **1** to show favour towards them. **2** to be a good omen ▫ *The gods are smiling on you today.*

smiley ▷ *noun* (***smileys***) *computing slang* a symbol created from a number of symbols on the keyboard (eg :-)) intended to look like a smiling face (sideways on), used to indicate irony.

smirch ▷ *verb* (***smirches, smirched, smirching***) **1** to make dirty; to soil or stain. **2** to damage or sully (a reputation, etc). ▷ *noun* (***smirches***) **1** a stain. **2** a smear on a reputation. ⓒ 15c: from French *esmorcher* to hurt.

smirk ▷ *verb* (***smirked, smirking***) to smile in a self-satisfied, affected or foolish manner. ▷ *noun* such a smile. • **smirking** *adj*. • **smirkingly** *adverb*. ⓒ Anglo-Saxon *smercian*.

smite ▷ *verb* (*past tense* ***smote*** /smoʊt/, *past participle* ***smitten*** /ˈsmɪtən/, *present participle* ***smiting***) *literary* **1** to strike or beat with a heavy blow or blows. **2** to kill. **3** to afflict. **4** to cause someone to fall immediately and overpoweringly in love ▫ *He could not fail to be smitten by such beauty.* **5** *intr* to come suddenly and forcefully ▫ *The king's authority smote down on him.* • **smiter** *noun*. • **smitten** *adj* in love; obsessed. ⓒ Anglo-Saxon *smitan* to smear.

smith ▷ *noun* **1** *in compounds* a person who makes articles in the specified metal ▫ *silversmith.* **2** a BLACKSMITH. **3** *in compounds* a person who makes skilful use of anything ▫ *wordsmith.* ⓒ Anglo-Saxon.

smithereens /smɪðəˈriːnz/ ▷ *plural noun, colloq* tiny fragments ▫ *She smashed it to smithereens.* ⓒ 19c: from Irish Gaelic *smidirín*, diminutive of *smiodar* fragment.

smithy /ˈsmɪðɪ/ ▷ *noun* (***smithies***) a blacksmith's workshop.

SMMT ▷ *abbreviation* Society of Motor Manufacturers and Traders.

smock ▷ *noun* **1** any loose shirt-like garment, usually of coarse cloth, worn over other clothes for protection especially by artists, etc. **2** a woman's long loose-fitting blouse. **3** *historical* a loose-fitting overall of coarse linen worn by farm-workers. Also called **smock-frock**. ⓒ Anglo-Saxon *smoc*.

smocking /ˈsmɒkɪŋ/ ▷ *noun* honeycomb-patterned stitching used on gathered or tucked material for decoration.

smog ▷ *noun* **1** a mixture of smoke and fog, especially in urban or industrial areas, produced by the burning of coal or other fuels. **2** a mixture of fog and motor vehicle exhaust fumes or other pollutants produced as a result of human activity. • **smoggy** *adj*. ⓒ Early 20c: from *smoke* + *fog*.

smoke ▷ *noun* **1** a visible cloud given off by a burning substance, and consisting of tiny particles of carbon dispersed in a gas or a mixture of gases, eg air. **2** visible fumes or vapours. **3** a cloud or column of fumes. **4** *colloq* the act or process of smoking tobacco ▫ *Got time for a smoke?* **5** *colloq* something that can be smoked, such as a cigarette or cigar. **6** (**the Smoke**) see THE BIG SMOKE. ▷ *verb* (***smoked, smoking***) **1** *intr* to give off smoke, visible fumes or vapours. **2** *tr & intr* to inhale and then exhale the smoke from burning tobacco or other substances in a cigarette, cigar, pipe, etc. **3** *tr & intr* to do this frequently, especially as a habit that is hard to break. **4** to cause oneself to be in a specific state by smoking. **5** to send or release smoke (especially in the wrong direction) ▫ *Oil lamps have a tendency to smoke.* **6** to preserve or flavour food by exposing it to smoke. **7** to fumigate or sterilize. **8** to blacken or taint by smoke. **9** to dry with smoke. • **smokable** *adj* fit or able to be smoked. • **go up in smoke** **1** to be completely destroyed by fire. **2** *colloq* said of plans, etc: to be ruined completely; to come to nothing. ⓒ Anglo-Saxon *smoca*.

■ **smoke someone** or **something out** to uncover them or it by persistent searching or investigation.

■ **smoke something out** to drive (an animal) out into the open by filling its burrow with smoke.

smoke alarm and **smoke detector** ▷ *noun* a device that gives a loud warning sound on detecting smoke from a fire in a room.

smoke-ball ▷ *noun* a shell emitting smoke as a screen for military operations, or to drive out an enemy.

smoke-bomb ▷ *noun* a bomb emitting smoke on exploding.

smoked /smoʊkt/ ▷ *adj* **1** cured or treated with smoke ▫ *smoked haddock.* **2** darkened by smoke.

smoke-dry ▷ *verb* to cure or dry using smoke. • **smoke-dried** *adj* ▫ *smoke-dried fish.*

smokehouse ▷ *noun* a building where meat or fish is cured by smoking, or where smoked meats are stored.

smokeless ▷ *adj* **1** said of a fuel: giving off little or no smoke when burned, eg coke. **2** said of an area: **a** where the use of smoke-producing fuel is prohibited; **b** where tobacco-smoking is prohibited.

smokeless zone ▷ *noun* an area, usually in an urban area, in which it is prohibited to produce smoke from any source, and where only smokeless fuels may be used.

smoker /ˈsmoʊkə(r)/ ▷ *noun* **1** someone who smokes tobacco products. **2** a railway carriage in which tobacco-smoking is permitted.

smokescreen ▷ *noun* **1** a cloud of smoke used to conceal the movements of troops, etc. **2** anything said or done to hide or deceive.

smokestack ▷ *noun* **1** a tall industrial chimney. **2** a funnel on a ship or steam train.

smoking /ˈsmoʊkɪŋ/ ▷ *noun* **1** the practice of inhaling the fumes from burning cigarettes or other forms of tobacco, known to be a causative factor in the development of several diseases, especially lung cancer. **2** a process used to preserve and improve the flavour of some foods (eg ham, some cheeses), which are exposed to wood smoke (usually from oak or ash) for long periods. ▷ *adj* where tobacco-smoking is allowed ▫ *a smoking-compartment.*

smoky /ˈsmoʊkɪ/ ▷ *adj* (***smokier, smokiest***) **1** giving out much or excessive smoke. **2** filled with smoke (especially tobacco smoke). **3** having a smoked flavour. **4** hazy, especially in colour ▫ *smoky blue.* **5** made dirty by smoke. • **smokily** *adverb*. • **smokiness** *noun*.

smolt /smoʊlt/ ▷ *noun* a young salmon migrating from fresh water to the sea. ⓒ 15c: Scots.

smooch /smuːtʃ/ *colloq* ▷ *verb* (***smooches, smooched, smooching***) *intr* **1** to kiss and cuddle. **2** to dance slowly while in an embrace. ▷ *noun* **1** the act of smooching. **2** a period of smooching. ⓒ 16c: variant of obsolete *smouch* to kiss.

smoochy /'smuːtʃɪ/ ▷ *adj* (***smoochier***, ***smoochiest***) said of music: sentimental and romantic.

smooth /smuːð/ ▷ *adj* (***smoother***, ***smoothest***) **1** having an even regular surface; not rough, coarse, bumpy or wavy. **2** having few or no lumps; having an even texture or consistency □ *smooth sauce.* **3** free from problems or difficulties □ *a smooth journey.* **4** characterized by steady movement and a lack of jolts and lurches □ *a smooth ferry crossing.* **5** not sharp or bitter □ *a smooth sherry.* **6** said of skin: having no hair, spots, blemishes, etc. **7** extremely charming, especially excessively or insincerely so □ *a smooth talker.* **8** *slang* very classy or elegant □ *a smooth dresser.* ▷ *verb* (***smoothed***, ***smoothing***) **1** (*also* **smooth something down** or **out**) to make it smooth □ *She smoothed out the sheets on the bed.* **2** (*often* **smooth over something**) to cause a difficulty, etc to seem less serious or important. **3** to free from lumps or roughness. **4** (*often* **smooth something away**) to remove (especially problems) by smoothing; to calm or soothe □ *A few words from him help smooth away my troubles.* **5** to make easier □ *smooth the way to promotion.* **6** *intr* to become smooth. ▷ *adverb* smoothly. ▷ *noun* **1** the act or process of smoothing. **2** the easy, pleasurable or trouble-free part or aspect (eg of a situation) □ *take the rough with the smooth.* **3** in racket sports: the side of the racket which, when spun and allowed to drop, determines who opens the game. • **smoothly** *adverb*. • **smoothness** *noun*. ⓔ Anglo-Saxon *smoth*.

smooth breathing see under BREATHING

smoothie or **smoothy** /'smuːðɪ/ ▷ *noun* (***smoothies***) *colloq* a person who is very elegant, charming or suave in dress or manner, especially one excessively or insincerely so.

smooth muscle see INVOLUNTARY MUSCLE

smooth snake ▷ *noun* a harmless European snake with smooth scales and a dark horizontal line on the side of its head.

smooth-talking, **smooth-spoken** and **smooth-tongued** ▷ *adj* **1** exaggeratedly and insincerely flattering. **2** charmingly persuasive. • **smooth-talk** *noun*. • **smooth-talker** *noun*.

smorgasbord /'smɔːgəsbɔːd, 'smɜː-/ ▷ *noun* a Swedish-style assortment of hot and cold savoury dishes served as a buffet. ⓔ 1920s: Swedish, from *smörgås* open sandwich + *bord* table.

smorzando /smɔːt'sandoʊ/ ▷ *adj, adverb, music* **1** gradually fading away. **2** growing slower and softer. ⓔ 18c: Italian, from *smorzare* to extinguish or tone down.

smote *past tense of* SMITE

smother /'smʌðə(r)/ ▷ *verb* (***smothered***, ***smothering***) **1** *tr & intr* to kill with or die from lack of air, especially with an obstruction over the mouth and nose; to suffocate. **2** to extinguish (a fire) by cutting off the air supply, eg by throwing a blanket over it. **3** to cover or smear something with a thick layer □ *She loved her bread smothered with jam* □ *smothered him with kisses.* **4** to give an oppressive or stifling amount to someone □ *She smothered the children with love.* **5** to suppress or contain □ *She managed to smother her laughter* □ *smother a rumour.* ▷ *noun* **1** thick floating dust. **2** dense smoke. **3** a welter or turmoil. • **smothered** *adj*. • **smotherer** *noun*. • **smothering** or **smothery** *adj*. • **smotheringly** *adverb*. ⓔ 12c: as *smorther*, related to Anglo-Saxon *smorian*.

smoulder /'smoʊldə(r)/ ▷ *verb* (***smouldered***, ***smouldering***) *intr* **1** to burn slowly or without flame. **2** said of emotions: to linger on in a suppressed and often hidden state □ *His grief is still smouldering.* **3** said of a person: to harbour suppressed and often hidden emotions □ *She sat smouldering in the corner.* ▷ *noun* a smouldering fire or emotion. • **smouldering** *noun, adj*. ⓔ 14c: as *smolder*.

smudge ▷ *noun* **1** a mark or blot caused or spread by rubbing. **2** a faint or blurred shape, eg an object seen from afar. ▷ *verb* (***smudged***, ***smudging***) **1** to make a smudge on or of something. **2** *intr* to become or cause a smudge □ *The ink has smudged* □ *These pens smudge easily.* • **smudger** *noun*. • **smudgily** *adverb*. • **smudginess** *noun*. • **smudgy** *adj*. ⓔ 15c: as *smogen*.

smug ▷ *adj* (***smugger***, ***smuggest***) arrogantly self-complacent or self-satisfied. • **smugly** *adverb*. • **smugness** *noun*. ⓔ 16c: from German dialect *smuck* neat.

smuggle /'smʌgəl/ ▷ *verb* (***smuggled***, ***smuggling***) **1** to take (goods) into or out of a country secretly and illegally, eg to avoid paying duty. **2** to bring, take or convey secretly, usually breaking a rule or restriction □ *He smuggled his notes into the exam.* • **smuggler** *noun*. • **smuggling** *noun*. ⓔ 17c: from German dialect *smuggeln*.

smut ▷ *noun* **1** soot. **2** a speck of dirt, soot, etc. **3** mildly obscene language, jokes, pictures or images □ *Enough of your smut!* **4 a** any of a group of parasitic fungi causing a serious disease of cereal crops, and characterized by the appearance of masses of black spores, resembling soot, on the leaves and other plant surfaces; **b** the disease caused by such a fungus. Compare RUST *noun* 4. ▷ *verb* (***smutted***, ***smutting***) **1** to dirty or affect with smut. **2** to become smutty. ⓔ 16c: as *smotten* to stain.

smutty /'smʌtɪ/ ▷ *adj* (***smuttier***, ***smuttiest***) **1** dirtied by smut. **2** mildly obscene □ *a smutty sense of humour.* • **smuttily** *adverb*. • **smuttiness** *noun*.

Sn ▷ *symbol, chem* tin.

snack ▷ *noun* a light meal often taken quickly, or a bite to eat between meals. ▷ *verb* (***snacked***, ***snacking***) *intr* to eat a snack. ⓔ 14c: perhaps from Dutch *snacken* to snap.

■ **snack on something** to make a light meal from it; to nibble at it □ *I snack on biscuits too much.*

snack bar and **snack counter** ▷ *noun* a café, kiosk or counter serving snacks.

snaffle /'snafəl/ ▷ *noun* (*in full* **snaffle-bit**) a simple bridle-bit for a horse. ▷ *verb* (***snaffled***, ***snaffling***) **1** to fit (a horse) with a snaffle. **2** to control using a snaffle. **3** *slang* to take sneakily or without permission; to steal. ⓔ 16c: from German and Dutch *snavel* mouth.

snafu /sna'fuː/ ▷ *noun, US slang, originally military* chaos. Also *as adj*. ⓔ 1940s: from situation normal: all fouled or fucked up.

snag ▷ *noun* **1** a problem or drawback □ *The snag is there is not enough funding.* **2** a protruding sharp or jagged edge on which clothes, etc could get caught. **3** a hole or tear in clothes (especially tights, stockings, etc) caused by such catching. **4** a part of a tree submerged in water, hazardous to boats. ▷ *verb* (***snagged***, ***snagging***) to catch or tear on a snag. • **snaggy** *adj*. ⓔ 16c: from Norse *snagi* peg.

snaggletooth /'snagəltuːθ/ ▷ *noun* a broken, irregular or projecting tooth. • **snaggletoothed** *adj*. ⓔ Early 19c: from SNAG + TOOTH.

snail ▷ *noun* **1** any of numerous marine, freshwater, and terrestrial molluscs belonging to the same class as slugs, but carrying a coiled or conical shell on their backs, into which the whole body can be withdrawn. **2** a sluggish person or animal. • **snail-like** *adj*. • **at a snail's pace** extremely slowly; at a very slow speed. ⓔ Anglo-Saxon *snæl*.

snail mail ▷ *noun, computing slang* the ordinary postal service, as opposed to electronic mail.

snake ▷ *noun* **1** any one of numerous species of a carnivorous reptile which has a long narrow body covered with scaly skin, and a forked tongue, and that differs from LIZARDS in that it lacks limbs, moveable eyelids or visible ears. **2** any long and flexible or winding thing or shape. **3** a SNAKE IN THE GRASS. **4** *formerly* the band within which the relative values of certain EC currencies were allowed to float. ▷ *verb* (***snaked***, ***snaking***) *intr* to move windingly or follow a winding course □ *The river* *snakes towards the sea.* • **snakelike** *adj.* ⓒ Anglo-Saxon *snaca*.

snakebird ▷ *noun* a DARTER.

snakebite ▷ *noun* **1** the wound or poisoned condition caused by the bite of a venomous snake. **2** *colloq* a drink of cider and beer or lager in equal measures.

snake-charmer ▷ *noun* a street entertainer who appears to induce snakes to perform rhythmical movements, especially by playing music.

snake in the grass ▷ *noun, colloq* a treacherous person; a friend revealed to be an enemy.

snakes and ladders ▷ *noun* a game played with counters and dice on a board marked with an ascending path on which ladders allow short cuts towards the finish and snakes force one to go back towards the starting-point.

snaky /'sneɪkɪ/ ▷ *adj* (*snakier, snakiest*) **1** like a snake, especially long, thin and flexible or winding. **2** treacherous or cruelly deceitful. • **snakily** *adverb.* • **snakiness** *noun.*

snap ▷ *verb* (*snapped, snapping*) **1** *tr & intr* to break suddenly and cleanly with a sharp cracking noise □ *He snapped the stick over his knee.* **2** *tr & intr* to make or cause to make a sharp noise. **3** *tr & intr* to move quickly and forcefully into place with a sharp sound □ *The lid snapped shut.* **4** *intr* to speak sharply in sudden irritation. **5** *colloq* to take a photograph of someone or something, especially spontaneously and with a hand-held camera. **6** *intr, colloq* to lose one's senses or self-control suddenly □ *When he answered me back I just snapped.* **7** *Amer football* to pass (the ball) from the line of the scrimmage back to the quarterback. ▷ *noun* **1** the act or sound of snapping. **2** *colloq* a photograph, especially taken spontaneously and with a hand-held camera. **3** a catch or other fastening that closes with a snapping sound. **4** a sudden bite. **5** a crisp biscuit or savoury. **6** a crisp and lively quality in style. **7** a COLD SNAP. **8** a card game in which all the cards played are collected by the first player to shout 'snap' on spotting a pair of matching cards laid down by consecutive players. **9** *Amer football* the play which involves the passing of the ball from the line of scrimmage back to the quarterback. ▷ *exclamation* **1** the word shouted in the card game (see *noun* 8 above). **2** the word used to highlight any matching pairs, circumstances, etc. ▷ *adj* taken or made spontaneously, without long consideration □ *a snap decision.* ▷ *adverb* with a snapping sound. • **snapping** *noun, adj.* • **snappingly** *adverb.* • **snap one's fingers 1** to make a short loud snapping sound by flicking one's fingers sharply, usually to attract attention. **2** to show contempt or defiance. • **snap someone's head** or **nose off** to answer irritably and rudely. • **snap out of it** *colloq* to bring oneself out of a state or condition, eg of sulking or depression. ⓒ 15c: from Dutch *snappen*.

■ **snap at someone** to speak abruptly with anger or impatience.

■ **snap at something 1** to make a biting or grasping movement towards it □ *The dog snapped at the biscuit in the boy's hand.* **2** to seize it eagerly.

■ **snap something off something** else to break something off it □ *She snapped the head off her doll.*

■ **snap someone up** to obtain them for employment, as a partner in a relationship, etc □ *You'd better move quick or she'll be snapped up.*

■ **snap something up** to acquire, purchase or seize it eagerly □ *He snapped up the opportunity.*

■ **snap up** to answer or interrupt rudely or sharply.

snapdragon ▷ *noun* any of various bushy perennial plants, native to Europe and N America, with spikes of large white, yellow, pink, red or purple two-lipped flowers. Also called ANTIRRHINUM.

snap-fastener ▷ *noun* a PRESS STUD.

snaplink see KARABINER

snapper ▷ *noun* **1** someone or something that snaps. **2** a deep-bodied fish found in tropical seas, some species of which are valuable food fish, so called because it has long conical front teeth and highly mobile jaws. **3** a SNAPPING-TURTLE. **4** *US* a party cracker. ⓒ 16c.

snapping-turtle ▷ *noun* a large aggressive American freshwater tortoise.

snappy /'snapɪ/ ▷ *adj* (*snappier, snappiest*) **1** irritable; inclined to snap. **2** smart and fashionable □ *a snappy dresser.* **3** lively □ *Play it at a snappy tempo.* • **snappily** *adverb.* • **snappiness** *noun.* • **Look snappy** or **Make it snappy!** *colloq* Hurry up!; Be quick about it!

snapshot ▷ *noun, colloq* a photograph, especially one taken spontaneously and with a hand-held camera.

snare ▷ *noun* **1** an animal trap, especially one with a string or wire noose to catch the animal's foot. **2** anything that traps or entangles. **3** anything that lures or tempts. **4** *surgery* a loop used for removing tumours, etc. **5 a** (in full **snare drum**) a medium-sized drum sitting horizontally, with a set of wires fitted to its underside that rattle sharply when the drum is struck; **b** the set of wires fitted to a snare drum. ▷ *verb* (*snared, snaring*) **1** to catch, trap or entangle in, or as if in, a snare. **2** *surgery* to remove (a tumour) using a snare. • **snarer** *noun.* • **snaring** *noun.* ⓒ Anglo-Saxon *sneare*.

snarl¹ ▷ *verb* (*snarled, snarling*) **1** *intr* said of an animal: to growl angrily, showing the teeth. **2** *tr & intr* to speak aggressively in anger or irritation. ▷ *noun* **1** an act of snarling. **2** a snarling sound or facial expression. • **snarler** *noun.* • **snarling** *noun, adj.* • **snarlingly** *adverb.* • **snarly** *adj.*

snarl² ▷ *noun* **1** a knotted or tangled mass. **2** a confused or congested situation or state. **3** a knot in wood. ▷ *verb, tr & intr* (*also* **snarl someone** or **something up** or **snarl up**) to make or become knotted, tangled, confused or congested. ⓒ 14c: related to SNARE.

snarl-up ▷ *noun, colloq* **1** a tangle. **2** any muddled or congested situation, especially a traffic jam.

snatch ▷ *verb* (*snatches, snatched, snatching*) **1** to seize or grab suddenly. **2** *intr* to make a sudden grabbing movement. **3** to pull suddenly and forcefully □ *She snatched her hand away from his.* **4** *colloq* to take or have as soon as the opportunity arises □ *We'll have to snatch a bite to eat.* ▷ *noun* (*snatches*) **1** an act of snatching. **2** a fragment overheard or remembered □ *She recalled a few snatches of conversation.* **3** a brief period □ *I caught snatches of the news now and then* □ *snatches of rest between long shifts.* **4** *colloq* a robbery □ *The snatch took place in broad daylight.* **5** *weightlifting* a type of lift in which the weight is raised from the floor to an overhead position in one movement. • **snatcher** *noun.* • **snatchily** *adverb.* • **snatchy** *adj.* ⓒ 13c: as *snacchen*.

snazzy /'snazɪ/ ▷ *adj* (*snazzier, snazziest*) *colloq* fashionably and often flashily smart or elegant □ *That's a snazzy little number you're wearing.* • **snazzily** *adverb.* • **snazziness** *noun.* ⓒ 1930s: perhaps from *snappy* + *jazzy*.

SNCF ▷ *abbreviation: Société Nationale des Chemins de Fer Français* (French), French national railways.

sneak ▷ *verb* (*sneaked* or (*colloq*) *snuck, sneaking*) **1** (*often* **sneak away, off, out**, *etc*) *intr* to move, go or depart quietly, furtively and unnoticed. **2** to bring or take secretly, especially breaking a rule or prohibition □ *He sneaked a girl into his room* □ *He tried to sneak a look at the letter.* **3** *intr, colloq* to inform about someone; to tell tales. **4** *slang* to steal. ▷ *noun, colloq* someone who sneaks; a tell-tale. ⓒ Anglo-Saxon *snican* to creep.

sneakers /'sniːkəz/ ▷ *plural noun, especially US* sports shoes; soft-soled, usually canvas, shoes.

sneaking /'sniːkɪŋ/ ▷ *adj* **1** said of a feeling, etc: slight but not easily suppressed □ *a sneaking suspicion he was* *cheating on me.* **2** secret; unrevealed □ *a sneaking admiration.* **3** underhand; deceptive. ● **sneakingly** *adverb.*

sneak thief ▷ *noun* a thief who enters premises through unlocked doors or windows, without actually breaking in.

sneaky /ˈsniːkɪ/ ▷ *adj* (***sneakier***, ***sneakiest***) done or operating with secretive unfairness or dishonesty; underhand. ● **sneakily** *adverb.* ● **sneakiness** *noun*

sneck *chiefly Scots & N Eng* ▷ *noun* a latch; a door-catch. ▷ *verb* (***snecked***, ***snecking***) to fasten with a sneck. ◷ 14c: from SNATCH.

sneer ▷ *verb* (***sneered***, ***sneering***) **1** (*often* **sneer at someone** or **something**) *intr* to show scorn or contempt, especially by drawing the top lip up at one side. **2** *intr* to express scorn or contempt. **3** to say scornfully or contemptuously. ▷ *noun* **1** an act of sneering. **2** an expression of scorn or contempt made with a raised lip, or in other ways. ● **sneerer** *noun.* ● **sneering** *noun, adj.* ● **sneeringly** *adverb.* ◷ 16c.

sneeze ▷ *verb* (***sneezed***, ***sneezing***) *intr* to blow air out through the nose suddenly, violently and involuntarily, especially because of irritation in the nostrils. ▷ *noun* an act or the sound of sneezing. ● **sneezer** *noun.* ● **sneezing** *noun.* ● **sneezy** *adj.* ● **not to be sneezed at** *colloq* not to be disregarded or overlooked lightly. ◷ Anglo-Saxon *fnesan.*

sneezewort /ˈsniːzwɜːt/ ▷ *noun* a species of yarrow whose dried leaves are powdered and used to cause sneezing.

snib *chiefly Scots* ▷ *noun* a small bolt or catch for a door or window-sash. ▷ *verb* (***snibbed***, ***snibbing***) to fasten with a snib. ◷ Early 19c: from German *snibbe* beak.

snick ▷ *noun* **1** a small cut; a nick. **2** *cricket* **a** a glancing contact with the edge of the bat; **b** the shot hit in this way. ▷ *verb* (***snicked***, ***snicking***) **1** to make a small cut in something. **2** *cricket* to hit with a snick. ◷ 16c: from Norse *snikka* to whittle.

snicker ▷ *verb* (***snickered***, ***snickering***) *intr* **1** to SNIGGER. **2** to say gigglingly. **3** to neigh or whinny. ▷ *noun* **1** a giggle. **2** a neigh or whinny. ◷ 17c.

snide ▷ *adj* **1** expressing criticism or disapproval in an offensive, sly or malicious manner. **2** counterfeit; sham. ● **snidely** *adverb.* ● **snideness** *noun.* ◷ 19c.

sniff ▷ *verb* (***sniffed***, ***sniffing***) **1** to draw in air with the breath through the nose. **2** *intr* to draw up mucus or tears escaping into the nose. **3** *intr* to draw in air through the nose in short sharp noisy bursts, eg when crying. **4** (*often* **sniff something** or **sniff at something**) *tr & intr* to smell it in this way. **5** to express disapprobation reticently by making a slight sound with the nose. **6** to snuffle. **7** to inhale the fumes from (a dangerous or addictive substance, eg a solvent). ▷ *noun* **1** an act or the sound of sniffing. **2** a smell. **3** a small quantity inhaled by the nose. **4** a slight intimation or suspicion. ● **sniffer** *noun.* ● **sniffing** *noun, adj.* ● **not to be sniffed at** *colloq* not to be disregarded or overlooked lightly □ *such good value that it's not an offer to be sniffed at.* ◷ 14c: imitating the sound.

> ■ **sniff at someone** or **something** to express contempt or derision for them or it.
>
> ■ **sniff someone** or **something out** to discover or detect them or it by, or as if by, the sense of smell.

sniffer dog ▷ *noun* a dog specially trained to search for or locate illicit or dangerous substances (eg illegal drugs, explosives, etc) by smell.

sniffle /ˈsnɪfəl/ ▷ *verb* (***sniffled***, ***sniffling***) *intr* to sniff repeatedly, eg because of having a cold. ▷ *noun* **1** an act or the sound of sniffling. **2** (*also* **the sniffles**) a slight cold. ● **sniffler** *noun.* ● **sniffly** *adj.* ◷ 17c: from SNIFF.

sniffy /ˈsnɪfɪ/ ▷ *adj* (***sniffier***, ***sniffiest***) *colloq* **1** contemptuous or disdainful, or inclined to be so. **2** sniffing repeatedly, or feeling that one wants to, especially because of having a cold. ● **sniffily** *adverb.* ● **sniffiness** *noun.*

snifter /ˈsnɪftə(r)/ ▷ *noun* **1** *slang* a drink of alcohol, especially alcoholic spirit; a tipple or dram. **2** *US* a brandy glass. ◷ 19c: from dialect *snift* to sniff.

snigger /ˈsnɪɡə(r)/ ▷ *verb* (***sniggered***, ***sniggering***) *intr* to laugh in a stifled or suppressed way, often derisively or mockingly. ▷ *noun* such a laugh. Also called SNICKER. ● **sniggerer** *noun.* ● **sniggering** *noun, adj.* ● **sniggeringly** *adverb.* ◷ 18c: an imitation of SNICKER.

snip ▷ *verb* (***snipped***, ***snipping***) to cut, especially with a single quick action or actions, with scissors. ▷ *noun* **1** an act or the action of snipping. **2** the sound of a stroke of scissors while snipping. **3** a small shred or piece snipped off. **4** a small cut, slit or notch. **5** (**snips**) small hand-shears used for cutting sheet metal. **6** *colloq* a bargain □ *It's a snip at £10.* **7** *colloq* a certainty; a thing easily done. **8** a small white or light patch or stripe on a horse, especially on its nose. ● **snipper** *noun.* ● **snipping** *noun.* ◷ 16c: from Dutch *snippen.*

snipe ▷ *noun* (***snipe*** or ***snipes***) **1** any of various wading birds with a long straight bill, relatively short legs and mottled and barred dark brown plumage. **2** a sniping shot, ie a shot at someone from a hidden position. **3** a quick verbal attack or criticism. ▷ *verb* (***sniped***, ***sniping***) *intr* **1** to shoot snipe for sport. **2** (*often* **snipe at someone**) **a** to shoot at them from a hidden position; **b** to criticize them bad-temperedly. ● **sniper** *noun* someone who shoots from a concealed position. ● **sniping** *noun.* ◷ 14c: from Norse *snipa.*

snippet /ˈsnɪpɪt/ ▷ *noun* **1** a scrap, eg of information, news, etc. **2** a little piece snipped off. ● **snippetiness** *noun.* ● **snippety** *adj.* ◷ 17c: from SNIP.

snitch *slang* ▷ *noun* (***snitches***) **1** the nose. **2** an informer. ▷ *verb* (***snitches***, ***snitched***, ***snitching***) **1** *intr* to betray others; to inform on them. **2** to steal; to pilfer. ● **snitcher** *noun* an informer. ◷ 18c.

snivel /ˈsnɪvəl/ ▷ *verb* (***snivelled***, ***snivelling***) *intr* **1** to whine or complain tearfully. **2** to have a runny nose. **3** to sniff or snuffle. **4** hypocritical cant. ▷ *noun* an act of snivelling. ● **sniveller** *noun.* ● **snivelly** *adj.* ◷ Anglo-Saxon *snofl* mucus.

SNO ▷ *abbreviation* **1** Scottish National Orchestra (now RSNO). **2** Scottish National Opera.

snob ▷ *noun* **1** someone who places too high a value on social status, treating those higher up the social ladder obsequiously, and those lower down the social ladder with condescension and contempt. **2** someone having similar pretensions as regards specific tastes □ *a wine snob* □ *an intellectual snob.* Compare INVERTED SNOB. ◷ 18c.

snobbery ▷ *noun* **1** snobbishness. **2** snobbish behaviour.

snobbish ▷ *adj* characteristic of a snob. ● **snobbishly** *adverb.* ● **snobbishness** *noun.*

snobby ▷ *adj* (***snobbier***, ***snobbiest***) snobbish. ● **snobbism** *noun.*

snoek see SNOOK[1]

snog *slang* ▷ *verb* (***snogged***, ***snogging***) *intr* to embrace, kiss and cuddle. ▷ *noun* a kiss and cuddle. ◷ 1950s.

snood /snuːd/ ▷ *noun* **1** a decorative pouch of netting or fabric worn by women on the back of the head, keeping the hair in a bundle. **2** a tube, usually made of a woollen material, worn as a hood. **3** *fishing* the length of fine line, gut, etc by which a baited fish hook is fixed to the line. **4** *historical* in Scotland: a hair band once worn by young unmarried women. ◷ Anglo-Saxon *snod.*

snook[1] or **snoek** /snuːk/ ▷ *noun* (***snook*** or ***snooks***; ***snoek***) any of several marine fishes. ⓒ 17c: from Dutch *snoek* pike.

snook[2] /snuːk/ ▷ *noun* the gesture of putting the thumb to the nose and waving the fingers as an expression of derision, contempt or defiance. • **cock a snook at someone** *colloq* **1** to make this gesture at them. **2** to express open contempt for them. ⓒ 19c.

snooker /ˈsnuːkə(r)/ ▷ *noun* **1** a game played with long leather-tipped sticks, or CUEs, 15 red balls, one white cue ball and six balls of other colours, the object being to use the white cue ball to knock the non-white balls in a certain order into any of the six pockets on the corners and sides of a large cloth-covered table, and to gain more points than the opponent. **2** in this game: a position in which the path between the white ball and the target ball is obstructed by another ball. ▷ *verb* (***snookered***, ***snookering***) **1** in snooker: to force (an opponent) to attempt to hit an obstructed target ball. **2** *colloq* to thwart (a person or a plan). ⓒ 19c.

snoop ▷ *verb* (***snooped***, ***snooping***) *intr* to go about sneakingly and inquisitively; to pry. ▷ *noun* **1** an act of snooping. **2** someone who snoops. • **snooper** *noun* a person who snoops. • **snoopy** *adj*. ⓒ 19c: from Dutch *snoepen* to eat or steal.

snooperscope ▷ *noun*, *US* a device which converts infrared radiation reflected from an object into a visible image, used for seeing in the dark. ⓒ 1940s.

snoot ▷ *noun*, *slang* the nose. ⓒ 19c: a variation of SNOUT.

snooty /ˈsnuːtɪ/ ▷ *adj* (***snootier***, ***snootiest***) *colloq* haughty; snobbish. • **snootily** *adverb*. • **snootiness** *noun*.

snooze /snuːz/ ▷ *verb* (***snoozed***, ***snoozing***) *intr* to sleep lightly; to doze. ▷ *noun* a brief period of light sleeping; a nap. • **snoozer** *noun*. • **snoozy** *adj*. ⓒ 18c: perhaps a combination of SNORE and DOZE.

snooze button ▷ *noun* a device on an alarm clock which stops the alarm and allows a few minutes respite before sounding again.

snore /snɔː(r)/ ▷ *verb* (***snored***, ***snoring***) *intr* to breathe heavily and with a snorting sound while sleeping. ▷ *noun* an act or the sound of snoring. • **snorer** *noun*. ⓒ 14c: imitating the sound.

snorkel /ˈsnɔːkəl/ and **schnorkel** /ˈʃnɔːkəl/ ▷ *noun* **1** a rigid tube through which air from above the surface of water can be drawn into the mouth while one is swimming just below the surface. **2** on a submarine: a set of tubes extended above the surface of the sea to take in air and release exhaust gases. ▷ *verb* (***snorkelled***, ***snorkelling***) *intr* to swim with a snorkel. • **snorkelling** *noun*. ⓒ 1940s: from German *Schnorchel*.

snort ▷ *verb* (***snorted***, ***snorting***) **1** *intr* said especially of animals: to force air violently and noisily out through the nostrils; to make a similar noise while taking air in. **2** *tr & intr* to express contempt or anger in this way. **3** *slang* to inhale (a powdered drug, especially cocaine) through the nose. ▷ *noun* **1** an act or the sound of snorting. **2** *colloq* a small drink of alcoholic spirit. **3** *slang* an amount of a powdered drug inhaled in one breath. • **snorting** *noun*, *adj*. • **snortingly** *adverb*. ⓒ 14c as *snorten*.

snorter ▷ *noun* **1** someone or something that snorts. **2** *colloq* anything exceptional, eg in size, strength, etc. ⓒ 17c.

snot ▷ *noun* **1** mucus of the nose. **2** a contemptible person. ⓒ Anglo-Saxon *gesnot*.

snotrag ▷ *noun*, *slang* a handkerchief.

snotty /ˈsnɒtɪ/ ▷ *adj* (***snottier***, ***snottiest***) *colloq* **1** covered or messy with nasal mucus □ *snotty-nosed kids*. **2** haughty or stand-offish; having or showing contempt □ *a snotty attitude*. **3** *derog* contemptible; worthless □ *I don't want your snotty advice*. • **snottily** *adverb*. • **snottiness** *noun*.

snout /snaʊt/ ▷ *noun* **1** the projecting nose and mouth parts of certain animals, eg the pig. **2** *colloq* the human nose. **3** any projecting part. **4** *slang* a cigarette; tobacco. **5** *slang* a police informer. • **snouted** *adj*. • **snouty** *adj* resembling a snout. ⓒ 13c: from German *snut*.

snow /snoʊ/ ▷ *noun* **1** precipitation in the form of aggregations of ice crystals falling to the ground in soft white flakes, or lying on the ground as a soft white mass. **2** a fall of this □ *There's been a lot of snow this year*. **3** any similar substance, such as carbonic acid snow which is frozen carbon dioxide. **4** *colloq* a flickering speckled background on a TV or radar screen, caused by interference or a poor signal. **5** *slang* cocaine. ▷ *verb* (***snowed***, ***snowing***) *intr* said of snow: to fall. • **be snowed under** be overwhelmed with work, etc. ⓒ Anglo-Saxon *snaw*.

■ **snow someone in** or **up** to isolate or block them with snow □ *We were snowed in for a week*.

snowball ▷ *noun* **1** a small mass of snow pressed hard together, often used for fun as a missile. **2** a drink made of advocaat and lemonade. ▷ *verb* (***snowballed***, ***snowballing***) **1** *tr & intr* to throw snowballs at someone or something. **2** *intr* to develop or increase rapidly and uncontrollably. • **not a snowball's chance (in hell** or **in an oven)** *colloq* absolutely no chance at all.

snowball tree ▷ *noun* a GUELDER ROSE.

snowberry ▷ *noun*, *bot* **1** any of various deciduous shrubs native to N America and W China, especially a N American species with simple leaves, small pinkish flowers and white spherical berry-like fruits. **2** the berry-like fruit produced by a N American species of this plant.

snow blindness ▷ *noun* severe but temporary impairment of eyesight caused by prolonged exposure of the eyes to bright sunlight reflected by snow. • **snow-blind** *adj* affected by snow blindness.

snowblower ▷ *noun* a snow-clearing machine which takes in the snow in front of it and blows it to the side of the road, path, etc.

snowboard ▷ *noun* a board resembling a skateboard without wheels, used on snow and guided with movements of the feet and body. ▷ *verb* (***snowboarded***, ***snowboarding***) *intr* to ski on a snowboard. • **snowboarder** *noun*. • **snowboarding** *noun*.

snowbound ▷ *adj* shut in or prevented from travelling because of heavy falls of snow.

snow bunting ▷ *noun* a small finch, native to northern regions, which has white plumage with black and brownish markings.

snowcap ▷ *noun* a cap of snow, as on the polar regions or a mountain-top. • **snowcapped** *adj* said especially of mountains: with a covering of snow on the top.

snow chain see TYRE CHAIN

snowdrift ▷ *noun* a bank of snow blown together by the wind.

snowdrop ▷ *noun* a bulbous early-flowering perennial plant with narrow strap-shaped bluish-green leaves and small solitary drooping white bell-shaped flowers.

snowfall ▷ *noun* **1** a fall of snow. **2** *meteorol* an amount of fallen snow in a given time □ *annual snowfall*.

snowfield ▷ *noun* a wide expanse of snow, especially one that is permanent.

snowflake ▷ *noun* any of the single small feathery clumps of crystals of frozen water vapour that make up snow.

snow goose ▷ *noun* a wild N American goose with white plumage and black wing-tips, a pink bill and pink legs, also occurring in a dark form with grey plumage, and a white head and neck.

snow leopard ▷ *noun* a large wild cat, now an endangered species, found in the mountains of Central Asia, which has long soft creamy or pale-grey fur patterned with black rosette spots. Also called **ounce**.

snowline ▷ *noun* the level or height on a mountain or other upland area above which there is a permanent covering of snow, or where snow accumulates seasonally.

snowman ▷ *noun* a figure, resembling a person, made from packed snow.

snowmobile /ˈsnoʊməbiːl/ ▷ *noun* a motorized vehicle, on skis or tracks, designed for travelling on snow.

snowplough ▷ *noun* **1** a large shovel-like device for clearing snow from roads or railway tracks. **2** a vehicle or train fitted with this. **3** *skiing* a position in which the skis are pointed together with the tips touching used as a means of slowing down.

snowshoe ▷ *noun* either of a pair of racket-like frameworks strapped to the feet for walking over deep snow.

snowstorm ▷ *noun* a heavy fall of snow, especially accompanied by a strong gale.

snow-white ▷ *adj* as white as snow.

snowy /ˈsnoʊɪ/ ▷ *adj* (***snowier***, ***snowiest***) **1** abounding or covered with snow. **2** white like snow. **3** pure. • **snowily** *adverb*. • **snowiness** *noun*.

snowy owl ▷ *noun*, *zool* an owl that inhabits tundra, northern marshes and Arctic islands, nests on the ground, and is so called because it has mainly white plumage.

SNP ▷ *abbreviation* Scottish National Party.

Snr or **snr** ▷ *abbreviation* senior.

snub ▷ *verb* (***snubbed***, ***snubbing***) **1** to insult by openly ignoring, rejecting or otherwise showing contempt. **2** to bring (a boat, unbroken horse, etc) to a sudden stop by means of a rope secured to a stake or post. ▷ *noun* an act of snubbing. ▷ *adj* short and flat; blunt. See also SNUB NOSE. • **snubbing** *noun*, *adj*. • **snubbingly** *adverb*. • **snubby** *adj*. ◷ 14c: from Norse *snubba* to scold.

snub nose ▷ *noun* a broad flat nose. • **snub-nosed** *adj* having a snub nose.

snuck see under SNEAK

snuff¹ ▷ *verb* (***snuffed***, ***snuffing***) **1** *intr* to draw in air violently and noisily through the nose. **2** *intr* to sniff; to smell at something doubtfully. **3** to examine or detect by sniffing. ▷ *noun* a sniff. ◷ 16c: from Dutch *snuffen* to snuffle.

snuff² ▷ *noun* **1** powdered tobacco for inhaling through the nose. **2** a pinch of snuff. ▷ *verb* (***snuffed***, ***snuffing***) *intr* to take snuff. • **snuffy** *adj* similar to, smelling of or soiled with snuff. • **up to snuff 1** not likely to be taken in; alert. **2** being of a high or suitable standard; up to scratch. ◷ 16c: from SNUFF¹.

snuff³ ▷ *verb* (***snuffed***, ***snuffing***) to snip off the burnt part of the wick of (a candle or lamp). ▷ *noun* the burnt part of the wick of a lamp or candle. • **snuff it** *slang* to die. ◷ 14c: as *snoffe*.

■ **snuff something out 1** to extinguish (a candle). **2** to put an end to it □ *tried to snuff out all opposition.*

snuffbox ▷ *noun* a small and often decorative lidded box, usually made of metal, for containing snuff.

snuffer /ˈsnʌfə(r)/ ▷ *noun* **1** a device with a cap-shaped part for extinguishing candles. **2** (**snuffers**) a device resembling a pair of scissors for removing snuffs from the wicks of candles or oil lamps.

snuffle /ˈsnʌfəl/ ▷ *verb* (***snuffled***, ***snuffling***) **1** *intr* to breathe, especially breathe in, through a partially blocked nose. **2** *tr & intr* to say or speak nasally. **3** *intr* to snivel. ▷ *noun* **1** an act or the sound of snuffling. **2** (**the snuffles**) *colloq* an obstructed condition of the nose; a slight cold. • **snuffler** *noun*. • **snuffling** *noun*, *adj*. ◷ 16c: see SNUFF¹.

snuff movie and **snuff film** ▷ *noun*, *slang* a pornographic film depicting scenes of violence and torture, and in which the climax is the actual murder of one of the unsuspecting participants.

snug ▷ *adj* (***snugger***, ***snuggest***) **1** warm, cosy and comfortable □ *a snug room.* **2** well protected and sheltered; not exposed □ *a snug boat.* **3** compact and comfortably organized □ *a snug kitchen.* **4** comfortably off; well provided for □ *a snug income.* **5** close-fitting □ *a snug dress.* ▷ *noun* a SNUGGERY. • **snugly** *adverb*. • **snugness** *noun*. ◷ 16c: perhaps from Norse *snoggr* short-haired.

snuggery /ˈsnʌgərɪ/ ▷ *noun* (***snuggeries***) *Brit* a small comfortable room or compartment in a pub.

snuggle /ˈsnʌgəl/ ▷ *verb* (***snuggled***, ***snuggling***) *intr* **1** (*usually* **snuggle down** or **in**) to settle oneself into a position of warmth and comfort. **2** (*sometimes* **snuggle up**) to hug close; to nestle. ◷ 17c: from SNUG.

SO ▷ *abbreviation* standing order.

so¹ ▷ *adverb* **1** to such an extent □ *so expensive that nobody buys it.* **2** to this, that, or the same extent; as □ *This one is lovely, but that one is not so nice.* **3** extremely □ *She is so talented!* **4** in that state or condition □ *promised to be faithful, and has remained so.* **5** also; likewise □ *She's my friend and so are you.* **6** used to avoid repeating a previous statement □ *You've to take your medicine because I said so.* ▷ *conj* **1** therefore; thereafter □ *He insulted me, so I hit him.* **2** (*also* **so that …**) in order that … □ *Lend me the book, so that I can read it* □ *Give me more time so I can finish it.* ▷ *adj* the case; true □ *You think I'm mad, but it's not so.* ▷ *exclamation* used to express discovery □ *So, that's what you've been doing!* • **and so on** or **and so forth** or **and so on and so forth** and more of the same; continuing in the same way. • **just so** neatly, precisely or perfectly □ *with her hair arranged just so.* • **or so** approximately □ *five or so days ago.* • **quite so** exactly right; just as you have said. • **so as to …** in order to …; in such a way as to …. • **so be it** used to express acceptance or defiant resignation. • **so far** to that, or to such an, extent or degree □ *I haven't managed to do any work so far.* • **so far so good** everything is fine up to this point. • **so much** or **many 1** such a lot □ *so much work to do!* **2** just; mere □ *politicians squabbling like so many children.* • **so much for …** nothing has come of …; that has disposed of or ruined … □ *So much for all our plans!* • **so much so** to such an extent (that). • **so so** moderate; average □ *How are you feeling? Oh, so so.* • **so to speak** or **to say** used as an apology for an unfamiliar or slightly inappropriate expression. • **so what?** *colloq* that is of no importance or consequence at all. ◷ Anglo-Saxon *swa*.

so² see SOH

soak ▷ *verb* (***soaked***, ***soaking***) **1** *tr & intr* to stand or leave to stand in a liquid for some time. **2** to make someone or something thoroughly wet; to drench or saturate. **3** (*also* **soak in** or **through something** or **soak through**) to penetrate or pass through □ *The rain soaked through my coat* □ *The spilt milk quickly soaked in.* **4** *colloq* to charge or tax heavily. **5** *intr*, *colloq* to drink especially alcohol to excess. ▷ *noun* **1** an act of soaking. **2** a drenching. **3** *colloq* a long period of lying in a bath. **4** *colloq* someone who habitually drinks a lot of alcohol. **5** a marshy location. • **soakage** *noun* liquid that has percolated. • **soaker** *noun*. • **soaking** *noun*. • **soakingly** *adverb*. • **soak up the sun** to sunbathe. ◷ Anglo-Saxon *socian*.

■ **soak something up** to absorb it □ *Tissue soaks up the water quickly* □ *He just soaks up knowledge.*

soakaway ▷ *noun* a depression in the ground into which water percolates.

soaked ▷ *adj* **1** (*also* **soaking**, **soaked through**) drenched; very wet (eg because of rain) □ ***He was soaked to the skin when he came in.*** **2** saturated or steeped. **3** *colloq* drunk.

so-and-so ▷ *noun* (***so-and-sos***) *colloq* **1** someone whose name one does not know or cannot remember □ ***He's gone with so-and-so.*** **2** a word in place of a vulgar word or oath □ ***You crafty little so-and-so!***

soap ▷ *noun* **1** a sodium or potassium salt of a FATTY ACID that is soluble in water and has detergent properties. **2** such a substance used as a cleaning agent in the form of a solid block, liquid or powder. **3** *colloq* a SOAP OPERA. ▷ *verb* (***soaped***, ***soaping***) to apply soap to something. ◷ Anglo-Saxon *sape*.

■ **soap someone up** *colloq* to charm or persuade them with flattery.

soapbox ▷ *noun* **1** a crate for packing soap. **2** an improvised platform for public speech-making, originally an upturned crate for carrying soap.

soap opera ▷ *noun* a radio or TV series concerning the domestic and emotional lives and troubles of a regular group of characters. ◷ originally applied to those sponsored in the USA by soap-manufacturing companies.

soapstone ▷ *noun* a soft usually grey or brown variety of the mineral talc, widely used for ornamental carvings. See also FRENCH CHALK.

soapsuds ▷ *plural noun* soapy water, especially when frothy.

soapwort /'soʊpwɜːt/ ▷ *noun* a tall herb, native to Europe, with pink or white flowers, and whose roots and leaves contain saponin. ◷ 16c.

soapy /'soʊpɪ/ ▷ *adj* (***soapier***, ***soapiest***) **1** like soap. **2** containing soap. **3** smeared with soap. **4** covered with soapsuds. **5** *slang* flattering. • **soapily** *adverb*. • **soapiness** *noun*.

soar ▷ *verb* (***soared***, ***soaring***) *intr* **1** to rise or fly high into the air. **2** to glide through the air at a high altitude. **3** to rise sharply to a great height or level □ ***soaring temperatures.*** **4** to increase rapidly in number. • **soaring** *noun*, *adj*. • **soaringly** *adverb*. ◷ 14c: from French *essorer* to expose to air by raising up, from Latin *ex* out + *aura* air.

sob ▷ *verb* (***sobbed***, ***sobbing***) **1** *intr* to cry uncontrollably with intermittent gulps for breath. **2** (*often* **sob out**) to say or tell something while crying in this way □ ***She sobbed out the whole story.*** **3** to bring (oneself) to a certain state, usually to sleep, by sobbing. ▷ *noun* a gulp for breath between bouts of crying. • **sobbing** *noun*, *adj*. • **sobbingly** *adverb*. ◷ 12c: imitating the sound.

sober /'soʊbə(r)/ ▷ *adj* **1** not at all drunk. **2** serious, solemn or restrained; not frivolous or extravagant. **3** suggesting sedateness or seriousness rather than exuberance or frivolity □ ***sober clothes*** □ ***sober colours.*** **4** plain; unembellished □ ***the sober truth.*** ▷ *verb* (***sobered***, ***sobering***) *tr & intr* **1** (*always* **sober down** or **sober someone down**) to become, or make someone, quieter, less excited, etc. **2** (*always* **sober up** or **sober someone up**) to become, or make someone, free from the effects of alcohol. • **sobering** *adj* causing someone to become serious or thoughtful □ ***a sobering thought.*** • **soberly** *adverb*. ◷ 14c: from Latin *sobrius*, from *se-* not + *ebrius* drunk.

sobriety /soʊ'braɪətɪ, sə-/ ▷ *noun* **1** the state of being sober, especially not drunk. **2** the state of being serious, solemn and calm. ◷ 15c: from Latin *sobrietas*, from *sobrius* SOBER.

sobriquet /'soʊbrɪkeɪ/ and **soubriquet** /'suːbrɪkeɪ/ ▷ *noun*, *literary* a nickname. ◷ 17c: French, meaning 'a chuck under the chin'.

sob-story ▷ *noun*, *colloq* a story of personal misfortune, which may or may not be true, told in order to gain sympathy.

Soc ▷ *abbreviation* **1** Socialist. **2** Society.

soca /'soʊkə/ ▷ *noun* a type of Caribbean calypso incorporating elements of American soul music. ◷ 20c: from *soul* + *calypso*.

so-called ▷ *adj* known or presented as such with the implication that the term is wrongly or inappropriately used □ ***a panel of so-called experts.***

soccer see under FOOTBALL

sociable /'soʊʃəbəl/ ▷ *adj* **1** fond of the company of others; friendly. **2** characterized by friendliness □ ***a sociable meeting.*** • **sociability** or **sociableness** *noun*. • **sociably** *adverb*. ◷ 16c: from Latin *sociabilis*, from SOCIAL.

social /'soʊʃəl/ ▷ *adj* **1** relating to or for people or society as a whole □ ***social policies.*** **2** relating to the organization and behaviour of people in societies or communities □ ***social studies.*** **3** tending or needing to live with others; not solitary □ ***social creatures.*** **4** intended for or promoting friendly gatherings of people □ ***a social club.*** **5** convivial; jovial. ▷ *noun* **1** a social gathering, especially one organized by a club or other group. **2** (**the social**) *colloq* social security. • **socially** *adverb*. • **socialness** *noun*. ◷ 16c: from Latin *sociare* to unite, from *socius* companion.

social action ▷ *noun*, *politics* action taken by an organized group or movement to achieve some reform or to promote a particular cause, outside the normal or formal channels of a government or political system, and aimed at gaining support from the wider public.

social anthropology ▷ *noun* the study of living societies with a view to establishing, by comparison, the range of variation in culture, social organization, institutions, etc, and the reasons for these differences.

social behaviourism ▷ *noun* in social psychology: a school of thought which holds that all observable social action is in response to the hidden needs, desires and beliefs of the deeper 'self'.

Social Chapter ▷ *noun* a section of the Maastricht Treaty, adopted by EU member states apart from the UK, setting out the social policy of the EU, concerning matters such as employment policies, living and working conditions, health and safety, equal opportunities for women, etc.

social cleansing ▷ *noun* the killing or forced removal of those considered socially undesirable from a particular area.

social climber ▷ *noun*, *often derog* someone who seeks to gain higher social status, often by despicable methods.

social contract and **social compact** ▷ *noun* an agreement, according to the theories of eg Hobbes, Locke and Rousseau, between individuals within a society to work together for the benefit of all, often involving the sacrifice of some personal freedoms.

social democracy ▷ *noun* a branch of socialism which emerged in the late 19c, and which supports gradual social change through reform within a framework of democratic politics rather than by revolutionary means.

social democrat ▷ *noun* **1** a supporter of social democracy. **2** (**Social Democrat**) a member of a Social Democratic party. • **social democratic** *adj*.

Social Democratic Party ▷ *noun* (abbreviation **SDP**) a UK political party formed in 1981 by four ex-Labour party members who then formed an electoral pact with the Liberals, and failing to break the two-party 'mould' of British politics merged with the Liberal Party in 1988, becoming the Social and Liberal Democrat Party, later the **Liberal Democrats**.

social engineering ▷ *noun* the application of theories and hypotheses of a social science to solve problems in society. ● **social engineer** *noun*.

social insurance ▷ *noun* state insurance by compulsory contributions against sickness, unemployment and old age.

socialism /ˈsoʊʃəlɪzəm/ ▷ *noun* a political doctrine or system which aims to create a classless society by removing the nation's wealth (land, industries, transport systems, etc) out of private and into public hands. ⓒ 1830s.

socialist /ˈsoʊʃəlɪst/ ▷ *noun* a supporter of socialism. ▷ *adj* relating to or characteristic of socialism. ● **socialistic** *adj*. ● **socialistically** *adverb*.

Socialist Realism ▷ *noun* the official form of art and literature in the former Soviet Union, and other Communist countries, distinct from SOCIAL REALISM, presenting an optimistic picture of the lives of the working people.

socialite /ˈsoʊʃəlaɪt/ ▷ *noun* someone who mixes with people of high social status.

sociality /soʊʃɪˈalɪtɪ/ ▷ *noun* (***socialities***) **1** the fact or quality of being social. **2** social relations, association or intercourse. **3** the inclination of people to engage in this.

socialization or **socialisation** /soʊʃəlaɪˈzeɪʃən/ ▷ *noun* **1** the act or process of socializing. **2** the process by which infants and young children become aware of society and their relationships with others.

socialize or **socialise** /ˈsoʊʃəlaɪz/ ▷ *verb* (***socialized***, ***socializing***) **1** *intr* to meet with people on an informal, friendly basis. **2** *intr* to mingle or circulate among guests at a party; to behave sociably. **3** to organize into societies or communities. **4** to make someone or something social.

social mobility ▷ *noun* the way individuals or groups move upwards or downwards from one status or class position to another within the social hierarchy.

social phobia ▷ *noun, psychol* an abnormal fear of interacting with other people, eg at meetings or social gatherings, or performing everyday activities in public, eg eating in a restaurant. ● **social phobic** *noun*.

social realism ▷ *noun, art* a form of art, especially before 1950, distinct from SOCIALIST REALISM, which presents a realistic picture of social and political conditions.

social sciences ▷ *plural noun* the subjects that deal with the organization and behaviour of people in societies and communities, including sociology, anthropology, economics and history.

social secretary ▷ *noun* someone responsible for organizing the social activities of a person, club, society, association, etc.

social security ▷ *noun* **1** a system by which members of a society pay money into a common fund, from which payments are made to individuals in times of unemployment, illness and old age. **2** a payment or scheme of payments from such a fund.

social services ▷ *noun* **1** services provided by local or national government for the general welfare of people in society, eg housing, education and health. **2** the public bodies providing these services.

social work ▷ *noun* work in any of the services provided by local government for the care of underprivileged people, eg the poor, the aged, people with disabilities, etc. ● **social worker** *noun*.

society /səˈsaɪətɪ/ ▷ *noun* (***societies***) **1** humankind as a whole, or a part of it such as one nation, considered as a single community. **2** a division of humankind with common characteristics, eg of nationality, race or religion. **3** an organized group or association, meeting to share a common interest or activity □ ***I'm a member of the gliding society.*** **4 a** the rich and fashionable section of the upper class; **b** the social scene of this class section; **c** *as adj* □ ***a society wedding.*** **5** *formal* company □ ***He prefers the society of women.*** **6** *ecol* a small plant community within a larger group. ⓒ 16c: from French *societe*, from Latin *societas*, from *socius* companion.

Society of Friends see THE RELIGIOUS SOCIETY OF FRIENDS

socio- /ˈsoʊsɪoʊ, ˈsoʊʃɪoʊ/ ▷ *combining form, signifying* social, or referring or relating to society or sociology.

sociobiology ▷ *noun, psychol* the integrated study of the biological basis of social behaviour, based on the assumption that all behaviour is adaptive.

socioeconomic ▷ *adj* referring or relating to social and economic aspects of something together.

sociolinguistics ▷ *singular noun* the study of the relationships between language and the society which uses it.

sociology /soʊsɪˈɒlədʒɪ, soʊʃɪ-/ ▷ *noun* the scientific study of the nature, structure and workings of human society. ● **sociological** *adj* **1** relating to or involving sociology. **2** dealing or concerned with social questions and problems of human society. ● **sociologist** *noun* an expert in sociology. ⓒ 1840s: from Latin *socius* companion + -LOGY.

sociometry /soʊsɪˈɒmətrɪ, soʊʃɪ-/ ▷ *noun* the study of interrelationships within social groups. ● **sociometric** *adj*.

sociopathy /soʊsɪˈɒpəθɪ, ˈsoʊʃɪ-/ ▷ *noun* any of various personality disorders characterized by asocial or antisocial behaviour. ● **sociopath** *noun*. ● **sociopathic** *adj*.

sock¹ ▷ *noun* **1** a fabric covering for the foot and ankle, sometimes reaching to or over the knee, worn inside a shoe or boot. **2** an insole placed inside a shoe to improve its fit. ● **pull one's socks up** *colloq* to make an effort to do better. ● **put a sock in it** *slang* to become silent; to be quiet. ⓒ Anglo-Saxon *socc* light shoe.

sock² ▷ *slang, verb* (***socked***, ***socking***) to hit with a powerful blow. ▷ *noun* a powerful blow. ● **sock it to someone** *slang* to make a powerful impression on them. ⓒ 17c.

socket /ˈsɒkɪt/ ▷ *noun* **1** a specially shaped hole or set of holes into which something is inserted or fitted □ ***an electrical socket*** □ ***a light socket.*** **2 a** *anatomy* a hollow structure in the body into which another part fits **b**) *as adj* □ ***a ball-and-socket joint.*** **3** *golf* the section of the head of a club to which the shaft is attached. ▷ *verb* (***socketed***, ***socketing***) **1** to provide with or place in a socket. **2** *golf* to strike with the socket. ● **socketed** *adj*. ⓒ 14c: from French *soket*, a diminutive of *soc*.

sockeye ▷ *noun* the blueblack salmon which inhabits coastal waters from Japan to California. ⓒ 19c: from American Indian *sukai* the fish of fishes, the native name on the Fraser River.

socle /ˈsoʊkəl, ˈsɒkəl/ ▷ *noun, archit* a plain projecting block or plinth at the base of a wall, column or pier. ⓒ 18c: French, from Italian *zoccolo*, from Latin *socculus*, a diminutive of *soccus* a shoe.

Socratic /sɒˈkratɪk/ ▷ *adj* referring or relating to the Greek philosopher Socrates, his philosophy, or his method of teaching or inquiry which was by a series of questions and answers.

Socratic irony ▷ *noun* the method of discussing a subject by claiming ignorance of it, forcing those present to make propositions which may then be queried.

sod¹ ▷ *noun* **1** a slab of earth with grass growing on it; a turf. **2** *poetic* the ground. ▷ *verb* (***sodded***, ***sodding***) to cover with sods. ⓒ 15c: from German *Sode*.

sod² ▷ *slang, noun* **1** a term of abuse for a person. **2** a person in general □ ***lucky sod.*** ▷ *verb* used as an exclamation of annoyance or contempt □ ***Sod you!*** ● **sod all** *slang* nothing at all. ⓒ 19c: a shortening of SODOMITE.

■ sod off *slang* (*sodas*) go away.

soda /'soudə/ ▷ *noun* **1** a common name given to any of various compounds of sodium in everyday use, eg SODIUM CARBONATE or BICARBONATE OF SODA. **2** *colloq* SODA WATER. **3** *N Amer, especially US* a fizzy soft drink of any kind. ◷ 16c: Latin.

soda ash ▷ *noun, chem* the common name for the commercial grade of anhydrous SODIUM CARBONATE.

soda bread ▷ *noun* bread in which the raising ingredient is baking soda rather than yeast.

soda fountain ▷ *noun, N Amer, especially US* **1** a counter in a shop from which fizzy drinks, ice-cream and snacks are served. **2** an apparatus for supplying soda water.

soda lime ▷ *noun, chem* a solid mixture of sodium or potassium hydroxide and calcium oxide, consisting of greyish-white granules that are used as a drying agent, and to absorb carbon dioxide gas.

sodality /soʊ'dalɪtɪ/ ▷ *noun* (*sodalities*) especially in the RC Church: a fellowship or fraternity. ◷ 16c: from Latin *sodalitas*, from *sodalis* comrade.

soda siphon see SIPHON *noun* 2.

soda water ▷ *noun* water made fizzy by the addition of carbon dioxide, widely used as a mixer with alcoholic spirits.

sodden /'sɒdən/ ▷ *adj* **1** heavy with moisture; saturated; thoroughly soaked. **2** said eg of bread: doughy; not thoroughly baked. **3** made lifeless or sluggish, especially through excessive consumption of alcohol □ ***a drink-sodden brain.*** ◷ 13c as *soden*: past tense of *sethen* to SEETHE.

sodding ▷ *adj, slang* a general term of disparagement and annoyance □ ***I'm fed up with this sodding car.***

sodium /'soudɪəm/ ▷ *noun, chem* (symbol **Na**, atomic number 11) a soft silvery-white metallic element used in alloys, as a reducing agent in chemical reactions, as a coolant in nuclear reactors, and in non-glare lighting, eg in street lamps, and also widely used in the form of its compounds, especially sodium chloride, in the chemical industry. ◷ Early 19c: from SODA.

sodium amytal see AMYTAL

sodium bicarbonate ▷ *noun, chem* (formula $NaHCO_3$) BICARBONATE OF SODA.

sodium borate see BORAX

sodium carbonate ▷ *noun, chem* (formula Na_2CO_3) a water-soluble white powder or crystalline solid, used as a water softener and food additive, in glass making, photography and in the manufacture of various sodium compounds. Also called **soda**. See also WASHING SODA, SODA ASH.

sodium chloride ▷ *noun, chem* (formula **NaCl**) a water-soluble white crystalline salt obtained from seawater and underground deposits of the mineral halite, used since ancient times for seasoning and preserving food, as a de-icing and water-softening agent and in the chemical industry. Also called COMMON SALT, ROCK SALT, SALT, TABLE SALT.

sodium hydroxide ▷ *noun, chem* (formula **NaOH**) a white crystalline solid that dissolves in water to form a highly corrosive alkaline solution, and is used in the manufacture of soap, detergents, pharmaceuticals, oven cleaners, rayon and paper, and in petroleum refining and the chemical industry. Also called **caustic soda**, SODA.

sodium lamp ▷ *noun* a street lamp using sodium vapour and giving a yellow light.

sodium nitrate ▷ *noun, chem* (formula $NaNO_3$) a water-soluble colourless crystalline solid that explodes at high temperatures, and is used in the manufacture of fireworks, matches, explosives, nitrate fertilizers and glass, and also as a food preservative, especially for cured meats.

Sodom /'sɒdəm/ ▷ *noun* a place of total depravity. ◷ 17c: named after the city in the Old Testament of the Bible which was demolished due to its evil and depravity.

sodomite /'sɒdəmaɪt/ ▷ *noun* (*sodomites*) someone who engages in sodomy.

sodomize or **sodomise** /'sɒdəmaɪz/ ▷ *verb* (***sodomized, sodomizing***) to practise sodomy on someone.

sodomy /'sɒdəmɪ/ ▷ *noun* **1** a form of sexual intercourse in which someone inserts a penis or similar object into the anus of a man or woman; buggery. **2** sexual intercourse between a person and an animal. ◷ 13c: from SODOM.

Sod's law ▷ *noun, slang* a facetious maxim stating that if something can go wrong it will, or that the most inconvenient thing that could happen is what is most likely to happen.

soever /soʊ'ɛvə(r)/ ▷ *adverb* generally used to extend or make indefinite the sense of something □ ***in any way soever.***

-soever /soʊ'ɛvə(r)/ ▷ *combining form, signifying* an indefinite kind; to any extent □ ***whysoever*** □ ***howsoever.***

sofa /'soufə/ ▷ *noun* (*sofas*) an upholstered seat with a back and arms, for two or more people. ◷ 17c: from Arabic *suffah*.

sofa bed ▷ *noun* a sofa designed to be converted into a bed as required.

soffit /'sɒfɪt/ ▷ *noun, archit* a term variously applied to the under surface of an arch, the underside of a stair, the underside of the top of a door or window opening, etc. ◷ 17c: from Italian *soffito*, ultimately from Latin *suffigere* to fasten beneath.

S. of S. ▷ *abbreviation, Bible* Song of Songs, or Song of Solomon.

soft ▷ *adj* **1** easily yielding or changing shape when pressed; pliable or malleable. **2** easily yielding to pressure. **3** easily cut. **4** said of fabric, etc: having a smooth surface or texture producing little or no friction. **5** pleasing or soothing to the senses; quiet □ ***a soft voice.*** **6** having little brightness; not glaring or brash □ ***soft colours.*** **7** kind or sympathetic, especially excessively so. **8** not able to endure rough treatment or hardship. **9** lacking strength of character; easily influenced. **10** *colloq* weak in the mind; simple □ ***soft in the head.*** **11** used especially in Liverpool: stupid or naive; weak □ ***Don't be soft!*** **12** said of a person: out of training; in an unfit condition. **13** weakly sentimental. **14** *mineralogy* easily scratched. **15** said of water: low in or free from mineral salts and so lathering easily. **16** said of coal: bituminous. **17** tender; loving or affectionate □ ***soft words.*** **18** *colloq* requiring little effort; easy □ ***a soft job.*** **19** said of diet: consisting of semi-liquid and easily-digestible foods. **20** said of drugs: not severely addictive. **21** SOFT-CORE. **22** with moderate rather than hardline or extreme policies □ ***the soft left.*** **23** *phonetics, non-technical* said of the consonants *c* and *g*: pronounced as a fricative as in *dance* and *age* respectively, rather than as a stop, as in *can* and *gate*. Compare HARD *adj*. **24** *finance* **a** said of prices, markets, etc: inclined to drop in value; **b** said of currency: not in great demand, usually due to a weakness in the BALANCE OF PAYMENTS system. **25** said of radiation: having short wavelengths and therefore not highly penetrating. **26** in computer typesetting and word-processing: referring to a space, hyphen (see SOFT HYPHEN) or page break that can be automatically removed when its environment changes to make it redundant. ▷ *adverb* softly; gently □ ***speaks soft.*** ● **softly** *adverb*. ● **softness** *noun*. ● **be** or **go soft on someone** *colloq* **1** to be lenient towards them. **2** to be infatuated with them. ● **soft spot** see separate entry. ◷ Anglo-Saxon *softe*.

softback ▷ *noun* a paperback. Also *as adj* □ ***softback edition.***

softball ▻ *noun* a game similar to baseball, played with a larger, softer ball which is pitched underarm, as opposed to overarm in baseball.

soft-boiled ▻ *adj* **1** said of eggs: boiled for a short while only, leaving the yolk soft. **2** *colloq* said of a person: soft-hearted.

soft-centred ▻ *adj* **1** said of sweets or chocolates: being soft in the middle. **2** said of a person: soft-hearted.

soft commodities ▻ *plural noun* foodstuffs, coffee, cotton, etc as opposed to metals.

soft-core ▻ *adj* said especially of pornography: graphic and blatant, but not explicit.

soft drink ▻ *noun* a non-alcoholic drink.

soften /'sɒfən/ ▻ *verb* (***softened***, ***softening***) *tr & intr* **1** to make or become soft or softer. **2** to make or become less severe □ *soften the blow*. • **softener** /'sɒfənə(r)/ *noun* a substance added to another to increase its softness, pliability, etc, such as fabric softener. • **softening** *noun*.

■ **soften someone up** *colloq* to prepare them for an unwelcome or difficult request.

■ **soften up** to wear down by continuous shelling and bombing.

softening of the brain ▻ *noun* **1** *pathol* a softening of the brain tissues, especially during old age. **2** *colloq* marked deterioration of the mental faculties.

soft focus ▻ *noun, photog, cinematog* the deliberate slight blurring of a picture or scene.

soft fruit ▻ *noun, Brit* small stoneless edible fruit, such as berries, currants, etc.

soft furnishings ▻ *plural noun* rugs, curtains, cushion covers and other articles made of fabric.

soft goods ▻ *plural noun, Brit* cloth or fabric, and articles made of cloth.

softhead ▻ *noun* a simpleton. • **soft-headed** *adj*.

soft-hearted ▻ *adj* kind-hearted and generous; compassionate.

soft hyphen ▻ *noun* in word-processing: a hyphen inserted in a word only if necessary for word division at the end of a line, but which would become redundant if the text were to be altered so that the whole word was on the same line.

soft iron ▻ *noun, chem* a form of iron with a low carbon content that is unable to retain magnetism and is used to make the cores of electromagnets, motors, generators and transformers.

soft landing ▻ *noun* **1** a landing by a spacecraft without uncomfortable or damaging impact. **2** the straightforward solution to a problem, especially an economic one.

soft lens ▻ *noun* a flexible CONTACT LENS of a HYDROPHYLIC material that allows some oxygen to reach the cornea.

soft line ▻ *noun* a flexible or lenient attitude, policy, etc.

soft loan ▻ *noun* a cheap or interest-free loan, usually made to a developing country.

softly-softly ▻ *adj* cautious or careful; delicate □ *a softly-softly approach*.

soft option ▻ *noun* the easier or easiest of two or several alternative courses of action.

soft palate ▻ *noun, anatomy* the fleshy muscular back part of the palate. Also called **velum**.

soft pedal ▻ *noun* a pedal on a piano pressed to make the tone less lingering or ringing, especially by causing the hammer to strike only one string.

soft-pedal ▻ *verb* **1** *colloq* to tone down, or avoid emphasizing or mentioning something □ *The government were soft-pedalling the scheme's disadvantages*. **2** *music* to play (the piano) using the soft pedal.

soft porn and **soft pornography** ▻ *noun, colloq* SOFT-CORE pornography in which sexual acts are not shown or described explicitly.

soft science ▻ *noun* any of the scientific disciplines in which rules or principles of evaluation are difficult to determine, such as social sciences. Compare HARD SCIENCE, PSEUDO-SCIENCE.

soft sell ▻ *noun* the use of gentle persuasion as a selling technique, rather than heavy-handed pressure. ▻ *adj* referring or relating to this kind of selling technique □ *the soft-sell approach*.

soft soap ▻ *noun* **1** a semi-liquid soap made containing potash. **2** *colloq* flattery or blarney. ▻ *verb* (**soft-soap**) *colloq* to speak flatteringly to someone, especially in order to persuade or deceive.

soft-spoken ▻ *adj* **1** having a soft voice, and usually a mild manner. **2** suave or smooth-tongued; plausible in speech.

soft spot ▻ *noun* **1** *colloq* a special liking or affection □ *has a soft spot for tall men* □ *has a soft spot for chocolate ice cream*. **2** an informal name for a FONTANELLE.

soft top ▻ *noun* a convertible car with a fabric roof.

soft touch ▻ *noun, colloq* someone easily taken advantage of or persuaded, especially into giving or lending money willingly.

software /'sɒftwɛə(r)/ ▻ *noun, computing* the programs that are used in a computer system (eg operating systems, and applications programs such as word-processing or database programs), and the magnetic disks, tapes, etc, on which they are recorded. Compare HARDWARE, LIVEWARE.

soft water ▻ *noun, chem* water that naturally contains very low levels of calcium and magnesium salts, or from which these salts have been removed artificially, so that it lathers easily with soap and does not cause scaling of kettles, boilers, etc.

softwood ▻ *noun* **1** *bot* the wood of a coniferous tree, eg pine, including some woods that are in fact very hard and durable. **2** *bot* any tree which produces such wood. Compare HARDWOOD.

softy or **softie** /'sɒftɪ/ ▻ *noun* (***softies***) *colloq* **1** someone who is easily upset. **2** a weakly sentimental, soft-hearted or silly person. **3** someone not able to endure rough treatment or hardship.

SOGAT ▻ *abbreviation* in the UK: Society of Graphical and Allied Trades.

soggy /'sɒgɪ/ ▻ *adj* (***soggier***, ***soggiest***) **1** thoroughly soaked or wet; saturated. **2** said of ground: waterlogged; boggy. **3** *colloq* spiritless or dejected. • **soggily** *adverb*. • **sogginess** *noun*. ◷ 16c: from dialect *sog* bog.

soh or **so** /soʊ/ or **sol** /sɒl/ ▻ *noun, music* in sol-fa notation: the fifth note or **dominant** of a major or minor scale. ◷ 14c: see SOL-FA.

soi-disant /swɑːdiː'zɑ̃/ ▻ *adj* self-styled; pretended or would-be. ◷ 18c: French, meaning 'calling oneself'.

soigné and ***soignée*** /'swɑːnjeɪ/ ▻ *adj* said of a male or female respectively: well-groomed; smart. ◷ Early 20c: French.

soil[1] ▻ *noun* **1** the mixture of fragmented rock, plant and animal debris that lies on the surface of the Earth, above the bedrock, containing water and air, as well as living organisms such as bacteria, fungi and invertebrates. **2** *literary* country; land □ *on foreign soil*. ◷ 14c: from French *suel*, from Latin *solum* ground.

soil[2] ▻ *verb* (***soiled***, ***soiling***) **1** to stain or make dirty. **2** to bring discredit on; to sully □ *soiled reputation*. ▻ *noun* **1** a spot or stain. **2** dirt. **3** dung; sewage. ◷ 13c: from French *souil* wallowing-place.

soil³ ▻ *verb* (***soiled, soiling***) to feed (cattle) on fresh-cut green food in order to purge or fatten them. ⓒ 17c: probably from SOIL².

soil horizon ▻ *noun, geol* a layer of soil that differs from adjacent layers in certain physical properties.

soil pipe ▻ *noun* an upright pipe which carries away waste water and sewage from a building into a sewer or drain.

soil profile ▻ *noun* a vertical section through the soil that needs a series of soil horizons extending from the surface to the bedrock from which the upper layers are derived.

soil science ▻ *noun* the scientific study of soil, its composition and its uses.

soirée or **soiree** /'swɑːreɪ/ ▻ *noun* **1** a formal party held in the evening. **2** an evening of entertainment of any kind. ⓒ 19c: French, meaning 'evening'.

soixante-neuf / *French* swasɑ̃tnœf/ and **sixty-nine** ▻ *noun* a sexual position in which both partners simultaneously orally stimulate each other's genitalia. ⓒ Early 20c: French, meaning 'sixty-nine', from the position adopted.

sojourn /'sɒdʒən, -ɜːn, 'sʌ-, 'soʊ-/ *formal* ▻ *noun* a short stay. ▻ *verb* (***sojourned, sojourning***) *intr* to stay for a short while. • **sojourner** *noun*. ⓒ 13c: from French *sojorner*, from Latin *sub* under + *diurnus* of a day, from *dies* day.

sol¹ see SOH

sol² ▻ *noun, chem* a type of colloid that consists of small solid particles dispersed in a liquid.

sol. ▻ *abbreviation* solution.

solace /'sɒləs/ ▻ *noun* **1** comfort in time of disappointment or sorrow. **2** a source of comfort. ▻ *verb* (***solaced, solacing***) **1** to provide with such comfort. **2** to bring relief from something. **3** *intr* to take comfort. ⓒ 13c: from French *solas*, from Latin *solari* to comfort in distress.

solar /'soʊlə(r)/ ▻ *adj* **1** referring or relating to the Sun. **2** relating to, by or using energy from the Sun's rays ▫ ***solar-powered.*** **3** *astron* said of time: determined by the Sun ▫ ***solar year.*** **4** *astron* influenced by the Sun. **5** *astrol* said of character, temperament, etc: influenced by the Sun. ⓒ 15c: from Latin *solaris*, from *sol* sun.

solar battery ▻ *noun, elec* a battery consisting of a number of solar cells.

solar cell ▻ *noun, elec* an electric cell that converts solar energy directly into electricity, used in pocket calculators, light meters, etc, and also used in arrays, known as **solar panels**, to power satellites and spacecraft. Also called **photovoltaic cell**.

solar day see DAY sense 1a

solar eclipse see under ECLIPSE

solar energy ▻ *noun* energy radiated from the Sun, mainly in the form of heat and light, that is required for PHOTOSYNTHESIS, and is also harnessed as a renewable energy source, eg in solar heating systems.

solar flare ▻ *noun, astron* a sudden release of energy in the vicinity of an active region on the Sun's surface, generally associated with a sunspot. Sometimes shortened to **flare**.

solarium /sə'lɛərɪəm/ ▻ *noun* (***solariums*** or ***solaria*** /-ə/) **1** a room or establishment equipped with sunbeds. **2** a sunbed. **3** a conservatory or other room designed to allow exposure to sunlight. ⓒ 19c: Latin, meaning 'sundial', from *sol* sun.

solar month ▻ *noun* one-twelfth of a SOLAR YEAR.

solar panel see under SOLAR CELL

solar plexus ▻ *noun, anatomy* an area in the abdomen in which there is a concentration of nerves radiating from a central point.

solar system ▻ *noun, astron* the Sun and the system of nine major planets (Mercury, Venus, Earth, Mars, Jupiter, Saturn, Uranus, Neptune and Pluto), together with their natural satellites, and the asteroids (minor planets), comets and meteors that revolve around it, held in their orbits by the Sun's gravitational pull.

solar wind ▻ *noun, astron* a stream of charged particles that flows outward from the Sun in all directions at speeds of over one million kph, passing the Earth and the other planets as it moves through the solar system.

solar year ▻ *noun, astron* the time taken for the Earth to complete one revolution around the Sun, ie 365 days, 5 hours, 48 minutes and 46 seconds. Also called **astronomical year, equinoctial year**.

solatium /soʊ'leɪʃɪəm/ ▻ *noun* (***solatia*** /-ə/) *formal* compensation for disappointment, inconvenience and disappointment. ⓒ 19c: Latin.

sold *past tense, past participle of* SELL

solder /'soʊldə(r), 'sɒldə(r)/ ▻ *noun, engineering* any of several alloys with a low melting point, often containing tin and lead, applied when molten to the joint between two metals to form an airtight seal. ▻ *verb* (***soldered, soldering***) to join (two pieces of metal) without melting them, by applying a layer of molten alloy to the joint between them and allowing it to cool and solidify. • **solderer** *noun*. • **soldering** *noun*. ⓒ 14c: from French *souldre*, from Latin *solidare* to strengthen.

soldering-iron ▻ *noun* a tool with a probe-like part, usually electrically heated, used to melt and apply solder.

soldier /'soʊldʒə(r)/ ▻ *noun* **1** a member of a fighting force, especially a national army. **2** a member of an army below officer rank. **3** someone of military skill. **4** a diligent worker for a cause. **5** an ant or white ant with strong jaws specially adapted for fighting. **6** any of various kinds of scarlet pugnacious or armoured animals, eg beetle, fish, etc. **7** *colloq* (**soldiers**) narrow strips of bread-and-butter or toast, especially for dipping into a soft-boiled egg. **8** *building* a brick laid upright in a wall. ▻ *verb* (***soldiered, soldiering***) *intr* to serve as a soldier. • **soldierly** *adverb*. ⓒ 13c: from French *soudier*, from *soude* pay, from Latin *solidus* a piece of money, the pay of a soldier.

▪ **soldier on** to continue determinedly in spite of difficulty and discouragement.

soldier of fortune ▻ *noun* someone willing to serve in any army that pays them; a mercenary.

sole¹ ▻ *noun* **1** the underside of the foot. **2** the underside of a shoe or boot, especially the part not including the heel. **3** the underside of a golf club head. **4** the flattish underside of various things. ▻ *verb* (***soled, soling***) to fit (a shoe or boot) with a sole. ⓒ 14c: French, from Latin *solea* sandal.

sole² ▻ *noun* (***sole*** or ***soles***) a flatfish with a slender brown body and both eyes on the left side of the head, found in shallow tropical and temperate waters, and highly prized as a food fish. ⓒ 14c: from Latin *solea*.

sole³ ▻ *adj* **1** alone; only. **2** exclusive ▫ ***has sole rights to the story.*** **3** *law* without a husband or wife. **4** *archaic* without another. ⓒ 14c: from Latin *solus* alone.

solecism /'sɒlɪsɪzəm/ ▻ *noun* **1** a mistake in the use of language; a breach of syntax, grammar, etc. **2** any absurdity, impropriety or incongruity. **3** an instance of bad or incorrect behaviour. • **solecistic** or **solecistical** *adj*. • **solecistically** *adverb*. ⓒ 16c: from Greek *soloikismos*, said to originate from the corruption of the Attic dialect among the Athenian colonists (*oikizein* to colonise) of *Soloi* in Cilicia.

solely /'soʊllɪ/ ▻ *adverb* **1** alone; without others ▫ ***solely to blame.*** **2** only; excluding all else ▫ ***done solely for profit.***

solemn /'sɒləm/ ▻ *adj* **1** done, made or carried out in earnest and seriousness ▫ ***a solemn vow.*** **2** being of a very serious and formal nature; suggesting seriousness □ *a solemn occasion.* **3** accompanied by an appeal to God, especially as an oath. **4** accompanied or marked by special (especially religious) ceremonies, pomp or gravity. **5** awe-inspiring. **6** glum or sombre in appearance. • **solemnly** *adverb.* • **solemnness** *noun.* ⓒ 14c: from French *solempne* from Latin *sollemnis* annual, customary or appointed.

solemnity /sə'lɛmnɪtɪ/ ▷ *noun* (***solemnities***) **1** the state of being solemn. **2** a solemn statement, sentiment, etc. **3** a solemn ceremony. ⓒ 13c: as *solempnete*, from Latin *sollemnitas*; see SOLEMN.

solemnize or **solemnise** /'sɒləmnaɪz/ ▷ *verb* (***solemnized, solemnizing***) **1** to celebrate (a religious event) with rites. **2** to perform (especially a marriage) with a formal or religious ceremony. **3** to make something solemn. • **solemnization** *noun.* ⓒ 14c: as *solempnise*, from Latin *sollemnis*; see SOLEMN.

solenoid /'soulənɔɪd, 'sɒl-/ ▷ *noun, physics* a cylindrical coil of wire that produces a magnetic field when an electric current is passed through it, and often contains a movable iron or steel core that can be used to operate a switch, relay, circuit breaker, etc. • **solenoidal** *adj.* ⓒ 19c: from Greek *solen* tube + -OID.

sol-fa /'sɒlfɑː/ ▷ *noun* a system of musical notation, either written down or sung, in which the notes of a scale are represented by the syllables *doh, re, mi, fah, soh, la, ti*. These names are mainly derived from the first syllables of words in a medieval Latin hymn. ▷ *verb* (***sol-fas, sol-faed, sol-faing***) *tr & intr* to sing to sol-fa syllables. Also called **tonic sol-fa**. ⓒ 16c: from *sol*, a form of SOH, + FAH.

solfatara /sɒlfə'tɑːrə/ ▷ *noun* (***solfataras***) a volcanic vent emitting only gases, especially one emitting acid gases, such as hydrochloric acid and sulphur dioxide, and water vapour. ⓒ 18c: named after Solfatara, a volcano near Naples, from Italian *solfo* sulphur.

solfeggio /sɒl'fɛdʒɪoʊ/ ▷ *noun* (***solfeggi*** /sɒl'fɛdʒiː/ or ***solfeggios***) *music* an exercise in sol-fa syllables. ⓒ 18c: Italian.

solicit /sə'lɪsɪt/ ▷ *verb* (***solicited, soliciting***) **1** *formal* to ask for something, or for something from someone □ *solicit aid from other countries* □ *solicited me for advice.* **2** *intr* said of a prostitute: to approach people with open offers of sex for money. **3** to invite or lure someone into illegal or immoral acts. **4** *intr* said of beggars: to importune or harass for money. **5** *formal* to require or call for someone or something. • **soliciting** *noun.* ⓒ 15c: from Latin *solicitare*, from *sollus* whole + *citus* aroused.

solicitation /səlɪsɪ'teɪʃən/ ▷ *noun* **1** an act of soliciting. **2** an earnest request. **3** an invitation.

solicitor /sə'lɪsɪtə(r)/ ▷ *noun* **1** in Britain: a lawyer who prepares legal documents, gives legal advice and, in the lower courts only, speaks on behalf of clients. **2** someone who solicits. **3** in N Amer: someone who canvasses. **4** in N Amer: someone responsible for legal matters in a town or city.

solicitor-advocate ▷ *noun, Scots law* a solicitor with the right to represent clients in the High Court or Court of Session.

Solicitor-General ▷ *noun* (***Solicitors-General***) **1** in England: the law-officer of the crown next in rank to the Attorney-General. **2** in Scotland: the law-officer of the crown next in rank to the Lord-Advocate.

solicitous /sə'lɪsɪtəs/ ▷ *adj* **1** (**solicitous about** or **for someone** or **something**) anxious or concerned about them. **2** (**solicitous to do something**) willing or eager to do it. • **solicitously** *adverb.* • **solicitousness** *noun.*

solicitude /sə'lɪsɪtʃuːd/ ▷ *noun* **1** anxiety or uneasiness of mind. **2** the state of being solicitous.

solid /'sɒlɪd/ ▷ *adj* **1** in a form other than LIQUID or GAS, and resisting changes in shape due to firmly cohering particles. **2** having the same nature or material throughout; uniform or pure □ *a solid oak table.* **3** not hollow; full of material □ *a solid chocolate egg.* **4** firmly constructed or attached; not easily breaking or loosening. **5** (*often* **solid for something**) unanimously in favour. **6** *geom* having or pertaining to three dimensions. **7** difficult to undermine or destroy; sound □ *solid support for the scheme.* **8** substantial; ample □ *a solid meal.* **9** without breaks; continuous □ *We waited for four solid hours.* **10** competent, rather than outstanding □ *a solid piece of work.* **11** said of a character: reliable; sensible. **12** said of a character: weighty; worthy of credit □ *He has a solid presence.* **13** financially secure; wealthy. ▷ *noun* **1** a solid substance or body. **2** *chem* a state of matter with a definite shape and in which the constituent molecules or ions can only vibrate about fixed positions, and are unable to move freely. **3** *geom* a three-dimensional geometric figure. **4** (**solids**) non-liquid food. **5** (**solids**) particles of solid matter in a liquid. • **solidity** /sə'lɪdɪtɪ/ *noun.* • **solidly** *adverb.* ⓒ 14c: from Latin *solidus.*

solid angle ▷ *noun, geom* a three-dimensional cone-shaped angle representing the region subtended at a point by a SURFACE (*noun* 4), as opposed to a line in the case of a PLANE ANGLE.

solidarity /sɒlɪ'darɪtɪ/ ▷ *noun* (***solidarities***) mutual support and unity of interests, aims and actions among members of a group.

solidify /sə'lɪdɪfaɪ/ ▷ *verb* (***solidifies, solidified, solidifying***) *tr & intr* to make or become solid. • **solidification** *noun.*

solid-state ▷ *adj* **1** *electronics* denoting an electronic device or component, eg a semiconductor or transistor, that functions by the movement of electrons through solids, and contains no heated filaments or vacuums. **2** *physics* concerned with the study of matter in the solid state, especially the electrical properties of semiconductors at the atomic level.

solidus /'sɒlɪdəs/ ▷ *noun* (***solidi*** /'sɒlɪdaɪ/) **1** a printed line sloping from right to left, eg separating alternatives, as in *and/or*; a stroke or slash mark. **2** *historical* a Roman gold coin. **3** *historical* a medieval silver coin. ⓒ 14c: from Latin *solidus (nummus)* a solid (coin).

soliloquize or **soliloquise** /sə'lɪləkwaɪz/ ▷ *verb* (***soliloquized, soliloquizing***) *intr* to speak a soliloquy. • **soliloquizer** *noun.* • **soliloquist** *noun.*

soliloquy /sə'lɪləkwɪ/ ▷ *noun* (***soliloquies***) **1** an act of talking to oneself, especially a speech in a play, etc in which a character reveals thoughts or intentions to the audience by talking aloud. **2** the use of such speeches as a device in drama. ⓒ 17c: from Latin *solus* alone + *loqui* to speak.

solipsism /'sɒlɪpsɪzəm/ ▷ *noun, philos* the theory that one's own existence is the only certainty. • **solipsist** *noun, adj.* • **solipsistic** *adj.* ⓒ 19c: from Latin *solus* alone + *ipse* self.

solitaire /sɒlɪ'tɛə(r)/ ▷ *noun* **1** any of several games for one player only, especially one whose object is to eliminate pegs or marbles from a board and leave only one. **2** a single gem in a setting on its own. **3** *N Amer, especially US* the card game PATIENCE. **4** a gigantic flightless bird related to the dodo, extinct since the 18th century. **5** an American or West Indian fly-catching thrush. ⓒ 14c: French.

solitary /'sɒlɪtərɪ/ ▷ *adj* **1** single; lone. **2** preferring to be alone; not social. **3** without companions; lonely. **4** remote; secluded. **5** *bot* growing single. **6** said of insects: not living in groups or colonies. ▷ *noun* (***solitaries***) **1** someone who lives alone, especially a hermit. **2** *colloq* solitary confinement. • **solitarily** *adverb.* • **solitariness** *noun.* ⓒ 14c: from Latin *solitarius*, from *solus* alone.

solitary confinement ▷ *noun* imprisonment in a cell by oneself.

solitude /'sɒlɪtʃuːd/ ▷ *noun* the state of being alone or secluded, especially pleasantly. ⓒ 14c: from Latin *solitudo*, from *solus* alone.

solmization or **solmisation** /sɒlmɪˈzeɪʃən/ ▻ *noun* in musical reference and training: a system in which syllables are used to designate the notes of a hexachord. ⓔ 18c: French, related to the terms SOL[1] + MI.

solo /ˈsoʊloʊ/ ▻ *noun* (***solos*** or ***soli*** /ˈsoʊliː/) **1** a piece of music, or a passage within it, for a single voice or instrument, with or without accompaniment. **2** any performance in which no other person or instrument participates. **3** a flight in which the pilot flies alone. **4** (*in full* **solo whist**) a card game based on WHIST, in which various declarations are made and the declarer does not have a partner. ▻ *adj* performed alone, without assistance or accompaniment. ▻ *adverb* alone □ ***fly solo.*** ▻ *verb* (***soloed, soloing***) *intr* **1** to fly solo. **2** to play a solo. ⓔ 17c: Italian, from Latin *solus* alone.

soloist /ˈsoʊloʊɪst/ ▻ *noun* someone who performs a solo or solos.

Solomon's seal ▻ *noun* a perennial plant with arching stems, oval leaves and white bell-shaped flowers that hang in clusters beneath the stem.

so long or **so-long** ▻ *exclamation, colloq* goodbye; farewell.

solo whist see under SOLO

solstice /ˈsɒlstɪs/ ▻ *noun* either of the times when the Sun is furthest from the equator: the longest day (**summer solstice**) around June 21 in the N hemisphere and the shortest day (**winter solstice**) around December 21 in the N hemisphere. • **solstitial** /sɒlˈstɪʃəl/ *adj* referring to or occurring at a solstice. ⓔ 13c: from Latin *solstitium* the standing still of the sun, from *sol* sun + *sistere, statum* to cause to stand.

soluble /ˈsɒljʊbəl/ ▻ *adj* **1** denoting a substance (a SOLUTE) that is capable of being dissolved in a liquid (a SOLVENT). **2** capable of being solved or resolved. • **solubility** *noun*. ⓔ 14c: from Latin *solubilis*.

solute /ˈsɒljuːt, sɒˈljuːt/ ▻ *noun, chem* any substance that is dissolved in a solvent, eg water to form a solution. ⓔ 15c: from Latin *solutus*, from *solvere, solutum* to loosen.

solution /səˈluːʃən, səˈljuːʃən/ ▻ *noun* **1** the process of finding an answer to a problem or puzzle. **2** the answer sought or found. **3** *chem* a homogeneous mixture consisting of a solid or gas (the SOLUTE) and the liquid (the SOLVENT) in which it is completely dissolved. **4** the act of dissolving or the state of being dissolved □ ***in solution.*** **5** the act of separating, or the separation of parts. **6** *math* in a mathematical equation: the value that one or more of the variables must have for that equation to be valid. ⓔ 14c: from Latin *solutio*.

solvation /sɒlˈveɪʃən/ ▻ *noun, chem* the interaction between the ions of a solute and the molecules of a solvent, which enables an ionic solid to dissolve in a solvent to form a solution, or to swell or form a gel in the presence of a solvent. ⓔ Early 20c: from SOLVE.

solve /sɒlv/ ▻ *verb* (***solved, solving***) **1** to discover the answer to (a puzzle) or a way out of (a problem). **2** to clear up or explain something. • **solvable** *adj*. • **solver** *noun*. ⓔ 15c: from Latin *solvere* to loosen.

solvent /ˈsɒlvənt/ ▻ *adj* able to pay all one's debts. ▻ *noun, chem* **1** in a solution: the liquid in which a solid or gas (the SOLUTE) is dissolved, eg water and organic chemicals such as ethanol (alcohol), ether, and acetone. **2** a substance which may act in this way, eg for dissolving and removing an unwanted substance such as glue. • **solvency** *noun* the ability to pay one's debts.

solvent abuse ▻ *noun* inhalation of the fumes given off by various solvents, eg adhesives, petrol or butane gas in cigarette-lighter refills, in order to induce euphoria, a practice that damages the brain and lungs and can be fatal. Also called GLUE-SNIFFING.

Som ▻ *abbreviation* Somerset.

soma[1] /ˈsoʊmə/ ▻ *noun* (***somas*** or ***somata*** /ˈsoʊmətə/) *biol* the body of a plant or animal, excluding its germ-cells. ⓔ 19c: Greek, meaning 'body'.

soma[2] or **Soma** /ˈsoʊmə/ ▻ *noun* **1** an intoxicating plant juice used in ancient Vedic ceremonies, personified as a god. **2** the plant yielding this juice. ⓔ 19c: Sanskrit.

somatic /soʊˈmatɪk/ ▻ *adj, medicine, biol* **1** referring or relating to the body, rather than the mind. **2** referring or relating to the body, as opposed to reproduction □ *somatic cells.* • **somatically** *adverb*. ⓔ 18c: from SOMA[1].

Somali /səˈmɑːlɪ/ ▻ *noun* (***Somalis***) **1** a group of Cushitic-speaking (see CUSHITIC LANGUAGES) peoples of Somalia and parts of Kenya, Ethiopia and Djibouti. **2** an individual belonging to this group of peoples.

somatogenic /soʊmətoʊˈdʒɛnɪk/ ▻ *adj, biol* originating in or developing from the body. ⓔ Early 20c.

somatotrophin /soʊmətoʊˈtroʊfɪn/ ▻ *noun, physiol* growth hormone. • **somatotrophic** *adj*. ⓔ 1940s.

somatotype /ˈsoʊmətoʊtaɪp/ ▻ *noun* a type consisting of a physical build paired with a particular temperament. ⓔ 1930s.

sombre /ˈsɒmbə(r)/ ▻ *adj* **1** sad and serious; grave. **2** dark and gloomy; melancholy. **3** said eg of colours: dark; drab. **4** suggesting seriousness, rather than light-heartedness. • **sombrely** *adverb*. • **sombreness** *noun*. ⓔ 18c: from French *sombre*, perhaps from Latin *sub* under + *umbra* shade.

sombrero /sɒmˈbrɛəroʊ/ ▻ *noun* (***sombreros***) a wide-brimmed straw or felt hat, especially popular in Mexico. ⓔ 16c: Spanish, from *sombra* shade.

some /sʌm/ ▻ *adj* **1** signifying an unknown or unspecified amount or number of something □ ***She owns some shares.*** **2** signifying a certain undetermined category □ ***Some films are better than others.*** **3** having an unknown or unspecified nature or identity □ ***some problem with the engine.*** **4** quite a lot of something □ ***We have been waiting for some time.*** **5** at least a little □ ***try to feel some enthusiasm.*** **6** *colloq* signifying a poor example of something □ ***Some friend you are!*** **7** *colloq* signifying an excellent or impressive example of something □ ***That was some shot!*** **8** *colloq* signifying a memorable or extraordinary example of something, not necessarily good or bad □ ***That was some evening!*** ▻ *pronoun* **1** certain unspecified things or people □ ***Some say he should resign.*** **2** an unspecified amount or number □ ***Give him some, too.*** ▻ *adverb* **1** to an unspecified extent □ ***play some more.*** **2** approximately □ ***some twenty feet deep.*** ⓔ Anglo-Saxon *sum*.

-some[1] /sʌm/ ▻ *suffix* **1** *forming adjectives, signifying* **a** inclined to cause or produce □ ***troublesome***; **b** inviting □ ***cuddlesome***; **c** tending to do, be or express something □ ***quarrelsome.*** **2** *forming nouns, signifying* a group of the specified number of people or things □ ***a foursome.*** ⓔ Anglo-Saxon *-sum*.

-some[2] /soʊm/ ▻ *suffix, forming nouns, signifying* a body □ ***chromosome.***

somebody ▻ *pronoun* **1** an unknown or unspecified person; someone. **2** someone of importance □ ***He always strove to be somebody.***

someday ▻ *adverb* at an unknown or unspecified time in the future.

somehow ▻ *adverb* **1** in some way not yet known. **2** for a reason not easy to explain. **3** (*also* **somehow or other**) in any way necessary or possible □ ***I'll get there somehow or other.***

someone ▻ *pronoun* somebody.

somersault or **summersault** /ˈsʌməsɔːlt, -sɒlt/ ▻ *noun* a leap or roll in which the whole body turns a complete circle forwards or backwards, leading with the head. ▻ *verb* (***somersaulted, somersaulting***) *intr* to perform such a leap or roll. ◷ 16c: from French *sombre saut*, from Latin *supra* over + *saltus* leap.

something ▷ *pronoun* **1** a thing not known or not stated □ *Take something to eat.* **2** an amount or number not known or not stated □ *something short of 1 000 people* □ *aged about 40 something.* **3** a person or thing of importance □ *make something of oneself.* **4** a certain truth or value □ *There is something in what you say.* **5** *colloq* (*also* **something else**) an impressive person or thing □ *That meal was really something!* □ *He really is something else!* ▷ *adverb* to some degree; rather □ *The garden looks something like a scrapyard.* • **something of a ...** a ... to some extent □ *She's something of a local celebrity.* • **something rotten, terrible, awful**, *etc* to an extreme degree □ *He teased me something rotten.*

-something ▷ *combining form* (combining with *twenty, thirty, forty*, etc) **1** *forming nouns* **a** indicating an unspecified or unknown number greater than or in addition to the combining number, as in *twentysomething*; **b** an individual or a group of people of this age, as in *he's a thirtysomething*, ie between the ages of 30 and 39. **2** *forming adjectives* referring or belonging to such a person or group. ◷ 1980s.

sometime ▷ *adverb* **1** at an unknown or unspecified time in the future or the past □ *I'll finish it sometime.* **2** *archaic* formerly. ▷ *adj* former; late □ *the sometime king.*

sometimes ▷ *adverb* occasionally; now and then.

somewhat ▷ *adverb* rather; a little □ *He seemed somewhat unsettled.* • **somewhat of ...** ... to some extent □ *He is somewhat of a liar.*

somewhere ▷ *adverb* in or to some place or degree, or at some point, not known or not specified.

somnambulate /sɒm'nambjʊleɪt/ ▷ *verb* (***somnambulated, somnambulating***) *intr* to walk in one's sleep. • **somnambulant** *adj.* ◷ 19c.

somnambulism /sɒm'nambjʊlɪzəm/ ▷ *noun* sleepwalking. • **somnambulist** *noun.* ◷ 18c: from Latin *somnus* sleep + *ambulare* to walk.

somniferous /sɒm'nɪfərəs/ and **somnific** /sɒm'nɪfɪk/ ▷ *adj* causing sleep. ◷ 17c: from Latin *somnifer*, from *somnus* sleep.

somnolent /'sɒmnələnt/ ▷ *adj, formal* sleepy or drowsy; causing sleepiness or drowsiness. • **somnolence** or **somnolency** *noun.* • **somnolently** *adverb.* ◷ 15c: as *sompnolence*, from Latin *somnolentia*, from *somnus* sleep.

son¹ /sʌn/ ▷ *noun* **1** a male child or offspring. **2** a descendant, or one so regarded or treated. **3** a male person closely associated with, or seen as developing from, a particular activity or set of circumstances □ *a son of the Russian revolution.* **4** a familiar and sometimes patronizing term of address used to a boy or man. **5** (**the Son**) *Christianity* the second person of the Trinity, Jesus Christ. ◷ Anglo-Saxon *sunu*.

son² /soʊn/ ▷ *noun* a style of Cuban music played with claves, bongo drums and guitar. ◷ Spanish, meaning 'sound'.

sonant /'soʊnənt/ *phonetics* ▷ *adj* said of a sound: voiced; syllabic. ▷ *noun* a voiced or syllabic sound. • **sonance** *noun.* ◷ 19c: from Latin *sonans, -antis*, present participle of *sonare* to sound.

sonar /'soʊnɑː(r)/ ▷ *noun* a system that is used to determine the location of underwater objects, eg submarines, shoals of fish, especially by transmitting ultrasound signals from the bottom of a ship and measuring the time taken for their echoes to return when they strike an obstacle. ◷ 1940s: from *so*und *n*avigation *a*nd *r*anging.

sonata /sə'nɑːtə/ ▷ *noun* (***sonatas***) a piece of classical music written in three or more movements for a solo instrument, especially the piano. ◷ 17c: Italian, from past participle of *sonare* to sound.

sonata form ▷ *noun, music* the plan or form most often used since c.1750 in the design of the first movement (and occasionally the slow movement and finale) of a sonata or symphony, divided into three basic sections: EXPOSITION, DEVELOPMENT and RECAPITULATION.

sonatina /sɒnə'tiːnə/ ▷ *noun* (***sonatinas***) a short sonata, usually one which is technically straightforward. ◷ 18c: Italian, a diminutive of SONATA.

sonde /sɒnd/ ▷ *noun* one of various devices for obtaining information about atmospheric and weather conditions at high altitudes. ◷ 1920s: French, meaning 'plumb line'.

son et lumière /sɒn eɪ 'luːmɪɛə(r), luːmɪ'ɛə(r)/ ▷ *noun* a dramatic night-time outdoor spectacle with lights, music and narration on a particular theme, often staged at and presenting the history of a famous building. ◷ 1960s: French, meaning 'sound and light'.

song ▷ *noun* **1** a set of words, short poem, etc to be sung, usually with accompanying music. **2** the music to which these words are set. **3** an instrumental composition of a similar form and character. **4** singing □ *poetry and song.* **5** a poem, or poetry in general. **6** the musical call of certain birds. **7** a habitual utterance, manner or attitude towards anything. • **going for a song** *colloq* at a bargain price. • **make a song and dance about something** *colloq* to make an unnecessary fuss about it. ◷ Anglo-Saxon *sang*.

songbird ▷ *noun* in the classification of the animal kingdom: any of a suborder of perching birds, most of which have a musical call, eg larks, thrushes, tits, etc.

songbook ▷ *noun* a book containing songs together with their music.

song cycle ▷ *noun* a set of songs connected by some common theme, often to words by a single poet.

songsmith ▷ *noun* a composer of songs.

songster /'sɒŋstə(r)/ ▷ *noun, old use* a talented male singer.

songstress /'sɒŋstrəs/ ▷ *noun, old use* a talented female singer.

song thrush ▷ *noun* a common thrush, native to Europe and W Asia, smaller than the mistle-thrush, and with a more lightly spotted breast, named because of its very distinctive song.

songwriter ▷ *noun* someone who composes music and sometimes also the words for, especially popular, songs.

sonic /'sɒnɪk/ ▷ *adj* **1** relating to or using sound or sound waves. **2** travelling at approximately the speed of sound. ◷ 1920s: from Latin *sonus*.

sonic barrier ▷ *noun* the technical term for SOUND BARRIER.

sonic boom and **sonic bang** ▷ *noun* a loud boom that is heard when an aircraft flying through the Earth's atmosphere reaches supersonic speed, ie when it passes through the sound barrier.

sonics /'sɒnɪks/ ▷ *singular noun* the study of the technological application of sounds, especially supersonic waves.

son-in-law ▷ *noun* (***sons-in-law***) the husband of one's daughter.

sonnet /'sɒnɪt/ ▷ *noun* a short poem with 14 lines of 10 or 11 syllables each and a regular rhyming pattern according to the scheme: the Italian sonnet consists of an OCTAVE and a SESTET, whereas the English sonnet consists of three QUATRAINS and ends with a rhyming COUPLET. ◷ 16c: from Italian *sonetto*, a diminutive of *suono*, from Latin *sonus* sound.

sonny /'sʌnɪ/ ▷ *noun* (***sonnies***) a familiar and often condescending term of address used to a boy or man.

sonobuoy /'soʊnoʊbɔɪ, 'sɒnoʊbɔɪ/ ▷ *noun* sonar equipment dropped to float on the sea, pick up underwater noise, eg from a submarine, and transmit bearings of the source to aircraft. ◐ 1940s.

son of a bitch or **sonofabitch** ▷ *noun* (***sons of bitches***) *especially US slang* **1** an abusive term of address. **2** a vulgar exclamation.

son of a gun ▷ *noun* (***sons of guns***) *slang* **1** a rogue or rascal. **2** an affectionate greeting.

sonogram /'sounəgram, 'sɒnə-/ ▷ *noun* **1** ▷ *acoustics* a visual representation of a sound, produced by a SONOGRAPH. **2** *medicine* a sonogram produced by ultrasonography. ◐ 1950s.

sonograph /'sounəgrɑːf, 'sɒnəgrɑːf/ ▷ *noun* a device for scanning and recording sound and its component frequencies. ◐ 1950s.

sonorant /'sɒnərənt/ ▷ *noun, phonetics* **1** a frictionless consonant or nasal (*l, r, m, n, ng*) capable of fulfilling a consonantal or vocalic function. **2** either of the consonants *w* and *y*, which have consonantal or vocalic functions. ◐ Early 20c: from Latin *sonorus*, from *sonus, sonoris*, from *sonare* to sound.

sonorous /'sɒnərəs, sə'nɔːrəs/ ▷ *adj* **1** sounding impressively loud and deep. **2** giving out a deep clear ring or sound when struck □ ***a sonorous bell.*** **3** said of language: impressively eloquent. • **sonority** /sə'nɒrɪtɪ/ and **sonorousness** *noun*. • **sonorously** *adverb*. ◐ 17c: from Latin *sonare* to sound.

sook /sʊk/ ▷ *noun* **1** *especially Austral colloq* a soft, timid or cowardly person. **2** *Brit dialect* someone who sucks up in a fawning or grovelling manner; a toady. ◐ 19c: perhaps from earlier *suck(-calf)* a hand-reared calf, influenced by the Scots pronunciation of SUCK.

soon /suːn/ ▷ *adverb* (***sooner, soonest***) **1** in a short time from now or from a stated time. **2** quickly; with little delay. **3** readily or willingly. • **as soon as ...** at or not before the moment when ... □ ***will pay you as soon as I receive the goods.*** • **as soon ... as ...** used to state that the first alternative is slightly preferable to the second □ ***He'd just as soon die as apologize to her.*** ◐ Anglo-Saxon *sona*.

sooner /'suːnə(r)/ ▷ *adverb* **1** earlier than previously thought. **2** preferably □ ***I'd sooner die than go back there.*** • **no sooner ... than ...** immediately after ... then ... □ ***No sooner had I mentioned his name than he appeared.*** • **no sooner said than done** said of a request, promise, etc: immediately fulfilled. • **sooner or later** eventually.

soot /sʊt/ ▷ *noun* a black powdery substance produced when coal or wood is imperfectly burned; smut. ▷ *verb* (***sooted, sooting***) to cover, smear or dirty with soot. ◐ Anglo-Saxon *sot*.

soothe /suːð/ ▷ *verb* (***soothed, soothing***) **1** to bring relief from (a pain, etc); to allay. **2** to comfort, calm or compose someone. **3** *intr* to have a calming, tranquillizing or relieving effect. • **soothing** *noun, adj*. • **soothingly** *adverb*. ◐ Anglo-Saxon *gesothian* to confirm as true.

soother /'suːðə(r)/ ▷ *noun* **1** a person or thing that soothes. **2** a baby's dummy teat.

soothsayer /'suːθseɪə(r)/ ▷ *noun* someone who predicts the future; a seer or diviner. • **soothsay** *verb* to foretell or divine. ◐ 14c: from archaic *sooth* truth + SAY.

sooty /'sʊtɪ/ ▷ *adj* (***sootier, sootiest***) **1** covered with soot. **2** like or consisting of soot. • **sootily** *adverb*. • **sootiness** *noun*.

SOP ▷ *abbreviation* standard operating procedure.

sop ▷ *noun* **1** (*often* **sops**) a piece of food, especially bread, dipped or soaked in a liquid, eg soup. **2** something given or done as a bribe or in order to pacify someone ◐ from the *Aeneid*, in which the Sibyl gave drugged sop to Cerberus in order to gain passage for Aeneas to Hades. **3** a feeble or spineless person. ▷ *verb* (***sopped, sopping***) *tr & intr* to soak or become soaked. ◐ Anglo-Saxon *sopp*.

■ **sop something up** to mop or soak it up.

sophism /'sɒfɪzəm/ ▷ *noun* a convincing but false argument or explanation, especially one intended to deceive. ◐ 14c: from Greek *sophisma* clever device, from *sophia* wisdom.

sophist /'sɒfɪst/ ▷ *noun* **1** someone who argues with shrewd but intentionally fallacious reasoning. **2** in ancient Greece: one of a class of public teachers of rhetoric, philosophy, etc. ◐ 16c: from Greek *sophia* wisdom.

sophistic /sɒ'fɪstɪk/ and **sophistical** ▷ *adj* **1** referring to or characteristic of a sophist or sophistry. **2** fallaciously subtle; specious. • **sophistically** *adverb*.

sophisticate ▷ *verb* /sə'fɪstɪkeɪt/ (***sophisticated, sophisticating***) **1** to make sophisticated. **2** to adulterate or falsify an argument; to make sophistic. **3** *intr* to practise sophistry. ▷ *noun* /sə'fɪstɪkət/ a sophisticated person. ◐ 14c: from Latin *sophisticare, sophisticatum* to adulterate.

sophisticated /sə'fɪstɪkeɪtɪd/ ▷ *adj* **1** said of a person: having or displaying a broad knowledge and experience of the world and its culture. **2** appealing to or frequented by people with such knowledge and experience. **3** said of a person: accustomed to an elegant lifestyle. **4** said especially of machines: complex; equipped with the most up-to-date devices □ ***sophisticated weaponry.*** **5** subtle; falsified □ ***sophisticated arguments.*** • **sophistication** /səfɪstɪ'keɪʃən/ *noun*.

sophistry /'sɒfɪstrɪ/ ▷ *noun* (***sophistries***) **1** plausibly deceptive or fallacious reasoning, or an instance of this. **2** the art of reasoning speciously.

sophomore /'sɒfəmɔː(r)/ ▷ *noun* (***sophomores***) *N Amer, especially US* a second-year student at a school or university. • **sophomoric** /sɒfə'mɒrɪk/ *adj*. ◐ 17c: from Greek *sophos* wise + *moros* foolish.

sopor /'soupɔː(r)/ ▷ *noun, pathol* an unnaturally deep sleep.

soporific /sɒpə'rɪfɪk/ ▷ *adj* **1** causing sleep or drowsiness. **2** extremely slow and boring □ ***a soporific speech.*** ▷ *noun* a sleep-inducing drug. ◐ 17c: from Latin *sopor* deep sleep + *facere* to make.

sopping /'sɒpɪŋ/ ▷ *adj* ▷ *adverb* (*also* **sopping wet**) thoroughly wet; soaking.

soppy /'sɒpɪ/ ▷ *adj* (***soppier, soppiest***) **1** *colloq* weakly sentimental. **2** thoroughly wet. • **soppily** *adverb*. • **soppiness** *noun*. ◐ 17c: from SOP.

sopranino /sɒprə'niːnou/ ▷ *noun* (***sopraninos*** or ***sopranini*** /-niː/) an instrument with a pitch higher than the corresponding soprano. Also *as adj*. ◐ Early 20c: Italian, a diminutive of SOPRANO.

soprano /sə'prɑːnou/ ▷ *noun* (***sopranos*** or ***soprani*** /-niː/) **1** a singing voice of the highest pitch for a woman or a boy. **2** a person having this voice pitch. **3** a musical part for such a voice. **4** a musical instrument high or highest in pitch in relation to others in its family. Also *as adj*. ◐ 18c: Italian, from Latin *supra* above.

sorb ▷ *noun* **1** SERVICE-TREE. **2** (*in full* **sorb-apple**) the fruit of this tree.

sorbefacient /sɔːbə'feɪʃənt/ ▷ *adj* causing or promoting absorption. Also *as noun*. ◐ 19c: from Latin *sorbere* to suck in + *faciens, facientis*, present participle of *facere* to make.

sorbet /'sɔːbeɪ, -bət/ ▷ *noun* a water ice. ◐ 16c: French, from Italian *sorbetto*, from Arabic *sharbah* drink.

sorbic acid ▷ *noun, chem* an acid obtained from the rowan-berry, used as a food preservative.

sorbitol /'sɔːbɪtɒl/ ▷ *noun, chem* (formula $C_6H_8(OH)_6$) a water-soluble white crystalline carbohydrate, used as a food additive and sweetening agent, and in cosmetics, toothpastes, resins and pharmaceuticals, and also used by diabetics as a substitute for sugar.

sorcery /'sɔːsərɪ/ ▷ *noun* **1** the art or use of magic, especially black magic that is associated with the power of evil spirits, supernatural forces, etc. **2** an instance of this kind of magic. **3** the spells that are used in this kind of magic. • **sorcerer** or **sorceress** *noun*. • **sorcerous** *adj*. ⓒ 14c: from French *sorcerie* witchcraft.

sordid /ˈsɔːdɪd/ ▷ *adj* **1** repulsively filthy; squalid. **2** morally revolting or degraded; ignoble □ ***a sordid affair.*** • **sordidly** *adverb*. • **sordidness** *noun*. ⓒ 16c: from French *sordide*, from Latin *sordidus*, from *sordere* to be dirty.

sordino /sɔːˈdiːnoʊ/ ▷ *noun* (***sordini*** /-niː/) *music* a mute on a musical instrument that is used to soften or deaden the sound. • **con sordino** or **con sordini** an instruction to the player of a musical piece that the following section should be played using a mute. • **senza sordino** or **senza sordini** an instruction to the player of a musical piece that the following section should be played without using a mute. ⓒ 18c: Italian, meaning 'mute', from Latin *surdus* deaf or noiseless.

sore ▷ *adj* **1** said of a wound, injury, part of the body, etc: painful or tender. **2** said of a blow, bite, sting, etc: painful or causing physical pain. **3** causing mental anguish, grief or annoyance □ ***a sore point.*** **4** *N Amer, especially US* angry or resentful □ ***got sore at the kids.*** **5** severe or urgent □ ***in sore need of attention.*** ▷ *noun* a diseased or injured spot or area, especially an ulcer or boil. ▷ *adverb* greatly □ ***be sore afraid.*** • **soreness** *noun*. • **stick out like a sore thumb** *colloq* to be awkwardly obvious or noticeable, especially by being different or out of place. ⓒ Anglo-Saxon *sar*.

sorely ▷ *adverb* acutely; very much □ ***I'm sorely tempted to tell her.***

sore point ▷ *noun* a subject that causes great anger, resentment, etc whenever it is raised.

sorghum /ˈsɔːgəm/ ▷ *noun* **1** any of several different varieties of grass, such as DURRA, that are related to the sugar cane and which are widely cultivated in Africa and parts of Asia as a cereal crop and a source of syrup. **2** *chiefly US* a type of molasses that is made from the syrup of one of these varieties of plant. ⓒ 16c: from Italian *sorgo*, from Latin *surgum*.

sori *plural of* SORUS

soroptimist or **Soroptimist** /səˈrɒptɪmɪst/ ▷ *noun* someone who is a member of Soroptimist International, a society founded in 1921 for professional and business women. ⓒ 1920s: from Latin *soror* sister + OPTIMIST.

sororal /səˈrɔːrəl/ and **sororial** /səˈrɔːrɪəl/ ▷ *adj* characteristic, or relating or referring to a sister or sisters □ ***a sororal bond.*** ⓒ 17c: from Latin *soror* sister.

sororicide /səˈrɒrɪsaɪd/ ▷ *noun* **1** the act of killing one's sister. **2** someone who has killed their sister. ⓒ 17c: from Latin *soror* sister + -CIDE.

sorority /səˈrɒrɪtɪ/ ▷ *noun* (***sororities***) a women's club or society, especially one affiliated to a US university, college or church. Compare FRATERNITY. ⓒ 16c: from Latin *soror* sister.

sorosis /səˈroʊsɪs/ ▷ *noun* (***soroses*** /-siːz/) *bot* a fleshy fruit, such as the pineapple or mulberry, that is formed from a large collection of flowers that grow in the shape of a spike around a pulpy stem. ⓒ 19c: from Greek *soros* a heap.

sorrel[1] /ˈsɒrəl/ ▷ *noun* **1** any of various low-growing perennial plants, many of which have spear-shaped leaves which give an acid taste. **2** the leaves of this plant, which are used in medicine and in cookery. ⓒ 15c: from French *sorele*, from *sur* sour.

sorrel[2] /ˈsɒrəl/ ▷ *adj* being reddish-brown or light chestnut in colour. ▷ *noun* **1** this colour. **2** a horse or other animal of this colour. ⓒ 15c: from French *sorel*, a diminutive of *sor* brown.

sorrow /ˈsɒroʊ/ ▷ *noun* **1** a feeling of grief or deep sadness, especially one that arises from loss or disappointment. **2** someone or something that is the cause of this. ▷ *verb* (***sorrowed, sorrowing***) *intr* to have or express such feeling. • **sorrower** *noun*. • **sorrowful** *adj*. • **sorrowfully** *adverb*. • **sorrowfulness** *noun*. • **sorrowing** *adj, noun*. ⓒ Anglo-Saxon *sorg*.

sorry /ˈsɒrɪ/ ▷ *adj* (***sorrier, sorriest***) **1** distressed or full of regret or shame, especially over something that one has done or said, something one feels responsible for, something that has happened, etc □ ***I'm sorry if I hurt you*** □ ***I'm sorry that you've had to wait.*** **2** (*usually* **sorry for someone**) full of pity or sympathy □ ***Everyone felt sorry for him when she left him.*** **3** pitifully bad □ ***in a sorry state.*** **4** contemptibly bad; worthless; extremely poor □ ***a sorry excuse.*** ▷ *exclamation* **1** given as an apology. **2** used when asking for something that has just been said to be repeated □ ***Sorry? What was that you said?*** • **sorrily** *adverb*. • **sorriness** *noun*. • **sorryish** *adj*. • **be, feel,** *etc* **sorry for oneself** to indulge in self-pity, especially in an excessive way. ⓒ Anglo-Saxon *sarig* wounded, from *sar* sore.

sort ▷ *noun* **1** a kind, type or class. **2** *colloq* a person □ ***not a bad sort.*** ▷ *verb* (***sorted, sorting***) **1** to arrange into different groups according to some specified criterion. **2** *colloq* to fix something or put it back into working order □ ***tried to sort the car himself.*** **3** *colloq* to deal with something, especially violently as a punishment. • **sortable** *adj*. • **sorter** *noun*. • **sorting** *noun, adj*. • **a sort of ...** a thing like a ... □ ***a cafetière — you know, a sort of pot for making coffee.*** • **of a sort** or **of sorts** of an inferior or untypical kind □ ***an author of a sort.*** • **nothing of the sort** no such thing □ ***I did nothing of the sort.*** • **out of sorts** *colloq* **1** slightly unwell. **2** peevish; bad-tempered. • **sort of** *colloq* rather; in a way; to a certain extent □ ***feeling sort of embarrassed.*** ⓒ 13c: French, from Latin *sors, sortis* a lot, from *sortiri* to divide or obtain by lots.

▪ **sort someone out 1** *colloq* to deal with them firmly and decisively and sometimes violently. **2** to put them right □ ***A good night's sleep will soon sort you out.***

▪ **sort something out 1** to separate things out from a mixed collection into a group or groups according to their kind. **2** to put things into order; to arrange them systematically or methodically □ ***sort out your priorities.*** **3** to resolve it.

sort

• Like **kind**, **sort** gives rise to a usage difficulty when it is followed by *of* with a plural noun and needs to be preceded by a demonstrative pronoun **this, that, these, those**. The grammatical sequences in use are as follows:

? *These sort of things sometimes come as a surprise.*

✓ *I was beginning to think about university and that sort of thing.*

✓ *Those sorts of factors (or factor) will always apply.*

• The first is sometimes rejected by language purists, but it is common, especially in speech.

☆ RECOMMENDATION: to avoid difficulty, use **this sort of** + singular noun, or **these sorts of** + singular or plural noun.

sortie /ˈsɔːtɪ/ ▷ *noun* (***sorties***) **1** a sudden attack by besieged troops. **2** an operational flight by a single military aircraft. **3** *colloq* a short return trip □ ***just going on a quick sortie to the shops.*** ▷ *verb* (***sortied, sortieing***) *intr* to make a sortie. ⓒ 17c: French, from *sortir* to go out.

sortilege /ˈsɔːtɪlɪdʒ/ ▷ *noun* the practice of predicting the future by drawing lots. • **sortileger** *noun*. • **sortilegy** *noun*. ⓒ 14c: French, from *sortilegus* a fortune teller.

sorus /ˈsɔːrəs/ ▷ *noun* (***sori*** /ˈsɔːraɪ/) *bot* **1** a cluster of sporangia on the under side of some fern leaves. **2** a similar structure in certain algae, lichens and fungi. ⓒ 19c: from Greek *soros* heap.

SOS /ɛsoʊ'ɛs/ ▷ *noun* (***SOSs***) **1** an internationally recognized distress call that is put out by a ship's or aircraft's radio-telegraphy system and which consists of these three letters repeatedly transmitted in Morse code. **2** *colloq* any call for help. ◷ Early 20c: in folk etymology, it is often popularly believed that this is an abbreviated form of *Save Our Souls*, but these three letters (represented by three dots, three dashes and three dots) were actually chosen because, in Morse code, they are the easiest to transmit and recognize.

so-so ▷ *adj, colloq* neither very good nor very bad; passable; middling. ▷ *adverb* in an indifferent or unremarkable way. ◷ 16c.

sostenuto /sɒstə'nuːtoʊ, -'njuːtoʊ/ ▷ *adverb* in a steady and sustained manner. ▷ ▷ *adj* steady and sustained. ▷ *noun* (***sostenutos***) a piece of music to be played in this way. ◷ 18c: Italian.

sot ▷ *noun, old use* someone who is drunk or who habitually drinks a lot of alcohol. • **sottish** *adj.* ◷ 16c in this sense; 11c meaning 'a fool'.

soteriology /sɒtɪərɪ'ɒlədʒɪ/ ▷ *noun, Christianity* the theological doctrine of salvation. • **soterial** /sɒ'tɪərɪəl/ or **soteriological** *adj.* ◷ 19c: from Greek *soteria* deliverance, from *soter* saviour + -LOGY.

sotto voce /'sɒtoʊ 'voʊtʃɪ, — 'voʊtʃeɪ/ ▷ *adverb* **1** in a quiet voice, so as not to be overheard. **2** *music* very softly. ◷ 18c: Italian, meaning 'below the voice'.

sou /suː/ ▷ *noun* (***sous***) **1** *formerly* a French coin of low value, which was later used to designate the five-centime piece. **2** *colloq* the smallest amount of money □ ***haven't a sou.*** ◷ Early 19c: French, from *sol*, from Latin *solidus* the name of a solid gold coin.

soubrette /suː'brɛt/ ▷ *noun* **1 a** a minor female part in a play, opera, etc, especially the role of a pert, impudent, flirtatious or intriguing maid; **b** an actress who plays this kind of part. **2** someone who behaves in this kind of way. ◷ 18c: French, meaning 'a lady's maid', from Provençal *soubreto* coy.

soubriquet see SOBRIQUET

souchong /suː'ʃɒŋ, -'tʃɒŋ/ ▷ *noun* a type of fine black China tea. See also LAPSANG. ◷ 18c: from Chinese *xiao-zhong* small sort.

souffle /'suːfəl/ ▷ *noun, medicine* a soft murmuring noise that can be heard coming from various body organs, eg by using a stethoscope. ◷ 19c: French, from *souffler*, from Latin *sufflare*, from SUB- + *flare* to blow.

soufflé /'suːfleɪ/ ▷ *noun* (***soufflés***) a light fluffy sweet or savoury dish that is made by gently combining egg yolks and other ingredients with stiffly beaten egg-whites, carefully putting the mixture into a cylindrical dish, leaving room at the top for it to expand, baking it in the oven and serving it immediately before the spectacular crown that has formed collapses. ◷ Early 19c: French, from *souffler*, from Latin *sufflare*, from SUB- + *flare* to blow.

sough[1] /saʊ, sʌf; *Scottish* suːx/ ▷ *noun* a sighing, rustling or murmuring sound that is made by the wind blowing through trees, etc. ▷ *verb* (***soughed***, ***soughing***) *intr*, *usually* said of the wind: to make this sound □ ***The wind soughed through the trees.*** ◷ Anglo-Saxon *swogan* to move with a rushing sound.

sough[2] /sʌf/ ▷ *noun* a small gutter or drain that allows water, sewage, etc to run off. ◷ 14c.

sought *past tense, past participle of* SEEK

sought-after ▷ *adj* desired; in demand.

souk, **suk**, **sukh** or **suq** /suːk/ ▷ *noun* an open-air market or market-place in Muslim countries, especially in N Africa and the Middle East. ◷ 19c: from Arabic *suq* market place.

soukous /'suːkʊs/ ▷ *noun* a central African style of dance music that originated in Zaire and which combines guitar, drumming and vocal melodies. ◷ 20c.

soul /soʊl/ ▷ *noun* **1 a** the spiritual, non-physical part of someone or something which is often regarded as the source of individuality, personality, morality, will, emotions and intellect, and which is widely believed to survive in some form after the death of the body; **b** this entity when thought of as having separated from the body after death, but which still retains its essence of individuality, etc. **2** emotional sensitivity; morality □ ***a singer with no soul*** □ ***cruelty committed by brutes with no soul.*** **3** the essential nature or an energizing or motivating force (of or behind something) □ ***Brevity is the soul of wit.*** **4** *colloq* a person or individual □ ***a kind soul.*** **5** (*also* **soul music**) a type of music that has its roots in Black urban rhythm and blues, and which has elements of jazz, gospel, pop, etc which tend to make it more mainstream than traditional blues. **6** *as adj* belonging, relating or referring to Black American culture □ ***soul food.*** • **the life and soul of the party,** *etc* see under LIFE. • **the soul of something** the perfect example of it; the personification of it □ ***She is the soul of discretion.*** ◷ Anglo-Saxon *sawol*.

soul brother ▷ *noun* **1** someone, especially a male, who shares a similar spirituality as someone else. **2** someone, especially a male, who shares the same racial roots as someone else. *Now* often shortened to **brother** or BRO'.

soul-destroying ▷ *adj* **1** said of a job, task, etc: extremely dull, boring or repetitive □ ***found the work in the factory utterly soul-destroying.*** **2** said of an on-going situation: difficult to tolerate or accept emotionally □ ***found being unemployed after doing her degree completely soul-destroying.***

soul food ▷ *noun* a style of cooking that originated with Black people in the Southern states of the US and which includes such things as chitterlings, corn bread, ham-bone soup, etc.

soulful ▷ *adj* having, expressing, etc deep feelings, especially of sadness. • **soulfully** *adverb*. • **soulfulness** *noun*.

soulless ▷ *adj* **1** having, showing, etc no emotional sensitivity, morality, etc. **2** said of a task, etc: lacking any need for human qualities; extremely monotonous or mechanical. **3** said of a place: bleak; lifeless. • **soullessly** *adverb*. • **soullessness** *noun*.

soul mate ▷ *noun* someone who shares the same feelings, thoughts, ideas, outlook, tastes, etc as someone else.

soul music ▷ *noun* see SOUL 5

soul-searching ▷ *noun* an act or instance or the process of critically examining one's own conscience, motives, actions, etc.

soul sister ▷ *noun* **1** a girl or woman who shares a similar spirituality as another. **2** a girl or woman who shares the same racial roots as another. *Now* often shortened to SISTER.

sound[1] ▷ *noun* **1** *physics* periodic vibrations that are propagated through a medium, eg air, as pressure waves, so that the medium is displaced from its equilibrium state. **2** the noise that is heard as a result of such periodic vibrations. **3** audible quality □ ***The guitar has a nice sound.*** **4** the mental impression created by something heard □ ***don't like the sound of that.*** **5** aural material, eg spoken commentary and music, accompanying a film or broadcast □ ***sound editor.*** **6** *colloq* volume or volume control, especially on a television set. **7** (*also* **sounds**) *colloq* music, especially pop music □ ***the sounds of the 60s.*** ▷ *verb* (***sounded***, ***sounding***) **1** *tr & intr* to produce or cause to produce a sound □ ***The bugle sounded as the emperor approached.*** **2** *intr* to create an impression in the mind □ ***sounds like fun.*** **3** to pronounce □ ***doesn't sound his h's.*** **4** to announce or signal with a sound □ ***sound the alarm.*** **5** *medicine* to examine by tapping or listening. See also SOUND[3] *verb* 2. ◷ 13c: from French *soner*, from Latin *sonare*, from *sonus* sound.

■ **sound off** *colloq* to state one's opinions, complaints, etc forcefully or angrily □ *Harry's sounding off about animal rights again.*

sound² ▷ *adj* **1** not damaged or injured; in good condition; healthy □ *The kitten was found safe and sound.* **2 a** sensible; well-founded; reliable □ *sound advice* □ *a sound investment*; **b** said of an argument, opinion, etc: well researched or thought through, logical and convincing. **3** acceptable or approved of. **4** severe, hard or thorough □ *a sound spanking.* **5** said of sleep: deep and undisturbed. ▷ *adverb* deeply □ *sound asleep.* ● **soundly** *adverb.* ● **soundness** *noun.* ⓒ Anglo-Saxon *gesund.*

sound³ ▷ *verb, tr & intr* **1** to measure the depth of (especially the sea). **2** *medicine* to examine (a hollow organ, etc) with a probe. See also SOUND¹ *verb* 5. ▷ *noun* a probe for examining hollow organs. ⓒ 14c: from French *sonder.*

■ **sound someone** or **something out** to try to discover or to make a preliminary assessment of (opinions, intentions, etc).

sound⁴ ▷ *noun* **1** a narrow passage of water that connects two large bodies of water or that separates an island and the mainland; a strait. **2** the SWIM-BLADDER of certain fish, such as the cod or sturgeon. ⓒ Anglo-Saxon *sund.*

sound barrier ▷ *noun, non-technical* the increase in drag that an aircraft experiences when it travels close to the speed of sound. See also SONIC BARRIER.

soundbite ▷ *noun* a short and succinct statement, especially one that has been deliberately extracted from a longer speech given by some public figure, and which is quoted on TV or radio or in the press because it can be used to epitomize a particular view, but which can often be misinterpreted because of the lack of contextualizing material.

sound-box ▷ *noun* the hollow body of a violin, guitar, etc.

soundcard ▷ *noun, computing* a printed circuit board that can be added to a computer to provide or enhance sound effects.

soundcheck ▷ *noun* the testing of sound equipment by playing a number of songs or parts of songs on stage before a concert to ensure that the balance of the sound from musicians, vocalists, etc is right in the auditorium. ▷ *verb, intr* to carry out a soundcheck □ *We'll soundcheck at 6 o'clock.*

sound effects ▷ *plural noun* artificially produced sounds that are used in film, broadcasting, theatre, etc, eg for authenticating the action, intensifying the suspense, etc.

sounding ▷ *noun* **1 a** the act or process of measuring depth, especially of the sea, eg by using echo; **b** an instance of doing this; **c (soundings)** measurements that are taken or recorded when doing this. **2 (soundings)** an area of sea close to the shore. **3** (*usually* **soundings**) a sampling of opinions or (eg voting) intentions.

sounding-board ▷ *noun* **1** (*also* **soundboard**) a thin board or piece of wood in a musical instrument such as a piano or violin that strengthens or amplifies the sound of the strings which pass over it. **2** a board over a stage or pulpit that is designed to direct the speaker's voice towards the audience. **3 a** a means of testing the acceptability or popularity of ideas or opinions; **b** someone or a group that is used for this purpose.

soundtrack ▷ *noun* **1 a** the recorded sound that accompanies a motion picture; **b** the band of magnetic tape that runs along the edge of a cinematographic film and which has the sound recorded on it. **2** a recording of the music from a film, broadcast, etc that is available in several formats, eg CD, cassette, vinyl, etc.

soup /suːp/ ▷ *noun* **1** a liquid food that is made by boiling meat, vegetables, grains, etc together in a stock or in water. **2 a** anything resembling soup, eg a thick liquid mixture; **b** a dense enveloping fog. See also PEA-SOUPER; **c** a rich mixture of organic material that is supposed to have once covered the Earth and from which life is believed to have emerged. Also called **primordial soup**. **3** *colloq, photog* the fluid that contains the chemicals for developing film. **4** *US colloq* nitroglycerine. ▷ *verb* (***souped***, ***souping***) (*usually* **soup up**) *colloq* to make changes to a vehicle or its engine in order to increase its speed or power. See also SOUPED-UP. ● **in the soup** *slang* in trouble or difficulty □ *got caught stealing and landed himself in the soup.* ● **soupy** *adj.* ⓒ 16c: from French *soupe* broth.

soupçon /ˈsuːpsɒn/ ▷ *noun, often humorous* the slightest amount; a hint or dash □ *Could I have a soupçon more of that delicious coffee, please?* ⓒ 18c: French, meaning 'suspicion'.

soup kitchen ▷ *noun* a place where volunteer workers supply free or very cheap food to people in need.

sour /ˈsaʊə(r)/ ▷ *adj* (***sourer***, ***sourest***) **1** having an acid taste or smell, similar to that of lemon juice or vinegar. **2** rancid or stale because of fermentation □ *sour milk.* **3** sullen; miserable; embittered □ *the sourest face I've ever seen.* **4** unpleasant, unsuccessful or inharmonious □ *The marriage turned sour.* **5** said of an alcoholic drink: with lemon or lime juice added to it □ *brandy sour.* ▷ *verb* (***soured***, ***souring***) *tr & intr* to make or become sour. ● **soured** *adj* □ *soured cream.* ● **souring** *noun.* ● **sourish** *adj.* ● **sourishly** *adverb.* ● **sourly** *adverb.* ● **sourness** *noun.* ⓒ Anglo-Saxon *sur.*

source /sɔːs/ ▷ *noun* **1** the place, thing, person, circumstance, etc that something begins or develops from; the origin. **2** a spring or place where a river or stream begins. **3 a** a person, a book or other document that can be used to provide information, evidence, etc; **b** someone or something that acts as an inspiration, model, standard, etc, especially in the realms of creativity. ▷ *verb* (***sourced***, ***sourcing***) **1** to acknowledge or mention as a source. **2** to originate in someone or something. ● **sourcing** *noun.* ● **at source** at the point of origin. ⓒ 14c: from French *sors*, from Latin *surgere* to rise.

sour cream ▷ *noun* cream that has been deliberately made sour by the addition of lactic acid bacteria and which is used in savoury dishes, sauces, dips, etc.

sourdough /ˈsaʊədoʊ/ ▷ *noun* **1 a** a piece of fermenting dough that is kept back to be used as a leaven in the next batch of bread-making; **b** a loaf of bread that has been made using this. **2** *colloq* an old-timer, especially, in Canada and Alaska, one who is an experienced pioneer or prospector.

sour grapes ▷ *noun* the assumption of a hostile or indifferent attitude towards something or someone, especially when it is motivated by envy, bitterness, resentment, etc □ *He says he wouldn't have taken the job anyway, but that's just sour grapes.*

sour mash ▷ *noun, US* **1** *brewing* MASH (*noun* 2) that has old mash added to it in order to increase acidity and promote fermentation. **2** *chiefly US* whiskey that has been distilled from this.

sourpuss ▷ *noun, colloq* a habitually sullen or miserable person. ⓒ 1940s: from SOUR + PUSS².

soursop /ˈsaʊəsɒp/ ▷ *noun* **1** an evergreen tree that is found in the W Indies. **2** the large sour pulpy fruit of this tree. ⓒ 17c: from SOUR 1 + SOP 1.

sousaphone /ˈsuːzəfoʊn/ ▷ *noun* a large brass instrument similar to the tuba but which encircles the player's body and has its bell facing forwards at head level. ⓒ 1920s: named after the American band leader and military-march composer, John Philip Sousa (1854–1932), who commissioned the first one.

sous-chef /ˈsuː ʃɛf/ ▷ *noun* a chef next in rank to the head chef in a hotel, restaurant, etc. ⓒ 19c: French *sous* under + CHEF.

souse /saʊs/ ▷ *verb* (***soused, sousing***) **1** to steep or cook something in vinegar or white wine. **2** to pickle. **3** to plunge in a liquid. **4** to make thoroughly wet; to drench. ▷ *noun* **1** an act of sousing. **2** the liquid in which food is soused. **3** *N Amer, especially US* any pickled food. **4** *colloq* a drunkard. • **sousing** *adj, noun.* ◷ 14c: from French *sous,* German *sulza,* from *sult-* salt.

soused ▷ *adj* **1** *slang* drunk. **2** pickled.

souslik see SUSLIK

soutache /suːˈtaʃ/ ▷ *noun* a narrow decorative braid or ribbon that is usually embroidered with flowers and sewn onto garments. ◷ 19c: French, from Hungarian *sujtas* braid for trimming.

soutane /suːˈtɑːn/ ▷ *noun, RC Church* a long plain robe or cassock that a priest wears. ◷ 19c: French, from Latin *subtus* under.

souter /ˈsuːtə(r)/ ▷ *noun, Scots & N England old use* someone whose job is to make or mend shoes; a cobbler or shoemaker. ◷ Anglo-Saxon *sutere,* from Latin *sutor* a cobbler.

souterrain /ˈsuːtəreɪn/ ▷ *noun* an underground chamber or passage. ◷ 18c: from French *sous* under + *terre* earth, modelled on Latin *subterraneus.*

south or **South** /saʊθ/ ▷ *noun* (*also* **the south** or **the South**) **1** one of the four main points of the compass which, if a person is facing the rising sun in the N hemisphere, is the direction that lies to their right. **2** the direction that is directly opposite north, ie 180° from the north and 90° from both east and west. **3 a** any part of the earth, a country, a town, etc that lies in this direction; **b** the southern states of the US thought of collectively □ *the rise of the Ku Klux Klan in the deep South.* **4** *cards, especially bridge* the person or position that corresponds to south on the compass. ▷ *adverb* towards the south. ▷ *adj* **1** belonging, referring or relating to, facing or lying in the south; on the side or in the part that is nearest the south □ *the constituency of Aberdeen South.* **2** in place names: denoting the southerly part □ *South America* □ *South Kensington.* **3** said of a wind: blowing from the south. • **southerly** see separate entry. • **south by east, west,** *etc* between south and the other specified direction □ *travel south by south-east.* ◷ Anglo-Saxon *suth.*

South African ▷ *adj* belonging or relating to South Africa, a republic that covers the southern tip of the African continent and which, until 1992, was shunned by much of the rest of the world because of its APARTHEID policy, or its inhabitants. ▷ *noun* a citizen or inhabitant of, or a person born in, South Africa. ◷ Early 19c.

South American ▷ *adj* belonging or relating to South America, the southern part of the American continent, or its inhabitants. ▷ *noun* an inhabitant of, or a person born in, South America. ◷ 18c.

southbound ▷ *adj* going or leading towards the south.

Southdown ▷ *noun* a type of sheep that has short fine wool and which is farmed for its high quality mutton. ◷ 18c: named after the area of the South Downs in Sussex and Hampshire, England.

south-east or **South-East** ▷ *noun* **1** the compass point or direction that is midway between south and east. **2 the south-east** or **the South-East** an area lying in this direction. ▷ *adverb* in this direction. ▷ *adj* belonging to, facing, coming from, lying in, etc the south-east.

southeaster ▷ *noun* a wind, usually a fairly strong one, that blows from the direction of the south-east.

south-easterly ▷ *adj* ▷ *adverb* **1** same as SOUTH-EAST *adj* and *adverb.* **2** said of the wind: blowing from the south-east. ▷ *noun* (***south-easterlies***) a wind that blows from the south-east.

south-eastern ▷ *adj* situated, lying on, coming from, towards, etc the south-east.

southeastward ▷ *adj* ▷ *adverb* towards the south-east. • **southeastwardly** *adj, adverb.* • **south eastwards** *adverb.*

southerly /ˈsʌðəlɪ/ ▷ *adj* **1** said of a wind, etc: coming from the south. **2** situated, looking, lying, etc towards the south. ▷ *adverb* to or towards the south. ▷ *noun* (***southerlies***) a southerly wind.

southern or **Southern** /ˈsʌðən/ ▷ *adj* **1** belonging, relating or referring to, or in, the south □ *southern hemisphere.* **2** (**Southern**) belonging, relating or referring to, or in, the southern states of the US □ *that epitome of the Southern belle, Scarlett O'Hara.* **3** being or facing in or directed towards the south □ *the southern slopes.* • **southernmost** *adj* situated farthest south.

the Southern Cross ▷ *noun, astron* a small but easily visible constellation of the southern hemisphere that has four bright stars marking the arms of a cross and which features on the flags of Australia and New Zealand. Also called **Crux.**

southerner or **Southerner** /ˈsʌðənə(r)/ ▷ *noun* someone who lives in or comes from the south, especially the southern part of England or of the USA.

southern hemisphere ▷ *noun* the half of the Earth that lies to the south of the equator.

the southern lights *plural noun* the AURORA AUSTRALIS.

southernwood ▷ *noun* an aromatic S European shrub of the wormwood genus. Also called OLD MAN.

southpaw /ˈsaʊθpɔː/ *colloq* ▷ *noun* someone whose left hand is more dominant than their right, especially a boxer. ▷ *adj* left-handed. ◷ 19c: from SOUTH *adj* 1 + PAW *noun* 2, originally a US baseball term that denoted a left-handed pitcher.

South Pole or **south pole** ▷ *noun* **1** (*usually* **the South Pole**) the southernmost point of the Earth's axis of rotation, which is in central Antarctica at latitude 90°S and longitude 0°. **2** *astron* see POLE 1 sense 2. **3** (**south pole**) the south-seeking pole of a magnet.

the South Sea ▷ *singular noun* and **the South Seas** ▷ *plural noun* the southern part of the Pacific Ocean. Also *as adj* □ *the South Sea Islands.*

south-south-east or **south-south east** ▷ *noun* the compass point or direction that is midway between south and south-east. ▷ *adverb* in this direction. ▷ *adj* belonging to, facing, coming from, lying in, etc the south-south-east.

south-south-west or **south-south west** ▷ *noun* the compass point or direction that is midway between south and south-west. ▷ *adverb* in this direction. ▷ *adj* belonging to, facing, coming from, lying in, etc the south-south-west.

southward /ˈsaʊθwəd, ˈsʌðəd/ and **southwards** ▷ *adverb, adj* towards the south. • **southwardly** *adverb.*

south-west or **South-West** /saʊθˈwɛst, saʊˈwɛst/ ▷ *noun* **1** the compass point or direction that is midway between south and west. **2** (**the south-west** or **the South-West**) an area lying in this direction. ▷ *adverb* in this direction. ▷ *adj* belonging to, facing, coming from, lying in, etc the south-west.

southwester /saʊθˈwɛstə(r), saʊˈwɛstə(r)/ ▷ *noun* **1** a wind that blows from the south-west. **2** a SOU'WESTER 1.

south-westerly ▷ *adj, adverb* **1** SOUTH-WEST *adj* and *adverb.* **2** said of the wind: blowing from the south-west. ▷ *noun* (***south-westerlies***) a wind that blows from the south-west.

south-western ▷ *adj* situated, lying on, coming from, towards, etc the south-west.

southwestward ▷ *adj, adverb* towards the south-west. • **southwestwardly** *adj, adverb* • **southwestwards** *adverb.*

souvenir /suːvəˈnɪə(r), ˈsuːvənɪə(r)/ ▷ *noun* something that is bought, kept or given as a reminder of a place, person, occasion, etc; a memento. ▷ *verb* (***souvenired, souveniring***) *colloq, euphemistic* to steal □ ***I just souvenired a couple of towels from the hotel.*** ⓒ 18c: French, meaning 'a memory'.

sou'wester /sɑʊˈwɛstə(r)/ ▷ *noun* **1** a type of oilskin or waterproof hat that has a large flap at the back and which is usually worn by seamen. **2** a SOUTHWESTER 1. ⓒ Early 19c: a shortened form of SOUTHWESTER.

sov ▷ *noun, colloq* a pound sterling □ ***not worth it for the few sovs I'd get.*** ⓒ Early 19c: a shortened form of SOVEREIGN (*noun* 2).

sovereign /ˈsɒvrɪn/ ▷ *noun* **1** a supreme ruler or head, especially a monarch. **2** a former British gold coin worth £1. ▷ *adj* **1** having supreme power or authority □ ***a sovereign ruler.*** **2** politically independent □ ***a sovereign state.*** **3** outstanding; unrivalled; utmost □ ***sovereign intelligence.*** **4** effective □ ***a sovereign remedy.*** ● **sovereignly** *adverb.* ⓒ 13c: from French *soverain.*

sovereign state see INDEPENDENCY

sovereignty ▷ *noun* (***sovereignties***) **1** supreme and independent political power or authority. **2** a politically independent state. **3** self-government.

soviet /ˈsoʊvɪət, ˈsɒvɪət/ ▷ *noun* **1** any of the councils that made up the local and national governments of the former Soviet Union. **2** any of the revolutionary councils in Russia prior to 1917. **3** (**Soviet**) a citizen or inhabitant of the former Soviet Union. ▷ *adj* (**Soviet**) belonging, relating or referring to the former Soviet Union. See also CIS. ⓒ Early 20c: from Russian *sovet* council.

sovietologist ▷ *noun* someone who studies, or is an expert in, the workings and history of the political, social and economic systems of the former USSR.

Soviet Union ▷ *noun, historical* a former federation of 15 Union Republics which, since its dissolution in 1991, have all become independent states, including Russia, Ukraine, the Baltic States, some states of central Asia and the Caucasus. See also CIS.

sow¹ /soʊ/ ▷ *verb* (***sowed, sown*** or ***sowed, sowing***) *tr & intr* **1** to scatter or place (plant seeds, a crop, etc) on or in the earth, in a plant pot, etc. **2** to plant (a piece of land) with seeds, a crop, etc □ ***sowed the upper field with barley.*** **3** to introduce or arouse □ ***sowed the seeds of doubt in his mind.*** ● **sower** *noun.* ● **sow one's wild oats** to indulge in a dissipated lifestyle, often having numerous sexual partners, especially for a relatively short period of time in one's youth. ● **sow the seeds of something** see under SEED. ⓒ Anglo-Saxon *sawan.*

sow² /sɑʊ/ ▷ *noun* **1 a** an adult female pig, especially one that has had a litter of piglets; **b** a female guinea pig; **c** the name given to the female of certain other animals, such as the mink. **2** *metallurgy* **a** the main channel that molten metal flows along towards the smaller channels or PIG (*noun* 5b); **b** a piece of metal that has solidified in one of these channels. ⓒ Anglo-Saxon *sugu.*

sox /sɒks/ ▷ *plural noun* a colloquial or commercial plural of SOCK that also appears in the names of some US sports (especially baseball) teams □ ***special offer on packs of sox*** □ ***the Boston Red Sox.*** ⓒ Early 20c.

soy /sɔɪ/ ▷ *noun* **1** (*also* **soy sauce**) a salty dark brown sauce that is made from soya beans which ferment for around six months and which is used especially in oriental fish dishes. **2** SOYA. ⓒ 17c: from Japanese *sho-yu,* from Chinese *jiang you* soy sauce.

soya /ˈsɔɪə/ and **soy** ▷ *noun* **1** any of numerous varieties of an annual plant of the pulse family, that are native to SW Asia but which are now more widely cultivated for their edible seeds. **2** (also called **soya bean**) the edible protein-rich seed of this plant, which is used in making soya flour, soya milk, bean curd, etc, and which yields an oil that is used as a cooking oil and in the manufacture of margarine, soap, enamels, paints, varnishes, etc. ⓒ 17c: Dutch, from SOY.

sozzled /ˈsɒzəld/ ▷ *adj, colloq* drunk. ⓒ 19c: from the obsolete *verb sozzle* to mix or mingle in a sloppy way.

SP ▷ *abbreviation* starting price.

sp ▷ *abbreviation*: *sine prole* (Latin), without issue.

sp. ▷ *abbreviation* (*plural* in sense 4 only ***spp***) **1** spelling. **2** special. **3** specific. **4** species.

spa /spɑː/ ▷ *noun* **1** a mineral water spring. **2** a town where such a spring is or was once located. ⓒ 16c: named after Spa, a town in Belgium.

SPAB ▷ *abbreviation* Society for the Protection of Ancient Buildings.

space ▷ *noun* **1** the limitless three-dimensional expanse where all matter exists. **2 a** a restricted portion of this; room □ ***no space in the garden for a pool;*** **b** *in compounds* □ ***a space-saving device.*** **3** an interval of distance; a gap □ ***sign in the space below*** □ ***If you don't know the answer, just leave a space.*** **4** any of a restricted number of seats, places, etc □ ***a space at our table*** □ ***only two spaces left on this course.*** **5** a period of time □ ***within the space of ten minutes.*** **6** (*also* **outer space**) all the regions of the Universe that lie beyond the Earth's atmosphere. **7** an area of a newspaper or a spot on TV or radio that is reserved for a specified use, purpose, etc □ ***sells advertising space.*** **8 a** the blank gap between printed or written words or letters; **b** *printing* a piece of metal that is used for producing this kind of gap. **9** *colloq* room for the unrestrained liberty to think, do, etc as one wants. ▷ *verb* (***spaced, spacing***) **1** to set or place at intervals □ ***spaced the interviews over three days.*** **2** to separate or divide with a space or spaces, eg in printing, etc. ● **spaced** see separate entry. ● **spaced out** see under SPACED. ● **spacer** *noun.* ● **spaceless** *adj.* ● **spacing** *noun.* See also SPACIOUS, SPATIAL. ⓒ 14c: from French *espace*, from Latin *spatium* space.

■ **space something out** to arrange it with intervals, or greater intervals, of distance or time between.

space age ▷ *noun* (*usually* **the space age**) the present era thought of in terms of being the time when space travel became possible. ▷ *adj* (**space-age**) **1** technologically very advanced. **2** having a futuristic appearance.

space-bar ▷ *noun* the long key that is usually situated below the character keys on the keyboard of a typewriter, word processor or computer and which gives a space in the text when it is pressed.

space blanket ▷ *noun* a lightweight plastic cover, often with one or both sides coated in aluminium foil, that is carried by climbers, mountaineers, marathon runners, etc and which can be used as an insulating body wrap when there is danger of exposure, hypothermia, exhaustion, etc.

space cadet ▷ *noun* **1** *colloq* someone who is or who appears to be in a more or less permanently drugged state. **2** a trainee astronaut.

space capsule ▷ *noun* a small manned or unmanned vehicle that is designed for travelling through space in order to gather information and transmit it back to Earth and which can usually be recovered when it re-enters the Earth's atmosphere.

spacecraft ▷ *noun* a manned or unmanned vehicle that is designed to travel in space or for orbiting the Earth.

spaced ▷ *adj* **1** (*also* **spaced out**) *colloq* being, acting, appearing to be, etc in a dazed, euphoric, stupefied or dreamlike state, especially one that is or seems to be induced by drugs □ ***That film was magic — it left me really spaced.*** **2** set, placed, arranged, occurring, etc at intervals □ ***Their children's ages are well spaced out.***

Space Invaders ▷ *noun, trademark* any of various video games in which the players' object is to use buttons or levers to try to fire at and destroy invading creatures that descend the screen.

spacelab ▻ *noun, astron* a self-contained research laboratory, especially one of the type developed by the European Space Agency and carried in the cargo bay of the NASA space shuttle.

spaceman and **spacewoman** ▻ *noun* someone who travels in space. See also ASTRONAUT.

space platform see SPACE STATION

space probe ▻ *noun, astron* an unmanned spacecraft that is designed to study conditions in space, especially on or around a planet or its natural satellites, and to transmit the information it gathers back to Earth.

space shuttle ▻ *noun* a reusable manned vehicle that takes off like a rocket but lands on a runway like an aircraft and which is designed to travel into space, especially one that can visit space stations that orbit the Earth or bases on the Moon in order to carry out tests, collect information, effect repairs, etc.

space sickness ▻ *noun* a collection of symptoms, similar to those of travel sickness, that astronauts experience during their first few days in space while their bodies are in the process of adapting to conditions of weightlessness.

space station ▻ *noun* a large orbiting artificial satellite, where crews of astronauts can live and carry out scientific and technological research in space over periods of weeks or months.

space suit ▻ *noun* a sealed and pressurized suit of clothing that is specially designed for space travel.

space-time and **space-time continuum** ▻ *noun* the three spatial dimensions of length, breadth and height, plus the dimension of time, thought of collectively, which allow an event, particle, etc to be specifically located.

space walk ▻ *noun* an act, instance or period of manoeuvring or other physical activity that occurs in space, outside a spacecraft, and which is undertaken by an astronaut who wears a pressurized space suit and who is usually still attached to the spacecraft by a lifeline.

space writer ▻ *noun* an author who is paid by the area that the copy takes up.

spacial see SPATIAL

spacing see under SPACE

spacio-temporal /speɪʃɪoʊ'tɛmpərəl/ ▻ *adj, physics, philos* **1** belonging to or existing in both space and time. **2** belonging to or being concerned with space-time.

spacious /'speɪʃəs/ ▻ *adj* having ample room or space; extending over a large area. • **spaciously** *adverb*. • **spaciousness** *noun*. Ⓒ 14c: from Latin *spatiosus*, from *spatium* space.

spade¹ ▻ *noun* **1 a** a long-handled digging tool with a broad metal blade which is designed to be pushed into the ground with the foot; **b** anything that is of a similar shape or used for a similar purpose, eg a child's plastic digging toy, or a knife-like implement used by whalers. **2** one spade's depth. ▻ *verb* (***spaded, spading***) to dig or turn over (ground) with a spade. • **spadelike** *adj*. • **spader** *noun*. • **call a spade a spade** to speak plainly and frankly. Ⓒ Anglo-Saxon *spadu*.

spade² ▻ *noun* (***spades***) **1** *cards* **a** one of the four suits of playing-card with a black spade-shaped symbol (♠), the others being the DIAMOND, HEART and CLUB; **b** a card of this suit □ *laid a spade and won the hand*; **c** (**spades**) one of the playing-cards of this suit. **2** *offensive slang* a black person, especially a male with very dark skin. Ⓒ 16c: from Italian *spada* a sword, from Greek *spathe* a broad flat piece of wood.

spadeful *noun* (***spadefuls***) the amount that can be carried on a spade.

spadework ▻ *noun* hard or boring preparatory work.

spadix /'speɪdɪks/ ▻ *noun* (***spadices*** /'speɪdɪsiːz/) *bot* a spike-shaped structure that consists of numerous tiny flowers on a fleshy axis and which is usually enclosed by a SPATHE. • **spadiceous** /speɪ'dɪʃəs/ *adj*. Ⓒ 18c: Latin, from Greek, meaning 'a torn-off palm branch'.

spag bol /spag 'bɒl/ ▻ *noun, colloq* a shortened form of SPAGHETTI BOLOGNESE.

spaghetti /spə'gɛtɪ/ ▻ *noun* **1** a type of pasta that is in the form of long thin solid string-like strands. **2** a dish made from this kind of pasta. Ⓒ 19c: Italian, from *spaghetto*, from *spago* a thin rope or cord.

spaghetti bolognese /spə'gɛtɪ bɒlə'neɪz, — boʊlən'jeɪz/ and **spaghetti alla bolognese** /— 'alə —/ ▻ *noun* a dish of spaghetti that is served with a sauce made from a tomato base with minced meat and added vegetables. Ⓒ 1940s: Italian, meaning 'from the city of Bologna'.

spaghetti junction ▻ *noun, Brit colloq* any complex motorway interchange where there is a great number of flyovers, etc so that it resembles the intertwined strands of cooked spaghetti. Ⓒ 1960s: first applied to a road setup of this kind near Birmingham.

spaghetti western ▻ *noun* a type of film, typically quite violent, which, although its subject is the American Wild West, is shot in Europe, usually in Italy or Spain, and which is usually filmed in widescreen with huge panoramic vistas, often having an international cast headed by an Italian director. Ⓒ 1960s: so called because of the Italian locations and the nationality of the directors.

spahi /'spɑːhɪː/ ▻ *noun, historical* **1** a member of the Turkish cavalry. **2** a member of the Algerian cavalry who served under French command. Ⓒ Late 19c in sense 2; 16c in sense 1: from Turkish *sipahi* soldier.

spake see SPEAK

spall /spɔːl/ ▻ *noun* a chip or splinter, especially one of rock or ore. ▻ *verb* (***spalled, spalling***) *mining* to chip, splinter or split or make (rock or ore) to chip, splinter or split before sorting or treating. Ⓒ 15c.

spallation /spɔː'leɪʃən/ ▻ *noun, physics* a nuclear reaction where there is a breakup of a nucleus into smaller parts, eg because it has been bombarded by an energetic nucleon or other particle. Ⓒ 1940s: from SPALL.

Spam or **spam¹** ▻ *noun, trademark* a type of tinned processed cold meat, mainly pork, with added spices. Ⓒ 1930s: probably from *sp*iced h*am*.

spam² *computing* ▻ *noun* electronic junk mail. ▻ *verb* (***spammed, spamming***) to send out electronic junk mail. Ⓒ 1990s: from SPAM.

span¹ ▻ *noun* **1 a** the distance, interval, length, etc between two points in space or time; **b** the length between the supports of a bridge, arch, pier, ceiling, etc; **c** the extent to which, or the duration of time for which, someone can concentrate, process information, listen attentively, etc; **d** the maximum distance between the tip of one wing and the tip of the other, eg in birds and planes; **e** *in compounds* □ ***wingspan*** □ ***timespan*** □ ***lifespan***. **2** a measure of length equal to the distance between the tips of thumb and little finger on an extended hand, which is conventionally taken as 9in (23cm). ▻ *verb* (***spanned, spanning***) **1 a** said of a bridge, pier, ceiling, rainbow, etc: to extend across or over, especially in an arched shape □ ***A rainbow spanned the sky***; **b** to bridge (a river, etc) □ ***spanned the river using logs.*** **2** to last □ ***The feud spanned more than 30 years.*** **3** to measure or cover, eg by using an extended hand. Ⓒ Anglo-Saxon *spann*.

span² ▻ *noun* **1** *naut* any of several kinds of ropes or chains that are used for securing, fastening, etc. **2** *US* a pair of horses or oxen, especially two that are very alike in size and colouring. Ⓒ 18c: from Dutch and German *spannen* to unite or fasten.

Spandex or **spandex** /'spandɛks/ ▻ *noun, trademark* **1** a synthetic elastic fibre made chiefly from polyurethane. **2** a fabric made from this. Ⓒ 1950s: from EXPAND.

spandrel or **spandril** /'spandrəl/ ▷ *noun, archit* **a** the triangular space between the curve of an arch and the enclosing mouldings, string-course, etc; **b** in 20c architecture: an infill panel below a window. 🕒 15c.

spangle /'spaŋgəl/ ▷ *noun* a small piece of glittering material, especially a sequin. ▷ *verb* (***spangled***, ***spangling***) **1** to decorate (eg a piece of clothing) with spangles. **2** *intr* to glitter. • **spangled** *adj*. See also STAR-SPANGLED BANNER. • **spangling** *noun, adj*. • **spangly** *adj*. 🕒 Anglo-Saxon *spang* a clasp.

Spaniard /'spanjəd/ ▷ *noun* a native, inhabitant or citizen of Spain. 🕒 14c: from French *Espaignart*.

spaniel /'spanjəl/ ▷ *noun* **1** any of various kinds of dog, such as the King Charles spaniel, cocker spaniel, springer spaniel, etc that have wavy coats and long silky dangly ears. The larger dogs were originally bred for retrieving game and all kinds are now popular as pets. **2** someone who behaves in a submissive, slavish or sycophantic manner. 🕒 14c: from French *espaigneul* Spanish dog.

Spanish /'spanɪʃ/ ▷ *adj* belonging or relating to Spain, the country in SW Europe which, together with Portugal, form the Iberian peninsula, or to its inhabitants or their language. ▷ *noun* **1** a citizen or inhabitant of, or person born in, Spain. **2** the official language of Spain, and also spoken in the southern USA and Central and S America. See also HISPANIC, SPANIARD. 🕒 13c.

Pronunciation of Spanish in English

- **ñ** is pronounced /nj/, as in **mañana**.
- **ch** is pronounced /tʃ/, as in **macho**.

The /ma'kɪzmoʊ/ pronunciation of **machismo** is incorrect; **ch** should not be pronounced /k/ in any Spanish loanword.

- **ll** is pronounced /j/, as in **Mallorca**.
- **j** is pronounced /x/, as in the name of the Spanish wine **Rioja**.
- **z** is pronounced /θ/ in European Spanish, as is **c** when followed by **i** or **e;** in American Spanish, both are pronounced /s/.

Spanish fly ▷ *noun* **1** a bright-green beetle. **2** a preparation made from the dried bodies of these beetles, which was formerly used for raising blisters and which was also believed to have aphrodisiac qualities. Also called **cantharides** /kan'θarɪdiːz/. 🕒 15c: so called because they are particularly abundant in Spain.

Spanish guitar ▷ *noun* a six-stringed acoustic guitar that is usually played in classical and folk music. Compare ELECTRIC GUITAR.

Spanish moss and **Spanish beard** ▷ *noun* an epiphytic tropical or subtropical plant that is found hanging in silvery greenish-blue strands from the branches of trees. 🕒 Early 19c.

Spanish omelette ▷ *noun* a type of omelette that contains diced vegetables such as potato, peppers, onion, tomato, etc and which is often served without being folded over.

Spanish onion ▷ *noun* a variety of large mild onion.

spank[1] ▷ *verb* (***spanked***, ***spanking***) to smack, usually on the buttocks with the flat of the hand, a slipper, belt, etc, often several times and as a punishment or a form of sexual gratification. ▷ *noun* such a smack. • **spanked** *adj*. 🕒 18c.

spank[2] ▷ *verb* (***spanked***, ***spanking***) (*often* **spank along** or **spank over**) said of a vehicle, horse, etc: to travel at a fairly quick pace. ▷ *noun* a quick pace. 🕒 Early 19c.

spanker ▷ *noun* **1** someone who smacks. **2** *naut* a FORE-AND-AFT sail on the MIZZENMAST of a sailing ship that is used for taking advantage of a following wind. **3** *colloq* a horse or vehicle that travels at a good pace. **4** something that is considered a particularly fine, large, etc example of its kind □ ***Mairi's new car's a real spanker.***

spanking[1] ▷ *noun* an act or instance or the process of delivering a series of smacks, eg as a punishment to a child or as a form of sexual gratification. 🕒 19c: from SPANK[1].

spanking[2] ▷ *adverb, colloq* absolutely; strikingly □ ***a spanking new watch.*** ▷ *adj, colloq* **1** brisk □ ***a spanking pace.*** **2** impressively fine; striking □ ***a spanking new car.*** 🕒 17c: from SPANK[2].

spanner /'spanə(r)/ ▷ *noun* a metal hand tool that has an opening (sometimes an adjustable one) or various sizes of openings at one or both ends and which is used for gripping, tightening or loosening nuts, bolts, etc. *US equivalent* WRENCH *noun* 3 • **a spanner in the works** a frustrating, annoying, irritating, etc person or thing. • **throw, put, chuck,** *etc* **a spanner in the works** to frustrate, annoy, irritate, etc, especially by causing a plan, system, etc that is already in place to change □ ***Harry's presence always puts a spanner in the works.*** 🕒 18c: German, from *spannen* to unite or fasten.

spar[1] ▷ *noun* **1** a strong thick pole of wood or metal, especially one used as a mast or beam on a ship. **2** *Scots* any smaller pole, bar, rail, etc □ ***The budgie fell off its spar.*** **3** (*sometimes* **SPAR**) *oil industry* an installation that is anchored above a submarine manifold and which is designed both for storing oil and for loading tankers. 🕒 1970s in sense 3; 14c, meaning a 'roof rafter'.

spar[2] ▷ *verb* (***sparred***, ***sparring***) *intr* (*often* **spar with someone** or **something**) **1 a** to box, especially in a way that deliberately avoids the exchange of heavy blows, eg for practice; **b** to box against an imaginary opponent, for practice. **2** to engage in lively and light-hearted argument, banter, etc. **3** said of game cocks: to fight with spurs (SPUR 3b). ▷ *noun* **1** an act or instance of sparring. **2** a boxing match. **3** a light-hearted argument, banter, etc. **4** a fight between game cocks using spurs. • **sparrer** *noun*. • **sparring** *noun, adj*. See also SPARRING PARTNER. 🕒 15c.

spar[3] ▷ *noun* **a** *combining form* any of various translucent non-metallic minerals, such as FELDSPAR and FLUORSPAR, that can be easily split into layers; **b** a particle or fragment of one of these minerals. • **sparry** *adj*. 🕒 16c: German.

sparable /'sparəbəl/and **sparrow-bill** ▷ *noun* a small headless nail that is used in the manufacture and mending of soles and heels of shoes and boots. 🕒 17c: a reduced form of *sparrow-bill*, so called because of the resemblance of the nail to the shape of a sparrow's beak.

sparaxis /spə'raksɪs/ ▷ *noun* any of several S African cormous plants that are related to the iris, that have jagged edges to their spathes and which are cultivated for their pretty star-shaped purple, red or orange flowers. 🕒 19c: Latin, from Greek *sparassein* to tear.

spare /speə(r)/ ▷ *adj* **1** kept for occasional use □ ***the spare room.*** **2** kept for use as a replacement □ ***a spare wheel.*** **3** available for use; additional; extra □ ***a spare seat next to me.*** **4** lean; thin. **5** frugal; scanty. **6** furious or distraught to the point of distraction □ ***He was going spare just 'cos he couldn't find his keys.*** ▷ *verb* (***spared***, ***sparing***) **1** to afford to give, give away or do without □ ***I can't spare the time.*** **2 a** to refrain from harming, punishing, killing or destroying □ ***spare his life*** □ ***spare their feelings***; **b** to avoid causing or bringing on something □ ***will spare your blushes.*** **3** to avoid incurring something □ ***no expense spared.*** ▷ *noun* **1** a duplicate kept in reserve for use as a replacement. **2** a spare tyre. **3** *ten-pin bowling* **a** the act of knocking down all ten pins with two bowls; **b** the score when this happens. • **sparely** *adverb*. • **spareness** *noun*. • **to spare** left over; surplus to what is required □ ***I have one cake to spare.*** 🕒 Anglo-Saxon *sparian*.

spare part ▷ *noun* a component for a car, machine, etc that is designed to replace an existing identical part that is lost or that has become worn or faulty.

spare-part surgery ▷ *noun, non-technical* treatment that involves replacing a damaged or diseased body part or organ with one from a donor or with a PROSTHESIS. ⓒ 1940s.

spare rib ▷ *noun* a cut of meat that consists of ribs, especially pork ribs, that have very little meat on them. ⓒ 16c: from German *ribbesper*.

spare room ▷ *noun* a room, especially a bedroom, that is generally not in use except for storage or when there are visitors.

spare time ▷ *noun* the hours that are spent away from work or other commitments, that can be spent doing what one wants to do.

spare tyre ▷ *noun* **1** an extra tyre for a motor vehicle, bicycle, etc that can be used to replace a punctured tyre. **2** *colloq* a roll of fat just above someone's waist.

sparge /spɑːdʒ/ ▷ *verb* (***sparged, sparging***) to sprinkle or moisten with water, especially in brewing. ⓒ 16c: from Latin *spargere* to sprinkle.

sparing /ˈspeərɪŋ/ ▷ *adj* **1** inclined to be economical or frugal, often to the point of inadequacy or meanness ▫ ***School cooks were sparing with raisins.*** **2** restrained, reserved or uncommunicative ▫ ***He's very sparing with the truth.*** • **sparingly** *adverb*. • **sparingness** *noun*.

spark¹ ▷ *noun* **1 a** a tiny red-hot glowing fiery particle that jumps out from some burning material; **b** a similar particle that is produced by the friction between two hard surfaces, such as metal and stone, a match and a matchbox, etc. **2 a** a flash of light that is produced by a discontinuous electrical discharge flashing across a short gap between two conductors; **b** this kind of electrical discharge, eg in the engine of a motor vehicle, etc where its function is to ignite the explosive mixture. **3** a trace, hint or glimmer ▫ ***showed not a spark of recognition.*** **4 a** a small precious stone, eg a diamond or ruby; **b** a particularly bright point in a precious stone. **5** (**sparks**) *colloq* a familiar name for an electrician, radio operator, etc. ▷ *verb* (***sparked, sparking***) *intr* to emit sparks of fire or electricity. • **sparky** *adj*. • **sparks will fly**, *etc* trouble, angry words, etc will ensue ▫ ***After the verdict sparks really began to fly.*** ⓒ Anglo-Saxon *spærca*.

■ **spark off** to stimulate, provoke or start ▫ ***The film sparked off great controversy.***

spark² ▷ *noun, often ironic* (*usually* **bright spark**) someone who is lively, witty, intelligent, etc ▫ ***What bright spark shut the dog out all night?*** ⓒ 16c: originally in the sense of 'a beautiful witty woman'.

spark coil ▷ *noun* an induction coil, especially one that energizes the spark plugs in an internal combustion-engine.

spark gap ▷ *noun, electronics* the space between two electrodes that a spark can jump across.

sparkle /ˈspɑːkəl/ ▷ *verb* (***sparkled, sparkling***) *intr* **1** to give off sparks. **2** to shine with tiny points of bright light ▫ ***Her eyes sparkled in the moonlight.*** **3** said of wine, mineral water, etc: to give off bubbles of carbon dioxide; to effervesce. **4** to be impressively lively or witty. ▷ *noun* **1** a point of bright shiny light; an act of sparkling; sparkling appearance. **2** liveliness; vivacity; wit. • **sparkly** *adj*. ⓒ 12c: from SPARK¹.

sparkler ▷ *noun* **1** a type of small firework that produces gentle showers of silvery sparks and which can be held in the hand. **2** *colloq* a diamond or other impressive jewel.

sparkling ▷ *adj* **1** said of wine, mineral water, etc: having a fizz that is produced by escaping carbon dioxide. Compare STILL. **2** said of eyes, gems, etc: having or giving off a sparkle. **3** said of a person, their conversation, etc: impressively lively or witty ▫ ***The speaker was in sparkling form.*** • **sparklingly** *adverb*.

spark plug and **sparking plug** ▷ *noun* an insulated device that is fitted to the cylinder head of an internal-combustion engine. Its function is to discharge a spark between the two electrodes at its end which results in the ignition of the explosive mixture of fuel and air in the cylinder.

sparrer and **sparring** see under SPAR²

sparring partner ▷ *noun* **1** someone that a boxer practises with. **2** someone that one can enjoy a lively argument with.

sparrow /ˈsparoʊ/ ▷ *noun* **1** any of various small grey or brown perching birds, such as the **house sparrow**, that have short conical beaks which are well adapted for cracking seeds, and which often congregate in large flocks in both urban and rural parts of the world. **2** *in compounds, denoting* any of various similar but unrelated small birds ▫ ***hedge sparrow.*** ⓒ Anglo-Saxon *spearwa*.

sparrow-bill see SPARABLE

sparrow-grass ▷ *noun, colloq* a popularized form of ASPARAGUS. ⓒ 17c.

sparrowhawk ▷ *noun* any of various small hawks found in Europe, Asia and N Africa which have a brownish upper plumage, a white breast barred with brown, short wings and a long tail, and which feed mainly on smaller birds.

sparrow hawk ▷ *noun* a small N American falcon that is closely related to the European kestrel.

sparry see under SPAR³

sparse /spɑːs/ ▷ *adj* (***sparser, sparsest***) thinly scattered or dotted about; scanty ▫ ***found his hair getting sparser by the month.*** • **sparsely** *adverb*. • **sparseness** *noun*. • **sparsity** *noun*. ⓒ 18c: from Latin *sparsus*, from *spargere* to scatter.

spartan /ˈspɑːtən/ ▷ *adj* **1** belonging, relating or referring to or characteristic of ancient Sparta, its inhabitants, customs, etc. **2 a** said of living conditions, upbringing, diet, a regime, etc: austere; frugal; harsh and basic; strict; simple; **b** disciplined; courageous; showing great endurance. ▷ *noun* **1** someone who shows these qualities. **2** a citizen or inhabitant of ancient Sparta. ⓒ 15c: from Latin *Spartanus*, from Sparta, a city in ancient Greece that was noted for its austerity and whose citizens were characterized by their courage and endurance in battle and by the simplicity and brevity of their speech.

spasm /ˈspazəm/ ▷ *noun* **1 a** a sudden uncontrollable contraction of a muscle or muscles; **b** an instance or the process of this. **2** a short period of activity; a spell. **3** a sudden burst (of emotion, etc) ▫ ***spasm of anger.*** ▷ *verb* (***spasmed, spasming***) to twitch or go into a spasm. ⓒ 15c: from Greek *spasmos* contraction.

spasmodic /spazˈmɒdɪk/ and **spasmodical** ▷ *adj* **1** being or occurring in, or consisting of, short periods; not constant or regular; intermittent ▫ ***spasmodic gunfire.*** **2** relating to or consisting of a spasm or spasms. • **spasmodically** *adverb* ▫ ***has only worked spasmodically since the accident.*** ⓒ 17c: from Latin *spasmodicus*, from Greek *spasmos* contraction.

spastic /ˈspastɪk/ ▷ *noun* **1** someone who suffers from CEREBRAL PALSY. **2** *offensive slang* someone who is thought of as being extremely clumsy, useless or stupid. Often shortened to **spaz** or **spazzy**. ▷ *adj* **1 a** affected by or suffering from cerebal palsy; **b** relating to, affected by, etc a spasm or spasms. **2** *offensive, slang* weak, clumsy, useless, stupid. • **spastically** *adverb*. • **spasticity** /spaˈstɪsɪtɪ/ *noun*. ⓒ 18c: from Latin *spasticus*, from Greek *spasmos* a spasm.

spastic paralysis ▷ *noun, formerly* a name for CEREBRAL PALSY.

spat¹ *past tense, past participle of* SPIT¹

spat² *colloq* ▷ *noun* **1** a splash or droplet of water, etc ▫ ***a few spits and spats of rain.*** **2** a trivial or petty fight or quarrel. ▷ *verb* (***spatted, spatting***) *intr* to engage in a trivial or petty fight or quarrel. ⓒ Early 19c.

spat[3] ▷ *noun* **1** (*usually* **spats**) *historical* a cloth covering that goes around the ankle and over the top of a shoe, originally to protect against splashes of mud and latterly, especially in the US in the 1920s and 1930s, as a fashion accessory. **2** a covering for the upper part of the wheel of an aircraft. ◷ Early 19c: an abbreviation of the obsolete *spatterdash* which was a type of long gaiter for protecting the trousers from mud splashes.

spat[4] ▷ *noun* the spawn of shellfish, especially oysters. ▷ *verb* (***spatted***, ***spatting***) said of oysters: to spawn. ◷ 17c.

spatchcock /ˈspatʃkɒk/ ▷ *noun* a chicken or game bird that has been split down the back, opened out and grilled flat. ▷ *verb* (***spatchcocked***, ***spatchcocking***) **1** to cook (a chicken, etc) in this way. **2** to slot in (a word, phrase, story, etc), especially inappropriately or incongruously. Compare SPITCHCOCK. ◷ 18c.

spate ▷ *noun* a sudden rush or increased quantity; a burst □ *received a spate of complaints.* ● **in spate** said of a river: in a swollen and fast-flowing state that is brought on by flooding or melting snow. ◷ 15c.

spathe /speɪð/ ▷ *noun, bot* a large bract that surrounds and protects the inflorescence or SPADIX of certain plant families such as the arums and palms. ● **spathaceous** /spəˈθeɪʃəs/ *adj.* ● **spathed** *adj.* ◷ 18c: from Latin *spatha*, from Greek *spathe* a broad blade.

spathic /ˈspaθɪk/ ▷ *adj* said of a mineral: having the qualities of a SPAR[3]. ● **spathose** /spaˈθoʊz/ *adj.* ◷ 18c: from German *spath* spar.

spatial or **spacial** /ˈspeɪʃəl/ ▷ *adj* belonging, referring or relating to space. ● **spatiality** /speɪʃɪˈalɪtɪ/ *noun.* ● **spatially** *adverb.* ◷ 19c: from Latin *spatium* space.

spatter /ˈspatə(r)/ ▷ *verb* (***spattered***, ***spattering***) *tr & intr* **1 a** said of mud, etc: to spray, cover, shower or splash in scattered drops or patches □ *The muddy water spattered the car* □ *A hail of bullets spattered the wall*; **b** to cause (mud, etc) to fly in scattered drops or patches □ *Don't speak with your mouth full — you're spattering food everywhere.* **2** to slander. ▷ *noun* **1** a quantity spattered; a sprinkling. **2** the act or process of spattering. ◷ 16c.

spatterdash /ˈspatədaʃ/ ▷ *noun* (***spatterdashes***) **1** *US* ROUGHCAST (*noun* 1). **2** (*usually* **spatterdashes**) *historical* a type of legging or gaiter that is used to protect the trousers from getting muddy. ◷ 17c.

spatula /ˈspatjʊlə/ ▷ *noun* (***spatulas***) **a** *cookery* an implement that has a broad blunt and often flexible blade and which can be used for a variety of purposes, such as stirring, spreading, mixing, turning foods during frying, etc; **b** *medicine* a simple flat, usually wooden, implement that is used for holding down the tongue during a throat examination, when a throat swab is being taken, etc. ● **spatular** *adj.* ◷ 16c: Latin, meaning 'broad blade', from *spatha* spathe.

spatulate /ˈspatjʊleɪt/ ▷ *adj* **1** said of fingers, etc: having a broad flat tip. **2** *bot* said of a leaf, sepal, etc: having a narrow base and a broad rounded tip. ◷ 18c.

spavin /ˈspavɪn/ ▷ *noun, vet medicine* **a** a condition in horses where there is swelling on the leg, in the region of either the shank bone or the hock bone; **b** the swelling that causes this condition. ◷ 15c: from French *espavain* swelling.

spawn ▷ *noun* **1 a** the cohering jelly-like mass or stream of eggs that amphibians, fish, molluscs, crustaceans, etc lay in water; **b** *in compounds* □ *frogspawn.* **2** *derisive* **a** something that is the product of or that is derived from something else and which, because it is not original, is regarded with a degree of contempt; **b** the offspring of someone or something that is held in contempt. ▷ *verb* (***spawned***, ***spawning***) **1** *intr* said of amphibians, fish, etc: to lay eggs. **2** to give rise to something; to lead to something □ *The film's success spawned several sequels.* **3** to give birth to someone or something □ *hard to believe she could have spawned such a lovely daughter.* **4** to produce □ *Scotland has spawned many famous people.* ● **spawned** *adj.* ● **spawner** *noun.* ● **spawning** *noun, adj.* ◷ 14c: from French *espandre* to shed.

spawning-ground and **spawning-bed** ▷ *noun* **1** a place at the bottom of a river, etc where fish, amphibians, etc regularly spawn. **2** a place where new ideas, techniques, developments, etc flourish or are encouraged □ *a spawning-ground for gossip.*

spay ▷ *verb* (***spayed***, ***spaying***) to remove the ovaries from (especially a domestic animal) in order to prevent it from breeding. ● **spayed** *adj.* ● **spaying** *noun.* ◷ 15c: from French *espeier* to cut with a sword.

spaz and **spazzy** see under SPASTIC

SPCK ▷ *abbreviation* Society for Promoting Christian Knowledge.

speak ▷ *verb* (***spoke*** or (*old use*) ***spake*** /speɪk/, ***spoken*** /ˈspoʊkən/, ***speaking***) **1** *tr & intr* **a** to utter words in an ordinary voice, as opposed to shouting, singing, screaming, etc; **b** to talk □ *speaks a load of rubbish.* **2** *intr* to have a conversation □ *We speak on the phone every night.* **3** *intr* to deliver a speech □ *spoke on the subject of rising urban crime.* **4** to communicate, or be able to communicate, in (a particular language) □ *He speaks French fluently.* **5** *intr* to convey meaning □ *Actions speak louder than words.* ▷ *combining form, forming nouns* talk or jargon of the specified kind □ *consultantspeak* □ *luvviespeak* □ *doublespeak.* ● **speakable** *adj.* ● **be on speaking terms** see under SPEAKING. ● **so to speak** in a way; as it were □ *had a bit of a tiff, so to speak.* ● **speak for itself** to have an obvious meaning; to need no further explanation or comment. ● **speak for oneself 1** to give one's own opinion or opinions. **2** to exclude others from what one is saying, referring to, etc. ● **speak for yourself** an expression that is used by someone who wants to be disassociated from what has just been said or from the implications of it □ *Speak for yourself! I'm not going into that dive.* ● **speak one's mind** to say what one thinks boldly, defiantly, without restraint, etc. ● **speak ill of someone or something** to criticize them or it; to blacken their or its name □ *Don't speak ill of the dead.* ● **speak the same language** see under LANGUAGE. ● **speak the truth** to tell no lies. ● **speak volumes** to be or act as a significant factor □ *The fact that he lied speaks volumes.* ● **to speak of** *usually with negatives* worth mentioning, considering, etc □ *received no education to speak of.* ● **speak well** or **highly of (someone** or **something)** to admire them or it. ◷ Anglo-Saxon *specan.*

■ **speak about something 1** to discuss it. **2** to put it forward, or think of it as a possibility, often without any further action, etc being taken □ *had often spoken about working abroad.*

■ **speak about someone** or **something** to gossip about them.

■ **speak for 1** to give an opinion on behalf of (another or others). **2** to articulate in either spoken or written words the commonly held feelings, beliefs, views, opinions, etc of (others) □ *Kurt Cobain's lyrics speak for the twentysomethings.*

■ **speak of someone** or **something 1** to make mention of or refer to them or it, especially casually, tentatively, etc □ *spoke of going to London for a few days.* **2** to explore or discuss, eg in a piece of writing or other non-verbal medium □ *Heaney's poetry often speaks of the insecurities the poet goes through.*

■ **speak out 1** to speak openly; to state one's views forcefully. **2** to speak more loudly.

■ **speak to someone 1** to have a conversation with them. **2** to reprimand them. **3** to be meaningful to them □ *That painting really speaks to me.*

■ **speak up** *intr* **1** to speak more loudly. **2** to make something known □ *If you've any objections, speak up now.*

■ **speak up for someone** or **something** **1** to vouch for or defend them or it. **2** to represent them or it.

■ **speak with someone** to talk to them.

speakeasy ▻ *noun* (***speakeasies***) *colloq* a bar or other place where alcohol was sold illicitly, especially one that operated during the period when the US prohibition laws were in force. ◑ 19c.

speaker ▻ *noun* **1** someone who speaks, especially someone who gives a formal speech. **2** a shortened form of LOUDSPEAKER. **3** (*usually* **the Speaker**) the person who presides over debate in a law-making assembly such as the House of Commons.

speaking ▻ *noun* an act, instance or the process of saying something. ▻ *adj* **1** able to produce speech □ *a speaking teddy bear.* **2** from or with regard to a specified point of view □ *Roughly speaking, the total cost will be about £100.* **3** *in compounds* having the ability to speak (a particular language) □ *Brazil is a Portuguese-speaking country.* **4** said of a portrait, etc: characterized by having a striking resemblance to its subject. • **be on speaking terms** to be sufficiently friendly or familiar to hold a conversation.

speaking clock ▻ *noun, Brit* a telephone service where callers can ring a number and hear a recorded message giving the exact time. ◑ 1930s.

spear¹ /spɪə(r)/ ▻ *noun* a weapon that consists of a long pole with a hard sharp point, usually a metal one, and which is thrown from the shoulder (eg at prey, fish or an enemy). ▻ *verb* (***speared***, ***spearing***) to pierce with a spear or something similar to a spear □ *managed to spear the pickled onion.* • **speared** *adj.* ◑ Anglo-Saxon *spere.*

spear² ▻ *noun* a spiky plant shoot, such as a blade of grass, an asparagus or broccoli shoot, etc. ◑ Early 19c; although an earlier now obsolete sense of 'a church spire' dates from 15c: from SPIRE.

spearfish ▻ *noun* see MARLIN

spearhead ▻ *noun* **1** the leading part or member of an attacking force. **2** the tip of a spear. ▻ *verb* to lead (a movement, campaign, attack, etc). ◑ 1930s as *verb*; 19c as *noun* 1; 15c as *noun* 2.

spearmint ▻ *noun* **1** a herbaceous perennial plant of the mint family with lance-shaped aromatic leaves and spikes of purple flowers. **2** the aromatic oil that is obtained from the leaves of this plant and which is used in cooking and as a flavouring in confectionery, toothpaste, etc. ◑ 16c: so named because of the shape of its leaves.

spec¹ /spɛk/ ▻ *noun, colloq* a commercial venture. • **on spec** as a speculation or gamble, in the hope of success □ *wrote on spec, asking for a job.* ◑ 18c: a shortened form of SPECULATION.

spec² ▻ *noun, colloq* a shortened form of SPECIFICATION. ◑ 1950s.

special /ˈspɛʃəl/ ▻ *adj* **1** distinct from, and usually better than, others of the same or a similar kind; exceptional □ *a special occasion* □ *She was very special to him.* **2** designed for a particular purpose □ *You can get a special program to do that.* **3** not ordinary or common □ *special circumstances.* **4** particular; great □ *make a special effort.* ▻ *noun* **1** something that is special, eg an extra edition of a newspaper, etc, an extra train that is put on over and above the time-tabled ones, an item offered at a low price, a dish on a menu, etc □ *put on four football specials.* **2** a special person, such as a member of the special police constabulary □ *The specials were drafted in to control the fans.* • **specially** *adverb.* • **specialness** *noun.* ◑ 13c: from Latin *specialis* individual or particular.

Special Branch ▻ *noun, Brit* the police department that deals with matters of political security.

specially

There is often confusion between **specially** and **especially**: **specially** means 'for a special purpose', as in □ *I made this cake specially for your birthday*, whereas **especially** means 'particularly, above all', as in □ *I like making cakes, especially for birthdays.* You will sometimes find **especially** used wrongly to mean **specially**:
✗ *He had driven up especially to collect her.*

special constable ▻ *noun* a member of a reserve police force who can be drafted in when necessary, eg when vast numbers of football fans are in town, in times of national emergency, etc.

special correspondent ▻ *noun, Brit* a journalist who has a remit to cover a particular area of news.

special delivery ▻ *noun* a delivery of post, etc outside normal delivery times.

Special Drawing Rights or **special drawing rights** ▻ *plural noun* an extra entitlement that allows member countries of the International Monetary Fund to draw currency from its assets and thereby increase their foreign exchange reserves. Often shortened to SDR or SDRs.

special education ▻ *noun* the branch of education that is there to help children who have learning difficulties or some form of physical or mental disability. See also SPECIAL NEEDS.

special effects ▻ *plural noun, cinematog* **1** the particular techniques, such as those that involve computer-generated graphics, simulated action scenes, elaborate make-up and costumes, skilled camera work, etc that are used in the making of films and TV programmes. **2** the resulting impact or illusion that these techniques produce. Sometimes shortened to **FX**, **sfx**.

special intention see INTENTION

specialism ▻ *noun* **1** a particular subject or area of study that someone specializes in. **2** the act of specializing in something.

specialist ▻ *noun* **1** someone whose work, interest or expertise is concentrated on a particular subject □ *Frank was the department's film noir specialist.* Opposite of GENERALIST. **2** an organism or species that is restricted to a narrow range of food and habitat preferences. • **specialistic** *adj.*

speciality /spɛʃɪˈalɪtɪ/ ▻ *noun* (***specialities***) **1** something such as a particular area of interest, a distinctive quality, a specified product, etc that a company, individual, etc has special knowledge of or that they especially excel in studying, teaching, writing about, producing, etc □ *Her speciality is ancient history* □ *The restaurant's speciality is seafood.* **2** a special feature, skill, characteristic, service, etc.

speciality, specialty

Speciality and **specialty** have virtually the same meaning. **Speciality** is the commoner form in British English, **specialty** in American English.

specialize or **specialise** /ˈspɛʃəlaɪz/ ▻ *verb* (***specialized***, ***specializing***) **1** (*also* **specialize in something**) **a** to be or become an expert in a particular activity, field of study, etc; **b** to devote a lot of time, effort, etc (to a particular activity) □ *He specializes in giving everyone a hard time.* **2** said of an organism, body part, etc: to adapt or become adapted for a specified purpose or to particular surroundings. • **specialization** *noun.* • **specializer** *noun.* ◑ 17c: from SPECIAL.

specialized or **specialised** ▻ *adj* **1** adapted, developed, modified, etc for a particular purpose or to particular surroundings □ *highly specialized plants that can live in arid conditions.* **2** highly specific; understood only by an expert in the field □ *a specialized knowledge of wine.*

special licence ▷ *noun* a licence that allows a marriage to take place outwith the normal hours or at short notice and usually without the normal legal formalities.

special needs ▷ *noun* a term for any of several conditions that can result in someone having learning difficulties.

special pleading ▷ *noun, law* the allegation of new facts in a case which offset those proposed by the opposite side rather than directly admitting or denying them.

special school ▷ *noun* a school where children with learning difficulties or physical or mental disabilities are taught.

specialty /'spɛʃəltɪ/ ▷ *noun* (***specialties***) **1** *chiefly US* a SPECIALITY. **2** *law* a deed that is a contractual document and which must be signed by its maker in the presence of a witness, or, if it is executed by a company, by a director and the secretary or by two directors, or executed by a seal if the company has one. ⓘ 15c in sense 2: from French *especialte*, from *especial* special.

specialty

See Usage Note at **speciality**.

speciation /spiːsɪ'eɪʃən/ ▷ *noun, biol* the process that involves the evolution of one or more species from an existing one, especially when it arises because of a geographical isolation from the parent species as has happened to many of the species found only on the island of Madagascar.

specie /'spiːʃiː, 'spiːʃɪ/ ▷ *noun* money in the form of coins as opposed to notes. • **in specie 1** in kind. **2** in coin. ⓘ 16c: Latin, meaning 'in kind'.

species /'spiːʃiːz, -siːz, -ʃɪz/ ▷ *noun* (***species***) **1 a** *biol* in taxonomy: any of the groups, *Canis familiaris* (the domestic dog), into which a GENUS (sense 1) is divided, the main criterion for grouping being that all the members should be capable of interbreeding and producing fertile offspring; **b** *biol* the members of one of these units of classification thought of collectively; **c** *loosely* any group of related plants or animals that share some common features or characteristics, but which do not technically form a taxonomic grouping. **2** *chem* a particular type of atom, molecule or ion. **3** any group whose members share certain features or characteristics. **4** (*usually* **species of**) a kind or type. ⓘ 16c: Latin, meaning 'kind, appearance', from *specere* to look.

speciesism /'spiːʃiːzɪzəm, 'spiːsiːzɪzəm/ ▷ *noun* the discrimination against, and exploitation of, animals by humans in the belief that humans are superior to all other species of animals and can therefore justify putting them to their own use. • **speciesist** *noun.* ⓘ 1970s: from SPECIES + -ISM and modelled on RACISM, etc.

specific /spə'sɪfɪk/ ▷ *adj* **1** particular; exact; precisely identified. **2** precise in meaning; not vague. ▷ *noun* **1** (*usually* **specifics**) a specific detail, factor or feature, eg of a plan, scheme, etc. **2** a drug that is used to treat one particular disease, condition, etc. • **specifical** *adj.* • **specifically** *adverb.* • **specificity** /spɛsɪ'fɪsɪtɪ/ *noun.* ⓘ 17c: from Latin *species* kind + -FIC.

specification /spɛsɪfɪ'keɪʃən/ ▷ *noun* **1 a** (*often* **specifications**) a detailed description of the type of methods, materials, dimensions, quantities, etc that are used in the construction, manufacture, building, planning, etc of something; **b** the standard, quality, etc of the construction, manufacture, etc of something □ *Saabs are built to high safety specifications.* **2** an act or instance or the process of specifying. **3** a document that details the particulars and projected use of an invention and which the person wanting to patent it draws up before submitting it to the proper authorities. ⓘ 17c: from SPECIFY.

specific gravity ▷ *noun* RELATIVE DENSITY

specific heat capacity see HEAT CAPACITY

specific resistance see RESISTIVITY

specify /'spɛsɪfaɪ/ ▷ *verb* (***specifies, specified, specifying***) **1** to refer to, name or identify precisely □ *The report does not specify who was to blame.* **2** (*usually* **specify that**) to state as a condition or requirement □ *The contract specified that the invoice must be paid at once.* • **specifiable** *adj.* • **specified** *adj.* • **specifier** *noun.* ⓘ 13c: from French *specifier*, from Latin *specificare* to describe or mention.

specimen /'spɛsɪmɪn/ ▷ *noun* **1** a sample or example of something, especially one that will be studied or put in a collection. **2** *medicine* a sample of blood, urine, tissue, etc that is taken so that tests can be carried out on it. **3** something that is regarded as typical of its kind; a part of something that is regarded as representative of it □ *Here is just one specimen of her artwork.* **4** *colloq* a person of a specified kind □ *an ugly specimen.* ⓘ 17c: Latin, from *specere* to see.

specious /'spiːʃəs/ ▷ *adj* **1** superficially or apparently convincing, sound or just, but really false, flawed or lacking in sincerity □ *specious arguments.* **2** outwardly attractive but possessing no real intrinsic value. • **speciosity** /spiːʃɪ'ɒsɪtɪ/ *noun.* • **speciously** *adverb.* • **speciousness** *noun.* ⓘ 14c: from Latin *speciosus* fair or beautiful, from *species* SPECIES.

speck /spɛk/ ▷ *noun* **1** a small spot, stain or mark □ *The carpet's blue with grey specks.* **2** (*usually* **speck of something**) a particle or tiny piece of it □ *a speck of dirt on your shirt.* ▷ *verb* (***specked, specking***) to mark with specks □ *a blue carpet specked with grey.* • **speckless** *adj.* • **specky** *adj.* ⓘ Anglo-Saxon *specca*.

speckle /'spɛkəl/ ▷ *noun* a little spot, especially one of several on a different-coloured background, eg on feathers, a bird's egg, etc. ▷ *verb* (***speckled, speckling***) to mark with speckles. ⓘ 15c: from Dutch *speckel* and related to SPECK.

speckled ▷ *adj* said especially of certain fish and birds or birds' eggs: covered or marked with specks or speckles □ *a speckled hen.*

specs /spɛks/ ▷ *plural noun, colloq* a shortened form of SPECTACLES.

spectacle /'spɛktəkəl/ ▷ *noun* **1** something that can be seen; a sight, especially one that is impressive, wonderful, disturbing, ridiculous, etc □ *The roses make a lovely spectacle.* **2** a display or exhibition, especially one that is put on for entertaining the public. **3** someone or something that attracts attention □ *Their squalid room was a revolting spectacle.* • **spectacled** *adj* said of certain animals and birds: having ringed markings around the eyes. • **make a spectacle of oneself** to behave in a way that attracts attention, especially ridicule or scorn. See also SPECTACLES. ⓘ 14c: from Latin *spectaculum*, from *specere* to look.

spectacled bear ▷ *noun* the only native S American bear which lives in forests in the W foothills of the Andes, and which has a small body with dark fur except for pale rings around its eyes. ⓘ 19c.

spectacles ▷ *plural noun* a frame that sits on the nose and which has two legs that fit behind the ears. It contains two lenses that are designed to correct defective eyesight. See also BESPECTACLED.

spectacular /spɛk'takjʊlə(r)/ ▷ *adj* **1** impressively striking to see or watch. **2** remarkable; dramatic; huge. ▷ *noun* a spectacular show or display, especially one with lavish costumes, sets, music, etc □ *an old-fashioned musical spectacular.* • **spectacularly** *adj.* • **spec-**

tacularity *noun*. ◎ 17c: from Latin *spectaculum* and related to SPECTACLE.

spectate /spɛk'teɪt/ ▻ *verb* (***spectated, spectating***) *intr* to be a spectator; to look on rather than participate. ◎ 1920s in this sense; 18c meaning 'to gaze at': formed from SPECTATOR.

spectator /spɛk'teɪtə(r)/ ▻ *noun* someone who watches an event or incident. • **spectatorial** /spɛktə'tɔːrɪəl/ *adj*. • **spectatorship** *noun*. ◎ 16c: Latin, from *spectare* to look.

spectator sport ▻ *noun* a sport or other activity that provides plenty of interest, excitement and involvement for those who are watching ▫ ***Sitting in a Parisian pavement café is a good spectator sport.*** ◎ 1940s.

specter the *US* spelling of SPECTRE

spectra *plural of* SPECTRUM

spectral /'spɛktrəl/ ▻ *adj* **1** relating to or like a spectre or ghost. **2** relating to, produced by or like a SPECTRUM. • **spectrality** *noun*. • **spectrally** *adverb*.

spectre or (*US*) **specter** /'spɛktə(r)/ ▻ *noun* (***spectres***) **1** a ghost or an apparition. **2** a haunting fear; the threat of something unpleasant ▫ ***The spectre of famine was never far away.*** ◎ 17c: French, from Latin *spectare*, from *specere* to look.

spectro- /spɛktroʊ, spɛk'trɒ/ ▻ *combining form, denoting* **1** a spectrum. **2** a spectrograph.

spectrochemistry ▻ *noun* the branch of chemistry that is concerned with the chemical analysis and interpretation of SPECTRA.

spectrogram ▻ *noun* a record, usually a photographic one, that is obtained from a spectrograph.

spectrograph ▻ *noun* a device that is designed to make a photographic or other type of visual record of a SPECTRUM. • **spectrographic** *adj*. • **spectrographically** *adverb*. • **spectrography** *noun*. See also MASS SPECTROGRAPH.

spectrometer ▻ *noun* a device that is designed to produce spectra, especially one that can measure wavelength, energy and intensity. • **spectrometric** /spɛktroʊ'mɛtrɪk/ *adj*. • **spectrometry** *noun*. See also MASS SPECTROMETER.

spectroscope ▻ *noun, chem* an optical device that is used to produce a spectrum for a particular chemical compound, allowing the spectrum to be observed and analysed in order to identify the compound, determine its structure, etc.

spectrum /'spɛktrəm/ ▻ *noun* (***spectra*** /–trə/ or ***spectrums***) **1** *physics* (*in full* **visible spectrum**) the band of colours (red, orange, yellow, green, blue, indigo and violet) that is produced when white light is split into its constituent wavelengths by passing it through a prism. **2** a continuous band or a series of lines representing the wavelengths or frequencies of electromagnetic radiation (eg visible light, X-rays, radio waves) emitted or absorbed by a particular substance. **3** any full range ▫ ***the whole spectrum of human emotions.*** ◎ 17c: Latin, meaning 'appearance'.

specular /'spɛkjʊlə(r)/ ▻ *adj* **1** belonging or relating to a mirror. **2** having the characteristics of a mirror. **3** belonging or relating to a SPECULUM. 16c.

speculate /'spɛkjʊleɪt/ ▻ *verb* (***speculated, speculating***) *intr* **1** (*often* **speculate on** or **about something**) to consider the circumstances or possibilities regarding it, usually without any factual basis and without coming to a definite conclusion. **2** to engage in risky financial transactions, usually in the hope of making a quick profit. ◎ 16c: from Latin *speculari, speculatus* to look out, from *specere* to see.

speculation ▻ *noun* **1** an act or instance, or the process or result, of speculating. **2** a risky investment of money for the sake of large profit.

speculative /'spɛkjʊlətɪv, -leɪtɪv/ ▻ *adj* **1 a** said of a theory, conjecture, etc: involving guesswork; **b** said of someone: tending to come to conclusions that have little or no foundation. **2** said of an investment, business venture: risky. • **speculatively** *adverb*. • **speculativeness** *noun*.

speculator /'spɛkjʊleɪtə(r)/ ▻ *noun* someone who speculates, especially financially.

speculum /'spɛkjʊləm/ ▻ *noun* (***specula*** /-lə/ or ***speculums***) **1** *optics* a mirror with a reflective surface usually of polished metal, especially one that forms part of a telescope. **2** *medicine* a device that is used to enlarge the opening of a body cavity so that the interior may be inspected. **3** a glossy coloured patch on the wings of some birds, especially certain ducks. ◎ 16c: Latin, meaning 'mirror', from *specere* to look at.

sped *past tense, past participle of* SPEED

speech ▻ *noun* **1** the act or an instance of speaking; the ability to speak. **2** a way of speaking ▫ ***slurred speech.*** **3** something that is spoken. **4** spoken language, especially that of a particular group, region, nation, etc ▫ ***Doric speech has very distinctive vowels.*** **5** a talk that is addressed to an audience. ◎ Anglo-Saxon *sprec*.

speech day ▻ *noun, Brit* in some schools, especially public schools in England: the day towards the end of the summer term when speeches are made and prizes handed out.

speechify ▻ *verb* (***speechifies, speechified, speechifying***) *intr, colloq* **1** to make a speech or speeches, especially of a long and tedious nature. **2** to talk in an over-formal, boring and pompous manner. • **speechifying** *noun*. ◎ 18c: from SPEECH.

speech impediment see IMPEDIMENT

speechless ▻ *adj* **1** *often euphemistic* temporarily unable to speak, because of surprise, shock, emotion, etc. **2** not able to speak at all. • **speechlessly** *adverb*. • **speechlessness** *noun*.

speech recognition ▻ *noun, computing* the understanding of an individual's speech patterns, or of continuous speech, by a computer.

speech therapist ▻ *noun* someone who is professionally qualified to provide speech therapy.

speech therapy ▻ *noun* the treatment of speech and language disorders, eg in deaf or brain-damaged children or in adults who have lost the ability to speak because of an accident, disease, etc.

speed ▻ *noun* **1** rate of movement or action, especially distance travelled per unit of time. **2** quickness; rapidity ▫ ***with speed.*** **3** a gear setting on a vehicle ▫ ***five-speed gearbox.*** **4** a photographic film's sensitivity to light. **5** *drug-taking slang* an AMPHETAMINE. ▻ *verb, intr* **1** (***sped, speeding***) to move quickly. **2** (***speeded, speeding***) to drive at a speed higher than the legal limit. • **speeder** *noun*. • **at speed** quickly. ◎ Anglo-Saxon *sped*.

▪ **speed up** or **speed something up** to increase in speed or make it increase in speed.

speedball ▻ *noun, slang* a mixture of cocaine and morphine or of cocaine and heroin.

speedboat ▻ *noun* a motor boat that has an engine designed to make it capable of high speeds.

speed bump ▻ *noun* a SLEEPING POLICEMAN.

speed camera ▻ *noun* a roadside camera which is triggered by cars that exceed the speed limit, enabling the police to use the photographs as evidence if they choose to prosecute.

speedfreak ▻ *noun, colloq* someone who habitually takes amphetamine.

speedily and **speediness** see under SPEEDY.

speeding ▻ *noun* **1** an act, instance or the process of going fast. **2** an act, instance or the process of going faster than the designated speed limit. ▷ *adj* moving, acting, etc fast □ *a speeding car.* • **be** or **get done for speeding** *colloq* to be caught, charged and fined for exceeding the speed limit in a vehicle.

speed limit ▷ *noun* the designated maximum speed a vehicle may legally travel at on a given stretch of road. • **break the speed limit** to drive faster than the designated speed limit.

speed merchant ▷ *noun, colloq* someone who habitually drives fast, usually faster than the designated speed limit, and especially someone who gets a thrill from doing this.

speedo ▷ *noun* (*speedos*) *colloq* a SPEEDOMETER.

speed of light ▷ *noun, physics* (symbol **c**) the constant and universal speed, exactly 2.99792458$10^8$ metres per second, at which electromagnetic waves, including visible light, travel through a vacuum.

speedometer /spiː'dɒmɪtə(r)/ ▷ *noun* (often shortened to **speedo**) a device which indicates the current speed that a motor vehicle is travelling at, and which often incorporates an odometer that displays the total mileage. Also (*colloq*) called **the clock**.

speedskating ▷ *noun* a sport that involves two competitors at a time racing each other many times round an oval ice track.

speed trap ▷ *noun* a stretch of road where police monitor the speed of vehicles, often with electronic equipment.

speedway ▷ *noun* **1** a sport or pastime that involves racing round a cinder track on lightweight motorcycles. **2** the track that is used for this. **3** *N Amer* a racetrack for cars. **4** *N Amer* a highway where vehicles are allowed to travel fast.

speedwell ▷ *noun* any of various low-growing annual or perennial plants with opposite lance-shaped or oval leaves and small bluish (or occasionally white) four-petalled flowers. ⓒ 16c.

speedy ▷ *adj* (*speedier, speediest*) fast; prompt; without delay. • **speedily** *adverb*. • **speediness** *noun*.

speiss /spaɪs/ ▷ *noun, metallurgy* the ARSENIDES and ANTIMONIDES that are produced during the smelting of cobalt and lead ores. ⓒ 18c: from German *Speise* food.

spelaean or **spelean** /spɪ'liːən/ ▷ *adj* said of an animal, etc: tending to live in a cave. ⓒ 19c: from Latin *spelaeus*, from *spaelaeum*, from Greek *spelaion* cave.

speleology or **spelaeology** /spelɪ'ɒlədʒɪ, spiː-/ ▷ *noun* **1** the scientific study of caves. **2** the activity or pastime of exploring caves. • **speleological** *adj*. • **speleologist** *noun*. ⓒ 19c: from French *spéléologie*, from Greek *spelaion* cave.

spell¹ ▷ *verb* (*spelt* or *spelled, spelling*) **1** to write or name (the constituent letters of a word or words) in their correct order. **2** said of letters: to form (a word) when written in sequence □ *How do you spell it? That's easy — I T spells 'it'.* **3** to indicate something clearly □ *His angry expression spelt trouble.* • **spellable** *adj*. • **speller** *noun*. • **spelling** see separate entry. ⓒ 13c: from French *espeller*, from German *spellen* and related to GOSPEL.

■ **spell something out 1** to read, write or speak (the constituent letters of a word) one by one. **2** to explain something clearly and in detail □ *The instructions spell out exactly how it's done.*

spell² ▷ *noun* **1** a set of words which, especially when spoken, is believed to have magical power, often of an evil nature □ *a magic spell.* **2** any strong attracting influence; a fascination □ *found the spell of her personality incredibly powerful.* • **cast a spell (on** or **upon someone)** to direct the words of a spell (towards them), especially in the hope that something bad will happen. • **under a spell** held by the influence of a spell that has been cast. • **under one's spell** captivated by their influence. ⓒ Anglo-Saxon, meaning 'narrative', from *spellian* to speak or announce.

spell³ ▷ *noun* **1** (*often* **for a spell** or **a spell of**) a period or bout of illness, work, weather, etc often of a specified kind □ *hope this spell of sunshine continues.* **2** *now chiefly Austral, NZ & N Eng dialect* an interval or short break from work. ▷ *verb* (*spelled, spelling*) *now chiefly Austral, NZ & N Eng dialect* **1** to replace or relieve someone at work. **2** *intr* to take an interval or short break from work. ⓒ Anglo-Saxon *spelian* to act for another.

spellbind /'spelbaɪnd/ ▷ *verb* to captivate, enchant, entrance or fascinate. • **spellbinder** *noun* someone, especially a politician, who has the ability to captivate, etc their audience. • **spellbinding** *adj*. • **spellbindingly** *adverb*. ⓒ Early 19c.

spellbound /'spelbaʊnd/ ▷ *adj* completely captivated, enchanted, entranced or fascinated.

spell-check ▷ *verb, wordprocessing* to run a program that will highlight any words in a section of text that differ in spelling from the words stored in its database.

spellican see SPILLIKIN

spelling ▷ *noun* **1** the ability to spell □ *His spelling is awful.* **2 a** a way a word is spelt □ *an American spelling*; **b** *as adj* □ *a spelling mistake* □ *spelling book.*

spelling-bee ▷ *noun* (*spelling-bees*) a competition where the object is to spell correctly as many words as possible.

spelling-checker and **spell-checker** ▷ *noun, wordprocessing* a program that is designed to highlight any words (in a section of text) that differ in spelling from the words stored in its database, so allowing one to find spelling errors.

spelt¹ *past tense, past participle of* SPELL¹

spelt² ▷ *noun* a type of grain which was once widely cultivated throughout Europe, but which has now largely been superseded by wheat, which it is related to, although it is still grown in some mountainous regions of S Europe. ⓒ Anglo-Saxon *spelta*.

spelter /'speltə(r)/ ▷ *noun* impure zinc that contains lead or other impurities. ⓒ 17c.

spelunker /spɪ'lʌŋkə(r)/ ▷ *noun* someone who takes part in the sport or activity of exploring caves; a potholer. • **spelunking** *noun*. ⓒ 1940s: from Latin *spelunca*, from Greek *spelynx* a cave.

spencer¹ /'spensə(r)/ ▷ *noun* **1** a short close-fitting men's overcoat that was worn around the turn of the 19c. **2** a type of thin woolly vest that was worn by women and girls for warmth in the winter. ⓒ Early 19c: from the Spencer family name.

spencer² /'spensə(r)/ ▷ *noun, naut* a type of FORE-AND-AFT sail that is set with a gaff on a square-rigger or barque. ⓒ Early 19c.

spend ▷ *verb* (*spent, spending*) **1** *tr & intr* (*often* **spend on**) to pay out (money, etc) eg on buying something new, for a service, repair, etc. **2** to use or devote (eg time, energy, effort, etc) □ *spent hours trying to fix the car.* **3** to use up completely; to exhaust □ *Her anger soon spends itself.* ▷ *noun* **1** an act or the process of spending (especially money) □ *went on a massive spend after winning the Lottery.* **2** an amount (of money) that is spent □ *allocated a £5 million spend for advertising.* • **spendable** *adj*. • **spender** *noun*. • **spending** *noun*. • **spent** *adj* used up; exhausted □ *a spent match.* • **spend a penny** *Brit euphemistic* to urinate or go to the toilet ⓒ from the charge sometimes levied for the use of public toilets. ⓒ Anglo-Saxon *spendan*, from Latin *expendere* to pay out.

spending money ▷ *noun* money that can be spent, especially on things that are not essential.

spendthrift ▷ *noun* someone who spends money freely, extravagantly and often wastefully.

sperm /spɜːm/ ▻ *noun* **1** a SPERMATOZOOAN. **2** SEMEN. ◷ 14c: from French *esperme* or from Latin *sperma*, from Greek *sperma* seed.

-sperm ▻ *combining form, bot, denoting* a seed ▫ *angiosperm.* • **-spermal** *combining form* forming adjectives ▫ *gymnospermal.* • **-spermous** *combining form* forming adjectives ▫ *angiospermous.*

spermaceti /spɜːməˈsiːtɪ/ ▻ *noun* a white translucent waxy substance that is present in a cavity in the snout of the sperm whale and which was formerly used for making candles, soap, cosmetics, ointments, etc. ◷ 15c: Latin, meaning 'whale sperm', from *sperma* seed + *ceti* of a whale, from the mistaken belief as to what the substance consists of.

spermatic /spɜːˈmatɪk/ ▻ *adj* belonging, relating or referring to sperm. • **spermatical** *adj.*

spermatid /ˈspɜːmətɪd/ ▻ *noun, zool* an immature male gamete that has developed from a SPERMATOCYTE and which, when mature, will become a SPERMATOZOON.

spermato- /spɜːˈmatoʊ, ˈspɜːmətoʊ/ or **sperma-** or **spermo-** ▻ *combining form, biol, denoting* **1** sperm. **2** seed. ◷ From Greek *sperma* seed.

spermatocyte ▻ *noun, zool* an immature male cell that has developed from a SPERMATOGONIUM and which itself divides, by meiosis, into four SPERMATID.

spermatogenesis ▻ *noun, zool* the formation and development of sperm in the testes. • **spermatogenetic** *adj.*

spermatogonium /spɜːmatoʊˈgoʊnɪəm/ ▻ *noun, zool* an immature male cell that, when it divides, gives rise to many SPERMATOCYTES.

spermatophore /ˈspɜːmətəfɔː(r), spəˈmatəfɔː(r)/ ▻ *noun, zool* in certain invertebrates, eg various molluscs, crustaceans, etc: the structure that contains a mass of spermatozoa. • **spermatophoric** /spɜːmatəˈfɔːrɪk/ *adj.* ◷ 19c.

spermatophyte and **spermophyte** ▻ *noun, bot* any seed-bearing plant. See also ANGIOSPERM, GYMNOSPERM. • **spermatophytic** *adj.* ◷ Late 19c.

spermatozoid /spɜːmətoʊˈzoʊɪd, spəˈmatoʊzoʊɪd/ ▻ *noun, bot* in certain plants: a mature male sex cell.

spermatozoon /spɜːmətoʊˈzoʊɒn/ ▻ *noun* (***spermatozoa*** /-ˈzoʊə/) *zool* in male animals: the small motile male gamete that locates, penetrates and fertilizes the female gamete, and which usually consists of a head containing a nucleus, and a long 'tail' that moves it forward. Often shortened to SPERM. • **spermatozoal** or **spermatozoan** or **spermatozoic** *adj.* ◷ 19c: from SPERMATO- + Greek *zoion* animal.

sperm bank ▻ *noun* a refrigerated store where semen is kept before it is used in artificial insemination.

sperm count ▻ *noun* **1** the mean number of sperm that are present in a sample of semen. **2** the test that determines this. ◷ 1940s.

spermicide /ˈspɜːmɪsaɪd/ ▻ *noun* a substance that can kill sperm and which is used in conjunction with various methods of barrier contraception, eg the condom and the diaphragm. • **spermicidal** *adj.*

spermo- see SPERMATO-

sperm oil ▻ *noun* oil that is obtained from the head of a sperm whale and which is used as a lubricant.

-spermous see -SPERM

sperm whale ▻ *noun* the largest of the toothed whales, with an enormous head and a square snout, which is now an endangered species, having been widely hunted as a source of spermaceti and ambergris. Also called CACHALOT. ◷ 19c: a shortened form of SPERMACETI.

spew /spjuː/ ▻ *verb* (***spewed***, ***spewing***) *tr & intr* **1** to vomit. **2** to pour or cause to pour or stream out ▫ *Obscenities spewed from his mouth.* ▻ *noun* vomit. • **spewer** *noun.* • **spewing** *noun, adj.* • **spew one's guts up** *slang* to vomit violently. ◷ Anglo-Saxon *spiowan* to spit.

SPF ▻ *abbreviation* sun protection factor.

sp. gr. ▻ *abbreviation* specific gravity.

sphagnum /ˈsfagnəm/ ▻ *noun* (***sphagna*** /ˈsfagnə/) any of numerous species of moss that grow on temperate boggy or marshy ground, which have a spongy structure that retains water, making them suitable for use as a packing material, eg for potting plants, and which form peat when they decay. Also called **bog moss** or **peat moss.** ◷ 18c: from Greek *sphagnos* moss.

sphalerite /ˈsfaləraɪt/ ▻ *noun, geol* a yellowish-brown to brownish-black mineral form of zinc sulphide, usually with a resinous lustre, that is the principal ore of zinc and also a source of cadmium. Also called **zinc blende.** ◷ 19c: from Greek *sphaleros* deceptive, so called because of its resemblance to GALENA.

sphere /sfɪə(r)/ ▻ *noun* **1** *math* **a** a round three-dimensional figure where all points on the surface are an equal distance from the centre; **b** the surface of this kind of figure. **2** a globe or ball. **3** a field of activity ▫ *Rugby's not really my sphere.* **4** a class or circle within society ▫ *We don't move in the same sphere any more.* **5 a** any body in the sky, such as a planet, star, etc; **b** *poetic* the sky itself; **c** any of the concentric shells that were once thought by astronomers to revolve around the Earth carrying the Moon, Sun, planets and fixed stars. • **spheral** *adj.* • **sphered** *adj.* • **sphereless** *adj.* • **spherelike** *adj.* ◷ 13c: from French *espere*, from Greek *sphaira* a globe.

-sphere /sfɪə(r)/ ▻ *combining form* **1** *denoting* the shape of a sphere ▫ *bathysphere.* **2** *denoting* an area around a planet ▫ *ionosphere.*

sphere of influence ▻ *noun* the range or extent over which a state or individual is, or is seen to be, dominant ▫ *extend one's sphere of influence.*

spherical /ˈsfɛrɪkəl/ and **spheric** ▻ *adj* **1** having or being in the shape of a sphere. **2** belonging, relating or referring to a sphere or spheres. • **sphericality** *noun.* • **spherically** *adverb.* • **sphericalness** or **sphericity** *noun.* ◷ 16c: from SPHERE.

spheroid /ˈsfɪərɔɪd/ ▻ *adj* characterized by having, or being in, almost the shape of a sphere. ▻ *noun* **1** a figure or body of this shape. **2** *math* **a** (*in full* **prolate spheroid**) a solid figure in the shape of an elongated sphere that is obtained by rotating an ellipse about its longer axis; **b** (*in full* **oblate spheroid**) a solid figure in the shape of a flattened sphere that is obtained by rotating an ellipse about its shorter axis. • **spheroidal** /sfɪəˈrɔɪdəl/ *adj.* • **spheroidicity** /sfɪərɔɪˈdɪsɪtɪ/ *noun.* ◷ 17c: from Latin *sphareoides*, from Greek *sphaira* a globe.

spherule /ˈsfɛrjuːl/ ▻ *noun* a small sphere. • **spherular** *adj.* ◷ 17c: from Latin *sphaerula*, a diminutive of *sphaera*, from Greek *sphaira* a globe.

sphincter /ˈsfɪŋktə(r)/ ▻ *noun, anatomy* a ring of muscle that, when it contracts, closes the entrance to a cavity in the body. • **sphincteral** or **sphincterial** or **sphincteric** /sfɪŋkˈtɛrɪk/ *adj.* ◷ 16c: from Greek *sphingein* to hold tight.

sphinx /sfɪŋks/ ▻ *noun* (***sphinxes*** /ˈsfɪŋksɪz/ or ***sphinges*** /ˈsfɪndʒiːz/) **1** (**Sphinx**) *Greek mythol* a monster, with the head of a woman and the body of a lion, which strangled travellers who could not solve its riddle and which was dashed to pieces on the rocks when it leapt from its lair in rage after Oedipus did give the correct answer to the riddle. **2** (*also* **Sphinx**) any stone carving or other representation in the form of a human head and lion's body, especially the huge recumbent statue near the Egyptian pyramids at Giza. **3** a mysterious or enigmatic person. • **sphinxlike** *adj.* ◷ 14c: Latin, from Greek, from *sphingein* to hold tight, because of the mythological monster's propensity for strangulation.

sphragistics /sfrəˈdʒɪstɪks/ ▻ *singular noun* the study of seals and signet rings. • **sphragistic** *adj.* ⓘ 19c: from French *sphragistique*, from Greek *sphragis* a seal.

sphygmogram /ˈsfɪgmoʊgram/ ▻ *noun, medicine* a record of variations in blood pressure and pulse beat. ⓘ 19c: from *sphygmos* a pulse, from *sphyzo* to beat.

sphygmograph /ˈsfɪgmoʊgrɑːf/ ▻ *noun, medicine* an instrument for recording variations in blood pressure and pulse beat. • **sphygmographical** *adj.* • **sphygmographically** *adverb.* • **sphygmography** /sfɪgˈmɒgrəfɪ/ *noun.* ⓘ 19c: from Greek *sphygmos* a pulse, from *sphyzo* to beat.

sphygmomanometer /sfɪgmoʊməˈnɒmɪtə(r)/ or **sphygmometer** /sfɪgˈmɒmətə(r)/ ▻ *noun, medicine* an instrument that consists of an inflatable cuff for the arm, which is connected to a column of mercury with a graduated scale and which is used for measuring blood pressure in the arteries. ⓘ 1880s: from Greek *sphygmos* a pulse, from *sphyzo* to beat.

spic[1], **spick** or **spik** ▻ *noun, offensive* **1** a name for a Spanish-speaking person from Central or S America or the Caribbean. **2** the form of the Spanish language that is spoken by someone from this area. ⓘ Early 20c: a shortened form of *spiggoty*, supposedly a rendering of the claim 'No spikee dee English'.

spic[2] see SPICK AND SPAN

spica /ˈspaɪkə/ ▻ *noun* (*spicae* /ˈspaɪsiː/ or *spicas* /ˈspaɪkəs/) **1** *bot* a flower spike or other part that resembles a spike. **2** *surgery* a bandage that is wrapped over in a series of V-shapes so that it resembles an ear of barley. • **spicate** /ˈspaɪkeɪt/ or **spicated** /spaɪˈkeɪtəd/ *adj, bot* having, forming or in a spike; relating to a spike. ⓘ 17c: Latin, meaning 'ear of grain'.

spiccato /spɪˈkɑːtoʊ/; *Italian* spikˈkato/ ▻ *adj, adverb, music* said of a style of STACCATO on stringed instruments: played with a kind of light controlled bouncing movement of the bow. ▻ *noun* (*spiccatos*) a piece of music or a series of notes played in this way. ⓘ 18c: Italian, meaning 'detached'.

spice ▻ *noun* **1** any of various aromatic or pungent substances, such as pepper, ginger, nutmeg, cloves, cinnamon, etc that are derived from plants and used for flavouring food, eg in sauces, curries, etc, and for drinks such as punch. **2** such substances collectively. **3** something that adds interest or enjoyment ◻ ***Variety is the spice of life.*** **4** (*usually* **a spice of something**) a trace of it ◻ ***Do I detect a spice of jealousy?*** ▻ *verb* (*spiced, spicing*) **1** to flavour with spice. **2** (*also* **spice up**) to add interest or enjoyment to something. • **spicy** or **spicey** see separate entry SPICY. ⓘ 13c: from French *espice*, from Latin *species* species.

spicebush ▻ *noun* an aromatic shrub that is native to America and which is related to the laurel family.

spiced ▻ *adj* flavoured with spices.

spick and span, **spic and span** or **spik and span** ▻ *adj* **1** neat, clean and tidy. **2** lacking any signs of wear and tear. ⓘ 17c: a shortened form of the obsolete *spick and span new*, from *spick* spike + Norse *spannyr* brand-new, from *spann* a chip or shaving + *nyr* new.

spicule /ˈspɪkjuːl/ ▻ *noun* **1** something that is small, sharp, hard and pointed, such as a splinter, a shard of glass, crystal or bone, etc. **2** *zool* a sharp pointed process, such as any of the needle-like projections that form the firm part of a sponge. **3** *bot* a small flower spike. **4** *astron* a spiked projection that can be seen in the corona of the Sun and which is caused by shooting jets of gas in the Sun's atmosphere. ⓘ 18c: French, from Latin *spiculum* a sharp point.

spicy or **spicey** /ˈspaɪsɪ/ ▻ *adj* (*spicier, spiciest*) **1** flavoured with or tasting or smelling of spices; pungent; piquant. **2** *colloq* characterized by, or suggestive of, scandal, sensation, impropriety, bad taste, etc ◻ ***Got any spicy gossip?*** • **spicily** *adverb.* • **spiciness** *noun.*

spider /ˈspaɪdə(r)/ ▻ *noun* **1 a** any of thousands of species of invertebrate animals that are found in virtually all habitats, which have eight legs and two main body parts with the head and thorax fused and joined to the abdomen at a narrow waist, and which, in most cases, can produce silk for spinning webs to trap their prey; **b** any similar related species such as the spider mite, harvest mite, etc. **2** something that resembles one of these creatures, such as a snooker rest which has long legs so that it can be used to arch over a ball, or an elasticated mesh for securing luggage on a car's roof rack, etc. See also ARACHNOPHOBIA. • **spider-like** *adj.* • **spidery** see separate entry. ⓘ Anglo-Saxon *spithra*, from *spinnan* to spin.

spiderman ▻ *noun* someone whose job is to do building work on high structures such as scaffolding, steeples, etc.

spider mite ▻ *noun* any one of various kinds of plant-eating mites, such as the RED SPIDER MITE.

spider monkey ▻ *noun* any one of several kinds of tropical American monkeys which have light slender bodies, extremely long limbs and a long prehensile tail. ⓘ 18c: so called because of their long spidery limbs and tails.

spider plant ▻ *noun* a perennial plant of the lily family which has long narrow striped leaves, a flower stalk that bears clusters of small white flowers and tufts of small leaves that are able to root on contact with the soil and develop into new plants. ⓘ 19c: so called because the little plantlets resemble spiders.

spiderwort see TRADESCANTIA

spidery /ˈspaɪdərɪ/ ▻ *adj* **1** thin and straggly ◻ ***spidery handwriting.*** **2** full of spiders.

spiegeleisen /ˈspiːgəlaɪzən/ ▻ *noun* a white cast-iron that contains manganese and which is used in the BESSEMER PROCESS for the manufacture of steel. ⓘ 19c: German, from *Spiegel* mirror + *Eisen* iron.

spiel /ʃpiːl, spiːl/ *colloq* ▻ *noun* a long rambling, often implausible, story, especially one that contains an excuse, one that the speaker hopes will divert attention from something else or one given as sales patter ◻ ***gave me this whole spiel about missing the train.*** ▻ *verb* (*spieled, spieling*) **1** to talk endlessly or glibly. **2** to reel off (a prepared statement, list, etc). • **spieler** *noun.* • **spieling** *noun.* ⓘ Late 19c: German, meaning 'play' or 'a game'.

spies *plural of* SPY

spiffing /ˈspɪfɪŋ/ ▻ *adj, Brit old colloq use* excellent; splendid. ⓘ 19c.

spiflicate or **spifflicate** /ˈspɪflɪkeɪt/ ▻ *verb* (*spiflicated, spiflicating*) *humorous* to destroy, overpower or beat (in a contest, fight, etc). • **spiflication** *noun.* ⓘ 18c.

spigot /ˈspɪgət/ ▻ *noun* **1** a peg or plug, especially one that is used for stopping the vent hole in a cask or barrel. **2 a** *US* a tap; **b** a tap for controlling the flow of liquid, eg in a cask, pipe, etc. **3** an end of a pipe that fits inside another to form a joint. ⓘ 14c.

spik see SPICK AND SPAN

spike[1] ▻ *noun* **1 a** any thin sharp point; **b** a pointed piece of metal, eg one of several on railings. **2 a** one of several pointed metal pegs that are set into the soles of running-shoes; **b** (**spikes**) a pair of running-shoes with spiked soles. **3** a large metal nail. **4** *drug-taking slang* a hypodermic needle. ▻ *verb* (*spiked, spiking*) **1** to strike, pierce or impale with a pointed object. **2** *colloq* **a** to make (a drink) stronger by adding alcohol or extra alcohol; **b** to lace (a drink) with a drug. • **spiked** *adj.* • **spiky** see separate entry. • **spike someone's guns** *colloq* to spoil their plans. ⓘ Anglo-Saxon *spicing*.

spike² ▻ *noun, bot* a pointed flower-head, such as that of the hyacinth, plantain, etc, which consists of a cluster of small individual flowers growing together around, or along one side of, an axis, with the youngest flowers at the tip and the oldest ones nearest the base. ◷ 16c in this sense; 13c, meaning 'ear of corn': from Latin *spica* ear of corn.

spikelet ▻ *noun, bot* a small spike such as those that form the inflorescences of many grasses, often enclosed by a pair of bracts.

spikenard /ˈspaɪknɑːd/ ▻ *noun* **1** an aromatic plant that is native to the Himalayas and which has rose-purple flowers and aromatic underground stems. **2** an aromatic oil or ointment that is prepared from the underground stem of this plant. Also called **nard.** **3** any of several N American plants, eg some of the ginseng family, that also have aromatic roots. ◷ 14c: from Latin *spica* a spike + *nardus* nard.

spiky /ˈspaɪkɪ/ ▻ *adj* (***spikier, spikiest***) **1** having spikes or pointed ends □ ***a spiky punk hairstyle.*** **2** *colloq* bad-tempered. ● **spikily** *adverb.* ● **spikiness** *noun.*

spill¹ ▻ *verb* (*past tense, past participle* ***spilt*** or ***spilled,*** *present participle* ***spilling***) **1** *tr & intr* to run or flow or cause (a liquid, etc) to run or flow out from a container, especially accidentally. **2** *intr* to come or go in large crowds, especially quickly □ ***The spectators spilled onto the pitch.*** **3** to shed (blood, especially that of other people) □ ***a terrible war in which a lot of blood was spilled.*** **4** *colloq* to throw from a vehicle or saddle. ▻ *noun* **1** an act of spilling. **2** *colloq* a fall, especially from a vehicle or horse. ● **spill the beans** *colloq* to reveal confidential information, either inadvertently or deliberately. ◷ Anglo-Saxon *spillan.*

■ **spill over** to overflow or go beyond. See also SPILLOVER.

spill² ▻ *noun* a thin strip of wood or twisted paper for lighting a fire, candle, pipe, etc. ◷ Early 19c.

spillage ▻ *noun* **1** the act or process of spilling. **2** something that is spilt or an amount spilt.

spillikin or **spilikin** /ˈspɪlɪkɪn/ and **spellican** /ˈspelɪkən/ ▻ *noun* **1** a small thin strip of wood, bone, etc. **2** (**spillikins**) a game where lots of these strips are heaped together and the object is to try and take one after another from the pile without disturbing the others. ◷ 18c: a diminutive of SPILL².

spillover ▻ *noun* **1** an overflowing. **2** a consequence or attendant side-effect. See also SPILL OVER at SPILL.

spilt see SPILL¹

spilth /spɪlθ/ ▻ *noun* **1** an act or the process of spilling. **2** something that is spilt or an amount spilt.

spin ▻ *verb* (*past tense, past participle* ***spun,*** *present participle* ***spinning***) **1** *tr & intr* to rotate or cause to rotate repeatedly, especially quickly □ ***We spun a coin to see who would go first.*** **2** to draw out and twist (fibres, etc) into thread. **3** **a** said of spiders, silkworms, etc: to construct (a web, cocoon, etc) from the silky thread they produce; **b** to tell (lies) □ ***spun a complex web of lies.*** **4** **a** to bowl, throw, kick, strike, etc (a ball) so that it rotates while moving forward, causing a change in the expected direction or speed; **b** said of a ball, etc: to be delivered in this way. **5** *intr* said of someone's head, etc: to have a revolving and disorientated sensation, especially one that is brought on by excitement, amazement, drugs or alcohol, etc. **6** to dry (washing) in a spin-dryer. **7** said of the wheels of a motor vehicle: to turn rapidly but without any forward momentum. **8** to play (a record, CD, cassette, etc) □ ***a station that spins mainly indie stuff.*** ▻ *noun* **1** an act or process of spinning or a spinning motion. **2** rotation in a ball thrown, struck, etc. **3** a nose-first spiral descent in an aircraft, especially one that is out of control. Also called **tailspin.** **4** *colloq* a short trip in a vehicle, for pleasure. **5** *colloq* an act of playing a record, etc. **6** said of information, a news report, etc, especially that of a political nature: a favourable bias □ ***The PR department will put a spin on it.*** ● **spinning** *noun, adj.* ● **spun** see separate entry. ● **spin a yarn, tale,** *etc* to tell a story, especially a long improbable one. ◷ Anglo-Saxon *spinnan.*

■ **spin out** **1** to prolong (an activity, etc). **2** to cause (something) to last longer through economical use.

■ **spin round** to turn around, especially quickly or unexpectedly.

spina bifida /ˈspaɪnə ˈbɪfɪdə, — ˈbaɪfɪdə/ ▻ *noun, pathol* a congenital defect where one or more vertebrae fail to surround the meninges and the spinal cord fully during the development of the embryo, leaving them exposed. It results in various degrees of disability, with severe cases manifesting permanent paralysis of the legs and mental retardation. ◷ 18c: Latin, from *spina* spine + *bifidus* split in two.

spinach /ˈspɪnɪtʃ, ˈspɪnɪdʒ/ ▻ *noun* **1** an annual plant that is native to Asia, but which is now widely cultivated in temperate regions for its edible leaves. **2** the young dark green crinkly or flat edible leaves of this plant which are particularly rich in iron and which are cooked and eaten as a vegetable or used raw in salads. ● **spinachy** *adj.* ◷ 16c: from French *espinache* spinach.

spinal ▻ *adj* belonging, relating or referring to the SPINE.

spinal anaesthesia ▻ *noun* anaesthesia of the lower half of the body which is achieved by injecting an anaesthetic beneath the ARACHNOID. See also EPIDURAL.

spinal canal ▻ *noun* the passage where the spinal cord lies and which runs the length of the spinal column.

spinal column ▻ *noun* the spine.

spinal cord ▻ *noun* a cord-like structure of nerve tissue that is enclosed and protected by the spinal column and which connects the brain to nerves in all other parts of the body. Together with the brain, it forms the CENTRAL NERVOUS SYSTEM.

spinal nerve ▻ *noun, anatomy* any of the 31 pairs of nerves that in humans arise from the spinal cord and extend to all parts of the body.

spinal tap ▻ *noun* a LUMBAR PUNCTURE.

spin bowler ▻ *noun, cricket* a bowler whose technique involves importing variations to the flight and/or SPIN (*noun* 2) of the ball.

spindle /ˈspɪndəl/ ▻ *noun* **1** **a** a rod with a notched or tapered end that is designed for twisting the thread in hand-spinning and which is the place where the spun thread is wound; **b** a similar device in a spinning wheel; **c** any of several similar devices in a spinning machine which twist the thread and wind it onto the bobbins. **2** a pin or axis which turns, or around which something else turns □ ***a record-player with a spindle for 10 singles.*** **3** a piece of wood that has been turned, especially one that is used as an upright member, eg in a banister or as a chair or table leg, etc. **4** *biol* a spindle-shaped structure of protein filaments that is formed during cell division and which serves to draw the newly divided chromosomes apart. **5** *in compounds* □ ***spindle-legged.*** ◷ Anglo-Saxon *spinel,* from *spinnan* to spin.

spindly /ˈspɪndlɪ/ ▻ *adj* (***spindlier, spindliest***) *colloq* long, thin and, often, frail-looking.

spin doctor ▻ *noun, colloq* someone, especially in politics, who tries to influence public opinion by putting a favourable bias on information when it is presented to the public or to the media. ● **spin-doctoring** *noun.* ◷ 1980s.

spindrift /ˈspɪndrɪft/ ▻ *noun* **1** spray that is blown from the crests of waves. **2** driving or driven snow, sand, etc. ◷ 17c: originally a Scots variation of the obsolete *spoondrift,* from *spoon* to be blown by the wind + DRIFT .

spin-dry ▷ *verb* (***spin-dried*** or ***spun-dry, spin-drying*** or ***spinning-dry***) to partly dry (wet laundry) in a spin dryer.

spin dryer or **spin drier** ▷ *noun* an electrically powered machine, which can either be part of a washing machine or free-standing, that takes some of the water out of wet laundry by spinning it at high speed in a revolving drum.

spine ▷ *noun* **1** in vertebrates: the flexible bony structure, consisting of a column of vertebrae connected by cartilage discs, that surrounds and protects the spinal cord and articulates with the skull, ribs and pelvic girdle. **2** the narrow middle section in the cover of a book that hides the part where the pages are fastened in and which often carries details of the title and/or author. **3** in certain plants and animals, eg cacti, hedgehogs, porcupines, etc: one of many sharply pointed structures that protect the plant or animal against predators. **4** *usually with negatives, colloq* courage; strength of character □ ***hasn't got the spine to answer back.*** ⌚ 15c: from French *espine*, from Latin *spina* thorn, prickle or backbone.

spine-chiller ▷ *noun* something, such as a frightening story, a thought, etc, that sends, or almost sends, shivers down one's spine. • **spine-chilling** *adj.*

spinel /spɪˈnɛl/ ▷ *noun* any of a group of hard glassy crystalline minerals of various colours, that contain oxides of magnesium, aluminium, iron, zinc or manganese and which are used as gemstones. ⌚ 16c: from French *espinelle*, from Latin *spina* thorn, because of the shape of the crystals.

spineless ▷ *adj* **1** invertebrate. **2** said of a plant or animal: having no spiny prickles. **3** *colloq* said of someone, their attitude, behaviour, etc: lacking courage or strength of character. • **spinelessly** *adverb.* • **spinelessness** *noun.*

spinet /spɪˈnɛt, ˈspɪnɪt/ ▷ *noun* a musical instrument like a small harpsichord. ⌚ 17c: from French *espinette*, from Italian *spinetta.*

spinnaker /ˈspɪnəkə(r)/ ▷ *noun* a large triangular sail set at the front of a yacht. ⌚ Late 19c.

spinner ▷ *noun* **1** someone or something that spins. **2** a spin dryer. **3** an angler's lure that has a projecting wing which makes it spin in the water when the line is pulled. **4** *cricket* **a** a spin bowler; **b** a ball that is bowled with spin. **5** a manufacturer or merchant of thread, etc.

spinneret ▷ *noun* **1** *zool* in spiders, silkworms, etc: a small tubular organ that produces the silky thread which they use in making webs, cocoons, etc. **2** a plate with several holes in it that is used in the manufacture of synthetic fibres.

spinney /ˈspɪnɪ/ ▷ *noun* (***spinneys***) a small wood or thicket, especially one that has a prickly undergrowth. ⌚ 16c: from French *espinei* a place full of thorns and brambles, from Latin *spina* thorn.

spinning-jenny /spɪnɪŋˈdʒɛnɪ/ ▷ *noun* a type of early spinning machine that has several spindles.

spinning top see TOP²

spinning-wheel ▷ *noun* a machine with a spindle driven by a wheel that is operated either by hand or by the foot and which is used, especially in the home, for spinning thread or yarn.

spin-off ▷ *noun* **1** a side-effect or by-product, especially one that is beneficial or valuable. **2** something that comes about because of the success of an earlier product or idea, eg a television series derived from a successful film.

spinose /spaɪˈnoʊs/ ▷ *adj, biol* said of a plant or animal, or of a specified body part: covered with spines; prickly.

spinous /ˈspaɪnəs/ ▷ *adj* **1** *biol* SPINOSE. **2** relating to or resembling a spine or thorn.

spinster /ˈspɪnstə(r)/ ▷ *noun* a woman, especially one who is middle-aged or older, who has never been married. • **spinsterhood** *noun.* • **spinsterish** *adj.* • **spinsterly** *adj.* ⌚ 14c as *spinnestere* a woman who spins thread.

spinule /ˈspaɪnjʊl/ *biol* ▷ *noun* a tiny spine or thorn. • **spinulose** or **spinulous** *adj.*

spiny /ˈspaɪnɪ/ ▷ *adj* (***spinier, spiniest***) **1** said of plants or animals: covered with spines; prickly. **2** troublesome; difficult to deal with □ ***a spiny problem.*** • **spininess** *noun.*

spiny anteater ▷ *noun* an ECHIDNA.

spiny lobster see LANGOUSTE

spiracle /ˈspaɪrəkəl/ and **spiraculum** /spaɪˈrakjʊləm/ ▷ *noun* (***spiracles*** or ***spiracula*** /spaɪˈrakjʊlə/) *zool* **1** any of various paired openings along the side of an insect's body that are used for breathing, each of which represents the external opening of a trachea. **2** the breathing hole in some fish, whales and sharks. ⌚ 17c: from Latin *spiraculum*, from *spirare* to breath.

spiraea or **spirea** /spaɪˈriːə/ ▷ *noun* (***spiraeas*** or ***spireas***) a deciduous northern temperate shrub of the rose family which has clusters of small white or pink flowers. ⌚ 17c: Latin, from Greek *speiraia* privet, from *speira* coil.

spiral /ˈspaɪərəl/ ▷ *noun* **1** the pattern that is made by a line winding outwards from a central point in circles or near-circles of regularly increasing size. **2** the pattern that is made by a line winding upwards or downwards from a specific point in circles or near-circles of the same or ever-increasing size, as if it were describing the shape of a cylinder or cone. **3** a curve or course that makes this kind of a pattern. **4** a gradual but continuous rise or fall, eg of prices, wages, etc. ▷ *adj* being in or having the shape or nature of a spiral □ ***a spiral staircase.*** ▷ *verb* (***spiralled, spiralling***; or (*US*) ***spiraled, spiraling***) **1** *intr* to follow a spiral course or pattern. **2** to make something into a spiral. **3** *intr* said especially of prices, wages, etc: to go up or down, usually quickly □ ***Prices were spiralling out of control.*** • **spiraliform** /spaɪəˈralɪfɔːm/ *adj.* • **spirality** *noun.* • **spiralled** or (*US*) **spiraled** *adj.* • **spirally** *adverb.* ⌚ 16c: from Latin *spiralis*, from Greek *speira* coil.

spiral galaxy ▷ *noun, astron* a class of galaxy that has older stars, etc in the centre, and structures called **spiral arms**, composed of dust, gas and younger stars, spiralling out from and around its nucleus. This is the shape and construction that the Milky Way is thought to have.

spire¹ /ˈspaɪə(r)/ ▷ *noun* **1** a tall thin structure tapering upwards to a point, especially the top of a tower on a church roof. Compare STEEPLE. **2** anything tall and tapering, eg a flower spike, the top of a tree, etc. ⌚ Anglo-Saxon *spir* shoot or sprout.

spire² /ˈspaɪə(r)/ ▷ *noun* **1** a coil or spiral; a single loop of a coil or spiral. **2** *zool* the top part of a spiral shell. • **spirated** *adj.* ⌚ 16c: from Greek *speira* coil.

spirit /ˈspɪrɪt/ ▷ *noun* **1** the animating or vitalizing essence or force that motivates, invigorates or energizes someone or something. **2** this force as an independent part of a person, widely believed to survive the body after death, and sometimes said to be visible as a ghost. **3** a supernatural being without a body □ ***Evil spirits haunted the house.*** **4** **a** temperament, frame of mind, etc, usually of a specified kind □ ***She always had a very independent spirit***; **b** the dominant or prevalent mood, attitude, etc □ ***tried to gauge public spirit***; **c** the characteristic essence, nature, etc of something □ ***the spirit of friendship*** □ ***the spirit of Christmas***; **d** courage □ ***team spirit***; **e** liveliness or vivacity □ ***enter into the spirit of the party***; **f** a person or thing that has a specified nature or quality □ ***thinks of himself as a free spirit.*** **5** the underlying essential meaning or intention, as distinct from literal interpretation □ ***in accordance with the spirit, not the letter, of the law.*** **6** a distilled alcoholic drink, eg whisky, brandy, gin, etc. **7** *chem* a volatile liquid obtained by distillation. ▷ *verb* (***spirited, spiriting***) **1** (*usually* **spirit something** or **someone away** or **off**) to carry or convey them mysteriously or magically. **2** (*usually* **spirit up**) to give or add determination, courage or liveliness. • **in good** or **high,** *etc* **spirits** in a happy, contented, etc mood. • **in spirit** as a presence that is perceived to be there □ ***I'll be with you in spirit, if not in person.*** • **out of spirits** sad or depressed. ⓘ 13c: from French *espirit*, from Latin *spiritus*, from *spirare* to breathe.

the Spirit see THE HOLY GHOST

spirited ▻ *adj* **1** full of courage or liveliness. **2** *in compounds* having or showing a specified kind of spirit, mood, attitude, etc □ ***high-spirited.*** • **spiritedly** *adverb*. • **spiritedness** *noun*.

spirit gum ▻ *noun* a quick-drying sticky substance that is especially used, eg by actors, for securing false facial hair.

spirit-lamp ▻ *noun* a lamp that burns methylated or other spirit as opposed to oil.

spirit level ▻ *noun* a device that consists of a flat bar with a short glass tube almost filled with liquid set inside it, and which is used for testing and ascertaining the horizontal or vertical levelness of a surface on which it is placed by seeing whether or not the large air bubble in the liquid lies precisely between two markings on the tube.

spirits of ammonia or **spirit of ammonia** ▻ *noun* SAL VOLATILE.

spirits of salt or **spirit of salt** ▻ *noun* hydrochloric acid in solution with water.

spirits of wine or **spirit of wine** ▻ *noun* alcohol.

spiritual /ˈspɪrɪtʃʊəl/ ▻ *adj* **1** belonging, referring or relating to the spirit or soul rather than to the body or to physical things. **2** belonging, referring or relating to religion; sacred, holy or divine □ ***a spiritual leader.*** **3 a** belonging, referring or relating to, or arising from, the mind or intellect; **b** highly refined in thought, feelings, etc. **4** belonging, referring or relating to spirits, ghosts, etc □ ***the spiritual world.*** ▻ *noun* (*also* **Negro spiritual**) a type of religious song that is characterized by voice harmonies and which developed from the communal singing traditions of Black people in the southern states of the USA. • **spirituality** *noun*. • **spiritually** *adverb*. • **spiritualness** *noun*. ⓘ 13c: from Latin *spiritualis*; see SPIRIT.

spiritualism ▻ *noun* **1 a** the belief that it is possible to have communication with the spirits of dead people, eg through a MEDIUM 3, a OUIJA board, etc. **b** the practice of this. **2** *philos* the doctrine that a person's spirit continues to exist after their physical death or that the spirit world is the only form of reality.

spiritualist ▻ *noun* someone who believes in or practises spiritualism. • **spiritualistic** *adj*.

spiritualize or **spiritualise** ▻ *verb* (***spiritualized, spiritualizing***) to make someone or something spiritual or more spiritual. • **spiritualization** *noun*. • **spiritualizer** *noun*.

spirituous ▻ *adj* **1** having a high alcohol content. **2** said of an alcoholic drink such as rum, whisky, etc: obtained by distillation. • **spirituosity** or **spirituousness** *noun*.

spirochaete /ˈspaɪərouki:t/ ▻ *noun, biol* any of a group of non-rigid spiral-shaped bacteria, many of which feed on dead organic matter, although some are parasitic and live in the intestines and genital regions of animals, causing various diseases, including syphilis in humans. ⓘ Late 19c: from Greek *speira* a coil + *chaite* long hair.

spirograph /ˈspaɪərougrɑ:f/ ▻ *noun, medicine* a device for measuring and recording breathing movements. ⓘ 19c: from Greek *speira* a coil.

spirogyra /spaɪərouˈdʒaɪərə/ ▻ *noun* a green alga which is found either floating or fixed to stones in ponds and streams and whose colour is due to its spiralling chloroplasts. ⓘ Late 19c: from Greek *speira* a coil + *gyros* circle.

spirt see SPURT

spit¹ ▻ *verb* (*past tense, past participle* ***spat*** or (*US*) ***spit***, *present participle* ***spitting***) **1 a** *tr & intr* to expel (saliva or phlegm) from the mouth; **b** *intr* to do this as a gesture of contempt □ ***spat in his face.*** **2** (*also* **spit out**) to eject (eg food) forcefully out of the mouth. **3** said of a fire, fat or oil in a pan, etc: to throw off (a spark of hot coal, oil, etc) in a spurt or spurts. **4** to speak or utter with contempt, hate, violence, etc. **5** *intr* said of rain or snow: to fall in light intermittent drops or flakes. **6** said especially of a cat: to make a hissing noise in anger, hostility, aggression, etc. ▻ *noun* **1** spittle; a blob of saliva or phlegm that has been spat from the mouth. **2** an act of spitting. • **spitter** *noun*. • **spitting** *noun, adj*. • **be, lie,** *etc* **in** or **within spitting distance (of)** to be very close by □ ***The flat's within spitting distance of the office.*** • **the spit** or **very spit** *colloq* an exact likeness; a spitting image □ ***She's the very spit of her mother.*** • **spit blood** to be utterly furious. • **spit it out** *colloq* usually said as a command: to say what one has been hesitating to say □ ***Come on, spit it out! Are you saying I'm a liar?*** ⓘ Anglo-Saxon *spittan*.

spit² ▻ *noun* **1 a** a long thin metal rod on which meat is skewered and held over a fire for roasting; **b** a similar device in a gas or electric cooker or oven. **2** a long narrow strip of land that juts out into the water. ▻ *verb* (***spitted, spitting***) **1** to put (a piece of meat, etc) on a spit. **2** to pierce or stab with something sharp. ⓘ Anglo-Saxon *spitu*.

spit³ ▻ *verb* (***spitted, spitting***) to dig or plant using a spade. ▻ *noun* a spade's depth or a spadeful. ⓘ Anglo-Saxon *spittan*.

spit and polish ▻ *noun, colloq* **1** the routine cleaning duties of a soldier, sailor, etc. **2** *often derog* exceptional cleanliness, tidiness, smartness, correctness, etc.

spit-and-sawdust ▻ *adj* basic; lacking luxury or refinement. ⓘ 1930s: from the sawdust that was formerly strewn on pub floors to absorb men's spit.

spitchcock /ˈspɪtʃkɒk/ ▻ *noun* an eel that is split down the middle, sometimes coated in breadcrumbs, and fried or grilled. ▻ *verb* (***spitchcocked, spitchcocking***) to cook (an eel, chicken, etc) in this way. Compare SPATCHCOCK. ⓘ 17c.

spite ▻ *noun* **1** the desire to intentionally and maliciously hurt or offend; ill-will. **2** an instance of this; a grudge. ▻ *verb* (***spited, spiting***) *chiefly* used in the infinitive form: to annoy, offend, thwart, etc intentionally and maliciously. • **in spite of** regardless; notwithstanding □ ***decided to go in spite of the rain.*** ⓘ 14c: from French *despit*; see DESPITE.

spiteful ▻ *adj* motivated by spite; vengeful; malicious. • **spitefully** *adverb*. • **spitefulness** *noun*.

spitfire ▻ *noun* someone who has a quick or fiery temper, especially a woman or girl. ⓘ 17c.

spitting image ▻ *noun, colloq* an exact likeness; a double.

spittle /ˈspɪtəl/ ▻ *noun* saliva, especially when it has been spat from the mouth; spit. ⓘ Anglo-Saxon *spatl*.

spittoon /spɪˈtu:n/ ▻ *noun* a container for spitting into, especially one that would formerly have been placed on the floor of a pub. ⓘ 19c: from SPIT *verb*¹ + *-oon* as in BALLOON, etc.

spitz /spɪts/ ▻ *noun* (***spitzes***) a breed of dog with a thick coat, a pointed foxy face, pricked ears and a tail that curls up over its back. ⓘ 19c: German, meaning 'pointed'.

spiv ▻ *noun, colloq* a man who sells, deals in, or is otherwise involved in the trading of, illicit, blackmarket or stolen goods, and who is usually dressed in a very flashy way. • **spivvy** *adj*. ⓘ 1930s.

splanchnic /ˈsplaŋknɪk/ ▻ *adj, anatomy* belonging, referring or relating to the VISCERA; intestinal. ⓘ 17c: from Latin *splanchnicus*, from Greek *splanchna* entrails.

splash ▻ *verb* (***splashes***, ***splashed***, ***splashing***) **1 a** to make (a liquid or semi-liquid substance) to fly around or land in drops; **b** *intr* said of a liquid or semi-liquid substance: to fly around or land in drops. **2** to make something wet or dirty (with drops of liquid or semi-liquid) □ *The bus splashed them with mud.* **3** to print or display something boldly □ *The photograph was splashed across the front page.* ▻ *noun* (***splashes***) **1** a sound of splashing. **2** an amount splashed. **3** a stain made by splashing. **4** an irregular spot or patch □ *splashes of colour.* **5** *colloq* a small amount of liquid; a dash □ *tea with just a splash of milk.* • **splashing** *noun, adj.* • **splashy** *adj.* • **make a splash** to attract a great deal of attention, especially deliberately or with outrageous behaviour. ⓘ 18c: from Anglo-Saxon *plasc.*

■ **splash about, around, in, into,** *etc* to make noisy splashes.

■ **splash down** said of the crew or capsule of a space rocket: to land at sea. See also SPLASHDOWN.

■ **splash out** or **splash out on something** *colloq* to spend a lot of money, especially extravagantly or ostentatiously □ *He splashed out on a fancy new car.*

splashdown ▻ *noun* the act or process of the crew or capsule of a space rocket landing at sea.

splat[1] ▻ *noun* the sound made by a soft wet object striking a surface. ▻ *adverb* with this sound □ *She gave him a custard pie splat in the face.* ▻ *verb* (***splatted***, ***splatting***) to hit, fall, land, etc with a splat. ⓘ Late 19c: a shortened form of SPLATTER.

splat[2] ▻ *noun* a flat, usually wooden, structure that forms the middle part of the back of a chair. ⓘ 19c.

splatter /ˈsplatə(r)/ ▻ *verb* (***splattered***, ***splattering***) **1** *tr & intr* (*often* **splatter something with something**) to make it dirty with lots of small scattered drops. **2** said of water, mud, etc: to wet or dirty □ *The mud splattered him from head to toe.* **3** to publicize, especially in a sensational way □ *News of their affair was splattered over every front page.* ▻ *noun* **1** a splashing sound, especially a repeated or continuous one. **2** a splash or spattering, eg of colour, mud, etc. ⓘ 18c.

splatter movie and **splatter film** ▻ *noun* a film that has a lot of on-screen violence and blood-spilling. Compare SNUFF MOVIE. ⓘ 1970s.

splatterpunk ▻ *noun* a genre of fiction that has a lot of graphically detailed violence and blood-spilling in it.

splay ▻ *verb* (***splayed***, ***splaying***) to spread (eg the fingers). ▻ *noun* a sloping surface that is at an oblique angle to a wall, especially one that widens the aspect of a window, door, etc. ▻ *adj* **1** broad and flat. **2** said of a foot, knee, etc: turned outwards. ⓘ 14c: from DISPLAY.

splay foot ▻ *noun* a foot that turns outwards, especially one that is broad and flat. • **splay-footed** *adj.*

spleen ▻ *noun* **1 a** a delicate organ which, in humans, is situated on the left side of the abdomen and beneath the diaphragm. It is involved in the production of LYMPHOCYTES, and it also destroys red blood cells that are no longer functional and acts as a reservoir for blood; **b** the equivalent organ in other animals. **2** bad temper; moroseness. **3** anger; spitefulness □ *vented his spleen by punching the wall.* • **splenetic** see separate entry. ⓘ 13c: from French *esplen*, from Latin *splen*; senses 2 and 3 came about from the belief that this organ was the seat of melancholy.

splendid /ˈsplɛndɪd/ ▻ *adj* **1** very good; excellent. **2** magnificent; impressively grand or sumptuous. • **splendidly** *adverb.* • **splendidness** *noun.* ⓘ 17c: from Latin *splendidus* shining or brilliant, from *splendere* to be bright.

splendiferous /splɛnˈdɪfərəs/ ▻ *adj, now colloq, humorous* splendid. • **splendiferously** *adverb.* • **splendiferousness** *noun.* ⓘ 15c: from Latin *splendorifer* carrying brightness.

splendour or (*US*) **splendor** /ˈsplɛndə(r)/ ▻ *noun* magnificence, opulence or grandeur. • **splendorous** or **splendrous** *adj.* ⓘ 15c: from French *esplendur*, from Latin *splendor*, from *splendere* to shine.

splenectomy /splɪˈnɛktəmɪ/ ▻ *noun* (***splenectomies***) *surgery* the removal of a diseased or damaged spleen. ⓘ 19c.

splenetic /splɪˈnɛtɪk/ ▻ *adj* **1** (*also* **splenic** /ˈsplɛnɪk, ˈspliːnɪk/) belonging, referring or relating to the spleen. **2** bad-tempered; spiteful; full of spleen. • **splenetical** *adj.* • **splenetically** *adverb.*

splenitis /splɪˈnaɪtəs/ ▻ *noun* inflammation of the spleen. ⓘ 18c: from SPLEEN + -ITIS.

splenius /ˈspliːnɪəs/ ▻ *noun* (***splenii*** /ˈspliːnɪaɪ/) *anatomy* either of the two large thick muscles in the back of the neck. • **splenial** *adj.* ⓘ 19c: from Latin *splenium*, from Greek *splenion* a bandage.

splice ▻ *verb* (***spliced***, ***splicing***) **1** to join (two pieces of rope) by weaving the strands of one into the other. **2** to join (two pieces of timber, etc) by overlapping and securing the ends. **3** to join the neatened ends of (two pieces of film, magnetic tape, wire, etc) using solder, adhesive, etc. ▻ *noun* a join made in one of these ways. • **splicer** *noun.* • **get spliced** *colloq* to get married. • **splice the mainbrace** *naut* **1** to give out or consume an extra portion of rum. **2** to start a drinking session. ⓘ 16c: from Dutch *splissen.*

spliff *colloq* ▻ *noun* **1** a cigarette that contains cannabis. Also called JOINT (sense 5). **2** cannabis. ▻ *verb* (***spliffed***, ***spliffing***) to smoke a cigarette that contains cannabis. • **spliffed** (*sometimes* **spliffed out**) *adj* high on cannabis. • **spliffer** *noun.* • **spliffing** *noun, adj.* ⓘ 1930s: West Indian.

spline ▻ *noun* **1** any of a number of rectangular keys that fit into the grooves in the shaft of a wheel and which allow for longitudinal movement. **2** a flexible instrument that is used for drawing curved lines. **3** a long thin narrow piece of wood, metal, plastic, etc. ▻ *verb* (***splined***, ***splining***) to fit with splines (*noun* 1). ⓘ 18c.

splint ▻ *noun* **1** a piece of rigid material that is strapped to a broken limb, etc to hold it in position while the bone heals. **2** a tumour or bony outgrowth that can develop on the leg, usually on the inside, of a horse, donkey, etc. **3** a strip of wood, etc. **4** a shortened form of SPLINT-COAL. **5** a SPILL[2]. ▻ *verb* (***splinted***, ***splinting***) to bind or hold (a broken limb, etc) in position using a splint (*noun* 1). ⓘ 13c: from Dutch *splinte.*

splint-coal ▻ *noun* a hard, highly bituminous coal that gives off a lot of heat. ⓘ 18c.

splinter /ˈsplɪntə(r)/ ▻ *noun* **1** a small thin sharp piece that has broken off a hard substance, eg wood or glass. **2** a fragment of an exploded shell, etc. ▻ *verb* (***splintered***, ***splintering***) *tr & intr* **1** to break into splinters. **2** said of a group, political party, etc: to divide or become divided □ *The party splintered over green issues.* • **splintery** *adj.* • **splinter-proof** *adj, military* able to withstand splinters, eg from bursting shells, bombs, etc. ⓘ 14c: Dutch, and related to SPLINT.

splinter-bar ▻ *noun* a cross-bar in a horse-drawn coach that the traces (TRACE[2]) are attached to. ⓘ 18c.

splinter group ▻ *noun* a small group, especially a political one, that is formed by individuals who have broken away from the main group, especially because of some disagreement, eg over policy, principles, etc.

splish ▻ *noun, verb informal* SPLASH.

split ▻ *verb* (***split***, ***splitting***) **1** *tr & intr* to divide or break or cause to divide or break apart or into, usually two, pieces, especially lengthways. **2** to divide or share, money, etc. **3** (*also* **split up**) *tr & intr* **a** to divide or separate into smaller amounts, groups, parts, etc; **b** to divide or separate or cause to divide or separate, eg because of disagreement, disharmony, etc □ *European policy split the party* □ *split up with his boyfriend.* See also SPLIT-UP. **4**

intr, colloq to go away or leave □ ***Let's split and go back for a smoke.*** **5** said of a ship: to be wrecked. ▷ *noun* **1 a** an act or the process of separating or dividing; **b** a division, especially of money, etc □ ***a two-way split on the Lottery winnings.*** **2** a lengthways break or crack. **3** a separation or division through disagreement. **4** a dessert that consists of fruit, especially a banana, sliced open and topped with cream and/or ice-cream, sauce, nuts, etc. **5** (**the splits**) an acrobatic leap or drop to the floor so that the legs form a straight line and each leg is at right angles to the torso. ▷ *adj* divided, especially in two. • **splitter** *noun.* • **splitting** see separate entry. • **split the difference 1** said of two people, groups, parties, etc: to come to a compromise where each makes an equal concession. **2** to divide a remaining amount equally. • **split hairs** to make or argue about fine and trivial distinctions. • **split one's sides** *colloq* to laugh uncontrollably. ⓘ 16c: from Dutch *splitten* to cleave.

■ **split away** or **split off** to separate from or break away from; to diverge □ ***split away from the rest of the group and found a short cut*** □ ***The road splits off to the right.***

■ **split on someone** *colloq* to inform on them, especially to someone in authority.

split capital trust ▷ *noun, finance* an investment trust that has several kinds of security with different rights and a limited life.

split end ▷ *noun* (*usually* **split ends**) hair that has divided at the end, usually as a result of the general condition of the hair being poor.

split infinitive ▷ *noun, grammar* an INFINITIVE that has an adverb or other word coming in between the particle *to* and the verb, as in *to really believe, to boldly go*, etc.

split infinitive

• A split infinitive occurs when the particle 'to' is separated, usually by an adverb, from the verb itself, as in *to really believe*. It has been a feature of English for centuries, and the superstition that it is necessarily incorrect or poor style arose in the mid-19c when attitudes to grammar were influenced by Classical models, especially Latin. The term 'split infinitive' is not found before the late 19c.

• There are occasions when a split infinitive seems clumsy, and then on stylistic grounds it is best to avoid it, eg □ *She went quickly to her room to hurriedly get her hairdrier into action* might be better put in the form □ *She went quickly to her room and hurriedly got her hairdrier into action.* In other cases, the close connection of adverb and verb requires them to come close together □ *He raised his other hand to gently caress her soft shoulders* □ *He was never one to idly beat about the bush.*

• Some modifying words like *only* and *really* have to come between *to* and the verb in order to achieve the right meaning, eg □ *Part of a personnel officer's job is to really get to know all the staff* □ *You've done enough to more than make up for it.*

☆ RECOMMENDATION: it is acceptable to use a split infinitive when the rhythm and meaning of the sentence call for it. Avoid the split infinitive if it is awkward, or rephrase the sentence. It is prudent to avoid the split infinitive when speaking or writing to prescriptively minded people.

split-level ▷ *adj* said of a house, room, etc: being on or having more than one level or floor.

split pea ▷ *noun* a dried pea that is split in half and used in soups, stews, etc.

split personality ▷ *noun* **1** a non-technical name for MULTIPLE PERSONALITY. **2** a propensity towards sudden mood swings.

split pin ▷ *noun* a type of pin that consists of a piece of metal doubled over to form a loop at the head and where the ends can be passed through a hole in a bolt and folded back to secure it firmly in place.

split screen ▷ *noun* a cinematic technique where two or more images are projected alongside each other, eg showing both participants in a telepone conversation.

split second ▷ *noun* a fraction of a second □ ***In a split second she was gone.***

split shift ▷ *noun* a period of work that is divided into two separate and distinct spells of duty, eg a waitress might work over breakfast time and then not come back on duty again until lunchtime.

splitting ▷ *adj* **1** said of a headache: very painful; severe. **2** said of a head: gripped by severe pain □ ***woke up and my head was absolutely splitting.*** See also EAR-SPLITTING.

split-up ▷ *noun* an act or the process of separation or division, especially of a couple who were sexually or romantically involved.

splodge and **splotch** ▷ *noun* a large splash, stain or patch. ▷ *verb* (***splodged, splodging***) *tr & intr* to mark with splodges. • **splodgily** *adverb.* • **splodginess** *noun.* • **splodgy** *adj.*

splosh ▷ *noun* ▷ *verb informal* SPLASH.

splurge /splɜːdʒ/ ▷ *noun* **1** an ostentatious display. **2** a bout of extravagance, eg a spending spree. ▷ *verb* (***splurged, splurging***) *tr & intr* to spend extravagantly or ostentatiously. • **splurgy** *adj.*

splutter /ˈsplʌtə(r)/ ▷ *verb* (***spluttered, spluttering***) **1** *intr* to put or throw out drops of liquid, bits of food, sparks, etc with spitting sounds. **2** *intr* to make intermittent noises or movements, especially as a sign of something being wrong □ ***The car spluttered to a halt.*** **3** *tr & intr* to speak or say haltingly or incoherently, eg through embarrassment □ ***could only splutter that he didn't know the answer.*** ▷ *noun* the act or noise of spluttering. • **splutterer** *noun.* • **spluttering** *adj, noun.* • **splutteringly** *adverb.* • **spluttery** *adj.* ⓘ 17c.

Spode or **spode** /spoʊd/ ▷ *noun, trademark* a type of fine china or porcelain. ⓘ 1860s: named after the English potter, Josiah Spode (1754–1827).

spoil ▷ *verb* (*past tense, past participle* ***spoilt*** or ***spoiled***, *present participle* ***spoiling***) **1** to impair, ruin or make useless or valueless. **2** to mar or make less enjoyable □ ***The contrived ending spoiled the film.*** **3 a** to treat someone or something in an indulgent way; **b** to harm (a child, pet, etc) by the kind of over-indulgence that will lead to selfish behaviour, unreasonable expectations of others, etc □ ***She is spoiling that boy — he never even has to tidy his room.*** **4** *intr* said of food: to become unfit to eat. **5** to deliberately deface (a ballot paper, voting slip, etc) in order to make it invalid. ▷ *noun* (*always* **spoils**) **1** possessions taken by force; plunder □ ***the spoils of war.*** **2** any benefits or rewards □ ***a company car — just one of the spoils of the new job.*** • **be spoiling for something** to seek out (a fight, argument, etc) eagerly. • **be spoiled** or **spoilt for choice** to have so many options or alternatives that it is hard to decide which to choose. ⓘ 13c: from French *espoillier*, from Latin *spoliare*, from *spolium* plunder or booty.

spoilage ▷ *noun* **1** an act or the process of spoiling. **2** decay or deterioration of food. **3** waste, especially waste paper caused by bad printing.

spoiled or **spoilt** ▷ *adj* **1** said of a child, pet, etc: selfish, demanding, greedy, etc, especially because of having been over-indulged, pampered, etc. **2** damaged, injured, marred, etc.

spoiler ▷ *noun* **1** a flap on an aircraft wing that is used for increasing drag and so assists in its descent by reducing the air speed. **2** a fixed horizontal structure on a car that is designed to put pressure on the wheels and so increase its roadholding capacity, especially at high speeds. **3** someone or something that spoils.

spoilsport ▷ *noun, colloq* someone who mars or detracts from the fun or enjoyment of others, especially by refusing to join in.

spoilt see SPOIL, SPOILED

spoke[1] *past tense of* SPEAK

spoke[2] /spoʊk/ ▷ *noun* **1** any of the radiating rods or bars that fan out from the hub of a wheel and attach it to the the rim. **2** any of the radial handles that project from the wheel for steering a ship, etc. **3** a rung of a ladder. ▷ *verb* (***spoked***, ***spoking***) to fit with a spoke or spokes. • **spoked** *adj.* • **put a spoke in someone's wheel** to upset their plans, especially intentionally or maliciously. ⓘ Anglo-Saxon *spaca*.

spoken /ˈspoʊkən/ ▷ *adj* **1** uttered or expressed in speech. **2** *in compounds* speaking in a specified way ◻ *well-spoken.* ▷ *verb*, past participle of SPEAK. • **be spoken for 1** to be reserved or taken ◻ *All the tickets have been spoken for.* **2** said of someone: to be married, engaged or in a steady relationship.

spokeshave ▷ *noun* a two-handled tool that is designed for planing curved surfaces. ⓘ 16c: from SPOKE[2] + SHAVE.

spokesman ▷ *noun* a male SPOKESPERSON. ⓘ 16c.

spokesperson ▷ *noun* (***spokespersons***) someone who is appointed to speak on behalf of other people, a specified group, a government, business, etc ◻ *a government spokesperson for defence.* ⓘ 1970s: a politically correct term that was coined in order to obviate the need to use gender-orientated words like SPOKESMAN and SPOKESWOMAN.

spokeswoman ▷ *noun* a female SPOKESPERSON. ⓘ 17c.

spoliation /spoʊlɪˈeɪʃən/ ▷ *noun* **1 a** an act, instance or the process of robbing, plundering, etc; **b** robbery. **2** *law* an act, instance or the process of destroying a document or of tampering with the contents of a document so that it can no longer be considered valid as evidence. • **spoliator** *noun.* • **spoliatory** /ˈspoʊlɪətərɪ/ *adj.* ⓘ 14c: from Latin *spoliare* to spoil.

spondaic /spɒnˈdeɪɪk/ ▷ *adj* **1** said of a verse or part of a verse: having spondees or being written predominately in spondees. **2** relating to spondees. **3** said of a hexameter: having a spondee as the fifth foot.

spondee /ˈspɒndiː/ ▷ *noun* (***spondees***) *prosody* a metrical foot of two long syllables or two stressed syllables and which in English verse tends to suggest weariness, depression, slowness, etc. ⓘ 14c: from Latin *spondeus*, from Greek *spondeios* a solemn drink offering.

spondulicks /spɒnˈdjuːlɪks, -ˈduːlɪks/ ▷ *plural noun, colloq, chiefly US* money; cash. ⓘ 19c.

spondylitis /spɒndɪˈlaɪtɪs/ ▷ *noun* inflammation of the vertebrae. ⓘ 19c: from Latin *spondylus* a vertebra + -ITIS.

sponge /spʌndʒ/ ▷ *noun* **1** any of several hundred different species of aquatic, usually marine, invertebrate primitive multicellular animals that consist of a large cluster of cells attached to a solid object such as a rock and which usually live in colonies. **2 a** a piece of the soft porous skeleton of this animal which is capable of holding comparatively large amounts of water and which remains soft when wet, making it particularly suitable for washing, bathing, cleaning, etc; **b** a piece of similarly absorbent synthetic material that is used in the same way. **3** sponge cake or pudding. **4** a wipe with a cloth or sponge in order to clean something ◻ *gave the baby's face a quick sponge.* **5** *colloq* someone who regularly drinks a lot. ▷ *verb* (***sponged***, ***sponging***) **1** to wash or clean with a cloth or sponge and water. **2** to mop up. **3** (*usually* **sponge off someone**) *colloq* to borrow money, etc from them, often without any intention of paying it back. **4** (*usually* **sponge on someone**) to survive by habitually imposing on someone else or others, expecting them to pay for things, etc ◻ *never works – just sponges on his mates.* **5** to go fishing or diving for sponges. • **spongeable** *adj.* • **throw in** or **up the sponge** or **towel** see under TOWEL. ⓘ Anglo-Saxon, from Greek *spongia*.

■ **sponge down** to clean something with a damp cloth or sponge.

sponge bag ▷ *noun* a small waterproof bag that toiletries are kept in, especially when travelling. Also called **toilet bag**.

sponge bath ▷ *noun* a BEDBATH.

sponge cake ▷ *noun* a light fluffy sweet cake that is made from flour, sugar and eggs, often with a buttercream or jam filling. Also called **Victoria sandwich**.

sponge finger ▷ *noun* a light sweet oblong biscuit, often used on the outside of puddings like CHARLOTTE RUSSE. Also called **lady's finger**.

sponger ▷ *noun, colloq* someone who survives by habitually imposing on other people, expecting them to pay for things, etc.

spongy /ˈspʌndʒɪ/ ▷ *adj* (***spongier***, ***spongiest***) soft and springy, and perhaps absorbent, like a sponge. • **spongily** *adverb.* • **sponginess** *noun.*

sponsion /ˈspɒnʃɪən/ ▷ *noun* **1** the act of becoming surety for another. **2** a solemn promise or pledge, especially one made on behalf of someone else. ⓘ 17c: from Latin *spondere, sponsum* to promise solemnly.

sponson /ˈspɒnsən/ ▷ *noun* **1 a** a structure that juts out from the deck of a boat and which provides a platform for a gun; **b** a similar structure on a paddle steamer where its function is to support the paddle-box. **2 a** an air-filled tank that is attached to the side of a canoe to minimize the chance of it capsizing; **b** a similar structure on a seaplane for improving its stability in the water. ⓘ 19c.

sponsor /ˈspɒnsə(r)/ ▷ *noun* **1** a person or organization that finances an event or broadcast in return for advertising. **2 a** someone who promises a sum of money to a participant in a forthcoming fund-raising event; **b** a company that provides backing for a team, especially in professional football, in return for the team displaying the company's name or logo on their shirts. **3** someone who offers to be responsible for another, especially in acting as a godparent. **4** someone who submits a proposal, eg for new legislation ◻ *sponsored the reform bill.* ▷ *verb* (***sponsored***, ***sponsoring***) to act as a sponsor for someone or something. • **sponsorial** /spɒnˈsɔːrɪəl/ *adj.* • **sponsorship** *noun.* ⓘ 17c: from Latin *spondere, sponsum* to promise solemnly.

sponsored ▷ *adj* **1** having a sponsor or sponsors. **2** said of an activity or event: financially supported by sponsors.

spontaneity /spɒntəˈneɪɪtɪ, –ˈniːɪtɪ/ ▷ *noun* natural or unrestrained reaction.

spontaneous /spɒnˈteɪnɪəs/ ▷ *adj* **1** unplanned and voluntary or instinctive, not provoked or invited by others. **2** occurring naturally or by itself, not caused or influenced from outside. **3** said of a manner or style: natural; not affected or studied. ⓘ 17c: from Latin *sponte* of one's own accord.

spontaneous combustion ▷ *noun* an act or instance or the process of a substance or body catching fire as a result of heat that is generated within it, as opposed to heat applied from outside.

spontaneous generation ▷ *noun, biol* the theory, now discredited, that living organisms, eg bacteria, can arise spontaneously from non-living matter.

spoof /spuːf/ *colloq* ▷ *noun* **1** a satirical imitation; a parody. **2** a light-hearted hoax or trick. ▷ *verb* (***spoofed***, ***spoofing***) to parody; to play a hoax. ⓘ Late 19c: coined by the British comedian, A Roberts (1852–1933), to designate a hoaxing game.

spook /spuːk/ *colloq* ▻ *noun* **1** a ghost. **2** *derog* a Black person. **3** *N Amer* a spy. ▻ *verb* (***spooked***, ***spooking***) **1** to frighten or startle. **2** to haunt. **3** to make someone feel nervous or uneasy. • **spookish** *adj.* ⓘ Early 19c: from German *spok* a ghost.

spooked ▻ *adj* frightened, startled or wary.

spooky ▻ *adj* (***spookier***, ***spookiest***) *colloq* **1** uncanny; eerie. **2** suggestive of ghosts or the supernatural. • **spookily** *adverb.* • **spookiness** *noun.*

spool /spuːl/ ▻ *noun* a small cylinder, usually with a hole down the centre and with extended rims at either end, on which thread, photographic film, tape, etc is wound; a reel. ⓘ 14c: from German dialect *spole* a reel.

spoon /spuːn/ ▻ *noun* **1** a metal, wooden or plastic utensil that has a handle with a round or oval shallow bowl-like part at one end and which is used for eating, serving or stirring food. **2** the amount a spoon will hold □ ***takes three spoons of sugar in coffee.*** **3** *drug-taking slang* two grams or one sixteenth of an ounce of heroin. ▻ *verb* (***spooned***, ***spooning***) **1** to lift or transfer (food) with a spoon. **2** *intr, old use* to kiss and cuddle □ ***You're never too old to spoon.*** • **be born with a silver spoon in one's mouth** to be born into a family with wealth and/or high social standing. • **wooden spoon** see separate entry. ⓘ Anglo-Saxon *spon.*

spoon-bait and **spoon-hook** ▻ *noun, fishing* a lure on a swivel that is used in the trolling for fish.

spoonbill ▻ *noun* any of several types of wading bird that are similar to the IBIS, and which have a long flat broad bill with a spoon-shaped tip which is used for sifting food from the water.

spoonerism /ˈspuːnərɪzəm/ ▻ *noun* an accidental slip of the tongue where the positions of the first sounds in a pair of words are reversed, such as *par cark* for *car park* or *shoving leopard* for *loving shepherd*, and which often results in an unintentionally comic or ambiguous expression. See also METATHESIS. ⓘ Late 19c: named after Rev. W A Spooner (1844–1930), an English clergyman, educationalist, and dean of New College, Oxford, whose rather nervous disposition led him to make such slips frequently and who became renowned at Oxford for doing so.

spoon-feed ▻ *verb* **1** to feed (eg a baby) with a spoon. **2 a** to supply someone with everything they need or require, so that any effort on their part is unnecessary; **b** to create a learning situation where information, etc is given out in such a way that the pupils or students do not have to put in any original thought or research.

spoonful ▻ *noun* (***spoonfuls***) **1** the amount a spoon will hold. **2** a small amount or number.

spoor /spʊə(r), spɔː(r)/ ▻ *noun* the track or scent left by an animal, especially an animal that is being hunted as game. ⓘ 19c: Afrikaans, from Dutch *spor* track.

sporadic /spəˈradɪk/ ▻ *adj* **1** occurring from time to time, at irregular intervals; intermittent. **2** said of a disease: occurring in isolated pockets; not epidemic. • **sporadically** *noun.* ⓘ 17c: from Greek *sporados* scattered.

sporangium /spɒˈrandʒɪəm/ ▻ *noun* (***sporangia*** /-dʒɪə/) *bot* in fungi and some plants: the hollow structure where the spores are produced. ⓘ 19c: from Greek *spora* seed + *angeion* receptacle.

spore /spɔː(r)/ ▻ *noun* one of the tiny reproductive bodies that are produced in vast quantities by some micro-organisms and certain non-flowering plants, such as ferns and mosses, and which are capable of developing into new individuals either immediately after being released by the parent or after lying dormant if adverse conditions prevail. ⓘ 19c: from Greek *spora* seed.

sporophyll or **sporophyl** /ˈspɔːrəfɪl, ˈspɒrəfɪl/ ▻ *noun, bot* in certain non-flowering plants, such as some mosses, ferns, etc: a leaf that bears sporangia and which, in many cases, has become so highly modified for this purpose that it no longer looks like a conventional leaf. ⓘ Late 19c: from Greek *spora* seed + *phyllon* leaf.

sporophyte /ˈspɔːrəfaɪt, ˈspɒrəfaɪt/ ▻ *noun, bot* in plants where the life cycle is characterized by ALTERNATION OF GENERATIONS: the plant that produces spores asexually. See also GAMETOPHYTE. • **sporophytic** /spɒrəˈfɪtɪk/ *adj.* • **sporophytically** *adverb.* ⓘ Late 19c: from Greek *spora* seed + -PHYTE.

sporran /ˈspɒrən/ ▻ *noun* a pouch for carrying money that is traditionally worn hanging from a belt in front of the kilt in Scottish Highland dress and which is usually made of leather or fur, sometimes with the face of an animal or tassels of animal fur on it. ⓘ Early 19c: from Gaelic *sporan* purse.

sport ▻ *noun* **1 a** an activity, pastime, competition, etc that usually involves a degree of physical exertion, eg football, tennis, squash, swimming, boxing, snooker, etc and which people take part in for exercise and/or pleasure; **b** such activities collectively □ ***enjoys watching sport on TV.*** See also SPORTS. **2** good-humoured fun □ ***It was just meant to be a bit of sport.*** **3** *colloq* **a** someone who is thought of as being fair-minded, generous, easy-going, etc □ ***Be a sport and lend me your car***; **b** someone who behaves in a specified way, especially with regard to winning or losing □ ***Even when he loses, he's a good sport***; **c** *Austral, NZ* a form of address that is especially used between men □ ***How's it going, sport?*** **d** *US* someone, especially a man, who dresses in a flashy way, likes to live well, spend lots of money and generally show off. **4** *literary* someone or something that is manipulated or controlled by outside influences; a plaything □ ***was but the sport of the gods.*** **5** *biol* an animal or, more usually, a plant that displays abnormal characteristics as a result of a mutation or that is strikingly different from the parent. **6** *slang* pleasure or success that is derived from hunting, shooting, fishing, etc □ ***bagged six grouse and had a good day's sport.*** ▻ *verb* (***sported***, ***sporting***) **1** to wear or display, especially proudly □ ***She sported a small tattoo.*** **2** *biol* to vary from, or produce a variation from, the parent stock. • **sportive** see separate entry. • **sporty** see separate entry. • **make sport of someone** or **something** *old use* to make fun of or ridicule them or it. ⓘ 15c: a shortened form of DISPORT.

sporting ▻ *adj* **1** belonging, referring or relating to sport □ ***Gun dogs are classed as sporting dogs.*** **2** said of someone, their behaviour, attitude, nature, etc: characterized by fairness, generosity, etc □ ***It was sporting of him to lend me the car.*** **3** keen or willing to gamble or take a risk □ ***I'm not a sporting man, but I like a bet on the Grand National.*** • **sportingly** *adverb.*

sporting chance ▻ *noun* (*usually* **a sporting chance**) a reasonable possibility of success.

sportive ▻ *adj* playful. • **sportively** *adverb.* • **sportiveness** *noun.*

sports ▻ *singular noun* **1** *Brit* in schools and colleges: a day or afternoon that each year is dedicated to competitive sport, especially athletics □ ***Parents may attend the school sports.*** **2** *as adj* belonging, referring or relating to sport □ ***sports pavilion.*** **3** *as adj* used in or suitable for sport □ ***sports holdall.*** **4** *as adj* casual □ ***sports jacket.***

sports car ▻ *noun* a small fast car, usually a two-seater, often with a low-slung body which has a roof that can be removed or folded back, and which has particularly quick acceleration.

sports ground ▻ *noun* an area of land that is used for outdoor sport, often one that has changing rooms, facilities for spectators, refreshment stands, etc.

sports jacket ▻ *noun* a man's jacket, often one made from tweed, that is meant for casual wear. Also called *N Amer, Austral & NZ* **sports coat**.

sportsman ▷ *noun* **1** a male sportsperson. **2** someone who plays fair, sticks to the rules and accepts defeat without any rancour or bitterness. • **sportsmanship** *noun.*

sportsmanlike ▷ *adj* said of someone, their behaviour, attitude, etc: characterized by fairness, observation of the rules, generosity in defeat, etc.

sportsperson ▷ *noun* (***sportspersons***) someone who takes part in sport, especially at a professional level.

sportswear ▷ *noun* clothes that are designed for or suitable for sport or for wearing casually.

sportswoman ▷ *noun* a female sportsperson.

sporty ▷ *adj* (***sportier, sportiest***) **1** said of someone: habitually taking part in sport, or being especially fond of, good at, etc sport. **2** said of clothes: casual; suitable for wearing when playing a sport □ *She looked so cute in her sporty little beret.* **3** said of a car: looking, performing or handling like a sports car. • **sportily** *adj.* • **sportiness** *noun.*

sporule /ˈspɒrjuːl/ ▷ *noun, biol* a small spore. • **sporular** *adj.*

spot ▷ *noun* **1** a small mark or stain. **2** a drop of liquid. **3** a small amount, especially of liquid. **4** an eruption on the skin; a pimple. **5** a place □ *found a secluded spot.* **6** *colloq* a small amount of work □ *did a spot of ironing.* **7** a place or period in a schedule or programme □ *a five-minute comedy spot.* **8** *colloq* a spotlight. **9** *snooker, billiards* a mark on the table where a specified ball is placed □ *had to put the black on pink ball's spot.* **10** a relatively dark patch on the sun. **11** *colloq* a place of entertainment □ *knew all the hot spots in town.* ▷ *verb* (***spotted, spotting***) **1** to mark with spots. **2** to see; to catch sight of something. **3** *usually in compounds* to watch for and record the sighting of (eg trains, planes, etc). **4** to search for (new talent). **5** *intr* said of rain: to fall lightly. **6** *snooker, billiards* to put (a ball) in its proper place on the table or, if that is not possible, to place it on the next available one. • **spotting** *noun.* • **-spotting** *noun, in compounds* □ *trainspotting.* • **high spot** see separate entry. • **in a spot** *colloq* in trouble or difficulty. • **knock spots off someone** or **something** *colloq* to be overwhelmingly better than them. • **on the spot 1** immediately and often without warning □ *Motorists caught speeding are fined on the spot.* **2** at the scene of some notable event. **3** in an awkward situation, especially one requiring immediate action or response □ *put someone on the spot.* • **soft spot, tight spot** and **weak spot** see separate entries. ⓒ 12c: from Norse *spotti* small bit.

spot cash ▷ *noun, colloq* money that is paid there and then.

spot check ▷ *noun* an inspection made at random and without warning. ▷ *verb* (**spot-check**) to carry out a random check □ *The police were spot-checking for worn tyres.*

spotless ▷ *adj* **1** absolutely clean. **2** unblemished □ *held a spotless driving licence.* • **spotlessly** *adverb.* • **spotlessness** *noun.*

spotlight ▷ *noun* **1** a concentrated circle of light that can be directed onto a small area, especially of a theatre stage. **2** a lamp that casts this kind of light. ▷ *verb* (***spotlit*** or ***spotlighted, spotlighting***) **1** to illuminate with a spotlight. **2** to direct attention to something; to highlight. • **be in the spotlight** to have the attention of others, the media, etc focused on (one or someone). • **put someone** or **something in the spotlight** to direct the attention of others, the media, etc onto them. ⓒ Early 20c.

spot-on ▷ *adj, Brit colloq* precisely what is required; excellent; very accurate.

spotted /ˈspɒtɪd/ ▷ *adj* **1** patterned or covered with spots. **2** stained; marked □ *wore a revolting tie spotted with tomato sauce.*

spotted dick ▷ *noun* a type of suet pudding that contains dried fruit which gives it a spotty look.

spotter ▷ *noun* **1** someone or something that keeps a vigilant watch.. **2** *usually in compounds* someone who watches for and records the sighting of trains, planes, etc.

spotty ▷ *adj* (***spottier, spottiest***) **1** marked with a pattern of spots. **2** said of someone's skin, especially that of the face, back, etc: covered in blemishes, pimples, etc. • **spottiness** *noun.*

spot-weld ▷ *verb* to join metal with single circular welds. ▷ *noun* a weld that is made in this way. • **spot-welder** *noun.*

spouse /spaʊs, spaʊz/ ▷ *noun* a husband or wife. ⓒ 13c: from Latin *sponsus,* from *spondere* to promise.

spout ▷ *noun* **1** a projecting tube or lip, eg on a kettle, teapot, jug, fountain, etc, that allows liquid to pass through or through which it can be poured. **2** a jet or stream of liquid, eg from a fountain or the blowhole of a whale. ▷ *verb* (***spouted, spouting***) **1** *tr & intr* to flow or make something flow out in a jet or stream. **2** *tr & intr* to speak or say, especially at length and boringly. **3** *intr* said of a whale: to squirt air through a blowhole. • **up the spout** *slang* **1** ruined or damaged beyond repair; no longer a possibility. **2** pregnant. ⓒ 14c.

sprain ▷ *verb* (***sprained, spraining***) to injure (a joint) by the sudden overstretching or tearing of a ligament or ligaments. ▷ *noun* such an injury, which can cause painful swelling that may take several months to heal. • **sprained** *adj.* ⓒ 17c.

sprang *past tense of* SPRING.

sprat ▷ *noun* a small edible fish of the herring family. • **a sprat to catch a mackerel 1** an enticement. **2** a small price to pay in the short-term to obtain a long-term gain. ⓒ Anglo-Saxon *sprot.*

sprawl ▷ *verb* (***sprawled, sprawling***) *intr* **1** to sit or lie lazily, especially with the arms and legs spread out wide. **2** to fall in an ungainly way. **3** to spread or extend in an irregular, straggling or untidy way □ *Huge writing sprawled across the blackboard.* ▷ *noun* **1** a sprawling position. **2** a straggling expansion, especially one that is unregulated, uncontrolled, etc □ *urban sprawl.* ⓒ Anglo-Saxon *spreawlian* to move convulsively.

spray¹ ▷ *noun* **1** a fine mist of small flying drops of liquid. **2** a liquid designed to be applied as a mist □ *hairspray.* **3** a device for dispensing a liquid as a mist; an atomizer or aerosol. **4** a shower of small flying objects □ *a spray of pellets.* ▷ *verb* (***sprayed, spraying***) **1** to squirt (a liquid) in the form of a mist. **2** to apply a liquid in the form of a spray to something □ *sprayed the car black.* **3** to subject someone or something to a heavy burst □ *sprayed the car with bullets.* **4** said of a male animal, eg a cat: to mark (territory) with urine. ⓒ 17c: from Dutch *sprayen.*

spray² ▷ *noun* **1 a** a small branch of a tree or plant which has delicate leaves and flowers growing on it; **b** any decoration that is an imitation of this. **2** a small bouquet of flowers. ⓒ 13c.

spray-gun ▷ *noun* a container with a trigger-operated aerosol attached, for dispensing liquid, eg paint, in spray form.

spray-on ▷ *adj* applied using an aerosol, etc.

spray-paint ▷ *noun* paint that is applied using an aerosol, etc. ▷ *verb* to cover something in paint, using an aerosol, etc. • **spray-painter** *noun.* • **spray-painting** *noun.* ⓒ Early 20c.

spread /sprɛd/ ▷ *verb* (***spread, spreading***) **1** *tr & intr* to apply, or be capable of being applied, in a smooth coating over a surface □ *spread the butter on the toast* □ *This butter spreads easily.* **2** (*also* **spread out** or **spread something out**) to extend or make it extend or scatter, often more widely or more thinly. **3** (*also* **spread something out**) to open it out or unfold it, especially to its full extent □ ***spread the sheet on the bed.*** **4** *tr & intr* to transmit or be transmitted or distributed □ ***Flies spread disease*** □ ***Rumours began to spread.*** **5 a** to separate or come undone or apart; **b** to force apart. ▷ *noun* **1 a** the act, process or extent of spreading; **b** coverage or expanse, area □ ***This mobile phone has a 98% spread.*** **2** a food in paste form, for spreading on bread, etc. **3 a** *originally* a pair of facing pages in a newspaper or magazine; **b** *loosely* an article in a newspaper or magazine □ ***a huge spread on Madonna.*** **4** *colloq* a lavish meal □ ***put on a scrumptious spread.*** **5 a** *N Amer* a farm and its lands, usually one given over to cattle-rearing; **b** a large house with extensive grounds. **6** *colloq* increased fatness around the waist and hips □ ***middle-age spread.*** **7** a cover, especially for a bed or table. **8** *stock exchange* the difference between the price that is bid for shares and the price they are offered at. ▷ *adj* **1** being in or having an extended, wide or open position. **2** *phonetics* said of a vowel such as the one in *spread*: articulated with the lips in an open as opposed to a rounded position. **3** said of a gemstone: flat and shallow. • **spreader** *noun*. • **spreading** see separate entry. • **spread it** or **oneself about** or **about a bit** *slang* to behave promiscuously. • **spread like wildfire** said of gossip, news, etc: to become widely known very quickly. • **spread oneself too thin** to commit oneself to too many things at once and so become unable to do any of them satisfactorily. • **spread one's wings** to attempt to broaden one's experience. ⓔ Anglo-Saxon *sprædan*.

■ **spread from** or **to somewhere** to extend or come from or to (a place, etc) □ ***Rain will spread from the west*** □ ***The unrest soon spread to all departments.***

spread-eagle ▷ *adj* (*also* **spread-eagled**) in a position where the arms and legs stretched out away from the body □ ***tripped up and lay spread-eagle on the floor.*** ▷ *noun* (**spread eagle**) **1** a figure of an eagle with outstretched wings, especially when used as an emblem of the USA. **2** *ice-skating* a glide made with the skates held heel to heel in a straight line. ▷ *verb* (***spread-eagled, spread-eagling***) **1** to lie or land, after a fall, etc, in a position with the arms and legs outstretched. **2** *ice-skating* to execute a spread eagle. **3** to spread someone's arms and legs apart and tie their wrists and ankles up to some kind of structure, eg a wagon wheel, and then beat them, as a form of punishment.

spreading ▷ *adj* **a** increasing in size, extent, etc □ ***Low pay fuelled the spreading discontent;*** **b** extending outwards □ ***under the spreading chestnut tree.***

spreadsheet ▷ *noun, computing* a program that displays a grid containing data in the form of figures, text, formulae, etc and whose function is to enable various mathematical, statistical, etc calculations to be done in business and financial planning, bookkeeping, analysis of experimental data, etc.

spree ▷ *noun* (***sprees***) a period of fun, extravagance or excess, especially one that involves spending a lot of money or drinking a lot of alcohol. ▷ *verb* (***spreed, spreeing***) to go on a spree. ⓔ 19c.

sprig ▷ *noun* a small shoot or twig. ▷ *verb* (***sprigged, sprigging***) to embroider or decorate with sprigs. • **sprigged** *adj*. ⓔ 14c.

sprightly /ˈspraɪtlɪ/ ▷ *adj* (***sprightlier, sprightliest***) **1 a** said of someone: lively and quick-witted; vivacious; **b** said of animals: quick-moving and spirited. **2** said of a piece of music or the manner a piece is played in: brisk, frisky and cheerful. • **sprightliness** *noun*. ⓔ 16c: from *spright*, a variant spelling of SPRITE.

spring ▷ *verb* (*past tense* ***sprang*** or (*US*) ***sprung***, *past participle* ***sprung***, *present participle* ***springing***) **1** *intr* to leap with a sudden quick launching action. **2** *intr* to move suddenly and swiftly, especially from a stationary position □ ***sprang into action.*** **3** to set off (a trap, etc) suddenly. **4** to fit (eg a mattress) with springs. **5** (*also* **spring something on someone**) to present or reveal something suddenly and unexpectedly □ ***sprang the idea on me without warning.*** **6** *slang* to engineer the escape of (a prisoner) from jail. **7** to jump over something □ ***sprang the fence.*** **8 a** *intr* said of wood or something wooden, eg a plank, mast, etc: to split, crack or become warped; **b** to split, crack or warp (wood or something wooden, eg a plank, mast, etc). ▷ *noun* **1 a** a metal coil that can be stretched or compressed, and which will return to its original shape when the pull or pressure is released, especially one where this can be done at a controlled rate so that it can be used to turn a mechanism, eg in a clock, watch, etc; **b** a similar device that is designed to absorb shock waves, eg in the shock absorbers of some motor vehicles, or to make seats, beds, etc comfortable and bouncy. **2** any place where water emerges from underground and flows on to the Earth's surface or into a body of water such as a lake. **3** (*also* **Spring**) the season between winter and summer, when most plants begin to grow, and usually thought of in the N hemisphere as consisting of the months from March to May inclusive, and in the S hemisphere as September to November. See also VERNAL. **c** an early stage of something □ ***in the spring of her career.*** **4** a sudden vigorous leap. **5 a** the ability of a material to return rapidly to its original shape after a distorting force, such as stretching, bending or compression, has been removed □ ***The elastic has lost its spring;*** **b** a lively bouncing or jaunty quality □ ***a spring in his step.*** • **springless** *adj*. • **springlike** *adj*. • **spring a leak** said of a boat, bucket, etc: to develop a hole so that water can flow in or out. • **spring to mind** to come into someone's thoughts immediately or suddenly □ ***His name doesn't spring to mind.*** ⓔ Anglo-Saxon *springan*.

■ **spring back** to return quickly to the original position.

■ **spring from somewhere** to develop or originate from (a place, etc) □ ***an idea that had sprung from one of his students.***

■ **spring to something** to come or rise to it, especially suddenly or quickly □ ***A beautiful smile sprang to her lips.***

■ **spring up** to appear or come into being suddenly □ ***New houses sprang up.***

spring balance ▷ *noun* a device that measures the weight of an object by gauging the extent of the downward pull on a large spring when the object is attached to it.

spring beetle see CLICK BEETLE

springboard ▷ *noun* **1 a** a long narrow pliable board that projects over a swimming pool and which is used in diving to give extra lift; **b** a similar but shorter board that is used in gymnastics and which is placed in front of a piece of apparatus to give extra height and impetus. **2** anything that serves to get things moving.

springbok /ˈsprɪŋbɒk/ ▷ *noun* (***springbok*** or ***springboks***) **1** (*also* **springbuck**) a type of South African antelope that is renowned for its high springing leap when it runs. **2 a** (**Springbok**) a nickname for a member of a S African sporting team, especially their national rugby union side; **b** (**the Springboks**) a nickname for any S African sporting team, but especially their national rugby union side. ⓔ Early 20c for sense 2; 18c for sense 1: from Afrikaans, from Dutch *springen* to spring + *bok* goat.

spring chicken ▷ *noun* 1 a very young chicken valued for its tender edible flesh. **2** *colloq* a young person. • **no spring chicken** no longer young □ ***She's no spring chicken — she must be coming up to forty.***

spring-clean ▷ *verb, tr & intr* to clean and tidy (a house) thoroughly, especially at the end of the winter. ▷ *noun* an act of doing this. • **spring-cleaning** *noun*. ⓔ 19c.

springe /sprɪndʒ/ ▷ *noun* a sprung snare that is used for trapping small wild animals and birds. ▷ *verb* (***springed, springeing***) **1** to set this kind of snare. **2** to catch something using this kind of snare. ⓔ 13c: related to SPRING.

spring equinox see under EQUINOX

springer spaniel ▻ *noun* either of two kinds of medium-sized dog, called the **English springer spaniel** (brown and white or black and white) and the **Welsh springer spaniel** (deep russet and white), which have a domed head and silky dangly ears. ◷ Early 19c.

spring halt ▻ *noun, vet medicine* a condition that affects horses and which is characterized by a jerky lameness, usually of the hind leg.

springier and **springiest** see SPRINGY

springing line ▻ *noun, archit* the level where an arch or vault comes out from its support.

spring-lock ▻ *noun* a lock that has a spring-loaded mechanism so that it can automatically be locked when closed, but which requires a key to open it.

spring mattress ▻ *noun* a type of mattress that is made up of a grid of connected spiral springs.

spring onion ▻ *noun* an immature onion that is picked when it is just a tiny white bulb with long thin green shoots, and which is usually eaten raw in salads.

spring roll ▻ *noun* a type of deep-fried folded Chinese pancake that can have a variety of fillings, such as vegetables, bamboo shoots, minced meat, prawns, etc.

springtail ▻ *noun* a primitive wingless insect that is found in soils or leaf litter, and which is able to leap by means of a forked springing organ that is folded up on the underside of its abdomen.

spring tide ▻ *noun* a tidal pattern that occurs twice a month when the Moon is full and again when it is new, ie at the time when the Earth, Moon and Sun are aligned so that the combined gravitational pull of the Moon and Sun makes high tides higher and low tides lower. Compare NEAP TIDE.

springtime and **springtide** ▻ *noun* the season of spring.

springy /ˈsprɪŋɪ/ ▻ *adj* (***springier***, ***springiest***) having the ability to readily spring back to the original shape when any pressure that has been exerted is released; bouncy; elastic; resilient. • **springily** *adverb*. • **springiness** *noun*.

sprinkle /ˈsprɪŋkəl/ ▻ *verb* (***sprinkled***, ***sprinkling***) **1** to scatter in, or cover with a scattering of, tiny drops or particles. **2** to arrange or distribute in a thin scattering □ ***The hillside was sprinkled with houses.*** ▻ *noun* **1** an act of sprinkling. **2 a** the amount that is sprinkled; **b** a very small amount. ◷ Anglo-Saxon *sprengan* to sprinkle.

sprinkler ▻ *noun* a person or device that sprinkles, especially one that sprinkles water over plants, a lawn, etc or one for extinguishing fires.

sprinkler system ▻ *noun* **1** an arrangement of overhead water pipes and nozzles for extinguishing fires and which is automatically set off by any substantial increase in temperature. **2** an arrangement of pipes for watering the land, eg large lawns, golf courses, vineyards, etc.

sprinkling ▻ *noun* a small amount of something, especially when it is thinly scattered.

sprint ▻ *noun* **1** *athletics* a race at high speed over a short distance. **2** a burst of speed at a particular point, usually the end, of a long race, eg in athletics, cycling, horse-racing, etc. **3** a fast run. ▻ *verb* (***sprinted***, ***sprinting***) *tr & intr* to run at full speed. ◷ 18c: from Norse *spretta* to jump up.

sprinter ▻ *noun* **1** an athlete, cyclist, etc who sprints. **2** a small bus or train that travels short distances.

sprit ▻ *noun* a small diagonal spar used to spread a sail. ◷ Anglo-Saxon *spreot* pole.

sprite ▻ *noun* **1** *folklore* a playful fairy; an elf or imp. **2** a number of PIXELS that can be moved around a screen in a group, eg those representing a figure in a computer game. ◷ 14c: from French *esprit* spirit.

spritsail /ˈsprɪtsəl/ ▻ *noun* a sail spread wide by a sprit.

spritz /ˈsprɪts/ ▻ *verb* (***spritzed***, ***spritzing***) to spray or squirt something □ ***spritz your brush with hairspray.*** ▻ *noun* an act or instance of this. ◷ 20c: from German *spritzen* to spray.

spritzer /ˈsprɪtsə(r)/ ▻ *noun* a drink of white wine and soda water. ◷ 1960s: from German *spritzen* to spray.

spritzig /ˈsprɪtsɪɡ/ ▻ *adj* said of wine: slightly sparkling. ▻ *noun* **1** a slightly sparkling, usually German, wine. **2** in wine-tasting: the slight prickle on the tongue that is given off by this kind of wine. ◷ 1940s: from German *spritzen* to spray.

sprocket /ˈsprɒkɪt/ ▻ *noun* **1** any of a set of teeth on the rim of a driving wheel, eg fitting into the links of a chain or the holes on a strip of film. **2** (*also* **sprocket wheel**) a wheel with sprockets. **3** a piece of wood used to build a roof out over the eaves. Also called **cocking piece**. ◷ 16c.

sprog ▻ *noun, slang* **1** a child. **2** a new recruit, especially one in the RAF.

sprout /sprɑʊt/ ▻ *verb* (***sprouted***, ***sprouting***) **1** *tr & intr* to develop (a new growth, eg of leaves or hair). **2** (*also* **sprout up**) to grow or develop; to spring up □ ***Cyber cafés are sprouting up everywhere.*** ▻ *noun* **1** a new growth; a shoot or bud. **2** a shortened form of BRUSSELS SPROUT. ◷ Anglo-Saxon *sprutan*.

spruce¹ /spruːs/ ▻ *noun* **1** any of several kinds of evergreen pyramid-shaped trees which have needle-like leaves and which can be distinguished from fir trees by the way their cones point downwards rather than up. **2** the valuable white-grained timber of this tree which is used in the manufacture of paper, boxes, etc and as a source of resin and turpentine. ◷ 17c: from *Pruce*, an obsolete name for Prussia, the former German state which originally supplied the timber.

spruce² /spruːs/ ▻ *adj* neat and smart, especially in appearance and dress. ▻ *verb* (***spruced***, ***sprucing***) (*usually* **spruce up**) to make oneself, someone or something neat and tidy. • **sprucely** *adverb*. • **spruceness** *noun*. ◷ 16c.

sprue¹ /spruː/ ▻ *noun* (***sprues***) **1** a vertical channel that leads into a mould and through which molten plastic or metal can be poured. **2** the solidified plastic or metal that collects in this kind of channel. ◷ 19c.

sprue² /spruː/ ▻ *noun* a tropical disease of unknown cause that affects the digestive tract and which is characterized by a sore tongue, severe diarrhoea, voluminous frothy stools, weight loss, anaemia and oedema. ◷ Early 19c: from Dutch *spruw*, from German *Spruwe* tumour.

spruik /spruːk/ ▻ *verb* (***spruiked***, ***spruiking***) *Austral & NZ slang* said especially of showmen, salesmen, etc: to speak in public, especially at length and using ornate language. • **spruiker** *noun*. ◷ Early 20c.

sprung /sprʌŋ/ ▻ *adj* fitted with a spring or springs. ▻ *verb, past tense, past participle of* SPRING.

sprung rhythm ▻ *noun, prosody* the name given to a type of strong stress METER where each FOOT (sense 8) has a stressed syllable which either stands alone or has a variable number of unstressed syllables attached to it and which are strung together in an arbitrary fashion so that the rhythm jumps about. ◷ 19c: coined by the poet Gerard Manley Hopkins (1844–89) to describe this kind of meter which he was particularly fond of using because he felt it was close to the rhythm of natural speech and also because he associated it with the meter of Anglo-Saxon and Middle English alliterative verse.

spry ▻ *adj* (***spryer***, ***spryest***) **1** lively; active. **2** light on one's feet; nimble. • **spryly** *adverb*. • **spryness** *noun*.

SPUC ▷ *abbreviation* Society for the Protection of the Unborn Child.

spud /spʌd/ ▷ *noun* **1** *colloq* a potato. **2** a small narrow digging tool with a chisel-shaped blade that is used for pulling up weeds, etc. ▷ *verb* (***spudded, spudding***) **1** to pull up (weeds) using a spud. **2** (*also* **spud in**) to start drilling an oil-well by boring a hole in the seabed. ◷ 14c as *spudde* short knife.

spud-bashing ▷ *noun, slang* the job of peeling lots of potatoes, especially as a punishment for some misdemeanour by a member of the armed forces.

spumante /spuːˈmantɪ, spjuː-/ ▷ *noun* a sparkling, usually sweet Italian wine. ◷ Early 20c: Italian, meaning 'sparkling', from *spumare* to froth.

spume /spjuːm/ ▷ *noun* foam or froth, especially on the sea. ▷ *verb* (***spumed, spuming***) *tr & intr* to foam or froth. • **spumy** *adj*. ◷ 14c: from Latin *spuma*, from *spuere* to spew.

spun ▷ *adj* **1** formed or made by a spinning process □ *spun gold*. **2** *in compounds* □ *home-spun*. ▷ *verb, past tense, past participle of* SPIN.

spunk ▷ *noun* **1** *colloq* courage; mettle. **2** *slang* semen. • **spunkily** *adverb*. • **spunkless** *adj*. • **spunky** *adj*. ◷ 19c as sense 2; 18c as sense 1; 16c in obsolete sense 'a spark'.

spun silk ▷ *noun* waste silk fibres, sometimes mixed with cotton, that are made into a fabric.

spun sugar ▷ *noun* sugar that has been teased into fine fluffy threads, eg in candy floss, cake decorations, etc.

spur /spɜː(r)/ ▷ *noun* **1** a device with a spiky metal wheel, fitted to the heel of a horse-rider's boot, which is used for pressing into the horse's side to make it go faster. **2** anything that urges or encourages greater effort or progress. **3 a** a spike or pointed part, eg on a cock's leg; **b** a similar but artifical part on a game cock; **c** any small spiky projection such as on the wing of certain birds or at the base of the corolla of some flowers. **4** a ridge of high land that projects out into a valley. **5 a** a short branch of a tree, especially a fruit tree; **b** a branch line or siding of a railway; **c** a side or slip road of a motorway, etc. **6 a** a breakwater; **b** a structure which helps prevent erosion on a riverbank, etc. ▷ *verb* (***spurred, spurring***) **1** to urge □ *The crowd spurred their team to victory*. **2** to press with spurs. **3** to hurry up. • **spurless** *adj*. • **spurry** *adj*. • **earn** or **win one's spurs 1** *formerly* to prove oneself worthy of a knighthood through acts of bravery. **2** to show one's proficiency at something and so attain distinction. • **on the spur of the moment** suddenly; on an impulse. ◷ Anglo-Saxon *spura*.

■ **spur someone** or **something on** to incite, encourage, provoke, etc them.

spurge /spɜːdʒ/ ▷ *noun* any of various plants which produce a bitter, often poisonous, milky juice that was formerly used as a laxative. ◷ 14c: from French *espurge*, from Latin *expurgare* to purge.

spur gear and **spur gearing** ▷ *noun* a type of gearing that consists of spur wheels.

spurge laurel ▷ *noun* an evergreen shrub that has yellowish-green flowers, thick glossy leaves and poisonous berries.

spurious /ˈspjʊərɪəs/ ▷ *adj* false, counterfeit or untrue, especially when superficially seeming to be genuine □ *made a spurious claim to the inheritance*. • **spuriously** *adverb*. • **spuriousness** *noun*. ◷ 17c: from Latin *spurius* illegitimate, false.

spurn /spɜːn/ ▷ *verb* (***spurned, spurning***) to reject (eg a person's love) scornfully. ▷ *noun* an act or instance of spurning. • **spurned** *adj*. • **spurning** *adj, noun*. ◷ Anglo-Saxon *spurnan*.

spurrey or **spurry** /ˈspʌrɪ/ ▷ *noun* (***spurries***) any of several varieties of annual plants or weeds, related to the pearlworts, which have very slender stems and leaves and small delicate flowers. ◷ 16c: from *spurrie*, the Dutch name for this plant.

spurt or **spirt** /spɜːt/ ▷ *verb* (***spurted, spurting***) *tr & intr* to flow out or make something flow out in a sudden sharp jet. ▷ *noun* **1** a jet of liquid that suddenly gushes out. **2** a short spell of intensified activity or increased speed □ *Business tends to come in spurts*. ◷ 16c.

spurtle or **spirtle** /ˈspɜːtəl/ ▷ *noun, Scots* **1** a wooden stick used for stirring porridge, soup, etc. **2** a long-handled utensil with a flat blade, used for turning oatcakes, scones, etc. ◷ 16c.

spur wheel ▷ *noun* a cog-wheel.

Sputnik or **sputnik** /ˈspʊtnɪk, ˈspʌt-/ ▷ *noun* an artificial satellite that orbits the Earth, especially one of those launched by the former Soviet Union between 1957 and 1961. ◷ 1950s: Russian, meaning 'travelling companion'. Sputnik 1 was the world's first artificial satellite, and Sputnik 2 carried the dog 'Laika', the first living creature to go into space.

sputter /ˈspʌtə(r)/ ▷ *verb* (***sputtered, sputtering***) **1** to SPLUTTER. **2 a** to remove metallic atoms from a cathode by positive ion bombardment; **b** to use the metal that has been removed in this way to give a thin metal coating to another surface, eg glass, plastic, another metal, etc. ▷ *noun* **1** to SPLUTTER. **2** disjointed, incomprehensible speech. **3** liquid, food particles, etc sprayed out of the mouth during this kind of speech. • **sputterer** *noun*. • **sputtery** *adj*. ◷ 16c: imitating the sound, from Dutch *sputeren*.

sputum /ˈspjuːtəm/ ▷ *noun* (***sputa*** /ˈspjuːtə/) a mixture of saliva, mucus and/or pus that is coughed up from the bronchial passages, and is indicative of an inflammatory disorder, especially in smoking-related conditions and other pulmonary conditions such as bronchitis, etc. Also called PHLEGM. ◷ 17c: Latin, meaning 'spit', from *spuere*, *sputum* to spit.

spy ▷ *noun* (***spies***) **1** someone who is employed by a government or organization to gather information about political enemies, competitors, etc. **2** someone who observes others in secret. ▷ *verb* (***spies, spied, spying***) **1** *intr* to act or be employed as a spy. **2** to catch sight of someone or something; to spot. • **I-spy** see separate entry. • **spy in the cab** *colloq* the lorry drivers' name for the TACHOGRAPH. • **spy in the sky** *colloq* an information-gathering satellite or aircraft. ◷ 13c: from French *espier*.

■ **spy on someone** or **something** to keep a secret watch on them or it.

■ **spy someone** or **something out 1** to discover or uncover them or it. **2** to make a detailed inspection of them or it.

spyglass ▷ *noun* a small hand-held telescope.

spyhole ▷ *noun* a small glass hole in a door that enables someone to see who is there before deciding to open the door; a peephole.

spy ring ▷ *noun* a network of spies who are known to each other and who work together.

spy story ▷ *noun* a popular genre of fiction where the narrative is set against a background of espionage, eg the James Bond stories of Ian Fleming.

sq ▷ *abbreviation* **1** square. **2** (**Sq.**) in addresses: Square.

Sq. and **sqn** ▷ *abbreviation* squadron.

sq. ▷ *abbreviation* **1** sequence. **2 a** the next one; **b** (***sqq***) *plural* the next ones. ◷ From Latin *sequens* and *sequentia*.

SQL ▷ *abbreviation, computing* structured query language, a standard programming language used to access information from databases.

squab /skwɒb/ ▷ *noun* **1** a young unfledged bird, especially a pigeon. **2** a short fat person. ▷ *adj* **1** said of a bird: newly hatched and unfledged. **2** said of a person: short and fat. • **squabby** *adj.* ⓒ 17c.

squabble /ˈskwɒbəl/ ▻ *verb* (***squabbled, squabbling***) *intr* to quarrel noisily, especially about something trivial. ▻ *noun* a noisy quarrel, especially a petty one. • **squabbler** *noun.* ⓒ 17c.

squacco /ˈskwɒkoʊ/ ▻ *noun* (***squaccos***) a small crested heron found in S Europe. ⓒ 17c: from Italian *sguacco*, a dialect word for this type of bird.

squad /skwɒd/ ▻ *noun* **1** a small group of soldiers, often twelve, who do drill formation together or who work together. **2** any group of people who work together in some specified field □ *drug squad.* **3** a set of players from which a sporting team is selected □ *Jess was included in the Scotland squad.* ⓒ 17c: from French *escouade*, from Spanish *escuadar* to square, because of the shape of the drill formation.

squad car ▻ *noun* a police car.

squaddy or **squaddie** ▻ *noun* (***squaddies***) *slang* an ordinary soldier; a private.

squadron /ˈskwɒdrən/ ▻ *noun* **1** a group of between 10 and 18 military aircraft which form the principal unit of an air force. **2** a group of warships sent on a particular mission. **3** a division of an armoured regiment of soldiers. • **squadroned** *adj.* ⓒ 16c: from Italian *squadrone* a group of soldiers in square formation; related to SQUAD.

squadron leader ▻ *noun* an air force officer who is in charge of a squadron and who ranks below WING COMMANDER. See table at RANK.

squalid /ˈskwɒlɪd/ ▻ *adj* **1** said especially of places to live: disgustingly filthy and neglected. **2** morally repulsive; sordid □ *gossip about their squalid affair.* • **squalidity** /skwɒˈlɪdɪtɪ/ *noun.* • **squalidly** *adverb.* • **squalidness** *noun.* See also SQUALOR. ⓒ 16c: from Latin *squalidus*, from *squalere* to be dirty.

squall¹ /skwɔːl/ ▻ *noun, meteorol* a sudden or short-lived violent gust of wind, usually accompanied by rain or sleet. ▻ *verb* (***squalled, squalling***) *intr* said of a wind: to blow in a squall. • **squally** *adj.* ⓒ 18c.

squall² /skwɔːl/ ▻ *noun* a loud cry; a yell. ▻ *verb* (***squalled, squalling***) *tr & intr* to yell. • **squaller** *noun.* ⓒ 17c.

squalor /ˈskwɒlə(r)/ ▻ *noun* the condition or quality of being disgustingly filthy. ⓒ 16c: Latin, meaning 'dirtiness', from *squalere* to be dry or dirty.

squama /ˈskweɪmə/ *biol* ▻ *noun* (***squamae*** /-miː/) a scale or scale-like structure. • **squamose** or **squamous** *adj.* ⓒ 18c: Latin, meaning 'scale'.

squander /ˈskwɒndə(r)/ ▻ *verb* (***squandered, squandering***) to use up (money, time, etc) wastefully. • **squanderer** *noun.* ⓒ 16c.

square /skwɛə(r)/ ▻ *noun* **1** a two-dimensional figure with four sides of equal length and four right angles. **2** anything shaped like this. **3** an open space in a town, usually roughly square in shape, and the buildings that surround it. **4** an L-shaped or T-shaped instrument which is used for measuring angles, drawing straight lines, etc. **5** the number that is formed when a number is multiplied by itself, eg the square of 2 (usually written 2^2) is 4. **6** *colloq* someone who has traditional or old-fashioned values, tastes, ideas, etc. ▻ *adj* **1** shaped like a square or, sometimes, like a cube □ *a square table* □ *a square box.* **2** used with a defining measurement to denote the area of something □ *The area of a rectangle whose sides are 2 feet by 3 feet would be 6 square feet.* **3** angular; less rounded than normal □ *a square jaw.* **4** measuring almost the same in breadth as in length or height. **5** fair; honest □ *a square deal.* **6** complete; outright □ *a square denial.* **7** set at right angles. **8** said of a pass in football, hockey, etc: driven across the pitch as opposed to ahead towards the goal. **9** said of a line of defence in football, hockey, etc: having all the players in a line across the pitch, usually a sign of poor tactical play. **10** *cricket* positioned at right angles to the wicket □ *played at square leg.* **11** *colloq, old use* having traditional or old-fashioned values, tastes, ideas, etc. ▻ *verb* (***squared, squaring***) **1** to make square in shape, especially to make right-angled. **2** to multiply (a number) by itself. **3** to pay off or settle (a debt). **4** to make the scores level in (a match). **5** to mark with a pattern of squares. **6** in football, hockey, etc: to drive (the ball, a pass, etc) across the pitch. ▻ *adverb* **1** solidly and directly □ *hit me square on the jaw.* **2** fairly; honestly. **3** said of the defence of a football, hockey, etc team: in a square position □ *The pass caught Rangers' defence square.* • **squarely** *adverb.* • **squareness** *noun.* • **squarer** *noun.* • **squarish** *adj.* • **all square** *colloq* **1** equal. **2** not in debt; with each side owing nothing. • **back to square one** *colloq* returned to the situation as it was before, with no progress having been made. • **square the circle** to do the impossible. • **square something with someone** to get their approval or permission for it. • **square up to someone** to prepare to fight them. • **square up to something** to prepare to tackle it, especially in a brave way. • **square with something** to agree or correspond with it. ⓒ 13c: from French *esquarre* to square.

■ **square up** to settle a bill, etc.

square-bashing ▻ *noun, slang* military drill on a barracks square.

square bracket ▻ *noun* either of a pair of characters ([]), chiefly used in mathematical notation or to contain special information eg comment by an editor of a text.

square dance *chiefly N Amer* ▻ *noun* any of various folk dances that are performed by couples in a square formation. ▻ *verb* (**square-dance**) *intr* to take part in this type of dance. • **square-dancer** *noun.* • **square-dancing** *noun.*

square deal ▻ *noun, colloq* an arrangement or transaction that is considered to be fair and honest by all the parties involved.

square-eyed ▻ *adj, humorous* said of someone who watches too much TV: having eyes or pupils shaped like the screen □ *It's a wonder you're not square-eyed watching all those soaps.*

square knot ▻ *noun* a REEF KNOT.

square leg ▻ *noun, cricket* **1** a fielding position level with the batsman, at some distance from him, and facing his back. **2** a fielder who takes up this position.

square meal ▻ *noun* a good nourishing meal.

the Square Mile ▻ *noun, Brit* the CITY.

square number ▻ *noun, math* an integer, such as 1, 4, 9, 16, 25, etc, that is the square of another integer.

square peg ▻ *noun* (*usually* **a square peg in a round hole**) something or someone that cannot or does not perform its or their function very well; a misfit.

square-rigged ▻ *adj* said of a sailing ship: fitted with large square sails set at right angles to the length of the ship. • **square-rigger** *noun* a ship with sails arranged like this. Compare FORE-AND-AFT.

square root ▻ *noun, math* (symbol √) a number or quantity that when multiplied by itself gives one particular number, eg 2 is the square root of 4, and 3 is the square root of 9.

square sail ▻ *noun* a more-or-less square sail supported by a yard which is generally at right angles to the mast.

squarial /ˈskweərɪəl/ ▻ *noun* a flat satellite dish for receiving programmes from British Satellite Broadcasting. ⓒ 1980s: a blend of SQUARE + AERIAL.

squarrose /skwaˈroʊs/ ▻ *adj, biol* rough; having scaly projections. ⓒ 18c: from Latin *squarrosus* scabby.

squash¹ /skwɒʃ/ ▻ *verb* (***squashes, squashed, squashing***) **1** to crush or flatten by pressing or squeezing. **2** *tr & intr* to force someone or something into a confined space □ *managed to squash all the washing into one bag.* **3** to suppress or put down (eg a rebellion). **4** to force someone into silence with a cutting reply. ▷ *noun* (***squashes***) **1** a concentrated fruit syrup, or a drink made by diluting this. **2** a crushed or crowded state. **3 a** SQUASH RACKETS; **b** SQUASH TENNIS. **4 a** an act or the process of squashing something; **b** the sound of something being squashed. • **squashable** *adj.* ◷ 17c: from French *esquasser* to crush.

squash² /skwɒʃ/ ▷ *noun, N Amer, especially US* **1** any of various trailing plants that have yellow funnel-shaped flowers and which are widely cultivated for their marrow-like gourds. **2** the fruit of any of these plants which can be cooked and used as a vegetable. ◷ 17c: from Narragansett (a Native American language) *askutasquash*.

squash rackets or **squash racquets** ▷ *noun* a game for either two or four players who use small-headed rackets to hit a little rubber ball around an indoor court with three solid walls and a back wall that is usually glass. The object is to make the ball rebound off the front wall above and below certain heights, while, at the same time, trying to make it as awkward as possible for the opponent to return the shot. Often shortened to SQUASH. ◷ 19c.

squash tennis ▷ *noun* a game similar to SQUASH RACKETS but played with larger rackets and an inflated ball. ◷ Early 20c.

squashy ▷ *adj* (***squashier, squashiest***) **1** soft and easily squashed. **2** wet and marshy. **3** marked by a flattened or squashed appearance. • **squashily** *adverb.* • **squashiness** *noun.*

squat /skwɒt/ ▷ *verb* (***squatted, squatting***) *intr* **1** to take up, or be sitting in, a low position with the knees fully bent and the weight on the soles of the feet. **2** said usually of a group of homeless people: to occupy an empty building without legal right. ▷ *noun* **1** a squatting position. **2 a** a building or part of a building that is unlawfully occupied; **b** the unlawful occupation of such a building. **3** a SQUAT THRUST. ▷ *adj* (*also* **squatty**) short and broad or fat. • **squatness** *noun.* ◷ 13c: from French *esquatir* to crush. The use of the word in connection with occupying buildings without legal right is not a recent coinage but was first used in the 19c.

■ **squat down** to crouch.

squatter /ˈskwɒtə(r)/ ▷ *noun* someone who unlawfully occupies a building, usually an empty one.

squat thrust ▷ *noun* a form of fitness exercise in which, from an all-fours position, the feet are repeatedly made to jump forwards so that the knees touch the elbows and then the legs are made to stretch out behind again.

squaw /skwɔː/ ▷ *noun, offensive* a Native American woman or wife. ◷ 17c: from Massachusett (a Native American language) *squa* woman.

squawk /skwɔːk/ ▷ *noun* **1** a loud harsh screeching noise, especially one made by a bird, eg a parrot. **2** a loud protest or complaint. ▷ *verb* (***squawked, squawking***) *intr* **1** to make a loud harsh screeching noise. **2** to complain loudly. • **squawker** *noun.* • **squawky** *adj.* • **squawkily** *adverb.* ◷ 19c: imitating the sound.

squawman ▷ *noun, derog* someone who is not of Native American origin and who has a Native American wife or partner.

squeak ▷ *noun* **1** a short high-pitched cry or sound, like that made by a mouse or a rusty gate. **2** (*also* **narrow squeak**) a narrow escape; a victory or success achieved by the slimmest of margins. ▷ *verb* (***squeaked, squeaking***) *tr & intr* **1** to utter a squeak or with a squeak. **2** to make something make a squeaking sound □ *squeaked the door closed.* • **squeaker** *noun.* ◷ 14c: imitating the sound.

■ **squeak through something** to succeed in it by a narrow margin.

squeaky ▷ *adj* (***squeakier, squeakiest***) characterized by squeaks or tending to squeak □ *a baby's squeaky toy* □ *a squeaky voice.* • **squeakily** *adverb.* • **squeakiness** *noun.*

squeaky clean ▷ *adj, colloq* **1** spotlessly clean. **2** virtuous, impeccable, above reproach or criticism, but often with an implication that this impression is superficial or for show. ◷ 1970s: originally used of newly-washed hair, which squeaks when it is being rinsed, etc.

squeal ▷ *noun* **1** a long high-pitched noise, cry or yelp, like that of a pig, a child, etc. **2** a screeching sound □ *The squeal of brakes was followed by a crunching noise.* ▷ *verb* (***squealed, squealing***) **1** *tr & intr* to utter a squeal or with a squeal. **2** *intr, colloq* to inform (on someone) or to report an incident (to the police or other authority). **3** *intr* to complain or protest loudly. ◷ 14c: imitating the sound.

squealer ▷ *noun* **1** someone or something that squeals. **2** a bird or animal that squeals, especially a piglet. **3** *colloq* an informer.

squeamish /ˈskwiːmɪʃ/ ▷ *adj* **1** slightly nauseous; easily made nauseous. **2** easily offended. • **squeamish about something** easily made nauseous by it; easily offended by it. • **squeamishly** *adverb.* • **squeamishness** *noun.* ◷ 15c: from French *escoymous*.

squeegee /ˈskwiːdʒiː/ ▷ *noun* (***squeegees***) **1** a device with a rubber blade for scraping water off a surface, eg a window, windscreen, vinyl floor, etc. **2** *photog* a roller for removing the water from prints in development. ▷ *verb* (***squeegeed, squeegeeing***) to use a squeegee to remove water from (a window, photographic print, etc). ◷ Early 20c; an earlier, now obsolete meaning 'a device for scraping mud from the side of roads' dates from 1840s: derived from SQUEEZE.

squeegie ▷ *noun* (***squeegies***) someone who washes the windscreens of cars stopped at traffic lights, in the hope of being tipped by drivers. ◷ A variant of SQUEEGEE.

squeeze ▷ *verb* (***squeezed, squeezing***) **1** to grasp or embrace tightly. **2** to press forcefully, especially from at least two sides. **3** to press or crush so as to extract (liquid, juice, toothpaste, etc). **4** to press gently, especially as an indication of affection, reassurance, etc □ *squeezed his hand.* **5** *tr & intr* to force or be forced into or through a confined space □ *Ten of us squeezed into a phone box.* **6** to put under financial pressure □ *squeezed his elderly mother for money for drugs.* **7** *bridge, whist* to play in a way that forces (an opponent) to discard a potentially winning card. ▷ *noun* **1** an act of squeezing. **2** a crowded or crushed state □ *It's a bit of a squeeze with four on the sofa.* **3** an amount (of fruit juice, etc) that is obtained by squeezing □ *a squeeze of lemon.* **4** a restriction, especially on spending or borrowing money. **5** (*also* **squeeze play**) *bridge, whist* a way of playing that forces an opponent to discard a potentially winning card. • **squeezable** *adj.* • **squeezability** *noun.* • **squeezer** *noun.* • **put the squeeze on someone** *colloq* to pressurize them into paying something. ◷ Anglo-Saxon *cwysan* to press.

■ **squeeze someone out** to force them from their position, especially by making things intolerable □ *squeezed them out with the high rents.*

■ **squeeze something out** **1** to force it from its place, container, etc. **2** to extract it, especially by exerting some form of pressure □ *They eventually squeezed a confession out of him.*

squeeze-box ▷ *noun, colloq* an accordion or concertina.

squeezer ▷ *noun* a person, device, machine, etc that squeezes something (especially fruit).

squeezy ▷ *adj* said of a bottle, container, etc: soft and flexible so that its contents can be squeezed out.

squelch ▷ *noun* (***squelches***) a loud gurgling or sucking sound made by contact with a thick sticky substance, eg wet mud. ▷ *verb* (***squelches, squelched, squelching***) *intr* **1** to walk through wet ground or with water in one's shoes and so make this sound. **2** to make this sound. ▷ *adverb* with a squelching sound □ *landed squelch in the mud.* • **squelcher** *noun.* • **squelchy** *adj.* ⓔ 17c: imitating the sound.

squib ▷ *noun* **1 a** a small firework that jumps around on the ground before exploding; **b** any firework. **2** a satirical criticism or attack; a lampoon. • **damp squib** a disappointing outcome to something, especially something that had been expected to go well. ⓔ 16c.

squid ▷ *noun* (***squid*** or ***squids***) **1** any of about 350 species of marine mollusc, related to the octopus and cuttlefish, which have a torpedo-shaped body supported by an internal horny plate, two well-developed eyes, eight sucker-bearing arms and two longer tentacles which they use to seize fish. Some are capable of changing colour to match their surroundings, and of emitting a cloud of dark ink when threatened by predators. **2** the flesh of this animal used as food. **3** see under OCTOPUSH. ⓔ 17c.

squidge ▷ *verb* (***squidged, squidging***) to squash; to squeeze together; to squelch. ⓔ 19c.

squidgy /ˈskwɪdʒɪ/ ▷ *adj* (***squidgier, squidgiest***) soft, pliant and sometimes soggy □ *Yuk! These sandwiches have gone all squidgy.* • **squidgily** *adverb.*

squiffy /ˈskwɪfɪ/ ▷ *adj* (***squiffier, squiffiest***) *old use* slightly drunk; tipsy. ⓔ 19c.

squiggle /ˈskwɪɡəl/ ▷ *noun* a wavy scribbled line. ▷ *verb* (***squiggled, squiggling***) **1** to wriggle. **2** to mark with wriggly lines. • **squiggly** *adj.* ⓔ Early 19c.

squill ▷ *noun* any of several perennial plants of the lily family that have small onion-like bulbs and white, blue or purply-blue flowers, especially the **sea onion** whose bulb flesh was formerly used medicinally as a diuretic and expectorant. ⓔ 15c.

squillion /ˈskwɪlɪən/ ▷ *noun* (***squillions*** or after a number ***squillion***) *colloq* a very large number. ⓔ 1980s: an arbitrary formation, modelled on MILLION and BILLION.

squinch ▷ *noun* (***squinches***) *archit* a small arch running diagonally across each corner of a square building or room, creating an octagonal base on which a tower or circular dome may be supported. ⓔ 19c in this sense; 16c, meaning 'a stone scuncheon'.

squint ▷ *noun* **1** *non-technical* the condition of having one or both eyes set slightly off-centre, preventing parallel vision. Also called STRABISMUS. **2** *colloq* a quick look; a peep □ *Gimme a quick squint at the paper.* ▷ *verb* (***squinted, squinting***) *intr* **1** to be affected by a squint. **2** to look with eyes half-closed; to peer. ▷ *adj* **1** having a squint. **2** *colloq* not being properly straight or centred. ▷ *adverb, colloq* in a way or manner that is not properly straight or centred □ *hung the picture squint.* • **squinter** *noun.* • **squinting** *noun, adj.* • **squintingly** *adverb.* ⓔ 16c.

squint-eyed ▷ *adj* affected by STRABISMUS.

squire ▷ *noun* **1** *historical* in England and Ireland: an owner of a large area of rural land, especially the chief landowner in a district. **2** *feudalism* a young man of good family who ranked next to a knight and who would attend upon him. **3** *colloq* a term of address especially used between men □ *Cor blimey, squire, is that your car?* ⓔ 13c: see ESQUIRE.

squirm ▷ *verb* (***squirmed, squirming***) *intr* **1** to wriggle along. **2** to feel or show embarrassment, shame, nervousness, etc often with slight wriggling movements of the body □ *Her accusations made him squirm with remorse.* ▷ *noun* a writhing or wriggling movement. • **squirmy** *adj.* ⓔ 17c.

squirrel /ˈskwɪrəl/ ▷ *noun* any of various medium-sized rodents that are found almost worldwide, which have a bushy tail, beady eyes and tufty ears, and which are noted for holding their food, mainly seeds and nuts, in their front paws as they feed. See also GREY SQUIRREL, RED SQUIRREL, FLYING SQUIRREL. ▷ *verb* (***squirrelled, squirrelling*** or (*chiefly US*) ***squirreled, squirreling***) (*often* **squirrel away** or **squirrel up**) to store or put away something for future use. ⓔ 14c: from Greek *skiouros*, from *skia* shade + *oura* tail.

squirt ▷ *verb* (***squirted, squirting***) **1 a** to shoot (a liquid, etc) out in a narrow jet □ *Martin squirted paint everywhere*; **b** *intr* said of a liquid, etc: to shoot out in a narrow jet □ *Paint squirted everywhere.* **2** *intr* to press the nozzle, trigger, etc of a container, etc so that liquid comes shooting out of it. **3** to cover something with a liquid □ *squirted the table with polish.* ▷ *noun* **1 a** an act or instance of squirting; **b** an amount of liquid squirted. **2** *colloq* a small, insignificant or despicable person, especially one who behaves arrogantly □ *Don't worry about a little squirt like Harry.* • **squirter** *noun.* • **squirting** *noun, adj.* ⓔ 15c: imitating the sound.

squish ▷ *noun* (***squishes***) a gentle splashing or squelching sound. ▷ *verb* (***squishes, squished, squishing***) **1** *intr* to make this sound; to move with this sound. **2** to crush (eg an insect, etc). • **squishy** *adj.* ⓔ 17c: imitating the sound.

squit ▷ *noun* **1** *colloq* an insignificant person. **2** *colloq* nonsense. **3** (**the squits**) *colloq* diarrhoea.

Sr[1] ▷ *abbreviation* **1** used after a name: Senior. **2** Señor. **3** Sir. **4** Sister.

Sr[2] ▷ *symbol, chem* strontium.

sr ▷ *symbol, geom* steradian.

SRC ▷ *abbreviation* Student Representative Council.

SRCh ▷ *abbreviation* State Registered Chiropodist.

Sri or **Shri** /ʃriː/ ▷ *noun* **1** *formerly* an honorific title that in India precedes the name of a deity or a distinguished person. **2** the Indian equivalent of MR. ⓔ 18c: Sanskrit, meaning 'majesty, holiness'.

Sri Lankan /ʃriː ˈlaŋkən/ ▷ *adj* belonging or relating to Sri Lanka (formerly called Ceylon), a republic in S Asia or to its inhabitants. ▷ *noun* a citizen or inhabitant of, or a person born in, Sri Lanka. See also SINHALESE.

SRN ▷ *abbreviation, Brit* State Registered Nurse.

SRO ▷ *abbreviation* **1** self-regulatory organization. **2** standing room only.

SRU ▷ *abbreviation* Scottish Rugby Union.

SS ▷ *abbreviation* **1** Saints. **2** *Schutzstaffel* (German), in the Nazi regime: an elite paramilitary unit, originally of bodyguards to party leaders, later of ruthless and feared enforcers of Nazi policy in all areas, of which the Gestapo formed a part ⓔ 1940s: German, meaning 'defence squadron'. **3** steamship.

SSD ▷ *abbreviation, Brit* Social Services Department.

SSE ▷ *abbreviation* south-south-east.

SSHA ▷ *abbreviation* Scottish Special Housing Association.

SSM ▷ *abbreviation* surface-to-surface missile.

SSP ▷ *abbreviation, Brit* statutory sick pay.

SSR ▷ *abbreviation, formerly* Soviet Socialist Republic.

SSSI ▷ *abbreviation, Brit* Site of Special Scientific Interest, an area that has been designated by the Nature Conservancy Council as being of special scientific interest because it contains particular flora, fauna, geology, etc.

SST ▷ *abbreviation* supersonic transport.

SSW ▷ *abbreviation* south-south-west.

St ▷ *abbreviation* **1** /sənt/ Saint. For entries using the abbreviation *St*, see under SAINT. **2** in addresses: Street.

st ▷ *abbreviation* stone (the imperial unit of weight).

stab ▷ *verb* (***stabbed***, ***stabbing***) **1 a** to wound or pierce with a sharp or pointed instrument or weapon; **b** said of a sharp instrument, etc: to wound or pierce; **c** to push (a sharp implement) into (someone or something). **2** (*often* **stab at something**) to make a quick thrusting movement with something sharp at something. **3** to produce a sharp piercing sensation □ *Her back pain stabs relentlessly.* ▷ *noun* **1** an act of stabbing. **2** a stabbing sensation □ *felt a sudden stab of pain.* • **stabber** *noun.* • **have** or **make a stab at something** to try to do it; to try to answer □ *I didn't really know the answer, but at least I made a stab at it.* ⓒ 14c.

stabbing ▷ *noun* an act or the action or process of using a sharp implement to cut, wound, etc. ▷ *adj* **1** said of a pain: sharp and sudden. **2** said of a remark, etc: hurtful.

stability /stəˈbɪlɪtɪ/ ▷ *noun* the state or quality of being stable. ⓒ 15c: from Latin *stabilitas*, see STABLE[1].

stabilize or **stabilise** /ˈsteɪbɪlaɪz/ ▷ *verb* (***stabilized***, ***stabilizing***) *tr & intr* to make or become stable or more stable. • **stabilization** *noun.*

stabilizer or **stabiliser** ▷ *noun* **1** one or more aerofoils used to give stability to an aircraft. **2** a device used to reduce rolling and pitching of a ship. **3** either of the two small wheels fitted to the back of a child's bicycle to give it added stability, and which can be removed after the child has mastered riding it. **4** any substance that prevents a compound, mixture or solution from changing its form or chemical nature. **5** a chemical substance that encourages food ingredients that would not otherwise mix well to remain together in a homogeneous state, eg as used in salad cream to prevent the separation of oil droplets. **6** *econ* any of various fiscal and monetary measures in a modern economic system which a government might take in order to try to keep the economy stable and reduce the effects of trade cycle fluctuations, eg by controlling interest rates, by cutting the guaranteed price of a commodity to farmers when production outstrips a certain level, etc.

stab in the back ▷ *noun* a devious or unscrupulous act of betrayal, especially one where the perpetrator has posed as a friend or ally of the victim. • **back-stabber** and **back-stabbing** see separate entries. • **stab someone in the back** to carry out this kind of act of betrayal.

stab in the dark ▷ *noun* an uninformed guess.

stable[1] /ˈsteɪbəl/ ▷ *adj* **1** firmly balanced or fixed; not likely to wobble or fall over. **2 a** firmly established; not likely to be abolished, overthrown or destroyed □ *a stable government*; **b** longstanding and committed □ *a stable and loving partnership.* **3 a** regular or constant; not erratic or changing; under control □ *The patient's condition is stable*; **b** said of someone or their disposition, judgement, etc: not likely to behave in an unpredictable manner; not fickle, moody, impulsive, etc. • **stableness** *noun.* • **stably** *adverb.* ⓒ 13c: from Latin *stabilis*, from *stare* to stand.

stable[2] /ˈsteɪbəl/ ▷ *noun* **1 a** a building where horses are kept. **2** a place where horses are bred and trained. **3** the horses that are under one particular trainer, thought of collectively □ *the Pitman stable.* **4** *colloq* a number of people or things with a common background or origin, eg a number of athletes trained by the same coach, a number of recording artistes whose work is distributed by the same record label, etc. ▷ *verb* (***stabled***, ***stabling***) **1** to put (a horse) into or back into its stable. **2** *tr & intr* to keep or be kept in a stable in a specified place. • **stabling** *noun* **1** the act of putting a horse into a stable. **2** accommodation for horses, etc. ⓒ 14c: from Latin *stabulum* standing room.

staccato /stəˈkɑːtoʊ/ *music* ▷ *adverb* in a short, abrupt manner. ▷ *adj* short and abrupt. ▷ *noun* (***staccatos***) a piece of music or a series of notes to be played in this way. ⓒ 18c: Italian, from *distaccare* to separate.

stack ▷ *noun* **1** a large pile. **2** a large pile of hay or straw. **3** (*sometimes* **stacks**) *colloq* a large amount □ *There's stacks to do in this resort.* **4 a** a large industrial chimney; **b** the chimneys of a house, factory, etc thought of collectively. **5** (**the stack** or **the stacks**) in a library: an area of dense bookshelving, often of the concertina type, where books that are not frequently requested are kept, and which is sometimes out-of-bounds to the public. **6** a hi-fi system where the individual components, such as the turntable, CD player, cassette deck, amplifier, etc are placed on top of each other. **7** *chiefly N Amer* an exhaust pipe on a truck that sticks up behind the driver's cab, rather than coming out at the back of the vehicle. ▷ *verb* (***stacked***, ***stacking***) **1** to arrange in a stack or stacks. **2** to pre-arrange (a deck of playing-cards) so that someone can have an advantage. **3** to arrange (circumstances, etc) to favour or disadvantage a particular person. **4** to arrange (aircraft that are waiting to land) into a queue in which each circles the airport at a different altitude. **5** to fill something □ *stacked the fridge with goodies.* • **stackable** *adj.* ⓒ 14c: from Norse *stakkr* haystack.

■ **stack something up** to pile (things) up on top of each other.

stacked ▷ *adj* **1** gathered into a pile. **2** filled or brimming (with a large amount or a large quantity). **3** *computing* said of an operation or task: put into a queue of similar tasks to wait until the computer is free to process it □ *a backlog of stacked printing jobs.* **4** said of cards, odds, etc: weighted or biased (in a specified direction) □ *The odds were stacked in our favour.* **5** (*also* **well-stacked**) *slang* said of a woman, usually by a man, with approval: endowed with a voluptuous figure, especially in having large breasts. **6** said of shoe heels: made from several layers of leather.

stacker ▷ *noun* **1** a person who stacks, especially someone employed to fill supermarket shelves. **2** a machine that stacks, especially an agricultural one that piles up hay, etc or one that piles up goods on a production line.

stadium /ˈsteɪdɪəm/ ▷ *noun* (***stadiums*** or ***stadia*** /-dɪə/) **1** a large sports arena in which the spectators' seats are arranged in rising tiers. **2** *Brit* a football ground □ *Pittodrie Stadium.* ⓒ 19c in sense 1; 17c, meaning 'a race course' originally one *stadium* in length, from Greek *stadion* 'an ancient Greek measure of length of about 1/8th of a mile.

stadium rock ▷ *noun* a type of guitar-based rock music, eg such as that played by *U2* and *Simple Minds*, which can often appear bombastic and anthemic, and is best suited to mass audiences in huge arenas or stadiums.

staff /stɑːf/ ▷ *noun* (*plural* in senses 1-3 ***staffs***, in senses 4-6 ***staffs*** or ***staves***) **1 a** the total number of employees working in an establishment or organization; **b** the employees working for or assisting a manager. **2** the teachers, lecturers, etc of a school, college, university, etc as distinct from the pupils or students. **3** *military* the officers assisting a senior commander, *as adj* □ *staff sergeant.* **4** any stick or rod, especially one that is carried in the hand as a sign of authority, dignity, etc. **5** (*also* **flagstaff**) a pole that a flag is hung from. **6** *music* a set of lines and spaces on which music is written. Also called STAVE. ▷ *verb* (***staffed***, ***staffing***) to provide (an establishment) with staff. ▷ *adj* employed on a permanent basis. • **staffed** *adj, in compounds* □ *found themselves understaffed.* ⓒ Anglo-Saxon *staf.*

staff

There is often uncertainty as to whether collective nouns such as **staff** should be followed by a singular or plural verb. Either is correct, depending on whether the group is being thought of as a single unit or as a number of individuals.

staff college ▷ *noun, military* a college where officers for staff appointments are trained.

staff corps ▷ *noun, military* a body of officers and men who assist a commanding officer and his staff.

staffer ▷ *noun, Brit informal* someone employed on a permanent basis, especially in journalism, as opposed to someone on a temporary contract or a freelance or casual worker.

staff nurse ▷ *noun* a qualified nurse of the rank below SISTER.

staff of life ▷ *noun* any staple food, but especially bread.

Staffs ▷ *abbreviation, English county* Staffordshire.

staff sergeant ▷ *noun, military* the senior sergeant in an army company. Often shortened to **staff**.

stag ▷ *noun* **1** an adult male deer, especially a red deer. **2** *stock exchange slang* someone who buys shares in the hope of selling them immediately for a profit. ▷ *adj* **1** relating to or intended for men only. **2** intended for men only, especially in being pornographic □ ***a stag film***. See also STAG NIGHT. Ⓢ Anglo-Saxon *stagga*.

stag beetle ▷ *noun* a large black or reddish-brown European beetle (up to 50mm in length) which takes its name from the males' large antler-like jaw parts.

stage ▷ *noun* **1 a** a platform on which a performance takes place, especially one in a theatre; **b** *in compounds* □ ***stage door*** □ ***stage craft***. **2 a** any raised area or platform; **b** a platform that is used for supporting something, eg in a microscope where it supports a slide; **c** a platform, especially one in a greenhouse, for putting plants on; **d** a platform that juts out from the land to allow for the transfer of passengers, goods, etc on and off vessels □ ***landing stage***. **3** the scene of a specified event □ ***a battle stage***. **4** any of several distinct and successive periods □ ***The project is at the planning stage***. **5** (**the stage**) the theatre as a profession or art form. **6 a** a part of a journey or route □ ***The last stage of the trip entails a short bus ride***; **b** *Brit* a major stop on a bus route, especially one that involves a change in ticket prices. Also called **fare stage**. **7** *colloq* a stagecoach. ▷ *verb* (***staged, staging***) **1** to present a performance of (a play). **2** to organize and put on something or set it in motion □ ***It was a huge undertaking to stage the festival***. **3** to prearrange something to happen in a particular way; to engineer □ ***tried to stage her colleague's downfall***. • **hold the stage** to contrive to be the centre of attention. • **in** or **by stages** gradually. • **on stage** performing □ ***He was on stage for three hours***. • **stage a comeback** said especially of a performer, actor, etc who has retired or whose career has been flagging: to make a determined effort to relaunch their popularity □ ***Sinatra stages a comeback every so often***. • **stage a strike** said of a workforce, etc: to refuse to work, especially temporarily in response to a specific grievance. • **stage left** or **right** at or on the left- or right-hand side of the stage when looking out at the audience. • **take the stage 1** to begin to act, perform, etc. **2** to come forward to speak to an assembled audience. Ⓢ 13c: from French *estage* storey or tier.

stagecoach ▷ *noun, formerly* a large horse-drawn coach carrying passengers and mail on a regular fixed route.

stagecraft ▷ *noun* the art of writing plays, especially competence in being able to handle the technicalities of the theatre skilfully.

stage directions ▷ *plural noun* the instructions that relate to actors' movements (eg when they should enter and exit the stage), sound and lighting effects, placement of props, etc, all of which are written as part of the script of a play.

stage-diving ▷ *noun* an act or the process of throwing oneself bodily off a stage head first into the audience and which is usually done by enthusiastic male fans at rock concerts.

stage door ▷ *noun* the back or side entrance to a theatre that is for the exclusive use of the performers and others connected with a production and where fans often hang about hoping to glimpse their idols.

stage fright ▷ *noun* nervousness felt by an actor or other performer or speaker when about to appear in front of an audience, especially for the first time.

stagehand ▷ *noun* someone who is responsible for moving scenery and props in a theatre.

stage-manage ▷ *verb* **1** to be the stage manager of (a play). **2** to prearrange for something to happen in a certain way, in order to create a particular effect; to engineer, especially in an underhand or devious way. • **stage-management** *noun*.

stage-managed ▷ *adj* engineered, especially in an underhand or devious way □ ***a stage-managed attack on the prime minister***.

stage manager ▷ *noun* someone who supervises the arrangement of scenery and props for a play.

stage name ▷ *noun* a name assumed by an actor, performer, etc.

stager ▷ *noun, informal* someone who has had plenty of experience in a specified field □ ***an old stager at sorting this kind of mess out***.

stage setting ▷ *noun, theat* MISE-EN-SCÈNE.

stage-struck ▷ *adj* filled with awe of the theatre, especially in having an overwhelming desire to become a stage actor.

stage whisper ▷ *noun* **1** an actor's loud whisper that is intended to be heard by the audience. **2** any loud whisper that is intended to be heard by people other than the person addressed.

stagey see STAGY

stagflation /stag'fleɪʃən/ ▷ *noun* inflation in an economy without the expected growth in employment or demand for goods. Ⓢ 1960s: a blend of *stag*nation + in*flation*.

stagger /'stagə(r)/ ▷ *verb* (***staggered, staggering***) **1** *intr* to walk or move unsteadily. **2** *informal* to cause extreme shock or surprise to someone. **3** to arrange (a series of things) so that they take place or begin at different times. ▷ *noun* the action or an act of staggering. Ⓢ 16c: from Norse *stakra* to push.

staggered ▷ *adj* arranged in such a way that the beginning, ending, etc do not coincide; alternate □ ***introduced staggered working hours***.

staggering ▷ *adj* amazing; shockingly surprising □ ***a staggering response to the appeal***. • **staggeringly** *adverb*.

staggers ▷ *singular noun* **1** a disease of the brain in horses and cattle that causes them to stagger. **2** (*often* **the staggers**) giddiness.

staginess see under STAGY

staging ▷ *noun* **1** scaffolding, especially the horizontal planks used for walking on; any temporary platform. **2** the act or process of putting on a play or other spectacle.

staging post ▷ *noun* a regular stopping place on a journey, now especially one on an air-route.

stagnant /'stagnənt/ ▷ *adj* **1** said of water: not flowing; dirty and foul-smelling because of a lack of movement. **2** not moving or developing; dull and inactive □ ***a stagnant market***. • **stagnantly** *adverb*. • **stagnance** or **stagnancy** *noun*. Ⓢ 17c: from Latin *stagnum* pond.

stagnate /stag'neɪt/ ▷ *verb* (***stagnated, stagnating***) *intr* to be or become stagnant. • **stagnation** *noun*. Ⓢ 17c: from Latin *stagnare, stagnatum* to stagnate.

stag night and **stag party** ▷ *noun* a night out for men only, especially one held to celebrate the end of bachelorhood of a man who is about to get married. Compare HEN PARTY.

stagy or **stagey** *N Amer, especially US* /'steɪdʒɪ/ ▷ *adj* (***stagier, stagiest***) theatrical; artificial or affectedly pretentious. • **stagily** *adverb*. • **staginess** *noun*.

staid ▻ *adj* serious or sober in character or manner, especially to the point of being dull. • **staidly** *adverb*. • **staidness** *noun*. ⓘ 16c: an obsolete past participle of STAY[1].

stain ▻ *verb* (***stained, staining***) **1** to make or become marked or discoloured, often permanently. **2** to change the colour of (eg wood) by applying a liquid chemical. **3** to tarnish or become tarnished □ ***The affair stained his previously good name.*** ▻ *noun* **1** a mark or discoloration. **2** a liquid chemical applied (eg to wood) to bring about a change of colour. **3** a cause of shame or dishonour □ ***a stain on his reputation.*** • **stainer** *noun*. • **stainless** *adj*. ⓘ 14c: from English *steynen* to paint.

stained glass ▻ *noun* decorative glass that has been coloured by a chemical process, and which is used especially in mosaics in church windows.

stainless steel ▻ *noun* any one of three types of STEEL that contain a high percentage of chromium (up to about 25%), making them resistant to rusting and abrasion and possessing a high tensile strength.

stair /stɛə(r)/ ▻ *noun* **1** any of a set of indoor steps connecting the floors of a building. **2** (*also* **stairs**) a set of these. • **below stairs** in the part of the house where the servants live and work. ⓘ Anglo-Saxon *stæger*.

staircase ▻ *noun* a set of stairs, often including the stairwell.

stairway ▻ *noun* a way into a building or part of a building that involves going up a staircase.

stairwell ▻ *noun* **1** the vertical shaft containing a staircase. **2** the floor area at the foot of a flight of stairs.

stake[1] ▻ *noun* **1** a stick or post, usually with one pointed end, that is knocked into the ground as a support, eg for a young tree or a fence. **2** (**the stake**) *formerly* **a** a post that is set into materials for a bonfire and which a person is tied to before being burned alive as a punishment; **b** this type of punishment □ ***sentenced to the stake.*** ▻ *verb* (***staked, staking***) to support or fasten to the ground with a stake. • **stake a claim** to assert or establish a right or ownership, especially to a piece of land. ⓘ Anglo-Saxon *staca*.

▪ **stake something out** **1** to mark the boundary of (a piece of land) with stakes, especially as a way of declaring ownership of it. **2** to keep (a building, etc under surveillance). See also STAKEOUT.

stake[2] ▻ *noun* **1** a sum of money risked in betting. **2** an interest, especially a financial one □ ***have a stake in the project's success.*** **3** (**stakes**) **a** a prize, especially in horse-racing, where the horses' owners put up the money that is to be won; **b** a race of this kind; **c** a specified area or sphere, especially one where there is pressure to appear to succeed □ ***It all depends on how he fares in the promotion stakes.*** ▻ *verb* **1** to risk, especially as a bet. **2** to support, especially financially □ ***staked the enterprise to the tune of £100 000.*** • **at stake** at risk; in danger. ⓘ 16c.

stakeholder ▻ *noun* **1** someone who holds the wager when a number of people place a bet together. **2 a** someone who has an interest or a STAKE[2] (*noun* 2) in something, especially an enterprise, business, etc; **b** *as adj* □ ***stakeholder economy.*** • **stakeholding** *noun*.

stakeholder society ▻ *noun, Brit* a society in which a culture is developed whereby everyone has a stake in its economic success and therefore has a vested interest in ensuring its success in terms of profitability, ethical considerations, etc, a concept promoted by the Labour party since 1995.

stakeout ▻ *noun, colloq* **1** an act or period of surveillance of a person, building, etc, usually carried out by the police or a private detective. **2** the house, etc where this kind of surveillance takes place.

stalactite /ˈstaləktaɪt/ ▻ *noun* an icicle-like mass of calcium carbonate that hangs from the roof of a cave, etc, and which is formed by water continuously dripping through and partially dissolving limestone rock. Compare STALAGMITE. • **stalactitic** /staləkˈtɪtɪk/ *adj*. ⓘ 17c: from Greek *stalaktos* a dripping.

stalag /ˈstalag; *German* ˈʃtalak/ ▻ *noun* during World War II: a prisoner-of-war camp set up by the Germans for non-commissioned officers and men. ⓘ 1940s: an abbreviation of the German *Stammlager* main camp.

stalagmite /ˈstaləgmaɪt/ ▻ *noun* a spiky mass of calcium carbonate that sticks up from the floor of a cave, etc, and which is formed by water containing limestone that drips from a stalactite. Compare STALACTITE. • **stalagmitic** *adj* /staləgˈmɪtɪk/ . ⓘ 17c: from Greek *stalagma* a drop.

stale[1] ▻ *adj* (***staler, stalest***) **1** said of food: past its best because it has been kept too long; not fresh and, therefore, unpalatable. **2** said of air: not fresh; musty. **3** said of words, phrases, ideas, etc: overused and no longer interesting or original. **4** said of an athlete, race horse, etc: out of condition because of over-training. **5** said of someone: lacking in energy because of overfamiliarity, boredom, etc with the job in hand. **6** said of news, gossip, etc: out-of-date. • **stalely** *adverb*. • **staleness** *noun*. ⓘ 14c.

stale[2] ▻ *noun* the urine of farm animals, especially horses and cattle. ▻ *verb* (***staled, staling***) said of horses and cattle: to urinate. ⓘ 15c.

stalemate ▻ *noun* **1** *chess* a position where either player cannot make a move without putting their king in check and which results in a draw. **2** a position in any contest or dispute where no progress can be made and no winner can emerge; a deadlock □ ***The staff and management had reached a stalemate over pay and conditions.*** ⓘ 18c.

Stalinism /ˈstɑːlɪnɪzəm/ ▻ *noun, politics* the political, economic and social principles and practices of Lenin's successor, especially his ruthless determination to transform the former USSR's economy from a poor agricultural one into a sophisticated industrialized one at any cost, that culminated in the country becoming a virtual dictatorship ruled by a monolithic government. • **Stalinist** *noun, adj*. Compare LENINISM, MARXISM. ⓘ 1920s: named after Josef Vissarionovich Dzhugashvili (1879–1953) who changed his name to *Stalin*, meaning 'man of steel', in 1913, and who, after expelling Trotsky from the communist party in 1929, ruled Russia until his death.

stalk[1] /stɔːk/ ▻ *noun* **1** *bot* **a** the main stem of a plant; **b** a stem that attaches a leaf, flower or fruit to the plant. **2** any slender connecting part. • **stalked** *adj*. • **stalkless** *adj*. ⓘ 14c.

stalk[2] /stɔːk/ ▻ *verb* (***stalked, stalking***) **1** to hunt, follow, or approach stealthily. **2** *intr* to walk or stride stiffly, proudly, disdainfully, etc □ ***stalked out of the meeting.*** **3** to pervade, penetrate or spread over (a place) □ ***After the murder, fear stalked the neighbourhood.*** ▻ *noun* **1** an act or the process of stalking. **2** a striding way of walking. • **stalking** *noun, adj*. ⓘ Anglo-Saxon *bistealcian* to move stealthily.

stalker ▻ *noun* **1** someone who stalks, especially game. **2** someone who follows another person, often with a sinister purpose.

stalking-horse ▻ *noun* **1** a horse or an imitation of a horse that a hunter hides behind while approaching game. **2** a person or thing that is used to conceal real plans or intentions, especially a planned attack; a pretext. **3** someone who puts himself or herself forward or who is put forward as a candidate for a post, especially a political one, in order to deflect votes from the candidate who is likely to win and so pave the way for some other candidate who has a good chance of winning at a subsequent ballot stage, at which point the stalking-horse will withdraw from the action □ ***John Redwood — a real contender or just a stalking-horse?***

stall¹ /stɔːl/ ⊳ *noun* **1** a compartment in a cowshed, stable, etc for housing a single animal. **2 a** a stand, often with a canopy, that is set up temporarily in a market place, bazaar, fête, etc for the purpose of selling goods; **b** *in compounds* □ ***stall-holder*** □ ***flower stall.*** **3** (**stalls**) the seats on the ground floor of a theatre or cinema. **4** an act or condition of a vehicle or its engine having stalled (*verb* 1). **5** said of an aircraft: an instance of sudden loss of control of the height it is flying at, caused either by a reduction in its air speed or by an increase in the angle of attack. **6** one of a row of public urinals which are screened off from their neighbours by small partitions. **7 a** a church seat with arms, especially one in the choir or chancel; **b** a pew without doors. **8** (**the stalls**) STARTING STALLS. **9 a** each of the fingers of a glove; **b** a FINGERSTALL. ⊳ *verb* (***stalled***, ***stalling***) **1** *tr & intr* **a** said of a motor vehicle or its engine: to cut out or make it cut out unintentionally, especially by not using the clutch properly; **b** to come, bring or be brought to a standstill □ ***Plans for the expansion had stalled.*** **2** to put (an animal) into a stall. **3** said of an aircraft: to go into a stall (*noun* 5) or to make it go into a stall. **4** *chiefly US* to stick or to make something stick in snow, mud, etc. ◎ Anglo-Saxon *steall* a standing place.

stall² /stɔːl/ ⊳ *verb* (***stalled***, ***stalling***) **1** to delay. **2** *intr* to do something in order to delay something else; to be evasive □ ***Quit stalling and answer the question.*** ⊳ *noun* an act of stalling; a delaying tactic. • **stall for time** to hold off doing something in the hope that things will change in one's favour. ◎ 16c: from obsolete *stale*, a decoy.

stall-feed ⊳ *verb* **1** to keep (an animal) in its stall and fatten it up before sending it to the slaughter. **2** said of an animal: to be kept in a stall for this purpose. ◎ 18c.

stallholder ⊳ *noun* someone who sells goods from a stall, especially a street market stall.

stallion /ˈstaljən/ ⊳ *noun* **1** an uncastrated adult male horse, especially one kept for breeding. See also FOAL, MARE. **2** *slang* a man of considerable sexual prowess. ◎ 14c: from French *estalon* stallion.

stalwart /ˈstɔːlwət/ ⊳ *adj* **1** strong and sturdy. **2** unwavering in commitment and support; reliable. ⊳ *noun* a long-standing and committed supporter, especially a political one □ ***the stalwarts of the right.*** • **stalwartly** *adverb*. • **stalwartness** *noun*. ◎ Anglo-Saxon *stælwierthe* serviceable.

stamen /ˈsteɪmən/ ⊳ *noun* (***stamens*** or ***stamina*** /ˈstamɪnə/) *bot* in flowering plants: the male reproductive structure, which consists of a stalk-like FILAMENT that supports a specialized double-celled chamber at its end (called the ANTHER) where the pollen grains are produced. • **staminiferous** /stamɪˈnɪfərəs/ *adj* having stamens. ◎ 17c: Latin, meaning 'warp' or 'thread'.

stamina /ˈstamɪnə/ ⊳ *noun* energy and staying power, especially of the kind that is needed to tackle and withstand prolonged physical or mental exertion. ◎ 18: the Latin plural of STAMEN.

staminate /ˈstamɪneɪt/ ⊳ *adj* said of certain flowering plants: having male reproductive parts, but no female ones. ◎ 19c: see STAMEN.

stammer /ˈstamə(r)/ ⊳ *verb* (***stammered***, ***stammering***) *tr & intr* to speak or say something in a faltering or hesitant way, often by repeating words or parts of words, usually because of indecision, heightened emotion or a pathological disorder that affects the speech organs or the nervous system. ⊳ *noun* a way of speaking that is characterized by this kind of faltering or hesitancy. • **stammerer** *noun*. • **stammering** *adj, noun*. • **stammeringly** *adverb*. ◎ Anglo-Saxon *stamerian*.

stamp ⊳ *verb* (***stamped***, ***stamping***) **1** *tr & intr* to bring (the foot) down with force □ ***stamped her feet in rage.*** **2** *intr* to walk with a heavy tread. **3 a** to imprint or impress (a mark or design); **b** to imprint or impress something with a mark or design, especially to show it has official approval or that the appropriate duty, fee, etc has been paid. **4** to fix or mark deeply □ ***The full horror of the event was stamped on his memory.*** **5** to prove to be; to characterize □ ***His lies stamp him as untrustworthy.*** **6** to fix a postage or other stamp on something. **7** to crush, grind or pound (ore, etc). ⊳ *noun* **1 a** a small piece of gummed paper bearing an official mark and indicating that a tax or fee has been paid, especially a POSTAGE STAMP; **b** a similar piece of gummed paper that is given away free, eg by petrol stations, and which can be collected until the requisite number of them is held, when they can be exchanged for a gift; **c** *colloq* a similar piece of gummed paper formerly stuck onto a card to record someone's National Insurance contributions. **2 a** a device for stamping a mark or design; **b** the mark or design that is stamped on something. **3** a characteristic mark or sign □ ***The crime bears the stamp of a professional.*** **4** an act or the process of stamping with the foot. • **stamper** *noun*. • **stamping** *adj, noun*. • **stamp of approval** an endorsement, either in physical or figurative terms □ ***Our proposal got management's stamp of approval*** □ ***The kite mark is a safety stamp of approval.*** ◎ Anglo-Saxon *stampian*.

■ **stamp on something** to bring one's foot down deliberately and heavily on top of it.

■ **stamp something out 1** to put out (a fire) by stamping on it. **2** to put an end to (an activity or practice, especially an illicit one) □ ***tried to stamp out the use of cocaine.*** **3** to quell it or put it down □ ***tried to stamp out the militants.*** **4** to eradicate (a disease) □ ***Rabies has now been stamped out.***

stamp album ⊳ *noun* a special book for keeping a collection of postage stamps in, especially unusual or foreign ones.

stamp collecting ⊳ *noun* an informal term for PHILATELY.

stamp collector ⊳ *noun* someone whose hobby, pastime, business, etc is PHILATELY.

stamp duty and **stamp tax** ⊳ *noun* a tax that is incurred when certain legal documents, eg those transferring ownership of property, are drawn up.

stampede /stamˈpiːd/ ⊳ *noun* **1** a sudden dash made by a group of startled animals, especially when they all go charging off in the same direction. **2** an excited or hysterical rush by a crowd of people. ⊳ *verb* (***stampeded***, ***stampeding***) *tr & intr* to rush or make (people or animals) rush in a herd or crowd. ◎ 19cs: from Spanish *estampida* a stamping.

stamp hinge see under HINGE

stamping-ground ⊳ *noun* someone's usual or favourite haunt or meeting place. ◎ 18c: originally said of the place a wild animal habitually returns to.

stamp mill ⊳ *noun* a machine operated pestle or series of pestles for crushing ores.

stance /stɑːns, stans/ ⊳ *noun* **1** point of view; a specified attitude towards something. **2 a** the position that the body of a person or an animal takes up □ ***She has a very upright stance***; **b** a position or manner of standing, eg when preparing to play a stroke in sport. ◎ 1960s in sense 1; 19c in sense 2; 16c in obsolete sense 'a standing place' from Latin *stare* to stand.

stanch see STAUNCH²

stanchion /ˈstɑːnʃən, ˈstan-/ ⊳ *noun* an upright beam or pole that functions as a support, eg in a window, ship, mine, etc. ◎ 14c: from French *estanchon*, from *estance* a prop.

stand ⊳ *verb* (***stood***, ***standing***) **1** *intr* to be in, remain in or move into an upright position supported by the legs or a base. **2** *tr & intr* to place or situate, or be placed or situated in a specified position □ ***stood the vase on the table.*** **3** *intr* to be a specified height □ ***The tower stands 300 feet tall.*** **4** to tolerate or put up with someone or something □ ***How***

can you stand that awful noise? **5** to be a candidate, eg in an election, etc □ *stood for S Aberdeen in the bi-election.* **6** *intr* to be in a specified state or condition □ *I stand corrected.* **7** *intr* to be in a position (to do something) □ *We stand to make a lot of money.* **8** *intr* to continue to apply or be valid □ *The decision stands.* **9** to withstand or survive something □ *stood the test of time.* ▷ *noun* **1** a base on which something sits or is supported. **2** a stall that goods or services for sale are displayed on. **3 a** a structure at a sports ground, etc which has sitting or standing accommodation for spectators; **b** a platform or similar structure; **c** (**the stand**) a witness box. **4 a** a rack, frame, etc where coats, hats, umbrellas, etc may be hung; **b** *in compounds* □ *hallstand.* **5** an opinion, attitude or course of action that is adopted resolutely □ *took a stand against animal testing.* **6** *cricket* a partnership between batsmen, expressed in terms of the time it lasts or the number of runs scored. **7** an act of resisting attack. **8** a stop on a tour made by a band, theatre company etc □ *at The King's for a two-week stand.* See also ONE-NIGHT STAND. • **make a stand** to adopt a determined attitude (against or towards something) □ *made a stand for higher pay.* • **Stand at ease!** a command given to soldiers on the parade ground, etc that allows them to assume a more relaxed position. • **stand at** or **to attention** to assume a very erect posture. • **stand guard** to keep a lookout for danger, an enemy, etc. • **stand on one's own feet** or **own two feet** to be or become independent. • **stand one's ground** to maintain a position resolutely; to refuse to give in. • **stand someone something** *colloq* to buy it for them □ *stood me lunch.* • **stand to reason** to be the logical or obvious assumption to make. • **stand trial** to go through the usual legal processes in order to establish guilt or innocence. • **take the stand** to enter a witness box and give evidence. ⓒ Anglo-Saxon *standan.*

■ **stand by 1** to be in a state of readiness to act. **2** to look on without taking the required or expected action □ *just stood by and never offered to help.* See also STAND-BY.

■ **stand by someone** to give them loyalty or support, especially when they are in difficulty.

■ **stand down 1** to resign, especially in favour of someone else. **2** to finish giving evidence from a witness box.

■ **stand for something 1** to be in favour of promoting it. **2** said of a symbol, letter, device, etc: to represent, mean or signify something □ *The red ribbon stands for AIDS awareness.* **3** to tolerate or allow it.

■ **stand in for someone** to act as a substitute for them. See also STAND-IN.

■ **stand off 1** to keep at a distance. **2** *naut* to steer away from (the shore or an obstacle). See also STAND-OFF.

■ **stand on** *naut* to continue on the same course.

■ **stand on something** to insist on it □ *We don't stand on ceremony.*

■ **stand out** to be noticeable or prominent.

■ **stand out for something** to persist in demanding or seeking (a concession, etc); to hold out.

■ **stand out for** or **against something** to remain resolutely in favour of or opposed to it.

■ **stand over someone** or **something** to watch them or it, especially in a supervisory or controlling manner.

■ **stand to** to be ready (to start work, etc).

■ **stand up 1** to assume a standing position. **2** to prove to be valid on examination □ *an argument that will stand up in court.* See also STAND-UP.

■ **stand someone up** *colloq* to fail to keep an appointment or date with them.

■ **stand up for someone 1** to back them in a dispute, argument, etc. **2** *chiefly US* to act as best man or be a witness at their wedding □ *Andy asked Bobby if he would stand up for him.*

■ **stand up for something** to support it.

■ **stand up to someone** to face or resist them.

■ **stand up to something** to withstand it (eg hard wear or criticism).

stand-alone ▷ *adj* said of a computer: able to work independently of a network or other system.

standard /ˈstandəd/ ▷ *noun* **1** an established or accepted model □ *Size 14 is the standard for British women.* **2** something that is basic and without any extra features, etc □ *This is the standard — the deluxe is gold-plated.* **3** something that functions as a model of excellence for other similar things to be compared to, measured or judged against □ *the standard by which all other dictionaries will be measured.* **4** (*often* **standards**) **a** a degree or level of excellence, value, quality, etc □ *Standards of living have fallen*; **b** a principle, eg of morality, integrity, etc □ *moral standards.* **5** a flag or other emblem, especially one carried on a pole □ *the royal standard.* See also STANDARD-BEARER. **6** an upright pole or support. **7** *colloq* something, especially a song, that has remained popular over the years □ *Julian Cope's set was a mixture of new stuff and old standards.* **8 a** the legally required weight for coins; **b** the fineness of the metal used in the minting of coins; **c** the commodity that the value of a country's other commodities and its monetary unit is based on □ *the gold standard.* **9** an unsupported tree, especially a fruit tree or shrub, as opposed to one that has been trained up an espalier, etc. **10** an authorized model of a unit of measurement or weight. ▷ *adj* **1** having features that are generally accepted as normal or expected; typical; average; unexceptional □ *A month's notice is standard practice.* **2** accepted as supremely authoritative □ *the standard text of Shakespeare.* **3** said of language: accepted as correct by educated native speakers. ⓒ 12c: from French *estandart* a gathering place for soldiers.

standard-bearer ▷ *noun* **1** someone who carries a flag. **2** the leader of a movement or cause.

standard deviation ▷ *noun, math* (abbreviation **SD**) a measurement frequently used in statistics, which is obtained by calculating the square root of the mean of the squared deviations that a set of observations show from the mean of the sample.

Standard English ▷ *noun* the variety of English perceived as being spoken by educated people, which is generally accepted as the correct form of the language. The term is usually avoided by linguists because it has a wide range of overlapping interpretations and is inherently judgemental. See also RECEIVED PRONUNCIATION.

standard error or **standard error of the mean** ▷ *noun, math* (abbreviation **SE** or **SEM**) a measurement widely used in statistics, which is obtained by dividing the STANDARD DEVIATION by the root of the number of observations.

standard gauge ▷ *noun* a railway system where the tracks are 4ft $8^1/_2$ins (1.435m) apart.

Standard grade ▷ *noun, Scottish* **1** an examination that replaced the O grade in 1986, taken in the fourth year of secondary school and designed to test pupils' ability to apply what they have been taught in practical ways as well as having a written component. **2 a** a subject that is offered or taken at this level; **b** a pass in a subject at this level.

Standard English

Standard English is the form of English generally used throughout the English-speaking world in education, the law-courts and government bodies, the media, and in all other forms of formal speech and writing.

It consists of those elements of vocabulary and grammar (not pronunciation) that are recognized and used by English-speakers across regional and national divides, although there is in fact no single regional community whose language conforms to it entirely, the language of each community having its own variance to a greater or lesser degree.

We can, then, only really say that a particular word or construction is or is not Standard English. Those words or constructions that are not Standard English are **non-standard**, which is not to say *substandard* or inferior. There is no difference in 'correctness' between *I ain't done nothing* and *I seen it* on the one hand, and *I haven't done anything* and *I saw it* on the other. Where they differ is in appropriateness: *I ain't done it yet* would be inappropriate in a business letter, but perfectly acceptable in informal speech.

standardize or **standardise** ▷ *verb* (***standardized***, ***standardizing***) to make (all the examples of something) conform in size, shape, etc. • **standardization** *noun*. • **standardizer** *noun*. ⌚ 19c.

standard lamp ▷ *noun* a lamp at the top of a pole which has a base that sits on the floor.

standard of living ▷ *noun* a measurement of the comparative wealth of a class or community, usually taken from their ability to afford certain commodities.

stand-by ▷ *noun* (***stand-by's*** or ***stand-bys***) **1 a** a state of readiness to act, eg in an emergency; **b** a person or thing that takes on this kind of role. **2 a** said of air travel: a system of allocating spare seats to passengers who do not have reservations, after all the booked seats have been taken; **b** a ticket that has been allocated in this way. • **on stand-by** ready and prepared to do something if necessary □ *The emergency team were on stand-by.*

stand-in ▷ *noun* a deputy or substitute.

standing ▷ *noun* **1** position, status, or reputation. **2** the length of time something has been in existence, someone has been doing something, etc □ *a professor of long standing.* ▷ *adj* **1** done, taken, etc in or from a standing position □ *a standing ovation.* **2** permanent; regularly used □ *a standing order.* **3** not moving □ *found some tadpoles in the standing water.*

standing committee ▷ *noun* a committee that is permanently in place to deal with a particular subject.

standing joke ▷ *noun* a subject that causes hilarity, derision or jeering whenever it is mentioned.

standing order ▷ *noun* **1** *finance* an instruction from an account-holder to a bank to make fixed payments from the account to a third party at regular intervals. Compare DIRECT DEBIT. **2** an order placed with a shopkeeper for a regular supply of something, eg a daily newspaper. **3** *military* a permanent or long-term rule. **4** (**standing orders**) regulations that govern the procedures that a legislative assembly adopts.

standing ovation ▷ *noun* a very enthusiastic response to a performance where the audience get out of their seats to clap, especially for a long time.

standing stone ▷ *noun* a large block of stone, usually one of several which were set upright in the ground in the late Neolithic and Early Bronze Ages to form a circle or other significant shape.

standing wave ▷ *noun, physics* a wave that results from interference between waves of the same wavelength that are travelling in opposite directions, eg on a guitar string, where a wave passes along the string and is reflected back along itself when it reaches the end of the string. Also called **stationary wave**.

stand-off ▷ *noun* **1** a stalemate or the condition of being in stalemate. **2** (*also* **stand-off half**) *rugby* a half-back who stands away from the scrum and acts as a link between the scrum-half and the three-quarters. Also called **fly half**, **halfback**. • **Mexican stand-off 1** a set of circumstances where someone has no opportunity of self-defence. **2** *colloq* a situation of deadlock, especially one where none of the parties involved stands to benefit from the lack of progress.

stand-offish ▷ *adj* unfriendly or aloof. • **stand-offishly** *adverb*. • **stand-offishness** *noun*.

standout ▷ *noun* someone or something that is of high quality.

standpipe ▷ *noun* a vertical pipe leading from a water supply, especially one that provides an emergency supply in the street when household water is cut off.

standpoint ▷ *noun* a point of view.

standstill ▷ *noun* a complete stop, with no progress being made at all □ *Traffic had come to a complete standstill.*

stand-up ▷ *adj* **1** in a standing position. **2** said of a verbal fight as well as a physical one: earnest; passionate; fervent. **3** said of a comedian: performing solo in front of a live audience and so likely to have to improvise with ad-libs and off-the-cuff jokes.

stanhope /'stanəp/ ▷ *noun* a light open one-seater carriage originally with two wheels but later commonly with four. ⌚ 19c: named after the Hon and Rev Fitzroy Stanhope (1787–1864), the person for whom the first one was made.

Stanislavsky method see under METHOD ACTING

stank *past tense of* STINK

Stanley knife /'stanlɪ —/ ▷ *noun, trademark* a type of very sharp knife with replaceable blades that is used for DIY purposes, eg cutting wallpaper, vinyl flooring, etc. ⌚ From Stanley, the name of the firm that manufactures it and other hand tools.

stannary /'stanərɪ/ ▷ *noun* (***stannaries***) a tin-mining district. ⌚ 15c: from Latin *stannum* tin.

stannic /'stanɪk/ ▷ *adj, chem* said of a compound: containing tin, especially in the tetravalent state. ⌚ 18c: from Latin *stannum* tin.

stannite /'stanaɪt/ ▷ *noun, mineralogy* sulphur of copper, iron and tin which usually occurs in tin-bearing veins. ⌚ 19c: from Latin *stannum* tin.

stannous /'stanəs/ ▷ *adj, chem* said of a compound: containing tin, especially in the bivalent state. ⌚ 19c: from Latin *stannum* tin.

stanza /'stanzə/ ▷ *noun* (***stanzas***) a verse in poetry. • **stanza'd** or **stanzaed** *adj*. • **stanzaic** /stan'zeɪɪk/ *adj*. ⌚ 16c: Italian, meaning 'stopping place'.

stapes /'steɪpiːz/ ▷ *noun* (*plural* ***stapes***) *anatomy* a small stirrup-shaped bone in the middle ear which, together with the MALLEUS and INCUS, transmits sound waves from the eardrum to the inner ear. Also called **stirrup bone**. ⌚ 17c: Latin, meaning 'stirrup'.

staphylococcus /stafɪloʊ'kɒkəs/ ▷ *noun* (***staphylococci*** /-'kɒksaɪ/) *biol* any of several pus-producing bacteria that are found on the skin and mucous membranes of humans and other animals, some of which can cause boils and abscesses, food poisoning, pneumonia and inflammation of the bone marrow. • **staphylococcal** *adj*. ⌚ 19c: from Greek *staphyle* bunch of grapes + *kokkos* a grain or berry, referring to their shape.

staple[1] /'steɪpəl/ ▷ *noun* **1** a squared-off U-shaped wire fastener for holding sheets of paper together and which is forced through the paper from a special device that has several of these loaded into it. **2** a U-shaped metal nail that is used to hold wires in place, to fasten a hasp to a post, etc. ▷ *verb* (***stapled, stapling***) to fasten or attach with a staple or staples. ⓒ Anglo-Saxon *stapol* post or support.

staple² /ˈsteɪpəl/ ▷ *adj* **1** principal; main □ *staple foods.* **2** said of a traded article, industry, etc of a specified individual, company, region, country, etc: rated and established as being of prime economic importance □ *Ship-building was once one of our staple industries.* ▷ *noun* **1** an economically important food, product, ingredient, industry, export, etc. **2** a major constituent of a particular community's diet. **3** the fibre of cotton, wool, etc thought of in terms of its quality and length. ▷ *verb* to grade (wool, cotton, etc) according to its quality and length. ⓒ 15c: from Dutch *stapel* shop or warehouse.

staple gun ▷ *noun* a hand-held tool that fires staples into a surface.

stapler /ˈsteɪplə(r)/ ▷ *noun* a device for driving staples (STAPLE¹ *noun* 1) through paper.

star ▷ *noun* **1 a** any celestial body that can be seen in a clear night sky as a twinkling white light, which consists of a sphere of gaseous material that is held together entirely by its own gravitational field, and which generates heat and light energy by means of nuclear fusion reactions deep within its interior; **b** used more loosely to refer to: any planet, comet or meteor, as well as any of these bodies. **2** a representation of such a body in the form of a figure with five or more radiating points, often used as a symbol of rank or excellence, as an award, etc. **3 a** a celebrity, especially in the world of entertainment or sport □ *movie star*; **b** a principal performer; **c** someone or something that is distinguished or thought well of in a specified field □ *Her brilliant paper made her the star of the conference*; **d** *colloq* anyone who shines at something □ *Fiona's a star — she got tickets for Julian Cope.* **4** (**the stars**) **a** the planets regarded as an influence on people's fortunes □ *believed his fate was in the stars*; **b** a horoscope □ *I'm going to win the Lottery according to my stars.* **5** an asterisk. **6** a white mark on the forehead of a horse, etc. ▷ *verb* (***starred, starring***) **1** *tr & intr* to feature someone as a principal performer or to appear in (a film, TV programme, theatre production, etc) as a principal performer. **2** to decorate something with stars. **3** to asterisk. • **starless** *adj.* • **starlike** *adj, adverb.* • **starry** see separate entry. • **see stars** to see spots of light before one's eyes, especially as a result of a heavy blow to the head. ⓒ Anglo-Saxon *steorra.*

star billing ▷ *noun* said of someone's name when it appears on a poster, flier, etc or in neon lights advertising a show, etc: the most prominent position, indicating they are the main attraction.

starboard /ˈstɑːbəd, ˈstɑːbɔːd/ ▷ *noun* the right side of a ship or aircraft as you look towards the front of it. ▷ *adj, adverb* relating to, on or towards the right side. Compare PORT². ⓒ Anglo-Saxon *steorbord* steering board.

starch ▷ *noun* (***starches***) **1 a** *biochem* a carbohydrate that occurs in all green plants, where it serves as an energy store, usually in the form of small white granules in seeds, tubers, etc; **b** the fine white powder form of this substance that is extracted from potatoes and cereals and which is widely used in the food industry; **c** a preparation of this substance used to stiffen fabrics and to make paper. **2** stiffness of manner; over-formality. ▷ *verb* (***starched, starching***) to stiffen with starch. • **starched** *adj.* • **starcher** *noun.* ⓒ Anglo-Saxon *stercan* to stiffen.

Star Chamber ▷ *noun* **1** *historical* **a** a suite of rooms in the palace of Westminster where members of the king's council and other dignitaries sat and held trials; **b** the court that sat in these rooms, which was very influential under the rules of James VI and I and Charles I and which administered its justice in a highly selective and tyrannical way until it was abolished in 1641. Also called **Court of Star-chamber**. **2** (*sometimes* **star chamber**) any decision, form of questioning, dispensation of justice, etc that is thought to be arbitrary, oppressive or tyrannical. ⓒ 14c.

starchy ▷ *adj* (***starchier, starchiest***) **1** like or containing starch. **2** said of someone's manner, demeanour, etc: over-formal; solemn and prudish. • **starchily** *adverb.* • **starchiness** *noun.*

star connection ▷ *noun, elec engineering* a Y-shaped connection in a three-phase load where one terminal of each phase is connected to a common point which is neutral. Also called **Y-connection**.

star-crossed ▷ *adj, literary* ill-fated; doomed never to be happy because the stars are in inauspicious positions □ *those star-crossed lovers, Dante and Beatrice.*

stardom ▷ *noun* the state of being a celebrity.

stardust ▷ *noun* an imaginary dust that blinds someone's eyes to reality and fills their thoughts with romantic illusions.

stare ▷ *verb* (***stared, staring***) *intr* said of someone or their eyes: to look with a fixed gaze. ▷ *noun* **1** an act of staring. **2** a fixed gaze. • **be staring someone in the face** **1** said of a solution, etc: to be readily apparent, but unnoticed. **2** said of a misfortune, etc: to be menacingly imminent. ⓒ Anglo-Saxon *starian.*

■ **stare someone out** or **down** to stare more fixedly at (someone staring back), causing them to look away.

starfish ▷ *noun* the popular name for any of numerous types of marine invertebrate animals that have a number of arms (usually five) radiating outward from a flattened central disc-like body.

star fruit ▷ *noun* a smooth-skinned yellow fruit, star-shaped in cross-section, which is produced by the CARAMBOLA, a SE Asian tree. ⓒ 1970s.

stargaze ▷ *verb intr* **1** to study the stars. **2** *colloq* to daydream. • **stargazer** *noun.* • **stargazing** *noun, adj.*

stark ▷ *adj* **1** barren or severely bare; harsh or simple □ *a stark treeless hillside.* **2** plain; unembellished □ *the stark truth.* **3** utter; downright □ *an act of stark stupidity.* ▷ *adverb* utterly; completely □ *stark staring bonkers.* • **starkly** *adverb.* • **starkness** *noun.* ⓒ Anglo-Saxon *stearc* hard or strong.

starkers ▷ *adj, colloq* **1** stark-naked. **2** stark raving mad.

stark-naked ▷ *adj* without any clothes on at all. ⓒ Anglo-Saxon *steort* tail + *nacod* naked.

starlet ▷ *noun* **1** a young film actress, especially one who is thought to have the potential to become a star of the future. **2** any young person who shows an outstanding aptitude in a specified field, eg in the world of sport, entertainment, etc.

starlight ▷ *noun* the light from the stars.

starling¹ /ˈstɑːlɪŋ/ ▷ *noun* a small common gregarious songbird which has dark glossy speckled feathers and a short tail. ⓒ Anglo-Saxon *stærling.*

starling² /ˈstɑːlɪŋ/ ▷ *noun* piles that are driven into a river bed to protect a bridge pier from floating debris, ice, etc. ⓒ 17c.

starlit ▷ *adj* lit by the stars.

star-nosed mole ▷ *noun* an amphibious mole that is found in the eastern states of N America, which has a ring of 22 pink fleshy tentacles around its muzzle which it uses as sensory organs to help it seek out food. ⓒ 19c: so called because of its ring of tentacles that form a star shape.

star ruby ▷ *noun* a ruby whose crystalline structure gives it a starlike appearance in reflected light.

starry ▻ *adj* (*starrier*, *starriest*) **1** relating to or like a star or the stars; filled or decorated with stars. **2** shining brightly. • **starrily** *adverb*. • **starriness** *noun*.

starry-eyed ▻ *adj* **1** naively idealistic or optimistic. **2** radiantly happy.

the Stars and Stripes ▻ *noun* the national flag of the US. Also called **the Star-Spangled Banner**.

star sapphire ▻ *noun* a sapphire whose crystalline structure gives it a starlike appearance in reflected light.

star shell ▻ *noun, military* a type of shell that is used to light up the night sky so that the position of the enemy is revealed.

star-ship ▻ *noun, science fiction* a big interstellar spacecraft that is manned by a large number of people who go off on voyages that can last years, and which effectively functions as a self-contained community for the storylines to be built around □ *the Star-Ship Enterprise*. Often shortened to **SS**.

the Star-Spangled Banner ▻ *noun* **1** the national anthem of the US. **2** THE STARS AND STRIPES.

star-spangled ▻ *adj* decorated with stars, especially glittering ones.

star-studded ▻ *adj* **1** *colloq* said of the cast of a film, theatre production, etc: featuring many well-known performers. **2** covered with stars.

star system ▻ *noun* **1** *astron* a group of stars thought of collectively; a galaxy. **2** the Hollywood practice of building up the profile of actors and actresses both on- and off-screen and of giving the leading parts in films to well-known names in hope of drawing a big audience and so increase the chance of a successful production. See also STUDIO SYSTEM.

START /stɑːt/ ▻ *abbreviation* Strategic Arms Reduction Talks or Treaty.

start ▻ *verb* (*started*, *starting*) **1** *tr & intr* to begin; to bring or come into being. **2** *tr & intr* to set or be set in motion, or put or be put into a working state □ *She started the car*. **3** to establish or set up □ *started his own business*. **4** to initiate or get going; to cause or set off □ *Harry started the quarrel*. **5** *intr* to begin a journey □ *started for home at midday*. **6** *intr* to flinch or shrink back suddenly and sharply, eg in fear or surprise. **7** *intr, colloq* to begin to behave in an annoying way, eg by picking a quarrel, making a noise, fighting, raising a disagreeable subject, etc □ *Come on, kids! Please don't start*. **8** said of someone's eyes: to bulge. **9** to drive (an animal) from a lair or hiding-place. ▻ *noun* **1** the first or early part. **2** a beginning, origin or cause. **3** the time or place at which something starts □ *made an early start*. **4** an advantage given or held at the beginning of a race or other contest □ *gave her a two metre start*. **5** a help in, or opportunity of, beginning, eg in a career □ *His uncle gave him a start in the business*. **6** a sudden flinching or shrinking back. • **for a start** as an initial consideration; in the first place. • **to start with 1** used to introduce a list, especially of complaints, objections, etc: as a first consideration. **2** in the beginning; in the first instance □ *She behaved very badly to start with*. Ⓒ Anglo-Saxon *styrten*.

■ **start as** or **start out as something** to begin a career, etc as it □ *started out as a doctor*.

■ **start off** or **out 1** to be initially □ *The film starts off in black and white*. **2** to begin a journey, etc □ *We started out yesterday*. **3** to begin (doing a specified thing or with a specified aim in mind) □ *started out camping, but the weather was too bad*.

■ **start something off 1** to be the cause of it □ *Anger over the tax started the riots off*. **2** to begin it.

■ **start on someone** to become suddenly and violently hostile towards them; to turn on them.

■ **start up** or **start something up 1** said of a car, engine, etc: to run or get it running. **2** to establish it; to put it into action □ *The mums started up their own playgroup*. See also START-UP.

■ **start with something** to have it at the beginning □ *The book starts with a gruesome murder*.

starter ▻ *noun* **1** an official who gives the signal for a race to begin. **2** any of the competitors, horses, greyhounds, etc that assemble for the start of a race. **3** (*also* **starter motor**) an electric motor that is used to start the engine of a motor vehicle. **4** the first course of a meal. • **for starters** *colloq* in the first place; for a start. • **under starter's orders** said of racehorses, greyhounds, athletes, etc: waiting for the official signal that the race can begin.

starting-block ▻ *noun, athletics* a device, usually one of a pair, that consists of a shaped block set at a backward sloping angle for athletes to rest their feet against while they are under starter's orders and which they use to push off against as a means of getting extra propulsion when the race, especially a sprint, starts.

starting gate ▻ *noun, horse-racing* a moveable barrier that stays down in front of the starting stalls until it is lifted at the beginning of a race.

starting price ▻ *noun* **1** *horse-racing* the final odds that are offered on a horse just before the race begins. **2** (abbreviation **SP**) the price that an item in an auction is initially offered at.

starting stalls ▻ *noun, horse-racing* a row of compartments where the runners and riders line up before the race gets under way.

startle /ˈstɑːtəl/ ▻ *verb* (*startled*, *startling*) **1** *tr & intr* to be or cause someone or something to be slightly shocked or surprised, often with an attendant jump or twitch. **2** to dismay or astonish □ *I was startled by the news of her death*. ▻ *noun* a slight shock or surprise. • **startler** *noun*. • **startled** *adj*. • **startling** *noun*. Ⓒ Anglo-Saxon *steartlian* to stumble or struggle.

star topology ▻ *noun, computing* a networking conformation where several computers or work stations are linked to a central control point, but not to each other.

start-up ▻ *adj* said of a mortgage, a loan for a new business, etc: designed for the new borrower, business person, etc, especially in being designed to make it easier for them to meet the repayments during the initial period.

star turn ▻ *noun* the principal item or performer in a show.

starvation /stɑːˈveɪʃən/ ▻ *noun* the state of ingesting too little food to provide energy for the adequate function of vital organs, prolongation of which leads to death.

starve ▻ *verb* (*starved*, *starving*) **1** *tr & intr* **a** to die or cause someone or something to die because of a long-term lack of food; **b** to suffer or cause someone or something to suffer because of a long-term lack of food. **2** *intr, colloq* to be very hungry. **3** to deprive someone or something of something that is vital □ *starved the project of funds*. • **starve to death** to deprive or be deprived of food for so long that death ensues. • **starved** *adj*. • **starving** *adj, noun*. Ⓒ Anglo-Saxon *steorfan* to die.

■ **starve someone into something** to force them into (behaviour of a particular kind) by withholding or preventing access to food □ *starved the rebels into submission*.

starveling /ˈstɑːvlɪŋ/ ▻ *noun* someone or something that looks weak and undernourished. ▻ *adj* less than adequate □ *starveling wages*.

Star Wars ▻ *noun* the colloquial name for the STRATEGIC DEFENCE INITIATIVE. Ⓒ 1980s: named after the George Lucas film of 1977.

starwort ▻ *noun* **1** another name for the STITCHWORT. **2** (*also* **water starwort**) an aquatic plant with a star-shaped rosette of leaves that are either submerged or partially submerged.

stash *slang* ▻ *verb* (***stashes***, ***stashed***, ***stashing***) to put into a hiding-place. ▻ *noun* (***stashes***) **1** a hidden supply or store of something, or its hiding-place. **2** *drug-taking slang* a supply of illegal drugs, especially cannabis. ⓘ 1940s as *noun* 2; 19c as *noun* 1; 18c as *verb*.

Stasi /ˈstɑːzɪ; *German* ʃtɑːzi/ ▻ *abbreviation* the name of the former East German secret police which was abolished in 1990. ⓘ 1990s: German, a shortened form of *Staatssicherheitsdienst* state security service.

stasis /ˈsteɪsɪs/ ▻ *noun* **1** *pathol* a condition where the normal circulation or flow of some body fluid, such as blood, urine, etc, has stopped. **2** a state of inactivity where no progress is being made. ⓘ 18c: Greek, meaning 'a standing state'.

stat ▻ *abbreviation* (*usually* **stats**) *colloq* statistic.

stat. ▻ *abbreviation* used especially in prescriptions: immediately. ⓘ 19c: from Latin *statim* immediately.

-stat ▻ *combining form, forming nouns, denoting* a device that gives a stationary or constant condition □ ***thermostat***. ⓘ From Greek *states* causing to stand.

state ▻ *noun* **1** the condition, eg of health, appearance, emotions, etc that someone or something is in at a particular time. **2** a territory governed by a single political body; a nation. **3** any of a number of locally governed areas making up a nation or federation under the ultimate control of a central government, as in the US. **4** (**the States**) the United States of America. **5** (*also* **State** or **the State**) **a** the political entity of a nation, including the government and all its apparatus, eg the civil service and the armed forces; **b** *as adj* relating to or controlled or financed by the State, or a federal state □ ***state police***; **c** *as adj* ceremonial □ ***a state visit by the Queen***. **5** *colloq* **a** an emotionally agitated condition □ ***He was in a right state***; **b** a confused or untidy condition □ ***What a state your room's in — tidy it up!*** ▻ *verb* (***stated***, ***stating***) **1** to express clearly, either in written or spoken form; to affirm or assert. **2** to specify. • **statable** *adj*. • **stated** *adj*. • **statehood** *noun*. • **lie in state** said of a dead person: to be ceremonially displayed to the public before burial. • **turn state's evidence** see under EVIDENCE. ⓘ 13c: from Latin *status*, from *stare* to stand.

State Department ▻ *noun, US* the FOREIGN OFFICE.

State Enrolled Nurse ▻ *noun, Brit* a nurse who is qualified to perform many, but not all, nursing tasks. Often shortened to SEN. See also STATE REGISTERED NURSE.

stateless ▻ *adj* having no nationality or citizenship.

stately ▻ *adj* (***statelier***, ***stateliest***) noble, dignified and impressive in appearance or manner. • **stateliness** *noun*.

stately home ▻ *noun* a large grand old house, especially one that is open to the public.

statement ▻ *noun* **1** a thing stated, especially a formal written or spoken declaration □ ***made a statement to the press***. **2 a** a record of finances, especially one sent by a bank to an account-holder detailing the transactions within a particular period; **b** an account that gives details of the costs of materials, services, etc and the amount that is due to be paid. **3** the act of stating.

state of affairs ▻ *noun* a situation or set of circumstances that pertains at a given time.

state of emergency ▻ *noun* the suspension of normal law and order procedures and the introduction of strict controls of the population, that usually involves the military, so that a crisis, revolution, etc can be contained.

state of play ▻ *noun* the situation at a specified moment □ ***What's the current state of play with this project?***

state of the art ▻ *noun* **1** the current level of advancement achieved by the most modern, up-to-date technology or thinking in a particular field. **2** (**state-of-the-art**) *as adj* □ ***state-of-the-art technology***.

State Registered Nurse ▻ *noun* a nurse who has taken advanced training and who is therefore qualified to perform all nursing tasks. Often shortened to SRN. See also STATE ENROLLED NURSE, REGISTERED GENERAL NURSE.

stateroom ▻ *noun* **1** a large room in a palace, etc that is used for ceremonial occasions. **2** a large private cabin on a ship.

the States ▻ *noun, colloq* a shortened form of THE UNITED STATES.

state school ▻ *noun* a school that is state-funded and where the education is free. Compare GRANT-MAINTAINED school, INDEPENDENT school, PUBLIC SCHOOL.

state's evidence ▻ *noun, US law* evidence that is given by an accomplice in a crime that is given voluntarily, usually in return for a promise of some form of immunity. • **turn state's evidence** to agree to give this kind of evidence. Compare QUEEN'S EVIDENCE.

Stateside or **stateside** *colloq* ▻ *adj* belonging, referring or relating to, or in, the USA. ▻ *adverb* to or towards the USA.

statesman ▻ *noun* an experienced and distinguished male politician. See also ELDER STATESMAN. • **statesmanlike** *adj*. • **statesmanship** *noun*.

statesperson ▻ *noun* a statesman or stateswoman.

stateswoman ▻ *noun* an experienced and distinguished female politician.

state trooper ▻ *noun, US* a member of a state police force.

static /ˈstatɪk/ ▻ *adj* (*also* **statical**) **1** not moving; stationary. **2** fixed; not portable. **3** tending not to move around or change. **4** relating to statics. Compare DYNAMIC. **5** characteristic of or relating to TV or radio interference. ▻ *noun* **1** (*in full* **static electricity**) an accumulation of electric charges that remain at rest instead of moving to form a flow of current, eg electricity produced by friction between two materials such as hair and a plastic comb. **2** a sharp crackling or hissing sound that interferes with radio and television signals, and which is caused by static electricity or atmospheric disturbance. • **statically** *adverb*. ⓘ 16c: from Greek *statikos* causing to stand.

statics ▻ *singular noun* the branch of mechanics that deals with the action of balanced forces on bodies such that they remain at rest or in unaccelerated motion. Compare DYNAMICS.

station /ˈsteɪʃən/ ▻ *noun* **1** a place where trains or buses regularly stop so that people can get off and on, goods can be loaded and unloaded, refuelling can be done, tickets bought, etc. **2 a** a local headquarters or depot, eg of a police force, etc; **b** *in compounds* □ ***fire station***. **3** *in compounds* a building equipped for some particular purpose □ ***power station*** □ ***petrol station***. **4 a** a radio or TV channel; **b** the building or organization that broadcasts particular radio or TV programmes. **5** a position in a specified structure, organization, etc □ ***ideas above his station***. **6** someone's calling, profession, etc. **7 a** a post or place of duty; **b** *in compounds* □ ***four workstations in the office***. **8** *Austral & NZ* a large farm that specializes in rearing sheep or cattle. **9** *biol* the habitat of an animal or plant. **10** (*also* **Station of the Cross**) *RC Church* any one of a series of images, usually fourteen in total, that depict the stages in Christ's journey to Calvary. ▻ *verb* (***stationed***, ***stationing***) to assign or appoint to a post or place of duty. ⓘ 14c: from Latin *statio*, from *stare* to stand.

stationary ▻ *adj* **1** not moving; still. **2** fixed; not changing; remaining in the same place. ⓘ 15c: from Latin *stationarius* belonging to a military station, from *statio* station.

stationary wave ▻ *noun, physics* a STANDING WAVE.

stationer ▻ *noun* a person or shop that sells stationery. ⓘ 14c: from Latin *stationarius* a person with a regular standing place, ie as opposed to an itinerant hawker.

stationery ▻ *noun* paper, envelopes, pens and other writing materials. Ⓒ 18c.

station house ▻ *noun, US* a police or fire station.

stationmaster ▻ *noun* the official who is in charge of a railway station.

station wagon *N Amer, especially US* ▻ *noun* an ESTATE CAR.

statistic /stəˈtɪstɪk/ ▻ *noun* a specified piece of information or data □ *He became just another statistic amongst drug-related deaths.* • **statistical** *adj.* • **statistically** *adverb.*

statistician /statɪˈstɪʃən/ ▻ *noun* someone who collects, analyses, prepares, etc statistics.

statistics ▻ *plural noun* (*sometimes* **stats**) items of related information that have been collected, collated, interpreted, analysed and presented to show particular trends. Also called **descriptive statistics**. ▻ *singular noun, math* the branch of mathematics concerned with drawing inferences from numerical data, based on probability theory, especially in so far as conclusions can be made on the basis of an appropriate sample from a population. See also VITAL STATISTICS. Ⓒ 18c: from German *Statistik* study of political facts and figures, from Latin *status* state.

stative /ˈsteɪtɪv/ *grammar* ▻ *adj* said of verbs: indicating a state as opposed to an action; *seem* and *like* would fall into this category, whereas *look* and *walk* would not. ▻ *noun* a verb of this kind. Ⓒ 19c: from Latin *stare* to stand.

stator /ˈsteɪtə(r)/ ▻ *noun* the part in an electric motor or generator that does not move. Compare ROTOR.

statoscope /ˈstatəskoʊp/ ▻ *noun* a very sensitive type of aneroid barometer that can detect and record minute changes in atmospheric pressure. Ⓒ Early 20c: from Greek *statos* standing + *skopeein* to look at.

statuary /ˈstatʃuːərɪ/ ▻ *noun* **1** statues collectively. **2** the art of sculpture. ▻ *adj* belonging or referring to statues or to the sculpting of them. Ⓒ 16c: from Latin *statua* a statue.

statue /ˈstatʃuː/ ▻ *noun* **1** a sculpted, moulded or cast figure, especially of a person or animal, usually life-size or larger, and often erected in a public place to commemorate someone famous. **2** (**statues**) a children's game in which the object is to stand as still as possible when the music stops. Also called **musical statues**. Ⓒ 14c: from Latin *statua*, from *stare* to stand.

statuesque /statʃʊˈɛsk/ ▻ *adj* said of someone's appearance: tall and well-proportioned; dignified and imposing. • **statuesquely** *adverb.* • **statuesqueness** *noun.* Ⓒ 19c: from STATUE + -ESQUE, modelled on PICTURESQUE.

statuette ▻ *noun* a small statue.

stature /ˈstatʃə(r)/ ▻ *noun* **1** the height of a person, animal, tree, etc. **2** greatness; eminence; importance. **3** the level of achievement someone has attained. Ⓒ 14c: from Latin *statura*, from *stare* to stand.

status /ˈsteɪtəs/ ▻ *noun* **1** rank or position in relation to others, within society, an organization, etc □ *social status.* **2** legal standing, eg with regard to adulthood, marriage, citizenship, etc. **3** a high degree or level of importance; prestige □ *Her huge salary reflects the status of the job.* Ⓒ 17c: Latin, from *stare* to stand.

status quo /steɪtəs ˈkwoʊ/ ▻ *noun* **1** (*usually* **the status quo**) the existing situation at a given moment. **2** (*also* **status quo ante**) /steɪtəs kwoʊ ˈantɪ/ the situation as it existed previously. Ⓒ 19c: Latin, meaning 'the state in which'.

status symbol ▻ *noun* a possession or privilege that represents prestige, wealth, high social standing, etc, but which is often seen by others as having more face value than real substance.

statute /ˈstatʃuːt/ ▻ *noun* **1 a** a law made by the legislative assembly of a country and recorded in a formal document. Also called *Brit* ACT OF PARLIAMENT; **b** the formal document where such a law is recorded. **2** a permanent rule drawn up by an organization, especially one that governs its internal workings or the conduct of its members. Ⓒ 13c: from Latin *statutum* decree, from *statuere* to set up.

statute-barred ▻ *adj* said of an action of law or an enforcement of a right: unable to be pursued because it has not been initiated within the legally prescribed time span.

statute book ▻ *noun* a formal written record of all the laws passed by a parliament, etc. • **on the statute book** approved and given legal status by parliament.

statute mile ▻ *noun* the legal term for a MILE (*noun* 1).

statute of limitations ▻ *noun* a statute that gives the prescribed legal time for bringing an action of law or enforcing a right.

statutory /ˈstatʃʊtərɪ, -trɪ/ ▻ *adj* **1** required or prescribed by law or a rule. **2** usual or regular, as if prescribed by law. • **statutorily** *adverb.*

statutory rape ▻ *noun, US* an act of sexual intercourse with someone, especially a girl, who is below the AGE OF CONSENT.

staunch¹ /stɔːntʃ/ ▻ *adj* **1** loyal; trusty; steadfast. **2** watertight. • **staunchly** *adverb.* • **staunchness** *noun.* Ⓒ 15c: from French *estanche* watertight.

staunch² /stɔːntʃ/ ▻ *verb* (**staunches, staunched, staunching**) to stop the flow of (something, such as blood from a wound, information, gossip, etc). Ⓒ 13c: from French *estanchier.*

stave /steɪv/ ▻ *noun* **1** any of the vertical wooden strips that are joined together to form a barrel, tub, boat hull, etc. **2** any bar, rod, shaft, etc, especially a wooden one, eg a rung on a ladder. **3** *music* a STAFF (*noun* 5). **4** a verse of a poem or song. ▻ *verb* (**staved** or **stove** /stoʊv/, **staving**) **1** (*often* **stave in**) **a** to smash (a hole, etc in something) □ *The door was staved in;* **b** to break (a stave or the staves of a barrel or boat). **2** (in this sense *past tense* only **staved**) (*often* **stave off**) **a** to delay the onset of something □ *tried to stave off his downfall by calling an election;* **b** to ward off something □ *staved her hunger with an apple.* **3** to fit or repair with staves. **4** *Scot* to accidently bend back (a finger or toe) and injure the joint at its base □ *staved my finger playing netball.* Ⓒ 14c: a back-formation from STAVES, a plural of STAFF.

staves see STAFF

stay¹ ▻ *verb* (**stayed, staying**) **1** *intr* to remain in the same place or condition, without moving or changing. **2 a** *intr* to reside temporarily, eg as a guest; **b** *Scot, intr* to live permanently □ *She's stayed in Edinburgh all her life.* **3** to suspend or postpone (eg legal proceedings). **4** to control or restrain (eg anger). ▻ *noun* **1** a period of temporary residence; a visit. **2** a suspension of legal proceedings or a postponement of a legally enforceable punishment □ *grant a stay of execution.* • **be here to stay** to be established as a permanent feature □ *looks like virtual reality's here to stay.* • **stay put** *colloq* to remain in the same place. • **stay still** to refrain from moving. • **stay the course** to have the stamina for something demanding □ *The job's really stressful — I doubt if she can stay the course.* Ⓒ 15c: from Latin *stare* to stand.

■ **stay away from someone** or **something** to keep some distance from them or it □ *I'd stay away from her — she's nothing but trouble.*

■ **stay for something** to remain for (a specified time or event).

■ **stay in** to remain indoors, especially as opposed to going out socially.

■ **stay on** to remain after the expected time for leaving.

■ **stay out** to be away from home.

■ **stay over** *colloq* to spend the night.

■ **stay to something** to remain long enough to take part in it □ *Can you stay to tea?*

■ **stay up** to remain out of bed, especially beyond one's usual bedtime.

■ **stay with something** to persevere with it.

stay² ▻ *noun* **1** a prop or support. **2** any of a number of strips of bone or metal sewn into a corset to stiffen it. **3** (**stays**) a corset stiffened in this way. ⓘ 16c: from French *estaye*, from *estayer* to stay.

stay³ ▻ *noun* a rope or cable that is used for anchoring something, eg a flagpole, mast, etc, and to keep it upright. ⓘ Anglo-Saxon *stæg*.

stay-at-home *colloq* ▻ *adj* tending to prefer the peaceful routine of domestic life to a busy and varied social life. ▻ *noun* a stay-at-home person.

stayer ▻ *noun, colloq* a person or animal who has great powers of endurance.

staying power ▻ *noun* stamina; endurance.

staysail ▻ *noun, naut* an auxiliary sail that is usually triangular.

stay stitching ▻ *noun* a line of stitches which are used to reinforce a seam and to prevent stretching and fraying.

STD ▻ *abbreviation* **1** sexually transmitted disease. This name has now replaced VD. **2** *Brit* subscriber trunk dialling.

STD code ▻ *noun, Brit* a telephone code for a town or other area that has to precede a subscriber's individual number if the caller is dialling from outside the area. ⓘ 20c: an abbreviation of subscriber trunk dialling.

Ste ▻ *abbreviation*: *Sainte* (French) a female saint.

stead /stɛd/ ▻ *noun* (*usually* **in someone's stead**) in place of them. • **stand someone in good stead** to prove useful to them. ⓘ Anglo-Saxon *stede* place.

steadfast /ˈstɛdfɑːst/ ▻ *adj* firm; resolute; determinedly unwavering. • **steadfastly** *adverb*. • **steadfastness** *noun*. ⓘ Anglo-Saxon *stede* place + *fæst* fixed.

Steadicam /ˈstɛdɪkam/ ▻ *noun, trademark* a hand-held film camera that has built-in shock absorbers, and which has a harness device so that the camera operator can attach it to their body allowing them to move over rough terrain where a DOLLY could not go, and yet still produce steady shots.

steading /ˈstɛdɪŋ/ ▻ *noun, Brit* **1** the outbuildings of a farm. **2** a farmhouse and its outbuildings. ⓘ 15c: from STEAD + -ING³.

steady /ˈstɛdɪ/ ▻ *adj* (*steadier*, *steadiest*) **1** firmly fixed or balanced; not tottering or wobbling. **2** regular; constant; unvarying □ *a steady job.* **3** stable; not easily disrupted or undermined. **4** having a serious or sober character. **5** continuous □ *a steady stream of traffic.* ▻ *verb* (*steadies*, *steadied*, *steadying*) *tr & intr* to make or become steady or steadier. ▻ *adverb* in a steady manner □ *steady as she goes.* ▻ *exclamation* (*also* **steady on!** or **steady up!**) used to urge someone to be careful or restrained. • **steadily** *adverb*. • **steadiness** *noun*. • **go steady with someone** *colloq* to have a steady romantic relationship with them. • **go steady with something** *colloq* to use it sparingly □ *Go steady with that whisky.* • **steady-as-she-goes** **1** *naut* used as a command of caution, especially by a captain to the crew, the 'she' being the ship. **2** careful and wary, often to the extent of appearing dull □ *gave a steady-as-she-goes performance.* • **steady-going** very reliable □ *Peter's always been a steady-going guy.* ⓘ 16c: from STEAD.

steady-state theory ▻ *noun, astron* in cosmology: a theory, now generally discredited, that hypothesizes that the universe has always existed and that it is constantly expanding with the continuous creation of matter. Compare BIG BANG, CONTINUOUS CREATION. ⓘ 1940s: coined by Thomas Gold (born 1920), Fred Hoyle (born 1915) and Hermann Bondi (born 1919).

steak /steɪk/ ▻ *noun* **1 a** a fine quality beef for frying or grilling; **b** a thick slice of this, often with a specifying term before or after it to indicate which part of the animal it has come from or how it is served □ *fillet steak* □ *steak diane.* Also called **beefsteak**. **2** beef that is cut into chunks and used for stewing or braising. **3** a thick slice of any meat or fish □ *salmon steaks.* ⓘ 15c: from Norse *steik* roast.

steak and kidney pie and **steak and kidney pudding** ▻ *noun* a traditional British pie or pudding with a filling of diced steak, usually stewing steak, and kidney in gravy.

steak au poivre /steɪk oʊ pwɑvrə/ ▻ *noun* a dish that consists of steak, usually rump or sirloin, served in a sauce that is made from peppercorns, stock, cream and brandy or wine.

steak diane /ˈsteɪk daɪˈan/ ▻ *noun* a dish that consists of steak served in a rich seasoned sauce.

steakhouse ▻ *noun* a restaurant that specializes in serving steaks.

steak knife ▻ *noun* a table knife with a serrated edge that is used for eating steaks.

steak tartare /— tɑːˈtɑː(r)/ ▻ *noun* a dish that consists of raw seasoned minced beef, or alternatively horse meat, and sometimes raw onions, bound together with raw egg.

steal /stiːl/ ▻ *verb* (*past tense* ***stole*** /stoʊl/ , *past participle* ***stolen***, *present participle* ***stealing***) **1** *tr & intr* to take away (another person's property) without permission or legal right, especially secretly. **2** to obtain something by cleverness or trickery □ *steal a kiss.* **3** to fraudulently present (another person's work, ideas, etc) as one's own. **4** *intr* to go stealthily □ *stole down to the basement.* ▻ *noun, colloq* **1** a bargain; something that can be easily obtained □ *The silk shirt was a steal at £25.* **2** *N Amer, especially US* an act of stealing. • **steal a bye** *cricket* to score a run without the batsman having touched the ball with either his bat or hand. • **steal a march on someone** to gain some kind of advantage over them, especially in a surreptitious or underhand way. • **steal someone's thunder** to present or use someone else's idea, plan, etc as one's own, thereby diverting attention from them and then wallow in the ensuing praise, adulation, etc. • **steal the show** to attract the most applause, attention, publicity, admiration, etc. ⓘ Anglo-Saxon *stelan*.

■ **steal away** to make off without being seen.

■ **steal over someone** to pervade them; to overcome them □ *Tiredness stole over her.*

Stealth /stɛlθ/ ▻ *noun US* the branch of military technology that is concerned with the development of aircraft, missiles, etc that can withstand detection by radar and other tracking systems. ⓘ 1970s.

stealth /stɛlθ/ ▻ *noun* **1** softness and quietness of movement in order to avoid being noticed. **2** secretive or deceitful behaviour. ⓘ 13c: from STEAL.

stealthy ▻ *adj* (*stealthier*, *stealthiest*) acting or done with stealth; furtive. • **stealthily** *adverb*. • **stealthiness** *noun*. ⓘ 17c: from STEALTH.

steam /stiːm/ ▻ *noun* **1 a** the colourless gas formed by vaporizing water at 100°C, which becomes visible in air due to suspended water droplets, and which can be used as a source of power or energy, eg in steam engines; **b** any similar vapour, especially one that is produced when an AQUEOUS liquid is heated. **2** *colloq* power, energy or speed □ *I haven't got the steam to climb any further.* **3** *as adj* **a** powered by steam □ *a steam generator;* **b** using steam □ *a* *steam iron*; **c** *humorous* old-fashioned □ ***a steam computer.*** ▷ *verb* (***steamed***, ***steaming***) **1** *intr* to give off steam. **2** to cook, etc using steam. **3** *intr* to move under the power of steam. **4** *intr*, *colloq* to go at speed □ ***steamed up the road to catch the bus.*** • **steamed** *adj.* • **be** or **get steamed up** or **all steamed up** *colloq* to be very angry or excited. • **full steam ahead** forward as fast as possible or with as much energy, enthusiasm, gusto, etc as possible. • **get up steam** said of the boiler of a steam ship, locomotive, etc: to be in the process of heating up. • **let off steam** to release bottled-up energy or emotions, eg anger. • **run out of steam** to become depleted of energy, power, enthusiasm, etc. • **steam open** to surreptitiously undo the seal of (a letter, especially one addressed to someone else) by directing steam at it. • **under one's own steam** unassisted by anyone else. ⌚ Anglo-Saxon.

■ **steam up** said of a transparent or reflective surface: to become clouded by tiny water droplets formed from condensed steam □ ***His glasses steamed up.***

■ **steam something up** to make it steam up.

steam bath ▷ *noun* **1** a steam-filled room or compartment where people relax and refresh themselves, often leaving the bath to cool off before re-entering. **2** a steam-filled chamber in a laboratory for sterilizing equipment.

steamboat ▷ *noun* a vessel that is driven by steam.

steam boiler ▷ *noun* a chamber where water is heated to produce steam in order to power a generator, engine, etc.

steamed-up ▷ *adj* said of windows, glasses, etc: clouded by condensed steam.

steam engine ▷ *noun* **1** an engine that is powered by steam from a boiler that is heated by a furnace. **2** a steam locomotive engine.

steamer ▷ *noun* **1** a ship whose engines are powered by steam. **2** a two-tier pot in which food in the upper tier is cooked by the action of steam from water heated in the lower tier. See also STEAMING.

steamie /ˈstiːmɪ/ ▷ *noun* (***steamies***) *Scots, formerly* a public building, generally in densely populated areas, where people could do their washing. ⌚ 1920s.

steaming ▷ *adj* **1** said of a liquid: very hot. **2** *colloq* very angry or upset. **3** *colloq* very drunk. ▷ *noun* **1** the act or process of cooking with steam. **2** *slang* a form of mugging that is carried out by gangs in busy places such as trains, the London underground, etc where they go charging through the rush-hour crowds or through the carriages grabbing people's bags, etc. • **steamer** *noun* a member of this kind of gang.

steam iron ▷ *noun* an electric iron that has a small built-in reservoir where water is heated to produce steam which is then released through holes in the base of the iron to dampen the clothes, etc and so make it easier to get the creases out.

steam jacket ▷ *noun, engineering* a casing that is placed around a vessel filled with steam so that the heat of the vessel is maintained. • **steam-jacketed** *adj.*

steam organ ▷ *noun* a CALLIOPE.

steamroller ▷ *noun* a large vehicle, originally and still often steam-driven, that has huge heavy solid metal cylinders for wheels so that when it is driven over newly made roads it smooths, flattens and compacts the surface. ▷ *verb, colloq* **1** to use overpowering force or persuasion to secure the speedy movement or progress of something, especially a parliamentary bill, etc. **2** to crush (opposition, etc). **3** to flatten (a road surface) using a steamroller.

■ **steamroller someone into something** to force or persuade them to do it, especially something they are reluctant to do.

steam turbine ▷ *noun, engineering* a turbine engine that is powered by steam, especially one that is used to drive an electricity generator in a power station.

steam whistle ▷ *noun, formerly* a kind of whistle that blows when a chain is pulled releasing steam through it, especially one of the type used on steam locomotives or in factories to signal the end of the working day.

steamy ▷ *adj* (***steamier***, ***steamiest***) **1** full of, clouded by, emitting, etc steam. **2** *colloq* salacious; sexy; erotic. • **steamily** *adverb.* • **steaminess** *noun.*

stearate /ˈstiːəreɪt/ ▷ *noun, chem* any of the salts or esters of stearic acid. ⌚ 19c.

stearic /stiːˈarɪk/ ▷ *adj* derived from, containing, etc fat. ⌚ 19c: from Greek *stear* fat or tallow.

stearic acid ▷ *noun, chem* (formula $\mathbf{CH_3(CH_2)_{16}COOH}$) a colourless fatty acid with a slight taste and odour that is commonly found in animal fats, as well as in some plants, and which is used as a lubricant and in the manufacture of pharmaceutical products, cosmetics, candles, soap, etc. Also called **octadecanoic acid**. ⌚ 19c.

stearin or **stearine** /ˈstiːərɪn/ ▷ *noun, chem* **1** any of the three glyceryl esters of stearic acid. Also called **tristearin**. **2** the solid part of a fat. Compare OLEIN. **3** (**stearine**) the commercial name for STEARIC ACID, especially when it is used in the manufacture of soap and candles. • **stearine** *adj.* ⌚ Early 19c.

steatite /ˈstiːətaɪt/ ▷ *noun* another name for SOAPSTONE. • **steatitic** /stiːəˈtɪtɪk/ *adj.* ⌚ 17c.

steatopygia /stiːətoʊˈpɪdʒɪə/ ▷ *noun* an excessive accumulation of fat on the buttocks and the backs of the thighs which is a genetic characteristic of certain races such as the Hottentots and the S African Bushmen, especially in the women of these peoples. ⌚ 19c; from Greek *stear* fat or tallow + *pyge* the rump or buttocks.

steatorrhoea or (*US*) **steatorrhea** /stiːətəˈrɪə/ ▷ *noun, pathol* the presence of excess fat in the stools, usually a sign of malabsorption due to some obstruction or disease. ⌚ 19c.

steed ▷ *noun* a horse, especially one that is lively and bold. ⌚ Anglo-Saxon *steda* stallion.

steel ▷ *noun* **1** any of a number of iron alloys that contain small amounts of carbon and, in some cases, additional elements, eg chromium, nickel, manganese, silicon, molybdenum, and which are used in the manufacture of motor vehicles, ships, bridges, machinery, tools, etc. **2** a rough-surfaced rod, made of this alloy, that knives are sharpened on by hand. **3** said especially of someone, their character, determination, etc: hardness, strength, etc □ ***a man of steel.*** ▷ *verb* (***steeled***, ***steeling***) (*usually* **steel oneself**) to harden oneself or prepare oneself emotionally, especially for something unpleasant or unwelcome. See also ALLOY STEEL, CARBON STEEL. ⌚ Anglo-Saxon *style*.

steel band ▷ *noun* a group, originally in the W Indies, who play music, usually CALYPSO music, on improvised percussion instruments that are made from oil or petrol drums which have had the tops specially beaten so that striking different areas produces different notes.

steel blue ▷ *noun* **1** a deep greyish-blue colour. **2** Also *as adj* □ ***a steel-blue suit.***

steel engraving ▷ *noun* **1** a method of engraving that uses steel plates. **2** an engraving that has been made using this technique.

steel grey or **steel gray** ▷ *noun* **1** a bluish grey. **2** Also *as adj* □ ***steel-grey eyes.***

steel wool ▷ *noun* thin strands of steel in a woolly mass that is used for polishing, scrubbing and scouring.

steelwork and **structural steelwork** ▷ *noun, building* welded steel beams and columns that are constructed to form the frames in large building projects such as office blocks and warehouses.

steelworker ▻ *noun* **1** someone whose job is to erect and weld steelwork. Also called **steel fixer**. **2** someone whose job is in a steelworks.

steelworks ▻ *singular or plural noun* a factory where steel is manufactured.

steely ▻ *adj* (***steelier***, ***steeliest***) **1** cold, hard and unyielding □ *a steely gaze.* **2** steel-blue. • **steeliness** *noun.*

steelyard /'stiːljɑːd/ ▻ *noun* a type of weighing machine that has one short arm that the object to be weighed is put onto and another longer graduated arm which has a single weight on it which is pushed along the arm until the balance is established. ⓒ 17c: from STEEL + YARD² 2.

steenbok or **steinbok** /'stiːnbɒk/ ▻ *noun* (***steenboks*** or ***steenbok***) a small S African antelope. ⓒ 18c: Dutch, from *steen* stone + *bok* buck.

steenbras /'stiːnbras/ ▻ *noun* any of several kinds of marine fish found especially in the estuaries of S African rivers and used as food. ⓒ 18c: Dutch, from *steen* stone + *brasem* bream.

steep¹ ▻ *adj* (***steeper***, ***steepest***) **1** sloping sharply. **2** *colloq* said of a price, rate, etc: unreasonably high. **3** *colloq* said of a story or someone's version of events: hard to believe. • **steepish** *adj.* • **steeply** *adverb.* • **steepness** *noun.* ⓒ Anglo-Saxon *steap.*

steep² ▻ *verb* (***steeped***, ***steeping***) *tr & intr* to soak something thoroughly in liquid. • **be steeped in something** **1** to be closely familiar with it, eg a specified subject, etc □ *He was steeped in classical Greek.* **2** to be deeply involved in it □ *a castle steeped in history.* • **steeper** *noun.* ⓒ 14c: from English *stepen.*

steepen /'stiːpən/ ▻ *verb* (***steepened***, ***steepening***) *tr & intr* to make or become steep or steeper.

steeple /'stiːpəl/ ▻ *noun* **1** a tower, especially one with a spire, that forms part of a church or temple. **2** the spire itself. • **steepled** *adj.* ⓒ Anglo-Saxon *stepel.*

steeplechase ▻ *noun* **1** a horse race round a course with hurdles, usually in the form of man-made hedges. **2** a track running race where athletes have to jump hurdles and, usually, a water jump. ▻ *verb, intr* to take part in a steeplechase. • **steeplechaser** *noun.* • **steeplechasing** *noun.* ⓒ 18c: so called because, in the original horse races, which were run across open country often from one village to the next, a church steeple would mark the end of the race.

steeplejack ▻ *noun* someone whose job is to construct and repair steeples and tall chimneys. ⓒ 19c.

steer¹ /stɪə(r)/ ▻ *verb* (***steered***, ***steering***) **1** *tr & intr* to guide or control the direction of (a vehicle or vessel) using a steering wheel, rudder, etc. **2** *intr* **a** to tend towards a specified direction □ *This car steers to the right*; **b** to move in a specified way □ *This car steers badly.* **3** to guide or encourage (someone, a conversation, etc) to move in a specified direction □ *steered the conversation round to the subject of money.* ▻ *noun, colloq* a piece of information, guidance, etc. • **steerable** *adj.* • **steerer** *noun.* • **steering** *noun.* • **steer clear of someone** or **something** *colloq* to avoid them or it. ⓒ Anglo-Saxon *styran.*

steer² /stɪə(r)/ ▻ *noun* a young castrated bull or male ox, especially one that is being reared for beef. ⓒ Anglo-Saxon *steor.*

steerage ▻ *noun* **1** *old use* the cheapest accommodation on board a passenger ship, traditionally near the rudder. **2** an act or the practice of steering.

steering column ▻ *noun* **1** in a motor vehicle: the shaft that has the steering wheel at one end and which connects up to the steering gear at the other. **2** in a bicycle: the shaft that has the handlebars at one end and which passes through the frame to the front forks.

steering committee ▻ *noun* **1** a committee that decides on the nature and order of topics to be discussed by a parliament, etc. **2** a committee in charge of the overall direction pursued by a business or other organization.

steering gear ▻ *noun* the mechanism that allows a motor vehicle, ship, etc to be guided in the desired direction.

steering-wheel ▻ *noun* a wheel that is turned by hand to direct the wheels of a vehicle or the rudder of a vessel.

steeve *naut* ▻ *noun* the angular elevation of a bowsprit, etc. ▻ *verb* (***steeved***, ***steeving***) **1** *tr* to incline (a bowsprit, etc) upwards at an angle to the horizon. **2** *intr* said of a bowsprit, etc: to incline upwards at an angle to the horizon. ⓒ 17c.

stegosaurus /stɛgə'sɔːrəs/ ▻ *noun* a herbivorous dinosaur measuring up to 7.5m in length, which lived during the late Jurassic and early Cretaceous periods and which had a small head, a high domed back with a double row of large vertical bony plates, short front legs and a long tail. ⓒ 19c: from Greek *stegos* roof + *saurus* lizard.

stein /staɪn; *German* ʃtaɪn/ ▻ *noun* a large metal or earthenware beer mug, often with a hinged lid. ⓒ 19c: German, meaning 'stone'.

steinbock /'stiːnbɒk/ ▻ *noun* **1** another name for the Alpine ibex. **2** an alternative spelling of STEENBOK. ⓒ 17c: German, meaning 'wild goat', from *Stein* stone + *Bock* buck.

stele /'stiːlɪ, 'stiːl/ or in sense 2 **stela** /'stiːlə/ ▻ *noun* (***stelae*** /'stiːliː/) **1** an ancient stone pillar or upright slab, usually carved or engraved. **2** *bot* the central cylinder in the stems and roots of vascular plants. • **stelar** *adj.* ⓒ 19c: Greek, meaning 'a standing stone'.

stellar /'stɛlə(r)/ ▻ *adj* **1** referring or relating to or resembling a star or stars. **2** referring or relating to the famous. ⓒ 17c: from Latin *stella* star.

stellarator /'stɛləreɪtə(r)/ ▻ *noun, physics* a twisted TORUS in which plasma can be confined by a magnetic field. ⓒ 1950s: from STELLAR + gener*ator*.

stellate /'stɛleɪt/ ▻ *adj* **1** shaped like a star. **2** used mostly in scientific contexts, eg said of the petals of certain flowers, various types of cells, crystals, starfish, etc: arranged in such a way as to have a central point with leaves, petals, arms, branches, etc radiating out from it. • **stellated** *adj.* • **stellately** *adverb.* ⓒ 17c: from Latin *stella* star.

stelliform /'stɛlɪfɔːm/ ▻ *adj* shaped like a star. ⓒ 18c: from Latin *stella* star.

stellular /'stɛljʊlə(r)/ and **stellulate** /'stɛljʊlət, –leɪt/ ▻ *adj* **1** shaped like a little star. **2** set or sprinkled with little stars. ⓒ 18c: from Latin *stella* star.

stem¹ ▻ *noun* **1 a** the central part of a plant that grows upward from its root; **b** the part that connects a leaf, flower or fruit to a branch. **2** any long slender part, eg of a written letter or musical note, of a wine glass or pipe, of the winder of a watch, etc. **3** *linguistics* the base form of a word that inflections are added to; for example *love* is the stem of *loved, lover, lovely, unloved*, etc and of *luvvie*, despite the distortion of the spelling. See also ROOT. **4** *genealogy* the major branch of a family. **5** *naut* the front part of a ship or the curved timber at a ship's prow. ▻ *verb* (***stemmed***, ***stemming***) *intr* **1** (**stem from something** or **someone**) to originate or derive from it or them □ *Resentment stems from their low wages and long hours.* **2** to remove the stems from (fruit, etc). **3** said of a boat, swimmer, bird, etc: to make headway (through the water, air, etc). • **stemless** *adj.* • **stemlet** *noun.* • **stemmed** *adj.* • **from stem to stern** **1** from one end of a boat to the other. **2** completely. ⓒ Anglo-Saxon *stemn.*

stem² ▻ *verb* (***stemmed, stemming***) **1** to stop (the flow of something) □ ***tried to stem the tide of Tory disaffection.*** **2** *intr, skiing* to slow down by pushing the heels apart. ▻ *noun* (*also* **stem turn**) *skiing* a breaking technique where the heels are pushed apart. ◷ 15c: from Norse *stemma.*

stem cell ▻ *noun, biol* any undifferentiated cell that subsequently gives rise to cells which have a specified function.

stem ginger ▻ *noun* crystallized pieces of the underground stem of ginger, often used in cake-making, preserves, etc.

stemma /ˈstɛmə/ ▻ *noun* (***stemmata*** /ˈstɛmətə/) a family tree or a diagrammatic representation of one. ◷ 19c: Greek, meaning 'garland'.

stemson /ˈstɛmsən/ ▻ *noun, naut* a curved timber that is fitted into the stem and keelson at the bow of a wooden vessel. ◷ 18c: from STEM + keel*son.*

stem stitch ▻ *noun, embroidery* a stitch that is made by slightly overlapping it with the previous stitch, and which is often used for embroidering thin lines such as the stems of plants.

stench ▻ *noun* (***stenches***) a strong and extremely unpleasant smell. ◷ Anglo-Saxon *stenc* a smell, either pleasant or unpleasant.

stench trap ▻ *noun* a device in a drain or sewer that is designed to prevent the rise of smelly gases.

stencil /ˈstɛnsɪl/ ▻ *noun* **1** a card or plate that has shapes cut out of it to form a pattern, letter, etc and which is put onto a surface, eg paper, a wall, etc, and ink or paint applied so that the cut-out design is transferred to the surface. **2** the design that is produced using this technique. ▻ *verb* (***stencilled, stencilling*** or (*US*) ***stenciled, stenciling***) **1** to mark or decorate (a surface) using a stencil. **2** to produce (a design, lettering, etc) using a stencil. • **stenciller** *noun.* • **stencilling** *noun.* ◷ 15c: from French *estinceller,* from Latin *scintilla* a spark or spangle.

Sten gun /stɛn —/ ▻ *noun* a lightweight portable submachine-gun. ◷ 1940s: from the initials of the names of its designers, Shepherd and Turpin + Br*en gun.*

stenograph /ˈstɛnəgraf, -grɑːf/ ▻ *noun* a kind of typewriter that produces shorthand and which is especially used for producing courtroom transcripts.

stenographer /stɪˈnɒgrəfə(r)/ ▻ *noun, N Amer, especially US* a shorthand typist.

stenography /stɪˈnɒgrəfɪ/ ▻ *noun* the skill or practice of writing in shorthand. • **stenographic** /stɛnoʊˈgrafɪk/ or **stenographical** *adj.* • **stenographically** *adverb.* ◷ 17c: from Greek *stenos* narrow + *graphein* to write.

stenosis /stɪˈnoʊsɪs/ ▻ *noun, pathol* the abnormal narrowing of a passageway, duct or canal. • **stenotic** /stɪˈnɒtɪk/ *adj.* ◷ 19c: Greek, from *stenos* narrow.

stentorian /stɛnˈtɔːrɪən/ ▻ *adj, literary* said of a voice: loud and strong. ◷ 17c: named after Stentor, a Greek herald in the Trojan War who, according to Homer, had a voice as loud as 50 men (*Iliad* 5.783–5).

Step or **step** ▻ *noun, trademark* an aerobics workout based on stepping onto and off a block of adjustable height, usually in choreographed moves in time to music. Also called **step aerobics**. ◷ 1990s.

step ▻ *noun* **1** a single complete action of lifting then placing down the foot in walking or running. **2** the distance covered in the course of such an action. **3** a movement of the foot (usually one of a pattern of movements) in dancing. **4** a single action or measure that is taken in proceeding towards an end or goal □ ***a step in the right direction.*** **5** (*often* **steps**) **a** a single (often outdoor) stair, or any stair-like support used to climb up or down; **b** (*also* **pair of steps**) a STEPLADDER. **c** a rung on a ladder. **6** the sound or mark of a foot being laid on the ground, etc in walking. **7** a degree or stage in a scale or series □ ***moved up a step on the payscale.*** **8** a way of walking; gait □ ***always has a bouncy step.*** **9** *naut* a block, frame, support, etc where the end of a mast, pivot, etc fits. **10** a hairstyle that has two distinctly separate layers. ▻ *verb* (***stepped, stepping***) **1** *intr* to move by lifting up each foot alternately and setting it down in a different place. **2** *intr* to go or come on foot □ ***Step right this way.*** **3** to perform (a dance) □ ***stepped the light fandango.*** **4** to raise (a mast, etc) and fit it into its support, frame, block, etc. **5** to arrange in such a way as to avoid overlap. • **stepper** *noun.* • **break step** to no longer be in step. • **in step 1** walking, marching, etc in time with others or with the music. **2** in harmony, unison, agreement, etc with another or others. • **keep step** to remain in step. • **out of step 1** not walking, marching, etc in time with others or with the music. **2** not in harmony, unison, agreement, etc with another or others. • **step by step** gradually. • **step into something** to enter into it or become involved in it, especially easily or casually □ ***stepped into a high-flying job.*** • **step into the breach** to take someone's place, especially when they unexpectedly leave or are unable to fulfil a role, etc. • **step on it** *colloq* to hurry up. • **step on someone** *colloq* to treat them harshly, contemptuously, etc. • **step on something** to put one's foot down on it. • **step out of line** to behave in an inappropriate way; to disobey or offend, especially in a minor way. • **take steps to** to take action in order to. • **watch one's step 1** to walk with careful steps in order to avoid danger, etc. **2** to proceed with caution, taking care not to anger, offend, etc others. ◷ Anglo-Saxon *steppe.*

■ **step down 1** to resign from a position of authority. **2** to reduce the rate, intensity, etc of something.

■ **step in 1** to take up a position or role as a substitute or replacement. **2** to intervene in an argument.

■ **step out 1** to walk quickly and confidently with long strides. **2** *colloq* to go out socially.

■ **step up** to increase the rate, intensity, etc of something. See separate entry STEP-UP.

step- ▻ *combining form, indicating* a family relationship that is through marriage or partnership as opposed to a blood relationship. ◷ Anglo-Saxon *steop* orphan.

stepbrother and **stepsister** ▻ *noun* a son or daughter of someone's step-parent.

stepchild, stepdaughter and **stepson** ▻ *noun* a child of someone's spouse or partner who is the offspring of a previous relationship.

stepfather ▻ *noun* a husband or partner of a person's mother who is not that person's biological father.

stephanotis /stɛfəˈnoʊtɪs/ ▻ *noun* a twining evergreen perennial plant that is a native of Madagascar, and which has glossy oval leaves and heavily scented white waxy tubular flowers which makes it popular as a house plant and in bridal bouquets. ◷ 19c: from Greek *stephanos* crown.

stepladder ▻ *noun* a short ladder with flat steps, not rungs, made free-standing by means of a supporting frame attached by a hinge at the ladder's top where there is usually a platform to stand on. Often shortened to STEPS.

stepmother ▻ *noun* a wife or partner of a person's father who is not that person's biological mother.

step-parent ▻ *noun* a stepfather or stepmother. • **step-parenting** *noun.*

steppe /stɛp/ ▻ *noun* an extensive dry grassy and usually treeless plain, especially one found in SE Europe and Asia extending east from the Ukraine through to the Manchurian plains of China. ◷ 17c: from Russian *step* lowland.

stepping-stone ▻ *noun* **1** a large stone that has a surface which is above the water level of a stream, etc and which can be used for crossing over to the other side. **2** something that functions as a means of progress □ *thought of the job as a stepping-stone to better things.*

stepson see under STEPCHILD

-ster ▷ *suffix, forming nouns, denoting* someone who is characterized by some specified trait, activity, membership of a group, etc □ *youngster*. Compare -STRESS.

steradian /stəˈreɪdɪən/ ▷ *noun* (abbreviation **sr**) *geom* the SI unit that is used for measuring solid (three-dimensional) angles. It is equal to the solid angle formed at the centre of a sphere when an area on the surface of the sphere, which is equal to the square of the sphere's radius, is joined to the centre. ◷ 19c: from Greek *stereos* solid + RADIAN.

stercoraceous /stɜːkəˈreɪʃəs/ ▷ *adj* containing, consisting of, referring or relating to FAECES. ◷ 18c: from Latin *stercus* dung.

stere /stɪə(r)/ ▷ *noun* a measurement used for timber and equal to a cubic metre (35.315 cubic feet). ◷ 18c: French, from Greek *stereos* solid.

stereo /ˈstɛrɪoʊ, ˈstɪːrɪoʊ/ ▷ *noun* **1** stereophonic reproduction of sound. **2** (*stereos*) a cassette player, record player, hi-fi system, etc that gives a stereophonic reproduction of sound. ▷ *adj* a shortened form of STEREOPHONIC. ◷ 1950s: from Greek *stereos* solid.

stereo- /stɛrɪoʊ/ or (before a vowel) **stere-** /stɛrɪ/ ▷ *combining form, forming words indicating* a solid or three-dimensional quality.

stereochemistry ▷ *noun, chem* the study of the three-dimensional arrangement of atoms within molecules, and the way in which such arrangements affect the chemical properties of the molecules. ● **stereochemical** *adj.* ● **stereochemically** *adverb.* ● **stereochemist** *noun.* ◷ 19c: from Greek *stereos* solid.

stereogram /ˈstɛrɪoʊgram/ ▷ *noun* **1** a picture, usually computer-generated, which at first does not seem to represent anything, but which, when it is looked at using one of several special techniques, forms an incredible 3-D image. **2** another word for STEREOGRAPH. **3** *Brit, formerly* in the sixties and seventies: a cabinet or unit that housed a record player, radio, speakers and record storage space; a stereo radiogram. ◷ 1990s in sense 1; 1950s in sense 3; 19c in sense 2.

stereograph /ˈstɛrɪoʊgrɑːf/ ▷ *noun* a picture or a pair of pictures that can give the impression that the represented object is in 3-D when viewed through special glasses or through a stereoscope. Also called STEREOGRAM. ● **stereographic** /stɛrɪoʊˈgrafɪk/ or ● **stereography** /stɛrɪˈɒgrəfɪ/ *noun.* ◷ 19c: from STEREO- + -GRAPH.

stereoisomer /stɛrɪoʊˈaɪsəmə(r), –zəmə(r)/ ▷ *noun, chem* an isomer that has the same chemical composition, molecular weight and structure but a different spacial arrangement of atoms as another. ● **stereoisomeric** *adj.* ● **stereoisomerism** /stɛrɪoʊaɪˈsɒmərɪzəm, -aɪˈzɒmərɪzəm/ *noun.* ◷ 19c.

stereometer /stɛrɪˈɒmɪtə(r)/ ▷ *noun* a device for measuring specific gravity. ● **stereometric** /stɛrɪoʊˈmɛtrɪk/ *adj.* ● **stereometrical** *adj.* ● **stereometrically** *adverb.* ● **stereometry** /stɛrɪˈɒmɪtrɪ/ *noun.* ◷ 19c.

stereophonic /stɛrɪoʊˈfɒnɪk/ ▷ *adj* said of a system for reproducing or broadcasting sound: using two or more independent sound channels leading to separate loudspeakers, in order to simulate the depth and physical separation of different sounds that would be experienced at a live performance. Often shortened to STEREO. ● **stereophonically** *adverb.* ● **stereophony** /stɛrɪˈɒfənɪ/ *noun.* ◷ 1920s.

stereoscope /ˈstɛrɪoʊskoʊp/ ▷ *noun* a binocular instrument that presents a slightly different view of the same object to each eye which produces an apparently 3-D image. ● **stereoscopic** /stɛrɪəˈskɒpɪk/ *adj.* ● **stereoscopically** *adverb.* ● **stereoscopy** /stɛrɪˈɒskəpɪ/ *noun.* ◷ 19c.

stereotype /ˈstɛrɪoʊtaɪp/ ▷ *noun* **1 a** an over-generalized and preconceived idea or impression of what characterizes someone or something, especially one that does not allow for any individuality or variation; **b** someone or something that conforms to such an idea, etc. **2** *printing* **a** a method of printing that involves using metal plates that have been cast from papier-mâché or plastic moulds which have been taken from the surface of a forme of type; **b** a solid metal plate of this kind. ▷ *verb* **1** to attribute over-generalized and preconceived characteristics to someone or something. **2 a** to make a stereotype plate; **b** to print using stereotype plates. ● **stereotyper** *noun.* ● **stereotypic** /stɛrɪoʊˈtɪpɪk/ *adj.* ● **stereotypical** *adj.* ● **stereotypically** *adverb.* ◷ 18c: from STEREO- + Latin *typus* bas relief.

stereotyped ▷ *adj* **1** said of opinions, etc: fixed, unchangeable; conventionalized, conforming to a stock image or cliché. **2** *printing* produced using a stereotype plate or plates.

stereotypy /stɛrɪoʊˈtaɪpɪ/ ▷ *noun* **1** the act or process of producing stereotype plates. **2** the persistent use of apparently meaningless or pointless words, actions, movements, etc that is characteristic of certain forms of mental illness. ◷ 19c.

steric /ˈstɛrɪk/ and **sterical** *chem* ▷ *adj* pertaining, referring or relating to the spacial arrangement of atoms in a molecule. ● **sterically** *adverb.* ◷ 19c: from Greek *stereos* solid.

sterile /ˈstɛraɪl, ˈstɛrɪl/ ▷ *adj* **1** biologically incapable of producing offspring, fruit or seeds. **2** free of germs. **3** producing no results; having no new ideas; lacking the usual attributes, qualities, etc. ● **sterilely** *adverb.* ● **sterility** /stəˈrɪlɪtɪ/ *noun.* ◷ 16c: from Latin *sterilis* barren.

sterilization or **sterilisation** /stɛrɪlaɪˈzeɪʃən/ ▷ *noun* **1** the treatment of food, surgical or laboratory equipment, etc with heat, chemicals or radiation in order to destroy all living micro-organisms. **2 a** *surgery* an operation that is performed, either through choice or for medical reasons, in order to stop someone having children and which usually involves a VASECTOMY in men or the cutting and tying of the FALLOPIAN tubes in women; **b** a similar operation that is performed on animals.

sterilize or **sterilise** ▷ *verb* (*sterilized, sterilizing*) **1** to make something germ-free. **2** to make someone or something infertile. ● **sterilizer** *noun.* ● **sterilizable** *adj.*

sterling /ˈstɜːlɪŋ/ ▷ *noun* **1** British money. **2 a** the official level of purity that silver must conform to, which is set at a minimum of 92.5 per cent; **b** *as adj* □ *sterling silver.* ▷ *adj* **1** good quality; worthy; reliable □ *gave a sterling performance.* **2** authentic; genuine. ◷ Anglo-Saxon *steorra* star, from the markings on early Norman pennies, + -LING.

stern[1] ▷ *adj* **1** extremely strict; authoritarian. **2** harsh, severe or rigorous. **3** unpleasantly serious or unfriendly in appearance or nature. ● **sternly** *adverb.* ● **sternness** *noun.* ◷ Anglo-Saxon *styrne.*

stern[2] ▷ *noun* **1** the rear of a ship or boat. **2** the tail or rump, especially of a sporting dog. ◷ 13c: from Norse *stjorn* steering.

sternal see under STERNUM

sternforemost ▷ *adverb, naut* backwards.

sternmost ▷ *adj, naut* nearest the stern.

sternport ▷ *noun, naut* an opening in the stern of a ship.

sternpost ▷ *noun, naut* an upright beam in the stern of a ship that supports the rudder.

stern sheets ▷ *plural noun, naut* the area, usually uncovered, towards the stern of a boat, especially the area that is behind any rowers.

sternum /ˈstɜːnəm/ ▷ *noun* (***sternums*** or ***sterna*** /-nə/) **1 a** *anatomy* in humans: the broad vertical bone in the chest that the ribs and collarbone are attached to. Also called **breastbone**; **b** the corresponding bone in other vertebrates. **2** *zool* in arthropods: the part of a body segment that faces towards the ground. • **sternal** *adj.* ⓘ 17c: from Greek *sternon* chest.

sternutation /stɜːnjʊˈteɪʃən/ ▷ *noun* an act of sneezing; a sneeze. ⓘ 16c: from Latin *sternuere* to sneeze.

sternutator ▷ *noun* something, especially a gas, that causes nasal irritation, often with attendant sneezing, coughing and tears. • **sternutative** or **sternutatory** *adj.*

steroid /ˈstɛrɔɪd, ˈstɪərɔɪd/ ▷ *noun* **1** *biochem* any of a large group of fat-soluble organic compounds, such as sterols, some sex harmones, bile acids, etc that have a complex molecular structure (17-carbon-atom, four-linked ring system), and which are important both physiologically and pharmacologically. **2** *medicine* a class of drug containing such a compound (eg corticosteroids). See ANABOLIC STEROID. • **steroidal** *adj.* ⓘ 1930s: from STEROL + -OID.

sterol /ˈstɪərɒl, ˈstɛrɒl/ ▷ *noun, biochem* any of a group of colourless waxy solid STEROID alcohols that are found in plants, animals and fungi, eg cholesterol. ⓘ Early 20c: a shortening of chole*sterol*, ergo*sterol*, etc.

stertorous /ˈstɜːtərəs/ ▷ *adj, formal* said of breathing: noisy; with a snoring sound. • **stertorously** *adverb.* • **stertorousness** *noun.* ⓘ 19c: from Latin *stertere* to snore.

stet /stɛt/ ▷ *noun* a conventionalized direction that is usually found in the margin of a manuscript or other text to indicate that something which has been changed or marked for deletion is to be retained in its original form after all. Compare SIC, DELE. ▷ *verb* (***stetted, stetting***) to put this kind of mark on a manuscript, etc. ⓘ 18c: Latin, meaning 'let it stand'.

stethoscope /ˈstɛθəskoʊp/ ▷ *noun, medicine* an instrument that consists of a small concave disc that has hollow tubes attached to it and which, when it is placed on the body, carries sounds, eg of the heart, lungs, etc, to earpieces. • **stethoscopic** /stɛθəˈskɒpɪk/ *adj.* • **stethoscopically** *adverb.* ⓘ 19c: from Greek *stethos* chest + -SCOPE.

stetson /ˈstɛtsən/ ▷ *noun* a man's broad-brimmed felt hat with a high crown, which is indented at the top and which is especially worn by cowboys, country-and-western singers, Texan oil magnates, etc. ⓘ 19c: named after the American hat-maker, John Stetson (1830–1906), who designed the hat.

stevedore /ˈstiːvədɔː(r)/ ▷ *noun* someone whose job is to load and unload ships; a docker. ▷ *verb* (***stevedored, stevedoring***) to load or unload (a ship or a ship's cargo). ⓘ 18c: from Spanish *estibador*, from *estibar* to pack or stow.

stew[1] /stjuː/ ▷ *verb* (***stewed, stewing***) **1** *tr & intr* to cook (especially meat) by long simmering. **2 a** to cause (tea) to become bitter and over-strong by letting it brew for too long; **b** *intr* said of tea: to become bitter and over-strong because it has been left brewing for too long. **3** *intr, colloq* to be in a state of worry or agitation. **4** *colloq* to become too hot, especially in a crowded, confined space. ▷ *noun* **1** a dish of food, especially a mixture of meat and vegetables, that has been cooked by stewing. **2** *colloq* a state of worry or agitation. • **stew in one's own juice** *colloq* to suffer the consequences of one's own, often ill-advised, actions. ⓘ 18c; although earlier, now obsolete senses of 'a heated room', 'a stove' and 'to take a very hot bath' date from 14c: from French *estuve* a sweat room.

stew[2] /stjuː/ ▷ *noun* **1** a pond or tank for fish. **2** an artificial oyster bed. ⓘ 14c: from French *estuier* to shut up, keep in reserve.

steward /ˈstjʊəd/ ▷ *noun* **1 a** someone whose job is to look after the needs of passengers on a ship or aircraft. See also FLIGHT ATTENDANT. **2** someone whose duties include supervising crowd movements during sporting events, gigs, public marches, etc. **3** someone whose job is to oversee the catering arrangements, etc in a hotel or club. **4** someone whose job is to manage another person's property and affairs, eg on a country estate. **5** a senior official who monitors a horse race and who has to adjudicate on photo-finishes, enquiries, etc. **6** a SHOP STEWARD. **7** a college caterer. ▷ *verb* (***stewarded, stewarding***) to serve as a steward of something. • **stewardship** *noun.* ⓘ Anglo-Saxon *stigweard* hall-keeper.

stewardess ▷ *noun* a female steward on a ship, aeroplane, etc. See also AIR HOSTESS, FLIGHT ATTENDANT.

stewed ▷ *adj* **1** said of meat, vegetables, fruit, etc: cooked by stewing □ ***stewed prunes.*** **2** said of tea: bitter and over-strong because it has been brewed for too long. **3** *colloq* drunk.

stg ▷ *abbreviation* sterling.

sthenic /ˈsθɛnɪk/ ▷ *adj* said of a disease or its symptoms: having excessive muscular strength or energy. ⓘ 18c: from ASTHENIC.

stibine /ˈstɪbaɪn/ ▷ *noun* a colourless poisonous gas that is slightly water-soluble. ⓘ 19c: from Latin *stibium* antimony + -INE[2].

stibnite /ˈstɪbnaɪt/ ▷ *noun* a grey mineral that is found in quartz veins and which is the chief ore of antimony. ⓘ 19c: from Latin *stibium* antimony + -ITE 3.

stich /ˈstɪk/ ▷ *noun* a piece of poetry or prose of a designated length; a line or verse. • **stichic** *adj.* ⓘ 18c: from Greek *stikhos* a row.

stichomythia /stɪkoʊˈmɪθɪə/ ▷ *noun, rhetoric* a form of quickfire hostile dialogue which was originally a feature of classical Greek drama but which has also been employed by modern dramatists, eg in *Richard III* IV. iv, and which is characterized by one speaker picking up a word, phrase or idea that has just been used by the other speaker and throwing it back at the original user, having in some way turned it around to their own advantage. ⓘ 19c: from Greek *stikhomythein* to speak alternate lines, from *stikhos* line + *mythos* speech.

stick[1] ▷ *noun* **1 a** a twig or thin branch of a tree; **b** **(sticks)** *colloq* the small hurdles of a steeplechase. **2 a** any long thin piece of wood; **b** *in compounds* a shaped piece of wood or other material which has a designated purpose □ ***hockey stick*** □ ***gear stick***; **c** a baton or wand, etc; **d** a bow for a fiddle or the wooden part of a bow. **3** a long thin piece of anything. **4** a piece of furniture, especially when it is one of few. **5** *colloq* verbal abuse, criticism or mockery. **6** **(the sticks)** *colloq* a rural area that is considered remote or unsophisticated. **7** *colloq* a person □ ***a funny old stick.*** **8 a** a group of bombs that are dropped from an aircraft one after the other over a target; **b** a group of parachutists that are dropped from an aircraft one after the other. ▷ *verb* (***sticked, sticking***) to support (a plant) using a stick or sticks. • **get hold of the wrong end of the stick** to misunderstand a situation, a statement, etc. • **give it some stick** *colloq* to put some force or effort into something. • **give someone stick** to criticize or punish them. • **in a cleft stick** in a dangerous or tricky position. • **up sticks** *colloq* to move away, especially without warning □ ***He just upped sticks and left.*** • **up the stick** *slang* pregnant. ⓘ Anglo-Saxon *sticca.*

stick[2] ▷ *verb* (***stuck, sticking***) **1 a** to push or thrust (especially something long and thin or pointed); **b** *colloq* to push or protrude (a hand, head, foot, etc) □ ***stick your feet into your trainers.*** **2** to fasten by piercing with a pin or other sharp object □ ***stick it up with drawing-pins.*** **3** *tr & intr* to fix, or be or stay fixed, with an adhesive. **4** *intr* to remain persistently □ ***an episode that sticks in my mind.*** **5** *tr & intr* to make or be unable to move; to jam, lock or lodge □ ***The car got stuck in the snow.*** **6** to confine □ ***stuck in the house all day.*** **7** *intr* said of criticism, etc: to continue to be considered valid. **8** *colloq* to place or put □

just stick it on the table. **9** *colloq* to bear or tolerate □ *could not stick it any longer.* **10** to cause to be at a loss; to baffle □ *He's never stuck for something to say.* • **be stuck on someone** or **something** and **get stuck into something** see under STUCK. • **stick at nothing** to act in a very ruthless manner. • **stick in one's throat** *colloq* to be extremely difficult to say or accept, usually for reasons of principle. • **stick it!** or **stick it up your jumper, arse,** *etc colloq* a contemptuous exclamation that is used when something is not wanted, not going one's way, etc. • **stick one's neck out** or **stick one's neck out for someone** or **something** to put oneself in a dangerous or tricky position for them or it. • **stick one's nose in** or **into something** to interfere or pry, or to interfere with it or pry into it, especially when it is none of one's business. • **stick out a mile** or **stick out like a sore thumb** to be glaringly obvious. • **stick something on someone** to put the blame for it onto them. • **stick to one's guns** to be adamant. ◷ 19c: from military use, literally 'to stay in one's position when under attack'. ◷ Anglo-Saxon *stician.*

■ **stick around** *colloq* to remain or linger.

■ **stick at something** to continue doggedly with it.

■ **stick by someone** or **something** to remain loyal or supportive towards them or it □ *She sticks by him no matter what he does.*

■ **stick someone for something** *colloq* to get them to pay for it.

■ **stick in** to start eating, etc □ *Stick in — the soup's getting cold.*

■ **stick on** *colloq* to put on (an item of clothing). See also STICK-ON.

■ **stick out 1** to project or protrude □ *His ears really stick out.* **2** to be obvious or noticeable; to stand out. **3** to endure □ *had to stick out the winter with hardly any supplies.*

■ **stick out for something** to continue to insist on it; to refuse to yield.

■ **stick to something 1** to remain faithful to it, eg a promise □ *stuck to the same story throughout the questioning.* **2** to keep to it, eg a matter under discussion without digressing.

■ **stick together** to remain loyal and supportive, especially in the face of some difficulty.

■ **stick up** *colloq* **1** to project upwards; to stand up. **2** to attach (a bill, poster, etc) to a wall, etc. **3** *colloq* to rob someone or something, especially at gunpoint □ *stuck up the liquor store.* See also STICK-UP.

■ **stick up for someone** or **oneself** to speak or act in their or one's own defence □ *quite capable of sticking up for myself.*

■ **stick someone with something** *colloq* to burden them with it □ *stuck her mother with watching the baby while she went out.*

stickability ▷ *noun, colloq* staying power; perseverance.

sticker ▷ *noun* **1** an adhesive label or small poster, card etc, especially one displaying a message or advertisement in a shop window, on a car, etc or that children swap and collect. **2** someone or something that sticks. **3** someone who perseveres with something.

sticking-plaster see PLASTER *noun* 2

sticking-point ▷ *noun* deadlock.

stick insect ▷ *noun* any of several kinds of tropical insect that have long slender bodies and legs which are camouflaged to look like twigs. Compare LEAF INSECT.

stick-in-the-mud ▷ *noun, colloq* someone who is opposed to anything new or adventurous and who is therefore seen as boring and dull.

stickleback /'stɪkəlbak/ ▷ *noun* a small spiny-backed fish that is found in many northern rivers. ◷ Anglo-Saxon *sticel* prick + BACK.

stickler ▷ *noun* (*usually* **a stickler for something**) someone who fastidiously insists on something. ◷ Anglo-Saxon *stihtan* to set in order.

stick-on ▷ *adj* with some form of adhesive already provided.

sticky ▷ *adj* (***stickier, stickiest***) **1** covered with something that is tacky or gluey. **2** able or likely to stick to other surfaces. **3** said of the weather: warm and humid; muggy. **4** *colloq* said of a situation, etc: difficult; awkward; unpleasant. ▷ *verb* (***stickies, stickied, stickying***) to make something sticky. • **stickily** *adverb.* • **stickiness** *noun.* • **come to** or **meet a sticky end** *colloq* to suffer an unpleasant end or death. • **be sticky about something** to act in an awkward, sometimes unpredictable, way over it □ *She can be a bit sticky about who she gives the keys to.*

sticky-fingered ▷ *adj, colloq* prone to stealing, shop-lifting or pilfering. • **sticky fingers** *noun* a thief.

sticky tape ▷ *noun* a strong tape that has an adhesive substance on one side and which is used for binding, fastening, joining, etc.

sticky wicket ▷ *noun, colloq* a difficult or awkward situation.

sties see under STY[1], STY[2]

stiff ▷ *adj* **1** not easily bent or folded; rigid. **2** said of limbs, joints, etc: lacking suppleness; not moving or bending easily. **3** said of a punishment, etc: harsh; severe. **4** said of a task, etc: difficult; arduous. **5** said of a wind: blowing strongly. **6** said of someone or their manner: **a** not natural and relaxed; over-formal; **b** *in compounds* □ *stiff-lipped.* **7** thick in consistency; viscous. **8** *colloq* said of an alcoholic drink: not diluted or only lightly diluted; strong. **9** said of a price: excessively high. ▷ *adverb, colloq* to an extreme degree □ *scared stiff.* ▷ *noun, slang* **1** a corpse. **2** something, especially a race-horse, that is destined to fail. • **stiffish** *adj.* • **stiffly** *adverb.* • **stiffness** *noun.* • **have** or **keep a stiff upper lip** to show or maintain self-control and resignation in the face of disappointment, difficulty, unpleasantness, etc. ◷ Anglo-Saxon *stif.*

stiffen ▷ *verb* (***stiffened, stiffening***) **1** *tr & intr* to make or become stiff or stiffer. **2** *intr* to become nervous or tense. • **stiffener** *noun.* • **stiffening** *adj, noun.*

stiff-necked ▷ *adj* arrogantly obstinate.

stiffware ▷ *noun, computing* software that is difficult or impossible to modify because it has been customized or there is incomplete documentation, etc.

stiffy or **stiffie** ▷ *noun* (***stiffies***) **1** *slang* an erect penis. **2** *Scots* someone who is physically not very fit or agile.

stifle[1] /'staɪfəl/ ▷ *verb* (***stifled, stifling***) **1 a** to suppress (a feeling or action) □ *stifled a laugh*; **b** to conceal □ *stifled the truth.* **2** *tr & intr* to experience or cause to experience difficulty in breathing, especially because of heat and lack of air. **3** to kill or nearly kill by stopping the breathing; to smother. **4** to stamp out □ *Police stifled the riot.* • **stifler** *noun.* ◷ 14c.

stifle[2] /'staɪfəl/ ▷ *noun* **1** the joint in the hind leg of a horse, dog or other four-legged animal that is between the femur and the tibia and which corresponds to the human knee. **2** *in compounds* □ *stifle-bone.* ◷ 14c.

stifling /'staɪflɪŋ/ ▷ *adj* **1** unpleasantly hot or airless. **2** overly oppressive. Also *as adverb.* • **stiflingly** *adverb.*

stigma /'stɪgmə/ ▷ *noun* (***stigmas***) **1** shame or social disgrace. **2** a blemish or scar on the skin. **3** *bot* in a flowering plant: the sticky surface that receives pollen and which is situated at the tip of the STYLE. **4** *zool* any of a variety of pigmented markings or spots, eg the wingspot of certain butterflies. • **stigmatic** *adj.* • **stigmatically**

adverb. ⓘ 16c: Greek, meaning 'brand', from *stizein* to mark with a tattoo.

stigmata /ˈstɪgmətə, -ˈmɑːtə/ ▻ *plural noun, Christianity* marks which are said to have appeared on the bodies of certain holy people and that are thought to resemble Christ's crucifixion wounds. • **stigmatic** or **stigmatist** *noun* someone marked by stigmata. ⓘ 17c: Greek plural of STIGMA.

stigmatism ▻ *noun* **1** the state or condition of not being affected by a defective lens. Compare ASTIGMATISM. **2** the condition that is caused by or is characteristic of stigmata.

stigmatize or **stigmatise** ▻ *verb* (***stigmatized***, ***stigmatizing***) to describe, regard, single out, etc someone as bad, shameful, etc. • **stigmatization** *noun*. • **stigmatizer** *noun*.

stilb ▻ *noun* a unit of luminance that is equal to one candela per square centimetre. ⓘ 1920s on the continent, although it is not attested in English until 1940s: from Greek *stilbe* lamp, from *stilbein* to glitter.

stilbene /ˈstɪlbiːn/ ▻ *noun, chem* a crystalline hydrocarbon that is used in the manufacture of dyes. ⓘ 19c: from Greek *stilbein* to glitter.

stilboestrol or (*N Amer*) **stilbestrol** /stɪlˈbiːstrəl/ ▻ *noun* a synthetic hormone that has oestrogenic properties. ⓘ 1930s: from Greek *stilbein* to glitter.

stile¹ ▻ *noun* a step, or set of steps, that is incorporated into a fence or wall so that people can cross but animals cannot. ⓘ Anglo-Saxon *stigel*.

stile² ▻ *noun* an upright spar in a wooden frame such as a door, window, wall panel, wainscot, etc. ⓘ 17c.

stiletto /stɪˈlɛtoʊ/ ▻ *noun* (***stilettos***) **1** (*in full* **stiletto heel**) a high thin heel on a woman's shoe. **2** *colloq* a shoe with such a heel. **3** a dagger with a narrow tapering blade. **4** a small pointed device that is used for making holes in cloth, leather, etc. ▻ *verb* (***stilettos*** or ***stilettoes***, ***stilettoed***, ***stilettoing***) to stab using a dagger of this kind. ⓘ 1950s in sense 1 & 2; 19c in sense 4; 17c in sense 3: Italian, a diminutive of *stilo* dagger, from Latin *stilus* a pen.

still¹ ▻ *adj* **1** motionless; inactive; silent. **2** quiet and calm; tranquil. **3** said of a drink: not having escaping bubbles of carbon dioxide. Compare SPARKLING. ▻ *adverb* **1** continuing as before, now or at some future time □ ***Do you still live in Edinburgh?*** **2** up to the present time, or the time in question; yet □ ***I still don't understand.*** **3** even then; nevertheless □ ***knows the dangers but still continues to smoke.*** **4** quietly and without movement □ ***sit still.*** **5** to a greater degree; even □ ***older still.*** ▻ *verb* (***stilled***, ***stilling***) **1** *tr & intr* to make or become still, silent, etc. **2** to calm, appease, or put an end to something □ ***Hugh's admission stilled the rumours.*** ▻ *noun* **1** stillness; tranquillity □ ***the still of the countryside.*** **2** a photograph, especially of an actor in, or a scene from, a cinema film, used for publicity purposes. • **stillness** *noun*. ⓘ Anglo-Saxon *stille*.

still² ▻ *noun* an apparatus for the distillation of alcoholic spirit. ⓘ 16c: from STILL¹ *verb* 1.

stillage ▻ *noun* **1** a frame, stand or stool for keeping things, eg casks, off the floor or ground. **2** a box-like container for transporting goods. ⓘ 16c.

stillbirth ▻ *noun* **1** the birth of a dead baby or fetus. **2** a baby or fetus that is dead at birth. ⓘ 18c.

stillborn ▻ *adj* **1** said of a baby or fetus: dead when born. **2** said of a project, etc: doomed from the start. ⓘ 17c.

still life ▻ *noun* **1 a** a painting, drawing or photograph of an object or objects, eg a bowl of fruit, rather than of a living thing; **b** *as adj* □ ***still-life photography.*** **2** this kind of art or photography. ⓘ 17c.

still room ▻ *noun* **1** a room where distilling is carried out. **2** a housekeeper's pantry in a large house.

Still's disease ▻ *noun, medicine* a form of rheumatoid arthritis that affects children's joints. ⓘ Early 20c: named after the English physician, Sir George F Still (1868–1941).

Stillson wrench ▻ *noun, trademark* a large adjustable wrench which has jaws that tighten when pressure is applied to the handle. ⓘ Early 20c: named after its American inventor, Daniel C Stillson (1830–1899).

stilt ▻ *noun* **1** either of a pair of long poles that have supports for the feet part of the way up so that someone can walk around supported high above the ground, and which were originally used for crossing marshy ground, but which are nowadays used by circus performers and children. **2** any of a set of props on which a building, jetty, etc is supported above ground or water level. **3** a long-legged wading bird that is related to the AVOCET and which is found in marshy places. Also called **stilt-bird** or **stilt-plover**. ▻ *verb* (***stilted***, ***stilting***) to raise or place on stilts or as though on stilts. • **stilting** *noun*. ⓘ 14c: English *stilte* a plough handle.

stilted ▻ *adj* **1** said of language: unnatural-sounding and over-formal. **2** laboured or jarring; not flowing □ ***a stilted conversation.*** **3** raised on stilts. • **stiltedly** *adverb*. • **stiltedness** *noun*. ⓘ 17c: from STILT.

stilted arch ▻ *noun, archit* an arch that has its SPRINGING LINE raised above IMPOST 2 level by vertical piers.

Stilton /ˈstɪltən/ ▻ *noun, trademark* either of two strong white English cheeses, one of which has blue veins, and which, since 1969, can only be made in Leicestershire, Derbyshire and Nottinghamshire. ⓘ 18c: named after Stilton, a town in Cambridgeshire, S England, where it was originally sold but not made.

stimulant /ˈstɪmjʊlənt/ ▻ *noun* **1** any substance, such as a drug, that produces an increase in the activity of a particular body organ or function, eg caffeine, nicotine, amphetamines. **2** anything that causes an increase in excitement, activity, interest, etc □ ***Praise can be a powerful stimulant.*** ▻ *adj* STIMULATING.

stimulate /ˈstɪmjʊleɪt/ ▻ *verb* (***stimulated***, ***stimulating***) **1** to cause physical activity, or increased activity, in (eg an organ of the body). **2** to initiate or get going. **3** to excite or arouse the senses of someone; to animate or invigorate them. **4** to create interest and enthusiasm in someone or something. • **stimulable** *adj*. • **stimulation** *noun*. • **stimulative** *adj, noun*. • **stimulator** *noun*. ⓘ 16c: from Latin *stimulare*, *stimulatum* to stimulate.

stimulating ▻ *adj* exciting; invigorating; arousing interest. • **stimulatingly** *adverb*.

stimulus /ˈstɪmjʊləs/ ▻ *noun* (***stimuli*** /-aɪ/) **1** something that acts as an incentive, inspiration, provocation, etc. **2** something, such as a drug, an electrical impulse, heat, light, etc, that causes a specific response in a cell, tissue, organ, etc. ⓘ 17c: Latin, meaning 'a goad'.

sting ▻ *noun* **1** a defensive puncturing organ that is found in certain animals and plants, which can inject poison or venom, eg the spine of a sting-ray, the hairs of a stinging nettle, etc. **2** the injection of poison from an animal or plant. **3** a painful wound resulting from the sting of an animal or plant. **4** any sharp tingling pain. **5** anything that is hurtful, eg a vicious insult □ ***felt the sting of her wicked words.*** **6** *slang* a trick, swindle or robbery. ▻ *verb* (***stung***, ***stinging***) **1** to pierce, poison or wound with a sting. **2** *intr* to produce a sharp tingling pain. **3** *slang* to cheat, swindle or rob; to cheat by overcharging □ ***stung him for 50 quid.*** • **stinged** *adj*. • **stinger** *noun*. • **stinging** *adj*. • **stingingly** *adverb*. • **stingless** *adj*. • **a sting in the tail** an unexpected turn of events, irony, unpleasantness, etc. • **sting someone into something** to goad or incite them into it. • **take the sting out of something** *colloq* to soften the pain of it. ⓘ Anglo-Saxon *stingan* to pierce.

stingaree /ˈstɪŋgəriː, stɪŋˈgəriː/ ▻ *noun* (***stingarees***) *N Amer, Austral* a popular name for the STINGRAY.

stinging nettle ▻ *noun* a NETTLE.

stingray /ˈstɪŋreɪ/ ▻ *noun* a RAY[2] with a long whip-like tail tipped with spikes which are capable of inflicting severe wounds.

stingy[1] /ˈstɪŋɪ/ ▻ *adj* (***stingier***, ***stingiest***) sharply painful.

stingy[2] /ˈstɪndʒɪ/ ▻ *adj* (***stingier***, ***stingiest***) ungenerous; mean; miserly. ● **stingily** *adverb*. ● **stinginess** *noun*. ◷ 17c.

stink ▻ *noun* **1** a strong and very unpleasant smell. **2** *colloq* an angry complaint or outraged reaction; a fuss. ▻ *verb* (*past tense* ***stank*** or ***stunk***, *past participle* ***stunk***, *present participle* ***stinking***) **1** *intr* to give off an offensive smell. **2** *intr*, *colloq* to be contemptibly bad or unpleasant □ *The idea of going with Harry stinks.* **3** *intr*, *colloq* to be morally suspect or disgusting □ *thought the deal stank from the beginning.* ● **stink to the heavens** or **high heavens 1** to emit a very offensive smell. **2** to be morally very suspect or disgusting. ● **kick up, raise** or **make a stink** to cause trouble, especially disagreeably and in public. ● **stink of something 1** to emit an offensive smell of it. **2** to be indicative of it □ *This stinks of double-dealing.* ◷ Anglo-Saxon *stincan* to smell.

■ **stink out** or **up** to fill (a room, etc) with an offensive smell.

stink bird see under HOATZIN

stink bomb ▻ *noun* a small bomb-like container that is thrown into busy places as a practical joke and which releases a foul-smelling gas or liquid when it breaks.

stinker ▻ *noun*, *colloq* **1** a very difficult task, question, etc. **2** *colloq* **a** someone who behaves in a dishonest, cheating or otherwise unscrupulous unpleasant way; **b** something that is very bad or of very poor quality □ *got a stinker of a cold.* **3** any of several kinds of smelly seabird that feed on carrion. **4** something or someone that emits an offensive smell.

stinkhorn ▻ *noun* any of several kinds of fungus that are found in woodland and which have a cap that is covered with a pungent-smelling slime that attracts insects which eat the slime and disperse the spores. ◷ 18c.

stinking ▻ *adj* **1** offensively smelly. **2** *colloq* very unpleasant, disgusting, etc. ▻ *adverb*, *colloq* extremely; disgustingly □ *stinking rich.* ● **stinkingly** *adverb*.

stinking camomile see MAYWEED

stinkwood ▻ *noun* **1** the name given to several trees that emit an offensive smell. **2** the wood of any of these trees. ◷ 18c.

stinky *colloq* ▻ *adj* (***stinkier***, ***stinkiest***) **1** offensively smelly. **2** devious; underhand. ▻ *noun* someone who emits an offensive smell. ● **stinkily** *adverb*.

stint[1] ▻ *verb* (***stinted***, ***stinting***) (**stint on**) to be mean or grudging in giving or supplying something □ *Don't stint on the booze for the party.* ▻ *noun* **1** an allotted amount of work or a fixed time for it □ *a twelve hour stint.* **2** a turn □ *did his stint yesterday.* ● **stinted** *adj*. ● **stintedly** *adverb*. ● **stintedness** *noun*. ● **stinter** *noun*. ● **stinting** *adj*. ● **stintingly** *adverb*. ● **without stint** liberally; unreservedly. ◷ Anglo-Saxon *styntan* to dull.

stint[2] ▻ *noun* a name for any of several small sandpipers such as the DUNLIN.

stipe /staɪp/ and **stipes** /ˈstaɪpiːz/ ▻ *noun* (***stipes*** or ***stipites*** /ˈstɪpɪtiːz/) **1** *bot* a stalk, especially one that supports a reproductive part such as a carpel or the cap of a fungus, or one that the leaflets of a fern or the fronds of seaweed are attached to. **2** *zool* in certain insects or crustaceans: any stalk-like appendage such as the secondary maxilla or an eyestalk. ● **stipitate** /ˈstɪpɪteɪt/ *adj*. ◷ 18c: French, from Latin *stipes* a post or tree trunk.

stipel /ˈstaɪpəl/ ▻ *noun*, *bot* one of a pair of small stipule-like appendages at the base of a leaflet. ● **stipellate** /stɪˈpɛlət, ˈstaɪpəleɪt/ *adj*. ◷ 19c: from French *stipelle*, from Latin *stipula*, a diminutive of *stipes* a post or tree trunk.

stipend /ˈstaɪpɛnd/ ▻ *noun* a salary or allowance, now especially one that is paid to a member of the clergy, but originally the pay of a soldier. ◷ 15c: from Latin *stipendium* tax.

stipendiary /staɪˈpɛndɪərɪ/ ▻ *adj* especially said of a member of the clergy: in receipt of a stipend. ▻ *noun* (***stipendiaries***) someone who receives a stipend.

stipendiary magistrate ▻ *noun*, *law* in England and Wales: a salaried and legally qualified magistrate who works in London and other large towns. They have far greater legal powers than most ordinary magistrates, who are generally lay people who receive only travelling expenses and a small allowance and have no formal legal training. ◷ 19c.

stipes see under STIPE

stipple /ˈstɪpəl/ ▻ *verb* (***stippled***, ***stippling***) **1** to paint, engrave or draw something in dots or dabs as opposed to using lines or masses of colour. See also POINTILLISM. **2** to give a finish of tiny raised bumps to (wet cement, plaster, etc) to create a grainy effect. ▻ *noun* **1** a pattern produced by stippling. **2** a painting, engraving, drawing, etc that has been produced using this technique. ● **stippled** *adj*. ● **stippler** *noun*. ◷ 17c: from Dutch *stippelen*, diminutive of *stippen* to dot.

stipulate[1] /ˈstɪpjʊleɪt/ ▻ *verb* (***stipulated***, ***stipulating***) **1** in a contract, agreement, etc: to specify as a necessary condition. **2** said of a party to an agreement, contract, etc: to insist on as a necessary condition. ● **stipulation** /stɪpjʊˈleɪʃən/ *noun*. ● **stipulator** *noun*. ● **stipulatory** *adj*. ◷ 17c.

stipulate[2] /ˈstɪpjʊleɪt, ˈstɪpjʊlət/ ▻ *adj*, *bot* said of a plant: characterized by the presence of stipules. ◷ 18c.

stipule /ˈstɪpjuːl/ ▻ *noun*, *bot* a small leaf-like structure, usually one of a pair, that is found at the base of some leaves or leaf stalks. ● **stipular** /ˈstɪpjʊlə(r)/ *adj*. ● **stipuled** *adj*. ◷ 18c: French, from Latin *stipula* straw or stubble.

stir[1] ▻ *verb* (***stirred***, ***stirring***) **1** to mix or agitate (a liquid or semi-liquid substance) by repeated circular strokes with a spoon or other utensil. **2** to arouse the emotions of someone; to move them. **3** to make or cause to make a slight or single movement □ *The baby stirred in her sleep.* **4** *intr* to get up after sleeping; to become active after resting. **5** to rouse (oneself) to action. **6** to evoke something □ *The photos stirred happy memories.* **7** *intr*, *colloq* to make trouble. ▻ *noun* **1** an act of stirring (a liquid, etc). **2** an excited reaction; a commotion □ *His arrest caused a real stir.* ● **stirless** *adj*. ● **stir it** to cause trouble. ◷ Anglo-Saxon *styrian*.

■ **stir from** to move away from □ *so frail now that she seldom stirs from her bed.*

■ **stir up something** to cause or provoke (eg trouble).

stir[2] ▻ *noun*, *slang* prison. ◷ 19c.

stir-crazy ▻ *noun*, *originally N Amer*, *especially US*, *slang* emotionally disturbed as a result of being confined, especially in prison, for a long time.

stir-fry ▻ *verb* to cook (small pieces of meat or vegetables or a mixture of both) lightly by brisk frying in a wok or large frying pan on a high heat with only a little oil. ▻ *noun* a dish of food that has been cooked in this way.

stirrer ▻ *noun* **1** someone or something that stirs. **2** *colloq* someone who enjoys making trouble or who deliberately goes about making trouble.

stirring ▻ *adj* **1** arousing strong emotions. **2** lively. ▻ *noun* an act of stirring. ● **stirringly** *adverb*.

stirrup /ˈstɪrəp/ ▻ *noun* **1** either of a pair of leather or metal loops which are suspended from straps that are attached to a horse's saddle and which are used as footrests for the rider. **2** any strap or loop that supports or passes under the foot □ ***ski-pants with stirrups.*** **3** *naut* a rope with an eyehole or THIMBLE (*sense* 2) at the end so that the FOOTROPE can be passed through it and supported by it. ◎ Anglo-Saxon *stigrap*, from *stige* ascent + *rap* rope.

stirrup bone ▷ *noun, non-technical* a stirrup-shaped bone in the middle ear which is technically called the STAPES.

stirrup cup ▷ *noun* an alcoholic drink that is given to someone, originally a rider, who is about to leave, especially someone who is going on a hunt.

stirrup pump ▷ *noun* a portable hand-operated pump that draws water from a bucket, etc, and which is used in fighting small fires.

stitch ▷ *noun* (***stitches***) **1** a single interlinking loop of thread or yarn in sewing or knitting. **2** a complete movement of the needle or needles to create such a loop. **3** *in compounds* any of various ways in which such loops are interlinked □ ***cross-stitch.*** **4** a sharp ache in the side resulting from physical exertion. **5** *non-technical* a SUTURE. ▷ *verb* (***stitches, stitched, stitching***) **1** to join, close, decorate, etc with stitches. **2** to sew. **3** *non-technical* to close a cut, wound, etc with stitches. • **stitched** *adj.* • **stitcher** *noun.* • **stitchery** *noun.* • **a stitch in time** an action, such as a repair, corrective measure, etc, that is taken just before any further damage is done. • **drop a stitch** *knitting* to accidently fail to knit it and so potentially leave a hole in the work. • **in stitches** *colloq* helpless with laughter. • **without a stitch** or **not a stitch** *colloq* without any clothing or no clothing at all. ◎ Anglo-Saxon *stice* prick.

■ **stitch someone up 1** *slang* to incriminate, trick, betray, double-cross, etc them. **2** *slang* to swindle or overcharge them □ ***The garage stitched him up by selling him four tyres when only two were worn.***

■ **stitch something up** to sew it together.

stitchwort /ˈstɪtʃwɜːt/ ▷ *noun, biol* a straggly perennial plant that has thin brittle stems, narrow leaves, and small white star-shaped flowers and which is found in woods and hedgerows throughout Europe. ◎ 13c: STITCH + WORT; so called because it was formerly used to treat a STITCH 4.

stoa /ˈstoʊə/ ▷ *noun* (***stoas*** or ***stoae*** /ˈstoʊiː/) *archit* a portico or roofed colonnade. ◎ 17c: Greek.

stoat /stoʊt/ ▷ *noun* a small flesh-eating mammal that is closely related to the weasel and which has a long slender body and reddish-brown fur with white underparts, although in northern regions the fur turns white in winter, during which time it is known as the ERMINE. ◎ 15c as *stote*.

stochastic /stoʊˈkastɪk/ ▷ *adj, statistics* random. • **stochastically** *adverb.* ◎ Early 20c in this sense; 17c, meaning 'pertaining to conjecture': from Greek *stokhastikos*, from *stokhazesthai* to aim at.

stocious or **stotious** /ˈstoʊʃəs/ ▷ *adj, colloq* drunk. ◎ 1930s.

stock ▷ *noun* **1** (*sometimes* **stocks**) goods or raw material that a shop, factory, warehouse, etc has on the premises at a given time □ ***Our stocks of packing material are getting low.*** **2** a supply kept in reserve □ ***an impressive stock of fine wine.*** **3** equipment or raw material in use. **4** liquid in which meat or vegetables have been cooked and which can then be used as a base for soup, a sauce, etc. **5** the shaped wooden or plastic part of a rifle or similar gun that the user rests against their shoulder. **6** farm animals; livestock. **7** the money raised by a company through the selling of shares. **8** the total shares issued by a particular company or held by an individual shareholder. **9** a group of shares bought or sold as a unit. **10** ancestry; descent □ ***of peasant stock.*** **11** any of various Mediterranean plants of the wallflower family that are cultivated for their bright flowers. **12** (**the stocks**) *formerly* a wooden device that was used for securing offenders who were held by the head and wrists or by the wrists and ankles, so that they could be displayed for public ridicule as a punishment, eg for drunkenness, whoring, etc. **13** reputation; standing. **14** the handle of a fishing rod, whip, etc. ▷ *adj* **1** being of a standard type, size, etc, constantly in demand and always kept in stock. **2** said of a phrase, etc: much used, especially so over-used as to be meaningless. ▷ *verb* (***stocked, stocking***) **1** to keep a supply for sale. **2** to provide with a supply □ ***stocked the drinks cabinet with expensive brandies.*** • **in stock** currently held for sale on the premises. • **out of stock** not currently held for sale on the premises, especially temporarily. • **take stock** to make an inventory of all stock held on the premises at a particular time. • **take stock of something** to make an overall assessment of one's circumstances, etc. ◎ Anglo-Saxon *stocc* stick.

■ **stock up on something** to acquire or accumulate a large supply of it.

stockade /stɒˈkeɪd/ ▷ *noun* a defensive fence or enclosure that is built of upright tall heavy posts. ▷ *verb* (***stockaded, stockading***) to protect or defend with a stockade. ◎ 17c: from Spanish *estacada*, from *estaca* a post.

stockbroker ▷ *noun* someone whose profession is to buy and sell stocks and shares on behalf of customers in return for a fee. Often shortened to **broker.** • **stockbrokerage** *noun.* • **stockbrokering** *noun.* ◎ 18c.

stock car ▷ *noun* a car that has been specially strengthened and modified for competing in a kind of track racing where deliberate ramming and colliding are allowed.

stock cube ▷ *noun* a small cube of compressed and concentrated meat or vegetable extract which is added to water to make stock for soups, sauces, gravies, etc.

stock exchange ▷ *noun* **1 a** a market where the trading of stocks and shares by professional dealers on behalf of customers goes on; **b** a building where this type of trading is done; **c** the traders in this type of market. **2** (*usually* **the stock exchange**) the level of prices in this type of market or the amount of activity that this type of market generates. See also FT INDEX, DOW JONES INDEX.

stockfish ▷ *noun* fish, especially cod or haddock, that is cured by being split and left to dry in the open air.

stock footage ▷ *noun* documentary, newsreel or feature film shots of action, crowd, etc scenes, or well-documented events, etc which are stored in a library or laboratory ready to be bought or rented by film companies who will insert them into a new film and thereby cut down on production costs.

stockily and **stockiness** see under STOCKY

stocking /ˈstɒkɪŋ/ ▷ *noun* **1** either of a pair of close-fitting coverings for women's legs which are made of fine semi-transparent nylon or silk and which can be either self-supporting or supported by suspenders. **2** a sock, especially one of the kind worn with highland dress. See also CHRISTMAS STOCKING. **3** the area of a bird's or animal's leg, especially when it has a distinctively different appearance from the rest of its body □ ***a black kitten with four white stockings.*** • **stockinged** *adj.* • **in stocking feet** or **soles** without shoes. ◎ 16c: from STOCK.

stocking filler ▷ *noun* a small, usually inexpensive, Christmas present.

stocking mask ▷ *noun* a piece of nylon stocking or tights that someone, eg a bank robber, pulls over their face in order to disguise their features.

stocking stitch ▷ *noun, knitting* a way of joining loops together that involves the alternation of plain and purl rows. ◎ Early 19c: so called because this is the way hosiery is made.

stock-in-trade ▷ *noun* **1 a** something that is seen as fundamental to a particular trade or activity; **b** *as adj* clichéd □ ***a story with stock-in-trade sentiments.*** **2** all the goods that a shopkeeper, etc has for sale.

stockist ▷ *noun* a person or shop that stocks a particular item or brand.

stockjobber ▷ *noun* **1** *formerly* someone who, until 1986, engaged in trading on the stock exchange by selling securities to brokers rather than dealing directly with the public. **2** *US* a contemptuous term for a stockbroker, especially one who is involved in unscrupulous dealings.

stockman ▷ *noun* **1** someone whose job is keeping, rearing, etc farm animals, especially cattle. **2** *US* a STOREMAN.

stock market ▷ *noun* the STOCK EXCHANGE.

stockpile ▷ *noun* a reserve supply that has been accumulated. ▷ *verb* to accumulate a large reserve supply. ◷ 1940s; although an earlier sense applied to 'a pile of coal or ore' dates from 19c.

stockroom ▷ *noun* a storeroom, especially in a shop.

stock-still ▷ *adj* ▷ *adverb* completely motionless. ◷ 15c.

stocktaking ▷ *noun* **1** the process of making a detailed inventory and valuation of all the goods, raw materials, etc that are held on the premises of a shop, factory, etc at a particular time. **2** the process of making an overall assessment eg of the present situation with regard to one's future prospects, etc.

stocky ▷ *adj* (***stockier***, ***stockiest***) said of a person or animal: broad, strong-looking and usually not very tall. ● **stockily** *adverb*. ● **stockiness** *noun*.

stockyard /'stɒkjɑːd/ ▷ *noun* a large yard or enclosure that is usually sectioned off into pens, where livestock are kept temporarily, eg before being auctioned.

stodge /stɒdʒ/ ▷ *noun* food that is heavy, filling and, usually, fairly tasteless. ▷ *verb* (***stodged***, ***stodging***) to stuff with food. ◷ 17c.

stodgy ▷ *adj* (***stodgier***, ***stodgiest***) **1** said of food: heavy and filling but usually fairly tasteless and unappetizing. **2** said of someone, their attitude, conversation, etc: boringly conventional or serious. ● **stodgily** *adverb*. ● **stodginess** *noun*. ◷ 19c; originally meaning 'thick', 'glutinous' or 'muddy'.

stoep /stuːp/ ▷ *noun, S Afr* a raised terraced verandah that runs along the front, and sometimes the sides, of a house. Compare STOOP². ◷ 18c: Dutch, related to STEP.

stoic /'stoʊɪk/ ▷ *noun* **1** someone who can repress emotions and show patient resignation under difficult circumstances. **2** (**Stoic**) *philos* a member of the Greek school of philosophy that was founded by Zeno around 300 BC. See also STOICISM. ◷ 14c: from Greek *Stoa Poikile* Painted Porch, the name of the place in Athens where Zeno taught.

stoical ▷ *adj* **1** accepting suffering or misfortune uncomplainingly. **2** indifferent to both pain and pleasure. ● **stoically** *adverb*.

stoichiometry or **stoicheiometry** /stɔɪkaɪ'ɒmətrɪ/ ▷ *noun* the branch of chemistry concerned with the relative proportions in which atoms or molecules react together to form chemical compounds. ● **stoichiometric** *adj*. ◷ Early 19c: from Greek *stoicheion* element.

stoicism /'stoʊɪsɪzəm/ ▷ *noun* **1 a** brave or patient acceptance of suffering and misfortune; **b** repression of emotion. **2** (**Stoicism**) the philosophy of the Stoics which was characterized by an emphasis on the development of self-sufficiency in the individual, whose duty was to conform only to the dictates of natural order to which all people belonged equally. ◷ 14c: from STOIC.

stoke ▷ *verb* (***stoked***, ***stoking***) **1** to put coal or other fuel on (eg a fire, the furnace of a boiler). **2** to arouse or intensify (eg passion or enthusiasm). ◷ 17c: from Dutch *stoken* to feed (a fire).

■ **stoke up** *colloq* to fill oneself with food.

■ **stoke something up** to fuel (a fire or furnace).

stokehold ▷ *noun* the boiler room on a steamship.

stoke-hole ▷ *noun* the space around the mouth of a furnace.

stoker ▷ *noun* someone whose job is to stoke a furnace, especially on a steamship or steam train.

stokes and *US* **stoke** ▷ *noun, physics* (symbol **St**) in the cgs system: the unit of KINEMATIC VISCOSITY. ◷ 1930s: named after the Irish-born physicist and mathematician, Sir George Stokes (1819–1903).

STOL /stɒl/ ▷ *noun* **1** a system that allows an aircraft to take off and land without the need for a long runway. **2** an aircraft that is fitted with this kind of system. Compare VTOL. ◷ 1960s: from *s*hort *t*ake-*o*ff and *l*anding.

stole¹ ▷ *noun* **1** a woman's scarf-like garment, often made of fur, that is worn around the shoulders. **2** a long narrow scarf-like ceremonial garment for various members of the clergy that is worn with both ends hanging down in front. ◷ Anglo-Saxon, from Greek *stellein* to array.

stole² *past tense of* STEAL

stolen *past participle of* STEAL

stolid /'stɒlɪd/ ▷ *adj* showing little or no interest or emotion; impassive. ● **stolidity** /stɒ'lɪdɪtɪ/ *noun*. ● **stolidly** *adverb*. ● **stolidness** *noun*. ◷ 17c: from Latin *stolidus* dull.

stollen /'stoʊlən; *German* 'ʃtɔlən/ ▷ *noun* a rich sweet fruit loaf that is traditionally served at Christmas and which contains dried fruit, glacé cherries, candied peel and often a layer of marzipan in the middle. ◷ Early 20c: German, meaning 'a post', so called because of its shape.

stolon /'stoʊlən/ ▷ *noun* **1** *bot* a stem that grows horizontally out of the base of certain plants and which has a node or nodes that can root and form new independent plants. Also called RUNNER. **2** *zool* a tubular outgrowth that is found in certain lower animals, eg in hydroid colonies, from which new individuals can arise. ◷ 17c: from Latin *stolo* a sucker of a plant.

STOLport ▷ *noun* an airport that is specifically designed for aircraft that only need a short runway. ◷ 1960s: from STOL + PORT¹.

stoma /'stoʊmə/ ▷ *noun* (***stomata*** /'stoʊmətə/) **1 a** *bot* one of many tiny pores that are found on the stems and leaves of vascular plants, each of which have two GUARD CELLS for the control and regulation of their functions, and which are the sites where water loss from the plant and gaseous exchange between plant tissue and the atmosphere take place; **b** *biol* any small opening or pore in the surface of a living organism. **2** *surgery* an artificial opening, especially one, such as a COLOSTOMY or an ILEOSTOMY, that is made for the excretion of waste matter which cannot be evacuated from the body in the normal way. ● **stomatal** or **stomatic** *adj*. ◷ 17c: Greek, meaning 'mouth'.

stomach /'stʌmək/ ▷ *noun* **1** in the alimentary canal of vertebrates: a large sac-like organ, sometimes, eg in ruminants, one of several, where food is temporarily stored until gastric juices and the contractions of the muscular walls partially digest the food to a semiliquid mass called CHYME. **2** *loosely* the area around the abdomen; the belly. **3** *formerly* disposition; pride; temper. ▷ *verb* (***stomached***, ***stomaching***) **1** *colloq* to bear or put up with □ ***can't stomach his arrogance.*** **2** to be able to eat, drink or digest easily □ ***find red meat very hard to stomach.*** See also GASTRIC. ● **stomachal** /'stɒməkəl/, **stomachic** /stə'makɪk/ or **stomachical** *adj*. ● **have the stomach for something** *colloq* to have the inclination, desire, courage, spirit, determination, etc for it □ ***has the***

stomach for dangerous sports. • **on a full** or **empty stomach** having just eaten or not having eaten for a while □ *You shouldn't drink on an empty stomach.* ⓒ 14c: from Greek *stomachos*, from *stoma* mouth.

stomach-ache and **tummy-ache** ▷ *noun* pain in the abdominal area, especially from indigestion, gastric flu, etc. Also called **stomach upset** or **upset stomach**.

stomacher ▷ *noun* an ornate covering for the chest and abdomen that was often decorated with jewels and which was worn by women underneath a laced bodice up until the end of the 19c. ⓒ 15c, when it was a garment worn by both men and women.

stomachful ▷ *noun* (***stomachfuls***) **1** the amount a stomach can hold. **2** an amount that is greater than can be tolerated □ *had an absolute stomachful of your lies.*

stomach pump ▷ *noun* a device that consists of a long tube which is inserted down the throat and into the stomach and which is used medically for sucking out the contents of the stomach, especially in cases of drug overdosing and other forms of suspected poisoning.

stomachy ▷ *adj* **1** having a large belly. **2** *colloq* prone to angry outbursts.

stomata and **stomatal** see under STOMA

stomatitis /stoʊməˈtaɪtəs/ ▷ *noun* inflammation of the mouth.

stomato- or before a vowel **stomat-** ▷ *combining form, indicating* the mouth or a part that looks or functions like a mouth. ⓒ From Greek *stoma* a mouth.

stomatology /stoʊməˈtɒlədʒɪ/ ▷ *noun* the study of the functions, diseases and structure of the mouth.

-stomous ▷ *combining form, denoting* a specified kind of mouth or a specified number of mouths □ *monostomous.*

stomp ▷ *verb* (***stomped***, ***stomping***) *intr* **1** to stamp or tread heavily. **2** to dance the stomp. ▷ *noun* **1 a** a kind of lively jazz dance that involves stamping movements; **b** a tune that is suitable for doing this kind of dance to; **c** the rhythm of this kind of tune. **2** a heavy thudding step. ⓒ 19c: originally a US dialectal variant of STAMP.

■ **stomp out** to march off or away from, especially in anger, disgust, etc.

-stomy ▷ *combining form, forming nouns denoting* a surgical operation where an artificial hole is created in an organ or where a permanent connection is formed between two internal body parts □ *ileostomy.* ⓒ From Greek *stoma* a mouth.

stone ▷ *noun* (***stones*** or in sense 7 ***stone***) **1** the hard solid material that rocks are made of. **2 a** a small fragment of rock, eg a pebble; **b** anything that resembles this □ *hailstone.* **3** *usually in compounds* a shaped piece of stone that has a designated purpose, eg millstone, paving stone, standing stone, milestone, tombstone, etc. **4** a gemstone. **5 a** the hard woody middle part of some fruits, eg peach, nectarine, plum, etc which contains the seed; **b** the hard seed of some other fruits such as the grape, date, etc. **6** a hard mass that sometimes forms in the gall bladder, kidney, etc, which often causes pain and which usually requires surgical removal. Also called **calculus**. **7** a UK measure of weight equal to 14 pounds or 6.35 kilograms. **8** a dull light grey colour. **9** a rounded piece of polished granite that is used in the game of CURLING. **10** *as adj* made of stoneware □ *a stone casserole dish.* **11** *printing* a flat table that is used for the imposition of pages. ▷ *verb* (***stoned***, ***stoning***) **1** to pelt with stones as a punishment. **2** to remove the stone from (fruit). ▷ *adverb, in compounds* completely □ *stone-cold.* • **stoneless** *adj.* • **stoner** *noun.* • **leave no stone unturned** to try all the possibilities imaginable or make every possible effort. • **a stone's throw** *colloq* a short distance. • **stone the crows!** or **stone me!** *colloq* an exclamation of bewilderment, shock, surprise, etc. ⓒ Anglo-Saxon *stan.*

Stone Age ▷ *noun* **1** the period in human history when tools and weapons were made of stone. **2** *as adj* **a** (**Stone-age** or **stone-age**) from or relating to this period □ *Stone-age remains*; **b** old-fashioned □ *stone-age technology.*

stone bass ▷ *noun* a large sea fish of the perch family that has spiny fins and which is found in the Mediterranean and the Atlantic. Also called **wreckfish**. ⓒ 17c.

stone-blind ▷ *adj* completely blind.

stonechat /ˈstoʊntʃat/ ▷ *noun* a small brownish European bird whose call is like stones knocking together.

stone circle ▷ *noun, archaeol* any of many circular or near-circular rings of prehistoric standing stones that are found throughout N Europe, which date from the late Neolithic and Early Bronze Ages and whose exact function is unknown.

stone-cold ▷ *adj* completely cold. • **stone-cold sober** absolutely sober.

stonecrop ▷ *noun* any of various species of succulent plant that are mostly native perennials of northern temperate regions and which have fleshy leaves and star-like yellow, white or red flowers. ⓒ Anglo-Saxon *stancrop*, so called because of its ability to thrive on rocks, old walls, etc, making it an ideal rockery plant.

stone curlew ▷ *noun* a large wading bird that looks like a plover and which nests on stony ground. Also called **thick knee**.

stone-cutter ▷ *noun* **1** someone skilled in the cutting or engraving of stones. **2** a machine that is used for dressing stone.

stoned ▷ *adj, slang* **1** in a state of drug-induced euphoria. **2** very drunk. **3** said of a fruit: with the stone removed. • **get stoned** to take drugs in order to reach a state of euphoria.

stone-dead ▷ *adj* completely without signs of life.

stone-deaf ▷ *adj* unable to hear at all.

stonefish ▷ *noun* a poisonous tropical sea fish that resembles a rock on the seabed when it lies in wait for its prey.

stonefly ▷ *noun* an insect that is found near water and whose larvae live under stones in streams.

stonefruit ▷ *noun* a fruit, such as the plum, peach, nectarine, cherry, etc, that has a fleshy edible part surrounding a woody stone which encloses a single seed; a DRUPE.

stoneground ▷ *adj* said of flour: produced by grinding between millstones.

stonemason ▷ *noun* someone who is skilled in shaping stone for building work. • **stonemasonry** *noun.*

stone pine ▷ *noun* a Mediterranean pine with umbrella-shaped branches and edible seeds or PINE NUTS.

stonewall ▷ *verb* **1** *tr & intr* to hold up progress, especially in parliament, intentionally, eg by obstructing discussion, giving long irrelevant speeches, etc. **2** *intr, cricket* said of a batsman: to bat extremely defensively. • **stonewaller** *noun.* ⓒ Early 20c in sense 2; 19c in sense 1.

stoneware ▷ *noun* a type of hard coarse pottery made from clay that has a high proportion of silica, sand or flint in it.

stonewashed ▷ *adj* said of new clothes or a fabric, especially denim: having a faded and worn appearance because of the abrasive action of the small pieces of pumice stone that they have been washed with.

stonework ▷ *noun* **1** a structure or building part that has been made out of stone. **2** the process of working in stone.

stonk *military slang* ▷ *noun* an intense artillery bombardment. ▷ *verb* (***stonked***, ***stonking***) to bombard with intense artillery fire. ⓒ 1940s; although an earlier dialectal meaning of 'a marble or the stake put up in a game of marbles' dates from 19c.

stonker ▻ *verb* (***stonkered***, ***stonkering***) *chiefly Austral & NZ slang* to put out of action; to thwart; to kill. • **stonkered** *adj* drunk. Ⓒ Early 20c: from STONK.

stonking ▻ *adj*, *colloq* excellent. ▻ *adverb* extremely □ *a stonking big cup of coffee.* Ⓒ 1980s.

stony or **stoney** /'stoʊnɪ/ ▻ *adj* (***stonier***, ***stoniest***) **1** covered with stones. **2** relating to or resembling stone or stones. **3** unfriendly; unfeeling; callous □ *a stony expression.* **4 a** fixed □ *a stony stare*; **b** unrelenting □ *a stony silence.* **5** *Brit colloq* a short form of STONY-BROKE. • **stonily** *adverb*. • **stoniness** *noun*.

stony-broke ▻ *adj*, *Brit colloq* absolutely without money; penniless.

stony-hearted ▻ *adj* callous and unfeeling. • **stony-heartedness** *noun*.

stood *past tense, past participle of* STAND

stooge /stuːdʒ/ ▻ *noun* **1** a performer whose function is to provide a comedian with opportunities for making jokes and who is often also the butt of the jokes. **2** an assistant, especially one who is given unpleasant tasks or who is exploited in some way. ▻ *verb* (***stooged***, ***stooging***) *intr* to act as a stooge for someone. Ⓒ Early 20c.

stook /stʊk/ ▻ *noun* a group of sheaves that are propped upright together in a field. ▻ *verb* (***stooked***, ***stooking***) to prop up (grain) in sheaves in a field. • **stooker** *noun*. Ⓒ 16c.

stookie /'stʊkɪ/ ▻ *noun* (***stookies***) *Scots* **1 a** plaster of Paris; **b** a plaster of Paris cast on a broken limb. **2** a slow, dull-witted person. • **stand like a stookie** to stand very still, especially in a transfixed or bemused way.

stool /stuːl/ ▻ *noun* **1** a simple seat without a back, usually with three or four legs. **2** a footstool. **3** faeces. **4 a** a felled tree stump, especially one that has new shoots sprouting from it; **b** the clump of new growth that sprouts from a felled tree stump. **5** *US* a hunter's decoy. ▻ *verb* (***stooled***, ***stooling***) **1** *intr* said of a felled tree stump, etc: to send up shoots. **2** to lure (wildfowl) using a decoy. • **fall between two stools** to lose two opportunities by hesitating between them or trying for both or to fail to achieve something because of failing to decide between alternative courses of action, etc. Ⓒ Anglo-Saxon *stol*.

stoolball ▻ *noun* an old-fashioned 11-a-side bat-and-ball game similar to cricket and rounders. Ⓒ 15c.

stool-pigeon ▻ *noun* **1** a police informer. **2** a decoy bird, originally a pigeon stuck to a stool, used by a hunter to lure others.

stoop[1] /stuːp/ ▻ *verb* (***stooped***, ***stooping***) **1** *intr* (*sometimes* **stoop down**) to bend the upper body forward and down. **2** *intr* to walk with head and shoulders bent forward. **3** said of a bird of prey: to swoop down. ▻ *noun* **1** a bent posture □ *walks with a stoop.* **2** a downward swoop. • **stooped** *adj* bent. • **stooping** *adj*. • **stoopingly** *adverb*. Ⓒ Anglo-Saxon *stupian*.

> ■ **stoop to something 1** to degrade oneself to do it □ *How could you stoop to shoplifting?* **2** to deign or condescend to do it.

stoop[2] /stuːp/ ▻ *noun*, *N Amer, especially US* an open platform, usually a wooden one, with steps leading up to it that runs along the front of a house and sometimes round the sides as well. Ⓒ 18c: from Dutch *stoep*.

stoop[3] an alternative spelling of STOUP

stop ▻ *verb* (***stopped***, ***stopping***) **1** *tr & intr* to bring or come to rest, a standstill or an end; to cease or cause to cease moving, operating or progressing. **2** to prevent. **3** to withhold or keep something back. **4** to block, plug or close something. **5** to deduct (money) from wages. **6** to instruct a bank not to honour (a cheque). **7** *intr*, *colloq* to stay or reside temporarily □ *stopped the night with friends.* **8** *music* to adjust the vibrating length of (a string) by pressing down with a finger. **9** *slang* to receive (a blow). ▻ *noun* **1** an act of stopping. **2** a regular stopping place, eg on a bus route. **3** the state of being stopped; a standstill. **4** a device that prevents further movement □ *a door stop.* **5** a temporary stay, especially when it is en route for somewhere else. **6** a shortened form of FULL STOP. **7 a** a set of organ pipes that have a uniform tone; **b** a knob that allows the pipes to be brought into and out of use; **c** a similar device on a harpsichord. **8** (*also* **f-stop**) any of a graded series of sizes that a camera's aperture can be adjusted to. **9** *phonetics* any consonantal sound that is made by the sudden release of air that has built up behind the lips, teeth, tongue, etc, eg the PLOSIVES and the AFFRICATES of English. • **stoppable** *adj*. • **stopping** *noun*. • **stopless** *adj*. • **pull out all the stops** to try one's best. • **put a stop to something** to cause it to end, especially abruptly. • **stop at nothing** to be prepared to do anything, no matter how unscrupulous, in order to achieve an aim, outcome, etc. • **stop the show** to be a great success. See also SHOW-STOPPER. Ⓒ Anglo-Saxon *stoppian*.

> ■ **stop something down** to reduce the size of the aperture in (a camera).
>
> ■ **stop off, in** or **by** to visit, especially on the way to somewhere else. See also STOP-OFF.
>
> ■ **stop out** *colloq* to stay away from home all night. See also STOPPING-OUT.
>
> ■ **stop something out** to selectively cover (parts of a cloth, printing plate, etc) so that special effects can be created in dyeing, etching, photographic development, etc.
>
> ■ **stop over** to make a break in a journey. See also STOP-OFF.
>
> ■ **stop short of something** to manage to refrain from doing, saying, etc it □ *just stopped short of calling her a thief.*
>
> ■ **stop up something** to plug (a hole, etc).

stop-and-search ▻ *adj* said of a police, army, etc policy: carrying out random searches of people, eg in the street, in order to control the carrying of weapons, drugs, etc, especially in times of civil unrest.

stop bath ▻ *noun*, *photog* a solution that negatives or prints are immersed in so that the action of a developer is halted.

stopcock ▻ *noun* a valve that controls the flow of liquid, gas, steam, etc in a pipe and which is usually operated by an external lever or handle.

stope ▻ *noun*, *mining* a horizontal step or notch in the wall of a pit. ▻ *verb* (***stoped***, ***stoping***) to mine in horizontal layers. • **stoping** *noun*. Ⓒ 18c.

stopgap ▻ *noun* a temporary substitute.

stop-go ▻ *adj*, *econ* said of an economic policy, etc: characterized by alternate periods of expansion in which unemployment falls and contraction in which inflation is contained. ▻ *noun* **1** a policy of this type. **2** the kind of economic cycle that this type of policy encourages. Ⓒ 1960s.

stop-off and **stop-over** ▻ *noun* a brief or temporary stop during a longer journey.

stoppage ▻ *noun* **1** an act of stopping or the state of being stopped. **2** an amount deducted from wages. **3** an organized withdrawal of labour, eg as in a strike.

stoppage time ▻ *noun*, *sport* the time added on at the end of either half of a football, rugby, etc match to compensate for time lost through injury, fouls, the ball being out of play, time-wasting, etc. See also INJURY TIME.

stopped *past tense, past participle of* STOP

stopper ▻ *noun* **1** a cork, plug or bung. **2** someone or something that stops something.

stopping-out ▷ *noun* the selective covering of parts of a cloth, printing plate, etc so that special effects can be created in dyeing, etching, photographic development, etc.

stop press ▷ *noun* **1** late news that can be placed in a specially reserved space of a newspaper even after printing has begun. **2** the space itself.

stopwatch ▷ *noun* a watch that is used for accurately recording the elapsed time in races, etc.

storage ▷ *noun* **1** the act of storing or the state of being stored. **2** space reserved for storing things. **3** *computing* the act or process of storing information in a computer's memory. **4** the amount that is charged for storing something, eg goods in a warehouse, furniture, etc. ● **put something into storage** to put it away temporarily until it is needed again. ⓒ 17c: from STORE.

storage battery ▷ *noun* an ACCUMULATOR (sense 1).

storage capacity ▷ *noun, computing* the maximum amount of information that can be held in a memory system.

storage device ▷ *noun, computing* any piece of equipment, such as a magnetic disk, that data can be stored on.

storage heater ▷ *noun* a device consisting of a metal outer casing that encloses a stack of bricks which accumulate and store heat (usually generated from overnight off-peak electricity) which is then slowly released by convection during the daytime.

storage heating ▷ *noun* a central heating system that uses storage heaters.

storax /ˈstɔːraks/ ▷ *noun* **1** any of several tropical or subtropical trees which have clusters of white showy flowers. **2** a resin obtained from these trees which smells of vanilla and which was formerly used in medicine and perfumery. ⓒ 14c.

store ▷ *noun* **1** a supply, usually one that is kept in reserve for use in the future. **2 a** *Brit* a shop, especially a large one that is part of a chain ▫ ***department store***; **b** *as adj* ▫ ***store detective***; **c** *in compounds* ▫ ***superstore***; **d** *N Amer, especially US* a small grocery that often also sells a wide variety of other goods. **3** (*also* **stores**) a place where stocks or supplies are kept, eg a warehouse. **4** a computer's MEMORY. ▷ *verb* (***stored***, ***storing***) **1** (*also* **store away** or **store up**) to put aside for future use. **2** to put something, eg furniture, into a warehouse for temporary safekeeping. **3** to put something into a computer's memory. ● **storable** *adj.* ● **stored** *adj.* ● **in store 1** kept in reserve; ready to be supplied. **2** destined to happen; imminent ▫ ***a surprise in store***. ● **set** or **lay store** or **great store by something** to value it highly. ⓒ 13c: from Latin *instaurare* to set up or restore.

store card ▷ *noun* a credit card that is issued by a department store for exclusive use in that store or any of its branches. Also called CHARGE CARD.

storefront ▷ *noun, N Amer, especially US* the façade of a shop or store.

storehouse ▷ *noun* a place where things are stored.

storekeeper ▷ *noun, N Amer, especially US* a person whose job is to look after a store or shop, keep track of supplies, order new stock, etc.

storeman ▷ *noun* a person whose job is to look after and monitor goods, etc that are kept in store.

storeroom ▷ *noun* **1** a room that is used for keeping thing in. **2** space for storing things.

storey or (*N Amer, especially US*) **story** /ˈstɔːrɪ/ ▷ *noun* (***storeys*** or ***stories***) a level, floor or tier of a building. ⓒ 14c.

storeyed or (*N Amer, especially US*) **storied** ▷ *adj, in compounds* having a specified number of floors.

stork ▷ *noun* **1** any of various species of large wading bird that are mostly found near water in warm regions of the world, which have long legs, a long bill and neck, and usually loose black and white plumage and which is related to the heron and ibis. **2** (**the stork**) a bird of this kind which is whimsically thought of as carrying a newborn baby suspended in a blanket from its bill and which is used euphemistically for the delivery of a baby. ⓒ Anglo-Saxon *storc*.

stork's bill ▷ *noun* any of several annual or biennial plants found in bare grassy places, especially near the seashore, many of which are quite sticky and strong smelling. ⓒ 16c: so called because of the long pointed shape of their fruit.

storm ▷ *noun* **1 a** an outbreak of violent weather, with severe winds and heavy falls of rain, hail or snow that is often accompanied by thunder and lightning **b** *in compounds* ▫ ***snowstorm***. **2** a violent reaction, outburst or show of feeling ▫ ***a storm of protest***. **3** a furious burst, eg of gunfire or applause. ▷ *verb* (***stormed***, ***storming***) **1** *intr* **a** to go or come loudly and angrily ▫ ***stormed out of the meeting***; **b** to come or go forcefully ▫ ***stormed through the defence to score***. **2** to say or shout something angrily ▫ ***stormed abuse at him***. **3** *military* to make a sudden violent attack on something ▫ ***stormed the embassy***. ● **storming** *noun, adj.* ● **stormless** *adj.* ● **a storm in a teacup** *colloq* a big fuss about something unimportant. ● **take someone** or **something by storm 1** to enthral or captivate them or it totally and instantly. **2** *military* to capture them or it by storming. ⓒ Anglo-Saxon *storm*.

stormbound ▷ *adj* **1** delayed, unable to proceed, cut off, etc because of bad weather. **2** said of a boat, etc: stuck in port because of bad weather.

storm centre ▷ *noun* **1** the place at the middle of a storm where air pressure is lowest. **2** any focus of trouble or controversy.

storm cloud ▷ *noun* **1** a big heavy dark-looking cloud that signals the approach of bad weather. **2** something that is seen as a bad omen.

storm cock ▷ *noun, colloq* another name for the MISTLE THRUSH. ⓒ Early 19c: so called because it was observed to sing in an agitated way just before storms broke.

storm-cone ▷ *noun, Brit* at airfields, etc: a canvas cone that is raised as warning of strong winds.

storm cuff ▷ *noun* an extra elasticated cuff on a jacket, etc that is designed to give added warmth and protection from the weather.

storm door ▷ *noun* an extra outer door that gives added protection in bad weather.

storm lantern see HURRICANE LAMP

storm petrel or **stormy petrel** ▷ *noun* **1** a small seabird with black or dark brown feathers and white underparts. See also PETREL. **2** someone who delights in bringing bad news, causing trouble, etc. ⓒ 18c: so called because sailors thought that their presence indicated that a storm was approaching.

stormtrooper ▷ *noun* **1** a soldier trained in methods of sudden violent attack. **2** *historical* a member of the *Sturmabteilung*, a branch of the Nazi army, who was trained to go in for quick assaults.

storm warning ▷ *noun* an announcement on TV or radio that gives travellers warning that bad weather can be expected.

storm window ▷ *noun* **1** an extra window that is fitted to give added protection in bad weather. **2** a type of dormer window.

stormy ▷ *adj* (***stormier***, ***stormiest***) **1** affected by storms or high winds. **2** said of a person or their temperament, etc or of circumstances, etc: characterized by violence, passion, emotion, tantrums, etc; unpredictable ▫ ***a stormy relationship***. ● **stormily** *noun*. ● **storminess** *noun*.

story¹ /'stɔːrɪ/ ▷ *noun* (***stories***) **1** a written or spoken description of an event or series of events which can be real or imaginary. **2** a SHORT STORY. **3** the plot of a novel, play, film, etc. See also STORYLINE. **4** an incident, event, etc that has the potential to be interesting, amusing, etc. **5** a news article. **6** *colloq* a lie. **7** history ◻ ***the story of rock***. ▷ *verb* (***stories, storied, storying***) to decorate (a pot, etc) with scenes that depict events from history, legend, etc. • **storied** *adj*. • **cut a long story short** to omit the finer details when telling something. • **the same story** or **same old story** an expression of exasperation at being fed the same, usually made-up, excuse, etc. • **the story goes** it is widely said or believed. ◷ 13c: from French *estorie*, from Latin *historia* history.

story² see STOREY

storyboard ▷ *noun* a series of sketches, photos, captions, etc that gives details of the order of the camera shots, angles, etc in the shooting of a cinematic, TV, animated, advertising, etc film.

storybook ▷ *noun* a book that contains a tale or a collection of tales, especially one for children. Also *as adj* ◻ ***a storybook ending***.

storyline ▷ *noun* the plot of a novel, play or film.

story-teller ▷ *noun* **1** someone who tells stories, especially someone who does this in conversation habitually or exceptionally well. **2** *colloq* a liar. • **story-telling** *noun, adj*.

stot /stɒt/ *Scots* ▷ *verb* (***stotted, stotting***) **1** to bounce or cause (a ball, etc) to bounce. **2** *intr* to stagger. • **stotting** *adj* drunk.

stotinka /stɒ'tɪŋkə/ ▷ *noun* (***stotinki*** /stɒ'tɪŋkɪ/) a Bulgarian unit of currency which is worth one-hundredth of a LEV. ◷ 19c.

stotter /'stɒtə(r)/ ▷ *noun, Scots* something or someone, especially a woman, that meets with approval.

stoup or **stoop** /stuːp/ ▷ *noun* a basin for holy water. ◷ 18c; 14c, meaning 'a pail or bucket': from Norse *staup* beaker.

stout ▷ *adj* (***stouter, stoutest***) **1 a** said of someone: well-built; on the fat side; **b** said of the stem of a plant, etc: thick. **2** hard-wearing; robust. **3** courageous; steadfastly reliable. ▷ *noun* dark beer that has a strong malt flavour. • **stoutish** *adj*. • **stoutly** *adverb*. • **stoutness** *noun*. ◷ 14c: from French *estout*, Dutch, meaning 'proud'.

stout-hearted ▷ *adj* courageous; steadfastly reliable. • **stout-heartedly** *adverb*. • **stout-heartedness** *noun*.

stove¹ ▷ *noun* **1** a domestic cooker. **2 a** any cooking or heating apparatus, eg an industrial kiln; **b** *in compounds* ◻ ***camping stove***. ◷ Anglo-Saxon *stofa* hot air bath.

stove² see STAVE.

stoved enamel ▷ *noun* a type of heatproof enamel that is made by heating it in a stove or kiln.

stovepipe ▷ *noun* **1** a metal funnel that takes smoke away from a stove. **2** (*in full* **stovepipe hat**) a tall cylindrical silk dress hat worn by men. ◷ 17c.

stovies /'stoʊvɪz/ ▷ *plural noun, Scot* a traditional dish of seasoned potatoes and onion that sometimes has leftover meat added to it and which is cooked slowly on top of the cooker. ◷ 19c: shortened form of *stoved tatties*, so called because it is cooked on the top of the STOVE1.

stow /stoʊ/ ▷ *verb* (***stowed, stowing***) **1** (*often* **stow something away**) to pack or store it, especially out of sight. **2** *naut* **a** to fill (the hold of a ship) with cargo; **b** to pack (sails, gear, etc) away. **3** to have room for something. • **stower** *noun*. • **stowing** *noun*. • **stow it!** *Brit colloq* stop it! ◷ Anglo-Saxon *stow* a place.

▪ **stow away** to hide on a ship, aircraft or vehicle in the hope of travelling free.

stowage /'stoʊɪdʒ/ ▷ *noun* **1** a place, charge, space, etc for stowing things. **2** the act or an instance of stowing. **3** the state of being stowed.

stowaway ▷ *noun* (***stowaways***) someone who hides on a ship, aeroplane, etc in the hope of being able to get to the destination undetected and so avoid paying the fare.

STP ▷ *abbreviation* **1** standard temperature and pressure, now called NTP. **2** *Sanctae Theologiae Professor* (Latin), Professor of Sacred Theology. **3** *trademark* scientifically treated petroleum, an additive for motor vehicles that is claimed to improve engine performance.

str ▷ *abbreviation* steamer.

str. ▷ *abbreviation* **1** strong. **2** straight.

strabismus /strə'bɪzməs/ ▷ *noun, medicine* the technical term for a SQUINT of the eye, which is caused by a muscular defect that prevents parallel vision. • **strabismal** or **strabismic** or **strabismical** *adj*. ◷ 17c: from Greek *strabos* squinting.

strad ▷ *noun, colloq* a short form of STRADIVARIUS.

straddle /'stradəl/ ▷ *verb* (***straddled, straddling***) **1** to have one leg or part on either side of something or someone ◻ ***straddled the horse***. **2** to part (the legs) widely. **3** *colloq* **a** to adopt a neutral or non-committal attitude towards something; **b** to seem to be in favour of or see the advantage of both sides of something at once. **4** to go across ◻ ***straddled the puddle*** ◻ ***The Net straddles the workplace and the home*** ◻ ***The problem of drug abuse straddles all sections of society***. ▷ *noun* **1** an act of straddling. **2** a stance or attitude that is non-committal. **3** *stock exchange* a transaction where the buyer has the privilege of either calling for or delivering stock at a fixed price. **4** *athletics* a high jump technique where the legs straddle the bar while the body is parallel to it. • **straddler** *noun*. ◷ 16c: related to STRIDE.

Stradivarius /stradɪ'vɛərɪəs/ ▷ *noun* a violin or other stringed instrument that was made by Antonio Stradivari Also shortened to STRAD. ◷ 19c: a Latinized form of the name of the Italian maker of stringed instruments, Antonio Stradivari (1644–1737), whose business was continued by his two sons.

strafe /streɪf, strɑːf/ ▷ *verb* (***strafed, strafing***) **1** to attack someone or something with heavy machine-gun fire from a low-flying aircraft. **2** *colloq* to punish someone severely. ▷ *noun* an attack or punishment. • **strafer** *noun*. ◷ 1915: from German *strafen* to punish, and adopted as British military slang from the World War I exhortation *Gott strafe England* God punish England.

straggle /'stragəl/ ▷ *verb* (***straggled, straggling***) *intr* **1** to grow or spread untidily. **2** to lag behind or stray from the main group or path, etc. • **straggling** *noun, adj*. • **stragglingly** *adverb*. ◷ 14c.

straggler ▷ *noun* **1** someone who trails along behind. **2** an animal that has become separated from the rest of the herd, flock, etc. **3** a plant or shoot that has grown too far or that has grown irregularly.

straggly ▷ *adj* (***stragglier, straggliest***) **1** said of a plant, etc: having long dangling stems, especially ones that do not produce many leaves. **2** said of a group of people, etc: spread out all over the place rather than in an orderly file. **3** said of hair: thin, wispy and messy-looking.

straight /streɪt/ ▷ *adj* (***straighter, straightest***) **1** not curved, bent, curly or wavy, etc ◻ ***straight hair***. **2** without deviations or detours; direct ◻ ***a straight road***. **3** level; horizontal; not sloping, leaning, or twisted ◻ ***Is the picture straight?*** ◻ ***a straight posture***. **4** frank; open; direct ◻ ***a straight answer***. **5** respectable; legitimate; not dishonest, disreputable, or criminal ◻ ***a straight deal***. **6** neat; tidy; in good order. **7** successive; in a row ◻ ***won three straight sets***. **8** said of a drink, especially alcoholic: undiluted; neat ◻ ***straight brandy***. **9** having all debts and favours paid back ◻ ***If you pay for the petrol, that'll make us straight***. **10** not comic; serious. **11** *colloq* conventional in tastes and opinions. **12** *colloq* heterosexual. **13** *slang* **a** not under the influence of drugs, alcohol, etc; **b** not in the habit of being under the influence of drugs, alcohol, etc.

▷ *adverb* **1** in or into a level, upright, etc position or posture ◻ ***Is the picture hung straight?*** **2** following an undeviating course; directly ◻ ***went straight home*** ◻ ***looked her straight in the eye.*** **3** immediately ◻ ***I'll come round straight after work.*** **4** honestly; frankly ◻ ***told him straight that it was over.*** **5** seriously ◻ ***played the part straight.*** ▷ *noun* **1** a straight line or part, eg of a race track ◻ ***doing 150mph down the straight.*** **2 a** someone who is conventional in their tastes and opinions; **b** *colloq* someone who is not in the habit of being under the influence of drugs, alcohol, etc. **3** *colloq* a heterosexual person. **4** *poker* **a** a running sequence of five cards, irrespective of suit; **b** a hand of this kind. Compare FLUSH[3]. • **straightish** *adj.* • **straightly** *adverb.* • **straightness** *noun.* • **get** or **go straight to the point** to discuss the important topic without any digressions. • **go straight** *colloq* to stop taking part in criminal activities and live an honest life. • **keep a straight face** to hold back from laughing. • **put someone straight** to let them know the way things really stand. • **straight away** immediately. • **straight off** without thinking, researching, etc ◻ ***couldn't say straight off.*** • **straight out** without any equivocation; bluntly ◻ ***asked her straight out if she was seeing someone else.*** • **straight talking** *colloq* conversation that is to the point and without any hidden agenda. • **straight-talking** *colloq* characterized by a lack of guile ◻ ***a straight-talking guy.*** • **straight up** *colloq* honestly; really. • **the straight and narrow** the honest, respectable, sober, etc way of life or behaving. ⓒ Anglo-Saxon *streht*, from *streccan* to stretch.

> ***straight***
>
> A word sometimes confused with this one is **strait**.

straight angle ▷ *noun* an angle of 180°.

straightedge ▷ *noun* a strip or stick that is used for testing the straightness of something or for drawing straight lines.

straighten ▷ *verb* (***straightened***, ***straightening***) *tr & intr* **1** to make or become straight. **2** (*sometimes* **straighten out something**) to resolve, disentangle, make something less complicated or put it into order ◻ ***straightened out their differences*** ◻ ***straightened out their finances*** ◻ ***straightened the living-room before the guests arrived.*** **3** *intr* (*often* **straighten up**) to stand upright, especially after bending down.

straight face ▷ *noun* an unsmiling expression which is usually hiding the desire to laugh ◻ ***When she talks about her budgies, I can hardly keep a straight face.***

straight fight ▷ *noun* a contest, eg a political one, where there are only two candidates or sides.

straight flush ▷ *noun* in poker, etc: a *flush* made up of five cards in sequence. Compare STRAIGHT (*noun* 4), ROYAL FLUSH.

straightforward ▷ *adj* **1** without difficulties or complications; simple. **2** honest and frank. • **straightforwardly** *adverb.* • **straightforwardness** *noun.*

straight man ▷ *noun* a comedian's stooge.

straight-out ▷ *adj, N Amer, especially US* **1** complete; unrestrained. **2** honest.

straight-to-video ▷ *adj* referring or relating to a film released on video without first being shown at a cinema or on TV, usually expected not to be very good. Also *as adverb*.

strain[1] ▷ *verb* (***strained***, ***straining***) **1** to injure or weaken (oneself or a part of one's body) through over-exertion. **2** *intr* to make violent efforts. **3** to make extreme use of or demands on something. **4** to pass something through or pour something into a sieve or colander. **5** to stretch or draw it tight. **6** (*usually* **strain at something**) to tug it forcefully. **7** *intr* to feel or show reluctance or disgust; to balk. ▷ *noun* **1** an injury caused by over-exertion, especially a wrenching of the muscles. **2** an act of forceful mental or physical perseverance or effort ◻ ***Talking to her is such a strain.*** **3** the fatigue resulting from such an effort. **4** mental tension; stress. **5** *physics* a measure of the deformation of an object when it is subjected to stress which is equal to the change in dimension, eg change in length, divided by the original dimension, eg original length. **6** (*also* **strains**) a melody or tune, or a snatch of one ◻ ***the strains of distant pipes.*** **7** one's tone in speech or writing. • **straining** *adj, noun.* ⓒ 13c: from French *estraindre*, from Latin *stringere* to stretch tight.

> ■ **strain something off** to remove it by the use of a sieve or colander.

strain[2] ▷ *noun* **1** a group of animals (especially farm livestock) or plants (especially crops) that is maintained by inbreeding, etc so that particular characteristics can be retained. **2** a group of bacteria or viruses of the same species that possess a particular characteristic that distinguishes them from other groups of the same species. **3** an inherited trait or tendency ◻ ***a strain of madness in the family.*** ⓒ Anglo-Saxon *streon* a begetting.

strained ▷ *adj* **1** said of an action, way of talking, someone's manner, etc: not natural or easy; forced. **2** said of an atmosphere, relations, etc: not friendly or relaxed; tense. **3** said of food: characterized by having been put through a sieve ◻ ***strained carrots.*** **4** said of a muscle, body part, etc: injured by overwork, etc ◻ ***a strained back.*** **5** tight; pushed to the extreme ◻ ***strained finances.***

strainer ▷ *noun* a small sieve or colander.

strait ▷ *noun* **1** (*often* **straits**) a narrow strip of water that links two larger areas of ocean or sea. **2** (**straits**) difficulty; hardship ◻ ***dire straits.*** ▷ *adj, old use* narrow; strict. ⓒ 13c: from French *estreit*, from Latin *strictus*, from *stringere* to draw tight.

> ***strait***
>
> A word sometimes confused with this one is **straight**.

straiten ▷ *verb* (***straitened***, ***straitening***) **1** to distress, especially financially. **2** to restrict. • **straitened** *adj* ◻ ***found themselves in straitened circumstances.*** ⓒ 17c: from STRAIT.

straitjacket ▷ *noun* **1** a jacket which has very long sleeves that can be crossed over the chest and tied behind the back and which is used for restraining someone who has violent tendencies. **2** anything that prevents freedom of development or expression.

strait-laced ▷ *adj* said of someone, their attitude, opinions, etc: strictly correct in moral behaviour and attitudes; prudish or puritanical.

strake ▷ *noun* **1** a section of the rim of a cartwheel. **2** *naut* any of several continuous planks or plates that form the side of a vessel and which run from the bow to the stern. **3** a strip. ⓒ 14c: related to Anglo-Saxon *streccan* to stretch.

stramonium /strəˈmoʊnɪəm/ ▷ *noun* **1** the THORN APPLE. **2** a preparation that is made from the leaves, flowers, seeds, etc of this plant and which is used in the treatment of asthma and nervous disorders. ⓒ 17c.

strand[1] /strand/ ▷ *verb* (***stranded***, ***stranding***) **1** to run (a ship) aground. **2** to leave someone in a helpless position, eg without transport. ▷ *noun, literary* a shore or beach. ⓒ Anglo-Saxon *strand* seashore.

strand[2] /strand/ ▷ *noun* **1** a single thread, fibre, length of hair, etc, either alone or twisted or plaited with others to form a rope, cord or braid. **2** a single element or component part. ⓒ 15c.

stranded /ˈstrandɪd/ ▻ *adj* **1** left without any money, means of transport, etc. **2** driven ashore, aground, etc.

strange /streɪndʒ/ ▻ *adj* **1** not known or experienced before. **2** unfamiliar or alien. **3** not usual, ordinary or predictable. **4** difficult to explain or understand; odd. **5** vaguely ill or ill at ease. **6** shy. **7** (*usually* **strange to something**) unfamiliar with it; inexperienced at it □ *I haven't driven for ages so I'm a bit strange to it.* **8** (*usually* **strange!**) an expression of wonder, surprise, etc. ● **strangely** *adverb.* ⓒ 13c: from French *estrange*, from Latin *extraneus* foreign.

strangeness ▻ *noun* **1** a strange quality. **2** *physics* the unexpected delay in the decay of HADRONS, in contrast to that expected from the large amount of energy released, represented by a quantum number, known as the **strangeness number**.

stranger /ˈstreɪndʒə(r)/ ▻ *noun* **1** someone that one does not know □ *a perfect stranger* □ *a total stranger.* **2** someone who comes from a different place, home town, family, etc. ● **a stranger to something** someone who is unfamiliar with or inexperienced in something □ *He's no stranger to trouble.*

strangle /ˈstraŋgəl/ ▻ *verb* (***strangled, strangling***) **1** to kill or attempt to kill by squeezing the throat with the hands, a cord, etc. **2** to hold back or suppress (eg a scream or laughter). **3** to hinder or stop (the development or expression of something) □ *The job strangled her creativity.* ● **strangler** *noun.* ⓒ 14c: from French *estrangler*, from Latin *strangulare*, from Greek *straggale* a halter.

stranglehold ▻ *noun* **1** a choking hold in wrestling. **2** a position of total control; a severely repressive influence.

strangles ▻ *singular noun, vet medicine* a contagious disease that affects horses, which is characterized by inflammation of the upper respiratory tract. ⓒ 17c: from STRANGLE.

strangulate /ˈstraŋgjʊleɪt/ ▻ *verb* (***strangulated, strangulating***) **1** *medicine* to press or squeeze so as to stop the flow of blood or air. **2** to STRANGLE. ● **strangulation** *noun.* ⓒ 17c: related to STRANGLE.

strangulated hernia ▻ *noun, medicine* a loop of intestine at the entrance to a HERNIA that has had its blood supply cut off or almost cut off and which can then become gangrenous, possibly resulting in death if untreated.

strangury /ˈstraŋgjʊrɪ/ ▻ *noun, pathol* a condition that is characterized by slow painful urination. ⓒ 14c: from Latin *stranguria*, from Greek *stranx* a drop squeezed out + *ouron* urine.

strap ▻ *noun* **1 a** a narrow strip of leather or fabric which can be used for hanging something from, carrying or fastening something, etc; **b** *in compounds* □ *watchstrap.* **2 a** (*also* **shoulder strap**) either of a pair of strips of fabric by which a garment hangs from the shoulders; **b** *in compounds* □ *bra-strap.* **3 a** a leather belt that is used for giving a beating as punishment; **b** (**the strap**) a beating of this kind, formerly used in some schools □ *got the strap for being cheeky.* **4** a loop that hangs down on a bus or train to provide a hand-hold for a standing passenger. ▻ *verb* (***strapped, strapping***) **1** (*also* **strap up**) to fasten or bind something with a strap or straps. **2** to beat something with a strap. ● **strapless** *adj.* ⓒ 16c: a dialect form of STROP.

■ **strap something on** to fix something on or secure it in place □ *strapped on his holster.*

■ **strap someone** or **something in** or **into something** to secure them or it with straps □ *strapped the baby into her safety seat.*

■ **strap something up** to bandage (eg a wound).

strap-hanger ▻ *noun, colloq* **1** a standing passenger on a bus, train, etc, especially one who holds onto a strap. **2** a commuter who uses public transport.

strap-on ▻ *adj* held in place by a strap or straps. ▻ *noun* a sex aid that can be secured to the body.

strapontin /straˈpɒntən; *French* strapɔ̃tɛ̃/ ▻ *noun* a seat, eg in a taxi, cinema, theatre, etc, that is usually folded up, but which can be flipped down for use.

strapped ▻ *adj* short of money. ● **strapped for something** in dire need of it, especially money, staff, etc □ *She's always strapped for cash.*

strapper ▻ *noun* a tall strong-looking person.

strapping ▻ *adj* tall and strong-looking.

strappy ▻ *adj* said of shoes, clothes, etc: distinguished by having lots of straps □ *a pair of pretty strappy sandals.*

strap-work ▻ *noun, archit* a type of decorative work found especially on ceilings, screens, etc where bands or fillets are folded, crossed and interwoven.

strata see STRATUM

stratagem /ˈstratədʒəm/ ▻ *noun* a trick or plan, especially one for deceiving an enemy or gaining an advantage. ⓒ 15c: from Greek *strategema* an act of generalship.

strategic /strəˈtiːdʒɪk/ ▻ *adj* **1** characteristic of or relating to strategy or a strategy. **2** said of weapons: designed for a direct long-range attack on an enemy's homeland, rather than for close-range battlefield use. ● **strategical** *adj.* ● **strategically** *adverb.* ⓒ 19c: from French *strategique*.

Strategic Defence Initiative ▻ *noun* (abbreviation **SDI**) a military defence programme that was initiated in 1983 by President Reagan to destroy enemy weapons in space using laser technology. Also called STAR WARS.

strategist /ˈstratədʒɪst/ ▻ *noun* someone who is skilled in strategy.

strategy /ˈstratədʒɪ/ ▻ *noun* (***strategies***) **1** the process of, or skill in, planning and conducting a military campaign. **2** a long-term plan for future success or development. ⓒ 17c: from French *strategie*, from Greek *strategia*, from *stratos* army + *agein* to lead.

strath /straθ/ ▻ *noun, Scottish* a broad flat valley with a river running through it. ⓒ 16c: from Gaelic *srath*.

strathspey /straθˈspeɪ/ ▻ *noun* (***strathspeys***) **1** a Scottish folk dance that has a similar format to the reel but with slower, more gliding steps. **2** a piece of music for this kind of dance. ⓒ 17c: named after Strathspey, the valley of the River Spey, in Scotland.

strati *plural of* STRATUS

stratification /stratɪfɪˈkeɪʃən/ ▻ *noun* **1** *geol* **a** the formation of layers of sedimentary matter on the Earth's crust; **b** the way in which these layers are arranged. **2** an act of stratifying or a stratified condition. ⓒ 18c; 17c, meaning 'the act of depositing in layers': from Latin *stratificare, stratificatum* to stratify.

stratiform /ˈstratɪfɔːm/ ▻ *adj* **1** *geol* said of rocks: characterized by having layers. **2** *meteorol* relating to or resembling a STRATUS cloud.

stratify /ˈstratɪfaɪ/ ▻ *verb* (***stratifies, stratified, stratifying***) **1** *geol* to deposit (rock) in layers or strata. **2** to classify or arrange things into different grades, levels or social classes. ● **stratified** *adj* □ *stratified rock* □ *a highly stratified society.* ● **stratification** *noun.* ⓒ 17c: from Latin *stratum* something laid down + *facere* to make.

stratigraphy /strəˈtɪgrəfɪ/ ▻ *noun, geol* the branch of geology that is concerned with the origin, composition and age of rock strata, especially sedimentary rocks and the sequence in which they have been laid down. ● **stratigrapher** or **stratigraphist** *noun.* ● **stratigraphic** or **stratigraphical** *adj.* ● **stratigraphically** *adverb.* ⓒ 19c: from Latin *stratum* a layer + -GRAPHY.

stratocumulus /stratoʊˈkjuːmjʊləs/ ▻ *noun* (***stratocumuli*** /-laɪ/) *meteorol* a cloud that occurs as a large globular or rolled mass. ◷ 19c: from Latin *strato-*, from *sternere* to lay down, + CUMULUS.

stratosphere /ˈstratəsfɪə(r)/ ▷ *noun, meteorol* the layer of the Earth's atmosphere that extends from about 12km to about 50km above the Earth's surface, which contains the ozone layer and which has a relatively constant temperature. It is situated above the TROPOSPHERE and below the MESOSPHERE. • **stratospheric** *adj.* ◷ Early 20c: from STRATUM + -SPHERE 2.

stratum /ˈstrɑːtəm, ˈstreɪtəm/ ▷ *noun* (***strata*** /–tə/) **1** a layer of sedimentary rock. **2** a layer of cells in living tissue. **3** a layer of the atmosphere or the ocean. **4** a level, grade or social class. • **stratal** or **stratose** *adj.* ◷ 16c: Latin, meaning 'something spread'.

stratus /ˈstreɪtəs/ ▷ *noun* (***strati*** /-taɪː/) *meteorol* a wide horizontal sheet of low grey layered cloud. ◷ Early 20c: Latin, from *sternere, stratum* to spread.

straw ▷ *noun* **1 a** the parts of cereal crops that remain after threshing, which may be ploughed back into the soil, burned as stubble or used as litter or feedstuff for animals, for thatching and weaving into hats, baskets, etc; **b** *as adj* ◻ ***a straw boater.*** **2** a single stalk of dried grass or cereal crop. **3** a thin hollow tube for sucking up a drink. **4** anything that has little or no value. **5 a** a pale yellow colour; **b** *as adj* ◻ ***straw-coloured.*** • **strawlike** *adj.* • **strawy** *adj.* • **clutch** or **grasp at straws** to resort to an alternative option, remedy, etc in desperation, even although it is unlikely to succeed. • **the last straw** see separate entry. • **draw straws** to decide on something by the chance picking of straws, one of which is significantly longer or shorter than the rest. • **draw, get, pick**, *etc* **the short straw** to be the person chosen to carry out an unpleasant task, etc. • **a straw in the wind** a tantalizing hint or indication of something. ◷ Anglo-Saxon *streaw*.

strawberry /ˈstrɔːbərɪ/ ▷ *noun* **1** any of various trailing perennial low-growing plants with white flowers, that propagate by means of runners or STOLONS and which are widely cultivated in temperate regions for their edible fruit. **2 a** the juicy red fruit of this plant, which consists of tiny pips or ACHENES (technically the true fruits) which are embedded in the surface of the swollen fleshy RECEPTACLE, and which is eaten raw, preserved by canning or freezing, made into jam and used as a flavouring in confectionery, etc; **b** *as adj* ◻ ***strawberry jam*** ◻ ***strawberry ice cream.*** **3 a** the flavour or colour of the fruit; **b** *as adj* ◻ ***strawberry pink.*** ◷ Anglo-Saxon *streawberige*.

strawberry blonde ▷ *adj* said mainly of human hair: reddish-blonde. ▷ *noun* a woman who has hair of this colour.

strawberry mark ▷ *noun* a reddish birthmark that appears on a newborn baby (especially on the face or scalp) shortly after birth and which usually grows during the first year to eighteen months, after which it tends to get smaller, often disappearing altogether.

strawberry tree ▷ *noun* a small evergreen tree of S Europe which has white or pink flowers and berries that look like strawberries.

straw man see MAN OF STRAW

straw poll and **straw vote** ▷ *noun* an unofficial vote, especially taken on the spot among a small number of people, to get some idea of the general opinion on a specified issue ◻ ***a straw poll on devolution.***

strawy see under STRAW

stray ▷ *verb* (***strays, strayed, straying***) *intr* **1** to wander away from the right path or place, usually unintentionally. **2** to move away unintentionally from the main or current topic in thought, speech or writing ◻ ***He usually strays a bit from the main topic during a lecture.*** **3** to depart from the accepted or required pattern of behaviour, living, etc. ▷ *noun* (***strays***) a homeless, ownerless, lost pet, farm animal, child, etc. ▷ *adj* **1** said of a pet, farm animal, child, etc: homeless; ownerless; lost ◻ ***a stray kitten.*** **2** not the result of a regular or intended process; random; casual ◻ ***stray gunfire.*** • **strayer** *noun.* • **waifs and strays** see separate entry. ◷ 13c: from French *estraier* to wander.

streak ▷ *noun* **1** a long irregular stripe or band. **2 a** a flash of lightning; **b** *as adj* ◻ ***streak lightning.*** **3** an element or characteristic ◻ ***a cowardly streak.*** **4** a short period; a spell ◻ ***a streak of bad luck.*** **5** *colloq* a naked dash through a public place. **6** *mineralogy* a distinctive coloured line of powder that is produced when a mineral is scratched or a similar line that is left by a mineral when it is rubbed on a surface that is harder than it is. **7** *bacteriol* a line of bacteria that is deliberately drawn across a medium so that the growing culture of micro-organisms can be studied. ▷ *verb* (***streaked, streaking***) **1** to mark with a streak or streaks. **2** *intr* to move at great speed; to dash. **3** *intr, colloq* to make a naked dash through a public place. • **streaked** *adj.* ◷ Anglo-Saxon *strica* stroke.

streaker ▷ *noun, colloq* someone who makes a naked dash in public.

streaking ▷ *noun, colloq* an act of running naked through a public place.

streaky ▷ *adj* (***streakier, streakiest***) **1** marked with streaks. **2** said of bacon: with alternate layers of fat and meat. **3** characterized by an unevenness of quality. • **streakily** *adverb.* • **streakiness** *noun.*

stream ▷ *noun* **1** a very narrow river; a brook, burn or rivulet. **2** any constant flow of liquid ◻ ***streams of tears.*** **3** anything that moves continuously in a line or mass ◻ ***a stream of traffic.*** **4** an uninterrupted and unrelenting burst or succession, eg of insults ◻ ***a stream of questions.*** **5** general direction, trend or tendency. **6** *Brit, education* any of several groups that pupils in some schools are allocated to, so that those of a broadly similar ability can be taught together. **7** a current ◻ ***the Gulf stream.*** ▷ *verb* (***streamed, streaming***) **1** *intr* to flow or move continuously and in large quantities or numbers ◻ ***Tears were streaming down his face.*** **2** *intr* to float or trail in the wind ◻ ***Her hair streamed out behind her.*** **3** *Brit* to divide (pupils) into streams. • **streaming** *noun, adj.* • **streamy** see separate entry. • **go, swim, sail**, *etc* **with the stream** to conform to the majority opinion. ◷ Anglo-Saxon *stream*.

streamer ▷ *noun* **1** a long paper ribbon used to decorate a room. **2** a roll of coloured paper that uncoils when thrown. **3** a long thin flag. **4** *journalism* a large bold headline. **5** a luminous band or beam of light, especially the kind that can be seen in an aurora.

streamline ▷ *verb* to make streamlined or more streamlined.

streamlined ▷ *adj* **1** said of a vehicle, aircraft, or vessel: shaped so as to move smoothly and efficiently with minimum resistance to air or water. **2** said of an organization, process, etc: extremely efficient, with little or no waste of resources, excess staff, unnecessary steps, etc.

streamlining ▷ *noun* **1** a condition of air or fluid flow such that no turbulence occurs. **2** the design of machinery or apparatus so that its shape creates a minimum of turbulence, either when moving (as in motor cars and aircraft) or when static (as in fixed structures that stand in a flow of air or water). **3** the refining of any system to optimize efficiency.

stream of consciousness ▷ *noun* **1** *psychol* the non-stop and often random flow of thoughts, ideas, emotions, etc that continuously bombard the waking mind. **2** the narrative technique first used by MODERNIST novelists such as Joyce and Woolf (although Henry James flirted with the idea in *The Portrait of a Lady* as early as 1881) that attempts to simulate this, eg by discarding conventional syntax, by clipping characters' thoughts to a bare minimum, by linking apparently unconnected thoughts, etc. ◷ 1890s: first coined by Henry James's brother, the American psychologist, William James (1842–1910) in *Principles of Psychology*, 1890.

streamy ▷ *adj* (*streamier*, *streamiest*) **1** *literary* said of an area: having lots of streams. **2** said of a nose: wet and runny, eg because of a cold, flu, etc. • **streaminess** *noun*.

street ▷ *noun* **1** (*also* in addresses **Street**) a public road with pavements and buildings at the side or sides, especially one in a town. **2** the road and the buildings together. **3** the area between the opposite pavements that is used by traffic. **4** the people in the buildings or on the pavements □ ***tell the whole street.*** **5** *as adj* **a** relating to, happening on, etc a street or streets □ ***street map*** □ ***street theatre***; **b** referring, relating, etc to modern urban culture □ ***streetwise*** □ ***street cred.*** • **be right up** or **up someone's street** *colloq* to be ideally suited to them. • **on the street** or **streets** *colloq* **1** homeless. **2** practising prostitution, especially soliciting. • **streets ahead of someone** or **something** *colloq* much more advanced than or superior to them. • **streets apart** very noticeably different. • **walk the streets 1** to walk from street to street. **2** to solicit as a prostitute on the street. ⓒ Anglo-Saxon *stræt*.

streetcar ▷ *noun, N Amer, especially US* a tram.

street cred ▷ *noun, colloq* (*in full* **street credibility**) approval of those in tune with modern urban culture □ ***That baseball cap really doesn't have any street cred nowadays.***

street hockey ▷ *noun* a form of hockey that is played on roller skates, first popularized in the USA but now also played in the UK. ⓒ 1960s: so called because it was first played by children on street corners, although it is now generally played in enclosed areas such as playgrounds.

streetlamp and **streetlight** ▷ *noun* a light, usually one of a series, at the top of a lamppost that lights up the road for motorists and pedestrians at night.

street-level ▷ *noun* **1** ground-floor level. **2** the level of being in touch with, functioning at the level of, working alongside, etc modern urban culture. **3** *as adj* □ ***a street-level apartment*** □ ***canvassed street-level opinion.***

street-sweeper ▷ *noun* someone whose job is to go round collecting up rubbish and sweeping the pavements.

street value ▷ *noun* the price something, such as illegal drugs, stolen goods, etc, is likely to go for when it is sold to the person who will use it □ ***seized cannabis with a street value of a million pounds.***

streetwalker ▷ *noun, colloq* a prostitute who solicits on the streets.

street-walking ▷ *noun* prostitution. ▷ *adj* belonging, referring or relating to prostitution.

streetwise and **street-smart** ▷ *adj, colloq* **1** experienced in and well able to survive the ruthlessness of modern urban life, especially in areas such as drugs, crime, etc. **2** cynical.

strelitzia /strəˈlɪtsɪə/ ▷ *noun* (*strelitzias*) any of several S African perennial plants that are related to the banana and grown for their big showy flowers. ⓒ 18c: named after the British queen, Charlotte of Mecklenburg-Strelitz (1744–1818).

strength ▷ *noun* **1** the quality or degree of being physically or mentally strong. **2** the ability to withstand pressure or force. **3** degree or intensity, eg of emotion or light. **4** potency, eg of a drug or alcoholic drink. **5** forcefulness of an argument. **6** a highly valued quality or asset. **7** the number of people, etc needed or normally expected in a group, especially in comparison to those actually present or available □ ***with the workforce only at half strength.*** • **go from strength to strength** to achieve a series of successes, each surpassing the last. • **on the strength of something** on the basis of it; judging by it. ⓒ Anglo-Saxon *strengthu*; related to STRONG.

strengthen ▷ *verb* (*strengthened*, *strengthening*) *tr & intr* to make or become strong or stronger. • **strengthener** *noun*. • **strengthening** *noun, adj*. ⓒ 14c.

strenuous /ˈstrɛnjʊəs/ ▷ *adj* **1** characterized by the need for or the use of great effort or energy. **2** performed with great effort or energy and therefore very tiring. • **strenuosity** /strɛnjʊˈɒsɪtɪ/ *noun*. • **strenuousness** *noun*. • **strenuously** *adj*. ⓒ 16c: from Latin *strenuus* brisk.

strep ▷ *adj, informal* a short form of STREPTOCOCCUS and STREPTOCOCCAL □ ***off school with a strep throat.***

streptococcus /strɛptoʊˈkɒkəs/ ▷ *noun* (*streptococci* /-ˈkɒksaɪ/) any of several species of bacterium that cause conditions such as scarlet fever and throat infections. • **streptococcal** /–kɒkəl/ or **streptococcic** /–ˈkɒksɪk/ *adj*. ⓒ 19c: from Greek *streptos* twisted + *kokkos* berry.

streptomycin /strɛptoʊˈmaɪsɪn/ ▷ *noun* an antibiotic used to treat various bacterial infections. ⓒ 1940s: from Greek *streptos* twisted + *mykes* fungus.

stress ▷ *noun* (*stresses*) **1** physical or mental overexertion. **2 a** pressure of adverse influences, circumstance, etc that disturbs the natural physiological balance of the body □ ***the stress of teaching***; **b** the condition that can result from being under this kind of pressure which manifests in physical, mental, emotional, etc disturbance □ ***had six weeks off work suffering from stress.*** **3** importance, emphasis or weight laid on or attached to something □ ***The stress was on speed not quality.*** **4** the comparatively greater amount of force that is used in the pronunciation of a particular syllable □ ***The stress is on the first syllable.*** **5** *physics* the force that is exerted per unit area on a body causing it to change its dimensions. ▷ *verb* (*stresses*, *stressed*, *stressing*) **1** to emphasize or attach importance to something. **2** to pronounce (a sound, word, etc) with emphasis. **3** to subject to mental or physical stress. • **stressful** *adj*. • **stressfully** *adverb*. • **stressless** *noun*. • **stressor** *noun*. ⓒ 14c: shortened form of DISTRESS.

■ **stress someone out** to put them under severe mental, emotional, etc pressure □ ***The job really stresses her out.*** See also STRESSED-OUT.

stressed ▷ *adj* said of a syllable: given a more forceful pronunciation than the other syllable or syllables in the same word.

stressed-out ▷ *adj* debilitated or afflicted by emotional, nervous or mental tension □ ***Harry was always completely stressed-out because of work.***

stress-mark ▷ *noun* a mark /ˈ/ that is used in phonetics and prosody to indicate a stressed syllable.

stretch ▷ *verb* (*stretches*, *stretched*, *stretching*) **1** *tr & intr* to make or become temporarily or permanently longer or wider by pulling or drawing out. **2** *intr* to extend in space or time. **3** *tr & intr* to straighten and extend the body or part of the body, eg when waking or reaching out. **4** *tr & intr* to make or become tight or taut. **5** *intr* to lie at full length. **6** *intr* to be extendable without breaking. **7** *tr & intr* to last or make something last longer through economical use. **8** (*also* **stretch out**) to prolong or last. **9** to make extreme demands on or severely test (eg resources or physical abilities) □ ***The course stretched even the brightest students.*** **10** to exaggerate (the truth, a story, etc). ▷ *noun* (*stretches*) **1** an act of stretching, especially (a part of) the body. **2** a period of time; a spell. **3** an expanse, eg of land or water. **4** capacity to extend or expand. **5** *horse-racing* a straight part on a race-track or course, especially the part that leads up to the finishing line. **6** *colloq* a difficult task or test □ ***a bit of a stretch to get there by six.*** **7** *slang* a term of imprisonment □ ***did a three year stretch for armed robbery.*** • **stretchable** *adj*. • **stretchability** *noun*. • **stretched** *adj*. • **stretchy** *adj* see separate entry. • **at a stretch 1** continuously; without interruption. **2** with difficulty. • **stretch a point 1** to agree to something not strictly in keeping with the rules; to bend the rules. **2** to exaggerate. • **stretch one's legs** to take a short walk to invigorate oneself after inactivity. ⓒ Anglo-Saxon *streccan*.

■ **stretch out** to extend (in space) □ ***stretched out his hand.***

■ **stretch over** **1** to last (in time) □ ***The training period stretches over 5 years.*** **2** to extend in length, area, etc □ ***Forests stretch over most of the island.***

stretcher ▷ *noun* **1** a device that is used for carrying a sick or wounded person in a lying position. **2** someone who stretches. **3** anything that is used for stretching something, eg gloves, shoes, a painter's canvas, etc. **4** a horizontal crossbar that is used in timbering. **5** *building* a brick, block or stone that is laid so that the longer side shows on the wall face. Compare HEADER. ▷ *verb* (***stretchered***, ***stretchering***) to carry someone on a stretcher. ⓒ 15c: from STRETCH.

■ **stretcher someone off** to carry (eg an injured football, rugby, etc player) away on a stretcher □ ***had to stretcher Gazza off after the tackle.***

stretcher-bearer ▷ *noun* someone who carries a stretcher.

stretch limo ▷ *noun, N Amer* an elongated and very luxurious car.

stretch marks ▷ *plural noun* whitish-grey marks on the skin, especially of the abdomen, thighs, breasts, etc, which indicate that the skin has been stretched, eg in pregnancy or rapid weight gain.

stretchy ▷ *adj* (***stretchier***, ***stretchiest***) said of materials, clothes, etc: characterized by having the ability or tendency to stretch. ● **stretchiness** *noun.*

stretto /ˈstrɛtoʊ/ ▷ *noun* (***strettos*** or ***stretti*** /–tiː/) *music* **1** in fugue: the overlapping of a second or subsequent voice with the one that goes before it so that subject and answer are brought more closely together and the excitement of the piece is increased. **2** (*also* **stretta** /–tə/) a passage, especially a coda, that is played in quicker time. ⓒ 18c: Italian, meaning 'narrow'.

strew /struː/ ▷ *verb* (*past tense* ***strewed***, *past participle* ***strewed*** or ***strewn***, *present participle* ***strewing***) **1** to scatter untidily □ ***Papers were strewn across the floor.*** **2** to cover with an untidy scattering □ ***The floor was strewn with papers.*** ● **strewer** *noun.* ⓒ Anglo-Saxon *streowian.*

strewth /struːθ/ ▷ *exclamation, chiefly Austral & NZ colloq* an expression of surprise or annoyance. ⓒ 19c: from *God's truth.*

stria /ˈstraɪə/ ▷ *noun* (***striae*** /ˈstraiiː/) *geol, biol* any of a series of parallel grooves in rock, or furrows or streaks of colour in plants and animals. ⓒ 17c: Latin, meaning 'a furrow'.

striated /ˈstraɪeɪtɪd, -ˈeɪtɪd/ ▷ *adj* marked with striae; striped.

striated muscle ▷ *noun, anatomy* a type of VOLUNTARY muscle that is attached to bones by tendons and which is composed of fibres that under a microscope can be seen to present alternate dark and light layers.

striation /straɪˈeɪʃən/ ▷ *noun* **1** the patterning of striae. **2** the condition of having striae.

stricken /ˈstrɪkən/ ▷ *adj, often in compounds* **1** deeply affected, especially by grief, sorrow, panic, etc □ ***horror-stricken.*** **2** afflicted by or suffering from disease, sickness, injury, etc □ ***a typhoid-stricken community.*** ⓒ 17c; 14c as the *past participle* of STRIKE.

strickle /strɪkəl/ ▷ *noun* **1** an implement for levelling off a measure of grain or for shaping the surface of a mould. **2** a tool for sharpening scythes. ⓒ Anglo-Saxon *stricel.*

strict ▷ *adj* (***stricter***, ***strickest***) **1** demanding obedience or close observance of rules; severe. **2** observing rules or practices very closely □ ***strict Catholics.*** **3** exact; precise □ ***in the strict sense of the word.*** **4** meant or designated to be closely obeyed □ ***strict instructions.*** **5** complete □ ***in the strictest confidence.*** ● **strictish** *adj.* ● **strictness** *noun.* ⓒ 16c: from Latin *strictus*, from *stringere* to bind tight.

strictly ▷ *adverb* **1** with or in a strict manner. **2** as a strict interpretation □ ***They have, strictly, broken the law.*** ● **strictly speaking** using or interpreting words in their STRICT (*adj* 3) sense □ ***Strictly speaking, the car park is for residents only.***

stricture /ˈstrɪktʃə(r)/ ▷ *noun* **1** a severe criticism. **2** *medicine* abnormal narrowing of a passage, especially the urethra, oesophagus or intestine. ● **strictured** *adj.* ⓒ 14c: from Latin *strictura* tightening.

stride ▷ *noun* **1** a single long step in walking. **2** the length of such a step. **3** a way of walking in long steps. **4** (*usually* **strides**) a measure of progress or development □ ***make great strides.*** **5** a rhythm, eg in working, playing a game, etc that someone or something aims for or settles into □ ***put me off my stride*** □ ***soon got into his stride.*** **6** (**strides**) *chiefly Austral slang* trousers. ▷ *verb* (*past tense* ***strode*** /stroʊd/, *past participle* ***stridden*** /ˈstrɪdən/, *present participle* ***striding***) **1** *intr* to walk with long steps. **2** *intr* to take a long step. **3** to step or extend over something □ ***easily strode the puddle.*** ● **strider** *noun.* ● **take something in one's stride** to achieve it or cope with it effortlessly, as if part of a regular routine. ⓒ Anglo-Saxon *stridan.*

strident /ˈstraɪdənt/ ▷ *adj* **1** said of a sound, especially a voice: loud and harsh. **2** loudly assertive □ ***a strident clamour for reforms.*** ● **stridence** /–dəns/ or **stridency** *noun.* ● **stridently** *adverb.* ⓒ 17c: from Latin *stridere* to creak.

stridor /ˈstraɪdə(r)/ ▷ *noun* **1** a harsh grating noise. **2** *medicine* a harsh whistling breathing noise that is caused by an obstruction in the respiratory tract.

stridulate /ˈstrɪdʒʊleɪt/ ▷ *verb* (***stridulated***, ***stridulating***) said of grasshoppers, cicadas, crickets, etc: to make a chirruping sound by rubbing certain body parts together. ● **stridulant** *adj.* ● **stridulantly** *adverb.* ● **stridulation** *noun.* ● **stridulator** *noun* **1** an insect that stridulates. **2** the body part it uses to do this. ● **stridulatory** *adj.* ● **stridulous** *adj.* ⓒ 19c: from Latin *stridulare, stridulatum*, from *stridere* to creak.

strife ▷ *noun* **1 a** bitter conflict or fighting; **b** *in compounds* □ ***strife-ridden Bosnia.*** **2** *colloq* trouble of any sort; hassle. ⓒ 13c: from French *estrif*, from *estriver* to strive.

striga /ˈstraɪgə/ ▷ *noun* (***strigae*** /ˈstraɪdʒiː/) **1** *bot* a stiff bristle, usually one of many that are arranged in rows. **2** *zool* a transverse stripe or streak. ● **strigose** /ˈstraɪgoʊs, ˈstrɪ-/ *adj.* ⓒ 18c: Latin, meaning 'a furrow'.

strigil /ˈstrɪdʒɪl/ ▷ *noun* **1** in ancient Greece and Rome: a scraper used to clean the skin after bathing. **2** in bees: a mechanism for cleaning the antennae. ⓒ 16c: from Latin *strigere* to touch lightly.

strike ▷ *verb* (***struck*** /strʌk/, ***striking***) **1** to hit someone or something; to give a blow to them. **2** to come or bring into heavy contact with someone or something □ ***The car struck the lamppost.*** **3** to make a particular impression on someone □ ***They struck me as a strange couple.*** **4** to come into one's mind; to occur to someone □ ***It struck me as strange.*** **5** to cause (a match) to ignite through friction. **6** *tr & intr* said of a clock: to indicate the time, eg on the hour, half-hour, quarter-hour, with chimes, etc □ ***The town hall clock strikes the hour and half-hour.*** **7** *intr* to happen suddenly □ ***Disaster struck.*** **8** *intr* to make a sudden attack. **9** to afflict someone suddenly; to cause to become by affliction □ ***The news struck him dumb.*** **10** to introduce or inject suddenly □ ***The thought struck terror into them.*** **11** to arrive at or settle (eg a bargain or a balance) □ ***struck a fair deal for the car.*** **12** to find a source of (eg oil, gold, etc). **13** *intr* to stop working as part of a collective protest against an employer, working conditions, pay, etc □ ***The factory has been striking for two weeks.*** **14** to dismantle (a camp). **15** to make (a coin) by stamping metal. **16** to adopt (a posture or attitude). **17** to lower (a flag). **18** *tr & intr* to draw (a line) in order to cross something out. ▷ *noun* **1** an act of hitting or dealing a blow. **2** a situation where a labour force refuses to work in order to protest against an employer, working conditions, pay, etc in the hope that, by doing this, their demands will be met. **3** a prolonged refusal to engage in a regular or expected activity, such as eating, in order to make some kind of a protest □ ***went on hunger strike.*** **4** a military attack, especially one that is carried out by aircraft □ ***a pre-emptive strike on the ground troops.*** **5** a discovery of a source, eg of gold, oil, etc. **6** *ten-pin bowling* the knocking down of all pins with a single ball. Compare SPARE *noun* 3. **7** *cricket* the position of being the batsman bowled at □ ***take strike.*** **8** *baseball* a ball that the batter has taken a swing at but missed. • **on strike** taking part in an industrial or other strike. • **strike it lucky** or **rich** to enjoy luck or become rich suddenly and unexpectedly. ⓒ Anglo-Saxon *strican*.

■ **strike at someone** or **something** to attempt to hit them or it.

■ **strike back** to retaliate.

■ **strike someone down 1** to afflict them with something □ ***He was struck down with MS in his twenties.*** **2** to cause to die.

■ **strike someone off 1** to remove (the name of a member of a professional body, eg a lawyer, doctor, accountant, etc) from the appropriate register, especially because of misconduct **2** to remove (someone's name from an official list, register, etc). See also BE STRUCK OFF at STRUCK.

■ **strike something off 1** to cancel (especially with a stroke of a pen) □ ***I like to strike off the crossword clues as I get the answers.*** **2** to remove it (especially by using a sword, axe, etc) □ ***struck off his head.***

■ **strike on something** to come upon or arrive at something (especially an idea) by chance.

■ **strike out 1** to attempt to injure, damage, etc, eg with a punch, abuse, criticism, etc) □ ***The cat struck out with her claws*** □ ***struck out at the press for their insensitivity.*** **2** *baseball* said of a batter: to be dismissed by means of three strikes (see STRIKE *noun* 8).

■ **strike someone out** *baseball* to dismiss (a batter) by means of three strikes.

■ **strike something out** to draw a line through (eg a name, etc) in order to to show a cancellation, removal, deletion, etc.

■ **strike out for something** to head towards it, especially in a determined way.

■ **strike up** said of a band, etc: to begin to play.

■ **strike something up** to start (eg a conversation, friendship, etc).

strikebound ▻ *adj* said of an area, a workplace, a transport system, etc: immobilized as a result of a strike or strikes by workers.

strike-breaker ▻ *noun* someone who continues to work while others STRIKE (*verb* 13), or who is brought in to do the job of a striking worker. Also called SCAB, BLACKLEG.

strike pay ▻ *noun* an allowance that is paid by a trade union to a member who is on strike.

striker ▻ *noun* **1** someone who takes part in a strike. **2** *football* a player who has an attacking role.

striking ▻ *adj* **1** impressive; arresting; attractive, especially in an unconventional way. **2** noticeable; marked □ ***a striking omission.*** **3** on strike. • **be** or **come within striking distance** to be close, possible, achievable, etc.

strimmer ▻ *noun, trademark* an electrically operated garden tool that trims grass by means of a plastic or metal cord revolving at high speed, designed for long grass around garden beds, alongside fences, etc.

string ▻ *noun* **1** thin cord, or a piece of this. **2** any of a set of pieces of stretched wire, catgut or other material that can vibrate to produce sound in various musical instruments such as the guitar, violin, piano, etc. See also STRINGED. **3** (**strings**) **a** the orchestral instruments in which sound is produced in this way, usually the violins, violas, cellos and double basses collectively; **b** the players of these instruments. **4** a group of similar things □ ***a string of racehorses.*** **5** a series or succession □ ***a string of disasters.*** **6** *computing* a group of characters that a computer can handle as a single unit. **7** one of several pieces of taut gut, etc that are used in sports rackets. **8** a set of things that are threaded together, eg beads, pearls, etc. **9** (**strings**) undesirable conditions or limitations □ ***no strings attached.*** **10** any cord-like thing, eg a nerve or tendon. **11** *US* a shoelace. ▻ *verb* (***strung, stringing***) **1** to fit or provide with a string or strings. **2** to tie with string. **3** to thread (eg beads) onto a string. **4** to remove the stringy parts from (a bean pod, etc). **5** to extend something in a string □ ***strung the onions.*** • **stringer** *noun* see separate entry. • **stringed** *adj* see separate entry. • **keep, get** or **have someone on a string** to control them or make them dependent, especially emotionally □ ***He'll do anything for her — she's got him on a string.*** • **pull strings** *colloq* to use one's influence, or relationships with influential people, to get something done. • **pull the strings** *colloq* to be the ultimate, although not usually apparent, controller of a situation or person. ⓒ Anglo-Saxon *streng*.

■ **string someone along** to keep them in a state of deception or false hope.

■ **string someone out** or **up** *colloq* to cause them to become tense, nervous or on edge. See also STRUNG-OUT.

■ **string something out 1** to extend or stretch it in a long line. **2** to make it last.

■ **string someone up** *colloq* **1** to kill them by hanging. **2** see *string someone out* above.

■ **string something up** to hang, stretch or tie it with string, or as if with string. See also STRUNG-UP.

string band ▻ *noun* a group of musicians who play stringed instruments.

string bass ▻ *noun* see DOUBLE BASS

string board ▻ *noun* a board that covers or supports the ends of steps in a wooden staircase.

string course ▻ *noun, building* a horizontal decorative band of brick or stone that runs along the wall of a building and which can sometimes indicate a floor level.

stringed /strɪŋd/ ▻ *adj* said of a musical instrument: having strings.

stringendo /strɪn'dʒɛndoʊ/ ▻ *adj* ▻ *adverb, music* an instruction to a musician to play with increasing speed and excitement. ⓒ 19c: Italian, from *stringere* to bind tight.

stringent /'strɪndʒənt/ ▻ *adj* **1** said of rules, terms, etc: severe; rigorous; strictly enforced. **2** marked by a lack of money. • **stringency** *noun*. • **stringently** *adverb*. ⓒ 17c: from Latin *stringere* to draw together.

stringer /'strɪŋə(r)/ ▻ *noun* **1** a horizontal beam in a framework. **2** a journalist employed part-time to cover a particular town or area. **3** someone or something that strings.

string piece ▻ *noun* a long heavy horizontal timber.

string quartet ▻ *noun* a musical ensemble that is made up of two violins, a cello and a viola.

string tie ▻ *noun* a very narrow necktie that is usually tied in a bow and worn with country-and-western clothes. Also called **bootlace tie**.

string vest ▻ *noun* a man's net-like vest.

stringy /'strɪŋɪ/ ▻ *adj* (***stringier, stringiest***) **1** like string, especially thin and thread-like. **2** said of meat or other food: full of chewy fibres. • **stringily** *adverb.* • **stringiness** *noun.*

strip¹ ▷ *verb* (***stripped*** /strɪpt/ , ***stripping*** /strɪpɪŋ/) **1** to remove (a covering, wallpaper, etc) by peeling or pulling it off □ ***usually strip the beds on Mondays.*** **2** to remove the surface or contents of something □ ***stripped the varnish.*** **3** *intr* to take one's clothes off. **4** to take to pieces; to dismantle □ ***stripped the engine.*** **5** *colloq* to rob □ ***Burglars had stripped the place clean.*** **6** to skin, peel or husk. **7** to squeeze the last drops of milk from (a cow's udder). **8** to remove the leaves from (a stalk). **9** *chem* to remove a constituent from (a substance) by boiling, distillation, etc. **10** to break the thread (of a screw) or the tooth (of a gear), etc. **11** to unload (especially a container or lorry). ▷ *noun* **1** an act of undressing. **2** a striptease performance. • **stripped** *adj* □ ***stripped pine.*** • **stripper** *noun* see separate entry. • **stripping** *noun.* ◷ Anglo-Saxon *strypan.*

■ **strip something down** to take it apart, eg to service or repair it. See also STRIPPED-DOWN.

■ **strip someone of something** to take it away from them □ ***stripped her of her dignity.***

■ **strip off** *colloq* to remove one's clothes.

■ **strip something off** to remove it □ ***stripped off the wallpaper.***

strip² ▷ *noun* **1 a** a long narrow, usually flat, piece of material, paper, land, etc; **b** *as adj* □ ***strip light***; **c** *in compounds* □ ***airstrip*** □ ***landing-strip.*** **2** *sport* lightweight distinctive clothing that is worn by a team □ ***Aberdeen's home strip is red.*** • **tear a strip off someone** to reprimand them severely and often angrily. ◷ 15c: from German *strippe* a strap.

strip cartoon ▷ *noun* a sequence of drawings, eg in a newspaper, magazine, etc, that tell a comic or adventure story. Also called COMIC STRIP.

strip club ▷ *noun* a club where striptease artistes perform.

stripe ▷ *noun* **1** a band of colour. **2** a chevron or coloured band on a uniform that indicates rank. ▷ *verb* (***striped*** /straɪpd/, ***striping*** /'straɪpɪŋ/) to mark with stripes. • **stripy** see separate entry. • **earn one's stripes** to have the experience, ability, etc to be rewarded, with greater responsibility, more money, higher status, etc. ◷ 15c: Dutch.

striped ▷ *adj* having, or marked with, stripes.

strip joint ▷ *noun, colloq* a place, usually a rather seedy bar, club, etc, where striptease artistes perform.

strip light and **strip lighting** ▷ *noun* a light or lighting that is given off by tube-shaped FLUORESCENT LIGHTS.

stripling /'strɪplɪŋ/ ▷ *noun, literary* a boy or youth. Also *as adj* □ ***stripling youths.*** ◷ 14c: from STRIP + -LING.

strippagram and **strippergram** ▷ *noun* **1** the delivering of a birthday, etc greeting by someone who performs a striptease for the recipient. **2** the striptease artist delivering such a greeting.

stripped-down ▷ *adj* having only the bare essentials.

stripper ▷ *noun* **1** *colloq* a striptease artiste. **2 a** a substance or appliance for removing paint, varnish, etc; **b** *in compounds* □ ***paint-stripper.***

strip search and **skin search** ▷ *noun* a thorough and often intimate search of someone's body after they have either been made to take off all their clothes or had them forcibly removed, in order that police, customs officials, etc can check for concealed or smuggled items, especially drugs. ▷ *verb* (**strip-search** and **skin-search**) to carry out a strip-search on a suspect. • **strip-searching** *noun* the practice of carrying out a strip-search. ◷ 1970s.

striptease ▷ *noun* **1 a** a type of titillating show where a performer slowly and gradually takes their clothes off one by one while moving in an erotic way to music; **b** an instance of this. ◷ 1930s.

stripy /'straɪpɪ/ ▷ *adj* (***stripier***, ***stripiest***) marked with stripes; striped. • **stripiness** *noun.*

strive ▷ *verb, intr* (*past tense* ***strove*** /stroʊv/, *past participle* ***striven*** /'strɪvən/, *present participle* ***striving***) **1** to try extremely hard; to struggle □ ***will strive to be the best in Scotland.*** **2** to contend; to be in conflict □ ***They strove with each other to get the manager's job.*** ◷ 13c: from French *estriver* to quarrel.

■ **strive against something** to fight against it □ ***strove against his addiction.***

strobe /stroʊb/ ▷ *noun* short form of **a** STROBE LIGHTING; **b** STROBOSCOPE; **c** STROBOSCOPIC. • **strobic** *adj* spinning or appearing to spin. ◷ 1940s: from Greek *strobos* whirling round.

strobe lighting ▷ *noun* **1** a type of powerful rapidly flashing light which creates an effect of jerky movement when it is directed on moving bodies, eg in a club, disco, party, etc. **2** the equipment that can produce this type of effect.

strobilus /stroʊ'baɪləs, strɒ-/ and **strobile** /'stroʊbaɪl/ (***strobiluses*** or ***strobili*** /-laɪ/ , and ***strobiles***) ▷ *noun, bot* the technical term for a CONE (*noun* 4). ◷ 18c: from Greek *strobile* a conical plug of lint, from *strobilos* a spinning top, whirl, pine cone.

stroboscope /'stroʊbəskoʊp/ ▷ *noun* an instrument that uses a flashing light to measure or set the speed of rotating shafts, propellers, etc and which, when the speed of the light is equal to that of the rotating object, makes the object appear to be stationary. • **stroboscopic** *adj.* ◷ 19c: from Greek *strobos* whirling + -SCOPE.

strode *past tense of* STRIDE

stroganoff or **stroganoff** /'strɒgənɒf/ ▷ *noun, cookery* a dish that is traditionally made with strips of sautéed fillet steak, onions and mushrooms, cooked in a lightly spiced, creamy white wine sauce and served with pilaf rice, although there are many variations on this, including one that uses only vegetables. Also called **beef stroganoff** or **boeuf stroganoff** /'bɜːf —/ . ◷ 1930s: named after the 19c Russian diplomat, Count Paul *Stroganov.*

stroke ▷ *noun* **1 a** any act or way of striking; **b** a blow. **2** *sport* **a** an act of striking a ball □ ***took six strokes at the par four***; **b** the way a ball is struck □ ***a well-timed ground stroke.*** See also STROKE PLAY. **3 a** a single movement with a pen, paintbrush, etc, or the line or daub produced; **b** *in compounds* □ ***downstroke.*** **4 a** a single complete movement in a repeated series, as in swimming or rowing; **b** the member of a rowing crew who sits at the other end from the cox and who sets the timing for the rowers; **c** *usually in compounds* a particular named style of swimming □ ***backstroke*** □ ***breaststroke.*** **5** the total linear distance travelled by a piston in the cylinder of an engine. **6 a** the action of a clock, etc striking, or the sound of this; **b** the time indicated or which would be indicated by a clock striking □ ***out the door on the stroke of five.*** **7** a gentle caress or other touching movement, eg when patting a dog, etc. **8** a sloping line used to separate alternatives in writing or print. Also called SOLIDUS. **9** *pathol* a sudden interruption to the supply of blood to the brain that results in loss of consciousness, often with accompanying temporary or permanent paralysis of one side of the body and loss of speech, caused by bleeding from an artery, tissue blockage of an artery or a blood clot. See also SUNSTROKE. **10** *colloq* the least amount of work □ ***hasn't done a stroke all day.*** ▷ *verb* (***stroked***, ***stroking***) **1** to caress in kindness or affection, often repeatedly. **2** to strike (a ball) smoothly and with seeming effortlessness. • **stroking** *adj, noun.* • **at a stroke** with a single action. • **on the stroke of one, five,** *etc* precisely at that particular time. • **a stroke of something** a significant or impressive instance of it, especially of genius or luck. •

with a single stroke or **a stroke of the pen** with one small action □ *wiped millions off the stock exchange with a single stroke of the pen.* ⓘ Anglo-Saxon *strac.*

stroke play ▷ *noun, golf* a method of scoring that involves counting up the number of strokes taken at all 18 holes so that the player with the lower or lowest score wins. Also *in compounds* □ *a stroke-play competition.* Compare MATCH PLAY.

stroll /stroʊl/ ▷ *verb* (***strolled, strolling***) *intr* to walk in a slow leisurely way. ▷ *noun* a leisurely walk. • **strolling** *adj* □ *a strolling minstrel.* • **stroll on!** an exclamation of surprise, disbelief, etc. ⓘ 17c.

stroller ▷ *noun* **1** someone who strolls. **2** a pushchair.

stroma /ˈstroʊmə/ ▷ *noun* (***stromata*** /–mətə/) **1** *anatomy* the supporting framework of a body part, organ, blood corpuscle or cell. **2** *bot* the dense framework of a CHLOROPLAST. **3** *bot* in fungi: a dense mass of hyphae (see HYPHA) where spores can develop. • **stromatic** /stroʊˈmatɪk/ or **stromatous** /ˈstroʊmətəs/ *adj.* ⓘ 19c: Latin, meaning 'a bed covering'.

strong ▷ *adj* (***stronger*** /ˈstrɒŋgə(r)/, ***strongest*** /ˈstrɒŋgɪst/) **1** exerting or capable of great force or power. **2** able to withstand rough treatment; robust. **3** said of views, etc: firmly held or boldly expressed. **4** said of taste, light, etc: sharply felt or experienced; intense; powerful. **5** said of coffee, alcoholic drink, etc: relatively undiluted with water or other liquid; concentrated. **6** said of an argument, etc: having much force; convincing. **7** said of language: bold or straightforward; rude or offensive. **8** said of prices, values, etc: steady or rising □ *a strong dollar.* **9** said of a syllable: stressed. **10** said of a group, etc: made up of about the specified number □ *a gang fifty strong.* **11** said of a colour: deep and intense. **12** said of a wind: blowing hard. **13** *grammar* said of a verb: characterized by vowel gradation in its conjugation as opposed to taking inflected endings, eg *swim, swam, swum.* Also called **vocalic**. Compare WEAK sense 17. **14** impressive □ *a strong candidate for the job.* **15** characterized by ability, stamina, good technique, etc □ *a strong swimmer.* **16** said of an urge, desire, feeling, etc: intense; powerful; overwhelming □ *a strong desire to tell her what really happened* □ *a strong feeling of distrust.* • **strongly** *adverb.* • **strongish** *adj.* • **come on strong** *colloq* to be highly persuasive or assertive, often in a way that others might find disconcerting. • **strong on something** excelling at it; well-skilled or versed in it □ *Jane's always been strong on languages.* • **going strong** *colloq* flourishing; thriving □ *He's still going strong at 95.* ⓘ Anglo-Saxon *strang.*

strongarm ▷ *adj, colloq* **1** aggressively forceful. **2** making use of physical violence or threats. ▷ *verb* to compel with aggressive forcefulness or threats of violence □ *strongarmed him into helping with the robbery.*

strongbox ▷ *noun* a safe, or other sturdy, usually lockable, box for storing money or valuables in.

strong drink ▷ *noun, colloq* any drink that contains alcohol.

stronghold ▷ *noun* **1** a fortified place of defence, eg a castle. **2** a place where there is strong support (eg for a political party) □ *a Labour stronghold.*

strong interaction and **strong force** ▷ *noun, physics* a transfer of energy between BARYONs and MESONs that is completed in about 10^{-23} seconds.

strong language ▷ *noun* **1** swearing. **2** impassioned and emphatic talk.

strong-minded ▷ *adj* resolutely determined. • **strong-mindedly** *adverb.* • **strong-mindedness** *noun.*

strong point ▷ *noun* **1** something that someone is especially good at □ *Maths was never my strong point.* **2** *military* a favourably situated fortified position that is easy to defend.

strongroom ▷ *noun* a room that is designed to be difficult to get into or out of so that valuables, prisoners, etc can be held for safekeeping.

strontium /ˈstrɒntɪəm, ˈstrɒnʃɪəm/ ▷ *noun, chem* (symbol **Sr**, atomic number 38) a soft silvery-white highly reactive metallic element that is a good conductor of electricity. It is used in certain alloys and, because of the bright red flame it gives off when burning, in flares and fireworks. ⓘ Early 19c: named after Strontian, the name of the parish in Argyllshire, Scotland where it was discovered.

strontium-90 ▷ *noun* the radioactive isotope of strontium, which occurs in radioactive fallout and is a recognized health hazard because it can become incorporated into bone.

strop[1] /strɒp/ ▷ *noun* a strip of coarse leather or other abrasive material that is used for sharpening razors. ▷ *verb* (***stropped, stropping***) to sharpen (a razor) on a strop. ⓘ Anglo-Saxon, from Latin *struppus* thong.

strop[2] /strɒp/ ▷ *noun, colloq* a bad temper, when the person concerned is awkward to deal with □ *came home in a teenage strop.* ▷ *verb* (***stropped, stropping***) *chiefly* **strop off**) *colloq* to go away from something in a bad temper □ *stropped off when he realised he wouldn't win the argument.* ⓘ Back formation from STROPPY.

strophe /ˈstroʊfɪ/ ▷ *noun, prosody* **1** in a Greek play: the song sung by the chorus as it moved towards one side, answered by the ANTISTROPHE. **2** part of any ODE answered in this way. **3** *loosely* a stanza. • **strophic** *adj.* ⓘ 17c: Greek, meaning 'a turn'.

stroppy /ˈstrɒpɪ/ ▷ *adj* (***stroppier, stroppiest***) *colloq* quarrelsome, bad-tempered and awkward to deal with. • **stroppily** *adverb.* • **stroppiness** *noun.* ⓘ 1950s: probably from OBSTREPEROUS.

strove *past tense of* STRIVE

struck /strʌk/ ▷ *verb, past tense, past participle of* STRIKE. • **be struck off** said of a member of a professional body, eg a lawyer, doctor, accountant: to have their name removed from the appropriate register, especially because of misconduct. • **struck on someone** or **something** *colloq* infatuated with them or it; enthusiastic about them or it.

structural ▷ *adj* belonging or relating to structure or a basic structure or framework. • **structurally** *adverb.*

structural formula ▷ *noun, chem* a formula that shows the exact arrangement of the atoms within a molecule of a chemical compound as well as its composition.

structuralism ▷ *noun* an approach to various areas of study, eg literary criticism and linguistics, which seeks to identify underlying patterns or structures, especially as they might reflect patterns of behaviour or thought in society as a whole.

structuralist ▷ *noun* someone who practices or believes in structuralism. ▷ *adj* relating to or characterized by structuralism □ *a structuralist reading of 'Ullyses'.*

structure /ˈstrʌktʃə(r)/ ▷ *noun* **1** the way in which the parts of a thing are arranged or organized. **2** a thing built or constructed from many smaller parts. **3** a building. ▷ *verb* (***structured, structuring***) to put into an organized form or arrangement. ⓘ 15c: from Latin *structura*, from *struere* to build.

strudel /ˈstruːdəl, *German* ʃtrudəl/ ▷ *noun* a baked roll of thin pastry with a filling of fruit, especially apple. ⓘ 19c: German, meaning 'whirlpool', from the way the pastry is rolled.

struggle /ˈstrʌgəl/ ▷ *verb* (***struggled, srtuggling***) *intr* **1** to strive vigorously or make a strenuous effort under difficult conditions. **2** to make one's way with great difficulty. **3** to fight or contend. **4** to move the body around violently, eg in an attempt to get free. ▷ *noun* **1** an act of struggling. **2** a task requiring strenuous effort. **3** a fight or contest. • **struggler** *noun*. • **struggling** *noun, adj*. • **strugglingly** *adverb*. ◷ 14c.

strum ▷ *verb* (***strummed***, ***strumming***) *tr & intr* to play (a stringed musical instrument, such as a guitar, or a tune on it) with sweeps of the fingers or thumb rather than with precise plucking. ▷ *noun* an act or bout of strumming. ◷ 18c: a word based on THRUM, imitating the sound made.

struma /ˈstruːmə/ ▷ *noun* (***strumae*** /–miː/) **1** *pathol* an abnormal swelling of the thyroid gland. Also called GOITRE. **2** SCROFULA. **3** *bot* a swelling, eg on a leafstalk, at the base of the spore-case in some mosses. • **strumatic** /strʊˈmatɪk/ or **strumose** /ˈstruːmoʊs/ or **strumous** /–məs/ *adj*. ◷ 16c: Latin, meaning 'a scrofulous tumour'.

strumpet /ˈstrʌmpət/ ▷ *noun, old use* a prostitute or a woman who engages in casual sex. ◷ 14c.

strung /strʌŋ/ ▷ *verb, past tense, past participle of* STRING. ▷ *adj* **1** said of a musical instrument: fitted with strings. **2 a** *in compounds*, said of a person or animal: characterized by a specified type of temperament □ *highly-strung*; **b** said of a musical instrument, etc: having strings of a specified kind □ *finely-strung*.

strung-out ▷ *adj, colloq* **1** addicted to or high on a drug □ *strung-out on cocaine*. **2** weakened or ill from drug dependence. **3** tense; nervous; on edge.

strung-up ▷ *adj, colloq* tense; nervous.

strut ▷ *verb* (***strutted***, ***strutting***) *intr* to walk in a proud or self-important way. ▷ *noun* **1** a strutting way of walking. **2** a bar or rod whose function is to support weight or take pressure; a prop. • **strut one's stuff** *colloq* **1** to dance in a sexually provocative way. **2** to flaunt a talent, attribute, etc. ◷ Anglo-Saxon *strutian*.

struthious /ˈstruːθɪəs/ ▷ *adj* relating or referring to or resembling the ostrich. ◷ 18c: from Latin *struthio* ostrich.

strychnine /ˈstrɪkniːn/ ▷ *noun* a deadly poison that is obtained from the seeds of a tropical Indian tree and which can be used medicinally in small quantities as a nerve or appetite stimulant. • **strychnic** *adj*. ◷ 19c: from Greek *strychnos* nightshade.

strychninism /ˈstrɪknɪnɪzəm/ and **strychnism** /ˈstrɪknɪzəm/ ▷ *noun* the condition that results from taking excessive amounts of strychnine.

stub ▷ *noun* **1** a short piece of something that remains when the rest of it has been used up, eg a cigarette, a pencil, etc. **2** the part of a cheque, ticket, receipt, etc that the holder retains as a record, proof of purchase, etc. **3** a stump of a tree, bush, etc. **4** anything that appears to be short, rounded and broken or worn down □ *spaniels with stubs for tails*. ▷ *verb* (***stubbed***, ***stubbing***) **1** to accidentally bump the end of (one's toe) against a hard surface. **2** (*usually* **stub out**) to extinguish (a cigarette or cigar) by pressing the end against a surface. • **stubby** see separate entry. ◷ Anglo-Saxon *stubb*.

stubbed ▷ *adj* **1** cut, broken or worn down. **2** said of a toe: injured because it has been accidently bumped against something hard. **3** short and blunted. **4** cleared of stubs.

stubble /ˈstʌbəl/ ▷ *noun* **1** the mass of short stalks left in the ground after a crop has been harvested. **2** a short early growth of beard. • **stubbled** or **stubbly** *adj*. ◷ 13c: from French *estuble*, from Latin *stipula* a stalk.

stubborn /ˈstʌbən/ ▷ *adj* **1** resolutely or unreasonably unwilling to change one's opinions, ways, plans, etc; obstinate. **2** determined; unyielding. **3** difficult to treat, remove, deal with, etc □ *stubborn stains*. • **stubbornly** *adverb*. • **stubbornness** *noun*. ◷ 14c.

stubby ▷ *adj* (***stubbier***, ***stubbiest***) **1** short and broad or thick-set. **2** small and worn down □ *a stubby pencil*. ▷ *noun, Austral colloq* a small squat bottle of beer or the beer contained in such a bottle. • **stubbily** *adverb*. • **stubbiness** *noun*.

STUC ▷ *abbreviation* Scottish Trades Union Congress.

stucco /ˈstʌkoʊ/ ▷ *noun* (***stuccos*** or ***stuccoes***) **1** a fine plaster that is used for coating indoor walls and ceilings and for forming decorative cornices, mouldings, etc. **2** a rougher kind of plaster or cement used for coating outside walls. ▷ *verb* (***stuccos*** or ***stuccoes***, ***stuccoed***, ***stuccoing***) to coat with or mould out of stucco. • **stuccoed** or **stucco'd** *adj*. ◷ 16c: Italian, from German *stucchi* coating.

stuck ▷ *adj* **1** unable to give an answer, reason, etc. **2** unable to move. ▷ *verb, past tense, past participle of* STICK[2]. • **be stuck for something** *colloq* to be in need of it or at a loss for it. • **be stuck with someone** to be unable to get rid of them □ *I was stuck with that neurotic Harry all night*. • **be, get,** *etc* **stuck with something** to be unable to get anyone else to do it □ *I was stuck with the washing-up*. • **get stuck in** *slang* to set about an activity with energy or aggression. • **stuck on someone** *colloq* fond of or infatuated with them.

stuck-up ▷ *adj, colloq* snobbish; conceited.

stud[1] ▷ *noun* **1** a rivet-like metal peg that is fitted on to a surface, eg of a garment, for decoration. **2** any of several peg-like projections on the sole of a sports boot or shoe that give added grip, when playing football, hockey, etc. **3** a type of small round plainish earring or nose-ring, sometimes set with a precious or semi-precious stone, that has a post that goes through a hole and which is usually fastened at the back with a butterfly. **4** a fastener consisting of two small discs on either end of a short bar or shank, eg for fixing a collar to a shirt. **5** a short form of PRESS STUD. ▷ *verb* (***studded***, ***studding***) to fasten or decorate with a stud or studs. ◷ Anglo-Saxon *studu* post.

stud[2] ▷ *noun* **1** a male animal, especially a horse, kept for breeding. **2** (*also* **stud farm**) a place where animals, especially horses, are bred. **3** a collection of animals kept for breeding. **4** *as adj* □ *stud-book*. **5** *colloq* a short form of STUD POKER. **6** *colloq* a man who has, or who sees himself as having, great sexual energy and prowess. • **at stud** or **out to stud** kept for breeding purposes. ◷ Anglo-Saxon *stod*.

studded /ˈstʌdɪd/ ▷ *adj* having lots of studs □ *a studded motorcycle jacket*. Also *in compounds* □ *a star-studded cast* □ *a sequin-studded frock*. • **studded with something** sprinkled with or covered in it or them □ *a sky studded with stars*.

studding sail /ˈstʌnsəl/ ▷ *noun, naut* a light narrow sail that is set at the outer edges of a square sail when the wind is light. Also called **stunsail**. ◷ 16c.

student /ˈstjuːdənt/ ▷ *noun* **a** someone who is following a formal course of study, especially in higher or further education, although the word is now often applied to secondary school pupils too; **b** *as adj* □ *student nurse*. • **a student of something** someone who has an informed interest in the specified subject. ◷ 14c: from French *estudiant*, from Latin *studere* to be zealous.

studied /ˈstʌdɪd/ ▷ *adj* **1** said of an attitude, expression, etc: carefully practised or thought through and adopted or produced for effect; unspontaneous and affected. **2** carefully considered □ *gave a studied report to the board*.

studio /ˈstʃuːdɪoʊ/ ▷ *noun* (***studios***) **1 a** the workroom of an artist or photographer; **b** *as adj* □ *studio flat*. **2 a** a room in which music recordings, or TV or radio programmes, are made; **b** *as adj* □ *studio audience*; **c** (*often* **studios**) the premises of a company making any of these. **3 a** a company that produces films □ *signed to the MGM studio*; **b** the premises where films are produced. ◷ Early 19c: Italian, meaning 'study', from Latin *studere* to be zealous.

studio couch ▷ *noun* a couch, often backless, that converts into a bed.

studio flat ▷ *noun* a small flat with one main room with open-plan living, eating, sleeping and often cooking areas.

studious /ˈstʃuːdɪəs/ ▷ *adj* **1** characterized by a serious hard-working approach, especially to study. **2** carefully attentive. • **studiously** *adverb*. • **studiousness** *noun*.

stud poker ▷ *noun* a form of poker in which bets are placed on hands where some of the cards are laid face up.

study /ˈstʌdɪ/ ▷ *verb* (***studies***, ***studied***, ***studying***) **1** *tr & intr* to set one's mind to acquiring knowledge and understanding, especially by reading, research, etc □ ***studied the effects of global warming*** □ ***studied hard to pass the exams.*** **2** to take an educational course in (a subject) □ ***studied French to A-level.*** **3** to look at or examine closely, or think about carefully □ ***studied her face.*** ▷ *noun* (***studies***) **1 a** the act or process of studying; **b** *as adj* □ ***a study group.*** **2** (**studies**) work done in the process of acquiring knowledge □ ***having to work interfered with her studies.*** **3** a careful and detailed examination or consideration □ ***undertook a careful study of the problem.*** **4** a work of art produced for the sake of practice, or in preparation for a more complex or detailed work. **5** a piece of music intended to exercise and develop the player's technique. **6** a private room where quiet work or study is carried out. 🕒 13c: from French *estudie*, from Latin *studium* zeal.

stuff ▷ *noun* **1 a** any material or substance □ ***the stuff that dreams are made of***; **b** something that is suitable for, relates to, or is characterized by whatever is specified □ ***kids' stuff*** □ ***hot stuff.*** **2** moveable belongings □ ***Hang on — I'll just get my stuff.*** **3** the characteristics that define someone, especially positive ones □ ***made of stronger stuff.*** **4** something that is thought of as stupid, worthless, etc □ ***a load of stuff and nonsense*** □ ***too much emphasis on all this PC stuff.*** **5** *old use* **a** cloth, especially woollen; **b** *as adj* □ ***a stuff gown.*** ▷ *verb* (***stuffed***, ***stuffing***) **1** to cram or thrust □ ***stuffed the clothes in the wardrobe.*** **2** to fill to capacity; to overfill. **3** to put something away □ ***stuffed the letter in the drawer.*** **4** to fill the hollow or hollowed-out part of something (eg a chicken, tomato, pepper, etc) with a mixture of other foods. **5** to fill out the disembodied skin of (an animal, bird, fish, etc) to recreate its living shape. See TAXIDERMY. **6** to feed (oneself) greedily □ ***stuffed himself until he felt sick.*** **7** (*also* **stuff up**) to block or clog something, eg a hole, the nose with mucus, etc. **8** *slang* to defeat someone convincingly. **9** *offensive* to have sexual intercourse with someone. • **and stuff** and other similar things. • **a tasty**, *etc* **bit** or **a bit of stuff** *colloq* someone who is thought of in terms of their sexual attractiveness □ ***That was a leggy bit of stuff you got off with last night.*** • **do one's stuff** *colloq* **1** to display one's talent or skill. **2** to perform the task that one is required to do □ ***You're always good at the music round — so go on, do your stuff.*** • **know one's stuff** *colloq* to have a thorough understanding of the specific subject that one is concerned or involved with. • **stuff it, you, them,** *etc slang* an expression of disgust, contempt, anger, dismissal, etc □ ***Well, I'm going anyway — so stuff you!*** □ ***You can stuff the job!*** 🕒 14c: from French *estoffe*, from *estoffer* to provide what is necessary.

stuffed ▷ *adj* **1** said of a food: having a filling □ ***stuffed aubergines.*** **2** said of a dead animal, bird, fish, etc: having had its internal body parts replaced by stuffing □ ***a stuffed tiger.*** **3** said of a toy, cushion, etc: filled with soft stuffing □ ***cuddled her stuffed kitten.*** **4** (*also* **stuffed-up**) said of the nose: blocked with mucus. • **get stuffed** *colloq* an exclamation expressing contempt, dismissal, anger, etc □ ***I'm not doing that — get stuffed!***

stuffed shirt ▷ *noun* a conservative or pompous person.

stuffing ▷ *noun* **1** any material that children's toys, cushions, animal skins, etc are filled with. **2** *cookery* any mixture which is used as a filling for poultry, vegetables □ ***sage and onion stuffing.*** • **knock the stuffing out of someone** to deprive them rapidly of strength, force, mental well-being, etc □ ***news of his arrest completely knocked the stuffing out of her.***

stuffy ▷ *adj* (***stuffier***, ***stuffiest***) **1** said of a room, atmosphere, etc: lacking fresh, cool air; badly ventilated. **2** said of someone or their attitude, etc: boringly formal, conventional or unadventurous; staid; pompous. **3** said of a nose: slightly blocked, eg because of a cold, hay fever, etc. • **stuffily** *adverb*. • **stuffiness** *noun*.

stultify /ˈstʌltɪfaɪ/ ▷ *verb* (***stultifies***, ***stultified***, ***stultifying***) **1** to make someone or something appear absurd, foolish, contradictory, etc. **2** to cause something to be useless, worthless, futile, etc. **3** to dull the mind of someone, eg with tedious tasks. **4** *law* to allege or prove someone or oneself to be insane and so unfit to plead or to be regarded as legally responsible, etc. • **stultification** *noun*. • **stultifier** *noun*. • **stultifying** *adj*. 🕒 18c: from Latin *stultus* foolish + *facere* to make.

stum /stʌm/ ▷ *noun* **1** a less common term for MUST[2]. **2** partly fermented grape juice that is added to a wine which has lost its strength, flavour, sharpness, etc in order to perk it up. ▷ *verb* (***stummed***, ***stumming***) to add stum to (a wine) and so restart the fermentation process. 🕒 17c: from Dutch *stom* dumb.

stumble /ˈstʌmbəl/ ▷ *verb* (***stumbled***, ***stumbling***) *intr* **1** to lose one's balance and trip forwards after accidentally catching or misplacing one's foot. **2** to walk unsteadily. **3** to speak with frequent hesitations and mistakes. **4** to make a mistake in speech or action. ▷ *noun* an act of stumbling. 🕒 14c as *stomble*.

■ **stumble across, into** or **upon something** to arrive at, find, come across, etc it by chance.

■ **stumble along** to go through life without much thought to the future.

stumbling-block ▷ *noun* **1** an obstacle or difficulty. **2** a cause of failure or faltering.

stumm see under SHTOOM

stump[1] ▷ *noun* **1** the part of a felled or fallen tree that is left in the ground. **2** the short part of anything, eg a limb, that is left after the larger part has been removed, used up, etc □ ***a little stump of a pencil.*** **3** *cricket* **a** any of the three thin vertical wooden posts that form the wicket; **b** (**stumps**) the whole wicket, including the bails. **4** *jocular* a leg. **5 a** a stumping walk; **b** the noise made by a stumping walk. **6** a tree stump or other platform that is used by someone giving a political speech. ▷ *verb* (***stumped***, ***stumping***) **1** to baffle or perplex. **2** *intr* to walk stiffly and unsteadily, or heavily and noisily. **3** *cricket* said of a fielder, especially a wicketkeeper: to dismiss (a batsman or batswoman) by disturbing the wicket with the ball while they are away from the crease. **4** to reduce to a stump. **5** to clear (land) of tree stumps. **6** *intr, N Amer, especially US* to go round making political speeches. • **stumper** *noun*. • **draw stumps 1** *cricket* to bring a match to an end. **2** to finish something. • **on the stumps** *N Amer, especially US* busy with political campaigning, especially by going round delivering speeches. • **stir one's stumps** to start moving, especially after a period of inactivity. 🕒 14c: from *stumpen* to stumble.

■ **stump up** *colloq* to pay.

stump[2] *art* ▷ *noun* a piece of cork or a roll of paper, leather, etc that is pointed at both ends and which is used for blurring chalk, charcoal, etc lines in order to achieve tonal gradations. Also called TORTILLON. ▷ *verb* (***stumped***, ***stumping***) to use a stump to produce gradations of tone. 🕒 18c.

stumpy ▷ *adj* (***stumpier***, ***stumpiest***) short and thick. • **stumpily** *adverb*. • **stumpiness** *noun*.

stun ▷ *verb* (***stunned***, ***stunning***) **1** to make someone unconscious, eg by a blow to the head. **2** to make someone unable to speak or think clearly, eg through shock. **3** *colloq* to impress someone greatly; to astound them. ▷ *noun* the act of stunning or state of being stunned. 🕒 13c: from French *estoner* to astonish.

stung *past tense, past participle of* STING

stun gun and **stun grenade** ▷ *noun* a weapon that is designed to stun temporarily rather than kill or cause serious injury.

stunk *past tense, past participle of* STINK

stunner ▷ *noun, colloq* someone or something that is extraordinarily beautiful, attractive, etc.

stunning ▷ *adj, colloq* **1** extraordinarily beautiful, attractive, etc. **2** extremely impressive. • **stunningly** *adverb.*

stunsail or **stuns'l** see STUDDING SAIL

stunt[1] ▷ *verb* (***stunted, stunting***) to curtail the growth or development of (a plant, animal, someone's mind, a business project, etc) to its full potential □ *Lack of water stunted the plants* □ *The recession stunted plans for expansion.* ▷ *noun* **1** an instance of growth or development being curtailed or a state of curtailed growth or development. **2** an animal or plant whose growth or development has been curtailed. • **stunted** *adj.* • **stuntedness** *noun.* ◷ Anglo-Saxon *stunt* dull or stupid.

stunt[2] ▷ *noun* **1** a daring act or spectacular event that is intended to show off talent or attract publicity. **2** a dangerous or acrobatic feat that is performed as part of the action of a film or television programme.

stuntman or **stuntwoman** ▷ *noun* someone who performs stunts, especially someone whose job is to act as a stand-in for a film actor.

stupa /'stuːpə/ ▷ *noun* (***stupas***) a domed monument that is used for housing Buddhist relics. ◷ 19c: Sanskrit.

stupe /stjuːp/ ▷ *noun* a piece of cloth that has been moistened with a medicinal substance and which is used for relieving pain, medicating wounds, etc. ▷ *verb* (***stuped, stuping***) to treat with a stupe. ◷ 14c: from Latin *stupa*, Greek *stuppe* flax, hemp or tow.

stupefacient /stʃuːpɪ'feɪʃɪənt/ ▷ *adj* said of a drug, etc: having a stupefying effect. ▷ *noun* a drug, etc of this kind. • **stupefactive** *adj.*

stupefaction /stʃuːpɪ'fakʃən/ ▷ *noun* **1** stunned surprise, astonishment, etc. **2** the act of stupefying or state of being stupefied; numbness.

stupefy /'stʃuːpɪfaɪ/ ▷ *verb* (***stupefies, stupefied, stupefying***) **1** to stun with amazement, fear, confusion or bewilderment. **2** to make someone senseless, eg with drugs or alcohol. • **stupefier** *noun.* • **stupefying** *noun, adj.* • **stupefyingly** *adverb.* ◷ 17c: from Latin *stupere* to be stunned + *facere* to make.

stupendous /stʃʊ'pɛndəs/ ▷ *adj* **1** astounding. **2** *colloq* astoundingly huge or excellent. • **stupendously** *adverb.* • **stupendousness** *noun.* ◷ 17c: from Latin *stupere* to be stunned.

stupid /'stʃuːpɪd/ ▷ *adj* **1** having or showing a lack of common sense, comprehension, perception, etc □ *a stupid mistake* □ *You stupid boy!* **2** slow to understand; dull-witted □ *I've always been stupid where maths is concerned.* **3** stunned or dazed, eg through amazement, lack of sleep, drugs, etc □ *The news just knocked me stupid.* **4** *colloq* silly; trivial; unimportant; ridiculous; boring □ *What are you wearing those stupid orange leggings for?* ▷ *noun, colloq* a stupid person. • **stupidly** *adverb.* • **stupidness** *noun.* ◷ 16c: from Latin *stupidus* senseless, from *stupere* to be stunned.

stupidity /stʃʊ'pɪdɪtɪ/ ▷ *noun* (***stupidities***) **1** a stupid state or condition; extreme foolishness. **2** a stupid action, comment, etc.

stupor /'stʃuːpə(r)/ ▷ *noun* **1** a state of unconsciousness or near-unconsciousness, especially one caused by drugs, alcohol, etc. **2** *colloq* a daze, especially one brought on by astonishment, sadness, lack of sleep, etc □ *She's been going around in a complete stupor since it happened.* • **stuporous** *adj.* ◷ 14c: Latin, from *stupere* to be stunned.

sturdy /'stɜːdɪ/ ▷ *adj* (***sturdier, sturdiest***) **1** said of limbs, etc: thick and strong-looking. **2** strongly built; robust. **3** healthy; vigorous; hardy. • **sturdily** *adverb.* • **sturdiness** *noun.* ◷ 14c; 13c in obsolete sense 'stern or harsh': from French *estourdi* stunned.

sturgeon /'stɜːdʒən/ ▷ *noun* a large long-snouted fish with rows of spines on its back that is common in the rivers and coastal waters of the N hemisphere and which is used as food and valued as the source of isinglass and true caviar. ◷ 13c: from French *esturgeon.*

Sturmabteilung /*German* 'ʃtʊrmaptaɪlʊŋ/ ▷ *noun, historical* (abbreviation **SA**) the Nazi assault troops. ◷ 1920s: German, from *Sturm* storm + *Abteilung* division.

Sturmer or **sturmer** /'stɜːmə(r)/ and **Sturmer Pippin** ▷ *noun* **1** a variety of crisp green-skinned eating apple that has creamy white flesh. **2** an apple of this variety. ◷ 19c: named after the village of Sturmer on the Essex-Suffolk border where the variety was first developed.

stushie or **stooshie** /'stuːʃɪ/ ▷ *noun, Scots* **1** a rumpus or row. **2** an excited, upset or anxious state □ *She was in a right stooshie when the cat died.* ◷ 19c.

stutter /'stʌtə(r)/ ▷ *verb* (***stuttered, stuttering***) *tr & intr* **1** to speak or say something in a faltering or hesitant way, often by repeating parts of words, especially the first consonant, usually because of indecision, heightened emotion or some pathological disorder that affects the speech organs or the nervous system. **2** to make short faltering noises □ *The engine stuttered into life.* ▷ *noun* **1** **a** a way of speaking that is characterized by this kind of faltering or hesitancy; **b** an instance of this kind of repetition. **2** a short faltering noise □ *the stutter of gunfire.* • **stutterer** *noun.* • **stuttering** *adj, noun.* • **stutteringly** *adverb.* ◷ 16c: from earlier *stutten* to stutter.

STV ▷ *abbreviation* **1** Scottish Television. **2** single transferable vote, a method of voting for proportional representation.

sty[1] ▷ *noun* (***sties***) **1** a pen where pigs are kept. **2** any filthy or disgusting place. ▷ *verb* (***sties, stied, stying***) to put or keep (a pig, etc) in a sty. ◷ Anglo-Saxon *stig* pen or hall.

sty[2] or **stye** ▷ *noun* (***sties*** or ***styes***) an inflamed swelling on the eyelid at the base of the lash. ◷ 15c: from *styanye* a rising, which was mistaken for 'sty on eye', from Anglo-Saxon *stigan* to rise.

Stygian /'stɪdʒɪən/ ▷ *adj* **1** belonging, referring or relating to the river Styx, which, in Greek mythology, was the river in Hades across which the souls of the dead were ferried by Charon. **2** *literary* **a** dark and gloomy; **b** hellish; **c** said of a promise, oath, etc: strongly binding. ◷ 16c: from Latin *Stygius*, from Greek *Stygios*, from *Styx* Styx.

style ▷ *noun* **1** a manner or way of doing something, eg writing, speaking, painting, designing buildings, etc. **2** a distinctive manner that characterizes a particular author, painter, film-maker, etc. **3** kind; type; make. **4** a striking quality, often elegance or lavishness, that is considered desirable or admirable □ *She dresses with style.* **5** the state of being fashionable □ *gone out of style.* **6** STYLUS (sense 2). **7** *bot* in flowers: the part of the CARPEL, which is usually elongated, that connects the STIGMA to the OVARY (*noun* 2). **8** *in compounds, forming adjectives and adverbs* □ *American-style fast food joints* □ *doggy-style.* ▷ *verb* (***styled, styling***) **1** to design, shape, groom, etc something in a particular way. **2** to name or designate someone □ *styled himself an expert.* ◷ 13c: from Latin *stilus* writing tool or literary style.

stylish ▷ *adj* elegant; fashionable. • **stylishly** *adverb.* • **stylishness** *noun.*

stylist ▷ *noun* **1** a trained hairdresser. **2** a writer, artist, etc who pays a lot of attention to style.

stylistic /staɪ'lɪstɪk/ ▷ *adj* relating to artistic or literary style. • **stylistically** *adverb.*

stylistics ▷ *singular noun, linguistics* the systematic study of style, especially literary, ranging from features of language which can be identified with an individual (eg Shakespeare's style, Joyce's style), to those which identify major occupation groups (eg legal style, journalistic style), and those characteristic of speakers and writers in particular situations (eg parliamentary style).

stylize or **stylise** /'staɪlaɪz/ ▷ *verb* (***stylizes, stylized, stylizing***) to give a distinctive, conventionalized or elaborate style to something so that an impression of unnaturalness is created. • **stylization** *noun*. • **stylized** *adj* conventionalized and unnaturalistic □ ***Cubism is a highly stylized art form***. • **stylizer** *noun*. ⓒ 19c: from STYLE + -IZE.

stylobate /'staɪləbeɪt/ ▷ *noun, archit* a continuous platform of masonry that supports a row of columns. ⓒ 17c: from Greek *stylobates*, from *stylos* a column + *bates*, from *bainein* to walk or tread.

stylometry /staɪ'lɒmətrɪ/ and **stylometrics** /-'metrɪks/ ▷ *singular noun* a method of studying literary style, frequency of word usage, etc by means of the statistical analysis of a text, usually with the aid of computer programs, which allows for the charting of historical changes in style, the investigation of questions of disputed literary authorship, the authentication or otherwise of written evidence, police statements, etc. • **stylometrist** *noun*. ⓒ 1940s: from Greek *stylos* style + *metron* a measure.

stylus /'staɪləs/ ▷ *noun* (***styluses*** or ***styli*** /-laɪ/) **1 a** a hard pointed device, usually made from diamond or sapphire, at the tip of the needle-like part of the cartridge at the end of the arm of a record-player, which picks up the sound from the record's grooves; **b** a similar device for recording information given out by electrocardiographs, seismographs, etc; **c** the cutting tool that is used to produce the grooves in a record. **2** (*also* **style**) **a** a pointed implement for engraving, drawing, writing, etc; **b** a type of ancient writing implement that has one pointed end for inscribing characters in wax tablets and a flat blunted end for making corrections and erasures. ⓒ 17c: from Latin *stilus*, which was incorrectly altered to *stylus*, a stake or pointed writing implement.

stymie /'staɪmɪ/ ▷ *verb* (***stymies, stymied, stymieing*** or ***stymying***) **1** to prevent, thwart, hinder or frustrate □ ***Plans for expansion were stymied by cash-flow problems***. **2** *golf, formerly* said of a player or their ball: to impede an opponent's putt by blocking their path to the hole. ▷ *noun* (***stymies***) **1** *golf, formerly* a situation on the green where an opponent's ball blocks the path between one's own ball and the hole, and which is no longer current because of a change in the rules which now allow for the use of markers. **2** any tricky or obstructed situation. • **stymied** *adj* placed in an awkward situation; unable to take the kind of action required or desired. ⓒ 19c.

styptic /'stɪptɪk/ *medicine* ▷ *adj* said of a drug or other substance: having the effect of stopping, slowing down or preventing bleeding, either by causing the blood vessels to contract or by accelerating the clotting of the blood. ▷ *noun* a drug or other substance has this type of effect and which is used in the treatment of minor cuts, as well as bleeding disorders such as haemophilia. ⓒ 14c: from Greek *styptikos*, from *styphein* to contract.

SU ▷ *abbreviation* **1** *IVR, formerly* Soviet Union. **2** strontium unit.

suable /'suːəbəl, 'sjuː-/ ▷ *adj* said of an offence, etc: able or liable to be pursued through the courts. • **suability** *noun*. ⓒ 16c: from SUE + -ABLE.

suave /swɑːv, sweɪv/ ▷ *adj* **1** said of someone, especially a man, or their manner, attitude, etc: polite, charming and sophisticated, especially in an insincere way. **2** *loosely* smart and fashionable. • **suavely** *adverb*. • **suavity** or **suaveness** *noun*. ⓒ 19c; 16c in obsolete sense 'sweet' or 'agreeable': from Latin *suavis* sweet.

sub *colloq* ▷ *noun* **1** a submarine. **2** a substitute player. **3** a small loan; an advance payment, eg from someone's wages to help them subsist. **4** a subeditor. **5** (*usually* **subs**) a subscription fee. **6** a subaltern. ▷ *verb* (***subbed, subbing***) **1** *intr* to act as a substitute. **2** *tr & intr* to subedit or work as a subeditor. **3** to lend (especially a small amount of money) □ ***Can you sub me a quid till tomorrow?*** ⓒ 17c.

sub- ▷ *prefix, meaning*: **1** under or below □ ***subaqua***. **2** secondary; lower in rank or importance □ ***sublieutenant***. **3** only slightly; imperfectly; less than □ ***subhuman***. **4** a part or division of the specified thing □ ***subcommittee***. See also SUR- 2. ⓒ Latin, meaning 'under' or 'near'.

subalpine ▷ *adj* **1** belonging or relating to the region at the foot of the Alps. **2** said especially of plants: inhabiting this region. ⓒ 17c.

subaltern /'sʌbəltən/ ▷ *adj* **1** inferior; lower in status, rank, etc. **2** *logic* said of a proposition: particular, especially in regard to a universal of the same quality. ▷ *noun* **1 a** any army officer below the rank of captain; **b** someone of inferior status, rank, etc. **2** *logic* a subaltern proposition. ⓒ 16c: from Latin *subalternus*, from SUB- 2 + *alter* another.

subaqua ▷ *adj* belonging, relating or referring to underwater activities □ ***subaqua diving***. ⓒ 1950s: from SUB- 1 + Latin *aqua* water.

subaquatic ▷ *adj* said of plants or, occasionally, animals: living under water; living partially under water and partially on land.

subaqueous ▷ *adj* adapted, designed etc for use, living, etc under water.

subatomic ▷ *adj* **1** smaller than an atom. **2** relating to an atom; existing or occurring in an atom. ⓒ 19c.

subatomic particle ▷ *noun, physics* a general term for any particle that is smaller than an atom, eg an ELECTRON, NEUTRON, PROTON, NEUTRINO, QUARK or MESON, all of which are either BOSONS or FERMIONS.

subatomics ▷ *singular noun* the study of subatomic particles, subatomic changes, etc.

Some words with *sub-* prefixed: see SUB-[2] for numbered senses specified below.

subabdominal *adj* sense 1.
subagency *noun* sense 4.
subantarctic *adj* sense 3.
subarctic *adj* sense 3.
subarid *adj* sense 3.
subaudible *adj* sense 3.
subbasement *noun* sense 1.
subbranch *noun* sense 4.
subbreed *noun* sense 2.
subcategory *noun* sense 2.
subcellular *adj* sense 3.
subclass *noun, taxonomy* sense 4.
subclause *noun, law, grammar* sense 2.
subcommittee *noun* senses 2 & 4.
subdean *noun* sense 2.
subdistrict *noun* sense 4.
subgroup *noun* senses 2 & 4.
subkingdom *noun, taxonomy* sense 4.
submicroscopic *adj* sense 3.
suboffice *noun* senses 2 & 4.
suborder *noun, taxonomy* sense 4.
subphylum *noun, taxonomy* sense 4.
subregion *noun* sense 4.
subsection *noun* sense 4.
subseries *noun* sense 4.
substandard *adj* sense 3.
subsurface *noun* sense 1.
subsystem *noun* senses 1 & 2.
subwarden *noun* sense 2.

subbed and **subbing** see under SUB

Subbuteo /sə'bjuːtɪoʊ/ ▷ *noun, trademark* a game where small footballing figures are flicked with the fingers to make contact with an oversized ball.

subclavian /sʌb'kleɪvɪən/ and **subclavicular** /sʌbklə'vɪkjʊlə(r)/ ▷ *adj, anatomy* below the CLAVICLE. ◷ 17c: from SUB- 1.

subclinical ▷ *adj, medicine* said of a disease, infection, etc: at the stage before the symptoms become discernable. • **subclinically** *adverb*. ◷ 1930s.

subconscious ▷ *noun* **1** the mental processes that go on below the level of conscious awareness. **2** *psychoanal* the part of the mind where memories, associations, experiences, feelings, etc are stored and from which such things can be retrieved to the level of conscious awareness. ▷ *adj* denoting mental processes which a person is not fully aware of □ *subconscious wish fulfilment*. • **subconsciously** *adverb*. • **subconsciousness** *noun*. ◷ 19c.

subcontinent ▷ *noun* a large part of a continent that is distinctive in some way, eg by its shape, culture, etc □ *the Indian subcontinent*. ◷ 19c.

subcontract ▷ *noun* /sʌb'kɒntrakt/ a secondary contract where the person or company that is initially hired to do a job then hires another to carry out the work. ▷ *verb* /sʌbkən'trakt/ (*also* **subcontract out**) to employ (a worker) or pass on (work) under the terms of a subcontract. • **subcontractor** *noun* a person or company employed under the terms of a subcontract. ◷ 19c.

subcontrary ▷ *adj, logic* said of a pair of propositions or the relationship between them: related in such a way that both cannot be false at once, but can both be true at the same time. ▷ *noun* a proposition of this kind. ◷ 17c.

subculture ▷ *noun* **1 a** a group within a society, especially one seen as an underclass, whose members share the same, often unconventional, beliefs, lifestyle, tastes, activities, etc; **b** the unconventional lifestyle, etc of one of these groups. **2** *biol* said of bacteria, etc: a CULTURE (*noun* 5) that is derived from another. • **subcultural** *adj*. ◷ 1930s for sense 1; 19c for sense 2.

subcutaneous /sʌbkjʊ'teɪnɪəs/ ▷ *adj, medicine* situated, used, introduced, etc under the skin. • **subcutaneously** *adverb*. • **subcutaneousness** *noun*. ◷ 17c: from SUB- 1 + Latin *cutis* skin.

subdeacon ▷ *noun, chiefly RC Church* a member of the clergy who is immediately below a deacon in rank and whose duties include helping the deacon, especially by preparing the sacred vessels for the celebration of the eucharist. ◷ 14c.

subdirectory ▷ *noun, computing* a directory of files that is contained within another directory, the parent directory. ◷ 1980s.

subdivide /sʌbdɪ'vaɪd, 'sʌb-/ ▷ *verb* to divide (especially something that is already divided) into even smaller parts. • **subdivider** *noun*. ◷ 15c.

subdivision ▷ *noun* **1** a second or further division. **2** a section that has been produced by subdividing. • **subdivisible** *adj*. • **subdivisional** *adj*. • **subdivisive** *adj*.

subdominant ▷ *noun, music* the note that comes immediately below the DOMINANT in a scale. Also *as adj* □ *subdominant chords*. ◷ 18c: from SUB- 1.

subdue /səb'dʒuː/ ▷ *verb* (***subdued***, ***subduing***) **1** to overpower and bring under control. **2** to suppress or conquer (feelings, an enemy, etc). **3** to reduce in intensity, eg colour, noise, etc; to tone down □ *A partition will help subdue the noise*. • **subduable** *adj*. • **subduably** *adverb*. • **subdual** *noun*. ◷ 14c: from Latin *subducere* to remove.

subdued ▷ *adj* **1** said of lighting, colour, noise, etc: not intense, bright, harsh, loud, etc; toned down. **2** said of a person: quiet, shy, restrained or in low spirits, especially uncharacteristically so. • **subduedly** *adverb*. • **subduedness** *noun*.

subedit /sʌb'ɛdɪt/ ▷ *verb, tr & intr* to prepare (copy) for the ultimate sanction of the editor-in-chief, especially on a newspaper. ◷ 19c.

subeditor ▷ *noun* someone whose job is to select and prepare material, eg articles, etc in a newspaper or magazine, for printing. • **subeditorial** *adj*. • **subeditorship** *noun*.

suber /'sjuːbə(r)/ ▷ *noun* another term for CORK or for the bark of the cork tree. • **subereous** /sjuː'bɪərɪəs/ or **suberic** /sjuː'bɛrɪk/ or **suberose** /'sjuːbəroʊs/ *adj*. ◷ Early 19c: Latin, meaning 'cork'.

suberate /'sjuːbəreɪt/ ▷ *noun, chem* a salt of SUBERIC ACID.

suberic acid ▷ *noun, chem* (formula **$HOOC(CH_2)_6COOH$**) an acid that is obtained from the action of nitric acid on cork.

suberin /'sjuːbərɪn/ ▷ *noun* the substance in cork which makes it water-repellant.

suberize or **suberise** /'sjuːbəraɪz/ ▷ *verb* (***suberized***, ***suberizing***) said of plant cell walls: to be impregnated with suberin and so become corky. • **suberization** *noun*. ◷ 19c.

subfamily ▷ *noun* in the taxonomy of plants, animals, languages, etc: a group within a FAMILY (senses 6 and 7) that consists of more than one GENUS. ◷ 19c.

subfloor ▷ *noun* a rough floor that functions as the foundation for the finished floor.

subframe ▷ *noun* the frame that supports the bodywork of a motor vehicle.

subfusc /'sʌbfʌsk/ ▷ *adj* dusky; sombre. ▷ *noun* dark formal clothes that are worn for examinations and at certain formal occasions at Oxford and Cambridge universities. ◷ 18c: from Latin *subfuscus* dark brown, from SUB- 3 + *fuscus* dark.

subgenus ▷ *noun* (***subgenera*** or ***subgenuses***) *biol* in the taxonomy of plants and animals: a category below a GENUS but higher than a SPECIES. • **subgeneric** *adj*. • **subgenerically** *adverb*. ◷ 19c.

subgrade ▷ *noun* the layer that lies below the foundations of a road, pavement or railway and which can either occur naturally or be constructed. ◷ 19c.

subheading and **subhead** ▷ *noun* a subordinate title in a book, chapter, article, etc. ◷ 19c.

subhuman ▷ *adj* **1** relating or referring to animals that are just below HOMO SAPIENS on the evolutionary scale. **2** said of a person or their behaviour, attitude, etc: barbaric; lacking in intelligence. ◷ 18c.

subito /'suːbɪtoʊ/ ▷ *adverb, music* suddenly, quickly or immediately. ◷ 18c: Italian, meaning 'sudden', from Latin *subire* to go stealthily.

subj. ▷ *abbreviation* **1** subject. **2** subjective or subjectively. **3** subjunctive.

subjacent /sʌb'dʒeɪsənt/ ▷ *adj* **1** underlying. **2** lying at a lower level. ◷ 16c: from SUB- 1 + Latin *jacere* to lie.

subject ▷ *noun* /'sʌbdʒɪkt/ **1 a** a matter, topic, person, etc that is under discussion or consideration or that features as the major theme in a book, film, play, etc; **b** the person that a biography is written about. **2** an area of learning that forms a course of study. **3** someone or something that an artist, sculptor, photographer, etc chooses to represent. **4** someone who undergoes an experiment, operation, form of treatment, hypnosis, psychoanalysis, etc. **5** someone who is ruled by a monarch, government, etc; a citizen □ *became an American subject*. **6** *grammar* a word, phrase or clause which indicates the person or thing that performs the action of an active verb or that receives the action of a passive verb, eg *The doctor* is the subject in *The doctor saw* *us*, and *We* is the subject in *We were seen by the doctor*. See also NOMINATIVE. **7** *music* the dominant pattern of notes that is repeated in a composition. Also called **theme**. ▻ *adj* /ˈsʌbdʒɪkt/ **1** (*often* **subject to something**) **a** liable; showing a tendency; prone ▫ *Harry is subject to huge mood swings*; **b** exposed; open ▫ *left himself subject to ridicule*; **c** conditional upon something. **2** dependent; ruled by a monarch or government ▫ *a subject nation*. ▻ *adverb* /ˈsʌbdʒɪkt/ (always **subject to**) conditionally upon something ▫ *You may go, subject to your parent's permission*. ▻ *verb* /səbˈdʒɛkt/ (***subjected, subjecting***) **1** (*usually* **subject someone** or **something to something**) to cause them or it to undergo or experience something unwelcome, unpleasant, etc ▫ *subjected them to years of abuse* ▫ *As a diver, he was constantly subjected to danger*. **2** to make (a person, a people, nation, etc) subordinate to or under the control of another. • **subjectless** *adj*. • **subjectship** *noun*. ⓒ 13c: from Latin *subjectus* or thrown under, inferior.

subject catalogue ▻ *noun* a catalogue where the books are arranged according to topics rather than alphabetically by title or author.

subjected /səbˈjɛktɪd/ ▻ *adj* under the domination of another ▫ *a subjected people*.

subject heading ▻ *noun* in an index, catalogue, etc: a caption under which all the related topics are collected and referenced.

subjection ▻ *noun* an act of domination; the state of being dominated ▫ *the subjection of women*.

subjective ▻ *adj* **1** based on personal opinion, thoughts, feelings, etc; not impartial. Compare OBJECTIVE. **2** *grammar* indicating or referring to the subject of a verb; nominative. • **subjectively** *adverb*. • **subjectiveness** *noun*.

subjectivism ▻ *noun, philos* the doctrine that all knowledge is subjective because there can never be an objective form of truth, perception, etc. • **subjectivist** *noun*. • **subjectivistic** *adj*. • **subjectivistically** *adverb*. ⓒ 19c.

subjectivize or **subjectivise** ▻ *verb* (***subjectivized, subjectivizing***) to make subjective or more subjective. • **subjectivization** *noun*.

subject matter ▻ *noun* the main topic, theme, etc of a book, publication, talk, etc.

subjoin /sʌbˈdʒɔɪn/ ▻ *verb* to add at the end of something written or spoken. • **subjunction** /səbˈdʒʌŋkʃən/ *noun*. ⓒ 16c: from Latin *subjungere* to join on as an addition.

sub judice /sʌb ˈdʒuːdɪsɪ/ ▻ *adj* said of a court case: under judicial consideration and therefore not to be publicly discussed or remarked on. ⓒ 17c: Latin, meaning 'under a judge'.

subjugate /ˈsʌbdʒəgeɪt/ ▻ *verb* (***subjugated, subjugating***) **1** said especially of one country, people, nation, etc in regard to another: to dominate them; to bring them under control ▫ *As a nation, the Poles have often been subjugated*. **2** to make someone obedient or submissive. • **subjugation** *noun*. • **subjugator** *noun*. ⓒ 15c: from Latin SUB- 1 + *jugum* yoke.

subjunctive *grammar* ▻ *adj* said of the mood of a verb: used in English for denoting the conditional or hypothetical (eg 'If he *were* in hospital, I would certainly visit him' or 'If I *were* you') or the mandatory (eg 'I insist he *leave* now'), although in other languages it has a wider application. ▻ *noun* **1** the subjunctive mood. **2** a verb in this mood. Compare INDICATIVE, CONDITIONAL, IMPERATIVE. • **subjunctively** *adverb*. ⓒ 16c: from Latin *subjungere* to subjoin.

sublease ▻ *verb* /sʌbˈliːs/ *tr & intr* to rent out (property one is renting from someone else) to another person. ▻ *noun* /ˈsʌbliːs/ an agreement to rent out a property in this way. • **sublessee** /sʌblɛˈsiː/ *noun* someone who holds a sublease on a property. • **sublessor** /sʌbˈlɛsə(r)/ *noun* someone who grants a sublease. ⓒ 19c.

sublet ▻ *verb* /sʌbˈlɛt/ *tr & intr* **1** to rent out (property one is renting from someone else) to another person. **2** to subcontract work. ▻ *noun* /ˈsʌblɛt/ **1** an agreement to rent out a property in this way. **2** an agreement to subcontract work. • **subletter** *noun*. • **subletting** *noun*. ⓒ 18c.

sublieutenant ▻ *noun* a naval officer, especially in the British Navy, who is immediately below lieutenant in rank. ⓒ 18c.

sublimate /ˈsʌblɪmeɪt/ ▻ *noun, chem* the solid product formed after SUBLIMATION. ▻ *verb* (***sublimated, sublimating***) **1** *chem* a less common term for SUBLIME (*verb* 1). **2** *psychol* to channel a morally or socially unacceptable impulse, especially a sexual one, towards something else, especially something creative, that is considered more appropriate. **3** to purify or refine. • **subliminated** *adj* ▫ *subliminated mercury* ▫ *subliminated desires*. ⓒ 16c: from Latin *sublimare, sublimatum* to elevate or exalt.

sublimation /sʌblɪˈmeɪʃən/ ▻ *noun* **1** *chem* the process whereby a solid forms a vapour without appearing in the liquid, ie intermediate, state. **2** *psychol* the channelling of a morally or socially unacceptable impulse towards something else, especially some form of creativity, that is considered more appropriate.

sublime /səˈblaɪm/ ▻ *adj* **1** said of someone: displaying the highest or noblest nature, especially in terms of their morality, intellectuality, spirituality, etc. **2** said of something in nature, art, etc: overwhelmingly great; supreme; awe-inspiring. **3** *loosely* unsurpassed. ▻ *noun* (**the sublime**) the ultimate or ideal example or instance. ▻ *verb* (***sublimed, subliming***) *tr & intr, chem* **1** to heat (a substance) and convert it from its solid state into a vapour or gas without an intermediate liquid stage, usually allowing it to resolidify. **2** said of a substance: to change from a solid to a vapour without passing through the liquid state. • **sublimely** *adverb*. • **sublimity** /səˈblɪmɪtɪ/ or **sublimeness** *noun*. • **go from the sublime to the ridiculous** to pass from something serious, elevated, etc to something silly or trivial. ⓒ 14c: from Latin *sublimis* in a high position.

subliminal /səbˈlɪmɪnəl/ ▻ *adj* existing in, resulting from, or targeting the area of the mind that is below the threshold of ordinary awareness. • **subliminally** *adverb*. ⓒ 19c: from SUB- 1 + Latin *limen* threshold.

subliminal advertising ▻ *noun* advertising that takes the form of pictures shown in the cinema or on TV for a split second only, the theory being that they will infiltrate the subconscious mind without the viewer registering them.

sublingual ▻ *adj* **1** situated below the tongue. **2** said of a pill: placed below the tongue. ⓒ 17c.

sublunary and **sublunar** ▻ *adj* **1** situated below the Moon. **2** influenced by the orbit of the Moon. **3** earthly. ⓒ 16c: from SUB- 1 + Latin *luna* the moon.

submachine-gun ▻ *noun* a lightweight portable machine-gun that can be fired from the shoulder or hip. ⓒ Early 20c.

submarginal ▻ *adj* **1** said of cells: near the edge of a body, organ, etc. **2** said of land: not economically viable for cultivation. ⓒ 1930s in sense 2; 19c in sense 1.

submarine /ˈsʌbməriːn, sʌbməˈriːn/ ▻ *noun* **1** a vessel, especially a military one, that is designed for underwater travel. **2** *chiefly US* a sandwich that is made from a long narrow bread roll. Also called **submarine sandwich**. Often shortened to **sub**. ▻ *adj* **1** said of plants, animals, etc: living under the sea. **2** used, fixed in place, etc underwater ▫ *North Sea submarine piping* ▫ *submarine warfare*. ⓒ 19c as noun 1; 1950s as noun 2; 17c as adjective.

submariner /sʌbˈmarɪnə(r)/ ▻ *noun* a member of the crew of a submarine.

submaxillary /–'maksɪlərɪ/ ▻ *adj* **1** situated under the lower jaw. **2** belonging, relating or referring to the lower jaw. ⓘ 18c.

submediant /sʌb'miːdɪənt/ ▻ *noun, music* in a major or minor scale: the sixth note above the TONIC. ⓘ 19c.

submerge and **submerse** ▻ *verb* (***submerged***, ***submerging***; ***submersed***, ***submersing***) **1** *tr & intr* to plunge or sink or cause to plunge or sink under the surface of water or other liquid. **2** to cover with water or other liquid. **3** to conceal or inhibit something □ *submerged his feelings*. **4** to overwhelm or inundate someone, eg with too much work. • **submergence** *noun*. • **submersion** *noun*. ⓘ 17c: from SUB- 1 + Latin *mergere* to plunge.

submerged and **submersed** ▻ *adj* **1** sunk. **2** *bot* said of plants or plant parts: growing underwater. **3** *informal* concealed or inhibited. **4** *informal* overwhelmed, especially by too much work.

the submerged tenth ▻ *noun* the nominal ten per cent of a population theoretically destined to remain in poverty.

submersible and **submergible** ▻ *adj* said of a vessel: designed to operate under water. ▻ *noun* a submersible vessel; a submarine. • **submersibility** *noun*. • **submergibility** *noun*.

submission ▻ *noun* **1** an act of submitting. **2** something, eg a plan, proposal, idea, view, etc, that is put forward for consideration or approval. **3 a** readiness or willingness to surrender; **b** *wrestling* a declaration of surrender that is made by a competitor when an opponent has caused them so much pain that they cannot continue the bout. ⓘ 15c: from Latin *submittere*, *submissum* to submit.

submissive ▻ *adj* willing or tending to submit; meek; obedient. • **submissively** *adverb*. • **submissiveness** *noun*.

submit /səb'mɪt/ ▻ *verb* (***submitted***, ***submitting***) **1** *intr* (*also* **submit to someone**) to surrender; to give in, especially to the wishes or control of another person; to stop resisting them. **2** *tr & intr* to offer (oneself) as a subject for an experiment, treatment, etc. **3 a** to offer, suggest or present (eg a proposal) for formal consideration by others; **b** to hand in (eg an essay or other piece of written work) for marking, correction, etc □ *He submitted the essay late*. **4** (*usually* **submit to someone**) to defer to someone or something □ *I submit to your better judgement*. • **submittable** or **submissible** *adj*. • **submitted** *adj*. • **submitter** *noun*. • **submitting** *noun*. ⓘ 14c: from Latin *submittere*, from *sub* beneath + *mittere* to send.

submucosa /sʌbmjuː'koʊsə/ ▻ *noun* (***submucosae*** /–siː/) *anatomy* the layer of tissue that lies below a mucus membrane. • **submucosal** or **submucous** *adj*. • **submucosally** *adverb*. ⓘ 19c.

submultiple ▻ *noun, math* a number that can be used for dividing another number an integral number of times leaving no remainder, eg 2 is a submultiple of 8. Also called ALIQUOT. ⓘ 17c: from Latin *sub-* denoting a ratio that is the opposite of the one expressed by a radical element + MULTIPLE.

subnormal ▻ *adj* said especially of someone's level of intelligence with regard to possible academic achievement: lower than normal. ▻ *noun, derog* someone of this type. • **subnormality** *noun*. • **subnormally** *adverb*. ⓘ Early 20c.

subnuclear ▻ *adj, physics* **1** relating to or occurring in the nucleus of an atom. **2** smaller than the nucleus of an atom. ⓘ 1960s.

suborbital ▻ *adj* **1** *anatomy* situated below the orbit of the eye. **2** said of a spaceship, missile, etc: not designed, capable, programmed, etc to do a complete orbit (of the Earth or other planet). ⓘ 19c in sense 1; 1950s in sense 2: from SUB- 1.

subordinate ▻ *adj* /sə'bɔːdɪnət/ (*often* **subordinate to someone**) lower in rank, importance, etc; secondary. ▻ *noun* /sə'bɔːdɪnət/ someone or something that is characterized by being lower or secondary in rank, status, importance, etc. ▻ *verb* /sə'bɔːdɪneɪt/ (***subordinated***, ***subordinating***) **1** to regard or treat someone as being lower or secondary in rank, status, importance, etc; to put someone into this kind of position. **2** to cause or force someone or something to become dependent, subservient, etc. • **subordinately** *adverb*. • **subordination** *noun*. • **subordinative** *adj*. ⓘ 15c: from SUB- 2 + Latin *ordo* rank.

subordinate clause ▻ *noun, grammar* a CLAUSE which cannot stand on its own as an independent sentence and which functions in a sentence in the same way as a noun, adjective or adverb, eg 'The book *that you gave me for Christmas* was fascinating' or '*What you see is what you get*'. Compare MAIN CLAUSE.

subordinating conjunction ▻ *noun, grammar* a CONJUNCTION, such as *until*, *when*, *if*, *where*, *because*, *though*, *in order to*, etc, that links a subordinate clause to another clause in a sentence. Compare CO-ORDINATING CONJUNCTION.

suborn /sə'bɔːn/ ▻ *verb* (***suborned***, ***suborning***) to persuade someone to commit perjury, a crime or other wrongful act, eg by bribing them. • **subornation** *noun*. • **suborner** *noun*. ⓘ 16c: from Latin *sub* secretly + *ornare* to equip.

subplot ▻ *noun* a minor storyline that runs parallel to the main plot in a novel, film, play, opera, etc and which often serves to comment on, emphasize or contrast the issues, themes, etc raised by main plot. ⓘ Early 20c.

subpoena /sə'piːnə, səb'piːnə/ ▻ *noun* (***subpoenas***) a legal document that orders someone to appear in a court of law at a specified time; a summons. ▻ *verb* (***subpoenas***, ***subpoenaed*** or ***subpoena'd***, ***subpoenaing***) to serve with a subpoena. ⓘ 15c: from Latin *sub poena* under penalty.

sub-post office ▻ *noun, Brit* a small post office that offers fewer services than a main post office and which is usually part of a general shop.

subreption /səb'rɛpʃən/ ▻ *noun* **1** *law & formal* the suppression or concealment of the truth in order to obtain some advantage. **2** any form of deception or misrepresentation. ⓘ 17c: from Latin *sub-* secretly + *rapere* to snatch.

subrogate /'sʌbrəgeɪt/ ▻ *verb* (***subrogated***, ***subrogating***) *law* to substitute (one party for another) as creditor with the attendant transfer of rights. • **subrogation** /–'geɪʃən/ *noun*. ⓘ 16c: from Latin *sub-* in place of + *rogare* to ask.

sub rosa /sʌb 'roʊzə/ ▻ *adverb* in secret. ⓘ 17c: Latin, meaning 'under the rose', from the ancient Roman tradition of having a rose at meetings, etc as a symbol that the participants were sworn to secrecy.

subroutine ▻ *noun, computing* a self-contained part of a computer program which performs a specific task and which can be called up at any time during the running of the main program. ⓘ 1940s.

subscribe /səb'skraɪb/ ▻ *verb* (***subscribed***, ***subscribing***) **1** *tr & intr* to contribute or undertake to contribute (a sum of money), especially on a regular basis. **2** (*usually* **subscribe to something**) to undertake to receive (regular issues of a magazine, etc) in return for payment □ *subscribes to 'The Economist'*. **3** (*usually* **subscribe to something**) to agree with or believe in (a theory, idea, etc) □ *subscribes to classical Marxism*. **4** to write one's name or put one's mark at the bottom of (a document, picture, etc). • **subscribable** *adj*. ⓘ 15c: from SUB- 1 + Latin *scribere* to write.

subscriber ▻ *noun* **1** someone who subscribes to something, eg a magazine. **2** someone who officially rents a telephone line.

subscriber trunk dialling ▷ *noun* (abbreviation **STD**) a telephone system in which customers can make long-distance calls directly, without the help of an operator.

subscript *printing* ▷ *adj* said of a character, especially one in chemistry and maths: set below the level of the line, eg the number 2 in H_2O. ▷ *noun* a character that is in this position. ⓒ 18c.

subscription ▷ *noun* **1 a** an act or instance of subscribing; **b** a payment made in subscribing; **c** *as adj* □ ***subscription TV.*** **2 a** *Brit* a set fee for membership of a society, club, etc; **b** *as adj* □ ***subscription fees.*** **3 a** an agreement to take a magazine, etc, usually for a specified number of issues; **b** the money paid for this. **4 a** an advance order, especially of a book before its official publication; **b** *as adj* □ ***a subscription copy.*** **5 a** the purchase of tickets for a series of operas, concerts, plays, etc in a batch in advance; **b** *as adj, denoting* a series of operas, concerts, plays, etc where tickets can be bought in the way □ ***a subscription concert.*** **6** an act of endorsement, sanction, etc. **7** a signature. ⓒ 15c: from SUBSCRIBE.

subscription TV see under PAY TV

subsea ▷ *adj* used especially in the North Sea oil industry: situated or occurring underwater; designed for use underwater □ ***subsea well systems.*** ▷ *adverb* below the sea □ ***can dive subsea to depths of 8 000 ft.*** ⓒ Early 20c.

subsequence ▷ *noun* **1** /ˈsʌbsɪkwəns/ **a** something that follows as a result of something else; **b** the fact or state of coming after something. **2** /sʌbˈsiːkwəns/ (*sometimes* **sub-sequence**) *math* a sequence that is contained in or that forms part of another sequence. ⓒ Early 20c in sense 2; 16c in sense 1.

subsequent /ˈsʌbsɪkwənt/ ▷ *adj* (*also* **subsequent to something**) happening after or following. • **subsequently** *adverb.* ⓒ 15c: from Latin *sub* near + *sequi* to follow.

subserve ▷ *verb* to help in furthering (a purpose, action, etc). ⓒ 17c: from SUB- 2 + Latin *servire* to serve.

subservient /sʌbˈsɜːvɪənt/ ▷ *adj* **1** ready or eager to submit to the wishes of others, often excessively so. **2** (*usually* **subservient to something**) functioning as a means to an end. **3** (*usually* **subservient to someone** or **something**) a less common term for SUBORDINATE (*adj*). • **subservience** or **subserviency** *noun.* ⓒ 17c: from SUB- 2 + Latin *servire* to serve.

subset ▷ *noun, math* a set (see SET² 2) that forms one part of a larger set, eg *set X* is said to be a subset of a *set Y* if all the members of *set X* can be included in *set Y*. ⓒ Early 20c.

subside /səbˈsaɪd/ ▷ *verb, intr* **1** said of land, buildings, etc: to sink to a lower level; to settle. **2** said of noise, feelings, wind, a storm, etc: to become less loud or intense; to die down. • **subsidence** /ˈsʌbsɪdəns, səbˈsaɪdəns/ *noun* the sinking of land, buildings, etc to a lower level □ ***couldn't get a mortgage because of the subsidence.*** ⓒ 17c: from SUB- 1 + Latin *sidere* to settle.

subsidiarity /sʌbsɪdɪˈarɪtɪ/ ▷ *noun* the principle that a central governing body will permit its member states, branches, local government, etc to have control over those issues, decisions, actions, etc that are deemed more appropriate to the local level. ⓒ 1930s: from SUBSIDIARY.

subsidiary /səbˈsɪdɪərɪ/ ▷ *adj* **1** of secondary importance; subordinate. **2** serving as an addition or supplement; auxiliary. ▷ *noun* (***subsidiaries***) **1** a subsidiary person or thing. **2** (*sometimes* **subsidiary of something**) a company controlled by another, usually larger, company or organization. • **subsidiarily** *adverb.* ⓒ 16c: from Latin *subsidium* auxilliary force.

subsidize or **subsidise** /ˈsʌbsɪdaɪz/ ▷ *verb* (***subsidized, subsidizing***) **1** to provide or support with a subsidy. **2** to pay a proportion of the cost of (a thing supplied) in order to reduce the price paid by the customer □ ***The company subsidized the meals in the canteen.*** **3** *loosely* to pay the expenses of someone. **4** *loosely* to top up something with money □ ***subsidized her grant by working in a bar.*** ⓒ 18c: from SUBSIDY.

subsidy /ˈsʌbsɪdɪ/ ▷ *noun* (***subsidies***) **1** a sum of money given, eg by a government to an industry, to help with running costs or to keep product prices low. **2** financial aid of this kind. **3** *Eng historical* money collected by the crown, usually in the form of duties on certain goods, often to finance specified projects such as wars. ⓒ 14c in sense 3, and meaning 'help' or 'assistance': from French *subside*, from Latin *subsidium* auxiliary force.

subsist /səbˈsɪst/ ▷ *verb* (***subsisted, subsisting***) *intr* **1** (*usually* **subsist on something**) to live or manage to stay alive by means of it. **2** (*usually* **subsist in something**) to be based on it; to consist of it □ ***The team's success subsists in their fitness.*** **3** to continue. ⓒ 16c: from Latin *subsistere* to stand still or firm.

subsistence /səbˈsɪstəns/ ▷ *noun* **1** the means of existence; livelihood. **2** *as adj* said of wages, diet, etc: meagre; barely enough to survive on □ ***a subsistence income.*** • **subsistent** *adj.*

subsistence allowance and **subsistence money** ▷ *noun* **1** an advance payment made to an employee to cover their immediate living expenses and which will be deducted from their next wage. **2** a payment made to an employee to cover their expenses while they are away from their usual place of work, eg attending a conference, training course, meeting, etc.

subsistence farming ▷ *noun* a type of farming in which almost all the produce is used to feed and support the farmer's family, leaving little or no surplus for selling.

subsistence level ▷ *noun* a standard of living in which the income is so low that only the bare necessities can be afforded.

subsistence wage ▷ *noun* an income that will only provide the bare necessities.

subsoil /ˈsʌbsɔɪl/ ▷ *noun, geol* the layer of soil that lies beneath the TOPSOIL and which contains clay minerals that have leached from the topsoil, but very little organic matter. ▷ *verb* to plough through the topsoil to an unusually deep level in order to loosen and turn over the subsoil. ⓒ 18c.

subsolar /sʌbˈsoulə(r)/ ▷ *adj* said of a point on the Earth's surface: directly below the Sun. ⓒ 19c.

subsonic /sʌbˈsɒnɪk/ ▷ *adj* relating to, being or travelling at speeds below the speed of sound. Compare INFRASONIC, SUPERSONIC, ULTRASONIC. ⓒ 1930s.

subspecies ▷ *noun, biol* in the taxonomy of plants, animals, etc: a subdivision of a species which shares many characteristics with the other subspecies, but which also displays some morphological differences which are usually brought about by geographical isolation. ⓒ 17c.

subst. ▷ *abbreviation* **1** *grammar* substantive. **2** substitute.

substance /ˈsʌbstəns/ ▷ *noun* **1** the matter or material that a thing is made of. **2** a particular kind of matter with a definable quality □ ***a sticky substance*** □ ***controlled substances.*** **3** the essence or basic meaning of something spoken or written. **4** touchable reality; tangibility □ ***Ghosts have no substance.*** **5** solid quality or worth □ ***food with no substance.*** **6** foundation; truth □ ***no substance in the rumours.*** **7** wealth and influence □ ***woman of substance.*** • **in substance** in actual fact. ⓒ 13c: from Latin *substantia*, from *sub* below + Latin *stare* to stand.

substantial /səbˈstanʃəl/ ▷ *adj* **1** considerable in amount, extent, importance, etc. **2** of real value or worth. **3** said of food: nourishing. **4** solidly built. **5** existing as a touchable thing; material; corporeal. **6** belonging or relating to something's basic nature or essence; essential. **7** wealthy and influential; well-to-do. • **substantiality** /-ʃɪ'alɪtɪ/ *noun*. • **substantially** *adverb*. ⓒ 14c: from SUBSTANCE.

substantialism /səb'stanʃəlɪzəm/ ▻ *noun, philos* the doctrine that states that there are substantial realities behind phenomena. • **substantialist** *noun*. ⓒ 19c.

substantialize or **substantialise** /səb'stanʃəlaɪz/ ▻ *verb* (***substantialized***, ***substantializing***) **1** to make something substantial. **2** to make something real. ⓒ 19c.

substantiate /səb'stanʃɪeɪt, -sɪeɪt/ ▻ *verb* (***substantiated***, ***substantiating***) to prove or support something; to confirm the truth or validity of something. • **substantiation** *noun*. ⓒ 19c; 17c, meaning 'to give form or real substance to something': from SUBSTANCE.

substantive /səb'stantɪv, 'sʌbstəntɪv/ ▻ *adj* **1** having or displaying significant importance, value, validity, solidity, independence, etc. **2** belonging or relating to the essential nature of something. **3** *grammar* expressing existence. **4** said of a dye: able to take effect without the use of a mordant. ▻ *noun, grammar* a noun or any linguistic unit that functions as a noun. • **substantival** /sʌbstən'taɪvəl/ *adj*. • **substantivally** *adverb*. • **substantively** *adverb*. • **substantiveness** *noun*. ⓒ 15c: from Latin *substantivus*, from *sub* below + *stare* to stand.

substantivize or **substantivise** /sʌb'stantɪvaɪz/ ▻ *verb* (***substantivized***, ***substantivizing***) *grammar* to turn (a verbal, adjectival, etc form) into a noun. ⓒ 19c.

substation ▻ *noun* **1** a building that is smaller, less important, etc than another one. **2** a place where high voltage electricity from a power station is converted from alternating to direct current, switched or transformed before being distributed to a network for supply to customers. ⓒ 19c.

substituent /səb'stɪtʃʊənt/ ▻ *noun, chem* an atom or group of atoms that take the place of another atom or group of atoms in a molecule or compound. ⓒ 19c.

substitute /'sʌbstɪtʃuːt/ ▻ *noun* someone or something that takes the place of, or is used instead of, another. Also *as adj* □ ***a substitute striker***. ▻ *verb* (***substituted***, ***substituting***) **1** (*usually* **substitute something for something else**) to use or bring something into use as an alternative, replacement, etc for something else. **2** (*usually* **substitute someone by** or **with someone else**) *informal or in error* to replace them □ ***Goram was substituted by Leighton in goal*** □ ***decided to substitute Goram with Leighton***. • **substitutable** *adj*. • **substitutability** *noun*. • **substitution** *noun*. • **substitutional** or **substitutionary** *adj*. • **substitutionally** *adverb*. • **substitutive** *adj*. • **substitutively** *adverb*. ⓒ 15c: from SUB- 1 + Latin *statuere* to set.

substitute

There is often confusion about which prepositions to use with **substitute** and **replace**. If X is put in place of Y, X is **substituted for** Y or **replaces** Y, and Y is **replaced by** or **replaced with** X.

substrate /'sʌbstreɪt/ ▻ *noun* **1** *biol* the material or medium (eg soil, rock, agar, etc) that a living organism, such as a plant, bacterium, lichen, crustacean, etc, grows on or is attached to, and which often provides it with nutrients and support. **2** *electronics* a piece of semiconductor material that gives support or insulation, especially in the manufacture of integrated circuits. **3** *biochem* the substance that an enzyme acts on during a biochemical reaction. **4** any surface that a substance, such as a paint, dye, ink, etc, can be applied to. **5** SUBSTRATUM. • **substrative** *adj*. ⓒ 19c: from SUBSTRATUM.

substratum /sʌb'strɑːtəm, sʌb'streɪtəm/ ▻ *noun* (***substrata*** /-tə/) **1** an underlying layer. **2** a foundation or foundation material. **3** a layer of soil or rock that lies just below the surface. • **substrative** or **substratal** *adj*. ⓒ 17c: from Latin *substernere, substratum*, from *sub* beneath + *sternere* to spread.

substructure ▻ *noun, archit* the part of a building or other construction that supports the framework. • **substructural** *adj*. ⓒ 18c: from SUB- 1.

subsume /səb'sjuːm, -suːm/ ▻ *verb* (***subsumed***, ***subsuming***) **1** (*often* **subsume under something**) to include (an example, instance, idea, etc) in or regard it as part of a larger, more general group, category, rule, principle, etc. **2** *loosely* to take it over. • **subsumable** *adj*. • **subsumption** /səb'sʌmpʃən/ *noun*. • **subsumptive** *adj*. ⓒ 19c in sense 1; 16c meaning 'to subjoin or add': from SUB- 1 + Latin *sumere* to take.

subteen ▻ *noun, N Amer* a child below the age of 13. Also *as adj* □ ***a class of subteen girls***. ⓒ 1950s.

subtenant ▻ *noun* someone who rents or leases a property from someone who already holds a lease for that propery. • **subtenancy** *noun*. ⓒ 15c: from SUB- 2.

subtend /səb'tɛnd/ ▻ *verb* **1** *geom* said of the line opposite a specified angle in a triangle or the chord of an arc: to be opposite and bounding. **2** *bot* to extend under (eg a bud, etc in a bract or leaf axil) and so enclose it. ⓒ 16c in sense 1; 19c in sense 2: from SUB- 1 + Latin *tendere* to stretch.

subterfuge /'sʌbtəfjuːdʒ, -fjuːʒ/ ▻ *noun* **1** a trick or deception that evades, conceals or obscures □ ***a clever subterfuge***. **2** trickery in general □ ***resorted to subterfuge***. ⓒ 16c: from Latin *subter-* secretly + *fugere* to flee.

subterranean /sʌbtə'reɪnɪən/ ▻ *adj* **1** situated, existing, operating, etc underground. **2** hidden; operating, working, etc in secret. ⓒ 17c: sense 1, from SUB- 1 + Latin *terra* earth.

subtext ▻ *noun* **1** the implied message that the author, director, painter, etc of a play, film, book, picture, etc creates, either consciously or subconsciously at a level below that of plot, character, language, image, etc and which can be discovered by the informed or attentive reader or viewer. **2** *more loosely* anything implied but not explicitly stated in ordinary speech or writing. ⓒ 1950s: from SUB- 2.

subtilize or **subtilise** /'sʌtɪlaɪz/ ▻ *verb* (***subtilized***, ***subtilizing***) **1** to refine. **2** to make subtle. **3** to argue subtly. **4** to make (the mind, senses, etc) more perceptive. • **subtilization** *noun*. • **subtilizer** *noun*. ⓒ 16c: from SUBTLE.

subtitle /'sʌbtaɪtəl/ ▻ *noun* **1** (*usually* **subtitles**) a printed translation of the dialogue of a foreign film that appears bit by bit at the bottom of the frame. **2** a subordinate title that usually expands on or explains the main title. ▻ *verb* (***subtitled***, ***subtitling***) to give a subtitle to (a literary work, film, etc). Compare DUB² *verb* 1. ⓒ 19c.

subtle /'sʌtəl/ ▻ *adj* (***subtler***, ***subtlest***) **1** not straightforwardly or obviously stated or displayed. **2** said of distinctions, etc: difficult to appreciate or perceive. **3** said of a smell, flavour, colour, etc: delicate; understated. **4** capable of making fine distinctions □ ***a subtle mind***. **5** carefully or craftily discreet or indirect. • **subtleness** *noun*. • **subtly** *adverb*. ⓒ 14c: from French *soutil*, from Latin *sub* below + *tela* web.

subtlety /'sʌtəltɪ/ ▻ *noun* (***subtleties***) **1** the state or quality of being subtle. **2** a subtle point or argument; subtle behaviour. **3** a fine distinction; the capability of being able to make fine distinctions; perceptiveness. ⓒ 14c.

subtonic ▻ *noun, music* the seventh note of a scale above the TONIC. Also called **leading note**. ⓒ 19c.

subtopia /sʌb'toʊpɪə/ ▻ *noun, Brit* an area of ugly suburban expansion into the rural landscape, especially when it swallows up traditional villages and so detracts from their character. • **subtopian** *adj*. ⓒ 1950s: a blend of *sub*urb + *utopia*.

subtotal ▻ *noun* the amount that a column of figures adds up to and which forms part of a larger total. ▻ *verb* to add up (this kind of column of figures). ⓒ Early 20c: from SUB- 2.

subtract /səb'trakt/ ▻ *verb* (***subtracted***, ***subtracting***) to take (one number, quantity, etc) away from another; to deduct. ● **subtracter** *noun*. ● **subtraction** *noun*. ● **subtractive** *adj*. ⓒ 16c: from Latin *sub* away + *trahere* to draw.

subtrahend /'sʌbtrəhɛnd/ ▻ *noun, math* the number or quantity that is to be subtracted from another. Compare MINUEND. ⓒ 17c: from Latin *subtrahendus*, from *subtrahere* to subtract.

subtropics ▻ *plural noun* the areas of the world that lie between the tropics and the temperate zone, and that have a near-tropical climate or experience tropical conditions for part of the year. ● **subtropical** or **subtropic** *adj*. ● **subtropically** *adverb*. ⓒ 19c.

subulate /'suːbjʊleɪt, -lɪt/ ▻ *adj* said especially of plant parts: narrow and tapering. ⓒ 18c: from Latin *subula* an awl.

suburb /'sʌbɜːb/ ▻ *noun* **1** a residential district that lies on the edge of a town or city. **2** (**the suburbs**) the outlying districts of a city thought of collectively ◻ *lives in the suburbs*. ⓒ 14c: from Latin *sub* near + *urbs* city.

suburban /sə'bɜːbən/ ▻ *adj* **1** belonging or relating to or situated in a suburb or the suburbs. **2** highly conventional in outlook; provincial and unsophisticated. ● **suburbanite** *noun*.

suburbanize or **suburbanise** /sə'bɜːbənaɪz/ ▻ *verb* (***suburbanized***, ***suburbanizing***) to make (an area) suburban. ● **suburbanization** /-'zeɪʃən/ *noun*.

suburbia /sə'bɜːbɪə/ ▻ *noun* the suburbs and its inhabitants and way of life thought of collectively, especially in terms of being characterized by conventional uniformity, provinciality, lacking sophistication, etc.

subvention /səb'vɛnʃən/ ▻ *noun* a grant or subsidy, especially a government-funded one. ● **subventionary** *adj*. ⓒ 15c: from French *subvencion*, from Latin *subvenire* to come to help.

subversion /səb'vɜːʃən/ ▻ *noun* **1** an act or instance of overthrowing a rule, law, government, etc. **2** the act or practice of subverting (usually a government).

subversive /sʌb'vɜːsɪv/ ▻ *adj* said of a person, action, thinking, etc: characterized by a likelihood or tendency to undermine authority. ▻ *noun* someone who is subversive; a revolutionary. ● **subversively** *adverb*. ● **subversiveness** *noun*. ⓒ 17c: from SUBVERT.

subvert /səb'vɜːt/ ▻ *verb* (***subverted***, ***subverting***) **1** to undermine or overthrow (especially eg a government or other legally established body). **2** to corrupt someone; to undermine (a principle, etc). ● **subverter** *noun*. ⓒ 14c: from Latin *subvertere* to overturn, from *sub* away + *vertere* to turn.

subviral /sʌb'vaɪərəl/ ▻ *adj* belonging or referring to or caused by a structural part of a virus. ⓒ 1960s.

subway /'sʌbweɪ/ ▻ *noun* (***subways***) **1** an underground passage or tunnel that pedestrians or vehicles can use for crossing under a road, railway, river, etc. **2** an underground passage for pipes and cables. **3** *chiefly N Amer, especially US* an underground railway. ⓒ 19c.

subzero /sʌb'zɪəroʊ/ ▻ *adj* said especially of a temperature: below zero degrees.

succedaneum /sʌksɪ'deɪnɪəm/ (***succedanea*** /-nɪə/) ▻ *noun, medicine* something, especially a drug, that can act as a substitute for something else, although it is usually not so effective as the one it replaces. ● **succedaneous** *adj*. ⓒ 17c: from Latin *succedaneus* succedaneous, from *succedere* to succeed.

succeed /sək'siːd/ ▻ *verb* (***succeeded***, ***succeeding***) **1** *intr* to achieve an aim or purpose ◻ *succeeded in his evil plan*. **2** *intr* to develop or turn out as planned. **3** *intr* (*also* **succeed in something**) to do well in a particular area or field ◻ *succeeded in getting four A's*. **4** *tr* to come next after something; to follow. **5** *tr & intr* (*also* **succeed to someone**) to take up a position, etc, following on from someone else ◻ *The Queen succeeded her father* ◻ *She succeeded to the throne*. ⓒ 14c: from Latin *succedere* to go after.

success /sək'sɛs/ ▻ *noun* (***successes***) **1** the quality of succeeding or the state of having succeeded. **2** any favourable development or outcome. **3** someone who attains fame, power, wealth, etc or is judged favourably by others ◻ *became an overnight success*. **4** something that turns out well or that is judged favourably by others ◻ *The party was a great success*. Also *as adj* ◻ *success rate* ◻ *success story*. ● **successless** *adj*.

successful ▻ *adj* **1** achieving or resulting in the required outcome ◻ *The rescue was successful*. **2** prosperous, flourishing ◻ *runs a very successful business*. ● **successfully** *adverb*. ● **successfulness** *noun*.

succession /sək'sɛʃən/ ▻ *noun* **1 a** a series of people or things that come, happen, etc one after the other; **b** the process or an instance of this. **2 a** the right or order by which one person or thing succeeds another; **b** the process or act of doing this. **3** *ecol* the process in which types of plant or animal communities sequentially replace one another until a stable CLIMAX community becomes established. ● **successional** *adj*. ● **successionally** *adverb*. ● **successionless** *adj*. ● **in succession** one after the other. ● **in quick succession** quickly one after the other.

successive /sək'sɛsɪv/ ▻ *adj* immediately following another or each other. ● **successively** *adverb*. ● **successiveness** *noun*.

successor /sək'sɛsə(r)/ ▻ *noun* someone who follows another, especially someone who takes over another's job, position, title, etc.

succinate /'sʌksɪneɪt/ ▻ *noun* a salt of succinic acid.

succinct /sək'sɪŋkt/ ▻ *adj* said of someone or of the way they write or speak: brief, precise and to the point; concise. ● **succinctly** *adverb*. ● **succinctness** *noun*. ⓒ 15c: from Latin *succinctus*, from *succingere* to gird from below.

succinic /sək'sɪnɪk/ ▻ *adj* belonging or relating to, or contained in or obtained from, amber. ⓒ 18c: from French *succinique*, from Latin *succinum* amber.

succinic acid ▻ *noun, chem* (formula **$HOOCCH_2CH_2COOH$**) a dibasic acid that occurs in plants and in various animal tissues where it plays an important part in metabolism.

succotash /'sʌkətaʃ/ ▻ *noun, N Amer* a traditional Native American dish that consists of under-ripe maize and beans boiled together, and which sometimes has red and green peppers or pork added to it. ⓒ 18c: from Narragansett *msiquatash* boiled whole kernels of corn.

Succoth see SUKKOTH

succour /'sʌkə(r)/ *formal* ▻ *noun* **1** help or relief in time of distress or need. **2** someone or something that gives this kind of help. ▻ *verb* (***succoured***, ***succouring***) to give help or relief to someone or something. ● **succourer** *noun*. ● **succourless** *adj*. ⓒ 13c: from French *succure*, from Latin *succurrere* to run to help.

succubus /'sʌkjʊbəs/ and **succuba** /-bə/ ▻ *noun* (***succubi*** /-baɪ/ or ***succubuses***; ***succubae*** /-biː/ or ***succubas***) a female evil spirit which was believed to have sexual intercourse with sleeping men and so conceive demonic children. Compare INCUBUS. ⓒ 14c: from Latin *succuba* prostitute, from *cubare* to lie.

succulent /'sʌkjʊlənt/ ▻ *adj* **1** full of juice; juicy; tender and tasty. **2** *bot* said of a plant: characterized by having thick fleshy leaves or stems. **3** *informal* attractive; inviting. ▷ *noun, bot* **1** a plant that is specially adapted to living in arid conditions by having thick fleshy leaves or stems or both which allow it to store water. **2** a plant that is similarly adapted to live in places, such as saltmarshes, where, although there is water present, the high levels of salts in the soil mean the plant cannot readily absorb it. ● **succulence** or **succulency** *noun*. ● **succulently** *adverb*. 🕔 17c: from Latin *succulentus*, from *sucus* juice.

succumb /sə'kʌm/ ▷ *verb* (***succumbed, succumbing***) *intr* (*often* **succumb to something**) **1** to give in to (eg pressure, temptation, desire, etc) ◻ *succumbed to her charms.* **2** to fall victim to or to die of (something, especially a disease, old age, etc). 🕔 15c: from Latin *cumbere* to lie down.

such ▷ *adj* **1** of that kind, or of the same or a similar kind ◻ *You cannot reason with such a person* ◻ *We ended up completely broke, such was our fate.* **2** so great; of a more extreme type, degree, extent, etc than is usual, normal, etc ◻ *got such a shock when she heard the news* ◻ *You've been such an idiot* ◻ *Such a shame you couldn't come to the party.* **3** of a type, degree, extent, etc that has already been indicated, spoken about, etc ◻ *I did no such thing.* ▷ *pronoun* a person or thing, or people or things, like that or those which have just been mentioned; suchlike ◻ *chimps, gorillas and such* ◻ *can't conceive that such was his intention.* ● **as such 1** in or by itself alone ◻ *Enthusiasm as such is not enough.* **2** as is usually thought of, described, etc ◻ *There's no spare bed as such, but you can use the sofa.* ● **such as** for example. ● **such as it is** for all its imperfection ◻ *You're welcome to use my car there, such as it is.* 🕔 Anglo-Saxon *swilc*.

such-and-such ▷ *adj* of a particular but unspecified kind. ▷ *pronoun* a person or thing of this kind.

suchlike ▷ *pronoun* things of the same kind ◻ *went to the chemist for soap, toothpaste and suchlike.* ▷ *adj* of the same kind ◻ *bought plenty of soap, toothpaste and suchlike things.*

suck ▷ *verb* (***sucked, sucking***) **1** *tr & intr* to draw (liquid) into the mouth. **2** to draw liquid from (eg a juicy fruit) with the mouth. **3** (*also* **suck something in** or **up**) to draw in by suction or an action similar to suction ◻ *the roots sucked up the water.* **4** to rub (eg one's thumb, a pencil, etc) with the tongue and inside of the mouth, using an action similar to sucking in liquids. **5** to draw the flavour from (eg a sweet) with squeezing and rolling movements inside the mouth. **6** to take milk (from a breast or udder) with the mouth. **7** *intr, N Amer slang* to be contemptible or contemptibly bad ◻ *That film really sucks!* ▷ *noun* an act or bout of sucking. ● **suck someone into something** to drag them into it ◻ *sucked her into his seedy world of prostitution.* 🕔 Anglo-Saxon *sucan*.

■ **suck something in** to pull in by a sucking action ◻ *sucked in her cheeks.*

■ **suck off** or **suck someone off** *slang* to perform cunnilingus or fellatio.

■ **suck up** to pull in by suction.

■ **suck up to someone** *colloq* to flatter them or be obsequious to them in order to gain favour.

sucker ▷ *noun* **1 a** someone or something that sucks; **b** *in compounds* ◻ *bloodsucker.* **2** *colloq* someone who is gullible or who can be easily deceived or taken advantage of. **3** (*usually* **sucker for something**) *colloq* someone who finds a specified type of thing or person irresistable ◻ *a sucker for chocolate ice cream.* **4** *zool* a specially adapted organ that helps an insect, sea creature, etc adhere to surfaces by suction so that it can feed, move, etc. **5** a rubber cup-shaped device that is designed to adhere to a surface by creating a vacuum. **6** *bot* a shoot that sprouts from the parent stem or root and which remains attached to the parent plant for nutrients until it is capable of independent existence. ▷ *verb* (***suckered, suckering***) **1** to remove the suckers (from a plant). **2** to deceive, cheat, trick or fool ◻ *suckered him out of £50.*

suckle /'sʌkəl/ ▷ *verb* (***suckled, suckling***) **1** to feed (a baby or young mammal) with milk from the nipple or udder. **2** *tr & intr* to suck milk from (a nipple or udder). ● **suckler** *noun*. 🕔 15c.

suckling ▷ *noun* **1 a** a baby or young animal that is still being fed with its mother's milk; **b** *as adj* ◻ *a suckling pig.* **2** an act or the process of feeding a baby or young animal with its mother's milk.

sucrose /'suːkroʊs, 'sjuː-/ ▷ *noun, biochem* (formula $C_{12}H_{22}O_{11}$) a white soluble crystalline sugar, found in most plants, that hydrolyses to a molecule of glucose linked to a molecule of fructose and which is extracted from sugar cane and sugar beet for use as a sweetener in food and drinks. Also called **sugar, cane-sugar**. 🕔 19c: from French *sucre* sugar.

suction /'sʌkʃən/ ▷ *noun* **1** an act, an instance or the process of sucking. **2 a** the production of an adhering or sucking force that is created by a difference or reduction in air pressure; **b** the amount of force that this creates. 🕔 17c: from Latin *sugere, suctum* to suck.

suction pump ▷ *noun* a pumping device for raising water, etc.

suctorial /sʌk'tɔːrɪəl/ ▷ *adj, zool* said of an organ or other body part: specially adapted for sucking or adhering. 🕔 19c: from Latin *sugere* to suck.

Sudanese /suːdə'niːz/ ▷ *adj* belonging or relating to the Sudan, a large Arabic-speaking country lying on the Red Sea in NE Africa, or its inhabitants. ▷ *noun* (***Sudanese***) a citizen or inhabitant of, or a person born in, the Sudan.

Sudanic /suː'danɪk/ ▷ *noun* a group of languages spoken in NE Africa. ▷ *adj* belonging or relating to these languages or to the country of Sudan.

sudarium /suː'dɛərɪəm, sjuː-/ ▷ *noun* (***sudaria*** /-rɪə/) **1** a cloth for mopping up sweat. **2** *RC Church* a VERONICA[2]. 🕔 17c: from Latin *sudare* to sweat.

sudatorium /suːdə'tɔːrɪəm, sjuː-/ ▷ *noun* (***sudatoria*** /–rɪə/) a hot room in a Roman bathhouse where the heat induces sweating. 🕔 18c: from Latin *sudare* to sweat.

sudatory /'suːdətərɪ, 'sjuː-/ ▷ *adj* relating to or producing sweat. ▷ *noun* (***sudatories***) a drug that has the effect of producing sweat. 🕔 16c: from Latin *sudare* to sweat.

sudden /'sʌdən/ ▷ *adj* happening or done quickly, without warning or unexpectedly. ● **suddenly** *adverb*. ● **suddenness** *noun*. ● **all of a sudden** without any warning; unexpectedly. 🕔 14c: from French *soudain*, from Latin *subire* to come or go stealthily.

sudden death ▷ *noun* a method of deciding a tied game, contest, quiz, etc by declaring the winner to be the first player or team to score, answer correctly, etc during a period of extra time or in a set of extra questions, etc. Also *as adj* ◻ *a sudden-death play-off.*

sudden infant death syndrome ▷ *noun* (abbreviation **SIDS**) *medicine* the sudden unexpected death, often at night, of an apparently healthy baby without any identifiable cause on clinical or post-mortem examination. Also (*non-technical*) called **cot death**.

sudorific /suːdə'rɪfɪk, sjuː-/ *medicine* ▷ *adj* said of a drug: causing sweating. ▷ *noun* a drug, remedy or substance that causes sweating. 🕔 17c: from Latin *sudor* sweat + *facere* to make.

suds /sʌdz/ ▷ *plural noun* **1** (*also* **soap-suds**) a mass of bubbles produced on water when soap or other detergent is dissolved. **2** water that has detergent in it. ● **sudsy** *adj*. 🕔 16c.

sue /suː, sjuː/ ▷ *verb* (***sued, suing***) *tr & intr* to take legal proceedings against (a person or company). ● **suer** *noun*. 🕔 13c: from French *sivre*, from Latin *sequi* to follow.

■ **sue for something** to make a claim for it.

■ **sue someone for something** to make a claim against them for it.

suede /sweɪd/ ▻ *noun* originally kidskin, but now any soft leather, where the flesh side is rubbed or brushed so that it has a velvety finish. ⓒ 19c: from French *gants de Suède* gloves from Sweden.

suet /'suːɪt, 'sjuːɪt/ ▻ *noun* hard fat from around the kidneys of sheep or cattle, used for making pastry, puddings, etc and in the manufacture of tallow. ● **suety** *adj.* ⓒ 14c: from Latin *sebum* fat.

suet pudding ▻ *noun* a type of boiled or steamed pudding that has a suet-based crust and a sweet or savoury filling.

Suff. ▻ *abbreviation, English county* Suffolk.

suffer /'sʌfə(r)/ ▻ *verb* (***suffered, suffering***) **1** *tr & intr* to undergo or endure (physical or mental pain or other unpleasantness). **2** *intr* to deteriorate (as a result of something). **3** to tolerate □ ***doesn't suffer fools gladly.*** **4** *old use* to allow □ ***suffer the little children to come unto me.*** ● **sufferable** *adj.* ● **sufferer** *noun.* ⓒ 13c: from Latin *sufferre* to endure.

■ **suffer for something** to undergo pain, punishment, unpleasantness, hardship, etc because of it □ ***He suffered for his crimes*** □ ***She suffered for her art.***

■ **suffer from something** to be afflicted with (an illness, condition, state, etc).

sufferance /'sʌfərəns/ ▻ *noun* consent that is given tacitly or that is understood to be given through the lack of objection. ● **on sufferance** with reluctant toleration.

suffering ▻ *noun* **1** pain, distress, etc. **2** the state or an example of undergoing pain, distress, etc.

suffice /sə'faɪs/ ▻ *verb* (***sufficed, sufficing***) **1** *intr* to be adequate, sufficient, good enough, etc for a particular purpose. **2** to satisfy. ● **sufficer** *noun.* ● **suffice it to say** it is enough to say. ⓒ 14c: from Latin *sufficere*, from SUB- 1 + *facere* to make.

sufficient /sə'fɪʃənt/ ▻ *adj* enough; adequate. ● **sufficiency** *noun.* ● **sufficiently** *adverb.* ⓒ 14c: from Latin *sufficere* to supply.

suffix /'sʌfɪks/ ▻ *noun* (***suffixes***) **1** *grammar* a word-forming element that can be added to the end of a word or to the base form of a word, eg as a grammatical inflection such as *-ed* or *-s* in *walked* and *monkeys* or in the formation of derivatives, such as *-less* and *-ly* in *helpless* and *lovely*. Compare AFFIX, INFIX, PREFIX. **2** *math* an INDEX that is placed below the other figures in an equation, etc, eg the *n* in x_n. Also called SUBSCRIPT. ▻ *verb* (***suffixes, suffixed, suffixing***) **1** *grammar* to attach something as a suffix to a word. **2** to add (a suffix) to something. ● **suffixation** *noun.* ⓒ 18c: from Latin *suffixus* fixed underneath, from *sub* under + *figere* to fasten.

suffocate /'sʌfəkeɪt/ ▻ *verb* (***suffocated, suffocating***) **1** *tr & intr* to kill or be killed by a lack of air, eg because the air passages are blocked or because of smoke inhalation, etc. **2** *intr* to experience difficulty in breathing because of heat and lack of air; to stifle. **3** to subject to an oppressive amount of something. ● **suffocating** *adj* □ ***suffocating heat.*** ● **suffocatingly** *adverb.* ● **suffocation** *noun.* ● **suffocative** *adj.* ⓒ 16c: from Latin *suffocare, suffocatum*, from *sub* under + *fauces* throat.

Suffolk /'sʌfək/ ▻ *noun* **1** a breed of black-faced sheep. **2** one animal of this breed. ⓒ 18c: from Suffolk, a county in East Anglia, in S England.

Suffolk punch ▻ *noun* a breed of small strong draught horse which has a chestnut coat and short legs. ⓒ 18c: from Suffolk, a county in East Anglia, in S England + PUNCH[4].

suffragan /'sʌfrəgən/ ▻ *noun* (*in full* **suffragan bishop** or **bishop suffragan**) **1** a bishop who is appointed to assist a diocesan bishop in running the diocese. **2** any bishop considered as subordinate to an archbishop or metropolitan. ● **suffraganship** *noun.* ⓒ 14c: French, from Latin *suffraganeus*, from *suffragium* suffrage.

suffrage /'sʌfrɪdʒ/ ▻ *noun* **1** the right to vote in political elections □ ***fought for universal suffrage.*** **2** the act of casting a vote. **3** a vote that is cast in support (of someone or something). **4** (*often* **suffrages**) a petitionary prayer or a prayer for the souls of the dead. ● **suffragism** *noun* the belief in or advocacy of voting rights, especially for women. ● **suffragist** *noun.* ⓒ 13c: from Latin *suffragium* a voting tablet, pebble, etc.

suffragette /sʌfrə'dʒɛt/ ▻ *noun* a woman who is in favour of or who campaigns for women having the same voting rights as men, especially one who acted militantly for this in Britain in the early years of the 20c. ● **suffragettism** *noun.* ⓒ 1906: from SUFFRAGE + -ETTE 1.

suffuse /sə'fjuːz/ ▻ *verb* (***suffused, suffusing***) (*often* **be suffused with something**) to be covered or spread over or throughout with (colour, light, liquid, etc) □ ***The sky was suffused with red*** □ ***His eyes were suffused with tears.*** ● **suffusion** *noun.* ● **suffusive** *adj.* ⓒ 16c: from Latin *suffundere, suffusum*, from *fundere* to pour.

Sufi /'suːfɪ/ ▻ *noun* (***Sufis***) a Muslim mystic ascetic. ⓒ 17c: from Arabic *sufi* man of wool, from *suf* wool (because of the woollen clothes worn by ascetics).

Sufism /'suːfɪzəm/ ▻ *noun, relig* an Islamic mystical movement which advocates a move away from the legalistic approach in Islam to a more personal relationship with God and whose adherents aspire to lose themselves in the ultimate reality of the Divinity by constant repetition of the name of God. ⓒ Early 19c: see SUFI.

sug ▻ *verb* (***sugged, sugging***) to sell or try to sell something to someone under the pretence of conducting market research. ● **sugging** *noun.* ⓒ Late 20c: from sell under the guise.

sugar /'ʃʊgə(r)/ ▻ *noun* **1** any of a group of white crystalline carbohydrates that are soluble in water, typically have a sweet taste and which are widely used as sweeteners in confectionery, desserts, soft drinks, etc. **2 a** the common name for SUCROSE; **b** *as adj* □ ***sugar candy*** □ ***sugar lump.*** **3** a measure of sugar □ ***takes three sugars in his tea.*** **4** *colloq* a term of endearment. ▻ *verb* (***sugared, sugaring***) **1** to sweeten something with sugar. **2** to sprinkle or coat something with sugar. ● **sugaring** *noun.* ● **sugarless** *adj.* ● **sugary** see separate entry. ● **sugar the pill** to make something unpleasant easier to deal with or accept. ⓒ 13c: from French *sucre*, from Arabic *sukkar*.

sugar beet ▻ *noun* a variety of beet that is widely cultivated in Europe and the USA for its large white conical root which contains up to 20 per cent sucrose, and which is the most important source of sugar in temperate regions. Compare SUGAR CANE.

sugar bird ▻ *noun* a S African bird with a long beak that is specially adapted for sucking nectar from flowers.

sugar candy ▻ *noun* **1** large crystals of sugar that are chiefly used for sweetening coffee, etc. **2** *N Amer* confectionery. Often shortened to CANDY.

sugar cane ▻ *noun* a tall tropical grass native to Asia, which is also cultivated in tropical and subtropical regions worldwide. It resembles bamboo and is one of the two main sources of sugar. Compare SUGAR BEET.

sugar daddy ▻ *noun, colloq* a wealthy elderly man who lavishes money and gifts on a friend who is much younger than him, especially in return for companionship or sex or both.

sugar diabetes ▻ *noun, non-technical* DIABETES MELLITUS.

sugared ▻ *adj* **1** sugar-coated; candied. **2** containing sugar.

sugar free ▻ *adj* containing no sugar, but instead often containing some form of artificial sweetener such as aspartame □ *sugar-free chewing gum*.

sugar gum ▻ *noun* a small Australian eucalyptus tree which has sweetish leaves that are used for feeding livestock.

sugariness see under SUGARY

sugar loaf ▻ *noun* **1** refined sugar that is moulded into a conical shape. Also called **loaf sugar**. **2** a hill, etc of similar shape.

sugar-lump and **sugar-cube** ▻ *noun* a compressed cube of sugar that is used for sweetening tea, coffee, etc and feeding to horses.

sugar-maple ▻ *noun* a N American maple tree that is cultivated for the sugar that is obtained from its sap.

sugar of lead ▻ *noun* a white poisonous crystalline compound of lead that is used in dyeing and in the manufacture of paints, varnishes, etc. Also called **lead acetate**.

sugar of milk see under LACTOSE

sugar pea and **sugar snap** ▻ *noun* (*in full* **sugar snap pea**) a variety of MANGETOUT that is fatter and rounder and in which the peas are more developed.

sugar-plum ▻ *noun* **1** *formerly* a small sweet made from flavoured boiled sugar. **2** something pleasant, eg a compliment, that is meant as a sweetner. **3** a term of endearment □ *my little sugar-plum*.

sugar sifter ▻ *noun* a container with a lid which has small holes in it and which is used for dusting cakes, etc with sugar.

sugar soap ▻ *noun* an alkaline substance that is used for cleaning or stripping paint.

sugar tongs ▻ *plural noun* small tongs that are used for lifting lumps of sugar from the sugar bowl to one's cup.

sugary ▻ *adj* **1** like sugar in taste or appearance. **2** containing much or too much sugar. **3** *colloq* exaggeratedly or insincerely pleasant or affectionate; cloying. • **sugariness** *noun*.

sugged and **sugging** see under SUG

suggest /sə'dʒɛst/ ▻ *verb* (***suggested***, ***suggesting***) **1** (*often* **suggest that something**) to put forward as a possibility or recommendation. **2** to create an impression of something; to evoke it □ *a painting that suggests the artist's anguish*. **3** to give a hint of something □ *an expression that suggests guilt*. ◷ 16c: from Latin *suggerere*, *suggestum* to put under, from *gerere* to bear or carry.

suggestible ▻ *adj* **1** easily influenced by suggestions made by others. **2** capable of being suggested. • **suggestibility** *noun*.

suggestion /sə'dʒɛstʃən/ ▻ *noun* **1 a** something that is suggested; a proposal, plan, recommendation, etc; **b** the act of suggesting. **2** a hint or trace □ *delicately flavoured with just a suggestion of coriander*. **3 a** the creation of a belief or impulse in the mind; **b** the process by which an idea, belief, etc can be instilled in the mind of a hypnotized person.

suggestive ▻ *adj* **1** (*often* **suggestive of something**) causing one to think of it; creating an impression of it. **2** capable of a tacitly erotic or provocative interpretation. • **suggestively** *adverb*. • **suggestiveness** *noun*.

suicidal /suːɪ'saɪdəl, sjuːɪ-/ ▻ *adj* **1** involving or indicating suicide. **2** characterized by behaviour that might result in suicide or ruin; irresponsibly rash or self-destructive. **3** said of a person: inclined or likely to commit suicide. • **suicidally** *adverb*.

suicide /'suːɪsaɪd, 'sjuːɪ-/ ▻ *noun* **1** the act or an instance of killing oneself deliberately, usually in the phrase **commit suicide**. **2** someone who deliberately kills or tries to kill himself or herself. **3** ruin or downfall, especially when it is unintentional □ *The minister's speech was political suicide*. **4** *as adj* □ *suicide bomber*. ◷ 17c: from Latin *sui* of oneself + -CIDE.

suing *present participle of* SUE

sui generis /suːiː 'dʒɛnərɪs/ ▻ *adj* unique. ◷ 18c: Latin, meaning 'of its own kind'.

suit /suːt, sjuːt/ ▻ *noun* **1** a set of clothes designed to be worn together, usually made from the same or contrasting material and which consists of a jacket and either trousers or a skirt and sometimes a waistcoat. **2** (*often in compounds*) an outfit worn on specified occasions or for a specified activity □ *wet suit* □ *suit of armour*. **3** any of the four groups (CLUBS, DIAMONDS, HEARTS or SPADES) that a pack of playing-cards is divided into. **4** a legal action taken against someone; a lawsuit. **5** *disparaging* a businessman. ▻ *verb* (***suited***, ***suiting***) **1** *tr & intr* to be acceptable to or what is required by someone. **2** to be appropriate to, in harmony with, or attractive to someone or something. • **suited** *adj* dressed in a suit. • **follow suit 1** to play a card of the same suit as the card first played. **2** to do the same as someone else has done. • **suit oneself** to do what one wants to do, especially without considering others. ◷ 13c: from French *sieute* a set of things, from *sivre* to follow.

suitable ▻ *adj* appropriate, fitting, proper, agreeable, etc. • **suitability** *noun*. • **suitableness** *noun*. • **suitably** *adverb*.

suitcase ▻ *noun* a stiffened portable travelling case that is used for carrying clothes.

suite /swiːt/ ▻ *noun* **1** a set of rooms forming a self-contained unit within a larger building □ *presidential suite* □ *bridal suite*. **2** a set of matching furniture, etc □ *bathroom suite* □ *three-piece suite*. **3** *music* a set of instrumental movements in related keys. **4** a group of followers or attendants. ◷ 17c: from French *sieute* a set of things, from *sivre* to follow.

suiting /'suːtɪŋ, 'sjuː-/ ▻ *noun* material that is used for making suits of clothes.

suitor /'suːtə(r), 'sjuː-/ ▻ *noun* **1** *old use* a man who woos a woman, especially with the intention of asking her to marry him. **2** someone who sues; a plaintiff. ◷ 14c: see SUIT.

suk or **sukh** an alternative spelling of SOUK

sukiyaki /suːkɪ'jakɪ/ ▻ *noun* a traditional Japanese dish which consists of vegetables, noodles and very thin strips of meat, usually beef, which are all sautéed together at the table, after which a sweet soy sauce is added. ◷ 1920s: Japanese, meaning 'grilled on a ploughshare' from the time when the people were forbidden to eat meat but continued to do so, secretly cooking strips of game outside using this quick method.

Sukkoth or **Succoth** /'sʊkout, 'sʊkouθ/ ▻ *noun* a Jewish harvest festival commemorating the period when the Israelites lived in tents in the desert during the Exodus from Egypt. Also called **Feast of Tabernacles**. ◷ Hebrew, meaning 'tents or huts'.

sulcus /'sʌlkəs/ ▻ *noun* (***sulci*** /'sʌlsaɪ/) *anatomy* a longitudinal furrow in a body part, especially the brain. • **sulcate** or **sulcated** *adj*.

sulf- and **sulfo-** see under SULPHO-

sulk ▻ *verb* (***sulked***, ***sulking***) *intr* to be silent, grumpy, unsociable, etc, especially because of some petty resentment, a feeling of being hard done by, etc. ▻ *noun* (*also* **the sulks**) a bout of sulking. ◷ 18c.

sulky ▻ *adj* (***sulkier***, ***sulkiest***) inclined to moodiness, especially when taking the form of grumpy silence, resentful unsociablility, etc. ▻ *noun* (***sulkies***) a light two-wheeled horse-drawn vehicle for one person. • **sulkily** *adverb*. • **sulkiness** *noun*. ◷ 18c: probably from Anglo-Saxon *aseolcan* to slack or be slow.

sullage /ˈsʌlɪdʒ/ ▻ *noun* refuse, sewage or other waste. ⓘ 16c.

sullen /ˈsʌlən/ ▻ *adj* **1** silently and stubbornly angry, serious, morose, moody or unsociable. **2** said of skies, etc: heavy and dismal. ● **sullenly** *adverb*. ● **sullenness** *noun*. ⓘ 16c.

sully /ˈsʌlɪ/ ▻ *verb* (***sullies***, ***sullied***, ***sullying***) **1** to tarnish or mar (a reputation, etc). **2** *now chiefly literary* to dirty something. ● **sullied** *adj*. ⓘ 16c.

sulph- see SULPHO-

sulpha or (*US*) **sulfa** /ˈsʌlfə/ ▻ *noun* any synthetic drug that is derived from sulphanilamide. ⓘ 1940s.

sulphadiazine or (*US*) **sulfadiazine** /sʌlfəˈdaɪəziːn/ ▻ *noun* an antibacterial drug used in the treatment of meningitis. ⓘ 1940s.

sulphanilamide or (*US*) **sulfanilamide** /sʌlfəˈnɪləmaɪd/ ▻ *noun* a SULPHONAMIDE drug formerly used topically to treat wounds, abcesses, infections, etc. ⓘ 1930s.

sulphate or (*US*) **sulfate** /ˈsʌlfeɪt/ ▻ *noun* a salt or ester of sulphuric acid. ▻ *verb* (***sulphated***, ***sulphating***) **1** to form a deposit of lead sulphate on something. **2** to treat or impregnate something with sulphur or a sulphate. ● **sulphation** *noun*. ⓘ 18c: French, from Latin *sulphur*.

sulphide or (*US*) **sulfide** /ˈsʌlfaɪd/ ▻ *noun* a compound that contains sulphur and another more electropositive element. ⓘ 19c.

sulphite or (*US*) **sulfite** /ˈsʌlfaɪt/ ▻ *noun* a salt or ester of sulphurous acid. ⓘ 18c.

sulpho- or (*US*) **sulfo-** /ˈsʌlfoʊ, sʌlˈfɒ/ or (before a vowel) **sulph-** or (*US*) **sulf-** ▻ *combining form, denoting* SULPHUR.

sulphonamide or (*US*) **sulfonamide** /sʌlˈfɒnəmaɪd/ ▻ *noun, chem* **1** an amide of a sulphonic acid. **2** *medicine* any of a group of drugs containing such a compound that prevent the growth of bacteria, formerly widely used to treat bacterial infections in humans, and to prevent infections of wounds and burns during World War II, but now largely superseded by antibiotics such as penicillin. ⓘ 19c: from SULPHONE + AMIDE.

sulphone or (*US*) **sulfone** /ˈsʌlfoʊn/ ▻ *noun* any substance that consists of two organic radicals combined with SULPHUR DIOXIDE. ● **sulphonic** /sʌlˈfɒnɪk/ *adj*. ⓘ 19c: from German *Sulfon*.

sulphur or (*US*) **sulfur** /ˈsʌlfə(r)/ ▻ *noun* (symbol **S**, atomic number 16) a yellow solid non-metallic element that occurs naturally in volcanic regions, areas around hot springs, in deposits deep underground and as a constituent of the amino acids cysteine and methionine, which are found in most proteins. Its main uses are in the vulcanization of rubber and the manufacture of sulphuric acid, fungicides, insecticides, gunpowder, matches, fertilizers and sulphonamide drugs. Also (*old use*) called BRIMSTONE. ▻ *verb* (***sulphured***, ***sulphuring***) to treat or fumigate using sulphur. ● **sulphuric** /sʌlˈfjʊərɪk/ *adj*. ● **sulphury** *adj*. ⓘ 14c: from French *soufre*, from Latin *sulfur*.

sulphurate or (*US*) **sulfurate** /ˈsʌlfjʊəreɪt/ ▻ *verb* (***sulphurated***, ***sulphurating***) to combine or treat with sulphur, eg in bleaching processes. Also called SULPHURIZE. ● **sulphuration** *noun*. ● **sulphurator** *noun*. ⓘ 18c.

sulphur-bottom ▻ *noun* a BLUE WHALE. ⓘ 18c: so called because of the yellow encrustation of diatoms on the whale's underbelly which forms during the breeding season in warmer waters and is lost again when it returns to polar seas.

sulphur dioxide ▻ *noun, chem* (formula SO_2) a colourless, pungent-smelling, toxic gas produced in the burning of fossil fuels and other sulphur-containing compounds. It is used as a reducing agent, as a bleach for paper and straw, as a food preservative, fumigant and solvent, and also in metal refining, paper pulping and the manufacture of sulphuric acid.

sulphureous or (*US*) **sulfureous** /sʌlˈfjʊərɪəs/ ▻ *adj* **1** SULPHUROUS. **2** sulphur-yellow in colour.

sulphuric acid or (*US*) **sulfuric acid** ▻ *noun, chem* (formula H_2SO_4) a colourless odourless oily liquid that is highly corrosive and strongly acidic when diluted with water. It is widely used in the manufacture of organic chemicals, fertilizers, explosives, detergents, paints and dyes and as a laboratory reagent; dilute sulphuric acid is used as an electrolyte in car batteries and for electroplating.

sulphurize or **sulphurise** or (*US*) **sulfurize** /ˈsʌlfjʊəraɪz/ ▻ *verb* (***sulphurized***, ***sulphurizing***) to SULPHURATE.

sulphurous or (*US*) **sulfurous** /ˈsʌlfərəs in senses 1 and 2, sʌlˈfjʊərəs in senses 3 and 4/ ▻ *adj* **1** relating to, like, or containing sulphur. **2** having a yellow colour like sulphur. **3** *chem* denoting any compound with sulphur in the tetravalent state such that SULPHUR DIOXIDE is always present. **4** denoting any compound with the characteristic odours of SULPHUR DIOXIDE and HYDROGEN SULPHIDE. ⓘ 18c.

sulphurous acid or (*US*) **sulfurous acid** /sʌlˈfjʊərəs —/ ▻ *noun, chem* (formula H_2SO_3) a colourless weakly acidic solution of SULPHUR DIOXIDE in water that acts as a reducing agent and is used as a bleach, antiseptic and preservative, and in brewing and wine-making, paper and textile manufacture and the refining of petroleum products. ⓘ 18c.

sulphur tuft ▻ *noun* a poisonous toadstool that has a sulphurous yellow cap.

sultan /ˈsʌltən/ ▻ *noun* **1** the ruler of any of various Muslim countries, especially the former ruler of the Ottoman empire. **2** a variety of small white domestic fowl that originated in Turkey and which has feathery legs and feet. ● **sultanate** *noun*. ● **sultanic** *adj*. ● **sultanship** *noun*. ⓘ 16c: Arabic, meaning 'king or sovereign'.

sultana /sʌlˈtɑːnə/ ▻ *noun* (***sultanas***) **1 a** a pale seedless raisin that is used in making cakes, puddings, etc; **b** the grape that this type of dried fruit comes from. **2** the wife, concubine, mother, sister or daughter of a sultan.

sultry /ˈsʌltrɪ/ ▻ *adj* (***sultrier***, ***sultriest***) **1** said of the weather: hot and humid; close. **2** characterized by a sensual, passionate or sexually suggestive appearance, manner, etc. ● **sultrily** *adverb*. ● **sultriness** *noun*. ⓘ 16c: from obsolete *sulter* to swelter.

sum ▻ *noun* **1 a** the total that is arrived at when two or more numbers, quantities, ideas, feelings, etc are added together □ ***The sum of four and two is six*** □ ***The sum of her resentments is detailed in the memo***; **b** *as adj* □ ***the sum total of his life's work***. **2** an amount of money, often a specified or particular one □ ***a ridiculous sum to pay*** □ ***the grand sum of 50p***. **3 a** an arithmetical calculation, especially of a basic kind; **b** (**sums**) *colloq* arithmetic □ ***I was never very good at sums***. ▻ *verb* (***summed***, ***summing***) to calculate the sum of something; ● **in sum** briefly; to sum up. ⓘ 13c: from French *summe*, from Latin *summa* top, from *summus* highest.

■ **sum up 1** to summarize before finishing a speech, argument, etc □ ***And so, to sum up, my main points are as follows ... .*** **2** said of a judge: to review the main points of a case for the jury before they retire to consider their verdict. See also SUMMING-UP.

■ **sum up someone** or **something 1** to express or embody the complete character or nature of them or it □ ***That kind of pettiness just sums her up.*** **2** to make a quick assessment of (a person, situation, etc).

sumac or **sumach** /ˈsuːmak, ˈsjuː-, ˈʃuː-/ ▻ *noun, bot* **1** any of several varieties of small trees or shrubs that are common across S Europe, Asia and NE America and which have a resinous milky sap, branches that have clusters of small flowers at the ends and small hairy single-seeded fruits. **2** the dried leaves and shoots of these plants which are used in dyeing and tanning. ⓘ 14c: French, from Arabic *summaq*.

Sumatran /sʊ'mɑːtrən/ ▷ *adj* belonging or relating to Sumatra, a mountainous island in W Indonesia, its inhabitants or their language. ▷ *noun* **1** a citizen or inhabitant of, or a person born in, Sumatra. **2** the language of Sumatra. ⓘ 18c.

Sumatran rhinoceros ▷ *noun* a species of rhinoceros found in Asia, which has two horns, and is unusual in that the young are covered with thick brown hair, which is gradually lost as the animal matures.

Sumerian /sʊ'mɪərɪən/ ▷ *adj* belonging or relating to Sumer, a district of the ancient civilization of Babylonia in Mesopotania, its non-Semitic inhabitants or their language. ▷ *noun* **1** a citizen or inhabitant of, or a person born in, Sumer. **2** the extinct language of Sumer. ⓘ 19c.

summa cum laude /'sʊmə kʊm 'laʊdeɪ/ ▷ *adverb, adj, chiefly US* said of a degree, a distinction in an exam, etc: of the highest standard. ⓘ Early 20c: Latin, meaning 'with highest praise'.

summarize or **summarise** /'sʌməraɪz/ ▷ *verb* (***summarized***, ***summarizing***) to make, present or be a summary of something; to state it concisely. • **summarist** *noun*. ⓘ 19c.

summary /'sʌmərɪ/ ▷ *noun* (***summaries***) a short account that outlines or picks out the main points. ▷ *adj* **1** done or performed quickly and without the usual attention to details or formalities. **2** *law* relating to the legal proceedings of a magistrates court or, in Scotland, a sheriff court and so relatively informal. • **summarily** *adverb* □ *The case was summarily dismissed.* • **summariness** *noun*. ⓘ 15c: from Latin *summarius* summary.

summary offence ▷ *noun, law* a common-law offence, eg a driving offence, petty theft, common assault and battery, that is considered minor enough to be tried in a magistrate's court or, in Scotland, a sheriff court rather than in the Crown Court before a jury. Compare INDICTABLE OFFENCE.

summation /sʌ'meɪʃən/ ▷ *noun* **1** the process of finding the sum; addition. **2** a summary or summing-up. • **summational** or **summative** *adj*. ⓘ 18c: from Latin *summare, summatum* to sum up.

summed *past tense, past participle of* SUM

summer[1] /'sʌmə(r)/ ▷ *noun* **1** (*also* **Summer**) the warmest season of the year, between spring and autumn, extending from about June to August in the N hemisphere and from about December to February in the S hemisphere. **2** the warm sunny weather that is associated with summer □ *a beautiful summer's day*. See also INDIAN SUMMER. **3** *astron* the period of the year between the SUMMER SOLSTICE and the AUTUMNAL EQUINOX (see under EQUINOX). **4** *literary* a time of greatest energy, happiness, etc; a heyday □ *in the summer of her life*. **5** (*usually* **summers**) *old use, poetic* a year, especially as thought of in terms of someone's age □ *an old lady of ninety summers*. ▷ *verb* (***summered***, ***summering***) **1** to pass the summer □ *summered in Nice*. **2** to put (livestock) to pasture for the summer □ *summered their sheep on the hillside*. • **summerlike** or **summery** *adj*. ⓘ Anglo-Saxon *sumer*.

summer[2] /'sʌmə(r)/ ▷ *noun* (*also* **summer-tree**) a horizontal load-bearing beam, especially one that supports the girders or joists of a floor or, less commonly, the rafters of a roof. ⓘ 14c: from French *sumer*, from *somier* pack-horse or beam, from Greek *sagma* a pack-saddle.

summerhouse ▷ *noun* any small building or shelter in a park or garden where people can sit during warm weather and which provides some shade.

summer job ▷ *noun* work that is undertaken for the summer months only, eg by students.

summer pudding ▷ *noun, Brit* a cold desert that is made from soft fruits and bread or sponge.

summersault see SOMERSAULT

summer school ▷ *noun, Brit* a course of study held during the summer vacation, eg one for Open University students or foreign students that is held at a university.

summer season ▷ *noun* the period of the year during the summer when certain businesses, eg hotels, holiday entertainment, etc, are at their busiest.

summer solstice ▷ *noun* the longest day of the year in either hemisphere, either (for the N hemisphere) when the Sun is at its most northerly point (usually 21 June), or (for the S hemisphere) when it is at its most southerly point (usually 22 December).

summertime ▷ *noun* the season of summer.

summer time ▷ *noun* **1** (*in full* **British summer time** or **British Summer Time**) *Brit* a system for extending the use of daylight during the period from the end of March to the third week of October by putting the clocks one hour ahead of Greenwich Mean Time. **2** any similar system in other countries.

summing *present participle of* SUM

summing-up ▷ *noun* a review of the main points, especially of a legal case by the judge before the members of the jury retire to consider their verdict.

summit /'sʌmɪt/ ▷ *noun* **1** the highest point of a mountain or hill. **2** the highest possible level of achievement or development, eg in a career. **3 a** *as adj* said of a meeting, conference, talks, etc: between heads of government or other senior officials, especially when it involves discussion of something of international significance □ *summit conference* □ *a meeting at summit level*; **b** such a meeting, conference, etc □ *the NATO summit on disarmament*. • **summitless** *adj*. ⓘ 15c: from French *sommette*, from Latin *summum* highest.

summon /'sʌmən/ ▷ *verb* (***summoned***, ***summoning***) **1** to order someone to come or appear, eg in a court of law as a witness, defendant, etc. **2** to order or request someone to do something; to call someone to something; to ask for something □ *summoned him to make the tea* □ *A bell summoned them to prayer* □ *had to summon help*. • **summonable** *adj*. • **summoner** *noun*. ⓘ 13c: from Latin *summonere* to warn secretly.

■ **summon up something** to gather or muster (eg one's strength or energy) □ *summoned up the nerve to tell him*.

summons ▷ *noun* (***summonses***) **1** a written order that legally obliges someone to attend a court of law at a specified time. **2** any authoritative order that requests someone to attend a meeting, etc or to do something specified. ▷ *verb* (***summonses***, ***summonsed***, ***summonsing***) *law* to serve someone with a summons. ⓘ 13c: from French *sumunse*, from Latin *summonere* to summon.

summum bonum /'sʌməm 'boʊnəm/ ▷ *noun* (***summa bona*** /-mə -nə/) the ultimate guiding principle of goodness in an ethical or moral value system. ⓘ 16c: Latin, meaning 'highest good'.

sumo /'suːmoʊ/ ▷ *noun* a style of traditional Japanese wrestling where contestants of great bulk try to force an opponent out of the unroped ring or to make them touch the floor with any part of their body other than the soles of the feet. ⓘ 19c: Japanese, from *sumafu* to wrestle.

sumotori /suːmoʊ'tɔːrɪ/ ▷ *noun* (***sumotoris***) a sumo wrestler. ⓘ 1970s: Japanese.

sump ▷ *noun* **1** a small depression inside a vehicle's engine that acts as a reservoir so that lubricating oil can drain into it. **2** any pit into which liquid drains or is poured. ⓘ 17c; 15c, meaning 'marsh': from Dutch *somp* a marsh.

sumptuary /'sʌmptʃʊərɪ/ ▷ *adj* **1** relating to or regulating expense. **2** said of a law, etc: controlling extravagance. ◷ 17c: from Latin *sumptuarius*, from *sumptus* cost, from *sumere* to consume or spend.

sumptuous /ˈsʌmptʃʊəs/ ▷ *adj* wildly expensive; extravagantly luxurious. • **sumptuosity** or **sumptuousness** *noun*. • **sumptuously** *adverb*. ◷ 15c: from Latin *sumptuosus*, from *sumptus* cost, from *sumere* to spend.

sum total ▷ *noun* the complete or final total.

Sun. ▷ *abbreviation* Sunday.

sun ▷ *noun* **1** (**the Sun**) the star that the planets revolve around and which gives out the heat and light energy necessary to enable living organisms to survive on Earth. **2** the heat and light of this star. **3** any star with a system of planets revolving around it. **4** someone or something that is regarded as a source of radiance, warmth, glory, etc. **5** *poetic* a day or a year. ▷ *verb* (***sunned***, ***sunning***) to expose (something or oneself) to the sun's rays. • **sunless** *adj*. • **sunlessness** *noun*. • **sunlike** *adj*. • **sunward** or **sunwards** or **sunwise** *adverb*. • **a touch of the sun** slight sunburn. • **catch the sun** to sunburn or tan in the sun □ *You're all red — you've really caught the sun.* • **think the sun shines out of someone's eyes, arse,** *etc* to consider them to be wonderful, infallible, etc. • **under the sun** anywhere on Earth. ◷ Anglo-Saxon *sunne*.

sun-and-planet ▷ *adj* said of a gearing system: designed so that one cog moves around another.

sun-baked ▷ *adj* said of ground, a road, etc: dried, hardened and often cracked due to prolonged exposure to hot sunshine.

sunbathe ▷ *verb, intr* to expose one's body to the sun in order to get a suntan. • **sunbather** *noun*. • **sunbathing** *noun*.

sunbeam ▷ *noun* a ray of sunlight.

sunbear ▷ *noun* a small black Malayan bear that has a white patch on its front. Also called **honey bear**.

sunbed ▷ *noun* **1** a device that has sun-lamps fitted above and often beneath a transparent screen and which someone can lie on in order to artificially tan the whole body. **2** a SUN-LOUNGER.

sunbelt ▷ *noun* **1** an area that has a warm sunny climate and which is therefore considered an ideal place to live. **2** (*often* **Sunbelt**) the southern states of the US.

sunbird ▷ *noun* a small brilliantly coloured tropical or subtropical bird that is found in Africa, Asia and Australia and which resembles the humming-bird.

sunblind ▷ *noun, Brit* an awning over the outside of a window that is designed to block out the Sun's rays.

sunblock ▷ *noun* a lotion, cream, etc that completely or almost completely protects the skin from the harmful effects of the Sun's rays.

sun-bonnet ▷ *noun* a hat that has a big brim and often a frill that extends down the back of the neck and which is worn, especially by babies, to protect against the Sun's rays.

sunbow ▷ *noun* a rainbow-like effect that is produced especially when the Sun shines on spraying water.

sunburn ▷ *noun* soreness and reddening of the skin caused by over-exposure to the Sun's rays. • **sunburnt** or **sunburned** *adj*.

sunburst ▷ *noun* **1** a sudden outbreak of strong sunshine, eg when the Sun appears from behind a cloud. **2** anything that looks like a shining sun with stylized radiating rays, eg an ornament, a piece of jewellery, a firework, etc.

sun cream ▷ *noun* a preparation that is used for protecting the skin against the Sun's rays or for promoting tanning.

sundae /ˈsʌndeɪ/ ▷ *noun* a portion of ice-cream topped with fruit, nuts, syrup, etc.

sundance ▷ *noun* a ritual dance that is performed by some Native American peoples in honour of the Sun and which often includes an element of self-torture.

Sunday /ˈsʌndeɪ/ ▷ *noun* **1** the first day of the week and for most Christians the day of worship and rest. **2** *colloq* a newspaper that is on sale on this day. • **a month of Sundays** a very long time. ◷ Anglo-Saxon *sunnandæg*, a translation of the Latin *dies solis*, from Greek *hemera heliou* day of the Sun.

Sunday best ▷ *noun, jocular* one's best clothes, formerly these considered the most suitable for wearing to church □ *You'd better put on your Sunday best when you go for the interview.*

Sunday driver ▷ *noun* someone who rarely drives but, when they do, it tends to be on country roads at the weekends and in a slow unskilled manner, which results in annoyance and frustration on the part of other drivers.

Sunday painter ▷ *noun* someone who draws or paints pictures as a hobby.

Sunday school ▷ *noun* a class for the religious instruction of children that is held on Sundays.

sundeck ▷ *noun* **1** an upper open deck on a passenger ship where people can sit in the sun. **2** *N Amer, Austral* a balcony or verandah that gets the sun.

sunder /ˈsʌndə(r)/ ▷ *verb* (***sundered***, ***sundering***) *archaic* to sever or separate. • **in sunder** apart or separate. ◷ Anglo-Saxon *syndrain*.

sundew ▷ *noun, bot* an insectivorous plant that grows in bogs where nitrogen is scarce and which has leaves that are covered with long sticky hairs so that it can trap and digest insects which act as a nitrogen supplement. ◷ 16c: so called because the digestive juices that the plant produces lie in glistening droplets that resemble dew.

sundial ▷ *noun* an instrument that uses sunlight to tell the time, by the changing position of the shadow that a vertical arm casts on a horizontal plate with graded markings that indicate the hours.

sun-disc ▷ *noun* a winged representation of the Sun that is used in certain religous iconography to designate the sun god, eg in ancient Egypt.

sundown ▷ *noun* sunset.

sundowner ▷ *noun* **1** *Austral, NZ* a tramp, originally one who arrives at a sheep station too late in the day to work but who still hopes to get food and lodgings. **2** *Brit colloq* an alcoholic drink that is taken around sunset.

sun dress ▷ *noun* a light sleeveless low-cut dress that is usually held up by narrow shoulder-straps.

sundried ▷ *adj* **1** dried or preserved by exposure to the sun rather than by artificial heating and therefore retaining more flavour □ *sundried tomatoes.* **2** said of bricks, clay, etc: dried in the sun.

sundry /ˈsʌndrɪ/ ▷ *adj* various; assorted; miscellaneous; several. ▷ *noun* (**sundries**) various small unspecified items; oddments. • **all and sundry** everybody. ◷ Anglo-Saxon *syndrig*.

sunfast ▷ *adj* said of a dye: not liable to fade when exposed to sunlight.

sunfish ▷ *noun* a name applied to a variety of different fish, most commonly to a type of large rounded marine fish that measures up to 3.5m (about $11\frac{1}{2}$ft) and weighs around 20 tonnes and which can be seen basking in the sun in tropical and temperate seas.

sunflower ▷ *noun* a annual plant that can grow to around 3m (about 10ft) in height and which produces large flattened circular flowerheads of up to 50cm (about 20in) diameter that have a great many closely-packed seeds in the middle and yellow petals radiating outwards. It is widely cultivated as a garden plant and for its seeds which are rich in edible oil.

sung *past participle of* SING

sunglasses /'sʌŋglɑːsɪz/ ▷ *plural noun* spectacles that have tinted lenses, which are worn to protect the eyes from sunlight. Also (*colloq*) called SHADES (see SHADE *noun* 11).

sun-god and **sun-goddess** ▷ *noun* **1** the Sun when it is thought of as a deity. **2** any god that has associations with the Sun.

sunhat ▷ *noun* a hat that has a wide brim and which is worn to shade the face from the rays of the Sun.

sunk *past participle of* SINK

sunken /'sʌŋkən/ ▷ *adj* **1** situated or fitted at a lower level than the surrounding area ◻ ***a sunken bath.*** **2** submerged in water ◻ ***sunken treasure.*** **3** said of eyes, cheeks, etc: abnormally fallen in, gaunt or hollow, eg because of ill health, old age, etc. 🕓 14c: a past participle of SINK.

sun-kissed ▷ *adj* having been warmed, bronzed, ripened, etc by the sun ◻ ***a sun-kissed beach*** ◻ ***a sun-kissed peach.***

sun-lamp ▷ *noun* **1** an electric lamp that emits rays, especially ultraviolet ray's, that are similar to natural sunlight and which is used therapeutically and for artificially tanning the skin. **2** *cinematog* a large film-making lamp that has a parabolic reflector so that it gives off a very bright light.

sunlight ▷ *noun* light from the Sun.

sunlit ▷ *adj* lit by the Sun.

sun lounge and **sun parlour** ▷ *noun, US* a room with large windows for letting in maximum sunlight.

sun-lounger ▷ *noun, Brit* a lightweight plastic sunbathing seat, sometimes with an upholstered covering, that can often be adjusted to a variety of positions and which usually supports the whole body. Also called SUNBED.

Sunna or **Sunnah** /'sʊnə, 'sʌnə/ ▷ *noun* a compilation of the sayings and deeds of Muhammad, which is a supplement to the KORAN for the more orthodox MUSLIM. 🕓 17c: Arabic, meaning 'form, way, course, rule'.

Sunni /'sʊnɪ, 'sʌnɪ/ **1** *singular noun* the more orthodox of the two main branches of the Islamic religion, which accepts the SUNNA as authoritative. Compare SHIA. **2** *noun* (***Sunni*** or ***Sunnis***) a Muslim of this branch of Islam. Also called **Sunnite**. • **Sunnism** *noun.* 🕓 17c: from Arabic *sunnah* rule.

sunny /'sʌnɪ/ ▷ *adj* (***sunnier***, ***sunniest***) **1** said of a day, the weather, etc: characterized by long spells of sunshine or sunlight. **2** said of a place, etc: exposed to, lit or warmed by plenty of sunshine ◻ ***a lovely sunny room.*** **3** cheerful; good-humoured ◻ ***her friendly sunny disposition.*** • **sunnily** *adverb.* • **sunniness** *noun.*

sunny side ▷ *noun* **1** the side of a street, road, house, etc that is more exposed to sunshine. **2** the cheerful aspect or point or view ◻ ***look on the sunny side of the issue.*** • **sunny side up** said of fried eggs: cooked without being flipped over onto the other side.

sunrise ▷ *noun* **1** the sun's appearance above the horizon in the morning. **2** the time of day when this happens. **3** the coloration of the sky at this time.

sunrise industry ▷ *noun* any new and rapidly expanding industry, especially one that involves computing, eletronics, etc.

sunroof ▷ *noun* a transparent panel in the roof of a car that lets sunlight in and that can usually open for ventilation.

sunscreen ▷ *noun* a preparation that protects the skin and minimizes the possibility of sunburn because it blocks out some or most of the Sun's harmful rays.

sunset ▷ *noun* **1** the sun's disappearance below the horizon in the evening. **2** the time of day when this happens. **3** the coloration of the sky at this time.

sunshade ▷ *noun* **1** a type of umbrella that is used as protection in strong sunshine; a parasol. **2** an awning.

sunshine ▷ *noun* **1** the light or heat of the Sun. **2** fair weather, with the Sun shining brightly ◻ ***There will be a mixture of sunshine and showers.*** **3** a place bathed in the light or heat of the sun ◻ ***We'll have our picnic over there in the sunshine.*** **4** an informal term of address, often used as part of a greeting or in a mockingly condescending or scolding tone. **5** a source of infectious happiness ◻ ***She was the sunshine in his life.*** **6** *as adj* ◻ ***sunshine yellow.*** • **sunshiny** *adj.*

sunspot ▷ *noun* **1** *astron* a relatively dark patch on the Sun's surface which indicates a transient cooler area that can measure anything from 100 to 100 000 miles in diameter and can last for a few hours or up to several months. It often appears as one of a cluster in 11 year cycles, has an intense magnetic field and is thought to be connected with magnetic storms on Earth. **2** *colloq* a holiday resort that is renowned for its sunny weather.

sunstroke ▷ *noun* a condition of collapse brought on by over-exposure to the sun and sometimes accompanied by fever.

suntan ▷ *noun* a browning of the skin through exposure to the sun or a sun-lamp. Also *as adj* ◻ ***suntan oil.*** Often shortened to TAN. • **sun-tanned** *adj* characterized by having a suntan; brown-skinned.

suntrap ▷ *noun, Brit* a sheltered sunny place.

sun-up ▷ *noun, US* sunrise.

sun visor ▷ *noun* **1** a flap at the top of a vehicle's windscreen that can be lowered to shield the driver's eyes from the Sun's rays. **2** a peaked shield that is worn on the head to protect the eyes from the Sun's rays.

sup[1] ▷ *verb* (***supped***, ***supping***) **1** to drink in small mouthfuls. **2** *colloq* to drink (alcohol). ▷ *noun* a small quantity, especially of something liquid; a sip ◻ ***put a wee sup of brandy in the coffee.*** 🕓 Anglo-Saxon *supan.*

sup[2] ▷ *verb* (***supped***, ***supping***) *old use* (*often* **sup off** or **on something**) to eat supper; to eat for supper. 🕓 13c: from French *soper* to take supper.

sup. ▷ *abbreviation* **1** superfine. **2** superior. **3** superlative. **4** supine. **5** supra. **6** supreme.

Sup. Ct. ▷ *abbreviation* **1** Superior Court. **2** Supreme Court.

super /'suːpə(r), 'sjuː-/ ▷ *adj* **1** (*also* **super duper**) *colloq* extremely good; excellent; wonderful. **2** *textiles* a short form of SUPERFINE. ▷ *exclamation* excellent! ▷ *noun* **1** something of superior quality or grade, eg petrol. **2** *colloq* a short form of SUPERINTENDENT. **3** *colloq* a SUPERNUMERARY, especially an extra in the theatre or on a film set. 🕓 19c: Latin, meaning 'above'.

super- /suːpə(r), sʊpə(r), sjuː-, sjʊ-/ ▷ *prefix, forming adjectives, nouns and verbs, denoting* **1** great or extreme in size or degree ◻ ***supermarket.*** **2** above, beyond or over ◻ ***superscript*** ◻ ***supernatural.*** **3** higher or more outstanding than usual ◻ ***superhero.*** Compare HYPER-. 🕓 Latin, meaning 'above, on top of, beyond, besides, in addition'.

Some words with *super-* prefixed: see SUPER- for numbered senses specified below.

superclass *noun, taxonomy* sense 2.
supercluster *noun* sense 2.
supercomputer *noun* sense 1.
supereminent *adj* sense 2.
superfamily *noun, taxonomy* sense 2.
supernormal *adj* sense 2.
superorder *noun, taxonomy* sense 2.
supersaturate *verb* sense 2.
superstate *noun* sense 1.
superstratum *noun* sense 2.

superable /'suːprəbəl, 'sjuː-/ ▷ *adj* said of a problem, difficulty, obstacle, etc: able to be overcome; surmountable. ⓒ 17c.

superabound ▷ *verb, intr* to be more, excessively or very plentiful. ⓒ 16c.

superabundant ▷ *adj* excessively or very plentiful. • **superabundance** *noun*. • **superabundantly** *adverb*. ⓒ 15c.

superadd ▷ *verb* to add something over and above. • **superaddition** *noun*. ⓒ 15c.

superannuate /suːpər'anjʊeɪt/ ▷ *verb* **1** to make (an employee) retire on a pension, eg because of illness, old age, etc. **2** to discard as too old for further use □ *superannuated the old computer in favour of a fancy multimedia one*. ⓒ 17c.

superannuated ▷ *adj* **1** said of a post, vacancy, job, etc: with a pension as an integral part of the employment package. **2** made to retire and given a pension; pensioned off. **3** old and no longer fit for use. ⓒ 17c: from Latin *annus* year.

superannuation ▷ *noun* **1** an amount that is regularly deducted from someone's wages as a contribution to a company pension. **2** the pension someone receives when they retire. **3** retirement □ *took early superannuation*. ⓒ 17c.

superb /sʊ'pɜːb, sjʊ-/ ▷ *adj* **1** *colloq* outstandingly excellent. **2** magnificent; majestic; highly impressive. • **superbly** *adverb*. • **superbness** *noun*. ⓒ 16c: from Latin *superbus* proud.

supercalifragilisticexpialidocious /'suːpəkalɪ'fradʒəlɪstɪk'ɛkspɪalə'doʊʃəs/ and **supercalifragilistic** ▷ *adj* absolutely stunningly fantastic. ⓒ 1964: first coined in a song title in the Walt Disney film *Mary Poppins*, although a music company and two songwriters instigated a lawsuit, which they lost, claiming to have used the word as early as 1949.

supercargo ▷ *noun* an officer in the merchant navy whose job is to oversee the cargo and any commercial or financial transactions associated with a voyage. • **supercargoship** *noun* the office of being a supercargo. ⓒ 17c: from the earlier form *supracargo*, from Spanish *sobrecargo*, from *sobre* over + *cargo* cargo.

supercharge ▷ *verb* **1** to increase the power and performance of (a vehicle engine). **2** (*usually* **supercharge with something**) to charge or fill (eg an atmosphere, a remark, etc) with an intense amount of an emotion, etc. ⓒ Early 20c.

supercharger ▷ *noun, engineering* a mechanical pump or compressor that is used to increase the amount of air taken into the cylinder of an internal combustion engine, in order to burn the fuel more rapidly and so increase the power output.

superciliary /suːpə'sɪlɪərɪ/ ▷ *adj, anatomy* **1** belonging or relating to the eyebrow. **2** situated over the eye. ⓒ 18c: from Latin *supercilium* eyebrow.

supercilious /suːpə'sɪlɪəs/ ▷ *adj* **1** arrogantly disdainful or contemptuous. **2** self-importantly judgemental. • **superciliously** *adverb*. • **superciliousness** *noun*. ⓒ 16c: from Latin *super cilium* eyebrow.

supercomputer ▷ *noun* a very powerful computer that is capable of performing more computations per second than most other computers. Since the processing power of computers changes so rapidly, what is a supercomputer one year will very likely not be considered such the following year. Supercomputing now often involves PARALLEL PROCESSING. • **super computing** *noun*.

superconductivity /suːpəkɒndʌk'tɪvɪtɪ/ ▷ *noun, physics* the property of having no electrical resistance that many metals and alloys display at temperatures close to absolute zero, and that other substances, such as ceramics, display at higher temperatures. • **superconducting** or **superconductive** *adj*. ⓒ Early 20c.

superconductor ▷ *noun, physics* a substance that displays superconductivity. ⓒ Early 20c: from SUPER- 2.

supercontinent ▷ *noun* any of the vast landmasses from which the continents were originally formed ⓒ 1950s.

supercool[1] ▷ *verb, physics* **1** to cool (a liquid) to a point below its usual freezing point without it becoming solid or crystallized. **2** *intr* said of a liquid: to be cooled without becoming solid or crystallized. • **supercooling** *noun*. ⓒ Late 19c.

supercool[2] ▷ *adj, colloq* very relaxed and sophisticated in an understated way. ⓒ 1970s.

super duper see under SUPER

superego ▷ *noun, psychoanal* in Freudian theory: that aspect of the psyche where someone's individual moral standards are internalized, especially parental and social ones that act as a censor on the EGO. It is associated with self-criticism and self-observation, often operating at an unconscious level, and it can be at odds with the person's conscious values. Compare ID. ⓒ 1920s.

superelevation ▷ *noun* the amount of elevation by which the outer edge of a curve on a road or railway exceeds the inner edge. ⓒ Late 19c.

supererogation /suːpərɛrə'geɪʃən/ ▷ *noun* **1** doing more than duty, circumstances, etc require. **2** *RC Church* the performance of prayers, devotions, good works, etc beyond those believed necessary for salvation, which are then held in store so that they can then be redistributed to those who have been deficient in these duties. • **supererogatory** /-ɪ'rɒgətərɪ/ *adj*. ⓒ 16c: from Latin *erogare* to pay out.

superfatted ▷ *adj* said of soap: containing extra fat. ⓒ Late 19c.

superfetation /suːpəfiː'teɪʃən/ ▷ *noun* **1** *physiol* **a** a conception in a uterus that is already pregnant with the result that two foetuses of different ages will develop simultaneously; **b** the condition of having two foetuses of different ages developing simultaneously in one uterus. **2** *bot* the fertilization of the same ovule by more than one kind of pollen. ⓒ 17c: from SUPER- 2 + Latin *fetus* a foetus.

superficial /suːpə'fɪʃəl/ ▷ *adj* **1** belonging or relating to, or on or near, the surface □ *a superficial wound*. **2** not thorough or in-depth; cursory □ *a superficial understanding*. **3** only apparent; not real or genuine □ *a superficial attempt to patch things up*. **4** lacking the capacity for sincere emotion or serious thought; shallow □ *a superficial person*. • **superficiality** *noun* (**superficialities**). • **superficially** *adverb*. • **superficialness** *noun*. ⓒ 14c: from Latin *superficies* surface.

superficial, superfluous

These words are sometimes confused with each other.

superfine ▷ *adj* **1** said of a product, etc: of very good quality. **2** said of someone, their attitude, behaviour, etc: over-refined, fastidiously elegant. ▷ *noun* (*usually* **superfines**) a commodity, especially cloth, that is of the highest quality. ⓒ 16c.

superfluidity ▷ *noun, physics* the property of flowing without friction or viscosity that the isotopes of liquid helium exhibit at certain low temperatures. ⓒ 1930s.

superfluity /suːpə'fluːɪtɪ, sjuː-/ ▷ *noun* (**superfluities**) **1** the state or fact of being superfluous. **2** something that is superfluous. **3** excess. ⓒ 14c: from SUPER- 2 + Latin *fluere* to flow.

superfluous /sʊ'pɜːflʊəs, sjʊ-/ ▷ *adj* **1** more than is needed or wanted. **2** (*sometimes* **superfluous to**

something) surplus; not or no longer needed □ *The six workers were superfluous* □ *Six workers were superfluous to their requirements.* • **superfluously** *adverb.* • **superfluousness** *noun.* ⓒ 15c: from Latin *superfluus* overflowing, from SUPER- 2.

super flyweight ▷ *noun, boxing, etc* a boxer weighing up to a maximum of 52 kg (115 lb).

supergiant ▷ *noun* a bright star that is enormous in size and low in density, such as Betelgeuse and Antares. ⓒ 1920s.

superglue ▷ *noun* a type of quick-acting extra strong adhesive. ▷ *verb* to bond something with superglue.

supergrass ▷ *noun, slang* someone who gives the police so much information that a large number of arrests follow, often in return for their own immunity or so that they will face lesser charges. ⓒ 1970s.

supergroup ▷ *noun* **1** a band, such as Queen, U2, The Grateful Dead, etc, that has great critical and usually financial success and which attracts huge audiences to their live gigs. **2** a band that is formed, usually temporarily, sometimes for a special purpose, for example to give a charity performance, which consists of famous rock musicians who do not normally play together. ⓒ 1970s.

superhero ▷ *noun* a character in a film, novel, cartoon, comic, etc that has extraordinary powers, especially for saving the world from disaster. ⓒ Early 20c.

superheterodyne /suːpəˈhɛtərədaɪn/ ▷ *adj, radio* denoting a radio receiver in which the frequency of the incoming signal is reduced by mixing it with another signal that is generated inside the receiver, making the resulting intermediate frequency easier to amplify and manipulate than the initial frequency. ▷ *noun* a radio receiver of this type. ⓒ 1920s.

super high frequency ▷ *noun, radio* (abbreviation **SHF**) a radio frequency in the range 3 000 to 30 000MHz. ⓒ 1940s.

superhighway ▷ *noun, US* **1** a wide road, with at least two carriageways going in either direction, that is meant for fast-moving traffic. **2** (*in full* **information superhighway**) electronic telecommunication systems collectively such as telephone links, cable and satellite TV, and computer networks, especially THE INTERNET, over which information in various digital forms can be transferred rapidly. ⓒ 1990s in sense 2; 1920s in sense 1.

superhuman ▷ *adj* beyond ordinary human power, ability, knowledge, etc. ⓒ 17c.

superimpose ▷ *verb* (*usually* **superimpose something on something else**) to lay or set (one thing) on top of another. • **superimposed** *adj* □ *a superimposed image.* • **superimposition** *noun.* ⓒ 18c.

superintend ▷ *verb* (***superintended, superintending***) *tr & intr* to look after and manage someone or something; to supervise. • **superintendence** or **superintendency** *noun.* ⓒ 17c: from Latin *superintendere.*

superintendent ▷ *noun* **1 a** *Brit* a police officer above the rank of chief inspector. Often shortened to SUPER; **b** *US* a high ranking police officer, especially a chief of police. **2** someone whose job is to look after and manage, eg a department, a group of workers, etc. **3** *N Amer* someone whose job is to act as caretaker of a building. • **superintendentship** *noun.*

superior /sʊˈpɪərɪə(r)/ ▷ *adj* (*often* **superior to someone** or **something**) **1** better in some way. **2** higher in rank or position □ *reported him to his superior officer* □ *Mother Superior.* **3** of high quality □ *a superior grade of flour.* **4** arrogant; self-important. **5** *printing* said of a character: set above the level of the line; superscript. **6** *bot* **a** said of a calyx: growing above the ovary; **b** said of an ovary: growing above the calyx. **7** *zool* said of a body part: growing or lying above (another body part) □ *the superior maxilliary.* ▷ *noun* **1** someone who is of higher rank or position. **2** the head of a religious community. **3** the feudal lord of a VASSAL. ⓒ 14c: Latin, literally 'higher'.

superiority /sʊpɪərɪˈɒrɪtɪ/ ▷ *noun* **1** the condition of being better, higher, greater than someone or something else. **2** pre-eminence □ *His lecture demonstrated his superiority in his field.*

superiority complex ▷ *noun, psychol* an over-inflated opinion of one's self-worth or status in relation to others which usually manifests in aggressively arrogant behaviour and which can often be a self-defensive response to feelings of inadequacy. Compare INFERIORITY COMPLEX sense1. ⓒ 1920s.

superior planet ▷ *noun, astron* any of the six planets, Mars, Jupiter, Saturn, Uranus, Neptune and Pluto, whose orbits around the Sun lie outside that of the Earth. ⓒ 16c.

superl. ▷ *abbreviation* superlative.

superlative /sʊˈpɜːlətɪv, sjʊ-/ ▷ *adj* **1** *grammar* said of adjectives or adverbs: expressing the highest degree of a particular quality, eg *nicest, prettiest, best, most beautiful, most recently.* **2** superior to all others; supreme. ▷ *noun, grammar* **1** a superlative adjective or adverb. **2** the superlative form of a word. Compare POSITIVE, COMPARATIVE 4. • **superlatively** *adverb.* • **superlativeness** *noun.* ⓒ 14c: from Latin *superlativus.*

superluminal /suːpəˈluːmɪnəl, sjuː-, -ljuːmɪnəl/ ▷ *adj* travelling at or having a speed that is greater than the speed of light. ⓒ 1950s.

superman ▷ *noun* **1** *philos* in NIETZSCHEAN terms: an ideal man as he will have evolved in the future, especially in having extraordinary strength, power, ability, etc. **2 a** (*often* **Superman**) a fictional character who can change from being a newspaper reporter to someone with superhuman powers, eg the ability to fly, which he uses to save people from danger and to fight evil and who is easily recognizable from his red and blue caped costume; **b** someone who has or thinks he has such exceptional powers □ *Get someone else to do it — you're not Superman, you know.* ⓒ Early 20c, from G B Shaw's *Man and Superman* (1903), although F W Nietzsche's term *Übermensch* is late 19c.

supermarket ▷ *noun* a large self-service store that sells food, household goods, etc. ⓒ 1920s.

super-middleweight see under MIDDLEWEIGHT

supermodel ▷ *noun* an extremely highly-paid female fashion model. ⓒ 1980s: from SUPER- 3.

supermundane ▷ *adj* having an unearthly quality or qualities, especially in being elevated, spiritual, etc. ⓒ 17c: from SUPER- 2.

supernatant /suːpəˈneɪtənt, sjuː-/ ▷ *adj* said of a liquid: swimming or floating on the surface of another liquid, a precipitate, sediment, etc. ▷ *noun, chem* a liquid of this kind. ⓒ 17c: from SUPER- 2 + Latin *natare* to swim, float.

supernatural ▷ *adj* **1** belonging or relating to or being phenomena that cannot be explained by the laws of nature or physics. **2** (**the supernatural**) the world of unexplained phenomena. • **supernaturalism** *noun.* • **supernaturalist** *noun.* • **supernaturally** *adverb.* ⓒ 16c: from Latin *supernaturalis,* from *natura* nature.

supernaturalize or **supernaturalise** ▷ *verb* to make someone or something supernatural or to give or attribute supernatural qualities to them or it.

supernova /suːpəˈnoʊvə, sjuː-/ ▷ *noun* (***supernovae*** /-viː/ or ***supernovas***) *astron* **1** a vast stellar explosion which takes a few days to complete and which results in the star becoming temporarily millions of times brighter than it was. It has two possible causes, one being a core implosion in a neutron star or BLACK HOLE at the end of its life and the other originating from WHITE DWARF components of paired stars. **2** a star that undergoes an explosion of either type. ⓒ 1930s.

supernumerary /suːpəˈnjuːmərərɪ, sjuː-/ ▷ *adj* additional to the normal or required number; extra. ▷ *noun* (***supernumeraries***) **1** someone or something that is extra or surplus to requirements. **2** an actor who does not have a speaking part. Often shortened to SUPER (*noun* 3). **3** someone who is not part of the regular staff, but who can be called on to work or serve, eg in the army or navy, when necessary. ⓒ 17c: from Latin *supernumerarius* the soldiers added to a legion after it is complete.

superordinate ▷ *adj* of higher grade, status, importance, etc. ▷ *noun* someone or something that is of higher grade, status, importance, etc. ⓒ 17c.

superoxide ▷ *noun, chem* **1** any of various chemical compounds that are very powerful oxidizing agents and contain the O_2^- ion, which is highly toxic to living tissues. **2** any oxide that reacts with hydrogen ions to form hydrogen peroxide and oxygen. ⓒ 1940s.

superphosphate ▷ *noun, chem* the most important type of phosphate fertilizer, made by treating calcium phosphate in the form of the mineral apatite, bone ash, or slag with sulphuric acid (which yields a fertilizer containing 16 to 20 per cent phosphorus) or phosphoric acid (which yields a fertilizer containing 45 to 50 per cent phosphorus). ⓒ 18c.

superphysical ▷ *adj* incapable of being explained in terms of physical causes. ⓒ 17c.

superpower ▷ *noun* a nation or state that has outstanding political, economic or military influence, especially the USA or the former USSR. ⓒ 1930s.

superscribe /suːpəˈskraɪb, sjuː-/ ▷ *verb* (***superscribed, superscribing***) **1** to write or engrave above something. **2** to address a letter. **3** to put one's name at the top of (a letter or other document). • **superscription** *noun*. ⓒ 16c: from Latin *super* above + *scribere* to write.

superscript *printing* ▷ *adj* said of a character: set above the level of the line that the other characters sit on, eg the number 2 in 10^2. ▷ *noun* a superscript character. ⓒ 19c: from Latin *super* above + *scribere* to write.

supersede /suːpəˈsiːd, sjuː-/ ▷ *verb* (***superseded, superseding***) **1** to take the place of (something, especially something outdated or no longer valid) □ ***CD-ROMs will supersede many reference books.*** **2** to adopt, appoint or promote in favour of another. • **supersedence** *noun*. • **superseder** *noun*. • **supersession** *noun*. ⓒ 15c: from Latin *super* above + *sedere* to sit.

supersonic ▷ *adj* **1** faster than the speed of sound. **2** said of aircraft: able to travel at supersonic speeds. • **supersonically** *adverb*. Compare INFRASONIC, SUBSONIC, ULTRASONIC. ⓒ 1930s; early 20c, meaning 'ULTRASONIC'.

superstar ▷ *noun* an internationally famous celebrity, especially from the world of film, popular music or sport. • **superstardom** *noun*. ⓒ 1920s.

superstition /suːpəˈstɪʃən, sjuː-/ ▷ *noun* **1** belief in an influence that certain (especially commonplace) objects, actions or occurrences have on events, people's lives, etc. **2** a particular opinion or practice based on such belief. **3** any widely held but unfounded belief. • **superstitious** *adj*. • **superstitiously** *adverb*. • **superstitiousness** *noun*. ⓒ 15c: from Latin *superstitio, -onis*.

superstore ▷ *noun* **1** a very large supermarket that often sells clothes, etc as well as food and household goods and which is usually sited away from the centre of town. **2** a very large store that sells a specified type of goods such as DIY products, electrical products, furniture, etc. ⓒ 1960s.

superstructure ▷ *noun* **1** a building thought of in terms of it being above its foundations. **2** anything that is based on or built above another, usually more important, part, eg those parts of a ship above the main deck. Compare INFRASTRUCTURE. • **superstructural** *adj*. ⓒ 17c.

supertanker ▷ *noun* a large ship for transporting oil or other liquid. ⓒ 1920s.

supertax ▷ *noun, colloq* a surtax. ⓒ Early 20c.

supertonic ▷ *noun, music* the note that is immediately above the TONIC. ⓒ Early 19c.

supervene /suːpəˈviːn, sjuː-/ ▷ *verb* (***supervened, supervening***) *intr* to occur as an interruption to some process, especially unexpectedly. • **supervention** /–ˈvɛnʃən/ *noun*. ⓒ 17c: from Latin *supervenire*.

supervise /ˈsuːpəvaɪz, ˈsjuː-/ ▷ *verb* (***supervised, supervising***) **1** to be in overall charge of (employees, etc). **2** to oversee (a task, project, etc). • **supervision** *noun*. ⓒ 16c: from Latin *supervidere*, from *super* over + *videre, visum* to see.

supervisor ▷ *noun* **1** someone who supervises. **2** someone whose job is to be in overall charge of (employees, etc); someone whose job is to oversee (a task, project, etc). **3** *Brit* someone whose job is to encourage and help a postgraduate student in their research. • **supervisory** *noun*.

superwoman ▷ *noun, colloq* a woman of exceptional ability, especially one who manages to successfully combine having a career and being a wife and mother. ⓒ 1970s in this sense, although an earlier sense of a feminized version of SUPERMAN sense 1 dates from the early 20c: from *Superwoman* (1976), the book written by Shirley Conran.

supinator /ˈsuːpɪneɪtə(r), ˈsjuː-/ ▷ *noun, anatomy* a muscle in the forearm or foreleg that allows the hand or foot to turn and face upwards. ⓒ 17c: from Latin *supinare, supinatum* to turn (the hand or foot) downwards.

supine /ˈsuːpaɪn, ˈsjuː-/ ▷ *adj* **1** lying on one's back. **2** passive. **3** lazy. ▷ *noun, grammar* said of a verbal noun in Latin: one of two forms that denote either purpose or motion. • **supinely** *adverb*. • **supineness** *noun*. ⓒ 16c: from Latin *supinus* lying face up.

supp. and **suppl.** ▷ *abbreviation* supplement.

supped *past tense, past participle of* SUP[1], SUP[2]

supper /ˈsʌpə(r)/ ▷ *noun* **1** an evening meal, especially a light one. **2** a late-night snack that usually consists of a drink, eg tea, cocoa, etc and toast, biscuits, etc that is taken just before bedtime and in addition to the main evening meal. • **supperless** *adj*. ⓒ 13c: from French *soper* supper.

supping *present participle of* SUP[1], SUP[2]

supplant /səˈplɑːnt/ ▷ *verb* (***supplanted, supplanting***) to take the place of someone, often by force or unfair means. • **supplantation** /sʌplɑːnˈteɪʃən/ *noun*. • **supplanter** *noun*. ⓒ 13c: from Latin *supplantare* to trip up, from *planta* sole of the foot.

supple /ˈsʌpəl/ ▷ *adj* (***suppler, supplest***) **1** said of a person, their joints, etc: bending easily; flexible. **2** said of a person's attitude, nature, etc: compliant; easily talked round to another's way of thinking. • **supplely** *adverb*. • **suppleness** *noun*. ⓒ 13c: French, from Latin *supplex* bending under.

supplement /ˈsʌpləmənt/ ▷ *noun* **1** something that is added to make something else complete or that makes up a deficiency □ ***vitamin supplement.*** **2** an extra section added to a book to give additional information or to correct previous errors. **3 a** a separate part that comes with a newspaper, especially a Sunday one; **b** a separate part that comes with a magazine, especially one that covers a specific topic. **4** an additional charge for a specified service, etc. **5** *math* the amount by which an angle or arc is less than 180°. ▷ *verb* (***supplemented, supplementing***) (*often* **supplement by** or **with something**) to add to something; to make up a lack of something. • **supplemental** *adj*. • **supplementally** *adverb*. • **supplementation** *noun* ⓒ 14c: from Latin *supplementum* a filling up, from *supplere* to supply.

supplementary /sʌpləˈmɛntərɪ/ ▷ *adj* additional; acting as or forming a supplement □ ***The tie in the quiz***

was resolved by a supplementary question. • **supplementarily** *adverb.*

supplementary angle ▷ *noun* one of a pair of angles whose sum is 180 degrees. Compare CONJUGATE ANGLE, COMPLEMENTARY ANGLE.

supplementary benefit ▷ *noun, Brit* a state allowance that was paid weekly to people on very low incomes in order to bring them up to a certain agreed level, replaced by INCOME SUPPORT in 1988.

suppletion /sə'pli:ʃən/ ▷ *noun, linguistics* an instance of or the fact of completing a grammatical paradigm or conjugation with a form that is etymologically unrelated to the base form, eg *went* in the series *go / goes / going / went / gone*, or *better* and *best* in *good, / better/ best.*

suppliant /'sʌplɪənt/ ▷ *adj* expressing or involving humble entreaty. ▷ *noun* someone who makes a humble entreaty. • **suppliance** *noun.* • **suppliantly** *adverb.* ⓘ 15c: French, from *suplier* to supply.

supplicate /'sʌplɪkeɪt/ ▷ *verb* (***supplicated, supplicating***) *tr & intr* **1** (*usually* **supplicate for something**) to humbly and earnestly request it. **2** (*usually* **supplicate someone for something**) to humbly and earnestly request them for it. • **supplicant** *noun.* • **supplicating** *adj.* • **supplicatingly** *adverb.* • **supplication** *noun.* • **supplicatory** *adj.* ⓘ 15c: from Latin *supplicare, supplicatum* to kneel, from *supplex* bending under.

supply /sə'plaɪ/ ▷ *verb* (***supplies, supplied, supplying***) **1 a** to provide or furnish (something believed to be necessary) □ *I'll supply the wine if you bring some beers*; **b** (*also* **supply someone with something**) to provide or furnish them with it □ *The garden supplied them with all their vegetables.* **2** to satisfy (something, eg a need); to make up (something, eg a deficiency). **3** *intr* said especially of a teacher or minister: to act as a temporary substitute. ▷ *noun* (***supplies***) **1** an act or instance of providing. **2** an amount provided, especially regularly. **3** an amount that can be drawn from and used; a stock. **4** (**supplies**) necessary food, equipment, etc that is stored, gathered, taken on a journey, etc. **5** a source, eg of water, electricity, gas, etc □ *cut off their gas supply.* **6** *econ* the total amount of a commodity that is produced and available for sale. Compare DEMAND *noun* 4. **7** someone, especially a teacher or minister, who acts as a temporary substitute. • **supplier** *noun.* • **in short supply** see under SHORT. ⓘ 14c: from French *soupleer*, from Latin *supplere* to fill up.

supply-side ▷ *adj, econ* applied to a type of policy that advocates low taxation in the belief that this will stimulate demand and increase the incentives to produce and invest more □ *supply-side economics.* • **supply-sider** *noun.* ⓘ 1970s.

support /sə'pɔːt/ ▷ *verb* (***supported, supporting***) **1** to keep something upright or in place. **2** to keep from falling. **3** to bear the weight of someone or something. **4** to give active approval, encouragement, money, etc to (an institution, belief, theory, etc); to advocate something. **5** to provide someone or something with the means necessary for living or existing □ *She supports a large family* □ *a salary that allows her to support a lavish lifestyle.* **6** to maintain a loyal and active interest in the fortunes of (a particular sport or team), eg by attending matches regularly. **7** to reinforce the accuracy or validity of (eg a theory, claim, etc) □ *The evidence supports the prosecution's case.* **8** to speak in favour of (a proposal, etc). **9** to play a part subordinate to (a leading actor). **10** to perform before (the main item in a concert, show, etc) □ *is supporting Aztec Camera.* **11** *computing* said of a computer, an operating system, etc: to allow for the use of (a specified language, program, etc). **12** to bear or tolerate something. ▷ *noun* **1** the act of supporting; the state of being supported. **2** someone or something that supports. **3** someone or something that helps, comforts, etc. **4 a** (*often* **the support**) a group, singer, film, etc that accompanies or comes on before the main attraction □ *The support was better than the main act*; **b** *as adj* □ *a different support band each night.* **5** *medicine* **a** something that is designed to take the strain off an injured or weak body part □ *a surgical support*; **b** *as adj* □ *support tights.* • **supportable** *adj.* • **supportability** *noun.* • **supportably** *adverb.* • **supporting** *adj, noun.* • **supportless** *adj.* • **in support of someone** or **something** advocating them or it; in favour, approval, etc of them or it; corroborating or reinforcing (an argument, theory, etc). ⓘ 14c: from French *supporter*, from Latin *supportare* to convey.

supporter ▷ *noun* **1** someone who is in favour of a cause, proposal, etc. **2** someone who gives a specified institution such as a sport, a team, a political party, etc their active backing, approval, promotion, etc □ *football supporters.*

support group ▷ *noun* **1** a collection of people who get together voluntarily with the aim of helping each other overcome a common specified trauma, difficulty, disease, etc. **2** a band that comes on before the main act at a live concert.

supportive ▷ *adj* providing support, especially active approval, encouragement, backing, etc □ *a bank that is supportive to new businesses.* • **supportively** *adverb.* • **supportiveness** *noun.*

suppose /sə'poʊz/ ▷ *verb* (***supposed, supposing***) **1** to consider something likely, even when there is a lack of tangible evidence for it to be so. **2** to think, believe, agree, etc reluctantly, unwillingly (that something could be true). **3** to assume, often wrongly □ *He supposed she wouldn't find out.* **4** (*often* **let us suppose**) to treat something as a fact for the purposes of forming an argument or plan □ *Let's suppose he's not coming.* **5** said of a theory, proposition, policy, etc: to require (some vital factor or assumption) to be the case before it can work, be valid, etc □ *Your idea for expansion supposes more money to be available.* • **supposable** *adj.* • **supposably** *adverb.* • **supposer** *noun.* • **supposing** *noun.* • **be supposed to be** or **do something** to be expected or allowed to be or do it □ *You're supposed to be an adult* □ *You were supposed to be here an hour ago* □ *You're not supposed to wear makeup to school.* • **I suppose so** an expression of reluctant agreement. • **just suppose ...?** or **(just) supposing ...?** What if ...?; How about ...? ⓘ 14c: from French *supposer*, from Latin *supponere* to place below.

supposed /sə'poʊzd, -zɪd/ ▷ *adj* generally believed to be so or true, but considered doubtful by the speaker □ *couldn't find him at his supposed address.* • **supposedly** /-zɪdlɪ/ *adverb.*

supposition /sʌpə'zɪʃən/ ▷ *noun* **1** the act of supposing. **2** something that is supposed; a mere possibility or assumption. **3** conjecture. • **suppositional** *adj.* • **suppositionally** *adverb.*

suppositious /sʌpə'zɪʃəs/ ▷ *adj* based on supposition; hypothetical. • **suppositiously** *adverb.* • **suppositiousness** *noun.*

suppository /sə'pɒzɪtərɪ/ ▷ *noun* (***suppositories***) *medicine* a soluble preparation of medicine that remains solid at room temperature, but which dissolves when it is inserted into the rectum (*in full* a **rectal suppository**) or into the vagina (*in full* a **vaginal suppository**), where its active ingredients are then released. ⓘ 14c: from Latin *suppositorium*, from *supponere* to place underneath.

suppress /sə'prɛs/ ▷ *verb* (***suppresses, suppressed, suppressing***) **1** to hold back or restrain (feelings, laughter, a yawn, etc). **2** to put a stop to something. **3** to crush (eg a rebellion). **4** to prevent (information, news, etc) from being broadcast, from circulating or from otherwise being made known. **5** to moderate or eliminate (interference) in an electrical device. **6** *psychol* to keep (a thought, memory, desire, etc) out of one's conscious mind. Compare REPRESS. • **suppressible** *adj.* • **suppressed** *adj.* • **suppressedly** /-sɪdlɪ/ *adverb.* • **suppression** *noun.* • **suppressive** *adj.* • **suppressively**

adverb. ⓒ 14c: from Latin *supprimere, suppressum* to restrain, from *premere* to press down.

suppressant ▻ *noun* a substance that suppresses or restrains, eg a drug that suppresses the appetite.

suppressor ▻ *noun* someone or something that suppresses something, especially a device for suppressing electrical interference.

suppurate /ˈsʌpjʊəreɪt/ ▻ *verb* (***suppurated, suppurating***) *intr* said of a wound, boil, cyst, ulcer, etc: to gather and release pus; to fester; to come to a head. • **suppurated** *adj.* • **suppuration** *noun.* • **suppurative** *adj.* ⓒ 16c: from Latin *suppurare, suppuratum,* from *pus* pus.

Supr. ▻ *abbreviation* Supreme.

supra /ˈsuːprə, ˈsjuː-/ ▻ *adverb* above, especially further up the page or earlier in the book. ⓒ 15c: Latin, meaning 'above'.

supra- /ˈsuːprə, sjuː-/ ▻ *prefix, denoting* above or beyond □ *supranational.* ⓒ Latin, meaning 'above'.

supramaxillary ▻ *adj* belonging or relating to the upper jaw.

supramundane ▻ *adj* above the world; beyond what is considered earthly.

supranational ▻ *adj* **1** belonging to or involving more than one nation. **2** said of authority, influence, etc: having the power to override national sovereignty.

supraorbital ▻ *adj, anatomy* said of a vein, artery, bone, nerve, etc: situated or occurring above the ORBIT of the eye.

suprarenal ▻ *adj, anatomy* situated above the kidney.

suprarenal gland ▻ *noun* ADRENAL GLAND.

supremacist /sʊˈprɛməsɪst, sjʊ-/ ▻ *noun* someone who promotes or advocates the belief that a particular group is in some way superior to all others, eg on grounds of race, gender, etc □ *white supremacist.* • **supremacism** *noun.* ⓒ 1940s.

supremacy /sʊˈprɛməsɪ, sjʊ-/ ▻ *noun* **1** supreme power or authority. **2** the state or quality of being supreme. ⓒ 16c.

supreme /sʊˈpriːm, sjʊ-/ ▻ *adj* **1** highest in rank, power, importance, etc; greatest □ *the Supreme Court.* **2** most excellent; best □ *supreme effort.* **3** greatest in degree; utmost □ *supreme stupidity.* • **supremely** *adverb.* • **supremeness** *noun.* ⓒ 16c: from Latin *supremus* highest, from *super* above.

suprême or **supreme** /sʊˈpriːm, sjʊ-, sʊˈprɛm/ ▻ *noun* **1** the boneless breast of a chicken or game bird with the wing still attached. **2 a** (*in full* **suprême sauce**) a rich VELOUTÉ sauce that has concentrated chicken consommé, butter and cream added to it, often served with chicken; **b** a dish, usually of chicken, coated in this kind of sauce □ *chicken suprême* □ *suprême of chicken.* ⓒ Early 19c: French, from Latin *supremus,* from *super* above.

Supreme Court or **supreme court** ▻ *noun* the highest court in a country, state, etc.

supreme sacrifice ▻ *noun, euphemistic old use* the act or an instance of someone giving up their life for their country, especially on the battlefield □ *Hugh made the supreme sacrifice on Flanders Field.*

Supreme Soviet ▻ *noun* in the former USSR: **1** the highest national ruling body **2** the national ruling body of one of the republics.

supremo /sʊˈpriːmoʊ, sjʊ-/ ▻ *noun* (***supremos***) *colloq* **1** a supreme head or leader. **2** a boss. ⓒ 1930s: from Spanish *generalísimo supremo* supreme general.

Supt. ▻ *abbreviation* Superintendent.

suq see SOUK

sur-[1] ▻ *prefix, signifying* over, above or beyond □ *surreal.* ⓒ From French *sur.*

sur-[2] ▻ *prefix* a form of SUB- that is used before some words beginning with *r* □ *surrogate.*

sura or **surah** /ˈsʊərə/ ▻ *noun* (***suras*** or ***surahs***) any one of the 114 chapters of the Koran. ⓒ 17c: from Arabic *surah* a rung or step.

surah /ˈsʊərə/ ▻ *noun* a soft twilled silk that is used in making dresses, blouses, scarves, etc. ⓒ 19c: from the French pronunciation of Surat, a port in W India famous for the manufacture of textiles.

sural /ˈsʊərəl/ ▻ *adj* belonging or relating to the calf of the leg □ *sural muscles.* ⓒ 17c: from Latin *suralis,* from *sura* calf.

surbahar /ˈsɜːbəhɑː(r)/ ▻ *noun* an Indian stringed instrument that is similar to the SITAR but larger. ⓒ 19c: the Bengali name for this instrument.

surbase /ˈsɜːbeɪs/ ▻ *noun, archit* an upper series of mouldings on a pedestal, skirting board, etc. ⓒ 17c.

surcharge /ˈsɜːtʃɑːdʒ/ ▻ *noun* **1** an extra charge, often as a penalty for late payment of a bill. **2** an alteration printed on or over something, especially a new valuation on a stamp. **3** an amount over a permitted load. ▻ *verb* **1** to impose a surcharge on someone. **2** to print a surcharge on or over something. **3** to overload something. **4** to saturate or fill something to excess. • **surcharged** *adj.* • **surcharger** *noun.* • **surchargement** *noun.* ⓒ 15c: from French *surcharger.*

surcingle /ˈsɜːsɪŋgəl/ ▻ *noun* a strap fastened round a horse's body to keep a blanket, pack, saddle, etc in place on its back. ⓒ 14c: from French *surcengle,* from Latin *cingere* to gird.

surd /sɜːd/ *math* ▻ *adj* said of a number: unable to be expressed in finite terms; irrational. ▻ *noun* **1** an IRRATIONAL NUMBER that is a root of a RATIONAL NUMBER, so can never be determined exactly, eg $\sqrt{3}$. **2** an arithmetic expression involving the sum or difference of such numbers, eg $\sqrt{3} + \sqrt{6}$. ⓒ 16c: from Latin *surdus* deaf.

sure /ʃʊə(r), ʃɔː(r)/ ▻ *adj* (***surer, surest***) **1** confident beyond doubt in one's belief or knowledge; convinced □ *felt sure he'd picked up the keys.* **2** undoubtedly true or accurate □ *a sure sign.* **3** reliably stable or secure □ *on a sure footing.* ▻ *adverb, colloq* certainly; of course. • **as sure as eggs is** or **are eggs** without the remotest doubt. • **as sure as fate** or **sure as fate** inevitably □ *put the washing out and, as sure as fate, down came the rain.* • **be sure and** to make certain to (do something) □ *Be sure and phone when you get there.* • **be sure of something** to be unquestionably certain or assured of it □ *wanted to be sure of the train times.* • **be** or **feel sure** or **very, so,** *etc* **sure of oneself** to act in a very self-confident way. • **be sure that** to be convinced that □ *I was sure that we'd agreed to meet on Friday.* • **be sure to** to be guaranteed or certain to (happen, etc) □ *Whenever we plan a picnic it's sure to rain.* • **for sure** *colloq* definitely; undoubtedly. • **make sure** to take the necessary action to remove all doubt or risk. • **sure enough** *colloq* in fact; as was expected. • **to be sure** certainly; admittedly. • **surenesss** *noun.* ⓒ 14c: from French *sur,* from Latin *securus* without care.

sure-fire ▻ *adj, colloq* destined to succeed; infallible.

sure-footed ▻ *adj* **1** not stumbling or likely to stumble. **2** not making, or not likely to make, mistakes. • **sure-footedly** *adverb.* • **sure-footedness** *noun.*

surely ▻ *adverb* **1** without doubt; certainly. **2** used in questions and exclamations: to express incredulous disbelief □ *Surely you knew he was just joking?* • **slowly but surely** slowly and steadily; inevitably.

sure thing ▻ *noun* something that is guaranteed to succeed. ▻ *exclamation* used to express spontaneous, enthusiastic, delighted, etc agreement □ *Sure thing! I'll be over in ten minutes!*

surety /ˈʃʊərətɪ/ ▻ *noun* (***sureties***) **1** someone who agrees to become legally responsible for another person's behaviour, debts, etc. **2 a** security, usually in the form of a sum of money, against loss, damage, etc or as a guarantee that a promise will be kept, eg that someone will turn up at court when they are supposed to; **b** something that is given to act as this type of security. • **stand surety for someone** to act as a surety for them. ◷ 14c: from French *surte*, from Latin *securus* without care.

surf ▻ *noun* **1** the sea as it breaks against the shore, a reef, etc. **2** the foam produced by breaking waves. **3** an act or instance of surfing. ▻ *verb* (***surfed, surfing***) **1** *intr* to take part in a sport or recreation where the object is to stand or lie on a long narrow board, try to catch the crest of a wave and ride it to the shore. **2** to browse through (the Internet) randomly. **3** *intr in compounds* to browse or flick through something randomly ◻ *channel-surf*. **4** *intr slang* to travel on the outside of a train. • **surfer** *noun* **1** someone who goes surfing. **2** someone who browses on the Internet. • **surfing** *noun* **1** the sport or recreation of riding a surfboard along on the crests of large breaking waves. **2** browsing on the Internet. • **surfy** *adj.* ◷ Early 20c as *verb* 1; 17c as *noun* 1, 2.

surface /'sɜːfɪs/ ▻ *noun* **1 a** the upper or outer side of anything, often with regard to texture or appearance; **b** the size or area of such a side. **2** the upper level of a body or container of liquid or of the land. **3** the external appearance of something, as opposed to its underlying reality ◻ *On the surface everything seems fine.* **4** *math* a geometric figure that is two-dimensional, having length and breadth but no depth. **5** *as adj* **a** at, on or relating to a surface ◻ *surface mail*; **b** superficial ◻ *surface appearances*. ▻ *verb* (***surfaced, surfacing***) **1** *intr* to rise to the surface of a liquid. **2** *intr* to become apparent; to come to light ◻ *The scandal first surfaced in the press.* **3** *intr, colloq* to get out of bed ◻ *never surfaces till the afternoon.* **4** to give the desired finish or texture to the surface of something. • **surfaced** *adj.* • **surfacer** *noun.* • **surfacing** *noun.* • **come to the surface 1** to rise to the top (of a liquid, body of water, etc) ◻ *The seal came to the surface for air.* **2** to become known, especially after having been hidden ◻ *The press made sure the scandal came to the surface.* • **scratch the surface 1** to begin to have a superficial understanding of or effect on something ◻ *measures that only scratch the surface of the drugs problem.* **2** to begin to investigate ◻ *You only need to scratch the surface to discover the sleaze.* ◷ 17c: French, from *sur* on + *face* face.

surface-active ▻ *adj, chem* said of a substance such as a detergent: capable of affecting the wetting or surface tension properties of a liquid. See also SURFACTANT. ◷ 1920s.

surface mail ▻ *noun* mail that is sent overland or by ship, as opposed to AIRMAIL.

surface noise ▻ *noun* undesirable and detrimental sounds that can be heard when a record is being played on slightly faulty equipment, eg a worn needle, or when the record itself is slightly damaged, eg with irregularities in the grooves.

surface structure ▻ *noun, grammar* in Chomskyan terms: a way of describing the syntactic elements of a sentence so that they can be put into a spoken or written form. Compare DEEP STRUCTURE. ◷ 1960s.

surface tension ▻ *noun, physics* the film-like tension on the surface of a liquid that is caused by the cohesion of its particles, which has the effect of minimizing its surface area. See also CAPILLARITY.

surface-to-air ▻ *adj, military* said of a rocket, missile, etc: designed to be launched from a base on the ground and fired at a target in the sky.

surface-to-surface ▻ *adj, military* said of a rocket, missile, etc: designed to be launched from a base on the ground and fired at a target that is also on the ground.

surface water ▻ *noun* water that is lying on a surface such as a road.

surfactant /sɜː'faktənt/ ▻ *noun, chem* **1** any soluble substance, such as a detergent, wetting agent, emulsifier, foaming agent, etc, that reduces the surface tension of a liquid, or reduces the surface tension between two liquids or between a solid and a liquid. **2** *zool* a substance secreted by the cells lining the alveoli of the lungs that prevents the walls of the alveoli from sticking together and the lungs from collapsing. ◷ 1950s: from *surface* + *active*.

surfbird ▻ *noun, N Amer* a Pacific shore bird related to the sandpiper.

surfboard ▻ *noun* a long narrow shaped fibreglass board that a surfer stands or lies on. ▻ *verb* to ride on a surfboard. • **surfboarder** *noun.* • **surboarding** *noun.* ◷ 1930s.

surfcasting ▻ *noun, angling* a form of fishing from the shore that involves casting into surf.

surfeit /'sɜːfɪt/ ▻ *noun* **1** (*usually* **surfeit of something**) an excess. **2** the stuffed or sickened feeling that results from any excess, especially over-eating or over-drinking. ▻ *verb* (***surfeited, surfeiting***) to indulge, especially in an excess of food or drink, until stuffed or disgusted. • **surfeited** *adj.* ◷ 13c: from French *surfait* excess.

surfer see under SURF

surfing see under SURF

surf scoter /— 'skoʊtə(r)/ and **surf duck** ▻ *noun, N Amer* a large black diving sea duck which in the adult male is distinguished by two white patches on its head. ◷ 19c.

surge /sɜːdʒ/ ▻ *noun* **1** a sudden powerful mass movement of a crowd, especially forwards. **2** a sudden sharp increase, eg in prices, electrical current, etc. **3** a sudden, often uncontrolled, rush of emotion ◻ *felt a surge of indignation.* **4** a rising and falling of a large area of sea, without individual waves; a swell. ▻ *verb* (***surged, surging***) *intr* **1** said of the sea, waves, etc: to move up and down or swell with force. **2** said of a crowd, etc: to move forward in a mass. **3** (*also* **surge up**) said of an emotion, etc: to rise up suddenly and often uncontrollably ◻ *sorrow surged up inside him.* **4** said of prices, electricity, etc: to increase, especially suddenly. **5** *naut* said of a rope wrapped around a capstan, etc: to slip back accidentally. • **surging** *adj, noun.* ◷ 15c: from Latin *surgere* to rise.

surgeon /'sɜːdʒən/ ▻ *noun* **1** a person who is professionally qualified to practise surgery. **2** a navy, army or military medical officer; a medical officer on board a ship. **3** *in compounds* a person qualified to treat something in the specified field ◻ *tree surgeon* ◻ *veterinary surgeon.* • **be** or **go under the surgeon's knife** to undergo a surgical operation. ◷ 14c: from French *surgien*; see also SURGERY.

surgeon fish ▻ *noun* a brightly coloured tropical marine fish that has spiny fins and knife-like appendages at its tail.

surgeon general ▻ *noun* (***surgeons general***) **1** *Brit, N Amer military* the chief medical officer in any of the services. **2** *US* the head of the Bureau of Public Health or of a state-level health service.

surgeon's knot ▻ *noun* a type of knot that is very similar to the REEF KNOT but with an extra twist at the start to prevent slippage and which is used in surgery for tying ligatures.

surgery /'sɜːdʒərɪ/ ▻ *noun* (***surgeries***) **1** the branch of medicine that is concerned with treating disease, disorder or injury by cutting into the patient's body to operate directly on or remove the affected part. **2** the performance or an instance of this type of treatment ◻ *The surgery took 10 hours.* **3** *Brit* **a** the place where a doctor, dentist, etc sees their patients and carries out treatment; **b** the time when they are available for consultation. **4** *Brit* **a** a place where a professional person such as an MP, lawyer, accountant, etc can be consulted, usually free of charge; **b** the time when they are available for consultation. Also *as* *adj* □ *during surgery hours.* ⓒ 14c: from French *surgerie*, from Latin *chirurgia*, from Greek *kheirurgia*, from *kheir* hand + *ergon* work.

surgical ▻ *adj* **1** belonging or relating to, involving, caused by, used in, or by means of surgery □ ***surgical instruments*** □ ***surgical fever.*** **2** said of a garment or appliance: designed to correct a deformity or to support a weak or injured body part □ ***surgical collar*** □ ***surgical boot.*** • **surgically** *adverb.*

surgical spirit ▻ *noun* methylated spirit that has small amounts of castor oil or oil of wintergreen, etc added to it and which is used for cleaning wounds and sterilizing medical equipment.

suricate /'sʊərɪkeɪt, 'sjʊ-/ ▻ *noun* a S African burrowing carnivore with a lemur-like face and four-toed feet. Also called **slender-tailed meerkat**. ⓒ 18c: from French *surikate.*

Surinamese /sʊərɪna'miːz, sjʊər-/ ▻ *adj* belonging or relating to Surinam, a republic on the NE Atlantic coast of S America, its inhabitants or their language. ▻ *noun* (***Surinamese***) a citizen, inhabitant of, or person born in, Surinam. ⓒ 1970s.

Surinam toad ▻ *noun* a PIPA.

surly /'sɜːlɪ/ ▻ *adj* (***surlier***, ***surliest***) grumpily bad-tempered; abrupt and impolite in manner or speech. • **surlily** *adverb.* • **surliness** *noun.* ⓒ 16c: from the obsolete *sirly*, meaning 'haughty', from SIR + -LY.

surmise /sə'maɪz/ ▻ *verb* (***surmised***, ***surmising***) to conclude something from the information available, especially when the information is incomplete or insubstantial. ▻ *noun* **1** a conclusion drawn from such information. **2** the act of drawing such a conclusion; conjecture. • **surmisable** *adj.* • **surmiser** *noun.* • **surmising** *noun.* ⓒ 15c: from French *surmettre* to accuse, from Latin *supermittere* accuse.

surmount /sə'maʊnt/ ▻ *verb* (***surmounted***, ***surmounting***) **1** to overcome (problems, obstacles, etc). **2** to be set on top of something; to crown. • **surmountable** *adj.* • **surmounted** *adj.* • **surmounter** *noun.* • **surmounting** *noun, adj.* ⓒ 14c: from French *surmonter*, from Latin *supermontare.*

surmullet /sə'mʌlɪt/ ▻ *noun* the red mullet. ⓒ 17c: from French *surmulet*, from *sor* reddish brown.

surname /'sɜːneɪm/ ▻ *noun* a family name or last name, as opposed to a forename or Christian name. Also called **last name**. ▻ *verb* (***surnamed***, ***surnaming***) **1** to give a specified last name. **2** to be called by a specified last name. ⓒ 14c: from SUR- + NAME 1, modelled on French *surnom.*

surpass /sə'pɑːs/ ▻ *verb* (***surpasses***, ***surpassed***, ***surpast***, ***surpassing***) **1** to go or be beyond in degree or extent; to exceed. **2** to be better than □ ***a holiday that surpassed all expectations.*** • **surpassable** *adj.* • **surpassed** *adj.* • **surpassing** *adj, noun.* ⓒ 16c: from French *surpasser* to pass over.

surplice /'sɜːplɪs/ ▻ *noun* a loose wide-sleeved white linen garment that is worn ceremonially by members of the clergy and choir singers over their robes. ⓒ 13c: from French *sourpeliz*, from Latin *superpellicium*, from *pellicia* fur coat.

surplus /'sɜːpləs/ ▻ *noun* (***surpluses***) **1 a** an amount that exceeds the amount required or used; an amount that is left over after requirements have been met; **b** *as adj* □ ***army surplus store.*** **2** *commerce* the amount by which a company's income is greater than expenditure. Compare DEFICIT. ▻ *adj* left over after needs have been met; extra. • **surplus to requirements 1** extra; in excess of what is needed. **2** *euphemistic* no longer needed or wanted. ⓒ 14c: French, from Latin *superplus*, from *plus* more.

surprise /sə'praɪz/ ▻ *noun* **1** a sudden, unexpected, astounding, amazing, etc event, factor, gift, etc. **2** a feeling of mental disorientation caused by something of this nature. **3 a** the act of catching someone unawares or off-guard; **b** the process of being caught unawares or off-guard. **4** *as adj* unexpected, sudden □ ***a surprise party.*** ▻ *verb* (***surprised***, ***surprising***) **1** to cause someone to experience surprise by presenting them with or subjecting them to something unexpected, amazing, etc □ ***surprised her with a kiss.*** **2** to come upon something or someone unexpectedly or catch unawares. **3** to capture or attack with a sudden unexpected manoeuvre. • **surpriser** *noun.* • **the surprise of one's life** a very big shock or surprise. • **surprise, surprise!** an exclamation indicating that something is or (*ironic*) is not a surprise. • **take someone by surprise** to catch them unawares or off-guard □ ***The news of the redundancies took everyone by surprise.*** ⓒ 15c: French, from *surprendre, surpris.*

surprised ▻ *adj* **1** taken unawares or off-guard. **2** shocked, startled, amazed. • **surprisedly** *adverb.* • **surprisedness** *noun.*

surprising ▻ *adj* unexpected, shocking or amazing; causing surprise □ ***a surprising number of people turned up.*** • **surprisingly** *adverb.* • **surprisingness** *noun.* • **be surprising** to be the source of shock, amazement, surprise, etc □ ***It's not surprising he's left her after what she did!***

surra /'sʊərə, 'sʌrə/ ▻ *noun* a tropical disease spread by horseflies, mainly affecting horses, but contractable by other domestic animals. It is characterized by fever, severe weight loss and anaemia, and is often fatal. ⓒ 19c: Marathi, meaning 'air breathed through the nostrils'.

surreal /sə'rɪəl/ ▻ *adj* **1** dreamlike; very odd or bizarre □ ***'Arizona Dream' is a totally surreal film.*** **2** being in the style of Surrealism □ ***Dali's surreal slithering watches.*** **3** (*usually* **the surreal**) a dreamlike world or state. • **surreality** /sərɪə'alɪtɪ/ *noun.* • **surreally** *adverb.* ⓒ 1930s: from SURREALISM.

surrealism /sə'rɪəlɪzəm/ ▻ *noun* **1** (*sometimes* **Surrealism**) a movement in art and literature that sprang up between the first and second World Wars, incorporating the nihilism of DADA. It was heavily influenced by FREUDIAN theories of psychoanalysis and its most prominent aim was to allow the artist's or writer's unconscious to be expressed with complete creative freedom. **2** an example of art or literature that has been influenced by or has a similarity to this movement. • **surrealist** *adj, noun.* • **surrealistic** *adj.* • **surrealistically** *adverb.* ⓒ Early 20c: from French *surréalisme*, first coined by the writer, Guillaume Apollinaire (1880–1918) in the notes to *Parade* in 1917.

surrender /sə'rɛndə(r)/ ▻ *verb* (***surrendered***, ***surrendering***) **1** *intr* **a** to accede or agree to an enemy's, the police's, etc demand for an end to resistance, hostilities, etc; **b** to admit defeat by giving oneself up to an enemy; to yield. **2** to give or hand over someone or something, either voluntarily or under duress □ ***weapons surrendered under the arms amnesty.*** **3** to lose or give up something □ ***surrendered all hope of being rescued.*** **4** to relinquish one's rights under an insurance policy and accept a smaller sum than the amount that would have been paid out had the policy been left to mature. ▻ *noun* an act, instance or the process of surrendering. • **surrenderer** *noun.* ⓒ 15c: from French *surrendre*, from *rendre* to give.

■ **surrender to something** to allow oneself to be influenced or overcome by a desire or emotion; to give in to it □ ***He surrendered to her beauty.***

surrender value ▻ *noun* said of an insurance policy: the amount that will be paid out if a policy is surrendered at a particular time before it matures.

surreptitious /sʌrəp'tɪʃəs/ ▻ *adj* secret, sneaky, clandestine, underhand. • **surreptitiously** *adverb.* • **surreptitiousness** *noun.* ⓒ 15c: from Latin *subreptitius*, from *sub* under + *rapere* to snatch.

surrey /'sʌrɪ/ ▻ *noun* (***surreys***) a type of four-wheeled horse-drawn carriage. ⓒ 19c: from *surrey cart*, named after the English county of Surrey where it was first made.

surrogate /ˈsʌrəgət/ ▷ *noun* someone or something that takes the place of or is substituted for another. • **surrogacy** or **surrogateship** *noun*. ⓘ 17c: from Latin *subrogare, subrogatum*, to substitute.

surrogate mother ▷ *noun* **1** a woman who carries and gives birth to a baby on behalf of another woman, especially one who becomes pregnant by artificial insemination with sperm from the other woman's partner or by the implantation of an egg taken from the other woman and fertilized *in vitro* with her partner's sperm. **2** a woman who acts as a mother to a child or children she did not give birth to.

surround /səˈraʊnd/ ▷ *verb* (***surrounded, surrounding***) to extend all around; to encircle. ▷ *noun* a border or edge, or an ornamental structure fitted round this. • **surrounding** *adj*. ⓘ 17c in the *verb* sense; 15c, meaning 'to overflow': from French *suronder* to overflow or abound, from Latin *undare* to rise in waves.

surrounded ▷ *adj* **1** encircled □ ***Give yourself up! We've got you surrounded!*** **2** (**surrounded by** or **with someone** or **something**) having it or them on all sides □ ***a house surrounded by beautiful scenery*** □ ***surrounded with rich and famous people.***

surroundings ▷ *plural noun* the places and/or things that are usually round about someone or something; environment □ ***preferred to live in rural surroundings.***

surround sound ▷ *noun* a system of recording or reproducing sound that uses three or more speakers or recording channels, designed to make recordings sound more like a live performance. ⓘ 1960s.

surtax /ˈsɜːtaks/ ▷ *noun* **1** an additional tax, especially one that is levied on incomes above a certain level. **2** an additional tax on something that already has a tax or duty levied on it. ▷ *verb* to levy such a tax on someone or something. ⓘ 19c: from French *surtaxe*.

surtitle /ˈsɜːtaɪtəl/ or (*especially US*) **supertitle** ▷ *noun* any of a sequence of captions that are projected onto a screen to the side of, or above, the stage during a foreign-language opera or play and which give a running translation of the libretto or dialogue as it is performed. ▷ *verb* to provide captions of this kind. ⓘ 1980s.

surveillance /səˈveɪləns/ ▷ *noun* (*often* **under surveillance** or **under the surveillance of someone** or **something**) a close watch over something (eg for security purposes) or someone (eg a suspected criminal) □ ***The police surveillance was called off*** □ ***The gallery was constantly under the surveillance of a complex system of video cameras.*** • **surveillant** *adj, noun*. ⓘ 19c: French, from *veiller*, from Latin *vigilare* to watch.

surveillance TV ▷ *noun* a system of closed-circuit television monitoring, usually for security purposes, eg in banks, supermarkets, etc, or in city centres or unattended locations.

survey ▷ *verb* /səːˈveɪ/ (***surveys, surveyed, surveying***) **1** to look at or examine at length or in detail, in order to get a general view. **2** to examine (a building) in order to assess its condition or value, especially on behalf of a prospective owner, mortgage lender, etc. **3** to measure land heights and distances in (an area) for the purposes of drawing a detailed map, plan, description, etc. **4** to canvas (public opinion) and make a statistical assessment of the replies. ▷ *noun* /ˈsɜːveɪ/ (***surveys***) **1** a detailed examination or investigation, eg to find out public opinion or customer preference. **2 a** an inspection of a building to assess condition or value; **b** the report that is drawn up after this has been done. **3 a** the collecting of land measurements for map-making purposes, etc; **b** the map, plan, report, etc that is drawn up after this has been done. • **surveying** *noun*. ⓘ 14c: from French *surveoir*, from Latin *videre* to see.

surveyor /səˈveɪə(r)/ ▷ *noun* **1** a person who is professionally qualified to survey land, buildings, etc. See also QUANTITY SURVEYOR. **2** *Brit* an official, especially one employed in local government, who oversees the maintenance, administration, finances, etc of a specified department. **3** someone whose job is to canvas public opinion and make a statistical assessment of the replies.

survival ▷ *noun* **1** said of an individual: the fact of continuing to live, especially after some risk that might have prevented this □ ***Her survival was due to the bravery of the firefighters.*** **2** said of a group or an institution: continued existence □ ***Many species depend on the rainforest for their survival.*** **3** something, such as an old custom, etc, that continues to be practised □ ***Up-Helly-Aa is a fine example of a survival of Viking tradition.*** • **survival of the fittest 1** *non-technical* the process or result of NATURAL SELECTION. **2** *colloq* the concept that in business, industry, academia, politics, etc the most able, determined, ambitious, etc will succeed, while those who are less able or less motivated will not.

survive /səˈvaɪv/ ▷ *verb* (***survived, surviving***) **1** *tr & intr* **a** to remain alive, especially despite (some risk that might prevent this) □ ***the only one to survive the tragedy*** □ ***plants that can survive in cold conditions***; **b** *informal* to come or get through (something arduous or unpleasant) □ ***It was a tough course, but I survived it.*** **2** to live on after the death of someone □ ***survived her husband by 10 years.*** **3** *intr* to remain alive or in existence □ ***How do they survive on such a small income?*** • **survivability** *noun*. • **survivable** *adj*. • **surviving** *adj, noun*. ⓘ 15c: from French *sourvivre*, from Latin *vivere* to live.

survivor ▷ *noun* **1** someone or something that survives. **2** someone who has it in their nature to come or get through adversity.

sus see SUSS

susceptibility /səseptɪˈbɪlɪtɪ/ ▷ *noun* (***susceptibilities***) **1** the state or quality of being susceptible. **2 a** the capacity or ability to feel emotions; **b** (**susceptibilities**) feelings; sensibilities.

susceptible /səˈseptɪbəl/ ▷ *adj* **1** (**susceptible to something**) prone to being, or likely to be, affected by it, eg bouts of illness, bad temper, etc □ ***always been susceptible to colds.*** **2** capable of being affected by strong feelings, especially of love. **3** (**susceptible to something**) capable of being influenced by something, eg persuasion. **4** (**susceptible of something**) open to it; able to admit it □ ***a ruling susceptible of several interpretations.*** • **susceptibly** *adverb*. • **susceptibleness** *noun*. ⓘ 17c: from Latin *suscipere, susceptum* to take up.

sushi /ˈsuːʃɪ/ ▷ *noun* (***sushis***) a Japanese dish of small rolls or balls of cold boiled rice that has been flavoured with vinegar and topped with egg, raw fish or vegetables. ⓘ 19c: Japanese, meaning 'it is sour'.

suslik /ˈsʌslɪk/ or **souslik** /ˈsuːslɪk/ ▷ *noun* a ground squirrel that is found in S Europe and parts of Asia. ⓘ 18c: Russian.

suspect ▷ *verb* /səˈspekt/ (***suspected, suspecting***) **1** to consider or believe likely. **2** to think (a particular person) possibly or probably guilty of a crime or other wrongdoing. **3** to doubt the truth or genuineness of someone or something. ▷ *noun* /ˈsʌspekt/ someone who is suspected of committing a crime, etc. ▷ *adj* /ˈsʌspekt/ thought to be possibly false, untrue or dangerous; dubious □ ***His excuse sounds pretty suspect to me.*** • **suspect someone of something** to believe they probably did it □ ***He suspected her of having an affair.*** ⓘ 14c: from Latin *suspicere, suspectum* to look up to or admire.

suspend /səˈspend/ ▷ *verb* (***suspended, suspending***) **1** to hang or hang up something. **2** to bring a halt to something, especially temporarily □ ***Services are suspended due to flooding.*** **3** to delay or postpone something. **4** to remove someone from a job, a team, etc temporarily, as punishment or during an investigation of a possible misdemeanour. **5** to keep (small insoluble solid particles) more or less evenly dispersed throughout a fluid (ie, a liquid or a gas). ⓒ 13c: from Latin *suspendere* to hang secretly.

suspended animation ▷ *noun* a state in which a body's main functions are temporarily slowed down to an absolute minimum, eg in hibernation.

suspended sentence ▷ *noun* a judicial sentence that is deferred for a set time providing the offender is of good behaviour throughout the period.

suspender ▷ *noun* **1** an elasticated strap that can be attached to the top of a stocking or sock to hold it in place. **2** (**suspenders**) *N Amer* braces for holding up trousers.

suspender-belt ▷ *noun* an undergarment with suspenders hanging from, is used for holding up stockings.

suspense /sə'spɛns/ ▷ *noun* **1** a state of nervous or excited tension or uncertainty. **2** tension or excitedness, especially as brought on by an eager desire to know the outcome of something. • **suspenseful** *adj.* • **keep someone in suspense** to deliberately delay telling them something or the outcome of something. ⓒ 15c: from French *suspens*, from Latin *suspendere* to suspend.

suspense account ▷ *noun, bookkeeping* an account that is used for temporarily recording items until it is decided where they will be permanently lodged.

suspension /sə'spɛnʃən/ ▷ *noun* **1** the act of suspending or the state of being suspended. **2** a temporary exclusion from an official position, work, school, college, etc, especially while allegations of misconduct are being investigated. **3** a temporary cessation ▫ ***suspension of hostilities.*** **4** a system of springs and shock absorbers that connects the axles of a vehicle to the chassis and absorbs some of the unwanted vibrations transmitted from the road surface. **5** a liquid or gas that contains small insoluble solid particles which are more or less evenly dispersed throughout it.

suspension bridge ▷ *noun* a bridge that has a road or rail surface hanging from vertical cables which are themselves attached to thicker cables stretched between towers.

suspensive ▷ *adj* **1** relating to or causing suspense. **2** having the effect of causing or the ability to cause a temporary exclusion, cessation, etc.

suspensory ▷ *adj* **1** having the ability to support something that is suspended. **2** *anatomy* said of a ligament, muscle, etc: having an organ or other body part suspended from it. **3** SUSPENSIVE 2.

suspicion /sə'spɪʃən/ ▷ *noun* **1** an act, instance or feeling of suspecting. **2** a belief or opinion that is based on very little evidence. **3** a slight quantity; a trace. • **suspicionless** *adj.* • **above suspicion** too highly respected to be suspected of a crime or wrongdoing. • **on suspicion** as a suspect ▫ ***held on suspicion of murder.*** • **under suspicion** suspected of a crime or wrongdoing. ⓒ 14c: from French *suspecioun*, from Latin *suspicio*, from *suspicere* to suspect.

suspicious ▷ *adj* **1** inclined to suspect guilt, wrongdoing, etc ▫ ***has a very suspicious nature.*** **2** inviting or arousing suspicion; dubious ▫ ***found the body in suspicious circumstances.*** • **suspiciously** *adverb.* • **suspiciousness** *noun.* ⓒ 14c: from French *suspecious*, from Latin *suspicio* suspicion.

suss or **sus** /sʌs/ *slang* ▷ *verb* (***susses, sussed, sussing***) **1** to discover, assess or establish something, especially by investigation or intuition ▫ ***soon sussed how the video worked.*** **2** to suspect something. ▷ *noun* **1** a suspect. **2** suspicion or suspicious behaviour. **3** shrewdness; sharp-wittedness. ⓒ 1930s: a shortened form of SUSPECT or SUSPICION.

■ **suss something out 1** to investigate, inspect or examine ▫ ***sussed out the nightlife.*** **2** to work out or understand ▫ ***couldn't suss out his motives.***

sustain /sə'steɪn/ ▷ *verb* (***sustained, sustaining***) **1** to keep going. **2** to withstand, tolerate or endure ▫ ***can sustain impacts even at high speed.*** **3** to bolster, strengthen or encourage ▫ ***had a whisky to sustain his nerves.*** **4** to suffer or undergo (eg an injury, loss, defeat, etc). **5** to declare that an objection in court is valid. **6** to support, ratify, back up (an argument, claim, etc). **7** to maintain or provide for something ▫ ***couldn't sustain her family on such a low salary.*** **8** to maintain or prolong ▫ ***another point to sustain the discussion.*** **9** to bear the weight of or support something, especially from below. • **sustainer** *noun.* • **sustaining** *adj, noun.* • **sustainment** *noun.* ⓒ 13c: from French *sustenir*, from Latin *sustinere*, from *sub* from below + *tenere* to hold or keep.

sustainable ▷ *adj* **1** capable of being sustained. **2** said of economic development, population growth, renewable resources, etc: capable of being maintained at a set level. • **sustainability** *noun.*

sustained ▷ *adj* kept up over a prolonged time, especially without wavering or flagging ▫ ***a sustained effort to make the deadline*** ▫ ***a sustained attack on the city.*** • **sustainedly** *adverb.*

sustained yield ▷ *noun, ecol* the amount of a natural resource, such as trees, fish, etc, that can safely be periodically removed or harvested without the risk of long-term depletion of the population. ⓒ Early 20c.

sustaining pedal ▷ *noun* a piano pedal operated by the right foot, which makes a sound more prolonged by holding off the dampers.

sustenance /'sʌstənəns/ ▷ *noun* **1 a** something, eg food or drink that nourishes the body or that keeps up energy or spirits; **b** the action or an instance of nourishment. **2** something that maintains, supports or provides a livelihood. ⓒ 13c: from French *sustenaunce*, and related to SUSTAIN.

susurrus /suː'sʌrəs, sjuː-/ and **sussuration** ▷ *noun, literary* a soft whispering or rustling sound. ⓒ 19c; *sussuration* from 15c: Latin, meaning 'humming, muttering or whispering'.

sutra /'suːtrə/ ▷ *noun* (***sutras***) **1** in Sanskrit literature: a set of aphorisms that relate to ritual, grammar, metre, philosophy, etc. **2** in Buddhist sacred literature: a collection of writings that includes the sermons of Buddha. ⓒ Early 19c: Sanskrit, meaning 'thread or rule'.

suttee or **sati** /'sʌtiː/ ▷ *noun* (***suttees*** or ***satis***) **1** *formerly* a Hindu custom that was abolished by the British authorities in India in 1829, in which a widow would sacrifice herself by being burned alive on her dead husband's funeral pyre. **2** a Hindu woman who sacrificed herself in this way. ⓒ 18c: from Sanskrit *sati* faithful wife, from *sat* good, wise, honest.

suture /'suːtʃə(r)/ ▷ *noun* **1 a** a stitch that joins the edges of a wound, surgical incision, etc together; **b** the joining of such edges together; **c** the thread, wire, etc that is used for this. **2** *anatomy* the junction or meeting point of two non-articulating bones, eg in the skull. ▷ *verb* (***sutured, suturing***) to sew up (a wound, surgical incision, etc). ⓒ 16c: French, from Latin *sutura*, from *suere* to sew.

suzerain /'suːzəreɪn/ ▷ *noun* **1** a nation, state or ruler that exercises some control over another state but which allows it to retain its own ruler or government. **2** a feudal lord. • **suzerainty** *noun.* ⓒ Early 19c: French, from Latin *subversus* upturned, and related to SOVEREIGN.

s.v. ▷ *abbreviation* **1** side valve. **2** used in referencing: *sub verbo* or *sub voce* (Latin), under the word or heading.

svelte /svɛlt/ ▷ *adj* slim or slender, especially in a graceful or attractive way. ⓒ Early 19c: French, from Latin *ex* out + *vellere* to pluck.

Svengali /svɛŋ'gɑːlɪ/ ▷ *noun* (***Svengalis***) someone who can exert great control or influence over someone else, usually for some evil or sinister reason or purpose. ⓒ Early 20c: the name of a character in the George Du

Maurier novel *Trilby* (1894) who is a musician and hypnotist.

SVQ ▷ *abbreviation* Scottish Vocational Qualification, a qualification awarded in the workplace by SCOTVEC for competence in job skills at any of five different levels from basic to university standard.

SW ▷ *abbreviation* **1** short wave. **2** south-west, or south-western.

swab /swɒb/ ▷ *noun* **1 a** a piece of cotton wool, gauze, etc that is used for cleaning wounds, applying antiseptics, taking a medical specimen, etc; **b** a medical specimen, eg of some bodily fluid, etc, that is taken for examination or testing. **2** a mop used for cleaning floors, ships' decks, etc. **3** *slang* a worthless person. ▷ *verb* (***swabbed, swabbing***) to use a swab or something like a swab for cleaning or mopping something (eg a wound, a ship's deck, etc); to clean or clean out with, or as if with, a swab. • **swabber** *noun*. ⓒ 17c: from Dutch *zwabberen* to mop.

swaddle /ˈswɒdəl/ ▷ *verb* (***swaddled, swaddling***) **1** to bandage. **2** to wrap (a baby) in swaddling-clothes. ⓒ Anglo-Saxon *swathel* bandage.

swaddling-clothes ▷ *plural noun, historical* strips of cloth wrapped round a newborn baby to restrict movement.

swag /swag/ ▷ *noun* **1** *slang* stolen goods. **2** *Austral* a traveller's pack or rolled bundle of possessions. **3 a** a garland of fruit, flowers or foliage that is hung between two points; **b** a representation of this, eg in plasterwork, as a design on wallpaper or fabric; **c** fabric that is hung to give this effect, eg at a window. ▷ *verb* (***swagged, swagging***) **1** *intr* to sway or sag. **2** to drape (eg curtain fabric) in swags. **3** *Austral* (*often* **swag it**) to travel around on foot with one's possessions in a bundle. ⓒ 16c.

swage /sweɪdʒ/ ▷ *noun* **1** a tool or die (see DIE²) that is used in the working and shaping of cold metal. **2** an ornamental moulding. ▷ *verb* (***swaged, swaging***) to work or shape (cold metal) using a swage. ⓒ 14c: from French *souage*.

swage block ▷ *noun* a block that has various holes, grooves, etc in it which is used in the working and shaping of cold metal.

swagger /ˈswagə(r)/ ▷ *verb* (***swaggered, swaggering***) *intr* **1** to walk with an air of self-importance. **2** to behave arrogantly. ▷ *noun* **1** a swaggering way of walking or behaving. **2** *colloq* the quality of being showily fashionable or smart. ▷ *adj, colloq* showily fashionable or smart. • **swaggerer** *noun*. • **swaggering** *noun, adj*. • **swaggeringly** *adverb*. ⓒ 18c.

swagger-stick ▷ *noun* a type of short cane that is carried by a military officer.

swagman and **swaggie** ▷ *noun, Austral* someone, especially an itinerant workman, who travels about on foot and who carries their belongings in a swag.

Swahili /swəˈhiːlɪ, swɑː-/ ▷ *noun* **1** a language that is widely spoken in E Africa both as a mother tongue and as a second language; it is thought to be an ARABIC-influenced pidgin of BANTU and is the official language of Kenya and Tanzania and a lingua franca in Uganda and Zaire. **2** (***Swahilis*** or ***Swahili***) a member of a people who speak this language and who live mainly in the area of the former state of Zanzibar. ▷ *adj* belonging or relating to this language or people. ⓒ 19c: Kiswahili, meaning 'pertaining to the coast', from Arabic *sahil* coast.

swain ▷ *noun, old use, poetic* **1** a country youth. **2** a young male lover or suitor. ⓒ Anglo-Saxon *swan*.

SWALK /swɔːlk/ ▷ *abbreviation* a message that is sometimes put on the back of an envelope, especially one that contains a love letter. ⓒ 1920s: Sealed With A Loving Kiss.

swallow¹ /ˈswɒloʊ/ ▷ *verb* (***swallowed, swallowing***) **1** to perform a muscular movement to make (food or drink) go from the mouth, down the oesophagus and into the stomach. **2** *intr* to move the muscles of the throat as if performing such an action, especially as a sign of emotional distress; to gulp. **3** (*also* **swallow something up**) to make it disappear or no longer be visible; to engulf or absorb it. **4** to stifle or repress (eg pride, tears, etc). **5** to accept or endure (eg an insult, affront, etc) meekly and without retaliation. **6** *colloq* to believe gullibly or unquestioningly. **7** to mumble. ▷ *noun* **1** an act of swallowing. **2** an amount swallowed at one time. • **swallower** *noun*. • **swallow one's pride** to behave humbly and do something which one would otherwise be reluctant to do. • **swallow one's words** to retract what one has said previously. ⓒ Anglo-Saxon *swelgan*.

swallow² /ˈswɒloʊ/ ▷ *noun* any of various small migratory fast-flying insect-eating birds that have long pointed wings and a long forked tail. • **one swallow does not make a summer** a single example of something positive does not necessarily mean that all subsequent similar instances will have the same outcome. ⓒ Anglo-Saxon *swalwe*.

swallow dive ▷ *noun* a dive during which the arms are held out to the side, at shoulder level, until just above the level of the water when they are pulled in to the sides and the diver enters the water head first.

swallowtail ▷ *noun* **1** a large colourful butterfly that has the back wings extended into slender tails. **2** a tail that is forked like a swallow's. **3** anything that resembles this kind of shape. **4** *as adj* □ *swallowtail coat*. • **swallowtailed** *adj* said especially of birds: having a deeply forked tail □ *swallowtailed duck* □ *swallowtailed kingfisher*.

swam *past tense of* SWIM

swami /ˈswɑːmɪ/ ▷ *noun* (***swamis*** or ***swamies***) an honorific title for a Hindu male religious teacher. ⓒ 18c: from Hindi *svami* lord or master.

swamp /swɒmp/ ▷ *noun* an area of land that is permanently waterlogged but which has a dense covering of vegetation, eg, in certain tropical regions, trees and shrubs, such as mangroves or, in the more temperate zones, willows or reeds. Also *as adj* □ *swamp fever*. ▷ *verb* (***swamped*** /swɒmpt/ , ***swamping***) **1** to overwhelm or inundate. **2** to cause (a boat) to fill with water. **3** to flood. • **swampy** (***swampier, swampiest***) *adj*. ⓒ 17c.

swan /swɒn/ ▷ *noun* **1** any of several species of a large graceful aquatic birds related to ducks and geese, which have a long slender elegant neck, powerful wings and webbed feet. See also COB¹, PEN⁴, CYGNET. **2** (**the Swan**) CYGNUS. ▷ *verb* (***swanned, swanning***) *intr, colloq* (*usually* **swan off, around, about**, *etc*) to spend time idly; to wander aimlessly or gracefully □ *justs swans off whenever she feels like it* □ *swans around in his Armani suit*. • **swanlike** *adj*. ⓒ Anglo-Saxon.

swank /swaŋk/ *colloq* ▷ *verb* (***swanked, swanking***) *intr* to boast or show off. ▷ *noun* flashiness, ostentation, etc; boastfulness. ▷ *adj* (***swanker, swankest***) *especially US* swanky. □ *Wow! What a swank car!* • **swanker** *noun*. • **swanking** *adj*. ⓒ 19c.

swanky ▷ *adj* (***swankier, swankiest***) *colloq* **1** boastful. **2** flashy, flamboyant, elaborate, fashionable, etc. • **swankily** *adverb*. • **swankiness** *noun*. ⓒ 19c.

swan neck ▷ *noun* a pipe, tube, etc that is moulded into an S-shape.

swannery ▷ *noun* a place where swans are kept or bred.

swan's-down ▷ *noun* **1** the very soft downy feathers of a swan used in trimming lingerie, etc and for powder puffs. **2** a type of thick cotton or woollen material that has a soft nap on one side.

swan song ▷ *noun* the last performance or piece of work that a musician, author, composer, artist, etc gives, writes, paints, etc before their death or retirement.

swan-upping ▷ *noun, Brit* **1** the act or custom of making a small nick in a swan's beak in order to show who it belongs to. **2** the annual ceremony of doing this to the royal cygnets on the River Thames. ⓒ 16c.

swap or **swop** /swɒp/ ▷ *verb* (***swapped, swapping, swopped ; swopping***) *tr & intr* to exchange or trade (something or someone) for another □ *They swapped shifts* □ *swapped his car for a newer model.* ▷ *noun* **1** an exchange or trading. **2** something that is exchanged or traded. **3** something that is suitable or offered as an exchange or a trade. • **swapper** *noun*. • **swapping** *noun*. ⓒ 13c: as *swappen*, to strike or to shake hands on a bargain.

SWAPO or **Swapo** /ˈswɑːpoʊ/ ▷ *abbreviation* South-West Africa People's Organization.

sward /swɔːd/ ▷ *noun* **1** a large, usually grassy, area of land. **2** turf. • **swarded** *adj*. ⓒ Anglo-Saxon *sweard* skin.

swarf /swɔːf/ ▷ *noun* **1** the grindings, filings or strips of waste that are produced in machine tooling. **2** the fine ribbons of plastic, wax, etc that are formed when grooves are cut into records (see RECORD *noun* 4). ⓒ 16c in sense 1; 1930s in sense 2.

swarm[1] /swɔːm/ ▷ *noun* **1** a large group of flying bees, led by a queen, that have left their hive in order to set up a new home. **2** any large group of insects or other small creatures, especially ones that are on the move. **3** a crowd of people, especially one that is on the move or that is in chaos. ▷ *verb* (***swarmed, swarming***) *intr* to gather, move, go, etc in a swarm. • **swarming** *adj, noun*. • **be swarming** or **be swarming with people** or **things** said of a place: to be crowded or overrun □ *That pub is absolutely swarming every night.* ⓒ Anglo-Saxon *swearm*.

swarm[2] /swɔːm/ ▷ *verb* (***swarmed, swarming***) *tr & intr* (*often* **swarm up something**) to climb (especially a rope or tree) by clasping with the hands and knees or feet. ⓒ 16c.

swarthy /ˈswɔːðɪ/ ▷ *adj* (***swarthier, swarthiest***) having a dark complexion. • **swarthily** *adverb*. • **swarthiness** *noun*. ⓒ 16c: from Anglo-Saxon *sweart* dark or black.

swash[1] /swɒʃ/ ▷ *verb* (***swashed, swashing***) **1** to move about in water making a splashing noise. **2** said of water: to pour or move with a splashing noise. ▷ *noun* a watery splashing noise. ⓒ 16c.

swash[2] /swɒʃ/ ▷ *noun* (***swashes***) **1** a figure or ornament in turning where the lines or mouldings lie at an oblique angle to the main axis of the piece of work. **2** a flourish on an old style of capital letter. **3** *as adj* □ *swash-work* □ *swash letter.* ⓒ 17c.

swashbuckler ▷ *noun* **1** a daring and flamboyant adventurer. **2** a type of highly stylized film, novel, etc that portrays exciting scenes of adventure usually in a romanticized historical setting such as feudalism, piracy, etc and which usually features scenes of flamboyant swordsmanship. • **swashbuckling** *adj*. ⓒ 16c: from SWASH[1] + BUCKLER.

swastika /ˈswɒstɪkə/ ▷ *noun* (***swastikas***) a plain cross with arms of equal length which are bent at right angles, usually clockwise, at or close to their mid point. The swastika is an ancient religious symbol, representing the sun and good-luck, and was also the adopted badge of the former German Nazi Party. ⓒ 19c: from Sanskrit *svastika*, from *svasti* wellbeing.

swat[1] /swɒt/ ▷ *verb* (***swatted, swatting***) to hit (especially a fly) with a heavy slapping blow. ▷ *noun* a heavy slap or blow. • **swatter** *noun* a device for swatting flies with, usually consisting of a long thin handle and a wide flat flexible head. ⓒ 18c: a US, Scottish and Northern English variant of *squat*.

swat[2] see SWOT

swatch /swɒtʃ/ ▷ *noun* (***swatches***) **1** a small sample, especially of fabric but also of wallpaper, carpet, etc. **2** (*also* **swatchbook**) a collection of samples (especially of fabric) bound together to form a sort of book.

swath /swɔːθ, swɒθ/ or **swathe** /sweɪð/ ▷ *noun* (***swaths*** or ***swathes***) **1 a** a strip of grass, corn, etc cut by a scythe, mower or harvester; **b** the width of this strip; **c** the cut grass, corn, etc left in such a strip. **2** a broad strip, especially of land. ⓒ Anglo-Saxon *swæth* track.

swathe /sweɪð/ ▷ *verb* (***swathed, swathing***) to bind or wrap someone or something in strips or bands of cloth or fabric, eg bandages. ▷ *noun* (***swathes***) a wrapping, especially a strip of cloth or fabric; a bandage. ⓒ Anglo-Saxon *swathian*.

sway ▷ *verb* (***swayed, swaying***) **1** *tr & intr* to swing, or make something swing, backwards and forwards or from side to side, especially slowly and smoothly. **2** *tr & intr* to lean or bend, or make something lean or bend, to one side or in one direction. **3** to persuade someone to take a particular view or decision, or dissuade them from a course of action. **4** *intr* (*usually* **sway towards something**) to incline towards a particular opinion. **5** *intr* to waver between two opinions or decisions. ▷ *noun* **1** a swaying motion. **2** control or influence. • **swaying** *noun, adj*. • **hold sway** to have authority or influence. ⓒ 15c in these senses: perhaps from Norse *sveigja* to bend.

sway-back ▷ *noun, vet medicine* **1** an abnormal downward curvature of the spine of an animal, especially a horse. **2** a disease of the nervous system in lambs, due to a copper deficiency in ewes, causing difficulty in walking or standing. • **sway-backed** *adj*.

Swazi /ˈswɑːzɪ/ ▷ *noun* (***Swazi*** or ***Swazis***) **1** a Bantu-speaking agricultural and pastoral people living in Swaziland, a kingdom in SE Africa, and in adjacent parts of southern Africa. **2** an individual belonging to this people. **3** their language. ▷ *adj* belonging or relating to this people or their language. ⓒ 19c: from the name of Mswazi, a 19c Swazi king.

swear /swɛə(r)/ ▷ *verb* (***swore*** /swɔː(r)/, ***sworn*** /swɔːn/, ***swearing***) **1** *intr* to use indecent or blasphemous language. **2** to assert something solemnly or earnestly, sometimes with an oath. **3** to promise solemnly, usually by taking an oath. **4** to take (an oath). ▷ *noun* an act of swearing □ *He went outside to have a good swear.* • **swearer** *noun*. • **swearing** *noun*. • **swear blind** *colloq* to assert emphatically. ⓒ Anglo-Saxon *swerian*.

■ **swear at someone** to speak to or shout at them in indecent or blasphemous language.

■ **swear by someone** or **something** **1** to appeal to (eg a deity or something precious or important) as a witness to a solemn promise or the truth of a statement. **2** *colloq* to have or put complete trust in it (eg a certain product or remedy) or item (eg a doctor or therapist).

■ **swear someone in** to introduce them formally into a post, or into the witness box, by requesting them to take an oath.

■ **swear off something** *colloq* to promise to renounce it or give it up.

■ **swear to something** to solemnly state it to be unquestionably true.

■ **swear someone to something** to bind them by a solemn promise □ *They swore her to secrecy.*

swear-word ▷ *noun* a word regarded as obscene or blasphemous.

sweat /swɛt/ ▷ *noun* **1** the salty liquid produced actively by the sweat glands and given out through the pores of the skin, especially in response to great heat, physical exertion, nervousness or fear. **2** the state, or a period, of giving off such moisture. **3** *colloq* any activity that causes the body to give off such moisture. **4** *colloq* any laborious activity. **5** moisture given out by or forming on the surface of any of various substances or objects. **6** *especially N Amer* *colloq* a SWEATSHIRT. **7** (**sweats**) *especially N Amer colloq* **a** SWEAT PANTS; **b** a SWEATSUIT. ▻ *verb* (***sweated*** or ***sweat, sweating***) **1** *intr* to give out sweat through the pores of the skin. **2** *intr* to release a sweat-like moisture, as cheese does when warm, or to gather condensed moisture on the surface, as a glass of cold liquid does. **3** *intr, colloq* to be nervous, anxious or afraid. **4** to give out (blood, sap, etc) like sweat or in a similar way to sweat. **5** to cook (eg meat or vegetables) slowly so as to release their juices. **6** to exercise (eg a racehorse) strenuously, to the point of producing sweat. **7** to force or extort money, information, etc from someone. • **in a sweat** or **in a cold sweat** *colloq* in a worried or anxious state. • **No sweat!** *slang* **1** That presents no problems. **2** Okay! • **sweat blood** *colloq* **1** to work extremely hard. **2** to be in a state of great anxiety. • **sweat it out** *colloq* to endure a difficult or unpleasant situation to the end, especially to wait for a long time in nervous anticipation. ⓔ Anglo-Saxon *swætan*.

■ **sweat something off** to remove (weight, fat, etc) by exercise that makes one sweat.

sweatband ▻ *noun* a strip of elasticated fabric worn around the wrist or head to absorb sweat when playing sports.

sweated labour ▻ *noun* **1** hard work for long hours with poor pay and conditions. **2** people carrying out such work.

sweater ▻ *noun* a knitted jersey or pullover, originally of a kind often worn before and after hard exercise.

sweat gland ▻ *noun* any of the minute curled tubes of the skin's EPIDERMIS growing down into the DERMIS which actively secrete sweat.

sweat pants ▻ *plural noun, especially N Amer* loose-fitting trousers made of a soft cotton fabric, with elasticated cuffs and an elasticated or drawstring waist, worn by athletes or as leisurewear.

sweatshirt ▻ *noun* a long-sleeved jersey of a thick soft cotton fabric, usually fleecy on the inside, originally worn for sports.

sweatshop ▻ *noun* a workshop or factory in which SWEATED LABOUR is used.

sweatsuit ▻ *noun* a loose-fitting suit of sweatshirt and trousers, usually tight-fitting at the wrists and ankles, worn by athletes or as leisurewear.

sweaty ▻ *adj* (***sweatier, sweatiest***) **1** causing sweat. **2** covered with sweat; wet or stained with sweat. **3** smelling of sweat.

Swede /swiːd/ ▻ *noun* a citizen or inhabitant of, or person born in, Sweden, a kingdom in N Europe. ⓔ 17c: from Dutch or Low German.

swede ▻ *noun* **1** an annual or biennial plant, widely cultivated in cool temperate regions for its edible root. **2** the swollen edible root of this plant, which has orange-yellow or whitish flesh and a purple, yellow or white skin, and can be cooked and eaten as a vegetable. ⓔ 19c: from *Swede*; the plant was introduced to Scotland from Sweden in the late 18c, and was originally known as the *Swedish turnip*.

Swedish /ˈswiːdɪʃ/ ▻ *adj* **1** belonging or relating to Sweden, a kingdom in N Europe, its inhabitants or their language. **2** (**the Swedish**) the citizens or inhabitants of, or people born in, Sweden; Swedes (see THE sense 4b). ▻ *noun* the official language of Sweden and one of the two official languages of Finland.

sweep ▻ *verb* (***swept, sweeping***) **1** (*also* **sweep something out** or **up**) to clean (a room, a floor, etc) with a brush or broom. **2** (*also* **sweep something away** or **off** or **up**) to remove (dirt, dust, etc) with a brush or broom. **3** (*usually* **sweep something aside** or **away**) to dismiss (ideas, suggestions, etc) or remove (problems, errors, etc) □ ***She swept aside their objections*** □ ***a need to sweep away the inadequacies of the past.*** **4** (*often* **sweep someone** or **something away, off, past,** *etc*) to take, carry or push them suddenly and with irresistible force □ ***The current swept the boat through the narrows.*** **5** (*often* **sweep someone** or **something off, up,** *etc*) to lift, gather or clear with a forceful scooping or brushing movement □ ***He swept the child into his arms.*** **6** *tr & intr* (*often* **sweep in, out,** *etc*) to move, pass or spread smoothly and swiftly, or strongly, or uncontrollably □ ***Strong winds were sweeping in from the sea*** □ ***A new fitness craze is sweeping the country*** □ ***Labour sweeps to victory in the local elections.*** **7** *intr* to walk, especially with garments flowing, impressively, arrogantly, angrily, etc □ ***She swept across the room in her silk pyjamas.*** **8** *tr & intr* to pass quickly over, making light contact □ ***Her dress swept the floor*** □ ***swept along the floor.*** **9** *intr* to extend curvingly and impressively □ ***The mountains swept down to the sea.*** **10** *intr* said of emotions, etc: to affect suddenly and overpoweringly □ ***She felt a chill sweep over her.*** **11** to force or inspire into taking an unwanted or unintended direction or course of action □ ***trying to sweep her into a quick resolution.*** **12** to have a decisive electoral win □ ***expecting to sweep the country in next week's elections.*** **13** to cast or direct (eg one's gaze) with a scanning movement. **14** to make extensive searches over (an area, especially the sea) for mines, ships, etc. **15** to make with a broad flourishing motion of the arms □ ***He swept a low bow.*** **16** *intr, football* to act as SWEEPER in a team □ ***the guy who sweeps for Norwich.*** ▻ *noun* **1** an act of sweeping. **2** a sweeping movement or action. **3** a sweeping line, eg of a road, or broad sweeping stretch, eg of landscape. **4** the range or area over which something moves, especially in a curving or circular path. **5** *colloq* a sweepstake. **6** *colloq* a chimney-sweep. **7** the cable towed by a minesweeper, used to clear mines from an area of sea. • **a clean sweep 1** a complete change or clear-out. **2** the winning of all prizes, awards, political seats, etc. • **sweep someone off their feet** to cause them to lose control of their thoughts, and especially to fall uncontrollably in love. • **sweep the board** see under BOARD. • **sweep something under the carpet** to hide or ignore something (especially unwelcome facts, difficulties, etc). ⓔ Anglo-Saxon *swapan*.

sweepback ▻ *noun, aeronautics, biol* **1** the form or state of a wing of an aircraft or bird that is angled towards the back as opposed to standing at right angles to the body. **2** the angle between the front edge of an aircraft's wing and a line at right angles to the body.

sweeper ▻ *noun* **1** someone who sweeps. **2** a device or machine used for sweeping. **3** *football* a player covering the whole area behind a line of defenders.

sweep hand and **sweep second hand** ▻ *noun, clock-making* a long hand on a clock or watch which indicates seconds or parts of seconds.

sweeping ▻ *adj* **1** said of a search, change, etc: wide-ranging and thorough. **2** said of a statement: too generalized; indiscriminate. **3** said of a victory, etc: impressive; decisive. ▻ *noun* (*usually* **sweepings**) something swept up. • **sweepingly** *adverb* **1** with a sweeping gesture or movement. **2** indiscriminately; comprehensively.

sweepstake ▻ *noun* **1** a system of gambling in which the prize money is the sum of the stakes of all those betting. **2** a horse race in which the owner of the winning horse receives sums of money put up by the owners of all the other horses. Also (*NAmer*) called **sweepstakes** *singular* or *plural noun*.

sweet ▻ *adj* **1** tasting like sugar; not sour, salty or bitter. **2** pleasing to any of the senses, especially smell and hearing. **3** likeable; charming □ ***He's so sweet when he smiles like that.*** **4** said of wine: having some taste of sugar or fruit; not dry. **5** *colloq* (*usually* **sweet on someone**) fond of them; infatuated with them. **6** said of air or water: fresh and untainted. **7** said of milk: fresh; not sour. **8** said of a picture: sentimentalized. **9** said of jazz or big-band music: played at a steady moderate tempo and without improvisations. **10** used as a general term of emphasis in certain expressions □ ***always goes her own sweet way*** □ ***does his own sweet will.*** ▷ *noun* **1** any small sugar-based confection that is sucked or chewed. **2** a pudding or dessert. **3** someone one loves or is fond of. ▷ *adverb* sweetly. ● **sweetly** *adverb.* ⓒ Anglo-Saxon *swete.*

sweet alyssum ▷ *noun* a plant belonging to the mustard family, related to ALYSSUM, with small white or purple scented flowers, widely cultivated as an ornamental plant.

sweet-and-sour ▷ *adj* **1** cooked in a sauce that includes both sugar and vinegar or lemon juice **2** *now especially* in Chinese cookery, cooked in a sauce that includes sugar, vinegar and soy sauce. ▷ *noun* a sweet-and-sour dish.

sweet bay see under BAY[4]

sweetbread ▷ *noun* the pancreas or thymus of a young animal, especially a calf, used as food.

sweet brier ▷ *noun* a species of wild rose, native to Europe and Asia, with sweet-scented foliage and single pink flowers. Also called EGLANTINE.

sweet chestnut see CHESTNUT

sweet cicely / — 'sɪsəlɪ/ ▷ *noun* **1** a perennial European plant that smells strongly of aniseed and has leaves divided into oval toothed segments and small white flowers. **2** the leaves of this plant which have a strong flavour resembling that of aniseed and are used as a seasoning in cooking, salads, etc. **3** the root of this plant, which can be cooked and eaten as a vegetable.

sweetcorn ▷ *noun* kernels of a variety of maize eaten young while still sweet.

sweeten ▷ *verb* (***sweetened, sweetening***) **1** to make (food) sweet or sweeter. **2** (*also* **sweeten someone up**) *colloq* to make them more agreeable or amenable, eg by flattery or bribery. **3** *colloq* to make (eg an offer) more acceptable or inviting, by making changes or additions. ● **sweetening** *noun* **1** the action of making food sweet or sweeter. **2** a substance used for making food sweet or sweeter.

sweetener ▷ *noun* **1** a substance used for sweetening food, especially one other than sugar. **2** *colloq* an inducement, usually illicit, added to an offer to make it more attractive, especially a bribe.

sweet Fanny Adams, **Fanny Adams** and **sweet FA** ▷ *noun, slang* nothing at all. Sometimes shortened to **FA**. ⓒ 19c: Fanny Adams is the name of a young woman murdered and cut up in 1867, and became services slang for tinned mutton; now used as a euphemism for FUCK ALL (see under FUCK).

sweetheart ▷ *noun* **1 a** a person one is in love with; **b** used as a term of endearment. **2** *obsolete* a lover; a person one has made love to.

sweetheart agreement, **sweetheart contract** and **sweetheart deal** ▷ *noun* an agreement between an employer and trade union officials, especially those of a local union branch, which is excessively favourable to the employer and usually to the advantage of the union officials but which is detrimental to the interests of the workers concerned.

sweetie or (*rarely*) **sweety** ▷ *noun* (***sweeties***) *colloq* **1** a sweet for sucking or chewing. **2** (*also* **sweetie-pie**) a term of endearment. **3** a lovable person. **4** (*usually* **Sweetie**) a large seedless citrus fruit with greenish-yellow skin, whose pulp is sweeter than that of the grapefruit.

sweetmeal ▷ *adj* said of biscuits: made of sweetened wholemeal.

sweetmeat ▷ *noun, old use* any small sugar-based confection or cake.

sweetness ▷ *noun* the state, or degree, of being sweet. ● **sweetness and light** *colloq* mildness, amiability and reasonableness.

sweet nothings ▷ *plural noun* the endearments that people in love say to each other.

sweet pea ▷ *noun* an annual climbing plant that has leaves with finely pointed leaflets and branched tendrils, and brightly coloured butterfly-shaped flowers with a sweet scent.

sweet pepper ▷ *noun* **1** a tropical American plant, widely cultivated for its edible fruit. **2** the hollow edible fruit of this plant, which can be eaten when red (or another colour such as orange or yellow) and ripe or when green and unripe. Also called **capsicum**.

sweet potato ▷ *noun* **1** a perennial S American plant with trailing or climbing stems, oval to heart-shaped leaves, and large purple funnel-shaped flowers. **2** the swollen edible root of this plant, which has sweet-tasting flesh surrounded by a red or purplish skin, and can be cooked and eaten as a vegetable.

sweetsop ▷ *noun* **1** a tropical American evergreen shrub with a sweet edible pulpy fruit. **2** the fruit of this shrub. Also called CUSTARD APPLE.

sweet spot ▷ *noun, sport* the place or spot on a tennis or squash racket, golf club, etc with which the ball should ideally make contact for the best effect and control.

sweet talk ▷ *noun, colloq* words, often flattery, intended to coax or persuade. ▷ *verb* **sweet-talk** *colloq* to coax or persuade, or to try to do so, eg with flattering words.

a sweet tooth ▷ *noun* a fondness for sweet foods. ● **sweet-toothed** *adj.*

sweet william /— 'wɪljəm/ ▷ *noun* a perennial European plant with dense compact heads of dark red, pink, white or spotted flowers, including many varieties grown as ornamental plants.

sweety see SWEETIE

swell ▷ *verb* (*past tense* ***swelled***, *past participle* ***swollen*** /'swoulən/ or ***swelled***, *present participle* ***swelling***) **1** *tr & intr* (*also* **swell up** or **out**, or **swell something up** or **out**) to become, or make something, bigger or fatter through injury or infection, or by filling with liquid or air. **2** *tr & intr* to increase or make something increase in number, size or intensity. **3** *intr* to become visibly filled with emotion, especially pride. **4** *intr* said of the sea: to rise and fall in smooth masses without forming individual waves. **5** *intr* said of a sound: to become louder and then die away. ▷ *noun* **1** a heaving of the sea without waves. **2** an increase in number, size or intensity. **3** an increase in volume of sound or music, followed by a dying away. **4** *old colloq* someone who dresses smartly and fashionably. **5** *old colloq* a prominent member of society. **6** *music* a device in organs and some harpsichords for increasing and decreasing the volume of sound. **7** a broad rounded hill; a piece of smoothly rising ground. ▷ *adj, exclamation, chiefly N Amer colloq* excellent. ● **swelling** *noun* an area of the body that is temporarily swollen as a result of injury or infection. ⓒ Anglo-Saxon *swellan.*

swell box ▷ *noun, music* **1** a part of an organ containing a set of pipes or reeds, with a shutter or shutters which can be opened or closed to vary the loudness of the sound. **2** a similar device in some harmoniums.

swelled head and **swell-headed** see SWOLLEN HEAD

swell organ ▷ *noun, music* in an organ: the pipes enclosed in the swell box.

swelter /'swɛltə(r)/ ▷ *verb* (***sweltered, sweltering***) *intr* to sweat heavily or feel extremely or oppressively hot. ▷ *noun* a sweltering feeling or state; sweltering weather. ● **sweltering** *adj* said of the weather: extremely or oppressively hot.

swept *past tense, past participle of* SWEEP

sweptback ▷ *adj, aeronautics* said of the wing of an aircraft: having SWEEPBACK.

sweptwing ▻ *adj, aeronautics* said of an aircraft: having sweptback wings.

swerve ▻ *verb* (***swerved***, ***swerving***) *intr* **1** to turn or move aside suddenly and sharply, eg to avoid a collision. **2** to deviate from a course of action. ▻ *noun* an act of swerving; a swerving movement. • **swerver** *noun*. • **swerving** *noun, adj*. ◷ 14c in this sense.

swift ▻ *adj* **1** fast-moving; able to move fast. **2** done, given, etc quickly or promptly. **3** acting promptly □ *His friends were swift to defend him.* ▻ *adverb* swiftly. ▻ *noun* any of various small fast-flying birds that have dark brown or grey plumage, long narrow pointed wings and a forked tail, and that feed, and sometimes mate, while in flight. • **swiftly** *adverb*. • **swiftness** *noun*. ◷ Anglo-Saxon *swift*.

swiftlet ▻ *noun* any member of a genus of small swifts, some species of which make nests from edible saliva-based gelatinous material, used in making a type of soup (BIRD'S NEST SOUP) greatly esteemed in parts of the Far East.

swig *colloq* ▻ *verb* (***swigged***, ***swigging***) *tr & intr* to drink in gulps, especially from a bottle. ▻ *noun* a large drink or gulp. ◷ 17c.

swill ▻ *verb* (***swilled***, ***swilling***) **1** (*also* **swill something out**) to rinse something by splashing water round or over it. **2** *colloq* to drink (especially alcohol) greedily. ▻ *noun* **1** any mushy mixture of scraps fed to pigs. **2** disgusting food or drink. **3** *colloq* a gulp of beer or other alcohol. ◷ Anglo-Saxon *swilian* to wash.

swim ▻ *verb* (***swam***, ***swum***, ***swimming***) **1** *intr* to propel oneself through water by moving the arms and legs or (in fish) the tail and fins. **2** to cover (a distance) or cross (a stretch of water) in this way □ *swam the Channel.* **3** to compete in (a race through water) by swimming. **4** to perform (a particular stroke) in swimming □ *swam breast stroke across the pool.* **5** *intr* to float. **6** *intr* to be affected by dizziness □ *His head was swimming.* **7** *intr* to move or appear to move about in waves or whirls. **8** to cause to swim; to take by swimming □ *have to swim the horses across the river.* ▻ *noun* **1** a spell of swimming. **2** the general flow of events. **3** a state of dizziness. **4** *fishing* a place or pool in a river, etc where fish are found. • **swimmable** *adj*. • **swimmer** *noun*. • **swimming** *noun*. • **in the swim** *colloq* up to date with, and often involved in, what is going on around one. • **swim with** or **against the stream** or **tide** to conform to, or go against, normal behaviour, current opinions, etc. ◷ Anglo-Saxon *swimman*.

■ **be swimming with something** to be flooded or awash with it □ *The kitchen is swimming with water.*

■ **be swimming in** or **with something** to have a great deal of it □ *absolutely swimming in milk.*

swim bladder ▻ *noun, zool* in bony fishes: an internal structure that can be filled with air and so used to control buoyancy of the fish in the water.

swimmeret /ˈswɪmərɛt/ and **swimming-leg** ▻ *noun, zool* any of a number of leg-like abdominal appendages on the body of many crustaceans, used in swimming and for carrying eggs.

swimming-bath ▻ *noun* or **swimming-baths** ▻ *plural noun* a swimming-pool, usually indoors.

swimming-costume ▻ *noun* a swimsuit.

swimmingly ▻ *adj, colloq* smoothly and successfully.

swimming-pool ▻ *noun* an artificial pool for swimming in.

swimsuit ▻ *noun* a garment worn for swimming.

swindle ▻ *verb* (***swindled***, ***swindling***) to cheat or trick someone in order to obtain money from them; to obtain (money, etc) by cheating or trickery. ▻ *noun* **1** an act of swindling. **2** anything that is not what it is presented as being. • **swindler** *noun*. ◷ 18c: the *verb* is a back-formation from *swindler*, which comes from German *Schwindler* someone who plans extravagant schemes, a cheat, from *schwindeln* to be giddy, to act extravagantly or to swindle.

swine ▻ *noun* (***swine*** in sense 1 or ***swines*** in sense 2) **1** a pig. **2** a despicable person. ◷ Anglo-Saxon *swin*.

swine fever ▻ *noun, vet medicine* a contagious and sometimes fatal viral disease of pigs.

swineherd ▻ *noun, old use* someone who looks after pigs.

swing ▻ *verb* (***swung***, ***swinging***) **1** *tr & intr* to move in a curving motion, pivoting from a fixed point □ *The door swung shut behind her* □ *gibbons swinging from tree to tree.* **2** *tr & intr* to move or make something move or turn with a sweeping or curving movement or movements □ *She swung the car into the driveway* □ *swung himself into the saddle.* **3** *tr & intr* to turn or make something turn around a central axis □ *He swung his chair round* □ *She swung round, surprised and a little wary.* **4** *intr* to move with a swaying movement or movements □ *She swung along through the meadows.* **5** *intr* to undergo, often suddenly or sharply, a change or changes of opinion, mood, fortune or direction □ *He swung between extremes of mood* □ *The match could have swung either way at that point.* **6** (*also* **swing someone round**) to persuade them to have a certain opinion □ *That should swing them round to our way of thinking.* **7** *colloq* to arrange or fix; to achieve the successful outcome of something □ *just needs a couple of free gifts to swing the sale.* **8 a** *colloq* to determine or settle the outcome of (eg an election in which voters were initially undecided); **b)** *intr* said of an electorate's voting pattern: to change in favour of a particular party □ *The vote has swung decisively to the Green Party.* **9** *tr & intr* (*often* **swing at someone** or **something**) **a** to attempt to hit or make a hit with a curving movement of a bat, etc □ *swung wildly at the ball*; **b** *colloq* to attempt to punch someone or make (a punch) with a curving arm movement □ *He swung a frustrated punch at the goalkeeper.* **10** *intr, colloq* said of a social function, etc: to be lively and exciting. **11** *intr, colloq* to enjoy oneself with vigour and enthusiasm. **12** *intr, colloq* to change sexual partners in a group, especially habitually. **13** *intr, colloq* to be hanged. **14** *tr & intr, music* to perform or be performed as swing (see *noun* 7 *below*). **15** *tr & intr, cricket* to cause (a ball) to move in a curving path; to move in such a path. ▻ *noun* **1** a seat suspended from a frame or branch for a child (or sometimes an adult) to swing on. **2** a change, usually a sudden and sharp change, eg in mood, support, success, etc. **3** a swinging stroke with a golf club, cricket bat, etc; the technique of a golfer. **4** a punch made with a curving movement □ *took a swing at him with her clenched fist.* **5** an act, manner or spell of swinging. **6** a swinging movement. **7** *music* **a** jazz or jazz-like dance music with a simple regular rhythm, popularized by bands in the 1930s; **b** *as adj* □ *swing band.* **8** *cricket* a curving movement of a bowled ball. **9** a change in the voting pattern of the electorate in a particular constituency, at a particular election, etc □ *a swing of 40% to Labour.* ▻ *adj* able to swing □ *a swing mirror.* • **in full swing** or **into full swing** at, or to, the height of liveliness. • **swing both ways** *colloq* to have sexual relations with both men and women, either consecutively or simultaneously; to be a bisexual. • **swing into action** to begin to move or act, especially decisively or enthusiastically. • **swing the lead** /lɛd/ *slang* to make up excuses to avoid work. • **swings and roundabouts** *colloq* a situation in which advantages and disadvantages, or successes and failures, are equal. • **the swing of things** the usual routine or pace of activity □ *get back into the swing of things after a month off work.* ◷ Anglo-Saxon *swingan*.

swingbeat ▻ *noun, music* a type of DANCE MUSIC (sense 2) influenced by hip-hop, rap music and rhythm and blues.

swingboat ▻ *noun* a boat-shaped swinging carriage in which rides are given at a fairground.

swing bowler ▷ *noun, cricket* a bowler who specializes or is skilled in imparting swing to a ball.

swing bridge ▷ *noun* a bridge that swings open to let boats through.

swing door ▷ *noun* a door, often one of a pair, hinged so as to open in both directions, usually swinging to a closed position automatically.

swingeing /ˈswɪndʒɪŋ/ ▷ *adj* hard to bear; severe, extensive. • **swingeingly** *adverb*. ⓒ Anglo-Saxon *swengan* to shake.

swinger /ˈswɪŋə(r)/ ▷ *noun, old slang use* **1** someone who has a very active social life, especially with much dancing and drinking. **2** a sexually promiscuous person (see SWING verb 12).

swinging ▷ *adj* **1** moving or turning with a swing. **2** *colloq old use* lively and exciting.

swingletree /ˈswɪŋgəltriː/ ▷ *noun* a crossbar, pivoted in the middle, to which the traces are attached in a cart, plough, etc. ⓒ 15c: from *swingle* the free-swinging part of a flail + TREE.

swingometer /swɪŋˈɒmɪtə(r)/ ▷ *noun, Brit, especially formerly* a device consisting of a dial and a movable pointer, designed to indicate the probable results (in terms of seats won and lost) from a swing of a given extent to or from a political party in an election.

swing-wing ▷ *adj, aeronautics* said of an aeroplane: having a wing whose angle to the fuselage can be varied during take-off, flight and landing. ▷ *noun* **1** an aeroplane wing whose angle to the fuselage can be varied during flight. **2** an aeroplane with such a wing.

swinish /ˈswaɪnɪʃ/ ▷ *adj* **1** like a swine. **2** filthy. **3** voracious. • **swinishly** *adverb*. • **swinishness** *noun*.

swipe ▷ *verb* (***swiped, swiping***) **1** to hit with a heavy sweeping blow. **2** (*usually* **swipe at someone** or **something**) to try to hit them or it. **3** *colloq* to steal. **4** to pass (a swipe card) through a device that electronically interprets the information encoded on the card. ▷ *noun* a heavy sweeping blow. ⓒ Anglo-Saxon *swipian* to beat.

swipe card ▷ *noun* a credit card, debit card, ID card, etc with information encoded on a magnetic strip that can be electronically interpreted when it is passed through a reader.

swirl ▷ *verb* (***swirled, swirling***) **1** *tr & intr* to flow or cause to flow or move with a whirling or circling motion. **2** said of the head: to be dizzy; to swim. ▷ *noun* **1** a whirling or circling motion. **2** a curling circling shape or pattern. • **swirling** *adj*. ⓒ 15c: probably from Scandinavian.

swish[1] ▷ *verb* (***swishes, swished, swishing***) *tr & intr* **1** to move with a brushing, rustling, rushing, hissing or whooshing sound. **2** to move or flick (especially a brush-like tail). ▷ *noun* (***swishes***) **1** a brushing, rustling, rushing, hissing or whooshing sound, or movement causing such a sound. **2** a movement or flick of a brush-like tail, etc. ⓒ 18c: imitating the sound.

swish[2] ▷ *adj, colloq* smart and stylish. ⓒ 19c: probably from SWISH[1].

Swiss ▷ *adj* belonging or relating to Switzerland, a republic in central Europe, to its inhabitants or to the German, French or Italian dialects spoken by them. ▷ *noun* (*plural* ***Swiss***) **1** a native or citizen of, or person born in, Switzerland. **2** any of the dialects of German, French or Italian spoken in Switzerland. ⓒ 16c: from French *suisse*.

Swiss cheese plant see under MONSTERA

Swiss roll ▷ *noun* a cylindrical cake made by rolling up a thin slab of sponge spread with jam or cream.

Switch ▷ *noun, trademark* a DEBIT-CARD service offered by a number of British banks. Also *as adj* □ *Switch card.* ⓒ 1990s.

switch ▷ *noun* (***switches***) **1** a manually operated or automatic device that is used to open or close an electric circuit, eg a lever or button that makes or breaks a pair of contacts. **2** a change. **3** an exchange or change-over, especially one involving a deception. **4** a long flexible twig or cane, especially one used for corporal punishment; a stroke with such a twig or cane. **5** a tool for beating eggs or cream; a whisk. **6** *cards* a change of suit. **7** a tress of hair, especially one of false hair used eg to give greater bulk to someone's natural hair. **8** a tuft of hair at the end of an animal's tail. **9** *N Amer* a set of railway points. ▷ *verb* (***switches, switched, switching***) **1** *tr & intr* to exchange (one thing or person for another), especially quickly and without notice in order to deceive. **2** *tr & intr* to transfer or change over (eg to a different system). **3** to beat with a switch. • **switched on** *colloq* **1** well informed or aware. **2** *old use* under the influence of drugs. ⓒ 16c, meaning 'riding whip': probably from German dialect *schwutsche* a long stick or Dutch *swijch* a branch.

■ **switch off** *colloq* to stop paying attention.

■ **switch something off** to turn (an appliance) off by means of a switch.

■ **switch someone on** *colloq* to make them aware of something.

■ **switch something on 1** to turn (an appliance) on by means of a switch. **2** *colloq* to bring on (eg charm or tears) at will in order to create the required effect.

switchback ▷ *noun* **1** a road with many twists and turns and upward and downward slopes. **2** a roller-coaster.

switchblade and **switchblade knife** ▷ *noun, especially N Amer* a FLICK KNIFE.

switchboard ▷ *noun* **1** a board on which incoming telephone calls are connected manually or electronically. **2** a board from which various pieces of electrical equipment are controlled.

swither /ˈswɪðə(r)/ *Scottish* ▷ *verb* (***swithered, swithering***) *intr* to hesitate; to be undecided; to consider possible alternatives. ▷ *noun* hesitation; indecision.

swivel /ˈswɪvəl/ ▷ *noun* **1** a joint between two parts enabling one part to turn or pivot freely and independently of the other. **2** *military* a swivel gun. ▷ *verb* (***swivelled, swivelling***) *tr & intr* to turn or pivot on a swivel or as if on a swivel. ⓒ Anglo-Saxon *swifan* to turn round.

swivel chair ▷ *noun* a chair in which the seat pivots on a shaft from the base and can be spun right round.

swivel gun ▷ *noun* a gun mounted on a swivel so that it can pivot round horizontally.

swizz ▷ *noun* (***swizzes***) *colloq* a thing that, in reality, is disappointingly inferior to what was cheatingly promised. ⓒ Early 20c: a shortening of *swizzle*.

swizzle /ˈswɪzəl/ ▷ *noun* **1** a swizz. **2** *colloq* a frothy cocktail with a rum or gin base. ▷ *verb* (***swizzled, swizzling***) *colloq* to cheat, let down, etc with a swizz. ⓒ 18c, meaning 'cocktail'.

swizzle-stick ▷ *noun* a thin stick used to stir cocktails and other drinks.

swollen *past participle of* SWELL

swollen head and **swelled head** ▷ *noun* conceitedness; excessive pride at one's own ability or achievements. • **swollen-headed** or **swell-headed** *adj*.

swoon ▷ *verb* (***swooned, swooning***) *intr* to faint, especially from over-excitement. ▷ *noun* an act of swooning. ⓒ 14c as *swowene*.

■ **swoon over someone** or **something** to go into raptures of adoration about them or it.

swoop ▷ *verb* (***swooped, swooping***) *intr* **1** to fly down with a fast sweeping movement. **2** to make a sudden forceful attack; to pounce. **3** (*usually* **swoop at someone** or **something**) to make a sudden and quick attempt to seize or get hold of them or it. **4** said of the stomach: to have a sudden sinking or dipping feeling. ▻ *noun* **1** an act of swooping. **2** a swooping movement or feeling. • **in one fell swoop** in one complete decisive action; all at one time. ⓘ Anglo-Saxon *swapan* to sweep.

swoosh ▻ *noun* (***swooshes***) the noise of a rush of air or water, or any noise resembling this. ▻ *verb* (***swooshes***, ***swooshed***, ***swooshing***) *intr* to make or move with such a noise. ⓘ 19c: probably imitating the sound made.

swop see SWAP

sword /sɔːd/ ▻ *noun* **1** a weapon like a large long knife, with a blade sharpened on one or both edges and usually ending in a point. **2** (**the sword**) violence or destruction, especially in war. **3** anything similar to a sword in shape, such as the long pointed upper jaw of a swordfish. • **cross swords with someone** to encounter them as an opponent; to argue or fight with them. • **put someone to the sword** *literary* to kill (prisoners, etc) with a sword or swords. ⓘ Anglo-Saxon *sweord*.

sword-bearer ▻ *noun* a public official whose function is to carry a ceremonial sword on special occasions.

swordbill and **sword-billed hummingbird** ▻ *noun* a species of hummingbird whose bill is longer than the head and body together.

sword dance ▻ *noun* **1** in Scotland: a dance, usually by a solo dancer, with steps over a cross formed by two swords or one sword and its scabbard laid on the ground. **2** in Northern England: a dance for a group of dancers carrying long flexible swords with which they perform a number of movements and create various patterns. • **sword-dancer** *noun*. • **sword-dancing** *noun*.

swordfish ▻ *noun* a large fast-swimming marine fish, so called because its upper jaw is prolonged into a long flat sword-shaped snout.

sword grass ▻ *noun* any of various species of grass, or of similar plants, with long, slender and usually sharp-edged leaves.

sword-guard ▻ *noun* the part of the hilt of a sword that protects the hand holding the sword.

sword of Damocles /— 'daməkliːz/ ▻ *noun, literary* any imminent danger or disaster. ⓘ 18c: from the story of Damocles in classical mythology, who was forced by the ruler of Syracuse to sit through a feast with a sword hanging by a single hair above his head in order that he should understand how uncertain and precarious life is even for those who have power and riches.

swordplay ▻ *noun* **1** the activity or art of fencing. **2** lively argument.

swordsman ▻ *noun* a man skilled in fighting with a sword. • **swordsmanship** *noun* skill in using a sword.

swordstick ▻ *noun* a hollow walking-stick containing a short sword or dagger.

swordtail ▻ *noun* any of various small brightly coloured freshwater fish, native to Central America and also a popular aquarium fish, so called because in the male the lower edge of the tail is prolonged to form a sword-like extension.

swore *past tense of* SWEAR

sworn ▻ *verb, past participle of* SWEAR. ▻ *adj* bound or confirmed by, or as if by, having taken an oath ◻ *sworn enemies*.

swot or **swat** /swɒt/ *colloq* ▻ *verb* (***swotted***, ***swotting***; ***swatted***, ***swatting***) *tr & intr* **1** to study hard and seriously. **2** (*also* **swot something up**) to study it intensively, especially at the last minute, ie just before an exam. ▻ *noun* **1** someone who studies hard, especially single-mindedly or in order to impress a teacher. **2** hard study; something which is hard to study ◻ *He finds maths a bit of a swot*. • **swotting** *noun*. ⓘ 19c: a variant of SWEAT.

SWOT analysis ▻ *noun, especially marketing* an analysis of the strengths and weaknesses of, the opportunities for, and the threats to, an organization, product, etc. ⓘ 1980s: acronym for *s*trengths, *w*eaknesses, *o*pportunities and *t*hreats.

swot card ▻ *noun* one of a set of cards on which the main points or key facts of a subject have been written, for ease of learning or revision eg before an examination.

SWP ▻ *abbreviation* Socialist Workers' Party.

SWRI ▻ *abbreviation* Scottish Women's Rural Institute.

swum *past participle of* SWIM

swung *past participle of* SWING

SY ▻ *abbreviation, IVR* Seychelles.

sybarite /'sɪbəraɪt/ ▻ *noun* someone devoted to a life of luxury and pleasure. • **sybaritic** /–'rɪtɪk/ *adj* luxurious. ⓘ 16c: originally an inhabitant of Sybaris, an ancient Greek city in S Italy, noted for its luxury.

sycamore /'sɪkəmɔː(r)/ ▻ *noun* **1** a large fast-growing deciduous tree with dark green leaves divided into five toothed lobes, yellowish flowers borne in long pendulous spikes, and two-winged fruits. **2** *N Amer* any of various plane trees native to America. **3** (*usually* **sycomore**) a kind of fig tree found in N Africa and the Middle East. **4** the wood of any of these trees, used for furniture-making, etc. ⓘ 13c: from Greek *sykomoros*, from *sykon* fig.

sycophant /'sɪkəfənt, -fant/ ▻ *noun* someone who flatters in a servile way; a crawler. • **sycophancy** *noun* the behaviour of a sycophant; flattery. • **sycophantic** *adj*. • **sycophantically** *adverb*. ⓘ 16c: from Greek *sykophantes* informer or swindler.

Sydenham's chorea /'sɪdənəmz —/ ▻ *noun, pathol* a disorder caused by an allergic reaction to bacterial infection, characterized by uncontrolled jerking and facial contortions, which most commonly affects children. ⓘ 19c: named after Thomas Sydenham (1624–89), English physician.

SYHA ▻ *abbreviation* Scottish Youth Hostels Association.

syllabary /'sɪləbərɪ/ ▻ *noun* (***syllabaries***) a writing system in which the symbols represent spoken syllables (although in fact some stand for single speech sounds).

syllabi *plural of* SYLLABUS

syllabic /sɪ'labɪk/ ▻ *adj* **1** relating to syllables or the division of words into syllables. **2** constituting a syllable or forming the core of a syllable. **3** said of verse or poetic metre: based on the number of syllables in a line, as opposed to the stress patterns of words or the lengths of the vowels in the words.

syllabicate /sɪ'labɪkeɪt/ ▻ *verb* (***syllabicated***, ***syllabicating***) to SYLLABIFY. • **syllabication** *noun*.

syllabify /sɪ'labɪfaɪ/ ▻ *verb* (***syllabifies***, ***syllabified***, ***syllabifying***) to divide (a word) into syllables. • **syllabification** *noun*.

syllable /'sɪləbəl/ ▻ *noun* **1** a segment of a spoken word consisting of one sound or of two or more sounds said as a single unit of speech (*segment* and *spoken* each consist of two syllables; *consisting* has three syllables). **2** the slightest word or sound ◻ *He hardly uttered a syllable all evening*. • **in words of one syllable** in simple language; frankly; plainly. ⓘ 14c: from Greek *syllabe*, literally 'something that is held or taken together'.

syllabub or **sillabub** /'sɪləbʌb/ ▻ *noun* a frothy dessert made by whipping a sweetened mixture of cream or milk and wine.

syllabus /'sɪləbəs/ ▻ *noun* (***syllabuses*** or ***syllabi*** /-baɪ/) **1** a series of topics prescribed for a course of study. **2** a booklet or sheet listing these. ⓘ 17c: from a misreading of Latin *sittybas*, from Greek *sittyba* book-label.

syllepsis /sɪ'lɛpsɪs/ ▻ *noun* (***syllepses*** /-siːz/) a figure of speech in which one word in a sentence stands in the same grammatical relationship to two or more words or phrases but with different senses, as does *in* in *She left home in tears and a taxi.* • **sylleptic** *adj.* ⓒ 16c: Greek, literally 'a taking together'.

syllogism /'sɪlədʒɪzəm/ ▻ *noun* an argument in which a conclusion, whether valid or invalid, is drawn from two independent statements using logic, as in *All dogs are animals, foxhounds are dogs, therefore foxhounds are animals.* • **syllogistic** *adj.* • **syllogistically** *adverb.* See also LOGIC, FALLACY. ⓒ 14c: from Greek *syllogismos* a reasoning together.

syllogize or **syllogise** /'sɪlədʒaɪz/ ▻ *verb* (***syllogized, syllogizing***) *tr & intr* to reason, argue or deduce by syllogisms.

sylph /sɪlf/ ▻ *noun* **1** in folklore: a spirit of the air. **2** a slender graceful woman or girl. ⓒ 17c: a word created in the 16c by Paracelsus, a Swiss alchemist.

sylph-like ▻ *adj* slim, like a sylph.

sylvan /'sɪlvən/ ▻ *adj, literary* relating to woods or woodland; wooded. ⓒ 16c: from Latin *silva* a wood.

symbiont /'sɪmbaɪɒnt, -bɪɒnt/ ▻ *noun, biol* either of two organisms living in a symbiotic relationship.

symbiosis /sɪmbaɪ'oʊsɪs, -bɪ'oʊsɪs/ ▻ *noun* (***symbioses*** /-siːz/) **1** *biol* a close association between two organisms of different species, usually to the benefit of both partners, and often essential for mutual survival. Compare MUTUALISM. **2** *psychol* a mutually beneficial relationship between two people who are dependent on each other. • **symbiotic** /-'ɒtɪk/ *adj* relating to or involving symbiosis. ⓒ 19c in these senses; 17c, meaning 'living together': from Greek *syn* together + *bios* life.

symbol /'sɪmbəl/ ▻ *noun* **1** a thing that represents or stands for another, usually something concrete or material representing an idea or emotion, eg the colour red representing danger. **2** a letter or sign used to represent a quantity, idea, object, operation, etc, such as the × used in mathematics to represent the multiplication process or £ used for pound sterling. **3** *psychol* an object or action which represents an unconscious or repressed conflict. • **symbolic** /–'bɒlɪk/ or **symbolical** *adj* **1** being a symbol of something; representing or standing for something. **2** relating to symbols or their use. • **symbolically** *adverb.* ⓒ 16c in senses 1 and 2; 15c, meaning 'creed', 'statement of doctrine': from Greek *symbolon* token.

symbolic interactionism ▻ *noun* a sociological theory which attempts to explain patterns of behaviour in terms of the meanings and symbols that people share in everyday interaction, and which emphasizes that mutual understanding depends on people continually checking and negotiating the meaning of what they say and how they behave.

symbolic logic ▻ *noun* a branch of logic which uses symbols instead of propositions and terms, as a means of clarifying reasoning.

symbolism ▻ *noun* **1** the use of symbols, especially to express ideas or emotions in literature, cinema, etc. **2** a system of symbols. **3** symbolic meaning or nature. **4** (*usually* **Symbolism**) a 19c movement in art and literature which made extensive use of symbols to indicate or evoke emotions or ideas. • **symbolist** *noun* an artist or writer who uses symbolism.

symbolize or **symbolise** /'sɪmbəlaɪz/ ▻ *verb* (***symbolized, symbolizing***) **1** to be a symbol of something; to stand for something. **2** to represent something by means of a symbol or symbols. • **symbolization** *noun.* • **symbolizer** *noun.*

symbology ▻ *noun* (***symbologies***) **1** the study or use of symbols. **2** symbols used.

symmetrical /sɪ'mɛtrɪkəl/ ▻ *adj* having symmetry. • **symmetrically** *adverb.*

symmetry /'sɪmətrɪ/ ▻ *noun* (***symmetries***) **1** exact similarity between two parts or halves, as if one were a mirror image of the other. **2** the arrangement of parts in pleasing proportion to each other; also, the aesthetic satisfaction derived from this. ⓒ 16c: from Greek *syn* together + *metron* measure.

sympathetic /sɪmpə'θɛtɪk/ ▻ *adj* **1** (*often* **sympathetic to someone** or **something**) feeling or expressing sympathy for them. **2** amiable, especially because of being kind-hearted. **3** acting or done out of sympathy; showing sympathy. **4** in keeping with one's mood or feelings; agreeable. **5** *biol* belonging or relating to the sympathetic nervous system. **6** *physics* denoting vibrations induced in one body by vibrations in another body. **7** *music* said of certain strings on some stringed instruments: not themselves plucked, bowed or hit but producing sound by vibrations induced in them by the vibrations of other strings. • **sympathetically** *adverb.*

sympathetic nervous system ▻ *noun, zool* in vertebrates: a subdivision of the AUTONOMIC NERVOUS SYSTEM, the activity of which tends to increase the heart rate, constrict blood vessels and generally prepare the body for action.

sympathize or **sympathise** ▻ *verb* (***sympathized, sympathizing***) *intr* **1** (*often* **sympathize with someone**) to feel or express sympathy for them. **2** (*often* **sympathize with someone** or **something**) to support or be in agreement with them. • **sympathizer** *noun.*

sympathy /'sɪmpəθɪ/ ▻ *noun* (***sympathies***) **1** (*often* **sympathy for** or **with someone**) an understanding of and feeling for the sadness or suffering of others, often shown in expressions of sorrow or pity. **2** (*often* **sympathies**) loyal or approving support for, or agreement with, an organization or belief. **3** affection between people resulting from their understanding of each other's personalities. ⓒ 16c: from Greek *syn* with + *pathos* suffering.

symphonic /sɪm'fɒnɪk/ ▻ *adj* said of music: suitable for performance by a symphony orchestra.

symphony /'sɪmfənɪ/ ▻ *noun* (***symphonies***) **1** a long musical work divided into several MOVEMENTs, played by a full orchestra. **2** an instrumental passage in a musical work which consists mostly of singing. **3** *literary* a pleasing combination of parts, eg shapes or colours. **4** a symphony orchestra. ⓒ 13c, meaning 'a musical work'; 17c: from Greek *syn* together + *phone* sound.

symphony orchestra ▻ *noun* a large orchestra capable of playing large-scale orchestral music.

symposium /sɪm'poʊzɪəm/ ▻ *noun* (***symposia*** /-zɪə/ or ***symposiums***) **1** a conference held to discuss a particular subject, especially an academic subject. **2** a collection of essays by different writers on a single topic. ⓒ 18c: from Greek *symposion* a drinking-party with intellectual discussion.

symptom /'sɪmptəm/ ▻ *noun* **1** *medicine* an indication of the presence of a disease or disorder, especially something perceived by the patient and not outwardly visible, eg pain, nausea, dizziness. **2** an indication of the existence of a, usually unwelcome, state or condition □ *The increase in crime is a symptom of moral decline.* ⓒ 14c: from Greek *symptoma* happening, attribute.

symptomatic /sɪmptə'matik/ ▻ *adj* **1** (*often* **symptomatic of something**) being a symptom of it; indicative of it. **2** belonging or relating to a symptom or symptoms. • **symptomatically** *adverb.*

symptomatize or **symptomatise** ▻ *verb* (***symptomatized, symptomatizing***) to be a symptom of something.

symptomatology ▻ *noun* (***symptomatologies***) *medicine* **1** the study of symptoms. **2** the symptoms of a patient or a disease taken as a whole.

symptomize or **symptomise** ▻ *verb* (***symptomized, symptomizing***) to SYMPTOMATIZE.

synagogue /'sɪnəgɒg/ ▻ *noun* **1** a Jewish place of worship and religious instruction. **2** a Jewish religious assembly or congregation. ◷ 12c: from Greek *synagoge* assembly.

synapse /'saɪnaps/ ▻ *noun, anatomy* in the nervous system: a region where one neurone communicates with the next, consisting of a minute gap across which nerve impulses are transmitted by means of a chemical substance known as a neurotransmitter. ◷ 19c: from Greek *synapsis* contact or junction.

synapsis /sɪ'napsɪs/ ▻ *noun* (***synapses*** /-siːz/) **1** *biol* the pairing of chromosomes of paternal and maternal origin during MEIOSIS. **2** *medicine* a synapse. • **synaptic** *adj.* ◷ 19c: Greek, meaning 'contact or junction'.

synch or **sync** /sɪŋk/ *colloq* ▻ *noun* synchronization, especially of sound and picture in film and television. ▻ *verb* (***synched***, ***synching***; ***synced***, ***syncing***) to synchronize.

synchro /'sɪŋkroʊ/ ▻ *noun, colloq, sport* synchronized swimming.

synchromesh /'sɪŋkroʊmɛʃ/ ▻ *noun* a gear system which matches the speeds of the gear wheels before they are engaged, avoiding shock and noise in gear-changing. ◷ 1920s: a shortening of *synchronized mesh*.

synchronic /sɪŋ'krɒnɪk/ ▻ *adj* **1** *linguistics* concerned with the study of a language as it exists at a particular point in time, without reference to its past history or development. Opposite of DIACHRONIC. **2** SYNCHRONOUS. • **synchronically** *adverb.* • **synchronicity** *noun.* ◷ 1920s in the linguistic sense, translating Ferdinand de Saussure's French term *synchronique*; 19c with the same meaning as *synchronous*: from Greek *syn* together + *chronos* time.

synchronize or **synchronise** /'sɪŋkrənaɪz/ ▻ *verb* (***synchronized***, ***synchronizing***) **1** *tr & intr* to happen or cause to happen, move or operate in exact time with (something else or each other). **2** to project (a film), or broadcast (a TV programme), so that the action, actors' lip movements, etc precisely match the sounds or words heard. **3** to set (clocks or watches) so that they show exactly the same time. • **synchronization** *noun.* • **synchronizer** *noun.* ◷ 17c: from Greek *syn* together + *chronos* time.

synchronized swimming ▻ *noun* a sport in which a swimmer or group of swimmers performs a sequence of gymnastic and balletic movements in time to music. Individual and group competitions have recently become official events in the Olympic Games.

synchronous /'sɪŋkrənəs/ ▻ *adj* **1** occurring at the same time; recurring with the same frequency. **2** said of the orbit of an artificial satellite: GEOSTATIONARY. • **synchronously** *adverb.*

synchrony /'sɪŋkrənɪ/ ▻ *noun* **1** the fact or state of being synchronous or synchronic; simultaneousness. **2** *linguistics* the state of a language or languages at a given time as a perspective for linguistic study.

synchrotron /'sɪŋkrətrɒn/ ▻ *noun, physics* a particle accelerator widely used in particle physics and designed to accelerate electrons and protons which travel around a hollow ring at increasing speed. ◷ 1940s: modelled on ELECTRON, from Greek *syn* together + *chronos* time.

syncline /'sɪŋklaɪn/ ▻ *noun, geol* a large generally U-shaped fold in the stratified rocks of the Earth's crust. ◷ 19c: from Greek *syn* together + *klinein* to cause to lean.

syncopate /'sɪŋkoʊpeɪt/ ▻ *verb* (***syncopated***, ***syncopating***) **1** to alter (the rhythm of music) by putting the stress on beats not usually stressed. **2** to shorten (a word) by syncope. • **syncopation** *noun* **1** syncopating. **2** the beat or rhythm produced by syncopating. • **syncopator** *noun.*

syncope /'sɪŋkəpɪ/ ▻ *noun* **1** *medicine* a sudden temporary loss of consciousness; a faint. **2** *linguistics* the dropping of a letter or syllable in the middle of a word, eg in *o'er*, the poetic version of *over*. ◷ 16c: from Greek *synkope* a cutting short.

sync pulse ▻ *noun* **1** *broadcasting* in a TV signal: a pulse transmitted at the beginning of each line and field to ensure the correct scanning rate on reception. **2** *cinema* in motion pictures: a series of signals linked to the camera frame rate recorded on the separate sound magnetic tape for subsequent matching to the picture.

syncretism /'sɪŋkrətɪzəm/ ▻ *noun* the merging or attempted reconciling of the beliefs and practices of different religions or philosophies. • **syncretist** *noun.* • **syncretistic** *adj.* ◷ 17c: from Greek *synkretismos* a confederation, originally a union of Cretans against a common enemy.

syncretize or **syncretise** /'sɪŋkrətaɪz/ ▻ *verb* (***syncretized***, ***syncretizing***) to treat, merge or deal with in a syncretistic way.

syndic /'sɪndɪk/ ▻ *noun* someone who represents a university, company or other body in business or legal matters. ◷ 17c: from Greek *syndikos* advocate or representative.

syndicalism ▻ *noun* a form of trade-unionism favouring the transfer of the ownership of factories, etc to the workers themselves. • **syndicalist** *noun.* ◷ 20c: from French *syndicalisme*, from Greek *syndikos* representative.

syndicate ▻ *noun* /'sɪndɪkət/ **1** any association of people or groups working together on a single project. **2** a group of business organizations jointly managing or financing a single venture. **3** an association of criminals organizing widespread illegal activities. **4** an agency selling journalists' material to a number of newspapers for publication at the same time. ▻ *verb* /-keɪt/ (***syndicated***, ***syndicating***) **1** to form into a syndicate. **2** to organize something by means of a syndicate. **3 a** to sell (an article, photograph, etc) for publication by a number of newspapers; **b** in the US: to sell (a programme) for broadcasting by a number of TV stations. • **syndication** *noun.* • **syndicator** *noun.* ◷ 17c: from French *syndicat*, from Greek *syndikos* representative.

syndrome /'sɪndroʊm/ ▻ *noun* **1** a group of signs or symptoms whose appearance together usually indicates the presence of a particular disease or disorder. **2** a pattern or series of events, observed qualities, etc characteristic of a particular problem or condition. ◷ 16c: from Greek *syndrome* a running together.

synecdoche /sɪ'nɛkdəkɪ/ ▻ *noun* a figure of speech in which a part of something is used to refer to or denote the whole thing, or the whole to refer to or denote a part, eg the use of *wiser heads* to mean *wiser people*. ◷ 15c: from Greek *synekdoche* a receiving together.

synergy /'sɪnədʒɪ/ or **synergism** /'sɪnədʒɪzəm/ ▻ *noun* **1** *pharmacol* the phenomenon in which the combined action of two or more compounds, especially drugs or hormones, is greater than the sum of the individual effects of each compound. **2** *physiol* the phenomenon in which the combined action of two or more muscles, nerves, etc, is greater than the sum of their individual effects. ◷ 19c in these senses; 17c, meaning 'co-operation': from Greek *synergia* co-operation.

synod /'sɪnəd, 'sɪnɒd/ ▻ *noun* **1 a** a local or national council of members of the clergy; **b** a meeting of this. **2** in the Presbyterian church system: a church court intermediate in status and responsibility between a PRESBYTERY and a GENERAL ASSEMBLY. ◷ 14c: from Greek *synodos* meeting.

synonym /'sɪnənɪm/ ▻ *noun* a word having the same, or very nearly the same, meaning as another. • **synonymous** /sɪ'nɒnɪməs/ *adj* (*often* **synonymous with something**) **1** having the same meaning. **2** very closely associated in the mind ◻ *For some, football is synonymous with hooliganism.* • **synonymy**

/sɪ'nɒnɪmɪ/ *noun*. ◷ 16c: from Greek *syn* with + *onyma*, a variant form of *onoma* name.

synopsis /sɪ'nɒpsɪs/ ▷ *noun* (***synopses*** /-siːz/) a brief outline, eg of the plot of a book; a summary. • **synoptic** *adj* being or like a synopsis; giving or taking an overall view. ◷ 17c: from Greek *syn* together + *opsis* view.

Synoptic Gospels ▷ *plural noun* the Gospels of Matthew, Mark and Luke. ◷ 19c: so called because they describe the events of Christ's life from a similar point of view..

synovia /sɪ'noʊvɪə, saɪ-/ ▷ *noun* the transparent liquid, produced by the synovial membranes of a joint, which serves to lubricate that joint. Also called **synovial fluid**.

synovial membrane ▷ *noun, anatomy* a membrane of connective tissue that lines tendon sheaths and capsular ligaments, and secretes synovia.

synovitis /saɪnoʊ'vaɪtɪs/ ▷ *noun, anatomy* inflammation of a synovial membrane.

synroc /'sɪnrɒk/ ▷ *noun* any of various types of synthetic rock developed to fuse with radioactive waste and hold it in a stable condition buried deep underground. ◷ 1970s: from *syn*thetic *roc*k.

syntax /'sɪntaks/ ▷ *noun* (***syntaxes***) **1 a** the positioning of words in a sentence and their relationship to each other; **b** the grammatical rules governing this. **2** the branch of linguistics that is concerned with the study of such rules. **3 a** the order and arrangement of elements in a logical statement, computer program, etc; **b** the rules governing these. • **syntactician** *noun* someone who studies syntax or is an expert on syntax. • **syntactic** or **syntactical** *adj*. • **syntactically** *adverb*. ◷ 17c: from Greek *syn* together + *tassein* to put in order.

synth ▷ *noun, music, colloq* short for SYNTHESIZER.

synthesis /'sɪnθəsɪs/ ▷ *noun* (***syntheses*** /-siːz/) **1** the process of putting together separate parts to form a complex whole. **2** the result of such a process. **3** *chem* any process whereby a complex chemical compound is formed from simpler compounds or elements, especially via a series of chemical reactions. **4** *linguistics* the indication of grammatical relationships by means of inflection (eg changes in the forms of words) rather than by word order and/or grammatical function words (such as prepositions). ◷ 18c in the chemical sense given here; 17c as a philosophical term meaning 'the process of arguing from causes or general principles to their effects or consequences': from Greek *syn* together + *thesis* a placing.

synthesize or **synthesise** /'sɪnθəsaɪz/ ▷ *verb* (***synthesized***, ***synthesizing***) **1** to combine (simple parts) to form (a complex whole). **2** *chem* to form (a compound, product, etc) by a process of chemical synthesis.

synthesizer or **synthesiser** ▷ *noun* **1** *music* an instrument that produces sound electronically, especially one able to produce the sounds of other instruments, comprising an integrated set of electronic devices for generating and modifying sounds and usually including one or more keyboards, oscillators, filters and devices for frequency and amplitude modulation. Also shortened to SYNTH. **2** someone who synthesizes something; a device for synthesizing something.

synthetic /sɪn'θɛtɪk/ ▷ *adj* **1** referring or relating to, or produced by, chemical synthesis; not naturally produced; man-made. **2** artificial or unreal □ ***the monochrome, synthetic appearance of the set for the play***. **3** not sincere; sham. **4** *linguistics* said of a language: using inflection (eg changes in the forms of words) rather than word order and/or grammatical words (such as prepositions) to indicate grammatical relationships. **5** integrating thoughts and ideas □ ***the synthetic power of his imagination***. ▷ *noun* a synthetic substance. • **synthetically** *adverb*. ◷ 17c as a term in philosophy, 18c as a term in chemistry; compare *synthesis*: from Greek *synthetikos* skilled at putting together.

syphilis /'sɪfɪlɪs/ ▷ *noun, medicine* a sexually transmitted disease caused by bacterial infection and characterized by painless ulcers on the genitals, fever and a faint red rash, which if left untreated may eventually result in heart damage, blindness, paralysis and death. • **syphilitic** *adj* relating to or affected with syphilis. ▷ *noun* someone infected with syphilis. ◷ 17c: named after Syphilus, the infected hero of a 16c Latin poem.

syphon see SIPHON

Syriac /'sɪrɪak/ ▷ *noun* **1** the ancient Aramaic dialect of Syria. **2** a modern form of this dialect, spoken by about one million people in the Middle East and the US. ▷ *adj* relating to or spoken or written in either of these dialects.

syringa /sɪ'rɪŋgə/ ▷ *noun* (***syringas***) **1** the name commonly, but technically incorrectly, used to refer to the mock orange shrub (see under PHILADELPHUS). **2** any of various species of plant belonging to a genus that includes the lilac. ◷ 17c: see SYRINGE.

syringe /sɪ'rɪndʒ, 'sɪ/ ▷ *noun* (***syringes*** /-dʒɪz/) **1** a medical instrument for injecting or drawing off liquid, consisting of a hollow cylinder with a plunger inside and a thin hollow needle attached. **2** a similar device used in gardening, cooking, etc. ▷ *verb* (***syringed***, ***syringing***) to clean, spray or inject using a syringe. ◷ 15c: from Greek *syrinx* tube.

syrinx /'sɪrɪŋks/ ▷ *noun* (***syringes*** /sɪ'rɪndʒɪz/ or ***syrinxes*** /'sɪrɪŋksɪz/) **1** a set of PANPIPES. **2** *zool* the sound-producing organ of a bird, consisting of several vibrating membranes. ◷ 17c: from Greek *syrinx* a reed or panpipes.

syrup /'sɪrəp/ ▷ *noun* **1** a sweet, sticky, almost saturated solution of sugar, widely used in cooking, baking, etc, and obtained from various plants, eg sugar cane, maple, or manufactured commercially, eg golden syrup. **2** a solution of sugar in water used to preserve canned fruit. **3** any sugar-flavoured liquid medicine. **4** *colloq* exaggerated sentimentality or pleasantness of manner. • **syrupy** *adj* **1** the consistency of or like syrup. **2** over-sentimental ◷ 14c: from Arabic *sharab* a drink.

systaltic /sɪ'staltɪk/ ▷ *adj* said especially of the heart: alternately contracting and dilating. Compare SYSTOLE. ◷ 17c: from Greek *systaltikos* depressing, from *syn* together + *stellein* to put.

system /'sɪstəm/ ▷ *noun* **1** a set of interconnected or interrelated parts forming a complex whole □ ***the transport system*** □ ***the human digestive system***. **2** an arrangement of mechanical, electrical or electronic parts functioning as a unit □ ***a stereo system***. **3** a way of working; a method or arrangement of organization or classification □ ***a more efficient filing system*** □ ***the capitalist system***. **4** efficiency of organization; methodicalness; orderliness □ ***You need to get some system into your exam revision***. **5** one's mind or body regarded as a set of interconnected parts □ ***get the anger out of your system***. **6** (**the system**) society, or the network of institutions that control it, usually regarded as an oppressive force. **7** *astron* a group of heavenly bodies consisting of a central body (eg a sun or a planet) and others (planets or moons respectively) which move around it under the influence of their mutual attraction □ ***the solar system***. **8** *geol* the basic unit of classification of rock strata formed during a single period of geological time, ranking above SERIES (sense 8) and characterized by its fossil content. **9** an interrelated body of doctrines or theories; a full and connected view of some branch of knowledge. • **all systems go** or **all systems are go** *colloq* everything is ready ◷ 20c: originally astronautics jargon. ◷ 17c: from Greek *systema*.

systematic /sɪstə'matɪk/ ▷ *adj* **1** making use of, or carried out according to, a clearly worked-out plan or method. **2** methodical. **3** *biol* referring or relating to systematics. • **systematically** *adverb*.

systematics ▷ *noun, biol* the scientific study of the classification of living organisms into a hierarchical series of groups which emphasizes their natural interrelationships.

systematize or **systematise** /ˈsɪstəmətaɪz/ ▻ *verb* (*systematized, systematizing*) to organize or arrange in a methodical way. • **systematization** *noun.*

system building ▻ *noun, archit* methods designed to increase the speed of construction by manufacturing component parts of a building ready for later assembly on site. Many modern buildings are constructed from prefabricated components, such as steel and timber frames, pre-formed roofing and exterior wall cladding, and windows.

system date ▻ *noun computing* the current date as specified by an operating system, used to record a user's operations or to begin preset programs, etc.

Système International d'Unités see SI

system engineering or **systems engineering** ▻ *noun* the branch of engineering that uses information technology in design applications.

systemic /sɪˈstiːmɪk, sɪˈste-/ ▻ *adj* **1** *biol* referring or relating to a whole organism. **2** *medicine* relating to or affecting the whole body. **3** *bot* said of a pesticide: not harmful to the plant, but absorbed into the sap and so rendering the whole plant resistant to attack by aphids, mites, etc. • **systemically** *adverb*.

systems analysis ▻ *noun* **1** the detailed analysis of all phases of activity of a commercial, industrial or scientific organization, usually with a computer, in order to plan more efficient methods and better use of resources. **2** *computing* the detailed investigation and analysis of some human task, usually in business, management, industry, etc, in order to determine whether and how it can be computerized, followed in appropriate cases by the design, implementation and evaluation of a computer system that can perform the task.

systole /ˈsɪstəlɪ/ ▻ *noun* (*systoles*) *medicine* contraction of the heart muscle, during which blood is pumped from the ventricle into the arteries. See also DIASTOLE. • **systolic** /sɪˈstɒlɪk/ *adj* relating to systole. ◷ 16c: from Greek *systole*, from *syn* together + *stellein* to place.

T

T[1] or **t** ▷ *noun* (*Ts, T's* or *t's*) **1** the twentieth letter of the English alphabet. **2** something shaped like a T, eg a pipe which is used to join three separate pipes together. ● **to a T** exactly; perfectly well.

T[2] ▷ *abbreviation* **1** *music* tenor. **2** *IVR* Thailand. **3** *physics* tesla.

T[3] ▷ *symbol, chem* tritium.

t ▷ *abbreviation* **1** *commerce* tare. **2** temperature. **3** ton. **4** tonne. **5** troy, or troy weight.

TA ▷ *abbreviation* Territorial Army.

Ta ▷ *symbol, chem* tantalum.

ta /tɑː/ ▷ *exclamation, Brit colloq* thank you. ◷ 18c: imitating a young child's pronunciation.

tab[1] ▷ *noun* **1** a small flap, tag, strip of material, etc attached to an article, for hanging it up, opening, holding or identifying it, etc. **2** a small strip of material attached to a garment for hanging it up. **3** *chiefly N Amer* a bill, eg in a restaurant, especially an account that is opened, eg at the beginning of an evening, and added to until it is settled at the end of the evening. **4** *chiefly N Amer* a price; cost. **5** *N Eng slang* a cigarette. ▷ *verb* (***tabbed, tabbing***) to fix a tab to something or someone. ● **keep tabs on someone** or **something** *colloq* to keep a close watch or check on them or it. ● **pick up the tab** *chiefly N Amer* to pay the bill. ◷ 19c: probably originally a dialect word.

tab[2] ▷ *noun* a key on a typewriter or word processor which sets and then automatically finds the position of the margins and columns needed to arrange information in a table. Also called **tabulator**. ◷ Early 20c: an abbreviation of TABULATOR.

tab[3] ▷ *noun* **1** a pill or drug, especially a small square of paper containing LSD or ECSTASY. **2** short for TABLET 1. ◷ 1960s.

tabard /'tabəd/ ▷ *noun* **1** a short loose sleeveless jacket or tunic, worn especially by a knight over his armour or, with the arms of the king or queen on the front, by a herald. **2** a woman's or girl's sleeveless or short-sleeved tunic or overgarment. ◷ 13c: from French *tabart*.

tabaret /'tabərɪt/ ▷ *noun* a type of silk fabric, used especially by upholsterers, with alternate stripes of watered and satin surface. ◷ 19c: perhaps from TABBY.

Tabasco /tə'baskoʊ/ ▷ *noun, trademark* a hot sauce made from a pungent type of red pepper and used as a flavouring. ◷ 19c: named after Tabasco, a river and state in Mexico.

tabbouleh /ta'buːleɪ/ ▷ *noun* a Mediterranean salad made with cracked wheat which has been moistened with water, lemon juice and olive oil, and mixed with chopped vegetables, especially tomatoes, cucumber and garlic. ◷ 1950s: from Arabic *tabbula*.

tabby /'tabɪ/ ▷ *noun* (***tabbies***) **1 a** (*also* **tabby cat**) a usually grey or brown cat with darker stripes; **b** any female domestic cat. **2** a kind of silk with irregular wavy shiny markings. ▷ *adj* characterized by dark stripes or wavy markings. ◷ 17c in sense 2: from French *tabis*, from *Al-Attabiyah* in Baghdad where the silk was first made; in sense 1b perhaps shortened from the female name Tabitha, as it is sometimes applied to old or elderly women, often thought to possess some cat-like qualities.

tabernacle /'tabənakəl/ ▷ *noun* **1** (*also* **Tabernacle**) the tent carried by the Israelites across the desert during the Exodus, used as a sanctuary for the Ark of the Covenant. See also SUKKOTH. **2** *RC Church* a receptacle in which the consecrated bread and wine are kept. **3** a place of worship of certain nonconformist Christian denominations. **4** *naut* a frame to support the foot of a mast. ◷ 13c: from Latin *tabernaculum* tent.

tabes /'teɪbiːz/ ▷ *noun, pathol* a wasting away of the body or parts of the body. ◷ 17c: Latin, meaning 'wasting away'.

tabla /'tablə, -lɑː/ ▷ *noun* (***tablas***) a pair of small drums played with the hands in Indian music. ◷ 19c: Hindi, from Arabic *tabl*.

tablature /'tablətʃə(r)/ ▷ *noun* a system of musical notation indicating the keys, frets, etc to be used rather than the pitch to be sounded, which is still used for the guitar and other fretted instruments. ◷ 16c: French, from Latin *tabula* a board.

table /'teɪbəl/ ▷ *noun* **1** a piece of furniture consisting of a flat horizontal surface supported by one or more legs. **2** the people sitting at a table. **3** the food served at a particular table or in a particular house □ ***keeps a good table.*** **4** a group of words or figures, etc arranged systematically in columns and rows. **5** a MULTIPLICATION TABLE □ ***learn your tables.*** **6** any flat level surface. **7** *historical* a slab of stone or wood inscribed with laws. **8** a TABLELAND. **9** a broad flat surface cut on a gem. ▷ *verb* (***tabled, tabling***) **1** *Brit* to put something forward for discussion. **2** *N Amer* to postpone discussion of (a bill, etc) indefinitely. **3** to make or enter something into a table; to tabulate. ● **at table** having a meal. ● **drink someone under the table** see under DRINK. ● **on the table** under discussion. ● **turn the tables on someone** to reverse a situation so that they are at a disadvantage where previously they had an advantage. ● **under the table** secretly; in a clandestine way. ◷ Anglo-Saxon *tabule*: from Latin *tabula* board or tablet.

tableau /'tabloʊ; *French* tablo/ ▷ *noun* (***tableaux*** /-bloʊz; *French* tablo/) **1** a picture or pictorial representation of a group or scene. **2** *theat* a moment or scene in which the action is frozen for dramatic effect. ◷ 17c: French, from *tablel* diminutive of *table* TABLE.

tableau vivant /*French* tablo vivɑ̃/ ▷ *noun* (***tableaux vivants*** /*French* tablo vivɑ̃/) a group of people on stage forming a silent motionless scene from history or literature, etc. ◷ 19c: French, literally 'living picture'.

tablecloth ▷ *noun* a cloth, often a decorative one, for covering a table, especially during meals.

table d'hôte /tɑːbəl 'doʊt; *French* tablədot/ ▷ *noun* (***tables d'hôte*** /'tɑːbəlz —; *French* tablədot/) a meal or menu with a set number of choices and a set number of courses offered for a fixed price, especially to residents in a hotel. Compare À LA CARTE. ◷ 17c: French, literally 'host's table'.

table football ▷ *noun* a version of football played on a table with plastic figures suspended on metal rods, which are spun to strike the ball.

tableland ▷ *noun, geol* a broad high plain or a plateau, usually with steep sides and rising sharply from the surrounding lowland.

table licence ▷ *noun* a licence to sell and serve alcohol only with meals.

table linen ▻ *noun* tablecloths and napkins collectively.

table mat ▻ *noun* a mat for protecting the surface of a table from the heat of dishes from the oven and warmed plates.

table napkin see NAPKIN

table salt ▻ *noun* fine salt suitable for use at meals.

tablespoon ▻ *noun* **1** a spoon which is larger than a DESSERTSPOON and is used for measuring and serving food. **2** (abbreviation **tbsp**) a TABLESPOONFUL.

tablespoonful ▻ *noun* (***tablespoonfuls***) the amount a tablespoon can hold.

tablet /'tablət/ ▻ *noun* **1** a small solid measured amount of a medicine or drug; a pill. **2** a solid flat piece of something, eg soap. **3** a slab of stone or wood on which an inscription may be carved. **4** *Scottish* a type of hard fudge made from sugar, butter and condensed milk, cut into smallish slabs when solid. ⓘ 14c: from French *tablete*, from Latin *tabula* board.

table tennis ▻ *noun* a game based on tennis played indoors on a table with small bats and a light hollow ball. Also called **ping-pong**.

tableware ▻ *noun* dishes, plates and cutlery, etc collectively for use at table.

tabloid /'tablɔɪd/ ▻ *noun* a newspaper with relatively small pages (approximately 12 × 16in, 30 × 40cm), especially one written in an informal and often sensationalist style and with many photographs. Often *as adj* □ ***the tabloid press*** □ ***tabloid television***. Compare BROADSHEET. ⓘ Early 20c in this sense; late 19c as a trademark for medicines produced in tablet form, from which sense the word came to be applied to anything produced in concentrated form, and in particular to newspapers that provide news coverage in a condensed informal style: from TABLET + -OID.

tabloid TV or **tabloid television** ▻ *noun* a form of TV which, like the tabloid press, features mainly short sensationalist stories. It is broadcast mainly by satellite and cable companies.

taboo or **tabu** /tə'buː/ ▻ *noun* (***taboos*** or ***tabus***) **1** anything which is forbidden or disapproved of for religious reasons or by social custom. **2** any system which forbids certain actions as being unclean or holy. ▻ *adj* forbidden or prohibited as being a taboo. ▻ *verb* (***taboos, tabooed, tabooing***; ***tabus, tabued, tabuing***) to forbid (a custom, or the use of a word, etc) as a taboo. ⓘ 18c: from Tongan *tabu*.

tabor /'teɪbə(r)/ ▻ *noun* **1** a small single-headed drum, used especially in the Middle Ages, played with one hand while the same player plays a pipe or fife with the other. **2** the player of such a drum. ⓘ 13c: from French *tabour*.

tabouret or *US* **taboret** /'tabərɛt/ *noun* **1** a low stool or seat. **2** a frame used to stretch out cloth which is being embroidered. ⓘ 17c: French, diminutive of *tabour* a TABOR.

tabular /'tabjʊlə(r)/ ▻ *adj* **1** arranged in systematic columns; in the form of or according to a table. **2** horizontally flattened. ⓘ 17c: from Latin *tabularis*, from *tabula* board.

tabula rasa /'tabjʊlə 'rɑːzə/ ▻ *noun* (***tabulae rasae*** /-liː -ziː/) **1** a mind not yet influenced by outside impressions and experience. **2** a smoothed or blank tablet; a clean slate. ⓘ 16c: Latin, literally 'scraped tablet'.

tabulate /'tabjʊleɪt/ ▻ *verb* (***tabulated, tabulating***) to arrange (information) in tabular form. ▻ *adj* /-lət/ flattened. • **tabulation** *noun*. ⓘ 18c in *verb* sense: from Latin *tabulare*, *tabulatum*, from *tabula* a board.

tabulator ▻ *noun* **1** a TAB[2]. **2** *computing, formerly* a machine which reads data from a computer storage device, especially punched cards, and prints it out on continuous sheets of paper.

tacamahac /'takəməhak/ ▻ *noun* **1** a gum-resin yielded by various tropical trees. **2** any tree which yields this resin. ⓘ 16c: from Aztec *tecomahiyac*.

tac-au-tac /'takoʊtak/ ▻ *noun, fencing* a parry combined with a riposte. ⓘ Early 20c: French, imitating the sound.

tacet /'teɪsɛt, 'takɛt/ ▻ *verb, music* used as a direction on a score: be silent or pause. ⓘ 18c: Latin, literally 'is silent', from *tacere* to be silent.

tache or **tash** /taʃ/ ▻ *noun* (***taches*** or ***tashes***) *colloq* a moustache.

tachism or **tachisme** /'taʃɪzəm/ ▻ *noun, art* a term used, especially in France, to describe a movement in mid-20c abstract painting in which paint was laid on in thick patches intended to be interesting in themselves, irrespective of whether a motif was represented. See also ACTION PAINTING. • **tachist** or **tachiste** *noun, adj*. ⓘ 1950s: from French *tache* blob (of paint).

tachograph /'takoʊgrɑːf/ ▻ *noun* a device which records the speed a vehicle travels at and the distance travelled in a particular period of time, used especially in lorries and coaches. ⓘ Early 20c: from Greek *tachos* speed.

tachometer /ta'kɒmətə(r)/ ▻ *noun* a device which measures the speed of a machine or vehicle, especially one that measures the speed of an engine in revolutions per minute. ⓘ Early 19c: from Greek *tachos* speed.

tachycardia /takɪ'kɑːdɪə/ ▻ *noun, pathol* abnormally rapid beating of the heart. ⓘ Late 19c: from Greek *tachys* swift + *kardia* heart.

tachygraphy /ta'kɪgrəfɪ/ ▻ *noun* shorthand, especially that as used by the ancient Greeks and Romans, or the abbreviated form of Greek and Latin used in medieval manuscripts. • **tachygrapher** *noun*. • **tachygraphic** /takɪ'grafɪk/ or **tachygraphical** *adj*. ⓘ 17c: from Greek *tachos* speed.

tacit /'tasɪt/ ▻ *adj* **1** silent; unspoken. **2** understood but not actually stated; implied. • **tacitly** *adverb*. • **tacitness** *noun*. ⓘ 17c: from Latin *tacitus*, from *tacere* to be silent.

taciturn /'tasɪtɜːn/ ▻ *adj* saying little; quiet and uncommunicative. • **taciturnity** *noun*. • **taciturnly** *adverb*. ⓘ 18c: from Latin *taciturnus*, from *tacere* to be silent.

tack[1] ▻ *noun* **1** a short nail with a sharp point and a broad flat head. **2** *N Amer* a drawing-pin. **3** a long loose temporary stitch used especially to hold material together while it is being sewn properly. **4** *naut* the direction of a sailing ship which is sailing into the wind at an angle, stated in terms of the side of the sail that the wind is blowing against □ ***on the starboard tack***. **5** *naut* a sailing ship's zigzag course formed by sailing with first one side of the sail to the wind and then the other. **6** a direction, course of action or policy □ ***to try a different tack***. **7** stickiness. ▻ *verb* (***tacked, tacking***) **1** (*sometimes* **tack something down** or **on**) to fasten or attach it with tacks. **2** to sew with long loose temporary stitches. **3** (*also* **tack something on**) to attach or add it as a supplement. **4** *intr, naut* said of a sailing ship or its crew: to sail into the wind at an angle with first one side of the sail to the wind and then the other, so as to sail in a zigzag course and be able to progress forwards. **5** *naut* to change the tack of (a ship) to the opposite one. **6** *intr* to change one's direction, course of action or policy abruptly. ⓘ 13c as *tak* a fastening.

tack[2] ▻ *noun* riding harness, saddle and bridle, etc for a horse. ⓘ 1930s: shortened from TACKLE.

tackle /'takəl/ ▻ *noun* **1** *sport* an act of trying to get the ball away from a player on the opposing team. **2** the equipment needed for a particular sport or occupation. **3** a system of ropes and pulleys for lifting heavy objects. **4** the ropes and rigging on a ship. ▻ *verb* (***tackled, tackling***) **1** to grasp or seize and struggle with something or someone, especially to try to restrain them. **2** to try to deal with or solve (a problem). **3** *tr & intr, sport* to try to get the ball from (a player on the opposing team). • **tackler** *noun.* ⓘ 13c as *takel* gear.

tacky¹ /'takɪ/ ▻ *adj* (*tackier, tackiest*) slightly sticky. • **tackily** *adverb.* • **tackiness** *noun.* ⓘ 18c: from TACK¹ *noun* 7.

tacky² /'takɪ/ ▻ *adj* (*tackier, tackiest*) *colloq* **1** shabby; shoddy. **2** vulgar; in bad taste. • **tackily** *adv.* • **tackiness** *noun.* ⓘ 19c; originally *US* meaning 'a weak or inferior quality horse'.

taco /'takoʊ, 'tɑː-/ ▻ *noun* (*tacos*) in Mexican cookery: a tortilla which is fried until crisp and stuffed with a filling, usually of meat. ⓘ 1940s: Mexican Spanish.

tact ▻ *noun* **1** an awareness of the best or most considerate way to deal with others so as to avoid offence, upset, antagonism or resentment. **2** skill or judgement in handling difficult situations; diplomacy. ⓘ 19c in these senses; 17c meaning 'touch': from Latin *tangere, tactum* to touch.

tactful ▻ *adj* showing or demonstrating tact. • **tactfully** *adverb.* • **tactfulness** *noun.*

tactic /'taktɪk/ ▻ *noun* a tactical manoeuvre. Compare TACTICS. ⓘ 18c in this sense.

tactical /'taktɪkəl/ ▻ *adj* **1** relating to or forming tactics. **2** skilful; well planned and well executed. **3** said of a bomb or missile, etc: used to support other military operations. • **tactically** *adverb.*

tactical voting ▻ *noun* the practice of voting for a candidate one does not support but who is the most likely to defeat another candidate that one supports even less.

tactician /tak'tɪʃən/ ▻ *noun* a person who is good at tactics or successful planning.

tactics /'taktɪks/ ▻ *singular or plural noun* **1** the art or science of employing and manoeuvring troops to win or gain an advantage over the enemy. **2** skill in or the art of using whatever means are available to achieve an end or aim. **3** the plans, procedure or means, etc followed. ⓘ 17c: from Greek *taktikos* concerning arrangement.

tactile /'taktaɪl/ ▻ *adj* **1** belonging or relating to, or having, a sense of touch. **2** perceptible to the sense of touch. ⓘ 17c: from Latin *tactilis*, from *tangere, tactum* to touch.

tactless ▻ *adj* lacking tact. • **tactlessly** *adverb.* • **tactlessness** *noun.*

tad ▻ *noun, colloq* **1** a small amount ▫ ***just a tad of milk in my tea.*** **2** a young lad. ⓘ 19c: perhaps shortened from **tadpole**.

tadpole /'tadpoʊl/ ▻ *noun* the larval (see LARVA) stage of many frogs and toads, which initially appears to consist of a small head and a tail. ⓘ 15c as *taddepol*: from *tadde* toad + *pol* head.

taekwondo or **tae kwon do** /taɪkwɒn'doʊ/ ▻ *noun* a Korean martial art and unarmed combat sport similar to karate. ⓘ 1960s: Korean *tae* kick + *kwon* fist + *do* method.

taenia /'tiːnɪə/ ▻ *noun* (*taeniae* /'tiːnɪiː/ or *taenias*) **1** *archit* the FILLET above the ARCHITRAVE of the DORIC order. **2** *anatomy* any ribbon-like structure. **3** any of various large tapeworms which are parasitic in humans. **4** in ancient Greece: a headband. ⓘ 16c: Latin, from Greek *tainia* ribbon.

Tafe /'teɪfiː/ ▻ *abbreviation* Technical and Further Education.

taffeta /'tafɪtə/ ▻ *noun* a stiff shiny fabric woven from silk or some silk-like material, eg rayon. ⓘ 14c: from Persian *taftan* to twist.

taffrail /'tafreɪl/ ▻ *noun, naut* a rail round a ship's stern. ⓘ 19c: from Dutch *tafereel* panel.

Taffy /'tafɪ/ ▻ *noun* (*Taffies*) *slang, often offensive* a Welshman. ⓘ 17c: from the supposed Welsh pronunciation of *Dafydd* David.

tag¹ ▻ *noun* **1** a piece of material, paper or leather, etc that carries information (eg washing instructions or price, etc) about the object to which it is attached. **2** an electronic device such as a bracelet or anklet which transmits radio signals and is used to supervise the movements of a prisoner or offender outside prison. **3** a metal or plastic point on the end of a shoelace or cord. **4** a loose hanging flap or piece of loose hanging cloth. **5** a trite or common quotation used especially for effect. **6** a verbal label applied to someone or something; an epithet ▫ ***It hardly justifies the 'discovery of the year' tag.*** **7** the final speech in a play, or refrain in a song, added to make the moral or point clear. **8** *colloq* a personal symbol or signature, often realized as a piece of graffiti. ▻ *verb* (*tagged, tagging*) **1** to put a tag or tags on something or someone. **2** to attach or fasten something. **3** (*usually* **tag along** or **on**, *etc*) *intr* to follow or accompany someone, especially when uninvited. ⓘ 15c.

tag² ▻ *noun* a children's game in which one child chases the others and tries to catch or touch one of them, who then becomes the chaser. Also called **tig**. ▻ *verb* (*tagged, tagging*) to catch or touch someone in, or as if in, the game of tag. ⓘ 18c.

Tagálog /tə'gɑːlɒg/ ▻ *noun* an Austronesian language spoken as a first language by c.12 million people on the island of Luzon in the Philippines. ▻ *adj* belonging or relating to, or spoken or written in, Tagálog. ⓘ Early 19c.

tagliatelle /taljə'tɛlɪ, taglɪə-/ ▻ *noun* **1** a type of pasta in the form of long narrow ribbons. **2** a dish made with this type of pasta. ⓘ 19c: Italian, from *tagliare* to cut.

tahini /tə'hiːnɪ/ ▻ *noun* a thick paste made from ground sesame seeds. ⓘ 1950s: from Arabic *tahana* to grind.

Tahitian /tə'hiːʃən/ ▻ *adj* belonging or relating to Tahiti, the largest island of French Polynesia in the S Pacific Ocean, or to its inhabitants or their language. ▻ *noun* **1** a citizen or inhabitant of, or person born in, Tahiti. **2** the official language of Tahiti. ⓘ 19c.

Tai /taɪ/ ▻ *noun* **1** a family of c.40 languages used in SE Asia, principally in Thailand, Laos, Vietnam and parts of China. **2** the languages that form this family. ▻ *adj* belonging or relating to this family, or the languages that form it. See also THAI.

t'ai chi ch'uan /taɪ tʃiː tʃwɑːn, — dʒiː —/ ▻ *noun* a Chinese system of exercise and self-defence in which good balance and co-ordination mean that minimum effort is used, developed especially by doing extremely slow and controlled exercises. Often shortened to **t'ai chi**. ⓘ 1960s: Chinese, meaning 'great art of boxing'.

taiga /'taɪgə/ ▻ *noun, geog* in northern parts of the N hemisphere: the large area of predominantly coniferous forest located south of the arctic and subarctic tundra regions. ⓘ 19c: Russian.

tail¹ /teɪl/ ▻ *noun* **1** the part of an animal's body that projects from the lower or rear end of the back to form a flexible appendage. **2** the feathers that project from the rear of a bird's body. **3** anything which has a similar form, function or position as a creature's tail ▫ ***shirt tail.*** **4** a lower, last or rear part ▫ ***the tail of the storm.*** **5** the rear part of an aircraft including the rudder and TAILPLANE. **6** *astron* the trail of luminous particles following a comet. **7** (**tails**) the reverse side of a coin, that side which does not bear a portrait or head. Compare HEADS at HEAD *noun* 21. **8** (**tails**) a TAILCOAT. **9** (**tails**) evening dress for men, usually including a tailcoat and white bow tie. **10** *colloq* someone who follows and keeps a constant watch on someone else. **11** *colloq* the buttocks. **12** *offensive slang* **a** women thought of as sexual objects; **b** the female genitalia. ▻ *verb* (*tailed, tailing*) **1** to remove the stalks (from fruit or vegetables). **2** to follow someone or something very closely. **3** to provide someone with a tail. **4** to join (objects or ideas, etc) with or as if with a tail. • **tailed** *adj* **1** having a tail. **2** with the tail removed. **3** *in compounds* having a tail of a specified kind. • **tailless** *adj*. • **turn tail** to turn round and run away. • **with one's tail between one's legs** completely defeated or humiliated. ⓔ Anglo-Saxon *tægel*.

▪ **tail away** or **off** to become gradually less, smaller or weaker.

tail² /teɪl/ *law* ▻ *noun* the limitation of who may inherit property to one person and that person's heirs, or to some other particular class of heirs. ▻ *adj* limited in this way. ⓔ 15c: from French *taillier* to cut.

tailback ▻ *noun* a long queue of traffic stretching back from an accident or roadworks, etc blocking the road.

tailboard ▻ *noun* a hinged or removable flap at the rear of a lorry, cart or wagon.

tailcoat ▻ *noun* a man's formal black jacket which is cut away below the waist in the front and has a long divided tapering tail which is slit to the waist.

tail end ▻ *noun* the very end or last part. • **tail-ender** *noun* someone coming at the very end.

tailgate ▻ *noun* **1** the rear door which opens upwards on a HATCHBACK vehicle. **2** the lower gate of a canal lock. **3** *N Amer* a TAILBOARD.

tailless see under TAIL¹

tail-light ▻ *noun, N Amer* a light, usually a red one, on the back of a car, train or bicycle, etc.

tailor /ˈteɪlə(r)/ ▻ *noun* someone who makes suits, jackets, trousers and overcoats, etc to measure, especially for men. ▻ *verb* (***tailored, tailoring***) **1** *tr & intr* to make and style (garments) so that they fit well. **2** to make something suitable for particular or special circumstances; to adapt it. **3** *intr* to work as a tailor. See also SARTORIAL. • **tailored** *adj* **1** tailor-made. **2** said of a person: dressed in clothes which fit well. ⓔ 13c: from French *taillour*, ultimately from Latin *taliare* to cut.

tailorbird ▻ *noun* a bird belonging to the warbler family, native to India and SE Asia, where it inhabits forests and cultivated land. ⓔ 18c: so called because it forms a nest from leaves by stitching them together with plant fibres, etc to form a pouch.

tailor-made ▻ *adj* **1** said of clothes: made by a tailor to fit a particular person. **2** perfectly suited or adapted for a particular purpose. ▻ *noun* (***tailor-mades***) **1** a tailor-made piece of clothing. **2** *colloq* a factory-made cigarette.

tailpiece ▻ *noun* **1** a piece at the end or tail. **2** a design or engraving at the end of a chapter in a book. **3** a strip of wood at the bottom of some stringed instruments (eg a violin) from which the strings are stretched across the bridge to the pegs.

tailplane ▻ *noun* a small horizontal wing at the rear of an aircraft.

tailspin ▻ *noun* **1** see SPIN *noun* 3. **2** *colloq* a state of great agitation.

tailstock ▻ *noun* a slidable casting mounted on a lathe, used to support the free end of the piece being worked on.

tail wind ▻ *noun* a wind blowing in the same direction as that in which a ship or aircraft, etc is travelling.

taint /teɪnt/ ▻ *verb* (***tainted, tainting***) **1** *tr & intr* to affect or be affected by pollution, putrefaction or contamination. **2** to contaminate morally; to infect with evil. **3** to affect or spoil something slightly with something considered bad. ▻ *noun* **1** a spot, mark or trace of decay, contamination, infection or something bad or evil. **2** a corrupt or decayed condition. • **tainted** *adj*. ⓔ 16c in *verb* sense 1: from French *teint*, from Latin *tingere* to dye.

'taint /teɪnt/ ▻ *contraction, slang* it is not.

taipan /ˈtaɪpan/ ▻ *noun* a highly venomous snake native to NE Australia and New Guinea, which is brown in colour with a paler head and feeds mainly on small mammals. ⓔ 1930s: an Aboriginal name.

taka /ˈtɑːkə/ ▻ *noun* (***takas***) the standard unit of currency of Bangladesh. ⓔ 1970s: Bengali.

take ▻ *verb* (***took*** /tʊk/, ***taken, taking***) **1** (*often* **take something down, off** or **out**, *etc*) to reach out for and grasp, lift or pull, etc (something chosen or known); to grasp or enter, etc something for use ▫ *take a book from the shelf.* **2** to carry, conduct or lead someone or something to another place. **3** to do or perform something ▫ *take a walk* ▫ *take one's revenge.* **4** to get, receive, occupy, obtain, rent or buy something. **5** to agree to have or accept something ▫ *take advice* ▫ *take office.* **6** to accept something as true or valid ▫ *take her word for it.* **7** to adopt or commit oneself to someone or something ▫ *take a decision.* **8** to endure or put up with someone or something ▫ *cannot take his arrogance.* **9** to need or require ▫ *It will take all day to finish.* **10** to use (eg a bus or train) as a means of transport. **11** to make (a written note of something) ▫ *take the minutes of the meeting.* **12** to make (a photographic record); to make a photographic record of someone or something ▫ *decided to take a few colour slides* ▫ *Shall I take you standing by the bridge?* **13** to study or teach (a subject, etc). **14** to remove, use or borrow something without permission. **15** to proceed to occupy something ▫ *take a seat.* **16** to come or derive from something or someone ▫ *a quotation taken from Camus.* **17** to have room to hold or strength to support something ▫ *The shelf won't take any more books.* **18** to consider someone or something as an example. **19** to consider or think of someone or something in a particular way; to mistakenly consider them to be someone or something ▫ *took her to be a teacher* ▫ *Do you take me for a fool?* **20** to capture or win. **21** (*usually* **be taken with someone**) to be charmed and delighted by them. **22** to eat or drink ▫ *take medicine* ▫ *I don't take sugar in coffee.* **23** to conduct or lead someone ▫ *This road will take you the station.* **24** to be in charge or control of something; to run ▫ *take the meeting.* **25** to react to or receive (news, etc) in a specified way. **26** to feel something ▫ *take pride in one's work.* **27** to turn to someone or something for (help or refuge, etc). **28** (*also* **take something away** or **off**) to subtract or remove it. **29** to go down or into something ▫ *took the first road on the left.* **30** to deal with or consider ▫ *take the first two questions together.* **31** *intr* to have or produce the expected or desired effect ▫ *The vaccination didn't take.* **32** *intr* said of seeds, etc: to begin to send out roots and grow. **33** to measure ▫ *take a temperature.* **34** *intr* to become suddenly (ill, etc). **35** to understand ▫ *I take him to mean he isn't coming.* **36** to have sexual intercourse with someone. ▻ *noun* **1** a scene filmed or piece of music recorded during an uninterrupted period of filming or recording. **2** the amount or number taken (eg of fish caught) at one time. **3** the amount of money taken in a shop or business, etc over a particular period of time ▫ *the day's take.* • **take a degree** to study for and obtain a university or college degree. • **take it 1** to be able to bear suffering, trouble or difficulty, etc ▫ *Tell me the worst. I can take it.* **2** to assume ▫ *I take it you can come.* • **take it from me** you can believe me. • **take it out of someone** *colloq* to exhaust their strength or energy. • **take it out on someone** *colloq* to vent one's anger or frustration on an innocent person. • **take it upon oneself** to take responsibility. • **take the air** *old use* to go for a walk. • **take to the air** said of young birds, etc: to start to fly. ⓔ Anglo-Saxon *tacan*.

▪ **take after someone** to resemble them in appearance or character.

■ **take against someone** to dislike them immediately.

■ **take someone apart** to criticize or defeat them severely.

■ **take something apart** to separate it into pieces or components.

■ **take someone back 1** to make them remember the past. **2** to receive back a former partner or lover, etc after an estrangement.

■ **take something back 1** to withdraw or retract (a statement or promise). **2** to regain possession of it. **3** to return it to an original or former position. **4** to return (something bought from a shop) for an exchange or refund.

■ **take someone down 1** to escort them to dinner. **2** to make them less powerful or self-important; to humble □ *take him down a peg or two.*

■ **take something down 1** to make a written note or record of it. **2** to demolish or dismantle it. **3** to lower it.

■ **take someone in 1** to include them. **2** to give them accommodation or shelter. **3** to deceive or cheat them.

■ **take something in 1** to include it. **2** to understand and remember it. **3** to make (a piece of clothing) smaller. **4** to do (paid work of a specified kind) in one's home □ *take in washing.* **5** to include a visit to (a place).

■ **take off 1** said of an aircraft or its passengers: to leave the ground. See also TAKE-OFF. **2** to depart or set out. **3** *colloq* said of a scheme or product, etc: to become popular and successful and expand quickly.

■ **take someone off 1** to imitate or mimic them, especially for comic effect. See also TAKE-OFF. **2** (**take oneself off**) to go away □ *took herself off to Paris for the weekend.*

■ **take something off 1** said especially of a piece of clothing: to remove it. **2** to deduct it. **3** to spend a period of time away from work on holiday, resting, etc □ *took two days off.*

■ **take on** *colloq* to be greatly upset or distraught.

■ **take someone on 1** to give them employment. **2** to challenge or compete with them □ *We took them on at snooker.*

■ **take something on 1** to agree to do it; to undertake it. **2** to acquire (a new meaning, quality or appearance, etc). **3** said of an aircraft, ship, etc: to admit (new passengers) or put (a new supply of fuel or cargo, etc) on board.

■ **take someone out 1** to go out with them or escort them in public. **2** *slang* to kill, defeat or destroy them.

■ **take something out 1** to remove or extract it. **2** to obtain it on application □ *take out a warrant.*

■ **take over** or **take something over** to assume control, management or ownership of it. See also TAKEOVER.

■ **take to someone** to develop a liking for them □ *took to him straight away.*

■ **take to something 1** to develop a liking for it. **2** to begin to do it regularly. **3** to turn to it as a remedy or for refuge □ *After the break-up, he took to drink.*

■ **take someone up** to become their patron or supporter.

■ **take something up 1** to lift or raise it. **2** to use or occupy (space or time). **3** to become interested in it and begin to do it □ *take up the violin.* **4** (*usually* **be taken up with something**) to be absorbed by it. **5** to shorten (a piece of clothing). **6** to resume (a story or account, etc) after a pause. **7** to assume or adopt □ *take up residence in July.* **8** to accept (an offer).

■ **take someone up on something 1** to accept their offer, proposal or challenge, etc. **2** to discuss (a point or issue) first raised by them.

■ **take up with someone** to become friendly with them; to begin to associate with them.

■ **take something up with someone** to discuss it with them.

takeaway ▷ *noun* **1** a cooked meal prepared and bought in a restaurant but taken away and eaten somewhere else, eg at home. **2** a restaurant which provides such meals. ▷ *adj* **1** said of cooked food: prepared in a shop or restaurant for the customer to take away. **2** said of a shop or restaurant: providing such meals. See also CARRY-OUT.

take-home pay ▷ *noun* the salary that one actually receives after tax, national insurance and pension contributions have been deducted.

take-off ▷ *noun* **1** an instance of an aircraft leaving the ground. **2** an act of imitating or mimicking, especially for comic effect. **3** a place from which one takes off or jumps, etc; a starting-point. See also TAKE OFF and TAKE SOMEONE OFF at TAKE.

takeover ▷ *noun* the act of taking control of something, especially of a company by buying the majority of its shares. See also TAKE OVER at TAKE.

taker ▷ *noun* someone who takes or accepts something, especially a bet, offer or challenge.

take-up ▷ *noun* the act or extent of claiming or accepting something, eg state benefit. See also TAKE SOMETHING UP at take.

take-up rate ▷ *noun* the number of people who claim a benefit to which they are entitled or who accept an offer.

taking ▷ *adj* attractive; charming. ▷ *noun* (**takings**) the amount of money taken at a concert or in a shop, etc; receipts.

tala /'tɑːlə/ ▷ *noun* (*talas*) a traditional rhythmic pattern in Indian music. Ⓒ 1940s: Sanskrit, meaning 'hand-clapping'.

talc /talk/ and **talcum** /'talkəm/ ▷ *noun* **1** *geol* a white, green or grey mineral form of MAGNESIUM SILICATE, one of the softest minerals, used in talcum powder and other cosmetics, in French chalk, lubricants and paper coatings, and as a filler in paints, plastics and rubber. **2** TALCUM POWDER. Ⓒ 16c: from Persian *talk*.

talcum powder ▷ *noun* a fine, often perfumed, powder made from purified talc, used on the body. Often shortened to **talc** or **talcum**.

tale ▷ *noun* **1** a story or narrative. **2** a false or malicious story or piece of gossip; a lie. • **tell tales** to disclose secret or private information, especially about another's wrongdoing, to someone in authority. • **tell tales out of school** to disclose confidential matters. Ⓒ Anglo-Saxon *talu*.

tale-bearer ▷ *noun* someone who repeats malicious or false gossip.

talent /'talənt/ ▷ *noun* **1** a special or innate skill, aptitude or ability, especially for art or music, etc. **2** high general or mental ability. **3** a person or people with such skill or ability. **4** *colloq* attractive members of the opposite sex as a group. **5** *historical* a measure of weight and unit of currency used eg by the ancient Greeks and Romans. • **talented** *adj*. Ⓒ Anglo-Saxon *talente*, from Latin *talentum*, from Greek *talanton* sum of money.

talent scout and **talent spotter** ▷ *noun* someone whose job is to find and recruit talented amateurs, especially singers and dancers, for professional engagements.

tales /ˈteɪliːz/ ▷ *noun, law* the filling up, from those who are present in court, of a vacancy in the number of jurors. ⓒ 14c: shortened from the Latin phrase *tales de circumstantibus* such of the bystanders.

talipes /ˈtalɪpiːz/ ▷ *noun, medicine or technical* CLUB FOOT. ⓒ 19c: Latin, from *talus* ankle + *pes* foot.

talisman /ˈtalɪzmən/ ▷ *noun* (***talismans***) a small object, such as a stone, supposed to have magic powers to protect its owner from evil, bring good luck or work magic; a charm or amulet. ● **talismanic** /-ˈmanɪk/ *adj.* ⓒ 17c: Spanish or French, from Arabic *tilsam*, from Greek *telesma* rite or consecrated object.

talk /tɔːk/ ▷ *verb* (***talked, talking***) **1** *intr* (*often* **talk to** or **with someone**) to express one's ideas, feelings and thoughts by means of spoken words, or by sign language, etc; to have a conversation or discussion. **2** to discuss; to speak about something □ ***Let's talk business.*** **3** *intr* to use or be able to use speech. **4** to express; to utter □ ***Don't talk nonsense!*** **5** *intr* to gossip. **6** *intr* to give away secret information. **7** to use (a language) or speak in it □ ***talk Dutch.*** **8** to get (oneself) into a certain state by talking □ ***talked themselves hoarse.*** **9** *intr* to have influence □ ***Money talks.*** **10** *intr* to give a talk or lecture □ ***Our guest speaker will talk on potholing.*** ▷ *noun* **1** a conversation or discussion. **2** (*often* **talks**) a formal discussion or series of negotiations. **3** an informal lecture. **4** gossip or rumour, or the subject of it □ ***the talk of the town.*** **5** fruitless or impractical discussion or boasting □ ***His threats are just talk.*** **6** a particular way of speaking or communicating □ ***baby talk.*** ● **talker** *noun.* ● **now you're talking** *colloq* now you are saying something I want to hear. ● **talk about ...** *colloq, often ironic* used to emphasize something as an extreme example □ ***Talk about expensive!*** ● **talk big** *colloq* to talk boastfully. ● **you can't talk** *colloq* you are in no position to criticize or disagree. ⓒ 13c.

■ **talk back** to answer rudely, impudently or boldly.

■ **talk someone down 1** to silence them by speaking more loudly or aggressively. **2** to help (a pilot or aircraft) to land by sending instructions over the radio.

■ **talk down to someone** to talk patronizingly or condescendingly to them.

■ **talk someone into** or **out of something** to persuade them to do or not to do it.

■ **talk something out 1** to resolve (a problem or difference of opinion) by discussion. **2** *Brit* to defeat (a bill or motion in parliament) by prolonging discussion of it until there is not enough time left to vote on it.

■ **talk something over** to discuss it thoroughly.

■ **talk someone round** to bring them to one's own way of thinking by talking persuasively.

■ **talk round something** to discuss all aspects of (a subject or problem, etc) without reaching a decision or coming to a conclusion.

talkative /ˈtɔːkətɪv/ ▷ *adj* talking a lot; chatty.

talkie /ˈtɔːkɪ/ ▷ *noun* (***talkies***) *dated colloq* a cinema film with sound, especially one of the first such films. ⓒ Early 20c: originally US, shortened from *talking movie*.

talking-point ▷ *noun* a subject for discussion.

talking-shop ▷ *noun* a place for discussion and argument as opposed to action.

talking-to ▷ *noun* (***talking-tos*** or ***-to's***) *colloq* a ticking-off; a scolding or reproof.

talk show ▷ *noun, especially N Amer* a CHAT SHOW.

tall ▷ *adj* **1** usually said of a person: above average height. **2** having a specified height □ ***six feet tall.*** **3** high □ ***a tall tree.*** **4** difficult to believe; extravagant □ ***a tall story.*** **5** difficult or demanding □ ***a tall order.*** ● **tallness** *noun.* ⓒ 15c, probably from Anglo-Saxon *getæl* swift or ready.

tallboy ▷ *noun* a tall chest of drawers, consisting of an upper and slightly smaller section standing on a larger lower one. ⓒ 18c.

tallith /ˈtalɪθ/ ▷ *noun* (***talliths*** or ***tallithim*** /-θiːm/) a shawl worn by Jewish men, especially for prayer. ⓒ 17c: Hebrew.

tallow /ˈtaloʊ/ ▷ *noun* hard fat from sheep and cattle which is melted down and used to make candles and soap, etc. ▷ *verb* (***tallowed, tallowing***) to cover or grease something with tallow. ⓒ 14c.

tally /ˈtalɪ/ ▷ *noun* (***tallies***) **1** an account or reckoning, eg of work done, debts, or the score in a game. **2** *historical* a stick in which notches were cut to show debts and accounts, and which could then be split in half lengthways so that each party had a record of the deal. **3** a distinguishing or identifying mark or label. **4** a counterpart; a corresponding part. **5** a mark representing a score or number. ▷ *verb* (***tallies, tallied, tallying***) **1** *intr* to agree, correspond or match □ ***Our results don't tally.*** **2** to count or mark (a number or score, etc) on, or as if on, a tally. **3** to provide something with a label. ⓒ 15c: from Latin *talea* stick.

tally clerk ▷ *noun* someone who checks a ship's cargo against an official list.

tally-ho /talɪˈhoʊ/ ▷ *exclamation* a cry to the hounds at a hunt when a fox has been sighted. ▷ *noun* (***tally-hos***) a cry of tally-ho. ▷ *verb* (***tally-hos, tally-hoed*** or ***-ho'd, tally-hoing***) *intr* to give a cry of tally-ho. ⓒ 18c: perhaps from French *taïnaut*, a hunting cry.

tallyman ▷ *noun* **1** someone who keeps a tally. **2** someone who sells goods on credit, especially from door to door.

Talmud /ˈtalmʊd/ ▷ *noun, Judaism* the body of Jewish civil and canon law. ● **Talmudic** or **Talmudical** *adj.* ● **Talmudism** *noun.* ● **Talmudist** *noun* a scholar of the Talmud. ⓒ 16c: Hebrew, meaning 'instruction'.

talon /ˈtalən/ ▷ *noun* **1** a hooked claw, especially of a bird of prey. **2** *facetious* a long fingernail. **3** in some card games: the cards which remain after the deal. **4** the part of a bolt of a lock that the key presses on when it is turned. **5** *archit* an OGEE. ⓒ 14c: French, from Latin *talus* heel or ankle.

talus /ˈteɪləs/ ▷ *noun* (***tali*** /-laɪ/) *anatomy* the ankle bone. ⓒ 17c: Latin, meaning 'ankle'.

tamable see under TAME

tamari /taˈmɑːrɪ/ ▷ *noun* a concentrated sauce made of soya beans and salt, used especially in Japanese cookery. ⓒ 1970s: Japanese.

tamarillo /taməˈrɪloʊ/ ▷ *noun* (***tamarillos***) the TREE TOMATO. ⓒ 1960s: originally NZ; an invented word.

tamarind /ˈtamərɪnd/ ▷ *noun* **1** a tropical evergreen tree which bears yellow flowers and brown seedpods. **2** the pod of this tree, containing seeds surrounded by a juicy acidic brown pulp which is used medicinally, as a flavouring and as a food preservative. ⓒ 16c: ultimately from Arabic *tamr-hindi* Indian date.

tamarisk /ˈtamərɪsk/ ▷ *noun* any of various evergreen shrubs and small trees native to the Mediterranean region and Asia, which have tiny scale-like leaves and dense cylindrical spikes of small pink or white flowers. ⓒ 15c: from Latin *tamariscus*.

tambour /ˈtambʊə(r)/ ▷ *noun* **1** a drum, especially the bass drum. **2** a frame for embroidery consisting of two hoops which hold the fabric taut while stitches are sewn. **3** embroidery done on such a frame. **4** on a desk or cabinet: a flexible top or front made from narrow strips of wood fixed closely together on canvas, the whole sliding in grooves. **5** *archit* a cylindrical stone forming the centre of a Corinthian or Composite CAPITAL². ▷ *verb* (***tamboured, tambouring***) to embroider something on a tambour. ⓒ 15c: French, meaning 'drum'.

tambourine /tambə'ri:n/ ▷ *noun* a musical instrument consisting of a circular frame, often with skin stretched tight over one side, with small discs of metal in the rim that jingle when it is struck with the hand. ◷ 16c: from Dutch *tamborijn* small drum, from French *tambour* drum.

tame ▷ *adj* (***tamer, tamest***) **1** said of animals: used to living or working with people; not wild or dangerous. **2** said of land, etc: changed by people from a natural wild state; cultivated. **3** docile, meek and submissive. **4** dull and unexciting; insipid ▫ ***a tame ending to the story.*** ▷ *verb* (***tamed, taming***) **1** to make (an animal) used to living or working with people. **2** to make meek and humble; to deprive someone or something of spirit; to subdue. • **tamable** or **tameable** *adj.* • **tamely** *adverb.* • **tameness** *noun.* • **tamer** *noun.* ◷ Anglo-Saxon *tam.*

Tamil /'tamɪl/ ▷ *noun* **1** a group of peoples living in S India and Sri Lanka. **2** an individual belonging to this group of peoples. **3** their language. ▷ *adj* belonging or relating to this group or their language. ◷ 18c.

tammy /'tamɪ/ ▷ *noun* (***tammies***) a tam-o'-shanter.

tam-o'-shanter /tamoʊ'ʃantə(r)/ ▷ *noun, Scottish* a flat round cloth or woollen cap which fits tightly round the brows and has a full crown, often with a bobble in the middle. ◷ 19c: named after the hero of Robert Burns's poem.

tamoxifen /tə'mɒksɪfɛn/ ▷ *noun, medicine* a drug that inhibits the effects of oestrogens, and is used in the treatment of specific advanced breast cancers and also to stimulate ovulation in the treatment of female infertility. ◷ 1970s.

tamp ▷ *verb* (***tamped, tamping***) **1** to fill up (a hole containing explosive) with earth or cement, etc before setting off the explosion. **2** to drive or force down (eg ballast on a railway) by repeated blows. **3** (*also* **tamp something down**) to pack (tobacco in a pipe or cigarette) into a tighter mass by tapping it or pushing it with a TAMPER[2] (sense 2) or a finger, etc. ◷ 19c: probably from *tampin,* an obsolete variant of TAMPION.

tamper[1] /'tampə(r)/ ▷ *verb* (***tampered, tampering***) *intr* (*usually* **tamper with something**) **1** to interfere or meddle, especially in a harmful way. **2** to attempt to corrupt or influence, especially by bribery. • **tamperer** *noun.* • **tampering** *noun.* ◷ 16c: a form of TEMPER.

tamper[2] ▷ *noun* **1** someone or something that tamps. **2** a device for pressing down tobacco in a pipe. **3** a casing around the core of a nuclear weapon to delay expansion and act as a neutron reflector.

tamper-evident ▷ *adj* said of packaging: designed in such a way that it is obvious when it has been tampered with.

tamper-proof ▷ *adj* said of a product or its packaging: designed in such a way that it is virtually impossible to tamper with it.

tampion /'tampɪən/ or **tompion** /'tɒmp-/ ▷ *noun* a plug, especially a protective plug placed in the muzzle of a gun when it is not in use. ◷ 17c in this sense: from French *tampon,* from *tapon* a plug of cloth.

tampon /'tampɒn/ ▷ *noun* a plug of cotton wool or other soft absorbent material inserted into a cavity or wound to absorb blood and other secretions, especially one for use in the vagina during menstruation. ▷ *verb* (***tamponed, tamponing***) to insert a tampon in something. ◷ 19c: French, from *tapon* a plug of cloth.

tam-tam /'tamtam/ ▷ *noun* a percussion instrument similar to a gong, but made of thinner metal and having no central boss, and whose sound varies depending on its size. ◷ 19c: perhaps from Hindi; see TOM-TOM.

tan[1] ▷ *noun* **1** the brown colour of the skin after exposure to the Sun's ultraviolet rays; a suntan. **2** a tawny-brown colour. **3** oak bark or other material, used especially for tanning hides. ▷ *adj* tawny-brown in colour. ▷ *verb* (***tanned, tanning***) **1** *tr & intr* to make or become brown in the sun. **2** to convert (hide) into leather by soaking it in a solution containing tannin, mineral salts or other chemicals. **3** *colloq* to beat someone or something. • **tanned** *adj.* • **tanning** *noun.* See also TANNED, TANNER1, TANNERY. ◷ Anglo-Saxon, from Latin *tannum* oak bark.

tan[2] ▷ *abbreviation, math* tangent.

tanager /'tanədʒə(r)/ ▷ *noun* any member of a S American family of birds, closely allied to the finches, the males of which have brightly coloured plumage. ◷ 17c: from Tupí *tangara.*

tandem /'tandəm/ ▷ *noun* **1** a type of long three-wheeled bicycle for two people, with two seats and two sets of pedals placed one behind the other. **2** a team of two horses harnessed one behind the other, or a carriage drawn by it. **3** any two people or things which follow one behind the other. ▷ *adverb* one behind the other, especially on a bicycle, or with two horses harnessed one behind the other. • **in tandem 1** with one behind the other. **2** together or in partnership. ◷ 18c: a pun on Latin *tandem,* meaning 'at length' or 'at last'.

tandoori /tan'dʊərɪ/ ▷ *noun* (***tandooris***) an Indian method of cooking food on a spit over charcoal in a clay oven. Especially *as adj* ▫ ***tandoori chicken.*** ◷ 1950s: from Hindi *tandoor* clay oven.

tang ▷ *noun* **1** a strong or sharp taste, flavour or smell. **2** a trace or hint. **3** the pointed end of a knife, sword or chisel, etc that fits into and is held firmly by the handle. ◷ 15c in sense 1: from Norse *tange* point.

tanga /'taŋgə/ ▷ *noun* (***tangas***) underpants for men or women which have no material at the sides other than the waistband. ◷ 20c: Portuguese, from Kimbundu (a language of Angola) *ntanga* loincloth.

tangelo /'tandʒəloʊ/ ▷ *noun* (***tangelos***) a hybrid between a TANGERINE and a POMELO. ◷ Early 20c.

tangent /'tandʒənt/ ▷ *noun* **1** *geom* a straight line that touches a curve at one point, and has the same GRADIENT (sense 3) as the curve at the point of contact. **2** (abbreviation **tan**) *trig* a FUNCTION (*noun* 4) of an angle in a right-angled triangle, defined as the length of the side opposite the angle divided by the length of the side adjacent to it. ▷ *adj* **1** belonging or relating to a tangent. **2** touching, without intersecting. • **at a tangent** in a completely different direction or course. ◷ 16c: from Latin *tangens, tangentis* touching.

tangential /tan'dʒɛnʃəl/ ▷ *adj* **1** belonging or relating to, or along a tangent. **2** not of central importance to something or someone; incidental; peripheral. • **tangentiality** *noun.* • **tangentially** *adverb.*

tangerine /tandʒə'ri:n/ ▷ *noun* **1** any of several varieties of a tree, native to Asia but widely cultivated in warm regions for its fruit. **2** the small edible fruit of this tree, similar to an orange, with sweet flesh surrounded by a bright orange rind. **3** the reddish-orange colour of this fruit. ▷ *adj* reddish-orange. ◷ 19c: named after Tangier, a port on the Moroccan coast.

tangible /'tandʒɪbəl/ ▷ *adj* **1** able to be felt by touch. **2** able to be grasped by the mind. **3** real or definite; material. • **tangibility** or **tangibleness** *noun.* • **tangibly** *adverb.* ◷ 16c: from Latin *tangibilis,* from *tangere* to touch.

tangle /'taŋgəl/ ▷ *noun* **1** an untidy and confused or knotted state or mass, eg of hair or fibres. **2** a confused or complicated state or situation. ▷ *verb* (***tangled, tangling***) **1 a** *intr* said especially of hair and fibres, etc: to become untidy, knotted and confused; **b** to make (hair or fibres, etc) so. **2** (*usually* **tangle with someone**) *colloq* to become involved with them, especially in conflict, a struggle or an argument. **3** *colloq* to trap or hamper the movement of someone or something. • **tangled** or **tangly** *adj.* ◷ 14c.

tango /'taŋgoʊ/ ▷ *noun* (***tangos***) **1** a Latin-American dance with dramatic stylized body positions and long pauses. **2** a piece of music composed for this dance. **3** (**Tango**) *communications* in the NATO alphabet: the word used to denote the letter 'T' (see table at NATO ALPHABET). ▷ *verb* (***tangos*** or ***tangoes***, ***tangoed***, ***tangoing***) *intr* to perform this dance. ⓒ Early 20c: American Spanish.

tangram /'taŋgram/ ▷ *noun* a Chinese puzzle consisting of a square cut into seven pieces that will fit in various forms. ⓒ 19c: perhaps from Chinese *Tang* Chinese + -GRAM.

tangy /'taŋɪ/ ▷ *adj* (***tangier***, ***tangiest***) with a fresh sharp smell or flavour. ⓒ 19c: from TANG.

tanh /tanʃ, tan'eɪtʃ, θan/ ▷ *noun*, *math* a conventional short form for hyperbolic tangent. See also HYPERBOLIC FUNCTION. ⓒ 20c: from TAN(GENT) + H(YPERBOLA).

tank ▷ *noun* **1** a large container for holding, storing or transporting liquids or gas. **2** a TANKFUL. **3** a heavy steel-covered vehicle armed with guns which moves on Caterpillar tracks. ▷ *verb* (***tanked***, ***tanking***) **1** to put or store something in a tank. **2** *slang* to defeat or thrash. **3** *intr* to move like a tank, especially quickly and heavily. ⓒ 17c: from Gujurati (an Indian language) *tankh* reservoir, and influenced by Portuguese *tanque* pond.

■ **tank up** or **tank someone up** *tr & intr*, *slang* to drink, or make someone drink, heavily and become very drunk.

■ **tank up** or **tank something up** *tr & intr*, *colloq* to fill up (a vehicle's tank) with petrol; to refuel.

tankard /'taŋkəd/ ▷ *noun* a large drinking-mug, usually made from silver, pewter or pottery, sometimes with a hinged lid, and used especially for drinking beer. ⓒ 15c; 14c meaning 'tub-like vessel'.

tanker ▷ *noun* **1** a ship or large lorry which transports liquid in bulk. **2** an aircraft which transports fuel and is usually able to refuel other aircraft in flight. ⓒ Early 20c.

tankful ▷ *noun* (***tankfuls***) the amount a tank can hold.

tank top ▷ *noun* a sleeveless knitted upper garment, with a low scooped or V neck, worn over a shirt, etc. ⓒ 1960s: modelled on *tank suit*, a one-piece bathing suit worn in the 1920s.

tanned ▷ *adj* **1** having a suntan. **2** said of hide: cured or treated. ▷ *verb*, *past tense*, *past participle of* TAN[1].

tanner[1] ▷ *noun* someone whose job is to tan leather. ⓒ Anglo-Saxon *tannere*.

tanner[2] ▷ *noun*, *Brit*, *old colloq* a sixpence. ⓒ Early 19c.

tannery ▷ *noun* (***tanneries***) a place where hides are tanned.

tannic acid /'tanɪk —/ and **tannin** /'tanɪn/ ▷ *noun* any of several substances obtained from certain tree barks and other plants, used in tanning leather, dyeing, ink-making and medicine (especially for treating burns), and which also occurs in, and gives a distinctive flavour to, red wine and tea. ⓒ 19c.

tanning see under TAN[1]

Tannoy /'tanɔɪ/ ▷ *noun*, *trademark* a communication system with loudspeakers, used for making announcements in public buildings, eg railway stations. ⓒ 1920s.

tansy /'tanzɪ/ ▷ *noun* (***tansies***) a perennial plant, native to Europe, with tubular yellow flowers in flat-topped clusters, whose aromatic leaves are used in cooking and formerly in medicine. ⓒ 15c: ultimately from Greek *athanasia* immortality.

tantalize or **tantalise** /'tantəlaɪz/ ▷ *verb* (***tantalized***, ***tantalizing***) to tease or torment someone by keeping something they want just out of reach. • **tantalization** *noun*. • **tantalizing** *adj*. • **tantalizingly** *adverb*. ⓒ 16c: from Tantalus, a king in Greek mythology who, as punishment for his crimes, had to stand in water which receded each time he stooped to drink it, overhung by grapes that drew back when he tried to reach them.

tantalum /'tantələm/ ▷ *noun*, *chem* (symbol **Ta**, atomic number 73) a hard bluish-grey metallic element with a high melting point, that is resistant to corrosion and is used to make certain alloys, especially for nuclear reactors, as well as electronic components, chemical equipment, and dental and surgical instruments. ⓒ 19c: named after Tantalus, due to the metal's inability to absorb acids; see TANTALIZE.

tantalus /'tantələs/ ▷ *noun* (***tantaluses***) a case for holding decanters of alcoholic drink so that they are visible but locked up. ⓒ 19c: named after Tantalus; see TANTALIZE.

tantamount /'tantəmaʊnt/ ▷ *adj* (*always* **tantamount to something**) producing the same effect or result as something; as good as it; equivalent to it □ *That's tantamount to blackmail!* ⓒ 17c: from Anglo-French *tant amunter* or Italian *tanto montare* to amount to as much.

tantara /tantə'rɑː/ ▷ *noun* (***tantaras***) a flourish or blast on a trumpet or horn. ⓒ 16c: imitating the sound.

Tantra or **tantra** /'tantrə/ ▷ *noun* (***Tantras*** or ***tantras***) any of a number of Hindu or Buddhist texts giving religious teaching and ritual instructions which may include descriptions of spells, magical formulas, mantras, meditative practices and rituals to be performed. • **Tantric** *adj*. • **Tantrism** *noun*. ⓒ 19c: Sanskrit, meaning 'thread' or 'doctrine'.

tantrum /'tantrəm/ ▷ *noun* an outburst of childish or petulant bad temper. ⓒ 18c.

Taoiseach /'tiːʃək, -ʃəx/ ▷ *noun* the prime minister of the Republic of Ireland. ⓒ 1930s: Irish Gaelic, meaning 'leader'.

Taoism /'taʊɪzəm, 'daʊ-/ ▷ *noun* **1** a Chinese philosophical system based on the teachings of Laozi (c.6c BC) and others, that advocates a life of simplicity and non-interference with the natural course of events. **2** a religion supposedly based on this system of philosophy, but also including magic, alchemy and the worship of many gods. • **Taoist** *noun*, *adj*. ⓒ 19c: from Chinese *dao* (formerly written *tao*) way.

tap[1] ▷ *noun* **1** a quick or light touch, knock or blow, or the sound made by this. **2** tap-dancing (see under TAP DANCE) □ *She teaches ballet and tap.* **3** a piece of metal attached to the sole and heel of a shoe for tap-dancing. ▷ *verb* (***tapped***, ***tapping***) **1** *tr & intr* to strike or knock lightly. **2** to strike or knock lightly on something. **3** (*also* **tap something out**) to produce it by tapping □ *tap out a message.* **4** (*sometimes* **tap at** or **on something**) to strike it with a light but audible blow. ⓒ 13c: from French *taper*.

tap[2] ▷ *noun* **1** a device consisting of a valve, with a handle for opening and shutting it, attached to a pipe for controlling the flow of liquid or gas. **2** a peg or stopper, especially in a barrel. **3** a receiver for listening to and recording private conversations, attached secretly to a telephone wire. **4** an act of attaching such a receiver to a telephone wire. **5** the withdrawal of fluid from a place, especially (*medicine*) from a cavity in the body □ *spinal tap.* **6** a screw for cutting an internal thread. ▷ *verb* (***tapped***, ***tapping***) **1** to get liquid from (a barrel or a cavity in the body, etc) by piercing it or opening it with, or as if with, a tap. **2** to let out (liquid) from a vessel by opening, or as if by opening, a tap. **3** to get sap from (a tree) by cutting into it. **4** to attach a receiver secretly to (a telephone wire) so as to be able to hear private conversations. **5** to start using (a source, supply, etc). **6** (*usually* **tap someone for something**) *colloq* to ask or obtain (money) from them. • **on tap 1** said of beer: stored in casks from which it is served. **2** ready and available for immediate use. ⓒ Anglo-Saxon *tæppa*.

tapas /'tapəs, -pəz/ ▷ *plural noun* light savoury snacks or appetizers, especially those based on Spanish foods and cooking techniques and served with drinks. ⓒ 20c: from Spanish *tapa*, literally 'cover' or 'lid'.

tap dance ▷ *noun* a dance performed wearing shoes with a piece of metal attached to the soles and toes so that the dancer's rhythmical steps can be heard clearly. ▷ *verb* (**tap-dance**) *intr* to perform a tap dance. • **tap-dancer** *noun*. • **tap-dancing** *noun*. ◷ 1920s.

tape ▷ *noun* **1** a narrow strip of woven cloth used for tying or fastening, etc. **2** (*also* **magnetic tape**) a strip of thin plastic or metal wound on spools, used for recording sounds or images. **3** anything which has been recorded on magnetic tape; a tape or video-recording. **4** (*also* **adhesive tape**) a strip of thin paper or plastic with a sticky surface, used for fastening or sticking, etc. **5** a string, strip of paper or ribbon stretched above the finishing line on a race track. **6** a tape-measure. ▷ *verb* (***taped***, ***taping***) **1** to fasten, tie or seal with tape. **2** *tr & intr* to record (sounds or images) on magnetic tape. • **have something or someone taped** *colloq* to understand it or them, or be able to deal with it or them. ◷ Anglo-Saxon *tæppe*.

tape deck ▷ *noun* a tape recorder and player used to record sound or video signals on to magnetic tape or to play back such a recording, usually forming part of an integrated sound system that may also include a CD player, record turntable, radio tuner, etc.

tape measure ▷ *noun* a length of plastic, cloth or thin flexible metal tape, marked for measuring in inches, feet and yards, or centimetres and metres.

taper /ˈteɪpə(r)/ ▷ *noun* **1** a long thin candle. **2** a long waxed wick or spill for lighting candles or fires. **3** a gradual lessening of diameter or width towards one end. ▷ *verb* (***tapered***, ***tapering***) *tr & intr* (*also* **taper off**) **1** to make or become gradually narrower towards one end. **2** to make or become gradually less. • **tapered** or **tapering** *adj*. ◷ Anglo-Saxon *tapor*.

tape-record ▷ *verb* to record (sounds) on magnetic tape.

tape recorder ▷ *noun* a machine that is used to record sound signals on magnetic tape, and play them back. See also VIDEO CASSETTE RECORDER. • **tape-recording** *noun*. ◷ 1930s.

tapestried ▷ *adj* covered or decorated with tapestry.

tapestry /ˈtapəstrɪ/ ▷ *noun* (***tapestries***) **1** a thick woven textile with an ornamental design (often a picture) on it, used for curtains, wall-hangings or chair coverings, etc. **2** embroidery, or an embroidery, usually done with wool on canvas, which imitates the designs and pictures and the heavy texture of tapestry. ◷ 15c: from French *tapisserie* carpeting.

tapeworm ▷ *noun* any of a group of segmented FLATWORMS that live as parasites in the intestines of humans and other vertebrates. ◷ 18c.

taphonomy /taˈfɒnəmɪ/ ▷ *noun* the study or science of how plants and animals die and become fossilized. • **taphonomist** *noun*. ◷ 1960s: from Greek *taphos* grave.

tapioca /tapɪˈoʊkə/ ▷ *noun* hard white grains of starch from the root of the CASSAVA plant, often made into a pudding with sugar and milk. ◷ 18c: Portuguese, from Tupí *tipioca* juice squeezed out (ie from the root).

tapir /ˈteɪpə(r), -pɪə(r)/ ▷ *noun* (***tapir*** or ***tapirs***) a brown or black-and-white nocturnal hoofed mammal with a long flexible snout, found near water in tropical forests of Central and S America and SE Asia, where it browses on water plants and low-growing vegetation on land. ◷ 18c: from Tupí *tapira*.

tappet /ˈtapɪt/ ▷ *noun*, *mech* a lever or projection that transmits motion from one part of a machine to another, especially in an internal-combustion engine from the CAMSHAFT to the valves. ◷ 18c: from TAP[1].

tapped and **tapping** see under TAP[1], TAP[2]

taproom ▷ *noun* a bar that serves alcoholic drinks, especially beer direct from casks. ◷ Early 18c.

taproot ▷ *noun*, *bot* a long straight main nutrient-storing root derived from the RADICLE and characteristic of some plants (eg carrot), from which smaller lateral roots develop and which allows perennial growth. ◷ 17c.

taps ▷ *singular noun* **1** *chiefly US* **a** a bugle call for lights out in army camps, etc; **b** the same bugle call used at military funerals. **2** in the Guide movement: a song sung at the end of a meeting or round a campfire in the evening.

tar[1] ▷ *noun* **1** a dark sticky pungent liquid obtained by distillation of coal or wood, or by petroleum-refining, which is used in road construction, as a wood preservative and also as a component of some antiseptics. **2** a similar substance, especially the residue formed from smoke from burning tobacco. ▷ *verb* (***tarred***, ***tarring***) to cover with tar. See also TARRY[2]. • **tar and feather someone** to cover them with tar and then feathers as a punishment. • **tarred with the same brush** possessing, or thought to possess, the same faults. ◷ Anglo-Saxon *teoru*.

tar[2] ▷ *noun*, *old colloq* a sailor. ◷ 17c: perhaps an abbreviation of **tarpaulin**, an old nickname for a seaman.

taramasalata /tarəməsəˈlɑːtə/ ▷ *noun* (***taramasalatas***) a creamy pink pâté made from the smoked roe of fish, especially cod, and olive oil and garlic. ◷ Early 20c: Greek, from *taramus* preserved roe + *salata* salad.

tarantella /tarənˈtɛlə/ ▷ *noun* (***tarantellas***) **1** a lively country dance from S Italy. **2** a piece of music for it. ◷ 18c: Italian, diminutive of Taranto, a town in S Italy.

tarantula /təˈrantʃʊlə/ ▷ *noun* (***tarantulas***) **1** a large European WOLF SPIDER. **2** any of a family of large tropical spiders with a fist-sized body and long hairy legs, which live in short burrows in the ground, and run down their prey instead of trapping it in webs. ◷ 16c: from Italian *tarantola*, from Taranto in S Italy where the wolf spider is common.

tarboosh /tɑːˈbuːʃ/ ▷ *noun* (***tarbooshes***) a FEZ. ◷ 18c: from Arabic *tarbush*.

tardigrade /ˈtɑːdɪgreɪd/ ▷ *noun* any of various minute and slow-moving freshwater ARTHROPODs, with a short plump body and eight legs. Also called **water bear**. ▷ *adj* belonging or relating to such creatures. ◷ 17c: from Latin *tardus* slow + *gradi* to step.

tardy /ˈtɑːdɪ/ ▷ *adj* (***tardier***, ***tardiest***) **1** slow to move, progress or grow; sluggish. **2** slower to arrive or happen than expected; late. • **tardily** *adverb*. • **tardiness** *noun*. ◷ 15c: from Latin *tardus* slow.

tare[1] ▷ *noun* **1** VETCH. **2** (*usually* **tares**) in older translations of the Bible: a weed which grows in cornfields. ◷ 14c.

tare[2] ▷ *noun* (abbreviation **t**) **1** the weight of the wrapping-paper or container in which goods are packed. **2** an allowance made for this. **3** the weight of a vehicle without its fuel, cargo or passengers. ◷ 15c: French, from Arabic *tarhah* that which is thrown away.

target /ˈtɑːgɪt/ ▷ *noun* **1** an object aimed at in shooting practice or competitions, especially a flat round board marked with concentric circles and with a bull's-eye in the centre. **2** any object or area fired or aimed at. **3** a person or thing which is the focus of ridicule or criticism. **4** a result aimed at; a goal. **5** *historical* a small buckler or round shield. ▷ *verb* (***targeted***, ***targeting***) **1** to direct or aim something. **2** to make (a person, place or thing) a target or the object of an attack. ◷ 14c: from French *targe* shield.

target language ▷ *noun*, *linguistics* **1** the language into which a text is translated. **2** the foreign language being learned.

Targum or **targum** /tɑːˈguːm, ˈtɑːgəm/ ▷ *noun*, *relig* an Aramaic version or paraphrase of the Hebrew Scriptures, probably originally composed orally (c.1c BC) when the Torah was read aloud in the synagogues. ◷ 16c: Chaldaean, meaning 'interpretation'.

tariff /ˈtarɪf/ ▷ *noun* **1** eg in a hotel: a list of prices or charges. **2** the tax or duty to be paid on a particular class of goods imported or exported. **3** a list of such taxes and duties. ▷ *verb* (***tariffed***, ***tariffing***) to set a tariff on something or someone. ⌚ 16c: from Italian *tariffa*, from Arabic *tarif* explanation.

tariff wall ▷ *noun* a barrier to the flow of imports made by high rates of customs duties.

tarlatan /'tɑːlətən/ ▷ *noun* an open transparent muslin, used for stiffening garments. ⌚ 18c: from French *tarlatane*.

tarmac /'tɑːmak/ ▷ *noun* **1** *trademark* tarmacadam. **2** a surface covered with tarmac, especially an airport runway. ⌚ Early 20c.

tarmacadam or **Tarmacadam** /tɑːmə'kadəm/ ▷ *noun, trademark* a mixture of small stones bound together with tar, used to make road surfaces, etc. Often shortened to **tarmac**. ⌚ Late 19c: from TAR[1] + *macadam*, named after John McAdam (1756–1836) a Scottish engineer.

tarn /tɑːn/ ▷ *noun* a small, often circular, mountain lake, especially one formed in a CIRQUE. ⌚ 14c: from Norse *tjörn*.

tarnish /'tɑːnɪʃ/ ▷ *verb* (***tarnishes***, ***tarnished***, ***tarnishing***) **1** *tr & intr* said of metal: to make or become dull and discoloured, especially through the action of air or dirt. **2** to spoil or damage something, eg someone's reputation. ▷ *noun* **1** a loss of shine or lustre. **2** a discoloured or dull film on the surface of metal. • **tarnishable** *noun*. ⌚ 16c: from French *ternir* to make dull.

taro /'tɑːroʊ/ ▷ *noun* (***taros***) *bot* a plant of the ARUM family, widely cultivated in the Pacific islands for its edible rootstock. ⌚ 18c: Polynesian.

tarot /'taroʊ/ ▷ *noun* **1** a pack of 78 playing-cards consisting of four suits of 14 cards and a fifth suit of 22 trump cards, now used mainly in fortune-telling. **2** any of the 22 trump cards in this pack, which are decorated with allegorical pictures. ⌚ 16c: French, from Italian *tarocco*.

tarpaulin /tɑː'pɔːlɪn/ ▷ *noun* **1** heavy canvas which has been made waterproof, especially with tar. **2** a sheet of this material. ⌚ 17c: from TAR[1] + PALL[1].

tarragon /'tarəgən/ ▷ *noun* **1** a bushy perennial plant native to Europe, with narrow lance-shaped leaves and small greenish-white flowers borne in globular heads arranged in groups. **2** the leaves of this plant, used to season vinegar and as a condiment to flavour salads, tartar sauce and other foods. ⌚ 16c: from French *targon*, from Arabic *tarkhun*.

tarry[1] /'tarɪ/ ▷ *verb* (***tarries***, ***tarried***, ***tarrying***) *intr* **1** to linger or stay in a place. **2** to be slow or late in coming, doing something, etc. • **tarrier** *noun*. ⌚ 14c.

tarry[2] /'tɑːrɪ/ ▷ *adj* (***tarrier***, ***tarriest***) like tar or covered with tar. • **tarriness** *noun*.

tarsal /'tɑːsəl/ *anatomy* ▷ *adj* relating to the bones of the tarsus. ▷ *noun* in terrestrial vertebrates: any of the bones that form the tarsus.

tarsus /'tɑːsəs/ ▷ *noun* (***tarsi*** /-saɪ/) **1** *anatomy* the seven bones forming the upper part of the foot and ankle. **2** *biol* in insects: the extremity of a limb, usually a five-jointed foot. **3** *anatomy* the firm connective tissue that supports and stiffens the eyelid. ⌚ 17c: Latin, from Greek *tarsos* the flat of the foot, or the eyelid.

tart[1] ▷ *adj* (***tarter***, ***tartest***) **1** sharp or sour in taste. **2** said of a remark, etc: brief and sarcastic; cutting. • **tartly** *adverb*. • **tartness** *noun*. ⌚ Anglo-Saxon *teart* rough.

tart[2] ▷ *noun* **1** a pastry case, especially one without a top, with a sweet or savoury filling. **2** *derog slang* a prostitute or a promiscuous person. ▷ *verb* (***tarted***, ***tarting***) (*always* **tart someone** or **something up**) *slang* to decorate or embellish them or it, especially in a showy or tasteless way. ⌚ 19c in sense 2; 13c in sense 1: from French *tarte*.

tartan /'tɑːtən/ ▷ *noun* **1** a distinctive checked pattern which can be produced with checks of different widths and different colours, especially one of the many designs which are each associated with a different Scottish clan. **2** a woollen cloth or garment woven with such a design. ⌚ 16c.

Tartar or **Tatar** /'tɑːtə(r)/ ▷ *noun* **1 a** *historical* a group of peoples, including Mongols and Turks, which overran Asia and parts of Europe in the Middle Ages; **b** a group of peoples related to the Turks now living especially in the republic of Tatarstan, Uzbekistan, Turkmenistan and W Siberia. **2** an individual belonging to these groups or peoples. **3** their language. ▷ *adj* belonging or relating to these groups or their language. ⌚ 14c: ultimately from Persian *Tatar*.

tartar[1] /'tɑːtə(r)/ ▷ *noun* **1** a hard deposit, consisting mostly of calcium salts, that forms on the teeth. **2** a deposit that forms a hard brownish-red crust on the insides of wine casks during fermentation. ⌚ 14c: from Latin *tartarum*, from Greek *tartaron*.

tartar[2] /'tɑːtə(r)/ ▷ *noun* a violent or fierce person. ⌚ 17c: from TARTAR.

tartaric acid ▷ *noun*, *chem* (formula **HOOCCH(OH)CH(OH)COOH**) an organic acid consisting of a white or colourless crystalline solid, that occurs naturally in many fruits, and is used in baking powder, food additives, dyeing, tanning and photographic chemicals. ⌚ Early 19c.

tartar sauce or **tartare sauce** /'tɑːtə(r) —/ ▷ *noun* mayonnaise flavoured with chopped pickles, capers, olives and parsley, often served as a dressing for fish. ⌚ 19c: from French *sauce tartare*, from TARTAR.

tarte tatin /tɑːt ta'tɛ̃/ ▷ *noun* a fruit pie, usually made with apples, cooked with a covering of caramelized pastry. The pie is then turned out upside down on the serving dish. ⌚ Named after a Mademoiselle Tatin who first made it.

tartrate see ARGOL

tartrazine /'tɑːtrəziːn/ ▷ *noun* a yellow powder, soluble in water, that is used as an artificial colouring in foods, drugs and cosmetics. ⌚ 19c: from TARTAR[1].

tarty ▷ *adj* (***tartier***, ***tartiest***) *derog, slang* **1** said of a woman or women's clothing: blatantly sexual or promiscuous. **2** cheap, showy and vulgar. ⌚ Early 20c.

Tas. ▷ *abbreviation, Austral state* Tasmania.

tash see TACHE

task /tɑːsk/ ▷ *noun* **1** a piece of work that is required to be done. **2** an unpleasant or difficult job; a chore. • **take someone to task** to scold or criticize them. ⌚ 13c: from French *tasque*, from Latin *taxa* tax.

task force ▷ *noun* **1** *military* a temporary grouping of different units, eg land, sea and air forces, under a single commander to undertake a specific mission. **2** any similar grouping of individuals for a specific purpose.

taskmaster and **taskmistress** ▷ *noun* a man or woman who sets and supervises the work of others, especially strictly or severely.

Tasmanian /taz'meɪnɪən/ ▷ *adj* belonging or relating to Tasmania, an island state of Australia in the S Pacific, or its inhabitants. ▷ *noun* a citizen or inhabitant of, or person born in, Tasmania. ⌚ 19c.

Tasmanian devil ▷ *noun* a small ferocious carnivorous marsupial now found only in Tasmania, with a black coat with white patches on the chest and hindquarters. ⌚ Late 19c.

Tasmanian wolf and **Tasmanian tiger** ▷ *noun* a carnivorous marsupial, perhaps still existing in some remote mountainous regions of Tasmania, with a light-brown coat with many dark vertical stripes across the hindquarters. Also called **thylacine** /'θaɪləsiːn/. ⌚ Late 19c.

Tass /tas/ ▷ *noun, historical* the official news agency of the former Soviet Union, replaced in 1992 by ITAR-TASS.

Ⓒ 1920s: an acronym of Russian *Telegrafnoe agentsvo Sovietskovo Soyuza* Telegraph Agency of the Soviet Union.

tassel /'tasəl/ ▻ *noun* **1** a decoration (eg on a curtain or cushion) consisting of a hanging bunch of threads held firmly by a knot at one end and loose at the other. **2** a tassel-like flower-head on some plants, especially maize. ▻ *verb* (***tasselled, tasselling***) **1** to adorn something with tassels. **2** *intr* said of maize: to grow tassels. Ⓒ 13c: French.

taste /teɪst/ ▻ *verb* (***tasted, tasting***) **1** *tr & intr* to perceive the flavour of (food, drink or some other substance) by means of the sensation produced on the surface of the tongue. **2** to try or test (a food or drink) by eating or drinking a small amount of it. **3** to be aware of or recognize the flavour of something. **4** (**taste of something**) to have a specified flavour □ ***This cake tastes of vanilla.*** **5** to eat or drink, especially in small quantities or with enjoyment □ ***I had not tasted food for days.*** **6** to experience □ ***taste defeat.*** ▻ *noun* **1** the particular sensation produced when food, drink or other substances are placed on the tongue. **2** the sense by which we perceive the flavour of food and drink, etc. **3** the quality or flavour of a food, drink or other substance that is perceived by this sense □ ***dislike the taste of onions.*** **4** an act of tasting or a small quantity of food or drink tasted. **5** a first, usually brief, experience of something □ ***a taste of what was to come.*** **6** the quality or flavour of something □ ***the sweet taste of victory.*** **7** a liking or preference □ ***a taste for exotic holidays.*** **8** the ability to judge and appreciate what is suitable, fine, elegant or beautiful □ ***a joke in poor taste.*** ● **tastable** *adj.* ● **to taste** as needed to give a pleasing flavour □ ***Add salt to taste.*** Ⓒ 13c: from French *taster* to touch.

taste bud ▻ *noun* any of four structurally similar types of sensory organs on the surface of the tongue which respond to the sensations of salt, sweet, sour (acid) and bitter. Ⓒ Late 19c.

tasteful ▻ *adj* showing good judgement or taste. ● **tastefully** *adverb.* ● **tastefulness** *noun.*

tasteless ▻ *adj* **1** lacking flavour. **2** showing a lack of good judgement or taste. ● **tastelessly** *adverb.* ● **tastelessness** *noun.*

taster ▻ *noun* **1** someone whose job is to taste and judge the quality of food or drink. **2** a sample of something.

-tastic ▻ *combining form, colloq, forming adjectives* indicating that something is fantastic with respect to the specified thing □ ***poptastic*** □ ***rocktastic.*** Ⓒ 1990s: modelled on FANTASTIC.

tasting ▻ *noun, often in compounds* a social event at which wine or some other food or drink is sampled □ ***a wine-tasting.***

tasty ▻ *adj* (***tastier, tastiest***) **1** having a good, especially savoury, flavour. **2** *colloq* interesting or attractive. ● **tastily** *adverb.* ● **tastiness** *noun.* Ⓒ 17c: from TASTE.

tat¹ ▻ *noun, Brit colloq* rubbish or junk. Ⓒ 20c; 19c meaning 'a rag'; compare TATTER.

tat² ▻ *verb* (***tatted, tatting***) *tr & intr* to make something by TATTING.

ta-ta /ta'tɑː/ ▻ *exclamation, Brit colloq* good-bye. Ⓒ 19c.

Tatar see TARTAR

tatter /'tatə(r)/ ▻ *noun* (*usually* **tatters**) a torn ragged shred of cloth, especially of clothing. ● **in tatters 1** said of clothes: in a torn and ragged condition. **2** said of an argument or theory, etc: completely destroyed. Ⓒ 14c: from Norse *torturr* rag.

tattered ▻ *adj* ragged or torn.

tattie /'tatɪ/ ▻ *noun* (***tatties***) *Scots* potato. Ⓒ 18c.

tattily, tattiness see under TATTY

tatting /'tatɪŋ/ ▻ *noun* **1** delicate knotted lace trimming made from sewing-thread and worked by hand with a small shuttle. **2** the process of making such lace. Ⓒ 19c.

tattle /'tatəl/ ▻ *noun* idle chatter or gossip. ▻ *verb* (***tattled, tattling***) **1** *intr* to chat or gossip idly. **2** to give away (secrets) by chatting idly or gossiping. ● **tattler** *noun.* Ⓒ 15c: from Dutch *tatelen.*

tattoo¹ /tə'tuː/ ▻ *verb* (***tattoos, tattooed, tattooing***) to mark (coloured designs or pictures) on (a person or part of the body) by pricking the skin and putting in indelible dyes. ▻ *noun* (***tattoos***) a design tattooed on the skin. ● **tattooer** or **tattooist** *noun.* Ⓒ 18c: from Tahitian *tatau.*

tattoo² /tə'tuː/ ▻ *noun* (***tattoos***) **1** a signal by drum or bugle calling soldiers to quarters, especially in the evening. **2** an outdoor military entertainment with marching troops, military bands, etc, usually given in the evening. **3** a rhythmic beating, tapping or drumming. Ⓒ 17c as *taptoo*: from Dutch *taptoe* shut the taps, from *tap* tap of a barrel + *toe* shut.

tatty /'tatɪ/ *colloq* ▻ *adj* (***tattier, tattiest***) shabby and untidy. ● **tattily** *adverb.* ● **tattiness** *noun.* Ⓒ 16c: probably from TATTER.

tau /tɑʊ/ ▻ *noun* the nineteenth letter of the Greek alphabet. See table at GREEK ALPHABET.

taught *past tense, past participle of* TEACH

taunt /tɔːnt/ ▻ *verb* (***taunting, taunted***) to tease, say unpleasant things to or jeer at someone in a cruel and hurtful way. ▻ *noun* a cruel, unpleasant and often hurtful or provoking remark. ● **taunting** *noun, adj.* ● **tauntingly** *adverb.* Ⓒ 16c.

taupe /toʊp/ ▻ *noun* a brownish-grey colour. ▻ *adj* brownish-grey. Ⓒ Early 20c: French, meaning 'mole'.

Taurus /'tɔːrəs/ ▻ *noun* (*plural* in sense 2b ***Tauruses***) **1** *astron* a constellation of the zodiac. **2** *astrol* **a** the second sign of the zodiac; **b** a person born between 21 April and 20 May, under this sign. See table at ZODIAC. ● **Taurean** /tɔː'rɪən/ *noun, adj.* Ⓒ 14c: Latin, meaning 'bull'.

taut /tɔːt/ ▻ *adj* (***tauter, tautest***) **1** pulled or stretched tight. **2** showing nervous strain or anxiety. **3** said of a ship: in good condition. Ⓒ 14c as *tought.*

tauten /'tɔːtən/ ▻ *verb* (***tautened, tautening***) *tr & intr* to make or become taut. Ⓒ Early 19c.

tautology /tɔː'tɒlədʒɪ/ ▻ *noun* (***tautologies***) **1** the use of words which repeat the meaning found in other words already used, as in *I myself personally am a vegetarian.* **2** *logic* a statement which is necessarily always true. ● **tautological** /tɔːtə'lɒdʒɪkəl/ or **tautologous** /-'tɒləgəs/ *adj.* ● **tautologically** *adverb.* Ⓒ 16c: from Greek *tautologos*, from *tauto* same + *legein* to say.

tautomerism /tɔː'tɒmərɪzəm/ ▻ *noun, chem* the existence of a substance as an equilibrium mixture of ISOMERS which have the properties of two different chemical groups and which can convert from one to the other, usually because a hydrogen atom is moving throughout the molecule. Ⓒ Late 19c: from Greek *tauto* same.

tavern /'tavən/ ▻ *noun* an inn or public house. Ⓒ 13c: from French *taverne*, from Latin *taberna* shed.

taverna /tə'vɜːnə/ ▻ *noun* (***tavernas***) **1** in Greece: a type of guesthouse with a bar, popular as holiday accommodation. **2** a Greek restaurant. Ⓒ 1940s: Greek.

taw¹ /tɔː/ ▻ *verb* (***tawed, tawing***) to prepare and dress (skins) to make leather, using an alum and salt solution rather than tannin. ● **tawer** *noun.* Ⓒ Anglo-Saxon *tawian* to prepare.

taw² /tɔː/ ▻ *noun* **1** a large or choice marble. **2** a game of marbles. **3** the line shot from at marbles. Ⓒ 18c.

tawdry /'tɔːdrɪ/ ▻ *adj* (***tawdrier, tawdriest***) cheap and showy and of poor quality. ● **tawdrily** *adverb.* ● **tawdriness** *noun.* Ⓒ 17c in this sense; 16c as obsolete *tawdry lace*: from *St Audrey lace* lace sold at fairs held on the feast day of St Audrey, ie 17 October.

tawny /ˈtɔːnɪ/ ▻ *noun* a yellowish-brown colour. ▻ *adj* (***tawnier***, ***tawniest***) yellowish-brown. ⓘ 14c: from French *tané*.

tawny owl ▻ *noun* a small nocturnal owl, native to Europe and Asia, with mottled brown plumage and a large rounded head.

taws or **tawse** /tɔːz/ ▻ *noun* (***tawses***) *chiefly Scots* a leather strap divided into strips at one end, formerly used for corporal punishment in schools. ⓘ 16c: plural of obsolete *taw* whip, from Anglo-Saxon *tawian* to tan leather.

tax ▻ *noun* (***taxes***) **1** a compulsory contribution towards a country's expenses raised by the government from people's salaries, property and from the sale of goods and services. **2** a strain, burden or heavy demand. ▻ *verb* (***taxes***, ***taxed***, ***taxing***) **1** to impose a tax on (a person or goods, etc) or take tax from (a salary). **2** to put a strain on, or make a heavy demand on, someone or something. **3** (*usually* **tax someone with something**) *formal* to accuse them of it. **4** *law* to assess (costs). • **taxable** *noun*. ⓘ 13c: from French *taxer*, from Latin *taxare* to appraise.

taxation ▻ *noun* **1** the act or system of imposing taxes. **2** the revenue raised by taxes.

tax-deductible ▻ *adj* said of expenses, etc: eligible for deduction from taxable income.

tax disc ▻ *noun* a paper disc displayed on a motor vehicle's windscreen to show that it has been duly taxed.

tax exile ▻ *noun* someone who lives abroad in a country with a lower tax rate than that of their native country, so as to avoid paying high taxes.

tax-free ▻ *adj*, *adverb* without payment of tax □ *tax-free shopping*.

tax haven ▻ *noun* a country or state with a low rate of taxation compared to one's own and which is therefore an attractive place to stay for wealthy people.

taxi /ˈtaksɪ/ ▻ *noun* (***taxis*** or ***taxies***) a car which may be hired together with its driver to carry passengers on usually short journeys, and which is usually fitted with a taximeter for calculating the fare. Also called **taxicab**. ▻ *verb* (***taxis*** or ***taxies***, ***taxied***, ***taxiing*** or ***taxying***) **1 a** *intr* said of an aircraft: to move slowly along the ground before or after take-off or landing; **b** to make (an aircraft) move in this way. **2** *tr & intr* to travel or cause someone or something to be conveyed in a taxi. ⓘ Early 20c: a shortening of *taximeter cab*.

taxidermy /ˈtaksɪdɜːmɪ/ ▻ *noun* the art of preparing, stuffing and mounting animal skins and birds so that they present a lifelike appearance. • **taxidermal** or **taxidermic** *adj*. • **taxidermist** *noun*. ⓘ 19c: from Greek *taxis* arrangement + *derma* skin.

taximeter /ˈtaksɪmiːtə(r)/ ▻ *noun* a meter fitted to a taxi which monitors the time taken and the distance travelled, and displays the fare due for the journey. ⓘ 19c: from French *taximètre*, from *taxe* tax + *mètre* meter.

taxing ▻ *adj* requiring a lot of mental or physical effort; demanding. ⓘ 1940s: from TAX *verb* 2.

taxi rank ▻ *noun* a place where taxis wait until hired.

taxis /ˈtaksɪs/ ▻ *noun* (***taxes*** /ˈtaksiːz/) **1** *biol* the movement of a single cell (eg a GAMETE, BACTERIUM or PROTOZOAN) in response to an external stimulus from a specific direction (eg light). **2** *surgery* the return to position of displaced parts by means of manual manipulation only. ⓘ 18c: Greek, meaning 'arrangement'.

taxonomy /takˈsɒnəmɪ/ ▻ *noun* (***taxonomies***) **1** *biol* the theory and techniques of describing, naming and classifying living and extinct organisms on the basis of the similarity of their anatomical and morphological features and structures, etc. **2** the practice or technique of classification. • **taxonomic** /taksəˈnɒmɪk/ *adj*. • **taxonomist** /takˈsɒnəmɪst/ *noun*. ⓘ 19c: from Greek *taxis* arrangement.

taxpayer ▻ *noun* someone who pays or is liable for tax or taxes.

tax return ▻ *noun* a yearly statement of one's income, from which the amount due in tax is calculated.

tax shelter ▻ *noun* a financial arrangement made in order to pay only the minimum taxation.

tax year ▻ *noun* FINANCIAL YEAR.

TB ▻ *abbreviation* tuberculosis.

Tb ▻ *symbol*, *chem* terbium.

tbsp ▻ *abbreviation* tablespoon, tablespoonful.

Tc ▻ *symbol*, *chem* technetium.

TCA see TRICARBOXYLIC ACID CYCLE

TCD ▻ *abbreviation* **1** *IVR* Chad (French name Tchad). **2** The Chambers Dictionary. **3** Trinity College, Dublin.

t-cell /ˈtiːsɛl/ ▻ *noun*, *medicine* a kind of LYMPHOCYTE that matures in the thymus gland in mammals and is responsible for cell immunity against viruses. ⓘ 1970: from *t*hymus-*cell*.

TCM ▻ *abbreviation* Trinity College of Music, London.

TCP ▻ *abbreviation*, *trademark* trichlorophenylmethyliodosalicyl, an antiseptic and disinfectant.

Te ▻ *symbol*, *chem* tellurium.

te or **ti** /tiː/ ▻ *noun* (***tes*** or ***tis***) *music* in SOL-FA notation: the seventh note of the major scale. ⓘ 19c: earlier *si*, from the initial sounds of *Sancte Iohannes* in a medieval Latin hymn, certain syllables and sounds of which were used in naming the notes of the scale.

tea /tiː/ ▻ *noun* (***teas***) **1** a small evergreen tree or shrub, with pointed leathery leaves and white fragrant flowers, cultivated in SE Asia and elsewhere for its leaves. **2** the dried leaves of this plant prepared for sale. **3** a beverage prepared by infusing the dried leaves of this plant with boiling water and which can then be served either hot or iced. **4** *in compounds* a similar drink made from the leaves or flowers of other plants □ *peppermint tea*. **5** a light afternoon meal at which tea, sandwiches and cakes are served. Also called **afternoon tea**. **6** *Brit* **a** a light cooked meal, usually less substantial than the midday meal, served early in the evening; **b** the main evening meal. See also HIGH TEA. ⓘ 17c: from Min Chinese *te*.

tea bag ▻ *noun* a small bag or sachet of thin paper containing tea, which is then infused in boiling water.

tea break ▻ *noun* a pause for tea or other refreshments during working hours.

tea caddy ▻ *noun* a small container for loose tea.

teacake ▻ *noun*, *Brit* a glazed currant bun, usually eaten toasted.

teach ▻ *verb* (***teaches***, ***taught***, ***teaching***) **1** to give knowledge to someone; to instruct someone in a skill or help them to learn. **2** *tr & intr* to give lessons in (a subject), especially as a professional. **3** said of circumstances or experience, etc: to make someone learn or understand, especially by example, experience or punishment □ *Experience had taught her to be cautious*. **4** to force home the desirability or otherwise of a particular action or behaviour, etc □ *That'll teach you to be more polite*. • **teachable** *adj*. • **teach one's grandmother to suck eggs** *colloq* to try to show someone more experienced than oneself how to do something they already know how to do. • **teach someone a lesson** to demonstrate and reinforce their mistake. • **teach school** *N Amer* to be a teacher in a school. ⓘ Anglo-Saxon *tæcan*.

teacher ▻ *noun* someone whose job is to teach, especially in a school.

tea chest ▻ *noun* a tall light wooden box in which tea is packed for export, or which is used for storing things in.

teach-in ▻ *noun* an informal lecture, demonstration and discussion, or a series of these given one after the other and usually on the same day, by experts in a particular subject.

teaching ▷ *noun* **1** the work or profession of a teacher. **2** (*often* **teachings**) something that is taught, especially guidance or doctrine.

teaching hospital ▷ *noun* a large hospital where medical students are taught.

tea cloth ▷ *noun* **1** a small cloth for decorating and protecting the surface of a table or trolley. **2** a tea towel.

tea cosy ▷ *noun* (***tea cosies***) a cover to keep a teapot warm.

teacup ▷ *noun* **1** a medium-sized cup used especially for drinking tea. **2** a TEACUPFUL.

teacupful ▷ *noun* (***teacupfuls***) the amount a teacup can hold.

tea dance ▷ *noun* a dance, usually held in the afternoon, at which tea is served. ⓒ 1920s.

teahouse ▷ *noun* a restaurant, especially in China or Japan, where tea and light refreshments are served.

teak /tiːk/ ▷ *noun* **1** a large evergreen tree, native to S India and SE Asia which is cultivated for its high-quality timber. **2** the heavy yellowish-brown wood of this tree, which is hard and durable and is used in furniture-making and shipbuilding, etc. ⓒ 17c: from Portuguese *teca*, from Malayalam (a S Indian language) *tekka*.

teal /tiːl/ ▷ *noun* (***teals*** or ***teal***) **1** any of several kinds of small freshwater duck closely related to the mallard, native to Europe, Asia and N America. **2** a dark greenish-blue colour. ▷ *adj* having this colour. ⓒ 14c.

tea leaf ▷ *noun* **1** a leaf of the tea plant, or a part of the leaf. **2** (**tea leaves**) the leaves remaining in the pot or cup after the tea made from them has been drunk. **3** *slang* a thief.

team /tiːm/ ▷ *noun* **1** a group of people who form one side in a game. **2** a group of people working together. **3** two or more animals working together, especially in harness. ▷ *verb* (***teamed***, ***teaming***) **1** *tr & intr* (*usually* **team up with someone**) to form a team for some common action. **2** to harness (horses or oxen, etc) together. **3** (*also* **team up**) to match (clothes). ⓒ Anglo-Saxon, meaning 'child-bearing' or 'offspring'.

team spirit ▷ *noun* willingness to work together as part of a team and suppress individual needs and desires.

teamster ▷ *noun* **1** a driver of a team of animals. **2** *N Amer, especially US* a lorry-driver. ⓒ 18c.

teamwork ▷ *noun* co-operation between those who are working together on a task.

teapot ▷ *noun* a pot with a spout and handle used for making and pouring tea.

tear¹ /tɪə(r)/ ▷ *noun* **1** a drop of clear saline liquid, secreted by the LACHRYMAL GLAND, that moistens and cleans the front of the eyeball, or overflows from it in response to irritation of the eye or as a result of emotion, especially sorrow. **2** any pear- or tear-shaped drop or blob. • **tearless** *noun*. • **in tears** crying; weeping. ⓒ Anglo-Saxon.

tear² /tɛə(r)/ ▷ *verb* (***tore*** /tɔː(r)/, ***torn*** /tɔːn/, ***tearing***) **1** to pull or rip something apart by force. **2** (*usually* **tear at something**) to pull it violently or with tearing movements. **3** to make (a hole, etc) by, or as if by, tearing or ripping. **4** *intr* to come apart; to be pulled or ripped apart □ *material that tears easily*. **5** (*often* **tear along, away, off,** *etc*) *intr* to rush; to move with speed or force. ▷ *noun* **1** a hole or other damage caused by tearing. **2** an act of tearing. **3** damage □ *wear and tear*. • **be torn between** to be unable to decide between (two or more options). • **tear a strip off someone** *colloq* to rebuke or reprimand them severely. • **tear one's hair out** to be in despair with impatience and frustration. ⓒ Anglo-Saxon *teran*.

■ **tear someone apart** to cause them severe suffering or distress.

■ **tear someone away** to remove or take them by force; to force or persuade them to leave.

■ **tear something down** to pull it down or demolish it using force.

■ **tear into someone** to attack them physically or verbally.

■ **tear something up 1** to tear it into pieces, especially to destroy it. **2** to remove it from a fixed position by violence or force.

tearaway /ˈtɛərəweɪ/ ▷ *noun, Brit colloq* an undisciplined and reckless young person.

teardrop ▷ *noun* **1** a single TEAR¹. **2** anything with a similar shape.

tear duct ▷ *noun* a short tube opening in the inner corner of the eye, for carrying tears to the eye or draining them into the nose. Also called **lachrymal duct**.

tearful /ˈtɪəfəl/ ▷ *adj* **1** inclined to cry or weep. **2** with much crying or weeping; covered with tears. **3** causing tears to be shed; sad. • **tearfully** *adverb*. • **tearfulness** *noun*. ⓒ 16c.

tear gas ▷ *noun* a gas which causes stinging blinding tears, and temporary loss of sight, used eg to control riots and in warfare, etc.

tearing /ˈtɛərɪŋ/ ▷ *adj* furious; overwhelming □ *a tearing hurry*.

tear-jerker ▷ *noun, colloq* a sentimental play, film or book, etc intended to make people feel sad and cry. • **tear-jerking** *adj* sentimental. ⓒ 1930s.

tearless see under TEAR¹

tearoom ▷ *noun* a restaurant where tea, coffee and cakes, etc are served.

tea rose ▷ *noun* any of various varieties of hybrid rose with pink or yellow flowers. ⓒ 19c: so called because its flowers are supposed to smell like tea.

tear-stained ▷ *adj* said of the face or cheeks: marked with the traces of tears.

tease /tiːz/ ▷ *verb* (***teased***, ***teasing***) **1** to annoy or irritate someone deliberately or unkindly. **2** to laugh at or make fun of someone playfully or annoyingly. **3** (*usually* **tease someone into something**) to persuade them to agree to it, especially by continual coaxing. **4** to arouse someone sexually without satisfying that desire. **5** to comb (wool, flax or hair, etc) to remove tangles and open out the fibres. **6** to raise a nap on (cloth) by scratching or brushing, especially with teasels. **7** to backcomb (hair). ▷ *noun* **1** someone or something that teases. **2** an act of teasing. ⓒ Anglo-Saxon *tæsan* to card.

■ **tease something out 1** to separate it from something in which it is entangled. **2** to clarify (an obscure point) by discussion, etc.

teasel, **teazel** or **teazle** /ˈtiːzəl/ ▷ *noun* **1** any of various biennial plants with white or mauve flower-heads surrounded by curved prickly BRACTS. **2** the dried flower-head of the teasel, used to raise the nap on cloth. **3** an artificial substitute for the teasel. ⓒ Anglo-Saxon *tæsel*.

teaser ▷ *noun* **1** a puzzle or tricky problem. **2** a person who enjoys teasing others. **3** an introductory advertisement intended to arouse people's curiosity as to the product being advertised.

teashop ▷ *noun* **1** a restaurant (usually a small one) where tea and light refreshments are served. **2** a shop where tea is sold.

teasing ▷ *noun* the act or practice of teasing. ▷ *adj* taunting; tantalizing. • **teasingly** *adverb*.

Teasmade /ˈtiːzmeɪd/ ▷ *noun, trademark* a small machine with an alarm clock or timer which automatically makes tea at a preset time. ⓒ 1930s.

teaspoon ⊳ *noun* **1** a small spoon for use with a teacup. **2** a TEASPOONFUL.

teaspoonful ⊳ *noun* (***teaspoonfuls***) the amount a teaspoon can hold.

teat ⊳ *noun* **1** the nipple of a breast or udder. **2** a piece of shaped rubber attached to a bottle through which a baby can suck milk. ◷ 13c: from French *tete*.

tea towel ⊳ *noun* a DISHTOWEL.

tea tray ⊳ *noun* a tray on which tea, usually with sandwiches and cakes, etc is served.

tea trolley ⊳ *noun* a small trolley from which tea, sandwiches, cakes, etc are served.

teazel or **teazle** see TEASEL

tec ⊳ *noun, colloq* a detective.

tech /tɛk/ ⊳ *noun, colloq* a technical college. ◷ Early 20c.

tech. ⊳ *abbreviation* **1** technical. **2** technology.

technetium /tɛk'niːʃɪəm/ ⊳ *noun, chem* (symbol **Tc**, atomic number 43) a radioactive metallic element that was first produced artificially by bombarding MOLYBDENUM with neutrons (now produced from URANIUM and PLUTONIUM), used in nuclear medicine for diagnostic purposes. ◷ 1940s: Latin, from Greek *technetos* artificial.

technic ⊳ *noun* **1** /'tɛknɪk, tɛk'niːk/ TECHNIQUE. **2** /'tɛknɪk/ TECHNICS. ◷ 17c: from Greek *technikos*, from *techne* 'art' or 'skill'.

technical /'tɛknɪkəl/ ⊳ *adj* **1** possessing knowledge of, specializing in or relating to a practical skill or applied science, especially those sciences which are useful to industry. **2** said especially of language: relating to a particular subject or requiring knowledge of a particular subject to be understood. **3** according to a strict interpretation of the law or rules. **4** belonging or relating to, or showing a quality of, technique. • **technically** *adverb*. • **technicalness** *noun*. ◷ 17c: from TECHNIC.

technical college ⊳ *noun* a college of further education that teaches practical skills and applied sciences that are necessary to industry and business. ◷ Late 19c.

technical drawing ⊳ *noun* **1** the drawing of plans, machinery, electrical circuits, etc done with compasses and rulers, etc for business and industry. **2** a drawing done for business or industry.

technical hitch ⊳ *noun* **1** a mechanical fault which causes a temporary halt to proceedings. **2** *loosely* a snag or problem.

technicality /tɛknɪ'kalɪtɪ/ ⊳ *noun* (***technicalities***) **1** a technical detail or term. **2** a usually trivial or petty detail caused by a strict interpretation of a law or rules. **3** the state of being technical.

technical knockout (abbreviation **TKO**) ⊳ *noun, boxing* a decision by a referee that a boxer has been defeated even though they have not been knocked out.

technician /tɛk'nɪʃən/ ⊳ *noun* **1** someone specialized or skilled in a practical art or science. **2** someone employed to do practical work in a laboratory.

Technicolor /'tɛknɪkʌlə(r)/ ⊳ *noun, trademark* a process of producing colour cinema film by placing several copies of a scene, each one produced using different colour filters, on top of each other. ◷ 1917.

technics ⊳ *singular or plural noun* TECHNOLOGY (*especially* sense 1). ◷ 19c; see TECHNIC.

technique /tɛk'niːk/ ⊳ *noun* **1** proficiency or skill in the practical or formal aspects of an art, especially painting, music and sport, etc. **2** mechanical or practical skill or method □ ***study the techniques of film-making.*** **3** a way of achieving one's purpose skilfully; a knack. ◷ 19c: French (as *adj*), from Greek *technikos*, from *techne* art.

techno ⊳ *noun* a style of DANCE MUSIC that makes use of electronic effects over a frenzied rhythm, and produces fast but often unmelodic sounds.

technobabble /'tɛknoʊbabəl/ ⊳ *noun, colloq* language that overuses technical jargon, eg specialized words, acronyms and abbreviations used in computing, etc. ◷ 1980s.

technocracy /tɛk'nɒkrəsɪ/ ⊳ *noun* (***technocracies***) the government of a country or management of an industry by technical experts. • **technocrat** /'tɛknoʊkrat/ *noun*. • **technocratic** *noun*. ◷ Early 20c.

technology /tɛk'nɒlədʒɪ/ ⊳ *noun* (***technologies***) **1** the practical use of scientific knowledge in industry and everyday life. **2** practical sciences as a group. **3** the technical skills and achievements of a particular time in history, of civilization or a group of people. • **technological** *adj*. • **technologically** *adverb*. • **technologist** *noun* someone skilled in technology and its applications. ◷ 17c: from Greek *technologia* systematic treatment, from *techne* 'art' or 'skill'.

technophile /'tɛknəfaɪl/ ⊳ *noun* someone who likes and advocates the use of new technology. • **technophilia** *noun*. • **technophilic** *adj*. ◷ 1960s.

technophobe /'tɛknəfoʊb/ ⊳ *noun* someone who dislikes or fears, and therefore avoids using, technology. • **technophobia** *noun*. • **technophobic** *adj*. ◷ 1960s.

technopop ⊳ *noun, music* pop music using synthesizers and other electronic equipment.

tectonics /tɛk'tɒnɪks/ ⊳ *singular noun* **1** *geol* the study of structures which form the Earth's crust and the forces which change it. See also PLATE TECTONICS. **2** the art or science of building and construction. ◷ 19c: from Greek *tekton* builder.

tectorial /tɛk'tɔːrɪəl/ ⊳ *adj, anatomy* forming a covering. ◷ 19c: from Latin *tectorius*, from *tegere*, *tectum* to cover.

tectrix /'tɛktrɪks/ ⊳ *noun* (***tetrices*** /-trɪsiːz/) ⊳ *noun, ornithol* a COVERT (*noun* 3). ◷ 19c: Latin, from *tegere*, *tectum* to cover.

Ted ⊳ *noun, Brit colloq* a Teddy boy. ◷ 1950s.

ted ⊳ *verb* (***tedded, tedding***) to spread out (newly-mown grass) for drying. • **tedder** *noun*. ◷ 15c: from Norse *thethja* to spread manure.

teddy¹ /'tɛdɪ/ ⊳ *noun* (***teddies***) (*in full* **teddy bear**) a child's stuffed toy bear. See also ARCTOPHILE. ◷ Early 20c: from 'Teddy', the pet-name of Theodore Roosevelt (1858–1919), who was well known as a bear hunter.

teddy² /'tɛdɪ/ ⊳ *noun* (***teddies***) a woman's one-piece undergarment consisting of a chemise and panties. ◷ 1920s: possibly from TEDDY¹.

Teddy boy ⊳ *noun, Brit colloq* an unruly or rowdy adolescent, especially one in the 1950s who dressed in Edwardian-style clothes, eg DRAINPIPE trousers and a long jacket. ◷ 1950s: from Teddy, a familiar form of the name Edward, because of their Edwardian style of dress.

Te Deum /tiː 'diːəm, teɪ 'deʊm/ ⊳ *noun* (***Te Deums***) a Latin hymn of praise and thanksgiving, or a musical setting of it. ◷ 10c: Latin, from its first words *Te Deum laudamus* You God we praise.

tedious /'tiːdɪəs/ ⊳ *adj* tiresomely long-winded or dull; monotonous. • **tediously** *adverb*. • **tediousness** *noun*. ◷ 15c: from Latin *taedium* weariness.

tedium /'tiːdɪəm/ ⊳ *noun* tediousness; boredom. ◷ 17c: from Latin *taedium* weariness.

tee¹ ⊳ *noun* (***tees***) a phonetic spelling for the letter *T*. See also T¹.

tee² ⊳ *noun* (***tees***) **1** *golf* **a** a small peg with a concave top, or a small pile of sand, used to support a ball when the first shot is taken at the beginning of a hole; **b** the small area of level ground from where this shot is taken. **2** a mark aimed at in quoits or curling. ▷ *verb* (***teed, teeing***) (*often* **tee up**) to place a golf ball on a tee ready to be played. Ⓒ 17c.

■ **tee off** *golf* to play the first shot of a hole.

tee-hee or **te-hee** ▷ *exclamation* expressing amusement or mirth. ▷ *noun* (***tee-hees***) a laugh or giggle. ▷ *verb* (***tee-heed, tee-heeing***) *intr* to laugh, especially in a derisive way. Ⓒ 14c: imitating the sound.

teem¹ ▷ *verb* (***teemed, teeming***) *intr* **1** (*usually* **teem with people** or **things**) to be full of them or abound in them □ *a resort teeming with tourists.* **2** to be present in large numbers; to be plentiful □ *Fish teem in this river.* Ⓒ Anglo-Saxon *teman* to give birth.

teem² ▷ *verb* (***teemed, teeming***) **1** *intr* (*usually* **teem down**) said of water, especially rain: to pour in torrents. **2** to pour out. Ⓒ 15c: from Norse *toema* to empty.

teen ▷ *noun* **1** (**teens**) the years of a person's life between the ages of 13 and 19. **2** (**teens**) the numbers from 13 to 19. **3** *colloq* a teenager. ▷ *adj* for or relating to teenagers. Ⓒ Anglo-Saxon *tien* ten.

-teen ▷ *suffix* used to form the numbers between 13 and 19. Ⓒ Anglo-Saxon: a form of TEN.

teenage /ˈtiːneɪdʒ/ ▷ *adj* **1** (*also* **teenaged**) in one's teens. **2** relating to or suitable for people in their teens. • **teenager** *noun*. Ⓒ 1920s.

teeny /ˈtiːnɪ/ and **teensy** /ˈtiːnzɪ/ ▷ *adj* (***teenier, teeniest; teensier, teensiest***) *colloq* tiny. Ⓒ 19c: from TINY.

teenybopper ▷ *noun, colloq* a young teenager, typically a girl, who enthusiastically follows the latest trends in clothes and pop music, and screams a lot at pop concerts. Ⓒ 1960s.

teeny-weeny /tiːnɪˈwiːnɪ/ or **teensy-weensy** /tiːnzɪˈwiːnzɪ/ ▷ *adj, colloq* very tiny. Ⓒ 19c.

teepee see TEPEE

tee shirt see T-SHIRT

teeter /ˈtiːtə(r)/ ▷ *verb* (***teetered, teetering***) *intr* **1** (*usually* **teeter about** or **along**, *etc*) to stand or move unsteadily; to wobble. **2** to hesitate or waver. Ⓒ 19c as *titeren.*

teeth *plural of* TOOTH

teethe /tiːð/ ▷ *verb* (***teethed, teething***) *intr* said of a baby: to develop or cut milk teeth. • **teething** *noun*. Ⓒ 14c.

teething ring ▷ *noun* a small hard ring, now usually made of plastic, for a baby to chew on while teething.

teething troubles ▷ *plural, noun* problems or difficulties in the early stages of a project, or with a new piece of machinery, etc.

teetotal /tiːˈtoʊtəl/ ▷ *adj* abstaining completely from alcoholic drink. • **teetotaller** *noun*. Ⓒ 19c: probably connected with 'total abstinence (from alcohol)' and popularly thought to have been coined by a campaigner for total abstinence in a speech in 1833.

teetotum /tiːˈtoʊtəm/ ▷ *noun, historical* a small spinning top with four sides, each of which is inscribed with a letter, to determine whether the person spinning it has lost or won. Ⓒ 18c: from *T* (the letter on one side) + Latin *totum* all the stakes, won by spinning a T.

tefillin or **tephillin** /təˈfɪlɪn, -ˈfiː-/ ▷ *plural noun, Judaism* **1** PHYLACTERIES. **2** the scriptural texts contained in them. Ⓒ 17c: from Hebrew *tephillah* prayer.

TEFL /ˈtɛfəl/ ▷ *abbreviation* Teaching English as a Foreign Language.

Teflon /ˈtɛflɒn/ ▷ *noun, trademark* another name for POLYTETRAFLUOROETHYLENE. Ⓒ 1945.

teg ▷ *noun* a sheep in its second year. Ⓒ 16c.

tegmen /ˈtɛgmən/ ▷ *noun* (***tegmina*** /-mɪnə/) **1** *bot* the inner coat of a seed covering. **2** *entomol* the leathery forewing of the cockroach or related insects. **3** any covering. Ⓒ 19c: Latin, from *tegere* to cover.

tegument ▷ *noun* an INTEGUMENT.

te-hee see TEE-HEE

tektite /ˈtɛktaɪt/ ▷ *noun* a type of small glassy stone found in several areas around the world, thought to be a result of meteoric impacts. Ⓒ 1920s: from Greek *tektos* molten.

tel¹ see TELL²

tel² ▷ *abbreviation* telephone, or telephone number.

telaesthesia /tɛlɪsˈθiːzɪə/ ▷ *noun, psychol* the apparent perception of distant objects or happenings by means other than the five recognized senses. Ⓒ 19c: from TELE- 1 + Greek *aisthesia* sensation.

tele- /tɛlɪ/ ▷ *combining form, signifying* **1** at, over, or to, a distance □ *telegram.* **2** television □ *teletext.* **3** telephone □ *telesales.* Ⓒ Greek, meaning 'far'.

tele-ad /ˈtɛlɪad/ ▷ *noun* an advertisement placed in a newspaper by telephone. Ⓒ 1970s.

telebanking ▷ *noun* a system which enables banking transactions to be carried out by means of a telecommunications network, most commonly achieved through a VIEWDATA system or an interactive computer link, or sometimes over an interactive cable TV network, with provision for the user to send signals to the bank. Ⓒ 1980s.

telecast /ˈtɛlɪkɑːst/ ▷ *verb, tr & intr* to broadcast by TV. ▷ *noun* a TV broadcast. • **telecaster** *noun*. Ⓒ 1930s.

telecommunication or **telecommunications** ▷ *noun* any process or group of processes that allows the transmission of audible or visible information, or data, over long distances by means of electrical or electronic signals, eg telephone, radio, TV, telegraph, fax, radar, etc. Ⓒ 1930s.

telecommuter ▷ *noun* someone who works at home and communicates with an office by telephone or computer link, etc. • **telecommuting** *noun* TELEWORKING.

teleconferencing ▷ *noun* the facility for conducting **teleconferences**, ie conferences or meetings between people in two or more remote locations by video, audio and/or computer links which allow communication in REAL TIME between the participants. Ⓒ 1950s.

telecottage ▷ *noun* a building situated in a rural area and equipped with computers and electronic communication links, used by a number of people for teleworking. • **telecottaging** *noun*. Ⓒ 1980s.

telegram /ˈtɛlɪgram/ ▷ *noun* a message sent by telegraph and delivered in printed form, now used (in the UK) only for messages sent abroad and replaced by TELEMESSAGE for inland messages. Ⓒ 19c: TELE- 1 + -GRAM.

telegraph /ˈtɛlɪgrɑːf/ ▷ *noun* a system of or instrument for sending messages or information to a distance, especially by sending electrical impulses along a wire. ▷ *verb* (***telegraphed, telegraphing***) **1** *tr & intr* to send (a message) to someone by telegraph. **2** to give a warning of (something which is to happen) without being aware of doing so. **3** *intr* to signal. • **telegrapher** /təˈlɛgrəfə(r)/ or **telegraphist** /təˈlɛgrəfɪst/ *noun*. Ⓒ 18c: from French *télégraphe* = TELE- 1 + -GRAPH.

telegraphese /tɛlɪgrɑːˈfiːz/ ▷ *noun* the jargon or abbreviated language typically used for telegrams. Ⓒ Late 19c.

telegraphic /tɛlɪˈgrafɪk/ ▷ *adj* **1** belonging or relating to, or sent by, telegraph or telegram. **2** concisely worded. • **telegraphically** *adverb*.

telegraphy /təˈlɛgrəfɪ/ ▷ *noun* the science or practice of sending messages by telegraph. Ⓒ 18c.

telekinesis /tɛlɪkaɪˈniːsɪs, -kɪˈniːsɪs/ ▷ *noun* **1** the moving of objects at a distance without using physical force, eg by willpower. **2** the apparent ability to move objects in this way. • **telekinetic** *adj.* Ⓒ Late 19c.

telemarketing ▷ *noun* a marketing system that uses the telephone to recruit and provide a service for prospective clients. Ⓒ 1980s.

Telemessage /ˈtɛlɪmɛsɪdʒ/ ▷ *noun, Brit trademark* a message sent by telex or telephone and delivered in printed form, replacing the telegram within the UK. Ⓒ 1981.

telemeter /təˈlɛmɪtə(r)/ ▷ *noun* an instrument that is used to take measurements, eg of meteorological data, and send the readings obtained, usually by means of electrical or radio signals, to a location remote from the site of measurement. ▷ *verb* to record and signal (data) in this way. • **telemetric** /-ˈmɛtrɪk/ *adj.* Ⓒ 19c.

telemetry /təˈlɛmətrɪ/ ▷ *noun* the practice of obtaining and sending data using a telemeter. Also called **remote sensing**.

teleology /tɛlɪˈɒlədʒɪ/ ▷ *noun* the doctrine that the universe, all phenomena and natural processes are directed towards a goal or are designed according to some purpose. • **teleological** *adj.* • **teleologist** *noun.* Ⓒ 18c: from Greek *telos* end.

telepathy /təˈlɛpəθɪ/ ▷ *noun* the apparent communication of thoughts directly from one person's mind to another's without using any of the five known senses. • **telepathic** /tɛlɪˈpaθɪk/ *adj.* • **telepathically** *adverb.* • **telepathist** /-ˈlɛp-/ *noun.* Ⓒ Late 19c.

telephone /ˈtɛlɪfoʊn/ ▷ *noun* **1** an instrument with a mouthpiece and an earpiece mounted on a handset, for transmitting human speech in the form of electrical signals or radio waves, enabling people to communicate with each other over a distance. **2** the system of communication that uses such an instrument. ▷ *verb* (***telephoned, telephoning***) **1** to seek or establish contact and speak to someone by telephone. **2** to send (a message, etc) by telephone. **3** *intr* to make a telephone call. Often shortened to **phone**. • **telephonic** /-ˈfɒnɪk/ *adj.* • **on the telephone 1** connected to the telephone system. **2** talking to someone by means of the telephone. Ⓒ 19c.

telephone box and **telephone booth** ▷ *noun* a small enclosed or partly-enclosed compartment containing a telephone for public use.

telephone directory and **telephone book** ▷ *noun* a book that lists the names, addresses and telephone numbers of telephone subscribers in a particular area. Also called **phone book**.

telephone exchange see EXCHANGE

telephone number ▷ *noun* **1** a combination of digits which identifies a particular telephone and can be dialled to make a connection with it. Often shortened to **number**. **2** (*usually* **telephone numbers**) *colloq* said especially of a salary or sales figures: a very large amount.

telephonic see under TELEPHONE

telephonist /təˈlɛfənɪst/ ▷ *noun* a telephone switchboard operator.

telephony /təˈlɛfənɪ/ ▷ *noun* the use or system of communication by means of the telephone. Ⓒ 19c.

telephoto ▷ *adj* TELEPHOTOGRAPHIC. ▷ *noun* (***telephotos***) a TELEPHOTO LENS or camera, or a photograph taken with one. Ⓒ Late 19c.

telephotography ▷ *noun* the photographing of distant objects with lenses which produce magnified images. • **telephotographic** *adj.* Ⓒ Late 19c.

telephoto lens ▷ *noun* a camera lens which produces magnified images of distant or small objects.

teleprinter ▷ *noun* (abbreviation **tpr**) an apparatus with a keyboard which types messages as they are received by telegraph and transmits them as they are typed. Ⓒ 1920s.

Teleprompter ▷ *noun, trademark* a device placed next to a TV camera or film camera and out of sight of the audience, which displays the script to the speaker, allowing them to read it while apparently looking into the camera. Ⓒ 1950s.

telesales ▷ *singular and plural noun* the selling of goods or services by telephone. Also called **teleselling**. Ⓒ 1960s.

telescope /ˈtɛlɪskoʊp/ ▷ *noun* **1** an optical instrument containing a powerful magnifying lens or mirror that makes distant objects appear larger. **2** a RADIO TELESCOPE. ▷ *verb* (***telescoped, telescoping***) **1** *intr* to be in the form of several cylinders which slide out of or into each other for opening and closing, like the sections of a folding telescope. **2** *tr & intr* to collapse part within part like a folding telescope. **3** *tr & intr* to crush or compress, or become crushed or compressed, under impact. Ⓒ 17c: from Italian *telescopio* or new Latin *telescopium*; see TELE-1 + -SCOPE.

telescopic /tɛlɪˈskɒpɪk/ ▷ *adj* **1** belonging or relating to, or like, a telescope; performed with a telescope. **2** able to be seen only through a telescope. **3** said of a lens: able to magnify distant objects. **4** made in sections which slide into each other. • **telescopically** *adverb.*

telescopic sight ▷ *noun* a small telescope used as a sight on a rifle.

teleshopping ▷ *noun* the purchase or ordering of goods from home, using an electronic communications network, with a list of goods available to the shopper displayed on a TV screen. Ⓒ 1980s.

teletext ▷ *noun* a non-interactive news and information service and type of VIDEOTEXT, eg CEEFAX, that is produced and regularly updated by a TV company, and can be viewed on TV sets fitted with a suitable receiver and decoder. See also VIEWDATA. Ⓒ 1970s.

telethon ▷ *noun* a TV programme, usually a day-long one, broadcast to raise money for charity. Ⓒ 1940s: from TELE- 2 modelled on MARATHON.

Teletype /ˈtɛlɪtaɪp/ ▷ *noun, trademark* a type of teleprinter. Ⓒ Early 20c.

televangelist /tɛlɪˈvandʒəlɪst/ ▷ *noun, especially US* an evangelical preacher who preaches and conducts religious services regularly on TV and often appeals for donations from viewers. Ⓒ 1970s: from TELE- 2 + EVANGELIST.

televise /ˈtɛlɪvaɪz/ ▷ *verb* (***televised, televising***) to broadcast something by television.

television /ˈtɛlɪvɪʒən/ ▷ *noun* (abbreviation **TV**) **1** an electronic system that is used to convert moving images and sound into electrical signals, which are then transmitted by radio waves or by cable to a distant receiver that converts the signals back to images and sound. **2** (*also* **television set**) a device with a picture tube and loudspeakers that is used to receive picture and sound signals transmitted in this way. **3** television broadcasting in general. Also *as adj* □ ***television programmes.*** Ⓒ Early 20c: TELE- 1 + VISION.

televisual ▷ *adj* belonging or relating to, or suitable for broadcast by, TV. • **televisually** *adverb.* Ⓒ 1920s.

teleworking ▷ *noun* working from home by means of an electronic communication link with an office. • **teleworker** *noun.* Ⓒ 1980s.

telex /ˈtɛlɛks/ ▷ *noun* (***telexes***) (*also* **Telex**) **1** *telecomm* an international telecommunications network that uses TELEPRINTERS and radio and satellite links to enable subscribers to the network to send messages to and receive messages from each other, often linking several receivers simultaneously. **2** a teleprinter used in such a network. **3** a message received or sent by such a network. See also FAX. ▷ *verb* (***telexes, telexed, telexing***) *tr & intr* to send a message to someone via such a network. Ⓒ 1930s: from *tele*printer + exchange.

tell[1] / ▻ *verb* (***told*** /toʊld/, ***telling***) **1** *tr & intr* to inform or give information to someone in speech or writing. **2** (*often* **tell of something**) *tr & intr* to relate or give an account of something. **3** to command or instruct. **4** to express something in words □ ***tell lies.*** **5** *tr & intr* to discover or distinguish □ ***You can tell it by its smell.*** **6** (*usually* **tell on someone**) *intr* to give away secrets about them. **7** to make it known or give away. **8** (*often* **tell on someone**) *intr* said of an ordeal, etc: to have a noticeable effect on them. **9** *tr & intr* to know or recognize something definitely □ ***I can never tell when he's lying.*** **10** to assure. **11**(*usually* **tell against someone**) *intr* said of evidence or circumstances, etc: to be unfavourable to a person's case or cause, etc. • **all told** in all; with all taken into account □ ***There were thirty all told.*** • **take a telling** to do as one is told without having to be asked again. • **you're telling me!** *colloq* an exclamation of agreement. ◷ Anglo-Saxon *tellan.*

■ **tell someone** or **something apart** or **tell something from something** to distinguish between them □ ***can't tell the twins apart.***

■ **tell someone off 1** to scold or reprimand them. **2** to count them off and detach them on some special duty.

tell[2] or **tel** ▻ *noun, archaeol* especially in the Middle East: an artificial mound or hill formed from the accumulated remains of former settlements. ◷ 19c: from Arabic *tall* hillock.

teller ▻ *noun* **1** someone who tells, especially someone who tells stories □ ***a teller of tales.*** **2** a bank employee who receives money from and pays it out to members of the public. **3** someone who counts votes.

telling ▻ *adj* producing a great or marked effect. • **tellingly** *adverb.* ◷ 19c.

telling-off ▻ *noun* a mild scolding. See TELL SOMEONE OFF at TELL[1].

telltale ▻ *noun* **1** someone who spreads gossip and rumours, especially about another person's private affairs or misdeeds. **2** any of various devices for recording or monitoring a process or machine, etc. ▻ *adj* revealing or indicating something secret or hidden □ ***telltale signs.*** ◷ 16c.

tellurian /tɛˈlʊərɪən, -ˈljʊərɪən/ ▻ *adj* belonging or relating to, or living on, the Earth. ▻ *noun* (**Tellurian**) especially in science fiction: an inhabitant of the Earth. ◷ 19c: from Latin *tellus* the earth.

telluric /tɛˈlʊərɪk, -ˈljʊərɪk/ ▻ *adj* **1** belonging or relating to, or coming from, the Earth. **2** belonging or relating to, or coming from the soil. **3** *chem* belonging or relating to tellurium in its high valency.

tellurium /tɛˈlʊərɪəm, -ˈljʊərɪəm/ ▻ *noun, chem* (abbreviation **Te**, atomic number 52) a brittle silvery-white element obtained from gold, silver and copper ores, which is added to alloys of lead or steel to increase their hardness. ◷ 19c: Latin, from *tellus* earth.

telly /ˈtɛlɪ/ ▻ *noun* (***tellies***) *colloq* **1** television. **2** a television set. ◷ 1930s.

telophase /ˈtɛloʊfeɪz/ ▻ *noun, biol* the final stage of cell division, occurring once in MITOSIS and twice in MEIOSIS, when the two sets of chromosomes aggregate at opposite poles of the spindle, and a nuclear membrane forms around each set, resulting in the production of two daughter nuclei. ◷ 19c: from Greek *telos* end.

telson /ˈtɛlsən/ ▻ *noun, zool* the hindmost segment on the abdomen of a crustacean or arachnid. ◷ 19c: Greek, meaning 'a limit'.

Telugu /ˈtɛluguː/ ▻ *noun* (***Telugu*** or ***Telugus***) **1** a Dravidian language of SE India and parts of Malaysia with c.35–55 million speakers. **2** someone who speaks this language. ▻ *adj* belonging or relating to this language or the people who speak it. ◷ 18c.

temazepam /təˈmazɪpam/ ▻ *noun* a drug used to treat insomnia, and as a sedative before operations. It is also often abused by drug addicts.

temerity /təˈmɛrɪtɪ/ ▻ *noun* rashness or boldness; an unreasonable lack of fear. ◷ 15c: from Latin *temeritas.*

temp ▻ *noun* an employee, especially a secretary, typist or other office worker, employed on a temporary basis. ▻ *verb* (***temped, temping***) *intr* to work as a temp. ◷ 1930s: short for TEMPORARY.

temp. ▻ *abbreviation* **1** temperature. **2** temporary.

temper /ˈtɛmpə(r)/ ▻ *noun* **1** a characteristic state of mind; mood or humour □ ***have an even temper.*** **2** a state of calm; composure; self-control □ ***lose one's temper.*** **3** a state of uncontrolled anger □ ***in a temper.*** **4** a tendency to have fits of uncontrolled anger □ ***She has quite a temper.*** **5** the degree of hardness and toughness of metal or glass. ▻ *verb* (***tempered, tempering***) **1** to soften something or make it less severe □ ***temper firmness with understanding.*** **2** *engineering* to heat a metal, hardened alloy (eg steel) or glass to a certain temperature and then allow it to cool slowly, in order to toughen it by reducing its hardness and making it less brittle. **3** to bring clay, plaster or mortar to the desired consistency by moistening it with water and kneading it. **4** to tune (the notes on a keyboard instrument) so that the intervals between them are correct. • **out of temper** irritable; peevish; fractious. ◷ Anglo-Saxon *temprian*: from Latin *temperare* to mix in due proportion.

tempera /ˈtɛmpərə/ ▻ *noun* (***temperas***) **1** a method of painting in which powdered pigment is mixed with an emulsion made usually of egg yolks and water. **2** an emulsion, especially one made with egg yolks and water, into which powdered pigments are mixed to produce paint. **3** a painting produced using tempera. ◷ 19c: from Italian *pingere a tempera* to paint in distemper.

temperament /ˈtɛmpərəmənt/ ▻ *noun* **1** a person's natural character or disposition which governs the way they behave and think. **2** a sensitive, creative and excitable or emotional personality. **3** *music* an adjustment made to the intervals between notes on an instrument's keyboard to allow the instrument to play in any key. ◷ 17c in sense 1; 15c in obsolete sense 'mixture': from Latin *temperamentum* a mixing in due proportion, in this case a mixing of the four HUMOURS believed in the Middle Ages to govern a person's physical and mental characteristics.

temperamental /tɛmpərəˈmɛntəl/ ▻ *adj* **1** given to extreme changes of mood; quick to show emotion, anger or irritability, etc. **2** said of a machine, etc: not working reliably or consistently. **3** belonging or related to, or caused by, temperament. • **temperamentally** *adverb.*

temperance /ˈtɛmpərəns/ ▻ *noun* **1** moderation or self-restraint, especially in controlling one's appetite or desires. **2** moderation in drinking, or complete abstinence from, alcohol. ◷ 14c: from Latin *temperantia* moderation or sobriety.

temperate /ˈtɛmpərət/ ▻ *adj* **1** moderate and self-restrained, especially in appetite, consumption of alcoholic drink, and behaviour. **2** not excessive; moderate. **3** said of a climate or region: characterized by mild temperatures, which are neither tropical nor polar. Compare INTEMPERATE. • **temperately** *adverb.* • **temperateness** *noun.* ◷ 14c: from Latin *temperatus.*

temperate zones ▻ *plural noun* those areas of the Earth with moderate climates, lying between the tropic of Cancer and the Arctic Circle, and the tropic of Capricorn and the Antarctic Circle.

temperature /ˈtɛmpərətʃə(r)/ ▻ *noun* **1** (abbreviation **t** or **temp.**) the degree of hotness or coldness of an object, body or medium, eg air or water, as measured by a thermometer. **2** *colloq* a body temperature above normal (37°C or 98.6°F), regarded as an indicator of ill health if it is significantly higher than normal □ ***He was sick and had a temperature.*** See also FEVER. ◷ 17c in sense 1; 16c in obsolete sense 'mixture': from Latin *temperatura* proportion.

tempest /ˈtɛmpɪst/ ⊳ *noun* **1** a violent storm with very strong winds. **2** a violent uproar. ◷ 13c: from Latin *tempestas* 'season' or 'storm'.

tempestuous /tɛmˈpɛstʃʊəs/ ⊳ *adj* **1** belonging or relating to, or like, a tempest; very stormy. **2** said of a person or behaviour, etc: violently emotional; passionate. • **tempestuously** *adverb*. • **tempestuousness** *noun*. ◷ 15c.

tempi *plural of* TEMPO

template /ˈtɛmpleɪt/ or **templet** /ˈtɛmplət/ ⊳ *noun* **1** a piece of metal, plastic or wood cut in a particular shape and used as a pattern when cutting out material or drawing, etc. **2** a small wooden beam or block placed in a wall to help spread and support the weight or load. **3** *biol* the coded instructions carried by a molecule for the formation of a new molecule of the same type. ◷ 17c: from Latin *templum* small piece of timber.

temple[1] /ˈtɛmpəl/ ⊳ *noun* **1** a building in which people worship, especially in ancient and non-Christian religions, and in some Christian sects such as the Mormons. **2** *historical* either of the two successive religious buildings built by the Jews in Jerusalem, one before and one after the exile in Babylon. **3** a place devoted to a particular purpose □ ***a temple to literature***. **4** *especially US* a synagogue, especially in Reform or Conservative Judaism. ◷ Anglo-Saxon *templ*: from Latin *templum*.

temple[2] /ˈtɛmpəl/ ⊳ *noun* either of the two flat parts of the head at the side of the forehead in front of the ear. See also TEMPORAL[2]. ◷ 14c: French, from Latin *tempus*.

temple[3] /ˈtɛmpəl/ ⊳ *noun* a device in a loom which keeps the cloth stretched. ◷ 15c: French, from Latin *templum* small piece of timber.

tempo /ˈtɛmpoʊ/ ⊳ *noun* (***tempos*** or ***tempi*** /-piː/) **1** the speed at which a piece of music should be or is played. **2** rate or speed. ◷ 18c: Italian, from Latin *tempus* time.

temporal[1] /ˈtɛmpərəl/ ⊳ *adj* **1** belonging or relating to time, often in being relatively short. **2** belonging or relating to worldly or secular life rather than to religious or spiritual life. **3** *grammar* relating to tense or the expression of time. • **temporally** *adverb*. ◷ 14c: from Latin *temporalis*, from *tempus* time.

temporal[2] /ˈtɛmpərəl/ ⊳ *adj* belonging, relating or close to the temples on either side of the head. ◷ 16c: from Latin *temporalis* belonging to the temples; see TEMPLE[2].

temporary /ˈtɛmpərərɪ/ ⊳ *adj* lasting, acting or used, etc for a limited period of time only. ⊳ *noun* (***temporaries***) a worker employed temporarily; a temp. • **temporarily** *adverb*. • **temporariness** *noun*. ◷ 16c: from Latin *temporarius*.

temporize or **temporise** /ˈtɛmpəraɪz/ ⊳ *verb* (***temporized***, ***temporizing***) *intr* **1** to avoid taking a decision or committing oneself to some course of action, in order to gain time and perhaps win a compromise. **2** to adapt oneself to circumstances or to what the occasion requires. • **temporization** *noun*. • **temporizer** *noun*. ◷ 16c: from Latin *tempus* time.

tempt ⊳ *verb* (***tempted***, ***tempting***) **1** to seek to attract and persuade someone to do something, especially something wrong or foolish. **2** to attract or allure. **3** (**be tempted to**) to be strongly inclined to do something. **4** to risk provoking, especially by doing something foolhardy □ ***tempt fate***. ◷ 13c: from French *tempter*, from Latin *temptare* 'to probe' or 'to test'.

temptation ⊳ *noun* **1** an act of tempting or the state of being tempted. **2** something that tempts.

tempter ⊳ *noun* **1** someone who tempts. **2** (**the Tempter**) *relig* the Devil.

tempting ⊳ *adj* attractive; inviting; enticing. • **temptingly** *adverb*.

temptress ⊳ *noun* (***temptresses***) a female tempter; an enticing woman. ◷ 16c.

tempura /ˈtɛmpʊrə, tɛmˈpʊərə/ ⊳ *noun*, *cookery* a Japanese dish of seafood or vegetables deep-fried in batter. ◷ 1920s: Japanese, from Portuguese *tempero* seasoning.

ten ⊳ *noun* **1 a** the cardinal number 10; **b** the quantity that this represents, being one more than nine. **2** any symbol for this, eg **10** or **X**. **3** the age of ten. **4** something, especially a garment or a person, whose size is denoted by the number 10. **5** the tenth hour after midnight or midday □ ***Come at ten*** □ ***10 o'clock*** □ ***10pm***. **6** a set or group of ten people or things. **7** a playing-card with ten pips □ ***He played his ten***. **8** a score of ten points. ⊳ *adj* **1** totalling ten. **2** aged ten. ◷ Anglo-Saxon.

tenable /ˈtɛnəbəl/ ⊳ *adj* **1** able to be believed, upheld or maintained. **2** said of a post or office: to be held or occupied for a specified period only or by a specified person. • **tenability** *noun*. ◷ 16c: from Latin *tenere* to hold.

tenacious /təˈneɪʃəs/ ⊳ *adj* **1** holding or sticking firmly. **2** determined; persistent; obstinate. **3** said of memory: retaining information extremely well; retentive. • **tenaciously** *adverb*. • **tenaciousness** *noun*. ◷ 17c: from Latin *tenax*, *tenacis*, from *tenere* to hold.

tenaculum /tɪˈnakjʊləm/ ⊳ *noun* (***tenacula*** /-lə/) a surgical hook, used for picking up blood vessels, etc. ◷ 17c: Latin, from *tenere* to hold.

tenancy /ˈtɛnənsɪ/ ⊳ *noun* (***tenancies***) **1** the temporary renting of property or land by a tenant. **2** the period during which property or land is so rented.

tenant /ˈtɛnənt/ ⊳ *noun* **1** someone who pays rent to another for the use of property or land. **2** an occupant. ⊳ *verb* (***tenanted***, ***tenanting***) to occupy (land, etc) as a tenant. • **tenanted** *adj*. ◷ 14c: French, from Latin *tenere* to hold.

tenant farmer ⊳ *noun* a farmer who farms land rented from another person, especially on an estate.

tenantry ⊳ *noun* **1** tenants collectively. **2** the state of being a tenant.

tench ⊳ *noun* (***tench*** or ***tenches***) a European freshwater fish belonging to the carp family, with a green or brownish body. ◷ 14c: from French *tenche*, from Latin *tinca*.

tend[1] ⊳ *verb* (***tended***, ***tending***) **1** to take care of or look after someone or something; to wait on or serve them. **2** (**tend to something**) to attend to it. • **tender** *noun* (see also TENDER[3]). ◷ 14c: variant of ATTEND.

tend[2] ⊳ *verb* (***tended***, ***tending***) *intr* **1** (*usually* **tend to** or **towards something**) to be likely or inclined to it. **2** to move slightly, lean or slope in a specified direction. ◷ 14c: from Latin *tendere* to stretch.

tendency /ˈtɛndənsɪ/ ⊳ *noun* (***tendencies***) **1** a likelihood of acting or thinking, or an inclination to act or think, in a particular way. **2** a general course, trend or drift. **3** a faction or group within a political party or movement. ◷ 17c.

tendentious /tɛnˈdɛnʃəs/ ⊳ *adj* characterized by a particular bias, tendency or underlying purpose. • **tendentiously** *adverb*. • **tendentiousness** *noun*.

tender[1] /ˈtɛndə(r)/ ⊳ *adj* **1** soft and delicate; fragile. **2** said of meat: easily chewed or cut. **3** easily damaged or grieved; sensitive □ ***a tender heart***. **4** easily hurt when touched, especially because of having been hurt before. **5** loving and gentle □ ***tender words***. **6** easily moved to love, pity or guilt, etc □ ***a tender conscience***. **7** youthful and vulnerable □ ***of tender years***. **8** requiring gentle or careful handling. • **tenderly** *adverb*. ◷ 13c: from French *tendre*, from Latin *tener*.

tender[2] /ˈtɛndə(r)/ ▷ *verb* (***tendered***, ***tendering***) **1** to offer or present (an apology or resignation, etc). **2** (*usually* **tender for something**) to make a formal offer to do (work or supply goods) for a stated amount of money and within a stated period of time. ▷ *noun* a formal offer, usually in writing, to do work or supply goods for a stated amount of money and within a stated period of time. • **put something out to tender** to invite tenders for (a job or undertaking). ◷ 16c: from Latin *tendere* to stretch.

tender[3] /ˈtɛndə(r)/ ▷ *noun* **1** *often in compounds* a person who looks after something or someone □ ***bartender***. **2** a small boat which carries stores or passengers to and from a larger boat. **3** a railway wagon attached to a steam-engine to carry fuel and water. See also TEND[1].

tenderfoot ▷ *noun* (***tenderfeet*** or ***tenderfoots***) an inexperienced newcomer or beginner. ◷ 19c.

tender-hearted ▷ *adj* kind and sympathetic; easily made to feel love or pity. • **tender-heartedly** *adverb*. • **tender-heartedness** *noun*.

tenderize or **tenderise** ▷ *verb* (***tenderized***, ***tenderizing***) to make (meat) tender by pounding it or by adding an acidic substance. • **tenderizer** *noun*. ◷ 1930s.

tenderloin ▷ *noun* a cut from the tenderest part of the loin of pork or beef, etc.

tendinitis or **tendonitis** /tɛndəˈnaɪtɪs/ ▷ *noun*, *pathol* inflammation of a tendon. ◷ Early 20c.

tendon /ˈtɛndən/ ▷ *noun*, *anatomy* a cord of strong fibrous tissue that joins a muscle to a bone or some other structure. ◷ 16c: from Latin *tendo*, *tendinis*.

tendril /ˈtɛndrɪl/ ▷ *noun*, *bot* a long, often spirally twisted, thread-like extension of a stem, leaf or PETIOLE, by means of which many climbing plants attach themselves to solid objects for support. • **tendrilled** *adj*. ◷ 16c.

tenebrism /ˈtɛnəbrɪzəm/ ▷ *noun*, *art* a 17c Italian and Spanish school of painting, characterized by large expanses of shadow. ◷ 1950s: from Italian *tenebroso* dark.

tenebrous /ˈtɛnəbrəs/ or **tenebrious** /təˈnɛbrɪəs/ ▷ *adj* dark; gloomy. ◷ 15c: from Latin *tenebrosus*, from *tenebrae* darkness.

tenement /ˈtɛnəmənt/ ▷ *noun* **1** *N Amer or Scottish* a large building divided into several self-contained flats or apartments. Also called **tenement building**. **2** a self-contained flat or room within such a building. **3** anything held, eg land or property, etc, by a tenant. • **tenemental** /-ˈmɛntəl/ *adj*. ◷ 14c: from Latin *tenementum*, from *tenere* to hold.

tenesmus /tɪˈnɛzməs/ ▷ *noun*, *medicine* a painful and ineffectual straining to relieve the bowel and bladder. ◷ 16c: from Greek *teinesmos*, from *teinein* to strain.

tenet /ˈtɛnɪt/ ▷ *noun* a belief, opinion or doctrine. ◷ 17c: Latin, meaning 'he or she holds', from *tenere* to hold.

tenfold ▷ *adj* **1** equal to ten times as much. **2** divided into or consisting of ten parts. ▷ *adverb* by ten times as much. ◷ Anglo-Saxon.

ten-gallon hat ▷ *noun*, *especially US* a hat worn by cowboys, with a broad brim and high crown. Compare STETSON. ◷ 1920s: often thought to be so called from the quantity of liquid such a hat could hold, but in fact probably from Spanish *galón* braid, referring to the decorative braiding round the hat.

Tenn. or **Ten.** see under TN

tenner /ˈtɛnə(r)/ ▷ *noun*, *colloq* **1** a £10 note. **2** *US* a $10 bill. ◷ 19c.

tennis /ˈtɛnɪs/ ▷ *noun* **1** (*also* **lawn tennis**) a game in which two players or two pairs of players use rackets to hit a small light ball across a net on a rectangular grass, clay or cement court. **2** REAL TENNIS. ◷ 14c: from French *tenetz* hold! or take!, from *tenir* to hold.

tennis court ▷ *noun* a court on which tennis is played.

tennis elbow ▷ *noun* painful inflammation of the elbow caused by over-exercise (typically by playing tennis) or overwork. ◷ 19c.

tenon /ˈtɛnən/ ▷ *noun* a projection at the end of a piece of wood, etc, formed to fit into a socket or MORTISE in another piece. ▷ *verb* (***tenoned***, ***tenoning***) **1** to fix with a tenon. **2** to cut a tenon in (a piece of wood, etc). ◷ 15c: French, from *tenir* to hold.

tenon saw ▷ *noun* a small fine-toothed saw, used especially for cutting tenons.

tenor /ˈtɛnə(r)/ ▷ *noun* **1 a** a singing voice of the highest normal range for an adult man; **b** a singer who has this voice. **2** an instrument, eg a viola, recorder or saxophone, with a similar range. **3** music written for a voice or instrument with such a range. **4** the general course or meaning of something written or spoken. **5** a settled or general course or direction, eg of a person's life. ◷ 13c: from French *tenour*, from Latin *tenere* to hold.

tenor clef ▷ *noun*, *music* the CLEF that fixes middle C on the fourth line of the STAFF.

tenosynovitis /tɛnoʊsaɪnoʊˈvaɪtəs/ ▷ *noun*, *pathol* inflammation and swelling of a tendon, usually associated with repetitive movements. ◷ 19c: from Greek *tenon* tendon + SYNOVITIS.

tenpin bowling ▷ *noun* a game in which ten skittles are set up at the end of an alley and a ball is rolled at them with the aim of knocking as many down as possible.

tense[1] /tɛns/ ▷ *noun*, *grammar* a form or set of forms of a verb showing the time of its action in relation to the time of speaking and whether that action is completed or not, eg PAST tense, PRESENT tense, FUTURE tense. ◷ 13c: from French *tens*, from Latin *tempus* time.

tense[2] /tɛns/ ▷ *adj* (***tenser***, ***tensest***) **1** feeling, showing or marked by emotional, nervous or mental strain. **2** tightly stretched; taut. ▷ *verb* (***tensed***, ***tensing***) *tr & intr* (*often* **tense up**) to make or become tense. • **tensely** *adverb*. • **tenseness** *noun*. ◷ 17c: from Latin *tendere*, *tensum* to stretch.

tensile /ˈtɛnsaɪl/ ▷ *adj* **1** able to be stretched. **2** relating to or involving stretching or tension. • **tensility** *noun*. ◷ 17c: from Latin *tensilis*.

tensile strength ▷ *noun*, *physics* a measure of the ability of a material to resist tension, equal to the minimum stress required to break it.

tension /ˈtɛnʃən/ ▷ *noun* **1** an act of stretching, the state of being stretched or the degree to which something is stretched. **2** mental or emotional strain, excitement or anxiety, usually accompanied by physical symptoms. **3** strained relations or underlying hostility between people or countries, etc. **4** *physics* a force which causes a body to be stretched or elongated. **5** *physics* ELECTROMOTIVE FORCE. **6** *knitting* the tightness or looseness of wool as one knits, measured as the number of stitches to the inch. ▷ *verb* (***tensioned***, ***tensioning***) to give the required tightness or tension to something. ◷ 16c: from Latin *tensio*, from *tendere*, *tensum* to stretch.

tent ▷ *noun* **1** a shelter made of canvas or other material supported by poles or a frame and fastened to the ground with ropes and pegs, that can be taken down and carried from place to place. **2** anything resembling a tent in form or function, such as a clear plastic device placed over the head and shoulders to control the oxygen supply to a sick person. ▷ *verb* (***tented***, ***tenting***) **1** *intr* to camp in a tent. **2** to cover or shelter something with a tent. ◷ 13c: from French *tente*, from Latin *tendere* to stretch.

tentacle /ˈtɛntəkəl/ ▷ *noun* **1** any of the long thin flexible appendages growing on the head or near the mouth of many invertebrate animals, eg the sea anemone and octopus, etc, used as sense organs or for defence, for grasping prey or for attachment to surfaces. **2** in certain insectivorous plants, eg the sundew: any of the sticky hairs on the leaves that serve to trap insects. • **tentacled** *adj.* • **tentacular** /tɛn'takjʊlə(r)/ *adj.* Ⓒ 17c: from Latin *tentaculum.*

tentative /'tɛntətɪv/ ▻ *adj* **1** not finalized or completed; provisional. **2** uncertain; hesitant; cautious. • **tentatively** *adverb.* • **tentativeness** *noun.* Ⓒ 16c: from Latin *tentare* to try.

tenter /'tɛntə(r)/ ▻ *noun* a frame on which cloth is stretched, especially so that it dries without losing its shape. ▻ *verb* (*tentered, tentering*) to stretch (cloth) on a tenter. Ⓒ 14c.

tenterhook ▻ *noun* a sharp hooked nail used for fastening cloth to a tenter. • **on tenterhooks** in a state of impatient suspense or anxiety. Ⓒ 15c.

tenth (often written **10th**) ▻ *adj* **1** in counting: **a** next after ninth; **b** last of ten. **2** in tenth position. **3** (**the tenth**) **a** the tenth day of the month; **b** *golf* the tenth hole. ▻ *noun* **1** one of ten equal parts. Also *as adj* □ ***a tenth share.*** **2** a FRACTION equal to one divided by ten (usually written $^1/_{10}$). **3** someone who comes tenth, eg in a race or exam □ ***He finished a respectable tenth.*** **4** *music* **a** an interval of an octave and a third; **b** a note at that interval from another. ▻ *adverb* tenthly. • **tenthly** *adverb* used to introduce the tenth point in a list. Ⓒ Anglo-Saxon; see TEN + -TH.

tenuous /'tɛnjʊəs/ ▻ *adj* **1** slight; with little strength or substance. **2** thin; slim. • **tenuously** *adverb.* • **tenuousness** *noun.* Ⓒ 16c: from Latin *tenuis* thin.

tenure /'tɛnjə(r)/ ▻ *noun* **1** the holding of an office, position or property. **2** the length of time an office, position or property is held. **3** the holding of a position, especially a university teaching job, for a guaranteed length of time or permanently. **4** the conditions by which an office, position or property is held. • **tenured** *adj.* • **tenurial** *adj.* Ⓒ 15c: from Latin *tenere* to hold.

tenuto /tɛ'nu:toʊ/ *music* ▻ *adverb* in a sustained manner. ▻ *adj* sustained. ▻ *noun* (*tenutos* or *tenuti* /-ti:/) a sustained note or chord. Ⓒ 18c: Italian.

tepee or **teepee** /'ti:pi:/ ▻ *noun* (*tepees*) a conical tent formed by skins stretched over a frame of poles, used by some Native Americans. Ⓒ 19c: from Dakota (Native American language) *tipi* dwelling.

tephillin see TEFILLIN

tephra /'tɛfrə/ ▻ *noun* (*tephras*) *geol* ash and debris ejected by a volcano during an eruption. Ⓒ 1960s: Greek, meaning 'ashes'.

tepid /'tɛpɪd/ ▻ *adj* **1** slightly or only just warm; lukewarm. **2** unenthusiastic. • **tepidity** *noun.* • **tepidly** *adverb.* Ⓒ 14c: from Latin *tepidus*, from *tepere* to be warm.

tequila /tə'ki:lə/ ▻ *noun* (*tequilas*) a Mexican spirit obtained from the agave plant, used as the basis for many alcoholic drinks. Ⓒ 19c: named after Tequila, a district in Mexico where it is produced.

ter- /tɜ:(r)/ ▻ *combining form, signifying* three; threefold; thrice. Ⓒ Latin *ter* thrice.

tera- /tɛrə, tɛ'ra/ ▻ *prefix, signifying* in the SI system: 10^{12} □ ***terawatt.*** Ⓒ From Greek *teras* monster.

terabyte ▻ *noun, computing* a unit of storage capacity equal to 2^{40} or 1 099 511 627 776 bytes.

teratogen /tɛ'ratədʒən, 'tɛrətə-/ ▻ *noun, medicine* a substance or procedure, eg a drug, disease or radiation, etc that interferes with the normal development of the fetus and leads to the development of physical abnormalities. • **teratogenic** *adj.* Ⓒ Early 20c: from Greek *teras, teratos* monster + -GEN.

teratogenesis /tɛrətoʊ'dʒɛnəsɪs/ ▻ *noun, pathol* congenital malformation as a result of exposure of the fetus to a TERATOGEN.

teratoid /'tɛrətɔɪd/ ▻ *adj, biol* monstrous; resembling a monster. Ⓒ 19c: from Greek.

teratoma /tɛrə'toʊmə/ ▻ *noun* (*teratomata* /-mətə/ or *teratomas*) *pathol* **1** a tumour consisting of tissue that is foreign to the place of growth. **2** a grossly deformed fetus. Ⓒ 19c: Latin, from Greek *teras, teratos* monster.

terbium /'tɜ:bɪəm/ ▻ *noun, chem* (symbol **Tb**, atomic number 65) a silvery metallic element that is a member of the LANTHANIDE series, and is used in semiconductor devices and phosphors. Ⓒ 19c: Latin, from Y*tterb*y in Sweden, where it was discovered.

terce /tɜ:s/ or **tierce** /tɪəs/ ▻ *noun, now especially RC Church* the third of the CANONICAL HOURS. Ⓒ 14c: from Latin *tertia pars* third part.

tercel /'tɜ:səl/ or **tiercel** /'tɪəsəl/ ▻ *noun* a male hawk. Ⓒ 14c: French, from Latin *tertius* third, perhaps because it is smaller than the female.

tercentenary or **tercentennial** ▻ *noun* a three-hundredth anniversary. ▻ *adj* relating to a period of three hundred years. Ⓒ 19c: from TER-.

tercet /'tɜ:sɪt/ ▻ *noun* a set of three lines in a poem which rhyme or which are connected by rhyme to a preceding or following group of three lines. Ⓒ 16c: from Italian *terzetto*, from *terzo* third.

terebinth see TURPENTINE TREE

teredo /tɛ'ri:doʊ/ ▻ *noun* (*teredos* or *teredines* /tɛ'ri:dɪni:z/) any of several bivalve molluscs which bore into wooden ships. Ⓒ 14c: from Greek *teredon* boring worm.

term ▻ *noun* **1** a word or expression, especially one used with a precise meaning in a specialized field □ ***a scientific term.*** **2** (**terms**) language used; a particular way of speaking □ ***in no uncertain terms.*** **3** a limited or clearly defined period of time □ ***her term of office.*** **4** the end of a particular time, especially the end of pregnancy when the baby is about to be born. **5** (**terms**) a relationship between people or countries □ ***be on good terms.*** **6** (**terms**) the rules or conditions of an agreement □ ***terms of sale.*** **7** (**terms**) fixed charges for work or a service. **8** one of the usually three divisions into which the academic year is divided. **9** the time during which a court is in session. **10** *math* a quantity which is joined to another by either addition or subtraction. **11** *math* one quantity in a series or sequence. **12** *logic* a word or expression which may be a subject or a predicate of a PROPOSITION. ▻ *verb* (*termed, terming*) to name or call. • **termly** *adverb, adj.* • **come to terms** to give way or submit; to yield. • **come to terms with someone** or **something** **1** to come to an agreement or understanding with them. **2** to find a way of living with or tolerating (some personal trouble or difficulty). • **in terms of …** in relation to …; using the language and value of … as a basis. Ⓒ 13c: from French *terme*, from Latin *terminus* boundary.

termagant /'tɜ:məgənt/ ▻ *noun* a scolding, brawling and overbearing woman. Ⓒ 17c: from French *Tervagan*, a mythical deity believed in the Middle Ages to be worshipped by Muslims and introduced into morality plays as a scolding overbearing character.

terminable /'tɜ:mɪnəbəl/ ▻ *adj* able to come or be brought to an end. • **terminability** or **terminableness** *noun.* • **terminably** *adverb.* Ⓒ 15c: from Latin *terminus* boundary.

terminal /'tɜ:mɪnəl/ ▻ *adj* **1** said of an illness: causing death; fatal. **2** said of a patient: suffering from an illness which will cause death. **3** *colloq* extreme; acute □ ***terminal laziness.*** **4** forming or occurring at an end, boundary or terminus. **5** **a** belonging or relating to a term; **b** occurring every term. ▻ *noun* **1** an arrival and departure building at an airport. **2** a large station at the end of a railway line or for long-distance buses and coaches. **3** a point in an electric circuit or electrical device at which the current leaves or enters it, or by which it may be connected to another device. **4** a device consisting usually of a keyboard and VDU, which allows a user to communicate with and use a distant computer. **5** an installation at the end of a pipeline or at a port where oil is stored and from where it is distributed. • **terminally** *adverb*. ⓒ 19c in *adj* sense 1; 15c in obsolete heraldic sense: from Latin *terminalis*, from *terminus* boundary.

terminal velocity ▷ *noun* the constant velocity, when resistive forces exactly balance applied force, reached by an object falling through a gas or liquid under the influence of gravity, and which when reached precludes further ACCELERATION.

terminate /ˈtɜːmɪneɪt/ ▷ *verb* (***terminated***, ***terminating***) **1** *tr & intr* to bring or come to an end. **2** *intr, formal* to end or conclude in a specified way or at a specified time. **3** to end (a pregnancy) artificially before its term. **4** to form a boundary or limit to something. **5** *intr, formal* said of public transport: to stop; to go no further □ *This train terminates at Vienna.* • **termination** *noun* **1** an act of ending or the state of being brought to an end. **2** an artificially induced miscarriage or abortion. **3** a final result. ⓒ 16c: from Latin *terminare*, *terminatum* to set a limit to.

terminate-and-stay-resident program ▷ *noun, computing* (abbreviation **TSR**) a program which remains in memory once activated, even while it is not running, and which can be reactivated quickly using a pre-set key, etc.

termination ▷ *noun* **1** someone or something that terminates. **2** an abortion (sense 1). **3** the ending or a result of something.

terminology /tɜːmɪˈnɒlədʒɪ/ ▷ *noun* (***terminologies***) the words and phrases used in a particular subject or field. • **terminological** *adj*. • **terminologically** *adverb*. • **terminologist** *noun*. ⓒ 19c: from Latin *terminus* term.

terminus /ˈtɜːmɪnəs/ ▷ *noun* (***termini*** /-naɪ/ or ***terminuses***) **1 a** the end of a railway line or bus route, usually with a station; **b** the station at this point. **2** an extreme or final point. **3** a stone marking a boundary. ⓒ 17c in sense 2; 16c in obsolete mathematical sense 'term': Latin, meaning 'boundary' or 'limit'.

termitarium /tɜːmɪˈtɛərɪəm/ ▷ *noun* (***termitaria***) a colony or nest of termites. ⓒ 19c.

termite /ˈtɜːmaɪt/ ▷ *noun* an ant-like social insect which lives in highly organized colonies, mainly in tropical areas, some of which feed on wood, causing damage to trees and buildings, etc. ⓒ 18c: from Latin *termites*, plural of *termes* white ant.

termly see under TERM

terms of reference ▷ *plural noun* a description or definition of the basis and scope of an undertaking or inquiry, etc.

tern ▷ *noun* any of several sea-birds related to the gulls, with grey and white plumage and a long forked tail. ⓒ 17c: from Scandinavian, eg Danish *terne*.

ternary /ˈtɜːnərɪ/ ▷ *adj* **1** containing three parts. **2** *math* said of a number system: using three as a base. ⓒ 15c: from Latin *ternarius* consisting of three.

terpene /ˈtɜːpiːn/ ▷ *noun, chem* any of three classes of unsaturated hydrocarbons, based on the ISOPRENE (formula C_5H_8) unit, that are present in plant resins and also form the main constituents of essential oils such as rose and jasmine oil. ⓒ 19c: from *terpentin*, an obsolete form of TURPENTINE.

terpsichorean /tɜːpsɪkəˈriːən/ ▷ *adj* relating to dancing. ⓒ 19c: from Terpsichore, the Muse of song and dance, from Greek *terpein* to enjoy + *choros* dance.

terr. or **ter.** ▷ *abbreviation* **1** terrace. **2** territory.

terrace /ˈtɛrəs/ ▷ *noun* **1** each one of a series of raised level banks of earth, like large steps on the side of a hill, used for cultivation. **2 a** a row of usually identical and connected houses, properly one overlooking a slope, or the street on to which they face; **b** (*usually* **Terrace**) in street names □ *South Inch Terrace.* **3** a raised level paved area by the side of a house. **4** (*usually* **terraces**) open areas rising in tiers round a sports ground, where spectators stand. ▷ *verb* (***terraced***, ***terracing***) to form something into a terrace or terraces. ⓒ 16c: from Latin *terracea*, from *terra* earth.

terrace house or **terraced house** ▷ *noun, Brit* a house which is part of a terrace.

terracotta /tɛrəˈkɒtə/ ▷ *noun* (***terracottas*** in sense 2) **1** an unglazed brownish-orange earthenware made from a mixture of sand and clay and used for pottery, statuettes and building. **2** an object made from this. **3** its brownish-orange colour. ▷ *adj* made of, or the colour of, terracotta. ⓒ 18c: Italian, meaning 'baked earth'.

terra firma /tɛrəˈfɜːmə/ ▷ *noun* dry land as opposed to water or air; solid ground. ⓒ 17c: Latin, meaning 'firm land'.

terrain /təˈreɪn/ ▷ *noun* a stretch of land, especially with regard to its physical features or as a battle area. ⓒ 18c: ultimately from Latin *terrenus*, from *terra* earth.

terrapin /ˈtɛrəpɪn/ ▷ *noun* **1** in the UK: any small freshwater turtle. **2** in the US: an edible turtle. ⓒ 17c: from a Native American language.

terrarium /təˈrɛərɪəm/ ▷ *noun* (***terraria*** or ***terrariums***) **1** an enclosed area or container in which small land animals are kept. **2** a large often globe-shaped sealed glass jar in which plants are grown. ⓒ 19c: from Latin *terra* earth, modelled on AQUARIUM.

terrazzo /tɛˈratsoʊ/ ▷ *noun* (***terrazzos***) a mosaic covering for concrete floors consisting of marble or other chips set in cement and then polished. ⓒ Early 20c: Italian, meaning 'terrace'.

terrestrial /təˈrɛstrɪəl/ ▷ *adj* **1** relating to dry land or to the Earth. **2** *denoting* animals or plants that live on dry land. **3** belonging or relating to this world; worldly; mundane. **4** said of broadcast signals: sent by a land transmitter as opposed to satellite. ▷ *noun* an inhabitant of the Earth. ⓒ 15c: from Latin *terrestris*, from *terra* earth.

terrible /ˈtɛrɪbəl/ ▷ *adj* **1** *colloq* very bad □ *a terrible singer.* **2** *colloq* very great; extreme □ *a terrible gossip.* **3** causing great fear or terror. **4** causing suffering or hardship and requiring great strength or fortitude □ *a terrible struggle.* ⓒ 15c: from Latin *terribilis*, from *terrere* to frighten.

terribly ▷ *adverb* **1** *colloq* very; extremely. **2** in a terrible way; to a great degree □ *hurts terribly.*

terrier /ˈtɛrɪə(r)/ ▷ *noun* any of several mostly small breeds of dog originally bred to hunt animals in burrows. ⓒ 15c: from French *chien terrier* dog of the earth.

terrific /təˈrɪfɪk/ ▷ *adj* **1** *colloq* marvellous; excellent. **2** *colloq* very great or powerful □ *a terrific storm.* **3** very frightening; terrifying. • **terrifically** *adverb*. ⓒ 17c: from Latin *terrificus* frightful.

terrify /ˈtɛrɪfaɪ/ ▷ *verb* (***terrifies***, ***terrified***, ***terrifying***) to make very frightened; to fill with terror. • **terrified** *adj*. • **terrifying** *adj*. ⓒ 16c: from Latin *terrificare*.

terrine /tɛˈriːn/ ▷ *noun* **1** an oval or round earthenware dish in which food may be cooked and served. **2** *cookery* food cooked or served in such a dish, especially pâté. ⓒ 18c: earlier form of TUREEN.

territorial /tɛrɪˈtɔːrɪəl/ ▷ *adj* **1** belonging or relating to a territory. **2** limited or restricted to a particular area or district. **3** said especially of birds and animals: likely to establish their own territory and defend it from others of the same species. ▷ *noun* (**Territorial**) *Brit* a member of the TERRITORIAL ARMY. • **territoriality** *noun*. • **territorially** *adverb*. ⓒ 17c.

Territorial Army (abbreviation **TA**) ▷ *noun* in the UK: a fully trained volunteer force intended to provide back-up to the regular army in cases of emergency.

territorial waters ▷ *noun* the area of sea surrounding a state which is considered to belong to that state.

territory /ˈtɛrɪtərɪ/ ▷ *noun* (***territories***) **1** a stretch of land; a region. **2** the land under the control of a ruler, government or state. **3** an area of knowledge, interest or activity □ *Grammar? That's George's territory.* **4** an area or district for which a travelling salesman or distributor is responsible. **5** an area which a bird or animal treats as its own and defends against others of the same species. **6** (*often* **Territory**) part of a country (usually a federal state such as the USA, Canada or Australia) with an organized government but without the full rights of a state. **7** (*often* **Territory**) a dependency. ◷ 15c: from Latin *territorium* the land round a town.

terror /ˈtɛrə(r)/ ▷ *noun* **1** very great fear or dread. **2** something or someone which causes such fear. **3** *colloq* a troublesome or mischievous person, especially a child. **4** a time of, or government by, terrorism. ◷ 14c: from Latin, from *terrere* to frighten.

terrorism /ˈtɛrərɪzəm/ ▷ *noun* the systematic and organized use of violence and intimidation to force a government or community, etc to act in a certain way or accept certain demands. • **terrorist** *noun, adj.* ◷ 18c.

terrorize or **terrorise** ▷ *verb* (***terrorized***, ***terrorizing***) **1** to frighten greatly. **2** to control or coerce someone by threatening violence. ◷ 19c.

terror-stricken ▷ *adj* in a state of great and uncontrollable fear.

terry /ˈtɛrɪ/ ▷ *noun* (***terries***) **1** an absorbent fabric with uncut loops on one side used especially for towels. **2** a baby's nappy made of this. ▷ *adj* made of this fabric □ *terry towelling.* ◷ 18c.

terse /tɜːs/ ▷ *adj* (***terser***, ***tersest***) **1** said of language: brief and concise; succinct. **2** abrupt and rude; curt. • **tersely** *adverb.* • **terseness** *noun.* ◷ 17c: from Latin *tergere*, *tersum* to wipe.

tertiary /ˈtɜːʃərɪ/ ▷ *adj* **1** third in order, degree, importance, etc. **2** said of education: coming after secondary, eg university or college. Compare PRIMARY, SECONDARY. **3** *chem* (abbreviation **tert.**) *denoting* complete replacement of hydrogen atoms in an organic molecule by other chemical groups. Compare PRIMARY, SECONDARY. **4** *chem, denoting* extraction of petroleum by high-pressure pumping into rock structures. **5** (**Tertiary**) *geol* relating to the first period of the Cenozoic era. **6** relating to rocks formed during this period. See also PRIMARY, SECONDARY. ▷ *noun* (***tertiaries***) **1** (**the Tertiary**) the first geological period of the CENOZOIC era. See table at GEOLOGICAL TIME SCALE. **2** *RC Church* a lay person who is affiliated to a monastic order and who follows a slightly modified form of that order's rule. ◷ 17c: from Latin *tertiarius*, from *tertius* third.

Terylene /ˈtɛrɪliːn/ ▷ *noun, trademark* a light tough synthetic fabric of polyester fibres. ◷ 1940s.

TESL ▷ *abbreviation* Teaching English as a Second Language.

tesla /ˈtɛslə/ ▷ *noun* (***teslas***) *physics* (abbreviation **T**) in the SI system: a unit of magnetic flux density, defined as a magnetic flux of one weber per square metre. ◷ 1950s: named after Nikola Tesla (1856–1943) the US physicist.

TESSA /ˈtɛsə/ ▷ *abbreviation, Brit finance* Tax-Exempt Special Savings Account.

tessellate /ˈtɛsəleɪt/ ▷ *verb* (***tessellated***, ***tessellating***) to form something into or mark it like a mosaic, especially with tesserae or checks. • **tessellated** *adj.* • **tessellation** *noun.* ◷ 18c: from Latin *tessella* small square piece of stone.

tessera /ˈtɛsərə/ ▷ *noun* (***tesserae*** /-riː/) a square piece of stone or glass, etc used in mosaics. ◷ 17c: from Latin *tessera*, from Greek *tesseres* four.

tessitura /tɛsɪˈtʊərə, -tjʊərə/ ▷ *noun* (***tessituras***) *music* the natural range of the pitch or compass of a particular voice, or of a vocal or instrumental part in a particular piece. ◷ 19c: Italian, meaning 'texture'.

test[1] ▷ *noun* **1** a critical examination or trial of a person's or thing's qualities or abilities, etc. **2** anything used as the basis of such an examination or trial, eg a set of questions or exercises. **3** a short minor examination, usually a written one □ *a spelling test.* **4** *sport* a TEST MATCH □ *lost the first test against Sri Lanka.* **5** *chem* anything used to distinguish, detect or identify a substance; a reagent. ▷ *verb* (***tested***, ***testing***) **1** to examine someone or something especially by trial. **2** *tr & intr* to examine (a substance) to discover whether another substance is present or not □ *test the water for microbes.* **3** *intr* to achieve a stated result in a test □ *tested negative for the virus.* • **testable** *adj.* ◷ 16c in sense 1; 14c meaning 'a vessel used in assaying': from French, from Latin *testum* earthenware pot.

test[2] ▷ *noun, biol* a hard outer covering or shell of certain invertebrates. ◷ 19c: from Latin *testa* tile.

testa ▷ *noun* /ˈtɛstə/ (***testae*** /-tiː/) *biol* the hard outer covering of a seed. ◷ 18c: Latin, meaning 'shell'.

testaceous /tɛˈsteɪʃəs/ ▷ *adj* **1** *biol* relating to or covered by a testa. **2** reddish-brown coloured.

testament /ˈtɛstəmənt/ ▷ *noun* **1 a** a written statement of someone's wishes, especially of what they want to be done with their property after death; **b** a will □ *her last will and testament.* **2** proof, evidence or tribute □ *a testament to her hard work.* **3** a covenant between God and humankind. **4** (**Testament**) **a** either of the two main divisions of the Bible, the Old Testament and the New Testament; **b** a copy of the New Testament. • **testamentary** /tɛstəˈmɛntərɪ/ *adj* **1** belonging or relating to a testament or will. **2** bequeathed or done by will. ◷ 14c: from Latin *testamentum*, from *testis* witness.

testate /ˈtɛsteɪt/ *law* ▷ *adj* having made and left a valid will. ▷ *noun* someone who dies testate. ◷ 15c: from Latin *testari*, *testatus* to make a will.

testator /tɛˈsteɪtə(r)/ ▷ *noun, law* someone who leaves a will at death. ◷ 14c: Latin.

testatrix /tɛˈsteɪtrɪks/ ▷ *noun* (***testatrixes*** or ***testatrices*** /-trɪsiːz/) *law* a female testator. ◷ 16c: Latin.

test case ▷ *noun, law* a case whose outcome will serve as a precedent for all similar cases in the future.

test drive ▷ *noun* a trial drive of a car by a prospective owner to test its performance. ▷ *verb* (**test-drive**) to take a car for a test drive.

testee /tɛsˈtiː/ ▷ *noun* (***testees***) someone who is tested or examined in some way. ◷ 1930s.

tester[1] ▷ *noun* **1** someone who tests. **2** a thing used for testing, especially a sample of a cosmetic in shops, for prospective buyers to test on the back of their hands.

tester[2] ▷ *noun* a canopy hanging over a bed, especially a four-poster bed. ◷ 14c: from Latin *testrum*, from *testa* a covering.

testes *plural of* TESTIS

testicle /ˈtɛstɪkəl/ ▷ *noun* a testis. • **testicular** /tɛˈstɪkjʊlə(r)/ *adj.* ◷ 15c: from Latin *testiculus*, diminutive of TESTIS.

testify /ˈtɛstɪfaɪ/ ▷ *verb* (***testifies***, ***testified***, ***testifying***) **1** *intr* to give evidence in court. **2** (*often* **testify to something**) to serve as evidence or proof of it. **3** *intr* to make a solemn declaration (eg of one's faith). **4** to declare solemnly □ *testify one's sorrow.* ◷ 14c: from Latin *testificari*, from *testis* witness.

testily see under TESTY

testimonial /tɛstɪˈmoʊnɪəl/ ▷ *noun* **1** a letter or certificate giving details of one's character, conduct and qualifications. **2** a gift presented (often in public) as a sign of respect or as a tribute to personal qualities or services. **3** *football* a match or series of matches held in honour of a player, usually towards the end of their playing career, with the proceeds being presented to them.

testimony /ˈtɛstɪmənɪ/ ▷ *noun* (***testimonies***) **1** a statement made under oath, especially in a law court. **2** evidence □ ***a testimony to her intelligence.*** **3** a declaration of truth or fact. **4** *Bible* the Ten Commandments as inscribed on the tablets of stone. ◷ 14c: from Latin *testimonium*, from *testis* witness.

testiness see under TESTY

testing ▷ *noun* the assessment of an individual level of knowledge or skill, etc by a variety of methods. ▷ *adj* **1** troublesome; difficult □ ***a testing time.*** **2** mentally taxing □ ***a testing question.***

testis /ˈtɛstɪs/ ▷ *noun* (***testes*** /ˈtɛstiːz/) *anatomy* in male animals: either of the two reproductive glands that produce sperm and are either internally or externally positioned, enclosed in the scrotum. ◷ 18c: Latin, meaning 'witness (of virility)'.

test match ▷ *noun* in various sports, especially cricket: a match forming one of a series played by the same two international teams. Often shortened to **test**.

testosterone /tɛˈstɒstəroʊn/ ▷ *noun, physiol* the main male sex hormone, a steroid that is secreted primarily by the testes, but also by the adrenal cortex and ovaries, which controls the growth and functioning of the male sex organs, and the appearance of male SECONDARY SEXUAL CHARACTERISTICS. ◷ 1930s: from *testis* + *sterol* + -ONE.

test paper ▷ *noun* **1** a list of questions forming a short minor examination. **2** paper which has been soaked in some substance so that it changes colour when it comes into contact with certain chemicals.

test pilot ▷ *noun* a pilot who tests new aircraft by flying them.

test tube ▷ *noun* a thin glass tube closed at one end, used in chemical tests or experiments.

test-tube baby ▷ *noun, medicine* **1** the popular name for a baby produced by IN-VITRO FERTILIZATION. **2** *formerly* a child born as a result of artificial insemination. ◷ 1930s.

testy /ˈtɛstɪ/ ▷ *adj* (***testier***, ***testiest***) irritable; bad-tempered; touchy. • **testily** *adverb*. • **testiness** *noun*. ◷ 16c; 14c in obsolete sense 'impetuous': from French *testif* headstrong.

tetanus /ˈtɛtənəs/ ▷ *noun* **1** *pathol* an infectious and potentially fatal disease, caused by the release of toxins from a bacterium, the spores of which are found in soil. Its main symptoms are fever and painful muscle spasms especially of the mouth and facial muscles. Also called **lockjaw**. **2** *physiol* any state of prolonged contraction of a muscle caused by rapidly repeated stimuli. ◷ 14c: from Greek *tetanos*, from *teinein* to stretch.

tetchy /ˈtɛtʃɪ/ ▷ *adj* (***tetchier***, ***tetchiest***) irritable; peevish. • **tetchily** *adverb*. • **tetchiness** *noun*. ◷ 16c.

tête-à-tête /teɪtəˈteɪt, tɛtəˈtɛt/ ▷ *noun* (***tête-à-têtes***) **1** a private conversation or meeting between two people. **2** a kind of sofa, designed for two people to sit almost face to face. ▷ *adj* private; intimate. ▷ *adverb* intimately □ ***They whispered tête-à-tête all evening.*** ◷ 17c: French, literally 'head to head'.

tether /ˈtɛðə(r)/ ▷ *noun* a rope or chain for tying an animal to a post or confining it to a particular spot. ▷ *verb* (***tethered***, ***tethering***) to tie or restrain with a tether. • **at the end of one's tether** having reached the limit of one's patience, strength or mental resources, etc. ◷ 14c: from Norse *tjothr*.

tetra /ˈtɛtrə/ ▷ *noun* (***tetras***) any of many small colourful freshwater fish from S and Central America, which are often kept in aquariums. ◷ 1930s: a shortening of the former genus name Tetragonopterus.

tetra- /ˈtɛtrə/ ▷ *combining form, signifying* four. ◷ Greek, meaning 'four'.

tetrachloromethane ▷ *noun, chem* (formula CCl_4) a toxic colourless pungent liquid, insoluble in water, formerly used as a solvent, a dry-cleaning reagent and in certain types of fire-extinguisher. Also called **carbon tetrachloride**.

tetracycline /tɛtrəˈsaɪkliːn/ ▷ *noun, medicine* any of a group of antibiotics of the same name, obtained from bacteria or synthesized and used to treat a wide range of bacterial infections, eg acne, respiratory infections and syphilis. ◷ 1950s: from TETRA- + CYCLIC + -INE[2].

tetrad /ˈtɛtrad/ ▷ *noun* a group of four. ◷ 17c: from Greek *tetras* four.

tetragon /ˈtɛtrəgən/ ▷ *noun, geom* a plane figure with four angles and four sides. • **tetragonal** /tɛˈtragənəl/ *adj*. ◷ 17c: from Greek *tetragonon*.

Tetragrammaton /tɛtrəˈgramətən/ ▷ *noun* the Hebrew name of God written using four letters, in the English alphabet given as either YHWH (Yahweh) or JHVH (Jehovah). ◷ 14c: from Greek *tetragrammatos* having four letters, from *tetra* four + *gramma* letter.

tetrahedron /tɛtrəˈhiːdrən/ ▷ *noun* (***tetrahedra*** or ***tetrahedrons***) *geom* a solid figure having four plane faces with three angles each. • **tetrahedral** *adj*. ◷ 16c: from Greek *tetraedron*.

tetralogy /tɪˈtralədʒɪ/ ▷ *noun* (***tetralogies***) **1** *historical* a group of four dramas, usually three tragic and one satiric. **2** any series of four related dramatic or operatic works. ◷ 17c.

tetrameter /tɛˈtramɪtə(r)/ ▷ *noun, poetry* a line of verse with four metrical feet. ◷ 17c: from Greek *tetrametros*.

tetraplegia see QUADRIPLEGIA

tetrapod /ˈtɛtrəpɒd/ ▷ *noun, zool* any animal with four limbs or derived from four-legged ancestors, including amphibians, reptiles, birds and mammals. ◷ 19c: from Greek *tetrapous* four-footed.

tetrastich /ˈtɛtrəstɪk/ ▷ *noun, poetry* a stanza or set of four lines. ◷ 16c: from Greek *tetrastichon*, from *stichos* row.

tetravalent /tɛtrəˈveɪlənt/ and **quadravalent** /kwɒdrə-/ ▷ *adj, chem* characterized by having a VALENCY of four. ◷ 19c: TETRA- + -VALENT.

Teuton /ˈtʃuːtən/ ▷ *noun* **1** any speaker of a Germanic language. **2** *historical* a member of an ancient Germanic tribe from N Europe. ◷ 18c: from Latin *Teutoni* or *Teutones* the Teutons.

Teutonic /tʃʊˈtɒnɪk/ ▷ *adj* **1** belonging or relating to the Germanic languages or peoples speaking these languages. **2** German. ▷ *noun* the parent language of the Teutons; early Germanic.

Tex. see TX

Tex-Mex /tɛksˈmɛks/ ▷ *adj* said of food, music, etc: typically Mexican but with elements either taken from, or adapted through contact with, Texan culture. ◷ 1940s: from *Texican* + *Mexican*.

text ▷ *noun* **1** the main body of printed words in a book as opposed to the notes and illustrations, etc. **2** the actual words of an author or piece of written work as opposed to commentary on them. **3** a short passage from the Bible taken as the starting-point for a sermon or quoted in authority. **4** a theme or subject. **5** a book, novel or play, etc that forms part of a course of study □ ***a set text.*** **6** *computing* the words written or displayed on a VDU. **7** a textbook. ◷ 14c: from Latin *texere*, *textum* to weave.

textbook ▷ *noun* **1** a book that contains the standard principles and information of a subject. **2** *as adj* conforming or as if conforming to the guidance of a textbook; exemplary □ ***textbook accountancy.***

textile /ˈtɛkstaɪl/ ▷ *noun* **1** any cloth or fabric made by weaving or knitting. **2** fibre or yarn, etc suitable for weaving into cloth. ▷ *adj* belonging or relating to manufacturing, or suitable for being woven into, such cloth. ⓒ 17c: from Latin *textilis*, from *texere*, *textum* to weave.

text linguistics ▷ *singular noun* the study of the structure of all forms of linguistic text which have a communicative function, eg essays, notices, scripts, conversations, etc.

textual /'tɛkstʃuəl/ ▷ *adj* belonging or relating to, found in, or based on, a text or texts. • **textually** *adverb*.

texture /'tɛkstʃə(r)/ ▷ *noun* **1** the way the surface of a material or substance feels when touched. **2** the way that a piece of cloth looks or feels, caused by the way in which it is woven. **3** the structure of a substance as formed by the size and arrangement of the smaller particles which form it, especially as seen, touched or tasted □ ***a crumbly texture.*** **4** the structure of a piece of music, writing, work of art, etc as formed by the individual parts which form it. ▷ *verb* (***textured, texturing***) to give a particular texture to (eg food or fabric). • **textural** *adj*. • **texturally** *adverb*. • **textured** *adj*. ⓒ 17c in these senses; 15c, meaning 'weaving': from Latin *texere*, *textum* to weave.

texturize or **texturise** ▷ *verb* (***texturized, texturizing***) to give a particular texture to (eg food or fabric). ⓒ 1950s.

TG ▷ *abbreviation* **1** *IVR* Togo. **2** transformational grammar.

TGWU ▷ *abbreviation* Transport and General Workers' Union.

Th ▷ *symbol, chem* thorium.

Th. ▷ *abbreviation* Thursday. Also written **Thur.**, **Thurs.**

-th¹ /θ/ or **-eth** /əθ/ ▷ *suffix* forming ordinal numbers and fractions from cardinal numbers □ ***fourth*** □ ***one fiftieth.*** ⓒ Anglo-Saxon *-tha* or *-the*.

-th² /θ/ ▷ *suffix, forming nouns, signifying* an action or process, or a state or condition □ ***warmth*** □ ***filth*** □ ***width.*** ⓒ Anglo-Saxon *-thu*, *-tho* or *-th*.

Thai /taɪ/ ▷ *adj* belonging or relating to Thailand, a kingdom in SE Asia, its inhabitants or their language. ▷ *noun* (***Thai*** or ***Thais***) **1** a citizen or inhabitant of, or person born in, Thailand. **2** the official language of Thailand. ⓒ Early 20c.

thalamus /'θaləməs/ ▷ *noun* (***thalami*** /-maɪ, -miː/) *anatomy* in the forebrain of vertebrates: either of two egg-shaped masses of grey matter that lie within the cerebral hemispheres, relaying sensory nerve impulses to the cerebral cortex. ⓒ 18c: Latin, from Greek *thalamos* inner room.

thalassaemia or *US* **thalassemia** /θalə'siːmɪə/ *noun, pathol* a hereditary disorder, most common in the Mediterranean region, characterized by the presence of an abnormal form of HAEMOGLOBIN in the red blood cells. ⓒ 1930s: from Greek *thalassa* sea + *haima* blood.

thalassotherapy /θaləsoʊ'θɛrəpɪ/ ▷ *noun, alternative medicine* a form of treatment to detoxify and relax the body, involving the application of mud and seaweed compresses, seawater baths and massage. ⓒ Late 19c: from Greek *thalassa* sea.

thalidomide /θə'lɪdəmaɪd/ ▷ *noun* a drug formerly used as a sedative but withdrawn in 1961 because it was found to cause malformation of the fetus if taken by the mother in early pregnancy. ⓒ 1950s.

thallium /'θalɪəm/ ▷ *noun, chem* (symbol **Tl**, atomic number 81) a soft bluish-white metallic element that is used in electronic equipment, experimental alloys and optical glass and whose toxic compounds are used as pesticides. ⓒ 19c: from Greek *thallos* a green shoot, so called because of the bright green line in its spectrum.

thallus /'θaləs/ ▷ *noun* (**thalluses** or ***thalli*** /'θalaɪ/) *biol* in fungi, lichens and seaweeds, etc: a flattened and sometimes branched structure that is not differentiated into stems, leaves and roots. • **thalloid** *adj*.

than /ðan, ðən/ ▷ *conj* **1** used to introduce the second part of a comparison, or that part which is taken as the basis of a comparison □ ***Nirvana are much better than Pearl Jam.*** **2** used to introduce the second, and usually less desirable or rejected, option in a statement of alternatives □ ***would rather go swimming than play football.*** **3** except; other than □ ***I'll be left with no alternative than to resign.*** ▷ *prep* in comparison with □ ***someone older than him.*** ⓒ Anglo-Saxon *thonne*.

than

For **than what** see Usage Note at **what**.

thanatology /θanə'tɒlədʒɪ/ ▷ *noun, medicine* the medical and legal study of death, its causes and related phenomena. ⓒ 19c: from Greek *thanatos* death + -LOGY.

thane ▷ *noun, historical* **1** in Anglo-Saxon England: a man holding land from the king or some other superior in exchange for military service. **2** in medieval Scotland: a man holding land from a Scottish king, but not in return for military service; a Scottish feudal lord. ⓒ Anglo-Saxon *thegn*.

thank ▷ *verb* (***thanked, thanking***) **1** to express gratitude to someone □ ***thanked him for his help.*** **2** to hold responsible for something □ ***has only himself to thank for the mess.*** ▷ *noun* (*usually* **thanks**) **1** gratitude or an expression of gratitude □ ***to express my thanks.*** **2** thank you □ ***Thanks for the present.*** • **no thanks to someone** or **something** in spite of them; no gratitude being due to them. • **thank God** or **goodness** or **heavens,** *etc* an expression of relief. • **thanks to …** as a result of …; because of … □ ***Thanks to Amy, we missed the train.*** • **thank you** a polite expression acknowledging a gift, help or offer. ⓒ Anglo-Saxon *thancian*.

thankful ▷ *adj* grateful; relieved and happy. • **thankfully** *adverb* **1** in a thankful manner. **2** in a way that invites one's thanks □ ***Thankfully, it didn't rain.*** • **thankfulness** *noun*.

thankless ▷ *adj* bringing no thanks, pleasure or profit. • **thanklessly** *adverb*. • **thanklessness** *noun*. ⓒ 16c.

thanksgiving ▷ *noun* **1** a formal act of giving thanks, especially to God. **2** (**Thanksgiving** or **Thanksgiving Day**) *N Amer* a public holiday for giving thanks, occurring on the fourth Thursday in November in the USA and the second Monday in October in Canada.

thankyou /'θaŋkjuː/ ▷ *noun* **1** an utterance of 'thank you'. **2** an instance of thanking someone, or anything that expresses thanks or gratitude, especially a gift. Also *as adj* □ ***a thankyou letter.***

that /ðat, ðət/ ▷ *adj* (*plural* ***those*** /ðoʊz/) **1** indicating the thing, person or idea already mentioned, specified or understood □ ***There's that girl I was telling you about.*** **2** indicating someone or something that is farther away or is in contrast □ ***not this book, but that one.*** ▷ *pronoun* (*plural* ***those***) **1** the person, thing or idea just mentioned, already spoken of or understood □ ***When did that happen?*** **2** a relatively distant or more distant person, thing or idea. ▷ *pronoun* used instead of *which*, *who* or *whom*, to introduce a relative clause which defines, distinguishes or restricts the person or thing mentioned in the preceding clause □ ***All the children that were late received detention.*** ▷ *conj* used to introduce a noun clause, or a clause showing reason, purpose, consequence or a result or expressing a wish or desire □ ***He spoke so quickly that I couldn't understand*** □ ***Oh, that the day would never end!*** ▷ *adverb* **1** to the degree or extent shown or understood □ ***won't reach that far.*** **2** *colloq or dialect* to such a degree that; so □ ***They are that unsociable they never leave the house.*** • **all that** *colloq* very □ ***not all that good.*** • **that's that** that is the end of the matter. ⓒ Anglo-Saxon *thæt*.

thatch ▷ *noun* (***thatches***) **1** a roof covering of straw or reeds, etc. **2** anything resembling such a roof, especially thick hair on the head. ▷ *verb* (***thatches, thatched, thatching***) *tr & intr* to cover (a roof or building) with thatch. • **thatcher** *noun*. ⓒ Anglo-Saxon *theccan*.

> ***that***
>
> Many people think that the relative pronoun **that** in constructions such as *The man that I met happened to be Philip's uncle* is informal and should be replaced by **who** or **whom** or **which** in formal contexts. In fact, **that** used in this way is acceptable in any context, as is the omission of **that** in *The man I met happened to be Philip's uncle*.

Thatcherism ▻ *noun* the policies and style of government associated with Margaret Thatcher between 1979 and 1990, characterized by MONETARISM, a commitment to private enterprise, opposition to trade unions, etc. • **Thatcherite** *noun, adj.* ⓘ 1970s.

thaw ▻ *verb* (***thawed, thawing***) **1 a** *intr* said of snow or ice: to melt; **b** to make (snow or ice) melt. **2 a** (*also* **thaw out**) *intr* said of anything frozen, eg food: to become unfrozen; to defrost; **b** (*also* **thaw something out**) to defrost (eg frozen food). **3** *intr* said of the weather: to be warm enough to begin to melt snow and ice □ ***It's beginning to thaw.*** **4** (*also* **thaw out** or **thaw something out**) *tr & intr, colloq* to make or become less stiff and numb with cold □ ***Come and thaw out by the fire.*** **5** (*also* **thaw out** or **thaw something out**) *tr & intr, colloq* to make or become more friendly or relaxed. ▻ *noun* **1** an act or the process of thawing. **2** a period of weather warm enough to begin to thaw ice and snow. **3 a** a lessening of tension and hostility and an increase in friendliness, especially between countries; **b** a lessening of repressive actions and controls by a government within a state. ⓘ Anglo-Saxon *thawian*.

the ▻ *definite article* **1** used to refer to a particular person or thing, or group of people or things, already mentioned, implied or known □ ***Pass me the CD.*** **2** used to refer to a unique person or thing □ ***the Pope.*** **3** used before a singular noun: *denoting* all the members of a group or class □ ***a history of the novel.*** **4** used before an adjective: *denoting* **a** something that is (a specified thing) □ ***the paranormal;*** **b** people who are (a specified thing) □ ***the poor.*** **5** used before certain titles and proper names. **6** used before an adjective or noun describing an identified person □ ***Robert the Bruce.*** **7** used after a preposition to refer to a unit of quantity or time, etc □ ***a car which does forty miles to the gallon*** □ ***paid by the hour.*** **8** *colloq* my; our □ ***I'd better check with the wife.*** ▻ *adverb* **1** used before comparative adjectives or adverbs to indicate (by) so much or (by) how much □ ***the sooner the better.*** **2** used before superlative adjectives and adverbs to indicate an amount beyond all others □ ***like this book the best.*** ⓘ Anglo-Saxon, meaning 'who', 'which' or 'that', replacing earlier *se* that.

theanthropic /θiːan'θrɒpɪk/ ▻ *adj* **1** both human and divine. **2** embodying deity in human forms. ⓘ 17c: from Greek *theos* a god + *anthropos* man.

thearchy /'θiːɑːkɪ/ ▻ *noun* (***thearchies***) **1** government by a god or gods. **2** a body of divine rulers. ⓘ 17c: from Greek *theos* a god + *archein* to rule.

theatre or *US* **theater** /'θɪətə(r)/ ▻ *noun* **1** a building or area outside specially designed for the performance of plays and operas, etc. **2** a large room with seats rising in tiers, eg for lectures. **3** (*also* **the theatre**) the writing and production of plays in general. **4** (**the theatre**) the world and profession of actors and theatre companies. **5** *Brit* a specially equipped room in a hospital where surgery is performed. **6** a scene of action or place where events take place □ ***theatre of war.*** **7** *N Amer* a cinema. ⓘ 14c: from Greek *theatron*, from *theaesthai* to see.

theatre-in-the-round ▻ *noun* (***theatres-in-the-round***) *theat* **1** a theatre in which a central stage is surrounded on all sides by the audience. **2** the style of staging plays in such a theatre. See also ARENA. ⓘ 1940s.

Theatre of the Absurd ▻ *noun* a term for certain plays of the 1950s, in which the absurdity and irrationality of the human condition was mirrored in a dramatic form of unreal situations without traditional narrative continuity or meaningful and coherent dialogue, as in works by Samuel Beckett, Eugène Ionesco, etc.

theatrical /θɪ'atrɪkəl/ ▻ *adj* **1** belonging or relating to theatres or acting. **2** said of behaviour or a gesture, etc: done only for effect; artificial and exaggerated. ▻ *noun* (**theatricals**) **1** dramatic performances. **2** insincere or exaggerated behaviour □ ***Less of the theatricals, please!*** • **theatricality** *noun*. • **theatrically** *adverb*.

thebaine /'θiːbeɪiːn/ ▻ *noun* a poisonous alkaloid obtained from opium. ⓘ 19c: from Latin *thebia* opium (as prepared at Thebes, the ancient Egyptian city).

theca /'θiːkə/ ▻ *noun* (***thecae*** /'θiːsiː/) **1** *bot* an enclosing sheath, case or sac. **2** *zool* a case or sheath enclosing an organ. ⓘ 17c: Latin, from Greek *theke* cover.

thee /ðiː/ ▻ *pronoun, old use or dialect, also relig* the objective form of *thou*. ⓘ Anglo-Saxon.

theft ▻ *noun* **1** stealing; an act of stealing someone else's property, with the intention of permanently depriving them of it. **2** something stolen. ⓘ Anglo-Saxon *thiefth*.

theine ▻ *noun* CAFFEINE.

their /ðɛə(r)/ ▻ *adj* **1** belonging or relating to them □ ***their opinion.*** **2** his or her □ ***Has everyone got their books with them?*** ⓘ 12c: from Norse *thierra*.

theirs /ðɛəz/ ▻ *pronoun* a person or thing that belongs to them □ ***That's theirs.*** • **of theirs** belonging to them.

theism /'θiːɪzəm/ ▻ *noun* the belief in the existence of God or a god, especially one revealed supernaturally to humans. Compare DEISM, AGNOSTICISM, ATHEISM. • **theist** *noun*. • **theistic** *adj*. ⓘ 17c: from Greek *theos* god.

them /ðɛm, ðəm/ ▻ *pronoun* **1** people or things already mentioned or spoken about, or understood from the context □ ***Just look at them giggling.*** **2** *colloq or dialect* those □ ***Them's the best, I reckon.*** **3** *colloq* him or her. **4** *old use* themselves. ▻ *adj, colloq or dialect* those □ ***I'll have one of them peppermints.*** ⓘ 12c: from Norse *thiem*.

theme /θiːm/ ▻ *noun* **1** the subject of a discussion, speech or piece of writing, etc. **2** *music* a short melody which forms the basis of a piece of music and which is developed and repeated with variations. **3** a repeated or recurring image or idea in literature or art. **4** a brief essay or written exercise. • **thematic** /θɪ'matɪk/ *adj*. • **thematically** *adverb*. ⓘ 13c: from Greek *thema*.

theme park ▻ *noun* a large amusement park in which all of the rides and attractions are based on a particular theme, such as outer space.

theme song and **theme tune** ▻ *noun* a song or melody that is associated with, and usually played at the beginning and end of, a film, TV or radio programme, or which is associated with a particular character.

themselves /ðəm'sɛlvz/ ▻ *pronoun* **1** the reflexive form of *they* and *them* □ ***They helped themselves.*** **2** used for emphasis □ ***They did it themselves.*** **3** their normal selves □ ***They aren't feeling quite themselves today.*** **4** *colloq* himself or herself □ ***Nobody needs to blame themselves.***

> ***themself***
>
> • **Themself** is beginning to appear as a gender-neutral reflexive pronoun, a singular form of **themselves** meaning 'himself or herself':
>
> **?** *You won't be the last man or woman who gets themself involved in a holiday romance.*
>
> • It is by no means fully accepted, and is best avoided when speaking or writing to prescriptively minded people. **Themselves** is more generally accepted in these contexts: see the Usage Note at **he or she**.

then /ðɛn/ ▻ *adverb* **1** at that time. **2** soon or immediately after that ◻ ***I looked at him, then turned away.*** **3** in that case; that being so; as a necessary consequence ◻ ***What would we do then?*** ◻ ***If you're tired, then you should rest.*** **4** also; in addition ◻ ***Then there's the cost to take into account.*** **5** used to continue a narrative after a break or digression ◻ ***By the time she got to the top, then, it had started to snow.*** **6** used especially at the end of questions which ask for an explanation or opinion, etc, or which ask for or assume agreement ◻ ***Your mind is made up, then?*** ▻ *noun* that time ◻ ***But until then, I think you should stay away.*** ▻ *adj* being or acting at that time ◻ ***the then Prime Minister.*** • **then and there** at that very time and on that very spot. Ⓒ Anglo-Saxon *thonne.*

thenar /ˈθiːnə(r)/ ▻ *noun, anatomy* the ball of muscle at the base of the thumb. Ⓒ 17c: Latin, from Greek.

thence /ðɛns/ ▻ *adverb, old use or formal* **1** from that place or time. **2** from that cause; therefore. Ⓒ 13c as *thennes*: from Anglo-Saxon *thanon* thence.

thenceforth and **thenceforward** ▻ *adverb, old use or formal* from that time or place forwards.

theo- /θiːoʊ, θɪˈɒ/ ▻ *combining form, signifying* belonging or relating to God or a god. Ⓒ From Greek *theos* god.

theobromine /θiːoʊˈbroʊmiːn, -ˈmaɪn, -mɪn/ ▻ *noun* an alkaloid found especially in the chocolate seed, used in medicine. Ⓒ 19c: from Latin *Theobroma* (the chocolate or cocoa genus) literally 'food of the Gods', from THEO- + Greek *broma* food.

theocracy /θɪˈɒkrəsɪ/ ▻ *noun* **1** government by a deity or by priests representing a deity. **2** a state ruled in this way. • **theocrat** /ˈθɪəkrat/ *noun.* • **theocratic** *adj.* • **theocratically** *adverb.* Ⓒ 17c.

theodolite /θɪˈɒdəlaɪt/ ▻ *noun, surveying* an instrument for measuring horizontal and vertical angles. Ⓒ 16c: from Latin *theodelitus.*

theolinguistics ▻ *singular noun* the study of language used in the theory and practice of religious belief, eg by theologians, biblical scholars, ministers and preachers, etc.

theologian /θɪəˈloʊdʒɪən/ ▻ *noun* someone who studies or is an expert in theology.

theological /θɪəˈlɒdʒɪkəl/ ▻ *adj* relating to or involving theology. • **theologically** *adverb.*

theology /θɪˈɒlədʒɪ/ ▻ *noun* **1** the study of God, religion, religious belief and revelation. **2** a particular system of theology and religion ◻ ***Catholic theology.*** Ⓒ 14c.

theorbo /θɪˈɔːboʊ/ ▻ *noun* (***theorbos***) a type of large LUTE widely used in the 17c, with fourteen strings above a fretted FINGERBOARD and ten additional unstopped bass strings. Ⓒ 17c: from Italian *tiorba.*

theorem /ˈθɪərəm/ ▻ *noun* a scientific or mathematical statement which makes certain assumptions in order to explain observed phenomena, and which has been proved to be correct. Ⓒ 16c: from Greek *theorema* subject for contemplation.

theoretical /θɪəˈrɛtɪkəl/ or **theoretic** ▻ *adj* **1** concerned with or based on theory rather than practical knowledge or experience. **2** existing in theory only; hypothetical. **3** dealing with theory only; speculative. • **theoretically** *adverb.*

theoretician /θɪərɛˈtɪʃən/ ▻ *noun* someone who specializes in or is concerned with the theoretical aspects of a subject rather than its practical use. Ⓒ Late 19c.

theorist /ˈθɪərɪst/ ▻ *noun* **1** someone who speculates or invents theories. **2** a theoretician. Ⓒ 17c.

theorize or **theorise** /ˈθɪəraɪz/ ▻ *verb* (***theorized, theorizing***) *intr* to devise theories; to speculate. Ⓒ 17c.

theory /ˈθɪərɪ/ ▻ *noun* (***theories***) **1** a series of ideas and general principles which seek to explain some aspect of the world ◻ ***theory of relativity.*** **2** an idea or explanation which has not yet been proved; a conjecture ◻ ***Well, my theory is he's jealous!*** **3** the general and usually abstract principles or ideas of a subject ◻ ***theory of music.*** **4 a** an ideal, hypothetical or abstract situation; **b** ideal, hypothetical or abstract reasoning ◻ ***a good idea in theory.*** Ⓒ 16c: from Greek *theoria*, from *theoreein* to view.

theosophy /θɪˈɒsəfɪ/ ▻ *noun* (***theosophies***) a religious philosophy based on the belief that a knowledge of God can be achieved through intuition, mysticism and divine inspiration, especially a modern movement which combines this with elements from Hinduism and Buddhism, such as a belief in reincarnation. • **theosophic** /θɪəˈsɒfɪk/ *adj.* • **theosophically** *adverb.* • **theosophist** /θɪˈɒsəfɪst/ *noun.* Ⓒ 17c: from THEO- + Greek *sophia* wisdom.

therapeutic /θɛrəˈpjuːtɪk/ ▻ *adj* **1** belonging or relating to, concerning, or contributing to, the healing and curing of disease. **2** bringing a feeling of general well-being. • **therapeutically** *adverb.* Ⓒ 17c: from Greek *therapeuein* to take care of or heal.

therapeutics ▻ *singular noun, medicine* the branch of medicine concerned with the treatment and cure of diseases. Ⓒ 17c.

therapy /ˈθɛrəpɪ/ ▻ *noun* (***therapies***) the treatment of physical, social or mental diseases and disorders by means other than surgery or drugs. Also *in compounds.* • **therapist** *noun* (*also in compounds*). Ⓒ 19c: from Greek *therapeuein* to take care of or heal.

there /ðɛə(r)/ ▻ *adverb* **1** at, in or to a place or position ◻ ***You can sit there.*** **2** at that point in speech, a piece of writing or a performance, etc ◻ ***Don't stop there.*** **3** in that respect ◻ ***I agree with him there.*** **4** (*also* /ðə(r)/) used to begin a sentence when the subject of the verb follows the verb instead of coming before it ◻ ***There are no mistakes in this.*** **5** used at the beginning of a sentence to emphasise or call attention to that sentence ◻ ***There goes the last bus.*** **6** used after a noun for emphasis ◻ ***That book there is the one you need.*** **7** *colloq or dialect* used between a noun and *this* or that, etc for emphasis ◻ ***that there tractor.*** ▻ *noun* that place or point. ▻ *exclamation* **1** used to express satisfaction, approval, triumph or encouragement, etc ◻ ***There! I knew he would come.*** **2** used to express sympathy or comfort, etc ◻ ***There, there! He's just not worth it.*** • **be there for someone** to be available to support them emotionally, particularly when most needed. • **have been there before** *slang* to have been in the same, especially unpleasant, situation before. • **there and then** at that very time and on that very spot. • **there you are 1** said when giving something to someone: this is what you need or want. **2** used to express satisfaction or triumph. Ⓒ Anglo-Saxon *thær.*

thereabouts /ðɛərəˈbaʊts, ˈðɛə-/ or **thereabout** ▻ *adverb* near that place, number, amount, degree or time.

thereafter /ðɛərˈaftə(r), -ˈɑːftə(r)/ ▻ *adverb, formal* from that time onwards.

thereby /ðɛəˈbaɪ, ˈðɛə-/ ▻ *adverb, formal* **1** by that means. **2** in consequence.

therefore /ˈðɛəfɔː(r)/ ▻ *adverb* for that reason; as a consequence.

therein /ðɛərˈɪn/ ▻ *adverb, formal* in or into that or it.

thereof /ðɛərˈɒv/ ▻ *adverb, formal* belonging or relating to, or from, that or it.

thereon /ðɛərˈɒn/ ▻ *adverb, formal* on or on to that or it.

thereto /ðɛəˈtuː/ ▻ *adverb, formal* to that or it; in addition.

thereunder /ðɛərˈʌndə(r)/ ▻ *adverb, formal* under that or it.

thereupon /ðɛərəˈpɒn, ˈðɛə-/ ▻ *adverb, formal* **1** on that matter or point. **2** immediately after it or that.

therm /θɜːm/ ▻ *noun* a unit of heat equal to 100 000 BRITISH THERMAL UNITs, used to measure the amount of gas supplied. ◷ 1920s in this sense: from Greek *therme* heat.

thermal /ˈθɜːməl/ ▻ *adj* **1** belonging or relating to, caused by, or producing heat. **2** said of clothing: designed to prevent the loss of heat from the body □ *thermal vest.* ▻ *noun* **1** a rising current of warm air, used by birds, gliders and hang-gliders to move upwards. **2** (**thermals**) thermal clothing, especially underwear. • **thermally** *adverb.* ◷ 18c: from Greek *therme* heat.

thermal barrier see HEAT BARRIER

thermal conductor see CONDUCTOR

thermal conductivity see CONDUCTIVITY

thermal imaging ▻ *noun* the visualization of objects and scenes by detecting and processing the infrared energy they emit.

Thermalite /ˈθɜːməlaɪt/ ▻ *noun, trademark* a manufactured material used to make building blocks, light and effective as insulation. ◷ 1940s.

thermalize or **thermalise** /ˈθɜːməlaɪz/ ▻ *verb* (***thermalized, thermalizing***) *tr & intr* to reduce the kinetic energy and speed of (fast NEUTRONS) in a nuclear reactor, or to undergo such a process. ◷ 1940s.

thermal printer ▻ *noun, computing* a printer which uses heat-sensitive paper, producing visible characters by the action of heated wires.

thermal reactor ▻ *noun* a nuclear reactor in which fission is induced mainly by low-energy neutrons.

thermion /ˈθɜːmɪən/ ▻ *noun, physics* an electrically charged particle emitted by an extremely hot or incandescent substance. • **thermionic** /-ˈɒnɪk/ *adj.* ◷ Early 20c: from Greek *therme* heat.

thermionic emission ▻ *noun, physics* the emission of electrons from a heated material, usually a metal surface.

thermionics /θɜːmɪˈɒnɪks/ ▻ *singular noun, physics* the branch of electronics concerned with the study of the processes involved in the emission of electrons from metal surfaces at high temperatures, and with the design of thermionic valves and electron guns. ◷ Early 20c.

thermionic valve ▻ *noun, electronics* a vacuum tube that emits electrons from an electrically heated cathode into a vacuum, formerly widely used in amplifiers, switches and other electrical devices.

thermistor /θɜːˈmɪstə(r)/ ▻ *noun, physics* a device with an electrical resistance that decreases rapidly as its temperature rises, used in electronic circuits for measuring or controlling temperature, eg electronic switches and thermometers. ◷ 1940s: a contraction of *thermal resistor.*

thermo- /θɜːmoʊ/ ▻ *prefix, signifying* heat. ◷ From Greek *therme* heat.

thermocouple ▻ *noun* a device for measuring temperature, consisting of two different metallic conductors welded together at their ends to form a loop. When the two junctions are kept at different temperatures, a voltage is generated between them, the size of which can be measured and is directly related to the temperature difference between the two junctions. ◷ Late 19c.

thermodynamics ▻ *singular noun, physics* the branch of physics concerned with the relationship between heat and other forms of energy, especially mechanical energy, and the behaviour of physical systems in which temperature is an important factor. • **thermodynamic** *adj.* • **thermodynamically** *adverb.* ◷ 19c.

thermoelectricity ▻ *noun* an electric current generated by a difference in temperature in an electric circuit, especially between a pair of junctions where two different metals are in contact, eg a thermocouple. • **thermoelectric** *adj.* ◷ 19c.

thermography /θɜːˈmɒgrəfɪ/ ▻ *noun* **1** a technique for the conversion of invisible heat energy into a visible picture, used for military purposes, and for nocturnal studies of wildlife. **2** *medicine* the analysis of heat emitted from the skin of a patient's body as infrared radiation, which is converted to a visible image representing warmer and cooler regions of the skin, and is used in the diagnosis of certain medical disorders, eg underlying tumours. **3** any process of writing or photographing, etc that involves the use of heat. ◷ 19c in sense 3; 1950s in senses 1 and 2.

thermoluminescence dating ▻ *noun, archaeol* a method of dating ancient pottery, burnt flint, calcite and sediments by measuring the energy accumulated in the crystal lattice of its inclusions of quartz, through the breakdown over time of naturally occurring uranium. ◷ 1960s.

thermometer /θəˈmɒmɪtə(r)/ ▻ *noun* an instrument for measuring temperature, often consisting of a narrow calibrated sealed glass tube filled with a liquid whose properties vary with temperature, eg mercury which expands as the temperature increases and contracts as it decreases. ◷ 17c.

thermonuclear ▻ *adj* **1** using or showing nuclear reactions which can only be produced at extremely high temperatures. **2** relating to or involving thermonuclear weapons. ◷ 1930s.

thermonuclear bomb see HYDROGEN BOMB

thermopile /ˈθɜːmoʊpaɪl/ ▻ *noun, physics* a device consisting of several THERMOCOUPLEs connected together, used to detect and measure the intensity of thermal radiation. ◷ 19c.

thermoplastic ▻ *noun, chem* a POLYMER that can be repeatedly softened and hardened, without any appreciable change in its properties, by heating and cooling it. ▻ *adj* denoting such a material. ◷ Late 19c.

Thermos /ˈθɜːməs/ or **Thermos flask** ▻ *noun, trademark* a kind of VACUUM FLASK. ◷ 1907: Greek, meaning 'hot'.

thermosetting ▻ *adj* said of plastics: that become permanently hard after a single melting and moulding. ◷ 1930s.

thermosphere /ˈθɜːməsfɪə(r)/ ▻ *noun, meteorol* the layer of the Earth's atmosphere situated above the MESOSPHERE, in which the temperature rises steadily with increasing height, although the actual heat content is very low because the air is so thin. Its lower limit is 80 km from ground level and includes the IONOSPHERE. • **thermospheric** *adj.* ◷ 1920s: from THERMO-.

thermostat /ˈθɜːməstat/ ▻ *noun* a device used to maintain the temperature of a system at a constant preset level, or which activates some other device when the temperature reaches a certain level. • **thermostatic** *adj.* • **thermostatically** *adverb.* ◷ 19c: from THERMO- + Greek *states* causing to stand.

thesaurus /θɪˈsɔːrəs/ ▻ *noun* (***thesauruses*** or ***thesauri*** /-raɪ/) **1** a book which lists words and their synonyms according to sense. **2** any book, eg a dictionary or encyclopedia, which gives information about a particular field, or quotations, etc. ◷ 18c: Latin, from Greek *thesauros* treasury.

these *plural of* THIS

thesis /ˈθiːsɪs/ ▻ *noun* (***theses*** /ˈθiːsiːz/) **1** a long written dissertation or report, especially one based on original research and presented for an advanced university degree such as the MSc, MLitt or PhD. **2** an idea or proposition to be supported or upheld in argument. **3** an unproved statement put forward as a basis for argument or discussion. ◷ 16c: Greek, meaning 'a setting down'.

thespian or *sometimes* **Thespian** /ˈθɛspɪən/ *adj* belonging or relating to tragedy, or to drama and the theatre in general. ▷ *noun, facetious* an actor or actress. ◷ 17c: from Thespis (lived c.534 BC), Greek poet and reputed founder of Greek tragedy.

Thess. ▷ *abbreviation* Book of the Bible: Thessalonians. See table at BIBLE.

theta /ˈθiːtə/ ▷ *noun* (*thetas*) the eighth letter of the Greek alphabet. See table at GREEK ALPHABET.

theurgy /ˈθiːɜːdʒɪ/ ▷ *noun* (*theurgies*) **1** magic by the agency of good spirits. **2** miraculous or divine intervention. ◷ 16c: from Greek *theourgeia* magic.

thew /θjuː/ ▷ *noun* (*thews* or *thewes*) *often in plural* **1** moral quality or strength. **2** muscular strength. ◷ Anglo-Saxon *theaw*.

they /ðeɪ/ ▷ *pronoun* **1** the people, animals or things already spoken about, being indicated, or known from the context. **2** people in general. **3** people in authority. **4** *colloq* he or she □ *Anyone can help if they want.* ◷ 12c: from Norse *their*.

they'd ▷ *contraction* **1** they had. **2** they would.

they'll ▷ *contraction* **1** they will. **2** they shall.

they're ▷ *contraction* they are.

they've ▷ *contraction* they have.

thi- see THIO-

thiamine /ˈθaɪəmiːn/ or **thiamin** /-mɪn/ ▷ *noun* VITAMIN B_1. ◷ 1930s: THI- + AMINE.

thick ▷ *adj* (*thicker, thickest*) **1** having a relatively large distance between opposite sides. **2** having a specified distance between opposite sides □ *one inch thick.* **3** having a large diameter □ *a thick rope.* **4** said of a line or handwriting, etc: broad. **5** said of liquids: containing a lot of solid matter □ *thick soup.* **6** having many single units placed very close together; dense □ *thick hair.* **7** difficult to see through □ *thick fog.* **8** (*usually* **thick with something**) covered with or full of it □ *a cake thick with chocolate.* **9** said of speech: not clear. **10** said of an accent: marked; pronounced. **11** *colloq* said of a person: stupid; dull. **12** (*usually* **thick with someone**) *colloq* friendly or intimate □ *He is very thick with the new manager.* **13** *colloq* unfair □ *That's a bit thick!* ▷ *adverb* thickly. ▷ *noun* **1** (**the thick**) the busiest, most active or most intense part □ *in the thick of the fighting.* **2** the thickest part of anything. • **thickly** *adverb*. • **as thick as thieves** very friendly. • **thick and fast** frequently and in large numbers. • **through thick and thin** whatever happens; in spite of any difficulties. ◷ Anglo-Saxon *thicce*.

thick ear see GIVE SOMEONE A THICK EAR at EAR

thicken /ˈθɪkən/ ▷ *verb* (*thickened, thickening*) **1** *tr & intr* to make or become thick or thicker. **2** *intr* to become more complicated □ *The plot thickens.* ◷ 15c.

thickening ▷ *noun* **1** something used to thicken liquid. **2** the process of making or becoming thicker. **3** a thickened part.

thicket /ˈθɪkət/ ▷ *noun* a dense mass of bushes and trees. ◷ Anglo-Saxon *thiccet*.

thickhead ▷ *noun* **1** *colloq* a stupid person. **2** any of a family of Australian and SE Asian songbirds, similar to the flycatcher and shrike. ◷ 19c.

thick-headed ▷ *adj, colloq* **1** stupid. **2** unable to think clearly because of a cold or too much alcohol, etc.

thick knee ▷ *noun* a STONE CURLEW

thickness ▷ *noun* **1** the state, quality or degree of being thick. **2** a layer. **3** the thick part of something.

thickset ▷ *adj* **1** heavily built; having a thick, short body. **2** growing or planted close together.

thick-skinned ▷ *adj* not easily hurt by criticism or insults; not sensitive.

thief /θiːf/ ▷ *noun* (*thieves* /ˈθiːvz/) a person who steals, especially secretly and usually without violence. • **thievish** *adj*. • **thievishly** *adverb*. • **thievishness** *noun*. ◷ Anglo-Saxon *theof*.

thieve /θiːv/ ▷ *verb* (*thieved, thieving*) *tr & intr* to steal. • **thieving** *noun*. ◷ Anglo-Saxon *theofian*.

thigh /θaɪ/ ▷ *noun* the fleshy part of the leg between the knee and hip in humans, or the corresponding part in animals. See also FEMORAL. ◷ Anglo-Saxon *theoh*.

thigh bone ▷ *noun* the FEMUR.

thimble /ˈθɪmbəl/ ▷ *noun* **1** a small metal, ceramic or plastic cap worn on the finger to protect it and push the needle when sewing. **2** a metal ring with a concave groove on the outside, fitted into a loop formed by splicing a rope in order to prevent chafing. ◷ Anglo-Saxon *thymel* originally meaning 'a covering for the thumb'.

thimbleful *noun* (*thimblefuls*) the amount a thimble will hold, especially used for a very small quantity of liquid.

thin ▷ *adj* (*thinner, thinnest*) **1** having a relatively short distance between opposite sides. **2** having a relatively small diameter □ *thin string.* **3** said of a line or handwriting, etc: narrow or fine. **4** said of people or animals: not fat; lean. **5** said of liquids: containing very little solid matter. **6** set far apart; sparse □ *thin hair.* **7** having a very low oxygen content □ *thin air.* **8** weak; lacking in body □ *thin blood.* **9** not convincing or believable □ *a thin disguise.* **10** *colloq* difficult; uncomfortable; unpleasant □ *have a thin time of it.* ▷ *adverb* thinly. ▷ *verb* (*thinned, thinning*) *tr & intr* (*often* **thin out**) to make or become thin, thinner, sparser or less dense. • **thinly** *adverb*. • **thinness** *noun*. • **thin on the ground** rare; few in number. ◷ Anglo-Saxon *thynne*.

thin air ▷ *noun* nowhere □ *disappear into thin air.*

thine /ðaɪn/ *old use or dialect, also relig* ▷ *pronoun* something which belongs to THEE. ▷ *adj* (sometimes used before a vowel instead of *thy*) belonging or relating to THEE. ◷ Anglo-Saxon *thin*.

thing ▷ *noun* **1** any object, especially one that is inanimate. **2** any object that cannot, need not or should not be named. **3** any fact, quality or idea, etc that can be thought about or referred to. **4** an event, affair or circumstance □ *Things are getting out of hand.* **5** a quality □ *Generosity is a great thing.* **6** *colloq* a person or animal, especially when thought of as an object of pity □ *Poor thing!* **7** a preoccupation, obsession or interest □ *She's got a real thing about Brad Pitt!* **8** what is needed or required □ *It's just the thing.* **9** an aim □ *The thing is to do better next time.* **10** (**things**) personal belongings, especially clothes. **11** (**things**) affairs in general □ *So, how are things?* • **do one's own thing** *colloq* to do what one likes doing best, or what it is natural for one to do. • **make a thing of something** to make a fuss about it or exaggerate its importance. • **one of those things** something that must be accepted or cannot be avoided. ◷ Anglo-Saxon.

thingummy /ˈθɪŋəmɪ/, **thingamy**, **thingummy-jig** and **thingummybob** ▷ *noun* (*thingummies, etc*) *colloq* someone or something whose name is unknown, forgotten or deliberately not used. ◷ 18c.

think ▷ *verb* (*thought* /θɔːt/, *thinking*) **1** (*often* **think about something**) *tr & intr* **a** to have or form ideas in the mind; **b** to have it as a thought in one's mind. **2** (*often* **think of someone** or **something**) *tr & intr* to consider, judge or believe them or it □ *I thought you were kidding!* □ *They think of themselves as great singers.* **3** (*often* **think of** or **about something**) *tr & intr* to intend or plan it; to form an idea of it □ *think about going to London* □ *couldn't think of being so unkind* □ *think no harm.* **4** (*often* **think of something**) *tr & intr* to imagine, expect or suspect it □ *I didn't think there would be any trouble.* **5** (*usually* **think of someone** or **something**) to keep them or it in one's mind; to consider them or it □ *think of the children first.* **6** (*usually* **think of something** or **to do something**) *tr & intr* **a** to remember it □ *couldn't think of his name;* **b** to consider it □ *I didn't think to tell her.* **7** (*often* **think of something**) to form or have an idea about it □ *think of a plan.* **8** to have one's mind full of something. **9** to bring someone or something into a specified condition by thinking □ *tried to think himself thin.* ▷ *noun, colloq* an act of thinking □ *have a good think.* • **thinker** *noun* someone who thinks, especially deeply and constructively or in a specified way. • **think better of something** or **someone 1** to change one's mind about it or them on further thought. **2** to think that they would not be so bad as to do something wrong □ *I thought better of him than that.* • **think highly, well** or **badly**, *etc* **of someone** to have a high, good or bad, etc opinion of them. • **think little of something** or **not think much of something** to have a very low opinion of it. • **think twice** to hesitate before doing something; to decide in the end not to do it. Ⓒ Anglo-Saxon *thencan.*

■ **think something out 1** to consider or plan it carefully. **2** to solve a problem by thinking about all the aspects of it.

■ **think something over** to consider all the advantages and disadvantages of an action or decision, etc; to reflect on it.

■ **think something through** to think carefully about all the possible consequences of a plan or idea, etc, especially so as to reach a conclusion as to its wisdom or value.

■ **think something up** to invent or devise it.

thinking ▷ *noun* **1** the act of using one's mind to produce thoughts. **2** opinion or judgement □ *What is your thinking on this?* ▷ *adj* said of people: using or able to use the mind intelligently and constructively. • **put on one's thinking-cap** *colloq* to think carefully or reflect, especially to try to solve a problem or come up with an idea.

think tank ▷ *noun, colloq* a group of experts who research an area to find solutions to problems and think up new ideas. Ⓒ 1950s.

thinner[1] ▷ *noun* a liquid such as turpentine that is added to paint or varnish to dilute it.

thinner[2] and **thinnest** see under THIN

thin-skinned ▷ *adj* sensitive; easily hurt or upset.

thio- /θaɪoʊ/ or before a vowel **thi-** ▷ *combining form, chem, denoting* the presence of sulphur in a compound. Ⓒ From Greek *theion* sulphur.

thiopentone sodium /θaɪoʊˈpɛntoʊn —/ or (*N Amer*) **thiopental sodium** /θaɪoʊˈpɛntəl —/ ▷ *noun* (formula $CH_{17}NaN_2O_2S$) a yellow-coloured barbiturate drug, used intravenously in solution as a general anaesthetic. Ⓒ 20c.

thiosulphate ▷ *noun, chem* an ester or salt of THIOSULPHURIC ACID, used in photography as a fixing agent. Ⓒ 19c.

thiosulphuric acid ▷ *noun, chem* (formula $H_2S_2O_3$) an unstable acid that readily decomposes and the sodium salt of which is SODIUM THIOSULPHATE.

third /θɜːd/ (often written **3rd**) ▷ *adj* **1** in counting: **a** next after second; **b** last of three. **2** in third position. **3** (**the third**) **a** the third day of the month; **b** *golf* the third hole. **4** in a motor vehicle, etc: referring to the third gear. ▷ *noun* **1** one of three equal parts. Also *as adj* □ *a third share.* **2** a FRACTION equal to one divided by three. (usually written ¹/₃). **3** (*also* **third gear**) the gear which is one faster than second in a gearbox, eg in a motor vehicle. **4** someone who comes third, eg in a race or exam □ *He finished a triumphant third.* **5** a third-class university degree. **6** *music* **a** an interval of three notes (counting inclusively) along the diatonic scale; **b** a note at that interval from another. ▷ *adverb* (*also* **thirdly**) used to introduce the third point in a list. Ⓒ Anglo-Saxon *thridda.*

third class ▷ *noun* **1** the class or rank next (especially in quality) after second. **2** (*also* **third**) a third-class honours degree from a university. ▷ *adj* (**third-class**) belonging or relating to the third class of anything.

third degree ▷ *noun* prolonged and intensive interrogation, usually involving physical and mental intimidation. ▷ *adj* (**third-degree**) *medicine, denoting* the most serious of the three degrees of burning, with damage to the lower layers of skin tissue. Ⓒ Early 20c.

third dimension ▷ *noun* the depth or thickness of an object which distinguishes a solid object from a flat one.

third estate see ESTATE 5

third party ▷ *noun, law* someone who is indirectly involved, or involved by chance, in a legal action or contract, etc between usually two PRINCIPALS. ▷ *adj* (**third-party**) said of insurance: covering damage done by or injury done to someone other than the insured.

third person see under PERSON 3

third-rate ▷ *adj* inferior; sub-standard.

the Third World ▷ *noun* the developing or underdeveloped countries in Africa, Asia and Latin America. Ⓒ 1960s.

thirst /θɜːst/ ▷ *noun* **1** the need to drink, or the feeling of dryness in the mouth that this causes. **2** a strong and eager desire or longing □ *a thirst for knowledge.* ▷ *verb* (***thirsted, thirsting***) *intr* **1** to have a great desire or long for something. **2** *old use* to be thirsty. Ⓒ Anglo-Saxon *thyrstan.*

thirsty ▷ *adj* (***thirstier, thirstiest***) **1** needing or wanting to drink. **2** eager or longing. **3** causing thirst. **4** said of land: lacking in moisture; arid. • **thirstily** *adverb.* • **thirstiness** *noun.*

thirteen /θɜːˈtiːn/ ▷ *noun* **1 a** the cardinal number 13; **b** the quantity that represents this, being one more than twelve, or the sum of ten and three. **2** any symbol for this, eg **13** or **XIII**. **3** the age of thirteen. **4** something, especially a garment or a person, whose size is denoted by the number 13. **5 a** a set or group of thirteen people or things; **b** *rugby league* a team of players. **6** a score of thirteen points. ▷ *adj* **1** totalling thirteen. **2** aged thirteen. Ⓒ Anglo-Saxon *threotine*; see THREE + -TEEN.

thirteenth (often written **13th**) ▷ *adj* **1** in counting: **a** next after twelfth; **b** last of thirteen. **2** in thirteenth position. **3** (**the thirteenth**) **a** the thirteenth day of the month; **b** *golf* the thirteenth hole. ▷ *noun* **1** one of thirteen equal parts. Also *as adj* □ *a thirteenth share.* **2** a FRACTION equal to one divided by thirteen (usually written ¹/₁₃). **3** someone who comes thirteenth, eg in a race or exam □ *He finished a dismal thirteenth.* ▷ *adverb* (*also* **thirteenthly**) used to introduce the thirteenth point in a list. Ⓒ Anglo-Saxon *threoteotha*; see THIRTEEN + -TH.

thirties ▷ *plural noun* **1** the period of time between one's thirtieth and fortieth birthdays □ *Martin is in his thirties.* **2** the range of temperatures between thirty and forty degrees □ *It must be in the thirties today.* **3** the period of time between the thirtieth and fortieth years of a century □ *born in the 30s.* Also *as adj* □ *a thirties hairstyle.*

thirtieth (often written **30th**) ▷ *adj* **1** in counting: **a** next after twenty-ninth; **b** last of thirty. **2** in thirtieth position. ▷ *noun* **1** one of thirty equal parts. Also *as adj* □ *a thirtieth share.* **2** a FRACTION equal to one divided by thirty. (usually written ¹/₃₀). **3** a person coming thirtieth, eg in a race or exam □ *He finished an exhausted thirtieth.* Ⓒ Anglo-Saxon *thritig*, see THIRTY + -TH.

thirty /ˈθɜːtɪ/ ▷ *noun* (***thirties***) **1 a** the cardinal number 30; **b** the quantity that this represents, being one more than twenty-nine, or the product of ten and three. **2** any symbol for this, eg **30** or **XXX**. Also *in compounds, forming adjectives and nouns,* with cardinal numbers between *one* and *nine* □ ***thirty-three.*** **3** the age of thirty. **4** something, especially a garment or person, whose size is denoted by the number 30. **5** a set or group of thirty people or things. **6** a score of thirty points. ▷ *adj* **1** totalling thirty. Also *in compounds, forming adjectives,* with ordinal numbers between *first* and *ninth* □ ***thirty-third.*** **2** aged thirty. See also THIRTIES, THIRTIETH. ⓒ Anglo-Saxon *thritig*; see THREE, -TY.

this /ðɪs/ ▷ *pronoun* (***these*** /ðiːz/) **1** a person, animal, thing or idea already mentioned, about to be mentioned, indicated or otherwise understood from the context. **2** a person, animal, thing or idea which is nearby, especially which is closer to the speaker than someone or something else. **3** the present time or place. **4** an action, event or circumstance □ ***What do you think of this?*** ▷ *adj* **1** being the person, animal, thing or idea which is nearby, especially closer than someone or something else □ ***this book or that one.*** **2** being the person, animal, thing or idea just mentioned, about to be mentioned, indicated or otherwise understood. **3** relating to today, or time in the recent past ending today □ ***this morning*** □ ***I've been ill these last few days.*** **4** *colloq* (used instead of *a* or the for emphasis) being a person, animal, thing or idea not yet mentioned □ ***then I had this bright idea.*** ▷ *adverb* to this (extreme) degree or extent □ ***I didn't think it would be this easy.*** • **this and that** *colloq* various minor unspecified actions or objects, etc. ⓒ Anglo-Saxon *thes.*

thistle /'θɪsəl/ ▷ *noun* **1** any of various annual or perennial plants with deeply indented prickly leaves and usually with globular purple, red or white flowerheads. **2** this plant as the national emblem of Scotland. ⓒ Anglo-Saxon.

thistledown ▷ *noun* the light fluffy hairs attached to thistle seeds.

thither /'ðɪðə(r)/ ▷ *adverb, old use, literary or formal* to or towards that place. ⓒ Anglo-Saxon *thider.*

thixotropy /θɪk'sɒtrəpɪ/ ▷ *noun, physics* the property of certain fluids, especially gels, which show a decrease in viscosity when stirred or shaken, eg non-drip paints. • **thixotropic** *adj.* ⓒ 1920s: from Greek *thixis* action of touching.

tho' /ðoʊ/ ▷ *conj, adverb, poetic* see THOUGH.

thole[1] /θoʊl/ and **tholepin** ▷ *noun* either one of a pair of pins in the side of a boat to keep an oar in place. Compare ROWLOCK. ⓒ Anglo-Saxon.

thole[2] /θoʊl/ ▷ *verb* (***tholed, tholing***) *Scots or old use* to endure or tolerate. ⓒ Anglo-Saxon *tholian* to suffer.

-thon see -ATHON

thong ▷ *noun* **1** a narrow strip of leather used eg to fasten something, or as the lash of a whip. **2** a type of skimpy undergarment or bathing costume, similar to a G-string. **3** (**thongs**) *N Amer, NZ, Austral* flip-flops. ⓒ Anglo-Saxon *thwang.*

thoracic /θɔː'rasɪk, θə-/ ▷ *adj* belonging or relating to, or in the region of, the thorax.

thoracic duct ▷ *noun, anatomy* the main lymphatic vessel running from the pelvic area up to the neck, its main function being the transportation of LYMPH and CHYLE from the smaller lymph vessels to the blood. 18c.

thorax /'θɔːraks/ ▷ *noun* (***thoraxes*** or ***thoraces*** /'θɔːrəsiːz/) **1** *anatomy, zool* in humans and other vertebrates: the part of the body between the head and abdomen; the chest. **2** *entomol* in insects: the middle section that bears the wings and legs. ⓒ 14c: Latin and Greek, meaning 'breastplate'.

thorium /'θɔːrɪəm/ ▷ *noun, chem* (symbol **Th**, atomic number 90) a silvery-grey radioactive metallic element used in X-ray tubes, photoelectric cells and sunlamps. Its isotope thorium-232 is used as a nuclear fuel in breeder reactors. ⓒ 19c: named after Thor, the Norse god of thunder.

thorn ▷ *noun* **1** a hard sharp point sticking out from the stem or branch of certain plants. **2** a shrub bearing thorns, especially a hawthorn. **3** a constant irritation or annoyance □ ***a thorn in one's side.*** **4** the Old English and Icelandic letter þ, pronounced /θ/ or /ð/ in Anglo-Saxon and /θ/ in Icelandic. ⓒ Anglo-Saxon.

thorn apple ▷ *noun* a poisonous plant belonging to the potato family, with a prickly capsule.

thorny ▷ *adj* (***thornier, thorniest***) **1** full of or covered with thorns. **2** difficult; causing trouble or problems □ ***a thorny question.***

thorough /'θʌrə/ ▷ *adj* **1** said of a person: extremely careful and attending to every detail. **2** said of a task, etc: carried out with great care and great attention to detail. **3** complete; absolute □ ***a thorough waste of time.*** • **thoroughly** *adverb.* ⓒ Anglo-Saxon *thurh*; compare THROUGH.

thorough bass see CONTINUO

thoroughbred ▷ *noun* **1** an animal, especially a horse, bred from the best specimens carefully developed by selective breeding over many years. **2** (**Thoroughbred**) a breed of racehorse descended from English mares and Arab stallions of the early 18c. **3** a racehorse belonging to this breed. ▷ *adj* **1** said of an animal, especially a horse: bred from the best specimens; pure-bred. **2** (**Thoroughbred**) belonging or relating to a Thoroughbred. ⓒ 18c.

thoroughfare ▷ *noun* **1** a public road or street. **2 a** a road or path that is open at both ends; **b** the right of passage through this. ⓒ 14c.

thoroughgoing ▷ *adj* **1** extremely thorough. **2** utter; out-and-out □ ***a thoroughgoing villain.*** ⓒ Early 19c.

thorp or **thorpe** /θɔːp/ ▷ *noun, archaic* mainly in place names: a village; a hamlet. ⓒ Anglo-Saxon.

those *plural of* THAT

thou[1] /ðaʊ/ ▷ *pronoun, old use or dialect, also relig* you (singular). ⓒ Anglo-Saxon *thu.*

thou[2] /θaʊ/ ▷ *noun* (***thous*** or ***thou***) **1** *colloq* a thousand. **2** a unit of length equal to one thousandth of an inch. ⓒ 19c.

though /ðoʊ/ ▷ *conj* **1** (*often* **even though**) despite the fact that □ ***I ate it up though I didn't like it.*** **2** if or even if □ ***I wouldn't marry him though he was the richest man in the world.*** **3** and yet; but □ ***We like the new car, though not as much as the old one.*** ▷ *adverb* however; nevertheless. • **as though ...** as if .... See also THO'. ⓒ Anglo-Saxon *theah*: from Norse *tho.*

thought /θɔːt/ ▷ *noun* **1** an idea, concept or opinion. **2** the act of thinking. **3** serious and careful consideration □ ***I'll give some thought to the problem.*** **4** the faculty or power of reasoning. **5** the intellectual ideas which are typical of a particular place, time or group, etc □ ***recent scientific thought.*** **6** intention, expectation or hope □ ***He arrived for work with no thought of redundancy.*** ▷ *verb, past tense and past participle of* THINK. ⓒ Anglo-Saxon *thoht.*

thoughtful ▷ *adj* **1** thinking deeply, or appearing to think deeply; reflective. **2** showing careful or serious thought □ ***a thoughtful reply.*** **3** thinking of other people; considerate □ ***such a thoughtful boy.*** • **thoughtfully** *adverb.* • **thoughtfulness** *noun.* ⓒ 13c.

thoughtless ▷ *adj* **1** not thinking about other people; inconsiderate. **2** showing a lack of careful or serious thought; rash. • **thoughtlessly** *adverb.* • **thoughtlessness** *noun.* ⓒ 16c.

thought transference ▷ *noun* telepathy.

thousand /'θaʊzənd/ ▷ *noun* (***thousands*** or ***thousand***) **1 a** the number 1 000; **b** the quantity that this represents, being the product of ten and one hundred. **2** any symbol for this, eg **1 000** or **M**. **3** anything having 1 000 parts, etc. **4** (*usually* **thousands**) *colloq, often loosely* a large unspecified number or amount. ▷ *adj* numbering 1 000. •

one in a thousand an extremely rare or special person or thing. ◷ Anglo-Saxon *thusend*.

thousandth ▻ *adj* **1** the last of 1 000 people or things. **2** the 1000th position in a sequence of numbers. ▻ *noun* one of 1 000 equal parts.

thrall /θrɔːl/ ▻ *noun* **1** someone who is in the power of another person or thing; a slave. **2** (*also* **thraldom** or **thralldom**) the state of being in the power of another person or thing; slavery □ ***be held in thrall by her beauty.*** ◷ Anglo-Saxon *thræl*.

thrash ▻ *verb* (***thrashes, thrashed, thrashing***) **1** to beat soundly, especially with blows or a whip. **2** to defeat thoroughly or decisively. **3** (*usually* **thrash about** or **around**, *etc*) *intr* to move around violently or wildly. **4** *tr & intr* to thresh (corn, etc). ▻ *noun* **1** an act of thrashing. **2** *colloq* a party. **3** *colloq* THRASH METAL music. • **thrashing** *noun*. ◷ Anglo-Saxon *therscan*.

■ **thrash something out** to discuss (a problem, etc) thoroughly to try to solve it.

thrasher ▻ *noun* any of various N American birds of the mockingbird family. ◷ Early 19c.

thrash metal ▻ *noun* a style of HEAVY METAL music, heavily influenced by punk and played at a very fast speed. ◷ 1980s.

thrawn /θrɔːn/ ▻ *adj, Scots* **1** twisted; misshapen. **2** perverse; sullen. ◷ 15c: an old form of THROWN.

thread /θrɛd/ ▻ *noun* **1** a very thin strand of silk, cotton or wool, especially when several such strands are twisted together for sewing. **2** any naturally formed, very thin strand of fibre, such as that forming a spider's web. **3** anything like a thread in length and narrowness. **4** the projecting spiral ridge round a screw or bolt, or in a nut. **5** a continuous connecting element or theme in a story or argument, etc □ ***I lost the thread of what he was saying.*** **6** a thin seam or vein of ore or coal. ▻ *verb* (***threaded, threading***) **1** to pass a thread through (eg the eye of a needle). **2** to pass (tape or film, etc) into or through something to put it into its correct position. **3** to string something on a thread or length of string. **4** *tr & intr* to make (one's way) carefully (through eg narrow streets or crowded areas). **5** to streak (hair or the sky, etc) with narrow patches of a different colour. **6** to provide (eg a bolt) with a screw thread. • **hang by a thread** to be in a very precarious or dangerous state or position. ◷ Anglo-Saxon.

threadbare ▻ *adj* **1** said of material or clothes: worn thin; shabby. **2** said of a person: wearing such clothes. **3** said of a word or excuse, etc: commonly used and meaningless; hackneyed; feeble. ◷ 14c.

thread mark ▻ *noun* a coloured mark, consisting of silk fibres, incorporated into bank notes to make counterfeiting difficult.

threadworm ▻ *noun* a worm which lives as a parasite in the large intestine of humans, mainly affecting children and causing very few symptoms apart from itching around the anus.

thready ▻ *adj* (***threadier, threadiest***) **1** resembling a thread; thread-like. **2** said of a someone's pulse: barely detectable.

threat /θrɛt/ ▻ *noun* **1** a warning that one is going to or might hurt or punish someone. **2** a sign that something dangerous or unpleasant is or may be about to happen. **3** a source of danger. ◷ Anglo-Saxon, meaning 'affliction'.

threaten ▻ *verb* (***threatened, threatening***) **1** to make or be a threat to someone or something. **2** to give warning of something, usually unpleasant or dangerous. **3** *intr* said of something unpleasant or dangerous: to seem likely to happen □ ***The storm threatened all day.*** • **threatening** *adj*. • **threateningly** *adverb*. ◷ 13c.

three ▻ *noun* **1 a** the cardinal number 3; **b** the quantity that this represents, being one more than two. **2** any symbol for this, eg **3** or **III**. **3** the age of three. **4** something, especially a garment or a person, whose size is denoted by the number 3. **5** the third hour after midnight or midday □ ***Come at three*** □ ***3 o'clock*** □ ***3pm.*** **6** a set or group of three people or things. **7** a playing-card with three pips □ ***He played his three.*** **8** a score of three points. ▻ *adj* **1** totalling three. **2** aged three. ◷ Anglo-Saxon *thrie*.

three-card trick ▻ *noun* a game in which players bet on which of three cards, turned face down and deftly manipulated, is the queen. Also called **find the lady**.

three cheers see under CHEER

three-D and **3-D** ▻ *noun* a three-dimensional effect or appearance. Also *as adj* □ ***3-D glasses.***

three-day event ▻ *noun, showjumping* a competition, usually held over three days, consisting of three sections: dressage, cross-country riding and showjumping.

three-decker ▻ *noun* **1** a ship with three gun-decks. **2** a sandwich made with three layers of bread.

three-dimensional ▻ *adj* **1** having or appearing to have three dimensions, ie height, width and depth. **2** said especially of fictional characters: developed or described in detail and therefore lifelike.

threefold ▻ *adj* **1** equal to three times as much. **2** divided into or consisting of three parts. ▻ *adverb* by three times as much. ◷ Anglo-Saxon.

the Three Kings see under MAGUS

three-legged race ▻ *noun* a race run between pairs of runners who have their adjacent legs tied together.

three-line whip ▻ *noun, politics* in the UK: a written notice, underlined three times to indicate its importance, to politicians belonging to a particular party that they must attend a vote in parliament and vote in the way in which they are instructed. ◷ Early 20c as *three-lined whip*.

threepence /'θrɛpəns, 'θrʌ-, 'θrɪ-/ ▻ *noun, Brit* before decimalization: the sum of three pence.

threepenny /'θrɛpənɪ, 'θrʌ-, 'θrɪ-/ ▻ *adj, Brit historical* **1** worth or costing threepence. **2** having little worth or value.

threepenny bit and **threepenny piece** ▻ *noun, Brit historical* a coin worth threepence.

three-ply ▻ *noun* anything which has three layers or strands bound together, especially wood or wool. ▻ *adj* having three layers or strands.

three-point landing ▻ *noun* an aircraft landing in which all three sets of wheels touch the ground simultaneously.

three-point turn ▻ *noun* a manoeuvre, usually done in three movements, in which a driver turns a motor vehicle using forward and reverse gears, so that it faces the opposite direction.

three-quarter ▻ *adj* being three-quarters of the full amount or length. ▻ *noun, rugby* any of the four players positioned between the full back and the scrum half and stand-off half.

three-ring circus ▻ *noun* **1** a circus with three rings in which simultaneous separate performances are given. **2** a showy or extravagant event. **3** a confusing or bewildering scene or situation.

the three Rs see under R[1]

threescore ▻ *noun, adj, archaic* sixty. • **threescore and ten** seventy. ◷ 14c: see SCORE (noun 5).

threesome ▻ *noun* **1** a group of three. **2** a game played by three people.

the Three Wise Men see under MAGUS

thremmatology /θrɛmə'tɒlədʒɪ/ ▻ *noun* the science of breeding domestic animals and plants. ◷ 19c: from Greek *thremma, thremmatos* nursling.

threnody /ˈθrɛnədɪ, ˈθriː-/ or **threnode** /-noʊd/ ▷ *noun* (*threnodies* or *threnodes*) a song or ode of lamentation, especially for a person's death. • **threnodial** or **threnodic** /-ˈnɒdɪk/ *adj*. • **threnodist** *noun*. ◷ 17c: from Greek *threnos* lament + *oide* song.

threonine /ˈθrɪənaɪn/ ▷ *noun, biochem* an AMINO ACID. ◷ 1930s: changed from Greek *erythron*, from *erythros* red.

thresh ▷ *verb* (*threshes, threshed, threshing*) **1** *tr & intr* to separate the grain or seeds from the stalks of cereal plants by beating. **2** to beat or strike. **3** *intr* (*often* **thresh about** or **around**) to move violently or wildly. ◷ Anglo-Saxon *therscan*.

thresher ▷ *noun* **1** a machine or person that threshes corn, etc. **2** a large shark, native to temperate and tropical seas worldwide, with a long whip-like tail.

threshing floor ▷ *noun* a hard floor on which grain is threshed.

threshing machine ▷ *noun* a machine used to thresh corn.

threshold /ˈθrɛʃhoʊld, ˈθrɛʃoʊld/ ▷ *noun* **1** a piece of wood or stone forming the bottom of a doorway. **2** any doorway or entrance. **3** a starting-point □ *on the threshold of a new career.* **4** the point, stage or level, etc at which something will happen or come into effect, etc. **5** *biol* the minimum intensity of a stimulus (eg pain) that is required to produce a response in a cell or organism, and below which there is no response. **6** *physics* the minimum value of a quantity or variable that must be reached before it has a specified effect. **7** in a pay agreement, etc: a point in the rise of the cost of living at which a wage-increase is prescribed. ◷ Anglo-Saxon *therscold*, from *thersan* to tread or thresh.

threw *past tense of* THROW

thrice /θraɪs/ ▷ *adverb, old use or literary* **1** three times. **2** three times as much. **3** greatly; highly. ◷ Anglo-Saxon *thriwa*.

thrift ▷ *noun* **1** careful spending, use or management of resources, especially money. **2** a wild plant with narrow bluish-green leaves and dense round heads of pink flowers, usually found near the coast. Also called **sea pink**. • **thriftless** *adj* not thrifty. ◷ 16c in these senses: Norse, meaning 'prosperity'.

thrift shop and **thrift store** ▷ *noun, especially US* a shop which sells second-hand goods, with the proceeds usually going to charity. ◷ 1940s.

thrifty ▷ *adj* (*thriftier, thriftiest*) showing thrift; economical; frugal. • **thriftily** *adverb*. • **thriftiness** *noun*.

thrill ▷ *verb* (*thrilled, thrilling*) **1** *tr & intr* to feel or make someone feel a sudden strong glowing, tingling or throbbing sensation, especially of excitement, emotion or pleasure. **2** *tr & intr* to vibrate or quiver. **3** *intr* said of a feeling: to pass quickly with a glowing or tingling sensation □ *Excitement thrilled through her.* ▷ *noun* **1** a sudden tingling feeling of excitement, happiness or pleasure. **2** something, eg an event, which causes such a feeling. **3** a shivering or trembling feeling caused especially by fear, terror or distress. • **thrilled** *adj* excited; delighted. • **thrilling** *adj*. • **thrillingly** *adverb*. ◷ Anglo-Saxon *thyrlian* to pierce.

thriller ▷ *noun* **1** an exciting novel, play or film, usually one involving crime, espionage or adventure. **2** an exciting situation or event □ *The cup final was a real thriller.*

thrips /θrɪps/ ▷ *noun* (*plural* ***thrips***) any of various minute black insects, which feed by sucking sap from plants and thereby often cause damage to crops. ◷ 18c: Greek, meaning 'woodworm'.

thrive ▷ *verb* (*throve* /θroʊv/ or *thrived, thriven* /ˈθrɪvən/ or *thrived, thriving*) *intr* **1** to grow strong and healthy. **2** to prosper or be successful, especially financially. • **thriving** *adj* prosperous; successful. ◷ 13c: from Norse *thrifask*, from *thrifa* to grasp.

thro' or **thro** /θruː/ ▷ *prep, adverb, adj* THROUGH.

throat /θroʊt/ ▷ *noun* **1** the top part of the windpipe. **2** the middle part of the PHARYNX, extending to the LARYNX. **3** the front part of the neck. **4** something that resembles a throat in form or function, especially a narrow passageway or opening. • **cut one's own throat** to cause one's own ruin or downfall. • **cut someone's throat** to kill or injure them by slitting open their throat. • **stick in one's throat** said of an unwelcome or unpalatable thought, etc: to be impossible to say, believe or accept. ◷ Anglo-Saxon.

throaty ▷ *adj* (*throatier, throatiest*) **1** said of a voice: deep and hoarse; husky. **2** *colloq* indicating a sore throat □ *She's feeling a bit throaty.* **3** coming from the throat. • **throatily** *adverb*. • **throatiness** *noun*.

throb ▷ *verb* (*throbbed, throbbing*) *intr* **1** to beat, especially with unusual force, in response to excitement, emotion, exercise or pain. **2** to beat or vibrate with a strong regular rhythm. ▷ *noun* a regular beat; pulse. ◷ 14c: probably imitating the sound.

throe /θroʊ/ ▷ *noun* (*usually* **throes**) a violent pang or spasm, especially during childbirth or before death. • **in the throes of something** involved in a difficult or painful struggle with it; suffering under it □ *in the throes of the storm.* ◷ Anglo-Saxon: from *throwian* to suffer.

> ***throe***
>
> There is sometimes a spelling confusion between **throe** and **throw**.

thrombin /ˈθrɒmbɪn/ ▷ *noun, biochem* an enzyme that causes the blood to clot by converting FIBRINOGEN into FIBRIN, which then forms a network of fibres. ◷ 19c: from *thrombus*.

thrombosis /θrɒmˈboʊsɪs/ ▷ *noun* (*thromboses* /-siːz/) *pathol* damage to the lining of a blood vessel, commonly inflammation, producing a THROMBUS. • **thrombotic** /-ˈbɒtɪk/ *adj*. ◷ 18c: Greek, meaning 'curdling'.

thrombus /ˈθrɒmbəs/ ▷ *noun* (*thrombi* /-baɪ/) *pathol* a blood clot which forms in an artery or vein, blocking blood circulation to surrounding tissues which may die or dislodge causing a STROKE (*noun* 9). ◷ 17c: from Greek *thrombos* clot.

throne /θroʊn/ ▷ *noun* **1** the ceremonial chair of a monarch or bishop, used on official occasions. **2** the office or power of the sovereign □ *come to the throne.* **3** *facetious, colloq* the toilet seat and bowl. **4** *relig* in the traditional medieval hierarchy of nine ranks of angels: an angel of the third-highest rank. Compare SERAPH, CHERUB, DOMINION, VIRTUE, POWER, PRINCIPALITY, ARCHANGEL, ANGEL. ▷ *verb* (*throned, throning*) to place someone on a throne; to enthrone. ◷ 13c: from Greek *thronos* seat.

throng ▷ *noun* a crowd of people or things, especially in a small space; a multitude. ▷ *verb* (*thronged, thronging*) **1** to crowd or fill □ *people thronging the streets.* **2** *intr* to move in a crowd; to come together in great numbers □ *The audience thronged into the theatre.* ◷ Anglo-Saxon *gethrang*.

throstle /ˈθrɒsəl/ ▷ *noun* **1** *poetic* a SONG THRUSH. **2** a machine for drawing, twisting and winding wool or cotton fibres. ◷ Anglo-Saxon.

throttle /ˈθrɒtəl/ ▷ *noun* **1 a** a valve which regulates the amount of fuel or steam, etc supplied to an engine; **b** the pedal or lever that controls this. **2** *now dialect* the throat or windpipe. ▷ *verb* (*throttled, throttling*) **1** to injure or kill by choking or strangling. **2** to prevent something from being said or expressed, etc; to suppress. **3** to control the flow of (fuel, steam, etc to an engine) using a valve. ◷ 14c: perhaps from THROAT.

> ■ **throttle back** or **down** to reduce the speed of an engine by using the throttle.

through or *N Amer* **thru** /θruː/ *prep* **1** going from one side or end of something to the other □ *a road through the village.* **2** from place to place within something; everywhere within it □ *searched through the house.* **3** from the beginning to the end of something □ *read through the magazine.* **4** *N Amer* up to and including □ *Tuesday through Thursday.* **5** because of something □ *lost his job through stupidity.* **6** by way of, means of or agency of something; by □ *related through marriage.* ▻ *adverb* **1** into and out of; from one side or end to the other □ *go straight through.* **2** from the beginning to the end. **3** into a position of having completed, especially successfully □ *sat the exam again and got through.* **4** to the core; completely □ *soaked through.* **5** *Brit* in or into communication by telephone □ *put the caller through.* ▻ *adj* **1** said of a journey, route, train or ticket, etc: going or allowing one to go all the way to one's destination without requiring a change of line or train, etc or a new ticket. **2** said of traffic: passing straight through an area or town, etc without stopping. **3** going from one surface, side or end to another □ *a through road.* • **be through** to have no further prospects or intentions in some regard □ *He is through as a businessman.* • **be through with someone** to have no more to do with them. • **be through with something** to have finished or completed it. • **through and through** completely. See also THRO'. Ⓒ Anglo-Saxon *thurh*; compare THOROUGH.

throughout /θruːˈaʊt/ ▻ *prep* **1** in all parts of something □ *We have decorated throughout the house.* **2** during the whole of something □ *They chattered throughout the film.* ▻ *adverb* **1** in every part; everywhere □ *a house with carpets throughout.* **2** during the whole time □ *remain friends throughout.*

throughput ▻ *noun* the amount of material put through a process, especially a computer or manufacturing process.

throve *a past tense of* THRIVE

throw /θroʊ/ ▻ *verb* (***threw*** /θruː/, ***thrown*** /θroʊn/, ***throwing***) **1** *tr & intr* to propel or hurl through the air with force, especially with a rapid forward movement of the hand and arm. **2** to move or hurl into a specified position, especially suddenly or violently. **3** to put into a specified condition, especially suddenly □ *threw them into confusion.* **4** to direct, cast or emit □ *a candle throwing shadows on the wall* □ *throw a glance.* **5** *colloq* to puzzle or confuse. **6** said of a horse: to make (its rider) fall off. **7** *wrestling, judo* to bring (one's opponent) to the ground. **8** to move (a switch or lever) so as to operate a mechanism. **9** to make (pottery) on a potter's wheel. **10** *colloq* to lose (a contest) deliberately, especially in return for a bribe. **11 a** *tr & intr* to roll (dice) on to a flat surface; **b** to obtain (a specified number) by throwing dice. **12** to have or suffer □ *throw a tantrum.* **13** to give (a party). **14** to deliver (a punch). **15** to cause (one's voice) to appear to come from elsewhere. ▻ *noun* **1** an act of throwing or instance of being thrown. **2** the distance something is thrown. **3** *colloq* an article, item or turn, etc □ *sell them at £2 a throw.* **4** *geol* the amount by which a fault in a stratum is displaced vertically. **5** a piece of fabric that is used to cover a piece of furniture, eg a settee, bed, etc, by placing it loosely over the furniture. • **throw in one's hand** *colloq* to give up or abandon what one is doing. • **throw in the towel** or **sponge** see under TOWEL. • **throw oneself into something** to begin doing it with great energy or enthusiasm. • **throw oneself on something** to rely or depend on (someone's goodwill, sympathies or mercy, etc). • **throw something open 1** to open it suddenly and widely. **2** to allow anyone to enter or take part in (a debate, etc). • **throw up one's hands** to raise them in the air quickly, usually as a sign of despair or horror, etc. Ⓒ Anglo-Saxon *thrawan* to twist.

■ **throw something about** or **around** to throw it in various directions; to scatter it.

■ **throw something away 1** to discard it or get rid of it. **2** to fail to take advantage of it; to waste or lose it through lack of care □ *He threw away his chance to become champion.* See also THROWAWAY.

■ **throw someone** or **something back** to delay or hinder their or its progress to a specified extent □ *The problem threw us back six months.*

■ **throw someone back on something** to force them to rely on it.

■ **throw back to something** to revert to some earlier, ancestral character or type. See also THROWBACK.

■ **throw something in 1** to include or add it as a gift or as part of a deal at no extra cost. **2** to contribute (a remark) to a discussion, especially casually. **3** (*also* **throw in**) *sport* to return (the ball) to play by throwing it in from the sideline. See also THROW-IN.

■ **throw something off 1** to get rid of it □ *throw off a cold.* **2** to write or say it in an offhand or careless way. **3** to remove (clothing) hurriedly.

■ **throw something on** to put on (clothing) hurriedly.

■ **throw someone out 1** to expel them. **2** to confuse or disconcert them.

■ **throw something out 1** to get rid of it; to reject or dismiss it. **2** to say it in a casual or offhand manner. **3** to cause it to extend or project, especially from a main body □ *throw out a new wing.*

■ **throw someone over** to leave or abandon them, especially a lover.

■ **throw people together** said of circumstances, etc: to bring them into contact by chance.

■ **throw something together** to construct it hurriedly or temporarily.

■ **throw up** *colloq* to vomit.

■ **throw something up 1** to give it up or abandon it. **2** to build or erect it hurriedly. **3** to bring up (eg a meal) by vomiting.

throw

There is sometimes a spelling confusion between **throw** and **throe**.

throwaway ▻ *adj* **1** meant to be thrown away after use. **2** said or done casually or carelessly □ *throwaway comments.*

throwback ▻ *noun* **1** someone or something that reverts back to earlier or ancestral characteristics □ *Mark? He's just a Fifties throwback.* **2** an instance of this. See also THROW BACK TO SOMETHING at THROW.

throw-in ▻ *noun, sport* in football and basketball, etc: an act of throwing the ball back into play from a sideline. See also THROW SOMETHING IN at THROW.

thru see THROUGH

thrum¹ ▻ *verb* (***thrummed, thrumming***) **1** *tr & intr* to strum idly on (a stringed instrument). **2** *intr* to drum or tap with the fingers. **3** *intr* to hum monotonously. ▻ *noun* repetitive strumming, or the sound of this. Ⓒ 16c: imitating the sound.

thrum² ▻ *noun* **1 a** an unwoven end of thread remaining on a loom when the woven fabric has been cut away; **b** a group of such threads. **2** any loose thread or fringe. ▻ *verb* (***thrummed, thrumming***) to furnish, cover or fringe something with thrums. Ⓒ 14c: Anglo-Saxon, as a combining form.

thrush¹ ▻ *noun* (***thrushes***) any of several common small or medium-sized songbirds, typically having brown feathers and a spotted chest. Ⓒ Anglo-Saxon *thrysce.*

thrush² ▻ *noun* **1** a fungal infection, especially common in children, which causes white blisters in the mouth, throat and lips. **2** a similar infection in the vagina. **3** an inflammation affecting the sole of a horse's hoof. Also called **aphtha**. ◷ 17c.

thrust ▷ *verb* (***thrust, thrusting***) **1** to push suddenly and violently. **2** (*usually* **thrust something on** or **upon someone**) to force them to accept it; to impose it on them. **3** (*usually* **thrust into** or **through**, *etc*) to force one's way. ▷ *noun* **1** a sudden or violent movement forward; a push or lunge. **2** *aeronautics* the force produced by a jet or rocket engine that propels an aircraft or rocket forward. **3** an attack or lunge with a pointed weapon; a stab. **4** an attack, especially by a military force on the enemy's territory, or a verbal attack on a person. **5** the strong continuous pressure that one part of an object exerts against another. **6** the main theme, message or gist, eg of an argument. **7** determination; drive. ◷ 12c: from Norse *thrysta*.

■ **thrust at something** to make a lunge at it.

■ **thrust through something** to pierce or stab it.

thrust stage ▷ *noun, theat* a stage that extends beyond the proscenium arch into the auditorium. ◷ 1960s.

thud ▷ *noun* a dull sound like that of something heavy falling to the ground. ▷ *verb* (***thudded, thudding***) *intr* to move or fall with a thud. ◷ Anglo-Saxon *thyddan* to strike.

thug ▷ *noun* **1** a violent or brutal person. **2** (**Thug**) *historical* a member of a religious organization of robbers and murderers in India. • **thuggery** *noun*. • **thuggish** *adj*. ◷ 19c: from Hindi *thag* 'thief' or 'cheat'.

thulium /ˈθjuːlɪəm, ˈθuː-/ ▷ *noun, chem* (symbol **Tm**, atomic number 69) a soft silvery-white metallic element that is a member of the LANTHANIDE series and is used as a source of X-rays and gamma rays. ◷ 19c: from Latin *Thule*, a northern region thought to be the most northerly in the world.

thumb /θʌm/ ▷ *noun* **1** in humans: the two-boned digit on the inner side of the hand, set lower than and at a different angle to the other four digits. **2** the part of a glove or mitten that covers this digit. **3** in other animals: the digit corresponding to the human thumb. ▷ *verb* (***thumbed, thumbing***) **1** (*often* **thumb through something**) *tr & intr* to turn over the pages of (a book or magazine, etc) to glance at the contents. **2** to smudge or wear something with the thumb. **3** (*usually* **thumb a lift** or **ride**) *tr & intr* to hitchhike □ ***I thumbed to London last week.*** • **all thumbs** awkward and clumsy. • **rule of thumb** see separate entry. • **thumb one's nose** to cock a snook (see under SNOOK[2]). • **thumbs down** a sign indicating failure, rejection or disapproval. • **thumbs up** a sign indicating success, best wishes for success, satisfaction or approval. • **under someone's thumb** completely controlled or dominated by them. ◷ Anglo-Saxon *thuma*.

thumb index ▷ *noun* a series of notches, each with a letter or word in them, cut into the outer edges of the pages of a book, etc to enable quick reference. ▷ *verb* (**thumb-index**) to provide (a book, etc) with a thumb index. ◷ Early 20c.

thumb nail ▷ *noun* **1** the nail on the thumb. **2** *as adj* brief and concise □ ***a thumb-nail sketch.***

thumbscrew ▷ *noun* **1** *historical* an instrument of torture which crushes the thumbs. **2** a type of screw with a head comprising two raised and flattened parts, which enable it to be turned using the thumb and forefinger.

thumbtack ▷ *noun, N Amer* a drawing-pin.

thump /θʌmp/ ▷ *noun* a heavy blow, or the dull sound of a blow. ▷ *verb* (***thumped, thumping***) **1** *tr & intr* to beat or strike with dull-sounding heavy blows. **2** *intr* to throb or beat violently. **3** (*also* **thump something out**) to play (a tune), especially on a piano, by pounding heavily on the keys. **4** (*usually* **thump along** or **around**, *etc*) to move with heavy pounding steps. ◷ 16c: imitating the sound.

thumping *colloq* ▷ *adj* very big □ ***a thumping lie.*** ▷ *adverb* very □ ***a pair of thumping great boots.*** ◷ 16c.

thunder /ˈθʌndə(r)/ ▷ *noun* **1** a deep rumbling or loud cracking sound heard after a flash of lightning, due to the lightning causing gases in the atmosphere to expand suddenly. **2** a loud deep rumbling noise. ▷ *verb* (***thundered, thundering***) **1** *intr* said of thunder: to sound or rumble. **2** *intr* to make a noise like thunder while moving □ ***tanks thundering over a bridge.*** **3** to say or utter something in a loud, often aggressive, voice. • **thundery** *adj*. • **steal someone's thunder** see under STEAL. ◷ Anglo-Saxon *thunor*.

thunderbolt ▷ *noun* **1** a flash of lightning coming simultaneously with a crash of thunder. **2** a sudden and unexpected event. **3** a supposed destructive stone or missile, etc falling to earth in a flash of lightning.

thunderclap ▷ *noun* **1** a sudden crash of thunder. **2** something startling or unexpected.

thundercloud ▷ *noun* a large cloud charged with electricity which produces thunder and lightning.

thunderflash ▷ *noun* a container, such as a blank shell, filled with explosive powder, which makes a flash and a loud explosion when detonated.

thunderhead ▷ *noun, chiefly US* a distinctively rounded mass of CUMULUS cloud projecting above the general cloud mass and usually the precursor of a storm.

thundering *colloq* ▷ *adj* very great □ ***a thundering idiot.*** ▷ *adverb* very □ ***a thundering great error.*** ◷ 16c.

thunderous ▷ *adj* **1** like thunder, especially in being very loud □ ***thunderous applause.*** **2** threatening or violent. • **thunderously** *adverb*. ◷ 16c.

thunderstorm ▷ *noun* a storm with thunder and lightning, usually accompanied by heavy rain.

thunderstruck ▷ *adj* completely overcome by surprise; astonished.

thundery see under THUNDER

Thur. or **Thurs.** ▷ *abbreviation* Thursday. Also written **Th.**

thurible see CENSER

Thursday /ˈθɜːzdɪ, -deɪ/ ▷ *noun* (abbreviation **Th.**, **Thur.**, **Thurs.**) the fifth day of the week. ◷ Anglo-Saxon *thunresdæg* the day of Thunor (the god of thunder).

thus /ðʌs/ ▷ *adverb* **1** in the way or manner shown or mentioned; in this manner. **2** to this degree, amount or distance □ ***thus far.*** **3** therefore; accordingly. ◷ Anglo-Saxon.

thwack ▷ *noun* **a** a blow with something flat; **b** the noise made by it. ▷ *verb* (***thwacked, thwacking***) to strike someone or something with such a noise. ◷ 16c: imitating the sound.

thwart /θwɔːt/ ▷ *verb* (***thwarted, thwarting***) to prevent or hinder someone or something. ▷ *noun* a seat for a rower that lies across a boat. ◷ 13c: from Norse *thvert* across.

thy /ðaɪ/ ▷ *adj, old use or dialect, also relig* belonging or relating to THEE. ◷ 12c: from THINE.

thylacine see under TASMANIAN WOLF

thyme /taɪm/ ▷ *noun* any of various herbs and shrubs, especially those whose aromatic-smelling leaves are used to season food. ◷ 14c: from French *thym*, from Greek *thymon*.

thymine /ˈθaɪmiːn/ ▷ *noun, biochem* a PYRIMIDINE derivative, which is one of the four bases found in the NUCLEIC ACID DNA. See also ADENINE, CYTOSINE, GUANINE. ◷ Late 19c: from Greek *thymos* thymus gland.

thymol /ˈθaɪmɒl/ ▷ *noun* a white crystalline compound obtained from THYME and used as an antiseptic. ◷ 19c.

thymus /ˈθaɪməs/ ▷ *noun* (***thymuses*** or ***thymi*** /-maɪ/) *anatomy* (*in full* **thymus gland**) in vertebrates: a gland just above the heart, which plays an important role in the development of the immune response to invasion of the body by PATHOGENs. ⓒ 17c: Latin, from Greek *thymos*.

thyroid /ˈθaɪərɔɪd/ ▷ *noun, physiol* (*in full* **thyroid gland**) in vertebrates: a shield-shaped gland situated in the neck, in front of the trachea, which secretes several hormones (including THYROXINE) which control growth, development and metabolic rate. See also ADAM'S APPLE. ▷ *adj* **1** belonging or relating to the thyroid gland or THYROID CARTILAGE. **2** shield-shaped. ⓒ 18c: from Greek *thyreoeides* shield-shaped.

thyroid cartilage ▷ *noun, anatomy* the principal cartilage in the larynx, which projects in men to form the Adam's apple.

thyroid hormone ▷ *noun, physiol* any of various hormones secreted by the thyroid gland that are required for normal mental and physical development, and for the growth and functioning of the body tissues.

thyroxine /θaɪˈrɒksiːn/ or **thyroxin** /-sɪn/ ▷ *noun* **1** *physiol* the principal hormone secreted by the THYROID GLAND. **2** a synthetic form of this compound, administered in order to treat underactivity of the thyroid gland.

thyself /ðaɪˈsɛlf/ ▷ *pronoun, old use or dialect, relig* **1** the reflexive form of *thou* and *thee*. **2** used for emphasis.

Ti ▷ *symbol, chem* titanium.

ti see TE

tiara /tɪˈɑːrə/ ▷ *noun* (*tiaras*) **1** a jewelled head-ornament similar to a crown, worn by women. **2** the pope's three-tiered crown. **3** *historical* a type of high headdress worn by the ancient Persians. ⓒ 16c: Latin, from Greek.

Tibetan /tɪˈbɛtən/ ▷ *adj* belonging or relating to Tibet, an autonomous region in SW China, or to its inhabitants or their language. ▷ *noun* **1** a citizen or inhabitant of, or person born in, Tibet. **2** the official language of Tibet. ⓒ 18c.

tibia /ˈtɪbɪə/ ▷ *noun* (*tibias* or *tibiae* /ˈtɪbiiː/) **1** *anatomy* **a** in the human skeleton: the inner and usually larger of the two bones between the knee and ankle; the shinbone; **b** the corresponding bone in other vertebrates. **2** *entomol* the fourth joint of an insect's leg. Compare FIBULA. • **tibial** *adj*. ⓒ 18c: Latin, meaning 'shinbone'.

tic ▷ *noun* a habitual nervous involuntary movement or twitch of a muscle, especially of the face. ⓒ 19c: French.

tic douloureux /tɪkduːləˈruː/ ▷ *noun, pathol* a disorder of the TRIGEMINAL NERVE, causing sudden attacks of pain in the face and forehead. Also called **trigeminal neuralgia**. ⓒ 19c: French, meaning 'painful twitching'.

tick¹ ▷ *noun* **1** a regular tapping or clicking sound, such as that made by a watch or clock. **2** *Brit colloq* a moment □ *Wait a tick.* **3** a small mark, usually a downward-sloping line with the bottom part bent upwards, used to show that something is correct, to mark off items on a list once they are dealt with, etc. Compare CROSS *noun* 1. ▷ *verb* (*ticked, ticking*) **1** *intr* said eg of a clock: to make a tick or ticks. **2** (*usually* **tick away**) *intr* said of time: to pass steadily. **3** to mark it with a written tick. *N Amer equivalent* CHECK. **4** (*often* **tick something off**) to count something (eg an item on a list) by marking a tick beside it. • **what makes someone tick** *colloq* their underlying character and motivation. ⓒ 15c *tek* a little touch.

■ **tick someone off** *colloq* to scold them.

■ **tick over 1** to function or work quietly and smoothly at a relatively gentle or moderate rate. **2** said of an engine: to idle.

tick² ▷ *noun* **1** any of several bloodsucking spider-like insects that live on the skin of some animals, eg dogs and cattle. **2** any of several bloodsucking flies that live on the skins of eg sheep and birds. ⓒ Anglo-Saxon *ticia*.

tick³ ▷ *noun* **1** the strong cover of a mattress, pillow or bolster. **2** short for TICKING. ⓒ 15c: from Greek *theke* case.

tick⁴ ▷ *noun, Brit colloq* credit □ *buy it on tick.* ⓒ 17c: a shortening of TICKET.

ticker ▷ *noun* **1** anything that ticks, eg a watch. **2** *colloq* the heart.

ticker tape ▷ *noun* **1** continuous paper tape with messages, especially up-to-date share prices, printed by a telegraph instrument. **2** this type of paper thrown from windows to welcome or meet a famous person.

ticket /ˈtɪkɪt/ ▷ *noun* **1** a printed piece of paper or card which shows that the holder has paid a fare, eg for travel on a bus or train, or for admission, eg to a theatre or cinema, or has the right to use certain services, eg a library. **2** an official notice issued to someone who has committed a motor offence, such as speeding or parking illegally. **3** a tag or label, especially one that shows the price and size, etc of the item to which it is attached. **4** *N Amer* a list of candidates put up for election by a political party. **5** the policies of a particular political party □ *was elected on the Republican ticket.* **6** *slang* a certificate discharging a soldier from the army. **7** *slang* a licence or permit, especially one allowing the holder to work as a ship's master or pilot. **8** *colloq* exactly what is required, proper or best □ *just the ticket.* ▷ *verb* (*ticketed, ticketing*) to give or attach a ticket or label to someone or something. ⓒ 17c: from French *estiquier* to attach or stick.

ticket collector ▷ *noun* someone whose job is to inspect tickets, especially those of people travelling on trains.

ticket day ▷ *noun, stock exchange* the day before SETTLING DAY, when the names of buyers are given to stockbrokers.

ticket office ▷ *noun* a kiosk, etc where tickets for shows or travel, etc can be purchased.

ticket of leave ▷ *noun, historical* a pass issued to convicts in Australia as a reward for good behaviour, in the form of parole which could be issued for four, six or eight years, depending on the length of the sentence and subject to certain restrictions.

ticket tout see TOUT (*noun* 1)

tickety-boo /tɪkɪtɪˈbuː/ ▷ *adj, dated Brit colloq* fine; satisfactory. ⓒ 1930s.

ticking ▷ *noun* a strong coarse, usually striped, cotton fabric used to make mattresses, pillows and bolsters, etc. Often shortened to **tick**.

ticking-off ▷ *noun, Brit colloq* a mild scolding. See also TICK SOMEONE OFF at TICK¹.

tickle /ˈtɪkəl/ ▷ *verb* (*tickled, tickling*) **1** to touch (a person or part of the body) lightly and so as to provoke a tingling or light prickling sensation or laughter. **2** *intr* said of a part of the body: to feel a tingling or light prickling sensation. **3** *colloq* to amuse or entertain. **4** to catch (a fish, especially a trout) by rubbing it gently underneath so that it moves backwards into one's hands. ▷ *noun* **1** an act of tickling. **2** a tingling or light prickling sensation. • **tickled pink** or **tickled to death** *colloq* very pleased or amused. • **tickle someone's fancy** to attract or amuse them in some way. ⓒ 14c.

ticklish ▷ *adj* **1** sensitive to tickling. **2** said of a problem, etc: difficult to manage or deal with; needing careful handling. • **ticklishly** *adverb*. • **ticklishness** *noun*.

tick-tack ▷ *noun* a system of communication based on hand signals, used by bookmakers at a racecourse to exchange information about the odds they are offering. ⓒ Late 19c slang.

tick-tack-toe ▷ *noun, N Amer* noughts and crosses. ⓒ 19c.

tidal /ˈtaɪdəl/ ▷ *adj* belonging or relating to, or affected by, tides. • **tidally** *adverb*.

tidal power ▷ *noun* **1** the generation of electricity by harnessing the energy of tidal flows. **2** the energy itself.

tidal wave ▷ *noun* **1** *non-technical* a popular name for a TSUNAMI. **2** *loosely* an unusually large ocean wave.

tidbit /'tɪdbɪt/ ▷ *noun, N Amer* a titbit.

tiddler /'tɪdlə(r)/ ▷ *noun, Brit colloq* **1** a small fish, especially a stickleback or a minnow. **2** any small person or thing. ◷ 19c: perhaps from *tittlebat* a childish form of STICKLEBACK and influenced by TIDDLY[2].

tiddly[1] /'tɪdlɪ/ ▷ *adj* (***tiddlier***, ***tiddliest***) *Brit colloq* slightly drunk. ◷ 19c meaning 'a drink'; early 20c as *adj*.

tiddly[2] /'tɪdlɪ/ ▷ *noun* (***tiddlier***, ***tiddliest***) *Brit colloq* little. ◷ 19c.

tiddlywinks /'tɪdlɪwɪŋks/ ▷ *singular noun* a game in which players try to flick small flat discs into a cup using larger discs. ◷ 19c: perhaps related to TIDDLY[1].

tide ▷ *noun* **1** the twice-daily rise and fall of the water level in the oceans and seas, caused by the gravitational pull of the Sun and especially the Moon. See also NEAP TIDE, SPRING TIDE. **2** the level of the water, especially the sea, as affected by this □ *high tide*. **3** a sudden or marked trend □ *the tide of public opinion*. **4** *in compounds* a time or season, especially of some festival □ *Whitsuntide*. ● *verb* (***tided***, ***tiding***) *intr* to drift with or be carried on the tide. ◷ Anglo-Saxon *tid*.

■ **tide someone over** to help them deal with a problem or difficult situation, etc for a time, until the problem, etc is resolved.

tidemark ▷ *noun* **1** a mark showing the highest level that the tide has reached or usually reaches. **2** *Brit colloq* a mark left on a bath which shows how high it was filled. **3** *Brit colloq* a dirty mark on the skin which shows the limit of washing.

tide table ▷ *noun* a table that gives the times of high and low tides at a particular place.

tidewater ▷ *noun* **1** water brought in by the tides. **2** *US* water affected by the tides.

tideway ▷ *noun* a channel in which a tide runs, especially that part of a river which has a tide.

tidings /'taɪdɪŋz/ ▷ *plural noun, old use* news. ◷ Anglo-Saxon *tidung*.

tidy /'taɪdɪ/ ▷ *adj* (***tidier***, ***tidiest***) **1** neat and in good order. **2** methodical. **3** *colloq* large; considerable □ *a tidy sum of money*. ▷ *noun* (***tidies***) **1** *often in compounds* a receptacle for odds and ends, especially one in a kitchen unit for waste scraps or on a desk for pens, paper-clips, etc □ *a sink-tidy* □ *a desk-tidy*. **2** *especially US* an ornamental cover for a chair-back. ▷ *verb* (***tidies***, ***tidied***, ***tidying***) (*also* **tidy something away** or **up**) to make it neat; to put things away or arrange them neatly. ● **tidily** *adverb*. ● **tidiness** *noun*. ◷ 18c in *adj* sense 1; 14c, meaning 'timely'.

tie /taɪ/ ▷ *verb* (***tied***, ***tying***) **1** to fasten with a string, ribbon or rope, etc. **2** to make (string, ribbon, etc) into a bow or knot, or to make a bow or knot in something. **3** *intr* to be fastened with a knot, string or ribbon, etc □ *a dress that ties at the back*. **4** (*usually* **tie with someone**) *intr* to have the same score or final position as another (competitor or entrant) in a game or contest, etc. **5** (*often* **tie someone down**) to limit or restrict the way they lead their life. **6** *music* **a** to mark (notes of the same pitch) with a curved line showing that they are to be played as a continuous sound rather than individually; **b** to play (notes of the same pitch) in this way. ▷ *noun* **1** a narrow strip of material worn, especially by men, round the neck under a shirt collar and tied in a knot or bow at the front. **2** a strip of ribbon, rope, cord or chain, etc for binding and fastening. **3** something that limits or restricts one's freedom. **4** a link or bond □ *ties of friendship*. **5 a** a match or competition, etc in which the result is an equal score for both sides; **b** the score or result achieved. **6** *Brit* a game or match to be played, especially in a knockout competition □ *The third round ties were all postponed*. **7** a rod or beam holding parts of a structure together. **8** *music* a curved line above two or more notes of the same pitch showing that they are to be played as a continuous sound rather than individually. **9** *N Amer* a railway sleeper. ● **tie someone in knots** and **tie the knot** see under KNOT1. ◷ Anglo-Saxon *tiegan*.

■ **tie someone down** to bind them to a decision or commitment.

■ **tie in** or **up with something** to be in or be brought into connection with it; to correspond or be made to correspond with it. See also TIE-IN.

■ **tie up** to moor or dock.

■ **tie someone** or **something up 1** to bind them securely. **2** to keep them busy. **3** to block or restrict their progress, movement or operation.

■ **tie something up 1** to attach and fasten it securely with string, especially to make it into a parcel with string. **2** to invest money or funds, etc so that it cannot be used for other purposes.

■ **tie up with something** see *tie in with something* above.

tie beam ▷ *noun, archit* a horizontal beam connecting the lower ends of rafters so that they do not move apart.

tie-break or **tie-breaker** ▷ *noun* an extra game, series of games or question that decides which of the competitors or teams is to win a match which has ended in a draw.

tie clip and **tie clasp** ▷ *noun* an ornamental clasp fixed to a tie to hold it in place.

tied cottage ▷ *noun, Brit* a cottage on an employer's land which is rented out to employees.

tied house ▷ *noun, Brit* a public house which may only sell the beer of a particular brewery.

tie-dye ▷ *noun* (*also* **tie-dyeing**) a technique of dyeing fabrics in which parts of the fabric are tied tightly to stop them absorbing the dye, which produces a kind of swirly pattern. ▷ *verb* to produce such patterns. ● **tie-dyed** *adj*. ◷ Early 20c.

tie-in ▷ *noun* (***tie-ins***) **1** a connection or link. **2** something which is presented at the same time as something else, especially a book which is published to coincide with a film or TV programme. See also TIE IN at TIE.

tie-pin ▷ *noun* an ornamental pin fixed to a tie to hold it in place.

tier /tɪə(r)/ ▷ *noun* any series of levels, ranks or grades, etc placed one above the other, eg of seats in a theatre. ▷ *verb* (***tiered***, ***tiering***) to place in tiers. ◷ 16c: from French *tire* sequence.

tierce /tɪəs/ ▷ *noun* **1** TERCE. **2** a sequence of three cards of the same suit. **3** a former measure of wine, equal to one-third of a PIPE[2]. **4** *music* the note two octaves and a third above a given note. **5** *fencing* **a** the third of eight parrying positions; **b** the corresponding thrust. ◷ 14c: from French *tiers*, from Latin *tertius* third.

tiercel see TERCEL

tiff ▷ *noun* **1** a slight petty quarrel. **2** a fit of bad temper. ▷ *verb* (***tiffed***, ***tiffing***) *intr* to have a tiff. ◷ 18c.

tiffany /'tɪfənɪ/ ▷ *noun* (***tiffanies***) a sheer silk-like gauze. ◷ 17c: from French *tifinie*, from Latin *theophania* Epiphany.

tiffin /'tɪfɪn/ ▷ *noun, Anglo-Indian* a light midday meal, especially as taken by members of the British Raj in India. ◷ 18c: from obsolete *tiff* to sip.

tig see under TAG[2]

tiger /'taɪgə(r)/ ▷ *noun* **1** a carnivorous animal, the largest member of the cat family, native to Asia and typically having a fawn or reddish coat, with black or brownish-black transverse stripes. See also TIGRESS. **2** a fierce cruel person. **3** *econ* a tiger economy. ▷ *adj, econ* said of a country's economy, originally of the economies of some East-Asian countries: having the potential to perform strongly. • **tigerish** *adj*. • **tigerishly** *adverb*. ◎ 13c: from French *tigre*, from Greek *tigris*.

tiger lily ▷ *noun* a tall lily, native to China and Japan, with orange petals spotted with black, widely cultivated as an ornamental garden plant.

tiger moth ▷ *noun* any of various relatively large moths, with a stout hairy body and brightly coloured wings marked with bold patterns.

tiger shark ▷ *noun* a voracious striped shark, found in the Indian Ocean.

tiger snake ▷ *noun* a deadly Australian snake, brown in colour with black crossbands.

tight /taɪt/ ▷ *adj* (***tighter, tightest***) **1** fitting very or too closely. **2** stretched so as not to be loose; tense; taut. **3** fixed or held firmly in place □ ***a tight knot***. **4** *usually in compounds* made so as not to let air or water, etc pass in or out □ ***watertight***. **5** difficult or posing problems □ ***in a tight spot***. **6** strictly and carefully controlled. **7** said of a contest or match: closely or evenly fought. **8** said of a schedule or timetable, etc: not allowing much time. **9** *colloq* mean; miserly. **10** *colloq* drunk. **11** said of money or some commodity: in short supply; difficult to obtain. **12** said of a band or team: that plays together in a disciplined way, making very few mistakes. ▷ *adverb* tightly; soundly; completely □ ***sleep tight***. • **tightly** *adverb*. • **tightness** *noun*. • **run a tight ship** to be in control of an efficient well-run organization or group and ensure that it remains so. ◎ 14c: probably an alteration of *thight*, from Norse *thettr*.

tighten ▷ *verb* (***tightened, tightening***) *tr & intr* to make or become tight or tighter. • **tighten one's belt** *colloq* to reduce one's spending and live more economically. • **tighten the screws** to increase the pressure on someone to do something. ◎ 18c.

tight-fisted ▷ *adj* mean and ungenerous with money.

tight-knit or **tightly-knit** ▷ *adj* closely organized or united.

tight-lipped ▷ *adj* with the lips firmly closed in determination to say or reveal nothing; uncommunicative.

tightrope ▷ *noun* **1** a tightly stretched rope or wire on which acrobats balance. **2** a difficult situation which requires careful handling if a potential disaster is to be avoided.

tights ▷ *plural noun* a close-fitting, usually nylon or woollen, garment which covers the feet, legs and body up to the waist, and is worn usually by women, as well as dancers and acrobats, etc.

tightwad ▷ *noun, colloq, especially N Amer* a skinflint; a miser. ◎ Early 20c.

tigon /'taɪgɒn/ or **tiglon** /'taɪglɒn/ ▷ *noun* the offspring of a tiger and lioness. ◎ 1920s; 1940s *tiglon*.

tigress /'taɪgrɪs/ ▷ *noun* (***tigresses***) **1** a female tiger. **2** a fierce or passionate woman.

tike see TYKE

tikka /'tiːkə, 'tɪkə/ ▷ *noun* (***tikkas***) in Indian cookery: meat that is marinated in yoghurt and spices and cooked in a clay oven. ◎ 1950s: Hindi.

tilde /'tɪldə, -deɪ/ ▷ *noun* a mark (~) placed over *n* in Spanish to show that it is pronounced *ny* and over *a* and *o* in Portuguese to show they are nasalized. ◎ 19c: Spanish, from Latin *titulus* TITLE.

tile ▷ *noun* **1** a flat thin slab of fired clay, or a similar one of cork or linoleum, used to cover roofs, floors and walls, etc. **2** a tube-shaped piece of clay used for building drains. **3** a small flat rectangular piece used in some games. ▷ *verb* (***tiled, tiling***) to cover something with tiles. • **tiler** *noun*. • **tiling** *noun*. • **on the tiles** having a wild time socially, usually including a lot of drinking and dancing. ◎ Anglo-Saxon *tigele*: from Latin *tegula*, from *tegere* to cover.

till¹ ▷ *prep* up to the time of □ ***wait till tomorrow***. ▷ *conj* up to the time when □ ***go on till you reach the station***. See also UNTIL. ◎ Anglo-Saxon *til*.

till² ▷ *noun* a container or drawer in which money taken from customers is put, now usually part of a CASH REGISTER. ◎ 17c; 15c meaning 'a drawer for valuables'.

till³ ▷ *verb* (***tilled, tilling***) to prepare and cultivate (land) for the growing of crops. • **tillable** *adj* arable. • **tiller** *noun*. ◎ Anglo-Saxon *tilian* to strive.

till⁴ ▷ *noun* stiff impervious clay; boulder clay. ◎ 17c.

tillage /'tɪlɪdʒ/ ▷ *noun* **1** the preparing and cultivating of land for crops. **2** land which has been tilled.

tiller¹ ▷ *noun* the lever used to turn the rudder of a boat. ◎ 14c: from French *telier* weaver's beam.

tiller² ▷ *noun* **1** a sapling. **2** a shoot growing from the bottom of the original stalk. **3** a SUCKER (*noun* 6). ◎ Anglo-Saxon *telgor* twig.

tiller³ see under TILL³

tilt ▷ *verb* (***tilted, tilting***) **1** *tr & intr* to slope or make something slope; to be or put in a slanting position. **2** (*often* **tilt at someone** or **something**) *intr* to charge at or attack them or it. **3** *intr* to fight on horseback with a lance; to joust. **4** to point (a lance) or attack with (a lance) as if in a joust. **5** to forge (steel, etc) using a tilt-hammer. ▷ *noun* **1** a slant; a sloping position or angle. **2** an act of tilting. **3** a joust. **4** a thrust, charge or attack with a lance during a joust. **5** an attack, disagreement or contest, especially a verbal one. • **tilter** *noun*. • **at full tilt** at full speed or with full force. ◎ Anglo-Saxon *tealt* tottering.

tilth ▷ *noun, agric* **1** the act or process of cultivation. **2** the physical condition of the soil surface after cultivation, eg after ploughing. ◎ Anglo-Saxon *tilthe*.

tilt-hammer ▷ *noun* a heavy pivoted hammer lifted by a cam, used in forging.

Tim. ▷ *abbreviation* Book of the Bible: Timothy. See table at BIBLE.

timbal or **tymbal** /'tɪmbəl/ ▷ *noun* a type of KETTLEDRUM. ◎ 17c: from French *timbale*, from Spanish *atabal*, from Arabic *at-tabl* the drum.

timbale /tɪm'bɑːl/ ▷ *noun* **1** *cookery* a dish of meat or fish, etc cooked in a cup-shaped mould or shell. **2** the mould used to make such a dish. ◎ 19c: see TIMBAL.

timber /'tɪmbə(r)/ ▷ *noun* **1** wood, especially wood prepared for building or carpentry. **2** trees suitable for this; forest or woodland. **3** a wooden beam in the framework of something, especially a ship or house. ▷ *exclamation* a warning cry that a tree has been cut and is about to fall. ▷ *verb* (***timbered, timbering***) **1** to provide with timber or beams. **2** to cover something in timber. • **timbering** *noun*. • **shiver my timbers** see under SHIVER. ◎ Anglo-Saxon.

timbered ▷ *adj* **1** built completely or partly of wood. **2** said of land: covered with trees; wooded.

timber line and **tree line** ▷ *noun* the line or level of high ground above which trees do not grow.

timber wolf ▷ *noun* a variety of wolf, with a grey, brindled coat, found especially in N America. Also called **grey wolf**.

timbre /'tambə(r)/ ▷ *noun* the distinctive quality of the tone produced by a musical instrument or voice, as opposed to pitch and loudness. ◎ 19c: French, meaning 'bell', from Greek *tympanon* drum.

timbrel /'tɪmbrəl/ ▷ *noun* a small tambourine. ◎ 16c: from French *timbre* bell.

time ▻ *noun* **1** the continuous passing and succession of minutes, days and years, etc. **2** a particular point in time expressed in hours and minutes, or days, months and years, and as can be read from a clock or watch, or told by a calendar. **3** any system for reckoning or expressing time □ ***Eastern European Time.*** **4** (*also* **times**) a point or period which is marked by some event or some particular characteristic □ ***at the time of her marriage*** □ ***Edwardian times.*** **5** *in compounds* the period required or available for, suitable for or spent doing a specified activity □ ***playtime.*** **6** an unspecified interval or period □ ***stayed there for a time.*** **7** one of a number or series of occasions or repeated actions □ ***been to Spain three times.*** **8** (**times**) expressing multiplication □ ***Three times two is six.*** **9** a period or occasion, especially a personal one, characterized by some quality or experience □ ***a good time*** □ ***hard times.*** **10** a particular period being considered, especially the present. **11** *colloq* a prison sentence □ ***do time.*** **12** an apprenticeship. **13** the point at which something ends, eg a match or game. **14** *Brit* the time when a public house must close. **15** the moment at which childbirth or death is expected. **16** the hours and days that one spends at work. **17** a rate of pay for work □ ***Saturdays pay double time.*** **18** *music* a specified rhythm or speed □ ***waltz time.*** **19** *music* the speed at which a piece of music is to be played. ▻ *verb* (***timed, timing***) **1** to measure the time taken by (an event or journey, etc). **2** to arrange, set or choose the time for something. **3** *tr & intr* to keep or beat time, or make something keep or beat time. • **against time** with as much speed as possible because of the need or wish to finish by a certain time. • **ahead of time** earlier than expected or necessary. • **all in good time** in due course; soon enough. • **all the time** continually. • **at times** occasionally; sometimes. • **behind time** late. • **behind the times** out of date; old-fashioned. • **for the time being** meanwhile; for the moment. • **from time to time** occasionally; sometimes. • **have no time for someone** or **something** to have no interest in or patience with them or it; to despise them or it. • **have the time of one's life** to enjoy oneself very much. • **in good time** early. • **in no time** very quickly. • **in one's own time 1** in one's spare time when not at work. **2** at the speed one prefers. • **in time** early enough. • **in time with someone** or **something** at the same speed or rhythm as them or it. • **keep time 1** to correctly follow the required rhythm of a piece of music. **2** said of a watch or clock: to function at an accurate speed. • **kill time** to pass time aimlessly while waiting on events. • **make good time** to travel as quickly as, or more quickly than, one had expected or hoped. • **no time at all** *colloq* a very short time. • **on time** at the right time; not late. • **pass the time of day** to exchange greetings and have a brief casual conversation. • **take one's time** not to hurry; to work as slowly as one wishes. • **time and time again** again and again; repeatedly. • **time out of mind** for longer than anyone can remember. ⓘ Anglo-Saxon *tima*.

time-and-motion study ▻ *noun* a study of the way work is done in a factory or company, etc with a view to increasing efficiency.

time bomb ▻ *noun* a bomb that has been set to explode at a particular pre-set time.

time capsule ▻ *noun* a box containing objects chosen as typical of the current age, buried or otherwise preserved for discovery in the future.

time clock ▻ *noun* an apparatus with a clock which stamps on cards (known as **timecards**) the time of arrival and departure of staff, especially in a factory.

time code ▻ *noun* a series of digitally coded signals that appear sequentially (as hours, minutes and seconds) on a magnetic tape of a video or audio recording, and sometimes on film, to provide specific identification and location of each frame, etc in editing and post-production.

time-consuming ▻ *adj* taking up a lot of or too much time.

time exposure ▻ *noun* **1** a photograph taken by exposing the film to the light for a relatively long period of time, usually a few seconds. **2** the process involved in producing such a photograph.

time-honoured ▻ *adj* respected and upheld because of custom or tradition.

timekeeper ▻ *noun* **1** someone who records the time, eg that worked by employees or taken by a competitor in a game. **2** a clock or watch, especially thought of in terms of its accuracy □ ***a good timekeeper.*** **3** someone thought of in terms of their punctuality. • **timekeeping** *noun.* ⓘ 17c, meaning 'timepiece'.

time lag ▻ *noun* the interval or delay between connected events or phenomena.

time-lapse photography ▻ *noun* a series of photographs taken of a subject at regular intervals and from the same viewpoint, to record some process or development (eg plant growth or cloud formation) with subsequent projection at normal speed providing a rapid presentation of changes which are slow or gradual in real time.

timeless ▻ *adj* **1** not belonging to or typical of any particular time or date. **2** unaffected by time; ageless; eternal. • **timelessly** *adverb.* • **timelessness** *noun.*

time limit ▻ *noun* a fixed length of time during which something must be completed.

timely /'taɪmlɪ/ ▻ *adj* (***timelier, timeliest***) coming at the right or a suitable moment; opportune. • **timeliness** *noun.*

time out ▻ *noun, N Amer* **1** a brief pause or period of rest. **2** *sport* a short break during a game or match, etc for discussion of tactics or for rest, etc.

timepiece ▻ *noun* an instrument for keeping time, such as a watch or clock.

timer ▻ *noun* **1** a device like a clock which switches an appliance on or off at pre-set times, or which makes a sound when a set amount of time has passed. **2** a person or instrument that records the time taken by someone or something.

timescale ▻ *noun* the time envisaged for the completion of a particular project or stage of a project.

time-served ▻ *adj* having completed an apprenticeship; fully trained □ ***a time-served electrician.***

timeserver ▻ *noun* someone who changes their behaviour or opinions to fit those held by people in general or by someone in authority. ⓘ 16c.

timeshare ▻ *noun* **1** the sharing of a property under a time-sharing scheme. **2** the property that is shared.

time-sharing ▻ *noun* **1** a scheme whereby someone buys the right to use a holiday home for the same specified period each year for an agreed number of years. **2** *computing* a system which allows many users with individual terminals to use a single computer at the same time.

time sheet ▻ *noun* a record of the time worked by a person on a daily, weekly or monthly basis, and often used as a basis for calculating pay.

time signal ▻ *noun* a signal, especially one broadcast on the radio, which gives the exact time of day.

time signature ▻ *noun, music* a sign consisting of two numbers one above the other (the lower one indicating the value of the note used as the basic beat and the upper one the number of these to the bar), placed after the key signature at the beginning of a piece of music to show the rhythm it is to be played in, or in the middle of a piece where the rhythm changes.

time slot ▻ *noun* **1** a particular period of time in the day or week allocated to a particular radio or TV programme. **2** a particular period of time assigned to some purpose, etc.

timetable ▻ *noun* **1** a list of the departure and arrival times of trains, coaches or buses, etc. **2** a plan showing the order of events, especially of classes in a school. ▻ *verb* to arrange or include something in a timetable; to schedule or plan.

time warp ▻ *noun* **1** in science fiction, etc: a hypothetical distortion in the time continuum, allowing someone to pass from the present to the past or the future, or to stand still in the present. **2** a state of apparent stoppage in time, in which styles or fashion, etc from a previous era are retained.

timeworn ▻ *adj* worn out through long use; old.

time zone ▻ *noun* any one of the 24 more or less parallel sections into which the world is divided longitudinally. All places within a given zone have the same standard time. ⓒ Early 20c.

timid ▻ *adj* (***timider***, ***timidest***) easily frightened or alarmed; nervous; shy. • **timidity** *noun*. • **timidly** *adj*. ⓒ 16c: from Latin *timidus*.

timing /'taɪmɪŋ/ ▻ *noun* the regulating and co-ordinating of actions and events to achieve the best possible effect, especially the regulating of the speed of dialogue, action and interaction between characters in a play or film, etc.

timocracy /taɪ'mɒkrəsɪ/ ▻ *noun* **1** a form of government in which ownership of property is a qualification for office. **2** a form of goverment in which ambition or desire of honour is a ruling factor. ⓒ 16c: from Greek *timokratia*, from *time* honour or worth.

timorous /'tɪmərəs/ ▻ *adj* very timid; frightened. • **timorously** *adverb*. • **timorousness** *noun*. ⓒ 15c: ultimately from Latin *timere* to fear.

timothy grass /'tɪməθɪ —/ ▻ *noun* a perennial grass used for fodder and pasture. Often shortened to **timothy**. ⓒ 18c: named after Timothy Hanson, who promoted its cultivation in America in the early 18c.

timpani or **tympani** /'tɪmpənɪ/ ▻ *plural noun* a set of two or three KETTLEDRUMS. • **timpanist** or **tympanist** *noun*. ⓒ 16c: Italian, plural of *timpano*.

tin ▻ *noun* **1** *chem* (symbol **Sn**, atomic number 50) a soft silvery-white metallic element obtained from ores such as CASSITERITE and used as a thin protective coating for steel, eg in 'tin' cans, and as a component of various alloys, eg bronze, pewter and solder. **2** an airtight metal container, often composed of steel coated with a thin layer of tin, used for storing food □ *a biscuit tin*. **3** any of several containers of different shapes and sizes made usually of tin or aluminium and in which food is cooked. **4** a TINFUL. **5** a strip of tin along the bottom of the front wall of a squash court. **6** *Brit slang* money. ▻ *adj* made of tin. ▻ *verb* (***tinned***, ***tinning***) **1** to pack (food) in tins; to can. **2** to cover or coat with tin. See also TINNY. ⓒ Anglo-Saxon.

tincture /'tɪŋktʃə(r)/ ▻ *noun* **1** a slight flavour, trace or addition. **2** a slight trace of colour; hue; tinge. **3** a solution of a drug in alcohol for medicinal use. ▻ *verb* (***tinctured***, ***tincturing***) to give a trace of a colour or flavour, etc to something. ⓒ 14c: from Latin *tinctura* dyeing.

tincture of iodine see IODINE

tinder /'tɪndə(r)/ ▻ *noun* dry material, especially wood, which is easily set alight and can be used as kindling. ⓒ Anglo-Saxon.

tinderbox ▻ *noun* **1** *historical* a box containing tinder, a flint and steel for striking a spark to light a fire. **2** a volatile and potentially dangerous situation.

tine /taɪn/ ▻ *noun* a slender prong or tooth, eg of a comb, fork or antler. ⓒ Anglo-Saxon *tind*.

tinea /'tɪnɪə/ ▻ *noun, pathol* RINGWORM. ⓒ 14c: Latin, meaning 'moth' or 'bookworm'.

tinfoil ▻ *noun* tin, aluminium or other metal in the form of very thin, paper-like sheets, used especially for wrapping food.

tinful ▻ *noun* (***tinfuls***) the amount a tin can hold.

ting ▻ *noun* a high metallic tinkling sound such as that made by a small bell. ▻ *verb* (***tinged***, ***tinging***) *tr & intr* to produce or make something produce this sound. ⓒ 15c: imitating the sound.

ting-a-ling ▻ *noun* a ringing or tinkling sound.

tinge /tɪndʒ/ ▻ *noun* **1** a trace or slight amount of colour. **2** a trace or hint of (eg a quality or feeling). ▻ *verb* (***tinged***, ***tinging***) **1** to give a slight colour to something or someone. **2** to give a trace or hint of a feeling or quality, etc to something or someone. ⓒ 15c: from Latin *tingere* to colour.

tingle /'tɪŋgəl/ ▻ *verb* (***tingled***, ***tingling***) *tr & intr* to feel or make someone or something feel a prickling or slightly stinging sensation, as with cold or embarrassment. ▻ *noun* a prickling or slightly stinging sensation. • **tingling** *adj*. ⓒ 14c: perhaps a variant of TINKLE.

tin god ▻ *noun* **1** a self-important pompous person. **2** someone or something held in excessively or unjustifiably high esteem.

tin hat ▻ *noun, colloq* a military steel helmet.

tinhorn *especially US, colloq* ▻ *noun* a cheap pretentious second-rate person. ▻ *adj* cheap and pretentious. ⓒ Late 19c.

tinier, **tiniest** and **tininess** see under TINY

tinker /'tɪŋkə(r)/ ▻ *noun* **1** a travelling mender of pots, pans and other household utensils; a gypsy. **2** *colloq* a mischievous or impish person, especially a child. ▻ *verb* (***tinkered***, ***tinkering***) *intr* **1** (*often* **tinker about** or **around**) to work in an unskilled way, meddle or fiddle with machinery, etc, especially to try to improve it. **2** to work as a tinker. ⓒ 13c.

tinkle /'tɪŋkəl/ ▻ *verb* (***tinkled***, ***tinkling***) **1** *tr & intr* to make, or cause something to make, a sound of or like the jingling of small bells. **2** *intr, colloq* to urinate. ▻ *noun* **1** a ringing or jingling sound. **2** *Brit colloq* a telephone call. **3** *colloq* an act of urinating. • **tinkly** *adj*. ⓒ 14c: imitating the sound.

tinned ▻ *adj* **1** coated or plated with tin. **2** preserved in tins; canned □ *tinned soup*.

tinnitus /'tɪnɪtəs, -'naɪtəs/ ▻ *noun, medicine* any noise (ringing, buzzing or whistling, etc) in the ears not caused by external sounds, frequently associated with deafness due to ageing or continuous exposure to loud noise, but also caused by ear infections or disease, high blood pressure or drugs. ⓒ 19c: from Latin *tinnire* to ring.

tinny ▻ *adj* (***tinnier***, ***tinniest***) **1** belonging to or resembling tin, especially in appearance or taste. **2** not solid and durable; flimsy; shoddy. **3** said of sound: thin and high-pitched. **4** *Austral & NZ slang* lucky. ▻ *noun* (***tinnies***) *Austral slang* a can of beer. • **tinnily** *adverb*. • **tinniness** *noun*.

tin-opener ▻ *noun* any of several different types of device for opening tins of food.

tin plate ▻ *noun* thin sheet iron or steel coated with tin. ▻ *verb* (**tin-plate**) to cover with a layer of tin.

tinpot ▻ *adj, Brit colloq* cheap or poor quality; paltry or contemptible □ *tinpot dictator*. ⓒ 19c.

tinsel /'tɪnsəl/ ▻ *noun* **1** a long strip of glittering coloured metal threads used as a decoration, especially at Christmas. **2** anything which is cheap and showy. ▻ *adj* belonging or relating to or resembling tinsel, especially in being cheap and showy. ▻ *verb* (***tinselled***, ***tinselling***; *US* ***tinseled***, ***tinseling***) **1** to adorn with, or as if with, tinsel. **2** to make something glittering or gaudy. • **tinselly** *adj*. ⓒ 16c: from French *estincele* a spark.

tinsmith ▻ *noun* a worker in tin and tin plate.

tint ▻ *noun* **1** a variety or (usually slightly) different shade of a colour. **2** a variety of a colour, especially one made softer by adding white. **3** a pale or faint colour used as a background for printing. **4** shading produced by engraving parallel lines close together. **5** a hair dye. ▻ *verb* (***tinted, tinting***) to give a tint to (eg hair); to colour slightly. ◷ 18c: from Latin *tingere, tinctum* to colour.

tintinnabulation /tɪntɪnabjʊ'leɪʃən/ ▻ *noun* a ringing of bells. ◷ 19c: from Latin *tintinnabulum* bell.

tiny /'taɪnɪ/ ▻ *adj* (***tinier, tiniest***) very small. ● **tininess** *noun*. ◷ 16c.

-tion /ʃən/ ▻ *suffix, forming nouns, signifying* action, result, condition or state, etc □ ***exploration*** □ ***condemnation***. ◷ From Latin *-tionem*.

tip[1] ▻ *noun* **1** the usually small pointed end of something. **2** a small piece forming an end or point □ ***a rubber tip on a walking-stick***. **3** a top or summit. **4** a tea leaf-bud. ▻ *verb* (***tipped, tipping***) **1** to put or form a tip on something. **2** to remove a tip from something. ● **on the tip of one's tongue** about to be said, but not able to be because not quite remembered. ● **tipped** *adj*. ◷ 15c as *noun* 1: from Norse *typpa*.

■ **tip something in** to attach (a loose sheet) into a book.

tip[2] ▻ *verb* (***tipped, tipping***) **1** (*also* **tip up** or **over**) *tr & intr* to lean or make something lean or slant. **2** (*also* **tip something out**) to remove or empty it from its container or a surface, etc by overturning or upsetting that container or causing that surface to slant. **3** *Brit* to dump (rubbish). ▻ *noun* **1** a place for tipping rubbish or coal, etc. **2** *colloq* a very untidy place. ◷ 14c meaning 'to overturn'.

■ **tip over** or **tip something over** to knock or fall over; to overturn.

tip[3] ▻ *noun* **1** a gift of money given to a servant or waiter, etc in return for service done well. **2** a piece of useful information; a helpful hint or warning. **3** a piece of inside information which may lead to financial gain, such as the name of a horse likely to win a race. ▻ *verb* (***tipped, tipping***) to give a tip to someone. ◷ 17c: perhaps a special use of TIP[4].

■ **tip someone off** to give them a piece of useful or secret information. See also TIP-OFF.

tip[4] ▻ *noun* a light blow or tap. ▻ *verb* (***tipped, tipping***) to hit or strike lightly. ● **tip the scales** to be the (usually small) fact, happening, etc which causes events to happen in a certain way, a certain decision to be made, etc. ◷ 15c.

tip-off ▻ *noun* (***tip-offs***) **1** a piece of useful or secret information, or the disclosing of this. **2** *basketball* the act or instance of the referee throwing the ball up into the air between two opposing players, each of whom tries to be the first to tip the ball in the direction of a team-mate. ◷ 1920s.

tip of the iceberg ▻ *noun* a small part of something much bigger, most of which is still to be discovered or dealt with.

tippet /'tɪpɪt/ ▻ *noun* **1** a shoulder-cape made from fur or cloth. **2** a long band of cloth or fur worn as part of some official costumes, eg by the clergy over the SURPLICE during morning and evening prayers. **3** *historical* a long narrow band of cloth worn as an attachment to a hood, etc. ◷ 14c: probably from TIP[1].

Tipp-Ex /'tɪpɛks/ ▻ *noun, trademark* a type of CORRECTING FLUID. ▻ *verb* (***Tipp-Exes, Tipp-Exed, Tipp-Exing***) to correct (text, etc) using Tipp-Ex. ◷ 1960s: from German *tippen* to type + Latin *ex* out.

tipple /'tɪpəl/ *colloq* ▻ *verb* (***tippled, tippling***) *tr & intr* to drink alcohol regularly, especially in relatively small amounts. ▻ *noun* alcoholic drink. ● **tippler** *noun*. ◷ 15c.

tipstaff ▻ *noun* (***tipstaffs*** or ***tipstaves*** /-steɪvz/) **1** a metal-tipped staff used as a symbol of office. **2** a SHERIFF OFFICER. ◷ 16c: a contraction of *tipped staff*.

tipster ▻ *noun* someone who gives tips, especially as to which horses to bet on. ◷ 19c.

tipsy /'tɪpsɪ/ ▻ *adj, colloq* (***tipsier, tipsiest***) slightly drunk; tiddly. ● **tipsily** *adverb*. ● **tipsiness** *noun*. ◷ 16c: probably from TIP[2].

tipsy cake ▻ *noun* a kind of sponge cake which is soaked with alcohol, eg wine or sherry, and often decorated with almonds.

tiptoe ▻ *verb* (***tiptoed, tiptoeing***) *intr* to walk quietly or stealthily on the tips of the toes. ▻ *noun* (*often* **tiptoes**) the tips of the toes. ▻ *adverb* (*usually* **on tiptoe**) on the tips of the toes. ◷ 14c as *noun*; 17c as *verb*.

tiptop *colloq* ▻ *adj, adverb* excellent; first-class. ▻ *noun* the very best; the height of excellence. ◷ 18c.

TIR ▻ *abbreviation*: *Transports Internationaux Routiers* (French), International Road Transport, a continental haulage organization.

tirade /taɪə'reɪd, tɪ-/ ▻ *noun* a long angry speech, harangue or denunciation. ◷ 19c: French, meaning 'a long speech'.

tire[1] /taɪə(r)/ *verb* (***tired, tiring***) **1** *tr & intr* to make or become physically or mentally weary and in need of rest. **2** (**tire of something** or **someone**) to lose patience with it or them; to have had enough of it or them; to become bored with it or them. ● **tiring** *adj*. ◷ Anglo-Saxon *teorian*.

tire[2] /taɪə(r)/ ▻ *noun* **1** a metal hoop placed round the rim of a wheel to bind it. **2** the *US* spelling of TYRE. ◷ 15c: from ATTIRE.

tired ▻ *adj* **1** wearied; exhausted. **2** (**tired of something** or **someone**) no longer interested in it or them; bored with it or them. **3** lacking freshness and showing the effects of time and wear, especially in being limp and grubby or hackneyed. ● **tiredly** *adverb*. ● **tiredness** *noun*.

tireless ▻ *adj* never becoming weary or exhausted. ● **tirelessly** *adverb*. ● **tirelessness** *noun*. ◷ 16c.

tiresome ▻ *adj* troublesome and irritating; annoying; tedious. ● **tiresomely** *adverb*. ● **tiresomeness** *noun*. ◷ 16c.

tiring see under TIRE[1]

tiro see TYRO

Tirolean see TYROLEAN

'tis /tɪz/ ▻ *contraction, old use or poetic* it is.

tisane /tɪ'zan/ ▻ *noun* a medicinal infusion of herbs, etc. ◷ 1930s: French.

'tisn't /'tɪzənt/ ▻ *contraction, old use or poetic* it is not.

tissue /'tɪʃuː, 'tɪsjuː/ ▻ *noun* **1** in an animal or plant: a group of cells with a similar structure and particular function. Often *in compounds* □ ***muscle tissue***. **2** a piece of thin soft disposable paper used as a handkerchief or as toilet paper. **3** (*also* **tissue paper**) fine thin soft paper, used eg for wrapping fragile objects. **4** fine thin delicate woven fabric. **5** an interwoven mass or collection □ ***a tissue of lies***. ◷ 14c: from French *tissu* woven cloth.

tissue culture ▻ *noun, biol* **1** the growth of isolated plant or animal cells, tissues or organs under controlled conditions in a sterile growth medium. **2** the tissue grown.

tit[1] ▻ *noun* any of several small agile songbirds. Also called **titmouse**. ◷ 16c.

tit[2] ▻ *noun* ● **tit for tat** blow for blow; with repayment of an injury by an injury. ◷ 16c.

tit[3] ▻ *noun* **1** *slang* a teat. **2** *coarse slang* a woman's breast. ◷ Anglo-Saxon *titt*.

Tit. ▻ *abbreviation* Book of the Bible: Titus. See table at BIBLE.

titan /'taɪtən/ ▻ *noun* someone or something of very great strength, size, intellect or importance. ◷ 19c: named after the Titans, in Greek mythology a family of giants, children of Earth and Heaven.

titanic /taɪˈtanɪk/ ▷ *adj* having great strength or size; colossal; gigantic. ⓒ 18c.

titanium /tɪˈteɪnɪəm/ ▷ *noun, chem* (symbol **Ti**, atomic number 22) a silvery-white metallic element used to make strong light corrosion-resistant alloys for components of aircraft and missiles, etc. ⓒ 18c: TITAN + -IUM.

titbit ▷ *noun* a choice or small tasty morsel of something, eg food or gossip. ⓒ 17c: from TIDE *noun* 4 + BIT[1].

titch or **tich** ▷ *noun* (***titches*** or ***tiches***) *Brit colloq* a very small person. ⓒ 19c: from Little Tich, the nickname of the music-hall comedian Harry Relph (1868–1928).

titchy ▷ *adj* (***titchier, titchiest***) *Brit colloq* very small.

titer the *US* spelling of TITRE.

titfer /ˈtɪtfə(r)/ ▷ *noun, rhyming slang* a hat. ⓒ 1930s: shortened from TIT FOR TAT.

tithe /taɪð/ ▷ *noun* **1** (*often* **tithes**) *historical* a tenth part of someone's annual income or produce, paid as a tax to support the church or clergy in a parish. **2** a tenth part. ▷ *verb* (***tithed, tithing***) **1** to demand a tithe or tithes from someone or something. **2** *tr & intr* to pay a tithe or tithes. ● **tithable** *adj*. ⓒ Anglo-Saxon *teotha*.

Titian /ˈtɪʃən/ ▷ *noun* a bright reddish-gold colour. ▷ *adj* Titian-coloured. ⓒ 19c: named after the painter Tiziano Vecellio (c.1490–1576).

titillate /ˈtɪtɪleɪt/ ▷ *verb* (***titillated, titillating***) **1** to excite someone or something gently, especially in a sexual way. **2** to tickle. ● **titillating** *adj*. ● **titillation** *noun*. ⓒ 17c: from Latin *titillare, titillatum*.

titivate or **tittivate** /ˈtɪtɪveɪt/ ▷ *verb* (***titivated, titivating***) *tr & intr, colloq* to smarten up or put the finishing touches to something or someone. ● **titivation** *noun*. ⓒ 19c: from earlier *tidivate*, from TIDY, modelled on ELEVATE, RENOVATE, etc.

titlark ▷ *noun* any bird belonging to the PIPIT family. ⓒ 17c.

title /ˈtaɪtəl/ ▷ *noun* **1** the distinguishing name of a book, play, work of art, piece of music, etc. **2** an often descriptive heading, eg of a chapter in a book or a legal document. **3** a word used before someone's name to show acquired or inherited rank, an honour, occupation or attainment. **4** a TITLE PAGE. **5** (**titles**) written material on film giving credits or dialogue, etc. **6** *law* a right to the possession or ownership of property. **7** *sport* a championship □ *St Johnstone won the title.* **8** a book or publication. **9** a book or publication as distinct from a copy and as listed in a catalogue. ▷ *verb* (***titled, titling***) to give a title to something or someone. ⓒ 13c: from Latin *titulus*.

titled ▷ *adj* having a title, especially one that shows noble rank.

title deed ▷ *noun* a document that proves legal ownership, especially of real property.

title-holder ▷ *noun* someone who holds a title, especially in sport.

title page ▷ *noun* the page at the beginning of a book which gives the name and address of the publisher, the title, author and cataloguing information, etc.

title role ▷ *noun* the role of the character in a play or film, etc from which it takes its name, eg *Macbeth*.

titmouse /ˈtɪtmaʊs/ ▷ *noun* a TIT[1]. ⓒ 14c.

titrate /ˈtaɪtreɪt/ ▷ *verb* (***titrated, titrating***) *chem* to determine the concentration of (a chemical substance in a solution) by titration. ⓒ 19c: from French *titre* title.

titration ▷ *noun, chem* a method of chemical analysis in which the concentration of a particular solution is determined, often electronically, by adding measured amounts of another solution of known concentration until the reaction between the two reaches its end-point, usually indicated by a change in colour of a dye.

titre or *US* **titer** /ˈtaɪtə(r), ˈtiːtə(r)/ *noun* **1** *chem* the concentration of a solution as determined by titration with a solution of known concentration. **2** *biol* the concentration of a particular virus present in a suspension. **3** the concentration of an ANTIBODY detectable in a sample of SERUM.

titter /ˈtɪtə(r)/ *colloq* ▷ *verb* (***tittered, tittering***) *intr* to giggle or snigger in a stifled way. ▷ *noun* a stifled giggle or snigger. ⓒ 17c: imitating the sound.

tittivate see TITIVATE

tittle /ˈtɪtəl/ ▷ *noun* **1** a small written or printed sign, mark or dot. **2** a very small particle. ⓒ 14c: from Latin *titulus* title.

tittle-tattle /ˈtɪtəltatəl/ ▷ *noun* idle or petty gossip or chatter. ▷ *verb* (***tittle-tattled, tittle-tattling***) *intr* to gossip or chatter idly. ⓒ 16c.

titty /ˈtɪtɪ/ ▷ *noun* (***titties***) *slang* TIT[3].

titubation /tɪtʃʊˈbeɪʃən/ ▷ *noun, pathol* staggering or unsteadiness, especially as a symptom of a cerebral or spinal disease. ⓒ 17c: from Latin *titubare* to stagger.

titular /ˈtɪtʃʊlə(r)/ ▷ *adj* **1** having the title of an office or position but none of the authority or duties. **2** belonging or relating to a title. ▷ *noun* **1** someone invested with a title. **2** someone who enjoys the bare title of an office, without the accompanying duties. ● **titularly** *adj*. ⓒ 17c: from Latin *titulus* title.

tizzy /ˈtɪzɪ/ or **tizz** ▷ *noun* (***tizzies*** or ***tizzes***) *colloq* a nervous highly excited or confused state. ⓒ 1930s.

T-junction ▷ *noun* a junction at which one road meets another at a right angle but does not cross it. ⓒ 1950s: from the shape (see T[1] *noun* 2).

TKO ▷ *abbreviation, boxing* technical knockout.

Tl ▷ *symbol, chem* thallium.

TLC ▷ *abbreviation, facetious* tender loving care.

TLS ▷ *abbreviation* Times Literary Supplement.

TM ▷ *abbreviation* transcendental meditation.

Tm ▷ *symbol, chem* thulium.

TN ▷ *abbreviation* **1** *US state* Tennessee. Also written **Tenn.** or **Ten. 2** *IVR* Tunisia.

TNT ▷ *abbreviation* trinitrotoluene.

TO ▷ *abbreviation* **1** Tax Officer. **2** telegraph office. **3** Transport Officer. **4** turn over.

to /tuː, tə/ ▷ *prep* **1** towards; in the direction of, or with the destination of somewhere or something □ *Let's go to the shop.* **2** used to express as a resulting condition, aim or purpose □ *boil the fruit to a pulp* □ *to my surprise.* **3** as far as; until □ *from beginning to end* □ *bears the scars to this day.* **4** used to introduce the INDIRECT OBJECT of a verb □ *He sent it to us.* **5** used to express addition □ *add one to ten.* **6** used to express attachment, connection, contact or possession □ *put his ear to the door* □ *the key to the lock.* **7** before the hour of □ *ten minutes to three.* **8** used to express response or reaction to a situation or event, etc □ *rise to the occasion* □ *dance to the music.* **9** used to express comparison or proportion □ *won by two goals to one* □ *second to none.* **10** used before an infinitive or instead of a complete infinitive □ *He asked her to stay but she didn't want to.* ▷ *adverb* **1** in or into a nearly closed position □ *pulled the window to.* **2** back into consciousness □ *He came to a few minutes later.* **3** near at hand. **4** in the direction required □ *hove to.* ● **to and fro** backwards and forwards. ● **toing and froing** movement backwards and forwards in an agitated way. ⓒ Anglo-Saxon.

toad ▷ *noun* **1** a tailless amphibian, with a short squat head and body, and moist skin which may contain poison glands which help to deter predators. **2** an obnoxious or repellent person. ⓒ Anglo-Saxon *tade*.

toadflax ▷ *noun* any of various perennial plants typically having narrow leaves resembling flax and spurred bright-yellow flowers. ⓒ 16c.

toad-in-the-hole ▷ *noun, Brit* a dish of sausages cooked in YORKSHIRE PUDDING batter. ⓒ 18c.

toadstool ▷ *noun* any of various fungi, most of which are poisonous or inedible, that produce a fruiting body consisting of an umbrella-shaped cap with SPORE-bearing gills on the underside. See also MUSHROOM. ⓒ 14c.

toady ▷ *noun* (***toadies***) someone who flatters someone else, does everything they want and hangs on their every word; a sycophant. ▷ *verb* (***toadies, toadied, toadying***) *tr & intr* (*usually* **toady to someone**) to flatter them and behave obsequiously towards them. • **toadyish** *adj.* • **toadyism** *noun.* ⓒ 19c: shortened from *toadeater* an assistant or servant to a charlatan, who would pretend to eat poisonous toads so that his master could show his expertise in ridding the body of poison.

toast ▷ *verb* (***toasted, toasting***) **1** to make something (especially bread) brown by exposing it to direct heat, eg under a grill. **2** *intr* said especially of bread: to become brown in this way. **3** *tr & intr* to make or become warm by being exposed to heat, eg a fire. **4** to drink ceremonially in honour of or to the health or future success of someone or something. ▷ *noun* **1** bread which has been browned by being exposed to direct heat, eg under a grill. **2 a** an act of drinking to someone's honour, health or future success; **b** someone whose honour, health or future success is drunk to. **3** a very admired person or thing □ *Her singing is the toast of the festival.* **4** the wish conveyed when drinking to someone's honour, etc. • **toasted** *adj.* ⓒ 14c: ultimately from Latin *torrere* to parch; sense 4 of the verb and senses 2, 3 and 4 of the noun reflect the idea that a woman's name (ie as the person whose health is being drunk to) would flavour the wine like spiced toast.

toaster ▷ *noun* an electric machine for toasting bread.

toastie /'toʊstɪ/ ▷ *noun, colloq* a toasted sandwich.

toasting-fork ▷ *noun* a fork with a long handle, used to toast bread in front of a fire.

toastmaster and **toastmistress** ▷ *noun* a man or woman who announces the toasts to be drunk at a ceremonial dinner.

toast rack ▷ *noun* a small rack for holding slices of toast.

tobacco /tə'bakoʊ/ ▷ *noun* (***tobaccos*** or ***tobaccoes***) **1** any of various plants, with large leaves which, in certain species, contain NICOTINE. **2** the dried leaves of this plant, which are used to make cigarettes, cigars, pipe tobacco and snuff. ⓒ 16c: from Spanish *tabaco*.

tobacconist /tə'bakənɪst/ ▷ *noun* a person or shop that sells tobacco, cigarettes, cigars and pipes, etc.

-to-be ▷ *adj, in compounds* future; soon to become □ *brides-to-be.*

toboggan /tə'bɒgən/ ▷ *noun* a long light sledge which curves up at the front, used for riding over snow and ice. ▷ *verb* (***tobogganed, tobogganing***) *intr* to ride on a toboggan. • **tobogganing** *noun.* • **tobogganer** or **tobogganist** *noun.* ⓒ 19c: from Canadian French *tabaganne*.

toby jug /'toʊbɪ —/ ▷ *noun* a type of jug, shaped like a stout man wearing a three-cornered hat. Often shortened to **toby**. ⓒ 19c: from the name Toby.

toccata /tɒ'kɑːtə/ ▷ *noun* (***toccatas***) a piece of music for a keyboard instrument intended to show off the performer's skill and touch in a series of runs and chords before breaking into a FUGUE. ⓒ 18c: Italian, from *toccare* to touch.

tocopherol /tɒ'kɒfərɒl/ ▷ *noun* VITAMIN E. ⓒ 1930s: from Greek *tokos* offspring + *pherein* to bear; so called because of its apparent necessity for reproduction.

tocsin /'tɒksɪn/ ▷ *noun* an alarm bell or warning signal. ⓒ 16c: French, from Provençal *tocar* to touch + *senh* signal.

tod ▷ *noun, Brit colloq,* usually used in the phrase • **on one's tod** alone. ⓒ 1930s: from rhyming slang *on one's Tod Sloan* on one's own; Tod Sloan (1874–1933) being a well-known jockey.

today /tə'deɪ/ ▷ *noun* **1** this day. **2** the present time. ▷ *adverb* **1** on or during this day. **2** nowadays; at the present time □ *It doesn't happen much today.* ⓒ Anglo-Saxon *to dæg*.

toddle /'tɒdəl/ ▷ *verb* (***toddled, toddling***) *intr* **1** to walk with unsteady steps, as or like a young child. **2** *colloq* to take a casual walk; to stroll or saunter. **3** (*usually* **toddle off**) *colloq* to leave; to depart. ▷ *noun* **1** a toddling walk. **2** *colloq* a casual walk or stroll. ⓒ 16c.

toddler ▷ *noun* a very young child who is just beginning or has just learnt to walk. ⓒ 18c.

toddy /'tɒdɪ/ ▷ *noun* (***toddies***) **1** a drink made of spirits, sugar, hot water, lemon juice and sometimes spices. **2** the sap obtained from various kinds of palm tree, which is fermented to produce an alcoholic beverage. ⓒ 17c: from Hindi *tari*, from *tar* palm.

to-do /tə'duː/ ▷ *noun* (***to-dos***) *colloq* a fuss, commotion or bustle. ⓒ 16c.

toe ▷ *noun* **1** in humans: any of the five digits at the end of each foot, whose main function is to assist balance and walking. **2** in other animals: the digit corresponding to the human toe. **3** the front part of a shoe or sock, etc that covers the toes. **4** the lower, often projecting, end of eg a tool or area of land. ▷ *verb* (***toed, toeing***) **1** to kick, strike or touch with the toes. **2** to provide (eg a stocking, sock or shoe) with a toe. • **on one's toes** alert and ready for action. • **toe the line** *colloq* to act according to the rules. • **tread on someone's toes** see under TREAD. • **turn up one's toes** *slang* to die. ⓒ Anglo-Saxon *ta*.

toecap ▷ *noun* a piece of reinforced metal or leather covering the toe of a boot or shoe.

toehold ▷ *noun* **1** a place where one's toes can grip, eg when climbing. **2** a small initial or beginning position. **3** *wrestling* a hold in which the toes are held and the foot is bent back or twisted.

toenail ▷ *noun* **1** a nail covering a toe. **2** *carpentry* a nail driven obliquely through something. ▷ *verb, carpentry* to fasten by driving a nail obliquely.

toerag ▷ *noun, Brit colloq* **1** a rascal. **2** a despicable or contemptible person. ⓒ 19c: originally meaning 'beggar', from the rags wrapped around beggars' feet and worn inside the shoes in place of socks.

toff ▷ *noun, Brit slang* an upper-class and usually smartly dressed person. ⓒ 19c: perhaps from *tuft* a titled undergraduate, from the gold tassel which was formerly worn on the cap.

toffee /'tɒfɪ/ ▷ *noun* (***toffees***) **1** a type of sticky sweet which can be chewy or hard, made by boiling sugar and butter. **2** an individual piece of this. • **do something for toffee** *with negatives* at all □ *He can't act for toffee!* ⓒ 19c: from earlier *taffy*.

toffee apple ▷ *noun* an apple on a stick, covered with a thin layer of toffee.

toffee-nosed ▷ *adj, Brit colloq* conceited; stuck-up.

tofu /'toʊfuː/ ▷ *noun* (***tofus***) a curd made from soya beans, with a creamy colour and bland flavour, used especially in Japanese cooking. ⓒ 19c: Japanese, from Chinese *dou fu* rotten beans.

tog[1] ▷ *noun* (**togs**) clothes. ▷ *verb* (***togged, togging***) *tr & intr* (*usually* **tog up** or **out**) to dress in one's best or warmest clothes. ⓒ 18c: a shortening of the obsolete slang *togemans* coat.

tog[2] ▷ *noun* a unit for measuring the warmth of fabrics, clothes and quilts, etc. ⓒ 1940s: perhaps from TOG[1].

toga /ˈtoʊɡə/ ▷ *noun* (***togas***) *historical* a loose outer garment, consisting of a large piece of cloth draped round the body, worn by a citizen of ancient Rome. • **togaed** or **toga'd** *adj*. ◷ 16c: Latin.

together /təˈɡɛðə(r)/ ▷ *adverb* **1** with someone or something else; in company ▫ ***travel together***. **2** at the same time ▫ ***all arrived together***. **3** so as to be in contact, joined or united. **4** by action with one or more other people ▫ ***Together we managed to persuade him***. **5** in or into one place ▫ ***gather together***. **6** continuously; at a time ▫ ***chatting on the phone for hours together***. **7** *colloq* into a proper or suitable order or state of being organized ▫ ***get things together***. ▷ *adj, colloq* well organized; competent. • **together with someone** or **something** as well or in addition to them or it. ◷ Anglo-Saxon *to gæthere*.

togetherness ▷ *noun* a feeling of closeness, mutual sympathy and understanding, and of belonging together.

toggle ▷ *noun* **1** a fastening, eg for garments, consisting of a small bar of wood or plastic, etc which will pass one way only through a loop of material or rope, etc. **2** a pin, bar or crosspiece placed through a link in a chain or a loop in a rope, etc to prevent the chain or rope, etc from slipping. **3** *computing* a keyboard command which turns a particular feature (eg bold type or read-only mode) alternately on or off. ▷ *verb* (***toggled, toggling***) **1** to provide or fasten something with a toggle. **2** *computing* **a** (*usually* **toggle on** or **off**) to turn a particular feature, eg bold type or read-only mode, alternately on and off using the same keyboard command; **b** *intr* to move between different features, modes or files, etc using a keyboard command. ◷ 18c: originally a nautical term.

toggle switch ▷ *noun* **1** *elec* a switch consisting of a projecting spring-loaded lever that can be moved to either of two positions, as a result of which an electric circuit is either opened or closed. **2** a TOGGLE (*noun* 3).

toil¹ ▷ *verb* (***toiled, toiling***) *intr* **1** to work long and hard; to labour. **2** to make progress or move forwards with great difficulty or effort. ▷ *noun* long hard work. ◷ 16c in this sense: from French *toiler* to contend.

toil² ▷ *noun* (*usually* **toils**) a trap or snare. ◷ 16c: from French *toile* cloth, from Latin *tela* web.

toile /twɑːl/ ▷ *noun* **1** a thin cotton or linen material used to make clothes. **2** an exclusive item of clothing made up using cheap material so that copies or alterations can be made. ◷ 19c: see TOIL².

toilet /ˈtɔɪlət/ ▷ *noun* **1** a LAVATORY. **2** (*also* **toilette**) the act of washing, dressing and arranging one's hair. **3** the cleansing of a part of the body after an operation or childbirth, etc. ◷ 17c in sense 2; 16c in obsolete sense 'a wrapper for clothes': from French *toilette* a little cloth.

toilet bag see SPONGE BAG

toilet paper and **toilet tissue** ▷ *noun* thin yet absorbent paper used for cleaning oneself after urination and defecation.

toilet roll ▷ *noun* a roll of toilet paper.

toiletry ▷ *noun* (***toiletries***) an article or cosmetic used when washing, arranging the hair, making up, etc.

toilet-training ▷ *noun* the training of young children to use the lavatory.

toilet water ▷ *noun* a light perfume similar to EAU-DE-COLOGNE.

toilsome ▷ *adj* involving long hard work. ◷ 16c.

tokamak /ˈtoʊkəmak/ ▷ *noun, physics* a toroidal apparatus for containing plasma by means of two magnetic fields. ◷ 1960s: from Russian acronym of *to*roidalnaya *ka*mera s *ma*gnitym polem 'toroidal chamber with a magnetic field'.

toke /toʊk/ *slang* ▷ *noun* a draw on a cigarette, especially one containing marijuana. ▷ *verb* (***toked, toking***) *intr* to take a draw on such a cigarette. • **toker** *noun*.

token /ˈtoʊkən/ ▷ *noun* **1** a mark, sign or distinctive feature. **2** anything that serves as a reminder or souvenir; a keepsake. **3** *especially in compounds* a voucher worth a stated amount of money which can be exchanged for goods of the same value ▫ ***book token***. **4** a small coin-like piece of metal or plastic which is used instead of money, eg in slot machines. ▷ *adj* nominal; of no real value ▫ ***token gesture***. • **by the same token** also; in addition; for the same reason. ◷ Anglo-Saxon *tacen*.

tokenism ▷ *noun* the principle or practice of doing no more than the minimum in a particular area, in pretence that one is committed to it, eg employing one black person in a company to avoid charges of racism. ◷ 1960s; see TOKEN *adj*.

Tok Pisin /tɒk ˈpɪzɪn/ ▷ *noun* an English-based Melanesian pidgin spoken by about 1 million people in Papua New Guinea. ◷ 1940s: Pidgin English, meaning 'talk pidgin'.

tolbooth or **tollbooth** /ˈtoʊlbuːð, ˈtɒl-/ ▷ *noun* **1** an office where tolls are or were collected. **2** *old Scots* a town hall. **3** *old Scots* a prison. ◷ 15c.

told *past tense, past participle of* TELL

tolerable /ˈtɒlərəbəl/ ▷ *adj* **1** able to be borne or endured. **2** fairly good. • **tolerability** *noun*. • **tolerableness** *noun*. • **tolerably** *adverb*.

tolerance /ˈtɒlərəns/ ▷ *noun* **1** the ability to be fair towards and accepting of other people's religious, political, etc beliefs or opinions. **2** the ability to resist or endure pain or hardship. **3** *medicine* the ability of someone to adapt to the effects of a prescribed or abused drug, so that increased doses are required to produce the same effect. **4** *biol* lack of reactivity to a particular ANTIGEN that would normally cause an immune response. **5** *biol* the ability of a plant or animal to survive extreme environmental conditions, eg drought or low temperature.

tolerant /ˈtɒlərənt/ ▷ *adj* **1** tolerating the beliefs and opinions of others. **2** capable of enduring unfavourable conditions, etc. **3** indulgent; permissive. **4** able to take drugs without showing serious side effects. • **tolerantly** *adverb*.

tolerate /ˈtɒləreɪt/ ▷ *verb* (***tolerated, tolerating***) **1** to bear or endure someone or something; to put up with it. **2** to be able to resist the effects of (a drug). **3** to treat fairly and accept (someone with different religious, political, etc beliefs or opinions). **4** to allow to be done or exist. ◷ 16c: from Latin *tolerare, toleratum*.

toleration ▷ *noun* **1** the act of tolerating. **2** the practice of allowing people to practise religions which are different to the established religion of the country. • **tolerationist** *noun*.

toll¹ /toʊl/ ▷ *verb* (***tolled, tolling***) **1** *tr & intr* to ring (a bell) with slow measured strokes. **2** said of a bell: to announce, signal or summon by ringing with slow measured strokes. ▷ *noun* the act or sound of tolling. ◷ 15c.

toll² /toʊl/ ▷ *noun* **1** a fee or tax paid for the use of some bridges and roads. **2** the cost in damage, injury or lives of some disaster. ◷ Anglo-Saxon.

tollbooth see TOLBOOTH

tollbridge ▷ *noun* a bridge which charges a toll to traffic wishing to use it.

toll-free see under FREEPHONE

tollgate ▷ *noun* a gate or barrier across a road or bridge which is not lifted until travellers have paid the toll.

tolu /ˈtoʊljuː/ ▷ *noun* a sweet-smelling balsam obtained from a S American tree, used in the manufacture of medicine and perfume. ◷ 17c: named after Santiago de Tolu, in Columbia where it first came from.

toluene /ˈtɒljʊiːn/ ▷ *noun, chem* (formula $C_6H_5CH_3$) a toxic organic compound, a colourless flammable liquid derived from benzene and used as an industrial solvent and as an intermediate in the manufacture of TNT, high-octane petrol and various other organic chemicals. ⓘ 19c: TOLU + -ENE.

tom ▷ *noun* a male of various animals, especially a male cat. ⓘ 18c: short form of the name Thomas.

tomahawk /'tɒməhɔːk/ ▷ *noun* a small axe used as a weapon by Native Americans. ⓘ 17c: from Algonquian *tamahaac*.

tomato /tə'mɑːtoʊ/ ▷ *noun* (***tomatoes***) **1** any of various annual plants cultivated worldwide for their fleshy fruit. **2** the round fleshy fruit of these plants, which can be red, orange or yellow and is eaten raw or cooked. ⓘ 17c: from Nahuatl *tomatl*.

tomb /tuːm/ ▷ *noun* **1** a chamber or vault for a dead body, especially one below the ground, and often one that serves as a monument; a grave. **2** a hole cut in the earth or rock for a dead body. **3** (**the tomb**) *poetic* death. ⓘ 13c: from Greek *tymbos*.

tombac /'tɒmbak/ ▷ *noun* an alloy of copper with a little zinc, used to make cheap jewellery. ⓘ 17c: French, from Malay *tambaga* copper.

tombola /tɒm'boʊlə/ ▷ *noun* (***tombolas***) a lottery in which winning tickets are drawn from a revolving drum. ⓘ 19c: from Italian *tombolare* to tumble.

tomboy ▷ *noun* a girl who dresses in a boyish way and who likes boisterous and adventurous activities supposedly more suited to boys. • **tomboyish** *adj.* • **tomboyishness** *noun*. ⓘ 16c.

tombstone ▷ *noun* an ornamental stone placed over a grave, on which the dead person's name and dates, etc are engraved.

tomcat ▷ *noun* a male cat.

Tom Collins ▷ *noun* a long drink made with gin, lemon or lime juice, soda water and sugar. ⓘ Early 20c.

Tom, Dick and Harry ▷ *noun* (*especially* **any** or **every Tom, Dick and Harry**) anybody at all; people in general. ⓘ Early 19c.

tome ▷ *noun* a large, heavy and usually learned book. ⓘ 16c: French, from Greek *tomos* slice.

tomentum /tə'mentəm/ ▷ *noun* (***tomenta*** /-tə/) **1** *bot* a matted down found on leaves, etc. **2** *anatomy* the deep layer of the PIA MATER, composed of many minute blood vessels. ⓘ 17c: Latin, meaning 'stuffing for cushions'.

tomfool ▷ *noun* an absolute fool. ⓘ 14c.

tomfoolery ▷ *noun* (***tomfooleries***) **1** stupid or foolish behaviour; nonsense. **2** an instance of it. ⓘ Early 19c.

Tommy ▷ *noun* (***Tommies***) *colloq* a private in the British army. ⓘ 19c: from Tommy Atkins, the name used on specimens of official forms.

tommygun ▷ *noun* a type of submachine-gun. ⓘ 1920s: named after J T Thompson (1860–1940), its American inventor.

tommy-rot ▷ *noun, colloq* absolute nonsense. ⓘ Late 19c.

tomography /toʊ'mɒgrəfɪ/ ▷ *noun, medicine* a diagnostic scanning technique, often referred to as a CT (computed tomography) or CAT (computer-aided tomography) scan, especially one involving the use of X-rays, in which a clear image of internal structures in a single plane of a body tissue is obtained. ⓘ 1930s: from Greek *tomos* cut.

tomorrow /tə'mɒroʊ/ ▷ *noun* **1** the day after today. **2** the future. ▷ *adverb* **1** on the day after today. **2** in the future. ⓘ Anglo-Saxon *to morgen*.

tompion see TAMPION

tomtit ▷ *noun* a tit, especially a bluetit. ⓘ 18c.

tom-tom ▷ *noun* a tall drum, usually with a small head, which is beaten with the hands. ⓘ 17c: from Hindi *tam-tam*, imitating the sound.

-tomy /təmɪ/ ▷ *combining form* (***-tomies***) *medicine, forming nouns, denoting* **1** removal by surgery □ ***appendectomy*** □ ***hysterectomy***. **2** a surgical incision □ ***laparotomy*** □ ***lobotomy***. **3** a cutting up □ ***anatomy***. **4** a division into parts □ ***dichotomy***. ⓘ From Greek *-tomia*, from *temnein* to cut.

ton /tʌn/ ▷ *noun* **1** (*in full* **long ton**) *Brit* a unit of weight equal to 2 240lb (approximately 1016.06kg). **2** (*in full* **short ton**) *N Amer* a unit of weight equal to 2 000lb (approximately 907.2kg). **3** (*in full* **metric ton**) a unit of weight equal to 1 000kg (approximately 2 204.6 lb). Also called **tonne**. **4** (*in full* **displacement ton**) a unit used to measure the amount of water a ship displaces, equal to 2 240 lb or 35 cubic feet of seawater. **5** (*in full* **register ton**) a unit (originally a *tun* of wine) used to measure a ship's internal capacity, equal to 100 cubic feet. **6** (*in full* **freight ton**) a unit for measuring the space taken up by cargo, equal to 40 cubic feet. **7** (*usually* **tons**) *colloq* a lot. **8** *colloq* a speed, score or sum, etc of 100. See also TONNAGE. ⓘ 14c: a variant of TUN.

tonal /'toʊnəl/ ▷ *adj* belonging or relating to tone or tonality.

tonality ▷ *noun* (***tonalities***) **1** *music* the organization of all of the notes and chords of a piece of music in relation to a single tonic. **2** the colour scheme and tones used in a painting.

tondo /'tɒndoʊ/ ▷ *noun* (***tondi*** /-diː/) *art* a circular painting or circular carving in relief. ⓘ 19c: Italian, meaning 'a round plate'.

tone ▷ *noun* **1** a musical or vocal sound with reference to its quality and pitch. **2** *music* a sound that has a definite pitch. **3** a quality or character of the voice expressing a particular feeling or mood, etc. **4** the general character or style of spoken or written expression. **5** *music* the interval between, or equivalent to that between, the first two notes of the major scale. **6** high quality, style or character □ ***His coarse jokes lowered the tone of the meeting.*** **7** the quality, tint or shade of a colour. **8** the harmony or general effect of colours. **9** firmness of the body, a bodily organ or muscle. ▷ *verb* (***toned, toning***) **1** (*also* **tone in**) *intr* to fit in well; to harmonize. **2** to give tone or the correct tone to something. **3** *intr* to take on a tone or quality. • **toneless** *adj.* • **tonelessly** *adverb.* ⓘ 14c: from Greek *tonos* tension.

■ **tone down** or **tone something down** to become, or make it, softer or less harsh in tone, colour or force, etc.

■ **tone up** or **tone something up** to become, or make it, stronger, healthier or more forceful, etc.

tone-deaf ▷ *adj* unable to distinguish accurately between notes of different pitch. • **tone-deafness** *noun*. ⓘ Late 19c.

tone language ▷ *noun* a language in which differing pitch levels, or tones, distinguish different words (as in Mandarin Chinese, where *ma* can mean 'mother', 'hemp', 'horse' or 'scold' depending on the tone used) or signal different grammatical features such as present and past tenses (as in some African languages).

toneme /'touniːm/ ▷ *noun, linguistics* one of two or more tones which serve to distinguish different words in a language. • **tonemic** *adj.* ⓘ 1920s: from TONE, modelled on PHONEME.

tonepad ▷ *noun, computing* an electronic device similar to a remote control for a TV, etc, which allows data to be input into a central computer from a distance, usually via a telephone link. ⓘ 1980s.

tone poem ▷ *noun* a piece of music not divided into movements and which is based on a story or literary or descriptive theme. ⓘ Early 20c.

tong ▷ *noun* a Chinese guild or secret society, especially one responsible for organized crime. ⌛ Late 19c: from Cantonese Chinese *tong* meeting hall.

tongs ▷ *plural noun* **1** a tool consisting of two arms joined by a hinge or pivot, for holding and lifting objects. **2** CURLING TONGS. ⌛ Anglo-Saxon *tang*.

tongue /tʌŋ/ ▷ *noun* **1** in certain animals: the fleshy muscular organ attached to the floor of the mouth, used for tasting, licking and swallowing, and in humans as the main organ of speech. **2** the tongue of some animals, eg the ox and sheep, used as food. **3** the ability to speak. **4** a particular language. **5** a particular manner of speaking ▫ *a sharp tongue.* **6** anything like a tongue in shape. **7** a narrow strip of land that reaches out into water. **8** the clapper in a bell. **9** a flap in the opening of a shoe or boot. **10** a projecting strip along the side of a board that fits into a groove in another. ▷ *verb* (***tongued***, ***tonguing***) **1** to touch or lick something with the tongue. **2** *intr, music* to play a wind instrument by TONGUING. **3** *music* to produce (notes) by tonguing. • **find one's tongue** to be able to speak again after a shock which has left one speechless. • **hold one's tongue** to say nothing; to keep quiet. • **lose one's tongue** to be left speechless with shock or horror, etc. • **speak in tongues** *relig* to speak in an unknown language or a language one has never learned. • **with one's tongue in one's cheek** or **tongue in cheek** with ironic, insincere or humorous intention. ⌛ Anglo-Saxon *tunge*.

tongue-and-groove joint ▷ *noun* a joint made between two pieces of wood, etc consisting of a projection along the side of one slotted into a groove along the side of the other.

tongue-lashing ▷ *noun* a severe verbal reprimand. ⌛ Late 19c.

tongue-tie ▷ *noun* a speech impediment caused by an abnormally small fold of skin under the tongue not allowing full movement of it. ⌛ 19c.

tongue-tied ▷ *adj* **1** unable to speak, especially because of shyness or embarrassment. **2** suffering from tongue-tie. ⌛ 16c.

tongue-twister ▷ *noun* a phrase or sentence that is difficult to say quickly, usually because it contains a series of similar consonant sounds, eg *She sells sea shells on the sea shore.* ⌛ Early 20c.

tonguing ▷ *noun, music* a way of playing a wind instrument which allows individual notes to be articulated separately by the tongue opening and blocking the passage of air. ▷ *verb, present participle of* TONGUE.

tonic /ˈtɒnɪk/ ▷ *noun* **1** a medicine that increases strength, energy and the general wellbeing of the body. **2** anything that is refreshing or invigorating. **3** TONIC WATER. **4** *music* the first note of a scale, the note on which a key is based. ▷ *adj* **1** increasing strength, energy and wellbeing. **2** invigorating. **3** *music* belonging or relating to the tonic scale. **4** producing tension, especially muscular, tension. ⌛ 17c: from Greek *tonikos*.

tonic sol-fa see SOL-FA

tonic spasm ▷ *noun, pathol* a prolonged uniform muscular spasm.

tonic water ▷ *noun* a carbonated soft drink flavoured with quinine, usually used as a MIXER with alcoholic drinks, especially gin. Often shortened to **tonic**.

tonight /təˈnaɪt/ ▷ *noun* the night of this present day. ▷ *adverb* on or during the night of the present day. ⌛ Anglo-Saxon *to niht*.

tonnage /ˈtʌnɪdʒ/ ▷ *noun* **1** the space available in a ship for carrying cargo, measured in tons. **2** the total carrying capacity of a country's merchant shipping, measured in tons. **3** a duty or tax on ships based on their cargo-carrying capacity. **4** a duty on cargo by the ton. ⌛ 14c: originally a tax or duty levied on each *tun* of wine carried by a ship; compare TON.

tonne see TON 3

tonner /ˈtʌnə(r)/ ▷ *noun, in compounds* with numbers: a ship or lorry, etc that can carry the specified number of tons ▫ *a 10-tonner.*

tonsil /ˈtɒnsɪl/ ▷ *noun, anatomy* either of two almond-shaped lumps of tissue at the back of the mouth, which produce LYMPHOCYTES. • **tonsillar** *adj.* ⌛ 17c: from Latin *tonsillae* (plural).

tonsillectomy /tɒnsɪˈlɛktəmɪ/ ▷ *noun* (***tonsillectomies***) a surgical operation to remove the tonsils. ⌛ Early 20c.

tonsillitis /tɒnsɪˈlaɪtɪs/ ▷ *noun, pathol* inflammation of the tonsils.

tonsorial /tɒnˈsoʊrɪəl/ ▷ *adj, often facetious* belonging or relating to barbers or hairdressing. ⌛ 19c: from Latin *tondere, tonsum* to clip or shave.

tonsure /ˈtɒnʃə(r)/ ▷ *noun* **a** in the RC church, until 1973: a shaved patch on the crown of a monk's or priest's head; **b** the act of shaving the crown of a monk's or priest's head as part of the rite of entering a monastic order or the priesthood; **c** a similar shaving of part or all of the hair in other Christian churches and other religions. ▷ *verb* (***tonsured***, ***tonsuring***) to shave the head of someone. • **tonsured** *adj.* ⌛ 14c: from Latin *tondere, tonsum* to clip or shave.

tontine /ˈtɒntiːn, -ˈtiːn/ ▷ *noun, finance* an ANNUITY scheme in which several subscribers share a common fund, with their individual benefits increasing as members die until only one member is left alive and receives everything, or until a specified date at which the proceeds will be shared amongst the survivors. ⌛ 18c: named after Lorenzo Tonti (c.1653), the Italian-born Parisian banker who invented it.

ton-up /ˈtʌnʌp/ *old slang* ▷ *adj* usually said of a motorcyclist: travelling or having travelled at more than 100mph, especially often and recklessly. ▷ *noun* a speed of more than 100mph. ⌛ 1960s: from TON 8.

too ▷ *adverb* **1** to a greater extent or more than is required, desirable or suitable ▫ *too many things to do.* **2** in addition; as well; also ▫ *loves Keats and likes Shelley too.* **3** what is more; indeed ▫ *They need a good holiday, and they'll get one, too!* **4** extremely ▫ *You're too generous!* ⌛ Anglo-Saxon: a stressed form of TO.

took *past tense of* TAKE

tool ▷ *noun* **1** an implement, especially one used by hand, for cutting or digging, etc, such as a spade or hammer, etc. **2** the cutting part of a MACHINE TOOL. **3** a thing used in or necessary to a particular trade or profession ▫ *Words are the tools of a journalist's trade.* **4** someone who is used or manipulated by another, especially for selfish or dishonest reasons. **5** *coarse slang* a penis. ▷ *verb* (***tooled***, ***tooling***) **1** to work or engrave (eg stone or leather) with tools. **2** (*also* **tool up** or **tool something up**) *tr & intr* to equip a factory, etc or become equipped with the tools needed for production. ⌛ Anglo-Saxon *tol*.

■ **tool along** or **around**, *etc colloq* to drive or ride casually.

toolbag and **toolbox** ▷ *noun* a bag or box for carrying and storing tools.

toolkit ▷ *noun* a set of tools, especially those required for a particular trade or purpose.

toolmaker ▷ *noun* someone who makes or repairs MACHINE TOOLS. • **toolmaking** *noun*.

toot ▷ *noun* **1** a quick sharp blast of a trumpet, whistle or horn, etc. **2** *US slang* a quantity of a drug, especially cocaine taken by inhalation. ▷ *verb* (***tooted***, ***tooting***) **1** *tr & intr* to sound or make (a trumpet or horn, etc) sound with a quick sharp blast. **2** *US slang* to inhale cocaine. ⓒ 16c: imitating the sound.

tooth /tuːθ/ ▷ *noun* (***teeth***) **1** in vertebrates: any of the hard structures, usually embedded in the upper and lower jaw bones, that are used for biting and chewing food. **2** in invertebrates: any similar structure that is used for rasping or grinding food, or that resembles a vertebrate tooth. **3** anything like a tooth in shape, arrangement or function, such as one of many equally spaced projections around the edge of a gear wheel or points on a comb. **4** *in compounds* an appetite or liking, especially for sweet foods □ *a sweet tooth.* **5** (**teeth**) enough power or force to be effective. ▷ *verb* (***toothed***, ***toothing***) **1** to provide something with teeth. **2** *intr* said of cogs: to interlock. • **toothless** *adj* **1** without teeth. **2** powerless or ineffective. • **get one's teeth into something** to tackle or deal with it vigorously or eagerly, etc. • **in the teeth of something** against it; in opposition to it. • **kick in the teeth** and **kick someone in the teeth** see under KICK. • **long in the tooth** *colloq* old. • **set someone's teeth on edge 1** to cause them a sharp pain in the teeth, eg when they eat something very cold. **2** to cause them to wince. **3** to irritate them severely. • **take the teeth out of something** to make it harmless. • **tooth and nail** fiercely and with all one's strength. ⓒ Anglo-Saxon *toth.*

toothache ▷ *noun* an ache or pain in a tooth, usually as a result of tooth decay.

toothbrush ▷ *noun* a brush for cleaning the teeth.

tooth fairy ▷ *noun* a fairy who supposedly takes a child's MILK TOOTH from underneath their pillow, where it has been placed after falling out, and leaves money in its place.

toothily and **toothiness** see under TOOTHY

toothpaste ▷ *noun* a paste used to clean the teeth.

toothpick ▷ *noun* a small sharp piece of wood or plastic, etc for removing food stuck between the teeth.

toothpowder ▷ *noun* a powder used to clean the teeth.

toothsome ▷ *adj* appetizing; delicious; attractive. ⓒ 16c.

toothy ▷ *adj* (***toothier***, ***toothiest***) showing or having a lot of teeth, especially large prominent ones □ *a toothy grin.* • **toothily** *adverb.* • **toothiness** *noun.* ⓒ 16c.

tootle /ˈtuːtəl/ ▷ *verb* (***tootled***, ***tootling***) *intr* **1** to toot gently or continuously. **2** (*usually* **tootle about** or **round**, *etc*) *colloq* to go about casually, especially by car. ▷ *noun* **1** a tootling sound. **2** *colloq* a trip or drive. ⓒ 19c.

tootsie or **tootsy** /ˈtʊtsɪ/ ▷ *noun* (***tootsies***) *colloq* **1** *children's or playful use* a foot. **2** a toe. **3** *US* a female lover; a sweetheart; a girl or woman. ⓒ 19c.

top¹ ▷ *noun* **1** the highest part, point or level of anything. **2 a** the highest or most important rank or position; **b** the person holding this. **3** the upper edge or surface of something. **4** a lid or piece for covering the top of something. **5** a garment for covering the upper half of the body, especially a woman's body. **6** the highest or loudest degree or pitch □ *the top of one's voice.* **7** (**the tops**) *colloq* the very best person or thing. **8** (*usually* **tops**) the part of a root vegetable that is above the ground. **9** *Brit, autos* TOP GEAR. ▷ *adj* at or being the highest or most important. ▷ *verb* (***topped***, ***topping***) **1** to cover or form the top of something, especially as a finishing or decorative touch. **2** to remove the top of something. **3** to rise above or be better than something; to surpass. **4** to reach the top of something. **5 a** *slang* to kill, especially by hanging; **b** (**top oneself**) to commit suicide. **6** *golf* to hit the upper half of (the ball). • **from top to toe** completely; from head to foot. • **on top of something 1** in control of it. **2** in addition to it. **3** very close to it. • **on top of the world** in the very best of spirits. • **top the bill** to head the list of performers in a show, as the main attraction. ⓒ Anglo-Saxon.

■ **top something off** to put a finishing or decorative touch to it.

■ **top something out** to put the highest stone on (a building).

■ **top something** or **someone up 1** to refill (someone's glass or a container, etc) that has been partly emptied. **2** to provide money to bring (a grant, wage or money supply, etc) to the required or desirable total.

top² ▷ *noun* a wooden or metal toy which spins on a pointed base. Also called **spinning top**. • **sleep like a top** to sleep very soundly. ⓒ Anglo-Saxon.

topaz /ˈtoʊpaz/ ▷ *noun* (***topazes***) **1** an aluminium silicate mineral, sometimes formed as enormous hard crystals, the pale yellow variety of which is most highly prized as a semi-precious gemstone. **2** the yellowish-brown colour of this gemstone. ▷ *adj* topaz-coloured. ⓒ 13c: from Greek *topazos.*

top boot ▷ *noun* a high boot with a band of different-coloured leather round the top.

top brass ▷ *noun, colloq* the highest-ranking officers or personnel, especially in the military.

topcoat ▷ *noun* an overcoat.

top coat ▷ *noun* a final coat of paint.

top dog ▷ *noun, colloq* the most important or powerful person in a group.

top drawer ▷ *noun* (*especially* **out of the top drawer**) the highest level, especially of society. Also (**top-drawer**) *as adj.*

top-dressing ▷ *noun* **1** manure or fertilizer applied to a growing crop. **2** the application of manure or fertilizer to a growing crop. **3** any superficial covering or treatment. • **top-dress** *verb* to put top-dressing on. ⓒ 18c.

tope¹ ▷ *verb* (***toped***, ***toping***) *intr, archaic* to drink alcohol to excess. • **toper** *noun.* ⓒ 17c: perhaps a variant of obsolete *top* to drink.

tope² ▷ *noun* a small shark, native to temperate and tropical seas, with a slender white and dark-grey body. ⓒ 17c.

topee see TOPI

top-flight ▷ *adj* belonging or relating to the best or highest quality. ⓒ 1930s.

topgallant /tɒpˈgalənt; *naut* təˈgalənt/ ▷ *noun* the mast or sail above the topmast and topsail. ⓒ 16c.

top gear ▷ *noun, Brit* the highest gear in a motor car or bike, etc. Often shortened to **top**.

top hat ▷ *noun* a tall cylindrical hat, often made of silk and worn as part of formal dress, usually by men.

top-heavy ▷ *adj* **1** disproportionately heavy in the upper part in comparison with the lower. **2** said of a company or administration, etc: employing too many senior staff in proportion to junior staff.

topi or **topee** /ˈtoʊpɪ/ ▷ *noun* (***topis*** or ***topees***) a lightweight hat, shaped like a helmet, worn in hot countries as protection against the sun. ⓒ 19c: Hindi, meaning 'hat'.

topiary /ˈtoʊpɪərɪ/ ▷ *noun* (***topiaries***) **1** the art of cutting trees, bushes and hedges into ornamental shapes. **2** an example of this. • **topiarian** *adj.* • **topiarist** *noun.* ⓒ 16c: from Latin *topia* landscape gardening.

topic /ˈtɒpɪk/ ▷ *noun* a subject or theme for a book, film or discussion, etc. ⓒ 16c: from Greek *ta topika,* the title of a work by Aristotle on reasoning from general considerations.

topical ▷ *adj* **1** relating to matters of interest at the present time; dealing with current affairs. **2** relating to a particular place; local. **3** belonging or relating to a topic or topics. **4** *medicine* said of an ointment or treatment, etc:

applied externally to the body. • **topicality** *noun*. • **topically** *adverb*.

topknot ▷ *noun* **1** *especially historical* a knot of ribbons, etc worn on the top of the head as decoration. **2** a tuft of hair, growing on top of the head. ⓘ 17c.

topless ▷ *adj* **1** having no top. **2** said of clothing: having no upper part; leaving the breasts exposed. **3** said of a woman: with her breasts exposed. **4** said of a place: where women go topless □ *topless beaches*.

topmast ▷ *noun, naut* the second mast, usually directly above the lower mast. ⓘ 15c.

topmost /'tɒpmoʊst/ ▷ *adj* the very highest of all.

top-notch ▷ *adj, colloq* the very best quality; superb. ⓘ Early 20c.

topography /tə'pɒgrəfɪ/ ▷ *noun* (**topographies**) **1 a** the natural and constructed features on the surface of land, such as rivers, mountains, valleys, bridges and railway lines; **b** a description or map of these; **c** the describing or mapping of such features. **2** the mapping or describing of the surface of any object or body. • **topographer** *noun*. • **topographic** /tɒpə'grafɪk/ or **topographical** *adj*. • **topographically** *adverb*. ⓘ 15c: from Greek *topos* place + *graphein* to describe.

topology /tə'pɒlədʒɪ/ ▷ *noun, geom* the branch of geometry concerned with those properties of a geometrical figure that remain unchanged even when the figure is deformed by bending, stretching or twisting, etc. • **topological** *adj*. • **topologically** *adverb*. ⓘ 17c: from Greek *topos* place + -LOGY.

toponymy /tə'pɒnəmɪ/ ▷ *noun* the study of place names. • **toponym** /'tɒpənɪm/ *noun* a placename. • **toponymic** *adj*. ⓘ 19c: from Greek *topos* place + *onyma* name.

topper ▷ *noun, colloq* **1** a top hat. **2** someone or something that excels.

topping ▷ *noun* something that forms a covering or garnish for food □ *cheese topping*. ▷ *adj, Brit dated colloq* excellent.

topple /'tɒpəl/ ▷ *verb* (**toppled**, **toppling**) *tr & intr* **1** (*also* **topple over**) to fall, or make someone or something fall, by overbalancing. **2** (*also* **topple over**) to make as if to fall by overbalancing, without actually falling. **2** to overthrow or be overthrown. ⓘ 16c: from TOP[1].

topsail /'tɒpseɪl; *naut* -səl/ ▷ *noun* a square sail set across the topmast. ⓘ 14c.

top-secret ▷ *adj* very secret, especially officially classified as such.

topside ▷ *noun* **1** a lean cut of beef from the rump. **2** the side of a ship above the waterline. ▷ *adj, adverb* on deck.

topsoil ▷ *noun* the uppermost layer of soil, rich in organic matter, where most plant roots develop. Compare SUBSOIL.

topspin ▷ *noun* a spin given to a ball by hitting it sharply on the upper half with a forward and upward stroke to make it travel higher, further or faster.

topsy-turvy /tɒpsɪ'tɜːvɪ/ ▷ *adj, adverb* **1** upside down. **2** in confusion. • **topsy-turvily** *adverb*. • **topsy-turviness** *noun*. ⓘ 16c: perhaps from TOP[1] + obsolete *terve* to turn over.

toque /toʊk/ ▷ *noun* **1** a small close-fitting brimless hat worn by women. **2** *historical* a type of cap popular in the 16c. ⓘ 16c: French.

tor /tɔː(r)/ ▷ *noun* a tower-like block of unweathered rock formed by erosion of surrounding weathered rock. Also called **corestone**. ⓘ Anglo-Saxon *torr*.

Torah /'tɔːrə/ ▷ *noun, Judaism* **1** the PENTATEUCH. **2** the scroll on which this is written, used in a synagogue. **3** the whole body of Jewish literature and law, both written and oral, and including the Old Testament and Talmud. ⓘ 16c: Hebrew, meaning 'instruction'.

torc see TORQUE 1

torch /tɔːtʃ/ ▷ *noun* (**torches**) **1** *Brit* a small portable light powered by electric batteries. **2** a piece of wood or bundle of cloth, etc which is set alight and used as a source of light. **3** any source of heat, light, illumination or enlightenment, etc. ▷ *verb* (**torches**, **torched**, **torching**) *colloq, especially N Amer* to set fire to something deliberately. • **carry a torch for someone** to feel love, especially unrequited love, for them. ⓘ 13c: from French *torche*.

torchbearer ▷ *noun* **1** someone who carries a torch. **2** someone who inspires and leads.

torchlight ▷ *noun* the light of a torch or torches.

torch song ▷ *noun* a song, especially popular in the 1930s, which expressed unrequited love in a mournful and sentimental way. • **torch singer** *noun*.

tore *past tense of* TEAR[2]

toreador /'tɒrɪədɔː(r)/ ▷ *noun* a bullfighter, especially one on horseback. See also MATADOR, PICADOR. ⓘ 17c: Spanish, from *torear* to bait a bull, from *toro* bull.

torero /tɒ'rɛəroʊ/ ▷ *noun* (**toreros**) a bullfighter, especially one on foot. ⓘ 18c: Spanish, from *toro* bull.

tori and **toric** see under TORUS

torment ▷ *noun* /'tɔːmɛnt/ **1** very great pain, suffering or anxiety. **2** something that causes this. ▷ *verb* /tɔː'mɛnt/ (**tormented**, **tormenting**) **1** to cause great pain, suffering or anxiety to someone or something. **2** to pester or harass (eg a child or animal). • **tormentor** *noun*. ⓘ 13c: from Latin *tormentum*.

tormentil /'tɔːməntɪl/ ▷ *noun* a perennial plant with clusters of bright-yellow flowers and an astringent woody root, which is used in herbal medicine. ⓘ 15c: from Latin *tormentum* torment, because it was used to numb pain.

torn ▷ *verb, past participle of* TEAR[2]. • **that's torn it!** an expression of annoyance indicating that something has happened to upset one's plans, etc.

tornado /tɔː'neɪdoʊ/ ▷ *noun* (**tornadoes**) **1** *meteorol* a violently destructive storm characterized by a funnel-shaped rotating column of air which can be seen extending downward from thunder clouds to the ground, tracing a narrow path across the land. **2** a violent outburst. ⓘ 16c: altered from Spanish *tronada* 'thunderstorm', influenced by *tornar* to turn.

toroid /'tɒrɔɪd/ ▷ *noun* a figure shaped like a TORUS. • **toroidal** *adj*.

torpedo /tɔː'piːdoʊ/ ▷ *noun* (**torpedoes** or **torpedos**) **1** a long self-propelling underwater missile which explodes on impact with its target (usually a ship) and can be fired from submarines, ships and aircraft. **2** (*also* **torpedo ray**) *zool* any of various cartilaginous fish, related to the skates and rays, that give off electric shocks. **3** *N Amer* a small container that holds an explosive charge, used in warfare as eg a firework or fog-signal. ▷ *verb* (**torpedoes**, **torpedoed**, **torpedoing**) **1** to attack with torpedoes. **2** to wreck or destroy (eg a plan). ⓘ 16c: Latin, meaning 'numbness' or 'electric ray'.

torpedo boat ▷ *noun* a small fast warship armed with torpedoes.

torpid /'tɔːpɪd/ ▷ *adj* **1** sluggish and dull; unenergetic. **2** unable to move or feel; numb. **3** said of a hibernating animal: dormant. • **torpidity** *noun*. • **torpidly** *adverb*. ⓘ 17c: from Latin *torpidus*.

torpor /'tɔːpə(r)/ ▷ *noun* the state of being torpid. ⓘ 17c: Latin.

torque /tɔːk/ ▷ *noun* **1** (*also* **torc**) *historical* a necklace made of metal twisted into a band, worn by the ancient

Britons and Gauls. **2** *physics* force multiplied by the perpendicular distance from a point about which it causes rotation, measured in newton-metres. ◷ 19c: from Latin *torquere* to twist.

torr /tɔː(r)/ ▷ *noun, physics* a unit of pressure equal to 133.32 pascals, used to measure very low pressures, eg in high-vacuum technology. ◷ 1950s: named after the Italian mathematician Evangelista Torricelli (1608–47).

torrefy /ˈtɒrɪfaɪ/ ▷ *verb* (***torrefies, torrefied, torrefying***) *technical* to dry or parch (ores or drugs, etc) by heat. ◷ 17c: from Latin *torrefacere* to dry by heat.

torrent /ˈtɒrənt/ ▷ *noun* **1** a great rushing stream or downpour of water or lava, etc. **2** a violent or strong flow, eg of questions or abuse. • **torrential** /təˈrɛnʃəl/ *adj.* ◷ 17c: from Latin *torrens, torrentis* boiling.

torrid /ˈtɒrɪd/ ▷ *adj* (***torrider, torridest***) **1** said of the weather: so hot and dry as to scorch the land. **2** said of land: scorched and parched by extremely hot dry weather. **3** passionate; intensely emotional. ◷ 16c: from Latin *torridus*.

torrid zone ▷ *noun* the area of the Earth lying between the TROPIC OF CANCER and the TROPIC OF CAPRICORN. ◷ 16c.

torsion /ˈtɔːʃən/ ▷ *noun* **1** the act or process of twisting something by applying force to one end while the other is held firm or twisted in the opposite direction (see TORQUE). **2** the state of being twisted in this way. • **torsional** *adj.* ◷ 16c in sense 1: from Latin *torsio, torsionis* from *torquere* to twist.

torso /ˈtɔːsoʊ/ ▷ *noun* (***torsos***) **1** the main part of the human body, without the limbs and head; the trunk. **2** a nude statue of this. ◷ 18c: Italian, from Latin *thyrsos* stalk.

tort ▷ *noun, law* any wrongful act, other than breach of contract, for which an action for damages or compensation may be brought. ◷ 14c: from Latin *tortum* wrong.

torte /tɔːt, ˈtɔːtə/ ▷ *noun* (***torten*** or ***tortes***) a rich sweet cake or pastry, often garnished or filled with fruit, nuts, cream or chocolate, etc. ◷ 18c: German.

tortelli /tɔːˈtɛlɪ/ ▷ *plural noun* small pasta parcels stuffed with various fillings, eg meat, cheese or vegetables.

tortellini /tɔːtəˈliːnɪ/ ▷ *plural noun* small pasta cases, often in the shape of rings, stuffed with various fillings, eg meat, cheese or vegetables. ◷ 1930s: Italian, diminutive plural of *tortello* cake.

torticollis /tɔːtɪˈkɒlɪs/ ▷ *noun, pathol* a twisted position of the head on the neck, due to muscular spasm, congenital injury to a neck muscle, etc. Also called **wryneck**. ◷ 19c: form Latin *tortus* twisted + *collum* neck.

tortilla /tɔːˈtiːjə/ ▷ *noun* (***tortillas***) a thin round Mexican maize cake cooked on a griddle and usually eaten hot, with a filling or topping of meat or cheese. ◷ 17c: Spanish, diminutive of *torta* cake.

tortillon /tɔːtiːˈɒn/ ▷ *noun* a STUMP².

tortoise /ˈtɔːtəs/ ▷ *noun* any of various slow-moving, toothless reptiles with a high domed shell into which the head, short scaly legs and tail can be withdrawn for safety. ◷ 14c: from Latin *tortuca*.

tortoiseshell and **turtle shell** ▷ *noun* **1** the brown and yellow mottled shell of a sea turtle, used in making combs, jewellery and decorative inlay in furniture. **2** a butterfly with mottled orange or red and brown or black wings. **3** a domestic cat with a mottled orange and creamy-brown coat. ▷ *adj* made of or mottled like tortoiseshell.

tortuous /ˈtɔːtʃʊəs/ ▷ *adj* **1** full of twists and turns. **2** not straightforward, especially in being devious or involved. • **tortuously** *adverb.* • **tortuousness** *noun.* ◷ 15c: from Latin *tortuosus*, from *torquere, tortum* to twist.

torture /ˈtɔːtʃə(r)/ ▷ *noun* **1** the infliction of severe pain or mental suffering, especially as a punishment or as a means of persuading someone to give information. **2 a** great physical or mental suffering; **b** a cause of this. ▷ *verb* (***tortured, torturing***) **1** to subject someone to torture. **2** to cause someone to experience great physical or mental suffering. **3** to force something out of its natural state or position; to distort. • **torturous** *adj.* • **torturously** *adverb.* ◷ 16c: from Latin *tortura* torment.

torus /ˈtɔːrəs/ ▷ *noun* (*tori* /ˈtɔːraɪ/) **1** *physics* a circular ring with a D-shaped cross-section used to contain plasma in NUCLEAR FISSION reactors. **2** *bot* the RECEPTACLE of a flower. **3** *geom* a solid curved surface with a hole in it, resembling a doughnut, obtained by rotating a circle about an axis lying in the same plane as the circle. • **toric** *adj.* See also TOROID. ◷ 16c: Latin, meaning 'bulge' or 'swelling'.

Tory /ˈtɔːrɪ/ ▷ *noun* (***Tories***) **1** a member or supporter of the British Conservative Party. **2** *historical* a member or supporter of a major English political party from the 17c to mid-19c which favoured royal authority over that of Parliament, supported the established Church and was against political and social reform, superseded by the Conservative Party. Compare WHIG. **3** *N Amer, historical* a supporter of the British Crown during the American Revolution. ▷ *adj* **1** relating to or supporting the Tories. **2** Conservative. • **Toryism** *noun.* ◷ 17c: from Irish Gaelic *tóraí* 'bandit' or 'outlaw'.

tosh ▷ *noun, colloq* twaddle; nonsense. ◷ 19c.

toss ▷ *verb* (***tossed, tossing***) **1** to throw something up into the air. **2** (*usually* **toss something away, aside** or **out**, *etc*) to throw it away or discard it casually or carelessly. **3** (*also* **toss about** or **around**, *etc*) *intr* to move restlessly or from side to side repeatedly. **4** (*also* **toss about**) *tr & intr* to be thrown or throw something from side to side repeatedly and violently □ ***a ship tossed by the storm.*** **5** to jerk (the head), especially as a sign of impatience or anger. **6** *tr & intr* **a** to throw (a spinning coin) into the air and guess which side will land facing up, as a way of making a decision or settling a dispute; **b** to settle a dispute with someone by tossing a coin □ ***toss him for the last cake.*** **7** to coat (food, especially salad) with oil or a dressing, etc by gently mixing or turning it. **8** said of a horse, etc: to throw (its rider). **9** said of an animal: to throw (a person) into the air with its horns. **10** (*also* **toss about** or **around**, *etc*) to discuss or consider (eg ideas) in, or as if in, light-hearted or casual debate. ▷ *noun* **1** an act or an instance of tossing. **2** a fall from a horse. **3** *slang* the slightest amount □ ***not give a toss.*** • **argue the toss** to dispute a decision. ◷ 16c.

■ **toss off** or **toss it off** *Brit, coarse slang* to masturbate.

■ **toss something off 1** to drink it quickly, especially in a single swallow. **2** to produce it quickly and easily.

■ **toss up** to throw a spinning coin into the air and guess which side will land facing upwards, as a way of making a decision or settling a dispute. See also TOSS-UP.

tosser ▷ *noun, Brit, course slang* a stupid or loathsome person. ◷ 1970s in this sense: from TOSS OFF.

toss-up ▷ *noun* **1** *colloq* an even chance or risk; something doubtful. **2** an act of tossing a coin.

tot¹ ▷ *noun* **1** a small child; a toddler. **2** a small amount of spirits □ ***a tot of whisky.*** ◷ 18c.

tot² ▷ *verb* (***totted, totting***) (*especially* **tot something up**) **1** to add it together. **2** *intr* said of money, etc: to increase. See also TOTTING-UP. ◷ 18c: an abbreviation of TOTAL.

total /ˈtoʊtəl/ ▷ *adj* whole; complete. ▷ *noun* the whole or complete amount, eg of various things added together. ▷ *verb* (***totalled, totalling***; *US* ***totaled, totaling***) **1** *tr & intr* to amount to a specified sum □ ***The figures totalled 385.*** **2** (*also* **total something up**) to add it up to produce a total.

3 *N Amer slang* to wreck or destroy (especially a vehicle) completely. ● **totally** *adverb*. ⓒ 14c: from Latin *totus* all.

total eclipse ▻ *noun, astron* an eclipse where all of the Sun or Moon is covered. Compare ANNULAR ECLIPSE, PARTIAL ECLIPSE.

total football ▻ *noun* the style of play popularized by the Dutch national team during the 1970s, involving a commitment to playing passing football, where all the players, including defenders, can be involved in attack.

totalitarian /toutalı'tɛərıən/ ▻ *adj* belonging or relating to a system of government by a single party which allows no opposition and which demands complete obedience to the State. ▻ *noun* someone in favour of such a system. ● **totalitarianism** *noun*. ⓒ 1920s.

totality /tou'talıtı/ ▻ *noun* (***totalities***) **1** completeness. **2** a complete number or amount.

Totalizator or **Totalisator** /toutəlaı'zeıtə(r)/ and **totalizer** or **totaliser** ▻ *noun* **1** a system of betting in which the total amount staked, minus tax, etc, is paid out to the winners in proportion to the size of their stake. **2** an automatic machine which records any bets made using this system and works out pay-outs and odds, etc. Often shortened to **Tote**. Also called PARI-MUTUEL.

total recall ▻ *noun* the power or ability to remember experiences accurately and in full detail.

tote /tout/ ▻ *verb* (***toted, toting***) *colloq* to carry, drag or wear something, especially something heavy. ⓒ 17c.

tote bag ▻ *noun* a large bag for carrying shopping.

totem /'toutəm/ ▻ *noun* **1** in Native American culture: a natural object, especially an animal, used as the badge or sign of a tribe or an individual. **2** an image or representation of this. ● **totemic** /-'tɛmık/ *adj*. ● **totemism** *noun*. ● **totemist** *noun*. ⓒ 18c: from Ojibwa (a Native American language).

totem pole ▻ *noun* **1** in Native American culture: a large wooden pole that has totems carved and painted on it, usually placed outside a house to ward off evil spirits and as a symbol of certain mystic sacred social rules, family relationships, etc. **2** *colloq* a hierarchical system ◻ ***not very high up on the social totem pole.***

tother and **t'other** /tʌðə(r)/ ▻ *adj, pronoun, Brit jocular or dialect* the other ◻ ***You grab that end and I'll get tother.*** ⓒ 13c: from *the tother*, from Anglo-Saxon *thet other* the other.

totter ▻ *verb* (***tottered, tottering***) *intr* **1** to walk or move unsteadily, shakily or weakly. **2** to sway or tremble as if about to fall. **3** said of a system of government, etc: to be on the verge of collapse. ▻ *noun* a weak and unsteady movement or gait. ● **totterer** *noun*. ● **tottering** *adj*. ● **totteringly** *adverb*. ● **tottery** *adj*. ⓒ 14c in this sense; 12c, meaning 'to swing'.

totted and **totting** see under TOT[2]

totting-up ▻ *noun* **1** an instance or the process of adding up. **2** *Brit* the scheme or arrangement which allows for the addition of penalty points to someone's driving licence for traffic offences, which can eventually lead to the holder being disqualified from driving. ⓒ 19c in sense 1; 1960s in sense 2: from TOT[2].

toucan /'tuːkən, -kan/ ▻ *noun* a tropical American fruit-eating bird with a huge beak and brightly coloured feathers. ⓒ 16c: from Tupí *tucana*.

touch /tʌtʃ/ ▻ *verb* (***touches, touched, touching***) **1** to bring something, such as a hand, into contact, usually lightly, with something else ◻ ***touched the radiator to check that it was on.*** **2 a** *tr & intr* to be in physical contact or come into physical contact with, especially lightly ◻ ***Make sure the seats don't touch the wallpaper;*** **b** to bring together in close physical contact ◻ ***They touched hands under the table.*** **3** *often with negatives* **a** to injure, harm or hurt ◻ ***It's not my fault, Mum — I never touched him!*** **b** to interfere with, move, disturb, etc ◻ ***Who's been touching my things?*** **c** to have dealings with, be associated with or be a party to something ◻ ***wouldn't touch that kind of job;*** **d** to make use of, especially as food or drink ◻ ***He never touches alcohol;*** **e** to use (eg money, etc) ◻ ***I don't touch the money in that account — it's my holiday money;*** **f** to approach in excellence; to be as good as; to compare to ◻ ***Nobody can touch her at chess.*** **4** to concern or affect; to make a difference to ◻ ***It's a matter that touches us all.*** **5** (*usually* **touch on** or **upon**) to deal with (a matter, subject, etc), especially in passing or not very thoroughly. **6** to affect with pity, sympathy, gratitude, quiet pleasure, etc ◻ ***The story of his sad life touched her heart.*** **7** to reach or go as far as, especially temporarily ◻ ***The temperature touched 100.*** **8 a** (*usually* **touch with**) to tinge, taint, mark, modify, etc slightly or delicately ◻ ***The sky was touched with pink*** ◻ ***a love that's touched with sorrow;*** **b** to make a usually slight, sometimes harmful, impression, effect, etc on something ◻ ***Frost had touched the early crop.*** **9** (*often* **touch in**) to mark, draw or paint with light strokes. ▻ *noun* **1** an act of touching or the sensation of being touched. **2** the sense by which the existence, nature, texture and quality of objects can be perceived through physical contact with the hands, feet, skin, lips, etc. **3** the particular texture and qualities of an object as perceived through contact with the hands, etc ◻ ***the silky touch of the fabric against her skin.*** **4** a small amount, quantity, distance, etc; a trace or hint ◻ ***move it left a touch.*** **5** a slight attack (eg of an illness). **6** a slight stroke or mark. **7** a detail which adds to or complements the general pleasing effect or appearance ◻ ***The flowers were an elegant touch.*** **8** a distinctive or characteristic style or manner ◻ ***need the expert's touch.*** **9** a musician's individual manner or technique of touching or striking the keys of a keyboard instrument or strings of a string instrument to produce a good tone. **10** an artist's or writer's individual style or manner of working. **11** the ability to respond or behave with sensitivity and sympathy ◻ ***have a wonderful touch with animals.*** **12** *sport* in rugby, etc: the ground outside the touchlines. **13** *slang* an act of asking for and receiving money from someone as a gift or loan. **14** *slang* someone who can be persuaded to give or lend money ◻ ***a soft touch.*** **15** a test with, or as if with, a touchstone. ● **get in touch (with)** to make contact or communicate (with) ◻ ***They got in touch by letter.*** ● **in touch (with) 1** in contact, communication, etc (with) ◻ ***We still keep in touch although we haven't seen each other for 20 years.*** **2** up to date ◻ ***keeps in touch with the latest news.*** **3** aware or conscious (of) ◻ ***in touch with her inner self.*** ● **into touch** *rugby* over the touchline. ● **lose one's touch** to become unfamiliar or out of practice ◻ ***I haven't played the piano for ages — I hope I haven't lost my touch.*** ● **lose touch (with) 1** to be no longer in contact, communication, etc (with) ◻ ***lost touch with them after they moved house.*** **2** to be no longer familiar (with) or well-informed (about) ◻ ***lost touch with what's happening in Bosnia.*** ● **lose touch with reality** to behave in an eccentric, mad, etc way. ● **out of touch (with) 1** not in contact, communication, etc (with) ◻ ***been out of touch with his brother for years.*** **2** not up to date (with) ◻ ***out of touch with the new technology.*** ● **touch wood 1** to lay a hand on something wooden, or to make as if to do this, eg by patting one's head, in the superstitious belief that this will ward off bad luck. **2** an expression that is used when this is done ◻ ***Oh! Touch wood! I hope she won't be there.*** ● **would not touch something with a bargepole** see under BARGEPOLE. ⓒ 13c: from French *tuchier*.

■ **touch down 1** said of an aircraft, spacecraft, etc: to land. **2** *rugby* to carry the ball over the goal-line and put it on the ground at a point that is either behind one's own goal-line as a defensive move or behind that of one's opponents to score a try. See also TOUCHDOWN.

■ **touch someone for something** *slang* to ask them for and receive (money), especially a specified amount, as a loan or gift ◻ ***touched him for 50 quid.***

■ **touch something off 1** to cause it to explode, eg by putting a match to it. **2** to cause it to begin; to trigger it □ *Police brutality touched off the riots.*

■ **touch on** to verge towards □ *That touches on the surreal.* See also *verb* 5 above.

■ **touch up 1** (*usually* **touch someone up**) *Brit slang* **a** to fondle them so as to excite them sexually; **b** to sexually molest them. **2** (*usually* **touch up something**) to improve it by adding small details, correcting or hiding minor faults, etc □ *touched up the painting so it looked as good as new.* See also TOUCH-UP.

touch and go ▻ *adj* very uncertain in outcome; risky □ *It was touch and go whether she'd survive.*

touchdown ▻ *noun* **1** the act, an instance or the process of an aircraft or spacecraft making contact with the ground when landing. **2** *Amer football* the act, an instance or the process of carrying the ball over the touchline or catching or gaining possession of it behind the goal line. It scores six points.

touché /'tuːʃeɪ/ ▻ *exclamation* **1** *fencing* expressing that a hit is acknowledged. **2** good-humoured acknowledgment of the validity of a point that is made either in an argument or in retaliation. ⓒ Early 20c: French, meaning 'touched'.

touched ▻ *adj* **1** having a feeling of pity, sympathy, quiet pleasure, etc. **2** *colloq* slightly mad.

touch-hole ▻ *noun* a small hole in a cannon or gun where the charge can be lit.

touchily, touchiness see under TOUCHY

touching ▻ *adj* causing feelings of pity or sympathy; moving □ *a touching story about a poor orphan.* ▻ *prep, old use* concerning; pertaining to. ● **touchingly** *adverb.* ● **touchingness** *noun.*

touch judge ▻ *noun, rugby* one of the two linesmen or lineswomen.

touchline ▻ *noun, sport, especially football & rugby* either of the two lines that mark the side boundaries of the pitch.

touch-me-not ▻ *noun* any of various plants that have seed pods which, when ripe, explode when touched. ▻ *adj* stand-offish □ *a real touch-me-not attitude.*

touchpaper ▻ *noun* paper that is steeped in saltpetre and which is used for lighting fireworks or firing gunpowder.

touch screen ▻ *noun, computing* a type of visual display unit screen that doubles as an input device and which is operated by pressing it with a finger.

touchstone ▻ *noun* **1** a hard black flint-like stone that is used for testing the purity and quality of gold and silver alloys according to the colour of the mark which is left when the alloy is rubbed on this stone. **2** a test or standard for judging the quality of something.

touch-type ▻ *verb, intr* to use a typewriter without looking at the keyboard. ● **touch-typing** *noun.* ● **touch-typist** *noun.* ⓒ 1940s.

touch-up ▻ *noun* (*touch-ups*) the act, an instance, or the process of, making small final improvements or of doing minor restorations. See also TOUCH UP at TOUCH.

touchwood ▻ *noun* dry or decayed wood which has been soften by fungi, making it particularly suitable for kindling fires.

touchy ▻ *adj* (*touchier, touchiest*) *colloq* **1** easily annoyed or offended. **2** needing to be handled or dealt with with care and tact. ● **touchily** *adverb.* ● **touchiness** *noun.*

tough /tʌf/ ▻ *adj* **1** strong and durable; not easily cut, broken, torn or worn out. **2** said of food, especially meat: difficult to chew. **3** said of a person, animal, etc: strong and fit and able to endure hardship. **4** difficult to deal with or overcome; testing □ *a tough decision.* **5** severe and determined; unyielding; resolute □ *a tough customer.* **6** rough and violent; criminal □ *a tough area.* **7** *colloq* unlucky; unjust; unpleasant □ *The divorce was tough on the kids.* ▻ *noun* a rough violent person, especially a bully or criminal. ▻ *adverb, colloq* aggressively; in a macho way □ *acts tough when he's with his mates.* ● **toughish** *adj.* ● **toughly** *adverb.* ● **toughness** *noun.* ● **get tough with someone** *colloq* to begin to deal with them more strictly or severely. ⓒ Anglo-Saxon *toh.*

■ **tough something out** (*often* **tough it out**) to withstand (a difficult, trying, etc situation) stoically or with great endurance, stamina, etc □ *lost his job and had to tough out the winter with hardly any money for heating.*

toughen ▻ *verb* (*toughened, toughening*) *tr & intr* (*also* **toughen up** or **toughen someone up**) to become, or make them, tough or tougher. ● **toughener** *noun.* ● **toughening** *adj, noun.* ⓒ 16c.

tough guy ▻ *noun* **1** someone who acts in an aggressively macho way. **2** someone who is perceived as being difficult to hurt, harm or dissuade from their course of action. ⓒ 1930s.

toughie ▻ *noun, colloq* **1** someone who is quite aggressive, violent, etc. **2** something, eg a question, problem, etc that is quite difficult to answer, solve, etc.

tough love ▻ *noun* the practice of keeping a loved one who has an addiction on a strict regime without any access to alcohol, drugs, etc while at the same time showing them love, care, sympathy, etc.

tough luck ▻ *noun* **1** a misfortune, disappointment, etc □ *It was tough luck not winning the quiz.* **2** misfortune in general, especially of the kind that deserves no sympathy □ *It's just your tough luck — you shouldn't drink and drive.* ▻ *exclamation* **1** expressing sympathy when something has gone wrong or not to plan. **2** expressing aggressive scorn □ *Well, tough luck! I'm not going, so you'll just have to go by yourself.*

toupee /tuː'peɪ/ ▻ *noun* (*toupees*) a small wig or hairpiece worn usually by men to cover a bald patch. ⓒ 18c: from French *toupet* tuft of hair.

tour /tʊə(r)/ ▻ *noun* **1 a** an extended journey round an area, country, etc with stops at various places of interest along the route and which usually returns to the starting-point at the end; **b** (**the Tour** or **the Grand Tour**) a journey through France, Germany, Switzerland and Italy that was formerly undertaken by wealthy or aristocratic young men as the culmination of their education. **2** a visit round a particular place □ *a tour of the cathedral.* **3** a journey round a place with frequent stops for business or professional engagements along the route, eg by a theatre company, a sports team visiting from abroad, a rock group, etc. **4 a** an official period of duty or military service, especially abroad □ *did a tour of duty in Germany*; **b** the time spent on this kind of duty or service. ▻ *verb* (*toured, touring*) *tr & intr* **1** to travel round (a place). **2** said of a theatre company, band, performer, etc: to travel from place to place giving performances. ● **on tour** said of a theatre company, band, performer, sports team, etc: playing a series of specified venues (around an area, country, etc). ● **touring** *adj, noun.* ⓒ 13c: from French *tor*, from Greek *tornos* tool for making circles.

touraco see TURACO

tour de force /tʊə də fɔːs/ (***tours de force*** /tʊə —/) ▻ *noun* a feat of strength or skill; an outstanding performance or effort □ *That was a wonderful meal — a veritable tour de force.* ⓒ 19c: French, meaning 'a feat of strength'.

Tourette's syndrome /tʊə'rɛts —/ ▻ *noun, medicine* a disorder characterized by severe and multiple nervous tics, a tendency to utter obscenities and to bark, grunt, etc, especially unexpectedly in public places. See also

COPROLALIA. ◎ 19c: named after the French neurologist G Gilles de la Tourette (1857–1904), who first described the disorder in 1885.

tourism ▷ *noun* **1** the practice of travelling to and visiting places for pleasure and relaxation. **2** the industry that is involved in offering various services for tourists, eg providing them with information on where to stay or eat, places of interest, etc, and which sometimes also books accommodation, travel, tours, theatre tickets, etc and organizes advertising campaigns, etc. ◎ 19c; originally a disparaging term.

tourist ▷ *noun* **1** someone who travels for pleasure and relaxation; a holiday-maker. **2** a member of a sports team that is visiting from abroad. ▷ *adj* relating or referring to or suitable for people on holiday ▫ ***tourist hotel.*** • **touristic** *adj.* • **touristically** *adverb.* • **touristy** *adj, usually derog* designed for, appealing to, frequented by or full of tourists.

tourist class ▷ *noun* the cheapest kind of passenger accommodation on a ship or in an aircraft.

tourist information office ▷ *noun* a building, office, etc where tourists can get information about where to stay, restaurants, local places of interest, events, etc and where they can also usually book accommodation.

tourist route ▷ *noun* a route, usually away from the motorways, where tourists will find places of interest, scenic countryside, etc.

Tourist Trophy ▷ *noun* an award given to the winner of the motorcycle races that are held annually on the Isle of Man. Often shortened to TT. ◎ 1907.

touristy see under TOURIST

tourmaline /ˈtʊəməliːn/ ▷ *noun, geol* any of a group of minerals found in transparent or coloured (pink, blue, green or black) crystalline form in granites and gneisses, used as semi-precious gemstones and, because of their refractive and electrical properties, in optical and electrical equipment. ◎ 18c: from Sinhalese *tormalliya* cornelian.

tournament /ˈtʊənəmənt, ˈtɔːn-/ ▷ *noun* **1** a competition, eg in tennis or chess, that usually involves many players taking part in heats for a championship. **2** *historical* in the Middle Ages: **a** a competition involving either pairs of knights or two groups of knights on horseback jousting with each other, usually with blunted lances and swords; **b** a meeting where this kind of competition takes place. See also TOURNEY. ◎ 13c: from French *torneiement.*

tournedos /ˈtʊənədoʊ/ ▷ *noun* (***tournedos*** /-doʊz/) a small round thick cut of beef fillet that is usually grilled or sautéed and served with a rich sauce, often on a crouton bed with pâté. Also called FILET MIGNON. ◎ 1870s: French, from *tourner* to turn + *dos* the back, reputedly because, when it was first served in French restaurants, it was considered such an unconventional dish that it had to be brought to the table 'behind the backs' of the customers.

tourney /ˈtʊənɪ/ ▷ *noun* (***tourneys***) a medieval tournament. ▷ *verb* (***tourneyed, tourneying***) *intr* to take part in a medieval tournament. ◎ 14c: from French *torneie*, from Latin *tornare* to turn.

tourniquet /ˈtʊənɪkeɪ, ˈtɔː-/ ▷ *noun* an emergency device that usually consists of a broad strip of cloth, etc which is wrapped around a limb and a bar which is then turned in the cloth to tighten it so that the flow of blood through an artery may be stopped (maximally for half an hour). ◎ 17c: French, from *tourner* to turn.

tour operator ▷ *noun* someone or a firm that organizes holidays for customers, especially package holidays.

tousle or **touzle** /ˈtaʊzəl/ ▷ *verb* (***tousled, tousling***) **1** to make (especially hair) untidy. **2** to tangle or dishevel. ▷ *noun* a tousled mass. • **tousled** *adj.* ◎ 15c: from obsolete *touse* to handle roughly.

tout /taʊt/ ▷ *verb* (***touted, touting***) **1** *intr* (*usually* **tout for something**) to persistently try to persuade people to buy something, give their support, etc ▫ ***tout for trade.*** **2** to advertise or praise strongly or aggressively. **3** *intr* to spy on racehorses in training to gain information about their condition and likely future performance. ▷ *noun* **1** (*in full* **ticket tout**) someone who buys up large numbers of tickets for a popular sporting event, concert, etc and sells them at inflated prices to members of the public. **2** someone who spies on racehorses in training and passes information about their condition, etc to people wishing to bet on them. **3** someone who touts for trade, especially persistently or aggressively. • **touter** *noun.* ◎ 18c; 15c slang, meaning 'to peep': from *tuten* to peep out.

tout de suite /*French* tu də sɥit/ and *colloq* **toot sweet** /tuːt swiːt/ ▷ *adverb* immediately. ◎ Late 19c: French, meaning 'at once'.

tovarisch, **tovarich** or **tovarish** /tɒˈvaːrɪʃ; *Russian* taˈvarʲɪʃtʃ/ ▷ *noun* in the former USSR: a comrade, often used as a form of address. ◎ Early 20c: from Russian *tovarishch* comrade.

tow[1] /toʊ/ ▷ *verb* (***towed, towing***) **1** to pull (a ship, barge, car, trailer, caravan, etc) by rope, chain, cable, etc behind the vehicle one is driving. **2** said of a vehicle: to pull (a ship, barge, car, etc) along by rope, chain or cable. ▷ *noun* **1** an act or the process of towing; the state of being towed. **2** something towed, eg a car. **3** *as adj* ▫ ***a tow-rope.*** • **towable** *adj.* • **towed** *adj.* • **tower** *noun.* • **towing** *adj, noun.* • **in tow 1** said of a vehicle: being towed. **2** said of a person: following or accompanying as a companion or escort ▫ ***She arrived late with several men in tow.*** • **on tow** said of a vehicle: being towed. • **under tow** said of a vessel: being towed. • **take someone in tow** to put them under one's protection, guidance, control, etc. ◎ Anglo-Saxon *togian.*

tow[2] /toʊ, taʊ/ ▷ *noun* coarse, short or broken fibres of flax, hemp or jute prepared for spinning into rope. • **towy** *adj.* • **tow-coloured**, **tow-head** and **tow-headed** see separate entries. ◎ Anglo-Saxon *tow-*, in compounds such as *towlic* threadlike.

towage /ˈtoʊɪdʒ/ ▷ *noun* **1** an act or the process of towing. **2** a fee for being towed.

toward /təˈwɔːd, twɔːd/ ▷ *prep* see TOWARDS. ▷ *adj, old use* in progress ▫ ***Have you heard what is toward?*** ◎ Anglo-Saxon *toweard*, from TO + -WARD.

towards /təˈwɔːdz, twɔːdz/ or **toward** ▷ *prep* **1** in the direction of ▫ ***turn towards him.*** **2** in relation or regard to ▫ ***showed no respect towards her boss.*** **3** as a contribution to ▫ ***donated £1 000 towards the cost of a new hospital.*** **4** near; just before ▫ ***towards midnight.*** ◎ Anglo-Saxon *toweard* future.

tow bar /toʊ —/ ▷ *noun* a device which is fitted to the back of a car or other vehicle so that a trailer, caravan, etc can to be hitched up to it and towed.

tow-coloured /taʊ -/ ▷ *adj* said especially of hair: very fair.

towel /ˈtaʊəl/ ▷ *noun* **1 a** a piece of absorbent cloth that is used for drying oneself, another person, etc ▫ ***a bath towel;*** **b** a piece of absorbent cloth that is used for drying something, eg dishes after they have been washed ▫ ***a tea towel.*** **2** *Brit dated* a SANITARY TOWEL. ▷ *verb* (***towelled, towelling***; *US* ***toweled, toweling***) **1** to rub, wipe or dry someone or something with a towel. **2** *slang* to thrash. • **throw, chuck, toss,** *etc* **in the towel** or **sponge** to admit defeat, originally in the literal boxing sense, but now applied to any defeat ▫ ***This relationship isn't working — we should just throw in the towel now.*** ◎ 13c: from French *toaille.*

towelling ▷ *noun* **1** a type of material that is formed with many tiny loops of, usually cotton, thread which makes it highly absorbent and therefore an ideal fabric for towels, bathrobes, etc. **2** *slang* a thrashing.

towel rail ▷ *noun* a frame or bar, sometimes heated, that towels can be hung on, especially in the bathroom.

tower /ˈtaʊə(r)/ ▻ *noun* **1 a** a tall narrow structure, usually circular or square in shape, that often forms part of a larger lower building such as a church or castle; **b** a tall free-standing structure built for a specified purpose, such as for defence, as a lookout, for housing machinery, etc □ ***a control tower.*** **2** a fortress, especially one with one or more towers □ ***the Tower of London.*** ▻ *verb* (***towered, towering***) *intr* **1** (*usually* **tower above something** or **someone**) to reach a great height, or rise high above it or them. **2** (*usually* **tower over someone**) to be considerably taller than them or to be intellectually superior to them. • **towered** *adj.* • **towering** see separate entry. ⓒ Anglo-Saxon *torr.*

tower block ▻ *noun, Brit* a very tall building that contains residential flats or offices.

towering ▻ *adj* **1** reaching a great height; very tall or elevated □ ***towering mountains.*** **2** said of rage, fury, a storm, the sea, etc: intense; violent. **3** very impressive, important or lofty □ ***a towering intellect.***

tower of strength ▻ *noun* someone who is a great help or support, especially in times of difficulty, hardship, etc.

tow-head /taʊ-/ ▻ *noun* someone who has very fair hair or tousled hair. • **tow-headed** *adj.*

towing rope, towline see TOW ROPE

town ▻ *noun* **1** an urban area with relatively defined boundaries and a name, smaller than a city but larger than a village. **2** the central shopping or business area in a neighbourhood □ ***went into town to buy new shoes.*** **3** the principal town in an area, or the capital city of a country, regarded as a destination □ ***We usually go to town on Thursdays.*** **4** the people living in a town or a city □ ***The whole town turned out when St Johnstone brought back the cup.*** **5** city or urban life in general as opposed to the countryside and rural life. **6** the permanent residents of a town as opposed to *gown*, the members of its university. • **go out on the town** *colloq* to enjoy the entertainments offered by a town, especially its restaurants and bars. • **go to town (on something)** *colloq* to do something very thoroughly or with great enthusiasm or expense. ⓒ Anglo-Saxon *tun* enclosure or manor.

town and gown ▻ *noun* the people of a town plus the members of its university, thought of collectively.

town centre ▻ *noun* the part of a town where most of the big shops and, usually, many of the important buildings such as the town hall, etc are situated.

town clerk ▻ *noun, Brit historical* until 1974, someone who served as secretary, chief administrator and legal advisor to a town council. ⓒ 14c.

town council ▻ *noun* the elected governing body of a town. • **town councillor** *noun.* ⓒ 17c.

town crier ▻ *noun, historical* someone whose job is to make public announcements on behalf of the town council in the streets, market place, etc of a town. ⓒ 17c.

townee or **townie** ▻ *noun* (***townees*** or ***townies***) *colloq, often derog* someone who lives in a town, especially as opposed to a member of a town's university or someone who lives in the countryside. ⓒ 19c.

town gas ▻ *noun* a type of manufactured flammable gas obtained from coal, formerly used as an industrial and domestic fuel (now largely superseded by NATURAL GAS). ⓒ Early 20c.

town hall ▻ *noun* the building where the official business of a town's administration is carried out.

town house ▻ *noun* **1** a terraced house, especially a fashionable one, and often with the living room on an upper floor. **2** someone's house in town as opposed to their country one. **3** *Scots* same as TOWN HALL.

town planning ▻ *noun* the planning and designing of the future development of a town, especially concerned with using land and resources to their best advantage and preserving the character of the architecture, etc. • **town planner** *noun.* ⓒ Early 20c.

townscape ▻ *noun* **1** the general appearance of, or visual impression created by, a town. **2** a picture of a town □ ***subtly coloured townscapes of Aberdeen.*** ⓒ 1930s in sense 1; 19c in sense 2.

townsfolk ▻ *plural noun* the people who live in a particular town or city.

township ▻ *noun* **1** *S Afr* an urban area that was formerly set aside for non-white citizens to live in. **2** *Brit historical* a division of a large parish. **3** *N Amer* a subdivision of a county that has some corporate powers over local administration. **4** *N Amer* an area of land or district that is six miles square and that contains 36 sections. **5** *Austral* a small town or settlement. ⓒ Anglo-Saxon *tunscipe*, from *tun* TOWN + *-scipe* -SHIP 3.

townsman and **townswoman** ▻ *noun* a man or woman who lives in a town or city.

townspeople ▻ *plural noun* the people who live in a town or city.

towpath /ˈtoʊpɑːθ/ and **towing path** ▻ *noun* a path that runs alongside a canal or river where a horse can walk while towing a barge.

tow rope, towing rope and **towline** /toʊ —/ ▻ *noun* a rope used to attach a vehicle or vessel that is on tow.

toxaemia or (*US*) **toxemia** /tɒkˈsiːmɪə/ ▻ *noun* **1** *medicine* a condition in which there are toxic substances present in the bloodstream, eg of the kind released from a local site of bacterial infection such as an abscess or that result from kidney failure. *Non-technical equivalent* **blood-poisoning**. **2** (*in full* **toxaemia of pregnancy**) a serious complication that sometimes occurs in late pregnancy or just after the birth and which is characterized by a sudden increase in the mother's blood pressure, OEDEMA and the presence of abnormally high levels of protein in the urine. Compare ECLAMPSIA, PRE-ECLAMPSIA. • **toxaemic** *adj.* ⓒ 19c: from Latin *toxicum* poison (see TOXIC) + *haima* blood.

toxic /ˈtɒksɪk/ ▻ *adj* **1** poisonous. **2** belonging, relating or referring to, characteristic of or caused by, a poison or toxin. • **toxically** *adverb.* ⓒ 17c: from Latin *toxicum* poison, from Greek *toxikon pharmakon* poison for the tips of arrows, from *toxon* bow.

toxicant /ˈtɒksɪkənt/ ▻ *noun* a substance that can produce poisonous or toxic effects.

toxicity /tɒkˈsɪsɪtɪ/ ▻ *noun* (***toxicities***) **1** the degree of strength of a poison. **2** the state of being poisonous.

toxicology ▻ *noun* the scientific study of poisons. • **toxicological** *adj.* • **toxicologically** *adverb.* • **toxicologist** *noun.* ⓒ 19c: from French *toxicologie.*

toxic shock syndrome ▻ *noun* (abbreviation **TSS**) *pathol* a potentially fatal condition in women that is characterized by flu-like symptoms, fever, vomiting, diarrhoea, muscle pains, etc and a drop in blood pressure, all of which are caused by staphylococcal blood-poisoning which is itself brought on because of the development of a toxin in a tampon that has been kept in the body for too long. ⓒ 1980s.

toxin ▻ *noun* **1** any poison that is produced by a micro-organism, especially one that is present in an animal or human and which stimulates the body to produce antibodies (see ANTIBODY) to fight the infection that results from its presence. **2** any naturally occurring plant or animal poison. ⓒ 19c: see TOXIC.

toxocara /tɒksəˈkɑːrə/ ▻ *noun, zool* any of various worms which parasitically infest the intestines of dogs and cats, and the larva of which can be transmitted, especially via faeces, to humans, resulting in the condition known as **toxocariasis** (/-ˈraɪəsɪs/) which often causes damage to the retina of the eye. • **toxocaral** *adj.* ⓒ 1940s: from *toxo-* (see TOXIC) + Greek *kara* head.

toxoid ▻ *noun, biol* a toxin that has been treated so as to remove its toxic properties without destroying its ability to stimulate the production of antibodies, eg chemically treated preparations of diphtheria and tetanus toxins used as vaccines.

toxoplasmosis /tɒksoʊplaz'moʊsɪs/ ▻ *noun* an infection of vertebrates, caused by a PROTOZOAN and transferred to humans through unhygienic food preparation, cat faeces, etc and varying widely in severity from presenting mild flu-like symptoms to being fatal, especially with unborn babies. ◷ 1930s: from Greek *toxon* bow + *plasso* to shape.

toy ▻ *noun* **1 a** an object that is made, especially for a child, to play with; **b** *as adj* being an imitation, especially of something that adults use ▫ *a toy gun.* **2** *often derog* something, especially a gadget, that is intended to be, or that is thought of as being, for amusement or pleasure rather than practical use. **3** something which is very small, especially a dwarf breed or variety of dog. ▻ *verb* (***toyed, toying***) *intr* **1** (*usually* **toy with**) to flirt or amuse oneself with someone or their feelings, etc. **2** (*usually* **toy with something**) to play with it in an idle, distracted, disinterested, etc way ▫ *toying with his food* ▫ *toyed with the idea of getting a new car* ▫ *toyed with his affections.* • **toyer** *noun.* • **toying** *adj, noun.* ◷ 16c, meaning 'an amorous sport': from *toye* dalliance.

toyboy ▻ *noun, colloq* a young man who is usually considered physically attractive and who has someone much older and wealthier than himself as his lover. ◷ 1980s.

tp ▻ *abbreviation* **1** township. **2** troop.

TPI ▻ *abbreviation* Town Planning Institute.

tpr ▻ *abbreviation* teleprinter.

TR ▻ *abbreviation, IVR* Turkey.

tr. ▻ *abbreviation* **1** transactions. **2** *grammar* transitive. **3** translator. **4** (*also* **trs**) *proofreading* transpose. **5** trustee.

trabecula /trə'bɛkjʊlə/ ▻ *noun* (***trabeculae*** /-liː/) **1** *anatomy* any beam-like structure, especially a supporting one that goes across a cavity or one that divides an organ, such as the heart, into chambers. **2** *bot* any similar structure that is found in some plant cavities. • **trabecular, trabeculate** /-ət/ or **trabeculated** *adj.* ◷ 19c: Latin, a diminutive of *trabs* beam.

trace¹ ▻ *noun* **1** a mark or sign that some person, animal or thing has been in a particular place. **2** a track or footprint. **3** a very small amount that can only just be detected ▫ *found traces of cocaine.* **4** a tracing. **5** a line marked by the moving pen of a recording instrument. **6** a visible line on a cathode-ray tube showing the path of a moving spot. **7** a supposed physical change in the brain or cells of the nervous system caused by learning. ▻ *verb* (***traced, tracing***) **1** to track and discover by or as if by following clues, a trail, etc. **2** to follow step by step ▫ *trace the development of medicine.* **3** to make a copy of (a drawing, design, etc) by covering it with a sheet of semi-transparent paper and drawing over the visible lines. **4** to outline or sketch (an idea, plan, etc). **5** (*also* **trace something back**) to investigate it and discover the cause, origin, etc of it, eg in a specified time, person, thing. • **traceability** *noun.* • **traceable** *adj.* • **traceably** *adverb.* • **traceless** *adj.* ◷ 14c: from French *tracier.*

trace² ▻ *noun* either of the two ropes, chains or straps that are attached to an animal's collar, etc so that it can pull a carriage, cart, etc. • **kick over the traces** see under KICK. ◷ 13c: French, from *trais.*

trace element ▻ *noun* **1** a chemical element that is only found in very small amounts. **2** a chemical element that living organisms require only in very small amounts for normal growth, development and general health, eg zinc, copper, molybdenum, and which can be toxic if they are absorbed in large quantities.

trace fossil ▻ *noun* a fossil that represents the track, trail, burrow, etc of an animal rather than the animal itself.

tracer ▻ *noun* **1 a** someone whose job is to trace, eg architectural, civil engineering, etc drawings; **b** a device that traces. **2** (*in full* **tracer bullet** or **tracer shell**) a bullet, shell, etc which leaves a smoke-trail behind it so that its flight path can be seen. **3** a substance, especially a radioactive element, whose course through the body, or effect on it, can be observed.

tracery ▻ *noun* (***traceries***) **1** ornamental open stonework used to form a decorative pattern, especially in the top part of a Gothic window. **2** a finely patterned decoration or design. • **traceried** *adj.*

trachea /trə'kɪə/ ▻ *noun* (***tracheae*** /-kɪiː/) **1** *anatomy* an air tube, usually stiffened by rings of cartilage, that extends from the LARYNX to the BRONCHUS of each lung. *Non-technical equivalent* **windpipe**. **2** *zool* in insects and arthropods: any of the openings on the surface of the body that function as specialized respiratory organs where air is absorbed into the blood and tissues. **3** *bot* any fluid-conducting vessel or duct in the woody tissue of plants, so called because they were once believed to serve the same function as the tracheae in insects, etc. See also PHLOEM, XYLEM. • **tracheal** or **tracheate** /-eɪt/ or **tracheated** *adj.* ◷ 15c: from Greek *tracheia arteria* rough artery.

tracheitis /trakiː'aɪtɪs, treɪ-/ ▻ *noun, medicine* inflammation of the trachea.

tracheostomy /trakɪ'ɒstəmɪ/ ▻ *noun* (***tracheostomies***) the creation of a temporary or permanent opening into the trachea after performing a TRACHEOTOMY. ◷ 1940s.

tracheotomy /trakɪ'ɒtəmɪ/ ▻ *noun* **a** a surgical incision through the front of the neck into the windpipe so that an alternative airway is made available when normal breathing is not possible; **b** an operation where this kind of incision is made. ◷ 18c.

trachoma /trə'koʊmə/ ▻ *noun, medicine* a contagious eye disease, common in the Third World, which is transmitted by flies carrying bacteria of the CHLAMYDIA family. The main symptoms are inflammation and scarring of the conjunctiva, redness and pain and, if left untreated, the disease may spread to the cornea and cause blindness. ◷ 17c: Greek, meaning 'roughness'.

trachyte /'trakaɪt, 'treɪ-/ ▻ *noun* any of several kinds of light-coloured rough volcanic rock. • **trachytic** /trə'kɪtɪk/ *adj.* ◷ 19c: French, from Greek *trachoma* roughness.

tracing /'treɪsɪŋ/ ▻ *noun* **1** a copy of a drawing, etc that is made on semi-transparent paper. **2** an act, instance or the process of making such a copy. ▻ *verb, present participle of* TRACE¹.

tracing-paper ▻ *noun* thin semi-transparent paper designed to be used for tracing drawings, etc.

track ▻ *noun* **1 a** a mark or series of marks that something leaves behind ▫ *a tyre track*; **b** a mark or series of marks, or a trail, that usually consists of footprints, and which indicates that a person, animal, etc has passed by; **c** a course of action, thought, etc that someone or something has taken ▫ *followed in her mother's tracks and studied medicine.* **2** a rough path, especially one that has been made by many people walking along it. **3** a specially prepared course, especially one that is used for racing ▫ *a race track.* **4** the branch of athletics that comprises all the running events. See also TRACK AND FIELD. **5** a railway line, ie the parallel rails, the space in between, and the sleepers and stones below. **6** a length of railing that something, such as a curtain, spotlight, etc, can move along. **7 a** the groove cut in a RECORD (*noun* 4) by the recording instrument; **b** an individual song, etc on an album, CD, cassette, etc; **c** one of several paths on magnetic recording tape that receives information from a single input channel; **d** one of a series of parallel paths on magnetic recording tape that contains a single sequence of signals; **e** a SOUNDTRACK; **f** *computing* an area on the surface of a magnetic disk where data can be stored and which is created during the process of formatting. **8** a line, path or course of travel, passage or movement □ *followed the track of the storm.* **9** the line or course of thought, reasoning, etc □ *couldn't follow the track of his argument.* **10** the predetermined line of travel of an aircraft. **11** the continuous band that heavy vehicles, eg tanks, mechanical diggers, etc, have instead of individual tyres and which allows them to travel over rough surfaces. **12** the distance between a wheel on one side of a vehicle and the corresponding wheel on the other side, taken by measuring the distance between the parts of the wheels which actually touch the ground. **13** (*usually* **tracks**) *drug-taking slang* a red mark, eg on someone's forearm, that indicates that they use or have used intravenous drugs. ▻ *verb* (***tracked***, ***tracking***) **1** to follow the marks, footprints, etc left by (a person or animal). **2** to follow and usually plot the course of (a spacecraft, satellite, etc) by radar. **3** *intr* (*often* **track in, out** or **back**) said of a television or film camera or its operator: to move, especially in such a way as to follow a moving subject, always keeping them or it in focus. See also TRACKING SHOT. **4** said of a stylus or laser beam: to extract information from (a recording medium, eg a vinyl record or a compact disc). **5** *intr* said of a vehicle's rear wheels: to run exactly in the course of the front wheels. • **across the tracks** *colloq* a socially disadvantaged area of town. • **cover one's tracks** to make an effort to ensure that one's motives, movements, etc cannot be easily discovered. • **in one's tracks** exactly where one is standing; right there and then □ *The news stopped her in her tracks.* • **keep,** or **lose, track of something** or **someone** to keep, or fail to keep, oneself informed about the progress, whereabouts, etc of them or it □ *Sorry I'm late — I lost all track of time.* • **make tracks** *colloq* to leave; to set out. • **off the beaten track** away from busy roads and therefore difficult to gain access to or find. • **on the right** or **wrong track** pursuing the right or wrong line of inquiry. • **on the track of someone** or **something** following, pursuing or looking for them or it. • **the wrong side of the tracks** a poor or disadvantaged urban area, especially one that is perceived as socially inferior. ⓒ 15c: from French *trac*.

■ **track someone** or **something down** to search for and find them or it after following clues, etc □ *managed to track down the address.*

track and field ▻ *noun* the branch of athletics that comprises all the running and jumping events plus the hammer, discus, javelin, shot put, etc.

trackball and **trackerball** ▻ *noun, computing* a ball mounted in a small box that is linked to a computer terminal and which can be rotated with the palm to move a cursor correspondingly on a screen.

trackbed ▻ *noun* the stony foundations that a railway track is laid on.

tracker dog ▻ *noun* a dog that is specially trained to search for eg missing people, criminals, etc. Compare SNIFFER DOG.

track event ▻ *noun, athletics* a running race. Compare FIELD EVENT.

tracking ▻ *noun* **1** the act or process of following someone or something. **2** the act or process of adding pre-recorded music to a motion picture as opposed to having a soundtrack of specially commissioned music. **3** *elec engineering* leakage of current between two insulated points caused by moisture, dirt, etc. ▻ *verb, present participle of* TRACK.

tracking shot ▻ *noun, cinematog* a type of shot in which the camera follows the movement of a subject, piece of action, etc usually by means of some kind of wheeled support such as a DOLLY. ⓒ 1940s: so called because the dolly that the camera is mounted on runs on tracks.

tracking station ▻ *noun* a site that is equipped with radar to follow and plot the courses of spacecraft, satellites, etc.

tracklist ▻ *noun* an index that gives such details as song titles, length, composer, etc of the tracks that appear on a CD, album, cassette, etc.

track record ▻ *noun* **1** *sport, especially athletics, cycling* **a** the best time or performance that has ever been recorded at a specified venue; **b** the best time or performance that someone has ever had recorded. **2** *colloq* someone's performance, achievements, etc in the past □ *Her CV shows an impressive track record.*

track shoe ▻ *noun* a running shoe that has a spiked sole.

tracksuit ▻ *noun* a suit, usually of soft warm material, worn by athletes, footballers, etc when exercising, or to keep the body warm before and after performing. Compare SHELL SUIT.

tract¹ ▻ *noun* **1** an area of land, usually of indefinite extent □ *large tracts of unpopulated wilderness.* **2** a system in the body that has a specified function and which consists of a series of connected organs and glands □ *the digestive tract.* **3** *old use* an extent of time. ⓒ 15c: from Latin *tractus* a drawing out.

tract² ▻ *noun* a short essay or pamphlet, especially one on the subject of religion, politics, etc, intended as a piece of propaganda. ⓒ 15c: from Latin *tractatus* a handling or discussion.

tractable /'traktəbəl/ ▻ *adj* **1** said especially of a child, animal, etc or their disposition: easily managed, controlled, etc; docile. **2** said of a material, etc: pliant. • **tractability** *noun*. • **tractably** *adverb*. ⓒ 15c: from Latin *tractare* to handle.

Tractarianism /trak'tɛərɪənɪzəm/ ▻ *noun* the religious movement which advocated the revival of high doctrine and ceremonial in the Church of England, which led to Anglo-Catholicism and ritualism. Also called **Oxford movement**. • **Tractarian** *noun, adj.* ⓒ 19c: from the *Tracts for the Times* (1833–41), a series of treatises which advocated a return to a more highly ritualized Church and opposed the liberal tendencies that the Reformation had started.

tractate /'trakteɪt/ ▻ *noun* a treatise. ⓒ 15c: from Latin *tractatus* a handling or treatise.

traction /'trakʃən/ ▻ *noun* **1** the action or process of pulling. **2** the state of being pulled or the force used in pulling. **3** *medicine* a process that involves steady pulling on a muscle, limb, etc using a series of pulleys and weights in order to correct some condition or problem. **4** the grip of a wheel, tyre, etc on a road surface, rail track, etc. • **tractional** *adj*. • **tractive** *adj*. • **in traction** *medicine* said of a person, one of their limbs, etc: being treated by steady pulling □ *had her leg in traction for six weeks.* ⓒ 17c: from Latin *tractio*.

traction engine ▻ *noun* a heavy steam-powered vehicle that was formerly used for pulling heavy loads, eg farm machinery. ⓒ 19c.

tractor /'traktə(r)/ ▻ *noun* **1** *chiefly agriculture* a slow-moving motor vehicle that has two large rear wheels and a high seat, and which is used especially for pulling farm machinery, heavy loads, etc. **2** (*also* **tractor unit**) a short vehicle with a cab and an extremely powerful engine, which is used to pull heavy loads such as the trailer of an articulated lorry. **3** another name for a TRACTION ENGINE. ⓒ Early 20c: Latin, from *trahere, tractum* to draw or drag.

tractor feed ▻ *adj* said of a printer, typewriter, etc: designed to take continuous paper with perforations that fit into cogs that roll the paper forward as printing progresses. ▻ *noun* a printer or typewriter of this kind.

trad *Brit colloq* ▷ *noun* a shortened form of **traditional jazz**, a style of jazz that follows on from the kind of music first played in the early 20c in New Orleans and which incorporates elements of DIXIELAND jazz. Compare MODERN JAZZ. ▷ *adj* a shortened form of TRADITIONAL.

trade ▷ *noun* **1 a** the act, an instance or the process of buying and selling; **b** buying and selling at an international level □ *foreign trade.* **2 a** a job, occupation or means of earning a living that involves skilled work, especially as opposed to professional or unskilled work □ *left school at 16 to learn a trade*; **b** the people and businesses that are involved in a specified job of this kind □ *the building trade.* **3 a** business and commerce, especially as opposed to a profession or the owning of landed property; **b** the people involved in this. **4** customers □ *the lunch-time trade.* **5** business at a specified time, for a specified market or of a specified nature □ *the tourist trade.* **6** (**trades**) the trade winds. ▷ *verb* (***traded, trading***) **1** *intr* to buy and sell; to engage in trading □ *trades in securities.* **2 a** to exchange (one commodity) for another; **b** to exchange (blows, insults, etc); **c** *colloq* to swap □ *traded a photo of Johnny Depp for one of Brad Pitt.* • **trader** see separate entry. • **trading** *noun, adj.* • **by trade** as a means of earning a living □ *a plumber by trade.* ⓒ 14c: originally meaning 'a course or path'.

■ **trade something in** to give something, eg a car, domestic appliance, etc, as part payment for something else, especially for a newer, more sophisticated etc version. See also TRADE-IN.

■ **trade something off** to give something in exchange for something else, usually as a compromise. See also TRADE-OFF.

■ **trade on something 1** to take unfair advantage of something, especially someone else's generosity, gullibility, etc □ *traded on his sister's popularity.* **2** to use something, eg a personal attribute, to one's advantage □ *trades on her good looks.*

trade agreement ▷ *noun* an international commercial treaty.

trade cycle ▷ *noun, econ* the recurrent fluctuation in buoyancy of a capitalist country's economy which results in periods of BOOM 2 and RECESSION.

trade deficit and **trade gap** ▷ *noun* the amount by which a country's VISIBLE imports outstrip its VISIBLE exports.

trade discount ▷ *noun* a sum of money or a percentage of the usual cost price that a trader, who is usually in the same kind of business as the buyer, deducts from the cost of goods or a service.

traded option ▷ *noun, stock exchange* an OPTION that can itself be bought and sold.

trade-in ▷ *noun* something, especially a used car or other vehicle, that is given, usually in part exchange, for another, especially one that is newer, in better condition, more sophisticated, etc. See also TRADE SOMETHING IN at TRADE.

trade journal ▷ *noun* a periodical that contains specialized information relevant to a specified trade, business, etc.

trademark ▷ *noun* **1** (*in full* **registered trademark**) a name, word or symbol, especially one that is officially registered and protected by law, which a company or individual uses as identification on all the goods made or sold by them. **2** a distinguishing characteristic or feature. ▷ *verb* **1** to label with a trademark. **2** to register as a trademark. • **trademarked** *adj.* ⓒ 16c.

tradename ▷ *noun* **1** a name that is given to an article or product, or a group of these, by the trade which produces them. **2** a name that a company or individual does business under. **3** a name that serves as a trademark □ *St Michael is the tradename of Marks and Spencer.* ⓒ 19c.

trade-off ▷ *noun* a balance or compromise that is struck, especially between two desirable but incompatible things, situations, etc. See also TRADE SOMETHING OFF at TRADE.

trade plates ▷ *noun* a set of temporary number plates that a garage, dealer, etc uses on an unregistered vehicle.

trade price ▷ *noun* the wholesale cost that a retailer pays for goods.

trader ▷ *noun* **1** someone who trades, often one who owns or runs a shop or market stall, or who trades in a particular group of goods. **2** *stock exchange* someone who trades privately on the stock exchange, as opposed to someone who does so on behalf of customers. **3** a ship used for trade.

trade route ▷ *noun* an established course that a trader, caravan, trading ship, etc takes.

tradescantia /tradɪ'skantɪə/ ▷ *noun* (***tradescantias***) any of several widely cultivated plants with attractive, often variegated, leaves and white, pink, blue or purple flowers. Also called **spiderwort**. ⓒ 17c: named after the English gardener, naturalist and traveller John Tradescant (c.1567–1637).

trade secret ▷ *noun* **1** an ingredient, technique, etc that a particular company or individual will not divulge because they see it as giving them an advantage over their rivals. **2** *humorous* any secret. ⓒ 19c.

tradesman and **tradeswoman** ▷ *noun* **1** a man or woman who is engaged in trading, eg a shopkeeper. **2** someone who follows a skilled trade, eg a plumber, electrician, etc.

tradespeople and **tradesfolk** ▷ *plural noun* people who are engaged in trade, especially shopkeepers, and their families.

Trades Union Congress ▷ *noun, Brit* a national organization that meets annually to discuss working conditions and the economy in the country at large, and which is made up of representatives of the individual trade unions. Often shortened to **TUC**.

trade union or **trades union** ▷ *noun* an organization for the employees of a specified profession, trade, or group of related trades, etc that exists to protect members' interests and to improve their pay, working conditions, etc. ⓒ 19c.

trade unionism ▷ *noun* the system, principles and practices of trade unions.

trade unionist ▷ *noun* a member of a trade union.

trade wind ▷ *noun* a wind that blows continually towards the equator and which, in the N hemisphere, is deflected westward by the eastward rotation of the earth. ⓒ 17c: from obsolete *blow trade* meaning 'to blow steadily in the same direction'.

trading see under TRADE

trading estate ▷ *noun, Brit* a specially designated area for industrial and/or commercial use.

trading post ▷ *noun* a store in a remote or sparsely populated region.

trading stamp ▷ *noun* a stamp that is given to a customer when they spend a specified amount of money on goods, a particular commodity, etc in a store, garage, etc, and which the customer then can collect, exchanging a set number of the stamps for a 'gift', usually something that the company issuing the trading stamp supplies.

tradition /trə'dɪʃən/ ▷ *noun* **1 a** something, such as a doctrine, belief, custom, story, etc, that is passed on from generation to generation, especially orally or by example; **b** the action or process of handing down something in this way. **2** a particular body of doctrines, beliefs, customs, etc that belongs to a specified group of people, religion, country, family, etc. **3** *colloq* an established, standard or usual practice or custom. **4** the continuous development of a body of artistic, literary or musical principles or conventions □ *'Thelma and Louise' follows in the tradition of the road movie.* **5** *Judaism* **a** one of a collection of unwritten regulations believed to have been handed down orally from generation to generation since God first gave them to Moses; **b** the whole collection of these regulations. **6** *Christianity* **a** one of a collection of unwritten teachings that are believed to have been handed down orally from generation to generation and which Roman Catholics believe come originally from Christ and the apostles; **b** the whole collection of these teachings. **7** *Islam* any of the collected sayings or deeds of Mohammed that are not contained in the Koran. • **traditionary** *adj.* • **traditionist** *noun.* • **traditionless** *adj.* • **break with tradition** to turn away from what is conventional, usual, expected, etc. ⓒ 15c: from Latin *traditio* handing over.

traditional ▻ *adj* **1** belonging, relating or referring to, based on or derived from tradition □ *morris dancers in their traditional costumes.* **2** see TRAD. • **traditionally** *adverb.* • **traditionality** *noun.*

traditionalism ▻ *noun* **1** adherence to or belief in tradition, often to an excessive degree. **2** a philosophical belief that religious knowledge and moral truth are obtained through divine revelation and are preserved and handed down by tradition.

traditionalist ▻ *noun* someone who subscribes to tradition, especially in a slavish way. ▻ *adj* belonging, relating or referring to, or involving, tradition □ *holds very traditionalist views on education.*

traditional jazz see TRAD sense 1

traduce /trə'dʒuːs/ ▻ *verb* (***traduces, traduced, traducing***) to say or write unpleasant things about someone or something; to malign or misrepresent them. • **traducement** *noun.* • **traducer** *noun.* ⓒ 16c: from Latin *traducere* to disgrace.

traffic /'trafɪk/ ▻ *noun* **1** the vehicles that are moving along a route. **2** the movement of vehicles, passengers, etc along a route. **3** illegal or dishonest trade □ *engaged in the traffic of cocaine.* **4** trade; commerce. **5** the transporting of goods or people on a railway, air or sea route, etc. **6** the goods or people transported along a route. **7** dealings or communication between groups or individuals. ▻ *verb* (***trafficked, trafficking***) **1** (*usually* **traffic in something**) to deal or trade in it, especially illegally or dishonestly. **2** *tr* to deal in (a particular type of goods). • **trafficker** *noun* someone who deals or trades in goods, usually illegal ones □ *drug trafficker.* • **trafficking** *noun.* ⓒ 16c: from French *traffique.*

traffic calming ▻ *noun* the intentional curbing of the speed of road vehicles by having humps, bends, narrowed passing places, etc on roads.

traffic cone ▻ *noun* a large plastic cone used for guiding traffic that is being diverted from its usual route.

traffic island see under ISLAND

traffic jam ▻ *noun* a queue of vehicles that are at a standstill, eg because of overcrowded roads, an accident, roadworks, etc.

trafficker see under TRAFFIC

traffic lights ▻ *plural noun* a system of red, amber and green lights which controls traffic at road junctions, pedestrian crossings, etc. Often shortened to **lights**.

traffic police ▻ *noun* the branch of the police involved in dealing with motoring offences and ensuring that traffic is flowing smoothly.

traffic warden ▻ *noun, Brit* someone whose job is to control the flow of traffic and the parking of vehicles in towns, and to put parking tickets on vehicles that infringe parking restrictions.

tragacanth /'tragəkanθ/ ▻ *noun* **1** any of several spiny low-growing shrubs that are found in E Asia and which produce a gum. **2** the gum that is produced by this type of plant and which is used in the manufacture of pills. ⓒ 16c: from Greek *tragos* goat + *akantha* thorn.

tragedian /trə'dʒiːdɪən/ ▻ *noun* **1** someone who specializes in acting tragic roles. **2** someone who writes tragedies. ⓒ 14c.

tragedienne /trədʒiːdɪ'ɛn/ ▻ *noun* an actress who specializes in tragic roles.

tragedy /'tradʒədɪ/ ▻ *noun* (***tragedies***) **1** a serious catastrophe, accident, natural disaster, etc. **2** *colloq* any sad event □ *an absolute tragedy when Aberdeen lost that goal.* **3** a serious play, film, opera, etc in which the PROTAGONIST is brought down, usually by a combination of events, circumstances, personal flaws, etc, and which often involves them having to examine, and try to come to terms with, the extent of their own culpability in how things turn out. See also CATHARSIS, HUBRIS. **4** such plays as a group or genre. Compare COMEDY. **5** *loosely* any sad play, film, book, etc, especially one that ends with an unnecessary or untimely death, but that does not necessarily have the conventional elements of classical tragedy. ⓒ 14c: from Greek *tragoidia*, from *tragos* goat + *oide* song.

tragic /'tradʒɪk/ and **tragical** ▻ *adj* **1** said especially of a death, disaster, accident, etc: very sad; intensely distressing. **2** *theat* belonging, referring or relating to, or in the style of, TRAGEDY (senses 3, 4) □ *a typical tragic dénouement.* • **tragically** *adverb.* ⓒ 16c: from Greek *tragikos*; see TRAGEDY.

tragic hero ▻ *noun* the PROTAGONIST of a tragedy, who should provoke feelings in the audience of pity (because the misfortune the protagonist suffers seems undeserved) and fear (because, in the protagonist, the audience recognize their own fallibility and vulnerability).

tragic irony ▻ *noun* a type of dramatic irony (see IRONY[1] sense 2) that involves the PROTAGONIST doing or saying something that actively contributes to their own downfall.

tragicomedy /tradʒɪ'kɒmədɪ/ ▻ *noun* (***tragicomedies***) **1** a play, film, event, etc that includes a mixture of both tragedy and comedy, especially one in which things have gone badly throughout, but which is resolved happily. **2** such plays as a group or genre. • **tragicomic** or **tragicomical** *adj.* • **tragicomically** *adverb.* ⓒ 16c: from Latin *tragicomoedia.*

tragopan /'tragəpan/ ▻ *noun* any of several types of Asian pheasant that have erect fleshy horns on their heads. ⓒ 17c: Latin, from Greek *tragos* goat + *Pan* the horned Greek god of flocks and shepherds.

trail ▻ *verb* (***trailed, trailing***) **1** *tr & intr* to drag or be dragged loosely along the ground or other surface. **2** *tr & intr* (*usually* **trail along, behind**, *etc*) to walk or move along slowly and wearily. **3** to drag (a limb, etc) especially slowly and wearily. **4** *tr & intr* to fall or lag behind in eg a race or contest □ *trailed their opponents by 20 points.* **5** to follow the track or footsteps of someone or something. **6** *tr & intr* **a** said of a plant or plant part: to grow so long that it droops over or along a surface towards the ground; **b** to encourage (a plant or plant part) to grow in this way. **7** to advertise (a forthcoming programme, film, etc) by showing chosen extracts, etc. ▻ *noun* **1** a track, series of marks, footprints, etc left by a passing person, animal or thing, especially one followed in hunting. **2** a rough path or track through a wild or mountainous area. **3** something that drags or is drawn behind. **4** the part of a gun carriage that rests on the ground when the LIMBER[2] is detached. ⓒ 14c, meaning 'to drag behind'.

■ **trail away** or **off** said especially of a voice or other sound: to become fainter.

trailblazer ▻ *noun* **1** someone who makes inroads into new territory; a pioneer. **2** an innovator in a particular field or activity. See also BLAZE A TRAIL under BLAZE[2].

trailblazing ▷ *noun* **1** the act or process of doing something innovatory. **2** the act or process of breaking new ground; pioneering. ▷ *adj* innovatory or pioneering.

trailer ▷ *noun* **1** a cart, usually with two wheels, that can be hooked up behind a car, etc, and which is used for carrying small loads, transporting small boats, etc. **2** the rear section of an ARTICULATED LORRY, as opposed to the tractor unit. **3** *N Amer* a caravan. **4** *cinema, TV, radio* a preview or foretaste, in the form of a brief excerpt or series of such excerpts from a film, programme, etc, that serves as advance publicity before its release or showing. **5** someone or something that trails behind. ▷ *verb* (***trailered, trailering***) *cinema, TV, radio* to advertise (a film, programme, etc) with a trailer. ◷ 19c: from TRAIL, except *noun* sense 4 and *verb* which date from 1920s, so called because in the cinema 'trailers' were shown after the main programme.

train ▷ *noun* **1 a** a string of railway carriages or wagons with a locomotive; **b** *loosely* a locomotive. **2** a back part of a long dress or robe that trails behind the wearer. **3** the attendants following or accompanying an important person. **4** a connected series of events, actions, ideas, thoughts, etc □ ***interrupted my train of thought.*** **5** a number of things in a string or connected line, eg a line of animals or vehicles carrying baggage. **6** a line of gunpowder, etc laid to fire a charge. **7** a set of connected wheels which act on each other to transmit motion. ▷ *verb* (***trained, training***) **1** to teach or prepare (a person or animal) for something through instruction, practice, exercises, etc. **2** *intr* to be taught, or prepare oneself to be taught, through instruction, practice, exercises, etc □ ***trained as a nurse.*** **3** (**train for something** or **train someone for something**) to prepare oneself or them for performance (eg in a sport) by instruction, practice, exercise, diet, etc □ ***trained for the marathon.*** **4** to point or aim (eg a gun) at or focus (eg a telescope) on a particular object or in a particular direction. **5** to make (a plant, tree, etc) grow in a particular direction □ ***train the ivy along the wall.*** **6 a** *intr* to travel by train; **b** (**train it**) to make a train journey. • **trainable** *adj.* ◷ 14c: from French *trahiner* to drag.

train-bearer ▷ *noun* someone who carries the train of another person's dress or robe.

trained ▷ *adj* **1** said of a person, animal, etc: having received training □ ***a trained nurse.*** **2** experienced □ ***can only be picked up by the trained eye.*** **3** said of a plant, tree, etc: made or encouraged to grow in a specified manner or place.

trainee ▷ *noun* (***trainees***) someone who is in the process of being trained for a particular job.

trainer ▷ *noun* **1** someone who trains racehorses, athletes, etc. **2** (**trainers**) *Brit* soft canvas or leather running shoes that have thick soles and no spikes, often worn just as casual shoes. *N Amer equivalent* **sneaker**. **3** a machine or device used in training, eg an aircraft with two sets of controls for training pilots. **4** a piece of gym equipment such as a rowing machine, exercise bike, etc.

training ▷ *noun* **1** the act or process of being prepared for something, of being taught or learning a particular skill and practising it until the required standard is reached □ ***go into training for the marathon.*** **2** the state of being physically fit □ ***out of training.***

train-spotter ▷ *noun* **1** someone whose hobby is to note the numbers of railway locomotives or rolling stock. **2** someone who is overly concerned with trivial details, matters, etc. • **train-spotting** *noun.*

traipse or **trapes** /treɪps/ ▷ *verb* (***traipsed, traipsing; trapesed, trapesing***) **1** *intr* to walk or trudge along idly or wearily □ ***traipsed round the shops.*** **2** *tr* to wander aimlessly □ ***traipsing the streets at one o'clock in the morning.*** ▷ *noun* a long tiring walk. ◷ 16c.

trait /treɪt/ ▷ *noun* an identifying feature or quality, especially one that distinguishes someone's character. ◷ 16c: French.

traitor /'treɪtə(r)/ ▷ *noun* **1** someone who betrays their country, sovereign, government, etc. **2** someone who betrays a trust. • **traitorous** *adj.* • **traitorously** *adverb.* ◷ 13c: from French *traitre.*

traitress ▷ *noun, old use* a female traitor.

trajectory /trə'dʒɛktərɪ/ ▷ *noun* (***trajectories***) **1** *physics* the curved path that a moving object describes, eg when it is projected into the air or when it is subjected to a given force or forces, etc. **2** *geom* a curve that passes through a set of given points, etc at a constant angle. ◷ 17c: from Latin *trajectorius* casting over.

tram ▷ *noun* **1** (*in full* **tramcar**) an electrically-powered passenger vehicle that runs on rails laid in the streets. *N Amer equivalent* **streetcar**. See also TROLLEY CAR. **2** a truck or wagon that runs on rails in a mine. ◷ 16c: from German *traam* shaft, eg of a wheelbarrow, or rung of a ladder.

tramline ▷ *noun* **1** (*usually* **tramlines**) either of a pair of rails that form the track for trams to run on. **2** the route that a tram takes. **3** (**tramlines**) *colloq* **a** the parallel lines at the sides of tennis and badminton courts; **b** the parallel lines at the back of a badminton court. ◷ 19c.

trammel /'traməl/ ▷ *noun* **1** (*usually* **trammels**) anything that hinders or prevents free action or movement □ ***trapped by the trammels of convention.*** **2** (*in full* **trammel net**) a type of long narrow triple-sectioned fishing net in which any fish that swims into the fine inner mesh carries the mesh through the coarse outer mesh where it becomes trapped in the pocket that is formed. ▷ *verb* (***trammelled, trammelling***; *US* ***trammeled, trammeling***) **1** to hinder, restrain or prevent free movement. **2** to catch or entangle, especially in a trammel. • **trammelled** *adj.* • **trammeller** *noun.* ◷ 15c: from French *tramail* a triple-meshed fishing or fowling net.

tramontana /trampn'tɑːnə/ ▷ *noun* a cold north wind that blows south from the Alps into Italy and the W Mediterranean. ◷ 17c: see TRAMONTANE.

tramontane /trampn'teɪn/ and **transmontane** ▷ *adj* **1** situated or living on the far side of a mountain, especially on the other side of the Alps from an Italian perspective. **2** uncultured. ▷ *noun* **1** a foreigner. **2** someone who lacks culture. **3** TRAMONTANA. ◷ 16c: from Italian *tramontano*, from Latin *transmontanus* from across the mountains.

tramp ▷ *verb* (***tramped, tramping***) **1** *intr* to walk with firm heavy footsteps. **2** *intr* to make a journey on foot, especially heavily or wearily □ ***tramp over the hills.*** **3** to walk heavily and wearily on or through □ ***tramp the streets.*** **4** to walk (a specified distance) heavily and wearily □ ***tramp six miles across the open moor.*** **5** *intr* to live as a tramp. **6** to tread or trample. ▷ *noun* **1** someone who has no fixed home or job and who often travels from place to place on foot doing odd jobs or begging. **2** a long and often tiring walk especially in the country. **3** the sound of heavy rhythmic footsteps. **4** (*in full* **tramp steamer**) a cargo boat with no fixed or regular route. **5** *slang* a promiscuous or immoral woman. **6** an iron plate on the sole of a shoe to protect it, eg when digging. ◷ 14c.

trampet or **trampette** /tram'pɛt/ ▷ *noun* a small trampoline.

trample ▷ *verb* (***trampled, trampling***) *tr & intr* **1** to tread on something heavily or roughly. **2** to press or be pressed down by treading or being trodden on. **3** to treat someone dismissively or with contempt □ ***trampled over their feelings.*** ▷ *noun* an act of trampling or the sound made by trampling. • **trampled** *adj.* • **trampler** *noun.* ◷ 14c: from TRAMP.

trampoline /trampə'liːn/ ▷ *noun* a piece of gymnastic equipment that consists of a sheet of tough canvas, nylon mesh, etc attached to a framework by strong springs and stretched tight, used by acrobats, gymnasts, children, etc for jumping on, performing somersaults, etc. ▷ *verb* (*trampolined*, *trampolining*) *intr* to jump, turn somersaults, etc on a trampoline. • **trampolinist** *noun*. ◷ 18c: from Italian *trampolino* springboard.

trampolining ▻ *noun* **1** an act or spell of using a trampoline. **2** the sport or pastime that involves using a trampoline.

tramway ▻ *noun* **1** a system of tracks for trams. **2** a tram system.

trance ▻ *noun* **1** a sleep-like or half-conscious state in which the ability to react to stimuli such as pain, etc is temporarily lost. **2** a dazed or absorbed state. **3** a state, usually self-induced, in which religious or mystical ecstasy is sometimes experienced. **4** the state that a medium can enter in order to make contact with the dead. **5** short for TRANCE MUSIC. ◷ 14c: from French *transe*.

trance music ▻ *noun* a type of repetitive electronic dance music.

tranche /trɑːnʃ/ ▻ *noun* **1** a part, piece or division of something □ ***The department is in the first tranche of the modularization process.*** **2** *econ* **a** an instalment of a loan; **b** part of a block of bonds, especially government stock. ◷ 16c: French, from *trancher* to cut.

trannie or **tranny** /'tranɪ/ ▻ *noun* (***trannies***) *Brit colloq, rather dated* a short form of TRANSISTOR RADIO.

tranquil /'traŋkwɪl/ ▻ *adj* serenely quiet or peaceful; undisturbed. • **tranquillity** or **tranquility** *noun*. • **tranquilly** *adverb*. • **tranquilness** *noun*. ◷ 17c: from Latin *tranquillus* quiet.

tranquillize, **tranquillise** or (*US*) **tranquilize** /'traŋkwɪlaɪz/ ▻ *verb* (***tranquillized***, ***tranquillizing***; ***tranquilized***, ***tranquilizing***) **1** to make or become calm, peaceful or less tense; to make or become calmer or more peaceful. **2** to give a tranquillizing drug to.

tranquillizer, **tranquilliser** or (*US*) **tranquilizer** ▻ *noun* someone or something that has a tranquillizing effect, especially any of several drugs that act on the central nervous system.

trans. ▻ *abbreviation* **1** transitive. **2** translated. **3** translation.

trans- ▻ *prefix, forming words, denoting* **1** across; beyond □ ***transatlantic***. **2** on, to or towards the other side of. **3** through. **4** into another state or place □ ***transform***. ◷ Latin, meaning 'across'.

transact /tran'zakt, trɑːn-, -'sakt/ ▻ *verb* (***transacted***, ***transacting***) to conduct or carry out (business). • **transactor** *noun*. ◷ 16c: from Latin *transigere*, *transactum* to drive through.

transactinide /tranz'aktɪnaɪd/ ▻ *adj, chem* referring or relating to radioactive elements with atomic numbers higher than the ACTINIDE series. ▻ *noun* such an element.

transaction ▻ *noun* **1** something, such as a business deal, that is settled or is in the process of being settled. **2** (**transactions**) the published reports of papers read, decisions taken, etc at a meeting of a learned society together with the records of any discussions arising from such a meeting. **3** an act of transacting.

transalpine /tranz'alpaɪn, trɑːnz-/ ▻ *adj* **1** situated or happening on the other side of the Alps, originally as viewed from a Roman or Italian stance. **2** built or stretching across the Alps. ◷ 16c: from Latin *transalpinus*.

transatlantic /tranzət'lantɪk, trɑːnz-/ ▻ *adj* **1** crossing, or designed for or capable of crossing, the Atlantic. **2 a** belonging, relating or referring to, originating from, or situated on the other side of, the Atlantic; **b** *N Amer* European; **c** *Brit* American.

transceiver /tran'siːvə(r), trɑːn-/ ▻ *noun* a piece of radio equipment designed to transmit and receive signals. ◷ 1930s.

transcend /tran'sɛnd, trɑːn'sɛnd/ ▻ *verb* (***transcended***, ***transcending***) **1** to be beyond the limits, scope, range, etc of something □ ***transcends the bounds of human endurance.*** **2** to surpass or excel. **3** to overcome or surmount □ ***transcend all difficulties.*** ◷ 16c: from Latin *transcendere*.

transcendent ▻ *adj* **1** excellent; surpassing others of the same or similar kind. **2** beyond ordinary human knowledge or experience. **3** said especially of a deity, etc: existing outside the material or created world and independent of it. Compare IMMANENT. • **transcendence** *noun*.

transcendental /transɛn'dɛntəl, trɑːn-/ ▻ *adj* **1** going beyond usual human knowledge or experience. **2** going beyond in excellence; surpassing or excelling. **3** supernatural or mystical. **4** vague, abstract or abstruse. • **transcendentally** *adverb*.

transcendentalism ▻ *noun* any philosophical system concerned with what is constant, innate and a priori, independent of and a necessary prerequisite to experience.

transcendental meditation ▻ *noun* a method of meditating that involves the, usually silent, repetition of a MANTRA (sense 1) to relieve anxiety, promote spiritual wellbeing and achieve physical and mental relaxation. Often shortened to TM. ◷ 1960s: first popularized in the West by the Maharishi Mahesh Yogi.

transcendental number ▻ *noun, math* any number that cannot be expressed as a ratio of two INTEGERS and which is not the root of an algebraic equation, eg π.

transcontinental /tranzkɒntɪ'nɛntəl, trɑːnz-/ ▻ *adj* said especially of a railway: extending across an entire continent. ▻ *noun* a railway that extends, train that travels, etc, across a continent.

transcribe /tran'skraɪb, trɑːn-/ ▻ *verb* (***transcribed***, ***transcribing***) **1** to write out (a text) in full, eg from notes □ ***The shorthand notes will be transcribed later.*** **2** to copy (a text) from one place to another □ ***transcribed the poem into her album.*** **3** to write out (a spoken text). **4** to transliterate. **5** *music* to arrange (a piece of music) for an instrument or voice that it was not originally composed for. **6** *broadcasting* **a** to record (a programme, etc) for reproducing at some later date; **b** to broadcast (a programme, etc that has been recorded in this way). **7** to record any form of information on a suitable storage medium. **8** *computing* to transfer data from one computer storage device to another, eg from tape to disk, or from the main memory of a computer to a storage device, or from a storage device to the main memory. • **transcriber** *noun*. ◷ 16c: from Latin *transcribere*.

transcript /'transkrɪpt, 'trɑːn-/ ▻ *noun* a written, typed or printed copy, especially a legal record of court proceedings. ◷ 13c: from Latin *transcriptum*.

transcription ▻ *noun* **1** the act or process of transcribing. **2** something that is transcribed; a transcript. **3** the act or process of representing speech sounds in writing, eg by using a phonetic alphabet. • **transcriptional** or **transcriptive** *adj*. ◷ 16c: Latin, from *transcriptio*.

transducer /tranz'dʒuːsə(r), trɑːnz-/ ▻ *noun* any device that converts energy from one form to another, eg a loudspeaker, where electrical energy is converted into sound waves. ◷ 1920s: from Latin *transducere* to transfer.

transept /'transɛpt, 'trɑːn-/ ▻ *noun* **1** in a cross-shaped building, especially a church: either of the two arms (the **north** and **south transepts**) that are at right angles to the NAVE. **2** the area formed by these two arms. • **transeptal** /tran'sɛptəl/ *adj*. ◷ 16c: from TRANS- sense 1 + Latin *saeptum* enclosure.

transexual see TRANSSEXUAL

transf. ▻ *abbreviation* transferred.

transfer ▻ *verb* /trans'fɜː(r), trɑːns-/ (***transferred***, ***transferring***) **1** *tr & intr* to move from one place, person, group, etc to another. **2** *intr* to change from one vehicle, line, passenger system, etc to another while travelling. **3** *law* to hand over (a title, rights, property, etc) to someone else by means of a legal document. **4** to transpose (a design, etc) from one surface to another. **5** *Brit* **a** *intr* said especially of a professional footballer: to change clubs; **b** said of a football club, manager, etc: to arrange for (a player) to go to another club. ▷ *noun* /ˈtransfɜː(r), ˈtrɑːns-/ **1** an act, instance or the process of transferring or the state of being transferred □ ***asked for a transfer to another department.*** **2** *Brit* a design or picture that can be transferred from one surface to another. **3** someone or something that is transferred. **4** *law* **a** the act of handing over, eg the legal right to property, etc, from one person to another; conveyance; **b** any document which records this kind of act. **5** *N Amer* a ticket that allows a passenger to continue a journey on another route, etc. ● **transferability** or **transferrability** *noun.* ● **transferable** or **transferrable** *adj.* ● **transferee** *noun.* ● **transferor** *noun, law.* ● **transferrer** *noun.* ⓒ 14c: from Latin *transferre*, from *ferre* to carry or bear.

transferable vote ▷ *noun* in proportional representation: a vote that is cast for another candidate if the voter's first-choice candidate is eliminated.

transference ▷ *noun* **1** the act or process of transferring from one person, place, group, etc to another. **2** *psychol* an act or the process of unconsciously transferring emotions, fears, anxieties, etc to someone or something else, especially to a psychoanalyst during therapy.

transfer fee ▷ *noun, Brit* the amount that one football club, etc agrees to pay to another for the transfer of a player.

transfer list ▷ *noun, Brit* a hypothetical list that details the names of professional footballers who are available for transfer □ ***Fergusson asked to be put on the transfer list.***

transferrin /transˈferɪn, trɑːns-/ ▷ *noun, biochem* any of several iron-transporting proteins in the blood. ⓒ 1940s: from Latin *ferrum* iron.

transfer RNA ▷ *noun* (abbreviation **tRNA**) *biol* a molecule of RIBONUCLEIC ACID whose function is to collect a specific amino acid in the CYTOPLASM and carry it to a RIBOSOME so that it can be used in the manufacture of protein. ⓒ 1960s.

transfiguration ▷ *noun* **1** a change in appearance, especially one that involves something becoming more beautiful, glorious, exalted, etc. **2** (**Transfiguration**) *Christianity* **a** the radiant change in Christ's appearance that is described in Matthew 17.2 and Mark 9.2-3; **b** a church festival held on 6 August to commemorate this. ⓒ 14c.

transfigure /transˈfɪgə(r), trɑːns-/ ▷ *verb* (***transfigured***, ***transfiguring***) to change or make someone or something change in appearance, especially in becoming more beautiful, glorious, exalted, etc. ● **transfigurement** *noun.* ⓒ 13c: from Latin *transfigurare* to change shape.

transfinite /transˈfaɪnaɪt, trɑːns-/ ▷ *adj* **1** beyond what is finite. **2** *math* said of a number: that exceeds all finite numbers. ⓒ Early 20c.

transfix /transˈfɪks, trɑːns-/ ▷ *verb* (***transfixes***, ***transfixed***, ***transfixing***) **1** to immobilize through surprise, fear, horror, etc. **2** to pierce through with, or as if with, a pointed weapon, instrument, etc. ● **transfixion** /-ˈfɪkʃən/ *noun.* ⓒ 16c: from Latin *transfigere*, *transfixum* to pierce through.

transform /ˈtransfɔːm, ˈtrɑːns-/ ▷ *verb* (***transformed***, ***transforming***) **1** **a** to change in appearance, nature, function, etc, often completely and dramatically □ ***Some fresh paint soon transformed the room***; **b** *intr* to undergo such a change. **2** *math* to change the form but not the value of (an equation or algebraic expression) by mathematical transformation. **3** *electronics* to change the voltage or type of (a current), eg from alternating to direct. ● **transformable** *adj.* ● **transformative** *adj.* ● **transformed** *adj.* ● **transforming** *adj, noun.* ⓒ 14c: from Latin *transformare*.

transformation /transfəˈmeɪʃən, trɑːns-/ ▷ *noun* **1** an act or instance or the process of transforming or being transformed. **2** a change of form, constitution, substance, etc. **3** *zool* any process that involves an animal changing its fundamental form; metamorphosis. **4** *math* an operation, eg a mapping one, that changes a set of elements or variables into another set with the same value, magnitude, etc. **5** *cytol* **a** the alteration that occurs in a eukaryotic cell (see EUKARYOTE) that changes it from its normal state into a malignant one; **b** the genetic alteration of a cell through the introduction of extraneous DNA. **6** *linguistics* in TRANSFORMATIONAL GRAMMAR: an operation whereby one syntactic structure is changed into another by applying specific rules that govern the moving, inserting, deleting and replacing of certain items, and which can be used to show the link between the DEEP STRUCTURE of a sentence and its SURFACE STRUCTURE. ● **transformational** *adj.* ⓒ 15c: from Latin.

transformational grammar ▷ *noun, linguistics* a system of GENERATIVE GRAMMAR in which elements or structures can be derived from others or related to others by using a set of rules to convert the underlying structure of a sentence into the form in which it will occur in the language.

transformer ▷ *noun* **1** *elec* an electromagnetic device designed to transfer electrical energy from one alternating current circuit to another, with an increase or decrease in voltage. **2** someone or something that transforms.

transfuse /transˈfjuːz, trɑːns-/ ▷ *verb* (***transfused***, ***transfusing***) **1** *medicine* **a** to transfer (blood or plasma) from one person or animal into the blood vessels of another; **b** to treat (a person or animal) with a transfusion of blood or other fluid. **2** to pass, enter, diffuse, etc through or over; to permeate □ ***Pink and orange patterns transfused the dawn sky.*** **3** to pour (fluid) from one receptacle to another. ● **transfuser** *noun.* ⓒ 15c: from Latin *transfundere*, *transfusum* to pour out.

transfusion /transˈfjuːʒən, trɑːns-/ ▷ *noun, medicine* **1** (*in full* **blood transfusion**) the process of introducing whole compatible blood directly into the bloodstream of a person or animal, eg to replace blood lost through injury, during surgery, etc. **2** a similar process where a component of whole blood, such as plasma, or a saline solution is used, eg to treat shock.

transgenic /transˈdʒɛnɪk/ ▷ *adj, genetics* said of a plant or animal: having had genetic material from another species artificially introduced. ⓒ Late 20c: from GENE.

transgress /tranzˈgrɛs, trɑːnz-/ ▷ *verb* (***transgresses***, ***transgressed***, ***transgressing***) **1** to break, breach or violate (divine law, a rule, etc). **2** to go beyond or overstep (a limit or boundary). ● **transgressive** *adj.* ● **transgressor** *noun.* ⓒ 16c: from Latin *transgredi*, *transgressus* to step across.

transgression ▷ *noun* **1** an act or instance of breaking a rule, divine law, etc. **2** a crime or sin. ● **transgressional** *adj.*

tranship /tranˈʃɪp, trɑːn-/ or **transship** /tranzˈʃɪp, trɑːnz-/ ▷ *verb, tr & intr* to transfer from one ship or form of transport to another. ● **transhipment** *noun.* ● **transhipper** *noun.* ● **transhipping** *noun.* ⓒ 18c.

transhumance /transˈhjuːməns, trɑːns-/ ▷ *noun* the moving of livestock to different grazing lands according to the season, eg when flocks are taken up to mountain pastures in summertime. ● **transhumant** *adj.* ⓒ Early 20c: from French *transhumer*.

transient /ˈtranzɪənt, ˈtrɑːn-/ ▷ *adj* lasting, staying, visiting, etc for only a short time; passing quickly. ▷ *noun* **1** a temporary resident, worker, etc. **2** a short sudden surge of voltage or current. ● **transience** or **transiency**

noun. • **transiently** *adverb*. ⓘ 17c: from Latin *transire* to cross over.

transistor /tran'zɪstə(r), trɑːn-/ ▻ *noun* **1** *electronics* in electronic circuits: a semiconductor device that has three or more electrodes, whose function is to act as a switch, amplifier or detector of electric current, eg in radio receivers, TV sets, etc. **2** (*in full* **transistor radio**) a small portable radio that has transistors instead of valves and tubes. ⓘ 1940s: from *trans*fer + re*sistor*.

transistorize or **transistorise** ▻ *verb* (***transistorized***, ***transistorizing***) to design or fit with a transistor or transistors rather than valves. • **transistorized** *adj*. • **transistorization** *noun*. ⓘ 1950s.

transit /'transɪt, 'trɑːn-/ ▻ *noun* **1** the act or process of carrying or moving goods, passengers, etc from one place to another. **2** a route or passage. **3** *N Amer, especially US* the transport of passengers or goods on public, usually local, routes. **4** *astron* **a** the passage of a heavenly body across a meridian; **b** the passage of a smaller heavenly body across a larger one, eg of a moon across its planet; **c** the passage of a satellite or its shadow across the disk of a planet. ▻ *verb* (***transited***, ***transiting***) to pass across or through. • **in transit** said of goods or passengers: in the process of being taken from or travelling from one place to another. ⓘ 15c: from Latin *transire*, *transitus* to go across.

transit camp ▻ *noun* a camp for the temporary accommodation of soldiers, refugees, etc who are on the way to their permanent destination.

transit instrument ▻ *noun, optics* a type of telescope on a single fixed horizontal axis of rotation that is designed for observing the passage of heavenly bodies across the meridian. ⓘ Early 19c.

transition /tran'zɪʃən, trɑːn-/ ▻ *noun* **1** a change or passage from one condition, state, subject, place, etc to another. **2** *music* a change from one key to another; a brief modulation. **3** *archit* the gradual change from one style to another, especially from NORMAN to EARLY ENGLISH. **4** *physics* a change of an atomic nucleus or orbital electron from one QUANTUM STATE to another where the emission or absorption of radiation is involved. • **transitional** or **transitionary** *adj*. • **transitionally** *adverb*. ⓘ 16c: from Latin *transitio* a going across.

transition element ▻ *noun, chem* in the periodic table: any of a group of metallic elements, eg copper, cobalt, iron, etc, that have only partially filled inner electron shells and therefore tend to show variable valency and form highly coloured compounds. Also called **transition metal**.

transitive /'transɪtɪv, 'trɑːn-, -zɪtɪv/ ▻ *adj* **1** *grammar* said of a verb: taking a DIRECT OBJECT, eg *They make lots of money*. Compare INTRANSITIVE, ABSOLUTE. **2** *logic, math* having the property whereby if there is a relation between item one and item two and the same relation is discernible between item two and item three, then there must be the same relation between item one and item three, eg if $a = b$ and $b = c$, then $a = c$. • **transitively** *adverb*. ⓘ 16c: from Latin *transitivus*.

transit lounge ▻ *noun* an area in an airport where passengers who are catching a connecting flight can wait.

transitory /'tranzɪtərɪ, 'trɑːn-, -sɪtərɪ, -trɪ/ ▻ *adj* short-lived; lasting only for a short time; transient. • **transitorily** *adverb*. • **transitoriness** *noun*. ⓘ 14c: from Latin *transitorius* having or following a passage.

transit visa ▻ *noun* a visa that allows someone to pass through a country but not to stay in it.

translate /trans'leɪt, trɑːnz-/ ▻ *verb* (***translated***, ***translating***) **1 a** to express (a word, speech, written text, etc) in another language, closely preserving the meaning of the original ▫ ***translated Umberto Eco's novel into English***; **b** *intr* to do this, especially as a profession ▫ ***translates for the EC***. **2** *intr* said of a written text, etc: to be able to be expressed in another language, format, etc ▫ ***Poetry doesn't always translate well***. **3** to put or express (eg an idea) in other terms, especially terms that are plainer or simpler than the original. **4** to interpret the significance or meaning of (an action, behaviour, etc) ▫ ***translated her expression as contempt***. **5** *tr & intr* to convert or be converted into; to show or be shown as ▫ ***need to translate their ideas into reality*** ▫ ***The price translates as roughly £50***. **6** *tr & intr* to change or move from one state, condition, person, place, etc to another. **7** *church* to transfer (a bishop) from one SEE to another. **8** to move (the relics of a saint) from one place to another. **9** *relig* to remove someone to heaven, especially without death. • **translatable** *adj*. ⓘ 13c: from Latin *transferre*, *translatum* to carry across.

translation ▻ *noun* **1** a word, speech, written text, etc that has been put into one language from another. **2** an act or instance or the process of translating. **3** *genetics* the process, which takes place on specialized structures called RIBOSOMEs, whereby the coded genetic information carried by messenger RNA molecules is used to specify the order in which individual amino acids are added to a growing chain of protein or polypeptide being manufactured within the cell. • **translational** *adj*.

translator ▻ *noun* someone whose job is to translate texts, speeches, etc from one language to another, especially someone who is professionally qualified to do this.

transliterate /tranz'lɪtəreɪt, trɑːnz-/ ▻ *verb* (***transliterated***, ***transliterating***) to replace (the characters of a word, name, text, etc) with the nearest equivalent characters of another alphabet. • **transliteration** *noun* **1** the process of transliterating. **2** a letter or word that has been transliterated. • **transliterator** *noun*. ⓘ 19c: from Latin *litera* letter.

translocate /tranzlou'keɪt, trɑːnz-/ ▻ *verb* (***translocated***, ***translocating***) **1** to move (especially wild animals) from one place to another. **2** to move (a substance in solution) from one part to another. In plants this occurs in the PHLOEM of the vascular system, and in animals it usually occurs by OSMOSIS. **3** *genetics* to move (part of a chromosome) to a different position. • **translocation** *noun*. ⓘ 17c.

translucent /trans'luːsənt, trɑːns-, -ljuːsənt/ ▻ *adj* **1** allowing light to pass diffusely; semi-transparent. **2** clear. • **translucence** or **translucency** *noun*. • **translucently** *adverb*. ⓘ 16c: from Latin *translucere*, from *lucere* to shine.

translunar /tranz'luːnə(r), trɑːnz-/ and **translunary** ▻ *adj* **1** situated beyond the Moon or beyond the Moon's orbit. **2** referring or relating to space travel or a trajectory that goes towards the Moon. **3** unearthly; insubstantial; visionary. ⓘ 17c.

transmigrate /tranzmaɪ'greɪt, trɑːnz-/ ▻ *verb, intr* **1** said of a soul: to pass into another body at or just after death. **2** to move from one home or abode to another; to migrate. • **transmigration** *noun*. • **transmigrator** *noun*. • **transmigratory** *adj*. ⓘ 17c: from Latin *transmigrare*, *transmigratum* to migrate.

transmigrationism ▻ *noun* the theory or doctrine of transmigration of the soul. • **transmigrationist** *noun* someone who believes in or who advocates this.

transmission /tranz'mɪʃən, trɑːnz-/ ▻ *noun* **1** an act or the process of transmitting or the state of being transmitted. **2** something that is transmitted, especially a radio or TV broadcast. **3** the system of parts in a motor vehicle that transfers power from the engine to the wheels. • **transmissional** *adj*. ⓘ 17c: from Latin *transmissio* sending across.

transmit /tranz'mɪt, trɑːnz-/ ▻ *verb* (***transmitted***, ***transmitting***) **1** to pass or hand on (especially a message, a genetic characteristic, an inheritance, or an infection or disease). **2** to convey (emotion, etc) ▫ ***a painting that transmits the artist's inner turmoil***. **3** *tr & intr* **a** to send out (signals) by radio waves; **b** to broadcast (a radio or television programme). **4** to allow (eg light, sound, heat, electricity, etc) to pass through; to act as a medium for. **5** to transfer (a force, power, etc) from one part, eg of an engine, mechanical system, etc, to another. • **transmissible** *adj.* • **transmissibility** *noun.* • **transmissive** *adj.* • **transmissivity** *noun.* • **transmittable** *adj.* • **transmittal** *noun.* Ⓒ 14c: from Latin *transmittere* to send across.

transmitter ▷ *noun* **1** someone or something that transmits. **2** the equipment that transmits the signals in radio and TV broadcasting. **3** *telecomm* the part of a telephone mouthpiece that converts sound waves into electrical signals. **4** *physiol* a NEUROTRANSMITTER.

transmogrify /tranz'mɒgrɪfaɪ, trɑːnz-/ ▷ *verb* (***transmogrifies***, ***transmogrified***, ***transmogrifying***) *humorous* to transform, especially in shape or appearance and often in a surprising or bizarre way. • **transmogrification** *noun.* Ⓒ 17c.

transmontane see TRAMONTANE

transmutation ▷ *noun* **1** the act or an instance or the process of transmuting; a change of form. **2** *physics* the changing of one element into another by nuclear bombardment or irradiation as opposed to spontaneous decay. **3** *alchemy* the changing of a base metal into gold or silver. • **transmutational** *adj.* • **transmutationist** *noun.*

transmute /tranz'mjuːt, trɑːnz-/ ▷ *verb* (***transmuted***, ***transmuting***) **1** to change the form, substance or nature of. **2** to change (one chemical element) into another. **3** *alchemy* to change (base metal) into gold or silver. • **transmutability** or **transmutableness** *noun.* • **transmutable** *adj.* • **transmutably** *adverb.* • **transmuter** *noun.* Ⓒ 15c: from Latin *transmutare* to change condition.

transnational ▷ *adj* extending beyond national boundaries or being of concern to more than one nation. ▷ *noun* a company that has interests in more than one country.

transoceanic /tranzoʊʃɪ'anɪk, trɑːnz-/ ▷ *adj* **1** existing or situated beyond an ocean. **2** relating to, capable of or concerned with ocean crossing □ ***transoceanic flights.***

transom /'transəm/ ▷ *noun* **1 a** a horizontal bar of wood or stone that divides a window; **b** a horizontal bar of wood or stone that goes across the top of a door or large window separating it from a small window or fanlight above it. **2** a lintel. **3** (*in full* **transom window**) a small window over the lintel of a door or larger window. **4** any of several crossbeams in the stern of a boat. • **transomed** *adj.* Ⓒ 14c.

transpacific ▷ *adj* **1** existing or situated beyond the Pacific ocean. **2** relating to, capable of or concerned with crossing the Pacific ocean.

transparency /trans'parənsɪ, trɑːns-, -'pɛərənsɪ/ ▷ *noun* (***transparencies***) **1** the quality or state of being transparent. **2** a small photograph on glass or rigid plastic mounted in a frame, designed to be viewed by placing it in a slide projector. Also called SLIDE. **3** a picture, print, etc on glass or other translucent background that can be seen when a light is shone behind it.

transparent /trans'parənt, trɑːns-, -'pɛərənt/ ▷ *adj* **1** able to be seen through; clear. **2** said of a motive, etc: easily understood or recognized; obvious; evident. **3** said of an excuse, pretence, disguise, etc: easily seen through. **4** said of a person, their character, etc: frank and open; candid. • **transparently** *adj.* • **transparentness** *noun.* Ⓒ 15c: from Latin *transparere*, from *parere* to appear.

transpersonal /trans'pɜːsənəl, trɑːns-/ ▷ *adj* **1** going beyond what is personal. **2** *denoting* a form of psychology or psychotherapy that emphasizes the use of mystical, psychical, spiritual, religious, etc experiences as a way of achieving greater self-awareness, potential, etc. Ⓒ Early 20c.

transpire /tran'spaɪə(r), trɑːn-/ ▷ *verb* (***transpired***, ***transpiring***) **1** *intr* said especially of something secret: to become known; to come to light. **2** *intr*, *loosely* to happen. **3** *tr & intr*, *bot* said of a plant: to release water vapour into the atmosphere, especially through the stomata on the lower surfaces of leaves. • **transpiration** /transpɪ'reɪʃən, trɑːns-/ *noun* **1** the act or process of transpiring. **2** emission of water vapour in plants. • **transpirable** *adj.* Ⓒ 16c: from Latin *transpirare*, from *spirare* to breathe.

transpire

Some people reject the use of **transpire** to mean 'to happen', but it is now well established.

transplant ▷ *verb* /trans'plɑːnt, trɑːns-/ (***transplanted***, ***transplanting***) **1** to take (living skin, tissue, an organ, etc) from someone and use it as an implant, either at another site in the donor's own body or in the body of another person. **2** to move (someone or something, especially a growing plant) from one place to another. ▷ *noun* /'trans-, 'trɑːns-/ **1** *surgery* an operation which involves an organ, skin, tissue, etc being transferred from one person or one part of the body to another. **2** something, especially an organ, skin, body tissue, plant, etc which has been transplanted or which is ready to be transplanted. • **transplantable** *adj.* • **transplantation** *noun.* • **transplanter** *noun.* • **transplanting** *noun.* Ⓒ 15c: from Latin *transplantare.*

transponder /trans'pɒndə(r), trɑːns-/ ▷ *noun* a radio and radar device that receives a signal and then sends out its own signal in response. Ⓒ 1940s: from *trans*mit + *respond.*

transport ▷ *verb* /trans'pɔːt, trɑːns-/ (***transported***, ***transporting***) **1** to carry (goods, passengers, etc) from one place to another. **2** *historical* to send (a criminal) to a penal colony overseas. **3** (*often* **be transported with**) to affect strongly or deeply □ ***was transported with grief.*** ▷ *noun* /'transpɔːt, 'trɑːns-/ **1** a system or business for taking people, goods, etc from place to place □ ***public transport.*** **2** a means of getting or being transported from place to place □ ***The car's in for repairs, so I haven't got transport at the moment.*** **3** (*often* **transports**) strong emotion, especially of pleasure or delight; ecstasy □ ***transports of joy.*** **4** a ship, aircraft, lorry, etc used to carry soldiers or military equipment and stores. **5** *historical* a criminal or convict who has been sentenced to transportation. • **transportability** *noun.* • **transportable** *adj.* Ⓒ 15c: from Latin *transportare* to carry across.

transportation ▷ *noun* **1** the act of transporting or the process of being transported. **2** a means of being transported; transport. **3** *historical* a form of punishment where convicted criminals were sent to overseas penal colonies.

transport café ▷ *noun*, *Brit* an inexpensive restaurant that is usually situated at or near the roadside and which caters especially for long-distance lorry drivers. *US equivalent* **truck stop**.

transporter ▷ *noun* **1** someone or something that transports. **2** a vehicle that caries other vehicles, large pieces of machinery, etc by road.

transpose /trans'poʊz, trɑːns-/ ▷ *verb* (***transposed***, ***transposing***) **1** to make (two or more things, letters, words, etc) change places. **2** to change the position of (an item) in a sequence or series. **3** *music* to perform or rewrite (notes, a piece of music, etc) in a different key from the original or intended key. **4** *math* to move (a term) from one side of an algebraic equation to the other and change the accompanying sign. • **transposable** *adj.* • **transposal** *noun.* • **transposer** *noun.* • **transposing** *adj*, *noun.* Ⓒ 14c: from French *transposer*, from *poser* to put.

transposing instrument ▷ *noun*, *music* **1** an instrument that incorporates a means for transposing notes into a different key. **2** an orchestral instrument which produces sounds that are in a different key from those that are written for it.

transposition /transpə'zɪʃən, trɑːns-/ ▻ *noun* **1** an act or the process of transposing or being transposed. **2** something that is transposed. • **transpositional** *adj.*

transputer /trans'pjuːtə(r), trɑːns-/ ▻ *noun, computing* a chip that is capable of all the functions of a microprocessor, including memory, and which is designed for parallel processing rather than sequential processing. Ⓒ 1970s: from *trans*istor + com*puter*.

transsexual or **transexual** /tran'sɛkʃʊəl, trɑːn-/ ▻ *noun* **1** someone who is anatomically of one sex but who adopts the characteristics, behaviour, etc usually perceived as typical of a member of the opposite sex, often as a prelude to having some form of medical treatment to alter their physical attributes. **2** someone who has had medical, hormonal and/or surgical treatment to alter their physical features so that they more closely resemble those of the opposite sex. ▻ *adj* **1** relating or referring to someone who has the physical characteristics of one gender, but the psychological characteristics, or a desire to be, of the opposite gender. **2** relating or referring to someone who has undergone medical treatment that results in any form of physical change of gender. • **transsexualism** *noun.* • **transsexuality** *noun.* Ⓒ 1940s.

transship ▻ *verb* see TRANSHIP

transubstantiate /transəb'stanʃɪeɪt, trɑːn-/ ▻ *verb, tr & intr* to change into another substance. Ⓒ 16c.

transubstantiation ▻ *noun* **1** the act or process of changing, or changing something, into something else. **2** *Christianity* especially in the Roman Catholic and Eastern Orthodox churches: **a** the conversion of the Eucharistic bread and wine, after they have been consecrated, into the body and blood of Christ, although there is no outward change in their appearance; **b** the doctrine which states that this happens. Compare CONSUBSTANTIATION. • **transubstantiationalist** *noun.* Ⓒ 14c; from TRANS- sense 4.

transude /tran'sjuːd/ ▻ *verb* (***transuded, transuding***) said of a fluid, especially a bodily fluid such as sweat: to ooze out, through pores or some permeable membrane. • **transudate** /-eɪt/ *noun* a fluid of this kind. • **transudation** *noun.* Ⓒ 17c: from Latin *sudare* to sweat.

transuranic /tranzjʊ'ranɪk, trɑːnz-/ ▻ *adj, chem* said of an element: having an atomic number greater than that of uranium, ie 93 or higher. Such elements are artificially manufactured and radioactive, most of them having short half-lives (see HALF-LIFE). Ⓒ 1930s: from TRANS- sense 1.

Transvaal daisy /trans'vɑːl —, trɑːns-/ ▻ *noun* a plant native to S Africa, popular as a cut flower because of its large brightly-coloured flowers in shades of orange, yellow, red and pink, which have hundreds of petals radiating from the centre. Ⓒ Early 20c: named after Transvaal, a province in S Africa.

transversal ▻ *noun, geom* a line that cuts a set of other lines.

transverse /'tranzvɜːs, 'trɑːnz-/ ▻ *adj* placed, lying, built, etc in a crosswise direction. • **transversely** *adverb.* Ⓒ 17: from Latin *transvertere*, from *vertere* to turn.

transverse wave ▻ *noun, physics* a wave, such as an electromagnetic one, where the disturbance of the medium occurs at right angles to the direction of propagation of the wave.

transvestite /tranz'vɛstaɪt, trɑːnz-/ ▻ *noun* someone, especially a man, who dresses in clothes that are conventionally thought of as being exclusive to people of the opposite sex and who may derive sexual pleasure from doing this. • **transvestism** or **transvestitism** *noun.* Ⓒ Early 20c: from Latin *vestire* to dress.

trap ▻ *noun* **1** a device or hole, usually baited, for catching animals, sometimes killing them in the process. **2** a plan or trick for surprising someone into speech or action, or catching them unawares □ ***a speed trap.*** **3** a trapdoor. **4** a bend in a pipe, especially a drainpipe, which fills with liquid to stop foul gases passing up the pipe. **5** a light, two-wheeled carriage which is usually pulled by a single horse. **6** a device for throwing a ball or clay pigeon into the air. **7** one of the box-like compartments that are set along the starting line of a greyhound race-track where the dogs wait before being released at the beginning of a race. **8** a bunker or other hazard on a golf course. **9** *slang* the mouth. **10** (**traps**) *jazz slang* drums or other percussion instruments. ▻ *verb* (***trapped, trapping***) **1** to catch (an animal) in a trap. **2** to catch someone out or unawares, especially with a trick. **3** to set traps in (a place). **4** to stop and hold in or as if in a trap. **5** *intr* to act as a TRAPPER. Ⓒ Anglo-Saxon *treppe*.

trapdoor ▻ *noun* a small door or opening in a floor, ceiling, theatre stage, etc that is usually set flush with its surface.

trapdoor spider ▻ *noun* any of several types of spider that build a burrow and cover it with a hinged door that they make from the silk threads they spin.

trapes see TRAIPSE

trapeze /trə'piːz/ ▻ *noun* a swing-like apparatus that consists of a short horizontal bar hanging on two ropes and is used by gymnasts and acrobats in their routines. Ⓒ 1860s: French, from Latin *trapezium* trapezium.

trapezium /trə'piːzɪəm/ ▻ *noun* (***trapeziums*** or ***trapezia*** /-zɪə/) **1** *Brit* a four-sided geometric figure that has one pair of its opposite sides parallel. **2** *N Amer* a four-sided geometric figure that has no parallel sides. **3** any four-sided geometric figure that is not a parallelogram. See also TRAPEZOID sense 1. • **trapezial** or **trapeziform** *adj.* Ⓒ 16c: Latin, from Greek *trapezion*, from *trapeza* table.

trapezius /trə'piːzɪəs/ and **trapezius muscle** ▻ *noun* (***trapeziuses*** or ***-zii*** /-zɪaɪ/) either of a pair of large flat triangular muscles that extend over the back of the neck and the shoulders. Ⓒ 18c: from the trapezium shape they form as a pair.

trapezoid /'trapɪzɔɪd, trə'piːzɔɪd/ ▻ *noun* **1** *Brit* a four-sided geometric figure that has no sides parallel. **2** *N Amer* a four-sided geometric figure that has one pair of its opposite sides parallel. See also TRAPEZIUM sense 1, 2. • **trapezoidal** *adj.* Ⓒ 16c: from Greek *trapezoeides*, from *trapeza* table.

trapped *past tense, past participle of* TRAP

trapper ▻ *noun* someone who traps wild animals, usually with the intention of selling their fur.

trapping *present participle of* TRAP

trappings ▻ *plural noun* **1** clothes or ornaments suitable for or indicative of a particular occasion, ceremony, status, office or person □ ***all the trappings of self-seeking materialism.*** **2** a horse's ceremonial or ornamental harness. Ⓒ 16c: from French *drap* cloth.

Trappist /'trapɪst/ ▻ *noun* a member of a branch of the Cistercian order of Christian monks who observe a severe rule which includes a vow of silence. Ⓒ Early 19c: from La Trappe, in Normandy, France, where the order was founded.

traps ▻ *plural noun, Brit* personal luggage. Ⓒ Early 19c: from French *drap* cloth.

trash ▻ *noun* **1 a** rubbish; waste material or objects; **b** *chiefly N Amer, especially US* domestic waste. **2** nonsense. **3** a worthless, contemptible, etc person or people □ ***white trash.*** **4 a** a worthless object or worthless objects; **b** art, literature, cinema, music, etc that is perceived as having little or no artistic, critical or creative merit. **5** *colloq* music. **6** the broken-off tops of plants or trees, especially sugar cane. ▻ *verb* (***trashes, trashed, trashing***) **1** *colloq* to wreck. **2** *colloq* **a** to expose as worthless; **b** to give (a film, novel, play, performance, etc) a very adverse review. **3** to remove the outer leaves of (sugar cane) to promote ripening. ⓒ 16c.

trashcan ▷ *noun, N Amer, especially US* a dustbin.

trashy ▷ *adj* (***trashier***, ***trashiest***) worthless; of poor quality ▫ *trashy novels*. ● **trashily** *adverb*. ● **trashiness** *noun*.

trattoria /tratəˈriːə, trəˈtɔːriːə/ ▷ *noun* (***trattorias*** or ***trattorie*** /-eɪ/) a restaurant, especially an informal one that serves Italian food. ⓒ 19c: Italian, from *trattore* host.

trauma /ˈtrɔːmə, ˈtraʊmə/ ▷ *noun* (***traumas*** or ***traumata*** /-mətə/) **1** *medicine* **a** a physical injury or wound; **b** a state of shock that is sometimes brought on by a physical injury or wound and which manifests in a lowering of the body's temperature, confusion, etc. **2** *psychiatry & psychoanal* **a** an emotional shock that may have long-term effects on behaviour or personality; **b** the condition that can result from this type of emotional shock. **3** *loosely* any event, situation, etc that is stressful, emotionally upsetting, etc. ⓒ 17c: Greek, meaning 'wound'.

traumatic /trɔːˈmatɪk, traʊ-/ ▷ *adj* **1** relating to, resulting from or causing physical wounds. **2** relating to, resulting from or causing a psychological shock that produces long-term effects. **3** *colloq* distressing; emotionally upsetting; frightening; unpleasant. ● **traumatically** *adverb*.

traumatism ▷ *noun* **1** the effects, state or condition that a physical or emotional trauma produces. **2** *loosely* any emotional shock or upsetting experience.

traumatize or **traumatise** ▷ *verb* (***traumatized***, ***traumatizing***) **1** to wound physically or emotionally ▫ *traumatized by events in his childhood*. **2** *loosely* to distress, upset or stun ▫ *traumatized by the heat*. ● **traumatization** *noun*. ● **traumatized** *adj*. ● **traumatizing** *adj, noun*. ⓒ Early 20c.

travail /ˈtraveɪl, ˈtravəl/ ▷ *noun* **1** painful or extremely hard work or labour. **2** the pain of childbirth; labour. ▷ *verb* (***travailed***, ***travailing***) *intr* **1** to work hard or with pain. **2** *old use* to be in labour; to suffer the pains of childbirth. ⓒ 13c: French, meaning 'painful effort'.

travel /ˈtravəl/ ▷ *verb* (***travelled***, ***travelling***; ***traveled***, ***traveling***) **1** *tr & intr* to go from place to place; to journey, especially abroad or far from home; to journey through, across or over (a region, country, etc) ▫ *travelled the world* ▫ *travelled through France*. **2** to journey across (a stated distance). **3** *intr* to be capable of withstanding a journey, especially a long one ▫ *not a wine that travels well*. **4** *intr* to journey from place to place as a sales representative. **5** *intr* to move ▫ *Light travels in a straight line*. **6** *intr* to move or pass deliberately, systematically, steadily, etc ▫ *Her eyes travelled over the horizon*. **7** *intr* said especially of machinery: to move along a fixed course. **8** *intr, colloq* to move quickly ▫ *You must have been really travelling to have got here so quickly*. ▷ *noun* **1** an act or process of travelling. **2** (*usually* **travels**) a journey or tour, especially abroad. **3** the range, distance, speed, etc of the motion of a machine or a machine part. ● **travelling** *adj* ▫ *travelling circus*. ⓒ 14c: from TRAVAIL.

travel agency ▷ *noun* a business that makes arrangements for travellers, holidaymakers, etc, eg by booking airline, coach, ship, train, etc tickets, hotel accommodation, etc, providing brochures, advice on the best deals, etc.

travel agent ▷ *noun* **1** someone whose job is to run a travel agency. **2** a TRAVEL AGENCY.

travelled ▷ *adj* **1** having made many journeys, especially abroad. **2** frequented by travellers ▫ *a well-travelled road*.

traveller ▷ *noun* **1** someone who travels. **2** *old use* a COMMERCIAL TRAVELLER. **3** *Brit colloq* a Gypsy. **4** short for NEW AGE TRAVELLER.

traveller's cheque ▷ *noun* a cheque for a specified amount that the bearer signs and can then exchange for currency, goods or services in another country when in that country.

traveller's joy ▷ *noun* a type of wild clematis with small white flowers that develop into fruits that have white feathery plumes.

travelling see under TRAVEL

travelling folk and **travelling people** ▷ *plural noun* people who have no fixed or permanent home and who usually choose to live in vans, caravans, etc leading an unconventional existence.

travelling rug ▷ *noun* a rug used for keeping travellers, spectators, etc warm or for sitting on outdoors.

travelogue /ˈtravəlɒg/ ▷ *noun* a film, article, talk, etc about travel, especially one that features someone's impressions of a trip to a particular place or region.

travel sickness ▷ *noun* nausea and vomiting brought on by the motion of travelling by car, boat, aircraft, etc.

traverse /ˈtravɜːs, trəˈvɜːs/ ▷ *verb* (***traversed***, ***traversing***) **1** to go across or through something. **2** to lie or reach across ▫ *A bridge traverses the deep gorge*. **3** *tr & intr* to climb, walk or ski at an angle across (a slope) rather than straight up or down. **4** *intr* to move sideways or to one side. **5** to examine or consider (a subject, problem, etc) carefully and thoroughly. **6** **a** to move (a large gun or its barrel) to one side while keeping it horizontal; **b** *intr* said of a large gun or its barrel: to move to one side. **7** to oppose or thwart. **8** to survey by traverse. ▷ *noun* **1** an act or the process of crossing or traversing. **2** a path or passage across eg a rock face or slope. **3** something that lies across. **4** a sideways movement. **5** the movement of the barrel of a large gun to one side while being kept horizontal. **6** a survey carried out by measuring straight lines from point to point and the angles between. **7** an obstruction. ● **traversable** *adj*. ● **traversal** *noun*. ● **traversed** *adj*. ● **traverser** *noun*. ● **traversing** *adj, noun* ⓒ 14c: from French *traverser*.

travertine /ˈtravərtɪn/ ▷ *noun* a type of white or light-coloured limestone rock often found as a deposit of hot, especially volcanic, springs and used as a building stone. ⓒ 16c: from Italian *travertino*.

travesty /ˈtravəstɪ/ ▷ *noun* (***travesties***) a ridiculous or crude distortion; a mockery or caricature ▫ *a travesty of justice* ▫ *believed that Hamlet in modern dress was a travesty*. ▷ *verb* (***travesties***, ***travestied***, ***travestying***) to make a travesty of. ⓒ 17c: from French *travestir* to disguise.

travesty role ▷ *noun* a theatrical part that is meant to be played by someone of the opposite sex.

travolator or **travelator** /ˈtravəleɪtə(r)/ ▷ *noun* a moving pavement that transports people or goods horizontally or at a slight incline, designed for use between busy concourses, eg at airports, railway stations, shopping malls, etc. Also called **moving walkway**. ⓒ 1950s: modelled on ESCALATOR and originally a proprietary name.

trawl ▷ *noun* **1** (*in full* **trawl-net**) a large bag-shaped net with a wide mouth, used for catching fish at sea. **2** a wide-ranging or extensive search ▫ *made a trawl through the library catalogue*. ▷ *verb* (***trawled***, ***trawling***) *tr & intr* **1** to fish (the sea, an area of sea, etc) using a trawl-net. **2** to search through (a large number of things, people, etc) thoroughly, especially before finding the one required ▫ *had to trawl through hundreds of applications*. ● **trawling** *noun*. ⓒ 17c as *noun*; 16c as *verb*: probably from Dutch *traghelen* to drag and *traghel* drag-net, perhaps from Latin *tragula* drag-net, ultimately from *trahere* to draw.

trawler ▷ *noun* **1** a fishing-boat used in trawling. **2** someone who trawls.

tray ▷ *noun* (***trays***) **1** a flat piece of wood, metal, plastic, etc, usually with a small raised edge, used for carrying dishes, crockery, etc. **2** a very shallow lidless box that forms a drawer in a wardrobe, trunk, etc or that is used for displaying articles in a cabinet, etc. ⓘ Anglo-Saxon *trig*.

trayful ▷ *noun* (***trayfuls***) the amount a tray can hold.

treacherous /ˈtrɛtʃərəs/ ▷ *adj* **1** said of someone, their conduct, etc: not to be trusted; ready or likely to betray. **2** hazardous or dangerous; unreliable or untrustworthy □ *Black ice made the roads treacherous.* • **treacherously** *adverb*. • **treacherousness** *noun*. ⓘ 14c: from French *trechier* to cheat.

treachery /ˈtrɛtʃərɪ/ ▷ *noun* (***treacheries***) **a** deceit, betrayal, cheating or treason; **b** an act or the process of this. ⓘ 13c: from French *trechier* to cheat.

treacle /ˈtriːkəl/ ▷ *noun* **1** the thick dark sticky liquid that remains after the crystallization and removal of sugar from extracts of sugar-cane or sugar-beet. Also called **black treacle**. **2** molasses. **3** anything that is overly sweet, cloying, sentimental, etc. • **treacly** *adj*. ⓘ 14c: from Greek *theriake antidotos* an antidote to the bites of wild beasts, from *therion* wild beast. The word gradually came to be applied to the sugary substance in which the antidote was taken rather than to the antidote itself.

tread /trɛd/ ▷ *verb* (***trod, trodden*** or ***trod, treading***) **1** *intr* (*usually* **tread on something**) to put a foot or feet on it; to walk or step on it □ *trod on the cat's tail.* **2** to step or walk on, over or along □ *trod the primrose path.* **3** to crush or press (into the ground, etc) with a foot or feet; to trample □ *treading ash into the carpet.* **4** to wear or form (a path, hole, etc) by walking. **5** to perform by walking. **6** *intr* (*usually* **tread on someone**) to suppress them; to treat them cruelly. **7** said of a male bird: to copulate with (a female bird). ▷ *noun* **1** a manner, style or sound of walking. **2** an act of treading. **3** the horizontal part of a stair where someone puts their foot. Compare RISER. **4** a mark made by treading; a footprint or track. **5 a** the thick, grooved and patterned surface of a tyre that grips the road and disperses rain water; **b** the depth of this surface. See also RETREAD. **6 a** the part of a wheel that comes into contact with a rail, the ground, etc; **b** the part of a rail that comes into contact with the wheels. **7** the part of a shoe's sole that touches the ground. • **treader** *noun*. • **treading** *noun*. • **tread on delicate** or **dangerous ground** or **tread on thin ice** to be or come perilously close to making a blunder, offending someone, etc. • **tread on air** to be or feel exhilarated. • **tread on someone's toes 1** to encroach on their sphere of influence, etc. **2** to offend them. • **tread the boards** to go on the stage; to act. • **tread water 1** to keep oneself afloat and upright in water by making a treading movement with the legs and a circular movement with the hands and arms. **2** to hold back from making a decision, taking progressive action, etc, usually temporarily □ *The company will have to tread water until sales improve.* ⓘ Anglo-Saxon *tredan*.

▪ **tread something down** to press it down firmly with the foot or feet.

▪ **tread in something** to put a foot in it.

▪ **tread something in** to grind, press or trample it (into the ground, floor, carpet, etc).

treadle /ˈtrɛdəl/ ▷ *noun* a foot pedal that can be pushed back and forward in a rhythmic motion and so produce the momentum to drive a machine, such as a sewing-machine or loom. ▷ *verb* (***treadled, treadling***) *intr* to work a treadle. ⓘ Anglo-Saxon *tredel* the step of a stair, related to TREAD.

treadmill ▷ *noun* **1** an apparatus for producing motion that consists of a large wheel turned by people (especially formerly prisoners) or animals treading on steps inside or around it. **2** a monotonous and dreary routine. **3** a piece of exercise equipment that consists of a continuous moving belt that is electrically driven and whose speed can be regulated to make the user walk, jog or run.

treason /ˈtriːzən/ ▷ *noun* **1** (*in full* **high treason**) disloyalty to or betrayal of one's country, sovereign or government. **2** any betrayal of trust or act of disloyalty. • **treasonable** *adj*. • **treasonableness** *noun*. • **treasonably** *adverb*. • **treasonous** *adj*. ⓘ 13c: from French *traison*, from Latin *traditio* a handing over.

treasure /ˈtrɛʒə(r)/ ▷ *noun* **1** wealth and riches, especially in the form of gold, silver, precious stones and jewels, etc which have been accumulated over a period of time and which can be hoarded. **2** anything of great value. **3** *colloq* **a** someone who is loved and valued, especially as a helper, friend, etc; **b** a term of affection □ *How are you today, treasure?* ▷ *verb* (***treasured, treasuring***) **1** to value greatly or think of as very precious □ *treasured him as a friend.* **2** (*usually* **treasure up**) to preserve or collect for future use or as valuable □ *treasured up all his old school photographs.* • **treasured** *adj*. ⓘ 12c: from French *tresor* treasure.

treasure hunt ▷ *noun* **1** a game where the object is to find a prize by solving a series of clues about its hiding place. **2** a hunt for treasure.

treasurer ▷ *noun* **1** the person in a club, society, etc who is in charge of the money and accounts. **2** an official who is responsible for public money, eg in a local council. • **treasurership** *noun*.

treasure-trove /— ˈtroʊv/ ▷ *noun* **1** *law* any valuable found hidden, eg in the earth, etc, which is of unknown ownership and therefore deemed to be the property of the Crown. **2** anything of value, especially something that unexpectedly gives great pleasure □ *This collection of short stories is a real treasure-trove of delights.* ⓘ 12c: from Anglo-French *tresor trové* treasure found, from French *tresor* treasure + *trover* to find.

treasury /ˈtrɛʒərɪ/ ▷ *noun* (***treasuries***) **1** (**Treasury**) **a** the government department in charge of a country's finances, especially the planning and implementation of expenditure policies, the collection of taxes, etc; **b** the officials who comprise this department; **c** the place where the money that this department collects is kept. **2** the income or funds of a state, government, organization, society, etc. **3** a place where treasure is stored. **4** a store of valued items, eg a book containing popular poems, stories or quotations. ⓘ 13c: from French *tresorie*, from *tresor* treasure.

Treasury bench ▷ *noun, Brit* the front bench in the House of Commons to the right of the Speaker, where the Prime Minister, Chancellor of the Exchequer and other senior members of the Government sit.

treat ▷ *verb* (***treated, treating***) **1** to deal with or behave towards someone or something in a specified manner □ *treat it as a joke.* **2** to care for or deal with (a person, illness, injury, etc) medically. **3** to put something through a process or apply something to it □ *treat the wood with creosote.* **4** to provide with food, drink, entertainment, a gift, etc at one's own expense □ *I'll treat you to lunch.* **5** *tr & intr* (*often* **treat of**) to deal with or discuss a subject, especially in writing. **6** *intr* (*usually* **treat with**) to negotiate with another nation, person, etc in order to settle a dispute, end a war, etc. ▷ *noun* **1** a gift, such as an outing, meal, present, etc, that one person gives to another. **2** any source of pleasure or enjoyment, especially when unexpected. • **treatable** *adj*. • **treater** *noun*. • **treating** *noun*. • **a treat** *colloq, sometimes ironic* very good or well □ *He looked a treat in his kilt.* ⓘ 13c: from French *traitier*, *tretier*, from Latin *tractare* to manage, from *trahere*, *tractum* to draw or drag.

treatise /ˈtriːtɪz, -tɪs/ ▷ *noun* a formal piece of writing that deals with a subject systematically and in depth. ⓘ 14c: from French *tretis*, from *traitier* to treat.

treatment ▷ *noun* **1 a** the medical or surgical care that a patient is given to cure an illness or injury. **2** an act or the manner or process of dealing with someone or something □ *rough treatment.* **3** a way of presenting something, especially in literature, music, art, etc □ *his sympathetic* *treatment of his women characters.* **4** the act, means or process of dealing with something, especially by using a chemical, biological, etc agent ◻ *Cold water is the best treatment for blood stains.* • **the (full) treatment** *colloq* the appropriate or usual way of dealing with someone or something, especially in its most complete, thorough or complicated form ◻ *The police took her in for questioning and gave her the full treatment.*

treaty /'triːtɪ/ ▻ *noun* (***treaties***) **1 a** a formal agreement between states or governments, especially one that ratifies a peace or trade agreement; **b** the document ratifying such an agreement. **2** an agreement between two parties or individuals, especially one that formalizes the purchase of property. ⓒ 14c: from French *traité*, from Latin *tractatus*, from *tractare*; see TREAT.

treble /'trɛbəl/ ▻ *noun* **1** anything that is three times as much or as many. **2** *music* **a** a soprano; **b** someone, especially a boy, who has a soprano singing voice; **c** a part written for this type of voice; **d** an instrument that has a similar range; **e** in a family of instruments: the member that has the highest range. **3** a high-pitched voice or sound. **4** the higher part of the audio frequency range of a radio, record, etc. **5** *betting* a type of cumulative bet that involves the better choosing three horses from three different races; the original stake money plus any winnings from the first race then goes on the horse from the second race, after which, if the second horse wins, the total is laid on the horse from the third race. Compare ACCUMULATOR. **6 a** (*darts*) the narrow inner ring of a dartboard, where scores are triple the number that is shown on the outside of the board; **b** a dart that hits the board in this area. **7** *sport* especially in football: the winning of three championships, cups, titles, etc in a single season. ▻ *adj* **1** three times as much or as many; threefold; triple. **2** belonging, relating or referring to, being or having a treble voice. **3** said of a voice: high-pitched. ▻ *adverb* with a treble voice ◻ *sing treble.* ▻ *verb* (***trebled, trebling***) *tr & intr* to make or become three times as much or as many. • **trebly** *adverb.* ⓒ 14c: French, from Latin *triplus* triple.

treble chance ▻ *noun, Brit* a type of football pools where draws, home wins and away wins are each accorded different values and winnings are paid out on the basis of how accurately punters can predict the number of matches falling into each of the three categories.

treble clef ▻ *noun, music* in musical notation: a sign (𝄞) that is put at the beginning of a piece of written music to place the note G (a fifth above middle C) on the second line of the staff.

trebuchet /'trɛbjʊʃɛt, treɪbuː'ʃeɪ/ ▻ *noun* **1** a large sling-like machine used during sieges in the Middle Ages, consisting of a counterpoised spar with a very heavy weight at one end and a spoon-shaped receptacle for missiles (such as stones) at the other; the missile end would be pulled down almost to ground level and then released, so firing the missiles up and forward. **2** a small accurate balance used for weighing light objects. ⓒ 13c: French, meaning 'a siege engine or bird-trap'.

trecento /treɪ'tʃɛntoʊ/ ▻ *noun* the fourteenth century, especially as thought of in terms of the style of Italian art and literature of that period. • **trecentist** *noun* an artist or author of this period. ⓒ 19c: Italian, meaning 'three hundred', shortened from *mille trecento* thirteen hundred.

tree ▻ *noun* (***trees***) **1** *bot* **a** a tall woody perennial plant that typically has one main stem or trunk and which, unlike a shrub, usually only begins to branch at some distance from the ground; **b** in extended use: any plant, eg the banana, plantain, palm, etc, that has a single non-woody stem which grows to a considerable height. **2** a FAMILY TREE. **3** *usually in compounds* **a** a frame or support, especially one made from wood ◻ *shoe tree*; **b** a branched structure that things can be hung on ◻ *ring tree.* **4** a CHRISTMAS TREE ◻ *lots of presents under the tree.* **5** *old use* **a** a cross that is used for crucifixion; **b** a gallows or gibbet. ▻ *verb* (***treed, treeing***) to drive or chase up a tree. • **treeless** *adj.* • **at the top of the tree** at the highest possible position, especially professionally, etc. • **out of one's tree** completely mad, especially in talking rubbish or behaving irrationally. • **up a tree** *N Amer colloq* in difficulties. See also ARBOREAL. ⓒ Anglo-Saxon *treow*.

tree creeper ▻ *noun* a small bird that runs up tree trunks looking for insects that live in the bark to eat.

tree diagram ▻ *noun, math & linguistics* a diagram that has a branching tree-like structure to represent the relationship between the elements.

tree fern ▻ *noun* a fern that is found in tropical regions and which has a tall thick woody stem covered in dead leaf bases with a crown of leaves at the top, so that it resembles a tree in size and shape.

tree frog ▻ *noun* any of several kinds of amphibian that have adapted to living in trees by having sucker-like discs on the fingers and toes to make climbing easier.

tree hopper ▻ *noun* any of several kinds of HOMOPTEROUS jumping insects that live on trees.

tree house ▻ *noun* a structure, usually made from odd bits of wood, etc, that is built into a tree and used by children, eg in games of make believe.

tree kangaroo ▻ *noun* any of several kinds of kangaroo that live in trees in New Guinea and N Australia and which, unlike their ground-dwelling relatives, have front and rear limbs of approximately the same length.

tree line see TIMBER LINE

tree-lined ▻ *adj* said of a street, etc: having trees along the pavement.

treen /triːn/ ▻ *adj* wooden; made from trees. ▻ *plural noun* wooden domestic articles, especially those that are antique. ⓒ Anglo-Saxon *treowen*, from *treow* a tree.

treenail or **trenail** /'triːneɪl/ ▻ *noun* a long cylindrical wooden pin used for fastening timbers together, eg in shipbuilding. ⓒ 13c.

tree of knowledge ▻ *noun* **1** *Bible* the tree in the garden of Eden that bore the forbidden fruit (Gen 2.9). **2** a figurative expression for knowledge in general.

tree of life ▻ *noun* a tree that symbolizes life or immortality, especially the one in the narrative of the creation of the world (Gen 2.9).

tree ring ▻ *noun* a distinct annular deposit that represents one year's growth and which can be seen in a cross-section of a tree trunk and used as a means of gauging the age of the tree.

tree shrew ▻ *noun* any of several small insectivorous SE Asian primates that have long bushy or tufted tails, large eyes and a long shrew-like face.

tree snake ▻ *noun* any of several different kinds of snake that spend much of their time in trees.

tree surgery ▻ *noun* the treatment and preservation of diseased or damaged trees, especially by using remedies that involve cutting off dead branches, filling cavities, providing supports, etc. • **tree surgeon** *noun.*

tree tomato ▻ *noun* **1** a type of S American shrub that produces oval red fruits. **2** a fruit of this shrub.

treetop ▻ *noun* the upper leaves and branches of a tree.

trefa /'treɪfə/ and **tref** /'treɪf/ ▻ *adj, Judaism* said of the flesh of an animal: not fit for human consumption because it has not been slaughtered in the prescribed way. Opposite of KOSHER. ⓒ 19c: from Hebrew *terephah* torn, which was applied to flesh torn off by wild animals, from *taraph* to tear.

trefoil /'trɛfɔɪl, 'triː-/ ▻ *noun* **1** a leaf which is divided into three sections. **2** any plant having such leaves, eg clover ◻ *bird's-foot trefoil.* **3** anything with three lobes or sections. **4** a carved ornament or decoration that has three lobes or sections. ▻ *adj* having three lobes or by being divided into three parts. ⓒ 15c: from Latin *trifolium*, from *folium* leaf.

trek ▻ *verb* (***trekked***, ***trekking***) *intr* **1** to make a long hard journey □ ***had to trek miles to the nearest phone.*** **2** *S Afr* **a** *historical* to make a journey by ox-wagon, especially a migrationary one; **b** said of an ox: to pull a load. ▻ *noun* **1** a long hard journey □ ***It's a bit of a trek to the shops.*** **2** *S Afr* a journey by ox-wagon. ● **trekker** *noun*. ⓒ 19c: from Afrikaans, from Dutch *trekken* to draw (a vehicle or load).

trellis /'trɛlɪs/ ▻ *noun* (***trellises***) (*in full* **trellis-work**) an open lattice framework of narrow interwoven strips of metal, wood, etc that is usually fixed to a wall and which is designed to support or train climbing plants, fruit trees, etc. ▻ *verb* (***trellises***, ***trellised***, ***trellising***) to provide or support with a trellis. ⓒ 14c: from French *trelis*.

trellis window see LATTICE WINDOW at LATTICE

trematode /'trɛmətoʊd/ ▻ *noun* any of several kinds of parasitic FLATWORM that have hooks or suckers and which live in the alimentary canals of animals and humans, eg flukes. ● **trematoid** *adj*. ⓒ 19c: from Greek *trematodes* perforated.

tremble ▻ *verb* (***trembled***, ***trembling***) *intr* **1** to shake or shudder involuntarily, eg with cold, fear, weakness, etc. **2** to quiver or vibrate □ ***The harebells trembled in the wind.*** **3** to feel great fear or anxiety □ ***trembled at the thought of having another interview.*** ▻ *noun* **1** a trembling movement; a shudder or tremor. **2** (**the trembles**) a disease of livestock, especially cattle and sheep, that is characterized by muscular weakness, shaking and constipation. ● **trembler** *noun*. ● **trembling** *adj, noun*. ● **tremblingly** *adverb*. ● **trembly** *adj* (***tremblier***, ***trembliest***) **1** agitated. **2** quivering. ● **all of a tremble 1** quivering all over, especially from fear, excitement, etc. **2** in an extremely agitated state. ● **go in fear and trembling of someone** or **something** *usually facetious* to be extremely afraid of them or it. ⓒ 14c: from French *trembler*.

trembling poplar ▻ *noun* another name for the ASPEN.

tremendous /trə'mɛndəs/ ▻ *adj* **1** *colloq* extraordinary, very good, remarkable, enormous, etc □ ***a tremendous relief.*** **2** awe-inspiring; terrible □ ***an accident involving a tremendous loss of lives.*** ● **tremendously** *adverb* □ ***tremendously grateful.*** ● **tremendousness** *noun*. ⓒ 17c: from Latin *tremendus* fearful, terrible.

tremolo /'trɛməloʊ/ ▻ *noun* (***tremolos***) *music* **1** a trembling effect achieved by rapidly repeating a note or notes, or by quickly alternating notes, eg on a stringed instrument, organ, etc. **2** a similar effect in singing. **3 a** (*also* **tremulant** /'trɛmjʊlənt/) a device in an organ that can be used for producing a tremolo or a vibrato; **b** (*in full* **tremolo arm**) the lever on an electric guitar that can be used to produce this effect. Compare VIBRATO. ⓒ 18c: Italian, meaning 'trembling'.

tremor /'trɛmə(r)/ ▻ *noun* **1** a shaking or quivering □ ***couldn't disguise the tremor in his voice.*** **2** (*in full* **earth tremor**) a minor earthquake. **3** a thrill, especially of fear or pleasure. ▻ *verb* (***tremored***, ***tremoring***) *intr* to shake. ⓒ 14c: French, from Latin *tremere* to tremble.

tremulous /'trɛmjʊləs/ ▻ *adj* **1** said of someone, their limbs, voice, etc: quivering, especially with fear, worry, nervousness, excitement, etc. **2** said of someone's disposition, etc: shy, retiring, fearful, anxious, etc. **3** said of a drawn line, writing, etc: that has been produced by a shaky or hesitant hand; wavy or squiggly. ● **tremulously** *adverb*. ● **tremulousness** *noun*. ⓒ 17c: from Latin *tremulus* trembling.

trenail see TREENAIL

trench ▻ *noun* (***trenches***) **1** a long narrow ditch in the ground. **2** *military* **a** a large scale version of this where the earth thrown up by the excavations is used to form a parapet to protect soldiers from enemy fire, shells, etc and which often incorporates rudimentary living quarters; **b** (**trenches**) a series of these that forms a defensive system. **3** a long narrow steep-sided depression in the floor of an ocean, especially one that runs parallel to a continent. ▻ *verb* (***trenches***, ***trenched***, ***trenching***) **1** to dig a trench or trenches. **2** to excavate a trench as fortification. **3** (*usually* **trench on** or **onto**) to come near, verge on or encroach. ⓒ 14c: from French *trenche* a cut.

trenchant /'trɛntʃənt/ ▻ *adj* **1** incisive; penetrating □ ***a trenchant mind.*** **2** forthright; vigorous □ ***a trenchant policy to improve efficiency.*** **3** *poetic* cutting; keen. ● **trenchancy** *noun*. ● **trenchantly** *adverb*. ⓒ 14c: from French, from *trencher* to cut.

trench coat ▻ *noun* **1** a type of long raincoat that is usually double-breasted, has a belt and sometimes epaulettes. **2** a type of military overcoat.

trencher /'trɛntʃə(r)/ ▻ *noun* **1** *historical* a wooden platter or board that is used for cutting or serving food. **2** (*in full* **trencher-cap**) a MORTARBOARD (sense 2). ⓒ 14c: from French *trenchour*, from *trencher* to cut.

trencherman ▻ *noun* someone who eats well, heartily or in a specified manner.

trench fever ▻ *noun* a highly contagious disease transmitted by lice, manifesting with such symptoms as headache, chills, rash, aching back and legs and a recurrent fever. ⓒ 1915: so called because it was common amongst soldiers in the trenches during World War I.

trench foot and **trench feet** ▻ *noun* a condition in which the feet become painfully swollen and blistered, often with some blackening of the tissue, and which is caused by long-term immersion in water or mud. ⓒ 1915: so called because soldiers in the trenches in World War I frequently suffered from this condition.

trench mortar ▻ *noun* a small mortar designed to launch bombs from one trench over to the enemy's trenches. ⓒ 1915.

trench warfare ▻ *noun* **1** protracted hostilities carried on between two opposing forces ensconced in trenches facing each other. **2** any drawn-out dispute where the opposing sides periodically launch attacks at each other □ ***ongoing trench warfare over rates of pay.*** ⓒ 1918.

trend ▻ *noun* **1** a general direction or tendency. **2** the current general movement in fashion, style, taste, etc. ▻ *verb* (***trended***, ***trending***) *intr* to turn or have a tendency to turn in a specified direction □ ***The road trends north.*** ⓒ Anglo-Saxon *trendan*.

trendsetter ▻ *noun* someone who starts off a fashion.

trendsetting ▻ *adj* innovative, especially in establishing something that becomes popular in the field of fashion.

trendy ▻ *adj* (***trendier***, ***trendiest***) *Brit colloq* **1** said of someone: following the latest fashions. **2** said of clothes, music, clubs, bars, etc: fashionable at a particular time. ▻ *noun* (***trendies***) someone who is, or who tries to be, at the forefront of fashion. ● **trendily** *adv*. ● **trendiness** *noun*.

trente-et-quarante /trɑ̃teɪka'rɑ̃t/ ▻ *noun* another name for the game ROUGE-ET-NOIR. ⓒ 17c: French, meaning 'thirty and forty' which are respectively the winning and losing numbers in the game.

trepan /trɪ'pan/ ▻ *noun, surgery* a type of small cylindrical saw that was formerly used for removing part of a bone, especially part of the skull. ▻ *verb* (***trepanned***, ***trepanning***) to remove (a piece of bone) with a trepan or a TREPHINE. ● **trepanation** *noun*. ● **trepanner** *noun*. ● **trepanning** *adj, noun*. ⓒ 15c: from Greek *trypanon* borer.

trepang /trɪ'paŋ/ ▻ *noun* any of several types of large SEA CUCUMBER especially prized by the Chinese for their dried body walls which are used as food. ⓒ 18c: from *tripang*, the Malay name for this creature.

trephine /trɪ'fiːn, -'faɪn/ ▷ *noun, surgery* an improved version of the trepan. ▷ *verb* (***trephined, trephining***) to remove (a circular piece of bone) with a trephine. • **trephination** /trɛfɪ'neɪʃən/ *noun*. • **trephiner** *noun*. ⌚ 17c: from Latin *tres fines* three ends, influenced by TREPAN.

trepidation /trɛpɪ'deɪʃən/ ▷ *noun* **1** fear; nervousness; unease; apprehension. **2** trembling, especially involuntary trembling of the limbs associated with certain paralyses. • **trepidatory** *adj*. ⌚ 17c: from Latin *trepidare* to be agitated or alarmed.

trespass /'trɛspəs/ ▷ *verb* (***trespasses, trespassed, trespassing***) *intr* (*usually* **trespass on** or **onto** or **upon someone** or **something**) **1** to enter (someone else's property) without the right or permission to do so. **2** to intrude on (someone's time, privacy, rights, etc). **3** *old use* to sin. ▷ *noun* **1** the act or process of entering someone else's property without the right or permission to do so. **2** an intrusion into someone's time, privacy, etc. **3** *old use* a sin. • **trespasser** *noun*. ⌚ 13c: from French *trespas* passing across.

tress ▷ *noun* (***tresses***) **1** a long lock or plait of hair. **2** (**tresses**) a woman's or girl's long hair. ▷ *verb* (***tresses, tressed, tressing***) to arrange (hair) in tresses. • **tressed** *adj*. • **tressy** *adj*. ⌚ 13c: from French *tresse* a braid of hair.

trestle /'trɛsəl/ ▷ *noun* **1** a type of supporting framework that has a horizontal beam the end of which rests on a pair of legs which slope outwards, eg the kind that a board can be put onto to form a table. **2** (*in full* **trestle-table**) a table that consists of a board supported by trestles. **3** (*in full* **trestlework**) a type of framework that consists of a series of wooden or metal trestles joined together to form a support for a bridge, viaduct, etc, especially one that carries a railway. ⌚ 14c: from French *trestel*.

trevally /trɪ'valɪ/ ▷ *noun* (***trevallies***) a name for several Australasian marine fish, especially the horse mackerels, that are used as food. ⌚ 19c.

trews /truːz/ ▷ *plural noun, Brit* trousers, especially ones that are close-fitting and made from tartan cloth. ⌚ 16c: from Irish *trius* and Gaelic *triubhas*; compare TROUSERS.

trey /treɪ/ ▷ *noun* (***treys***) the three in cards or on a dice. ⌚ 14c: from French *treis* three.

TRH ▷ *abbreviation* Their Royal Highnesses.

tri- /traɪ, trɪ/ ▷ *combining form, denoting* **1** three or three times □ ***triangle*** □ ***tri-weekly***. **2** *chem* three atoms, groups, radicals, etc □ ***triacid***. ⌚ From Latin and Greek *tri*, a form of Latin *tres* and Greek *treis* three.

triable /'traɪəbəl/ ▷ *adj* **1** capable of or liable to being tried in a court of law. **2** able to be tested or attempted. ⌚ 15c.

triacid /traɪ'asɪd/ ▷ *adj, chem* said of a BASE (sense 6): capable of combining or reacting with three molecules of a monobasic acid. ⌚ 1940s.

triad /'traɪad/ ▷ *noun* **1** any group of three people or things. **2** *music* a chord that consists of three notes, usually a base note and those notes a third and a fifth above it. **3** (*sometimes* **Triad**) **a** the Western name for any of several Chinese secret societies, especially of the kind that operate in foreign countries and are involved in organized crime, drug-trafficking, extortion, etc. Also called **Triad Society**. **b** a member of such a society. **4** in Welsh literature: a form of composition where sayings, stories, etc about related subjects are grouped into threes. • **triadic** *adj*. ⌚ 16c: from Greek *trias* group of three.

trial /'traɪəl/ ▷ *noun* **1** a legal process in which someone who stands accused of a crime or misdemeanour is judged in a court of law. **2 a** an act or the process of trying or testing; a test; **b** *as adj* provisional; experimental □ ***on a trial basis***. **3** trouble, worry or vexation; a cause of this □ ***Her son is a great trial to her***. **4** *sport* a preliminary test of the skill, fitness, etc of a player, athlete, etc, especially one undertaken by a manager, coach, etc before deciding to offer them a job, a team place, etc. **5** a test of a vehicle's performance held especially over rough ground or a demanding course. **6** a competition, usually over rough ground, to test skills in handling high-performance cars or motorcycles. **7** (*usually* **trials**) any competition in which the skills of animals are tested □ ***sheepdog trials***. **8** an attempt. ▷ *verb* (***trialled, trialling; US trialed, trialing***) *tr & intr* to put (a new product, etc) to the test □ ***trialled the new TV sitcom in our area***. • **trialist** or **triallist** *noun*. • **on trial 1** in the process of undergoing legal action in court □ ***on trial for murder***. **2** in the process of undergoing tests or examination before being permanently accepted or approved. • **stand trial** see under STAND. • **trial and error** the process of trying various methods, alternatives, etc until a correct or suitable one is found □ ***got there by trial and error***. ⌚ 16c as *noun*; 1980s as *verb*: French.

trial balance ▷ *noun, bookkeeping* a statement that is periodically drawn up in order to test the accuracy of the entries of all the debits and credits in a double-entry ledger. The total of the credit entries should tally with that of the debit entries; if this is not the case, it indicates that some mistake has been made. ⌚ 19c.

trial run ▷ *noun* a test of a new product, etc, especially in order to assess its effectiveness, potential, capacity, etc prior to an official launch.

triangle /'traɪaŋgəl/ ▷ *noun* **1** *geom* a two-dimensional figure that has three sides and three internal angles which always total 180°. **2** anything of a similar shape. **3** a simple musical percussion instrument made from a metal bar which has been bent into a trianglular shape with one corner left open and which is played by striking it with a small metal hammer. **4** an emotional relationship or love affair that involves three people □ ***involved in an eternal triangle***. **5** (*in full* **warning triangle**) a fluorescent triangular sign that is placed at the roadside to warn other road users of a broken-down vehicle, an accident or other hazard. **6** a right-angled triangular drawing instrument that is used for drawing lines, especially ones which are at 90°, 60°, 45° and 30°. ⌚ 14c: from Latin *triangulus* three-cornered.

triangular /traɪ'aŋgjʊlə(r)/ ▷ *adj* **1** shaped like a triangle. **2** said of an agreement, treaty, competition, etc: involving three people or parties. • **triangularity** *noun*. • **triangularly** *adverb*.

triangulate /traɪ'aŋgjʊleɪt/ ▷ *verb* (***triangulated, triangulating***) **a** to mark off (an area of land) into a network of triangular sections with a view to making a survey; **b** to survey (a triangularly divided area of land), eg in map-making. • **triangulation** *noun*.

triangulation point see under TRIGONOMETRICAL POINT

Triassic /traɪ'asɪk/ *geol* ▷ *adj* **1** belonging, relating or referring to the earliest period of the Mesozoic era when the first dinosaurs, large sea reptiles and small mammals appeared and conifers became widespread, forming luxuriant forests. See table at GEOLOGICAL TIME SCALE. **2** the name for the series of rock strata that lies beneath the JURASSIC and above the PERMIAN. ▷ *noun* this period or rock system. ⌚ 19c: from Latin *trias* TRIAD, so called because the period is divisible into three distinct sections.

triathlon /traɪ'aθlɒn/ ▷ *noun* an athletic contest that consists of three events, usually swimming, running and cycling. • **triathlete** *noun*. ⌚ 1970s: from TRI- and modelled on DECATHLON.

triatomic /traɪə'tɒmɪk/ ▷ *adj, chem* having three atoms in the molecule. • **triatomically** *adverb*. ⌚ 19c.

tribade /'trɪbəd/ ▷ *noun* a lesbian, especially one who takes part in **tribadism**, a sexual practice usually involving two women who adopt a position one on top of the other and rub their genitals together. ⌚ 17c: French, from Greek *tribein* to rub.

tribalism ▷ *noun* **1** the system of tribes as a way of organizing society. **2** the feeling of belonging to a tribe.

tribe ▷ *noun* **1** a group of people, families, clans or communities who share social, economic, political, etc ties and often a common ancestor and who usually have a common culture, dialect and leader. **2 a** *often derog or jocular* a large group of people or things with a shared interest, profession, etc □ ***a whole tribe of protesters***; **b** any group of things that have something in common. **3** *historical* any of the three divisions of the ancient Romans, namely the Latins, Etruscans and Sabines. **4** *historical* any of the twelve divisions of the Israelites, each of which was believed to be descended from one of the twelve patriarchs. **5 a** *biol* in plant and animal classification: a subdivision of a family, usually thought of as being made up of several closely related genera; **b** *loosely* any related animals, plants, etc □ ***a member of the finny tribe.*** • **tribal** *adj.* • **tribally** *adverb.* ◷ 13c: from Latin *tribus* one of the divisions of the ancient Roman people.

tribesman and **tribeswoman** ▷ *noun* a man or woman who belongs to a tribe.

tribespeople ▷ *noun* the members of a tribe, especially when thought of collectively.

tribo- /'traɪboʊ, 'trɪboʊ/ ▷ *combining form, denoting* rubbing, friction. ◷ From Greek *tribein* to rub.

tribo-electricity ▷ *noun* a type of electricity generated by friction. ◷ Early 20c.

tribology /traɪ'bɒlədʒɪ/ ▷ *noun* the branch of science and technology that deals with the study of friction, wear, lubrication, etc. • **tribologist** *noun.* ◷ 1960s.

triboluminescence ▷ *noun* the emission of light produced by rubbing, pressure, etc as opposed to light produced during a rise in temperature. • **triboluminescent** *adj.* ◷ 19c.

tribometer /traɪ'bɒmɪtə(r)/ ▷ *noun* an instrument designed for measuring the amount of friction generated when two surfaces rub together. ◷ 18c.

tribrach /'traɪbrak/ ▷ *noun* (***tribrachs***) *prosody* a type of metrical foot that consists of three unstressed or short syllables. • **tribrachic** /traɪ'brakɪk/ *adj.* ◷ 16c: from Latin *tribrachys*, from Greek *brachys* short.

tribulation /trɪbjʊ'leɪʃən/ ▷ *noun* **1** great sorrow, trouble, affliction, misery, etc. **2** a cause or source of this. ◷ 13c: from Latin *tribulatio*.

tribunal /traɪ'bjʊnəl, 'trɪbjʊnəl/ ▷ *noun* **1** a court of justice. **2** *Brit* a board of people who have been appointed to inquire into a specified matter or dispute and to adjudicate or give judgement on it □ ***took her case to the rent tribunal.*** See also INDUSTRIAL TRIBUNAL. **3** a seat or bench in a court for a judge or judges. ◷ 16c: Latin, from *tribunus* head of a tribe.

tribune[1] /'trɪbjuːn/ ▷ *noun* **1** *historical* **a** (*in full* **tribune of the people**) a high official who was elected by the ordinary people of ancient Rome to represent them and defend their rights, etc, especially against the interests of the wealthier patricians; **b** (*in full* **military tribune**) one of the six officers who shared the leadership of a Roman legion, each of whom was in charge for a spell of two months. **2** anyone who acts as a champion or defender of the rights of the common people. • **tribunate** or **tribuneship** *noun.* ◷ 14c: from Latin *tribunus* head of a tribe.

tribune[2] /'trɪbjuːn/ ▷ *noun* **1 a** the apse in a Christian basilica where the bishop's throne sits; **b** the bishop's throne itself. **2** a raised area, dais or stand. **3** a raised area or gallery with seats, especially in a church. ◷ 17c: French, from Latin *tribuna*, from *tribunal* a seat of judgement.

Tribune group ▷ *noun, Brit* a group of Labour MPs who share and advocate radical left-wing socialist policies and views. • **Tribunism** *noun.* • **Tribunite** *noun, adj.* ◷ 1960s: from *Tribune*, the title of a weekly paper that was founded in 1937 to promote these views.

tributary /'trɪbjʊtərɪ/ ▷ *noun* (***tributaries***) **1** a stream or river that flows into a larger river or a lake. **2** *historical* a person or nation that pays tribute to another. ▷ *adj* **1** said of a stream or river: flowing into a larger river or a lake. **2** *historical* **a** paid or owed as tribute; **b** said of a speech, prayer, gift, etc: paying tribute. ◷ 14c: from Latin *tributarius*, from *tribuere* to assign, give or pay.

tribute /'trɪbjuːt/ ▷ *noun* **1** something, eg a speech, gift, etc, that is said or given as an expression of praise, thanks, admiration, affection, etc. **2** a sign or evidence of something valuable, effective, worthy of praise, etc; a testimony □ ***Her success was a tribute to all her hard work.*** **3** *historical* **a** a sum of money that is regularly paid by one nation or ruler to another in return for protection, peace, security, etc or as an acknowledgement of submission; **b** *feudalism* a payment or other donation that is made by a vassal to a lord in homage or rent; **c** the obligation to pay tribute. ◷ 14c: from Latin *tributum*, from *tribuere* to assign.

tricameral /traɪ'kamərəl/ ▷ *adj* said of a parliament, legislative body, etc: having three chambers. ◷ From Latin *camera* chamber.

tricarboxylic acid cycle /traɪkɑːbɒk'sɪlɪk — —/ ▷ *noun, biochem* another name for KREBS CYCLE. Often shortened to **TCA cycle**.

trice ▷ *noun* • **in a trice** in a very short time; almost immediately. ◷ 15c: from Dutch *trijsen* to pull, hoist or haul.

tricentenary /traɪsɛn'tiːnərɪ/ ▷ *noun* a TERCENTENARY.

triceps /'traɪsɛps/ ▷ *noun* (***tricepses*** or ***triceps***) any muscle that is attached in three places, especially the large muscle at the back of the upper arm which allows the elbow to bend and straighten. ◷ 16c: Latin, from *ceps*, from *caput* head.

triceratops /traɪ'sɛratɒps/ ▷ *noun* (***triceratopses***) a four-legged herbivorous dinosaur that had a bony frill round the back of its neck, one horn over each eye and one on its nose. ◷ 19c: Latin, from Greek *trikeratos* three-horned + *ops* face.

trich- see TRICHO-

trichiasis /trɪ'kaɪəsɪs/ ▷ *noun, medicine* a condition in which hairs grow in an abnormal direction, eg when this affects the eyelashes causing irritation to the eye. ◷ 17c: Latin, from Greek *trichiasis*, from *trichos* hair.

trichina /'trɪkɪnə, trɪ'kaɪnə/ ▷ *noun* (***trichinae*** /-niː/) a type of tiny parasitic NEMATODE worm that infests the gut of humans and other mammals, producing larvae that form cysts in muscular tissue. • **trichinous** *adj.* ◷ 19c: from Greek *trichinos* of hair.

trichinosis /trɪkɪ'noʊsɪs/ ▷ *noun, medicine* a disease that is caused by entry of the pork roundworm into the digestive system usually as a result of eating raw or under-cooked pork that was infested with the worm's larvae, the main symptoms being nausea, diarrhoea and fever accompanied by pain and stiffness in the muscles. ◷ 19c: from Greek *trichinos* of hair.

trichloroethanal /traɪklɔːroʊ'ɛθənəl/ ▷ *noun* CHLORAL.

trichloroethylene /traɪklɔːroʊ'ɛθəliːn/ ▷ *noun, chem* (formula $\mathbf{C_2HCl_3}$) a colourless liquid used as an industrial solvent. ◷ 19c.

trichloromethane see under CHLOROFORM

tricho- /'trɪkəʊ, 'traɪkəʊ/ or before a vowel **trich-** ▷ *combining form, denoting* hair. ◷ From Greek *thrix*, *trichos* hair.

trichology /trɪ'kɒlədʒɪ/ ▷ *noun* the branch of medicine that deals with the scientific study of the hair and its diseases. • **trichological** *adj.* • **trichologist** *noun* an expert in trichology. ◷ 19c.

trichome /'trɪkoum, 'traɪ-/ ▷ *noun, bot* any outgrowth, such as a prickle, hair or scale, from the epidermis of a plant. ⓘ 19c: from Greek *trichoma* growth of hair.

trichomonad /trɪkou'mɒnəd/ ▷ *noun* any of several kinds of flagellate parasitic PROTOZOANs that can infest the urinary, digestive and reproductive tracts in humans, cattle and birds. ⓘ 19c: from Latin *monad*, from Greek *monas* unity.

trichomoniasis /trɪkoumə'naɪəsɪs/ ▷ *noun, pathol* any of several diseases in humans and other mammals that are caused by TRICHOMONADs infesting the reproductive, urinary or digestive tracts, especially a type of sexually transmitted disease in women that is characterized by vaginal irritation and is sometimes accompanied by a frothy discharge. ⓘ Early 20c.

trichopteron /traɪ'kɒptərɒn/ ▷ *noun* (***trichoptera*** /-rə/) any of several small moth-like insects that have hairy wings and whose larvae develop in water. Also called **caddis fly**. ● **trichopterous** *adj* belonging, relating or referring to this type of insect. ⓘ 19c: from Greek *ptera* a wing.

trichosis /trɪ'kousɪs, traɪ-/ ▷ *noun* any disorder or disease of the hair. ⓘ 17c: Greek, meaning 'growth of hair'.

trichotomy /traɪ'kɒtəmɪ/ ▷ *noun* a sharp division into three parts, categories, etc, eg the Christian concept of humans being made up of body, soul and spirit. ● **trichotomous** *adj*. ● **trichotomously** *adverb*. ⓘ 17c: from Greek *tricha* in three parts, modelled on DICHOTOMY.

trichroic /traɪ'krouɪk/ ▷ *adj* said especially of crystals: having or showing three different colours. ● **trichroism** /'traɪkrouɪzəm/ *noun*. ⓘ 19c: from Greek *chros* colour.

trichromat /traɪ'kroumat/ ▷ *noun* someone who has normal colour vision.

trichromatic /traɪkrou'matɪk/ ▷ *adj* **1** having or using three colours. **2 a** belonging or relating to or having the fundamental three colours of red, green and violet; **b** able to see these three colours, ie having normal colour vision. ● **trichromatism** *noun*. ⓘ 19c: from Greek *chroma* colour.

trick ▷ *noun* **1** something which is done or said to cheat, deceive, fool or humiliate someone. **2 a** a deceptive appearance, especially one caused by the light; an illusion; **b** *as adj* □ ***trick photography***. **3** a mischievous act or plan; a prank or joke. **4 a** a clever or skilful act or feat which astonishes, puzzles or amuses; **b** *as adj* □ ***played a trick shot***. **5** a peculiar habit or mannerism □ ***He has a trick of always saying inappropriate things***. **6** a special technique or knack □ ***a trick of the trade***. **7** a feat of skill which can be learned. **8** the cards played in one round of a card game and which are won by one of the players. **9** *slang* a prostitute's client. **10** *naut* a period of duty at the helm. ▷ *verb* (***tricked***, ***tricking***) **1** to cheat, deceive or defraud. **2** (**trick someone into** or **out of something**) to make them do as one wants, or to gain something from them, by cheating or deception. ● **be up to one's tricks again** or **old tricks (again)** *colloq* to be acting in the characteristic, expected or usual way, especially by misbehaving. ● **do the trick** *colloq* to do or be what is necessary to achieve the required result. ● **How's tricks?** *colloq* a casual greeting that is equivalent to 'How are things going?'. ● **turn a trick** *slang* said of a prostitute: to have sex with a client. ⓘ 15c: from Norman French *trique*.

■ **trick out** or **up** to dress or decorate in a fancy way.

trick cyclist ▷ *noun* **1** an acrobat who performs stunts on a bicycle or monocycle, eg in a circus. **2** *colloq* a psychiatrist.

trickery /'trɪkərɪ/ ▷ *noun* (***trickeries***) **1** an act, instance, or the practice, of deceiving or cheating. **2** the use of tricks.

trickle /'trɪkəl/ ▷ *verb* (***trickled***, ***trickling***) *tr & intr* **1** to flow or make something flow in a thin slow stream or drops. **2** to move, come or go slowly and gradually. ▷ *noun* a thin slow stream, flow or movement. ⓘ 14c: originally said of tears.

trick or treat ▷ *noun, chiefly N Amer* the children's practice of dressing up on Hallowe'en to call at people's houses for small gifts, threatening to play a trick on them if they are not given one.

trickster ▷ *noun* someone who deceives, cheats or plays tricks.

tricky ▷ *adj* (***trickier***, ***trickiest***) **1** difficult to handle or do; needing skill and care. **2** inclined to trickery; sly; deceitful. **3** clever in tricks; resourceful; adroit. ● **trickily** *adverb*. ● **trickiness** *noun*.

triclinic /traɪ'klɪnɪk/ ▷ *adj, mineralogy* said of crystalline forms: having three unequal axes that are obliquely inclined. ⓘ 19c: from Greek *klinein* to slope.

tricolour or (*US*) **tricolor** ▷ *noun* /'trɪkələ(r)/ a three-coloured flag, especially one with three equal stripes of different colours, such as the French and Irish flags. ▷ *adj* /'traɪkʌlə(r)/ having or being of three different colours. ● **tricoloured** *adj*. ⓘ 18c: from Latin *tricolor*.

tricorne or **tricorn** /'traɪkɔːn/ ▷ *adj* having three horns or corners. ▷ *noun* a type of three-cornered COCKED HAT that has the brim turned back on three sides. ⓘ 19c: French, from Latin *tricornis* three-horned.

tricot /'triːkou/ ▷ *noun* **1** a hand-knitted woollen fabric. **2** a soft, slightly ribbed cloth for women's garments. ⓘ 15c: French, meaning 'knitting'.

tricuspid /traɪ'kʌspɪd/ ▷ *adj* having three points or cusps. ▷ *noun* **1** something, such as a tooth, leaf, etc, that has three points or cusps. **2** a valve in the heart that has three segments. ⓘ 17c: from Latin *tricuspis* three-pointed.

tricycle /'traɪsɪkəl/ ▷ *noun* **1** a three-wheeled, usually pedal-driven vehicle. Often shortened to **trike**. **2** *formerly* a light, three-wheeled car designed to be used by a disabled person. ▷ *verb* (***tricycled***, ***tricycling***) *intr* to ride a tricycle. ● **tricyclist** *noun*. ⓘ 19c: French, from Greek *kuklos* circle.

trident /'traɪdənt/ ▷ *noun* **1** *historical* a spear with three prongs. **2** (**Trident**) a type of ballistic missile that is fired from a nuclear submarine. ● **tridental** /traɪ'dɛntəl/ or **tridentate** /traɪ'dɛnteɪt/ *adj*. ⓘ 16c in sense 1; 1972 in sense 2: from Latin *tridens* three-toothed.

Tridentine /traɪ'dɛntaɪn, trɪ-/ ▷ *adj* relating to the Council of Trent (1545–63) or the traditional Catholic beliefs and doctrines reaffirmed there as a reaction to Protestantism and the Reformation. ▷ *noun* a member of the RC Church who follows the traditional doctrine affirmed at the Council of Trent. ⓘ 16c: from Latin *Tridentum* Trent, Trento in N Italy.

triecious see TRIOECIOUS

tried ▷ *verb, past tense, past participle of* TRY. ▷ *adj* tested and proved to be good, efficient, etc. **2** having had one's patience put to strain □ ***sorely tried***.

triennial /traɪ'ɛnɪəl/ ▷ *adj* **1** happening once every three years. **2** lasting for three years. ▷ *noun* **1** a period of three years. **2** an event that recurs every three years. ● **triennially** *adverb*. ⓘ 17c: from Latin *triennis*, from *triennium* a span of three years.

triennium /traɪ'ɛnɪəm/ ▷ *noun* (***trienniums*** or ***triennia*** /-nɪə/) a period of three years. ⓘ 1840s: Latin, meaning 'a span of three years'.

tries see under TRY

trier ▷ *noun* **1** someone who perseveres at something, especially something they have little talent or aptitude for □ ***Jane isn't very good at maths, but she is a trier.*** **2** someone who tries out food. **3** someone who is officially appointed to determine whether or not a challenge made to a juror has any foundation. ⓘ 14c: from TRY *verb*.

trifacial nerve see TRIGEMINAL NERVE

trifecta ▷ *noun* a betting system requiring that the horses which finish first, second and third in a race are selected in the correct order. Compare QUINELLA, PERFECTA, QUADRELLA.

trifid /ˈtraɪfɪd/ ▷ *adj, biol* split or divided into three parts or lobes. ⓘ 18c: from Latin *trifidus* in three.

trifle /ˈtraɪfəl/ ▷ *noun* **1** anything that has little or no value. **2** a very small amount. **3** *Brit* a type of dessert that usually consists of a layer of sponge-cake soaked in sherry, followed by a layer of jelly and fruit, topped with custard and whipped cream. ▷ *verb* (***trifled, trifling***) **1** (*usually* **trifle with**) **a** to treat (someone, their feelings, etc) frivolously, insensitively or with a lack of seriousness or respect; **b** to talk or think about (a proposition, idea, project, etc) idly or not very seriously. **2** (*usually* **trifle away**) to spend or pass (time, energy, money, resources, etc) frivolously. • **trifler** *noun*. • **a trifle** slightly, rather; to a small extent □ *He's a trifle upset.* ⓘ 13c: from French *trufle*, from *trufe* mockery, deceit.

trifling ▷ *adj* **1** unimportant; trivial. **2** frivolous. • **triflingly** *adverb*.

trifocal /traɪˈfoukəl/ ▷ *adj* **1** said of a lens: having three different focal lengths. **2** said of a pair of spectacles: having lenses of this kind. ▷ *noun* (**trifocals**) spectacles that have lenses of this kind. ⓘ 19c.

trifoliate /traɪˈfoulɪət/ ▷ *adj* **1** said of a compound leaf: made up of three leaflets. **2** said of a plant: having leaves of this kind. ⓘ 18c: from Latin *foliatus* leaved.

triforium /traɪˈfɔːrɪəm/ ▷ *noun* (***triforia*** /-ɪə/) a gallery or arcade that runs along the top of the arches at the sides of the nave, choir and sometimes the transepts in some large churches and cathedrals. ⓘ 18c.

triform /ˈtraɪfɔːm/ and **triformed** ▷ *adj* having or consisting of three different parts. ⓘ 15c: from Latin *forma* form.

trifurcate ▷ *verb* /ˈtraɪfəkeɪt/ (***trifurcated, trifurcating***) *tr & intr* to divide or branch into three parts. ▷ *adj* /traɪˈfɜːkeɪt/ (*also* **trifurcated** /ˈtraɪ-/) divided into three branches, prongs or forks. • **trifurcation** *noun*. ⓘ 18c: from Latin *furca* a fork.

trig[1] ▷ *noun, colloq* a short form of TRIGONOMETRY.

trig[2] *old or dialectal use* ▷ *adj* said of a person or place: smart or tidy in appearance. ▷ *verb* (***trigged, trigging***) to smarten or tidy up. ⓘ 16c: from Norse *tryggr* faithful, trusty, secure.

■ **trig out** to dress or decorate □ *trigged himself out in his Sunday best.*

trigeminal /traɪˈdʒemɪnəl/ ▷ *adj, anatomy* belonging or relating to the trigeminal nerve. ⓘ 19c: from Latin *trigeminus* born three together.

trigeminal nerve and **trigeminus** /traɪˈdʒemɪnəs/ ▷ *noun* (***trigemini*** /-naɪ/) *anatomy* in vertebrates: either of the fifth and largest pair of cranial nerves, each of which is divided into three branches known as the optical, maxillary and mandibular nerves. Also called **trifacial nerve**. ⓘ 19c.

trigeminal neuralgia see TIC DOULOUREUX

trigger /ˈtrɪgə(r)/ ▷ *noun* **1** a small lever which can be squeezed and released in order to set a mechanism going, especially one that fires a gun. **2** something that starts off a train of events, actions, reactions, etc. ▷ *verb* (***triggered, triggering***) **1** (*also* **trigger off**) to start (a train of events, actions, reactions, etc) in motion. **2** to pull a trigger or other firing mechanism (of a gun, detonating device, etc). ⓘ 17c: from Dutch *trekker* a trigger, from *trekken* to pull.

trigger finger ▷ *noun* **1** *colloq* the forefinger, especially of the right hand, ie the finger that is most commonly used to pull the trigger of a gun. **2** a condition where extending or flexing the finger or fingers can only be achieved with forced jerky movements.

triggerfish ▷ *noun* a type of tropical marine fish that gets its name from the fact that its second dorsal fin can depress the spines on the first fin in a way that resembles the action of a trigger against the hammer in a gun.

trigger-happy ▷ *adj, colloq* said of a person, their nature, attitude, etc: **1** ready or likely to shoot (a gun, etc) without thinking of the consequences or with very little provocation. **2** keen or likely to react, either physically or verbally, in a violent, rash, irresponsible, etc way. • **trigger-happiness** *noun*. ⓘ 1940s.

triglyceride /traɪˈglɪsəraɪd/ ▷ *noun, biochem* any of a large number of chemical compounds that are present in most fats and oils and which consist of a glycerol molecule combined with three acid radicals. ⓘ 19c.

triglyph /ˈtraɪglɪf/ ▷ *noun, archit* in the frieze of a Doric entablature: a block or tablet that has three parallel vertical grooves and which usually alternates with a METOPE. • **triglyphic** *adj*. ⓘ 16c: from Latin *triglyphus*, from Greek *glyphe* a carving.

trigon /ˈtraɪgɒn/ ▷ *noun* **1** a triangle. **2** *music* a type of ancient triangular lyre or harp. **3** *astrol* any one of the four groups of three star signs, ie fire, water, earth or air. ⓘ 16c: from Greek *trigonon* triangle.

trigonal /ˈtraɪgənəl/ ▷ *adj* **1** belonging or relating to a trigon. **2** triangular. **3** *biol* triangular in cross-section. **4** belonging or relating to the crystal system characterized by having three equal axes which are equally inclined and not perpendicular. • **trigonally** *adverb*. ⓘ 16c.

trigonometrical point ▷ *noun* a fixed reference point, often one that is on a hilltop and marked by a small pyramidal structure or a pillar, which is used in surveying, map-making, etc. Also called **trig point**, **triangulation point**.

trigonometric function /trɪgənəˈmetrɪk —/ and **trigonometric ratio** ▷ *noun, math* any function of an angle that is defined by the relationship between the angles and sides in a right-angled triangle, eg sine, cosine, tangent, secant, cosecant, cotangent.

trigonometry /trɪgəˈnɒmətrɪ/ ▷ *noun, math* the branch of mathematics that is concerned with the relationships between the sides and angles of triangles, especially by use of the TRIGONOMETRIC FUNCTIONS. ⓘ 17c: from Greek *trigonon* triangle + *metron* measure.

trigraph /ˈtraɪgrɑːf/ and **trigram** /ˈtraɪgram/ ▷ *noun* a combination of three letters or characters that represents a single sound. ⓘ 19c: from Greek *graphe* writing.

trike /traɪk/ see under TRICYCLE

trilateral /traɪˈlatərəl/ ▷ *adj* **1** three-sided. **2** said of talks, an agreement, treaty, etc: involving three parties, nations, countries, etc. ▷ *noun* a three-sided figure. • **trilateralism** *noun*. • **trilateralist** *noun*. • **trilaterally** *adverb*. ⓘ 17c: from Latin *latus* side.

trilby /ˈtrɪlbɪ/ ▷ *noun* (***trilbies***) *Brit* a soft felt hat with an indented crown and narrow brim. ⓘ 19c: named after the heroine of George du Maurier's novel *Trilby* (1894) who wore this type of hat.

trilingual /traɪˈlɪŋgwəl/ ▷ *adj* **1** said of someone: able to speak three languages fluently. **2** written or spoken in three languages. • **trilingualism** *noun*. ⓘ 19c: from Latin *lingua* tongue.

trill ▷ *noun* **1** *music* a sound that is produced by repeatedly playing or singing a note and a note above in rapid succession. **2** a warbling sound made by a songbird. **3** a consonant sound, especially an 'r' sound, that is made by rapidly vibrating the tongue. ▷ *verb* (***trilled, trilling***) *tr & intr* to play, sing, pronounce, etc something with a trill. ⓘ 17c: from Italian *trillare* to quaver or warble.

trillion /ˈtrɪlɪən/ ▷ *noun* **1** (*plural* ***trillion***) **a** *chiefly N Amer* a million million (10^{12}). *British equivalent* **billion**. **b** (*plural* ***trillion***) *chiefly Brit* a million million million (10^{18}). *N Amer* *equivalent* **quintillion**. **2** (*usually* **trillions**) *colloq* an enormous number or amount. • **trillionth** *adj, noun.* ⓒ 17c: French, modelled on BILLION.

trillium /'trɪlɪəm/ ▻ *noun* any of several beautiful low-growing perennial spring-flowering wild plants of the lily family, native to N America with three leaves, three green sepals and three showy petals. ⓒ 18c: Latin, based on Linnaeus's alteration of the Swedish *trilling* triplet.

trilobate /traɪ'loʊbeɪt, 'traɪləbeɪt/ and **trilobated** ▻ *adj, biol* said especially of a leaf: having or consisting of three lobes. ⓒ 18c: from Greek *lobos* ear lobe.

trilobite /'traɪləbaɪt, 'trɪ-/ ▻ *noun* **1** *zool* any of several types of extinct marine arthropod which had a flat oval body with an exoskeleton that was divided lengthwise into three lobes. **2** the fossilized remains of this animal which show it to have been abundant in the Cambrian to the Permian periods. • **trilobitic** /-'bɪtɪk/ *adj.* ⓒ 19c: from Greek *trilobos* three-lobed.

trilogy /'trɪlədʒɪ/ ▻ *noun* (***trilogies***) **1** a group of three plays, novels, poems, operas, etc that are usually related in some way, eg by theme, by having a particular character or characters in all three, etc. **2** *Greek theat* a group of three tragedies that would have been performed at the festival of Dionysus at Athens. ⓒ 17c: from Greek *trilogia*, from *logos* word, reason.

trim ▻ *verb* (***trimmed, trimming***) **1** to make something neat and tidy, especially by clipping. **2** (*also* **trim away** or **off**) to remove by, or as if by, cutting □ *trim hundreds of pounds off the cost.* **3** to make less by, or as if by, cutting □ *trim costs.* **4** to decorate with ribbons, lace, ornaments, etc □ *trimmed the dress with pink velvet.* **5** to adjust the balance of (a ship, submarine or aircraft) by moving its cargo, ballast, etc. **6** to arrange (a ship's sails) to suit the weather conditions. **7** *intr* to hold a neutral or middle course between two opposing individuals or groups. **8** *intr* to adjust one's behaviour to suit current trends or opinions, especially for self-advancement. ▻ *noun* **1 a** a haircut that is intended to neaten up an existing hairstyle rather than radically change the style; **b** the act or process of giving or having this type of haircut. **2** proper order or condition □ *in good trim.* **3** material, ornaments, etc used as decoration. **4** the decorative additions to a car, including the upholstery, internal and external colour scheme, and chrome and leather accessories. **5** the set or balance of a ship on the water. **6** said of a ship: the state of being ready, especially with the sails in proper order, for sailing. **7** the inclination of an aircraft in flight, especially with reference to the horizon. **8** parts removed by trimming. ▻ *adj* (***trimmer, trimmest***) **1** in good order; neat and tidy. **2** clean-cut; slim. • **trimmer** see separate entry. ⓒ Anglo-Saxon *trymian* to strengthen.

trimaran /'traɪməran/ ▻ *noun* a boat that has three hulls side by side. ⓒ 1940s: from TRI- sense 1 + cata*maran*.

trimer /'traɪmə(r)/ ▻ *noun, chem* a substance whose molecules are formed from three molecules of a MONOMER. • **trimeric** /traɪ'merɪk/ *adj.* ⓒ 1920s: from Greek *meros* part.

trimerous /'trɪmərəs/ ▻ *adj, bot* said of a flower, leaf, etc: having three parts or being in a group of three. ⓒ 19c: from Greek *meros* part.

trimester /trɪ'mestə(r), traɪ-/ ▻ *noun* **1** a period of three months, eg one of the three such periods of human gestation. **2** *especially N Amer* a period of approximately three months which is the length of an academic term. • **trimestrial** /-'mestrɪəl/. ⓒ 19c: from Latin *trimestris* lasting three months.

trimeter /'trɪmɪtə(r), 'traɪ-/ ▻ *noun, prosody* a line of verse that has three metrical feet. ⓒ 16c: from Latin *trimetrus* having three metrical measures.

trimmed *past tense, past participle of* TRIM

trimmer ▻ *noun* **1** someone or something that trims. **2** someone who adjusts their behaviour, attitude, opinions, etc to conform more closely with current trends in order to gain an advantage, self-advancement, etc. **3** a short horizontal beam on a floor where the ends of joists fit. ⓒ 16c: from TRIM.

trimming ▻ *noun* **1** ribbon, lace, etc that is attached to clothes, furniture, etc for a decorative effect □ *a tablecloth with lace trimming.* **2** (**trimmings**) **a** the traditional or usual accompaniments of a meal or specified dish □ *turkey with all the trimmings*; **b** the expected accessories, perks, etc that come with something □ *an executive post with all the trimmings — company car, private health scheme, etc.* **3** (**trimmings**) the parts cut or trimmed off □ *swept up the hair trimmings.* ▻ *verb, present participle of* TRIM.

trimonthly /traɪ'mʌnθlɪ/ ▻ *adj* lasting for three months or occurring every three months.

trimorphism /traɪ'mɔːfɪzəm/ ▻ *noun, biol, crystallog* the property or condition of existing in three distinct forms. • **trimorphic** or **trimorphous** *adj.* ⓒ 19c: from Greek *trimorphos* in three forms.

trimurti or **Trimurti** /trɪ'mʊətɪ/ ▻ *noun* the Hindu trinity of gods, Brahma, Shiva and Vishnu. ⓒ 19c: from Sanskrit *tri* three + *murti* shape.

Trin. ▻ *abbreviation* Trinity.

trine ▻ *adj* **1** triple; threefold; in three parts. **2** *astrol* said of two heavenly bodies with regard to ASPECT (sense 5): separated by one third of the zodiac, ie 120°, and so thought to be having a favourable influence. ▻ *noun* **1** *astrol* a trine aspect. **2** a group of three; a triad; something that has three parts to it. • **trinal** or **trinary** *adj.* ⓒ 14c: from Latin *trinus* threefold.

Trinidadian /trɪnɪ'dadɪən, -'deɪdɪən/ ▻ *adj* belonging or relating to Trinidad, an island in the W Indies. ▻ *noun* a citizen or inhabitant of, or someone born in, Trinidad. ⓒ Early 20c.

Trinitarian /trɪnɪ'teərɪən/ ▻ *noun* someone who believes in the doctrine of the Trinity. ▻ *adj* relating to or believing in the doctrine of the Trinity. Compare UNITARIAN. • **Trinitarianism** *noun.* ⓒ 17c: from Latin *trinitarius*; see TRINITY.

trinitrotoluene /traɪnaɪtroʊ'tɒljuiːn/ and **trinitrotoluol** /-'tɒljʊɒl/ ▻ *noun, chem* (formula $C_6H_2(CH_3)(NO_2)_3$) a highly explosive yellow crystalline solid that is used as an explosive and in certain photographic chemicals and dyes. Often shortened to TNT. ⓒ Early 20c.

trinity /'trɪnɪtɪ/ ▻ *noun* (***trinities***) **1** the state of being three. **2** a group of three. **3** (**Trinity**) *Christianity* the unity of the Father, Son and Holy Spirit in a single Godhead. **4** (**Trinity**) TRINITY SUNDAY. **5** (**Trinity**) TRINITY TERM. ⓒ 13c: from Latin *trinitas*.

Trinity House ▻ *noun, Brit* an association that formerly regulated shipping, but which is now chiefly concerned with the licensing of pilots and the erection and maintainance of lighthouses and buoys around the coasts of England and Wales. ⓒ 16c.

Trinity Sunday ▻ *noun* the Sunday after WHIT SUNDAY, kept as a festival in honour of the Trinity. Often shortened to **Trinity**.

Trinity term ▻ *noun* the university or law term that begins after Easter. Often shortened to **Trinity**.

trinket /'trɪŋkɪt/ ▻ *noun* a small ornament or piece of jewellery, especially one that is of little value. • **trinketry** *noun.* ⓒ 16c.

trinomial /traɪ'noʊmɪəl/ ▻ *adj* having three terms or names. ▻ *noun* a scientific or mathematical expression that has three parts to it, eg, in taxonomy, the genus, species and subspecies of an organism or, in algebra, an equation with three terms. • **trinomialism** *noun.* • **trinomialist** *noun.* ⓒ 18c: modelled on BINOMIAL.

trio /'tri:oʊ/ ▻ *noun* (***trios***) **1** a group or set of three. **2** *music* **a** a group of three instruments, players or singers; **b** a piece of music composed for such a group. **3** *music* a contrastive central section of a minuet, scherzo or march. ⓒ 18c: French, from Italian *tre* three, influenced by DUO.

triode /'traɪoʊd/ ▻ *noun, electronics* **1** (*in full* **triode valve**) a thermionic valve that has three electrodes. **2** a semiconductor that has three terminals. ⓒ Early 20c: from TRI- sense 1 + Greek *hodos* way.

trioecious or **triecious** /traɪ'i:ʃəs/ ▻ *adj, bot* said of a plant: occurring in three different sexual forms, ie male, female and hermaphrodite. ⓒ 18c: from Greek *oikos* house.

triolet /'traɪoʊlɛt/ ▻ *noun, poetry* a verse of eight lines that rhyme *abaaabab* in which the first line is repeated as the fourth and seventh lines and the second line is repeated as the eighth. ⓒ 17c: French, a diminutive of TRIO.

trioxide /traɪ'ɒksaɪd/ ▻ *noun, chem* an oxide that contains three atoms of oxygen. ⓒ 19c.

trip ▻ *verb* (***tripped, tripping***) **1** *tr & intr* (*also* **trip over** or **up**) to stumble or make someone stumble. **2** *tr & intr* (*also* **trip up**) to make or cause to make a mistake. **3** to catch someone out, eg in a fault or mistake. **4** *intr* (*often* **trip along**) to walk, skip or dance with short light steps. **5** *intr* to move or flow smoothly and easily □ ***words tripping off the tongue***. **6** *intr* to take a trip or excursion. **7** *intr, colloq* to experience the hallucinatory effects of a drug, especially LSD. **8** *tr & intr* to activate or cause (a device or mechanism) to be activated, especially suddenly. **9** to perform (a dance) with quick light agile steps. ▻ *noun* **1 a** a short journey or excursion, especially for pleasure and usually to a place and back again; **b** a journey of any length. **2** a stumble; the act or process of accidentally catching the foot. **3** a short light step or skip. **4** a part or catch that can be struck in order to activate a mechanism. **5** an error or blunder. **6** *colloq* a hallucinatory experience, especially one that is brought on by taking a drug, eg LSD □ ***a bad trip***. **7** *colloq* an intensely emotional experience. See also EGO TRIP. ● **tripper**, **trippy** see separate entries. ● **trip the light fantastic** *jocular* to dance. ⓒ 15c: from French *triper* to strike with the foot, to dance.

tripartite /traɪ'pɑ:taɪt/ ▻ *adj* **1** divided into or composed of three parts. **2** said of talks, an agreement, etc: involving, concerning, ratified by, etc three parts, groups, people, nations, etc. ● **tripartitely** *adverb*. ● **tripartition** *noun*. ⓒ 15c: from Latin *tripartitus* in three parts.

tripe ▻ *noun* **1** parts of the stomach of a cow or sheep, used as food. **2** *colloq* nonsense; rubbish. ⓒ 14c: French, meaning 'the entrails of an animal'.

trip hammer ▻ *noun* a large powered hammer that is raised by a cam and then allowed to drop under gravity.

trip hop ▻ *noun* a type of music consisting mainly of instrumental, mellow GROOVEs, developed chiefly in the UK. It takes rhythms from HIP-HOP and adds psychedelic and dub effects. ⓒ 1990s.

triphthong /'trɪfθɒŋ/ ▻ *noun* **1** *phonetics* a sequence of three vowel sounds in the same syllable that are pronounced together, eg those in the word *flower* /flaʊə(r)/. **2** *non-technical* a TRIGRAPH. ● **triphthongal** *adj*. ⓒ 16c: from Greek *phthongos* voice; modelled on DIPHTHONG.

triple /'trɪpəl/ ▻ *adj* **1** three times as great, as much or as many. **2** made up of three parts or things. **3** *music* having three beats to the bar. ▻ *verb* (***tripled, tripling***) *tr & intr* to make or become three times as great, as much or as many. ▻ *noun* **1 a** an amount that is three times greater than the original, usual, etc amount; **b** a measure (of spirits) that is three times greater than a single measure. **2** a group or series of three. ● **triply** *adverb*. ⓒ 14c: French, from Latin *triplus* threefold.

triple crown ▻ *noun* **1** *Brit horse-racing* victory in the *Two Thousand Guineas*, the *Derby* and the *St Leger* in the same season. **2** *Brit rugby union & hockey* in the home championships between England, Ireland, Scotland and Wales: victory by one team over all three opponents in the same season. **3** the Pope's tiara.

triple jump ▻ *noun* an athletic event that involves competitors trying to cover the greatest distance with a hop, followed by a skip and then a jump.

triple point ▻ *noun, physics* the temperature and pressure at which the solid, liquid and vapour phases of a particular substance, or of any combinations of these phases (eg two solids and a liquid) can coexist in equilibrium.

triplet /'trɪplət/ ▻ *noun* **1** one of three children or animals born to the same mother at one birth. **2** a group or set of three. **3** *music* a group of three notes played in the time usually given to two. **4** a group of three rhyming verses in a poem. ⓒ 18c: from TRIPLE, modelled on DOUBLET.

triple time ▻ *noun* musical time with three beats to the bar.

triplicate ▻ *adj* /'trɪplɪkət/ **1** having three parts which are exactly alike. **2** being one of three identical copies. **3** tripled. ▻ *noun* /'trɪplɪkət/ any of three identical copies or three parts which are exactly alike. ▻ *verb* /'trɪplɪkeɪt/ (***triplicated, triplicating***) **1** to make three copies of. **2** to multiply by three. ● **triplication** *noun*. ● **in triplicate** three times; with three separate copies of the same document. ⓒ 15c: from Latin *triplicare*, *triplicatum* to triple.

tripling *present participle of* TRIPLE

triploid /'trɪplɔɪd/ *biol* ▻ *adj* said of an organism or cell: having three times the HAPLOID number of chromosomes. ▻ *noun* an organism or cell of this kind. ⓒ Early 20c: from Greek *triplous* threefold.

triply see TRIPLE

tripod /'traɪpɒd/ ▻ *noun* **1** a type of stand that has three legs and which is designed for supporting something, eg a camera, compass, etc. **2** a stool or table with three legs or feet. **3** *Greek hist* a pot with three legs at the shrine of Apollo at Delphi where the priestess sat to deliver oracles. ● **tripodal** /'trɪpədəl/ *adj*. ⓒ 17c: from Greek *tripous* three-footed.

tripos /'traɪpɒs/ ▻ *noun* **1** the final honours examination in the BA degree at Cambridge University. **2** the list of successful candidates in this examination. ⓒ 19c: from Latin *tripus* tripod.

tripped and **tripping** see under TRIP

tripper ▻ *noun* **1** *Brit* someone who goes on a journey for pleasure; a tourist □ ***day trippers***. **2** *colloq* someone who experiences the hallucinatory effects of a drug, eg LSD.

trippy ▻ *adj* (***trippier, trippiest***) said of music, film camerawork, etc: producing psychadelic effects that are similar to those experienced after taking a drug such as LSD. ⓒ 1960s: from TRIP *verb* 7, *noun* 6.

triptane /'trɪpteɪn/ ▻ *noun* a type of powerful hydrocarbon used in high-octane aviation fuel. ⓒ 1940s: from TRI- sense 1 + (BU)TANE.

triptych /'trɪptɪk/ ▻ *noun* **1** a picture or carving that covers three panels joined together by hinges to form a single work of art, often used as an ALTARPIECE. See also DIPTYCH. **2** a set of three writing tablets joined together by hinges or ties. ⓒ 18c: from Greek *triptychos* consisting of three layers, and modelled on 'diptych'.

triptyque /trɪp'ti:k/ ▻ *noun* a type of international pass for a motor vehicle that allows it to go through customs. ⓒ Early 20c: French, so called because the original versions were cards that folded in three parts; see TRIPTYCH.

trip-wire ⊳ *noun* a hidden wire that sets off a mechanism of some kind, eg an alarm, bomb, etc, when someone trips over it.

trireme /ˈtraɪəriːm/ ⊳ *noun* a type of ancient galley, originally Greek but later also adopted by the Romans, that had three banks of rowers on each side and which was principally used as a warship. ⌚ 17c: from Latin *triremis*, from *remus* oar.

trisect /traɪˈsɛkt/ ⊳ *verb* (***trisected***, ***trisecting***) to divide something into three parts, usually of equal size. • **trisection** *noun*. • **trisector** *noun*. ⌚ 17c: from Latin *secare* to cut.

trishaw /ˈtraɪʃɔː/ ⊳ *noun* a type of three-wheeled vehicle driven by pedals, commonly used in Asian cities as a taxi. ⌚ 1940s: from TRI- sense 1 + *rickshaw*.

triskaidekaphobia /trɪskaɪdɛkəˈfoʊbɪə/ ⊳ *noun* fear of the number thirteen. ⌚ Early 20c: from Greek *treiskaideka* thirteen.

triskelion /trɪˈskɛlɪən/ and **triskele** /trɪˈskiːl/ ⊳ *noun* a symbol that has three bent limbs or lines radiating from a common centre, eg the emblem of the Isle of Man. ⌚ 19c: from Greek *skelos* leg.

trismus see LOCKJAW

trisomy /ˈtraɪsəmɪ/ ⊳ *noun, medicine* a condition in which there is an extra copy of a chromosome in the cell nuclei, eg **trisomy-21** which is associated with DOWN'S SYNDROME. • **trisomic** /traɪˈsoʊmɪk/ *adj, noun*. ⌚ 1920s: from TRI- sense 1 + -SOME sense 2.

tristearin see under STEARIN

tristesse /*French* tʀistɛs/ ⊳ *noun* sadness. ⌚ 14c: French.

trisyllable /traɪˈsɪləbəl/ ⊳ *noun* a word or metrical foot of three syllables. • **trisyllabic** /traɪsɪˈlabɪk/ *adj*. ⌚ 16c.

trite ⊳ *adj* said of a remark, phrase, etc: having no meaning or effectiveness because it has been repeated or used so often; hackneyed. • **tritely** *adverb*. • **triteness** *noun*. ⌚ 16c: from Latin *tritus* worn, common.

tritheism /ˈtraɪθiːɪzəm/ ⊳ *noun* belief in three gods, especially the belief that the Trinity is composed of three distinct gods. • **tritheist** *noun*. • **tritheistic** or **tri-theistical** *adj*. ⌚ 17c.

tritiate /ˈtrɪtɪeɪt, -ʃɪeɪt/ ⊳ *verb* (***tritiated***, ***tritiating***) to introduce tritium to (a substance) and replace an ordinary atom of hydrogen with it. • **tritiation** *noun*. ⌚ 1940s: from TRITIUM.

triticum /ˈtrɪtɪkəm/ ⊳ *noun* any of several types of cereal grass, eg wheat. ⌚ 19c: from Latin, meaning 'wheat'.

tritium /ˈtrɪtɪəm, -ʃɪəm/ ⊳ *noun, chem* (symbol **^{3}H, T**) a radioactive isotope of hydrogen that has two neutrons as well as one proton in its nucleus and which is used in fusion reactors and as an isotopic label or tracer. ⌚ 1930s: from Greek *tritos* third.

Triton /ˈtraɪtən/ ⊳ *noun* **1** *Greek mythol* a type of minor sea-god usually depicted with the upper body of a man and the lower body of a fish or dolphin and carrying a trident and a conch. **2** any of several large marine GASTROPODs that have conch-like shells. ⌚ 16c: originally the name of the Greek sea-god, the son of Amphitrite and Poseidon.

triton /ˈtraɪtən/ ⊳ *noun* a nucleus of a tritium atom which is composed of one proton and two neutrons. ⌚ 1940s: from TRITIUM.

tritone /ˈtraɪtoʊn/ ⊳ *noun, music* an AUGMENTED (sense 2) FOURTH (*noun* sense 4a) interval, which is comprised of three tones. ⌚ 17c: from Greek *tritonos* of three tones.

triturate /ˈtrɪtjʊreɪt/ ⊳ *verb* (***triturated***, ***triturating***) to grind or rub to a powder. • **trituration** *noun*. • **triturator** *noun*. ⌚ 17c: from Latin *triturare*, *trituratum* to thresh.

triumph /ˈtraɪʌmf/ ⊳ *noun* **1** a great or notable victory, success, achievement, etc. **2** the joy or feeling of elation that is felt after winning a great victory, etc. **3** *Roman hist* the procession that would accompany a general on his return to Rome after a great victory over a foreign enemy. ⊳ *verb* (***triumphed***, ***triumphing***) *intr* **1** (*usually* **triumph over**) to win a victory or be successful; to prevail. **2** *Roman hist* to celebrate a triumph. **3** to rejoice in a feeling of triumph over someone; to exult. • **triumphal** /traɪˈʌmfəl/ *adj*. • **triumpher** *noun*. • **triumphing** *adj, noun*. ⌚ 14c: from Latin *triumphus*.

triumphalism ⊳ *noun* an attitude of righteous pride and self-congratulation over the defeat of a perceived evil. • **triumphalist** *adj, noun*.

triumphal arch ⊳ *noun, archit* a stone monument, usually in the form of a free-standing gateway, that commemorates a military victory, eg the Arc de Triomphe in Paris commemorating Napoleon's victories.

triumphant ⊳ *adj* **1** having won a victory or achieved success. **2** exultant; feeling or showing great joy or elation because of a victory, success, achievement, etc. • **triumphantly** *adverb*.

triumvir /traɪˈʌmvɪə(r)/ ⊳ *noun* (***triumviri*** /-raɪ/ or ***triumvirs***) **1** someone who shares an official position, power, authority, etc equally with two other people. **2** *Roman hist* someone who is part of a triumvirate. • **triumviral** *adj*. ⌚ 16c: Latin, from *triumviri* of three men.

triumvirate /traɪˈʌmvərеɪt/ ⊳ *noun* a group of three people who share an official position, power, authority, etc equally. • **triumviral** *adj*. ⌚ 16c: originally, in ancient Rome, the name given to the coalition between Caesar, Pompey and Crassus in 60 BC (the 'first triumvirate') and later to the joint rule from 43 BC of Caesar, Antony and Lepidus (the 'second triumvirate').

triune /ˈtraɪjuːn/ ⊳ *adj* said of a godhead, especially the Trinity: three in one. ⌚ 17c: from TRI- sense 1 + Latin *unus* one.

trivalent /traɪˈveɪlənt/ ⊳ *adj, chem* having a valency of three. • **trivalence** or **trivalency** *noun*. ⌚ 19c: from Latin *valere* to be worth.

trivet /ˈtrɪvɪt/ ⊳ *noun* **1** a three-legged stand or bracket that can be hooked on to a grate and which is used as a support for cooking vessels over a fire. **2** a stand that a hot dish, pot, teapot, etc is placed on, eg at the table. ⌚ Anglo-Saxon *trefet*.

trivia /ˈtrɪvɪə/ ⊳ *plural noun* **1** unimportant or petty matters or details. **2** useless information. ⌚ Early 20c: Latin, plural of TRIVIUM; influenced in sense by TRIVIAL.

trivial /ˈtrɪvɪəl/ ⊳ *adj* **1** having or being of very little importance or value. **2** said of a person: only interested in unimportant things; frivolous. **3** commonplace; ordinary. ⊳ *noun* **1** (*usually* **the trivial**) trivial things collectively. **2** (*usually* **trivials**) something that is considered trivial. • **trivially** *adverb*. • **trivialness** *noun*. ⌚ 15c: from Latin *trivialis*, from TRIVIUM.

triviality /trɪvɪˈalɪtɪ/ ⊳ *noun* (***trivialities***) **1** the state or condition of being trivial. **2** something that is trivial.

trivialize or **trivialise** ⊳ *verb* (***trivialized***, ***trivializing***) to make or treat something as if it were unimportant, worthless, etc. • **trivialization** *noun*. ⌚ 19c.

Trivial Pursuit ⊳ *noun, trademark* a type of board game that involves players progressing by correctly answering questions on geography, entertainment, history, art and literature, science and nature, and sport and leisure. ⌚ 1970s.

trivium /ˈtrɪvɪəm/ ⊳ *noun, historical* the three liberal arts, ie grammar, rhetoric and logic, that formed part of a medieval university course and which were considered less important than the QUADRIVIUM. ⌚ 19c: Latin, meaning 'a place where three roads or ways meet'.

tri-weekly ⊳ *adj* **a** occurring, being published, etc every three weeks; **b** occurring, being published, etc three times per week. ▻ *adverb* **a** every three weeks; **b** three times per week. ▻ *noun* **a** a publication that comes out every three weeks; **b** a publication that comes out three times per week. ◷ 19c.

-trix /trɪks/ ▻ *suffix* (***-trices*** /trɪˈsiːz/ or ***-trixes*** /trɪksəz/) *especially law, denoting* a feminine agent corresponding to the masculine *-tor*, eg *executor, executrix*.

tRNA ▻ *abbreviation* transfer RNA.

trocar /ˈtroʊkɑː(r)/ ▻ *noun, surgery* an instrument that has a perforator enclosed in a tube, used for drawing off fluid from a body cavity, etc, eg in conditions such as oedema. ◷ 18c: from French *trocart, troisquart*, from *trois* three + *carre* side or face, and so called because of the triangular shape of the instrument.

trochaic /troʊˈkeɪɪk/ ▻ *adj, prosody* **1** said of a verse, rhythm, etc: consisting mainly of TROCHEES. **2** said of a metrical foot: consisting of one long or stressed syllable followed by one short or unstressed one. ◷ 16c: from TROCHEE.

trochal /ˈtrɒkəl/ ▻ *adj, zool* resembling or shaped like a wheel. ◷ 19c: from Greek *trochos* a wheel.

trochanter /troʊˈkantə(r)/ ▻ *noun* **1** *anatomy* any bony process where muscles are attached to the upper part of the thigh bone. **2** *zool* in insects: the second leg joint. • **trochanteric** /troʊkanˈtɛrɪk/ *adj*. ◷ 17c in sense 1: from Greek *trochanter*, from *trechein* to run.

troche /troʊʃ/ ▻ *noun* a flat round medicinal tablet that is usually dissolved on the tongue. ◷ 16c: from Greek *trochiskos* a little wheel.

trochee /ˈtroʊkiː/ ▻ *noun, prosody* a metrical foot of one long or stressed syllable followed by one short or unstressed one. • **trochaic** see separate entry. ◷ 16c: from Greek *trochaios pous* running foot.

trochlea /ˈtrɒkliːə/ ▻ *noun, anatomy* any bony or cartilaginous structure that functions or looks like a pulley and which has a tendon or bone articulating with it or sliding over it, eg the one at the elbow end of the humerus. • **trochlear** *adj*. ◷ 17c: from Greek *trochileia* a set of pulleys.

trochlear nerve ▻ *noun, anatomy* in vertebrates: either of the fourth pair of cranial nerves which are the motor nerves of the superior oblique muscles of the eye.

trochoid /ˈtroʊkɔɪd/ ▻ *noun, geom* the curve that a fixed point on the radius, but not on the circumference, of a circle describes as the circle rolls along a straight line or along another circle. ▻ *adj* **1** (*also* **trochoidal**) *geom* characteristic of a trochoid. **2** *anatomy* said of a bone in a pivot joint: articulating with another bone with a rotary motion. ◷ 18c: from Greek *trochoeides* circular.

trod ▻ *verb, past tense, past participle of* TREAD

trodden *past participle of* TREAD

troglodyte /ˈtrɒglədaɪt/ ▻ *noun* **1** someone who lives in a cave, especially in prehistoric times. **2** *colloq* someone who has little to do with the outside world and who is therefore thought to be rather eccentric and out of touch. • **troglodytic** /-ˈdɪtɪk/ or **troglodytical** *adj*. • **troglodytism** /-ˈdaɪtɪzəm/ *noun*. ◷ 16c: from Greek *troglodytes*, from *trogle* a hole + *dyein* to creep into.

trogon /ˈtroʊgɒn/ ▻ *noun* any of several different kinds of tropical birds that have brightly coloured plumage and long tails. ◷ 18c: from Greek *trogein* to gnaw.

troika /ˈtrɔɪkə/ ▻ *noun* (***troikas***) **1 a** a type of Russian vehicle drawn by three horses abreast; **b** a team of three horses harnessed abreast. **2** any group of three people working as a team, especially when they have an equal share of power. ◷ 19c: Russian.

troilism /ˈtrɔɪlɪzəm/ ▻ *noun* any form of sexual activity where three people are involved simultaneously. • **troilist** *adj*. ◷ 1940s.

Trojan /ˈtroʊdʒən/ ▻ *noun* **1** *historical* a citizen or inhabitant of ancient Troy in Asia Minor. **2** someone who works, fights, etc extremely hard or courageously ◻ ***working like a Trojan***. ▻ *adj* belonging or relating to ancient Troy or its inhabitants or citizens. ◷ 14c: from Latin *Troianus*.

Trojan Horse ▻ *noun* **1** *historical* the hollow wooden horse that the Greeks used to infiltrate Troy. **2** someone or something that undermines from within an organization, etc, especially when the intention is to bring about the downfall of an enemy, rival, etc. **3** *computing* a program that contains hidden instructions that can lead to the destruction or corruption of data under certain conditions, but which, unlike a VIRUS, does not replicate itself. ◷ 16c.

troll[1] /troʊl/ ▻ *noun, Scand mythol* an ugly, evil-tempered, human-like creature that can take the form of either a dwarf or a giant. ◷ 19c: Norse and Swedish.

troll[2] /troʊl/ ▻ *verb* (***trolled, trolling***) **1** *tr & intr* to fish by trailing bait on a line through water. **2** *intr, old use* to stroll or saunter. ▻ *noun* the bait used in trolling, or a line holding this. ◷ 14c: from *trollen* to roll or stroll.

trolley /ˈtrɒlɪ/ ▻ *noun* (***trolleys***) **1** *Brit* a small cart or basket on wheels that is used for conveying luggage, shopping, etc. **2** *Brit* a small table, usually with a shelf underneath, mounted on castors or wheels, used for conveying food, crockery, etc in the home or a restaurant. **3** a bed on wheels for transporting patients in hospital. **4** *Brit* a small wagon or truck running on rails. **5** a TROLLEY WHEEL. **6** *Brit* a TROLLEY BUS. **7** *N Amer* a TROLLEY CAR. • **off one's trolley** *colloq* daft; crazy. ◷ 19c: probably from TROLL[2].

trolley bus ▻ *noun* a public transport vehicle that is powered from overhead electric wires by means of a pole and a trolley wheel.

trolley car ▻ *noun, N Amer* a public transport vehicle that runs on rails like a tram and is powered by overhead electric wires using a trolley wheel.

trolley wheel ▻ *noun* a small grooved wheel which collects current from an overhead electric wire and transmits it down a pole to power the vehicle underneath.

trollop /ˈtrɒləp/ ▻ *noun* **1 a** a promiscuous or disreputable girl or woman; **b** a prostitute. **2** a slovenly or untidy girl or woman. • **trollopy** *adj*. • **trolloping** *adj, noun*. ◷ 17c.

trombone /trɒmˈboʊn/ ▻ *noun* **a** a type of brass musical wind instrument that has tubes that can slide in and out of each other to alter the pitch of notes; **b** someone who plays this instrument especially in an orchestra ◻ ***The trombones stood up***. • **trombonist** *noun*. ◷ 18c: Italian, from *tromba* trumpet.

trommel /ˈtrɒməl/ ▻ *noun, mining* a rotating cylindrical sieve used for cleaning or sizing ore. ◷ 19c: German, meaning 'drum'.

trompe or **tromp** /trɒmp/ ▻ *noun* a device in a furnace that produces a blast of air by using a column of water to force air into a receiver where it is compressed before going into the blast-pipe. ◷ 19c: French, meaning 'trumpet'.

trompe l'oeil /trɒmp ˈlɜːj/ ▻ *noun* (***trompe l'oeils***) a painting or decoration which gives a convincing illusion of reality. ◷ 19c: French, meaning 'deceives the eye'.

-tron /trɒn/ ▻ *suffix, physics, forming nouns, denoting* **1** a thermionic valve or electron tube ◻ ***klystron***. **2** a subatomic particle ◻ ***positron***. **3** a particle accelerator ◻ ***cyclotron***. ◷ 1930s: from electron.

troop ▻ *noun* **1** (**troops**) armed forces; soldiers. **2** a group or collection, especially of people or animals. **3** a division of a cavalry or armoured squadron. **4** a large group of Scouts that is divided into patrols. ▻ *verb* (***trooped, trooping***) *intr* (*usually* **troop along, off, in**, *etc*) to move as a group. • **troop the colour** *Brit* to parade a regiment's flag ceremonially. ◷ 16c: from Latin *troppus* a flock.

trooper ▻ *noun* **1** a private soldier, especially one in a cavalry or armoured unit. **2** a cavalry soldier's horse. **3** *especially US* a policeman mounted on a horse or motorcycle. **4** *Brit* a troop-ship. ● **swear like a trooper** to be in the habit of using language that is liberally sprinkled with strong expletives.

troop-ship ▻ *noun* a ship that is designed for transporting military personnel.

tropaeolum /troʊ'piːələm/ ▻ *noun* (***tropaeola*** /-lə/ or ***tropaeolums***) *bot* any of several types of trailing or climbing plants that have yellow or orange trumpet-shaped flowers, some of which are grown for their ornamental value and a species of which is commonly called nasturtium. ⓒ 18c: Latin.

trope /troʊp/ ▻ *noun* a word or expression that is used in a figurative way, eg a METAPHOR. ● **tropic** /'troʊpɪk/ *adj.* ⓒ 16c: from Latin *tropus* a figure of speech.

trophy /'troʊfɪ/ ▻ *noun* (***trophies***) **1** a cup, medal, plate, etc awarded as a prize for victory or success in some contest, especially in sport. **2** something which is kept in memory of a victory or success, eg in hunting. **3** a memorial of victory, especially in ancient Greece or Rome, originally captured weapons, armour and other spoils, set up on or near the field of victory. **4** a representation of such a memorial, eg on a medal or monument. ⓒ 16c: from Greek *tropaion*, from *trope* a turning, defeat, from *trepein* to turn.

tropic /'trɒpɪk/ ▻ *noun* **1** either of two lines of latitude that encircle the earth at 23° 27′ north (the **tropic of Cancer**) and 23° 27′ south (the **tropic of Capricorn**) of the equator. **2** (**the tropics** or **the Tropics**) the parts of the Earth that lie between these two circles. ▻ *adj* **1** TROPICAL. **2** see under TROPE. ⓒ 14c: from Greek *tropikos* relating to the apparent turning of the Sun at a solstice.

tropical ▻ *adj* **1** relating to, found in or originating from the tropics. **2** very hot ▫ *a tropical climate.* **3** passionate. **4** luxuriant ▫ *tropical rainforest.* ● **tropically** *adverb.*

tropical rainforest and **rainforest** ▻ *noun* the richest natural terrestrial environment in relation to BIOMASS and species, found in hot humid equatorial regions and providing much of the oxygen for plant and animal respiration, the clearing of which may cause global warming contributing to the GREENHOUSE EFFECT.

tropism /'troʊpɪzəm/ ▻ *noun, biol* the change of direction of an organism, especially a plant or plant part, in response to an external stimulus such as gravity, light or heat: plant roots grow vertically downward in response to gravity (**positive geotropism**) and they grow away from the light (**negative phototropism**), whereas shoots grow towards the light (**positive phototropism**) and away from the soil (**negative geotropism**). ⓒ 19c: from Greek *tropos* a turn.

troposphere /'trɒpəsfɪə(r)/ ▻ *noun, meteorol* the lowest atmospheric layer, which extends from the Earth's surface to a height of about 8km over the Poles rising to about 17km over the Equator and is characterized by having temperatures that steadily decrease as the height increases. It is situated below the STRATOSPHERE. ● **tropospheric** *adj.* ⓒ 1930s: from Greek *tropos* turn.

Trot /trɒt/ ▻ *noun, derog colloq* **1** a Trotskyist. **2** any supporter of the extreme left. ⓒ 1960s: a short form of TROTSKYIST.

trot ▻ *verb* (***trotted, trotting***) **1** *intr* said of a horse: to move at a steady, fairly fast pace, moving each diagonally opposite pair of legs together in a bouncy kind of walk. **2** to make (a horse) move in this way. **3** *intr* to move or proceed at a steady, fairly brisk pace ▫ *The pig trotted up to the chicken house.* ▻ *noun* **1** the pace at which a horse, rider, etc moves when trotting. **2** an act or the process of trotting. **3** (**the trots**) *colloq* a euphemistic name for an ongoing bout of diarrhoea. ● **on the trot** *colloq* **1** one after the other. **2** continually moving about; busy. ⓒ 13c: from French *troter*.

■ **trot out** to go out ▫ *He's not in — he's just trotted out to the library.*

■ **trot something out** *colloq* to produce (a story, article, excuse, etc), especially habitually or repeatedly and without much thought, effort, etc ▫ *trots out the same boring lectures every year.*

troth /troʊθ, trɒθ/ ▻ *noun, old use* faith or fidelity. ● **plight one's troth** to make a solemn promise, especially to commit oneself to a betrothal or marriage. ⓒ Anglo-Saxon *treowth* truth.

Trotskyism /'trɒtskɪɪzəm/ ▻ *noun* the political, economic and social principles and practices of Leon Trotsky, especially his interpretation of MARXISM, which he saw as advocating world-wide socialist revolution. Compare LENINISM, STALINISM. ⓒ 1920s: from Leon Trotsky, the name adopted by Lev Davidovich Bronstein (1879–1940), the Jewish Russian revolutionary and politician.

Trotskyist /'trɒtskɪɪst/ or **Trotskyite** /'trɒtskɪaɪt/ *often derog* ▻ *noun* someone who is a supporter of Trotskyism. ▻ *adj* belonging or relating to or involving Trotskyism.

trotter ▻ *noun* **1 a** a pig's foot; **b** (*usually* **pigs' trotters**) pigs' feet used as food. **2** a horse trained to trot in harness. **3** someone or something that trots.

troubadour /'truːbədʊə(r), -dɔː(r)/ ▻ *noun* **1** *historical* one of a group of lyric poets in S France and N Italy during the 11c–13c who wrote, usually in Provençal, about a highly idealized form of love. **2** a poet or singer, especially one whose topic is love. ⓒ 18c: French, from Provençal *trobador*, from *trobar* to find, invent or compose in verse.

trouble /'trʌbəl/ ▻ *noun* **1 a** distress, worry or concern; **b** a cause of this. **2** bother or effort, or a cause of this ▫ *go to a lot of trouble* ▫ *The dog was no trouble.* **3** a problem or difficulty ▫ *Your trouble is that you're too generous.* **4 a** (*usually* **troubles**) public disturbances and unrest; **b** (**the Troubles**) a term used to describe the periods of civil war and unrest from 1919 to 23 and since 1969 in N Ireland. **5 a** illness or weakness ▫ *heart trouble*; **b** malfunction; failure ▫ *engine trouble.* ▻ *verb* (***troubled, troubling***) **1** to cause distress, worry, concern, anger, sadness, etc to ▫ *What's troubling you?* **2** to cause physical distress or discomfort to ▫ *His weak knee always troubled him.* **3** used especially in polite requests: to put someone to the inconvenience of (doing, saying, etc something) ▫ *Could I trouble you to open the window a little?* **4** *intr* to make any effort or take pains ▫ *He didn't even trouble to tell me what had happened.* **5** to disturb or agitate (eg the surface of water). ● **be asking for trouble** *colloq* to behave in a way likely to bring problems or difficulties. ● **in trouble** in difficulties, especially because of doing something wrong or illegal. ● **look for trouble** to actively and aggressively seek out an argument or fight. ● **take trouble** or **take the trouble** to make an effort (to do something, especially to do it well). ⓒ 13c: from French *trubler*, from Latin *turbidus* full of confusion, disturbed.

trouble and strife ▻ *noun, cockney rhyming slang* wife.

troubled /'trʌbəld/ ▻ *adj* agitated, disturbed, etc or reflecting, showing, having experienced, etc some kind of trouble ▫ *a troubled look on her face* ▫ *the victim of a troubled childhood.* ● **troubled waters** a state of agitation, confusion, disruption, etc ▫ *guided the company through potentially troubled waters.*

troublemaker ▻ *noun* someone who continually, and usually deliberately, causes trouble, worry, problems, etc to others ▫ *She's a right troublemaker — always spreading nasty rumours.*

troubleshoot ▻ *verb* **1 a** to trace and mend a fault (in machinery, etc); **b** to identify and solve problems. **2** to mediate (in disputes, etc). ● **troubleshooter** *noun.* ● **troubleshooting** *noun, adj.* ⓒ Early 20c: originally applied to the tracing of faults in telegraph or telephone wires.

troublesome ▷ *adj* slightly worrying, annoying, difficult, etc. • **troublesomely** *adverb*.

trouble spot ▷ *noun* a place where unrest, conflict, civil war, etc flares up, especially frequently or on a regular basis □ *N Ireland has been one of the world's worst trouble spots this century.*

troublous ▷ *adj, old use, literary* full of troubles; disturbed.

trough /trɒf/ ▷ *noun* **1** a long narrow open container that animal feed or water is put into. **2** a channel, drain or gutter. **3** a long narrow hollow between the crests of two waves. **4** *meteorol* a long narrow area of low atmospheric pressure. Compare RIDGE 5. **5** a low point in an economic recession. **6** any low point. ⌚ Anglo-Saxon *trog*.

trounce ▷ *verb* (***trounced, trouncing***) to beat or defeat completely; to thrash □ *Aberdeen trounced Rangers four nil.* • **trouncing** *noun*. ⌚ 16c.

troupe /truːp/ ▷ *noun* a group or company of performers. ⌚ 19c: French, from Latin *troppus* troop.

trouper ▷ *noun* **1** a member of a troupe. **2** an experienced, hard-working and loyal colleague.

trousers /'traʊzəz/ ▷ *plural noun* **1** an outer garment for the lower part of the body, reaching from the waist and covering each leg separately, usually down to the ankle. **2** (**trouser**) *as adj* □ *trouser press.* • **be, get,** *etc* **caught with one's trousers down** *colloq* to be embarrassed and taken by surprise. • **wear the trousers** *colloq* to be the dominant member of a household who makes the decisions. ⌚ 16c: from Irish *trius* and Scottish Gaelic *triubhas* trews, and influenced by 'drawers' (see DRAWER sense 3).

trouser suit ▷ *noun* a woman's suit, consisting of a jacket and trousers. Also (*N Amer*) called **pant suit**.

trousseau /'truːsoʊ/ ▷ *noun* (***trousseaux*** /'truːsoʊ/ or ***trousseaus*** /-soʊz/) a set of new clothes, linen, etc that is traditionally bought by a woman who is engaged to be married and which she keeps for her wedding and married life. See also BOTTOM DRAWER. ⌚ 19c: French, meaning 'a little bundle'.

trout ▷ *noun* (***trout*** or ***trouts***) **1 a** any of several freshwater fish of the salmon family that are highly valued as food and by anglers; **b** any of various similar but unrelated fish. **2** *derog* an unpleasant, interfering old person, usually a woman. ⌚ Anglo-Saxon *truht*.

trove see TREASURE-TROVE

trowel /'traʊəl/ ▷ *noun* **1** a small hand-held tool with a flat blade that is used for applying and spreading mortar, plaster, etc. **2** a similar tool with a blade that is slightly curved in on itself and which is used for potting plants, etc. ▷ *verb* (***trowelled, trowelling***) to use a trowel, eg to apply, spread, etc (plaster, etc). • **lay it on with a trowel** to act in an overly sycophantic way; to use excessive flattery. ⌚ 14c: from French *truel*.

troy /trɔɪ/ ▷ *noun* (*in full* **troy weight**) a system of weights used for precious metals and gemstones in which there are 12 ounces or 5 760 grains to the pound. ⌚ 14c: from Troyes, in France.

truant /'truənt/ ▷ *noun* someone who stays away from school or work without good reason or without permission. Also *as adj*. ▷ *verb* (***truanted, truanting***) *intr* to be a truant. • **truancy** *noun*. • **play truant** to stay away from school without good reason and without permission. ⌚ 13c: French, related to Welsh *truan* a wretch.

truce ▷ *noun* **1** an agreement to stop fighting, usually temporarily. **2** a temporary break in fighting, hostilities, feuding, etc. • **call a truce** to agree to an end of hostilities, fighting, feuding, etc. ⌚ 14c: from Anglo-Saxon *treow* truth.

truck[1] ▷ *noun* **1** *Brit* an open railway wagon for carrying goods. **2** *chiefly N Amer* a lorry. **3** a frame with four or more wheels that supports a railway carriage. **4** any wheeled vehicle, trolley or cart for moving heavy goods. **5** a type of steerable axle on a skateboard. ▷ *verb* (***trucked, trucking***) **1 a** to put on or into a truck; **b** to transport by truck. **2** *intr, chiefly N Amer* to work as a truck driver. ⌚ 17c.

truck[2] ▷ *noun* **1** exchange of goods; commercial dealings. **2** payment of wages in goods rather than money. **3** *colloq* small goods or wares. **4** *colloq* odds and ends □ *Clear all the marbles and other truck off the floor.* **5** *especially US* market-garden produce, such as vegetables and fruit. ▷ *verb* (***trucked, trucking***) *intr* to give (goods) in exchange; to barter. • **have no truck with someone** or **something** to avoid them or it; to have nothing to do with them or it. ⌚ 13c: from French *troquer* to exchange.

trucker ▷ *noun, N Amer* someone whose job is to drive a lorry, especially over long distances.

trucking ▷ *noun* the process of transporting (goods, etc) by trucks.

truckle /'trʌkəl/ ▷ *noun* (*in full* **truckle-bed**) a low bed, usually on wheels, that can be stored away when not in use under a larger bed. ▷ *verb* (***truckled, truckling***) *intr* to submit or give in passively or weakly. ⌚ 14c: from Greek *trochileia* a system of pulleys.

truck stop ▷ *noun* a place, usually just off a highway, where truck drivers can get fuel, food and drinks and, sometimes, a bed, shower and basic supplies. *Brit equivalent* TRANSPORT CAFÉ.

truculent /'trʌkjʊlənt/ ▷ *adj* aggressively defiant, quarrelsome or discourteous. • **truculence** *noun*. • **truculently** *adverb*. ⌚ 16c: from Latin *truculentus*.

trudge ▷ *verb* (***trudged, trudging***) **1** *intr* (*usually* **trudge through, along, over,** *etc*) to walk with slow and weary steps □ *trudged through the snow.* **2** to cover (a stated distance, ground, etc) slowly and wearily □ *had to trudge three miles to the nearest shops.* ▷ *noun* a long and tiring walk. ⌚ 16c.

true ▷ *adj* **1** agreeing with fact or reality; not false or wrong. **2** real; genuine; properly so called □ *The spider is not a true insect.* **3** accurate or exact □ *The photograph doesn't give a true idea of the size of the building.* **4** faithful; loyal □ *a true friend* □ *be true to one's word.* **5** conforming to a standard, pattern, type or expectation □ *behaved true to type.* **6** in the correct position; well-fitting; accurately adjusted. **7** said of a compass bearing: measured according to the Earth's axis and not magnetic north. **8** honest; sincere □ *twelve good men and true.* ▷ *adverb* **1** certainly □ *True, she isn't very happy here.* **2** truthfully. **3** faithfully. **4** honestly. **5** accurately or precisely. **6** accurately in tune □ *sing true.* **7** conforming to ancestral type □ *breed true.* ▷ *verb* (***trued, truing***) to bring or restore (eg machinery) into an accurate or required position. • **truly** see separate entry. • **come true** said of a dream, hope, wish, etc: to happen in reality; to be fulfilled. • **out of true** not in the correct position; not straight or properly balanced. • **true to form** said of someone, their behaviour, etc: conforming to what is normal for them or expected of them. ⌚ Anglo-Saxon *treow*.

true-blue *Brit* ▷ *adj* **a** extremely loyal; **b** staunchly orthodox. ▷ *noun* (**true blue**) someone who is unwavering in their support of something, especially the Conservative Party or the Royal Family.

true love ▷ *noun* **1** (*sometimes* **true-love**) someone who is very much loved by another person; a sweetheart. **2** love that is considered to be deep and lasting.

true north ▷ *noun* the direction of the north pole (rather than the direction of MAGNETIC NORTH).

true rib ▷ *noun* a rib that is joined to the breastbone. Compare FALSE RIB, FLOATING RIB.

truffle /'trʌfəl/ ▷ *noun* **1** any of several dark round fungi that grow underground and which are considered a delicacy. **2** a type of chocolate sweet that usually has a centre made with cream, butter, chocolate and some kind of flavouring, eg rum, and is shaped into a ball and dusted with cocoa. ⓒ 16c: French.

trug ▷ *noun, Brit* a shallow rectangular basket with a handle, used for carrying flowers, fruit, vegetables, small garden tools, etc. ⓒ 16c.

truism /ˈtruːɪzəm/ ▷ *noun* a statement that is so obviously true that it requires no discussion; a platitude. • **truistic** *adj.* ⓒ 18c: from TRUE.

truly ▷ *adverb* **1** really. **2** genuinely; honestly. **3** faithfully. **4** accurately; exactly. **5** properly; rightly.

trumeau /ˈtruːmoʊ/ ▷ *noun* (***trumeaux*** /ˈtruːmoʊz/) *archit* a stone pillar or a section of wall that divides a doorway, etc. ⓒ 19c: French, meaning 'calf of the leg'.

trump¹ ▷ *noun* **1 a** (**trumps**) the suit of cards that is declared to be of a higher value than any other suit; **b** (*also* **trump card**) a card of this suit. **2** a secret advantage. **3** *colloq* a helpful, reliable, fine, etc person. ▷ *verb* (***trumped, trumping***) **1 a** to defeat (an ordinary card, a trick with no trumps or an opponent) by playing a trump; **b** *intr* to lay a trump card when an opponent has led with another suit. **2** to win a surprising victory or advantage over (a person, plan, idea, etc). • **come up** or **turn up trumps** *colloq* **1** to be unexpectedly useful or helpful in difficult circumstances. **2** to turn out to be better than expected. ⓒ 16c: a variant of TRIUMPH.

■ **trump something up** to invent or make up false evidence, accusations, etc.

trump² ▷ *noun, old use, poetic* a trumpet. • **the last trump** *relig* the trumpet call to waken the dead on the Day of Judgement. ⓒ 13c: from French *trompe* trumpet.

trumped-up ▷ *adj* said of evidence, an accusation, etc: invented or made up; false.

trumpery /ˈtrʌmpərɪ/ ▷ *noun* (***trumperies***) **1** showy but worthless articles. **2** rubbish. ▷ *adj* showy but worthless. ⓒ 15c: from French *tromperie*, from *tromper* to deceive.

trumpet /ˈtrʌmpɪt/ ▷ *noun* **1 a** a brass musical wind instrument with a narrow tube and flared bell and a set of valves; **b** a similar but simpler instrument that is used, especially by the military, for signalling, fanfares, etc. **2** the corona of a daffodil. **3** any conical device designed to amplify sound, eg an EAR-TRUMPET. **4** the loud cry of an elephant. ▷ *verb* (***trumpeted, trumpeting***) **1** *intr* said of an elephant: to make a loud cry. **2** *intr* to blow a trumpet. **3** to make known or proclaim loudly. • **trumpeter** *noun.* • **trumpeted** *adj.* • **trumpeting** *adj, noun.* • **blow one's own trumpet** to boast about one's own skills, achievements, etc. ⓒ 13c: from French *trompette*.

trumpet call ▷ *noun* **1** a signal or summons on a trumpet. **2** any urgent call to action.

trumpeter swan ▷ *noun* a black-billed American swan, the largest of the world's swans. ⓒ 19c.

truncate ▷ *verb* /trʌŋˈkeɪt/ (***truncated, truncating***) to cut something, eg a tree, word, piece of writing, etc, so as to shorten it. ▷ *adj* /ˈtrʌŋkeɪt/ (*also* **truncated**) said eg of a leaf: having the base or tip cut square. • **truncated** *adj* □ *gave a truncated version of his lecture.* • **truncately** *adverb.* • **truncation** *noun.* ⓒ 15c: from Latin *truncare*, *truncatum* to shorten.

truncheon /ˈtrʌntʃən/ ▷ *noun* **1** a short thick heavy stick that police officers carry and which is used in self-defence or for subduing the unruly, eg in riots, difficult arrest situations, etc. *US equivalent* NIGHT-STICK. **2** a staff of authority or office. ⓒ 14c: from French *tronchon* stump.

trundle /ˈtrʌndəl/ ▷ *verb* (***trundled, trundling***) *tr & intr* to move or roll, or make something move or roll, heavily and clumsily. ▷ *noun* an act or the process of trundling. ⓒ Anglo-Saxon *trendel*.

trunk ▷ *noun* **1** the main stem of a tree without the branches and roots. **2** the body of a person or animal, discounting the head and limbs. **3** the main part of anything. **4** a large rigid box or chest, usually with a hinged lid, used for storing or transporting things, eg clothes, personal items, etc. **5** *N Amer* the boot of a car. **6** the long, muscular nose of an elephant. **7** (**trunks**) men's close-fitting shorts or pants worn especially for swimming. **8** a major body structure, such as a blood vessel, nerve, etc, as opposed to one of its branches. **9** an enclosed duct or shaft for cables, ventilation, etc. ⓒ 15c: from Latin *truncus* a main stem of a tree.

trunk call ▷ *noun, Brit old use* a long-distance telephone call.

trunk line ▷ *noun* **1** a main telephone line between large towns or cities. **2** a main railway line.

trunk road ▷ *noun* a main road between large towns.

truss ▷ *noun* (***trusses***) **1** a framework, eg of wooden or metal beams, that supports a roof, bridge, etc. **2** a belt, bandage, etc worn to support a hernia. **3** a bundle of hay or straw that can be of various weights, eg 56lbs for old hay, 60lbs for new hay or 36lbs for straw. **4** a cluster of flowers or fruit at the top of a main stalk or stem. **5** *archit* a large CORBEL. ▷ *verb* (***trusses, trussed, trussing***) **1** (*often* **truss up**) to tie up or bind tightly. **2** to tie up the legs of (a pig, rabbit, etc), or the wings and legs of (a chicken, etc), before cooking. **3** to support (a roof, bridge, etc) with a truss. • **trussed** *adj.* • **trusser** *noun.* • **trussing** *noun.* ⓒ 13c: from French *trousser*.

trust ▷ *noun* **1** belief or confidence in, or reliance on, the truth, goodness, character, power, ability, etc of someone or something. **2** charge or care □ *The child was placed in my trust.* **3** the state of being responsible for the conscientious performance of some task □ *be in a position of trust.* **4** a task assigned to someone in the belief that they will perform it well and conscientiously. **5** credit □ *put it on trust.* **6** an arrangement by which money or property is managed by one person for the benefit of someone else. **7** the amount of money or property managed by one person for the benefit of another. **8** a group of business firms working together to control the market in a particular commodity, beat down competition, and maximize profits. ▷ *verb* (***trusted, trusting***) **1** *tr & intr* (*usually* **trust someone** or **trust in someone**) to have confidence or faith in them; to depend or rely on them □ *We can trust her to do a good job.* **2** to allow (someone) to use or do something in the belief that they will behave responsibly, honestly, etc □ *I wouldn't trust him with your new car.* **3** (*usually* **trust something** or **someone to someone**) to give them into the care of that person □ *trusted the children to their grandfather.* **4** *tr & intr* to be confident; to hope or suppose □ *I trust you had a good journey.* **5** to give credit to someone, especially in business. • **trustable** *adj.* • **truster** *noun.* • **in trust** said of money, property, etc: under the care, safe-keeping, management, etc of a legally appointed person. • **on trust** on credit. • **take something** or **someone on trust** to accept or believe it or them without verification. • **trust to luck** to hope for a fortunate outcome, especially when a matter is out of one's control. • **trust you, her, him, them,** *etc colloq* a expression that is given when someone does something predictable or something predictable happens □ *Trust it to rain when we planned a picnic.* ⓒ 13c: from Norse *traust*.

trustee /trʌsˈtiː/ ▷ *noun* (***trustees***) **1** someone who manages money or property for someone else. **2** a member of a group of people managing the affairs and business of a company or institution. • **trusteeship** *noun.*

trustful ▷ *adj* **1** having confidence or trust in others. **2** lacking in suspicion. • **trustfully** *adverb.* • **trustfulness** *noun.*

trust fund ▷ *noun* money or property that is held in trust, eg until the owner comes of age.

trusting ▷ *adj* showing trust or having a trustful nature. • **trustingly** *adverb.* • **trustingness** *noun.*

trustworthy /ˈtrʌstwɜːðɪ/ ▻ *adj* able to be trusted or depended on; reliable. • **trustworthily** *adverb*. • **trustworthiness** *noun*.

trusty ▻ *adj* (***trustier***, ***trustiest***) *old use* **1** able to be trusted or depended on □ *my trusty sword.* **2** loyal □ *a trusty servant.* ▻ *noun* (***trusties***) a trusted person, especially a convict who is granted special privileges for good behaviour. • **trustily** *adverb*. • **trustiness** *noun*.

truth /truːθ/ ▻ *noun* **1** the quality or state of being true, genuine or factual. **2** the state of being truthful; sincerity; honesty. **3** that which is true. **4** that which is established or generally accepted as true □ *scientific truths.* **5** strict adherence to an original or standard. • **God's (honest) truth** something that is absolutely true. • **in truth** really, actually. • **to tell the truth** or **truth to tell** to be frank or honest □ *To tell the truth, I really can't stand her.* ◷ Anglo-Saxon *treowth*.

truth drug and **truth serum** ▻ *noun* any of various substances that are supposed to have the effect of making someone tell the truth.

truthful ▻ *adj* **1** said of a person: telling the truth. **2** true; realistic. • **truthfully** *adverb*. • **truthfulness** *noun*.

try ▻ *verb* (***tries***, ***tried***, ***trying***) **1** *tr & intr* to attempt or make an effort; to seek to attain or achieve. **2** (*also* **try out**) to test something or experiment with it in order to assess its usefulness, value, quality, etc. **3 a** to conduct the legal trial of someone □ *tried him for murder*; **b** to examine all the evidence of and decide (a case) in a law court. **4** to exert strain or stress on □ *try the limits of his patience.* ▻ *noun* (***tries***) **1** an attempt or effort. **2** *rugby* the act of carrying the ball over the opponent's goal line and touching it down on the ground, scoring three points in Rugby League or five in Rugby Union and entitling the scoring side to attempt a CONVERSION. • **triable**, **trier** see separate entries. • **try one's hand at something** to see if one can do it, especially at a first attempt. • **try it on** *Brit colloq* to attempt to deceive someone, or to test their patience or tolerance. See also TRY-ON. ◷ 13c: from Latin *triare* to sift or pick out.

▪ **try something on** to put on (clothes, shoes, etc) in order to check the fit, appearance, etc.

▪ **try out** to go, eg to a football, rugby, hockey, etc team, and have trials in the hope of being asked to join the team □ *Phil tried out for Aberdeen when he was only 14.* See also TRY-OUT.

▪ **try something out** to test its qualities, capabilities, etc □ *tried out a new brand of coffee.* See also TRY-OUT.

trying ▻ *adj* causing strain or anxiety; stretching one's patience to the limit.

try-on ▻ *noun* (***try-ons***) *Brit colloq* an attempt to deceive or to test someone's patience.

try-out ▻ *noun* (***try-outs***) *colloq* a test or trial.

trypanosome /ˈtrɪpənəsoʊm/ ▻ *noun* any of several parasitic protozoans that are spread by insects and infest the blood of vertebrates causing SLEEPING SICKNESS and other diseases. • **trypanosomal** or **trypanosomic** /-ˈsɒmɪk/ *adj*. ◷ 19c: from Greek *trypanon* borer + *soma* body.

trypanosomiasis /trɪpənəsoʊˈmaɪəsɪs/ ▻ *noun* a disease, such as SLEEPING SICKNESS, that is spread by insect bites and caused by a trypanosomic infestation of the blood.

trypsin /ˈtrɪpsɪn/ ▻ *noun*, *biochem* a digestive enzyme secreted by the pancreas and which converts proteins into peptones. • **tryptic** *adj*. ◷ 19c: from Greek *tripsis* rubbing (because it was first obtained by rubbing down the pancreas with glycerine).

tryptophan /ˈtrɪptoʊfan/ or **tryptophane** /-feɪn/ ▻ *noun*, *biochem* an essential amino acid found in proteins. ◷ 19c.

trysail /ˈtraɪsəl/ ▻ *noun* a small strong FORE-AND-AFT sail used in stormy weather. ◷ 18c: TRY + SAIL.

tryst /trɪst, traɪst/ *old use or literary* ▻ *noun* **1** an arrangement to meet someone, especially a lover. **2** the meeting itself. **3** (*also* **trysting-place**) the place where such a meeting takes place. ▻ *verb* (***trysted***, ***trysting***) *intr* (*usually* **tryst with**) to arrange a meeting, especially a secret one. ◷ 14c: from French *triste* a hunter's waiting-place.

tsar, **czar** or **tzar** /zɑː(r), tsɑː(r)/ ▻ *noun* **1** *historical* the title of the former emperors of Russia. **2** a despot or tyrant. • **tsardom** *noun*. • **tsarism** *noun*. • **tsarist** *noun*, *adj*. ◷ 16c: Russian, from Latin *Caesar* the family name of the earliest Roman emperors.

tsarevitch, **czarevitch** or **tzarevitch** /ˈzɑːrɪvɪtʃ, ˈtsɑː-/ ▻ *noun* (***tsarevitches***) *historical* the title of a son of a Russian emperor, especially the eldest son. ◷ 18c: Russian, meaning 'son of a tsar'.

tsarevna, **czarevna** or **tzarevna** /zɑːˈrevnə, tsɑː-/ ▻ *noun* (***tsarevnas***) *historical* **1** the daughter of a tsar. **2** the wife of a tsarevitch. ◷ 19c: Russian, meaning 'daughter of a tsar'.

tsarina, **czarina** or **tzarina** /zɑːˈriːnə, tsɑː-/ ▻ *noun* (***tsarinas***) *historical* **1** the title of a former Russian empress. **2** the title of a wife or widow of a tsar. ◷ 18c: probably from German *Zarin*; the Russian feminine form of TSAR is *tsaritsa*.

TSB ▻ *abbreviation* Trustee Savings Bank.

tsetse /ˈtsɛtsɪ/ ▻ *noun* (***tsetses***) (*in full* **tsetse fly**) any of several kinds of African fly which feed on human and animal blood and which transmit several dangerous diseases including SLEEPING SICKNESS. ◷ 19c: the Tswana (a southern African language) name for this kind of fly.

T-shirt or **tee shirt** /ˈtiːʃɜːt/ ▻ *noun* a type of light short-sleeved collarless top, usually made from knitted cotton. ◷ 1920s: so called because of its shape when laid out flat.

tsp ▻ *abbreviation* (***tsps***) teaspoon or teaspoonful.

T-square /ˈtiːskwɛə(r)/ ▻ *noun* a type of T-shaped ruler used for drawing and testing right angles.

TSR ▻ *abbreviation*, *computing* terminate-and-stay-resident.

TSS ▻ *abbreviation* toxic shock syndrome.

tsunami /tsʊˈnɑːmɪ/ ▻ *noun* (***tsunamis***) a type of fast-moving and often very destructive high wave caused by some form of movement in the Earth's surface, eg a volcanic eruption, landslide, etc. Sometimes referred to as a **tidal wave** although it is not associated with the tides. ◷ 19c: Japanese, from *tsu* harbour + *nami* wave.

Tswana /ˈtswɑːnə/ ▻ *noun* (***Tswana*** or ***Tswanas***) **1 a** a S African people who live mainly in Botswana and the surrounding area; **b** someone who belongs to this people. **2** (*also called* **Setswana**) the Bantu language that is spoken by this people. ▻ *adj* belonging or relating to this people or their language. ◷ 1930s: the native name for this people, their language, etc.

TT ▻ *abbreviation* **1 a** teetotal; **b** teetotaller. **2** Tourist Trophy. **3** *IVR* Trinadad and Tobago. **4** tuberculin tested.

TTL ▻ *abbreviation* through-the-lens, *denoting* a system of metering light in cameras.

Tuareg /ˈtwɑːrɛg/ ▻ *noun* **1 a** a nomadic people who live in the western and central Sahara; **b** someone who belongs to this people. **2** the Berber language spoken by this people. ▻ *adj* belonging or relating to this people or their language. ◷ 19c: the native name for this people, their language, etc.

tuatara /tʊəˈtɑːrə/ ▻ *noun* (***tuataras***) a type of rare lizard-like reptile once native throughout New Zealand but now found only on certain islands off the mainland. ◷ 19c: Maori, from *tua* on the back + *tara* spine.

tub ▷ *noun* **1** any of various large, low, round, wooden, metal or plastic containers, usually for holding water. **2** a small round plastic or cardboard container for cream, ice-cream, yoghurt, margarine, etc. **3** a TUBFUL ▫ *ate a whole tub of ice-cream himself.* **4** (*in full* **bathtub**) a bath. **5** *colloq* a slow and often clumsy boat. **6** *mining* an open-topped wooden or metal box on wheels that is used for transporting coal or ore from the face to the surface. ▷ *verb* (***tubbed***, ***tubbing***) **1** to soak, bathe, wash, etc in a tub. **2** to put or enclose in a tub. • **tubbable** *adj* able to be washed in a tub. • **tubber** *noun.* ⓒ 14c: from English *tubbe*.

tuba /'tʃuːbə/ ▷ *noun* (***tubas***) **1** a type of bass brass musical wind instrument that has three to five valves, a mouthpiece set at right angles, a conical bore and a wide bell that points upward. **2** someone who plays this instrument, especially in an orchestra ▫ *The tubas stood up.* ⓒ 19c: Latin and Italian *tuba*, originally the name for a straight Roman war trumpet.

tubby /'tʌbɪ/ ▷ *adj* (***tubbier***, ***tubbiest***) *colloq* **1** said of a person: plump; podgy. **2** shaped or sounding like a tub. • **tubbiness** *noun.* ⓒ 19c: from TUB.

tube /tʃuːb/ ▷ *noun* **1** a long hollow cylinder which can be flexible or rigid and which is designed for holding or conveying air, liquids, etc. See also INNER TUBE. **2** a body structure of similar shape and design in an animal or plant ▫ *bronchial tubes.* **3** a squeezable, approximately cylindrical container that is made from soft metal or plastic with a cap at one end, and that contains a paste, a semi-liquid substance, etc. **4** *Brit* **a** an underground railway system, especially the London one; **b** (*in full* **tube train**) an underground train. Compare SUBWAY. **5 a** a cathode ray tube; **b** *colloq* a television set. **6** *N Amer* a thermionic valve. **7** *surfing* the rounded hollow that a breaking wave forms between its crest and the trough ▫ *tried to shoot the tube.* **8** *colloq* an extremely stupid person. ▷ *verb* (***tubed***, ***tubing***) **1** to fit with a tube or tubes. **2** to enclose in a tube. • **tubal** *adj.* • **tubed** *adj.* • **tubelike** *adj.* • **tubiform** *adj.* • **go down the tubes** *colloq* to fail dismally; to be ruined. ⓒ 17c: from Latin *tubus* pipe.

tubectomy /tʃuː'bɛktəmɪ/ ▷ *noun* (***tubectomies***) *surgery* the removal of a Fallopian tube.

tube foot ▷ *noun* in ECHINODERMS: any of the small tubelike protrusions that are used in locomotion, respiration or the ingestion of food.

tubeless ▷ *adj* **1** without a tube or tubes. **2** said of a tyre: not having an INNER TUBE.

tuber /'tʃuːbə(r)/ ▷ *noun* **1** *bot* **a** a swollen rounded underground stem or RHIZOME, such as that of the potato, where food is stored allowing the plant to survive from one growing season to the next, and which may also have buds or 'eyes' on the surface which can develop into new plants; **b** a similar structure that is formed from a root, eg that of a dahlia. **2** *anatomy* a thickened region or swelling. • **tuberiferous** /-'rɪfərəs/ or **tuberiform** /'tʃuː-/ *adj.* ⓒ 17c: Latin *tuber* a swelling.

tubercle /'tʃuːbəkəl/ ▷ *noun* **1** a small round swelling or lump, eg on a bone. **2** a small round swelling in an organ, especially one in the lung that is caused by a bacillus and which is characteristic of tuberculosis. • **tubercled** *adj.* ⓒ 16c: from Latin *tuberculum* small swelling.

tubercle bacillus ▷ *noun* the type of bacillus that causes tuberculosis.

tubercular /tʃʊ'bɜːkjʊlə(r)/ ▷ *adj* (*also* **tuberculous** /tʃʊ'bɜːkjʊləs/) **1** affected by or suffering from tuberculosis. **2** belonging or relating to, or having, tubercles. ▷ *noun* someone who is suffering from tuberculosis.

tuberculate /tʃʊ'bɜːkjʊleɪt/ ▷ *adj* affected by or covered with tubercles. • **tuberculated** *adj.* • **tuberculation** *noun.*

tuberculin /tʃʊ'bɜːkjʊlɪn/ ▷ *noun* a sterile liquid preparation that is extracted from a culture of the bacillus which causes tuberculosis, used to test for the disease and also formerly in its treatment.

tuberculin-tested (abbreviation **TT**) ▷ *adj* said of milk: produced by cows that have been tested for and certified free from tuberculosis.

tuberculosis /tʃʊbɜːkjʊ'loʊsɪs/ ▷ *noun* (abbreviation **TB**) any of various infectious diseases of humans and animals that are caused by the tubercle bacillus and which are characterized by the formation of tubercles, eg **pulmonary tuberculosis** which affects the lungs (formerly known as **consumption**) or **scrofula** which affects the lymphatic system. ⓒ 19c: from Latin *tuberculum* small swelling.

tuberculous see TUBERCULAR

tuberose¹ /'tʃuːbəroʊs/ ▷ *noun* a plant that has large creamy-white funnel-shaped flowers and a tuberous root and which is valued for its strong sweet perfume. ⓒ 17c: from Latin *tuberosa*, the name for this type of plant.

tuberose² see TUBEROUS

tuberous /'tʃuːbərəs/ or **tuberose** /'tʃuːbəroʊs/ ▷ *adj* **1** having tubers. **2** relating to or like a tuber. • **tuberosity** /-'rɒsɪtɪ/ *noun.*

tuberous root ▷ *noun* a thick fleshy root that resembles a true tuber but which has no buds or 'eyes'.

tube worm ▷ *noun* any of several types of worm that construct a tubelike hole, usually of sand, to live in.

tubful ▷ *noun* (***tubfuls***) the amount a tub can hold.

tubing /'tʃuːbɪŋ/ ▷ *noun* **1** a length of tube or a system of tubes. **2** material that tubes can be made from. ▷ *verb, present participle of* TUBE.

tub-thumper ▷ *noun, colloq* a passionate or ranting public speaker or preacher. • **tub-thumping** *adj, noun.*

tubular /'tʃuːbjʊlə(r)/ ▷ *adj* **1** made or consisting of tubes or tube-shaped pieces. **2** shaped like a tube.

tubular bells ▷ *noun* a set of brass tubes of differing lengths that have been tuned to different pitches and suspended in a large frame in the same arrangement as a keyboard. They are used in orchestral and operatic music and are played by striking them with a short mallet to simulate the sounds of bells. ⓒ Early 20c.

tubule /'tʃuːbjuːl/ ▷ *noun* a small tube in the body of an animal or plant. ⓒ 17c: from Latin *tubulus*, a diminutive of *tubus* a tube.

TUC ▷ *abbreviation, Brit* Trades Union Congress.

tuck ▷ *verb* (***tucked***, ***tucking***) **1** (*usually* **tuck in, into, under, up**, *etc*) to push or fold something into a specified position ▫ *tucked the note into the envelope* ▫ *tucked her hair under her hat.* **2** to make a tuck or tucks in (a piece of material, clothing, etc). **3** to carry out a cosmetic operation to tighten a flabby part, smooth out wrinkles or remove fat. ▷ *noun* **1** a flat pleat or fold sewn into a garment or piece of material, especially one that shortens it, makes it tighter or has a decorative effect. **2** *Brit colloq* food, especially sweets, cakes, etc, eaten by children as snacks. **3** (*in full* **tuck position**) *gymnastics, diving, trampolining, etc* a position where the knees are drawn up towards the chin and the hands hug the shins. **4** *downhill skiing* a type of squatting position where the skier hugs the poles close to the body to minimize wind resistance. **5** a cosmetic operation to tighten a flabby part, smooth out wrinkles or remove fat ▫ *had a tummy tuck.* See also NIP AND TUCK. ⓒ Anglo-Saxon *tucian* to disturb.

■ **tuck something away** *colloq* **1** to eat (large quantities of food), especially heartily and with enjoyment. **2** to store or conceal, especially in a place that is difficult to find ▫ *Their cottage was tucked away from prying eyes.*

■ **tuck in** (*also* **tuck into something**) *colloq* to eat heartily or greedily ▫ *tucked into a huge plate of chips.*

■ **tuck someone in** *colloq* to put someone to bed, make them cosy by pulling the covers, duvet, etc snugly around them, and often give them a goodnight kiss.

■ **tuck someone up** to pull or bring covers, a duvet, etc closely around them ▫ *You should tuck yourself up in bed with a hot toddy.*

■ **tuck something up** to draw or put it into a folded position ▫ *tucked her legs up*

tuck box ▻ *noun* a container for food, especially one that has treats in it and which is used by children at boarding school.

tucker¹ ▻ *noun* **1** someone or something that tucks. **2** *historical* a piece of material, lace, etc that is drawn or fastened over the bodice of a low-cut dress. **3** *colloq* food. • **best bib and tucker** *colloq* best clothes. ⓒ 15c: from TUCK.

tucker² ▻ *verb* (***tuckered***, ***tuckering***) (*usually* **tucker out**) to tire. • **tuckered-out** *adj.* ⓒ 19c: from TUCK.

tuckerbag and **tuckerbox** ▻ *noun, chiefly Austral & NZ* a bag or box used for carrying food.

tuck-in ▻ *noun, colloq* a big feast.

tuck shop ▻ *noun, Brit* a small shop that sells sweets, cakes, pastries, etc in or near a school.

Tudor /ˈtʃuːdə(r)/ ▻ *adj* **1 a** belonging or relating to the royal family which ruled England from 1485 to 1603; **b** belonging or relating to this period in English history, ie the reigns of Henry VII, Henry VIII, Edward VI, Mary I and Elizabeth I. **2** denoting the style of architecture that was prominent during this period, having visible external HALF-TIMBER work (usually set in white plaster or brick), lattice windows, extensive internal wood panelling and often fancy plasterwork on the ceiling, cornices, etc. ▻ *noun* a member of the House of Tudor. • **Tudoresque** /-ˈɛsk/ or **Tudor-style** *adj.* ⓒ 18c: from the Welsh surname *Tewdwr*, the family name of Henry Tudor who married Henry V's widow Catherine.

Tudor rose ▻ *noun* a conventionalized figure of a rose that Henry VII adopted as an emblem and which was used in Tudor architecture, decoration, heraldry, etc. It symbolically combined the red rose of the House of Lancaster and the white rose of the House of York.

Tues or **Tues.** ▻ *abbreviation* (*also* **Tue** or **Tue.**) Tuesday.

Tuesday /ˈtʃuːzdɪ, -deɪ/ ▻ *noun* the third day of the week, the day after Monday but before Wednesday. ⓒ Anglo-Saxon *Tiwesdaeg* Tiw's day, from Tiw, the Teutonic god of war.

tufa /ˈtuːfə, ˈtʃuːfə/ ▻ *noun* (***tufas***) *geol* a type of white spongy porous rock that forms in a calcium carbonate incrustation in areas around springs, streams, etc that are rich in lime. • **tufaceous** /tuːˈfeɪʃəs, tʃuː-/ *adj.* ⓒ 19c in this sense; 18c as a generic term for porous rock: Italian, from Latin *tofus* soft stone.

tuff ▻ *noun* rock that is largely composed of fine volcanic fragments and dust. • **tuffaceous** /tʌˈfeɪʃəs/ *adj.* ⓒ 19c in this sense; 16c, meaning any light porous rock: from Latin *tofus* soft stone.

tuffet /ˈtʌfət/ ▻ *noun* **1** a small grassy mound. **2** a low seat. ⓒ 16c: a variant of TUFT.

tuft ▻ *noun* **1** a small bunch or clump of grass, hair, feathers, wool, etc attached or growing together at the base. **2** *anatomy* a group of small blood vessels. ▻ *verb* (***tufted***, ***tufting***) **1** to grow or form in a tuft or tufts. **2** *upholstery* to use thread to draw two sides of (a cushion, mattress, etc) together so that the padding is secured and a regular pattern of depressions is produced, each depression then being covered with a button or a tuft of threads. • **tufting** *noun.* • **tufty** *adj* (***tuftier***, ***tuftiest***). ⓒ 14c.

tufted ▻ *adj* **1** having, forming or growing in a tuft or tufts. **2** said of a bird: having a tuft of feathers on its head.

tufted duck ▻ *noun* a freshwater European duck that has black or brown and white feathers and, in the males, a drooping black crest.

tug ▻ *verb* (***tugged***, ***tugging***) *tr & intr* **1** (*sometimes* **tug at** or **on**) to pull sharply or strongly ▫ *tugged the money from her pocket* ▫ *Spike tugs at the lead until he gets to the park.* **2** to tow (a ship, barge, oil platform, etc) with a tugboat. ▻ *noun* **1 a** a strong sharp pull; **b** a sharp or sudden pang of emotion. **2** a hard struggle. **3** (*in full* **tugboat**) a small boat with a very powerful engine, for towing larger ships, barges, oil platforms, etc. **4** an aircraft designed to tow a glider into the air. • **tugger** *noun.* • **tugging** *adj, noun.* • **tug at someone's heartstrings** to touch their deepest feelings, emotions, etc. ⓒ 13c as *toggen*: from Anglo-Saxon *teon* to tow.

tug-of-love ▻ *noun* (***tugs-of-love***) *Brit colloq* a dispute over the guardianship of a child, eg between divorced parents.

tug-of-war ▻ *noun* (***tugs-of-war***) **1** a contest in which two people or teams pull at opposite ends of a rope and try to haul their opponents over a centre line. **2** any hard struggle between two opposing sides.

tugrik /ˈtuːgriːk/ ▻ *noun* the standard unit of currency of Mongolia. ⓒ 1930s: Mongolian, meaning 'disk'.

tui /ˈtuːiː/ ▻ *noun* (***tuis***) a type of New Zealand HONEY-EATER that has glossy black feathers with a distinctive tuft of white ones at its throat, renowned as a mimic of human voices and of other songbirds. Also called **parson bird**. ⓒ 19c: the Maori name for this bird.

tuition /tʃʊˈɪʃən/ ▻ *noun* **1** teaching or instruction, especially when paid for, or in a college or university ▫ *driving tuition.* **2** the fee levied or paid for teaching or instruction. • **tuitional** or **tuitionary** *adj.* ⓒ 16c in this sense; 13c, meaning 'custody or care': from Latin *tuitio* guard or guardianship.

tularaemia or (*US*) **tularemia** /tuːləˈriːmɪə, tʃuː-/ ▻ *noun* a type of infectious disease that affects rodents and rabbits and which can be transmitted to humans by infected insects or by handling infected animals or their flesh. The symptoms include fever, chills, headache and muscle pain. • **tularaemic** *adj.* ⓒ 1920s: named after Tulare County in California where it was first recorded + Greek *haima* blood.

tulip /ˈtʃuːlɪp/ ▻ *noun* **1** any of several spring-flowering perennial plants which each have an underground bulb and produce a single cup-shaped flower on a long stem. **2** a flower of this plant. **3** *as adj, denoting* something that is shaped like a tulip ▫ *tulip wine glasses.* ⓒ 16c: from the Turkish pronunciation of Persian *dulband* turban.

tulip root ▻ *noun* a disease that affects the roots of oats, characterized by a nodular swelling at the base of the stem which is caused by a type of tiny nematoid worm. ⓒ 18c.

tulip tree ▻ *noun* any of various N American trees, especially those of the magnolia family, that have tulip-like flowers.

tulip wood ▻ *noun* the pale fine-grained wood of the tulip tree which is used by cabinet makers in making furniture and in veneers. ⓒ 19c.

tulle /tʃuːl, tuːl/ ▻ *noun* a delicate thin netted cloth made of silk or rayon that was popularly used, especially in the 19c, for making veils, dresses, hats, etc. ⓒ 19c: named after the town of Tulle in SW France where it was first made.

tum ▻ *noun, Brit colloq* the stomach. ⓒ 19c: a short form of TUMMY.

tumble /'tʌmbəl/ ▷ *verb* (***tumbled***, ***tumbling***) **1** *tr & intr* (*often* **tumble down, over**, *etc*) to fall or make someone or something fall headlong, especially suddenly or clumsily. **2** *intr* to fall or collapse suddenly, especially in value or amount. **3** *tr & intr* (*often* **tumble about, around**, *etc*) to roll over and over or toss around helplessly □ *The kids tumbled around in the garden.* **4** *intr* to perform as an acrobat, especially turning somersaults. **5** *intr* to move or rush in a confused hasty way □ *tumble out of the car.* **6** to rumple or disorder □ *tumble the bedclothes.* **7** (*also* **tumble to something**) *colloq* to understand, realize or become aware of, especially suddenly □ *tumbled to their intentions.* **8** to dry (wet laundry) in a tumble-drier. ▷ *noun* **1** an act of tumbling. **2** a fall. **3** a somersault. **4** a confused or untidy state or heap. • **tumbling** *noun, adj.* • **take a tumble to oneself** *colloq* to take a look at one's situation and do something to improve it □ *It's two years since he left school and he's never had a job — I wish he'd take a tumble to himself.* ⓒ Anglo-Saxon *tumbian*.

tumbledown ▷ *adj* said of a building, etc: falling to pieces; ramshackle.

tumble-dry ▷ *verb, tr & intr* to dry in a tumble-dryer.

tumble-dryer or **tumble-drier** ▷ *noun* an electrically powered machine that can be either part of a washing machine or free-standing, which is used for drying wet laundry by tumbling it around in a current of warm air.

tumbler ▷ *noun* **1 a** a flat-bottomed drinking cup without a stem or handle, usually of glass or plastic; **b** a TUMBLERFUL. **2** an acrobat, especially one who performs somersaults. **3** *colloq* a tumble-dryer. **4** the part of a lock which holds the bolt in place until it is moved by a key. **5** the part of a firearm which is released by the trigger and forces the hammer forward. **6** (*in full* **tumbler-box**) a machine with a revolving drum in which gemstones are polished.

tumblerful ▷ *noun* (***tumblerfuls***) the amount a tumbler can hold.

tumbleweed ▷ *noun* a name for various plants that grow in arid areas, especially in the US and Australia, and which in late summer become so dried up that they curl into a ball and snap off above the root to be blown about in the wind. ⓒ 19c.

tumbling see under TUMBLE

tumbling-barrel ▷ *noun* a TUMBLER sense 6.

tumbrel or **tumbril** /'tʌmbrəl/ ▷ *noun* **1** a two-wheeled cart that can be tipped over backwards to empty its load. **2** *historical* a similar type of cart that was used during the French Revolution to take people who had been sentenced to death to the guillotine. **3** *historical* a two-wheeled covered military cart that was used for carrying ammunition and other supplies. ⓒ 15c, meaning 'cart'; found earlier as the name of an instrument of punishment: from French *tomberel*.

tumefy /'tʃuːmɪfaɪ/ ▷ *verb* (***tumefies***, ***tumefied***, ***tumefying***) to swell or puff up. • **tumefacient** /-'feɪʃənt/ *adj.* • **tumefaction** /-'fakʃən/ *noun.* ⓒ 16c: from French *tumefier*.

tumescent /tʃu'mɛsənt/ ▷ *adj* swollen or becoming swollen, especially with blood as a response to sexual stimulation. • **tumescence** *noun.* • **tumescently** *adverb.* ⓒ 19c: from Latin *tumescere* to begin to swell up.

tumid /'tʃuːmɪd/ ▷ *adj* **1** said of an organ or body part: swollen, enlarged or bulging, especially abnormally so. **2** said of writing, speech, etc: bombastic; inflated. • **tumidity** or **tumidness** *noun.* • **tumidly** *adverb.* ⓒ 16c: from Latin *tumidus*, from *tumere* to swell.

tummy /'tʌmɪ/ ▷ *noun* (***tummies***) *colloq* **1** a name for the stomach. **2** a type of upset stomach that is associated with foreign travel □ *spent most of the holiday suffering from Spanish tummy.* ⓒ 19c: a childish pronunciation of STOMACH.

tummy-ache see STOMACH-ACHE

tummy-button see under BELLY BUTTON

tumour or (*US*) **tumor** /'tʃuːmə(r)/ ▷ *noun* **1** *pathol* an abnormal growth of benign or malignant cells that develops in, or on the surface of, normal body tissue. **2** any abnormal swelling that is not caused by bacterial infection or inflammation. • **tumorous** *adj.* ⓒ 16c: from Latin *tumor*, from *tumere* to swell.

tumult /'tʃuːmʌlt/ ▷ *noun* **1** a great or confused noise, eg as made by a crowd; an uproar. **2** a violent or angry commotion or disturbance. **3** a state of extreme confusion, agitation, etc □ *a mind in tumult.* ⓒ 15c: from Latin *tumultus* commotion.

tumultuous /tʃu'mʌltʃuəs/ ▷ *adj* **1** noisy and enthusiastic □ *his usual tumultuous welcome.* **2** disorderly; unruly. **3** agitated. • **tumultuously** *adverb.* • **tumultuousness** *noun.*

tumulus /'tʃuːmjʊləs, 'tʊmʊlʊs/ ▷ *noun* (***tumuli*** /-laɪ/) *archaeol* an ancient burial mound or barrow. • **tumular** *adj.* ⓒ 17c: Latin, from *tumere* to swell.

tun ▷ *noun* **1** a large cask for holding liquid, eg ale, beer or wine. **2** *historical* the amount that this kind of cask holds, usually thought of as 216 imperial gallons or 252 old wine-gallons, used as a measure for liquids. ▷ *verb* (***tunned***, ***tunning***) to put or store (liquid, eg ale, beer or wine) in a tun. ⓒ Anglo-Saxon *tunne*.

tuna¹ /'tʃuːnə, 'tuːnə/ ▷ *noun* (***tuna*** or ***tunas***) (*in full* **tuna fish**) **1** any of several large marine fish that live in warm and tropical seas and are related to the mackerel. **2** the flesh of this fish. Also (*Brit*) called TUNNY. ⓒ 19c.

tuna² /'tʃuːnə, 'tuːnə/ ▷ *noun* (***tunas***) **1** any of various types of PRICKLY PEAR that are taller and more tree-like than most other varieties and which originate from Central America and the West Indies. **2** the fruit of this plant. ⓒ 16c: thought to be a Haitian word that has passed through Spanish and into English.

tundra /'tʌndrə/ ▷ *noun* (***tundras***) *geog* any of the vast relatively flat treeless zones that lie to the south of the polar ice cap in America and Eurasia where the subsoil is permanently frozen. ⓒ 19c: the Lapp name for this kind of region.

tune /tʃuːn/ ▷ *noun* **1** a pleasing succession of musical notes; a melody. **2** the correct, or a standard, musical pitch. ▷ *verb* (***tuned***, ***tuning***) **1** *tr & intr* (*also* **tune up**) to adjust (a musical instrument or instruments, their keys or strings, etc) to the correct or a standard pitch. **2 a** to adjust (a radio, TV, video recorder, etc) so that it can pick up signals from a specified frequency, station; **b** *intr* (*usually* **tune in**) to have a radio adjusted to receive a specified signal, station, DJ, etc and listen to it or them □ *tunes in to Chris Evans every morning.* **3** to adjust (an engine, machine, etc) so that it runs properly and efficiently. See also FINE-TUNE. • **tuning** *noun.* • **call the tune** *colloq* to be in charge. • **change one's tune** to change one's attitude, opinions, approach or way of talking. • **in tune 1** said of a voice or musical instrument: having or producing the correct or a required pitch □ *sing in tune.* **2** having the same pitch as other instruments or voices □ *The two guitars are not in tune.* • **in tune with someone** or **something** being aware of and able to relate to them or it □ *in tune with public opinion.* • **out of tune 1** not having or producing the correct or a required pitch. **2** not having the same pitch as other instruments or voices. • **out of tune with someone** or **something** not being aware of and able to relate to them or it □ *completely out of tune with the latest technology.* • **to the tune of** *colloq* to the (considerable) sum or total of □ *had to shell out to the tune of 500 quid for the car repairs.* • **tunable** or **tuneable** *adj.* ⓒ 14c: a variant of TONE.

tuneful ▷ *adj* **1** having a good, clear, pleasant, etc tune; melodious. **2** full of music. • **tunefully** *adverb.* • **tunefulness** *noun.*

tuneless ▷ *adj* lacking a good, pleasant, etc tune; not melodious. • **tunelessly** *adverb.* • **tunelessness** *noun.*

tuner /ˈtʃuːnə(r)/ ▷ *noun* **1** someone whose job is tuning instruments, especially pianos. **2** *electronics* an electronic circuit that acts as a filter for radio or television broadcast signals, by selecting one specific frequency, eg the channel selector on a television set. **3** a knob, dial, etc, that is used to adjust a radio to different wavelengths corresponding to different stations. **4** a radio that is part of a stereo sound system.

tuner-amplifier ▷ *noun* a unit that combines a radio tuner and an amplifier.

tung /tʌŋ/ ▷ *noun* **1** (*in full* **tung tree**) any of three types of tree that are native to China and Japan and which are grown commercially for the oil in their seeds. Also called **tung-oil tree**. **2** (*in full* **tung oil**) the oil extracted from the seeds of any of these trees, which is waterproof and particularly quick drying, making it suitable for use in paints, varnishes, printing inks, etc. ◷ 19c: from Chinese *tong* a tung tree.

tungsten /ˈtʌŋstən/ ▷ *noun, chem* (symbol **W**, atomic number 74) a very hard silvery-white metallic element that occurs naturally in scheelite and is notable for its very high melting point. It is used in the manufacture of filaments of electric light bulbs, X-ray tubes and TV sets and in steel alloys that are used in turbine blades and cutting tools. Also called **wolfram**. ◷ 18c: Swedish, from *tung* heavy + *sten* stone.

tungsten lamp ▷ *noun* a type of electrically powered lamp that has a tungsten filament which, when heated to incandescence, produces light.

Tungus /ˈtʊŋʊs, ˈtʊŋgʊs/ ▷ *noun* (***Tungus*** or ***Tunguses***) **1** a Mongolian people of E Siberia. **2** an individual who belongs to this people. **3** the Altaic language that is spoken by this people. • **Tungusic** *adj*. ◷ 17c: the Yakut name for this people.

tunic /ˈtʃuːnɪk/ ▷ *noun* **1** a close-fitting, usually belted jacket which forms part of the uniform of the military, police, security services, etc. **2** **a** a loose garment, often sleeveless, that covers the upper body usually coming down as far as the hip or knee and sometimes belted or gathered at the waist; **b** a garment of this kind as worn in ancient Greece and Rome; **c** a garment of this kind as worn by men in the Middle Ages; **d** a garment of this kind as worn, especially by women, with a blouse or T-shirt over trousers; **e** (*in full* **gym tunic**) a garment of this kind as worn by schoolgirls. **3** *anatomy* a membrane that envelops or lines a body organ. **4** *bot* **a** a concentric layer of a bulb; **b** a covering membrane of one of these layers. • **tunicked** *adj*. ◷ Anglo-Saxon, from Latin *tunica* a tunic.

tunicle /ˈtʃuːnɪkəl/ ▷ *noun* a garment similar to the DALMATIC that a subdeacon wears over the ALB (or which a bishop wears between the alb and the dalmatic) at celebrations of the Eucharist. ◷ 15c: a diminutive of TUNIC.

tuning see under TUNE

tuning fork ▷ *noun* a small device used for tuning musical instruments and testing acoustics, etc, consisting of a stem with two prongs at the top which, when made to vibrate, produce a specified musical note. ◷ 18c: invented in 1711 by the English trumpeter John Shore (c.1662–1752).

Tunisian /tʃuːˈnɪzɪən/ ▷ *adj* **a** belonging or relating to Tunisia, a republic in N Africa; **b** belonging or relating to Tunisia's capital city, Tunis, or to its inhabitants. ▷ *noun* a citizen or inhabitant of, or someone born in, Tunisia or Tunis. ◷ 19c.

tunned *past tense, past participle of* TUN

tunnel /ˈtʌnəl/ ▷ *noun* **1** a constructed underground passage through or under some obstruction, eg a hill, river, road, etc, allowing access for pedestrians, vehicles, trains, etc. **2** an underground passage that a burrowing animal, such as a mole, digs, often one of a connected series. **3** a period of difficulty, problems, stress or exceptionally hard work ▫ ***After years of poverty they could at last see the light at the end of the tunnel.*** ▷ *verb* (***tunnelled***, ***tunnelling***; (*US*) ***tunneled***, ***tunneling***) **1** *intr* (*often* **tunnel through, under**, *etc*) to make a tunnel through, under, etc (a hill, river, road, etc). **2** to make (a tunnel or passageway) through, under, etc a hill, river, road, etc. **3** (**tunnel one's way**) to make one's way by digging a tunnel. • **tunneller** *noun*. • **tunnelling** *adj, noun*. ◷ 15c: from French *tonel* cask.

tunnel-of-love ▷ *noun* a type of fairground amusement where people, especially courting couples, take a trip through a darkened tunnel on a train or boat.

tunnel vision ▷ *noun* **1** a medical condition in which one is unable to see objects on the periphery of the field of vision. **2** **a** the inability or unwillingness to consider other opinions, viewpoints, etc; **b** single-minded determination.

tunning *present participle of* TUN

tunny /ˈtʌnɪ/ ▷ *noun* (***tunnies***) (*in full* **tunny-fish**) *especially Brit* tuna. ◷ 16c: from French *thon* tuna.

tup *Brit* ▷ *noun* **1** a ram. **2** the face of a steam-hammer, pile-driver, etc that does the striking. ▷ *verb* (***tupped***, ***tupping***) said of a ram: to copulate with (a ewe). ◷ 14c.

tupelo /ˈtʃuːpɪloʊ/ ▷ *noun* (***tupelos***) any of several large deciduous N American trees, eg the American gum tree, that grow in the swamps and on the river banks in the southern states. ◷ 18c: a Native North American name for this tree.

Tupí /tuːˈpiː, ˈtuːpiː/ ▷ *noun* (***Tupí*** or ***Tupís***) **1** a group of Native American peoples who live in the Amazon basin. **2** an individual who belongs to one of these peoples. **3** the language of these peoples. ▷ *adj* belonging or relating to these peoples or their language. • **Tupían** *adj, noun*. ◷ 19c.

tupik /ˈtuːpɪk/ ▷ *noun* a type of traditional seal or caribou skin tent or hut that Inuits in the Canadian Arctic use for shelter during the summer. ◷ 19c: from Inuit *tupiq*.

tupped, tupping see under TUP

tuppence, tuppenny see TWOPENCE, TWOPENNY

Tupperware /ˈtʌpəwɛə(r)/ ▷ *noun, trademark* a brand of plastic kitchenware, eg storage containers, serving dishes, gadgets, etc, that is sold by agents on a commission basis through holding parties in people's homes. ◷ 1950s: named after Earl S Tupper, President of Tupper Corporation + WARE sense 1.

tuque /tuːk/ ▷ *noun* a type of Canadian tubular cap that is closed at both ends and which is worn by tucking one end inside itself to form the part where the head goes while the other end is left free. ◷ 19c: Canadian French *toque* a small cap or bonnet.

turaco or **touraco** /ˈtʊərəkoʊ/ ▷ *noun* (***turacos***) any of several varieties of large African fruit-eating birds that are noted for the vivid scarlets, blues and greens of their feathers and their prominent crests. ◷ 18c: from French *touraco* or Dutch *toerako*.

turban /ˈtɜːbən/ ▷ *noun* **1** a type of headdress formed by wrapping a long cloth sash around the head or a cap and which is worn especially by Muslim and Sikh men. **2** a woman's hat that looks similar to this. • **turbaned** *adj*. ◷ 16c: probably a Turkish pronunciation of *dulband*, the Persian name for this kind of headdress.

turbary /ˈtɜːbərɪ/ ▷ *noun* (***turbaries***) **1** an area of land that has been designated as a place where peat may be dug. **2** in England: (*in full* **common of turbary**) the legal right to cut peat from a designated piece of land. ◷ 14c: from Latin *turbaria*, from *turba* turf.

turbellarian /tɜːbəˈlɛərɪən/ ▷ *noun, zool* a type of flatworm that lives in salt or fresh water and which propels itself along by the cilia (see CILIUM) that cover its body, producing little whirlpools in the water. ▷ *adj* belonging or relating to this type of flatworm. ◷ 19c: from Latin *turbella*, a diminutive of *turba* a crowd.

turbid /ˈtɜːbɪd/ ▷ *adj* **1** said of liquid, etc: cloudy; not clear. **2** said of air, clouds, etc: thick or dense ◻ ***a turbid fog.*** **3** said of a piece of writing, the construction of an argument, etc: confused; disordered; unclear. • **turbidity** or **turbidness** *noun*. • **turbidly** *adverb*. ◷ 17c: from Latin *turbidus* full of confusion, from *turba* a crowd.

turbinate /ˈtɜːbɪnət/ ▷ *adj* **1** like a spinning top. **2** *zool* said of the shells of certain molluscs: spiral. **3** *bot* shaped like an inverted cone with a narrow base and a wider top. **4** *anatomy* said especially of certain nasal bones: scroll-shaped. • **turbinal** *adj*. • **turbinated** *adj*. • **turbination** *noun*. ◷ 17c: Latin *turbinatus*, from *turbo* a whirlwind.

turbine /ˈtɜːbaɪn, -bɪn/ ▷ *noun* any of several types of power-generating machine that have a rotating wheel driven by water, steam, gas, etc. ◷ 19c: French, from Latin *turbo* whirlwind.

turbit /ˈtɜːbɪt/ ▷ *noun* a fancy variety of domestic pigeon that has a squat body, a short beak and a frill around its neck and breast. ◷ 17c: perhaps from Latin *turbo* a spinning-top.

turbo /ˈtɜːboʊ/ ▷ *noun* (***turbos***) **1** a short form of TURBOCHARGER. **2 a** *colloq* a car fitted with a turbocharger; **b** *as adj* ◻ ***drives around in her turbo Saab.***

turbo- /ˈtɜːboʊ/ ▷ *combining form, forming words, denoting* something that has, or is driven by, a turbine. ◷ from Latin *turbo* whirlwind.

turbocharge ▷ *verb* (***turbocharged, turbocharging***) to fit (an engine) with a turbocharger. • **turbocharged** *adj*.

turbocharger ▷ *noun* a type of SUPERCHARGER driven by a turbine which is itself powered by the exhaust gases of the engine. Often shortened to TURBO.

turbofan ▷ *noun* **1** a jet engine driven by a gas turbine in which part of the power developed is used to drive a fan which blows air out of the exhaust and so increases thrust. **2** an aircraft powered by this kind of engine.

turbojet ▷ *noun* **1** (*in full* **turbojet engine**) a type of gas turbine that uses exhaust gases to provide the propulsive thrust in an aircraft. **2** an aircraft powered by this kind of engine.

turboprop ▷ *noun* **1** a jet engine in which the turbine drives a propeller. **2** an aircraft powered by this kind of engine.

turbot /ˈtɜːbət/ ▷ *noun* (***turbot*** or ***turbots***) **1** a large flatfish that has bony tubercles instead of scales and eyes on the left side of its head and which is highly valued as food. **2** a name applied to other similar fish. ◷ 13c: from French *tourbout*.

turbulence /ˈtɜːbjʊləns/ ▷ *noun* **1** a disturbed, wild or unruly state. **2** *meteorol* stormy weather caused by disturbances in atmospheric pressure. **3** *physics* **a** the irregular movement of particles in a liquid or gas that causes continual changes in the magnitude and direction of motion, eg during the flow of air across an aircraft wing or the movement of a liquid through a pipe; **b** the resulting effect of this. ◷ 16c: from Latin *turbulentia* agitation.

turbulent /ˈtɜːbjʊlənt/ ▷ *adj* **1** violently disturbed; wild; unruly ◻ ***She's had a turbulent life.*** **2** *meteorol* stormy. **3** causing disturbance or unrest. • **turbulently** *adverb*.

Turcoman see TURKOMAN

turd ▷ *noun* **1** *colloq* a lump of excrement. **2** *slang* a term of contempt or abuse used for someone who is considered worthless, despicable, etc. ◷ Anglo-Saxon *tord*.

tureen /tʃʊˈriːn, təˈriːn/ ▷ *noun* a large deep dish with a cover that food, especially soup or vegetables, is served from at table. ◷ 18c: from French *terrine* a large circular earthen dish.

turf ▷ *noun* (***turfs*** or ***turves***) **1 a** the surface of an area of grassland that consists of a layer of grass, weeds, matted roots, etc plus the surrounding earth; **b** a square piece that has been cut from this. **2** a slab of peat used as fuel. **3** (**the turf**) horse-racing, a race-course or the racing world generally. **4** *colloq* **a** an area of activity, operation, influence, etc; territory ◻ ***thinks of the computing department as his own turf;*** **b** *chiefly US* the area of a city that a criminal, detective, prostitute, etc works ◻ ***We shouldn't go in — that's the 14th Precinct's turf.*** ▷ *verb* (***turfed, turfing***) to cover (an area of land, garden, etc) with turf. • **turfed** *adj*. ◷ Anglo-Saxon *tyrf*.

■ **turf out** *Brit colloq* to throw out, eject or expel.

turf accountant ▷ *noun*, *Brit* **a** a BOOKMAKER; **b** a betting shop.

turfy ▷ *adj* (***turfier, turfiest***) **1** resembling, covered in, associated with or consisting of turf. **2** relating to or characteristic of horse-racing; horsey. • **turfiness** *noun*.

turgescent /tɜːˈdʒɛsənt/ ▷ *adj* **1** becoming swollen, growing bigger, etc. **2** said of a plant cell: becoming distended with fluid. • **turgescence** *noun*. ◷ 17c: from Latin *turgescere* to begin to swell.

turgid /ˈtɜːdʒɪd/ ▷ *adj* **1** swollen; inflated or distended. **2** said of language: sounding important but meaning very little; pompous. **3** said of a plant cell: distended with fluid. • **turgidity** *noun*. • **turgidly** *adverb*. ◷ 17c: from Latin *turgidus*, from *turgere* to swell.

turgor /ˈtɜːgə(r)/ ▷ *noun*, *bot* the rigidity of a plant's cells. ◷ 19c: from Latin *turgere* to swell.

turion /ˈtʃʊrɪən/ ▷ *noun* an underground bud that gives rise to a new shoot. ◷ 17c: from Latin *turio* a shoot.

Turk /tɜːk/ ▷ *noun* **1 a** a citizen or inhabitant of, or someone born in, the modern state of Turkey, a republic that straddles SE Europe and W Asia; **b** a citizen or inhabitant of, or someone born in, the former OTTOMAN Empire. **2** someone who speaks a Turkic language. **3** *derog* a wild or unmanageable person. See also YOUNG TURK. ◷ 16c: Persian and Arabic.

turkey /ˈtɜːkɪ/ ▷ *noun* (***turkeys***) **1** a large gamebird indigenous to woodland in N and Central America but now farmed in most parts of the world. It has dark plumage with a greenish sheen, a bald blue or red head with red wattles and the male has a fanlike tail. **2** the flesh of this bird used as food, particularly at Christmas and (in the USA) at Thanksgiving when it is usually roasted. **3** *N Amer colloq* a stupid or inept person. **4** *N Amer colloq* a play, film, etc that is a complete failure. • **cold turkey** see separate entry. • **talk turkey** *N Amer colloq* **1** to talk bluntly or frankly. **2** to talk business. ◷ 16c: originally applied to a GUINEA FOWL imported from Turkey but later wrongly used to designate the American bird.

turkey buzzard and **turkey vulture** ▷ *noun* a type of American carrion-eating vulture that has a baldish head and dark feathers. ◷ 17c: so called because it resembles the turkey.

turkey cock ▷ *noun* a male turkey. Also called **gobbler**.

turkey hen ▷ *noun* a female turkey.

Turkey red ▷ *noun* **1** a bright scarlet dye obtained from the roots of the MADDER and used in colouring cotton. **2** cotton that has been coloured with this type of dye. ◷ 18c.

Turki /ˈtɜːkɪ, ˈtʊəkiː/ ▷ *noun* (*plural* ***Turki*** or ***Turkis*** in sense 2) **1** the Turkic languages thought of collectively, especially those of central Asia. **2** someone who belongs to a Turkic-speaking people. ▷ *adj* belonging or relating to the Turkic languages or to Turkic-speaking people. ◷ 18c.

Turkic /ˈtɜːkɪk/ ▷ *noun* the family of Ural-Altaic languages that Turkish, Tatar, Uzbek, etc belong to. ▷ *adj* belonging or relating to this family of languages or the people who speak them. ◷ 19c.

Turkish /ˈtɜːkɪʃ/ ▷ *adj* belonging or relating to Turkey, its people, language, etc. ▷ *noun* the official language of Turkey, belonging to the Altaic family of languages. ◷ 16c.

Turkish bath ▷ *noun* **1** a type of bath that is taken in a room filled with hot steam or air to induce sweating and which is followed by washing, massaging and finally a cold shower. **2** the room, rooms or building where this takes place. ◷ 17c.

Turkish carpet and **Turkey carpet** ⊳ *noun* a richly coloured wool carpet with a bold design and a dense pile that resembles velvet. ◷ 16c.

Turkish coffee ⊳ *noun* **1** strong black, usually very sweet, coffee, served with the grounds. **2** a cup of this. ◷ 19c.

Turkish delight ⊳ *noun* a sticky jelly-like cube-shaped sweet usually flavoured with ROSE-WATER and dusted with icing sugar. ◷ 19c.

Turkmen /ˈtɜːkmɪn/ ⊳ *noun* (***Turkmens*** or ***Turkmen***) **1** a member of various Turkic-speaking peoples who live in the area to the east of the Caspian Sea, including Turkmenistan and parts of Iran and Afghanistan. **2** the language these people speak. ⊳ *adj* belonging or relating to these people or their language. ◷ 1920s.

Turkoman or **Turcoman** /ˈtɜːkoumən/ same as TURKMEN. ◷ 16c.

Turk's cap ⊳ *noun* a type of lily that has brightly coloured flowers with turned-back petals which give the appearance of a turban. ◷ 17c.

Turk's head ⊳ *noun* a type of ornamental knot that looks like a turban. ◷ 19c.

turmeric /ˈtɜːmərɪk/ ⊳ *noun* **1** an E Indian plant of the ginger family. **2** the aromatic underground stem of this plant which, when dried and powdered, is used as a spice (eg in curry powder) and as a yellow dye. ◷ 16c.

turmeric paper ⊳ *noun, chem* paper that has been impregnated with turmeric and which is used to test for alkalis which, if present, will turn the paper brown. It can also be used to test for boric acid which will turn the paper a reddish brown.

turmoil /ˈtɜːmɔɪl/ ⊳ *noun* wild confusion, agitation or disorder; upheaval. ◷ 16c.

turn ⊳ *verb* (***turned, turning***) **1** *tr & intr* to move or go round in a circle or with a circular movement □ *turned the key and opened the door.* **2** *tr & intr* to change or make someone or something change position so that a different side or part comes to the top, front, etc □ *turn the pages slowly* □ *turn to face the sun.* **3** to put something into a specified position by, or as if by, inverting it; to tip out □ *turned the dough on to the table.* **4** *intr* to change direction or take a new direction □ *turn left at the corner.* **5** *tr & intr* to direct, aim or point, or be directed, aimed or pointed □ *turned his thoughts to the problems at work.* **6** to go round □ *turned the corner too fast.* **7** *tr & intr* to become or make someone or something become or change to something specified □ *Fame turned him into a real show-off* □ *love which turned to hate* □ *turn nasty.* **8** *tr & intr* to change or make someone or something change colour □ *The shock turned his hair white* □ *The leaves begin to turn in September.* **9** *tr & intr* said of milk, etc: to make or become sour. **10** to shape something using a lathe or potter's wheel. **11** to perform with a rotating movement □ *turn somersaults.* **12** *intr* to move or swing around a point or pivot □ *a gate turning on its hinge* □ *turn on one's heels.* **13** to pass the age or time of □ *turned forty this year* □ *It's turned midnight.* **14** to appeal to or have recourse to someone or something for help, support, relief, etc □ *turned to drink after the divorce* □ *always turns to me for advice.* **15** to come to consider or pay attention to something or to doing something □ *The conversation turned to politics.* **16** *tr & intr* **a** said of the stomach: to feel nausea or queasiness; **b** to cause (the stomach) to become nauseous or queasy □ *That scene is enough to turn your stomach.* **17** to translate □ *turned Camus's unfinished work into English.* **18** to remake (part of a piece of clothing, sheet, etc) by putting the worn outer part on the inside □ *turn a collar.* **19** to express, especially elegantly □ *always turning compliments.* **20** *intr* said of the tide: to begin to flow in the opposite direction. **21** to make (a profit, etc). ⊳ *noun* **1** an act, instance or the process of turning; a complete or partial rotation □ *a turn of the wheel.* **2** a change of direction, course or position □ *The road takes a turn to the right.* **3** a point or place where a change of direction occurs □ *The house is just past the turn in the road.* **4** a direction, tendency or trend □ *the twists and turns of the saga.* **5** a change in nature, character, condition, course, etc □ *an unfortunate turn of events.* **6** an opportunity or duty that comes to each of several people in rotation or succession □ *her turn to bat.* **7** inclination or tendency □ *a pessimistic turn of mind.* **8** a distinctive style or manner □ *a blunt turn of phrase.* **9** an act or service of a specified kind, usually good or malicious □ *always doing good turns for others.* **10** *colloq* a sudden feeling of illness, nervousness, shock, faintness, etc □ *gave her quite a turn.* **11** a short walk or ride □ *went for a turn round the garden.* **12 a** each of a series of short acts or performances, eg in a circus or variety theatre; **b** a performer who does one of these acts. **13** a single coil or twist of eg rope or wire. **14** *music* an ornament in which the principal note is preceded by that next above it and followed by that next below it. **15** *golf* the place on the course or the stage of play after the ninth hole when the players start heading back to the clubhouse □ *They were all square at the turn.* • **at every turn** everywhere, at every stage; continually. • **by turns** see *in turn* below. • **in one's turn** when it is one's turn, chance, etc. • **in turn** or **by turns** one after the other in an orderly or pre-arranged manner □ *The class took the gerbil home at weekends in turn.* • **not know where** or **which way to turn** to be completely confused as to how to act, behave, etc. • **on the turn 1** said of the tide: starting to change direction. **2** said of milk: on the point of going sour. • **out of turn 1** out of the correct order or at the wrong time □ *played his shot out of turn.* **2** inappropriately, discourteously, etc □ *He apologized for speaking out of turn.* • **not turn a hair** see under HAIR. • **serve its turn** to be adequate for the job in hand. • **take a turn for the better** or **the worse** to improve, or deteriorate, especially slightly □ *took a turn for the better after she was given the medicine* □ *The weather took a turn for the worse.* • **take turns** or **take it in turns** said especially of two or more people or things: to do something alternately or one after another □ *took it in turns to cook the dinner.* • **the turn of the month, year, century,** *etc* the end of one month, year, century, etc and the beginning of the next. • **to a turn** to exactly the right degree; to perfection □ *The steak was done to a turn.* • **turn a blind eye** see under BLIND. • **turn a deaf ear** see under DEAF. • **turn (and turn) about** one after the other; each taking a turn. • **turn in one's grave** said of a dead person: to be thought certain to have been distressed or offended, had they been alive, by circumstances such as those now in question. • **turn one's ankle** to twist it or strain it slightly. • **turn one's back on someone** or **something 1** to leave them or it for good. **2** to have no more to do with them or it □ *says he's turned his back on drugs.* • **turn one's hand to something** to undertake a task, etc or have the ability for it □ *She's very talented and can turn her hand to most things.* • **turn on one's heels** see under HEEL. • **turn over a new leaf** see under LEAF. • **turn Queen's** or **King's** or **state's evidence** see under EVIDENCE. • **turn the other cheek** to refuse to engage in any form of retaliation. • **turn a someone's head** to make them conceited, smug, snobbish, etc. • **turn someone** or **something loose** to set them or it free. • **turn the corner** see under CORNER. • **turn tail** to flee. • **turn the tables (on someone)** see under TABLE. • **turn the tide** to cause a change or reversal, eg in events, thinking, etc. • **turn a trick** see under TRICK. • **turn turtle** see under TURTLE. • **turn up one's nose (at something)** see under NOSE. ◷ Anglo-Saxon *turnian* and 13c French *torner.*

■ **turn about** to move so as to face a different direction.

■ **turn against someone** to become hostile or unfriendly towards them □ *She turned against him after she discovered his lies.*

■ **turn someone against someone else** to make them become hostile or unfriendly towards them □ *His lies turned her against him.*

■ **turn aside** or **turn something aside** to look away or turn (one's eyes, gaze, face, concentration, etc) to another direction.

■ **turn away** to move or turn to face in the opposite direction.

■ **turn someone away** to send them away.

■ **turn something away** to reject or refuse to accept or consider it □ *turned away his pleas for leniency.*

■ **turn back** to begin to go in the opposite direction □ *We turned back because of heavy snow.*

■ **turn someone** or **something back** to make them or it begin to go in the opposite direction □ *The occupying forces turned back the aid convoy.*

■ **turn something back** to fold over or back □ *turned back the beds.*

■ **turn down somewhere** or **turn something down somewhere** to head or place in a downwards direction □ *The car turned down the lane.*

■ **turn someone** or **something down** to refuse or reject (them, an application, etc) □ *turned him down at the interview* □ *She turned down the job.*

■ **turn something down 1** to reduce the level of light, noise, etc produced by it by, or as if by, using a control □ *Turn that telly down — it's far too loud!* **2** to fold it or them down or back □ *turned down the bedclothes.*

■ **turn in 1** to bend, fold, incline, etc inwards. **2** *colloq* to go to bed.

■ **turn someone** or **something in** to hand them or it over, eg to someone in authority □ *turned in the wallet he found to the police.*

■ **turn something in** to give, achieve, etc (a specified kind of performance, score, etc).

■ **turn off** to leave a straight course or a main road □ *The car turned off at the lights.* See also TURN-OFF.

■ **turn off somewhere 1** said of a side road: to lead from (a main road). **2** said of a person or vehicle: to leave (a main road). See also TURN-OFF.

■ **turn someone off** *colloq* to make them feel dislike or disgust, or to lose (especially sexual) interest □ *The violent scenes really turned me off.* See also TURN-OFF.

■ **turn something off 1** to stop (the flow of water, electricity, etc) by using, or as if by using, a knob, tap, button, switch, etc. **2** to make (a machine, appliance, etc) stop functioning, working, etc by using, or as if by using, a knob, switch, etc □ *turned off the microwave.*

■ **turn on** *colloq* to cause feelings such as a heightened sense of awareness, especially with hallucinogenic drugs □ *They smoke dope and turn on most weekends.*

■ **turn on someone** or **something 1** to attack them or it physically or verbally, usually suddenly or violently □ *The dogs turned on each other.* **2** to depend on them or it □ *The whole argument turns on a single point.*

■ **turn someone on** *colloq* to make them feel excitement, pleasure, interest, etc. See also TURN-ON.

■ **turn something on 1** to start (the flow of water, electricity, etc) by using, or as if by using, a knob, tap, button, switch, etc. **2** to make (a machine, appliance, etc) start functioning, working, etc by using, or as if by using, a knob, switch, etc.

■ **turn out 1** to happen or prove to be □ *She turned out to be right.* **2** to finally be □ *It turned out all right in the end.* **3** to gather or assemble, eg for a public meeting or event □ *Hundreds of people turned out to vote.* See also TURN-OUT. **4** *colloq* to get out of bed.

■ **turn someone out 1** to send them away; to make them leave; to expel them □ *The bouncers turned the trouble makers out of the club.* **2** to dress, equip, groom, etc □ *He always turns the kids out nicely.* See also TURN-OUT. **3** to call (soldiers, a guard, etc) for duty.

■ **turn something out 1** to bend, fold, incline, etc it outwards. **2** to switch off (a light, etc). **3** to make, manufacture, etc (usually specified quantities of goods or produce) □ *They turn out around 50 cars a week.* See also TURN-OUT. **4** *Brit* to empty, clear, etc (a room, drawer, pocket, etc), especially for cleaning or to check the contents □ *The police made him turn out his pockets.*

■ **turn over 1** to roll oneself over when in a lying position. **2** said of an engine: to start running at low speed.

■ **turn someone over** *colloq* to surrender or transfer them (to an other person, an authority, etc) □ *turned the thief over to the police.*

■ **turn something over 1** to start (an engine) running at low speed. **2** to turn it so that the hidden or reverse side becomes visible or faces upwards □ *turn over the page.* **3** to consider it, especially thoughtfully, carefully, etc □ *turned over his proposal in her mind.* **4** *slang* to rob it □ *turned over the off-licence.* **5** to handle or do business to a specified amount of (money, etc) □ *The business turns over five million pounds per year.* See also TURNOVER.

■ **turn round 1** to turn to face in the opposite direction □ *Peter, turn round and pay attention.* **2** said of a loaded vehicle, ship, etc: to arrive, be unloaded, loaded with new cargo, passengers, etc and depart again □ *The ship turned round in two hours.* **3** to adopt a different policy, opinion, etc.

■ **turn something round** to receive and deal with or process (a matter, the arrival of loaded vehicles, etc) in a specified manner, time, etc □ *We're able to turn an order round in an hour* □ *The ship was turned round in two hours.*

■ **turn to someone** or **something** to use it or them, eg as a form of comfort, etc □ *turned to drugs.*

■ **turn to something** to begin (a task, undertaking, etc).

■ **turn up 1** to appear or arrive □ *Hardly anyone turned up for the match.* **2 a** to be found, especially by accident or unexpectedly □ *The kitten turned up safe and well;* **b** to discover or reveal.

■ **turn something up 1** to increase the flow, intensity, strength, volume, etc, eg of (sound, light, etc produced by a machine) by, or as if by, turning a knob □ *turned up the music.* **2** to shorten (a piece of clothing or its hem) by folding part of it up and stitching it in place.

turnabout ▷ *noun* **1** an act of turning to face the opposite way. **2** a complete change or reversal of direction, opinion, policy, etc.

turnaround ▷ *noun* **1 a** an act or the operation of processing something, eg through a manufacturing procedure; **b** the time that this takes. **2 a** an act or the operation of unloading and reloading a vehicle or ship; **b** the time that this takes. **3** a TURNABOUT (sense 2).

turncoat ▷ *noun* someone who turns against or leaves his or her party, principles, etc and joins the opposing side.

turner ▷ *noun* **1** someone or something that turns. **2** someone whose job is to work with a lathe.

turning ▷ *noun* **1** a place where one road branches off from another. **2** a road which branches off from another. **3** the art or process of using a lathe to form curves in wood, metal, etc. **4** (**turnings**) the shavings that come from an object as it is turned on a lathe.

turning-circle ▷ *noun* the smallest possible circle in which a vehicle can turn round.

turning-point ▷ *noun* a time, place, event at which there is a significant change or something crucial happens □ *Her promotion was the turning-point in her career.*

turnip /'tɜːnɪp/ ▷ *noun* **1** a plant of the cabbage family which has a large round white or yellowish root. **2** the root of this vegetable used as food or animal fodder. • **turnipy** *adj*. See also SWEDE. ◷ 16c.

turnkey /'tɜːnkiː/ ▷ *noun* (***turnkeys***) *historical* someone who keeps the keys in a prison; a gaoler. ▷ *adj* said of a contract, etc: stipulating that the contractor will provide and install all that is necessary and will leave everything fully operational.

turn-off ▷ *noun* (***turn-offs***) **1** a road that branches off from a main road. **2** *colloq* someone or something that causes dislike, disgust or revulsion □ *Beards are such a turn-off.*

turn of phrase ▷ *noun* (***turns of phrase***) a way of talking, especially when it is distinctive □ *has an amusing turn of phrase.*

turn of speed ▷ *noun* (***turns of speed***) ability to move quickly □ *showed an unexpected turn of speed.*

turn-on ▷ *noun* (***turn-ons***) *colloq* someone or something that causes excitement or interest, especially of a sexual nature.

turn-out ▷ *noun* (***turn-outs***) **1** the number of people who collectively attend a meeting, celebration, event, etc □ *a poor turn-out at the match.* **2** the number of people voting in an election. **3** an outfit or set of clothes or equipment. **4** the quantity of goods produced or on display.

turnover ▷ *noun* **1** the total value of sales in a business during a certain time. **2** the rate at which stock is sold and replenished. **3** the rate at which money or workers pass through a business □ *They pay rotten wages so there is a high staff turnover.* **4** *biol* in a living organism, eg in bone tissue: the synthesis, degradation and replacement of body constituents. **5** *biol* the measure of the amount of a substance reacting with an ENZYME in a given time. **6** *biol* in an ECOSYSTEM: the rate at which members of a population of plants or animals that are lost as a result of death or emigration are being replaced by reproduction or by the immigration of new members. **7** a small pastry with a fruit or jam filling □ *a yummy apple turnover.*

turnpike ▷ *noun* **1** *historical* **a** a gate or barrier that goes across a road or bridge and which is lifted only after travellers have paid the toll; **b** a road that has this type of barrier and toll system. Sometimes shortened to PIKE. **2** *N Amer* a motorway where drivers must pay a toll. ◷ 15c.

turnstile ▷ *noun* a gate that has revolving metal arms which allow only one person to pass through at a time, especially one for controlling admissions, eg to a football ground, etc.

turntable ▷ *noun* **1** the revolving platform on a record-player where records are placed. **2** a revolving platform used for turning railway engines and other vehicles.

turn-up ▷ *noun* (***turn-ups***) *Brit* the bottom of a trouser-leg folded back on itself.

turn-up for the book ▷ *noun, colloq* (*also* **a (real) turn-up for the book(s)**) an unexpected and usually pleasant surprise; a surprising piece of good luck.

turpentine /'tɜːpəntaɪn/ ▷ *noun* **1** a thick oily resin obtained from certain trees, eg pines. **2** (*in full* **oil** or **spirit of turpentine**) a clear ESSENTIAL OIL distilled from this resin and used in many commercial products, especially solvents, paint thinners and in medicine. Often shortened to **turps**. ◷ 14c: from Latin *terebinthina*.

turpentine tree ▷ *noun* a small Mediterranean tree that yields a resin that can be distilled to give turpentine. Also called **terebinth**.

turpeth /'tɜːpɪθ/ ▷ *noun* **1** an E Indian plant of the morning glory family. **2** a cathartic drug prepared from the root of this plant. ◷ 14c: from Latin *turpethum*.

turpitude /'tɜːpɪtʃuːd/ ▷ *noun, formal* vileness; depravity □ *moral turpitude.* ◷ 15c: from Latin *turpitudo*.

turquoise /'tɜːkwɔɪz, 'tɜːkwɑːz/ ▷ *noun* **1** an opaque semi-precious stone that comes in varying shades of light blue or greenish blue and which consists of hydrated copper aluminium phosphate. It is valued as a gemstone and ornamental material. **2 a** the greenish blue colour of this stone; **b** *as adj* □ *a turquoise bathroom suite.* ◷ 14c: from French *pierre turquoise* Turkish stone; so called because it was first brought to Europe from Persia through Turkey or Turkestan.

turret /'tʌrɪt/ ▷ *noun* **1** a small tower, usually rounded in shape and projecting from a wall of a castle or other building. **2** (*in full* **gun-turret**) a small revolving tower-like structure on a warship, tank, etc that has a gun mounted on it. **3** the part of a lathe that holds the cutting tools and which can be rotated so that the required tool can be selected. • **turreted** *adj*. ◷ 14c: from French *tourette*, a diminutive of *tour* a tower.

turret lathe ▷ *noun* a lathe that has an attachment in which various dies or cutting tools are held and which can be rotated so that the required tool is selected for use.

turtle /'tɜːtəl/ ▷ *noun* **1** any of several marine and freshwater reptiles with bodies enclosed in a bony shell similar to that of the tortoises, but which have flippers or webbed toes, making them excellent swimmers. **2** *N Amer* applied more generally to include the tortoise and terrapin. **3** the flesh of these reptiles used as food. **4** *computing* a type of cursor that is is moved around in on-screen drawing and plotting. • **turn turtle** said of a boat, etc: to turn upside down; to capsize. ◷ 17c: from Latin *tortuca* a tortoise.

turtledove ▷ *noun* **1** any of several kinds of wild doves that are noted for their soft cooing and for the affectionate way they behave towards their mates and young. **2 a** someone who is gentle and loving; **b** a term of endearment. ◷ 14c.

turtle graphics ▷ *singular noun, computing* on-screen drawing and plotting that involves using a TURTLE (sense 4).

turtle-neck ▷ *noun* **1** a round close-fitting neckline that comes up higher than a CREW NECK but not so high as a POLO NECK. **2** a jumper, etc that has this kind of neckline. **3** *as adj* □ *a turtle-neck T-shirt.* • **turtle-necked** *adj*. ◷ Late 19c.

turtleshell see TORTOISESHELL

turtle soup ▷ *noun* a type of soup made from the harder parts of the sea turtle and traditionally flavoured with a combination of aromatic herbs, eg basil, marjoram, chervil, savory and fennel. Compare MOCK TURTLE SOUP.

turves see TURF

Tuscan /'tʌskən/ ▷ *adj* **1** belonging or relating to Tuscany, the region around Florence in central Italy, or to its inhabitants or their language. **2** *archit, denoting* the simplest of the five orders of classical architecture, similar to DORIC but with the shaft of the column unfluted and minimal decoration on the capital and entablature. See also CORINTHIAN, IONIC, COMPOSITE. ▷ *noun* a citizen or inhabitant of, or someone born in, Tuscany. ◷ 16c: from Latin *Tuscanus* belonging to the Tusci, the Etruscans.

tusche /tʊʃ/ ▷ *noun* a greasy black water-repellent liquid used for drawing the design in LITHOGRAPHY and as the blocking medium in silk-screen printing. ◷ 19c: German, from *tuschen* to touch up with colour.

tush[1] /tʌʃ/ ▷ *exclamation*, *old use* expressing disgust, contempt, disapproval, etc. ◷ 15c: imitating the sound.

tush[2] /tʊʃ/ ▷ *noun* (***tushes***) *chiefly US colloq* the backside □ *Get off your tush and go find some work.* ◷ 1960s: from Yiddish *tokhes*, from Hebrew *tahat* beneath.

tush[3] /tʌʃ/ ▷ *noun* (***tushes***) **1** a horse's canine tooth. **2** a type of small narrow tusk that is found in some kinds of Indian elephant. ◷ 17c: from Anglo-Saxon *tusc* tusk.

tusk ▷ *noun* one of a pair of long, curved, pointed teeth which project from the mouth area of certain animals, eg the elephant, walrus, narwhal and wild boar. • **tusked** or **tusky** *adj*. • **tuskless** *adj*. ◷ Anglo-Saxon *tusc*.

tusker ▷ *noun* an elephant, walrus, wild boar, etc that has especially well-developed tusks.

tusk shell ▷ *noun* **1** any of several kinds of mollusc that have long pointed tubular shells. **2** a shell of this kind.

tusser /ˈtʌsə(r)/ and **tussore** /ˈtʌsɔː(r)/ ▷ *noun* **1** (*in full* **tusser silk**) a type of coarse brownish silk. **2** the silkworm that produces this kind of silk. ◷ 17c: from Hindu and Urdu *tasar*.

tussive /ˈtʌsɪv/ ▷ *adj*, *medicine* relating or referring to, or caused by, a cough. ◷ 19c: from Latin *tussis* a cough.

tussle /ˈtʌsəl/ ▷ *noun* a verbal or physical struggle or fight. ▷ *verb* (***tussled***, ***tussling***) *intr* to engage in a tussle. ◷ 15c: from Scots and N English *touse* to pull or shake about.

tussock /ˈtʌsək/ ▷ *noun* a clump of grass or other vegetation. • **tussocked** *adj*. • **tussocky** *adj*. ◷ 16c.

tussock grass ▷ *noun* any of several tall-growing grasses of the S hemisphere that have a great number of stems sprouting from a central point. ◷ 19c.

tussore see TUSSER

tut /tʌt/ or **tut-tut** ▷ *exclamation* expressing mild disapproval, annoyance or rebuke. ▷ *verb* (***tutted***, ***tutting***) *intr* to express mild disapproval, annoyance or rebuke by saying 'tut' or 'tut-tut'. ▷ *noun* an act of saying 'tut' or 'tut-tut'. ◷ 16c: a conventionalized spelling that imitates the sound made by clicking the tongue against the back of the upper front teeth or gums and which can also be represented by **tch** or **tsk**.

tutelage /ˈtʃuːtɪlɪdʒ/ ▷ *noun* **1** the state or office of being a guardian. **2** the state of being under the care of a guardian. **3** tuition or instruction, especially as given by a tutor. ◷ 17c: from Latin *tutela* guardianship.

tutelary /ˈtʃuːtɪlərɪ/ and **tutelar** ▷ *adj* **1** having the power or role of a guardian. **2** belonging or relating to a guardian. **3** giving protection. ◷ 17c: from Latin *tutelaris* guardian.

tutor /ˈtʃuːtə(r)/ ▷ *noun* **1** a university or college teacher who teaches undergraduate students individually or in small groups, or who is responsible for the general welfare and progress of a certain number of students. **2** a private teacher □ *my piano tutor.* **3** *Brit* an instruction book. ▷ *verb* (***tutored***, ***tutoring***) *tr & intr* **1** to act or work as a tutor to someone. **2** to discipline. • **tutee** *noun* (***tutees***) someone who is tutored. • **tutorage** *noun*. • **tutoring** *noun*. • **tutorship** *noun*. ◷ 14c: Latin, meaning 'a watcher'.

tutorial /tʃʊˈtɔːrɪəl/ ▷ *noun* **1** a period of instruction when a university or college tutor and an individual student or small group of students meet, usually to discuss an assignment, lectures, etc. **2** a lesson that is intended to be worked through by a learner at their own pace, eg one that teaches the user how to use a computing program □ *found the Windows tutorials really useful.* ▷ *adj* belonging or relating to a tutor or tuition by a tutor □ *forgot his tutorial exercise.* • **tutorially** *adverb*. ◷ 20c in *noun* sense 1; 18c, meaning 'relating to a legal guardian': from Latin *tutor* a watcher.

tutsan /ˈtʌtsən/ ▷ *noun* a plant of the ST JOHN'S WORT family, formerly used in healing wounds, etc. ◷ 15c.

tutti /ˈtʊtɪ/ *music* ▷ *adverb* with all the instruments and singers together. ▷ *noun* (***tuttis***) a passage to be played or sung by all the instruments and singers together. ◷ 18c: Italian, plural of *tutto* all.

tutti-frutti /tuːtɪˈfruːtiː/ ▷ *noun* an ice cream or other sweet that contains or is flavoured with mixed fruits. ◷ 19c: Italian, meaning 'all fruits'.

tut-tut see TUT

tutty /ˈtʌtɪ/ ▷ *noun* impure zinc oxide that collects in the flues of zinc-smelting furnaces and which is used in powder form as a polish. ◷ 14c: from Arabic *tutiya* oxide of zinc.

tutu /ˈtuːtuː/ ▷ *noun* a very short protruding skirt that consists of layers of stiffened frills of net, etc and is worn by female ballet dancers. ◷ Early 20c: French, from *cucu*, a diminutive of *cul* the buttocks.

tu-whit tu-whoo /tʊˈwɪt tʊˈwuː/ ▷ *noun* a conventionalized representation of an owl's hoot. ◷ 16c: imitating the sound.

tuxedo /tʌkˈsiːdoʊ/ ▷ *noun* (***tuxedos*** or ***tuxedoes***) *chiefly N Amer* **1** a DINNER-JACKET. **2** an evening suit with a dinner-jacket. Often shortened to **tux**. ◷ 19c: named after a fashionable country club at Tuxedo Park, New York.

tuyère or **tuyere** /twɪə(r), twaɪə(r)/ and **twyer** /twaɪə(r)/ ▷ *noun* a nozzle that the blast of air is forced through in a forge or furnace. ◷ 17c: from French *toiere*, from *tuyau* a pipe.

TV ▷ *abbreviation* television.

TV dinner ▷ *noun* a prepared convenience meal, usually frozen and suitable for heating in a microwave, which can be eaten while watching TV.

TVEI ▷ *abbreviation*, *Brit* Technical and Vocational Education Initiative, a scheme that is intended to make more job-oriented and technological courses available to school students.

TV movie ▷ *noun* a film made for TV, and not intended for cinema release.

TVP ▷ *abbreviation* textured vegetable protein, a form of protein obtained from vegetable sources, such as soya beans, made to resemble minced meat in look and texture and used as a substitute for meat.

TWA ▷ *abbreviation* Trans-World Airlines.

twaddle /ˈtwɒdəl/ *colloq* ▷ *noun* nonsense; senseless or silly writing or talk. ▷ *verb* (***twaddled***, ***twaddling***) *intr* to speak or write nonsense. • **twaddler** *noun*. • **twaddling** *adj*, *noun*. • **twaddly** *adj*. ◷ 18c.

twain /tweɪn/ ▷ *noun* ▷ *adj*, *old use* two. ◷ Anglo-Saxon *twegen*, from *twa* two.

twang ▷ *noun* **1** a sharp ringing sound like that produced by plucking a tightly-stretched string or wire. **2** a nasal quality or tone of voice. **3** *colloq* a local or regional intonation. ▷ *verb* (***twanged***, ***twanging***) *tr & intr* **1** to make or cause to make a twang. **2** *often derog* to play (a musical instrument or a tune) casually, informally, etc □ *twangs away on his guitar for hours.* • **twanging** *adj*, *noun*. • **twangingly** *adverb*. • **twangy** *adj* (***twangier***, ***twangiest***). ◷ 16c: imitating the sound.

'twas /twɒz, twəz/ ▷ *contraction*, *old use or poetic* it was □ *'twas a great pity.* ◷ 17c.

twat /twat, twɒt/ ▷ *noun*, *coarse slang* **1** the female genitals. **2** a term of contempt for someone who is considered worthless, unpleasant, despicable, etc. ◷ 17c.

tweak ▷ *verb* (***tweaked***, ***tweaking***) **1** to get hold of and pull or twist something with a sudden jerk. **2** to make fine adjustments to (eg to a computer program, the workings of an engine, etc). ▷ *noun* an act or instance, or the process, of tweaking □ ***It'll work if you give that button a tweak.*** • **tweaker** *noun.* ◷ 17c.

twee ▷ *adj, Brit colloq, disparaging* affectedly or pretentiously pretty, sweet, cute, quaint, sentimental, etc. • **tweely** *adverb.* • **tweeness** *noun.* ◷ Early 20c: from *tweet*, a childish pronunciation of SWEET.

tweed ▷ *noun* **1 a** a thick roughish woollen cloth, usually with coloured flecks, used for making suits, jackets, skirts, etc and often identified with the town, area, etc where it is produced □ ***Harris tweed.*** **2** (**tweeds**) clothes, eg a suit, that are made of this material. ◷ 19c: originally a trade name which was a misreading of Scots *tweel* meaning 'twill' and which became reinforced by the name of the River Tweed in the Borders along which many of the factories that first produced the cloth were situated.

tweedy ▷ *adj* (***tweedier, tweediest***) **1** relating to or like tweed. **2** relating to or typical of people who enjoy the outdoors and taking part in such pastimes as fishing, shooting, hillwalking, etc and who are, by tradition, characterized by the wearing of tweed clothes. Also called GREEN-WELLIE. • **tweedily** *adverb.* • **tweediness** *noun.*

'tween ▷ *contraction, old use* between. ◷ 14c.

'tween-decks ▷ *noun, naut* a sailors' term for the space between two decks. ◷ 19c: in full, 'between the decks'.

tweet ▷ *noun* a melodious chirping sound made by a small bird. ▷ *verb* (***tweeted, tweeting***) *intr* to chirp melodiously. ◷ 19c: imitating the sound.

tweeter ▷ *noun, electronics* a loudspeaker that is designed to reproduce high-frequency sounds. Compare WOOFER. ◷ 1930s.

tweezers ▷ *plural noun* a small pair of pincers for pulling out individual hairs, holding small objects, etc. ◷ 16c: from obsolete *tweeze*, meaning 'a surgeon's case of instruments'.

twelfth (often written **12th**) ▷ *adj* **1** in counting: **a** next after eleventh; **b** last of twelve; **c** in twelfth position. **2** (**the twelfth**) **a** the twelfth day of the month □ ***I don't get paid till the twelfth***; **b** (*golf*) the twelfth hole □ ***scored a double bogey at the twelfth.*** ▷ *noun* **1** one of twelve equal parts. Also *as adj* □ ***a twelfth share.*** **2** a FRACTION equal to one divided by twelve (usually written $^{1}/_{12}$). **3** *music* **a** an interval of an OCTAVE and a FIFTH (*noun* 5); **b** a note at that interval from another. ▷ *adverb* used to introduce the twelfth point in a list. • **twelfthly** *adverb.* ◷ Anglo-Saxon *twelfta.*

Twelfth Day ▷ *noun* **1** 6 January, the twelfth day after Christmas. **2** the festival of EPIPHANY.

twelfth man ▷ *noun, cricket* a reserve member of a team.

Twelfth Night ▷ *noun* the evening before the twelfth day after Christmas (5 January) or the evening of the day itself (6 January).

twelve ▷ *noun* **1 a** the cardinal number 12; **b** the quantity that this represents, being one more than eleven. **2** any symbol for this, eg **12** or **XII**. **3** the age of 12. **4** something, especially a garment or a person, whose size is denoted by the number 12. **5** (*also* **12 o'clock, 12am** or **12pm**) midnight or midday □ ***stopped at twelve for lunch.*** **6** a set or group of 12 people or things. **7** a score of 12 points. **8** *Brit* a film that has been classified as being suitable only for people aged twelve or over. ▷ *adj* **1** totalling 12. **2** aged 12. ◷ Anglo-Saxon *twelf.*

twelvefold ▷ *adj* **1** 12 times as much or as many. **2** divided into or consisting of 12 parts. ▷ *adverb* by 12 times as much □ ***prices had increased twelvefold.*** ◷ Anglo-Saxon.

twelve-hour clock ▷ *noun* a system of referring to the time by separately numbering each hour in each of the twelve-hour periods after midnight and after midday. The periods are usually distinguished by the abbreviations A.M. and P.M. respectively. The number of minutes past each hour is indicated after a stop or colon, eg 12:45a.m. means 45 minutes after midnight. Compare TWENTY-FOUR-HOUR CLOCK.

twelve-inch and **12 inch** ▷ *noun* a RECORD (*noun* 4) which is played at 45 rpm and which usually has an extended version of a track previously released as a SEVEN-INCH on it.

twelvemo /ˈtwɛlvmoʊ/ (***twelvemos***) see DUODECIMO

twelvemonth ▷ *noun, old use* a year.

twelve-tone ▷ *adj, music* belonging or relating to music based on a pattern formed from the 12 notes of the CHROMATIC SCALE.

twenties ▷ *plural noun* **1** the period of time between one's 20th and 30th birthdays □ ***They are both in their twenties.*** **2** the range of temperatures between 20 and 30 degrees □ ***It was in the high twenties every day.*** **3** the period of time between the 20th and 30th years of a century □ ***the roaring twenties.***

twentieth /ˈtwɛntɪəθ/ (often written **20th**) ▷ *adj* **1** in counting: **a** next after nineteenth; **b** last of twenty. **2** (**the twentieth**) the twentieth day of the month. ▷ *noun* **1** one of twenty equal parts. Also *as adj* □ ***a twentieth share.*** **2** a FRACTION equal to one divided by twenty (usually written $^{1}/_{20}$).

twenty /ˈtwɛntɪ/ ▷ *noun* (***twenties***) **1 a** the cardinal number 20; **b** the quantity that this represents, being one more than 19. **2** any symbol for this, eg **20** or **XX**. **3** the age of 20. **4** something, especially a garment or a person, whose size is denoted by the number 20. **5** a set or group of 20 people or things. **6** a score of 20 points. **7** a bank note worth 20 pounds. ▷ *adj* **1** totalling 20. **2** aged 20. • **twentyish** *adj.* ◷ Anglo-Saxon *twentig.*

twenty-first ▷ *noun, colloq* a twenty-first birthday, often thought of as a RITE OF PASSAGE or an important landmark in the transition from adolescence to adulthood □ ***got a lovely watch for her twenty-first.***

twenty-four-hour ▷ *adj* said of an illness, etc: lasting a relatively short time □ ***a twenty-four-hour flu bug.***

twenty-four-hour clock ▷ *noun* a system of referring to the time by numbering each of the hours after midnight from zero to 23. The number of minutes past each hour is indicated after the hour, sometimes with a stop or colon, eg 0045 means 45 minutes after midnight. Compare TWELVE-HOUR CLOCK.

twenty-one see under PONTOON^{2}

twenty-twenty (often written **20/20**) ▷ *adj* **1** said of someone's vision: normal. **2** said of perception or hindsight: sharp and insightful.

twerp or **twirp** /twɜːp/ ▷ *noun, colloq* a silly or contemptible person. ◷ 1920s:.

twibill /ˈtwaɪbɪl, ˈtwɪbəl/ ▷ *noun* **1** *historical* a battle-axe that has a double blade. **2** a MATTOCK. ◷ Anglo-Saxon.

twice ▷ *adverb* **1** two times □ ***Twice two is four.*** **2** on two occasions. **3** double in amount or quantity □ ***twice as much.*** ◷ Anglo-Saxon *twiges.*

twiddle /ˈtwɪdəl/ ▷ *verb* (***twiddled, twiddling***) **1** to twist something round and round □ ***twiddle the knob on the radio.*** **2** to play with or twist something round and round idly □ ***She always twiddles her hair.*** ▷ *noun* **1** an act of twiddling. **2** a curly mark or ornamentation. • **twiddler** *noun.* • **twiddling** *adj, noun.* • **twiddly** *adj.* • **twiddle one's thumbs 1** to move one's thumbs in a circular movement round and round each other, usually as a sign of boredom. **2** to have nothing to do. ◷ 16c: perhaps from TWIRL, TWIST, TWITCH, FIDDLE.

twig^{1} ▷ *noun* **1** a small shoot or branch of a tree, bush, etc. **2** something that resembles this, eg a small blood vessel. • **twigged** *adj.* • **twiglet** *noun.* • **twiggy** *adj* (***twiggier, twiggiest***). ◷ Anglo-Saxon.

twig² ▻ *verb* (***twigged***, ***twigging***) *tr & intr, Brit colloq* **1** to understand (a joke, situation, etc), especially suddenly. **2** to perceive or observe. ⓒ 18c: from Irish Gaelic *tuigim* I understand.

twilight /'twaɪlaɪt/ ▻ *noun* **1** the faint diffused light in the sky when the sun is just below the horizon, especially the kind that can be seen just after sunset, but also the kind that can be seen just before sunrise. **2** the time of day when this occurs □ *arranged to meet at twilight.* **3** dim light or partial darkness. **4** a period or state when full understanding, knowledge, perception, etc is lacking. **5** a period of decline in strength, health or importance, especially after a period of vigorous activity □ *the twilight of his life.* ▻ *adj* **1** belonging, relating or referring to, or occurring at, twilight □ *in her twilight years.* **2** shadowy; dim □ *twilight images on the edge of consciousness.* **3** not fully part of society; not quite within the law □ *twilight enterprises.* ⓒ Anglo-Saxon *twi* two + LIGHT.

twilight world ▻ *noun* a lifestyle or section of society that deviates from the way most people live, especially if not quite within the law □ *lives in a twilight world of drugs and crime.*

twilight zone ▻ *noun* **1** a decaying area of a city or town situated typically between the main business and commercial area and the suburbs. **2** any indefinite or intermediate state or position.

twilit /'twaɪlɪt/ and **twilighted** /'twaɪlaɪtɪd/ ▻ *adj* lit by or as if by twilight.

twill ▻ *noun* a strong fabric woven in such a way that it has a surface pattern of parallel diagonal ridges. ▻ *verb* (***twilled***, ***twilling***) to weave (fabric) with a twill. • **twilled** *adj.* ⓒ Anglo-Saxon *twilic* woven of double thread.

twin ▻ *noun* **1** either of two people or animals that are born at the same time and have the same mother. See IDENTICAL (sense 3), FRATERNAL (sense 2). **2** either of two people or things that are very like each other or closely associated to each other. **3** (**the Twins**) the constellation GEMINI. **4** *chem* (*in full* **twin crystal**) a compound crystal consisting of two crystals or parts of crystals which have grown together so that each one or part is a mirror image of the other. ▻ *adj* being one of a pair or consisting of very similar or closely connected parts. ▻ *verb* (***twinned***, ***twinning***) **1** *tr & intr* to bring or come together closely or intimately. **2** to link (a town) with a counterpart in another country to encourage cultural, social and economic exchanges and co-operation. **3** *intr* to give birth to twins. **4** *tr & intr, chem* to form into or grow as a twin crystal. • **twinned** *adj.* • **twinning** *noun.* ⓒ Anglo-Saxon *twinn.*

twin bed ▻ *noun* one of a pair of matching single beds. • **twin-bedded** *adj* □ *a twin-bedded room.*

twin-cam ▻ *adj* said especially of a car engine: equipped with two CAMSHAFTs.

twine ▻ *noun* **1** strong string or cord made from two or more threads of cotton, hemp, etc twisted together. **2** a coil or twist. **3** an act of twisting or clasping. ▻ *verb* (***twined***, ***twining***) **1** to twist together; to interweave. **2** to form by twisting or interweaving. **3** *tr & intr* to twist or coil round □ *Ivy twined itself round the old tree trunk.* • **twined** *adj.* • **twiner** *noun.* • **twining** *adj, noun.* • **twiningly** *adverb.* • **twiny** *adj* (***twinier***, ***twiniest***). ⓒ Anglo-Saxon *twin* double or twisted thread.

twin-engined ▻ *adj* having a pair of engines.

twinge /twɪndʒ/ ▻ *noun* **1** a sudden sharp stabbing or shooting pain. **2** a sudden sharp pang of emotional pain, bad conscience, etc. ▻ *verb* (***twinged***, ***twinging*** or ***twingeing***) *tr & intr* to feel or make someone feel a sharp pain or pang. ⓒ Anglo-Saxon *twengan* to pinch.

twinkle /'twɪŋkəl/ ▻ *verb* (***twinkled***, ***twinkling***) **1** *intr* said of a star, etc: to shine with a bright, flickering light. **2** *intr* said of the eyes: to shine or sparkle with amusement, mischief, etc. **3** to give off (light) with a flicker. ▻ *noun* **1** a gleam or sparkle in the eyes. **2** a flicker or glimmer of light. **3** an act of twinkling. • **in a twinkle** or **twinkling**, or **in the twinkle** or **twinkling of an eye** in a moment or very short time. • **twinkler** *noun.* • **twinkling** *adj, noun.* • **twinkly** *adj* (***twinklier***, ***twinkliest***). ⓒ Anglo-Saxon *twinclian.*

twinset ▻ *noun, Brit* a woman's matching sweater and cardigan.

twin town ▻ *noun* a town which is linked to another town abroad to encourage cultural, social and economic exchanges and co-operation.

twin tub ▻ *noun* a type of washing machine that has two separate drums, one for washing and one for spinning the laundry dry. Compare AUTOMATIC, WASHER-DRYER.

twirl ▻ *verb* (***twirled***, ***twirling***) *tr & intr* to turn, spin or twist round □ *twirled across the dancefloor.* ▻ *noun* **1** an act of twirling □ *did a twirl to show off her new dress.* **2** a curly mark or ornament, eg a flourish made with a pen. • **twirler** *noun.* • **twirly** *adj* (***twirlier***, ***twirliest***). ⓒ 16c: from *twist* + *whirl.*

twirp see TWERP

twist ▻ *verb* (***twisted***, ***twisting***) **1** *tr & intr* to wind or turn round, especially by moving only a single part or by moving different parts in opposite directions □ *twist the knob* □ *He twisted round in his seat.* **2** *intr* to follow a winding course □ *The road twists through the mountains.* **3** *tr & intr* to wind around or together □ *twist the pieces of string together.* **4** to force or wrench out of the correct shape or position with a sharp turning movement □ *twisting his ankle as he fell.* **5** to distort the form, meaning, implication or balance of something □ *twisted his face into an ugly sneer* □ *twisted her words.* **6** (*often* **twist something off**) to remove or break off with a sharp turning movement. **7** to form something by winding or weaving. **8** *intr* to dance the twist. **9** *tr & intr* to take or give a spiral or coiled form (to). ▻ *noun* **1** an act or the process of twisting. **2** something that is formed by twisting or being twisted. **3** a turn or coil; a bend. **4** a sharp turning movement which pulls something out of shape; a wrench. **5** an unexpected event, development or change, eg of direction □ *a twist in the plot.* **6** a distortion of form, nature or meaning. **7** an eccentricity or perversion. **8** a length of thread, cord, silk, etc formed by twisting two or more strands together. **9 a** a twisted roll of bread; **b** a twisted roll of tobacco; **c** a curl of citrus peel that is used to flavour a drink □ *served with a twist of lemon.* **10** a piece of paper that has its ends twisted together to form a small packet, especially one that contains a collection of small items such as sweets. **11** (*usually* **the twist**) a dance that was popular during the 1960s and which involves making twisting movements of the legs and hips. • **twistable** *adj.* • **twisting** *adj, noun.* • **get one's knickers in a twist** see under KNICKERS. • **round the twist** *colloq* mad; crazy. • **twist someone's arm** *colloq* to apply pressure, especially moral pressure, to someone to make them act in the way one wants. • **twist** or **wind someone round one's little finger** to manipulate or dominate them unscrupulously. • **twist the knife in the wound** see under KNIFE. ⓒ 14c: from English *twisten* to divide.

twist drill ▻ *noun* a drill bit that is used in metal working and which has two grooves that run from the point along the shank to help keep the drill clear of swarf and shavings.

twisted ▻ *adj* **1** full of twists; coiled or distorted □ *a tree with knarled and twisted branches.* **2** *colloq* said of someone or their mind: emotionally disturbed or perverted □ *a film that would appeal to twisted minds.*

twister ▻ *noun* **1** *Brit colloq* a dishonest or deceiving person; a swindler. **2** *N Amer colloq* a tornado. **3** someone who dances the twist. **4** in cricket, billiards, tennis, etc: a twisting ball or shot.

twist-off ▻ *adj* said of a lid, top, etc: able to be removed without using an opener □ ***The beer now comes with a handy twist-off top.***

twisty ▷ *adj* (***twistier, twistiest***) **1** full of twists or turns □ ***a dangerous twisty road.*** **2** dishonest □ ***He's a bit of a twisty character.***

twit[1] ▷ *noun, colloq* a fool or idiot. ◷ 1930s.

twit[2] ▷ *verb* (***twitted, twitting***) to tease, reproach or criticize, usually with good humour or affection. ◷ 16c: from Anglo-Saxon *ætwitan*, from *æt* at + *witan* to blame.

twitch ▷ *verb* (***twitches, twitched, twitching***) **1** *intr* said of a muscle, limb, etc: to move involuntarily with a spasm □ ***My eye has been twitching all day.*** **2** *tr & intr* to move with quick sudden actions □ ***The guinea pig twitched his nose.*** **3** to pull or pluck something sharply or jerkily. **4** to hurt with a nip or pinch. ▷ *noun* (***twitches***) **1** a sudden involuntary spasm of a muscle, limb, etc. **2** a sudden sharp jerky movement □ ***the twitches of the rabbit's nose.*** **3** a sharp pang, eg of pain, conscious, etc. **4** a noose that is used for restraining a horse during a veterinary examination or operation. • **twitching** *adj, noun.* ◷ 12c.

twitcher ▷ *noun* **1** someone or something that twitches. **2** *colloq* a bird-watcher whose aim is to spot as many rare birds as possible.

twitch grass ▷ *noun* another name for COUCH[2]. Often shortened to **twitch**.

twitchy ▷ *adj* (***twitchier, twitchiest***) *colloq* **1** nervous, anxious or restless □ ***a twitchy smile*** □ ***been feeling twitchy about the interview.*** **2** characterized by twitching □ ***a twitchy eye.*** • **twitchily** *adverb.*

twite ▷ *noun* a small brown moorland bird of the linnet family that lives in N Britain and Scandanavia, migrating south in large flocks in the summer. ◷ 16c: imitating the sound of the bird's call.

twitter /ˈtwɪtə(r)/ ▷ *noun* **1** a light repeated chirping sound made by especially small birds. **2** *colloq* a nervous or excited state □ ***Just the sound of his voice can make me go all of a twitter.*** ▷ *verb* (***twittered, twittering***) **1** *intr* said especially of a bird: to make a light repeated chirping sound or similar high-pitched trembling sounds. **2** to say or utter with such a chirping sound. **3** *intr* to make small nervous or excited movements. **4** (*also* **twitter on** or **away**) to talk rapidly and often trivially. • **twitterer** *noun.* • **twittering** *adj, noun.* • **twitteringly** *adverb.* • **twittery** *adj.* ◷ 14c: imitating the sound.

'twixt /twɪkst/ ▷ *prep, old use* a shortened form of BETWIXT □ ***There's many a slip 'twixt cup and lip.***

twizzle /ˈtwɪzəl/ ▷ *verb* (***twizzled, twizzling***) *tr & intr* to spin round rapidly. ▷ *noun* a twist or turn. ◷ 18c.

two /tuː/ ▷ *noun* **1 a** the cardinal number 2; **b** the quantity that this represents, being one more than one. **2** any symbol for this, eg **2** or **II**. **3** the age of two. **4** something, such as a shoe size, that is denoted by the number 2. **5** the second hour after midnight or midday □ ***The meeting is at two*** □ ***2 o'clock*** □ ***2pm.*** **6** a set or group of two. **7** a playing-card with two pips □ ***had to lay down his two.*** Compare DEUCE[1]. **8** a score of two points. ▷ *adj* **1** totalling two. **2** aged two. • **in two** in or into two pieces. • **in two ticks** or **two shakes (of a lamb's tail)** in a moment. • **or two** an indefinite small number □ ***I'll just be a minute or two.*** • **two or three** or **two-three** approximately two or three or between two and three □ ***worked here for two-three years.*** • **put two and two together** to come to a conclusion, usually an obvious one, from the available evidence. • **that makes two of us** *colloq* the same is true of me too. • **two a penny** so common as to be almost worthless. • **two by two** in pairs. • **two can play at that game** a taunt or threat which implies that the speaker will resort to the same devices, tactics, etc as the person addressed has used. See also SECOND, BI-, BINARY, DOUBLE, DUAL, TWICE. ◷ Anglo-Saxon *twa*.

two-bit ▷ *adj, originally N Amer colloq* cheap; petty; small-time.

two-by-four ▷ *noun* **a** timber that measures approximately 2″ thick by 4″ wide; **b** a length of timber of this size.

two-dimensional ▷ *adj* **1** having, or appearing to have, breadth and length but no depth. **2** having little depth or substance □ ***His portrayal of Hamlet was totally two-dimensional.***

two-edged ▷ *adj* **1** double-edged. **2** having both advantageous and disadvantageous functions, side-effects, outcomes, etc.

two-faced ▷ *adj* deceitful; hypocritical; insincere.

twofold ▷ *adj* **1** twice as much or as many. **2** divided into or consisting of two parts. ▷ *adverb* by twice as much.

two-handed ▷ *adj* **1** having, needing or being meant for two hands or people □ ***a two-handed saw.*** **2** able to use both hands equally well.

two-horse race ▷ *noun* a contest in which only two entrants have a realistic chance of winning.

twopence *Brit* ▷ *noun* **1** (/ˈtʌpəns/; *also* **tuppence**) the sum of two pence, especially before the introduction of decimal coinage. **2** /tuːˈpɛns/ a decimal coin of the value of two pence. • **not care** or **give twopence** (/ˈtʌpəns/) *colloq* not to care at all □ ***don't give tuppence for what you think.***

twopenny or **tuppenny** /ˈtʌpənɪ/ *Brit* ▷ *adj* **1** worth or costing twopence. **2** *colloq* cheap; worthless. • **twopenny-halfpenny** or **tuppenny-ha'penny** (/-ˈheɪpnɪ/) *disparaging* almost worthless □ ***I don't want your nasty tuppenny-ha'penny present.***

two-piece ▷ *adj* said of a suit, bathing costume, etc: consisting of two matching or complementary pieces or parts. ▷ *noun* a two-piece suit, etc.

two-ply ▷ *adj* consisting of two strands or layers □ ***two-ply wool*** □ ***two-ply wood.*** ▷ *noun* (***two-plies***) knitting wool or yarn that consists of two strands of wool twisted together.

two-seater ▷ *noun* **1** a vehicle or aircraft that has only two seats. **2** a settee, etc that is designed to accommodate two people. **3** *as adj* □ ***a two-seater plane.***

two-sided ▷ *adj* **1** having two sides which differ from each other. **2** controversial; having two aspects.

twosome ▷ *noun* **1** a game, dance, etc for two people. **2** a pair of people together; a couple □ ***make a lovely twosome.***

two-step ▷ *noun* a ballroom dance in duple time, or a piece of music for it □ ***did the military two-step.***

two-stroke ▷ *adj* said of an internal-combustion engine: taking one upward movement and one downward movement of the piston to complete the power cycle. ▷ *noun* an engine or vehicle that works in this way.

two-time ▷ *verb* (***two-timed, two-timing***) *tr & intr, colloq* **1** to deceive or be unfaithful to (a husband, wife, lover, etc). **2** to swindle or double-cross. • **two-timer** *noun.* • **two-timing** *adj, noun.* ◷ 1920s.

two-tone ▷ *adj* having two colours, or two shades of the same colour, or two sounds □ ***a car with a two-tone trim*** □ ***a two-tone alarm.***

two-up ▷ *noun, Austral* a game in which two coins are tossed and bets are made on both falling heads up or both falling tails up.

two-way ▷ *adj* **1** said of a street, etc: having traffic moving in both directions. **2** said of a radio, etc: able to send and receive messages. **3** having two sides sharing equal participation, responsibility, gains, etc □ ***held two-way talks on disarmament.*** **4** said of a switch, wiring, etc:

designed so that the electricity can be switched on or off from either of two points. **5** able to be used in two ways.

two-way mirror ▷ *noun* a mirror designed so that it looks and functions like a normal mirror from one side but allows someone on the other side to see through it.

two-wheeler ▷ *noun* a vehicle, such as a bicycle, that has two wheels.

twyer see TUYÈRE

TX ▷ *abbreviation, US state* Texas.

-ty[1] ▷ *suffix, forming nouns, denoting* quality or condition □ ***safety*** □ ***certainty.***

-ty[2] ▷ *suffix, denoting* tens □ ***ninety.***

tycoon /taɪ'kuːn/ ▷ *noun* **1** someone who has power and influence, eg in business, industry, politics, etc; a magnate. **2** *historical* a title used by the Japanese when describing their SHOGUN to foreigners. ⓒ 19c: from Japanese *taikun* great prince.

tying *present participle of* TIE

tyke ▷ *noun* **1** a dog, especially a mongrel. **2** *Brit colloq* a rough or coarse person. **3** *Brit colloq* a small child, especially a naughty or cheeky one □ ***Stop pulling the cat's tail, you little tyke.*** **4** *Brit colloq* someone who comes from or was born in Yorkshire. **5** *Austral & NZ offensive slang* a Roman Catholic. • **tykish** *adj.* ⓒ 14c: from Norse *tik* a bitch; sense 5 is assimilated from *teague*, from *Tadgh*, a common name in Ireland.

tylopod /'taɪlɒpɒd/ ▷ *noun* any ruminant mammal, such as the camel or llama, that has pads on its feet rather than hoofs. ▷ *adj* belonging, referring or relating to this kind of mammal. ⓒ 19c: from Greek *tulos* knob, or *tule* cushion + -POD.

tympan /'tɪmpan/ ▷ *noun, printing* a device in a printing press that fits between the PLATEN and the sheet that is to be printed, so as to soften and equalize the pressure. ⓒ 16c in this sense; 9c, meaning 'a drum': from Latin *tympanum* a drum.

tympana *plural of* TYMPANUM

tympani see TIMPANO

tympanic /tɪm'panɪk/ ▷ *adj* **1** belonging or relating to, or in the region of, the EARDRUM. **2** belonging or relating to, or functioning as, a drum.

tympanic membrane see under EARDRUM

tympanist see under TIMPANO

tympanites /tɪmpə'naɪtiːz/ ▷ *noun, medicine* distension of the abdomen caused by excess gas in the intestinal or peritoneal cavity. • **tympanitic** /-'nɪtɪk/ *adj.* ⓒ 14c: from Greek *tympanites*, from *tympanon* a drum.

tympanum /'tɪmpənəm/ ▷ *noun* (***tympana*** /-nə/ or ***tympanums***) **1** *anatomy* **a** the cavity of the middle ear; **b** another term for the TYMPANIC MEMBRANE or any similar structure. **2** *archit* the recessed usually triangular face of a PEDIMENT. **3** *archit* **a** the area between the LINTEL of a doorway or window and an arch over it; **b** a carving on this area. **4** a drum or drumhead. ⓒ 17c: Latin, from Greek *tympanon* a drum.

the Tynwald /'tɪnwəld, taɪnwəld/ ▷ *noun* the parliament of the Isle of Man. ⓒ 15c: from Norse *thing-vollr* place of assembly, from *thing* assembly + *vollr* field.

typ. see TYPO

type /taɪp/ ▷ *noun* **1** a class or group of people, animals or things which share similar characteristics; a kind or variety. **2** the general character, nature or form of a particular class or group. **3** *colloq* a person, especially of a specified kind □ ***the silent type*** □ ***He's not really my type.*** **4** a person, animal or thing that is a characteristic example of its group or class. **5** *printing* **a** a small metal block with a raised letter or character on one surface that is used for printing; **b** a set of such blocks; **c** a set of such blocks that give printing of a specified kind □ ***italic type.*** **6** printed letters, characters, words, etc □ ***a leaflet with bold red type.*** **7** *biol* in taxonomy: **a** the group whose essential characteristics serve to define the next highest grouping and which normally gives the family its name; **b** *as adj* □ ***type genus;*** **c** (*in full* **type specimen**) the actual specimen or individual that the description of a new species or genus is based on and from which the species usually takes its name. **8** a figure or device on either side of a coin. **9** *Christian theol* a person, object or event in the Old Testament that in some way prefigures or symbolizes someone or something that is revealed in the New Testament. ▷ *verb* (***typed, typing***) **1** (*sometimes* **typewrite**) *tr & intr* to write (words, text, etc) using a typewriter or word processor. **2** to be a characteristic example or type of something; to typify. **3** *medicine, biol* to allocate to a type; to classify □ ***typed the blood sample for cross-matching.*** • **typing** see separate entry. • **typist** see separate entry. ⓒ 15c: from Greek *typos* a blow or impression.

typecast ▷ *verb* (***typecast, typecasting***) to put (an actor or actress) regularly in the same kind of part, usually because they have had previous box-office success in similar roles or because they fit the physical requirements of the role □ ***angry about always being typecast as a dumb bimbo.*** ▷ *adj* said of an actor or actress: regularly cast in the same kind of part.

typeface ▷ *noun, printing* **1** a set of letters, characters, etc of a specified design or style. **2** the part of the type that is inked or the impression this leaves.

type founder ▷ *noun, printing* someone whose job is designing and casting metallic type.

type metal ▷ *noun* an alloy of lead and antimony, usually with tin or bismuth, that is used for casting printing type.

typescript ▷ *noun* any typewritten document, manuscript or copy.

typeset ▷ *verb* (***typeset, typesetting***) *printing* to arrange (type) or set (a page, etc) in type ready for printing.

typesetter ▷ *noun* **1** someone whose job is to set type ready for printing. **2** a machine that does this.

type specimen see TYPE *noun* sense 7c

typewrite see TYPE *verb* sense 1

typewriter ▷ *noun* a machine with a keyboard the keys of which the user strikes to produce characters on paper. • **typewriting** *noun.*

typewritten ▷ *adj* said of a document, etc: produced using a typewriter.

typhlitis /tɪ'flaɪtɪs/ ▷ *noun, medicine* inflamation of the caecum. • **typhlitic** /tɪ'flɪtɪk/ *adj.* ⓒ 19c: Latin, from Greek *typhlon* CAECUM OR BLIND GUT + -ITIS.

typhoid /'taɪfɔɪd/ ▷ *noun* **1** (*in full* **typhoid fever**) *medicine* a serious and sometimes fatal infection of the digestive system caused by the bacillus *Salmonella typhi* which is transmitted through contaminated food and drinking water, characterized by fever, a rash of red spots on the front of the body, abdominal pain and sometimes delirium. **2** a similar infection in animals. ▷ *adj* relating to or resembling TYPHUS. • **typhoidal** *adj.* ⓒ 19c: so called because the fever was thought to be related to TYPHUS.

typhoon /taɪ'fuːn/ ▷ *noun, meteorol* a cyclonic tropical storm that occurs over the W Pacific Ocean, the South China Sea and the surrounding areas, usually during the period from July to October. • **typhonic** /taɪ'fɒnɪk/ *adj.* ⓒ 16c: from Chinese *da feng* great wind, altered under the influence of Greek *typhon* whirlwind, from the name in Greek mythology of the fire-breathing giant Typhon, believed to be buried under Mount Etna.

typhus /'taɪfəs/ ▷ *noun, medicine* any of a group of infectious diseases that are caused by RICKETTSIAE and transmitted to humans by lice carried by rodents. The main symptoms are fever, severe headache, a reddish-purple rash and delirium, and the disease is most prevalent in overcrowded and insanitary living conditions. Also called **typhus fever**. • **typhous** *adj*. ⓘ 18c: Latin, from Greek *typhos* smoke or stupour.

typical /'tɪpɪkəl/ ▷ *adj* **1** having or showing the usual features, traits, etc, or being a characteristic or representative example □ *We take in about £1000 on a typical day.* **2 a** (*often* **typical of**) displaying the usual or expected behaviour, attitude, etc □ *It's typical of him to be late*; **b** an exclamation expressing disdain, frustration, etc □ *Typical! It always rains when we plan a picnic.* **3** *biol* in taxonomy: belonging or relating to, or being a representative or characteristic specimen or type. **4** symbolic or prefiguring. • **typicality** *noun*. • **typically** *adverb*. ⓘ 17c: from Latin *typicalis*.

typify /'tɪpɪfaɪ/ ▷ *verb* (***typifies, typified, typifying***) **1** to be an excellent or characteristic example of something. **2** to represent by a type or symbol; to symbolize. • **typification** *noun*. • **typifier** *noun*. ⓘ 17c: from Latin *typus* + *facere* to make.

typing ▷ *noun* **1 a** the act or process of using a typewriter; **b** the state or quality of something that has been produced using a typewriter □ *poor typing.* **2** the act or process of classifying, eg blood.

typist ▷ *noun* **1** someone whose job is to type. **2** someone who uses a typewriter or word processor □ *I'm not a very fast typist.*

typo /'taɪpoʊ/ ▷ *noun* (***typos***) *colloq* **a** an error made in the typesetting of a text, such as the use of one letter in place of another; **b** a typographer. Sometimes shortened to TYP. ⓘ 19c: an abbreviation of *typographical error* or *typographer*.

typographer ▷ *noun* **1** someone whose job is to set type; a compositor. **2** someone who is skilled in the art of printing.

typography /taɪ'pɒgrəfɪ/ ▷ *noun* **1** the art or occupation of setting type and arranging texts for printing. **2** the style and general appearance of printed matter. • **typographic** /taɪpə'grafɪk/ and **typographical** *adj*. • **typographically** *adverb*. ⓘ 17c: from French *typographie*.

Tyr ▷ *symbol* tyrosine

tyrannical /tɪ'ranɪkəl/, **tyrannic** and **tyrannous** /'tɪrənəs/ ▷ *adj* **1** belonging or relating to, or like, a tyrant. **2** oppressive; despotic. • **tyrannically** and **tyrannously** *adverb*.

tyrannize /'tɪrənaɪz/ or **tyrannise** ▷ *verb* (***tyrannized, tyrannizing***) *tr & intr* to rule or treat in a cruel, unjust and oppressive way. ⓘ 16c: from Latin *tyrannizare* to act like a tyrant.

tyrannosaurus /tɪranə'sɔːrəs, taɪ-/ and **tyrannosaur** /tɪ'ranəsɔː(r), taɪ-/ ▷ *noun* the largest flesh-eating dinosaur, which reached a height of around 6m and a length of about 15m and lived during the Cretaceous period on a diet that consisted mainly of herbivorous dinosaurs. It walked on its hind legs which had powerful claws for killing its prey, and had relatively small and ineffectual front legs. ⓘ Early 20c: from Greek *tyrannos* tyrant + *sauros* lizard, modelled on DINOSAUR.

tyranny /'tɪrənɪ/ ▷ *noun* (***tyrannies***) **1** the use of cruelty, injustice, oppression, etc to enforce authority or power. **2 a** absolute, cruel and oppressive government by a single tyrant or group of tyrannical people; **b** a state under such government; **c** a period when this kind of government rules. **3** a cruel, unjust or oppressive act. ⓘ 14c: from French *tyrannie*.

tyrant /'taɪərənt/ ▷ *noun* **1** a cruel, unjust and oppressive ruler with absolute power. **2** someone who uses authority or power cruelly and unjustly. ⓘ 13c: French, from Greek *tyrannos* a tyrant, originally a term for an absolute ruler of a city state who had seized power illegally.

tyre or (*US*) **tire** ▷ *noun* **1** a rubber ring that fits around the outside edge of the wheel of a vehicle such as a bicycle, pram, wheelbarrow, etc to give traction and help minimize the effect of bumps and hollows in road surfaces. **2** (*in full* **pneumatic tyre**) a type of hollow rubber tyre that has an inner tube filled with compressed air and a tread that is specially designed to provide good roadholding and efficient water dispersal in the rain. **3** a band of steel, iron, etc fitted around the rim of a cartwheel or the wheel of a railway vehicle to strengthen it. ⓘ 18c: a variant of 15c *tire* a headdress, from ATTIRE.

tyre chain ▷ *noun* a type of chain fastened round the tyre of a vehicle to improve roadholding and help prevent skidding in snow. Also called **snow chain**. ⓘ 1950s.

tyre gauge ▷ *noun* a piece of equipment used for measuring the air pressure in a pneumatic tyre.

Tyrian /'tɪrɪən/ ▷ *adj* belonging or relating to Tyre, once an important ancient Phoenician seaport, but now a small market town in S Lebanon. ▷ *noun* a citizen or inhabitant of, or someone born in, Tyre. ⓘ 16c: from Latin *Tyrius*.

Tyrian purple and **Tyrian red** ▷ *noun* **1** a dye prepared from molluscs and which the ancient city of Tyre was once famous for producing. **2** the colour of this dye.

tyro or **tiro** /'taɪəroʊ/ ▷ *noun* (***tyros***) a novice or beginner. ⓘ 17c: from Latin *tiro* a young soldier, a recruit.

Tyrolean or **Tirolean** /tɪrə'liːən/ (*also* **Tyrolese** or **Tirolese**) ▷ *adj* **1** belonging or relating to the Tyrol, an E Alpine region that lies mainly in W Austria, although the southern part was ceded to Italy after World War I. **2** belonging or relating to Tyrol, a province in the E Alpine region of W Austria. **3** belonging or relating to the inhabitants of this region or province, or to their language. ▷ *noun* **1** a citizen or inhabitant of, or someone born in, the Tyrol or the province of Tyrol. **2** the dialect of German that is spoken around this area. ⓘ 19c: from *Tyrol*.

Tyrolean hat ▷ *noun* a man's soft felt hat with a turned-up brim and a small feather cockade at one side.

tyrosinase /taɪroʊsɪ'neɪz/ ▷ *noun* an enzyme that works as the catalyst in the conversion of tyrosine to the pigment melanin. ⓘ 19c: from TYROSINE.

tyrosine /'taɪəroʊsiːn, 'tɪ-/ ▷ *noun* (symbol **Tyr**) *biochem* an amino acid found in proteins and which is the precursor of certain hormones, eg adrenaline, thyroxine, and of the pigment melanin. ⓘ 19c: from Greek *tyros* cheese.

tzar, **tzarevitch**, **tzarevna**, **tzarina** see TSAR, TSAREVITCH, TSAREVNA, TSARINA

tzatziki /tsat'siːkɪ/ ▷ *noun* a Greek dip made of yoghurt and chopped cucumber, flavoured with mint and garlic. ⓘ 20c: modern Greek, from Turkish *cacik*.

tzigane /tsɪ'gɑːn/ ▷ *noun* a Hungarian Gypsy. Also *as adj*. ⓘ 18c: French, from Hungarian *cigány* gypsy.

U

U¹ or **u** /juː/ *noun* (***Us***, ***U's*** or ***u's***) **1** the twenty-first letter of the English alphabet. **2** anything shaped like the letter.

U² /juː/ *adj*, *Brit colloq* said especially of language: typical of or acceptable to the upper classes. Compare NON-U.

U³ *abbreviation* **1** unionist. **2** united. **3** *Brit* universal, denoting a film designated as suitable for people of all ages. **4** *IVR* Uruguay.

U⁴ *symbol, chem* uranium.

UAE ⊳ *abbreviation* United Arab Emirates.

UAR ⊳ *abbreviation* United Arab Republic.

UB40 ⊳ *abbreviation* in the UK: unemployment benefit form 40, a registration card issued by the Department of Employment to an unemployed person. See also UNEMPLOYMENT BENEFIT.

U-bend ⊳ *noun* an air-trap in the form of a U-shaped bend in a pipe, especially a waste pipe.

Übermensch /'yːbəmɛnʃ/ ⊳ *noun* (***Übermenschen*** /-ʃən/) *philos* the German source word for SUPERMAN (sense 1), often used in academic and literary English. ◷ Early 20c: German, literally 'beyond man'.

ubiety /jʊ'baɪətɪ/ ⊳ *noun* the state or condition of being in a definite place; location. ◷ 17c: from Latin *ubi* where.

ubiquinone /jʊ'bɪkwɪnoʊn/ ⊳ *noun, biochem* a quinone involved in the transfer of electrons during cell respiration. ◷ 1950s: from *ubi*quitous + QUINONE.

ubiquitous /jʊ'bɪkwɪtəs/ ⊳ *adj* existing, found or seeming to be found everywhere at the same time; omnipresent. • **ubiquitously** *adverb*. • **ubiquitousness** *noun*. ◷ 19c: from UBIQUITY.

ubiquity /jʊ'bɪkwɪtɪ/ ⊳ *noun* **1** existence everywhere at the same time; omnipresence. **2** (*also* **Ubiquity**) *theol* the omnipresence of Christ. ◷ 16c: from Latin *ubique* everywhere.

U-boat ⊳ *noun* a German submarine, used especially in World Wars I and II. ◷ Early 20c: from German *U-boot*, short for *Unterseeboot*, literally 'undersea-boat'.

UBR ⊳ *abbreviation* Uniform Business Rate.

u.c. ⊳ *abbreviation* upper case.

UCAS /'juːkas/ ⊳ *abbreviation* in the UK: Universities and Colleges Admissions Service, an organization which administers entry to universities and colleges, formed in 1993 by an amalgamation of UCCA and PCAS.

UCATT ⊳ *abbreviation* Union of Construction, Allied Trades and Technicians.

UCCA /'ʌkə/ ⊳ *abbreviation* Universities Central Council on Admissions, an organization which formerly administered entry to universities in the UK, now part of UCAS.

UCW ⊳ *abbreviation* Union of Communication Workers.

UDA ⊳ *abbreviation* Ulster Defence Association, a Northern Irish Loyalist paramilitary organization.

udder /'ʌdə(r)/ ⊳ *noun* in certain mammals, eg cows, goats, etc: the bag-like structure, with two or more teats, containing the mammary glands that secrete milk. ◷ Anglo-Saxon *uder*.

UDF ⊳ *abbreviation* United Democratic Front, a South African organization of anti-apartheid groups.

UDI ⊳ *abbreviation* Unilateral Declaration of Independence.

UDM ⊳ *abbreviation* Union of Democratic Mineworkers.

udometer /jʊ'dɒmɪtə(r)/ ⊳ *noun* a rain-gauge. ◷ 19c: from Latin *udus* wet.

UDR ⊳ *abbreviation* Ulster Defence Regiment.

UEFA /juː'eɪfə, -'iːfə/ ⊳ *abbreviation* Union of European Football Associations.

uey or **U-ey** /'juːɪ/ ⊳ *noun* (***ueys*** or ***U-eys***) *Austral slang* a U-turn. ◷ 1970s.

UFC ⊳ *abbreviation* Universities Funding Council.

UFO or **ufo** /juːɛf'oʊ, 'juːfoʊ/ (***UFOs*** or ***ufos***) *noun* an unidentified flying object, any unrecognizable flying vehicle presumed to be from another planet or outer space. See also FLYING SAUCER. ◷ 1950s.

ufology /jʊ'fɒlədʒɪ/ ⊳ *noun* the study of UFOs. • **ufological** *adj*. • **ufologist** *noun*.

ugh /ʌx, ʌg, ɜːx, ɜːg/ ⊳ *exclamation* expressing dislike or disgust. ⊳ *noun* used to represent the sound of a cough or grunt. ◷ 18c.

ugli /'ʌglɪ/ ⊳ *noun, trademark* (***uglis*** or ***uglies***) **1** a large juicy citrus fruit with a thick wrinkled yellow-red skin, that is a cross between a grapefruit, a Seville orange and a tangerine. It is either eaten fresh or used in jams or preserves to give a sweet-sour flavour. **2** the plant that produces this fruit, native to the W Indies. ◷ 1930s: from *ugly*, because of the fruit's appearance.

uglify /'ʌglɪfaɪ/ ⊳ *verb* (***uglifies***, ***uglified***, ***uglifying***) to make something ugly; to disfigure it. • **uglification** *noun*. ◷ 16c.

ugly /'ʌglɪ/ ⊳ *adj* (***uglier***, ***ugliest***) **1** unpleasant to look at; extremely unattractive. **2** morally repulsive or offensive. **3** threatening, or involving danger or violence ▫ *an ugly situation*. **4** angry; bad-tempered ▫ *an ugly mood*. • **uglily** *adverb*. • **ugliness** *noun*. ◷ 13c: from Norse *uggligr* to be feared, from *ugga* fear or dread.

ugly duckling ⊳ *noun* someone or something, initially thought ugly or worthless, that later turns out to be outstandingly beautiful or highly valued. ◷ 19c: from *The Ugly Duckling*, the title of a story about a cygnet in a brood of ducklings, by Hans Christian Andersen.

Ugric /'uːgrɪk, 'juː-/ ⊳ *adj* belonging or relating to the branch of the FINNO-UGRIC languages that includes Hungarian, or to the people who speak it. ⊳ *noun* **1** the branch of Finno-Ugric that includes Hungarian. **2** someone who speaks one of these languages. Also called **Ugrian**. ◷ 19c: from *Ugri* a name coined by Russian writers for a group of peoples living to the east of the Ural mountains.

UHF ⊳ *abbreviation*, *radio* ultrahigh frequency.

uh-huh /'ʌhʌ/ ⊳ *exclamation* **1** expressing agreement, affirmation, etc. **2** used as a less emphatic form of 'yes'.

uhlan /'uːlɑːn, 'juː-/ ⊳ *noun*, *historical* in certain European armies, especially the Polish or, later, German armies: a light cavalryman or lancer. ◷ 18c: French, from German *Uhlan*, from Polish *ulan*, *hulan*, from Turkish *oglan* young man.

UHT ⊳ *abbreviation* **1** ultra-heat-treated. **2** ultrahigh temperature.

uhuru /uː'huːruː/ ⊳ *noun*, *especially E Afr* **1** freedom, eg from slavery. **2** national independence. ◷ 1960s: Swahili meaning 'freedom'.

uillean pipes /ˈuːlɪən —/ ▷ *plural noun* bagpipes in which the bag is inflated by squeezing bellows under the arm. Also called **union pipes**. ⓘ 19c: from Irish *píob uilleann*, from *píob* pipe + *uilleann* of the elbow.

uitlander /ˈeɪtlandə(r), ˈɔɪtlandə(r)/ ▷ *noun* (*sometimes* **Uitlander**) *S Afr* a foreigner, originally a British person who went to the Transvaal or Orange Free State before the Boer War of 1899–1902. ⓘ 19c: Afrikaans, from Dutch, meaning 'outlander' or 'foreigner'.

UK ▷ *abbreviation* United Kingdom.

UKAEA ▷ *abbreviation* United Kingdom Atomic Energy Authority.

ukase /jʊˈkeɪz/ ▷ *noun* **1** a command issued by a supreme ruler, especially the Tsar in Imperial Russia. **2** any arbitrary decree or command. ⓘ 18c: from Russian *ukaz* order, from *ukazat* to order or decree.

uke /juːk/ ▷ *noun, colloq* short form of UKULELE. ⓘ Early 20c.

Ukrainian /jʊˈkreɪnɪən/ ▷ *adj* belonging or relating to Ukraine, a republic of SE Europe that borders the Black Sea (formerly a republic of the USSR), its inhabitants or their language. ▷ *noun* **1** a citizen or inhabitant of, or person born in, Ukraine. **2** the official language of Ukraine, a Slavonic language closely related to Russian. ⓘ 19c: from an obsolete Russian word *ukraina* frontier regions, from *u* at + *krai* edge.

ukulele or **ukelele** /jʊkəˈleɪlɪ/ ▷ *noun* a small guitar, usually with four strings, that developed in Hawaii from an earlier Portuguese instrument. ⓘ 19c: Hawaiian, literally 'jumping flea'.

ULA or **ula** ▷ *abbreviation, computing* uncommitted logic array.

ulcer /ˈʌlsə(r)/ ▷ *noun* **1** *pathol* a persistent open sore, often accompanied by inflammation, on the surface of the skin or of the mucous membranes lining a body cavity. **2** a continuing source of evil or corruption. • **ulcered** *adj*. • **ulcerous** *adj*. ⓘ 14c: from Latin *ulcus, ulceris*, related to Greek *helkos* a sore.

ulcerate /ˈʌlsəreɪt/ ▷ *verb* (***ulcerated, ulcerating***) *tr & intr* to form or cause an ulcer on or in a part of the body. • **ulceration** *noun*. • **ulcerative** *adj*.

-ule /juːl/ ▷ *suffix, forming nouns, denoting* a diminutive; smallness □ ***nodule*** □ ***globule***. ⓘ From Latin *-ulus* a diminutive suffix.

ulema /ˈuːlɪmə/ ▷ *noun* (***ulemas***) in a Muslim country or society: **1** the body of professional theologians who are regarded as the authority on religious law. **2** a member of this body. ⓘ 17c: from Arabic *ulama*, plural of *alim* learned.

-ulent /jʊlənt/ ▷ *suffix, forming adjectives, denoting* full of; with much □ ***fraudulent***. • **-ulence** *suffix, forming nouns*. ⓘ From Latin *-ulentus*.

ullage /ˈʌlɪdʒ/ ▷ *noun* **1** the amount of wine, etc by which a container falls short of being full. **2** the quantity of liquid lost from a container through leakage, evaporation, etc. **3 a** the part of a fuel tank, especially that of a rocket, that is not filled with fuel; **b** the volume or capacity of this part. **4** *slang* the dregs remaining in a glass, etc. ⓘ 15c: from French *eullage*, from *euillier* to fill a barrel or cask, from Latin *oculus* eye, used in the sense 'bung-hole'.

ulna /ˈʌlnə/ ▷ *noun* (***ulnae*** /-niː/ or ***ulnas***) *anatomy* **1** the thinner and longer of the two bones of the human forearm. Compare RADIUS (sense 5). **2** the corresponding bone in the forelimb or wing of other vertebrates. • **ulnar** *adj* □ ***ulnar nerve***. ⓘ 16c: Latin, meaning 'elbow' or 'arm'.

ulotrichous /jʊˈlɒtrɪkəs/ *anthropol* ▷ *adj* having hair that is tightly curled. ▷ *noun* someone with this kind of hair. ⓘ 19c: from Latin *Ulotrichi* (the classification applied to those with this type of hair), from Greek *oulos* curly + *thrix, trichos* hair.

ulster /ˈʌlstə(r)/ ▷ *noun* a man's loose heavy double-breasted overcoat, often worn with a belt. ⓘ 19c: named after Ulster in Northern Ireland, where such coats were first made.

Ulsterman and **Ulsterwoman** ▷ *noun* a citizen or inhabitant of, or person born in, Ulster.

ult. ▷ *abbreviation* **1** ultimate or ultimately. **2** ultimo.

ulterior /ʌlˈtɪərɪə(r)/ ▷ *adj* **1** said of motives, etc: beyond or other than what is apparent or admitted. **2** coming later; in the future; subsequent. **3** situated beyond a particular point or line; on the further side. • **ulteriorly** *adverb*. ⓘ 17c: Latin, meaning 'further' or 'more distant', from *uls* beyond.

ultima /ˈʌltɪmə/ ▷ *noun* (***ultimas***) *linguistics* the last syllable of a word. ⓘ Early 20c: Latin feminine of *ultimus* last.

ultimate /ˈʌltɪmət/ (abbreviation **ult.**) *adj* **1** last or final in a series or process. **2** most important; greatest possible. **3** fundamental; basic. **4** *colloq* best; most advanced. ▷ *noun* **1** the final point; the end or conclusion. **2** (**the ultimate**) *colloq* the best; the most advanced of its kind □ ***the ultimate in computer technology***. • **ultimately** *adverb* (abbreviation **ult.**) in the end; finally. • **ultimateness** *noun*. ⓘ 17c: from Latin *ultimus* last, from *ulter* distant or far.

ultimatum /ʌltɪˈmeɪtəm/ ▷ *noun* (***ultimatums*** or ***ultimata*** /-tə/) **1** in a dispute, negotiations, etc: a final statement from one of the parties involved to another, declaring an intention to take hostile action unless specified conditions are fulfilled. **2** any final terms, demand, etc. ⓘ 18c: Latin neuter of *ultimatus* ULTIMATE.

ultimo /ˈʌltɪmoʊ/ ▷ *adj* (abbreviation **ult.**) used mainly in formal correspondence: of or during last month □ ***your letter of the tenth ultimo***. Compare PROXIMO. ⓘ 17c; 16c in obsolete sense 'the last day (of a specified month)': from Latin *ultimus* last.

ultimogeniture /ʌltɪmoʊˈdʒɛnɪtʃə(r)/ ▷ *noun, law* the right of the youngest child of a family to succeed or to inherit a title or property. ⓘ 19c: from Latin *ultimus* last, modelled on PRIMOGENITURE.

ultra /ˈʌltrə/ ▷ *adj* **1** said of a person or party: holding extreme opinions, especially in political matters. **2** *colloq* extremely good; marvellous. ▷ *noun* (***ultras***) someone who holds extreme opinions, especially in political or religious matters. ⓘ 19c: originally meaning 'ultra-royalist', with reference to early 19c France, an abbreviation of French *ultra-royaliste*.

ultra- /ʌltrə/ ▷ *prefix, denoting* **1** beyond in place, range or limit □ ***ultra-microscopic***. **2** extreme or extremely □ ***ultra-Conservative*** □ ***ultra-modern***. ⓘ From Latin *ultra* beyond.

ultracentrifuge *chem* ▷ *noun* a very high-speed type of centrifuge, used to separate colloidal and large-molecular solutions. ▷ *verb* to spin (a solution, etc) in an ultracentrifuge. • **ultracentrifugal** *adj*. ⓘ 1920s.

ultrafiche ▷ *noun* a sheet of microfilm similar to a microfiche but with a much greater number of microcopied records on it. See also MICROFICHE. ⓘ 1970s: from French *fiche* a small card or slip of paper.

ultra-heat-treated ▷ *adj* (abbreviation **UHT**) said of milk, etc: sterilized by exposure to very high temperatures, and thus with its shelf-life increased.

ultrahigh frequency ▷ *noun* (abbreviation **UHF**) a radio frequency between 300 and 3 000MHz.

ultraism /ˈʌltrəɪzəm/ ▷ *noun* extreme principle, opinion or measure. • **ultraist** *noun, adj*. ⓘ 19c.

ultramarine ▷ *noun* **1** a deep-blue pigment used in paints, originally made by grinding lapis lazuli. **2** the colour of this pigment. ▷ *adj* **1** of the colour ultramarine. **2** *rare* from or situated beyond the sea. ⓘ 16c: from Latin *ultramarinus*, from *ultra* beyond + *mare* sea, so called because the lapis lazuli, used to make the pigment, was imported from Asia.

ultramicro- ▻ *prefix, denoting* smaller than MICRO-, or dealing with quantities smaller than MICRO- □ *ultramicrochemistry.*

ultramicroscope ▻ *noun* a microscope with strong illumination from the side, used to observe ultramicroscopic objects by the scattering of light through them. • **ultramicroscopy** *noun.* Ⓒ Early 20c.

ultramicroscopic ▻ *adj* **1** too small to be visible under an ordinary microscope. **2** relating to an ultramicroscope or its use. • **ultramicroscopically** *adverb.*

ultramontane /ʌltrəˈmɒnteɪn/ ▻ *adj* **1** situated or relating to an area beyond a mountain range, especially the Alps. **2** *RC Church* relating or belonging to a faction which is in favour of supreme papal authority on doctrinal matters. ▻ *noun* **1** someone who lives beyond a mountain range, especially the Alps. **2** *RC Church* a member of the ultramontane faction. • **ultramontanism** *noun.* See also VATICANISM. • **ultramontanist** *noun.* Ⓒ 16c: from Latin *ultramontanus*, from *mons, montis* mountain.

ultramundane /ʌltrəˈmʌndeɪn/ ▻ *adj* beyond the physical world or beyond the limits of our solar system. 16c: from Latin *ultramundanus*, from *mundus* world.

ultrasonic ▻ *adj* relating to or producing ultrasound. Compare INFRASONIC, SUPERSONIC, SUBSONIC. • **ultrasonically** *adverb.* Ⓒ 1920s.

ultrasonics ▻ *plural noun* ultrasonic waves; ultrasound. ▻ *singular noun* the branch of physics that deals with the study of ultrasound. Ⓒ 20c.

ultrasound ▻ *noun* sound consisting of waves with frequencies higher than 20 000Hz, and therefore above the upper limit of normal human hearing. It is widely used in medical diagnosis (especially during pregnancy when X-rays would be damaging), in sonar systems, for cleaning industrial tools, and for detecting flaws and impurities in metals. Ⓒ 1920s.

ultrasound scan ▻ *noun* a medical examination of an internal part, especially a fetus, by directing ultrasound waves through it to produce an image on a screen. • **ultrasound scanner** *noun* the device used to make such an examination.

ultrastructure ▻ *noun, biol* the molecular structure of cell organelles examined by electronmicroscopy. Ⓒ 1930s.

ultraviolet *adj* (abbreviation **UV**) **1** denoting electromagnetic radiation with wavelengths in the range 4 to 400nm, ie in the region between violet light and X-rays. **2** relating to or involving ultraviolet radiation or its use. ▻ *noun* the ultraviolet part of the spectrum. Ⓒ 19c.

ultra vires /ˈʌltrə ˈvaɪəriːz/ ▻ *adverb, adj, law* beyond the powers or legal authority of a person, corporation, etc. Ⓒ 18c: Latin, meaning 'beyond the powers or strength'.

ululate /ˈjuːljʊleɪt, ˈʌl-/ ▻ *verb* (***ululated, ululating***) *intr* to howl, wail or screech. • **ululant** *adj.* • **ululation** *noun.* Ⓒ 17c: from Latin *ululare, ululatum* to howl.

um /ɜːm, əm, ʌm/ ▻ *exclamation* expressing hesitation, uncertainty, etc. ▻ *noun* an utterance of 'um'. ▻ *verb* (***ummed, umming***) *intr* to make the sound 'um', expressing hesitation, etc. Ⓒ 17c.

umbel /ˈʌmbəl/ ▻ *noun, bot* a flower-head, characteristic of plants of the **Umbelliferae** family, eg cow parsley and hogweed, in which a cluster of flowers with stalks of equal length arise from the same point on the main stem. • **umbellar** /ʌmˈbelə(r)/ *adj.* • **umbellate** /ˈʌmbɛleɪt/ *adj.* Ⓒ 16c: from Latin *umbella* sunshade, a diminutive of *umbra* shade.

umbelliferous /ʌmbəˈlɪfərəs/ ▻ *adj, bot* denoting or belonging to plants which typically have flowers arranged in umbels. • **umbellifer** /ʌmˈbɛlɪfə(r)/ *noun* any plant of this family. Ⓒ 17c: from Latin *umbella* (see UMBEL) + *ferre* to carry or bear.

umber /ˈʌmbə(r)/ ▻ *noun* **1** a dark yellowish-brown earthy mineral containing oxides of iron and manganese, used to make pigments. **2** any of these pigments or the brownish colours produced by them. ▻ *adj* referring to the colour of umber; dark brown. Ⓒ 16c: from French *terre d'ombre* or Italian *terra di ombra* shadow earth, from Latin *umbra* shade or shadow, or from *Umbra* feminine of *Umber* UMBRIAN.

umbilical /ʌmˈbɪlɪkəl, -ˈlaɪkəl/ ▻ *adj* relating to the umbilicus or the umbilical cord.

umbilical cord ▻ *noun* **1** a long flexible tube-like organ by which a fetus is attached to the placenta and through which it receives nourishment. **2** any cable, tube, servicing line, etc through which essential supplies are conveyed, eg that attached to a rocket vehicle or spacecraft during preparations for its launch, or the lifeline that connects astronauts to their spacecrafts during a spacewalk.

umbilicate /ʌmˈbɪlɪkət/ ▻ *adj* **1** with a navel or umbilicus. **2** navel-like. • **umbilication** *noun.*

umbilicus /ʌmˈbɪlɪkəs, -ˈlaɪkəs/ ▻ *noun* (***umbilici*** /ʌmˈbɪlɪsaɪ, -ˈlaɪsaɪ/ or ***umbilicuses*** /-siːz/) **1** *anatomy* the navel. **2** *biol* a small, usually central, depression or navel-like hole, such as that at the base of a shell. Ⓒ 17c: Latin, meaning 'navel'.

umble pie /ˈʌmbəl —/ ▻ *noun* HUMBLE PIE

umbles /ˈʌmbəlz/ ▻ *plural noun, archaic* the entrails (the liver, heart, lungs, etc) of an animal, especially a deer. Ⓒ 14c: from French *nombles*, from Latin *lumbulus*, diminutive of *lumbus* loin.

umbo /ˈʌmboʊ/ ▻ *noun* (***umbones*** /ʌmˈboʊniːz/ or ***umbos***) **1** the central boss of a shield. **2** *zool* the protuberant oldest part of a bivalve shell. **3** *bot* a knob or protuberance on the cap of certain fungi. **4** *anatomy* a projection on the inner surface of the eardrum where the malleus is attached. • **umbonal** *adj.* • **umbonate** *adj.* Ⓒ 18c: Latin, meaning 'the boss of a 'shield', 'knob' or 'protuberance'.

umbra /ˈʌmbrə/ ▻ *noun* (***umbrae*** /ˈʌmbriː/ or ***umbras***) **1** the central and darkest part of a shadow. **2 a** any shadow; **b**) *astron* the shadow cast by the moon on the earth during an eclipse of the sun. **3** the darker inner part of a sunspot. • **umbral** *adj.* Ⓒ 17c; 16c in sense 'ghost' or 'phantom': Latin, meaning 'shade' or 'shadow'.

umbrage /ˈʌmbrɪdʒ/ ▻ *noun* **1** (*especially* **give** or **take umbrage**) anoyance; offence. **2** *archaic, literary* **a** the shadow cast or shade provided by trees, etc; **b** the foliage of trees, as something that provides shade. Ⓒ 15c: from French *ombrage*, from Latin *umbra* shade or shadow.

umbrageous /ʌmˈbreɪdʒəs/ ▻ *adj* **1 a** providing shade; **b** shaded, eg by trees, etc. **2** said of a person: suspicious or tending to take offence easily. Ⓒ 16c.

umbrella /ʌmˈbrɛlə/ ▻ *noun* (***umbrellas***) **1** a device carried to give shelter from rain, etc, consisting of a rounded fabric canopy supported on a lightweight, usually metal, collapsible framework of ribs fitted around a central stick or handle. This allows it to be folded down to form a slim cylinder when not in use. **2** anything that resembles an open umbrella in form or function. **3** *bot* a part of a plant that resembles an open umbrella. **4** *zool* the circular or flattened bell-shaped body of a jellyfish. **5** *military* a protective screen or shield of fighter aircraft or gunfire. **6** *US military slang* a parachute. **7** something, such as an organization, that provides protection or overall cover for a number of others. ▻ *adj* **1** referring to something that covers or protects a number of things □ *an umbrella organization.* **2** said of a word, term, etc: general; covering several meanings or ideas. Ⓒ 17c: from Italian *ombrella*, diminutive of *ombra* shade; see UMBRA.

umbrella bird ▻ *noun* any of three species of bird with black plumage, native to tropical forests of S America. It has a crest of raised feathers on the crown of its head which, when opened during courtship, resembles an umbrella.

umbrella group and **umbrella organization** ▷ *noun* an organization that represents and supports separate smaller bodies with common interests.

umbrella stand ▷ *noun* a stand or receptacle for holding closed umbrellas, walking sticks, etc in an upright position.

umbrella tree ▷ *noun* any of various trees with leaves or branches arranged in an umbrella-like formation, especially a type of N American magnolia.

Umbrian /ˈʌmbrɪən/ ▷ *noun* **1** a citizen or inhabitant of, or person born in, Umbria, a province in central Italy, especially a member of the Italic people who inhabited this area in pre-Roman times. **2** the extinct language of this people. **3** a painter of the Umbrian school, an Italian Renaissance school of painting to which Raphael belonged. ▷ *adj* **1** relating or belonging to Umbria or its inhabitants. **2** relating to the ancient Umbrian language. **3** relating or belonging to the Umbrian school of painting. ◷ 17c: from Latin *Umber* or *Umbria*.

umiak or **oomiak** /ˈuːmɪak/ ▷ *noun* a large open boat made from a wooden frame covered with stretched skins, typically paddled by women. ◷ 18c: from Inuit *umiaq*.

UMIST /ˈjuːmɪst/ ▷ *abbreviation* University of Manchester Institute of Science and Technology.

umlaut /ˈʊmlɑʊt/ ▷ *noun* in Germanic languages: **1** a change in the pronunciation of a vowel under the influence of a front vowel in a following syllable (especially in a suffix). **2** a mark consisting of two dots placed above a vowel (eg *ö* or *ä*) that undergoes or has undergone this change. ◷ 19c: German, from *um* around + *Laut* sound.

umpire /ˈʌmpaɪə(r)/ ▷ *noun* **1** an impartial person who supervises play in various sports, eg cricket and tennis, enforcing the rules and deciding disputes. **2** someone who judges or decides a dispute or deadlock; an arbitrator. ▷ *verb* (***umpired***, ***umpiring***) *tr & intr* to act as umpire in a match, dispute, etc. ◷ 15c originally as *noumpere*, by mistaken division of *a noumpere*: from French *nompere*, from *non-* not + *per*, *pair* peer or equal.

umpteen /ʌmpˈtiːn, ˈʌmptiːn/ ▷ *adj*, *colloq* very many; innumerable □ ***I've told you umpteen times!*** ● **umpteenth** *noun, adj* the latest or last of very many □ ***For the umpteenth time, I don't know!*** ◷ Early 20c: from earlier *umpty* (modelled on twen*ty*, etc) a great deal + *-teen*.

UN ▷ *abbreviation* United Nations.

un or **'un** /ʌn, ən/ ▷ *pronoun, dialect, colloq* one □ ***That's a nice 'un.*** ◷ 19c: a spelling that is supposed to reflect dialectal or informal pronunciation.

un- /ʌn/ ▷ *prefix* **1** *added to adjectives, nouns and adverbs, denoting* the opposite of the base word; not. **2** *added to verbs, denoting* **a** a reversal of an action, process or state □ ***uncurl*** □ ***unharness***; **b** an intensification of the base word □ ***unloosen***. **3** *added to nouns, forming verbs, chiefly archaic, denoting* release or removal from or deprivation of □ ***ungarter*** □ ***unfrock***. ◷ Anglo-Saxon.

unable ▷ *adj* (*chiefly* **unable to do something**) not able; not having sufficient strength, skill or authority (to do something). ◷ 14c.

unaccompanied ▷ *adj* **1** not accompanied; not escorted or attended. **2** *music* without instrumental accompaniment. ◷ 16c.

unaccomplished ▷ *adj* **1** not accomplished; not achieved or completed. **2** said of a person: without social or intellectual accomplishments. ◷ 16c.

unaccountable ▷ *adj* **1** impossible to explain. **2** said of a person: difficult to make out; puzzling in character. **3** not answerable or accountable. ● **unaccountability** *noun*. ● **unaccountably** *adverb*. ◷ 17c.

unaccounted ▷ *adj* (*usually* **unaccounted for**) **1** unexplained. **2** not included in an account.

unaccustomed ▷ *adj* **1** not usual or customary; unfamiliar. **2** (*usually* **unaccustomed to something**) not used or accustomed to it. ● **unaccustomedness** *noun*. ◷ 16c.

una corda /uːnə ˈkɔːdə/ ▷ *adj, adverb, music* said of the piano: played using the soft (left) pedal. ◷ 19c: Italian, meaning 'one string' since only one of the three strings tuned to each note is struck by the hammer when the soft pedal is used.

unactable ▷ *adj* unable to be acted; not suitable for theatrical performance. ● **unactability** *noun*. ◷ 19c.

unadopted ▷ *adj* **1** not adopted. **2** said of a road, etc: not maintained, repaired, etc by a local authority. ◷ 17c.

unadulterated ▷ *adj* **1** pure; not mixed with anything else. **2** sheer; complete. ◷ 17c.

unadvisable 1 said of a person: not open to advice; obstinate. **2** said of a course of action, etc: INADVISABLE. ● **unadvisableness** *noun*. ● **unadvisably** *adverb*. ◷ 17c.

unadvised ▷ *adj* **1** not advised; without advice. **2** unwise; ill-advised. ● **unadvisedly** *adverb*. ● **unadvisedness** *noun*. ◷ 14c.

unaffected ▷ *adj* **1** sincere or genuine, not affected; free from pretentiousness. **2** not affected or influenced. ● **unaffectedly** *adverb*. ● **unaffectedness** *noun*. ◷ 16c.

unalienable ▷ *noun* INALIENABLE.

Some words with *un-* prefixed, all of which refer to UN- sense 1 unless specified otherwise below.

unabashed *adj.*
unabated *adj.*
unabbreviated *adj.*
unabridged *adj.*
unacademic *adj.*
unaccented *adj.*
unaccentuated *adj.*
unacceptability *noun.*
unacceptable *adj.*
unacceptableness *noun.*
unacceptably *adverb.*
unacclimatized or **unacclimatised** *adj.*
unaccommodated *adj.*
unaccommodating *adj.*
unaccredited *adj.*
unachievable *adj.*
unacknowledged *adj.*
unacquainted *adj.*
unacted *adj.*
unadaptable *adj.*
unadapted *adj.*
unaddressed *adj.*
unadjusted *adj.*
unadorned *adj.*
unadventurous *adj.*
unadvertised *adj.*
unaesthetic *adj.*
unaffectionate *adj.*
unaffiliated *adj.*
unaffordable *adj.*
unafraid *adj.*
unaided *adj.*
unaimed *adj.*
unaired *adj.*
unalarmed *adj* sense 2.
unaligned *adj.*
unalike *adj.*
unallayed *adj.*
unalleviated *adj.*
unallied *adj.*
unallotted *adj.*
unallowable *adj.*
unalterability *noun.*
unalterable *adj.*
unalterably *adverb.*
unaltered *adj.*
unamazed *adj.*

unalloyed ▻ *adj* **1** not alloyed; pure. **2** said of joy, pleasure, etc: pure; sheer; not mixed with feelings of sadness or anxiety. ◷ 17c.

un-American ▻ *adj* **1** not in accordance with American character, ideas, feeling, tradition, etc. **2** disloyal to, or against the interests or ideals of, the US. ● **un-Americanism** *noun*. ◷ 19c.

unanimity /juːnəˈnɪmɪtɪ/ ▻ *noun* the state of being unanimous; unanimous agreement. ◷ 15c: from French *unanimité*; see UNANIMOUS.

unanimous /jʊˈnanɪməs/ ▻ *adj* **1** all in complete agreement; of one mind. **2** said of an opinion, decision, etc: shared or arrived at by all, with none disagreeing. ● **unanimously** *adverb*. ◷ 17c: from Latin *unanimus*, from *unus* one + *animus* mind.

unannounced ▻ *adj* not announced; unexpectedly or without warning. ◷ 18c.

unapprehended ▻ *adj* **1** not understood. **2** not having been arrested.

unapproachable ▻ *adj* **1** out of reach; inaccessible. **2** with a manner that discourages familiarity; aloof; unfriendly; stand-offish. **3** beyond rivalry. ● **unapproachableness** *noun*. ● **unapproachably** *adverb*. ◷ 16c.

unappropriated /ʌnəˈproʊprɪeɪtɪd/ ▻ *adj* **1** not set aside for a particular purpose. **2** not taken into anyone's possession. ◷ 18c.

unapt ▻ *adj* **1** (*usually* **unapt for something**) not fitted for it; unsuitable. **2** lacking in aptitude; slow. **3** (*sometimes* **unapt to do something**) not readily inclined or accustomed to do it. ● **unaptly** *adverb*. ● **unaptness** *noun*. ◷ 14c.

unarmed ▻ *adj* **1** not armed; without weapons. **2** said of an animal: without claws, horns, etc. **3** said of a plant: without spines, prickles, etc. ◷ 13c.

unasked-for ▻ *adj* not sought or invited.

unassailable ▻ *adj* **1** not able to be assailed or attacked. **2** not able to be challenged or denied; irrefutable. ● **unassailably** *adverb*. ◷ 16c.

unassuming ▻ *adj* modest or unpretentious. ● **unassumingly** *adverb*. ● **unassumingness** *noun*. ◷ 18c.

unattached ▻ *adj* **1** not attached, associated or connected, especially to a particular group, organization, etc. **2** not in a steady romantic or sexual relationship. ◷ 18c; 15c in obsolete legal sense 'not arrested or seized by authority'.

unattended ▻ *adj* **1** not accompanied or watched over. **2** (*usually* **unattended by** or **with something**) not resulting from or occurring with a particular thing, circumstance, etc. **3** (*often* **unattended to**) not listened to or paid attention. ◷ 17c.

unau /ˈjuːnɔː/ ▻ *noun* the two-toed sloth. ◷ 18c: French, from Tupí.

unavailing ▻ *adj* said of efforts, etc: futile; of no avail. ● **unavailingly** *adverb*. ◷ 17c.

una voce /ˈjuːnəˈvoʊsiː/ ▻ *adverb* with one voice; unanimously. ◷ 16c: Latin, from *unus* one + *vox* voice.

unavoidable ▻ *adj* not able to be avoided; inevitable. ● **unavoidability** and **unavoidableness** *noun*. ● **unavoidably** *adverb*. ◷ 16c.

unaware ▻ *adj* with no knowledge (of something); not aware or conscious (of it). ▻ *adverb* unawares. ● **unawareness** *noun*. ◷ 16c.

> ***unaware, unawares***
>
> These words are often confused with each other.

unawares ▻ *adverb* **1** unexpectedly; by surprise. **2** without knowing or realizing; inadvertently. ● **catch** or **take someone unawares** to catch or take them off guard; to surprise them. ◷ 16c.

unbacked ▻ *adj* **1** said eg of a chair: without a back. **2** without backing; unsupported; unendorsed. **3** said of a racehorse, etc: not betted on. ◷ 16c.

unbalance ▻ *verb* **1** to throw someone or something off balance. **2** to upset someone's mental balance; to derange them. ▻ *noun* lack of balance or (mental) stability. ◷ 19c.

unbalanced ▻ *adj* **1** not in a state of physical balance. **2** lacking mental balance; deranged. **3** said eg of a view or judgement: lacking impartiality; biased. **4** *bookkeeping* not adjusted so as to show balance of debtor and creditor. ◷ 17c.

unbar ▻ *verb* **1** to remove a bar or bars from (a door, gate, etc). **2** to unfasten or open (a door, etc). ◷ 14c.

unbearable ▻ *adj* not bearable; intolerable or unendurable. ● **unbearably** *adverb*. ◷ 15c.

unbeatable ▻ *adj* not able to be beaten or defeated; unsurpassable. ● **unbeatably** *adverb*. ◷ 19c.

unbeaten ▻ *adj* **1** not beaten, especially not defeated or surpassed. **2** *cricket* not out. ◷ 13c.

unbecoming ▻ *adj* (*also* **unbecoming for** or **to someone**) **1** not becoming; not suited to the wearer or

Some words with *un-* prefixed, all of which refer to UN- sense 1 unless specified otherwise below.

unambiguous *adj.*
unambiguously *adverb.*
unambitious *adj.*
unambitiously *adverb.*
unambivalent *adj.*
unamended *adj.*
unamiable *adj.*
unamplified *adj.*
unamused *adj.*
unamusing *adj.*
unannotated *adj.*
unanswerable *adj.*
unanswered *adj.*
unanticipated *adj.*
unapologetic *adj.*
unapologetically *adverb.*

unapparent *adj.*
unappealable *adj.*
unappealing *adj.*
unappealingly *adverb.*
unappeasable *adj.*
unappeased *adj.*
unappetizing or **unappetising** *adj.*
unapplied *adj.*
unappointed *adj.*
unappreciated *adj.*
unappreciative *adj.*
unapproved *adj.*
unarguable *adj.*
unarguably *adverb.*
unarticulated *adj.*

unartificial *adj.*
unartistic *adj.*
unartistically *adverb.*
unascertained *adj.*
unashamed *adj.*
unashamedly *adverb.*
unasked *adj.*
unaspirated *adj.*
unaspiring *adj.*
unassertive *adj.*
unassertively *adverb.*
unassertiveness *noun.*
unassigned *adj.*
unassimilated *adj.*
unassisted *adj.*
unassociated *adj.*

showing them to advantage. **2** said of behaviour, etc: not appropriate or fitting; unseemly. • **unbecomingly** *adverb*. • **unbecomingness** *noun*. ◷ 16c.

unbeknown /ʌnbɪˈnoʊn/ or **unbeknownst** /-nst/ ▷ *adverb* **1** (*usually* **unbeknown** or **unbeknownst to someone**) unknown to them; without their knowledge. **2** without being known; unobserved. ◷ 17c.

unbelief ▷ *noun* disbelief; lack of belief, especially of religious belief. ◷ 12c.

unbelievable ▷ *adj* **1** too unusual or unexpected to be believed. **2** *colloq* remarkable; astonishing. • **unbelievability** or **unbelievableness** *noun*. • **unbelievably** *adverb*. ◷ 16c.

unbeliever ▷ *noun* someone who does not believe, especially in a particular religion. ◷ 16c.

unbelieving ▷ *adj* not believing, especially in a particular religion; without belief. • **unbelievingly** *adverb*. ◷ 16c.

unbend ▷ *verb* **1** to release the tension from or unstring (a bow). **2** *tr & intr* to relax (one's mind, behaviour, etc) from stiffness or formality; to make or become affable. **3** *naut* **a** to unfasten (a sail) from a yard or stay; **b** to cast loose (a cable) or untie (a rope, etc). **4** *tr & intr* to straighten or release something from a bent or curved position. • **unbendable** *adj*. ◷ 13c.

unbending ▷ *adj* **1** not bending; unyielding or inflexible. **2** strict or severe. • **unbendingly** *adverb*. • **unbendingness** *noun*. ◷ 17c.

unbent ▷ *adj* **1** not bent or bowed. **2** not overcome or vanquished.

unbiased or **unbiassed** ▷ *adj* not biased; unprejudiced or impartial. • **unbiasedly** *adverb*. • **unbiasedness** *noun*. ◷ 17c.

unbidden /ʌnˈbɪdən/ ▷ *adj* **1** not commanded or ordered; spontaneous or voluntary. **2** not invited or solicited. ◷ Anglo-Saxon.

unbind ▷ *verb* **1** to release or free someone from a bond or restraint. **2** to unfasten or undo (a bond, manacle, etc). ◷ Anglo-Saxon.

unbinding ▷ *noun* **1** the action of releasing from a bond or restraint. **2** the action of unfastening a bond. ▷ *adj* not binding.

unblinking ▷ *adj* without blinking; not showing emotion, especially fear; unflinching. • **unblinkingly** *adverb*. ◷ 20c.

unblown ▷ *adj* **1** not blown. **2** said of a flower: still at the bud stage.

unblushing ▷ *adj* **1** not blushing. **2** unashamed; shameless or brazen. • **unblushingly** *adverb*. ◷ 16c.

unbolt ▷ *verb* to unfasten or open (a door, etc) by undoing or drawing back a bolt. ◷ 15c.

unbolted¹ *adj* not fastened with a bolt or bolts. ◷ 16c.

unbolted² *adj* said of grain, flour, etc: not sifted; coarse. ◷ 16c.

unborn ▷ *adj* **1** said of a baby: not yet born; still in the womb. **2** not yet in existence; belonging to or in the future. ◷ Anglo-Saxon.

unbosom /ʌnˈbʊzəm/ ▷ *verb* (***unbosomed***, ***unbosoming***) **1** to reveal or confess something. **2** *intr* (*often* **unbosom oneself**) to speak openly about what is on one's mind; to free oneself of worries or troubles by talking about them. ◷ 16c.

unbound ▷ *adj* **1** not bound or restrained. **2** loose; not tied or fastened with a band, etc. **3** said of a book: without binding. ◷ Anglo-Saxon.

unbounded ▷ *adj* **1** without bounds or limits. **2** unchecked; unrestrained. • **unboundedly** *adverb*. • **unboundedness** *noun*. ◷ 16c.

unbowed /ʌnˈbaʊd/ ▷ *adj* **1** not bowed or bent. **2** not conquered or forced to yield. ◷ 14c.

unbridled ▷ *adj* **1** said of a horse: not wearing a bridle. **2** said of speech, emotion, etc: fully and freely felt or expressed; unrestrained.

un-British ▷ *adj* not British, especially not in accordance with British characteristics, traditions, etc. ◷ 18c.

unbroken ▷ *adj* **1** not broken; intact. **2** uninterrupted; continuous or undisturbed. **3** undaunted; not subdued in spirit or health. **4** said of a horse or other animal: not broken in; untamed. **5** said of a (sporting) record: not surpassed. • **unbrokenly** *adverb*. • **unbrokenness** *noun*. ◷ 13c.

unbundle ▷ *verb* **1** to remove something from a bundle; to unpack it. **2** to price and sell (the constituents of a larger package of goods or services) separately. **3** *commerce* to break (a company, organization, etc) down into its constituent businesses or assets before re-organizing it or selling it off. • **unbundler** *noun*. ◷ 17c.

unburden ▷ *verb* **1** to remove a load or burden from someone or something. **2** (*often* **unburden oneself**) to relieve (oneself or one's mind) of worries, secrets, etc by confessing them to another person. ◷ 16c.

unbutton ▷ *verb* **1** to undo the button or buttons on (a garment). **2** to unbend; to relax or become confidential. •

Some words with *un-* prefixed, all of which refer to UN- sense 1 unless specified otherwise below.

unassorted *adj*.
unatoned *adj*.
unattackable *adj*.
unattainable *adj*.
unattained *adj*.
unattempted *adj*.
unattested *adj*.
unattractive *adj*.
unattractively *adverb*.
unattractiveness *noun*.
unattributable *adj*.
unattributably *adverb*.
unattributed *adj*.
unattributively *adverb*.
unauthentic *adj*.
unauthoritative *adj*.
unauthorized or **unauthorised** *adj*.
unavailability *noun*.
unavailable *adj*.
unavowed *adj*.
unavowedly *adverb*.
unawakened *adj*.
unawed *adj*.
unbanked *adj*.
unbankable *adj*.
unbaptized or **unbaptised** *adj*.
unbefitting *adj*.
unbefriended *adj*.
unbegotten *adj*.
unbeholden *adj*.
unbeloved *adj*.
unbelt *verb*.
unbelted *adj*.
unbetrayed *adj*.
unbettered *adj*.
unbiblical *adj*.
unbiddable *adj*.
unblameable or **unblamable** *adj*.
unblameably or **unblamably** *adverb*.
unblamed *adj*.
unbleached *adj*.
unblemished *adj*.
unblended *adj*.
unblessed *adj*.
unblock *verb* sense 2.

---

unbuttoned *adj* **1** without a button or buttons. **2** with the buttons undone. **3** informal; unrestrained; confidential. ⓘ 14c.

uncalled-for ▷ *adj* said of a remark, etc: not warranted or deserved, especially unjustifiably rude or aggressive.

uncanny /ʌn'kanɪ/ ▷ *adj* **1** weird, strange or mysterious, especially in an unsettling or uneasy way. **2** said eg of skill or ability: beyond what is considered normal for an ordinary human being. • **uncannily** *adverb*. • **uncanniness** *noun*. ⓘ 19c.

uncap ▷ *verb* **1** *tr & intr* to remove a cap from (the head or another person). **2** to remove the cap or top from (a bottle, container, etc). **3** to remove the upper limit or restriction, eg on a currency's value. • **uncapped** *adj*, *sport* never having played for a national team. ⓘ 16c.

uncared-for ▷ *adj* not well looked-after; neglected. ⓘ 16c.

unceasing ▷ *adj* not ceasing; never-ending. • **unceasingly** *adverb*. ⓘ 14c.

unceremonious ▷ *adj* **1** without ceremony; informal. **2** with no regard for politeness or dignity; direct and abrupt. • **unceremoniously** *adverb*. • **unceremoniousness** *noun*. ⓘ 16c.

uncertain ▷ *adj* **1** not sure, certain or confident. **2** not definitely known or decided. **3** not to be depended upon. **4** likely to change. **5** (*often* **uncertain of something**) lacking confidence; hesitant. • **uncertainly** *adverb*. • **uncertainty** *noun* (***uncertainties***) **1** the state or condition of being uncertain. **2** something that is uncertain. • **in no uncertain terms 1** unambiguously. **2** strongly; emphatically. ⓘ 14c.

uncertainty principle ▷ *noun, physics* the theory that it is impossible to determine the exact position and the momentum of a moving particle simultaneously. Also called **Heisenberg uncertainty principle**.

unchain ▷ *verb* **1** to release something from a chain or chains; to set free. **2** to remove the chain from something. ⓘ 16c.

uncharted ▷ *adj* **1** said of territory, etc: **a** not fully explored or mapped in detail; **b** not shown on a map or chart. **2** said of a non-physical area, a subject area, etc: not yet examined or fully investigated. ⓘ 19c.

unchartered ▷ *adj* **1** not holding or provided with a charter. **2** unauthorized. ⓘ 19c.

unchecked ▷ *adj* **1** not restrained. **2** not checked or verified. ⓘ 15c.

unchristian ▷ *adj* **1** said of a person, community, etc: not Christian; without Christian priciples or feeling. **2** not in accordance with the principles or spirit of Christianity; uncharitable or uncaring. • **unchristianly** *adverb*. ⓘ 16c.

unchurch ▷ *verb* **1** to remove or exclude someone from a church; to excommunicate them. **2** to remove the status of church from (a building). See also DECONSECRATE. ⓘ 17c.

uncial /'ʌnsɪəl/ ▷ *adj* said of a form of writing: in large rounded letters with flowing strokes, of a kind used in ancient manuscripts. ▷ *noun* **1** an uncial letter or form of writing. **2** a manuscript written in uncials. ⓘ 17c: from Latin *uncia* a twelfth part or inch; see OUNCE.

uncircumcised ▷ *adj* **1** not circumcised. **2** not Jewish; gentile. **3** not spiritually purified. • **uncircumcision** *noun*. ⓘ 14c.

uncivil /ʌn'sɪvəl/ ▷ *adj* discourteous; rude or impolite. • **uncivility** *noun*. • **uncivilly** *adverb*. ⓘ 16c.

uncivilized or **uncivilised** ▷ *adj* **1** said of a people, tribe, etc: not civilized. **2** uncultured; rough. • **uncivilizable** *adj*. ⓘ 17c.

unclasp ▷ *verb* **1** to unfasten the clasp or clasps on something. **2** *tr & intr* to relax one's clasp or grip (on something). ⓘ 16c.

unclassified ▷ *adj* **1** not classified. **2** said of information: not classified as secret. **3** said of a road: minor; not classified by the Department of Transport as a motorway, A-road or B-road. • **unclassifiable** *adj*. ⓘ 19c.

uncle /'ʌŋkəl/ ▷ *noun* **1** the brother or brother-in-law of a father or mother. **2** the husband of an aunt. **3** *colloq* a form of address used by a child to a male friend of their parents. **4** *slang* a pawnbroker. See also AVUNCULAR. ⓘ 13c: from French *oncle, uncle*, from Latin *avunculus* maternal uncle.

unclean ▷ *adj* **1** morally or spiritually impure. **2** said of an animal: regarded for religious reasons as impure and unfit to be used as food. **3** not clean; dirty or foul. • **uncleanness** *noun*. ⓘ Anglo-Saxon.

uncleanly ▷ *adverb* /ʌn:kli:nlɪ/ in an unclean manner. ▷ *adj* /ʌn'klɛnlɪ/ *archaic or formal* unclean; characterized by a lack of cleanliness. • **uncleanliness** /-'klɛnlɪnəs/ *noun*. ⓘ Anglo-Saxon.

Uncle Sam ▷ *noun, colloq* the United States, its government or its people. ⓘ 19c: perhaps a humorous interpretation of the letters *US*.

Uncle Tom ▷ *noun, offensive* **1** a Black person who behaves subserviently to Whites. **2** someone who is thought of as betraying or being disloyal to their cultural or social background. ▷ *adj* designating or

---

Some words with *un-* prefixed, all of which refer to UN- sense 1 unless specified otherwise below.

unblooded *adj*.	**unbuilt** *adj*.	**uncashed** *adj*.
unbloodied *adj*.	**unburied** *adj*.	**uncatalogued** *adj*.
unbookish *adj*.	**unburned** or **unburnt** *adj*.	**uncaught** *adj*.
unbothered *adj*.	**unbusinesslike** *adj*.	**uncelebrated** *adj*.
unblunted *adj*.	**unbuttered** *adj*.	**uncensored** *adj*.
unbrace *verb* sense 2.	**uncaged** *adj*.	**uncensured** *adj*.
unbranched *adj*.	**uncalculated** *adj*.	**uncertificated** *adj*.
unbranded *adj*.	**uncalculating** *adj*.	**uncertified** *adj*.
unbreached *adj*.	**uncandid** *adj*.	**unchallengeable** *adj*.
unbreakable *adj*.	**uncandidly** *adverb*.	**unchallengeably** *adverb*.
unbribable *adj*.	**uncandidness** *noun*.	**unchallenged** *adj*.
unbridgeable *adj*.	**uncanonical** *adj*.	**unchangeable** *adj*.
unbridged *adj*.	**uncanonized** or **uncanonised** *adj*.	**unchanged** *adj*.
unbrotherly *adj*.		**unchanging** *adj*.
unbruised *adj*.	**uncaring** *adj*.	**unchangingly** *adverb*.
unbuckle *verb* sense 2.	**uncarpeted** *adj*.	**unchaperoned** *adj*.

characteristic of such a person. • **Uncle Tomery** or **Uncle Tomism** *noun* Uncle Tom behaviour. Also written **Uncle Tommery** and **Uncle Tommism.** ⓒ 19c: from the name of the hero of Harriet Beecher Stowe's novel *Uncle Tom's Cabin* (1851–2).

unclimbable ▷ *adj* said of a mountain face, etc: too difficult to climb.

unclimbed ▷ *adj* said of a mountain, or a specified mountain face, etc: not known to have been climbed before.

unclog ▷ *verb* to free something from an obstruction; to unblock it. ⓒ 17c.

unclose ▷ *verb* **1** *tr & intr* to open. **2** *rare* to reveal or make known. ⓒ 14c.

unclothe ▷ *verb* **1** to remove the clothes from someone. **2** to uncover or reveal something. ⓒ 14c.

unco /ˈʌŋkə/ *Scots* ▷ *adj* **1** strange; weird; unusual. **2** unknown; not previously encountered. ▷ *adverb* very; extremely. ▷ *noun* (***uncos***) something strange or new. ⓒ 14c: a dialect variant of UNCOUTH.

uncoil ▷ *verb, tr & intr* to untwist or unwind something, or to become untwisted. ⓒ 18c.

uncomfortable ▷ *adj* **1** not comfortable. **2** feeling, involving or causing discomfort or unease. • **uncomfortableness** *noun.* • **uncomfortably** *adverb.*

uncomfy ▷ *adj, colloq* uncomfortable. ⓒ 19c.

uncommitted ▷ *adj* not bound or pledged to support any particular party, policy, action, etc. ⓒ 19c; 14c in sense 'not entrusted or delegated'.

uncommitted logic array (abbreviation **ULA** or **ula**) *noun, computing* a microchip, the standardized logic circuits of which are all connected during manufacture and selectively disconnected later to the customer's specification.

uncommon ▷ *adj* **1** rare or unusual. **2** uncommon in amount or degree; remarkably great; extreme. ▷ *adverb, archaic* uncommonly □ *The wine was uncommon good.* • **uncommonly** *adverb* in an uncommon way or to an uncommon degree; unusually. • **uncommonness** *noun.* ⓒ 17c; 16c in obsolete sense 'not possessed in common'.

uncommunicative ▷ *adj* not communicative; not inclined to talk, express opinions, etc. • **uncommunicativeness** *noun.* ⓒ 17c.

uncomplicated ▷ *adj* not complicated; straightforward. ⓒ 18c.

uncompromising ▷ *adj* **1** unwilling to compromise or submit. **2** sheer; out-and-out. • **uncompromisingly** *adverb.* • **uncompromisingness** *noun.* ⓒ 19c.

unconcern ▷ *noun* lack of concern or interest; indifference. ⓒ 18c.

unconcerned ▷ *adj* **1** lacking concern or interest; indifferent. **2** not anxious; untroubled. **3** *rare* not involved. • **unconcernedly** /ʌnkənˈsɜːnɪdlɪ/ *adverb.* ⓒ 17c.

unconditional ▷ *adj* **1** not conditional; with no conditions or limits imposed. **2** complete or absolute. • **unconditionally** *adverb.* ⓒ 17c.

unconditioned ▷ *adj* **1** not subject to conditions or limitations. **2** said of a person, response, etc: not conditioned by learning or experience; innate. **3** *philos* not restricted by conditions; infinite; absolute. **4** not put into the required condition or state. • **unconditionedness** *noun.* ⓒ 17c.

unconformable ▷ *adj* **1** not conformable or conforming. **2** *geol* said of rock: made up of recent rock strata overlying different and older strata. • **unconformability** *noun, chiefly geol.* • **unconformably** *adverb, chiefly geol.* ⓒ 16c.

unconscionable /ʌnˈkɒnʃənəbəl/ ▷ *adj* **1** said of a person, behaviour, etc: without conscience; unscrupulous. **2** outrageous; unthinkable. **3** unreasonably excessive. • **unconscionably** *adverb.* ⓒ 16c.

unconscious ▷ *adj* **1** said of a person or animal: in a state of insensibility, characterized by loss of awareness of the external environment, and inability to respond to sensory stimuli. **2** (*usually* **unconscious of something**) not actively thinking about it; unaware of it. **3** said of a quality, emotion, etc: not recognized as being present within oneself; referring to something that a person is unaware of. **4** said of an action, behaviour, etc: characterized by lack of awareness; unintentional; not deliberate. **5** *psychol* relating to or produced by the unconscious. ▷ *noun* (**the unconscious**) *psychol* in psychoanalysis: the part of the mind that contains memories, thoughts and feelings of which one is not consciously aware, but which may be manifested as dreams, psychosomatic symptoms or certain patterns of behaviour. • **unconsciously** *adverb.* • **unconsciousness** *noun.* ⓒ 18c.

unconstitutional ▷ *adj* not allowed by or consistent with a nation's constitution. • **unconstitutionalism** or **unconstitutionality** *noun.* • **unconstitutionally** *adverb.* ⓒ 18c.

unconventional ▷ *adj* not conventional; not conforming to the normal or accepted standards, rules, etc; unusual. • **unconventionality** *noun.* • **unconventionally** *adverb.* ⓒ 19c.

Some words with *un-* prefixed, all of which refer to UN- sense 1 unless specified otherwise below.

uncharacteristic *adj.*
uncharged *adj.*
uncharitable *adj.*
uncharitableness *noun.*
uncharitably *adverb.*
unchaste *adj.*
uncheered *adj.*
uncheerful *adj.*
unchewed *adj.*
unchivalrous *adj.*
unchoke *verb* sense 2.
unchosen *adj.*
unchronicled *adj.*
unclad *adj.*
unclaimed *adj.*
unclear *adj.*
uncleared *adj.*
unclearly *adverb.*
unclench *verb* sense 2.
unclinch *verb* sense 2.
unclouded *adj.*
uncluttered *adj.*
uncollected *adj.*
uncoloured *adj.*
uncombed *adj.*
uncomely *adj.*
uncommercial *adj.*
uncompassionate *adj.*
uncompelled *adj.*
uncompelling *adj.*
uncompensated *adj.*
uncompetitive *adj.*
uncomplaining *adj.*
uncomplainingly *adverb.*
uncompleted *adj.*
uncompliant *adj.*
uncomplying *adj.*
uncomplimentary *adj.*
uncompounded *adj.*
uncomprehended *adj.*
uncomprehending *adj.*
unconcealed *adj.*
unconcluded *adj.*
unconducive *adj.*
unconfident *adj.*
unconfined *adj.*
unconfirmed *adj.*
uncongenial *adj.*

uncool ▷ *adj, colloq* **1** unsophisticated; not smart or fashionable. **2** tense or excitable. ⓒ 20c.

uncoordinated ▷ *adj* **1** not coordinated. **2** said eg of a person's movements: lacking coordination; clumsy or awkward. ⓒ 19c.

uncork ▷ *verb* **1** to remove the cork from (a bottle, etc). **2** *colloq* to release (eg emotion) from a pent-up state. ⓒ 18c.

uncountable ▷ *adj* **1** not able to be counted; innumerable. **2** *linguistics* said of a noun: that cannot be used with the indefinite article or form a plural.

uncounted ▷ *adj* **1** not counted. **2** not able to be counted; innumerable. ⓒ 15c.

uncouple ▷ *verb* **1** to undo the coupling of, or between (two or more things); to disconnect or release. **2** *intr* to become unfastened or disconnected.

uncouth /ʌn'kuːθ/ ▷ *adj* coarse or awkward in behaviour, manners or language; uncultured or lacking refinement. • **uncouthly** *adverb*. • **uncouthness** *noun*. ⓒ Anglo-Saxon *uncuth* unfamiliar (eg with social graces).

uncover ▷ *verb* **1** to remove the cover or top from something. **2** to reveal or expose something. **3** to drive (eg a fox) out of cover. **4** *intr, archaic* to take off one's hat as a mark of respect.

uncovered ▷ *adj* **1** not covered; bare; revealed or exposed. **2** not wearing a hat. **3** not protected by insurance.

uncross ▷ *verb* to change or move something from a crossed position □ *uncrossed his legs*. ⓒ 16c.

uncrossed ▷ *adj* **1** not crossed. **2** not wearing or marked with a cross. **3** not blocked or obstructed, etc. **4** said of a cheque: not marked with the two parallel lines that indicate that it must be paid into a bank account. • **uncrossable** *adj*. ⓒ 16c.

uncrowned ▷ *adj* **1** said of a monarch: not yet crowned. **2** with a specified status but not a formal title; denoting an acknowledged master or expert in something □ *the uncrowned king of swindlers*.

UNCSTD ▷ *abbreviation* United Nations Conference on Science and Technology for Development.

UNCTAD /'ʌŋktad/ ▷ *abbreviation* United Nations Conference on Trade and Development.

unction /'ʌŋkʃən/ ▷ *noun* **1** *Christianity* **a** the act of ceremonially anointing a person with oil; **b** the oil used. **2** ointment of any kind. **3** anything that soothes, such as words or thoughts. **4** the kind of sincerity in language or tone of voice that provokes, or is the result of, deep emotion. **5** affected charm, sincerity or religious feeling. ⓒ 14c: from Latin *unctio, unctionis*, from *unguere, unctum* to anoint.

unctuous /'ʌŋktʃuəs/ ▷ *adj* **1** insincerely and excessively charming. **2** oily; greasy. • **unctuosity** and **unctuousness** *noun*. • **unctuously** *adverb*. ⓒ 14c: see UNCTION.

uncured ▷ *adj* **1** said of food, especially meat and fish: not dried, salted or smoked. **2** said of an illness, etc: not cured or remedied.

uncut ▷ *adj* **1** not cut. **2** said of a book: **a** with the pages not (yet) cut open; **b** with the margins untrimmed. **3** said of a book, film, etc: with no parts cut out; unabridged. **4** said of a gemstone, especially a diamond: not cut into a regular shape. **5** said of illegal drugs: not adulterated; pure.

undamped /ʌn'dampt/ ▷ *adj* **1** said of a person, hopes, etc: not discouraged or subdued. **2** said of a wave, oscillation, etc: not damped; with unrestricted motion. ⓒ 18c.

undaunted ▷ *adj* not daunted; not discouraged or put off. • **undauntedly** *adverb*. • **undauntedness** *noun*.

undead /ʌn'dɛd/ ▷ *adj* **1** said eg of a vampire, zombie, etc: supposedly dead but still able to move around, etc. **2** (**the undead**) those who are undead in general or as a group (see THE sense 4b). ⓒ 15c.

undeceive ▷ *verb* to free someone from a mistaken belief; to reveal the truth to them. • **undeceivable** *adj* incapable, not able to be deceived. • **undeceived** *adj* **1** not deceived or misled. **2** freed from a mistaken belief. • **undeceiver** *noun*. ⓒ 16c.

undecideable ▷ *adj* **1** not able to be decided. **2** *math, logic* said of a proposition, etc: not able to be formally proved or disproved within a given system. ▷ *noun* something that is undecidable. • **undecidability** *noun*. ⓒ 17c.

undecided ▷ *adj* **1** said of a problem, question, etc: not (yet) decided; not settled. **2** said of a person: not (yet) having decided or not able to decide; hesitating or irresolute. • **undecidedly** *adverb*. • **undecidedness** *noun*. ⓒ 16c.

undeniable ▷ *adj* **1** not able to be denied; unquestionably or obviously true. **2** clearly and indisputably excellent. • **undeniableness** *noun*. • **undeniably** *adverb*. ⓒ 16c.

under /'ʌndə(r)/ ▷ *prep* **1 a** below or beneath something but not in contact with it □ *under the table*; **b** below or beneath something and in contact with it □ *under the*

Some words with *un-* prefixed, all of which refer to UN- sense 1 unless specified otherwise below.

unconnected *adj*.
unconquerable *adj*.
unconquered *adj*.
unconscientious *adj*.
unconscientiously *adverb*.
unconsecrated *adj*.
unconsidered *adj*.
unconsolable *adj*.
unconsolidated *adj*.
unconstrained *adj*.
unconstricted *adj*.
unconsumed *adj*.
unconsummated *adj*.
uncontaminated *adj*.
uncontested *adj*.
uncontradicted *adj*.
uncontrived *adj*.
uncontrollable *adj*.
uncontrolled *adj*.
uncontroversial *adj*.
unconverted *adj*.
unconvinced *adj*.
unconvincing *adj*.
unconvincingly *adverb*.
uncooked *adj*.
unco-operative *adj*.
unco-operatively *adverb*.
uncorrected *adj*.
uncorroborated *adj*.
uncorrupted *adj*.
uncovenanted *adj*.
uncreative *adj*.
uncritical *adj*.
uncritically *adverb*.
uncropped *adj*.
uncrowded *adj*.
uncrumple *verb* sense 2.
uncrushed *adj*.
uncrystallized or **uncrystallised** *adj*.
uncultivated *adj*.
uncultured *adj*.
uncurbed *adj*.
uncurl *verb* sense 2.
uncurtailed *adj*.
undamaged *adj*.
undamned *adj*.
undated *adj*.

book. **2** at the foot of □ ***under the column***. **3** less than; short of □ ***under 10 per cent***. **4** lower in rank than. **5** during the reign or administration of □ ***under Queen Elizabeth II***. **6** subjected to, receiving or sustaining □ ***under consideration*** □ ***under pressure***. **7** in the category or classification of. **8** known by □ ***goes under the name of***. **9** according to □ ***under the terms of the agreement***. **10** in view of; because of □ ***under the circumstances***. **11** propelled by □ ***under sail***. **12** said of a field: planted with (a particular crop). **13** *astrol* within the influence of (a particular sign of the zodiac). ▷ *adverb* **1** in or to a lower place, position or rank. **2** into a state of unconsciousness. ▷ *adj* **1** lower. **2** subordinate. ● **under lock and key** see under KEY[1]. ● **under one's belt** see under BELT[1]. ● **under the knife** see under KNIFE. ● **under way** **1** said of a process, activity, project, etc: in progress; having been instigated. **2** *naut* said of a vessel: in motion. ◷ Anglo-Saxon.

under- ▷ *combining form* forming words meaning: **1** beneath or below □ ***underfoot***. **2** too little in quantity or degree; insufficient or insufficiently □ ***underexposed*** □ ***underpaid***. **3** lower in rank or importance □ ***under-secretary***. **4** less than □ ***underbid***. **5** less or lower than expectations or potential □ ***underdeveloped***.

underachieve ▷ *verb, intr* to be less successful than expected, especially academically; to fail to fulfil one's potential. ● **underachievement** *noun*. ● **underachiever** *noun*. ◷ 1950s.

underact ▷ *verb, tr & intr* **1** to play (a part) with insufficient emphasis. **2** to act or play (a part) with little emphasis or in an understated way. ◷ 17c.

underactivity ▷ *noun* reduced or insufficient activity. ● **underactive** *adj*. ◷ 20c.

under-age ▷ *adj* **1** said of a person: below an age required by law; too young □ ***At seventeen he was under age***. **2** said of an activity, etc: carried on by an under-age person □ ***under-age drinking***.

underarm ▷ *adj* **1 a** said of a style of bowling in sports, especially cricket, or of a service in tennis, etc: performed with the arm kept below the level of the shoulder; **b** said of a person: using this style of bowling, service, etc. **2** said eg of a bag, case, etc: placed or held under the arm. **3** relating to or for the armpit. ▷ *adverb* with an underarm style or action. ▷ *noun* the armpit. ◷ 19c.

underbelly /ˈʌndəbɛlɪ/ ▷ *noun* **1** the part of an animal's belly that faces or is nearest the ground. **2** any underside that approximately resembles this, eg that of a car. **3** (*also* **soft underbelly**) any unprotected part vulnerable to attack. **4** an unattractive subculture □ ***the sleazy underbelly of New York***. ◷ 17c.

underbid ▷ *verb* **1** *intr* to make an offer that is too low. **2** to offer a lower bid than (another person, other people, etc). **3** *tr & intr, bridge* to bid (a hand) lower than is justified by its value. ▷ *noun, bridge* **1** a bid too low to be valid. **2** a bid less than the hand is worth. ● **underbidder** *noun* **1** someone who underbids. **2** the bidder next below the highest bidder, especially at an auction. ◷ 17c.

underblanket ▷ *noun* a blanket of warm material (now also an ELECTRIC BLANKET) placed under the bottom sheet of a bed rather than being used as a covering. ◷ 19c.

underbody ▷ *noun* the underside of eg an animal's body or a motor vehicle.

underbred ▷ *adj* /ʌndəˈbrɛd/ **1** ILL-BRED. **2** said of an animal: not pure bred. ▷ *noun* /ˈʌndəbrɛd/ an underbred person or animal. ● **underbreeding** *noun*. ◷ 17c.

underbuy ▷ *verb* **1** to buy less of something than required. **2** to buy something at a lower price than that paid by others. **3** to buy something at a price below its true value.

undercapitalize or **undercapitalise** ▷ *verb* to provide (a commercial enterprise) with too little capital to allow it to operate efficiently. ● **undercapitalization** *noun*. ◷ 20c.

undercard ▷ *noun, boxing* a programme of matches supporting the main event. ◷ 20c.

undercarriage ▷ *noun* **1** the landing gear of an aircraft, including wheels, shock absorbers, etc, used to take the impact on landing and support the aircraft on the ground. **2** the supporting framework or chassis of a carriage or vehicle. ◷ 20c in sense 1; 18c in sense 2.

undercart ▷ *noun, colloq* UNDERCARRIAGE (sense1).

undercharge ▷ *verb* **1** to charge someone too little money. **2** to put an insufficient charge in (eg an electrical circuit or explosive device). ◷ 17c.

underclad ▷ *adj, old use* UNDERCLOTHED. ◷ 17c.

underclass ▷ *noun* a subordinate social class, especially a class of people disadvantaged in society through poverty, unemployment, etc. ◷ Early 20c.

undercliff ▷ *noun* a terrace formed from material that has fallen from a cliff. ◷ 19c.

underclothed ▷ *adj* not sufficiently clothed. ◷ 19c.

underclothes ▷ *plural noun* (*also* **underclothing**) UNDERWEAR. ◷ 19c.

undercoat ▷ *noun* **1 a** a layer of paint applied as preparation for the top or finishing coat; **b** the kind of paint used. **2** UNDERFUR. **3** a coat worn under another. ▷ *verb* to apply an undercoat to (a surface). ◷ 17c.

Some words with *un-* prefixed, all of which refer to UN- sense 1 unless specified otherwise below.

undecipherable *adj*.
undeclared *adj*.
undefeated *adj*.
undefended *adj*.
undefiled *adj*.
undefinable *adj*.
undefined *adj*.
undemanding *adj*.
undemocratic *adj*.
undemonstrative *adj*.
undenied *adj*.
undependable *adj*.
undeserved *adj*.
undeserving *adj*.
undesired *adj*.
undestroyed *adj*.
undetectable *adj*.
undetected *adj*.
undeterred *adj*.
undeveloped *adj*.
undeviating *adj*.
undeviatingly *adverb*.
undiagnosed *adj*.
undifferentiated *adj*.
undignified *adj*.
undiminished *adj*.
undimmed *adj*.
undiplomatic *adj*.
undirected *adj*.
undiscerned *adj*.
undiscerning *adj*.
undisciplined *adj*.
undisclosed *adj*.
undiscovered *adj*.
undiscriminating *adj*.
undisguised *adj*.
undisguisedly *adverb*.
undismayed *adj*.
undisposed *adj*.
undisputed *adj*.
undisputedly *adverb*.
undissolved *adj*.
undistinguishable *adj*.
undistinguished *adj*.
undistributed *adj*.
undisturbed *adj*.
undivided *adj*.
undivulged *adj*.

undercook ▷ *verb* to cook (food) insufficiently or for too short a time. ◷ 19c.

undercover ▷ *adj* working, carried out, etc in secret □ *an undercover agent.* ▷ *adverb* in secret □ *working undercover for the KGB.* ◷ 20c; 19c in sense 'under cover' or 'sheltered'.

undercroft ▷ *noun* an underground chamber or vault, such as the crypt of a church. ◷ 14c: from Dutch *crofte* a vault, cavern, etc, from Latin *crypta* crypt.

undercurrent ▷ *noun* **1** an unseen current under the (often still) surface of a body of water. **2** an underlying trend or body of opinion, especially if different from the one generally perceived. ◷ 17c.

undercut ▷ *verb* /ʌndəˈkʌt/ **1** to offer goods or services at a lower price than (a competitor). **2** to cut away the underside of something. **3** *sport* to apply backspin to (a ball). ▷ *noun* /ˈʌndəkʌt/ **1** the action or an act of cutting underneath something. **2** a part that is cut away underneath. **3** the underside of a sirloin, ie the fillet. **4** a notch cut in the trunk of a tree on the side to which it is intended to fall. **5** *sport* a stroke that gives a ball backspin.

underdeveloped ▷ *adj* **1** insufficiently developed; immature or undersized. **2** said of a country: with resources inadequately used, a low standard of living and, usually, also lacking capital and social organization to advance. **3** *photog* not sufficiently developed to produce a normal image. ◷ 19c.

underdo ▷ *verb* to do something incompletely or inadequately, especially to cook (food) insufficiently or (too) lightly. • **underdone** *adj.* ◷ 18c.

underdog ▷ *noun* **1** the person who is losing or who is defeated in a fight, contest, etc. **2** the competitor in a contest, etc who is considered unlikely to win. **3** anyone in adversity. ◷ 19c.

underdrawing ▷ *noun* an outline drawing or sketch done on canvas, etc before paint is applied. ◷ 20c.

underdress /ʌndəˈdrɛs/ *verb* to dress too plainly or with insufficient formality for a particular occasion. • **underdressed** *adj.*

underdrive ▷ *noun* a gear that transmits to the driving shaft a speed less than engine speed. ◷ 1920s.

underemphasize or **underemphasise** ▷ *verb* to emphasize something insufficiently. • **underemphasis** *noun.* ◷ 20c.

underemployed ▷ *adj* **1** given less work than could realistically be done. **2** given work that fails to make good use of the skills possessed.

underemployment ▷ *noun* **1** insufficient use of something. **2** a situation where too large a part of a labour force is unemployed.

underestimate ▷ *verb* /ʌndərˈɛstɪmeɪt/ to make too low an estimate of (someone's or something's value, capacity, extent, etc). ▷ *noun* /ʌndərˈɛstɪmət/ an estimate that is too low. • **underestimation** *noun.* ◷ 19c.

underexpose ▷ *verb* **1** *photog* to expose (a film, plate or paper) for too little time or to too little light, resulting in a darkened photograph. **2** to fail to expose someone or something to sufficient publicity. • **underexposed** *adj.* • **underexposure** *noun.* ◷ 19c.

underfeed ▷ *verb* to give (a person or animal) too little food. ◷ 17c.

underfelt ▷ *noun* an old type of underlay, made of felt. ◷ 19c.

underfloor ▷ *adj* situated, operating, etc beneath the floor □ *underfloor heating.* ◷ 19c.

underfoot /ʌndəˈfʊt, ˈʌndəfʊt/ ▷ *adverb* **1** beneath the foot or feet; on the ground. **2** in a position of inferiority or subjugation. **3** *colloq* in the way; always present and causing inconvenience.

underframe see SUBFRAME

underfund ▷ *verb* to provide (an organization, public service, etc) with insufficient funding to carry out all the planned activities. • **underfunded** *adj.* • **underfunding** *noun.* ◷ 1920s.

underfur ▷ *noun* a layer of short dense fur that grows under the longer outer layer of an animal's fur or coat. ◷ 19c.

undergarment ▷ *noun* any garment worn under other clothes, especially an item of underwear. ◷ 16c.

underglaze ▷ *noun* **1** in ceramics: a glaze applied to form a surface which can be decorated and over which a second glaze is applied. **2** a pigment, decoration, etc applied to porcelain, etc before a glaze is applied. ▷ *adj* **1** relating to or suitable for an underglaze. **2** applied or done before glazing. ◷ 19c.

undergo ▷ *verb* to endure, experience or be subjected to something. ◷ Anglo-Saxon *undergan.*

undergraduate ▷ *noun* someone studying for a first degree in a higher education establishment. Sometimes shortened to **undergrad**. ◷ 17c.

underground ▷ *noun* /ˈʌndəgraʊnd/ **1** (*often* **the underground**; *also* **Underground**) a system of electric trains running in tunnels below ground. **2** a secret paramilitary organization fighting a government or

Some words with *un-* prefixed, all of which refer to UN- sense 1 unless specified otherwise below.

undocumented *adj.*	**unemotional** *adj.*	**unenlightened** *adj.*
undomesticated *adj.*	**unemotionally** *adverb.*	**unentered** *adj.*
undrained *adj.*	**unemphatic** *adj.*	**unenterprising** *adj.*
undrinkable *adj.*	**unemptied** *adj.*	**unentertaining** *adj.*
undubbed *adj.*	**unenclosed** *adj.*	**unenthusiastic** *adj.*
undyed *adj.*	**unencumbered** *adj.*	**unenvied** *adj.*
uneatable *adj.*	**unending** *adj.*	**unequipped** *adj.*
uneaten *adj.*	**unendingly** *adverb.*	**unescorted** *adj.*
unedited *adj.*	**unendangered** *adj.*	**unessential** *adj.*
uneducable *adj.*	**unendowed** *adj.*	**unethical** *adj.*
uneducated *adj.*	**unendurable** *adj.*	**unethically** *adverb.*
unelectable *adj.*	**unendurably** *adverb.*	**un-European** *adj.*
unelected *adj.*	**unengaged** *adj.*	**unexaggerated** *adj.*
unemancipated *adj.*	**un-English** *adj.*	**unexamined** *adj.*
unembarrassed *adj.*	**un-Englishness** *noun.*	**unexcelled** *adj.*
unembellished *adj.*	**unenjoyable** *adj.*	**unexcitable** *adj.*

occupying force. **3** any artistic movement seeking to challenge or overturn established and mainstream (usually social as well as artistic) views and practices. ▷ *adj* /ˈʌndəgraʊnd/ **1** existing or operating below the surface of the ground □ *an underground station.* **2** referring or relating to any political or artistic underground □ *underground music.* ▷ *adverb* /ʌndəˈgraʊnd/ **1** to a position below ground level. **2** into hiding □ *went underground immediately after the robbery.*

undergrown ▷ *adj* not fully grown or developed.

undergrowth ▷ *noun* a thick growth of shrubs and bushes among trees. ⓔ 17c.

underhand ▷ *adj* **1** secretively deceitful or dishonest; sly. **2** *sport* UNDERARM. ▷ *adverb* in an underhand way. ▷ *noun* **1** an underhand ball. **2** underhand bowling. ⓔ 16c.

underhanded ▷ *adverb* /ʌndəˈhandɪd/ UNDERHAND. ▷ *adj* /ˈʌndəhandɪd/ **1** UNDERHAND. **2** short of workers; undermanned. • **underhandedly** *adverb*. • **underhandedness** *noun*. ⓔ 19c.

underhung /ʌndəˈhʌŋ, ˈʌndəhʌŋ/ ▷ *adj* **1** said of a lower jaw: protruding beyond the upper jaw. **2** said of a person: with an underhung jaw. ⓔ 17c.

underlay /ʌndəˈleɪ/ ▷ *verb* to lay underneath something, or support or provide with something laid underneath. ▷ *noun* /ˈʌndəleɪ/ a thing laid underneath another, especially felt or rubber matting laid under a carpet for protection.

underlie ▷ *verb* **1** to lie underneath something. **2** to be the hidden cause or meaning of (an attitude, event, etc), beneath what is apparent, visible or superficial.

underline ▷ *verb* **1** to draw a line under (eg a word or piece of text). **2** to emphasize. ⓔ 16c.

underling /ˈʌndəlɪŋ/ ▷ *noun, derog* a subordinate.

underlying ▷ *adj* **1** lying under or beneath. **2** present though not immediately obvious □ *his underlying intentions.* **3** fundamental; basic □ *the underlying causes.*

undermanned ▷ *adj* provided with too few workers; understaffed.

undermentioned ▷ *adj* mentioned or named below or later in the text. ⓔ 17c.

undermine ▷ *verb* (**undermined**, **undermining**) **1** to weaken or destroy something, especially gradually and imperceptibly □ *undermined his confidence.* **2** to dig or wear away the base or foundation of (land, cliffs, etc). **3** to tunnel or dig beneath (a wall, etc). • **underminer** *noun*. • **undermining** *adj, noun*. • **underminingly** *adverb*.

undermost /ˈʌndəmoʊst/ ▷ *adj* lowest. ▷ *adverb* in or to the lowest position; underneath. ⓔ 16c.

undernamed ▷ *adj* named or specified below or later in the text. ⓔ 16c.

underneath /ʌndəˈniːθ/ ▷ *prep, adverb* beneath or below; under. ▷ *adj* lower. ▷ *noun* a lower or downward-facing part or surface. ⓔ Anglo-Saxon *underneothan*, from UNDER + *neothan* below.

undernote ▷ *noun* **1** an undertone. **2** a suggestion. ⓔ 19c.

undernourished ▷ *adj* insufficiently nourished; living on less food than is necessary for normal health and growth. • **undernourishment** *noun*. ⓔ Early 20c.

underpaid ▷ *adj* not paid sufficiently; paid less than is due. ⓔ 19c.

underpants ▷ *plural noun* a man's undergarment covering the body from the waist or hips to (especially the tops of) the thighs. ⓔ 20c.

underpart ▷ *noun* **1** (*usually* **underparts**) the lower side, especially the underside, or part of the underside, of an animal, bird, etc. **2** *theat* any less important part in a play. ⓔ 17c.

underpass ▷ *noun, originally US* **1** a tunnel for pedestrians under a road or railway; a subway. **2** a road or railway passing under another.

underpay ▷ *verb* to pay less than is required or deserved. • **underpayment** *noun*. ⓔ 19c.

underpeopled ▷ *adj* not sufficiently peopled; underpopulated. ⓔ 17c.

underperform ▷ *verb* **1** *intr* **a** to perform less well than expected; **b** said of an investment: to be less profitable than expected. **2 a** to perform less well than (another); **b** said of an investment: to be less profitable than (another investment). • **underperformance** *noun*. • **underperformer** *noun*. ⓔ 1970s.

underpin ▷ *verb* **1** to support (a structure) from beneath, usually temporarily, with brickwork or a prop. **2** to support or corroborate. • **underpinning** *noun*. ⓔ 16c.

underplay ▷ *verb* **1** *intr, cards* to lead or follow suit with a lower card while holding a higher one. **2** *tr & intr* to underact; to perform (a role) in a deliberately restrained or understated way. **3** to understate or play down the importance of something; not to emphasize it too strongly. ⓔ 19c.

underpopulated ▷ *adj* with a very low or insufficient population.

Some words with *un-* prefixed, all of which refer to UN- sense 1 unless specified otherwise below.

unexcited *adj.*
unexciting *adj.*
unexercised *adj.*
unexperienced *adj.*
unexpiated *adj.*
unexpired *adj.*
unexplainable *adj.*
unexplained *adj.*
unexploded *adj.*
unexplored *adj.*
unexposed *adj.*
unexpressed *adj.*
unexpurgated *adj.*
unextended *adj.*
unfaded *adj.*
unfading *adj.*
unfaltering *adj.*
unfalteringly *adverb.*
unfashionable *adj.*
unfashionably *adverb.*
unfatherly *adj.*
unfeasible *adj.*
unfed *adj.*
unfeigned *adj.*
unfeminine *adj.*
unfenced *adj.*
unfermented *adj.*
unfertilized or **unfertilised** *adj.*
unfetter *verb* sense 2.
unfilled *adj.*
unfilmable *adj.*
unfinished *adj.*
unfired *adj.*
unfished *adj.*
unfitting *adj.*
unfixed *adj.*
unflagging *adj.*
unflaggingly *adverb.*
unflattering *adj.*
unflatteringly *adverb.*
unflavoured or (*US*) **unflavored** *adj.*
unflustered *adj.*
unfocused or **unfocussed** *adj.*
unforced *adj.*
unforeseeable *adj.*
unforeseen *adj.*

underprepared ▷ *adj* not sufficiently prepared, eg for an exam, etc.

underpriced ▷ *adj* with too low a price.

underprivileged ▷ *adj* **1** deprived of the basic living standards and rights enjoyed by most people in society. **2** (**the underprivileged**) underprivileged people in general or as a group (see THE sense 4b).

underproduction ▷ *noun* production of less of a commodity, etc than is required or possible. ◷ 19c.

underquote ▷ *verb* **1** to quote a lower price than (another person). **2** to quote a lower price (for goods, services, etc) than that quoted by others. ◷ 19c.

underrate ▷ *verb* to rate or assess something at too low a worth or value than it deserves; to have too low an opinion of something. ◷ 16c.

underrepresented ▷ *adj* said especially of a minority social group or a specified type or specimen: not present in sufficient numbers, eg to accurately reflect opinions, statistics, etc.

underripe and **underripened** ▷ *adj* said especially of fruit: not sufficiently ripe. ◷ 18c.

underscore ▷ *verb* **1** to score or draw a line under something. **2** to stress or emphasize something. ▷ *noun* a line inserted or drawn under a piece of text. ◷ 18c.

undersea ▷ *adj* **1** situated or lying below the surface of the sea. **2** intended for use below the surface of the sea. ▷ *adverb* below the sea or the surface of the sea. ◷ 17c.

underseal ▷ *noun* /ˈʌndəsiːl/ an anti-rusting substance painted on to the underside of a motor vehicle. ▷ *verb* /ʌndəˈsiːl/ to apply such a substance to (a vehicle) in order to seal the metal for protection. ◷ 1940s.

under-secretary ▷ *noun* a subordinate to a SECRETARY OF STATE, especially a junior minister or senior civil servant. • **under-secretaryship** *noun*. ◷ 17c.

undersell ▷ *verb* **1** to sell goods or services at a lower price than (a competitor). **2** to sell (goods, etc) at less than their real value or for less than the usual price. • **underseller** *noun*. ◷ 17c.

undersexed ▷ *adj* experiencing sexual desire less frequently or less intensely than is considered normal. ◷ 1930s.

undershirt ▷ *noun* **1** a man's undergarment, usually of cotton and with or without sleeves. **2** *chiefly N Amer* a vest. ◷ 17c.

undershoot ▷ *verb* **1** said of an aircraft: to land short of (a runway). **2** to fall short of (a target, etc). ◷ 17c.

undershot ▷ *adj* **1** said of a water wheel: driven by the weight of a flow of water that passes under rather than over the wheel. **2** having the lower jaw protruding beyond the upper; underhung. ◷ 17c.

underside ▷ *noun* the downward-facing side or surface. ◷ 17c.

undersigned ▷ *adj* whose names are signed below □ *we, the undersigned, …* ◷ 17c.

undersized ▷ *adj* referring to something of less than the usual size. ◷ 18c.

underskirt ▷ *noun* a thin skirt-like undergarment worn under a dress or skirt; a petticoat. ◷ 19c.

underslung ▷ *adj* **1** suspended or supported from above. **2** said of a vehicle chassis: extending below the axles. ◷ 20c.

underspend ▷ *verb* /ʌndəˈspɛnd/ to spend less than (a budget allows or a specified amount). ▷ *noun* /ˈʌndəspɛnd/ **1** the action or an act of underspending. **2** the amount that remains unspent from an allocated budget, etc.

understaffed /ʌndəˈstɑːft/ ▷ *adj* said of a business, organization, etc: provided with too few members of staff. • **understaffing** *noun*. ◷ 19c.

understand ▷ *verb* **1** to grasp the meaning of (a subject, words, a person, a language, etc) □ *I've never understood trigonometry* □ *I could understand him when he spoke more slowly* □ *Do you understand Polish?* **2** to make out the significance, cause, etc of something □ *I don't understand what all the fuss is about.* **3** to have sympathetic awareness of someone or something □ *I fully understand your point of view.* **4** to infer from the available information □ *He got the sack? I understood that he'd resigned.* **5** to mentally put in (a word or words) □ *A relative pronoun is understood to be there.* • **understand each other** or **one another** **1** to know and accept each other's opinions, feelings, etc. **2** to agree. ◷ Anglo-Saxon.

understandable ▷ *adj* **1** capable of being understood. **2** reasonable. • **understandability** *noun*. • **understandably** *adverb*.

understanding ▷ *noun* **1** the act of understanding or the ability to understand. **2** someone's perception or interpretation of information received. **3** an informal agreement. **4** a sympathetic harmony of viewpoints. **5** a condition agreed upon □ *on the understanding that you stay for six months.* ▷ *adj* sympathetic to, or keenly aware of, the feelings and opinions of others. • **understandingly** *adverb*.

Some words with *un-* prefixed, all of which refer to UN- sense 1 unless specified otherwise below.

unforetold *adj*.
unforgettable *adj*.
unforgettably *adverb*.
unforgiveable *adj*.
unforgiven *adj*.
unforgiving *adj*.
unforgotten *adj*.
unformed *adj*.
unformatted *adj*.
unformulated *adj*.
unforthcoming *adj*.
unfortified *adj*.
unframed *adj*.
unfranked *adj*.
unfree *adj*.
unfrequented *adj*.
unfrightened *adj*.
unfrozen *adj*.
unfruitful *adj*.
unfulfilled *adj*.
unfunded *adj*.
unfunny *adj*.
unfurnished *adj*.
unfussy *adj*.
ungallant *adj*.
ungathered *adj*.
ungauged *adj*.
ungenerous *adj*.
ungenerously *adverb*.
ungenial *adj*.
ungentle *adj*.
ungentlemanly *adj*.
ungifted *adj*.
ungird *verb* sense 2.
unglamorous *adj*.
unglazed *adj*.
unglossed *adj*.
ungloved *adj*.
ungraceful *adj*.
ungracious *adj*.
ungraciously *adverb*.
ungraded *adj*.
ungrammatical *adj*.
ungrateful *adj*.
ungratefully *adverb*.
ungrazed *adj*.
ungrounded *adj*.
ungrudging *adj*.

understate ▷ *verb* **1** to describe something as being less or more moderate than is really the case. **2** to express something in very restrained or moderate terms, often for ironic or dramatic effect. • **understatement** *noun* **1** something that is understated. **2** the quality of being understated in dress, appearance, etc. • **understater** *noun*. ◷ 19c.

understated ▷ *adj* **1** referring to something that understates. **2** said of clothes, someone's appearance, etc: effective through simplicity; not over-embellished or showy. ◷ 20c.

understeer ▷ *verb, intr* said of a motor vehicle: to have a tendency to turn less sharply than it should, given the degree by which the steering wheel is turned. ▷ *noun* a tendency in a motor vehicle to understeer.

understrength ▷ *adj, sport* said of a team: unable to field their best players, eg because of injury, suspension, etc.

understood ▷ *adj* **1** implied but not expressed or stated. **2** realized without being, or needing to be, openly stated. ▷ *verb, past tense, past participle of* UNDERSTAND.

understudy /ˈʌndəstʌdɪ/ ▷ *verb* **1** to study or prepare (a role or part) so as to be able to replace the actor or actress who usually plays that part, in case of absence, etc. **2** *tr & intr* to act as understudy to (an actor or actress). ▷ *noun* (***understudies***) **1** an actor or actress who understudies a role. **2** any person who is trained to replace another in case of absence, etc.

undersubscribed ▷ *adj* said of a share issue, etc: not having enough people prepared to subscribe to it.

undertake ▷ *verb* **1** to accept (a duty, responsibility or task). **2** to promise or agree. **3** *colloq* to drive illegally by using the nearside lane to pass a slow-moving vehicle. ◷ 12c as *undertaken* to entrap; 1980s in sense 3.

undertaker ▷ *noun* a person whose job is to organize funerals and prepare the bodies of the dead for burial or cremation.

undertaking ▷ *noun* **1** a duty, responsibility or task undertaken. **2** a promise or guarantee. **3** the work of an undertaker. **4 a** using the nearside lane to pass a slow-moving vehicle; **b** an instance of this.

under-the-counter ▷ *adj* said of goods: obtained or sold illicitly, surreptitiously, etc.

underthings /ˈʌndəθɪŋz/ ▷ *plural noun* underclothes, especially a woman's or girl's. ◷ 19c.

underthrust ▷ *noun, geol* a fault in which one mass of rock is moved under another relatively static layer. ◷ 19c.

undertone ▷ *noun* **1** a quiet tone of voice. **2** an underlying quality, emotion or atmosphere. **3** a subdued sound or shade of a colour. ◷ 18c.

undertow /ˈʌndətoʊ/ ▷ *noun* **1** the strong current that flows away from the shore underneath a breaking wave. **2** any undercurrent that flows in the opposite direction to the surface current. ◷ 19c.

undertrick ▷ *noun, bridge* a trick by which the declarer falls short of their contract. ◷ Early 20c.

underuse ▷ *noun* /ʌndəˈjuːs/ **1** insufficient use of resources, a facility, etc. **2** use that is below the optimum level, capacity, frequency, etc. ▷ *verb* /ʌndəˈjuːz/ **1** to make insufficient use of (resources, a facility, etc). **2** to use something below the optimum level, capacity, frequency, etc. ◷ 1960s.

underutilize or **underutilise** ▷ *verb* to underuse. • **underutilization** *noun*. ◷ 1950s.

undervalue ▷ *verb* **1** to place too low a value on something. **2** to appreciate something insufficiently. • **undervaluation** *noun*. • **undervaluer** *noun*. ◷ 16c.

undervest ▷ *noun* an undergarment worn on the upper part of the body; a VEST (sense1). ◷ 19c.

underwater ▷ *adj* **1** situated, carried out, happening, etc under the surface of the water. **2** *naut* below the water line of a vessel. ▷ *adverb* below the surface of the water.

underwear ▷ *noun* clothes, eg bras, pants, etc, worn under shirts, trousers, dresses and skirts, etc, and usually next to the skin. ◷ 19c.

underweight ▷ *noun* /ˈʌndəweɪt/ **1** lack or insufficiency of weight. **2** an underweight person. **3** the condition of weighing less than is normal or healthy for one's height, build, etc. ▷ *adj* /ʌndəˈweɪt/ **1** lacking in weight; not heavy enough. **2** said of a person: weighing less than is normal or healthy for their height, build, etc. ◷ 17c.

underwhelm ▷ *verb* (***underwhelmed, underwhelming***) *jocular* to fail to impress or make any impact on someone. ◷ 1950s: modelled on OVERWHELM.

underwing ▷ *noun* **1** the hindwing of an insect. **2** any of various moths with distinctively coloured hindwings, eg the **red underwing** or the **yellow underwing**. **3** the underside of a bird's wing. **4** the underside of an aeroplane wing. ◷ 16c.

underwired ▷ *adj* said of a bra: with a thin band of wire under each cup. See WONDERBRA.

underwood ▷ *noun* undergrowth. ◷ 14c.

Some words with *un-* prefixed, all of which refer to UN- sense 1 unless specified otherwise below.

unguided *adj.*
ungummed *adj.*
unhampered *adj.*
unhandy *adj.*
unhardened *adj.*
unharmed *adj.*
unharmful *adj.*
unharmonious *adj.*
unharness *verb* sense 2.
unharvested *adj.*
unhatched *adj.*
unhaunted *adj.*
unheated *adj.*
unheeded *adj.*
unheedful *adj.*
unheeding *adj.*
unhelped *adj.*
unhelpful *adj.*
unheralded *adj.*
unheroic or **unheroical** *adj.*
unheroically *adverb.*
unhesitating *adj.*
unhesitatingly *adverb.*
unhewn *adj.*
unhindered *adj.*
unhitch *verb* sense 2.
unhonoured *adj.*
unhoped-for *adj.*
unhopeful *adj.*
unhoused *adj.*
unhuman *adj.*
unhung *adj.*
unhurried *adj.*
unhurriedly *adverb.*
unhurt *adj.*
unhygienic *adj.*
unhyphenated *adj.*
unidentifiable *adj.*
unidiomatic *adj.*
unignorable *adj.*
unilluminated *adj.*
unilluminating *adj.*
unillumined *adj.*
unillustrated *adj.*
unimaginable *adj.*
unimaginably *adverb.*
unimaginative *adj.*
unimaginatively *adverb.*

underworld ▷ *noun* **1** *mythol* a world imagined to lie beneath the Earth's surface, the home of the souls of the dead. **2** the antipodes. **3** a hidden sphere of life or stratum of society, etc, especially the world of criminals and organized crime. ⓒ 17c.

underwrite /ʌndəˈraɪt, ˈʌndəraɪt/ ▷ *verb* **1** to write (words, figures, etc) beneath other written matter. **2** to agree to finance (a commercial venture) and accept the loss in the event of failure. **3** to agree to buy, or find a buyer for, leftover shares from (a sale of shares to the public). **4** to issue (an insurance policy), accepting the risk involved. **5** *intr* to practise as an underwriter.

underwriter ▷ *noun* **1** a person or organization that underwrites insurance. **2** a person or organization that underwrites shares or bonds. ⓒ 17c.

undescended ▷ *adj, medicine* said of a testicle: remaining in its fetal position in the abdomen instead of descending into the scrotum. ⓒ 19c.

undesigned ▷ *adj* not meant; unintentional.

undesirable ▷ *adj* not desirable; unpleasant or objectionable in some way. ▷ *noun* someone or something that is considered undesirable. • **undesirability** or **undesirableness** *noun*. • **undesirably** *adverb*. ⓒ 17c.

undetermined ▷ *adj* **1** not authoritatively settled or concluded. **2** not yet known or ascertained. **3** not limited. **4** irresolute; undecided. ⓒ 15c.

undies /ˈʌndɪz/ ▷ *plural noun, colloq* items of underwear, especially women's bras, pants, etc. ⓒ Early 20c: from *underwear* or *underclothes*, etc.

undigested ▷ *adj* **1** not digested. **2** said of information, etc: not properly considered or thought through.

undiluted ▷ *adj* **1** not diluted. **2** complete; utter □ *told a pack of undiluted lies.*

undine /ˈʌndiːn/ ▷ *noun* a nymph; a female water spirit. ⓒ 17c: coined by Paracelsus, the Swiss-born physician and writer (1493–1541), from Latin *unda* a wave.

undo /ʌnˈduː/ ▷ *verb* (***undoes, undid, undone, undoing***) **1** *tr & intr* to open, unfasten or untie (something). **2** to cancel or reverse the doing of something, or its effect or result; to annul. **3** *facetious or literary* to bring about the downfall or ruin of someone or something. ⓒ Anglo-Saxon *undon*.

undock ▷ *verb* **1 a** said eg of a space shuttle, etc: to separate from another craft in space; **b** to separate (two space craft) in space. **2** to bring (a ship) out of a dock.

undoing ▷ *noun* **1** the act or action of unfastening, untying, opening etc. **2 a** downfall or ruin; **b** the cause of it. • **be the undoing of someone** to bring about their downfall □ *Alcohol will be the undoing of her.* Opposite of BE THE MAKING OF SOMEONE (at MAKING).

undone¹ ▷ *adj* not done; not achieved; unfinished or incomplete. ⓒ 14c.

undone² ▷ *adj* **1** unfastened, untied, etc. **2** reversed; annulled. **3** destroyed; ruined □ *I am undone!* • **come undone 1** to become unfastened, untied, etc; to open. **2** to go wrong; to come up against problems or difficulties.

undoubted ▷ *adj* beyond doubt or question; clear; evident. • **undoubtedly** *adverb* without doubt; certainly. ⓒ 15c.

undramatic ▷ *adj* **1** not dramatic. **2** low key; subdued; not sensational.

undraped ▷ *adj* **1** not covered by draping. **2** naked.

undreamed /ʌnˈdriːmd/ or **undreamt** /ʌnˈdrɛmt, ʌnˈdrɛmpt/ ▷ *adj* (*usually* **undreamed-of** or **undreamt-of**) not even imagined or dreamed of, especially thought never to be likely or possible. • **undreamable** *adj*. ⓒ 17c.

undress ▷ *verb* **1** to take the clothes off oneself (or another person). **2** *intr* to take one's clothes off. **3** to remove the dressing from (a wound). ▷ *noun* **1** nakedness, or near-nakedness □ *walked out of the bathroom in a state of undress.* **2** casual or informal dress. **3** *military* ordinary uniform as opposed to full military dress (as worn on ceremonial occasions). ⓒ 16c.

undressed ▷ *adj* **1** said of hair: not styled, combed, etc. **2** said of stone, animal hide, etc: not treated, prepared or processed for use. **3** said of food, especially salad: without a dressing. **4** not wearing clothes; partially or completely naked. **5** *military* not wearing formal dress or full dress uniform. • **get undressed** to take off one's clothes.

undue ▷ *adj* **1 a** unjustifiable; improper; **b** inappropriately or unjustifiably great; excessive □ *undue criticism.* **2** *rare* said of a debt, etc: not due or owing. • **unduly** *adverb* **1** unjustifiably. **2** excessively; unreasonably. ⓒ 14c.

undue influence ▷ *noun, law* a strong influence over another person, especially when it is considered to have prevented that person from exercising free will.

undulant /ˈʌndʒʊlənt/ and **undulating** /-leɪtɪŋ/ ▷ *adj* rising and falling like waves. ⓒ 19c: from UNDULATE.

undulant fever ▷ *noun, medicine* a remittent fever often so mild that it passes unnoticed, caused by the bacterium which produces BRUCELLOSIS in animals and is transmitted to humans by unpasteurized goat's or cow's milk. ⓒ 19c.

Some words with *un-* prefixed, all of which refer to UN- sense 1 unless specified otherwise below.

unimaginativeness *noun*.
unimagined *adj*.
unimpaired *adj*.
unimpassioned *adj*.
unimpeded *adj*.
unimportance *noun*.
unimportant *adj*.
unimposing *adj*.
unimpressed *adj*.
unimpressible *adj*.
unimpressionable *adj*.
unimpressive *adj*.
unincorporated *adj*.
unindexed *adj*.
uninfected *adj*.
uninflamed *adj*.
uninflammable *adj*.
uninflected *adj*.
uninfluenced *adj*.
uninfluential *adj*.
uninformative *adj*.
uninformed *adj*.
uninhabitable *adj*.
uninhabited *adj*.
uninhibited *adj*.
uninitiated *adj*.
uninjured *adj*.
uninspired *adj*.
uninspiring *adj*.
uninstructed *adj*.
uninstructive *adj*.
uninsured *adj*.
unintegrated *adj*.
unintellectual *adj*.
unintelligent *adj*.
unintelligible *adj*.
unintelligibly *adverb*.
unintended *adj*.
unintentional *adj*.
unintentionally *adverb*.
uninteresting *adj*.
uninterestingly *adverb*.
uninterrupted *adj*.
uninventive *adj*.
uninvested *adj*.
uninvestigated *adj*.
uninvited *adj*.
uninviting *adj*.

undulate /ˈʌndʒʊleɪt/ ▷ *verb* (***undulated, undulating***) **1** *tr & intr* to move or to make something move in or like waves. **2** *tr & intr* to have or to give something a wavy surface, form, etc. ▷ *adj* (*also* /ˈʌndʒʊlət/) *chiefly bot, zool* wavy; with a wavy margin, surface, etc. • **undulated** *adj.* • **undulator** *noun.* • **undulatory** /–leɪtərɪ/ *adj.* ⓒ 17c: from Latin *unda* a wave.

undulation /ʌndʒʊˈleɪʃən/ ▷ *noun* **1** the action of undulating. **2** a wave-like motion or form. **3** waviness. **4** a wave.

unduly see under UNDUE

undying /ʌnˈdaɪɪŋ/ ▷ *adj* referring to something that does not die; everlasting; eternal. • **undyingly** *adverb.* ⓒ 14c.

unearned ▷ *adj* not deserved or merited. ⓒ 13c.

unearned income ▷ *noun* income, such as dividends and interest earned on savings or from property, that is not remuneration for work done.

unearth ▷ *verb* **1** to dig something up out of the ground. **2** to drive (eg a fox) from its earth or burrow. **3** to discover something by investigation, or by searching or rummaging; to bring it to light. ⓒ 15c.

unearthed ▷ *adj* **1** dug up. **2** discovered; brought to light. **3** *elec* not earthed.

unearthly ▷ *adj* **1** not of this Earth; heavenly or sublime. **2** supernatural; weird; ghostly; mysterious. **3** *colloq* ridiculous or outrageous, especially outrageously early □ *at an unearthly hour.* • **unearthliness** *noun.* ⓒ 17c.

unease ▷ *noun* lack of ease; discomfort or apprehension.

uneasy /ʌnˈiːzɪ/ ▷ *adj* (***uneasier, uneasiest***) **1** nervous, anxious or unsettled; ill at ease. **2** unlikely to prove lasting; unstable. **3** causing anxiety; unsettling. **4** not conducive to physical comfort. • **uneasily** *adverb.* • **uneasiness** *noun.* ⓒ 13c.

uneconomic ▷ *adj* not economic; not in accordance with the principles of sound economics, especially unprofitable. ⓒ 20c.

uneconomical ▷ *adj* not economical; wasteful. • **uneconomically** *adverb.* ⓒ 19c.

unedifying ▷ *adj* not edifying, especially not morally or aesthetically uplifting; degrading or degraded. • **unedifyingly** *adverb.* ⓒ 17c.

unemployable ▷ *adj* unable or unfit for paid employment. ▷ *noun* someone who is unemployable. • **unemployability** *noun.* ⓒ 19c.

unemployed ▷ *adj* **1** without paid employment; jobless. **2** not in use or not made use of. **3** (**the unemployed**) unemployed people in general or as a group (see THE sense 4b). ⓒ 17c.

unemployment ▷ *noun* **1** the state or condition of being unemployed. **2** the number or percentage of unemployed people in a particular region, country, etc. ⓒ 19c.

unemployment benefit ▷ *noun, Brit* a regular payment made to an unemployed person through the national insurance scheme, replaced by Job Seekers Allowance in October 1996.

unenforceable ▷ *adj* said of a law, contract, etc: not able to be enforced, especially legally. • **unenforceability** *noun.* ⓒ 19c.

unenforced ▷ *adj* not enforced. ⓒ 17c.

unenviable ▷ *adj* not to be envied; not provoking envy, especially because unpleasant or disagreeable □ *an unenviable task.* • **unenviably** *adverb.* ⓒ 17c.

unequal ▷ *adj* **1** not equal in quantity, value, rank, size, etc. **2** said of a contest, etc: not evenly matched or balanced. **3** (*usually* **unequal to something**) unable to carry it out, deal with it, etc; inadequate. **4** not uniform; varying. • **unequally** *adverb.* ⓒ 16c.

unequalled ▷ *adj* without equal; not matched by any other; supreme.

unequivocal ▷ *adj* clearly stated or expressed; unambiguous. • **unequivocally** *adverb.* ⓒ 18c.

unerring ▷ *adj* **1** not missing the mark or target; sure or certain. **2** consistently true or accurate; never making an error. • **unerringly** *adverb.* • **unerringness** *noun.* ⓒ 17c.

UNESCO /juːˈnɛskoʊ/ ▷ *abbreviation* United Nations Educational, Scientific and Cultural Organization.

uneven ▷ *adj* **1** said of a surface, etc: not smooth or flat; bumpy. **2** said of a contest: with contestants or sides poorly matched; unequal. **3** not uniform; inconsistent; varying. **4** not equal; not matched or corresponding. • **unevenly** *adverb.* • **unevenness** *noun.* ⓒ Anglo-Saxon *unefen.*

uneventful ▷ *adj* during which nothing interesting or out of the ordinary happens; uninteresting or routine. • **uneventfully** *adverb.* • **uneventfulness** *noun.* ⓒ 19c.

unexampled /ʌnɪgˈzɑːmpəld/ ▷ *adj* **1** unprecedented. **2** unequalled; unparalleled. ⓒ 17c.

unexceptionable ▷ *adj* impossible to criticize or object to; completely satisfactory, suitable, etc. •

Some words with *un-* prefixed, all of which refer to UN- sense 1 unless specified otherwise below.

uninvoked *adj.*
uninvolved *adj.*
un-ionized or **un-ionised** *adj.*
unironed *adj.*
unissued *adj.*
unjoined *adj.*
unjust *adj.*
unjustifiable *adj.*
unjustifiably *adverb.*
unjustified *adj.*
unjustly *adverb.*
unjustness *noun.*
unkept *adj.*
unkissed *adj.*
unknit *verb* sense 2.
unknot *verb* sense 2.
unknowable *adj.*
unlabelled *adj.*
unlaboured or (*US*) **unlabored** *adj.*
unladen *adj.*
unladylike *adj.*
unlaid *adj.*
unlamented *adj.*
unlatch *verb* sense 2.
unlawful *adj.*
unlawfully *adverb.*
unleased *adj.*
unlet *adj.*
unlettable *adj.*
unliberated *adj.*
unlicensed *adj.*
unlighted *adj.*
unlikable or **unlikeable** *adj.*
unliterary *adj.*
unlivable or **unliveable** *adj.*
unlosable or **unloseable** *adj.*
unlovable or **unloveable** *adj.*
unloved *adj.*
unloving *adj.*
unmaintainable *adj.*
unmaintained *adj.*
unmalleable *adj.*
unmanageable *adj.*
unmanaged *adj.*
unmanfully *adverb.*
unmarked *adj.*
unmarketable *adj.*

unexceptionably *adverb* **1** in an unexceptionable way. **2** without exception. ⓒ 17c.

unexceptional ▷ *adj* **1** not admitting or forming an exception. **2** ordinary; run-of-the-mill. • **unexceptionally** *adverb*. ⓒ 18c.

unexecuted ▷ *adj* not put into operation; not carried out.

unexhausted ▷ *adj* not finished or used up.

unexpected ▷ *adj* not expected; surprising; unforeseen. • **unexpectedly** *adverb*. • **unexpectedness** *noun*. ⓒ 16c.

unexploited ▷ *adj* **1** not exploited. **2** said eg of a resource, etc: not used to full potential.

unfailing ▷ *adj* **1** remaining constant; never weakening or failing. **2** continuous. **3** certain; sure. • **unfailingly** *adverb*. ⓒ 14c.

unfair ▷ *adj* **1** not fair or just; inequitable. **2** involving deceit or dishonesty. • **unfairly** *adverb*. • **unfairness** *noun*. ⓒ 17c; Anglo-Saxon *unfæger*, meaning 'not pleasing to the eye' or 'ugly'.

unfaithful ▷ *adj* **1** not faithful to a sexual partner, usually by having a sexual relationship with someone else. **2** not loyal. **3** not true to a promise. **4** said of a translation, interpretation, etc: not accurate as a copy or reproduction; not true to the original. **5** without religious faith; unbelieving. • **unfaithfully** *adverb*. • **unfaithfulness** *noun*. ⓒ 14c.

unfamiliar ▷ *adj* **1** not (already or previously) known, experienced, etc. **2** strange; unusual. **3** (*usually* **unfamiliar with something**) said of a person: not familiar or well acquainted with it. • **unfamiliarity** *noun*. • **unfamiliarly** *adverb*. ⓒ 16c.

unfancied ▷ *adj* said of a racehorse, greyhound, sporting team, competition: not thought likely to win or do well.

unfasten ▷ *verb* **1** to undo or release something from a fastening. **2** *intr* to open or become loose. • **unfastened** *adj* **1** released from fastening. **2** not fastened; loose. ⓒ 13c.

unfathered ▷ *adj* **1** without a father or an acknowledged father. **2** unknown or obscure, especially of source, origin, etc. ⓒ 16c.

unfathomable ▷ *adj* **1** unable to be understood or fathomed; incomprehensible. **2** too deep or vast to measure or fathom. • **unfathomableness** *noun*. • **unfathomably** *adverb*. • **unfathomed** *adj* **1** unsounded; of unknown depth or meaning. **2** not fully explored or understood. ⓒ 17c.

unfavourable or (*US*) **unfavorable** *adj* **1** not favourable; adverse or inauspicious. **2** said of features, appearance, etc: ill-favoured; disagreeable or unattractive. • **unfavourableness** *noun*. • **unfavourably** *adverb*. ⓒ 16c.

unfavourite or (*US*) **unfavorite** *adj* least favourite. ⓒ 20c.

unfazed ▷ *adj*, *colloq* not fazed; not disconcerted or perturbed. • **unfazable** or **unfazeable** *adj* imperturbable. ⓒ 19c: originally US.

unfeeling ▷ *adj* **1** without physical feeling or sensation. **2** unsympathetic; hard-hearted. • **unfeelingly** *adverb*. • **unfeelingness** *noun*. ⓒ Anglo-Saxon in sense 1; 16c in sense 2.

unfettered ▷ *adj* not controlled or restrained. ⓒ 17c.

unfilial ▷ *adj* not becoming of a son or daughter.

unfiltered ▷ *adj* **1** not filtered. **2** said of a cigarette: without a filter.

unfit ▷ *adj* **1** (*often* **unfit for** or **to** or **to do something**) said of a person: not suitably qualified for it; not good enough; incompetent. **2** (*often* **unfit for something**) said of a thing: not suitable or appropriate for it. **3** not fit; not in good physical condition. • **unfitly** *adverb*. • **unfitness** *noun*. ⓒ 16c.

unfitted ▷ *adj* **1** not adapted or suited (for, to or to do something). **2** not provided or equipped with fittings.

unfix ▷ *verb* **1** to loosen or release something; to detach it. **2** to unsettle or disturb. ⓒ 16c.

unflappable ▷ *adj*, *colloq* never becoming agitated, flustered or alarmed; always remaining calm under pressure. • **unflappability** *noun*. • **unflappably** *adverb*. ⓒ 1950s.

unfledged ▷ *adj* **1** said of a bird: not yet fledged; not yet having developed adult flight feathers. **2** young and inexperienced. **3** relating to or characteristic of youth and inexperience. ⓒ 16c.

unflinching ▷ *adj* not flinching; showing a fearless determination in the face of danger or difficulty. • **unflinchingly** *adverb*. ⓒ 18c.

unfold ▷ *verb* **1** to open out the folds of something; to spread it out. **2** *intr* to open out or be spread out. **3** to reveal (a mystery, idea, etc); to make something clear. **4** *intr* to develop or be revealed gradually. • **unfolded** *adj* **1** not folded. **2** opened or spread out from a folded state. • **unfolder** *noun*. ⓒ Anglo-Saxon.

unforced ▷ *adj* **1** not compelled. **2** natural.

Some words with *un-* prefixed, all of which refer to UN- sense 1 unless specified otherwise below.

unmarred *adj*.
unmarriageable *adj*.
unmarried *adj*.
unmatchable *adj*.
unmatched *adj*.
unmatriculated *adj*.
unmatured *adj*.
unmeant *adj*.
unmeasurable *adj*.
unmeasured *adj*.
unmechanical *adj*.
unmechanized or **unmechanised** *adj*.
unmediated *adj*.
unmelodious *adj*.
unmelted *adj*.
unmemorable *adj*.
unmentioned *adj*.
unmercenary *adj*.
unmerited *adj*.
unmetaphorical *adj*.
unmethodical *adj*.
unmetrical *adj*.
unmilitary *adj*.
unmissed *adj*.
unmistaken *adj*.
unmixed *adj*.
unmodernized or **unmodernised** *adj*.
unmodified *adj*.
unmodulated *adj*.
unmolested *adj*.
unmotherly *adj*.
unmotivated *adj*.
unmounted *adj*.
unmourned *adj*.
unmovable or **unmoveable** *adj*.
unmown *adj*.
unmusical *adj*.
unmusically *adverb*.
unnail *verb* sense 2.
unnameable or **unnamable** *adj*.
unnamed *adj*.
unnavigable *adj*.
unnavigated *adj*.
unneeded *adj*.

unfortunate ▷ *adj* **1** unlucky; suffering misfortune or ill-luck. **2** resulting from or constituting bad luck □ *an unfortunate injury*. **3** regrettable. ▷ *noun* an unfortunate person. ● **unfortunately** *adverb* **1** in an unfortunate way; unluckily. **2** it's unfortunate that ...; I'm sorry to say ... □ *Unfortunately he can't come*. ◷ 16c.

unfounded ▷ *adj* said of allegations, ideas, rumours, etc: not based on fact; without foundation; groundless. ● **unfoundedly** *adverb*. ● **unfoundedness** *noun*. ◷ 17c.

unfreeze ▷ *verb* **1** *tr & intr* to thaw or cause something to thaw. **2** to free (eg prices, wages or funds) from a restriction or control imposed, eg by a government. ◷ 1940s in sense 2; 16c in sense 1.

unfriended ▷ *adj, rare & literary* without friends; friendless. ◷ 16c.

unfriendly ▷ *adverb* **1** not friendly; somewhat hostile. **2** not favourable. ● **unfriendliness** *noun*. ◷ 15c.

unfrock ▷ *verb* (***unfrocked***, ***unfrocking***) to defrock; to deprive (someone in holy orders) of ecclesiastical office or function. ◷ 17c.

unfurl ▷ *verb, tr & intr* to open, spread out or unroll something from a rolled-up or tied-up state. ◷ 17c.

unfurnished ▷ *adj* said especially of a rented property: lacking furniture.

ungainly /ʌnˈgeɪnlɪ/ ▷ *adj* (***ungainlier***, ***ungainliest***) awkward and ungraceful in movement; clumsy. ● **ungainliness** *noun*. ◷ 17c: from obsolete *gainly* graceful.

unget-at-able or **ungetatable** /ʌngɛtˈatəbəl/ ▷ *adj, colloq* inaccessible; unreachable. ◷ 19c.

ungettable /ʌnˈgɛtəbəl/ ▷ *adj* unattainable. ◷ 16c.

ungodly ▷ *adj* **1** wicked or sinful; irreligious. **2** *colloq* outrageous, especially outrageously early □ *at an ungodly hour*. ● **ungodliness** *noun*. ◷ 16c.

ungovernable ▷ *adj* said especially of a person's temper, etc: uncontrollable; not able to be restrained. ● **ungovernability** *noun*. ● **ungovernably** *adverb*. ● **ungoverned** *adj*. ◷ 17c.

ungraspable ▷ *adj* **1** not able to grasped by hand. **2** not able to be understood.

ungreen ▷ *adj* **1** said of government, industrial, etc policy or practice: lacking consideration for the environment. **2** harmful to the environment.

ungual /ˈʌŋgwəl/ ▷ *adj* **1** *anatomy* relating to, like or affecting the fingernails or toenails. **2** *zool* relating to an animal's claw or hoof. ▷ *noun* **1** an ungual phalanx or bone. **2** a nail, claw or hoof. ◷ 19c: from Latin *unguis* nail.

unguarded ▷ *adj* **1** without guard; unprotected. **2** said of speech, behaviour, etc: **a** showing a lack of caution or alertness; **b** revealing. **3** unscreened; not provided with a safety device, etc. ● **unguardedly** *adverb*. ● **unguardedness** *noun*. ◷ 16c.

unguent /ˈʌŋgwənt/ ▷ *noun* ointment or salve. ◷ 15c: from Latin *unguentum*, from *unguere* to anoint.

unguiculate /ʌŋˈgwɪkjʊlət/ ▷ *adj* **1** *bot* said of a petal: with a clawlike base. **2** *zool* **a** said of mammals: with claws or nails; **b** said of an organ, part, etc: clawlike. ▷ *noun* an unguiculate mammal. ◷ 19c: from Latin *unguiculus* fingernail or toenail, diminutive of UNGUIS.

unguis /ˈʌŋgwɪs/ ▷ *noun* (***ungues*** /ˈʌŋgwiːz/) **1** *zool* a nail or claw. **2** *bot* the clawlike base of a petal. ◷ 18c: Latin, meaning 'nail' or 'claw'.

ungulate /ˈʌŋgjʊlət/ *chiefly, zool* ▷ *adj* **1** with the form of a hoof; hoof-shaped. **2** said of a mammal: hoofed. ▷ *noun* a hoofed mammal. ◷ 19c: from Latin *ungula* hoof or claw.

unhallowed ▷ *adj* **1** said of ground, etc: not formally hallowed or consecrated. **2** not of a hallowed character; unholy. ◷ Anglo-Saxon.

unhand ▷ *verb, archaic or jocular* to let go of someone; to release them from one's grasp or take one's hands off them. ◷ 17c.

unhandy ▷ *adj* **1** awkward; difficult to handle or manage. **2** not skilled with the hands.

unhappy ▷ *adj* **1** sad; in low spirits; miserable. **2** bringing sadness; unfortunate □ *an unhappy ending to the film*. **3** inappropriate; infelicitous □ *an unhappy choice of words*. ● **unhappily** *adverb* **1** in an unhappy way; sadly or miserably. **2** unfortunately; regrettably. **3** unsuccessfully. ● **unhappiness** *noun*. ◷ 14c.

UNHCR ▷ *abbreviation* **1** United Nations High Commission for Refugees. **2** United Nations High Commissioner for Refugees. ◷ 1950s.

unhealthy ▷ *adj* **1** not conducive to health; harmful. **2** suffering from, or showing evidence of, ill health. **3** flouting or corrupting moral standards. **4** causing or likely to cause anxiety or worry; psychologically damaging □ *an unhealthy attitude*. **5** *colloq* dangerous to life. ● **unhealthily** *adverb*. ● **unhealthiness** *noun*. ◷ 16c.

unheard ▷ *adj* **1** not heard; not perceived with the ear. **2** not listened to; not heeded; ignored. **3** *law* not granted a hearing in court, etc. **4** UNHEARD-OF. ◷ 14c.

unheard-of ▷ *adj* **1** not known to have ever happened or been done before; unprecedented. **2** not at all famous; unknown □ *an unheard-of comedian*.

Some words with *un-* prefixed, all of which refer to UN- sense 1 unless specified otherwise below.

unneedful *adj*.
unneighbourly or (*US*) **unneighborly** *adj*.
unnoted *adj*.
unnoticeable *adj*.
unnoticed *adj*.
unnoticing *adj*.
unnourishing *adj*.
unobjectionable *adj*.
unobliging *adj*.
unobscured *adj*.
unobservable *adj*.
unobservant *adj*.
unobserved *adj*.
unobstructed *adj*.
unobstructive *adj*.
unobtainable *adj*.
unobtained *adj*.
unobtrusive *adj*.
unoffended *adj*.
unoffending *adj*.
unofficious *adj*.
unoiled *adj*.
unopened *adj*.
unopposed *adj*.
unordained *adj*.
unordered *adj*.
unoriginal *adj*.
unornamented *adj*.
unorthodox *adj*.
unorthodoxly *adverb*.
unorthodoxy *noun*.
unostentatious *adj*.
unostentatiously *adverb*.
unowned *adj*.
unoxidized or **unoxidised** *adj*.
unpaid *adj*.
unpainted *adj*.
unpaired *adj*.
unpalatable *adj*.
unpapered *adj*.
unpardonable *adj*.
unpardonably *adverb*.
unpardoned *adj*.
unpasteurized or **unpasteurised** *adj*.
unpatented *adj*.
unpatriotic *adj*.

unhinge ▷ *verb* **1 a** to remove (a door, etc) from its hinges; **b** to remove the hinges from (a door, etc). **2** to unbalance or derange (a person or a person's mind). **3** to disrupt (a process, etc) or throw it into a state of confusion. **4** to detach or separate (one thing from another). • **unhinged** *adj* **1** said of a door, etc: **a** removed from its the hinges; **b** with its hinges removed. **2** said of a person: deranged; crazy □ *Harry has been unhinged for years now.* ⓒ 17c.

unhip ▷ *adj, colloq* not hip; not trendy or fashionable. ⓒ 20c.

unhistoric ▷ *adj* not historic. • **unhistorically** *adverb.*

unhistorical 1 not historical. **2** not based on or in accordance with history. • **unhistorically** *adverb.* ⓒ 17c.

unholy ▷ *adj* **1** not holy or sacred. **2** wicked; sinful; irreligious. **3** *colloq* outrageous; dreadful. • **unholiness** *noun.* ⓒ Anglo-Saxon *unhalig.*

unholy alliance ▷ *noun* an alliance (especially a political one) that seems unnatural or unlikely, eg because it is between adversaries, sometimes formed for malicious purposes against a third party.

unhook ▷ *verb* **1** to remove or free something from a hook or hooks. **2** to unfasten the hook or hooks of (eg a dress or other garment). **3** *intr* to unfasten or become unfastened. ⓒ 17c.

unhorse ▷ *verb* **1** to throw or force (a rider) off a horse. **2** *archaic* to overthrow or dislodge (a person), eg from a position of power. **3** to unharness a horse or horses from a horse-drawn vehicle, etc. ⓒ 14c.

unhouseled /ʌnˈhɑʊzəld/ ▷ *adj, archaic* not having received the Eucharist. ⓒ 16c: from obsolete *housel* to admininster the sacrament, from Anglo-Saxon *husl.*

uni /ˈjuːnɪ/ ▷ *noun, colloq* short form of UNIVERSITY.

uni- /juːnɪ/ ▷ *combining form, signifying* one; a single □ *unidirectional.* ⓒ From Latin *unus* one.

Uniat /ˈjuːnɪət/ or **Uniate** /ˈjuːnɪɪt, ˈjuːnɪeɪt/ ▷ *adj* belonging, referring or relating to any church in eastern Europe and the Near East that acknowledges papal supremacy but retains its own customs, practices, liturgy, etc. ▷ *noun* a member of such a church. • **Uniatism** *noun.* ⓒ 19c: from Russian *uniyat,* from *uniya* union, from Latin *unus* one.

uniaxial ▷ *adj* **1** said of plants: with one main unbranched axis. **2** said of a crystal: with one optical axis. • **uniaxially** *adverb.* ⓒ 19c: see AXIAL.

unicameral ▷ *adj* said of a parliamentary system: with only one law-making body or chamber. • **unicameralism** *noun.* • **unicameralist** *noun.* • **unicamerally** *adverb.* ⓒ 19c: from Latin *camera* a chamber or room.

UNICEF /ˈjuːnɪsɛf/ ▷ *abbreviation* **1** United Nations Children's Fund. **2** *formerly* United Nations International Children's Emergency Fund.

unicellular ▷ *adj, biol* said of organisms or structures, eg bacteria, protozoa and many spores: consisting of a single cell. • **unicellularity** *noun.* ⓒ 19c.

unicorn /ˈjuːnɪkɔːn/ ▷ *noun* **1** a mythical animal in the form of a horse (usually a white one) with a long straight spiralled horn growing from its forehead. **2** *heraldry* a representation of such an animal, especially as a charge or supporter of the Royal Arms of Great Britain or of Scotland. ⓒ 13c: from French *unicorne,* from Latin *unicornis* one-horned, from *unus* one + *cornu* horn.

unicycle ▷ *noun* a cycle consisting of a single wheel with a seat and pedals attached, used especially by acrobats in circus performances, etc. • **unicyclist** *noun.* ⓒ 19c.

unidentified ▷ *adj* **1** not identified. **2** too strange to identify. • **unidentifiable** *adj.* • **unidentifiably** *adverb.* ⓒ 19c.

unidentified flying object see UFO

unidirectional ▷ *adj* with movement or operating in one direction only. • **unidirectionality** *noun.* • **unidirectionally** *adverb.* ⓒ 19c.

UNIDO /juːˈniːdoʊ/ ▷ *abbreviation* United Nations Industrial Development Organization.

unifiable and **unifier** see under UNIFY

unification /juːnɪfɪˈkeɪʃən/ ▷ *noun* **1** an act or the process of unifying or uniting. **2** the state of being unified □ *The unification of East and West Germany took place in 1990.* • **unificationist** *noun* someone who advocates unification. • **unificatory** *adj.* ⓒ 19c.

Unification Church ▷ *noun* an evangelistic religious and political movement which advocates the importance of family life and which is well known for its mass wedding ceremonies where up to 8 000 couples get married at the same time. Its members are sometimes referred to as **Moonies**. ⓒ 1970s: formed in 1954 in Korea by Sun Myung Moon (born 1920), hence the name given to his followers.

unified field ▷ *noun, physics* an ultimate basis on which some physicists seek to bring the workings of all natural phenomena within a single field.

uniflorous /juːnɪˈflɔːrəs/ ▷ *adj, bot* bearing only one flower. ⓒ 18c.

Some words with *un-* prefixed, all of which refer to UN- sense 1 unless specified otherwise below.

unpatronized or **unpatronised** *adj.*
unpatronizing or **unpatronising** *adj.*
unpaved *adj.*
unpayable *adj.*
unpeaceable *adj.*
unpeaceful *adj.*
unperceivable *adj.*
unperceived *adj.*
unperceptive *adj.*
unperfected *adj.*
unperforated *adj.*
unperformed *adj.*
unperfumed *adj.*
unperjured *adj.*
unperplexed *adj.*
unpersuadable *adj.*
unpersuaded *adj.*
unpersuasive *adj.*
unperturbed *adj.*
unphilosophic or **unphilosophical** *adj.*
unpicked *adj.*
unpierced *adj.*
unpitied *adj.*
unpitying *adj.*
unplanted *adj.*
unplayable *adj.*
unpleasing *adj.*
unpleasurable *adj.*
unpliable *adj.*
unploughed or (*US*) **unplowed** *adj.*
unpoetic or **unpoetical** *adj.*
unpoetically *adverb.*
unpoised *adj.*
unpolarized or **unpolarised** *adj.*
unpoliceable *adj.*
unpoliced *adj.*
unpolitic *adj.*
unpolitical *adj.*
unpolluted *adj.*
unpopulated *adj.*
unposed *adj.*
unposh *adj.*
unposted *adj.*

unifoliate ▷ *adj, bot* with only one leaf. 🕒 19c.

uniform /ˈjuːnɪfɔːm/ ▷ *noun* **1** distinctive clothing, always of the same colour, cut, etc, worn by all members of a particular organization or profession, eg by schoolchildren or soldiers. **2** a single set of such clothing. **3** the recognizable appearance, or a distinctive feature or way of dressing, that is typical of a particular group of people. **4** (**Uniform**) *communications* in the NATO alphabet: the word used to denote the letter 'U' (see table at NATO ALPHABET). ▷ *adj* **1** unchanging or unvarying in form, nature or appearance; always the same, regardless of changes in circumstances, etc. **2** alike all over or throughout. **3** with the same form, character, etc as another or others; alike or like. **4** forming part of a military or other uniform. ▷ *verb* (***uniformed***, ***uniforming***) **1** to make (several people or things) uniform or alike. **2** to fit out or provide (a number of soldiers, etc) with uniforms. • **uniformed** *adj* wearing a uniform. • **uniformly** *adverb*. • **uniformness** *noun*. 🕒 16c: from French *uniforme* or Latin *uniformis*, from *unus* one + *forma* form or shape.

uniformitarianism /juːnɪfɔːmɪˈtɛərɪənɪzəm/ ▷ *noun, geol* the principle which states that the results of past geological events resemble the results of geological processes and phenomena occurring in the present, and can be explained by them. • **uniformitarian** *noun* someone who supports this principle. ▷ *adj* relating to uniformitarianism or uniformitarians. 🕒 19c.

uniformity /juːnɪˈfɔːmɪtɪ/ ▷ *noun* **1** the state or fact of being uniform; conformity or similarity between several things, constituent parts, etc; sameness. **2** monotony; lack of variation. 🕒 15c.

unify /ˈjuːnɪfaɪ/ ▷ *verb* (***unifies***, ***unified***, ***unifying***) to bring (two or more things) together to form a single unit or whole; to unite. • **unifiable** *adj*. • **unification** see separate entry. • **unifier** *noun*. 🕒 16c: from French *unifier* or Latin *unifacere*, from Latin *unus* one + *facere* to make.

unilateral /juːnɪˈlatərəl/ ▷ *adj* **1** occurring on, affecting or involving one side only. **2** affecting, involving or done by only one person or group among several ◻ *unilateral disarmament*. **3** *law* said of a contract, obligation, etc: entered into, binding, affecting, etc only one party. **4** *bot* with parts of a plant, eg leaves, flowers, etc, situated on one side of an axis only. • **unilaterality** *noun*. • **unilaterally** *adverb*. 🕒 19c: see LATERAL.

Unilateral Declaration of Independence ▷ *noun* (abbreviation **UDI**) a declaration of independence made by a dependent state without the agreement of the state that protects it.

unilateralism ▷ *noun* a policy or the practice of unilateral action, especially of unilateral nuclear disarmament. • **unilateralist** *noun* a supporter or advocate of unilateralism. ▷ *adj* relating to or involving unilateralism. 🕒 1920s.

unilingual /juːnɪˈlɪŋgwəl/ ▷ *adj* relating to, in or using one language only; monolingual. • **unilingually** *adverb*. 🕒 19c.

unimpeachable ▷ *adj* indisputably reliable or honest; impossible to blame, find fault with, etc. • **unimpeachably** *adverb*. 🕒 18c.

unimproved ▷ *adj* **1** not improved; not made better. **2** said of land: not cultivated, cleared, built upon, etc. **3** not put to use or taken advantage of. 🕒 17c.

uninflected ▷ *adj* **1** *grammar* said of a language, word, etc: not characterized by INFLECTION (sense 1). **2** *music* not modulated. **3** not bent inwards.

uninterested ▷ *adj* not interested; indifferent. • **uninterestedly** *adverb*. • **uninterestedness** *noun*. See also DISINTERESTED. 🕒 18c.

> ***uninterested***
>
> See Usage Note at **disinterested**.

uninteresting ▷ *adj* boring; not able to raise, or capable of raising, any interest. • **uninterestingly** *adverb*.

the Union ▷ *noun* **1 a** the uniting of the Scottish and English crowns in 1603 or of the Scottish and English parliaments in 1707; **b** the resulting regnal or political unit that was formed after these events. **2 a** the uniting of the parliaments of Great Britain and Ireland in 1801; **b** the resulting political unit that was formed after this event and which lasted until 1920. **3 a** the uniting of Great Britain and N Ireland in 1920; **b** the regnal and political unit that has been in place since then. **4** the United States of America. **5 a** the collection of northern US states which fought against the south in the American Civil War; **b** (**Union**) *as adj* ◻ *Union soldiers*.

union /ˈjuːnjən, ˈjuːnɪən/ ▷ *noun* **1 a** the action or an act of uniting two or more things; **b** the state of being united. **2** a united whole. **3** *surgery* the growing together in healing of the parts of a broken bone, sides of a wound, etc. **4** *formal* **a** marriage; the state of wedlock; **b** sexual intercourse. **5** an association, confederation, etc of people or groups for a common (especially political) purpose. **6** agreement or harmony. **7** a league or association, especially a TRADE UNION. **8 a** a device representative of union on a flag; **b** the same device used separately as a flag, such as the Union Jack. **9** a device that connects one thing with another, especially a connecting part for pipes, etc. **10** (*also* **Union**) **a** an organization concerned

Some words with *un-* prefixed, all of which refer to UN- sense 1 unless specified otherwise below.

unpracticable *adj*.
unpredictability *noun*.
unpredictable *adj*.
unpredictableness *noun*.
unpredictably *adverb*.
unpredicted *adj*.
unpremeditated *adj*.
unprepared *adj*.
unprescribed *adj*.
unpresentable *adj*.
unpressed *adj*.
unpressurized *adj*.
unpresuming *adj*.
unpresumptuous *adj*.
unpretending *adj*.
unpretentious *adj*.
unpriced *adj*.
unprimed *adj*.
unprinted *adj*.
unprivileged *adj*.
unproblematic *adj*.
unprocessed *adj*.
unproclaimed *adj*.
unprocurable *adj*.
unproductive *adj*.
unprofessed *adj*.
unprofitable *adj*.
unprofitably *adverb*.
unprogressive *adj*.
unprohibited *adj*.
unpromising *adj*.
unprompted *adj*.
unpronounceable *adj*.
unpronounced *adj*.
unpropitious *adj*.
unprotected *adj*.
unprotesting *adj*.
unprovable or **unproveable** *adj*.
unproved *adj*.
unproven *adj*.
unprovided *adj*.
unprovoked *adj*.
unpublished *adj*.
unpunctual *adj*.
unpunctuated *adj*.
unpunishable *adj*.
unpunished *adj*.

with the interests and welfare of the students in a college, university, etc; **b** the building that houses such an organization, often also the site of canteen and recreational facilities, etc. **11** a textile fabric made from more than one kind of fibre. **12** *math* (symbol ⋃) **a** a SET[2] (*noun* 2) comprising all the members (but no others) of two or more smaller sets; **b** the operation of forming such a set. See also INTERSECTION sense 5. **13** *historical* in 19c England: a number of parishes united for the administration of the poor laws. **14** in the Indian subcontinent: a local administrative unit made up of several villages. ⓒ 15c: from French, from Latin *unio*, *unionis* oneness or unity, from Latin *unus* one.

union catalogue ▷ *noun* a catalogue that lists all the publications held at several co-operating libraries.

Union flag see under UNION JACK

unionism or **Unionism** ▷ *noun* **1** advocacy of combination into one body for the purposes of social or political organization. **2** *US* advocacy of or adherence to union between the States. **3** advocacy of or adherence to the principles of the former Unionist Party of Great Britain and Ireland or of any party advocating the continued political union of Great Britain and Northern Ireland. **4** advocacy of or support for continued political union between Scotland, England and Wales. **5** adherence to the principles and practices of trade unions. ⓒ 19c.

unionist ▷ *noun* **1** an advocate or supporter of unionism, especially as a system of social or political organization. **2** (**Unionist**) a supporter of the federal union of the United States, especially at the time of the American Civil War. **3** (*sometimes* **Unionist**) **a** before 1920: a supporter of the Union of all Ireland and Great Britain; **b** since 1920: a supporter of the union of Great Britain and Northern Ireland. **4** a supporter of the continued political union between Scotland, England and Wales. **5** an advocate or supporter of trade unions; a trade-unionist. ▷ *adj* (*sometimes* **Unionist**) relating to unionists or to unionism. See also LOYALIST. ⓒ 18c.

unionize or **unionise** ▷ *verb* (***unionized, unionizing***) **1** to organize (a workforce) into a trade union or trade unions. **2** to subject to the rules of a trade union. **3** to recruit (a person or people) into a trade union. **4** *intr* to join or constitute a trade union. • **unionization** *noun*. • **unionized** *adj* said of a workforce or a workplace: organized into a trade union or trade unions, or accepted by management as being so. ⓒ 19c.

Union Jack ▷ *noun* (*also* **Union flag**) the national flag of the United Kingdom, combining the crosses of St Andrew, St George and St Patrick.

union pipes see under UILLEAN PIPES

union shop ▷ *noun* an establishment, factory, trade, etc in which the employees must belong to a trade union or join one within a specified period of time.

uniparous /juːˈnɪpərəs/ ▷ *adj* **1** *zool* relating to or characterized by producing only one offspring at any one birth. **2** *bot* said of a cyme: producing one lateral branch only at each node. ⓒ 17c: from Latin *parus*, from *parere* to bear or give birth to.

uniped /ˈjuːnɪpɛd/ ▷ *noun* a person or creature with only one foot or leg. ▷ *adj* with only one foot or leg. ⓒ 19c: from UNI- + Latin *pes, pedis* foot.

unipod /ˈjuːnɪpɒd/ ▷ *noun, photog* a one-legged stand or support for a camera. ⓒ 1930s: from Greek *pous, podos* foot, modelled on TRIPOD.

unipolar ▷ *adj* **1** with, relating to, or using one magnetic or electronic pole only. **2** *biol* said of a nerve cell, etc: with one pole or process only. **3** *electronics* said of a transistor: involving conduction by charge carriers of one polarity only. **4** *psychiatry* said of an illness or disorder: characterized by episodes of either a depressive or manic nature but not both. • **unipolarity** *noun*. ⓒ 19c: UNI- + POLAR.

unique /jʊˈniːk/ ▷ *adj* **1** sole or solitary; of which there is only one. **2** referring to something that is the only one of its kind; without equal; unparalleled, especially in excellence. **3** (*usually* **unique to someone** or **something**) referring to something that belongs solely to, or is associated solely with, them or it. **4** *colloq, loosely* extremely unusual; excellent. ▷ *noun* **1** anything, especially formerly a coin or medal, of which there is only one example or copy. **2** a person or thing that is without equal, especially in excellence. • **uniquely** *adverb*. • **uniqueness** *noun*. ⓒ 17c: from French, from Latin *unicus* alone of its kind or without equal, from *unus* one.

> ***unique***
>
> • **Unique** is commonly qualified by words like **absolutely, completely, more, most, very**, although some people object to this, regarding **unique** as something absolute in itself □ *The atmosphere of the occasion was absolutely unique* □ *Surely no one had more unique or peaceful surroundings in which to work than we did.*
>
> ☆ RECOMMENDATION: Avoid (in particular) using **more, most** and **very** with **unique** when writing or speaking to people who are likely to be precise about the use of language.

unisex ▷ *adj* suited to, for use by, or wearable by, both men and women □ *a unisex sauna*. ⓒ 1960s.

Some words with *un-* prefixed, all of which refer to UN- sense 1 unless specified otherwise below.

unpurged *adj.*
unpurified *adj.*
unquantifiable *adj.*
unquantified *adj.*
unquelled *adj.*
unquenchable *adj.*
unquenched *adj.*
unquotable *adj.*
unrated *adj.*
unratified *adj.*
unreachable *adj.*
unreached *adj.*
unreactive *adj.*
unrealistic *adj.*
unrealistically *adverb.*
unrealizable or
unrealisable *adj.*
unrealized or **unrealised** *adj.*
unreasoned *adj.*
unreceived *adj.*
unreceptive *adj.*
unreciprocated *adj.*
unreclaimable *adj.*
unreclaimed *adj.*
unrecognizable or **unrecognisable** *adj.*
unrecognized or **unrecognised** *adj.*
unrecommended *adj.*
unrecompensed *adj.*
unreconciled *adj.*
unreconstructed *adj.*
unrecorded *adj.*
unrecoverable *adj.*
unrecovered *adj.*
unrectified *adj.*
unredeemable *adj.*
unredeemed *adj.*
unreduced *adj.*
unrefined *adj.*
unreflected *adj.*
unreflecting *adj.*
unreflective *adj.*
unreformable *adj.*
unreformed *adj.*
unrefreshed *adj.*
unrefreshing *adj.*
unregarded *adj.*

unisexual ▻ *adj* **1** relating to or restricted to one sex only. **2** *bot, zool* said of certain organisms: with either male or female reproductive organs but not both. **3** unisex. • **unisexuality** *noun*. • **unisexually** *adverb*. ⓘ 19c.

UNISON /ˈjuːnɪsən/ ▻ *noun* in the UK: an amalgamated trade union for public service workers, formed in 1993 from COHSE, NALGO and NUPE. ⓘ 1990s.

unison /ˈjuːnɪsən/ ▻ *noun* **1** *music* the interval between two notes of the same pitch, or which are one or more octaves apart. **2** the state of acting all in the same way at the same time. **3** (*usually* **in unison**) complete agreement. • **unisonal, unisonant** or **unisonous** *adj*. ⓘ 16c: from Latin *unus* one + *sonus* sound.

unit /ˈjuːnɪt/ ▻ *noun* **1** a single item or element regarded as the smallest subdivision of a whole; a single person or thing. **2** a set of mechanical or electrical parts, or a group of workers, performing a specific function within a larger construction or organization. **3** a standard measure of a physical quantity, such as time or distance, specified multiples of which are used to express its size, eg an SI unit. **4** *non-technical* a kilowatt-hour. **5** any whole number less than 10. **6** any subdivision of a military force. **7 a** an item of furniture that combines with others to form a set; **b** a set of such items. **8** *pharmacol* the amount of a drug, vaccine, etc that is required to produce a specific effect. **9** a standard measure used to calculate alcohol intake, equivalent to 9 grams of absolute alcohol, approximately equivalent to a pint of beer, etc, a glass of wine, a measure of spirits, etc. **10** *finance* the smallest measure of investment in a UNIT TRUST. **11** *N Amer, Austral, NZ* short form of HOME UNIT. ▻ *adj* relating to the quantity of one, eg unit mass. ⓘ 16c: from Latin *unus* one, perhaps modelled on DIGIT; see also UNITY.

UNITA /juːˈniːtə/ ▻ *abbreviation*: *União Nacional para a Independência Total de Angola* (Portuguese), National Union for the Total Independence of Angola. ⓘ 1960s.

unitard /ˈjuːnɪtɑːd/ ▻ *noun* a close-fitting one-piece garment of stretchable fabric that covers the body from neck to feet. ⓘ 1960s: from UNI-, modelled on LEOTARD.

Unitarian /juːnɪˈtɛərɪən/ ▻ *noun* **1** a member of a religious group originally comprising Christians who believed God to be a single entity rather than a Trinity of Father, Son and Holy Spirit, now including members holding a broad spectrum of beliefs. **2** any non-Christian monotheist, especially a Muslim. **3** (**unitarian**) a supporter or advocate of some belief based on unity or union, eg political centralization. ▻ *adj* **1** relating to or characteristic of Unitarians. **2** (**unitarian**) relating or pertaining to unity or political centralization. • **Unitarianism** or **unitarianism** *noun*. ⓘ 17c.

unitary /ˈjuːnɪtərɪ/ ▻ *adj* **1** relating to, characterized by or based on unity. **2** referring or relating to the nature of a unit; individual. **3** relating to a unit or units. ⓘ 19c.

unit cost ▻ *noun* the actual cost of producing one item.

unite /jʊˈnaɪt/ ▻ *verb* (***united, uniting***) **1** *tr & intr* to make or become a single unit or whole. **2** *tr & intr* to bring or come together in a common purpose or belief. **3** to have or exhibit (features, qualities, etc) in combination. **4** *tr & intr* to join in marriage. • **uniter** *noun*. • **uniting** *noun, adj*. ⓘ 15c: from Latin *unire, unitum* to join together, from *unus* one.

united ▻ *adj* **1** referring to something that has or has been united; joined together or combined. **2** relating or pertaining to, or resulting from, two or more people or things in union or combination. **3** (*usually* **United**) often in the names of churches, societies, etc and of football clubs: made up of or resulting from the union of two or more parts. • **unitedly** *adverb*. • **unitedness** *noun*. ⓘ 16c.

United Kingdom ▻ *noun* (abbreviation **UK**) (*in full* **United Kingdom of Great Britain and Northern Ireland**) since 1922: the official title for the kingdom comprising England, Wales, Scotland and Northern Ireland.

> ***United Kingdom***
>
> See Usage Note at **Britain**.

United Nations ▻ *singular or plural noun* (abbreviation **UN**) an association of independent states formed in 1945 to promote peace and international co-operation.

United Reformed Church ▻ *noun* a church formed by the union in 1972 of the Presbyterian Church in England and the Congregational Church in England and Wales.

United States ▻ *singular or plural noun* (*in full* **United States of America**) (abbreviation **US** or **USA**) a federal republic mostly in N America, comprising 50 states and the District of Columbia.

unitholder ▻ *noun* someone who holds a unit of securities in a UNIT TRUST.

unitive /ˈjuːnɪtɪv/ ▻ *adj* **1** *Christianity* with the quality of uniting spiritually to God. **2** uniting; harmonizing. **3** characterized by unity or union. ⓘ 16c.

unitize or **unitise** /ˈjuːnɪtaɪz/ ▻ *verb* (***unitized, unitizing***) **1** to form something into a unit; to unite or make one. **2** to package (cargo) into unit loads. **3** *finance* to convert (an investment trust) into a unit trust. •

Some words with *un-* prefixed, all of which refer to UN- sense 1 unless specified otherwise below.

unregistered *adj.*
unregulated *adj.*
unrehearsed *adj.*
unrelated *adj.*
unrelaxed *adj.*
unreliable *adj.*
unrelieved *adj.*
unremarkable *adj.*
unremarked *adj.*
unremembered *adj.*
unremorseful *adj.*
unremovable *adj.*
unremunerative *adj.*
unrenewed *adj.*
unrenowned *adj.*
unrepealed *adj.*
unrepairable *adj.*
unrepaired *adj.*
unrepeatable *adj.*
unrepentant *adj.*
unrepenting *adj.*
unreported *adj.*
unrepresentative *adj.*
unrepresented *adj.*
unreprieved *adj.*
unreproachful *adj.*
unreproducible *adj.*
unreproductive *adj.*
unreproved *adj.*
unrequested *adj.*
unresentful *adj.*
unreserve *noun.*
unresisting *adj.*
unresolvable *adj.*
unresolved *adj.*
unrespected *adj.*
unresponsive *adj.*
unrested *adj.*
unrestrainable *adj.*
unrestrained *adj.*
unrestrainedly *adverb.*
unrestricted *adj.*
unreturnable *adj.*
unreturned *adj.*
unrevealed *adj.*
unrevealing *adj.*
unrevenged *adj.*
unrevised *adj.*

unitization *noun*. ⓘ 19c in sense 1; 20c in senses 2 and 3: from UNIT.

unit-linked ▷ *adj* said eg of an equity, pension plan, etc: having a return that reflects the rise and fall of the prices of the investment funds to which it is linked.

unit of account ▷ *noun* a monetary unit used as a basis of exchange or comparison, or as a unit in accounting, but which does not necessarily correspond to any actual currency.

unit price ▷ *noun* the price per unit of goods supplied.

unit pricing ▷ *noun* a method of pricing foodstuffs, etc by showing the cost per agreed unit, eg kilogram or pound, as well as or instead of the price of the item.

unit trust ▷ *noun* **1** an investment scheme in which clients' money is invested in various companies, with the combined shares purchased divided into units which are allocated in multiples to each client according to the individual amount invested. **2** a financial organization operating such a scheme.

unity /'juːnɪtɪ/ ▷ *noun* (***unities***) **1** the state or quality of being one; oneness. **2** a single unified whole. **3** the act, state or quality of forming a single unified whole from two or more parts. **4** agreement; harmony; concord. **5** *math* the number or numeral 1. **6** a quantity, value, etc equivalent to one for the purposes of calculation or measurement. **7** uniformity or coherence. **8** *theat* any one of the three principles of classical drama, whereby the action of the play should be limited to a single location (**unity of place**), all the events should be such as could happen within a single day (**unity of time**), and nothing should be admitted that is not directly relevant to the development of a single plot (**unity of action**). ⓘ 13c: from French *unité*, from Latin *unitas*, from *unus* one.

Univ. ▷ *abbreviation* University.

univalent ▷ *adj* **1** *chem* MONOVALENT. **2** said of a chromosome during meiosis: not paired with its homologue. • **univalence** or **univalency** *noun*. ⓘ 19c.

univalve *zool* ▷ *adj* **1** with one valve or shell. **2** said of a mollusc: with a shell that is in one piece, lacking a hinge as in a BIVALVE. ▷ *noun* **1** an undivided shell. **2** a mollusc whose shell is composed of a single piece. ⓘ 17c.

universal /juːnɪ'vɜːsəl/ ▷ *adj* **1** relating to the universe. **2** relating to, typical of, affecting, etc the whole world or all people. **3** relating to, typical of, affecting, etc all the people or things in a particular group. **4** *colloq* widespread; general; all-round ▫ *won universal approval*. **5** *logic* said of a statement or proposition: asserting something about all the members of a class. Compare PARTICULAR. **6** said of a language, especially an artificial one, etc: intended to be used as a means of communication by speakers of different languages throughout the world. **7** covering or knowledgeable in a wide range of subjects, activities, interests, etc. **8** said of a machine, tool, etc: designed for, or adjustable to, a wide range of uses, sizes, etc; not restricted to one purpose, position, etc. **9** (abbreviation **U**) in film classification: suitable for everyone. ▷ *noun* **1** something that is universal. **2** *philos* a general term or concept, or the nature or type signified by such a term. **3** *logic* a universal proposition. **4** *linguistics* a basic feature or rule that is found generally in natural languages. **5** a film that has been classified as suitable for everyone. • **universally** *adverb*. • **universalness** *noun*. ⓘ 14c: from French *universel* or Latin *universalis*, from *universus*; see UNIVERSE.

universal indicator ▷ *noun, chem* a mixture of several chemical indicators, used to measure the pH (relative acidity or alkalinity) of a solution, that shows a whole range of different colours corresponding to different pH values.

Universalism ▷ *noun, theol* the doctrine of or belief in universal salvation, ie the ultimate salvation of all mankind. • **Universalist** *noun, adj*.

universalism ▷ *noun* **1** a universal feature, characteristic, etc. **2** UNIVERSALITY.

universality /juːnɪvɜː'salɪtɪ/ ▷ *noun* the state or quality of being universal.

universalize or **universalise** /juːnɪ'vɜːsəlaɪz/ ▷ *verb* (***universalized***, ***universalizing***) **1** to make something universal. **2** to bring something into universal use. • **universalization** *noun*. ⓘ 17c.

universal joint and **universal coupling** ▷ *noun* a joint or coupling, especially between two rotating shafts, that allows movement in all directions.

universe /'juːnɪvɜːs/ ▷ *noun* **1** *astron* **a** (**the Universe**) all existing space, energy and matter, ie the whole of space and all the galaxies, stars, planets, moons, asteroids and other bodies contained within it; the cosmos. **b** a star system; a galaxy. **2** a domain; a sphere of activity, interest, etc. **3** the world; all people. ⓘ 16c; 14c in obsolete form *in universe*, meaning 'universally' or 'of universal application': from French *univers*, from Latin *universum* the whole world, from *universus* all together, literally 'turned into one', from *unus* one + *vertere* to turn.

universe of discourse ▷ *noun, logic* all the objects, ideas, etc that are expressed or implied in a discussion.

university /juːnɪ'vɜːsɪtɪ/ ▷ *noun* (***universities***) **1** a higher education institution with the authority to award

Some words with *un-* prefixed, all of which refer to UN- sense 1 unless specified otherwise below.

unrevoked *adj.*	**unsaleable** *adj.*	**unscratched** *adj.*
unrevolutionary *adj.*	**unsalted** *adj.*	**unscreened** *adj.*
unrewarded *adj.*	**unsanctioned** *adj.*	**unseaworthy** *adj.*
unrewarding *adj.*	**unsanitary** *adj.*	**unseconded** *adj.*
unrhymed *adj.*	**unsatisfactory** *adj.*	**unsecured** *adj.*
unrhythmical *adj.*	**unsatisfied** *adj.*	**unseeing** *adj.*
unrhythmically *adverb.*	**unsatisfying** *adj.*	**unsegmented** *adj.*
unridable or **unrideable** *adj.*	**unsaved** *adj.*	**unsegregated** *adj.*
unridden *adj.*	**unscalable** *adj.*	**unselected** *adj.*
unrifled *adj.*	**unscaled** *adj.*	**unselective** *adj.*
unrisen *adj.*	**unscarred** *adj.*	**unselfconscious** *adj.*
unroadworthy *adj.*	**unscented** *adj.*	**unsensational** *adj.*
unromantic *adj.*	**unscheduled** *adj.*	**unsentenced** *adj.*
unruled *adj.*	**unscholarly** *adj.*	**unsentimental** *adj.*
unrumpled *adj.*	**unschooled** *adj.*	**unserviceable** *adj.*
unsalaried *adj.*	**unscientific** *adj.*	**unset** *verb* sense 2, *adj.*

degrees at bachelor, master and doctoral level (traditionally in academic, non-vocational subjects but now also in technical and vocational areas) and usually having research facilities. **2** the buildings, staff or students of such an institution. Sometimes (*colloq*) shortened to UNI. • **universitarian** *adj*. ◷ 14c: from French *université*, from Latin *universitas* the whole, the entire number, the universe, and (in later and medieval Latin) a society or guild, from *universus*; see UNIVERSE.

univocal /juːnɪˈvoʊkəl, jʊˈnɪvəkəl/ ⊳ *adj, chiefly logic* said of a word or term: with one meaning only; unambiguous. ⊳ *noun* a univocal word or term. • **univocalic** *adj*. • **univocality** *noun*. • **univocally** *adverb*. ◷ 16c.

UNIX or **Unix** /ˈjuːnɪks/ ⊳ *noun, trademark, computing* a type of operating system designed to handle large file transfers and allow multi-user access of data. ◷ 1970s: from UNI-, modelled on *Multics*, an operating system developed in the 1960s.

unjoint ⊳ *verb* to disjoint; to dislocate. ◷ 14c.

unjointed ⊳ *adj* **1** disjointed; incoherent. **2** without joints. ◷ 16c.

unkempt /ʌnˈkɛmpt/ ⊳ *adj* **1** said of hair: uncombed. **2** said of general appearance: untidy; dishevelled. • **unkemptly** *adverb*. ◷ 18c: a variant of earlier *unkembed*, from Anglo-Saxon *cemban* to comb.

unkind ⊳ *adj* unsympathetic, cruel or harsh. • **unkindly** *adverb*. • **unkindness** *noun*. ◷ 14c in this sense; 13c in obsolete sense 'strange' or 'foreign'.

unknowing ⊳ *adj* **1** not knowing; ignorant. **2** (*often* **unknowing of something**) ignorant or unaware of it. **3** unwitting. • **unknowingly** *adverb*. ◷ 14c.

unknown ⊳ *adj* **1** not known; unfamiliar. **2** not at all famous. ⊳ *noun* **1** an unknown person or thing. **2** (*usually* **the unknown**) something that is unknown, undiscovered, unexplored, etc. • **unknownness** *noun*. ◷ 13c.

unknown quantity ⊳ *noun* a person or thing whose precise identity, nature or influence is not known or cannot be predicted.

Unknown Soldier and **Unknown Warrior** ⊳ *noun* an unidentified soldier, representative of the members of a country's armed forces who have been killed in war, for whom a tomb is established to serve as a memorial.

unlace ⊳ *verb* **1** to undo or loosen the lace or laces of (shoes, etc). **2** to unfasten or remove garments, etc from (oneself or someone else) by undoing the laces or lacing. ◷ 14c.

unlawful assembly ⊳ *noun, law* a meeting of three or more people that is considered likely to cause a breach of the peace or endanger the public.

unlay ⊳ *verb* to untwist (a rope, cable, etc) into its separate strands. ◷ 18c.

unleaded /ʌnˈlɛdɪd/ ⊳ *adj* **1** not covered, weighted, etc with lead. **2** (*also* **lead-free**) said of petrol: free from lead additives, eg antiknocking agents. ⊳ *noun* unleaded petrol. ◷ 17c.

unlearn ⊳ *verb* **1** to try actively to forget something learned; to rid the memory of it. **2** to free oneself from (eg an acquired habit). ◷ 15c.

unlearned[1] /ʌnˈlɜːnɪd/ ⊳ *adj* not well educated; uneducated. • **unlearnedly** *adverb*. • **unlearnedness** *noun*.

unlearned[2] /ʌnˈlɜːnd/ or **unlearnt** /ʌnˈlɜːnt/ ⊳ *adj* **1** said of a lesson, etc: not learnt. **2** said of a skill, etc: not acquired by learning; instinctive; innate.

unleash ⊳ *verb* **1** to release (eg a dog) from a leash. **2** to release or give free expression to (eg anger). ◷ 17c.

unleavened /ʌnˈlɛvənd/ ⊳ *adj* said of bread: not leavened; made without yeast, and therefore rather flat and hard. ◷ 16c.

unless /ʌnˈlɛs/ ⊳ *conj* if not; except when; except if □ *Unless you come in now you won't get any tea.* ◷ 15c as the prepositional phrase *on less*, meaning 'on a lesser footing or on a lower condition (than)'; first used as a preposition and conjunction in the 16c.

unlettered ⊳ *adj* **1** uneducated. **2** illiterate. ◷ 14c.

unlike ⊳ *prep* **1** different from □ *Unlike her, he's going shopping today.* **2** not typical or characteristic of □ *It's unlike her to be late.* ⊳ *adj* not like or alike; different; dissimilar. • **unlikeness** *noun*. ◷ 13c.

unlikely ⊳ *adj* **1** not expected or likely to happen. **2** not obviously suitable; improbable. **3** probably untrue; implausible. • **unlikeliness** or **unlikelihood** *noun*. ◷ 14c.

unlimber ⊳ *verb* to remove (a gun) from its limber in preparation for use. ◷ 19c.

unlimited ⊳ *adj* **1** not limited or restricted. **2** *loosely* very great or numerous. • **unlimitedly** *adverb*. • **unlimitedness** *noun*. ◷ 15c.

unlined[1] ⊳ *adj* free from or not marked with lines □ *a youthful unlined face* □ *unlined paper.* ◷ 19c in sense 2; 16c in sense 1.

Some words with *un-* prefixed, all of which refer to UN- sense 1 unless specified otherwise below.

unsewn *adj.*
unsexy *adj.*
unshakeable or **unshakable** *adj.*
unshaken *adj.*
unshapely *adj.*
unshared *adj.*
unsharpened *adj.*
unshaved *adj.*
unshaven *adj.*
unshed *adj.*
unshell *verb* sense 2.
unsheltered *adj.*
unshielded *adj.*
unshockable *adj.*
unshocked *adj.*
unshod *adj.*
unshrinkable *adj.*
unshrinking *adj.*
unsigned *adj.*
unsinkable *adj.*
unsized *adj.*
unskilful or (*US*) **unskillful** *adj.*
unskimmed *adj.*
unslakeable *adj.*
unsleeping *adj.*
unsliced *adj.*
unsmiling *adj.*
unsocketed *adj.*
unsoiled *adj.*
unsold *adj.*
unsolicited *adj.*
unsolicitous *adj.*
unsolid *adj.*
unsolvable *adj.*
unsolved *adj.*
unsorted *adj.*
unsought *adj.*
unsounded *adj.*
unsown *adj.*
unspecialized or **unspecialised** *adj.*
unspecific *adj.*
unspecified *adj.*
unspectacular *adj.*
unspent *adj.*
unspilled or **unspilt** *adj.*

unlined[2] ⊳ *adj* said of a garment, etc: without any lining.

unlisted ⊳ *adj* **1** not entered on a list. **2** *stock exchange* **a** *originally* said of securities: not dealt in on the Stock Exchange; **b** *now* designating a securities market in smaller companies admitted for trading on the Stock Exchange but which do not have to comply with the rules or requirements for listed securities. **3** *chiefly N Amer* said of a telephone number: ex-directory. ◷ 17c.

unlit ⊳ *adj* not lit; without lights or lighting. ◷ 19c.

unlived-in ⊳ *adj* not lived in; not homely or comfortable □ *That cottage looks unlived-in.*

unload ⊳ *verb* **1** *tr & intr* to remove (a load or cargo) from (a vehicle, ship, etc). **2** *tr & intr* to discharge (cargo, freight, etc). **3** to free or relieve someone or something of a load or burden. **4** to relieve (oneself or one's mind) of troubles or anxieties by telling them to another; to get rid of (troubles) in this way. **5** to remove the charge of ammunition from (a gun) without firing it. **6** to dispose or get rid of (something undesirable). • **unloader** *noun.* ◷ 16c.

unlock ⊳ *verb* **1** to undo the lock of (a door, etc). **2** to free someone or something from being locked up. **3** to release or reveal (eg emotions, etc) □ *The accident unlocked the memory of her father's death.* **4** to explain or find the key to (a puzzle, etc). **5** *intr* to become unlocked. • **unlockable** *adj.* • **unlocked** *adj.* ◷ 15c.

unlooked-for ⊳ *adj* **1** unexpected. **2** not deliberately encouraged or invited.

unloose or **unloosen** ⊳ *verb* **1** to make something less tight; to loosen it. **2** to set free; to release. ◷ 14c.

unlovely ⊳ *adj* unattractive; unpleasant or ugly. • **unloveliness** *noun.* ◷ 14c.

unlucky ⊳ *adj* **1** bringing, resulting from or constituting bad luck. **2** having, or tending to have, bad luck. **3** regrettable. • **unluckily** *adverb* **1** in an unlucky way; as a result of bad luck. **2** I am sorry to say; regrettably. • **unluckiness** *noun.* ◷ 16c.

unmade ⊳ *adj* **1** not yet made. **2** said of a bed: with bedclothes not arranged neatly. **3** said of a road: with no proper surface (eg of tarmac).

unmade-up ⊳ *adj* **1** said of a person: not wearing make-up. **2** not made up.

unmake ⊳ *verb* **1** to cancel or destroy the (especially beneficial) effect of something. **2** to depose someone from office or a position of authority. **3** to change the nature or quality of something. ◷ 15c.

unman ⊳ *verb, old use, literary* **1** to cause someone to lose self-control, especially to overcome with emotion. **2** to deprive someone of their virility; to emasculate. • **unmanned** *adj.* ◷ 16c.

unmanly ⊳ *adj* **1** not manly; not virile or masculine. **2** weak or cowardly. • **unmanliness** *noun.* ◷ 15c.

unmanned ⊳ *adj* said especially of a vehicle or spacecraft: without personnel or a crew, especially controlled remotely or automatically; not manned.

unmannered ⊳ *adj* **1** without affectation or pretention. ◷ 16c.

unmannerly ⊳ *adj* ill-mannered; impolite. ⊳ *adverb, archaic* in an unmannerly way; impolitely or rudely. • **unmannerliness** *noun.* ◷ 14c.

unmapped ⊳ *adj* **1** not appearing on a geographical or chromosome map. **2** unexplored; untried □ *entering unmapped territory.*

unmask ⊳ *verb, tr & intr* **1** to remove a mask or disguise from (oneself or someone else). **2** to reveal the true identity or nature of (oneself or someone else). • **unmasker** *noun.* ◷ 16c.

unmeaning ⊳ *adj* **1** without any aim or purpose. **2** without meaning or significance. • **unmeaningly** *adverb.* • **unmeaningness** *noun.* ◷ 17c.

unmentionable ⊳ *adj* not fit to be mentioned or talked about, especially because considered indecent. ⊳ *noun* **1** (**unmentionables**) *humorous* underwear. **2** (*often* **unmentionables**) someone or something that cannot or should not be mentioned. • **unmentionableness** *noun.* • **unmentionably** *adverb.* ◷ 19c.

unmerciful ⊳ *adj* **1** merciless; not merciful. **2** unpleasantly great or extreme. • **unmercifully** *adverb.* • **unmercifulness** *noun.* ◷ 15c.

unmet ⊳ *adj* said of a target, quota, etc: not achieved.

unminded /ʌnˈmaɪndɪd/ ⊳ *adj* unheeded; unregarded. ◷ 16c.

unmindful ⊳ *adj* (*often* **unmindful of something**) not mindful of it; careless or heedless of it. • **unmindfully** *adverb.* • **unmindfulness** *noun.* ◷ 14c.

unmissable ⊳ *adj* said of a TV programme, film, etc: too good to be missed. ◷ 1930s.

unmistakable or **unmistakeable** ⊳ *adj* too easily recognizable to be mistaken for anything or anyone else; certain; unambiguous. • **unmistakably** or **unmistakeably** *adverb.* ◷ 17c.

Some words with *un-* prefixed, all of which refer to UN- sense 1 unless specified otherwise below.

unspoiled or **unspoilt** *adj.*
unspoken *adj.*
unsponsored *adj.*
unspool *verb* sense 2.
unsporting *adj.*
unsportsmanlike *adj.*
unspotted *adj.*
unsprung *adj.*
unstable *adj.*
unstably *adverb.*
unstabilized or **unstabilised** *adj.*
unstacked *adj.*
unstaffed *adj.*
unstainable *adj.*
unstained *adj.*
unstamped *adj.*
unstarched *adj.*
unstated *adj.*
unstatesmanlike *adj.*
unstaunchable *adj.*
unsteadfast *adj.*
unstereotyped *adj.*
unsterile *adj.*
unsterilized or **unsterilised** *adj.*
unstifled *adj.*
unstinted *adj.*
unstinting *adj.*
unstirred *adj.*
unstitch *verb* sense 2.
unstopper *verb* sense 2.
unstrained *adj.*
unstrap *verb* sense 2.
unstressed *adj.*
unstriated *adj.*
unstriped *adj.*
unstuffed *adj.*
unstuffy *adj.*
unstylish *adj.*
unsubduable *adj.*
unsubdued *adj.*
unsubjugated *adj.*
unsublimated *adj.*
unsubmerged *adj.*
unsubmissive *adj.*
unsubmitting *adj.*
unsubscribed *adj.*

unmitigated ▻ *adj* **1** not lessened or made less severe. **2** unqualified; absolute; out-and-out □ *an unmitigated disaster.* • **unmitigatedly** *adverb.* ⓒ 16c in sense 1; 19c in sense 2.

unmoor ▻ *verb* **1** to release or free (a vessel) from moorings. **2** *intr* to cast off moorings. ⓒ 15c in sense 1; 17c in sense 2.

unmoral ▻ *adj* not moral; with no relation to morality; amoral. • **unmorality** *noun.* • **unmorally** *adverb.* ⓒ 19c.

unmoved ▻ *adj* **1** still in the same place. **2** not persuaded. **3** not affected by emotion; calm. ⓒ 14c.

unmoving ▻ *adj* **1** still; stationary. **2** lacking the power to affect the emotions.

unmurmuring ▻ *adj* not murmuring, especially not complaining. ⓒ 18c.

unmuzzle ▻ *verb* **1** to remove the muzzle from (a dog, etc). **2** to free (a person, organization, etc) from control or censorship. • **unmuzzled** *adj.* ⓒ 17c.

unnatural ▻ *adj* **1** contrary to the way things usually happen in nature; contrary to the physical nature of humans or animals. **2** abnormal. **3** said of a sexual act, vice, etc: considered to be immoral and unacceptably indecent. **4** contrary to ordinary human nature, especially intensely evil or cruel. **5** insincere; affected. • **unnaturally** *adverb.* • **unnaturalness** *noun.*

unnecessary ▻ *adj* **1** not necessary. **2** more than is expected or required □ *spoke with unnecessary caution.* • **unnecessarily** *adverb.* • **unnecessariness** *noun.* ⓒ 16c.

unnerve ▻ *verb* **1** to deprive of strength; to weaken. **2** to deprive someone of courage or confidence; to make them feel ill at ease or disconcerted. • **unnervingly** *adverb* disquietingly; unsettlingly. ⓒ 17c.

unnil- /ʌnnɪl/ ▻ *combining form, chem* used to form names of recently discovered elements of atomic numbers 104–109. ⓒ See UN- and NIL.

unnilennium /ʌnnɪl'ɛnɪəm/ ▻ *noun, chem* (symbol **Une**, atomic number 109) an artificially manufactured radioactive chemical element that belongs to the transactinide series. See also MEITNERIUM.

unnilhexium /ʌnnɪl'hɛksɪəm/ ▻ *noun, chem* (symbol **Unh**, atomic number 106) an artificially manufactured radioactive chemical element that belongs to the transactinide series. See also RUTHERFORDIUM and SEABORGIUM.

unniloctium /ʌnnɪl'ɒktɪəm/ ▻ *noun, chem* (symbol **Uno**, atomic number 108) an artificially manufactured radioactive chemical element that belongs to the transactinide series. See also HAHNIUM.

unnilpentium /ʌnnɪl'pentɪəm/ ▻ *noun, chem* (symbol **Unp**, atomic number 105) an artificially manufactured radioactive metallic element that has six isotopes, all with half-lives of a fraction of a second. See also HAHNIUM, NIELSBOHRIUM and JOLIOTIUM.

unnilquadium /ʌnnɪl'kwɒdɪəm/ ▻ *noun, chem* (symbol **Unq**, atomic number 104) a radioactive metallic element, formed by bombarding CALIFORNIUM with carbon nuclei. It has 10 isotopes with half-lives of up to 70 seconds. See also RUTHERFORDIUM, KURCHATOVIUM and DUBNIUM.

unnilseptium /ʌnnɪl'sɛptɪəm/ ▻ *noun, chem* (symbol **Uns**, atomic number 107) an artificially manufactured radioactive chemical element. See also BOHRIUM.

unnumbered ▻ *adj* **1** too numerous to be counted; innumerable. **2** not marked with or given a number.

UNO ▻ *abbreviation* United Nations Organization.

unoccupied ▻ *adj* **1** not doing any work or engaged in any activity; idle. **2** said of a building, etc: without occupants or inhabitants; empty. **3** said of a country, region, etc: not occupied by foreign troops.

unofficial ▻ *adj* **1** not officially authorized or confirmed. **2** not official or formal in character. **3** said of a strike: not called or sanctioned by the strikers' trade union. • **unofficially** *adverb.* ⓒ 18c.

unorganized or **unorganised** ▻ *adj* **1** not organized; not brought into an organized state or form. **2 a** said of a workforce: not formed into or represented by a trade union; **b** said of a company, etc: without or not recognizing a trade union for its workers. See also DISORGANIZED. ⓒ 17c.

Unp ▻ *symbol* unnilpentium.

unpack ▻ *verb* **1** to take something out of a packed state. **2** to empty (eg a suitcase, bag, etc) of packed contents. **3** *computing* to UNZIP (sense 3). ⓒ 15c.

unpaged ▻ *adj* said of a book: with unnumbered pages. ⓒ 19c.

unpalatable ▻ *adj* said of food, drink, etc: not having a pleasant taste. **2** said of a suggestion, idea, film scene, etc: unacceptable; distasteful.

unparalleled ▻ *adj* so remarkable as to have no equal or parallel. ⓒ 16c.

unparliamentary ▻ *adj* not in accordance with the established procedures by which, or with the spirit in which, a parliament is conducted. • **unparliamentarily** *adverb.* • **unparliamentariness** *noun.* ⓒ 17c.

Some words with *un-* prefixed, all of which refer to UN- sense 1 unless specified otherwise below.

unsubsidized or **unsubsidised** *adj.*
unsubstantiated *adj.*
unsubtle *adj.*
unsuccessful *adj.*
unsuccessfully *adverb.*
unsuitable *adj.*
unsuited *adj.*
unsullied *adj.*
unsummoned *adj.*
unsupervised *adj.*
unsupportable *adj.*
unsupported *adj.*
unsupportive *adj.*
unsuppressed *adj.*
unsure *adj.*
unsurfaced *adj.*
unsurpassable *adj.*
unsurpassed *adj.*
unsurprised *adj.*
unsurprising *adj.*
unsusceptible *adj.*
unsuspecting *adj.*
unsuspicious *adj.*
unsustainable *adj.*
unsustained *adj.*
unsustaining *adj.*
unswayed *adj.*
unsweetened *adj.*
unswept *adj.*
unsworn *adj.*
unsymmetrical *adj.*
unsympathetic *adj.*
unsympathizing or **unsympathising** *adj.*
unsystematic *adj.*
unsystematized or **unsystematised** *adj.*
untack *verb* sense 2.
untainted *adj.*
untalented *adj.*
untameable or **untamable** *adj.*
untamed *adj.*
untanned *adj.*
untapped *adj.*
untarnished *adj.*
untasted *adj.*

unpeg ▻ *verb* **1** to unfasten something by removing a peg or pegs from it. **2** to allow (prices, etc) to rise and fall freely. ⓘ 17c.

unpeople ▻ *verb* to empty (an area, etc) of people; to depopulate. ⓘ 16c.

unperson ▻ *noun* someone whose existence is officially denied or ignored and who is deemed not to have existed, often to the extent that their name is removed from official records. ▻ *verb* (*unpersoned*, *unpersoning*) to make someone into an unperson. • **unpersoned** *adj.* ⓘ 1949: first used by the English writer George Orwell (1903–50) in his novel *Nineteen Eighty-four.*

unpick ▻ *verb* **1** to undo (stitches). **2** to take (a sewn or knitted article, seam, etc) to pieces by undoing the stitching.

unpickupable /ʌnpɪk'ʌpəbəl/ ▻ *adj, colloq* said of a book: so tedious or difficult that it proves impossible to continue reading it. Compare UNPUTDOWNABLE. ⓘ 1980s.

unpin ▻ *verb* **1** to remove a pin or pins from something. **2** *tr & intr* to undo or unfasten by removing pins.

unplaced ▻ *adj* said eg of a racehorse, greyhound, athlete, etc: not one of the first three, or sometimes four, to finish a race.

unplanned ▻ *adj* **1** not planned or scheduled □ *made an unplanned stopover in Paris.* **2** said of a pregnancy: accidental, either because of a lack of contraceptive or because a contraceptive method has failed.

unplayable ▻ *adj* **1** not able to be played. **2** *sport* said of a ball: impossible to hit, kick, return, etc.

unpleasant ▻ *adj* not pleasant; disagreeable. • **unpleasantly** *adverb.* • **unpleasantness** *noun* **1** the quality of being unpleasant. **2** *euphemistic* an unpleasant incident, especially a disagreement involving open hostility.

unplug ▻ *verb* **1** to unblock or unstop (something that is plugged or blocked). **2** to disconnect (an electrical appliance) by removing its plug from a socket. **3** to remove a plug (of an electrical appliance) from a socket. ⓘ 18c.

unplumbed ▻ *adj* **1** said of a building, etc: without plumbing. **2** unfathomed; unsounded. **3** not fully understood. • **unplumbable** *adj.* ⓘ 17c.

unpointed ▻ *adj* **1** not sharp or drawn to a point or points. **2** said of masonry, brickwork etc: not having the joins filled with cement or mortar.

unpolled /ʌn'pould/ ▻ *adj* **1** not having voted at an election. **2** not included in an opinion poll. ⓘ 19c.

unpolished ▻ *adj* **1** not polished. **2** unrefined; not cultured or sophisticated.

unpopular ▻ *adj* not popular; not popular or liked by an individual or by people in general. • **unpopularity** *noun.* • **unpopularly** *adverb.* ⓘ 17c.

unpractical ▻ *adj* with no practical skills; not good at practical tasks. • **unpracticality** *noun.* • **unpractically** *adverb.* Compare IMPRACTICAL. ⓘ 17c.

unpractised or (*US*) **unpracticed** ▻ *adj* **1** with little or no practice, experience or skill. **2** not, or not yet, put into practice. ⓘ 16c.

unprecedented /ʌn'presɪdentɪd/ ▻ *adj* **1** without precedent; not known to have ever happened before. **2** unparalleled. • **unprecedentedly** *adverb.* ⓘ 17c.

unprejudiced ▻ *adj* free from prejudice; impartial. • **unprejudicedly** *adverb.* • **unprejudicedness** *noun.* ⓘ 17c.

unprepossessing ▻ *adj* **1** unappealing; unattractive. **2** not creating or likely to create a good impression. ⓘ 19c.

unprincipled ▻ *adj* without or showing a lack of moral principles. • **unprincipledness** *noun.* ⓘ 17c.

unprintable ▻ *adj* not fit to be printed, especially because of being obscene or libellous. • **unprintably** *adverb.* ⓘ 19c.

unprofessional ▻ *adj* **1** not in accordance with the rules governing, or the standards of conduct expected of, members of a particular profession. **2** amateur. **3** not belonging to or having the necessary qualifications for a particular profession. • **unprofessionally** *adverb.* ⓘ 19c.

UNPROFOR or **Unprofor** /'ʌnprəfɔː(r)/ ▻ *abbreviation* United Nations Protection Force.

unprotected ▻ *adj* **1** not protected. **2** said of an act of sexual intercourse: performed without the use of a condom.

unputdownable /ʌnput'daunəbəl/ ▻ *adj, colloq* said of a book: so absorbing that it proves difficult to stop reading it. Compare UNPICKUPABLE. ⓘ 1980s.

Unq ▻ *symbol* unnilquadium.

unqualified ▻ *adj* **1** not having any formal qualifications; lacking the formal qualifications required for a particular job, etc. **2** not limited or moderated in any way. **3** absolute; out-and-out □ *an unqualified success.* **4** not competent. • **unqualifiable** *adj.* • **unqualifiedly** *adverb.* ⓘ 16c.

unquestionable ▻ *adj* beyond doubt or question. • **unquestionability** *noun.* • **unquestionably** *adverb.* ⓘ 17c.

Some words with *un-* prefixed, all of which refer to UN- sense 1 unless specified otherwise below.

untaxed *adj.*
unteachable *adj.*
untempted *adj.*
untended *adj.*
untenured *adj.*
untested *adj.*
untether *verb* sense 2.
untethered *adj.*
untheorized *adj.*
unthanked *adj.*
unthankful *adj.*
unthoughtful *adj.*
unthought-of *adj.*
unthreatened *adj.*
unthreatening *adj.*
unthrifty *adj.*
untilled *adj.*
untinged *adj.*
untiring *adj.*
untiringly *adverb.*
untitled *adj.*
untouristy *adj.*
untouched *adj.*
untraceable *adj.*
untraced *adj.*
untraditional *adj.*
untrained *adj.*
untrammelled *adj.*
untransferable *adj.*
untranslatable *adj.*
untransmissable *adj.*
untransmitted *adj.*
untravelled or (*US*)
untraveled *adj.*
untreatable *adj.*
untreated *adj.*
untrendy *adj.*
untried *adj.*
untrimmed *adj.*
untrodden *adj.*
untroubled *adj.*
untrusting *adj.*
untrustworthy *adj.*
untucked *adj.*
untuneful *adj.*
untwine *verb* sense 2.
untwist *verb* sense 2.
untwisted *adj.*

unquestioned ▻ *adj* **1** not questioned or interrogated. **2** not examined or inquired into. **3** not called into question; undisputed. 🕓 17c.

unquestioning ▻ *adj* not arguing or protesting; done, accepted, etc without argument, protest or thought. • **unquestioningly** *adverb*. 🕓 19c.

unquiet *literary* ▻ *adj* **1** anxious; ill at ease; restless. **2** characterized by disturbance or disorder. ▻ *noun* disquiet; disturbance or unrest. • **unquietly** *adverb*. • **unquietness** *noun*.

unquote ▻ *verb* to indicate (in speech) the end of something that was said by someone else. Compare QUOTE (*verb* 7b). 🕓 1930s.

unquoted ▻ *adj* said of a company: not quoted on the Stock Exchange. 🕓 19c.

unravel ▻ *verb* **1** to separate out the strands of (a knitted or woven fabric). **2** to take something out of a tangled state. **3** to explain or make clear (something confusing or obscure, a mystery, etc). **4** *intr* to become unravelled. 🕓 17c.

unread /ʌn'red/ ▻ *adj* **1** said of a book, etc: not having been read. **2** said of a person: not well-read; not educated or instructed through reading.

unreadable ▻ *adj* **1** too difficult or tedious to read. **2** illegible. **3** said of facial expression, a remark, etc: uninterpretable. • **unreadability** or **unreadableness** *noun*. 🕓 19c.

unready ▻ *adj* **1** not ready. **2** not acting quickly; hesitant. • **unreadily** *adverb*. • **unreadiness** *noun*.

unreal ▻ *adj* **1** not real; illusory or imaginary. **2** *colloq* **a** exceptionally strange; incredible; **b** amazing; excellent. • **unreality** *noun*. • **unreally** *adverb*. • **unrealness** *noun*. 🕓 17c in sense 1; 20c in sense 2.

unreason ▻ *noun* lack of reason or reasonableness.

unreasonable ▻ *adj* **1** not influenced by, based on, or in accordance with reason or good sense. **2** immoderate; beyond what is reasonable or fair. • **unreasonableness** *noun*. • **unreasonably** *adverb*.

unreasoning ▻ *adj* not reasoning; showing lack of reasoning; irrational. • **unreasoningly** *adverb*. 🕓 18c.

unreel ▻ *verb* **1** to unwind something from a reel. **2** *intr* to become unwound. 🕓 16c.

unregenerate ▻ *adj* **1** not regenerate; unrepentant; unreformed. **2** adhering obstinately to one's own opinions. ▻ *noun* an unregenerate person. • **unregeneracy** *noun*. • **unregenerated** *adj*. • **unregenerately** *adverb*. 🕓 16c.

unreleased ▻ *adj* **1** not released. **2** said of a film, music recording, etc: not having had a public showing.

unrelenting ▻ *adj* **1** refusing to change viewpoint or a chosen course of action. **2** not softened by feelings of mercy or pity. **3** constant; relentless; never stopping. • **unrelentingly** *adverb*. • **unrelentingness** *noun*. 🕓 16c.

unreligious ▻ *adj* **1** not religious. **2** not relating to or concerned with religion; secular. • **unreligiously** *adverb*.

unremitting /ʌnrɪ'mɪtɪŋ/ ▻ *adj* **1** not easing off or abating. **2** constant; never stopping. • **unremittingly** *adverb*. • **unremittingness** *noun*. 🕓 18c.

unrequited ▻ *adj* /ʌnrɪ'kwaɪtɪd/ said especially of love: not returned. 🕓 16c.

unreserved ▻ *adj* **1** not booked or reserved. **2** open and sociable in manner; showing no shyness or reserve. **3** not moderated or limited; unqualified. • **unreservedly** *adverb*. • **unreservedness** *noun*. 🕓 16c.

unrest ▻ *noun* **1** a state of (especially public) discontent bordering on riotousness. **2** anxiety; unease.

unriddle ▻ *verb* to solve or explain (a riddle, mystery, etc). • **unriddler** *noun*. 🕓 16c.

unrig ▻ *verb* **1** to remove all the rigging from (a ship). **2** *intr* to remove or take down rigging. **3** *archaic or dialect* to undress (someone or oneself). 🕓 16c.

unrighteous ▻ *adj* **1** sinful or wicked. **2** not right or fair; unjust. • **unrighteously** *adverb*. • **unrighteousness** *noun*. 🕓 Anglo-Saxon.

unrip ▻ *verb* to rip open. 🕓 16c.

unripe ▻ *adj* **1** not (yet) fully developed; not matured. **2** said of fruit, etc: not (yet) ready to be harvested or eaten; not ripe. • **unripened** *adj*. • **unripeness** *noun*. 🕓 Anglo-Saxon.

unrivalled or (*US*) **unrivaled** *adj* far better than any other; unequalled. 🕓 16c.

unroll ▻ *verb* **1** to open something out from a rolled state. **2** *intr* to become unrolled. **3** *tr & intr* to become or make something visible or known; to unfold gradually.

unrounded ▻ *adj* **1** not rounded. **2** *phonetics* said especially of a vowel: articulated with the lips spread. 🕓 16c.

Some words with *un-* prefixed, all of which refer to UN- sense 1 unless specified otherwise below.

untypical *adj*.
unurgent *adj*.
unusable *adj*.
unutilized or **unutilised** *adj*.
unuttered *adj*.
unvaccinated *adj*.
unvalued *adj*.
unvanquishable *adj*.
unvanquished *adj*.
unvaried *adj*.
unvarying *adj*.
unventilated *adj*.
unverifiable *adj*.
unverified *adj*.
unviable *adj*.
unviewed *adj*.
unviolated *adj*.
unvisited *adj*.
unwalled *adj*.
unwanted *adj*.
unwarlike *adj*.
unwarmed *adj*.
unwarned *adj*.
unwarped *adj*.
unwatched *adj*.
unwatchful *adj*.
unwavering *adj*.
unwaveringly *adverb*.
unwaxed *adj*.
unweakened *adj*.
unwearable *adj*.
unwearied *adj*.
unweary *adj*.
unwearying *adj*.
unwebbed *adj*.
unwedded or **unwed** *adj*.
unweeded *adj*.
unwelcome *adj*.
unwelcoming *adj*.
unwhipped *adj*.
unwinged *adj*.
unwinking *adj*.
unwinnable *adj*.
unwiped *adj*.
unwithered *adj*.
unwitnessed *adj*.
unwomanly *adj*.
unwooded *adj*.
unworkable *adj*.
unworkmanlike *adj*.
unworn *adj*.
unworried *adj*.
unwounded *adj*.
unwrinkled *adj*.
unwrought *adj*.
unyielding *adj*.

unruffled ▻ *adj* **1** said of a surface: smooth or still. **2** said of a person: not agitated or flustered. • **unrufflable** *adj*. • **unruffledness** *noun*. ◷ 17c.

unruly /ʌn'ruːlɪ/ ▻ *adj* (***unrulier***, ***unruliest***) disobedient or disorderly, especially habitually. • **unruliness** *noun*.

UNRWA /'ʌnrə/ ▻ *abbreviation* United Nations Relief and Works Agency.

Uns ▻ *symbol* unnilseptium.

unsaddle ▻ *verb* **1** to take the saddle off (a horse). **2** to throw (a rider) from a horse; to unhorse.

unsafe ▻ *adj* **1** not safe or secure; dangerous. **2** said of a verdict, conclusion or decision: based on insufficient or suspect evidence. ◷ 16c.

unsaid ▻ *adj* not said, expressed, spoken, etc, especially when it might have been or should have been. See also UNSAY. ◷ Anglo-Saxon.

unsaturated ▻ *adj, chem* **1** said of an organic chemical compound: containing at least one double or triple bond between its carbon atoms, eg unsaturated fats. **2** said of a solution: not containing the maximum amount of a solid or gas (SOLUTE) that can be dissolved in it. • **unsaturation** *noun*. ◷ 18c.

unsavoury or (*US*) **unsavory** *adj* unpleasant or distasteful; offensive. • **unsavourily** *adverb*. • **unsavouriness** *noun*.

unsay ▻ *verb* (***unsaid***, ***unsaying***) to take back or withdraw (something said, eg a statement, etc) ▫ *Given the response, he just wanted to unsay the confession.* • **unsayable** *adj*. See also UNSAID. ◷ 15c.

unscathed /ʌn'skeɪðd/ ▻ *adj* **1** not harmed or injured. **2** without harm, injury or damage.

unschooled ▻ *adj* **1** not educated. **2** not skilled or trained in a specified field or area.

unscramble ▻ *verb* **1** to interpret (a coded or scrambled message). **2** to take something out of a jumbled state and put it in order. • **unscrambler** *noun* a device that unscrambles coded or scrambled messages. ◷ 1920s.

unscrew ▻ *verb* **1** to remove or loosen something by taking out a screw or screws, or with a twisting or screwing action. **2** to loosen (a screw or lid). **3** *intr* to be removed or loosened by turning a screw or screws. **4** *intr* said of a screw or lid: to be loosened or removed by a turning action. ◷ 17c.

unscripted ▻ *adj* **1** said of a speech, etc: made or delivered without a prepared script. **2** said of comments, remarks, etc that are made eg in a TV show: not in the script; unplanned. ◷ 20c.

unscrupulous ▻ *adj* without scruples or moral principles. • **unscrupulously** *adverb*. • **unscrupulousness** *noun*. ◷ 19c.

unseal ▻ *verb* **1** to remove or break open the seal of (a letter, container, etc). **2** to free or open (something that is closed as if sealed). ◷ Anglo-Saxon.

unsealed ▻ *adj* not sealed; not closed, marked, etc with a seal.

unseasonable ▻ *adj* **1** (*also* **unseasonal**) said especially of the weather: not appropriate to the time of year. **2** coming at a bad time; inopportune. • **unseasonableness** *noun*. • **unseasonably** *adverb*.

unseasoned ▻ *adj* **1** said of food: without seasonings. **2** not matured ▫ *unseasoned timber.* **3** not habituated through time or experience. ◷ 16c.

unseat ▻ *verb* **1** said of a horse: to throw or knock (its rider) off. **2** to remove someone from an official post or position, especially from a parliamentary seat ▫ *was unseated at the last general election.* ◷ 16c in sense 1; 19c in sense 2.

unseeded ▻ *adj* **1** *sport, especially tennis* not placed among the top players in the preliminary rounds of a tournament. ◷ 20c.

unseemly ▻ *adj* (***unseemlier***, ***unseemliest***) not seemly; not becoming or fitting, especially because of being indecent. • **unseemliness** *noun*.

unseen ▻ *adj* **1** not seen or noticed. **2** said of a text for translation: not seen or prepared in advance. ▻ *noun* **1** an unseen text for translation in an examination. **2** the translation of such a text.

unselfish ▻ *adj* **1** having or showing concern for others. **2** generous. • **unselfishly** *adverb*. • **unselfishness** *noun*. ◷ 17c.

unsettle ▻ *verb* **1** to make someone ill at ease; to disturb, discompose, confuse or disconcert them. **2** *intr* to become unsettled. ◷ 16c.

unsettled ▻ *adj* **1** lacking stability. **2** frequently changing or moving from place to place. **3** undecided or unresolved. **4** said of the weather: changeable; unpredictable. **5** not relaxed or at ease. **6** said of a debt: unpaid. • **unsettledness** *noun*. ◷ 16c.

unsex ▻ *verb, chiefly literary* to deprive someone of their gender, sexuality or the typical attributes of their gender. ◷ 17c.

unshackle ▻ *verb* **1** to release someone from a shackle or shackles; to remove a shackle from them. **2** to set them free. **3** *naut* to remove a shackle from (a chain, etc). ◷ 16c.

unshaped ▻ *adj* **1** not shaped. **2** ill-formed. **3** not finished; incomplete. ◷ 16c.

unsheathe ▻ *verb* **1** to draw (especially a sword, knife, etc) from a sheathe. **2** to remove something as if from a sheathe or covering; to uncover.

unship ▻ *verb* **1** to unload or disembark from a ship. **2** *naut* to detach or remove something from a fixed place or usual position. **3** to unseat (a rider).

unsighted ▻ *adj* **1** said of a gun: without sights. **2** without a clear view; prevented from seeing, especially because of an obstruction. **3** without sight; blind.

unsightly ▻ *adj* (***unsightlier***, ***unsightliest***) not pleasant to look at; ugly. • **unsightliness** *noun*.

unskilled ▻ *adj* **1** lacking skill; inexpert. **2** not having or requiring any special skill or training ▫ *unskilled jobs.* ◷ 16c in sense 1; 19c in sense 2.

unsling ▻ *verb* **1** to remove something from a sling or from a slung position. **2** to remove the sling or slings from something. ◷ 17c.

unsmoked ▻ *adj* **1** said of bacon, etc: not cured by smoking. **2** not used up by smoking ▫ *an unsmoked cigar.*

unsnap ▻ *verb* **1** to undo or unfasten the snap or snaps of something. **2** to release or unfasten something by such an action. ◷ 19c.

unsnarl ▻ *verb* to untangle or free something from snarls.

unsociable ▻ *adj* **1** said of a person: disliking or avoiding the company of other people. **2** not conducive to social intercourse. • **unsociability** or **unsociableness** *noun*. • **unsociably** *adverb*. ◷ 16c.

unsocial ▻ *adj* **1** annoying, or likely to annoy, other people; antisocial. **2** said of working hours: falling outside the normal working day. ◷ 18c.

unsophisticated ▻ *adj* **1** not experienced or worldly; naive. **2** free from insincerity or artificiality. **3** lacking refinement or complexity; basic. **4** unadulterated; pure. • **unsophisticatedly** *adverb*. • **unsophisticatedness** *noun*. • **unsophistication** *noun*. ◷ 17c.

unsound ▻ *adj* **1** not reliable; not based on sound reasoning ▫ *an unsound argument.* **2** not firm or solid. • **unsoundly** *adverb*. • **unsoundness** *noun*. • **of unsound mind** mentally ill; insane.

unsounded[1] ▻ *adj* **1** not uttered. **2** not caused to make a noise.

unsounded[2] ▻ *adj* not fathomed.

unsparing ▻ *adj* **1** giving generously or liberally. **2** showing no mercy; unrelenting. • **unsparingly** *adverb*. • **unsparingness** *noun*. ⓘ 16c.

unspeakable ▻ *adj* **1** not able to be expressed in words; indescribable. **2** too bad, wicked or obscene to be spoken about. **3** not to be spoken about; unmentionable. • **unspeakably** *adverb*.

unsteady ▻ *adj* **1** not secure or firm. **2** said of behaviour, character, etc: not steady or constant; erratic. **3** not regular or even. **4** said of movement, a manner of walking, etc: unsure or precarious. • **unsteadily** *adverb*. • **unsteadiness** *noun*. ⓘ 16c.

unstick ▻ *verb* **1** to free or separate something that is stuck to something else. **2** *colloq* **a** *intr* said of an aircraft: to take off; **b** to make an aircraft take off. ⓘ 18c in sense 1; 20c in sense 2.

unstop ▻ *verb* **1** to free something from being stopped or blocked. **2** to draw out the stop or stopper from something. **3** to draw out the stops on (an organ).

unstoppable ▻ *adj* unable to be stopped or prevented. • **unstoppably** *adverb*. ⓘ 19c.

unstopped ▻ *adj* **1** not stopped or obstructed. **2** *phonetics* said of a sound: articulated without closure of the vocal tract.

unstreamed ▻ *adj* said of schoolchildren: not divided into classes according to ability. ⓘ 1960s.

unstring ▻ *verb* **1** to relax or remove the string or strings of (a bow, a musical instrument, etc). **2** to detach or remove (eg beads, etc) from a string. **3** to weaken (a person, a person's nerves, etc) emotionally. **4** *intr* said of the nerves: to relax or weaken. ⓘ 16c.

unstructured ▻ *adj* without any formal structure or organization. ⓘ 20c.

unstrung ▻ *adj* **1** said of a stringed instrument: with strings removed. **2** unnerved. See also UNSTRING.

unstuck ▻ *adj* loosened or released from a stuck state. • **come unstuck** *colloq* said of a person, plan, etc: to suffer a setback; to go wrong. See also UNSTICK.

unstudied ▻ *adj* **1** not affected; natural and spontaneous. **2** (*usually* **unstudied in something**) without skill or training in it.

unsubstantial ▻ *adj* **1** with no basis or foundation in fact. **2** without material substance. **3** lacking strength or firmness. • **unsubstantiality** *noun*. • **unsubstantially** *adverb*.

unsung ▻ *adj* **1** said of someone, an achievement, etc: not praised or recognized □ *an unsung hero*. **2** not (yet) sung.

unsuspected ▻ *adj* **1** not suspected; not under suspicion. **2** not known or supposed to exist. • **unsuspectedly** *adverb*. • **unsuspectedness** *noun*. ⓘ 15c.

unswerving ▻ *adj* not deviating from a belief or aim; steadfast. • **unswervingly** *adverb*. ⓘ 17c.

untangle ▻ *verb* **1** to disentangle something; to free something from a tangled state. **2** to clear something of confusion.

untaught ▻ *adj* **1** without education or instruction; ignorant. **2** not aquired through instruction; innate or spontaneous.

untempered ▻ *adj* said of metal: not brought to the correct hardness or consistency.

untenable ▻ *adj* **1** said of an opinion, theory, argument, etc: not able to be maintained, defended or justified. **2** said of a position, office, etc: not able to be occupied or enjoyed. • **untenability** or **untenableness** *noun*. • **untenably** *adverb*. ⓘ 17c.

Untermensch /'ʊntəmɛnʃ/ ▻ *noun* (***Untermenschen***) someone who is considered inferior; especially in Nazi Germany, someone of racial inferiority. Compare ÜBERMENSCH. ⓘ 1960s: German, literally 'under man'.

unthinkable ▻ *adj* **1** too unusual to be likely; inconceivable. **2** too unpleasant to think about. • **unthinkableness** *noun*. • **unthinkably** *adverb*.

unthinking ▻ *adj* **1** inconsiderate; thoughtless. **2** careless. • **unthinkingly** *adverb*. • **unthinkingness** *noun*. ⓘ 17c.

unthread ▻ *verb* **1** to take the thread out of (a needle, etc). **2** to find one's way through or out of (a maze, etc). ⓘ 16c.

untidy ▻ *adj* not tidy; messy or disordered. ▻ *verb* to make untidy. • **untidily** *adverb*. • **untidiness** *noun*.

untie ▻ *verb* **1** to undo (a knot, parcel, etc) from a tied state. **2** *intr* said of a knot, etc: to come unfastened. **3** to remove the constraints on something; to set something free. ⓘ Anglo-Saxon.

until /ʌn'tɪl/ ▻ *prep* **1** up to the time of □ *worked until 8*. **2** up to the time of reaching (a place); as far as □ *slept until Paris*. **3** *with negatives* before □ *not until Wednesday*. ▻ *conj* **1** up to the time that □ *He waited until she emerged with the money*. **2** *with negatives* before □ *not until I say so*. ⓘ 13c as *untille*; see TILL[1].

untimely ▻ *adj* **1** happening before the proper or expected time □ *an untimely death*. **2** coming at an inappropriate or inconvenient time. • **untimeliness** *noun*.

unto /'ʌntʊ/ ▻ *prep, archaic or literary* to.

untogether ▻ *adj, colloq* **1** not well organized. **2** lacking self-possession. ⓘ 20c.

untold ▻ *adj* **1** not told. **2** too severe to be described. **3** too many to be counted.

untouchable ▻ *adj* **1** not to be touched or handled. **2** discouraging physical contact. **3** above the law. **4** unable to be matched; unrivalled. ▻ *noun* **1** an untouchable person or thing. **2** *formerly* in India: a member of the lowest social class or caste whose touch was regarded by members of higher castes as a contamination. • **untouchability** or **untouchableness** *noun*. • **untouchably** *adverb*. ⓘ 16c.

untoward /ʌntə'wɔːd/ ▻ *adj* **1** inconvenient; unfortunate. **2** adverse; unfavourable. **3** difficult to manage; unruly or intractable. **4** unseemly; improper. • **untowardly** *adverb*. • **untowardness** *noun*. ⓘ 16c.

untrue ▻ *adj* **1** not true. **2** not accurate. **3** unfaithful. • **untruly** *adverb*. ⓘ Anglo-Saxon.

untruss ▻ *verb* to unfasten or release something from, or as if from, a truss.

untruth ▻ *noun* **1** the fact or quality of being untrue. **2** something that is untrue; a lie.

untruthful ▻ *adj* not truthful; lying or untrue. • **untruthfully** *adverb*. • **untruthfulness** *noun*.

untuck ▻ *verb* to free (a person, bedclothes, etc) from being tucked in. ⓘ 17c.

untuned ▻ *adj* **1** not tuned. **2** not in tune; discordant. **3** said of an electronic device, eg a radio, etc: not tuned to one particular frequency; able to receive signals of a wide range of frequencies. ⓘ 16c in sense 1 and 2; 20c in sense 3.

untutored ▻ *adj* **1** uneducated; untaught. **2** unsophisticated. ⓘ 16c.

untypable /ʌn'taɪpəbəl/ ▻ *adj, medicine, biol* unable to be assigned to a particular type. ⓘ 1950s.

unused ▻ *adj* **1** /ʌn'juːzd/ brand new; never used. **2** /ʌn'juːst/ (*always* **unused to something**) not used or accustomed to it.

unusual ▻ *adj* not usual; uncommon; rare. • **unusually** *adverb*. ⓘ 16c.

unutterable ▷ *adj* so extreme or intense as to be impossible to express in words. • **unutterableness** *noun*. • **unutterably** *adverb*. ⓒ 16c.

unvarnished ▷ *adj* **1** said of an account, report, etc: not exaggerated or embellished. **2** not covered with varnish. ⓒ 17c in sense 1; 18c in sense 2.

unveil ▷ *verb* **1** to remove a veil from (one's own or someone else's face). **2** to remove a curtain or other covering from (a plaque, monument, etc) as part of a formal opening ceremony. **3** to reveal something or make it known for the first time. • **unveiling** *noun* **1** the action or an act of removing a veil. **2** the ceremony of opening or presenting something new for the first time.

unversed ▷ *adj* (*usually* **unversed in something**) not experienced in it. ⓒ 17c.

unvoiced /ʌnˈvɔɪst/ ▷ *adj* **1** not spoken. **2** *phonetics* said of a sound: pronounced without vibrating the vocal cords, like 'p'; voiceless.

unwaged ▷ *adj* **1** said of work: unpaid. **2** said of a person: **a** not in paid employment; out of work; **b** doing unpaid work; **c** (**the unwaged**) people who are not in paid work, generally or collectively (see THE sense 4b) □ *The unwaged get in for free.* ⓒ 16c.

unwarrantable ▷ *adj* not warrantable; unjustifiable. • **unwarrantability** or **unwarrantableness** *noun*. • **unwarrantably** *adverb*. ⓒ 17c.

unwarranted ▷ *adj* **1** not warranted; not justified. **2** not authorized. ⓒ 16c.

unwary /ˈʌnwɛərɪ/ ▷ *adj* not wary; careless or incautious; not aware of possible danger. • **unwarily** *adverb*. • **unwariness** *noun*. ⓒ 16c.

unwashed ▷ *adj* not washed; not clean. • **the great unwashed** *colloq, jocular* the lower classes; the masses.

unwatchable ▷ *adj* **1** not watchable. **2** too disturbing or too boring, etc to watch.

unweighed ▷ *adj* **1** said of goods, quantities, etc: not weighed. **2** said of words, opinions, etc: not carefully considered.

unwell ▷ *adj* not well; ill.

unwept ▷ *adj* **1** said of a person: not wept for; unlamented. **2** said of tears: not shed. ⓒ 16c.

unwholesome ▷ *adj* **1** not conducive to physical or moral health; harmful. **2** said of a person: of dubious character or morals. **3** diseased; not healthy-looking. **4** said of food: of poor quality. • **unwholesomeness** *noun*.

unwieldy /ʌnˈwiːldɪ/ ▷ *adj* **1** said of an object: large and awkward to carry or manage; cumbersome. **2** said of a person: clumsy; not graceful in movement; awkward or ungainly. • **unwieldily** *adverb*. • **unwieldiness** *noun*.

unwilling ▷ *adj* **1** reluctant; loath. **2** done, said, etc reluctantly. • **unwillingly** *adverb*. • **unwillingness** *noun*. ⓒ Anglo-Saxon.

unwind /ʌnˈwaɪnd/ ▷ *verb* **1** to undo, slacken, untwist, etc something that has been wound or coiled up. **2** *intr* said of something that has been wound or coiled up: to come undone, to slacken, untwist, etc. **3** *tr & intr, colloq* to make or become relaxed.

unwise ▷ *adj* not prudent; ill-advised; foolish. • **unwisely** *adverb*. • **unwiseness** *noun*. ⓒ Anglo-Saxon.

unwished ▷ *adj* (*usually* **unwished for**) **1** unwelcome; uninvited. **2** not wanted or desired. ⓒ 16c.

unwitting ▷ *adj* **1** not realizing or being aware. **2** done without being realized or intended. • **unwittingly** *adverb*. • **unwittingness** *noun*. ⓒ Anglo-Saxon: see WIT².

unwonted /ʌnˈwoʊntɪd/ ▷ *adj* not usual or habitual. • **unwonted to something** not used or accustomed to it. • **unwontedly** *adverb*. • **unwontedness** *noun*. ⓒ 16c.

unworldly ▷ *adj* **1** not relating or belonging to this world; otherwordly. **2** not concerned with material things. **3** unsophisticated; naive. • **unworldliness** *noun*. ⓒ 18c.

unworthy ▷ *adj* **1** (*often* **unworthy of something**) not deserving or worthy of it. **2** (*often* **unworthy of someone** or **something**) not worthy or befitting to (a person's character, etc). **3** without worth; of little or no merit or value. **4** said of treatment, etc: not warranted; undeserved or worse than is deserved. • **unworthily** *adverb*. • **unworthiness** *noun*.

unwound *past tense, past participle of* UNWIND

unwrap ▷ *verb* **1** to remove the wrapping or covering from something; to open something by removing its wrapping. **2** *intr* said of something that is wrapped: to become unwrapped; to have the covering come off.

unwritten ▷ *adj* **1** not recorded in writing or print. **2** said of a rule or law: not formally enforceable, but traditionally accepted and followed.

unyoke ▷ *verb* **1** to release (an animal) from a yoke or harness. **2** to disconnect or unfasten. **3** to set free; to liberate. ⓒ Anglo-Saxon.

unzip ▷ *verb* **1** to unfasten or open (a garment, etc) by undoing a zip. **2** *intr* to open or come apart by means of a zip. **3** (*also* **unpack**) *computing* to convert (data that has been compressed in order to save storage space) into a less compressed form. ⓒ 1930s.

UP ▷ *abbreviation* United Press.

up ▷ *prep* at or to a higher position on, or a position further along □ *climbed up the stairs* □ *walking up the road.* ▷ *adverb* **1** at or to a higher position or level □ *lift it up* □ *turn up the volume* □ *prices went up.* **2** at or to a place higher up, or a more northerly place. **3** in or to a more erect position □ *stood up.* **4** fully or completely □ *use up* □ *eat up.* **5** into the state of being gathered together □ *saved up for it* □ *parcel up the presents.* **6** in or to a place of storage or lodging □ *put them up for the night.* **7** out of bed □ *got up.* **8** to or towards □ *went up to the town* □ *travelling up to London* □ *walked up to him.* **9** *formal* to or at university □ *up at Oxford.* ▷ *adj* (*comparative* ***upper***, *superlative* ***uppermost*** or ***upmost***; see also separate entries) **1** placed in, or moving or directed to, a higher position. **2** out of bed □ *He's not up yet.* **3** having an advantage; ahead □ *two goals up* □ *£5 up after the first bet.* **4** said of a road: under repair. **5** appearing in court □ *up before the judge.* **6** said of the sun: visible above the horizon. **7** relating to or providing (especially rail) transport to, rather than away from, a major place, especially London □ *the up train* □ *the up line.* ▷ *verb* (***upped***, ***upping***) **1** to raise or increase something □ *upped the price.* **2** *intr, colloq* to start boldly or unexpectedly saying or doing something; to get up (and do something) □ *He upped and left her.* ▷ *noun* **1** a success or advantage. **2** a spell of good luck or prosperity. • **be well up on** or **in something** to have a thorough knowledge of it. • **it's all up with someone** *colloq* there is no hope for them. • **not up to much** *colloq* not good at all; no good. • **on the up-and-up** *colloq* **1** steadily becoming more successful. **2** honest; on the level. • **something's up** something is wrong or amiss. • **up against someone** or **something** **1** situated or pressed close against them. **2** facing the difficulties, etc associated with them; having to cope with them. • **up and about** or **up and doing** out of bed and active. • **up for something** **1** presented or offered for (eg discussion or sale). **2** under consideration for (a job or post). **3** prepared and eager to do it □ *We're going out clubbing. Are you up for it, too?* • **up to someone** their responsibility; dependent on them □ *It's up to you.* • **up to something** **1** immersed or embedded as far as □ *up to his eyes in work.* **2** capable of; equal to □ *Are you up to meeting them?* **3** thinking about doing or engaged in doing □ *was up to his usual tricks* □ *What are you up to?* **4** as good as □ *not up to his usual standard.* **6** as many or as much as □ *up to two weeks.* • **up to speed** **1** as fast as is appropriate for something (eg a competition in a race, a schedule, etc). **2** proficient or efficient at something;

knowledgeable about it. • **up top** *colloq* (in) the head or mind. • **up to the minute** completely up to date. • **up with** 1 abreast of. 2 even with. 3 an expression of enthusiastic approval or support □ *Up with Christmas!* • **Up yours!** *coarse slang* an expression of strong refusal, defiance, contempt, etc. • **What's up?** What's the matter? What's wrong? ⓘ Anglo-Saxon *up* or *upp*.

up- ▷ *prefix, signifying* up, upper or upward.

up-anchor ▷ *verb, intr, naut* to weigh anchor.

up-and-coming ▷ *adj* beginning to become successful or well known.

up-and-down ▷ *adj* 1 undulating. 2 moving or working both, or alternately, up and down.

up-and-over ▷ *adj* said of a door, etc: raised to a horizontal position when opened.

up-and-under see GARRYOWEN

Upanishad /uː'panɪʃad/ ▷ *noun* any of a number of Sanskrit philosophical treatises comprising the last section of the VEDA. See also ATMAN. ⓘ 19c: Sanskrit, from *upa* near + *ni-sad* sit down.

upbeat /'ʌpbiːt/ ▷ *adj, colloq* cheerful; optimistic. ▷ *noun, music* 1 an unstressed beat, especially the last in a bar and so coming before the downbeat. 2 the upward gesture by a conductor which marks this. ⓘ 19c.

upbraid /ʌp'breɪd/ ▷ *verb* (***upbraided***, ***upbraiding***) to scold or reproach someone. • **upbraiding** *noun*. • **upbraidingly** *adverb*. ⓘ Anglo-Saxon *upbregdan*: see BRAID.

upbringing /'ʌpbrɪŋɪŋ/ ▷ *noun* the all-round instruction and education of a child, which influences their character and values. ⓘ 16c.

upchuck /'ʌptʃʌk/ *N Amer slang* ▷ *verb* to vomit. ▷ *noun* vomit. ⓘ 1920s.

upcoming ▷ *adj, colloq, especially N Amer* forthcoming; approaching.

up-country ▷ *noun* the inland part or regions of a country. ▷ *adj, adverb* to or in the regions away from the coast; inland. ⓘ 17c.

update ▷ *verb* /ʌp'deɪt/ to make or bring something or someone up to date. ▷ *noun* /'ʌpdeɪt/ 1 an act of updating. 2 something that is updated. • **updatable** or **updateable** *adj*. • **updater** *noun*. ⓘ 1960s: originally US.

up-end ▷ *verb* 1 *tr & intr* to turn or place something, or become turned or placed, upside down. 2 to put something into disorder or disarray. ⓘ 19c.

upfront ʌp'frʌnt/ *colloq* ▷ *adj* (*also* **up-front**) 1 candid; open. 2 said of money: paid in advance. ▷ *adverb* (*also* **up front**) 1 candidly; openly. 2 said of money or a payment: in advance. ⓘ 1960s.

upgrade ▷ *verb* /ʌp'greɪd/ 1 to promote someone. 2 to increase the grade or status of (a job or post). 3 to improve the quality of (machinery, equipment, a computer or its memory, etc), especially by adding or replacing features, components, etc. ▷ *noun* /'ʌpgreɪd/ 1 *N Amer* an upward slope; an incline. 2 an act or the process of upgrading something. 3 an upgraded version of something, eg a piece of machinery or equipment. 4 a thing that upgrades something, eg an additional feature, etc. ▷ *adverb, N Amer* uphill. • **on the upgrade** 1 rising. 2 improving or getting better. ⓘ 19c: originally US.

upheaval /ʌp'hiːvəl/ ▷ *noun* 1 a change or disturbance that brings about great disruption. 2 *geol* see UPLIFT *noun* 4. ⓘ 19c.

upheave ▷ *verb* 1 to heave or lift something up, especially forcibly. 2 *intr* to rise or be lifted up. ⓘ 14c.

uphill ▷ *adj* 1 sloping upwards; ascending. 2 said of a task, etc: requiring great and sustained effort; arduous. ▷ *adverb* 1 up a slope. 2 against problems or difficulties. ▷ *noun* an upward slope; an ascent or incline. ⓘ 16c.

uphold ▷ *verb* 1 to support (an action), defend (a right) or maintain (the law), especially against opposition. 2 to declare (eg a court judgement or verdict) to be correct or just; to confirm. 3 to hold something up; to support it. • **upholder** *noun*. ⓘ 13c.

upholster /ʌp'hoʊlstə(r)/ ▷ *verb* (***upholstered***, ***upholstering***) to fit (chairs, sofas, etc) with upholstery. ⓘ 19c: originally US, back-formation from UPHOLSTERER or UPHOLSTERY.

upholstered ▷ *adj* fitted with upholstery. • **well-upholstered** *jocular* said of a person: fat.

upholsterer ▷ *noun* a person who upholsters furniture, especially as their profession. ⓘ 17c: from obsolete *upholster* a maker of or dealer in furniture.

upholstery /ʌp'hoʊlstərɪ/ ▷ *noun* 1 the springs, stuffing and covers of a chair or sofa. 2 the work of an upholsterer. ⓘ 17c.

UPI ▷ *abbreviation* United Press International.

upkeep /'ʌpkiːp/ ▷ *noun* 1 the task or process of keeping something in good order or condition; maintenance. 2 the cost of doing this. ⓘ 19c.

upland /'ʌplənd/ ▷ *noun* (*often* **uplands**) a high or hilly region. ▷ *adj* relating to or situated in such a region. ⓘ 16c.

uplift ▷ *verb* /ʌp'lɪft/ 1 to lift something up; to raise it. 2 to fill (a person or people) with an invigorating happiness, optimism or awareness of the spiritual nature of things. 3 *chiefly formal Scots* to pick up; to collect. ▷ *noun* /'ʌplɪft/ 1 the action or result of lifting up. 2 a morally or spiritually uplifting influence, result or effect. 3 support given by a garment, especially a bra, that raises part of the body, especially the breasts. 4 (*also* **upheaval**) *geol* the process or result of land being raised, eg as in a period of mountain-building. • **uplifting** *adj* cheering; inspiring with hope. ⓘ 14c.

uplighter /'ʌplaɪtə(r)/ and **uplight** /'ʌplaɪt/ ▷ *noun* a type of lamp or wall light placed or designed so as to throw light upwards. ⓘ 1960s.

upload /ʌp'loʊd/ ▷ *verb, tr & intr, computing* to send (data, files, etc) from one computer to another, eg by means of a telephone line and modem. ⓘ 20c.

up-market ▷ *adj* relating to or suitable for the more expensive end of the market; high in price, quality or prestige □ *lives in an up-market area of town.* ⓘ 1970s.

upmost see UPPERMOST

upon /ə'pɒn/ ▷ *prep* on or on to. • **upon my word!** *old use* an exclamation of surprise. ⓘ 12c.

upped *past tense, past participle of* UP

upper /'ʌpə(r)/ ▷ *adj* 1 higher; situated above. 2 high or higher in rank or status. 3 (*with capital* when part of a name) upstream, farther inland or situated to the north. 4 (*with capital* when part of a name) *geol, archaeol* designating a younger or late part or division, deposit, system, etc, or the period during which it was formed or deposited. ▷ *noun* 1 the part of a shoe above the sole. 2 the higher of two people, objects, etc. 3 *slang* a drug that induces euphoria. • **on one's uppers** *colloq* extremely short of money; destitute. ⓘ 14c: comparative of UP.

upper atmosphere ▷ *noun, meteorol* the upper part of the Earth's atmosphere, especially that part above the troposphere.

upper-case *printing* ▷ *adj* (abbreviation **u.c.**) referring or relating to capital letters, as opposed to small or LOWER-CASE letters. ▷ *noun* (**upper case**) a letter or letters of this kind □ *wrote the sign all in upper case.* ⓘ 17c: see LOWER-CASE.

upper chamber see UPPER HOUSE

upper class ▷ *noun* the highest social class; the aristocracy. Also *as adj* □ *upper-class etiquette.*

upper crust ▻ *noun, colloq* the upper class.

uppercut /ˈʌpəkʌt/ ▻ *noun* a forceful upward blow with the fist, usually under the chin. ▻ *verb* (***uppercut, uppercutting***) *tr & intr* to hit someone with an uppercut.

upper hand ▻ *noun* (*usually* **the upper hand**) a position of advantage or dominance. • **have, get, take,** *etc* **the upper hand** to obtain control.

upper house and **upper chamber** ▻ *noun* (*often* **Upper House** and **Upper Chamber**) the higher but normally smaller part of a two-chamber (bicameral) parliament, such as the HOUSE OF LORDS in the UK.

uppermost /ˈʌpəmoust/ or **upmost** ▻ *adj, adverb* at, in or into the highest or most prominent position. ⓒ 15c: superlative forms of UP.

upper regions ▻ *plural noun* (*usually* **the upper regions**) **1** heaven or the heavens. **2** the sky.

upper works ▻ *plural noun, naut* the parts of a vessel above the main deck when fully laden.

upping *present participle of* UP

uppish /ˈʌpɪʃ/ ▻ *adj* **1** arrogant or snobbish. **2** pretentious. • **uppishly** *adverb*. • **uppishness** *noun*. ⓒ 18c: from UP + -ISH.

uppity /ˈʌpɪtɪ/ ▻ *adj, colloq* self-important; arrogant; uppish. • **uppitiness** *noun*. ⓒ 19c: from UP.

upraise /ʌpˈreɪz/ ▻ *verb, chiefly literary* to raise or lift something up; to elevate it. ⓒ 14c.

uprate /ʌpˈreɪt/ ▻ *verb* to upgrade something; to increase its rate, value, performance, etc. ⓒ 1960s.

upright /ˈʌpraɪt/ ▻ *adj* **1** standing straight up; erect or vertical. **2** possessing integrity or moral correctness. ▻ *adverb* into an upright position. ▻ *noun* **1** a vertical (usually supporting) post or pole. **2** an UPRIGHT PIANO. • **uprightly** *adverb*. • **uprightness** *noun*. ⓒ Anglo-Saxon *upriht*.

upright piano ▻ *noun* a piano with strings arranged vertically in a case above the keyboard. Compare GRAND PIANO.

uprise *chiefly poetic* ▻ *verb* /ʌpˈraɪz/ to rise up. ▻ *noun* /ˈʌpraɪz/ **1** the action of rising to a higher level or position. **2** an increase in wealth, importance, etc. ⓒ 17c.

uprising /ˈʌpraɪzɪŋ/ ▻ *noun* a rebellion or revolt. ⓒ 16c.

uproar /ˈʌprɔː(r)/ ▻ *noun* an outbreak of noisy and boisterous behaviour, especially angry protest. ⓒ 16c: from Dutch *oproer*, from *oproeren* to stir up.

uproarious /ʌpˈrɔːrɪəs/ ▻ *adj* **1** making, or characterized by, an uproar. **2** said of laughter: loud and unrestrained. **3** provoking such laughter; very funny. • **uproariously** *adverb*. • **uproariousness** *noun*. ⓒ 19c.

uproot /ʌpˈruːt/ ▻ *verb* **1** to displace (a person or people) from their usual surroundings or home ◻ ***Many Bosnians were uprooted by the war.*** **2** to pull (a plant) out of the ground completely, with the root attached. **3** to eradicate or destroy something completely. **4** to move away from a usual location or home ◻ ***uprooted and moved to the country.*** ⓒ 16c.

uprush ▻ *verb* /ʌpˈrʌʃ/ *intr, poetic* to rush up. ▻ *noun* /ˈʌprʌʃ/ a sudden upward rush or flow, eg of emotion, ideas, etc. ⓒ 19c.

ups-a-daisy /ˈʌpsədeɪzɪ/ or **upsy-daisy** /ˈʌpsɪ-/ ▻ *exclamation* expressing encouragement to a child who is being helped up or who is getting up, eg after a fall. ⓒ 19c.

ups and downs ▻ *plural noun* **1** rises and falls. **2** spells of alternating success and failure; changes of fortune.

upscale /ˈʌpskeɪl/ ▻ *adj, US colloq* pertaining to or designed to appeal to the wealthier in society; upmarket. ⓒ 1960s.

upset ▻ *verb* /ʌpˈsɛt/ **1** to disturb or distress someone emotionally. **2** to ruin or spoil (eg plans, etc). **3** to disturb the proper balance or function of (a person's stomach or digestion). **4** to disturb something's normal balance or stability. **5** *tr & intr* to knock something over or overturn. **6** to defeat or overthrow (an opponent), especially unexpectedly. ▻ *noun* /ˈʌpsɛt/ **1** a disturbance or disorder, eg of plans, the digestion, etc. **2** an unexpected result or outcome, eg of a contest. ▻ *adj* **1** /ʌpˈsɛt/ emotionally distressed, angry or offended, etc. **2** /ʌpˈsɛt, ˈʌpsɛt/ disturbed ◻ ***an upset stomach.*** • **upsetter** *noun*. • **upsetting** *adj*. • **upsettingly** *adverb*.

upset price ▻ *noun* the lowest price acceptable for something that is for sale, and the price at which bidding starts at an auction; a reserve price.

upshot /ˈʌpʃɒt/ ▻ *noun* **1** (*often* **the upshot**) the final outcome or ultimate effect; the result or consequence, often of a particular course of action or series of events. **2** *archery* the final shot in a match. ⓒ 16c.

upside /ˈʌpsaɪd/ ▻ *noun* **1** the upper part or side of anything. **2** *colloq* a positive or favourable aspect.

upside down ▻ *adj* (*also* **upside-down**) **1** with the top part at the bottom; upturned or inverted. **2** *colloq* in complete confusion or disorder ◻ ***The room was completely upside down half an hour ago.*** ▻ *adverb* **1** in an inverted way or manner ◻ ***Why does buttered toast always fall upside down on the floor?*** **2** in a completely confused or disordered way. ⓒ 14c as *up so doun* or *upsedoun*, perhaps with *so* meaning 'as if'.

upside-down cake ▻ *noun* a kind of sponge cake, baked with fruit at the bottom and turned upside down before it is served.

upsides ▻ *adverb* (*usually* **upsides with someone**), *Brit colloq* even with them, especially through revenge or retaliation. ⓒ 18c.

upsilon /ˈʌpsɪlɒn/ ▻ *noun* **1** the twentieth letter of the Greek alphabet. See table at GREEK ALPHABET. **2** a short-lived heavy subatomic particle produced when beryllium nuclei are bombarded with high-energy protons. ⓒ 17c: from Greek *u psilon* simple or slender *u*, so called to avoid confusion with the diphthong *oi* which was pronounced the same in late Greek.

upstage ▻ *adverb* /ʌpˈsteɪdʒ/ **1** on, at or towards the back of a theatre stage. **2** *colloq* in an arrogant or haughty manner. ▻ *adj* /ˈʌpsteɪdʒ/ **1** situated, occurring at or towards, or relating to, the back of a theatre stage. **2** *slang* arrogant or haughty. ▻ *noun* the back of a theatre stage, the part furthest from the audience. ▻ *verb* /ʌpˈsteɪdʒ/ **1** said of an actor: to move upstage and force (another actor) to turn their back to the audience. **2** *colloq* to direct attention away from someone on to oneself; to outshine them. **3** *colloq* to treat someone in an arrogant or haughty manner. ⓒ 19c.

upstairs ▻ *adverb* /ʌpˈstɛəz/ **1** up the stairs; to or on an upper floor or floors of a house, etc. **2** *colloq* to or in a senior or more senior position. **3** *colloq* mentally; in the head. ▻ *adj* /ˈʌpstɛəz/ (*also* **upstair**) on or relating to an upper floor or floors. ▻ *noun* /ʌpˈstɛəz/ **1** an upper floor or the upper floors of a building, especially the part of a house above the ground floor. **2** *chiefly historical* **a** the upper floors of a house, as opposed to the servants' quarters; **b** the occupants, usually the householder and their family, of this part of a house. ⓒ 16c.

upstanding ▻ *adj* **1** standing up. **2** said of a person: honest; respectable; trustworthy ◻ ***an upstanding member of society.*** **3** with a healthily erect posture; vigorous; upright. • **be upstanding** *formal* a direction to all the people present, eg in a court of law or at a formal dinner or function, to rise to their feet. ⓒ Anglo-Saxon.

upstart ▻ *noun, derog* someone who has suddenly acquired wealth or risen to a position of power or importance, especially one who is considered arrogant, or not to have the appropriate qualifications for such a position. ▻ *adj* **1** newly or suddenly come into existence.

2 belonging or relating to someone who is an upstart; typical or characteristic of an upstart. ⓘ 16c.

upstate *US* ▷ *adverb* /ʌp'steɪt/ in, to or towards the part of a state remotest from, and usually to the north of, the principal city of the state. ▷ *adj* /'ʌpsteɪt/ in, relating to, or characteristic of this part of a state. ▷ *noun* /'ʌpsteɪt/ the remoter, and usually northern, part of a state. • **upstater** *noun*. ⓘ Early 20c.

upstream ▷ *adverb* /ʌp'striːm/ **1** towards the source of a river or stream and against the current. **2** in the oil and gas industries: at or towards the source of production, especially at a stage in the extraction and production process before the raw material is ready to be refined. ▷ *adj* /'ʌpstriːm/ **1** situated towards the source of a river or stream. **2** in the oil and gas industries: relating to the stages of production before the raw material is ready to be refined. ⓘ 17c.

upstretched ▷ *adj* said especially of the arms: stretched upwards. ⓘ 16c.

upstroke ▷ *noun* **1 a** an upward stroke or movement, especially of a pen or brush; **b** the mark made by such a movement. **2** the upward movement of a piston in a reciprocating engine. ⓘ 19c.

upsurge ▷ *noun* a sudden sharp rise or increase; a surging up ▫ *The upsurge of violence developed into full-scale rioting.* • **upsurgence** *noun* ▫ *an upsurgence of neo-facism in central Europe.* ⓘ 1920s.

upsweep ▷ *noun* **1** a sweep or curve upwards; a raising up. **2** an upswept hairstyle. ⓘ 19c in sense 1; 1940s in sense 2.

upswept ▷ *adj* **1** made clear or thrown up by sweeping. **2 a** with an upward sweep or curve; **b** said of hair or a hairstyle: brushed upwards. ⓘ 18c in sense 1; 1940s in sense 2.

upswing ▷ *noun* **1** *econ* a recovery in the trade cycle or a period during which this occurs. **2** a swing or movement upwards, or a period of increase or improvement. ⓘ 1930s.

upsy-daisy see UPS-A-DAISY

uptake ▷ *noun* **1** a pipe or flue with upward current. **2** an act of lifting up. **3** the act of taking up or accepting something on offer, or the extent of this. • **quick** or **slow on the uptake** *colloq* quick or slow to understand or realize something. ⓘ 19c.

up-tempo or **uptempo** ▷ *adj, adverb, music* with or at a fast tempo. ⓘ 1940s.

upthrow ▷ *noun* **1** an uplift; a raising up. **2** *geol* (*also* **upthrust**) **a** the upward movement of the relatively raised strata on one side of a fault; **b** the extent of this movement. ⓘ 19c.

upthrust ▷ *noun* **1** an upward thrust or push. **2** *geol* **a** the action or an instance of thrusting up, especially by volcanic action; **b** an UPTHROW 2. **3** *physics* the upward force exerted by a liquid that tends to make an object immersed in it float. ⓘ 19c.

uptight ▷ *adj, colloq* **1** nervous; anxious; tense. **2** angry; irritated. **3** strait-laced; conventional. ⓘ 1960s.

uptime ▷ *noun* the time when a computer or similar device is operating. ⓘ 1950s.

up to date or **up-to-date** ▷ *adj* **1** containing all the latest facts or information. **2** knowing or reflecting the latest trends.

uptown *chiefly N Amer* ▷ *adverb* in, into or towards the part of a town or city that is away from the centre, usually the more prosperous or residential area. ▷ *adj* situated in, relating, or belonging to or characteristic of this part of a town or city. ▷ *noun* the uptown part of a town or city. • **uptowner** *noun*. ⓘ 19c.

upturn ▷ *noun* /'ʌptɜːn/ **1** an upheaval. **2** an increase in (especially economic) activity; an upward trend. ▷ *verb* /ʌp'tɜːn/ **1** to turn something over, up or upside-down. **2** to direct or cast (eg the face or eyes) upwards. **3** *intr* to turn or curve upwards. • **upturned** *adj*.

UPU ▷ *abbreviation* Universal Postal Union.

upward ▷ *adverb* (*usually* **upwards**) to or towards a higher place, a more important or senior position, or an earlier era. ▷ *adj* moving or directed upwards, to a higher position, etc. • **upwardly** *adverb*. • **upwardness** *noun*. • **upwards of ...** more than ... ▫ *upwards of a thousand people.* ⓘ Anglo-Saxon *upweard*.

upwardly mobile ▷ *adj* moving, or in a position to move, into a higher social class or income bracket. • **upward mobility** *noun*.

upwind /ʌp'wɪnd/ ▷ *adverb* **1** against the direction of the wind; into the wind. **2** in front in terms of wind direction; with the wind carrying one's scent towards eg an animal one is stalking. ▷ *adj* /'ʌpwɪnd/ going against or exposed to the wind. ⓘ 19c.

uracil /'jʊərəsɪl/ ▷ *noun, biochem* one of the bases, derived from pyrimidine, that is present in the nucleic acid RNA. ⓘ Early 20c.

uraemia or (*US*) **uremia** /jʊə'riːmɪə/ *noun, medicine* the presence of excessive amounts of urea and other nitrogenous waste products in the blood, one of the first symptoms of kidney failure. • **uraemic** or (*US*) **uremic** *adj* **1** relating to or characterized by uraemia. **2** said of a person: affected by uraemia. ⓘ 19c: from Greek *ouron* urine + *haima* blood.

Ural-Altaic /jʊərəlal'teɪɪk/ ▷ *noun* a supposed group of related languages of eastern Europe and northern Asia, comprising the URALIC and ALTAIC language families. ▷ *adj* **1** referring or relating to this group of languages and their speakers. **2** relating to the area of the Ural Mountains which separate Europe and Asia and the Altai Mountains in central Asia.

Uralic /jʊə'ralɪk/ and **Uralian** /jʊə'reɪlɪən/ ▷ *noun* a family of languages descended from an ancestor spoken in the N Ural Mountains over 7 000 years ago, comprising the FINNO-UGRIC family and SAMOYED (sense 2). ▷ *adj* **1** in or relating to these languages. **2 a** relating to or inhabiting the area of the Ural Mountains, a range in Russia which forms the north-eastern boundary of Europe with Asia; **b** relating to the inhabitants of this area.

Uranian /jʊə'reɪnɪən/ *adj* relating to the planet Uranus, the seventh planet from the sun, discovered by Herschel in 1781. ▷ *noun* an imaginary inhabitant of the planet Uranus. ⓘ 19c: from Latin *Uranus*, from Greek *Ouranos*, literally 'the sky', in mythology, the husband of Gaia (Earth) and father of Kronos (Saturn).

uraninite /jʊə'ranɪnaɪt/ ▷ *noun, geol* a hard, slightly greasy, black, brown, grey or greenish mineral form of uranium oxide that is often associated with thorium, lead, radium or the rare earth elements. It is the principal ore of uranium and is highly radioactive. ⓘ 19c.

uranium /jʊə'reɪnɪəm/ ▷ *noun, chem* (symbol **U**, atomic number 92) a dense silvery-white radioactive metallic element, originally discovered in pitchblende in 1789, but now mainly obtained from the ore URANINITE. It is chiefly used to produce nuclear energy, as a fuel for nuclear reactors and nuclear weapons, by fission of the isotope uranium-235. • **uranic** *adj*. ⓘ 18c: named after the planet Uranus, discovered shortly before the metal; see URANIAN.

urano- /jʊərənoʊ, jʊərə'nɒ/ ▷ *combining form, denoting* **1** the sky or the heavens. **2** *medicine* the roof of the mouth; the palate. ⓘ From Greek *ouranos*; see URANIAN.

uranography /jʊərə'nɒgrəfɪ/ ▷ *noun* the branch of astronomy that deals with the description and mapping of the stars, constellations, etc. • **uranographer** *noun*. • **uranographic** /-'grafɪk/ or **uranographical** *adj*. ⓘ 17c: from Greek *ouranographia*.

urate /ˈjʊəreɪt/ ▷ *noun, chem* any salt or ester of uric acid. • **uratic** /jʊəˈratɪk/ *adj.* ⓒ 19c.

urban /ˈɜːbən/ ▷ *adj* **1** relating or belonging to, constituting, or characteristic of a city or town □ *the urban landscape.* **2** living in a city or town □ *an urban fox.* Compare RURAL. ⓒ 17c: from Latin *urbanus*, from *urbs* city.

urbane /ɜːˈbeɪn/ ▷ *adj* **1** with refined manners; suave; courteous. **2** sophisticated; civilized; elegant. • **urbanely** *adverb.* • **urbaneness** *noun.* ⓒ 16c: from French *urbain* or from Latin *urbanus* of the town; see URBAN.

urban guerrilla ▷ *noun* someone who carries out terrorist activities in urban areas.

urbanism /ˈɜːbənɪzəm/ ▷ *noun* **1** the urban way of life. **2** the study of this. • **urbanist** *noun* someone who is expert in, or who studies, the urban way of life. ⓒ 19c.

urbanity /ɜːˈbanɪtɪ/ ▷ *noun* (***urbanities***) **1** the quality of being URBANE; refinement or elegance of manner, etc. **2** (**urbanities**) civilities; courtesies. **3 a** the state or character of a city or town; **b** urban life. ⓒ 16c: from French *urbanité* or from Latin *urbanitas*; see URBAN.

urbanize or **urbanise** /ˈɜːbənaɪz/ ▷ *verb* (***urbanized***, ***urbanizing***) to make (an area) less rural and more townlike. • **urbanization** *noun.* ⓒ 19c.

urban myth ▷ *noun* an amusing story or anecdote, perhaps with an element of truth to it, that is so frequently retold that it becomes common knowledge, eg the belief that traffic police select cars to stop for speeding by their colour so that they conform to the same order as the coloured balls to be potted in snooker. ⓒ 1980s.

urban renewal ▷ *noun* the clearing and redevelopment of slums, etc, in large cities and towns.

urceolate /ˈɜːsɪəlɪt/ ▷ *adj, chiefly biol* shaped like a pitcher or urn. ⓒ 18c: from Latin *urceolus*, diminutive of *urceus* pitcher.

urchin /ˈɜːtʃɪn/ ▷ *noun* **1** a mischievous child. **2** a dirty raggedly dressed child. **3** a SEA URCHIN. **4** *archaic* a hedgehog. ▷ *adj* relating to or like an urchin. ⓒ 14c: from French *herichon*, *heriçon*, from Latin *ericius* hedgehog.

Urdu /ˈʊəduː, ʊəˈduː, ˈɜː-/ ▷ *noun* an Indo-Aryan language, the official literary language of Pakistan, also spoken in Bangladesh and among Muslims in India. It is related to Hindi and has many words from Arabic and Persian. ▷ *adj* in or relating to this language. ⓒ 18c: from Persian and Urdu *(zaban i) urdu* (language of) the camp, from Persian *urdu*, from Turkish *ordu* camp.

-ure /jʊə(r)/ ▷ *suffix, forming nouns, denoting* **1** an action, process or result □ ***seizure.*** **2** official position □ ***prefecture.*** **3** a collective group □ ***legislature.*** ⓒ French, from Latin *-ura*.

urea /jʊəˈrɪə, ˈjʊərɪə/ ▷ *noun, biochem* (formula $CO(NH_2)_2$) a compound, white and crystalline when purified, formed during amino-acid breakdown in the liver of mammals, and excreted in the urine. It is also manufactured synthetically for use as a component of plastics, pharmaceuticals, fertilizers and animal-feed additives. • **ureal** or **ureic** *adj.* ⓒ 19c: from French *urée*, from Greek *ouron* urine.

urea-formaldehyde ▷ *noun* a type of plastic, resin or foam, produced by condensation of urea with formaldehyde and often used in cavity insulation. ▷ *adj* relating to or denoting this substance. ⓒ 1920s.

urea resin ▷ *noun* a thermosetting resin made by heating urea and aldehyde, usually formaldehyde.

ureide /ˈjʊərɪaɪd/ ▷ *noun, chem* any of various acyl derivatives of urea. ⓒ 19c.

uremia and **uremic** *US* spellings of URAEMIA, *etc*

ureter /jʊəˈriːtə(r)/ ▷ *noun, anatomy* one of the two tubes through which urine is carried from the kidneys to the bladder. • **ureteral** or **ureteric** /jʊərɪˈterɪk/ *adj.* ⓒ 16c: from French *uretère* or Latin *ureter*, from Greek *ourein* to urinate.

urethane /ˈjʊərəθeɪn/ ▷ *noun* **1** *chem* a crystalline amide used eg in pesticides and formerly as an anaesthetic. **2** short form of POLYURETHANE. ⓒ 19c: from UREA + ETHYL.

urethra /jʊəˈriːθrə/ ▷ *noun* (***urethras*** or ***urethrae*** /-riː/) *anatomy* the tube through which urine passes from the bladder out of the body and which, in males, also conveys semen. • **urethral** *adj.* ⓒ 17c: from Greek *ourethra*, from *ourein* to urinate.

urethritis /jʊərɪˈθraɪtɪs/ ▷ *noun, medicine* inflammation of the urethra. • **urethritic** /-ˈθrɪtɪk/ *adj.* ⓒ 19c.

urethroscope /jʊəˈriːθrəskoʊp/ ▷ *noun, medicine* an instrument for examining the urethra. • **urethroscopic** *adj.* • **urethroscopy** *noun.* ⓒ 19c.

urge /ɜːdʒ/ ▷ *verb* (***urged***, ***urging***) **1** (*also* **urge someone on**) to persuade someone forcefully or incite them (to do something). **2** to beg or entreat someone (to do something). **3 a** (*usually* **urge that …**) to earnestly advise or recommend that …; **b** (*usually* **urge something**) to earnestly recommend it □ *urged prudence.* **4** to drive or hurry (onwards, forwards, etc). ▷ *noun* a strong impulse, desire or motivation (to do something). • **urger** *noun.* ⓒ 16c: from Latin *urgere*.

urgent /ˈɜːdʒənt/ ▷ *adj* **1** requiring or demanding immediate attention, action, etc; pressing. **2** said of a request, etc: forcefully and earnestly made. • **urgency** /ˈɜːdʒənsɪ/ *noun.* • **urgently** *adverb.* ⓒ 15c: French, from Latin *urgere* to urge.

-uria /jʊərɪə/ ▷ *suffix, forming nouns, denoting* abnormal or diseased conditions of the urine □ ***dysuria.*** • **-uric** *suffix, forming adjectives.* ⓒ From Greek *-ouria*, from *ouron* urine.

urial or **oorial** /ˈʊərɪəl/ ▷ *noun* a Himalayan wild sheep with long curved horns and reddish wool. ⓒ 19c: from Punjabi *urial* or *hureal*.

uric /ˈjʊərɪk/ ▷ *adj* relating to, present in, or derived from, urine. ⓒ 18c.

uric acid ▷ *noun, biochem* (formula $C_5H_4N_4O_3$) an organic acid, a product of protein metabolism, present in urine and blood.

uridine /ˈjʊərɪdiːn/ ▷ *noun, biochem* a pyrimidine NUCLEOSIDE based on uracil and ribose, obtained from RNA. ⓒ Early 20c.

urinal /jʊəˈraɪnəl, ˈjʊərɪnəl/ ▷ *noun* **1** any receptacle or sanitary fitting, especially one attached to a wall, designed for men to urinate into. **2** a vessel for urine, especially one for use by an incontinent or bedridden person. ⓒ 19c: French, from Latin *urina* urine.

urinalysis /jʊərɪˈnalɪsɪs/ ▷ *noun* (***urinalyses*** /-siːz/) analysis of urine, eg to detect disease, drugs, etc. ⓒ 19c.

urinary /ˈjʊərɪnərɪ/ ▷ *adj* **1** relating to urine or the passing of urine. **2** containing or contained in urine. **3** relating to or affecting the organs and structures that excrete and discharge urine. ▷ *noun* (***urinaries***) a reservoir for urine. ⓒ 16c.

urinate /ˈjʊərɪneɪt/ ▷ *verb* (***urinated***, ***urinating***) *intr* to discharge urine. • **urination** *noun.* ⓒ 16c.

urine /ˈjʊərɪn/ ▷ *noun* the yellowish slightly acidic liquid consisting mainly of water and containing urea, uric acid, and other nitrogenous waste products filtered from the blood by the kidneys. • **urinous** /ˈjʊərɪnəs/ *adj.* ⓒ 14c: French, from Latin *urina*, related to Greek *ouron* urine.

urinogenital /jʊərɪnoʊˈdʒenɪtəl/ or **urogenital** /jʊəroʊ-/ ▷ *adj* relating or pertaining to, or affecting, both the urinary and genital functions or organs. ⓒ 19c.

urn ▷ *noun* **1** a vase or vessel with a rounded body, usually a small narrow neck and a base or foot. **2** such a vase used to contain the ashes of a dead person. **3** a large cylindrical metal container with a tap and an internal heating element, used for heating water or making large quantities of tea or coffee. ◎ 14c: from Latin *urna*, from *urere* to burn.

urnfield /'ɜːnfiːld/ *archaeol* ▷ *noun* a late Bronze Age cemetery of individual graves with urns containing ashes. ▷ *adj* said of several Bronze Age peoples, cultures, etc: characterized by this method of burial.

uro-¹ /jʊəroʊ, jʊə'rɒ/ or (before a vowel) **ur-** ▷ *combining form, denoting* urine or the urinary tract. ◎ From Greek *ouron* urine.

uro-² /jʊəroʊ, jʊə'rɒ/ ▷ *combining form, denoting* tail; posterior part. ◎ From Greek *oura* tail.

urodele /'jʊəroudiːl/ *zool* ▷ *noun* (*also* **urodelan** /-'diːlən/) any amphibian of the order **Urodela**, eg a newt or salamander, which is characterized by having a tail in the adult stage. ▷ *adj* belonging or relating to this order. ◎ 19c: from French *urodèle*, from Greek *oura* tail + *delos* clear or evident.

urogenital see URINOGENITAL

urography /jʊə'rɒgrəfɪ/ ▷ *noun, medicine* radiological examination of the urinary tract. ● **urographic** *adj.* ◎ 1920s.

urology /jʊə'rɒlədʒɪ/ ▷ *noun, medicine* the branch of medicine that deals with the study and treatment of diseases and disorders of the male and female urinary tracts, and of the male genital tract. ● **urologic** or **urological** *adj.* ● **urologist** *noun.* ◎ 19c.

uropygium /jʊərə'pɪdʒɪəm/ ▷ *noun, zool* the rump of a bird, that supports the tail feathers. ● **uropygial** *adj.* ◎ 18c: Latin, from Greek *ouropygion*, from *oura* tail + *pyge* rump.

urostyle /'jʊəroustaɪl/ ▷ *noun, zool* in certain of the lower vertebrates: a prolongation of the last vertebra in frogs, toads and certain other amphibians. ◎ 19c: from URO-² + Greek *stylos* column.

Ursa Major /'ɜːsə —/ ▷ *noun* a N hemisphere constellation whose seven brightest stars form the PLOUGH. Also called **the Great Bear**. ◎ 14c: Latin, meaning 'greater she-bear'.

Ursa Minor /'ɜːsə —/ ▷ *noun* a N hemisphere constellation whose brightest star is the POLE STAR. Also called **the Little Bear**. ◎ 16c: Latin, meaning 'lesser she-bear'.

ursine /'ɜːsaɪn/ ▷ *adj* **1** belonging, relating or referring to a bear or bears. **2** bearlike. ◎ 16c: from Latin *ursinus*, from *ursus* bear.

urtica /'ɜːtɪkə, ɜː'taɪkə/ ▷ *noun* (***urticas***) any plant of the nettle genus; a stinging nettle. ● **urticaceous** /-'keɪʃəs/ *adj.* ◎ 17c: Latin, from *urere* to burn.

urticaria /ɜːtɪ'keərɪə/ ▷ *noun, medicine* an allergic skin reaction with raised red or white itchy patches. Also called **nettle rash** or **hives**. ● **urticarial** *adj.* ◎ 18c: from URTICA.

urticate /'ɜːtɪkeɪt/ ▷ *verb* (***urticated, urticating***) *tr & intr* to sting. ● **urtication** *noun* a stinging or itching sensation. ◎ 19c: from Latin *urticare, urticatum* to sting, from *urtica* nettle.

Uruguayan /jʊərə'gwaɪən/ ▷ *adj* belonging or relating to Uruguay, a Spanish-speaking republic on the Atlantic coast of S America, or to its inhabitants, culture, etc. ▷ *noun* a citizen or inhabitant of, or person born in, Uruguay. ◎ 19c.

urus see AUROCHS

US ▷ *abbreviation* **1** Under-Secretary. **2** United States (of America).

us ▷ *pronoun* **1** the speaker or writer together with another person or other people; the object form of *we* □ ***asked us the way*** □ ***give it to us.*** **2** all or any people; one □ ***Computers can help us to work more efficiently.*** **3** *colloq* **a** me □ ***Give us a hand;*** **b** ourselves □ ***looks like we'll make us a pile of dough.*** **4** *formal* used by monarchs, etc: me. ● **be us** *colloq* to be suited to us □ ***Breakdancing is just not us.*** ◎ Anglo-Saxon.

> **us**
>
> See Usage Note at **we**.

USA ▷ *abbreviation* **1** United States of America. **2** United States Army.

usable or **useable** /'juːzəbəl/ ▷ *adj* able to be used. ● **usability** *noun.* ● **usableness** *noun.*

USAF ▷ *abbreviation* United States Air Force.

usage /'juːsɪdʒ, 'juːzɪdʒ/ ▷ *noun* **1** the act or way of using, or fact of being used; use; employment. **2** custom or practice. **3 a** the way that the vocabulary, constructions, etc of a language are actually used in practice; **b** an example of this. **4** the amount or quantity of use, or the rate at which something is used. ◎ 14c: from French, from Latin *usus* use.

usance /'juːzəns/ ▷ *noun, commerce* the time allowed for the payment of bills of exchange, especially foreign ones.

USDAW ▷ *abbreviation* Union of Shop, Distributive and Allied Workers.

use ▷ *verb* /juːz/ (***used, using***) **1** to put to a particular purpose. **2** to consume; to take something as fuel. **3** to treat someone as a means to benefit oneself; to exploit them. **4** *slang* to take (eg drugs or alcohol) regularly. **5** *old use* to behave (well or badly) towards someone. ▷ *noun* /juːs/ **1** the act of using. **2** the state of being (able to be) used □ ***go out of use*** □ ***not in use.*** **3** a practical purpose a thing can be put to. **4** the quality of serving a practical purpose □ ***It's no use complaining*** □ ***Is this spanner any use?*** **5** the ability or power to use something (eg a limb) □ ***lost the use of her leg after the accident.*** **6** the length of time a thing is, will be or has remained serviceable □ ***should give you plenty of use.*** **7** the habit of using; custom. ● **have no use for something** or **someone 1** to have no need of it or them. **2** *colloq* to dislike or despise it or them. ● **make use of someone** to exploit them. ● **make use of something** to put it to a practical purpose. ● **use by** said of perishable food: recommended to be consumed by the specified date □ ***use by Dec 99.*** Also *as adj* □ ***The use-by date was clearly marked.*** ● **used to something** or **someone** or **to doing** or **being something** accustomed to it or them, or to doing or being it □ ***She's not used to working so fast*** □ ***used to being in charge of two hundred people*** □ ***The puppies haven't got used to us yet.*** See also separate entry USED TO. ● **used up** *colloq* tired or exhausted. ◎ 13c: from French *user*, from Latin *usus*, from *uti* to use.

■ **use something up 1** to exhaust supplies, etc. **2** to finish off an amount left over.

used /juːzd/ ▷ *adj* not new; second-hand □ ***a used car.***

used to /'juːstə/ ▷ *auxiliary verb* used with other verbs to express habitual actions or states that took place in the past □ ***They used to be friends, but they aren't any more*** □ ***He didn't use to be as grumpy as he is now.*** See note.

> **used to**
>
> ● There is often uncertainty about the correct negative form of **used to.** The following are all acceptable (note that when an auxiliary verb is used, it is **did**, not **had**):
>
> ✓ *He used not to do it.*
>
> ✓ *He usedn't to do it.*
>
> ✓ *He didn't use to do it.*
>
> ● The following are usually considered incorrect:
>
> ✗ *He usen't to do it.*
>
> ✗ *He didn't used to do it.*

useful /ˈjuːsfəl/ ▷ *adj* **1** able to be used advantageously; serving a helpful purpose; able to be put to various purposes. **2** *colloq* skilled or proficient □ *Booth put in a useful performance for Aberdeen.* • **usefully** *adverb.* • **usefulness** *noun.* • **come in useful** to prove to be useful. ⓒ 16c.

useless /ˈjuːslɪs/ ▷ *adj* **1** serving no practical purpose. **2** (*often* **useless at something**) *colloq* not at all proficient □ *I've always been useless at maths.* • **uselessly** *adverb.* • **uselessness** *noun.* ⓒ 16c.

user /ˈjuːzə(r)/ ▷ *noun* **1** someone who uses a specified facility such as a leisure centre, a computer network, etc. **2** someone who regularly takes a specified drug □ *a heroin user.*

user-friendly ▷ *adj* said especially of a computer system: designed to be easy or pleasant to use, or easy to follow or understand □ *user-friendly software.* • **user-friendliness** *noun.*

usher /ˈʌʃə(r)/ ▷ *noun* **1 a** someone whose job is to show people to their seats, eg in a theatre, cinema, etc; **b** someone whose function is to direct wedding guests to their seats in church, and to look after them generally. **2** an official in a court of law who guards the door and maintains order. **3** an official who escorts, or introduces people to, dignitaries on ceremonial occasions. **4** *archaic* a schoolmaster's assistant; a teacher. ▷ *verb* (***ushered, ushering***) **1** (*usually* **usher someone in** or **out**) to conduct or escort them, eg into or out of a building, room, etc. **2** (*usually* **usher something in**) *formal or literary* to be a portent of it; to herald it □ *technology that will usher in a new age of communication.* ⓒ 14c: from French *ussier*, from Latin *ostiarius* doorkeeper, from *ostium* door.

usherette /ʌʃəˈrɛt/ ▷ *noun* a woman who shows people to their seats in a theatre or cinema. ⓒ 1920s: see USHER.

USIA ▷ *abbreviation* United States Information Agency.

USM ▷ *abbreviation, stock exchange* Unlisted Securities Market.

USN ▷ *abbreviation* United States Navy.

USS ▷ *abbreviation* **1** United States Senate. **2** United States Ship or Steamer.

USSR ▷ *abbreviation, historical* Union of Soviet Socialist Republics. See SOVIET UNION.

usual /ˈjuːʒʊəl/ ▷ *adj* done, happening, etc most often; customary □ *took the usual route to work.* ▷ *noun* **1** something which is usual, customary, etc. **2** (*usually* **the** or **my usual**) *colloq* the thing regularly requested, done, etc, especially the drink that someone regularly or most often orders. • **usually** *adverb* ordinarily; normally. • **usualness** *noun.* • **as usual** as regularly happens; as is or was usual. ⓒ 14c: French, from Latin *usus* use.

usufruct /ˈjuːzjʊfrʌkt/ *law* ▷ *noun* the right to use and profit from another's property, as long as the property is not damaged or diminished in any way. ▷ *verb* (***usufructed, usufructing***) to hold (property) in usufruct. • **usufructuary** /-ˈfrʌktʃʊərɪ/ ▷ *noun* someone who holds property in usufruct. ▷ *adj* relating to usufruct. ⓒ 17c: from Latin *usufructus*, from Latin *usus et fructus* use and enjoyment.

usurer /ˈjuːʒərə(r)/ ▷ *noun* someone who lends money, especially one who charges exorbitant rates of interest. ⓒ 13c: see USURY.

usurp /jʊˈzɜːp/ ▷ *verb* (***usurped, usurping***) **1** to take possession of (eg land) or assume (eg power, authority, a title, etc) by force, without right or unjustly. **2** to encroach on something (eg someone else's rights, territory, sphere of interest, etc). • **usurpation** *noun.* • **usurper** *noun.* ⓒ 14c: from French *usurper*, from Latin *usurpare* to take possession for use.

usury /ˈjuːʒərɪ/ ▷ *noun* (***usuries***) **1** the practice of lending money at an unfairly or illegally high rate of interest. **2** such a rate of interest. • **usurious** /jʊˈzjʊərɪəs/ *adj* **1** relating to or involving usury. **2** said of interest: excessive. **3** practising usury; charging excessive interest. ⓒ 14c: from Latin *usuria*, from *usus* USE.

USW ▷ *abbreviation, radio* **1** ultrashort wave or waves. **2** ultrasonic wave or waves.

UT ▷ *abbreviation* **1** Universal Time. **2** *US state* Utah. Also written **Ut**.

ut /uːt, ʌt/ ▷ *noun, music* the syllable (now called DOH) once generally used for the first note of a scale and for the note C. ⓒ 14c: Latin, meaning 'that'; see GAMUT.

UTC ▷ *abbreviation* Universal Time Co-ordinates, used in telecommunications for GMT.

ute /juːt/ ▷ *noun, Austral & NZ colloq* short form of UTILITY TRUCK or UTILITY VEHICLE. ⓒ 1940s.

utensil /jʊˈtɛnsɪl/ ▷ *noun* an implement or tool, especially one for everyday or domestic use □ *cooking utensils.* ⓒ 14c: from French *utensile*, from Latin *utensilis* 'fit for use' or 'useful', from *uti* to use.

uterine /ˈjuːtəraɪn/ ▷ *adj* **1** *medicine* relating to, in the region of or affecting the uterus. See also INTRAUTERINE. **2** said of siblings: born of the same mother but different fathers. ⓒ 15c: French, from Latin *uterus* UTERUS.

uterus /ˈjuːtərəs/ ▷ *noun* (***uteri*** /-raɪ/) *technical* the WOMB (sense 1). ⓒ 17c: Latin.

utilitarian /jʊtɪlɪˈtɛərɪən/ ▷ *adj* **1** intended to be useful rather than beautiful. **2** concerned too much with usefulness and not enough with beauty; strictly or severely functional. **3** relating to or characterized by utilitarianism. ▷ *noun* a believer in utilitarianism. ⓒ 18c: from UTILITY.

utilitarianism ▷ *noun, ethics* a set of values based on the belief that an action is morally right if it benefits the majority of people. ⓒ 19c.

utility /jʊˈtɪlɪtɪ/ ▷ *noun* (***utilities***) **1** usefulness; practicality. **2** something that is useful. **3** *philos* the power of someone or something to satisfy the needs or wants of the majority of people. **4** *econ* the ability of a commodity to satisfy human needs or wants. **5** a PUBLIC UTILITY. **6** *computing* a program designed to carry out a routine function. ▷ *adj* **1** designed for usefulness or practicality, rather than beauty. **2** said of a breed of dog: originally bred to serve a practical purpose or to be useful. ⓒ 14c: from French *utilité*, from Latin *utilitas*, from *uti* to use.

utility room ▷ *noun* a room, especially one in a private house, where things such as a washing machine, freezer, etc are kept.

utility truck and **utility vehicle** ▷ *noun, Austral, NZ* a small truck, pick-up or van designed to carry both passengers and goods. Often shortened to **ute**.

utilize or **utilise** /ˈjuːtɪlaɪz/ ▷ *verb* (***utilized, utilizing***) to make practical use of something; to use it. • **utilizable** *adj.* • **utilization** *noun.* • **utilizer** *noun.* ⓒ 19c: from French *utiliser*, from Italian *utilizzare*, from Latin *uti* to use.

utmost /ˈʌtmoʊst/ ▷ *adj* **1** greatest possible in degree, number or amount □ *of the utmost urgency.* **2** furthest or most remote in position; outermost. ▷ *noun* **1** (*often* **the utmost**) the greatest possible amount, degree or extent. **2** the best or greatest, eg in terms of power, ability, etc □ *tried his utmost to win.* ⓒ Anglo-Saxon *utemest*, from *ute* out + double superlative suffix *-m-est*.

Utopia or **utopia** /jʊˈtoʊpɪə/ ▷ *noun* (***Utopias*** or ***utopias***) any imaginary place, state or society of idealized perfection. ⓒ 16c: Latin, meaning 'no-place', from Greek *ou* not + *topos* a place; the title of a book by Sir Thomas Moore (1477–1535), describing the narrator's search for the perfect form of government.

Utopian or **utopian** ▷ *adj* relating to Utopia, to a utopia or to some unrealistically ideal place, society, etc. ▷ *noun* **1** an inhabitant of Utopia. **2** someone who advocates idealistic or impracticable social reforms. • **Utopianism** *noun*. ⓒ 16c.

utricle /'juːtrɪkəl/ ▷ *noun* **1** *anatomy, zool* a small cell, bag or bladder-like structure, especially the larger of the two parts of the membranous labyrinth of the inner ear. **2** *bot* any of various bladder-like structures. • **utricular** *adj*. ⓒ 18c: from French *utricule*, or from Latin *utriculus* small bag, diminutive of *uter* a bag or leather bottle.

utter¹ /'ʌtə(r)/ ▷ *verb* (***uttered, uttering***) **1** to give audible vocal expression to (an emotion, etc); to emit (a sound) with the voice □ ***uttered a piercing cry***. **2** to speak or say; to express something in words. **3** *law* to put (counterfeit money) into circulation. • **utterable** *adj*. • **utterer** *noun*. ⓒ 14c: from Dutch *uteren* to show or make known.

utter² /'ʌtə(r)/ ▷ *adj* complete; total; absolute □ ***utter disbelief***. • **utterly** *adverb*. • **utterness** *noun*. ⓒ 15c: from Anglo-Saxon *uterra* outer, comparative of *ut* out.

utterance /'ʌtərəns/ ▷ *noun* **1** the act of uttering or expressing something with the voice. **2** the ability to utter; the power of speech. **3** a person's manner of speaking. **4** something that is uttered or expressed. **5** *linguistics* an uninterrupted stretch of speech that is in some way isolated from, or independent to, what proceeds and follows it.

uttermost /'ʌtəmoust/ ▷ *adj, noun* UTMOST.

U-turn ▷ *noun* **1** a manoeuvre in which a vehicle is turned to face the other way in a single continuous movement, the turn making the shape of a U. **2** a complete reversal of direction, eg of government policy.

UV ▷ *abbreviation* ultraviolet.

UV-A or **UVA** ▷ *abbreviation* ultraviolet A, ultraviolet radiation with a range of 320–380 nanometres.

uvarovite /uː'vɑːrəvaɪt/ ▷ *noun, mineralogy* an emerald-green variety of garnet, found in deposits of chromium. ⓒ 19c: from German *Uvarovit*, named after Count Sergei Semenovich Uvarov (1785–1855), a Russian author and statesman.

UV-B or **UVB** ▷ *abbreviation* ultraviolet B, ultraviolet radiation with a range of 280–320 nanometres.

UVF ▷ *abbreviation* Ulster Volunteer Force.

uvula /'juːvjʊlə/ ▷ *noun* (***uvulas*** or ***uvulae*** /-liː/) *anatomy* the small fleshy part of the soft palate that hangs over the back of the tongue at the entrance to the throat. • **uvular** *adj* **1** relating to the uvula. **2** *phonetics* said of a consonantal sound: produced by the articulation of the back of the tongue with the uvula. ▷ *noun, phonetics* a uvular consonant such as the 'r' of some French speakers. ⓒ 14c: Latin, literally 'small grape', from Latin *uva* grape.

UWIST /'juːwɪst/ ▷ *abbreviation* University of Wales Institute of Science and Technology.

uxorial /ʌk'sɔːrɪəl/ ▷ *adj* **1** relating or pertaining to a wife or wives. **2** UXORIOUS. ⓒ 19c: from Latin *uxor* wife.

uxoricide /ʌk'sɔːrɪsaɪd, ʌg'zɔː-/ ▷ *noun* **1** a man who kills his wife. **2** the act of killing one's wife. • **uxoricidal** *adj*. ⓒ 19c: from Latin *uxor* wife + -CIDE.

uxorious /ʌk'sɔːrɪəs/ ▷ *adj* excessively or submissively fond of one's wife. • **uxoriously** *adverb*. • **uxoriousness** *noun*. ⓒ 16c: from Latin *uxoriosus*, from *uxor* wife.

Uzbek /'ʊzbɛk, 'ʌz-/ ▷ *noun* (***Uzbek*** or ***Uzbeks***) **1 a** a member of a Turkic people of central Asia; **b** a citizen or inhabitant of, or person born in, Uzbekistan, a republic in central Asia. **2** the official Turkic language of Uzbekistan. ▷ *adj* belonging or relating to the republic, its inhabitants, or their language. ⓒ 17c.

V

V[1] /viː/ or **v** ▷ *noun* (*Vs, V's* or *v's*) **1** the twenty-second letter of the English alphabet. **2** *also in compounds* an object or mark shaped like the letter V □ *V-sign*. See also VEE.

V[2] ▷ *abbreviation* **1** *IVR* Vatican City. **2** victory. **3** volt.

V[3] ▷ *symbol* **1** *chem* vanadium. **2** the Roman numeral for 5.

v or **v.** ▷ *abbreviation* **1** velocity. **2** verb. **3** versus. **4** very. **5** *vide* (Latin), see, refer to. **6** volume.

V-1 and **V-2** ▷ *noun* respectively a robot flying bomb and a long-range rocket-powered missile, used by the German army in World War II especially to bomb S England. ⊙ 1940s: an abbreviation of German *Vergeltungswaffe* reprisal bomb.

VA ▷ *abbreviation* **1** *US state* Virginia. Also written **Va. 2** (Royal Order of) Victoria and Albert.

vac ▷ *noun, colloq* short for VACATION, especially between terms at a university or college.

vacancy /ˈveɪkənsɪ/ ▷ *noun* (*vacancies*) **1** the state of being vacant; emptiness. **2** an unoccupied job or post. **3** an unoccupied room in a hotel or guesthouse. **4** lack of thought.

vacant /ˈveɪkənt/ ▷ *adj* **1** empty or unoccupied. **2** having, showing or suggesting an absence of thought, concentration or intelligence. **3** said of a period of time: not assigned to any particular activity. • **vacantly** *adverb*. ⊙ 13c: from Latin *vacare* to be empty.

vacant possession ▷ *noun* applying to a house, flat, etc: the state of being ready for occupation immediately after purchase, the previous occupiers having already left.

vacate /ˈveɪkeɪt, və-/ ▷ *verb* (*vacated, vacating*) **1** to make something empty; to empty something out. **2** *tr & intr* to leave or cease to occupy (a house or an official position). • **vacatable** *adj*. ⊙ 17c: from Latin *vacare, vacatum* to be empty.

vacation /vəˈkeɪʃən, veɪ-/ ▷ *noun* **1** *N Amer, especially US* a holiday. **2** a holiday between terms at a university, college or court of law. ▷ *verb* (*vacationed, vacationing*) *intr, N Amer, especially US* to take a holiday. • **vacationist** *noun* someone taking a holiday. ⊙ 14c: from French, from Latin *vacatio* freedom or exemption, from *vacare* to be empty.

vaccinate /ˈvaksɪneɪt/ ▷ *verb* (*vaccinated, vaccinating*) to administer to a person or an animal a vaccine that gives immunity from a disease; to INOCULATE. ▷ **vaccination** *noun*. • **vaccinator** *noun*.

vaccine /ˈvaksiːn/ ▷ *noun* **1** *medicine* a preparation containing killed or weakened (attenuated) bacteria or viruses, or serum containing specific antibodies, used in vaccination to confer temporary or permanent immunity to a bacterial or viral disease by stimulating the body to produce antibodies to a specific bacterium or virus. **2** *medicine, historical* cowpox virus, or lymph containing it, used for inoculation against smallpox. **3** *computing* a piece of software designed to detect and remove computer viruses (see VIRUS 5) from a floppy disk, program, etc. • **vaccinal** *adj*. ⊙ 18c: from *viriolae vaccinae* cowpox, the title of a paper (1798) by E Jenner, from Latin *vacca* cow.

vaccinia /vakˈsɪnɪə/ ▷ *noun* **1** cowpox. **2** in humans: a mild or localized reaction to inoculation with the vaccinia virus against smallpox. ⊙ 19c: from Latin *vaccinus* vaccine.

vacherin / *French* vaʃʀɛ̃/ ▷ *noun* a dessert made of a ring of meringue or almond paste filled with ice cream or whipped cream.

vacillate /ˈvasɪleɪt/ ▷ *verb* (*vacillated, vacillating*) *intr* to change opinions or decisions frequently; to waver. • **vacillating** *adj*. • **vacillatingly** *adverb*. • **vacillation** *noun*. ⊙ 16c: from Latin *vacillare, vacillatum*.

vacua see under VACUUM

vacuity /vaˈkjuːɪtɪ/ ▷ *noun* (*vacuities*) **1** the state or quality of being vacuous. **2** a foolish thought or idea. **3** *formal* an empty space.

vacuole /ˈvakjuoul/ ▷ *noun, biol* a space within the cytoplasm of a living cell that is filled with air or liquid and, in plant cells only, is surrounded by a membrane that controls the movement of substances into and out of that space. • **vacuolar** *adj*. • **vacuolation** *noun*. ⊙ 19c: French, meaning 'little vacuum'.

vacuous /ˈvakjuəs/ ▷ *adj* **1** unintelligent; stupid; inane. **2** said of a look or expression: blank; conveying no feeling or meaning. **3** empty. **4** having no meaning or purpose. • **vacuity** see separate entry. • **vacuousness** *noun*. • **vacuously** *adverb*. ⊙ 17c: from Latin *vacuus* empty.

vacuum /ˈvakjuəm, ˈvakjuːm/ ▷ *noun* (*vacuums* or *technical* ***vacua*** /ˈvakjuə/) **1** a space from which all matter has been removed. **2** a space from which all or almost all air or other gas has been removed. **3** a feeling or state of emptiness. **4** a condition of isolation from outside influences. **5** *colloq* a VACUUM CLEANER. **6** *as adj* relating to, containing or operating by means of a vacuum □ *a vacuum pump*. ▷ *verb* (*vacuumed, vacuuming*) *tr & intr, colloq* to clean with a vacuum cleaner. 16c: from Latin *vacuus* empty.

vacuum brake ▷ *noun* a brake in the working of which suction by vacuum supplements the pressure applied by the operator, especially a braking system of this type applied simultaneously throughout a train.

vacuum-clean ▷ *verb, tr & intr* to clean with a vacuum cleaner.

vacuum cleaner ▷ *noun* an electrically powered cleaning device that lifts dust and dirt by suction. See also HOOVER, VACUUM. ⊙ Early 20c.

vacuum flask ▷ *noun* **1** a container for preserving the temperature of liquids, especially drinks, consisting of a double-skinned glass bottle with a vacuum sealed between the layers, fitted inside a protective metal or plastic container. **2** a container serving the same function made of plastic. See also THERMOS. ⊙ Early 20c.

vacuum-packed ▷ *adj* said especially of prepacked food: sealed in a container from which most of the air has been removed. ⊙ 1950s.

vacuum tube ▷ *noun* **1** *elec* an electron tube containing an electrically heated electrode (the CATHODE) that emits electrons which flow through a vacuum to a second electrode (the ANODE). Also called VALVE. **2** a THERMIONIC VALVE.

VAD ▷ *abbreviation* Voluntary Aid Detachment, an organization of British volunteer nurses who served in World War I. ▷ *noun* a member of this organization.

vade-mecum /vɑːdɪˈmeɪkum/ ▷ *noun* a handbook of practical information carried for frequent reference. ⊙ 17c: Latin, literally 'go with me'.

vagabond /ˈvagəbɒnd/ ▻ *noun* someone with no fixed home who lives an unsettled wandering life, especially someone regarded as lazy or worthless. ▻ *adj* wandering; roving. Ⓒ 15c: French, from Latin *vagari* to wander.

vagal see under VAGUS

vagary /ˈveɪgərɪ/ ▻ *noun* (***vagaries***) an unpredictable and erratic act or turn of events. Ⓒ 16c: from Latin *vagari* to wander.

vagi *plural of* VAGUS

vagina /vəˈdʒaɪnə/ ▻ *noun* (***vaginas*** or ***vaginae*** /-niː/) **1** in the reproductive system of most female mammals: the muscular canal that leads from the cervix of the uterus to the exterior of the body. **2** *bot* a sheath around the stem at the base of a leaf. • **vaginal** *adj*. Ⓒ 17c: Latin, meaning 'sheath'.

vaginismus /vadʒɪˈnɪzməs/ ▻ *noun, medicine* painful spasmodic contraction of the muscles surrounding the vagina which may be associated with fear of or aversion to sexual intercourse, or may have physical causes.

vaginitis /vadʒɪˈnaɪtɪs/ ▻ *noun, pathol* inflammation of the vagina.

vagrant /ˈveɪgrənt/ ▻ *noun* someone who has no permanent home or place of work. ▻ *adj* **1** wandering; roving. **2** uncertain; unsettled. • **vagrancy** *noun*. • **vagrantly** *adverb*. Ⓒ 15c: probably from French *wakerant* roaming.

vague /veɪg/ ▻ *adj* (***vaguer***, ***vaguest***) **1** indistinct or imprecise. **2** thinking, expressing or remembering without clarity or precision. • **vaguely** *adverb*. • **vagueness** *noun*. Ⓒ 16c: from Latin *vagus* wandering.

vagus /ˈveɪgəs/ (***vagi*** /-dʒaɪ/) *anatomy* in vertebrates: the tenth cranial nerve, branches of which carry motor nerve fibres to many internal organs, such as the heart, lungs, stomach, kidneys and liver. • **vagal** *adj*. Ⓒ 19c: from Latin *vagus* wandering.

vain ▻ *adj* **1** having too much pride in one's appearance, achievements or possessions; conceited. **2** having no useful effect or result; futile. • **in vain** without success; fruitlessly. • **take someone's name in vain** to refer to them in a disrespectful way, especially in anger or surprise. • **vainly** *adverb*. • **vainness** *noun*. See also VANITY. Ⓒ 13c: from French, from Latin *vanus* empty.

vainglory ▻ *noun, literary* extreme boastfulness; excessive pride in oneself. • **vainglorious** *adj*. • **vaingloriously** *adverb*. Ⓒ 13c: from French *vaine gloire*.

valance /ˈvaləns/ ▻ *noun* a decorative strip of fabric hung over a curtain rail or round the frame of a bed. • **valanced** *adj* trimmed with a valance. Ⓒ 15c: possibly from French *valer* to descend.

vale ▻ *noun, literary* a VALLEY. Ⓒ 13c: from French *val*, from Latin *vallis*.

valediction /valɪˈdɪkʃən/ ▻ *noun* **1** the act of saying farewell; a farewell. **2** a valedictory speech, etc. Ⓒ 17c: from Latin *vale* farewell + *dicere* to say.

valedictory /valɪˈdɪktərɪ/ ▻ *adj* signifying or accompanying a farewell ◻ ***a valedictory speech***. ▻ *noun* (***valedictories***) *US* a farewell speech made by a graduand.

valence electron ▻ *noun, chem* an electron in one of the outer shells of an atom that participates in the formation of chemical bonds with other atoms, resulting in the production of molecules.

valency /ˈveɪlənsɪ/ or (*especially N Amer*) **valence** *noun* (***valencies***; ***valences***) *chem* a positive or negative whole number that denotes the combining power of an atom of a particular element, equal to the number of hydrogen atoms or their equivalent with which it could combine to form a compound. For example, in water (H_2O), oxygen has a valency of two. Ⓒ Late 19c in this sense; 17c in obsolete sense 'power' or 'strength', from Latin *valentia* strength or capacity.

-valent /veɪlənt, vələnt/ ▻ *combining form, chem, forming adjectives* referring to the specified valency or an element within a compound ◻ ***trivalent***. Ⓒ Modelled on EQUIVALENT.

valentine /ˈvaləntaɪn/ ▻ *noun* **1** a card or other message given, often anonymously, as a token of love or affection on ST VALENTINE'S DAY. **2** the person it is given to. Ⓒ 14c.

valerian /vəˈlɪərɪən, vəˈlɛərɪən/ ▻ *noun* **1 a** any of a family of small flowering plants of Europe and Asia with pinnate leaves, toothed leaflets, pink tubular flowers borne in dense terminal heads, and rhizome roots; **b** a sedative drug derived from the root. **2** (*in full* **red valerian**) a related plant native to the N hemisphere which has oval leaves and red or white spurred flowers. • **valeric** *adj*. Ⓒ 14c: from Latin *valeriana herba*, from the name *Valerius*.

valeric acid ▻ *noun* PENTANOIC ACID.

valet /ˈvaleɪ, ˈvalɪt/ ▻ *noun* **1** a man's personal servant, who attends to his clothes, dressing, etc. **2** a man who carries out similar duties in a hotel. ▻ *verb* (***valeted***, ***valeting***) **1** *intr* to work as a valet. **2** to clean the bodywork and interior of (a car) as a service. Ⓒ 16c: French, related to VARLET.

valet parking ▻ *noun, especially N Amer* a service offered at a restaurant, airport, hotel, etc when a customer's car is taken away to, and brought back from, a parking place by an attendant. Ⓒ 1960s.

valeta see VELETA

valetudinarian /valɪtʃuːdɪˈnɛərɪən/ *formal* ▻ *adj* **1** relating to or suffering from a long-term or chronic illness. **2** anxious about one's health; hypochondriac. ▻ *noun* a valetudinarian person. • **valetudinarianism** *noun*. Ⓒ 18c: from Latin *valetudo* state of health.

Valhalla /valˈhalə/ ▻ *noun, Scand mythol* the palace of bliss where the souls of slain heroes feast for eternity with Odin, the supreme creator. Ⓒ 18c: from Norse *Valhöll*, from *valr* the slain + *höll* hall.

valiant /ˈvalɪənt/ ▻ *adj* outstandingly brave and heroic. • **valiantly** *adverb*. Ⓒ 14c: from French *vailant*, from Latin *valere* to be strong.

valid /ˈvalɪd/ ▻ *adj* **1** said of an argument, objection, etc: **a** based on truth or sound reasoning; **b** well-grounded; having some force. **2** said of a ticket or official document: **a** legally acceptable for use ◻ ***a valid passport***; **b** not having reached its expiry date ◻ ***The ticket is still valid.*** **3** said of a contract: drawn up according to proper legal procedure. • **validity** *noun*. • **validly** *adverb*. Ⓒ 16c: from Latin *validus* strong, from *valere* to be strong.

validate /ˈvalɪdeɪt/ ▻ *verb* (***validated***, ***validating***) **1** to make (a document, a ticket, etc) valid, eg by marking it with an official stamp. **2** to confirm the validity of something. • **validation** *noun*.

valine /ˈveɪliːn, ˈvaliːn/ ▻ *noun, biochem* an AMINO ACID. Ⓒ Early 20c: from VALERIC ACID.

valise /vəˈliːz; *N Amer* vəˈliːs/ ▻ *noun, now chiefly N Amer, especially US* a small overnight case or bag. Ⓒ 17c: French, meaning 'suitcase'.

Valium /ˈvalɪəm/ ▻ *noun, trademark* DIAZEPAM, a type of tranquillizing drug. Ⓒ 1960s.

Valkyrie /ˈvalkɪrɪ, valˈkɪərɪ/ ▻ *noun* (***Valkyries***) *Scand mythol* a handmaiden of Odin, one of twelve who accompanied the souls of slain heroes to VALHALLA. Ⓒ 18c: from Norse *Valkyrja*, from *valr* the slain + *kjosa* to choose.

valley /ˈvalɪ/ ▻ *noun* (***valleys***) **1** a long flat area of land, usually containing a river or stream, flanked on both sides by higher land, eg hills or mountains. **2** any trough or hollow between ridges, eg on an M-shaped roof. Ⓒ 13c: from French *valee*, from *val*, from Latin *vallis* valley.

vallum /ˈvaləm/ ▻ *noun, archaeol* a rampart or earthwork. Ⓒ 17c: from Latin *vallus* stake.

valonia /və'louniə/ ▷ *noun* a tanning material consisting of the acorns of an oak, especially of the Levantine oak. ⓘ 18c: from Italian *vallonea*, from Greek *balanos* an acorn.

valorize or **valorise** /'valəraɪz/ ▷ *verb* (***valorized, valorizing***) to fix or stabilize the price of (a commodity, etc), especially by a policy imposed by a government or other controlling body. • **valorization** *noun*. ⓘ 1920s, from obsolete *valor* the value of something: Latin.

valour or (*N Amer*) **valor** /'valə(r)/ *noun* courage or bravery, especially in battle. • **valorous** *adj*. • **valorously** *adverb*. ⓘ 15c: French, from Latin *valor*, from *valere* to be strong.

valuable /'valjuːəbəl/ ▷ *adj* having considerable value or usefulness. ▷ *noun* (*usually* **valuables**) personal possessions of high financial or other value. • **valuableness** *noun*. • **valuably** *adverb*.

valuation /valju'eɪʃən/ ▷ *noun* **1** an assessment of the monetary value of something, especially from an expert or authority. **2** the value arrived at. • **valuational** *adj*.

value /'valjuː/ ▷ *noun* **1** worth in monetary terms. **2** the quality of being useful or desirable; the degree of usefulness or desirability. **3** the exact amount of a variable quantity in a particular case. **4** the quality of being a fair exchange □ *value for money*. **5** (**values**) moral principles or standards. **6** *math* a quantity represented by a symbol or set of symbols. **7** *music* the duration of a note or rest. ▷ *verb* (***valued, valuing***) **1** to consider something to be of a certain value, especially a high value; to esteem. **2** to assess the value of something. • **valueless** *adj*. • **valuer** *noun*. ⓘ 14c: French, from *valoir*, from Latin *valere* to be worth.

value added and **added value** ▷ *noun, econ* the difference between the overall cost of a manufacturing or marketing process and the final value of the goods.

value-added tax ▷ *noun, Brit* (abbreviation **VAT**) a tax on goods and services sold which is calculated on the difference between the cost of raw materials and production, and the market value of the final product. ⓘ 1970s.

valued ▷ *adj* considered valuable or precious; highly prized.

value judgement ▷ *noun* an assessment of worth or merit based on personal opinion rather than objective fact.

valuta /vɑː'ljuːtə, -'luːtə/ ▷ *noun* the comparative value of one currency with respect to another. ⓘ 19c: Italian, from Latin *valere* to be worth something.

valvate /'valveɪt/ ▷ *adj* **1** with a valve or valves. **2** *biol* **a** taking place by means of valves □ *valvate dehiscence*; **b** meeting at the edges without overlapping.

valve /valv/ ▷ *noun* **1 a** any device that regulates the flow of a liquid or gas through a pipe by opening or closing an aperture; **b** any such device that allows flow in one direction only. **2** *anatomy* in certain tubular organs: a flap of membranous tissue that allows flow of a body fluid, such as blood, in one direction only, eg the valves in the heart and veins. **3** *electronics* a THERMIONIC VALVE. **4** any of a set of finger-operated devices that control the flow of air through some brass musical instruments producing different notes. **5** *bot* any of the sections that are formed when a capsule or other dry fruit opens to shed its seeds at dehiscence. **6** *zool* either half of the hinged shell of a bivalve mollusc such as a cockle or clam. • **valved** *adj*. ⓘ 14c: from Latin *valva* folding door.

valvular /'valvjʊlə(r)/ ▷ *adj* **1** having valves. **2** functioning as a valve.

vamoose /və'muːs/ ▷ *verb* (***vamoosed, vamoosing***) *intr, N Amer, especially US slang* to depart hurriedly; to clear off. Usually used as an *exclamation* □ *Vamoose!* ⓘ 19c: from Spanish *vamos* let us go.

vamp¹ *colloq* ▷ *noun* a woman who flaunts her sexual charm, especially in order to exploit men. ▷ *verb* (***vamped, vamping***) **1** to seduce (a man) with intent to exploit him. **2** *intr* to behave like a vamp. ⓘ Early 20c: a shortening of VAMPIRE.

vamp² ▷ *noun* the part of a shoe or boot that covers the toes. ▷ *verb* (***vamped, vamping***) to improvise (a simple musical accompaniment). See also REVAMP. ⓘ 13c: from French *avanpié* forefoot, from *avant* before + *pié* foot.

■ **vamp something up 1** to refurbish it or do it up; to prepare something old or out-of-date for re-use by making alterations. **2** to make it up from bits and pieces.

vampire /'vampaɪə(r)/ ▷ *noun* **1** a dead person who supposedly rises from the grave at night to suck the blood of the living. **2** someone who ruthlessly exploits others. **3** a VAMPIRE BAT. • **vampiric** *adj*. • **vampirism** *noun*. ⓘ 18c: French, from Hungarian *vampir*, of Slavonic origin.

vampire bat ▷ *noun* any of various species of small bat native to the forests of Central and S America that pierce the skin of animals and humans with their sharp canine and incisor teeth and suck their blood.

van¹ ▷ *noun* **1** a commercial road vehicle with luggage space at the rear, lighter than a lorry or truck. **2** (*also* **luggage van**) *Brit* a railway carriage in which luggage and parcels are carried, often also where the guard travels. ⓘ 19c: a shortening of CARAVAN.

van² ▷ *noun* **1** a vanguard. **2** the forefront □ *in the van of progress*. ⓘ 17c: a shortening of VANGUARD.

vanadium /və'neɪdɪəm/ ▷ *noun, chem* (symbol **V**, atomic number 23) a soft silvery-grey metallic element that is used to increase the toughness and shock resistance of steel alloys, eg for components of cars. ⓘ 19c: named by the Swedish chemist Sefström after *Vanadis*, a name of the Norse goddess Freyja.

Van Allen belt ▷ *noun, astron* either of two rings of intense radiation that encircle the Earth at distances of about 1000km to 5000km and 15000km to 25000km, consisting of electrically charged particles trapped by the Earth's magnetic field, the outer zone consisting mainly of electrons and the inner one of protons. ⓘ 1950s: named after James Van Allen (born 1914), US physicist.

V&A or **V and A** ▷ *abbreviation, colloq* in Britain: the Victoria and Albert Museum, London.

Vandal /'vandəl/ ▷ *noun, historical* a member of a Germanic people who overran Gaul, Spain, N Africa and Rome in the 4c-5c, destroying churches, manuscripts, etc in the process. ▷ *adj* relating to the Vandals. ⓘ 16c: from Latin *Vandalus*, the name given to these people, from Germanic.

vandal /'vandəl/ ▷ *noun* someone who wantonly damages or destroys personal and public property. • **vandalism** *noun*. ⓘ 17c: from VANDAL.

vandalize or **vandalise** ▷ *verb* (***vandalized, vandalizing***) to inflict wilful and senseless damage on (property, etc).

van der Waals' force /van də 'wɑːlz —, — 'vɑːlz —/ ▷ *noun, physics* any of the weak attractive forces that exist between atoms or molecules. ⓘ 19c: named after Johannes Diderik van der Waals (1837–1923), Dutch physicist.

vandyke or **Vandyke** /van'daɪk, 'vandaɪk/ ▷ *noun* **1** (*in full* **vandyke collar**) a broad collar with the edge cut into deep points. **2** (*in full* **vandyke beard**) a short pointed beard. ⓘ 18c: named after Sir Anthony Van Dyke (1599–1641), a Flemish painter in whose portraits these features typically appear.

vane ▷ *noun* **1** a WEATHERVANE. **2** each of the blades of a windmill, propeller or revolving fan. **3** a sight on an observing or surveying instrument. **4** the flat part of a bird's feather. • **vaned** *adj*. • **vaneless** *adj*. ⓘ 15c: from obsolete *fane* flag or weathercock.

vanguard /'vaŋgɑːd, 'van-/ ▻ *noun* **1** the part of a military force that advances first. **2 a** a person or group that leads the way, especially by setting standards or forming opinion; **b** a leading position ▫ ***in the vanguard of discovery.*** ⓘ 15c: from French *avant-garde* advance guard.

vanguardism ▻ *noun* the condition of being or practice of positioning oneself in the vanguard of a political, cultural, artistic, etc movement.

vanilla /və'nɪlə/ ▻ *noun* **1 a** a Mexican climbing orchid having large fragrant white or yellow flowers followed by pod-like fruits; **b** (*in full* **vanilla pod**) its fruit. **2** a flavouring substance obtained from the pod, used in ice cream, chocolate and other foods. ▻ *adj* **1** flavoured with or like vanilla ▫ ***vanilla ice cream.*** **2** *colloq* ordinary; plain. ⓘ 17c: from Spanish *vainilla* small pod, from Latin *vagina* sheath.

vanillin /və'nɪlɪn/ ▻ *noun* the aromatic principle of vanilla, $C_8H_8O_3$, used in perfumes, and pharmaceuticals.

vanish /'vanɪʃ/ ▻ *verb* (***vanishes, vanished, vanishing***) **1** *intr* to disappear suddenly. **2** *intr* to cease to exist; to die out. **3** to make something disappear ▫ ***The magician vanished the swords.*** **4** *intr, math* to become zero. ⓘ 14c:from Latin *evanescere*, from *ex* from + *vanus* empty.

vanishing cream ▻ *noun* moisturizing cream that leaves no trace on the skin.

vanishing point ▻ *noun* **1** the point at which parallel lines extending into the distance appear to meet. **2** the point at which something disappears completely.

vanitas /'vanɪtas/ ▻ *noun, art* a type of still-life picture, produced mainly by 17c Dutch artists, in which symbolic motifs such as skulls, hourglasses and old books feature as reminders of the vanity of earthly pleasures and the transience of human life and aspirations. ⓘ Early 20c in this sense; 16c as an exclamation of disillusionment or pessimism: from a phrase in the Vulgate (Eccles. 1.2): *vanitas vanitatum, omnia vanitas* vanity of vanities, all is vanity.

vanity /'vanɪtɪ/ ▻ *noun* (***vanities***) **1** the quality of being vain or conceited. **2** a thing one is conceited about. **3** futility or worthlessness. ⓘ 13c: from Latin *vanitas.*

vanity bag or **vanity case** ▻ *noun* a woman's small case for cosmetics.

vanity publishing ▻ *noun* publication by the author at their own expense.

vanity unit ▻ *noun* a piece of furniture combining a dressing-table and washbasin.

vanquish /'vaŋkwɪʃ/ ▻ *verb* (***vanquishes, vanquished, vanquishing***) *literary* **1** to defeat or overcome someone. **2** *intr* to be victor. • **vanquishable** *adj.* • **vanquisher** *noun.* ⓘ 14c: from Latin *vincere* to conquer.

vantage /'vɑːntɪdʒ/ ▻ *noun* short for ADVANTAGE *noun* 4. ⓘ 13c in archaic sense *advantage*, from French *avantage* advantage.

vantage point ▻ *noun* a position affording a clear overall view or prospect.

vapid /'vapɪd/ ▻ *adj* **1** dull; uninteresting; insipid. **2** having little taste, colour or smell. • **vapidity** /va'pɪdɪtɪ/ *noun.* • **vapidly** *adverb.* • **vapidness** *noun.* ⓘ 17c: from Latin *vapidus* flat-tasting.

vapor the *N Amer* spelling of VAPOUR.

vaporetto /vapə'rɛtoʊ/ ▻ *noun* (***vaporettos*** or ***vaporetti*** /-tiː/) a small ship (originally steam, now motor) that plies the canals in Venice. ⓘ 1920s: Italian, meaning 'steamboat'.

vaporize or **vaporise** /'veɪpəraɪz/ ▻ *verb* (***vaporized, vaporizing***) **1** to convert something into vapour. **2** *intr* to become vapour; to evaporate. **3** to destroy something by reducing it to vapour. • **vaporizable** *adj.* • **vaporization** *noun.* • **vaporizer** *noun.*

vapour or (*N Amer*) **vapor** /'veɪpə(r)/ *noun* **1** a substance in the form of a mist, fume or smoke, especially one coming off from a solid or liquid. **2** *chem* a gas that can be condensed to a liquid by pressure alone, without being cooled, consisting of atoms or molecules, dispersed in the air, that have evaporated from the surface of a substance that normally (ie at standard temperature and pressure) exists in the form of a liquid or solid ▫ ***water vapour.*** **3** (**the vapours**) *old use* a feeling of depression, or of faintness, formerly thought to be caused by gases in the stomach. ▻ *verb* (***vapoured, vapouring***) *intr* **1** to rise as vapour; to evaporate. **2** to brag or talk idly. • **vaporous** *adj.* • **vaporously** *adverb.* • **vaporousness** *noun.* • **vapourish** *adj.* • **vapoury** *adj.* ⓘ 14c: from Latin *vapor* steam.

vapour density ▻ *noun* the density of a gas or vapour relative to that of a reference gas, usually hydrogen, at the same temperature and pressure.

vapour pressure ▻ *noun, physics* the pressure exerted by the atoms or molecules of a vapour with its liquid or solid form.

vapour trail ▻ *noun* a white trail of condensed water vapour from the engine exhausts of a high-flying aircraft.

varactor /və'raktə(r)/ ▻ *noun, electronics* a two-electrode semiconductor device in which capacitance varies with voltage. ⓘ 1950s: from *varying reactor.*

variable /'vɛərɪəbəl/ ▻ *adj* **1** referring to something that varies or tends to vary; not steady or regular; changeable. **2** referring to something that can be varied or altered. ▻ *noun* **1** a thing that can vary unpredictably in nature or degree. **2** a factor which may change or be changed by another. **3** *math* in an algebraic expression or equation: a symbol, usually a letter, for which one or more quantities or values may be substituted, eg in the expression $3x$, x is a variable. **4** *astron* a VARIABLE STAR. • **variability** or **variableness** *noun.* • **variably** *adverb.* ⓘ 14c: French, from Latin *variabilis*, from *variare* to VARY.

variable costs ▻ *plural noun, econ* costs which, unlike FIXED COSTS, vary with the level of production, eg the costs of raw materials, fuel used, etc.

variable interest rate ▻ *noun* a rate of interest on a loan, etc that varies with the market rate of interest.

variable star ▻ *noun* a star whose brightness changes over a period of time.

variance ▻ *noun* **1** the state of being different or inconsistent ▫ ***There was some variance between them.*** **2** *statistics* a quantity equal to the square of the standard deviation. • **at variance with something** in disagreement or conflict with it. ⓘ 14c: from Latin *varientia* difference, related to VARY.

variant ▻ *noun* **1** a form of a thing that varies from another form, eg the ending of a story or one of several permissible spellings of a word. **2** an example that differs from a standard. ▻ *adj* **1** different. **2** differing from a standard.

variate ▻ *noun, statistics* the variable quantity which is being studied.

variation ▻ *noun* **1** the act or process of varying or changing. **2** something that varies from a standard. **3** the extent to which something varies from a standard. **4** a passage of music in which the main melody is repeated with some, usually only slight, changes. **5** *biol* differences in characteristics, eg size or colouring, between individual members of the same plant or animal species, due to environmental differences, differences in genetic make-up, or (more often) both. **6** differences in characteristics between parents and their offspring, due to mutations, or more often to the rearrangement of genetic material that occurs during sexual reproduction. **7** *ballet* a solo dance. • **variational** *adj.* ⓘ 14c: French, from Latin *variatio*, from *variare* to VARY.

varicella /varɪ'sɛlə/ ▻ *noun, medicine* chickenpox. ⓘ 18c: an irregular diminutive of VARIOLA.

varices *plural of* VARIX

varicoloured /ˈvɛərɪkʌləd/ ▻ *adj* having different colours in different parts. ◷ 17c: from Latin *varius* various + COLOUR.

varicose /ˈvarɪkəs/ *pathol*, ▻ *adj* **1** said of a superficial vein: abnormally swollen and twisted so that it produces a raised and often painful knot on the skin surface, usually of the legs. **2** said of an ulcer: formed as a result of the development of a varicosity. • **varicosity** *noun* **1** being varicose. **2** an abnormally swollen vein. ◷ 18c: from Latin *varicosus*, from *varix* varicose vein.

varicotomy /varɪˈkɒtəmɪ/ ▻ *noun* (**varicotomies**) the surgical removal of a VARIX.

varied see under VARY

variegate /ˈvɛərɪgeɪt, ˈvɛərɪəgeɪt/ ▻ *verb* (**variegated, variegating**) to alter the appearance of something, especially with patches of colours. • **variegation** *noun.* ◷ 17c: from Latin *variegatus*, from *varius* changing.

variegated ▻ *adj, bot* said of leaves or flowers: marked with patches of two or more colours.

varies see under VARY

variety /vəˈraɪətɪ/ ▻ *noun* (**varieties**) **1** any of various types of the same thing; a kind or sort. **2** the quality of departing from a fixed pattern or routine; diversity. **3** a plant or animal differing from another in certain characteristics, but not enough to be classed as a separate species; a race, breed or strain. **4 a** a form of theatrical entertainment consisting of a succession of acts of different kinds; **b** *as adj* □ *variety show* □ *variety entertainment*. Compare VAUDEVILLE. ◷ 16c: from Latin *varietas* difference or diversity.

varifocals /vɛərɪˈfoʊkəlz/ ▻ *plural noun* a pair of glasses with **varifocal** lenses, whose variable focal lengths allow a wide range of focusing distances. Compare BIFOCALS.

variform /ˈvɛərɪfɔːm/ ▻ *adj* referring to something whose shape or form may vary. ◷ 17c: from Latin *vari-*, from *varius* changing.

variola /vəˈraɪələ/ ▻ *noun, medicine* smallpox. • **variolar** *adj.* ◷ 18c: Latin, meaning 'pustule' or 'pox', from *varius* various or spotted.

variometer /vɛərɪˈɒmɪtə(r)/ ▻ *noun* **1** an instrument for comparing magnetic forces. **2** *electronics* a variable inductor composed of two connected coils, one rotating inside the other. **3** *aeronautics* an instrument that indicates by a needle the rate of climb and descent.

variorum /vɛərɪˈɔːrəm/ ▻ *adj* said of an edition of a text: including the notes of earlier commentators or editors or including variant meanings. ▻ *noun* a variorum edition. ◷ 18c: from Latin *cum notis variorum* with the notes of various commentators.

various /ˈvɛərɪəs/ ▻ *adj* **1** several different □ *worked for various companies.* **2** different; disparate; diverse □ *Their interests are many and various.* • **variously** *adverb.* • **variousness** *noun.* ◷ 16c: from Latin *varius* changing.

varistor /vəˈrɪstə(r)/ ▻ *noun* a two-electrode semiconductor used to short-circuit transient high voltages in delicate electronic devices. ◷ 1930s: from *variable* + *resistor*.

varix /ˈvɛərɪks, ˈva-/ ▻ *noun* (**varices** /-rɪsiːz/) *medicine* **1** an abnormally dilated, lengthened and tortuous vein, artery or lymphatic vessel. **2** dilation of a blood vessel. ◷ 14c: Latin, meaning 'varicose vein'.

varlet /ˈvɑːlət/ ▻ *noun, old use* **1** a menial servant. **2** a rascal or rogue. ◷ 15c: French, a variant form of *vaslet* VALET.

varmint /ˈvɑːmɪnt/ ▻ *noun, N Amer, especially US* **1** *slang* a troublesome animal or person. **2** vermin. ◷ 16c: a variant form of VERMIN.

varnish /ˈvɑːnɪʃ/ ▻ *noun* (**varnishes**) **1** an oil-based liquid containing resin, painted on a surface such as wood to give a hard transparent and often glossy finish. **2** any liquid providing a similar finish □ *nail varnish.* **3** a superficial attractiveness or impressiveness, especially masking underlying shoddiness or inadequacy; a gloss. ▻ *verb* (**varnishes, varnished, varnishing**) **1** to apply varnish to something. **2** to make something superficially appealing or impressive. • **varnisher** *noun.* • **varnishing** *noun.* ◷ 14c: from French *vernis*, from Latin *veronix* sandarach.

varsity /ˈvɑːsɪtɪ/ ▻ *noun* (**varsities**) *colloq* **1** *Brit* a university, especially with reference to sport. **2** *N Amer* the principal team representing a college in a sport. ◷ 19c: a colloquial abbreviation of UNIVERSITY.

varus /ˈvɛərəs/ ▻ *adj, pathol* said of a foot or hand: displaced from normal alignment so as to deviate towards the midline of the body. ◷ 18c: Latin, meaning 'bent' or 'bow-legged'.

varve /vɑːv/ ▻ *noun, geol* a seasonal deposit of clay in still water, used to determine Ice Age chronology. ◷ Early 20c: from Swedish *varv* layer.

vary /ˈvɛərɪ/ ▻ *verb* (**varies, varied, varying**) **1** *intr* to change, or be of different kinds, especially according to different circumstances. **2** *tr & intr* to make or become less regular or uniform and more diverse. • **varied** *adj* having variety; diverse. • **varying** *noun, adj.* • **varyingly** *adverb.* ◷ 15c: from Latin *variare* to vary.

vas /vas/ ▻ *noun* (**vasa** /ˈveɪsə/) *anatomy, biol* a vessel, tube or duct carrying liquid. • **vasal** *adj.* ◷ 16c: from Latin *vas* vessel.

vascular /vaskjuːlə(r)/ ▻ *adj, biol* **1** relating to the blood vessels of animals or the sap-conducting tissues (XYLEM and PHLOEM) of plants. **2** composed of or provided with such vessels. ◷ 17c: from Latin *vasculum*, from *vas* vessel.

vascular bundle ▻ *noun, bot* in higher plants such as flowering plants, conifers and ferns: any of numerous thin strands of VASCULAR TISSUE running upwards through the roots and stem and extending into the leaves, composed of both XYLEM and PHLOEM (as in the stem) or either (as in the roots).

vascular disease ▻ *noun* any of various diseased conditions of the blood vessels.

vascular tissue ▻ *noun, biol* tissue within which water, nutrients and other materials are transported from one part of a living organism to another, ie the blood vessels of animals, and the XYLEM and PHLOEM of plants.

vas deferens /vas ˈdɛfərenz/ ▻ *noun* (**vasa deferentia** /ˈveɪzə dɛfəˈrɛnʃɪə/) *biol* the duct from each testicle that carries spermatozoa to the penis. ◷ 16c: from Latin *deferre* to carry away.

vase /vɑːz; *US* veɪz/ ▻ *noun* an ornamental glass or pottery container, especially one for holding cut flowers. ◷ 17c: French, from Latin *vas* vessel.

vasectomy /vəˈsɛktəmɪ/ ▻ *noun* (**vasectomies**) *medicine* a surgical operation involving the tying and cutting of the VAS DEFERENS as a means of sterilization. ◷ Late 19c: from Latin *vas* VAS + -ECTOMY.

Vaseline /ˈvasəliːn/ ▻ *noun, trademark* an ointment consisting mainly of PETROLEUM JELLY. ◷ Late 19c: based on German *Wasser* water + Greek *elaion* oil.

vaso- /veɪzoʊ/ ▻ *combining form, medicine, denoting* a duct or vessel. ◷ From Latin *vas* vessel.

vasoconstrictor ▻ *noun, physiol* any agent, such as a hormone, drug or nerve, that stimulates blood vessels to contract so that they become narrower. ◷ Late 19c.

vasodilator ▻ *noun, physiol* any agent, such as a hormone, drug or nerve that stimulates blood vessels to dilate so that they become wider. ◷ Late 19c.

vasopressin /veɪzoʊˈprɛsɪn/ ▻ *noun, physiol* a hormone released by the pituitary gland that increases blood pressure and the absorption of water by the kidneys so that less water is excreted from the body. ◷ 1920s.

vassal /ˈvasəl/ ▷ *noun* **1** *feudalism* someone acting as a servant to, and fighting on behalf of, a medieval lord in return for land or protection or both. **2** a person or nation dependent on or subservient to another. **3** *Scots law* someone holding land from a superior in return for a payment of FEU-DUTY. ▷ *adj* in the relationship or state of a vassal; subordinate □ ***vassal state***. ◷ 13c: from Latin *vassus* servant.

vassalage ▷ *noun, feudalism* **1** the state of being a vassal **2** a system of using vassals.

vast /vɑːst/ ▷ *adj* **1** extremely great in size, extent or amount. **2** *colloq* considerable; appreciable □ ***a vast difference***. ▷ *noun, literary* an immense tract; a boundless or empty expanse of space or time. • **vastly** *adverb*. • **vastness** *noun*. ◷ 16c: from Latin *vastus* desolate or huge; compare WASTE.

VAT or **Vat** /vat, viːeɪˈtiː/ ▷ *abbreviation, Brit* value-added tax.

vat ▷ *noun* **1** a large barrel or tank for storing or holding liquids, often used for fermentation, dyeing or tanning. **2** a liquid containing VAT DYE. ▷ *verb* (***vatted, vatting***) to put something into, or treat it in, a vat. ◷ Anglo-Saxon *fæt*.

vat dye ▷ *noun* an insoluble dye contained in a reduced, colourless, soluble liquid in which textiles are soaked, after which they take up the colour through oxidation when exposed to the air. • **vat-dyed** *adj*.

Vatican /ˈvatɪkən/ ▷ *noun* (*usually* **the Vatican**) **1** a collection of buildings on Vatican Hill in Rome, including the palace and official residence of the pope, set up as an independent papal state called **Vatican City** in 1929. **2** the authority of the pope. ◷ 16c: from Latin *Mons Vaticanus* Vatican Hill.

Vaticanism ▷ *noun* the system of theology and ecclesiastical government based on absolute papal authority. Compare ULTRAMONTANISM. • **Vaticanist** *noun*.

Vatman ▷ *noun, Brit colloq* an employee of the Customs and Excise Board responsible for administering, assessing and collecting VAT.

vaudeville /ˈvɔːdəvɪl, ˈvoʊ-/ ▷ *noun, N Amer, especially US* **1** variety entertainment (see VARIETY sense 4). **2** a music hall. • **vaudevillian** *adj, noun*. ◷ 18c: French, originally applied to 15c songs composed in *Vau de Vire* in Normandy.

vault¹ /vɔːlt/ ▷ *noun* **1** an arched roof or ceiling, especially in a church. **2** an underground chamber used for storage or as a burial tomb. **3** a wine cellar. **4** a fortified room for storing valuables, eg in a bank. **5** *poetic* the sky or heaven. ▷ *verb* (***vaulted, vaulting***) **1** to build something in the shape of an arch. **2** to provide (a building) with an arched roof or ceiling. ◷ 14c: from French *voute*, from Latin *volvere* to roll.

vault² /vɔːlt/ ▷ *verb* (***vaulted, vaulting***) *tr & intr* to spring or leap over something, especially assisted by the hands or a pole. ▷ *noun* an act of vaulting. ◷ 16c: from French *voulter*, from Latin *volvere* to roll.

vaulting¹ ▷ *adj* a series of vaults (see VAULT¹ *noun* 1) considered collectively.

vaulting² ▷ *adj* **1** for vaulting or relating to vaulting (see VAULT²). **2** especially referring to ambition or pride: excessive or immoderate.

vaulting-horse ▷ *noun* a padded wooden block on legs, vaulted over by gymnasts.

vaunt /vɔːnt/ ▷ *verb* (***vaunted, vaunting***) *tr & intr* to boast or behave boastfully about something. ▷ *noun* a boast. • **vaunter** *noun*. • **vaunting** *noun, adj*. • **vauntingly** *adverb*. ◷ 14c: from Latin *vanitare*, from *vanus* vain.

vavasour /ˈvavəsʊə(r)/ ▷ *noun, feudalism* a knight, noble, etc with vassals under him who is himself the vassal of a greater noble. ◷ 14c: French, from Latin *vavassor*, probably from *vassus vassorum* vassal of vassals.

vb ▷ *abbreviation* verb.

VC ▷ *abbreviation* **1** Vatican City. **2** vice-chancellor. **3** Victoria Cross.

VCR ▷ *abbreviation* video cassette recorder.

VD ▷ *abbreviation* venereal disease.

VDQS ▷ *abbreviation*: *vins délimités de qualité supérieure* (French), wines of superior quality from approved vineyards, the interim wine quality designation between VIN DE PAYS and APPELLATION CONTRÔLÉE.

VDU ▷ *abbreviation* visual display unit.

've /v/ ▷ *contraction* (usually after pronouns) have □ ***we've*** □ ***they've***.

veal ▷ *noun* the flesh of a calf, used as food. ◷ 14c: from French *veel*, from Latin *vitulus* calf.

Vectian /ˈvɛktɪən/ ▷ *adj, geol* referring or relating to the Isle of Wight or the specific geological formation which it is part of. ◷ 19c: from Latin *Vectis*, name given to the Isle of Wight.

vector /ˈvɛktə(r)/ ▷ *noun* **1** *math* a quantity which has both magnitude and direction, eg force, velocity, acceleration, often represented by an arrow pointing in an appropriate direction, whose length is proportional to its magnitude. Compare SCALAR, PARALLELOGRAM OF VECTORS. **2** *aeronautics* the course of an aircraft or missile. **3** *medicine* any agent, such as an insect, that is capable of transferring a PATHOGEN from one organism to another, eg from an animal to man, usually without itself contracting the disease, eg the vector of the malaria parasite is the ANOPHELES mosquito. **4** *biol* in genetic engineering: a vehicle used to transfer DNA from one organism to another to make RECOMBINANT DNA. **5** *computing* **a** a one-dimensional sequence of elements within a matrix; **b** such a sequence having a single identifying code or symbol, especially one acting as an INTERMEDIATE ADDRESS. ▷ *verb* (***vectored, vectoring***) to direct (an aircraft in flight) to the required destination, especially when the directions are given from the ground. ◷ 18c: Latin, meaning 'carrier'.

Veda /ˈveɪdə/ ▷ *noun* (***Vedas***) any one, or all of, four ancient holy books of the Hindus consisting of the **Rig-veda**, **Sama-veda**, **Yajur-veda** and **Athara-veda**. • **Vedist** *noun*. See also VEDIC. ◷ 18c: Sanskrit, meaning 'knowledge'.

vedalia /vɪˈdeɪlɪə/ ▷ *noun* (***vedalias***) an Australian ladybird used as a means of BIOLOGICAL CONTROL.

Vedanta /vɪˈdɑːntə, -də/ ▷ *noun* a system of Hindu philosophy founded on the VEDA, influenced mainly by the UPANISHADS. • **Vedantic** *adj*. ◷ 18c: Sanskrit, from *veda* VEDA + *anta* end.

VE day /viː iː deɪ/ ▷ *noun* Victory in Europe day, 8 May, the day marking the Allied victory in Europe in 1945.

Vedda /ˈvɛdə/ ▷ *noun* (***Veddas***) **1** an aboriginal people of Sri Lanka. **2** a member of this people. ◷ 17c: Sinhalese, meaning 'hunter'.

Vedic /ˈveɪdɪk/ ▷ *adj* relating to the Hindu VEDA. ▷ *noun* the old Sanskrit language used in the Vedas. ◷ 19c: from Sanskrit *veda* knowledge.

Vedist see under VEDA

veduta /veˈduːtə/ ▷ *noun* (***vedute*** /-teɪ/) *art* a painting depicting a panoramic view of a place, usually a city, in a topographically accurate and decorative manner, popular especially in the 18c. ◷ Early 20c: Italian, meaning 'view'.

vee ▷ *noun* (**vees**) **1** a representation of the twenty-second letter of the English alphabet, V. **2** an object or mark shaped like the letter V. **3** *sometimes in compounds* shaped like the letter V ◻ *vee-neck.* See also V[1].

veer ▷ *verb* (**veered**, **veering**) *intr* **1** to move abruptly in a different direction ◻ *The car veered off the road into the ditch.* **2** said of the wind: to change direction clockwise in the northern hemisphere and anticlockwise in the southern. **3** *naut* to change course, especially away from the wind. ▷ *noun* a change of direction. ⓒ 16c: from French *virer* to turn.

veg[1] /vɛdʒ/ ▷ *noun* (*plural* **veg**) *colloq* a vegetable or vegetables ◻ *a meal of meat and two veg.* ⓒ 19c: short for VEGETABLE.

veg[2] /vɛdʒ/ ▷ *verb* (**vegges**, **vegged**, **vegging**) *intr* (*usually* **veg out**) *colloq* to be inactive or engage in mindless activity, especially after a period of over-exertion ◻ *She vegges out every evening in front of the telly.* ⓒ 1980s: short for VEGETATE.

vegan /ˈviːgən/ ▷ *noun* someone who does not eat meat, fish, dairy products or any foods containing animal fats or extracts, such as eggs, cheese and honey, often also avoiding using wool, leather and other animal-based substances. ▷ *adj* **1** referring to or for vegans. **2** said of a meal or diet: excluding such foods. • **veganism** *noun.* Compare VEGETARIAN, LACTOVEGETARIAN. ⓒ 1940s: from *vegetarian* + -AN.

vegeburger /ˈvɛdʒɪbɜːgə(r)/ ▷ *noun* a flat cake resembling and served like a hamburger, made with vegetables, soy beans, etc instead of meat. ⓒ Late 20c: from VEGETARIAN, modelled on HAMBURGER.

vegetable /ˈvɛdʒtəbəl, ˈvɛdʒɪtəbəl/ ▷ *noun* **1 a** a plant or any of its parts, other than fruits and seeds, that is used for food, eg roots, tubers, stems or leaves; **b** the edible part of such a plant. **2** *loosely* used to refer to some fruits that are used for food, eg tomato, marrow. **3** *offensive, colloq* a person almost totally incapable of any physical or mental activity because of severe brain damage. **4** *derog, colloq* a dull uninteresting person. ▷ *adj* for, relating to, or composed of vegetables. ⓒ 14c: from Latin *vegetabilis*, from *vegetus* lively.

vegetable kingdom ▷ *noun* the division of natural objects which consists of vegetables or plants.

vegetable marrow see MARROW

vegetable oil ▷ *noun* any of various oils obtained from plants, used especially in cooking and cosmetics.

vegetable oyster see SALSIFY

vegetable wax ▷ *noun* a wax secreted by various plants that protects their surface from moisture loss.

vegetal /ˈvɛdʒɪtəl/ ▷ *adj* consisting of or relating to vegetables or to plant life in general. ⓒ 14c: from Latin *vegetalis*, from *vegetare* to animate.

vegetarian /vɛdʒɪˈtɛərɪən/ ▷ *noun* someone who does not eat meat or fish. ▷ *adj* **1** referring to or for vegetarians. **2** denoting food or a diet that contains no meat or fish. • **vegetarianism** *noun.* Compare LACTOVEGETARIAN, VEGAN. ⓒ 19c: from VEGETABLE.

vegetate /ˈvɛdʒɪteɪt/ ▷ *verb* (**vegetated**, **vegetating**) *intr* **1** said of a person: to live a dull inactive life. See also VEG[2]. **2** to live or grow as a vegetable. ⓒ 18c in sense 1; 17c in sense 2: from Latin *vegetare*, *vegetatum* to animate.

vegetation ▷ *noun* **1** *bot* a collective term for plants. **2** *bot* the plants of a particular area which may be very diverse or belong to just one or a few species, depending on climatic conditions, the nature of the soil and human activity.

vegetative ▷ *adj* **1** referring to plants or vegetation. **2** *biol* denoting asexual reproduction in plants or animals, as in bulbs, corms, yeasts, etc. **3** *bot* denoting a phase of plant growth as opposed to reproduction. **4** *biol* denoting unconscious or involuntary bodily functions as resembling the process of vegetable growth. • **vegetatively** *adverb.* • **vegetativeness** *noun.*

vegetative nervous system ▷ *noun* the nervous system that regulates involuntary bodily activity, such as the secretion of the glands, the beating of the heart, etc.

vegetative propagation ▷ *noun, bot* any form of asexual reproduction in plants, such as reproduction without the formation of seeds, giving rise to new plants known as clones which are genetically identical to the parent plant.

veggie or **vegie** /ˈvɛdʒɪ/ ▷ *noun, colloq* **1** a vegetarian. **2** a vegetable. Also written **veggy**.

vehemence /ˈvɪəməns, ˈviːhə-/ ▷ *noun* strong and forceful feeling.

vehement /ˈvɪəmənt, ˈviːhə-/ ▷ *adj* expressed with strong feeling or firm conviction; forceful; emphatic. • **vehemently** *adverb.* ⓒ 15c: from Latin *vehemens* eager.

vehicle /ˈviːɪkəl/ ▷ *noun* **1** a conveyance for transporting people or things, especially a self-powered one. **2** someone or something used as a means of communicating ideas or opinions ◻ *newspapers as vehicles for political propaganda.* **3** *medicine* a neutral substance in which a drug is mixed in order to be administered, eg a syrup. **4** a substance in which a pigment is transferred to a surface as paint, eg oil or water. ⓒ 17c: from Latin *vehere* to carry.

Vehicle Registration Document see LOGBOOK

vehicular /vəˈhɪkjʊlə(r)/ ▷ *adj* relating to or for the use of vehicles ◻ *no vehicular access.*

veil /veɪl/ ▷ *noun* **1** a fabric covering for a woman's head or face, forming part of traditional dress in some societies. **2** a covering of fine netting for a woman's head, which may be attached to a hat or headdress, worn for decoration or ceremonially, eg by a bride. **3** the hoodlike part of a nun's habit. **4** (**the veil**) *literary* the vocation of a nun. **5** anything that covers or obscures something ◻ *a veil of secrecy.* ▷ *verb* (**veiled**, **veiling**) **1** to cover something, or cover the face of someone, with a veil ◻ *She veiled herself before going out.* **2** to conceal or partly conceal; to disguise or obscure something ◻ *veiled his threats in pleasantries.* • **veiled** *adj* ◻ *veiled threats.* • **draw a veil over something** to conceal it discreetly; to avoid mentioning it. • **take the veil** to become a nun. ⓒ 13c: from French VEILE, from Latin *velum* curtain.

veiling ▷ *noun* **1** material for making veils. **2** in Islam: the custom of covering the face practised by women.

vein /veɪn/ ▷ *noun* **1** *anatomy* any blood vessel, apart from the PULMONARY VEIN, that carries deoxygenated blood back towards the heart. **2** *anatomy, loosely* any blood vessel. **3** a thin sheetlike deposit of one or more minerals, eg quartz, deposited in a fracture or joint in the surrounding rock. **4** a streak of different colour, eg in cheese. **5** in a leaf: any of a large number of thin branching tubes containing the vascular tissues. **6** in an insect: any of the tubes of chitin that stiffen and support the membranous structure of the wings. **7** a mood or tone ◻ *written in a sarcastic vein.* **8** a distinct characteristic present throughout; a streak. ▷ *verb* (**veined**, **veining**) to form veins or the appearance of veins in something. • **veined** *adj.* • **veinlet** *noun.* • **veiny** *adj.* ⓒ 14c: from French *veine*, from Latin *vena* vein.

vela *plural of* VELUM

velamen /vəˈleɪmən/ ▷ *noun* (**velamina** /-mɪnə/) *bot* a multi-layered covering of dead cells on some aerial roots. ⓒ Late 19c: Latin, from *velare* to cover.

velar /ˈviːlə(r)/ ▷ *adj* **1** referring to or attached to the VELUM. **2** *phonetics* said of a sound: produced by the back of the tongue brought close to, or in contact with, the soft palate. ▷ *noun, phonetics* a sound produced in this way, such as /k/ and /g/ .

velarize or **velarise** /ˈviːləraɪz/ ▷ *verb* (**velarized**, **velarizing**) to pronounce (a sound that is usually non-velar) with the back of the tongue brought close to the soft palate. • **velarization** *noun*.

Velcro /ˈvɛlkroʊ/ ▷ *noun, trademark* a fastening material consisting of two nylon surfaces, one of tiny hooks, the other of thin fibres, which bond tightly when pressed together but are easily pulled apart. ⓒ 1960s: from French *velours croché* hooked velvet.

veld or **veldt** /fɛlt, vɛlt/ ▷ *noun* a wide grassy plane with few or no trees, especially in S Africa. ⓒ 18c: Dutch, meaning 'field'.

veleta or **valeta** /vəˈliːtə/ ▷ *noun* (***veletas*** or ***valetas***) a ballroom dance or dance tune with a fast waltz-like rhythm. ⓒ Early 20c: Spanish, meaning 'weathercock'.

vellum /ˈvɛləm/ ▷ *noun* **1** a fine kind of parchment, originally made from calfskin. **2** a manuscript written on such parchment. **3** thick cream-coloured writing-paper resembling such parchment. ▷ *adj* made of, resembling or printed on vellum. ⓒ 15c: from French *velin*, from *veel* calf.

veloce /vəˈloʊtʃeɪ/ ▷ *adverb, adj, music* with great rapidity. ⓒ Italian, from Latin *velox* quick.

velocipede /vəˈlɒsɪpiːd/ ▷ *noun, historical* an early form of bicycle propelled by pushing of the rider's feet along the ground. ⓒ 19c: from French *vélocipède*, from Latin *velox, velocis* quick + *pes, pedis* foot.

velocity /vəˈlɒsɪtɪ/ ▷ *noun* (***velocities***) **1** *technical* rate of motion, ie distance per unit of time, in a particular direction, being a vector quantity. **2** *loosely* speed. Compare SPEED. ⓒ 16c: from Latin *velocitas*, from *velox* swift.

velodrome /ˈvɛlədroʊm/ ▷ *noun* a building containing a cycle-racing track. ⓒ Early 20c: French, from *vélo*, modelled on HIPPODROME.

velour or **velours** /vəˈlʊə(r)/ ▷ *noun* any fabric with a velvet-like pile, used especially for upholstery. Also *as adj*. ⓒ 18c: from French *velours* VELVET.

velouté /vəˈluːteɪ/ or **veloutée sauce** ▷ *noun, cookery* a smooth white sauce made with stock. ⓒ 19c: French, meaning 'velvety'.

velum /ˈviːləm/ ▷ *noun* (***vela*** /-lə/ or ***velums***) **1** an integument or membrane. **2** *anatomy* the SOFT PALATE. **3** the membrane joining the rim of a young toadstool with the stalk. • **velar** see separate entry. ⓒ 18c: Latin, meaning 'veil' or 'sail'.

velvet /ˈvɛlvət/ ▷ *noun* **1** a fabric, usually cotton, nylon or silk, with a very short soft closely woven pile on one side. **2** the soft skin that covers the growing antlers of deer and is rubbed off as they mature. ▷ *adj* **1** made of velvet. **2** soft or smooth like velvet. • **velvety** *adj*. • **on velvet** *colloq* in a comfortable position of safety or wealth. ⓒ 14c: from Latin *velvettum*, from *villus* tuft or shaggy hair.

velveteen /ˈvɛlvɪtiːn, -ˈtiːn/ ▷ *noun* cotton fabric with a velvet-like pile. Also *as adj* □ ***a velveteen dress***. ⓒ 18c.

velvet glove ▷ *noun* apparent gentleness or lenience concealing strength or firmness, especially with allusion to the phrase *an iron hand in a velvet glove*.

Ven. ▷ *abbreviation* Venerable.

vena /ˈviːnə/ ▷ *noun* (***venae*** /-niː/) *anatomy* a vein. ⓒ 14c: Latin, meaning 'vein'.

vena cava /ˈviːnə ˈkeɪvə/ ▷ *noun* (***venae cavae*** /-niː -viː/) *anatomy* either of the two large veins, the **superior vena cava** and the **inferior vena cava**, that carry deoxygenated blood to the right ATRIUM of the heart. ⓒ 16c: Latin, meaning 'hollow vein'.

venal /ˈviːnəl/ ▷ *adj* **1** said of a person: willing to be persuaded by corrupt means, especially bribery. **2** said of behaviour: dishonest; corrupt. • **venality** *noun*. • **venally** *adverb*. ⓒ 17c: from Latin *venum* goods for sale.

venation /vɪˈneɪʃən/ ▷ *noun* **1** *biol* the arrangement of veins in the wing of an insect. **2** *bot* the arrangement of veins in the leaf of a plant. **3** such veins collectively. • **venational** *adj*. ⓒ 19c: from Latin *vena* vein.

vend ▷ *verb* (***vended, vending***) to sell or offer (especially small wares) for sale. ⓒ 17c: from Latin *vendere* to sell.

vendace /ˈvɛndəs/ ▷ *noun* **1** a freshwater white fish found in lakes in SW Scotland. **2** a freshwater white fish found in lakes in NW England. ⓒ 18c: probably from French *vendese* dace.

vendee /vɛnˈdiː/ ▷ *noun* (***vendees***) *law* a buyer, especially of property.

vendetta /vɛnˈdɛtə/ ▷ *noun* (***vendettas***) **1** a bitter feud in which the family of a murdered person takes revenge by killing the murderer or one of their relatives. **2** any long-standing bitter feud or quarrel. ⓒ 19c: Italian, from Latin *vindicta* revenge.

vendible /ˈvɛndɪbəl/ ▷ *adj* referring to something that may be sold, offered for sale or that is easily marketable. ▷ *noun* something that is for sale. • **vendibility** *noun*.

vending machine ▷ *noun* a coin-operated machine that dispenses small articles such as snacks, condoms, cigarettes. ⓒ 19c.

vendor or (*rarely*) **vender** /ˈvɛndə(r)/ *noun* **1** *law* a seller, especially of property. **2** a VENDING MACHINE.

veneer /vəˈnɪə(r)/ ▷ *noun* **1** a thin layer of a fine material, especially wood, fixed to the surface of an inferior material to give an attractive finish. **2** a false or misleading external appearance, especially of a favourable quality □ ***a veneer of respectability***. ▷ *verb* (***veneered, veneering***) to put a veneer on something. • **veneerer** *noun*. • **veneering** *noun*. ⓒ 18c: from German *furnieren*, from French *fornir* to furnish.

venepuncture or **venipuncture** /ˈvɛnɪpʌŋktʃə(r)/ ▷ *noun, medicine* the puncturing of a vein with a hypodermic needle in order to draw off a sample of blood or inject a drug. ⓒ 1920s: from Latin *vena* vein + PUNCTURE.

venerable /ˈvɛnərəbəl/ ▷ *adj* **1** deserving to be greatly respected or revered, especially on account of age or religious association. **2** (**Venerable**) **a** *C of E* given as a title to an archdeacon; **b** *RC Church* given as a title to a person due to be declared a saint. • **venerableness** *noun*. • **venerably** *adverb*. ⓒ 15c: from Latin *venerabilis*, from *venerari* to revere.

venerate /ˈvɛnəreɪt/ ▷ *verb* (***venerated, venerating***) to regard someone or something with deep respect or awe; to revere someone or something. • **veneration** *noun*. ⓒ 17c: from Latin *venerari, veneratus* to adore or revere.

venereal /vəˈnɪərɪəl/ ▷ *adj* **1** said of a disease or infection: transmitted by sexual intercourse. **2** relating to, resulting from, or for the treatment of such diseases. ⓒ 15c: from Latin *venereus*, from *Venus* Roman goddess of love.

venereal disease ▷ *noun, medicine* (abbreviation **VD**) former name for a SEXUALLY TRANSMITTED DISEASE.

venereology /vənɪərɪˈɒlədʒɪ/ ▷ *noun* the study and treatment of venereal diseases. • **venereological** *adj*. • **venereologist** *noun*. ⓒ 19c.

venesection /ˈvɛnɪsɛkʃən/ ▷ *noun* the surgical incision of a vein. Also called PHLEBOTOMY. ⓒ 17c: from Latin *vena* vein.

Venetian /vəˈniːʃən/ ▷ *adj* relating or belonging to Venice, a city in NE Italy. ▷ *noun* **1** a citizen or inhabitant of, or person born in, Venice. **2** a VENETIAN BLIND. ⓒ 15c: from Latin *Venetia* Venice.

Venetian blind ▷ *noun* a window blind consisting of horizontal slats strung together, one beneath the other, and tilted to let in or shut out light. ⓒ 19c.

vengeance /ˈvɛndʒəns/ ▷ *noun* punishment inflicted as a revenge; retribution. • **with a vengeance 1**

forcefully or violently. **2** to a great degree. ◷ 13c: French, from Latin *vindicare* to avenge.

vengeful ▻ *adj* **1** eager for revenge. **2** carried out in revenge. ● **vengefully** *adverb*. ● **vengefulness** *noun*. ◷ 16c: from obsolete *venge* to avenge.

venial sin /ˈviːnɪəl —/ ▻ *noun* a sin that is pardonable or excusable. Compare MORTAL SIN. ◷ 13c: from Latin *venialis* pardonable, from *venia* pardon.

venipuncture see VENEPUNCTURE

venison /ˈvɛnɪsən, -zən/ ▻ *noun* the flesh of a deer, used as food. ◷ 13c: from French *venaison*, from Latin *venari* to hunt.

venite /vɪˈnaɪtɪ/ ▻ *noun* the 95th Psalm, beginning *Venite exultemus* O come, let us rejoice. ◷ 13c.

Venn diagram ▻ *noun, math* a diagram that is used to illustrate the relationships between mathematical sets, which are denoted by circles, with intersecting sets being indicated by two or more overlapping circles, and a subset being shown as a smaller circular area within a circle. The whole diagram is enclosed by a rectangle representing the universal set. ◷ 19c: named after John Venn (1834–1923), British logician.

venom /ˈvɛnəm/ ▻ *noun* **1** a poisonous liquid that some creatures, including scorpions and certain snakes, inject in a bite or sting. **2** spitefulness, especially in language or tone of voice. ● **venomed** *adj*. ◷ 13c: from French *venim*, from Latin *venenum* poison.

venomous /ˈvɛnəməs/ ▻ *adj* **1** said of snake, etc: **a** having the ability to poison; poisonous; **b** inflicting venom. **2** said of a person or their behaviour, etc: spiteful. ● **venomously** *adverb*. ● **venomousness** *noun*.

venose /ˈviːnoʊs/ ▻ *adj* with very marked veins; veiny. ◷ 17c: from Latin *venosus* veiny.

venous /ˈviːnəs/ ▻ *adj* **1** relating to or contained in veins. **2** said of blood: deoxygenated and, in humans, dark red in colour. ● **venosity** /viːˈnɒsɪtɪ/ *noun*. ◷ 17c: from Latin *vena* vein.

vent¹ ▻ *noun* a slit in a garment, especially upwards from the hem at the back, for style or ease of movement. ◷ 15c: from French *fente* slit.

vent² ▻ *noun* **1** an opening that allows air, gas or liquid into or out of a confined space. **2** the passage inside a volcano through which lava and gases escape. **3** *biol* the anus of a bird or other small animal. **4** a chimney flue. **5** the opening in a parachute canopy through which air escapes at a controlled rate. ▻ *verb* (***vented***, ***venting***) **1** to make a vent in something. **2** to let something in or out through a vent. **3** to release and express (especially emotion) freely □ ***vented his frustration shaking his fists***. **4** *intr* said of a beaver or otter: to take breath or rise for breath. ● **give vent to something** to express one's feelings or emotions openly. ◷ 16c: from French *éventer* to expose to air.

venter /ˈvɛntə(r)/ ▻ *noun* **1** *anatomy, zool* **a** the abdomen; **b** a swelling or protuberance. **2** *bot* the upper side or surface of a leaf, etc. ◷ 16c: Latin, meaning 'abdomen'.

ventil /ˈvɛntɪl/ ▻ *noun, music* **1** a valve in a wind instrument. **2** a valve in an organ for controlling the wind supply to various stops. ◷ 19c: German, from Latin *ventile* shutter, from *ventus* wind.

ventilate /ˈvɛntɪleɪt/ ▻ *verb* (***ventilated***, ***ventilating***) **1** to allow fresh air to circulate throughout (a room, building, etc). **2** to cause (blood) to take up oxygen. **3** to supply air to (the lungs). **4** to expose (an idea, etc) to public examination or discussion. ● **ventilable** *adj*. ● **ventilation** *noun*. ● **ventilative** *adj*. ◷ 15c: from Latin *ventilare*, *ventilatum* to fan, from *ventus* wind.

ventilator ▻ *noun* **1** a device that circulates or draws in fresh air. **2** a machine that ventilates the lungs of a person whose respiratory system is damaged.

ventral /ˈvɛntrəl/ ▻ *adj* **1** denoting the lower surface of an animal that walks on four legs, of any invertebrate, or of a structure such as a leaf or wing. **2** denoting the front surface of the body of an animal that walks upright, eg a human being. **3** denoting a structure that is situated on or just beneath such a surface. Compare DORSAL. ● **ventrally** *adverb*. ◷ 18c: from Latin *venter* VENTER.

ventral fin ▻ *noun* either of the paired fins on the belly of a fish.

ventricle /ˈvɛntrɪkəl/ ▻ *noun, anatomy* **1** in mammals: either of the two lower chambers of the heart which have thick muscular walls. **2** in vertebrates: any of several cavities within the brain, connecting it to the spinal cord, and containing cerebrospinal fluid. ● **ventricular** *adj*. ◷ 14c: from Latin *ventriculus*, diminutive of *venter* abdomen.

ventricose /ˈvɛntrɪkoʊs/ ▻ *adj, bot, zool* distended or swollen in the middle, at the side or round the base. ◷ 18c: from Latin *venter* abdomen.

ventriloquism /vɛnˈtrɪləkwɪzəm/ ▻ *noun* the art of speaking in a way that makes the sound appear to come from elsewhere, especially a dummy's mouth. ● **ventriloquist** *noun*. ◷ 18c: from Latin *venter* abdomen + *loqui* to speak.

ventriloquize or **ventriloquise** /vɛnˈtrɪləkwaɪz/ ▻ *verb* (***ventriloquized***, ***ventriloquizing***) *intr* to perform ventriloquism.

venture /ˈvɛntʃə(r)/ ▻ *noun* **1** an exercise or operation involving danger or uncertainty. **2** a business project, especially one involving risk or speculation. **3** an enterprise attempted. ▻ *verb* (***ventured***, ***venturing***) **1** *tr & intr* to be so bold as to; to dare □ ***ventured to criticize the chairman***. **2** to put forward or present (a suggestion, etc) in the face of possible opposition □ ***ventured a different opinion*** □ ***ventured that it might be the wrong decision***. **3** to expose someone or something to danger or chance; to risk. ◷ 15c: shortening of ADVENTURE.

■ **venture on something** to attempt something dangerous.

■ **venture out** or **forth** *intr* to dare to go out, especially outdoors □ ***reluctant to venture out in bad weather***.

venture capital ▻ *noun* money supplied by individual investors or business organizations for a new, especially speculative, business enterprise. Also called **risk capital**. ◷ 1940s.

venturer ▻ *noun* **1** someone who takes part in a venture or enterprise. **2** *historical* a participant in a trading scheme.

Venture Scout ▻ *noun* a member of the senior branch of the Scout movement, for 16- to 20-year-olds. ● **Venture Scouting** *noun*. ◷ 1960s: prior to that known as a Rover Scout.

venturesome ▻ *adj* **1** prepared to take risks; enterprising. **2** involving danger; risky.

Venturi and **Venturi tube** /vɛnˈtjʊərɪ —/ ▻ *noun* (***Venturis*** or ***Venturi tubes***) a tube or duct which is narrow in the middle and wider at both ends, used in measuring the flow rate of fluids, as a means of accelerating air flow, or to alter pressure. ◷ 19c: named after G B Venturi (1746–1822), Italian physicist.

venue /ˈvɛnjuː/ ▻ *noun* **1** the chosen location for a sports event, a concert or other entertainment. **2** *law* **a** the place where a court case is to be tried; **b** the district from which the jurors are chosen. **3** a meeting-place. ◷ 19c in sense 1; 14c in obsolete sense 'a coming on, in order to attack': from Latin *venire* to come.

venule /ˈvɛnjuːl/ ▻ *noun, biol* **1** a branch of a vein in an insect's wing. **2** any of the small-calibre blood vessels into which the capillaries empty and which join up to form veins. ◷ 19c: from Latin *venula*, diminutive of *vena* vein.

Venus /'viːnəs/ ▷ *noun* **1** *astron* the second planet from the Sun, clearly visible from the Earth as a bright morning and evening star, its orbit lying between those of Mercury and Earth. **2** a beautiful woman. ◎ Anglo-Saxon, from the Latin name of the goddess of love, from *venus, veneris* desire.

Venus flytrap ▷ *noun* an insectivorous plant native to the bogs of N and S Carolina with leaves consisting of two parts hinged together which shut when an insect touches the inner surface of the leaf, trapping the insect.

Venusian /vɪ'njuːzɪən/ ▷ *noun, science fiction* an inhabitant of the planet VENUS, or their language. ▷ *adj* belonging or relating to, or supposedly coming from, the planet Venus.

Venus's comb ▷ *noun* an umbelliferous plant with long-beaked fruits set like comb teeth.

Venus's flowerbasket ▷ *noun* a deep-sea sponge with a skeleton of glassy spicules.

veracious /və'reɪʃəs/ ▷ *adj, formal* truthful. • **veraciously** *adverb*. ◎ 17c.

veracity /və'rasɪtɪ/ ▷ *noun, formal* truthfulness. ◎ 17c: from Latin *verax, veracis*, from *verus* true.

veracity

A word often confused with this one is **voracity**.

veranda or **verandah** /və'randə/ ▷ *noun* (***verandas*** or ***verandahs***) a sheltered terrace attached to a house or other building. ◎ 18c: from Hindi *varanda*, probably from Portuguese *varanda* balcony.

veratrine /'vɛrətriːn, -trɪn/ ▷ *noun* a toxic compound obtained from SABADILLA seeds, formerly used as a counter-irritant in the treatment of neuralgia and rheumatism. ◎ 19c: from Latin *verax*, *veratum* hellebore + INE².

verb ▷ *noun* (abbreviation **vb, v**) a word or group of words that belongs to a grammatical class denoting an action, experience, occurrence or state, eg *do, feel, happen, love*. See also AUXILIARY VERB. ◎ 14c: from Latin *verbum* word.

verbal ▷ *adj* **1** relating to or consisting of words □ *verbal abuse*. **2** spoken, not written □ *verbal communication*. **3** *grammar* relating to or derived from a verb or verbs. **4** literal; word-for-word. **5** talkative; articulate. ▷ *noun* **1** a word, especially a noun, derived from a verb. **2** *Brit slang* an oral statement, especially an arrested suspect's confession of guilt, made to the police, or claimed by them to have been made. **3** *Brit slang* an insult; abuse. • **verbally** *adverb* □ *communicated with them verbally*.

verbalism ▷ *noun* excessive attention paid to words used, rather than to ideas expressed, especially in literary criticism; literalism. • **verbalist** *noun*.

verbalize or **verbalise** ▷ *verb* (***verbalized, verbalizing***) **1** to express (ideas, thoughts, etc) in words. **2** *intr* to use too many words; to be verbose. **3** to turn (any word) into a verb. • **verbalization** *noun*.

verbal diarrhoea see LOGORRHOEA sense 2

verbal noun ▷ *noun* a form of a verb that functions as a noun, eg '*to err* is human' and '*swimming* keeps you fit'. Compare GERUND.

verbatim /vɜː'beɪtɪm/ ▷ *adj, adverb* using exactly the same words; word-for-word. ◎ 15c: Latin.

verbena /vɜː'biːnə/ ▷ *noun* (***verbenas***) **1** any of a group of plants of mild and tropical climates with clusters of fragrant white, pink, red or purplish tubular flowers, used in herbal medicine and cosmetics. **2** any of various related plants, especially the **lemon verbena**, native to Chile with lemon-scented foliage and small two-lipped purplish flowers. ◎ 16c: Latin, meaning 'sacred bough', referring in Roman times to leaves of certain plants, such as olive, myrtle, laurel, etc, which had a sacred character and were used in religious ceremonies.

verbiage /'vɜːbɪɪdʒ/ ▷ *noun* **1** the use of language that is wordy or needlessly complicated, and often meaningless. **2** such language. ◎ 18c: from French *verbeier* to chatter.

verbose /vɜː'bous/ ▷ *adj* using or containing too many words; boringly or irritatingly long-winded. • **verbosely** *adverb*. • **verboseness** or **verbosity** /vɜː'bɒsɪtɪ/ *noun*. ◎ 17c: from Latin *verbosus*, from *verbum* word.

verboten /fə'boutən; *German* fɛə'boːtən/ ▷ *adj* forbidden; not allowed. ◎ Early 20c: German.

verdant /'vɜːdənt/ ▷ *adj* **1** covered with lush green grass or vegetation. **2** of a rich green colour. **3** naïve or unsophisticated; gullible; green. • **verdancy** *noun*. • **verdantly** *adverb*. ◎ 16c: from French *verdeant*, from Latin *viridis* green.

verd-antique /vɜːd—/ ▷ *noun* a dark-green stone, a BRECCIA of serpentine containing calcite, a green porphyry, or other similar stones. ◎ 18c: French, meaning 'antique green'.

verdelho /və'dɛljuː/ ▷ *noun* (***verdelhos***) **1** a white Madeira. **2** the white grape from which it is made, grown originally in Madeira, now also in Portugal, Sicily, Australia and S Africa. ◎ 19c: Portuguese.

verdict ▷ *noun* **1** a decision arrived at by a jury in a court of law. **2** any decision, opinion or judgement. See also FORMAL VERDICT, OPEN VERDICT. ◎ 13c: from Latin *veredictum* truly said.

verdigris /'vɜːdɪgriː, -griːs/ ▷ *noun, chem* **1** a blueish-green coating of basic copper salts, especially copper carbonate, that forms as a result of corrosion when copper, brass or bronze surfaces are exposed to air and moisture for long periods. **2** basic copper acetate. ◎ 14c: from French *verd de Grece* green of Greece.

verdure /'vɜːdjə(r), -dʒə(r)/ ▷ *noun, literary* **1** lush green vegetation. **2** the rich greenness of such vegetation. • **verdured** covered with verdure. • **verdureless** *adj*. • **verdurous** *adj*. ◎ 14c: from French *verd* green, from Latin *viridis* green.

Verey light see VERY LIGHT

verge¹ /vɜːdʒ/ ▷ *noun* **1** a limit, boundary or border. **2** a strip of grass bordering a road. **3** a point or stage immediately beyond or after which something exists or occurs □ *on the verge of tears*. **4** *archit* a roof projecting beyond the gable. ▷ *verb* (***verged, verging***) to serve as the border or boundary of something. ◎ 16c in sense 1, which referred to the area of jurisdiction of the holder of an office symbolized by a rod; 15c, meaning 'a rod as an emblem of office': French, from Latin *virga* rod.

■ **verge on something** to be close to being or becoming something specified □ *enthusiasm verging on obsession*.

verge² /vɜːdʒ/ ▷ *verb* (***verged, verging***) *intr* to slope or incline in a specified direction. Compare CONVERGE, DIVERGE. ◎ 17c: from Latin *vergere* to bend.

■ **verge to** or **towards something** to move or tend to move towards it.

verger /vɜːdʒə(r)/ ▷ *noun, chiefly C of E* **1** a church official who assists the minister and acts as caretaker. **2** an official who carries the ceremonial staff of a bishop or other dignitary. ◎ 15c: from Latin *virga* rod; compare VERGE¹.

verglas /'vɛəglɑː/ ▷ *noun* a thin transparent coating of ice on eg rock. ◎ 19c: French, from *verre* glass + *glas*, related to *glace* ice.

veridical /və'rɪdɪkəl/ ▷ *adj* **1** coinciding with fact. **2** said of a dream or vision: corresponding exactly with what has happened or with what happens later. • **veridicality** *noun*. ◎ 17c: from Latin *veridicus*, from *verus* true + *dicere* to say.

verify /ˈvɛrɪfaɪ/ ▷ *verb* (***verifies, verified, verifying***) **1** to check or confirm the truth or accuracy of something. **2** to assert or prove the truth of something. **3** *law* to testify to the truth of something; to support (a statement). ● **verifiability** *noun*. ● **verifiable** *adj*. ● **verification** *noun*. ● **verifier** *noun*. ⓒ 14c: from Latin *verus* true.

verily /ˈvɛrɪlɪ/ ▷ *adverb, old use* truly; really. ⓒ 13c: related to VERY.

verisimilitude /vɛrɪsɪˈmɪlɪtʃuːd/ ▷ *noun, formal* **1** appearing to be real or true. **2** a statement or proposition that sounds true but may not be. ● **verisimilar** *adj* probable; likely. ⓒ 17c: from French, from Latin *verus* true + *similis* like.

verism /ˈvɛrɪzəm, ˈvɪər-/ ▷ *noun, art history* **1** use of everyday contemporary material, including what is ugly or sordid, in art and literature; a form of REALISM (sense 2). **2** the theory supporting this. ● **verist** *adj, noun*. ● **veristic** *adj*. ⓒ 19c: from Latin *verus* true.

verismo /vɛˈrɪzmoʊ/ ▷ *noun, music* a style of opera drawing on themes from everyday life, especially of certain Italian operas of the early 20c. ⓒ Early 20c: Italian.

veritable /ˈvɛrɪtəbəl/ ▷ *adj, formal* accurately described as such; real □ ***a veritable genius!*** ● **veritably** *adverb*. ⓒ 15c: French, from Latin *verus* true.

vérité see CINÉMA VÉRITÉ

verity /ˈvɛrɪtɪ/ ▷ *noun* (***verities***) **1** a true statement, especially one of fundamental wisdom or importance; a maxim. **2** truthfulness. ⓒ 14c: from French *vérité*, from Latin *veritas*.

verjuice /ˈvɜːdʒuːs/ ▷ *noun* **1** the acidic juice of unripe fruit. **2** sourness; bitterness. ⓒ 14c: from French *verjus*, from *vert* green + *jus* juice.

verkrampte /fəˈkramptə/ *historical* in South Africa: ▷ *adj* referring to rigidly conservative political attitudes, especially with regard to apartheid and particularly those of an Afrikaner nationalist. ▷ *noun* someone with such attitudes. ⓒ 1960s: Afrikaans, meaning 'restricted'.

verligte /fəˈlɪxtə/ *historical* in South Africa: ▷ *adj* referring to liberal, politically enlightened attitudes, especially with regard to apartheid and particularly those of an Afrikaner nationalist. ▷ *noun* someone with such attitudes. ⓒ 1960s: Afrikaans, meaning 'enlightened'.

vermeil /ˈvɜːmeɪl/ ▷ *noun* **1** gilt bronze or silver gilt. **2** bright red; scarlet; vermilion. ▷ *adj* referring to or having this colour. ⓒ 14c: French, from Latin *vermiculus* small worm.

vermes *plural of* VERMIS

vermi- /vɜːmɪ-, vəˈmɪ-/ ▷ *combining form, denoting* worm. ⓒ From Latin *vermis* worm.

vermian see under VERMIS

vermicelli /vɜːmɪˈtʃɛlɪ, -ˈsɛlɪ/ ▷ *noun* **1** pasta in very thin strands, thinner than spaghetti. **2** (*also* **chocolate vermicelli**) tiny splinters of chocolate used for decorating desserts and cakes. ⓒ 17c: Italian, meaning 'little worms'.

vermicide /ˈvɜːmɪsaɪd/ ▷ *noun* a worm-killing agent.

vermicular /vɜːˈmɪkjʊlə(r)/ ▷ *adj* **1** resembling a worm in movement or form. **2** *pathol* relating to or caused by intestinal worms. **3** *archit* vermiculate. ⓒ 17c: from Latin *vermiculus*, diminutive of *vermis* worm.

vermiculate /vɜːˈmɪkjʊlət/ and **vermiculated** ▷ *adj* **1** *archit* decorated with irregular shallow channels like worm tracks. **2** worm-eaten.

vermiculite /vɜːˈmɪkjʊlaɪt/ ▷ *noun* an altered mica that curls before a blowpipe flame and expands greatly at high temperature, forming a water-absorbent substance. This material is used as a base in which seed plants are grown and also used as insulating material.

vermiculture ▷ *noun* the farming of earthworms, eg as bait for fishing.

vermiform ▷ *adj* like a worm; worm-shaped. ⓒ 18c.

vermiform appendix ▷ *noun, anatomy* a small blind tube leading off the CAECUM, part of the large intestine. Usually shortened to **appendix**.

vermilion /vəˈmɪlɪən/ ▷ *noun* **1** a bright scarlet colour. **2** a pigment of this colour consisting of sulphide of mercury; cinnabar. ▷ *adj* referring to or having this colour. ⓒ 13c: from French *vermeillon*, from VERMEIL.

vermin /ˈvɜːmɪn/ ▷ *singular or plural noun* **1** a collective name for wild animals that spread disease or generally cause a nuisance, especially rats and other rodents. **2** detestable people. ● **verminous** *adj* **1** like vermin; parasitic; vile. **2** infested with vermin. ⓒ 14c: from Latin *vermis* worm.

vermis /ˈvɜːmɪs/ ▷ *noun* (***vermes*** /-miːz/) *anatomy* a wormlike structure, such as the **vermis cerebelli**, the central lobe of the cerebellum. ● **vermian** *adj*. ⓒ 19c: Latin, meaning 'worm'.

vermouth /ˈvɜːməθ, vəˈmuːθ/ ▷ *noun* an alcoholic drink consisting of wine flavoured with aromatic herbs, originally wormwood. ⓒ 19c: French, from German *Wermut* wormwood.

vernacular /vəˈnakjʊlə(r)/ ▷ *noun* (*usually* **the vernacular**) **1** the native language of a country or people, as opposed to a foreign language that is also in use. **2** the form of a language as commonly spoken, as opposed to the formal or literary language. **3** the language or jargon of a particular group. **4** *humorous* slang or indecent language. ▷ *adj* **1** referring to or in the vernacular. **2** local; native □ ***vernacular architecture***. ● **vernacularly** *adverb*. ⓒ 17c: from Latin *vernaculus* native.

vernal /ˈvɜːnəl/ ▷ *adj* **1** relating to or appropriate to spring; happening or appearing in spring. **2** *poetic* youthful. ● **vernally** *adverb*. ⓒ 16c: from Latin *vernalis*, from *vernus* referring to spring, from *ver* spring.

vernal equinox ▷ *noun, astron* spring equinox.

vernalization or **vernalisation** ▷ *noun, bot* the process by which germinating seeds or seedlings are exposed to low temperatures in order to ensure that they flower subsequently. ⓒ 1930s: from Russian *yarovizatsiya*, translated and modelled on VERNAL.

vernation /vɜːˈneɪʃən/ ▷ *noun* the arrangement of the leaves in a bud. ⓒ 18c: from Latin *vernare* to become springlike.

vernicle /ˈvɜːnɪkəl/ ▷ *noun, RC Church* a VERONICA² (sense 1). ⓒ 14c: from French *veronicle*, from Latin *veronica*, referring to St Veronica.

vernier /ˈvɜːnɪə(r)/ ▷ *noun* a small sliding device on some measuring instruments, eg barometers and theodolites, used to measure fractions of units. ⓒ 18c: named after Pierre Vernier (1580–1637), French mathematician.

veronica¹ /vəˈrɒnɪkə/ ▷ *noun* (***veronicas***) a plant of the foxglove family, native to temperate and cold regions, with small blue, pink or white flowers, including the SPEEDWELL. ⓒ 16c: Latin, from the name Veronica.

veronica² /vəˈrɒnɪkə/ ▷ *noun* (***veronicas***) **1** *RC Church* **a** a cloth bearing the face of Christ; **b** a similar representation of the face of Christ; **c** a medal or badge bearing this, worn by pilgrims. **2** *bullfighting* a movement in which the matador slowly swings the open cape away from the charging bull, encouraging him to follow it. Also called **vernicle** or **sudarium**. ⓒ 1920s in sense 2; 18c in sense 1: from the name of St Veronica, on whose handkerchief an impression of Christ's face is believed to have miraculously appeared after His face was wiped with it on His way to Calvary.

verruca /vəˈruːkə/ ▷ *noun* (***verrucas*** or ***verrucae*** /-ˈruːsiː/) **1** *pathol* a wart, especially one on the sole of the foot. **2** *bot* a wartlike growth. ● **verrucose** /ˈvɛrʊkoʊs, -vəˈruː-/ *adj*. ● **verrucous** /ˈvɛrʊkəs, vəˈruː-/ *adj*. ⓒ 16c: Latin, meaning 'wart'.

versant /ˈvɜːsənt/ ▻ *noun* the general slope of land. ◷ 19c: French, from *verser* to turn over, from Latin *versare*.

versatile /ˈvɜːsətaɪl/ ▻ *adj* **1** adapting easily to different tasks. **2** having numerous uses or abilities. **3** *bot, zool* moving freely on a support ▫ *versatile antler.* • **versatilely** *adverb.* • **versatileness** or **versatility** *noun.* ◷ 17c: from Latin *versatilis*, from *vertere* to turn.

verse ▻ *noun* **1** a division of a poem; a stanza. **2** poetry, as opposed to prose. **3** a poem. **4** a division of a song. **5** any of the numbered subdivisions of the chapters of the Bible. ◷ Anglo-Saxon *fers*, from Latin *versus* line or row.

versed ▻ *adj* (*always* **versed in something**) familiar with it or skilled in it ▫ *well versed in chemistry.*

versed sine ▻ *noun, math* a trigonometrical function of an angle equal to one minus the cosine. Often shortened to **versin** or **versine** /ˈvɜːsaɪn/.

versicle /ˈvɜːsɪkəl/ ▻ *noun* **1** in liturgy: a verse said or sung by a minister and responded to by the congregation. **2** a short verse. • **versicular** /vɜːˈsɪkjʊlə/ *adj.* ◷ 14c: from Latin *versiculus*, diminutive of *versus*.

versicoloured /ˈvɜːsɪkʌləd/ ▻ *adj* diversely or changeably coloured. ◷ 18c: from Latin *versicolor*, from *vertere, versum* to change + *color* colour.

versify /ˈvɜːsɪfaɪ/ ▻ *verb* (***versifies, versified, versifying***) **1** *intr* to write poetry. **2** to express something as, or turn it into, a poem. • **versification** *noun.* • **versifier** *noun.* ◷ 14c: from Latin *versificare* to put into verse.

versin or **versine** see under VERSED SINE

version /ˈvɜːʃən/ ▻ *noun* any of several types or forms in which a thing exists or is available, eg a particular edition or translation of a book, or one person's account of an incident. • **versional** *adj.* ◷ 16c: from Latin *versio, versionis*, from *vertere* to turn.

vers libre /vɛə ˈliːbrə; *French* vɛʀ libʀ/ ▻ *noun* (***vers libres*** /vɛə ˈlibrə; *French* vɛʀ libʀ/) FREE VERSE. • **verslibrist** /vɛəˈliːbrɪst/ *noun* a writer of FREE VERSE.

verso /ˈvɜːsoʊ/ ▻ *noun* (***versos***) *printing* **1** the back of a loose sheet of printed paper. **2** the left-hand page of two open pages. Compare RECTO. ◷ 19c: Latin, from *verso folio* turned leaf.

versus /ˈvɜːsəs/ ▻ *prep* **1** (abbreviation **vs, v**) in a contest or lawsuit: against. **2** *colloq* in comparison to. ◷ 15c: Latin.

vertebra /ˈvɜːtəbrə/ ▻ *noun* (***vertebrae*** /-breɪ, -briː/) *anatomy* in vertebrates: any of the small bones or cartilaginous segments that form the backbone, each vertebra containing a central canal through which the spinal cord passes. • **vertebral** *adj.* ◷ 17c: Latin, from *vertere* to turn.

vertebral column ▻ *noun* the SPINE.

vertebrate /ˈvɜːtəbreɪt, -brɪt/ ▻ *noun, zool* any animal, including fish, amphibians, reptiles, birds and mammals, that has a backbone consisting of bony or cartilaginous vertebrae enclosing a spinal cord. ▻ *adj* relating to an animal that has a backbone. ◷ 19c.

vertebration /vɜːtəˈbreɪʃən/ ▻ *noun* division into vertebrae or vertebra-like segments.

vertex /ˈvɜːtɛks/ ▻ *noun* (***vertexes*** or ***vertices*** /-tɪsiːz/) **1** the highest point; the peak or summit. **2** *geom* **a** the point opposite the base of a geometric figure, eg the pointed tip of a cone; **b** the point where the two sides forming an angle meet in a POLYGON, or where three or more surfaces meet in a POLYHEDRON; **c** the intersection of a curve with its axis. **3** *astron* the ZENITH. **4** *anatomy* the crown of the head. ◷ 16c: Latin, meaning 'summit' or 'whirlpool'.

vertical /ˈvɜːtɪkəl/ ▻ *adj* **1** perpendicular to the horizon; upright. **2** running from top to bottom, not side to side. **3** referring to a vertex or at a vertex. **4** relating to, involving or running through all levels within a hierarchy, all stages of a process, etc, rather than just one. ▻ *noun* a vertical line or direction. • **vertically** *adverb.* • **verticality** or **verticalness** *noun.*

vertical angles ▻ *plural noun, geom* opposite angles, which are equal to each other, formed by intersecting lines.

vertical circle ▻ *noun* a GREAT CIRCLE of the heavens passing through the ZENITH and the NADIR.

vertical integration ▻ *noun, commerce* a business situation in which a company expands by buying up its suppliers or its customers or both, thus controlling all the processes of production, from raw materials through to sale of the final product.

vertically challenged ▻ *adj, euphemistic* of less than average height.

vertical take-off ▻ *noun* a take-off by an aircraft directly upwards from a stationary position. See also VTOL.

verticil /ˈvɜːtɪsɪl/ ▻ *noun, bot* a set of parts arranged in a circle around an axis. • **verticillate** /vəˈtɪsɪlət/ *adj.* ◷ 18c: from Latin *verticillus*, diminutive of *vertex* VERTEX.

vertiginous /vɜːˈtɪdʒɪnəs/ ▻ *adj* **1** so high or whirling as to bring on vertigo; dizzying. **2** relating to vertigo. • **vertiginously** *adverb.* • **vertiginousness** *noun.*

vertigo /ˈvɜːtɪgoʊ/ ▻ *noun* (***vertigos, vertigoes*** or ***vertigines*** /vɜːˈtɪdʒɪniːz/) a whirling sensation felt when the sense of balance is disturbed; dizziness; giddiness. ◷ 16c: Latin, meaning 'turning', from *vertere* to turn.

vertu see VIRTU

vervain /ˈvɜːveɪn/ ▻ *noun* a wild VERBENA native to Europe, Asia and N Africa having square stems, opposite leaves and small white, lilac or purple flowers borne in long slender spikes, formerly used medicinally and believed to have magical powers. ◷ 14c: from French *vervaine*, from Latin *verbena* VERBENA.

verve ▻ *noun* great liveliness or enthusiasm, especially that which animates a poet or artist. ◷ 17c: French, meaning 'loquaciousness', from Latin *verba* words.

vervet /ˈvɜːvɪt/ ▻ *noun* an African guenon monkey. ◷ 19c: French.

very /ˈvɛrɪ/ ▻ *adverb* **1** to a high degree or extent ▫ *very kind.* **2** (used with *own, same* and with superlative adjectives) absolutely; truly ▫ *my very own room* ▫ *the very same day* ▫ *my very best effort.* ▻ *adj* (used for emphasis) **1** absolute ▫ *the very top.* **2** precise; actual ▫ *this very minute.* **3** most suitable ▫ *That's the very tool for the job.* **4** mere ▫ *shocked by the very thought.* • **not very** not at all; the opposite of. • **very good** or **very well** expressions of consent and approval. ◷ 13c: from French *veri*, from Latin *verus* true.

very high frequency ▻ *noun* (abbreviation **VHF**) **1** a band of radio frequencies between 30 and 300MHz. **2** a radio frequency lying between these frequencies.

Very light or **Verey light** /ˈvɛrɪ —, ˈvɪərɪ —/ ▻ *noun* a coloured flare fired from a pistol, as a signal or to illuminate an area. ◷ Early 20c: invented by E W Very (1852–1910), US naval ordnance officer.

very low frequency ▻ *noun* (abbreviation **VLF**) **1** a band of radio frequencies between 3 and 30kHz. **2** a radio frequency lying between these frequencies.

Vesak or **Wesak** /ˈvɛsaːk/ ▻ *noun* the most widely celebrated of Buddhist festivals, held in May to commemorate the birth, enlightenment and death of Buddha. ◷ 1920s: from Sanskrit *vaisakha* the name of a month.

vesica /ˈvɛsɪkə/ ▻ *noun* (***vesicae*** /-sɪsiː/) *anatomy* a bladder or sac, especially the urinary bladder. • **vesical** *adj.* ◷ 17c: Latin, meaning 'bladder' or 'blister'.

vesicant /ˈvɛsɪkənt/ ▻ *adj* blistering. ▻ *noun* anything that causes blisters.

vesicate /ˈvɛsɪkeɪt/ ▻ *verb* (***vesicated, vesicating***) *tr & intr* to raise blisters on (the skin, etc), or become blistered. ● **vesication** *noun*. ● **vesicatory** *adj, noun*. ⓒ 17c.

vesicle /ˈvɛsɪkəl/ ▻ *noun* **1** *biol* any small sac or cavity, especially one filled with fluid, within the cytoplasm of a living cell. **2** *medicine* a small blister in the skin containing SERUM, usually associated with herpes, eczema or other skin disorders. **3** *geol* a cavity formed by trapped gas bubbles during the solidification of molten lava. ⓒ 16c: from Latin *vesicula*, diminutive of *vesica* bladder.

vespers /ˈvɛspəz/ ▻ *singular noun*, **1** *now especially RC Church* the sixth of the CANONICAL HOURS, taking place towards evening. **2** an evening service in some Christian churches; evensong. ⓒ 17c: from Latin *vesper* evening.

vessel /ˈvɛsəl/ ▻ *noun* **1** a container, especially for liquid. **2** a ship or large boat. **3** a tube or duct carrying liquid, eg blood or sap, in animals and plants. ⓒ 13c: French, from Latin *vascellum* small vessel, from *vasis* a vessel.

vest ▻ *noun* **1** an undergarment for the top half of the body. **2** *US, Austral* a waistcoat. ▻ *verb* (***vested, vesting***) *intr* to put on ecclesiastical robes. ⓒ 15c: from French *vestir*, from Latin *vestire* to clothe, from Latin *vestis* clothing.

■ **vest something in someone** or **someone with something** to give or bestow legally or officially □ ***by the power vested in me*** □ ***The chairman is vested with absolute authority.***

vestal /ˈvɛstəl/ ▻ *adj* **1** virginal; chaste. **2** referring to or consecrated to the Roman goddess Vesta. ▻ *noun* **1** a chaste woman, especially a nun. **2** a VESTAL VIRGIN. ⓒ 15c: from Latin *vestalis* of Vesta, the Roman goddess of the hearth and home.

vestal virgin ▻ *noun, historical* in ancient Rome: one of the patrician virgins consecrated to Vesta, who kept the sacred fire burning on her altar.

vested /ˈvɛstɪd/ ▻ *adj, law* usually said of property or money held in trust: recognized as belonging to a person, although not perhaps available to them until some future date.

vested interest ▻ *noun* **1** an interest a person has in the fortunes of a particular system or institution because that person is directly affected or closely associated, especially financially. **2** a person or company with such an interest.

vestibule /ˈvɛstɪbjuːl/ ▻ *noun* **1** an entrance hall. **2** *anatomy* a cavity that serves as entrance to another, especially that of the inner ear. ● **vestibular** /vɛˈstɪbjʊlə(r)/ *adj*. ⓒ 17c: from Latin *vestibulum* entrance court.

vestige /ˈvɛstɪdʒ/ ▻ *noun* **1** a slight amount; a hint or shred. **2** a surviving trace of what has almost disappeared. **3** *biol* a small functionless part in an animal or plant, once a fully developed organ in ancestors. ● **vestigial** /vəˈstɪdʒɪəl/ *adj*. ⓒ 17c: from Latin *vestigium* footprint.

vestment /ˈvɛstmənt/ ▻ *noun* **1** any of various garments worn ceremonially by members of the clergy and church choir. **2** any ceremonial robe. ⓒ 13c: from Latin *vestimentum*, from *vestire* to clothe.

vestry /ˈvɛstrɪ/ ▻ *noun* (***vestries***) **1** a room in a church where the vestments are kept, often also used for meetings, Sunday school classes, etc. **2** *historical* **a** a meeting of church members or their elected representatives; **b** the committee of such members who meet for parish business. ● **vestral** *adj*. ⓒ 14c: probably from French *vestiarie*, from Latin *vestis* clothing.

vesture /ˈvɛstʃə(r)/ ▻ *noun, poetic* clothing; garments. ⓒ 14c: from Latin *vestiarium*, from *vestis* clothing.

vet[1] ▻ *noun* short for VETERINARY SURGEON. ▻ *verb* (***vetted, vetting***) to examine or investigate (especially a person) thoroughly; to check someone for suitability or reliability for a particular activity, especially a job which requires a high degree of loyalty or trust. See also POSITIVE VETTING. ⓒ 19c.

vet[2] ▻ *noun, colloq N Amer, especially US* short for VETERAN □ ***a war vet.*** ⓒ 19c.

vetch ▻ *noun* (***vetches***) any of various climbing plants of the pea family native to northern temperate regions and S America, with blue or purple flowers the pods of which are often used as fodder. Also called **tare**. ⓒ 14c: from French *veche*, from Latin *vicia*.

vetchling /ˈvɛtʃlɪŋ/ ▻ *noun* any plant of the SWEET-PEA genus, related to the vetch.

veteran /ˈvɛtərən/ ▻ *noun* **1** someone with many years of experience in a particular activity. **2** an old and experienced member of the armed forces. **3** *N Amer, especially US* an ex-serviceman or -woman. **4** *as adj* **a** old; experienced; **b** referring to veterans or for veterans. ⓒ 16c: from Latin *veteranus* old.

veteran car ▻ *noun* a very old motor car, specifically one made before 1905. Compare VINTAGE CAR.

Veterans' Day ▻ *noun* 11 November, a public holiday in the USA in honour of veterans of all wars, originally instituted as ARMISTICE DAY after World War I, and known by that name until 1954.

veterinary /ˈvɛtərɪnərɪ/ ▻ *adj* concerned with diseases of animals. ▻ *noun* (***veterinaries***) *colloq* a veterinary surgeon. ⓒ 18c: from Latin *veterinarius*, from *veterinae* cattle.

veterinary surgeon or (*N Amer*) **veterinarian** /vɛtərɪˈnɛərɪən/ *noun* a person qualified to treat diseases of animals.

veto /ˈviːtoʊ/ ▻ *noun* (***vetoes***) **1 a** the right to formally reject a proposal or forbid an action, eg in a law-making assembly; **b** the act of using such a right. **2** *colloq* any prohibition or refusal of permission. ▻ *verb* (***vetoes, vetoed, vetoing***) **1** to formally and authoritatively reject or forbid. **2** *loosely* to forbid. ⓒ 17c: from Latin *veto* I forbid.

Vet. Surg. ▻ *abbreviation* Veterinary Surgeon.

vex ▻ *verb* (***vexes, vexed, vexing***) **1** to annoy or irritate someone. **2** to worry someone. ● **vexing** *adj*. ⓒ 15c: from Latin *vexare* to shake or annoy.

vexation /vɛkˈseɪʃən/ ▻ *noun* **1** the state or feeling of being vexed. **2** a thing that vexes.

vexatious /vɛkˈseɪʃəs/ ▻ *adj* **1** vexing; annoying; troublesome. **2** said of a law action: brought on insufficient grounds, with the intention merely of annoying the defendant. ● **vexatiously** *adverb*. ● **vexatiousness** *noun*.

vexed /vɛkst/ ▻ *adj* **1** annoyed; angry; troubled. **2** said of an issue, etc: much discussed or debated □ ***vexed question.***

vexillum /vɛkˈsɪləm/ ▻ *noun* (***vexilla*** /-lə/) **1** *ornithol* the series of barbs on the sides of the shaft of a feather. **2** *bot* the large upper petal of a papilionaceous flower. **3** *historical* a Roman standard.

VG ▻ *abbreviation* vicar-general.

vg ▻ *abbreviation* very good.

VGA ▻ *abbreviation, computing* video graphics array, a computer monitor screen display system able to display several colours at a resolution of 640×480 pixels.

VHF ▻ *abbreviation, radio* very high frequency.

VHS ▻ *abbreviation* video home system, a video cassette recording system.

via /ˈvaɪə, ˈvɪə/ ▻ *prep* by way of or by means of; through □ ***travelled from Edinburgh to London via York*** □ ***sent it via head office.*** ⓒ 18c: Latin, meaning 'way'.

viable /ˈvaɪəbəl/ ▻ *adj* **1** said of a plan, etc: having a chance of success; feasible; practicable. **2** said of a plant, etc: able to exist or grow in particular conditions. **3** said of a fetus or baby: able to survive independently outside the womb. • **viability** *noun*. ⓘ 19c: French, from Latin *vita* life.

viaduct /'vaɪədʌkt/ ▻ *noun* a bridge-like structure of stone arches supporting a road or railway across a valley, etc. ⓘ 19c: from Latin *via* way + *ducere* to lead, modelled on AQUEDUCT.

vial see PHIAL

viands /'vaɪəndz/ ▻ *plural noun, formal* items of food; provisions. ⓘ 14c: from French *viande* food, from Latin *vivenda*, from *vivere* to live.

viaticum /vaɪ'atɪkəm/ ▻ *noun* (***viaticums*** or ***viatica*** /-kə/) **1** *RC Church* the Eucharist given to a dying person. **2** *formal* provisions for a journey. ⓘ 16c: Latin, from *via* way.

vibes /vaɪbz/ ▻ *plural noun* **1** (*also* **vibe** *singular noun*) *colloq* feelings, sensations or an atmosphere experienced or communicated □ ***bad vibes in the room*** □ ***got a really bad vibe from her***. Also (*in full*) **vibrations**. **2** the VIBRAPHONE. ⓘ 1960s in sense 1; 1940s in sense 2.

vibex /'vaɪbɛks/ ▻ *noun* (***vibices*** /vaɪ'baɪsiːz/) *medicine* a streak under the skin due to the leakage of blood. ⓘ 18c: Latin, meaning 'weal'.

vibrant /'vaɪbrənt/ ▻ *adj* **1** extremely lively or exciting; made strikingly animated or energetic. **2** said of a colour: strong and bright. **3** vibrating. • **vibrancy** *noun*. • **vibrantly** *adverb*. ⓘ 16c: from Latin *vibrare*, related to VIBRATE.

vibraphone /'vaɪbrəfoʊn/ ▻ *noun, music, especially jazz* a percussion instrument with pitched keys set over tuned resonating tubes and electrically driven rotating metal discs which produce a vibrato effect. • **vibraphonist** *noun*. ⓘ 1920s: from VIBRATE + -PHONE.

vibrate /vaɪ'breɪt/ ▻ *verb* (***vibrated, vibrating***) **1** *tr & intr* to move a short distance back and forth very rapidly. **2** *intr* to ring or resound when struck. **3** *intr* to shake or tremble. **4** *intr* to swing back and forth; to oscillate. • **vibratory** *adj*. ⓘ 17c: from Latin *vibrare*, *vibratum* to tremble.

vibration ▻ *noun* **1** a vibrating motion. **2 a** a single movement back and forth in vibrating; **b** *sometimes* a half of this period, ie either of the back or forward movements. **3** (**vibrations**) *colloq* VIBES. • **vibrational** *adj*. • **vibrationless** *adj*. ⓘ Late 19c.

vibrato /vɪ'brɑːtoʊ/ ▻ *noun* (***vibratos***) *music* a faint trembling effect in singing or the playing of string and wind instruments, achieved by vibrating the throat muscles or the fingers. Compare TREMOLO. ⓘ 19c: Italian, from Latin *vibratus* vibrated.

vibrator ▻ *noun* **1** any device that produces a vibrating motion, eg for massage. **2** a battery-powered vibrating dildo.

vibrissa /vaɪ'brɪsə/ ▻ *noun* (***vibrissae*** /-siː/) **1** a tactile bristle, such as a cat's whisker. **2** a vaneless feather at the corner of a bird's beak. **3** a bristle or hair, as in the nostril. ⓘ 17c: from Latin *vibrare* to vibrate.

Vic. ▻ *abbreviation* **1** Vicar. **2** Vicarage.

vicar /'vɪkə(r)/ ▻ *noun* **1** *C of E* the minister of a parish. **2** *RC Church* a bishop's deputy. • **vicarship** *noun*. ⓘ 13c: from French *vicaire*, from Latin *vicarius* deputy or substitute.

vicarage /'vɪkərɪdʒ/ ▻ *noun* a vicar's residence or benefice.

vicar-apostolic ▻ *noun, RC Church* a member of the clergy appointed, with the rank of bishop, to a country with no established church structure.

vicar-general ▻ *noun, RC Church* an official who assists a bishop in administrative matters.

vicarial /vɪ'kɛərɪəl, vaɪ-/ ▻ *adj* **1** referring to or serving as a vicar. **2** delegated.

vicariate /vɪ'kɛərɪət/ ▻ *adj* delegated. ▻ *noun* the office, authority, time of office or sphere of a vicar.

vicarious /vɪ'kɛərɪəs, vaɪ-/ ▻ *adj* **1** experienced not directly but through witnessing the experience of another person □ ***vicarious pleasure in seeing his children learn***. **2** undergone on behalf of someone else. **3** standing in for another. **4** said of authority, etc: delegated to someone else. • **vicariously** *adverb*. • **vicariousness** *noun*. ⓘ 17c: from Latin *vicarius* substituted.

vicarious sacrifice ▻ *noun* the suffering and death of Christ held by orthodox Christians to be accepted by God in lieu of the punishment to which guilty humankind is liable.

Vicar of Christ ▻ *noun, RC Church* the pope, regarded as representative of Christ on earth.

vice[1] or (*N Amer*) **vise** /vaɪs/ ▻ *noun* a tool with heavy movable metal jaws, usually fixed to a bench, for gripping an object being worked on. ⓘ 15c: French *vis* screw.

vice[2] /vaɪs/ ▻ *noun* **1** a habit or activity considered immoral, evil or depraved, especially involving prostitution or drugs. **2** such activities collectively. **3** a bad habit; a fault in one's character. ⓘ 13c: French, from Latin *vitium* blemish.

vice[3] /'vaɪsɪ/ ▻ *prep* **1** in place of. **2** following on from or succeeding. ⓘ 18c: Latin, meaning 'by turn'.

vice- /vaɪs/ ▻ *combining form, denoting* next in rank to; acting as deputy for □ ***vice-admiral*** □ ***vice-president***. ⓘ 17c: related to VICE[3].

vice-admiral *noun* an officer in the navy. See table at RANK.

vice-chamberlain ▻ *noun* the Lord Chamberlain's deputy and assistant.

vice-chancellor ▻ *noun* **1** the deputy chancellor of a British university, responsible for most administrative duties. **2** in the US: a chancery judge acting in place of a chancellor. • **vice-chancellorship** *noun*.

vice-consul ▻ *noun* **1** a consul's deputy. **2** an official who acts as consul in a less important district. • **vice-consulate** *noun*. • **vice-consulship** *noun*.

vicegerent /vaɪs'dʒɛrənt, -dʒɪərənt/ ▻ *noun* someone appointed to act in place of a superior. ▻ *adj* acting in this capacity. • **vicegerency** *noun*. ⓘ 16c: from VICE[3] + Latin *gerere* to manage.

vicennial /vaɪ'sɛnɪəl/ ▻ *adj* **1** lasting, or coming at the end of, twenty years. **2** occurring every twenty years. ⓘ 18c: from Latin *vicennium*, from *vicies* twenty times + *annus* a year.

vice-president ▻ *noun* **1** a president's deputy or assistant. **2** an officer next below the president.

viceregal /vaɪs'riːgəl/ ▻ *adj* relating to a viceroy. • **viceregally** *adverb*.

viceregent /vaɪs'riːdʒənt/ ▻ *noun* a substitute for a regent.

vicereine /vaɪs'reɪn, 'vaɪsrɛn/ ▻ *noun* **1** a viceroy's wife. **2** a female viceroy. ⓘ 19c: from French *vicereine*, from *reine* queen.

vice ring ▻ *noun* criminals working together as a group to organize illegal activities, especially prostitution.

viceroy /'vaɪsrɔɪ/ ▻ *noun* (***viceroys***) a male governor of a province or colony ruling in the name of, and with the authority of, a monarch or national government. • **viceroyalty** or **viceroyship** *noun*. ⓘ 16c: French, from *roi* king.

vicesimal, vicesimo- see under VIGESIMAL

vice squad ▻ *noun* a branch of the police force that investigates crimes relating to VICE[2], especially prostitution, gambling, etc.

vice versa /vaɪs 'vɜːsə, 'vaɪsɪ —/ ▻ *adj* with the order or correspondence reversed; the other way round

□ *from me to you and vice versa.* ⓒ 17c: Latin, meaning 'the position being reversed'.

vicinity /və'sɪnɪtɪ/ ▷ *noun* (***vicinities***) **1** a neighbourhood. **2** the area immediately surrounding. **3** the condition of being close; nearness. ⓒ 16c: from Latin *vicinus* neighbour.

vicious /'vɪʃəs/ ▷ *adj* **1** violent or ferocious. **2** spiteful or malicious. **3** extremely severe or harsh. **4** said of reasoning, etc: incorrect or faulty; unsound. • **viciously** *adverb*. • **viciousness** *noun*. ⓒ 14c: from Latin *vitiosus* faulty.

vicious circle ▷ *noun* **1** a situation in which any attempt to resolve a problem creates others which in turn recreate the first one. **2** an incorrect form of reasoning in which one proposition is supposedly proved on the basis of another which itself depends for its proof on the truth of the first. Compare VIRTUOUS CIRCLE.

vicissitude /vɪ'sɪsɪtʃuːd/ ▷ *noun* an unpredictable change of fortune or circumstance. • **vicissitudinous** *adj*. ⓒ 16c: from Latin *vicissim* by turns.

victim /'vɪktɪm/ ▷ *noun* **1** a person or animal subjected to death, suffering, ill-treatment or trickery. **2** a person or animal killed in a sacrifice or ritual. ⓒ 15c: from Latin *victima* beast for sacrifice.

victimize or **victimise** /'vɪktɪmaɪz/ ▷ *verb* (***victimized***, ***victimizing***) **1** to single someone or something out for hostile, unfair or vindictive treatment. **2** to cause someone or something to be a victim. • **victimization** *noun*. • **victimizer** *noun*.

victimless ▷ *adj* referring to a crime involving no injured party, such as prostitution, minor traffic offences, etc. ⓒ 1960s: originally US.

victor /'vɪktə(r)/ ▷ *noun* **1** the winner or winning side in a war or contest. **2** (**Victor**) *communications* in the NATO alphabet: the word used to denote the letter 'V' (see table at NATO ALPHABET). ⓒ 14c: Latin, from *vincere, victum* to conquer.

victoria /vɪk'tɔːrɪə/ ▷ *noun* (***victorias***) a large oval red and yellow variety of plum with a sweet flavour. Also called **victoria plum**. ⓒ 1860s: named after Queen Victoria.

Victoria Cross ▷ *noun* (abbreviation **VC**) a bronze MALTESE CROSS, the highest decoration in recognition of outstanding bravery in battle awarded to British and Commonwealth armed forces. ⓒ 1856: established in that year by Queen Victoria.

Victorian /vɪk'tɔːrɪən/ ▷ *adj* **1** relating to or characteristic of Queen Victoria or the period of her reign (1837–1901). **2** said of attitudes or values: **a** typical of the strictness, prudery or conventionality associated with this period; **b** typical of the hypocrisy and bigotry often thought to underlie these values. ▷ *noun* **1** someone who lived during this period. **2** someone with Victorian attitudes or values. • **Victorianism** *noun*. ⓒ 1830s.

Victoriana or **victoriana** /vɪktɔːrɪ'ɑːnə/ ▷ *plural noun* objects from, or in a style typical of, the Victorian period in Britain, especially bric-à-brac.

Victoria sandwich see under SPONGE CAKE

victorious /vɪk'tɔːrɪəs/ ▷ *adj* **1** having won a war or contest □ *the victorious army*. **2** referring to, marking or representing a victory □ *a victorious outcome*. • **victoriously** *adverb*. • **victoriousness** *noun*.

victory /'vɪktərɪ/ ▷ *noun* (***victories***) **1** success against an opponent in a war or contest. **2** an occurrence of this. ⓒ 14c: from Latin *victoria*, from *victor* VICTOR.

victual /'vɪtəl/ ▷ *verb* (***victualled***, ***victualling***; *US* ***victualed***, ***victualing***) **1** to supply with victuals. **2** *intr* to obtain supplies. **3** *intr* said of animals: to eat victuals. See also VICTUALS.

victualler or (*US*) **victualer** /'vɪtələ(r)/ *noun, formal* **1** a shopkeeper selling food and drink. **2** (*in full* **licensed victualler**) *Brit* a publican licensed to sell food and alcoholic liquor for consumption on the premises. **3** a ship carrying supplies for another ship.

victuals /'vɪtəlz/ ▷ *plural noun* (*occasionally* **victual**) food; provisions. ⓒ 14c: from Latin *victualis*.

vicuña or **vicuna** /vɪ'kuːnjə, vɪ'kjuː-, vaɪ-, -nə/ ▷ *noun* (***vicuñas***) **1** a ruminant mammal belonging to the camel family native to high grassland in the Andes Mountains of S America, resembling a LLAMA but smaller and slenderer with a light-brown coat and a yellowish-red bib. **2** a cloth or yarn made from its wool. ⓒ 17c: Spanish, from Quechua *wikúña* the name of this animal.

vid ▷ *noun* short for VIDEO.

vide ▷ /'vaɪdiː/ ▷ *verb* (abbreviation **vid.**) used as an instruction in a text: refer to or see, eg a particular page-number or section. ⓒ 16c: Latin, imperative singular of *videre* to see.

videlicet see VIZ

video /'vɪdɪoʊ/ ▷ *noun* (***videos***) **1** short for VIDEO CASSETTE. **2** short for VIDEO CASSETTE RECORDER □ *Have you set the video?* **3** a film or programme pre-recorded on video cassette □ *now available as a video*. **4** the process of recording, reproducing or broadcasting of visual, especially televised, images on magnetic tape. **5** the visual rather than audio elements of a TV broadcast. ▷ *adj* relating to the process of or equipment for recording by video. ▷ *verb* (***videos***, ***videoed***, ***videoing***) to make a video cassette recording of (a TV programme, a film, etc). ⓒ 1930s: Latin, from *videre* to see, modelled on AUDIO.

video camera ▷ *noun, photog* a portable camera that records moving visual images directly on to videotape, which can then be played back on a video cassette recorder and viewed on the screen of a television receiver. Compare CAMCORDER. ⓒ 1970s.

video cassette ▷ *noun* a cassette containing videotape, for use in a video cassette recorder.

video cassette recorder ▷ *noun* (abbreviation **VCR**) a machine for recording on magnetic tape the sound and video signals of a TV broadcast, so that they can be played back on a standard TV receiver at a later date, also used to play back pre-recorded tapes of motion pictures.

videoconference ▷ *noun* a live discussion between groups of people in different locations using electronically linked telephones and video screens. • **videoconferencing** *noun*. ⓒ 1970s.

video disc ▷ *noun* a disc on which visual images and sound can be recorded for playing back on a TV or similar apparatus. ⓒ 1970s.

videofit ▷ *noun* a type of IDENTIKIT picture put together using a database of electronic images manipulated on a computer screen.

video game ▷ *noun* any electronically operated game involving the manipulation of images produced by a computer program on a visual display unit, such as a computer screen, a TV screen, a GAME BOY, etc. ⓒ 1970s.

video nasty ▷ *noun, colloq* an explicitly shocking violent or pornographic film available as a video cassette. ⓒ 1980s.

video-on-demand *noun* (abbreviation **VOD**) a service by which films, TV programmes, etc can be viewed by individual subscribers accessing a film by telephone or other electronic link (see SUPERHIGHWAY 2) with the supplier. Current technology would allow such a service, but the present infrastructure (eg the suitability of most telephone lines) is not yet sufficient for a widespread service. ▷ *adj* referring or relating to such a service.

videophone ▷ *noun* a communication device like a telephone which transmits a visual image as well as sound. ⓒ 1950s, but the phones themselves are only now becoming more extensively used as technological advances allow less bulky and expensive equipment to be produced.

video RAM or **VRAM** ▷ *noun, computing* video random access memory, a part of a computer's memory in which data controlling the visual display is stored, sometimes physically separate from the main memory.

video recorder ▷ *noun* a VIDEO CASSETTE RECORDER.

videotape ▷ *noun* magnetic tape on which visual images and sound can be recorded.

videotext ▷ *noun* any system in which computerized information is displayed on a TV screen, eg TELETEXT or VIEWDATA.

video-wall ▷ *noun* a number of TV screens placed together, each showing either the same programme, etc, or part of a picture so that the whole wall makes up one large image.

vidimus /ˈvaɪdɪməs/ ▷ *noun* an attested copy; an inspection, eg of accounts, etc. ◯ 16c: Latin, meaning 'we have seen', from *videre* to see.

vie /vaɪ/ ▷ *verb* (***vies, vied, vying***) *intr* (*often* **vie with someone for something**) to compete or struggle with them for some gain or advantage. ◯ 16c: from French *envier* to challenge or invite.

Viennese /vɪəˈniːz/ ▷ *adj* referring to Vienna, the capital of Austria. ▷ *noun* (*plural* ***Viennese***) a citizen or inhabitant of, or person born in, Vienna.

Vietnamese /vɪɛtnəˈmiːz/ ▷ *noun* **1** (*plural* ***Vietnamese***) a citizen or inhabitant of, or person born in, Vietnam, a republic in SE Asia. **2** an Austro-Asiatic language spoken by c.50 million people in Vietnam, Laos and Cambodia. ▷ *adj* belonging or relating to Vietnam, its people or their language.

view /vjuː/ ▷ *noun* **1** an act or opportunity of seeing without obstruction □ *a good view of the stage.* **2** something, especially a landscape, seen from a particular point □ *a magnificent view from the summit.* **3** a range or field of vision □ *out of view.* **4** a scene recorded in photograph or picture form. **5** a description or impression □ *The book gives a view of life in Roman times.* **6** an opinion; a point of view □ *Can we have your view on homelessness?* **7** a way of considering or understanding something □ *a short-term view of the situation.* **8** (**View**) used in street names □ *Atlantic View.* ▷ *verb* (***viewed, viewing***) **1** to see or look at something. **2** to inspect or examine something □ *viewed the house that was for sale.* **3** to consider or regard something. **4** *tr & intr* to watch (a programme) on TV; to watch TV. ● **have something in view** to have it as a plan or aim. ● **in view of something** taking account of it; because of it. ● **on view** displayed for all to see or inspect. ● **take a dim view of something** to regard it disapprovingly or unfavourably. ● **with a view to something** with the hope or intention of achieving it □ *bought the house with a view to retiring there.* ◯ 15c: from French *veue* saw, from *veoir* to see, from Latin *videre.*

viewable ▷ *adj* **1** able to be seen. **2** sufficiently interesting to be looked at or watched.

viewdata ▷ *noun* a system by which computerized information can be displayed on a TV screen by means of a telephone link with a computer source.

viewer ▷ *noun* **1** any device used for viewing something, especially a photographic slide. **2** someone who views something, especially TV.

viewfinder ▷ *noun* a device that forms part of a camera showing the FIELD OF VISION covered by the lens. Also shortened to FINDER.

viewing ▷ *noun* an act or opportunity of seeing or inspecting something, eg an exhibition or a house for sale □ *Viewing is on Thursdays from 6pm.*

viewpoint ▷ *noun* **1 a** an interpretation of facts received; **b** an opinion or point of view; a standpoint. **2** a location or a position which is particularly good for admiring scenery.

vigesimal /vaɪˈdʒɛsɪməl/ or **vicesimal** /vaɪˈsɛ-/ ▷ *adj* based on the number twenty. ● **vigesimo-quarto** or **vicesimo-quarto** *printing* twenty-four-mo. See -MO. ◯ 17c: from Latin *vigesimus* twentieth, from *viginti* twenty.

vigil /ˈvɪdʒɪl/ ▷ *noun* **1** a period of staying awake, usually to guard or watch over a person or thing. **2** a stationary, peaceful demonstration for a specific cause. **3** the day before a major religious festival, traditionally spent in prayer. **4** a night-time religious service or session of prayer. ◯ 13c: from Latin *vigila,* from *vigil,* meaning 'awake' or 'watchful'.

vigilance /ˈvɪdʒɪləns/ ▷ *noun* the state of being watchful or observant. ◯ 16c: from Latin *vigilare* to keep awake.

vigilance committee ▷ *noun* in the US: an unauthorized body which, in the absence or inefficiency of the regular government, exercises powers of arrest, punishment, etc.

vigilant ▷ *adj* ready for possible trouble or danger; alert; watchful. ● **vigilantly** *adverb.*

vigilante /vɪdʒɪˈlantɪ/ ▷ *noun* (***vigilantes*** /-tɪz/) **1** a member of an organization looking after the interests of a group threatened in some way, especially a self-appointed and unofficial policeman. **2** in the US: a member of a VIGILANCE COMMITTEE. ● **vigilantism** *noun.* ◯ 19c: originally US, from Spanish, meaning 'vigilant'.

vignette /viːnˈjɛt/ ▷ *noun* **1** a decorative design on a book's title page, traditionally of vine leaves. **2** a photographic portrait with the background deliberately faded. **3** a short literary essay, especially one describing a person's character. ▷ *verb* (***vignetted, vignetting***) to make a vignette of something or someone. ● **vignettist** *noun.* ◯ 19c: French, meaning 'little vine'.

vigorish /ˈvɪgərɪʃ/ ▷ *noun, US slang* **1** a percentage of a gambler's winnings taken by the bookmaker, organizers of a game, etc. **2** excessive interest charged on a loan. ◯ Early 20c: probably Yiddish, from Russian *vyigrysh* profit or winnings.

vigoro /ˈvɪgəroʊ/ ▷ *noun* (***vigoros***) *Austral* a 12-a-side game with similarities to cricket and baseball. ◯ 1930s: from VIGOROUS.

vigorous /ˈvɪgərəs/ ▷ *adj* **1** strong and active. **2** forceful; energetic □ *had a vigorous approach to life.* ● **vigorously** *adverb.* ● **vigorousness** *noun.*

vigour or (*N Amer*) **vigor** /ˈvɪgə(r)/ *noun* **1** great strength and energy of body or mind. **2** liveliness or forcefulness of action. **3** in plants, etc: healthy growth. ◯ 14c: from Latin *vigor,* from *vigere* to be strong.

vihara /viːˈhɑːrə/ ▷ *noun* (***viharas***) a Buddist or Jain temple, monastery or nunnery. ◯ 17c: Sanskrit, meaning 'dwelling place'.

viking /ˈvaɪkɪŋ/ ▷ *noun* (*often* **Viking**) any of the Scandinavian seafaring peoples who raided and settled in much of NW Europe between the 8c and 11c. Also *as adj* □ *Viking ship.* ◯ 19c: from Norse *vikingr,* perhaps from Anglo-Saxon *wicing* pirate.

vile /vaɪl/ ▷ *adj* (***viler, vilest***) **1** morally evil or wicked. **2** physically repulsive; disgusting. **3** *colloq* extremely bad or unpleasant. ● **vilely** *adverb.* ● **vileness** *noun.* ◯ 13c: from French *vil,* from Latin *vilis* worthless or base.

vilification /vɪlɪfɪˈkeɪʃən/ ▷ *noun* verbal abuse; defamation.

vilify /ˈvɪlɪfaɪ/ ▷ *verb* (***vilifies, vilified, vilifying***) to say insulting or abusive things about someone or something; to malign or defame someone. ● **vilifier** *noun.* ◯ 16c in this sense; 15c in sense 'to lower in value': from Latin *vilificare* to make worthless or base.

villa /ˈvɪlə/ ▷ *noun* (***villas***) **1** in ancient Rome: a large country house or mansion. **2** *Brit* a good-sized, especially detached suburban house. **3** a country residence. **4** a holiday home, especially one abroad. ◷ 17c: Latin, meaning 'country house'.

village /ˈvɪlɪdʒ/ ▷ *noun* **1** a group of houses, shops and other buildings, smaller than a town and larger than a hamlet, especially in or near the countryside. **2** the people living in it, regarded as a community □ ***The village has started to gossip about the Vicar's imminent departure.*** **3** a residential complex for participants in a major, usually international, sporting event □ ***Olympic village.*** **4** *N Amer* a small municipality which has limited powers. ● **villager** *noun.* ◷ 14c: French, from Latin *villaticus*, from *villa* VILLA.

villain /ˈvɪlən/ ▷ *noun* **1** the principal wicked character in a story. **2** any violent, wicked or unscrupulous person. **3** *colloq* a criminal. ◷ 14c: originally meaning 'a rustic', from French *vilein*, from Latin *villanus* worker on a country estate.

villain of the piece ▷ *noun* **1** the villain in a story. **2** someone responsible for some trouble or mischief.

villainous ▷ *adj* **1** like or worthy of a villain □ ***villainous deeds.*** **2** *colloq* extremely bad □ ***a villainous storm.*** ● **villainously** *adverb.* ● **villainousness** *noun.*

villainy ▷ *noun* (***villainies***) **1** wicked or vile behaviour. **2** an act of this kind.

-ville /vɪl/ ▷ *combining form, signifying* a supposed world or place characterized by the specified quality, etc □ ***sleazeville*** □ ***squaresville.***

villein /ˈvɪlən/ ▷ *noun, historical, feudalism* a peasant worker bound to a lord and showing allegiance to him. ● **villeinage** *noun.* ◷ 14c: from French *vilein* serf; see VILLAIN.

villus /ˈvɪləs/ ▷ *noun* (***villi*** /ˈvɪlaɪ/) **1** *anatomy* any of many tiny fingerlike projections that line the inside of the small intestine and absorb the products of digestion. **2** *bot* a long soft hair. ● **villiform** /ˈvɪlɪfɔːm/ *adj.* ● **villous** *adj.* ◷ 18c: Latin, meaning 'shaggy hair'.

vim ▷ *noun, colloq* energy; liveliness. ◷ 19c: perhaps from Latin *vis* force.

vimana /vɪˈmɑːnə/ ▷ *noun* (***vimanas***) **1** the central shrine of an Indian temple with a pyramidal roof. **2** *mythol* a chariot of the gods. ◷ 19c: Sanskrit, meaning 'a marking out'.

vina /ˈviːnə/ ▷ *noun* (***vinas***) an Indian stringed instrument with a fretted fingerboard over two gourds. ◷ 18c: Sanskrit and Hindi.

vinaigrette /vɪneɪˈgret, vɪnə-/ ▷ *noun* **1** (*also* **vinaigrette sauce**) a type of salad dressing made by mixing oil, vinegar and seasonings, especially mustard. **2** a small ornate bottle used for holding smelling-salts. ◷ 19c: French, from *vinaigre* vinegar.

vincible /ˈvɪnsɪbəl/ ▷ *adj, literary* able to be overcome or defeated. ● **vincibility** *noun.* ◷ 16c: from Latin *vincibilis*, from *vincere* to overcome.

vinculum /ˈvɪŋkjʊləm/ ▷ *noun* (***vincula*** /-lə/) **1** *math* a horizontal line placed above part of an equation as an alternative to brackets. **2** *anatomy* a tendinous band. ◷ 17c: Latin, from *vincire* to bind.

vindaloo /vɪndəˈluː/ ▷ *noun* (***vindaloos***) a hot Indian curry, usually made with meat, poultry or fish. ◷ 19c: probably from Portuguese *vin d'alho* wine and garlic sauce.

vin de pays /van du peɪˈiː/ ; *French* van dy pei/ ▷ *noun* country or local wine.

vindicate /ˈvɪndɪkeɪt/ ▷ *verb* (***vindicated, vindicating***) **1** to clear someone of blame or criticism. **2** to show something to have been worthwhile or justified □ ***The year's results vindicated their cautious planning.*** **3** to maintain or uphold (a point of view, cause, etc). ● **vindicable** *adj.* ● **vindication** *noun.* ● **vindicative** *adj.* ● **vindicator** *noun.* ● **vindicatory** /ˈvɪn-/ *adj.* ◷ 17c: from Latin *vindicare, vindicatum*, from *vindex* claimant.

vindictive /vɪnˈdɪktɪv/ ▷ *adj* **1** feeling or showing spite or hatred. **2** seeking revenge. ● **vindictively** *adverb.* ● **vindictiveness** *noun.* ◷ 17c: from Latin *vindicta* vengeance; see VINDICATE.

vindictive damages ▷ *plural noun, law* damages which are awarded as punishment to the defendant as well as compensation to the plaintiff.

vine ▷ *noun* **1** any of various woody climbing plants that produce grapes. **2** any climbing or trailing plant, including ivy. ● **viny** *adj.* ◷ 13c: from French *vigne*, from Latin *vinea*, from *vinum* wine.

vine-dresser ▷ *noun* a person whose job it is to trim and cultivate vines.

vinegar /ˈvɪnɪgə(r)/ ▷ *noun* **1** a sour liquid consisting of a dilute solution of acetic acid, which is produced by the bacterial fermentation of alcoholic beverages such as cider or wine and is used as a condiment and preservative. **2** bad temper or peevishness. ● **vinegarish** *adj.* ● **vinegary** *adj.* ◷ 13c: from French *vinaigre*, from *vin* wine + *aigre* sour.

vineyard /ˈvɪnjəd, -jɑːd/ ▷ *noun* a plantation of grape-bearing vines, especially for wine-making.

vingt-et-un / *French* vɛ̃teœ̃/ ▷ *noun, cards* PONTOON². ◷ 18c: French, meaning 'twenty-one'.

vinho verde /ˈviːnoʊ ˈvɜːdɪ/ ▷ *noun* a light sharp young Portuguese wine. ◷ 19c: Portuguese, literally 'green wine'.

viniculture /ˈvɪnɪkʌltʃə(r)/ ▷ *noun* the cultivation of grapes for wine-making. ● **vinicultural** *adj.* ● **viniculturist** *noun.* ◷ 19c: from Latin *vinum* wine + CULTURE.

vino /ˈviːnoʊ/ ▷ *noun* (***vinos***) *slang* wine, especially of poor quality. ◷ 20c in this sense: Spanish and Italian, meaning 'wine'.

vin ordinaire /van ɔːdɪˈnɛə(r)/ ▷ *noun* inexpensive table wine for everyday use. ◷ 19c: French, meaning 'ordinary wine'.

vinous /ˈvaɪnəs/ ▷ *adj* **1** belonging or relating to, or resembling, wine. **2** caused by or indicative of an excess of wine □ ***a vinous complexion.*** ● **vinosity** *noun.* ◷ 17c: from Latin *vinosus*, from Latin *vinum* wine.

vintage /ˈvɪntɪdʒ/ ▷ *noun* **1** the grape-harvest of a particular year. **2** the wine produced from a year's harvest. **3** the time of year when grapes are harvested. **4** a particular period of origin, especially when regarded as productive □ ***literature of a postwar vintage.*** ▷ *adj* **1** said of wine: good quality and from a specified year. **2** typical of someone's best work or most characteristic behaviour □ ***That remark was vintage Churchill.*** **3** outdated; unfashionable. ◷ 15c: influenced by VINTNER, from Norman French, from Latin *vindemia*, from *vinum* wine + *demere* to remove.

vintage car ▷ *noun, Brit* an old motor car, specifically one built between 1919 and 1930. Compare VETERAN CAR.

vintner /ˈvɪntnə(r)/ ▷ *noun, formal* a wine-merchant. ◷ 15c: from French *vinetier*, from Latin *vinetarius*, from *vinum* wine.

viny see under VINE

vinyl /ˈvaɪnɪl/ ▷ *noun* **1** any of a group of tough plastics manufactured in various forms, eg paint additives and carpet fibres. **2 a** *colloq* plastic records (see RECORD *noun* 4) regarded collectively, as distinct from cassettes and compact discs; **b** *as adj* □ ***vinyl record.*** ◷ 19c: from Latin *vinum* wine + -YL.

viol /ˈvaɪəl/ ▷ *noun* any of a family of Renaissance stringed musical instruments played with a bow. ◷ 15c: from French *vielle*, from Provençal *viola*.

viola¹ /vɪ'oʊlə/ ▷ *noun* (*violas*) **1** a musical instrument of the violin family, larger than the violin and lower in pitch. **2** someone who plays the viola. ⓘ 18c: Italian and Spanish.

viola² /'vaɪələ/ ▷ *noun* (*violas*) any of various perennial plants native to temperate regions, including the violet and pansy. ⓘ 18c in this sense: Latin, meaning 'violet'.

violate /'vaɪəleɪt/ ▷ *verb* (*violated*, *violating*) **1** to disregard or break (a law, agreement or oath). **2** to treat (something sacred or private) with disrespect; to profane. **3** to disturb or disrupt (eg a person's peace or privacy). **4** to rape or sexually abuse someone. • **violable** *adj*. • **violation** *noun*. • **violator** *noun*. ⓘ 15c: from Latin *violare, violatum* to treat violently.

violence /'vaɪələns/ ▷ *noun* **1** the state or quality of being violent. **2** violent behaviour. • **do violence to someone** or **something 1** to harm them or it physically. **2** to spoil or ruin them or it. **3** to distort their meaning or significance. ⓘ 13c: from Latin *violentus*, from *vis* force.

violent /'vaɪələnt/ ▷ *adj* **1** marked by or using extreme physical force. **2** using or involving the use of such force to cause physical harm. **3** impulsively aggressive and unrestrained in nature or behaviour. **4** intense; extreme; vehement ▫ *They took a violent dislike to me.* • **violently** *adverb*.

violet /'vaɪələt/ ▷ *noun* **1** any of various flowering perennial plants, native to temperate regions, with large purple, blue or white petals. **2** any of various similar but unrelated plants, eg the African violet. **3** a bluish-purple colour. ▷ *adj* violet-coloured. ⓘ 14c: from French *violette*, diminutive of *viole*, from Latin *viola*.

violin /vaɪə'lɪn, 'vaɪ-/ ▷ *noun* **1** a four-stringed musical instrument with a shaped body, which is usually held with one end under the chin and played with a bow. **2** any of the violinists in an orchestra or group ▫ *first violin.* See also FIDDLE (sense 1). • **violinist** *noun*. ⓘ 16c: from Italian *violino* little viol.

violist /'vaɪəlɪst, vɪ'oʊlɪst/ ▷ *noun* someone who plays the viol or viola.

violoncello /vaɪələn'tʃɛloʊ/ ▷ *noun* (*violoncellos*) *formal* a CELLO. • **violoncellist** *noun*. ⓘ 18c: Italian, diminutive of *violone* double bass viol.

VIP ▷ *abbreviation* very important person.

viper /'vaɪpə(r)/ ▷ *noun* **1** any of a large family of poisonous snakes found in Europe, Asia and Africa with long tubular fangs through which venom is injected into the prey. **2** an ADDER. **3** a treacherous or spiteful person. • **viperish** *adj*. • **viperous** *adj*. ⓘ 16c: from Latin *vipera*, from *vivus* alive + *parere* to bring forth.

viper's bugloss ▷ *noun* a stiff bristly plant with intensely blue flowers.

virago /vɪ'rɑːgoʊ, vɪ'reɪ-/ ▷ *noun* (*viragoes* or *viragos*) *literary* **1** a loudly fierce or abusive woman. **2** a heroic or masculine woman. ⓘ 11c: Latin, meaning 'manlike woman'.

viral /'vaɪərəl/ ▷ *adj* belonging or relating to or caused by a virus.

virement /'vaɪəmənt/ ▷ *noun, finance* the authorized transference of funds from one account to another. ⓘ Early 20c: French, from *virer* to turn.

virga /'vɜːgə/ ▷ *singular or plural noun* (*virgae* /-giː/) *meteorol* trails of water, drops or ice particles coming from a cloud, which evaporate before reaching the ground. ⓘ 1940s: Latin, meaning 'rod'.

virgin /'vɜːdʒɪn/ ▷ *noun* **1** a person, especially a woman, who has never had sexual intercourse. **2** a member of a religious order of women sworn to chastity. **3** (**the Virgin**) *RC Church* a name for Mary, the mother of Jesus Christ. **4** (**Virgin**) a portrait or statue of Mary. **5** (**Virgin**) *astron, astrol* same as VIRGO. ▷ *adj* **1** never having had sexual intercourse; chaste. **2** in its original state; never having been used. ⓘ 13c: from Latin *virgo* maiden.

virginal¹ /'vɜːdʒɪnəl/ ▷ *adj* **1** belonging or relating or appropriate to a virgin. **2** in a state of virginity.

virginal² /'vɜːdʒɪnəl/ ▷ *noun* a keyboard instrument, used in the 16c and 17c, like a small harpsichord but with strings set at right angles to the keys. ⓘ 16c: perhaps so called because it was mostly played by young women.

Virgin Birth ▷ *noun, Christianity* the birth of Christ to the Virgin Mary, regarded as an act of God. See also IMMACULATE CONCEPTION.

virgin forest ▷ *noun* a forest in its natural state.

Virginia creeper ▷ *noun* a N American climbing-plant, closely related to the vine, whose foliage turns bright red in autumn.

virginity /vɜː'dʒɪnɪtɪ/ ▷ *noun* (*virginities*) the state of being a virgin.

Virgo /'vɜːgoʊ/ ▷ *noun* (*plural* in sense 2b *Virgos*) **1** *astron* a constellation of the zodiac. **2 a** *astrol* the sixth sign of the zodiac; **b** a person born between 23 August and 22 September, under this sign. See table at ZODIAC. • **Virgoan** *noun, adj*. ⓘ 14c: Latin, meaning 'virgin'.

virgo intacta /vɜːgoʊ ɪn'taktə/ ▷ *noun* a woman who has never had sexual intercourse. ⓘ 18c: Latin.

virgule /'vɜːgjuːl/ ▷ *noun* another word for SOLIDUS (sense 1). ⓘ 19c: French, meaning 'comma', from Latin *virgula*, diminutive of *virga* rod.

viridescent /vɪrɪ'dɛsənt/ ▷ *adj* greenish. • **viridescence** *noun*. ⓘ 19c: from Latin *viridescere* to become green.

virile /'vɪraɪl, -rɪl/ ▷ *adj* **1** said of a man: having a high level of sexual desire. **2** displaying or requiring qualities regarded as typically masculine, especially physical strength. **3** said of a man: able to produce children. **4** relating to or possessing the features of a mature adult male. • **virility** *noun*. ⓘ 15c: from Latin *virilis*, from *vir* man.

virology /vaɪ'rɒlədʒɪ/ ▷ *noun, medicine* the branch of microbiology concerned with the study of viruses and viral diseases. • **virological** *adj*. • **virologist** *noun*.

virtu or **vertu** /vɜː'tuː/ ▷ *noun* (*virtus* or *vertus*) **1 a** a love of works of fine art or curiosities; **b** such items collectively. **2** the distinctive and usually moral worth found in a person or thing. ⓘ 18c: Italian, from Latin *virtus* VIRTUE.

virtual /'vɜːtʃʊəl/ ▷ *adj* **1** being so in effect or in practice, but not in name ▫ *a virtual state of war.* **2** nearly so; almost but not quite ▫ *the virtual collapse of the steel industry.* **3** *computing slang* referring or relating to interaction, connection, use, etc via THE INTERNET ▫ *pay by virtual money.* **4** *computing* said of memory or storage: appearing to be internal but actually transferred a segment at a time as required from (and to) back-up storage into (and out of) the smaller internal memory. ⓘ 17c in sense 1: from Latin *virtualis*, related to VIRTUE.

virtually ▷ *adverb* **1** in practice, though not strictly speaking ▫ *was virtually in charge.* **2** almost; nearly.

virtual pet see CYBERPET

virtual reality ▷ *noun* (abbreviation **VR**) a computer simulation of a real or artificial environment that gives the user the impression of actually being within the environment and interacting with it, eg by way of a special visor that contains two tiny television screens and special gloves fitted with sensors, which are worn by the user.

virtue /'vɜːtʃuː/ ▷ *noun* **1** a quality regarded as morally good ▫ *He has many virtues, including honesty.* **2** moral goodness; righteousness. **3** an admirable quality or desirable feature ▫ *The virtue of this one is its long life.* **4** virginity, especially in women. **5** *Christianity* in the traditional medieval hierarchy of nine ranks of angels: an angel of the fifth-highest rank. Compare SERAPH, CHERUB, THRONE, DOMINION, POWER, PRINCIPALITY, ARCHANGEL, ANGEL. • **by** or **in virtue of something** because of it; on account of it. • **make a virtue of necessity** to do something unpleasant with a good grace, from a sense of duty or obligation. ⓒ 13c: from French *vertu*, from Latin *virtus* 'manliness' or 'bravery'.

virtuoso /vɜːtʃʊ'oʊsoʊ, -zoʊ/ ▷ *noun* (***virtuosos***) **1 a** someone with remarkable artistic skill, especially a brilliant musical performer; **b** *as adj* ▫ ***a virtuoso performance.*** **2** someone with a great knowledge or collection of fine art. • **virtuosity** *noun*. ⓒ 17c: Italian, meaning 'skilful', from Latin *virtuosus* virtuous.

virtuous /'vɜːtʃʊəs/ ▷ *adj* **1** possessing or showing virtue; morally sound. **2** said especially of a woman: chaste. • **virtuously** *adverb*. • **virtuousness** *noun*.

virtuous circle ▷ *noun* a situation in which one element improves the conditions of others which in turn improve the conditions of the first. Compare VICIOUS CIRCLE.

virulent /'vɪrʊlənt, 'vɪrjʊ-/ ▷ *adj* **1** said of a disease: having a rapidly harmful effect. **2** said of a disease or the organism causing it: extremely infectious. **3** said of a substance: highly poisonous. **4** bitterly hostile; acrimonious. • **virulence** *noun*. ⓒ 14c: from Latin *virulentus* venomous, from *virus* VIRUS.

virus /'vaɪərəs/ ▷ *noun* **1** an infectious particle, consisting of a core of DNA or RNA enclosed in a protein shell, only visible under an electron microscope, that invades the cells of animals, plants and bacteria, and can only survive and reproduce within such cells. **2** the organism that causes and transmits an infectious disease. **3** *loosely* a disease caused by such an organism. **4** anything that damages or corrupts. **5** (*in full* **computer virus**) a self-replicating program that attaches to a computer system, spreading to other systems via a network and when activated, often at a later date, can corrupt or destroy data stored on the hard disk. • **viral** see separate entry. ⓒ 16c: Latin, meaning 'slimy liquid'.

vis /vɪs/ ▷ *noun* force; power. ⓒ 17c: Latin.

Vis. ▷ *abbreviation* Viscount.

visa /'viːzə/ ▷ *noun* (***visas***) a permit stamped into a passport, or a similar document, allowing the holder to enter or leave the country which issues it. ▷ *verb* (***visaed, visaing***) to stamp (a passport, etc) with a visa. ⓒ 19c: French, from Latin, from *videre, visum* to see.

visage /'vɪzɪdʒ/ ▷ *noun, literary* **1** the face. **2** the usual expression of a face; a countenance. ⓒ 14c: French, from Latin *visus* face.

vis-à-vis /viːzɑː'viː/ ▷ *prep* in relation to something or someone; with regard to them. ▷ *adverb* face-to-face. ▷ *noun* (***vis-à-vis***) a counterpart or opposite number. ⓒ 18c: French, from Latin *visus* face.

viscacha /vɪ'skatʃə/ or **vizcacha** /vɪ'zka-/ ▷ *noun* (***viscacha*** or ***viscachas***) a burrowing rodent native to S America, that resembles a chinchilla but is slightly larger. ⓒ 17c: Spanish, from Quechua *huiscacha*.

viscera /'vɪsərə/ ▷ *plural noun, anatomy* the internal organs of the body, especially those found in the abdominal cavity. See also VISCUS. ⓒ 17c: Latin, plural of *viscus* internal organ.

visceral /'vɪsərəl/ ▷ *adj* **1** belonging or relating to the viscera. **2** belonging or relating to the feelings, especially the basic human instincts as distinct from the intellect.

viscid /'vɪsɪd/ ▷ *adj* **1** glutinous; sticky. **2** said of a surface, especially a leaf: clammy and covered with a sticky secretion. • **viscidity** *noun*. ⓒ 17c: from Latin *viscum* bird-lime.

viscose /'vɪskoʊs/ ▷ *noun* **1** cellulose in a viscous state, able to be made into thread. **2** RAYON made from such thread. ⓒ Late 19c.

viscosity /vɪs'kɒsɪtɪ/ ▷ *noun* (***viscosities***) (symbol η) **1** a measure of the resistance of a fluid to flow, caused by internal friction which results in different rates of flow in different parts of the liquid, eg treacle has a higher viscosity than water. **2** a quantity expressing this, measured in units of PASCAL or POISE.

viscount /'vaɪkaʊnt/ ▷ *noun* **1** a member of the British nobility ranked below an earl and above a baron. **2** *historical* an officer who acted as administrative deputy to an earl; a sheriff. • **viscountcy** or **viscounty** (***viscountcies*** or ***viscounties***) *noun*. • **viscountship** *noun*. ⓒ 14c: from French *visconte*.

viscountess /'vaɪkaʊntɪs/ ▷ *noun* **1** the wife or widow of a viscount. **2** a woman of the rank of viscount in her own right.

viscous /'vɪskəs/ ▷ *adj* **1** with a thick semi-liquid consistency; not flowing easily. **2** said of liquid: sticky. • **viscously** *adverb*. • **viscousness** *noun*. ⓒ 14c: from Latin *viscosus* sticky, from *viscum* bird-lime.

viscus /'vɪskəs/ ▷ *noun* (*plural* ***viscera*** /'vɪsərə/) *medicine* any one of the body's large internal organs. See also VISCERA. ⓒ 18c: Latin.

vise the *N Amer* spelling of VICE[1].

Vishnu /'vɪʃnuː/ ▷ *noun, Hinduism* the second god of the Hindu TRIMURTI, believed to appear in many incarnations and regarded by some worshippers as the saviour. ⓒ 18c: Sanskrit.

visibility /vɪzɪ'bɪlɪtɪ/ ▷ *noun* **1** the state or fact of being visible. **2** the range in which one can see clearly in given conditions of light and weather ▫ ***poor visibility*** ▫ ***visibility down to 20 yards.***

visible /'vɪzɪbəl/ ▷ *adj* **1** able to be seen. **2** able to be realized or perceived; apparent ▫ ***his visible discomfort.*** **3** *econ* relating to actual goods rather than services. • **visibleness** *noun*. • **visibly** *adverb*. ⓒ 14c: from Latin *visibilis*, from *videre* to see.

visible exports ▷ *plural noun* goods which are sold abroad by traders. Compare INVISIBLE *adj* 3.

visible horizon see HORIZON

visible panty line see under VPL

visible spectrum ▷ *noun, physics* the range of wavelengths of electromagnetic radiation that can be seen by the human eye, ie visible light, ranging from about 390nm to 780nm.

Visigoth /'vɪzɪgɒθ/ ▷ *noun, historical* a member of the Western Goths, who formed settlements in France and Spain in the 5c and whose kingdom in Spain lasted until the 8c. Compare OSTROGOTH. ⓒ 17c: from Latin *Visigothus*, with the first element perhaps meaning 'west'.

vision /'vɪʒən/ ▷ *noun* **1** the ability or faculty of perceiving with the eye; sight. **2** an image conjured up vividly in the imagination. **3** the ability to perceive what is likely, and plan wisely for it; foresight. **4** an image communicated supernaturally, especially by God; an apparition. **5 a** the picture on a TV screen; **b** the quality of such a picture. **6** someone or something of overwhelming beauty ▫ ***a vision in pink taffeta.*** • **visional** *adj*. ⓒ 13c: from Latin *visio* sight, from *videre, visum* to see.

visionary /'vɪʒənərɪ/ ▷ *adj* **1** showing or marked by great foresight or imagination. **2** possible only in the imagination; impracticable; fanciful. **3** capable of seeing supernatural images or apparitions. ▷ *noun* (***visionaries***) a visionary person. • **visionariness** *noun*.

vision mixer ▷ *noun* in video and film production: **1** a person whose job is to blend or combine different camera images, by switching from one to another in order to create the visual effects required by the director. **2** the operator of this equipment.

visit /'vɪzɪt/ ▷ *verb* (***visited, visiting***) **1** *tr & intr* to go or come to see (a person or place) socially or professionally.

2 *tr & intr* to go or come to stay with someone temporarily. **3** (*usually* **visit something on someone**) to inflict (harm or punishment) on them. **4** to enter the mind of someone temporarily. **5** (*usually* **visit someone with something**) *old use* to afflict or trouble them □ *The plague visited the villagers with dire consequences.* **6** *N Amer colloq* (*usually* **visit with someone**) to have a chat with them. ▷ *noun* **1** an act of visiting; a social or professional call. **2** a temporary stay. **3** a sightseeing excursion. • **visitable** *adj.* ◷ 13c: from Latin *visitare*, from *visere* to go to see.

visitant ▷ *noun* **1** *relig* a person appearing in a supernatural vision; an apparition. **2** a VISITOR (sense 2).

visitation ▷ *noun* **1** an official visit or inspection. **2** an event regarded as a divine punishment or reward. **3** an instance of seeing a supernatural vision. **4** (**the Visitation**) **a** the visit made by the Virgin Mary to her cousin Elizabeth (Luke 1.39–56); **b** the Christian festival commemorating this, held on 2 July. **5** *informal* an unduly long or wearisome visit.

visitatorial /vɪzɪtə'tɔːrɪəl/ or **visitorial** /vɪzɪ'tɔːrɪəl/ ▷ *adj* belonging or relating to an official visit or visitation.

visiting card ▷ *noun* a card with one's name, address, etc printed on it, which is left instead of a formal visit. *N Amer equivalent* CALLING CARD.

visitor ▷ *noun* **1** someone who visits a person or place. **2** (*also* **visitant**) a migratory bird present in a place for a time □ *winter visitors.*

visitors' book ▷ *noun* a book in which visitors to a hotel, museum, etc write their names and addresses and often any comments they have regarding their visit.

visitor's passport ▷ *noun, formerly* in the UK: a type of passport, usually issued by post offices and valid for one year, allowing holders to visit certain countries for a period not exceeding three months. It was phased out in December 1995.

visor or **vizor** /'vaɪzə(r)/ ▷ *noun* **1** the movable part of a helmet, covering the face. **2** a SUN VISOR. ◷ 14c: from French *viser*, from *vis* face.

vista /'vɪstə/ ▷ *noun* (*vistas*) **1** a view into the distance, especially one bounded narrowly on both sides, eg by rows of trees. **2** a mental vision extending over a lengthy period of time into the future or past. ◷ 17c: Italian, meaning 'view', from Latin *videre*, *visum* to see.

visual /'vɪʒʊəl/ ▷ *adj* **1** relating to or received through sight or vision □ *a visual image.* **2** creating vivid mental images □ *visual poetry.* **3** creating a strong impression through what is seen, rather than what is said or heard □ *a very visual play.* ▷ *noun* **1** a rough sketch of the layout of an advertisement. **2** (*usually* **visuals**) a drawing, piece of film, etc as distinct from the words or sounds accompanying it. • **visually** *adverb.* ◷ 15c: from Latin *visualis*, from *visus* sight.

visual aid ▷ *noun* a picture, film or other visual material used as an aid to teaching or presenting information.

visual arts ▷ *plural noun* (*usually* **the visual arts**) the art-forms painting, sculpture, film, etc, as opposed to literature, music, etc.

visual display unit ▷ *noun* (abbreviation **VDU**) a screen on which information from a computer is displayed.

visualize or **visualise** /'vɪʒʊəlaɪz/ ▷ *verb* (***visualized***, ***visualizing***) to form a clear mental image of someone or something. • **visualization** *noun*.

visually challenged ▷ *adj, euphemistic* blind.

visual purple see RHODOPSIN

vital /'vaɪtəl/ ▷ *adj* **1** relating to or essential for life □ *the vital organs.* **2** determining life or death, or success or failure □ *a vital error.* **3** essential; of the greatest importance. **4** full of life; energetic. ▷ *noun* (**vitals**) the vital organs, including the brain, heart and lungs. • **vitally** *adverb.* ◷ 14c: from Latin *vitalis*, from *vita* life.

vital capacity ▷ *noun, physiol* the volume of air that can be expelled from the lungs after taking the deepest breath possible.

vitality /vaɪ'talɪtɪ/ ▷ *noun* **1** liveliness and energy. **2** the state of being alive; the ability to stay alive.

vitalize or **vitalise** /'vaɪtəlaɪz/ ▷ *verb* (***vitalized***, ***vitalizing***) to fill someone with life or energy. • **vitalization** *noun*.

vital spark ▷ *noun* the important principle of life in humans.

vital statistics ▷ *plural noun* **1** statistics concerning births, marriages, deaths and other matters relating to population. **2** *colloq* a woman's bust, waist and hip measurements.

vitamin /'vɪtəmɪn, 'vaɪ-/ ▷ *noun* any of various organic compounds that occur in small amounts in many foods, are also manufactured synthetically and are essential in small amounts for the normal growth and functioning of the body. Only the B complex and vitamin C are water-soluble and hence are excreted, requiring regular replacement. ◷ Early 20c: from Latin *vita* life + AMINE.

vitamin A ▷ *noun* a fat-soluble organic compound found in liver, fish oils, dairy products and egg yolk, required for normal growth and especially the functioning of the light-sensitive rods and cones of the retina. Also called **retinol** /'rɛtɪnɒl/.

vitamin B_1 *noun* a member of the vitamin B complex found in yeast, wheat germ, peas, beans and green vegetables, a deficiency of which causes BERIBERI. Also called **thiamine** /'θaɪəmiːn/. Previously called **aneurin**.

vitamin B_2 *noun*, a member of the vitamin B complex, found in eg yeast, liver and green vegetables, which is required to promote growth in children, and also used as a yellow or orange food colouring. Also called **riboflavin** /raɪboʊ'fleɪvɪn/ or **riboflavine** /-viːn/.

vitamin B_6 pɪrɪ'dɒksiːn/ *noun* any of three interconvertible organic compounds in the vitamin B complex found in milk, eggs, liver, cereal grains, yeast and fresh vegetables, required for the metabolism of amino acids. Also called **pyridoxine** /.

vitamin B_7 *noun* a member of the vitamin B complex found in liver, yeast extracts, cereals, peas and beans, and is essential for human nutrition and prevention of PELLAGRA. Also called **nicotinic acid** /nɪkə'tɪnɪk—/ and **niacin** /'naɪəsɪn/.

vitamin B_{12} *noun* three active forms of the vitamin B complex found in eggs, milk and liver, and required for the metabolism of fatty acids, DNA synthesis and the formation of red blood cells (and hence prevention of pernicious anaemia). Also called **cyanocobalamin** /saɪənoʊkə'baləmɪn/.

vitamin B complex ▷ *noun* any of a group of closely inter-related, but distinctly different, water-soluble substances, no one capable of replacing another as a vitamin, found in yeast, liver and wheat germ, and referred to either by individual B numbers, eg VITAMIN B_1, VITAMIN B_2, or by specific names, eg thiamine, riboflavin.

vitamin C ▷ *noun* a white crystalline water-soluble organic compound found in fresh fruits, especially citrus fruits and blackcurrants, potatoes and green vegetables, required for the maintenance of healthy bones, cartilage and teeth. Also called **ascorbic acid** /ə'skɔːbɪk —/.

vitamin D ▷ *noun* a complex of vitamin D_2 (**calciferol**), provitamin D_2 (**ergosterol**) and vitamin D_3 (**cholecalciferol**), found in fish liver oils, egg yolk and milk, and required for the deposition of adequate amounts of calcium and phosphates in the bones (and hence to prevent RICKETS) and teeth.

vitamin E ▷ *noun* any of various related fat-soluble organic compounds found in wholemeal flour, wheat germ and green vegetables, and which may be required for maintenance of the structure of cell membranes. Also called **tocopherol** /tɒˈkɒfərɒl/.

vitamin H ▷ *noun* BIOTIN.

vitamin K ▷ *noun* either of two fat-soluble organic compounds (vitamins K_1 and K_2) found in green leafy vegetables, and also manufactured by bacteria in the intestines, required for the production of several proteins involved in blood clotting.

vitamin P ▷ *noun* BIOFLAVONOID.

vitiate /ˈvɪʃɪeɪt/ ▷ *verb* (***vitiated, vitiating***) **1** to impair the quality or effectiveness of (eg an argument); to make something faulty or defective. **2** to make (eg a legal contract) ineffectual or invalid. • **vitiation** /vɪʃɪˈeɪʃən/ *noun*. • **vitiator** *noun*. ⓒ 16c: from Latin *vitiare*, from *vitium* blemish.

viticulture /ˈvɪtɪkʌltʃə(r)/ ▷ *noun* the cultivation of grapes for making wine; viniculture. • **viticultural** *adj*. • **viticulturist** *noun*. ⓒ 19c: from Latin *vitis* vine + CULTURE.

vitiligo /vɪtɪˈlaɪgoʊ/ ▷ *noun, pathol* a condition in which irregular patches of the skin lose colour and turn white. ⓒ 17c: Latin, meaning a skin eruption.

vitreous /ˈvɪtrɪəs/ ▷ *adj* **1** relating to or consisting of glass. **2** like glass in hardness, sheen or transparency □ *vitreous china*. • **vitreousness** *noun*. ⓒ 17c: from Latin *vitreus*, from *vitrum* glass.

vitreous humour ▷ *noun, anatomy* a gelatinous substance inside the eye, between the lens and the retina. Compare AQUEOUS HUMOUR.

vitrescent /vɪˈtrɛsənt/ ▷ *adj* tending to become glass or capable of being turned into glass. • **vitrescence** *noun*.

vitriform /ˈvɪtrɪfɔːm/ ▷ *adj* resembling glass in form or appearance.

vitrify /ˈvɪtrɪfaɪ/ ▷ *verb* (***vitrifies, vitrified, vitrifying***) *tr & intr* to make into or become glass or something like glass, especially by heating. • **vitrification** /-fɪˈkeɪʃən/ *noun*. ⓒ 16c: from French *vitrifier*, from Latin *vitrum* glass + *facere* to make.

vitriol /ˈvɪtrɪəl/ ▷ *noun* **1** concentrated sulphuric acid. **2** a sulphate of a metal, originally one of a glassy appearance. **3** extremely bitter or hateful speech or criticism. ⓒ 14c: from Latin *vitriolum*, from *vitrum* glass.

vitriolic /vɪtrɪˈɒlɪk/ ▷ *adj* extremely bitter or hateful, especially with reference to speech or criticism.

vitta /ˈvɪtə/ ▷ *noun* (*vittae* /ˈvɪtiː/) **1** *bot* a thin elongated cavity containing oil found in the PERICARPS of some fruits. **2** *zool* a stripe of colour. ⓒ 19c in these senses: Latin, meaning 'a band worn round the head'.

vituperate /vɪˈtʃuːpəreɪt, vaɪ-/ ▷ *verb* (***vituperated, vituperating***) **1** to attack someone with abusive criticism or disapproval. **2** *intr* to use abusive language. • **vituperation** *noun*. • **vituperative** *adj*. ⓒ 16c: from Latin *vituperare*, *vituperatum* to blame, from *vitium* a fault + *parare* to prepare.

viva[1] /ˈviːvə/ ▷ *exclamation* long live (someone or something named) □ *viva Rodriguez!* ⓒ 17c: Spanish and Italian, meaning 'live'.

viva[2] /ˈvaɪvə/ ▷ *noun* (*vivas*) a VIVA VOCE. ▷ *verb* (***vivas, vivaed, vivaing***) to examine someone orally. ⓒ 19c: Latin, shortened from VIVA VOCE.

vivace /vɪˈvɑːtʃɪ/ *music* ▷ *adverb* in a lively manner. ▷ *adj* lively. ▷ *noun* (*vivaces*) a piece of music to be played in this way. ⓒ 17c: Italian.

vivacious /vɪˈveɪʃəs, vaɪˈ-/ ▷ *adj* attractively lively and animated, especially with reference to a person. • **vivaciously** *adverb*. • **vivacity** /vɪˈvasɪtɪ/ or **vivaciousness** *noun*. ⓒ 17c: from Latin *vivax* lively, from *vivere* to live.

vivarium /vaɪˈvɛərɪəm/ ▷ *noun* (***vivariums*** or ***vivaria*** /-rɪə/) any place or enclosure in which live animals are kept, especially in conditions resembling their natural habitat. ⓒ 16c: Latin, from *vivere* to live.

viva voce /ˈvaɪvə ˈvoʊtʃɪ/ ▷ *adverb* in speech; orally. ▷ *noun* (*viva voces*) an oral examination, usually for an academic qualification. Often shortened to VIVA. ⓒ 16c: Latin, meaning 'by the living voice'.

vivid /ˈvɪvɪd/ ▷ *adj* **1** said of a colour: strong and bright. **2** creating or providing a clear and immediate mental picture □ *gave a vivid account of the incident* □ *She has a vivid imagination.* **3** said of a person: full of life; vivacious. • **vividly** *adverb*. • **vividness** *noun*. ⓒ 17c: from Latin *vividus* lively, from *vivere* to live.

vivify /ˈvɪvɪfaɪ/ ▷ *verb* (***vivifies, vivified, vivifying***) **1** to endue something with life. **2** to make something more vivid or startling. • **vivification** *noun*. ⓒ 16c: from French *vivifier*, from Latin *vivificare*, from *vivus* living.

viviparous /vɪˈvɪpərəs, vaɪ-/ ▷ *adj* **1** *zool* said of an animal: giving birth to live young that have developed within the mother's body, as in humans and most other mammals. Compare OVIPAROUS and OVOVIVIPAROUS. **2** *bot* denoting a form of asexual reproduction in which new young plants start to develop on the parent plant while still attached to it, as in the spider plant and certain grasses. • **viviparity** /vɪvɪˈparɪtɪ/ *noun*. • **viviparously** *adverb*. • **viviparousness** *noun*. ⓒ 17c: from Latin *vivus* alive + *parere* to produce.

vivisect /ˈvɪvɪsɛkt, -ˈsɛkt/ ▷ *verb* (***vivisected, vivisecting***) to perform vivisection on (an animal, etc). • **vivisector** *noun*.

vivisection ▷ *noun* **1** *strictly* the practice of dissecting living animals for experimental purposes. **2** *loosely* used to refer to any form of ANIMAL EXPERIMENTATION. • **vivisectional** *adj*. ⓒ 18c: from Latin *vivus* living + *secare* to cut.

vivisectionist ▷ *noun* **1** someone who performs vivisection. **2** someone who advocates the use of vivisection as being useful or necessary for science.

vixen /ˈvɪksən/ ▷ *noun* **1** a female fox. **2** a fierce or spiteful woman. • **vixenish** or **vixenly** *adj*. ⓒ Anglo-Saxon *fyxen*.

viz. /vɪz/ ▷ *adverb* (*in full* **videlicet** /vɪˈdeɪlɪsɛt/) used especially in writing: namely; that is. ⓒ 16c: an abbreviation of Latin *videlicet*, from *videre* to see + *licet* it is allowed.

vizcacha see VISCACHA

vizier /vɪˈzɪə(r), ˈvɪzɪə(r)/ ▷ *noun* a high-ranking government official in certain Muslim countries, especially in Turkey during the Ottoman Empire. • **vizierate** *noun*. • **vizierial** *adj*. ⓒ 16c: from Turkish *vezir*, from Arabic *wazir* porter, hence a bearer of a burden.

vizor see VISOR

vizsla /ˈvɪʒlə/ ▷ *noun* (*vizslas*) a breed of Hungarian hunting dog with a smooth red or rust-coloured coat. ⓒ 1940s: named after a town in Hungary.

VLF ▷ *abbreviation, radio* very low frequency.

VMH ▷ *abbreviation* Victoria Medal of Honour.

VN ▷ *abbreviation, IVR* Vietnam.

V-neck ▷ *noun* **1** the open neck of a garment cut or formed to a point at the front. **2** a garment, especially a pullover, with such a neck. ▷ *adj* (*also* **V-necked**) □ *a red V-neck jumper*.

VOA ▷ *abbreviation* Voice of America.

voc. ▷ *abbreviation* vocative.

vocab /ˈvoʊkab/ ▷ *noun, colloq* vocabulary.

vocable /ˈvoʊkəbəl/ ▻ *noun, linguistics* **1** a spoken word or single sound in a word. **2** a spoken or written word regarded as a series of sounds or letters, rather than as a unit of meaning. ⓘ 16c: from Latin *vocabulum*, from *vocare* to call.

vocabulary /vəˈkabjʊlərɪ, voʊ-/ ▻ *noun* (***vocabularies***) **1** the words used in speaking or writing a particular language. **2** the words, or range of words, known to or used by a particular person or group. **3** a list of words with translations in another language alongside. **4** a range of artistic or stylistic forms and techniques. ⓘ 16c: from Latin *vocabularius*, from *vocabulum* VOCABLE.

vocal /ˈvoʊkəl/ ▻ *adj* **1** relating to or produced by the voice. **2** expressing opinions or criticism freely and forcefully □ *She was very vocal in her support for the homeless.* **3** *phonetics* voiced. ▻ *noun* (**vocals**) the parts of a musical composition that are sung, as distinct from the instrumental accompaniment. • **vocally** *adverb*. ⓘ 14c: from Latin *vocalis*, from *vox* voice.

vocal cords ▻ *noun, anatomy* in mammals: the two folds of tissue within the larynx that vibrate and produce sound when air is expelled from the lungs.

vocalic /voʊˈkalɪk/ ▻ *adj* belonging or relating to, or containing, a vowel or vowels.

vocalise¹ /voʊkəˈliːz/ ▻ *noun, music* an exercise in which a vowel sound is sung over and over, usually to develop control over pitch and tone.

vocalise² see VOCALIZE

vocalism ▻ *noun* **1** the use of the voice as in singing or speaking. **2 a** a vowel sound; **b** a system of vowels.

vocalist ▻ *noun* a singer, especially in a pop group or jazz band.

vocalize or **vocalise** /ˈvoʊkəlaɪz/ ▻ *verb* (***vocalized, vocalizing***) **1** to utter or produce something with the voice. **2** to express in words; to articulate. **3** to VOWELIZE. **4** *intr* to sing on a vowel or vowels. • **vocalization** *noun*.

vocally see under VOCAL

vocation /voʊˈkeɪʃən/ ▻ *noun* **1** a particular occupation or profession, especially one regarded as needing dedication and skill. **2** a feeling of being especially suited for a particular type of work. **3** *relig* a divine calling to adopt a religious life or perform good works. • **vocational** *adj*. • **vocationally** *adverb*. ⓘ 15c: from Latin *vocare* to call.

vocational education ▻ *noun* education aimed at preparing students for their present or future employment, which may take place in colleges of further education, universities or in the workplace itself and is increasingly being offered to secondary school pupils in the form of work experience.

vocative /ˈvɒkətɪv/ *grammar* ▻ *noun* (abbreviation **voc.**) **1** in some languages, eg Latin and Greek: the form or CASE of a noun, pronoun or adjective used when a person or thing is addressed directly. **2** a noun, etc in this case. ▻ *adj* belonging to or in this case. ⓘ 15c: from Latin *vocativus*, from *vocare* to call.

vociferate /vəˈsɪfəreɪt/ ▻ *verb* (***vociferated, vociferating***) *tr & intr, formal* **1** to exclaim loudly and forcefully. **2** to shout or cry in a loud voice; to bawl. ⓘ 17c: from Latin *vociferari, vociferatus*, from *vox* voice + *ferre* to carry.

vociferous /vəˈsɪfərəs/ ▻ *adj* **1** loud and forceful, especially in expressing opinions. **2** noisy. • **vociferously** *adverb*. • **vociferousness** *noun*.

vocoder /voʊˈkoʊdə(r)/ ▻ *noun* a type of synthesizer used to impose human speech patterns onto the sound of musical instruments. ⓘ 1930s: from *voice coder*.

VOD ▻ *abbreviation* video on demand.

Vodafone /ˈvoʊdəfoʊn/ ▻ *noun, trademark* in the UK: **1** a system of mobile telecommunications using cellular radio. **2** a cellular phone used in this system.

vodka /ˈvɒdkə/ ▻ *noun* (***vodkas***) **1** a clear alcoholic spirit of Russian origin, traditionally made from rye, but sometimes from potatoes. **2** a drink of this □ *Do you fancy a vodka?* ⓘ 19c: Russian, literally 'little water' from *voda* water.

voe /voʊ/ ▻ *noun* in Orkney and Shetland: a bay; a creek. ⓘ 17c: from Norse *vagr*.

vogue /voʊg/ ▻ *noun* **1** (*usually* **the vogue**) the current fashion or trend in any sphere. **2** a period of being fashionable or popular □ *The little black dress has enjoyed a long vogue.* • **voguish** *adj*. • **in vogue** in fashion. ⓘ 16c: French, meaning 'fashion' or 'rowing', from Italian *vogare* to row.

vogue word ▻ *noun* a word that is currently fashionable.

voice /vɔɪs/ ▻ *noun* **1** a sound produced by the vocal organs and uttered through the mouth, especially by humans in speech or song. **2** the ability to speak; the power of speech □ *lost his voice.* **3** a way of speaking or singing peculiar to each individual □ *couldn't recognize the voice.* **4** a tone of speech reflecting a particular emotion □ *in a nervous voice.* **5** the sound of someone speaking □ *heard a voice.* **6** the ability to sing, especially to sing well □ *has no voice* □ *has a lovely voice.* **7** expression in the form of spoken words □ *gave voice to their feelings.* **8** a means or medium of expression or communication □ *newspapers as the voice of the people.* **9** *grammar* the status or function of a verb in being either ACTIVE or PASSIVE. ▻ *verb* (***voiced, voicing***) **1** to express something in speech □ *He voiced his disapproval.* **2** *phonetics* to pronounce (a sound) with a vibration of the vocal cords. • **give voice to something** to express it. • **in good voice** singing well. • **with one voice** unanimously. ⓘ 13c: from French *vois*, from Latin *vox*.

voice box ▻ *noun, colloq* the larynx.

voiced ▻ *adj* **1** expressed in speech. **2** *phonetics* pronounced with a vibration of the vocal cords, as in *z, d, b*. **3** *in compounds* having a specified tone, style, etc of voice □ *husky-voiced* □ *sweet-voiced.*

voiceless ▻ *adj* **1** without a voice. **2** *phonetics* produced without vibration of the vocal cords, as in *s, t, p*. • **voicelessly** *adverb*. • **voicelessness** *noun*.

Voice of America ▻ *noun* (abbreviation **VOA**) the branch of the US Information Agency that broadcasts news and entertainment programmes to the world.

voice-over ▻ *noun* (***voice-overs***) the voice of an unseen narrator in a film, TV advertisement or programme, etc. ⓘ 1940s.

voiceprint ▻ *noun* an electronically recorded visual representation of speech, indicating frequency, amplitude and duration.

void /vɔɪd/ ▻ *adj* **1** not valid or legally binding □ *declared the contract null and void.* **2** containing nothing; empty or unoccupied. **3** (*usually* **void of something**) lacking in it □ *void of humour.* ▻ *noun* **1** an empty space. **2** a space left blank or unfilled. **3** a feeling of absence or emptiness strongly felt. **4** (*usually* **void in something**) *cards* lacking (cards of a particular suit) □ *void in hearts.* ▻ *verb* (***voided, voiding***) **1** to make empty or clear. **2** to invalidate or nullify. **3** to empty (the bladder or bowels). • **voidable** *adj*. • **voidness** *noun*. ⓘ 13c: from French *voide* empty.

voidance ▻ *noun* **1** a vacancy in a benefice. **2 a** an act of voiding or emptying; **b** the state of being voided.

voile /vɔɪl, vwɑːl/ ▻ *noun* any very thin semi-transparent fabric. ⓘ 19c: French, meaning 'veil'.

voix céleste /vwaː sɪˈlɛst/ ▻ *noun, music* an organ stop producing a soft tremulous sound. Also called **vox angelica** /vɒks anˈdʒɛlɪkə/. ⓘ 19c: French, meaning 'heavenly voice'.

vol. or **vol** ▻ *abbreviation* **1** volume. **2** volunteer. **3** voluntary.

volant /'voʊlənt/ ▻ *adj* **1** *zool* **a** belonging or relating to flight; **b** able to fly. **2** *heraldry* represented as flying. **3** *poetic* nimble. ◷ 16c: French, from *voler* to fly, from Latin *volare*.

volatile /'vɒlətaɪl/ ▻ *adj* **1** changing quickly from a solid or liquid into a vapour. **2** explosive. **3** easily becoming angry or violent. **4** said of a situation, etc: liable to change quickly, especially verging on violence. **5** *computing* said of a memory: not able to retain data after the power supply has been cut off. ▻ *noun* a volatile substance. • **volatileness** or **volatility** *noun*. ◷ 17c in sense 1; 12c in obsolete sense 'birds': from Latin *volatilis*, from *volare* to fly.

volatile oil see ESSENTIAL OIL

volatilize or **volatilise** /vɒ'latɪlaɪz, 'vɒlə-/ ▻ *verb* (***volatilized, volatilizing***) *tr & intr* to change from a solid or liquid into a vapour. • **volatilization** *noun*. • **volatilizable** *adj*.

vol-au-vent /'vɒloʊvɑ̃/ ▻ *noun* a small round puff-pastry case with a savoury filling. ◷ 19c: French, literally 'flight in the wind'.

volcanic /vɒl'kanɪk/ ▻ *adj* **1** relating to or produced by a volcano or volcanoes. **2** easily erupting into anger or violence □ *a volcanic temper.*

volcano /vɒl'keɪnoʊ/ ▻ *noun* (***volcanoes***) **1** any of various vents in the Earth's crust through which MAGMA is or has previously been forced out onto the surface, forming various structures but usually taking the form of a conical hill due to the build up of solidified lava. **2** a situation or person likely to erupt into anger or violence. ◷ 17c: Italian, from Latin *Vulcanus* Roman god of fire.

volcanology see VULCANOLOGY

vole /voʊl/ ▻ *noun* a small rodent related to the lemming, with a small tail, blunt snout and smaller eyes and ears, found in Europe, Asia, N Africa and N America. ◷ 19c: originally *vole-mouse*, from Norwegian *voll* field + *mus* mouse.

volition /və'lɪʃən/ ▻ *noun* the act of willing or choosing; the exercising of one's will □ *She did it of her own volition.* • **volitional** *adj*. • **volitionally** *adverb*. ◷ 17c: French, from Latin *volitio*, from *volo* I wish.

volitive /'vɒlɪtɪv/ ▻ *adj* **1** belonging or relating to the will. **2** originating in the will.

volley /'vɒlɪ/ ▻ *noun* (***volleys***) **1 a** a firing of several guns or other weapons simultaneously; **b** the bullets, missiles, etc discharged. **2** an aggressive outburst, especially of criticism or insults. **3** *sport* a striking of the ball before it bounces. ▻ *verb* (***volleys, volleyed, volleying***) **1** *tr & intr* to fire (weapons) in a volley. **2** *tr & intr, sport* to strike (a ball) before it bounces. **3** to utter (words, oaths, etc) in an aggressive outburst. • **volleyer** *noun*. ◷ 16c: from French *volée*, from Latin *volare* to fly.

volleyball ▻ *noun, sport* **1** a game for two teams of six players each, in which a large ball is volleyed back and forth over a high net with the hands. **2** the ball used in the game.

volt[1] /voʊlt/ ▻ *noun* (symbol **V**) in the SI system: a unit of electric potential, the difference in potential that will carry a current of one ampere across a resistance of one ohm. ◷ 19c: named after the Italian physicist Alessandro Volta (1745–1827).

volt[2] or **volte** /vɒlt/ ▻ *verb* (***volted, volting***) *fencing* to make a volt. ▻ *noun* **1** *fencing* a sudden movement or leap to avoid a thrust. **2 a** *dressage* a gait of a horse going sideways round a centre; **b** a track made by a horse doing this. ◷ 17c: from French, from Italian *volta* turn.

voltage ▻ *noun, elec* potential difference expressed as a number of volts.

voltaic cell see under PRIMARY CELL

voltaic pile /vɒl'teɪɪk —/ ▻ *noun* a type of early battery, devised by Allesandro Volta (1745–1827) comprising a number of flat VOLTAIC CELLS in SERIES, the ELECTROLYTE being absorbed into paper discs.

voltameter /vɒl'tamətə(r)/ ▻ *noun* an instrument used formerly for measuring electric charge.

volte see VOLT[2]

volte-face /vɒlt'fɑːs/ ▻ *noun* a sudden and complete reversal of opinion or policy. ◷ 19c: French, meaning 'turning face'.

voltmeter ▻ *noun, elec* an instrument that measures electromotive force in volts.

voluble /'vɒljʊbəl/ ▻ *adj* **1** speaking or spoken insistently, uninterruptedly or with ease. **2** tending to talk at great length. • **volubility** /-'bɪlɪtɪ/ *noun*. • **volubly** *adverb*. ◷ 16c: from Latin *volubilis*, from *volvere* to roll.

volume /'vɒljuːm/ ▻ *noun* **1** the amount of three-dimensional space occupied by an object, gas or liquid. **2 a** loudness of sound; **b** the control that adjusts it on a radio, hi-fi system, etc. **3 a** a book, whether complete in itself or one of several forming a larger work; **b** *in compounds, as adj* □ *a six-volume encyclopedia.* **4** an amount or quantity, especially when large □ *the volume of traffic.* • **speak volumes** to be very significant; to say a lot □ *The look on his face spoke volumes.* ◷ 14c: from French, from Latin *volumen* 'roll' or 'scroll', from *volvere* to roll.

volumetric analysis ▻ *noun, chem* a method of chemical analysis in which the unknown concentration of a solution of known volume is determined, usually by TITRATION.

voluminous /və'luːmɪnəs, -'ljuː-/ ▻ *adj* **1** said of clothing: flowing or billowing out; ample. **2** said of a writer: producing great quantities of writing. **3** said of writing: enough to fill many volumes. • **voluminously** *adverb*. • **voluminousness** *noun*. ◷ 17c: from Latin *voluminosus*, from *volumen* VOLUME.

voluntarism ▻ *noun* the philosophical doctrine that the will dominates the intellect as the most important factor in the universe or the individual.

voluntary /'vɒləntərɪ/ ▻ *adj* **1** done or acting by free choice, not by compulsion. **2** working with no expectation of being paid or otherwise rewarded. **3** said of work: unpaid. **4** said of an organization: staffed by unpaid workers; supported by donations of money freely given. **5** said of a movement, muscle or limb: produced or controlled by the will. **6** spontaneous; carried out without any persuasion. ▻ *noun* (***voluntaries***) a piece of music, usually for an organ, played before, during or after a church service. • **voluntarily** *adverb*. ◷ 14c: from Latin *voluntarius*, from *voluntas* will.

voluntary-aided school ▻ *noun* a state school which is funded mainly by the local education authority, with the Church providing the rest of the funding and therefore having a say in the religious education policy of the school.

voluntary-controlled school ▻ *noun* a state school funded completely by the local education authority.

voluntaryism ▻ *noun* **1** the principle or practice of relying on voluntary action and not coercion. **2** the practice or system of maintaining the Church by voluntary offerings, instead of by the aid of the state. **3** the principle or system of maintaining voluntary schools.

voluntary muscle ▻ *noun, anatomy* muscle that is under conscious control and produces voluntary movements by pulling against the bones of the skeleton to which it is attached by means of tendons. See also STRIATED MUSCLE. Compare INVOLUNTARY MUSCLE.

Voluntary Service Overseas ▻ *noun* (abbreviation **VSO**) a charity founded in 1958 to send skilled volunteers to work for two-year periods in developing countries, with the host government providing a living allowance and accommodation, and the charity providing the briefing, airfare and a grant.

volunteer /vɒlən'tɪə(r)/ ▻ *verb* (***volunteered, volunteering***) **1** *tr & intr* (*often* **volunteer for something**) to offer one's help or services freely, without being persuaded or forced. **2** *intr* to go into military service by choice, without being conscripted. **3** to give (information, etc) unasked. **4** *colloq* to assign someone to perform a task or give help without first asking them ▫ *I'm volunteering you for playground duty.* ▻ *noun* **1** someone who volunteers. **2** someone carrying out voluntary work. **3** a member of a non-professional army of voluntary soldiers set up during wartime. ⓒ 17c: from French *voluntaire*, from Latin *voluntarius* VOLUNTARY.

voluptuary /və'lʌptʃʊərɪ/ ▻ *noun* (***voluptuaries***) someone addicted to luxury and sensual pleasures. ▻ *adj* promoting or characterized by luxury and sensual pleasures. ⓒ 17c: from Latin *voluptas* pleasure.

voluptuous /və'lʌptʃʊəs/ ▻ *adj* **1** relating to or suggestive of sensual pleasure. **2** said of a woman: full-figured and sexually attractive; curvaceous. • **voluptuously** *adverb*. • **voluptuousness** *noun*. ⓒ 14c: from Latin *voluptas* pleasure.

volute /və'ljuːt, vɒ-/ ▻ *noun* **1** a spiral. **2** *archit* **a** a scroll carved in stone, especially at the top of an IONIC column; **b** a smaller scroll found in COMPOSITE and CORINTHIAN columns. **3** one single twist in a spiral shell. ⓒ 17c: from Latin *volvere, volutum* to roll.

vomit /'vɒmɪt/ ▻ *verb* (***vomited, vomiting***) **1** *tr & intr* to eject the contents of the stomach forcefully through the mouth through a reflex action; to be sick. **2** to emit or throw something out with force or violence. ▻ *noun* the contents of the stomach ejected during the process of vomiting. ⓒ 14c: from Latin *vomere*.

voodoo /'vuːduː/ ▻ *noun* (***voodoos***) **1** witchcraft of a type originally practised by the Black peoples of the West Indies and southern US. **2** the beliefs and practices of the religious cult that developed it, including serpent-worship and human sacrifice. ▻ *verb* (***voodoos, voodooed, voodooing***) to bewitch someone or something using, or as if using, voodoo methods. ⓒ 19c: from *vodu* (in various W African languages) spirit or demon.

Voortrekker /'fʊətrɛkə(r)/ ▻ *noun* **1** one of the Boer farmers from Cape Colony who took part in the Great Trek into the Transvaal in 1836 and following years, establishing the independent republics of the Orange Free State and the South African Republic. **2** a member of an Afrikaner Scout-type movement. ⓒ 19c: from Dutch *voor* before + *trekken* TREK.

voracious /və'reɪʃəs/ ▻ *adj* **1** eating or craving food in large quantities. **2** extremely eager in some respect ▫ *a voracious reader.* • **voraciously** *adverb*. • **voracity** /və'rasɪtɪ/ *noun*. ⓒ 17c: from Latin *vorare* to devour.

> ***voracity***
>
> A word often confused with this one is **veracity**.

vortex /'vɔːtɛks/ ▻ *noun* (***vortexes*** or ***vortices*** /-tɪsiːz/) **1** a whirlpool or whirlwind; any whirling mass or motion. **2** a situation or activity into which all surrounding people or things are helplessly and dangerously drawn. • **vortical** /'vɔːtɪkəl/ *adj*. • **vortically** *adverb*. ⓒ 17c: Latin, meaning 'a whirlpool', from *vortere* to turn.

vorticism /'vɔːtɪsɪzəm/ ▻ *noun, art* a British movement in painting developed from futurism, which blended cubism and expressionism, and emphasized the complications of machinery that characterize modern life. • **vorticist** *noun*. ⓒ 19c.

votary /'voʊtərɪ/ ▻ *noun* (***votaries***) **1** someone bound by solemn vows to a religious life. **2** someone dedicated to a particular cause or activity; a devout follower. • **votarist** *noun*. ⓒ 16c: from Latin *vovere, votum* to vow.

vote /voʊt/ ▻ *noun* **1** a formal indication of choice or opinion, eg in an election or debate. **2** the right to express a choice or opinion, especially in a national election ▫ *Asylum seekers do not have a vote.* **3** a choice or opinion expressed formally, eg by a show of hands, a mark on a BALLOT PAPER, etc ▫ *a vote in favour of the motion.* **4** the support given by a certain sector of the population, or to a particular candidate or group, in this way ▫ *He'll attract the middle-class vote.* ▻ *verb* (***voted, voting***) **1** *intr* to cast a vote in an election ▫ *Have you voted yet?* **2** to decide, state, grant or bring about something by a majority of votes ▫ *They voted that the tax be abolished* ▫ *voted to accept the proposal* ▫ *voted £100 for the project.* **3** *colloq* to declare or pronounce by general consent ▫ *The show was voted a success.* **4** *colloq* to propose or suggest something ▫ *I vote that we go for a swim.* • **voter** *noun*. • **votable** *adj*. • **vote with one's feet** to indicate one's dissatisfaction with a situation or condition by leaving. ⓒ 14c: from Latin *votum* wish, from *vovere* to vow.

> ■ **vote someone** or **something down** to reject or defeat them or it by voting.
>
> ■ **vote for** or **against something** or **someone** to cast a vote in favour of or in opposition to (a proposal, candidate, etc).
>
> ■ **vote someone in** to appoint them by voting; to elect them ▫ *voted the Green candidate in.*
>
> ■ **vote someone into, out of, off,** *etc* **something** to appoint or elect them to or from a particular post ▫ *voted off the committee* ▫ *voted out of the White House.*
>
> ■ **vote someone out** to dismiss them from office ▫ *was voted out.*

vote of confidence and **vote of no confidence** ▻ *noun* a vote taken to show whether the majority support or disapprove of a person or group in authority or leadership, especially the government.

votive /'voʊtɪv/ ▻ *adj, relig* done or given in thanks to a deity, or to fulfil a vow or promise. ⓒ 16c: from Latin *votivus*, from Latin *vovere* to vow.

vouch /vaʊtʃ/ ▻ *verb* (***vouches, vouched, vouching***) **1** *intr* (*usually* **vouch for someone** or **something**) to give a firm assurance or guarantee of their authenticity, trustworthiness, etc. **2** to give (evidence) in support of a statement, assertion, etc. ⓒ 16c in these senses; 14c in legal sense 'to summon': from French *voucher* to call upon to defend.

voucher ▻ *noun* **1** a ticket or paper serving as proof, eg of the purchase or receipt of goods. **2** *especially in compounds* a ticket worth a specific amount of money, exchangeable for goods or services up to the same value ▫ *gift voucher.* **3** someone who vouches for someone or something.

voucher scheme ▻ *noun, education* a scheme giving parents a voucher equivalent in value to the average cost of a child's education, which they are then entitled to 'spend' at the school of their choice

vouchsafe /vaʊtʃ'seɪf/ ▻ *verb* (***vouchsafed, vouchsafing***) *tr & intr, literary* **1** to agree or condescend to do, give, grant or allow. **2** (*usually* **vouchsafe to do something**) to condescend to do it. ⓒ 14c.

voussoir /vuː'swɑː(r)/ ▻ *noun, archit* one of the wedge-shaped stones that form part of the centre line of an arch. Also called **arch stone**. ▻ *verb* (***voussoired, voussoiring***) to form (an arch) with voussoirs. ⓒ 18c: French, from Latin *volsorium*, from *volvere* to roll.

vow /vaʊ/ ▻ *noun* (***vows***) **1** a solemn and binding promise, especially one made to or in the name of a deity. **2** (*often* **vows**) a solemn or formal promise of fidelity or affection ▫ *marriage vows.* **3** (*usually* **baptismal vows**) the promises made at baptism by the person being baptized, or by their sponsors or parents. ▻ *verb* (***vowed,***

vowing) *tr & intr* to promise or declare solemnly, or threaten emphatically; to swear. ◷ 13c: from French *vou*, from Latin *votum* VOTE.

vowel /ˈvaʊəl/ ▻ *noun* **1** any speech-sound made with an open mouth and no contact between mouth, lips, teeth or tongue. **2** a letter of the alphabet, used alone or in combination, representing such a sound, in English, eg *a*, *e*, *i*, *o*, *u*, *ai*, *oa* and in some words *y*. Compare CONSONANT. ◷ 14c: from French *vouel*, from Latin *vocalis* vocal, from *vox* voice.

vowel gradation ▻ *noun* another word for ABLAUT.

vowelize or **vowelise** ▻ *verb* (***vowelized***, ***vowelizing***) to mark the vowel points in (a shorthand, Hebrew, etc text). Also called VOCALIZE.

vowel point ▻ *noun* a mark inserted into a text using a consonantal alphabet, as in Hebrew, Arabic, etc to indicate a vowel sound.

vox angelica see under VOIX CÉLESTE

vox humana /vɒks hjuːˈmɑːnə/ ▻ *noun, music* an organ stop producing tones which resemble the human voice. ◷ 18c: Latin, meaning 'human voice'.

vox pop ▻ *noun, broadcasting* **1** popular opinion derived from comments given informally by members of the public. **2** an interview in which such opinions are expressed. ◷ 1960s: shortened from VOX POPULI.

vox populi /vɒks ˈpɒpjʊliː, -laɪ/ ▻ *noun* public opinion; popular belief. ◷ 16c: Latin, meaning 'voice of the people'.

voyage /ˈvɔɪɪdʒ/ ▻ *noun* **1** a long journey to a distant place, especially by air or sea. **2** a journey into space. ▻ *verb* (***voyaged***, ***voyaging***) *intr* to go on a voyage; to travel. • **voyager** *noun*. ◷ 13c: from French *voiage*, from Latin *viaticum* provision for a journey.

voyeur /vwɑːˈjɜː(r)/ ▻ *noun* **1** someone who derives gratification from furtively watching the sexual attributes or activities of others. **2** someone who observes, especially with fascination or intrusively, the feelings, actions, etc of others. • **voyeurism** *noun*. • **voyeuristic** *adj*. ◷ 20c: French, from *voir* to see.

VP ▻ *abbreviation* Vice-President.

VPL ▻ *abbreviation* visible panty line, the top or bottom of knickers, etc that can be seen as an indentation through outer clothing, eg in tight-fitting jeans, etc.

VR ▻ *abbreviation* **1** *Victoria Regina* (Latin), Queen Victoria. **2** virtual reality.

VRAM see VIDEO RAM

V. Rev. ▻ *abbreviation* Very Reverend.

VRI ▻ *abbreviation*: *Victoria Regina et Imperatrix* (Latin), Victoria, Queen and Empress.

vroom /vruːm, vrʊm/ *colloq* ▻ *noun* power, drive and energy □ *He's got vroom.* ▻ *verb* (***vroomed***, ***vrooming***) *intr* **1** to travel at speed □ *Pat vroomed along the motorway.* **2** to rev (a car engine) □ *He always vrooms the engine at the traffic lights.* ◷ 1960s: originally US, imitating the roaring sound of a car.

VS ▻ *abbreviation* Veterinary Surgeon.

vs or **vs.** ▻ *abbreviation* versus.

V-shaped ▻ *adj* referring to an object or mark shaped in the form of a V.

V-sign ▻ *noun, Brit* a sign made by raising the first two fingers and clasping the other fingers and the thumb in against the palm, an expression of victory with the palm turned outwards or an offensive gesture of contempt with the palm inwards. ◷ 1940s: meaning 'victory sign', first used in July 1941 by Victor de Lavelaye, working for the Belgium section of the BBC, to indicate no surrender, and particularly used to signify victory at the end of World War II.

VSO ▻ *abbreviation* Voluntary Service Overseas.

VSOP ▻ *abbreviation* very special old pale, a port, sherry or brandy between 20 and 25 years old.

VT ▻ *abbreviation, US state* Vermont. Also written **Vt.**

VTOL /ˈviːtɒl/ ▻ *noun* **1** a system that allows an aircraft to take off and land vertically. **2** an aircraft that is fitted with this system. See also VERTICAL TAKE-OFF. Compare STOL, HOTOL. ◷ 1960s: from *v*ertical *t*ake-*o*ff and *l*anding.

VTR ▻ *abbreviation* videotape recorder.

vulcanite /ˈvʌlkənaɪt/ ▻ *noun* hard black vulcanized rubber.

vulcanize or **vulcanise** /ˈvʌlkənaɪz/ ▻ *verb* (***vulcanized***, ***vulcanizing***) to treat natural or artificial rubber with various concentrations of sulphur or sulphur compounds at high temperatures for specific times, so as to harden it and increase its elasticity. • **vulcanization** *noun*. ◷ 19c: from Latin *Vulcanus* Roman god of fire.

vulcanology /vʌlkəˈnɒlədʒɪ/ or **volcanology** /vɒl-/ ▻ *noun* the scientific study of volcanoes and volcanic phenomena. • **vulcanological** *adj*. • **vulcanologist** *noun*.

vulg. ▻ *abbreviation* vulgar.

vulgar /ˈvʌlgə(r)/ ▻ *adj* **1** marked by a lack of politeness or social or cultural refinement; coarse. **2** belonging or relating to the form of a language commonly spoken, rather than formal or literary language; vernacular. • **vulgarly** *adverb*. ◷ 15c: from Latin *vulgaris*, from *vulgus* the people.

vulgar fraction ▻ *noun* a fraction expressed in the form of a numerator above a denominator, rather than in decimal form. Compare DECIMAL FRACTION.

vulgarian /vʌlˈgeɪrɪən/ ▻ *noun* a vulgar person, especially one who is rich.

vulgarism ▻ *noun* **1** a vulgar expression in speech. **2** an example of vulgar behaviour.

vulgarity /vʌlˈgarɪtɪ/ ▻ *noun* (***vulgarities***) **1** coarseness in speech or behaviour. **2** an instance of it.

vulgarize or **vulgarise** /ˈvʌlgəraɪz/ ▻ *verb* (***vulgarized***, ***vulgarizing***) **1** to make something vulgar. **2** to make something common or popular, or spoil it in this way. • **vulgarization** *noun*.

Vulgar Latin ▻ *noun* any of the spoken varieties of Latin in the early Common Era, as opposed to literary classical Latin.

Vulgate /ˈvʌlgeɪt, -gət/ ▻ *noun* **1** a Latin version of the Bible prepared mainly by St Jerome in the 4c, and later twice revised. **2** (**vulgate**) a comparable accepted text of any other book or author. **3** (**vulgate**) commonly used or accepted speech. ◷ 17c: from Latin *vulgata* (*editio*) popular (edition) (of the Bible), so called from its common use in the Roman Catholic church.

vulnerable /ˈvʌlnərəbəl/ ▻ *adj* **1** easily hurt or harmed physically or emotionally. **2** easily tempted or persuaded. **3** (*often* **vulnerable to something** or **someone**) unprotected against physical or verbal attack from them. **4** *bridge* said of a side that has won a game towards the rubber: liable to increased bonuses or penalties. • **vulnerability** or **vulnerableness** *noun*. • **vulnerably** *adverb*. ◷ 17c: from Latin *vulnerabilis*, from *vulnerare* to wound.

vulnerary /ˈvʌlnərərɪ/ ▻ *adj* **1** belonging or relating to wounds. **2** useful in healing wounds. ▻ *noun* (***vulneraries***) a vulnerary drug, medicine, etc. ◷ 16c: from Latin *vulnerarius*, from *vulnus* wound.

vulpine /ˈvʌlpaɪn, -pɪn/ ▻ *adj* **1** belonging or relating to, or resembling, a fox. **2** *formal* cunning like a fox. ◷ 17c: from Latin *vulpinus*, from *vulpes* fox.

vulture /ˈvʌltʃə(r)/ ▻ *noun* **1** any of various large carnivorous birds with brown or black plumage, long broad wings, a bare head and a strongly curved beak, which feed on carrion. **2** an American vulture or condor, sometimes referred to as a buzzard. **3** someone who exploits the downfall or death of another. See also CULTURE VULTURE. ⓔ 14c: from French *voltour*, from Latin *vultur*.

vulva /ˈvʌlvə/ ▷ *noun* (*vulvas*) *anatomy* the two pairs of labia surrounding the opening to the vagina; the external female genitals. • **vulval** *adj*. • **vulvar** *adj*. ⓔ 16c: Latin, meaning 'wrapping' or 'womb'.

vv ▷ *abbreviation* **1** versus. **2** vice versa.

VW ▷ *abbreviation* **1** Very Worshipful. **2** Volkswagen, a German car manufacturer ⓔ 1950s: German, meaning 'people's car'.

Vw ▷ *abbreviation* used in street names: View.

vying *present participle of* VIE

W

W¹ or **w** /ˈdʌbəljuː/ ▷ *noun* (***Ws***, ***W's*** or ***w's***) the twenty-third letter of the English alphabet.

W² ▷ *symbol, chem* the element called tungsten or wolfram.

W³ ▷ *abbreviation* **1** watt. **2** Welsh. **3** West. **4** Western. **5** winter. **6** women. **7** said of clothing size: women's. **8** won, the Korean currency unit. **9** *physics* work.

w ▷ *abbreviation* **1** week. **2** weight. **3** *cricket* wicket. **4** wide. **5** width. **6** wife. **7** with.

WA ▷ *abbreviation* **1** *US state* Washington. Also written **Wash.** **2** West Africa. **3** *Austral state* Western Australia.

WAAC or **Waac** /wak/ ▷ *abbreviation, historical* Women's Army Auxiliary Corps (now WRAC).

WAAF /waf/ ▷ *abbreviation, historical* Women's Auxiliary Air Force (now WRAF).

wacko /ˈwakoʊ/ *colloq* ▷ *adj* mad or crazy; eccentric. ▷ *noun* (***wackos***) a mad, crazy or eccentric person. ◷ 1970s: from WACKY.

wacky or **whacky** /ˈwakɪ/ ▷ *adj* (***wackier***, ***wackiest***; ***whackier***, ***whackiest***) *colloq, originally N Amer, especially US* mad or crazy; eccentric. • **wackily** *adverb*. • **wackiness** *noun*. ◷ 1930s: dialect, meaning 'left-handed' and 'fool'.

wad /wɒd/ ▷ *noun* **1** a compressed mass of soft material used for packing, padding or stuffing, etc. **2** a disc of felt or paper (originally a plug of paper or tow) for keeping the charge in a cannon or gun. **3** *Brit slang* a sandwich, cake or bun. **4** a compact roll or bundle of banknotes, etc. ▷ *verb* (***wadded***, ***wadding***) **1** to roll or form something into a wad. **2** to stuff or pad out something. **3** to stuff a wad into something. ◷ 16c: from Latin *wadda*.

wadding ▷ *noun* **1** material used as padding or stuffing. **2** a piece of this material. **3** material used for making wads for cannons or guns.

waddle /ˈwɒdəl/ ▷ *verb* (***waddled***, ***waddling***) *intr* **1** said of a duck: to sway from side to side in walking. **2** *derog* said of a person: to walk in a similar way. ▷ *noun* **1** the act of waddling. **2** a clumsy rocking movement. • **waddler** *noun*. • **waddling** *adj*. ◷ 14c.

waddy /ˈwɒdɪ/ ▷ *noun* (***waddies***) a wooden club used in warfare by Australian Aboriginals. ▷ *verb* (***waddies***, ***waddied***, ***waddying***) to strike someone using a waddy. ◷ 19c.

wade ▷ *verb* (***waded***, ***wading***) *tr & intr* to walk through something, especially deep water, which does not allow easy movement of the feet; to cross (a river, etc) by wading. ▷ *noun* the act of wading. ◷ Anglo-Saxon *wadan* to go.

- **wade in** to involve oneself unhesitatingly and enthusiastically in a task, etc.
- **wade into someone** to attack or criticize them fiercely.
- **wade through something** to make one's way laboriously through it □ *wading through legal documents.*

wader ▷ *noun* **1** someone or something that wades. **2** any long-legged bird that wades in marshes, or along the shores of rivers, lakes or seas. **3** (**waders**) thigh-high waterproof boots used by anglers, etc.

wadi or **wady** /ˈwɒdɪ/ ▷ *noun* (***wadies***) a rocky river bed in N Africa and Arabia, dry except during the rains. ◷ 19c: Arabic.

wafer /ˈweɪfə(r)/ ▷ *noun* **1** a thin light finely layered kind of biscuit, baked between **wafer-irons** or **wafer-tongs**, served eg with ice cream. **2** *Christianity* a thin disc of unleavened bread or rice paper served to communicants at Holy Communion. **3** a thin disc of adhesive material used instead of a seal on documents, etc. **4** *computing* a thin disc of silicon from which chips are cut. ▷ *verb* (***wafered***, ***wafering***) to close, fasten or stick with a wafer. • **wafery** *adj*. ◷ 14c: Dutch, a variant of *wafel* waffle.

waffle¹ /ˈwɒfəl/ ▷ *noun, cookery* a light-textured cake made of batter, with a distinctive grid-like surface pattern formed by the hinged iron mould (called a **waffle iron**) in which it is baked. ◷ 18c: from Dutch *wafel*.

waffle² /ˈwɒfəl/ *colloq* ▷ *verb* (***waffled***, ***waffling***) *intr* **1** (*also* **waffle on**) to talk or write at length but to little purpose. **2** to waver or vacillate. ▷ *noun* talk or writing of this kind. • **waffler** *noun*. ◷ 19c: originally Scots and N England dialect.

waft /wɒft, wɑːft/ ▷ *verb* (***wafted***, ***wafting***) *tr & intr* to float or make something float or drift gently, especially through the air. ▷ *noun* **1** the action of wafting. **2** a whiff, eg of perfume. **3** *naut* **a** a flag or substitute hoisted as a signal; **b** the act of displaying such a signal. ◷ 16c: back formation from obsolete *wafter* escort vessel, from German or Dutch *wachter* guard.

wag ▷ *verb* (***wagged***, ***wagging***) **1** *tr & intr* to wave to and fro vigorously. **2** said of a dog: to wave (its tail) as a sign of pleasure. **3** said of a dog's tail: to wave as a sign of pleasure. **4** to shake (one's finger) up and down at someone, while giving advice, a warning or rebuke. **5** *intr* said of the tongue, chin or beard: to move in light or gossiping chatter. **6** *slang* to play truant. ▷ *noun* **1** a wagging movement. **2** a habitual joker or a wit; someone with a roguish sense of humour. • **waggish** *adj* amusing; mischievous. ◷ Anglo-Saxon *wagian*.

wage ▷ *verb* (***waged***, ***waging***) to engage in or fight (a war or battle). ▷ *noun* **1** (*often* **wages**) a regular, especially daily or weekly rather than monthly, payment from an employer to an employee, especially an unskilled or semi-skilled one. Compare SALARY. **2** (**wages**) *singular & plural, literary* reward, recompense or repayment □ *The wages of sin is death.* ◷ 14c: from French *wagier* to pledge.

wage differential ▷ *noun* the difference in wages paid to different classes of workers in an industry, or to workers doing similar jobs in different industries or areas.

wage-earner ▷ *noun* **1** someone who works for wages. **2** the person who earns the money that supports, or helps to support, the household. • **wage-earning** *noun*.

wage-freeze ▷ *noun* a fixing of wages at a certain level for some time ahead.

wage packet ▷ *noun* **1** a small envelope in which a worker's wages are issued. **2** *loosely* a worker's wages.

wager /ˈweɪdʒə(r)/ ▷ *noun* **1** a bet on the outcome or result of something. **2** the act of making such a bet. ▷ *verb* (***wagered***, ***wagering***) to bet; to stake something in a bet. • **wagerer** *noun*. ◷ 14c: from French *wagier* to pledge.

wage slave ▷ *noun* a person dependent on a low wage or salary.

wagged, **wagging** and **waggish** see under WAG

waggle /ˈwagəl/ ▷ *verb* (***waggled***, ***waggling***) *tr & intr* to move or make something move to and fro. ▷ *noun* a wobble or wobbling motion. • **waggly** *adj*. ⓒ 16c: from WAG.

Wagnerian /vɑːgˈnɪərɪən/ ▷ *adj* **1** referring or relating to the music or musical theories of the German composer Richard Wagner (1813–1883), especially to his MUSICAL DRAMAS which are notable for the sumptuousness of their production and the intensity of emotion they can generate. **2 a** lavishly splendid, **b** highly dramatic. **3** said of a woman: domineering; having great physical presence as well as a forceful personality. ▷ *noun* **1** a devotee of Wagner's music. **2** someone who has specialized knowledge of his music or musical theories. ⓒ 19c.

wagon or **waggon** /ˈwagən/ ▷ *noun* **1** a four-wheeled vehicle, often horse-drawn, used especially for carrying loads; a cart. **2** an open truck or closed van for carrying railway freight. **3** *colloq* a car, especially an estate car. **4** a tea trolley. • **wagoner** *noun* the driver of a wagon. • **on the wagon** *colloq* temporarily abstaining from alcohol. • **off the wagon** *colloq* no longer abstaining from alcohol. ⓒ 16c: from Dutch *wagen*.

wagonette /wagəˈnɛt/ ▷ *noun* a kind of horse-drawn carriage with one or two seats positioned crosswise in the front, and two back seats positioned lengthwise and facing each other. ⓒ 19c.

wagon-lit / *French* vagɔ̃li/ ▷ *noun* (***wagon-lits*** /-li/) a sleeping-carriage on a continental train. ⓒ 19c.

wagonload ▷ *noun* **1** the load carried by a wagon. **2** a large amount.

wagon train ▷ *noun, historical* a train of wagons, usually horse-drawn, used by pioneer settlers to travel into new territory.

wagtail ▷ *noun* any of various birds so called because of the constant wagging motion of their long tails. ⓒ 16c.

wahine /wɑːˈhiːnɛ/ ▷ *noun* (*plural* ***wahine***) a Maori woman. ⓒ 19c: Maori.

wahoo /waˈhuː/ ▷ *noun* (***wahoos***) a large fast-moving marine food and game fish, related to the mackerel. ⓒ Early 20c.

wah-wah /ˈwɑːwɑː/ ▷ *noun, music* the sound effect produced on a brass instrument by inserting and removing the MUTE (*noun* 3), imitated on an electric guitar by varying the amplification level. ⓒ 1920s: imitating the sound.

waif /weɪf/ ▷ *noun* **1** an orphaned, abandoned or homeless child. **2** any pathetically undernourished-looking person. **3** something unclaimed and apparently ownerless, eg a stray animal, or objects cast up by the tide. • **waif-like** *adj*. ⓒ 14c: French, probably from Norse *veif* any flapping or waving thing.

waifs and strays ▷ *plural noun* **1** homeless and destitute people, especially children. **2** unclaimed articles; odds and ends.

wail ▷ *noun* **1** a prolonged and high-pitched mournful or complaining cry. **2** any sound resembling this. ▷ *verb* (***wailed***, ***wailing***) **1** *tr & intr* to make, or utter something with, such a cry. **2** said eg of a siren: to make a similar noise. **3** to grieve over someone or something. • **wailer** *noun*. • **wailing** *noun, adj*. • **wailingly** *adverb*. ⓒ 14c.

wain ▷ *noun, usually poetic, often in compounds* an open wagon, especially for hay or other agricultural produce □ ***haywain***. ⓒ Anglo-Saxon *wægen, wæn*, from *wegen* to carry.

wainscot /ˈweɪnskɒt, -skət/ ▷ *noun* **1** wooden panelling or boarding covering the lower part of the walls of a room. **2** fine oak used for wall panelling. • **wainscoting** or **wainscotting** *noun*. ⓒ 14c: from Dutch *wagen-schot* wagon partition.

waist ▷ *noun* **1** the narrow part of the human body between the ribs and hips. **2** the part of a garment that covers this. **3** a narrow middle part of an insect, such as a wasp. **4** a narrow middle part of an object, such as a violin. **5** the middle part of a ship. • **waisted** *adj, often in compounds* having a waist, often of a specified kind □ ***high-waisted***. ⓒ Anglo-Saxon *wæstm* form or figure.

waistband ▷ *noun* the reinforced strip of cloth on a skirt or trousers, etc that fits round the waist.

waistcoat /ˈweɪskoʊt, ˈwɛskət, ˈweɪstkoʊt/ ▷ *noun* **1** a close-fitting sleeveless garment, usually waist-length, worn especially by men under a jacket. **2** a similar garment worn by women. *N Amer equivalent* VEST. ⓒ 16c.

waistline ▷ *noun* **1** the line marking the waist. **2** the measurement of a waist.

wait ▷ *verb* (***waited***, ***waiting***) **1** *intr* said of a task, etc: to remain temporarily undealt with □ ***That can wait.*** **2** (*also* **wait about** or **around**) to be or remain in a particular place in readiness. **3** to postpone action for (a period of time). **4** to await (one's turn, etc). **5** *colloq* to delay eating (a meal) till someone arrives □ ***won't wait dinner.*** **6** *intr* to park one's vehicle briefly at the kerb, etc □ ***no waiting.*** **7** *intr* to serve as a waiter or waitress. **8** *dialect* to wait for someone. • **lie in wait** or **lay wait** to be in hiding ready to surprise or ambush someone. • **you wait!** an expression used to warn or threaten. • **wait on** *Austral, NZ* be patient; hold back □ ***Wait on, I'll come too.*** ⓒ 12c: from French *waitier* or *guaitier*, from German *wahten* to watch.

■ **wait for something** to delay action or remain in a certain place in expectation of, or readiness for it.

■ **wait on someone 1** to serve them with food as a waiter or waitress. **2** to act as a servant or attendant to them.

■ **wait up** *US* to slow down or wait □ ***Wait up, I can't run that fast.***

■ **wait up for someone** to delay going to bed at night waiting for their arrival or return, or some other event.

Waitangi Day /waɪˈtʌŋɪ —/ ▷ *noun* 6 February, the national day of New Zealand, commemorating the Treaty of Waitangi made between Britain and the Maori chiefs in 1840.

waiter and **waitress** ▷ *noun* a man or woman who serves people with food at a hotel or restaurant, etc.

waiting-list ▷ *noun* a list of people waiting for something currently unavailable, eg accommodation or surgery.

waiting-room ▷ *noun* a room for people to wait in, eg at a railway station or doctor's surgery.

waive ▷ *verb* (***waived***, ***waiving***) **1** *law* to refrain from insisting upon something; to voluntarily give up (a claim or right, etc). **2** to refrain from enforcing (a rule or penalty, etc). • **waiver** *noun* **1** the act, or an act, of waiving. **2** a written statement formally confirming this. ⓒ 13c: from French *weyver* to abandon.

wake[1] ▷ *verb* (***woke*** /woʊk/, ***woken*** /woʊkən/, ***waking***) **1** (*also* **wake someone up** or **wake up**) *tr & intr* **a** to rouse or be roused from sleep; **b** to stir or be stirred out of a state of inactivity or lethargy, etc. **2** *intr* to stay awake at night; to keep watch or stay vigilant. **3** to disturb (eg a night or silence, etc) with noise. ▷ *noun* **1** a watch or vigil kept beside a corpse. **2** *dialect* an annual holiday. **3** *historical* the feast of the dedication of a church, formerly kept by watching all night. • **waking** *noun, adj*. ⓒ Anglo-Saxon *wacan* to become awake, and *wacian* to stay awake.

■ **wake up** or **wake someone up to something** to become or make them aware of (a fact, circumstance or situation, etc).

wake, waken, awake, awaken

These four verbs are virtually synonymous, with **wake** the most commonly used. All can be used with or without an object; all can be used both in the literal sense 'to rouse from sleep' and in the figurative sense 'to arouse or provoke (feelings)'. The only difference between them is that **awake** and **awaken** are never followed by **up**.

wake² ▷ *noun* a trail of disturbed water left by a ship, or of disturbed air left by an aircraft. • **in one's wake** wherever one has been. • **in the wake of someone** or **something** coming after them; resulting from them. ◷ 16c: from Norse *vök* a hole or channel in the ice.

wakeful ▷ *adj* **1** not asleep or unable to sleep. **2** said of a night: sleepless. **3** vigilant or alert; watchful. • **wakefully** *adverb*. • **wakefulness** *noun*. ◷ 16c.

waken /ˈweɪkən/ ▷ *verb* (*wakened*, *wakening*) **1** *tr & intr* to rouse or be roused from sleep. **2** *tr & intr* to rouse or be roused from inactivity or lethargy. ◷ Anglo-Saxon *wæcnan*.

■ **waken to something** to become aware of (a fact or situation, etc).

waking hours ▷ *noun* the part of the day during which one is normally awake.

WAL ▷ *noun, IVR* (West Africa) Sierra Leone.

wale ▷ *noun* **1** a raised mark on the skin; a WEAL¹. **2** a ridge on the surface of cloth, eg the rib on corduroy. **3** *naut* a course of planking running along the top edge of a ship's side. ▷ *verb* (*waled*, *waling*) **1** to create wales by striking. **2** to make, provide with or secure something with wales. ◷ Anglo-Saxon *walu* ridge.

walk /wɔːk/ ▷ *verb* (*walked*, *walking*) **1** *intr* to move along in some direction on foot, moving one's feet alternately and always having one or other foot on the ground. **2** to do this for exercise. **3** *intr* to go or travel on foot. **4** to travel (a distance) by walking. **5** to go about (the streets or countryside, etc) on foot; to ramble. **6** to lead, accompany or support (someone who is on foot). **7** to take (a dog) out for exercise. **8** *intr, old use* to live one's life or behave in a specified manner □ *walk in fear*. **9** *intr, colloq* to disappear or go away; to be stolen □ *my pen has walked*. **10** *tr & intr* said of a ghost: to roam or haunt. ▷ *noun* **1** the motion, or pace of walking. **2** an outing or journey on foot, especially for exercise. **3** a perambulation in procession. **4** a distance walked or for walking. **5** a person's distinctive manner of walking. **6** a path, especially a broad one; a promenade. **7** a route for walking. **8** a tree-bordered avenue. **9** a WALK OF LIFE. **10** a district or round walked by a postman, policeman or hawker, etc. • **walk all over someone** *colloq* to treat them inconsiderately or arrogantly; to take advantage of them. • **walk it** *colloq* to succeed or win easily. • **walk on air** to feel euphoric and light-hearted; to be elated. • **walk tall** *colloq* to be proud; to have and show self-respect. • **walk the plank** see under PLANK. • **walk the streets 1** to wander about aimlessly, or in search of work. **2** to be a prostitute. ◷ Anglo-Saxon *wealcan*.

■ **walk away from someone** *colloq* to outdistance them.

■ **walk away from something 1** to ignore or abandon (a commitment or responsibility, etc). **2** to escape unhurt from (an accident, etc).

■ **walk away with something** *colloq* to win (a prize or reward) effortlessly.

■ **walk into something 1** to collide or meet with (eg a joke) unexpectedly. **2** to involve oneself in trouble or difficulty through one's own unwariness.

■ **walk off** said of a person or animal: to depart.

■ **walk off something** to get rid of (unpleasant thoughts or feelings, etc) by walking.

■ **walk off with something 1** to win (a prize or reward) effortlessly. **2** *colloq* to steal it.

■ **walk out 1** said of factory workers, etc: to leave the workplace in a body, in declaration of a strike. See also WALKOUT. **2** to depart abruptly, especially in protest.

■ **walk out on someone** to abandon or desert them.

■ **walk out with someone** *old use* to court someone of the opposite sex.

■ **walk over 1** to cross or traverse. **2** to win an uncontested race. **3** *colloq* to have an easy or effortless victory or success. See also WALKOVER.

walkabout ▷ *noun* **1** a casual stroll through a crowd of ordinary people by a celebrity, especially a member of the royal family or a politician, etc. **2** *Austral* a walk alone in the bush by an Australian Aboriginal. • **go walkabout 1** *Austral* to walk alone in the bush. **2** to become lost or mislaid. ◷ Early 20c.

walkathon /ˈwɔːkəθɒn/ ▷ *noun* a long-distance walk, either as a race or in aid of charity. ◷ 1930s: from *walk* + mar*athon*.

walker ▷ *noun* **1** someone who walks, especially for pleasure. **2** someone who takes part in walking races. **3** (*also* **babywalker**) a device which helps babies learn to walk. **4** a WALKING FRAME.

walkies ▷ *plural noun, colloq* a walk for a dog. Also *as adverb* □ *My pen has gone walkies*. ◷ 1930s.

walkie-talkie or **walky-talky** /wɔːkɪˈtɔːkɪ/ ▷ *noun* (*walkie-talkies*) *colloq* a portable two-way radio carried by police, etc. ◷ 1930s.

walking ▷ *adj* **1** in human form □ *a walking encyclopedia*. **2** for the use of walkers □ *walking shoes*.

walking-frame ▷ *noun* a device used to support an elderly or infirm person while walking.

walking papers ▷ *plural noun, slang* orders to leave; dismissal. ◷ 19c.

walking-stick ▷ *noun* **1** a stick or cane used for support or balance in walking. **2** *US* a STICK INSECT.

walking wounded ▷ *noun* **1** said of casualties: not requiring stretchers or not confined to bed. **2** *colloq* people experiencing problems, especially psychological or emotional ones.

Walkman /ˈwɔːkmən/ ▷ *noun* (*Walkmans* or *Walkmen*) *trademark* a small portable audio cassette recorder and/or radio with headphones, designed for personal use while walking or travelling, etc. ◷ 1980s.

walk of life ▷ *noun* someone's occupation or profession; a sphere of action.

walk-on ▷ *adj* said of a part in a play or opera, etc: not involving any speaking or singing.

walkout ▷ *noun* a sudden departure, especially of a workforce in declaration of a strike. See also WALK OUT at WALK.

walkover ▷ *noun* **1** *colloq* an easy victory. **2** a race with only one competitor, where to win one merely has to complete the course. See also WALK OVER at WALK.

walkway ▷ *noun* a paved path or passage for pedestrians.

walky-talky see WALKIE-TALKIE

wall /wɔːl/ ▷ *noun* **1** a solid vertical brick or stone construction serving eg as a barrier, territorial division or protection. **2** the vertical side of a building or room. **3** (**walls**) fortifications. **4** anything in some way suggestive of a wall □ *a wall of fire* □ *a wall of secrecy*. **5** *biol* **a** an outer covering, eg of a cell; **b** the side of a hollow organ or cavity. **6** a sheer rock face. **7** an unsurmountable barrier such as that experienced physically and psychologically by long-distance runners. ▷ *verb* (*walled*, *walling*) **1** to surround something with, or as if with, a wall. **2** to fortify something with, or as if with, a wall. **3** (*usually* **wall something off** or **in**) to separate or enclose it with a wall □ *That garden has been walled off for years.* • **walled** *adj.* • **go to the wall** said of a business: to fail or go under. • **have one's back to the wall** to be making one's last desperate stand. • **up the wall** *colloq* angry; crazy or mad. • **walls have ears** a warning or advice to speak discreetly; you may be overheard anywhere. ⓒ Anglo-Saxon *weall*, from Latin *vallum* rampart.

■ **wall something** or **someone up 1** to block (an opening) with, or seal it or them behind, brickwork, etc. **2** to imprison them in this way.

wallaby /ˈwɒləbɪ/ ▷ *noun* (***wallabies*** or ***wallaby***) **1** any of several species of a plant-eating marsupial, belonging to the same family as the kangaroo, and native to Australia and Tasmania. **2** (**the Wallabies**) *colloq* the Australian national Rugby Union football team. ⓒ 18c: from Aboriginal *wolaba*.

wallah or **walla** /ˈwɒlə/ ▷ *noun, Anglo-Indian, in compounds* a person who performs a specified task □ *the tea wallah.* ⓒ 18c: from Hindi *-wala* an adjectival suffix.

wallaroo /wɒləˈruː/ ▷ *noun* (***wallaroos*** or ***wallaroo***) a large kind of kangaroo. ⓒ 19c: from Aboriginal *wolaru*.

wall bars ▷ *plural noun* a series of horizontal wooden bars supported by uprights lining the walls of a gymnasium.

wallet /ˈwɒlɪt/ ▷ *noun* **1** a flat folding case, often made of leather, for holding banknotes, etc and carried in the pocket or handbag. **2** any of various kinds of folders or envelopes, especially plastic ones, for holding papers, etc. ⓒ 14c.

walleye ▷ *noun* **1** an eye in which the iris has a pale chalky appearance. **2** an eye that squints away from the nose, so that an abnormal amount of the white shows. • **walleyed** *adj* **1** having a walleye. **2** having a staring or blank expression, or bland appearance. ⓒ 16c: from Norse *wagleygr*.

walleyed pike ▷ *noun* a large fish, up to 90cm long, that is closely related to the perch and resembles the pike, native to rivers and lakes of eastern N America.

wallflower ▷ *noun* **1** a sweet-smelling plant with yellow, orange or red flowers, widely cultivated as an ornamental garden plant. Also called GILLYFLOWER. **2** *colloq* someone who sits all evening at the edge of the dance floor, waiting in vain to be asked to dance. ⓒ 16c; 19c in sense 2.

wallies *plural of* WALLY

Walloon /wɒˈluːn/ ▷ *noun* **1** a member of the French-speaking population of S Belgium. **2** their language, a dialect of French. ▷ *adj* relating to or belonging to the Walloons. Compare FLEMISH. ⓒ 16c: from French *Wallon*, literally 'foreigner'.

wallop /ˈwɒləp/ *colloq* ▷ *verb* (***walloped***, ***walloping***) **1** to hit or strike someone or something vigorously. **2** to defeat or thrash someone or something soundly. ▷ *noun* **1** a hit or a thrashing. **2** a powerful impression. **3** *Brit slang* beer. • **walloper** *noun* **1** someone or something that wallops. **2** *Austral slang* a policeman. ⓒ 14c: from French *waloper* to gallop.

walloping ▷ *noun* a thrashing. ▷ *adj* great; whopping.

wallow /ˈwɒloʊ/ ▷ *verb* (***wallowed***, ***wallowing***) *intr* (*often* **wallow in something**) **1** to lie or roll about (in water or mud, etc). **2** to revel or luxuriate (in admiration, etc). **3** to indulge excessively (in self-pity, etc). **4** said of a ship: to roll from side to side making poor headway. **5** said of an enterprise or project, etc: to fail to progress with speed and efficiency. ▷ *noun* **1** the act of wallowing. **2** the place, or the dirt, in which an animal wallows. • **wallower** *noun.* • **wallowing** *noun, adj.* ⓒ Anglo-Saxon *wealwian*.

wallpaper ▷ *noun* **1** paper, often coloured or patterned, used to decorate the interior walls and ceilings of houses, etc. **2** *colloq, often derog* something of a bland or background nature, lacking in originality or significance. ▷ *verb* (***wallpapered***, ***wallpapering***) to cover (walls) or the walls of (a room) with wallpaper. ⓒ 19c.

wall plate ▷ *noun, building* a horizontal piece of timber or rolled steel on top of a wall, etc to support the ends of the joists, etc.

wall-to-wall ▷ *adj* **1** said of carpeting: covering the entire floor of a room. **2** *facetious* widespread or ever-present; inescapable. ⓒ 1940s.

wally /ˈwɒlɪ/ ▷ *noun* (***wallies***) *Brit colloq* an ineffectual, stupid or foolish person. ⓒ 1960s: from the name *Walter*.

walnut /ˈwɔːlnʌt/ ▷ *noun* **1** any of various deciduous trees found in N temperate regions, with large compound leaves, cultivated for their timber and edible nut. **2** the round nut yielded by this tree, consisting of a wrinkled two-lobed seed, rich in protein and fat, surrounded by a hard shell. **3** the hard durable dark-brown or black wood of this tree, which has an attractive grain and is highly prized for furniture-making, cabinetwork and panelling. ⓒ Anglo-Saxon *wealhhnutu* foreign nut.

walrus /ˈwɔːlrəs, ˈwɒl-/ ▷ *noun* (***walruses*** or ***walrus***) a large carnivorous marine mammal related to the seal, with thick wrinkled skin, webbed flippers and two long tusks, which is found in the northern waters of the Atlantic and Pacific oceans. ⓒ 17c: Dutch, from Swedish *hvalross*, literally 'whale-horse'.

walrus moustache ▷ *noun* a thick drooping moustache.

waltz /wɔːlts, wɒ-/ ▷ *noun* (***waltzes***) **1** a slow or fast ballroom dance in triple time, in which the dancers spin round the room. **2** a piece of music for this dance or in this style. ▷ *verb* (***waltzes***, ***waltzed***, ***waltzing***) *intr* **1** to dance a waltz. **2** (*often* **waltz in** or **off**) *colloq* to go or move with vivacity and easy confidence □ *She just waltzed in and took over.* • **waltz Matilda** see under MATILDA. ⓒ 18c: from German *Walzer*, from *walzen* to roll or dance.

waltzer ▷ *noun* **1** someone who waltzes. **2** a type of fairground roundabout in which passengers sit in small round cars that are spun while rotating. ⓒ 1960s in sense 2.

wampum /ˈwɒmpəm, ˈwɔː-/ ▷ *noun, historical* shells strung together for use as money among the Native Americans. ⓒ 17c: a shortening of Algonquian *wampumpeag* white string of beads.

WAN ▷ *abbreviation* **1** *computing* wide area network, a computer network that operates over a wide area and is therefore normally dependent on telephone lines or other long-distance links rather than cables. Compare LAN. **2** *IVR* (West Africa) Nigeria.

wan /wɒn/ ▷ *adj* (***wanner***, ***wannest***) **1** pale and pinched-looking, especially from illness, exhaustion or grief. **2** said of stars, etc: faint; dim. • **wanly** *adverb.* • **wanness** *noun.* ⓒ Anglo-Saxon *wann* dusky or lurid.

wand /wɒnd/ ▷ *noun* **1** a slender rod used by magicians, conjurors and fairies, etc for performing magic. **2** a conductor's baton. **3** a rod carried as a symbol of authority. **4** *dialect* a slender young shoot; a flexible cane or switch, used in basketmaking. ⓒ 12c: from Norse *vöndr* shoot.

wander /ˈwɒndə(r)/ ▷ *verb* (***wandered***, ***wandering***) **1** to walk, move or travel about, with no particular destination; to ramble. **2** to stray or deviate, eg from the right path, or from the point of an argument, etc. **3** said of a stream, etc: to follow a meandering course. **4** said of people or their wits, etc: to become confused, incoherent or irrational, eg in delirium or advanced age. **5** said of one's thoughts, etc: to flit randomly. ▷ *noun* a ramble or stroll. • **wanderer** *noun.* • **wandering** *noun, adj.* • **wanderingly** *adverb.* ⓒ Anglo-Saxon *wandrian*.

wandering Jew ▷ *noun* **1** *folklore* a Jew who was unable to die, condemned to wander till the Day of Judgment, because of an insult made to Christ on the way to the Crucifixion. **2** any of various kinds of trailing or creeping plants.

wanderlust /ˈwɒndəlʌst/ ▷ *noun* an urge to rove or travel; a desire to move from place to place. ◎ 19c: German, from *wandern* to travel + *Lust* desire.

wanderoo /wɒndəˈruː/ ▷ *noun* (***wanderoos***) **1** a LANGUR from Sri Lanka. **2** the lion-tailed macaque monkey from the Malabar coast of India. ◎ 17c: from Sinhalese *wanderu* monkey.

wandoo /ˈwɒnduː/ ▷ *noun* (***wandoos***) a W Australian eucalyptus with white bark and durable wood. ◎ Late 19c: Aboriginal.

wane /weɪn/ ▷ *verb* (***waned, waning***) *intr* **1** said of the Moon: to appear to grow narrower as the Sun illuminates less of its surface. **2** to decline in glory, power or influence, etc. ▷ *noun* **1** the process of waning or declining. **2** the time during which this takes place. **3** a defective edge or corner on a plank of wood. • **waney** or **wany** *adj*. • **on the wane** decreasing or declining. ◎ Anglo-Saxon *wanian* to lessen.

wangle /ˈwaŋgəl/ *colloq* ▷ *verb* (***wangled, wangling***) **1** to contrive or obtain something by persuasiveness. **2** to manipulate something. ▷ *noun* an act of wangling. • **wangler** *noun*. ◎ 19c: perhaps from WAGGLE + dialect *wankle* wavering.

wank *coarse slang* ▷ *verb* (***wanked, wanking***) *intr* to masturbate. ▷ *noun* masturbation. • **wanker** *noun* **1** someone who masturbates. **2** *derog* a worthless contemptible person. ◎ 1940s.

Wankel engine /ˈwaŋkəl —/ ▷ *noun* a rotary automobile engine which has an approximately triangular central rotor turning in a close-fitting oval-shaped chamber rather than conventional pistons and cylinders, and has very few moving parts. ◎ 1959: named after Felix Wankel (1902–88), the German engineer who invented it.

wannabe or **wannabee** /ˈwɒnəbiː/ ▷ *noun* (***wannabes***) *colloq* **1** someone who admires and imitates the appearance, mannerisms and habits, etc of another person. **2** someone who aspires, usually ineffectually, to a particular lifestyle or image. ◎ 1980s: a shortening of *want to be*.

wanner, **wanness** and **wannest** see under WAN

want /wɒnt/ ▷ *verb* (***wanted, wanting***) **1** to feel a need or desire for something. **2** to need to be dealt with in a specified way □ *The bin wants emptying.* **3** *colloq* ought; need □ *You want to take more care.* **4** *colloq* to need (a certain treatment, etc) □ *He wants his head examined.* **5** (*often* **want for something**) to feel the lack of it □ *That kid wants for nothing.* **6** to require the presence of someone or something □ *You are wanted next door.* **7** to desire someone sexually. ▷ *noun* **1** a need or requirement. **2** a lack □ *a want of discretion.* **3** a state of need; destitution. • **wanter** *noun*. • **for want of something** in the absence of it. • **in want of something** needing it. • **want to do something** or **want someone to do something** to wish or require that it be done. ◎ 12c: from Norse *vanta* to be lacking.

■ **want in** or **out**, *etc*: *colloq* to desire to get in or out, etc.

> ***want***
>
> There is often a spelling confusion between **want** and **wont**.

want ad ▷ *noun, chiefly US* a small advertisement, especially in a newspaper, specifying goods, property or employment, etc required by the advertiser. *Brit equivalent* CLASSIFIED ADVERTISEMENT or **small ad**.

wanted ▷ *adj* **1** needed or desired. **2** said of a person: being sought by the police on suspicion of having committed a crime, etc.

wanting ▷ *adj* **1** missing; lacking. **2** not up to requirements □ *has been found wanting.* • **wanting in something** not having enough of it.

wanton /ˈwɒntən/ ▷ *adj* (***wantoner, wantonest***) **1** thoughtlessly and needlessly cruel. **2** motiveless □ *wanton destruction.* **3** sexually immoral; lewd or licentious. **4** unrestrained or prodigal. **5** *old use* playfully fanciful; whimsical. ▷ *noun, old use* a wanton woman. • **wantonly** *adverb*. • **wantonness** *noun*. ◎ Anglo-Saxon *wan-* not + *togen* disciplined.

wany see under WANE

wapiti /ˈwɒpɪtɪ/ ▷ *noun* (***wapiti*** or ***wapitis***) a type of large N American deer, reddish in colour with a light patch on its rump, and with large branched antlers. Also (*N Amer*) called **elk**. ◎ 19c: Shawnee, meaning 'white deer'; it was erroneously called 'elk' by white settlers.

war /wɔː(r)/ ▷ *noun* **1** an open state of armed conflict, especially between nations. Compare COLD WAR. **2** a particular armed conflict. **3** a conflict between states, or between parties within a state. See also CIVIL WAR. **4** fighting as a science. **5** open hostility between people. **6** any long-continued struggle or campaign. **7** fierce rivalry or competition in business. ▷ *verb* (***warred, warring***) *intr* **1** to fight wars. **2** to conflict one with another. • **at war** participating in armed conflict. • **go to war** to begin an armed conflict. • **have been in the wars** *colloq* to have, or show signs of having, sustained injuries. ◎ 12c: from German *werra* quarrel.

waratah /ˈwɒrətə/ ▷ *noun* any of a genus of Australian shrubs with flamboyant scarlet flowers. ◎ 18c: Aboriginal.

war baby ▷ *noun* a baby born during a war.

warble¹ /ˈwɔːbəl/ ▷ *verb* (***warbled, warbling***) *tr & intr* **1** said of a bird: to sing melodiously. **2** said of a person: to sing in a high tremulous voice; to trill. **3** to express, or extol, in poetry or song. ▷ *noun* the act of warbling. ◎ 14c: from French *werbler*.

warble² /ˈwɔːbəl/ ▷ *noun* **1** a swelling on a horse's back, caused by the rubbing of a saddle. **2** a swelling under the hide of horses or cattle, especially one caused by a warble fly larva. ◎ 16c: perhaps from Swedish *varbulde* boil.

warble fly ▷ *noun* any of various species of fly whose larvae cause painful warbles on the hide of horses or cattle.

warbler ▷ *noun* **1** someone or something that warbles. **2** any of several small insect-eating songbirds with dull green, brown or grey upper plumage and lighter underparts, and a slender pointed bill, found from W Europe to Australia.

war bride ▷ *noun* a soldier's bride, met as a result of wartime movements or postings.

war correspondent ▷ *noun* a journalist sent to a scene of war so as to give first-hand reports of the events.

war crime ▷ *noun* a crime committed during, and in connection with, a war, especially ill-treatment of prisoners or massacre of civilians, etc. • **war criminal** *noun*.

war cry ▷ *noun* **1** a cry used to rally or encourage troops, or as a signal for charging. **2** a slogan or watchword.

ward /wɔːd/ ▷ *noun* **1** a room in a hospital with beds for patients. **2** the patients in a ward collectively. **3** any of the areas into which a town, etc is divided for administration or elections. **4** a division or department of a prison. **5** care or guardianship; custody. **6** *law* someone, especially a minor, under the protection of a guardian or court. **7** a projection inside a lock that fits into a notch in its key, ensuring that the lock cannot be turned by the wrong key. ▷ *verb* (***warded, warding***) (*usually* **ward something off**)

1 to fend off, turn aside, or parry (a blow). **2** to keep (trouble, hunger or disease, etc) away. ⓒ Anglo-Saxon *weard* protector.

-ward see -WARDS

war dance ▷ *noun* a dance performed by primitive tribes before going into battle, or after victory.

warden /ˈwɔːdən/ ▷ *noun* **1** someone in charge of a hostel, student residence or old people's home, etc. **2** *in compounds* a public official responsible in any of various ways for maintaining order □ ***traffic warden*** □ ***game warden***. **3** *N Amer* the officer in charge of a prison. **4** a CHURCHWARDEN (sense 1). ⓒ 13c: from French *wardein*.

warder /ˈwɔːdə(r)/ and **wardress** /ˈwɔːdrəs/ ▷ *noun* **1** *Brit* a prison officer. **2** a man or woman who guards someone or something. ⓒ 14c: from French *warder* to guard.

wardrobe /ˈwɔːdroʊb/ ▷ *noun* **1** a tall cupboard in which clothes are kept. **2** a personal stock of garments and accessories. **3** the stock of costumes belonging to a theatrical company. **4** a department in a royal or noble household in charge of robes, clothing and jewellery, etc. ⓒ 14c: from French *garderobe*.

wardrobe mistress and **wardrobe master** ▷ *noun* the woman or man in charge of the costumes of a theatrical company, or of an individual actor or actress.

wardroom ▷ *noun* the officers' quarters on board a warship.

-wards /wədz/ or **-ward** /wəd/ ▷ *combining form, signifying* direction □ ***backwards*** □ ***toward***. ⓒ Anglo-Saxon *-weardes*, genitive of *-weard* towards.

ware /wɛə(r)/ ▷ *noun* **1** *in compounds* manufactured goods of a specified material or for a specified range of use □ ***glassware*** □ ***kitchenware***. **2** *often in compounds* a particular type of pottery. **3** (**wares**) goods that one has for sale. ⓒ Anglo-Saxon *waru*.

warehouse ▷ *noun* **1** a large building or room for storing goods. **2** a large, usually wholesale, shop. ▷ *verb* (***warehoused***, ***warehousing***) to deposit or store in a warehouse, especially a BONDED WAREHOUSE. ⓒ 14c.

warehouseman ▷ *noun* someone employed to keep or work in a warehouse or wholesale store.

warehouse party ▷ *noun* an ACID HOUSE party held in a large otherwise unused building away from main residential areas. ⓒ 1980s.

warehousing ▷ *noun* **1** the act of depositing goods in a warehouse. **2** *stock exchange* the practice of covertly building up a block of company shares, using one or more front companies, etc to obtain shares on behalf of the true purchaser.

warfare /ˈwɔːfɛə(r)/ ▷ *noun* **1** the activity or process of waging or engaging in war. **2** armed or violent conflict. ⓒ 15c.

warfarin /ˈwɔːfərɪn/ ▷ *noun* a crystalline substance used in medicine as an anticoagulant, either to prevent the clotting of blood or to break up existing clots, and otherwise as a poison for rats, etc. ⓒ 1940s: from *W*isconsin *A*lumni *R*esearch *F*oundation + coum*arin*.

war game ▷ *noun* **1** a mock battle or military exercise that provides training in tactics, etc. **2** an elaborate game in which players use model soldiers, etc to enact historical or imaginary battles.

warhead ▷ *noun* the front part of a missile or torpedo etc that contains the explosives. ⓒ Late 19c.

warhorse ▷ *noun* **1** *historical* a powerful horse on which a knight rode into battle. **2** an old soldier or politician. **3** a standard, frequently used and over-familiar musical composition, etc.

warier, **wariest**, **warily** and **wariness** see under WARY

warlike ▷ *noun, adj* **1** fond of fighting; aggressive or belligerent. **2** relating to war; military.

warlock /ˈwɔːlɒk/ ▷ *noun* a wizard, male magician or sorcerer. ⓒ Anglo-Saxon *warloga* a breaker of an agreement, from *war* a compact + *leogan* to lie.

warlord ▷ *noun* a powerful military leader.

warm /wɔːm/ ▷ *adj* (***warmer***, ***warmest***) **1** moderately, comfortably or pleasantly hot. **2** said eg of clothes: providing and preserving heat. **3** said of work: making one hot. **4** said of a person: kind-hearted and affectionate. **5** said of an environment, etc: welcoming and congenial. **6** enthusiastic; whole-hearted. **7** *old use* vehement; indignant. **8** said of a colour: suggestive of comfortable heat, typically containing red or yellow. **9** said of a trail or scent: still fresh enough to follow. **10** in a children's game, etc: close to guessing correctly or finding the thing sought. **11** *old use* said of one's situation: awkward or dangerous. ▷ *verb* (***warmed***, ***warming***) **1** *tr & intr* to make or become warm or warmer. **2** (*usually* **warm to something**) to gain in enthusiasm for (a task) as one performs it. **3** (*usually* **warm up** or **warm something up**) **a** to become or make it warm or warmer; **b** to re-heat (food); **c** said of a party, etc: to become or make it livelier; **d** said of an engine: to reach, or bring it up to, an efficient working temperature. • **warmly** *adverb*. ⓒ Anglo-Saxon *wearm*.

▪ **warm to someone** to gain in affection or approval for them.

▪ **warm up** to exercise the body gently in preparation for a strenuous work-out, race or athletic contest, etc. See also WARM-UP.

warm-blooded ▷ *adj* **1** *zool* said of an animal: HOMOEOTHERMIC. **2** said of a person: passionate, impulsive or ardent. ⓒ 18c.

warm boot ▷ *noun, computing* a reboot activated by pressing a computer's reset key or a combination of keys, rather than by switching off and on again at the power source. Compare COLD BOOT.

war memorial ▷ *noun* a monument erected to commemorate members of the armed forces, especially those from a particular locality, who died in war.

warm front ▷ *noun, meteorol* the edge of a mass of warm air advancing against a mass of cold air.

warm-hearted ▷ *adj* kind, affectionate and generous; sympathetic. • **warm-heartedly** *adverb*. • **warm-heartedness** *noun*. ⓒ 16c.

warming-pan ▷ *noun, historical* a long-handled lidded pan, usually made of copper or brass, that was filled with hot coals and placed in a bed to warm it up. ⓒ 15c.

warmonger ▷ *noun* someone who tries to precipitate war, or who generates enthusiasm for it. ⓒ 16c.

warmth /wɔːmθ/ ▷ *noun* **1** the condition of being warm. **2** moderate, pleasant or comfortable heat. **3** the sensation of such heat. **4** affection or kind-heartedness. **5** passion; vehemence. **6** strength or intensity.

warm-up ▷ *noun* the act of gently exercising the body in preparation for a strenuous work-out, a race or an athletic contest, etc.

warn /wɔːn/ ▷ *verb* (***warned***, ***warning***) **1** (*usually* **warn someone of** or **about something**) to make them aware of (possible or approaching danger or difficulty). **2** to advise someone strongly. **3** to rebuke or admonish someone, with the threat of punishment for a repetition of the offence. **4** (*often* **warn someone against someone** or **something**) to caution them. **5** to inform someone in advance □ ***warned him she might be late***. • **warner** *noun*. ⓒ Anglo-Saxon *wearnian*.

▪ **warn someone off** to order them to go or keep away, often with threats.

warning ▷ *noun* **1** a caution against eg danger. **2** something that happens, or is said or done, that serves to warn against this. ▷ *adj* intended or serving to warn □ *a warning shot.*

warning coloration ▷ *noun, zool* brightly coloured patterns that occur on some animals, especially poisonous, unpalatable or stinging insects, eg the black-and-yellow stripes on the abdomen of the wasp.

warning triangle see under TRIANGLE

warp /wɔːp/ ▷ *verb* (***warped, warping***) *tr & intr* **1** said of wood and other hard materials: to become, or make it become, twisted out of shape through the shrinking and expanding effects of damp or heat, etc. **2** to become, or make something, distorted, corrupted or perverted. **3** to misinterpret something; deliberately to give a false meaning to something. **4** to turn something from the right course. **5** *naut* to move (a vessel) by hauling on a rope fixed to a position on a wharf. ▷ *noun* **1** the state or fact of being warped. **2** an unevenness or twist in wood, etc. **3** a distorted or abnormal twist in personality, etc. **4** a shift or displacement in a continuous dimension, especially time. **5** *naut* a rope used for warping a vessel. **6** *weaving* the set of threads stretched lengthways in a loom, under and over which the widthways set of threads (the WEFT or WOOF[2]) are passed. ● **warped** *adj.* ● **warper** *noun.* ⓒ Anglo-Saxon *weorpan* to throw.

warpaint ▷ *noun* **1** paint put on the face and body by primitive peoples when going to war. **2** *sport* paint put on the face in similar fashion by sportsmen, eg American footballers, when the team plays a match. **3** *colloq* full-dress or finery. **4** *colloq* a woman's make-up.

warpath ▷ *noun* the march to war, especially (*historical*) among Native Americans. ● **on the warpath 1** setting off to fight. **2** *colloq* in angry pursuit; in an angry mood.

warplane ▷ *noun* any aircraft designed or intended for use in warfare.

warragal see WARRIGAL

warrant /ˈwɒrənt/ ▷ *noun* **1** a written legal authorization for doing something, eg arresting someone, or searching property. **2** someone who gives this authorization. **3** a certificate such as a licence, voucher or receipt, that authorizes, guarantees or confirms something. **4** a justification □ *has no warrant for such an accusation.* **5** *military* a certificate appointing a warrant officer. ▷ *verb* (***warranted, warranting***) **1** to justify something. **2** *old use* to assert something with confidence; to be willing to bet on it. **3** to guarantee (goods, etc) as being of the specified quality or quantity; to confirm as genuine or worthy, etc. ● **I** or **I'll warrant** I've no doubt; for certain. ⓒ 13c: from French *warant.*

warrantable ▷ *adj* **1** that may be permitted; justifiable. **2** said of deer: being of sufficient age to be hunted. ● **warrantably** *adverb.* ⓒ 16c.

warrantee /wɒrənˈtiː/ ▷ *noun* (***warrantees***) someone to whom a warranty is given. ⓒ 17c.

warrant officer ▷ *noun* (abbreviation **WO**) in the armed services: an officer ranked between a commissioned and non-commissioned officer. ⓒ 17c.

warrantor /wɒrənˈtɔː(r)/ or **warranter** ▷ *noun, law* someone who gives a warrant or warranty. ⓒ 17c.

warranty /ˈwɒrəntɪ/ ▷ *noun* (***warranties***) **1** an assurance of the quality of goods being sold, usually with an acceptance of responsibility for repairs during an initial period of use. See also GUARANTEE. **2** an undertaking or assurance expressed or implied in certain contracts. **3** an authorization or justification. ⓒ 14c.

warred *past tense, past participle of* WAR

warren /ˈwɒrən/ ▷ *noun* **1** an underground labyrinth of interconnecting rabbit burrows. **2** the rabbits living in such a labyrinth. **3** an overcrowded dwelling or district. **4** any maze of passages. ⓒ 14c: from French *warenne.*

warrigal or **warragal** /ˈwɒrɪgəl, ˈwɒrɪgəl/ ▷ *noun, Austral* **1** the wild dog or dingo. **2** a wild horse. ▷ *adj* wild; savage. ⓒ 19c: Aboriginal.

warring *present participle of* WAR

warrior /ˈwɒrɪə(r)/ ▷ *noun* **1** a skilled fighting man, especially one belonging to earlier times. **2** any distinguished soldier or veteran. **3** someone notable for strength of spirit or indomitability. ⓒ 13c: from French *werreieor.*

warship ▷ *noun* a ship armed with guns, etc for use in naval battles.

wart /wɔːt/ ▷ *noun* **1** a small and usually hard benign growth with a horny surface, transmitted by a virus, and found on the skin, especially of the fingers, hands and face. **2** a small protuberance on a plant surface or the skin of an animal. ● **warty** *adj.* ● **warts and all** *colloq* with any blemishes or defects showing and accepted. ⓒ Anglo-Saxon *wearte.*

warthog ▷ *noun* a large wild pig, native to Africa south of the Sahara, with a greyish-brown skin, wart-like lumps on its face, sparse shaggy hair, a bristly mane and two pairs of backward-curving tusks. ⓒ 19c.

wartime ▷ *noun* a period during which a war is going on.

Warwicks. ▷ *abbreviation, English county* Warwickshire.

wary /ˈwɛərɪ/ ▷ *adj* (***warier, wariest***) **1** alert, vigilant or cautious; on one's guard. **2** distrustful or apprehensive. **3** (*often* **wary of something** or **someone**) cautious; suspicious of it or them □ *Be wary of such invitations.* ● **warily** *adverb.* ● **wariness** *noun.* ⓒ Anglo-Saxon *wær* to beware.

was *past tense of* BE

wash /wɒʃ/ ▷ *verb* (***washes, washed, washing***) **1** to cleanse someone or something with water or other liquid, and usually soap or detergent. **2** *intr* to cleanse oneself, or one's hands and face, with water, etc. **3** *intr* said of a fabric or dye: to withstand washing without change or damage. **4** *tr & intr* (*usually* **wash off** or **out**, *etc* or **wash something off** or **out**, *etc*) said of dirt or a stain: to be removed, or remove it, through washing. **5** *tr & intr* said of an animal: to lick (itself or its young, etc) clean. **6** to moisten or wet (eg an injured part). **7** (*usually* **wash against** or **over something**) said of a river, the sea, waves, etc: to flow against or over (a place or land feature, etc). **8** said of flowing water: to erode or gouge out (a channel, etc) in the landscape. **9** to cover (a surface, eg a wall) with a thin layer of metal. **10** in watercolour painting: to cover (paper) with a thin layer of watery paint or ink. **11** *intr, colloq* to stand the test; to bear investigation □ *That excuse just won't wash.* **12** *mining* to separate (ore) from earth with a flow of water. **13** *literary* to spread over something. ▷ *noun* (***washes***) **1** the process of washing or being washed. **2** this process undertaken by a laundry. **3** a quantity of clothes, etc for washing, or just washed. **4** the breaking of waves against something; the sound of this. **5** the rough water or disturbed air left by a ship or aircraft. **6** *often in compounds* a lotion or other preparation for cleansing or washing □ *facewash.* **7** kitchen slops or brewery waste, etc for giving to pigs. **8** *art* a thin application of water colour. ● **come out in the wash 1** said of a mark or stain, etc: to disappear after washing. **2** *colloq* to turn out satisfactorily, or become intelligible, in the end. ● **wash one's hands of something** or **someone** to abandon responsibility for it or them. ⓒ Anglo-Saxon *wæscan.*

■ **wash something away 1** to remove it by washing. **2** said of flowing water: to carry it off by force.

■ **wash something down 1** said of a liquid: to carry something downwards; to wash it away. **2** to wash it from top to bottom. **3** to ease (a pill) down one's throat, or accompany or follow (food), with a drink.

■ **wash up** or **wash something up** to wash the dishes and cutlery after a meal.

Wash. see under WA

washable ▷ *adj* said especially of clothes: able to be washed without damage.

washbasin and **washhand basin** ▷ *noun* a shallow sink in which to wash one's face and hands.

washboard ▷ *noun* **1** a corrugated board for rubbing clothes on while washing them. **2** the same board used as a percussion instrument in certain types of music. **3** a thin plank on a boat's gunwale to prevent the sea from breaking over.

washcloth and **washrag** ▷ *noun, N Amer* a FACE CLOTH.

washday ▷ *noun* a day, often the same day each week, on which one's washing is done.

washed-out ▷ *adj* **1** *colloq* said of a person: worn out and pale; lacking in energy. **2** said of the colour in a fabric: faded by, or as if by, washing. **3** said of an outdoor occasion, eg a sports match: cancelled because of rain or other bad weather. See also WASHOUT. ⓒ 19c.

washed-up ▷ *adj* **1** *colloq* said of a person: exhausted; lacking in energy. **2** *slang* done for; at the end of one's resources. **3** said of plans, etc: to have come to nothing. **4** (*especially* **all washed-up**) *slang* finished; unsuccessful. ⓒ 1920s.

washer ▷ *noun* **1** someone who washes. **2** a washing machine. **3** a flat ring of rubber or metal for keeping a joint or nut secure.

washer-dryer or **washer-drier** ▷ *noun* a washing machine with a tumble-dryer built in. Compare TWIN TUB.

washerwoman and **washerman** ▷ *noun, historical* a man or woman paid to wash clothes.

washhouse ▷ *noun, historical* **1** an outhouse or basement room for washing clothes. **2** a public building for washing clothes.

washier, washiest see under WASHY

washing ▷ *noun* **1** the act of cleansing, wetting or coating with liquid. **2** clothes to be, or which have just been washed.

washing line ▷ *noun* a CLOTHESLINE.

washing machine ▷ *noun* a machine for washing clothes and bed linen, etc. ⓒ 18c.

washing powder and **washing liquid** ▷ *noun* a powdered or liquid detergent for washing clothes.

washing soda ▷ *noun* SODIUM CARBONATE crystals, used dissolved in water for washing and cleaning.

washing-up ▷ *noun* **1** the washing of dishes and cutlery, etc after a meal. **2** dishes and cutlery, etc for washing.

washout ▷ *noun* **1** *colloq* a flop or failure. **2** *colloq* a useless person. **3** a rained-off event, eg a match. See also WASHED-OUT.

washrag see WASHCLOTH

washroom ▷ *noun, N Amer* a lavatory.

washstand ▷ *noun, historical* a small table in a bedroom for holding a jug and basin for washing one's hands and face.

washy /ˈwɒʃɪ/ ▷ *adj* (***washier, washiest***) *colloq* **1** said of a drink: watery or weak, usually excessively so. **2** feeble; lacking liveliness or vigour. **3** said of colours: faded-looking or pallid. ⓒ 16c.

wasn't /ˈwɒzənt/ ▷ *contraction* was not.

WASP or **Wasp** /wɒsp/ ▷ *noun, N Amer, often derog* a white person representing the most privileged class in US society. ⓒ 1950s: from *W*hite *A*nglo-*S*axon *P*rotestant.

wasp /wɒsp/ ▷ *noun* any of numerous social or solitary stinging insects which have slender black-and-yellow striped bodies and narrow waists, belonging to the same order as bees and ants, and found worldwide. • **waspy** *adj* (***waspier, waspiest***). ⓒ Anglo-Saxon *wæsp*.

waspish /ˈwɒspɪʃ/ ▷ *adj* sharp-tongued; caustic or venomous. • **waspishly** *adverb*. • **waspishness** *noun*. ⓒ 16c.

wasp nest, **wasp's nest** or **wasps' nest** ▷ *noun* **1** the nest of, or a community of, wasps. **2** *colloq* a place crammed full of enemies or very angry people.

wasp waist ▷ *noun* a slender waist. • **wasp-waisted** *adj*.

wassail /ˈwɒseɪl, ˈwɒsəl/ ▷ *noun, old use* **1** a festive bout of drinking. **2** a toast made at such an occasion. **3** a liquor with which such toasts were made, especially an ale made with roasted apple, sugar and nutmeg. ▷ *verb* (***wassailed, wassailing***) **1** to hold a wassail. **2** to go from house to house at Christmas singing carols and festive songs. • **wassailer** *noun*. ⓒ 13c: from Norse *ves heill* be in good health.

Wassermann's test /ˈvasəmanz —/ and **Wassermann's reaction** ▷ *noun, medicine* a blood test for syphilis. ⓒ Early 20c: named after A P von Wassermann, (1866–1925), the German bacteriologist.

wast /wɒst/ ▷ *verb, old use or dialect, 2nd person singular past tense of* BE, used with the pronoun THOU. 17c.

wastage /ˈweɪstɪdʒ/ ▷ *noun* **1** the process of wasting; loss through wasting. **2** the amount lost through wasting. **3** loss through use or natural decay, etc. **4** (*especially* **natural wastage**) reduction of staff through retirement or resignation, as distinct from dismissal or redundancy.

waste /weɪst/ ▷ *verb* (***wasted, wasting***) **1** to use or spend something purposelessly or extravagantly; to squander. **2** *intr* to be used to no, or little, purpose or effect. **3** to fail to use, make the best of or take advantage of (an opportunity, etc). **4** to throw away (something unused or uneaten, etc). **5** to offer (advice or sympathy, etc) where it is unheeded or unappreciated. **6** (*also* **waste away**) *tr & intr* to lose or cause someone to lose flesh or strength. **7** *intr* to be diminished, used up or impaired by degrees. **8** *tr & intr* to wear out or tire, or become worn out or tired. **9** *chiefly US slang* to attack, kill or murder someone. **10** to treat something as waste material. **11** *old use* to devastate (territory); to lay (an area) waste. ▷ *adj* **1** rejected as useless, unneeded or excess to requirements. **2** said of ground: lying unused, uninhabited or uncultivated. **3** *physiol* denoting material excreted from the body, usually in the urine or faeces. ▷ *noun* **1** the act or an instance of wasting, or the condition of being wasted. **2** failure to take advantage of something ▫ *a waste of talent*. **3** material that is no longer needed in its present form and must be processed, eg household waste and nuclear waste. **4** refuse; rubbish. **5** *physiol* matter excreted from the body. **6** a devastated or barren region. **7** (*often* **wastes**) a vast tract of uncultivated land or expanse of ocean, etc. • **go** or **run to waste** to be wasted. • **lay something waste** to devastate it. ⓒ 12c: from French *wast*.

waste bin and **waste basket** see WASTEPAPER BASKET

wasted ▷ *adj* **1** not exploited; squandered. **2** worn out; exhausted. **3** shrunken or emaciated; gaunt. **4** *slang* extremely drunk, or high on drugs.

waste disposal ▷ *noun* the depositing of waste from domestic, industrial or agricultural sources.

wasteful ▷ *adj* causing waste; extravagant. • **wastefully** *adverb*. • **wastefulness** *noun*.

waste ground ▷ *noun* a piece of land lying unused in a built-up area. *Can equivalent* WASTELOT.

wasteland ▷ *noun* **1** a desolate and barren region. **2** a place or point in time that is culturally, intellectually and spiritually empty.

waste paper ▷ *noun* used paper discarded as rubbish.

wastepaper basket, **wastepaper bin**, **waste bin** and (*N Amer*) **waste basket** ▷ *noun* a basket or other container for waste paper and other refuse.

waste pipe ▷ *noun* a pipe that carries waste material or surplus water from a sink.

waste product ▷ *noun* **1** useless material produced during a manufacturing process, etc which is discarded on the completion of that process. **2** a substance excreted from the body during the metabolic and physiological processes.

waster ▷ *noun* **1** an idler, good-for-nothing or wastrel. **2** a person or thing that wastes.

wasting asset ▷ *noun* any asset, especially a natural one such as a mine, which has a limited life, and whose value decreases with its depletion.

wastrel /ˈweɪstrəl/ ▷ *noun* an idle spendthrift; a good-for-nothing. ⓒ 19c.

wat /wɒt/ ▷ *noun* a Thai Buddhist temple or monastery. ⓒ 19c: from Sanskrit *vata* enclosed ground.

watch /wɒtʃ/ ▷ *verb* (***watches***, ***watched***, ***watching***) **1** *tr & intr* to look at or focus one's attention on someone or something that is moving or doing something, etc. **2** *tr & intr* to pass time looking at or observing (TV, a programme, entertainment or sports event, etc). **3** to keep track of, follow or monitor (developments, progress, etc). **4** to keep (eg a building or person) under observation or surveillance. **5** *intr* to keep vigil; to remain awake or on the alert. **6** (*also* **watch for something**) **a** to await one's chance; to be on the alert to take advantage of (an opportunity); **b** to look out for or guard against it. **7** to keep checking on something, in case controlling measures or adjustments are necessary. **8** to pay proper attention to something □ *watch where you're going!* ▷ *noun* (***watches***) **1** a small timepiece, usually worn strapped to the wrist (also called a WRISTWATCH) or on a chain in the waistcoat pocket or attached to clothing. **2** the activity or duty of watching or guarding. **3** a wake; a vigil kept beside a corpse. **4** *naut* **a** any of the four-hour shifts during which particular crew members are on duty; **b** those on duty in any such shift. **5** *old use* a body of sentries on look-out duty; a watchman or body of watchmen. **6** *historical* a division of the night, especially one of fixed time. ● **keep a watch on something** or **someone** to keep it or them under observation. ● **on the watch for something** seeking or looking out for it. ● **watch it!** be careful! ● **watch oneself** *colloq* to take care in one's behaviour or actions. ● **watch one's step 1** to step or advance with care. **2** *colloq* to act cautiously or warily; to take care not to arouse suspicion or cause offence, etc. ⓒ Anglo-Saxon *wæccan* or *wacian* to watch.

■ **watch out** to be careful.

■ **watch out for something** or **someone** to be on one's guard against it or them; to look out for them.

■ **watch over someone** or **something** to guard, look after or tend to them or it.

-watch ▷ *combining form, signifying* vigilance exercised by a community over some aspect of the environment, especially as a professed brief of a TV programme □ *crimewatch* □ *naturewatch.*

watchable ▷ *adj* **1** able to be watched. **2** *colloq* said of an entertainment, especially a TV programme: enjoyable and interesting to watch; worth watching.

watchcase ▷ *noun* an outer protective case for a watch.

watch chain ▷ *noun* a chain for securing a watch to one's clothing.

watchdog ▷ *noun* **1** a dog kept to guard premises, etc. **2** a person or organization that guards against unacceptable standards, inefficiency or illegality, etc in governmental or commercial operations by closely monitoring their procedures.

watchful ▷ *adj* alert, vigilant and wary. ● **watchfully** *adverb.* ● **watchfulness** *noun.*

watchglass ▷ *noun* **1** a piece of glass that covers the face of a watch. **2** a small curved glass dish used in laboratories for holding small quantities of solutions, etc.

watching brief ▷ *noun* **1** an instruction to a barrister to follow a case on behalf of a client not directly involved. **2** a responsibility for observing developments, etc in a specific area.

watchmaker ▷ *noun* someone who makes and repairs watches and clocks. ● **watchmaking** *noun, adj.*

watchman ▷ *noun* **1** (*also* **nightwatchman**) a man employed to guard premises at night. **2** a man employed to guard the streets at night.

watchnight ▷ *noun* in Protestant churches: **1** the night of Christmas Eve or New Year's Eve. **2** (*in full* **watchnight service**) a church service lasting through midnight on these nights. ⓒ 18c.

watchspring ▷ *noun* the mainspring of a watch.

watchstrap ▷ *noun* a strap for fastening a watch round the wrist.

watchtower ▷ *noun* a tower from which a sentry keeps watch.

watchword ▷ *noun* **1** a catchphrase or slogan that encapsulates the principles of a party, group or profession, etc. **2** *old use* a password.

water /ˈwɔːtə(r)/ ▷ *noun* **1** (formula H_2O) a colourless odourless tasteless liquid that freezes to form ice at 0°C and boils to form steam at 100°C, at normal atmospheric pressure. **2** (*also* **waters**) an expanse of this, with varying degrees of impurity; a sea, lake or river, etc. **3** the surface of a body of water. **4** (**waters**) the sea round a country's coasts, considered part of its territory □ *in British waters.* **5** the level or state of the tide, as in HIGH TIDE and LOW TIDE. **6** *in compounds* a solution of a specified substance in water □ *rosewater.* **7** (**the waters**) water at a spa, etc, containing minerals and generally considered good for one's health. **8** *physiol* **a** any of several fluids secreted by the body, especially urine, sweat, tears, etc; **b** saliva. **9** any liquid that resembles or contains water, eg rain. **10** a dose of water given to a plant or animal. **11** (**waters**) the amniotic fluid that surrounds the fetus in the womb. **12** a wavy sheen effect on fabric, especially silk or satin. **13** the degree of brilliance and transparency of a diamond. **14** quality or class; excellence. See *of the first* or *finest water* below. **15** *finance* an increase in a company's stock issue without an increase in assets to back it up. ▷ *verb* (***watered***, ***watering***) **1** to wet, soak or sprinkle something with water. **2** to irrigate (land). **3** to dilute (wine, etc). **4** *intr* said of the mouth: to produce saliva in response to a stimulus activated by the expectation of food. **5** *intr* said of the eyes: to fill with tears in response to irritation. **6** *tr & intr* to let (animals) drink; said of animals: to drink □ *fed and watered.* **7** to wet (plants) with water. **8** to give a wavy appearance to the surface of (fabric), by wetting and pressing □ *watered silk.* **9** *finance* to increase (the debt of a company) by issuing new stock without a corresponding increase in assets. ● **waterer** *noun.* ● **waterless** *adj.* ● **watery** see separate entry. ● **by water** by water transport, eg ship. ● **hold water** said of an explanation, etc: to prove sound; to be valid. ● **in deep water** in trouble, danger or difficulty. ● **keep one's head above water** to remain out of difficulty or trouble. ● **like a fish out of water** ill at ease; uncomfortable in a particular environment. ● **like water** *colloq* in large quantities; freely or lavishly. ● **like water off a duck's back** said of a rebuke or scolding, etc: having no effect at all; making no impression. ● **make someone's mouth water** to make their saliva flow; to stimulate their appetite for something. ● **of the first** or **finest water** being of the highest class; first-class or prize. ● **pass water** to urinate. ● **pour oil on troubled waters** to take measures to calm a turbulent situation. ● **still waters run deep** a calm and quiet exterior often conceals strong emotions, obstinacy or cunning, etc. ● **test the water** or **waters** to test for a response to an intended course of action. • **throw cold water on** or **over something** *colloq* to be discouraging or unenthusiastic about (an idea, etc). • **tread water** see under TREAD. • **under water** beneath the surface of the water. • **water under the bridge** experiences that are past and done with. ⓒ Anglo-Saxon *wæter*.

■ **water something down 1** to dilute or thin it with water □ *to water down the wine.* **2** to reduce the impact of it; to make it less controversial or offensive. See also WATERED-DOWN.

water bag ▷ *noun* a bag made of leather, skin or canvas, etc used for holding water.

water bailiff ▷ *noun* an official whose duty is to enforce bylaws relating to fishing, or to prevent poaching in protected waters.

water-based ▷ *adj* said of a substance, etc: having water as its principal component.

water bear ▷ *noun* a TARDIGRADE.

waterbed ▷ *noun* **1** a waterproof mattress filled with water. **2** a bed equipped with this. ⓒ 19c.

water beetle ▷ *noun* any of a large number of beetles that live on or in water, and have fringed legs by means of which they swim easily.

water bird ▷ *noun* a swimming or wading bird.

water biscuit ▷ *noun* a thin plain biscuit made from water and flour, usually eaten with cheese, etc.

water blister ▷ *noun* a blister that contains a watery fluid, rather than pus or blood.

water boatman ▷ *noun* a predatory aquatic bug that swims upside-down in water, using its paddle-like hindlegs to propel itself forward and its forelegs to grasp prey.

waterborne ▷ *adj* **1** floating on water. **2** carried or transported by water. **3** said of an infection, etc: transmitted by means of water.

water bottle ▷ *noun* a leather, glass or plastic bottle for carrying drinking water, used by hikers and cyclists, etc.

waterbuck ▷ *noun* any of several antelopes with long ridged horns and which inhabit swampy areas in Africa.

water buffalo ▷ *noun* the common domestic buffalo, native to India, Sri Lanka and SE Asia, which has large ridged horns that curve backwards, and is often used as a draught animal.

water bus ▷ *noun* a passenger boat that sails regularly across a lake or along a river, etc.

water butt ▷ *noun* a large barrel left standing out of doors for collecting rainwater.

water cannon ▷ *noun* a hosepipe that sends out a powerful jet of water, used for dispersing crowds.

Water Carrier and **Water Bearer** ▷ *noun, astron, astrol* AQUARIUS

water chestnut ▷ *noun* **1** an aquatic annual plant, native to Asia, Africa and warm parts of Europe, which produces white flowers and triangular woody fruits. **2 a** a sedge, grown in China, that produces edible tubers; **b** the tuber of this plant, eaten as a vegetable, especially in Chinese and Japanese cuisine.

water clock ▷ *noun* a clock powered by means of flowing water.

water closet ▷ *noun* (abbreviation **WC**) **1** a lavatory whose pan is mechanically flushed with water. **2** a small room containing such a lavatory. ⓒ 18c.

watercolour or (*US*) **watercolor** *noun* **1** paint thinned with water rather than oil. **2** a painting done using such paint. • **watercolourist** *noun* an artist who works in watercolours. ⓒ 16c.

water-cooled ▷ *adj* said of an engine, etc: cooled by circulating water.

water cooler ▷ *noun* a device for cooling by means of water, or for keeping water cool.

watercourse ▷ *noun* **1** a stream, river or canal. **2** the bed or channel along which any of these flow.

watercraft ▷ *singular noun* **1** a boat. **2** skill in swimming, handling boats, or in water sports generally. ▷ *plural noun* boats collectively.

watercress ▷ *noun* **1** a perennial plant with hollow creeping stems and dark-green leaves divided into several pairs of oval leaflets, that grows in watery regions. **2** its sharp-tasting leaves that are used in salads and soups, etc. ⓒ 14c.

water cure ▷ *noun* HYDROTHERAPY; HYDROPATHY.

water cycle ▷ *noun, geog* the continuous cycle in which water evaporates from the sea into the atmosphere, where it later condenses and falls back to the land as rain and snow, etc, when it either evaporates straight back into the atmosphere or runs back into the sea by rivers.

water-diviner ▷ *noun* someone who detects, or attempts to detect, underground sources of water, usually with a DIVINING-ROD. See also DOWSE[1].

watered-down ▷ *adj* **1** very diluted. **2** modified or attenuated; reduced in force or vigour. See also WATER DOWN at WATER.

waterer see under WATER

waterfall ▷ *noun* a sudden interruption in the course of a river or stream where water falls more or less vertically, in some cases for a considerable distance, eg over the edge of a plateau or where overhanging softer rock has been eroded away.

water flea ▷ *noun* a DAPHNIA.

waterfowl ▷ *singular noun* a bird that lives on or near water, especially a swimming bird such as a duck or swan, typically having webbed feet, a medium to long neck, short legs, narrow pointed wings and a broad flattened bill. ▷ *plural noun* swimming birds collectively.

waterfront ▷ *noun* the buildings or part of a town that lie or lies along the edge of a river, lake or sea.

water gas ▷ *noun* an explosive and toxic gaseous mixture, consisting mainly of carbon monoxide and hydrogen, obtained by passing steam, or steam and air, over incandescent coke or other source of carbon.

Watergate ▷ *noun* **1** the US political scandal in 1972 involving an attempted break-in at the Democratic Party headquarters (the Watergate building, Washington DC) by agents employed by President Richard Nixon's re-election organization, a scandal magnified by the subsequent attempted cover-up by senior White House officials who had approved the break-in. **2** any similar political or public scandal, especially one involving corruption, or abuse or misuse of power. ⓒ 1970s.

water gate ▷ *noun* **1** a floodgate. **2** a gate that opens into a river or other watercourse.

water gauge or (*US*) **water gage** ▷ *noun* a device for measuring the quantity or height of water in a vessel, etc.

waterglass ▷ *noun* a solution of potassium or sodium silicate in water, used as protective coating, an adhesive, and *especially formerly* for preserving eggs.

water hammer ▷ *noun* **1** a wave of increased pressure travelling through water in a pipe caused by a sudden stoppage or change in the water flow, eg when the tap is shut off. **2** the loud concussion and noise caused by this.

waterhole ▷ *noun* (*also* **watering hole**) a pool or spring in a dried-up or desert area, where animals can drink.

water ice ▷ *noun* sweetened fruit juice or purée frozen and served as a dessert; a sorbet.

watering can ▷ *noun* a container with a handle and spout used for watering plants.

watering hole ▷ *noun* **1** a waterhole. **2** *slang* a public house.

watering place ▷ *noun* **1** a place where animals may obtain water. **2** *historical* a spa or other resort where people go to drink mineral water or bathe.

water jacket ▷ *noun* **1** a casing containing water placed round eg the cylinder block of an internal-combustion engine to keep it cool. **2** *chem* a similar casing, usually glass, part of a DISTILLATION apparatus.

water jump ▷ *noun* in a steeplechase, etc: a jump over a water-filled ditch or pool, etc.

water level ▷ *noun* **1** the height reached by the surface of a body of still water. **2** the level below which the ground is waterlogged; a water table. **3** a waterline.

waterless see under WATER

water lily ▷ *noun* any of various aquatic perennial plants with large flat circular leaves and white, pink, red or yellow cup-shaped flowers that float on the surface of still or very slow-moving water. ◷ 15c.

waterline ▷ *noun* the level reached by the water on the hull of a floating vessel when under different conditions of loading.

waterlogged /ˈwɔːtəlɒgd/ ▷ *adj* **1** saturated with water. **2** said of a boat: so filled or saturated with water as to be unmanageable.

Waterloo /wɔːtəˈluː/ ▷ *noun* the challenge that finally defeats someone. • **meet one's Waterloo** to be finally and decisively defeated. ◷ 19c: named after the battle of Waterloo where Napoleon was finally defeated in 1815.

water main ▷ *noun* a large underground pipe that carries a public water supply.

waterman ▷ *noun* **1** a man who plies a boat for hire; a boatman. **2** a skilled oarsman.

watermark ▷ *noun* **1** the limit reached by the sea at high or low tide; a waterline. **2** a manufacturer's distinctive mark in paper, visible only when the paper is held up to the light. ▷ *verb* to impress (paper) with a watermark.

water meadow ▷ *noun* a meadow kept fertile by periodic flooding from a stream.

watermelon ▷ *noun* **1** a large round or ovoid fruit native to Africa, with a hard leathery green skin and sweet juicy pink or red flesh containing many black seeds. **2** the trailing vine with deeply lobed leaves and yellow funnel-shaped flowers that bears this fruit. ◷ 17c.

water milfoil ▷ *noun* an aquatic plant with whorls of finely divided leaves.

watermill ▷ *noun* a mill whose machinery is driven by a waterwheel.

water moccasin see MOCCASIN

water nymph ▷ *noun, mythol* a nymph which inhabits water, especially a NAIAD in Greek mythology.

water of crystallization ▷ *noun, chem* water that is chemically incorporated in definite proportions in crystalline compounds called HYDRATES, which can be removed by heating, usually resulting in crystal destruction.

water pipe ▷ *noun* **1** a pipe for conveying water. **2** a HOOKAH.

water pistol ▷ *noun* a toy pistol that fires squirts of water.

water plantain ▷ *noun* a marsh plant with plantain-like leaves and clustered white or pink flowers.

water pollution ▷ *noun, ecol* the contamination of any body of water with industrial waste, sewage and other materials that are considered to be detrimental to living organisms.

water polo ▷ *noun* **1** a seven-a-side ball game for swimmers, in which the object is to score goals by propelling the ball into the opposing team's goal. **2** a similar game for canoeists.

water power ▷ *noun* **1** the power generated by moving water used to drive machinery either directly or indirectly, eg turbines for generating hydroelectricity. **2** the source of such power.

waterproof ▷ *adj* impenetrable by water; treated or coated so as to resist water ▫ *a waterproof anorak.* ▷ *verb* to treat (fabric, etc) so as to make it waterproof. ▷ *noun* a waterproof outer garment. ◷ 18c; 19c as *verb*.

water pump ▷ *noun* a pump for raising water.

water rail ▷ *noun* the common RAIL[3], a long-beaked wading bird which inhabits marshy areas of Europe.

water rat ▷ *noun* **1** *Brit* any of various unrelated small rat-like rodents that live near water, especially the WATER VOLE. **2** *US* the MUSKRAT.

water rate ▷ *noun* a charge made for the use of the public water supply.

water-repellent ▷ *adj* said of a fabric, etc: treated so as not to absorb water.

water-resistant ▷ *adj* resistant to penetration by water.

watershed ▷ *noun* **1** the line that separates two river basins. **2** a crucial point after which events take a different turn. ◷ Early 19c.

waterside ▷ *noun* the edge of a river, lake or sea.

water-ski ▷ *noun* a ski on which to glide over water, towed by a powered boat. ▷ *verb, intr* to travel on water skis. • **water-skier** *noun*. • **water-skiing** *noun*. ◷ 1930s.

water snake ▷ *noun* any of various kinds of snake that inhabit fresh water.

water softener ▷ *noun* a substance or device used in water to remove minerals, especially calcium, that cause hardness and prevent lathering.

water-soluble ▷ *adj* able to be dissolved in water.

water sports ▷ *plural noun* **1** sports practised on or carried out in the water, eg swimming and water-skiing, etc. **2** *slang* sexual arousal and gratification associated with urination.

waterspout ▷ *noun* **1** *meteorol* a tornado that occurs over open water, mainly in the tropics, and consists of a rotating column of water and spray. **2** *meteorol* a torrential downpour of rain. **3** a pipe, etc from which water spouts.

water supply ▷ *noun* **1** the obtaining and distribution of water to a town or community, etc. **2** the amount of water distributed in this way.

water table ▷ *noun* **1** *geol* the level below which porous rocks are saturated with water. **2** *archit* a moulding, especially in the string course of a building, designed to direct water outwards so that it does not flow down the wall below.

water thrush ▷ *noun* either of two kinds of N American warbler with brownish backs and striped underparts.

watertight ▷ *adj* **1** so well sealed as to be impenetrable by water. **2** said of an argument, etc: without any apparent flaw, weakness or ambiguity, etc; completely sound. ◷ 14c.

water torture ▷ *noun* a form of torture, especially one in which water drips or is poured slowly and incessantly on the victim's forehead.

water tower ▷ *noun* a tower that supports an elevated water tank, from which water can be distributed at uniform pressure.

water vapour ▷ *noun* water in the form of an air dispersion, especially where evaporation has occurred at a temperature below boiling point.

water vole ▷ *noun* any of several species of vole, native to Europe, Asia and N America, most of which burrow into the banks of streams and ponds.

waterway ▷ *noun* a navigable channel, eg a canal or river, used by ships or smaller boats either for travel or for conveying goods.

waterwheel ▷ *noun* a wheel that is turned by the force of flowing or falling water on blades or buckets around its rim, formerly used as a source of energy to drive machinery, etc, but now largely superseded by the turbine.

waterwings ▷ *plural noun* an inflatable device that supports the chest, or a pair of inflatable armbands, used by people learning to swim. ⓒ Early 20c.

waterworks ▷ *noun* **1** *singular* an installation where water is purified and stored for distribution to an area. **2** *plural, euphemistic* one's bladder and urinary system. **3** *plural, facetious* tears; weeping. • **turn on the waterworks** to start crying or weeping.

watery ▷ *adj* (***waterier, wateriest***) **1** relating to, consisting of or containing water. **2** containing too much water; over-diluted; weak or thin. **3** said of the sky, Sun or sunlight: weak and pale; having a rainy appearance. **4** said of eyes: moist; inclined to water. **5** said of a smile, etc: half-hearted; feeble. • **wateriness** *noun*.

watt /wɒt/ ▷ *noun* (symbol **W**) *physics* in the SI system: a unit of power, defined as the power that gives rise to the production of energy at the rate of one joule per second. ⓒ Late 19c: named after James Watt (1736–1819), the Scottish engineer.

wattage /ˈwɒtɪdʒ/ ▷ *noun* an amount of electrical power expressed in watts.

watt-hour ▷ *noun* a unit of electrical energy, the amount of work done by one watt in one hour.

wattle /ˈwɒtəl/ ▷ *noun* **1** rods or branches, etc forming eg a framework for a wall, fences or roofs, especially when interwoven. **2** a loose fold of skin hanging from the throat of certain birds, fish and lizards. **3** any of various acacia trees, especially one native to Australia, with leaves divided into numerous tiny leaflets, and many tiny yellow flowers in rounded or catkin-like clusters. ▷ *verb* (***wattled, wattling***) **1** to bind something with wattle or twigs. **2** to form something from wattle. • **wattled** *adj*. ⓒ Anglo-Saxon.

wattle and daub ▷ *noun* wattle plastered with mud or clay, used as a building material.

wattmeter ▷ *noun, physics* an instrument for measuring the power consumption (usually in watt-hours or units) in an alternating-current electric circuit.

waul or **wawl** /wɔːl/ ▷ *verb* (***wauled, wauling; wawled, wawling***) *intr* to cry in the manner of a cat or newborn baby. ▷ *noun* such a cry. ⓒ 16c: imitating the sound.

wave /weɪv/ ▷ *verb* (***waved, waving***) **1** *intr* to move (one's hand) to and fro in greeting, farewell or as a signal. **2** to hold up and move (some other object) in this way for this purpose. **3** to say (*especially* goodbye) in this way. **4** *tr & intr* to move or make something move or sway to and fro. **5** (*especially* **wave someone on** or **through**) to direct them with a gesture of the hand. **6** *intr* said of hair: to have a gentle curl or curls. **7** to put a gentle curl into (hair) by artificial means. ▷ *noun* **1 a** any of a series of moving ridges on the surface of the sea or some other body of water; **b** such a ridge as it arches and breaks on the shore, etc. **2** an act of waving the hand, etc. **3** *physics* a regularly repeated disturbance or displacement in a medium eg water or air. **4** any of the circles of disturbance moving outwards from the site of a shock, such as an earthquake. **5** a loose soft curl, or series of such curls, in the hair. **6** a surge or sudden feeling of an emotion or a physical symptom. **7** a sudden increase in something □ ***a crime wave*** □ ***a heat wave***. **8** an advancing body of people. **9** any of a series of curves in an upward-and-downward curving line or outline. • **waved** *adj*. • **make waves** to create a disturbance or cause trouble, etc; to aggravate a situation. ⓒ Anglo-Saxon *wafian* to wave.

■ **wave someone** or **something aside** to dismiss them or it as unimportant or intrusive.

■ **wave someone off** to watch and wave as they go off on a journey.

waveband ▷ *noun, radio* a range of frequencies in the electromagnetic spectrum occupied by radio or TV broadcasting transmission of a particular type.

wave energy see WAVE POWER

waveform and **waveshape** ▷ *noun, physics* a graph that shows the variation of amplitude of an electrical signal, or other wave, against time.

wave function ▷ *noun, physics* a mathematical equation in QUANTUM MECHANICS, that represents the space and time variations in amplitude for a wave system.

wavelength ▷ *noun, physics* **1** the distance between two successive peaks or two successive troughs of a wave. **2** the length of the radio wave used by a particular broadcasting station. • **on the same wavelength** said of two or more people: speaking or thinking in a way that is mutually compatible.

wave mechanics ▷ *plural noun, physics* the area of QUANTUM MECHANICS that deals with the wave aspect of the behaviour of radiations.

wave power and **wave energy** ▷ *noun* energy or power derived from the movement of the ocean waves, especially when used for the generation of electricity.

waver /ˈweɪvə(r)/ ▷ *verb* (***wavered, wavering***) *intr* **1** to move to and fro. **2** to falter, lessen or weaken, etc. **3** to hesitate through indecision; to vacillate. **4** said of the voice: to become unsteady through emotion, etc. **5** to shimmer or flicker. **6** to vary or fluctuate between extremes. • **waverer** *noun*. • **wavering** *adj*. • **waveringly** *adverb*. ⓒ 14c: from Norse *vafra* to flicker.

waveshape see WAVEFORM

wavy ▷ *adj* (***wavier, waviest***) **1** said of hair: full of waves. **2** said of a line or outline: curving alternately upward and downward. • **wavily** *adverb*. • **waviness** *noun*.

wawl see WAUL

wax[1] ▷ *noun* (***waxes***) **1** *chem* any of a wide variety of solid or semi-solid lipids, either natural or synthetic, that are typically shiny, have a low melting point, are easily moulded when warm, and are insoluble in water. **2** beeswax. **3** sealing-wax. **4** the sticky yellowish matter that forms in the ears. ▷ *verb* (***waxes, waxed, waxing***) to use or apply a natural or mineral wax on something, eg prior to polishing. ⓒ Anglo-Saxon *weax*.

wax[2] ▷ *verb* (***waxes, waxed, waxing***) *intr* **1** said of the Moon: to appear larger as more of its surface is illuminated by the Sun. **2** to increase in size, strength or power. **3** *facetious* to become eg eloquent or lyrical in one's description of something. • **wax and wane** to increase and decrease in alternating sequence. ⓒ Anglo-Saxon *weaxan* to grow.

wax[3] ▷ *noun* (***waxes***) *dated Brit colloq* a fit of anger; a temper. • **in a wax** irate; incensed. ⓒ 19c.

waxberry ▷ *noun* **1** the WAX MYRTLE. **2** the waxy-surfaced fruit from this plant.

waxbill ▷ *noun* any of various small seed-eating birds with coloured bills resembling sealing-wax in colour.

waxcloth ▷ *noun, old use* **1** OILCLOTH. **2** LINOLEUM.

waxen ▻ *adj* **1** made of or covered with wax. **2** similar to or resembling wax. **3** easily impressed or penetrated like wax.

wax flower ▻ *noun* any of several Australian plants with waxy pink five-petalled flowers.

wax myrtle ▻ *noun* a US shrub that bears small waxy berries. Also called **bayberry**, **waxberry**.

wax palm ▻ *noun* CARNAUBA (sense 1).

wax paper ▻ *noun* paper covered with a thin layer of white wax to make it waterproof.

wax plant ▻ *noun* any of several climbing plants native to Australia and E Asia, with clusters of waxy white or pink star-shaped flowers and fleshy leaves.

wax tree ▻ *noun* a tree, such as the wax myrtle, from which wax is obtained.

waxwing ▻ *noun* a songbird of the N hemisphere, which has a crested head, greyish-brown plumage with a black tail, and red wax-like marks on the tips of its wings.

waxwork ▻ *noun* **1** a lifelike model, especially of a famous person or a celebrity, made of wax. **2** an object modelled from wax. **3** (**waxworks**) an exhibition of either or both of these. ⓒ 17c.

waxy ▻ *adj* (***waxier***, ***waxiest***) similar to or resembling wax in appearance or feel. • **waxily** *adverb*. • **waxiness** *noun*.

way ▻ *noun* (**ways**) **1 a** a route, entrance or exit, etc that provides passage or access somewhere; **b** the passage or access provided. **2** the route, road or direction taken for a particular journey. **3** *often in compounds* a track or road. **4** (**Way**) used in street names. **5** *often in compounds* a direction of motion □ *a one-way street* □ *a two-way radio*. **6** an established position □ *the wrong way up* □ *the other way round*. **7** a distance in space or time □ *a little way ahead*. **8** one's district □ *if you're round our way*. **9** the route or path ahead; room to move or progress. **10** a means. **11** a distinctive manner or style. **12** a method. **13** (**ways**) customs or rituals. **14** a characteristic piece of behaviour. **15** a habit or routine. **16** a typical pattern or course □ *It's always the way*. **17** a mental approach □ *different ways of looking at it*. **18** a respect □ *correct in some ways*. **19** an alternative course, possibility or choice, etc. **20** a state or condition. **21** scale. **22** progress; forward motion □ *made their way through the crowds*. **23** *naut* headway; progress or motion through the water □ *made little way that day*. **24** (**ways**) *engineering* the machined surfaces of the top of a lathe bed on which the carriage slides. **25** *engineering* the framework of timbers on which a ship slides when being launched. ▻ *adverb*, *colloq* far; a long way □ *met way back in the 60s*. • **across** or **over the way** on or to the other side of something, eg a street □ *I just live across the way*. • **be on** or **get on one's way** to make a start on a journey. • **by the way** incidentally; let me mention while I remember. • **by way of ...** as a form or means of ... □ *He grinned by way of apology*. • **by way of somewhere** by the route that passes through it. • **come someone's way** said of an opportunity, etc: to become available to them, especially unexpectedly. • **divide something three** or **four**, *etc* **ways** to divide it into three or four, etc parts. • **get** or **have one's own way** to do, get or have what one wants, often as opposed to what others want. • **give way 1** to collapse or subside. **2** to fail or break down under pressure, etc. **3** to yield to persuasion or pressure. • **go all** or **the whole way with someone** *slang* to have sexual intercourse with them. • **go one's own way** to do or behave as one likes, especially in a manner different from others. • **go out of one's way** to make special efforts; to do more than is needed. • **go someone's way** said eg of circumstances: to favour them. • **have a way with someone** or **something** to be good at dealing with them. • **have a way with one** *colloq* to have an attractive manner. • **have it both ways** to benefit from two actions, situations or arguments, etc, each of which excludes the possibility or validity, etc of the others. • **have it** or **everything one's way** or **one's own way** to get one's way in something or everything, especially with disregard for the advice or opinions of others. • **in a bad way** *colloq* in a poor or serious condition; unhealthy. • **in a big way** *colloq* with enthusiasm; on a large or grandiose scale. • **in a way** from a certain viewpoint; to some extent. • **in its**, *etc* **own way** as far as it, etc goes; within limits. • **in no way** not at all. • **in the way of something** in the nature of it □ *not much in the way of cash*. • **lead** or **show the way** to act as a guide or inspiration to others. • **learn one's way around** to accustom oneself to one's new environment or duties, etc. • **look the other way** to ignore or pretend not to notice something. • **lose the** or **one's way** to leave one's intended or known route by mistake. • **make one's way 1** to go purposefully. **2** to progress or prosper □ *making her way in life*. • **make way for someone** or **something 1** to stand aside, or make room, for them or it. **2** to be replaced by them or it. • **no two ways about it** that's certain; no doubt about it. • **no way** *slang* absolutely not. • **on the way out** becoming unfashionable. • **on the way to ...** progressing towards ... □ *well on the way to becoming a millionaire*. • **one way and another** considering certain aspects or features, etc of something □ *It's been a good year, one way and another*. • **out of the way 1** situated so as not to hinder or obstruct anyone. **2** remote; in the middle of nowhere. • **pay one's way** to pay one's own debts and living expenses. • **put someone out of the way** to kill them. • **put someone in the way of something** to contrive to make it available to them. • **see one's way to** or **clear to doing something** to be able and willing to do it. • **that's the way!** a formula of encouragement or approval. • **the, this** or **that way** the manner or tendency of a person's feelings or wishes, etc □ *Do you really want it this way?* □ *I didn't know you felt that way*. • **under way** in motion; progressing. ⓒ Anglo-Saxon *weg*.

waybill ▻ *noun* a list that gives details of goods or passengers being carried by a public vehicle.

wayfarer ▻ *noun, old use or poetic* a traveller, especially on foot. • **wayfaring** *noun, adj*.

wayfaring-tree ▻ *noun* a large shrub, native to Europe and Asia, with white flowers and berries that turn red and eventually black, common in hedges.

waylay /weɪˈleɪ/ ▻ *verb* **1** to lie in wait for and ambush someone. **2** to wait for and delay someone with conversation. • **waylayer** *noun*. ⓒ 16c: WAY + LAY².

wayleave ▻ *noun* permission given to pass over another's ground or property, usually on payment of a fee. ⓒ 15c: WAY + LEAVE².

waymark ▻ *noun* a signpost; something that serves as a guide for a traveller.

way of life ▻ *noun* a style or conditions of living; the living of one's life according to certain principles.

way-out ▻ *adj, slang* **1** excitingly unusual, exotic or new. **2** excellent.

-ways /weɪz/ ▻ *combining form, forming adjectives and adverbs, denoting* direction or manner □ *lengthways* □ *edgeways*.

ways and means ▻ *plural noun* **1** methods for obtaining funds to carry on a government. **2** methods and resources for carrying out and fulfilling any purpose.

wayside ▻ *noun* the edge of a road, or the area to the side of it. ▻ *adj* growing, situated or lying near the edge of roads. • **fall by the wayside** to fail or give up in one's attempt to do something; to drop out.

wayward /ˈweɪwəd/ ▻ *adj* undisciplined or self-willed; headstrong, wilful or rebellious. • **waywardly** *adverb*. • **waywardness** *noun*. ⓒ 14c: from AWAY + -WARD.

wazir /wɑːˈzɪə(r)/ ▻ *noun* a VIZIER. ⓒ 18c: Arabic.

Wb ▻ *symbol* weber.

WBA ▷ *abbreviation* World Boxing Association.

WBC ▷ *abbreviation* World Boxing Council.

WBO ▷ *abbreviation* World Boxing Organization.

WC ▷ *abbreviation* **1** (*WCs* or *WC's*) water closet. **2** West Central.

WCC ▷ *abbreviation* World Council of Churches.

W/Cdr or **W/C** ▷ *abbreviation* Wing Commander.

WD ▷ *abbreviation* **1** *IVR* Dominica, Windward Islands. **2** War Department. **3** Works Department.

we /wiː, wɪ/ ▷ *pronoun*, used as the subject of a verb: **1** to refer to oneself in company with another or others □ *We went to a party last night.* **2** to refer to people in general □ *the times we live in.* **3** used by a royal person, and by writers and editors in formal use: to refer to themselves or the authority they represent. **4** *patronizing* to mean 'you' □ *How are we feeling today?* Ⓒ Anglo-Saxon.

> ***we***
>
> Take care not to use **we** for **us**: say □ *They're laying on a party for us workers*, just as you would say *for us*, not *for we*.

WEA ▷ *abbreviation* Workers' Educational Association.

weak ▷ *adj* (*weaker, weakest*) **1** lacking physical strength. **2** lacking in moral or mental force. **3** not able to support or sustain a great weight. **4** not functioning effectively. **5** liable to give way. **6** lacking power. **7** *commerce* dropping in value. **8** too easily influenced or led by others. **9** yielding too easily to temptation. **10** lacking full flavour. **11** said of an argument: unsound or unconvincing; inconclusive. **12** faint □ *a weak signal.* **13** half-hearted □ *a weak smile.* **14** *phonetics* said of a sound or accent: having little force. **15** said of a verse line: having the accent on a normally unstressed syllable. **16** (*sometimes* **weak on** or **in something**) defective in some respect; having insufficient of something. **17** *grammar* said of a verb: inflected by the addition of a regular suffix rather than by a change in the main vowel, eg *talk, talked*. Compare STRONG sense 13. • **weakly** *adverb*. Ⓒ 13c: from Norse *veikr*.

weaken /ˈwiːkən/ ▷ *verb* (*weakened, weakening*) **1** *tr & intr* to make or become weaker. **2** *intr* to yield to pressure or persuasion. • **weakener** *noun*. Ⓒ 16c.

the weaker sex ▷ *noun, derog* women.

weak-kneed ▷ *adj, colloq* cowardly; feeble.

weakling /ˈwiːklɪŋ/ ▷ *noun* **1** a sickly or physically weak person or animal. **2** someone weak in a certain respect □ *a moral weakling.* Ⓒ 16c.

weakly /ˈwiːklɪ/ ▷ *adj* (*weaklier, weakliest*) sickly; not strong or robust. • **weakliness** *noun*. Ⓒ 16c.

weak-minded ▷ *adj* **1** having feeble intelligence. **2** lacking will or determination. • **weak-mindedly** *adverb*. • **weak-mindedness** *noun*.

weak moment ▷ *noun* a momentary lapse of self-discipline.

weakness ▷ *noun* (*weaknesses*) **1** the condition of being weak. **2** a fault or failing; a shortcoming. **3** (*often* **a weakness for something**) a particular, usually indulgent, liking for it.

weak point, **weak side** and **weak spot** ▷ *noun* **1** the side or point in which someone is most easily influenced or liable to temptation. **2** a side or point in anything at which it is susceptible to error or attack, etc.

weak-willed ▷ *adj* lacking a strong will; irresolute; easily tempted.

weal¹ /wiːl/ ▷ *noun* a long raised reddened mark on the skin caused eg by a slash with a whip or sword. Ⓒ 19c: a variant of WALE.

weal² /wiːl/ ▷ *noun, old use* **1** welfare or wellbeing. **2** (*especially* **the public, general** or **common weal**) the wellbeing, interest and prosperity of the country. Ⓒ Anglo-Saxon *wela* wealth or bliss.

weald /wiːld/ ▷ *noun, archaic or poetic* an area of open or forested country. Ⓒ Anglo-Saxon.

wealth /wɛlθ/ ▷ *noun* **1** riches, valuables and property, or the possession of them. **2** abundance of resources □ *the country's mineral wealth.* **3** a large quantity □ *a wealth of examples.* Ⓒ Anglo-Saxon *wela*; see WEAL².

wealth tax ▷ *noun* a tax paid on personal property and riches when their value exceeds a specific amount.

wealthy ▷ *adj* (*wealthier, wealthiest*) **1** possessing riches and property; rich or prosperous. **2** (**wealthy in something**) well supplied with it; rich in it. • **wealthily** *adverb*. • **wealthiness** *noun*. Ⓒ 14c.

wean /wiːn/ ▷ *verb* (*weaned, weaning*) **1** to accustom (a baby or young mammal) to taking food other than its mother's milk. **2** to gradually break someone of a bad habit, etc □ *how to wean him off drugs.* Ⓒ Anglo-Saxon *wenian* to accustom.

weaner ▷ *noun* a young animal, especially a pig, that has recently been weaned.

weapon /ˈwɛpən/ ▷ *noun* **1** an instrument or device used to kill or injure people, usually in a war or fight. **2** something one can use to get the better of others □ *Patience is our best weapon.* • **weaponed** *adj*. • **weaponless** *adj*. Ⓒ Anglo-Saxon *wæpen*.

weaponry ▷ *noun* (*weaponries*) weapons collectively; armament. Ⓒ 19c.

wear¹ /wɛə(r)/ ▷ *verb* (**wore** /wɔː(r)/, **worn**, **wearing**) **1** to be dressed in something, or have it on one's body. **2** to have (one's hair or beard, etc) cut a certain length or in a certain style. **3** to have (a certain expression). **4** to display or show something. **5** said of a ship: to fly (a flag). **6** *intr* said of a carpet or garment: to become thin or threadbare through use. **7** to make (a hole or bare patch, etc) in something through heavy use. **8** *intr* to bear intensive use; to last in use. **9** *colloq* to accept (an excuse or story, etc) or tolerate (a situation, etc). **10** to tire □ *worn to a frazzle.* ▷ *noun* **1** the act of wearing or state of being worn. **2** *often in compounds* clothes suitable for a specified purpose, person or occasion, etc □ *menswear* □ *evening wear.* **3** the amount or type of use that clothing or carpeting, etc gets □ *subjected to heavy wear.* **4** damage caused through use. See also WEAR AND TEAR. • **wearer** *noun*. • **wearing thin 1** becoming thin or threadbare. **2** said of an excuse, etc: becoming unconvincing or ineffective through overuse. • **the worse for wear 1** showing signs of wear. **2** showing signs of exhaustion or intoxication, etc. Ⓒ Anglo-Saxon *werian*.

> ■ **wear away** or **wear something away** to become or make something thin, or to disappear or make something disappear completely, through rubbing or weathering, etc.
>
> ■ **wear down** or **wear something down** to become reduced or consumed, or to reduce or consume something, by constant use, rubbing, friction, etc.
>
> ■ **wear someone down** to tire or overcome them, especially with persistent objections or demands.
>
> ■ **wear off** said of a feeling or pain, etc: to become less intense; to disappear gradually.
>
> ■ **wear on** said of time: to pass.
>
> ■ **wear on someone** to irritate them.
>
> ■ **wear out** or **wear something out** to become unusable or make it unusable through use. See also WORN OUT.
>
> ■ **wear someone out** to tire them completely; to exhaust them.

■ **wear through** said of clothing, etc: to develop a hole through heavy wear.

wear² /wɛə(r)/ ▻ *verb* (**wore** /wɔː(r)/, **worn**, **wearing**) *naut* **1** to bring (a ship) to another course by turning the helm towards the wind. **2** *intr* said of a ship: to turn towards the wind. ⓒ 17c.

wearable ▻ *adj* capable of being worn; good for wearing. • **wearability** *noun*.

wear and tear ▻ *noun* damage sustained in the course of continual or normal use. See also WEAR *noun* 4.

wearing ▻ *adj* exhausting or tiring. ⓒ Early 19c: from WEAR¹ *verb* 10.

wearisome /ˈwɪərɪsəm/ ▻ *adj* tiring, tedious or frustrating. • **wearisomely** *adverb*. ⓒ 15c.

weary /ˈwɪərɪ/ ▻ *adj* (**wearier**, **weariest**) **1** tired out; exhausted. **2** (*usually* **weary of something**) tired by it; fed up with it. **3** tiring, dreary or irksome; wearing. ▻ *verb* (**wearies**, **wearied**, **wearying**) **1** *tr & intr* to make or become weary. **2** (*usually* **weary of something**) *intr* to get tired of it. • **wearily** *adverb*. • **weariness** *noun*. ⓒ Anglo-Saxon *werig*.

■ **weary for someone** or **something** *Scots* to long for them or it.

weasel /ˈwiːzəl/ ▻ *noun* **1** a small nocturnal carnivorous mammal, closely related to the stoat and found in most N temperate regions, with a slender body, short legs and reddish-brown fur with white underparts. **2** *colloq* a furtive, treacherous or sly person. ▻ *verb* (**weaselled**, **weaselling**; *US* **weaseled**, **weaseling**) to equivocate. • **weaselly** *adj*. ⓒ Anglo-Saxon *wesle*.

■ **weasel out of, on** or **round**, *etc* **something** *colloq* to extricate oneself or circumvent (an obligation or responsibility, etc) especially indefensibly.

weasel words ▻ *plural noun* words used to deliberately make statements evasive or misleading. ⓒ Early 20c: such words suck the meaning out of neighbouring words in the way a weasel sucks the contents out of an egg, leaving the shell empty.

weather /ˈwɛðə(r)/ ▻ *noun* the atmospheric conditions in any area at any time, with regard to sun, cloud, temperature, wind and rain, etc. ▻ *adj*, *especially naut* on the side exposed to the wind. ▻ *verb* (**weathered**, **weathering**) **1** *tr & intr* to expose or be exposed to the effects of wind, Sun and rain, etc; to alter or be altered in colour, texture and shape, etc through such exposure. **2** to come safely through (a storm or difficult situation). **3** *naut* to get to the windward side of (a headland, etc). **4** *archit* to set or slope (a roof or surface, etc) to keep the rain out. • **weathered** *adj*. • **keep a weather eye open** to keep alert for developments. • **make heavy weather of something** to make its progress unnecessarily slow and difficult. • **under the weather** *colloq* not in good health; slightly unwell. ⓒ Anglo-Saxon *weder*.

weatherbeaten and **weather-worn** ▻ *adj* **1** said of the skin or face: tanned or lined by exposure to sun and wind. **2** worn or damaged by exposure to the weather.

weatherboard ▻ *noun* **1** a sloping board fitted to the bottom of a door or window, etc to exclude rain. **2** any of a series of overlapping horizontal boards covering an exterior wall. ▻ *verb* to fit something with such boards or planks. • **weatherboarding** *noun*. ⓒ 16c.

weather-bound ▻ *adj* detained, or prevented from happening, etc, by bad weather.

weather chart see WEATHER MAP

weathercock ▻ *noun* **1** a weathervane in the form of a farmyard cock. **2** *derog* a fickle unreliable person who frequently and easily changes loyalties. ⓒ 14c.

weather eye ▻ *noun* **1** the eye as the means by which someone forecasts the weather. **2** an eye watchful for developments. See also KEEP A WEATHER EYE OPEN at WEATHER.

weather forecast ▻ *noun* a forecast of the weather based on meteorological observations.

weather-gage or **weather-gauge** ▻ *noun*, *naut* position to the windward. Opposite of LEE-GAGE.

weather glass ▻ *noun* a glass or device that indicates the changes in the weather; a barometer.

weathering ▻ *noun*, *geol* the physical disintegration and chemical decomposition of rocks on or just beneath the Earth's surface, with little or no transport of the altered rock material, which occurs as a result of exposure to wind, rain, humidity, extremes of temperature (eg frost), atmospheric oxygen, etc.

weatherman, **weathergirl** and **weatherlady** ▻ *noun*, *colloq* a man or woman who presents the weather forecast on radio or television.

weather map and **weather chart** ▻ *noun* a map that shows meteorological conditions over a large area of country.

weatherproof ▻ *adj* designed or treated so as to keep out wind and rain. ▻ *verb* to make something weatherproof. ⓒ 17c.

weather side ▻ *noun* the windward side.

weather station ▻ *noun* a station where meteorological phenomena are observed.

weather strip and **weatherstripping** ▻ *noun* a thin piece of material fixed along a door or window to keep out the wind and cold.

weathervane ▻ *noun* a revolving arrow that turns to point in the direction of the wind, having a fixed base with arms for each of the four compass points, mounted eg on a church spire. See also WEATHERCOCK. ⓒ 18c.

weather window ▻ *noun* a period of time when the weather is suitable for a particular purpose, eg oil-drilling.

weather-wise ▻ *adj* **1** skilful in forecasting the changes in the weather. **2** quick to sense or determine what turn events will take. ▻ *adverb* with regard to the weather conditions.

weather-worn see WEATHERBEATEN

weave¹ ▻ *verb* (**wove** /woʊv/, **woven** /woʊvən/, **weaving**) **1** *tr & intr* to make (cloth or tapestry) in a loom, passing threads under and over the threads of a fixed warp; to interlace (threads) in this way. **2** to depict something by weaving. **3** to construct anything eg a basket or fence, by passing flexible strips in and out between fixed canes, etc; to make something by interlacing or intertwining. **4 a** to devise (a story or plot, etc); **b** to work (details or facts, etc) into a story, etc. **5** said of a spider: to weave or spin (a web). ▻ *noun* the pattern, compactness or texture of the weaving in a fabric. • **weaver** *noun* **1** someone who weaves. **2** a WEAVERBIRD. ⓒ Anglo-Saxon *wefian*.

weave² ▻ *verb* (**weaved**, **weaving**) *intr* to move to and fro, or wind in and out. • **get weaving** *colloq* to get busy; to hurry. ⓒ 16c.

weaverbird ▻ *noun* (*also* **weaver**) a small passerine bird with a conical bill, found in Africa and Asia, that has bright plumage during the breeding season, and is so called because of the elaborate nests it weaves.

web ▻ *noun* **1** a network of slender threads constructed by a spider to trap insects. **2** a membrane that connects the toes of a swimming bird or animal. **3** *printing* a continuous roll of paper fed through rollers in an offset lithographic printing process. Also called **web offset**. **4** any intricate network □ *a web of lies*. **5** a thin metal plate or sheet. **6 a** (**the Web**) short for WORLD WIDE WEB; **b** *as adj* □ *Web page* □ *Web site*. ▻ *verb* (**webbed**, **webbing**) **1** *intr* to make or weave a web. **2** to envelop or connect with a web. ⓒ Anglo-Saxon *webb*.

webbed ▻ *adj* **1** having a web. **2** said of fingers or toes: partially joined together by a membrane of skin.

webbing ▷ *noun* **1** strong jute or nylon fabric woven into strips for use as belts, straps and supporting bands in upholstery. **2** the membrane that connects fingers or toes in webbed hands or feet.

weber /ˈveɪbə(r), ˈwiːbə(r)/ ▷ *noun, physics* (symbol **Wb**) in the SI system: a unit of magnetic flux (the total size of a magnetic field). 🕓 19c: named after Wilhelm Weber (1804–91), German physicist.

web-footed and **web-toed** ▷ *adj* said of swimming birds, etc: having webbed feet. • **webfoot** *noun*.

web offset see WEB *noun* 3

website ▷ *noun, computing* a person or organization's location on the WORLD WIDE WEB. 🕓 1990s.

Wed. or **Weds.** ▷ *abbreviation* Wednesday.

wed ▷ *verb* (**wedded** or **wed**, **wedding**) **1** *tr & intr, old use* to marry. **2** *old use* to join someone in marriage. **3** (*usually* **wed one thing to** or **with another**) to unite or combine them □ *wed firmness with compassion*. 🕓 Anglo-Saxon *weddian* to promise or marry.

we'd /wiːd, wɪd/ ▷ *contraction of* we had, we would or we should.

wedded ▷ *adj* **1** married. **2** in marriage. • **wedded to something** devoted or committed to it.

wedding ▷ *noun* **1** a marriage ceremony, or the ceremony together with the associated celebrations. **2** *in compounds* any of the notable anniversaries of a marriage, eg *silver wedding*. 🕓 Anglo-Saxon *weddung*.

wedding anniversary ▷ *noun* the anniversary of someone's wedding day.

wedding breakfast ▷ *noun* the celebratory meal served after a wedding ceremony and before the newly married couple leave for their honeymoon.

wedding cake ▷ *noun* a rich iced fruit cake usually in several tiers, served to wedding guests at a reception.

wedding day ▷ *noun* the day of a marriage.

wedding dress ▷ *noun* the dress worn by a bride on her wedding day.

wedding march ▷ *noun* a piece of music in march time played to accompany the entrance of the bride into the church, and at the close of the wedding ceremony.

wedding ring ▷ *noun* a ring, especially in a plain gold band, given by a bridegroom to his bride, or by a bride and bridegroom to each other, and worn as an indication of married status.

wedge ▷ *noun* **1** a piece of solid wood, metal or other material, tapering to a thin edge, that is driven into eg wood to split it, pushed into a narrow gap between moving parts to immobilize them, or used to hold a door open, etc. **2** anything shaped like a wedge, usually cut from something circular. **3** a shoe heel in the form of a wedge, tapering towards the sole. **4** *golf* a club with a steeply angled wedge-shaped head for lofting the ball. ▷ *verb* (**wedged**, **wedging**) **1** to fix or immobilize something in position with, or as if with, a wedge. **2** to thrust, insert or squeeze, or be pushed or squeezed like a wedge □ *wedged herself into the corner*. • **wedged** *adj*. • **wedgy** *adj*. • **drive a wedge between people** to cause ill-feeling or division between people who were formerly friendly or united. • **the thin end of the wedge** something that looks like the small beginning of a significant, usually unwanted, development. 🕓 Anglo-Saxon *wecg*.

Wedgwood /ˈwɛdʒwʊd/ ▷ *noun, trademark* a type of pottery made in factories near Stoke-on-Trent, the most distinctive type consisting of white classical figures applied over a blue background. 🕓 18c: named after Josiah Wedgwood (1730–95), an English potter.

wedlock /ˈwɛdlɒk/ ▷ *noun* the condition of being married. • **born out of wedlock** born to parents not married to each other. 🕓 Anglo-Saxon *wedlac*.

Wednesday /ˈwɛnzdɪ, ˈwɛdənzdɪ, -deɪ/ ▷ *noun* (abbreviation **Wed.** or **Weds.**) the fourth day of the week. 🕓 Anglo-Saxon *Wodnes dæg* the day of Woden, the chief god of the Germanic peoples.

wee[1] ▷ *adj* (**weer**, **weest**) *especially Scots* small; tiny. 🕓 Anglo-Saxon *wæg* weight.

wee[2] and **wee-wee** *colloq* ▷ *verb* (**wees**, **weed**, **weeing**) *intr* to urinate. ▷ *noun* (**wees**) **1** an act of urinating. **2** urine. 🕓 1930s.

weed ▷ *noun* **1** any plant that grows wild and has no specific use or aesthetic value. **2** any plant growing where it is not wanted, especially one that is thought to hinder the growth of cultivated plants such as crops or garden plants. **3** *often in compounds* a plant growing in fresh or salt water □ *pondweed* □ *seaweed*. **4** *slang* marijuana. **5** (**the weed**) *slang* tobacco. **6** *derog* a skinny, feeble or ineffectual man. ▷ *verb* (**weeded**, **weeding**) **1** *tr & intr* to uproot weeds from (a garden or flowerbed, etc). **2** (*also* **weed out**) to identify and eliminate (eg those who are unwanted or ineffective from an organization or other group). • **weeder** *noun*. • **weeding** *noun*. • **weedless** *adj*. 🕓 Anglo-Saxon *weod*.

weedkiller ▷ *noun* a substance, usually a chemical preparation, used to kill weeds.

weeds and **widow's weeds** ▷ *plural noun, old use* the black mourning clothes worn by a widow. 🕓 Anglo-Saxon *wæd* garment.

weedy ▷ *adj* (**weedier**, **weediest**) **1** overrun with weeds. **2** said of a plant: straggly in growth. **3** *derog* said of a person: having a weak or lanky build. **4** *derog* feeble or ineffectual; having an insipid character. • **weediness** *noun*.

week ▷ *noun* **1** a sequence of seven consecutive days, usually beginning on Sunday. **2** any period of seven consecutive days. **3** (*also* **working week**) the working days of the week, as distinct from the WEEKEND. **4** the period worked per week □ *works a 45-hour week*. **5** (**weeks**) an indefinitely long period of time □ *I haven't seen you for weeks!* ▷ *adverb* by a period of seven days before or after a specified day □ *We leave Tuesday week*. • **Friday** or **Saturday**, *etc* **week** the Friday or Saturday, etc after the next one. • **a week last Friday** or **Saturday**, *etc* the Friday or Saturday, etc before the last one. • **a week on** or **next Friday** or **Saturday**, *etc* the Friday or Saturday, etc after the next one. • **a week, two weeks**, *etc* **today** one week, two weeks, etc from today. • **a week tomorrow** or **tomorrow week** one week after the following day. • **week in, week out** endlessly; relentlessly. 🕓 Anglo-Saxon *wice*.

weekday ▷ *noun* any day except Sunday, or except Saturday and Sunday.

weekend ▷ *noun* the period from Friday evening to Sunday night. See also LONG WEEKEND.

weekender ▷ *noun* **1** someone who goes away from home at weekends. **2** *Austral slang* a cottage used at weekends. **3** *chiefly US* a small boat used for leisure at weekends.

weekly ▷ *adj* occurring, produced or issued every week, or once a week. ▷ *adverb* **1** every week. **2** once a week. ▷ *noun* (**weeklies**) a magazine or newspaper published once a week.

weeknight ▷ *noun* the evening or night of a weekday.

ween ▷ *verb* (**weened**, **weening**) *archaic* to think or believe. 🕓 Anglo-Saxon *wenan*.

weeny /ˈwiːnɪ/ ▷ *adj* (**weenier**, **weeniest**) *colloq* used especially by a child: very small; tiny. 🕓 18c: a combination of WEE + TINY or TEENY.

weep ▷ *verb* (**wept**, **weeping**) **1** *intr* to shed tears as an expression of grief or other emotion. **2** to express something while, or by, weeping □ *She wept her goodbyes*. **3** *tr & intr* said of a wound or seal, etc: to exude matter; to ooze. **4** to drip or rain. ▷ *noun* a bout of weeping. ⓒ Anglo-Saxon *wepan*.

■ **weep for something** or *poetic* **weep something** to lament or mourn it.

weeper ▷ *noun* **1 a** someone who weeps; **b** *historical* a hired mourner. **2** a reproduction of a mourner on a graveyard monument. **3** something worn to indicate mourning, such as a scarf or veil.

weeping ▷ *adj* said of a tree variety: having low-drooping branches.

weeping willow ▷ *noun* an ornamental Chinese willow with long drooping branches. ⓒ 18c.

weepy or **weepie** ▷ *adj* (*weepier*, *weepiest*) **1** tearful. **2** said of a film or novel, etc: that makes one weep; poignant or sentimental. ▷ *noun* (*weepies*) *colloq* a film or novel, etc of this kind. • **weepily** *adverb*. • **weepiness** *noun*.

weer, **weest** see WEE[1]

weever /ˈwiːvə(r)/ ▷ *noun* a fish with sharp poisonous spines in the area of the dorsal fin and gills. ⓒ 17c: from French *wivre* serpent, from Latin *vipera*.

weevil /ˈwiːvəl/ ▷ *noun* **1** any of several beetles with an elongated proboscis that may be as long as the rest of the body, which both as adult and larva can damage fruit, grain, nuts and trees. **2** any insect that damages stored grain. • **weevily** *adj*. ⓒ Anglo-Saxon *wifel*.

wee-wee see WEE[2]

wef ▷ *abbreviation* with effect from.

weft ▷ *noun*, *weaving* **1** the threads that are passed over and under the fixed threads of the warp in a loom. **2** the thread carried by the shuttle (also called **woof**). ⓒ Anglo-Saxon.

weigela /ˈwaɪgɪlə, -ˈgiːlə, -ˈdʒiːlə/ ▷ *noun* (*weigelas*) an Asian deciduous shrub with large showy pink, purplish or white flowers. ⓒ 19c: named after C E von Weigel (1748–1831), German botanist.

weigh /weɪ/ ▷ *verb* (*weighed*, *weighing*) **1** to measure the weight of something. **2** *tr & intr* to have (a certain weight). **3** (*often* **weigh something out**) to measure out a specific weight of it. **4** (*often* **weigh something up**) **a** to consider or assess (facts or possibilities, etc); **b** to balance it in one's hand so as to feel its weight. **5** to raise (the anchor) of a ship before sailing. • **weighable** *adj*. • **weigher** *noun*. ⓒ Anglo-Saxon *wegan*.

■ **weigh in** said of a wrestler or boxer before a fight, or of a jockey after a race: to be weighed officially. See also WEIGH-IN.

■ **weigh in with something** *colloq* to contribute (a comment, etc) to a discussion.

■ **weigh on** or **upon someone** to oppress them.

■ **weigh someone down** to burden, overload or oppress them.

■ **weigh with someone** to impress them favourably.

weighbridge ▷ *noun* an apparatus for weighing vehicles with their loads, consisting of a metal plate set into a road surface and connected to a weighing device.

weigh-in ▷ *noun* the official weighing of a wrestler, boxer or jockey. See also WEIGH IN at WEIGH.

weight /weɪt/ ▷ *noun* **1** the heaviness of something; the amount that it weighs. **2** *physics* the gravitational force, measured in NEWTONs, acting on a body. Compare MASS[1]. **3** any system of units for measuring and expressing weight. **4** a piece of metal of a standard weight, against which to measure the weight of other objects. **5** *often in compounds* a heavy object used to compress, hold down or counterbalance something. **6** a heavy load. **7** *athletics* a heavy object for lifting, throwing or tossing. **8** (**weights**) weightlifting or weight-training. **9** a standard amount that a boxer, etc should weigh. See table. **10** a mental burden. **11** strength or significance in terms of amount. **12** the main thrust or force. **13** influence, authority or credibility. **14** *slang* a set measure of a drug, especially an illegal one. **15** *statistics* **a** the frequency of an element within a frequency distribution; **b** the number denoting this. ▷ *verb* (*weighted*, *weighting*) **1** to add weight to something, eg to restrict movement. **2** (*often* **weight something down**) to hold it down in this way. **3** to burden or oppress someone. **4** to assign a handicap weight to (a horse). **5** to arrange or organize something so as to have an unevenness or bias □ *a tax system weighted in favour of the wealthy*. **6** *statistics* to attach numbers indicating their relative frequency to (items in a frequency distribution). • **gain** or **put on weight** to become fatter; to increase one's body size. • **lose weight** to become thinner; to decrease one's body size. • **pull one's weight** to do one's full share of work, etc. • **throw one's weight about** *colloq* to behave in an arrogant or domineering manner. • **throw one's weight behind something** to give one's full support to it. • **worth one's weight in gold** exceptionally useful or helpful. ⓒ Anglo-Saxon *wiht*.

Weight Divisions in Professional Boxing

Name	Maximum weight
heavyweight	any weight
cruiserweight/junior-heavyweight	88 kg/195 lb
light-heavyweight	79 kg/175 lb
super-middleweight	77 kg/170 lb
middleweight	73 kg/160 lb
light-middleweight/ junior-middleweight	70 kg/154 lb
welterweight	67 kg/147 lb
light-welterweight/ junior-welterweight	64 kg/140 lb
lightweight	61 kg/135 lb
junior-lightweight/ super-featherweight	59 kg/130 lb
featherweight	57 kg/126 lb
super-bantamweight/ junior-featherweight	55 kg/122 lb
bantamweight	54 kg/118 lb
super-flyweight/ junior-bantamweight	52 kg/115 lb
flyweight	51 kg/112 lb
light-flyweight/ junior-flyweight	49 kg/108 lb
mini-flyweight/straw-weight/ minimum weight	under 48 kg/105 lb

weighted mean see MEAN[3]

weightier and **weightiest** see under WEIGHTY

weighting ▷ *noun* a supplement to a salary, usually to compensate for high living costs □ *London weighting*. ⓒ 1940s in this sense.

weightless ▷ *adj* **1** weighing nothing or almost nothing. **2** said of an astronaut, etc in space: not subject to the Earth's gravity, so able to float freely.

weightlessness /ˈweɪtləsnəs/ ▷ *noun* **1** the condition of a freely falling body at the beginning of the fall when its INERTIA exactly balances the GRAVITATIONAL force. **2** the condition of a body at an infinite distance from another body such that there is no GRAVITATIONAL force acting on it.

weightlifting ▷ *noun* a sport in which competitors lift, or attempt to lift, a barbell which is made increasingly heavier as the competition progresses, ending only when the competitor is not able to lift it. • **weightlifter** *noun* someone who specializes in weightlifting.

weight-training ▷ *noun* muscle-strengthening exercises performed with the aid of adjustable weights and pulleys.

weightwatcher ▷ *noun* someone who is attempting to lose weight by careful dieting, especially one who regularly attends meetings of an association of people with a similar desire to lose weight. • **weightwatching** *noun*.

weighty /ˈweɪtɪ/ ▷ *adj* (***weightier, weightiest***) **1** heavy. **2** important or significant; having much influence. **3** grave; worrying. • **weightily** *adverb*. • **weightiness** *noun*. ⓒ 15c.

weir /wɪə(r)/ ▷ *noun* **1** a shallow dam constructed across a river to control its flow. **2** a fence of stakes built across a river or stream to catch fish. ⓒ Anglo-Saxon *wer* enclosure.

weird /wɪəd/ ▷ *adj* (***weirder, weirdest***) **1** eerie or supernatural; uncanny. **2** queer, strange or bizarre. **3** *colloq* odd or eccentric. • **weirdly** *adverb*. • **weirdness** *noun*. ⓒ Anglo-Saxon *wyrd* fate.

weirdo /ˈwɪədoʊ/ and **weirdie** /ˈwɪədɪ/ ▷ *noun* (***weirdos, weirdoes*** or ***weirdies***) *derog colloq* someone who behaves or dresses bizarrely or oddly. ⓒ 1950s; late 19c *weirdie*.

Weismannism /ˈvaɪsmanɪzəm/ ▷ *noun*, *biol* the doctrine that acquired characteristics are not genetically inherited. ⓒ Late 19c: named after August Weismann (1834–1914), a German biologist.

welch see WELSH

welcome /ˈwɛlkəm/ ▷ *verb* (***welcomed, welcoming***) **1** to receive (a guest or visitor, etc) with a warm greeting or kind hospitality. **2** to encourage (visits from a specified person or thing) □ *We welcome coach parties.* **3** to invite (suggestions or contributions, etc). **4** to approve of (an action, etc). **5** to respond with pleasure to something. ▷ *exclamation* expressing pleasure on receiving someone. ▷ *noun* **1** the act of welcoming. **2** a reception □ *a cool welcome.* ▷ *adj* **1** warmly received. **2** gladly permitted or encouraged (to do or keep something). **3** much appreciated. • **welcoming** *adj*. • **welcomingly** *adverb*. • **outstay one's welcome** to stay too long. • **welcome someone** or **something with open arms** to receive them or it warmly, gladly, gratefully or thankfully. • **wear out one's welcome** to stay too long or call too often. • **you're welcome!** used in response to thanks: not at all; it's a pleasure. ⓒ Anglo-Saxon *wilcuma* a welcome guest.

weld¹ ▷ *verb* (***welded, welding***) **1** *engineering* to join (two pieces of metal) by heating them to melting point and fusing them together, or by applying pressure alone, producing a stronger joint than soldering. **2** to unite or blend something together firmly. ▷ *noun* a joint between two metals formed by welding. • **weldable** *adj*. • **weldability** *noun*. • **welder** or **weldor** *noun* a person or device that welds. ⓒ 16c: a past participle of obsolete *well* to melt or weld.

weld² ▷ *noun* **1** a scentless species of mignonette that yields a yellow dye. **2** the dye itself. ⓒ 14c.

welfare /ˈwɛlfɛə(r)/ ▷ *noun* **1** the health, comfort, happiness and general wellbeing of a person or group, etc. **2** social work concerned with helping those in need, eg the very poor. Also called **welfare work**. **3** financial support given to those in need. • **on welfare** *chiefly US* receiving financial help from the government or a charity, etc. ⓒ 14c: from WELL¹ + FARE.

welfare economics ▷ *singular noun* an economic theory devoted to studying how best to distribute the gross national product and a nation's wealth among competing claimants, and the extent to which government interferes with market forces.

welfare state ▷ *noun* a system in which the government uses tax revenue to look after citizens' welfare, with the provision of free healthcare, old-age pensions and financial support for the disabled or unemployed. ⓒ 1940s.

well¹ ▷ *adverb* (***better, best***) **1** competently; skilfully. **2** satisfactorily. **3** kindly or favourably. **4** thoroughly, properly or carefully. **5** fully or adequately. **6** intimately □ *don't know her well.* **7** successfully; prosperously. **8** approvingly. **9** attractively. **10** by a long way □ *well past midnight.* **11** justifiably □ *can't very well ignore him.* **12** conceivably; quite possibly □ *may well be right.* **13** understandably □ *if she objects, as well she may.* **14** very much □ *well worth doing.* **15** *usually colloq* used in combination for emphasis □ *I'm jolly well going to* □ *I was well pleased!* ▷ *adj* (***better, best***) **1** healthy. **2** in a satisfactory state. **3** sensible; advisable □ *would be well to check.* ▷ *exclamation* **1** used enquiringly in expectation of a response or explanation, etc. **2** used variously in conversation, eg to resume a narrative, preface a reply, express surprise, indignation or doubt, etc. • **all very well** *colloq* said as an objecting response to a consoling remark: satisfactory or acceptable but only up to a point □ *It's all very well to criticize.* • **as well 1** too; in addition. **2** (*also* **just as well**) for all the difference it makes □ *I may as well tell you.* **3** (*also* **just as well**) a good thing; lucky □ *It was just as well you came when you did.* • **as well as …** in addition to … • **be as well to do something** to be sensible to do it. • **do well out of something** to profit from it. • **leave** or **let well alone** not to interfere in things that are satisfactory as they are. • **mean well** to have helpful or kindly intentions. • **very well** an expression of acceptance in complying with an order or accepting a point, etc. • **well and good** used to show acceptance of facts or a situation. • **well and truly** thoroughly; completely. • **well away 1** making rapid progress; far away. **2** *colloq* drunk or asleep, etc. • **well done!** an expression used to congratulate someone on an achievement, etc. • **well enough** satisfactory within limits. • **well off 1** wealthy; financially comfortable. **2** fortunate; successful. • **well out of something** *colloq* fortunate to be free of it. • **well up in something** *colloq* having a thorough knowledge of it. • **well, well** expressing surprise. • **well worth something** definitely worth it. ⓒ Anglo-Saxon *wel*.

well² ▷ *noun* **1** a lined shaft that is sunk from ground level to a considerable depth below ground in order to obtain a supply of water, oil or gas, etc. **2** a natural spring of water, or a pool fed by it. **3** *especially in compounds* a shaft, or shaft-shaped cavity, eg that made through the floors of a building to take a staircase or lift □ *stairwell.* **4** *naut* an enclosure in a ship's hold round the pumps. **5** *in compounds* a reservoir or receptacle □ *inkwell.* **6** *Brit law* the open space in the centre of a law court. **7** a plentiful source of something. ▷ *verb* (***welled, welling***) *intr* (*often* **well up**) said of a liquid: to spring, flow or flood to the surface. ⓒ Anglo-Saxon *wella*.

we'll /wiːl, wɪl/ ▷ *contraction* we will; we shall.

well acquainted ▷ *adj* **1** having intimate personal knowledge. **2** (**well acquainted with someone** or **something**) familar with them.

> ***well***
>
> • In compounds such as **well intentioned** and **well prepared**, a hyphen is used when the compound comes before the noun it qualifies, as in □ *a well-intentioned person* □ *a well-prepared meal.*
>
> • When the compound comes after a verb such as **be**, it is usually not hyphened, as in □ *they were well intentioned* □ *the meal was well prepared.*
>
> • Idiomatic expressions such as **well-heeled** are usually hyphenated in all positions. See Usage Note at **hyphen**.

well adjusted ▷ *adj* **1** emotionally and psychologically sound. **2** having a good adjustment.

well advised ▷ *adj* sensible; prudent.

well appointed ▷ *adj* said of a house, etc: well furnished or equipped.

well balanced ▷ *adj* **1** satisfactorily proportioned. **2** sane, sensible and stable.

well behaved ▷ *adj* behaving with good manners or due propriety.

wellbeing ▷ *noun* the state of being healthy and contented, etc; welfare.

well beloved ▷ *adj* very dear; greatly loved. ▷ *noun* a greatly loved person.

well born ▷ *adj* descended from an aristocratic family □ *a well-born young man.*

well bred ▷ *adj* **1** having good manners; showing good breeding. **2** said of animals: being of good stock.

well built ▷ *adj* **1** strongly built. **2** said of a person: with a muscular or well-proportioned body.

well chosen ▷ *adj* often said of words: carefully chosen, usually for a positive effect.

well conducted ▷ *adj* **1** properly organized or managed. **2** said of a person: acting or behaving properly.

well connected ▷ *adj* having influential or aristocratic friends and relations.

well covered ▷ *adj* plump or fleshy.

well defined ▷ *adj* clearly and precisely determined.

well deserved ▷ *adj* properly merited or earned.

well designed ▷ *adj* **1** said of living accommodation, furniture, etc: having a functional design. **2** having a clear, skilled and professional design.

well developed ▷ *adj* **1** said of an organism, etc: having developed to an advanced state; mature. **2** large or generous in size.

well disposed ▷ *adj* inclined to be friendly, agreeable or sympathetic.

well-done ▷ *adj* said of food, especially beef: thoroughly cooked. Compare MEDIUM *adj* 3, RARE[2].

well dressed ▷ *adj* very smart and presentable; wearing stylish clothes □ *a well-dressed woman.*

well earned ▷ *adj* thoroughly deserved or merited □ *a well-earned break.*

well educated ▷ *adj* having received a good education, usually to an advanced level □ *a well-educated man.*

well endowed ▷ *adj, colloq* **1** said of a man: having a large penis. **2** said of a woman: having large breasts.

well established ▷ *adj* said of a company or habit, etc: deep seated; strongly or permanently formed or founded.

well favoured ▷ *adj* good-looking.

well fed ▷ *adj* **1** having been given plenty of usually nutritious food. **2** plump.

well formed ▷ *adj* **1** well-proportioned; shapely □ *a well-formed figure.* **2** *linguistics* said eg of a sentence: correct according to the established rules of grammar. **3** (*also* **well-formed formula**) *logic* said of a series of numbers or symbols: corresponding or complying to set rules in a logical system.

well founded ▷ *adj* **1** built on secure foundations. **2** said of suspicions, etc: justified; based on good grounds □ *a well-founded belief.*

well groomed ▷ *adj* said of a person: with a smart and neat appearance □ *a well-groomed image.*

well grounded ▷ *adj* **1** said of an argument, etc: soundly based; well founded. **2** (*usually* **well grounded in something**) having had a good basic education or training in it.

wellhead ▷ *noun* **1** the source of a stream; a spring. **2** an origin or source. **3** the rim or structure round the top of a well.

well-heeled ▷ *adj, colloq* prosperous; wealthy.

well hung ▷ *adj* **1** said of meat or game: hung long enough to mature. **2** *slang* said of a man: having sizeable genitals.

well informed ▷ *adj* **1** having sound and reliable information on something particular. **2** full of varied knowledge.

wellington /ˈwɛlɪŋtən/ and **wellington boot** ▷ *noun* **1** a waterproof rubber or plastic boot loosely covering the foot and calf. **2** a riding-boot that covers the knee, but is cut away at the back allowing the knee to bend. ◷ 19c: named after the first Duke of Wellington (1769–1852).

Wellingtonia /wɛlɪŋˈtoʊnɪə/ ▷ *noun, popularly* the SEQUOIA. ◷ 19c.

well intentioned ▷ *adj* having or showing good intentions, but often having an unfortunate effect.

well judged ▷ *adj* neatly and correctly calculated; judicious □ *a well-judged aim.*

well-knit ▷ *adj* **1** said of a person: sturdily and compactly built. **2** compactly or soundly constructed.

well known ▷ *adj* **1** said especially of a person: familiar or famous; celebrated □ *a well-known celebrity.* **2** fully known or understood.

well liked ▷ *adj* popular; liked in general □ *a well-liked girl.*

well loved ▷ *adj* said of a person: thought of with great affection; well beloved □ *a well-loved person.*

well made ▷ *adj* **1** cleverly and competently made, produced, constructed, etc. **2** said of a person or animal: strongly built; well proportioned.

well mannered ▷ *adj* polite; courteous.

well marked ▷ *adj* obvious, decided or evident; recognizeable.

well matched ▷ *adj* said of two people: able to be or live, etc together harmoniously.

well meaning and **well meant** ▷ *adj* well intentioned.

well-nigh ▷ *adverb* almost; nearly.

well oiled ▷ *adj* **1** *colloq* drunk. **2** smoothly mechanical from thorough practice.

well ordered ▷ *adj* properly arranged; carefully organized.

well paid ▷ *adj* **1** said of a particular job: paying a high salary. **2** said of a person: receiving a high salary in their job.

well placed ▷ *adj* **1** in a good or favourable position for some purpose. **2** holding a position senior or intimate enough to gain information, etc.

well prepared ▷ *adj* **1** carefully prepared. **2** having prepared diligently for (an exam, etc).

well preserved ▷ *adj* **1** in good condition; having little or no decay. **2** youthful in appearance; showing few signs of age.

well read ▷ *adj* having read and learnt much.

well rounded ▷ *adj* **1** pleasantly plump. **2** having had a broadly based and balanced upbringing and education. **3** well constructed and complete.

well spent ▷ *adj* said of time or money, etc: spent usefully or profitably.

well spoken ▷ *adj* having a courteous, fluent and usually refined way of speaking.

wellspring ▷ *noun* **1** a spring or fountain. **2** any rich or bountiful source. ◷ Anglo-Saxon.

well-stacked see STACKED 5

well thought of ▷ *adj* approved of or esteemed; respected.

well thought out ▷ *adj* skilfully and meticulously reasoned and arranged.

well thumbed ▷ *adj* said of a book: showing marks of repeated use and handling □ *a well-thumbed dictionary.*

well timed ▷ *adj* timely or judicious; opportune □ *a well-timed comment.*

well-to-do ▷ *adj* wealthy; financially comfortable. ⓒ 19c.

well travelled ▷ *adj* having travelled often and to many different locations.

well tried ▷ *adj* found reliable from frequent testing.

well trodden ▷ *adj* often followed or walked along; much used or frequented.

well turned ▷ *adj* **1** *old use* attractively formed □ *a well-turned ankle.* **2** neatly and delicately expressed □ *That phrase was well turned.*

well upholstered ▷ *adj, facetious* said of a person: plump or fat.

well versed ▷ *adj* thoroughly trained; knowledgeable □ *He is well versed in law.*

well-wisher ▷ *noun* someone concerned for one's welfare. ⓒ 16c.

well-woman clinic ▷ *noun, medicine* a clinic that specializes in the diagnosis and treatment of minor gynaecological and sexual disorders, and also offers advice on related health matters. *Male equivalent* **well-man clinic**. ⓒ 1980s.

well worn ▷ *adj* **1** much worn or used; showing signs of wear □ *a well-worn pullover.* **2** said of an expression, etc: over-familiar from frequent use; trite.

welly or **wellie** ▷ *noun* (**wellies**) *colloq* a WELLINGTON. Also called **welly-boot**. • **give it welly** or **some welly** *slang* **1** in a motor vehicle: to put one's foot down heavily on the accelerator. **2** to put a great deal of effort or energy into something.

Welsh ▷ *noun* **1** a citizen or inhabitant of, or someone born in, Wales. **2** the official Celtic language of Wales. ▷ *adj* belonging or referring to Wales, its inhabitants or their language. ⓒ Anglo-Saxon *welisc*, from *wealh* Briton or foreigner.

welsh or **welch** ▷ *verb* (**welshes**, **welshed**, **welshing**; **welches**, **welched**, **welching**) **1** *intr* (*usually* **welsh on something**) to fail to pay one's debts or fulfil one's obligations. **2** *intr* (*usually* **welsh on someone**) to fail to keep one's promise to them. **3** to cheat in such a way. • **welsher** *noun.* ⓒ 19c.

Welsh dresser ▷ *noun* a dresser with open shelves that rests on cupboards and drawers.

Welsh harp ▷ *noun* a large harp with three rows of strings.

Welshman and **Welshwoman** ▷ *noun* a man or woman from Wales.

Welsh rabbit or **Welsh rarebit** ▷ *noun, cookery* a dish consisting of melted cheese, usually with butter, ale and seasoning mixed in, served on toast. Also called **rarebit**. ⓒ 18c.

welt ▷ *noun* **1** a reinforcing band or border fastened to an edge, eg the ribbing at the waist of a knitted garment. **2** *shoemaking* a strip of leather fitted round the upper, as a means of attaching it to the sole. **3** a WEAL[1] raised by a lash or blow. ▷ *verb* (**welted**, **welting**) **1** to fit a welt. **2** to beat or thrash someone or something. ⓒ 15c as *welte* or *walt.*

welter /ˈwɛltə(r)/ ▷ *noun* **1** a state of turmoil or confusion. **2** a confused mass. ▷ *verb* (**weltered**, **weltering**) *intr* **1** to lie, roll or wallow. **2** *poetic* to be or lie soaked in a liquid, especially blood. ⓒ 13c: from Dutch *welteren.*

welterweight ▷ *noun* **1** a class for boxers and wrestlers of not more than a specified weight (66.7kg in professional boxing; similar but different weights in amateur boxing and wrestling). **2** a boxer or wrestler of this weight. ⓒ Late 19c: probably from WELT.

wen[1] ▷ *noun* **1** *pathol* a sebaceous cyst on the skin, usually of the scalp. **2** an enormous congested city. • **the great wen** London. ⓒ Anglo-Saxon *wenn* a swelling or wart.

wen[2] see WYN

wench /wɛntʃ/ ▷ *noun* (**wenches**) **1** *facetious* a girl; a woman. **2** a servant girl. **3** *archaic* a prostitute. ▷ *verb* (**wenches**, **wenched**, **wenching**) *intr* **1** to associate with prostitutes. **2** to go courting or associate with girls. ⓒ Anglo-Saxon *wencel* a child.

wend ▷ *verb* (**wended**, **wending**) *archaic or literary* to go or direct (one's course). • **wend one's way** to go steadily and purposefully on a route or journey. ⓒ Anglo-Saxon *wendan.*

Wendy house ▷ *noun* **1** a small playhouse for children constructed of vinyl or cloth, usually erected indoors. **2** a similar playhouse for outdoors, constructed of wood. ⓒ 1940s: from the house built for Wendy in J M Barrie's play *Peter Pan.*

Wensleydale /ˈwɛnzlɪdeɪl/ ▷ *noun* **1** a white crumbly variety of cheese made in Wensleydale. **2** a breed of long-woolled sheep originally developed in Wensleydale. ⓒ 19c: named after Wensleydale, North Yorkshire.

went *past tense of* GO

wentletrap /ˈwɛntəltrap/ ▷ *noun* a gastropod mollusc with a spiral shell with many deep whorls crossed by elevated ribs. ⓒ 18c: from Dutch wenteltrap a winding staircase.

wept *past tense, past participle of* WEEP

were *past tense of* BE

we're /wɪə(r)/ ▷ *contraction* we are.

weren't /wɜːnt/ ▷ *contraction* were not.

werewolf /ˈwɛəwʊlf, ˈwɪə-/ ▷ *noun, folklore* someone who is changed, or changes at free will, into a wolf, usually at full moon. ⓒ Anglo-Saxon *werwulf* man-wolf.

wert /wɜːt/ ▷ *verb, old use or dialect, 2nd person singular past tense of* BE, used with the pronoun THOU. ⓒ 17c: from WERE, influenced by ART[2] and WAST.

Wesak see VESAK

Wesleyan /ˈwɛzlɪən/ *Christianity* ▷ *adj* **1** referring or relating to John Wesley (1703–91). **2** referring or relating to Methodism, the Protestant movement founded by him. ▷ *noun* a follower of Wesley or Methodism. • **Wesleyanism** *noun.* ⓒ 18c.

the West ▷ *noun* **1** the countries of Europe and N America, in contrast to those of Asia. **2** *old use* the non-communist bloc as distinct from the communist or former communist countries of the East. **3** the part of the US to the west of the Mississippi. **4** *historical* the western part of the Roman Empire or Holy Roman Empire.

west ▷ *noun* **1** the quarter of the sky in which the sun sets. **2** one of the four chief points of the compass, the other three being NORTH, SOUTH and EAST. **3** any part of the Earth, a country or town, etc lying in the direction of the west. ▷ *adj* **1** in the west; on the side that is on or nearer the west. **2** said of a wind: situated towards or blowing from the west. ▷ *adverb* toward the west. • **go west** *colloq* **1** to be lost or destroyed; to die. **2** said eg of a business: to collapse. ⓒ Anglo-Saxon.

westbound ▷ *adj* going or leading towards the west.

west by north and **west by south** ▷ *noun* $11^1/_4$; degrees north or south from due west.

the West Country ▷ *noun* the SW counties of England, namely Somerset, Devon and Cornwall.

westering ▷ *adj* said especially of the Sun: sinking towards the west.

westerly ▷ *adj* **1** said of a wind: coming from the west. **2** looking, lying, etc towards the west. ▷ *adverb* to or towards the west. ▷ *noun* (***westerlies***) **1** a westerly wind. 2 (**the westerlies** or **the Westerlies**) *meteorol* winds that blow west to east, most often over the middle latitudes of both hemispheres. In the N hemisphere the westerlies blow from the SW, and in the S hemisphere they blow from the NW.

western /'wɛstən/ ▷ *adj* **1** situated in the west. **2** facing or directed towards the west. **3** belonging to the west. **4** (**Western**) belonging to THE WEST. ▷ *noun* (**Western**) a film or novel featuring cowboys in the west of the USA, especially during the 19c.

Western Church ▷ *noun* the Latin Church, having its ritual and doctrine from Rome, as distinguished from the Eastern or Greek Church.

westerner /'wɛstənə(r)/ ▷ *noun* **1** someone who lives in or comes from the west of anywhere, especially the western part of the USA. **2** (**Westerner**) someone who lives in or comes from THE WEST.

Western hemisphere ▷ *noun* the hemisphere of the Earth that contains the Americas.

westernize or **westernise** ▷ *verb* (***westernized, westernizing***) to make or become like the people of Europe and America in customs, or like their institutions, practices or ideas. • **westernization** *noun*. ◷ 19c.

westernmost ▷ *adj* situated furthest west.

western roll ▷ *noun, athletics* a style of high jumping, taking off from the inside foot, twisting the body while in the air, and so clearing the bar face downwards.

West Germanic see GERMANIC

West Highland white terrier ▷ *noun* a breed of small muscular terrier developed in Scotland, with a thick coat of straight white hair, a rounded head, and short pointed erect ears. ◷ Early 20c.

West Indian ▷ *adj* belonging or relating to the West Indies, a large archipelago separating the Gulf of Mexico and the Caribbean Sea from the Atlantic Ocean. ▷ *noun* a citizen or inhabitant of, or someone born in, the West Indies. ◷ 17c.

Westminster /'wɛsmɪnstə(r), 'west-/ ▷ *noun* the British parliament. ◷ Early 20c: named after the London borough where the Houses of Parliament are situated..

west-north-west and **west-south-west** ▷ *noun* (abbreviation **WNW** and **WSW**) 22½ degrees north or south from the west.

westward /'wɛstwəd/ or **westwards** ▷ *adverb, adj* towards the west.

wet ▷ *adj* (***wetter, wettest***) **1** covered or soaked in water, rain, perspiration, or other liquid. **2** said of the weather: rainy. **3** said of paint, cement or varnish, etc: not yet dried. **4** covered with tears. **5** said of a baby: having a urine-soaked nappy. **6** *derog slang* said of a person: feeble; ineffectual. **7** *Brit derog* in politics: moderately Conservative, especially as judged by more right-wing Conservatives. **8** *N Amer historical* allowing the sale of alcoholic drink. **9** *chem* said of processes and methods, etc: using liquid. **10** said of natural gases: containing large amounts of liquid constituents. ▷ *noun* **1** moisture. **2** rainy weather; rain □ *Don't stay outside in the wet!* **3** *derog slang* a feeble ineffectual person. **4** *colloq* in politics: a moderate Conservative. **5** *colloq* an alcoholic drink; a dram. ▷ *verb* (***wet*** or ***wetted, wetting***) **1** to make someone or something wet; to splash or soak them or it. **2** to urinate involuntarily on something. • **wetly** *adverb*. • **wetness** *noun*. • **wet behind the ears** *colloq* immature or inexperienced. • **wet oneself 1** to make oneself wet by urinating inadvertently. **2** to be so excited or frightened, etc as to be on the point of urinating inadvertently. • **wet one's whistle** *colloq* to take an alcoholic drink. • **wet the baby's head** *colloq* to celebrate the baby's birth with drinks, usually alcoholic ones. • **wet through** completely wet. ◷ Anglo-Saxon *wæt*.

> ***wet***
>
> There is often a spelling confusion between **wet** and **whet**.

wet-and-dry-bulb thermometer ▷ *noun* a hygrometer consisting of two thermometers, one with a dry bulb, the other with the bulb kept moist.

wetback ▷ *noun, US colloq* an illegal Mexican immigrant worker. ◷ 1940s: so called because they swim the Rio Grande to get into the US.

wet blanket ▷ *noun* a dreary and pessimistic person who dampens the enthusiasm and enjoyment of others; a killjoy. ◷ 19c.

wet dream ▷ *noun* an erotic dream that causes the involuntary ejaculation of semen. ◷ 1920s.

wet fly ▷ *noun, angling* a fly for use on or under water.

wether /'wɛðə(r)/ ▷ *noun* a castrated ram. ◷ Anglo-Saxon.

wetland ▷ *noun* (*often* **wetlands**) a region of marshy land.

wet look ▷ *adj* **1** said of a garment or fabric, etc: made of a glossy material, usually PVC, giving the appearance of being wet. **2** said of hair: with the appearance of being wet from the application of a certain type of gel. ▷ *noun* such a material or gel. ◷ 1960s.

wet monsoon see under MONSOON

wet nurse ▷ *noun* a woman employed to breastfeed another's baby. ◷ 18c.

wet pack ▷ *noun* **1** a medical treatment involving the wrapping of a person in blankets or sheets dampened with warm or cold water. **2** the dampened material used for this treatment.

wet rot ▷ *noun bot* **1** a form of decay in timber caused by certain fungi which develop in wood that is alternately wet and dry. **2** the fungi that cause this. Compare DRY ROT.

wet suit ▷ *noun* a tight-fitting rubber suit that is permeable by water, but conserves body heat, worn by divers and canoeists, etc.

wetted, **wetter**, **wettest** and **wetting** see under WET

wetting agent ▷ *noun, chem* a substance (eg soap) that, when added to water, reduces its surface tension so that it is more readily spread over or absorbed by the materials it is applied to.

we've /wiːv, wɪv/ ▷ *contraction* we have.

wf ▷ *abbreviation, printing* wrong fount.

WFTU ▷ *abbreviation* World Federation of Trade Unions.

whack /wak/ *colloq* ▷ *verb* (***whacked, whacking***) to hit something or someone sharply and resoundingly. ▷ *noun* **1** a sharp resounding blow. **2** the sound of this. **3** one's share of the profits or work, etc □ *haven't had their whack yet.* • **have a whack at something** to try it; to have a go at it. • **out of whack** *especially Austral & US* out of order. • **top, full** or **the full whack** the highest price, wage or rate, etc. ◷ 18c: imitating the sound.

whacked or **whacked-out** ▷ *adj, colloq* exhausted; worn out. ◷ Early 20c.

whacker ▷ *noun, colloq* something big of its kind, especially a blatant lie. ◷ 19c.

whacking *colloq* ▷ *noun* a beating. ▷ *adj* enormous; huge. ▷ *adverb* extremely. ◷ Early 19c.

whacko /ˈwakoʊ/ ▻ *exclamation, Brit slang* expressing surprise or delight. Ⓒ 1940s.

whacky see WACKY

whale[1] ▻ *noun* (**whale** or **whales**) any of various large marine mammals of the order Cetacea. They are distributed worldwide and have a torpedo-shaped body, two flippers, flat horizontal tail blades, and a blowhole on the top of the head for breathing. ▻ *verb* (**whaled, whaling**) *intr* to hunt whales. • **whaling** *noun*. • **a whale of a ...** *colloq* a hugely enjoyable (time or evening, etc). Ⓒ Anglo-Saxon *hwæl*.

whale[2] ▻ *verb* (**whaled, whaling**) *chiefly US slang* to thrash someone or something; to strike them or it violently. Ⓒ 18c.

whaleboat ▻ *noun* (*also* **whaler**) **1** a long narrow boat, sharp at both ends, originally used in pursuit of whales. **2** a similar boat carried on larger ships as a lifeboat.

whalebone ▻ *noun* the light flexible horny substance consisting of the baleen plates of toothless whales, used especially formerly for stiffening corsets, etc.

whale oil ▻ *noun* oil obtained from whale blubber.

whaler ▻ *noun* a person or ship engaged in hunting and killing whales (**whaling**).

whale shark ▻ *noun* the largest of all fishes, widely distributed in surface waters of tropical seas, which feeds mainly on small planktonic organisms.

wham ▻ *noun* a resounding noise made by a hard blow. ▻ *verb* (**whammed, whamming**) **1** to hit or make something hit with a wham. **2** to crash or bang □ *The car whammed into the back of the truck.* Also *as exclamation & adverb*. Ⓒ 18c: imitating the sound.

whammy /ˈwamɪ/ ▻ *noun* (**whammies**) *originally US colloq* **1** an unfortunate or malevolent influence. **2** a stunning or powerful blow, or (*usually* **double whammy**) two such blows. Ⓒ 1940s, meaning a spell cast by someone's evil eye (a *double whammy* being one cast by both eyes): from US cartoon strip *Li'l Abner*.

whang ▻ *noun* **1** a resounding noise. **2** a blow. ▻ *verb* (**whanged, whanging**) **1** to make, or hit with, a whang. **2** *intr* to hit or make something hit with a whang. Also *as exclamation & adverb*. Ⓒ 16c: imitating the sound.

whangee /waŋˈiː/ ▻ *noun* (**whangees**) **1** any of several grasses related to bamboo, native to China and Japan. **2** a walking cane made from the stem of such a plant. Ⓒ 18c: probably from Chinese *huang* yellow + *li* bamboo.

wharf /wɔːf/ ▻ *noun* (**wharfs** or **wharves**) a landing-stage built along a waterfront for loading and unloading vessels. Ⓒ Anglo-Saxon *hwearf* bank or shore.

wharfage /ˈwɔːfɪdʒ/ ▻ *noun* **1** dues paid for the use of a wharf. **2** accommodation for vessels at a wharf.

wharfie /ˈwɔːfɪ/ ▻ *noun* (**wharfies**) *Austral & NZ colloq* someone who works at the shore; a wharf labourer.

wharfinger /ˈwɔːfɪndʒə(r)/ ▻ *noun* the owner or supervisor of a wharf. Ⓒ 16c.

what /wɒt/ ▻ *adj, pronoun* **1** used in questions, indirect questions and statements, identifying, or seeking to identify or classify, a thing or person □ *What street are we in?* □ *Tell me what flowers these are* □ *I've just realized what man you meant.* **2** used in exclamations expressing surprise, sympathy or other emotions □ *What! You didn't pass?* □ *What a fool!* □ *What she has to put up with!* **3** used as a relative pronoun or adjective: that or those which; whatever; anything that □ *It is just what I thought* □ *They gave what money they could.* **4** used to introduce a suggestion or new information □ *I know what — let's go to the zoo!* **5** used to ask for a repetition or confirmation of something said □ *What? I didn't catch what you said.* ▻ *adverb* used in questions, indirect questions and statements: to how great an extent or degree? □ *What does that matter?* • **give someone what for** *colloq* to scold or punish them. • **know what it is** to know and understand what is involved in a particular action or experience; to have experienced or suffered it □ *He knows what it is to be bullied.* • **know what's what** *colloq* to know what really goes on or what counts, etc; to know the truth of the matter. • **so what?** or **what of it?** *colloq* why is that important? • **what about ...?** an expression used to make a suggestion or ask an opinion, etc □ *What about stopping for a drink first?* • **what else?** could anything else be the case? • **what ... for?** for what reason ...? to what purpose ...? □ *What did you do that for?* • **what have you** *colloq* other such things; whatnot □ *CDs, records, tapes or what have you.* • **what if ...? 1** what would it matter if ...? □ *What if she did leave for good?* **2** what would happen if ...? □ *What if he doesn't come back?* • **what is more** or **what's more** more to the point ...; in addition ... □ *They came, and what's more, they stayed all evening.* • **what ... like?** a request for a description or opinion on someone or something □ *What does he look like?* □ *What was the theatre like?* • **what next?** often said in despair: what is to be done next? what will happen next? • **what now? 1** what can be done now? what other options are there? **2** what is the meaning of this latest interruption? what is wrong now? • **what of ...? 1** what comes or follows from ...? **2** what is the news of ...? • **what of it?** see *so what?* above. • **what the hell** an expression of indifference or abandoned caution □ *Oh what the hell, I'll buy both of them.* • **what then?** what would be the consequence? • **what's new?** *colloq* **1** tell me the latest news. **2** there's nothing new about that! □ *She's drunk again. So what's new!* • **what's up?** what's the matter? is something wrong? • **what's with ...?** *colloq* what's the matter with ...? • **what with** because of ...; taking account of ... □ *We were exhausted, what with the delays and everything.* Ⓒ Anglo-Saxon *hwæt*.

> ***what***
>
> • **What** and **which** may both be used when asking questions about a choice, as in □ *What/Which is the best way to cook rice?* although **which** generally implies a choice from a known or limited number of options, whereas **what** is used when the choice is unlimited or unspecified.
>
> • Take care not to add a **what** after **than** in comparative constructions such as □ *He can play faster than I can.* **What** should only follow **than** when it means 'that which' or 'the things which', as in □ *Those are better than what we saw in the shops yesterday.*

what-d'you-call-it and **what's-its-name** ▻ *noun, colloq* a thing whose name you can't remember.

whatever ▻ *pronoun, adj* **1** (*also* **what ever**) used as an emphatic form of WHAT □ *Whatever shall I do?* **2** anything □ *Take whatever you want.* **3** no matter what □ *I must finish, whatever happens.* **4** *with negatives* at all □ *has nothing whatever to do with you.* **5** *colloq* some or other □ *has disappeared, for whatever reason.* **6** used to express uncertainty □ *a didgeridoo, whatever that is.* • **... or whatever** *colloq* ... or some such thing □ *Use tape, glue or whatever.* Ⓒ 14c.

whatnot /ˈwɒtnɒt/ ▻ *noun* **1** a stand with shelves for ornaments, etc. **2** *colloq* a whatsit. **3** *colloq* and other similar things □ *grammar and whatnot.* Ⓒ 16c; early 19c in sense 1.

what's-his-name, what's-her-name, what's-its-name, whatsisface and **whatsit** ▻ *noun, colloq* used as a substitute for an unknown or forgotten name for a person or thing.

whatsoever ▻ *adj, pronoun* **1** *old use or literary* whatever; what. **2** *with negatives* at all □ *none whatsoever.* Ⓒ 13c.

whaup / *Scots* hwɔːp/ ▻ *noun* a CURLEW. Ⓒ 16c: imitating its cry.

wheat ▷ *noun* **1** a cereal grass which is the most important cereal crop in terms of harvested area, native to the Middle East but now cultivated in temperate regions worldwide. **2** the grain of this plant, which provides white or brown flour. ◎ Anglo-Saxon *hwæte*.

wheatear ▷ *noun* any of various small migratory songbirds of the thrush family, native to Europe, W Asia, Africa and N America, which have light grey plumage with a conspicuous white rump, and black and white wings and tail. ◎ 16c: probably changed from *white arse*.

wheaten ▷ *adj* **1** made of wheat flour or grain. **2** having the colour of ripe wheat. **3** wholemeal.

wheat germ ▷ *noun* the vitamin-rich germ or embryo of wheat, present in the grain.

wheatmeal ▷ *noun* wheat flour containing most of the powdered whole grain (bran and germ), but not as much as WHOLEMEAL flour.

wheatsheaf ▷ *noun* a sheaf of wheat.

Wheatstone bridge /ˈwiːtstən —/ ▷ *noun, physics* an electric circuit, consisting of four resistors connected in a loop, for measuring the resistance of one resistor of unknown value by comparing it with three other resistors of known values. ◎ 19c: popularized by Sir Charles Wheatstone (1802–75), a British physicist.

whee ▷ *exclamation* expressing excitement or delight. ◎ Late 19c.

wheedle /ˈwiːdəl/ ▷ *verb* (***wheedled***, ***wheedling***) *tr & intr* to coax or cajole someone; to persuade them by flattery. • **wheedler** *noun*. ◎ 17c.

▪ **wheedle something out of someone 1** to obtain it by coaxing. **2** to cheat them of it by cajolery.

wheel ▷ *noun* **1** a circular object or frame rotating on an axle, used eg for moving a vehicle along the ground. **2** such an object serving as part of a machine or mechanism. **3** an object similar to or functioning like a wheel, eg a spinning-wheel or waterwheel. **4** a STEERING-WHEEL. **5** a POTTER'S WHEEL. **6** a rotating firework; a CATHERINE WHEEL. **7** (**wheels**) *colloq* a motor vehicle for personal use. **8** (**wheels**) the workings of an organization, etc ▫ *the wheels of justice*. **9** (*usually* **the wheel**) *historical* a circular instrument of torture on which the victim was stretched. **10** *betting* a disc or drum on the results of whose random spin bets are made ▫ *a roulette wheel*. **11** a circling or pivoting movement, eg of troops. **12** any progression that appears to go round in a circle. **13** a circular design. **14** a FERRIS WHEEL. **15** *poetry* one or more short lines at the end of a stanza. **16** a trip, usually a brief one, in a wheeled contraption ▫ *went out for a wheel in the pram*. ▷ *verb* (***wheeled***, ***wheeling***) **1** to fit something with a wheel or wheels. **2** to push (a wheeled vehicle or conveyance) or to push someone or something in or on it ▫ *He wheeled the bike outside*. **3** to make something move in a circular course. **4** *intr* said of troops or birds, etc: to sweep round in a curve around a pivot. **5** see *wheel about* below. **6** to change one's mind abruptly. • **at** or **behind the wheel 1** in the driver's seat of a car, boat, etc. **2** in charge. • **wheel and deal** to engage in tough business dealing or bargaining. • **wheels within wheels** said of a situation in which a complexity of influences is at work. ◎ Anglo-Saxon *hweol*.

▪ **wheel about** and **wheel round** to turn around suddenly; to pivot on one's heel.

▪ **wheel something forward** or **out 1** to suggest (an idea, etc) that has often been considered before. **2** to bring it forward or out.

wheel and axle ▷ *noun* one of the mechanical powers, in its primitive form a cylindrical axle on which a wheel, concentric with the axle, is firmly fastened, the power being applied to the wheel, and the weight attached to the axle.

wheel animalcule ▷ *noun, zool* a ROTIFER. ◎ 19c.

wheelbarrow ▷ *noun* a hand-pushed cart with a wheel in front and two handles and legs at the rear.

wheelbase ▷ *noun* the distance between the front and rear axles of a vehicle.

wheelchair ▷ *noun* a chair with wheels in which invalids or disabled people can be conveyed or convey themselves.

wheel clamp ▷ *noun* a locking device fitted to the wheel or wheels of an illegally parked vehicle in order to immobilize it, and removed only after the payment of a fine. • **wheel clamping** *noun*. ◎ 1980s.

wheeler-dealing ▷ *noun* tough dealing and bargaining in pursuit of one's political or business interests. See also WHEEL AND DEAL at WHEEL. • **wheeler-dealer** *noun*. ◎ 1950s.

wheelhouse ▷ *noun* the shelter on a ship's bridge in which the steering-gear is housed.

wheelie ▷ *noun* (***wheelies***) *Brit* a trick performed on a motorbike or bicycle in which the front wheel is lifted off the ground, either while stationary or in motion. ◎ 1960s.

wheelie bin or **wheely bin** ▷ *noun, Brit* a large dustbin in a wheeled frame. ◎ 1980s.

wheel of Fortune ▷ *noun, mythol* the wheel believed to be spun by Fortune, the emblem of mutability, consequently bringing about indiscriminate changes in people's lives.

wheel spin ▷ *noun* the rotation of the wheels of a vehicle as a result of reduced road-surface frictional force, causing a spin without any forward movement of the vehicle.

wheel window ▷ *noun* a ROSE WINDOW.

wheelwright /ˈwiːlraɪt/ ▷ *noun* a craftsman who makes and repairs wheels and wheeled carriages. ◎ 13c.

wheesht see WHISHT

wheeze ▷ *verb* (***wheezed***, ***wheezing***) **1** *intr* to breathe in a laboured way with a gasping or rasping noise, when suffering from a lung infection, etc. **2** to speak, or attempt to speak, with such a sound. ▷ *noun* **1** a wheezing breath or sound. **2** *colloq* a bright idea; a clever scheme. • **wheezer** *noun*. • **wheezy** *adj*. • **wheezily** *adverb*. • **wheeziness** *noun*. ◎ 15c: from Norse *hvæsa* to hiss.

whelk¹ ▷ *noun* any of various large predatory marine snails with a pointed spirally-coiled shell, especially the common whelk, native to the coasts of Europe and N America. ◎ Anglo-Saxon *weoloc*.

whelk² ▷ *noun* a pimple, spot or protruberance. ◎ Anglo-Saxon *hwylca*, from *hwelian* to suppurate.

whelp ▷ *noun* **1** the young of a dog or wolf; a puppy. **2** an impudent boy or youth. **3** *naut* a ridge running longitudinally on the barrel or drum of a capstan or windlass to control the cable. ▷ *verb* (***whelped***, ***whelping***) *intr* **1** to give birth to puppies or cubs. **2** *derog* said of a woman: to give birth. ◎ Anglo-Saxon *hwelp*.

when ▷ *adverb* used in questions, indirect questions and statements: at what time?; during what period?; at which time. ▷ *conj* **1** at the time, or during the period, that. **2** as soon as. **3** at any time that; whenever. **4** but just then. **5** at which time. **6** in spite of the fact that; considering that ▫ *Why just watch when you could be dancing?* ▷ *pronoun* **1** what or which time ▫ *They stayed talking, until when I can't say* ▫ *since when she hasn't spoken to me*. **2** used as a relative pronoun: at, during, etc which time ▫ *an era when life was harder*. • **say when** *colloq* used specifically when pouring a drink: tell me when to stop. ◎ Anglo-Saxon *hwænne*.

whence /wɛns/ *old use, formal or literary* ▷ *adverb, conj* **1** used in questions, indirect questions and statements: from what place?; from which place ▫ *enquired whence they had come*. **2** used especially in statements: from what cause or circumstance □ *can't explain whence the mistake arose.* **3** to the place from which □ *returned whence they had come.* ▷ *pronoun* which place □ *the town from whence he came.* ⓒ 13c as *hwannes.*

whenever /wɛnˈɛvə(r)/ ▷ *conj* **1** at any or every time that □ *gets furious whenever he doesn't get his way.* **2** (*also formal* **whensoever**) if ever; no matter when □ *I'll be here whenever you need me.* ▷ *adverb* **1** (*also* **when ever**) an emphatic form of WHEN □ *Whenever could I have said that?* **2** used to indicate that one does not know when □ *at Pentecost, whenever that is.* ● **... or whenever** *colloq* ... or some such or comparable time. ⓒ 14c.

where /wɛə(r)/ ▷ *adverb* used in questions, indirect questions and statements: **1** in, at or to which place; in what direction □ *Where is she going?* □ *I don't know where this road takes us.* **2** in what respect □ *showed me where I'd gone wrong.* **3** from what source □ *Where did you get information like that?* ▷ *pronoun* what place? □ *Where have you come from?* ▷ *conj* **1** in, at or to the, or any, place that □ *went where he pleased.* **2** in any case in which □ *keep families together where possible.* **3** the aspect or respect in which □ *That's where you are wrong.* **4** and there □ *stopped at Hull, where we picked up Jane.* ● **tell someone where to get off** *colloq* to tell them that their behaviour is unwelcome or unacceptable and will not be tolerated. ● **where does he** or **she**, *etc* **get off!** *colloq* who does he or she, etc think they are! ● **where it's at** *slang* the scene of what is considered to be the most important, exciting or trendy place, etc. ● **where someone is coming from** or **where someone is** *dated slang* what they are saying or getting at; what their view or opinion is. ⓒ Anglo-Saxon *hwær.*

whereabouts ▷ *adverb* where or roughly where? ▷ *singular or plural noun* the position or rough position of a person or thing.

whereafter ▷ *conj, formal or old use* after which.

whereas /wɛərˈaz/ ▷ *conj* **1** when in fact □ *She thought she'd failed, whereas she'd done well.* **2** but, by contrast □ *I'm a pessimist, whereas my husband is an optimist.* ⓒ 14c.

whereat /wɛərˈat/ ▷ *adverb, conj, formal or old use* at which; at what?

whereby /wɛəˈbaɪ/ ▷ *pronoun* by means of which.

wherefore /ˈwɛəfɔː(r)/ ▷ *conj, adverb, formal, old use or law* for what reason? why? ▷ *noun* a reason □ *the whys and wherefores.*

wherein /wɛərˈɪn/ *formal, old use or law* ▷ *adverb, conj* in what place?; in what respect? □ *Wherein is the justification?* ▷ *pronoun* in which place or thing.

whereof /wɛərˈɒv/ ▷ *pronoun, formal or old use* of which; of what □ *the circumstances whereof I told you.*

whereon /wɛərˈɒn/ ▷ *pronoun, formal or old use* on which; on what?

whereupon /wɛərəˈpɒn/ ▷ *conj* at which point; in consequence of which.

wherever /wɛərˈɛvə(r)/ ▷ *pronoun* any or every place that □ *I'll take it to wherever you like.* ▷ *conj* **1** in, at or to whatever place □ *They were welcomed wherever they went.* **2** no matter where □ *I won't lose touch, wherever I go.* Also *formal or old use* **wheresoever**. ▷ *adverb* **1** (*also* **where ever**) an emphatic form of WHERE □ *Wherever can they be?* **2** used to indicate that one does not know where □ *the Round House, wherever that is.* ● **... or wherever** *colloq* ... or some such place. ⓒ 13c.

wherewithal /ˈwɛəwɪðɔːl/ and **wherewith** ▷ *pronoun, old use* with which. ▷ *noun* (**the wherewithal**) the means or necessary resources, especially money. ⓒ 16c.

wherry /ˈwɛrɪ/ ▷ *noun* (*wherries*) **1** a long light rowing boat, especially for transporting passengers. **2** a light barge. ⓒ 15c.

whet ▷ *verb* (*whetted, whetting*) **1** to sharpen (a bladed tool) by rubbing it against stone, etc. **2** to arouse or intensify (someone's appetite, interest or desire). ▷ *noun* **1** the act of whetting. **2** something that whets the appetite, etc. ● **whetter** *noun.* ⓒ Anglo-Saxon *hwettan.*

> ***whet***
>
> There is often a spelling confusion between **whet** and **wet**.

whether /ˈwɛðə(r)/ ▷ *conj* **1** used to introduce an indirect question □ *asked whether it was raining.* **2** used to introduce an indirect question involving alternative possibilities □ *was uncertain whether he liked her or not.* **3** (*also* **whether or no** or **not**) used to state the certainty of something, whichever of two circumstances applies □ *promised to marry her, whether or not his parents agreed* □ *the rules, whether fair or unfair, are not our concern.* ⓒ Anglo-Saxon *hwæther.*

whetstone ▷ *noun* **1** a stone for sharpening bladed tools. **2** something that WHETs the appetite, etc. ⓒ Anglo-Saxon *hwetstan.*

whew /hjuː/ ▷ *exclamation, colloq* expressing relief or amazement. ⓒ 16c.

whey /weɪ/ ▷ *noun* the watery content of milk, separated from the curd in making cheese and junket, etc. Compare CURD. ⓒ Anglo-Saxon *hwæg.*

whey face ▷ *noun* a pale or white face. ● **whey-faced** *adj* pale, especially with terror.

which ▷ *adj, pronoun* **1** used in questions, indirect questions and statements: to identify or specify a thing or person, usually from a known set or group □ *can't decide which book is better* □ *Which did you choose?* **2** used to introduce a defining or identifying relative clause □ *animals which hibernate* □ *the evidence on which it is based.* **3** used to introduce a commenting clause, used chiefly in reference to things or ideas rather than people □ *The house, which lies back from the road, is painted red.* **4** used in a relative clause, meaning 'any that' □ *Take which books you want* □ *Tell me which you fancy.* ● **which is which?** said of two or more virtually indistinguishable people or things, etc: which is the one, which is the other? ⓒ Anglo-Saxon *hwilc.*

whichever ▷ *pronoun, adj* **1** the one or ones that; any that □ *Take whichever are suitable* □ *Take whichever coat fits better.* **2** according to which □ *at 10.00 or 10.30, whichever is more convenient.* **3** no matter which □ *I'll be satisfied, whichever you choose.* **4** used to express uncertainty □ *It's in the 'To Do' folder, whichever that is.*

whicker /ˈwɪkə(r)/ ▷ *verb* (*whickered, whickering*) *intr* said of a horse: to neigh or whinny. ▷ *noun* a neigh or whinny. ⓒ 17c: imitating the sound.

whidah see WHYDAH

whiff ▷ *noun* **1** a puff or slight rush of air or smoke, etc. **2** a slight inhalation or exhalation. **3** a slight smell. **4** a hint or trace □ *at the first whiff of scandal.* **5** *slang* a cigarette or cigar. ▷ *verb* (*whiffed, whiffing*) **1** to puff or blow something in whiffs. **2** to inhale or smell. **3** *intr* to move with, or as if with, a puff of air. **4** *intr* to smell, especially to smell unpleasant. ● **whiffy** *adj.* ⓒ 16c: imitating the sound.

whiffle /ˈwɪfəl/ ▷ *verb* (*whiffled, whiffling*) **1** *intr* to blow in puffs or light wafts, especially like the wind. **2** to move as if blown by a puff □ *The leaves whiffled in the breeze.* **3** *intr* to make a slight whistling, puffing or rustling sound. **4** *intr* to talk idly. **5** *intr* to vacillate; to think or behave erratically or fitfully. **6** to prevaricate or speak evasively. ● **whiffling** *noun, adj.* ⓒ 16c: imitating the sound.

whiffletree see WHIPPLETREE

Whig *historical* ▷ *noun* **1** a member of one of the main British political parties that emerged 1679–80, agitating for the exclusion of James, the Duke of York (later James VII and II) from the throne, on the grounds of his Catholicism. The party was superseded in 1830 by the LIBERAL PARTY. Compare TORY. **2** a Scottish Presbyterian in the 17c. **3** in the US: someone in the colonial period who was opposed to British rule; a supporter of the American Revolution. **4** in the US: a member of the party formed from the survivors of the old National Republican party and other elements, first given this name in 1834. ▷ *adj* composed of, referring or relating to the Whigs. ● **Whiggery** or **Whiggism** *noun* Whig principles. ● **Whiggish** *adj.* ● **Whiggishly** *adverb.* ⓒ 17c: probably from *whiggamore*, the name for a 17c Scottish Presbyterian rebel, from *whig* to urge forward + *mere* mare or horse.

while /waɪl/ ▷ *conj* **1** at the same time as □ ***She held the bowl while I stirred.*** **2** for as long as; for the whole time that □ ***guards us while we sleep.*** **3** during the time that □ ***happened while we were abroad.*** **4** whereas □ ***He likes camping, while she prefers sailing.*** **5** although □ ***While I see your point, I still cannot agree.*** ▷ *adverb* at or during which □ ***all the months while I was ill.*** ▷ *noun* a space or lapse of time □ ***after a while.*** ▷ *verb* (***whiled, whiling***) (*often* **while away something**) to pass (time or hours, etc) in a leisurely or undemanding way. ● **all the while** during all the time that. ● **every once in a while** or **once in a while** now and then; sometimes but not often. ● **for a while** for a long time □ ***I haven't been to the cinema for a while.*** ● **in a while** or **little while** in a short time □ ***I'm going out in a while anyway.*** ● **in between whiles** during the intervals. ● **make it worth someone's while** *colloq* to reward them well for their trouble. ● **worth while** or **one's while** worth one's time and trouble. ⓒ Anglo-Saxon *hwil.*

whilst /waɪlst/ ▷ *conj* WHILE.

whim /wɪm/ ▷ *noun* a sudden fanciful idea; a caprice. ⓒ 17c: shortened from *whim-wham* a toy.

whimbrel /'wɪmbrəl/ ▷ *noun* a species of small curlew. ⓒ 16c.

whimper /'wɪmpə(r)/ ▷ *verb* (***whimpered, whimpering***) **1** *intr* to cry feebly or plaintively. **2** to say something plaintively. **3** to say something in a whining or querulous manner. ▷ *noun* a feebly plaintive cry. ● **whimperer** *noun.* ● **whimpering** *noun, adj.* ● **whimperingly** *adverb.* ⓒ 16c: imitating the sound.

whimsical /'wɪmzɪkəl/ ▷ *adj* **1** delicately fanciful or playful. **2** odd, weird or fantastic. **3** given to having whims. ● **whimsicality** *noun.* ● **whimsically** *adverb.*

whimsy or **whimsey** /'wɪmzɪ/ ▷ *noun* (***whimsies***) **1** quaint or fanciful humour. **2** a whim. ▷ *adj* (***whimsier, whimsiest***) quaint or odd. ● **whimsily** *adverb.* ● **whimsiness** *noun.* ⓒ 17c.

whin[1] ▷ *noun* GORSE. ⓒ 15c.

whin[2] ▷ *noun* WHINSTONE. ⓒ 14c.

whine ▷ *verb* (***whined, whining***) **1** *intr* to whimper. **2** *intr* to cry fretfully. **3** *intr* to complain peevishly or querulously. **4** to speak in a thin, ingratiating or servile voice. **5** to say something peevishly. ▷ *noun* **1** a whimper. **2** a continuous shrill or high-pitched noise. **3** an affected, thin and ingratiating nasal tone of voice. ● **whiner** *noun.* ● **whining** *noun, adj.* ● **whiningly** *adverb.* ● **whiny** *adj.* ⓒ Anglo-Saxon *hwinan.*

whinge ▷ *verb* (***whinged, whingeing***) *intr, colloq* to complain irritably; to whine. ▷ *noun* a peevish complaint. ● **whingeing** *noun, adj.* ● **whinger** *noun.* ⓒ Anglo-Saxon *hwinsian* to whine.

whinny /'wɪnɪ/ ▷ *verb* (***whinnies, whinnied, whinnying***) *intr* said of a horse: to neigh softly. ▷ *noun* (***whinnies***) a gentle neigh. ⓒ 16c: imitating the sound.

whinstone /'wɪnstoun/ ▷ *noun* **1** *geol* quartz-dolerite or quartz-basalt igneous rock. **2** a piece of this type of rock.

whip ▷ *noun* **1** a lash with a handle for driving animals or punishing people. **2** a stroke administered by, or as if by, such a lash. **3** a whipping action or motion. **4** someone accustomed to using, or proficient with, a whip, especially a driver or coachman. **5** *politics* a member of a parliamentary party responsible for members' discipline, and for their attendance to vote on important issues. **6** *politics* a notice sent to members by a party whip requiring their attendance for a vote, urgency being indicated (*in compounds*) by the number of underlinings □ ***a three-line whip.*** **7** a dessert of any of various flavours made with beaten egg-whites or cream. **8** a WHIPPER-IN. **9** a simple form of hoisting apparatus consisting of a single rope and block. ▷ *verb* (***whipped, whipping***) **1** to strike or thrash with a whip. **2** to punish someone with lashes or smacking. **3** to lash someone or something with the action or force of a whip □ ***a sharp wind whipped their faces.*** **4** *tr & intr* to move or make something move with a sudden or whip-like motion □ ***the branch whipped back.*** **5** (*usually* **whip something off** or **out**, *etc*) to take or snatch it □ ***whipped out a revolver.*** **6** *tr & intr* to move smartly □ ***whipped out of sight.*** **7** to rouse, goad, drive or force into a certain state □ ***whipped the crowd into a fury.*** **8** *colloq* to steal. **9** to beat (egg-whites or cream, etc) until stiff. **10** to make (egg-whites) frothy by rapidly stirring and turning them with a whisk or similar utensil. **11** to wind cord round (a rope, etc) to prevent fraying. **12** to oversew; to sew using whipstitch. **13** *colloq* to outdo, outwit or defeat. ● **whipper** *noun.* ● **whipping** *noun, adj.* ● **a fair crack of the whip** see under CRACK. ⓒ 13c.

■ **whip something up 1** to arouse (support, enthusiasm or other feelings) for something. **2** to prepare (a meal, etc) at short notice.

whipbird ▷ *noun* either of two types of Australian songbird that make a sound like the crack of a whip. ⓒ 19c.

whipcord ▷ *noun* **1** strong fine tightly twisted cord, as used for making whips. **2** cotton or worsted cloth with a diagonal rib, used chiefly for making dresses, suits and coats. ⓒ 14c.

whipgraft ▷ *verb, hortic* to graft by fitting a tongue cut on the SCION to a slit cut slopingly in the **stock**, a plant for inserting grafts. ▷ *noun* such a graft. ● **whipgrafting** *noun.* ⓒ 17c.

whip hand ▷ *noun* **1** the hand that holds the whip. **2** (*often* **the whip hand**) the advantage in a situation. ⓒ 17c.

whiplash ▷ *noun* **1** the springy end of a whip. **2** the lash of a whip, or the motion it represents. **3** (*also* **whiplash injury**) a popular term for a neck injury caused by the sudden jerking back of the head and neck, especially as a result of a motor vehicle collision.

whipped *past tense, past participle of* WHIP

whipper-in ▷ *noun* (***whippers-in***) an assistant to a huntsman, who controls the hounds. ⓒ 18c.

whippersnapper ▷ *noun, colloq* an insignificant and cheeky young lad or any lowly person who behaves impudently. ⓒ 17c.

whippet /'wɪpɪt/ ▷ *noun* a small slender breed of dog, resembling a greyhound but with a slightly deeper body, developed in northern England and probably produced by cross-breeding small greyhounds with terriers. ⓒ 17c.

whipping *present participle of* WHIP

whipping boy ▷ *noun* **1** someone who is blamed for the faults and shortcomings of others. **2** *historical* a boy who is educated with a prince and given whatever beatings the prince has deserved. ⓒ 17c.

whipping cream ▷ *noun* cream with enough butterfat in it to allow it to thicken when whipped.

whippletree and (*N Amer*) **whiffletree** ▷ *noun* the crosspiece of a carriage or plough, etc which is made so as to swing on a pivot and to which the traces of a harnessed animal are fixed. Also called SWINGLETREE. ⓒ 18c.

whippoorwill /ˈwɪppʊəwɪl, ˈwɪppə-/ ▻ *noun* a species of NIGHTJAR, native to N America, named after its characteristic repetitive call which can be heard at dusk or just before dawn. ⓒ 18c.

whippy /ˈwɪpɪ/ ▻ *adj* (***whippier***, ***whippiest***) said of a stick or cane: springy; flexible. • **whippiness** *noun*. ⓒ 19c.

whip-round ▻ *noun, colloq* a collection of money hastily made among a group of people. ⓒ Late 19c.

whipsaw ▻ *noun* a narrow saw used for dividing timber lengthways, usually set in a frame and worked by two people, one at each end. ▻ *verb* **1** to cut something with a whipsaw. **2** *US slang* to defeat or disadvantage someone in two ways.

whip scorpion ▻ *noun* an arachnid that slightly resembles a true scorpion, but usually has a whip-like appendage instead of a sting at the rear of the body.

whip snake ▻ *noun* any of various long slender snakes resembling a whiplash.

whipstitch ▻ *noun* a small overcasting stitch.

whipstock ▻ *noun* the rod or handle of a whip.

whir see WHIRR

whirl ▻ *verb* (***whirled***, ***whirling***) **1** *intr* to spin or revolve rapidly. **2** *tr & intr* to move with a rapid circling or spiralling motion. **3** *tr & intr* to move or make something move along with great speed, on or as if on wheels. **4** *intr* said of the head: to feel dizzy from excitement, etc. ▻ *noun* **1** a circling or spiralling movement or pattern. **2** a round of intense activity; commotion. **3** a dizzy or confused state □ ***a whirl of emotion***. • **whirler** *noun*. • **whirling** *noun, adj*. • **give something a whirl** *colloq* to try it out; to give it a go. ⓒ 13c: from Norse *hvirfla* to turn.

whirligig /ˈwɜːlɪgɪg/ ▻ *noun* **1** a spinning toy, especially a top. **2** a merry-go-round. **3** anything that spins or revolves rapidly. **4** a dizzying round of activity or progression of events, etc. **5** (*in full* **whirligig beetle**) a water beetle, so called because it whirls round on the surface of ponds. ⓒ 15c.

whirlpool ▻ *noun* a violent circular eddy of water that occurs in a river or sea at a point where several strong opposing currents converge. ⓒ 16c.

whirlwind ▻ *noun* **1** a violently spiralling column of air over land or sea, sometimes extending upwards to a height of several hundred feet. **2** anything that moves in a similarly rapid and usually destructive way. ▻ *adj* referring or relating to anything that developed rapidly or violently □ ***a whirlwind courtship***. ⓒ 14c.

whirlybird /ˈwɜːlɪbɜːd/ ▻ *noun, colloq* a helicopter. ⓒ 1950s.

whirr or **whir** ▻ *noun* a rapid drawn-out whirling, humming or vibratory sound. ▻ *verb* (***whirred***, ***whirring***) **1** *intr* to turn or spin with a whirring noise. **2** to make something move with this sound. ⓒ 14c.

whisht /hwɪʃt/, **whist** /wɪst/ or **wheesht** /hwiːʃt/ *chiefly Scottish* ▻ *verb, intr* to be quiet; to keep silent. Also *as exclamation*. ▻ *noun* hush or silence; a whisper. • **hold** or **keep one's whisht** *Scottish* to be quiet or keep silent. ⓒ 16c: imitating the sound.

whisk ▻ *verb* (***whisked***, ***whisking***) **1** to transport someone or something rapidly □ ***was whisked into hospital***. **2** to move something with a brisk waving motion. **3** to beat (egg-whites or cream, etc) until stiff. ▻ *noun* **1** a whisking movement or action. **2** a hand-held implement for whisking egg-whites or cream, etc. **3** a bundle of grass or twigs, etc for swatting flies or sweeping dust. ⓒ 14c.

■ **whisk someone off** or **away** to take them away quickly.

■ **whisk something off** or **away** to brush or sweep it lightly off or away.

whisker /ˈwɪskə(r)/ ▻ *noun* **1** any of the long coarse hairs that grow round the mouth of a cat or mouse, etc. **2** (**whiskers**) a man's beard. **3** the tiniest possible margin; a hair's breadth □ ***won by a whisker***. **4** a very thin strong fibre or filament made by growing a crystal. **5** someone or something that whisks. • **whiskered** or **whiskery** *adj*. ⓒ 15c.

whisky or (*Irish & N Amer, especially US*) **whiskey** /ˈwɪskɪ/ *noun* (***whiskies*** or ***whiskeys***) **1** an alcoholic spirit distilled from a fermented mash of cereal grains, eg barley, wheat or rye. **2** a drink of this. **3** (**Whisky**) *communications* in the NATO alphabet: the word used to denote the letter 'W' (see table at NATO ALPHABET). ⓒ 18c: from Gaelic *uisge beatha*, literally 'water of life'.

whisper /ˈwɪspə(r)/ ▻ *verb* (***whispered***, ***whispering***) **1** *tr & intr* to speak or say something quietly, breathing rather than voicing the words. **2** *tr & intr* to speak or say something in secrecy or confidence. **3** *tr & intr* to spread a rumour; to rumour □ ***It's whispered that she's leaving him***. **4** *intr* said of a breeze, etc: to make a rustling sound in leaves, etc. ▻ *noun* **1** a whispered level of speech. **2** (*often* **whispers**) a rumour or hint; whispered gossip. **3** a soft rustling sound. • **whisperer** *noun*. • **whispering** *noun*. ⓒ Anglo-Saxon *hwisprian*.

whispering campaign ▻ *noun* an attack launched by means of furtively spread rumours.

whispering gallery and **whispering dome** ▻ *noun* a gallery or dome constructed in such a way that a whisper or slight sound is carried to an unusual distance.

whist¹ ▻ *noun* a card game, usually for two pairs of players, in which the object is to take a majority of 13 tricks, each trick over six scoring one point. ⓒ 17c: altered from its earlier form *whisk* under the influence of WHIST² because of the silence during play.

whist² see WHISHT

whist drive ▻ *noun* a gathering for playing WHIST, with a change of partner after every four games.

whistle /ˈwɪsəl/ ▻ *noun* **1 a** a shrill sound produced through pursed lips or through the teeth, used to signal or to express surprise, etc; **b** the act of making this sound. **2** any of several similar sounds, eg the call of a bird or the shrill sigh of the wind. **3** a small hand-held device used for making a similar sound, used especially as a signal, eg as blown by a referee to regulate play on the pitch. **4** any of several devices which produce a similar sound by the use of steam, eg a railway locomotive or a kettle. **5** a simple wind instrument consisting of a wooden or metal pipe with finger holes. ▻ *verb* (***whistled***, ***whistling***) **1** *tr & intr* to produce a whistle through pursed lips or teeth; to perform (a tune), signal or communicate with this sound. **2** (*often* **whistle up someone** or **something**) to summon them or it with a whistle. **3** *tr & intr* to blow or play on a whistle. **4** *intr* said of a kettle or locomotive: to emit a whistling sound. **5** *intr* said of the wind: to make a shrill sound. **6** *tr & intr* said of a bird: to sing. **7** *intr* said of a bullet, etc: to whizz through the air. • **blow the whistle on someone** or **something** *colloq* **1** to expose them (or their illegal or dishonest practices) to the authorities. **2** to declare it to be illegal. See also WHISTLE-BLOWER. • **as clean, clear** or **dry as a whistle** very clean, clear or dry. • **wet one's whistle** *colloq* to have a drink; to quench one's thirst. • **whistle down the wind 1** to abandon something or let it go. ⓒ 17c: from the practice of casting a hawk off down the wind. **2** to talk to no purpose. • **whistle in the dark** to do something (eg whistle or talk brightly) to quell or deny one's fear. ⓒ Anglo-Saxon *hwistlian* to whistle.

■ **whistle for something** *colloq* to expect it in vain.

whistle-blower ▻ *noun, colloq* a person who informs on someone or something.

whistler ▻ *noun* **1** someone or something that whistles. **2** a large type of marmot. **3** *radio* a whistling sound that descends in pitch, caused by the radiation produced by lightning flashes.

whistle-stop ▻ *adj* **1** said of a politician's tour: on which a number of short stops are made, originally at railway stations, to deliver an electioneering address or a **whistle-stop speech** to local communities. **2** said of any tour: very rapid, with a number of brief stops. ◎ 1950s; 1930s as *noun*, meaning a place at which the train only stops if signalled to by a whistle.

Whit ▻ *noun* Whitsuntide. ▻ *adj* related or belonging to Whitsuntide.

whit ▻ *noun, with negatives* the least bit; the smallest particle imaginable □ *not a whit worse*. ◎ 15c: a variant of *wight* creature.

white ▻ *adj* (***whiter***, ***whitest***) **1** having the colour of snow, the colour that reflects all light. **2** (*often* **White**) **a** said of people: belonging to one of the pale-skinned races; **b** referring or relating to such people. **3** abnormally pale, eg from shock or illness. **4** said eg of a rabbit or mouse: albino. **5** said of hair: lacking pigment, as in old age. **6** said of a variety of anything, eg grapes: pale-coloured, as distinct from darker types. **7** said of wine: made from white grapes or from skinned black grapes. **8 a** said of flour: having had the bran and wheat germ removed; **b** said of bread: made with white flour. **9** said of coffee or tea: with milk or cream added. **10** auspicious; fortunate or favourable. **11** said of glass, etc: transparent or colourless. **12** *poetic* said of the soul, etc: pure or purified from sin; innocent. **13** said of one's morals, etc: pure; innocent. **14** said of a witch: not malevolent; only using her powers for good purposes. ▻ *noun* **1** the colour of snow. **2** white colour or colouring matter, eg paint. **3** white clothes. **3** (*often* **White**) a white person. **4** (*in full* **egg-white**) the clear fluid surrounding the yolk of an egg; albumen. **5** the white part of the eyeball, surrounding the iris. **6** a white butterfly. **7** *games* **a** something white, eg a playing-piece in chess or draughts, a ball in snooker, or ring on an archery target; **b** the player of the white pieces in a board game. **8** (**whites**) **a** household linen; **b** white clothes, eg as worn for cricket or tennis. • **whitely** *adverb*. • **whiteness** *noun*. • **bleed someone white** to drain or deprive them gradually of resources or wealth, etc. • **whiter than white** extremely white; very pure. ◎ Anglo-Saxon *hwit*.

white admiral ▻ *noun* a butterfly of the same genus as the RED ADMIRAL, with white bands across its wings.

white ant ▻ *noun* a termite.

whitebait /ˈwaɪtbeɪt/ ▻ *noun* (*plural* ***whitebait***) the young of any of various silvery fishes, especially herrings and sprats, abundant in shallow coastal waters and estuaries, and which are often fried and eaten whole.

whitebeam ▻ *noun* a small tree whose leaves are white and downy on the underside.

white blood cell and **white corpuscle** ▻ *noun* a colourless blood cell containing a nucleus, whose main functions are to engulf invading micro-organisms and foreign particles, to produce antibodies, or to remove cell debris from sites of injury and infection. Also called **leucocyte**.

whiteboard ▻ *noun* a board, used for teaching or presentation purposes, similar to a BLACKBOARD, but with a white plastic surface for writing on using felt-tipped pens.

White Canon ▻ *noun* a PREMONSTRATENSIAN.

white Christmas ▻ *noun* a Christmas day on which there is snow.

white-collar ▻ *adj* referring to or denoting a class of workers, eg clerks or other professions, who are not engaged in manual labour. Compare BLUE-COLLAR. ◎ 1920s.

whited sepulchre /ˈwaɪtɪd —/ ▻ *noun, formal or literary* someone who is professedly righteous but inwardly wicked; a hypocrite. ◎ 16c: from the Bible, Matthew 23.27.

white dwarf ▻ *noun, astron* a small dense hot star that has reached the last stage of its life, having exhausted the nuclear fuel in its central core and started to collapse under its own gravity. Compare RED GIANT. ◎ 1920s.

white elephant ▻ *noun* a possession or piece of property that is useless or unwanted, especially one that is inconvenient or expensive to keep. ◎ 19c: so called because of the practice of the kings of Siam of giving this honourable but onerous gift to any courtier they wished to ruin.

White Ensign see under ENSIGN

white-eye ▻ *noun* a species of songbird of the Old World with a conspicuous ring of minute white feathers around its eye.

whiteface ▻ *noun* white face make-up, especially as worn by clowns.

white feather ▻ *noun* a symbol of cowardice. • **show the white feather** to behave in a cowardly fashion. ◎ 18c: so called because a white feather in the tail of a game bird was a sign of poor breeding and consequently of poor fighting skills.

white finger ▻ *noun, medicine* a symptom of RAYNAUD'S DISEASE, in which arterial spasms reduce the blood flow to the fingers.

white fish ▻ *noun* a general name for edible sea fish, including whiting, cod, sole, haddock and halibut.

white flag ▻ *noun* the signal used for offering surrender or requesting a truce.

whitefly ▻ *noun* a small sap-sucking bug, whose body and wings are covered with a white waxy powder.

White Friar or **white friar** ▻ *noun* a member of the Carmelite order of monks. ◎ 15c: so called because of their white garments.

white frost see HOARFROST

white gold ▻ *noun* a pale lustrous alloy of gold containing platinum, palladium, nickel or silver, giving it a white colour.

white goods ▻ *noun* **1** household linen. **2** large kitchen appliances such as washing machines, refrigerators and cookers, traditionally white in colour. Compare BROWN GOODS.

whitehead ▻ *noun* a pimple or pustule with a white top. ◎ 1930s.

white heat ▻ *noun* **1** the energy contained in a metal, etc such that white light is emitted. **2** *colloq* an extremely intense state of enthusiasm, activity or excitement □ *the white heat of technology*.

white hope ▻ *noun* someone of whom great achievements and successes are expected. ◎ Early 20c, meaning a white boxer to challenge an established black champion.

white horse ▻ *noun* (*often* **white horses**) a white wave crest on a choppy sea.

white-hot ▻ *adj* **1** said of a metal, etc: so hot that white light is emitted. **2** intense; passionate.

white knight ▻ *noun* someone who rescues a company financially, especially from an unwanted takeover bid. ◎ 1980s in this sense.

white-knuckle ▻ *adj, colloq* indicating extreme anxiety, alarm or terror, especially in **white-knuckle ride**, an exhilarating and terrifying fairground ride, especially the roller-coaster.

white lead ▻ *noun* a lead compound (especially carbonate but also sulphate and silicate) in the form of a white powder, used in paint and putty.

white-leg ▻ *noun, pathol* a form of PHLEBITIS occurring after childbirth. Also called **milk-leg**.

white lie ▻ *noun* a forgivable lie, especially one told to avoid hurting someone's feelings.

white light ▻ *noun* light, such as that of the sun, that contains all the wavelengths in the visible range of the spectrum.

white line ▻ *noun* a longitudinal line on a road, either continuous or broken, to separate lanes of traffic. ▻ *verb, intr* to put white markings on (a road). See also LINE *verb* 1.

whitely see under WHITE

white magic ▻ *noun* magic used only for beneficial purposes, eg to oppose evil or cure disease.

white matter ▻ *noun, anatomy* pale fibrous nerve tissue in the brain and spinal cord. Compare GREY MATTER sense 1. ⓒ 19c.

white meat ▻ *noun* **1** pale-coloured meat, eg veal, rabbit, chicken and turkey. See also RED MEAT. **2** in poultry: the paler meat of the breast. Compare DARK MEAT.

white metal ▻ *noun* **1** any of various alloys that contain large amounts of tin, antimony or lead. **2** a copper ore containing about 75% copper, obtained in copper smelting operations.

whiten ▻ *verb* (***whitened, whitening***) *tr & intr* to make or become white or whiter; to bleach. • **whitening** *noun*. ⓒ 14c.

whitener ▻ *noun* **1** someone or something that whitens. **2** an artificial substitute for milk in tea or coffee.

whiteness see under WHITE

white noise ▻ *noun* sound waves that contain a large number of frequencies of roughly equal intensity.

white-out ▻ *noun* **1** a phenomenon in snowy weather in poor visibililty conditions when the overcast sky blends imperceptively with the white landscape. **2** a dense blizzard. ⓒ 1940s: modelled on BLACKOUT.

white paper ▻ *noun* (*also* **White Paper**) in the UK: a government policy statement printed on white paper, issued for the information of parliament. Compare COMMAND PAPER, GREEN PAPER.

white pepper ▻ *noun* light-coloured pepper made from peppercorns from which the dark outer husk has been removed.

white pudding ▻ *noun* a spicy sausage made from oatmeal and suet.

White Russian ▻ *noun* a BELORUSSIAN.

the whites see under LEUCORRHOEA

white sale ▻ *noun* a sale of household linen goods at a reduced price.

white sauce ▻ *noun* a thick sauce made from flour, fat and a liquid such as milk or stock.

white slave ▻ *noun* a girl or woman held against her will, and forced into prostitution. • **white slaver** *noun*. • **white slavery** *noun*.

white spirit ▻ *noun* a colourless liquid distilled from petroleum and containing a mixture of hydrocarbons, used as a solvent and thinner for paints and varnishes.

white sugar ▻ *noun* refined sugar. Compare BROWN SUGAR.

whitethorn ▻ *noun* the HAWTHORN.

whitethroat ▻ *noun* any of several types of WARBLER with white throat feathers.

white tie ▻ *noun* **1** a white bow tie worn as part of men's formal evening dress. **2** as an instruction on an invitation: formal evening dress for men.

whitewash ▻ *noun* **1** (*also* **limewash**) a mixture of lime and water, used to give a white coating to walls, especially outside walls. **2** measures taken to cover up a disreputable affair or to clear a stained reputation, etc. ▻ *verb* **1** (*also* **limewash**) to coat something with whitewash. **2** to clean up or conceal (eg a disreputable affair). **3** *colloq* in a game: to beat (the opponent) so decisively that they fail to score at all. ⓒ 16c as *verb*.

white water ▻ *noun* **1** the foaming water as in rapids. **2** shoal water near the shore; breakers.

white whale ▻ *noun* a large toothed whale with a rounded white body, related to the dolphin and native to arctic waters. Also called **beluga**.

whitewood ▻ *noun* **1** any of various trees with a light-coloured timber, eg the tulip tree. **2** unstained wood; wood prepared for staining. ⓒ 17c.

whitey or **whity** ▻ *noun, colloq, often derog* usually used by a black person: a white person; white people as a race. Also written **Whitey**.

whither /ˈwɪðə(r)/ *old use or poetic* ▻ *adverb* **1** to what place? ▫ *Whither did they go?* **2** in what direction?; towards what state? ▫ *whither education?* ▻ *conj, pronoun* **1** to the, or any, place that; towards which ▫ *went whither he was bid.* **2** towards which place ▫ *Some miles away lay London, whither they journeyed.* ⓒ Anglo-Saxon *hwider*.

whithersoever /wɪðəsoʊˈɛvə(r)/ ▻ *conj, formal or old use* to whatever place.

whiting[1] /ˈwaɪtɪŋ/ ▻ *noun* (*plural* ***whiting***) a small edible fish related to the cod, native to shallow inshore waters of northern Europe. ⓒ 15c as *hwitling*: so called because of its white colour.

whiting[2] ▻ *noun* ground and washed white chalk, used in putty, whitewash and silver-cleaner. ⓒ 15c.

whitish ▻ *adj* somewhat white; nearly white.

whitlow /ˈwɪtloʊ/ ▻ *noun* an inflammation of the finger or toe, especially near the nail. ⓒ 14c as *whitflawe* white flaw.

Whitsun /ˈwɪtsən/ and **Whitsuntide** ▻ *noun* in the Christian church: the week beginning with Whit Sunday, particularly the first three days. ▻ *adj* relating to, or observed at, Whitsuntide. ⓒ 13c.

Whit Sunday or **Whitsunday** ▻ *noun* PENTECOST (sense 1). ⓒ Anglo-Saxon *hwita sunnandæg* white Sunday, because traditionally those newly baptized wore white robes.

Whitsunday ▻ *noun* **1** WHIT SUNDAY. **2** a Scottish QUARTER DAY, falling on 28 May.

whittle /ˈwɪtəl/ ▻ *verb* (***whittled, whittling***) **1** to cut, carve or pare (a stick or piece of wood, etc) with a knife. **2** to shape or fashion something by this means. • **whittler** *noun*. ⓒ Anglo-Saxon *thwitan* to cut.

▪ **whittle something away** to consume it bit by bit; to eat away at it or erode it.

▪ **whittle something down** to reduce it gradually or persistently.

whity see WHITEY

whizz or **whiz** ▻ *verb* (***whizzes, whizzed, whizzing***) *intr* **1** to fly through the air, especially with a whistling or hissing noise. **2** to move rapidly. ▻ *noun* (***whizzes***) **1** a whistling or hissing sound. **2** *colloq* someone with an exceptional and usually specific talent for something; an expert. **3** *drug-taking slang* SPEED (sense 5). ⓒ 16c: imitating the sound.

▪ **whizz through something** *colloq* to work through or complete it quickly.

whizz-bang ▻ *noun* **1** *World War I slang* a light shell of a very high velocity so that its flight was heard only for a split second before its explosion on landing. **2** a firework that is reminiscent of this.

whizz kid, **whiz kid** or **wiz kid** ▻ *noun, colloq* someone who achieves success quickly and early, through ability, inventiveness, dynamism or ambition. ◷ 1940s.

WHO ▻ *abbreviation* World Health Organization.

who /huː/ ▻ *pronoun* **1** used in questions, indirect questions and statements: which or what person; which or what people □ ***Who is at the door?*** □ ***asked who else he had seen.*** **2** used as a relative pronoun to introduce a defining clause □ ***the boy who was on the train.*** **3** used as a RELATIVE pronoun to add a commenting clause □ ***Julius Caesar, who was murdered in 44 BC.*** ● **know who's who** to know the important people and what they do. ◷ Anglo-Saxon *hwa*.

whoa /woʊ/ ▻ *exclamation* a command to stop, especially to a horse. ◷ 15c.

who'd /huːd/ ▻ *contraction* **1** who would. **2** who had.

whodunit or **whodunnit** /huːˈdʌnɪt/ ▻ *noun, colloq* a detective novel or play, etc; a mystery. ◷ 1920s: from *who done it?*, a non-standard form of *who did it?*

whoever ▻ *pronoun* **1** (*also* **who ever**) used in questions, indirect questions and statements as an emphatic form of WHO or WHOM □ ***Whoever is that at the door?*** □ ***ask whoever you like.*** **2** no matter who □ ***I don't want to see them, whoever they are.*** **3** used to indicate that one does not know who □ ***St Fiacre, whoever he was.*** ● **... or whoever** *colloq* ... or some other such person or people.

whole /hoʊl/ ▻ *noun* **1** all the constituents or components of something □ ***He ate the whole of it*** □ ***the whole of the time.*** **2** something complete in itself, especially something consisting of integrated parts. ▻ *adj* **1** comprising all of something; no less than the whole; entire □ ***The concert lasted four whole hours*** □ ***The whole street heard you.*** **2** in one piece □ ***swallowed it whole.*** **3** unbroken □ ***only two cups left whole.*** **4** said of food: processed as little as possible. **5** *colloq* huge; vast □ ***a whole pile of work to do.*** **6** *old use* healthy; well □ ***the miracle that made him whole.*** **7** said of a sister or brother: having both parents in common. ▻ *adverb, colloq* completely; altogether; wholly □ ***found a whole new approach.*** ● **wholeness** *noun*. ● **a whole lot** *colloq* a great deal □ ***I feel a whole lot better.*** ● **as a whole** in general; taken as a complete group, etc rather than as individuals. ● **go the whole hog** see under HOG. ● **on the whole** considering everything. ◷ Anglo-Saxon *hal* healthy.

whole cloth ▻ *noun* cloth in its full manufactured size.

wholefood ▻ *noun* (*sometimes* **wholefoods**) food which is processed or treated as little as possible, and produced without the use of any fertilizers or pesticides, etc. ◷ 1960s.

wholegrain ▻ *adj* said of bread and flour, etc: made from the complete grain, with no parts discarded during manufacture.

wholehearted ▻ *adj* sincere and enthusiastic. ● **wholeheartedly** *adverb*.

wholemeal and **wholewheat** ▻ *adj* **1** said of flour: made from the entire wheat grain. **2** said of bread: made from wholemeal flour.

whole number ▻ *noun, math* **1** an INTEGER. **2** an integral number, being one without fractions. **3** a natural number (1, 2, 3, etc).

wholesale ▻ *noun* the sale of goods in large quantities to a retailer. ▻ *adj, adverb* **1** buying and selling, or concerned with buying and selling in this way. Compare RETAIL. **2** on a huge scale and without discrimination □ ***wholesale destruction.*** ● **wholesaler** *noun*. ◷ 15c as *noun*.

wholesome /ˈhoʊlsəm/ ▻ *adj* **1** attractively healthy. **2** promoting health □ ***wholesome food.*** **3** *old use* morally beneficial. **4** sensible; prudent □ ***a wholesome respect for the sea.*** ● **wholesomely** *noun*. ● **wholesomeness** *noun*. ◷ 13c.

whole-tone scale ▻ *noun, music* either of two scales produced by beginning on one of any two notes a chromatic semitone apart and ascending or descending in whole tones for an octave.

wholewheat see WHOLEMEAL

wholly /ˈhoʊllɪ, ˈhoʊlɪ/ ▻ *adverb* completely; altogether □ ***not wholly satisfied with the job they did.***

whom /huːm/ ▻ *pronoun* used as the object of a verb or preposition (but often replaced by WHO, especially in less formal usage): **1** in seeking to identify a person □ ***Whom do you want?*** □ ***To whom are you referring?*** **2** as a relative pronoun in a defining clause □ ***I am looking for the man whom I met earlier.*** **3** used as a relative pronoun to introduce a commenting clause □ ***The man, whom I met earlier, has left.*** ◷ Anglo-Saxon *hwam*.

whomever ▻ *pronoun, formal or old use* used as the object of a verb or preposition to mean 'any person or people that' □ ***I will write to whomever they appoint.*** Also **whomsoever**.

whoop /wuːp/ ▻ *noun* **1** a loud cry of delight, joy or triumph, etc. **2** /huːp/ a noisy indrawn breath typical in whooping cough. ▻ *verb* (***whooped***, ***whooping***) *tr & intr* **1** to utter or say something with a whoop. **2** to summon or urge something or someone on by whooping. ● **whoop it up** *colloq* to celebrate noisily. ◷ 14c.

whoopee ▻ *exclamation* /wʊˈpiː/ expressing exuberant delight. ▻ *noun* /ˈwʊpiː, ˈwuːpiː/ (***whoopees***) **1** exuberant delight or excitement. **2** a cry indicating this. ● **make whoopee** *colloq* **1** to celebrate exuberantly. **2** to make love. ◷ 19c; 1920s as *noun*.

whoopee cushion ▻ *noun* a rubber cushion filled with air, which makes a noise like the breaking of wind when sat on.

whooper swan or **whooper** ▻ *noun* a swan, common in N Europe and Asia, that is easily distinguished by its straight neck and yellow-and-black bill. ◷ 19c: so called because it makes loud whooping calls when in flight.

whooping cough ▻ *noun, pathol* a highly contagious disease that mainly affects children, characterized by bouts of violent coughing followed by a sharp drawing in of the breath which produces a characteristic 'whooping' sound. *Technical equivalent* **pertussis**. ◷ 18c.

whoops /wʊps, wuːps/ and **whoops-a-daisy** ▻ *exclamation* expressing surprise or concern, eg when one has a slight accident, makes an error, etc or sees someone else do so.

whoosh or **woosh** /wʊʃ/ ▻ *noun* (***whooshes***) the sound of, or like that made by, something passing rapidly through the air. ▻ *verb* (***whooshes***, ***whooshed***, ***whooshing***) to move with or make such a sound. ◷ Early 20c: imitating the sound.

whop /wɒp/ ▻ *verb* (***whopped***, ***whopping***) *colloq* **1** to hit or thrash someone. **2** to defeat someone soundly; to surpass them. **3** to throw or pull something suddenly or violently. ▻ *noun* a blow or bump; the sound made by either of these. ◷ 14c: a variant of dialect *wap*.

whopper ▻ *noun, colloq* **1** anything very large of its kind. **2** a blatant lie. ◷ 18c.

whopping ▻ *adj, colloq* huge; enormous; unusually large. ▻ *noun* a thrashing. ◷ 17c.

whore /hɔː(r)/ ▻ *noun, offensive* **1** a prostitute. **2** a sexually immoral or promiscuous woman. ▻ *verb* (***whored***, ***whoring***) *intr* **1** said of a man: to have sexual relations with prostitutes. **2** said of a woman: to be a prostitute. ● **whorish** *adj*. ● **whorishly** *adverb*. ● **whorishness** *noun*. ◷ Anglo-Saxon *hore*.

■ **whore after something** to pursue (an unworthy, dishonest or selfish goal).

who're /huːər/ ▻ *contraction* who are.

whorehouse ▻ *noun* a brothel.

whorl /wɔːl, wɜːl/ ▷ *noun* **1** *bot* a COROLLA. **2** *zool* one complete coil in the spiral shell of a mollusc, the number of which indicates the shell's age. **3** a type of fingerprint in which there is a spiral arrangement of the ridges on the skin. **4** any type of convolution. ● **whorled** *adj.* ⓔ Anglo-Saxon *hwyrfel*.

whortleberry /ˈwɜːtəlbɛrɪ, -bərɪ/ ▷ *noun* a dark-blue edible berry; a bilberry. See also HUCKLEBERRY. ⓔ 16c: a variant of American dialect *hurtleberry*.

who's /huːz/ ▷ *contraction* **1** who is. **2** who has.

whose /huːz/ ▷ *pronoun, adj* **1** used in questions, indirect questions and statements: belonging to which person or people □ *Whose is this jacket?* □ *We do not know whose these are.* **2** used as a relative adjective to introduce a defining clause: of whom or which □ *buildings whose foundations are sinking.* **3** used as a relative adjective to add a commenting clause □ *my parents, without whose help I could not have succeeded.* **4** used as a relative adjective, meaning 'whoever's' or 'whichever's' □ *Take whose advice you will.*

whose

- **Whose** is correctly used to mean both 'of whom' and 'of which', as in □ *the boy whose father is a policeman* □ *the book whose pages are torn.*
- Note that **who else's** is more common than **whose else**, because **who else** is regarded as a unit and **whose else** is more awkward to say.
- Note also that **who's**, which is pronounced the same way as **whose** and is sometimes confused with it, is a contraction of **who is** or **who has**, as in □ *Who's there?* □ *I'm looking for the person who's taken my pen.*

whosoever ▷ *pronoun, formal or old use* used in statements: WHOEVER.

why /waɪ/ ▷ *adverb* used in questions, indirect questions and statements: for what reason. ▷ *conj* for, or because of, which □ *no reason why I should get involved.* ▷ *exclamation* **1** expressing surprise, indignation, impatience or recognition, etc □ *Why, you little monster!* **2** used to challenge an implied criticism □ *Why, have you any objection?* ▷ *noun* (*whys*) a reason. See also THE WHYS AND WHEREFORES. ● **why not** used to make or agree to a suggestion □ *Like a drink? Why not!* ⓔ Anglo-Saxon *hwi*.

whydah or **whidah** /ˈwaɪdə, ˈwɪdə/ and **widow bird** ▷ *noun* any of various African weaverbirds, with mostly black plumage, and very long tail feathers. ⓔ 18c: originally WIDOW BIRD, but later named after *Whydah* (now *Ouidah*) a town in Benin.

the whys and wherefores ▷ *plural noun* all the reasons.

WI ▷ *abbreviation* **1** West Indies. **2** *US state* Wisconsin. Also written **Wis.** **3** in the UK: Women's Institute.

wick ▷ *noun* the twisted string running up through a candle or lamp and projecting at the top, that burns when lit and draws up the wax or inflammable liquid into the flame. ● **dip one's wick** *slang* said of a man: to have sexual intercourse with someone. ● **get on someone's wick** *slang* to be a source of irritation to them. ⓔ Anglo-Saxon *weoce*.

wicked /ˈwɪkɪd/ ▷ *adj* (*wickeder, wickedest*) **1** evil or sinful; immoral. **2** mischievous, playful or roguish. **3** *slang* excellent or cool; admirable. Also *as exclamation*. **4** *colloq* bad □ *wicked weather.* **5** (**the wicked**) wicked people as a group (see THE 4b). ● **wickedly** *adverb.* ● **wickedness** *noun.* ⓔ 13c: from Anglo-Saxon *wicca* wizard.

wicker /ˈwɪkə(r)/ ▷ *noun* **1** a small pliant twig, cane, etc. **2** wickerwork. ▷ *adj* **1** said of a fence or basket, etc: made of interwoven twigs, canes or rushes, etc. **2** encased in wickerwork. ⓔ 14c: Scandinavian.

wickerwork ▷ *noun* articles made from wicker; basketwork of any kind.

wicket /ˈwɪkɪt/ ▷ *noun* **1** *cricket* **a** a row of three small wooden posts stuck upright in the ground behind either crease; **b** the playing area between these; **c** a batsman's stand at the wicket; **d** a batsman's dismissal by the bowler □ *45 runs for two wickets.* **2** (*in full* **wicket gate** or **wicket door**) a small door or gate, especially one that can open separately within a large door or gate. **3** *US* a small opening or window with a grille, eg at a ticket office or bank. ● **get** or **take**, *etc* **a wicket** to bowl a batsman out, or have them put out in any way as a result of one's bowling. ● **keep wicket** to be wicketkeeper. ● **on a good** or **sticky wicket** in a valuable or difficult position. ⓔ 13c: from French *wiket*.

wicketkeeper ▷ *noun, cricket* the fielder who stands immediately behind the wicket.

widdershins see WITHERSHINS

wide ▷ *adj* (*wider, widest*) **1** large in extent from side to side. **2** measuring a specified amount from side to side □ *three feet wide.* **3** said of the eyes: open to the fullest extent. **4** said eg of a door or window: opened as wide as possible. **5** said of a range or selection, etc: covering a great variety □ *There's a wide choice of films on.* **6** extensive; widespread □ *wide support.* **7** said of clothing: not tight-fitting; loose or baggy □ *a wide skirt.* **8** general, as opposed to particular □ *consider the wider implications.* **9** (**wide of something**) off the mark □ *his aim was wide of the target.* **10** *slang* lax in morals. ▷ *adverb* **1** over an extensive area, especially in the phrase **far and wide**. **2** to the fullest extent □ *with legs wide apart.* **3** off the mark □ *His aim went wide.* ▷ *noun, cricket* a ball bowled out of the batsman's reach. ● **widely** see separate entry. ● **wideness** *noun.* ● **widish** *adj.* ● **wide awake** fully awake or alert. ● **wide of the mark** **1** off target. **2** far or astray from the truth. ● **wide open** **1** open to the fullest extent. **2** *colloq* vulnerable; exposed to attack. ⓔ Anglo-Saxon *wid*.

-wide ▷ *combining form, indicating* throughout the extent of something □ *nationwide* □ *worldwide.*

wide-angle ▷ *adj, photog, cinematog* said of a shot, an effect, etc: taken with, or resulting from being taken with, a wide-angle lens.

wide-angle lens ▷ *noun, photog, cinematog* a camera lens with an angle of 60° or more and a short focal length, which takes pictures that cover a wider area than a normal lens, but with some distortion.

wide body and **wide bodied** ▷ *adj* said of an aircraft: that has a wide fuselage.

wide boy ▷ *noun, colloq* a shrewd but dishonest operator, especially in business undertakings.

wide-eyed ▷ *adj* **1** showing great surprise. **2** naive or credulous.

widely ▷ *adverb* **1** over a wide area or range. **2** to a great extent. **3** by a large number of people □ *a widely accepted theory.* **4** extremely; greatly □ *a widely differing attitude.*

widen /ˈwaɪdən/ ▷ *verb* (*widened, widening*) *tr & intr* to make, or become, wide or wider. ● **widener** *noun.* ⓔ 17c.

wide-ranging ▷ *adj* said of interests, discussions, etc: covering a large variety of subjects or topics.

wide receiver ▷ *noun, Amer football* a member of the offence whose task is to catch and run with the ball.

wide-screen ▷ *adj, cinematog* said of a film or a specific film print, video release, etc: having an ASPECT RATIO of 1.66: 1 (in Europe) or 1.85: 1 (in US), which makes it an ideal medium for showing huge panoramic vistas, used eg in Westerns and road movies. ▷ *noun* (**wide screen**) **1** a film, film print, video release, etc in this format. **2** a cinema screen that is wider and more concave than a conventional one. ⓔ 1950s.

widescreen TV ▷ *noun* a TV set which has a picture width to height ratio of 16:9 as opposed to the common standard of 4:3.

widespread ▷ *adj* **1** extending over a wide area. **2** affecting or involving large numbers of people. ⓒ 18c.

widgeon see WIGEON

widget /ˈwɪdʒɪt/ ▷ *noun* **1** a device attached to the bottom of cans of draught beer so that when it is poured it has a proper head and resembles a glass of beer as poured from a tap in a pub. **2** a gadget; any small manufactured item or component. ⓒ 1920s: perhaps an alteration of GADGET.

widish see under WIDE

widow /ˈwɪdoʊ/ ▷ *noun* **1** a woman whose husband is dead and who has not remarried. **2** *colloq, in compounds* a woman whose husband spends much time away from her on a specified pursuit □ ***golf widows.*** **3** an extra hand in some card games. **4** *printing* a short last line at the end of a paragraph which stands at the top of a page or column of print. ▷ *verb* (***widowed, widowing***) **1** to leave or make someone a widow or widower. **2** (**widow someone of something**) to strip them of it (especially something valued). ● **widowhood** *noun.* ⓒ Anglo-Saxon *widewe.*

widow bird see WHYDAH

widower ▷ *noun* a man whose wife is dead, and who has not remarried.

widow's peak ▷ *noun* a point of hair over the forehead, resembling the cusped front of a cap formerly worn by widows. ⓒ 19c.

widow's weeds see under WEEDS

width /wɪdθ/ ▷ *noun* **1** extent from side to side; breadth. **2** (*also* **wideness**) the condition of being wide. **3** the distance from side to side across a swimming-pool □ *swam ten widths.* **4** the stretch from side to side of a piece of cloth. ⓒ 17c.

widthways and **widthwise** ▷ *adverb, adj* across the width.

wield /wiːld/ ▷ *verb* (***wielded, wielding***) **1** to brandish or use (a tool or weapon, etc). **2** to have or exert (power, authority or influence, etc). ● **wielder** *noun.* ⓒ Anglo-Saxon *wieldan* to control.

wieldy /ˈwiːldɪ/ ▷ *adj* (***wieldier, wieldiest***) easy to wield; manageable. ⓒ 14c.

Wiener schnitzel /ˈviːnə ˈʃnɪtsəl/ ▷ *noun, cookery* a veal cutlet coated in eggs and breadcrumbs and then fried. ⓒ 19c: German, meaning 'Viennese cutlet'.

wife /waɪf/ ▷ *noun* (***wives*** /waɪvz/) **1** the woman to whom a man is married; a married woman. **2** *often in compounds* a woman □ ***housewife*** □ ***fishwife.*** ● **wifehood** *noun.* ● **wifely** *adj.* ⓒ Anglo-Saxon *wif.*

wife-swapping ▷ *noun, colloq* a form of sexual activity in which married couples exchange partners temporarily. ⓒ 1950s.

wig¹ ▷ *noun* an artificial covering of natural or synthetic hair for the head to conceal baldness or as a fashion accessory, a disguise, as period costume or as part of a specific uniform, as for a judge or barrister. ● **wigged** *adj.* ● **wigless** *adj.* ⓒ 17c: a short form of PERIWIG.

wig² ▷ *verb* (***wigged, wigging***) *colloq* to scold someone severely. ● **wigging** *noun* a scolding. ⓒ 17c.

wigeon or **widgeon** /ˈwɪdʒən/ ▷ *noun* (***wigeon*** or ***wigeons***; ***widgeon*** or ***widgeons***) any of various freshwater dabbling ducks, native to Europe, Asia, N Africa and the New World, having long pointed wings and a wedge-shaped tail. ⓒ 16c: from French *vigeon.*

wiggle /ˈwɪgəl/ ▷ *verb* (***wiggled, wiggling***) *tr & intr, colloq* to move or cause something to move, especially jerkily, from side to side or up and down. ▷ *noun* **1** an act of wiggling. **2** a wiggling motion. **3** a line, eg one drawn by a pen or pencil, with a twist or bend in it. ● **wiggler** *noun.* ⓒ 13c: from Dutch *wiggelen* to totter.

wiggly /ˈwɪgəlɪ/ ▷ *adj* (***wigglier, wiggliest***) **1** wriggly. **2** wavy; bendy □ ***a wiggly line.***

wigwag /ˈwɪgwag/ ▷ *verb, intr* **1** to twist about. **2** to signal by means of flag semaphore. ▷ *noun* an act of wigwagging. ⓒ 16c.

wigwam /ˈwɪgwam/ ▷ *noun* **1** a domed Native American dwelling made of a framework of arched poles covered with skins, bark or mats. **2** *loosely* a tepee. **3** a similar tent-like structure for children to play in. ⓒ 17c: from Abenaki (Native American language) *wikewam* house.

wilco /ˈwɪlkoʊ/ ▷ *exclamation* in signalling and telecommunications, etc: expressing compliance or acknowledgement of instructions. ⓒ 1930s: from 'I *will co*mply'.

wild /waɪld/ ▷ *adj* (***wilder, wildest***) **1** said of animals: untamed or undomesticated; not dependent on humans. **2** said of plants: growing in a natural uncultivated state. **3** said of country: desolate, rugged, inhospitable or uninhabitable. **4** said of peoples: savage; uncivilized. **5** unrestrained; uncontrolled □ ***wild fury.*** **6** frantically excited. **7** distraught □ ***wild with grief.*** **8** dishevelled; disordered □ ***wild attire.*** **9** said of the eyes: staring; distracted or scared-looking. **10** said of weather: stormy. **11** said of plans or hopes, etc: crazy; impracticable or unrealistic. **12** said of a guess: very approximate, or quite random. **13** *colloq* furious; extremely angry. **14** *slang* enjoyable; terrific. ▷ *noun* **1** (**the wild**) a wild animal's or plant's natural environment or life in it □ ***returned the cub to the wild.*** **2** (**wilds**) lonely, sparsely inhabited regions away from the city. ● **wildish** *adj.* ● **wildly** *adverb.* ● **wildness** *noun.* ● **run wild 1** said of a garden or plants: to revert to a wild, overgrown and uncultivated state. **2** said eg of children: to live a life of freedom, with little discipline or control. ● **wild about someone** or **something** intensely fond of or keen on them or it. ● **wild and woolly** unrefined or unpolished; crude. ⓒ Anglo-Saxon *wilde.*

wild boar ▷ *noun* a wild pig of Europe, NW Africa and S Asia, with prominent tusks, which is the direct ancestor of the domestic pig.

wild card ▷ *noun* **1** someone allowed to compete in a sports event, despite lacking the usual or stipulated qualifications. **2** *computing* a symbol, eg an asterisk, that can be used to represent any character or set of characters in a certain position, in order to identify text strings with variable contents. **3** *cards* a card that is able to be allocated any rank or value.

wildcat ▷ *noun* (***wildcats*** or ***wildcat***) **1** (*often* **wild cat**) an undomesticated cat of Europe and Asia, which has a longer stouter body and longer legs than the domestic cat, and a thick bushy tail. **2** (*often* **wild cat**) any of several small or medium-sized cats, eg lynx and ocelot, as opposed to the lion, tiger, leopard, cheetah and other large cats. **3** a short-tempered, fierce and aggressive person. **4** an exploratory oil well. ▷ *adj* **1** said of an industrial strike: not called or approved by a trade union. **2** said of a business scheme: financially unsound or risky; speculative. **3** said of an oil well: exploratory; experimental.

wild dog ▷ *noun* any of several wild species of dog, especially the DINGO.

wildebeest /ˈwɪldəbiːst, ˈvɪl-/ ▷ *noun* (***wildebeest*** or ***wildebeests***) either of two species of large antelope that live in herds on the grassland of Africa, having a large head, thick neck and large curved horns. Also called GNU. ⓒ 19c: Afrikaans, from Dutch *wilde* wild + *beest* ox.

wilderness /ˈwɪldənəs/ ▷ *noun* **1** an uncultivated or uninhabited region. **2** any desolate or pathless area. **3** an overgrown tangle of weeds, etc. **4** a part of a garden or estate deliberately left wild for romantic effect. **5** *politics* the state of being without office or influence after playing a leading role. **6** a large confused or confusing assemblage. **7** any daunting maze. ● **a voice crying in the wilderness** someone with an important message or warning that goes unheeded, in allusion to Matthew 3.3. ⓒ 13c: from Anglo-Saxon *wilddeoren* of wild beasts.

wildfire ▷ *noun* **1** a highly flammable liquid originally used in warfare. **2** a sweeping destructive fire. ● **spread like wildfire** said of disease or rumour, etc: to spread rapidly and extensively.

wildfowl ▷ *singular or plural noun* a game bird or game birds, especially waterfowl. ● **wildfowler** *noun* someone who hunts and kills wildfowl. ● **wildfowling** *noun*.

wild-goose chase ▷ *noun* a search that is bound to be unsuccessful and fruitless. ⓒ 16c.

wild horse ▷ *noun* **1** an untamed or undomesticated horse. **2** (**wild horses**) *colloq* the greatest possible persuasion or influence ◻ *Wild horses could not drag me back to that place.*

wild hyacinth ▷ *noun* the BLUEBELL.

wilding ▷ *noun* **1** a wild crab apple. **2** any plant that grows wild or without cultivation. **3** a wild animal. ● **go wilding** *US* said of a gang of youths: to roam the streets violently attacking, robbing and rampaging.

wildish see under WILD

wildlife ▷ *noun* wild animals, birds and plants in general.

wildlife park ▷ *noun* a safari park.

wildly see under WILD

wild man ▷ *noun* **1** an uncivilized person; a savage. **2** in politics: someone with extreme or radical views.

wild oat ▷ *noun* any of several tall perennial weeds related to the cultivated oat. ● **sow one's wild oats** said especially of young men: to live a life of debauchery, indulgence and excesses before settling down to a more decent and dignified life.

wild pansy see HEARTSEASE

wild rice ▷ *noun* a tall aquatic grass that yields rice-like seeds.

wild type ▷ *noun* the form of a species typically that occurs under natural breeding conditions, as distinct from mutant types.

Wild West and **the Wild West** ▷ *noun, historical* the part of the US west of the Mississippi, settled during the 19c and legendary for the adventures of its cattlemen and the struggle to gain territory from the Native American population. ⓒ 19c.

wildwood ▷ *noun, chiefly poetic* wild, uncultivated or unfrequented woodland.

wile ▷ *noun* **1** (**wiles**) charming personal ways. **2** a piece of cunning or trickery; a ruse, manoeuvre or stratagem. ▷ *verb* (*wiled*, *wiling*) (*usually* **wile someone away** or **into something**) to lure or entice them. ⓒ Anglo-Saxon *wil*.

▪ **wile away something** to pass (time) pleasantly; to while away (time).

wilful or *US* **willful** /ˈwɪlfəl/ *adj* **1** deliberate; intentional. **2** headstrong, obstinate or self-willed. ● **wilfully** *adverb*. ● **wilfulness** *noun*. ⓒ Anglo-Saxon.

wilier, **wiliest** and **wiliness** see under WILY

will¹ ▷ *auxiliary verb* expressing or indicating: **1** the future tense of other verbs, especially when the subject is *you, he, she, it* or *they* ◻ *They will no doubt succeed.* **2** intention or determination, when the subject is *I* or *we* ◻ *We will not give in.* **3** a request ◻ *Will you please shut the door?* **4** a command ◻ *You will apologize to your mother immediately!* **5** ability or possibility ◻ *The table will seat ten.* **6** readiness or willingness ◻ *Any of our branches will exchange the goods.* **7** invitations ◻ *Will you have a coffee?* **8** what is bound to be the case ◻ *The experienced teacher will know when a child is unhappy.* **9** what applies in certain circumstances ◻ *An unemployed youth living at home will not receive housing benefit.* **10** an assumption or probability ◻ *That will be Paul at the door.* **11** obstinate resistance to advice ◻ *She will leave her clothes on the floor.* **12** choice or desire ◻ *Make what you will of that.* See also SHALL, WON'T, WOULD. ⓒ Anglo-Saxon *wyllan*.

will² ▷ *noun* **1** the power of conscious decision and deliberate choice of action ◻ *free will* ◻ *exercise one's will.* **2** one's own preferences, or one's determination in effecting them ◻ *a clash of wills* ◻ *against my will.* **3** desire or determination ◻ *the will to live.* **4** a wish or desire. **5 a** instructions for the disposal of a person's property, etc after death; **b** the document containing these. **6** *in compounds* one's feeling towards someone else ◻ *felt no ill-will towards her.* ▷ *verb* (*willed*, *willing*) **1** to try to compel someone by, or as if by, exerting one's will ◻ *willed herself to keep going.* **2** *formal* to desire or require that something be done, etc ◻ *Her Majesty wills it.* **3** to bequeath something in one's will. ● **at will** as and when one wishes. ● **with a will** eagerly; enthusiastically. ● **with the best will in the world** *with negatives* no matter how willing one is or how hard one tries. ⓒ Anglo-Saxon *willa*.

willed ▷ *adj* **1** having a will. **2** given or disposed of by will. **3** *in compounds* having a will of a particular kind ◻ *weak-willed.*

willet /ˈwɪlɪt/ ▷ *noun* (*plural* ***willet***) a large N American bird of the snipe family. ⓒ 18c: imitating the sound of its cry.

willie and **willies** see WILLY

the willies /ˈwɪlɪz/ ▷ *plural noun, colloq* the creeps; a feeling of anxiety or unease. ⓒ 19c.

willing /ˈwɪlɪŋ/ ▷ *adj* **1** ready, glad or not disinclined to do something. **2** eager and co-operative. **3** voluntarily given. ● **willingly** *adverb*. ● **willingness** *noun*. ⓒ 14c.

will-o'-the-wisp /wɪləðəˈwɪsp/ ▷ *noun* (***will-o'-the-wisp*** or ***will-o'-the-wisps***) **1** a light sometimes seen over marshes, caused by the combustion of marsh gas. Also called **ignis fatuus**. **2** any elusive or deceptive person. **3** any elusive thing, such as an unattainable goal. ⓒ 17c: literally 'Will of the torch', from *Will* short for the name William + WISP.

willow /ˈwɪloʊ/ ▷ *noun* **1** a deciduous tree or shrub found mainly in the N hemisphere, generally growing near water, and having slender flexible branches, narrow leaves, and spikes or CATKINS of male and female flowers. **2** the durable yellowish-brown wood of this tree, which is used to make cricket bats, wicker baskets, high-quality drawing charcoal and furniture. ⓒ Anglo-Saxon *welig*.

willow herb ▷ *noun* any of various perennial plants, native to temperate and alpine regions, having narrow to lance-shaped leaves, and usually pink, rose-purple or white flowers. Also called FIREWEED.

willow pattern ▷ *noun* a design used on pottery, usually in blue on a white background, showing a Chinese landscape with a willow tree, bridge and figures. ⓒ 19c.

willowy ▷ *adj* said of a person, especially a woman: slender and graceful. ⓒ 18c.

willpower ▷ *noun* the determination, persistence and self-discipline needed to accomplish something. ⓒ 19c.

willy or **willie** /ˈwɪlɪ/ ▷ *noun* (***willies***) *colloq* a penis. See also THE WILLIES. ⓒ Early 20c.

willy-nilly /ˈwɪlɪˈnɪlɪ/ ▷ *adverb* whether one wishes or not; regardless. ▷ *adj* occurring or taking place willy-nilly. ⓒ 17c: originally *will I, nill I*, meaning 'will I, will I not'.

wilt¹ ▷ *verb* (*wilted*, *wilting*) *intr* **1** *bot* said of a plant organ or tissue: to droop or become limp because there is insufficient water to maintain the individual cells in a turgid state. **2** to droop from fatigue or heat. **3** to lose courage or confidence. ▷ *noun* **1** the act or process of wilting. **2** *bot* one of a number of plant diseases, often caused by fungal infection, in which wilting is the main sign. ◷ 17c: a variant of *wilk* to wither.

wilt² ▷ *verb, old use or relig, 2nd person singular of* WILL¹ used with the pronoun THOU.

Wilts. ▷ *abbreviation, English county* Wiltshire.

wily /'waɪlɪ/ ▷ *adj* (***wilier, wiliest***) cunning; crafty or devious. • **wiliness** *noun.* ◷ 13c: from WILE.

WIMP /wɪmp/ ▷ *abbreviation, computing* windows, icons, menus (or mouse), printer, a user-friendly computer interface which allows the user to operate system commands by clicking on symbols on the screen instead of typing out codes. ◷ 1980s.

wimp /wɪmp/ *colloq* ▷ *noun* a feeble person. ▷ *verb* (***wimped, wimping***) *intr* (*always* **wimp out**) to back out of doing something through feebleness. • **wimpish** *adj.* • **wimpishly** *adverb.* • **wimpishness** *noun.* ◷ 1960s.

wimple /'wɪmpəl/ ▷ *noun* a veil folded around the head, neck and cheeks, originally a women's fashion and still worn as part of a nun's dress. ▷ *verb* (***wimpled, wimpling***) **1** to wrap in or hide (eg a head) with a wimple. **2** to lay or set (eg a veil) in folds. ◷ Anglo-Saxon *wimpel* neck-covering.

Wimpy /'wɪmpɪ/ ▷ *noun, trademark* a type of hamburger. ◷ 1930s: named after J W Wimpy, a character in the *Popeye* cartoons.

win ▷ *verb* (***won, winning***) **1** *tr & intr* to be victorious or come first in (a contest, race or bet, etc). **2** *tr & intr* to beat an opponent or rivals in (a competition, war, conflict or election, etc). **3** to compete or fight for, and obtain (a victory or prize, etc). **4** to obtain something by struggle or effort. **5** to earn and receive or obtain something. **6** *old use* to gain the hand of someone in marriage. **7** to secure something for someone. **8** to open up (a new portion of a coal seam). ▷ *noun, colloq* a victory or success. • **winnable** *adj.* • **winner** see separate entry. • **win by a head** or **a short head** to win very narrowly. • **you can't win** there's no way to succeed, or to please someone, etc. ◷ Anglo-Saxon *winnan.*

■ **win someone over** or **round** to persuade them over to one's side or opinion.

■ **win through** or **out** to be successful, or succeed in getting somewhere, after a struggle.

wince /wɪns/ ▷ *verb* (***winced, wincing***) *intr* to shrink back, start or grimace, eg in pain or anticipation of it; to flinch. ▷ *noun* a start or grimace in reaction to pain, etc. • **wincer** *noun.* • **wincingly** *adverb.* ◷ 13c: from French *wencier* or *guenchier.*

winceyette /wɪnsɪ'ɛt/ ▷ *noun* a soft cotton cloth with a raised brushed surface on both sides. ◷ 1920s: from Scots *wincey* a linen or cotton cloth with a mixture of wool.

winch ▷ *noun* (***winches***) **1** a reel or roller round which a rope or chain is wound for hoisting or hauling heavy loads; a windlass. **2** a crank or handle for setting a wheel, axle or machinery in motion. ▷ *verb* (***winches, winched, winching***) (*usually* **winch something up** or **in**) to hoist or haul it with a winch. ◷ Anglo-Saxon *wince.*

wind¹ /wɪnd/ ▷ *noun* **1** the movement of air, especially horizontally, across the Earth's surface as a result of differences in atmospheric pressure between one location and another. **2** a current of air produced artificially, by a fan, etc. **3** an influence that seems to pervade events ◻ ***a wind of change.*** **4** one's breath or breath supply ◻ ***short of wind.*** **5** the scent of game or, for animals, the scent of a hunter or predator, carried by the wind. **6** gas built up in the intestines; flatulence. **7** empty, pompous or trivial talk. **8 a** the wind instruments of an orchestra; **b** (*also* **winds**) the players of these. ▷ *verb* (***winded, winding***) **1** to deprive someone of breath temporarily, eg by a punch or fall. **2** to burp (a baby). • **before the wind** said of a ship: sailing with the wind coming from behind it. • **break wind** to discharge intestinal gas through the anus. • **cast, fling** or **throw something to the winds 1** to scatter or throw it away recklessly. **2** to abandon (caution, restraint or prudence, etc). • **down wind from something** receiving, or able to receive, air laden with the smell or pollutants, etc from it. • **get wind of something** to have one's suspicions aroused or hear a rumour, especially of something unfavourable or unwelcome. • **get the wind up** *colloq* to become nervous, anxious or alarmed. • **get one's second wind** to sufficiently recover one's breath after an initial exertion to carry on with ease. • **in the wind** about to happen. • **like the wind** swiftly. • **put the wind up someone** *colloq* to make them nervous, anxious or alarmed. • **sail close to** or **near the wind** see under SAIL. • **see which way the wind blows** to assess current opinions or likely developments, etc. • **take the wind out of someone's sails** to thwart their confident progress; to deflate or humble them. • **wind** or **winds of change** a pervasive influence bringing change. ◷ Anglo-Saxon.

wind² /waɪnd/ ▷ *verb* (***wound*** /waʊnd/, ***winding***) **1** (*often* **wind round** or **up**) *tr & intr* to wrap or coil, or be wrapped or coiled. **2** *tr & intr* to progress on a path with many twists and turns. **3** (*also* **wind something up**) to tighten the spring of (a clock, watch or other clockwork device) by turning a knob or key. ▷ *noun* **1** the state of being wound. **2** a turn, coil or twist. ◷ Anglo-Saxon *windan.*

■ **wind down 1** said of a clock or clockwork device: to slow down and stop working. **2** said of a person: to begin to relax, especially after a spell of tension, stress or work.

■ **wind something down 1** to lower it by turning a handle. **2** to reduce the resources and activities of (a business or enterprise).

■ **wind up** *colloq* to end up ◻ ***He wound up in jail.***

■ **wind someone up 1** to make them tense, nervous or excited. **2** *colloq* to taunt or tease them. See also WIND-UP.

■ **wind something up 1** to raise it by turning a handle. **2** to conclude or close down a business or enterprise.

windage /'wɪndɪdʒ/ ▷ *noun* **1** the deflection of a missile, eg a bullet, caused by wind. **2** the extent of deflection caused. **3** the difference between the diameter of the bore of a gun and the missile, to allow for the release of gas. ◷ 18c.

windbag ▷ *noun, colloq* **1** an excessively talkative person who communicates little of any value. **2** the bellows of a bagpipe.

wind band ▷ *noun* a musical ensemble made up of WIND INSTRUMENTS.

windborne ▷ *adj* said of pollen, seeds, etc: carried by the wind.

windbound ▷ *adj* said of a ship, etc: prevented from sailing by contrary winds.

windbreak ▷ *noun* a barrier, eg in the form of a screen, fence or line of trees, that provides protection from the wind.

windburn ▷ *noun* inflammation and soreness of the skin caused by overexposure to the wind.

windcheater ▷ *noun* a windproof tightly-fitted jacket, usually made of close-woven fabric. ◷ 1940s.

windchill ▷ *noun, meteorol* the extra chill given to air temperature by the wind.

windchill factor ▷ *noun, meteorol* the measurement made of the cooling effect of the wind on air temperature.

wind cone see WINDSOCK

winder /'waɪndə(r)/ ▷ *noun* **1** someone or something that winds (see WIND2). **2** any device for winding, eg a windlass. **3** a device for winding a clock, etc. **4** any type of twisting plant. **5** a triangular step at the turn of a stair, or in a spiral staircase.

windfall ▷ *noun* **1** a fruit, especially an apple, blown down from its tree. **2** an unexpected or sudden financial gain, or any other piece of good fortune.

wind farm ▷ *noun* a concentration of wind-driven turbines generating electricity.

wind gauge ▷ *noun* **1** an ANEMOMETER. **2** a device fitted to a gun in order to determine the allowance to be made for the force of the wind. **3** *music* a gauge for measuring the pressure of wind in an organ.

windier, **windiest**, **windily** and **windiness** see under WINDY

winding-sheet /'waɪndɪŋ —/ ▷ *noun* a sheet for wrapping a corpse in; a shroud.

wind instrument ▷ *noun* a musical instrument such as a clarinet, flute or trumpet, played by blowing air through it, especially the breath. ⓒ 16c.

windjammer /'wɪnddʒamə(r)/ ▷ *noun* **1** *historical* a large fast merchant sailing-ship. **2** a windcheater. ⓒ Late 19c.

windlass /'wɪndləs/ ▷ *noun* a drum-shaped axle round which a rope or chain is wound for hauling or hoisting weights. ▷ *verb* (***windlasses***, ***windlassed***, ***windlassing***) to haul or hoist something using a windlass. ⓒ 14c: from Norse *windass*, from *vinda* to wind + *ass* beam.

wind machine ▷ *noun, chiefly theat* a device that produces wind and/or the sound of wind.

windmill ▷ *noun* **1** a mechanical device operated by wind-driven sails or VANEs that revolve about a fixed shaft, formerly used in W Europe to mill flour, now used in many developing countries to pump water (eg for land drainage) and to generate electricity. **2** a toy with a set of plastic or paper sails mounted on a stick, that revolve in the wind. ▷ *verb* to move, or make something move, like the vanes of a windmill. • **tilt at windmills** to attack imaginary opponents ⓒ with reference to Cervantes' hero Don Quixote, who in a crazed state gave battle to windmills, thinking them to be knights. ⓒ 13c.

window /'wɪndoʊ/ ▷ *noun* **1** an opening in a wall to look through, or let in light and air, consisting of a wooden or metal frame fitted with panes of glass; a pane. **2** the frame itself. **3** the area immediately behind a shop's window, in which goods on sale are displayed. **4** a glass-covered opening, eg at a railway or theatre, at which to purchase one's ticket. **5** a gap in a schedule, etc available for some purpose. **6** a chance to observe or experience something. **7** an opening in the front of an envelope, allowing the address written on the letter inside to be visible. **8** a WEATHER WINDOW. **9** a LAUNCH WINDOW. **10** *computing* an enclosed rectangular area displayed on the VDU of a computer, which can be used as an independent screen. • **out** or **out of the window** finished with or done for; abandoned. ⓒ 13c: from Norse *windauga* literally 'wind eye'.

window box ▷ *noun* a box fitted along an exterior window ledge, for growing plants in.

window cleaner ▷ *noun* **1** someone who makes their living by cleaning windows. **2** the soap or detergent used for cleaning windows.

window-dressing ▷ *noun* **1** the art of arranging goods in a shop window. **2** the art or practice of giving something superficial appeal by skilful presentation. • **window-dresser** *noun*.

window ledge see WINDOWSILL

windowpane ▷ *noun* a sheet of glass set in a window.

window sash ▷ *noun* a frame in which panes of glass are set.

window seat ▷ *noun* **1** a seat placed in the recess of a window. **2** on a train or aeroplane, etc: a seat next to a window.

window-shopping ▷ *noun* **1** the activity of looking at goods in shop windows as an alternative to buying them. **2** *colloq* the act of eyeing up a person or people, but without any serious intention or desire. • **window-shop** *verb*. • **window-shopper** *noun*.

windowsill and **window ledge** ▷ *noun* the interior or exterior ledge that runs along the bottom of a window.

windpipe ▷ *noun, anatomy* the TRACHEA.

windpower ▷ *noun* a renewable energy source derived from winds in the Earth's atmosphere, used to generate electricity.

windscreen ▷ *noun* the large sheet of curved glass at the front of the motor vehicle. *N Amer equivalent* WINDSHIELD.

windscreen-wiper ▷ *noun* a device fitted to the windscreen of a motor vehicle, consisting of a rubber blade on an arm which moves in an arc, to keep the windscreen clear of rain and snow, etc.

windsock and **wind cone** ▷ *noun* an open-ended cone of fabric flying from a mast, eg at an airport, which shows the direction and speed of the wind.

windstorm ▷ *noun* a storm consisting of very strong winds.

windsurfing ▷ *noun* the sport of riding the waves on a sailboard; sailboarding. • **windsurf** *verb*. • **windsurfer** *noun*. ⓒ 1960s: from US trademark Windsurfer, a sailboard.

windswept ▷ *adj* **1** exposed to strong winds. **2** dishevelled from, or showing the effects of, exposure to the wind.

wind tunnel ▷ *noun, aeronautics* an experimental chamber in which fans blow a controlled stream of air past stationary models of aircraft, cars or trains, etc or their components, in order to test their aerodynamic properties by simulating the effects of movement through air.

wind-up /'waɪndʌp/ ▷ *noun* **1** the taunting or teasing of someone, eg the playing of a practical joke on them. See also WIND SOMEONE UP at WIND2. **2** the close or ending of something, eg a film.

windward /'wɪndwəd/ ▷ *noun* the side of a boat, etc facing the wind. ▷ *adj* on this side.

windy ▷ *adj* (***windier***, ***windiest***) **1** exposed to, or characterized by, strong wind. **2** suffering from, producing or produced by flatulence. **3** *colloq* said of speech or writing: long-winded or pompous. **4** *colloq* nervous; uneasy. • **windily** *adverb*. • **windiness** *noun*.

wine ▷ *noun* **1** an alcoholic drink made from the fermented juice of grapes. **2** a similar drink made from other fruits or plants, etc. **3** the dark-red colour of red wine. ▷ *verb* (***wined***, ***wining***) **1** to entertain someone with wine. **2** *intr* to take wine. • **wine and dine** to partake of, or treat someone to, a meal, usually accompanied by wine. See also WINY. ⓒ Anglo-Saxon *win*.

wine bar ▷ *noun* a bar which specializes in the selling of wine and often food.

wine bottle ▷ *noun* a glass bottle of a standard size for wine, holding 75cl (26⅔ fl oz).

wine cellar ▷ *noun* **1** a cellar in which to store wines. **2** the stock of wine stored there.

wine cooler ▷ *noun* an ice-filled receptacle for cooling wine in bottles, ready for serving.

wine glass ▻ *noun* **1** a drinking-glass typically consisting of a small bowl on a stem, with a wide base flaring out from the stem. **2** the capacity of this; a wineglassful.

wineglassful ▻ *noun* (*wineglassfuls*) the amount a wineglass can hold.

wine list ▻ *noun* a list of the wines available, eg in a restaurant.

winepress ▻ *noun* in the manufacture of wine: a machine in which grapes are pressed to extract the juice.

winery /'waɪnərɪ/ ▻ *noun* (*wineries*) *chiefly US* a place where wine is prepared and stored. ◷ Late 19c.

wineskin ▻ *noun, historical* the skin of a goat or sheep sewn up and used for holding wine.

wine tasting ▻ *noun* **1** the sampling of a variety of wines. **2** a gathering specifically for this. • **wine taster** *noun.*

wine vault ▻ *noun* **1** a vaulted WINE CELLAR. **2** a place where wine is tasted or drunk.

wine vinegar ▻ *noun* vinegar which has been made from wine, as opposed to malt.

winey see WINY

wing ▻ *noun* **1** one of the two modified forelimbs of a bird or bat that are adapted for flight. **2** one of two or more membranous outgrowths that project from either side of the body of an insect enabling it to fly. **3** one of the flattened structures that project from either side of an aircraft body. **4** any of the corner sections of a vehicle body, forming covers for the wheels. **5** a part of a building projecting from the central or main section ▫ *the west wing.* **6** the left or right flank of an army or fleet in battle formation. **7** *sport* in football and hockey, etc: **a** either edge of the pitch; **b** the player at either extreme of the forward line. **8** (**wings**) *theat* the area at each side of a stage, where performers wait to enter, out of sight of the audience. **9** a group with its own distinct views and character, within a political party or other body. See also LEFT WING, RIGHT WING. **10** in the RAF: a unit consisting of several squadrons. **11** (**wings**) in the RAF: a qualified pilot's badge. **12** (**wings**) *literary* a miraculous surge of speed. **13** *bot* any of various flat or projecting sections of a plant. ▻ *verb* (*winged* /wɪŋd/, *winging*) **1** (*often* **wing one's way**) to make one's way by flying, or with speed. **2** to wound (a bird) in the wing or a person in the arm or shoulder; to wound someone or something superficially. **3** *poetic* to fly or skim lightly over something. **4** to send (eg an arrow) swiftly on its way. • **winged** *adj.* • **wingless** *adj.* • **in the wings** *theat* waiting for one's turn to perform. • **on the wing** flying; in flight. • **spread** or **stretch one's wings 1** to use one's potential fully. **2** to escape from a confining environment in order to do this. • **take wing** *poetic* to fly off. • **under someone's wing** under their protection or guidance. ◷ 12c: from Norse *vængre.*

wingbeat ▻ *noun* the beat or flap of a bird's or insect's wings.

wing case ▻ *noun* the horny case or cover over the wings of some insects.

wing chair ▻ *noun* an armchair that has a high back with projections on both sides.

wing collar ▻ *noun* a stiff collar worn upright with the points turned down.

wing commander ▻ *noun* an officer in the airforce. See table at RANK.

wingding /'wɪŋdɪŋ/ ▻ *noun, chiefly US slang* **1** a wild or boisterous party. **2** a drug-addict's seizure. **3** a faked seizure. ◷ 1920s: a rhyming combination based on WING.

winged words /'wɪŋɪd —/ ▻ *plural noun, literary* meaningful words spoken, uttered or flying from one person to another. ◷ 17c: imitating the Homeric phrase *epea pteroenta.*

winger ▻ *noun, sport* in football and hockey, etc: a player in wing position.

wing forward see under FLANKER

wing mirror ▻ *noun* a rear-view mirror attached to the wing, or more commonly the side, of a motor vehicle.

wing nut ▻ *noun* a metal nut easily turned on a bolt by the finger and thumb by means of its flattened projections. Also called BUTTERFLY NUT.

wingspan and **wingspread** ▻ *noun* the distance from tip to tip of the wings of an aircraft, or of a bird's wings when outstretched.

winier, **winiest** see under WINY

wink ▻ *verb* (*winked, winking*) *tr & intr* **1** to shut an eye briefly as an informal or cheeky gesture or greeting. **2** said of lights and stars, etc: to flicker or twinkle. ▻ *noun* **1** an act of winking. **2** a quick flicker of light. **3** a short spell of sleep. Also called **forty winks**. • **winking** *noun, adj.* • **winkingly** *adverb.* • **easy as winking** *colloq* very easily indeed. • **tip someone the wink** *colloq* to give them a useful hint or valuable information, etc, especially in confidence. ◷ Anglo-Saxon *wincian.*

> ■ **wink at something** to ignore (an offence or improper procedure) deliberately; to pretend not to notice it.

winker ▻ *noun* **1** someone or something that winks. **2** *colloq* a flashing direction-indicator on a motor vehicle. **3** (*usually* **winkers**) horses' BLINKERS. ◷ 16c.

winkle /'wɪŋkəl/ ▻ *noun* **1** a small edible snail-shaped shellfish; a periwinkle. **2** *slang* the penis. ▻ *verb* (*winkled, winkling*) (*always* **winkle something out**) to force or prise it out. ◷ 16c: from PERIWINKLE[2].

winkle-picker ▻ *noun, colloq* a shoe with a long narrow pointed toe, especially popular during the Mod era (see MOD[1]) of the early 1960s.

winnable see under WIN

winner ▻ *noun* **1** a person, animal or vehicle, etc that wins a contest or race. **2** said of an idea or proposition, etc: full of potential; likely to be popular or successful.

winning ▻ *adj* **1** attractive or charming; persuasive. **2** securing victory. ▻ *noun* (**winnings**) money or prizes won, especially in gambling. ▻ *verb, present participle of* WIN. • **winningly** *adverb.*

winning-post ▻ *noun, horse-racing* the post marking the point where a race finishes.

winnow /'wɪnoʊ/ ▻ *verb* (*winnowed, winnowing*) **1** to separate chaff from (grain) by blowing a current of air through it or fanning it. **2** to sift (evidence, etc). • **winnower** *noun.* ◷ Anglo-Saxon *windwian.*

> ■ **winnow something out 1** to blow (chaff) from grain. **2** to identify and reject what is unwanted from a group or mass.

wino /'waɪnoʊ/ ▻ *noun* (*winos*) *slang* someone, especially a down-and-out, addicted to cheap wine; an alcoholic. ◷ Early 20c.

winsome /'wɪnsəm/ ▻ *adj, old use* charming; captivating. • **winsomely** *adverb.* • **winsomeness** *noun.* ◷ Anglo-Saxon *wynsum* joyous.

winter /'wɪntə(r)/ ▻ *noun* **1** (also **Winter**) the coldest season of the year, coming between autumn and spring, in the Northern hemisphere from November or December to February or March. **2** *astron* the time from the WINTER SOLSTICE in December to the SPRING EQUINOX (see under EQUINOX) in March. **3** (*often* **winters**) *literary* a year, especially in reference to a person's age ▫ *fifty winters.* ▻ *adj* **1** referring, relating or belonging to winter ▫ *a winter dish.* **2** said of plants, crops and fruit, etc: sown in autumn so as to be reaped in the following winter. ▻ *verb* (*wintered, wintering*) **1** *intr* to spend the winter in a specified place, usually other than one's normal home. **2**

to feed and keep (animals) through the winter. ⓘ Anglo-Saxon.

winter aconite ▷ *noun* a plant of the buttercup family, usually grown for its early-blossoming yellow flowers.

winter cherry ▷ *noun* **1** a CHINESE LANTERN (sense 2). **2** the fruit from this plant.

winter garden ▷ *noun* **1** an ornamental garden planted with evergreens. **2** a conservatory with flowers that blossom in the winter.

wintergreen ▷ *noun* **1** any of various creeping evergreen plants, native to northern temperate and arctic regions of N America, which have oval leaves and drooping bell-shaped pink or white flowers. **2** (*in full* **oil of wintergreen**) the aromatic oil obtained from this plant, which can be used medicinally or as a flavouring.

winterize or **winterise** ▷ *verb* (***winterized, winterizing***) *especially US* to make (a car, etc) suitable for use in wintry conditions. • **winterization** *noun*. ⓘ 1930s.

winter solstice ▷ *noun* the shortest day of the year, when the Sun reaches its lowest point in the N hemisphere (usually 21 December), or the highest point in the S hemisphere (usually 21 June).

winter sports ▷ *noun* open-air sports held on snow or ice, such as skiing and ice-skating.

wintertime ▷ *noun* the season of winter.

wintry /ˈwɪntrɪ/ or **wintery** ▷ *adj* (***wintrier, wintriest***) **1** said of weather, etc: like or characteristic of winter. **2** unfriendly, cold or hostile. ⓘ Anglo-Saxon wintrig.

winy or **winey** /ˈwaɪnɪ/ ▷ *adj* (***winier, winiest***) having a wine-like flavour.

wipe ▷ *verb* (***wiped, wiping***) **1** to clean or dry something with a cloth, etc. **2** to dry (dishes). **3** (*often* **wipe something away, off, out** or **up**) to remove it by wiping. **4** *computing, etc* **a** to clear (magnetic tape or a disk) of its contents; **b** to erase (the content) from a disk or magnetic tape. **5** to remove or get rid of something □ *wiped the incident from his memory.* **6** to pass (a cloth, etc) over, or rub (a liquid, etc) on to, a surface. **7** *Austral colloq* to discard (a person, idea or proposition, etc). **8** *tr & intr* to clean oneself with toilet paper after urinating or defecating. ▷ *noun* **1** the act of cleaning something by rubbing □ *Give the table a quick wipe.* **2** the act of wiping oneself. **3** *slang* a handkerchief. **4** a piece of fabric or tissue, usually specially treated, for wiping and cleaning eg wounds. **5** *cinematog* a style of editing in which the picture on the screen appears to be pushed or wiped off the screen by the following one. • **wipe the floor with someone** to defeat them completely. ⓘ Anglo-Saxon *wipian*.

■ **wipe something down** to wipe it (especially something vertical or upright).

■ **wipe out** *slang* to fall from a surfboard or skis, etc. See also WIPEOUT.

■ **wipe someone out** *slang* to kill or murder them.

■ **wipe something out 1** to clean out the inside of it. **2** to remove or get rid of it. **3** to destroy or obliterate it.

wipeout ▷ *noun* **1** *slang* a fall from a surfboard or skis, etc. **2** *colloq* a complete failure or disaster; total destruction. **3** the interruption of one radio signal by another, making reception impossible. ⓘ 1920s in sense 3.

wiper ▷ *noun* **1** someone or something that wipes. **2** a WINDSCREEN-WIPER. **3** *electronics* a moving arm for making a selected contact out of a number of possible connections.

wire ▷ *noun* **1** metal drawn out into a narrow flexible strand. **2** a length of this, usually wrapped in insulating material, used for carrying an electric current. **3** *telecomm* a cable that connects point with point. **4** *old use* a telegram or telegraph. **5** a fence or barrier, etc made of wire; wire netting. **6** *originally US horse-racing* the wire stretched across the track at the finishing line. ▷ *verb* (***wired, wiring***) **1 a** to send a telegram to someone; **b** to send (a message) by telegram. **2** (*also* **wire something up**) **a** to fit up or connect up (an electrical apparatus or system, etc) with wires; **b** to fasten or secure it with wire. **3** to catch (an animal) in a trap. • **wirer** *noun*. • **get one's wires crossed** to misunderstand or be confused about something. ⓘ Anglo-Saxon *wir*.

■ **wire away** or **in** to act or work with vigour.

wire brush ▷ *noun* **1** a brush with wire bristles, for cleaning dirt off suede shoes and rust off metal, etc. **2** *music* a brush with long bristles which are scraped against side drums or cymbals.

wire cloth ▷ *noun* a cloth or mesh of closely woven wire.

wirecutter ▷ *noun* a tool, similar to pliers in shape, for cutting through wire.

wired ▷ *adj, slang* highly-strung; stressed-out.

wiredraw ▷ *verb* to draw (metal) into wire by pulling it through successively smaller holes in a series of hard steel dies (see DIE²). • **wiredrawer** *noun*. • **wiredrawing** *noun*. ⓘ 17c.

wire gauge ▷ *noun* **1** a disc or plate with graded indents representing standard sizes, with which to measure the diameter of a wire. **2** the diameter of a particular piece of wire.

wire gauze ▷ *noun* a stiff close fabric made of fine wire.

wire grass ▷ *noun* **1** a type of fine meadow grass. **2** any type of other grass with wiry stems.

wire-haired ▷ *adj* said of a breed of dog: with a coarse, usually wavy coat.

wireless /ˈwaɪələs/ ▷ *noun, old use* **1** a radio. **2** (*also* **wireless telegraphy** or **wireless telephony**) the transmission of signals by means of electromagnetic waves generated by high-frequency alternating currents, therefore dispensing with the need for conducting wires between transmitter and receiver.

wire netting ▷ *noun* wires twisted into a network for use as fencing, etc.

wirepuller ▷ *noun* someone, especially a politician, who, in their own interests, exerts an influence which is felt but not seen; an intriguer. • **wirepulling** *noun*. ⓘ 19c.

wire rope ▷ *noun* a rope made from wires twisted together.

wirestripper ▷ *noun* a tool for stripping the protective insulation from wires.

wiretap ▷ *verb* to tap (a telephone) or the telephone of (a person). ⓘ Early 20c.

wire wheel ▷ *noun* a wheel, especially on a sports car, in which the rim is connected to the hub by wire spokes.

wire wool ▷ *noun* a mass of fine wire used for scouring.

wireworm ▷ *noun* the hard-bodied worm-like larva of the CLICK BEETLE, which lives in soil where it is extremely destructive to plant roots.

wiring ▷ *noun* **1** the arrangement of wires that connects the individual components of electric circuits into an operating system, eg the mains wiring of a house. **2** the act of securing with, connecting with, or communicating by wire. ▷ *verb, present participle of* WIRE.

wiry ▷ *adj* (***wirier, wiriest***) **1** said of a person: of slight build, but strong and agile. **2** resembling wire. **3** said of hair: coarse and wavy. • **wirily** *adverb*. • **wiriness** *noun*.

Wis. see under WI

wisdom /ˈwɪzdəm/ ▷ *noun* **1** the quality of being wise. **2** the ability to make sensible judgements and decisions, especially on the basis of one's knowledge and experience; prudence and common sense. **3** learning; knowledge. **4** the weight of informed opinion □ *the* *current wisdom on capital punishment.* **5** *old use* wise sayings. ⊙ Anglo-Saxon.

wisdom tooth ▷ *noun* in humans: any of the last four molar teeth to come through, at the back of each side of the upper and lower jaw. ⊙ 19c: so called because they are cut in early adulthood.

wise[1] ▷ *adj* (***wiser***, ***wisest***) **1** having or showing wisdom; prudent; sensible. **2** learned or knowledgeable. **3** astute, shrewd or sagacious. **4** *in compounds* knowing the ways of something □ ***streetwise*** □ ***worldly-wise.*** • **wisely** *adverb.* • **be wise to something** *colloq* to be aware of or informed about it. • **none the wiser** knowing no more than before. • **put someone wise** *colloq* to give them necessary information. ⊙ Anglo-Saxon *wis.*

■ **wise up to someone** or **something** *colloq* to find out the facts about them or it.

wise[2] ▷ *noun, old use* way □ ***in no wise to blame.*** ⊙ Anglo-Saxon, meaning 'manner'.

-wise ▷ *combining form, signifying* **1** direction or manner □ ***clockwise*** □ ***otherwise.*** **2** respect or relevance □ ***money-wise*** □ ***business-wise.*** ⊙ From WISE[2].

wiseacre /'waɪzeɪkə(r)/ ▷ *noun, derog* **1** someone who assumes an air of superior wisdom. **2** a WISE GUY. ⊙ 16c: from Dutch *wijsegghher* soothsayer.

wisecrack ▷ *noun* a smart, clever or knowing remark. ▷ *verb* to make a wisecrack. ⊙ 1920s.

wise guy ▷ *noun, colloq* someone who is full of smart and cocky comments; a know-all. ⊙ Late 19c.

wisely see under WISE

wise man ▷ *noun, old use* **1** a wizard. **2** one of the Magi.

wish ▷ *verb* (***wishes***, ***wished***, ***wishing***) **1** to want; to have a desire. **2** to desire, especially vainly or helplessly (that something were the case). **3** to express a desire for (luck, success, happiness, etc) to come to someone. **4** to demand or want something, or to do something. **5** to say (good afternoon, etc) to someone. ▷ *noun* (***wishes***) **1** a desire. **2** (*usually* **wishes**) what one wants to be done, etc. **3** (**wishes**) a hope expressed for someone's welfare □ ***best wishes.*** **4** in fairy tales and traditional ritual, etc: the stating of a desire in expectation or hope of its being magically fulfilled. • **wisher** *noun.* • **wish someone joy of something** *usually ironic* to wish them well of (some liability or commitment, etc that the speaker is glad to be rid of). ⊙ Anglo-Saxon *wyscan.*

■ **wish for something** **1** to long for it, especially in vain. **2** to make a wish for it.

■ **wish someone well** **1** to wish them success or good fortune. **2** to bear them no ill-will.

■ **wish something on someone** **1** *with negatives* to desire it to be inflicted on them □ ***I wouldn't wish it on my worst enemy.*** **2** *colloq* to impose or inflict it on them □ ***I expect she'll wish herself on us for Christmas.***

wishbone ▷ *noun* a V-shaped bone in the breast of poultry, formed by fused clavicles. *Technical equivalent* FURCULA. ⊙ 19c: so called because of the tradition in which two people pull the clavicles apart, and whoever holds the longer part is said to have their wish granted.

wishful ▷ *adj* **1** having a desire or wish. **2** eager or desirous. • **wishfully** *adverb.* • **wishfulness** *noun.*

wish-fulfilment ▷ *noun, psychol* the satisfaction of a subconscious desire by means of dreams or daydreams, etc.

wishful thinking ▷ *noun* an over-optimistic expectation that something will happen, arising from one's desire that it should. • **wishful thinker** *noun.*

wishing well ▷ *noun* a well that is thought to make wishes come true if they are expressed after casting a coin into it.

wishy-washy /'wɪʃɪwɒʃɪ/ ▷ *adj* **1** said eg of colours: pale and insipid. **2** lacking character; bland. **3** watery; weak. ⊙ 17c.

wisp ▷ *noun* **1** a strand; a thin fine tuft or shred. **2** something slight or insubstantial. **3** a twisted bunch used as a torch. ⊙ 14c.

wispy /'wɪspɪ/ ▷ *adj* (***wispier***, ***wispiest***) wisp-like; light, fine and insubstantial in texture. • **wispily** *adverb.* • **wispiness** *noun.*

wist see WIT[2]

wisteria /wɪ'stɪərɪə/ or **wistaria** /wɪ'steərɪə/ ▷ *noun* (***wisterias***) a deciduous climbing shrub, native to E Asia and N America, which has leaves divided into leaflets, and lilac, violet or white flowers borne in long pendulous clusters. ⊙ 19c: named after Caspar Wistar (1761–1818), the American anatomist.

wistful ▷ *adj* sadly or vainly yearning. • **wistfully** *adverb.* • **wistfulness** *noun.* ⊙ 18c in this sense; 17c in obsolete sense 'intent'.

wit[1] ▷ *noun* **1** the ability to express oneself amusingly; humour. **2** someone who has this ability. **3** humorous speech or writing. **4** (*also* **wits**) common sense or intelligence or resourcefulness □ ***will he have the wit to phone?*** • **at one's wits' end** *colloq* reduced to despair; completely at a loss. • **have** or **keep one's wits about one** to be, or stay, alert. • **live by one's wits** to live by cunning. • **scared**, *etc* **out of one's wits** extremely scared, etc. ⊙ Anglo-Saxon, meaning 'mind' or 'thought'.

wit[2] ▷ *verb* (*1st and 3rd person present tense* ***wot***, *past tense and past participle* ***wist***, *present participle* ***witting***) *archaic* to know how; to discern. • **to wit** *law* that is to say; namely. ⊙ Anglo-Saxon *witan* to know.

witch /wɪtʃ/ ▷ *noun* (***witches***) **1** someone, especially a woman, supposed to have magical powers used usually, but not always, malevolently. **2** a frighteningly ugly or wicked old woman or hag. **3** a dangerously or irresistibly fascinating woman. ▷ *verb* (***witches***, ***witched***, ***witching***) to bewitch. • **witchlike** *adj.* ⊙ Anglo-Saxon *wicca.*

witchcraft ▷ *noun* **1 a** magic or sorcery of the kind practised by witches; **b** the use of this. **2** a bewitching charm or enchantment.

witch doctor ▷ *noun* a member of a tribal society who is believed to have magical powers, and to be able to use them to cure or harm people.

witch elm see WYCH-ELM

witchery ▷ *noun* (***witcheries***) **1** the activities of witches. **2** a bewitching or spellbinding charm or influence; fascination.

witches' broom ▷ *noun, bot* a dense tuft of poorly developed branches formed on a woody plant, caused by an infection.

witchetty /'wɪtʃətɪ/ ▷ *noun* (***witchetties***) (*in full* **witchetty grub**) *Austral* any of the large grubs of species of certain moths, eaten by the Aboriginals. ⊙ 19c: Aboriginal.

witch hazel and **wych hazel** ▷ *noun* **1** a N American shrub with narrow-petalled yellow flowers. **2** an astringent lotion produced from the bark of this shrub, used to treat bruises, etc. ⊙ Anglo-Saxon *wice.*

witch hunt ▷ *noun* the hunting down and persecution of an individual or number of individuals, for alleged political or other types of heresy, or behaviour considered dangerous to society, etc.

with /wɪð, wɪθ/ ▷ *prep* **1** in the company of someone □ ***went with her.*** **2** used after verbs of partnering, co-operating, associating, etc □ ***danced with him*** □ ***plays with Celtic.*** **3** used after verbs of mixing □ ***mingled with the crowd.*** **4** by means of; using □ ***raised it with a crowbar.*** **5** used after verbs of covering, filling, etc □ ***plastered with mud*** □ ***filled with rubbish.*** **6** used after verbs of providing □ *equipped with firearms.* **7** as a result of something □ *shaking with fear.* **8** bearing; announcing □ *rang with bad news.* **9** in the same direction as something □ *drift with the current.* **10** at the same time or rate as something □ *Discretion comes with age.* **11** used after verbs of conflict □ *quarrelled with her brother.* **12** used after verbs of agreeing, disagreeing, and comparing □ *compared with last year.* **13** used in describing someone or something □ *a man with a limp.* **14** used in stating manner □ *won with ease.* **15** because of having something □ *With your talents, you'll surely get the job.* **16** in spite of having something □ *With all his money he's still unhappy.* **17** in or under (the specified circumstances) □ *I can't go abroad with my mother so ill.* **18** featuring; starring □ *'Seven' with Brad Pitt.* **19** in the care of someone □ *leave the key with the neighbours.* **20** used after verbs of parting □ *dispensed with his crutches.* **21** regarding □ *What shall we do with this?* □ *can't do a thing with my hair.* **22** used after adverbs and adverbial phrases in exclamations expressing a wish or order □ *Down with tyranny!* □ *Into bed with you!* **23** *colloq* understanding □ *Are you with me?* **24** loyal to or supporting someone or something □ *We're with you all the way.* • **in with someone** *colloq* friendly or associated with them. • **with it** *colloq* **1** fashionable; trendy. **2** aware of or comprehending what is going on or being said. • **with that** at that point …; thereupon … □ *With that, Daniel left the room.* ⓒ Anglo-Saxon.

withal /wɪˈðɔːl/ *literary or old use* ▻ *adverb* **1** as well; into the bargain. **2** for all that; nevertheless. ▻ *prep* with □ *flesh to bait fish withal.* ⓒ 12c.

withdraw /wɪðˈdrɔː, wɪθ-/ ▻ *verb* (***withdrew***, ***withdrawn***, ***withdrawing***) **1** *intr* to move somewhere else, especially more private □ *withdrew into her bedroom.* **2** *intr* to leave; to go away □ *We tactfully withdrew.* **3** *tr & intr* said of troops: to move back; to retreat or order to retreat. **3** to pull something in or back. **4** to take (money) from a bank account for use. **5** *tr & intr* to back out or pull out of an activity or contest, etc. **6** to take back or retract (a comment) that one regrets saying. **7** (*usually* **withdraw from something**) *intr* to stop oneself taking a drug to which one is addicted. **8** *intr* to become uncommunicative or unresponsive. **9** to discontinue or cancel something. ⓒ 13c.

withdrawal ▻ *noun* **1** the act or process of withdrawing. **2** (*usually* **make a withdrawal**) a removal of funds from a bank account. **3** *medicine* the breaking of an addiction to drugs, etc, with associated physical and psychological symptoms. **4** a retreat into silence and self-absorption. **5** (*in full* **withdrawal method**) an unreliable method of contraception in which the penis is removed from the vagina before ejaculation has occurred. Also called COITUS INTERRUPTUS.

withdrawal symptom ▻ *noun* **1** *medicine* any of a number of symptoms such as pain, nausea, sweating or depression, experienced by someone who is deprived of a drug or other substance to which they have become addicted. **2** *colloq* any of a number of symptoms experienced by someone deprived of anyone or anything to which they are accustomed.

withdrawn ▻ *adj* **1** said of a person or their manner, etc: unresponsive, shy or reserved. **2** said of a place: secluded; isolated.

withe /wɪð, wɪθ, waɪð/ ▻ *noun* **1** (*also* **withy**) a pliable branch or twig, especially one from the willow tree. **2** a band of twisted twigs. ▻ *verb* (***withed***, ***withing***) to bind with a withe or withes. ⓒ Anglo-Saxon *withthe*.

wither /ˈwɪðə(r)/ ▻ *verb* (***withered***, ***withering***) **1** *tr & intr* said of plants: to fade or make them fade, dry up and die. **2** (*sometimes* **wither away**) *tr & intr* to fade or make something fade and disappear. **3** *tr & intr* to shrivel or make something shrivel and decay. **4** to humble or disconcert someone with a glaring or scornful, etc expression. • **withered** *adj.* • **withering** *adj.* • **witheringly** *adverb.* ⓒ 13c: possibly a variant of WEATHER.

withers /ˈwɪðəz/ ▻ *plural noun* the ridge between the shoulder blades of a horse. ⓒ 16c.

withershins /ˈwɪðəʃɪnz/ and **widdershins** /ˈwɪdəʃɪnz/ ▻ *adverb, Scots* in the contrary direction; contrary to the course of the Sun. Opposite of DEASIL. ⓒ 16c: from German *weddersins*, from *wider* against + *sin* direction.

withhold ▻ *verb* **1** to refuse to give or grant something □ *withheld evidence.* **2** to hold back something □ *withholding payment.* • **withholder** *noun.* ⓒ 12c.

within /wɪˈðɪn, wɪˈθɪn/ ▻ *prep* **1** inside; enclosed by something □ *within these four walls.* **2** not outside the limits of something; not beyond □ *within sight.* **3** in less than (a certain time or distance) □ *finished within a week.* ▻ *adverb* **1** inside □ *apply within.* **2** *old use* indoors □ *There is someone within.* **3** *old use or literary* in the mind, soul or heart, etc. • **within reach** said of an object or goal, etc: positioned so as to be obtainable or attainable without much (more) effort, difficulty or loss of time. ⓒ Anglo-Saxon *withinnan*.

withing *present participle of* WITHE

without /wɪˈðaʊt, wɪˈθaʊt/ ▻ *prep* **1** not having the company of someone □ *She went home without him.* **2** deprived of someone or something □ *He can't live without her.* **3** not having something □ *a blue sky without a cloud.* **4** lacking something □ *books without covers.* **5** not (behaving as expected or in a particular way) □ *answered without smiling* □ *did it without being told.* **6** not giving or showing, etc something □ *complied without a murmur.* **7** free from something □ *admitted it without shame.* **8** not encountering (some possible circumstance) □ *managed without difficulty* □ *completed the rescue without anyone getting hurt.* **9** not having (something required); in neglect of (a usual procedure) □ *entered without permission* □ *imprisoned without trial.* **10** not using; not having the help of something □ *opened it without a key* □ *found our way without a map.* **11** not needing; while not doing or needing to do something □ *swimming a length without coming up for air.* **12** if it had not been for someone or something □ *would have died without their help.* **13** *old use or literary* outside □ *without the walls.* ▻ *adverb, old use* outside □ *He is without.* ⓒ Anglo-Saxon *withutan*.

withstand ▻ *verb* **1** to maintain one's position or stance against someone or something. **2** to resist or brave something □ *withstanding the storm* □ *withstood his insults.* • **withstander** *noun.* ⓒ Anglo-Saxon.

withy /ˈwɪðɪ/ ▻ *noun* (***withies***) **1** any type of willow. **2** a WITHE. ⓒ Anglo-Saxon withig.

witless ▻ *adj* **1** stupid or brainless; lacking wit, sense or wisdom. **2** crazy. • **witlessly** *adverb.* • **witlessness** *noun.* ⓒ Anglo-Saxon *witleas*, from WIT[1].

witness /ˈwɪtnəs, -nɪs/ ▻ *noun* (***witnesses***) **1** someone who sees, and can therefore give a direct account of, an event or occurrence, etc. **2** someone who gives evidence in a court of law. **3** someone who adds their own signature to confirm the authenticity of a signature just put on a document, etc. **4** proof or evidence of anything. ▻ *verb* (***witnesses***, ***witnessed***, ***witnessing***) **1** to be present as an observer at (an event or occurrence, etc). **2** to add one's own signature to confirm the authenticity of (a signature on a document, etc). **3** *intr* to give evidence. **4** said of a period or place, or of a person: to be the setting for, or to live through certain events. ▻ *prep* as shown by □ *Politicians do not get everything right, witness the poll tax.* • **witnesser** *noun.* • **bear witness to something** **1** to be evidence of it. **2** to give confirmation of it. • **be witness to something** to be in a position to observe it. ⓒ Anglo-Saxon *witnes*, from *witan* to know.

■ **witness something** or **witness to something** to confirm it □ *I can witness to his generosity.*

witness box and **witness stand** ▻ *noun* the enclosed stand from which a witness gives evidence in a court of law.

witter /'wɪtə(r)/ ▻ *verb* (***wittered, wittering***) *intr* (*usually* **witter on**) to talk or mutter ceaselessly and ineffectually. ◷ 19c: probably a variant of *whitter* to chatter.

witticism /'wɪtɪsɪzəm/ ▻ *noun* a witty remark or comment. ◷ 17c: coined by the English poet John Dryden (1631–1700), from WITTY, modelled on CRITICISM.

witting /'wɪtɪŋ/ ▻ *adj, rare* conscious; deliberate. • **wittingly** *adverb*. ◷ Anglo-Saxon *witan* to know.

witty /'wɪtɪ/ ▻ *adj* (***wittier, wittiest***) **1** able to express oneself cleverly and amusingly. **2** *old use or dialect* clever; intelligent. • **wittily** *adverb*. • **wittiness** *noun*. ◷ Anglo-Saxon, from WIT[1].

wivern see WYVERN

wives *plural of* WIFE

wizard /'wɪzəd/ ▻ *noun* **1** someone, especially a man, supposed to have magic powers; a magician or sorcerer. **2** *dated colloq* (*often* **a wizard at** or **with something**) someone extraordinarily skilled in a particular way. ▻ *adj* **1** referring or relating to a wizard or magic. **2** *dated, colloq* marvellous. • **wizardry** *noun* sorcery. ◷ 15c as *wisard*, from *wis* WISE.

wizen /'wɪzən/ ▻ *verb* (***wizened, wizening***) *tr & intr* to make or become dry and shrivelled. • **wizened** and **wizen** *adj* shrivelled or wrinkled, especially with age. ◷ Anglo-Saxon *wisnian* to dry up.

wiz kid see WHIZZ KID

wk ▻ *abbreviation* **1** week. **2** work.

wks ▻ *abbreviation* weeks.

WMO ▻ *abbreviation* World Meteorological Organization.

WNO ▻ *abbreviation* Welsh National Opera.

WNP ▻ *abbreviation* Welsh National Party.

WNW ▻ *abbreviation* west-north-west.

WO ▻ *abbreviation* Warrant Officer.

woad /woʊd/ ▻ *noun* **1** a cruciferous plant from whose leaves a blue dye is obtained. **2** this dye, used by the ancient Britons to paint their bodies. ◷ Anglo-Saxon *wad*.

wobbegong /'wɒbɪgɒŋ/ ▻ *noun* an Australian brown shark with a patterned back. Also called **carpet shark**. ◷ 19c: Aboriginal.

wobble /'wɒbəl/ ▻ *verb* (***wobbled, wobbling***) **1** *tr & intr* to rock or make something rock, sway or shake unsteadily. **2** to move or advance in this manner □ *wobbled down the street*. **3** *intr* said of the voice: to be unsteady. **4** *intr* to be undecided; to waver. ▻ *noun* a wobbling, rocking or swaying motion. • **wobbler** *noun* **1** someone or something that wobbles. **2** *colloq* a WOBBLY. ◷ 17c: from German *wabbeln*, from Norse *vafla* to waver.

wobble board ▻ *noun, Austral* a sheet of hardboard used as a type of musical instrument, played by flexing it to produced certain sound effects.

wobbly ▻ *adj* (***wobblier, wobbliest***) unsteady; shaky; inclined to wobble. ▻ *noun* (***wobblies***) *colloq* a fit of anger; a tantrum. • **wobbliness** *noun*. • **throw a wobbly** *colloq* to have a tantrum; to rage. ◷ 1970s as *noun*.

wodge ▻ *noun, colloq* a large lump, wad or chunk. ◷ Early 20c: a variant of WEDGE.

woe /woʊ/ ▻ *noun* (***woes***) **1** grief; misery. **2** (*often* **woes**) affliction; calamity. ▻ *exclamation, old use* expressing grief. • **woe betide ...** *old use, facetious* may evil befall, or evil will befall whoever offends or acts in some specified way □ *Woe betide anyone who disturbs him*. • **woe is me** *old use* alas! ◷ Anglo-Saxon *wa*.

woebegone /'woʊbɪgɒn/ ▻ *adj* dismal-looking; showing sorrow. ◷ 14c: from *begone* surrounded.

woeful ▻ *adj* **1** mournful; sorrowful. **2** causing woe □ *a woeful story*. **3** disgraceful; pitiful □ *a woeful lack of interest*. • **woefully** *adverb*. • **woefulness** *noun*.

wog[1] ▻ *noun, Brit offensive slang* any non-white person. ◷ 1920s, originally used only of Arabs: perhaps from GOLLIWOG.

wog[2] ▻ *noun, Austral colloq* any illness or infection, eg influenza. ◷ 1930s.

woggle /'wɒgəl/ ▻ *noun* a ring, usually of leather or plastic, through which Cubs, Scouts and Guides, etc thread their neckerchiefs. ◷ 1930s.

wok ▻ *noun* an almost hemispherical pan used in Chinese cookery. ◷ 1950s: Cantonese Chinese.

woke *past tense of* WAKE

woken *past participle of* WAKE

wold /woʊld/ ▻ *noun* a tract of open rolling upland. ◷ Anglo-Saxon *wald* or *weald* forest.

wolf /wʊlf/ ▻ *noun* (***wolves***) **1** a species of carnivorous mammal belonging to the dog family which hunts in packs, and has erect ears, a long muzzle and a long bushy tail. **2** any similar animal. **3** *colloq* a man with an insatiable appetite for sexual conquests. **4** a greedy or cunning person. **5** *music* a dissonance heard in a keyboard instrument not tuned by equal temperament. **6** (*also* **wolf note**) *music* an extraneous discordant sound made by the bow on a stringed instrument. ▻ *verb* (***wolfed, wolfing***) **1** (*usually* **wolf something down**) *colloq* to gobble it quickly and greedily. **2** *intr* to hunt for wolves. • **wolfish** *adj*. • **wolfishly** *adverb*. • **wolflike** *adj*. • **cry wolf** to give a false alarm, usually repeatedly. • **keep the wolf from the door** to ward off hunger or poverty. • **throw** or **fling someone** or **something to the wolves** to abandon them or it to certain destruction. • **wolf in sheep's clothing** a dangerous or powerful person who appears to be harmless. ◷ Anglo-Saxon.

wolfcub ▻ *noun* **1** a young wolf. **2** (**Wolfcub**) *formerly* a Cub Scout.

wolffish ▻ *noun* any genus of fierce and voracious saltwater fishes.

wolfhound ▻ *noun* any of several large breeds of domestic dog, such as the Irish wolfhound, formerly used for hunting wolves.

wolf note see WOLF *noun 6*

wolf pack ▻ *noun* **1** a group of wolves hunting together. **2** a group of submarines or aircraft sent out to attack enemy targets.

wolfram /'wʊlfrəm/ ▻ *noun, chem* TUNGSTEN. ◷ 18c: German.

wolfsbane see under ACONITE

wolf spider ▻ *noun* a spider of the genus to which the true tarantula belongs, and which chases its prey rather than trapping it in a web. Also called **hunting spider**.

wolf whistle ▻ *noun* a loud whistle used as an expression of admiration for the appearance of the person to whom it is directed. ▻ *verb* (**wolf-whistle**) to whistle at someone in this way. ◷ 1940s.

wolverine or **wolverene** /'wʊlvəriːn/ ▻ *noun* **1** a large carnivorous animal of the weasel family, which inhabits forests in N America and Eurasia. Also called **glutton**. **2** the fur of this animal. ◷ 16c as *wolvering*: from WOLF.

wolves *plural of* WOLF

woman /'wʊmən/ ▻ *noun* (***women*** /'wɪmɪn/) **1** an adult human female. Opposite of MAN. **2** women generally; the female sex. **3** *in compounds* **a** a woman associated with a specified activity □ *policewoman* □ *markswoman*; **b** a woman who is a native of a specified country or place □ *Irishwoman*. **4** one's wife or girlfriend. **5** *derog* a man who displays characteristics considered more typical of a woman. **6** (**the woman**) feminine instincts. **7** *old use* a female servant or domestic daily help. **8** *old use* a female attendant to a queen, etc. ▻ *adj* female □ *a woman doctor*. • **womanhood** *noun*. • **womanlike** *adj*. • **kept woman** a mistress. • **the little woman** *patronizing* one's wife. ⓒ Anglo-Saxon *wifman*, from *wif* wife + *man* human being.

womanish ▷ *adj, derog* **1** associated with women. **2** said of a man, his behaviour or appearance: effeminate; unmanly. • **womanishly** *adverb*. • **womanishness** *noun*.

womanize or **womanise** /ˈwʊmənaɪz/ ▷ *verb* (**womanized**, **womanizing**) **1** *intr, derog colloq* said of a man: to pursue and have casual affairs with women. **2** *tr & intr* to make or become effeminate. • **womanizer** *noun*. ⓒ 16c in sense 2.

womankind ▷ *noun* (*also* **womanhood**) women generally; the female sex.

womanly ▷ *adj* (**womanlier**, **womanliest**) **1** having characteristics specific to a woman; feminine. **2** considered natural or suitable to a woman. • **womanliness** *noun*.

woman of the streets ▷ *noun* a whore or prostitute.

woman of the world ▷ *noun* **1** a woman of fashion or of worldly wisdom. **2** a woman who is familiar with and makes allowances for the ways of the world.

womb /wuːm/ ▷ *noun* **1** *anatomy* the organ in female mammals in which the young develop after conception and remain till birth. *Technical equivalent* UTERUS. **2** a place of origin ◻ *the womb of civilization*. **3** *literary* a deep dark centre ◻ *in the womb of the earth*. ⓒ Anglo-Saxon *wamb*.

wombat /ˈwɒmbat/ ▷ *noun* a nocturnal marsupial of Australia and Tasmania, well adapted for burrowing, with a compact body, short legs, a large flat head and no tail. ⓒ 18c: from Aboriginal *wambat*.

women *plural of* WOMAN

womenfolk ▷ *plural noun* **1** women generally. **2** the female members of a family or society.

Women's Institute ▷ *noun* (abbreviation **WI**) in the UK: an organization for women, especially from rural areas, which holds regular meetings for social and cultural activities and demonstrations of craftwork, etc.

women's liberation ▷ *noun* (*also* with capitals) a movement started by women, and forming part of the women's movement, aimed at freeing them from the disadvantages and irregularities they suffer in a male-dominated society. Often shortened to **women's lib**. ⓒ 1960s.

women's movement ▷ *noun* (*also* with capitals) the movement with the object of achieving equality for women with men, eg with regard to job opportunities, pay, legal status, etc.

women's rights ▷ *plural noun* the rights of women giving them, or aimed at giving them, equality with men, particularly concerning job prospects and pay, etc.

womera see WOOMERA

won[1] /wɒn/ ▷ *noun* (*plural* **won**) the standard monetary unit of currency in both N and S Korea. ⓒ Early 20c: from Korean *wan*.

won[2] *past tense, past participle of* WIN

wonder /ˈwʌndə(r)/ ▷ *noun* **1** the state of mind produced by something extraordinary, new or unexpected; amazement or awe. **2** something that is a cause of awe, amazement or bafflement; a marvel or prodigy. ▷ *adj* notable for accomplishing marvels ◻ *a wonder drug*. ▷ *verb* (**wondered**, **wondering**) **1** *tr & intr* to be curious ◻ *wondered about her background* ◻ *wondering where you'd gone*. **2** (*also* **wonder at something**) to be amazed or surprised by it ◻ *shouldn't wonder she felt ill* ◻ *I wonder at you sometimes!* **3** to be uncertain or undecided; to feel doubt. **4** used politely to introduce requests ◻ *I wonder if you could help me?* • **wonderer** *noun*. • **wonderment** *noun*. • **do** or **work wonders** to achieve marvellous results. • **no, little** or **small wonder** it is hardly surprising. • **wonders never** or **will never cease** *colloq* an expression of surprise at some unexpected but welcome development. ⓒ Anglo-Saxon *wundor*.

Wonderbra ▷ *noun, trademark* an underwired bra with side padding, designed to give uplift and a more conspicuous cleavage. ⓒ 1970s: first manufactured by Gossard.

wonderful ▷ *adj* **1** arousing wonder; extraordinary. **2** excellent; splendid. • **wonderfully** *adverb*.

wondering ▷ *adj* full of wonder ◻ *a wondering expression*. • **wonderingly** *adverb*.

wonderland ▷ *noun* **1** an imaginary place full of marvels. **2** a scene of strange unearthly beauty.

wonder-struck and **wonder-stricken** ▷ *adj* struck with wonder or astonishment at something.

wondrous /ˈwʌndrəs/ ▷ *adj* wonderful, strange or awesome ◻ *a wondrous sight*. • **wondrously** *adverb*. • **wondrousness** *noun*.

wonga /ˈwɒŋgə/ ▷ *noun, slang* money. ⓒ 20c.

wonk /wɒŋk/ ▷ *noun, derog, slang* a serious or studious person, especially someone who is interested in a trivial or unfashionable subject.

wonky /ˈwɒŋkɪ/ ▷ *adj* (**wonkier**, **wonkiest**) *Brit colloq* **1** unsound, unsteady or wobbly. **2** crooked or awry; uneven. • **wonkily** *adverb*. • **wonkiness** *noun*. ⓒ 1920s: a variant of dialect *wanky*.

wont /woʊnt, wɒnt/ *chiefly formal, literary or old use* ▷ *adj* habitually inclined; accustomed ◻ *He is wont to retire to bed early*. ▷ *noun* a habit that one has ◻ *It was her wont to rise early*. ▷ *verb, tr & intr* (**wont** or **wonts**, **wont** or **wonted**, **wonting**) to become, or make someone become, accustomed. • **wonted** *adj* customary. ⓒ Anglo-Saxon *gewunod* accustomed.

> **wont**
>
> There is often a spelling confusion between **wont** and **want**.

won't /woʊnt/ ▷ *contraction* will not.

woo ▷ *verb* (**wooed**, **wooing**) **1** *old use* said of a man: to try to win the love and affection of (a woman) especially in the hope of marrying her. **2** to try to win the support of someone ◻ *woo the voters*. **3** to pursue or seek (eg fame, success or fortune). • **wooer** *noun*. • **wooing** *noun, adj*. • **wooingly** *adverb*. ⓒ Anglo-Saxon *wogian*.

wood /wʊd/ ▷ *noun* **1** *bot* the hard tissue beneath the bark, that forms the bulk of woody trees and shrubs. *Technical equivalent* XYLEM. **2** this material obtained from trees and used for building timber, fencing and furniture-making, etc. **3** (*also* **woods**) an expanse of growing trees. **4** firewood. **5** *golf* a club with a head traditionally made of wood, now usually of metal, used for driving the ball long distances. **6** *bowls* a bowl. **7** casks or barrels made of wood, for wine or beer ◻ *matured in wood*. ▷ *adj* made of, or using, wood. ▷ *verb* (**wooded**, **wooding**) to cover (land, etc) with trees. • **wooded** *adj*. • **wooden** and **woody** see separate entries. • **not see the wood for the trees** to fail to grasp the broad issue because of over-attention to details. • **out of the woods** free at last of trouble or danger. • **touch wood** see under TOUCH. ⓒ Anglo-Saxon *wudu*.

wood alcohol ▷ *noun* METHANOL.

wood anemone ▷ *noun* any type of anemone that grows in woods, with a single whorl of leaves and a white flower.

woodbine /ˈwʊdbaɪn/ ▷ *noun* honeysuckle. ⓒ Anglo-Saxon *wudubinde*.

woodblock ▷ *noun* **1** a woodcut. **2** a flat block of wood used for surfacing floors. **3** *music* a hollow piece of wood tapped with a drumstick to produce a knocking sound (also called **Chinese block**).

woodcarving ▻ *noun* **1** the process of carving in wood. **2** an object or decoration carved in wood. • **woodcarver** *noun*.

woodchip ▻ *noun* **1** a chip of wood. **2** (*in full* **woodchip paper**) paper incorporating chips of wood for texture, used for decorating walls.

woodchuck ▻ *noun* a N American marmot. Also called **groundhog**. ⓔ 17c: from Cree (Native American language) *otchek* marten.

woodcock ▻ *noun* a long-billed game bird related to the snipe, but with a bulkier body and shorter, stronger legs. ⓔ Anglo-Saxon wudecoc.

woodcut ▻ *noun* **1** a design cut into a wooden block. **2** a print taken from this. ⓔ 17c.

woodcutter ▻ *noun* **1** someone who fells trees and chops wood. **2** someone who makes woodcuts. • **woodcutting** *noun*.

wooden /'wʊdən/ ▻ *adj* (*woodener, woodenest* only in senses 2, 3 and 4) **1** made of or resembling wood. **2** said of an actor, performance, etc: stiff, unnatural and inhibited; lacking expression and liveliness. **3** clumsy or awkward. **4** said especially of a facial expression: blank; expressionless. • **woodenly** *adverb*.

wood engraving ▻ *noun* **1** a design for printing, etched into the surface of a block. **2** an impression taken from this. **3** the art of cutting and producing such designs. • **wood engraver** *noun*. ⓔ Early 19c.

wooden-headed ▻ *adj* dull-witted; unintelligent. • **wooden-headedness** *noun*.

wooden horse see TROJAN HORSE

wooden overcoat ▻ *noun, slang* a coffin.

wooden spoon ▻ *noun* a booby prize. ⓔ Early 19c: from the wooden spoon presented to the person who came bottom in the mathematical tripos list at Cambridge University.

wood fibre ▻ *noun* fibre obtained from wood, used especially in papermaking.

woodgrouse ▻ *noun* a CAPERCAILLIE.

woodland ▻ *noun* (*also* **woodlands**) an area of land planted with relatively short trees that are more widely spaced than those in a forest. Also *as adj*. • **woodlander** *noun*.

woodlark ▻ *noun* a species of lark that habitually perches in trees, and tends to sing in flight.

woodlouse ▻ *noun* a crustacean with a grey oval plated body, found in damp places, under stones and bark, etc. Also (in Scotland) called **slater**.

woodman or **woodsman** ▻ *noun* **1** a woodcutter. **2** a forest officer.

wood nightshade see WOODY NIGHTSHADE

wood nymph ▻ *noun, mythol* a nymph who lives in the woods; a dryad or hamadryad.

woodpecker ▻ *noun* any of several species of tree-dwelling bird found in woodland areas, which have a straight pointed chisel-like bill used to bore into tree bark in search of insects and to drill nesting holes. ⓔ 16c.

woodpigeon ▻ *noun* a common pigeon that lives in woods, with a white marking round its neck. Also called **ring-dove**.

woodpile ▻ *noun* a pile of wood, especially that intended to be used as firewood.

wood pulp ▻ *noun* wood fibres that have been chemically and mechanically pulped for papermaking.

woodruff /'wʊdrʌf/ ▻ *noun* a sweet-smelling plant with small white flowers and whorled leaves. ⓔ Anglo-Saxon *wuduroffe*.

woodscrew ▻ *noun* a tapered screw for fastening together pieces of wood, or wood and metal, etc.

woodshed ▻ *noun* a shed for storing wood and tools, etc. • **something nasty in the woodshed** *colloq* an unpleasant or shocking experience in one's past, especially one kept secret ⓔ from the novel *Cold Comfort Farm* (1932) by Stella Gibbons.

woodsman see WOODMAN

wood sorrel ▻ *noun* a plant with trifoliate leaves and white or rose-tinted flowers.

wood spirit ▻ *noun* a crude methyl alcohol yielded by wood.

wood stain ▻ *noun* a substance for staining wood.

wood tar ▻ *noun* a product of destructive distillation of wood, especially pine, containing a complex mixture of hydrocarbons including phenols.

wood warbler ▻ *noun* **1** a greenish-yellow European warbler. **2** a similar bird, the American warbler.

woodwind ▻ *noun* **1** orchestral WIND INSTRUMENTS made, or formerly made, of wood, including the flute, oboe, clarinet and bassoon. **2 a** the section of the orchestra composed of these; **b** (*also* **woodwinds**) the players of these. ⓔ 19c.

woodwork ▻ *noun* **1** the art of making things out of wood; carpentry. **2** the wooden parts of any structure. • **woodworker** *noun*. • **crawl out from the woodwork** said of someone or something undesirable: to make themselves or their presence known. ⓔ 17c.

woodworm ▻ *noun* (*woodworm* or *woodworms*) **1** the larva of any of several beetles, that bores into wood. **2** the condition of wood caused by this.

woody ▻ *adj* (*woodier, woodiest*) **1** said of countryside: wooded; covered in trees. **2** resembling, developing into, or composed of wood ◻ ***plants with woody stems***. **3** similar to wood in texture, smell or taste, etc. • **woodiness** *noun*.

woody nightshade or **wood nightshade** ▻ *noun* a Eurasian purple-flowered climbing plant with poisonous red berries.

woof[1] /wʊf/ ▻ *noun* the sound of, or an imitation of, a dog's bark. ▻ *verb* (*woofed, woofing*) *intr* to bark. ⓔ 19c.

woof[2] /wʊf/ ▻ *noun, weaving* **1** the weft. **2** the texture of a fabric. ⓔ Anglo-Saxon *owef*, later *oof*, with *w* added by association with WEFT and WARP.

woofer /'wʊfə(r)/ ▻ *noun, electronics* a large loudspeaker for reproducing low-frequency sounds. Compare TWEETER. ⓔ 1930s.

woofter see POOFTER

wool /wʊl/ ▻ *noun* **1** the soft wavy hair of sheep and certain other animals. **2** this hair spun into yarn for knitting or weaving. **3** fabric or clothing woven or knitted from this yarn. **4** anything that is light and fleecy like wool. **5** *in compounds* fluffy, curly or tangled material resembling this ◻ ***steel wool***. **6** short coarse human hair. ▻ *adj* **1** made of wool. **2** relating to wool or its production. • **wool-like** *adj*. • **pull the wool over someone's eyes** *colloq* to deceive them ⓔ probably referring to pulling someone's wig over their eyes when robing them. ⓔ Anglo-Saxon *wull*.

wool fat ▻ *noun* LANOLIN.

wool-gathering ▻ *noun* absent-mindedness; day-dreaming. ⓔ 16c: from the occupation of gathering wool from around the hedges, etc.

woollen or (*US*) **woolen** *adj* **1** made of or relating to wool. **2** producing, or dealing in, goods made of wool. ▻ *noun* **1** (*often* **woollens**) a woollen, especially knitted, garment. **2** a woollen fabric.

woolly or (*US*) **wooly** /'wʊlɪ/ *adj* (*woollier, woolliest*) **1** made of, similar to, or covered with wool or wool-like fibres, etc; fluffy and soft. **2** vague and muddled; lacking in clarity ◻ ***woolly thinking*** ◻ ***woolly-minded*** ◻ ***woolly argument***. ▻ *noun* (*woollies*) *colloq* a woollen, usually knitted garment. • **woolliness** *noun*.

woolly bear ▷ *noun* **1** the hairy caterpillar of any of several moths, including the tiger moth. **2** the larva of the carpet beetle.

woolsack ▷ *noun* (*also* **Woolsack**) *Brit* **1** the seat of the Lord Chancellor in the House of Lords, which is a large square wool-stuffed sack covered with scarlet. **2** the office of Lord Chancellor. ◷ 16c in sense 1.

woolshed ▷ *noun, Austral, NZ* a large shed for shearing sheep and baling wool.

wool stapler ▷ *noun* **1** someone who deals in wool. **2** someone who classifies wool.

woomera /ˈwuːmərə/ or **womera** /ˈwɒmərə/ ▷ *noun* (***woomeras***) *Austral* a notched stick used by the Aboriginals to launch a dart or spear with greater force. ◷ 19c: from Dharuk (Australian Aboriginal language) *wumara*.

woosh see WHOOSH

woozy /ˈwuːzɪ/ ▷ *adj* (***woozier, wooziest***) *colloq* **1** dazed or stupefied; having blurred senses, due to drink or drugs, etc. **2** confused; dizzy. **3** vague or woolly. • **woozily** *adverb*. • **wooziness** *noun*. ◷ 19c: perhaps a combination of *woolly* and *dizzy*.

wop ▷ *noun, offensive slang* a member of a Latin or Mediterranean race, especially an Italian. ◷ Early 20c: probably from Italian dialect *guappo* swaggerer, from Spanish *guapo* bold or handsome.

Worcester sauce /ˈwʊstə —/ or **Worcestershire sauce** /ˈwʊstəʃə —/ ▷ *noun* a strong-tasting sauce used as a seasoning, made with soy sauce, vinegar and spices. ◷ 17c: from Worcester in England, where it was originally made.

word /wɜːd/ ▷ *noun* **1** the smallest unit of spoken or written language that can be used independently, usually separated off by spaces in writing and printing. **2** a brief conversation on a particular matter. **3** any brief statement, message or communication □ *a word of caution.* **4** news or notice □ *any word of Jane?* □ *She sent word she'd arrive tomorrow.* **5** a rumour □ *The word is he's bankrupt.* **6** one's solemn promise. **7** an order □ *expects her word to be obeyed.* **8** a word given as a signal for action □ *Wait till I give the word.* **9** what someone says or said □ *remembered her mother's words.* **10** (**words**) language as a means of communication □ *impossible to convey in words.* **11** (**words**) an argument or heated discussion; verbal contention □ *We had words when he returned.* **12** (**words**) discussion in contrast to action □ *Words alone will get us nowhere.* **13** (**words**) **a** the lyrics of a song, etc; **b** the speeches an actor must learn for a particular part. **14** (**the Word**) *Christianity* the teachings contained in the Bible. **15** a watchword □ *mum's the word.* **16** *computing* **a** a group of bits or bytes that can be processed as a single unit by a computer, the size of a word varying according to the size of the computer; **b** in word processing: any group of characters separated from other such groups by spaces or punctuation, whether or not it is a real word. **17** *in compounds* used after a letter and preceded by THE (sense 4a) *indicating* something unmentionable or taboo beginning with that letter □ *the m-word* (for 'marriage') □ *the c-word* (for 'cancer'). ▷ *verb* (***worded, wording***) to express something in carefully chosen words. • **a good word** a recommendation, praise, etc □ *not a good word to say about anyone.* • **as good as one's word** careful to keep one's promise. • **a word in someone's ear** a confidential or private conversation. • **break one's word** to fail to keep or fulfil one's promise. • **by word of mouth** see under WORD OF MOUTH. • **have a word with someone** to speak with them, usually for a specific reason. • **have no words for someone** or **something** to be at a loss to describe or express them or it. • **have words with someone** *colloq* to quarrel with them. • **in a word** briefly; in short. • **in other words** saying the same thing in a different way. • **in so many words** explicitly; bluntly. • **my word** or **upon my word** an exclamation of surprise. • **not the word for it** not a strong enough expression for it □ *Stupid isn't the word for it.* • **of many** or **few words** inclined to be talkative or reserved. • **put in a good word for someone** to recommend or mention them favourably to someone who could benefit them in some way. • **put words into someone's mouth** to attribute or supply to them words that they did not, or do not intend to, use. • **say the word** to give one's consent or approval for some action to proceed. • **take someone at their word** to take their offer or suggestion, etc literally. • **take someone's word for it** to accept what they say as true, without verification. • **take the words out of someone's mouth** to say exactly what they were about to say. • **the last word 1** the final, especially conclusive, remark or comment in an argument. **2** the most up-to-date design or model, or most recent advance in something. **3** the finest example of eg a particular quality, etc □ *the last word in good taste.* • **too funny** or **stupid,** *etc* **for words** *colloq* exceptionally or extremely funny or stupid, etc. • **word for word** said of a statement, etc: repeated in exactly the same words, or translated into exactly corresponding words; verbatim. • **word of honour** see separate entry. • **words fail me** I am unable to express my feelings or reaction. ◷ Anglo-Saxon.

wordage /ˈwɜːdɪdʒ/ ▷ *noun* (***wordages***) **1** words generally, especially text as opposed to pictures. **2** the quantity of words or length of text, etc.

word association ▷ *noun* **1** *psychol* a technique that involves the presentation of a word to a patient or subject, who then has to respond immediately with the first word that comes to mind on hearing the stimulus word. This technique is meant to draw out features of the subconscious. **2** a game utilizing a similar process, involving a group of people where one starts off by presenting a word, and the next person says the first word that they associate with that word, and so on throughout the group.

word-blindness ▷ *noun* **1** ALEXIA. **2** DYSLEXIA. • **word-blind** *adj*.

wordbook ▷ *noun* a book containing lists of words; a dictionary or vocabulary.

wordclass ▷ *noun, grammar* a set of words that share the same grammatical property, or are all the same PART OF SPEECH.

wordfinder ▷ *noun* a book designed as a tool for finding a required word; a thesaurus.

wordgame ▷ *noun* any game or puzzle in which words are constructed or deciphered, etc.

wording ▷ *noun* **1** the choice and arrangement of words used to express something. **2** the words used in this arrangement.

word of honour ▷ *noun* a promise or assurance which cannot be broken without disgrace.

word of mouth ▷ *noun* spoken, as opposed to written, communication. • **by word of mouth** through spoken word or conversation.

word order ▷ *noun* the ordering of words in a sentence or phrase, etc.

word-perfect ▷ *adj* **1** able to repeat something accurately from memory. **2** said of a recitation, etc: faultless.

word play ▷ *noun* verbal ambiguity exploited to produce puns and witty repartee.

word processor ▷ *noun* (abbreviation **WP**) *computing* a computer application dedicated completely to the input, processing, storage and retrieval of text. • **word-processing** *noun* the production of text using a word processor. Also *as adj*. ◷ 1970s.

wordsearch ▷ *noun* a wordgame consisting of a square filled with letters arranged in rows, within which are hidden various words.

wordsmith ▻ *noun* **1** *sometimes ironic* an articulate user of words. **2** a coiner of words. ⌚ Late 19c.

word wrapping or **wordwrap** ▻ *noun, computing* in word-processing: a facility that ensures that a word which is too long to fit into the end of a line of text is automatically put to the start of the following line. ⌚ 1970s.

wordy ▻ *adj* (*wordier, wordiest*) using or containing too many words; long-winded, especially pompously so. • **wordily** *adverb*. • **wordiness** *noun*.

wore *past tense of* WEAR[1], WEAR[2]

work /wɜːk/ ▻ *noun* **1** physical or mental effort made in order to achieve or make something, eg labour, study, research, etc. **2** employment □ *out of work*. **3** one's place of employment □ *He leaves work at 4.30*. **4** tasks to be done □ *She often brings work home with her*. Also *in compounds* □ *housework*. **5** the product of mental or physical labour □ *His work has improved* □ *a lifetime's work*. **6** a manner of working, or WORKMANSHIP. **7 a** any literary, artistic, musical, or dramatic composition or creation; **b** (**works**) the entire collection of such material by an artist, composer or author, etc. **8** anything done, managed, made or achieved, etc; an activity carried out for some purpose □ *works of charity*. **9** *old use* needlework. **10** *in compounds* things made in the material or with the tools specified; the production of such things □ *basketwork*. **11** *in compounds* the parts of a building, etc using a specified material □ *stonework*. **12** (**works**) *often in compounds* building or repair operations □ *roadworks*. **13** (**works**) *often in compounds* a rampart or defense □ *earthworks*. **14** (**works**) *colloq* the operating parts of eg a watch or machine; the mechanism. **15** (**works**) *often in compounds* the place of manufacture of a specified product □ *gasworks*. **16** (**the works**) *colloq* everything possible, available or going; the whole lot □ *She has a headache, fever, cold — the works!* **17** *physics* the transfer of energy that occurs when force is exerted on a body to move it, measured in JOULES. ▻ *adj* relating to, or suitable for, etc work □ *work clothes*. ▻ *verb* (*worked, working*) **1** *intr* to do work; to exert oneself mentally or physically; to toil, labour or study. **2** *tr & intr* to be employed or have a job. **3** to impose tasks on someone; to make them labour □ *She works her staff hard*. **4** *tr & intr* to operate, especially satisfactorily □ *Does this radio work?* **5** *intr* said of a plan or idea, etc: to be successful or effective. **6** *intr* to function in a particular way □ *That's not how life works*. **7** *intr* said of a craftsman: to specialize in the use of a specified material □ *He works in brass*. **8** to shape or fashion (metals or other materials); to make by doing this □ *earrings worked in silver*. **9** to cultivate (land). **10** to extract materials from (a mine). **11** to knead (eg dough). **12** to cover (an area) as a salesman, etc. **13** to sew or embroider, etc. **14** to achieve (miracles, wonders, etc). **15** *colloq* to manipulate (a system or rules, etc) to one's advantage. **16** *tr & intr* to make (one's way), or shift or make something shift gradually □ *work one's way forward* □ *worked the nail out of the wall*. **17** *intr* said eg of a screw: to become gradually (loose or free, etc). **18** *intr* said of the face or features: to move uncontrollably with emotion; to contort. **19** to exercise (a part of the body). **20** *intr* said of a liquid: to ferment. **21** to earn (one's sea passage) by unpaid work on board. • **workless** *adj*. • **all in a day's work** not being any more work or trouble than usual. • **give someone the works** *colloq* to use every measure available in dealing with them, by way of eg punishment, coercion or welcome. • **have one's work cut out** *colloq* to be faced with a challenging task. • **make short work of something** or **someone** to deal with it or them rapidly and effectively. • **a … piece** or **bit of work** *colloq* a person, especially with regard to an unfavorable aspect of character or disposition □ *He's a nasty piece of work*. • **work to rule** to reduce efficiency by working strictly to official working rules, especially as a form of industrial action. ⌚ Anglo-Saxon *weorc*.

■ **work at something** to apply oneself to it.

■ **work in** said of workers protesting against closure or redundancy, etc: to occupy work premises and take over the running of the business. See also WORK-IN.

■ **work something in 1** to add and mix (an ingredient) into a mixture. **2** to find a place for it; to fit it in □ *I'll work an appointment in somehow*.

■ **work something off** to get rid of (energy or the effects of a heavy meal) by energetic activity.

■ **work on someone** *colloq* to use one's powers of persuasion on them.

■ **work on something 1** to try to perfect or improve it. **2** to use it as a basis for one's decisions and actions □ *working on that assumption*.

■ **work out 1** to be successfully achieved or resolved □ *It'll all work out in the end*. **2** to perform a set of energetic physical exercises □ *She's working out at the gym*. See also WORKOUT.

■ **work something out** to solve it; to sort or reason it out.

■ **work someone over** *slang* to beat them up.

■ **work someone up** to excite or agitate them.

■ **work something up** to summon up (an appetite, enthusiasm or energy, etc).

■ **work up to something** to approach (a difficult task or objective) by gradual stages.

workable ▻ *adj* **1** said of a scheme, etc: able to be carried out; practicable. **2** said eg of a material or mineral source: able to be worked. • **workability** or **workableness** *noun*.

workaday ▻ *adj* **1** ordinary or mundane; commonplace. **2** suitable for a work day; practical or everyday.

workaholic ▻ *noun, colloq* someone addicted to work. ⌚ 1960s: from WORK, modelled on ALCOHOLIC.

workbasket, **workbag** and **workbox** ▻ *noun* a basket or box for holding sewing materials and implements.

workbench ▻ *noun* a table, usually a purpose-built one, at which a mechanic or craftsman, etc works.

workbook ▻ *noun* **1** a book of exercises, often with spaces included for the answers. **2** a book containing a record of jobs undertaken, in progress or completed.

workday see WORKING DAY

worked ▻ *adj* having been treated or fashioned in some way, especially embroidered or ornamented.

worker ▻ *noun* **1** someone who works. **2** someone employed in manual work. **3** an employee as opposed to an employer. **4** a female social insect, eg a honeybee or ant, that is sterile and whose sole function is to maintain the colony and forage for food. Compare QUEEN, DRONE.

worker priest ▻ *noun* in the RC Church: a priest who works part-time in a secular job so as to understand the problems of lay people better.

work ethic ▻ *noun* the general attitude of a specific group towards work, especially one (the **Protestant work ethic**) which places a high moral value on hard work.

work experience ▻ *noun* a scheme arranged for school pupils or leavers, where they work unpaid with a company or organization, etc for a short time in order to gain experience.

workfare ▻ *noun, US* an unemployment benefit scheme under which the payment recipients are required to do work of some kind, usually some form of public service. ⌚ 1960s: from WORK, modelled on WELFARE.

workforce ▻ *noun* the number of workers engaged in a particular industry, factory, etc; the total number of workers potentially available. ⌚ 1940s.

workhorse ▷ *noun* **1** a horse used for labouring purposes rather than for recreation or racing, etc. **2** a person, machine or anything else heavily depended on to carry out arduous work.

workhouse ▷ *noun, historical* **1** a house where any work or manufacture is carried out. **2** an institution where the poor can be housed and given work to do. ◷ 17c.

work-in ▷ *noun* the occupation of work premises by employees, especially in protest at closure or redundancy, etc. See also WORK IN at WORK.

working ▷ *noun* **1** the act or process of shaping, making, effecting or solving, etc. **2** (*also* **workings**) the operation or mode of operation of something. **3** a written record of the steps taken to reach the answer of a mathematical problem. **4** (**workings**) excavations at a mine or quarry. ▷ *adj* **1** said of a period of time: devoted to work, or denoting that part that is devoted to work. **2** adequate for one's purposes □ *a working knowledge of French.* • **in working order** functioning properly.

working capital ▷ *noun* money used to keep a business, etc going.

working class ▷ *noun* the wage-earning section of the population, employed especially in manual labour. Also (**working-class**) *as adj.* ◷ 19c.

working day or (*N Amer*) **workday** *noun* **1** a day on which people go to work as usual. **2** the part of the day during which work is done.

working drawing ▷ *noun* a drawing that contains the details of the construction or assembly of something, used as a guide by the builders.

working hours ▷ *plural noun* the period of the day during which work is normally done, and shops and offices, etc are open.

working hypothesis ▷ *noun* an assumption on which a plan or action is based.

working lunch ▷ *noun* a lunch arranged as an alternative to a formal meeting for the discussion of business.

working majority ▷ *noun, politics* a majority sufficient to enable a party in office to carry through its legislative programme without the risk of parliamentary defeat.

working model ▷ *noun* a model of a machine that can do, on a smaller scale, the same work as the machine.

working party ▷ *noun* a group of people appointed to investigate and report on something.

working week or (*N Amer*) **workweek** *noun* **1** the period in the week during which work is normally done. **2** any week in which such work is done, especially as opposed to eg holidays.

workload ▷ *noun* the amount of work to be done by a person or machine, especially in a specified time.

workman /ˈwɜːkmən/ ▷ *noun* **1** a man employed to do manual work. **2** anyone performing a craft.

workmanlike ▷ *adj* suitable to, or characteristic of, a good or skilful workman.

workmanship ▷ *noun* **1** the skill of a craftsman. **2** the degree of expertise or skill shown in making something, or of the refinement of finish in the finished product.

workmate ▷ *noun colloq* someone who works with another or others in their place of work; a fellow-worker or colleague.

work of art ▷ *noun* **1** a painting or sculpture of high quality. **2** anything constructed or composed with obvious skill and elegance.

workout ▷ *noun* a session of physical exercise or training. See also WORK OUT (sense 2) at WORK.

workpeople ▷ *plural noun* workers who are engaged in manual labour.

workpiece ▷ *noun* an object that is being or has been worked on with a machine or tool.

workplace ▷ *noun* an office, factory, etc.

workroom ▷ *noun* a room in which work, usually of a specific kind, is done.

works council and **works committee** ▷ *noun, chiefly Brit* a body on which representatives of both employer and employee meet to deal with labour relations within a business.

worksheet ▷ *noun* **1** a paper or form detailing work being planned or already in operation. **2** a sheet of paper used especially by students for roughly calculating or solving problems.

workshop ▷ *noun* **1** a room or building where construction and repairs are carried out. **2 a** a course of study or work, especially of an experimental or creative kind, for a group of people on a particular project □ *a theatre workshop.* **b** the people participating in such a course. ◷ 16c.

workshy ▷ *adj, colloq* lazy; inclined to avoid work. ◷ Early 20c.

workspace ▷ *noun* the area required for one's work, eg a desk, office, room, etc.

workstation ▷ *noun* **1** in an office, etc: **a** a computer terminal, usually comprising a keyboard, screen and processor; **b** someone's seat at such a terminal. **2** in a production line: a position at which a particular job is done.

work study ▷ *noun* an investigation of the most efficient way of doing a job, especially with regard to time and effort.

work surface and **worktop** ▷ *noun* a flat surface constructed along the top of kitchen installations such as fridge and cupboards, on which to prepare food, etc.

work to rule ▷ *verb, intr* said of workers: to scrupulously observe all the regulations for the express purpose of slowing down work, as a form of industrial action. • **work-to-rule** *noun* a period of working to rule by employees.

workwear ▷ *noun* clothing worn specifically for work, especially overalls, issued to factory workers, etc.

workweek see WORKING WEEK

world /wɜːld/ ▷ *noun* **1** the Earth. **2** the people inhabiting the Earth; humankind □ *tell the world.* **3** any other planet or potentially habitable heavenly body. **4** human affairs □ *the present state of the world.* **5** (*also* **World**) a group of countries characterized in a certain way □ *the Third World* □ *the New World.* **6** (*also* **World**) the people of a particular period, and their culture □ *the Ancient World.* **7** a state of existence □ *in this world or the next.* **8** (**the world**) human existence, especially regarded as oppressive and materialistic, or as distinct from spiritual or intellectual life □ *escape from the world of today.* **9** someone's individual way of life or range of experience □ *He's in a world of his own.* **10** an atmosphere or environment □ *enter a world of make-believe.* **11** a particular area of activity □ *the world of politics.* **12** a class of living things □ *the insect world.* **13** *colloq* a great deal; a lot □ *did her a world of good* □ *We are worlds apart.* ▷ *adj* relating to, affecting, or important throughout, the whole world. • **all the world and his wife** *colloq* everybody; a large number of people. • **be** or **mean all the world to someone** to be important or precious to them. • **the best of both worlds** the benefits of both alternatives with the drawbacks of neither. • **bring someone into the world** to give birth to or deliver (a baby). • **come into the world** to be born. • **come** or **go up** (or **down**) **in the world** to rise (or fall) in social status. • **for all the world as if …** exactly as if … • **in the world** used for emphasis □ *How in the world ...?* □ *without a care in the world.* • **it's a small world** *colloq* an indication of surprise or interest, etc at an unexpected and unlikely coincidence. • **not for the world** not for anything. • **on top of the world** *colloq* supremely happy. • **out of this world** *colloq* extraordinarily fine; marvellous. • **the world is your**, *etc* **oyster** the world and its opportunities all await you, etc. • **think the world of someone** to love or admire them immensely. ◎ Anglo-Saxon *weorold*.

World Bank ▷ *noun, colloq* a popular name for the International Bank for Reconstruction and Development, an agency of the United Nations set up in 1945 to make loans to poorer countries.

world-beater ▷ *noun, colloq* a person or a product, etc that is supreme in its class. • **world-beating** *adj*.

world-class ▷ *adj, sport* being among or competing against those of the highest standard in the world.

World Cup ▷ *noun, especially football* an international competition, taking place every four years, in which teams from several countries in the world compete, usually having qualified in preliminary rounds.

world-famous ▷ *adj* well known throughout the world.

world language ▷ *noun* **1** a language designed for international use. **2** a language used widely internationally.

worldling ▷ *noun* someone who is devoted to worldly pursuits and possessions; a worldly person. ◎ 16c.

worldly ▷ *adj* (*worldlier, worldliest*) **1** relating to this world; material, as opposed to spiritual or eternal □ *worldly possessions.* **2** over-concerned with possessions, money, luxuries, etc; materialistic. **3** shrewd about the ways of the world; knowing and sophisticated in outlook; worldly-wise. • **worldliness** *noun*.

worldly-minded ▷ *adj* having the mind focused on the present world and material possessions, etc. • **worldly-mindedness** *noun*.

worldly-wise ▷ *adj* knowledgeable about life; having the wisdom of those experienced in, and affected by, the ways of the world; cynical or not easily impressed.

world music ▷ *noun* popular folk music originating in non-western, especially African, cultures.

world power ▷ *noun* a state, group of states or institution, etc strong enough to have influence in world affairs and politics.

World Series ▷ *noun, baseball* a set of annual championship matches played in the US.

world-shaking and **world-shattering** ▷ *adj, colloq* extremely important or significant; momentous.

world war ▷ *noun* a war in which most of the major world powers take part, especially WORLD WAR I or WORLD WAR II.

World War I, the Great War and **First World War** ▷ *noun* the war (1914–18) in which the Central Powers (Germany, Austria-Hungary, Turkey and Bulgaria) were defeated by the Allies (Britain, France, Italy, Russia and later the US).

World War II and **Second World War** ▷ *noun* the war (1939–45) in which the Axis Powers (Germany, Italy and Japan) were defeated by the Allies (mainly Britain and countries of the British Commonwealth, the US and the then USSR).

worldweary ▷ *adj* tired of the world; bored of life. • **worldweariness** *noun*.

worldwide ▷ *adj, adverb* extending or known throughout the world.

World Wide Web ▷ *noun* (abbreviation **WWW**) a network of HYPERMEDIA files containing HYPERLINKS from one file to another over THE INTERNET, which allows the user to browse files containing related information from all over the world. ◎ 1990s.

WORM ▷ *abbreviation, computing* write once read many, a CD system that allows the user to store their own data, and then read it as often as they wish.

worm /wɜːm/ ▷ *noun* **1** *zool* any member of several unrelated groups of small soft-bodied limbless invertebrates that are characteristically long and slender, either cylindrical and segmented (eg the EARTHWORM) or flat (eg the TAPEWORM). **2** any superficially similar but unrelated animal, eg the larva of certain insects. **3** a maggot or worm thought to devour dead bodies in the grave. **4** a mean, contemptible, weak or worthless person. **5** *mech* the spiral thread of a screw. **6** anything that corrupts, gnaws or torments. **7** (**worms**) *pathol* any disease characterized by the presence of parasitic worms in the intestines of humans or animals. **8** *computing* an unauthorized computer program, differing from a virus in that it is an independent program rather than a piece of coding, designed to sabotage a computer system, especially by reproducing itself throughout a computer network. ▷ *verb* (*wormed, worming*) **1** to move or crawl like a worm. **2** (*also* **worm something out**) to extract (information, etc) little by little □ *wormed the secret out of them.* **3** to treat (an animal that has worms) especially to rid it of these. **4** to rid (a plant) of worms. • **wormer** *noun*. • **wormlike** *adj*. • **worm one's way** to wriggle or manoeuvre oneself gradually □ *wormed their way to the front.* • **worm one's way into something** to insinuate oneself into someone's favour or affections, etc. ◎ Anglo-Saxon *wyrm*.

wormcast ▷ *noun* a coiled heap of sand or earth excreted by a burrowing earthworm or lugworm.

worm-eaten ▷ *adj* **1** said eg of furniture: riddled with wormholes. **2** worn out; old.

worm gear ▷ *noun, mech* **1** a gear consisting of a shaft with a spiral thread that engages with and drives a toothed wheel. **2** (*also* **worm wheel**) the toothed wheel driven in this way.

wormhole ▷ *noun* a hole left by a burrowing grub, in eg furniture, books or fruit. • **wormholed** *adj*.

worm's eye view ▷ *noun* a view seen from a low or humble position.

wormwood ▷ *noun* **1** a bitter-tasting herb from which the flavouring for absinthe is obtained. **2** acute bitterness or chagrin, or a cause of this. ◎ Anglo-Saxon *wermod*.

wormy ▷ *adj* (*wormier, wormiest*) **1** similar to or full of worms. **2** relating to worms. **3** grovelling or sycophantic. • **worminess** *noun*.

worn[1] /wɔːn/ ▷ *adj* **1** haggard with weariness. **2** showing signs of deterioration through long use or wear. **3** exhausted. **4** too badly worn to be any further use; threadbare. ▷ *verb, past participle of* WEAR[1].

worn[2] *past participle of* WEAR[2]

worn out ▷ *adj* **1** damaged or rendered useless by wear. **2** extremely weary; exhausted. See also WEAR SOMETHING OR SOMEONE OUT at WEAR[1].

worriment /ˈwʌrɪmənt/ ▷ *noun, chiefly US colloq* worry; anxiety.

worrisome /ˈwʌrɪsəm/ ▷ *adj* **1** causing worry; perturbing or vexing. **2** said of a person: inclined to worry.

worry /ˈwʌrɪ/ ▷ *verb* (*worries, worried, worrying*) **1** *intr* to be anxious; to fret. **2** to make someone anxious. **3** to bother, pester or harass someone. **4** said of a dog: **a** to tear and pull something about with its teeth; **b** to chase and bite (sheep, etc). **5** (*often* **worry at something**) to try to solve (a problem, etc). ▷ *noun* (*worries*) **1** a state of anxiety. **2** a cause of anxiety. **3** the act of biting and pulling about with the teeth by a dog. • **worried** *adj*. • **worriedly** *adverb*. • **worrier** *noun*. • **worrying** *noun, adj*. • **worryingly** *adverb*. • **not to worry** *colloq* there is no cause for worry or alarm; never mind. ⓒ Anglo-Saxon *wyrgan* to strangle.

■ **worry along** or **through** to continue or progress, regardless of any problems or difficulties.

worry beads ▻ *noun* a string of beads for fiddling with, as a means of relieving mental tension and calming the nerves. ⓒ 1950s.

worryguts and (*especially US*) **worrywart** ▻ *singular noun, colloq* someone who worries unnecessarily and excessively.

worse /wɜːs/ ▻ *adj* **1** more bad □ *to be blind or deaf – which is worse?* **2** more ill. **3** more grave, serious or acute. **4** inferior in standard. ▻ *noun* something worse □ *Worse was to follow.* ▻ *adverb* less well; more badly □ *He's doing worse at school.* • **could** or **might do worse than** ... should consider (doing something) □ *You could do worse than end up with him.* • **go from bad to worse** to get worse; to deteriorate. • **none the worse for** ... unharmed by (an accident or bad experience, etc). • **the worse for something** showing the bad effects of it. • **the worse for wear 1** worn or shabby from use. **2** in poor condition. **3** drunk. • **worse off** in a worse situation, especially financially. ⓒ Anglo-Saxon *wyrsa*, the adjective form used as a comparative of BAD.

worsen /ˈwɜːsən/ ▻ *verb* (**worsened**, **worsening**) *tr & intr* to make or become worse. ⓒ 13c.

worship /ˈwɜːʃɪp/ ▻ *verb* (**worshipped**, **worshipping**) **1** *tr & intr* to honour (God or a god) with praise, prayer, hymns, etc. **2** to love or admire someone or something, especially blindly; to idolise them or it. **3** to glorify or exalt (material things, eg money). ▻ *noun* **1 a** the activity of worshipping; **b** the worship itself. **2** a religious service in which God or a god is honoured □ *morning worship.* **3** the title used to address or refer to a mayor or magistrate, usually in the form of **His** or **Her Worship** or **Your Worship**. • **worshipper** *noun*. ⓒ Anglo-Saxon *weorthscipe*, meaning 'worthship'.

worshipful ▻ *adj* **1** full of or showing reverence or adoration. **2** *old use* worthy of worship or honour. **3** (*usually* **Worshipful**) used as a term of respect in the titles of certain dignitaries. **4** worshipping; adoring. • **worshipfully** *adverb*. • **worshipfulness** *noun*.

worst /wɜːst/ ▻ *adj* **1** most bad, awful or unpleasant, etc. **2** most grave, severe, acute or dire. **3** most inferior; lowest in standard. ▻ *noun* **1** the worst thing, part or possibility. **2** the most advanced degree of badness. ▻ *adverb* most severely; most badly. ▻ *verb* (**worsted**, **worsting**) to defeat someone; to get the better of them. • **at its**, *etc* **worst** in the worst state or severest degree. • **at worst** or **at the worst 1** in the worst possible circumstances. **2** taking the most unfavourable or pessimistic view. • **do your worst** an indignant expression rejecting or defying a threat, etc. • **get the worst of** or **come off worst in something** to lose a fight or argument, etc. • **if the worst comes to the worst** if the worst happens. ⓒ Anglo-Saxon *wyrst*, the adjective form used as a superlative of BAD and ILL.

worsted /ˈwɜːstɪd/ ▻ *noun* **1** a fine strong twisted yarn spun out from long combed wool. **2** fabric woven from this. ⓒ 13c: named after Worstead, a village in Norfolk.

wort /wɜːt/ ▻ *noun* **1** *in compounds* a plant □ *liverwort.* **2** *brewing* a dilute solution or infusion of malt, fermented to make beer and whisky. ⓒ Anglo-Saxon *wyrt* plant or root.

worth /wɜːθ/ ▻ *noun* **1** value, importance or usefulness. **2** financial value. **3** the quantity of anything that can be bought for a certain sum, accomplished in a certain time, etc. ▻ *adj* **1** having a value of a specified amount. **2** *colloq* having money and property to a specified value. **3** justifying, deserving, meriting, repaying or warranting something □ *worth consideration.* • **for all one is worth** with all one's might. • **for all it's**, *etc* **worth** to the utmost. • **for what it's**, *etc* **worth** worthless though it, etc may be □ *You have my support, for what it's worth.* • **worth it** worthwhile. ⓒ Anglo-Saxon *weorth*.

worthless ▻ *adj* **1** having no value or significance. **2** having no merit or virtue; useless. • **worthlessly** *adverb*. • **worthlessness** *noun*.

worthwhile ▻ *adj* **1** worth the time, money or energy expended. **2** useful, beneficial or rewarding.

worthy /ˈwɜːðɪ/ ▻ *adj* (**worthier**, **worthiest**) **1** admirable, excellent or deserving. **2** *in compounds* **a** in good condition; fit for a specified use □ *roadworthy*; **b** deserving of a specified thing □ *trustworthy* □ *noteworthy*. ▻ *noun* (**worthies**) **1** *often patronizing* an esteemed person; a dignitary. **2** someone of notable and eminent worth. • **worthily** *adverb*. • **worthiness** *noun*. • **worthy of someone** suitable or appropriate for them. • **worthy of something** deserving it.

wot see under WIT²

wotcher /ˈwɒtʃə(r)/ ▻ *exclamation, slang* a greeting. ⓒ 19c: developed from the earlier phrase *what cheer?*, meaning 'how are you?'.

would /wʊd/ ▻ *auxiliary verb*, used: **1** in reported speech, as the past tense of WILL¹ □ *said she would leave at 10.* **2** to indicate willingness, readiness, or ability □ *was asked to help, but wouldn't* □ *The radio just would not work.* **3** to express probability □ *They would surely have heard.* **4** to indicate habitual action □ *would always telephone at six.* **5** to imply that some happening is predictable or unsurprising □ *'She refused, but I suppose she would.'* **6** to suggest obstinate resistance to advice □ *He would have his own way.* **7** to express frustration at some happening □ *It would rain, just as we're setting out.* **8** to express the probable outcome of a particular condition □ *In your place, I would have told her.* **9** to make polite invitations, offers or requests □ *Would you ring her back?* **10** to express a desire □ *I wish she would stop talking.* **11** in politely expressing and seeking opinions □ *I would suggest* □ *Would you not agree?* • **would that** ... *old use* if only ... □ *Would that I were twenty again.* See also SHOULD. ⓒ Anglo-Saxon *wolde*, past tense of *wyllan*.

would-be ▻ *adj* hoping, aspiring or professing to be a specified thing □ *a would-be actor.* ⓒ 14c.

wouldn't /ˈwʊdənt/ ▻ *contraction* would not.

wound¹ *past tense, past participle of* WIND²

wound² /wuːnd/ ▻ *noun* **1** any local injury to living tissue of a human, animal or plant, caused by an external physical means such as cutting, piercing, crushing or tearing. **2** an incision made by a surgeon. **3** an injury caused to pride, feelings or reputation, etc. ▻ *verb* (**wounded**, **wounding**) *tr & intr* **1** to inflict a wound on (a person, creature or limb, etc). **2** to injure (feelings, etc). • **wounding** *noun, adj*. ⓒ Anglo-Saxon *wund*.

wounded ▻ *adj* **1** hurt or injured, eg in a fight. **2** said of feelings: hurt. **3** (**the wounded**) injured people as a group (see THE 4b), especially those from a battle or fight.

woundwort ▻ *noun* any of several plants of the mint family, popularly believed to have wound-healing properties. ⓒ 16c.

wove *past tense of* WEAVE¹

woven *past participle of* WEAVE¹

wove paper ▻ *noun* a type of paper with a fine, uniformly smooth surface, made on a fine wire gauze sieve or mould.

wow¹ /waʊ/ *colloq* ▻ *exclamation* (*also* **wowee**) an exclamation of astonishment, admiration or wonder. ▻ *noun* a huge success. ▻ *verb* (**wowed**, **wowing**) to impress or amaze hugely. ⓒ 19c: originally Scots.

wow² /waʊ/ ▻ *noun, electronics* a repeated waver in the pitch of reproduced sound, usually caused by an irregularity in the operating speed of the recording or reproducing apparatus. ⓒ 1930s: imitating the sound.

wowser /ˈwaʊzə(r)/ ▻ *noun, Austral slang* **1** a puritanical person who tries to interfere with the pleasures of others; a spoilsport. **2** a teetotaller. ◎ Early 20c: from English dialect *wow*, meaning 'to complain'.

WP ▻ *abbreviation* **1** word processing. **2** word processor.

wp ▻ *abbreviation* weather permitting.

wpb ▻ *abbreviation* wastepaper basket.

WPC ▻ *abbreviation* Woman Police Constable.

wpm ▻ *abbreviation* words per minute.

WRAC ▻ *abbreviation* Women's Royal Army Corps.

wrack /rak/ ▻ *noun* **1** a type of seaweed, especially one of the large brown varieties, floating, cast-up or growing on the beach. **2** destruction or devastation. **3** a wreck or wreckage. ◎ 14c, meaning 'a wreck', and so later 'something cast up on the beach': from Dutch or German *wrak*; in sense 2, a variant of RACK².

WRAF ▻ *abbreviation* Women's Royal Air Force.

wraith /reɪθ/ ▻ *noun* **1** a ghost; a spectre. **2** any apparition, especially of a living person, believed to appear shortly before their death; a similar apparition appearing shortly after someone's death. **3** an extremely thin and pale person. • **wraithlike** *adj*. ◎ 16c: originally Scots.

wrangle /ˈraŋgəl/ ▻ *verb* (***wrangled, wrangling***) **1** *intr* to quarrel, argue or debate noisily or bitterly. **2** to obtain, persuade or spend time by wrangling. **3** *US* to herd (horses or cattle). ▻ *noun* **1** the act of disputing noisily. **2** a bitter dispute. • **wrangling** *noun, adj*. ◎ 14c: from German *wrangeln*.

wrangler ▻ *noun* **1** someone who disputes, especially angrily and noisily. **2** *US* a herdsman, especially of horses. **3** *Brit* in the University of Cambridge: a student who has gained first-class honours in the final mathematics examinations. ◎ 16c.

wrap /rap/ ▻ *verb* (***wrapped, wrapping***) **1** to fold or wind something round someone or something. **2** (*also* **wrap something up**) to cover or enfold it. **3** *literary* to embrace someone. ▻ *noun* **1** a warm garment, especially a shawl or stole for the shoulders. **2** a protective covering. **3** a wrapper. **4** *cinematog, TV* the completion of filming or recording, or the end of a session of filming or recording. • **keep something under wraps** *colloq* to keep it secret. • **take the wraps off something** *colloq* to reveal it to the public for the first time. • **wrapped up in someone** or **something** absorbed in them or it; engrossed by them or it. ◎ 14c.

▪ **wrap round 1** said eg of a piece of clothing: to pass right round with an overlap. See also WRAPAROUND 1. **2** *computing* said of text on a screen: to start a new line automatically as soon as the last character space on the previous line is filled. See also WRAPAROUND 2.

▪ **wrap something round oneself** or **someone** to draw or pull (a garment) close round them □ *She wrapped the scarf round her neck* □ *She wrapped the coat round his shoulders.*

▪ **wrap something round** something to crash (a vehicle) into (a post or tree, etc).

▪ **wrap up 1** to dress warmly □ *Wrap up warm before you leave!* **2** *slang* to be quiet.

▪ **wrap something up 1** *colloq* to finish it off or settle it finally. **2** to put and secure wrapping paper around it, especially a gift.

wraparound or **wrapround** ▻ *adj* **1** (*also* **wrapover**) said of clothing, eg a skirt or blouse: designed to wrap round with one edge overlapping the other and usually tied. **2** said of a windscreen or the cover of a book, etc: curving round in a uniform strip. ▻ *noun* **1** *computing* on a VDU: the automatic division of input into lines. See also WRAP ROUND 2 at WRAP. **2** *printing* a plate of flexible material, such as rubber, plastic or metal, that wraps round a cylindrical plate.

wrapper ▻ *noun* **1** someone or something that wraps. **2** a paper or cellophane cover round a packet or sweet, etc. **3** a paper band put round a newspaper or magazine for posting. **4** the dust jacket of a book. **5** a woman's loose dressing gown or negligee. **6** a high quality tobacco leaf encasing a cigar.

wrapping ▻ *noun* (*usually* **wrappings**) any of various types of cover, wrapper or packing material.

wrapping paper ▻ *noun* paper, either strong and coarse for sending packages through the post, or decorative for presenting a package as a gift.

wrasse /ras/ ▻ *noun* (***wrasses*** /ˈrasɪz/ or ***wrasse***) a brightly coloured bony sea fish with thick lips and powerful teeth. ◎ 17c: from Cornish *wrach*.

wrath /rɒθ/ ▻ *noun* **1** violent anger; resentment or indignation. **2** *literary* a fit of anger or fury. ◎ Anglo-Saxon *wræththo*.

wrathful ▻ *adj* **1** *literary* angry. **2** arising from, expressing or characterized by wrath. • **wrathfully** *adverb*. • **wrathfulness** *noun*.

wreak /riːk/ ▻ *verb* (***wreaked, wreaking***) **1** (*especially* **wreak havoc**) to cause (damage or chaos, etc) on a disastrous scale. **2** to take (vengeance or revenge) ruthlessly on someone. **3** to give unrestrained expression to (one's anger or hatred). **4** *archaic* to avenge. • **wreaker** *noun*. ◎ Anglo-Saxon *wrecan*.

wreath /riːθ/ ▻ *noun* (***wreaths*** /riːθs, riːðz/) **1** a ring-shaped garland of flowers and foliage placed on a grave or memorial as a tribute. **2** a similar garland hung up as a decoration, eg at Christmas. **3** *heraldry* a representation of such a garland beneath a crest. **4** a victor's crown of especially laurel leaves. **5** (*usually* **wreaths**) a ring, curl or spiral of smoke, mist, etc. **6** a single twist or coil in a helical object. ◎ Anglo-Saxon *writha* something coiled.

wreathe /riːð/ ▻ *verb* (***wreathed, wreathing***) **1** *intr* to coil, twine or intertwine. **2** to form something by twisting; to twist together. **3** to hang or encircle something with flowers, etc. **4** to cover or surround something (in smoke or mist, etc). **5** *intr* said of smoke, etc: to curl, coil or spiral. • **wreathed in smiles** smiling broadly or joyously. ◎ 16c.

wreck /rɛk/ ▻ *noun* **1** the destruction, especially accidental, of a ship at sea. **2** a hopelessly damaged sunken or grounded ship. **3** a crashed aircraft or a ruined vehicle. **4** *colloq* someone in a pitiful state of fitness or mental health. **5** something in so advanced a state of deterioration that it cannot be salvaged. **6** *colloq* a mess or shambles. **7** (*usually* **wreck of something**) the remains of something destroyed □ *a wreck of his former self.* ▻ *verb* (***wrecked, wrecking***) **1** to break or destroy something. **2** to spoil (plans, hopes, a holiday, relationship, etc). **3** to cause the wreck of (a ship, etc). **4** to involve someone or something in a wreck. • **wrecking** *noun, adj*. ◎ 13c: from Danish *wræce*.

wreckage /ˈrɛkɪdʒ/ ▻ *noun* **1** the act of wrecking. **2** the remains of things that have been wrecked. **3** wrecked material.

wrecked ▻ *adj, slang* said of a person: **1** extremely drunk, or heavily under the influence of drugs or a drug. **2** extremely tired. ◎ 1960s.

wrecker ▻ *noun* **1** someone or something that wrecks. **2** someone who criminally ruins anything. **3** *historical* someone who deliberately causes a wreck in order to plunder the wreckage. **4** *N Amer* a person or business whose job is to demolish buildings or vehicles, etc. **5** *N Amer* a breakdown vehicle.

wreckfish see STONE BASS

Wren /rɛn/ ▻ *noun* **1** a member of the Women's Royal Naval Service. **2** (**the Wrens**) the service itself. ◎ Early 20c: from the initials WRNS.

wren /rɛn/ ▷ *noun* **1** a very small songbird with short wings and a short erect tail. **2** any of several related small birds. ⓘ Anglo-Saxon *wrenna.*

wrench /rɛntʃ/ ▷ *verb* (***wrenches***, ***wrenched***, ***wrenching***) **1** (*often* **wrench something off** or **out**) to pull or twist it violently. **2** to sprain (an ankle, etc). **3** to twist or distort (a meaning). ▷ *noun* (***wrenches***) **1** an act or instance of wrenching. **2** a violent pull or twist. **3** an adjustable spanner-like tool for gripping and turning nuts and bolts, etc. **4** a painful parting or separation. ⓘ Anglo-Saxon *wrencan.*

■ **wrench someone away** to force them to leave.

wrest /rɛst/ ▷ *verb* (***wrested***, ***wresting***) **1** to turn or twist something. **2** to pull or wrench something away, especially from someone else's grasp or possession. **3** to extract (a statement or promise, etc) with force or difficulty. **4** to grab (victory) from the expected victor. **5** to distort or twist (words) from their true meaning. ▷ *noun* **1** the act of wresting. **2** *archaic* a wrench-like key for tuning a piano, harpsichord or harp, etc. • **wrester** *noun.* ⓘ Anglo-Saxon *wræstan.*

wrestle /ˈrɛsəl/ ▷ *verb* (***wrestled***, ***wrestling***) **1** *tr & intr* **a** to fight by trying to grip, throw and pinion one's opponent; **b** to force someone into some position in this way; **c** to do this as a sport. **2** *intr* to struggle intensely. **3** *intr* to move or proceed with great effort. **4** (*usually* **wrestle with something**) to apply oneself keenly to it. ▷ *noun* **1** a spell of wrestling. **2** a struggle. • **wrestler** *noun.* ⓘ Anglo-Saxon *wrestlian.*

■ **wrestle with** or **against someone** or **something** to struggle or fight with, or confront them or it.

wrestling ▷ *noun* **1** the activity of wrestlers. **2** the sport or exercise, governed by certain fixed rules, in which two people WRESTLE (*verb* 1).

wretch /rɛtʃ/ ▷ *noun* (***wretches***) **1** a miserable, unfortunate and pitiful person. **2** a worthless and despicable person. **3** *humorous* a shamelessly wicked person. ⓘ Anglo-Saxon *wrecca.*

wretched /ˈrɛtʃɪd/ ▷ *adj* **1** pitiable. **2** miserable, unhappy, distressed or distraught. **3** inferior or poor; humble or lowly. **4** infuriating. • **wretchedly** *adverb.* • **wretchedness** *noun.* ⓘ 13c.

wrick see RICK[2]

wriggle /ˈrɪɡəl/ ▷ *verb* (***wriggled***, ***wriggling***) **1** *tr & intr* to twist to and fro. **2** *tr & intr* to make (one's way) by this means. **3** *tr & intr* to move, advance or make (one's way) sinuously or deviously. ▷ *noun* a wriggling action or motion. • **wriggler** *noun.* • **wriggling** *noun.* • **wriggly** *adverb.* ⓘ 15c: from German *wriggeln.*

■ **wriggle out of something** to manage cleverly to evade or escape from (an awkward situation or disagreeable obligation, etc).

wright /raɪt/ ▷ *noun, usually in compounds* a maker, creator or repairer, usually of a specified thing □ *playwright* □ *shipwright.* ⓘ Anglo-Saxon *wryhta.*

wring /rɪŋ/ ▷ *verb* (***wrung*** /rʌŋ/, ***wringing***) **1** (*also* **wring something out**) to force liquid from it by twisting or squeezing. **2** to force (information or a consent, etc) from someone. **3** to break (the neck) of a bird, etc by twisting. **4** to keep clasping and twisting (one's hands) in distress or agitation. **5** to crush (someone's hand) in one's own, by way of greeting. **6** to tear at (the heart as the supposed seat of the emotions). • **wringing wet** soaking wet; saturated. ⓘ Anglo-Saxon *wringan.*

wringer ▷ *noun, historical* a machine with two rollers for squeezing water out of wet clothes.

wrinkle[1] /ˈrɪŋkəl/ ▷ *noun* **1** a crease or line in the skin, especially of the face, appearing with advancing age. **2** a slight crease or ridge in any surface. **3** a minor problem or difficulty to be smoothed out. ▷ *verb* (***wrinkled***, ***wrinkling***) *tr & intr* to develop or make something develop wrinkles. ⓘ Anglo-Saxon *wrinclian* to wind round.

wrinkle[2] /ˈrɪŋkəl/ ▷ *noun, colloq* a useful tip or trick; a handy hint. ⓘ Anglo-Saxon *wrenc* trick.

wrinkly ▷ *adj* (***wrinklier***, ***wrinkliest***) having or full of wrinkles. ▷ *noun* (*usually* **wrinklies**) *derog* an elderly person. ⓘ 16c; 1970s as *noun.*

wrist /rɪst/ ▷ *noun* **1** *anatomy* in terrestrial vertebrates: the joint formed by the RADIUS and three of the small bones of the hand. *Technical equivalent* CARPUS. **2** *anatomy* the region surrounding this joint. **3** the part of a sleeve that covers this. **4** a wrist pin. ⓘ Anglo-Saxon.

wristband ▷ *noun* **1** a band or part of the sleeve that covers the wrist. **2** a band worn round the wrist for a specific reason, eg at swimming pools, etc to show that the wearer has paid in order to make use of flumes, etc.

wristlet /ˈrɪstlət/ ▷ *noun* **1** a decorative or supporting band for the wrist, a bracelet. **2** a handcuff.

wrist pin ▷ *noun, mech* a pin joining the end of a connecting rod to the end of a piston rod.

wristwatch ▷ *noun* a WATCH (*noun* 1) worn strapped to the wrist.

wristy ▷ *adj* (***wristier***, ***wristiest***) said of a shot in golf, tennis, etc: made with extensive use of the wrist or wrists.

writ[1] /rɪt/ ▷ *noun* **1** a legal document issued by a court in the name of a sovereign, by which someone is summoned, or required to do or refrain from doing something. **2** *archaic* a writing. • **serve a writ on someone** to deliver a summons to them. ⓘ Anglo-Saxon in sense 2.

writ[2] ▷ *verb, archaic past tense, past participle of* WRITE. • **writ large 1** written in large letters. **2** on a large scale; very obvious.

write /raɪt/ ▷ *verb* (*past tense* ***wrote*** /roʊt/, *past participle* ***written*** /ˈrɪtən/, *present participle* ***writing***) **1** *tr & intr* to mark or produce (letters, symbols, numbers, words, sentences, etc) on a surface, especially paper, usually using a pen or pencil. **2 a** to compose or create (a book or music, etc) in manuscript, typescript or on computer, etc; **b** to be the author or composer of (a book or music, etc). **3** *intr* to compose novels or contribute articles to newspapers, etc, especially as a living. **4** to inscribe or engrave (a surface). **5** to make or fill in (a document or form, etc). **6** *tr & intr* to compose (a letter, etc) □ *I must write to him.* **7** to say or express in a letter, article or book, etc. **8** to put up-to-date information in (a diary, etc). **9** to include (a condition, etc) in a contract, or will, etc. **10** to underwrite (an insurance policy). **11** to fill (pages or sheets, etc) with writing. **12** to display clearly □ *Guilt was written all over his face.* **13** to decree or foretell. **14** *computing* to transfer (data) to a memory or storage device. ⓘ Anglo-Saxon *writan.*

■ **write something down 1** to put it down or record it in writing. **2** to reduce its accounting value. See also WRITE-DOWN.

■ **write down to someone** to write in a simplified style for their benefit.

■ **write in** to write a letter formally to an organization, TV programme, etc.

■ **write off** to write and send a letter of request □ *I wrote off for a catalogue.*

■ **write something off 1** to damage a vehicle (in a crash) beyond repair. See also WRITE-OFF. **2** to cancel (a debt). **3** to discontinue (a project, etc) because it is likely to fail. **4** to dismiss something as being of no importance.

■ **write something out 1** to write it in full; to copy or transcribe it. **2** to remove a character or scene from a film or serial, etc.

■ **write something up** 1 to write or rewrite it in a final form. 2 to bring (a diary or accounts, etc) up to date. 3 to write about it or review it, especially approvingly. See also WRITE-UP.

write-down ▷ *noun, business* a reduction in the book value of an asset, etc. ◷ 1930s.

write-off ▷ *noun* something that is written off, especially a motor vehicle involved in an accident. ◷ Early 20c.

writer ▷ *noun* **1** someone who writes, especially as a living; an author. **2** someone who has written a particular thing. **3** someone who writes music. **4** a WRITER TO THE SIGNET. **5** in Scotland: an ordinary legal practioner in a country town. **6** a professional clerk or scribe. **7** someone who paints lettering for signs. ◷ Anglo-Saxon.

writer's block ▷ *noun* a temporary lack of enthusiasm and imagination that affects fiction writers.

writer's cramp ▷ *noun* painful muscular cramp of the hand brought on by intensive writing.

Writer to the Signet ▷ *noun* (abbreviation **WS**) a member of an ancient society of solicitors in Scotland who formerly had the exclusive right to prepare all summonses and other writs relating to the supreme court of justice, and still have the exclusive privilege of preparing crown writs.

write-up ▷ *noun* an written or published account, especially a review in a newspaper or magazine, etc. ◷ Late 19c.

writhe /raɪð/ ▷ *verb* (***writhed***, ***writhing***) *intr* **1** to twist violently, especially in pain or discomfort; to squirm. **2** *colloq* to feel painfully embarrassed or humiliated. ▷ *noun* the action of writhing; a twist or contortion. • **writhing** *noun, adj*. • **writhingly** *adverb*. ◷ Anglo-Saxon *writhan* to twist.

writing ▷ *noun* **1** written or printed words. **2** handwriting. **3 a** a literary composition; **b** the art or activity of literary composition. **4** (*usually* **writings**) literary work. **5** a form of script □ *Chinese writing.* • **in writing** said of a promise or other commitment: in written form, especially as being firm proof of intention, etc.

writing case ▷ *noun* a portable case for carrying materials, eg paper and envelopes, etc, for writing.

writing desk ▷ *noun* a desk with a surface (sometimes a sloping one) for writing on, and usually compartments and divisions for stationery and papers, etc.

the writing on the wall and *US* **the handwriting on the wall** ▷ *noun* an occurrence or sign foretelling downfall or disaster. ◷ 13c: a reference from the Bible, Daniel 5.5.

writing pad ▷ *noun* a pad of paper for writing letters.

writing paper ▷ *noun* paper for writing letters on.

written /ˈrɪtən/ ▷ *adj* expressed in writing, and so undeniable □ *a written undertaking* □ *written law.* ▷ *verb, past participle of* WRITE.

written law ▷ *noun* statute law, as distinguished from common law.

the written word ▷ *noun* written language, as distinct from spoken language.

WRNS ▷ *abbreviation* Women's Royal Naval Service. See also WREN.

wrong /rɒŋ/ ▷ *adj* **1** not correct. **2** mistaken. **3** not appropriate or suitable. **4** not good or sensible; unjustifiable. **5** morally bad; wicked. **6** defective or faulty. **7** amiss; causing trouble, pain, etc. **8** said of one side of a fabric or garment, etc: intended as the inner or unseen side. **9** not socially acceptable. ▷ *adverb* **1** incorrectly. **2** improperly; badly. ▷ *noun* **1** whatever is not right or just. **2** any injury done to someone else. **3** *law* an offence, either against an individual (**private wrong**) or against the public or society (**public wrong**). ▷ *verb* (***wronged***, ***wronging***) **1** to treat someone unjustly; to do wrong to someone. **2** to judge unfairly. **3** to deprive someone of some right; to defraud. • **wronger** *noun*. • **wrongly** *adverb* in the wrong direction or way. • **wrongness** *noun*. • **don't get me wrong** *colloq* don't misinterpret or misunderstand me. • **get on the wrong side of someone** *colloq* to antagonize them; to make them displeased or annoyed with one. • **get out of bed on the wrong side** to get up in the morning in a bad mood. • **get something wrong 1** to give the incorrect answer to it, or do it incorrectly. **2** to misunderstand it. • **go wrong 1** said of plans, etc: to fail to go as intended. **2** to make an error. **3** to stray morally; to fall into bad ways. **4** said of a mechanical device: to stop functioning properly. • **in the wrong** guilty of an error or injustice. ◷ Anglo-Saxon *wrang*.

wrongdoer ▷ *noun* someone guilty of an evil, immoral or illegal act. • **wrongdoing** *noun* evil or wicked action or behaviour. ◷ 14c.

wrongfoot ▷ *verb* (***wrongfooted***, ***wrongfooting***) **1** *tennis, etc* to catch (one's opponent) off balance by making an unpredictable shot, etc to a point away from the direction in which they are moving or preparing to move. **2** to contrive to place (an opponent in a dispute, etc) at a tactical or moral disadvantage; to disconcert them. ◷ 1920s.

wrongful ▷ *adj* unlawful; unjust. • **wrongfully** *adverb*. • **wrongfulness** *noun*.

wrong-headed ▷ *adj* obstinate and stubborn, adhering wilfully to wrong principles and/or policy. • **wrong-headedly** *adverb*. • **wrong-headedness** *noun*.

wrongly see under WRONG

wrong number ▷ *noun* **1** a telephone number that a caller is connected to in error, especially through misdialling. **2** a call that involves such a misconnection.

wrote *past tense of* WRITE

wroth /roʊθ, rɒθ/ ▷ *adj, old use* angry; full of wrath. ◷ Anglo-Saxon *wrath*.

wrought /rɔːt/ ▷ *adj* **1** *old use* made, formed or shaped; fashioned. **2** *old use* decorated or ornamented. **3** said of metal: beaten into shape with tools, as distinct from being cast. ◷ 13c: an old *past participle* of WORK.

wrought iron ▷ *noun* a malleable form of iron with a very low carbon content, but containing small amounts of slag as evenly distributed threads or fibres that render it tough and ductile. Also (**wrought-iron**) *as adj*.

wrought-up ▷ *adj* over-excited; in an agitated condition.

WRP ▷ *abbreviation* Workers' Revolutionary Party.

wrung *past tense and past participle of* WRING

WRVS ▷ *abbreviation* Women's Royal Voluntary Service.

wry /raɪ/ ▷ *adj* (***wryer***, ***wryest***) **1** said eg of a smile: slightly mocking or bitter; ironic. **2** said of a facial expression: with the features distorted or twisted into a grimace, in reaction to a bitter taste, etc. **3** said of humour: dry. **4** twisted to one side; awry. • **wryly** *adverb*. • **wryness** *noun*. ◷ Anglo-Saxon *wrigian* to turn or twist.

wrybill ▷ *noun* a New Zealand bird related to the plover, with a bill that bends sideways which it uses to obtain food from under stones.

wryneck ▷ *noun* **1** a small woodpecker, native to Europe, Asia and N Africa, with a mottled greyish-brown plumage, a short bill and a long tail, and which twists its head to look backwards over its shoulder when alarmed. **2** *pathol* TORTICOLLIS.

WS ▷ *abbreviation* **1** *IVR* Western Samoa. **2** Writer to the Signet.

WSW ▷ *abbreviation* west-south-west.

wt ▷ *abbreviation* weight.

wunderkind /ˈvʊndəkɪnt/ ▷ *noun* (***wunderkinds*** or ***wunderkinder*** /-kɪndə(r)/) **1** a child prodigy. **2** someone who shows great talent and achieves remarkable success early in life. ◎ Late 19c: German, literally 'wonder child'.

wurst /vʊəst, wɜːst/ ▷ *noun* any of various types of large German or Austrian sausage. ◎ Late 19c: from German, meaning 'something rolled', related to Latin *vertere* to turn.

wuss /wʊs/ or **wussy** ▷ *noun* (***wusses*** or ***wussies***) *N Amer slang* a weakling; a feeble person. • **wussy** *adj.*

wuthering /ˈwʌðərɪŋ/ ▷ *adj* **1** said of wind: to blow strongly and with a roaring sound. **2** said of a place: characterized by windy weather of this kind. ◎ 19c: from dialect *wuther* to roar or bluster; related to Norse *hvitha* squalt.

WV ▷ *abbreviation* **1** *IVR* St Vincent, Windward Islands. **2** *US state* West Virginia. Also written **W.Va.**

WVS ▷ *abbreviation, historical* Women's Voluntary Service (now WRVS).

WWF ▷ *abbreviation* World Wide Fund for Nature (*formerly* World Wildlife Fund).

WWW or (in Web addresses) **www** ▷ *abbreviation* World Wide Web.

WY ▷ *abbreviation, US state* Wyoming. Also written **Wy.** or **Wyo.**

Wy ▷ *abbreviation* in street names: Way.

Wyandot or **Wyandotte** /ˈwaɪəndɒt/ ▷ *noun* (***Wyandots*** or ***Wyandot***) **1** a member of a Native American tribe. **2** the language spoken by this tribe. **3** (*usually* **Wyandotte**) a medium-sized breed of domestic fowl of American origin. ◎ 18c: from French *Ouendat*, from the tribal name *Wendat*.

wych-elm or **witch elm** /ˈwɪtʃɛlm/ ▷ *noun* a deciduous tree of the elm family, native to N Europe and Asia, that has a broadly domed crown, arching lower branches and smooth grey bark that becomes darker and ridged with age. ◎ Anglo-Saxon *wice* a tree with pliant branches.

wych hazel see WITCH HAZEL

wyn or **wynn** /wɪn/ ▷ *noun* a rune ƿ with the value of modern English *w*, adopted into the Anglo-Saxon alphabet. See also WEN. ◎ Anglo-Saxon *wynn* joy (of which *w* is the initial letter).

wynd /waɪnd/ ▷ *noun, Scottish* a narrow lane or alley leading off a main street in a town. ◎ 15c: from WIND².

Wyo. see under WY

WYSIWYG or **wysiwyg** /ˈwɪzɪwɪg/ ▷ *acronym, computing* what you see is what you get, indicating that the type and characters appearing on screen are as they will appear on the print-out. ◎ 1980s.

wyvern or **wivern** /ˈwaɪvən/ ▷ *noun, heraldry* a fictitious monster with wings, two legs and a barbed tail, that combines the characteristics of a dragon and griffin. ◎ 17c: from Norse *wivre*, from Latin *vipera* VIPER

X

X¹ or **x** /ɛks/ ▻ *noun* (*Xs, X's* or *x's*) **1** the twenty-fourth letter of the English alphabet. **2** anything shaped like an X. **3** an unknown or unnamed person.

X² ▻ *symbol* **1** *math* (*usually* **x**) an unknown quantity; the first of a pair or group of unknown quantities. See also Y³, Z³. **2** the Roman numeral for 10. **3** a film classified as suitable for people over the age of 17 (in the USA) or 18 (in the UK; now replaced by '18'). **4** a mark used **a** to symbolize a kiss; **b** to indicate an error; **c** as the signature of an illiterate person, etc. **5** Christ, as in XMAS. ⓘ from X = chi, letter of the Greek alphabet, and the first letter of *Christos*, the Greek form of *Christ*.

xanth- /zanθ/ or (before a consonant) **xantho-** ▻ *combining form, technical, denoting* yellow. ⓘ From Greek *xanthos* yellow.

xanthene /ˈzanθiːn/ ▻ *noun* (*xanthenes*) *chem* a white or yellowish crystalline compound, used as a fungicide and as a source of various dyes. ⓘ Early 20c.

xanthoma /zanˈθoʊmə/ ▻ *noun* (*xanthomata* /-mətə/ or *xanthomas*) *medicine* a small yellowish lump or swelling in the skin, often on the eyelid, formed by deposits of fat, and usually a symptom of high blood cholesterol levels. ⓘ 19c.

x-axis ▻ *noun, math* in a graph: the horizontal axis along which the x-coordinate is plotted. See also Y-AXIS, Z-AXIS.

X-chromosome ▻ *noun, biol* the sex chromosome that when present as one half of an identical pair determines the female sex in most animals, including humans. See also Y-CHROMOSOME.

Xe ▻ *symbol, chem* xenon.

xeno- /zɛnoʊ, zɛˈnɒ/ or (before a vowel) **xen-** ▻ *combining form, denoting* **1** strange; foreign. **2** stranger; foreigner. ⓘ From Greek *xenos*.

xenoglossia /zɛnoʊˈglɒsɪə/ ▻ *noun* in psychical research: the spontaneous use of a language which the speaker has never heard or learned. Compare GLOSSOLALIA. ⓘ 1980s: from XENO- + Greek *glossa* tongue.

xenolith ▻ *noun, geol* a piece of foreign material that occurs within a body of igneous rock. ⓘ 20c.

xenon /ˈzɛnɒn, ˈziːnɒn/ ▻ *noun, chem* (symbol **Xe**, atomic number 54) an element, a colourless odourless inert gas, one of the NOBLE GASes, used in fluorescent lamps, photographic flash tubes, and lasers. ⓘ 19c: from Greek *xenos* stranger.

xenophobia ▻ *noun* intense fear or dislike of foreigners or strangers. • **xenophobe** *noun*. • **xenophobic** *adj*. ⓘ Early 20c.

xero- /zɪəroʊ, zɪəˈrɒ/ or (before a vowel) **xer-** ▻ *combining form, signifying* dry. ⓘ From Greek *xeros* dry.

xerography /zɪəˈrɒgrəfɪ/ ▻ *noun* an electrostatic printing process used to make photocopies of printed documents or illustrations. • **xerographic** *adj*. ⓘ 1940s.

xerophthalmia /zɪərɒfˈθalmɪə/ ▻ *noun, pathol* an abnormal condition in which the conjunctiva of the eye becomes dry and lustreless, caused by a dietary deficiency of vitamin A. ⓘ 17c: Latin, from Greek.

xerophyte /ˈzɪəroʊfaɪt/ ▻ *noun, bot* a plant that is adapted to grow under conditions where water is very scarce and that often shows structural modifications, eg swollen stems or leaves reduced to spines. ⓘ 1890s.

Xerox /ˈzɪərɒks/ ▻ *noun* (*Xeroxes*) *trademark* **1** a type of xerographic process. **2** a copying-machine using this process. **3** a photocopy made by such a process. ▻ *verb* (*usually* **xerox**) (*xeroxes, xeroxed, xeroxing*) to photocopy something using this process. ⓘ 1950s: see XEROGRAPHY.

Xhosa /ˈkoʊsə, -zə ˌhoʊ-/ ▻ *noun* (*Xhosa* or *Xhosa*) **1** a group of Bantu-speaking peoples of the Transkei and Ciskei, S Africa. **2** an individual belonging to this group of peoples. **3** their language. ▻ *adj* belonging or relating to this group or their language. • **Xhosan** *adj*.

xi /ksaɪ/ ▻ *noun* (*xis*) the fourteenth letter of the Greek alphabet. See table at GREEK ALPHABET.

Xmas /ˈɛksməs, ˈkrɪsməs/ ▻ *noun, informal* Christmas. ⓘ 18c: X² sense 5 + -MAS.

X-ray ▻ *noun* **1** an electromagnetic ray which can pass through many substances that are opaque to light, producing on photographic film an image of the object passed through. **2** a photograph taken using X-rays. **3** a medical examination using X-rays. **4** (**Xray**) *communications* in the NATO alphabet: the word used to denote the letter 'X' (see table at NATO ALPHABET). ▻ *verb* (*X-rayed, X-raying*) to take a photograph of something using X-rays. ⓘ 1890s: X² (called X because at the time of their discovery in 1895, the nature of the rays was unknown) + RAY¹.

X-ray astronomy ▻ *noun, astron* the study of X-ray emissions from celestial objects, using instruments mounted on rockets or satellites.

X-ray crystallography ▻ *noun, chem* the study of the arrangement of atoms within a crystal by analysis of the X-RAY DIFFRACTION pattern.

X-ray diffraction ▻ *noun, chem* the characteristic interference pattern produced when X-rays are passed through a crystal, often used to determine the arrangement of atoms within crystals.

xylem /ˈzaɪləm/ ▻ *noun, bot* the woody tissue that transports water and mineral nutrients from the roots to all other parts of a plant, and also provides structural support. Compare PHLOEM. ⓘ 19c: German, from Greek *xylon* wood.

xylene /ˈzaɪliːn/ and **xylol** /ˈzaɪlɒl/ ▻ *noun, chem* (formula $C_6H_4(CH_3)_2$) a colourless liquid hydrocarbon obtained from coal tar, etc, and used as a solvent and in the preparation of specimens for microscopy and the manufacture of organic chemical compounds. ⓘ 19c.

xylo- /zaɪloʊ, zaɪˈlɒ/ or (before a vowel) **xyl-** ▻ *combining form, signifying* wood. ⓘ From Greek *xylon* wood.

xylophone /ˈzaɪloʊfoʊn/ ▻ *noun* (*xylophones*) a musical instrument consisting of a series of wooden or sometimes metal bars of different lengths, played by being struck by wooden hammers. • **xylophonist** /zaɪˈlɒfənɪst/ *noun*. ⓘ 19c.

Y

Y[1] or **y** /waɪ/ ▷ *noun* (***Ys, Y's*** or ***y's***) **1** the twenty-fifth letter of the English alphabet. **2** anything shaped like the letter Y □ ***Y-junction.***

Y[2] ▷ *abbreviation* yen.

Y[3] ▷ *symbol* **1** *chem* yttrium. **2** *math* (*usually* **y**) the second of two or three unknown quantities. See also X[2], Z[3].

the Y ▷ *noun, colloq* **1** the YMCA. **2** the YWCA. ◷ 20c abbreviation.

y see under Y[3]

-y[1] /ɪ/ ▷ *suffix, forming adjectives* (***-ier, -iest***) *signifying* full of; characterized by; having the quality of; keen on, etc □ ***spotty*** □ ***icy*** □ ***shiny*** □ ***horsey.*** ◷ From Anglo-Saxon *-ig.*

-y[2] or **-ey** /ɪ/ ▷ *suffix, forming nouns* (*plural* ***-ies***) *indicating* **1** a diminutive or term of affection □ ***doggy*** □ ***daddy.*** **2** someone or something with a specified characteristic □ ***fatty.*** ◷ Originally Scots, used in familiar forms of names.

-y[3] /ɪ/ ▷ *suffix, forming nouns* (*plural* ***-ies***) *signifying* **1** a quality or state □ ***jealousy*** □ ***modesty.*** **2** an action □ ***entreaty*** □ ***expiry.*** ◷ From French *-ie.*

yacht /jɒt/ ▷ *noun* a boat or small ship, usually with sails and often with an engine, built for racing or cruising. ◷ 16c: from Dutch *jachtschip* chasing ship.

yacht club ▷ *noun* a club for yacht-owners.

yachting ▷ *noun* sailing in yachts, especially as a sport.

yachtsman and **yachtswoman** ▷ *noun* a person who sails a yacht.

yack or **yak** *derog slang* ▷ *exclamation* imitating the sound of persistent annoying chatter. ▷ *verb* (***yacked, yacking; yakked, yakking***) *intr* to talk at length and often foolishly or annoyingly. ▷ *noun* persistent, foolish or annoying chatter. ◷ 1950s.

yackety-yak /jakətɪ'jak/ ▷ *exclamation, verb, noun* YACK.

yah /jɑː/ ▷ *exclamation* **1** expressing scorn or contempt. **2** *colloq* often attributed to an upper-class or affected speaker: yes.

yahoo[1] /jɑː'huː/ ▷ *noun* (***yahoos***) a lout or ruffian. ◷ 18c: named after the brutish characters that looked like humans in Swift's *Gulliver's Travels.*

yahoo[2] /jaː'huː, jə'huː/ ▷ *exclamation* expressing happiness, excitement, etc.

Yajur-veda see VEDA

yak[1] ▷ *noun* (***yaks*** or ***yak***) a large ox-like Tibetan mammal with a stocky body, a thick shaggy black coat, humped shoulders, a white muzzle and large upward-curving horns. ◷ 18c: from Tibetan *gyag.*

yak[2] see YACK

yakitori /jakɪ'tɔːrɪ/ ▷ *noun, cookery* a Japanese dish of boneless pieces of chicken grilled on skewers and basted with a thick sweet sauce of sake, mirin and soy sauce. ◷ 1960s: Japanese, from *yaki* grill + *tori* bird.

yakked and **yakking** see under YACK

Yakut /jɑː'kuːt/ ▷ *noun* **1** a Turkic people of NE Siberia. **2** an individual belonging to this group. **3** their language. ▷ *adj* belonging or relating to this group. ◷ 18c: Russian.

Yale lock /jeɪl —/ ▷ *noun, trademark* a type of lock operated by a flat key with a notched upper edge (a **Yale key**). ◷ 19c: named after Linus Yale (1821–68), US locksmith.

y'all see under YOU

yam ▷ *noun* **1** any of various perennial climbing plants cultivated in tropical and subtropical regions for their thick edible tubers. **2** the thick starchy tuber of some species of this plant, a major food crop in SE Asia, W Africa, and Central and S America. **3** *N Amer* a sweet potato. ◷ 17c: from Portuguese *inhame.*

yammer /'jamə(r)/ ▷ *verb* (***yammered, yammering***) **1** *intr* to complain whiningly; to grumble. **2** *intr* to talk loudly and at length. **3** to say something, especially as a complaint, loudly and at length. ▷ *noun* the act or sound of yammering. ◷ 15c as *yamer*: from Anglo-Saxon *geomrian.*

yang see under YIN

Yank ▷ *noun, colloq* a person from the US. ◷ 18c: short form of YANKEE.

yank *colloq* ▷ *noun* a sudden sharp pull. ▷ *verb* (***yanked, yanking***) *tr & intr* to pull suddenly and sharply. ◷ 19c: originally US.

Yankee /'jaŋkɪ/ ▷ *noun* (***Yankees***) **1** *Brit colloq* a person from the US. **2** *N Amer, especially US* a person from New England or from any of the northern states of America. **3** *communications* in the NATO alphabet: the word used to denote the letter 'Y' (see table at NATO ALPHABET). ◷ 18c: perhaps from Dutch *Jan Kees* John Cheese, the nickname given by the New York Dutch to the British settlers in Connecticut.

yap ▷ *verb* (***yapped, yapping***) *intr* **1** said of a puppy or small dog: to give a high-pitched bark. **2** *derog colloq* said of a person: to talk continually in a shrill voice, often about trivial matters. ▷ *noun* a short high-pitched bark. • **yapper** *noun.* • **yapping** *noun.* ◷ 17c as *yapping*: imitating the sound.

yappy ▷ *adj* (***yappier, yappiest***) said of a dog: inclined to yap.

the Yard ▷ *noun, colloq* New Scotland Yard, the headquarters of the London Metropolitan Police.

yard[1] ▷ *noun* **1** in the imperial system: a unit of length equal to 3 feet (0.9144m). **2** *naut* a long beam hung on a mast, from which to hang a sail. ◷ Anglo-Saxon *gierd* rod.

yard[2] ▷ *noun* **1** *often in compounds* an area of enclosed ground associated with a building. **2** *often in compounds* an area of enclosed ground used for a special industrial purpose □ ***a shipyard.*** **3** *N Amer* a garden. ◷ Anglo-Saxon *geard* fence or enclosure.

yardage ▷ *noun* (***yardages***) the length (or (*rare*) the area or volume) of something, measured in yards.

yard-arm ▷ *noun, naut* either of the tapering end-sections of a YARD[1]).

Yardie ▷ *noun* (***Yardies***) a member of a criminal organization, originally from and based in Kingston, Jamaica, that is involved in drug-dealing and related crime. ◷ 1980s: from Jamaican English *yard* a home, dwelling, or (by Jamaicans abroad) Jamaica.

yardstick ▷ *noun* **1** a standard for comparison. **2** a stick exactly one YARD[1] long, used for measuring.

yarmulka or **yarmulke** /'jɑːməlkə/ ▷ *noun* (***yarmulkas*** or ***yarmulkes***) a skullcap worn by Jewish men on ceremonial or ritual occasions, and at all times by the orthodox. ◷ 20c: Yiddish.

yarn ▷ *noun* **1** thread spun from wool, cotton, etc. **2** a story or tale, often a lengthy and incredible one. **3** *colloq* a lie. • **spin someone a yarn** *colloq* to tell them a long or untruthful story. ◷ Anglo-Saxon *gearn*.

yarrow /ˈjaroʊ/ ▷ *noun* a creeping perennial plant, formerly used widely in herbal medicine, with finely divided aromatic leaves and white or pink flower-heads in dense flat-topped clusters. ◷ Anglo-Saxon *gearwe*.

yashmak /ˈjaʃmak/ ▷ *noun* a veil worn by Muslim women that covers the face below the eyes. ◷ 19c: from Arabic *yashmaq*.

yaw ▷ *verb* (***yawed, yawing***) **1** *intr* said of a ship: to move temporarily from, or fail to keep to, the direct line of its course. **2** *intr* said of an aircraft: to deviate horizontally from the direct line of its course. **3** *intr* to move unsteadily; to zigzag. **4** to make (a boat or aircraft) yaw. ▷ *noun* an act of yawing. ◷ 16c.

yawl ▷ *noun* **1** a type of small fishing- or sailing-boat, especially one with two masts. **2** a ship's small boat, usually with four or six oars. ◷ 17c: from Dutch *jol*.

yawn ▷ *verb* (***yawned, yawning***) *intr* **1** to open one's mouth wide and take a deep involuntary breath when tired or bored. **2** said of a hole, gap, etc: to be or become wide open. ▷ *noun* **1** an act or an instance of yawning. **2** *colloq* a boring or tiresome event, person, etc. • **yawning** *adj* said of a hole, etc: wide; large. ◷ Anglo-Saxon *ganian* to yawn, and *geonian* to gape widely.

yaws /jɔːz/ ▷ *singular noun, pathol* an infectious skin disease of tropical countries, characterized by red ulcerating sores. ◷ 17c.

y-axis ▷ *noun, math* in a graph: the vertical axis along which the y-coordinate is plotted. See also X-AXIS, Z-AXIS.

Yb ▷ *symbol, chem* ytterbium.

YC *Brit* ▷ *abbreviation* Young Conservatives. ▷ *noun* (***YCs***) a member of the Young Conservatives.

Y-chromosome ▷ *noun, biol* the smaller of the two sex chromosomes, whose presence determines the male sex in most animals. See also X-CHROMOSOME.

Y-connection see STAR CONNECTION

yd ▷ *abbreviation* yard, or yards.

ye¹ /jiː, jɪ/ ▷ *pronoun, archaic or dialect* you (plural). ◷ Anglo-Saxon *ge*.

ye² /jiː, jɪ/ ▷ *definite article, old or affected use* the □ ***Ye Olde Englishe Tea Shoppe.*** ◷ 15c: from the use of *y* by medieval printers as a substitute for the old letter þ which represented the *th*-sound.

yea /jeɪ/ *formal or old use* ▷ *exclamation* yes. ▷ *noun* (***yeas***) **a** a yes; **b** a person who has voted or is voting yes. See also AYE. ◷ Anglo-Saxon *gea*.

yeah /jɛ, jɛə/ ▷ *exclamation, colloq* yes.

year /jɪə(r), jɜː(r)/ ▷ *noun* **1 a** the period of time the Earth takes to go once round the Sun, about 365 ¹/₄ days; **b** the equivalent time for any other planet. 2 (*also* **calendar year**) the period between 1 January and 31 December, 365 days in a normal year, 366 days in a leap year. **3** any period of twelve months. **4** a period of less than 12 months during which some activity is carried on □ ***an academic year runs from September to June.*** **5** a period of study at school, college, etc over an academic year □ ***She's in third year now.*** **6** students at a particular stage in their studies, considered as a group □ ***had a meeting with the third year this morning.*** See also YEARS. **7** *colloq, in compounds* a student belonging to a specified year □ ***He's a second-year now.*** • **since the year dot** used when exaggerating a period of time: since the beginning of time. • **year in, year out** happening, done, etc every year, with tedious regularity. ◷ Anglo-Saxon *gear*.

yearbook ▷ *noun* a book of information updated and published every year, especially one that records the events, etc of the previous year.

yearling ▷ *noun* **1 a** an animal which is a year old; **b** a racehorse during the calendar year following the 1 January after its birth. **2** *finance* a bond that matures after one year. Also *as adj.* ▷ *adj* said of an animal: one-year-old.

yearlong ▷ *adj* lasting all year.

yearly ▷ *adj* **1** happening, etc every year. **2** valid for one year. ▷ *adverb* every year. See also ANNUAL.

yearn /jɜːn/ ▷ *verb* (***yearned, yearning***) *intr* **1** (**yearn for** or **after something** or **to do something**) to feel a great desire for it; to long for it. **2** to feel compassion. • **yearner** *noun*. • **yearning** *noun, adj*. • **yearningly** *adverb*. ◷ Anglo-Saxon *giernan* to desire.

year of grace and **year of our Lord** ▷ *noun, Christianity* or *archaic* used in giving dates in the Christian era. See also AD.

year-on-year ▷ *adj, econ* said of figures: set against figures for the equivalent period in the previous year.

year-round ▷ *adj* open all year; lasting throughout the year.

years ▷ *plural noun* **1** age □ ***He is wise for his years.*** **2** *colloq* a very long time □ ***She's been coming for years.*** **3** some period of time in the past or future □ ***in years gone by.***

yeas *plural of* YEA

yeast ▷ *noun* **1** any of various single-celled fungi that are capable of fermenting carbohydrates, widely used in the brewing and baking industries, and in genetic and biochemical research. **2** something that is a catalyst for change. ◷ Anglo-Saxon *gist*.

yeast-plant ▷ *noun, bot, brewing, etc* a yeast that causes fermentation in saccharine fluids.

yeasty ▷ *adj* (***yeastier, yeastiest***) **1** consisting, tasting or smelling of yeast. **2** frothy. **3** trivial.

yell ▷ *noun* (***yelled, yelling***) a loud shout or cry. ▷ *verb* (***yelled, yelling***) *tr & intr* to shout or cry out. ◷ Anglo-Saxon *gellan*.

yellow /ˈjɛloʊ/ ▷ *adj* (***yellower, yellowing***) **1** of the colour of gold, butter, egg-yolk, a lemon, etc. **2** *derog, colloq* cowardly. **3** *often offensive* when used as a term of racial description: having a yellow or yellowish skin. **4** said of journalism: sensationalist. ▷ *noun* **1** any shade of the colour of gold, butter, egg-yolk, etc. **2** something, eg material or paint, that is yellow in colour. ▷ *verb* (***yellowed, yellowing***) *tr & intr* to make or become yellow. • **yellowish** *adj*. • **yellowness** *noun*. • **yellowy** *adj*. ◷ Anglo-Saxon *geolu*.

yellow alert ▷ *noun* a security alert one stage less serious than a RED ALERT.

yellow-belly *slang* ▷ *noun* a coward. • **yellow-bellied** *adj*.

yellow card ▷ *noun* **1** *football* a yellow-coloured card shown by the referee as a warning to a player being cautioned for a serious violation of the rules. Compare RED CARD. **2** any similar cautionary warning, or a symbol of such a warning.

yellow fever ▷ *noun, pathol* an acute viral disease of tropical America and W Africa, transmitted by the bite of a mosquito and causing high fever, jaundice and haemorrhaging.

yellowhammer ▷ *noun* a large brightly-coloured bunting with a yellow head and underparts, streaky brown plumage on its back and wings, a chestnut back and rump, and a long notched tail.

yellow jersey ▷ *noun* in the Tour de France cycle race: any of the jerseys awarded to and worn in turn by each winner of a stage.

yellow line ▷ *noun* a yellow-painted line on a road indicating restrictions in parking and waiting.

Yellow Pages ▷ *plural noun, trademark* a telephone directory, or a section of one, printed on yellow paper, in which entries are classified and arranged in sub-sections according to the nature of the trade or profession of the individuals or companies listed and the services they offer.

the yellow peril ▷ *noun dated, facetious* **1** the perceived danger that Asiatic peoples, especially the Chinese, might conquer the West and destroy Western civilization. **2** the Chinese or Japanese. ◎ 1890s.

yellow ribbon ▷ *noun* in the US: a symbol of welcome for those returning home after having undergone some danger. ◎ Originally a decoration on US cavalrymen's tunics, given to a sweetheart as a favour.

yellow spot see FOVEA

yellow streak ▷ *noun* a tendency to cowardice.

yelp ▷ *verb* (*yelped, yelping*) *intr* said of a dog, etc: to give a sharp sudden cry. ▷ *noun* such a cry. • **yelper** *noun*. ◎ Anglo-Saxon *gielpan* to boast.

yen[1] ▷ *noun* (*plural* **yen**) the standard unit of currency of Japan. ◎ 19c: from Japanese *en*, from Chinese *yuan* dollar.

yen[2] *colloq* ▷ *noun* a desire. ▷ *verb* (*yenned, yenning*) *intr* (*usually* **yen for something**) to feel a longing or craving for it. ◎ 19c: from Cantonese Chinese *yan* craving.

yeoman /ˈjoʊmən/ ▷ *noun* (*yeomen*) **1** *historical* a farmer who owned and worked his own land, often serving as a foot-soldier when required. **2** *military* a member of the YEOMANRY (sense 2). ◎ 14c as *yoman*; perhaps from earlier *yongman* young man.

yeoman of the guard ▷ *noun* a member of the oldest corps of the British sovereign's personal bodyguard. Also called BEEFEATER.

yeomanry /ˈjoʊmənrɪ/ ▷ *noun* (*yeomanries*) **1** *historical* the class of land-owning farmers. **2** a volunteer cavalry force formed in the 18c, now mechanized and forming part of the TERRITORIAL ARMY.

yep ▷ *exclamation, colloq* yes.

yerba maté /ˈjɜːbə —/ and **yerba** ▷ *noun* (*yerba matés* or *yerbas*) MATÉ. ◎ 19c: Spanish, meaning 'herb maté'.

yes ▷ *exclamation* used to express agreement or consent. ▷ *noun* (*yesses*) an expression of agreement or consent. ◎ Anglo-Saxon *gese* or *gise*, from *gea* or *ge* yea + *si* let it be.

yeshiva /jəˈʃiːvə/ ▷ *noun* (*yeshivas* or *yeshivoth* /-vɒt/) *Judaism* **1** a school for the study of the TALMUD. **2** a seminary for the training of rabbis. **3** an orthodox Jewish elementary school. ◎ 19c: from Hebrew *yeshibhah* a sitting.

yes-man ▷ *noun, derog* someone who always agrees with the opinions and follows the suggestions of a superior, employer, etc, especially to curry favour with them.

yesses *plural of* YES

yesterday /ˈjɛstədeɪ/ ▷ *noun* (*yesterdays*) **1** the day before today. **2** *often in plural* the recent past. ▷ *adverb* **1** on the day before today. **2** in the recent past. ◎ Anglo-Saxon *giestran dæg*.

yesteryear /ˈjɛstəjɪə(r)/ ▷ *noun, literary* **1** the past in general. **2** last year. ◎ 1871: coined by D G Rossetti to translate French *antan* in François Villon's famous line '*Mais où sont les neiges d'antan?*'.

yestreen /jɛˈstriːn/ ▷ *adverb, literary Scottish* yesterday evening. ◎ 16c: contracted from *yestereven* yesterday evening.

yet ▷ *adverb* **1** (*also* **as yet**) up till now or then; by now or by that time □ ***He had not yet arrived.*** **2** at this time; now □ ***You can't leave yet.*** **3** at some time in the future; before the matter is finished; still □ ***She may yet make a success of it.*** **4** (used for emphasis with *another, more,* or a comparative) even; still □ ***yet bigger problems*** □ ***yet another mistake.*** ▷ *conj* but; however; nevertheless. • **nor yet ...** and not ... either. • **yet again** once more. ◎ Anglo-Saxon *giet*.

yeti /ˈjɛtɪ/ ▷ *noun* (*yetis*) an ape-like creature supposed to live in the Himalayas. Also called **abominable snowman**. See also BIGFOOT. ◎ 1930s: from Tibetan.

yew /juː/ ▷ *noun* **1** any of various cone-bearing evergreen trees or shrubs with reddish-brown flaky bark and narrow flattened dark-green leaves. **2** the hard close-grained reddish-brown wood of this tree, formerly the source of the finest longbows. ◎ Anglo-Saxon *iw*.

> ***yew***
>
> There is sometimes a spelling confusion between **yew** and **ewe**.

Y-fronts ▷ *plural noun* men's or boys' underpants with a Y-shaped front seam.

YHA ▷ *abbreviation* Youth Hostels Association.

Yid or **yid** ▷ *noun, offensive* a Jew. ◎ 19c: from YIDDISH.

Yiddish /ˈjɪdɪʃ/ ▷ *noun* a language spoken by many Jews, based on medieval German, with elements from HEBREW and several other, especially SLAVONIC, languages. ▷ *adj* consisting of, or spoken or written in, this language. ◎ 19c: from German *jüdisch* Jewish.

Yiddisher or **yiddisher** ▷ *adj* Jewish. ▷ *noun* a Jew.

yield /jiːld/ ▷ *verb* (*yielded, yielding*) **1** to produce (an animal product such as meat or milk, or a crop). **2** *finance* to give or produce (interest, etc) □ ***Shares yield dividends.*** **3** to produce (a specified quantity of a natural or financial product). **4** *tr & intr* to give up or give in; to surrender. **5** *intr* to break or give way under force or pressure. ▷ *noun* **1** the amount produced. **2** the total amount of a product produced by an animal or plant, or harvested from a certain area of cultivated land. **3** finance the return from an investment or tax. ◎ Anglo-Saxon *gieldan* to pay.

yielding ▷ *adj* **1** submissive. **2** flexible. **3** able or tending to give way. • **yieldingly** *adverb*. • **yieldingness** *noun*.

yield point ▷ *noun, engineering* said of iron and annealed steels: the level of stress at which substantial deformation suddenly takes place.

yikker /ˈjɪkə(r)/ ▷ *verb* (*yikkered, yikkering*) *intr* said of a bird or animal: to utter sharp little cries. ◎ 1950s: imitating the sound.

yin /jɪn/ ▷ *noun* in traditional Chinese philosophy, religion, medicine, etc: one of the two opposing and complementary principles, being the negative, feminine, dark, cold and passive element or force (as opposed to the positive, masculine, light, warm and active **yang** /jaŋ/). ◎ 17c: Chinese *yin* dark, and *yang* bright.

yippee /jɪˈpiː/ ▷ *exclamation, colloq* expressing excitement, delight, etc.

the yips ▷ *noun, sport, especially golf* a quivering of the muscles caused by tension, experienced before attempting a putt, etc. ◎ 20c.

-yl /ɪl/ ▷ *suffix, chem forming nouns, denoting* a radical or group □ ***methyl.*** ◎ From Greek *hyle* matter.

ylang-ylang /iːlaŋˈiːlaŋ/ ▷ *noun* **1** an evergreen tree, native to Malaysia and the Philippines, with large elliptical leaves and dull-yellow fragrant flowers whose oil (**macassar oil**) is used in perfumes and aromatherapy. **2** the perfume or aromatherapy oil itself. ◎ 19c: from Tagálog.

ylem /ˈaɪləm/ ▷ *noun, physics* in the big bang theory: the original substance from which the elements developed. ◎ A reinvention in the 1940s of 14c *ylem* matter, ultimately from Greek *hyle* wood or material.

YMCA ▷ *abbreviation* Young Men's Christian Association, a charity providing accommodation and other services, originally for young men and boys, but increasingly now for both sexes. Compare YWCA. ▷ *noun* (***YMCAs***) a hostel run by the YMCA. See also THE Y.

-yne /aɪn/ ▷ *suffix, chem, forming nouns, denoting* an organic compound that contains a triple bond □ ***alkyne.*** ◷ Altered from -INE[2].

yo /joʊ/ ▷ *exclamation* **1** used to call someone's attention. **2** used as a greeting. **3** *especially US* used in answer to a call: present; here. ◷ 15c as a call to hounds.

yob ▷ *noun, slang* a bad-mannered aggressive young person (usually male); a lout or hooligan. • **yobbish** *adj.* • **yobbishness** *noun.* ◷ 19c: back-slang for *boy*.

yobbo /'jɒboʊ/ ▷ *noun* (***yobbos***) *slang* a YOB.

yodel /'joʊdəl/ ▷ *verb* (***yodelled, yodelling***) *tr & intr* to sing (a melody, etc), changing frequently from a normal to a falsetto voice and back again. ▷ *noun* an act of yodelling. • **yodeller** *noun.* • **yodelling** *noun.* ◷ 19c: from German dialect *jodeln*.

yoga /'joʊgə/ ▷ *noun* (*plural* in sense 2 ***yogas***) **1** a system of Hindu philosophy showing how to free the soul from reincarnation and reunite it with God. **2** any of several systems of physical and mental discipline based on this, especially (in western countries) a particular system of physical exercises. • **yogic** *adj.* ◷ 19c: Sanskrit, meaning 'union'.

yogh /jɒg, jɒx/ ▷ *noun* a letter ȝ used in writing Middle English, representing either a consonantal *y* or a *gh* sound. ◷ 14c.

yoghurt, **yogurt** or **yoghourt** /'jɒgət, 'joʊ-/ ▷ *noun* a type of semi-liquid food made from fermented milk, now often flavoured with fruit. ◷ 17c: Turkish.

yogi /'joʊgɪ/ and **yogin** /-gɪn/ ▷ *noun* (***yogis*** or ***yogins***) a person who practises the YOGA philosophy and the physical and mental disciplines associated with it. ◷ 17c as *loggue*: Hindi.

yogini /joʊ'gɪnɪ/ ▷ *noun* (***yoginis***) a female yogi. ◷ 19c: Sanskrit.

yogurt see YOGHURT

YOI ▷ *abbreviation* young offender institution.

yoicks /jɔɪks/ ▷ *exclamation* **1** in fox-hunting: used to urge on the hounds. **2** used generally to express excitement.

yoke ▷ *noun* (***yokes***) **1** a wooden frame placed over the necks of oxen to hold them together when they are pulling a plough, cart, etc. **2** a frame placed across a person's shoulders, for carrying buckets. **3** something oppressive; a great burden □ ***the yoke of slavery.*** **4** *dressmaking, etc* the part of a garment that fits over the shoulders and round the neck. **5** a pair of animals, especially oxen. ▷ *verb* (***yoked, yoking***) (*always* **yoke something to another** or **yoke two things together**) **1** to join them under or with a yoke (sense 1). **2** to join or unite them. ◷ Anglo-Saxon *geoc*.

yoke, yolk

These words are sometimes confused with each other.

yokel /'joʊkəl/ ▷ *noun, derog* an unsophisticated person from the country, usually a male. ◷ 19c.

yolk /joʊk/ ▷ *noun* **1** in the eggs of birds and some reptiles: the yellow spherical mass of nutritive material. **2** *cookery, etc* this yellow part of an egg, as distinct from the WHITE (sense 4). Also called **egg-yolk, yolk of egg.** ◷ Anglo-Saxon *geolca*, from *geolu* yellow.

yolk sac ▷ *noun, zool* the yolk-containing sac that is attached to the embryo by the **yolk-stalk**, a short stalk by means of which nutrients from the yolk may pass into the alimentary canal of the embryo.

Yom Kippur /jɒm kɪ'pʊə(r)/ ▷ *noun* an annual Jewish religious festival devoted to repentance for past sins, and celebrated with fasting and prayer. Also called **Day of Atonement**. ◷ 19c: Hebrew *yom* day + *kippur* atonement.

yon ▷ *adj, literary or dialect* that or those □ ***Do you see yon fellow?*** ◷ Anglo-Saxon *geon*.

yonder /'jɒndə(r)/ ▷ *adverb* in or at that place over there. ▷ *adj* situated over there. • **the wide blue yonder** the far distance. ◷ 13c.

yoni /'joʊniː/ ▷ *noun* (***yonis***) *Hinduism* **1** the female genitalia. **2** a representation of these as an object of worship, symbolic of the goddess Sakti. ◷ 18c: Sanskrit.

yonks /jɒŋks/ ▷ *noun, colloq* • **for yonks** *usually with negatives* for a long time; for ages □ ***I haven't seen him for yonks.***

yoo-hoo /'juːhuː/ ▷ *exclamation, colloq* used to attract someone's attention.

yore /jɔː(r)/ and **days of yore** ▷ *noun, literary or archaic* times past or long ago. ◷ Anglo-Saxon *geara* formerly.

yorker /'jɔːkə(r)/ ▷ *noun, cricket* a ball pitched to a point directly under the bat. ◷ 19c: probably from the name Yorkshire.

Yorkie or **yorkie** /'jɔːkɪ/ ▷ *noun* (***Yorkies*** or ***yorkies***) a Yorkshire terrier.

Yorkist *historical* ▷ *noun* a supporter of the House of York in the Wars of the Roses. Compare LANCASTRIAN. ▷ *adj* relating to the House of York.

Yorks. ▷ *abbreviation* Yorkshire.

Yorkshire fog ▷ *noun, bot* a grass with greyish-green leaves covered with soft hair, and long white, green, pink or purple spikelets borne in dense hairy flower-heads.

Yorkshire pudding ▷ *noun* a baked PUDDING of unsweetened batter, especially and traditionally cooked and served with roast beef. ◷ 18c: named after Yorkshire in England.

Yorkshire terrier ▷ *noun* a very small terrier with a long straight coat of fine brown and bluish-grey hair that reaches the ground, and large erect ears. Often shortened to YORKIE.

Yoruba /'jɒrʊbə/ ▷ *noun* (***Yoruba*** or ***Yorubas***) **1** a group of Kwa-speaking peoples of SW Nigeria and Benin, W Africa. **2** an individual belonging to this group of peoples. **3** their language. ▷ *adj* belonging or relating to this group or their language. ◷ 19c: native name.

you /juː, jʊ, jə/ ▷ *pronoun* **1** the person or people, etc spoken or written to, with or without others □ ***When are you all coming to visit us?*** **2** any or every person □ ***You don't often see that nowadays.*** • **something is you** or **really**, *etc* **you** *colloq* it suits you □ ***That hat is really you.*** • **you-all** or **y'all** *US, especially Southern* you (*plural*) □ ***You-all take care now.*** • **you know who** or **what** someone or something that the speaker does not want to name. ◷ Anglo-Saxon *eow*, originally accusative and dative of *ge* YE.

you'd /juːd, jʊd/ ▷ *contraction* **1** you would. **2** you had.

you'll /juːl, jʊl/ ▷ *contraction* **1** you will. **2** you shall.

young /jʌŋ/ ▷ *adj* (***younger*** /'jʌŋgə(r)/, ***youngest*** /-gɪst/) **1** in the first part of life, growth, development, etc; not old. **2** (**the young**) young people in general (see THE 4b). **3** (*often* **their**, *etc* **young**) said usually of animals or birds: their, etc offspring □ ***Some birds feed their young on insects.*** **4** (placed before the name) the younger of two people of the same name. **5** (**Young**) used in titles of subsections of political parties or other organizations which are run by and for younger members, and hence also applied to the younger members themselves □ ***Young Farmers Association*** □ ***He's a Young Conservative.*** **6** in the early stages ◻ *The night is young.* • **youngish** /ˈjʌŋɪʃ, -gɪʃ/ *adj.* • **with young** said of animals: pregnant. ◷ Anglo-Saxon *geong*.

young blood ▷ *noun* new people with fresh ideas.

young fustic ▷ *noun* **1** the wood of any of several European trees. **2** see FUSTIC sense 2.

young lady and **young woman** ▷ *noun, dated or facetious* a girlfriend. Compare YOUNG MAN.

young man ▷ *noun, dated or facetious* a boyfriend. Compare YOUNG LADY.

young offender ▷ *noun, Brit* a law-breaker aged between 16 and 21.

young offender institution ▷ *noun, Brit* (abbreviation **YOI**) an establishment for the detention of YOUNG OFFENDERS who are given custodial sentences.

young person ▷ *noun, law* a person aged between 14 and 17.

the Young Pretender ▷ *noun* a nickname for Charles Edward Stuart (1720–88). ◷ 18c: so called because he pretended to (ie claimed) the British throne; his father, James Francis Edward (1688–1766), son of James II, was called *the Old Pretender*.

youngster ▷ *noun, colloq* a young person.

Young Turk ▷ *noun* **1** a radical rebellious member of any organization. **2** *historical* in Turkey: a member of the group of modernizing and westernizing reformers that brought about the revolution of 1908.

young woman see YOUNG LADY

your /jɔː(r), jʊə(r)/ ▷ *adj* **1** belonging to you. **2** *colloq, often derog* usual; ordinary; typical ◻ *Your politicians nowadays have no principles.* ◷ Anglo-Saxon *eower*, genitive of *ge* ye.

you're /jɔː(r), jʊə(r)/ ▷ *contraction* you are.

Your Highness see under HIGHNESS 1

Your Holiness see under HOLINESS 2

Your Honour see under HONOUR

yours /jɔːz, jʊəz/ ▷ *pronoun* **1** something belonging to you. **2** (*also* **yours faithfully**, **sincerely** or **truly**) conventional expressions written before a signature at the end of a letter. See also separate entry YOURS TRULY. • **of yours** (a specified thing, relation, etc) belonging to you ◻ *a book of yours.*

yourself /jɔːˈsɛlf, jəˈsɛlf/ ▷ *pronoun* (*plural* ***yourselves***) **1** the reflexive form of YOU. **2** used for emphasis ◻ *you yourself* ◻ *Are you coming yourself?* **3** your normal self ◻ *don't seem yourself this morning.* **4** (*also* **by yourself**) alone; without help ◻ *Can you reach it yourself?*

yours truly ▷ *pronoun, colloq* used to refer to oneself, especially with irony or affected condescension ◻ *Then yours truly had to go and fetch it.* ◷ 19c: from its use at the end of a letter (see under YOURS).

Your Worship see under WORSHIP

youth /juːθ/ ▷ *singular noun* **1** the state, quality or fact of being young. **2** the early part of life, often specifically that between childhood and adulthood. **3** the enthusiasm, rashness, etc associated with people in this period of life. **4** (*plural* ***youths*** /juːðz/) a boy or young man. **5** (*singular or plural noun*) young people in general ◻ *The youth of today expect too much.*

youth club ▷ *noun* a place or organization providing leisure activities for young people.

youth custody centre ▷ *noun, Brit* a place where a YOUNG OFFENDER is detained and given education and training.

youthful ▷ *adj* **1** young, especially in manner or appearance. **2** said of someone who is not young: young-looking, or having the energy, enthusiasm, etc of a young person. **3** referring to, associated with or suitable for, youth ◻ *youthful pleasures.* • **youthfully** *adverb.* • **youthfulness** *noun.*

youth hostel ▷ *noun* a hostel providing simple overnight accommodation, especially one that belongs to the Youth Hostels Association.

youth hosteller ▷ *noun* someone who stays at YOUTH HOSTELS, especially regularly.

Youth Training Scheme see YTS

you've /juːv, jʊv/ ▷ *contraction* you have.

yowl /jaʊl/ ▷ *verb* (***yowled***, ***yowling***) *intr* said especially of an animal: to howl or cry sadly. ▷ *noun* such a howl. • **yowling** *noun.* ◷ 14c as *yuhel*.

yo-yo /ˈjoʊjoʊ/ ▷ *noun* (***yo-yos***) **1** a toy consisting of a pair of wooden, metal or plastic discs joined at their centre with a deep groove between them, and with a piece of string attached to and wound round the joining axis within the groove, the toy being repeatedly made to unwind from the string by the force of its weight and rewind by its momentum. **2** someone or something regarded as like a yo-yo in some way, eg because it moves up and down, varies or fluctuates continuously. ▷ *verb* (***yo-yoed***, ***yo-yoing***) *intr* to rise and fall repeatedly; to fluctuate repeatedly in any way. ◷ Originally (1915) a trademark: apparently Filipino, applied to a similar device, but literally meaning 'come come'.

yr ▷ *abbreviation* **1** year. **2** younger. **3** your.

yrs ▷ *abbreviation* **1** years. **2** in letter-writing: yours (see YOURS 2).

YT ▷ *abbreviation, Canadian province* Yukon Territory.

YTS ▷ *abbreviation* Youth Training Scheme, a British government-sponsored scheme to give training and work-experience to unemployed school-leavers.

ytterbium /ɪˈtɜːbɪəm/ ▷ *noun, chem* (symbol **Yb**, atomic number 70) a soft silvery lustrous metallic element belonging to the LANTHANIDE series, used in lasers, and for making steel and other alloys. ◷ 19c: named after Ytterby, a quarry in Sweden where it was discovered.

yttrium /ˈɪtrɪəm/ ▷ *noun, chem* (symbol **Y**, atomic number 39) a silvery-grey metallic element used in alloys to make superconductors and strong permanent magnets. ◷ 19c: from the same source as YTTERBIUM.

YU ▷ *abbreviation, IVR* Yugoslavia.

yuan /jʊˈɑːn/ ▷ *noun* (*plural* ***yuan***) the standard unit of currency of the People's Republic of China. ◷ 20c (the unit was introduced in 1914): Chinese, literally 'round thing'.

yucca /ˈjʌkə/ ▷ *noun* (***yuccas***) any of various tropical and subtropical American plants with a short thick trunk, stiff narrow sword-shaped leaves and waxy white bell-shaped flowers in large pyramidal clusters. ◷ 17c; 16c as *yuca*, meaning 'cassava': Carib.

yuck or **yuk** *colloq* ▷ *noun* a disgusting mess; filth. ▷ *exclamation* expressing disgust or distaste. • **yucky** or **yukky** *adj* (***yuckier***, ***yuckiest***; ***yukkier***, ***yukkiest***). ◷ 1960s.

Yugoslav /ˈjuːgoʊslɑːv/ ▷ *adj* belonging or relating to the republic of Yugoslavia in SE Europe (now consisting only of the republics of Serbia and Montenegro but before the civil war of the 1990s also containing Slovenia, Croatia, Bosnia-Herzegovina and Macedonia) or its inhabitants. ▷ *noun* **1** a citizen or inhabitant of, or person born in, Yugoslavia. **2** *rare* SERBO-CROAT. • **Yugoslavian** *adj, noun.* ◷ 19c: Serbo-Croat, from *jug* south + SLAV.

yuko /ˈjuːkoʊ/ ▷ *noun* (***yukos***) *judo* an award of five points. ◷ Japanese.

Yule /juːl/ ▷ *noun* (***Yules***) *old, literary & dialect* **1** Christmas. **2** (*also* **Yuletide**) the Christmas period. ◷ Anglo-Saxon *geol*.

yummy /ˈjʌmɪ/ ▻ *adj* (***yummier***, ***yummiest***) *colloq* delicious. ⓒ 20c: from YUM-YUM.

yum-yum /jʌmˈjʌm/ ▻ *exclamation* expressing delight at or appreciative anticipation of something, especially delicious food. ⓒ 19c: imitating the sound of the jaws opening and closing.

yup /jʌp, jəp/ ▻ *exclamation, colloq* same as YEP.

yuppie or **yuppy** /ˈjʌpɪ/ ▻ *noun* (***yuppies***) *derog, colloq* an ambitious young professional person working in a city job. • **yuppiedom** *noun*. ⓒ 1980s: from *y*oung *u*rban *p*rofessional, or *y*oung *u*pwardly-mobile *p*rofessional.

yuppie flu ▻ *noun, colloq, non-technical* any of various long-term debilitating disorders, often characterized by chronic fatigue, eg ME.

yuppify ▻ *verb* (***yuppifies***, ***yuppified***, ***yuppifying***) **1** to alter (usually a place) so as to conform to yuppie taste. **2** to turn someone into a yuppie. • **yuppification** *noun*.

yurt /juət/ ▻ *noun* a light circular tent of skins or felt on a framework of poles, used by nomads in Central Asia and Siberia. ⓒ 18c as *yourt*: from Russian *yurta*.

YV ▻ *abbreviation, IVR* Venezuela.

YWCA ▻ *abbreviation* Young Women's Christian Association. Compare YMCA. ▻ *noun* (***YWCAs***) a hostel run by the YWCA. See also THE Y.

Z

Z[1] or **z** /zɛd; *N Amer* ziː/ ▷ *noun* (***Zs, Z's*** or ***z's***) **1** the twenty-sixth and last letter of the English alphabet. **2** anything shaped like a Z.

Z[2] ▷ *abbreviation* **1** zaire, or zaires. **2** *IVR* Zambia.

Z[3] ▷ *symbol, math* (*usually* **z**) the third of three unknown quantities. See also X[3], Y[3].

Z[4] ▷ *symbol* **1** *chem* atomic number. **2** *physics* impedance.

z see Z[1], Z[3]

ZA ▷ *abbreviation, IVR Zuid Afrika* (Afrikaans), South Africa.

zabaglione /zabal'jounɪ/ ▷ *noun* (***zabagliones***) *cookery* a dessert made from egg-yolks, sugar and wine (usually Marsala), whisked together over a gentle heat. Also called **zabaione** /zabaɪ-/. 19c: Italian.

zag, **zagged** and **zagging** see under ZIG

zaire /zɑː'ɪə(r)/ ▷ *noun* (***zaires*** or ***zaire***) the standard unit of currency of Zaire. 1960s.

Zairean /zɑː'ɪərɪən/ ▷ *adj* belonging or relating to Zaire, a republic in central Africa, or its inhabitants. ▷ *noun* a citizen or inhabitant of, or person born in, Zaire. 1970s.

zakat /za'kɑːt/ ▷ *noun, Islam* the tax of $2\frac{1}{2}$ per cent payable as alms by all Muslims, levied annually on income and capital. 19c: Persian, from Arabic *zakah.*

Zambian /'zambɪən/ ▷ *adj* belonging or relating to Zambia, a republic in southern Africa, or its inhabitants. ▷ *noun* a citizen or inhabitant of, or person born in, Zambia.

ZANU /'zɑːnuː/ ▷ *abbreviation* Zimbabwe African National Union.

zany /'zeɪnɪ/ ▷ *adj* (***zanier, zaniest***) amusingly crazy. • **zanily** *adverb*. • **zaniness** *noun*. 16c, meaning 'a clown's stooge': from *Zanni*, a N Italian dialect form of *Gianni* or *Giovanni* John, name of a servant who plays the clown in commedia dell'arte.

zap ▷ *verb* (***zapped, zapping***) *colloq* **1** to hit, destroy or shoot something, especially suddenly. **2** *computing* to delete all the data in (a file) or from (the main memory of a computer). **3** *intr* to change TV channels frequently using a remote-control device. **4** *tr & intr* to move quickly or suddenly. • **zapping** *noun*. 1940s: imitation of the sound.

zapper ▷ *noun, colloq* a REMOTE CONTROL (sense 2) for a TV or video recorder.

ZAPU /'zɑːpuː/ ▷ *abbreviation* Zimbabwe African People's Union.

zarzuela /θɑːθʊ'eɪlɑː/ ▷ *noun* a type of popular Spanish opera, either comic or serious, with spoken dialogue. 19c: probably from *La Zarzuela*, a royal palace near Madrid, where productions were first staged in the 17c.

z-axis ▷ *noun, math* in 3-dimensional graphs: the vertical axis at right angles to the X-AXIS and Y-AXIS, along which the z-coordinate is plotted.

zeal ▷ *noun* great, and sometimes excessive, enthusiasm or keenness. 14c as *zele*: from Greek *zelos.*

zealot /'zɛlət/ ▷ *noun* **1** *often derog* a single-minded and determined supporter of a political cause, religion, etc. **2** (**Zealot**) *historical* a member of **the Zealots**, a militant Jewish sect in the first century AD, which was violently opposed to Roman rule in Palestine. • **zealotry** *noun*. 13c as *zelote*: from Greek *zelotes* in sense 2.

zealous /'zɛləs/ ▷ *adj* enthusiastic; keen. • **zealously** *adverb*. • **zealousness** *noun*. 16c: from medieval Latin *zelosus*; see ZEAL + -OUS.

zebra /'zɛbrə, əziː-/ ▷ *noun* (***zebras*** or ***zebra***) a stocky black-and-white striped African mammal with a stubby mane, related to the horse and ass. 16c: from an African language.

zebra crossing ▷ *noun, Brit* a pedestrian crossing marked by black and white stripes on the road. See also PELICAN CROSSING. 1950s.

zebroid /'ziːbrɔɪd/ ▷ *noun* a cross between a horse and a zebra. ▷ *adj* resembling a zebra. 1890s: ZEBRA + -OID.

zebu /'ziːbjuː, -buː/ ▷ *noun* (***zebus*** or ***zebu***) a species of domestic cattle, native to S Asia, with a light-coloured coat, large upturned horns, long pendulous ears and a prominent hump on its shoulders, used as a draught animal. 18c: from French *zébu.*

Zech. ▷ *abbreviation*, Book of the Bible: Zechariah. See table at BIBLE.

zed ▷ *noun, Brit* **1** the name of the letter Z. *N Amer equivalent* ZEE. **2** (**zeds**) *slang* sleep. • **catch some zeds** *slang* to get some sleep. 15c: from French *zède*, from Greek *zeta*; sense 2 derives from the use of zzz to represent (in cartoons, etc) the sound of someone sleeping. Compare ZIZZ.

zedoary /'zɛdouərɪ/ ▷ *noun* (***zedoaries***) a plant of the GINGER family, native to parts of Asia, with aromatic bitter rootstocks which are used as a drug, as a condiment and in making perfume. 15c as *zeduary*: from Arabic *zedwar.*

zee /ziː/ ▷ *noun* (***zees***) *N Amer* the name of the letter Z. 17c: modelled on the pronunciation of the names of other consonant letters, eg B, G, T.

Zeitgeist /'zaɪtgaɪst/ ▷ *noun* (*also* **zeitgeist**) the spirit of the age; the attitudes or viewpoint of a specific period. 19c: German.

zek ▷ *noun* an inmate of a USSR prison or labour camp. 1960s: Russian slang, possibly from *zk*, abbreviation of *zaklyuchënnyi* prisoner.

Zen and **Zen Buddhism** ▷ *noun* a school of Buddhism which stresses the personal experience of enlightenment based on a simple way of life, close to nature, and simple methods of meditation. Compare MAHAYANA, HINAYANA. 18c: Japanese, from Sanskrit *dhyana* meditation.

zenana /zɛ'nɑːnə/ ▷ *noun* (***zenanas***) in India, Iran, etc: a part of a house in which women and girls are secluded, corresponding to the HAREM in Arabic-speaking Muslim countries. 18c: from Persian *zanana*, from *zan* woman.

Zend-Avesta /zɛnd —/ ▷ *noun* the Zoroastrian sacred writings, comprising the scriptures (the *Avesta*) and a commentary on them (the *Zend*). 17c as *Zundavastaw*: from Persian *zand* commentary + *avastak* text.

zenith /'zɛnɪθ, 'ziː-/ ▷ *noun* **1** *astron* the point on the celestial sphere diametrically opposite the NADIR and directly above the observer. Also called **vertex**. **2** the highest point. 14c as *cinit* or *cenith*, etc: ultimately from Arabic *samt-ar-ras* direction of the head.

zenithal projection /'zɛnɪθəl, 'ziː-/ ▷ *noun, geog* a type of map projection in which the plane of projection is tangential to the sphere.

zeolite /'ziːəlaɪt/ ▷ *noun* (***zeolites***) *geol* any of numerous hydrated aluminosilicate minerals, usually containing sodium, potassium, or calcium, widely used as 'molecular sieves' for separating substances, and as water softeners. • **zeolitic** /-ˈlɪtɪk/ *adj.* ◎ 18c: from Greek *zeein* to boil (in allusion to the fact that many swell up when heated with a blowpipe).

Zeph. ▻ *abbreviation* Book of the Bible: Zephaniah. See table at BIBLE.

zephyr /ˈzɛfə(r)/ ▻ *noun, literary* a light gentle breeze. ◎ Anglo-Saxon as *zefferus*: from Greek *Zephyros* the west wind.

zeppelin or **Zeppelin** /ˈzɛpəlɪn/ ▻ *noun* a cigar-shaped airship of the type originally designed by the German Count Zeppelin in 1900.

zero /ˈzɪəroʊ/ ▻ *noun* (***zeros***) **1** the number, figure or symbol 0. **2** the point on a scale eg on a thermometer which is taken as the base from which measurements may be made □ ***5 degrees below zero***. See also ABSOLUTE ZERO. **3** zero hour. ▻ *adj* **1** being of no measurable size. **2** *colloq* not any; no □ ***She has zero confidence.*** ▻ *verb* (***zeroes***, ***zeroed***, ***zeroing***) to set or adjust something to zero. ◎ 17c: from French *zéro*, from Arabic *sifr*.

■ **zero in on something** **1** to aim for it; to move towards it. **2** to focus one's attention on it. **3** to aim a weapon at it.

zero-coupon bond ▻ *noun, stock exchange* a bond that carries no interest, but has a redemption value higher than its issue price.

zero grazing ▻ *noun, agric* a feeding system, often used on intensively stocked farms, where freshly cut grass is fed to livestock which are confined in a building, yard or paddock.

zero hour ▻ *noun* **1** the exact time fixed for something to happen. **2** the time at which a military operation, etc is fixed to begin.

zero option ▻ *noun* **1** in nuclear arms negotiations: a proposal to limit or abandon the deployment of shorter-range nuclear missiles if the opposing side does likewise. **2** a proposal to abandon a specific range or category of something.

zero-rate ▻ *verb* to assess (goods, etc) at a zero rate of VAT.

zero-rated ▻ *adj* said of goods: on which the buyer pays no VAT, and on which the seller can claim back any VAT they have paid.

zeroth /ˈzɪəroʊθ/ ▻ *adj, math, etc* in a series: coming before what would normally be regarded as the first term. ◎ 19c: modelled on eg FOURTH, FIFTH.

zero-zero ▻ *adj, meteorol, aeronautics* applied to conditions in which cloud ceiling and horizontal visibility are both zero.

zero-zero option ▻ *noun* in nuclear arms negotiations: a proposal that extends the ZERO OPTION to include also intermediate (300–600ml or 483–966km) range missiles.

zest ▻ *noun* **1** keen enjoyment; enthusiasm. **2** something that adds to one's enjoyment of something. **3** *cookery* the coloured outer layer of the peel of an orange or lemon, or the oil contained in it, used for flavouring. **4** piquancy; agreeably sharp flavour. ◎ 17c in sense 3: from French *zeste*.

zestful ▻ *adj* keen; enthusiastic. • **zestfully** *adverb*. • **zestfulness** *noun*.

zesty ▻ *adj* (***zestier***, ***zestiest***) **1** piquant; agreeably sharp-tasting. **2** lively; enthusiastic.

ZETA or **Zeta** /ˈziːtə/ ▻ *abbreviation* zero-energy thermonuclear apparatus, used in the study of controlled thermonuclear reactions.

zeta /ˈziːtə/ ▻ *noun* (***zetas***) the sixth letter of the Greek alphabet. See table at GREEK ALPHABET.

zeugma /ˈzjuːgmə/ ▻ *noun* (***zeugmas***) *grammar* a figure of speech in which a word, usually an adjective or verb, is applied to two nouns although strictly it is appropriate to only one of them, or it has a different sense with each, as in *weeping eyes and hearts*. ◎ 16c: Greek, meaning 'yoking together'.

ziff ▻ *noun, Austral & NZ slang* a beard. ◎ 20c.

ZIFT or **Zift** /zɪft/ ▻ *abbreviation, medicine* zygote intrafallopian transfer, a technique in which a fertilized egg is inserted into the recipient's fallopian tube. Compare GIFT.

zig and **zag** ▻ *noun* either of the alternative directions on a zigzag course, or the change to either of them. ▻ *verb* (***zigged***, ***zigging***; ***zagged***, ***zagging***) *intr* to veer sharply in either of the alternative directions on a zigzag course. ◎ 18c for both: the syllables of ZIGZAG used separately.

ziggurat /ˈzɪgʊrat/ ▻ *noun* in ancient Mesopotamia: a pyramid-like temple, consisting of many storeys each of which is smaller than the one below. ◎ 19c: from Assyrian *ziqqurratu* mountain-top.

zigzag ▻ *noun* **1** (*usually* **zigzags**) two or more sharp bends to alternate sides in a path, etc. **2** a path, road, etc with a number of such bends. ▻ *adj* **1** having sharp bends to alternate sides. **2** bent from side to side alternately. ▻ *verb* (***zigzagged***, ***zigzagging***) *intr* to move in a zigzag direction. ▻ *adverb* in a zigzag direction or manner. ◎ 18c: French.

zilch /zɪltʃ/ ▻ *noun, slang* nothing. ◎ 1960s.

zillion /ˈzɪlɪən/ ▻ *noun, colloq* a very large but unspecified number. ◎ 1940s: modelled on MILLION, BILLION, etc.

Zimbabwean /zɪmˈbɑːbwɪən/ ▻ *adj* belonging or relating to Zimbabwe (formerly Southern Rhodesia and later Rhodesia), a republic in SE Africa, or its inhabitants. ▻ *noun* a citizen or inhabitant of, or person born in, Zimbabwe.

Zimmer or **zimmer** /ˈzɪmə(r)/ and **Zimmer frame** or **zimmer frame** ▻ *noun, trademark* a tubular metal frame, used as a support for walking by the disabled or infirm. ◎ 1950s: the name of the original manufacturer.

zinc /zɪŋk/ ▻ *noun, chem* (symbol **Zn**, atomic number 30) a brittle bluish-white metallic element used in dry batteries and various alloys, and as a corrosion-resistant coating to galvanize steel. ◎ 17c as *zinke*: from German *Zink*.

zinc blende see SPHALERITE

zincite /ˈzɪŋkaɪt/ ▻ *noun, geol* a yellow, orange or dark-red mineral form of zinc oxide, often also containing small amounts of manganese, that is an important ore of zinc. ◎ 19c.

zinc ointment ▻ *noun* a soothing antiseptic ointment composed of a mixture of zinc oxide and a suitable base such as lanolin or petroleum jelly.

zinc oxide ▻ *noun* a white crystalline solid, widely used as an antiseptic and astringent in skin ointments and cosmetics, and as a pigment in paints, plastics and ceramics.

zinc white ▻ *noun* ZINC OXIDE used as a pigment in paint.

zine /ziːn/ ▻ *noun, slang* **1** a magazine, especially one aimed at a special-interest group. **2** *in compounds* such a magazine aimed at the specified special-interest group □ ***fanzine*** □ ***teen-zine*** □ ***queer-zine*** □ ***cyber-zine***. ◎ 1990s: a shortening of MAGAZINE.

zineb /ˈzɪnəb/ ▻ *noun* an organic fungicide and insecticide sprayed on cereal grasses, fruit trees, etc. ◎ 1950s: from *zinc* ethylene *b*isdithiocarbamate, its chemical name.

zing ▻ *noun* **1** a short high-pitched humming sound, eg that made by a bullet or vibrating string. **2** *colloq* zest or vitality. ▻ *verb* (***zinged***, ***zinging***) *intr* to move very quickly, especially while making a high-pitched hum. • **zingy** *adj, colloq* full of zest; lively. ◷ 20c: imitating the sound.

zinger /ˈzɪŋə(r)/ ▷ *noun, colloq, especially US* **1** an exceptional example of its kind. **2** a one-liner; a punchline. **3** an unexpected turn of events.

zinnia /ˈzɪnɪə/ ▷ *noun* (***zinnias***) any of various annual plants, native to Mexico and S America, with whorled or opposite leaves and brightly coloured daisy-like flower-heads. ◷ 18c: named after J G Zinn (1727–59), German botanist.

Zionism /ˈzaɪənɪzəm/ ▷ *noun* the movement which worked for the establishment of a national homeland in Palestine for Jews and now supports the state of Israel. ◷ 19c: from Zion, one of the hills in Jerusalem, and hence allusively Jerusalem itself.

Zionist ▷ *noun* **1** a supporter of Zionism. **2** a member of one of the Africanized pentecostal churches of southern Africa. ▷ *adj* characteristic of or supporting Zionism.

zip[1] ▷ *noun* **1** a ZIP FASTENER. *N Amer equivalent* ZIPPER. Also *in compounds* □ ***zip-neck*** □ ***zip-top***. **2** *colloq* energy; vitality. **3** a whizzing sound. ▷ *verb* (***zipped, zipping***) **1** *tr & intr* (*also* **zip up**) to fasten, or be fastened, with a zip fastener. **2** *intr* to make, or move with, a whizzing sound. **3** *computing* to convert (a file, etc) into a compressed form in order to save storage space. ◷ 19c as *verb* 2 and *noun* 3; 1920s as *noun* 1: imitating the sound it makes.

zip[2] ▷ *noun, US slang* zero; nothing. ◷ Early 20c.

zip- ▷ *combining form, used with a following adverb, forming adjectives, denoting* able to be added, removed, inserted, etc by means of a zip □ ***zip-on*** □ ***zip-off*** □ ***zip-in***.

zip code ▷ *noun* in the US: a postal code consisting of a five- or nine-figure number. *Brit equivalent* POSTCODE. ◷ 1960s: from *Z*one *I*mprovement *P*lan.

zip fastener ▷ *noun* a device for fastening clothes, bags, etc, in which two rows of metal or nylon teeth are made to fit into each other when a sliding tab is pulled along them.

zipper *N Amer* ▷ *noun* a zip fastener. ▷ *verb* (***zippered, zippering***) to fasten with a zipper.

zippy ▷ *adj* (***zippier, zippiest***) *colloq* lively; quick.

zircaloy or **Zircoloy** /ˈzɜːkəlɔɪ/ ▷ *noun* (***zircaloys*** or ***Zircoloys***) an alloy of zirconium with tin, chromium and nickel, widely used, especially in the nuclear power industry, for its heat- and corrosion-resistant properties. ◷ 1950s.

zircon /ˈzɜːkɒn/ ▷ *noun, geol* a hard mineral form of zirconium silicate, which is the main ore of zirconium, and occurs in colourless varieties that are used as semi-precious gemstones. ◷ 18c as *circon*: originally from Persian *zargun* golden.

zirconium /zɜːˈkoʊnɪəm/ ▷ *noun, chem* (symbol **Zr**, atomic number 40) a silvery-grey metallic element that is resistant to corrosion and absorbs neutrons, used in certain alloys and as a coating for fuel rods in nuclear reactors. ◷ 19c: from ZIRCON.

zit ▷ *noun, slang* a pimple. ◷ 1960s.

zither /ˈzɪðə(r)/ ▷ *noun* a musical instrument consisting of a flat wooden sound-box, one section of which has frets on it, over which strings (usually metal ones) are stretched, the instrument being played resting on a table or on the player's knees. ◷ 19c: German.

zizz or **ziz** /zɪz/ *slang* ▷ *noun* (***zizzes***) a nap; a sleep. ▷ *verb* (***zizzes, zizzed, zizzing***) *intr* to have a nap. ◷ 19c, meaning 'a buzzing sound': imitative, and perhaps partly based on *zzz*, the conventional representation of snoring or the heavy breathing of a sleeper in strip cartoons; see also ZED sense 2.

Zl. ▷ *abbreviation* zloty, or zlotys.

zloty /ˈzlɒtɪ/ ▷ *noun* (***zloty*** or ***zlotys***) the standard unit of currency of Poland. ◷ 20c: Polish, from *zloto* gold.

Zn ▷ *symbol, chem* zinc.

zodiac /ˈzoʊdɪak/ ▷ *noun* **1** (**the zodiac**) *astron* the band of sky that extends 8° on either side of the Sun's ECLIPTIC, divided into 12 equal parts, each of which once contained one of the zodiacal constellations, though some no longer do. **2** *astrol* a chart or diagram (usually a circular one), representing this band of sky and the **signs of the zodiac** contained within it (see table). • **zodiacal** /zoʊˈdaɪəkəl/ *adj*. ◷ 14c: from French *zodiaque*, from Greek *zoidiakos*, from *zoidion* a figure of a small animal.

zombie or **zombi** /ˈzɒmbɪ/ ▷ *noun* (***zombies*** or ***zombis***) **1** *derog, colloq* a slow-moving, stupid, unresponsive or apathetic person. **2** a corpse brought to life again by magic. ◷ 19c in sense 2; 1930s in sense 1: from Kongo (W African language) *zumbi* fetish.

zonal /ˈzoʊnəl/ ▷ *adj* **1** relating to a zone or zones. **2** arranged in zones.

zone /zoʊn/ ▷ *noun* **1** an area or region of a country, town, etc, especially one marked out for a special purpose or by a particular feature. **2** *geog* any of the five horizontal bands into which the Earth's surface is divided by the Arctic Circle, the Tropic of Cancer, the Tropic of Capricorn and the Antarctic Circle. ▷ *verb* (***zoned, zoning***) **1** (*also* **zone something off**) to divide it into zones; to mark it as a zone. **2** to assign to a particular zone. ◷ 15c: from Greek *zone* girdle.

zonk ▷ *verb* (***zonked, zonking***) *colloq* to hit with a sharp or firm impact. ◷ 1950s: imitating the sound of the impact.

■ **zonk out** *tr & intr* to collapse or make someone collapse into unconsciousness or in exhaustion.

zonked and **zonked out** ▷ *adj* **1** *colloq* exhausted. **2** *slang* under the influence of drugs or alcohol.

zoo /zuː/ ▷ *noun* (***zoos***) a garden or park where wild animals are kept for the purpose of study, breeding of rare species for conservation, etc, and where they are usually on show to the public. ◷ 19c: a shortening of ZOOLOGICAL GARDEN.

zoo- /zoʊoʊ, zoʊə, zuə, zoʊˈɒ, zuˈɒ/ ▷ *combining form, scientific, denoting* animal. ◷ From Greek *zoion* animal.

zoogeography ▷ *noun* the scientific study of the geographical distribution of animal species. • **zoogeographic** *adj*. ◷ 19c.

zoological /zuəˈlɒdʒɪkəl, zoʊə-/ ▷ *adj* referring or relating to ZOOLOGY. • **zoologically** *adverb*.

zoological garden ▷ *noun, formal* a ZOO.

zoology /zuˈɒlədʒɪ, zoʊ-/ ▷ *noun* the scientific study of animals, including their structure, function, behaviour, ecology, evolution and classification. • **zoologist** *noun* a scientist who specializes in zoology. ◷ 17c.

zoom ▷ *verb* (***zoomed, zooming***) **1** *tr & intr* (*often* **zoom over, past**, *etc*) to move or cause something to move very quickly, making a loud low-pitched buzzing noise. **2** *intr* (*usually* **zoom away, off**, *etc*) to move very quickly. **3** *intr* to increase quickly □ ***Prices have zoomed in the past year.*** ▷ *noun* the act or sound of zooming. ◷ 19c, meaning 'to make a buzzing noise', but soon transferring its meaning from the sound made by bees to their speed of movement.

■ **zoom in** or **zoom (a camera) in on someone** or **something** said of a camera or its operator: to close up on them using a zoom lens.

■ **zoom out** or **zoom (a camera) out** said of a camera or its operator: to open out a shot after a close-up.

zoom lens ▷ *noun* a type of camera lens which can be used to make a distant object appear gradually closer or

Signs of the Zodiac

further away without the camera being moved and without loss of focus.

zoophyte /ˈzoʊəfaɪt/ ▷ *noun, zool* any of various invertebrate animals which resemble plants, such as sponges, corals and sea anemones. ◷ 17c.

zooplankton ▷ *noun, zool* the part of the plankton that is composed of passively drifting or floating microscopic animals. • **zooplanktonic** *adj*. ◷ Early 20c.

zoot suit /ˈzuːt suːt/ ▷ *noun, slang* a type of man's suit popular in the late 1940s, with padded shoulders, fitted waist, long jacket, and trousers tapering to very narrow bottoms.

Zoroastrian /zɒroʊˈastrɪən/ ▷ *noun* a follower of Zoroastrianism. ▷ *adj* relating to or characteristic of Zoroastrianism.

Zoroastrianism ▷ *noun* an ancient religion of Persian origin founded or reformed by Zoroaster (c.630–c.553 BC), which teaches the existence of two continuously opposed divine beings, one good and the other evil.

zoster /ˈzɒstə(r)/ ▷ *noun* **1** *pathol* the disease called herpes zoster; SHINGLES. **2** an ancient Greek waist-belt for men. ◷ 18c in sense 1: from Greek *zoster* girdle.

zouk /zuːk/ ▷ *noun* a style of dance music originating in the French Antilles, which combines Latin American, African and Western disco rhythms. ◷ 20c: French.

zounds /zaʊndz, zuːndz/ ▷ *exclamation, archaic* used in oaths, etc: expressing astonishment or annoyance. ◷ 17c: from *God's wounds.*

ZPG ▷ *abbreviation, social science* zero population growth, an absence of any increase or decrease in a population over a specified period.

Zr ▷ *symbol, chem* zirconium.

ZRE ▷ *abbreviation, IVR* Zaire.

zucchetto /tsʊˈkɛtoʊ/ ▷ *noun* (***zucchettos***) the skullcap worn by Roman Catholic clergy, varying in colour according to their rank. ◷ 19c: Italian diminutive of *zucca* a pumpkin, or (*slang*) someone's head.

zucchini /zʊˈkiːnɪ/ ▷ *noun* (***zucchini*** or ***zucchinis***) *especially N Amer & Austral* a courgette. ◷ 1920s: Italian.

Zulu /ˈzuːluː/ ▷ *noun* (***Zulu*** or ***Zulus***) **1** a Bantu people of S Africa. **2** an individual belonging to this people. **3** their language. **4** *communications* in the NATO alphabet: the word used to denote the letter 'Z' (see table at NATO ALPHABET). ▷ *adj* belonging or relating to this people or their language. ◷ 19c.

Zuni or **Zuñi** /ˈzuːnjiː, ˈsuːnjiː/ ▷ *noun* (***Zuni*** or ***Zunis***) **1** a Native American Pueblo people from New Mexico and Arizona in the US South-West. **2** an individual belonging to this people. **3** their language. ▷ *adj* belonging or relating to this people or their language. ◷ 19c.

ZW ▷ *abbreviation, IVR* Zimbabwe.

Zwinglian /ˈtsvɪŋlɪən/ ▷ *noun, Christianity* a follower of Huldreich Zwingli (1484–1531), Swiss Protestant reformer, who disagreed with Luther in rejecting the doctrine of the presence of Christ in the Eucharist. ▷ *adj* relating or referring to Zwingli, his beliefs, or his followers and adherents. ◷ 16c.

zwitterion /ˈtsvɪtəraɪən/ ▷ *noun, chem* an ion that carries both a positive and a negative charge. • **zwitterionic** /-aɪˈɒnɪk/ *adj.* ◷ 20c: from German *zwitter* hybrid.

zygo- /zaɪgoʊ, zaɪˈgɒ, zɪˈgɒ/ or (before a vowel) **zyg-** *combining form, denoting* **1** a union. **2** a pair. ◷ From Greek *zygon* yoke.

zygote /ˈzaɪgoʊt/ ▷ *noun, biol* the cell that is formed as a result of the fertilization of a female gamete by a male gamete. • **zygotic** /-gɒtɪk/ *adj.* ◷ 19c: from Greek *zygon* yoke.

zymase /ˈzaɪmeɪs/ ▷ *noun, chem* any enzyme that catalyses the fermentation of carbohydrates to ETHANOL. ◷ 19c.

zymo- /zaɪmoʊ, zaɪˈmɒ/ or (before a vowel) **zym-** *combining form, denoting* fermentation □ ***zymology***. ◷ From Greek *zyme* leaven.

zymotic /zaɪˈmɒtɪk/ ▷ *adj* **1** relating to or causing fermentation. **2** medicine, *old use* relating to, causing or like an infectious disease. ◷ 19c: from Greek *zymotikos* causing fermentation.